Directory of
Special Libraries and
Information Centers

ISSN 0731-633X

Directory of Special Libraries and Information Centers

16th Edition

A Guide to More Than 20,800 Special Libraries,
Research Libraries, Information Centers, Archives, and Data Centers
Maintained by Government Agencies, Business, Industry, Newspapers,
Educational Institutions, Nonprofit Organizations, and Societies in
the Fields of Science and Engineering, Medicine, Law, Art, Religion,
the Social Sciences, and Humanities.

1993

DEBRA M. KIRBY
Editor

JOANNA M. ZAKALIK
Associate Editor

VOLUME 1
PART 2
N-Z
(Entries 10,949-20,851)
Appendixes and Subject Index

 **Gale Research Inc.** · *DETROIT* · *LONDON*

Amy Lucas, *Senior Editor*

Debra M. Kirby, *Editor*

Eric G. Carlson and Joanna M. Zakalik, *Associate Editors*
Sandra Doran and Christine Mathews, *Assistant Editors*

Research Staff

Victoria B. Cariappa, *Research Manager*
Gary J. Oudersluys, *Research Supervisor*
Lisa Lantz, *Editorial Associate*
Melissa E. Brown, Daniel L. Day, Charles A. Jewell, Richard A. Lawson,
L. Philip Naud, Phyllis Shepherd, Patricia A. Taraskiewicz, and Tracie A. Wade,
Editorial Assistants

Production Staff

Mary Beth Trimper, *Production Director*
Shanna Heilveil, *Production Assistant*

Arthur Chartow, *Art Director*
Cynthia Baldwin, *Graphic Designer*
C.J. Jonik, *Keyliner*

Benita L. Spight, *Data Entry Supervisor*
Gwendolyn S. Tucker, *Data Entry Group Leader*
Marjorita Onyekuru and Constance J. Wells, *Data Entry Associates*

Theresa A. Rocklin, *Supervisor of Editorial Programming Services*
Donald G. Dillaman, *Programming Consultant*

The paper used in this publication meets the minimum requirements
of American National Standard for Information Sciences—
Permanence Paper for Printed Library Materials, ANSI Z39.48-1984.

Library of Congress Catalog Number 84-640165
ISBN 0-8103-7661-X (set)
ISBN 0-103-7743-8 (Part 2)
ISSN 0731-633X

Printed in the United States of America

Published simultaneously in the United Kingdom
by Gale Research International Limited
(An affiliated company of Gale Research Inc.)

Contents

Volume 1, Part 1

Volume 1, Part 2

User's Guide

Volume 1 of the *Directory of Special Libraries and Information Centers* consists of descriptive listings, appendixes, and the Subject Index. It is published in two parts:

- Part 1 contains entries A through M
- Part 2 contains entries N through Z, seven appendixes, and the Subject Index.

Descriptive Listings

Entries within the main section of *DSL* are arranged in alphabetical order; libraries associated with a company, institution, agency, or association are grouped under the official name of the parent organization. Several exceptions to the alphabetical arrangement exist:

–The libraries of the U.S. Department of Veterans Affairs (formerly the U.S. Veterans Administration) are subarranged geographically.

–The information units of the Environmental Protection Agency as well as some other U.S. government agencies and departments are listed numerically by region.

–Some United States state supreme courts are arranged numerically by judicial district.

–Libraries within a university system with more than one campus are grouped alphabetically by campus. For instance, the University of Wisconsin, Madison libraries appear together as a group before libraries situated at the University of Wisconsin, Milwaukee.

–Federal governmental units are listed under the country of origin; for example, entries for the National Library of Canada are found in the Cs as Canada—National Library of Canada.

More than 7,750 cross-references are interfiled throughout the listings to direct the user to main entries. Cross-references are supplied for libraries well known by an acronym, libraries with multiple sponsors, facilities with memorial or bilingual names, libraries of subsidiaries of large corporations, and many governmental agencies.

The fictitious entry shown below is followed by a brief description of the individual components of the listing. Each numbered item is explained in the descriptive paragraph bearing the same number.

---

[1] ★562★ **[2]** **Agricultural Research Center, Inc.— [3] Library [4]** (Agri; Biol Sci)
[5] 789 Minnesota Ave.   **[6]** Phone: (913)237-8884
Kansas City, KS 66101   **[7]** Margaret Miller-Holmes, Dir.
[8] **Founded:** 1972. **[9]** **Staff:** Prof 6; Other 12. **[10]** **Subjects:** Agronomy, plant breeding, soil fertility, entomology, dairy science, animal health. **[11]** **Special Collections:** Biotechnology Research Collection (24 VF drawers of technical reports). **[12]** **Holdings:** 75,000 books; 150 bound periodical volumes; 85 microfiche; 100 reels of microfilm; 250 AV programs; 6500 internal and technical reports; 4689 government documents. **[13]** **Subscriptions:** 75 journals and other seials; 12 newspapers. **[14]** **Services:** interlibrary loan; copying; SDI; library open to the public for reference use only. **[15]** **Automated Operations:** Computerized cataloging, acquisitions, serials, and circulation. **[16]** **Computerized Information Services:** OCLC, DIALOG Information Services; Ag-viser (internal database; BITNET (electronic mail service). Performs searches on fee basis. Contact Person: Winston C. Darnay, Online Serv.Libn., 237-8871. **[17]** **Networks/Consortia:** Member of Bibliographical Center for Research, Rocky Mountain Region, Inc. (BCR). **[18]** **Publications:** Library Newsletter, quarterly—to selected agricultural libraries; New Acquisitions List, monthly—for internl distribution only. **[19]** **Special Catalogs:** Catalog of Biotechnology Research Collection (loose-leaf). **[20]** **Special Indexes:** Indexes to AV programs and internal and technicl reports (card). **[21]** **Remarks:** FAX (913) 237-8888. Telex: 924421. Electronic mail address(es): HOLMES@ARC (BITNET). Maintains a branch library in Lawrence, KS. **[22]** **Formerly:** Farming Resources Corporation. **[23]** **Formed by the merger of:** Technical Information Center and Corporte Library. **[24]** **Also Known As:** ARC. **[25]** **Staff:** Martin Lessner, Chf., Tech.Serv.; Don H. Bunny, Chf., Pub.Serv.; Kathleen O'Brien, Libn.; Derek Morrison, Libn.; Miranda Kern, Libn.

---

1 **Entry Number.** The entries in *DSL* are numbered sequentially. The sequential entry number (rather than the page number) is used in the Subject Index to refer to an entry, and also follows the entry title in *Volume 2, Geographic and Personnel Indexes.*

2 **Name of Organization.** Name of parent organization, society, or agency that sponsors or is served by the library or information center. Independent libraries and centers and those commonly known by a distinct name are entered directly under the library's name. Cross-references are included in the body of the work for those libraries which may be known by two or more distinct names.

3 **Name of Library or Information Center.** Descriptive and memorial names are given as reported. Otherwise, the appropriate generic term is used, e.g., library, archives, collection, or information center. In many cases, the generic term has been supplied by the editors and the inclusion of the term "library" may not indicate the existence of a formal library.

4 **Principal Subject Keyword.** The major subject or type of material represented by the collection as a whole. When there are two areas of equal importance, both are indicated. If a collection has more than four major subjects or is general in scope, no keyword is used. The keywords offer a classification by broad subject category only; each library's more specialized interests are mentioned in the body of each listing. Both the general key words and specialized interests are used as headings in the subject index. The following keywords are employed:

Agri	-Agriculture	Info Sci	-Information science
Area-Ethnic	-Area ethnic	Law	-Law
Art	-Art	Med	-Medicine
Aud-Vis	-Audiovisual	Mil	-Military
Biol Sci	-Biological sciences	Mus	-Music
Bus-Fin	-Business and finance	Plan	-Planning
Comp Sci	-Computer science	Publ	-Publishing
Educ	-Education	Rare Book	-Rare book
Energy	-Energy	Rec	-Recreation
Env-Cons	-Environment and conservation	Rel-Phil	-Religion and philosophy
Food-Bev	-Food and beverages	Sci-Engr	-Science and engineering
Geog-Map	-Geography and maps	Soc Sci	-Social sciences
Hist	-History	Theater	-Theater
Hum	-Humanities	Trans	-Transportation

5 **Mailing Address.** The permanent mailing address of the library or center. In some instances this will differ from the headquarters address of the parent organization and the physical location of the library. When there is a separate location address, it is given under "Remarks" (see item 21).

6 **Phone Number.** Area code and telephone number. Alternate phone numbers are listed under "Remarks" (see item 21). Extensions are not provided, since they are subject to frequent change.

7 **Head of Library or Information Center.** Name and title of the person directly in charge of the library or information center. Where no librarian has been identified or where there is no position as such, the name of the administrative officer may be given. When the directorship is shared by two persons, the names of both individuals are provided in the "Staff Names" section (see item 25).

8 **Founding Date.** Year when library or information center was established, either formally or informally.

9 **Number of Staff.** Number of individuals directly engaged in the operation of the library or center on a regular basis. Part-time employees are included but student assistants and other occasional help generally are not. Professional staff includes librarians, bibliographers, subject specialists, information specialists, and other related specialists. Semiprofessionals and clerical assistants are grouped in the second category. Distinction between professional and nonprofessional staff is made by the respondents. Where the differentiation is not made, the total number of staff is listed.

10 **Subjects.** Terms specifically designating the most important subjects represented in the collection as a whole.

11 **Special Collections.** Separately grouped collections of unusual or notable interest that are identifiable by subject, form, name of donor, or distinctive name.

12 **Holdings.** Quantitative data concerning collections. Numbers of books, bound periodical volumes, pamphlets, and technical reports are given separately when supplied by respondents. When the term "volumes" is used, it generally indicates bound units or collections of bound and unbound items which have been accessioned and cataloged. Unbound material is indicated either by unit count, number of vertical file (VF) drawers, linear shelf feet, or cubic storage space. Estimates rather than the exact statistics have frequently been given. Holdings of nonbook materials are also indicated whenever of significant size and importance.

13 **Subscriptions.** Figures generally represent the number of journal and serial titles, not separate copies, received by paid subscription, gift, and exchange. Newspaper subscriptions are given separately.

14 **Services.** Most special libraries provide bibliographic or reference services primarily for their own sponsoring organizations. For these, an appropriate statement of service limitations is given. When the library or center provides some form of access to outside clientele, it is so indicated. When services offered are of an unusual nature they are noted and indication is given whether such services are for internal or external use. Entries for libraries which honor interlibrary loan requests include the appropriate information, as do those for libraries with copying or reproducing facilities. Normally, copying services to outside users are on a fee basis. Some libraries now charge for interlibrary loans and this information is included when supplied by respondent.

15 **Automated Operations.** Computerized library management functions such as public access catalog, cataloging, circulation, acquisitions, and serials, are identified here.

16 **Computerized Information Services.** Indicates a special library's access to online information systems, such as MEDLINE, DIALOG Information Services, LEXIS, etc. CD-ROMs, internally produced databases, and electronic mail services are also listed. Also included here are fee policies for online searches the library may perform for the public, and the name and telephone number of the contact person.

17 **Networks/Consortia.** Lists the special library's memberships in formal or informal groups involved in cooperative sharing of library resources on the local, regional, or national level. Acronyms are used for networks and consortia which are familiar to the library profession (e.g., CLASS, ILLINET).

18 **Publications.** Periodical, serial, and other publications issued or prepared by the library or information center are included. Title, frequency, and basis of distribution are indicated when known.

19 **Special Catalogs.** Unique and unusual catalogs which are locally prepared and maintained, including card, book, computer printout, and other formats.

20 **Special Indexes.** Unique and unusual indexes which are locally prepared and maintained.

21 **Remarks.** Additional information not adaptable to the standard entry format, including historical data, explanatory notes, and descriptions of unusual activities. Corporate affiliations are often noted here. Also included is the address of a special library's location when it differs from the mailing address in item 5, and any toll-free telephone numbers, alternate telephone numbers, telex numbers, telefacsimile numbers, and electronic mail addresses. Facsimile correspondence should be addressed to the attention of the special library or information center because in some cases the number listed is that of the overall organization or general library.

22 **Formerly.** Former name and/or location of a special library or its parent organization when there is a recent change of name and/or location under which they were formerly listed. Crossreferences are generally supplied from the former names.

23 **Formed By the Merger of.** When the special library has been created by the merger of two or mo[r]e units previously listed as separate entries, the names of the components are identified here. Merge[r]s of parent organizations which affect the special library are also noted.

24 **Also Known As.** Variant names of a special library or its parent organization, including translations [of] non-English names if provided by the respondent. Cross-references from these are provided whe[re] needed.

25 **Staff Names.** Names and titles of professional and supervisory personnel in the special library [or] information center. Only principal members of the professional staff are listed for operations with larg[e] staff.

Appendixes

The descriptive listings are followed by seven appendixes that group specific types of special libraries. Listings typically include library name, address, and telephone number. Entries within each appendix are arranged geographically. The appendixes are:

Appendix A - Networks and Consortia lists organizations involved in cooperative efforts to share resources. Listings also may include contact person and notes covering former and alternate names, the names of member organizations, references to other listings in *DSL*, and address rotation schedules. The appendix is followed by a cumulative index to all cited networks and consortia and their alternate names.

Appendix B - Regional and Subregional Libraries for the Blind and Physically Handicapped identifies libraries that cooperate with the Library of Congress in providing free library services to persons who are unable to read or use standard printed material because of visual or physical impairment. Listings may also include contact name, notes covering services offered or geographic area served, alternate, toll-free, TTY, and TDD numbers.

Appendix C - Patent and Trademark Depository Libraries lists libraries that are designated as patent depository libraries by the U.S. Patent and Trademark Office and are open to the public.

Appendix D - Regional Government Depository Libraries identifies libraries that make federal government information available to the public through participation in the U.S. Government Printing Office's Depository Library Program.

Appendix E - United Nations Depository Libraries lists libraries throughout the world that house documents and publications issued by the United Nations.

Appendix F - World Bank Depository Libraries identifies libraries providing free and public access to materials produced by or for the World Bank. Telephone, facsimile, telex, and contact names are given for selected entries.

Appendix G - European Community Depository Libraries lists libraries throughout the United States that maintain European Community document collections.

Subject Index

The Subject Index employs more than 4,000 terms and cross-references to classify the major fields of interest of each library described in the listing portion of *DSL*.

While the index is based on terms provided by librarians describing the subject interests of their collections, the editors exercised considerable selection and interpretation to arrive at standard headings. Cross-references link synonyms and related terms. *Library of Congress Subject Headings* was used as a professional guide but was not followed in all cases.

The Subject Index refers users to entry numbers, not page numbers. Entry numbers following a subject term are arranged geographically as follows: United States entries are arranged by state code; Canadian entries are arranged by province or territory code; and International entries are arranged b[y] country code. A key to the state, province, and country codes precedes the index.

Abbreviations

Acq.	-Acquisitions	Coop.	-Cooperating, Cooperation, Cooperative
Act.	-Acting	Coord.	-Coordinating, Coordination, Coordinator
Actv.	-Activities, Activity	Corp.	-Corporate, Corporation
Adm.	-Administration, Administrative, Administrator	Coun.	-Council
Adv.	-Advisor	Couns.	-Counsel, Counseling, Counselor
AFB	-Air Force Base	Ct.	-Court
Aff.	-Affairs	Ctr.	-Center, Centre
Agri.	-Agricultural, Agriculture	Ctrl.	-Central
AHEC	-Area Health Education Center	Cur.	-Curator, Curatorial
Amer.	-American	Curric.	-Curricular, Curriculum
ANGB	-Air National Guard Base	Cust.	-Custodian
Anl.	-Analysis, Analyst, Analytical	Dept., Depts.	-Department, Departmental, Departments
APO	-Army Post Office		
Arch.	-Architect, Architectural, Architecture	Des.	-Design, Designer
Archeo.	-Archeological, Archeologist, Archeology	Dev.	-Development, Developmental
Archv.	-Archival, Archives, Archivist	Dir.	-Director
ART	-Accredited Record Technician	Dissem.	-Dissemination
Assn.	-Association	Dist.	-District
Assoc.	-Associate	Distr.	-Distribution, Distributor
Asst.	-Assistant	Div.	-Division, Divisional
Att.	-Attorney	Doc., Docs.	-Document, Documentalist(e), Documentation, Documents
Aud.	-Audio		
AV	-Audiovisual	DOD	-U.S. Department of Defense
Ave.	-Avenue	DOE	-U.S. Department of Energy
B.P.	-Boite Postale	Dp.	-Deputy
Bd.	-Board	Dr.	-Doctor,Drive
Biblio.	-Bibliotechnicien(ne), Bibliothecaire	E.	-East
Bibliog.	-Bibliographer, Bibliographic, Bibliographical, Bibliography	Econ.	-Economic(s)
		Ed.	-Editor, Editorial
Biol.	-Biological, Biologist, Biology	Educ.	-Education, Educational, Educator
Biomed.	-Biomedical, Biomedicine	Engr.	-Engineer, Engineering
Bk.,Bks.	-Book, Books	Env.	-Environment, Environmental
Bldg.	-Building	Exch.	-Exchange
Blvd.	-Boulevard	Exec.	-Executive
Br.	-Branch	Expy.	-Expressway
Bro.	-Brother	Ext.	-Extended, Extension, External
Bur.	-Bureau	Fac.	-Facilitator, Facility, Faculty
Bus.	-Business	Fed.	-Federal, Federation
C.P.	-Caixa Postal, Caja Postale, Case Postale, Casetta Postale	Fin.	-Finance, Financial
		Fl.	-Floor
Capt.	-Captain	Fld.	-Field
Cart.	-Cartographer, Cartographic, Cartography	Found.	-Foundation
Cat.	-Catalog, Cataloger, Cataloging	FPO	-Fleet Post Office
CD-ROM	-Compact Disk Read-Only Memory	Fr.	-Father
Cedex	-Courrier d'Entreprise a Distribution Exceptionnelle	Ft.	-Fort
Ch.	-Chair, Child, Children, Children's	FTS	-Federal Telephone System
Chem.	-Chemical, Chemist, Chemistry	Fwy.	-Freeway
Chf.	-Chief	G.P.O.	-General Post Office
Chm.	-Chairman	Gen.	-General
Circ.	-Circulation	Geneal.	-Genealogical, Genealogist, Genealogy
Ck.	-Clerk	Geog.	-Geographer, Geographic, Geographical, Geography
Class.	-Classical, Classification, Classified	Geol.	-Geological, Geologist, Geology
Clghse.	-Clearinghouse	Govt.	-Government, Governmental
Clin.	-Clinical	Hd.	-Head
Co.	-Company	Hea.	-Health
Col.	-Colonel	Hist.	-Historian, Historic, Historical, History
Coll.	-Collection(s), College	Hndcp.	-Handicap, Handicapped
COM	-Computer Output Microfilm/Microfiche	Hon.	-Honorable, Honorary
Comm.	-Committee	Hosp.	-Hospital
Commn.	-Commission	HQ	-Headquarters
Commnr.	-Commissioner	Hum.	-Humanities
Commun.	-Communication(s), Community	Hwy.	-Highway
Comp.	-Computer, Computerized, Computing	ILL	-Interlibrary Loan
Cons.	-Conservation, Conservator, Consultant, Consulting	Illus.	-Illustrated, Illustration, Illustrative, Illustrator
Cont.	-Continuing, Control	Indiv.	-Individual

Indus.	-Industrial, Industry	Prov.	-Province, Provincial
Info.	-Information, Informational	Psych.	-Psychiatric, Psychiatry, Psychological, Psychology
Inst.	-Institute, Institution, Institutional	Pub.	-Public
Instr.	-Instruction, Instructional, Instructor	Publ.	-Published, Publisher, Publishing
Int.	-Internal	Pubn., Pubns.	-Publication, Publications
Interp.	-Interpretation, Interpreter, Interpretive	R&D	-Research and Development
Intl.	-International	Rd.	-Reader(s), Road
Jnl.	-Journal	Rec.	-Record(s), Recreation
Jr.	-Junior	Ref.	-Reference
Kpr.	-Keeper	Reg.	-Region, Regional, Registrar
KWIC	-Keyword in Context	Rel.	-Relations, Religion, Religious
KWOC	-Keyword out of Context	Rep.	-Representative
Lab., Labs.	-Laboratory, Laboratories	Repro.	-Reproduction
Lang.	-Language(s)	Res.	-Research, Researcher
LATCH	-Literature Attached to the Chart (Medical)	Resp.	-Responsible
LCDR	-Lieutenant Commander	Ret.	-Retired, Retrieval
Ldr.	-Leader	Rev.	-Reverend
Leg.	-Legal, Legislation, Legislative, Legislator, Legislature	Rm., Rms.	-Room, Rooms
		Rpt.	-Report(s)
Lib., Libs.	-Library, Libraries	Rsrc., Rsrcs.	-Resource, Resources
Libn.	-Librarian	Rte.	-Route
Lit.	-Literary, Literature	S.	-South
Ln.	-Lane	S/N	-Sin Numero
LRC	-Learning Resource(s) Center	Sch.	-School
Lrng.	-Learning	Sci.	-Science(s), Scientific, Scientist
Lt.	-Lieutenant	SDI	-Selective Dissemination of Information
LTC	-Lieutenant Colonel	Sec.	-Secretary
Maint.	-Maintenance	Sect.	-Section
Maj.	-Major	Sel.	-Selection
Math.	-Mathematical, Mathematics	Ser.	-Serial(s)
Med.	-Medical, Medicine	Serv.	-Service(s)
Mfg.	-Manufacturing	Sgt.	-Sergeant
Mgr.	-Manager	SLA	-Special Libraries Association
Mgt.	-Management	Soc.	-Social, Society
Mil.	-Military	Spec.	-Special, Specialist, Specialized
Mktg.	-Marketing	Sq.	-Square
Mng.	-Managing	Sr.	-Senior, Sister
Ms., Mss.	-Manuscript, Manuscripts	St.	-Saint, Street
Mt.	-Mount	Sta.	-Station
Mtls.	-Materials	Stat.	-Statistical, Statistics
Mus.	-Music, Musical	Ste.	-Sainte, Societe
Musm.	-Museum	Sts.	-Saints, Streets
Myth.	-Mythology	Stud.	-Student(s), Studies, Study
N.	-North	Succ.	-Succursale
Natl.	-National	Sup.	-Support, Supporting
NCME	-Network for Continuing Medical Education	Supt.	-Superintendent
No.	-Number, Numero	Supv.	-Supervising, Supervisor, Supervisory
Nurs.	-Nursing	Sys.	-System(s)
Off.	-Office, Officer	Tchg.	-Teaching
Oper.	-Operations, Operator	TDD	-Telecommunications/Telephone Device for the Deaf
Org.	-Organization, Organizational	Tech.	-Technical, Technological, Technology
P.O.	-Post Office	Techn.	-Technician
P.R.	-Public Relations	Theol.	-Theological, Theology
Per.	-Periodical(s)	Tpke.	-Turnpike
Perf.	-Perform, Performing	Trans.	-Transportation
Pers.	-Personnel	Transl.	-Translation, Translator
Pharm.	-Pharmaceutical, Pharmacy	Treas.	-Treasurer
Photo.	-Photograph(s), Photographer, Photographic	Trng.	-Training
Photodup.	-Photoduplication	TTY	-Teletypewriter
Pict.	-Pictorial, Picture(s)	U.N.	-United Nations
Pk.	-Park	U.S.	-United States
Pkwy.	-Parkway	UNESCO	-United Nations Educational, Scientific, and Cultural Organization
Pl.	-Place		
Plan.	-Planner, Planning	Univ.	-University
Pres.	-President	Unpubl.	-Unpublished
Presrv.	-Preservation	V.P.	-Vice President
Prin.	-Principal	Vet.	-Veteran(s), Veterinary
Proc.	-Process, Processing, Processor	VF	-Vertical File(s)
Prod.	-Product, Production	Vis.	-Vision, Visual
Prof.	-Professional, Professor	Vol., Vols.	-Volume, Volumes
Prog.	-Program(s), Programmer, Programming	W.	-West
Proj.	-Project(s)		

Directory of Special Libraries and Information Centers

VOLUME 1, PART 2

N-Z

Appendixes and Subject Index

N

★ 10949 ★
N.S. Community College - Halifax Campus - Library (Educ)
1825 Bell Rd.   Phone: (902)424-7972
Halifax, NS, Canada B3H 2Z4   Debbie Costelo, Libn.
Founded: 1949. **Staff:** Prof 1; Other 1. **Subjects:** Vocational and technical trades, business administration, data processing, secretarial science, library technology. **Holdings:** 27,500 books; 2000 pocketbooks; 68 films; 173 AV programs; 137 videotapes. **Subscriptions:** 200 journals and other serials. **Services:** Interlibrary loan; copying; library open to the public with restrictions. **Computerized Information Services:** QL Systems; Envoy 100 (electronic mail service). **Remarks:** FAX: (902)424-0553. Electronic mail address(es): ILL.NSHVH (Envoy 100).

NAACP Legal Defense Fund - Law Library
See: National Association for the Advancement of Colored People - NAACP Legal Defense and Educational Fund - Law Library (11049)

Nabisco Brands, Inc.
See: RJR Nabisco - Nabisco Brands, Inc. (13959)

★ 10950 ★
Nabisco Brands Ltd. - Research Centre - Library
1101 Walker's Line
Burlington, ON, Canada L7N 2G4
Subjects: Food science, waste water technology, pesticides. **Special Collections:** History of canning industry in Canada; International CODEX files (food industry). **Holdings:** 800 books; 600 bound periodical volumes. **Remarks:** Currently inactive.

David Nabow Library
See: Duke Power Company (5036)

★ 10951 ★
NAC RE Corporate Library (Bus-Fin)
1 Greenwich Plaza
P.O. Box 2568
Greenwich, CT 06836   Phone: (203)622-5316
     Sheila Repice, Libn.
Founded: 1985. **Subjects:** Reinsurance, insurance. **Holdings:** 700 books; 1000 reports; 1000 annual statements. **Subscriptions:** 300 journals and other serials; 5 newspapers. **Services:** Interlibrary loan; library not open to the public. **Computerized Information Services:** DIALOG Information Services, LEXIS, NEXIS, Dow Jones News/Retrieval, Human Resource Information Network (HRIN). **Remarks:** FAX: (203)622-1494.

NAES College
See: Native American Educational Services Inc. (11336)

★ 10952 ★
Nagoya American Center - USIS Library (Educ)
Nagoya Kokusai Senta Bldg., 6th Fl.
1-47-1 Nagono, Nakamura-ku
Nagoya 450, Japan   Phone: 52 5818641
Founded: 1972. **Staff:** 1. **Subjects:** International relations, economics, U.S. society, arts, American literature, environmental issues. **Holdings:** 5000 books; microfiche; microfilm. **Subscriptions:** 120 journals and other serials; 3 newspapers. **Services:** Copying; library open to the public. **Computerized Information Services:** DIALOG Information Services. **Remarks:** Maintained or supported by the U.S. Information Agency. Focus is on materials that will assist peoples outside the United States to learn about the United States, its people, history, culture, political processes, and social milieux. **Staff:** Mrs. Kazuyo Watanabe, Lib.Spec.

★ 10953 ★
Nagoya Daigaku Sugakuka - Toshoshitsu (Sci-Engr)
Furocho, Chikusa-ku
Nagoya 464-01, Aichi, Japan   Phone: 52 7815111
     S. Mukai
Founded: 1942. **Staff:** Prof 3; Other 1. **Subjects:** Mathematics. **Special Collections:** D. Hilbert Collection (off-prints of mathematics journals). **Holdings:** 70,000 books and bound periodical volumes. **Subscriptions:** 350 journals and other serials. **Services:** Interlibrary loan; copying; library open to the public for reference use only. **Computerized Information Services:** DIALOG Information Services.

★ 10954 ★
Naiad Press, Inc. - Lesbian and Gay Archives (Soc Sci, Publ)
Box 10543   Phone: (904)539-5965
Tallahassee, FL 32302   Donna J. McBride, Hd.Libn.
Founded: 1960. **Staff:** Prof 1; Other 1. **Subjects:** Lesbian, gay, and feminist literature. **Holdings:** 18,000 books; 1000 bound periodical volumes; 4000 unbound periodicals; 450 manuscripts; 8 boxes of clippings; 300 videotapes. **Subscriptions:** 62 journals and other serials; 111 newspapers. **Services:** Interlibrary loan (limited); copying; archives open to the public by request. **Publications:** The Lesbian in Literature, 1981; Black Lesbians: An Annotated Bibliography, 1981. **Special Indexes:** The Lesbian Periodicals Index, 1986. **Remarks:** FAX: (904)539-9731.

★ 10955 ★
NAIOP, The Association for Commercial Real Estate - NAIOP Information Center (Bus-Fin)
1215 Jefferson Davis Hwy., Suite 100   Phone: (703)979-3400
Arlington, VA 22202   Dorothy Gray, Dir., Info.Serv.
Founded: 1985. **Staff:** Prof 1. **Subjects:** Commercial real estate and allied topics. **Special Collections:** Commercial Real Estate Marketing Collection, 1985 to present (500 brochures and video cassettes). **Holdings:** 400 books; slides. **Subscriptions:** 90 journals and other serials. **Services:** Center open to the public by appointment. **Computerized Information Services:** DIALOG Information Services; library records (internal database). **Publications:** NAIOP Information Center Research Review, quarterly - to members. **Remarks:** FAX: (703)979-3409. **Formerly:** National Association of Industrial & Office Parks.

★ 10956 ★
(Nairobi) American Cultural Center - USIS Library (Educ)
Natl. Bank Bldg.
Harambee Ave.
P.O. Box 30143
Nairobi, Kenya
Remarks: Maintained or supported by the U.S. Information Agency. Focus is on materials that will assist peoples outside the United States to learn about the United States, its people, history, culture, political processes, and social milieux.

★ 10957 ★
Naismith Memorial Basketball Hall of Fame - Edward J. and Gena G. Hickox Library (Rec)
1150 W. Columbus Ave.
Box 179
Springfield, MA 01101-0179   Phone: (413)781-6500
     Wayne Patterson, Res.Spec.
Staff: Prof 1. **Subjects:** Men's and women's basketball - amateur, scholastic, collegiate, professional, international. **Special Collections:** William G. Mokray Collection (691 books, guides, scrapbooks). **Holdings:** 3000 books; 31 VF drawers of photographs; 68 VF drawers of news clippings, pamphlets, reports, statistics; 16 VF drawers of collegiate, professional, international game programs, including all-star and tournament games; complete set of basketball guides. **Subscriptions:** 18 journals and other serials. **Services:** Copying; library open to the public by appointment. **Publications:** Official Hall of Fame Book - for sale; Newsletter, quarterly. **Remarks:** FAX: (413)781-1939.

★ 10958 ★
Nalco Chemical Company - Library and Information Services (Sci-Engr)
1 Nalco Center   Phone: (708)305-2402
Naperville, IL 60563-1198   Stephen Boyle, Supv.
Founded: 1928. **Staff:** Prof 3; Other 4. **Subjects:** Chemistry, water treatment, polymer science. **Holdings:** 8000 books; 10,000 bound periodical volumes;

28 VF drawers of bulletins, reprints, photocopies; 12 VF drawers of internal research reports; 20 VF drawers of technical data; 24 VF drawers of patents; 4000 unbound journals; microfilm. **Subscriptions:** 400 journals and other serials. **Services:** Interlibrary loan; copying; services open to the public by appointment. **Automated Operations:** Computerized serials and circulation. **Computerized Information Services:** DIALOG Information Services, LEXIS, PFDS Online, Chemical Abstracts Service (CAS); internal databases. **Networks/Consortia:** Member of DuPage Library System. **Publications:** Acquisitions bulletin, bimonthly. **Remarks:** FAX: (708)305-2876. **Staff:** C. Nitsche, Sr.Info.Sci.; J.D. Brown, Bus.Info.Spec.; D. Portmann, Info.Sci.

★ 10959 ★
Nalco Chemical Company - Sugar Land Library (Sci-Engr)
Box 87   Phone: (713)263-7445
Sugar Land, TX 77478   Margaret Hayes
Founded: 1987. **Staff:** 1. **Subjects:** Chemistry, petroleum production, oil refining, polymer science. **Holdings:** 4000 books; 3000 bound periodical volumes. **Subscriptions:** 85 journals and other serials. **Services:** Library open to the public by appointment for reference use only. **Computerized Information Services:** Internal database. **Publications:** Acquisitions List - for internal distribution only. **Remarks:** FAX: (713)263-7865.

★ 10960 ★
Namibia - National Archives of Namibia (Hist)
Private Bag 13250   Phone: 61 293385
Windhoek 9000, Namibia   Brigitte Lan
Founded: 1939. **Staff:** Prof 5; Other 8. **Subjects:** Namibian history, library and information sciences, historical colonial law. **Special Collections:** C.J.C. Lemmer Collection of Namibiana (1100 items). **Holdings:** 5900 books; 156 periodical series; 106 reports; 6000 linear meters of archival items; 3212 microfiche; 2673 reels of microfilm; 10,000 photographs; 6000 maps; 2500 AV items. **Subscriptions:** 8 journals and other serials; 3 newspapers. **Services:** Copying; archives open to the public for reference use only. **Computerized Information Services:** ICL Status (internal database). **Publications:** List of archival materials; Central Register of Theses on Namibia; ARCHEIA source publications. **Remarks:** Alternate telephone number(s): 61 293377.

★ 10961 ★
Namibia Scientific Society - Library (Area-Ethnic)
P.O. Box 67   Phone: 61 225372
Windhoek 9000, Namibia   J. Klusener, Libn.
Founded: 1925. **Staff:** 2. **Subjects:** Namibia - history, natural sciences, archeology, ethnology, zoology, botany, geology. **Holdings:** 7000 volumes. **Subscriptions:** 3 journals and other serials. **Services:** Interlibrary loan; SDI; library open to the public. **Formerly:** South West Africa Scientific Society. **Staff:** A. Benseler.

★ 10962 ★
Nanaimo Daily Free Press - Library (Publ)
223 Commercial St.
Box 69   Phone: (604)753-3451
Nanaimo, BC, Canada V9R 5K5   Wayne Campbell, Mng.Ed.
Subjects: Newspaper reference topics. **Holdings:** Newspaper, 1874 to present, on microfilm. **Services:** Library open to the public. **Remarks:** FAX: (604)753-8730.

★ 10963 ★
Nanaimo & District Museum Society - Nanaimo Centennial Museum - Archives (Hist)
100 Cameron Rd.
Nanaimo, BC, Canada V9R 2X1   Phone: (604)753-1821
Founded: 1964. **Staff:** 3. **Subjects:** History - local Native Canadian groups, coal mining, Nanaimo area, fishing and logging industries. **Special Collections:** Local historical photographs; diorama depicting traditional Native life style; restored and fully furnished miner's cottage; extensive Chinese artifact collection. **Holdings:** 1000 volumes; 8000 photographs; 150 maps; 8000 archival materials. **Subscriptions:** 10 journals and other serials; 3 newspapers. **Services:** Copying; archives open to the public for reference use only with supervision. **Publications:** Nanaimo Story of a City, 1983.

★ 10964 ★
Nanjing Botanical Garden - Sun Yat-Sen Memorial - Library (Biol Sci)
Nanjing 210014, Jiangsu Province,   Phone: 42 432126
  People's Republic of China   Ding-Fa Xu
Founded: 1954. **Staff:** 6. **Subjects:** Botany; plant taxonomy; horticulture; plants for medical use; plant protection, ecology, physiology, breeding; environmental protection; chemistry; agronomy. **Special Collections:** Plant taxonomy; flowers. **Holdings:** 42,446 volumes, books, periodicals; 171 microforms and AV programs. **Subscriptions:** 437 journals and other serials. **Services:** Interlibrary loan; copying; international book exchange. **Publications:** Journal of Plant Resource and Environment, quarterly. **Remarks:** FAX: 25 432074. Telex: 34025 ISSAS CN. **Staff:** Ding-Fa Xu; Su-Qin Zhang; Hui-Hui Yu; Nai-Cheng Xu; Ming-Yi Sun; Hou-Jun Wu.

★ 10965 ★
Nanjing University - Library (Area-Ethnic)
Hankou Lu
Nanjing, Jiangsu Province, People's   Phone: 25 634651
  Republic of China   Zhong-wen Bao, Univ. V.P./Libn.
Founded: 1902. **Staff:** 131. **Subjects:** Orientalism, bibliography, archeology. **Special Collections:** Chinese ancient books (1452 titles; 20,428 volumes); district histories, especially Jiangsu and Sichuan provinces (3500 titles; 38,000 volumes); books of rubbings from stone inscriptions (2,300 titles). **Holdings:** 3.1 million volumes. **Subscriptions:** 6000 journals and other serials. **Services:** Copying; library open to the public for research. **Special Catalogs:** Catalogue of Remarkable Editions of Chinese Ancient Books Held by the Library; Catalogue of District Histories Held by the Library. **Remarks:** 25 307965. Telex: 34151 PRCNU CN. **Staff:** Xian-zhen Ma, Vice Dir.; Ke-yi Yang, Vice Dir.; Peiguo Yuan, Assoc.Res.Libn.; Bo-lian Lu, Assoc.Res.Libn.; Qin-Qi Zheng, Assoc.Res.Libn.; Hong-xiang Ma, Assoc.Res.Libn.; Si-ai Wang, Assoc.Res.Libn.; Jirong Xu, Hd. of Off.; Zhu-ying Wang, Hd. of Circ.Dept.; Zhi-zhong Fan, Hd. of Circ.Dept.; Yuan-huan Chen, Hd. of Acq.Dept.; Yi Liu, Hd. pf Per.Dept.; Yi-fei Jiang, Hd. of Chinese Dept.

★ 10966 ★
Nantucket Historical Association - Research Center (Hist)
Broad St.
Box 1016   Phone: (508)228-1655
Nantucket, MA 02554   Jacqueline K. Haring, Cur.
Founded: 1894. **Staff:** Prof 2; Other 2. **Subjects:** Nantucket and maritime history, whaling. **Special Collections:** Logbooks (327); account and letter books; original documents connected with whaling; Nantucket and maritime history. **Holdings:** 5000 volumes; pamphlets; 308 manuscript collections; 750 linear feet of research materials; 21,000 photographs and AV programs; maps; architectural drawings; scrapbooks. **Services:** Copying; center open to adults. **Computerized Information Services:** Internal database. Performs searches free of charge. **Publications:** Guide to Manuscript Collections - for sale. **Special Indexes:** Subject access card file. **Staff:** Amy Rokioki, Res.Libn.; Peter MacGlashan, AV Libn.

★ 10967 ★
Nantucket Maria Mitchell Association - Library (Sci-Engr)
2 Vestal St.   Phone: (508)228-9198
Nantucket, MA 02554   Dr. M. Jane Stroup, Libn.
Founded: 1902. **Staff:** Prof 1; Other 1. **Subjects:** Astronomy, biology, chemistry, general science, mathematics, biography, Nantucket topics. **Special Collections:** Maria Mitchell Memorabilia (Maria Mitchell's personal library). **Holdings:** 12,000 books; 1236 bound periodical volumes. **Subscriptions:** 49 journals and other serials. **Services:** Interlibrary loan; copying; library open to the public.

★ 10968 ★
Nanville Corporation - The Information Center (Med)
P.O. Box 5108   Phone: (303)978-5374
Denver, CO 80217   Barbara Norton, Chf.Libn.
Founded: 1974. **Staff:** Prof 1; Other 2. **Subjects:** Occupational health, toxicology, industrial hygiene and safety, pollution, carcinogens, chemistry, engineering, buildings materials, business, health, safety. **Special Collections:** Asbestos, silica, and man-made vitreous fibers; medical-scientific papers (38 lateral file drawers). **Holdings:** 8000 books and government agency reports; 26 VF drawers of internal reports; 14 VF drawers of patents. **Subscriptions:** 164 journals and other serials. **Services:** Center not open to the public. **Computerized Information Services:** BRS Information Technologies, DIALOG Information Services, MEDLINE,

LEXIS, NEXIS, Dow Jones News/Retrieval, VU/TEXT Information Services, STN International; internal database. **Publications:** Infosource, monthly - for internal distribution only; current awareness bulletins. **Remarks:** FAX: (303)978-5094. Library located at 10100 W. Ute St., Littleton, CO 80127. **Formed by the merger of:** Manville Sales Corporation - HS & E/Technical Information Center and its Technical Information Center. **Staff:** Pat Klug, Int.Rec.Spec.; Roseanne Grow, Ref.Asst.

★ 10969 ★
Napa County Historical Society - Library (Hist)
Goodman Library Bldg.
1219 1st St.   Phone: (707)224-1739
Napa, CA 94559   Jess Doud, Exec.Dir.
Founded: 1975. **Staff:** 12. **Subjects:** Napa County history. **Holdings:** 2500 books; 3000 pictures; 210 boxes of newspaper clippings and ephemera; 50 linear feet of scrapbooks, diaries, manuscripts; artifacts and tools; Napa Register, 1954 to present; Napa Journal, 1890-1960; St. Helena Star, 1975 to present; Napa Valley Times, 1985-1989. **Subscriptions:** 2 newspapers. **Services:** Copying; library open to the public. **Publications:** Gleanings and Sketches, annual - to members or for sale. **Staff:** Dorothy Soderholm, Libn.; Helen Roberts, Photo.Archv.; Diane Ballard, Adm.Asst.

★ 10970 ★
Napa County Law Library (Law)
Old Courthouse
825 Brown St.   Phone: (707)253-4436
Napa, CA 94559   Maxine Oellien, Law Libn.
Subjects: Law. **Holdings:** Figures not available. **Services:** Library open to the public for reference use only.

★ 10971 ★
Napa State Hospital - Wrenshall A. Oliver Professional Library (Med)
2100 Napa-Vallejo Hwy.   Phone: (707)253-5477
Napa, CA 94558   Barbara Fetesoff, Sr.Libn.
Founded: 1875. **Staff:** Prof 1; Other 1. **Subjects:** Psychiatry, psychiatric social work, psychiatric nursing, neurology, clinical psychology. **Special Collections:** Argens Memorial Collection (history of psychiatry and psychology); Laskay Collection (contemporary psychotherapies). **Holdings:** 9000 books; 901 bound periodical volumes; 800 tape cassettes. **Subscriptions:** 128 journals and other serials. **Services:** Interlibrary loan; copying; library open to mental health professionals. **Computerized Information Services:** MEDLARS. **Networks/Consortia:** Member of National Network of Libraries of Medicine - Pacific Southwest Region, Northern California and Nevada Medical Library Group (NCNMLG). **Publications:** Recent Additions to the Library.

★ 10972 ★
Napa Valley Genealogical & Biographical Society - Library (Hist)
Box 385   Phone: (707)252-9829
Napa, CA 94559   Dolores Hibbert, Libn.
Founded: 1975. **Subjects:** Genealogy. **Special Collections:** Horace Davis Collection (books; vital records). **Holdings:** 5000 books; Hartford Times; family and surname files. **Services:** Copying; library open to the public on fee basis. **Publications:** Wine Press (newsletter), monthly. **Remarks:** Library located at 1701 Menlo Ave., Napa, CA.

★ 10973 ★
Napa Valley Wine Library Association - Library (Food-Bev)
1492 Library Ln.   Phone: (707)963-5244
St. Helena, CA 94574   Mrs. Clayla Davis, Lib.Dir.
Founded: 1962. **Staff:** 7. **Subjects:** Grapes, viticulture, wine and winemaking. **Special Collections:** Wine labels (1500). **Holdings:** 6000 books; 200 bound periodical volumes; 12 VF drawers; 99 reels of microfilm. **Subscriptions:** 80 journals and other serials. **Services:** Interlibrary loan; copying; library open to the public. **Automated Operations:** Computerized circulation. **Computerized Information Services:** OCLC; OnTyme Electronic Message Network Service (electronic mail service). **Networks/Consortia:** Member of North Bay Cooperative Library System (NBCLS). **Publications:** Napa Valley wine library bibliography. **Remarks:** Library located at St. Helena Public Library, 1492 Library Lane. FAX: (707)963-5264. Electronic mail address(es): STHEL (OnTyme Electronic Message Network Service). **Staff:** Joyce Milton, Asst.Lib.Dir.; Allie LaCentra, Pub.Serv.Libn.

★ 10974 ★
Naperville Sun - Sun News Library (Publ)
9 W. Jackson Ave.   Phone: (708)355-0063
Naperville, IL 60566   Laurie K. Kagann, News Libn.
Founded: 1986. **Staff:** Prof 1; Other 1. **Subjects:** Newspaper reference topics. **Holdings:** 100 bound volumes of Sun newspapers; back issues of Sun newspapers on microfilm. **Services:** Interlibrary loan; copying; library open to the public with restrictions. **Computerized Information Services:** Internal database. **Networks/Consortia:** Member of DuPage Library System. **Publications:** Newsletter - for internal distribution only. **Remarks:** FAX: (708)355-2432.

★ 10975 ★
Naples Daily News - Library (Publ)
1075 Central Ave.   Phone: (813)263-4796
Naples, FL 33940   Gerald Johnson, Libn.
Founded: 1969. **Staff:** Prof 1. **Subjects:** Newspaper reference topics. **Holdings:** 200 books; 230,000 news clippings; 6500 photographs. **Subscriptions:** 3 journals and other serials. **Services:** Interlibrary loan; library not open to the public. **Remarks:** FAX: (813)263-4816.

★ 10976 ★
Naprstek Museum of Asian, African and American Cultures - Library (Area-Ethnic)
Betlemske nam 1   Phone: 2 227691
CS-110 00 Prague, Czechoslovakia   Dr. Jakub Karfik
Founded: 1862. **Staff:** Prof 4; Other 1. **Subjects:** Ethnology; non-European cultures, arts, and literature; archeology; numismatics. **Special Collections:** Historical photos (40,000); historical interior (1500 items); graphics (10,000); library prints and newspapers (7000 volumes); archives of foreign Czechoslovaks (40,000 items); archives of Czech travelers (15,000 items). **Holdings:** 80,000 books; 10,000 bound periodical volumes; 60,000 archives. **Subscriptions:** 300 journals and other serials. **Services:** Interlibrary loan; copying; library open to the public for reference use only. **Special Catalogs:** Catalog of the prints and periodicals of foreign Czechoslovaks. **Remarks:** Alternate telephone number(s): 2 227692. **Also Known As:** Naprstkova Muzeum Asijskych Africkych a Americkych Kultur - Knihovna.

Naprstkovo Muzeum Asijskych Africkych a Americkych Kultur - Knihovna
See: **Naprstek Museum of Asian, African and American Cultures - Library** (10976)

J.T. Naramore Library
See: **Larned State Hospital** (8954)

★ 10977 ★
Narcotic & Drug Research Inc. - Resource Center (Med)
11 Beach St., 2nd Fl.   Phone: (212)966-8700
New York, NY 10013-2429   Betty Gee, Rsrc.Ctr.Coord.
Founded: 1976. **Staff:** Prof 2; Other 2. **Subjects:** Drug abuse, addiction treatment, pharmacology, counseling, training, AIDS. **Special Collections:** NIDA and OSAP pamphlets and reports. **Holdings:** 1500 books; 8000 VF materials; 150 computer searches. **Subscriptions:** 75 journals and other serials. **Services:** Copying; center open to the public by appointment for reference use only. **Computerized Information Services:** DIALOG Information Services. **Networks/Consortia:** Member of Regional Alcohol and Drug Abuse Resource Network (RADAR), New York Metropolitan Reference and Research Library Agency, Substance Abuse Librarians and Information Specialists (SALIS). **Remarks:** The center will provide printed material on substance abuse on request. FAX: (212)941-1539. **Staff:** Judith M. Lukin.

NARIC
See: **National Rehabilitation Information Center** (11265)

Narodni Lekarska Knihovna
See: **Czechoslovakia - National Library of Medicine** (4515)

Narodni Muzej - Biblioteka
See: **Yugoslavia - National Museum in Belgrade** (20829)

★ 10978 ★
Naropa Institute - Library (Rel-Phil, Hum)
2130 Arapahoe   Phone: (303)444-0202
Boulder, CO 80302   Tere Winters, Libn.
Founded: 1974. **Staff:** Prof 1; Other 1. **Subjects:** Buddhism, contemporary poetry. **Special Collections:** Lecture tapes of religious teachers and poets (3800); Tibetan Religious Texts. **Holdings:** 26,000 books. **Subscriptions:** 200 journals and other serials. **Services:** Interlibrary loan; library open to the public on fee basis. **Computerized Information Services:** OCLC. **Remarks:** FAX: (303)444-0410. **Staff:** Kathy Pope.

★ 10979 ★
NASA - Ames Research Center - Dryden Flight Research Facility - Library (Sci-Engr)
Box 273   Phone: (805)258-3702
Edwards AFB, CA 93523   Karen Puffer, Libn.
Staff: Prof 1; Other 1. **Subjects:** Flight research, aerodynamics, flight testing and systems, aerospace medicine and human factors, instrumentation, aerostructures, propulsion, data systems. **Holdings:** 3500 books; 2400 bound periodical volumes; microfiche; reports. **Subscriptions:** 120 journals and other serials. **Services:** Interlibrary loan; copying; library open to the public with restrictions. **Automated Operations:** Computerized cataloging, acquisitions, serials, and circulation. **Computerized Information Services:** DIALOG Information Services, NASA/RECON; NASAMAIL (electronic mail service). **Networks/Consortia:** Member of NASA Aerospace Research Information Network (ARIN). **Remarks:** FAX: (805)258-5244. Alternate telephone number(s): 258-3127.

★ 10980 ★
NASA - Ames Research Center - Library (Sci-Engr, Comp Sci)
Moffett Field, Mail Stop 202-3   Phone: (415)604-6325
Mountain View, CA 94035-1000   Mary Walsh, Chf., Lib.Br.
Founded: 1940. **Staff:** Prof 11; Other 12. **Subjects:** Aeronautics, astrophysics, geophysics, aerospace sciences, life sciences, fluid mechanics and dynamics, computers and simulation, navigation and control, mathematics, physics. **Special Collections:** NACA and NASA documents, 1915 to present. **Holdings:** 104,000 books; 75,000 bound periodical volumes; 101,000 technical reports; 980,000 technical reports on microfiche. **Subscriptions:** 1700 journals and other serials. **Services:** Interlibrary loan; library open to the public for reference use only. **Automated Operations:** Computerized cataloging. **Computerized Information Services:** DTIC, NASA/RECON, DIALOG Information Services, MEDLINE, OCLC; ARIN (internal database); OnTyme Electronic Message Network Service, DIALMAIL (electronic mail services). **Networks/Consortia:** Member of NASA Aerospace Research Information Network (ARIN). **Special Catalogs:** Catalog of NACA and NASA documents on 16mm microfilm, 1915-1962. **Remarks:** Alternate telephone number(s): 604-6325. FAX: (415)604-4988. **Staff:** Esther Johnson, Life Sci.Libn.; Betsy Sandford, Hd. Cat.Libn.; Doreen Cohen Lib.Proj.Mgr.; Deirdre Campbell, Lib.Proj.Mgr.; Donna Yung, Cat.Libn.; Dan Pappas, Ref.Libn.; Eric Scholl, Ref.Libn.; Robert Schwier, Ref.Libn.; Catherine Andrejak, Acq.Libn.; Jeanette Johnson, Info.Sci.Libn.

★ 10981 ★
NASA - Computer Software Management & Information Center (COSMIC) (Comp Sci)
University of Georgia
382 E. Broad St.   Phone: (404)542-3265
Athens, GA 30602   Pat Mortenson, Mktg.Coord.
Founded: 1966. **Staff:** Prof 8; Other 10. **Subjects:** NASA-developed computer software. **Holdings:** 1200 computer programs. **Services:** Software distribution. **Computerized Information Services:** InterNet, BITNET (electronic mail services). **Special Catalogs:** COSMIC Software Catalog, annual; Microcomputer Catalog. **Remarks:** FAX: (404)542-4807. Electronic mail address(es): COSMIC@UGA (BITNET); SERVICE@COSSACK.COSMIC.UGA.EDU (InterNet).

★ 10982 ★
NASA - Goddard Institute for Space Studies - Library (Sci-Engr)
2880 Broadway   Phone: (212)678-5613
New York, NY 10025   Dahlia Oller, Mgr.
Founded: 1961. **Staff:** Prof 1; Other 1. **Subjects:** Physics, astronomy, astrophysics, meteorology, remote sensing. **Holdings:** 12,000 books; 7500 bound periodical volumes; 700 technical reports. **Subscriptions:** 250 journals and other serials. **Services:** Library open to institute scientists and staff. **Automated Operations:** Computerized circulation. **Computerized Information Services:** OCLC, NASA/RECON, DIALOG Information Services; BITNET (electronic mail service). **Networks/Consortia:** Member of NASA Aerospace Research Information Network (ARIN). **Remarks:** FAX: (212)678-5552. Electronic mail address(es): OPLIB@NASAGISS (BITNET).

★ 10983 ★
NASA - Goddard Space Flight Center - Library (Sci-Engr, Comp Sci)
Greenbelt, MD 20771   Phone: (301)286-7218
     Janet D. Ormes, Hd., Lib.Br.
Founded: 1959. **Staff:** Prof 5; Other 26. **Subjects:** Astronomy, physics, earth sciences, climatology, mathematics, computers, communication. **Holdings:** 70,000 books; 50,000 bound periodical volumes; 200,000 NASA reports on microfiche. **Subscriptions:** 1300 journals and other serials. **Services:** Interlibrary loan; copying; library open to the public. **Automated Operations:** Computerized public access catalog, cataloging, acquisitions, serials, and circulation. **Computerized Information Services:** OCLC, DIALOG Information Services, STN International, NASA/RECON; CD-ROM. **Networks/Consortia:** Member of NASA Aerospace Research Information Network (ARIN), FEDLINK. **Remarks:** FAX: (301)286-4217. **Staff:** John Boggess, Dp.Br.Hd.

★ 10984 ★
NASA - Headquarters S & T Library (Sci-Engr)
600 Independence Ave., S.W.
Code DBD-3   Phone: (202)453-8545
Washington, DC 20546   Joseph Langdon, Hd.Libn.
Founded: 1958. **Staff:** Prof 10; Other 5. **Subjects:** Aerospace, science, technology and policy-related social science, management. **Holdings:** 15,000 books; 400 bound periodical volumes; 2500 bound volumes of reports; 2000 unbound reports; 859,000 NASA microfiche. **Subscriptions:** 400 journals and other serials. **Services:** Interlibrary loan; library open to the public for research subject to security regulations. **Automated Operations:** Computerized public access catalog, acquisitions, cataloging, and circulation. **Computerized Information Services:** NASA/RECON, OCLC, Washington Alert Service, DIALOG Information Services, NewsNet, Inc., NEXIS, LEXIS, DataTimes, Aerospace Database. **Networks/Consortia:** Member of FEDLINK, NASA Aerospace Research Information Network (ARIN). **Remarks:** FAX: (202)755-9234 or (202)755-9235. **Staff:** Harry Needleman, Proj.Mgr.; Chris Ivancin, Cat.Libn.; John Vogel, Info.Sys.Mgr.; Marlene Duckworth, Acq.Libn.; Lynn Newbill, Lib.Mgr.; Joyce Stipe, Hd. of Ref.; Beverly Lehrer, Ref.Libn.; Tricia Porth, Ref.Libn.; Char Moss, Spec.Coll.Libn.

★ 10985 ★
NASA - John F. Kennedy Space Center - Library (Sci-Engr)
NWSI   Phone: (407)867-3600
Kennedy Space Center, FL 32899   W.G. Cooper, Hd.Libn.
Founded: 1962. **Staff:** Prof 8; Other 8. **Subjects:** Aerospace sciences. **Special Collections:** Kennedy Space Center Reports; archives; photograph collection. **Holdings:** 25,000 books; 4628 bound periodical volumes; 85,000 technical reports; 1.1 million microfiche; 255,000 specifications and standards; 20 VF drawers of pamphlets. **Subscriptions:** 3200 journals and other serials. **Services:** Interlibrary loan; copying (both limited); NASA SDI program; library open to the public with approval of proper KSC/NASA authority. **Computerized Information Services:** DIALOG Information Services, NASA/RECON, MEDLARS, NEXIS. **Networks/Consortia:** Member of NASA Aerospace Research Information Network (ARIN), Central Florida Library Consortium (CFLC), Florida Library Network (FLN). **Special Indexes:** Shuttle Index for the Space Transportation System; KSC Index of Specifications and Standards; Index to the Spaceport News. **Remarks:** FAX: (407)867-4534. **Staff:** D. Guelzow, Hd., Proc.; C. Wood, Hd., Rd./Ref.Serv.; D. Atkins, Hd., Docs.; K. Nail, Archv.; L. Lee, Specifications.

★ 10986 ★

NASA - Langley Research Center - Technical Library (Sci-Engr)
MS 185   Phone: (804)864-2356
Hampton, VA 23665-5225   George Roncaglia, Hd., Tech.Lib.Br.
Founded: 1920. **Staff:** Prof 18; Other 18. **Subjects:** Aeronautics, space
sciences and technology, engineering, physics and chemistry, electronics and
control, structural mechanics and materials, atmospheric sciences, computer
science, administration and management. **Holdings:** 95,500 books; 63,625
bound periodical volumes; 1.33 million microfiche; 1.33 million technical
reports; 254 audio cassettes; 1775 motion pictures; 426 video cassettes.
Subscriptions: 1226 journals and other serials. **Services:** Interlibrary loan;
copying; SDI; library open to the public. **Automated Operations:**
Computerized cataloging, acquisitions, serials, circulation, and ILL.
Computerized Information Services: NASA/RECON, RLIN, DIALOG
Information Services, DTIC, OCLC, NewsNet, Inc., WILSONLINE,
British Lending Library, STN International; NASAMAIL (electronic mail
service). Performs searches free of charge for NASA/RECON. Contact
Person: H. Garland Gouger, Subj. Searches. **Networks/Consortia:** Member
of NASA Aerospace Research Information Network (ARIN). **Publications:**
New Books, Documents, Journals, and Calls for Papers (acquisitions list).
Remarks: FAX: (804)864-2375. **Also Known As:** Floyd Thompson Library.
Staff: Carolyn E. Floyd, Ref.; Linn Landis, Circ./Acq.; Cecelia
Grzeskowiak, ILL; Carolyn Helmetsie, Ser.

★ 10987 ★

NASA - Lewis Research Center - Library (Sci-Engr, Energy)
21000 Brookpark Rd.   Phone: (216)433-5767
Cleveland, OH 44135   Leona T. Jarabek, Chf., Lib.Br.
Founded: 1942. **Staff:** Prof 7; Other 18. **Subjects:** Aeronautical and space
propulsion; space power, technology, communications; materials and
structures; energy sources. **Holdings:** 77,000 books; 31,400 bound periodical
volumes; 65,000 reports; 380,000 microfiche; 480 microfilm boxes.
Subscriptions: 1036 journals and other serials. **Services:** Interlibrary loan;
copying; SDI; library open to qualified persons. **Automated Operations:**
Computerized public access catalog, cataloging, and circulation.
Computerized Information Services: NASA/RECON, DIALOG
Information Services, STN International, PFDS Online, DTIC; internal
database; NASAMAIL (electronic mail service). **Networks/Consortia:**
Member of FEDLINK, NASA Aerospace Research Information Network
(ARIN). **Publications:** Lewis Library Services, April 1989; Library Journal
Holdings, april 1990. **Remarks:** FAX: (216)433-5777. **Staff:** Susanne F.
Oberc, Hd., Acq.; Jaclyn R. Facinelli, Acq. & User Serv.Libn.; Melanie C.
Long, Contract Serv.Libn.; Gregory Square, Ref.Libn.; Freya Turner, Cat.
& Ref.Libn.; Irene Shaland, Cat. & Ref.Libn.

★ 10988 ★

**NASA - Lyndon B. Johnson Space Center - Scientific & Technical
    Information Center Library/JM2** (Sci-Engr)
Houston, TX 77058   Phone: (713)483-4248
                                                 Laura Chiu, Lib.Supv.
Founded: 1962. **Staff:** Prof 8; Other 14. **Subjects:** Space sciences, space
vehicles, life sciences, space medicine, space shuttles, space station,
astronomy, astrophysics, navigation and guidance, telemetry, mathematics,
physics. **Holdings:** 42,000 books; 68,900 bound periodical volumes; 249,808
technical reports; 912,000 microfiche; 280 AV materials. **Subscriptions:** 500
journals and other serials. **Services:** Interlibrary loan; library not open to the
public. **Automated Operations:** Computerized public access catalog,
cataloging, and circulation. **Computerized Information Services:** NASA/
RECON, OCLC; CD-ROMs; DIS (Document Index System); internal
database). Performs searches. **Networks/Consortia:** Member of FEDLINK,
NASA Aerospace Research Information Network (ARIN). **Publications:**
JSC Technical Library User's Guide - available upon request. **Remarks:**
FAX: (713)483-2527. **Formerly:** Its Technical Library/JM2. **Staff:** Tom
Calkins, Info.Spec.; Carol Hoover, Info.Spec.; Sylvia Hu, Info.Spec. Lead;
Mary Jackson, Info.Spec. Lead; Aimee Patterson, Info.Spec.; Bob Guz,
NASA/JSC Libn.; Mary Wilkerson, ILL Libn.; John Stansbury, Auto
Lib.Libn.; Suzanne Daumas, Acq.Libn.

★ 10989 ★

NASA - Marshall Space Flight Center - MSFC Library (Sci-Engr)
Code CN22   Phone: (205)544-4524
Marshall Space Flight Center, AL 35812   Deborah R. Wills, Libn.
Founded: 1960. **Staff:** Prof 1; Other 2. **Subjects:** Space flight, astronautics,
space processing, engineering, science. **Holdings:** 4500 books; 820 bound
periodical volumes; 80,000 documents; 700,000 NASA microfiche; NASA
Information Center for Freedom of Information. **Subscriptions:** 125 journals
and other serials. **Services:** Library not open to the public. **Computerized
Information Services:** DIALOG Information Services, NASA/RECON.
Networks/Consortia: Member of NASA Aerospace Research Information
Network (ARIN).

★ 10990 ★

NASA - Wallops Flight Facility - Technical Library 250 PT 9 (Sci-Engr)
Wallops Island, VA 23337   Phone: (804)824-1540
                                                 Bobbi Eddy, Lib.Adm.
Founded: 1959. **Staff:** Prof 2; Other 3. **Subjects:** Aerospace, electronics,
mathematics, engineering, technology, physics. **Holdings:** 18,801 books;
4699 bound periodical volumes; 655,724 microfiche; 27,719 technical
reports. **Subscriptions:** 345 journals and other serials. **Services:** Interlibrary
loan; library open to the public by appointment. **Automated Operations:**
Computerized public access catalog, cataloging, and circulation.
Computerized Information Services: NASA/RECON, DIALOG
Information Services, OCLC. **Networks/Consortia:** Member of NASA
Aerospace Research Information Network (ARIN). **Publications:** Booster
(new books list), monthly - for internal distribution only. **Remarks:** FAX:
(804)824-1716.

NASA - World Data Center A - Rockets & Satellites
See: **World Data Center A - Rockets & Satellites - National Space
    Science Data Center** (20616)

NASA Industrial Application Center (NIAC)
See: **University of Southern California** (19342)

NASA Industrial Applications Center (NIAC)
See: **University of Pittsburgh** (19219)

★ 10991 ★

NASA Library - John C. Stennis Space Center (Sci-Engr, Comp Sci)
Bldg. 1100, Rm. S170A   Phone: (601)688-3244
Stennis Space Center, MS 39529-6000   Hannah Cake, Chf.Libn.
Founded: 1964. **Staff:** Prof 2; Other 2. **Subjects:** Remote sensing, computers,
cryogenics, electronics, environmental science and technology, marine
science, space technology. **Holdings:** 10,000 books; 3300 reports.
Subscriptions: 300 journals and other serials. **Services:** Interlibrary loan;
copying; SDI; library open to the public on request. **Automated Operations:**
Computerized public access catalog, cataloging, and circulation.
Computerized Information Services: BRS Information Technologies, PFDS
Online, NASA/RECON, DIALOG Information Services, OCLC;
NASAMAIL (electronic mail service). **Networks/Consortia:** Member of
FEDLINK, NASA Aerospace Research Information Network (ARIN).
Remarks: Alternate telephone number(s): (601)688-1358. FAX: (601)688-
1482. **Staff:** Erlinda Nye, Asst.Chf.Libn.

NASA Space Life Sciences Archive
See: **Houston Academy of Medicine - Texas Medical Center Library**
    (7445)

NASA Teacher Resource Center
See: **Murray State University - Libraries** (10871)

NASA Technical Information Center
See: **Technology Transfer Society** (16047)

★ 10992 ★

NASA/University of Kentucky - Technology Applications Center
109 Kinkead Hall
Lexington, KY 40506-0057
Founded: 1976. **Subjects:** Aerospace, engineering, business, patents.
Holdings: 200 books; 20 bound periodical volumes; 80,000 reports on
microfiche. **Remarks:** Currently inactive.

C.H. Nash Museum Library
See: **Memphis State University** (10069)

★ 10993 ★
Nashoba Community Hospital - Medical Library (Med)
200 Groton Rd.   Phone: (508)772-0200
Ayer, MA 01432   Mary Ann Finnegan, Libn.
Staff: Prof 1; Other 2. **Subjects:** Medicine, nursing. **Holdings:** 500 books;
400 bound periodical volumes. **Subscriptions:** 35 journals and other serials.
Services: Interlibrary loan; copying; library open to local health
professionals and students only. **Networks/Consortia:** Member of Central
Massachusetts Consortium of Health Related Libraries (CMCHRL).

★ 10994 ★
Nashotah House Seminary - Library (Rel-Phil)
2777 Mission Rd.   Phone: (414)646-3371
Nashotah, WI 53058-9793   Michael J. Tolan, Libn.
Founded: 1842. **Staff:** Prof 1; Other 2. **Subjects:** Theology, Bible, church
history. **Holdings:** 70,000 books; 13,500 bound periodical volumes.
Subscriptions: 250 journals and other serials. **Services:** Interlibrary loan;
copying; library open to the public with restrictions. **Automated Operations:**
Computerized cataloging. **Computerized Information Services:** OCLC.
Networks/Consortia: Member of Library Council of Metropolitan
Milwaukee, Inc. (LCOMM), Southeastern Wisconsin Information
Technology Exchange (SWITCH). **Formerly:** Nashotah House - Library.

★ 10995 ★
Nashua Corporation - Technical Library (Sci-Engr)
44 Franklin St.   Phone: (603)880-2537
Nashua, NH 03061   Kay Marquis, Tech.Lib.Supv.
Founded: 1963. **Staff:** Prof 2. **Subjects:** Magnetic media, polymers, paper
converters, toners, tapes, labels. **Holdings:** 5500 books; 200 bound periodical
volumes; reports; patents; foreign patents; annual reports. **Subscriptions:**
125 journals and other serials; 7 newspapers. **Services:** Interlibrary loan;
library not open to the public. **Computerized Information Services:**
DIALOG Information Services; internal database. **Remarks:** FAX:
(603)880-2541.

★ 10996 ★
Nashua Memorial Hospital - Health Sciences Library (Med)
8 Prospect St.
P.O. Box 2014
Nashua, NH 03061-2014   Phone: (603)883-5521
                                 Janis Isaacson Silver, Libn.
Staff: Prof 1. **Subjects:** Medicine, nursing, and allied health sciences.
Holdings: 1000 books; 1920 bound periodical volumes; 30 videotapes; 600
VF items. **Subscriptions:** 131 journals and other serials. **Services:**
Interlibrary loan; copying; library open to the public by appointment for
research only. **Computerized Information Services:** NLM, BRS Information
Technologies; DOCLINE (electronic mail service). Performs searches on fee
basis.

★ 10997 ★
Nashua Peace Center - Library (Soc Sci)
22 Meade St.   Phone: (603)889-0049
Nashua, NH 03060   Thomas R. Wall, Dir.
Founded: 1985. **Subjects:** Peace, economic justice, war tax resistance,
nonviolence, Central America, nuclear power, alternative energy. **Holdings:**
500 books; 200 bound periodical volumes; photographs; slide shows; posters;
videotapes. **Subscriptions:** 19 journals and other serials. **Services:** Library
open to the public by appointment. **Computerized Information Services:**
Internal database.

★ 10998 ★
Nashua Public Library - Chandler Memorial Library and Ethnic Center
   (Area-Ethnic)
257 Main St.   Phone: (603)594-3415
Nashua, NH 03060   Margaret Merrigan, Libn.
Staff: Prof 3; Other 1. **Subjects:** Ethnic groups in the U.S., foreign languages.
Special Collections: French collection; Lithuanian collection. **Holdings:**
7000 books. **Subscriptions:** 42 journals and other serials; 14 newspapers.
Services: Interlibrary loan; center open to the public. **Networks/Consortia:**
Member of Nashua Area Materials Exchange (NAME). **Publications:**
Calendar of events, bimonthly.

★ 10999 ★
Nashville Banner - Library (Publ)
1100 Broadway   Phone: (615)259-8225
Nashville, TN 37202   Sally Moran, Libn.
Founded: 1938. **Staff:** Prof 1; Other 2. **Subjects:** Newspaper reference topics.
Holdings: 400 books; 50,000 photographs; clippings. **Services:** Library not
open to the public.

★ 11000 ★
Nashville and Davidson County Metropolitan Planning Commission -
   Library (Plan)
Lindsley Hall
730 2nd Ave., S.   Phone: (615)862-7150
Nashville, TN 37201   Maxie Starks
Staff: Prof 1. **Subjects:** Urban planning, demography, economics,
environment, transportation, zoning, census. **Special Collections:**
Commission archives; Citizen's Resource Center. **Holdings:** 7550 books; 45
bound periodical volumes; 250 documents and archival materials; U.S.
Bureau of Census studies. **Subscriptions:** 214 journals and other serials.
Services: Interlibrary loan; library open to the public. **Computerized
Information Services:** Internal database. **Publications:** Acquisition List,
monthly; Agency Books and Reports. **Remarks:** FAX: (615)259-6268.

★ 11001 ★
Nashville Metropolitan Department of Public Health - Lentz Health
   Center Library (Med)
311 23rd Ave., N.   Phone: (615)862-5900
Nashville, TN 37203   Feli C. Propes, Libn.
Founded: 1967. **Staff:** Prof 1. **Subjects:** Internal medicine, public health,
nursing, environmental health. **Holdings:** 2000 volumes. **Subscriptions:** 123
journals and other serials. **Services:** Interlibrary loan; library not open to the
public. **Computerized Information Services:** DIALOG Information
Services, MEDLARS. **Networks/Consortia:** Member of Tennessee Health
Science Library Association (THeSLA). **Publications:** Current Serials List,
annual. **Remarks:** FAX: (615)340-5665.

★ 11002 ★
Nashville State Technical Institute - Library (Educ)
120 White Bridge Rd.   Phone: (615)353-3555
Nashville, TN 37209   Carolyn Householder, Hd.
Founded: 1970. **Staff:** Prof 6; Other 5. **Subjects:** Electronic data processing,
science and engineering technology, business, architecture, photography.
Holdings: 36,000 books; 406 bound periodical volumes; 9540 microfiche.
Subscriptions: 462 journals and other serials; 10 newspapers. **Services:**
Interlibrary loan; copying; center open to the public for reference use only.
Automated Operations: Computerized cataloging, acquisitions, serials,
circulation, and reserves. **Computerized Information Services:** DIALOG
Information Services. **Networks/Consortia:** Member of SOLINET.
Remarks: FAX: (615)353-3558. **Staff:** James R. Veatch, Hd., Tech.Serv.;
Harriet Dunn, Pub.Serv.; Charles May, Pub.Serv.Libn.; Pepper Bruce,
Pub.Serv.; Sara Maxwell, Lrng.Lab.Coord.

Nasjonalgalleriets Bibliotek
See: **Norwegian National Gallery - Library** (12114)

Nassau Academy of Medicine
See: **Nassau County Medical Society - Nassau Academy of Medicine**
   (11007)

★ 11003 ★
Nassau Community College - New York State Health Film Collection
   (Aud-Vis)
Garden City, NY 11530   Phone: (516)222-7406
                                       Arthur L. Friedman, Cur.
Staff: Prof 2; Other 1. **Subjects:** Health. **Holdings:** 2334 16mm films;
filmstrips; slides; overhead transparencies. **Services:** Interlibrary loan;
collection open to the public. **Special Catalogs:** Film catalogs, irregular - free
upon request. **Remarks:** FAX: (516)222-7607.

★11004★
Nassau County Department of Health - Division of Laboratories & Research - Medical Library (Med)
209 Main St.   Phone: (516)483-9158
Hempstead, NY 11550   Douglas S. Lieberman, Libn.
Founded: 1959. **Staff:** Prof 1. **Subjects:** Laboratory diagnosis, communicable diseases, environmental health. **Holdings:** 1000 books; 2500 bound periodical volumes; 1800 microfilm cartridges; microfiche of previous two years of journals. **Subscriptions:** 60 journals and other serials. **Services:** Interlibrary loan; library not open to the public. **Computerized Information Services:** MEDLARS. **Networks/Consortia:** Member of Medical & Scientific Libraries of Long Island (MEDLI), Long Island Library Resources Council. **Remarks:** FAX: (516)248-6576.

★11005★
Nassau County Department of Health - Library (Med)
240 Old Country Rd., Rm. 613   Phone: (516)535-3470
Mineola, NY 11501   Douglas S. Lieberman, Libn.
Staff: 1. **Subjects:** Public health. **Holdings:** 1000 books; 259 reels of microfilm of journals; microfiche; Nassau County Department of Health publications, monthly and annual reports. **Subscriptions:** 60 journals and other serials. **Services:** Interlibrary loan; copying; library open to the public for reference use only. **Computerized Information Services:** MEDLINE. **Networks/Consortia:** Member of Medical & Scientific Libraries of Long Island (MEDLI), Long Island Library Resources Council. **Remarks:** FAX: (516)248-6576.

Nassau County Department of Recreation and Parks - Tackapausha Museum
See: **Tackapausha Museum** (15978)

★11006★
Nassau County Medical Center - Health Sciences Library (Med)
2201 Hempstead Tpke.   Phone: (516)542-3542
East Meadow, NY 11554   William F. Casey, Lib.Dir.
Founded: 1935. **Staff:** Prof 3; Other 5. **Subjects:** Medicine, nursing, and allied health sciences. **Special Collections:** Pathology; radiology. **Holdings:** 9000 books; 6000 bound periodical volumes; 100 AV programs. **Subscriptions:** 700 journals and other serials. **Services:** Interlibrary loan; library open to the public for reference use only. **Computerized Information Services:** CD-ROMs (MEDLINE, CINAHL, HealthLine, CANCERLIT). **Networks/Consortia:** Member of Medical Library Center of New York (MLCNY), Medical & Scientific Libraries of Long Island (MEDLI), BHSL. **Remarks:** FAX: (516)542-5788. **Staff:** Joan S. Hust, Med.Libn.; Sharon Barton, Med.Libn.

★11007★
Nassau County Medical Society - Nassau Academy of Medicine - John N. Shell Library (Med)
1200 Stewart Ave.   Phone: (516)832-2320
Garden City, NY 11530   Mary L. Westermann, Cons.
Founded: 1964. **Staff:** Prof 1; Other 3. **Subjects:** Medicine, psychiatry, nursing. **Special Collections:** Consumer health. **Holdings:** 8000 books; 45,000 bound periodical volumes; 3 VF drawers. **Subscriptions:** 500 journals and other serials. **Services:** Interlibrary loan; copying; SDI; library open to the public for reference use only. **Computerized Information Services:** DIALOG Information Services, MEDLARS. Performs searches on fee basis. **Networks/Consortia:** Member of Medical & Scientific Libraries of Long Island (MEDLI). **Remarks:** FAX: (516)832-8183.

Nassau County Museum Reference Library - Long Island Studies Institute
See: **Hofstra University - Library - Special Collections** (7316)

★11008★
Nassau County Planning Commission - Library (Plan)
400 County Seat Dr.   Phone: (516)535-5953
Mineola, NY 11501   Robert A. Gaiser, Sr.Plan.
Founded: 1950. **Staff:** Prof 1. **Subjects:** Planning, population, environment, industry, zoning, land use, conservation, transportation, history. **Special Collections:** Census (60 printouts). **Holdings:** 5000 volumes. **Services:** Library open to the public. **Computerized Information Services:** Internal database. **Publications:** Annual Report; Data Book; Census volumes; professional reports. **Remarks:** FAX: (516)535-3839.

★11009★
Nassau County Police Department - Police Academy - Library (Law)
Cross St.
Williston Park, NY 11596   Phone: (516)573-7000
Staff: 3. **Subjects:** Police science, criminal justice. **Holdings:** Books; periodicals; 6 VF drawers. **Services:** Library not open to the public.

★11010★
Nassau County Supreme Court - Law Library (Law)
100 Supreme Court Dr.   Phone: (516)535-3883
Mineola, NY 11501   James J. Lodato, Prin. Law Libn.
Founded: 1968. **Staff:** Prof 2; Other 9. **Subjects:** Law. **Holdings:** 288,968 books; 12,627 reels of microfilm; 150,082 microfiche; 14,411 microcards. **Subscriptions:** 1358 journals and other serials. **Services:** Library open to the public. **Automated Operations:** Computerized cataloging. **Computerized Information Services:** OCLC. **Publications:** Ex Libris; Nassau Lawyer, monthly. **Remarks:** Alternate telephone number(s): 535-3884. **Staff:** Barbara Oberlander, Law Libn.

Nassau Educational Resource and Planning Center (NERPC)
See: **Board of Cooperative Educational Services of Nassau County (BOCES)** (1923)

Natchez Trace Parkway
See: **U.S. Natl. Park Service** (17757)

★11011★
Nathan Associates, Inc. - Library (Bus-Fin)
2101 Wilson Blvd., Suite 1200   Phone: (703)516-7750
Arlington, VA 22201   Rhea C. Austin, Libn.
Staff: Prof 1. **Subjects:** Economics - antitrust, telecommunications, international. **Holdings:** 5000 books; 100 bound periodical volumes; 15,000 pamphlets and government documents. **Subscriptions:** 300 journals and other serials; 6 newspapers. **Services:** Interlibrary loan; library open to other libraries by special permission. **Computerized Information Services:** DIALOG Information Services, Data-Star, Dun & Bradstreet Business Credit Services, NEXIS, OCLC, ORBIT Search Service, Dow Jones News/Retrieval, WILSONLINE. **Remarks:** FAX: (703)351-6162. Telex: 248 482 NATC UR. **Formerly:** Robert R. Nathan Associates, Inc. - RRNA Research Library, located in Washington, DC.

★11012★
Natick Historical Society - Library (Hist)
Bacon Free Library Bldg.   Phone: (508)653-6730
South Natick, MA 01760   Anne K. Schaller, Dir.
Founded: 1870. **Staff:** Prof 1; Other 3. **Subjects:** Local history, vital records of Massachusetts towns. **Special Collections:** Harriet Beecher Stowe Collection; John Eliot Indian Bible; Horatio Alger Collection; Henry Wilson Collection (U.S. Vice-President under Ulysses S. Grant); old natural history books. **Holdings:** 500 books. **Services:** Copying; library open to the public for reference use only. **Publications:** The Arrow, quarterly - to members only. **Staff:** Iola C. Scheufele, Cur./Libn.

★11013★
National 4-H Council - Resource Center (Soc Sci)
7100 Connecticut Ave.   Phone: (301)961-2881
Chevy Chase, MD 20815   Margaret L. Emerson, Cons.
Founded: 1977. **Staff:** Prof 1; Other 1. **Subjects:** History of 4-H, citizenship, leadership, youth development, current 4-H projects. **Special Collections:** Historical information on National 4-H Service Committee, National 4-H Foundation, National 4-H Congress, National 4-H Conference; International Four-H Youth Exchange. **Holdings:** 1200 books; 50 bound periodical volumes; 280 file drawers; 5 storage cabinets of films, tapes, slides; 12 shelves of photographs; 56 shelves of printed educational materials. **Services:** Interlibrary loan; copying; center open to the public with permission. **Special Catalogs:** Subject catalog of studies concerning 4-H and the U.S.D.A. Cooperative Extension System (card). **Remarks:** Alternate telephone number(s): 961-2879. FAX: (301)961-2937.

★11014★
National Abortion Federation - Resource Center (Soc Sci)
1436 U St., N.W., Suite 103
Washington, DC 20009　　　　　Phone: (202)667-5881
Founded: 1977. **Staff:** 1. **Subjects:** Abortion, contraception, sexuality, sociology, health, medicine, sexually transmitted diseases. **Holdings:** 225 volumes; symposia publications; 5000 clippings; audiocassettes. **Subscriptions:** 5 journals and other serials; 3 newspapers. **Services:** Center not open to the public. **Computerized Information Services:** Internal database. **Remarks:** FAX: (202)667-5890.

★11015★
National Academic Advising Association - Archives (Educ)
Iowa State University
204 Carver Hall　　　　　Phone: (515)294-4729
Ames, IA 50011　　　　　James D. Beatty, Archv.
Founded: 1981. **Staff:** Prof 1. **Subjects:** Academic advisement. **Holdings:** 2 cubic feet of archival materials. **Services:** Archives open to scholars for reference use only.

★11016★
National Academy of Design - Library and Archives (Art)
1083 Fifth Ave.　　　　　Phone: (212)369-4880
New York, NY 10128　　　　　Barbara S. Krulik, Dp.Dir.
Founded: 1826. **Subjects:** American art, art history. **Holdings:** 4250 volumes. **Services:** Library and archives open to students and scholars by appointment. **Remarks:** FAX: (212)360-6795.

National Academy of Engineering
See: **National Research Council** (11268)

National Academy of Sciences
See: **National Research Council** (11268)

National Academy of Sciences of Buenos Aires - Darwinian Institute of Botany
See: **Darwinian Institute of Botany** (4618)

★11017★
National Academy of Social Insurance - Library (Soc Sci)
505 Capitol Ct., N.E., Suite 300　　　　　Phone: (202)547-9592
Washington, DC 20002　　　　　Pamela Larson, Exec.Dir.
Founded: 1987. **Subjects:** Social insurance, social security, workman's compensation, unemployment insurance, health care financing. **Holdings:** 1500 volumes; legislative histories. **Subscriptions:** 5 journals and other serials. **Services:** Interlibrary loan; copying; library open to the public. **Remarks:** FAX: (202)547-9595. **Staff:** Alison J. Rapping, Commun.Dir.

★11018★
National Adoption Center - Information Services (Soc Sci)
1218 Chestnut St.　　　　　Phone: (215)925-0200
Philadelphia, PA 19107　　　　　Carolyn Johnson
Founded: 1980. **Staff:** Prof 1; Other 1. **Subjects:** Adoption, foster care, child welfare. **Special Collections:** Special needs adoption; black adoption recruitment; foster care; searching for birthparents; adoption legislation; employee adoption benefits information. **Holdings:** 5000 books; 180 unbound materials; 60 AV programs. **Subscriptions:** 130 journals and newsletters; 5 newspapers. **Services:** Interlibrary loan; SDI; copying; services open to the public. **Computerized Information Services:** National Adoption Network. **Publications:** Adoption information packet for libraries. List of other publications - available on request. **Remarks:** Toll-free telephone number(s): (800)862-3678.

★11019★
National Aeronautic Association - Library (Sci-Engr)
1815 N. Ft. Myer Dr., Suite 700　　　　　Phone: (703)527-0226
Arlington, VA 22209　　　　　Arthur W. Greenfield, Jr.
Founded: 1905. **Staff:** Prof 1; Other 2. **Subjects:** Aviation. **Special Collections:** World and U.S. aviation records. **Holdings:** Completed dossiers on record flights. **Services:** Library not open to the public. **Publications:** NAA Newsletter, 6/yr; World and United States Aviation and Space Records, annual - both to members. **Remarks:** FAX: (703)527-0229.

National Aeronautics and Space Administration
See: **NASA** (10980)

★11020★
National Aftermarket Audit Company - Library (Trans)
P.O. Box 1509
Duxbury, MA 02331　　　　　Phone: (617)934-6577
Subjects: Vehicles - registration, parts replacement, aftermarket analysis. **Holdings:** 2000 bound volumes. **Subscriptions:** 20 journals and other serials. **Computerized Information Services:** Internal databases. **Publications:** Aftermarket Statistical Yearbook, annual.

National Agricultural Library
See: **U.S.D.A.** (17203)

National Agro-Industrial Union (of Bulgaria)
See: **Bulgaria - National Agro-Industrial Union** (2348)

National AIDS Committee (of Vietnam)
See: **Vietnam - Department of Hygiene and Environment - National AIDS Committee - Library** (19838)

National Air and Space Museum
See: **Smithsonian Institution Libraries** (15277)

★11021★
National Alliance of Senior Citizens - Library (Soc Sci)
2525 Wilson Blvd.　　　　　Phone: (202)986-0117
Arlington, VA 22201　　　　　Peter Luciano, Exec.Dir.
Staff: 8. **Subjects:** Aging, economics, political theory, reference, legal services, taxation, national defense, housing, welfare services, Social Security, Medicare, crime, criminal justice reform, women's equity. **Holdings:** 1850 books; 100 bound periodical volumes; extensive government hearings. **Services:** Library not open to the public. **Publications:** The Senior Guardian, monthly; Seniors, U.S.A., quarterly.

National Animal Disease Center
See: **U.S.D.A. - Agricultural Research Service** (17188)

National Anthropological Archives
See: **Smithsonian Institution** (15263)

★11022★
National Anti-Vivisection Society - Library (Soc Sci)
53 W. Jackson Blvd., Suite 1550　　　　　Phone: (312)427-6065
Chicago, IL 60604-3703　　　　　Michael J. Bello, Ph.D., Dir. of Educ.
Subjects: Vivisection. **Holdings:** Figures not available. **Remarks:** FAX: (312)427-6524. Society conducts educational program to acquaint the public with the "problems of vivisection of animals" and to teach the methods and means of alternatives to vivisection. Compiles statistics on laboratory experiments using animals, the purpose and cost of such experiments, and other facts.

★11023★
National Aquarium in Baltimore - A. Carter Middendorf Library (Biol Sci)
501 E. Pratt St., Pier 3　　　　　Phone: (301)659-4257
Baltimore, MD 21202　　　　　Cathy Womack, Staff Libn.
Founded: 1982. **Staff:** Prof 1; Other 3. **Subjects:** Marine science - fish, invertebrates, and mammals; tropical birds and rainforests. **Holdings:** 1500 books; NOAA Reports. **Subscriptions:** 50 journals and other serials. **Services:** Interlibrary loan; library not open to the public. **Computerized Information Services:** DIALOG Information Services. **Networks/Consortia:** Member of PALINET. **Remarks:** FAX: (301)576-8238.

National Archives of Bangladesh
See: **Bangladesh - National Archives of Bangladesh** (1465)

National Archives of Canada
See: **Canada - National Archives of Canada** (2770)

National Archives Collection of Afro-American Artists
See: **State University of New York - Syracuse Educational Opportunity Center - Paul Robeson Library** (15725)

National Archives of Finland
See: **Finland - National Archives** (5708)

National Archives (of Honduras)
See: **Honduras - National Archives** (7364)

National Archives of Iceland
See: **Thjodskjalasafn Islands** (16311)

National Archives of India
See: **India - National Archives of India** (7744)

National Archives (of Ireland)
See: **Republic of Ireland - National Archives** (13828)

National Archives of Namibia
See: **Namibia - National Archives of Namibia** (10960)

National Archives (of Nepal)
See: **Nepal - National Archives** (11391)

National Archives of Norway
See: **Norway - National Archives of Norway** (12104)

National Archives of Pakistan
See: **Pakistan - National Archives of Pakistan** (12694)

★11024★
National Archives & Records Administration - Center for Electronic Records (Hist)
8th & Constitution Ave., N.W.
Washington, DC 20408   Ken Thibodeau, Dir.
Founded: 1968. **Staff:** 30. **Subjects:** United States history, United States politics and government, Vietnam conflict, economics, demographics, finance, education, health services, international relations, military sciences, science, and technology. **Holdings:** 11,500 data sets. **Computerized Information Services:** NNXA Management Information System, Reference Management Sysytem, Reproduction System, Preservation Log, Tape administration, Preservation Evaluation System (internal databases). **Publications:** Partial and Preliminary Title List of Holdings; Information About the Center for Electronic Records (leaflet); Information About Electronic Records in the National Archives for Prospective Researchers (leaflet); reference information papers on various subjects. **Staff:** Margaret O. Adams; Bruce I. Ambacher; Thomas E. Brown; Ross J. Cameron; L. Mark Conrad; Dianne L. Dimkoff; Fynnette L. Eaton; Lee A. Gladwin; Linda J. Henry; Theodore J. Hull; Chauncey B. Jessup; Nancy Y. McGovern; Martha J. Merselis; Richard A. Noble; P. Dian Palmer; Crystal I. Revelle; Roberta S. Thornton; James A. Whittington.

★11025★
National Archives & Records Administration - Center for Legislative Archives (NNL) (Hist)
8th & Pennsylvania Ave., N.W.   Phone: (202)501-5350
Washington, DC 20408   Dr. Michael L. Gillette, Div.Dir.
Founded: 1988. **Subjects:** United States - history, politics, government. **Special Collections:** Publications of the U.S. Government (record group 287), 1789 to 1979. **Holdings:** 2.4 million items. **Services:** Copying; Center open to the public with restrictions. **Remarks:** FAX: (202)219-2176.

★11026★
National Archives & Records Administration - Library (NNRS-L) (Hist, Rare Book)
8th & Pennsylvania Ave., N.W.   Phone: (202)501-5415
Washington, DC 20408   Sharon Fawcett, Ref.Serv.Br.Chf.
Founded: 1934. **Staff:** Prof 7; Other 6. **Subjects:** United States biography, history, politics, and governement; archives, manuscripts and records management. **Special Collections:** Archives Library Information Center's collection of professional literature (160 linear feet); government publications, including congressional materials. **Holdings:** Branch contains over 200,000 items and is composed of three major collections. The first is a special collection on American biography, history, politics and government (2500 reference books). The second is the Archives Library Information Center (ALIC); its holdings are collected, organized, and made available as a service provided by the National Archives for the entire records community. The third collection consists of federal government publications arranged by the Superintendent of Documents classification system; publications selected for this collection relate to the organization, functions, duties, and history of federal agencies. **Subscriptions:** 700 journals and other serials. **Services:** Interlibrary loan of non-reference library holdings; copying; ALIC reference services by phone, mail, or in person; library open to the public with research pass. **Automated Operations:** Computerized cataloging and acquisitions. **Computerized Information Services:** RLIN, DIALOG Information Services, OCLC, WILSONLINE; Archives Library Information Center (ALIC; internal database). Performs searches free of charge for ALIC patrons. Contact: (202)501-5423. **Networks/Consortia:** Member of FEDLINK. **Publications:** Subject bibliographies; accession lists; ALIC Notes (newsletter), quarterly; catalogs; indexes. **Remarks:** FAX: (202)501-5005. Alternate telephone number(s): 501-5421. **Staff:** J. Thomas Converse, Chf.Libn.; Maryellen Trautman, Govt.Docs.Libn.; Lida Holland Churchville, ALIC Libn.; John Cornelius, Cat.; Caroline Ladeira, Ref.Libn.; Veronica Williams, Acq.Libn.; Jeff Hartley, Ref.Libn.

★11027★
National Archives & Records Administration - National Archives (Hist, Aud-Vis)
8th & Constitution Ave., N.W.   Phone: (202)501-5400
Washington, DC 20408   Dr. Don W. Wilson, Archv.
Founded: 1934. **Staff:** 625. **Subjects:** United States history, archives and manuscripts, genealogical research, government publications, United States politics and government. **Special Collections:** Printed Archives of the Federal Government (GPO Collection); Gift Collection; Polar Archives; film collections. **Holdings:** 1.64 million cubic feet of textual cartographic, audiovisual, and machine readable records, 1774 to present: 4 billion documents; 235,000 reels of microfilm; 170,000 reels of motion picture film; 180,000 sound recordings; 7 million still pictures; 2 million maps and charts; 9 million aerial photographs; 6000 magnetic computer electronic data sets. **Subscriptions:** 700 journals and other serials. **Services:** Copying; archives open to the public. **Publications:** List of publications - available on request. **Special Catalogs:** List of Special Catalogs - available on request. **Special Indexes:** List of Special Indexes - available on request. **Remarks:** FAX: (202)501-5005.

★11028★
National Archives & Records Administration - National Archives - Alaska Region (Soc Sci)
654 W. 3rd Ave., Rm. 012   Phone: (907)271-2441
Anchorage, AK 99501   Thomas E. Wiltsey
Founded: 1991. **Staff:** Prof 4. **Subjects:** U.S. District Courts, Bureau of Indian Affairs, Alaska Road Commision, Bureau of Land Management, U.S. Customs Service, Military. **Special Collections:** Records of federal agencies in Alaska. **Holdings:** 8000 cubic feet of archival items; 5000 sheets of microfiche; 53,000 reels of microfilm. **Subscriptions:** 6 journals and other serials. **Services:** Copying; library open to the public. **Publications:** Funding aids, inventories, guides to records and film holdings. **Remarks:** FAX: (907)271-2442. Alternate telephone number(s): (907)271-2443.

★ 11029 ★
National Archives & Records Administration - National Archives -
  Cartographic & Architectural Branch (Geog-Map, Plan)
8th & Pennsylvania Ave., N.W.   Phone: (703)756-6700
Washington, DC 20408   John A. Dwyer, Chf.
Founded: 1935. **Staff:** Prof 8; Other 8. **Subjects:** United States - history,
politics, government; cartography; aerial photography; maps; architectural
and engineering drawings. **Holdings:** 2 million maps and charts; 9 million
aerial photographs; 500,000 architectural and engineering drawings; 500
cubic feet of survey field notebooks and census enumeration district
descriptions; acquired or produced by federal agencies as part of their official
activities, including material relating to military operations, explorations,
public land surveys, and various civil works. **Subscriptions:** 15 journals and
other serials. **Services:** Copying; branch open to the public. **Computerized
Information Services:** Internal databases. **Publications:** Guides; inventories;
lists - limited supply is available for free distribution to libraries. **Remarks:**
Research room is located at 841 S. Pickett St., Alexandria, VA. **Staff:**
Charles E. Taylor, Supv., Proj.; Robert E. Richardson , Supv., Ref.

★ 11030 ★
National Archives & Records Administration - National Archives -
  Central Plains Region (Hist)
2312 E. Bannister Rd.   Phone: (816)926-6272
Kansas City, MO 64131   Diana L. Duff, Dir.
Founded: 1968. **Staff:** Prof 5; Other 7. **Subjects:** Noncurrent administrative
and program records of historical and informational value accessioned from
Federal Agencies in the states of Iowa, Nebraska, Kansas, Missouri, North
Dakota, and South Dakota. **Special Collections:** Pre-1900 records from the
Bureau of Customs, Geological Survey, Internal Revenue Service, Forest
Service, U.S. Coast Guard, U.S. Attorneys and Marshals, Weather Bureau,
U.S. Army Engineers; Bureau of Indian Affairs Reservations located in the
present states of North and South Dakota, Minnesota, Nebraska, and
Kansas, 1850-1965; United States District and Territorial Courts, 1824-
1965. **Holdings:** 30,000 cubic feet of records. **Services:** Copying; reference
service; reading rooms and research room open to the public. **Computerized
Information Services:** Archival Information Service (internal database).
Publications: Guide to Research in the Central Plains Region (book).
Special Catalogs: In-ho use archives inventories and shelf lists. **Remarks:**
FAX: (816)926-6235. **Staff:** Mark A. Corriston, Asst.Dir.

★ 11031 ★
National Archives & Records Administration - National Archives - Great
  Lakes Region (Hist)
7358 S. Pulaski Rd.   Phone: (312)581-7816
Chicago, IL 60629   Peter W. Bunce, Dir.
Founded: 1969. **Staff:** Prof 4; Other 5. **Subjects:** Federal Government
records for Illinois, Wisconsin, Michigan, Indiana, Ohio, Minnesota. **Special
Collections:** U.S. Circuit and District Courts, 1806-1974; Army Corps of
Engineers, 1833-1974; Bureau of Indian Affairs, 1870-1962; Internal
Revenue Service, 1867-1919; Immigration and Naturalization Service, index
to Chicago-area naturalizations, 1840-1950; Argonne National Laboratory,
1946-1970; U.S. Circuit Court of Appeals, 6th and 7th Circuits, 1891-1965;
War Manpower Commission, 1941-1945; Fish and Wildlife Service, 1880-
1969; Soil Conservation Service, 1953-1959; U.S. Attorneys precedent case
files, 1905-1971; Chinese immigration case files, 1894-1940; duplicate copies
of naturalizations in Cook County (IL) courts, 1871-1906; War Assets
Administration, 1945-1952; U.S. Coast Guard unit logs, 1959-1981; Federal
Highway Administration, 1920-1960; Bureau of Marine Inspection and
Navigation, 1850-1968; Public Health Service, Cleveland Marine Hospital,
1878-1922; Agricultural Research Service, 1937-1966; Selective Service
System, 1917-1919; Office of Housing Expediter, 1942-1953; Railroad
Retirement Board, 1938-1988; General Land Office (Bureau of Land
Management), 1800-1888; U.S. Naval Districts (9th) & Shore
Establishments (Great Lakes Naval Training Station; Glenview, IL Naval
Air Station & Naval Reserve Training Command), 1914-1957; U.S. Food
Administration, 1917-1919; National Mediation Board (Train Board files),
1921-1934; Farmers Home Administration, 1935-1947; Farm Credit
Administration, 1944-1951; National Archives Gift Collection (papers of
Federal judges), 1919-1977; Lewis Flight Propulsion Laboratory, Cleveland,
OH, 1943-1951; National War Labor Board, 1946-1947; Office of
Quartermaster General, 1874-1939; Committee on Fair Employment
Practice, 1941-1946. **Holdings:** 57,230 cubic feet of records; 40,000 reels of
microfilm. **Services:** Copying; genealogy workshops; teachers' workshops;
exhibit program; archives open to the public with restrictions. **Computerized
Information Services:** NARS A-1 (internal database). **Publications:** Guide
to Records in the National Archives - Great Lakes Region; Microfilm
Publications in the National Archives - Great Lakes Region - both available
on request. **Staff:** Shirley J. Burton, Asst.Dir.; Donald W. Jackanicz,
Archv.; Beverly Watkins, Archv.

★ 11032 ★
National Archives & Records Administration - National Archives - Mid-
  Atlantic Region (Hist)
9th & Market Sts.   Phone: (215)597-3000
Philadelphia, PA 19107   Robert J. Plowman, Dir.
Founded: 1969. **Staff:** Prof 7. **Subjects:** Archives and records of federal
agencies located in Pennsylvania, Delaware, Maryland, Virginia, and West
Virginia. **Special Collections:** Records of U.S. District Court, U.S. Court of
Appeals for 3rd and 4th Circuit, U.S. Corps of Engineers, Bureau of Census,
National Park Service, Bureau of Mines, U.S. Attorneys and Marshals,
Bureau of Customs. **Holdings:** 42,000 cubic feet of federal government
archives; 27,500 reels of microfilm. **Services:** Copying; branch open to the
public with restrictions, dependent on agency regulations. **Special Catalogs:**
List of microfilm holdings; list of textual record holdings. **Remarks:** FAX:
(215)597-2303. **Staff:** Joseph J. Sheehan, Asst.Dir.

★ 11033 ★
National Archives & Records Administration - National Archives -
  Motion Picture, Sound, & Video Branch (Aud-Vis)
7th St. & Pennsylvania Ave., N.W.   Phone: (202)501-5449
Washington, DC 20408   William T. Murphy, Br.Chf.
Founded: 1934. **Staff:** Prof 8; Other 21. **Subjects:** United States - history,
politics, government; archival resources - AV materials, sound recordings,
moving pictures. **Special Collections:** Records of U.S. Government military
and civilian agencies; Ford Motor Company Film Collection; Universal
Newsreel; March of Time Stock Film Library; National Public Radio
Collection; Milo Ryan Phonoarchive; League of Nations; American Town
Meeting of the Air; Longines' Chronoscope; Harmon Foundation; Country
Music Time; ABC Radio News Collection; MacNeil-Lehrer Reports.
Holdings: 170,000 motion pictures; 180,000 sound recordings; 45,000 video
recordings from U.S. Government agencies, private news organizations,
other documentary producers. **Subscriptions:** 11 journals and other serials.
Services: Interlibrary loan (limited); copying; branch open to the public.
Automated Operations: Computerized cataloging, preservation, and
inventory. **Computerized Information Services:** INFOCEN, BASIS
(internal databases). Contact Person: Charles De Arman, Supv.Libn.
Remarks: FAX: (202)501-5778. **Staff:** Leslie C. Waffen, Supv.Archv.; Alan
Lewis, Supv.-AV Spec.

★ 11034 ★
National Archives & Records Administration - National Archives - New
  England Region (Hist)
380 Trapelo Rd.   Phone: (617)647-8100
Waltham, MA 02154   James K. Owens, Dir.
Founded: 1969. **Staff:** Prof 3; Other 3. **Subjects:** Noncurrent permanent
federal government records for agencies located in Vermont, New
Hampshire, Massachusetts, Connecticut, Rhode Island, Maine. **Holdings:**
19,000 cubic feet of records of federal agencies in New England, 1789-1977:
U.S. District and Circuit Courts, U.S. Court of Appeals, customs and Coast
Guard activities, Life Saving Service Stations Logs, Naval Shore
Establishments including Boston and Portsmouth, NH naval shipyards,
Bureau of Public Roads, U.S. Army Corps of Engineers, and War
Manpower Commission (World War II); Office of Scientific Research and
Development (Harvard/MIT Labs); 65,000 reels of microfilm of National
Archives publications; U.S. Census reports, 1790-1910, on microfilm;
records of other federal agencies and bureaus. **Subscriptions:** 12 journals and
other serials. **Services:** Copying; branch open to the public. **Computerized
Information Services:** National Archives - Archival Information System
(internal database). **Publications:** Guide to Records in the National
Archives - New England Region; Microfilm Publications in the National
Archives - New England Region; Sources for Family History in the National
Archives - New England Region (leaflet) - to the public. **Staff:** Stanley
Tozeski, Archv.; Helen Engle, Archv.

★ 11035 ★
National Archives & Records Administration - National Archives -
  Northeast Region (Hist)
Bldg. 22-MOT Bayonne   Phone: (201)823-7252
Bayonne, NJ 07002   Robert C. Morris, Dir.
Founded: 1970. **Staff:** Prof 6; Other 5. **Subjects:** Permanently valuable
records of federal agencies in New York State, New Jersey, Puerto Rico, and
The Virgin Islands, 1790-1978. **Holdings:** 58,000 cubic feet of archival
materials; 42,000 reels of National Archives microfilm. **Services:** Copying;
branch open to the public for research. **Computerized Information Services:**
NARS-5, NARS-A1 (internal databases). **Remarks:** FAX: (201)823-7251.
Staff: John J. Celardo, Asst.Dir.; Joel Buckwald, Sr.Arch.; Francis Butkus,
Archv.;   Gregory   Plunges,   Archv.Techn.;   Arlene   Lukaszewski,
Archv.Techn.

★ 11036 ★

National Archives & Records Administration - National Archives - Pacific Northwest Region (Hist)
6125 Sand Point Way
Seattle, WA 98115

Phone: (206)526-6507
Phillip E. Lothyan, Dir.

Founded: 1969. **Staff:** 6. **Subjects:** Historical records of agencies of the Federal Government for Washington, Oregon, Idaho, and Montana; Bureau of Customs; Bureau of Land Management; Bureau of Indian Affairs; U.S. Army Corps of Engineers; U.S. District Courts; Bonneville Power Administration. **Special Collections:** Census records for all states and territories, 1790-1920. **Holdings:** 60,000 cubic feet of records; 50,000 reels of microfilm. **Services:** Copying; branch open to the public with restrictions. **Publications:** Guide, 1988; Preliminary Inventories; Special Lists; Research Opportunities at the National Archives - Seattle Branch, 1985. **Remarks:** Alternate telephone number(s): 526-6347. **Staff:** Joyce Justice, Archv.; Susan Karren, Asst.Dir.

★ 11037 ★

National Archives & Records Administration - National Archives - Pacific Sierra Region (Hist)
1000 Commodore Dr.
San Bruno, CA 94066

Phone: (415)876-9009
Waverly B. Lowell, Dir.

Founded: 1969. **Staff:** Prof 5; Other 4. **Subjects:** Archival records of the Federal Government in Nevada (except Clark County), Northern California, Hawaii, the Pacific Ocean areas. **Special Collections:** Records of the government of American Samoa; records of the Bureau of Indian Affairs, California and Nevada; Chinese immigration records; records of naval shipyards at Pearl Harbor, HI, and Mare Island, CA; records relating to World War II industry, labor, housing, and racial discrimination in employment; records of Federal district courts in Northern California, Hawaii, and Nevada, and of the U.S. Court of Appeals for the Ninth Circuit; records relating to scientific anf technical research in agriculture, aviation, civil and military engineering, fisheries, forestry, high-energy physics, river basins, and waterways; record s relating to maritime history; records relating to migratory labor. **Holdings:** 32,000 cubic feet of original records; 31,000 reels of microfilm. **Subscriptions:** 6 journals and other serials. **Services:** Copying; branch open to the public. **Computerized Information Services:** Chinese Immigration to Hawaii, 1898-1947; Official Logbooks of Merchant Vessels, San Francisco, 1942-1957 (internal databases). **Publications:** Guide to Records; Chinese Studies in Federal Records; Microfilm Publications Concerning Spanish Private Land Grant Claims; reference information papers on Federal records relating to ethnic groups, science, technology, natural resources, the environment, and World War II; reference information paper on records of Federal district and appellate courts. **Special Indexes:** Admiralty case files of the U.S. District Court for the Northern District of California, 1850-1900 (microfilm). **Remarks:** FAX: (415)876-0920. **Staff:** Kathleen O'Connor, Archv. ; Richard Boyden, Archv.

★ 11038 ★

National Archives & Records Administration - National Archives - Pacific Southwest Region (Hist)
24000 Avila Rd.
Box 6719
Laguna Niguel, CA 92677-6719

Phone: (714)643-4241
Diane S. Nixon, Reg.Dir.

Founded: 1969. **Staff:** Prof 4; Other 6. **Subjects:** Inactive and noncurrent Federal Government records for Arizona, Clark County, Nevada, and Southern California. **Special Collections:** Pre-presidential materials of Richard Nixon; National Archives microfilm publications of national significance; records of Bureau of Indian Affairs, Bureau of Land Management, Bureau of Customs, U.S. Navy, U.S. District Courts. **Holdings:** 20,000 cubic feet of original records. **Services:** Copying; branch open to the public with restrictions. **Publications:** Guide to the National Archives - Pacific Southwest Region. **Remarks:** Alternate telephone number(s): 643-4242; 643-4706. FAX: (714)643-4500. **Staff:** Suzanne Dewberry, Archv.; Fred W. Klose, Archv.; Laura McCarthy, Archv.

★ 11039 ★

National Archives & Records Administration - National Archives - Rocky Mountain Region (Hist)
Denver Federal Center, Bldg. 48
Denver, CO 80225

Phone: (303)236-0817
Joel Barker, Dir.

Founded: 1969. **Staff:** Prof 3; Other 3. **Subjects:** Archival records of the federal government for Arizona, Colorado, Montana, Wyoming, North Dakota, South Dakota, New Mexico, Utah. **Special Collections:** Records of 30 federal agencies, including the U.S. District Courts, Bureau of Land Management, Bureau of Reclamation (reclamation projects in 17 western

states), Bureau of Indian Affairs, National Bureau of Standards. **Holdings:** 20,000 cubic feet of archives; 60,000 reels of microfilm; census on microfilm. **Services:** Copying; reference service to federal agencies and researchers; branch open to the public. **Remarks:** FAX: (303)236-9297. **Staff:** Eileen Bolger, Asst.Dir.; Joan Howard, Archv.

★ 11040 ★

National Archives & Records Administration - National Archives - Southeast Region (Hist)
1557 St. Joseph Ave.
East Point, GA 30344

Phone: (404)763-7477
Gayle P. Peters, Dir.

Founded: 1969. **Staff:** Prof 4; Other 9. **Subjects:** Historically valuable records, 1716-1978, of the Federal Government from field offices and courts in North Carolina, South Carolina, Tennessee, Kentucky, Georgia, Florida, Alabama, Mississippi. **Special Collections:** Records of World War I Selective Service System for the entire United States; Tennessee Valley Authority, 1933-1973; Atomic Energy Commission, Oak Ridge, Tennessee, 1943-1960. **Holdings:** 45,000 cubic feet of records; 46,000 reels of microfilm. **Services:** Copying; branch open to the public. **Computerized Information Services:** National Archives A-1 (internal database). **Publications:** Research Opportunities and list of microfilm available, biennial - to mailing list. **Special Catalogs:** Catalog of Federal Court records; shelf list finding aids on material in regional archives and in Records Center. **Remarks:** FAX: (404)763-7815. **Staff:** Charles R. Reeves, Archv.; Mary Ann Hawkins, Archv.; David Hilkert, Archv.

★ 11041 ★

National Archives & Records Administration - National Archives - Southwest Region (Hist)
501 Felix at Hemphill, Bldg. 1
Box 6216
Fort Worth, TX 76115

Phone: (817)334-5525
Kent Carter, Dir., Archv.Br.

Founded: 1969. **Staff:** Prof 3; Other 5. **Subjects:** Inactive records of U.S. government agencies in Texas, Oklahoma, Arkansas, New Mexico, Louisiana. **Special Collections:** U.S. census reports, 1790-1910; index to Civil War records; passenger records from various ports; Bureau of Indian Affairs records from the state of Oklahoma. **Holdings:** 56,000 cubic feet of records; 40,000 reels of microfilm. **Services:** Copying; archives open to the public except for restricted records. **Staff:** Barbara Rust, Archv.; Meg Hacker, Archv.

★ 11042 ★

National Archives & Records Administration - National Audiovisual Center - Customer Services (Aud-Vis)
8700 Edgeworth Dr.
Capitol Heights, MD 20743-3701

Phone: (301)763-1896
George H. Ziener, Dir.

Founded: 1974. **Staff:** 45. **Subjects:** Alcohol, drugs, business and government management, career education, environment, energy conservation, foreign language instruction, industrial safety, information science, nursing, science, special and vocational education, consumer education, engineering, dentistry, medicine, emergency medical services, fire/law enforcement, flight/meteorology, social sciences, space. **Holdings:** 10,000 titles of slide sets, audiotapes, filmstrips, multimedia kits, video cassettes, 16mm films. **Subscriptions:** 30 journals and other serials. **Services:** Open to the public by appointment. **Automated Operations:** Computerized cataloging. **Computerized Information Services:** Defense Audiovisual Information System (DAVIS). Performs searches free of charge. Contact Person: Thomas Raines, Database Mgr. **Publications:** Information lists in 20 areas - free upon request. **Special Catalogs:** Media Resource Catalog, 1990, 1991. **Remarks:** FAX: (301)763-6025. TDD: (301) 763-4385.

★ 11043 ★

National Archives & Records Administration - National Personnel Records Center (Mil)
9700 Page Blvd.
St. Louis, MO 63132-5100

Phone: (314)538-4201
David L. Petree, Dir.

Founded: 1952. **Staff:** 500. **Subjects:** Service and medical records of persons who have served in the Armed Forces, noncurrent records of organizations which have been a part of the military establishment, personnel and medical records of former federal civilian employees. **Holdings:** 1.8 million cubic feet of military and personnel records (MPR) and organizational records; 1.9 million cubic feet of civilian personnel records (CPR) and agency organizational records. **Services:** Library not open to the public. **Remarks:** The National Personnel Records Center (MPR) maintains and services the records of separated military personnel of the Army (1912 to present), Navy

(1885 to present), Air Force (1947 to present), Marine Corps (1905 to present), Coast Guard (1906 to present). The National Personnel Records Center (CPR) maintains and services the personnel and medical records of former federal civilian employees; it is located at 111 Winnebago St., St. Louis, MO 63118-4199. **Staff:** Paul D. Gray, Asst.Dir., CPR; Wayne N. Wallace, Asst.Dir., MPR.

★ 11044 ★
National Archives & Records Administration - Nixon Presidential Materials Staff (Hist)
Washington, DC 20408   Phone: (703)756-6498
                                        Clarence F. Lyons, Jr., Act.Dir.
Founded: 1976. **Staff:** Prof 12; Other 10. **Subjects:** U.S. history, President Richard M. Nixon, White House. **Special Collections:** White House Central File; White House Special File; Staff Member and Office Files; National Security Files; Federal records; donated materials. **Holdings:** 950 Nixon White House tapes; 435,000 White House photographs; 700 hours of motion picture film; 4082 video recordings; 4469 audio recordings; 30,000 Presidential gifts. **Services:** Copying; 4.5 million pages of documents, 60 hours of Nixon White House tapes, and virtually the entire audiovisual collection are open for public research. **Computerized Information Services:** Internal database. **Publications:** Finding aids; lists. **Remarks:** FAX: (703)756-6407. Research room located at 845 S. Pickett St., Alexandria, VA.

National Archives & Records Administration - Presidential Libraries
See: **U.S. Presidential Libraries** (17921)

★ 11045 ★
National Archives & Records Administration - Still Picture Branch (Aud-Vis)
8th St. and Pennsylvania Ave., N.W.
NNSP-18N   Phone: (202)501-5455
Washington, DC 20408   Elizabeth L. Hill, Chf.
Founded: 1935. **Staff:** Prof 9; Other 14. **Subjects:** AV materials; still photography; posters; United States - history, politics, government. **Special Collections:** Included in the wide-ranging files are historical photographs from such agencies as: American Commission for the Protection and Salvage of Artistic and Historic Monuments in War Areas, 1943-1946 (German destruction of monuments; vandalism of historic buildings; architectural damage caused by war activities in Europe and Japan; works of art); Department of Defense, 1775-1982 (Army, Navy, Air Force, Marine Corps personnel, activities, installations, ordnance, transport; includes Revolutionary War, Mathew Brady Civil War photographs, western exploration, surveys, settlement, minor military expeditions, Spanish-American War, World War I, history of flight, scenic photographs, recruiting and war loan posters, effects of atomic bombing of Japan, occupation of Germany and Japan, U.S. Navy and U.S. Army photographs of World War II, the Korean War, and Vietnam War); Harmon Foundation Collection of Photographs, 1922-1966 (art works by black American and African artists; prominent black Americans; foreign art objects; activities of blacks on campuses of southern colleges; exhibits of black artists' works and art workshops); Department of the Interior, 1850-1973 (geological surveys; western land development; coastal fishing; wildlife; power; irrigation; soil conservation projects; national parks and recreation; U.S. territories; Indian affairs; Antarctic exploration; Bureau of Mines activities and Russell Lee photographs of coal mining activities in 1946); NASA, 1920-1965 (history of aviation and rocketry research and development; lunar surface photographs); Tennessee Valley Authority, 1933-1941 (dams, scenery, recreational areas; Lewis Hine photographs of families forced to leave their land); Department of the Treasury, 1917-1977 (posters for war bonds and E bonds campaigns; stills from World War I promotional movies; Bureau of Engraving and printing activities; Office of War Information, 1940-1950 (World War II military operations and U.S. home front; U.S. and foreign posters; international conferences and personalities; views of American life and culture for foreign distribution). **Holdings:** 7 million archival photographs from U.S. Federal Government agencies which document American and world cultural, social, environmental, economic, technological, political history of a nong overnmental nature as well as activities of military and civilian governmental agencies; historical photographs of precursors of contemporary governmental activity. **Services:** Copying; branch open to the public for reference use only. **Computerized Information Services:** TextBank (internal database). **Publications:** Guide to the Holdings of the Still Pictures Branch of the National Archives (1990). **Special Catalogs:** War and Conflict: Selected Images from the National Archives, 1795-1970. **Staff:** Fred Pernell, Asst.Chf., Ref.; Ed McCarter, Asst.Chf., Proj.; Dale Connelly, Archv.

★ 11046 ★
National Archives & Records Administration - Washington National Records Center (Hist)
4205 Suitland Rd., Rm. 121   Phone: (301)763-7000
Suitland, MD 20409   Ferris E. Stovel, Dir.
Founded: 1968. **Staff:** Prof 125. **Subjects:** Records of U.S. Government agencies in the District of Columbia, Maryland, Virginia, West Virginia; records of the United States Army, Air Force, and Navy worldwide. **Holdings:** 3.1 million cubic feet of records. **Subscriptions:** 15 journals and other serials. **Services:** Access to information is obtained by contacting the Federal agency that created the records. **Computerized Information Services:** Internal databases. Performs searches free of charge. Contact Person: Andrew Jones.

★ 11047 ★
National Arthritis and Musculoskeletal and Skin Diseases Information Clearinghouse (Med)
9000 Rockville Pike
Box AMS   Phone: (301)495-4484
Bethesda, MD 20892   Phyllis Payne, Info.Spec.
Founded: 1978. **Staff:** Prof 1; Other 1. **Subjects:** Arthritis; rheumatic, skin, and musculoskeletal diseases; sports medicine. **Holdings:** 11,000 database records. **Subscriptions:** 30 journals and other serials; 50 newspapers. **Services:** Clearinghouse serves health professionals involved in the diagnosis, treatment, and education of patients. **Computerized Information Services:** Combined Health Information Database (CHID), available through BRS Information Technologies. **Publications:** Bibliographies; catalogs; directories, biblioprofiles; Memo (newsletter), quarterly - to mailing list. **Remarks:** FAX: (301)587-4352. Clearinghouse identifies and disseminates information about print and nonprint materials for professional and patient education in the rheumatic, musculoskeletal, skin diseases, and sports injuries. It is funded by U.S. Department of Health and Human Services, U.S. National Institutes of Health, and National Institute of Arthritis and Musculoskeletal and Skin Diseases. **Also Known As:** AMS Information Clearinghouse.

★ 11048 ★
National Asphalt Pavement Association - Charles R. Foster Technical Library (Plan, Trans)
5100 Forbes Blvd.
Lanham, MD 20706-4413   Phone: (301)731-4748
Founded: 1976. **Subjects:** Hot mix asphalt technology and applications, highway engineering. **Special Collections:** Archive of NAPA publications. **Holdings:** Manuals; selected reports (Transportation Research Board, Federal Highway Administration, Federal Aviation Administration, Transport and Road Research Laboratory); selected proceedings; foreign asphalt association publications; 30 VF drawers. **Subscriptions:** 75 journals and other serials. **Remarks:** Holdings are not cataloged.

National Association of Accountants
See: **Institute of Management Accountants - Library** (7955)

★ 11049 ★
National Association for the Advancement of Colored People - NAACP Legal Defense and Educational Fund - Law Library (Law, Soc Sci)
99 Hudson St., 16th Fl.   Phone: (212)219-1900
New York, NY 10013   Donna Gloeckner
Subjects: Civil rights law - discrimination against blacks, other racial minorities, and women in employment, education, housing, and other areas. **Holdings:** 15,000 volumes.

★ 11050 ★
National Association of Animal Breeders - Library (Agri)
401 Bernadette Dr.
Box 1033   Phone: (314)445-4406
Columbia, MO 65205   Gordon A. Doak, Pres.
Subjects: Cattle breeding, artificial breeding, physiology of reproduction, artificial insemination industry. **Holdings:** 300 books; 40 bound periodical volumes. **Subscriptions:** 50 journals and other serials. **Services:** Library not open to the public. **Remarks:** FAX: (314)446-2279.

★ 11051 ★
National Association of Anorexia Nervosa and Associated Disorders, Inc. - Library (Med)
Box 7
Highland Park, IL 60035
Phone: (708)831-3438
Vivian Meehan, Adm.Dir.
Founded: 1976. **Subjects:** Anorexia nervosa, bulimia, bulimarexia, other eating disorders. **Holdings:** Figures not available. **Services:** Library not open to the public. **Publications:** Quarterly newsletter; information packets - to educational institutions, health facilities and professionals, victims of anorexia nervosa/bulimia and their families. **Remarks:** FAX: (708)433-4632. Association provides referrals. All services are free.

★ 11052 ★
National Association of Boards of Pharmacy - Library (Med)
1300 Higgins Rd., Suite 103
Park Ridge, IL 60068-5743
Phone: (708)698-6227
Carmen A. Catizone, Exec.Dir.
Founded: 1904. **Subjects:** Pharmacy - law and regulation, education, licensure. **Holdings:** Figures not available. **Remarks:** FAX: (708)698-0124.

★ 11053 ★
National Association of Broadcasters - Library and Information Center (Info Sci)
1771 N St., N.W.
Washington, DC 20036
Phone: (202)429-5490
Susan M. Hill, V.P.
Founded: 1946. **Staff:** Prof 3; Other 2. **Subjects:** Radio and television broadcasting and allied subjects. **Holdings:** 9500 volumes. **Subscriptions:** 220 journals and other serials. **Services:** Library open to the public by appointment on fee basis. **Computerized Information Services:** DIALOG Information Services, NewsNet, Inc., VU/TEXT Information Services, WILSONLINE, DataTimes, Burrelle's Broadcast Database, Global Scan. **Publications:** Broadcasting Bibliography: A Guide to the Literature of Radio and Television (3rd ed.). **Remarks:** FAX: (202)775-3520. **Staff:** Ann Cardace, Dir.; Myra Weinberg, Libn.; Janice B. Hauck, Libn.

National Association of College Wind and Percussion Instructors Research Center
See: **University of Maryland, College Park Libraries - Music Library** (18821)

★ 11054 ★
National Association of Conservation Districts - Conservation Film Service (Aud-Vis)
408 E. Main St.
League City, TX 77573
Phone: (713)332-3402
Ruth Chenhall, Educ.-Info. Spec.
Founded: 1967. **Staff:** Prof 2. **Subjects:** Conservation - water, soil, education; water quality; natural resources; wildlife. **Holdings:** 150 films, slides, and videotapes. **Subscriptions:** 16 journals and other serials. **Services:** Service open to the public. **Special Catalogs:** Audio-Visual Publication Catalog, available to conservation districts and the public - free. **Remarks:** FAX: (713)332-5259.

★ 11055 ★
National Association of Convenience Stores - NACS Information Center (Bus-Fin)
1605 King St.
Alexandria, VA 22314-2792
Phone: (703)684-3600
Marie Cavanagh, Dir.
Founded: 1988. **Staff:** Prof 1; Other 1. **Subjects:** Convenience stores, retail trade, petroleum marketing, food service. **Holdings:** 500 books; video cassettes; market research; VF drawers; training and educational materials. **Subscriptions:** 100 journals and other serials; 5 newspapers. **Services:** Interlibrary loan; center open to the public by appointment. **Automated Operations:** Computerized public access catalog. **Computerized Information Services:** DIALOG Information Services. Performs searches on fee basis. **Publications:** Manuals, research reports, state of the industry reports. **Remarks:** FAX: (703)836-4564.

★ 11056 ★
National Association for Core Curriculum, Inc. - Library (Educ)
404 White Hall
Kent State University
Kent, OH 44242
Phone: (216)672-2792
Dr. Gordon F. Vars, Exec.Sec.-Treas.
Staff: 1. **Subjects:** Core curriculum, interdisciplinary studies, block-time programs, humanities programs, education. **Holdings:** 50 books; 1 file drawer of clippings; 150 curriculum guides; 35 audiotapes. **Services:** Library open to the public by appointment. **Publications:** The Core Teacher (newsletter), quarterly; Core Today; curriculum guides and bulletins; A Bibliography of Research on the Effectiveness of Block-Time, Core and Interdisciplinary Programs, 1991. **Special Indexes:** Selected References on Block-Time, Core and Interdisciplinary Programs, 1991.

★ 11057 ★
National Association of Corporate Directors - Library (Bus-Fin)
1707 L St., N.W., Suite 560
Washington, DC 20036
Phone: (202)775-0509
John M. Nash, Pres.
Founded: 1977. **Subjects:** Corporate governance. **Holdings:** 400 volumes. **Services:** Library open to the public by appointment. **Publications:** Directors Monthly.

★ 11058 ★
National Association of Corrosion Engineers - Library (Sci-Engr)
1440 S. Creek Dr.
Box 218340
Houston, TX 77218
Phone: (713)492-0535
C.K. Donahoo, Info.Spec.
Founded: 1945. **Subjects:** Corrosion, metallurgy, nonmetals, materials science, chemistry, electrochemistry, coatings, economics. **Holdings:** 7500 books; 130,000 NACE documents. **Subscriptions:** 25 journals and other serials. **Services:** not open to the public by appointment. **Computerized Information Services:** (internal database). Performs searches on fee basis. **Special Indexes:** Abstracts (online). **Remarks:** FAX: (713)492-8254. Telex: 792310. **Also Known As:** NACE.

★ 11059 ★
National Association for Creative Children and Adults - Library (Educ)
8080 Springvalley Dr.
Cincinnati, OH 45236
Phone: (513)631-1777
Ann Fabe Isaacs, Hd.
Subjects: Creativity, giftedness, talent, art, music, writing. **Holdings:** Figures not available. **Subscriptions:** 30 journals and other serials. **Services:** Library open to the public by appointment. **Publications:** The Creative Child and Adult Quarterly - for sale; list of additional publications - available upon request. **Special Indexes:** Annual and cumulative indexes for The Creative Child and Adult Quarterly. **Also Known As:** NACCA.

National Association for Hispanic Elderly
See: **Asociacion Nacional Por Personas Mayores** (1127)

★ 11060 ★
National Association of Hispanic Publications - Library
1219 Palo Verde
Carson City, NV 89701
Founded: 1982. **Subjects:** Hispanic publishing and journalists. **Holdings:** 170 Hispanic newspapers, newsletters, magazines, journals. **Remarks:** Currently inactive.

★ 11061 ★
National Association of Home Builders - NAHB Library (Plan)
15th & M Sts., N.W.
Washington, DC 20005
Phone: (202)822-0203
Kimberly G. Allen, Chf.Libn.
Founded: 1955. **Staff:** Prof 2; Other 1. **Subjects:** Technical, social, and financial aspects of homebuilding. **Holdings:** 10,000 books; 20,000 pamphlets and trade catalogs. **Subscriptions:** 200 journals and other serials. **Services:** Interlibrary loan; copying; library open to the public. **Computerized Information Services:** DIALOG Information Services; NAHB-NET (internal database). **Publications:** Library Bulletin, quarterly with annual cumulation; Homes and Homebuilding. **Remarks:** FAX: (202)861-2153.

★ 11062 ★
National Association of Hosiery Manufacturers - Library (Bus-Fin)
447 S. Sharon Amity Rd.
Charlotte, NC 28211
Phone: (704)365-0913
Sid Smith, Pres. & Chf.Exec.Off.
Subjects: Hosiery - statistics, industry standards, regulatory bulletins. **Holdings:** Figures not available. **Services:** Library open to association staff and members. **Publications:** Magazine, monthly. **Remarks:** FAX: (704)362-2056.

★ 11063 ★
National Association of Independent Insurers - NAII Insurance Library (Bus-Fin)
2600 River Rd.
Des Plaines, IL 60018-3286
Phone: (708)297-7800
Holly Grossman, Info.Serv.Supv.
Staff: Prof 1; Other 1. **Subjects:** Insurance, law. **Holdings:** 4000 books. **Subscriptions:** 250 journals and other serials; 6 newspapers. **Services:** Interlibrary loan. **Computerized Information Services:** DIALOG Information Services, LEXIS, NEXIS, DataTimes. Performs searches.

National Association of Industrial & Office Parks
See: **NAIOP, The Association for Commercial Real Estate** (10955)

★ 11064 ★
National Association for Industry-Education Cooperation - Library
(Educ)
235 Hendricks Blvd.
Buffalo, NY 14226-3304   Phone: (716)834-7047
Subjects: Industry involvement in education. **Holdings:** 1340 books; 45
bound periodical volumes; 2 AV programs; 89 manuscripts. **Services:**
Library open to members. **Remarks:** FAX: (716)834-7047.

★ 11065 ★
National Association of Insurance Commissioners - NAIC Support and
Services Office - Research Library (Bus-Fin, Law)
120 W. 12th St., Suite 1100   Phone: (816)842-3600
Kansas City, MO 64105   Angela Anthony, Lib.Mgr.
Founded: 1970. **Staff:** Prof 2; Other 1.5. **Subjects:** Insurance - regulation,
law, business. **Special Collections:** NAIC Proceedings, 1871 to present.
Holdings: 10,000 volumes. **Subscriptions:** 150 serials. **Services:** Library not
open to the public. **Automated Operations:** Computerized cataloging and
serials. **Computerized Information Services:** DIALOG Information
Services, LEXIS, NEXIS, ELSS (Electronic Legislative Search System),
DataTimes, OCLC EPIC. **Networks/Consortia:** Member of Missouri
Library Network Corp. (MLNC). **Remarks:** FAX: (816)471-7004. **Staff:**
Crystal Cameron, Res.Libn.

★ 11066 ★
National Association of Investigative Specialists - Library (Law)
Box 33244   Phone: (512)928-8190
Austin, TX 78764   Ralph D. Thomas, Dir.
Founded: 1984. **Subjects:** Private investigation, social science, criminal law.
Holdings: 250 volumes. **Computerized Information Services:** Internal
database; EasyLink (electronic mail service). **Publications:** Private
Investigation Manuals. **Remarks:** Library located at 8107 Springdale, Suite
101, Austin, TX 78724. FAX: (512)928-4544. Electronic mail address(es):
62814262 (EasyLink).

★ 11067 ★
National Association for Legal Support of Alternative Schools - Library
Box 2823   Phone: (505)471-6928
Santa Fe, NM 87504-2823   Ed Nagel
Founded: 1972. **Subjects:** Educational law and legislation, alternative
education. **Holdings:** 4200 books; 3100 bound periodical volumes.

★ 11068 ★
National Association of Letter Carriers - Information Center (Bus-Fin)
100 Indiana Ave., N.W.   Phone: (202)393-4695
Washington, DC 20001   Candace Main Rush, Info.Spec.
Founded: 1984. **Staff:** 2. **Subjects:** Letter carriers, postal system, labor,
economics, politics. **Special Collections:** Union publications collection.
Holdings: 400 volumes; 350 AV programs; U.S. Postal Service documents.
Subscriptions: 200 journals and other serials; 6 newspapers. **Services:**
Interlibrary loan; copying; center open to the public by appointment.
Automated Operations: Computerized acquisitions, cataloging, and
circulation. **Computerized Information Services:** DIALOG Information
Services, ORBIT Search Service, LEXIS, NEXIS, Human Resource
Information Network (HRIN).

★ 11069 ★
National Association of Manufacturers - Library (Bus-Fin)
1331 Pennsylvania Ave., N.W., Suite 1500-North   Phone: (202)637-3000
Washington, DC 20004-1703   Joni Hodgson, Libn.
Subjects: Business, economics. **Holdings:** Government documents; legal
reports; digests. **Services:** Library open to the public by appointment.

★ 11070 ★
National Association of Mutual Insurance Companies - NAMIC Library
(Bus-Fin)
3601 Vincennes Rd.
Box 68700
Indianapolis, IN 46268   Phone: (317)875-5250
Founded: 1977. **Staff:** Prof 1. **Subjects:** Mutual companies; insurance - farm,
crop, property and casualty; association management. **Holdings:** 300 titles.
Subscriptions: 2 newspapers. **Services:** Interlibrary loan; copying; library
open to the public. **Remarks:** FAX: (317)879-8408.

★ 11071 ★
National Association of Parliamentarians - Non-Profit Educational
Association - Library (Soc Sci)
6601 Winchester Ave., Suite 260   Phone: (816)356-5604
Kansas City, MO 64133-4600   Cathy Dehoney, Off.Mgr.
Staff: Prof 1. **Subjects:** Parliamentary procedure. **Holdings:** 500 books; 200
bound periodical volumes; reports. **Services:** Center open to the public for
reference use only. **Formerly:** Its Technical Information Center.

National Association of Precancel Collectors, Inc.
See: **Chester Davis Memorial Library** (4640)

National Association for the Preservation & Perpetuation of Storytelling
See: **National Storytelling Resource Center** (11307)

★ 11072 ★
National Association of Private, Nontraditional Schools & Colleges -
NAPNSC Accreditation Library and Clearinghouse Information
Center (Educ)
182 Thompson Rd.   Phone: (303)243-5441
Grand Junction, CO 81503   H. Earl Heusser, Ed.D., Exec.Dir.
Founded: 1974. **Staff:** Prof 3. **Subjects:** Curriculum development and
evaluation; private school accreditation; education - nontraditional,
alternative, special purpose; teaching and learning strategies. **Special
Collections:** Criteria and Standards for Regional and National Specialized
Accrediting Agencies and Associations (15 reports); Institutional Self
Studies; bound masters' and doctoral theses and dissertations (including
abstracts) of graduates of NAPNSC accredited member institutions (329).
Holdings: 1302 books. **Subscriptions:** 18 journals and other serials. **Services:**
Copying; center open to the public for reference use only. **Publications:** List
of publications - available on request. **Remarks:** Maintains an 11 member
accrediting commission and provides clearinghouse information for private
alternative education at all levels. **Staff:** Dolly Heusser, Psy.D., Co-Dir.;
Dawn S. Crawford, Exec.Sec./Treas.

★ 11073 ★
National Association for Professional Saleswomen - Library
5520 Cherokee Ave., Suite 200
Alexandria, VA 22312
Founded: 1980. **Subjects:** Business and sales. **Remarks:** Currently inactive.

★ 11074 ★
National Association of Purchasing Management, Inc. - Information
Center (Bus-Fin)
Box 22160   Phone: (602)752-6276
Tempe, AZ 85285-2160   Kathleen R. Little, Libn.
Founded: 1968. **Staff:** 1. **Subjects:** Purchasing, materials management,
inventory management, vendor relations. **Special Collections:** Doctoral
dissertations on aspects of purchasing; NAPM and other archives on
purchasing. **Holdings:** 1000 books; 14 VF drawers of clippings, reports,
NAPM serials, allied publications on purchasing. **Subscriptions:** 102
journals and other serials. **Services:** Copying; center open to the public by
appointment. **Computerized Information Services:** DIALOG Information
Services. **Remarks:** FAX: (602)752-7890.

★ 11075 ★
National Association of Realtors - Library (Bus-Fin, Plan)
430 N. Michigan Ave.   Phone: (312)329-8292
Chicago, IL 60611-4087   Karen J. Switt, Dir., Lib.Info.Serv.
Founded: 1923. **Staff:** Prof 7; Other 7. **Subjects:** Real estate, architecture,
city planning. **Holdings:** 20,000 volumes; 75,000 pamphlets. **Subscriptions:**

700 journals and other serials. **Services:** Interlibrary loan; library open to the public on fee basis. **Automated Operations:** Computerized cataloging, serials, and circulation. **Computerized Information Services:** LEXIS, NEXIS, DIALOG Information Services. Performs searches on fee basis. **Networks/Consortia:** Member of ILLINET. **Publications:** Bibliography series, irregular; Library manual. **Special Catalogs:** Thesaurus of Subject Terms. **Special Indexes:** Real Estate Index, 1975-1985; Real Estate Index, 1985-1987. **Remarks:** Alternate telephone number(s): 329-8293. FAX: (312)329-5960. **Staff:** Rosanne A. Zambrow, Hd., Tech.Serv.; John D. Krukoff, Hd., User Serv.; Elizabeth Beckman, Info.Spec.; Tracy Jones, Cat.; Gordon Gilespie, Indexer; Marilyn Heneghan, Archv.

★11076★
National Association of Securities Dealers - Library (Bus-Fin)
1735 K St., N.W.   Phone: (202)728-8000
Washington, DC 20006   Joseph R. Hardiman, Pres.
Founded: 1939. **Subjects:** Securities; commercial standards and fair practice in the over-the-counter securities market. **Holdings:** 5000 volumes. **Services:** Interlibrary loan; library not open to the public. **Computerized Information Services:** National Association of Securities Dealers Automated Quotations (NASDAQ).

★11077★
National Association for Sport & Physical Education - Media Resource Center (Educ)
Dept. of Physical Education
University of South Carolina   Phone: (803)777-3172
Columbia, SC 29208   Dr. Richard C. Hohn, Dir.
Staff: Prof 2. **Subjects:** Physical education, sports, physical fitness, intramurals, dance and career related information. **Holdings:** 200 audio- and videotapes. **Services:** Copying; center open to the public with restrictions on a fee for service basis. **Remarks:** Affiliated with the American Alliance for Health, Physical Education, Recreation and Dance.

National Association of State Approved Colleges & Universities
See: **American Council for University Planning & Academic Excellence** (553)

★11078★
National Association of State Emergency Medical Services Directors - Sam Channell National EMS Clearinghouse
P.O. Box 11910
Iron Works Pike
Lexington, KY 40578
Defunct. Holdings absorbed by Emergency Care Information Center.

★11079★
National Association of Suggestion Systems - Library (Bus-Fin)
111 E. Wacker Dr., Suite 200   Phone: (312)616 1100
Chicago, IL 60601   George M. Otto, Exec.Dir.
Founded: 1942. **Staff:** 4. **Subjects:** Suggestion systems, employee involvement programs, promotional programs. **Holdings:** Manuals; employee booklets; special studies and reports. **Services:** Library not open to the public. **Remarks:** FAX: (312)616-0226.

★11080★
National Association for Visually Handicapped - Library (Aud-Vis)
22 W. 21st St.   Phone: (212)889-3141
New York, NY 10010   Ann Illuzzi, Libn.
Founded: 1982. **Subjects:** General collection for the visually impaired. **Holdings:** 2000 large-print books. **Services:** Library open to the public. **Publications:** Large Print Loan Library.

★11081★
National Association of Watch and Clock Collectors, Inc. - Watch & Clock Museum of the NAWCC - Library (Sci-Engr)
514 Poplar St.   Phone: (717)684-8261
Columbia, PA 17512   Eileen B. Doudna, Libn.
Founded: 1977. **Staff:** Prof 1. **Subjects:** Horology. **Special Collections:** Hamilton Watch Company business records (73 bound volumes; 10 cubic feet of documents; 352 reels of microfilm). **Holdings:** 3340 books; 570 bound periodical volumes; 21,000 patents; 505 reels of microfilm; 30 VF drawers; archive boxes of manuscripts, catalogs, ephemera. **Subscriptions:** 43 journals and other serials. **Services:** Copying; library open to the public for reference use only. **Computerized Information Services:** Horological patents, BULLETIN index, Jewelers' Circular index (internal databases). Performs searches on fee basis. **Publications:** Horological Literature Available from the NAWCC Lending Library, irregular - to members. **Remarks:** FAX: (717)684-0878.

★11082★
National Association for Year-Round Education - Library (Educ)
6401 Linda Vista Rd.   Phone: (619)276-5296
San Diego, CA 92111   Dr. Charles E. Ballinger, Exec.Dir.
Founded: 1972. **Staff:** 1. **Subjects:** Year-round education - research, feasibility studies, legislation, models, curriculum, program. **Holdings:** Books; pamphlets; brochures; unbound periodicals; clippings. **Services:** Library open to the public by arrangement. **Publications:** The Year-Rounder (newsletter), quarterly; Annual Directory; occasional papers. **Remarks:** The aim of the association is "to aid and assist local, state and national organizations in the research, collection, evaluation, design and implementation of year-round education." An alternate telephone number is 292-3679.

★11083★
National Astronomical Observatory, Mizusawa - Library (Sci-Engr)
Hoshi-ga-oka 2-12   Phone: 197 227111
Mizusawa 023, Iwate, Japan   Mr. Y. Tamura, Libn.
Subjects: Geodynamics, Earth's rotation, astronomy, geophysics. **Holdings:** 57,000 volumes. **Subscriptions:** 140 journals and other serials. **Services:** Library not open to the public. **Remarks:** FAX: 197 227120. Telex: 837628 ILSMIZ J. Maintained by Japan - Ministry of Education, Science, and Culture. **Formerly:** International Polar Motion Service - IPMS Library.

National Atomic Museum
See: **U.S. Dept. of Energy - Albuquerque Operations Office** (17229)

★11084★
National Audubon Society - Aullwood Audubon Center and Farm - Library (Biol Sci)
1000 Aullwood Rd.   Phone: (513)890-7360
Dayton, OH 45414   Evelyn Pereny, Libn.
Founded: 1957. **Subjects:** Natural history, environmental education, agriculture. **Holdings:** 2000 books. **Services:** Copying; library open to the public for reference use only.

★11085★
National Audubon Society - Library (Biol Sci)
950 Third Ave.   Phone: (212)546-9108
New York, NY 10022   Barbara Linton, Libn.
Founded: 1905. **Subjects:** Ornithology, conservation of natural resources, natural history. **Holdings:** 3,000 volumes; 1000 reports. **Subscriptions:** 50 journals and other serials. **Services:** Library not open to the public.

National Automobile Museum - Library
See: **William F. Harrah Foundation** (6912)

National Automotive History Collection
See: **Detroit Public Library** (4826)

National Autonomous University of Mexico
See: **Universidad Nacional Autonoma de Mexico** (17990)

★11086★
National Bank of Alaska - Heritage Library and Museum (Hist)
Box 100600   Phone: (907)265-2834
Anchorage, AK 99510-0600   Gail L. Hollinger, Cur./Libn.
Founded: 1968. **Staff:** Prof 1. **Subjects:** Northwest coast, subarctic and arctic area - history, geography, anthropology, ethnology, exploration, resources. **Special Collections:** Alaska Collection (400 volumes of old reference books and early maps); Alaskan art and artifacts. **Holdings:** 2500 books; 1000 bound periodical volumes. **Subscriptions:** 3 journals and other serials. **Services:** Copying; library open to the public for reference use only. **Remarks:** FAX: (907)265-2043.

★ 11087 ★
National Bank of Canada - Documentation Centre (Bus-Fin)
600, rue de la Gauchetiere, W., 11th Fl.   Phone: (514)394-6157
Montreal, PQ, Canada H3B 4L2   Agathe Sabourin, Hd.
Founded: 1982. **Staff:** Prof 1; Other 1. **Subjects:** Banking, finance, business, commerce, economics, statistics. **Holdings:** 1000 books. **Subscriptions:** 480 journals and other serials; 13 newspapers. **Services:** Interlibrary loan; copying; center open to the public by appointment. **Automated Operations:** Computerized serials. **Computerized Information Services:** DIALOG Information Services, Info Globe, Dow Jones News/Retrieval, Infomart Online, InvesText. **Publications:** Bulletin des acquisitions, monthly; Choix d'articles recents, monthly - for internal distribution only. **Remarks:** FAX: (514)394-8471. **Also Known As:** Banque Nationale du Canada.

★ 11088 ★
National Baseball Hall of Fame and Museum, Inc. - National Baseball Library (Rec)
Box 590   Phone: (607)547-2101
Cooperstown, NY 13326   Thomas R. Heitz, Libn.
Founded: 1939. **Staff:** Prof 1; Other 8. **Subjects:** Baseball. **Special Collections:** August Hermann correspondence; A.G. Mills correspondence; George Weiss; Lou Perini Collection; Roger Angell Collection; Negro baseball collection; official records of the major leagues. **Holdings:** 10,000 books; 750 bound periodical volumes; 1500 pamphlets; 25,000 player data cards; 150,000 photographs; 150 VF drawers of biographical clippings; 1000 videotapes; 700 reels of microfilm; 1100 reels of motion picture film. **Subscriptions:** 85 journals and other serials; 9 newspapers. **Services:** Copying; 16mm film rental library; genealogical research; inquiries answered; library open to the public by appointment. **Computerized Information Services:** Museum and Library Accession Records (internal database). **Networks/Consortia:** Member of South Central Research Library Council (SCRLC). **Publications:** Bibliographies, occasional. **Remarks:** FAX: (607)547-4094. **Staff:** Patricia Kelly, Photo.Coll.Mgr.; Bill Deane, Res.Assoc.

★ 11089 ★
National Biomedical Research Foundation - Library (Med)
Georgetown University Medical Center
3900 Reservoir Rd., N.W.   Phone: (202)687-2121
Washington, DC 20007   JoAnn Ahern, Adm.
Founded: 1960. **Staff:** Prof 1. **Subjects:** Biochemistry, evolution, proteins, nucleic acids, origins of life, pattern recognition, biomedical engineering and instrumentation, mathematics, computer technology, computerized radiology, computers in biology and medicine, health operations research. **Holdings:** 4000 books; 8 VF drawers of staff publications reprints. **Subscriptions:** 130 journals and other serials. **Services:** Interlibrary loan; copying; library open to the public with permission. **Computerized Information Services:** MEDLINE. **Remarks:** FAX: (202)687-1662. Affiliated with Georgetown University Medical School.

National Board of Antiquities (of Finland)
See: **Finland - National Ministry of Education - National Board of Antiquities** (5711)

★ 11090 ★
National Broadcasting Company, Inc. - NBC News Archives (Info Sci)
30 Rockefeller Plaza, Rm. 922   Phone: (212)664-3797
New York, NY 10112   Nancy Cole, Dir., News Archv.
Staff: Prof 5; Other 21. **Subjects:** Current and historic events. **Holdings:** 200 million feet of newsfilm; 50 million feet of stock shot footage; news video cassettes; NBC news documentaries. **Subscriptions:** 12 journals and other serials. **Services:** Archives open to buyers of newsfilm/tape. **Automated Operations:** Computerized cataloging. **Computerized Information Services:** Internal database. **Remarks:** FAX: (212)957-8917.

★ 11091 ★
National Broadcasting Company, Inc. - Records Administration Information and Archives (Info Sci)
30 Rockefeller Plaza, Rm. 1508 W.   Phone: (212)664-2690
New York, NY 10112   Catherine Lim, Sr.Adm.
Staff: Prof 3; Other 2. **Subjects:** NBC radio and television broadcast history. **Special Collections:** Radio masterbooks and logs; television masterbooks. **Holdings:** 2000 bound periodical volumes; 7060 reels of microfilm; 34 VF drawers of broadcasting indexes; 5900 audiotapes; 3000 radio and television audio cassettes. **Services:** Copying; archives open to the public with restrictions. **Staff:** Vera Mayer, V.P., Info.Serv.; Debra Levinson, Mgr., Info.Serv.

★ 11092 ★
National Broadcasting Company, Inc. - Reference Library (Info Sci)
30 Rockefeller Plaza, Rm. 1426   Phone: (212)664-5307
New York, NY 10112-0001   Vera Mayer, V.P., Info.Serv.
Founded: 1930. **Staff:** Prof 10; Other 2. **Subjects:** Broadcasting, politics and government, current events, business, economics, marketing, advertising. **Special Collections:** NBC history. **Holdings:** 17,000 books; 650 bound periodical volumes; 8800 reels of microfilm; 170 VF drawers of clippings. **Subscriptions:** 225 journals and other serials; 16 newspapers. **Services:** Copying; SDI; library open to NBC and General Electric employees, to librarians by appointment, and to the public on a fee basis. **Automated Operations:** Computerized cataloging, acquisitions, serials, and circulation. **Computerized Information Services:** DIALOG Information Services, BRS Information Technologies, NEXIS, VU/TEXT Information Services, Dow Jones News/Retrieval, NewsNet, Inc., WILSONLINE, CQ Washington Alert Service, DataTimes, Info Globe, LEXIS, BASELINE, Reuter TEXTLINE, FT PROFILE, CompuServe Information Service, InvesText, USNI Military Database, Burrelle's Broadcast Database. Performs searches on fee basis. **Remarks:** Alternate telephone number(s): 664-5721. FAX: (212)582-7734. **Also Known As:** NBC. **Staff:** Debra Levinson, Mgr., Lib.Info.Sys.; Jerry Bornstein, Sr.Res.; Judy Freidman, Sr. Res; Svetlana Shakner, Sr. Res.; Joan Levinstein, Sr.Res.; Sandra Newman, Res.Libn.; Carolyn Wilder, Res.Libn.; Judy Ganeles, Res.Libn.; Ramona Perry-Jones, Res.Libn.; Gerard Middleton, Res.Libn.; Ruth Tenenbaum, Res.Libn.; Celine Wojtala, Res.Libn.

National Building Technology Centre (of Australia)
See: **Australia - Commonwealth Scientific and Industrial Research Organization (CSIRO) - Division of Building Construction and Engineering - National Building Technology Centre** (1324)

★ 11093 ★
National Cable Television Institute - Resource Center (Info Sci)
Box 27277   Phone: (303)761-8554
Denver, CO 80227   Roland D. Hieb, Exec.Dir.
Subjects: Technical careers in cable television, satellite earth station technology. **Holdings:** Figures not available. **Services:** Library not open to the public. **Remarks:** FAX: (303)761-8556.

National Cancer Institute
See: **U.S. Natl. Institutes of Health** (17627)

★ 11094 ★
National Capital Historical Museum of Transportation - Library (Trans)
P.O. Box 4007   Phone: (301)384-6088
Silver Spring, MD 20914-0007   Neil Otchin, Cur.
Founded: 1979. **Staff:** 2. **Subjects:** Street railways, railroads, transportation. **Holdings:** 650 books, photograph collections, and other publications. **Services:** Library open to the public for reference use only with curator's approval. **Computerized Information Services:** Internal database.

National Capital Park-East - Douglass Private Collection
See: **U.S. Natl. Park Service - Frederick Douglass National Historic Site - Library** (17716)

★ 11095 ★
National Car Rental System, Inc. - Business Information Center
7700 France Ave., S.
Minneapolis, MN 55435-5296
Defunct.

National Cartographic Information Center
See: **Virginia (State) Department of Mines, Minerals, and Energy** (19886)

National Cartoonists Society Archives
See: **Ohio State University - Cartoon, Graphic, and Photographic Arts Research Library** (12299)

National Catholic Press and Library for the Visually Handicapped
See: Xavier Society for the Blind (20675)

National Catholic Rural Life Conference Archives
See: Marquette University - Department of Special Collections and
University Archives - Manuscript Collections Memorial Library (9709)

★ 11096 ★
National Catholic Stewardship Council - Information Center (Rel-Phil)
1275 K St., N.W., Suite 980   Phone: (202)289-1093
Washington, DC 20005   Matthew R. Paratore, Natl.Dir.
Staff: 2. **Subjects:** Stewardship-ministries; fundraising; data for diocesan/parish councils, finance committees, stewardship committees. **Holdings:** Figures not available. **Services:** Library not open to the public. **Publications:** Newsletter, quarterly; Stewardship Kit for Increased Offertory and Time and Talent; Wills Awareness Seminar Kit; Renewal Stewardship Kit; Annual Stewardship Conference presentations/cassettes. **Remarks:** FAX: (202)682-9018.

National Center for Agricultural Utilization Research
See: U.S.D.A. - Agricultural Research Service - National Center for
Agricultural Utilization Research - Library (17189)

★ 11097 ★
National Center for Appropriate Technology - Library (Energy)
3040 Continental Dr.
Box 3838   Phone: (406)494-4572
Butte, MT 59702   Rose C. Sullivan, Libn.
Founded: 1977. **Staff:** Prof 3; Other 1. **Subjects:** Appropriate technology, solar and wind energy, building technology, agriculture, biomass, superinsulation, community and economic development. **Holdings:** 6000 books; 96 VF drawers; 1 cabinet of blueprints. **Subscriptions:** 500 journals and other serials. **Services:** Interlibrary loan; copying; library open to the public with restrictions on circulation. **Computerized Information Services:** DIALOG Information Services. **Publications:** List of publications - available upon request. **Remarks:** FAX: (406)494-2905. **Staff:** Gerry Durkin, Rsrc.Spec.; Ilen Stoll, Rsrc.Spec.

★ 11098 ★
National Center for Atmospheric Research - High Altitude Observatory Library (Sci-Engr)
P.O. Box 3000
Boulder, CO 80307   Phone: (303)497-1516
Founded: 1960. **Staff:** 1. **Subjects:** Solar physics, astronomy, astrophysics, geophysics, mathematics, physics. **Holdings:** 7000 books; 6000 bound periodical volumes; reports. **Subscriptions:** 160 journals and other serials. **Services:** Interlibrary loan; copying; library open to the public for reference use only. **Automated Operations:** Computerized public access catalog, cataloging, serials, and circulation. **Remarks:** FAX: (303)497-1170.

★ 11099 ★
National Center for Atmospheric Research - Library (Sci-Engr)
Box 3000   Phone: (303)497-1180
Boulder, CO 80307-3000   Karon M. Kelly, Mgr., Info.Sup.Serv.
Founded: 1962. **Staff:** Prof 3; Other 6. **Subjects:** Meteorology, physics, mathematics, computer science, chemistry, oceanography, electrical and mechanical engineering. **Holdings:** 22,000 books; 15,000 bound periodical volumes; 20,000 indexed technical reports; 47,000 indexed technical reports on microfiche. **Subscriptions:** 630 journals and other serials. **Services:** Interlibrary loan; copying; SDI; current awareness; library open to the public. **Automated Operations:** Computerized public access catalog, cataloging, acquisitions, serials, and circulation (SIRSI). **Computerized Information Services:** DIALOG Information Services, OCLC. **Networks/Consortia:** Member of Bibliographic Center for Research, Rocky Mountain Region, Inc. (BCR), Central Colorado Library System (CCLS). **Publications:** Weekly bulletin of acquisitions. **Remarks:** FAX: (303)497-1170. **Formerly:** Its Mesa Library. **Staff:** Gayl Gray, Pub.Serv.Libn.; Terry Murray, Tech.Serv.Libn.

National Center for Chronic Disease Prevention and Health Promotion
See: U.S. Centers for Disease Control (17128)

★ 11100 ★
National Center for Computer Crime Data (Comp Sci)
1222 17th St., Suite B
Santa Cruz, CA 95062   Phone: (408)475-4457
                              Jay J. BloomBecker, Dir.
Founded: 1978. **Staff:** 4. **Subjects:** Computer crime, security, ethics. **Special Collections:** Case histories of computer crimes (800 files). **Holdings:** 200 books; legal documents. **Subscriptions:** 20 journals and other serials; 5 newspapers. **Services:** Interlibrary loan; copying; center open to the public. **Remarks:** FAX: (408)475-5336.

★ 11101 ★
National Center for Constitutional Studies - Library
5288 S. 320 West, No. B-158
Salt Lake City, UT 84107
Subjects: United States Constitution, constitutional principles, states' rights. **Holdings:** 5000 volumes; research file; biographical archives. **Remarks:** Currently inactive.

National Center for Death Education
See: Mount Ida College - Wadsworth Learning Resource Center (10805)

★ 11102 ★
National Center for Education in Maternal and Child Health - Library (Med)
38th & R St., N.W.
Washington, DC 20057   Phone: (202)625-8400
                     Olivia K. Pickett, Dir., Info.Serv.
Founded: 1982. **Staff:** Prof 3. **Subjects:** Maternal and child health - genetics, prenatal care, adolescent health, chronic illness/disability, developmental disabilities, infant mortality, nutrition, violence and injury prevention, child health. **Holdings:** 5000 books; ephemeral literature; organization files. **Subscriptions:** 50 journals and other serials. **Services:** Library open to health professionals; responds to requests from the public. **Computerized Information Services:** BRS Information Technologies; Organization database, bibliographic database, Special Projects of Regional and National Significance (SPRANS) database (internal databases). **Publications:** List of publications - available on request. **Remarks:** FAX: (202)625-8404. Branch of U.S. Public Health Service - Health Resources and Services Administration. Affiliated with Bureau of Maternal and Child Health and Resources Development.

★ 11103 ★
National Center for Health Statistics - Clearinghouse on Health Indexes (Med)
6525 Belcrest Rd.
Presidential Rm. 1070
Hyattsville, MD 20782-2003   Phone: (301)436-7035
                              Pennifer Erickson, Chf.
Staff: Prof 2; Other 1. **Subjects:** Health statistics, quality of life assessment, cost of illness studies. **Holdings:** 3000 reprints and original manuscripts. **Services:** SDI; clearinghouse open to the public by appointment. **Computerized Information Services:** NLM; Health Index Info (internal database). **Publications:** Bibliography on Health Indexes. **Remarks:** Center is part of U.S. Public Health Service. **Staff:** Anita Powell, Lib.Serv. & Tech.Info.

★ 11104 ★
National Center for Juvenile Justice - Technical Assistance Resource Center (Law)
701 Forbes Ave.   Phone: (412)227-6950
Pittsburgh, PA 15219   Hunter Hurst, Dir.
Subjects: Juvenile justice, courts, computer applications to the juvenile court, management information systems. **Holdings:** 1500 volumes of administrative manuals, blueprints, evaluations, and other applied documents. **Computerized Information Services:** National Juvenile Court Data Archive, Automated Juvenile Law Archive (internal databases). Performs searches on fee basis. **Special Indexes:** Kindex: An Index to Legal Periodical Literature Concerning Children (print, online); Index to Technical Assistance Resource Center Materials (online).

National Center for Research in Vocational Education
See: ERIC Clearinghouse on Adult, Career, and Vocational Education
(5395)

★ 11105 ★
**National Center for Science Education - William V. Mayer Creation/
Evolution Resource Center** (Sci-Engr)
2530 San Pedro Ave., No. D   Phone: (510)843-3393
Berkeley, CA 94702-2013   Eugenie C. Scott, Ph.D.
Founded: 1984. **Staff:** Prof 1. **Subjects:** Creationism, evolution, religious
right, anti-evolutionism, science education policy. **Holdings:** Books;
technical and popular articles; documents; debate transcripts; book reviews.
Services: Copying; center open to the public; answers telephone queries.
Publications: NCSE Reports (newsletter), quarterly; Creation/Evolution
(journal), biannual. **Remarks:** FAX: (510)843-2237. Center is a pro-
evolution clearinghouse and information center.

National Center of Scientific and Technological Information (of Israel)
See: Israel - National Center of Scientific and Technological Information
(8264)

★ 11106 ★
National Center for Social Policy & Practice - Information Center (Soc
Sci)
7981 Eastern Ave.   Phone: (301)565-0333
Silver Spring, MD 20910   Charlotte Reppy, Dir. of Info.Serv.
Founded: 1982. **Staff:** Prof 2; Other 1. **Subjects:** Social work - practice,
administration, education; health and social policy; social welfare. **Holdings:**
3500 books; 100 bound periodical volumes; 600 conference tapes; 1000 other
cataloged items. **Subscriptions:** 250 journals and other serials; 35
newspapers and newsletters. **Services:** Interlibrary loan; copying; center
open to the public by appointment. **Computerized Information Services:**
Social Work Abstracts Database, available through BRS Information
Technologies. Performs searches on fee basis. **Remarks:** Alternate telephone
number(s): 495-7207. FAX: (301)495-0842. Toll-free telephone number(s):
is (800)-638-8799.

National Center for Standards and Certification Information
See: U.S. Natl. Institute of Standards and Technology (17621)

★ 11107 ★
National Center for State Courts - Library (Law)
300 Newport Ave.   Phone: (804)253-2000
Williamsburg, VA 23187-8798   Erick Baker Low, Libn.
Founded: 1973. **Staff:** Prof 3; Other 2. **Subjects:** Judicial administration,
state courts, criminal justice. **Holdings:** 27,000 books and pamphlets; 4000
microforms; NCSC project archives. **Subscriptions:** 400 journals and other
serials. **Services:** Interlibrary loan; copying; library open to the public by
permission. **Automated Operations:** Computerized cataloging and ILL.
Computerized Information Services: DIALOG Information Services,
OCLC, LEXIS, WESTLAW. **Networks/Consortia:** Member of CAPCON
Library Network, Criminal Justice Information Exchange Group.
Publications: Selected List of Recent Acquisitions. **Remarks:** FAX:
(804)220-0449. **Staff:** Peggy W. Rogers, Acq.Libn.; Ruth Etheredge, Cat.

★ 11108 ★
**National Center for State Courts - Northeastern Regional Office -
Donald J. Hurley Library** (Law)
2 Dundee Park   Phone: (508)470-1881
Andover, MA 01810-3743   Jeanette Erard, Adm.Asst.
Staff: Prof 1. **Subjects:** Judicial administration, court information systems,
criminal justice data management. **Special Collections:** National
commission reports; bibliography of the National Institute of Law
Enforcement and Criminal Justice publications. **Holdings:** 3060 volumes;
general rules; NCSC publications and reports. **Subscriptions:** 55 journals
and other serials. **Services:** Interlibrary loan; library open to the public.
Remarks: FAX: (508)474-8088.

★ 11109 ★
**National Center for the Study of Collective Bargaining in Higher
Education and the Professions - Elias Lieberman Higher Education
Contract Library** (Bus-Fin)
17 Lexington Ave.
Box 322   Phone: (212)387-1510
New York, NY 10012   Joel M. Douglas, Dir.
Staff: Prof 4. **Subjects:** Collective bargaining, higher education, health
professions, faculty unions, arbitration, grievance procedures. **Holdings:** 800
books; 400 faculty contracts from universities and colleges in the U.S. and
Canada; 100 Yeshiva-related court document files; 400 arbitration awards;
U.S. Department of Labor documents; dissertations; leaflets; bulletins.
Subscriptions: 50 journals and other serials; 5 newspapers. **Services:**
Interlibrary loan; copying; SDI; center open to the public for reference use
only. **Computerized Information Services:** DIALOG Information Services
(through Baruch College). Performs searches on fee basis. **Publications:** List
of publications - available on request. **Remarks:** Affiliated with Baruch
College of the City University of New York.

★ 11110 ★
**National Center for the Study of Corporal Punishment & Alternatives in
the Schools - Library** (Educ)
Temple University
253 Ritter Annex   Phone: (215)787-6091
Philadelphia, PA 19122   Irwin A. Hyman, Dir.
Subjects: Corporal punishment, discipline, classroom management.
Holdings: 1000 books, pamphlets, research reports; 2000 clippings; 25
dissertations. **Services:** Copying; library open to members. **Publications:**
Discipline, semiannual - by subscription. **Special Indexes:** Cross referenced
files of newspaper clippings describing corporal punishment incidents.

National Center for Toxicological Research
See: U.S. Food & Drug Administration (17510)

**National Centre for Training and Education in Prosthetics and Orthotics
(of Great Britain)**
See: University of Strathclyde (19357)

★ 11111 ★
National Center on Women and Family Law, Inc. - Information Center
(Law)
799 Broadway, Rm. 402   Phone: (212)674-8200
New York, NY 10003   Laurie Woods, Dir.
Founded: 1979. **Staff:** 6. **Subjects:** Battered women and law, marital rape,
rape, single mothers, divorce, custody, child snatching, child and wife
support. **Holdings:** 500 books; 50 VF drawers; 200 resource packets.
Subscriptions: 1500 newspapers. **Services:** Center not open to the public.
Publications: Newsletter, bimonthly. **Remarks:** FAX: (212)533-5104.

★ 11112 ★
**National Chamber of Commerce for Women, Inc. - Elizabeth Lewin
Business Library & Information Center** (Bus-Fin)
10 Waterside Plaza, Suite 6H   Phone: (212)685-3454
New York, NY 10010-2610   Maggie Rinaldi, Dir.
Founded: 1977. **Staff:** 2. **Subjects:** Law and women, labor-management
relations, small business, consumerism, women in education. **Holdings:** 1800
books; 650 bound periodical volumes; 100 cassette tapes; 800 market
research reports and proposals; 500 annual reports and quarterly brochures;
2 VF drawers of press clippings. **Subscriptions:** 10 journals and other serials.
Services: Center not open to the public. **Computerized Information Services:**
Internal database. Performs searches on fee basis. **Publications:** National
Chamber of Commerce for Women Research Digest, monthly - to members.

National Christian Resource Center
See: Bethesda Lutheran Home (1788)

★ 11113 ★
National City Bank - Investment Library (Bus-Fin)
Box 5756   Phone: (216)575-2546
Cleveland, OH 44101-0756   Laura O. Cannon, Res.Libn.
Staff: Prof 1; Other 2. **Subjects:** Security analysis, banking, finance.
Holdings: 1038 books; 150 bound periodical volumes; technical reports.
Subscriptions: 83 journals and other serials; 6 newspapers. **Services:** Library
not open to the public. **Automated Operations:** Computerized circulation.
Computerized Information Services: Internal database. **Remarks:** FAX:
(214)575-3122.

National Civic League, Inc. - Murray Seasongood Library
See: University of Colorado--Denver - Auraria Library - Archives and
Special Collections (18510)

★11114★
National Clearing House of Rehabilitation Training Materials (Educ)
816 W. 6th St.
Oklahoma State University   Phone: (405)624-7650
Stillwater, OK 74078-0435   Paul G. Gaines, Proj.Dir.
Founded: 1961. **Staff:** 4.5. **Subjects:** Rehabilitation training and counselor
skills, disabilities, special needs education, vocational rehabilitation, service
delivery. **Special Collections:** Publications of the Institute on Rehabilitation
Issues; publications of the Special Study Groups of Rehabilitation Problems,
1947-1983; World Rehabilitation Fund. **Holdings:** 3500 titles in hardcopy
or microfiche; 2000 microfiche; AV programs. **Services:** Copying;
clearinghouse open to rehabilitation professionals and students. **Automated
Operations:** Computerized acquisitions and holdings lists. **Publications:**
NCHRTM Memorandum (annotated bibliographic newsletter), quarterly -
to mailing list. **Remarks:** FAX: (405)624-0695. **Staff:** Jo Heiliger, Coord./
Libn.

National Clearinghouse on Aging - Service Center for Aging Information
See: Chippewa Valley Technical College - Technology Resource Center-
Library (3617)

★11115★
National Clearinghouse for Alcohol and Drug Information - Library
(Med)
Box 2345   Phone: (301)468-2600
Rockville, MD 20852   Lisa Swanberg, Dir., Lib. & Info.Serv.
Founded: 1987. **Staff:** Prof 6; Other 3. **Subjects:** Alcohol and other drug
abuse prevention. **Holdings:** 900 books; 19,000 cataloged items; 93,000
accessioned items. **Subscriptions:** 90 journals and other serials; 8
newspapers. **Services:** Interlibrary loan; copying; SDI; library open to the
public for reference use only. **Computerized Information Services:** Online
systems; internal database. **Publications:** Prevention Pipeline: An Alcohol
and Drug Awareness Service, bimonthly; subject area bibliographies; Fact
Sheets; guide to audiovisual materials; NCADI resource guides on various
topics. **Remarks:** FAX: (301)468-6433. Toll-free telephone number(s):
(800)729-6686. TDD: (800)487-4889. Clearinghouse is a branch of U.S.
Public Health Service - Office for Substance Abuse Prevention and is
operated under contract by Social & Health Services, Ltd. **Staff:** Kristan
Allen; Roger Bryant; John Fay; Lynn Hallard; Susan Caffery.

★11116★
National Clearinghouse for Bilingual Education (Educ)
1118 2nd St., N.W.   Phone: (800)321-NCBE
Washington, DC 20037   Joel Gomez, Dir.
Founded: 1978. **Staff:** 11. **Subjects:** Bilingual education, English as a second
language. **Special Collections:** Department of Education Title VII, Part C,
Bilingual Research Study Reports Archive (250 reports); Title VII-produced
classroom materials collection (1000 volumes). **Holdings:** 17,500 books and
reports; 400 dissertations. **Subscriptions:** 50 journals and other serials.
Services: Clearinghouse will answer telephone inquiries. **Computerized
Information Services:** Produces National Clearinghouse for Bilingual
Education (NCBE) databases. Performs searches free of charge.
Publications: Forum (newsletter), bimonthly - available on request; program
information guides; occasional papers series, irregular. **Remarks:** FAX:
(202)429-9766. Maintained by George Washington University, and located
at the Center for Applied Linguistics.

National Clearinghouse for Commuter Programs
See: University of Maryland, College Park (18808)

National Clearinghouse on Election Administration
See: U.S. Federal Election Commission (17491)

★11117★
National Clearinghouse for Legal Services - Library (Law)
407 S. Dearborn   Phone: (312)939-3830
Chicago, IL 60605   Katherine Stevenson, Hd.Libn.
Founded: 1967. **Staff:** Prof 1. **Subjects:** Legal services, public welfare,
housing, employment, schools and education, mental health, public utilities,
consumer law, juveniles. **Holdings:** 3000 books; 150 bound periodical
volumes; 48,000 cases of litigation materials; 5000 nonlitigation materials.
Subscriptions: 150 journals and other serials. **Services:** Copying; library
open to the public by appointment. **Publications:** Clearinghouse Review, 12/
year - free to Legal Services attorneys. **Special Catalogs:** Clearinghouse
Publications in Print, 13/year. **Special Indexes:** Clearinghouse Review
Cumulative Index: 1967-1984.

★11118★
National Clearinghouse on Marital and Date Rape (Soc Sci)
2325 Oak St.   Phone: (510)524-1582
Berkeley, CA 94708   Laura X, Exec.Dir.
Staff: Prof 1; Other 1. **Subjects:** Rape - marital, date, cohabitation,
legislation; marital rape legislation and prosecution. **Holdings:** 20 books;
1000 files of briefs, testimony, clippings, reports, newsletters, studies,
research, dissertations. **Subscriptions:** 10 journals and other serials.
Services: Copying; center open to the public for consultation on fee basis by
telephone. **Publications:** Bibliographic Guide to the Files on Marital Rape;
Newsletter; Summary of Greta Rideout's Story; pamphlet; sociolegal case
chart; prosecution statistics chart; state law chart. **Remarks:** Affiliated with
the Women's History Research Center, Inc. Holdings housed at University
of Illinois - Women's Studies Library. Publications available from them as
well.

National Climatic Data Center
See: U.S. Natl. Oceanic & Atmospheric Administration - National
Environmental Satellite, Data, & Information Services - National
Climatic Data Center (17654)

★11119★
National Coalition Against the Misuse of Pesticides - Library (Env-
Cons)
530 7th St., S.E.
Washington, DC 20003   Phone: (202)543-5450
Subjects: Pesticides - public health and safety, environmental problems,
economic problems. **Holdings:** 2000 volumes. **Remarks:** FAX: (202)543-
4791.

★11120★
National Coffee Association of U.S.A. - Library (Food-Bev)
110 Wall St., 13th Fl.   Phone: (212)344-5596
New York, NY 10005-3801   George E. Boecklin, Pres.
Founded: 1911. **Subjects:** Coffee, caffeine. **Holdings:** 6000 volumes of
scientific and medical literature.

★11121★
National College - Thomas Jefferson Learning Resource Center (Educ)
321 Kansas City St.   Phone: (605)394-4943
Rapid City, SD 57701   LeAnn Dean, LRC Dir.
Founded: 1964. **Staff:** Prof 1. **Subjects:** Accounting, word processing,
electronics, management, finance, taxation, data processing, marketing,
animal health, airlines, travel, medical assistance, paralegal. **Special
Collections:** American Enterprise Institute depository. **Holdings:** 33,000
books; 1425 AV programs; pamphlets; microforms. **Subscriptions:** 275
journals and other serials; 10 newspapers. **Services:** Interlibrary loan;
copying; computer workstations available; center open to the public.
Automated Operations: Computerized cataloging. **Computerized
Information Services:** OCLC. **Networks/Consortia:** Member of MINITEX
Library Information Network, South Dakota Library Network (SDLN).

National College of Art and Design (of Norway)
See: Norway - National College of Art and Design - Library (12105)

★ 11122 ★
National College of Chiropractic - Learning Resource Center (Med)
200 E. Roosevelt Rd.   Phone: (708)268-6616
Lombard, IL 60148   Joyce Whitehead, Dir.
Founded: 1963. **Staff:** Prof 4; Other 7. **Subjects:** Chiropractic, manipulation, anatomy, radiology, neurology, physiology, orthopedics. **Holdings:** 16,750 books; 8900 bound periodical volumes; 725 AV program titles; 2100 reels of microfilm. **Subscriptions:** 540 journals and other serials. **Services:** Interlibrary loan; copying; center open to the public. **Automated Operations:** Computerized cataloging. **Computerized Information Services:** NLM, BRS Information Technologies; OnTyme Electronic Message Network Service (electronic mail service). Performs searches on fee basis. **Networks/Consortia:** Member of National Network of Libraries of Medicine - Greater Midwest Region, Chiropractic Library Consortium (CLIBCON), Fox Valley Health Science Library Consortium (FVHSL), ILLINET. **Publications:** Topical bibliographies; acquisition lists. **Remarks:** FAX: (708)268-6618. Electronic mail address(es): CLASS.CLIBCON09 (OnTyme Electronic Message Network Service). **Staff:** Jane Plass, Hd. of Lib.; Russell Iwami, Ref.Libn.; Sheila Corman, Tech.Serv.Libn.

★ 11123 ★
National College of District Attorneys - Law Center (Law)
Law Center
University of Houston
Houston, TX 77204-6380   Phone: (713)747-6232
Staff: Prof 1; Other 1. **Subjects:** Constitutional law, functions of the prosecutor, trial techniques, scientific evidence. **Holdings:** Figures not available. **Services:** Center open to prosecuting attorneys. **Remarks:** FAX: (713)749-2567.

★ 11124 ★
National College of Naturopathic Medicine - Library (Med)
11231 S.E. Market   Phone: (503)255-4860
Portland, OR 97216   Friedhelm Kirchfeld, Libn.
Founded: 1978. **Staff:** Prof 1. **Subjects:** Naturopathy, homeopathy, nutrition, physiotherapy, botanical medicine, acupuncture, clinical and basic sciences. **Holdings:** 7500 books; 600 bound periodical volumes. **Subscriptions:** 103 journals and other serials. **Services:** Interlibrary loan; copying; library open to the public with restrictions.

National Colonial Farm
See: **Accokeek Foundation** (48)

★ 11125 ★
National Commission for Judicial Reform - Library (Law)
P.O. Box 1105
Staunton, VA 24401   Eustace Mullins
Founded: 1989. **Staff:** Prof 2. **Subjects:** Law - general, civil, international, tax, constitutional; history of law. **Special Collections:** Ezra Pound Collection. **Holdings:** 4000 books. **Subscriptions:** 12 journals and other serials; 6 newspapers. **Services:** Library not open to the public. **Publications:** Annual reports.

National Commission on Nuclear Safety and Safeguards (of Mexico)
See: **Mexico - National Commission on Nuclear Safety and Safeguards**
   (10241)

★ 11126 ★
National Committee for Adoption - Library (Soc Sci)
1930 17th St., N.W.
Washington, DC 20009-6207   Phone: (202)328-1200
Subjects: Adoption - voluntary agencies, adoptive parents, adoptees, birthparents, maternity services; legislation for the adoption process; infertility. **Holdings:** 2000 volumes and files; statistics. **Remarks:** FAX: (202)332-0935. Alternate telephone number(s): National Adoption Hotline, (202)628-8072.

★ 11127 ★
National Concrete Masonry Association - Library (Plan)
2302 Horse Penn Rd.   Phone: (703)713-1900
Herndon, VA 22071   Connie Filanowski, Libn.
Subjects: Masonry engineering and energy conservation. **Holdings:** 4000 volumes. **Services:** Interlibrary loan; Library not open to the public. **Remarks:** FAX: (703)713-1910.

★ 11128 ★
National Confederation of Dominican Workers - Library (Soc Sci)
Ave. Duarte 270
Santo Domingo, Dominican Republic   Phone: (809)682-5754
Subjects: Dominican workers - economic and social welfare. **Holdings:** 1000 volumes. **Also Known As:** Confederacion Nacional de Trabajadores Dominicanos.

★ 11129 ★
National Conference of Christians and Jews - Paula K. Lazrus Library
   of Intergroup Relations
71 Fifth Ave., Suite 1100
New York, NY 10003   Phone: (212)206-0006
Subjects: Intergroup relations, interreligious relations, religion and public affairs, race relations. **Special Collections:** Early works on intergroup relations; materials from the presidential election of 1960. **Holdings:** 2000 books; 300 pamphlets. **Remarks:** Archival material housed at University of Minnesota - Social Welfare History Archives, c/o Wilson Library, Minneapolis, MN 55455. Currently inactive.

★ 11130 ★
National Conference on Ministry to the Armed Forces - Chaplains
   Memorial Library (Rel-Phil)
4141 N. Henderson Rd., Suite 13
Arlington, VA 22203   Phone: (703)276-7905
Founded: 1963. **Staff:** 1.7. **Subjects:** Military chaplaincy, religion in the armed forces, church and state relations and the chaplaincy. **Holdings:** 655 volumes; 85 journals and publications. **Subscriptions:** 15 journals and other serials. **Computerized Information Services:** Library not open to the public. **Computerized Information Services:** Internal database. **Remarks:** FAX: (703)276-7906. **Staff:** Clifford T. Weathers; Maureen Francis.

★ 11131 ★
National Conference on Soviet Jewry - Research Bureau (Rel-Phil)
Ten E. 40th St., Suite 907   Phone: (212)679-6122
New York, NY 10016   Martin A. Wenick, Exec.Dir.
Founded: 1971. **Subjects:** Soviet Jewry - emigration, culture; U.S.-U.S.S.R. relations. **Special Collections:** Case histories of individual Soviet Jewish refuseniks and prisoners of conscience. **Holdings:** 100 books; periodical volumes; 32 VF drawers of files and clippings; 30 loose-leaf books. **Subscriptions:** 45 journals and other serials; 35 newspapers. **Services:** Copying; bureau open to the public with restrictions. **Publications:** Emigration Update and Statistics, weekly; Newsbreak, weekly - both by subscription. **Remarks:** FAX: (212)686-1193. Telex: 237311 NCSJ. **Also Known As:** NCSJ. **Staff:** Mark Levin, Assoc.Exec.Dir.

★ 11132 ★
National Conference of State Legislatures - Library (Law)
1560 Broadway, Suite 700
Denver, CO 80202-5140   Phone: (303)830-2200
Subjects: State legislatures - quality, effectiveness, voice in federal decision-making, interstate communication, cooperation. **Holdings:** 3000 volumes; statistics. **Services:** Library not open to the public. **Computerized Information Services:** Produces LEGISNET. **Remarks:** FAX: (303)863-8003.

National Congress of Parents and Teachers
See: **National PTA** (11255)

★11133★
National Conservatory of Arts and Crafts - National Institute for Information Science - Library (Info Sci)
292, rue Saint-Martin
F-75141 Paris Cedex 3, France
Phone: 1 40272516
Adriana Lopez-Vroz, Doc.
Subjects: Information science. Holdings: 5500 bound volumes; 2000 theses. Subscriptions: 100 journals and other serials. Services: Library open to Institute students, documentalists, and other information professionals. Computerized Information Services: Produces Bulletin Bibliographique INTD Data Base. Publications: Bulletin Bibliographique INTD, monthly. Remarks: FAX: 1 42719329. Telex: CNAM 240 247. Also Known As: Conservatoire National des Arts et Metiers - Institut National des Techniques de la Documentation.

★11134★
National Corrugated Steel Pipe Association - Library (Sci-Engr)
2011 Eye St., N.W., 5th Fl.
Washington, DC 20006
Phone: (202)223-2217
Corwin L. Tracy, Chf.Engr.
Founded: 1956. Subjects: Corrugated steel drainage pipes, drainage, materials. Holdings: 1000 volumes, pieces of technical literature, research data. Services: Library not open to the public. Remarks: FAX: (202)457-9121.

★11135★
National Cotton Council of America - Library (Biol Sci)
1918 N. Parkway
Memphis, TN 38112
Phone: (901)274-9030
Jerry Armour, Info.Sys.Spec.
Founded: 1946. Staff: Prof 1. Subjects: Cotton. Holdings: 800 books; 150 bound periodical volumes; 50 VF drawers. Subscriptions: 300 journals and other serials. Services: Copying; library open to the public by appointment. Computerized Information Services: DIALOG Information Services, CompuServe Information Service; internal database. Remarks: FAX: (901)725-0510.

★11136★
National Council Against Health Fraud - Library (Med)
P.O. Box 1276
Loma Linda, CA 92354
Phone: (714)824-4690
Founded: 1977. Subjects: Consumer protection in health marketplace; health - fraud, misinformation, quackery. Holdings: 500 books; 30 reports; topic files. Services: Library open to the public for reference use only. Publications: Resource Lists of Health Information; NCAHF Newsletter; NCAHF Bulletin Board; Recommended Antiquackery Publications.

★11137★
The National Council on the Aging, Inc. - Ollie A. Randall Library (Soc Sci)
409 3rd St., S.W., No. 200
Washington, DC 20024
Phone: (202)479-1665
Founded: 1950. Staff: Prof 2; Other 2. Subjects: Aging, retirement, economics, employment, community organization, legislation, nursing homes, senior centers, health care. Special Collections: Ollie A. Randall papers. Holdings: 12,000 volumes; 16 VF drawers; 34 VF drawers of archival materials. Subscriptions: 300 journals and other serials. Services: Interlibrary loan; copying; library open to the public. Publications: Abstracts in Social Gerontology: Current Literature on Aging, - by subscription; bibliographies - for sale. Remarks: Alternate telephone number(s): 479-6669. FAX: (202)479-0735.

National Council on Alcoholism, Inc. - Yvelin Gardner Alcoholism Library
See: Rutgers University - Rutgers Center of Alcohol Studies (14172)

★11138★
National Council of Farmer Cooperatives - Library
50 F St., N.W., Suite 900
Washington, DC 20001
Founded: 1925. Subjects: Farmer cooperatives. Holdings: 5000 volumes. Remarks: Affiliated with Agricultural Cooperative Development International. Currently inactive.

National Council of Jewish Women Volunteers - Jewish Community Center of Greater Minneapolis
See: Jewish Community Center of Greater Minneapolis (8382)

★11139★
National Council for Medical Research - Library (Med)
P.O. Box 1105
Staunton, VA 24401
E.C. Mullins
Founded: 1987. Staff: Prof 2. Subjects: History of medicine; organized medicine in the United States; health care - alternative, government. Special Collections: Josephson Collection; Mendelsohn Collection. Holdings: 800 books. Subscriptions: 8 journals and other serials; 3 newspapers. Services: Library not open to the public. Publications: Annual reports - available by subscription.

★11140★
National Council of the Paper Industry for Air & Stream Improvement, Inc. - Library (Env-Cons)
260 Madison Ave.
New York, NY 10016
Phone: (212)532-9000
Dr. Isaiah Gellman, Pres.
Founded: Staff: 1. 1942. Subjects: Environmental quality management. Holdings: 10,000 documents. Subscriptions: 25 journals and other serials. Services: Library open to personnel only. Remarks: FAX: (212)779-2849.

★11141★
National Council of Savings Institutions - Library (Bus-Fin)
1101 15th St., N.W., Suite 400
Washington, DC 20005
Phone: (202)857-3100
Cheryl Smith
Founded: 1983. Staff: Prof 1. Subjects: Savings institutions, bank operations, general banking, finance, mortgage finance. Holdings: 1500 books; 133 bound periodical volumes; 60 drawers of clippings, unbound reports, documents. Subscriptions: 125 journals and other serials; 9 newspapers. Services: Interlibrary loan; copying; library open to the public with special permission of librarian. Computerized Information Services: LEXIS, NEXIS. Remarks: FAX: (202)659-4816.

National Council of Scientific and Technical Research (of Argentina) - Darwinian Institute of Botany
See: Darwinian Institute of Botany (4618)

National Council of Scientific and Technological Development (of Brazil) - Brazilian Institute for Information in Science and Technology
See: Brazil - National Council of Scientific and Technological Development - Brazilian Institute for Information in Science and Technology (2095)

National Council of Scientific and Technological Development (of Brazil) - Emilio Goeldi Museum
See: Emilio Goeldi Museum (6519)

National Council of Scientific and Technological Development (of Brazil) - National Institute of Amazon Research
See: National Institute of Amazon Research (11206)

★11142★
National Council of Senior Citizens - Information Center (Soc Sci)
1331 F St., N.W.
Washington, DC 20004
Phone: (202)347-8800
Brien Kinkel, Info.Spec.
Founded: 1961. Staff: Prof 1. Subjects: Gerontology, legislative issues affecting the elderly. Holdings: 2500 books; 12 VF cabinets. Subscriptions: 200 journals and other serials. Services: Interlibrary loan; library open to the public. Computerized Information Services: DIALOG Information Services, Washington Alert (Congressional Quarterly). Publications: Bimonthly acquisitions list. Remarks: FAX: (202)624-9595. Staff: Christopher Papps, Lib.Serv.Coord.

★ 11143 ★
National Council of Teachers of English - Library (Educ)
1111 Kenyon Rd.   Phone: (217)328-3870
Urbana, IL 61801   Carolyn H. McMahon, Libn.
Founded: 1912. **Staff:** Prof 1. **Subjects:** English language teaching,
curriculum, language, education, communication, teacher training, speech,
computers, teaching English as an international language, language arts,
reading, literature. **Special Collections:** NCTE monographs (1400 titles);
NCTE journals and newsletters; NCTE archives. **Holdings:** 4500 books; 275
bound periodical volumes; 200 boxes of archival material; 300 cassette tapes.
Subscriptions: 175 journals and other serials; 6 newspapers. **Services:**
Interlibrary loan; copying; SDI; library open to the public for reference use
only. **Computerized Information Services:** DIALOG Information Services.
Performs searches on fee basis. Contact Person: Millie Davis, 328-3870, ext.
220. **Networks/Consortia:** Member of Lincoln Trail Libraries System
(LTLS). **Remarks:** FAX: (217)328-9645.

★ 11144 ★
National Council of Teachers of Mathematics - Teacher/Learning Center
   (Educ)
1906 Association Dr.   Phone: (703)620-9840
Reston, VA 22091   Kelly Fox, Adm.Asst.
Staff: 5. **Subjects:** Mathematics. **Holdings:** 2000 volumes; 500
microcomputer programs; 70 AV programs; 100 games and other
instructional aids. **Services:** Copying; center open to the public.
Computerized Information Services: CompuServe Information Service.
Remarks: FAX: (703)476-2970.

National Council on Year-Round Education
See: National Association for Year-Round Education (11082)

★ 11145 ★
National Council of YMCAs of Japan - Library (Soc Sci)
2-3-18, Nishiwaseda
Shinjuku-ku
Tokyo 169, Japan   Phone: 33 2030171
                                              Hiroshi Yoshinaga
Founded: 1905. **Subjects:** Individual and community development, social
justice, voluntarism, youth in Japan, social service activities, Christian
Movement in Japan, YMCA history. **Holdings:** 10,000 volumes. **Services:**
Copying; library open to the public. **Remarks:** FAX: 33 2070226. Telex:
232992 YMCA JP.

National Courts' Library
See: U.S. Court of Appeals for the Federal Circuit (17161)

★ 11146 ★
National Cowboy Hall of Fame & Western Heritage Center - Research
   Library of Western Americana (Hist)
1700 N.E. 63rd St.   Phone: (405)478-2250
Oklahoma City, OK 73111   Bobby Weaver
Founded: 1965. **Subjects:** Cowboys and Western history. **Special
Collections:** South American Gaucho. **Holdings:** 10,000 books. **Services:**
Library open to the public for reference use only.

★ 11147 ★
National Crime Prevention Institute - Information Center (Soc Sci)
University of Louisville, Shelby Campus   Phone: (502)588-6987
Louisville, KY 40292   Barbara R. Bomar, Asst.Dir.
Founded: 1973. **Staff:** Prof 2. **Subjects:** Crime prevention through
environmental design, security systems, community participation. **Special
Collections:** Juvenile Delinquents/Habitual Juvenile Offenders (250
documents). **Holdings:** 1200 books; 300 bound periodical volumes; 2000
crime prevention programs; 50,000 brochures; 50 films. **Subscriptions:** 100
journals and other serials. **Services:** Copying; center open to the public with
restrictions. **Remarks:** FAX: (502)588-6990.

National Criminal Justice Reference Service
See: U.S. Dept. of Justice - National Institute of Justice (17260)

National Dairy Shrine Museum
See: Hoard Historical Museum - Library (7297)

National Defense College of Canada
See: Canada - National Defence - Fort Frontenac Library (2783)

National Defense University
See: U.S. Natl. Defense University (17609)

National Diet Library (of Japan)
See: Japan - National Diet Library (8334)

★ 11148 ★
National Digestive Diseases Information Clearinghouse (Med)
Box NDDIC
9000 Rockville Pike
Bethesda, MD 20892   Phone: (301)468-6344
Founded: 1980. **Staff:** Prof 4; Other 1. **Subjects:** Digestive diseases.
Holdings: 100 books; 500 patient education booklets and pamphlets.
Subscriptions: 15 journals and other serials. **Services:** Clearinghouse not
open to the public. **Computerized Information Services:** BRS Information
Technologies, DIALOG Information Services, MEDLARS, CHID
(Combined Health Information Database). Performs searches free of charge
for CHID. **Publications:** Fact sheets on selected digestive disease topics - free
upon request. **Special Catalogs:** CHID Search Reference Guide; CHID
Word List; Digestive Diseases Organizations: Lay and Voluntary; Digestive
Diseases Organizations: Professional. **Remarks:** Maintained by National
Institute of Diabetes and Digestive and Kidney Diseases, U.S. National
Institutes of Health, and U.S. Department of Health and Human Services.
Staff: Frances Heilig, Info.Spec.

National Economic Development & Law Center
See: National Housing Law Project/National Economic Development &
   Law Center (11196)

★ 11149 ★
National Economic Research Associates, Inc. - Library (Bus-Fin)
555 S. Flower St., Suite 4100   Phone: (213)628-0131
Los Angeles, CA 90071   Annie S. Lam, Anl.
Founded: 1975. **Staff:** Prof 1; Other 1. **Subjects:** Antitrust law, energy,
economics. **Holdings:** 3500 books; 30 bound periodical volumes; 8 VF
drawers of internal reports; 2 VF drawers of trade regulation case decisions.
Subscriptions: 123 journals and other serials. **Services:** Interlibrary loan;
library not open to the public. **Automated Operations:** Computerized
cataloging. **Computerized Information Services:** DIALOG Information
Services, LEXIS, DRI/McGraw-Hill, Reuters Information Services
(Canada), Dow Jones News/Retrieval. **Publications:** Newsletter - for
internal distribution only. **Remarks:** FAX: (213)628-9368. **Also Known As:**
NERA. **Staff:** Sue G. Yee, Asst.Libn.

★ 11150 ★
National Economic Research Associates, Inc. - Library (Energy)
1800 M St., N.W.   Phone: (202)466-3510
Washington, DC 20036   C. Christopher Pavek, Libn.
Founded: 1965. **Staff:** Prof 2. **Subjects:** Petroleum, natural gas, energy,
economics, antitrust, public utilities. **Holdings:** 5000 books; Wall Street
Journal, 1973 to present, on microfilm. **Subscriptions:** 300 journals and
other serials. **Services:** Interlibrary loan; library not open to the public.
Automated Operations: Computerized cataloging and acquisitions.
Computerized Information Services: DIALOG Information Services,
LEXIS, NEXIS, Dow Jones News/Retrieval, VU/TEXT Information
Services. **Publications:** Library Letter, monthly. **Remarks:** FAX: (202)466-
3605.

★ 11151 ★
National Economic Research Associates, Inc. - Library (Energy)
123 Main St., 8th Fl.   Phone: (914)681-7200
White Plains, NY 10601   Joan Houghton, Hd.Libn.
Founded: 1960. **Staff:** Prof 2; Other 1. **Subjects:** Energy, public utilities,
economics, environmental studies, antitrust, telecommunications. **Holdings:**
5000 books; U.S. Government documents; New York Stock Exchange and
American Stock Exchange companies annual reports, 1977-1987, on
microfiche. **Subscriptions:** 300 journals and other serials. **Services:**
Interlibrary loan; copying; library open to the public with restrictions.
Automated Operations: Computerized circulation. **Computerized
Information Services:** DIALOG Information Services, Mead Data Central,
WESTLAW, DRI/McGraw-Hill, Interactive Data Services, Inc., Dow
Jones News/Retrieval, NewsNet, Inc., VU/TEXT Information Services,
OCLC EPIC. **Remarks:** FAX: (914)681-7953; (914)681-7925. A subsidiary
of Marsh and McLennan, Inc. **Staff:** Kathy Mason-Page, Libn.

★11152★
National Ecumenical Coalition, Inc. - Library (Rel-Phil, Soc Sci)
4300 Old Dominion Dr., Suite 502   Phone: (703)522-9759
Arlington, VA 22207-3246   Bro. Scott R. Desmond, S.J.
Staff: Prof 22. **Subjects:** Civil and constitutional rights, ecumenical programs, juvenile delinquency, drug abuse, law, gay rights, AIDS advocacy, human rights, Equal Rights Amendment (ERA), refugee programs. **Holdings:** 6000 books; 7500 bound periodical volumes; 340 boxes of civil rights archives; 51 boxes of gay rights archives; 200 boxes of ecumenical archives; U.N. publications. **Subscriptions:** 350 journals and other serials; 72 newspapers. **Services:** Library not open to the public. **Automated Operations:** Computerized cataloging and serials. **Publications:** N.E.C. Today, monthly - by subscription; bibliography on civil rights, gay rights, AIDS education, ecumenical organizations, and drug abuse (computer printout).

★11153★
National Educational Resource Center of the Jewish Education Service of North America, Inc. (Area-Ethnic)
730 Broadway   Phone: (212)529-2000
New York, NY 10003-9540   Caren N. Levine, Dir.
Founded: 1978. **Staff:** Prof 1; Other 1. **Subjects:** Jewish education, Holocaust, Israel, Bible, Jewish life cycle, youth movements. **Special Collections:** Uncopyrighted teacher-designed classroom materials. **Holdings:** 1000 file boxes of educational materials on 47 subjects. **Services:** Center open to the public by appointment. **Publications:** NERCatalog. **Remarks:** Educational information available on request. FAX: (212)529-2009.

National Emergency Training Center
See: **Federal Emergency Management Agency** (5626)

★11154★
National Employee Services & Recreation Association - Information Center (Rec)
2400 S. Downing Ave.   Phone: (708)562-8130
Westchester, IL 60154   Patrick B. Stinson, Exec.Dir.
Founded: 1941. **Subjects:** Employees - activities, sports, recreation, facilities, travel, fitness, wellness, preretirement planning, assistance programs, productivity, day care. **Holdings:** 50 volumes. **Services:** Center open to the public for reference use only. **Automated Operations:** Computerized circulation. **Publications:** List of publications - available on request. **Remarks:** FAX: (708)562-8436.

★11155★
National Employment Law Project - Library (Law)
475 Riverside Dr., Suite 240   Phone: (212)870-2121
New York, NY 10115   Deborah Hassan, Lib.Info.Mgr.
Staff: Prof 1. **Subjects:** Employment law. **Holdings:** 3000 volumes; 12 filing cases of legal case materials. **Subscriptions:** 50 journals and other serials. **Services:** Library open to legal services personnel only. **Special Catalogs:** Employment law dealing with employment problems of the poor (card).

★11156★
National Endowment for the Arts - Arts Library (Art)
1100 Pennsylvania Ave., N.W.   Phone: (202)682-5485
Washington, DC 20506   M. Christine Morrison, Libn.
Founded: 1971. **Staff:** Prof 1. **Subjects:** Folk arts, dance, design, arts in education, literature, museums, music, public policy and arts, theater, visual arts, arts management, law and art, history of government and the arts, history of the National Endowment for the Arts. **Holdings:** 7000 books; 10 VF drawers of pamphlets. **Subscriptions:** 150 journals. **Services:** Interlibrary loan; library open to the public by appointment. **Computerized Information Services:** DIALOG Information Services, OCLC. **Remarks:** FAX: (202)682-5610. **Staff:** Jeanne E. McConnell.

★11157★
National Endowment for the Arts - Library
Office of the General Counsel
1100 Pennsylvania Ave., N.W.
Washington, DC 20506
Defunct. Holdings absorbed by general library.

★11158★
National Endowment for the Humanities - Library (Hum)
1100 Pennsylvania Ave., N.W.   Phone: (202)786-0244
Washington, DC 20506   Enayet Rahim, Libn.
Founded: 1971. **Staff:** Prof 1; Other 2. **Subjects:** Humanities, education, history, language and linguistics, religion, philosophy, ethics, contemporary culture, biography, jurisprudence, politics and government. **Special Collections:** Books resulting from National Endowment for the Humanities' funding; documents relating to the history of the endowment; Jefferson lecture manuscripts. **Holdings:** 10,000 books. **Subscriptions:** 200 journals and other serials; 6 newspapers. **Services:** Interlibrary loan; copying; library open to the public by appointment. **Computerized Information Services:** DIALOG Information Services, WILSONLINE, OCLC. **Networks/Consortia:** Member of FEDLINK. **Publications:** Acquisitions list, bimonthly; periodical list, annual. **Remarks:** FAX: (202)786-0243.

National Energy Information Center
See: **U.S. Dept. of Energy - Energy Information Administration** (17232)

National Energy Software Center
See: **Argonne National Laboratory** (976)

★11159★
National Enquirer - Research Department Library (Publ)
600 S.E. Coast Ave.   Phone: (407)586-1111
Lantana, FL 33464   Martha Moffett, Res.Libn.
Founded: 1956. **Staff:** Prof 2. **Subjects:** Entertainment, biography, directories. **Special Collections:** Personality Clip Files. **Holdings:** 3500 books; back issues of the Enquirer, 1926 to present, on microfilm. **Subscriptions:** 16 journals and other serials; 12 newspapers. **Services:** Library not open to the public. **Computerized Information Services:** NEXIS, LEXIS, DataTimes, CompuServe Information Service, BASELINE. **Special Indexes:** Index to National Enquirer; Clip Files Annual Index. **Remarks:** FAX: (407)547-1017. **Staff:** Frances B. Jacobson, Libn.

★11160★
National Environmental Health Association - Library (Med)
720 S. Colorado Blvd., Suite 970, South Tower
Denver, CO 80222   Phone: (303)756-9090
Staff: 14. **Subjects:** Environmental health concerns, environmental protection. **Holdings:** 1000 volumes. **Services:** Library not open to the public. **Computerized Information Services:** Internal database. **Remarks:** FAX: (303)691-9490.

National Environmental Satellite, Data, & Information Services
See: **U.S. Natl. Oceanic & Atmospheric Administration - National Environmental Satellite, Data, & Information Services - National Climatic Data Center** (17654)

★11161★
National Epilepsy Library (Med)
4351 Garden City Dr., Suite 406   Phone: (301)459-3700
Landover, MD 20785   Bonnie Kessler, Dir.
Founded: 1982. **Staff:** Prof 4. **Subjects:** Social, psychological, medical aspects of epilepsy; neurology. **Special Collections:** Archives of the Epilepsy Movement. **Holdings:** 1000 books; 60,000 microfiche; 200 reports. **Subscriptions:** 125 journals and other serials. **Services:** Interlibrary loan; library open to the public by appointment. **Computerized Information Services:** Produces NEL Database. **Remarks:** Maintained by Epilepsy Foundation of America. Toll-free telephone number(s): is 800-332-4050. FAX: (301)577-2684. Telex: 467106 EFA CI. **Staff:** Robyn Ertwine, Assoc.Dir.; Deborah Judy, Asst.Libn.; Martina Darragh, Asst.Libn.

National Evangelical Lutheran Church Archives
See: **Concordia Historical Institute - Department of Archives and History** (4115)

National Exhibition Centre
See: **Rodman Hall Arts Centre/National Exhibition Centre** (14028)

National Farmers Union Archives
See: **University of Colorado--Boulder - Western Historical Collections/ University Archives** (18508)

★ 11162 ★
National Federation of Abstracting and Information Services (Info Sci)
1429 Walnut St., 13th Fl.   Phone: (215)563-2406
Philadelphia, PA 19102-3206   Ann Marie Cunningham, Exec.Dir.
Founded: 1958. **Staff:** Prof 3; Other 3. **Subjects:** Information science. **Publications:** NFAIS Newsletter, monthly - by subscription; Report Series, quarterly; Membership Directory, annual. **Remarks:** The federation is a group of secondary information producers, distributors, users, and related organizations. Its purpose is to serve the worldwide information community through education, research, and publication. FAX: (215)563-2848. **Staff:** Wendy Wicks, Pubns.Mgr.; Eileen Cleveland, Promotions Coord.

National Federation of Business and Professional Women's Clubs, Inc. of the U.S.A.
See: **Business and Professional Women's Foundation** (2404)

★ 11163 ★
National Federation of Local Cable Programmers - Library (Info Sci)
666 11th St., N.W., Suite 806   Phone: (202)393-2650
Washington, DC 20001   T. Andrew Lewis, Exec.Dir.
Founded: 1977. **Staff:** Prof 2; Other 1. **Subjects:** Cable television - community access, local origination, legislation, industry, franchising. **Special Collections:** Archives of the history of the formation of community access in the United States. **Services:** Library not open to the public. **Publications:** Community Television Review, bimonthly. **Remarks:** FAX: (202)393-2653.

National Film Board of Canada
See: **Canada - National Film Board of Canada** (2793)

★ 11164 ★
National Fire Protection Association - Charles S. Morgan Technical Library (Sci-Engr)
Batterymarch Park   Phone: (617)984-7445
Quincy, MA 02269-9101   Arlene C. Barnhart, Libn.
Founded: 1945. **Staff:** Prof 1; Other 2. **Subjects:** Fire prevention and protection, fire protection engineering and research, arson investigation, fire services management, flammability of materials, model building codes. **Special Collections:** NFPA Published Archives (includes the National Fire Codes historical file; 192 shelf feet); voluntary industrial standards (43 shelf feet). **Holdings:** 5300 books; 11,300 technical reports; 129 film and videocassette titles; 11,000 microfiche; 210 reels and cartridges of microfilm; 325 tapes. **Subscriptions:** 300 journals and other serials. **Services:** Copying; library open to the public by appointment. **Computerized Information Services:** CompuServe Information Service; CASPR's MLS System (internal database). Performs searches on fee basis. **Publications:** Acquisitions Update, monthly - for internal distribution and institutions in the fire protection field. **Special Indexes:** Index of National Board of Fire Underwriters (NBFU) and NFPA codes. **Remarks:** FAX: (617)984-7060.

National Firearms Museum
See: **National Rifle Association of America - National Firearms Museum** (11274)

National Fisheries Contaminant Research Center
See: **U.S. Fish & Wildlife Service** (17499)

National Fisheries Research Center
See: **U.S. Fish & Wildlife Service** (17501)

★ 11165 ★
National Flag Foundation - Flag Plaza Library (Hist)
Flag Plaza   Phone: (412)261-1776
Pittsburgh, PA 15219   George F. Cahill, Pres.
Founded: 1968. **Staff:** Prof 1. **Subjects:** History of the American flag, flag courtesy and display. **Special Collections:** Historic Flags of America (original art and text; 42 scenes); Bicentennial salutes by preeminent Americans (65); Bicentennial salutes by America's great cartoonists (50); One Hundred Years Ago (painting, circa 1876). **Holdings:** 250 books; 15 bound periodical volumes; 10 charts; 400 pamphlets; 10 35mm films. **Subscriptions:** 3000 journals and other serials. **Services:** Designs flag-related programs; research inquiries on flag history and flag display; library open to the public. **Publications:** List of publications - available on request. **Staff:** Anthony A. Martin, Libn.

★ 11166 ★
National Fluid Power Association - Information Center (Sci-Engr)
3333 N. Mayfair Rd.
Milwaukee, WI 53222   Phone: (414)778-3344
Founded: 1980. **Staff:** 1. **Subjects:** Industrial fluid power, communication, fluid, lubricants and sealing devices, pressure rating, pumps, motors, power units and reservoirs, filtration and contamination, cylinders, compressors, valves, hose and tube, fittings. **Special Collections:** Proceedings of National Conferences on Fluid Power, 1955 to present; Economic Outlook Conference Proceedings, 1979-1987. **Holdings:** 550 books; 145 National Fluid Power standards; 500 International Standard Organization publications; 200 American National Standards; 20 standards of the American Society for Testing and Materials. **Subscriptions:** 50 journals and other serials; 5 newspapers. **Services:** Interlibrary loan; copying; SDI; center open to association members. **Computerized Information Services:** DIALOG Information Services. **Publications:** Newsletter - for internal distribution only; Fluid Power Market News, monthly - to participants of the Confidential Shipments Statistics only; Reporter - available by subscription. **Remarks:** Alternate telephone number(s): 778-3369. FAX: (414)778-3361. Telex: 70455.

National Flute Association Music Library
See: **University of Arizona - Music Collection** (18224)

★ 11167 ★
National Food Processors Association - Library (Food-Bev)
1401 New York Ave., N.W., Suite 400   Phone: (202)639-5900
Washington, DC 20005   Alice McDonald, Hd.Libn.
Subjects: Processed food industry, food packaging, labeling information. **Holdings:** 2000 volumes.

★ 11168 ★
National Food Processors Association - National Food Laboratory - Library (Food-Bev)
6363 Clark Ave.
Box 2277   Phone: (510)828-1440
Dublin, CA 94568   Marian Marquardt, Libn.
Staff: Prof 1. **Subjects:** Food and thermal processing/engineering, analytical chemistry, microbiology, product development, federal and state regulations, sensory evaluation, sanitation. **Holdings:** 2600 books; 1000 bound periodical volumes; 181 reels of microfilm of journals; 17 VF drawers of patents; 5 years of Federal Register on microfiche; 40 VF drawers of clippings and pamphlets (uncataloged). **Subscriptions:** 88 journals and other serials. **Services:** Interlibrary loan; library not open to the public. **Computerized Information Services:** DIALOG Information Services. Performs searches on fee basis. **Remarks:** Includes the holdings of the Foremost Dairies Company Research Department Library. FAX: (510)833-8795.

★ 11169 ★
National Football Foundation - College Football Hall of Fame - Library (Rec)
Kings Island, OH 45034   Phone: (513)398-5410
                                       Pat Harmon, Cur.
Founded: 1978. **Staff:** Prof 1. **Subjects:** College football. **Holdings:** 3000 books; game programs; college media guides; films. **Services:** Copying; library open to the public by appointment. **Computerized Information Services:** Biographies of Famous Players and Coaches (internal database). **Publications:** Footballetter (newsletter) - distributed to National Football Foundation participating members. **Remarks:** FAX: (513)398-4892.

National Football Museum
See: **Pro Football Hall of Fame** (13392)

★11170★
National Foreign Language Center at Johns Hopkins University -
  Reference Center
1619 Massachusetts Ave., N.W., 4th Fl.
Washington, DC 20036
Founded: 1987. **Subjects:** Foreign language pedagogy and education policy, less commonly-taught languages. **Special Collections:** Newsletters of organizations engaged in the promotion of foreign languages and cultures. **Holdings:** 1000 books; 500 reports. **Remarks:** Currently inactive.

National Forest Products Association - Archives
See: **Forest History Society, Inc. - Library and Archives** (5979)

★11171★
National Forest Products Association - Information Center (Biol Sci)
1250 Connecticut Ave., N.W., 2nd Fl.   Phone: (202)463-2736
Washington, DC 20036   Shirley Vines, Mgr.
Founded: 1962. **Staff:** Prof 2. **Subjects:** Forest management and economics, wood construction, wood technology, Congressional information. **Holdings:** 4000 books; 80 bound periodical volumes; 24 VF drawers of pamphlets and documents; 1500 scientific and technical reports. **Subscriptions:** 100 journals and other serials. **Services:** Interlibrary loan; copying; center open to the public by appointment; some files are for internal use only. **Remarks:** Alternate telephone number(s): 463-2700. FAX: (202)463-2785.

★11172★
National Foundation for Consumer Credit - Library
8611 Second Ave., Suite 100
Silver Spring, MD 20910
Subjects: Consumer credit, credit counseling, credit research and education. **Remarks:** Currently inactive.

★11173★
National Foundation of Funeral Service - Beryl L. Boyer Library (Sci-Engr)
2250 E. Devon Ave., Suite 250
Des Plaines, IL 60018   Phone: (708)827-6337
Founded: 1945. **Subjects:** Funeral service, mortuary management, death customs, burial, bereavement, embalming, mortuary science, restorative art. **Special Collections:** Frank K. Fairchild Collection; Clarence E. Smith Collection; Dr. Charles A. Renouard Collection; Harry G. Samson Collection. **Holdings:** 3100 books; 300 bound periodical volumes; 300 prints and pamphlets. **Subscriptions:** 48 journals and other serials. **Services:** Library open to responsible adults for reference only. **Remarks:** FAX: (708)827-6342. **Formerly:** Located in Evanston, IL.

★11174★
National Foundation for Gifted and Creative Children - Library (Educ)
395 Diamond Hill Rd.   Phone: (401)738-0937
Warwick, RI 02886   Marie Friedel, Exec.Dir.
Staff: Prof 1; Other 1. **Subjects:** Gifted children, creative children, misuse of prescription drugs, physical chemistry and biology, science, humanities, music, art, creative writing. **Special Collections:** Case histories of individual gifted and creative children; statistical studies. **Holdings:** 2500 books; 1000 unbound periodicals; 45 notebooks of newspaper clippings, 1968 to present; test scores of 800 children; 200 records of prescription drugs given to children. **Subscriptions:** 10 journals and other serials. **Services:** Library open to parents and professionals. **Publications:** Newsletter, bimonthly.

National Foundation for History of Chemistry
See: **University of Pennsylvania - National Foundation for History of**
  Chemistry - Library (19190)

National Foundation of Political Sciences - Center for Advanced Studies
  on Modern Africa and Asia
See: **Center for Advanced Studies on Modern Africa and Asia** (3205)

★11175★
National Funeral Directors Association - Learning Resource Center (Sci-Engr)
11121 W. Oklahoma Ave.   Phone: (414)541-2500
Milwaukee, WI 53227-4096   Debra Pass, Dir. of Educ.
Founded: 1882. **Staff:** Prof 1. **Subjects:** Dying and death, grief and mourning, funeral customs, embalming, business practices. **Holdings:** 600 books; films. **Services:** Copying; center open to the public by appointment. **Remarks:** FAX: (414)541-1909. **Staff:** Kathleen A. Walczak.

★11176★
National Gallery of Art - Department of Education Resources (Art, Aud-Vis)
Fourth and Constitution Ave., N.W.   Phone: (202)842-6273
Washington, DC 20565   Ruth R. Perlin, Hd.
Staff: Prof 9; Other 10. **Subjects:** Western European and American painting, sculpture, decorative arts, and folk arts; themes of temporary exhibitions. **Holdings:** 46 slide program titles; 28 videocassette programs; 47 film titles; 10 closed captioned videocassettes titles; 1 videodisc title; 2 teaching packets. **Services:** Slide programs, films, and video cassettes distributed on a free-loan basis to schools, colleges, libraries, civic groups, and individuals; will respond to written inquiries. **Computerized Information Services:** Learning Link. **Special Catalogs:** Catalog - free upon request. **Remarks:** FAX: (202)789-2681. **Staff:** Leo J. Kasun, Rsrc.Prog.Prod.Spec.; Christopher With, Coord. Art Info.; Carol Lippitt, Chf. Booking/Shipping Ck.

★11177★
National Gallery of Art - Gallery Archives (Art)
Washington, DC 20565   Phone: (202)842-6614
                                          Maygene Daniels, Hd.
Founded: 1984. **Staff:** Prof 6. **Subjects:** History and development of gallery, architecture of gallery buildings. **Holdings:** Historic files; 10,000 photographs; 20,000 architectural plans; oral histories. **Services:** Copying; archives open to the public. **Remarks:** FAX: (202)842-2356. **Staff:** Richard Saito, Arch.Archv.; Martha Shears, Ref.Archv., Anne Ritchie, Oral Hist.

★11178★
National Gallery of Art - Index of American Design (Art)
Sixth and Constitution Ave., N.W.   Phone: (202)842-6605
Washington, DC 20565   Ruth E. Fine
Founded: 1941. **Staff:** Prof 2. **Subjects:** Watercolor renderings of American decorative and folk arts from the colonial period to 1900. **Holdings:** 17,000 watercolors; photographs; color microfiche of collection and accompanying catalog. **Services:** Slide programs; open to the public by appointment. **Computerized Information Services:** Internal database. **Publications:** The Index of American Design. **Remarks:** FAX: (202)842-2356. **Staff:** Charlie Ritchie, Asst.Cur.; Carlotta Owens, Asst.Cur.

★11179★
National Gallery of Art - Library (Art)
Sixth and Constitution Ave., N.W.   Phone: (202)842-6511
Washington, DC 20565   Neal Turtell, Exec.Libn.
Founded: 1941. **Staff:** Prof 13; Other 23. **Subjects:** Art, architecture, decorative arts, European and American painting and sculpture, drawing, prints. **Special Collections:** Artist biographies; sale catalogs; exhibition catalogs; Leonardo da Vinci; museum and private collection catalogs; catalogs raisonne. **Holdings:** 162,000 books; 28,000 bound periodical volumes; 330 VF drawers; 60,000 titles in microform. **Subscriptions:** 958 journals and other serials. **Services:** Interlibrary loan; copying; library open to college students and qualified researchers. **Automated Operations:** Computerized public access catalog, cataloging, acquisitions, serials, and circulation. **Computerized Information Services:** OCLC, DIALOG Information Services, RLIN, ArtQuest, WILSONLINE. **Networks/Consortia:** Member of FEDLINK. **Publications:** Guide to National Gallery of Art Microfilm Holdings. **Remarks:** FAX: (202)408-8530. **Staff:** Lamia Doumato, Hd., Rd.Serv.; Frances Lederer, Ref.Libn.; Roger Lawson, Hd.Cat.; Jane Collins, Cat.; Trudy Olivetti, Cat.; Catherine Quinn, Cat.; Marsha Spieth, Cat.; Gail Rubenstein, Cat.; Anna Rachwald, Hd., Order Sect.; Caroline Backlund, Coll.Dev.; Roberta Geier, VF/Microform.

★ 11180 ★
National Gallery of Art - Photographic Archives (Art, Aud-Vis)
4th and Constitution Ave., N.W.   Phone: (202)842-6026
Washington, DC 20565   Ruth R. Philbrick, Cur.
Staff: Prof 6; Other 2. **Subjects:** Western European art and architecture, early Christian era to present; American art and architecture; ancient art. **Holdings:** 1.35 million photographs and negatives; 4.8 million microforms. **Services:** Archives open to graduate students and qualified researchers. **Automated Operations:** VLTS Inc. **Staff:** Jerry Mallick, Cat./Adm.; Richard Hutton, Cat.; Andrea Gibbs, Cat.; Karen Weinberger, Cat.; Barbara Chabrowe, Cat.Spec.Proj.

★ 11181 ★
National Gallery of Art - Slide Library (Art, Aud-Vis)
4th and Constitution Ave., N.W.   Phone: (202)842-6100
Washington, DC 20565   Nicholas Martin, Act. Slide Libn.
Founded: 1978. **Staff:** Prof 4. **Subjects:** Western European and American painting and sculpture, graphic arts, decorative arts, architecture, ancient architecture and art (Egyptian, Greek, Roman). **Special Collections:** Medieval Illuminated Manuscripts from U.S. and European Libraries; Mark Rothko Collection. **Holdings:** 140,000 slides. **Services:** Interlibrary loan; library open to the public. **Automated Operations:** VTLS, Inc. **Publications:** Slide Classification Manual. **Staff:** Thomas O'Callaghan, Asst. Slide Libn.; Mary Wassermann, Asst. Slide Libn.

National Gallery of Canada
See: Canada - National Gallery of Canada (2802)

National Gallery of Iceland
See: Iceland - National Gallery of Iceland (7637)

National Gallery of Prague
See: Czechoslovakia - National Gallery of Prague (4514)

★ 11182 ★
National Gardening Association - Library (Biol Sci)
180 Flynn Ave.   Phone: (802)863-5962
Burlington, VT 05401   Charlie Nardozzi, Horticulturist
Founded: 1979. **Staff:** 1. **Subjects:** Gardening - vegetable, fruit, ornamental; plant and soil science. **Holdings:** 1200 books. **Subscriptions:** 20 journals and other serials. **Services:** Library open to members only. **Remarks:** FAX: (802)863-5962

★ 11183 ★
National Genealogical Society - Library (Hist)
4527 17th St., N.   Phone: (703)525-0050
Arlington, VA 22207-2363   Robert J.C.K. Lewis, Libn.
Founded: 1903. **Staff:** Prof 1; Other 5. **Subjects:** Genealogy, local history, bibliography, biography. **Special Collections:** Manuscript collections of former members. **Holdings:** 18,000 books; 2000 bound periodical volumes; 100 boxes of manuscript materials; 40 VF drawers of documents, clippings, pamphlets; microfilm; microfiche. **Subscriptions:** 40 journals and other serials. **Services:** Copying; library open to the public. **Computerized Information Services:** OCLC. **Publications:** National Genealogical Society Quarterly; National Genealogical Society Newsletter, bimonthly; 54 special publications, book list revised 1988 with supplement, 1989.

National Geodetic Information Center
See: U.S. Natl. Oceanic & Atmospheric Administration (17655)

★ 11184 ★
National Geographic Society - Film Library (Aud-Vis)
1600 M St., N.W.   Phone: (202)857-7659
Washington, DC 20036   Patricia Gang, Dir., Film Lib.
Founded: 1972. **Staff:** 10. **Subjects:** Wildlife, animal behavior, lands and peoples of the world, science, technology, exploration, recreational activities. **Special Collections:** National Geographic research grant documentaries (film); NGS television productions (250); NGS educational films (210); out-takes from NGS's television and educational film productions (10 million feet of 16mm film); Explorer cable television program segments and out-takes; magnetic sound tapes. **Services:** Copying; library open to qualified researchers by appointment. **Remarks:** FAX: (202)775-6141.

★ 11185 ★
National Geographic Society - Illustrations Library (Aud-Vis)
17th & M Sts., N.W.   Phone: (202)857-7493
Washington, DC 20036   Maura Mulvihill, Dir.
Founded: 1919. **Staff:** Prof 6; Other 30. **Subjects:** Photographs, transparencies, and artwork of subjects suitable for use in National Geographic publications. **Special Collections:** Herbert G. Ponting (Antarctic); George Shiras 3rd (wildlife); Joseph F. Rock (China); Robert F. Griggs (Mt. Katmai, Alaska); Hiram Bingham (Machu Picchu, Peru); Bradford Washburn (Yukon); Society's Space Collection of NASA space probe and Skylab missions. **Holdings:** 10.3 million published and indexed transparencies, photographs, original paintings. **Services:** Library for the exclusive use of the society and its publications. **Automated Operations:** Computerized circulation and videodisc picture research system. **Computerized Information Services:** Internal databases. **Special Catalogs:** Thesaurus (subject authority file created by the Illustrations Library to fulfill its unique needs). **Remarks:** FAX: (202)775-6141. **Staff:** Fern L. Dame, Illus.Lib n.; Carolyn J. Harrison, Asst.Dir.; Eudora L. Babyak, Asst.Dir., Circ.; Robin E. Siegel, Cons.; William D. Perry, Asst.Dir., Res.Cat. and Pict.Sel.

★ 11186 ★
National Geographic Society - Library (Geog-Map)
17th & M Sts., N.W.   Phone: (202)857-7787
Washington, DC 20036   Susan M. Fifer Canby, Dir.
Founded: 1920. **Staff:** Prof 9; Other 19. **Subjects:** Geography, United States, American history, polar region, photography, natural history. **Special Collections:** General A.W. Greely's Polar Library (1600 items); complete set of Hakluyt Society publications; National Geographic Society Research and Exploration Collection (6127 reports). **Holdings:** 65,000 books; 4800 bound periodical volumes; 90 file cabinets containing 2 million clippings, pamphlets, documents; 135,000 map sheets. **Subscriptions:** 820 journals and other serials; 17 newspapers. **Services:** Interlibrary loan (limited); copying; library open to the public for reference use only. **Automated Operations:** Computerized cataloging. **Computerized Information Services:** OCLC, Burrelle's, DIALOG Information Services, NEXIS, DataTimes, VU/TEXT Information Services, CompuServe Information Service; ORBIS (Online Reference and Bibliographic Information System; internal database); Dialcom, Inc. (electronic mail service). **Networks/Consortia:** Member of CAPCON Library Network. **Publications:** Library Brochure; Library News (newsletter), monthly. **Remarks:** FAX: (202)429-5735. Electronic mail address(es): 134:N6L3710 (Dialcom, Inc.). **Staff:** David Beveridge, Asst.Dir.; Ellen Briscoe, Asst.Dir.

National Geological Library (of the People's Republic of China)
See: People's Republic of China - National Geological Library (12928)

National Geophysical Data Center - Solar-Terrestrial Physics Division
See: World Data Center A - Solar-Terrestrial Physics (20617)

★ 11187 ★
National Graduate University - Library (Soc Sci)
1101 N. Highland St.   Phone: (703)527-4800
Arlington, VA 22201   Dr. Jean K. Boek, Lib.Comm.Chm.
Founded: 1967. **Staff:** Prof 1; Other 2. **Subjects:** Management, gerontology, human services, American democracy, procurement. **Holdings:** 27,000 books; 678 bound periodical volumes; 650 reports and manuscripts. **Subscriptions:** 23 journals and other serials. **Services:** Interlibrary loan; copying; SDI; library open to the public by appointment for reference use only. **Remarks:** FAX: (703)524-4013.

★ 11188 ★
National Grocers Association - Library (Bus-Fin)
1825 Samuel Morse Dr.   Phone: (703)437-5300
Reston, VA 22090   Stu Zlotnikoff, V.P. of Commun. & Mktg.
Staff: Prof 2. **Subjects:** Food store operation. **Holdings:** 700 volumes; 6 VF drawers. **Services:** Library not open to the public.

★ 11189 ★
National Ground Water Information Center (Sci-Engr, Env-Cons)
6375 Riverside Dr.   Phone: (614)761-3222
Dublin, OH 43017   Kevin B. McCray, Dir.
Founded: 1960. **Staff:** Prof 4. **Subjects:** Ground water, water well technology, hydrogeology, environmental pollution. **Holdings:** 20,000 books; 10,000 microfiche. **Subscriptions:** 300 journals and other serials. **Services:** Interlibrary loan; copying; library open to the public for reference use only. **Automated Operations:** Computerized cataloging. **Computerized Information Services:** OCLC, DIALOG Information Services; produces Ground Water On-Line, Legislative Data Base, and 11 other databases. Performs searches on fee basis. **Networks/Consortia:** Member of OHIONET. **Publications:** NGWIC Update, quarterly. **Remarks:** FAX: (614)761-3446. **Staff:** Janet Bix, Chf.Libn.; Kathy Stumpf, Libn.; Betty Grimes, Libn.

★ 11190 ★
National Guard Association of the United States - Library (Mil)
1 Massachusetts Ave., N.W.
Washington, DC 20001   Phone: (202)789-0031
Subjects: Military history. **Holdings:** 4500 volumes.

★ 11191 ★
National Hamiltonian Party - Hamiltonian Library (Hist)
510 W. Shiawassee Ave.   Phone: (313)629-0292
Fenton, MI 48430   Michael Kelly, Libn.
Founded: 1965. **Staff:** 1. **Subjects:** American political history, National Hamiltonian Party, American political campaigns, minor political parties, Alexander Hamilton. **Special Collections:** Kelly Collection (political documents and campaign material from American presidential campaigns, 1824 to present). **Holdings:** 916 books; 15,000 pieces of political memorabilia. **Subscriptions:** 10 journals and other serials. **Services:** Interlibrary loan; library open to the public by appointment. **Formerly:** Located in Flushing, MI.

★ 11192 ★
National Hardwood Lumber Association - Library (Agri)
Box 34518   Phone: (901)377-1818
Memphis, TN 38184-0518   Ernest J. Stebbins, Exec.Mgr.
Founded: 1898. **Subjects:** Hardwood lumber; grading rules. **Special Collections:** Historic records of grading rules. **Holdings:** 100 volumes. **Services:** Copying; library open to members of NHLA. **Remarks:** FAX: (901)382-6419.

★ 11193 ★
National Heart, Lung, and Blood Institute - Education Programs' Information Center (Med)
University Research Corporation
4733 Bethesda Ave., Suite 530   Phone: (301)951-3260
Bethesda, MD 20814   Jory Barone, Ctr.Mgr.
Founded: 1972. **Staff:** Prof 5; Other 2. **Subjects:** High blood pressure, cholesterol, smoking, health education, cardiovascular risk reduction, blood resources, asthma. **Holdings:** 2050 books; 235 periodicals; 8000 periodical articles; 1000 pamphlets; 2000 documents. **Subscriptions:** 190 journals and other serials. **Services:** Interlibrary loan; copying; center open to the public. **Computerized Information Services:** BRS Information Technologies, Combined Health Information Database (CHID). Contact Person: Sue Innes, Info.Serv.Coord. **Publications:** Bibliographies, brochures, directories, reports, and publications for health professionals. **Special Catalogs:** Abstracts of the literature (online). **Remarks:** FAX: (301)951-3269. Program operated by the U.S. National Institutes of Health.

National Herbarium of the Netherlands
See: **Netherlands - National Herbarium of the Netherlands** (11409)

National Highway Traffic Safety Administration
See: **U.S. Natl. Highway Traffic Safety Administration** (17610)

★ 11194 ★
National Hispanic University - National Hispanic Center for Advanced Studies and Policy - Library (Educ)
262 Grand Ave.   Phone: (510)451-0511
Oakland, CA 94806   Barbara Fukai, Libn.
Founded: 1981. **Staff:** Prof 1; Other 1. **Subjects:** Bilingual education, general education, business administration, health sciences, liberal arts. **Special Collections:** Bilingual education covering pre-school through 12th grade. **Holdings:** 5000 books; 1000 bound periodical volumes. **Subscriptions:** 20 journals and other serials. **Services:** Interlibrary loan; library open to the public at librarian's discretion. **Publications:** State of Hispanic America, Vol. 1-6; **Special Catalogs:** Catalogue on Bilingual Educational Aides for Teachers. **Remarks:** FAX: (510)451-4NHU.

National Historical Fire Foundation - Hall of Flame
See: **Hall of Flame** (6845)

★ 11195 ★
National Home Study Council - Library (Educ)
1601 18th St., N.W.   Phone: (202)234-5100
Washington, DC 20009   Michael P. Lambert, Exec.Dir.
Subjects: Home study, correspondence and vocational education. **Holdings:** 500 books and periodicals. **Services:** Copying; library open to the public by appointment. **Remarks:** FAX: (202)332-1386.

National Housing Center Library
See: **National Association of Home Builders** (11061)

★ 11196 ★
National Housing Law Project/National Economic Development & Law Center - Library (Soc Sci)
1950 Addison St.   Phone: (510)548-9400
Berkeley, CA 94704   Leonard Claudio, Lib.Mgr.
Founded: 1969. **Staff:** 1. **Subjects:** Housing, community economic development, health services, law. **Holdings:** 5000 books; 8000 handbooks, regulations, government documents. **Subscriptions:** 44 journals and other serials. **Services:** Copying; library open to the public by appointment for reference use only.

★ 11197 ★
National Humanities Center - Library (Hum)
7 Alexander Dr.
Box 12256   Phone: (919)549-0661
Research Triangle Park, NC 27709-2256   Walter Alan Tuttle, Libn.
Founded: 1978. **Staff:** Prof 2; Other 1. **Subjects:** Humanities. **Holdings:** 900 volumes. **Services:** Library not open to the public. **Automated Operations:** Computerized cataloging and serials. **Computerized Information Services:** DIALOG Information Services, OCLC. **Networks/Consortia:** Member of SOLINET. **Remarks:** Electronic mail address(es): NHC@UNCECS.EDU **Staff:** Rebecca B. Vargha, Assoc.Libn.

★ 11198 ★
National Hunters Association, Inc. - Library (Rec)
P.O. Box 820   Phone: (919)365-7157
Knightdale, NC 27545-0820   D.V. Smith, Pres.
Founded: 1976. **Subjects:** Hunting rights in the U.S. and around the world, hunter safety, preservation of an adequate supply of game, wilderness survival, game control, firearm safety. **Holdings:** Figures not available. **Remarks:** Library located on Hwy. 64, east of Raleigh, NC.

National Hurricane Center
See: **U.S. Natl. Oceanic & Atmospheric Administration - National Hurricane Center - Library** (17656)

★ 11199 ★
National Indian Brotherhood - Assembly of First Nations - Resource Centre (Area-Ethnic)
55 Murray St., 5th Fl.   Phone: (613)236-0673
Ottawa, ON, Canada K1N 5M3   Kelly Whiteduck
Founded: 1973. **Staff:** Prof 1; Other 2. **Subjects:** First nations government, land claims, constitutional status, aboriginal rights. **Holdings:** 10,000 books; 4000 documents on microfiche. **Subscriptions:** 100 journals and other serials; 15 newspapers. **Services:** Interlibrary loan; copying; center open to the public for reference use only. **Special Catalogs:** The Key: Indian Control of Indian Information (book). **Remarks:** FAX: (613)238-5780.

National Indian Law Library
See: **Native American Rights Fund** (11337)

★ 11200 ★
National Information Center for Children and Youth with Disabilities (Educ)
Box 1492   Phone: (703)893-6061
Washington, DC 20013   Lana Ambler, Info.Serv.Coord.
Founded: 1982. **Staff:** Prof 9; Other 2. **Subjects:** Disabilities and special education. **Holdings:** 1000 books; vertical files. **Subscriptions:** 400 journals and other serials. **Services:** Information and referral services; center open to the public by appointment. **Computerized Information Services:** BRS Information Technologies; SpecialNet, Southern California Answering Network (SCAN; electronic mail services). **Publications:** Transition Summary, annual; News Digest, 3/year - both to the public. **Remarks:** Toll-free telephone number(s): (800)555-9955. TDD: (703)893-8614. **Staff:** Eve Robins, Info.Spec.; Roxanne Rice, Info.Spec.; Joan Kemper, Info.Spec.; Debbie Szanto, Info.Spec.; Sue Ferguson, Info.Spec.

★ 11201 ★
National Information Center on Deafness (Educ)
Gallaudet University
800 Florida Ave., N.E.   Phone: (202)651-5051
Washington, DC 20002   Loraine DiPietro, Dir.
Founded: 1980. **Staff:** Prof 4; Other 1. **Subjects:** Deafness, hearing loss, Gallaudet University. **Holdings:** 75 books; 5 VF drawers of subject files; 6 VF drawers of deafness agencies/organizations files. **Services:** Access to Gallaudet University Library, which houses world's largest deafness collection; accepts requests for information made in person, by telephone, or by letter; center open to the public. **Publications:** Fact sheets; resource listings; reading lists; information packets; list of 800 other publications - all available on request. **Remarks:** FAX: (202)651-5054. TDD: 651-5052. Main telephone number is also TDD accessible. **Staff:** Arlynn Joffe, Sr.Info.Spec.; Cheryl Barto, Coord., Info.Serv.

National Information Center for Educational Media
See: **Access Innovations, Inc.** (46)

★ 11202 ★
National Information Center for Special Education Materials (Educ)
Box 40130   Phone: (505)265-3591
Albuquerque, NM 87196   Marjorie Hlava
Subjects: Special education. **Holdings:** 40,000 abstracts. **Computerized Information Services:** DIALOG Information Services, BRS Information Technologies. **Special Indexes:** List of indexes - available on request. FAX: (505)256-1080. Toll-free telephone number(s): (800)468-3453.

National Information Centre for Textile and Allied Subjects
See: **Ahmedabad Textile Industry's Research Association** (142)

National Injury Information Clearinghouse
See: **Consumer Product Safety Commission** (4244)

★ 11203 ★
National Insitute of Industrial Environment and Hazards - Library (Sci-Engr, Env-Cons)
B.P. 7   Phone: 44 556422
F-60550 Verneuil en Hallatte, France   Eliane Palat, Libn.
Staff: 8. **Subjects:** Safety and hygiene in mines and industries; occupational health; environmental protection; chemistry. **Holdings:** 25,000 volumes. **Subscriptions:** 700 journals and other serials; 8 newspapers. **Services:** Interlibrary loan; copying; library open to the public by appointment. **Computerized Information Services:** DIALOG Information Services, ESA/IRS, STN International, Questel, BELINDAS, NLM, CEDOCAR Europeenne de Donnees; G.CAM; COLIVER, CHADOCC (internal databases). **Remarks:** FAX: 44 556399. Institute is part of the French Ministry of the Environment. **Formerly:** Centre d'Etudes et Recherches de Charbonnages de France; Coal Mining Research and Development Center of France. **Also Known As:** Institut National de L'Environment Industriel et des Risques (INERIS). **Staff:** Marie-Claude Buck; Nicole Leveque.

★ 11204 ★
National Institute on Aging - Gerontology Research Center Library (Soc Sci, Med)
4940 Eastern Ave.   Phone: (301)558-8125
Baltimore, MD 21224-2137   Joanna Chen Lin, Hd., Lib. Unit
Founded: 1968. **Staff:** Prof 1; Other 3. **Subjects:** Aging research, gerontology and geriatrics, psychology, biochemistry, biomedical research, molecular genetics, neurobiology, Alzheimer's disease. **Special Collections:** Aging collections (150 journals; 5000 books). **Holdings:** 9000 books; 10,000 bound periodical volumes; 500 unbound reports and statistics. **Subscriptions:** 500 journals and other serials. **Services:** Interlibrary loan; library open to the public for reference use only. **Automated Operations:** Computerized cataloging, serials, and literature searching. **Computerized Information Services:** DIALOG Information Services, OCLC, BRS Information Technologies, NLM, REMO, CCOD; CD-ROM (MEDLINE). **Networks/Consortia:** Member of Maryland Association of Health Science Librarians (MAHSL), FEDLINK, National Network of Libraries of Medicine - Southeastern/Atlantic Region. **Remarks:** Institute is a branch of U.S. Public Health Service - National Institutes of Health.

★ 11205 ★
National Institute on Alcohol Abuse and Alcoholism - NIAAA Research Library (Med)
1400 Eye St., N.W., C/CSR, Inc.   Phone: (202)842-7600
Washington, DC 20005   June Picciano, Info.Serv.Mgr.
Founded: 1972. **Staff:** Prof 4; Other 3. **Subjects:** Biomedical and psychosocial aspects of alcohol research. **Special Collections:** Classified abstracts of alcohol-related literature. **Holdings:** 2000 books; 72,000 accessioned items. **Subscriptions:** 200 journals and other serials. **Services:** Library open to the public by appointment. **Automated Operations:** Computerized cataloging, acquisitions, and serials. **Computerized Information Services:** BRS Information Technologies, DIALOG Information Services; internal database. **Networks/Consortia:** Member of Substance Abuse Librarians and Information Specialists (SALIS). **Publications:** Alcohol Health & Research World, quarterly; Alcohol Alert. **Remarks:** FAX: (202)842-0418. NIAAA is part of the U.S. Department of Health and Human Services. **Staff:** Gail Chotoff.

National Institute of Allergy & Infectious Diseases
See: **U.S. Natl. Institutes of Health** (17628)

★ 11206 ★
National Institute of Amazon Research - Library (Biol Sci)
Estrada do Aleixo
C.P. 478   Phone: 92 6423432
69000 Manaus, Amazonas, Brazil   Alvaro Alves Vieira, Libn.
Founded: 1955. **Subjects:** Amazon region - botany, ecology, agronomy, natural resources, tropical silviculture, tropical diseases, limnology. **Holdings:** 284,849 volumes. **Subscriptions:** 630 journals and other serials. **Services:** Copying; SDI; library open to the public, but only local residents may borrow materials. **Publications:** Currents Summary; Bol.Bilbiographyc. **Remarks:** FAX: 92 6421706. Telex: 922269. Maintained by National Council of Scientific and Technological Development - Secretary of Science & Technology. **Also Known As:** Instituto Nacional de Pesquisas da Amazonia. **Staff:** Alcinea Fernandes Nogueira; Ana Luiza Belem Rebello; Eurijader De Oliveira Veras; Francisca Ines De Rocha Barros; Idalcia Ennes Vara; Julieta Da Costa Lima; Maria De Lourdes Davila De Andrade Lima; Maria De Matias Fernandes Oliveira; Raimunda Silva Neves; Silvia Lessi; Waldizia Paula De Lima; Yeda Video De Sousa; Gloria De Oliveira Batista.

National Institute of Arthritis and Musculoskeletal and Skin Diseases -
AMS Information Clearinghouse
See: **National Arthritis and Musculoskeletal and Skin Diseases**
Information Clearinghouse (11047)

★11207★
National Institute of Arthritis and Muskuloskeletal and Skin Diseases -
Office of Scientific and Health Communication (Med)
Bldg. 31, Rm. 4C05
NIH/NIAMS
9000 Rockville Pike   Phone: (301)496-8188
Bethesda, MD 20892   Constance Raab, Dir.
Staff: Prof 1; Other 2. **Subjects:** Clinical and laboratory research dealing
with the various arthritic, rheumatic, and collagen diseases, the metabolic
diseases including diabetes, digestive diseases, orthopedics, dermatology,
hematology, nutrition, endocrine disorders, urology, and renal disease
including research and development of the artificial kidney. Basic research
includes biochemistry, nutrition, pathology, histochemistry, chemistry,
pharmacology, toxicology, and physical, chemical, and molecular biology.
Holdings: Figures not available. **Services:** Office of Health Research Reports
collects and disseminates scientific information about current research
carried on at the institute and by its grantees in nonfederal research centers.
Remarks: A branch of U.S. Public Health Service - National Institutes of
Health.

National Institute of Corrections
See: **U.S. Dept. of Justice - Bureau of Prisons - National Institute of**
Corrections (17253)

National Institute of Demographic Studies (of France)
See: **France - National Institute of Demographic Studies** (6070)

★11208★
National Institute of Dental Research - Management Information
Section (Med)
5333 Westbard Ave.   Phone: (301)496-7220
Bethesda, MD 20016   Carla Flora, Chf.
Staff: Prof 1; Other 7. **Subjects:** Dental research. **Holdings:** 10,000 project
summaries; 1500 technical reports on microfiche. **Services:** Copying; office
open to the public with restrictions. **Computerized Information Services:**
BRS Information Technologies, PaperChase, DTIC, DIALOG Information
Services; NIDR ONLINE, RIF (internal databases); DIALMAIL,
BITNET (electronic mail services). **Publications:** List of publications -
available upon request. **Remarks:** FAX: (301)496-9241. Institute is a branch
of U.S. Public Health Service - National Institutes of Health. **Formerly:** Its
Research Data and Management Information.

National Institute of Diabetes and Digestive and Kidney Diseases -
National Digestive Diseases Information Clearinghouse
See: **National Digestive Diseases Information Clearinghouse** (11148)

National Institute on Disability and Rehabilitation Research
See: **FES Information Center - Library** (5675)

National Institute on Disability & Rehabilitation Resources
See: **National Rehabilitation Information Center** (11265)

★11209★
National Institute on Drug Abuse - Addiction Research Center Library
(Med)
Box 5180   Phone: (301)550-1488
Baltimore, MD 21224   Mary Pfeiffer, Libn.
Staff: Prof 1; Other 1. **Subjects:** Pharmacology, psychology, psychiatry,
biochemistry, neurochemistry, psychopathology, chemistry, substance
abuse, AIDS. **Holdings:** 7000 books; 2500 bound periodical volumes; 21,000
reprint articles. **Subscriptions:** 450 journals and other serials. **Services:**
Interlibrary loan; copying; SDI; library open to the public at librarian's
discretion. **Automated Operations:** DOCLINE. **Computerized Information**
Services: DIALOG Information Services, MEDLINE, OCLC, BRS
Information Technologies, Loansome Doc. **Networks/Consortia:** Member
of Maryland Association of Health Science Librarians (MAHSL), Substance
Abuse Librarians and Information Specialists (SALIS). **Publications:** Book
Acquisitions; Reprint Acquisitions, both monthly; Current Awareness
Service, weekly. **Remarks:** FAX: (301)550-1438. Institute is a branch of U.S.
Public Health Service - Alcohol, Drug Abuse and Mental Health
Administration. **Also Known As:** NIDA Addiction Research Center.

★11210★
National Institute of Environmental Health Sciences - Library (Med,
Biol Sci)
Box 12233
Research Triangle Park, NC 27709   W. Davenport Robertson, Lib.Dir.
Founded: 1966. **Staff:** Prof 5; Other 4. **Subjects:** Pharmacology, toxicology,
mutagenesis, teratogenesis, cell biology, carcinogenesis, environmental
health. **Holdings:** 22,500 books; 2700 bound periodical volumes; 20,000
unbound periodical volumes; 2500 reels of microfilm; 3500 microfiche; 8 VF
drawers of manuscripts; 200 reports on microfiche; 5 file drawers of internal
reprints. **Subscriptions:** 800 journals and other serials. **Services:** Interlibrary
loan; copying; SDI; library open to the public. **Automated Operations:**
Computerized public access catalog, cataloging, acquisitions, serials, and
circulation. **Computerized Information Services:** DIALOG Information
Services, BRS Information Technologies, STN International, OCLC, PFDS
Online, NLM; EasyLink, BITNET, LINX Courier (electronic mail
services). **Networks/Consortia:** Member of FEDLINK, North Carolina
Information Network (NCIN). **Publications:** NIEHS Library Newsletter,
monthly - for internal distribution only; NIEHS Bibliography, annual - free
upon request. **Remarks:** FAX: (919)541-0669. Electronic mail address(es):
ROBERTSON@NIEHS (BITNET). Institute is a branch of U.S. Public
Health Service - National Institutes of Health. **Staff:** Ellen Leadem,
Tech.Serv.Libn.;   Ralph Hester, Tech.Info.Spec.;   Larry Wright,
Info.Rsrcs.Libn.

National Institute for Environmental Studies (of Japan)
See: **Japan - Environment Agency - National Institute for Environmental**
Studies - Environmental Information Center (8329)

★11211★
National Institute of Governmental Purchasing, Inc. - Specifications
Library (Bus-Fin)
115 Hillwood Ave.   Phone: (703)533-7300
Falls Church, VA 22046   Leslie S. Jackson, Dir., Tech.Serv.Div.
Founded: 1946. **Staff:** Prof 1; Other 1. **Subjects:** Governmental purchasing.
Holdings: Files of specifications. **Services:** Interlibrary loan; copying; library
open to the public on a fee basis. **Publications:** NIGP Technical Bulletin,
6/year. **Remarks:** FAX: (703)532-0915.

National Institute of Health and Family Welfare (of India)
See: **India - National Institute of Health and Family Welfare** (7745)

National Institute of Justice
See: **U.S. Dept. of Justice** (17259)

National Institute for Medical Research (of Tanzania)
See: **Tanzania - National Institute for Medical Research** (16006)

★11212★
National Institute of Mental Health - Neuroscience Research Center/
Neuropsychiatric Research Hospital - Library (Med)
W.A.W. Bldg., Rm. 115
St. Elizabeth's Hospital   Phone: (202)373-6071
Washington, DC 20032   LaVerne Corum, Hd.Libn.
Founded: 1967. **Staff:** Prof 2. **Subjects:** Neuroscience, psychopharmacology,
psychiatry, pharmacology, biochemistry, psychology. **Special Collections:**
Vertical file of reprints of papers by former and present research staff (2500).
Holdings: 5700 books; 11,000 bound periodical volumes; 18 drawers of
journals on microfilm and microfiche; 5 drawers of audio cassettes.
Subscriptions: 301 journals and other serials. **Services:** Interlibrary loan;
copying; SDI; library open to the public with restrictions. **Computerized**
Information Services: DIALOG Information Services, MEDLINE.
Remarks: Alternate telephone number(s): 373-6073. **Staff:** Dera Tompkins,
Asst.Libn.

National Institute of Metrology (of Romania)
See: **Romania - National Institute of Metrology** (14050)

★ 11213 ★
National Institute of Municipal Law Officers - Library (Soc Sci)
1000 Connecticut Ave., N.W., Suite 902   Phone: (202)466-5424
Washington, DC 20036   Mark Hessel, Sr. Staff Att.
Subjects: Municipal law, city codes, ordinances, treatises, briefs and opinions. **Holdings:** Figures not available. **Services:** Library open to members only. **Remarks:** FAX: (202)785-0152.

National Institute for Occupational Safety & Health
See: **U.S. Natl. Institute for Occupational Safety & Health** (17611)

National Institute of Occupational Safety and Health (of Spain)
See: **Spain - Ministry of Labour - National Institute of Occupational Safety and Health** (15564)

National Institute of Oceanography (of India)
See: **India - National Institute of Oceanography** (7746)

★ 11214 ★
National Institute for Petroleum & Energy Research (NIPER) - Library (Energy)
Box 2128   Phone: (918)337-4371
Bartlesville, OK 74005   Josh Stroman, Hd.Libn.
Founded: 1927. **Staff:** Prof 2; Other 2. **Subjects:** Petroleum and natural gas technology, enhanced oil recovery, chemistry, automotive fuels, thermodynamics. **Special Collections:** Technical Oil Mission War Reports; Oklahoma oil well log file. **Holdings:** 20,000 books; 9800 bound periodical volumes; 25,000 government reports; 2200 society reports; 3000 microfilm cartridges; 391 microfiche and microcards. **Subscriptions:** 275 journals and other serials. **Services:** Interlibrary loan; copying (limited); library open to the public with restrictions. **Automated Operations:** Computerized cataloging and ILL. **Computerized Information Services:** DIALOG Information Services, PFDS Online, STN International, OCLC. **Networks/Consortia:** Member of FEDLINK. **Remarks:** FAX: (918)337-4365. Telex: 910 841 2521 CHNWWBRV. Electronic mail address(es): 23827 (DIALMAIL).

National Institute for Psychosocial Factors and Health (of Sweden)
See: **Sweden - Karolinska Institute** (15906)

★ 11215 ★
National Institute for Public Policy - NIPP Research Library (Mil, Soc Sci)
3031 Javier Rd., Suite 300   Phone: (703)698-0563
Fairfax, VA 22031   Colin S. Gray, Pres.
Staff: Prof 6; Other 11. **Subjects:** Nuclear strategy and theory, arms control, military history, foreign affairs, U.S. defense policy. **Holdings:** 12,000 volumes; 100 reports. **Subscriptions:** 47 journals and other serials. **Services:** Interlibrary loan; library not open to the public. **Publications:** Information Series, monthly; Strategy (newsletter), monthly.

National Institute of Roman Studies (of Italy)
See: **Italy - Ministry of Cultural Affairs - National Institute of Roman Studies** (8281)

National Institute for Scientific Research (of Portugal)
See: **Portugal - National Institute for Scientific Research** (13262)

★ 11216 ★
National Institute for the Study of the Theater (of Argentina) - Library (Theater)
Avenida Cordoba 1199   Phone: 1 45881
1055 Buenos Aires, Bs. As., Argentina   Osvaldo Calatayud, Dir.
Founded: 1936. **Staff:** 9. **Subjects:** National theater of Argentina and Latin America - heritage and history. **Holdings:** 15,000 volumes; historic manuscript file; documents; pictures; costumes. **Subscriptions:** 25 journals and other serials; 30 newspapers. **Services:** Copying; library open to the public. **Remarks:** Maintained by Argentina - Secretariat of Culture. **Also Known As:** Instituto Nacional de Estudios del Teatro. **Staff:** Jorge Lima, Libn.

★ 11217 ★
National Institute for Urban Wildlife - Library (Env-Cons)
10921 Trotting Ridge Way   Phone: (301)596-3311
Columbia, MD 21044   Louise E. Dove, Wildlife Biol.
Staff: 1. **Subjects:** Urban wildlife, land use, wildlife management. **Holdings:** 500 books; 1000 bound periodical volumes; 500 slides; 150 maps; 4000 pamphlets, catalogs, newspaper clippings, reprints. **Subscriptions:** 100 journals and other serials. **Services:** Library open to the public by appointment. **Publications:** Urban Wildlife News (newsletter), quarterly - to members; Planning for Wildlife in Cities & Suburbs; Annotated Bibliography on Planning and Management for Urban-Suburban Wildlife; attracting backyard wildlife informational leaflets - for sale; Planning for Urban Fishing and Waterfront Recreation - for sale; A Guide to Urban Wildlife Management - for sale; Urban Wetlands for Stormwater Control & Wildlife Enhancement - for sale; Urban Wildlife Manager's Notebook (informational leaflet), quarterly - to members and for sale; Wildlife Habitat Conservation Teacher's Pac Series (10 titles) - for sale; Proceedings of a National Symposium on Urban Wildlife (held in 1986) - for sale; Wildlife Reserves and Corridors in the Urban Environment - for sale.

★ 11218 ★
National Institute of Victimology - Library (Soc Sci)
2333 N. Vernon St.
Arlington, VA 22207-4036   Phone: (703)536-1750
Subjects: Victim/witness programs, victim/witness services, problems and needs of crime victims. **Holdings:** 3500 volumes; file collection of research, statistics, and publications.

National Institutes of Health
See: **U.S. Natl. Institutes of Health** (17626)

National Interfaith Coalition on Aging Archives
See: **Marquette University - Department of Special Collections and University Archives - Manuscript Collections Memorial Library** (9709)

★ 11219 ★
National Interfraternity Conference - Library (Educ)
3901 W. 86th St., Suite 390   Phone: (317)872-1112
Indianapolis, IN 46268   Jonathan J. Brant, Exec.V.P.
Founded: 1909. **Staff:** 6. **Subjects:** College fraternities, scholarship programs, fraternity statistics, fraternity operational procedures. **Holdings:** 500 books. **Subscriptions:** 50 journals and other serials. **Services:** Library open to the public by appointment. **Remarks:** FAX: (317)872-1134.

★ 11220 ★
National Investigations Committee on Unidentified Flying Objects (Sci-Engr)
14617 Victory Blvd., Suite 4   Phone: (818)989-5942
Van Nuys, CA 91411   Dr. Frank E. Stranges, Pres.
Staff: Prof 3; Other 3. **Subjects:** Unidentified flying objects, space, science, law, religion, astronomy. **Holdings:** 10 manuscripts; 4 16mm films; 1000 slides; clippings. **Services:** Collection open to the public by appointment. **Remarks:** FAX: (818)989-5942.

National Jewish Archive of Broadcasting
See: **Jewish Museum** (8401)

★ 11221 ★
National Jewish Center for Immunology and Respiratory Medicine - Gerald Tucker Memorial Medical Library (Med, Biol Sci)
1400 Jackson St.   Phone: (303)398-1483
Denver, CO 80206   Rosalind F. Dudden, Libn.
Staff: Prof 1; Other 2. **Subjects:** Respiratory diseases, molecular and cellular biology, immunology, allergy, asthma, tuberculosis. **Holdings:** 3000 books; 10,500 bound periodical volumes. **Subscriptions:** 340 journals and other serials. **Services:** Interlibrary loan; copying; library open to the public with restrictions. **Automated Operations:** Computerized cataloging, serials, and ILL (DOCLINE). **Computerized Information Services:** DIALOG Information Services, WILSONLINE, BRS Information Technologies, NLM, PHILSOM, OCLC. **Networks/Consortia:** Member of Colorado Council of Medical Librarians.

★11222★

National Jewish Information Service for the Propagation of Judaism -
Research Library and Archives (Rel-Phil)
3761 Decade St.   Phone: (702)454-5872
Las Vegas, NV 89121   Rachel D. Maggal, P.R. Dir./Asst.Ed.
Founded: 1960. **Staff:** 2. **Subjects:** Propagation of Judaism, Jewish
missionary activities, Judaica, comparative religion. **Special Collections:**
Conversions to Judaism in history and literature. **Holdings:** 1000 books.
Subscriptions: 12 journals and other serials. **Services:** Translation of
periodical articles from major European magazines; questions on Judaism
answered through the mail; library open to the public by appointment for
reference use only. **Publications:** Voice of Judaism, annual - to members or
by donation. **Staff:** Rabbi Moshe M. Maggal, Founder & Pres./Ed.

★11223★

National Journal Library (Publ)
1730 M St., N.W., Suite 1100   Phone: (202)857-1492
Washington, DC 20036   Rose Marie Pool, Dir. of Info.Serv.
Founded: 1969. **Staff:** Prof 3. **Subjects:** Federal government legislation and
activities. **Holdings:** 1500 books; 110 VF drawers of news clippings;
congressional documents and government serials. **Subscriptions:** 300
journals and newsletters; 14 newspapers. **Services:** Interlibrary loan;
copying; reference and bibliographic services for reporters and National
Journal subscribers; library open to the public by appointment.
Computerized Information Services: NEXIS, LEGI-SLATE. **Publications:**
National Journal. **Remarks:** FAX: (202)833-8069. **Staff:** Colita Glivens,
Lib.Asst.

★11224★

National Judicial College - Law Library (Law)
University of Nevada   Phone: (702)784-6039
Reno, NV 89557   Clara S. Kelly, Libn.
Founded: 1965. **Staff:** Prof 1; Other 6. **Subjects:** Courts, law, judicial
administration and education. **Special Collections:** Judges' manuals and
benchbooks; pattern jury instructions; court rules; U.S. selective depository
library. **Holdings:** 73,000 volumes. **Subscriptions:** 650 journals and other
serials. **Services:** Interlibrary loan; copying. **Computerized Information**
Services: WESTLAW, LEXIS. **Remarks:** FAX: (702)784-4234.

★11225★

National Labor Relations Board - Law Library (Bus-Fin, Law)
1717 Pennsylvania Ave., N.W., Rm. 900   Phone: (202)251-7126
Washington, DC 20570   Kenneth E. Nero, Adm.Libn.
Founded: 1937. **Staff:** Prof 3; Other 6. **Subjects:** Law, labor law, labor
relations, labor history, economics, political science. **Special Collections:**
The library is a national resource for the literature of the U.S. primary labor
relations law and allied subjects. It includes nearly everything published by
and about the National Labor Relations Board and the National Labor
Relations Act, as amended. **Holdings:** 45,000 volumes. **Subscriptions:** 300
journals and other serials. **Services:** Interlibrary loan; SDI; library open to
the public for reference use only on request. **Automated Operations:**
Computerized cataloging. **Computerized Information Services:** DIALOG
Information Services, LEGI-SLATE, Dun & Bradstreet Business Credit
Services, OCLC. **Publications:** New Books & Current Labor Articles,
bimonthly; Bibliography of the Labor Management Relations Act, 1947, as
amended, biennial supplements; Recommended Publications for the
National Labor Relations Board Regional Office Libraries, irregular. **Also**
Known As: NLRB. **Staff:** Susan L. Harlem, Libn.; Audrey Stewart, Libn.

National Laboratories of Industrial Development
See: **Laboratorios Nacionales de Fomento Industrial** (8861)

National Law Center
See: **George Washington University - National Law Center** (20009)

National Lawyers Guild Archives
See: **Meiklejohn Civil Liberties Institute - Library** (10023)

★11226★

National League of Cities - Municipal Reference Service (Soc Sci)
1301 Pennsylvania Ave., N.W.
Washington, DC 20004   Phone: (202)626-3130
Founded: 1924. **Staff:** Prof 4. **Subjects:** Municipal government and
administration, citizen participation, community development,
environmental quality, housing, intergovernmental relations, public revenue
and finance, urban affairs, transportation. **Special Collections:** Serials and
reports of state leagues of cities; city codes, reports, ordinances. **Holdings:**
25,000 books; 300 bound periodical volumes; census data; 42 shelves of
archival materials. **Subscriptions:** 400 journals and other serials. **Services:**
Interlibrary loan; copying (limited); service open to members only.
Computerized Information Services: DIALOG Information Services, Local
Exchange; Local Exchange (electronic mail service). **Publications:** Urban
Affairs Abstracts, monthly - by subscription. **Remarks:** FAX: (202)626-
3043. Contains the holdings of Public Technology Inc. - Information Center.
Staff: Kathryn Shane McCarty, Dir., Info.Serv.; Gail B. Jackson,
Sr.Info.Spec.; Dennis K. Rosser, Info.Spec.; Thomas E. Mann,
Tech.Serv.Libn.

★11227★

National Legal Center for the Medically Dependent and Disabled -
Library and Information Center (Law)
50 S. Meridian St, Suite 605   Phone: (317)632-6245
Indianapolis, IN 46204-3541   Tom Marzen
Subjects: Persons with disabilities, Baby Doe, death and dying, euthanasia,
discrimination based on disability. **Holdings:** 400 books. **Subscriptions:** 20
journals and other serials. **Services:** Copying; library open to the public.
Publications: Issues in Law and Medicine; The Medical Treatment Rights
of Children with Disabilities. **Remarks:** FAX: (317)632-6542.

★11228★

National Legal Research Group, Inc. - Library (Law)
2421 Ivy Rd.
P.O. Box 7187   Phone: (804)977-5790
Charlottesville, VA 22906   Russell T. Payne
Founded: 1983. **Staff:** 3. **Subjects:** Law. **Holdings:** 24,000 bound volumes.
Services: Library not open to the public. **Computerized Information**
Services: WESTLAW, LEXIS. Performs searches for attorneys on a fee
basis. **Publications:** Report from Counsel (newsletter), quarterly; Equitable
Distribution Journal, monthly; Product Liability Trends, monthly; Supreme
Court Researcher, monthly when Court is in session; South Carolina
Appellate Digest. **Remarks:** Toll-free telephone number(s): (800)727-6574.
FAX: (804)295-4667.

★11229★

National Lekotek Center - Library (Educ)
2100 Ridge Ave.   Phone: (708)328-0001
Evanston, IL 60201   Therese Wehman, Assoc.Exec.Dir.
Founded: 1980. **Staff:** 20. **Subjects:** Infant stimulation, fine motor
coordination and development, language development, reading,
mathematics, visual perception, musical play. **Special Collections:** Toys
designed and adapted for severely disabled children; computer hardware and
software suitable for children with special needs. **Holdings:** 3500 toys, books,
computer materials, and other items. **Subscriptions:** 10 journals and other
serials. **Services:** Center open to families of children with special needs.
Computerized Information Services: Database listing software for disabled
children. **Publications:** Toys for Growing; Adapted Toy Plan Books I, II,
and III; Lekotek Play Guide for Children with Special Needs; The Innotek
Software Resource Guide; Using the Computer to Teach Children with
Special Needs; Effective Methods for Using Computers with Children with
Special Needs (videotape) - all for sale. **Remarks:** Lekotek provides services
for handicapped children and their families. Leaders trained in special
education select toys to suit the child's abilities and work with the child on
an individual basis. Its technology division, Innotek, focuses on the use of
computers with children who have diabilities. Lekotek resource centers are
located throughout the United States. FAX: (708)328-5514. **Staff:** Pam
Ross, Dir. of Innotek; Mary Ellen Van Ness, Libn.

National Library (of Algeria)
See: **Algeria - Bibliotheque Nationale** (349)

The National Library and Archives of Ethiopia
See: Ethiopia - The National Library and Archives of Ethiopia (5469)

National Library of Australia
See: Australia - National Library of Australia (1333)

National Library for the Blind (of Great Britain)
See: Great Britain - National Library for the Blind (6685)

National Library of Bulgaria
See: Bulgaria - Committee of Culture - St. Cyril and St. Methodius
   National Library (2345)

National Library of Canada
See: Canada - National Library of Canada (2803)

National Library of China
See: People's Republic of China - The National Library of China (12929)

National Library of Economics in the Federal Republic of Germany
See: Germany - National Library of Economics in Germany (6451)

National Library (of the Faeroe Islands)
See: Faeroe Islands - Foroya Landsbokasavn (5550)

National Library of Finland
See: University of Helsinki - Library (18635)

National Library of Greece
See: Greece - National Library of Greece (6715)

National Library of International Trade
See: U.S. International Trade Commission - National Library of
   International Trade (17594)

National Library of Ireland
See: Republic of Ireland - Department of the Taoiseach (13827)

National Library of the Islamic Republic of Iran
See: Iran - National Library of the Islamic Republic of Iran (8243)

National Library of Jamaica
See: Jamaica - National Library of Jamaica (8321)

National Library of Malaysia
See: Malaysia - National Library of Malaysia (9569)

National Library of Malta
See: Malta - National Library of Malta (9576)

National Library of Medicine
See: U.S. National Library of Medicine (17629)

National Library of the Netherlands
See: Netherlands - Koninklijke Bibliotheek (11402)

National Library of New Zealand
See: New Zealand - National Library of New Zealand (11739)

National Library of Nigeria
See: Nigeria - National Library of Nigeria (11808)

National Library of Paraguay
See: Paraguay - Biblioteca Nacional del Paraguay (12736)

National Library (of the Philippines)
See: Philippines - National Library - Special Collections (13002)

National Library (of Poland)
See: Poland - Biblioteka Narodowa (13161)

The National Library for Psychology and Education (of Sweden)
See: Sweden - The National Library for Psychology and Education
   (15909)

National Library of Scotland
See: Scotland - National Library of Scotland (14953)

National Library of Scotland
See: Scotland - National Library of Scotland - Scottish Science Library
   (14954)

National Library Service for the Blind and Physically Handicapped
See: Library of Congress (9132)

National Library Service (of Lesotho)
See: Lesotho - National Library Service (9069)

National Library Service (of Malawi)
See: Malawi - National Library Service (9567)

National Library Services Board (of Sri Lanka)
See: Sri Lanka - National Library Services Board (15626)

National Library (of Singapore)
See: Singapore - Ministry of Information and the Arts (15189)

National Library of Sweden
See: Sweden - Royal Library - National Library of Sweden (15911)

National Library of Thailand
See: Thailand - National Library of Thailand (16293)

★ 11230 ★
National Life Insurance Company - Library (Bus-Fin)
National Life Dr.   Phone: (802)229-3278
Montpelier, VT 05604   Diana J. Yahyazadeh, Law Lib.Mgr.
Staff: Prof 1. **Subjects:** Law, insurance, business, economics. **Special
Collections:** Archives (historical material relating to company). **Holdings:**
16,500 books; 225 bound periodical volumes; 32 VF drawers of pamphlets
and clippings. **Subscriptions:** 291 journals and other serials. **Services:**
Interlibrary loan; copying; library open to the public with restrictions.

★11231★
National Livestock and Meat Board - Meat Industry Information Center
(Food-Bev)
444 N. Michigan Ave.   Phone: (312)467-5520
Chicago, IL 60611   William D. Siarny, Jr., Dir.
Founded: 1976. **Staff:** Prof 1; Other 1. **Subjects:** Meat, nutrition, food economics, cookery. **Special Collections:** Archives of the American Meat Science Association; Meat Board Archives. **Holdings:** 5000 books; 600 reports; 28 VF drawers of reprints, clippings, government documents. **Subscriptions:** 400 journals and other serials; 8 newspapers. **Services:** Interlibrary loan; copying; center open to industry members by appointment. **Computerized Information Services:** Online systems; EasyLink (electronic mail service). **Networks/Consortia:** Member of ILLINET, National Network of Libraries of Medicine - Greater Midwest Region, Illinois Health Libraries Consortium, Chicago Library System. **Remarks:** FAX: (312)467-9729.

★11232★
National Louis University - West Suburban Campus Library (Educ)
IS331 Grace St.   Phone: (708)691-9390
Lombard, IL 60148   Jane Wilson Adickes
Staff: 2. **Subjects:** Education, health and human services, business education. **Special Collections:** W.S. Gray Research Collection in Reading (on microfiche). **Holdings:** 10,000 books. **Subscriptions:** 5 newspapers. **Services:** Interlibrary loan; copying; library open to the public for reference use only. **Computerized Information Services:** CD-ROM (ERIC, PsychLit, Periodicals Abstrats Ondisc). **Networks/Consortia:** Member of ILLINET. **Remarks:** FAX: (708)629-3838. The main library is located in Evanston, Illinois.

★11233★
National Lucht en Ruimtevaartlaboratorium - NLR - Bibliotheek (Sci-Engr)
Postbus 153
NL-8300 AD Emmeloord, Netherlands   Phone: 5274 8317
     C.W. De Jong
Founded: 1919. **Staff:** Prof 7; Other 2. **Subjects:** Aerospace, aerodynamics, flight informatics, structures and materials, remote sensing, spaceflight technology. **Holdings:** 12,000 books; 60,000 reports including NACA, NASA, ARC reports; 30,000 microfiche. **Subscriptions:** 950 journals and other serials. **Services:** Interlibrary loan; library not open to the public. **Computerized Information Services:** ESA/IRS, DIALOG Information Services, STN International, BLAISE. **Remarks:** FAX: 5274 8210. Library located at Voorsterweg 31, NL-8316 PR Marknesse, Netherlands.

National Marine Fisheries Service
See: **U.S. Natl. Marine Fisheries Service** (17630)

National Marine Mammal Laboratory
See: **U.S. Natl. Marine Fisheries Service** (17635)

★11234★
National Maritime Museum - J. Porter Shaw Library (Hist, Trans)
Bldg. E, 3rd Fl.
Fort Mason
San Francisco, CA 94123   Phone: (415)556-9870
     David Hull, Prin.Libn.
Founded: 1959. **Staff:** Prof 3; Other 2. **Subjects:** Maritime history, especially Pacific Ocean; nautical technology; navigation; local history. **Special Collections:** Oral histories (400 taped interviews); John Lyman Reading Room; John Lyman Maritime Collection; San Francisco Marine Exchange vessel movement records, 1903-1960 (70,000 cards; 80 ledgers); photographic collection (250,000 images); ship plans (10,000); ship registers, 1780-1985. **Holdings:** 15,000 volumes; 3500 bound periodical volumes; 2900 logbooks; 700 nautical charts and maps; 600 cubic feet of archival material; 70 VF drawers of reports, pamphlets, clippings, and ephemera; 260 scrapbooks. **Subscriptions:** 150 journals and other serials. **Services:** Interlibrary loan; copying; library open to the public for reference use only. **Automated Operations:** Computerized cataloging and serials. **Computerized Information Services:** DataTimes, DIALOG Information Services, OCLC, CIN. **Networks/Consortia:** Member of FEDLINK. **Remarks:** FAX: (415)556-1624. Maintained by U.S. National Park Service - San Francisco Maritime National Historical Park. **Staff:** Herbert H. Beckwith, Asst.Prin.Libn.; Irene Stachura, Ref.Libn.

National Medical Enterprises - Lutheran Medical Center
See: **Lutheran Medical Center** (9462)

★11235★
National Medium Miners Association - Library (Sci-Engr)
Calle Pedro Salazar Esq. Presbitero
Medina 600
Casilla Postale 6094
La Paz, Bolivia   Phone: 2 354125
Subjects: Bolivian mining industry, labor relations. **Holdings:** 1500 volumes. **Remarks:** Telex: 3377 ASOMIN BV. **Also Known As:** Asociacion Nacional de Mineros Medianos.

★11236★
National Mental Health Association - Clifford Beers Memorial Library
(Med)
1021 Prince St.
Alexandria, VA 22314-2971   Phone: (703)684-7722
Founded: 1950. **Subjects:** Mental health for laymen, voluntary public agencies. **Holdings:** 1500 books. **Remarks:** Toll-free telephone number(s): (800)969-NMHA. FAX: (703)684-5968.

National Meteorological Library (of Great Britain)
See: **Great Britain - National Meteorological Library & Archive** (6687)

National Mine Health and Safety Academy
See: **U.S. Dept. of Labor - Mine Safety & Health Administration** (17272)

★11237★
National Minority AIDS Council - Library (Med)
300 I St., N.E., Suite 400   Phone: (202)544-1076
Washington, DC 20002   Anita Taylor
Staff: 1. **Subjects:** AIDS issues relating to minorities population. **Holdings:** 30 books; 40 reports. **Subscriptions:** 20 journals and other serials; 5 newspapers. **Services:** Library open to the public. **Remarks:** FAX: (202)544-0378. Telex: 940103 WU PUBTLX BSN.

★11238★
National Moving and Storage Association - Library (Trans)
1500 N. Beauregard St.
Alexandria, VA 22311   Phone: (703)671-8813
Founded: 1967. **Subjects:** Moving and storage, trends in the household goods industry. **Holdings:** 150 books; 70 bound periodical volumes; training manuals; videotapes. **Subscriptions:** 10 journals and other serials; 3 newspapers. **Services:** Copying; library open to the public by appointment. **Remarks:** FAX: (703)671-6712. **Staff:** Joyce McDowell, Dir. of Pub.Aff.; Eileen Clark.

★11239★
National Multiple Sclerosis Society - Information Resource Center and Library (Med)
205 E. 42nd St., 3rd Fl.   Phone: (212)986-3240
New York, NY 10017   Margaret Calvano, Dir., Lib. & Info.Serv.
Founded: 1984. **Staff:** Prof 6; Other 2. **Subjects:** Medical research; medical, psychosocial, socioeconomic aspects of multiple sclerosis. **Holdings:** 1000 books; 15,000 indexed reprints; client service materials; professional and lay pamphlets. **Subscriptions:** 120 journals and other serials. **Services:** Interlibrary loan; center open to the public by appointment. **Computerized Information Services:** DIALOG Information Services, BRS Information Technologies; internal database. Performs searches free of charge. **Remarks:** Toll-free telephone number(s): (800)624-8236. FAX: (212)986-7981. **Staff:** Amber LaMann, Database/Sys.Mgr.; Ann Palmer, Asst.Dir.; Cynthia Weniger, Info.Serv.Assoc.; Julie Berger, Sr.Info.Assoc.; Mary Patricia Rogers, Info.Serv.Assoc.

National Municipal League Archives
See: **University of Colorado--Denver - Auraria Library - Archives and Special Collections** (18510)

National Museum of American Art
See: Smithsonian Institution (15265)

National Museum of American History - Archives Center
See: Smithsonian Institution - National Museum of American History - Archives Center (15269)

National Museum of American History - Library
See: Smithsonian Institution Libraries (15278)

National Museum of Antiquities of Scotland - Library
See: Scotland - National Museums of Scotland - Library (14955)

National Museum in Belgrade - Library
See: Yugoslavia - National Museum in Belgrade (20829)

National Museum of Bhutan - Reference Library
See: Bhutan - National Museum of Bhutan - Reference Library (1810)

★ 11240 ★
National Museum of Iceland - Library (Hist)
Sudurgotu 41
P.O. Box 1489   Phone: 1 9128888
IS-101 Reykjavik, Iceland   Groa Finnsdottir, Libn.
Founded: 1863. **Staff:** Prof 1. **Subjects:** Cultural history, archeology, architecture, ethnology, textiles, art. **Holdings:** 9000 books; 200 bound periodical volumes; 40 videotapes. **Subscriptions:** 300 journals and other serials. **Services:** Interlibrary loan; copying; SDI; library open to university students and researchers. **Remarks:** FAX: 1 9128967.

National Museum of Natural History
See: Smithsonian Institution Libraries (15279)

★ 11241 ★
National Museum of Racing - Library (Rec)
Union Ave.
Saratoga Springs, NY 12866   Phone: (518)584-0400
Subjects: Thoroughbred horse racing. **Holdings:** 800 books. **Services:** Library not open to the public. **Publications:** Hall of Fame books.

★ 11242 ★
National Museum of Science and Technology - Library (Sci-Engr)
P.O. Box 9724
Ottawa Terminal   Phone: (613)991-2981
Ottawa, ON, Canada K1G 5A3   Hilary Perrott, Libn.
Founded: 1967. **Staff:** Prof 2; Other 6. **Subjects:** Space, communications, ground transportation, history of Canadian science and technology, agriculture, forestry, surveying, marine transportation, energy, physical sciences, graphic arts, computer technology history. **Holdings:** 20,000 books; 2500 bound periodical volumes. **Subscriptions:** 340 journals and other serials. **Services:** Interlibrary loan; SDI; library open to the public for reference use only. **Automated Operations:** Computerized cataloging, serials, and acquisitions. **Computerized Information Services:** UTLAS, DIALOG Information Services, CAN/OLE, DOBIS Canadian Online Library System; Envoy 100 (electronic mail service). **Publications:** Acquisitions list, monthly. **Remarks:** FAX: (613)990-3636. Electronic mail address(es): ILL.OONMST (Envoy 100). **Formerly:** Canada - National Museums of Canada - National Museum of Science and Technology. **Also Known As:** Musee National des Sciences et de la Technologie.

★ 11243 ★
National Museum of Transport - Transportation Reference Library (Trans, Info Sci)
3015 Barrett Station Rd.   Phone: (314)965-7998
St. Louis, MO 63122   Capt. W.S. Streckfus
Founded: 1944. **Staff:** Prof 1; Other 1. **Subjects:** Transportation and communication. **Holdings:** 20,000 books; 6000 bound periodical volumes; 2000 pamphlets; 9 VF drawers of pamphlets; extensive collection of photographs, blueprints, phonograph records, movie films, slides. **Subscriptions:** 200 journals and other serials. **Services:** Library open to qualified users by appointment. **Publications:** Occasional papers.

★ 11244 ★
National Museum of Women in the Arts (NMWA) - NMWA Library and Research Center (Art)
1250 New York Ave., N.W.   Phone: (202)783-5000
Washington, DC 20005   Krystyna Wasserman, Dir., Lib. & Res.Ctr.
Founded: 1982. **Staff:** Prof 1.5; Other 1. **Subjects:** Art by women - painting, sculpture, printmaking, photography, book art. **Special Collections:** Women artists (14,000 vertical files); artists' books (120); collection of bookplates by women; personal library of Irene Rice Pereira; Archives of the International Conference of Women Artists in Copenhagen, 1985. **Holdings:** 6000 volumes; manuscripts; artists' correspondence; slides; 1100 institution files; 400 subject files. **Subscriptions:** 70 journals and other serials. **Services:** Library open to scholars and students by appointment. **Computerized Information Services:** RLIN; internal database. **Publications:** The NMWA News (newsletter), quarterly - to members. **Special Indexes:** Index to group exhibition catalogs - for internal distribution only. **Remarks:** FAX: (202)393-3235. **Staff:** Reiko Yoshimura, Cat.; Kathryn Phillips, Cat.

National Museums of Scotland
See: Scotland - National Museums of Scotland - Library (14955)

National Naval Medical Center
See: U.S. Navy - National Naval Medical Center (17805)

★ 11245 ★
National Network of Youth Advisory Boards, Inc. - Technical Assistance Library (Soc Sci)
Ocean View Branch
P.O. Box 402036   Phone: (305)532-2607
Miami Beach, FL 33140   Stuart Alan Rado, Dir.
Staff: 1. **Subjects:** Youth involvement and employment, child abuse, juvenile justice, substance abuse, education. **Holdings:** 500 books; manuals. **Services:** Library not open to the public. **Publications:** Resources list giving information on organizations concerned with all aspects of youth - available on request (with stamped, self-addressed envelope).

National Nuclear Data Center
See: Brookhaven National Laboratory (2220)

National Ocean Service
See: U.S. Natl. Oceanic & Atmospheric Administration (17657)

National Oceanic & Atmospheric Administration
See: U.S. Natl. Oceanic & Atmospheric Administration (17650)

National Oceanographic Data Center
See: U.S. Natl. Oceanic & Atmospheric Administration - National Environmental Satellite, Data, & Information Service - National Oceanographic Data Center (17653)

National Opinion Research Center
See: University of Chicago - National Opinion Research Center (NORC) (18456)

National Optical Astronomy Observatories
See: Kitt Peak National Observatory (8753)

National Optical Astronomy Observatories - National Solar Observatory
See: National Solar Observatory (11299)

★ 11246 ★
National Organization for Raw Materials - Information Center (Agri)
Box 9547   Phone: (816)737-0064
Kansas City, MO 64133   Charles Walters, Jr., Pres.
Founded: 1968. **Staff:** Prof 1. **Subjects:** Raw materials, agricultural parity prices. **Holdings:** Transcripts of NORM convention speeches; audiotapes; videotapes. **Services:** Copying; center open to the public by appointment. **Publications:** NORM books.

★11247★
National Organization for River Sports - Resource Center (Rec)
314 N. 20th St.   Phone: (719)473-2466
Colorado Springs, CO 80904   Mary McCurdy, Rsrc.Ctr.Mgr.
Founded: 1978. **Subjects:** Whitewater rivers, whitewater river running.
Holdings: 450 books; 45 maps. **Subscriptions:** 75 journals and other serials;
2 newspapers. **Services:** Center open to the public for reference use only by
appointment; telephone inquiries accepted. **Automated Operations:**
Computerized public access catalog. **Remarks:** Contains many out-of-print
and obscure books. **Remarks:** FAX: (719)475-1752.

**National Organization of Scientific Research (of Algeria) - Applied
Economics Studies and Research Center for Development**
See: **Algeria - National Organization of Scientific Research - Applied
Economics Studies and Research Center for Development** (350)

★11248★
**National Outdoor Leadership School - Outdoor Education Resource
Library** (Rec)
288 Main St.
Box AA   Phone: (307)332-6973
Lander, WY 82520   John Gookin, Curric.Mgr.
Founded: 1965. **Staff:** Prof 1; Other 2. **Subjects:** Outdoor education - skills
and techniques, safety, medicine, backpacking, communication, climbing,
sailing, hiking. **Special Collections:** Baja California and Mexico;
Washington and North Cascades; Alaska and Denali; Wyoming;
Waddington Range (Canada); Kenya; the Southwest and Canyonlands;
environmental accidents, disease, and illness. **Holdings:** 2000 books; 500
unbound periodicals; films; slides. **Subscriptions:** 50 journals and other
serials; 10 newspapers. **Services:** Library not open to the public.
Publications: NOLS Newsletter, every other month - to community
residents. **Remarks:** FAX: (307)332-3631.

National Parent Teacher Association
See: **National PTA** (11255)

★11249★
National Parents' Resource Institute for Drug Education, Inc. (Med)
The Hurt Bldg., Suite 210
50 Hurt Plaza   Phone: (404)577-4500
Atlanta, GA 30303   Rebecca Lewis
Founded: 1977. **Subjects:** Drug abuse prevention, drug education and
research, drug treatment centers, parent groups. **Holdings:** Archival
materials. **Subscriptions:** 30 journals and other serials. **Services:** Institute
open to the public. **Computerized Information Services:** Internal database.
Publications: PRIDE (newsletter), quarterly - to mailing list. **Remarks:**
PRIDE is a resource, information, conference, training organization
providing current research information on drug abuse and referrals to drug
treatment centers. Drug informaion available through a touch tone
telephone. FAX: (404)688-6937. **Also Known As:** PRIDE.

National Park Service
See: **U.S. Natl. Park Service** (17661)

★11250★
National Parks and Conservation Association - Library (Env-Cons)
1776 Massachusetts Ave., N.W., 2nd Fl.   Phone: (202)223-6722
Washington, DC 20036   Paul C. Pritchard, Pres.
Subjects: National parks, conservation. **Holdings:** 3000 volumes. **Services:**
Library open to members only. **Remarks:** FAX: (202)659-0650

National Peking Library Rare Book Collection
See: **University of Michigan - Asia Library** (18854)

National Personnel Records Center
See: **National Archives & Records Administration** (11043)

★11251★
National Pest Control Association - Library (Biol Sci)
8100 Oak St.   Phone: (703)573-8330
Dunn Loring, VA 22027   Harvey S. Gold, Exec. V.P.
Subjects: Entomology, pest control. **Holdings:** 2000 volumes. **Services:**
Library not open to the public. **Remarks:** FAX: (703)573-4116.

National Portrait Gallery
See: **Smithsonian Institution - National Museum of American Art/
National Portrait Gallery** (15268)

★11252★
National Presbyterian Church - William S. Culbertson Library (Rel-Phil)
4101 Nebraska Ave., N.W.   Phone: (202)537-0800
Washington, DC 20016   Elizabeth W. Stone, Libn.
Founded: 1966. **Staff:** Prof 2. **Subjects:** Religion, theology. **Special
Collections:** Religious children's literature. **Holdings:** 5500 books; 150
bound periodical volumes; 480 cassettes. **Subscriptions:** 36 journals and
other serials. **Services:** Interlibrary loan; copying; library open to the public
for reference use only. **Automated Operations:** Computerized public access
catalog. **Publications:** Special bibliographies; Current Contents of
Periodicals. **Staff:** Edward A. Johnson, Chm., Lib.Comm.

★11253★
National Press Club - Eric Friedheim Library (Info Sci)
529 14th St., N.W.   Phone: (202)662-7523
Washington, DC 20045   Barbara Vandegrift, Dir./Libn.
Founded: 1984. **Staff:** Prof 3; Other 2. **Subjects:** Current events; journalism
- craft, history; print and broadcast media. **Special Collections:** Archives of
the National Press Club, 1908 to present; Archives of Washington Press
Club (Women's National Press Club, 1919-1985); photographs; cartoons
(original art). **Holdings:** 2500 books; audio and video cassettes; microfilm;
government documents. **Subscriptions:** 155 journals and other serials; 69
newspapers. **Services:** Interlibrary loan; copying; audio cassette copying
(fee); library open to journalists and press researchers on fee basis.
Computerized Information Services: NEXIS, VU/TEXT Information
Services, DataTimes, Compuserve, Prodigy; internal databases; Dialcom
Inc. (electronic mail service). Performs searches on fee basis. **Publications:**
The Record (newsletter) - by subscription; finding aids for archive-
manuscript collections; library brochure. **Special Catalogs:** Audio cassette
inventory. **Remarks:** FAX: (202)879-6725. **Staff:** Robert Garber, Ref.Libn.
; Barbara Van Woerkom, Ref.Libn.

★11254★
**National Psychological Association for Psychoanalysis - George Lawton
Memorial Library** (Med)
150 W. 13th St.
New York, NY 10011   Phone: (212)924-7440
Founded: 1958. **Staff:** Prof 1. **Subjects:** Psychoanalysis, psychology.
Holdings: 2000 volumes. **Subscriptions:** 25 journals and other serials.
Services: Library not open to the public.

★11255★
National PTA - Information Resource Center (Educ)
700 N. Rush St.   Phone: (312)787-0977
Chicago, IL 60611-2571   Julia A. Van, Info.Res.Spec.
Staff: Prof 1; Other 1. **Subjects:** Parental involvement in education; health;
education; child safety and protection. **Special Collections:** National
Congress of Parents and Teachers Resource Center. **Subscriptions:** 575
journals and other serials. **Services:** Center not open to the public. **Also
Known As:** National Parent Teacher Association.

★11256★
National Public Radio - Broadcast Library (Info Sci)
2025 M St., N.W.   Phone: (202)822-2064
Washington, DC 20036   Jacqueline Gilbert, Hd.Libn.
Founded: 1973. **Staff:** Prof 4; Other 2. **Subjects:** News and current events,
drama, music. **Holdings:** 95,000 audiotapes; 7000 phonograph records.
Services: Copying (limited); library open to the public with restrictions.
Automated Operations: Computerized cataloging. **Special Catalogs:**
Catalog of NPR programs (online, printout). **Remarks:** FAX: (202)822-
4329. After 5 years NPR transfers its programs to the Library of Congress
and the National Archives. **Also Known As:** NPR. **Staff:** Lisa Reginbal,
News Libn.; William Sugar, News Libn.

★ 11257 ★
National Publications Library (Med)
1207 S. Oak St.   Phone: (217)333-4600
Champaign, IL 61820   M. Jocelyn Armstrong, Supv.
Founded: 1945. **Staff:** 1. **Subjects:** Physical and sensory impairments, rehabilitation concerning persons with physical and sensory impairments. **Special Collections:** Elmer Joseph Collection of Rehabilitation Journals and Newsletters. **Holdings:** 300 volumes. **Subscriptions:** 50 serials and newsletters. **Services:** Library open to students and researchers by appointment and for reference use only. **Automated Operations:** Computerized public access catalog. **Networks/Consortia:** Member of ILLINET. **Remarks:** Maintained by Division of Rehabilitation Education, University of Illinois at Urbana-Champaign. **Remarks:** FAX: (217)244-6784. **Staff:** Jing Qiu.

★ 11258 ★
National Radio Astronomy Observatory - Library (Sci-Engr)
520 Edgemont Rd.   Phone: (804)296-0211
Charlottesville, VA 22903   Ellen N. Bouton, Libn.
Founded: 1957. **Staff:** Prof 2. **Subjects:** Astronomy, physics, mathematics, engineering, computer science, general science. **Holdings:** 11,300 monographs; 18,680 bound periodical volumes; 650 linear feet of observatory publications; 458 reels of microfilm; 4800 microfiche; 3 VF drawers of reprints; 2200 star charts. **Subscriptions:** 302 journals and other serials. **Services:** Interlibrary loan; copying; library open to qualified users. **Automated Operations:** Computerized public access catalog and cataloging. **Computerized Information Services:** DIALOG Information Services, STN International, OCLC, Set of Identifications, Measurements and Bibliography for Astronomical Data (SIMBAD); internal database; BITNET, Space Physics Analysis Network (SPAN) (electronic mail services). **Networks/Consortia:** Member of FEDLINK. **Publications:** Acquisitions list, monthly; NRAO reprint series list, annual; RAPsheet, biweekly - all to qualified users. **Remarks:** FAX: (804)296-0278. Maintains small collections in Green Bank, WV, Tucson, AZ, and Socorro, NM. **Staff:** Mary Jo Hendricks, Asst.Libn., Charlottesville; Julie Lagoyda, Asst.Libn., Socorro.

★ 11259 ★
The National Railroad Construction and Maintenance Association, Inc. - Technical Reference Library (Trans)
10765 Woodwatch Circle   Phone: (612)942-8825
Eden Prairie, MN 55347   Daniel Foth, Exec. V.P.
Staff: 2. **Subjects:** Railroad - construction, maintenance, rehabilitation, removal. **Holdings:** 2000 volumes. **Services:** Library not open to the public. **Remarks:** FAX: (612)942-8947.

★ 11260 ★
National Railway Historical Society - Atlanta Chapter - Southeastern Railway Museum Library (Trans)
3966 Buford Hwy.
P.O. Box 1267   Phone: (404)476-2013
Duluth, GA 30136-1267   Jamie Reid, Cur./Libn.
Founded: 1959. **Staff:** 1. **Subjects:** Railroads; steam locomotives and boilers; railroad history; trolley and interurban railways. **Holdings:** 650 books; 2000 bound periodical volumes; 550 documents; 10 AV programs; 150 nonbook items; 5 manuscripts. **Subscriptions:** 450. **Services:** Copying; library open to the public by appointment for reference use only.

★ 11261 ★
National Railway Historical Society - Library of American Transportation (Hist)
P.O. Box 58153   Phone: (215)557-6606
Philadelphia, PA 19102-8153   Linda M. Burshtin, Libn.
Founded: 1977. **Staff:** Prof 2. **Subjects:** Railroads, trolleys, transportation. **Special Collections:** National Railway Bulletin (1936 to present). **Holdings:** 2000 books; 90 bound periodical volumes. **Subscriptions:** 50 journals and other serials. **Services:** Library open to the public for reference use only. **Staff:** Hugh R. Gibb.

★ 11262 ★
National Railway Historical Society - Mohawk and Hudson Chapter - Lawrence R. Lee Memorial Library (Hist)
32 Berkshire Dr.   Phone: (518)477-7168
East Greenbush, NY 12061   Paul R. Brustman, Libn.
Founded: 1978. **Staff:** Prof 1. **Subjects:** Railroads - history, literature. **Holdings:** 520 books; 75 bound periodical volumes. **Subscriptions:** 10 journals and other serials. **Services:** Library not open to the public.

★ 11263 ★
National Recreation and Park Association - Joseph Lee Memorial Library and Information Center (Rec)
2775 S. Quincy St.
Arlington, VA 22206
Founded: 1980. **Staff:** 1. **Subjects:** Public recreation, park services, leisure time use, conservation, therapeutic recreation. **Special Collections:** Archives for NRPA and predecessor organizations. **Holdings:** 1068 books; 145 bound periodical volumes; 55 rolls of microfilm; 230 cubic feet of archival material. **Subscriptions:** 15 journals and other serials. **Services:** Copying; center open to the public by appointment. **Computerized Information Services:** ISAR (internal database). **Formerly:** Located in Alexandria, VA.

National Reference Center for Bioethics Literature
See: **Georgetown University - Kennedy Institute of Ethics** (6377)

★ 11264 ★
National Rehabilitation Hospital - Learning Resource Center (Med)
102 Irving St., N.W.   Phone: (202)877-1995
Washington, DC 20010   Margaret Texidor, Ph.D.
Founded: 1986. **Staff:** 2. **Subjects:** Rehabilitation. **Holdings:** 500 books. **Subscriptions:** 76 journals and other serials. **Services:** Interlibrary loan; center not open to the public. **Computerized Information Services:** MEDLARS. **Special Catalogs:** Audio-Visual Catalog. **Remarks:** FAX: (202)726-8512. **Staff:** Diane Cooper, Lib.Cons.

★ 11265 ★
National Rehabilitation Information Center (Med)
8455 Colesville Rd., Suite 935   Phone: (301)588-9284
Silver Spring, MD 20910-3319   Mark Odum, Dir.
Founded: 1977. **Staff:** Prof 9; Other 3. **Subjects:** Rehabilitation of persons with mental or physical disabilities. **Special Collections:** RSA/NIDRR Collection (materials prepared under grants from Rehabilitation Services Administration/Department of Education and the National Institute on Disability and Rehabilitation Research, 1958 to present). **Holdings:** 30,000 listings. **Subscriptions:** 350 journals and other serials. **Services:** Copying; document delivery; center open to the public. **Automated Operations:** Computerized cataloging. **Computerized Information Services:** BRS Information Technologies; internal databases. Performs searches. **Publications:** NARIC Quarterly; NARIC Guide to Disability and Rehabilitation Periodicals; Directory of Rehabilitation Librarians and Information Professionals. **Remarks:** Toll-free telephone number(s) is (800)346-2742. TDD users may use same telephone numbers. FAX: (301)587-1967. **Also Known As:** NARIC. **Staff:** Jacquie Sein, Acq.Spec.; Theresa Craig, Info.Spec.; Louise Elmquist, Info.Spec.; Roland Fagan, Info.Spec.

★ 11266 ★
National Religious Vocation Conference - Library (Rel-Phil)
1603 S. Michigan Ave., Suite 400   Phone: (312)663-5454
Chicago, IL 60616   Mary Ann Hamer, Adm.Asst.
Founded: 1968. **Staff:** 3. **Subjects:** Church-related careers. **Holdings:** 125 audiocassettes; 5 statistical studies and research documents. **Services:** Interlibrary loan; copying; library open to the public. **Publications:** Woman Song I (1986); Woman Song II (1987); Who's Entering Religious Life (1987); Turning Parables and Paradigms (1986); Horizon, quarterly; Directory of Resources; Woman Song III (1989). **Remarks:** FAX: (312)663-5030.

★11267★
National Renewable Energy Laboratory - Library (Energy)
1617 Cole Blvd. Phone: (303)231-1415
Golden, CO 80401 Joseph F. Chervenak, Mgr.
Founded: 1977. **Staff:** Prof 6; Other 3. **Subjects:** Renewable energy - solar, wind, ocean, biomass, photovoltaics; energy conservation; biotechnology; solid state physics. **Holdings:** 20,000 books; 50,000 bound periodical volumes; 30,000 technical reports; 10,000 patents; 500,000 reports on microfiche. **Subscriptions:** 450 journals and other serials; 5 newspapers. **Services:** Interlibrary loan; copying; current alert; library open to researchers by appointment. **Automated Operations:** Computerized public access catalog, cataloging, circulation, and serials. **Computerized Information Services:** DIALOG Information Services, ORBIT Search Service, RLIN, OCLC, BRS Information Technologies, Chemical Abstracts Service (CAS), DOE Energy Data Base (ITIS), CQ Washington Alert Service; internal database. **Networks/Consortia:** Member of FEDLINK, Central Colorado Library System (CCLS). **Publications:** Serials Holdings List, irregular; library brochure. **Remarks:** The National Renewable Energy Laboratory operates under contract to the U.S. Department of Energy. FAX: (303)231-1422. **Formerly:** Solar Energy Research Institute - SERI Technical Library. **Staff:** Nancy Greer, Sr.Libn.; Al Berger, Ref.; Soon Duck Kim, Cat./ILL.

★11268★
National Research Council - Library (Sci-Engr)
2101 Constitution Ave., N.W. Phone: (202)334-2125
Washington, DC 20418 Pamela C. Pangburn, Mgr.
Staff: Prof 6; Other 3.5. **Subjects:** Science policy. **Special Collections:** Publications of the National Academy of Sciences - National Research Council, National Academy of Engineering, and Institute of Medicine. **Holdings:** 200,000 books and bound reports. **Subscriptions:** 600 journals and other serials; 6 newspapers. **Services:** Interlibrary loan; copying; SDI; library open to the public by appointment. **Automated Operations:** Computerized public access catalog, cataloging, acquisitions, serials, and circulation. **Computerized Information Services:** DIALOG Information Services, PFDS Online, BRS Information Technologies, Integrated Technical Information System (ITIS), Dow Jones News/Retrieval, Mead Data Central, NLM, OCLC, DataTimes, NEXIS, LEXIS, EPIC; CD-ROM; Academy Information Rerieval System (AIRS) (internal database); DIALMAIL, BITNET, Easy Net (electronic mail services). **Networks/Consortia:** Member of Interlibrary Users Association (IUA); FEDLINK. **Publications:** NewsLetter, bimonthly; NRC Periodicals Holdings Union List, quarterly; NRC Reference Holdings Union List, annual; Pathfinders; brochure; New Acquisitions List, monthly. **Remarks:** FAX: (202)334-1651. Library serves the staff and members of the National Academy of Sciences, the National Academy of Engineering, and the Institute of Medicine committees. **Staff:** Lynda Browne, Assoc.Libn., Cat.; Janet Ewing, Assoc.Libn., Ref.; Laura Baird, Assoc.Libn., Ref.; Sue Little Page, Info.Anl.; Sally Ann Carr, Asst.Libn., ILL.

★11269★
National Research Council - Transportation Research Board Library
(Trans)
2101 Constitution Ave., N.W. Phone: (202)334-2989
Washington, DC 20418 Barbara L. Post, Libn.
Founded: 1946. **Staff:** Prof 2. **Subjects:** Transportation - engineering, planning, geology, law, safety, economics, environment; traffic engineering. **Special Collections:** Transportation Research Board publications (complete collection). **Holdings:** 17,000 books, bound periodical volumes, reports; VF drawers. **Subscriptions:** 400 journals and other serials. **Services:** Interlibrary loan; copying; library open to the public. **Automated Operations:** Computerized circulation. **Computerized Information Services:** DIALOG Information Services, OCLC; internal databases. Performs searches on fee basis. Contact Person: Suzanne Crowther. **Networks/Consortia:** Member of FEDLINK. **Publications:** Periodicals List, biennial. **Special Catalogs:** Author/title catalog of Transportation Research Board publications (online). **Special Indexes:** Index to Transportation Research News, 1987 to present (online). **Remarks:** FAX: (202)334-2527. **Staff:** Yvonne Williams.

★11270★
National Research Council - Transportation Research Information
Service (Trans)
Transportation Research Board
2101 Constitution Ave., N.W. Phone: (202)334-2995
Washington, DC 20418 Jerome T. Maddock, Mgr.
Founded: 1967. **Staff:** Prof 5; Other 3. **Subjects:** Highway transport, mass transit, operations, planning, design and maintenance, construction.

Holdings: 350,000 machine readable abstracts of technical literature; 4500 machine readable resumes of ongoing research projects. **Services:** SDI; service open to the public. **Computerized Information Services:** DIALOG Information Services, Transportation Research Information Services (TRIS), International Road Research Documentation (IRRD); BITNET (electronic mail service). Performs searches on fee basis. Contact Person: Suzanne Crowther, User Serv.Rep. **Publications:** Highway Research Abstracts, quarterly; Hot Topics, monthly; Urban Transportation Abstracts, annual; Highway Safety Literature, annual. **Remarks:** FAX: (202)334-2527. Telex: 710 822 9589. Electronic mail address(es): JMADDOCK@NAS (BITNET). **Staff:** Nancy Dagenhart, Info.Spec.; Mrs. Rukmini Seevaratnam, Info.Spec.; Shirley Morin, Comp.Serv.; Jack Chen, Software Dev.; Arthur B. Mobley, Database Dev.

National Resource Center on Child Abuse and Neglect
See: **American Humane Association - American Association for**
Protecting Children (620)

★11271★
National Resource Center for Consumers of Legal Services -
Clearinghouse (Law)
1444 Eye St., NW 8th Fl. Phone: (202)842-3503
Washington, DC 20005 Tom Chiancone, Asst.Dir.
Founded: 1974. **Staff:** Prof 2. **Subjects:** Group and prepaid legal services, lawyer advertising, legal clinics, consumer education. **Holdings:** 1000 volumes; 25 VF drawers of documents and clippings. **Subscriptions:** 25 journals and other serials. **Services:** Copying; clearinghouse open to the public with restrictions. **Publications:** Legal Plan Letter, biweekly; list of additional publications - available on request. **Remarks:** FAX: (202)842-4354. **Staff:** Bill Bolger, Exec.Dir.

National Resource Center for Family Support Programs
See: **Family Resource Coalition** (5591)

★11272★
National Restaurant Association - Information Service and Library
(Food-Bev)
1200 17th St., N.W. Phone: (202)331-5900
Washington, DC 20036 Larry Himelfarb, Lib.Mgr.
Founded: 1976. **Staff:** Prof 5; Other 2. **Subjects:** Foodservice industry, restaurants, cookery, public health. **Special Collections:** Menu Collection. **Holdings:** 4000 books; 1300 subject clipping files; annual reports. **Subscriptions:** 250 journals and other serials. **Services:** Library open to non-members and students by appointment only. **Computerized Information Services:** DIALOG Information Services; Dineline (internal database). **Publications:** Foodservice Information Abstracts, biweekly - by subscription. **Remarks:** FAX: (202)331-2429. **Staff:** Elizabeth Baker, Libn.; Susan Aylward, Sr.Info.Spec.; Diane Byler, Info.Spec.; Sharon Jones, Info.Spec.

★11273★
National Reye's Syndrome Foundation - Library (Med)
426 N. Lewis
P.O. Box 829
Bryan, OH 43506 Phone: (419)636-2679
Staff:. 1.5. **Subjects:** Reye's Syndrome - awareness, guidance, treatment, research. **Special Collections:** Journal of the NRSF (up to 1986). **Holdings:** Bound periodicals; reports; brochures. **Services:** Library open to the public.

★11274★
National Rifle Association of America - National Firearms Museum -
Library (Mil)
1600 Rhode Island Ave., N.W. Phone: (202)828-6198
Washington, DC 20036 Doug Wicklund, Cur.
Subjects: Firearms, arms technology, cartridges/reloading, military history. **Holdings:** 2000 books. **Services:** Library open to the public by appointment. **Remarks:** FAX: (202)223-2691.

★ 11275 ★
National Rifle Association of America - NRA-ILA Library (Rec)
1600 Rhode Island Ave., N.W., 7th Fl.   Phone: (202)828-6332
Washington, DC 20036   Janet Greer
Founded: 1976. **Staff:** Prof 2. **Subjects:** Criminal justice, legislation, natural resources, firearms and hunting issues. **Holdings:** 1100 books; 250 linear feet of newspaper clippings; 150 linear feet of vertical file materials. **Subscriptions:** 77 journals and other serials; 8 newspapers. **Services:** Library for the use of Association staff only. **Automated Operations:** INMAGIC. **Publications:** Library Pack - a daily collection of relevant news articles. **Remarks:** FAX: (202)861-0306. **Also Known As:** NRA. **Staff:** Virginai Hurst, Asst.Libn.

★ 11276 ★
National Rifle Association of America - NRA Technical Library (Rec)
470 Spring Park Pl., Suite 1000
Herndon, VA 22070   Pete Dickey, Tech.Ed.
Founded: 1946. **Staff:** 1. **Subjects:** Firearms, ammunition, hunting, military ordnance, antique arms. **Holdings:** 1500 books. **Services:** Library not open to the public.

★ 11277 ★
National Right to Life Committee - Library (Soc Sci)
419 7th St., N.W., Suite 500
Washington, DC 20004   Phone: (202)626-8800
Founded: 1981. **Subjects:** Abortion, euthanasia, and infanticide. **Holdings:** 1000 books, pamphlets, brochures, and audiovisual materials; vertical file containing 20,000 items. **Subscriptions:** 20 journals and other serials; 6 newspapers. **Services:** Copying; library open to the public by appointment.

★ 11278 ★
National Rural Electric Cooperative Association - Norris Memorial Library (Energy)
1800 Massachusetts Ave., N.W., GMO-26   Phone: (202)857-9787
Washington, DC 20036   Chuck Rice, Lib.Serv.Spec.
Founded: 1963. **Staff:** Prof 1; Other 1. **Subjects:** Rural electrification, electric power, energy policy. **Special Collections:** Congressional documents; Electric Power Research Institute reports (100). **Holdings:** 25,000 volumes; 500 subject files; 375 reels of microfilm; 7 drawers of microfiche. **Subscriptions:** 600 journals and other serials; 7 newspapers. **Services:** Interlibrary loan (limited); copying; library open to the public by appointment. **Computerized Information Services:** DIALOG Information Services, EPIC. **Networks/Consortia:** Member of CAPCON Library Network. **Publications:** Library Acquisitions List, irregular. **Remarks:** Alternate telephone number(s): (202)857-9788.

★ 11279 ★
National Safety Council - Library (Sci-Engr)
444 N. Michigan Ave.   Phone: (312)527-4800
Chicago, IL 60611   Robert J. Marecek, Mgr.
Founded: 1913. **Staff:** Prof 6; Other 1. **Subjects:** Accident prevention, traffic safety, industrial health, all aspects of safety and safety research. **Special Collections:** National Safety Council Archives. **Holdings:** 4000 books; 700 bound periodical volumes; 70,000 other cataloged items; 21,000 research reports; 700 reels of microfilm; 5000 microfiche. **Subscriptions:** 250 journals and other serials. **Services:** Interlibrary loan; copying; library open to the public with prior contact suggested. **Computerized Information Services:** Online systems; NSCL Database (internal database). **Networks/Consortia:** Member of National Network of Libraries of Medicine - Greater Midwest Region. **Special Indexes:** Historical Index to the Industrial Data Sheets. **Remarks:** FAX: (312)527-9381. **Staff:** Violeta Bernadas, Coord., Ref./ILL; Lucinda Fuller, Coord., Per./Archv./Indexing.

National Scholastic Press Association
See: **Associated Collegiate Press/National Scholastic Press Association** (1135)

★ 11280 ★
National School Boards Association - Library (Educ)
1680 Duke St.   Phone: (703)838-6731
Alexandria, VA 22314-3407   Susan R. Fournier, Mgr., Info.Serv.
Founded: 1973. **Staff:** Prof 2. **Subjects:** Educational administration, board governance, education policy development, school district management.

Special Collections: State School Board Association publications; Education Policies Clearinghouse (8 VF drawers of sample policies from local school boards in the U.S. and Canada). **Holdings:** 4000 books and reports; 8 VF drawers of current information on issues in public elementary and secondary education. **Subscriptions:** 200 journals and other serials; 9 newspapers. **Services:** Interlibrary loan; copying; SDI; library open to the public by appointment. **Computerized Information Services:** BRS Information Technologies, VU/TEXT Information Services, OCLC. **Networks/Consortia:** Member of CAPCON Library Network. **Publications:** NSBA Fact Sheet on Elementary and Secondary Education Statistics. **Remarks:** FAX: (703)683-7590. Alternate telephone number(s): (703)838-6722.

National School Safety Center
See: **Pepperdine University** (12938)

National Science Council (of Taiwan)
See: **Taiwan - National Science Council** (15986)

National Science Film Library (of Canada)
See: **Canadian Film Institute** (2929)

★ 11281 ★
National Science Foundation - Library (Sci-Engr, Biol Sci)
1800 G St., N.W.   Phone: (202)357-7811
Washington, DC 20550   Janell C. Walker, Hd.
Founded: 1951. **Staff:** Prof 2; Other 1. **Subjects:** Basic and applied science and technology; biological sciences; environmental policy; physics; computer and information sciences; mathematics; astronomical, atmospheric, earth, ocean, and polar sciences; chemistry; engineering; science and engineering education; science policy; technological innovations; materials research; social sciences; economics, research and development management. **Holdings:** 15,000 books; 650 bound periodical volumes. **Subscriptions:** 700 journals and other serials; 5 newspapers. **Services:** Interlibrary loan; copying; library open to the public. **Automated Operations:** Computerized cataloging and serials. **Computerized Information Services:** OCLC, DIALOG Information Services. **Networks/Consortia:** Member of FEDLINK. **Publications:** Periodicals Received, annual; Library Reading List, quarterly; Library Guide, irregular. **Remarks:** FAX: (202)357-7745. **Staff:** Richard P. Scott, Cat.; Florence E. Heckman, Ref.Libn.

National Science Foundation - National Solar Observatory
See: **National Solar Observatory** (11299)

★ 11282 ★
National Science Foundation - Polar Information Program (Sci-Engr)
Division of Polar Programs   Phone: (202)357-7817
Washington, DC 20550   Guy G. Guthridge, Mgr.
Founded: 1962. **Staff:** Prof 2; Other 2. **Subjects:** Antarctic research and operations, Arctic research. **Holdings:** 500 books; 20 bound periodical volumes; 51,000 antarctic titles on microfiche. **Subscriptions:** 30 journals and other serials. **Services:** Program open to the public for reference use only. **Computerized Information Services:** SCIENCEnet, SprintMail (electronic mail services). **Publications:** Current Antarctic Literature; Antarctic Journal of the United States; Arctic Research of the United States. **Remarks:** FAX: (202)357-9422. **Staff:** Winifred Reuning, Writer-Ed.

★ 11283 ★
National Science Teachers Association - Glenn O. Blough Library (Educ)
1742 Connecticut Ave., N.W.   Phone: (202)328-5800
Washington, DC 20009   Phyllis Marcuccio, Chf.Libn.
Founded: 1978. **Staff:** Prof 1; Other 2. **Subjects:** Science, curriculum materials. **Special Collections:** Glenn O. Blough Science Textbook Collection (75 sets of textbooks and curriculum guides). **Holdings:** 2145 books; 21 bound periodical volumes; 10 boxes of archival material; 1000 other cataloged items. **Subscriptions:** 60 journals and other serials. **Services:** Interlibrary loan; library open to the public by appointment. **Remarks:** FAX: (202)328-0974.

National Scientific and Technological Documentation Center (of Bolivia)
See: **Bolivia - National Scientific and Technological Documentation Center** (1949)

National Sea Grant Depository
See: **U.S. Natl. Oceanic & Atmospheric Administration - National Sea Grant College Program** (17658)

★ 11284 ★
National Self-Help Clearinghouse (Soc Sci)
25 W. 43rd St., Rm. 620
New York, NY 10036   Phone: (212)642-2944
Founded: 1976. **Staff:** 2. **Subjects:** Self-help groups, activities, research. **Holdings:** 7 VF drawers; bibliographic material. **Subscriptions:** 20 journals and other serials; 40 newspapers. **Services:** Clearinghouse open to the public by appointment. **Publications:** Self-Help Reporter - for sale. **Staff:** Frank Riessman, Co-Dir.; Audrey Gartner, Co-Dir.

National Severe Storms Laboratory
See: **U.S. Natl. Oceanic & Atmospheric Administration** (17659)

★ 11285 ★
National Sheriffs' Association - Education and Resource Center (Law)
1450 Duke St.   Phone: (703)836-7827
Alexandria, VA 22314-3490   Julia Stanton Gigante, Dir., Info.Serv.
Staff: 1. **Subjects:** Law enforcement, corrections, criminal justice. **Special Collections:** Jail policy manuals and contract law enforcement; periodicals on law enforcement and criminal justice. **Holdings:** 5500 books; victim/witness information. **Subscriptions:** 75 journals and other serials. **Services:** Library open to the public by appointment. **Remarks:** Alternate telephone number(s): 836-7827. FAX: (703)683-6541.

National Sisters Vocation Conference Archives
See: **Marquette University - Department of Special Collections and University Archives - Manuscript Collections Memorial Library** (9709)

★ 11286 ★
National Ski Hall of Fame and Museum - Roland Palmedo National Ski Library (Rec)
Box 191
Ishpeming, MI 49849   Phone: (906)486-9281
Founded: 1954. **Staff:** 2. **Subjects:** Skiing. **Special Collections:** Roland Palmedo Collection (300 volumes). **Holdings:** 1200 volumes; 20 VF drawers of reports, pamphlets, clippings; 175 films. **Subscriptions:** 7 journals and other serials. **Services:** Copying; library open to the public for reference use only. **Staff:** Deborah Arbelius, Libn.; Kenneth P. Luostari, Libn.

★ 11287 ★
National Small Business Benefits Association - Library (Bus-Fin)
2244 N. Grand Ave. E.   Phone: (217)544-0881
Springfield, IL 62702   Delvan McKinnley
Staff: 6. **Subjects:** Small businesses. **Holdings:** 300 volumes. **Services:** Library not open to the public. **Computerized Information Services:** Internal database. **Remarks:** FAX: (217)544-5816.

National Small Flows Clearinghouse - Library
See: **U.S. Environmental Protection Agency** (17470)

★ 11288 ★
National Soaring Museum - Joseph C. Lincoln Memorial Library & Ralph S. Barnaby Archives (Rec)
Harris Hill, R.D. 3   Phone: (607)734-3128
Elmira, NY 14903   Charles D. Smith, Ph.D., Exec.Dir.
Founded: 1972. **Staff:** Prof 3; Other 4. **Subjects:** Soaring, aviation. **Special Collections:** Joseph C. Lincoln Collection (166 books and papers on soaring). **Holdings:** 200 books; 90 bound periodical volumes; 5 manuscripts; 4 document sets; 2 files of papers and documents on sailplanes; 2 boxes of Mountain Wave Project manuscripts; 1 case of Warren Eaton documents and newsclips; 2 cases of historical soaring photographs. **Subscriptions:** 75 journals and other serials. **Services:** Library not open to the public. **Networks/Consortia:** Member of Regional Conference of Historical Agencies. **Staff:** Mary D. Flasphaler, Dir. of Musm.Serv.

★ 11289 ★
National Society, Daughters of the American Revolution - Aloha Chapter - DAR Memorial Library (Hist)
1914 Makiki Heights Dr.   Phone: (808)621-7681
Honolulu, HI 96822   Jean G. Rigler, Libn.
Staff: Prof 1; Other 10. **Subjects:** Family genealogies, state and regional history, colonial genealogy. **Special Collections:** Barbour Collection (92 reels of microfilm); Genealogical Collection; census records (most states); historical state collections; family histories; family manuscripts (100); family records (1000; on microfiche); patriotic organization records. **Holdings:** 6000 books; 350 bound periodical volumes. **Subscriptions:** 10 journals and other serials. **Services:** Copying; library open to the public.

★ 11290 ★
National Society, Daughters of the American Revolution - Hannah Weston Chapter - Burnham Tavern Museum (Hist)
2 Free St.   Phone: (207)255-4432
Machias, ME 04654   Valdine C. Atwood, Chm.
Founded: 1910. **Subjects:** Local history. **Special Collections:** Machias Valley area collection (records; ledgers; daybooks; chapter books, 1901 to present). **Holdings:** 300 volumes. **Services:** Museum open to the public.

★ 11291 ★
National Society, Daughters of the American Revolution - Library (Hist)
1776 D St., N.W.   Phone: (202)879-3229
Washington, DC 20006-5392   Eric G. Grundset, Lib.Dir.
Founded: 1896. **Staff:** Prof 6; Other 11. **Subjects:** Genealogy, U.S. local history, U.S. history, American Indian history, American women's history. **Special Collections:** Genealogies; United States, state, county, local histories; published rosters of Revolutionary War soldiers; published vital records; cemetery inscriptions; Bible records; transcripts of various county records (such as wills), compiled by the Genealogical Records Committees of DAR; published archives of some of the thirteen original states; abstracts of some Revolutionary War pension files; American Indian history, genealogy, culture; U.S. City Directory Collection, 20th century. **Holdings:** 110,000 books; 10,000 bound periodical volumes; 250,000 files of manuscript material, genealogical records, pamphlets. **Subscriptions:** 550 journals and other serials. **Services:** Copying; library open to the public on a fee basis. **Automated Operations:** Computerized cataloging. **Special Catalogs:** DAR Library Catalog, volume 1: Family Histories and Genealogies, 1982; supplement to volume 1, 1984; volume 2: State and Local Histories and Records, 1986; volume 3: Acquisitions 1985-1991, 1991. **Remarks:** FAX: (202)879-3252. **Staff:** Marilyn A. Duncan, Asst.Libn., Ref.Serv.; Bertha G. Mutz, Libn., Tech.Serv.

★ 11292 ★
National Society, Daughters of Utah Pioneers - Library (Hist)
300 N. Main St.   Phone: (801)538-1050
Salt Lake City, UT 84103-1699   Louise C. Green, Pres.
Subjects: History of Utah and Western states. **Holdings:** 1000 volumes; 50,000 documents on microfilm. **Services:** Copying; library open to descendants of Utah Pioneers. **Special Catalogs:** Artifacts and documents catalog (online).

★ 11293 ★
National Society of Insurance Premium Auditors - Library (Bus-Fin)
15404 R St.
Box 323   Phone: (402)496-4700
Boys Town, NE 68010   Betty Gerdes, Sec.Treas.
Founded: 1975. **Staff:** 1. **Subjects:** Policy auditing to determine insurance premiums. **Holdings:** Manuals; textbooks; pamphlets; reference articles; videotapes; slides. **Services:** Interlibrary loan; library not open to the public.

★ 11294 ★
National Society for Internships and Experiential Education - National Resource Center for Experiential and Service Learning (Educ)
3509 Haworth Dr., Suite 207   Phone: (919)787-3263
Raleigh, NC 27609-7229   Barbara E. Baker, Prog.Assoc.
Founded: 1971. **Staff:** 6. **Subjects:** Education - experiential, higher, secondary, service-learning; cooperative; internships; program design and administration. **Holdings:** 1000 books; 12,000 conference papers, manuscripts, reports, video- and audiotapes. **Subscriptions:** 1250 journals and other serials. **Services:** Copying; library open to the public.

Publications: Combining Service and Learning: A Resource Book for Community and Public Service; Preparing Humanists for Work: A National Study of Undergraduate Internships in the Humanities; Strengthening Experiential Education within Your Institution; Knowing and Doing: Learning from Experience; A Guide to Environmental Internships: How Environmental Organizations Can Use Internships Effectively; NSIEE Occasional Papers; PANEL Resource Papers. **Staff:** Sally A. Migliore, Assoc.Exec.Dir.; Annette Wofford, Off.Mgr.; Rich Ungerer, Sr.Assoc.; Allen Wutzdorff, Exec.Dir.

★11295★
National Society to Prevent Blindness - Conrad Berens Library (Med)
500 E. Remington Rd.   Phone: (708)843-2020
Schaumburg, IL 60173   Pamela Gerali, Dir.Prog.Serv.
Staff: Prof 1; Other 1.5. **Subjects:** Ophthalmology, optometry, eye health and safety; association management. **Special Collections:** NSPB Archives. **Holdings:** 3000 volumes; 21 VF drawers of reports, pamphlets, clippings, association reports, bulletins, state health reports. **Subscriptions:** 100 journals and other serials. **Services:** Library open to researchers, health professionals, and public by appointment. **Networks/Consortia:** Member of North Suburban Library System (NSLS). **Remarks:** FAX: (708)843-8458. Toll-free telephone number(s): (800)221-3004.

★11296★
National Society of Professional Engineers - Information Center (Sci-Engr)
1420 King St.   Phone: (703)684-2810
Alexandria, VA 22314   Donald G. Weinert, Exec.Dir.
Staff: 2. **Subjects:** Engineering (nontechnical) - manpower, salary, ethics, registration, legislation, law, allied subjects. **Holdings:** 1500 books; 35 VF drawers of documents and reports. **Subscriptions:** 100 journals and other serials. **Services:** Library not open to the public. **Remarks:** FAX: (703)836-4875. **Staff:** Lisa Boccetti, Dir., Info.Ctr.

★11297★
National Society of the Sons of the American Revolution - Genealogy Library (Hist)
1000 S. 4th St.   Phone: (502)589-1776
Louisville, KY 40203   Michael A. Christian, Libn.
Founded: 1926. **Staff:** Prof 1. **Subjects:** American history and genealogy, Revolutionary War, Colonial America. **Special Collections:** Daughters of the American Revolution Lineage Book Collection; Sons of the American Revolution Archives; state census record indexes; George Washington Collection. **Holdings:** 20,000 books; 2000 periodicals; 1400 pamphlets; 5300 microforms. **Subscriptions:** 20 journals and other serials. **Services:** Copying; library open to the public on a fee basis. **Automated Operations:** Computerized public access catalog, cataloging, acquisitions, and serials. **Also Known As:** Sons of the American Revolution. **Staff:** Robert A. Lentz, Exec.Dir., N.S. SAR.

★11298★
National Society of the Sons of the American Revolution - New Jersey Society - S.A.R. Library (Hist)
101 W. 9th Ave.   Phone: (908)245-1777
Roselle, NJ 07203   Howard W. Wiseman, Libn.
Founded: 1889. **Staff:** Prof 1. **Subjects:** Genealogy, Revolutionary War history and biography, local history, patriotic organizations. **Holdings:** 2000 books; 1000 bound periodical volumes; 1000 other cataloged items. **Services:** Copying; library open to the public on a limited schedule. **Special Indexes:** Index of each member and his ancestral Revolutionary War veteran, 1889 to present (card).

National Soil Dynamics Laboratory
See: **U.S.D.A. - Agricultural Research Service** (17190)

★11299★
National Solar Observatory - Technical Library (Sci-Engr)
Sunspot, NM 88349   Phone: (505)434-7024
                                               John Cornett, Libn.
Founded: 1960. **Staff:** Prof 1. **Subjects:** Solar astronomy, physics, optics. **Holdings:** 3500 books; 7000 bound periodical volumes; 2000 observatory

technical reports and preprints; 10 VF drawers of staff publications. **Subscriptions:** 110 journals and other serials. **Services:** Interlibrary loan; copying; library open to the public with restrictions. **Automated Operations:** Computerized cataloging and ILL. **Computerized Information Services:** DIALOG Information Services, STN International, OCLC; NSO Publications Bibliography (internal database); InterNet (electronic mail service). **Networks/Consortia:** Member of FEDLINK. **Publications:** Acquisitions list, quarterly. **Special Catalogs:** Serial holdings (book). **Remarks:** FAX: (505)434-7029; 434-7024. Telex: 1561030. Electronic mail address(es): jcornett@noao.edu (InterNet). The observatory is a division of the National Optical Astronomy Observatories, under contract with the National Science Foundation.

National Space Science Data Center
See: **World Data Center A - Rockets & Satellites - National Space Science Data Center** (20616)

★11300★
National Space Society - Von Braun-Oberth Memorial Library (Sci-Engr)
922 Pennsylvania Ave., S.E.   Phone: (202)543-1900
Washington, DC 20003   Lorraine Hughes
Founded: 1987. **Subjects:** Space - development, program history, transportation, long range plans. **Special Collections:** Repository of the archival L5 NEWS & Space Frontier (1975-1987); Space World magazine. **Holdings:** 500 books; 1000 other cataloged items. **Services:** Copying; library open to the public by appointment. **Remarks:** FAX: (202)546-4189.

★11301★
National Speleological Society - NSS Library (Sci-Engr)
1 Cave Ave.   Phone: (205)852-1300
Huntsville, AL 35810   William W. Torode, NSS Libn.
Founded: 1940. **Staff:** 1. **Subjects:** Speleology, geology, cave exploration, biospeleology, archeology. **Special Collections:** Foreign publications on speleology; "largest collection of American Cave Club literature in the world"; collection of foreign cave club newsletters. **Holdings:** 3000 books; 1000 periodical volumes; 4000 items in author reprint file; newspaper clippings, pamphlets, abstracts, paperbacks about recreational and scientific speleology. **Subscriptions:** 166 foreign and 200 American exchange publications. **Services:** Copying; library open to NSS members only.

★11302★
National Sporting Library, Inc. (Rec)
Box 1335   Phone: (703)687-6542
Middleburg, VA 22117   Laura Rose, Libn.
Founded: 1954. **Staff:** Prof 2. **Subjects:** Field sports - thoroughbred racing and breeding, foxhunting, beagling, polo, horse shows and allied activities, fishing, shooting, falconry, cockfighting. **Special Collections:** Thomas Holden White Polo Collection; Huth-Lonsdale-Arundel Collection of 16th-19th century books on horses; H.T. Peters' American Sporting Art Books; Durell Derrydale Collection; Sharp Beagling and Foxhunting Collection; Wells Dealer's Catalogue Collection. **Holdings:** 12,000 books; 1500 bound periodical volumes; 20 boxes of Harry Worcester Smith Papers; sporting paintings and prints; 120 reels of microfilm of sporting periodicals. **Services:** Interlibrary loan; copying; library open to the public for reference use only. **Computerized Information Services:** OCLC. **Publications:** National Sporting Library Newsletter, 2/year - to members of Friends of the National Sporting Library. **Special Indexes:** Indexes of N.Y. Sporting Magazine, U.S. Sporting Magazine, Spirit of the Times, 1831-1861; American Turf Register and Sporting Magazine, 1829-1844. **Staff:** Laura Rose, Libn.; June Ruhsam, Libn.

★11303★
National Standards Association, Inc. - Techinfo (Sci-Engr)
1200 Quince Orchard Blvd.   Phone: (301)590-2352
Gaithersburg, MD 20878   Doug Hansen, Supv., Tech.Info.
Founded: 1946. **Subjects:** Military and federal standards and specifications, industry standards. **Special Collections:** National Aerospace Standards (2900); Department of Defense Index of Specifications and Standards documents (45,000). **Holdings:** 250,000 specifications and standards; government and industrial technical documents. **Services:** Library open to the public with restrictions. **Automated Operations:** Computerized cataloging and acquisitions. **Computerized Information Services:** DIALOG Information Services. Performs searches on fee basis. **Publications:** National Aerospace Standards (NAS), 10/year; Metric National Aerospace Standards, 6/year; Standards and Specifications Information Bulletin, weekly; AN, AND & MS Drawings & Handbooks, monthly; Identified Sources of Supply, annual. **Special Indexes:** Indexes and supplements to NAS, NA, AN, AND & MS; Identified Sources of Supply. **Remarks:** FAX: (301)990-8378. Toll-free telephone number(s): is (800)638-8094.

National Standards Council of American Embroiderers - NSCAE Library
See: Council of American Embroiderers (4358)

★ 11304 ★
National Starch and Chemical Company - Information Resources (Sci-Engr)
10 Finderne Ave.
Box 6500   Phone: (201)685-5082
Bridgewater, NJ 08807   Marianne Vago, Info.Rsrcs.Supv.
Founded: 1954. **Staff:** Prof 2. **Subjects:** Organic chemistry, physical chemistry, inorganic chemistry, chemical technology, physics. **Holdings:** 4000 books; 7000 bound periodical volumes; 25 VF drawers of patents and technical reports. **Subscriptions:** 300 journals and other serials. **Services:** Interlibrary loan; copying. **Computerized Information Services:** STN International, DIALOG Information Services, MEDLARS.

★ 11305 ★
National Steel Corporation - Technical Research Center - R & D Technical Library (Sci-Engr)
1745 Fritz Dr.   Phone: (313)676-6750
Trenton, MI 48183   Susan K. Smith, Sr.Res.Libn.
Founded: 1960. **Staff:** Prof 1; Other 2. **Subjects:** Chemistry, metallurgy, steel, business. **Holdings:** 4000 books; 3500 bound periodical volumes. **Subscriptions:** 330 serials. **Services:** Interlibrary loan; library not open to the public. **Automated Operations:** Computerized public access catalog, cataloging, acquisitions, serials, and circulation. **Computerized Information Services:** DIALOG Information Services, STN International, Dow Jones News/Retrieval, NEXIS, Maxwell Online, Inc., EBSCONET, OCLC, QL Systems; DIALMAIL (electronic mail service). **Networks/Consortia:** Member of Michigan Library Consortium (MLC). **Remarks:** FAX: (313)676-2030.

★ 11306 ★
National Stereoscopic Association - Oliver Wendell Holmes Stereoscopic Research Library (Aud-Vis)
Eastern College   Phone: (215)688-3300
St. Davids, PA 19087-3696   Dr. William Allen Zulker, Cur./Libn.
Staff: Prof 1; Other 1. **Subjects:** Stereoscopic photography. **Holdings:** 530 volumes; 4 VF drawers of unbound documents; 30,000 stereoscopic views; 2 VF drawers. **Subscriptions:** 12 journals and other serials. **Services:** Copying; library open to the public by appointment. **Computerized Information Services:** BRS Information Technologies, OCLC. **Remarks:** FAX: (215)341-1375.

★ 11307 ★
National Storytelling Resource Center (Hum)
Box 309   Phone: (615)753-2171
Jonesborough, TN 37659   Jimmy Neil Smith, Dir.
Founded: 1975. **Staff:** 13. **Subjects:** Storytelling. **Holdings:** 850 audiotapes; 780 videotapes; 5500 journals. **Services:** Center open to the public. **Publications:** Storytelling Magazine, quarterly; Yarnspinner (newsletter), monthly. **Special Catalogs:** National Catalog of Storytelling. **Special Indexes:** National Directory of Storytelling (lists individual storytellers, storytelling activities, and storytelling organizations). **Remarks:** FAX: (615)753-9331. **Also Known As:** National Association for the Preservation & Perpetuation of Storytelling (NAPPS). **Staff:** Sandra Moore, Archv.

★ 11308 ★
National Stroke Association - Stroke Information and Referral Center (Med)
300 E. Hampden Ave., Suite 240   Phone: (303)762-9922
Englewood, CO 80110-2654   Thelma Edwards, RN, Dir., Prog.Dev.
Founded: 1984. **Staff:** Prof 1; Other 5. **Subjects:** Stroke - prevention, medical care, rehabilitation, research, resocialization. **Holdings:** 100 books; 10 videotapes; 85 booklets, brochures, articles; 20 VF drawers. **Subscriptions:** 100 newspapers and newsletters. **Publications:** Be Stroke Smart (newsletter), quarterly; list of publications - both available on request. **Remarks:** FAX: (303)762-1190.

★ 11309 ★
National Sudden Infant Death Syndrome Resource Center (Med)
8201 Greensboro Dr., Suite 600
McLean, VA 22102-3810   Phone: (703)821-8955
Founded: 1985. **Subjects:** Sudden Infant Death Syndrome, infant mortality, apnea, perinatal grief and loss. **Services:** Center open to the public by appointment. **Computerized Information Services:** Internal database. **Publications:** Subject-specific publications (Sudden Infant Death Syndrome, monitoring, family grief and loss); newsletter; fact sheets; bibliographies; educational and resource materials. **Remarks:** FAX: (703)821-2098. **Formerly:** National Sudden Infant Death Syndrome Clearinghouse.

★ 11310 ★
National Swedish Institute for Building Research - Library (Plan)
P.O. Box 785   Phone: 10 02 20
S-801 29 Gavle, Sweden   Lena Berntler, Libn.
Subjects: Building, planning, architecture. **Holdings:** 25,000 books. **Subscriptions:** 400 journals and other serials. **Services:** Interlibrary loan; copying; library open to the public. **Computerized Information Services:** DIALOG Information Services, ESA/IRS, ARAMIS, BYGGDOK. **Remarks:** FAX: 26-118154. Telex: 47396 BYGGFO. **Also Known As:** Statens Institut for Byggnadsforskning.

National Szechenyi Library
See: Hungary - National Szechenyi Library - Centre for Library Science and Methodology (7557)

★ 11311 ★
National Taiwan University - Medical Library (Med)
1 Jen Ai Rd, Sec 1   Phone: 2 3911301
Taipei 10013, Taiwan   Huei-chu Chang
Founded: 1900. **Staff:** Prof 12; Other 3. **Subjects:** Medicine, dentistry, nursing, public health, pharmacy. **Special Collections:** Taiwanese medical journals. **Holdings:** 77,855 books; 69,909 bound periodical volumes; 264 microfiche; 39 reels of microfilm; AV materials. **Subscriptions:** 1600 journals and other serials; 10 newspapers. **Services:** Interlibrary loan; copying; library open to the public. **Computerized Information Services:** DIALOG Information Services, MEDLARS; NTOMG (internal database). Contact Person: T-Shion Yu. **Remarks:** FAX: 2 3938354.

★ 11312 ★
National Taxpayers Union - Library (Bus-Fin)
325 Pennsylvania Ave., S.E.   Phone: (202)543-1300
Washington, DC 20003   Pete Sepp
Founded: 1969. **Subjects:** National taxpayer movements, constitutional amendment for a balanced budget, IRS abuses, congressional spending ratings. **Holdings:** 750 books; 50 reports; archival items. **Subscriptions:** 7 journals and other serials. **Services:** Library open to the public with restrictions, must inquire by telephone. **Remarks:** FAX: (202)546-2086.

★ 11313 ★
National Tay-Sachs and Allied Diseases Association - Library (Med)
2001 Beacon St., Suite 304   Phone: (617)277-4463
Brookline, MA 02146   Debi Gutter
Founded: 1986. **Staff:** 3. **Subjects:** Grief counseling, Tay-Sachs' disease, lysosomal storage diseases. **Holdings:** 100 books; 10,000 newspaper clippings. **Services:** Library open to the public. **Remarks:** FAX: (617)277-0134. **Formerly:** Located in Newton, MA.

National Technical Information Centre and Library (of Hungary)
See: Hungary - National Technical Information Centre and Library (7558)

National Technical Institute for the Deaf
See: Rochester Institute of Technology (13982)

National Technological Library of Denmark
See: Denmark - National Technological Library of Denmark (4767)

National Telecommunications Center (of France) - Interministerial Documentation Service
See: **France - National Telecommunications Research Center - Interministerial Documentation Service** (6071)

★ 11314 ★
National Theatre School of Canada - Theatrical Library (Theater)
5030 Saint-Denis St.   Phone: (514)842-7954
Montreal, PQ, Canada H2J 2L8   Wolfgang R. Noethlichs, Hd.Libn.
Founded: 1941. **Staff:** Prof 2; Other 3. **Subjects:** Plays in French and English, theater, fine arts, architecture, performing arts. **Holdings:** 40,000 volumes; 100 VF drawers; records. **Subscriptions:** 60 journals and other serials. **Services:** Interlibrary loan; copying; library open to the public on a subscription basis. **Remarks:** FAX: (514)842-5661.

National Track & Field Hall of Fame
See: **Athletics Congress of the U.S.A.** (1232)

National Track & Field Hall of Fame - Historical Research Library
See: **Butler University - Irwin Library - Hugh Thomas Miller Rare Book Room** (2416)

★ 11315 ★
National Training Center of Polygraph Science - Library (Law)
200 W. 57th St.   Phone: (212)755-5241
New York, NY 10019   Richard O. Arther, Sch.Dir.
Founded: 1958. **Staff:** Prof 3; Other 2. **Subjects:** Polygraphs, lie detection. **Special Collections:** All issues of the Journal of Polygraph Science. **Holdings:** Figures not available. **Services:** Library not open to the public. **Publications:** Journal of Polygraph Science, bimonthly.

National Transportation Agency of Canada
See: **Canada - National Transportation Agency of Canada** (2829)

★ 11316 ★
National Tropical Botanical Garden - Library (Biol Sci)
P.O. Box 340
Lawai   Phone: (808)332-7324
Kauai, HI 96765   Richard E. Hanna, Libn.
Founded: 1972. **Staff:** 1. **Subjects:** Tropical botany, tropical horticulture, ethnobotany, natural history. **Special Collections:** Botanical print collection (4000); Victorian horticultural/botanical periodical collection (100 volumes). **Holdings:** 7500 books; 5000 periodical volumes; 3000 slides. **Subscriptions:** 200 journals and other serials; 4 newspapers. **Services:** Copying (limited); library open to the public for reference use only. **Computerized Information Services:** Internal database. **Remarks:** FAX: (808)332-9765.

★ 11317 ★
National Trust Company - Reference Library (Law, Bus-Fin)
1 Adelaide St., E., 3rd Fl.
Toronto, ON, Canada M5C 2W8   Phone: (416)361-3611
Founded: 1971. **Staff:** 2. **Subjects:** Law; trusts and estates. **Special Collections:** Annual reports of the National Trust Company. **Holdings:** 3200 books; 3500 annual reports of outside companies. **Subscriptions:** 150 journals and other serials; 8 newspapers. **Services:** Library not open to the public.

National Trust for Historic Preservation - Chesterwood
See: **Chesterwood** (3492)

National Trust for Historic Preservation - Cliveden
See: **Cliveden** (3841)

National Trust for Historic Preservation Library Collection
See: **University of Maryland, College Park Libraries - Architecture Library** (18810)

★ 11318 ★
National University - Law Library (Law)
8380 Miramar Rd.   Phone: (619)492-5180
San Diego, CA 92126-4431   Larry D. Dershem, Dir.
Founded: 1979. **Staff:** Prof 2; Other 4. **Subjects:** State and federal law. **Special Collections:** Advocacy. **Holdings:** 60,000 books; U.S. Government selective depository; California State depository. **Subscriptions:** 300 journals and other serials. **Services:** Interlibrary loan; library open to the public. **Automated Operations:** Computerized cataloging, acquisitions, serials, and circulation. **Computerized Information Services:** DIALOG Information Services, WESTLAW, LEXIS, NEXIS, CompuMark. Performs searches on fee basis. **Publications:** Beginner's Guide to the Law Library. **Remarks:** FAX: (619)492-5181. **Staff:** Elizabeth J. Carroll.

★ 11319 ★
National University of Singapore - Chinese Language and Research Center (Hum, Soc Sci)
10 Kent Ridge Crescent   Phone: 7722016
Singapore 0511, Singapore   Koh Thong Ngee, Libn.
Subjects: Chinese linguistics, humanities, social sciences. **Holdings:** 300,000 volumes. **Subscriptions:** 400 journals and other serials. **Remarks:** Library holdings are in Chinese. FAX: 7773571. Telex: 33943 UNISPO.

★ 11320 ★
National Urban League - Research Department - Library (Soc Sci)
1111 14th St., N.W., Suite 600   Phone: (202)898-1604
Washington, DC 20005   Billy Tidwell, Dir. of Res.
Subjects: U.S. social and economic conditions, blacks, poor minorities. **Holdings:** 1000 volumes; U.S. Department of Commerce and Bureau of Census information. **Services:** Library not open to the public. **Remarks:** FAX: (202)408-1965.

National Vaccine & Serum Institute (of the People's Republic of China)
See: **People's Republic of China - National Vaccine & Serum Institute** (12930)

★ 11321 ★
National Victim Center - Library (Soc Sci)
2111 Wilson Blvd., Suite 300   Phone: (703)276-2880
Arlington, VA 22209   Diane Alexander, Libn.
Founded: 1986. **Staff:** Prof 2. **Subjects:** Victims of violent crimes, legislation, national and local victim organizations. **Holdings:** 10,000 books and articles. **Subscriptions:** 76 journals and other serials. **Services:** Library open to the public. **Publications:** National Library Resource Project on Crime Victimization. **Special Catalogs:** Victims of Violent Crime. **Remarks:** FAX: (703)276-2889. **Formerly:** Located in Fort Worth, TX. **Staff:** Gary Markham.

★ 11322 ★
The National Volunteer Center (Soc Sci)
736 Jackson Pl., N.W.   Phone: (202)408-5162
Washington, DC 20503   Melissa Kirnman, Dir., Info.Serv.
Founded: 1979. **Staff:** 1. **Subjects:** Volunteerism, corporate volunteerism, citizen participation, philanthropy, nonprofit management. **Holdings:** 10,000 published and unpublished documents. **Subscriptions:** 10 journals and other serials. **Services:** Free library research service for associates; fee for nonassociates. **Publications:** Voluntary Action Leadership; Volunteering; Volunteer Readership; Volnet - biweekly electronic newsmagazine; The Workplace in the Community. **Formerly:** Located in Arlington, VA.

National Water Data Exchange and Water Data Storage and Retrieval System
See: **U.S. Geological Survey - Water Resources Division - National Water Data Exchange and Water Data Storage and Retrieval System** (17545)

National Water Data Storage & Retrieval System
See: **U.S. Geological Survey - Water Resources Division - National Water Data Exchange and Water Data Storage and Retrieval System** (17545)

National Water Information Clearinghouse
See: **U.S. Geological Survey - Water Resources Division - National Water Information Clearinghouse** (17546)

National Weather Service
See: **U.S. Natl. Weather Service** (17796)

★11323★
National Wetlands Technical Council - Library (Env-Cons)
1616 P St., N.W., Suite 200   Phone: (202)939-3800
Washington, DC 20036   Steve Mattox, Exec.Sec.
Founded: 1977. **Subjects:** Wetlands science, management, and law. **Holdings:** 150 volumes. **Remarks:** FAX: (202)328-5002. Affiliated with Environmental Law Institute.

★11324★
National Wildflower Research Center - Library (Biol Sci)
2600 FM 973 N.   Phone: (512)929-3600
Austin, TX 78725   Beth Anderson, Rsrc. Botanist
Founded: 1982. **Subjects:** North American flora, native plant landscaping, ecology, restoration, wildlife gardening, botany, conservation, sustainable agriculture. **Holdings:** 1000 books; 12,000 images on slides. **Subscriptions:** 50 journals and other serials. **Services:** Library open to the public by appointment for reference use only. **Publications:** Listing of native plant nurseries and seed companies; list of recommended native plants for landscaping; list of other organizations and resources for each state. **Remarks:** FAX: (512)929-0513. **Staff:** Bonnie Crozier, Rsrc. Botanist.

★11325★
National Wildlife Federation - George Preston Marshall Memorial Library (Env-Cons)
8925 Leesburg Pike   Phone: (703)790-4446
Vienna, VA 22184   Sharon Levy, Libn.
Founded: 1960. **Staff:** Prof 1. **Subjects:** Wildlife, natural resources, conservation, ecology, environment. **Special Collections:** Endangered species collection. **Holdings:** 5000 books. **Subscriptions:** 400 journals and other serials. **Services:** Interlibrary loan; copying; library open to the public for reference use only. **Computerized Information Services:** DIALOG Information Services, DataTimes. **Remarks:** FAX: (703)442-7332.

★11326★
National Woman's Christian Temperance Union - Frances E. Willard Memorial Library (Soc Sci)
1730 Chicago Ave.   Phone: (708)864-1396
Evanston, IL 60201   Alfred H. Epstein
Founded: 1939.**Staff:** Prof 1. **Subjects:** History of temperance; biographies of temperance leaders; influence of alcohol, tobacco, and narcotics on the human body; history of prohibition; alcohol education; history of women's movement; social reform history. **Special Collections:** Works by and about Frances Willard (correspondence; journals; scrapbooks). **Holdings:** 5000 books; 500 bound periodical volumes; photographs; archives; song books; reports; documents. **Subscriptions:** 15 journals and other serials. **Services:** Research by mail; library open to the public with restrictions.

★11327★
National Woman's Party - Florence Bayard Hilles Library
144 Constitution Ave., N.E.
Washington, DC 20002
Special Collections: Susan B. Anthony rare books. **Holdings:** 4000 volumes; suffrage materials, 1913-1920, on microfilm; equal rights archival material, 1920-1927. **Remarks:** Currently inactive.

★11328★
National Women's Health Network - Women's Health Information Service - Library (Med)
1325 G St., N.W.
Washington, DC 20005   Phone: (202)347-1140
Subjects: Women's health issues - general, abortion, breast cancer, cervical cancer, childbirth, contraceptives, menopause, occupational and environmental health, osteoporosis, pregnancy, premenstrual syndrome, sexually transmitted diseases, teen pregnancy, toxic shock syndrome, women and alcohol. **Holdings:** Figures not available. **Services:** Library open to the public by appointment.

★11329★
National Wrestling Hall of Fame - Library (Rec)
405 W. Hall of Fame Ave.   Phone: (405)377-5243
Stillwater, OK 74075   Bob Dellinger, Dir.
Founded: 1976. **Subjects:** Wrestling history, Olympics, sports medicine, biographies of wrestlers and coaches. **Holdings:** 421 books; 50 bound periodical volumes. **Services:** Copying; library open to museum visitors.

★11330★
National Writers Club - Library (Hum)
1450 S. Havana, Suite 620   Phone: (303)751-7844
Aurora, CO 80012   James Lee Young, Exec.Dir.
Founded: 1940. **Staff:** 3. **Subjects:** Writing, biographies of writers, markets for written work. **Special Collections:** Retrospective collection of "little" magazines. **Holdings:** 3000 books. **Subscriptions:** 20 journals and other serials. **Services:** Interlibrary loan; library open to the public by appointment. **Remarks:** FAX: (303)751-8593.

★11331★
National Writers Group - Library (Soc Sci)
11537 34th Ave., N.E.   Phone: (206)365-1624
Seattle, WA 98125-5613   Mike Perry, Ed.
Founded: 1983. **Staff:** 1. **Subjects:** German euthanasia program, medical ethics, resistance to Nazism, abortion, Holocaust. **Holdings:** 1000 books. **Subscriptions:** 15 journals and other serials. **Services:** Copying; library open to the public by appointment. **Computerized Information Services:** Internal database (German medicine and medical ethics, 1900-1950); GEnie (electronic mail service). Performs searches. **Remarks:** Electronic mail address(es): M.PERRY1 (GEnie).

★11332★
National Yiddish Book Center - Library (Area-Ethnic, Hum)
Old East Street School
Box 969   Phone: (413)256-1241
Amherst, MA 01004   Aaron Lansky, Pres.
Founded: 1980. **Staff:** 9. **Subjects:** Yiddish publications. **Special Collections:** Aliza Greenblatt Collection (women Yiddish writers); Sandler Collection (American Jewish experience); Flexer Collection (Russian socialist literature); Jakob Rosner Collection (100 photographs). **Holdings:** 900,000 books. **Subscriptions:** 10 journals and other serials; 5 newspapers. **Services:** Worldwide distribution of out-of-print Yiddish books; library open to the public. **Automated Operations:** Computerized cataloging. **Computerized Information Services:** Internal database. Performs searches on fee basis. Contact Person: Neil Zagorin, Dir., Yiddish Lib.Dev.Prog. **Publications:** The Book Peddler (newsletter), semiannual. **Special Catalogs:** Yiddish Book News (catalog of newly accessioned out-of-print Yiddish books) - available on request. **Remarks:** FAX: (413)253-4261. **Staff:** Nansi S. Glick, Asst.Dir.; Pearl-Anne Margalit, Volunteer Coord.; Carie Sipowicz, Membership Coord.

★11333★
National Youth Orchestra Association of Canada - Library (Mus)
1032 Bathurst St.   Phone: (416)532-4470
Toronto, ON, Canada M5R 3G7   Herbert C. Meyer, Gen.Mgr.
Subjects: Orchestra and chamber music. **Special Collections:** National Youth Orchestra performance tapes and video cassettes; historic orchestral recordings. **Holdings:** 175 linear feet of scores, sheet music, performance materials; 200 linear feet of recordings, tapes, cassettes. **Subscriptions:** 10 journals and other serials. **Services:** Copying; library open to the public with restrictions. **Publications:** Who We Are And What We Do (information booklet).

National Zoological Park
See: **Smithsonian Institution Libraries** (15282)

Nationalities Culture Palace - Library
See: **China Nationality Library** (3606)

★ 11334 ★
Nationwide Mutual Insurance Company - Library/Corporate Archives
(Bus-Fin)
One Nationwide Plaza
P.O. Box 1559   Phone: (614)249-6343
Columbus, OH 43216   Victoria Blackford, Chf.Libn.
Founded: 1950. **Staff:** Prof 3; Other 4. **Subjects:** Business management, insurance, cooperative movement. **Special Collections:** Corporate archives (550 linear feet of records; 350 films and videotapes; 2500 photographs; fire marks and memorabilia). **Holdings:** 10,000 books; 12 VF drawers. **Subscriptions:** 250 journals and other serials; 10 newspapers. **Services:** Library open to the public for reference use only on request. **Automated Operations:** Computerized cataloging, acquisitions, and serials. **Computerized Information Services:** DIALOG Information Services, Columbus News Index (CNI), Insurance Information Institute (III), LEXIS, NEXIS; internal databases; DIALMAIL (electronic mail service). **Networks/Consortia:** Member of Columbus Area Libraries Information Council of Ohio (CALICO). **Remarks:** FAX: (614)249-2218. **Staff:** Dr. Robert Bober, Corp.Archv./Rec.Adm.

Native American Artists Archive and Resource Collection
See: **Heard Museum - Library and Archives** (7085)

★ 11335 ★
Native American Center for the Living Arts, Inc. - Library (Area-Ethnic)
25 Rainbow Blvd.   Phone: (716)284-2427
Niagara Falls, NY 14303   Elwood Green, Musm.Dir./Coll.Cur.
Founded: 1981. **Staff:** Prof 1. **Subjects:** Native American history and education; art of North, Central, and South America; museology. **Special Collections:** Smithsonian Institution Bureau of American Ethnology Reports (30 volumes); educational resources (50 titles); native periodicals. **Holdings:** 800 books; 200 bound periodical volumes; 65 newsprint periodicals; 5000 slides; 2500 newspaper clippings; 30 native music and oral history tapes; 5 films; 15 videotapes. **Subscriptions:** 10 journals and other serials; 20 newspapers. **Services:** Copying; library open to the public for reference use only by appointment. **Publications:** Turtle Quarterly Magazine, 4/year - by subscription. **Remarks:** The center's Education Department resources are included in the library holdings.

★ 11336 ★
Native American Educational Services Inc. - Central Library and
Resource Center (Area-Ethnic)
2838 W. Peterson   Phone: (312)761-5000
Chicago, IL 60659   Anne Valdez, Libn.
Staff: Prof 2. **Subjects:** Indian community development, education, human services, history, culture and religion, government and Indian law, economic development. **Special Collections:** Sol Tax Collection; Armin Beck Special Collection. **Holdings:** 5000 books; 500 pamphlets; 1000 articles; studies; papers; 37 linear feet archives. **Subscriptions:** 30 journals and other serials; 25 newspapers. **Services:** Copying; Library open to the public for reference use only. **Publications:** Reservation/Urban Learning Exchange, irregular. **Remarks:** FAX: (312)761-3808. **Also Known As:** NAES College. **Staff:** David Beck, Archv.

Native American Research Library
See: **Navajo Nation Library System** (11352)

★ 11337 ★
Native American Rights Fund - National Indian Law Library (Law,
Area-Ethnic)
1522 Broadway   Phone: (303)447-8760
Boulder, CO 80302-6296   Deana J. Harragarra Waters, Law Libn.
Founded: 1972. **Staff:** Prof 3; Other 5. **Subjects:** Federal Indian law, U.S. government-Indian relations, Indians. **Special Collections:** Indian Legal Materials and Resources (5000 documents). **Holdings:** 7500 books; 35 bound periodical volumes. **Subscriptions:** 77 journals and other serials; 101 newspapers. **Services:** Interlibrary loan; copying; library open to the public for reference use only. **Computerized Information Services:** Internal database. Performs searches on fee basis. **Publications:** Bibliography on Indian Economic Development. **Special Catalogs:** National Indian Law Library Catalogue, every 5 years - by subscription. **Special Indexes:** Index to Indian Claims Commission Decisions (book). **Staff:** Bernita Wendelin, Cat.Libn.; Mary Mousseau, Libn.

★ 11338 ★
Native Americans for a Clean Environment - Resource Office (Env-Cons)
Box 1671   Phone: (918)458-4322
Tahlequah, OK 74465   Lance Hughes, Exec.Dir.
Subjects: Nuclear energy - waste and waste routes, facilities, health effects; national environmental issues; area issues. **Special Collections:** Sequoyah Fuels Facility, Gore, Oklahoma; Nuclear Regulatory Commission listings, hearings, permits. **Holdings:** Figures not available. **Services:** Copying; office will respond to telephone and written inquiries.

★ 11339 ★
NATO - Office of Information and Press - Library (Soc Sci)
Office Nb 123   Phone: 2 7285022
B-1110 Brussels, Belgium   Eliane Baetens, Libn.
Founded: 1948. **Staff:** Prof 3. **Subjects:** Politics, military science, arms controls and disarmament, economics, applied sciences, computer sciences. **Holdings:** 20,000 books; 1500 bound periodical volumes. **Subscriptions:** 800 journals and other serials; 20 newspapers. **Services:** Interlibrary loan; copying; library open to the public with prior consent. **Computerized Information Services:** Internal databases. **Publications:** Thematic bibliographies; acquisitions list, monthly; magazine selections; library guide; serials guide. **Remarks:** FAX: 2 7285457. Telex: 23-867.

Natsionalen Agrarno-Promishlen Suyuz - Selskostopanska Akademiya -
Tsentur za Naouchno-Technicheska i Ikonomicheska Infomatsiya
See: **Bulgaria - National Agro-Industrial Union** (2348)

Natural Gas Supply Information Center
See: **Colorado School of Mines - Arthur Lakes Library** (3947)

Natural Gas Supply Information Center
See: **University of Alabama - Natural Gas Supply Information Center**
(18165)

Natural Hazards Research and Applications Information Center
See: **University of Colorado--Boulder - Institute of Behavioral Science**
(18499)

★ 11340 ★
Natural History Museum - Department of Library Services (Biol Sci)
Cromwell Rd.   Phone: 71 938 9191
London SW7 5BD, England   Mr. R. Banks, Hd. of Lib.Serv.
Founded: 1881. **Staff:** 33. **Subjects:** Natural history, zoology, botany, entomology, paleontology, mineralogy, ornithology. **Special Collections:** Linnaeus; Tweeddale; Owen; Sowerby; Gunther; Rothschild. **Holdings:** 800,000 books; 22,000 periodical titles; 20,000 microforms; 72,000 maps; 375,000 prints and drawings; 20,000 manuscripts. **Subscriptions:** 9000 journals and other serials. **Services:** Copying; department open to the public by appointment. **Computerized Information Services:** DIALOG Information Services, BLAISE Online Services. Performs searches on fee basis. Contact Person: Ms. Harvey, 71 9388949. **Publications:** A Short History of the Libraries and List of Manuscripts and Original Drawings in the British Museum (Natural History). **Special Catalogs:** A Catalogue of the Richard Owen Collection of Palaeontological and Zoological Drawings in the British Museum (Natural History); Catalogue of the Drawings from Captain Cook's First Voyage; list of manuscripts and drawings; catalog of portraits. **Remarks:** FAX: 71 9389290. **Staff:** Miss Philbert, Dp.Hd., Lib.Serv.; John C. Thackray, Archv.; Malcolm A. Beasley, Botany Lib.; Julia Hickey, Botany Lib.; Julie M.V. Harvey, Entomology Lib.; Kathy Martin, Entomology Lib.; Ann Datta, Gen. and Zoology Lib.; Carol Gokce, Gen. and Zoology Lib.; Paul Cooper, Gen. and Zoology Lib.; Effie Warr, Zoological Musm., Lib., TRING; Neil H. Thomson, Hd., Info.Sys.Sect.; Martin Fisk, Sys.Libn./Telecom.Mgr.; Michael J.D. Willsher, Hd., Tech.Serv.; Mrs. Gill Cornelius, Hd., Cat./Acq.; Audrey Meenan, Cat./Acq.; Zara J.X. Frenkiel, Cat./Acq.; Annette Klaczak, Cat./Acq.; Paula Packman, Cat./Acq.

★ 11341 ★
Natural History Museum of Los Angeles County - Research Library
(Sci-Engr, Hist, Biol Sci)
900 Exposition Blvd.   Phone: (213)744-3387
Los Angeles, CA 90007   Donald W. McNamee, Chf.Libn.
Founded: 1921. **Staff:** Prof 2; Other 2. **Subjects:** Life sciences - botany, entomology, ornithology, mammalogy, herpetology, ichthyology, malacology; earth sciences - vertebrate and invertebrate paleontology, mineralogy, invertebrate zoology; anthropology; Southwestern history; military history; business and industrial history; cartography; photography; performing arts. **Special Collections:** Los Angeles Theatre programs (pre-1900); Southern California newspaper collection (pre-1900; 350 titles); Lepidopterists' Society Library; Southern California Academy of Science Library; Bookplate Collection; Natural History Art and Illustration. **Holdings:** 50,000 books; 100,000 bound periodical volumes; 20,000 maps; 5000 pamphlets; manuscripts; 300 environmental impact reports for Los Angeles County; 857 reels of microfilm. **Subscriptions:** 3291 journals and other serials. **Services:** Interlibrary loan; copying; library open to the public. **Automated Operations:** Computerized cataloging and serials. **Computerized Information Services:** DIALOG Information Services, OCLC. **Special Indexes:** Chronological index to newspapers. **Remarks:** FAX: (213)746-2999. **Staff:** Jennifer L. Edwards, Asst.Libn.

★ 11342 ★
Natural History Museum of Los Angeles County - Seaver Center for Western History Research (Hist)
900 Exposition Blvd.   Phone: (213)744-3359
Los Angeles, CA 90007   Dr. Errol Stevens, Hd., Seaver Ctr.
Founded: 1981. **Staff:** Prof 5. **Subjects:** History of Los Angeles, Southern California, and the American West. **Special Collections:** Photographs of the Southwest and Los Angeles (200,000 images); 2000 linear feet of manuscripts and other material relating to Los Angeles history. **Holdings:** 7000 books; 2000 bound periodical volumes; 500 reels of microfilm; 2500 maps, 16th-20th centuries. **Subscriptions:** 80 journals and other serials. **Services:** Copying; center open to the public by appointment. **Automated Operations:** Computerized cataloging. **Staff:** Janet Evander, Sr.Coll.Mgr.; M. Guy Bishop, Ref.Serv.; John Cahoon, Photo.Spec.; Don McNamee, Libn.

★ 11343 ★
Natural History Society of Maryland - Library
2643 N. Charles St.   Phone: (301)235-6116
Baltimore, MD 21218   Haven Kolb
Founded: 1929. **Subjects:** Natural history and biology. **Special Collections:** Bird books; depository for Smithsonian Institution and Maryland Geological Survey. **Holdings:** Figures not available. **Remarks:** Currently inactive.

Natural Resources Institute - NRI Library
See: **Great Britain - Overseas Development Administration - Natural Resources Institute - NRI Library** (6691)

★ 11344 ★
Natural Rights Center - Library (Law)
156 Drakes Ln.
Summertown, TN 38483   Phone: (615)964-3992
Founded: 1980. **Staff:** 1. **Subjects:** Environment, nuclear energy, chemicals, weapons, defense. **Holdings:** 5000 volumes. **Subscriptions:** 25 journals and other serials. **Services:** Library reading room open to the public. **Remarks:** Affiliated with Plenty - U.S.A.

★ 11345 ★
Nature Center for Environmental Activities - Reference Library (Env-Cons)
P.O. Box 165   Phone: (203)227-7253
Westport, CT 06881   Mary Lou Amirault, Libn.
Staff: Prof 1; Other 3. **Subjects:** Natural history, environment, ecology. **Holdings:** 3000 books; 150 bound periodical volumes; 6 VF drawers of pamphlets on natural history; 9 VF drawers of pamphlets on the environment; unbound periodicals. **Subscriptions:** 65 journals and other serials. **Services:** Library not open to the public.

★ 11346 ★
Nature Conservancy - Long Island Chapter - Uplands Farm Environmental Center (Env-Cons)
250 Lawrence Hill Rd.   Phone: (516)367-3225
Cold Spring Harbor, NY 11724   Andrew Walker, Dir.
Staff: 1. **Subjects:** Conservation, land preservation, natural history, terrestrial and freshwater ecology, endangered species, Long Island environment. **Special Collections:** Natural Diversity Collection; Long Island Freshwater and Terrestrial Ecology Collection. **Holdings:** 2000 books; 2000 slides. **Services:** Interlibrary loan; center open to the public. **Publications:** L.I. Chapter Newsletter, 4/year; The Nature Conservancy News, 6/year.

★ 11347 ★
Nature Conservancy - Montana Natural Heritage Program (Env-Cons)
State Library Bldg.
1515 E. 6th Ave.   Phone: (406)444-3009
Helena, MT 59620   David Genter, Coord.
Founded: 1985. **Staff:** Prof 5. **Subjects:** Rare plants and animals, natural communities, public lands. **Special Collections:** Site data on rare plants and animals and natural communities; collection of published, unpublished, and other documents on biological diversity, community classifications, and ecological inventory in Montana. **Holdings:** 6000 computer records; 18 legal file cabinets; 5000 topographic maps. **Subscriptions:** 38 journals and other serials. **Services:** Program open to the public with restrictions. **Computerized Information Services:** Natural Heritage Databases (internal databases). **Special Indexes:** Index to plant and animal species in North America and Latin America (printout). **Remarks:** FAX: (406)444-5612.

Nature Conservancy - New York Natural Heritage Program
See: **New York State Department of Environment Conservation** (11649)

★ 11348 ★
Naturhistorisches Museum - Bibliothek (Biol Sci)
Bernastr 15   Phone: 31 431839
CH-3005 Berne 32, Switzerland   Mrs. Verena Andres
Founded: 1930. **Subjects:** Zoology, earth sciences. **Holdings:** 16,000 books; 8000 bound periodical volumes. **Subscriptions:** 30 journals and other serials; 2 newspapers. **Services:** Interlibrary loan; copying; library open to the public. **Computerized Information Services:** SIBIL.

★ 11349 ★
The Naturopathy Institute - Library (Med)
P.O. Box 56
Malverne, NY 11565   Dr. Edgar A. Kinon, N.D., Dir.
Founded: 1984. **Staff:** Prof 1. **Subjects:** Naturopathy, nutrition, natural healing sciences, radiesthesia/radionics, botanical medicine, anatomy, physiology. **Special Collections:** Rare works on Albert Abrams, M.D. and Ruth Drown, D.C. (original and reprinted); original books by Bernarr Macfadden and Henry Lindlahr, M.D.; old osteopathic and chiropractic texts. **Holdings:** 850 books; 1000 nonbook items. **Subscriptions:** 7 journals and other serials. **Services:** Library will provide information for a fee to mail correspondents. **Publications:** Reprints of published articles by E.A. Kinon, N.D., research reports - for sale.

★ 11350 ★
Naucno Issledovatelskij Institut Selskogo Chozjajstva - Biblioteka (Agri)
Krasnodar 12, Russia   Phone: 22184
                                              Lyubov Victorovna Abakumova
Founded: 1956. **Staff:** Prof 3. **Subjects:** Wheat, barley, maize, hemp, legumes used for grain, fodder grasses, agrotechnics, plant protection, economics, farm mechanization. **Special Collections:** Entsiklopedicheskij slovar, 1890-1904 (82 volumes); Bolshaya Entsiclopedia, 1903-1909 (22 volumes); Trudy po priklandoi botanike, genetike i selektsii, 1910-1991. **Holdings:** 32,972 books; 36,896 bound periodical volumes; 952 reports; 41 reels of microfilm; 772 translations; 3749 booklets. **Subscriptions:** 80 journals and other serials; 18 newspapers. **Services:** Interlibrary loan; library open to visiting scientists and graduate and post-graduate students. **Publications:** Bibliography. **Remarks:** FAX: 8612 562274. Telex: 279117 AQVA SU.

★ 11351 ★
Nauman, Smith, Shissler, & Hall - Library
122 Market St., 5th Fl.   Phone: (717)236-3010
Harrisburg, PA 17108   Cathy Smith, Lib.Dir.
Remarks: No further information was supplied by respondent.

★ 11352 ★
Navajo Nation Library System (Area-Ethnic)
Drawer K   Phone: (602)871-6376
Window Rock, AZ 86515   Irving Nelson, Mgr.
Founded: 1941. **Staff:** Prof 1; Other 10. **Subjects:** Navajos, Indians of the Southwest, Indians of North America, archeology, Arizona history. **Special Collections:** Navajo History; Native American Research Library; J.L. Correll Collection (30 filing cabinets); Navajo Times (80 acid-free boxes). **Holdings:** 22,000 books; 1000 manuscripts; 60 films; 250 tape recordings; microfilm. **Subscriptions:** 80 journals and other serials. **Services:** Interlibrary loan; copying; facsimile services; library open to the public. **Automated Operations:** Computerized cataloging. **Computerized Information Services:** CD-ROM. **Special Indexes:** Navajo Times index (tribal newspaper); ONEO Oral History Index. **Remarks:** Alternate telephone number are 871-7303; FAX: (602)871-7304. Maintains two branch libraries in Window Rock, AZ, and one branch library in Navajo, NM.

NAVFs edb- senter for humanistisk forskning
See: **Norwegian Computing Center for the Humanities** (12113)

★ 11353 ★
Navistar International Transportation Corporation - Research Services (Trans)
455 N. Cityfront Plaza, 9th Fl.   Phone: (312)836-2061
Chicago, IL 60611   N. Maria Nemeth, Res.Serv.Adm.
Founded: 1990. **Staff:** Prof 1; Other 1. **Subjects:** Trucks, engines, foundries. **Special Collections:** Archives; law library. **Holdings:** 5000 linear feet of archives. **Subscriptions:** 160 journals and other serials, 8 newspapers. **Services:** Archives open to qualified researchers. **Automated Operations:** Computerized cataloging. **Computerized Information Services:** DIALOG Information Services, LEXIS, NEXIS; internal database. **Remarks:** FAX: (312)836-2192. Telex: 190090 NAV UT.

Navy
See: **U.S. Navy**

★ 11354 ★
Navy League of Canada - National Office - Library (Mil)
2323 Riverside Dr., 8th Fl.   Phone: (613)993-5415
Ottawa, ON, Canada K1H 8L5   G.G. Armstrong
Founded: 1970. **Staff:** 1. **Subjects:** Maritime defense, marine-based industry, marine environment and training. **Special Collections:** Navy League of Canada Archives. **Holdings:** Figures not available. **Subscriptions:** 20 journals and other serials. **Services:** Library open to members of affiliated organizations. **Remarks:** The Navy League of Canada Library is mainly a collection of current reference materials for use in the league's publications, briefs, and submissions. Alternate telephone number(s): (613)998-0447. FAX: (613)990-8701.

NAWDEX
See: **U.S. Geological Survey - Water Resources Division - National Water Data Exchange and Water Data Storage and Retrieval System** (17545)

Bernard Naylor Archives
See: **University of Victoria - McPherson Library - Music & Audio Collection** (19488)

★ 11355 ★
Nazarene Bible College - Trimble Library (Rel-Phil)
Box 15749   Phone: (719)596-5110
Colorado Springs, CO 80935   Roger M. Williams, Lib.Adm.
Founded: 1967. **Staff:** Prof 1; Other 8. **Subjects:** Bible, theology, Christian education, music. **Special Collections:** Wesley Collection. **Holdings:** 43,559 books; 3289 bound periodical volumes; 1761 books on microfiche; 8247 cassettes, phonograph records, slides, filmstrips; 8 VF drawers of pamphlets. **Subscriptions:** 236 journals and other serials; 5 newspapers. **Services:** Interlibrary loan; copying; SDI; library open to the public for reference use only. **Remarks:** FAX: (719)550-9437.

★ 11356 ★
Nazarene Theological Seminary - William Broadhurst Library (Rel-Phil)
1700 E. Meyer Blvd.   Phone: (816)333-6255
Kansas City, MO 64131   William C. Miller, Dir. of Lib.Serv.
Founded: 1945. **Staff:** Prof 2; Other 8. **Subjects:** Theology, Biblical studies, Christian education, missions, practics, philosophy, church history, philology. **Special Collections:** History of the Church of the Nazarene; Wesleyana-Methodism. **Holdings:** 83,000 volumes; 14,000 microforms. **Subscriptions:** 465 journals and other serials. **Services:** Interlibrary loan; copying; library open to the public. **Automated Operations:** Computerized cataloging and acquisitions. **Computerized Information Services:** DIALOG Information Services, WILSONLINE, OCLC. Performs searches on fee basis. **Networks/Consortia:** Member of Kansas City Theological Library Association (KCTLA), Kansas City Metropolitan Library Network (KCMLN), Missouri Library Network Corp. (MLNC). **Remarks:** FAX: (816)822-9025. **Staff:** Debra Bradshaw, Cat.Libn.

★ 11357 ★
Nazareth College of Rochester - Lorette Wilmot Library - Special Collections (Hum)
Box 18950
4245 East Ave.   Phone: (716)586-2525
Rochester, NY 14618-0950   Richard A. Matzek, Lib.Dir.
Founded: 1957. **Staff:** 21. **Special Collections:** Chesterton Collection (300 volumes); Belloc Collection (250 volumes); Baring Collection (100 volumes); Sitwell Collection (150 volumes); Byrne Collection (Auburn, NY, imprints; 200 volumes); Thomas Merton Collection (250 volumes). **Services:** Interlibrary loan; copying; SDI; collections open to the public for reference use only. **Automated Operations:** Computerized cataloging and circulation. **Computerized Information Services:** DIALOG Information Services, BRS Information Technologies, NLM, OCLC. Performs searches on fee basis. **Contact Person:** Scott S. Smith, Dir., Rd.Serv./Lib.Sys., 586-2525, ext. 452. **Networks/Consortia:** Member of Rochester Regional Library Council (RRLC). **Remarks:** FAX: (716)248-8766. **Staff:** Sheila A. Smyth, Dir., Tech.Serv.; Janet B. Smith, Acq.Libn.; Jennifer Burr, Ref.Coord.; Madeleine Tainton, Dir., Media Serv.

★ 11358 ★
Nazareth Hospital - Medical Library (Med)
2601 Holme Ave.   Phone: (215)335-6273
Philadelphia, PA 19152   Steven Carl Brown, Libn.
Founded: 1940. **Staff:** 1. **Subjects:** Medicine, surgery, allied health sciences. **Holdings:** 3731 books; 2951 bound periodical volumes; nursing materials; 125 pamphlets; 35 VF drawers; 684 cassettes. **Services:** Library not open to the public.

NBC
See: **National Broadcasting Company, Inc.** (11090)

★ 11359 ★
NBD Bank, NA - Library Services Department (Bus-Fin)
611 Woodward Ave.   Phone: (313)225-2840
Detroit, MI 48226   Carolyn Woodrow, Mgr., Lib.Serv.
Founded: 1955. **Staff:** Prof 2.5; Other 2. **Subjects:** Banking, finance, economics, business and management. **Special Collections:** Federal Reserve Bank publications. **Holdings:** 5000 books; 100 VF drawers of pamphlets and clippings; 500 reels of microfilm; 200 theses; 125 titles on microfiche. **Subscriptions:** 600 journals and other serials; 6 newspapers. **Services:** Library open to SLA members with prior approval. **Automated Operations:** Computerized cataloging and routing. **Computerized Information Services:** DIALOG Information Services, Dow Jones News/Retrieval, VU/TEXT Information Services, NEXIS. **Staff:** Joan Martin, Libn.

★ 11360 ★
NBS/Lowry Inc. - Corporate Library
P.O. Box 28100
San Diego, CA 92198-0100
Founded: 1980. Subjects: Wastewater treatment, water systems, land development, flood control. Holdings: 1000 books; 50 bound periodical volumes; 5000 government documents; 50 maps; 1600 internal publications. Remarks: Currently inactive.

NC Aquarium/Pine Knoll Shores - Bogue Banks Library
See: Bogue Banks Library (1943)

★ 11361 ★
NC Aquarium/Roanoke Island - Roanoke Island Library (Biol Sci)
Airport Rd.
Box 967   Phone: (919)473-3493
Manteo, NC 27954   Pat Raves, Educ.
Founded: 1976. Staff: 1. Subjects: Marine and coastal studies. Holdings: 3000 volumes. Subscriptions: 37 journals and other serials. Services: Copying; library open to the public for reference use only. Remarks: FAX: (919)473-1980. Operated by the North Carolina State Department of Administration - Office of Marine Affairs.

★ 11362 ★
Ncorthern Institute for Resource Studies - Library (Bus-Fin)
3330 22nd Ave.   Phone: (604)562-2131
Prince George, BC, Canada V2N 1P8   Katherine Plett, Res.Off.
Founded: 1983. Staff: 1. Subjects: Economic development in northern British Columbia - mining, smelting, forestry, energy-based industries. Holdings: 2000 volumes. Services: Library open to institute members. Automated Operations: Computerized cataloging. Computerized Information Services: DOBIS Canadian Online Library System, CAN/OLE, DIALOG Information Services, UTLAS; Envoy 100 (electronic mail service). Performs searches on fee basis. Publications: N.I.R.S. addresses/essays/lectures series, irregular. Remarks: FAX: (604)561-5845. Electronic mail address(es): CNC.LIB (Envoy 100).

★ 11363 ★
NCR Canada Ltd - MIRS Library (Comp Sci)
320 Front St., W.   Phone: (416)351-2105
Toronto, ON, Canada M5V 3C4   Jill Lococo, MIRS Libn.
Founded: 1975. Staff: Prof 1; Other 1. Subjects: Computer industry, business. Holdings: 1200 reference manuals; 100 books; 200 VF drawers of reference material; 100 videotapes; annual reports; brochures; slides; scripts. Subscriptions: 200 journals and other serials. Services: Library not open to the public. Publications: MIRS NEWS FLASH(newsletter), monthly - for internal distribution only. Remarks: FAX: (416)351-2006.

★ 11364 ★
NCR Corporation - Engineering & Manufacturing Division - Library (Comp Sci)
16550 W. Bernardo Dr.   Phone: (619)485-3291
San Diego, CA 92127   Mary Lou Nagle, Libn.
Staff: Prof 1. Subjects: Computers, mathematics, science, management, business. Holdings: 5500 books; 6000 bound periodical volumes; 1500 documents and microfiche. Subscriptions: 83 journals and other serials. Services: Interlibrary loan; library not open to the public. Remarks: FAX: (619)485-3788.

★ 11365 ★
NCR Corporation - SE-SD Library (Comp Sci)
9900 Old Grove Rd.   Phone: (619)693-5473
San Diego, CA 92131   Mary M. Hill, Libn.
Staff: Prof 1. Subjects: Business and management, computers, communications, data management, programming language. Holdings: 2000 books; 800 external technical reports; 400 pieces of internal documentation; 700 IBM documents. Subscriptions: 150 journals and other serials; 6 newspapers. Services: Interlibrary loan; library not open to the public. Automated Operations: Computerized cataloging, serials, and circulation. Computerized Information Services: DIALOG Information Services. Special Catalogs: NCR Union List of Periodicals. Remarks: FAX: (619)693-5705.

★ 11366 ★
NCR Corporation - Technical Library (Bus-Fin, Comp Sci)
Engineering & Manufacturing-Dayton
Building EMD, 3rd Fl.   Phone: (513)445-7032
Dayton, OH 45479   Vicki Anderson, Libn.
Founded: 1958. Staff: 1. Subjects: Computers, data processing, electronics, engineering, management, banking. Special Collections: Management and computer literature (250 items). Holdings: 7500 books; 3000 bound periodical volumes; 300 other cataloged items. Subscriptions: 160 journals and other serials. Services: Interlibrary loan; copying; library open to the public by request. Computerized Information Services: DIALOG Information Services. Networks/Consortia: Member of Southwestern Ohio Council for Higher Education (SOCHE). Remarks: FAX: (513)445-7191.

★ 11367 ★
NCR Corporation - Technical Library (Comp Sci)
3325 Platt Springs Rd.   Phone: (803)796-9250
West Columbia, SC 29170   Charlotte Burlingane, Libn.
Staff: Prof 1. Subjects: Computers, management. Holdings: 1500 books; 3 VF drawers; 2 drawers of standards. Subscriptions: 70 journals and other serials. Services: Interlibrary loan; library not open to the public. Automated Operations: Computerized circulation and inventory. Computerized Information Services: DIALOG Information Services; internal database. Publications: NCR Library Network Newsletter, bimonthly - for internal distribution only.

★ 11368 ★
NDC/Federal Systems, Inc. - Technical Publications Department - Library
1300 Piccard Dr., Suite 101
Rockville, MD 20850-4303
Defunct.

★ 11369 ★
Neal, Gerber & Eisenberg - Law Library (Law)
2 N. LaSalle St., Suite 2300   Phone: (312)269-8000
Chicago, IL 60602   Nina Cunningham, Ph.D., Hd.Libn./Info.Serv.Dir.
Founded: 1988. Staff: Prof 1; Other 3. Subjects: Law - securities, taxation, labor, litigation, general corporate. Holdings: 32,000 books; 540 bound periodical volumes; internal legal memoranda; pamphlets; tax legislation. Subscriptions: 440 journals and other serials. Services: Interlibrary loan; library not open to the public. Computerized Information Services: WESTLAW, Dow Jones News/Retrieval, DIALOG Information Services, LEXIS, Dun & Bradstreet Business Credit Services, Hannah Information Systems, Disclosure Information Group, State Net 50; internal databases. Publications: Catalog UPDATE, 4/year - both for internal distribution only; Labor Law (newsletter); Association Law (newsletter). Special Catalogs: Pamphlet File and Brief Bank. Remarks: FAX: (312)269-1747. Formerly: Neal, Gerber, Eisenberg & Lurie.

J.A.W. Neander Library
See: Ambrose Swasey Library (15904)

Neatby Library
See: Canada - Agriculture Canada (2644)

Nebraska Archives of Medicine
See: University of Nebraska at Omaha - Medical Center - McGoogan Library of Medicine (19010)

★ 11370 ★
Nebraska Arts Council - Library (Art)
State Office Bldg.
1313 Farnan-On-The-Mall   Phone: (402)595-2122
Omaha, NE 68102-1873   Michelle E. Pope
Founded: 1965. Subjects: Art, art and the government, art in schools and education, music, drama, museums, crafts, literature, visual arts, folk arts. Holdings: 750 books; 75 bound periodical volumes; 19 films; 7 slide sets; 8 videotapes; 24 audiocassettes. Subscriptions: 6 journals and other serials; 2 newspapers. Services: Library open to the public. Remarks: FAX: (402)595-2217.

Nebraska Career Information System
See: University of Nebraska, Lincoln (19002)

★ 11371 ★
Nebraska Christian College - Library - Special Collections (Rel-Phil)
1800 Syracuse Ave.   Phone: (402)371-5960
Norfolk, NE 68701   Maria S. Johnson
Founded: 1945. **Staff:** Prof 1; Other 2. **Subjects:** Biblical studies, theology, church history, philosophy, Christian education, religion. **Special Collections:** Gunderson Collection (rare Bibles; 400 volumes); Guy B. Dunning Library (religious studies; 200 volumes). **Holdings:** 24,000 books; 1200 bound periodical volumes; 1500 archival items. **Subscriptions:** 130 journals and other serials; 2 newspapers. **Services:** Interlibrary loan; copying; library open to the public.

★ 11372 ★
Nebraska College of Technical Agriculture - Library (Biol Sci)
404 E. 7th St.
Box 69   Phone: (308)367-4124
Curtis, NE 69025-0069   Delroy L. Hemsath
Founded: 1965. **Staff:** Prof 1. **Subjects:** Animal science, horticulture, agronomy. **Holdings:** 2000 books; 400 reels of microfilm. **Subscriptions:** 160 journals and other serials; 10 newspapers. **Services:** Interlibrary loan; library open to the public. **Computerized Information Services:** Nebraska Libraries Communications System (NELCMS), Instructional Resources Information System (IRIS).

★ 11373 ★
Nebraska Legislative Council - Legislative Reference Library (Soc Sci)
1201 State Capitol
Box 94945   Phone: (402)471-2221
Lincoln, NE 68509   Jo Casullo, Coord., Lib.Serv.
Founded: 1980. **Staff:** Prof 2; Other 1. **Subjects:** Policy - state government, agriculture, groundwater; statistical data; economic development; human services. **Holdings:** 7000 books; 2000 journal articles. **Subscriptions:** 335 journals and other serials; 9 newspapers. **Services:** Interlibrary loan; library not open to the public. **Automated Operations:** Computerized cataloging, acquisitions, public access catalog, serials, circulation, and ILL. **Computerized Information Services:** OCLC, DIALOG Information Services, Legislative Information System (LIS), WESTLAW; internal databases. **Networks/Consortia:** Member of NEBASE, Nebraska Library Loan & Information Exchange (NELLIE). **Publications:** Legislative Reference Library Acquisitions List, monthly - for internal distribution only. **Special Catalogs:** Annotated Periodicals List; Published Interim Study Reports, 1938-1986; Research Division Publications. **Staff:** Patricia Sloan, Leg.Ref.Libn.

★ 11374 ★
Nebraska Methodist Hospital - John Moritz Library (Med)
8303 Dodge St.   Phone: (402)390-4611
Omaha, NE 68114   Angela Armer, Lrng.Rsrcs.Mgr.
Founded: 1951. **Staff:** Prof 3; Other 1. **Subjects:** Medicine, nursing, and allied health sciences. **Special Collections:** American Journal of Nursing, 1900 to present. **Holdings:** 7649 books; 3586 bound periodical volumes; 10 VF drawers of pamphlets and reprints. **Subscriptions:** 535 journals and other serials. **Services:** Interlibrary loan; copying; library open to the public for reference use only. **Computerized Information Services:** BRS Information Technologies, PaperChase, NLM. **Publications:** Library Newsletter, monthly; Current Awareness Review Editor - both for internal distribution only.

Nebraska State Data Center
See: University of Nebraska, Omaha - Center for Public Affairs Research - Library (19006)

★ 11375 ★
Nebraska (State) Department of Roads - Technical Research Library (Trans)
1500 Nebraska Hwy. 2
Box 94759   Phone: (402)479-4316
Lincoln, NE 68509-4759   Anne L. White, Libn.
Founded: 1979. **Staff:** Prof 1. **Subjects:** Roads, traffic, environment, safety, transportation, bridges. **Special Collections:** Historical roads collection. **Holdings:** 10,000 books. **Subscriptions:** 150 journals and other serials. **Services:** Interlibrary loan; copying; library open to the public with restrictions. **Automated Operations:** Computerized public access catalog and cataloging. **Computerized Information Services:** EasyNet; AASHTO (electronic mail service). **Publications:** Monthly Listing of Acquisitions. **Remarks:** FAX: (402)479-4325. Electronic mail address(es): HTO 10028 (AASHTO).

★ 11376 ★
Nebraska (State) Game and Parks Commission - Library (Biol Sci)
2200 N. 33rd St.   Phone: (402)471-0641
Lincoln, NE 68503   Barbara Voeltz, Libn.
Founded: 1970. **Subjects:** Wildlife, fishery management, recreation, planning, horticulture, chemistry, environmental protection. **Holdings:** 5000 books; 500 bound periodical volumes; 6400 cataloged reprints and pamphlets; 8000 uncataloged reprints and pamphlets; 1500 maps. **Subscriptions:** 30 journals and other serials. **Services:** Interlibrary loan; copying; library open to the public. **Remarks:** Alternate telephone number(s): 471-5587.

★ 11377 ★
Nebraska State Historical Society - Department of Reference Services - Archives (Hist)
Box 82554   Phone: (402)471-4771
Lincoln, NE 68501   Andrea I. Paul, Dir.Ref.Serv. State Archv.
Founded: 1905. **Staff:** Prof 4; Other 12. **Subjects:** Nebraska - history, politics, agriculture, Western Indians. **Holdings:** 15,000 cubic feet of state and local archives; 8000 cubic feet of manuscripts; 28,000 reels of microfilm of newspapers, 1854-1991. **Subscriptions:** 700 journals and other serials; 200 newspapers. **Services:** Copying; archives open to the public. **Publications:** Guides to the State Archives, issued periodically. **Remarks:** FAX: (402)471-3100. **Staff:** Paul Eisloeffel, Cur. of Mss. and AV Coll.; Steve Wolz, P.R. Rec.Off.; Cathy Atwood, Cons.Spec.; Ann Billesbach, Ref.Spec.

★ 11378 ★
Nebraska State Historical Society - Department of Reference Services - Library (Hist)
1500 R St.
Box 82554   Phone: (402)471-4751
Lincoln, NE 68501   Andrea I. Paul, Dir., Ref.Serv.
Founded: 1878. **Staff:** Prof 3; Other 5.5. **Subjects:** Nebraska history, Indians of the Great Plains, archeology, Great Plains history, genealogy. **Holdings:** 80,000 volumes; 563 sets of Sanborn Fire Insurance maps of Nebraska; 2000 maps and 400 atlases relating to Nebraska, 1854 to present; 2500 photographs in Solomon D. Butcher Photograph Collection of Sod Houses; 465 photographs in John A. Anderson Photograph Collection of Brule Sioux; 247,000 other photographs; Nebraska state government publications repository, 1905 to present; 15,000 volumes of genealogical materials. **Subscriptions:** 230 journals and other serials. **Services:** Interlibrary loan (copies only); copying; library open to the public. **Automated Operations:** Computerized cataloging. **Networks/Consortia:** Member of NEBASE. **Remarks:** FAX: (402)471-3100. **Staff:** John E. Carter, Cur., Photo.; Cindy Steinhoff-Drake, Lib.Oper.Mgr.; Ann Billesbach, Ref.Spec.

★ 11379 ★
Nebraska State Historical Society - Fort Robinson Museum - Research Library (Hist)
Box 304   Phone: (308)665-2852
Crawford, NE 69339   Tom Buecker, Cur.
Founded: 1970. **Subjects:** Nebraska history. **Holdings:** Fort Robinson records on microfilm; Red Cloud and Spotted Tail Agency records; diaries and interview manuscripts; newspapers of Crawford and Chadron, Nebraska. **Services:** Library open to the public for reference use only by appointment.

★ 11380 ★
Nebraska State Historical Society - John G. Neihardt Center - Research Library (Area-Ethnic)
Elm and Washington Sts.
Box 344   Phone: (402)648-3388
Bancroft, NE 68004   Lori Utecht, Cur.
Founded: 1976. **Staff:** Prof 1; Other 1. **Subjects:** John G. Neihardt; American Indian culture and religion; Missouri River; fur trade; Nebraska and Plains history. **Special Collections:** First editions, essays, and reviews of works by John Neihardt (1 VF drawer); Bancroft Blade, June 21, 1904 to August 9, 1907 (2 reels of microfilm). **Holdings:** 202 books; 74 bound periodical volumes; 100 audiotapes and transcripts; 1 VF drawer of pamphlets and photographs; 3 dissertations; clipping files. **Services:** Library open to the public for reference use only.

★ 11381 ★
Nebraska State Historical Society - Willa Cather Historical Center -
   Archives (Hum)
338 N. Webster St.
Box 326   Phone: (402)746-3285
Red Cloud, NE 68970   John R. Lindahl, Cur.
Founded: 1955. **Staff:** Prof 1; Other 6. **Subjects:** Willa Cather's life and art,
the lives of real people who are prototypes of Cather's characters. **Holdings:**
400 books; 20 bound periodical volumes; 200 periodicals containing articles
dealing with Cather and her works; 250 letters; 10 rare manuscripts about
Cather; 1900 photographs; 700 pages of clippings; 175 reels of microfilm.
Services: Copying (limited); archives open to the public.

★ 11382 ★
Nebraska State Library (Law)
Capitol Bldg., 3rd Fl. S.
Box 98910   Phone: (402)471-3189
Lincoln, NE 68509   Reta Johnson, Dp. State Libn.
Founded: 1854. **Staff:** Prof 1; Other 2. **Subjects:** Law, current Nebraska
census. **Holdings:** 127,000 volumes; state and federal documents pertaining
to law. **Subscriptions:** 230 journals and other serials. **Services:** Copying; mail
service to attorneys and judges; library open to the public for reference use
only. **Remarks:** Library is under the direction of the Nebraska State
Supreme Court and serves the court, state agencies, and attorneys.

★ 11383 ★
Nebraska (State) Library Commission (Info Sci, Aud-Vis)
1420 P St.   Phone: (402)471-2045
Lincoln, NE 68508-1683   Rod Wagner, Dir.
Founded: 1901. **Staff:** Prof 25; Other 23. **Subjects:** Library science,
bibliography. **Special Collections:** Nebraska State Publications
Clearinghouse (63,144). **Holdings:** 25,000 books; 13,359 AV programs;
156,000 talking books, cassettes, and braille items; U.S. Government
documents depository (269,183 government documents). **Subscriptions:** 552
journals and other serials. **Services:** Interlibrary loan; copying; library open
to the public. **Automated Operations:** Computerized cataloging, circulation,
and ILL. **Computerized Information Services:** DIALOG Information
Services, BRS Information Technologies, WILSONLINE, OCLC; CD-
ROMS; ALANET, Nebraska Libraries Communications System
(NELCMS) (electronic mail services). **Networks/Consortia:** Member of
NEBASE. **Publications:** NLCommunication, bimonthly; Overtones, 6/year;
What's Up Doc, monthly; NEBASE NEWS, 10/year; NEBASE: From
Here & There, 10/year; Nebraska Library Directory, annual; Interlibrary
Loan Directory. **Special Catalogs:** Nebraska State Publications Checklist,
bimonthly; NEON - Nebraska State Database on OCLC; Nebraska Union
List of Serial Titles; Interlibrary Loan Directory; List of Reference Tools for
Public Libraries. **Remarks:** FAX: (402)471-2083. **Staff:** Nancy Busch,
Dp.Dir.; Dave Oertli, Hd., Lib. for Blind/Phys.Hndcp.; Jim Minges, Hd.,
Lib.Info.Dev.; Doreen Kuhlmann, Bus.Mgr. Jacqueline Mundell, Hd.,
Lib.Info.Serv. and NEBASE.

★ 11384 ★
Nebraska (State) Natural Resources Commission - Planning Library
   (Env-Cons)
301 Centennial Mall, S.
Box 94876   Phone: (402)471-2081
Lincoln, NE 68509-4876   Jerry Wallin, Hd., Plan.Sect.
Subjects: Water resources - Nebraska, regional, national. **Holdings:** 4000
books. **Subscriptions:** 20 journals and other serials. **Services:** Library open
to the public with restrictions.

Nebraska Vocational Curriculum Resource Center
See: **University of Nebraska at Kearney - Nebraska Vocational**
   Curriculum Resource Center (19009)

★ 11385 ★
NEC America - Switching Systems Divison - Technical Document Center
   (Info Sci)
1525 Walnut Hill Ln.   Phone: (214)518-5180
Irving, TX 75038   Michiko K. Adams, Mgr.
Founded: 1980. **Staff:** Prof 1; Other 9. **Subjects:** Telecommunications.
Special Collections: Worldwide telecommunications. **Holdings:** Figures not
available. **Subscriptions:** 140 journals and other serials; 10 newspapers.
Services: Interlibrary loan; center not open to the public. **Automated
Operations:** Computerized cataloging and circulation. **Computerized
Information Services:** DIALOG Information Services, OCLC. **Remarks:**
FAX: (214)518-5200.

Nederlands Bureau voor Bibliotheekwezen en Informatieverzorging
   (NBBI)
See: **Netherlands Organization for Libraries and Information Services -**
   Library (11414)

Nederlands Openluchtmuseum - Bibliotheek
See: **Netherlands Opendir Museum - Library** (11412)

Nederlands Organisatie voor Toegepast Natuurwetenschappelijk
   Onderzoek
See: **Netherlands Organization for Applied Scientific Research** (11413)

Arthur Neef Law Library
See: **Wayne State University** (20118)

Negro Historical Society of Nebraska
See: **Great Plains Black Museum** (6700)

★ 11386 ★
Neighborhood Playhouse School of the Theatre - Irene Lewisohn Library
   (Theater)
340 E. 54th St.   Phone: (212)688-3770
New York, NY 10022   Alice G. Owen, Libn.
Founded: 1945. **Staff:** Prof 1. **Subjects:** Drama, theater, biography,
literature. **Special Collections:** Neighborhood Playhouse-iana (12 books; 2
VF drawers; file of photographs). **Holdings:** 5323 volumes; 573 typescripts;
870 scores; 3 VF drawers of pamphlets, clippings, pictures; 4 VF drawers
of scenes; 1 VF drawer of sheet music. **Subscriptions:** 15 journals and other
serials. **Services:** Permission may be requested to consult material not
available elsewhere. **Publications:** Reading List; Memo from the Librarian,
both irregular - both for internal distribution only. **Special Indexes:** Scene
index (cards).

John G. Neihardt Center
See: **Nebraska State Historical Society** (11380)

Balmer Neilly Library
See: **Connaught Laboratories, Ltd.** (4174)

Neilson Dental Library
See: **University of Manitoba** (18792)

Victoria Nelli Memorial Library
See: **Central City Business Institute** (3335)

★ 11387 ★
Nelson-Atkins Museum of Art - Slide Library (Aud-Vis, Art)
4525 Oak St.   Phone: (816)561-4000
Kansas City, MO 64111-1873   Jan McKenna, Slide Libn.
Founded: 1933. **Staff:** Prof 1; Other 1. **Subjects:** Oriental, Occidental, and
Native art - architecture, sculpture, bronzes, painting, ceramics, decorative
arts, furniture, textiles. **Holdings:** 70,000 slides. **Services:** Library not open
to the public.

★ 11388 ★
Nelson-Atkins Museum of Art - Spencer Art Reference Library (Art)
4525 Oak St.
Kansas City, MO 64111-1873   Phone: (816)751-1216
Founded: 1933. **Staff:** Prof 2; Other 6. **Subjects:** Art and art history, Oriental
and Occidental art with emphasis on Chinese painting and history,
decorative arts, artists. **Special Collections:** John H. Bender Library of
Prints and Drawings; Oriental Library; Henry Moore Photograph Archive
and Study Center; auction and sales catalogs. **Holdings:** 60,000 volumes; 64
VF drawers of material by artist and subject; 1062 periodical titles.
Subscriptions: 561 journals and other serials. **Services:** Interlibrary loan;
copying; library open to the public for reference use only. **Automated
Operations:** Computerized cataloging and ILL. **Computerized Information
Services:** RLIN, BITNET (electronic mail services). **Networks/Consortia:**
Member of Kansas City Metropolitan Library Network (KCMLN),
Missouri Library Network Corp. (MLNC). **Remarks:** FAX: (816)561-7154.
Electronic mail address(es): BM.N2C (RLIN); bm.n2c@RLG (BITNET).
Staff: Jian Shen, Asian Proj.Cat.

Dr. Kenneth O. Nelson Library of the Health Sciences
See: Perry Memorial Hospital (12951)

Florence L. Nelson Memorial Library
See: Trinity Lutheran Hospital (16513)

★ 11389 ★
Nelson Industries, Inc. - Corporate Technical Library (Sci-Engr)
Box 600   Phone: (608)873-4370
Stoughton, WI 53589-0600   Larry J. Eriksson, Ph.D., Res.
Founded: 1975. **Staff:** 1. **Subjects:** Acoustics, noise control, signal processing, environmental control, mechanical engineering, filtration. **Holdings:** 1500 books; 200 bound periodical volumes; 200 reports. **Subscriptions:** 125 journals and other serials; 10 newspapers. **Services:** Interlibrary loan; library not open to the public. **Remarks:** FAX: (608)873-1550. Telex: 26 5433.

Margery H. Nelson Medical Library
See: St. Christopher's Hospital for Children (14260)

Nelson Museum
See: Kootenay Museum Association and Historical Society (8789)

P.C. Nelson Memorial Library
See: Southwestern Assemblies of God College (15537)

★ 11390 ★
Waldemar S. Nelson and Company, Inc. - Library (Sci-Engr)
1200 St. Charles Ave.   Phone: (504)523-5281
New Orleans, LA 70130   Mary Sudduth, Libn.
Founded: 1945. **Staff:** Prof 1. **Subjects:** Engineering, environment, project management, construction management. **Holdings:** 7000 books; 100 volumes on microfilm; computer software. **Subscriptions:** 100 journals and other serials. **Services:** Library not open to the public. **Remarks:** FAX: (504)523-4587.

Nemser-Scarf Reading Room
See: Pennsylvania Hospital - Department for Sick and Injured - Medical Library (12848)

★ 11391 ★
Nepal - National Archives (Rare Book)
Ramshah Path   Phone: 212778
Kathmandu, Nepal   Prof. Balram Das Dangol, Dir.
Founded: 1967. **Staff:** Prof 25; Other 20. **Subjects:** Ancient Hindu, Buddhist learning and philosophy, astrology, Dharma, rituals, Aurveda, Jamba, Tibetan texts. **Holdings:** 10,000 books; 30,000 manuscripts; 125,000 reels of microfilm; government noncurrent documents; rubbings of ancient inscriptions; legal deeds on palm leaf. **Services:** Copying; archives open to the public for reference use only. **Computerized Information Services:** Internal database (under development). **Publications:** Abhilekh, annual. **Remarks:** National Archives are said to be the oldest library of Nepal.

★ 11392 ★
Ner Israel Rabbinical College - Library (Rel-Phil)
400 Mt. Wilson Ln.   Phone: (301)484-7200
Baltimore, MD 21208   Rabbi Richard Goldenberg, Libn.
Staff: Prof 2. **Subjects:** Religion, theology, sociology, education. **Special Collections:** Ancient religious tomes. **Holdings:** 15,582 volumes. **Subscriptions:** 20 journals and other serials; 5 newspapers. **Services:** Copying (limited); library open to the public for reference use only with special permission.

★ 11393 ★
Nerco, Inc. - Corporate Library (Energy)
500 N.E. Multnomah   Phone: (503)731-6600
Portland, OR 97232   Melanie R. Birnbach, Libn.
Founded: 1979. **Staff:** Prof 1; Other 1. **Subjects:** Coal mining, minerals, energy, business and economics. **Holdings:** 1200 books. **Subscriptions:** 225 journals and other serials; 6 newspapers. **Services:** Interlibrary loan; library open to the public for reference use only. **Automated Operations:** Computerized cataloging. **Computerized Information Services:** OCLC, Dun & Bradstreet Business Credit Services, Dow Jones News/Retrieval, LEXIS, NEXIS, DIALOG Information Services, The Source, Global Report. **Remarks:** FAX: (503)241-2819.

★ 11394 ★
Nesbitt Memorial Hospital - Library (Med)
562 Wyoming Ave.   Phone: (717)288-1411
Kingston, PA 18704   Katherine L. McCrea, Libn.
Staff: Prof 1. **Subjects:** Medicine, nursing, paramedical sciences. **Holdings:** 3000 books; 380 bound periodical volumes. **Subscriptions:** 150 journals and other serials. **Services:** Interlibrary loan; copying; SDI; library open to the public with permission. **Computerized Information Services:** DIALOG Information Services, NLM. **Networks/Consortia:** Member of Health Information Library Network of Northeastern Pennsylvania (HILNNEP), National Network of Libraries of Medicine - Middle Atlantic Region, Northeastern Pennsylvania Bibliographic Center (NEPBC).

★ 11395 ★
Nesbitt Thomson Deacon Inc. - Library (Bus-Fin)
355, rue St-Jacques ouest   Phone: (514)282-5967
Montreal, PQ, Canada H2Y 1P1   Miss L. Cahill, Libn.
Founded: 1920. **Staff:** Prof 1; Other 1. **Subjects:** Stocks and bonds, investments, corporation and government finance, money market. **Holdings:** 75 books; 35 VF drawers of annual reports, prospectuses; 50 VF drawers of company files, clippings, pamphlets, government documents, studies. **Subscriptions:** 25 journals and other serials; 20 newspapers. **Services:** Interlibrary loan; library open to the public by appointment only. **Publications:** Research studies. **Remarks:** Alternate telephone number(s): 282-5968. FAX: (514)282-5853.

★ 11396 ★
Nesbitt Thomson Deacon Inc. - Research Department - Library
150 King St., W., 21st Fl.   Phone: (416)586-3912
Toronto, ON, Canada M5H 3W2   James Parker, Libn.
Founded: 1986. **Staff:** 2. **Subjects:** Investment. **Special Collections:** Annual Reports Collection (Canadian Public Companies). **Holdings:** 50 books; 1000 reports. **Subscriptions:** 200 journals and other serials, 15 newspapers. **Services:** Library not open to the public. **Computerized Information Services:** Internal database. **Remarks:** FAX: (416)586-4293.

★ 11397 ★
Neshaminy-Warwick Presbyterian Church - Library (Rel-Phil)
Bristol & Meetinghouse Rds.   Phone: (215)343-6060
Warminster, PA 18974   Bernard E. Deitrick, Libn.
Founded: 1958. **Staff:** 8. **Subjects:** Religion, local history. **Special Collections:** Rare books concerning William Tennent and the Log College. **Holdings:** 6650 books; cassette tapes; videocassettes; phonograph records; filmstrips. **Subscriptions:** 24 journals and other serials. **Services:** Library open to the public on a limited schedule.

★ 11398 ★
Nestle Food Company - SIC (Food-Bev)
800 N. Brand Blvd.   Phone: (818)549-6041
Glendale, CA 91203   Yelta Hucks, Sr.Sec.
Staff: Prof 1. **Subjects:** Food, marketing, business. **Holdings:** Figures not available. **Subscriptions:** 52 journals and other serials. **Services:** Center not open to the public. **Computerized Information Services:** DIALOG Information Services, InvesText. **Remarks:** FAX: (213)549-6912. **Formerly:** Nestle USA - Strategic Information Center.

Nestle USA - Strategic Information Center
See: Nestle Food Company (11398)

★ 11399 ★
Netherlands - Bibliotheek van het Algemeen Rijksarchief (Hist)
Prins Willem Alexanderhof 20   Phone: 70 3814381
NL-2595 The Hague, Netherlands   M. Abrahamse
Founded: 1811. **Staff:** Prof 2. **Subjects:** History. **Holdings:** 40,000 books; 20,000 bound periodical volumes. **Subscriptions:** 350 journals and other serials. **Services:** Copying; library open to the public. **Remarks:** FAX: 70 3473231. **Formerly:** Algemeen Rijksarchief's-Gravenhage.

★ 11400 ★
Netherlands - Central Bureau of Statistics - Library (Soc Sci)
P.O. Box 959   Phone: 70 3375818
NL-2270 AZ Voorburg, Netherlands   T. Vreugdenhil, Libn.
Founded: 1899. **Staff:** Prof 21; Other 9. **Subjects:** Worldwide statistical data. **Holdings:** 390,000 volumes; 78,000 bound periodical volumes; 100,000 microfiche. **Subscriptions:** 9500 journals and other serials. **Services:** Interlibrary loan; copying; SDI; library open to the public. **Automated Operations:** Computerized public access catalog, cataloging, and journal routing. **Computerized Information Services:** EUROSTAT, RCC. **Remarks:** FAX: 70 3877429. Telex: 32692 CBS NL.

★ 11401 ★
Netherlands - Education Department - Economisch-Historische Bibliotheek (Bus-Fin)
Cruquiusweg 31   Phone: 20 6685866
NL-1019 AT Amsterdam, Netherlands   Dr. J.J. Seegers
Subjects: History - economic, accounting. **Special Collections:** Accountancy prior to 1850 (3000 titles); history of economic thought. **Holdings:** 75,000 books; 25,000 bound periodical volumes; 10,000 documents. **Subscriptions:** 150 journals and other serials. **Services:** Interlibrary loan; copying; library open to the public. **Special Catalogs:** Economisch-Historische Katalogi; Katalogi bronnenoverzichten. **Remarks:** FAX: 20 6654181.

★ 11402 ★
Netherlands - Koninklijke Bibliotheek (Hum, Soc Sci, Law, Info Sci)
P.O. Box 90407
NL-2509 LK The Hague, Netherlands   Phone: 70 3140911
Staff: 230. **Subjects:** Humanities, philosophy, psychology, religion, law, sociology, economics, language and literature, history and fine art, geography, education, political science. **Special Collections:** Medieval manuscripts; incunabula and post-incunabula; bookbindings; historical collection of paper; chess and draughts literature. **Holdings:** 2.25 million bound volumes; 160,000 microforms; 7000 manuscripts. **Subscriptions:** 14,500 periodicals. **Services:** Interlibrary loan; copying; library open to the public. **Publications:** Treasures of the Royal Library; Bibliography of Cartographic Materials in the Netherlands; special bibliographies. **Special Catalogs:** Cumulatieve Catalogus; Centrale catalogus van Periodieken (Union Catalog of Periodicals; book); exhibition catalogs. **Remarks:** FAX: 703140450. Telex: 34402 KBNL. **Formerly:** Netherlands - Royal Library. **Also Known As:** National Library of the Netherlands.

★ 11403 ★
Netherlands - Ministry of Agriculture, Nature Management and Fisheries - International Institute for Land Reclamation and Improvement - Library (Agri)
Postbus 45   Phone: 8370 76733
NL-6700 AA Wageningen, Netherlands   Ir. G. Naber, Hd.Libn.
Founded: 1945. **Staff:** 6. **Subjects:** Soil science, water management, hydrology, irrigation and drainage, remote sensing, land-use planning, recreation, landscape, environmental management. **Holdings:** 50,000 books; 16,000 bound periodical volumes. **Subscriptions:** 1500 journals and other serials. **Services:** Interlibrary loan; copying; SDI; library open to the public. **Automated Operations:** Computerized public access catalog, cataloging, and circulation. **Computerized Information Services:** ESA/IRS, DIMDI, DIALOG Information Services, PFDS Online; AGRALIN (Agricultural Literature Information System in the Netherlands) (internal database); electronic mail service. Performs searches on fee basis. **Publications:** Attenderingsbulletin Bibliotheek Staringgebouw: land, soil, water, 6/year. **Remarks:** FAX: 8370 11524. Telex: 75230 VISI NL. **Staff:** Mrs. L.A. Trouw, Doc.; P. Heikamp, Desk Off.

Netherlands - Ministry of Development Cooperation/Ministry of Education - Institute of Social Studies
See: **Institute of Social Studies - Library (7977)**

★ 11404 ★
Netherlands - Ministry of Foreign Affairs - Translations Branch - Terminology and Documentation Section - Library (Info Sci)
P.O. Box 20061
Bezuidenhoutseweg 67
NL-2500 EB The Hague, Netherlands   Phone: 70 3485520
Founded: 1970. **Subjects:** Terminology - law, agreements and treaties, government, finance and economics, European political cooperation, development aid, the Netherlands. **Holdings:** 5000 volumes; 10,000 documents; sets of laws. **Subscriptions:** 60 journals and other serials. **Computerized Information Services:** Produces Terminological Data Bank (available online through EURODICAUTOM - ECHO). **Also Known As:** Ministerie van Buitenlandse Zaken - Hoofdafdeling Vertalingen. **Staff:** M. Fabbricotti; H. Hunicke; R. van Mannen.

★ 11405 ★
Netherlands - Ministry of Justice - Library and Documentation Center (Law)
Schedeldoekshaven 100
Kamer L420
Postbus 20301   Phone: 70 3706934
NL-2500 EH The Hague, Netherlands   E. Van Zelst
Staff: Prof 15; Other 4. **Subjects:** Law, governmental publications, criminology, jurisprudence. **Holdings:** 120,000 books; microfiche. **Services:** Interlibrary loan; copying; SDI; library open to the public. **Computerized Information Services:** RCC, Celex, Datalex. **Publications:** Documented articles and books, biweekly. **Remarks:** FAX: 70 3707941.

Netherlands - Ministry of Social Affairs - International Information Center and Archives for the Women's Movement
See: **International Information Center and Archives for the Women's Movement (8121)**

★ 11406 ★
Netherlands - Ministry of Transport, Public Works, and Water Management - Library (Trans)
Plesmanweg 1
Postbus 20901   Phone: 70 3517086
NL-2500 EX The Hague, Netherlands   M.J. Nicasie
Founded: 1945. **Staff:** Prof 12; Other 9. **Subjects:** Transportation, transport policy, traffic. **Holdings:** 50,000 books; 31,000 reels of microfilm. **Services:** Interlibrary loan; copying; library open to the public for reference use only. **Computerized Information Services:** VENW-LIS (internal database). **Remarks:** FAX: 70 3516868. Telex: 32562 (MINVWNL).

★ 11407 ★
Netherlands - Ministry of Welfare, Public Health, and Culture - Library (Soc Sci, Med)
P.O. Box 5406
Sir W Churchill-laan 366   Phone: 703405676
NL-22890HK Rijswijk, Netherlands   B. Robert Klaverstijn
Founded: 1965. **Staff:** Prof 23; Other 5. **Subjects:** Health, welfare, cultural affairs. **Special Collections:** Dutch governmental reports; Parliamentary documents. **Holdings:** 105,000 books. **Subscriptions:** 960 journals and other serials; 40 newspapers. **Services:** Interlibrary loan; copying. **Computerized Information Services:** MINISTERIE WVC. **Publications:** Health in the Netherlands. **Remarks:** FAX: 703405044.

★ 11408 ★
Netherlands - Museum Boerhaave - Rijksmuseum voor de Geschiedenis van de Natuurwetenschappen en van de Geneeskunde - Bibliotheek (Biol Sci, Med)
Lange St Agnietenstraat 10
Postbus 11280   Phone: 71 214224
NL-2301 EG Leiden, Netherlands   H.J.F.M. Leechburch Auwers
Founded: 1928. **Staff:** Prof 2. **Subjects:** History of science, history of medicine. **Special Collections:** Historical collection of Koninklijke Nederlandse Chemische Vereniging (History of Chemistry, 2000 volumes); seventeenth and eighteenth century books of Leiden Observatory (500 volumes). **Holdings:** 25,000 books; 2500 bound periodical volumes; 8000 prints; 500 archival items. **Subscriptions:** 130 journals and other serials. **Services:** Interlibrary loan; copying; library open to the public. **Remarks:** FAX: 71 120344.

★ 11409 ★
Netherlands - National Herbarium of the Netherlands - Library (Biol Sci)
Rapenburg 70-74
P.O. Box 9514   Phone: 71 273513
NL-2300 RA Leiden, Netherlands   C.W.J. Lut, Libn.
Subjects: Plant systematics, plant geography. **Holdings:** 30,000 books; 90,000 reprints and pamphlets; 100,000 microfiche. **Subscriptions:** 2500 journals and other serials. **Services:** Library open to the public. **Remarks:** FAX: 71 273511. Maintained by Leiden State University. **Also Known As:** Rijksherbarium.

Netherlands - National Library
See: **Netherlands - Koninklijke Bibliotheek** (11402)

★ 11410 ★
Netherlands - Netherlands Foreign Trade Agency - Library (Bus-Fin)
Bezuidenhoutseweg 151   Phone: 70 797221
NL-2594 AG The Hague, Netherlands   J.H. Ypma, Hd.
Staff: Prof 14; Other 26. **Subjects:** Economics, international trade, foreign investment. **Holdings:** 150,000 volumes. **Subscriptions:** 1800 journals and other serials. **Services:** Library open to businesses, government agencies, and students. **Computerized Information Services:** DIALOG Information Services, Belgian Information and Dissemination Service (BELINDIS); produces Foreign Trade & Econ Abstracts; DIALMAIL (electronic mail service). Performs searches on fee basis. **Remarks:** FAX: 070 797878. Telex: 31099 ECOZA NL. Electronic mail address(es): HUMMELINK (DIALMAIL).

Netherlands - Royal Academy of Sciences
See: **Royal Academy of Sciences - Netherlands Institute for Developmental Biology** (14092)

Netherlands - Royal Library
See: **Netherlands - Koninklijke Bibliotheek** (11402)

Netherlands - Royal Netherlands Academy of Arts and Sciences
See: **Royal Netherlands Academy of Arts and Sciences** (14126)

★ 11411 ★
Netherlands - State Museum - Library (Art)
Jan Luykenstraat 1A   Phone: 20 732121
NL-1071 XZ Amsterdam, Netherlands   G.J. Koot, Dir.
Founded: 1885. **Staff:** Prof 5; Other 5. **Subjects:** Fine art, decorative art. **Special Collections:** Auction catalogs (Waller Fund, 1722-1932); architecture collection (A.N. Godefroy, 1897). **Holdings:** 200,000 books; 10,000 bound periodical volumes; 40,000 auction catalogs. **Subscriptions:** 700 journals and other serials. **Services:** Copying; library open to the public. **Remarks:** FAX: 20 6798146.

Netherlands Institute for Developmental Biology
See: **Royal Academy of Sciences - Netherlands Institute for Developmental Biology** (14092)

Netherlands Museum - Archives
See: **(Holland) Joint Archives of Holland** (7328)

★ 11412 ★
Netherlands Opendir Museum - Library (Art, Soc Sci)
Schelmseweg 89   Phone: 85 576255
NL-6816 SJ Arnhem, Netherlands   H. Lunenborg, Libn.
Founded: 1918. **Staff:** Prof 2; Other 1. **Subjects:** Ethnology, folklore, traditional costume, industrial archeology, tradition, ceramics. **Special Collections:** 18th-19th century children's books (2000). **Holdings:** 35,000 books; 10,000 bound periodical volumes; 660 microfiche; 10 reels of microfilm. **Subscriptions:** 451 journals and other serials. **Services:** Interlibrary loan; copying; library open to the public for reference use only. **Computerized Information Services:** Internal database. **Publications:** List of acquisitions. **Also Known As:** Nederlands Openluchtmuseum - Bibliotheek.

★ 11413 ★
Netherlands Organization for Applied Scientific Research - Central Office Library (Sci-Engr)
P.O. Box 297   Phone: 70 496500
NL-2501 BD Grallenhage, Netherlands   Mrs. T. Wagemakers, Dir.
Subjects: Applied research and development in the areas of industrial technology, energy, environment, food and nutrition. **Holdings:** 16,000 volumes. **Subscriptions:** 600 journals and other serials; 10 newspapers. **Services:** Interlibrary loan; copying; library open to the public. **Remarks:** Library located at Juliana van Stolberglann 148, NL-2595 CL The Hague, Netherlands. FAX: 70 3855700. Telex: 31660 tnogv nl. **Also Known As:** Nederlands Organisatie voor Toegepast Natuurwetenschappelijk Onderzoek; TNO.

★ 11414 ★
Netherlands Organization for Libraries and Information Services - Library (Info Sci)
19 Burgemeester van Karnebeeklaan   Phone: 70 3607833
NL-2585 BA The Hague, Netherlands   W.A.M. Leys
Founded: 1971. **Subjects:** Information handling - scientific, technical. **Holdings:** 4500 volumes. **Subscriptions:** 100 journals and other serials. **Services:** Interlibrary loan; copying; library open to the public by appointment. **Publications:** Annual reports. **Remarks:** FAX: 70 3615011. **Also Known As:** Nederlands Bureau voor Bibliotheekwezen en Informatieverzorging (NBBI).

Netherlands Organization for Scientific Research - Stichting Mathematisch Centrum
See: **Center for Mathematics and Computer Science** (3267)

Helen Nettleton Library
See: **Owyhee County Historical Complex - Helen Nettleton Library** (12640)

★ 11415 ★
Network of Educational Innovation for Development in Africa - Library (Educ)
B.P. 3311
Dakar, Senegal
Subjects: Educational innovation, education and productive work, education for rural development, systems administration and supervision. **Holdings:** 2000 volumes. **Also Known As:** Reseau d'Innovations Educatives pour le Developpement en Afrique.

Rabbi Neuhaus Library
See: **Telshe Yeshiva - Rabbi A.N. Schwartz Library** (16078)

★ 11416 ★
Neuropsychiatric Research Institute - Library (Med)
700 1st Ave., S.   Phone: (701)239-1620
Fargo, ND 58103   Diane Nordeng, Libn.
Founded: 1977. **Staff:** Prof 1. **Subjects:** Neurosurgery, neurology, psychiatry, neuropsychology. **Holdings:** 416 books; 1878 bound periodical volumes. **Subscriptions:** 32 journals and other serials. **Services:** Interlibrary loan; copying; library open to allied medical personnel. **Computerized Information Services:** MEDLINE; EasyLink, DOCLINE (electronic mail services). **Networks/Consortia:** Member of Valley Medical Network (VMN). **Remarks:** FAX: (701)239-1639.

★ 11417 ★
Neurosciences Institute of the Neurosciences Research Program - Library (Med)
Smith Hall Annex
Rockefeller University
1230 York Ave.   Phone: (212)570-8975
New York, NY 10021-6399   Stephanie Gregerman, Bibliog.
Staff: 1. **Subjects:** Neurosciences, brain sciences, neurobiology. **Holdings:** 3000 books. **Subscriptions:** 50 journals and other serials. **Services:** Library open to scholars in the field by special arrangement. **Computerized Information Services:** DIALOG Information Services. **Publications:** Bibliographies; reference lists; accessions lists; bibliographies of issues of Neurosciences Research Program Bulletin. **Remarks:** FAX: (212)570-7628. Maintained by the Neurosciences Research Foundation.

Nevada Architectural Archives
See: **University of Nevada--Reno - Special Collections Department/University Archives (19022)**

★ **11418** ★
Nevada County Historical Society - Searls Historical Library (Hist)
214 Church St.   Phone: (916)265-5910
Nevada City, CA 95959   Edwin L. Tyson, Libn.
Founded: 1972. **Staff:** Prof 1; Other 1. **Subjects:** Nevada County history. **Holdings:** 3480 books; 50 bound periodical volumes; 350,000 documents, pamphlets, vertical file materials; 240 maps and charts; 50 tape recordings; 2500 photographs. **Services:** Copying; library open to the public with restrictions.

★ **11419** ★
Nevada County Law Library (Law)
Courthouse Annex   Phone: (916)265-1475
Nevada City, CA 95959   Vera Butisbauch, Law Libn.
Staff: Prof 2. **Subjects:** Law. **Holdings:** 5000 books. **Services:** Interlibrary loan; copying; library open to the public with restrictions. **Staff:** Kathleen R. Pinaglia, Asst. Law Libn.

★ **11420** ★
Nevada Habilitation Center - Library
Ashland at Highland
Nevada, MO 64772
Founded: 1972. **Subjects:** Mental retardation. **Holdings:** 1000 books. **Remarks:** Currently inactive.

★ **11421** ★
Nevada Historical Society - Library (Hist)
1650 N. Virginia St.   Phone: (702)688-1190
Reno, NV 89503-1799   Peter L. Bandurraga, Dir.
Founded: 1904. **Staff:** 7. **Subjects:** Nevada history, mining, Indians, agriculture, water, gambling, transportation and communication. **Holdings:** 30,000 books; 5000 bound periodical volumes; 3000 manuscript collections; 5000 reels of microfilm; 250,000 photographs; 50,000 maps; manuscripts; photographs; government documents. **Subscriptions:** 260 journals and other serials. **Services:** Copying; limited written research by mail; library open to the public. **Publications:** Nevada Historical Society Quarterly. **Special Indexes:** An Index to the Publications of the Nevada Historical Society, 1907-1971. **Staff:** M. Lee Mortensen, Res.Libn.; Eric Moody, Cur. of Mss.

★ **11422** ★
Nevada Mental Health Institute - Library (Med)
480 Galletti Way   Phone: (702)688-2055
Sparks, NV 89431-5574   Robert D. Armstrong, Libn.
Founded: 1968. **Staff:** Prof 1. **Subjects:** Psychiatry, psychology, mental health, psychiatric nursing. **Holdings:** 5500 books; 500 government documents; 2000 pamphlets and reports; 450 audio cassettes. **Subscriptions:** 40 journals and other serials. **Services:** Interlibrary loan; copying; library open to health professionals and students. **Networks/Consortia:** Member of National Network of Libraries of Medicine - Pacific Southwest Region, Northern California and Nevada Medical Library Group (NCNMLG), Nevada Medical Library Group (NMLG).

★ **11423** ★
Nevada State Department of Transportation - Map Section (Geog-Map)
1263 S. Stewart St., Rm. 206
Carson City, NV 89712   Phone: (702)687-3451
Subjects: Maps, geographic names. **Holdings:** Figures not available. **Services:** Library not open to the public. **Special Indexes:** Map indexes - available upon request.

★ **11424** ★
Nevada State Library and Archives (Info Sci)
Capitol Complex   Phone: (702)687-5160
Carson City, NV 89710   Joan G. Kerschner, State Libn.
Founded: 1859. **Staff:** Prof 16; Other 21. **Subjects:** Public administration, history of Nevada, business. **Special Collections:** Nevada Collection; state, county, and municipal documents (55,000); Regional Library for the Blind and Physically Handicapped. **Holdings:** 47,627 books; 12,596 bound periodical volumes; 250,000 U.S. Government publications; 15,233 reels of microfilm of Nevada newspapers. **Subscriptions:** 504 journals and other serials; 60 newspapers. **Services:** Interlibrary loan; copying; archives open to the public. **Automated Operations:** Computerized cataloging and circulation. **Computerized Information Services:** DIALOG Information Services, RLIN, VU/TEXT Information Services, OCLC, WILSONLINE, DataTimes; ALANET (electronic mail service). Performs searches. Contact Person: Joyce C. Lee, Asst. State Libn. **Networks/Consortia:** Member of Information Nevada, CLASS. **Publications:** Info Connection; Official Publications List. **Special Catalogs:** Nevada Statewide Union catalog. **Remarks:** FAX: (702)887-2630. Electronic mail address(es): ALA0736 (ALANET). **Staff:** Bill Strader, Lib.Dev.Off.; Betty McNeal, State Data Ctr.Libn.; Allison Cowgill, Hd. of Ref.; Ann Brinkmeyer, Hd., Tech.Serv.; Patricia Deadder, Doc.Libn.; Sherry Evans, Cat.Libn.; Leslie Peterson, Talking Books Libn.; Joyce Cox, Ref.Libn.; Millie Syring, ILL Libn.; Bonnie Buckley, Adm.Serv.; Guy Rocha, State Archv./Rec.Adm.; Jeffrey Kintop, Archv.; Robert van Straten, Rec.Mgr.; Emmy Bell, Literacy Coord.; Diane Baker, Cons.

★ **11425** ★
Nevada State Library and Archives - Division of Archives and Records (Info Sci)
3579 Highway 50 E.   Phone: (702)687-5210
Carson City, NV 89710   Guy L. Rocha, Archv. & Rec.Adm.
Founded: 1965. **Staff:** Prof 6; Other 6. **Subjects:** Nevada state history and government. **Special Collections:** Nevada and Utah state, local, and government records; territorial records; state government records center (6000 cubic feet). **Holdings:** 6400 books; photographs; portraits; maps; drawings; sketches. **Services:** Copying; archives open to the public. **Computerized Information Services:** RLIN. **Remarks:** FAX: (702)887-2630. **Staff:** Jeffrey M. Kintop, State Archv.Mgr.; Robert van Straten, State Rec.Mgr.; Bill Bowden, Rec.Mgr.; Christopher Driggs, Archv.; George Earnhart, Rec.Mgr.

★ **11426** ★
Nevada State Museum - Library (Hist)
Capitol Complex
600 N. Carson St.   Phone: (702)687-4810
Carson City, NV 89710   Robert A. Nylen, Cur. of Hist.
Founded: 1939. **Staff:** 18. **Subjects:** Nevada history, historical artifacts. **Special Collections:** Site files on threatened and endangered plants of Nevada; anthropological papers; Virginia & Truckee Railroad ledgers and reports. **Holdings:** 650 volumes. **Subscriptions:** 20 journals and other serials. **Services:** Copying; library open to students and researchers by appointment. **Publications:** Newsletter, quarterly; Popular Series, irregular. **Remarks:** FAX: (702)687-4168. **Staff:** Gloria J. Harjes; (702)687-4168.

★ **11427** ★
Nevada State Supreme Court - Law Library (Law)
Supreme Court Bldg., Capitol Complex Phone: (702)687-5140
Carson City, NV 89710   Susan Southwick, Law Libn.
Founded: 1973. **Staff:** Prof 4; Other 2. **Subjects:** Law. **Holdings:** 79,907 volumes; 13,664 volumes on microfiche. **Subscriptions:** 342 journals and other serials. **Services:** Interlibrary loan; copying; library open to the public with restrictions. **Automated Operations:** Computerized public access catalog. **Computerized Information Services:** WESTLAW, DIALOG Information Services, LEXIS. Performs searches on fee basis. **Publications:** New Titles List, irregular - to local legal community. **Staff:** Kathleen Harrington, Asst.Libn.; Charlyn Lewis, Libn.IV.

C.W. Nevel Memorial Library
See: **Lutheran Medical Center (9460)**

Louise Nevelson Archives
See: **William A. Farnsworth Library and Art Museum (5604)**

★ 11428 ★
Neville Chemical Company - Library (Energy)
2800 Neville Rd.   Phone: (412)331-4200
Pittsburgh, PA 15225-1496   John E. Henderson, Libn.
Founded: 1949. **Staff:** 1. **Subjects:** Petroleum hydrocarbon resins. **Special Collections:** U.S. patents on petroleum hydrocarbon resins. **Holdings:** 1500 books. **Subscriptions:** 300 journals and other serials. **Services:** Interlibrary loan; copying; library open to the public by appointment. **Computerized Information Services:** DIALOG Information Services, STN International. **Remarks:** FAX: (412)777-4234. Telex: 216315.

★ 11429 ★
Neville Public Museum - Library (Art)
210 Museum Pl.   Phone: (414)448-4460
Green Bay, WI 54303   Ann L. Koski, Dir.
Founded: 1915. **Staff:** Prof 1. **Subjects:** Museum studies, art, earth sciences, history and anthropology with regional and state emphasis. **Special Collections:** Photograph collection (black/white prints and negatives). **Holdings:** 4500 books. **Subscriptions:** 100 journals and other serials. **Services:** Copying; library open to the public by appointment for reference use only. **Staff:** Louise C. Pfotenhauer, Libn.

★ 11430 ★
Neville Public Museum - Photograph & Film Collection (Art, Aud-Vis)
210 Museum Pl.   Phone: (414)448-4460
Green Bay, WI 54303   Ann L. Koski, Dir.
Founded: 1915. **Staff:** 1. **Subjects:** Art, earth sciences, museum studies, history and anthropology with regional and state emphasis. **Special Collections:** Photograph Collection. **Holdings:** 4480 bound materials; 1.5 million negatives and prints. **Subscriptions:** 100 journals and other serials. **Services:** Copying; library open to the public by appointment for reference use only. **Staff:** Louis C. Pfotenhauer.

George P. Nevitt Library
See: **Paine Art Center and Arboretum (12689)**

★ 11431 ★
New Alchemy Institute - Library (Energy)
237 Hatchville Rd.   Phone: (508)564-6301
East Falmouth, MA 02536   Betty Green, Site Info.Coord.
Founded: 1969. **Staff:** Prof 1. **Subjects:** Organic agriculture, energy conservation, renewable energy resources. **Special Collections:** U.S. Department of Energy documents (solar, wind, and renewable energy resources; 1500 reports). **Holdings:** 2500 volumes; 50 other cataloged items. **Subscriptions:** 60 journals and other serials. **Services:** Copying; library open to members.

★ 11432 ★
New America Makers - Library (Aud-Vis)
475 30th St.   Phone: (415)695-2904
San Francisco, CA 94110   Joanne Kelly, Co-Dir.
Founded: 1970. **Staff:** 1. **Subjects:** Video, dance, individual artists. **Holdings:** 500 volumes. **Subscriptions:** 100 journals and other serials. **Services:** Library open to the public by appointment.

★ 11433 ★
New Bedford Free Public Library - Genealogy Room (Hist)
613 Pleasant St.   Phone: (508)991-6275
New Bedford, MA 02740   Paul Albert Cyr, Cur.
Staff: Prof 1; Other 1. **Subjects:** Genealogy of New England, Massachusetts town histories, history of New Bedford and vicinity, French-Canadian and Acadian genealogy. **Special Collections:** Leonard Papers (Dartmouth Genealogy); Pierce Papers (Bristol Genealogy); Paul Cuffe Papers; Quakeriana. **Holdings:** 5000 books; 500 bound periodical volumes; 1250 reels of microfilm of New Bedford newspapers and city documents. **Subscriptions:** 18 journals and other serials. **Services:** Interlibrary loan (microfilm only); copying; room open to the public for reference use only. **Automated Operations:** Computerized public access catalog and cataloging. **Publications:** Paul Cuffe Papers (microfilm). **Special Indexes:** New Bedford newspaper index (card).

★ 11434 ★
New Bedford Free Public Library - Melville Whaling Room (Hist)
613 Pleasant St.   Phone: (508)999-6291
New Bedford, MA 02740   Paul Albert Cyr, Cur.
Founded: 1962. **Staff:** 1; Other 1. **Subjects:** Whaling - New Bedford, New England, United States. **Special Collections:** Whaling logs of 495 voyages; J. & W.R. Wing Collection (business records, 1840-1920); C.W. Morgan Collection (business records, 1818-1850) C.R. Tucker Collection, 1838-1867; G.H. Hussey Collection, 1845-1865. **Holdings:** 650 books; 35 bound periodical volumes; 120 pamphlets; 1025 volumes of whaling manuscripts, logs, journals, account books; 6700 crew lists; 11,000 custom house records; 300 reels of microfilm; 100 photographs, prints, paintings. **Services:** Interlibrary loan (limited); copying; research; room open to the public for reference use only. **Publications:** Birth of a Whaleship; Addendum to Starbuck and Whaling Masters. **Special Indexes:** Card index of men who signed on whaleships (200,000 entries); voyage abstracts (37,000 entries); index to whaling manuscripts (microfilm).

★ 11435 ★
New Bedford Law Library (Law)
Superior Court House
441 County St.   Phone: (508)992-8077
New Bedford, MA 02740   Margaretha E.H. Birknes, Law Libn.
Founded: 1894. **Staff:** Prof 1. **Subjects:** Law. **Holdings:** 35,000 volumes. **Services:** Interlibrary loan; copying; library open to outside users for research only. **Remarks:** Part of the Massachusetts State Trial Court; Marnie Warner, Law Library Coordinator.

★ 11436 ★
New Bedford Standard-Times Library (Publ)
555 Pleasant St.   Phone: (508)997-7411
New Bedford, MA 02740   Maurice G. Lauzon, Libn.
Founded: 1890. **Staff:** Prof 1. **Subjects:** Local history, newspaper reference topics. **Holdings:** Clippings; local newspapers. **Services:** Library open to law and investigative users. **Remarks:** FAX: (508)997-7852.

New Bedford Whaling Museum - Library
See: **Old Dartmouth Historical Society - Whaling Museum Library (12383)**

★ 11437 ★
New Britain General Hospital - Health Science Library (Med)
100 Grand St.   Phone: (203)224-5011
New Britain, CT 06050   Linda A. LaRue, Lib.Dir.
Founded: 1946. **Staff:** Prof 1; Other 2. **Subjects:** Medicine, surgery, obstetrics and gynecology, pediatrics, cardiology. **Special Collections:** History of Medicine Collection (130 texts); History of Nursing; patient education. **Holdings:** 3000 books; 9000 bound periodical volumes; pamphlets; videotapes; films; slides; Audio-Digest tapes. **Subscriptions:** 240 journals and other serials. **Services:** Interlibrary loan (fee); library open to the public by appointment. **Automated Operations:** Computerized cataloging. **Computerized Information Services:** MEDLARS, BRS Information Technologies, OCLC. **Networks/Consortia:** Member of Connecticut Association of Health Science Libraries (CAHSL).

★ 11438 ★
New Britain Museum of American Art - Library (Art)
56 Lexington St.   Phone: (203)229-0257
New Britain, CT 06052   Jane Darnell, Res.Libn.
Founded: 1972. **Subjects:** American art. **Special Collections:** Illustration collection. **Holdings:** 500 books 65 linear feet of vertical files. **Subscriptions:** 7 journals and other serials. **Services:** Library open to the public by appointment for reference use only; mail inquiries answered.

★ 11439 ★
(New Brunswick) Alcoholism and Drug Dependency Commission of New Brunswick - Chemical Dependency Library
65 Brunswick St.
Fredericton, NB, Canada E3B 2H4
Defunct. Holdings absorbed by New Brunswick Department of Health & Community Services - Library.

★ 11440 ★
New Brunswick College of Craft and Design - Library (Educ)
P.O. Box 6000   Phone: (506)453-2305
Fredericton, NB, Canada E3B 5H1   Barbara Smith, Volunteer Libn.
Founded: 1976. **Subjects:** Crafts and and allied subjects. **Holdings:** 2200
books; videotapes; slides. **Subscriptions:** 30 journals and other serials.
Services: Library not open to the public. **Remarks:** FAX: (506)457-7352.
Formerly: New Brunswick Craft School.

New Brunswick Craft School
See: **New Brunswick College of Craft and Design** (11440)

★ 11441 ★
New Brunswick Department of Agriculture - Library (Agri)
P.O. Box 6000
Fredericton, NB, Canada E3B 5H1   Phone: (506)453-2666
Founded: 1966. **Subjects:** Agriculture science and industry, statistics.
Holdings: 528 brochures and pamphlets. **Services:** Library not open to the
public, pamphlets are supplied to farmers on request at no charge. **Remarks:**
FAX: (506)453-7170.

New Brunswick Department of Commerce & Technology
See: **New Brunswick Department of Economic Development & Tourism**
(11442)

★ 11442 ★
New Brunswick Department of Economic Development & Tourism -
  Central Files & Library (Bus-Fin)
P.O. Box 6000   Phone: (506)453-2187
Fredericton, NB, Canada E3B 5H1   Jane A. Phillips, Supv.
Staff: 1. **Subjects:** Foreign and domestic trade, statistics. **Holdings:** 1500
books; 1450 bound periodical volumes; reports and studies; catalogs;
directories; statistical data. **Subscriptions:** 145 journals and other serials; 42
newspapers. **Services:** Interlibrary loan; library open to the public for
reference use only. **Remarks:** FAX: (506)457-4845. **Formerly:** New
Brunswick Department of Commerce & Technology.

★ 11443 ★
New Brunswick Department of Education - Library (Educ)
King's Place, 3rd Fl.
P.O. Box 6000   Phone: (506)453-3229
Fredericton, NB, Canada E3B 5H1   Judith Colter, MLIS
Founded: 1979. **Staff:** Prof 1; Other 1. **Subjects:** Education, administration.
Holdings: 7600 books; 60 bound periodical volumes; 3900 reports and
studies; 1100 curriculum guides; 900 government documents. **Subscriptions:**
465 journals and other serials; 16 newspapers. **Services:** Interlibrary loan;
library open to the public for reference use only. **Automated Operations:**
Computerized cataloging and circulation. **Computerized Information
Services:** DOBIS Canadian Online Library System, PHOENIX; internal
database; Envoy 100 (electronic mail service). **Publications:** Library
Updates, monthly - to staff and provincial government libraries and
universities. **Remarks:** FAX: (506)453-3325. Electronic mail address(es):
ILL.NBFED (Envoy 100).

★ 11444 ★
New Brunswick Department of the Environment - Library (Env-Cons)
P.O. Box 6000   Phone: (506)453-3700
Fredericton, NB, Canada E3B 5H1   Gail Darby, Lib.Mgr.
Founded: 1972. **Staff:** 1. **Subjects:** Industrial waste, sewage treatment, air
pollution, water resources, environmental impact assessment, pesticides.
Special Collections: New Brunswick government reports on environmental
subjects. **Holdings:** 8000 books; 240 bound periodical volumes; 4 VF drawers
of articles. **Subscriptions:** 100 journals and other serials. **Services:**
Interlibrary loan; library open to the public for reference use only.
Computerized Information Services: Envoy 100 (electronic mail service).
Publications: Monthly Accessions List - to staff, other departments, and
interested firms. **Remarks:** FAX: (506)453-3843. Electronic mail
address(es): NB.DEPT.ENVIR (Envoy 100).

★ 11445 ★
New Brunswick Department of Health & Community Services - Library
  (Med)
Carleton Place, 3rd Fl.
P.O. Box 5100
Fredericton, NB, Canada E3B 5G8   Phone: (506)453-2536
Founded: 1982. **Staff:** 1. **Subjects:** Health, medicine, social services.
Holdings: 9000 books; 260 bound periodical volumes. **Subscriptions:** 75
journals and other serials. **Services:** Interlibrary loan; copying; library open
to the public. **Remarks:** FAX: (506)453-2958. Contains the holdings of the
former (New Brunswick) Alcoholism and Drug Dependency Commission
of New Brunswick - Chemical Dependency Library.

New Brunswick Department of Municipalities, Culture and Housing
See: **New Brunswick Library Service** (11450)

★ 11446 ★
New Brunswick Department of Natural Resources and Energy - Library
  (Biol Sci, Sci-Engr)
Hugh John Flemming Forestry Complex
P.O. Box 6000   Phone: (506)453-5478
Fredericton, NB, Canada E3B 5H1   Samuel Inch, Libn.
Founded: 1987. **Staff:** Prof 1; Other 1. **Subjects:** Forestry, fisheries, wildlife
management, land use, mines and geology, energy. **Holdings:** 30,000 books;
5000 bound periodical volumes; 250 annual reports; 40 shelf units of
pamphlets; 60 shelf units of technical reports; departmental archives.
Subscriptions: 203 journals and other serials. **Services:** Interlibrary loan;
library open to the public with restrictions. **Automated Operations:**
Computerized public access catalog, cataloging, acquisitions, serials, and
circulation. **Computerized Information Services:** DIALOG Information
Services, CAN/OLE, Info Globe; internal database; Envoy 100 (electronic
mail service). **Publications:** Acquisition List, monthly - local distribution;
Catalogue of Departmental Publications, annual - national and international
distribution. **Remarks:** FAX: (506)453-4279. Electronic mail address(es):
ILL.NBFNR (Envoy 100).

★ 11447 ★
New Brunswick Department of Transportation - Library (Trans)
P.O. Box 6000   Phone: (506)453-2535
Fredericton, NB, Canada E3B 5H1   Bonnie Ellis, Libn.
Founded: 1974. **Staff:** Prof 1; Other 1. **Subjects:** Transportation - general
and history. **Holdings:** 5000 books. **Subscriptions:** 150 journals and other
serials. **Services:** Interlibrary loan; copying; library open to the public.
Automated Operations: Computerized cataloging. **Computerized
Information Services:** DOBIS Canadian Online Library System; Phoenix
(internal database). **Publications:** Recent accessions, bimonthly.

★ 11448 ★
New Brunswick Electric Power Commission - Reference Center (Sci-
  Engr)
515 King St.
P.O. Box 2000   Phone: (506)458-4444
Fredericton, NB, Canada E3B 4X1   Julie A. Robinson, Libn.
Founded: 1965. **Staff:** 1. **Subjects:** Engineering, accounting, management,
psychology, law, economics, energy. **Holdings:** 6400 books; 70 bound
periodical volumes. **Subscriptions:** 447 journals and other serials; 43
newspapers. **Services:** Interlibrary loan; center open to the public. **Also
Known As:** Commission d'Energie Electrique du Nouveau Brunswick.

★ 11449 ★
New Brunswick Legislative Assembly - Legislative Library (Law, Soc
  Sci)
Legislative Bldg.
P.O. Box 6000   Phone: (506)453-2338
Fredericton, NB, Canada E3B 5H1   Eric L. Swanick, Leg.Libn.
Founded: 1841. **Staff:** Prof 10; Other 4. **Subjects:** Political science,
economics, history, social affairs, management. **Special Collections:** New
Brunswickana. **Holdings:** 32,000 volumes; government documents.
Subscriptions: 500 journals and other serials. **Services:** Interlibrary loan;
copying; library open to the public. **Computerized Information Services:**
DIALOG Information Services, QL Systems, Info Globe, DOBIS Canadian
Online Library System, CAN/OLE, Infomart Online, The Financial Post
DataGroup; Envoy 100 (electronic mail service). Performs searches on fee
basis. Contact Person: Margaret Pacey, Ref.Libn. **Publications:** New
Brunswick Government Documents, a checklist, quarterly and annual - free
upon request; Selected Accessions List, 6/year. **Remarks:** FAX: (506)453-
7154. Electronic mail address(es): ILL.NBFL (Envoy 100). **Staff:** Jean-
Claude Arcand, Cat.; Janet McNeil, Govt.Pubns.Libn.

★ 11450 ★
New Brunswick Library Service (Info Sci)
P.O. Box 6000   Phone: (506)453-2354
Fredericton, NB, Canada E3B 5H1   Jocelyne LeBel, Dir.
Staff: Prof 6; Other 8. **Subjects:** Library science. **Holdings:** 1494 monograph
titles. **Subscriptions:** 96 journals and other serials. **Services:** Interlibrary
loan; service not open to the public. **Automated Operations:** Computerized
cataloging (INLEX). **Computerized Information Services:** Envoy 100
(electronic mail service). **Publications:** Liaison: News of the New Brunswick
Public Library System, 3/year; Regional and Public Libraries Statistics,
annual. **Special Catalogs:** Union catalog of public library holdings in the
province. **Remarks:** FAX: (506)453-2416. Electronic mail address(es):
ILL.NBFC JL.NBLS (Envoy 100). Acts as a central cataloging office and
clearinghouse for New Brunswick public libraries. Maintained by New
Brunswick Department of Municipalities, Culture and Housing. **Staff:**
Jocelyne Thompson, Asst.Dir.; Joyce Waterhouse, Hd., Tech.Serv.; Eunice
Stringer, Libn.; Lucie Laperriere, Libn.

★ 11451 ★
New Brunswick Museum - Library and Archives Department (Art, Hist)
277 Douglas Ave.   Phone: (506)693-1196
Saint John, NB, Canada E2K 1E5   Carol Rosevear, Hd.Libn.
Founded: 1842. **Staff:** Prof 2; Other 2. **Subjects:** Fine arts, New Brunswick
history, shipping, natural science. **Special Collections:** Ganong Library
(1000 volumes); Webster Canadiana Collection (10,000 volumes). **Holdings:**
55,000 volumes; 200 linear meters of manuscripts; 3000 maps; 200 reels of
microfilm. **Subscriptions:** 200 journals and other serials. **Services:**
Interlibrary loan (limited); copying; department open to the public on a
limited schedule.

★ 11452 ★
New Brunswick Office of the Ombudsman - Library (Soc Sci)
P.O. Box 6000   Phone: (506)453-2789
Fredericton, NB, Canada E3B 5H1   M. St-Pierre, Asst. to Ombudsman
Founded: 1967. **Staff:** Prof 1. **Subjects:** Ombudsmanship. **Holdings:** Figures
not available. **Subscriptions:** Library not open to the public. **Services:**
Library open to the public for reference use only.

★ 11453 ★
(New Brunswick) Provincial Archives of New Brunswick (Hist)
P.O. Box 6000   Phone: (506)453-3288
Fredericton, NB, Canada E3B 5H1   Marion Beyea, Prov.Archv.
Founded: 1968. **Staff:** Prof 13; Other 16. **Subjects:** Government, industry,
business, judiciary, genealogy, local history. **Holdings:** 25,000 cubic feet of
government records and private manuscripts in the Historical Division;
50,000 cubic feet of government records in the Records Center; 175,000
photographs; 60,000 maps; 140,000 plans and architectural drawings; audio
recordings. **Services:** Interlibrary loan (microforms); copying; archives open
to the public. **Remarks:** FAX: (506)453-3288. **Staff:** Burton Glendenning,
Mgr., Admin.; Thomas Parker, Rec.Mgr.; Dale Cogswell, Mgr., Govt.Rec.;
Fred Farrell, Mgr., Mss. and AV; Allen Doiron, Mgr., Cart. and Pub.Serv.;
Harold Holland, Mgr., Consrv.Div.

★ 11454 ★
(New Brunswick) Research and Productivity Council - Information
   Centre (Bus-Fin, Sci-Engr)
921 College Hill Rd.   Phone: (506)452-1381
Fredericton, NB, Canada E3B 6Z9   Virginia Jackson, Coord.
Founded: 1965. **Staff:** 2. **Subjects:** Geology and mineralogy, food science,
mechanical   engineering,   computer-aided   design/computer-aided
manufacture, analytical chemistry, entomology, metallurgy, nondestructive
testing, aquaculture, electronic engineering. **Holdings:** 12,500 books; 200
bound periodical volumes; 500 journal titles with back issues. **Subscriptions:**
200 journals and other serials. **Services:** Interlibrary loan; copying; library
open to the public with restrictions. **Automated Operations:** Computerized
cataloging. **Computerized Information Services:** DIALOG Information
Services, CAN/OLE, Infomart Online, Info Globe; internal database;
Envoy 100 (electronic mail service). Performs searches on fee basis.
Publications: Alert, quarterly - free to mailing list. **Special Catalogs:** Library
Serials Holdings (book). **Remarks:** FAX: (506)452-1395. Electronic mail
address(es): NBFRP.ILL (Envoy 100).

★ 11455 ★
New Brunswick Theological Seminary - Gardner A. Sage Library (Rel-
   Phil)
21 Seminary Pl.   Phone: (908)247-5243
New Brunswick, NJ 08901-1159   Rev. Renee S. House, Libn.
Founded: 1784. **Staff:** Prof 2; Other 2. **Subjects:** Theology, church history,
Biblical studies, classics. **Special Collections:** Dutch Church Collection;
archives of Reformed Church in America; Leiby Collection. **Holdings:**
142,580 books; 10,738 bound periodical volumes. **Subscriptions:** 300
journals and other serials. **Services:** Interlibrary loan; copying; library open
to the public with identification. **Automated Operations:** Computerized
circulation and acquisitions. **Computerized Information Services:** RLIN.
Remarks: FAX: (908)249-5412. **Staff:** Carol Kinsey, Circ.; Marilyn Strauss,
Accessions/Per.; Lynn Berg, Tech.Serv.

★ 11456 ★
New Canaan Historical Society - Library (Hist)
13 Oenoke Ridge   Phone: (203)966-1776
New Canaan, CT 06840   Marilyn O'Rourke, Libn.
Founded: 1889. **Staff:** Prof 1. **Subjects:** Genealogy; history - local, state, New
England. **Special Collections:** Noyes Family Papers, 1750-1900 (10,000
cataloged items); Silliman Family Papers, 1792-1972 (750 cataloged items);
Hoyt Nursery Papers, 1823-1971; Stephen B. Hoyt, Jr. Family Papers, 1877-
1961; Paul W. Prindle Collection of Weed Genealogical Papers. **Holdings:**
4000 books; 300 bound periodical volumes; local newspapers, 1868 to
present, on microfilm; 4000 biography cards; 852 manuscripts.
Subscriptions: 31 journals and other serials. **Services:** Copying; library open
to the public. **Networks/Consortia:** Member of Southwestern Connecticut
Library Council (SWLC). **Publications:** Annuals, 1943 to present; Philip
Johnson in New Canaan: the Glass House and John Rogers and the Rogers
Groups; Portrait of New Canaan, the History of a Connecticut Town; A
New Canaan Private in the Civil War; The Merrit Parkway, annual. **Special
Indexes:** Subject index to local newspapers (card); file of names of New
Canaan early settlers and later residents (card); updated house list.

New Castle Business School
See: **Erie Business Center South** (5414)

★ 11457 ★
New Castle County Law Library (Law)
Public Bldg./Courthouse   Phone: (302)577-2437
Wilmington, DE 19801   Rene Yucht, Hd.Libn.
Founded: 1911. **Staff:** Prof 1; Other 1. **Subjects:** Law. **Holdings:** 30,000
volumes. **Subscriptions:** 35 journals and other serials. **Services:** Copying;
library open to the public. **Computerized Information Services:** LEXIS,
WESTLAW; internal databases.

★ 11458 ★
New Castle Public Library - Pennsylvania History Room (Hist)
207 E. North St.   Phone: (412)658-6659
New Castle, PA 16101   John Walter, Dir.
Staff: 12. **Subjects:** Pennsylvania history and genealogy. **Special Collections:**
Pennsylvania census, 1790-1910 (microfilm). **Holdings:** 6763 volumes.
Subscriptions: 200 journals and other serials; 6 newspapers. **Services:**
Interlibrary loan; copying; room open to the public with identification.
Automated   Operations: Computerized   cataloging.   **Computerized
Information Services:** OCLC. **Networks/Consortia:** Member of Pittsburgh
Regional Library Center (PRLC). **Remarks:** FAX: (412)658-9012.

★ 11459 ★
New Castle State Developmental Center - Library (Med)
100 Van Nuys Rd.
New Castle, IN 47362   Phone: (317)529-0900
Staff: 1. **Subjects:** Psychiatry, neurology, general medicine, physiology,
nursing. **Holdings:** 600 books. **Subscriptions:** 25 journals and other serials.
Services: Library open to the public for reference use only.

New Church Theological School
See: **Swedenborg School of Religion** (15915)

★ 11460 ★
New College of California - New College Library (Hum, Soc Sci)
50 Fell St.   Phone: (415)626-1694
San Francisco, CA 94102-5298   Janet Talleman, Dir.
Founded: 1973. **Staff:** Prof 2; Other 3. **Subjects:** Law, alternative humanities, psychology, poetics, women's studies, homosexuality/lesbianism, minorities, Third World. **Special Collections:** Modern American poetry. **Holdings:** 30,000 books; unbound periodicals. **Subscriptions:** 100 journals and other serials. **Services:** Interlibrary loan; library not open to the public. **Automated Operations:** Computerized cataloging, serials, and circulation. **Computerized Information Services:** DIALOG Information Services, WESTLAW, OCLC; internal database. Performs searches on fee basis. Contact Person: Dale Soules, Ref./Comp. **Staff:** David Smith, Law Libn.; Lucia Tanyag, Assoc. Law Libn.; Michael Yockey, Hd., Tech.Serv.; Everett Moore, Circ.; Dale Soules, Hum.Ref.

★ 11461 ★
New Community College of Baltimore - Libraries/Media Services (Hist)
Bard Library
2901 Liberty Heights Ave.   Phone: (301)396-0432
Baltimore, MD 21215   Bruce Carroll
Founded: 1947. **Staff:** Prof 4; Other 6. **Subjects:** Black history, health science, Baltimore and Maryland history, technology. **Special Collections:** Baltimore is Best Collection. **Holdings:** 85,483 books; 125,000 pamphlets (uncataloged); 12,500 reels of microfilm; 20,000 nonprint materials. **Subscriptions:** 436 journals and other serials. **Services:** Interlibrary loan; copying; library open to the public for reference use only. **Automated Operations:** Computerized acquisitions, circulation, and shelflist files. **Computerized Information Services:** WILSONLINE; CD-ROM (Academic Index, General Periodicals Ondisc); Microcat (internal database). **Remarks:** Includes holdings of Business and Continuing Education Center Library located at Lombard at Market Place, Baltimore, MD 21202; phone: 396-1860. **Formerly:** Community College of Baltimore. **Staff:** Phil Hurd, Hd. of Media Serv.; Stephanie Reidy, Coll.Dev.Libn.; Virgie Williams, Hd. of Circ.; Maria Rodriguez, Pub.Serv./Libn.; Sukuntulla Dhanesar, Per.Libn.

★ 11462 ★
(New Delhi) American Center - USIS Library (Area-Ethnic)
24, Kasturba Gandhi Marg   Phone: 11 3314251
New Delhi 110 001, Delhi, India   Ms. Heera Kapasi, Lib.Dir.
Founded: 1946. **Staff:** 15. **Subjects:** International relations, political science, economics, literatue, arts. **Special Collections:** U.S. Federal Statutes, 1789 to present; U.S. Foreign Relations Documents, 1933 to present. **Holdings:** 27,000 books; 1000 bound periodical volumes; 398 microfiche. **Subscriptions:** 5 newspapers. **Services:** Interlibrary loan; copying; SDI; library open to the public. **Computerized Information Services:** Internal databases. **Publications:** Article Alert; Recent Additions to American Center Library; Subject bibliographies. **Remarks:** FAX: 11 3329499. Telex: 031-65269 USEM IN. Maintained or supported by the U.S. Information Agency. Focus is on materials that will assist peoples outside the United States to learn about the United States, its people, history, culture, political processes, and social milieux. **Staff:** Mr. Kunwar Prem; Mrs. Saroj Bhatia; Mrs. Veena Chawla; Mr. Madan Mohan Janveja; Mrs. Ranjana Bhatnagar; Mrs. Anjali Gupta; Ms. Naintara Kumar; Mrs. Dipika Naik; Ms. Girija Tickoo; Mr. Udai Singh Rawat; Mrs. Shashi Sareen; Mr. Kripa Shankar Sharma; Mrs. Chetna Khera.

★ 11463 ★
The New England - Corporate Library (Bus-Fin)
501 Boylston St.   Phone: (617)578-2307
Boston, MA 02117   Adrienne Korman, Dir.
Founded: 1935. **Staff:** Prof 4; Other 4. **Subjects:** Life insurance, employee benefit plans, pensions, financial products, business and finance. **Special Collections:** The New England Archives. **Holdings:** 18,000 volumes; 36 VF drawers of pamphlets and reports. **Subscriptions:** 500 journals and other serials; 6 newspapers. **Services:** Interlibrary loan; SDI; library open to the public for reference use only. **Automated Operations:** Computerized cataloging, acquisitions, serials, and circulation. **Computerized Information Services:** DIALOG Information Services, NEXIS, PFDS Online, BRS Information Technologies, VU/TEXT Information Services, Dow Jones News/Retrieval. **Publications:** Selected Readings, biweekly - for internal distribution only; Monitor: a competitive newsletter, monthly. **Special Catalogs:** Data from Selected Readings. **Remarks:** FAX: (617)536-7083. **Staff:** George Hart, Info.Cons.; Pamela Shrago, Info.Cons.; Phyllis Steele, Archv.

New England Air Museum Reference Library
See: **Connecticut Aeronautical Historical Association** (4175)

★ 11464 ★
New England Aquarium - Library (Biol Sci)
Central Wharf   Phone: (617)973-5237
Boston, MA 02110-3309   Dot Wensink, Libn.
Founded: 1982. **Staff:** Prof 1. **Subjects:** Ichthyology, marine mammalogy, invertebrate zoology, oceanography, coastal and environmental studies, ecology, conservation. **Holdings:** 4000 books; 360 subject heading files. **Subscriptions:** 55 periodicals; 190 newsletters. **Services:** Interlibrary loan; library open to the public by appointment only. **Automated Operations:** Computerized acquisitions. **Computerized Information Services:** Internal database. **Publications:** Aquasphere, quarterly; Aqualog (newsletter) - both to members; Aqualines (newsletter) - for internal distribution only. **Remarks:** FAX: (617)720-5098; (617)723-6207.

★ 11465 ★
New England Baptist Hospital - Health Sciences Library (Med)
125 Parker Hill Ave.   Phone: (617)738-5830
Boston, MA 02120   Paul Esty Woodard, Ph.D., Chf.Med.Libn.
Founded: 1963. **Staff:** Prof 2; Other 4. **Subjects:** Medicine, orthopedics, history of medicine, nursing, history of nursing. **Special Collections:** M.N. Smith-Peterson Collection (48 volumes on orthopedics and the history of medicine). **Holdings:** 6717 books; 3500 bound periodical volumes. **Subscriptions:** 153 journals and other serials. **Services:** Interlibrary loan; library open to physicians, nurses, and scholars only. **Computerized Information Services:** NLM; internal database. **Networks/Consortia:** Member of Boston Biomedical Library Consortium, National Network of Libraries of Medicine - New England Region, Libraries and Information for Nursing Consortium (LINC), Massachusetts Health Sciences Libraries Network (MaHSLiN). **Remarks:** FAX: (617)731-5742. **Staff:** Sharon S. Regen, Libn.

★ 11466 ★
New England Board of Higher Education - Library (Educ)
45 Temple Pl.   Phone: (617)357-9620
Boston, MA 02111   Sue Klemer, Res.Assoc.
Staff: Prof 3. **Subjects:** New England - higher education, economy, and business development, research and development, education/training, higher education and international economic competitiveness, minority issues in higher education. **Holdings:** 500 volumes. **Subscriptions:** 70 journals and other serials. **Services:** Library open to the public with restrictions. **Staff:** Judith Beachler, Dir., Res.

New England Brick Company Archives
See: **Cambridge Historical Society - Library** (2601)

★ 11467 ★
New England Coalition on Nuclear Pollution - Library (Env-Cons)
P.O. Box 545
Brattleboro, VT 05302   Phone: (802)257-0336
Founded: 1971. **Staff:** 1. **Subjects:** Nuclear power, nuclear war, radiation, alternate energy, energy conservation, radiation health. **Holdings:** 1000 books; 1000 reprints, unbound periodicals, and manuscripts; government documents; alternate press publications. **Subscriptions:** 50 journals and other serials. **Services:** Interlibrary loan; copying (both limited); library open to the public. **Publications:** On the Watch (newsletter), irregular.

★ 11468 ★
New England College of Optometry - Library (Med)
420 Beacon St.   Phone: (617)236-6263
Boston, MA 02115   Lynne A. Silvers, Lib.Dir.
Founded: 1894. **Staff:** Prof 3; Other 5. **Subjects:** Optometry, ophthalmology. **Holdings:** 10,000 books; 2800 bound periodical volumes; 4 VF drawers of pamphlets; 8 VF drawers of reprints; 500 35mm color slides; 450 audiotape cassettes; 97 video cassettes; 82 slide/tape sets; 18 slide sets; 15 realia. **Subscriptions:** 275 journals and other serials. **Services:** Interlibrary loan; copying; SDI; library open to the public for reference use only. **Automated Operations:** Computerized cataloging. **Computerized Information Services:** BRS Information Technologies, LION, DIALOG Information Services; MEDLINK, DOCLINE (electronic mail services). Performs searches on fee basis. **Networks/Consortia:** Member of Association of Visual Science Librarians (AVSL). **Publications:** Acquisitions List, irregular - for internal distribution and other optometry libraries. **Remarks:** FAX: (617)424-9202.

★ 11469 ★
New England Conservatory of Music - Harriet M. Spaulding Library
(Mus)
33 Gainsborough St.   Phone: (617)262-1120
Boston, MA 02115   Jean A. Morrow, Dir. of Libs.
Founded: 1959. **Staff:** Prof 4; Other 4. **Subjects:** Music and music literature, acoustics, humanities, social sciences. **Special Collections:** Americana (music, manuscripts, Boston Classicists, letters, memorabilia, 18th century psalmody); Preston Collection of letters of great musicians; Elise Hall Collection of French music manuscripts; A.G. Morse Collection of opera piano scores; Voice of Firestone kinescopes and performance materials. **Holdings:** 70,000 books and scores; 20,000 sound recordings; 150 video recordings; 240 theses; 200 reels of microfilm; publications and documents on Boston musical life and history of the conservatory. **Subscriptions:** 250 journals and other serials. **Services:** Interlibrary loan; copying; library open to the public for reference use. **Automated Operations:** Computerized public access catalog, circulation, and cataloging. **Computerized Information Services:** Fenway Libraries Online (internal database). **Networks/Consortia:** Member of Fenway Library Consortium (FLC), Boston Area Music Libraries (BAML), NELINET, Inc. **Publications:** Recently Cataloged, quarterly. **Remarks:** FAX: (617)262-0500. Also maintains the Idabelle Firestone Audio Library, 290 Huntington Ave., Boston, MA 02115. **Staff:** Patrick Maxfield, Libn.; Richard Vallone, Pub.Serv.Libn.; Kenneth Pristash, Audio Libn.; Paul Beaudoin, Acq.; Victoria Nelson, Asst.Aud.Libn.; Craig Thomas, Asst. to Cat.; Thomas Cox, Bindery Supv.

★ 11470 ★
New England Deaconess Hospital - Horrax Library (Med)
185 Pilgrim Rd.   Phone: (617)732-8311
Boston, MA 02215   Paul Vaiginas, Libn.
Founded: 1959. **Staff:** Prof 1; Other 3. **Subjects:** General medicine, diabetes, cancer, renal disease, cardiology, surgery. **Special Collections:** Horrax Collection on Neurosurgery (212 books). **Holdings:** 3300 books; 3500 bound periodical volumes; 850 audio cassettes. **Subscriptions:** 252 journals and other serials. **Services:** Interlibrary loan; library open to the public with permission. **Networks/Consortia:** Member of Boston Biomedical Library Consortium.

★ 11471 ★
New England Deposit Library (Info Sci)
135 Western Ave.   Phone: (617)782-8441
Allston, MA 02134   Morris I. Hyman, Mgr.
Founded: 1942. **Staff:** Prof 1; Other 1. **Holdings:** Figures not available. **Services:** Library open to the public with permission. **Remarks:** This is a depository for research and reference materials from 7 contributing libraries in the greater Boston area.

★ 11472 ★
New England Fire & History Museum - Library and Archives (Hist)
1439 Main St., Rte. 6A   Phone: (508)896-5711
Brewster, MA 02631   Eugene I. Morris, Dir. of Musm.
Founded: 1972. **Staff:** 1. **Subjects:** Fire history and engineering, apothecary history, blacksmithing, historical events, Civil War. **Special Collections:** Principles of Fire Rating & Analysis of Risks (25 volumes); Charles Dominge Insurance Rating Series (1st edition); Antique Blacksmithing Collection; rare fire histories. **Holdings:** 646 books; 200 bound periodical volumes; 300 booklets. **Services:** Interlibrary loan; library open to the public by appointment. **Publications:** Siren Soundings - to members and interested individuals. **Staff:** Barbara Burger.

★ 11473 ★
New England Governors' Conference, Inc. - Reference Library (Energy, Bus-Fin)
76 Summer St.   Phone: (617)423-6900
Boston, MA 02110   Fran Larson, Exec.Sec.
Staff: Prof 1; Other 2. **Subjects:** Energy, transportation, economic development, hazardous waste, tourism. **Special Collections:** New England Regional Commission reports (2000); New England River Basins Commission reports (complete set); Canadian Affairs. **Holdings:** 10,000 volumes; 100 bound periodical volumes. **Subscriptions:** 28 journals and other serials. **Services:** Interlibrary loan; copying; library open to the public for reference use only.

★ 11474 ★
New England Historic Genealogical Society - Library (Hist)
99-101 Newbury St.
Boston, MA 02116   Phone: (617)536-5740
Founded: 1845. **Staff:** Prof 4; Other 28. **Subjects:** Genealogy and family history, local history, vital records, heraldry. **Special Collections:** New England family and local histories; Eastern Canadian family and local histories; genealogical research materials. **Holdings:** 125,000 volumes; 7000 reels of microfilm; 3500 linear feet of manuscripts; city directories; vital records; diaries; regimental histories; church histories. **Subscriptions:** 420 periodicals. **Services:** Copying; research; lectures and seminars; library open to the public on a fee basis. **Automated Operations:** Computerized cataloging and serials. **Computerized Information Services:** OCLC, Sydney Library Systems, MARCIVE. **Publications:** New England Historical and Genealogical Register, quarterly; Nexus (newsletter), 5/year; monographs. **Remarks:** FAX: (617)536-7307. **Staff:** Alexander Kamphuis, Dir., User Serv.; George F. Sanborn, Jr., Dir., Tech.Serv.; Marie E. Daly, Bus.Mgr.; Gary B. Roberts, Dir. of Pubns.; Nathaniel S. Shipton, Archv.; Marilyn Burke, Tech.Serv.Libn.; Scott A. Bartley, Cur., Mss.

★ 11475 ★
New England Medical Center - Elizabeth S. Makkay Library (Med)
750 Washington St.
Box 395   Phone: (617)956-5497
Boston, MA 02111   Nancy B. Duggan, Libn.
Founded: 1979. **Staff:** Prof 1. **Subjects:** Psychiatry, psychology, social work. **Holdings:** 1500 books; 500 bound periodical volumes; 100 AV programs; 1000 reprints. **Subscriptions:** 38 journals and other serials. **Services:** Interlibrary loan; copying; library open to those affiliated with the Department of Psychiatry. **Computerized Information Services:** NLM, MEDLINE.

New England Mutual Life Insurance Company
See: **The New England (11463)**

★ 11476 ★
New England Power Company - Technical Information Center (Energy)
25 Research Dr.   Phone: (508)366-9011
Westborough, MA 01582   Rita M. Jones
Founded: 1947. **Staff:** Prof 1. **Subjects:** Engineering, environmental sciences, alternative energy sources, management, economics. **Special Collections:** Alternative energy forms (biomass, hydro, solar, wind). **Holdings:** 3400 books; 125,000 microfiche. **Subscriptions:** 280 journals and other serials. **Services:** Interlibrary loan; copying (limited); SDI; center open to the public by appointment. **Automated Operations:** Computerized cataloging, serials, and circulation. **Computerized Information Services:** DIALOG Information Services, PFDS Online. **Special Indexes:** KWIC index to all cataloged items (card).

New England Regional Primate Research Center
See: **Harvard University - New England Regional Primate Research Center (6985)**

New England Round Table of Children's Librarians Archives
See: **Boston Public Library (1991)**

★ 11477 ★
New England School of Law - Library (Law)
154 Stuart St.   Phone: (617)422-7288
Boston, MA 02116   Frank S.H. Bae, Dir.
Founded: 1908. **Staff:** Prof 7; Other 9. **Subjects:** Law. **Special Collections:** U.S. and Massachusetts legal materials, 17th century to present. **Holdings:** 224,250 volumes. **Subscriptions:** 2870 journals and other serials. **Services:** Library open to qualified persons on request for reference use. **Automated Operations:** Computerized cataloging. **Computerized Information Services:** WESTLAW, LEXIS, NEXIS, Dow Jones News/Retrieval, DIALOG Information Services, VU/TEXT Information Services, OCLC, RLIN, USC Current, EPIC, State Net, QUIC/LAW. **Networks/Consortia:** Member of New England Law Library Consortium (NELLCO), NELINET, Inc. **Publications:** New England School of Law Library Guide; list of recent acquisitions. **Remarks:** FAX: (617)422-7303. **Staff:** Anne Acton, Asst.Libn.; Susan Tatelman, Rd.Serv.; Barry Stearns, Sr.Ref.Libn.; Kyle Kelly, Tech.Serv.Libn.; Wendy Cohen, Govt.Doc.Libn.; Sandra Lamar, Ref.Libn.

★ 11478 ★
New England Telephone Learning Center - Resource Center (Bus-Fin)
280 Locke Dr.   Phone: (508)460-4695
Marlborough, MA 01752   Robert Johnson, Supv.
Founded: 1973. **Staff:** Prof 1; Other 1. **Subjects:** Training for management, instructional systems and techniques, management. **Holdings:** 4000 books; 15,000 microfiche; company documents; 6 VF drawers of pamphlets; 400 videotapes and films; 200 audiotapes. **Subscriptions:** 100 journals and other serials; 8 newspapers. **Services:** Interlibrary loan; copying; SDI; center open to the public by appointment. **Computerized Information Services:** DIALOG Information Services. **Publications:** Bibliography series; News Notes; Course Lists - all for internal distribution, NYNEX corporate offices, and New York Telephone facilities.

★ 11479 ★
New England Wholesalers Assn. - Lending Library (Sci-Engr)
262 Main St.
Box 638   Phone: (508)478-8621
Milford, MA 01757-0638   Maurice A. Desmarais, Exec. V.P.
Founded: 1985. **Subjects:** Plumbing, heating, air conditioning, industrial pipe, wholesale distribution. **Holdings:** 300 surveys and reports, training manuals, management and sales texts. **Subscriptions:** 5 journals and other serials. **Services:** Library open to the public with restrictions (deposit required). **Remarks:** FAX: (508)473-0302.

★ 11480 ★
New England Wild Flower Society, Inc. - Lawrence Newcomb Library
  (Biol Sci)
Hemenway Rd.
Framingham, MA 01701   Phone: (508)877-7630
Founded: 1969. **Staff:** Prof 2. **Subjects:** Native plants, botany, natural history, wild flower gardening. **Special Collections:** Publications of Native Plant Societies and Botanical Clubs; state, regional and some foreign wild flower guides and technical floras. **Holdings:** 3000 books; pamphlets; 16 VF drawers; 20,000 slides in Wild Flower Slide Collection. **Subscriptions:** 10 journals and other serials. **Services:** Interlibrary loan; copying; SDI; slide set loans and sales; reference questions accepted; library open to the public for reference use only with borrowing privileges for members. **Computerized Information Services:** Internal database. **Publications:** A Comprehensive Bibliography of Publications About Gardening With Native Plants; Botanical Clubs and Native Plant Societies of the U.S.; "Readsources" book reviews. **Remarks:** FAX: (508)877-3658. Alternate telephone number(s): (617)237-4924. **Staff:** Mary M. Walker, Libn.; John Benson, Libn.; Jean Baxter, Slide Libn.

★ 11481 ★
New England Wireless & Steam Museum, Inc. - Library (Sci-Engr)
697 Tillinghast Rd.   Phone: (401)884-1710
East Greenwich, RI 02818   Robert W. Merriam, Dir.
Founded: 1964. **Staff:** 1. **Subjects:** Wireless, telegraph, early electricity, telephone, steam engineering, gas/hot air engines. **Special Collections:** Lloyd Espenshied Collection of textbooks (wireless and telegraph); Thorn Mayes and Edward Raser Collections of textbooks (wireless and telegraph). **Holdings:** Figures not available. **Services:** Library not open to the public. **Publications:** 1876-1976 Corliss Centennial folder; Wireless Communication in the U.S., the Early Operating Companies.

★ 11482 ★
New Hampshire Antiquarian Society - Museum and Library (Hist)
R.R. 5, Box 251 Main St.   Phone: (603)746-3825
Hopkinton, NH 03229   Kathleen Belko, Exec.Dir.
Founded: 1875. **Staff:** 2. **Subjects:** New Hampshire, especially Hopkinton and adjacent towns. **Special Collections:** Music books, 1722-1860; complete file of Hopkinton town reports; New Hampshire registers and almanacs; file of Hopkinton vital records, 1737 to present (6000 cards); early schools and textbooks; Indian artifacts; early clocks; old and family Bibles; early New Hampshire pottery jugs; folk art portraits. **Holdings:** 1400 volumes; deeds; military records; town warrants; early sermons and newspapers; revolutionary diaries; manuscripts. **Services:** Library open to the public on a limited schedule or by appointment. **Publications:** "A Walk Through Two Villages", book of photographs, 1990. **Staff:** Mildred T. Rice; Priscilla Bohanan.

★ 11483 ★
New Hampshire College - Shapiro Library (Bus-Fin)
2500 N. River Rd.   Phone: (603)668-2211
Manchester, NH 03106-1394   Richard Pantano, Lib.Dir.
Founded: 1963. **Staff:** Prof 7; Other 7. **Subjects:** Economics, accounting, computer sciences, business management, finance, taxes, marketing and retailing, hotel/resort/tourism, community economic development, mathematics, fashion merchandising. **Special Collections:** Business Teacher Education (800 items); New Hampshiriana (100 volumes); federal and state documents depository (40,161 items); New Hampshire Business Education Association Archives; New England Business Education Association Archives. **Holdings:** 78,269 books; 590 bound periodical volumes; 1349 sound recordings; 1320 art slides; 6869 reels of microfilm; 6 VF drawers of archival materials; 143,764 microfiche; 637 videotapes and films. **Subscriptions:** 921 journals and other serials; 28 newspapers. **Services:** Interlibrary loan; copying; library open to the public. **Computerized Information Services:** DIALOG Information Services, VU/TEXT Information Services. **Networks/Consortia:** Member of New Hampshire College & University Council Library Policy Committee (NHCUC). **Publications:** Acquisitions list - for internal distribution and consortium use standing order list; Periodical List; Periodical Subject List - for internal distribution only. **Remarks:** FAX:: (603)645-9685. **Staff:** Patricia A. Beaton, Ref./Govt.Doc.; Carol West, Ref./Per.; Deborah Wilcox, Tech.Serv.Libn.; David Dillman, AV Dir.; Edward Daniels, Ref./Circ.Libn.

New Hampshire Governor's Energy Office - Energy Information Center
See: **New Hampshire Governor's Office of Energy and Community Services** (11484)

★ 11484 ★
New Hampshire Governor's Office of Energy and Community Services -
  Library (Energy)
57 Regional Dr.
Concord, NH 03301-8519   Phone: (603)271-2611
Founded: 1973. **Staff:** 23. **Subjects:** Energy - data, policy, conservation. **Special Collections:** Solar energy information. **Holdings:** Binders; reports; manuscripts. **Subscriptions:** 25 journals and other serials. **Services:** Center open to the public by appointment. **Publications:** List of publications - available on request. **Remarks:** FAX: (603)271-2615. Toll-free telephone number(s): (800)735-2964. **Formerly:** New Hampshire Governor's Energy Office - Energy Information Center.

★ 11485 ★
New Hampshire Historical Society - Library (Hist)
30 Park St.   Phone: (603)225-3381
Concord, NH 03301   William Copeley, Libn.
Founded: 1823. **Staff:** Prof 3. **Subjects:** New Hampshire history, New England history and genealogy, architecture and decorative arts of New England. **Special Collections:** Eighteenth and nineteenth century account books and diaries; papers of Daniel Webster, Franklin Pierce, General John Sullivan, William E. Chandler, Josiah Bartlett; New Hampshire maps. **Holdings:** 50,000 volumes; 2000 volumes of early New Hampshire newspapers; 40,000 photographs of New Hampshire towns and people. **Subscriptions:** 150 journals and other serials. **Services:** Interlibrary loan (limited); copying; library open to the public on a fee basis. **Computerized Information Services:** OCLC. **Publications:** Historical New Hampshire, quarterly; Newsletter, quarterly. **Special Catalogs:** Manuscript catalog. **Special Indexes:** Genealogy index; New Hampshire Notables index (card). **Remarks:** FAX: (603)224-0463. **Staff:** Debbie Tapley, Asst.Libn.; Betsy Hamlin-Morin, Mss.Libn.

★ 11486 ★
New Hampshire Hospital - Professional Library (Med)
105 Pleasant St.   Phone: (603)271-5422
Concord, NH 03301   Linda McCracken, Libn.
Founded: 1880. **Staff:** Prof 1; Other 1. **Subjects:** Psychiatry, psychology, geriatrics, nursing, neurology, social work. **Holdings:** 3500 books; 250 videotapes; 5 cassettes; 8 microfiche. **Subscriptions:** 131 journals and other serials. **Services:** Interlibrary loan; library open to the public. **Automated Operations:** Computerized public access catalog and ILL (DOCLINE). **Computerized Information Services:** DIALOG Information Services, MEDLINE. Performs searches on fee basis. **Networks/Consortia:** Member of National Network of Libraries of Medicine - New England Region, Merrimack Valley/Lakes Region Health Science Librarians, BHSL. **Remarks:** Alternate telephone number(s): (603)271-5422 (ILL).

New Hampshire Society of Genealogists - Rockingham County Chapter
  Library
See: Rockingham Society of Genealogists - Library (14006)

★ 11487 ★
New Hampshire (State) Department of Cultural Affairs - Law Library
  (Law)
Supreme Court Bldg.
Noble Dr.
Concord, NH 03301-6160   Phone: (603)271-3777
Staff: Prof 1; Other 1. Subjects: Law. Holdings: 90,000 volumes.
Subscriptions: 105 journals and other serials. Services: Interlibrary loan;
copying; library open to the public. Computerized Information Services:
WESTLAW. Performs searches on fee basis. Special Indexes: Index of
proposed state legislation (online). Remarks: FAX: (603)271-2168. Staff:
Norma Jane Lyman, Asst. Law Libn.

★ 11488 ★
New Hampshire (State) Department of Education - Computer &
  Statistical Services (Educ)
101 Pleasant St.   Phone: (603)271-2778
Concord, NH 03301   Sallie D. Fellows, Dir.
Staff: 4. Subjects: New Hampshire education and comparative education
statistics. Holdings: Federal and compiled state reports. Services: Copying;
services open to the public. Publications: Annual statistics of New
Hampshire Public Schools.

★ 11489 ★
New Hampshire (State) Department of State - Division of Records
  Management & Archives (Hist)
71 S. Fruit St.   Phone: (603)271-2236
Concord, NH 03301   Frank C. Mevers, State Archv.
Staff: Prof 2. Subjects: State and county archives. Services: Copying;
archives open to the public for reference use. Remarks: FAX: (603)271-
2272. Staff: Andrew S. Taylor, Rec.Mgr.

★ 11490 ★
New Hampshire (State) Department of Transportation - Library (Trans)
Morton State Office Bldg., Rm. 101
Hazen Dr.
Box 483   Phone: (603)271-2515
Concord, NH 03301-0483   Ted Dickerson, Fiscal and Policy Prog.
Founded: 1990. Staff: 1. Subjects: Civil engineering, highway research,
traffic engineering. Holdings: 5000 books; 2000 bound periodical volumes;
2000 reports; 100 manuscripts. Subscriptions: 25 journals and other serials;
2 newspapers. Services: Library open to the public.

★ 11491 ★
New Hampshire (State) Division of Forests and Lands - Fox Forest
  Library (Biol Sci)
Box 1175   Phone: (603)464-3453
Hillsboro, NH 03244-1175   J.B. Cullen, Chf., Forest Info. & Plan.
Founded: 1933. Staff: Prof 1. Subjects: Forestry, entomology, fire, ecology.
Special Collections: Herbarium. Holdings: Figures not available. Services:
Library not open to the public. Publications: Fox Forest Notes; Fox Forest
Bulletins, both occasional.

★ 11492 ★
New Hampshire State Library (Info Sci)
20 Park St.   Phone: (603)271-2393
Concord, NH 03301-6303   Kendall F. Wiggin, State Libn.
Founded: 1716. Staff: Prof 18; Other 41. Subjects: History, government
documents, political science, law. Special Collections: Children's Historical
Collection; New Hampshire history and genealogy. Holdings: 450,100
books; 16,011 manuscripts; 5271 scores; 12,500 reels of microfilm; 71,770
microcards; 114,000 microfiche; 653 motion pictures; 500 sound recordings.
Subscriptions: 850 journals and other serials; 44 newspapers. Services:
Interlibrary loan; copying; library open to the public. Automated
Operations: Computerized cataloging and serials. Computerized
Information Services: DIALOG Information Services, OCLC; internal
database. Networks/Consortia: Member of New Hampshire College &
University Council Library Policy Committee (NHCUC), NELINET, Inc.,
Capital Area Library Network (Calnet). Publications: Granite State
Libraries, bimonthly; Public Library Statistics, annual - both to library
community; Issues and Trends, monthly - to state legislature; Reference
Roundtable, quarterly. Remarks: FAX: (603)271-2205; 271-2397. Staff:
John McCormick, Supv., Ref/Info.Sect.; Charles LeBlanc, Supv., Network
Serv.Sect.; Judith Kimball, Supv., Dev.Serv.Sect.; Eileen Keim, Supv.,
Hndcp./Inst.Sect.; Eleanor O'Donnell, Supv., Tech.Serv.Sect.

★ 11493 ★
New Hampshire State Library - Children's Literature Special Collection
  (Hum)
20 Park St.   Phone: (603)271-2394
Concord, NH 03301   Kendall F. Wiggin
Founded: 1889. Subjects: Children's literature. Special Collections:
Children's Historical Collection (5000 books, 1850 to present). Services:
Library open to the public for reference use only. Remarks: FAX: (603)271-
2205.

★ 11494 ★
New Hampshire (State) Public Utilities Commission - Library (Energy)
8 Old Suncook Rd.   Phone: (603)271-2431
Concord, NH 03301   Debra Howland, Libn.
Founded: 1980. Staff: Prof 1. Subjects: Energy - policies, resources, research
and development. Special Collections: Electric Power Research Institute
Rate Design Study. Holdings: 1000 books; 350 bound periodical volumes;
300 Interstate Commerce Commission reports; U.S. Nuclear Regulatory
Commission releases and rulings; New Hampshire Supreme Court decisions.
Subscriptions: 30 journals and other serials; 7 newspapers. Services:
Interlibrary loan; copying; library open to the public with restrictions.

★ 11495 ★
New Hampshire Technical College - Learning Resources Center (Educ)
277R Portsmouth Ave.
Box 365   Phone: (603)772-1194
Stratham, NH 03885-0365   David B. Washburn, MLS, Dir., LRC
Founded: 1970. Staff: Prof 1; Other 1. Subjects: Nursing, allied health,
applied sciences. Holdings: 11,500 books; 14,000 microfiche. Subscriptions:
110 journals and other serials. Services: Interlibrary loan; copying; library
open to the public with restrictions. Networks/Consortia: Member of
Health Science Libraries of New Hampshire & Vermont (HSL-NH/VT).
Publications: Library Handbook, annual - to new students.

★ 11496 ★
New Hampshire Technical College - Library (Educ)
1 College Dr.   Phone: (603)542-7744
Claremont, NH 03743   Phil Prever, Libn.
Founded: 1968. Staff: Prof 1; Other 2. Subjects: Technology, basic health
sciences. Special Collections: New Hampshire history (146 volumes).
Holdings: 11,000 books; film loops; filmstrips; records; cassettes.
Subscriptions: 85 journals and other serials; 10 newspapers. Services:
Interlibrary loan; library open to the public with restrictions. Computerized
Information Services: CD-ROMs.

★ 11497 ★
New Hampshire Technical College - Library (Educ)
Prescott Hill   Phone: (603)524-3207
Laconia, NH 03246   Patty Miller, Libn.
Founded: 1968. Staff: Prof 1. Subjects: Industrial electricity, electrical
construction, automotive/marine technologies, administrative support/
information processing, fire protection, graphic arts, accounting, business
management, paralegal. Holdings: 9985 books; 256 cassettes; 154 filmstrips;
videotapes; 21 titles on microfiche; 152 reels of microfilm; 147 overhead
transparencies; 4120 slides. Subscriptions: 110 journals and other serials.
Services: Interlibrary loan; copying; library open to the public.
Computerized Information Services: CD-ROM. Remarks: FAX: (603)524-
8084.

★ 11498 ★
New Hampshire Technical College - Library (Educ)
505 Amherst St.
P.O. Box 2052   Phone: (603)882-6923
Nashua, NH 03061   William A. McIntyre, Ed.D., Dir. of Lrng.Rsrcs
Staff: Prof 2. Subjects: Business, electronics, machine tools, secretarial
studies, police science, automotive technology, aviation. Holdings: 12,000
books. Subscriptions: 125 journals and other serials. Services: Library open
to the public.

New Hampshire Water Resource Research Center
See: University of New Hampshire (19033)

★11499★
New Harmony Workingmen's Institute - Library and Museum (Soc Sci)
407 W. Tavern St.
Box 368   Phone: (812)682-4806
New Harmony, IN 47631   Ruth I. Roat, Dir.
Founded: 1838. **Staff:** 2. **Subjects:** Owen-Maclure Community, communal society, 19th century education, women's rights, music and drama, 19th century scientists. **Special Collections:** Manuscript Collection, 1814-1940. **Holdings:** 22,000 books. **Services:** Archives open to researchers with restrictions and by appointment.

★11500★
New Haven Colony Historical Society - Whitney Library (Hist)
114 Whitney Ave.   Phone: (203)562-4183
New Haven, CT 06510-1025 James W. Campbell, Libn. and Cur. of Mss.
Founded: 1862. **Staff:** Prof 4. **Subjects:** Local history and genealogy. **Special Collections:** Dana Scrapbooks of New Haven (150 volumes). **Holdings:** 30,000 volumes; 500 maps; 4800 architectural drawings; processed manuscript collection including New Haven County Superior Court documents, 1789-1905; New Haven Clock Company papers, 1853-1946; New Haven Water Company papers, 1820-1895; United Church papers, 1742-1970; Woman's Seamen's Friend Society of Connecticut records, 1859-1968; papers of the Ingersoll, Morris, and Twining families; New Haven city and county documents, 1648-1900; New Haven Board of Education records, 1799-1970; school records, 1715-1963; New Haven YWCA records, 1880 to present; Maritime Collection, 1721-1887; Harbor Collection, 1750-1925; Military Collection, 1737-1945; Civil War Collection, 1861-1931; family papers; corporate records; national and local historic figures A-Z, 1638-1976. **Subscriptions:** 61 journals and other serials. **Services:** Copying; library open to adults for research only (nonmembers on a fee basis). **Special Indexes:** Finding aids to manuscript collection and archives - for sale. **Staff:** Ruth Knowlton, Cat.; Carol McHugh-Grieger, Archv.; James English, Indexer.

New Holland Inc.
See: **Ford New Holland** (5967)

New Ideas - Interior Design Center Library
See: **Armstrong World Industries, Inc.** (1061)

New Jersey Alcohol/Drug Resource Center and Clearinghouse
See: **Rutgers University - Rutgers Center of Alcohol Studies - New Jersey Alcohol/Drug Resource Center and Clearinghouse** (14173)

★11501★
New Jersey Education Association - Research Library (Educ)
180 W. State St.
Box 1211   Phone: (609)599-4561
Trenton, NJ 08607   E. Lynne Van Buskirk, Assoc.Dir., Res.
Staff: Prof 1; Other 1. **Subjects:** New Jersey education including statistics and school law; school finance; teacher negotiations; collective bargaining. **Special Collections:** George H. Reavis Reading Area (complete set of Phi Delta Kappa materials). **Holdings:** 1000 books; 60 VF drawers of pamphlets; National Education Association publications; NJEA research bulletins and circulars; contracts from 512 New Jersey school districts. **Subscriptions:** 250 journals and other serials. **Services:** Interlibrary loan (limited); copying; library open to the public. **Special Indexes:** Index to the NJEA Review (book); Subject Index to New Jersey Commissioner of Education Decisions (loose-leaf notebook).

★11502★
New Jersey Geological Survey - Information Center (Sci-Engr)
CN-029
29 Arctic Pkwy.   Phone: (609)292-2576
Trenton, NJ 08625   Daniel R. Dombroski, Prin.Geol.
Founded: 1835. **Staff:** Prof 1. **Subjects:** Geology, topography, ground water, geodetic control, geophysics, mineral resources. **Holdings:** Geologic reports and open report files; survey publications, 1835 to present. **Services:** Copying; center open to the public by appointment.

★11503★
New Jersey Historical Society - Library (Hist)
230 Broadway   Phone: (201)483-3939
Newark, NJ 07104   Rosalind Libbey, Dir.
Founded: 1845. **Staff:** Prof 4; Other 1. **Subjects:** New Jersey history, genealogy of New Jersey and neighboring states. **Holdings:** 70,000 books; 3000 bound periodical volumes; 1600 manuscript groups; 400 newspaper titles; maps. **Subscriptions:** 150 journals and other serials. **Services:** Copying; library open to the public for reference use only. **Automated Operations:** Computerized cataloging. **Computerized Information Services:** OCLC. **Networks/Consortia:** Member of Essex Hudson Regional Library Cooperative. **Publications:** Guide to Manuscript Collections of the New Jersey Historical Society, 1979 (book). **Remarks:** FAX: (201)483-1988. **Staff:** Janet W. Koch, Cons.; Elsa Meyers, Cat.; Nancy Blankenhorn, Ref.; Jessica Peters, Geneal.Spec.

New Jersey Hospital Association at the Center for Health Affairs - Health Research and Educational Trust of New Jersey
See: **Health Research and Educational Trust of New Jersey** (7080)

★11504★
New Jersey Institute of Technology - Robert W. Van Houten Library (Sci-Engr)
323 Dr. Martin Luther King Blvd.   Phone: (201)596-3206
Newark, NJ 07102   Anne M. Buck, Univ.Libn.
Founded: 1881. **Staff:** Prof 8; Other 9. **Subjects:** Engineering, physical sciences, management, architecture. **Holdings:** 103,000 books; 42,700 bound periodical volumes; 3360 reels of microfilm. **Subscriptions:** 1701 journals and other serials. **Services:** Interlibrary loan; copying; library open to the public. **Automated Operations:** Computerized cataloging and circulation. **Computerized Information Services:** OCLC, DIALOG Information Services; CD-ROM. **Networks/Consortia:** Member of PALINET. **Publications:** List of periodicals, annual. **Special Catalogs:** Catalog of dissertations and theses. **Remarks:** An alternate telephone number is 596-3000. FAX: (201)643-5601. **Staff:** Ellen Callanan, Cat.Dept.Hd.; Betsy Reidinger, Per.Libn.; Golda Lask, Acq.Libn.; Doreen Mettle, Circ.Libn.; Christine Zembicki, Hd.Ref.Libn.; Steve Maricic, ILL Libn.

★11505★
New Jersey (State) - Roebling Building Library (Educ)
20 W. State St., CN 542
Trenton, NJ 08625   Phone: (609)984-1666
                                          Maxine Goldsmith, Adm.
Founded: 1988. **Staff:** Prof 1.5; Other 1. **Subjects:** Higher education, insurance, commerce, banking. **Special Collections:** Retrospective collection of New Jersey college catalogs; New Jersey State Data Center materials. **Holdings:** 200 books; 10,000 reports; 1000 archival items. **Subscriptions:** 150 journals and other serials; 8 newspapers. **Services:** Interlibrary loan; copying; library open to the public by appointment. **Computerized Information Services:** DIALOG Information Services, OCLC. Performs searches. **Publications:** Monthly checklist of publications. **Remarks:** FAX: (609)984-9300. **Staff:** Joan Gaylord.

★11506★
New Jersey (State) Board of Public Utilities - Library
2 Gateway Center, 9th Fl.
Newark, NJ 07102
Defunct.

New Jersey State Data Center - Cumberland County Department of Planning and Development
See: **Cumberland County Department of Planning and Development - Library** (4473)

★11507★
New Jersey (State) Department of Education - Division of Vocational Education - Northeast Curriculum Coordination Center (Educ)
Crest Way   Phone: (201)290-1900
Aberdeen, NJ 07747   Martha J. Pocsi, Ed.D., Dir.
Staff: Prof 2; Other 1. **Subjects:** Vocational, technical, career, and consumer/homemaker education; curriculum development. **Special Collections:** Vocational curriculum and assessment instruments;

educational microcomputer software; bilingual vocational curriculum, refugee materials, occupational task lists. **Holdings:** 20,000 books; 16 VF drawers; 4200 AV programs; 350,000 ERIC documents on microfiche, 1966 to present. **Services:** Interlibrary loan; copying; center open to the public. **Automated Operations:** Computerized cataloging. **Computerized Information Services:** BRS Information Technologies; Dialcom Inc. (electronic mail service). Performs searches. Contact Person: Catherine Liapes, Coord. **Publications:** Northeast Network Communique, 3/year. **Remarks:** Center is one of six vocational curriculum centers in the National Network for Curriculum Coordination in Vocational-Technical Education, and serves the northeast region of the United States (including Puerto Rico and the Virgin Islands). FAX: (201)290-9678. **Staff:** Quentin Van Buren, Res.Coord.

New Jersey State Department of Education - New Jersey State Library
See: New Jersey State Library (11514)

★ 11508 ★
New Jersey (State) Department of Environmental Protection and Energy - Information Resource Center (Env-Cons)
CN-409
432 E. State St.   Phone: (609)984-2249
Trenton, NJ 08625   Maria Baratta, Lib.Mgr.
Founded: 1987. **Staff:** Prof 2; Other 1. **Subjects:** Toxic substances; hazardous waste; pollution - water, air, soil; carcinogens; mutagens; teratogens; water resources. **Special Collections:** International Agency for Research on Cancer (IARC) monograph series; EPA documents; NJDEPE documents. **Holdings:** 2500 books; 4500 technical documents; 12 VF drawers of Chemical Reference Files; 5 VF drawers. **Subscriptions:** 125 journals and other serials. **Services:** Interlibrary loan; copying; center open to the public by appointment. **Automated Operations:** Computerized cataloging. **Computerized Information Services:** MEDLARS, OCLC, DIALOG Information Services, LEXIS, NEXIS. **Networks/Consortia:** Member of PALINET, Central Jersey Health Science Libraries Association (CJHSLA). **Publications:** Serials List, annual; Services Brochure, irregular; Acquisition List, quarterly. **Remarks:** FAX: (609)292-3298. **Formerly:** New Jersey Department of Environmental Protection. **Staff:** Dorothy Alibrando, Libn.

★ 11509 ★
New Jersey (State) Department of Health - Division of Occupational/ Environmental Health - Information Center (Med)
Health Agricultural Bldg. CN 360
John Fitch Plaza   Phone: (609)633-2039
Trenton, NJ 08625   Suzanne Ficara, Res.Sci.
Founded: 1987. **Staff:** Prof 1. **Subjects:** Occupational health and safety; industrial hygiene; epidemiology; medicine - environmental, occupational; toxicology; pesticides; public health. **Special Collections:** New Jersey Right-to-Know Fact Sheets. **Holdings:** 500 books; 200 subject files; government documents. **Subscriptions:** 31 journals and other serials. **Services:** Center not open to the public. **Computerized Information Services:** DIALOG Information Services, MEDLARS, Public Health Network (PHN). **Remarks:** FAX: (609)292-0584.

★ 11510 ★
New Jersey (State) Department of Labor - Library (Bus-Fin)
John Fitch Plaza, CN 943, Rm. 211   Phone: (609)292-2035
Trenton, NJ 08625   Jennifer C. McAdoo, Libn.
Founded: 1967. **Staff:** Prof 1; Other 1. **Subjects:** Labor - economics, welfare, laws, legislation; unemployment insurance; economic development; census. **Special Collections:** Labor law reports; Employment Practices; New Jersey Administrative Code. **Holdings:** 2000 books; 200 bound periodical volumes; 800 U.S. documents; 1200 state documents; 33 VF drawers of pamphlets, reports, reprints; 2000 other cataloged items; industrial directories; study guides; census publications. **Subscriptions:** 345 journals and other serials; 5 newspapers. **Services:** Interlibrary loan; copying; library open to the public with restrictions. **Computerized Information Services:** Department of Commerce Electronic Bulletin Board. **Networks/Consortia:** Member of (New Jersey) Regional Library Cooperatives. **Publications:** Selected New Items, monthly. **Remarks:** FAX: (609)292-9563. **Staff:** Shirley Yenner, Prin.Asst.Libn.

★ 11511 ★
New Jersey (State) Department of Law and Public Safety - Attorney General's Library (Law)
Hughes Justice Complex, CN115   Phone: (609)292-4958
Trenton, NJ 08625   Moira O. Strong, Chf., Res.Serv.
Staff: Prof 5; Other 4. **Subjects:** Federal and state law. **Holdings:** 35,000 volumes. **Subscriptions:** 100 journals and other serials; 5 newspapers. **Services:** Library not open to the public. **Computerized Information Services:** LEXIS, NEXIS, WESTLAW, LEGI-SLATE, DIALOG Information Services, DataTimes. **Remarks:** FAX (609)633-6555. **Staff:** Judy Assenheimer, Libn.; Helen Leavitt, Libn.; Marilyn Money, Libn.; Antonia Constant, Libn.

★ 11512 ★
New Jersey (State) Department of Public Advocate - Newark Branch Library (Law)
31 Clinton St., 10th Fl.
P.O. Box 46004   Phone: (201)877-1264
Newark, NJ 07102   Kevin M. Hale
Founded: 1974. **Staff:** Prof 1. **Subjects:** Rate counsel - law, regulated industry, public utilities, hospitals, insurance, criminal law, mental health law. **Holdings:** 4500 books; 150 bound periodical volumes; reports; 3 audiovisual kits. **Subscriptions:** 15 journals and other serials; 3 newspapers; 12 newsletters. **Services:** Library not open to the public; accepts telephone inquiries from other libraries on a limited basis. **Computerized Information Services:** WESTLAW. **Remarks:** FAX: (201)624-1047. **Formerly:** Its Division of Rate Counsel - Library.

★ 11513 ★
New Jersey State League of Municipalities - Bureau of Municipal Information (Plan)
407 W. State St.   Phone: (609)695-3481
Trenton, NJ 08618   Albert J. Wolfe, Bur.Chf.
Founded: 1917. **Staff:** Prof 2; Other 1. **Holdings:** Local ordinances and administrative codes; reports; articles. **Services:** Interlibrary loan; bureau not open to the public. **Publications:** New Jersey Municipalities Magazine, 9/year. **Remarks:** FAX: (609)695-0151.

★ 11514 ★
New Jersey State Library (Info Sci)
185 W. State St., CN520
Trenton, NJ 08625-0520   Phone: (609)292-6220
Founded: 1796. **Staff:** Prof 39; Other 68. **Subjects:** Law, New Jersey history and newspapers, political science, public administration, genealogy. **Special Collections:** Library for the Blind and Handicapped; New Jerseyana; manuscripts; Foundation Center depository; U.S. Government documents selective depository. **Holdings:** 750,000 volumes. **Subscriptions:** 2800 journals and other serials. **Services:** Interlibrary loan; copying; consultant services and grant administration for libraries; library open to the public with restrictions. **Automated Operations:** Computerized cataloging, acquisitions, serials, and circulation. **Computerized Information Services:** OCLC, RLIN, LEXIS, NEXIS, BRS Information Technologies, DIALOG Information Services; ALANET, OnTyme Electronic Message Network Service (electronic mail services). Performs searches on fee basis. **Publications:** Checklist of Official New Jersey Publications, bimonthly - limited distribution; Impressions (newsletter), monthly; New Jersey Public Library Statistics, annual. **Special Catalogs:** New Jersey Documents card catalog; Genealogy: New Jersey Family Names. **Remarks:** FAX: (609)984-7900. Electronic mail address(es): ALA0256 (ALANET). Maintained by New Jersey State Department of Education. Library coordinates a statewide, cooperative multitype library network. **Staff:** Elizabeth Breedlove, Hd., Tech.Serv.; Marya Hunsicker, Hd., Lib. for the Blind; Donna Dziedzic, Asst. State Libn.; Oliver Gillock, Jr., Coord., Plan. & Dev.

★ 11515 ★
New Jersey State Library - Bureau of Law and Reference (Law, Soc Sci)
185 W. State St.
CN 520   Phone: (609)292-6220
Trenton, NJ 08625-0520   Donna Dziedzic, Act. State Libn.
Founded: 1796. **Staff:** Prof 19; Other 19. **Subjects:** Law, political science, social science, New Jerseyana, library science. **Special Collections:** New Jersey documents; Foundation Collection; genealogy. **Holdings:** 460,000 volumes; 35 file cabinets of pamphlets and clippings; 26 microfilm cabinets; 21,700 reels of microfilm; 18 microfiche cabinets; 495,000 microfiche. **Subscriptions:** 2645 journals and other serials; 50 newspapers. **Services:**

Interlibrary loan; copying; open to the public. **Computerized Information Services:** DataTimes, DIALOG Information Services, INFOBANK, LEXIS, NEXIS, WESTLAW, OCLC, RLIN, DataTimes, NewsNet, Inc., VU/TEXT Information Services, BRS Information Technologies; CD-ROMs (Infotrac, Legaltrac, CIRR, LePac-Government Documents, Grolier Electronic Encyclopedia, Census Test Discs 1&2); ALANET (electronic mail service). **Publications:** Accessions List, biweekly; Selected New Books, monthly; Checklist of Official New Jersey Publications, irregular. **Special Indexes:** Index to Supreme and Superior Court Cases. **Remarks:** The telephone number of the Law Library is 292-6230. FAX: (609)984-7901 (Governmental Reference); (609)984-7901 (Law Library). Electronic mail address(es): ALA0256 (ALANET). Division of the New Jersey State Department of Education. **Staff:** Robert Bland, Coord., Law; Janet Tuerff, Coord., Ref.

★11516★
New Jersey State Museum - Library (Hum)
New Jersey State Library
185 W. State St.
CN 520   Phone: (609)292-6300
Trenton, NJ 08625   Louise Minervino, Libn.
Founded: 1890. **Subjects:** Art, cultural history, archeology, ethnology, natural and space sciences. **Holdings:** 2500 volumes. **Subscriptions:** 25 journals and other serials. **Services:** Students and researchers may study books on museum premises only by advance reservation. **Computerized Information Services:** Questor, Muse (internal databases). **Remarks:** FAX: (609)777-1242.

New Jersey Vocational Education Resource Center
See: New Jersey (State) Department of Education - Division of Vocational Education (11507)

★11517★
New Kuban Education & Welfare Association - Library (Area-Ethnic)
Don Rd.   Phone: (609)697-2255
Buena, NJ 08310   Anthony Sienczenko, Pres.
Founded: 1972. **Staff:** 1. **Subjects:** Cossack history and traditions. **Holdings:** 1100 volumes. **Subscriptions:** 3 journals and other serials. **Services:** Library open to the public by appointment.

★11518★
New Liskeard College of Agricultural Technology - Northern Ontario Agricultural Resource Centre (Agri)
Hwy. 11B, Box G   Phone: (705)647-6738
New Liskeard, ON, Canada P0J 1P0   Corinna Hoogenhoud, Libn.
Founded: 1981. **Staff:** 1.5. **Subjects:** Agriculture, Northern Ontario. **Holdings:** 8000 books; 700 AV programs. **Subscriptions:** 300 journals and other serials. **Services:** Copying; library open to Northern Ontario residents. **Automated Operations:** Computerized cataloging and circulation. **Computerized Information Services:** Sydney, Alis (internal databases). **Publications:** News from NOARC; North Ontario NORFACTS - both to Northern Ontario residents only. **Special Catalogs:** Custom book and AV listings - available on request. **Remarks:** FAX: (705)647-7008. Maintained by Ontario Ministry of Agriculture and Food.

★11519★
New London County Historical Society - Library (Hist)
11 Blinman St.   Phone: (203)443-1209
New London, CT 06320   William E. Hare, II, Cur.
Founded: 1871. **Staff:** Prof 1. **Subjects:** Local history and genealogy. **Special Collections:** Shaw Collection (Revolutionary period); Caulkins Collection. **Holdings:** 5000 books; 400 antique newspapers; 50 early town and county records; 3000 pieces of family correspondence; 15 ships' logs; 50 feet of manuscripts; 25 early account books. **Services:** Copying; library open to the public by appointment. **Special Catalogs:** Shaw Collection (card); manuscripts (card).

★11520★
New London Day - Library (Publ)
41 Eugene O'Neill Dr.   Phone: (203)442-5599
New London, CT 06320   Clare M. Peckham
Staff: Prof 1. **Subjects:** Newspaper reference topics. **Holdings:** Newspaper clippings.

★11521★
New Mexico Institute of Mining and Technology - New Mexico Tech Library (Sci-Engr)
Campus Station   Phone: (505)835-5614
Socorro, NM 87801   Betty Reynolds, Lib.Dir.
Founded: 1889. **Staff:** Prof 2; Other 7. **Subjects:** Geology, mining, petroleum, chemistry, physics, mathematics, ground-water hydrology, geophysics, computer science. **Holdings:** 90,000 books; 80,000 bound periodical volumes; 177,000 government documents (depository); 11,000 maps; theses. **Subscriptions:** 1000 journals and other serials; 10 newspapers. **Services:** Interlibrary loan; copying; library open to the public. **Automated Operations:** Computerized public access catalog, cataloging, acquisitions, and serials. **Computerized Information Services:** BRS Information Technologies, STN International, DIALOG Information Services, OCLC. Performs searches on fee basis. **Networks/Consortia:** Member of AMIGOS Bibliographic Council, Inc. **Remarks:** FAX: (505)835-5754. **Formerly:** Its Martin Speare Memorial Library. **Staff:** Louise Dano, ILL; Betsy Kraus, Pub.Serv.Libn.; Kathleen Le Febre, Govt.Docs.

★11522★
New Mexico Military Institute - J. Penrod Toles Learning Center - Paul Horgan Library (Hist)
101 W. College   Phone: (505)624-8380
Roswell, NM 88201-5173   M. Bruce McLaren, Dir.
Founded: 1893. **Staff:** Prof 3; Other 5. **Subjects:** Liberal arts. **Special Collections:** J.P. White Napoleon Collection (250 volumes). **Holdings:** 60,000 books; 3500 bound periodical volumes; 30 VF drawers. **Subscriptions:** 250 journals and other serials; 25 newspapers. **Services:** Interlibrary loan; copying; library open to the public for reference use only. **Automated Operations:** Computerized public access catalog, cataloging, and circulation. **Computerized Information Services:** DIALOG Information Services. Performs searches on fee basis. Contact Person: Jerry Klopfer, Lib./Media Spec., 624-8382. **Remarks:** FAX: (505)624-8390. **Staff:** Kathy Flanary, Lib. Media Spec.

★11523★
New Mexico School for the Deaf - Library (Educ)
1060 Cerrillos Rd.   Phone: (505)827-6743
Santa Fe, NM 87503   Carla Fenner, Libn.
Founded: 1945. **Staff:** Prof 1; Other 1. **Subjects:** Deafness, sign language. **Holdings:** 10,000 books; 260 bound periodical volumes. **Subscriptions:** 48 journals and other serials. **Services:** Interlibrary loan; copying; library open to the public. **Publications:** New Mexico Progress (newsletter), monthly - available on request. **Remarks:** FAX: (505)827-6739.

★11524★
New Mexico School for the Visually Handicapped - Library and Media Center (Aud-Vis)
1900 White Sands Blvd.   Phone: (505)437-3505
Alamogordo, NM 88310   Bill Davis, Media Coord.
Staff: Prof 2; Other 11. **Special Collections:** Visually handicapped. **Holdings:** 11,000 books in braille and print; 4400 AV programs; 7500 textbooks in special media and instructional aids for the visually handicapped. **Subscriptions:** 46 journals and other serials. **Services:** Library open to public schools, New Mexico agencies for pre-college students, and the public with restrictions. **Computerized Information Services:** APH-CARL; internal databases; CD-ROMS; SpecialNet (electronic mail service). Performs searches free of charge. **Remarks:** FAX: (505)437-7851. **Staff:** Wanda West, Libn.

(New Mexico State) 13th Judicial District Law Library
See: New Mexico State University - 13th Judicial District Law Library (11532)

★11525★
New Mexico (State) Department of Environment - Environment Library (Env-Cons)
1190 St. Francis Dr., S1350
P.O. Box 26110   Phone: (505)827-2633
Santa Fe, NM 87502   Jacqueline M. Calligan, Libn.Sr.
Founded: 1980. **Staff:** Prof 1. **Subjects:** Ground water protection, surface water protection, hazardous waste disposal, radiation protection, occupational health and safety, air quality protection. **Holdings:** 700 books;

154 bound periodical volumes; 6500 reports and documents. **Subscriptions:** 35 journals and other serials. **Services:** Copying; library open to the public for reference use only. **Automated Operations:** Computerized ILL. **Computerized Information Services:** DIALOG Information Services; internal databases. **Publications:** Library News (new arrival list and journal tables of contents), monthly - for internal distribution only. **Formerly:** New Mexico (State) Department of Health & Environment - Environmental Improvement Division - EID Library.

New Mexico (State) Department of Health & Environment - Environmental Improvement Division - EID Library
See: New Mexico (State) Department of Environment - Environment Library (11525)

★11526★
New Mexico (State) Department of Hospitals - Las Vegas Medical Center - Medical and Staff Library (Med)
Box 1388   Phone: (505)454-2111
Las Vegas, NM 87701   Bonnie S. Hatch, Dir., Lib.Serv.
Founded: 1964. **Staff:** Prof 1; Other 1. **Subjects:** Medicine, psychiatry, clinical psychology, psychoanalysis and therapy, hospital management. **Holdings:** 3000 volumes; 905 bound periodical volumes; 155 videocassettes; 75 audiocassettes. **Subscriptions:** 100 journals and other serials. **Services:** Interlibrary loan; library open to New Mexico health care providers. **Automated Operations:** Computerized cataloging. **Computerized Information Services:** NLM, DIALOG Information Services. Performs searches on fee basis. **Networks/Consortia:** Member of National Network of Libraries of Medicine - South Central Region, New Mexico Consortium of Biomedical and Hospital Libraries. **Publications:** Synergy, monthly - to TALON members; LVMC Reporter (in-house newsletter); La Palabra de la Verdad: The True Word (mental health flyer) - both free upon request. **Remarks:** FAX: (505)454-2136. **Staff:** Bettina M. Romero.

★11527★
New Mexico (State) Energy, Minerals and Natural Resources Department - Library (Energy)
2040 S. Pacheco   Phone: (505)827-5913
Santa Fe, NM 87505   Margaret D. Cordovano, ·Libn.
Founded: 1978. **Staff:** Prof 1. **Subjects:** Energy, New Mexico geology, mining and minerals. **Special Collections:** New Mexico Environmental Impact Statements. **Holdings:** 2435 books; 8750 technical reports; 950 microfiche; 24 VF drawers. **Subscriptions:** 337 journals and other serials. **Services:** Interlibrary loan; copying; library open to the public. **Computerized Information Services:** DIALOG Information Services. **Publications:** Library Letter. **Remarks:** FAX: (505)438-3855. Telex: 14383855.

★11528★
New Mexico State Highway and Transportation Department - Research Bureau Library (Trans)
Box 1149   Phone: (505)827-5534
Santa Fe, NM 87504-1149   Dinah Lea Jentgen, Libn.
Founded: 1981. **Staff:** Prof 1. **Subjects:** Transportation - planning, safety, engineering, statistics, environmental impacts. **Special Collections:** Departmental publications (1200 titles). **Holdings:** 10,000 books; 50 bound periodical volumes; 25 internal manuscripts; 5000 reports. **Subscriptions:** 25 journals and other serials. **Services:** Interlibrary loan; copying; library open to the public with restrictions. **Automated Operations:** Computerized cataloging. **Computerized Information Services:** DIALOG Information Services, OCLC EPIC. Performs searches free of charge. **Networks/Consortia:** Member of FEDLINK. **Publications:** Transpo-Topics (newsletter), quarterly - to New Mexico local governmental agencies and other interested groups. **Remarks:** FAX: (505)827-3214.

★11529★
New Mexico (State) Legislative Council Service - Library (Soc Sci)
State Capitol, Rm. 311   Phone: (505)984-9600
Santa Fe, NM 87503   Ann Bancroft, Libn.
Founded: 1951. **Staff:** Prof 1. **Subjects:** Government, taxation, public finance, law. **Holdings:** 4000 books; 25 bound periodical volumes; 6000 pamphlets; clippings. **Subscriptions:** 35 journals and other serials. **Services:** Library open to the public. **Computerized Information Services:** WESTLAW. **Publications:** Biennial Report, limited edition - free upon request. **Remarks:** FAX: (505)984-9610.

★11530★
New Mexico State Library (Info Sci)
325 Don Gaspar   Phone: (505)827-3800
Santa Fe, NM 87503   Karen J. Watkins, State Libn.
Founded: 1929. **Staff:** Prof 16; Other 42. **Subjects:** Public administration, management, education, literature, history, biography. **Special Collections:** Professional Library Science material. **Holdings:** 100,000 books; 900,000 federal and state documents (Federal Regional Depository); ERIC microfiche collection. **Subscriptions:** 634 journals and other serials; 57 newspapers. **Services:** Interlibrary loan; copying; library open to the public. **Automated Operations:** Computerized cataloging and ILL. **Computerized Information Services:** DIALOG Information Services, OCLC. Performs searches on fee basis for New Mexico libraries. **Networks/Consortia:** Member of AMIGOS Bibliographic Council, Inc. **Publications:** Hitchhiker, weekly. **Remarks:** FAX: (505)827-3888. **Staff:** Paul A. Agriesti, Adm.Libn.; Harold Bogart, Adm.Libn., Automation & Tech.Serv.; Nancy Fischer, Adm.Libn., Info.Serv.; Scott Sheldon, Adm.Libn.; Norma McCallan, Southwest State Doc.; Laurie Chaney, Fed.Docs.

★11531★
New Mexico State Records Center and Archives - Archives (Hist)
404 Montezuma St.   Phone: (505)827-8860
Santa Fe, NM 87503   J. Richard Salazar, Chf., Archv.Serv.
Founded: 1960. **Staff:** Prof 4; Other 2. **Subjects:** New Mexico state history, Southwestern history. **Special Collections:** Spanish and Mexican Archives of New Mexico; New Mexico Territorial Archives; New Mexico Statehood Archives. **Holdings:** 4000 books; 300 bound periodical volumes. **Subscriptions:** 4 journals and other serials. **Services:** Copying; archives open to the public. **Publications:** Spanish, Mexican, Territorial Archives of New Mexico. **Special Indexes:** Photograph index. **Remarks:** FAX: (505)827-8809. **Staff:** Al Regensberg, Archv.; Sandy Macias, Archv.; Ron Montoya, Archv.

★11532★
New Mexico State University - 13th Judicial District Law Library (Law)
1500 3rd St.   Phone: (505)287-7981
Grants, NM 87020   Fred Wilding-White, Libn.
Subjects: Law. **Holdings:** 8146 books. **Services:** Copying; library open to the public. **Remarks:** FAX: (505)287-7992.

★11533★
New Mexico State University - Grants Library (Bus-Fin)
1500 3rd St.   Phone: (505)287-7981
Grants, NM 87020   Fred Wilding-White, Libn.
Subjects: Business, computers. **Special Collections:** Southwest history. **Holdings:** 34,022 books; 798 bound periodical volumes; 2350 documents; 28,000 nonbook items. **Services:** Interlibrary loan; copying; library open to the public. **Special Catalogs:** Audio-visual catalog. **Remarks:** FAX: (505)287-7992.

★11534★
New Mexico State University - Library - Rio Grande Historical Collections (Hist)
Box 30006   Phone: (505)646-4727
Las Cruces, NM 88003-0006   Austin Hoover, Univ.Archv.
Staff: Prof 2; Other 2. **Subjects:** New Mexico State University; history of New Mexico, 1800 to present. **Special Collections:** Noncurrent records of New Mexico State University; New Mexico collection (records of organizations; papers of individuals and families; ephemera; AV programs; programs concerning education, farming, ranching, water resources management, mining, transportation, business and commerce, politics and government, social and cultural affairs, pioneer life; collections total 4500 cubic feet). **Holdings:** Manuscripts; archives; microfilm. **Services:** Copying; collections open to the public. **Computerized Information Services:** Internal databases. **Remarks:** FAX: (505)646-4335.

★11535★
New Mexico State University - Water Resources Research Institute (Sci-Engr)
P.O. Box 30001, Dept. 3167   Phone: (505)646-4337
Las Cruces, NM 88003   Leslie Blair, Info.Coord.
Staff: 1. **Subjects:** New Mexico water resources and geology, surface water, ground water. **Holdings:** 1000 books; 20 bound periodical volumes; 8000 reports; maps. **Services:** Copying; library open to the public for reference use only. **Remarks:** FAX: (505)646-6418.

★ 11536 ★
New Mexico Supreme Court - Law Library (Law)
Supreme Court Bldg.
Drawer L   Phone: (505)827-4850
Santa Fe, NM 87504   Thaddeus Bejnar, Dir.
Founded: 1852. Staff: Prof 3; Other 4. Subjects: Law. Special Collections:
Spanish and Mexican colonial laws to 1850. Holdings: 180,000 volumes; 50
reels of microfilm of territorial land claim cases; 78,000 microfiche.
Subscriptions: 395 journals and other serials. Services: Interlibrary loan;
copying; library open to the public. Computerized Information Services:
WESTLAW, LEXIS, DIALOG Information Services. Publications: New
Mexico Legal Forms for prose litigants. Special Indexes: Index to New
Mexico Attorney General Opinions. Remarks: FAX: (505)827-4853. Staff:
Kevin M. Lancaster, Assoc.Libn.; Michael Poulson, Assoc.Libn.

New Mexico Tech Library
See: New Mexico Institute of Mining and Technology (11521)

★ 11537 ★
New Milford Hospital - Health Sciences Library (Med)
21 Elm St.   Phone: (203)355-2611
New Milford, CT 06776   Susan E. Hays, Libn.
Staff: Prof 1. Subjects: Medicine, nursing, allied health sciences. Holdings:
1200 books; 878 bound periodical volumes; 75 periodical titles on
microfiche. Subscriptions: 106 journals and other serials. Services:
Interlibrary loan; copying; library open to the public by appointment.
Computerized Information Services: MEDLARS. Performs searches on fee
basis. Networks/Consortia: Member of Northwestern Connecticut Health
Science Library Consortium (NW-CT-HSL), Connecticut Association of
Health Science Libraries (CAHSL). Publications: Library Letters,
bimonthly - for internal distribution only. Remarks: FAX: (203)350-9515.
(attention librarian).

New Music Festival Archives
See: Bowling Green State University (2039)

★ 11538 ★
New Orleans Baptist Theological Seminary - John T. Christian Library
(Rel-Phil)
4110 Seminary Pl.   Phone: (504)282-4455
New Orleans, LA 70126   Ken Taylor, Dir.
Founded: 1917. Staff: Prof 4; Other 14. Subjects: Bible, theology, Baptists,
preaching, missions, religious education, church music. Special Collections:
R.G. Lee Collection; William Carey Library (microfilm); Keith Collection
(church music). Holdings: 201,176 volumes; 12,333 Baptist annuals and
minutes; 6043 VF materials; 2873 pamphlets, tracts, manuscripts; 17,119
microforms; 25,402 AV programs; 730 curriculum materials. Subscriptions:
993 journals and other serials. Services: Interlibrary loan; copying; library
open to the public for reference use only. Automated Operations:
Computerized cataloging. Computerized Information Services: DIALOG
Information Services, OCLC EPIC. Networks/Consortia: Member of
SOLINET. Remarks: FAX: (504)944-4455. Staff: Connie Pong, Cat.;
Raymond Legendre, ILL; Dr. Harry Eskew, Mus.Libn; Dr. Janice Meier,
Circ.

★ 11539 ★
New Orleans Museum of Art - Felix J. Dreyous Library (Art)
City Park
P.O. Box 19123   Phone: (504)488-2631
New Orleans, LA 70179   Carl O. Penny, Ph.D., Libn.
Founded: 1971. Staff: Prof 1. Subjects: Photography, African art, Japanese
painting, glass, American and European 19th and 20th century painting,
pre-Columbian art, silver, Faberge. Special Collections: Rare and limited-
edition illustrated books. Holdings: 18,000 books; 1400 bound periodical
volumes; 9000 auction catalogs and museum publications; 300 file boxes of
pamphlets; 12,000 35mm slides; 23 VF drawers of living artist files.
Subscriptions: 100 journals and other serials. Services: Interlibrary loan;
copying; library open to museum members and general public by
appointment. Special Indexes: Index to New Orleans Artists, 1805-1940 (15
volumes). Remarks: FAX: (504)484-6662.

★ 11540 ★
New Orleans Psychoanalytic Institute, Inc. - Library (Med)
3624 Coliseum St.   Phone: (504)899-5815
New Orleans, LA 70115   Dr. Denise Dorsey, Chm.
Founded: 1950. Staff: 1. Subjects: Psychoanalysis. Holdings: 650 books; 500
bound periodical volumes. Subscriptions: 13 journals and other serials.
Services: Library not open to the public. Staff: Kellie Barnes.

★ 11541 ★
New Orleans Public Library - Business and Science Division (Bus-Fin,
Sci-Engr, Soc Sci)
219 Loyola Ave.   Phone: (504)596-2580
New Orleans, LA 70140-1016   Jean Jones, Hd.
Founded: 1958. Staff: Prof 9; Other 2. Subjects: Business, consumerism,
science, technology, education, careers, social sciences. Special Collections:
Federal document depository collection (600,000 items); Louisiana
Cooperating Collection of Foundation Center (600 items). Holdings: 76,000
volumes; 3000 college catalogs on microfiche; 2500 annual and 10K reports,
1978-1989; 2000 business and career pamphlets. Services: Interlibrary loan;
copying; division open to the public. Automated Operations: Computerized
public access catalog, cataloging, acquisitions, and circulation.
Computerized Information Services: OCLC, Louisiana Numerical Register,
DIALOG Information Services; CD-ROM (Compact Disclosure, Health
Reference Center). Performs searches on fee basis. Networks/Consortia:
Member of SOLINET. Remarks: FAX: (504)596-2655. Staff: Pamela
Barrows, Govt.Docs.Libn.; Joseph Clark, Asst.Hd., Bus. & Sci. Div.

★ 11542 ★
New Orleans Public Library - Foreign Language Division (Hum)
219 Loyola Ave.   Phone: (504)596-2585
New Orleans, LA 70140-1016   Norka Diaz, Hd.
Founded: 1972. Staff: Prof 1; Other 1. Subjects: Spanish, French, German,
Vietnamese, Chinese popular and classical literature. Special Collections:
Applied sciences in Spanish (100 volumes); children's books in Spanish (100
volumes). Holdings: 13,500 books. Subscriptions: 15 journals and other
serials. Services: Interlibrary loan; copying; library open to the public.
Remarks: FAX: (504)596-2609.

★ 11543 ★
New Orleans Public Library - Louisiana Division (Hist)
219 Loyola Ave.   Phone: (504)596-2610
New Orleans, LA 70140-1016   Collin B. Hamer, Jr., Div.Hd.
Founded: 1946. Staff: Prof 8.5; Other 4. Subjects: New Orleans archives,
1769 to present; New Orleans newspapers, 1802 to present; Louisiana state
documents; books by Louisianians; books on Louisiana subjects. Special
Collections: Carnival (Mardi Gras) Collection (11,000 items); Genealogy
Collection (3350 volumes; 7650 reels of microfilm; City Archives Collection
(15,900 volumes; 4400 reels of microfilm; 500 reels of 16mm sound and silent
film; 450 videotapes; 3500 cubic feet of manuscripts; 1575 blueprints);
Orleans Parish Civil Court Collection, 1805-1927 (4000 cubic feet; 2200
reels of microfilm; Orleans Parish Criminal Court Records, 1830-1931 (625
cubic feet; 800 volumes). Holdings: 33,250 books; 2200 newspapers; 14,000
reels of microfilm; 3000 maps; 46,700 Louisiana and New Orleans
photographs; 30,000 Louisiana state documents; 6300 newsreels from
WVUE-TV. Subscriptions: 330 journals and other serials; 23 newspapers.
Services: Interlibrary loan; copying; microfilming; division open to the
public with restrictions. Automated Operations: Computerized cataloging,
acquisitions, serials, and circulation. Computerized Information Services:
OCLC. Publications: Genealogical Material in the New Orleans Public
Library; How to Research the History of Your House (or Other Building)
in New Orleans - both for sale. Special Indexes: Louisiana Biography Index
containing obituaries appearing in New Orleans newspapers, 1804-1972 and
biographies appearing in books (700,000 cards); News Index to news items
in local papers concerning Louisiana and Louisianians, 1804-1963 (600,000
cards); index to photograph collection; Blueprint Index to Nonresidential
Buildings, 1896-1987. Remarks: FAX: (504)596-2609. Staff: J. Rodney
Smith, Asst.Hd./Docs.Libn.; Wayne M. Everard, Archv.

★ 11544 ★
New Orleans Public Library - Periodicals, Art, & Recreation Division
(Art, Mus, Rec)
219 Loyola Ave.   Phone: (504)596-2565
New Orleans, LA 70140-1016   Margaret Roberts, Hd.
Founded: 1957. Staff: Prof 7.5; Other 4. Subjects: Fine arts, music, costume,
sports, recreation, periodicals. Special Collections: Early New Orleans and

southern sheet music. **Holdings:** 38,100 books; 4 VF drawers of pamphlets; 4630 audio cassettes; 481 compact discs; 100,000 mounted pictures in 11 file cabinets; 25,000 phonograph records; 3000 circulating catalog scores; 1105 video cassettes; periodicals on microfilm and microfiche; newspapers; CD-ROM indexes. **Subscriptions:** 1669 journals and other serials; 46 newspapers. **Services:** Interlibrary loan; copying; SDI; division open to the public. **Automated Operations:** Computerized public access catalog, cataloging, acquisitions, and circulation. **Computerized Information Services:** DIALOG Information Services. Performs searches on fee basis. **Remarks:** Alternate telephone number(s): 596-2567. FAX: (504)596-2671. **Staff:** Marilyn Wilkins, Art & Mus.Spec.

New Orleans Town Gardeners Garden Library
See: Tulane University - Southeastern Architectural Archive (16565)

New Place Rare Book Library
See: Shakespeare Society of America (15072)

★ 11545 ★
New Providence Historical Society - Library (Hist)
1350 Springfield Ave.   Phone: (201)464-5798
New Providence, NJ 07974   Dorothy Mason, Hd., Archv./Lib.
Staff: 5. **Subjects:** Local history and current events. **Holdings:** 197 loose-leaf binders; 39 loose-leaf photograph albums; 83 oral history tapes with 50 transcriptions; VF drawers. **Services:** Library open to the public for reference use only. **Computerized Information Services:** Internal databases. **Publications:** Turkey Tracks, quarterly.

New Readers Press
See: Laubach Literacy International, Inc. - Library (8973)

★ 11546 ★
New River Community College - Learning Resource Center - Library (Hum, Soc Sci)
P.O. Drawer 1127   Phone: (703)674-3627
Dublin, VA 24084   Roberta S. White, Coord., Lib.Serv.
Founded: 1960. **Staff:** Prof 2; Other 2.5. **Subjects:** American literature, social sciences, U.S. history, business, computers, nursing. **Special Collections:** Collection for the Hearing Impaired (600 volumes). **Holdings:** 29,000 books; 40,000 microfiche; 10,000 reels of microfilm; 2000 media items. **Subscriptions:** 230 journals and other serials; 7 newspapers. **Services:** Interlibrary loan; copying; library open to the public. **Computerized Information Services:** ABI/INFORM; CD-ROM (Periodical Abstracts Ondisc). **Remarks:** FAX: (703)674-3626.

New Rochelle Historical Society - Library
See: Thomas Paine National Historical Association (of New Rochelle) (12690)

★ 11547 ★
New Rochelle Hospital Medical Center - Health Science Library (Med)
16 Guion Pl.   Phone: (914)632-5000
New Rochelle, NY 10802   Mary F. Shanahan, Lib.Dir.
Founded: 1950. **Staff:** Prof 1; Other 2. **Subjects:** Surgery, medicine, nursing, graphics. **Special Collections:** Nursing history. **Holdings:** 3000 books; 10,000 bound periodical volumes; 300 tapes; 100 AV programs; staff reprints. **Subscriptions:** 300 journals and other serials. **Services:** Interlibrary loan; copying; library open to the public by appointment. **Computerized Information Services:** MEDLINE, BRS Information Technologies. Performs searches free of charge. **Networks/Consortia:** Member of Health Information Libraries of Westchester (HILOW), Medical Library Center of New York (MLCNY), National Network of Libraries of Medicine - Middle Atlantic Region, New York Metropolitan Reference and Research Library Agency. **Publications:** quarterly Library Newsletter. **Remarks:** FAX: (914)576-4028. **Staff:** Laura Wright, AV Dir.

New School Institute
See: Temple University - Esther Boyer College of Music - New School Institute (16146)

New School for Social Research - Parsons School of Design
See: Parsons School of Design (12768)

★ 11548 ★
New School for Social Research - Raymond Fogelman Library (Soc Sci)
65 Fifth Ave.   Phone: (212)741-7902
New York, NY 10003   Gail Persky, Lib.Dir.
Founded: 1919. **Staff:** Prof 4; Other 8. **Subjects:** Psychology, political science, economics, sociology, philosophy, anthropology. **Special Collections:** Husserl Archives (unpublished notebooks of Edmond Husserl). **Holdings:** 153,500 volumes. **Subscriptions:** 1010 journals. **Services:** Interlibrary loan; copying; library open to the public with restrictions. **Automated Operations:** Computerized public access catalog, cataloging, acquisitions, serials, and circulation. **Computerized Information Services:** RLIN. **Networks/Consortia:** Member of Research Library Association of South Manhattan, Research Libraries Information Network (RLIN). **Remarks:** FAX: (212)229-5359. **Staff:** Margaret Rose Hedrich; Carmen Hendershott; Leslie Meyers.

★ 11549 ★
New Song Library (Mus)
P.O. Box 295   Phone: (413)586-9485
Northampton, MA 01061   Johanna Halbeisen, Dir.
Founded: 1980. **Staff:** Prof 1. **Subjects:** Folk songs on social justice issues - peace, environment, civil rights, women's rights, labor unions, nuclear power, lesbian/gay rights, economic justice. **Special Collections:** Woody Guthrie and Pete Seeger collections; People's Music Weekend Archive (175 tapes). **Holdings:** 250 books; 17 bound periodical volumes; 1500 phonograph records; 1600 cassette tapes. **Services:** Library open to members only.

New South Wales - State Library of New South Wales
See: State Library of New South Wales - Special Collections (15688)

★ 11550 ★
New South Wales Roads and Traffic Authority - Library (Sci-Engr)
260 Elizabeth St., Ground Fl.   Phone: 2 2186520
Surry Hills, NSW 2010, Australia   Karen Sinclair-Smith, Mgr., Lib.Serv.
Staff: 9. **Subjects:** Civil and traffic engineering. **Special Collections:** Road safety. **Holdings:** 83,000 books; 200 microforms. **Services:** Interlibrary loan; copying; library open to the public for reference use only. **Computerized Information Services:** DIALOG Information Services, TRIS, ESA/IRS, AUSTRALIS, AUSINET. **Remarks:** FAX: 2 2186938. Telex: AA 21825. **Formerly:** Located in Sydney, NSW, Australia.

New Thought Archive
See: Southern Methodist University - Perkins School of Theology - The Bridwell Library (15503)

New Virginia Review Library
See: Virginia Commonwealth University - James Branch Cabell Library (19861)

New Westminster Museum
See: Irving House Historic Centre and New Westminster Museum (8252)

★ 11551 ★
New Year Shooters and Mummers Museum - Library (Theater)
2nd St. and Washington Ave.   Phone: (215)336-3050
Philadelphia, PA 19147   Jack A. Cohen, Lib.Coord.
Founded: 1976. **Staff:** Prof 3; Other 3. **Subjects:** Mumming. **Special Collections:** Costume collection, 1800s to present (1500). **Holdings:** 115 volumes; 20 manuscripts; 150 video cassettes; 325 magnetic tapes and sound recordings; 3000 photographs and slides; documents; news clippings. **Services:** Copying; library open to the public by appointment. **Staff:** Margaret Boritz, Cur.

★ 11552 ★
New York Academy of Medicine - Library (Med)
2 E. 103rd St.   Phone: (212)876-8200
New York, NY 10029   Arthur Downing, Act.Libn.
Founded: 1847. **Staff:** Prof 19; Other 39. **Subjects:** Medicine, allied health sciences, health statistics. **Special Collections:** Medical Americana; history of medicine; medical biography; rare books; health reports; food and cookery. **Holdings:** 696,951 bound volumes; 182,928 pamphlets; 141 incunabula; 2227 manuscripts; 494 reels of microfilm; 250,245 portraits; 25,543 illustrations; 14,429 separate portraits. **Subscriptions:** 2900 journals and other serials. **Services:** Interlibrary loan (fee); document delivery, library open to the public for reference use only. **Automated Operations:** Integrated library system. **Computerized Information Services:** NLM, BRS Information Technologies, DIALOG Information Services, WILSONLINE; EasyLink (electronic mail service). Performs searches on fee basis. **Networks/Consortia:** Member of Medical Library Center of New York (MLCNY), SUNY/OCLC Library Network, New York State Interlibrary Loan Network (NYSILL), National Network of Libraries of Medicine - Middle Atlantic Region. **Publications:** History of Medicine Series; Collection Development Policy. **Special Catalogs:** Author Catalog of the Library; Author Catalog - First and Second Supplements; Subject Catalog of Library; Subject Catalog - First Supplement; Portrait Catalog of the Library; Illustration Catalog of the Library; Catalog of Biographies in the Library. **Remarks:** FAX: (212)722-7650. Headquarters of Middle Atlantic Regional Medical Library Program. **Staff:** Mark Salamon, Adm.Sys.; Donald Clyde, ILL; Gerald Goss, Cat.; Elaine Schlefer, Presrv.; Sheila Paul, Ref.; Ann Pasquale, Spec.Coll.; Mary Mylenki, Reg.Med.Lib.Prog.

New York Aquarium Library
See: **Osborn Laboratories of Marine Sciences - New York Aquarium Library** (12588)

★ 11553 ★
New York Association for the Blind - Lighthouse Library (Aud-Vis)
800 2nd Ave.   Phone: (212)808-0077
New York, NY 10017   Mike Buttner, Contact
Staff: Prof 1; Other 2. **Subjects:** Blindness and visual impairment, handicaps. **Holdings:** 2000 books; 2000 volumes in braille; 400 large print books; 1700 talking books on disc and cassette; 8 VF drawers. **Subscriptions:** 110 journals and other serials. **Services:** Library open to the public.

★ 11554 ★
New York Botanical Garden - Library (Biol Sci, Env-Cons)
Bronx, NY 10458   Phone: (212)220-8751
                                            John F. Reed, V.P., Educ./Dir., Lib.
Founded: 1896. **Staff:** Prof 11; Other 18. **Subjects:** Systematic botany, horticulture, environmental sciences, landscape design. **Special Collections:** Manuscripts, letters, and archives (2361 linear feet); Pre Linnean collection; Darwiniana; Botanical Art (10,000 items); Lord Burnham Architectural Drawings. **Holdings:** 196,962 volumes; 9000 periodical titles; 7000 nursery catalogs and seed lists; 108,509 scientific reprints and pamphlets; 28,097 microforms; 100,000 photographs and slides; 3600 artifacts. **Subscriptions:** 2000 journals and other serials. **Services:** Interlibrary loan; copying; library open to the public. **Automated Operations:** Computerized cataloging. **Computerized Information Services:** DIALOG Information Services, OCLC; DOCLINE, SCIENCEnet (electronic mail services). Performs searches on fee basis. Contact Person: Bernadette Callery, Res.Libn., 220-8753. **Networks/Consortia:** Member of New York Metropolitan Reference and Research Library Agency, New York State Interlibrary Loan Network (NYSILL). **Publications:** Bibliographies and indexes. **Remarks:** FAX: (212)220-6504. Electronic mail address(es): NYBG (SCIENCEnet). **Staff:** Rose Li, Assoc.Libn.; Susan Fraser, Spec.Coll.Libn.; Harry Chapman, Assoc.Libn.; Jane Brennan, Asst.Libn.; Marie Long, Asst.Ref.Spec.; Katy Enders, Asst.Libn.; Marianne Block, Ser./Exch.; Grace Courtney, Cat.; Yelena Bunin, Asst.Libn.; Marjorie Madsen, Asst.Libn.; Dora Galitzi, Plant Info.Off.; Judith Reed, Bookbinder/Cons.; Elaine DiLorenzo, Admin.Asst.

★ 11555 ★
New York Chiropractic College - Library (Med)
2360 State Rte. 89
P.O. Box 800
Seneca Falls, NY 13148-0800   Phone: (315)568-3244
                                                      Dan Kanaley, Act.Dir.
Founded: 1919. **Staff:** Prof 3; Other 2. **Subjects:** Health sciences, basic sciences, chiropractic. **Special Collections:** Palmer Series and other rare chiropractic material. **Holdings:** 9000 books. **Subscriptions:** 332 journals and other serials. **Services:** Interlibrary loan; SDI; library open to the public for reference use only. **Computerized Information Services:** BRS Information Technologies; CD-ROM (MEDLINE); OnTyme Electronic Message Network Service (electronic mail service). Performs searches on fee basis. **Networks/Consortia:** Member of Chiropractic Library Consortium (CLIBCON), BHSL. **Publications:** Shelf Notes (newsletter), quarterly; Monthly Acquisitions List; Research Aids (flyers). **Remarks:** FAX: (315)568-3015. Electronic mail address(es): CLIBCON010 (OnTyme Electronic Message Network Service). **Formerly:** Located in Glen Head, NY. **Staff:** Eilene Moeri, Media Libn.

★ 11556 ★
New York City Board of Education - Division of Bilingual Education - Resource Library (Educ)
131 Livingston St., Rm. 204   Phone: (718)935-3905
Brooklyn, NY 11201   Carmen Gloria Burgos, Libn.
Founded: 1973. **Staff:** Prof 1; Other 1. **Subjects:** Bilingual and bicultural education, English as a second language. **Special Collections:** Puerto Rican Heritage Collection. **Holdings:** 53,000 books; 410 curriculum guides; 1500 ERIC microfiche; 220 proposals; 3 VF drawers of reports; 9 VF drawers of clippings and articles; AV programs. **Subscriptions:** 46 journals and other serials. **Services:** Interlibrary loan; library open to the public. **Remarks:** The language groups served include Spanish, Italian, French, Haitian-Creole, Chinese, Greek, Portuguese, Indochinese, Korean, and Russian. **Formerly:** Its Office of Bilingual Education.

★ 11557 ★
New York City Board of Education - Special Education Teachers Resource Center (Educ)
55 E. 120th St., Rms. 300 & 302   Phone: (212)534-6500
New York, NY 10035   Roberta Berger, Libn.
Founded: 1968. **Staff:** 2. **Subjects:** Language arts, science, teacher education, social studies, early childhood, mathematics. **Special Collections:** Media materials; computer hardware and software. **Holdings:** New York State Department of Education publications. **Services:** Center open to the public. **Publications:** Newsletter - for internal distribution only.

★ 11558 ★
New York City Department of Records and Information Services - Municipal Archives (Hist)
31 Chambers St.   Phone: (212)566-5292
New York, NY 10007   Kenneth R. Cobb, Dir.
Founded: 1950. **Staff:** Prof 12; Other 8. **Subjects:** New York City history, municipal government, New York City government history. **Special Collections:** Brooklyn Bridge Drawings (12,000); New York Building Record collection (2000 cubic feet; 4000 drawings); Central Park Drawings (1400). **Holdings:** 75,000 cubic feet of historic city government records; 50,000 photographs. **Services:** Copying; archives open to the public. **Computerized Information Services:** RLIN. **Remarks:** FAX: (212)385-0984. **Staff:** Evelyn Gonzalez, Ref.Supv.

★ 11559 ★
New York City Department of Records and Information Services - Municipal Reference and Research Center (Soc Sci)
31 Chambers St., Rm. 112
New York, NY 10007   Phone: (212)566-4284
Founded: 1913. **Staff:** Prof 5; Other 4. **Subjects:** New York City - history, government, laws, politics, finance, economy, sociology. **Special Collections:** Civil service (40 VF drawers); neighborhood information files (8 VF drawers); street name file (18 drawers). **Holdings:** 77,500 books; 4200 bound periodical volumes; 30,000 VF materials; 55 drawers of microfilm and microfiche; 20 VF drawers of political information files; 4 VF drawers of New York State materials. **Subscriptions:** 39 journals and other serials; 12 newspapers. **Services:** Interlibrary loan; copying; center open to the public for reference use only. **Computerized Information Services:** Legislative Retrieval System (LRS), RLIN, LOGIN; Citylaw (internal database). **Networks/Consortia:** Member of New York Metropolitan Reference and Research Library Agency, Research Libraries Information Network (RLIN). **Special Indexes:** Index to local laws; index to departmental rules and regulations; Index to Mayor's Executive Orders. **Remarks:** FAX: (212)385-4809. **Staff:** Stephanie C. Makler, Chf., Tech.Serv.; Devra L. Zetlan, Chf., Pub.Serv.

★ 11560 ★
New York City Health and Hospitals Corporation - Coler Memorial Hospital - Health Sciences Library (Med)
Roosevelt Island   Phone: (212)848-6071
New York, NY 10044   Martin M. Leibovici, Dir.
Founded: 1964. **Staff:** Prof 1. **Subjects:** Medical sciences, rehabilitation medicine, psychiatry, geriatrics and gerontology, nursing, audiology and speech. **Holdings:** 1500 volumes; Audio-Digest tapes; Network for Continuing Medical Education videotapes. **Subscriptions:** 112 journals and other serials. **Services:** Interlibrary loan; copying; library open to the public when staff member is present. **Networks/Consortia:** Member of New York Metropolitan Reference and Research Library Agency. **Remarks:** Alternate telephone numbers are 848-7071 and 848-6070. FAX: (212)848-6945.

★ 11561 ★
New York City Human Resources Administration - Library (Soc Sci)
109 E. 16th St.   Phone: (212)420-7652
New York, NY 10003   Harold W. Benson, Libn.
Founded: 1945. **Staff:** Prof 1; Other 3. **Subjects:** Public welfare, social work, child welfare, poverty, homeless, ethnic studies, public administration, employment, income maintenance. **Holdings:** 14,500 volumes; 75 VF drawers; 5000 titles of uncataloged reports and pamphlets. **Subscriptions:** 200 journals and other serials; 6 newspapers. **Services:** Interlibrary loan; copying; library open to the public. **Computerized Information Services:** DIALOG Information Services, OCLC. **Publications:** Library Bulletin, bimonthly. **Remarks:** Alternate telephone number(s): 420-7653.

★ 11562 ★
New York City Human Resources Administration - Medical Assistance Program - MAP Library
11-17 Beach St., 6th Fl. N.W.
New York, NY 10013
Defunct.

★ 11563 ★
New York City Law Department - Corporation Counsel's Library (Soc Sci)
100 Church St., Rm. 6B1   Phone: (212)788-1609
New York, NY 10007   Evania A. Thompson, Chf. Law Libn.
Staff: Prof 3; Other 5. **Subjects:** Federal, state, and municipal government. **Holdings:** 100,000 volumes; microfilm; ultrafiche. **Subscriptions:** 30 journals and other serials. **Services:** Library not open to the public. **Computerized Information Services:** WESTLAW. **Remarks:** FAX: (212)732-9546. **Staff:** Judith D. Sonds, Dp. Law Libn.; James B. Potext, Ref.Libn.; Anthony Fagbore, Lib.Assoc./Circ.Supv.

★ 11564 ★
New York City Office of Chief Medical Examiner - Milton Helpern Library of Legal Medicine (Med)
520 First Ave.   Phone: (212)447-2030
New York, NY 10016   Malvin Vitriol, Med.Libn.
Founded: 1962. **Subjects:** Legal medicine, forensic pathology, forensic toxicology, forensic serology, criminology, forensic immunology. **Special Collections:** Papers of Dr. Milton Helpern; forensic and legal dentistry collection (books and articles). **Holdings:** 4500 books; 928 bound periodical volumes; 480 microfiche; 58 reels of microfilm; 16 VF drawers; 136 tapes; vertical files. **Subscriptions:** 41 journals and other serials. **Services:** Interlibrary loan; copying; library open to forensic science professionals. **Computerized Information Services:** MEDLINE. **Networks/Consortia:** Member of Medical Library Center of New York (MLCNY). **Remarks:** FAX: (212)779-1297.

★ 11565 ★
New York City Police Department - Training Resource Center (Law)
235 E. 20th St., Rm. 639
New York, NY 10003   Phone: (212)477-9723
Staff: Prof 2; Other 2. **Subjects:** Criminal justice, police science, law, social science, history of New York City Police Department, forensic science. **Holdings:** 11,000 books; 50 periodical titles; p80 N.Y.P.D. annual reports, 1892-1969; (incomplete set) 56 VF drawers of pamphlets and clippings; 345 masters' theses; 3 VF drawers of N.Y.P.D. crime statistics; microfiche. **Subscriptions:** 30 journals and other serials; 5 newspapers. **Services:** Interlibrary loan; copying; center open to the public by permission. **Publications:** Library Newsletter, quarterly - for internal distribution only. **Remarks:** Alternate telephone number(s): (212)477-9742. **Staff:** Ina E. Sinclair, Staff Anl.

★ 11566 ★
New York City Public Health Laboratories - William Hallock Park Memorial Library (Med, Biol Sci)
455 First Ave.   Phone: (212)447-2584
New York, NY 10016   Shirley Chapin, Libn.
Founded: 1900. **Staff:** Prof 1; Other 1. **Subjects:** Virology, applied immunology, biochemistry, bacteriology, genetics, laboratory diagnosis, microbiology, cytobiology, toxicology. **Special Collections:** New York City health reports, 1866 to present. **Holdings:** 28,000 books and bound periodical volumes; microcards; 5 VF drawers of archival materials. **Subscriptions:** 265 journals and other serials. **Services:** Interlibrary loan; copying; library open to the public by appointment. **Computerized Information Services:** MEDLARS, DIALOG Information Services; DOCLINE (electronic mail service). **Networks/Consortia:** Member of Medical Library Center of New York (MLCNY), New York Metropolitan Reference and Research Library Agency.

★ 11567 ★
New York City Technical College of City University of New York - Library (Sci-Engr)
300 Jay St.   Phone: (718)260-5470
Brooklyn, NY 11201   Darrow Wood, Chf.Libn. & Dept.Chm.
Founded: 1947. **Staff:** Prof 14; Other 8. **Subjects:** Paramedical sciences, graphic arts, hotel and restaurant management, Afro-American studies, engineering technology, business fields. **Holdings:** 161,555 books; 5156 bound periodical volumes; 108 VF drawers of pamphlet material; 3 VF drawers of menus; 15 VF drawers of pictures; 15 VF drawers of career material; 15 VF drawers of company history; 9051 reels of microfilm; 1934 phonograph records; 797 8mm film loops; 327 audio tapes; 795 videocassettes. **Subscriptions:** 918 journals and other serials; 15 newspapers. **Services:** Interlibrary loan; copying; library open to the public for reference use only. **Automated Operations:** Computerized public access catalog and cataloging. **Computerized Information Services:** OCLC, BRS Information Technologies, ACADEMIC INDEX, MAGAZINE ASAP. **Networks/Consortia:** Member of New York Metropolitan Reference and Research Library Agency, Academic Libraries of Brooklyn (ALB). **Publications:** Library Notes, irregular; Library Alert, irregular; Library Basics, irregular - all to faculty and to others on request. **Remarks:** FAX: (718)260-5467. **Staff:** Paul T. Sherman, Adm. & Personnal Serv.Libn.; Joan Grassano, Coord., Ref.Serv.; Morris Hounion, Cat.; Sharon Swacker, Acq.; Jacqueline Jefferson, Coord., Bibliog.Instr.; Oliver Bright, Coord., AV & Comp.Serv.; Betty Brenner, Ser.; Bonnie Hack, On-Line Serv.; Nancy Gonzalez, Circ.

★ 11568 ★
New York City Transit Authority - Law Library (Law, Trans)
130 Livingston St.
12th Fl.   Phone: (718)330-4330
Brooklyn, NY 11201   Rhonda Hogan-Brock, Mgr., Legal Lib. and Rec.
Staff: Prof 1; Other 1. **Subjects:** Law, New York City Rapid Transit history. **Holdings:** 20,000 volumes. **Services:** Library not open to the public. **Computerized Information Services:** WESTLAW. **Remarks:** FAX: (718)858-1610.

★ 11569 ★
New York College of Osteopathic Medicine - Medical Library (Med)
c/o New York Institute of Technology   Phone: (516)626-6943
Old Westbury, NY 11568   G. Flanzraich, Chf.Med.Libn.
Staff: Prof 1; Other 7. **Subjects:** Medicine. **Special Collections:** Archives of Osteopathic Medical History. **Holdings:** 4000 books. **Subscriptions:** 250 journals and other serials. **Services:** Interlibrary loan; copying; library open to NYCOM students, faculty, and staff only. **Automated Operations:** Computerized public access catalog. **Computerized Information Services:** MEDLINE. **Networks/Consortia:** Member of Long Island Library Resources Council. **Publications:** Acquisition list; NYCOM Library Newsletter. **Remarks:** FAX: (516)626-7439.

★ 11570 ★
New York College of Podiatric Medicine - Medical Library (Med)
53-55 E. 124th St., 2nd Fl.   Phone: (212)410-8020
New York, NY 10035   James Provenzano, Lib.Dir.
Founded: 1930. **Staff:** Prof 1. **Subjects:** Podiatry, medicine, orthopedics, physical medicine, basic sciences. **Holdings:** 10,000 volumes; reprints of journal articles; slides; audiotapes; video cassettes; microfilm; pamphlets. **Subscriptions:** 300 journals and other serials. **Services:** Interlibrary loan; copying; library open to the public for reference use only by request. **Networks/Consortia:** Member of National Network of Libraries of Medicine - Middle Atlantic Region, Manhattan-Bronx Health Sciences Library Consortia, New York Metropolitan Reference and Research Library Agency. **Publications:** Acquisitions lists; journals holdings list. **Remarks:** FAX: (212)876-9426.

★11571★
New York County District Attorney's Office Library (Law)
One Hogan Place
New York, NY 10013
Phone: (212)335-9749
Barbara B. Rosengarten, Libn.
Founded: 1905. **Staff:** Prof 1; Other 3. **Subjects:** Criminal law. **Holdings:** 25,000 books; 600 bound periodical volumes. **Subscriptions:** 40 journals and other serials. **Services:** Interlibrary loan; library not open to the public. **Computerized Information Services:** LEXIS, WESTLAW; Brief Bank (internal database). **Networks/Consortia:** Member of National Network of Libraries of Medicine - Middle Atlantic Region. **Publications:** Current Articles in Criminal Law and Procedure, monthly - for internal distribution only. **Remarks:** FAX: (212)335-9288.

★11572★
New York County Lawyers' Association - Library (Law)
14 Vesey St.
New York, NY 10007
Phone: (212)267-6646
Alison Alifano
Staff: Prof 4; Other 5. **Subjects:** Law. **Special Collections:** Records and briefs, New York Appellate Division and Court of Appeals. **Holdings:** 183,000 volumes. **Subscriptions:** 300 journals and other serials. **Services:** Library not open to the public. **Computerized Information Services:** LEXIS, WESTLAW, DIALOG Information Services. **Remarks:** FAX: (212)285-4482. **Staff:** Martha Pascual, Tech.Serv.Libn.; Bruce Millard, Hd. of Ref.Serv.

★11573★
New York County Surrogate's Court - Law Library (Law)
31 Chambers St., Rm. 401
New York, NY 10007
Phone: (212)374-8275
Nadine A. Dubson, Libn.
Staff: Prof 1. **Subjects:** Law. **Holdings:** 12,500 volumes. **Services:** Library not open to the public.

★11574★
New York Daily News - Daily News Library (Publ)
220 E. 42nd St.
New York, NY 10017
Phone: (212)210-6395
Faigi Rosenthal, Hd.Libn.
Founded: 1919. **Staff:** Prof 2; Other 13. **Subjects:** Newspaper reference topics. **Holdings:** 5000 books; 20,000 microfiche; 2000 pamphlets; 10 million clippings; 5 million pictures; 600,000 negatives; New York Daily News, 1919 to present, on microfilm; New York Times, 1951 to present, on microfilm. **Subscriptions:** 27 journals and other serials. **Services:** Library not open to the public. **Computerized Information Services:** NEXIS, VU/TEXT Information Services. **Remarks:** Alternate telephone number(s): 210-6395. FAX: (212)989-4394. **Staff:** Peter Edelman, Hd.Asst.Libn.

★11575★
New York Downtown Hospital - Elisha Walker Staff Library (Med)
170 William St.
New York, NY 10038
Phone: (212)312-5229
Annette Leyden, Dir.
Staff: Prof 1. **Subjects:** Medicine, surgery, nursing. **Holdings:** 4500 volumes; 105 bound journals; reprints; catalogs; reports. **Subscriptions:** 125 journals and other serials. **Services:** Interlibrary loan; library not open to the public. **Computerized Information Services:** MEDLARS. Performs searches on fee basis. **Networks/Consortia:** Member of Medical Library Center of New York (MLCNY), Manhattan-Bronx Health Sciences Library Consortia. **Remarks:** FAX: (212)312-5929. **Formerly:** New York Infirmary Beekman Downtown Hospital.

★11576★
New York Eye and Ear Infirmary - Bernard Samuels Library (Med)
310 E. 14th St.
New York, NY 10003
Phone: (212)979-4431
Carolyn Stafford, Dir.
Founded: 1950. **Staff:** Prof 1. **Subjects:** Ophthalmology, otolaryngology, plastic surgery. **Holdings:** 1300 books; 1300 bound periodical volumes; pamphlets. **Subscriptions:** 52 journals and other serials. **Services:** Interlibrary loan; library not open to the public. **Computerized Information Services:** NLM, BRS Information Technologies. **Networks/Consortia:** Member of Manhattan-Bronx Health Sciences Library Consortia, New York Metropolitan Reference and Research Library Agency.

★11577★
New York Genealogical and Biographical Society - Genealogical Research Library (Hist)
122 E. 58th St.
New York, NY 10022
Phone: (212)755-8532
Gunther E. Pohl, Cons. Trustee Libn.
Founded: 1869. **Staff:** Prof 2; Other 2. **Subjects:** Genealogy, biography, local history. **Special Collections:** New York State church, town, and other records; family Bible records. **Holdings:** 67,800 volumes; 22,700 manuscripts; 2255 reels of microfilm; 6565 microfiche. **Subscriptions:** 750 journals and other serials. **Services:** Copying; library open to the public with restrictions. **Publications:** Accession lists; serials lists. **Remarks:** FAX: (212)754-4218. **Staff:** Betty Hall Payne, Assoc.Libn., Oper.

★11578★
New-York Historical Society - Library (Hist)
170 Central Park, W.
New York, NY 10024
Phone: (212)873-3400
Jean Ashton, Dir. of the Lib.
Founded: 1804. **Staff:** 30. **Subjects:** American art, history of the North American continent, New York City and state, naval history, New York genealogy. **Special Collections:** American Almanacs; American Genealogy; American Indian (accounts of and captivities); Early American Imprints; Early Travels in America; Early American Trials; Circus in America (Leonidas Westervelt); Civil War Regimental Histories and Muster Rolls; Jenny Lind (Leonidas Westervelt); Maps; Military History (Military Order of the Loyal Legion of the United States, Commandery of the State of New York); Military History and Science (Seventh Regiment Military Library); Naval and Marine History (Naval History Society); 18th and 19th Century New York City and State Newspapers; Slavery and the Civil War; Spanish American War (Harper); manuscript collections including Horatio Gates, Alexander McDougall, Rufus King, American Fur Company, Livingston Family, American Art Union, American Academy of the Fine Arts. **Holdings:** 635,000 books; 2 million manuscripts; 150,000 pamphlets; 25,000 broadsides; 1 million prints and photographs; 30,000 maps. **Subscriptions:** 400 journals and other serials. **Services:** Copying; library open to nonmembers on fee basis. **Automated Operations:** Computerized public access catalog and cataloging. **Networks/Consortia:** Member of Research Libraries Information Network (RLIN). **Special Catalogs:** Manuscript catalog. **Remarks:** FAX: (212)874-8706. **Staff:** Duane Watson, Assoc.Libn., Presrv.; Roberta Pilehe, Cons.; Margaret Heilbrun, Cur., Mss.; Mariam Touba, Newspaper Libn.; Pedro Figueredo, Hd., Cat.

★11579★
New York Hospital-Cornell Medical Center - Medical Archives (Med, Hist)
1300 York Ave.
New York, NY 10021
Phone: (212)746-6072
Adele A. Lerner, Archv.
Founded: 1975. **Staff:** Prof 1. **Subjects:** Medical education; health care; history - medicine, nursing, psychiatry; women's history. **Special Collections:** New York Hospital-Cornell Medical Center records, 1927 to present; Society of the New York Hospital records, 1771 to present; Cornell University Medical College records, 1898 to present; Cornell University Graduate School of Medical Sciences records, 1952 to present; Cornell University-New York Hospital School of Nursing records, 1877-1979; Society of the Lying-In Hospital of the City of New York records, 1799 to present; Manhattan Maternity and Dispensary records, 1905-1939; Nursery for the Children of Poor Women and Nursery and Child's Hospital records, 1854-1910; New York Infant Asylum records, 1865-1910; New York Nursery and Child's Hospital records, 1910-1947; New York Asylum for Lying-In Women records, 1823-1899; Women's Medical Association of New York City records, 1902 to present; American Medical Women's Association Archives, 1915 to present (76 linear feet); Vincent du Vigneaud papers (45.2 linear feet); Walsh McDermott papers (20 linear feet); George N. Papanicolaou papers; Connie M. Guion papers; George J. Heuer papers; Philip Reichert Collection of Diagnostic Instruments (500 medical instruments and artifacts); Medical and Surgical Case Books, 1808-1932; photograph and print collection (20,000 items). **Holdings:** 4600 linear feet of archival materials and manuscripts; 217 films; 22 videotapes; 844 audiotapes and cassettes. **Subscriptions:** 8 journals and other serials (for archival reference). **Services:** Copying; archives open to the public by appointment. **Computerized Information Services:** OnTyme Electronic Message Network Service (electronic mail service). **Publications:** An Introduction to the Medical Archives of the New York Hospital-Cornell Medical Center, 1976. **Special Catalogs:** In-house finding aids; Registers. **Remarks:** FAX: (212)746-6494. Electronic mail address(es): CLASS.CORNELLMED (OnTyme Electronic Message Network Service). Maintained by Cornell University Medical College. Affiliated with the C.V. Starr Biomedical Information Center.

★ 11580 ★
New York Hospital-Cornell Medical Center - Oskar Diethelm Historical
  Library (Med)
525 E. 68th St.
New York, NY 10021   Phone: (212)746-3727
Founded: 1936. **Staff:** 1. **Subjects:** History of psychiatry before 1950,
philosophy, psychology. **Special Collections:** History of Psychiatry
Reference Library (8700 volumes); early doctoral dissertations on
psychiatric topics (241); hospital annual reports (2720); Archives of
Psychiatry (300 cubic feet of archival materials and manuscripts). **Holdings:**
18,000 books; 3850 bound periodical volumes; 695 philosophy and
psychology materials; 123 reels of microfilm. **Subscriptions:** 45 journals and
other serials. **Services:** Library open to qualified researchers for reference use
only on application. **Staff:** Eric T. Carlson.

★ 11581 ★
New York Hospital-Cornell Medical Center, Westchester Division -
  Medical Library (Med)
21 Bloomingdale Rd.   Phone: (914)997-5897
White Plains, NY 10605   Marcia A. Miller, Med.Libn.
Founded: 1823. **Staff:** Prof 1; Other 2. **Subjects:** Psychiatry, clinical
psychology, psychoanalysis, psychiatric nursing. **Holdings:** 7000 books;
5000 bound periodical volumes; 19 VF drawers of reprints and pamphlets;
800 audiotapes; 39 videotapes. **Subscriptions:** 163 journals and other serials.
Services: Interlibrary loan; copying; SDI; library open to hospital staff.
Computerized Information Services: MEDLARS, BRS Information
Technologies; DOCLINE (electronic mail service). **Networks/Consortia:**
Member of Health Information Libraries of Westchester (HILOW),
Medical Library Center of New York (MLCNY), National Network of
Libraries of Medicine - Middle Atlantic Region. **Special Indexes:**
Specialized indexes to literature of medicine, psychiatry, psychology, and
psychoanalysis. **Remarks:** FAX: (914)997-5861.

New York Infirmary Beekman Downtown Hospital
See: New York Downtown Hospital (11575)

★ 11582 ★
New York Institute for Special Education - Walter Brooks Library
  (Educ, Aud-Vis)
999 Pelham Pkwy.   Phone: (212)519-7000
Bronx, NY 10469   Harriet Rothstein, Hd.Libn.
Founded: 1832. **Staff:** Prof 2. **Subjects:** Special education. **Holdings:** 6600
ink-print books; 14,750 braille books; 650 talking books; 5000 pamphlets;
10 VF drawers; 205 filmstrips; 200 tapes. **Subscriptions:** 111 journals and
other serials. **Automated Operations:** Computerized public access catalog
and circulation. **Computerized Information Services:** Internal databases.
Staff: Mary Coppinger, Libn.

★ 11583 ★
New York Institute of Technology - Education Hall - Art & Architecture
  Library (Art, Plan)
Wheatley Rd.   Phone: (516)686-7579
Old Westbury, NY 11568   Clare Cohn, Br.Libn.
Staff: Prof 1.5; Other 1. **Subjects:** Architecture, art, interior design, urban
planning, building technology, engineering, photography. **Special
Collections:** Architecture slides (32,500); architectural plans and drawings
(451); local history and architecture collection; Sweet's catalogs. **Holdings:**
15,992 books; 3700 bound periodical volumes; 224 maps; 22 films; 41
videotapes; 198 theses; 1249 reels of microfilm; 77 cassettes; 12 VF drawers
of clippings. **Subscriptions:** 251 journals and other serials. **Services:**
Interlibrary loan (through Central Library); copying; library open to the
public for reference use only. **Automated Operations:** Computerized
cataloging. **Computerized Information Services:** Access to DIALOG
Information Services. Performs searches on fee basis. Contact Person: Jeff
Feinsilver, 686-7568. **Special Indexes:** Subject index to clipping files, theses,
maps, and periodicals not indexed. **Remarks:** Alternate telephone
number(s): (516)686-7422. **Staff:** Aurorita Intal; Maria Serra.

★ 11584 ★
New York Institute of Technology - Wisser Memorial Library (Sci-Engr,
  Bus-Fin)
Northern Rd.   Phone: (516)686-7657
Old Westbury, NY 11568   Dr. Constance Woo, Dir. of Libs.
Staff: Prof 13; Other 15. **Subjects:** Business; labor and industrial relations;
computer science; energy; engineering; architecture; fine arts; mechanical,

electrical, and computer technology; communication arts; clinical nutrition.
Holdings: 177,700 books; 27,200 bound periodical volumes; 24,000 reels of
microfilm; 385,000 microfiche; 33 VF cabinets; ERIC documents.
Subscriptions: 3300 journals and other serials. **Services:** Interlibrary loan
(fee); copying; library open to the public for reference use only.
Computerized Information Services: DIALOG Information Services, BRS
Information Technologies; CD-ROMs (InfoTrac, ABI/INFORM).
Networks/Consortia: Member of Long Island Library Resources Council,
New York Metropolitan Reference and Research Library Agency.
Publications: Library News; Newly Cataloged Acquisitions. **Remarks:**
FAX: (516)626-2914. Maintains branch libraries at 1855 Broadway, New
York, NY 10023 and Central Islip, NY 11722. **Staff:** Marjorie Shapiro,
Tech.Serv.Div.; Marilyn Koplik, Br.Libn., Old Westbury; Rosemary
Feeney, Br.Libn., Central Islip; Merlene Jackson, Br.Libn., New York City;
Clare Cohn, Br.Libn., Educ. Hall.

★ 11585 ★
New York Law Institute - Library (Law)
120 Broadway, Rm. 932   Phone: (212)732-8720
New York, NY 10271   Nancy G. Joseph, Libn.
Founded: 1828. **Staff:** Prof 2; Other 14. **Subjects:** Law. **Special Collections:**
Records and briefs of the New York Court of Appeals and Supreme Court,
Appelate Division, 1st, 2nd, 3rd, and 4th departments; legal Americana.
Holdings: 250,000 books; 25,000 bound periodical volumes; loose-leaf
serials; microfilm; microfiche; periodicals. **Services:** Library open to the
public with restrictions. **Automated Operations:** Computerized cataloging
and serials. **Computerized Information Services:** LEXIS, WESTLAW, LRS.
Remarks: FAX: (212)406-1204. **Staff:** David Orenstein, Asst.Libn.

★ 11586 ★
New York Law School - Library (Law)
57 Worth St.   Phone: (212)431-2333
New York, NY 10013   Joyce D. Saltalamachia, Lib.Dir.
Founded: 1891. **Staff:** Prof 10; Other 13. **Subjects:** Law. **Holdings:** 336,000
books. **Subscriptions:** 3000 journals and other serials. **Services:** Interlibrary
loan; library not open to the public. **Automated Operations:** Computerized
cataloging. **Computerized Information Services:** DIALOG Information
Services, OCLC, LEXIS, WESTLAW. **Networks/Consortia:** Member of
New York Metropolitan Reference and Research Library Agency.
Publications: Contents of Current Legal Periodicals, weekly; New
Acquisitions List, monthly - both for internal distribution only. **Remarks:**
FAX: (212)431-2327. **Staff:** William R. Mills, Assoc.Libn.; Joseph Molinari,
Hd., Pub.Serv.; Paul Mastrangelo, Tech.Serv.Coord.

★ 11587 ★
New York Life Insurance Company - Law Library (Law)
51 Madison Ave., Rm. 10SB   Phone: (212)576-6458
New York, NY 10010   Margaret Butler, Law Libn.
Founded: 1946. **Staff:** Prof 1. **Subjects:** Law. **Holdings:** 25,000 volumes.
Subscriptions: 90 journals and other serials; 3 newspapers. **Services:**
Interlibrary loan; library not open to the public. **Remarks:** FAX: (212)576-
8339.

★ 11588 ★
New York Medical College - Medical Sciences Library (Med)
Basic Sciences Bldg.
New York Medical College   Phone: (914)993-4200
Valhalla, NY 10595   Donald E. Roy, Dir.
Founded: 1972. **Staff:** Prof 8; Other 7. **Subjects:** Basic science, clinical
medicine. **Special Collections:** History of medicine; rare books in medicine
and science. **Holdings:** 35,200 books; 118,000 bound periodical volumes; 65
VF drawers; 616 microfiche; 410 reels of microfilm; 32 audiotapes; 702
videotapes. **Subscriptions:** 1200 journals and other serials. **Services:**
Interlibrary loan; copying; library open to health professionals who purchase
a special membership. **Automated Operations:** Computerized cataloging,
acquisitions, and serials. **Computerized Information Services:** OCLC,
ERIC, MEDLARS, DIALOG Information Services, BRS Information
Technologies; CD-ROM (MEDLINE); LINX Courier, DOCLINE
(electronic mail services). Performs searches on fee basis. Contact Person:
Rita Lee, Hd., Info.Serv., 993-4210. **Networks/Consortia:** Member of
Medical Library Center of New York (MLCNY), National Network of
Libraries of Medicine - Middle Atlantic Region, New York State
Interlibrary Loan Network (NYSILL), Health Information Libraries of
Westchester (HILOW), New York Metropolitan Reference and Research
Library Agency. **Publications:** Libraryline, irregular. **Remarks:** Alternate
telephone number(s): 993-4203. FAX: (914)993-4191. **Staff:** Luiza
Balthazar, Hd., Info.Proc.; Phyllis Niles, Hd., Ser.; Arlene Miller, Hd.,
Circ.; Anthony Artale, Hd., ILL; Christine Hunter, Cat.; Kathleen Conrad,
ILL Coord.

★ 11589 ★
New York Metropolitan Transportation Council - Library
One World Trade Center, 82nd Fl. E.
New York, NY 10048
Founded: 1961. **Subjects:** Regional planning, transportation, economic development, census, grants, ecology, air pollution, land use, open space, master plans. **Holdings:** 7000 books; 10,000 technical reports. **Remarks:** Currently inactive.

New York Natural Heritage Program
See: **New York State Department of Environment Conservation** (11649)

★ 11590 ★
New York Post - Library (Publ)
210 South St.   Phone: (212)815-8200
New York, NY 10002   Merrill F. Sherr, Hd.Libn.
Founded: 1920. **Staff:** Prof 4; Other 6. **Subjects:** Newspaper reference topics. **Holdings:** 5000 books; 10,000 pamphlets; 10 million clippings; 1.4 million pictures. **Services:** Library not open to the public. **Remarks:** FAX: (212)732-4241.

★ 11591 ★
New York Psychoanalytic Institute - Abraham A. Brill Library (Med)
247 E. 82nd St.   Phone: (212)879-6900
New York, NY 10028   Maria Astifidis, Libn.
Founded: 1932. **Staff:** Prof 1; Other 2. **Subjects:** Psychoanalysis, psychiatry. **Special Collections:** Works of Sigmund Freud in all available translations; Kris Memorial Collection (books in allied fields); archives and oral history. **Holdings:** 50,000 volumes. **Subscriptions:** 55 journals and other serials. **Services:** Interlibrary loan; copying; SDI; library open to the public. **Automated Operations:** Computerized cataloging, serials, and circulation. **Computerized Information Services:** DIALOG Information Services; JOURLIT/JOURLOOK (internal database). **Networks/Consortia:** Member of National Network of Libraries of Medicine (NN/LM), New York Metropolitan Reference and Research Library Agency.

★ 11592 ★
New York Public Library - Andrew Heiskell Library for the Blind and Physically Handicapped (Aud-Vis)
40 W. 20th St.   Phone: (212)206-5400
New York, NY 10011   Barbara Nugent, Reg.Br.Libn.
Founded: 1895. **Staff:** Prof 9; Other 17. **Holdings:** 504,500 items including braille, talking books, and cassettes. **Services:** A designated Regional Library of the National Library Service for the Blind and Physically Handicapped for readers residing in New York City and Long Island. Materials and appropriate equipment loaned to eligible individuals and institutions. Provides bibliographic, reference, consultant, reader guidance, outreach, and agency referral services. Message recording service, 24 hours a day at (212)206-5425. Training and assistance in the use of the Kurzweil Reading Machine and other aids by appointment, Audio Book studio. **Automated Operations:** Computerized circulation. **Publications:** Informational brochures; newsletter (large-print and braille), semiannual; bibliographies - available on request. **Remarks:** FAX: (212)206-5418. **Formerly:** Its Regional Library for the Blind and Physically Handicapped.

★ 11593 ★
New York Public Library - Annex Section - Newspapers and Other Research Materials Collection (Info Sci)
521 W. 43rd St.   Phone: (212)714-8520
New York, NY 10036   Richard L. Hill, First Asst., Annex
Founded: 1911. **Staff:** Prof 1; Other 12. **Subjects:** Extensive coverage of New York City newspapers (English and foreign language); selective coverage for United States and principal foreign countries. **Holdings:** 2 million city directories, telephone directories, periodicals, public documents, other materials; 15,000 bound volumes of newspapers; 125,000 reels of microfilm. **Subscriptions:** 164 newspapers. **Services:** Copying. **Networks/Consortia:** Member of Research Libraries Information Network (RLIN), New York Metropolitan Reference and Research Library Agency, New York State Interlibrary Loan Network (NYSILL).

★ 11594 ★
New York Public Library - Annex Section - Patents Collection (Sci-Engr)
521 W. 43rd St.   Phone: (212)714-8529
New York, NY 10036   Richard L. Hill, First Asst., Annex
Founded: 1911. **Staff:** 3. **Subjects:** Complete U.S. and British patents, extensive holdings from France, Germany, Belgium, Denmark, and Sweden, abstracts from other nations, complete files of U.S. indexes. **Holdings:** 100,000 volumes; 5500 reels of microfilm; 4800 microfiche. **Subscriptions:** 52 journals and other serials. **Services:** Copying; collection open to the public. **Computerized Information Services:** U.S. Patent Classification System. **Networks/Consortia:** Member of Research Libraries Information Network (RLIN), New York Metropolitan Reference and Research Library Agency, New York State Interlibrary Loan Network (NYSILL).

★ 11595 ★
New York Public Library - Arents Collection of Books in Parts (Hum)
Fifth Ave. & 42nd St., Rm. 324
New York, NY 10018   Phone: (212)930-0801
Founded: 1957. **Staff:** 1. **Subjects:** Books issued in installments or parts in original format, unbound parts as issued. **Holdings:** 1500 books; autograph letters, original drawings, manuscripts related to works issued in parts. **Services:** Open to qualified researchers by card of admission secured in Special Collections Office.

★ 11596 ★
New York Public Library - Arents Tobacco Collection (Biol Sci)
Fifth Ave. & 42nd St., Rm. 324
New York, NY 10018   Phone: (212)930-0801
Founded: 1944. **Staff:** 1. **Subjects:** Tobacco, herbals, history, medicine, law. **Special Collections:** Autograph letters; manuscripts; first editions of English and American drama, poetry, prose containing mention of tobacco; selected tobacco ephemera. **Holdings:** 13,000 books and manuscripts; 150,000 cards and pieces of ephemera. **Services:** Open to qualified researchers by card of admission secured in Special Collections Office.

★ 11597 ★
New York Public Library - Belmont Regional Library - Enrico Fermi Cultural Center - Italian Heritage Collection (Area-Ethnic)
610 E. 186th St.   Phone: (212)933-6410
Bronx, NY 10458   Mary Rinato Berman, Reg.Libn.
Founded: 1981. **Staff:** Prof 5; Other 6. **Subjects:** Italian heritage and contribution to American ideals; immigration. **Special Collections:** Italian language books (2800); Italian/American biographies from newspapers and periodicals. **Holdings:** 42,291 books; 141 filmstrips; 1667 recordings; 1003 video cassettes. **Subscriptions:** 78 journals and other serials; 10 newspapers. **Services:** Center open to the public; reference assistance available on-site only. **Remarks:** FAX: (212)365-8756.

★ 11598 ★
New York Public Library - Berg Collection (Hum)
Fifth Ave. & 42nd St., Rm. 318, 320   Phone: (212)930-0802
New York, NY 10018   Francis O. Mattson, Cur.
Founded: 1940. **Staff:** Prof 3. **Subjects:** English and American literature of 15th-20th centuries. **Holdings:** 25,000 books; 77,000 letters and manuscripts. **Services:** Collection open by card of admission only. **Networks/Consortia:** Member of Research Libraries Information Network (RLIN), New York Metropolitan Reference and Research Library Agency. **Special Catalogs:** Five-volume catalog published in 1969 with a two-volume supplement in 1983. **Remarks:** Incorporates libraries of Dr. Albert A. Berg, W.T.H. Howe, and Owen D. Young.

★ 11599 ★
New York Public Library - Carl H. Pforzheimer Shelley and His Circle Collection (Hum)
Fifth Ave. & 42nd St., Rm. 319
New York, NY 10018   Phone: (212)930-0717
Founded: 1986. **Staff:** Prof 2. **Subjects:** Outstanding English literature material on Shelley and his circle, including Byron, Leigh Hunt, Peacock, Godwin, Thomas Moore, women writers of 1790-1840 (Mary Wollstoncraft, Mary Hays, Lady Blessington). **Holdings:** 13,000 books; 8000 manuscripts; 6 VF drawers. **Subscriptions:** 45 journals and other serials. **Services:** Collection open to scholars on approval of application. **Special Catalogs:** Shelley and His Circle 1773-1822 (in progress). **Remarks:** FAX: (212)302-4815. **Staff:** Dr. D.H. Reiman, Ed.; Stephen S. Wagner, Bibliog.

★ 11600 ★
New York Public Library - Chatham Square Regional Branch Library -
Chinese Heritage Collection (Area-Ethnic)
33 E. Broadway   Phone: (212)964-6598
New York, NY 10002   Virginia Swift, Reg.Libn.
Founded: 1903. **Staff:** Prof 5; Other 5. **Subjects:** Chinese Heritage
Collections. **Special Collections:** Chinese heritage; history of Chinatown.
Holdings: 39,707 books; 190 filmstrips; 2205 sound recordings.
Subscriptions: 80 journals and other serials. **Services:** Interlibrary loan;
copying; library open to the public. **Remarks:** FAX: (212)385-7850.

★ 11601 ★
New York Public Library - Countee Cullen Regional Branch Library -
African-American Heritage Collection (Area-Ethnic)
104 W. 136th St.   Phone: (212)491-2070
New York, NY 10030   Phyllis G. Mack, Reg.Libn.
Founded: 1905. **Staff:** Prof 5; Other 4. **Subjects:** Ethnic heritage, African and
African-American heritage and culture. **Special Collections:** James Weldon
Johnson Collection of Children's Books on the Black Experience. **Holdings:**
68,178 books; 2642 recordings; 1020 videocassettes. **Subscriptions:** 55
journals and other serials; 12 newspapers. **Services:** Interlibrary loan;
copying; library open to the public. **Remarks:** FAX: (212)491-6541.
Formerly: Its Ethnic Heritage Collection.

★ 11602 ★
New York Public Library - Donnell Library Center
20 W. 53rd St.   Phone: (212)621-0665
New York, NY 10019   Anne J. Hofmann, Chf.Libn.
Founded: 1955. **Staff:** Prof 37.5; Other 41. **Holdings:** 329,253 books.
Services: Interlibrary loan; copying; library open to the public.
Computerized Information Services: InfoTrac; CD-ROM (National
Newspaper Index). **Remarks:** "Donnell Library Center provides reference,
advisory, and lending services. It provides the most extensive service to
children and young adults within The New York Public Library, through
its Central Children's Room and Nathan Straus Young Adult Library. The
system's major holdings in film and video and in foreign language materials
are contained in Donnell's Media Center and in the Foreign Language
Library. The Donnell Library Center also includes a large Adult Lending
Library, Reference Library, and a large collection of recordings in the Media
Center. An auditorium offers a wide diversity of programs without charge
to persons of all ages." FAX: (212)245-5272. **Staff:** Robert Bellinger,
Assoc.Chf.Libn.

★ 11603 ★
New York Public Library - Donnell Library Center - Central Children's
Room (Hum)
20 W. 53rd St.   Phone: (212)621-0636
New York, NY 10019   Angeline Moscatt, Supv.Libn.
Founded: 1911. **Staff:** Prof 3. **Subjects:** 20th century fiction and nonfiction,
folklore, histories of children's literature, foreign languages. **Special**
Collections: Historical collection of children's literature; Mary Gould Davis
- Folklore; Erica Davies - autographed copies; Winnie the Pooh and friends
(original toys). **Holdings:** 112,495 books; 600 bound periodical volumes;
4471 phonograph records and cassettes; 206 filmstrips; vertical files of
clippings and pamphlets; 200 computer software programs. **Services:**
Interlibrary loan; copying; room open to the public; appointment must be
made to use rare book collection. **Remarks:** FAX: (212)245-5272.

★ 11604 ★
New York Public Library - Donnell Library Center - Foreign Language
Library (Hum)
20 W. 53rd St.   Phone: (212)621-0641
New York, NY 10019   Bosiljka Stevanovic, Supv.Libn.
Founded: 1955. **Staff:** Prof 5; Other 1. **Subjects:** Books in more than 80
foreign languages with emphasis on classical and contemporary literature in
the languages represented. **Holdings:** 133,528 books, including bilingual
dictionaries, foreign language grammars and encyclopedias (for reference
only); magazines of general interest. **Services:** Interlibrary loan; telephone
reference; library open to the public. **Remarks:** FAX: (212)245-5272.

★ 11605 ★
New York Public Library - Donnell Library Center - Media Center
(Aud-Vis)
20 W. 53rd St.   Phone: (212)621-0609
New York, NY 10019   Marie Nesthus, Prin.Libn.
Founded: 1958. **Staff:** Prof 8; Other 8. **Subjects:** General collection of short
documentary and feature-length films for children, young adults, adults;
recordings of classical music, jazz, musical comedy, folk music; recordings
of drama, poetry, speeches, documentaries in English and languages other
than English; instructional recordings for learning English and over 40
European, African, Oriental languages; instructional recordings for steno-
dictation, typing, spelling, Morse code, yoga, dance. **Special Collections:**
Pamphlet collection of filmographies and sources of 16mm films. **Holdings:**
1541 books; 5000 pamphlets; 8150 16mm sound films; 3500 video cassettes;
32,000 phonograph records, cassettes, compact discs of classical and
international popular music, language instruction, literature. **Subscriptions:**
34 journals and other serials. **Services:** Films, video cassettes, and compact
discs loaned to nonprofit organizations (not schools) and individuals in New
York City; reference materials available for use within the library; Film/
Video Study Center for viewing films and video cassettes; viewing equipment
available for use by appointment; center open to the public. **Publications:**
Film Catalog, Video Catalog - for sale. **Remarks:** FAX: (212)245-5272.

★ 11606 ★
New York Public Library - Donnell Library Center - Nathan Straus
Young Adult Library (Hum)
20 W. 53rd St.   Phone: (212)621-0633
New York, NY 10019   Joanne Rosario, Supv.Libn.
Founded: 1941. **Staff:** Prof 3. **Subjects:** Young adult literature. **Special**
Collections: Historical collection of young adult books; reference copies of
books appearing on New York Public Library's Books for the Teen Age list
(1250); Learners Advisory Service for Teenagers. **Holdings:** 12,069 books;
8 VF drawers of pamphlets; recreational materials; games; 154 software
programs. **Subscriptions:** 67 journals and other serials. **Services:** Interlibrary
loan; library open to the public. **Computerized Information Services:** GIS
Educational Service (internal database). **Remarks:** FAX: (212)245-5272.

★ 11607 ★
New York Public Library - Early Childhood Resource and Information
Center (Educ)
66 Leroy St., 2nd Fl.   Phone: (212)929-0815
New York, NY 10014   Hannah Nuba, Supv.Libn.
Founded: 1978. **Staff:** Prof 1.5. **Subjects:** Early childhood and parent
education, prenatal care, parent-child activities, language and intellectual
development, multicultural and multilingual education, adoption and foster
care. **Special Collections:** Adult collection on child development, parenting,
education, and special needs; circulating collection of books and puzzles for
young children. **Holdings:** 14,597 books; 72 noncirculating filmstrip kits; 72
noncirculating films; 359 sound recordings; 132 videocassettes.
Subscriptions: 45 journals and other serials. **Services:** Center open to the
public; offers free workshops (September-May).

★ 11608 ★
New York Public Library - Economic and Public Affairs Division (Bus-
Fin, Soc Sci)
Fifth Ave. & 42nd St., Rm. 228   Phone: (212)930-0750
New York, NY 10018   John V. Ganly, Chf.
Founded: 1911. **Staff:** Prof 15; Other 16. **Subjects:** Government
publications, demography, advertising, marketing, labor, industry, banking,
insurance. **Special Collections:** Government publications of national, state,
and municipal jurisdictions throughout the world and of intergovernmental
organizations; census and statistical information; Henry George Collection.
Holdings: 1.5 million books; 1.5 million microforms. **Subscriptions:** 11,000
journals and other serials. **Services:** Interlibrary loan; copying; division open
to the public. **Automated Operations:** Computerized cataloging.
Computerized Information Services: DIALOG Information Services,
WESTLAW, WILSONLINE, Questel, Legislative Retrieval Systems
(LRS). Performs searches on fee basis. Contact Person: Jacqueline Lavalle,
930-0755. **Networks/Consortia:** Member of Research Libraries Information
Network (RLIN), New York Metropolitan Reference and Research Library
Agency, New York State Interlibrary Loan Network (NYSILL). **Remarks:**
Public Affairs Information Service is housed in this division but is not part
of the library. **Staff:** Erminio D'Onofrio, Docs.Libn.

New York Public Library - General Library & Museum of the
Performing Arts at Lincoln Center
See: New York Public Library for the Performing Arts (11635)

★11609★
New York Public Library - General Research Division (Hum)
Fifth Ave. & 42nd St.   Phone: (212)930-0831
New York, NY 10011   Beth Diefendorf, Chf.
Founded: 1911. **Staff:** Prof 34.5; Other 16. **Subjects:** Anthropology, archeology, bibliography, biography, geography, history, languages and literatures of the world (except collections in Jewish, Slavonic, and Oriental Divisions), philology, philosophy, printing, publishing, psychology, religion, sports. **Special Collections:** Spaulding Collection (baseball); David McKelvy White Collection (Spanish Civil War); folklore of the Americas; Indians of the Western Hemisphere; chess collection; small press poetry; Southwest Americana; World Wars I and II. **Holdings:** 2.7 million volumes. **Subscriptions:** 11,000 periodicals. **Services:** Copying; division open to the public for reference use only. **Automated Operations:** Computerized public access catalog. **Computerized Information Services:** DIALOG Information Services, Questel, WILSONLINE, RLIN, OCLC, VU/TEXT Information Services; internal databases; CD-ROMs; ALANET (electronic mail service). Performs searches on fee basis. Contact Person: John Hawker, 930-0826. **Networks/Consortia:** Member of Research Libraries Information Network (RLIN), New York Metropolitan Reference and Research Library Agency, New York State Interlibrary Loan Network (NYSILL).

★11610★
**New York Public Library - Hunt's Point Regional Branch Library -
Hispanic Heritage Collection** (Area-Ethnic)
877 Southern Blvd.   Phone: (212)617-0338
Bronx, NY 10459   Margaret Hetley, Reg.Libn.
Founded: 1929. **Staff:** Prof 5; Other 5.5. **Subjects:** Spanish language and literature, Puerto Rican culture, literary criticism in English and Spanish. **Special Collections:** Hispanic Heritage Collection (10,000 volumes). **Holdings:** 50,000 books; 27 bound periodical volumes; 1222 sound recordings; 583 filmstrips; 478 videocassettes; 30 periodicals on microfiche; 119 software programs. **Subscriptions:** 175 journals and other serials; 7 newspapers. **Services:** Interlibrary loan; copying; library open to the public. **Remarks:** FAX: (212)893-3491.

★11611★
New York Public Library - Jewish Division (Area-Ethnic, Rel-Phil)
Fifth Ave. & 42nd St., Rm. 84   Phone: (212)930-0601
New York, NY 10018   Leonard S. Gold, Chf.
Founded: 1897. **Staff:** Prof 7; Other 3. **Subjects:** General works in Hebrew and Yiddish; Jewish history, literature, and traditions (in various languages). **Special Collections:** Rare Hebrew books including 40 incunabula; early kabbalistic and ethical tracts; illuminated Ketubot (marriage contracts); Yizkor (memorial) books. **Holdings:** 233,000 volumes; newspapers; periodicals; microfilm; microfiche. **Services:** Division open to the public. **Networks/Consortia:** Member of Research Libraries Information Network (RLIN), New York Metropolitan Reference and Research Library Agency, New York State Interlibrary Loan Network (NYSILL), Council of Archives and Research Libraries in Jewish Studies (CARLJS). **Remarks:** FAX: (212)921-2546.

★11612★
New York Public Library - Map Division (Geog-Map)
Fifth Ave. & 42nd St., Rm. 117   Phone: (212)930-0587
New York, NY 10018   Alice C. Hudson, Chf.
Staff: Prof 4; Other 1. **Subjects:** History of cartography; techniques of map making; gazetteers; state, county, historical, and real estate atlases; city plans; travel; American maps and atlases, 1700 to present; European maps, 1600 to present; topographical surveys; thematic maps; oil company road maps; 17th century Dutch atlases. **Special Collections:** Scrapbook collection of small-size sheet maps (on microfilm); New York City real estate atlases. **Holdings:** 12,459 atlases and folded maps in binders; 4928 volumes; 400,000 sheet maps. **Subscriptions:** 84 journals and other serials. **Services:** Copying. **Automated Operations:** Computerized cataloging. **Networks/Consortia:** Member of Research Libraries Information Network (RLIN), New York Metropolitan Reference and Research Library Agency, New York State Interlibrary Loan Network (NYSILL). **Remarks:** FAX: (212)869-7824. **Staff:** April Carlucci, Asst.Chf.; Nancy A. Kandoian, Map Cat.; Julie Zelman, Map Ref.Libn.; Sonia Moss, Tech.Asst.

★11613★
New York Public Library - Microforms Division (Soc Sci)
Fifth Ave. & 42nd St.   Phone: (212)930-0838
New York, NY 10018   Thomas Bourke, Chf.
Founded: 1980. **Staff:** Prof 2; Other 5.5. **Subjects:** Literature, psychology, social science, science. **Special Collections:** FBI files on the Assassination of President Kennedy; American Civil Liberties Union papers; History of Women Collection; History of Photography Collection; papers pertaining to the Amistad Schooner case. **Holdings:** 170,000 reels of microfilm; 400,000 microfiche; 103,309 microcards; city directories; newspapers. **Subscriptions:** 4000 journals and other serials; 200 newspapers. **Services:** Interlibrary loan (limited); copying; division open to the public. **Automated Operations:** Computerized cataloging and acquisitions. **Computerized Information Services:** DIALOG Information Services, RLIN. **Networks/Consortia:** Member of Research Libraries Information Network (RLIN), New York Metropolitan Reference and Research Library Agency, New York State Interlibrary Loan Network (NYSILL).

★11614★
New York Public Library - Mid-Manhattan Library
455 Fifth Ave.   Phone: (212)340-0833
New York, NY 10016   Robert Goldstein, Chf.Libn.
Founded: 1970. **Staff:** Prof 69.5; Other 71.5. **Holdings:** 732,424 books; 38,000 bound periodical volumes; 4.8 million pictures; 8808 nonmusical cassettes; 501 filmstrips; 3292 videocassettes; 25 software programs. **Subscriptions:** 5000 journals and other serials; 45 newspapers. **Services:** Interlibrary loan; copying; library open to the public. **Automated Operations:** Computerized public access catalog and cataloging. **Computerized Information Services:** DIALOG Information Services. **Networks/Consortia:** Member of New York Metropolitan Reference and Research Library Agency. **Remarks:** "The Mid-Manhattan Library, which opened on October 26, 1970, is the central library of the New York Public Library's Branch Library System. It provides a needed transition between the level of service provided by the neighborhood branches and borough centers and that provided through the vast scholarly archival collections of the Research Libraries of the New York Public Library. Mid-Manhattan Library's primary function is to serve, through open shelf collections, the serious adult reader and the college undergraduate student. The collections of this library are housed in a History and Social Sciences Department; a Literature and Language Department, which includes the Art and Picture Collections and Popular Library, a general circulation collection; a Science and Business Department; and the General Reference Service (see entries below). The departments contain both reference and circulating materials. In addition, there are a number of special collections and services administered by the departments. The library has strong holdings in serials, especially those appearing in the standard indexes. It provides online database searches in all departments. Its catalog is computer-produced, in book form, and online." FAX: (212)679-5695. **Staff:** Eric Steele, Assoc.Chf.Libn.

★11615★
New York Public Library - Mid-Manhattan Library - Art Collection
(Art)
455 Fifth Ave.   Phone: (212)340-0871
New York, NY 10016   Frances Novack, Supv.Libn.
Founded: 1956. **Staff:** Prof 4. **Subjects:** Fine arts, architecture, graphic art, photography. **Holdings:** 34,176 books; 2000 bound periodical volumes; 200 reels of microfilm of periodicals; 20 VF drawers of clippings and catalogs. **Subscriptions:** 110 journals and other serials. **Services:** Copying; collection open to the public. **Remarks:** FAX: (212)679-5695.

★11616★
**New York Public Library - Mid-Manhattan Library - Art and Literature
Department** (Hum)
455 Fifth Ave.   Phone: (212)340-0873
New York, NY 10016   Robert Foy, Sr.Coord.Libn.
Founded: 1970. **Staff:** Prof 7; Other 6. **Subjects:** English and American literature, French and Spanish literature, other foreign literatures in translation, linguistics, languages and language learning. **Holdings:** 152,357 books; 5500 bound periodical volumes; 6770 language and nonmusic audiocassettes; 10,000 volumes of English literature on microfiche; 7000 periodical volumes in microform. **Subscriptions:** 510 journals and other serials. **Services:** Interlibrary loan; copying; closed circuit television enlarger; department open to the public. **Computerized Information Services:** DIALOG Information Services; CD-ROM (MLA International Bibliography). Performs searches free of charge. **Remarks:** FAX: (212)679-5695. This department administers literature, art and picture collections, and the popular library. **Formerly:** Its Literature and Language Department. **Staff:** Deborah Hirsch, Supv.Libn.

★ 11617 ★
New York Public Library - Mid-Manhattan Library - General Reference Service/Education Collection (Educ)
455 Fifth Ave.   Phone: (212)340-0863
New York, NY 10016   Barbara Shapiro, Sr.Coord.Libn.
Founded: 1970. **Staff:** Prof 17; Other 16. **Special Collections:** U.S. and foreign college catalogs (4000). **Holdings:** 30,554 books; 8000 bound periodical volumes; ERIC microfiche, 1966 to present. **Subscriptions:** 650 journals and other serials; 39 newspapers. **Services:** Copying; open to the public. **Computerized Information Services:** DIALOG Information Services, InfoTrac, ERIC, Peterson's College Database; CD-ROMs (Dissertation Abstracts Ondisc, Education Index, General Periodicals Index-Public Library Edition, National Newspaper Index, Biography Index). **Remarks:** FAX: (212)679-5695. This department administers general reference services, telephone reference service, and specialized services in the fields of education, job information, learner's advisory, and service for the disabled. The above telephone numbe r is for General Reference Service. The number for Education is 340-0864. **Staff:** Wol Sue Lee, First Asst.; Barbara Berliner, Telephone Ref.Serv.; Georgia Donati, Job Info.Ctr.

★ 11618 ★
New York Public Library - Mid-Manhattan Library - History and Social Sciences Department (Hist, Soc Sci)
455 Fifth Ave.   Phone: (212)340-0887
New York, NY 10016   Donna Abbaticchio, Sr.Prin.Libn.
Founded: 1970. **Staff:** Prof 9; Other 5. **Subjects:** History, psychology, sociology, law, religion, philosophy. **Special Collections:** New York City history (3500 volumes); Microbook Library of American Civilization (ultrafiche). **Holdings:** 270,776 books; 10,500 bound periodical volumes; 60 VF drawers of pamphlets; selective government depository. **Subscriptions:** 2000 journals and other serials. **Services:** Interlibrary loan; copying; department open to the public. **Computerized Information Services:** DIALOG Information Services, InfoTrac, Legaltrac; CD-ROMs (PsycLIT, General Periodicals Index-Public Library Edition, Sociofile). **Remarks:** FAX: (212)679-5695. **Staff:** Edith Ostrowsky, First Asst.

★ 11619 ★
New York Public Library - Mid-Manhattan Library - Job Information Center (Educ)
455 Fifth Ave.   Phone: (212)340-0836
New York, NY 10016   Georgia Donati, Supv.Libn.
Founded: 1975. **Staff:** Prof 4; Other 1. **Subjects:** Career planning, job search techniques, resume writing, educational and vocational guidance. **Special Collections:** Civil Service study guides; national clipping files of job ads; business directories; career-oriented periodicals; college and university directories; continuing education information. **Holdings:** 8851 books. **Subscriptions:** 40 journals and other serials; 6 newspapers. **Services:** Copying; center open to the public. **Computerized Information Services:** DISCOVER (internal database). **Remarks:** FAX: (212)679-5695. **Formerly:** Its Learner's Advisory Service and Job Information Center.

★ 11620 ★
New York Public Library - Mid-Manhattan Library - Picture Collection (Aud-Vis)
455 Fifth Ave.   Phone: (212)340-0877
New York, NY 10016   Mildred P. Wright, Supv.Libn.
Founded: 1915. **Staff:** Prof 5; Other 9. **Subjects:** Comprehensive subject coverage in the following areas: costume, flora and fauna, history, geographic views, design. **Holdings:** 698 books; 4.7 million classified pictures. **Services:** Copying; collection open to the public with valid library card, except for classroom use or exhibition. **Remarks:** FAX: (212)679-5695.

★ 11621 ★
New York Public Library - Mid-Manhattan Library - Popular Library
455 Fifth Ave.   Phone: (212)340-0837
New York, NY 10016   Elena Bivona, Supv.Libn.
Founded: 1970. **Staff:** Prof 6; Other 3. **Subjects:** General collection. **Special Collections:** Large-print books. **Holdings:** 77,309 books; 3292 videocassettes. **Services:** Copying; library open to the public. **Remarks:** FAX: (212)679-5695.

★ 11622 ★
New York Public Library - Mid-Manhattan Library - Project Access (Aud-Vis)
455 Fifth Ave.   Phone: (212)340-0843
New York, NY 10016   Betsy Crenshaw, Sr.Libn.
Founded: 1979. **Staff:** Prof 1; Other 1. **Subjects:** The disabled - blind, deaf, learning and mobility impaired. **Special Collections:** Directory collection of organizations, services, equipment, and information sources for the disabled; access guides. **Holdings:** 238 books; 10 VF drawers of pamphlet material concerning the disabled. **Subscriptions:** 20 journals and other serials. **Services:** Library open to the public; special equipment, including Kurzweil reading machine, available for use by appointment. **Computerized Information Services:** DIALOG Information Services; VISTA, VERT PLUS (internal databases). **Publications:** Bibliographies - available on request. **Special Indexes:** Subject index to organizations, services, equipment, information sources, and AV materials for and about the disabled (card). **Remarks:** FAX: (212)679-5695. TDD: (212)340-0931.

★ 11623 ★
New York Public Library - Mid-Manhattan Library - Science/Business Department (Sci-Engr, Biol Sci, Bus-Fin)
455 Fifth Ave.   Phone: (212)340-0883
New York, NY 10016   Frederick Dusold, Sr.Prin.Libn.
Founded: 1970. **Staff:** Prof 12; Other 6. **Subjects:** Life sciences, pure and applied sciences, mathematics, economics, insurance, management. **Holdings:** 155,637 books; 15,000 bound periodical volumes; 12,000 volumes of periodicals in microform; 2380 cassettes; 480 filmstrips. **Subscriptions:** 1450 journals and other serials; 6 newspapers. **Services:** Interlibrary loan; copying; department open to the public. **Computerized Information Services:** DIALOG Information Services, InfoTrac, MEDLINE; CD-ROMs (Business Periodicals Ondisc, General BusinessFile, General Periodicals Index-Public Library Edition). Performs searches free of charge. **Remarks:** The above telephone number is for the Science Department. The number for the Business Department is 340-0884. FAX: (212)679-5695. **Staff:** Edmond Fursa, Supv.Libn./Bus.Coll.

★ 11624 ★
New York Public Library - Miriam and Ira D. Wallach Division of Art, Prints & Photographs - Art and Architecture Collection (Art)
Fifth Ave. & 42nd St., Rm. 313   Phone: (212)930-0834
New York, NY 10018   Paula Baxter, Chf.
Staff: Prof 5; Other 2. **Subjects:** Architecture, painting, drawing, sculpture, costume, applied arts, ceramics, interior decoration, Oriental art. **Holdings:** 230,000 volumes and pamphlets; 100,000 clippings (arranged by name of artist). **Services:** Collection open to the public for reference use only. **Networks/Consortia:** Member of Research Libraries Information Network (RLIN), New York Metropolitan Reference and Research Library Agency, New York State Interlibrary Loan Network (NYSILL). **Staff:** Robert Rainwater, Asst.Dir., Art Div.

★ 11625 ★
New York Public Library - Miriam and Ira D. Wallach Division of Art, Prints & Photographs - Prints & Photographs Room (Art)
Fifth Ave. & 42nd St., Rm. 308
New York, NY 10018   Phone: (212)930-0817
Founded: 1900. **Staff:** Prof 6; Other 3. **Subjects:** Original prints, 15th century to present, with emphasis on 19th century French and American prints; representative examples of contemporary American and international printmakers; photography, 1839 to present. **Special Collections:** Stokes and Eno Collections (American views); Japanese prints; printmaking, print collecting, and graphic arts; Dennis Collection (80,000 stereographs). **Holdings:** 175,000 prints; 200,000 original photographs. **Services:** Room open to qualified researchers by card of admission secured in Special Collections Office. **Staff:** Roberta Waddell, Kpr. of Prints; Julia Van Haaften, Cur. of Photo.

★ 11626 ★
New York Public Library - Oriental Division (Area-Ethnic)
Fifth Ave. & 42nd St., Rm. 219   Phone: (212)930-0845
New York, NY 10018   John M. Lundquist, Chf.
Founded: 1897. **Staff:** Prof 8; Other 5.5. **Subjects:** Language, literature, history, archeology, and religion of the Orient (includes China, Japan, Korea, Tibet, South Asia, Central Asia, the Middle East, and the ancient Middle East). **Special Collections:** Arabic manuscripts; Japanese technical periodicals; Mason Collection of Chinese Mohammedan literature; Manchu

language materials; materials from the Schiff Collection; 19th and 20th century missionary, traveler, and explorer accounts; Egyptology and Assyriology (includes rare 19th century material); Bibliographie Papyrologique Index; rare Chinese books and manuscripts (Ming and Ching) from the library of James Legge (handwritten manuscripts); rare materials illustrating the history of printing in India; Armenian holdings; editions of texts in several Oriental languages (origin als and translations); runs of early Orientalist periodicals; Tibetan language collections. **Holdings:** 250,000 books; 650 pamphlets; 3740 reels of microfilm. **Subscriptions:** 1170 journals and other serials; 47 newspapers. **Services:** Division open to the public for reference use only. **Networks/Consortia:** Member of Research Libraries Information Network (RLIN), New York Metropolitan Reference and Research Library Agency, New York State Interlibrary Loan Network (NYSILL). **Special Catalogs:** Dictionary catalog of the Oriental Collection (1960, 16 volumes; 1976, 8 volumes). **Staff:** Usha Bhasker, First Asst., S. Asia Sec.Hd.; Todd Thompson, Middle East Sec.Hd.; Chung-Soo Kim, E. Asia Sec.Hd.

New York Public Library - Performing Arts Research Center - Billy Rose Theatre Collection
See: **New York Public Library for the Performing Arts (11634)**

New York Public Library - Performing Arts Research Center - Dance Collection
See: **New York Public Library for the Performing Arts - Dance Collection (11636)**

New York Public Library - Performing Arts Research Center - Music Division
See: **New York Public Library for the Performing Arts - Music Division (11637)**

New York Public Library - Performing Arts Research Center - Rodgers & Hammerstein Archives of Recorded Sound
See: **New York Public Library for the Performing Arts (11638)**

★ 11627 ★
New York Public Library - Rare Books & Manuscripts Division - Manuscripts and Archives Section (Hist)
476 Fifth Ave., Rm. 324   Phone: (212)930-0801
New York, NY 10018   Mary B. Bowling, Cur. of Mss.
Staff: Prof 9; Other 5. **Subjects:** New York and American political, social, and literary history from the colonial era to present. **Special Collections:** New York Public Library Historical Archives; American Revolutionary sources; colonial Americana; 19th and 20th century social, political, literary, and personal collections of correspondence; extensive collection of diaries; early merchants account-books; papers of engineers and inventors of the late 19th century; Shakers and Shaker communities; editorial files of periodicals published in New York City; New York World's Fairs, 1939-1940 and 1964-1965. **Holdings:** 25,000 linear feet of manuscripts; personal papers; organizational records. **Services:** Open by appointment to qualified researchers by card of admission secured in Special Collections Office. **Remarks:** FAX: (212)302-4815. **Staff:** Robert Sink, Archv.

★ 11628 ★
New York Public Library - Rare Books & Manuscripts Division - Rare Book Collection (Rare Book)
Fifth Ave. & 42nd St.
New York, NY 10018   Phone: (212)930-0801
Staff: Prof 4; Other 1. **Subjects:** Early voyages and travels; Americana, especially before 1801. **Special Collections:** Early Bibles, including Gutenberg Bible; Bunyan's Pilgrim's Progress; Oscar Lion Collection of Walt Whitman; broadsides (20,000); 18th century American newspapers; modern fine printing. **Holdings:** 110,000 books; 2350 bound periodical volumes; 1750 volumes of bound newspapers; type facsimiles, bindings, ephemera. **Services:** Open to qualified researchers by card of admission secured in Special Collections office. **Publications:** Studies, bibliographies, and lists, irregular.

★ 11629 ★
New York Public Library - Schomburg Center for Research in Black Culture (Area-Ethnic)
515 Malcolm X Blvd.   Phone: (212)491-2200
New York, NY 10037-1801   Howard Dodson, Chf.
Founded: 1926. **Staff:** Prof 30; Other 33. **Subjects:** Social sciences, humanities, the black experience throughout the world. **Special Collections:** Haitian Collection; African and Caribbean music; works of Harlem Renaissance authors and artists. **Holdings:** 102,000 volumes; 3200 archival record groups; 10,000 recordings; 300,000 photographs; 600 videotapes; 5000 hours of oral history; 30,000 reels of microfilm; 40,000 microfiche; paintings; sculpture; drawings; prints; African artifacts. **Subscriptions:** 1000 journals and other serials. **Services:** Copying; center open to adults for reference use. **Computerized Information Services:** RLIN. **Networks/ Consortia:** Member of Research Libraries Information Network (RLIN), New York Metropolitan Reference and Research Library Agency, New York State Interlibrary Loan Network (NYSILL). **Publications:** The Schomburg Center Journal, quarterly. **Special Indexes:** Kaiser Index to Black Resources, 1940 to present (card, online); clipping files (microfiche); local data bases; vertical file holdings, 1925-1974 (microfiche), 1975 to present (paper). **Remarks:** The Center sponsors two Scholar-in-Residency Programs supported by the Ford Foundation and NEH, as well as the bi-annual Clarence L. Holte Literary Prize. FAX: (212)491-6760. **Staff:** Diana Lachatanere, Hd., MMS, Archv., Rare Bks.; Sharon Howard, Hd., Acq. and Tech.Serv.; James B. Murray, Hd., Moving Images, Rec. Sound; Deborah Willis, Hd., Photo. and Prints/Exhibition Coord.; Harold Anderson, Pub.Rel.Off.; Roberta Yancy, Dev.Off.

★ 11630 ★
New York Public Library - Science and Technology Research Center (Sci-Engr)
Fifth Ave. & 42nd St., Rm. 121   Phone: (212)930-0574
New York, NY 10018   Elizabeth Bentley, Chf.
Founded: 1911. **Staff:** Prof 10; Other 9. **Subjects:** Aeronautics, astronautics, astronomy, automobiles, chemistry, communications, computers, cookery, earth sciences, electricity, electronics, engineering (all branches), food technology, industrial arts, mathematics, metallurgy, meteorology, mining, navigation, paper, petroleum, physics, plastics, radio, railroads, rubber, science history, shipbuilding, technology history, textiles. **Special Collections:** William B. Parsons Transportation Engineering Collection (1200 titles of early works). **Holdings:** 1.2 million volumes; 50,000 pamphlet sets and reports. **Subscriptions:** 4500 journals and other serials. **Services:** Copying; reference service by phone and letter; center open to the public for reference use only. **Automated Operations:** Computerized cataloging and acquisitions. **Computerized Information Services:** DIALOG Information Services, NewsNet, Inc., STN International, WILSONLINE, Questel; ALANET (electronic mail service). **Networks/Consortia:** Member of Research Libraries Information Network (RLIN), New York Metropolitan Reference and Research Library Agency, New York State Interlibrary Loan Network (NYSILL). **Publications:** New Technical Books, 6/year - by subs cription. **Remarks:** Alternate telephone number(s): 930-0575. FAX: (212)869-7824. Science-technology materials in Oriental or Slavonic languages are available in the Oriental Division (room 219) or in the Slavic and Baltic Division (room 216).

★ 11631 ★
New York Public Library - Slavic and Baltic Division (Area-Ethnic)
Fifth Ave. & 42nd St., Rm. 217   Phone: (212)930-0714
New York, NY 10018-2788   Edward Kasinec, Chf.
Founded: 1898. **Staff:** Prof 11; Other 6. **Subjects:** Slavic and Baltic literature and linguistics; history (especially Russian Imperial regimental histories and history of Russian revolutionary movements, history of Alaska and her peoples); economics and political science; philosophy; archeology; folklore; art and architecture; ethnology of Baltic, Slavic, and Soviet Central Asian peoples. **Special Collections:** Periodicals of the Imperial and early Soviet periods; Slavic rare books, including early Polonica; especially strong in Russian imprints before 1860 and original photographs, many from the Russian Imperial collections, including the library of Tsarskoye Selo. **Holdings:** 289,468 volumes; 13,562 microforms. **Subscriptions:** 1245 journals; 155 newspapers. **Services:** Copying; replies to written and telephone inquiries; division open to the public for reference use only. **Automated Operations:** Computerized cataloging. **Computerized Information Services:** DIALOG Information Services, RLIN; CATNYP (internal database). **Networks/Consortia:** Member of Research Libraries Information Network (RLIN), New York Metropolitan Reference and Research Library Agency, New York State Interlibrary Loan Network (NYSILL). **Special Catalogs:** Dictionary Catalog of the Slavic Collection (44 volumes); Bibliographic Guide to Soviet and East European Studies (26

volumes, 1979 to present). **Remarks:** Alternate telephone numbers are 930-0941 and 930-0713. The number for current periodical inquiries is 930-0715. FAX: (212)921-2546 or 869-8094, attention: Kasinec.

★ 11632 ★
New York Public Library - Spencer Collection (Rare Book)
Fifth Ave. & 42nd St., Rm. 308   Phone: (212)930-0818
New York, NY 10018   Robert Rainwater, Cur.
Subjects: Rare, illustrated books and illuminated manuscripts in fine bindings, showing the history of book illustration and the book arts in the West from the Middle Ages to the present; work from China, Japan, India, Arabia, Persia. **Holdings:** 7000 books; 1500 manuscripts. **Services:** Collection open to qualified researchers by card of admission secured in Special Collections Office.

★ 11633 ★
New York Public Library - United States History, Local History and Genealogy Division (Hist)
Fifth Ave. & 42nd St., Rm. 315N   Phone: (212)930-0828
New York, NY 10018   Ruth A. Carr, Chf.
Staff: Prof 5; Other 1.5. **Subjects:** U.S. history; county, city, town histories of the United States; European and American genealogy and heraldry; works on names and flags of the world. **Special Collections:** Photographic views of New York City (54,000); postcards and scrapbooks of U.S. local views; Lewis W. Hine Collection (443 prints and negatives); local history ephemera; U.S. election campaign materials. **Holdings:** 106,000 volumes. **Subscriptions:** 1424 journals and other serials. **Services:** Copying; division open to the public. **Automated Operations:** Computerized public access catalog, cataloging, and acquisitions. **Computerized Information Services:** DIALOG Information Services. **Networks/Consortia:** Member of Research Libraries Information Network (RLIN), New York Metropolitan Reference and Research Library Agency, New York State Interlibrary Loan Network (NYSILL). **Staff:** Barbara Hillman, Libn. IV; Asa Rubenstein, Libn. II; Robert Scott, Libn. II; Lawrence Gundersen, Libn. II; Zoe Collier, Libn. II.

★ 11634 ★
New York Public Library for the Performing Arts - Billy Rose Theatre Collection (Theater)
40 Lincoln Center Plaza   Phone: (212)870-1639
New York, NY 10023   Bob Taylor, Cur.
Founded: 1931. **Staff:** Prof 9; Other 15. **Subjects:** Stage, cinema, marionettes and puppets, industrial shows, circus, amusement parks, fairs, carnivals, night club and cabaret, radio and television. **Special Collections:** Robinson Locke Collection; Hiram Stead Collection; Henin Collection; Chamberlain and Lyman Brown Theatrical Agency Collection; Archives of the Vandamm and White Studios; Society of American Magicians; Universal Pictures Still Books; Townsend Walsh Collection; George Becks Collection; Archives of Radio Writers Guild; Archives of Lambs Club, NY; scrapbooks, office records, memorabilia of performing artists, writers, and professional organizations, including: Brooks Atkinson, David Belasco, Katharine Cornell, Helen Hayes, Klaw and Erlanger, R.H. Burnside, Burl Ives, Betty Comden and Adolph Green, Maurice Evans, Jerome Lawrence and Robert E. Lee, Cheryl Crawford, Harold Clurman, Edward Albee, The Living Theatre, The Actor's Workshop (San Francisco), Vivian Beaumont Theater, New York (under Jules Irving's management), Chelsea Theatre Center, Leland Hayward, Sophie Tucker, Playwrights Company, Clifford Odets, Alexander H. Cohen, Neighborhood Playhouse (New York), Group Theatre, Montgomery Clift, Rosamond Gilder, John Golden, Hallie Flanagan, Victor Moore, Bert Lahr, Harold Prince, Alan Schneider, Elliott Nugent, Nancy Hamilton, Israel Horovitz, Jean Dalrymple, Paul Muni, Robert Patrick, Carolyn Leigh, Dorothy Fields, Shepperd Strudwick, Richard Rodgers, Richard and Edie Barstow, Dorothy Stickney. The theatre collection maintains active clipping files on personnel in all areas of the performing arts within its purview, on theater buildings, producing organizations, corporate bodies, amateur theatre and cinema groups, college and university theatre and cinema organizations, and several hundred subject headings. Original designs for stage, cinema, and television by famous designers including: Boris Aronson, Howard Bay, Jo Mielziner, Ladislaus Czettel, Robert Edmond Jones, Bonnie Cashin, Lucinda Ballard, Aline Bernstein, John Boyt, Claude Bragdon, Millia Davenport, Raoul Pene Du Bois, Motley, Mstislav Dobujinsky, Alexandra Exter, David Ffolkes, Simon Lissim, Norman Bel Geddes, Donald Oenslager, Raymond Sovey, Rouben Ter-Arutunian, Irene Sharaff, Sergei Soudeikine; original drawings by Alex Gard, Al Frueh, Al Hirschfeld, Milton Marx, Bert Green. An additional dimension has been added to the collection through an archive of productions and dialogues on videotape. **Holdings:** 39,000 monographs

and bound periodical volumes; 34,550 prompt books and typescripts, including scripts for motion pictures, radio, and television; 32,400 scrapbooks and portfolios; 20 million clippings; 8350 scenery and costume designs; 25,150 posters; 4000 blueprints and plans; 3200 reels of microfilm; 5300 microfiche; 2 million prints, photographs, cinema stills; 850,000 letters and business papers; 1315 videotapes of productions and interviews. **Subscriptions:** 574 journals and other serials. **Services:** Interlibrary loan; copying (both limited); collection open to the public. **Networks/Consortia:** Member of Research Libraries Information Network (RLIN), New York Metropolitan Reference and Research Library Agency, New York State Interlibrary Loan Network (NYSILL). **Special Catalogs:** Printed book catalog and nonbook catalog. **Remarks:** FAX: (212)787-3852. **Formerly:** New York Public Library - Performing Arts Research Center.

★ 11635 ★
New York Public Library for the Performing Arts - Circulating Collections (Mus, Theater)
40 Lincoln Center Plaza   Phone: (212)870-1630
New York, NY 10023-7498   Susan Sommer, Chf.Libn.
Founded: 1965. **Staff:** Prof 15; Other 20. **Subjects:** Music, drama, dance, performing arts. **Special Collections:** Orchestra Collection (4525 parts); Children's Collection; museum which mounts special exhibits, but does not comprise a permanent collection. **Holdings:** 238,570 books; 2250 bound periodical volumes; 96 VF drawers; 100,000 scores; 77,397 sound recordings; 2774 videocassettes. **Subscriptions:** 274 journals and other serials. **Services:** Copying; library open to the public. **Networks/Consortia:** Member of New York Metropolitan Reference and Research Library Agency, Library Information and Online Network (LIONS). **Publications:** Special subject bibliographies and discographies. **Special Indexes:** Song index (card); play analytics. **Remarks:** FAX: (212)870-1704. **Formerly:** New York Public Library - General Library & Museum of the Performing Arts at Lincoln Center. **Staff:** Kristen Shuman, Prin.Libn.; Janice Frank, Supv. Drama Libn.; John L. Hildreth, Supv.Rec.Libn.; Pamela McKay, Sr. Dance Libn.; Elizabeth Long, Sr.Ch.Libn.; Josephine Chan Yung, Supv.Mus.Libn.

★ 11636 ★
New York Public Library for the Performing Arts - Dance Collection (Art, Theater)
40 Lincoln Center Plaza   Phone: (212)870-1657
New York, NY 10023   Madeleine Nichols, Cur.
Founded: 1944. **Staff:** Prof 10.5; Other 6.5. **Subjects:** All forms of dance. **Special Collections:** Jerome Robbins Archive of the Recorded Moving Image (dance films and videotapes); Cia Fornaroli Toscanini (rare ballet history; 15,000 items); Lincoln Kirstein (rare dance history); Fania Marinoff (5000 photographs by Carl Van Vechten); Roger Pryor Dodge (Nijinsky photographs); George Platt Lynes (American ballet; 3000 negatives); Robert W. Dowling (Albert E. Kahn photographs of Galina Ulanova); Constantine (American ballet; 2300 photographs and negatives); Denishawn (American dance; 50,000 items); Ruth St. Denis (10,000 items); Ted Shawn (8000 items); Humphrey-Weidman (modern dance; 5000 items); Doris Humphrey (7000 items); Jose Limon Collection; Helen Tamiris Collection; Hanya Holm (modern dance in Europe and America; 1200 items) ; Irma Duncan (Isadora Duncan memorabilia); Craig-Duncan Collection (400 Isadora Duncan manuscripts); Loie Fuller Collection; American Ballet Theatre Archives; Ballet Russe de Monte Carlo-Serge Denham Collection; Astruc-Dyagilev (Dyagilev Ballets Russes; 1300 documents); Irving Deakin (American ballet); Ruth Page Collection; Claire Holt Collection on Indonesian dance (9000 items); Agnes De Mille Collection (8000 items); Eugene Loring Collection (1200 items); Rouben Ter-Arutunian Collection (70,000 items). **Holdings:** 40,000 books; 2000 original drawings and stage designs; 1.1 million manuscripts; 1600 reels of microfilm; 7000 videotape titles; 2700 motion picture film titles; 1600 oral history tapes; 2200 scrapbooks; 400,000 clippings and reviews; 250,000 photographs; 150,400 photographic negatives; 4500 posters; 6000 prints; 92,500 programs. **Subscriptions:** 75 journals and other serials. **Services:** Copying; collection open to public. **Networks/Consortia:** Member of Research Libraries Information Network (RLIN), New York Metropolitan Reference and Research Library Agency, New York State Interlibrary Loan Network (NYSILL). **Publications:** The Dance Collection: Descriptive Leaflet; Isadora Duncan, Pioneer in the Art of Dance, by Irma Duncan, 1958; When All the World was Dancing: Rare and Curious Books from the Cia Fornaroli Collection, by Marian Eames, 1958 (2nd edition, 1971); Famed for Dance: Essays on the Theory and Practice of Theatrical Dancing in England, 1660-1740, by Ifan Kyrle Fletcher, Selma Jeanne Cohen, and Roger Lonsdale, 1960; New York's First Ballet Season, 1792, by Lillian Moore, 1961; The Professional Appearances of Ruth St. Denis and Ted Shawn: a Chronology and an Index of Dances, 1906-1932, by Christena L. Schlundt, 1962; Stravinsky and the Dance: a Survey of Ballet Productions, 1910-1962, by

Selma Jeanne Cohen, introduction by Herbert Read, 1962; Dancing in Prints, a Portfolio of Twelve Etchings, Engravings and Lithographs, 1634-1870, with Commentary by Marian Eames, 1964; Bournonville's London Spring, by Lillian Moore, 1965; Images of the Dance, Historical Treasures of the Dance Collection, 1581-1861, by Lillian Moore, 1965; The Professional Appearances of Ted Shawn & His Men Dancers: a Chronology and an Index of Dances, 1933-1940, by Christena L. Schlundt, 1967; The Papers of Gabriel Astruc, 1864-1938, a Register, by Nicki N. Ostrom, 1971; Tamiris, a Chronicle of Her Dance Career, 1927-1955, by Christena L. Schlundt, 1972; Your Isadora, by Francis Steegmuller, 1974; The Doris Humphrey Collection: an Introduction and Guide, by Andrew Wentink, 1973; Asian Dance Images from the Spencer Collection: an Exhibition at Lincoln Center, New York, 1977; the Ruth Page Collection: an Introduction and Guide to Manuscript Materials through 1970, by Andrew Wentink, 1980 (in Bulletin of Research in the Humanities, NYPL, 83:1, Spring 1980). **Special Catalogs:** Dictionary Catalog of the Dance Collection, 10 volumes, 1974 (annual supplements); Stravinsky and the Theatre: a Catalog of Decor and Costume Designs for Stage Productions of His Works, 1910-1962, 1963; WPA Card Index of Ethnic and Folkdance Material, circa 1936; International Dance Film and Videotape Festival Catalog, 1981. **Remarks:** Alternate telephone number(s): 870-1658. FAX: (212)787-3852. **Formerly:** New York Public Library - Performing Arts Research Center - Dance Collection.

★ 11637 ★
New York Public Library for the Performing Arts - Music Division (Mus)
40 Lincoln Center Plaza   Phone: (212)870-1650
New York, NY 10023   Jean Bowen, Chf.
Founded: 1911. **Staff:** Prof 11.5; Other 9. **Subjects:** Opera, orchestral and chamber music, folk music, complete works of standard composers, monumenta devoted to special schools, theory, harmony, criticism, instruments, libretti, sheet music, music for dance. **Special Collections:** Drexel Collection and Rare Book and Manuscript Collection; Americana Collection; Beethoven Collection; Toscanini Memorial Archives (microfilm reproductions of European composers' manuscripts). **Holdings:** 400,000 books and bound scores; 5500 bound periodical volumes; 50,000 manuscripts; 700,000 pieces of sheet music; 60,000 photographs; 2 million clippings and programs; 6000 fine prints. **Subscriptions:** 750 journals. **Services:** Division open to adults. **Computerized Information Services:** CATNYP (catalog; internal database). **Networks/Consortia:** Member of Research Libraries Information Network (RLIN), New York Metropolitan Reference and Research Library Agency, New York State Interlibrary Loan Network (NYSILL). **Special Indexes:** Vocal music index; biographical file; program note and first performance index (all on cards). **Formerly:** New York Public Library - Performing Arts Research Center - Music Division.

★ 11638 ★
New York Public Library for the Performing Arts - Rodgers & Hammerstein Archives of Recorded Sound (Mus, Aud-Vis)
40 Lincoln Center Plaza   Phone: (212)870-1663
New York, NY 10023   Donald McCormick, Cur.
Founded: 1963. **Staff:** Prof 6; Other 10. **Subjects:** Sound and video recordings and allied materials. **Special Collections:** Benedict Stambler Memorial Collection of Recorded Jewish Music (5000 items); Jan Holcman Collection of Recorded Piano Music (2200 items); Rosalyn Tureck Archives (500 hours of tape); Metropolitan Opera Broadcast Archives; WNYC (municipal radio station) Archives; Association of German Broadcasters (400 hours of tape); Marian McPartland's Piano Jazz Radio Series (90 hours of tape); Metropolitan Opera (120 Mapleson cylinders); Toscanini Legacy; WNEW Collection (20,000 popular music recordings). **Holdings:** 4500 books; 1200 bound periodical volumes; 2000 phonograph record and manufacturers' catalogs and notebooks; 150 linear feet of unbound periodicals, catalogs, notebooks; 480,000 phonograph records, discs, tapes, cylinder and wire recordings; 1350 reels of microfilm; 400 video cassettes. **Subscriptions:** 120 journals and other serials. **Services:** Archives open to the public for professional or serious research. **Networks/Consortia:** Member of Research Libraries Information Network (RLIN), New York Metropolitan Reference and Research Library Agency, New York State Interlibrary Loan Network (NYSILL). **Special Indexes:** Discography index (card); musical theater recordings (inventory list). **Formerly:** New York Public Library - Performing Arts Research Center - Rodgers & Hammerstein Archives of Recorded Sound. **Staff:** Christine Hoffman, First Asst.; Adrian Cosentini, Audio Engr.

★ 11639 ★
New York Road Runners Club - Albert H. Gordon Library (Rec)
9 E. 89th St.   Phone: (212)860-4455
New York, NY 10128   Kenny Herbert, Libn.
Founded: 1983. **Staff:** Prof 1; Other 3. **Subjects:** Running, fitness, sports medicine, triathlon. **Special Collections:** Ted Corbitt Archives (papers of the first president of the New York Road Runners Club). **Holdings:** 600 books; 4000 American and international running publications; medical journals; video cassettes; articles. **Services:** Copying; library open to the public. **Publications:** New York Running News, bimonthly - to the public. **Remarks:** Library located at 9 E. 89th St., New York, NY 10128. FAX: (212)860-9754. Telex: 238093 NYRRC.

★ 11640 ★
New York Society Library (Hist)
53 E. 79th St.   Phone: (212)288-6900
New York, NY 10021   Mark Piel, Libn.
Founded: 1754. **Staff:** Prof 9; Other 5. **Subjects:** Fiction, biography, Americana, New York City history and early newspaper files, 19th century travel. **Special Collections:** John Winthrop Collection of chemistry and alchemy; Goodhue Papers (letters and documents of distinguished Americans, early 19th century); Hammond Fiction Collection, 1750-1830. **Holdings:** 210,000 books; 1100 bound periodical volumes. **Subscriptions:** 80 journals. **Services:** Interlibrary loan (for members); copying; library open to nonmembers for reading and reference. **Computerized Information Services:** OCLC. **Publications:** Annual Report; Monthly New Books. **Staff:** Sharon Brown, Asst.Libn.

★ 11641 ★
New York Society of Model Engineers - Library (Rec)
341 Hoboken Rd.
Carlstadt, NJ 07072   Phone: (201)939-9212
Staff: 1. **Subjects:** Railroading and model railroading. **Holdings:** Books; periodicals. **Services:** Library not open to the public.

★ 11642 ★
New York Society of Security Analysts - Library (Bus-Fin)
71 Broadway, 2nd Fl.   Phone: (212)344-8450
New York, NY 10006   T. Wayne Whipple, CFA, Exec.Dir.
Founded: 1937. **Staff:** 8. **Subjects:** Public corporations. **Holdings:** 600 audio cassettes, videotapes, and written transcriptions of corporate presentations. **Services:** Library not open to the public. **Computerized Information Services:** First Call, InvesText, Corporate Industry Research Reports Index BRS Information Technologies, DIALOG Information Services, Data-Star, PFDS Online, Dow Jones News/Retrieval, Source Telecomputing Corporation, NewsNet, Inc. **Remarks:** FAX: (212)809-6439. Affiliated with Association for Investment Management and Research. **Staff:** Carol Morgan.

New York State Agricultural Experiment Station
See: **Cornell University - New York State Agricultural Experiment Station** (4325)

★ 11643 ★
New York State Archaeological Association - Library (Soc Sci)
657 East Ave.
Box 1480   Phone: (716)271-4320
Rochester, NY 14603-1480   Ms. Lee Kemp, Libn.
Subjects: Archeology, anthropology. **Special Collections:** Regional Northeast archeology. **Holdings:** 3000 books. **Subscriptions:** 50 journals and other serials. **Services:** Library (at Rochester location) open to the public with restrictions. **Remarks:** Library located at Lower Hudson Chapter, NYSAA, c/o MALFA, Muscoot Park, Route 100, Katonah, NY 10536. Library volumes dating to 1950 are housed at the Rochester Museum and Science Center Library.

New York State Archeological Association - Van Epps-Hartley Chapter - Archives
See: **Mohawk-Caughnawaga Museum - Library** (10588)

★ 11644 ★

New York State Bronx Criminal-Family Courts - Library (Law)

215 E. 161st St., Rm. 9-5A　　　Phone: (212)590-2931
Bronx, NY 10451　　　Mary T. Rooney, Sr. Law Libn.
Staff: Prof 1; Other 1. **Subjects:** Criminal and family law. **Holdings:** 15,000 books. **Subscriptions:** 73 serials. **Services:** Interlibrary loan; library open to the public by appointment. **Remarks:** FAX: (212)590-2857. **Formerly:** New York State Criminal-Family Courts.

New York State Bureau of Historic Sites
See: New York (State) Office of Parks, Recreation and Historic Preservation - Palisades Region (11682)

New York State College of Agriculture & Life Sciences
See: Cornell University - Albert R. Mann Library (4302)

★ 11645 ★

New York State College of Ceramics at Alfred University - Samuel R. Scholes Library of Ceramics (Sci-Engr, Art)

Harder Hall　　　Phone: (607)871-2492
Alfred, NY 14802-1297　　　Bruce E. Connolly, Dir.
Founded: 1947. **Staff:** Prof 5; Other 7. **Subjects:** Ceramic science, technology, art; industrial, mechanical, electrical engineering; pottery; glass; fine art; sculpture; materials; design. **Special Collections:** Hostetter Collection (glass); Barringer Collection (ceramics); Bancroft Collection (science and engineering); Silverman Collection (ceramic art); McBurney Collection (brick); Shand Collection (glass); Spretnak Collection (metallurgy); College of Ceramics Archives (170 shelf feet); Charles F. Binns papers (30 shelf feet); NCECA Archives (26 shelf feet); James T. Robson technical papers (ceramic technology). **Holdings:** 55,346 books; 31,265 bound periodical volumes; 8699 other cataloged items; 61,095 government documents, hardcopy and microfiche; 600 microtexts; 4000 serial monographs; 127,377 slides; 200 videotapes; 209 audiocassettes; 256 videocassettes. **Subscriptions:** 981 journals and other serials. **Services:** Interlibrary loan; copying; library open to the public. **Automated Operations:** Computerized cataloging, serials, and ILL. **Computerized Information Services:** DIALOG Information Services, PFDS Online, OCLC EPIC; BITNET (electronic mail service). Performs searches on fee basis. Contact Person: Paul T. Culley, Tech.Ref.Libn. **Networks/Consortia:** Member of South Central Research Library Council (SCRLC), SUNY/OCLC Library Network. **Special Indexes:** Ceramic art index (online); card indexes to ceramics, glass, materials science, and engineering. **Remarks:** FAX: (607)871-2349. Electronic mail address(es): FCONNOLL@CERAMICS (BITNET). **Staff:** Martha A. Mueller, Cat. & Ser.; Elizabeth Gulacsy, Ref./Archv.; Carla C. Freeman, Vis.Rsrcs./Art Ref.; Paul T. Culley, Tech.Ref.

New York State College of Human Ecology
See: Cornell University - Albert R. Mann Library (4302)

New York State College of Veterinary Medicine at Cornell University
See: Cornell University - Flower Veterinary Library (4311)

★ 11646 ★

New York State Court of Appeals - Library (Law)

Eagle St.　　　Phone: (518)455-7700
Albany, NY 12207-1905　　　Elizabeth Frances Murray, Law Libn.
Staff: Prof 1; Other 1. **Subjects:** Law. **Holdings:** 70,000 volumes. **Subscriptions:** 431 journals and other serials. **Services:** Library not open to the public. **Computerized Information Services:** WESTLAW, LEXIS, NEXIS, Legislative Retrieval System, VU/TEXT Information Services, DIALOG Information Services, OCLC EPIC.

★ 11647 ★

New York (State) Department of Audit Control - Library (Bus-Fin, Law)

Alfred E. Smith Office Bldg.　　　Phone: (518)473-5960
Albany, NY 12236　　　Richard Conety, Lib.Ck.
Founded: 1948. **Staff:** 1. **Subjects:** Law, statistics, finance, accounting. **Holdings:** 3300 books; 420 bound periodical volumes; 1500 pamphlets and departmental reports. **Subscriptions:** 25 journals and other serials. **Services:** Interlibrary loan; copying; library open to the public for reference use only. **Computerized Information Services:** WESTLAW.

★ 11648 ★

New York (State) Department of Economic Development - Library (Bus-Fin)

1 Commerce Plaza　　　Phone: (518)474-5664
Albany, NY 12245　　　Barbara S. Beverley, Dir.
Founded: 1943. **Staff:** Prof 1; Other 1. **Subjects:** Economic research, business. **Special Collections:** Census reports. **Holdings:** 15,500 books; 1000 microfiche, 300 reels of microfilm. **Subscriptions:** 500 journals and other serials; 20 newspapers. **Services:** Library open to the public for reference use only. **Computerized Information Services:** DIALOG Information Services, VU/TEXT Information Services, OCLC, ISIS. **Publications:** Library bulletin - for internal distribution only. **Remarks:** FAX: (518)474-1512.

New York State Department of Education - North Country Reference & Research Resources Council
See: North Country Reference & Research Resources Council (11918)

★ 11649 ★

New York State Department of Environment Conservation - New York Natural Heritage Program (Env-Cons)

700 Troy-Schenectady Rd.　　　Phone: (518)783-3932
Latham, NY 12110-2400　　　Rachel Pleuthner, Info.Mgr.
Founded: 1985. **Staff:** 5. **Subjects:** Botany, ecology, floras, faunas, natural communities, rare species, zoology. **Special Collections:** Natural area inventories. **Holdings:** 1500 books. **Services:** Program open to the public by appointment. **Computerized Information Services:** Biological Conservation Data System (internal database). **Publications:** The Natural Communities of New York (lists of rare species and natural communities in New York). **Remarks:** FAX: (518)783-3916. Jointly maintained by The Nature Conservancy and the New York State Department of Environment Conservation. **Staff:** Kathryn Schneider, Coord./Zoologist; Carol Reschke, Ecologist; Steven Young, Botanist; Diane Thomson, Info.Mgt.Asst.

New York State Department of Health - Roswell Park Cancer Institute
See: Roswell Park Cancer Institute (14087)

★ 11650 ★

New York (State) Department of Health - Wadsworth Center for Laboratories and Research Library (Med, Biol Sci)

Empire State Plaza　　　Phone: (518)474-6172
Albany, NY 12201-0509　　　Thomas Flynn, Lib.Dir.
Founded: 1914. **Staff:** Prof 5; Other 5. **Subjects:** Public health, bacteriology, biochemistry, birth defects, child health, clinical labs, communicable diseases, cytology, environmental health, epidemiology, laboratory animals, mycology, pathology, radiology, sanitary engineering, toxicology, veterinary medicine, virology, zoonoses. **Special Collections:** Bibliographies on Coxsackie virus; nystatin; AIDS. **Holdings:** 20,500 books; 33,500 bound periodical volumes; 600 linear feet of U.S. and New York State Government publications; 180 linear feet of reference materials. **Subscriptions:** 1200 journals and other serials. **Services:** Interlibrary loan; copying; library open to health professionals by permission. **Automated Operations:** Computerized cataloging. **Computerized Information Services:** OCLC, BRS Information Technologies, NLM, STN International, DIALOG Information Services; CD-ROMs; DOCLINE, ALANET. **Publications:** Library Information Bulletin, monthly - for internal distribution only. **Remarks:** FAX: (518)474-8590. **Staff:** Jane D. Allen, Sr.Libn., Rd.Serv.; Rae Clark, Sr.Libn., Tech.Serv.; Cindy Yochym, Sr.Libn., Ser.

★ 11651 ★

New York (State) Department of Labor - Labor Research Library (Bus-Fin)

Bldg. 12, Rm. 492
Averill Harriman State Office Campus　　　Phone: (518)457-1292
Albany, NY 12240-0013　　　Kathleen J. Grimes, Sr.Libn.
Founded: 1970. **Staff:** Prof 1; Other 1. **Subjects:** Employment, unemployment, statistics. **Special Collections:** History of department. **Holdings:** 25,000 books; 12 VF drawers; government documents. **Subscriptions:** 78 journals and other serials. **Services:** Interlibrary loan; copying; library open to the public. **Computerized Information Services:** Internal databases. **Networks/Consortia:** Member of New York State Interlibrary Loan Network (NYSILL). **Special Catalogs:** New York State documents (card, printout). **Remarks:** FAX: (518)457-0620.

★ 11652 ★
New York (State) Department of Labor - Library (Bus-Fin)
1 Main St., Rm. 950   Phone: (718)797-7718
Brooklyn, NY 11201   R. Ashley Hibbard, Sr.Libn.
Founded: 1907. **Staff:** Prof 1; Other 1. **Subjects:** Economic and business conditions, personnel management, unions, fringe benefits, unemployment insurance, wages and hours, labor legislation, vocational education and guidance, interviewing and counseling, occupational health and safety, women in industry, apprenticeship. **Special Collections:** Women's Trade Union League; releases of state labor departments; state labor laws; New York State industrial code rules; International Labour Office publications. **Holdings:** 48,000 books; 1545 bound periodical volumes; 10,000 government documents; 5000 pamphlets; 275 reels of microfilm; 2700 microfiche; 408 VF drawers. **Subscriptions:** 175 journals and other serials. **Services:** Interlibrary loan; copying; SDI; library open to the public for materials not available in public or college libraries. **Publications:** Selected Additions List, quarterly - for internal distribution. **Remarks:** FAX: (718)797-7704.

★ 11653 ★
New York (State) Department of Law - Library (Law)
The Capitol   Phone: (518)474-3840
Albany, NY 12224   Judith Brown, Chf., Law Lib.Serv.
Founded: 1944. **Staff:** Prof 5; Other 8. **Subjects:** Law. **Special Collections:** Opinions of the Attorney General of New York, allied material. **Holdings:** 125,000 volumes; 900 bound periodical volumes. **Subscriptions:** 225 journals and other serials. **Services:** SDI; library open to personnel from other state agencies; library open to other professionals with special permission. **Automated Operations:** Computerized cataloging. **Computerized Information Services:** OCLC, WESTLAW, BRS Information Technologies. **Special Catalogs:** Department of Law briefs and records. **Remarks:** Above figure for holdings includes collections at branch libraries in Binghamton, Buffalo, Harlem, Hauppauge, Mineola, New York City, Plattsburgh, Poughkeepsie, Rochester, Syracuse, Utica, White Plains, and Watertown. **Staff:** Lily Kouo, Sr.Libn., Tech.Serv.; Tina Rovelli, Sr.Libn., Tech.Serv.; Linda Stopard, Sr.Libn., Ref.; Franette Sheinwald, NYC Sr.Libn.

★ 11654 ★
New York (State) Department of Law - New York City Library (Law)
120 Broadway, Rm. 2520   Phone: (212)341-2012
New York, NY 10271   Fran Sheinwald, Sr.Libn.
Staff: Prof 1; Other 2. **Subjects:** Law. **Special Collections:** Opinions of the Attorney General of New York, 1892 to present. **Holdings:** 20,000 volumes. **Subscriptions:** 52 journals and other serials. **Services:** Library open to members of the law department and other state agencies. **Computerized Information Services:** WESTLAW.

★ 11655 ★
New York (State) Department of Motor Vehicles - Research Library (Trans)
Swan St. Bldg., Rm. 418
Empire State Plaza
Albany, NY 12228   Phone: (518)473-5467
                                   Gerald Ellsworth, Sr.Libn.
Founded: 1960. **Staff:** Prof 1; Other 1. **Subjects:** Traffic accident and management research; driver education and improvement; drinking driver rehabilitation; vehicle and traffic safety; vehicle and traffic laws; vehicle registration and driver licensing. **Special Collections:** Traffic law and highway safety; driver education films. **Holdings:** 43,000 books and documents; 232 bound periodical volumes; 20,000 unbound reports and manuscripts; 416 slides; 103 prints; 20 audiotapes; 161 titles on videocassettes and 16mm film; 23 filmstrips; 80 VF drawers; 1000 microforms; 400 maps and charts. **Subscriptions:** 20 journals and other serials. **Services:** Interlibrary loan (limited); library open to the public for reference use only and by appointment. **Networks/Consortia:** Member of Capital District Library Council for Reference & Research Resources (CDLC). **Special Catalogs:** Traffic Safety Film Catalog, irregular - limited distribution to the public. **Remarks:** FAX: (518)473-1930.

★ 11656 ★
New York (State) Department of Social Services - Social Services Department Library 10-D (Soc Sci)
40 N. Pearl St.   Phone: (518)473-8072
Albany, NY 12243   Madeline Raciti, Libn.
Remarks: No further information was supplied by respondent.

★ 11657 ★
New York (State) Department of State - Office of Fire Prevention and Control - Academy of Fire Science - Library (Sci-Engr)
600 College Ave.
Box 811   Phone: (607)535-7136
Montour Falls, NY 14865   Diana Zell Robinson, Libn.
Staff: Prof 1. **Subjects:** Fire protection, prevention, and control; occupational safety; fire department administration and management; codes, standards, and regulations; emergency medical services; consumer safety; hazardous materials; arson prevention and control; history of fire service in New York State. **Holdings:** 5450 books; 185 bound periodical volumes; 16 VF drawers; 150 microfiche. **Subscriptions:** 130 journals and other serials. **Services:** Interlibrary loan; copying; answers to mail and telephone inquiries; library open to the public. **Computerized Information Services:** BRS Information Technologies, DIALOG Information Services, FIREDOC, New York State Library Catalog, OCLC; internal database. Performs searches free of charge. **Networks/Consortia:** Member of South Central Research Library Council (SCRLC). **Publications:** Acquisitions list; bibliographics. **Special Indexes:** Index to fire, rescue, EMS, and public safety journal articles. **Remarks:** The academy is the shipping point for New York State's largest collection of fire training and fire safety films and videotapes. FAX: (607)535-4841.

★ 11658 ★
New York (State) Department of Taxation & Finance - Tax Library (Bus-Fin)
State Campus, Taxation & Finance Bldg.
Bureau of Research & Statistics   Phone: (518)457-3512
Albany, NY 12227   Kim P. Murphy, Libn.
Founded: 1946. **Staff:** Prof 1. **Subjects:** Taxation, public finance, population. **Holdings:** 14,149 books; 4774 bound periodical volumes; 100 VF drawers. **Subscriptions:** 106 journals and other serials. **Services:** Interlibrary loan; copying; library open to the public for reference use only.

★ 11659 ★
New York (State) Department of Transportation - Map Information Unit (Geog-Map)
State Office Campus
Bldg. 4, Rm. 105   Phone: (518)457-3555
Albany, NY 12232   Paul McElligott, Mapping Technl.
Staff: Prof 1; Other 3. **Subjects:** Maps, aerial photography. **Holdings:** 100,000 aerial photographs; 5000 maps. **Services:** Unit open to the public. **Publications:** Inventory of Aerial Photography & Other Remotely Sensed Imagery of New York State, 1983, revised semiannually. **Special Indexes:** Map indexes. **Remarks:** Unit is the New York State affiliate of the U.S. Geological Survey's Earth Science Information Center (ESIC). FAX: (518)457-5933.

★ 11660 ★
New York (State) Department of Transportation - Public Transportation Library (Trans)
State Campus Bldg. 4, Rm. 212
1220 Washington Ave.   Phone: (518)457-8320
Albany, NY 12232   Jinny Williams
Founded: 1962. **Staff:** Prof 2. **Subjects:** Transportation planning. **Holdings:** 20,000 books; 400 unbound periodical volumes. **Subscriptions:** 100 journals and other serials. **Services:** Interlibrary loan; copying; library open to the public with restrictions. **Computerized Information Services:** DIALOG Information Services. **Staff:** Richard J. Zabinski, Hd., Travel/Energy Unit.

★ 11661 ★
New York (State) Division of Housing and Community Renewal - Reference Room (Soc Sci)
1 Fordham Plaza, 4th Fl.
Bronx, NY 10458   Phone: (212)519-5912
Founded: 1941. **Staff:** 1. **Subjects:** Housing - laws and titles, building codes; mobile housing; housing for elderly; neighborhood preservation. **Holdings:** 2000 books; slides; microfilm; microfiche. **Subscriptions:** 30 journals and other serials. **Services:** Library not open to the public. **Remarks:** FAX: (212)519-5840. **Staff:** Carole L. Williams.

★11662★
New York (State) Electric and Gas Corporation - Corporate Library
(Energy)
4500 Vestal Pkwy., E.
P.O. Box 3607
Binghamton, NY 13902-3607   Jorette Anne Martin, Libn.
Phone: (607)729-2551
Founded: 1954. **Staff:** Prof 1; Other 1. **Subjects:** Public utilities, energy, environment, electrical engineering, management, natural gas. **Holdings:** 2127 books. **Subscriptions:** 252 journals and other serials; 24 newspapers. **Services:** Interlibrary loan; library not open to the public. **Automated Operations:** Computerized public access catalog and serials. **Computerized Information Services:** DIALOG Information Services, Dun & Bradstreet Business Credit Services, Knight-Ridder Unicom, Dow Jones News/ Retrieval. **Networks/Consortia:** Member of South Central Research Library Council (SCRLC). **Publications:** Library News, quarterly. **Remarks:** FAX: (607)798-8317.

New York State Health Film Collection
See: Nassau Community College (11003)

★11663★
New York (State) Historical Association - Library (Hist)
Lake Rd.
Box 800
Cooperstown, NY 13326   Amy Barnum, Libn.
Phone: (607)547-2509
Founded: 1899. **Staff:** Prof 3; Other 3. **Subjects:** New York State history, central New York genealogy, American social history and art, agricultural history. **Special Collections:** Page Collection of James Fenimore Cooper (first editions); Louis C. Jones Folklore Archives (14 cubic feet); Harold W. Thompson Folklore Archives (32 cubic feet). **Holdings:** 65,000 books; 10,000 bound periodical volumes; 2500 linear feet of manuscripts. **Subscriptions:** 200 journals and other serials. **Services:** Interlibrary loan; copying; library open to the public; collections open to the public for reference use only. **Networks/Consortia:** Member of South Central Research Library Council (SCRLC). **Publications:** Guide to Historical Resources in Otsego County, New York depositories. **Special Catalogs:** Manuscript holdings cataloged on RLIN. **Staff:** Eileen O'Brien, Spec.Coll.; Wayne Wright, Tech.Serv.

★11664★
New York State Institute for Basic Research in Developmental
Disabilities - Library (Med)
1050 Forest Hill Rd.
Staten Island, NY 10314   Lawrence Black, Assoc.Libn.
Phone: (718)494-5407
Founded: 1968. **Staff:** Prof 1; Other 1. **Subjects:** Neurology, neurophysiology, neurochemistry, neuropathology, genetics, virology, immunology. **Holdings:** Figures not available. **Subscriptions:** 200 journals and other serials. **Services:** Library not open to the public. **Networks/ Consortia:** Member of Medical Library Center of New York (MLCNY), SUNY/OCLC Library Network. **Remarks:** FAX: (718)494-6660.

★11665★
New York State Legislative Library (Law)
State Capitol, Rm. 337
Albany, NY 12224-0345   Ellen Breslin, Contact
Phone: (518)455-4000
Staff: Prof 3; Other 6. **Subjects:** Law, New York State legislation. **Holdings:** 50,030 volumes; New York State documents. **Subscriptions:** 300 journals and other serials; 80 newspapers. **Services:** Library not open to the public. **Automated Operations:** Computerized cataloging and acquisitions. **Computerized Information Services:** WESTLAW, LEXIS, DIALOG Information Services, BRS Information Technologies, WILSONLINE, VU/TEXT Information Services; Legislative Retrieval System (LRS). **Remarks:** FAX: (518)463-0218. **Staff:** Frances Murray, Info.Sys.Libn.; James Giliberto, Doc.Libn.

★11666★
New York State Library (Info Sci)
Cultural Education Center
Empire State Plaza
Albany, NY 12230   Jerome Yavarkovsky, Dir.
Phone: (518)474-7646
Founded: 1818. **Staff:** Prof 89; Other 119. **Subjects:** Education, science, technology, art, architecture, economics, sociology, current affairs, bibliography, New York State documents, New York State newspapers, law,

medicine, state and local history, genealogy, heraldry. **Special Collections:** Almanacs; American imprints and bookplates; Fourth of July orations; World War posters; Shakers; New York State documents; Washington eulogies. **Holdings:** 7.2 million books, bound periodical volumes, manuscripts, pamphlets; patents; microfilm; microcards; pictures; maps. **Subscriptions:** 20,250 journals and other serials; 111 newspapers. **Services:** Interlibrary loan; copying; library open to the public. **Automated Operations:** Computerized cataloging, acquisitions, serials, and circulation. **Computerized Information Services:** BRS Information Technologies, DIALOG Information Services, LEXIS, NEXIS, NLM; ALANET (electronic mail service). **Networks/Consortia:** Member of New York State Interlibrary Loan Network (NYSILL). **Publications:** Bookmark, quarterly; Checklist of Official Publications of the State of New York, monthly. **Remarks:** FAX: (518)474-5786. Electronic mail address(es): ALA0198 (ALANET). **Staff:** Joseph F. Shubert, State Libn. & Asst.Commnr.; Elizabeth Lane, Hd., Coll.Acq.; J. Vanderveer Judd, Hd., Coll.Mgt.; Lee Stanton, Hd., Ref.; Mary Redmond, Hd., Leg./Govt.Serv.

★11667★
New York State Library - Core Reference Services (Info Sci)
Cultural Education Center
Empire State Plaza
Albany, NY 12230   Jean Hargrave, Supv.Libn.
Phone: (518)473-4636
Founded: 1818. **Staff:** Prof 23; Other 10. **Subjects:** New York State and North American history; bibliography; biography; literature; language; fine and applied arts; library science; genealogy; philosophy; religion; grantsmanship; law - federal, state, foreign; political science; public administration; legislative organization; intergovernmental relations; state and regional planning; education; science; medicine and allied health sciences; technology. **Special Collections:** Foundation Center Regional Collection; New York State newspapers, 18th-20th centuries; city directories; 19th century American periodicals; census records; local and family histories; legislative background material; individual and collected trials; constitutional convention materials from other states; records and briefs of U.S. Supreme Court, 1874 to present; early rare books; virtually complete collection of Blackstone and Kent commentaries; session laws of all 50 states (complete); appeal records of all appellate courts of New York State; Bill Jacket Collection (laws of New York), 1921-1982; New York State publications; New York State Legislative Bills, 1830 to present (microfilm); National Technical Information Service (NTIS) reports (microfiche); all U.S. patents (depository library); foreign patents in chemistry, plastics, metallurgy, refractories and ceramics (1971-1985; microfilm); Department of Energy reports (microfiche); NASA reports (microfiche); U.S. Government Printing Office publications (depository and nondepository); Rand reports; standards and specifications. **Holdings:** 2.1 million books; 11 million manuscripts and archival materials; 5.1 million microforms. **Subscriptions:** 20,250 journals and other serials. **Services:** Interlibrary loan; copying; reference services and borrowing privileges extended to State government and legislative personnel; section open to the public for reference use only. **Automated Operations:** Computerized public access catalog, cataloging, acquisitions, serials, and circulation. **Computerized Information Services:** OCLC, DIALOG Information Services, Mead Data Central, WILSONLINE, BRS Information Technologies, NEXIS, NLM. Performs searches on fee basis (free to State government employees). **Networks/Consortia:** Member of New York State Interlibrary Loan Network (NYSILL), Research Libraries Information Network (RLIN), National Network of Libraries of Medicine - Middle Atlantic Region. **Remarks:** FAX: (518)474-5786. **Staff:** Soumaya Baaklini, Assoc.Libn. and Coord. of Online Serv.; Christine Bain, Assoc.Libn.; Sally Legendre, Assoc.Libn.; Linda Braun, Ref.Libn.; Virginia Camerman, Ref.Libn.; Ruth Clayman, Ref.Libn.; Lynn Eggleston, Ref.Libn.; Michael Esposito, Ref.Libn.; Evelyn Galante, Ref.Libn.; Maureen Gross, Ref.Libn.; Nancy Horan, Ref.Libn.; Henry Ilnicki, Ref.Libn.; Campbell Lathey, Ref.Libn.; Cindy Lyon, Ref.Libn.; Allan Raney, Ref.Libn.; Glenis Ratcliff, Ref.Libn.; Elaine Clark, Ref.Libn.; Cindy Stark, Ref.Libn.; Theresa Strasser, Ref.Libn.; Dawn Tybur, Ref.Libn.; Yvonne Teitsworth, Ref.Libn.; Melinda Yates, Ref.Libn.

★11668★
New York State Library - Legislative and Governmental Services (Soc
Sci)
Cultural Education Center
Empire State Plaza
Albany, NY 12230   Mary Redmond, Prin.Libn.
Phone: (518)474-3940
Staff: Prof 6; Other 5. **Services:** Provides special and enhanced services, bibliographic research, and other publications to the legislature and state government; provides advice and assistance to selective federal and New York State depository libraries. **Computerized Information Services:**

BITNET (electronic mail service). **Publications:** Legislative Trends (annotated listing of selected recent acquisitions), 9/year; Topic (highly selective subject reading lists); Spotlight (one page subject researchers' guides); Sources (lists of special/specialized materials and formats available); bibliographies on subjects of legislative interest for the legislature. **Remarks:** FAX: (518)474-5786; 474-5163. Electronic mail address(es): USERGLN9@RPITSMTS (BITNET). Operates a service point for the legislature in the Legislative Office Building. **Staff:** Robert Allan Carter, Sr.Libn.; Marilyn Douglas, Sr.Libn. Miriam Bogen, Sr.Libn.; Cynthia Conway, Sr.Libn.

★11669★
New York State Library - Manuscripts and Special Collections (Hist)
Cultural Education Center
Empire State Plaza   Phone: (518)474-4461
Albany, NY 12230   James Corsaro, Assoc.Libn.
Founded: 1818. **Staff:** Prof 4; Other 2. **Subjects:** History - New York, U.S., local; cartography; historic iconography. **Special Collections:** Historical manuscripts and archives (11 million); rare books (47,000). **Holdings:** 5400 books; 450 bound periodical volumes; 4800 war posters; 4000 broadsides; 35,000 prints, glass negatives, pictures; 35,000 pieces of sheet music; 180,000 maps; 6000 reels of microfilm; 1300 atlases. **Subscriptions:** 15 journals and other serials. **Services:** Interlibrary loan; copying; exhibits; collections open to the public. **Automated Operations:** Computerized cataloging. **Computerized Information Services:** OCLC, RLIN; RLIN (electronic mail service). **Networks/Consortia:** Member of New York State Interlibrary Loan Network (NYSILL), Research Libraries Information Network (RLIN). **Publications:** Brochures on collections and services. **Remarks:** FAX: (518)474-5786. Electronic mail address(es): (Corsaro)[RLIN-BM.N2A (RLIN). **Staff:** Billie Aul, Sr.Libn.; Fred Bassett, Sr.Libn.; Paul Mercer, Archv. I.

★11670★
New York State Library for the Blind and Visually Handicapped (Aud-Vis)
Cultural Education Center
Empire State Plaza   Phone: (518)474-5935
Albany, NY 12230   Jane Somers, Assoc.Libn.
Founded: 1896. **Staff:** Prof 8; Other 14. **Subjects:** Recreational and informational reading materials in special media collections. **Holdings:** 39,000 titles (542,791 copies). **Subscriptions:** 70 journals and other serials. **Services:** Interlibrary loan; postage-free mail circulation of books and magazines in braille and on disc and cassettes; player machines available for loan; readers advisory, reference, and referral services by telephone and mail; library open to qualified residents of New York State (excluding New York City and Long Island); deposit collection service to institutions with eligible patrons. **Automated Operations:** Computerized cataloging, acquisitions, serials, and circulation. **Networks/Consortia:** Member of National Library Service for the Blind & Physically Handicapped (NLS). **Publications:** Upstate Update (newsletter); Sublending Agency News; School News. **Remarks:** FAX: (518)474-5786. **Staff:** Frank Conron, Sr.Libn.; Dave Gosda, Assoc.Libn.; Peter Douglas, Sr.Libn.; Edith Bensen, Sr.Libn.; Cassandra Hamm, Sr.Libn.; Scott Briggs, Sr.Libn.; Larry Zimmer, Coord. of Vol.Serv.

★11671★
New York (State) Museum and Science Service - Museum Library (Sci-Engr)
Cultural Education Center, Rm. 3128
Empire State Plaza   Phone: (518)473-4636
Albany, NY 12230   Alta Beach, Libn.
Founded: 1932. **Staff:** Prof 1. **Subjects:** General science, geology, paleontology, biology, anthropology. **Special Collections:** John M. Clarke Collection; Winifred Goldring Collection. **Holdings:** Museum reports; government documents; society publications. **Services:** Library not open to the public.

★11672★
New York (State) Nurses Association - Library (Med)
2113 Western Ave.   Phone: (518)456-5371
Guilderland, NY 12084   Warren G. Hawkes, Lib.Dir.
Founded: 1972. **Staff:** Prof 1; Other 2. **Subjects:** Nursing and allied health fields, labor, collective bargaining. **Special Collections:** Association archival materials. **Holdings:** 7500 books; 695 bound periodical volumes; New York State nursing school catalogs (complete set); 6 VF drawers of pamphlets.

Subscriptions: 275 journals and other serials. **Services:** Interlibrary loan; copying; library open to the public with restrictions. **Computerized Information Services:** BRS Information Technologies. Performs searches on fee basis. **Networks/Consortia:** Member of Capital District Library Council for Reference & Research Resources (CDLC), National Network of Libraries of Medicine - Middle Atlantic Region. **Publications:** Memorandum to Staff, irregular - for internal distribution only. **Remarks:** FAX: (518)456-0697.

New York State Office of Court Administration - Bronx Criminal-Family Courts Library
See: **New York State Bronx Criminal-Family Courts - Library** (11644)

★11673★
New York (State) Office of Mental Health - Binghamton Psychiatric Center - Professional Library (Med)
425 Robinson St.   Phone: (607)773-4316
Binghamton, NY 13901   Martha A. Mason, Sr.Libn.
Staff: Prof 1. **Subjects:** Psychiatry, child psychiatry, community mental health, psychology, child psychology, group psychotherapy, mental illness, general medicine, psychoanalysis, social services, family therapy. **Holdings:** 3450 books, bound periodicals, and pamphlets; 400 cassette tapes. **Subscriptions:** 63 journals and other serials. **Services:** Interlibrary loan; copying; library open to professionals, students, and community agency staff. **Automated Operations:** Computerized public access catalog, and ILL (DOCLINE). **Computerized Information Services:** OCLC. **Networks/Consortia:** Member of South Central Research Library Council (SCRLC). **Remarks:** Alternate telephone number(s): 773-4308. FAX: (607)773-4411.

New York State Office of Mental Health - Creedmoor Psychiatric Center
See: **Creedmoor Psychiatric Center** (4424)

★11674★
New York (State) Office of Mental Health - Nathan S. Kline Institute for Psychiatric Research - Health Sciences Library (Med)
Bldg. 37   Phone: (914)365-2000
Orangeburg, NY 10962   Lois Cohan, Lib.Dir.
Founded: 1952. **Staff:** Prof 1; Other 3. **Subjects:** Psychiatry, psychopharmacology, biomedical computers, psychology, biochemistry, mental health, neurochemistry, neuroscience. **Holdings:** 19,000 books; 21,000 bound periodical volumes; 18 VF drawers; 12 VF drawers of pamphlets, brochures, and catalogs. **Subscriptions:** 350 journals and other serials. **Services:** Interlibrary loan; copying; library open to the public by appointment. **Computerized Information Services:** BRS Information Technologies, MEDLARS; internal database. Performs searches on fee basis. Contact Person: Sharon Sternbach, Lib.Asst. **Networks/Consortia:** Member of Southeastern New York Library Resources Council (SENYLRC), Health Information Libraries of Westchester (HILOW). **Publications:** Publications of the staff, biennial.

★11675★
New York (State) Office of Mental Health - Research Resource Center Library (Med)
44 Holland Ave.   Phone: (518)474-7167
Albany, NY 12229   Paul G. Hillengas, Libn.
Staff: Prof 1. **Subjects:** Psychiatry, psychology, mental hygiene, sociology. **Holdings:** 4000 books; 8000 unbound periodicals; 2258 reprints. **Subscriptions:** 103 journals and other serials. **Services:** Interlibrary loan; copying; library open to the public for reference use only. **Networks/Consortia:** Member of Capital District Library Council for Reference & Research Resources (CDLC).

★11676★
New York (State) Office of Mental Health - Rochester Psychiatric Center - Professional Library (Med)
1600 South Ave.
Rochester, NY 14620   Phone: (716)473-3230
Staff: 1. **Subjects:** Psychiatry, nursing. **Holdings:** 5320 books; 21 bound periodical volumes; 275 Audio-Digest tapes. **Subscriptions:** 33 journals and other serials. **Services:** Interlibrary loan; copying; library open to the public by appointment. **Computerized Information Services:** Internal databases. **Networks/Consortia:** Member of Rochester Regional Library Council (RRLC).

★ 11677 ★
New York (State) Office of Mental Health - St. Lawrence Psychiatric Center - Professional Library (Med)
Sta. A   Phone: (315)393-3000
Ogdensburg, NY 13669   Eleanor Cunningham, Lib.Techn.
Staff: 1. **Subjects:** Nursing, psychiatry, general medicine. **Holdings:** 5493 volumes; 110 VF folders of clippings; 71 videotapes; 1100 nonprint materials. **Subscriptions:** 200 journals and other serials; 15 newspapers. **Services:** Interlibrary loan; library not open to the public. **Computerized Information Services:** BRS Information Technologies, OCLC. **Networks/Consortia:** Member of North Country Reference and Research Resources Council (NCRRRC). **Publications:** Gifts & Exchange, semiannual. **Remarks:** FAX: (315)393-0725.

★ 11678 ★
New York (State) Office of Mental Retardation and Developmental Disabilities - Reference Center (Med)
44 Holland Ave.   Phone: (518)474-4613
Albany, NY 12229   Kathryn J. Jasenski, Sec.
Staff: Prof 1. **Subjects:** Mental retardation, developmental disabilities, community-based services, foster care, residential services. **Special Collections:** Historical records (state services; late 1800s to present). **Holdings:** 1000 books; 1000 other cataloged items; archival materials; records; photographs. **Subscriptions:** 66 journals and other serials. **Services:** Interlibrary loan; copying; center open to the public for reference use only. **Networks/Consortia:** Member of Capital District Library Council for Reference & Research Resources (CDLC).

★ 11679 ★
New York (State) Office of Parks, Recreation and Historic Preservation - Field Services Bureau - Library
Agencies Tower No. 1
Empire State Plaza
Albany, NY 12238   Phone: (518)474-0479
Subjects: Architectural history, historic preservation, historic archeology, New York State and local history. **Services:** Library not open to the public.

★ 11680 ★
New York (State) Office of Parks, Recreation & Historic Preservation - Fort Ontario State Historic Site - Library (Hist)
1 E. 4th St.   Phone: (315)343-4711
Oswego, NY 13126   Paul A. Lear, Jr., Act. Historic Site Mgr.
Founded: 1948. **Staff:** Prof 2; Other 7. **Subjects:** History - military, American, state, local; Oswego military fortifications; architecture and furniture; Fort Ontario. **Special Collections:** World War II use of Fort Ontario as refugee center. **Holdings:** 1200 volumes; 200 bound periodical volumes; 30 reels of microfilm; 300 photographs; 4 cases of vertical files; 6000 slides; manuscripts; unbound reports; magnetic tapes. **Services:** Copying; library open to the public for reference use only. **Computerized Information Services:** Internal database. **Staff:** Patricia Sivers, Park & Rec. Aide III.

★ 11681 ★
New York (State) Office of Parks, Recreation & Historic Preservation - John Jay Homestead State Historic Site - Library (Hist)
Box AH   Phone: (914)232-5651
Katonah, NY 10536   Linda M. McLean, Mgr.
Founded: 1959. **Staff:** Prof 2. **Subjects:** Jay Family, New York State history, antislavery, Westchester County history. **Special Collections:** Antislavery pamphlets of William Jay and John Jay II; archival materials from the Jay family, 18th-20th centuries (5000 items). **Holdings:** 4000 volumes. **Services:** Special arrangements can be made for use of the material by qualified scholars at the site. **Remarks:** The bulk of this collection consists of the library of John Jay (first Chief Justice of the United States) and four generations of his descendants.

★ 11682 ★
New York (State) Office of Parks, Recreation and Historic Preservation - Palisades Region - Washington's Headquarters State Historic Site - Library (Hist)
84 Liberty St.
P.O. Box 1783
Newburgh, NY 12551-1476   Phone: (914)562-1195
    Tom Hughes, Hist. Site Mgr.
Founded: 1850. **Staff:** Prof 1.25. **Subjects:** George Washington, American Revolution, local history. **Special Collections:** Timothy Pickering papers (100 pieces); Abraham Miller papers (75 pieces); Clinton Papers; George Washington papers. **Holdings:** 700 books; 2500 manuscripts. **Services:** Library open to the public by appointment only. **Also Known As:** New York State Bureau of Historic Sites. **Staff:** Mel Johnson, Hist. Site Asst.

★ 11683 ★
New York (State) Office of Parks, Recreation and Historic Preservation - Senate House State Historic Site - Library & Archives (Hist)
296 Fair St.   Phone: (914)338-2786
Kingston, NY 12401   Rich Goring, Mgr.
Founded: 1946. **Staff:** Prof 3. **Subjects:** Art and local history, genealogy. **Special Collections:** Hoes Collection; VanGaasbeek Collection; Vanderlyn Collection; Elting Collection; DeWitt Collection. **Holdings:** 975 books; 1000 bound periodical volumes; 200 pamphlets; 25,000 manuscripts, maps, clippings, land grants, and deeds. **Services:** Copying; library open to the public by appointment. **Special Indexes:** Vanderlyn Index; DeWitt Index.

★ 11684 ★
New York State Psychiatric Institute - Research Library (Med)
722 W. 168th St.   Phone: (212)960-5670
New York, NY 10032   David Lane, Lib.Dir.
Founded: 1896. **Staff:** Prof 3; Other 3. **Subjects:** Psychiatry, neurology, psychology, neuropathology. **Special Collections:** Sigmund Freud Memorial Collection (800 volumes). **Holdings:** 20,000 books; 21,000 bound periodical volumes; 300 dissertations and theses; 500 dissertations on microfilm; 1000 microfiche reports and journal volumes. **Subscriptions:** 600 journals and other serials. **Services:** Interlibrary loan; copying (limited); orientation lectures; library open to the public with restrictions. **Computerized Information Services:** DIALOG Information Services, BRS Information Technologies, PFDS Online, MEDLARS, Lithium Library, Institute for Scientific Information (ISI). **Networks/Consortia:** Member of Medical Library Center of New York (MLCNY). **Publications:** ReLPI Bulletin, irregular; ReLPI Handbook - limited distribution. **Staff:** John Harrison, ILL.

New York State School of Industrial and Labor Relations
See: **Cornell University - New York State School of Industrial and Labor Relations (4326)**

★ 11685 ★
New York State Supreme Court - 1st Judicial District - Criminal Law Library (Law)
100 Centre St., 17th Fl.   Phone: (212)374-5615
New York, NY 10013   David G. Badertscher, Prin. Law Libn.
Staff: Prof 2; Other 5. **Subjects:** Criminal law; New York state law; criminology; court administration and management; information science. **Special Collections:** Trial transcripts for New York State Supreme Court - 1st Judicial District. **Holdings:** 110,000 volumes. **Subscriptions:** 150 journals and other serials. **Services:** Interlibrary loan; library open to the public by appointment. **Automated Operations:** Computerized cataloging, acquisitions, and serials **Computerized Information Services:** WESTLAW, Legislative Retrieval System (LRS); CompuServe Information Service (electronic mail service). **Networks/Consortia:** Member of New York Metropolitan Reference and Research Library Agency. **Remarks:** FAX: (212)374-5770. Electronic mail address(es): 7161,2434 (CompuServe Information Service). **Staff:** Sonia Penich, Sr. Law Libn.

★ 11686 ★
New York State Supreme Court - 2nd Judicial District - Law Library (Law)
360 Adams St., Rm. 349   Phone: (718)643-8080
Brooklyn, NY 11201   Jatindra N. Mukerji, Prin. Law Libn.
Staff: 5. **Subjects:** Law. **Special Collections:** Forensic medicine; records and briefs of cases in New York Court of Appeals and all appellate divisions. **Holdings:** 269,043 volumes; 5992 reels of microfilm; 112,615 microfiche cards; 7799 ultrafiche cards; 191 cassettes. **Subscriptions:** 775 journals and other serials. **Services:** Interlibrary loan; library open to members and court personnel only. **Also Known As:** Law Library in Brooklyn. **Staff:** Paul C. Henrich, Sr. Law Libn.; Louis J. Romeo, Sr. Law Libn.; Brenda E. Pantell, Law Libn.

★ 11687 ★
New York State Supreme Court - 2nd Judicial District - Law Library (Law)
County Court House   Phone: (718)390-5291
Staten Island, NY 10301   Philip A. Klingle, Sr. Law Libn.
Founded: 1920. **Staff:** Prof 1; Other 1. **Subjects:** Law. **Holdings:** 75,000 books; 185 feet of vertical files of reports, pamphlets, clippings. **Subscriptions:** 55 journals and other serials. **Services:** Copying; library open to the public for reference use only. **Computerized Information Services:** OCLC.

★ 11688 ★
New York State Supreme Court - 3rd Judicial District - Emory A. Chase Memorial Library (Law)
Greene County Court House
320 Main St.   Phone: (518)943-2230
Catskill, NY 12414   Mr. Eric Maurer
Founded: 1908. **Staff:** Prof 1. **Subjects:** Law. **Special Collections:** New York State Law; Greene County Survey Maps/Books of C.H. Vanorden. **Holdings:** 12,000 volumes. **Subscriptions:** 167 journals and other serials; 2 newspapers. **Services:** Interlibrary loan; copying; library open to the public for reference use only. **Remarks:** FAX: (518)943-7763.

★ 11689 ★
New York State Supreme Court - 3rd Judicial District - Hamilton Odell Library (Law)
Sullivan County Court House   Phone: (914)794-1547
Monticello, NY 12701   Edith Schop, Law Libn.
Staff: Prof 1. **Subjects:** Law. **Holdings:** 9000 volumes. **Subscriptions:** 2 newspapers. **Services:** Library open to the public. **Remarks:** FAX: (914)791-6170.

★ 11690 ★
New York State Supreme Court - 3rd Judicial District - Law Library (Law)
Court House   Phone: (518)828-3206
Hudson, NY 12534   Emily M. Wildey, Law Lib.Ck.
Staff: Prof 1. **Subjects:** Law. **Holdings:** 5000 volumes. **Services:** Library open to the public for reference use only. **Remarks:** FAX: (518)828-2101.

★ 11691 ★
New York State Supreme Court - 3rd Judicial District - Law Library (Law)
Court House
Box 3535   Phone: (914)339-5680
Kingston, NY 12401   Harriett Straus, Libn.
Staff: Prof 1. **Subjects:** Law. **Holdings:** 17,000 volumes. **Services:** Copying; library open to the public.

★ 11692 ★
New York State Supreme Court - 3rd Judicial District - Law Library (Law)
Court House, 2nd St. Annex
Rensselaer County   Phone: (518)270-3717
Troy, NY 12180   Karlye Ann Gill Pillai, Law Libn.
Founded: 1908. **Staff:** Prof 1; Other 1.5. **Subjects:** Federal and state law. **Holdings:** 39,950 books; 105,900 microfiche. **Subscriptions:** 420 journals and other serials. **Services:** Copying; library service to prisoners; library open to the public with restrictions. **Automated Operations:** Computerized cataloging. **Computerized Information Services:** Legislative Retrieval System (LRS), WESTLAW, OCLC EPIC.

★ 11693 ★
New York State Supreme Court - 4th Judicial District - Joseph F. Egan Memorial Supreme Court Library (Law)
612 State St.   Phone: (518)382-3310
Schenectady, NY 12307   Patricia L. North, Law Libn.
Staff: Prof 1. **Subjects:** Law. **Holdings:** 26,000 books; 2000 bound periodical volumes. **Services:** Copying; library open to the public with restrictions.

★ 11694 ★
New York State Supreme Court - 4th Judicial District - Law Library (Law)
Warren County Municipal Center   Phone: (518)761-6442
Lake George, NY 12845   James D. Summa, Jr., Law Lib.Ck.
Founded: 1923. **Staff:** 1. **Subjects:** Law. **Holdings:** 31,000 books. **Services:** Copying; library open to the public.

★ 11695 ★
New York State Supreme Court - 4th Judicial District - Law Library (Law)
City Hall
474 Broadway   Phone: (518)584-4862
Saratoga Springs, NY 12866   Linda E. Macica
Founded: 1866. **Staff:** Prof 1. **Subjects:** Law. **Special Collections:** Saratoga Springs City Directories, 1884 to present. **Holdings:** 20,000 volumes. **Services:** Library open to the public with restrictions. **Computerized Information Services:** LRS (Legislative Retrieval System).

★ 11696 ★
New York State Supreme Court - 5th Judicial District - Law Library (Law)
Court House
E. Oneida St.   Phone: (315)342-0550
Oswego, NY 13126   Janice Drumm, Law Lib.Ck.
Founded: 1920. **Staff:** Prof 2. **Subjects:** Law - federal, state, county, city; medicine. **Special Collections:** New York State Reporters, 1891; Series Law of New York, 1853-1899 (Session Laws); records of all departments of the New York State Appellate and North Eastern Division (microfilm); Federal Reporter and Federal Supplement, 1st and 2nd series (microfilm); New York Law Journal (microfilm). **Holdings:** 25,000 books; 30 drawers of microfiche; periodicals. **Services:** Interlibrary loan; copying; library open to the public for reference use only. **Computerized Information Services:** WESTLAW. **Remarks:** FAX: (315)342-0195. **Staff:** Mary Jane Lower, Sr.Off. Typist.

★ 11697 ★
New York State Supreme Court - 5th Judicial District - Law Library (Law)
Oneida County Court House   Phone: (315)798-5703
Utica, NY 13501   Mary M. Anthony, Law Libn.
Founded: 1875. **Staff:** Prof 1; Other 3. **Subjects:** Law. **Special Collections:** Special Trials of the Century; history of law; Utica city directories, 1841 to present; proceedings of Utica Common Council; late 18th-early 19th century American legal treatises. **Holdings:** 60,000 volumes; 2000 bound periodical volumes; official documents from New York and the federal government; advance sheets from the courts; microfiche; ultrafiche. **Subscriptions:** 100 journals and other serials. **Services:** Interlibrary loan; copying; library open to the public. **Automated Operations:** Computerized cataloging. **Computerized Information Services:** WESTLAW, Legislative Retrieval System (LRS); internal database. Performs searches free of charge. **Networks/Consortia:** Member of Central New York Library Resources Council (CENTRO). **Publications:** Book lists. **Remarks:** FAX: (315)797-0531.

★ 11698 ★
New York State Supreme Court - 5th Judicial District - Law Library (Law)
Court House   Phone: (315)785-3064
Watertown, NY 13601   Patrica B. Donaldson, Libn.
Founded: 1914. **Staff:** 2. **Subjects:** Law. **Holdings:** 26,000 volumes. **Subscriptions:** 36 journals and other serials. **Services:** Interlibrary loan; library open to the public for reference use only. **Computerized Information Services:** OCLC, WESTLAW, Commerce Clearing House, Inc. (CCH). **Remarks:** FAX: (315)785-8179.

★ 11699 ★
New York State Supreme Court - 6th Judicial District - Law Library (Law)
Court House Square
Delhi, NY 13753   Phone: (607)746-3959
Staff: Prof 1. **Subjects:** Law. **Holdings:** 8000 books; 10 drawers of microfiche (Records and Briefs; New York Law Reports, 1st series); 16 boxes of ultrafiche (American Law Reports, 1st and 2nd series; Federal Reporter, 1st series; Federal Reporter, 2nd series, volumes 1-750; Federal Supplement; New York Supplement, 1st series; New York Supplement, 2nd series, volumes 1-450). **Services:** Library open to the public. **Automated Operations:** Computerized cataloging. **Remarks:** FAX: (607)746-3253.

★ 11700 ★

New York State Supreme Court - 6th Judicial District - Law Library
(Law)
Hazlett Bldg.   Phone: (607)737-2983
Elmira, NY 14901   Laurie A. Hubbard, Libn.
Founded: 1895. **Staff:** Prof 1. **Subjects:** Law. **Special Collections:** New York State and Federal Collections; treatises. **Holdings:** 25,000 volumes. **Subscriptions:** 10 journals and other serials; 3 newspapers. **Services:** Library open to the public with restrictions on borrowing. **Computerized Information Services:** WESTLAW, OCLC. **Remarks:** FAX: (607)732-8879.

★ 11701 ★

New York State Supreme Court - 6th Judicial District - Law Library
(Law)
5 Maple St.   Phone: (607)334-9463
Norwich, NY 13815   Margaret S. Reed, Libn.
Staff: 1. **Subjects:** Law. **Holdings:** 12,000 volumes. **Subscriptions:** 5 journals and other serials. **Services:** Library open to the public for reference use only. **Remarks:** FAX: (607)336-9463.

★ 11702 ★

New York State Supreme Court - 7th Judicial District - Law Library
(Law)
Cayuga County Court House
Auburn, NY 13021   Phone: (315)253-1279
Staff: Prof 1. **Subjects:** Law. **Holdings:** 19,000 volumes. **Subscriptions:** 12 journals and other serials. **Services:** Library open to the public with restrictions.

★ 11703 ★

New York State Supreme Court - 7th Judicial District - Law Library
(Law)
County Office Bldg.
3 Pulteney Square E.   Phone: (607)776-9631
Bath, NY 14810   Kristine E. Gilbert, Law Libn.
Founded: 1940. **Staff:** Prof 1. **Subjects:** Law. **Holdings:** 12,000 volumes. **Services:** Copying; library open to the public with restrictions. **Computerized Information Services:** WESTLAW.

★ 11704 ★

New York State Supreme Court - 8th Judicial District - Law Library
(Law)
92 Franklin St., 4th Fl.   Phone: (716)852-0712
Buffalo, NY 14202   James R. Sahlem, Prin. Law Libn.
Founded: 1863. **Staff:** Prof 2; Other 3. **Subjects:** Law. **Holdings:** 264,000 volumes. **Subscriptions:** 224 journals and other serials. **Services:** Interlibrary loan; copying; library open to the public. **Computerized Information Services:** OCLC; LRS (New York State legislative document retrieval system; internal database). Performs searches on fee basis. **Remarks:** FAX: (716)852-3510. **Staff:** Jeannine A. Lee, Law Libn.

★ 11705 ★

New York State Supreme Court - 9th Judicial District - Joseph F. Barnard Memorial Law Library Association (Law)
Court House
10 Market St.   Phone: (914)431-1815
Poughkeepsie, NY 12601   Catherine A. Maher, Sr. Law Lib.Ck.
Founded: 1904. **Staff:** 1. **Subjects:** Law. **Holdings:** 15,000 books; 4600 ultrafiche; appellate records and briefs on microfiche. **Subscriptions:** 258 journals and other serials. **Services:** Library open to the public. **Computerized Information Services:** WESTLAW.

★ 11706 ★

New York State Supreme Court - 9th Judicial District - Law Library
(Law)
Newburgh Free Library
255 Main St.
Goshen, NY 10924   Phone: (914)294-5151
Staff: 1. **Subjects:** Law. **Holdings:** Figures not available. **Services:** Library open to the public. **Remarks:** Maintains Orange County Law Library, Government Center, 265 Main St., Goshen, NY 10924.

★ 11707 ★

New York State Supreme Court - 9th Judicial District - Law Library
(Law)
Westchester County Court House
111 Grove St., 9th Fl.   Phone: (914)285-3900
White Plains, NY 10601   Sonja C. Davis, Prin. Law Libn.
Founded: 1908. **Staff:** Prof 2; Other 3. **Subjects:** Law. **Holdings:** 300,000 volumes; Records on Appeal of 4 Appellate Departments and Court of Appeals. **Subscriptions:** 140 journals and other serials. **Services:** Library open to the public.

★ 11708 ★

New York State Supreme Court - 10th Judicial District - Law Library
(Law)
Criminal Courts Bldg.
220 Center Dr.   Phone: (516)852-1887
Riverhead, NY 11901-3312   Lynn C. Fullshire, Prin. Law Libn.
Founded: 1928. **Staff:** Prof 2; Other 4. **Subjects:** Law - federal, state, Suffolk County, town. **Holdings:** 100,000 volumes; New York Law Journal, 1956 to present, on microfilm; checklist of official publications of New York State, 1975 to present, on microfilm; New York Court of Appeals Records and Briefs, 36 NY 2nd to present, on microfilm. **Subscriptions:** 963 journals and other serials; 4 newspapers. **Services:** Copying; library open to the public. **Automated Operations:** Computerized cataloging. **Computerized Information Services:** OCLC, Legislative Retrieval System (LRS), DataTimes. **Networks/Consortia:** Member of Long Island Library Resources Council. **Remarks:** FAX: (516)852-1782. The Civil Court Law Library is located at Griffing Ave.; it is not open to the public. **Staff:** Michele M. Warner, Law Libn.

★ 11709 ★

New York State Supreme Court - 11th Judicial District - Law Library
(Law)
General Court House
88-11 Sutphin Blvd.   Phone: (718)520-3140
Jamaica, NY 11435   Andrew J. Tschinkel, Prin. Law Libn.
Founded: 1911. **Staff:** Prof 4; Other 2. **Subjects:** Law. **Holdings:** 100,000 books; 10,000 bound periodical volumes; 141,756 fiche; 3443 16mm films; 735 35mm films; 5250 ultrafiche; New York state document depository; 800 reels of microfilm of legislative documents. **Subscriptions:** 1500 journals and other serials. **Services:** Library open to the public. **Automated Operations:** Computerized cataloging. **Computerized Information Services:** WESTLAW, InfoMaster, New York Legislative Retrieval System (LRS); CCIS (Civil Case Information Service - New York State courts; internal database); EasyLink (electronic mail service). **Networks/Consortia:** Member of SUNY/OCLC Library Network. **Staff:** Robert Cambridge, Sr. Law Libn.; John Butler, Law Libn.; Armine Lalayan, Law Libn.

★ 11710 ★

New York State Supreme Court - 11th Judicial District - Law Library
(Law)
Supreme Court Bldg.
125-01 Queens Blvd.   Phone: (718)520-3541
Kew Gardens, NY 11415   Andrew J. Tschinkel, Libn.
Subjects: Law. **Holdings:** 20,000 volumes. **Services:** Library open to judges, staff, and attorneys.

★ 11711 ★

New York State Supreme Court - Appellate Division, 1st Judicial Department - Law Library (Law)
27 Madison Ave.   Phone: (212)340-0400
New York, NY 10010   Stephen R. Grotsky, Libn.
Founded: 1900. **Staff:** 3. **Subjects:** Law. **Holdings:** 75,000 volumes. **Services:** Library not open to the public. **Computerized Information Services:** WESTLAW, LEXIS. **Staff:** Robert C. Gelber, Asst.Libn.

★ 11712 ★

New York State Supreme Court - Appellate Division, 3rd Judicial Department - Law Library (Law)
Justice Bldg., Empire State Plaza
Capitol Station, Box 7288   Phone: (518)486-4578
Albany, NY 12224   Ronald J. Milkins, Libn.
Subjects: Law. **Holdings:** 100,000 volumes. **Services:** Library not open to the public.

★ 11713 ★
New York State Supreme Court - Appellate Division, 4th Judicial Department - Law Library (Law)
525 Hall of Justice
Rochester, NY 14614
Phone: (716)428-1070
David Voisinet, Prin. Law Libn.
Founded: 1849. **Staff:** Prof 3; Other 4. **Subjects:** Law, legislative intent, local history. **Special Collections:** Briefs and records in the Court of Appeals and the four departments of the Appellate Division of the State of New York and in the U.S. Court of Appeals for the 2nd Circuit; Chancellor Walworth Library of the Court of Chancery, 1613-1837 (imprints). **Holdings:** 250,000 volumes. **Subscriptions:** 500 journals and other serials; 5 newspapers. **Services:** Interlibrary loan; copying; library open to the public. **Computerized Information Services:** WESTLAW, LRS, OCLC; NYS Data Center (electronic mail service). **Networks/Consortia:** Member of Rochester Regional Library Council (RRLC). **Remarks:** FAX: (716)428-1073. **Staff:** Robert R. Gutz, Sr. Law Libn.; Maryanne Clark, Asst. Law Libn.; Judy Weiner, Asst. Law Libn.

★ 11714 ★
New York State Supreme Court - Library (Law)
Broome County Court House, Rm. 107
Binghamton, NY 13901
Phone: (607)778-2119
Judy A. Lauer, Law Libn.
Founded: 1859. **Staff:** Prof 1; Other 2. **Subjects:** New York and federal law. **Holdings:** 45,000 books; 1975 bound periodical volumes; 4600 volumes of ultrafiche; 45 microfiche; 3480 reels of microfilm. **Subscriptions:** 140 journals and other serials. **Services:** Interlibrary loan; copying; library open to the public. **Computerized Information Services:** OCLC, WESTLAW, LRS (Legislative Retrieval System). **Networks/Consortia:** Member of South Central Research Library Council (SCRLC), New York State Unified Court Law Libraries Association. **Remarks:** FAX: (607)772-8331.

★ 11715 ★
New York State Supreme Court - Library (Law)
500 Court House
Syracuse, NY 13202
Phone: (315)435-2063
Susan M. Wood, Prin. Law Libn.
Founded: 1849. **Staff:** Prof 4; Other 3. **Subjects:** Law. **Special Collections:** Early English case law; records and briefs of the 4th Appellate Division and other New York State Court of Appeals, 1900 to present; shared federal depository; extensive New York and U.S. legal materials. **Holdings:** 107,000 books; 5000 bound periodical volumes; 48,000 microforms. **Subscriptions:** 600 journals and other serials. **Services:** Interlibrary loan; copying; library open to the public. **Automated Operations:** Computerized cataloging. **Computerized Information Services:** WESTLAW, Legislative Retrieval System (LRS). Performs searches free of charge on LRS only. **Networks/Consortia:** Member of Central New York Library Resources Council (CENTRO), SUNY/OCLC Library Network. **Remarks:** FAX: (315)425-9635. **Staff:** Carmen E. Brigandi, Law Libn.; Cynthia J. Kesler, Law Libn.; Mary Beth Dunn, Law Libn.

★ 11716 ★
New York State Workers' Compensation Board - Library (Law)
180 Livingston St., Rm. 622
Brooklyn, NY 11248
Phone: (718)802-6600
Donald H. Holley, Assoc.Att.
Founded: 1944. **Staff:** Prof 2. **Subjects:** Workers' compensation law - legislation, statistics, medical aspects. **Special Collections:** Workers' compensation laws of other states. **Holdings:** 5000 books; 100 bound periodical volumes. **Services:** Library open to attorneys and board staff for reference use only. **Publications:** Workers' Compensation Law; Volunteer Firemen's Benefit Law.

★ 11717 ★
New York Stock Exchange - Research Library (Bus-Fin)
11 Wall St.
New York, NY 10005
Phone: (212)656-2491
Ellen Duttweiler, Libn.
Founded: 1935. **Staff:** Prof 1; Other 1. **Subjects:** Banking and finance, business and economics. **Special Collections:** Publications of other domestic and foreign exchanges. **Holdings:** 4000 books; 3000 pamphlets; 75 VF drawers. **Subscriptions:** 75 journals and other serials. **Services:** Interlibrary loan; library not open to the public. **Computerized Information Services:** NEXIS, DIALOG Information Services, Dow Jones News/Retrieval. **Remarks:** FAX: (212)656-5045.

★ 11718 ★
New York Telephone Company - Legal Department Library (Law, Info Sci)
1095 Avenue of the Americas
New York, NY 10036
Phone: (212)395-6158
Staff: Prof 1. **Subjects:** Law, communications. **Holdings:** 17,500 volumes. **Subscriptions:** 30 journals and other serials. **Services:** Library not open to the public. **Computerized Information Services:** LEXIS.

★ 11719 ★
New York Theological Seminary - Library (Rel-Phil)
5 W. 29th St.
New York, NY 10001
Phone: (212)532-4012
Eleanor Soler, Libn.
Founded: 1900. **Staff:** Prof 1; Other 1. **Subjects:** Bible, theology, pastoral counseling, parish ministry, African-American church studies, women in the church. **Holdings:** 20,000 volumes; 700 audio cassettes; 20 video cassettes; 300 Spanish books; 200 Korean books; 2 drawers of periodicals on microfiche. **Subscriptions:** 40 journals and other serials. **Services:** Interlibrary loan; copying; library open to the public for reference use only.

★ 11720 ★
New York Times - Library (Publ)
229 W. 43rd St.
New York, NY 10036
Phone: (212)556-7428
Linda Amster
Staff: 9. **Subjects:** Journalism, New York City, politics, history, biography. **Special Collections:** Times Books repository; Arno Books repository. **Holdings:** 60,000 books; archival items; microfiche; microfilm. **Subscriptions:** 350 journals and other serials; 20 newspapers. **Services:** Library not open to the public. **Computerized Information Services:** NEXIS.

New York Times Group - Santa Rosa Press Democrat
See: Santa Rosa Press Democrat (14819)

★ 11721 ★
New York University - Conservation Center - Library (Art)
14 E. 78th St.
New York, NY 10012
Phone: (212)772-5800
Robert Stacy
Staff: Prof 1. **Subjects:** Conservation and restoration of works of art. **Holdings:** 9000 books; 5000 bound periodical volumes. **Subscriptions:** 250 journals and other serials. **Services:** Interlibrary loan; copying; library open to the public by appointment. **Automated Operations:** Computerized cataloging. **Computerized Information Services:** Chemical Industry Notes (CIN), Association of Research Libraries Newsletter (ARLN). **Remarks:** FAX: (212)772-5807.

★ 11722 ★
New York University - David B. Kriser Dental Center - John & Bertha E. Waldmann Memorial Library (Med)
345 E. 24th St.
New York, NY 10010
Phone: (212)998-9794
Roy C. Johnson, Libn.
Staff: Prof 2; Other 8. **Subjects:** Dentistry, allied health sciences. **Special Collections:** Weinberger, Blum, Mestal Collection on Dental History. **Holdings:** 12,000 books; 22,000 bound periodical volumes; 88 volumes of masters' theses; 4 VF drawers of archival materials. **Subscriptions:** 449 journals and other serials. **Services:** Interlibrary loan; library not open to the public. **Automated Operations:** Computerized cataloging and serials. **Computerized Information Services:** PaperChase; EasyLink, DOCLINE (electronic mail services). **Networks/Consortia:** Member of Medical Library Center of New York (MLCNY), National Network of Libraries of Medicine (NN/LM), National Network of Libraries of Medicine - Middle Atlantic Region. **Publications:** Library Newsletter, 3/year - for internal distribution only. **Special Catalogs:** Audiovisual Materials Catalog (booklet). **Remarks:** FAX: (212)995-3529. **Staff:** Maureen Wren, Assoc.Libn.

★ 11723 ★
New York University - Fales Library - Division of Special Collections (Hum)
Elmer Holmes Bobst Library
70 Washington Square, S.
New York, NY 10012
Phone: (212)998-2599
Frank Walker, Cur.
Founded: 1957. **Staff:** Prof 1. **Subjects:** British and American literature. **Special Collections:** Robert Frost Library; Lewis Carroll; Erich Maria Remarque Papers; New American Library Archives; Elizabeth Robins Papers; Coleman Dowell Papers. **Holdings:** 148,000 books; 2000 bound periodical volumes; 30,000 manuscripts. **Services:** Collections open to scholars by appointment.

★ 11724 ★
New York University - Institute of Fine Arts - Slide and Photographic
  Collection (Art, Aud-Vis)
1 E. 78th St.   Phone: (212)772-5821
New York, NY 10021   Jenni Rodda, Cur., Vis.Rsrcs.
Staff: 4.25. **Subjects:** European drawing, painting, sculpture, architecture; art of the Low Countries; antique art known to the Renaissance. **Special Collections:** Offner (Florentine painting); Coor (Sienese painting); Berenson (Italian painting); D.I.A.L. (art of the Low Countries; 11,000 items); I Tatti Archive (13,000 items); Gernsheim corpus (60,000 drawings); Bartsch prints (10,000); Offner corpus (50,000 items); census of antique works of art known to Renaissance artists; Frank Caro Collection. **Holdings:** 200 books; 5 bound periodical volumes; 6 archival materials. **Subscriptions:** 3 journals and other serials. **Services:** Collection open to qualified researchers by appointment only. **Remarks:** FAX: (212)772-5807. **Staff:** Dorothy Simon, Asst.Cur.; Christa Blackwood, Photographer.

★ 11725 ★
New York University - Institute of Fine Arts - Stephen Chan Library of
  Fine Arts (Art)
1 E. 78th St.   Phone: (212)772-5826
New York, NY 10021   Sharon Chickanzeff, Dir.
Founded: 1938. **Staff:** Prof 2; Other 4. **Subjects:** History of art, architectural history, archeology, art technology and conservation of art. **Holdings:** 112,000 books; 14,000 bound periodical volumes; 10,000 microforms. **Subscriptions:** 676 journals and other serials. **Services:** Interlibrary loan; copying; library open to scholars by appointment. **Automated Operations:** Computerized public access catalog and cataloging. **Computerized Information Services:** RLIN; BOBCAT (internal database). **Networks/Consortia:** Member of Research Libraries Information Network (RLIN), New York Metropolitan Reference and Research Library Agency. **Special Catalogs:** Library Catalog of the Conservation Center of the Institute of Fine Arts, New York University. **Remarks:** FAX: (212)772-5807. **Staff:** Max Marmor, Ref.Libn.; Elizabeth Dansky, Acq.; Robert Stacy, Cons.Ctr.

★ 11726 ★
New York University - Medical Center - Department of Environmental
  Medicine - Library (Med)
Long Meadow Rd.   Phone: (914)351-4232
Tuxedo, NY 10987   Christine M. Singleton, Res.Libn.
Staff: Prof 1; Other 1. **Subjects:** Environmental medicine and science, cancer research, air and water pollution, industrial health, radiobiology and toxicology. **Holdings:** 6500 books; 7000 bound periodical volumes. **Subscriptions:** 150 journals and other serials. **Services:** Interlibrary loan; library not open to the public. **Computerized Information Services:** DIALOG Information Services, NLM, STN International. **Networks/Consortia:** Member of Southeastern New York Library Resources Council (SENYLRC). **Remarks:** FAX: (914)351-4825.

★ 11727 ★
New York University - Medical Center - Frederick L. Ehrman Medical
  Library (Med)
550 First Ave.   Phone: (212)340-5393
New York, NY 10016   Karen Brewer, Lib.Dir.
Staff: Prof 13; Other 20. **Subjects:** Medicine, allied health sciences. **Special Collections:** Heaton Collection on the history of medicine; Archives. **Holdings:** 162,000 volumes. **Subscriptions:** 2019 journals and other serials. **Services:** Interlibrary loan; library not open to the public. **Automated Operations:** Computerized public access catalog, cataloging, acquisitions, and serials. **Computerized Information Services:** BRS Information Technologies, DIALOG Information Services, MEDLINE, OCLC; BITNET (electronic mail service). **Networks/Consortia:** Member of Medical Library Center of New York (MLCNY). **Publications:** Newsletter. **Remarks:** FAX: (212)995-8196. Electronic mail address(es): BREWER@MCCLBO.MED.NYU.EDU (BITNET). **Staff:** Jean Reibman, Assoc.Dir.; N.J. Wolfe, Hd., Access Serv., Dorice Horne, Hd.Educ.Serv.

★ 11728 ★
New York University - Medical Center - Goldwater Memorial Hospital -
  Health Sciences Library (Med)
Franklin D. Roosevelt Island   Phone: (212)750-6749
New York, NY 10044   Martin M. Leibovici, Lib.Dir.
Founded: 1939. **Staff:** Prof 1; Other 2. **Subjects:** General medicine, rehabilitation medicine, geriatrics, chronic disease. **Holdings:** 3800 books; 6000 bound periodical volumes; 850 AV programs; 4 VF drawers.

Subscriptions: 342 journals and other serials. **Services:** Interlibrary loan; copying; library open to scholars by appointment. **Automated Operations:** Computerized cataloging and ILL. **Computerized Information Services:** BRS Information Technologies, MEDLINE; DOCLINE (electronic mail service). **Networks/Consortia:** Member of Medical Library Center of New York (MLCNY), New York Metropolitan Reference and Research Library Agency, National Network of Libraries of Medicine - Middle Atlantic Region. **Publications:** Acquisitions lists; Periodical Holdings; AV Collection lists.

★ 11729 ★
New York University - Real Estate Institute - Jack Brause Library
  (Bus-Fin)
11 W. 42nd St., 5th Fl.   Phone: (212)790-1325
New York, NY 10036   Jan Horah, Dir.
Founded: 1983. **Staff:** Prof 1; Other 3. **Subjects:** Real estate in New York and metropolitan area. **Special Collections:** Stephen W. Brenner Hospitality Collection. **Holdings:** 1000 books; 300 bound periodical volumes; files on real estate topics and neighborhood data; zoning maps and resolutions; ownership directories; space surveys. **Subscriptions:** 100 journals and other serials; 10 newspapers. **Services:** Library open to the public. **Computerized Information Services:** DIALOG Information Services, RLIN; BOBCAT (internal database). **Special Indexes:** Real estate periodicals index; periodical index to 100 subscriptions. **Remarks:** FAX: (212)790-1680.

★ 11730 ★
New York University - Salomon Center for the Study of Financial
  Institutions - Library (Bus-Fin)
90 Trinity Place   Phone: (212)285-6100
New York, NY 10006   Mary Jaffier
Founded: 1971. **Staff:** 2. **Subjects:** Finance, economics. **Holdings:** 200 books; 300 other cataloged items. **Subscriptions:** 50 journals and other serials. **Services:** Library not open to the public.

★ 11731 ★
New York University - School of Law Library (Law)
40 Washington Square, S., Rm. 109   Phone: (212)998-6300
New York, NY 10012   Leslie Rich, Law Libn.
Founded: 1860. **Staff:** Prof 16; Other 52. **Subjects:** Law. **Holdings:** 825,000 volumes and volume equivalents. **Subscriptions:** 6800 journals and other serials. **Services:** Interlibrary loan; copying for law firms. **Automated Operations:** Computerized cataloging, circulation, acquisitions, and serials. **Computerized Information Services:** LEXIS, RLIN, WESTLAW, DIALOG Information Services; CD-ROM (LegalTrac, WILSONDISC, Martindale-Hubbell Law Directory). **Networks/Consortia:** Member of Legal Information Network of New York. **Remarks:** Alternate telephone number(s): 998-6363. FAX: (212)995-3477. **Staff:** Carol Alpert, Media/Ref.Libn.; Mary Burgos, Ser.Libn.; Julia Bidden, Acq.Libn.; Camille Broussard, Coll.Serv./Ref.Libn.; Ronald Brown, Res./Ref.Libn.; Mary Chapman, Assoc.Libn., Tech.Serv.; Elizabeth Evans, Comp./Ref. Libn.; Gretchen Feltes, Cons./Ref.Libn.; Aura Marina Flores, Spec.Coll.Mgr.; Aurora Ioanid, Cat.; Orley Jones, Automated Sys.Libn.; Blanka Kudej, Assoc.Libn., Spec.Coll.; Maria Okonska, Cat.; Viji Nittor, Tech.Serv.Mgr.; Radu Popa, Intl.Ref.Libn.; Sara Pritchett, Adm.Coord.; Jay Shuman, Ref.Libn.; Stuart Spore, Hd., Cat./Automated Sys.

★ 11732 ★
New York University - Stearn Graduate School of Business
  Administration - Library (Bus-Fin)
19 Rector St., 2nd Fl.   Phone: (212)285-6230
New York, NY 10006   Carol Falcione, Dir.
Founded: 1920. **Staff:** Prof 5; Other 9. **Subjects:** Finance, accounting, management, international business, computer applications. **Holdings:** 94,000 volumes; 219,000 microforms. **Subscriptions:** 1800 journals and other serials. **Services:** Interlibrary loan; library open to the SLA members by arrangement only. **Automated Operations:** Computerized cataloging and circulation. **Computerized Information Services:** BRS Information Technologies, DIALOG Information Services, Dow Jones News/Retrieval, RLIN, ABI/INFORM, Disclosure Incorporated, Predicasts, F & S Text; CD-ROM (General BusinessFile). **Networks/Consortia:** Member of Research Libraries Information Network (RLIN), New York Metropolitan Reference and Research Library Agency. **Staff:** Bill Sils, Access; Alicia Estes, Ref.Libn.; Mary Jean Pavelsek, Ref.Libn.; Elizabeth Thompson, Ref.Libn.

★ 11733 ★
New York University - Tamiment Library (Soc Sci, Bus-Fin)
70 Washington Square, S.
New York, NY 10012
Phone: (212)998-2630
Dorothy Swanson
Founded: 1956. **Staff:** Prof 3; Other 4. **Subjects:** History of labor and unionism; radical and reform movements. **Special Collections:** Meyer London Memorial Library of the Rand School of Social Science; Eugene V. Debs Collection; American Socialist Society Collection; B. Charney Vladeck papers; Fund for the Republic Communism Collection; Robert F. Wagner Labor Archives; Oral History of the American Left (OHAL); Jacob and Bessye Blaufarb Videotape Library. **Holdings:** 58,517 volumes; 14,891 microforms; 500,000 items in special collections; 200 VF drawers of pamphlets; 5488 linear feet of manuscript collections. **Subscriptions:** 563 journals and other serials. **Services:** Interlibrary loan; library open to the public for research. **Publications:** Tamiment Library Bulletin; New York Labor Heritage; OHAL Newsletter. **Staff:** Debra Bernhardt, Archv.; Peter Filardo, Archv.; Gail Malmgreen, Archv.

★ 11734 ★
New York University - United Nations Collection (Soc Sci)
Elmer Holmes Bobst Library
70 Washington Square, S.
New York, NY 10012
Phone: (212)998-2610
Carol Falcione, Hd., Soc.Sci./Docs.
Founded: 1946. **Staff:** Prof 1; Other 2. **Subjects:** United Nations and League of Nations; Specialized Agencies of the United Nations; other international organizations. **Holdings:** 90,000 document items in hardcopy, including UN official records and sales publications (bound), UN mimeographed documents (bound and unbound), publications of the UN specialized agencies, League of Nations, and other international organizations (bound and unbound); microfiche collections, including National Statistical Compendia, annual reports of the world's central banks, the complete Index to International Statistics, Latin American historical statistics, United Nations Conference on Trade & Development/UNCTAD (5132 microfiche), Organization of American States/OAS (1600 microfiche); League of Nations documents (547 reels of microfilm) ; International Monetary Fund/IMF materials (6 reels of microfilm). **Subscriptions:** 530 journals and other serials. **Services:** Copying; collection open to the public. **Staff:** Susan Shiroma, Ref.Libn.

★ 11735 ★
New York Zoological Society - Library (Biol Sci)
185th St. & Southern Blvd.
Bronx, NY 10460
Phone: (212)220-6874
Steven P. Johnson, Supv.Libn./Archv.
Founded: 1899. **Staff:** Prof 1. **Subjects:** Conservation biology, zoo biology. **Holdings:** 5000 books; 2000 bound periodical volumes; 800 linear feet of archival materials. **Subscriptions:** 200 journals and other serials. **Services:** Interlibrary loan; copying; library open to the public by appointment for reference use only. **Automated Operations:** Computerized public access catalog and cataloging. **Computerized Information Services:** DIALOG Information Services, OCLC; internal databases; CD-ROM (Wildlife and Fish Worldwide); DIALMAIL (electronic mail service). **Networks/Consortia:** Member of New York Metropolitan Reference and Research Library Agency. **Publications:** Guide to the archives of the New York Zoological Society (1982) - available on request. **Remarks:** FAX: (212)220-7114.

New York Zoological Society - New York Aquarium Library
See: **Osborn Laboratories of Marine Sciences - New York Aquarium Library** (12588)

★ 11736 ★
New Zealand - Department of Scientific and Industrial Research - Library (Biol Sci, Agri)
Fitzherbert W.
Private Bag
Palmerston North, New Zealand
Phone: 6 3568019
Steven A. Northover, Libn.
Staff: 3.5. **Subjects:** Plant and pasture improvement in New Zealand and worldwide; agronomy; ecology; molecular genetics; seed technology; plant breeding; plant nutrition; biotechnology - bioprocessing, controlled release, rumen physiology, wine microbiology, wool growth, animal feeding; plant physiology - fruit tree physiology, tree crops, climate change research, general. **Holdings:** 36,000 volumes. **Subscriptions:** 500 journals and other serials. **Services:** Interlibrary loan; copying; SDI; library open to the public upon application to staff at arrival. **Computerized Information Services:** DIALOG Information Services, STN International, NZBN (New Zealand Bibliographic Network); SIRIS (internal database). **Remarks:** FAX: 6 3561130.

★ 11737 ★
New Zealand - Department of Scientific and Industrial Research - Mt. Albert Research Centre (Biol Sci)
120 Mt. Albert Rd.
Private Bag
Auckland, New Zealand
Phone: 9 893660
Mrs. J.C.C. Muggeridge
Founded: 1973. **Staff:** Prof 4. **Subjects:** Entomology, mycology, fungi, fruit tree horticulture, plant/insect virology, plant/insect bacteriology, fruit processing. **Special Collections:** David Sharp Entomological Collection; Actindia Collection (3000 items). **Holdings:** 22,000 books; 71,000 periodical volumes; archives; 430 microfiche; 580 reels of microfilm; 24 maps; 34 videocassettes. **Subscriptions:** 1171 journals and other serials. **Services:** Interlibrary loan; copying; library open to the public for reference use only. **Computerized Information Services:** DIALOG Information Services; LIBRA, ACTINDIA D-BASE, BUGS (internal databases). **Publications:** Accessions lists; Distributors of Fauna of New Zealand. **Remarks:** FAX: 9 863330.

New Zealand - Embasssy
See: **Embassy of New Zealand - Library** (5324)

★ 11738 ★
New Zealand - Ministry of Forestry - Forest Research Institute - Library (Agri, Biol Sci)
Private Bag 3020
Rotorua, New Zealand
Phone: 73 475899
Beryl Anderson, Libn.
Founded: 1947. **Staff:** Prof 3; Other 1. **Subjects:** Forest health, improvement, management, resources; wood technology; production forestry; pulp and paper. **Holdings:** 250,000 books and monographs; 8000 microfiche. **Subscriptions:** 1600 journals and other serials. **Services:** Interlibrary loan; copying; SDI; library open to the public. **Automated Operations:** Computerized cataloging, serials, and journal circulation. **Computerized Information Services:** DIALOG Information Services, PFDS Online, INFOS (Information Network for Official Statistics), STN International. Performs searches on fee basis. **Contact Person:** Marilla Mullon, Dp.Libn. **Publications:** Accessions list, monthly - to staff and selected libraries. **Remarks:** FAX: 73 479380. **Staff:** Judy Prictor, Asst.Libn.

★ 11739 ★
New Zealand - National Library of New Zealand - Alexander Turnbull Library (Area-Ethnic, Hum)
P.O. Box 12349
Wellington, New Zealand
Phone: 4 4743000
Ms. M. Calder, Chf.Libn.
Founded: 1919. **Staff:** 51. **Subjects:** New Zealand, Pacific, John Milton, English literature, voyages and travels, printing and the book. **Special Collections:** John Milton and the Seventeenth Century. **Holdings:** 247,286 books; 2700 linear meters of periodicals; 92,906 microforms; 47,217 linear meters of manuscripts; 662 bays of newspapers. **Subscriptions:** 5239 journals and other serials. **Services:** Copying; library open to the public. **Computerized Information Services:** New Zealand Bibliographic Network. Performs searches free of charge. **Contact Person:** Miss J. Horncy, Rd.Educ.Libn. **Publications:** National Register of Archives and Manuscripts; Turnbull Library Record; Descriptive Catalogue of the Milton Collection; Victoria's Furthest Daughters: A Bibliography of Published Sources for the Study of Women in New Zealand, 1830-1914; Solomon Islands Bibliography (to 1980); Women's Words: A Guide to Manuscripts and Archives in the Alexander Turnbull Library Relating to Women in the 19th Century; Katherine Mansfeld: Manuscripts in the Alexander Turnbull Library; The Collection of Douglas Lilburn; Manuscripts in the Alexander Turnbull Library; Directory of New Zealand Photograph Collections. **Special Catalogs:** Catalog of prints and books published by the Alexander Turnbull Library, 1989 - free upon request from the Library Office. **Remarks:** FAX: 4 4743035. **Staff:** Sharon Dell, Asst.Chf.Libn./Kpr., Spec.Coll.; Philip Rainer, Kpr., Printed Coll.; David Colquhoun, Cur.Mss./Archv.; Bruce Ralston, Mgr., Ref.; Joan McCracken, Libn., Pict.Ref.Serv.; Marian Minson, Cur., Drawings/Prints; John Sullivan, Cur., Photo.Archv.; Kate Olsen, Cart.Cur.; Darea Sherratt, Acq.Libn.; Clark Stiles, Newspaper Cur.; Robert Petre, Spec. Printed Coll.Libn.; Robyn Bell, Supv.Cat.; Jim Sullivan, Mgr., Oral Hist.Ctr.; Ewan Hyde, Ser.Libn.; John Etheridge, Sys.Mgr.; Wharehuia Hemara, Maori Subject Spec.; Jill Palmer, Mus.Libn.

★ 11740 ★
New Zealand - National Museum of New Zealand - Hector Library
(Env-Cons, Hist)
Buckle St
POB 467   Phone: 4 3859609
Wellington, New Zealand   Manuela C. Angelo
Founded: 1865. **Staff:** 3. **Subjects:** Natural environment, ethnology, history - New Zealand, Pacific. **Special Collections:** Carter Collection; G.V. Hudson Bequest (entomology; 62 volumes); W.M. Swainson Collection (natural science; 18 volumes). **Holdings:** 20,500 books; 5234 bound periodical volumes; 67 microfiche; 30 reels of microfilm; 1961 maps. **Subscriptions:** 1668 journals and other serials. **Services:** Interlibrary loan; copying; SDI; library open to the public; appointments preferred. **Automated Operations:** Inmagic. **Computerized Information Services:** Kiwinet, NZBN. **Remarks:** FAX: 04 3857157.

★ 11741 ★
Newark Beth Israel Medical Center - Dr. Victor Parsonnet Memorial Library (Med)
201 Lyons Ave.   Phone: (201)926-7233
Newark, NJ 07112   Betty L. Garrison, Chf.Libn.
Staff: Prof 1. **Subjects:** Medicine, surgery, cardiology, oncology, pediatrics, dentistry. **Special Collections:** Dr. Victor Parsonnet rare book collection. **Holdings:** 1200 books; 5500 bound periodical volumes; 180 video cassettes; 540 cassettes. **Subscriptions:** 225 journals and other serials. **Services:** Interlibrary loan; library not open to the public. **Computerized Information Services:** MEDLARS. **Networks/Consortia:** Member of Cosmopolitan Biomedical Library Consortium (CBLC), Health Sciences Library Association of New Jersey (HSLANJ), BHSL, National Network of Libraries of Medicine - Middle Atlantic Region, Essex Hudson Regional Library Cooperative. **Remarks:** Alternate telephone number(s): (201)926-7441. FAX: (201)923-4280. **Staff:** Nancey Ryder-Cunningham, ILL.

★ 11742 ★
Newark Board of Education - Teachers' Professional Library (Educ)
Harold Wilson School
190 Muhammad Ali Blvd.
Newark, NJ 07108   Phone: (201)733-6488
Staff: Prof 1. **Subjects:** Education. **Holdings:** 4600 books; minutes and reports of Board of Education. **Subscriptions:** 113 journals and other serials. **Services:** Library open to the public with restrictions. **Publications:** Read, See and Hear - to Newark teachers; School Library Notes - to Newark librarians. **Staff:** Binnie McIntosh.

★ 11743 ★
Newark Museum - Museum Library (Art)
49 Washington St.
Box 540   Phone: (201)596-6622
Newark, NJ 07101   Margaret Di Salvi, Libn.
Founded: 1926. **Staff:** Prof 1. **Subjects:** American painting and sculpture, decorative arts, Oriental arts, classical art, ethnological materials, natural sciences, numismatics. **Special Collections:** Tibetan Collection (rare and out-of-print books on Tibetan art, decorative arts, and culture; 500 books). **Holdings:** 28,000 volumes; 10,000 pamphlets; 25,000 black/white photographs; 3000 slides; 450 color transparencies. **Subscriptions:** 200 journals and other serials. **Services:** Interlibrary loan (limited); library open to the public for reference use only. **Networks/Consortia:** Member of Essex Hudson Regional Library Cooperative. **Remarks:** FAX: (201)642-0459.

★ 11744 ★
Newark Public Library - Art and Music Division (Art, Mus)
5 Washington St.
Box 630   Phone: (201)733-5648
Newark, NJ 07101-0630   Frances M. Beiman, Supv.Libn.
Staff: Prof 4; Other 2. **Subjects:** Art and art history, architecture, decorative arts, photography, costume history, music history, music theory and practice, biography. **Holdings:** 70,000 books; 15,000 scores and song books; 1800 portfolios of design; 1 million pictures; 19,000 slides; 2500 music recordings; 3000 compact discs; 300 trade catalogs. **Subscriptions:** 300 journals and other serials. **Services:** Interlibrary loan; copying; department open to the public. **Automated Operations:** Computerized public access catalog, cataloging, acquisitions, and circulation. **Computerized Information Services:** OCLC EPIC, BRS Information Technologies, DIALOG Information Services, NEXIS, ORBIT Search Service, VU/TEXT Information Services, WILSONLINE, DataTimes. Performs searches on fee

basis. **Networks/Consortia:** Member of New Jersey Library Network, Essex Hudson Regional Library Cooperative. **Special Catalogs:** Picture Collection Subject Headings (book). **Special Indexes:** New Jersey Architectural Index (microfiche); Index to "Cartoonists Profile," (typescripts), Popular Songs Database (printout), and "New Jersey Music and Arts." **Remarks:** FAX: (201)733-5648. **Staff:** Barry Redlich, Prin.Libn.

★ 11745 ★
Newark Public Library - Business Information Center (Bus-Fin)
34 Commerce St.
Newark, NJ 07102   Phone: (201)733-7779
Founded: 1904. **Staff:** Prof 5; Other 3. **Subjects:** Business, accounting, insurance, advertising and marketing, investments, money and banking. **Special Collections:** Directories (city, trade, telephone, foreign); business histories; corporate annual reports. **Holdings:** 10,000 books. **Subscriptions:** 700 journals and other serials; 8 newspapers. **Services:** Interlibrary loan (limited); copying; center open to the public. **Automated Operations:** Computerized cataloging, acquisitions, and circulation. **Computerized Information Services:** DIALOG Information Services, InfoTrac; CD-ROM (COMPACT DISCLOSURE, Dun's Million Dollar Disc, General BusinessFile). **Networks/Consortia:** Member of New Jersey Library Network, Essex Hudson Regional Library Cooperative. **Remarks:** FAX: (201)733-5750. **Staff:** Donald Lewis, Prin.Libn.; Stuart Spier, Sr.Libn.; Dale Colston, Prin.Libn.; Maureen Ritter, Supv.Libn.; Yoshiko Ishii, Asst.Libn.

★ 11746 ★
Newark Public Library - Humanities Division (Hum)
5 Washington St.
Box 630   Phone: (201)733-7820
Newark, NJ 07101-0630   Sallie Hannigan, Supv.Libn.
Staff: Prof 5; Other 2. **Subjects:** Literature, language, literary criticism, biography, bibliography, religion, philosophy, history, geography, psychology, librariana, travel, film, theater, television, sports and recreation, encyclopedias, dictionaries. **Special Collections:** Black literature, history, and biography; Granger Collection of Poetry and Anthologies; Puerto Rican Reference Collection; Travel Collection (books; pamphlets; clippings). **Holdings:** 130,000 books; 1000 bound periodical volumes; 1000 maps; dictionaries and encyclopedias in Spanish, Italian, French, German, Russian; information file. **Subscriptions:** 630 journals and other serials. **Services:** Interlibrary loan; copying; telephone and in-person reference available in Spanish; division open to the public. **Automated Operations:** Computerized public access catalog, cataloging, acquisitions, and circulation. **Computerized Information Services:** BRS Information Technologies, DIALOG Information Services, ORBIT Search Service, VU/TEXT Information Services, NEXIS, WILSONLINE, OCLC EPIC, DataTimes. Performs searches on fee basis. **Networks/Consortia:** Member of New Jersey Library Network, Essex Hudson Regional Library Cooperative. **Remarks:** FAX: (201)733-5648. **Staff:** Leslie Kahn, Prin.Libn.; Maureen Ritter, Prin.Libn.

★ 11747 ★
Newark Public Library - New Jersey Reference Division (Hist)
5 Washington St.
Box 630   Phone: (201)733-7776
Newark, NJ 07101-0630   George S. Hawley, Supv.Libn.
Staff: Prof 5; Other 3. **Subjects:** New Jersey, Newark, Essex County history and laws; current affairs; travel and description; biography (genealogy excluded). **Special Collections:** New Jersey Author-Imprints; Stephen Crane Collection (388 secondary source items relating to Crane and the Stephen Crane Association, defunct 1941); DeLagerberg Collection (manuscript drawings and newspaper clippings relating to New Jersey architecture); New Jersey and Newark Picture Collection (37,000 photographs of buildings and people; 2500 postcards); Berg Collection (1800 photographs of Newark street scenes); Dorer Collection (3000 negatives from Newark newspapers); HABS drawings (includes entire state); Newark Evening News Collection, 1912-1972 (800,000 black/white photographs; 1.5 million clippings; 400 handwritten indexes); U.S. and New Jersey state census on microfilm. **Holdings:** 22,000 books; 1300 bound periodical volumes; 1250 unbound periodical volumes; 5000 reels of microfilm of New Jersey newspapers; 55 VF drawers of clippings in 4000 subject folders; 42,000 documents; 3500 maps; videotapes of New Jersey network and WWOR nighly news broadcasts since 1984. **Subscriptions:** 300 journals and other serials; 19 newspapers. **Services:** Interlibrary loan (limited); copying (hardcopy and microfilm); photo lab copies of prints owned by institution; division open to the public. **Automated Operations:** Computerized public access catalog, cataloging, acquisitions, and circulation. **Computerized Information**

Services: BRS Information Technologies, DataTimes, DIALOG Information Services, NEXIS, OCLC EPIC, ORBIT Search Service, VU/TEXT Information Services, WILSONLINE. Performs searches on fee basis. **Networks/Consortia:** Member of New Jersey Library Network, Essex Hudson Regional Library Cooperative. **Publications:** New Jersey Bibliographer; local subject list; compilation of walking tour guides. **Special Indexes:** New Jersey Periodical Notes (periodical index); New Jersey Illustration Index (160,000 card picture index to loose pictures and pictures in books) ; Star Ledger (Newark, NJ) Index, 1971 to present (65,000 card index); New Jersey Folklore Index; New Jersey Law Journal Index (biographical entries); Newark and New Jersey Association File; New Jersey Author File; New Jersey Lake File. **Remarks:** Alternate telephone number(s): 733-7775. **FAX:** (201)733-5648. **Staff:** Robert Blackwell, Prin.Libn.; Simone Galik, Prin.Libn.

★ 11748 ★
Newark Public Library - Popular Library Division (Area-Ethnic)
5 Washington St.
Box 630   Phone: (201)733-7784
Newark, NJ 07101-0630   Delores Whitehead, Supv.Libn.
Staff: Prof 7; Other 8. **Subjects:** General fiction, popular nonfiction, black studies, foreign languages, job and career information. **Special Collections:** African American room, Sala Hispanoamericana; French, German, Italian, Polish, Portuguese, Russian, and Yiddish language collections; 20,000 volumes in Spanish. **Holdings:** 60,000 books; 30 films; 2000 video cassettes; 500 phonograph records; 1500 audio cassettes; 550 large print titles. **Subscriptions:** 25 journals and other serials; 10 newspapers. **Services:** Interlibrary loan; copying; division open to the public. **Automated Operations:** Computerized public access catalog, cataloging, acquisitions, and circulation. **Computerized Information Services:** DIALOG Information Services, BRS Information Technologies, NEXIS, OCLC EPIC, ORBIT Search Service, VU/TEXT Information Services, WILSONLINE, DataTimes. Performs searches on fee basis. Contact Person: James Capuano, Prin.Libn., 733-7814. **Networks/Consortia:** Member of New Jersey Library Network, Essex Hudson Regional Library Cooperative. **Publications:** Monthly film list - to registered borrowers. **Special Indexes:** Index of books into films. **Remarks:** FAX: (201)733-5648. **Staff:** Paul Williams, Prin.Libn., African American Room; Ingrid Betancourt, Prin.Libn., Foreign Languages.

Newark Public Library - Pure, Applied and Social Science Division
See: **Newark Public Library - Social Sciences, Sciences and U.S. Government Publications Division** (11749)

★ 11749 ★
Newark Public Library - Social Sciences, Sciences and U.S. Government Publications Division (Sci-Engr, Soc Sci)
5 Washington St.
Box 630   Phone: (201)733-7782
Newark, NJ 07101-0630   James E. Capuano, Supv.Libn.
Staff: Prof 5; Other 2. **Subjects:** Social science, education, science, consumer affairs, applied technology. **Special Collections:** U.S. patent specifications and drawings, 1790 to present; American National Standards Institute (ANSI) standards (24 VF drawers); U.S. Government Documents Regional Depository. **Holdings:** 100,000 books; 50,000 bound periodical volumes. **Subscriptions:** 750 journals and other serials. **Services:** Interlibrary loan; copying; division open to the public. **Automated Operations:** Computerized public access catalog, cataloging, acquisitions, and circulation. **Computerized Information Services:** DIALOG Information Services, BRS Information Technologies, NEXIS, OCLC EPIC, ORBIT Search Service, VU/TEXT Information Services, WILSONLINE, DataTimes, U.S. Patent Classification System. Performs searches on fee basis. **Networks/Consortia:** Member of New Jersey Library Network, Essex Hudson Regional Library Cooperative. **Remarks:** Alternate telephone number(s): 733-7815. **FAX:** (201)733-5648. **Formerly:** Its Pure, Applied and Social Science Division. **Staff:** Donald Fostel, Prin.Libn.; Paul Pattwell, Prin.Libn., U.S. Govt.Docs.

★ 11750 ★
Newark Public Library - Special Collections Division (Art, Rare Book)
5 Washington St.
Box 630   Phone: (201)733-7732
Newark, NJ 07101-0630   William J. Dane, Supv.Libn.
Staff: Prof 2. **Subjects:** Graphic arts, lithography (Fine Prints), rare books, history of printing, incunabula, manuscripts, bookbinding, illustration of books. **Special Collections:** Fine Prints (18,000); Artists' books (500);

autographs (1100); bookplates (2500); Rabin and Krueger Archives (artist biographies); John Tasker Howard Collection (American music); shopping bags (1000); posters (4000); portfolios of plates of design (2000); historic greeting cards (holidays, Valentines, and others; 1500); trade catalogs (300); postcards (4000); Richard C. Jenkinson Collection of finely printed books (3600 books and manuscripts); rare books (3500); Bruce Rogers Collection (600 books and related letters); maps and atlases (500); incunabula (25). **Holdings:** 11,000 books. **Subscriptions:** 10 journals and other serials. **Services:** Division open to the public by appointment. **Special Catalogs:** Jenkinson Collection Catalogs I and II (books); Hidden Treasures: Japanese Art from the Newark Public Library (1991). **Special Indexes:** Old Print Shop Portfolio. **Remarks:** Alternate telephone number(s): (201)733-7837. FAX: (201)733-5648. **Staff:** Nancy J. Gresko-Knight.

★ 11751 ★
Newark United Methodist Church - Library (Rel-Phil)
69 E. Main St.
Box 595   Phone: (302)368-8774
Newark, DE 19715   Marietta J. Garrett, Libn.
Founded: 1955. **Staff:** 1. **Subjects:** Religion, Methodist Church history. **Special Collections:** Biographies of Methodist pioneers. **Holdings:** 2500 books; recordings; filmstrips. **Services:** Library not open to the public.

★ 11752 ★
Newberry Library (Hum)
60 W. Walton St.   Phone: (312)943-9090
Chicago, IL 60610   Charles T. Cullen, Libn.
Founded: 1887. **Staff:** Prof 42; Other 60. **Subjects:** European, English, and American history and literature; local and family history; church history; Italian Renaissance; expansion of Europe; philology; bibliography; history and theory of music; history of cartography. **Special Collections:** History of Printing; Western Americana; American Indian; Midwest manuscripts; Sherwood Anderson; music; Melville Collection; railroad archives. **Holdings:** 1.4 million volumes; 5 million manuscripts; 225,000 microforms; 150,000 pieces of sheet music and scores. **Subscriptions:** 1500 journals and other serials. **Services:** Copying; library open to the public with identification. **Computerized Information Services:** OCLC, Association of Research Libraries (ARL). **Networks/Consortia:** Member of ILLINET. **Publications:** General Guide to the Collections in the Newberry Library; An Uncommon Collection of Uncommon Collections; Newberry Library Center for the History of the American Indian Bibliographical Series; newsletter; bulletins. **Staff:** Mary Wyly, Assoc.Libn.; Richard H. Brown, Academic V.P.

Newcomb College Center for Research on Women
See: **Tulane University - Newcomb College Center for Research on Women** (16563)

Josiah T. Newcomb Library
See: **Broome County Historical Society - Josiah T. Newcomb Library** (2251)

Lawrence Newcomb Library
See: **New England Wild Flower Society, Inc.** (11480)

★ 11753 ★
Newcomen Society of the United States - Thomas Newcomen Library in Steam Technology & Industrial History (Hist)
412 Newcomen Rd.   Phone: (215)363-6600
Exton, PA 19341   Nancy Arnold, Libn./Cur.
Founded: 1965. **Staff:** Prof 1. **Subjects:** History of steam and steam technology; business and industrial history. **Holdings:** 3500 books; 300 bound periodical volumes; 1100 trade catalogs. **Subscriptions:** 59 journals and other serials. **Services:** Interlibrary loan; copying; library open to the public for reference use only. **Remarks:** FAX: (215)363-0612.

★ 11754 ★
Newfoundland Department of Education - Learning Resources
  Distribution Centre (Aud-Vis, Educ)
Bldg. 951, Pleasantville   Phone: (709)729-2619
St. John's, NF, Canada A1A 1R2   Frank Cholette, Mgr. of
                                     Lrng.Rsrcs.Ctr.
Founded: 1946. **Staff:** Prof 1; Other 6. **Subjects:** All subjects relative to K-12 curriculum. **Holdings:** 9000 films; 5000 videotapes. **Services:** Audiotape and videotape copying; slide/tape presentations; materials available to public, priority given to schools. **Automated Operations:** Computerized cataloging and circulation. **Special Catalogs:** Instructional Materials Catalogue, annual - free to schools. **Remarks:** FAX: (709)729-2177. **Staff:** Jewel Cousens, Libn.

★ 11755 ★
Newfoundland Department of Environment and Lands - Parks Division
  Library (Rec)
P.O. Box 8700
St. John's, NF, Canada A1B 4J6   Phone: (709)576-2429
Subjects: Parks, Natural Heritage. **Holdings:** Figures not available. **Subscriptions:** 15 journals and other serials. **Services:** Library not open to the public. **Remarks:** FAX: (709)576-1930.

★ 11756 ★
Newfoundland Department of Forestry and Agriculture - Library (Env-
  Cons)
Herald Bldg.
Box 2006   Phone: (709)637-2307
Corner Brook, NF, Canada A2H 6J8   Bruce Boland, Libn.
Founded: 1984. **Staff:** Prof 1. **Subjects:** Forest management, products, marketing and utilization, protection, fires, insects, and history; forestry history; silviculture; land use policy. **Special Collections:** Departmental publications; provincial government legislation. **Holdings:** 3260 books; 4 filing cabinets of pamphlets. **Subscriptions:** 44 journals and other serials. **Services:** Interlibrary loan; copying; library open to the public with restrictions. **Publications:** Monthly List of Additions to the Library - for internal distribution only. **Remarks:** FAX: (709)637-2403.

Newfoundland Department of Health - Public Health Nursing Division
See: **St. John's and District Health Unit** (14335)

★ 11757 ★
Newfoundland Department of Justice - Law Library (Law)
Confederation Bldg.   Phone: (709)729-2861
St. John's, NF, Canada A1B 4J6   Mona B. Pearce, Law Libn.
Staff: Prof 1. **Subjects:** Law. **Holdings:** 20,000 books. **Subscriptions:** 90 journals and other serials. **Services:** Interlibrary loan; library not open to the public. **Computerized Information Services:** QL Systems, LEXIS, WESTLAW. Performs searches on fee basis. **Remarks:** Library is central reference library for all Newfoundland court libraries, which maintain small working collections. FAX: (709)729-2129.

★ 11758 ★
Newfoundland Department of Mines and Energy - Energy Resources
  Centre (Energy)
Atlantic Place, 6th Fl.
P.O. Box 8700   Phone: (709)729-2416
St. John's, NF, Canada A1B 4J6   Mary Varghese, Libn.
Founded: 1983. **Staff:** Prof 1; Other 1. **Subjects:** Petroleum and natural gas, geology, energy and technology, energy economics, renewable energy, energy management, housing information, energy and environment. **Holdings:** 4000 books; 600 pamphlets on energy-related topics; 53 video cassettes; 800 slides; 300 photographs. **Subscriptions:** 154 journals and other serials. **Services:** Interlibrary loan; SDI; center open to the public for reference use only. **Computerized Information Services:** CAN/OLE. **Publications:** Energy Information Guide, annual - to the public. **Special Catalogs:** Videotape library catalog. **Remarks:** FAX: (709)729-2508.

★ 11759 ★
Newfoundland Department of Mines and Energy - Geological Survey
  Branch Library (Sci-Engr)
P.O. Box 8700   Phone: (709)729-6487
St. John's, NF, Canada A1B 4J6   Sudarshan Sachdev, Libn.
Founded: 1950. **Staff:** Prof 1; Other 1. **Subjects:** Earth sciences, mining. **Holdings:** 700 textbooks; 3000 technical reports; 11,000 geological documents/technical files on Newfoundland and Labrador; 4000 maps. **Subscriptions:** 80 journals and other serials; 6 newspapers. **Services:** Interlibrary loan; copying; library open to the public with restrictions on confidential documents. **Computerized Information Services:** DIALOG Information Services, CAN/OLE, RESORS (Remote Sensing On-line Retrieval System), GEOSCAN Database. Performs searches on fee basis. Contact Person: Catherine Patey, Geol. **Special Indexes:** GEOSCAN Newfoundland and Labrador National Topographical System Index (microfiche, hardcopy), irregular; GEOSCAN Newfoundland and Labrador keyword, author, and drill hole indexes (microfiche) - both for sale. **Remarks:** FAX: (709)729-3493.

★ 11760 ★
Newfoundland Department of Municipal & Provincial Affairs -
  Provincial Planning Office - Library (Plan)
Confederation Bldg., West Block
P.O. Box 8700   Phone: (709)729-5406
St. John's, NF, Canada A1B 4J6   Rosemary Eddy, Adm.Off.
Staff: 1. **Subjects:** Municipal planning and legislation, housing, natural resources, laws and statutes, environmental assessment. **Special Collections:** Newfoundland municipal plans and zoning regulations. **Holdings:** 2000 books. **Subscriptions:** 35 journals and other serials. **Services:** Copying; library open to the public. **Computerized Information Services:** Internal database. **Publications:** Measures in Effect (update of municipal status of communities), annual. **Remarks:** FAX: (709)729-2609. Municipal plans available for purchase.

Newfoundland and Labrador Development Corporation Ltd.
See: **Enterprise Newfoundland and Labrador** (5371)

★ 11761 ★
Newfoundland and Labrador Hydro Corporation - Library (Sci-Engr)
Hydro Place, Columbus Dr.
P.O. Box 12400   Phone: (709)737-1287
St. John's, NF, Canada A1B 4K7   Valerie Benson, Libn.
Founded: 1990. **Staff:** 1.5. **Subjects:** Hydro-power - engineering, environment, law, and allied subjects. **Holdings:** Figures not available. **Subscriptions:** 104 journals and other serials; 12 newspapers. **Services:** Interlibrary loan; copying. **Computerized Information Services:** DIALOG Information Services, CAN/OLE. **Remarks:** FAX: (709)737-1902. **Formerly:** Its Information Resource Centre.

★ 11762 ★
Newfoundland Legislative Library (Soc Sci)
House of Assembly, Confederation Bldg.
P.O. Box 8700   Phone: (709)729-3604
St. John's, NF, Canada A1B 4J6   N.J. Richards, Leg.Libn.
Staff: 3. **Special Collections:** Government documents; Newfoundlandiana. **Holdings:** Figures not available. **Services:** Library open to the public with special permission if material not available elsewhere. **Remarks:** This is a small library set up to provide assistance to the House of Assembly and the cabinet.

★ 11763 ★
Newfoundland Power - Research Centre (Trans)
55 Kenmount Rd.
P.O. Box 8910   Phone: (709)737-2936
St. John's, NF, Canada A1B 3P6   Susanna P. Duke, Supv., Res.Ctr.
Staff: 2. **Subjects:** Transportation, safety, Canadian statistics, finance, accounting, public utilities. **Holdings:** 500 books; company annual reports, 1924 to present; 500 reels of microfilm of company records; newspaper clippings. **Subscriptions:** 88 journals and other serials; 6 newspapers. **Services:** Library open to students. **Computerized Information Services:** QL Systems, CAN/OLE. **Remarks:** FAX: (709)737-5832.

★11764★
(Newfoundland) Provincial Archives of Newfoundland and Labrador (Hist)
Colonial Bldg.
Military Rd.   Phone: (709)729-3065
St. John's, NF, Canada A1C 2C9   David J. Davis, Prov.Archv.
Founded: 1958. Staff: Prof 5; Other 8. Subjects: Newfoundland - history, economic history, folklore, sociology, geography, genealogy. Special Collections: Parish registers from churches throughout Newfoundland; British and French records relating to Newfoundland (586 reels of microfilm). Holdings: 180 linear feet of books and booklets; 1200 bound periodical volumes; 11,480 linear feet of archival materials (manuscripts, maps, government documents); 10,000 photographs. Subscriptions: All newspapers published in Newfoundland. Services: Copying; archives open to the public. Computerized Information Services: Internal database. Special Catalogs: Inventories; finding aids. Remarks: FAX: (709)729-0578. Staff: Shelley Smith, Archv.; Howard C. Brown, Archv.; Anthony P. Murphy, Archv.; Ann Devlin-Fischer, Archv.

★11765★
(Newfoundland) Provincial Public Libraries Service (Area-Ethnic, Info Sci)
Arts & Culture Centre
Administration Office
Allandale Rd.   Phone: (709)737-3964
St. John's, NF, Canada A1B 3A3   Pearce J. Penney, Prov.Dir.
Founded: 1936. Staff: Prof 19; Other 206. Special Collections: Newfoundlandiana (20,000 items). Holdings: 1.14 million volumes. Subscriptions: 800 journals and other serials; 40 newspapers. Services: Interlibrary loan; copying; library open to the public. Automated Operations: Computerized cataloging. Computerized Information Services: UTLAS; Envoy 100 (electronic mail service). Publications: Library Footnotes, quarterly; Annual Report of the Provincial Public Libraries Board. Special Indexes: Newfoundland newspaper index. Remarks: FAX: (709)737-3009. Electronic mail address(es): ADMIN.NPL (Envoy 100). Above data includes the main library, 3 branch libraries, the Provincial Reference & Resource Library in St. John's, and 101 libraries elsewhere in the province - all maintained by Public Library Services. Formerly: Newfoundland Public Library Services.

★11766★
Newfoundland Teachers' Association - Library (Educ)
3 Kenmount Rd.   Phone: (709)726-3223
St. John's, NF, Canada A1B 1W1   Judy Handrigan, Libn.
Subjects: Education. Holdings: 3000 books; reports; archives. Services: Interlibrary loan; copying. Remarks: FAX: (709)726-4302.

★11767★
Newfoundland Telephone Company, Ltd. - Information Resources Centre (Sci-Engr)
Fort William Bldg., 5th Fl.
P.O. Box 2110   Phone: (709)739-2841
St. John's, NF, Canada A1C 5H6   Clarissa Dicks, Corp. Commun. Officer
Remarks: No further information was supplied by respondent.

★11768★
Newhouse Galleries, Inc. - Library
19 E. 66th St.
New York, NY 10021   Phone: (212)879-2700
Services: Library not open to the public. Remarks: No further information was supplied by respondent.

★11769★
Newington Children's Hospital - Professional Library (Med)
181 E. Cedar St.   Phone: (203)667-5380
Newington, CT 06111   Julie Lueders, Dir.
Founded: 1970. Staff: Prof 1; Other 1. Subjects: Orthopedics, pediatrics, nursing. Holdings: 2600 books; 3100 bound periodical volumes. Subscriptions: 125 journals and other serials. Services: Interlibrary loan; copying; library open to the public with restrictions. Automated Operations: Computerized cataloging and serials. Computerized Information Services: MEDLARS, BRS Information Technologies. Networks/Consortia: Member of Connecticut Association of Health Science Libraries (CAHSL).

Newkirk Medical Library
See: Hanover General Hospital (6893)

★11770★
Newman Catholic Student Center - Timothy Parkman Religious Library (Rel-Phil)
1615 E. 2nd St.   Phone: (602)327-6662
Tucson, AZ 85719   Fr. Micheal Sherwin, Hd.Libn.
Founded: 1952. Staff: Prof 2. Subjects: Catholic religion, theology, philosophy, psychology. Holdings: 7500 books; 250 bound periodical volumes. Subscriptions: 38 journals and other serials; 5 newspapers. Services: Interlibrary loan; library open to center staff, University of Arizona students, local religious, and registered members of the center community. Publications: List of new acquisitions. Staff: Sr. Dominic, Cat.Libn.

Newman Center
See: University of Minnesota - Newman Center (18926)

Newman Collection
See: Mount St. Mary's College (10811)

Jean & Dorothy Newman Library
See: University of Toronto - Centre for Industrial Relations (19432)

★11771★
Newman Theological College - Library (Rel-Phil)
15611 St. Albert Trail, R.R. No. 8   Phone: (403)447-2993
Edmonton, AB, Canada T5L 4H8   Ellen Fagan, Libn.
Founded: 1917. Staff: Prof 1; Other 2. Subjects: Roman Catholic theology, Christian authors, scripture studies, church law, Canadiana, philosophy. Holdings: 26,500 books; 5000 bound periodical volumes. Subscriptions: 200 journals and other serials. Services: Copying; library open to the public at librarian's discretion. Remarks: FAX: (403)447-2685.

★11772★
Newmarket Historical Society - Stone School Museum Collections (Hist)
Granite St.   Phone: (603)659-3652
Newmarket, NH 03857   Sylvia Fitts Getchell, Cur.
Founded: 1966. Subjects: Newmarket history, textile mills, shoe shops. Holdings: 200 books; 50 old mill and store ledgers; hotel registers; surveying notebooks; 10 AV programs; photographs. Services: Library open to the public.

★11773★
Newport Aeronautical Sales - Library (Trans)
23221 Peralta Dr., No. A   Phone: (714)454-2588
Laguna Hills, CA 92653   George M. Posey, III, V.P., Res.
Founded: 1970. Staff: Prof 2; Other 3. Subjects: Aircraft. Special Collections: U.S. Air Force, Navy, and Army aircraft technical manuals on early and late revision aircraft and systems. Holdings: 80,000 manuals; engineering drawings. Subscriptions: 25 journals and other serials. Services: Copying; library open to the public. Computerized Information Services: Internal database. Remarks: FAX: (714)454-8288. Telex: 69 2493.

Christopher B. Newport Information Resource Center
See: Sprint International - Christopher B. Newport Information Resource Center (15616)

★11774★
Newport Harbor Art Museum - Library (Art)
850 San Clemente Dr.   Phone: (714)759-1122
Newport Beach, CA 92660   Ruth E. Roe, Libn.
Staff: Prof 1. Subjects: Contemporary and California arts and artists. Holdings: 200 books; 1000 art exhibition catalogs; 4 VF drawers of clippings and ephemera in field of art. Subscriptions: 12 journals and other serials. Services: Library open to students and museum professionals by appointment only.

★ 11775 ★
Newport Historical Society - Library (Hist)
82 Touro St.   Phone: (401)846-0813
Newport, RI 02840   Bertram Lippincott, III, Geneal./Libn.
Founded: 1853. **Staff:** Prof 1. **Subjects:** Newport and Rhode Island history and genealogy, architecture, decorative arts, religion, gilded age cottages and families. **Special Collections:** Manuscript material relating to 18th century colonial merchants; church records; photographs; records of the Newport Town Council. **Holdings:** 14,000 books; 200 boxes of manuscripts; 100 scrapbooks; newspapers on microfilm. **Subscriptions:** 10 journals and other serials. **Services:** Interlibrary loan (limited); copying; library open to the public. **Networks/Consortia:** Member of Rhode Island Library Network (RHILINET). **Special Catalogs:** Catalogs of genealogy, building-house, ships, captains (card). **Special Indexes:** Genealogy index, house index, mansion index.

★ 11776 ★
Newport Hospital - Ina Mosher Health Sciences Library (Med)
Friendship St.   Phone: (401)846-6400
Newport, RI 02840   Tosca N. Carpenter, Hd.Libn.
Founded: 1958. **Staff:** Prof 1; Other 1. **Subjects:** Medicine, nursing, allided health sciences. **Holdings:** 4500 volumes; 56 newsletters; 15 VF drawers; 10 tape journals. **Subscriptions:** 160 journals and other serials. **Services:** Interlibrary loan; copying; SDI; library open to the public for reference use only. **Computerized Information Services:** MEDLARS. **Networks/Consortia:** Member of Rhode Island Library Network (RHILINET), Association of Rhode Island Health Sciences Librarians (ARIHSL), BHSL, North Atlantic Health Science Libraries (NAHSL).

★ 11777 ★
Newport News Daily Press, Inc. - Library (Publ)
7505 Warwick Blvd.   Phone: (804)247-4882
Newport News, VA 23607   Melissa L. Oakley, Lib.Supv.
Founded: 1961. **Staff:** Prof 6; Other 1. **Subjects:** Newspaper reference topics. **Holdings:** 1450 books; 96 VF drawers of clippings; 14 VF drawers of reports and pamphlets; 1436 reels of microfilm of the newspaper; 75 VF drawers of photographs; 15 VF drawers of negatives. **Subscriptions:** 30 journals and other serials; 18 newspapers. **Services:** Interlibrary loan; copying; library open to the public with restrictions. **Computerized Information Services:** VU/TEXT Information Services, DIALOG Information Services; TEQLIB, SAVE (internal databases). **Publications:** Quarterly Library Memo - for internal distribution only. **Remarks:** FAX: (804)245-8618. **Staff:** Kim Dougherty, Lib.Ck.; Elizabeth Joines, Libn.; Sandra Dudley, Lib.Ck.; Carolyn Snare, Lib.Ck.

Newport News Shipbuilding
See: **Tenneco, Inc.** (16152)

★ 11778 ★
News America Publications, Inc. - TV Guide Microfilm Library (Publ)
4 Radnor Corporate Center   Phone: (215)293-8947
Radnor, PA 19088   Cathy Johnson, Microfilm Coord.
Staff: 2. **Subjects:** Television. **Holdings:** TV Guide, 1953-1990, on microfilm. **Services:** Library not open to the public. **Special Indexes:** TV Guide 25 Year Index, 1953-1977, with annual supplements. **Formerly:** Triangle Publications, Inc. - TV Guide Microfilm Library.

★ 11779 ★
News Group Boston, Inc. - Boston Herald Library (Publ)
P.O. Box 2096   Phone: (617)426-3000
Boston, MA 02106   John R. Cronin, Libn.
Staff: Prof 1; Other 5. **Subjects:** Newspaper reference topics. **Holdings:** 750 books; 275 file cabinets of news clippings and photographs; microfilm. **Subscriptions:** 10 journals and other serials; 30 newspapers. **Services:** Interlibrary loan; copying; library open to the public at librarian's discretion. **Computerized Information Services:** DataTimes, NEXIS. **Remarks:** FAX: (617)542-1314; 542-1315.

★ 11780 ★
The News-Journal Company - Library (Publ)
P.O. Box 15505   Phone: (302)324-2898
Wilmington, DE 19850   Charlotte Walker, Chf.Libn.
Founded: 1954. **Staff:** Prof 3; Other 2. **Subjects:** News - local, national. **Special Collections:** Company archives. **Holdings:** 1500 books; 92 VF drawers of photographs and art; city directories; 10 million clippings. **Subscriptions:** 150 journals and other serials; 10 newspapers. **Services:** Library open to the public by appointment only. **Remarks:** FAX: (302)324-5509. **Staff:** Anne Haslam, Libn.; Cecilia James, Libn.

★ 11781 ★
News and Observer Publishing Company - News Research Center (Publ)
215 S. McDowell St.   Phone: (919)829-4580
Raleigh, NC 27602   Lany W. McDonald, Dir.
Founded: 1964. **Staff:** Prof 3; Other 8. **Subjects:** Newspaper reference topics. **Holdings:** Books; news clippings; photographs. **Services:** Library not open to the public. **Computerized Information Services:** NEXIS, VU/TEXT Information Services, DataTimes, DIALOG Information Services, USNI Military Database, TOXNET, OCLC, Burrelle's Broadcast Database. **Publications:** The News and Observer, July 1990 to present (online) - available through DataTimes. **Staff:** Teresa G. Leonard; Denise Henry.

Newsbank-Urban Affairs Library
See: **Chicago Public Library Central Library - Social Sciences Division** (3535)

★ 11782 ★
Newsday, Inc. - Library (Publ)
235 Pine Lawn Rd.   Phone: (516)454-2330
Melville, NY 11747   Mary Ann Skinner, Dir.
Staff: Prof 12; Other 14.5. **Subjects:** Newspaper reference topics. **Special Collections:** Long Island history. **Holdings:** 6000 books; 1 million photographs and negatives. **Subscriptions:** 100 journals and other serials; 10 newspapers. **Services:** Library not open to the public. **Automated Operations:** Computerized cataloging, acquisitions, and serials. **Computerized Information Services:** DIALOG Information Services, NEXIS, Reuters Information Services (Canada) Limited, VU/TEXT Information Services, DataTimes; BASIS (internal database). Performs searches on fee basis. Contact Person: Elizabeth Whisnant, Lib.Mgr., 454-2338. **Remarks:** FAX: (516)454-2342. **Staff:** Karen Van Rossem, NYC Lib.Mgr.; Elizabeth Whosnent, LI Lib.Mgr.; David Hoffman, Libn.; Carolyn Brook, NY Libn.; Peter Johnson, Libn.; Dorothy Guadagno, Libn.; Christine Baird, NY Libn.; Christine Merkle, DC Res.; Kathy Sweeney, Photo Libn.; Lillian Marx, Photo Libn.; Eileen Effrat, Libn.; Iris Quigley, Libn.

★ 11783 ★
Newspaper Advertising Bureau, Inc. - Information Center (Bus-Fin)
1180 Avenue of the Americas   Phone: (212)704-4549
New York, NY 10036   Ann Brady, Hd., Info.Ctr.
Staff: 2. **Subjects:** Advertising, marketing, newspapers. **Holdings:** 600 books; 48 bound periodical volumes; 26 shelves of government publications; 20 VF drawers of clippings and pamphlets. **Subscriptions:** 90 journals and other serials. **Services:** Interlibrary loan; center open to the public for reference use only on request. **Remarks:** Alternate telephone number(s): 921-5080. FAX: (212)704-4616.

★ 11784 ★
Newspaper Guild - Heywood Broun Library (Publ)
8611 2nd Ave.   Phone: (301)585-2990
Silver Spring, MD 20910   David J. Eisen, Dir. of Res. & Info.
Founded: 1957. **Subjects:** Works of Heywood Broun; labor relations; labor unions; newspaper industry; First Amendment. **Holdings:** 850 books. **Subscriptions:** 50 journals and other serials. **Services:** Copying; library open to the public by appointment.

★ 11785 ★
Newsweek, Inc. - Library (Publ)
444 Madison Ave.   Phone: (212)350-4680
New York, NY 10022-6999   Peter Salber, Lib.Dir.
Founded: 1933. **Staff:** Prof 7; Other 12. **Subjects:** Current affairs; history; biography; politics; statistics; international affairs; specific departmental

subject fields: music, press, religion, education, entertainment, science, art, books, business, medicine, and sports. **Holdings:** 36,000 books; 475 bound periodical volumes; 710 pamphlets; 1785 VF drawers of biographical and subject materials; 3600 reels of microfilm. **Subscriptions:** 472 journals and other serials; 37 newspapers. **Services:** Interlibrary loan (limited); library not open to the public. **Computerized Information Services:** DataTimes, BASELINE, InfoMaster, LEGI-SLATE, VU/TEXT Information Services, DIALOG Information Services, NEXIS. **Networks/Consortia:** Member of New York Metropolitan Reference and Research Library Agency. **Publications:** Weekly Acquisitions List. **Remarks:** FAX: (212)350-4131. **Staff:** Mata Stevenson, Ref.Libn.; Ron Wilson, Ref.Libn.; Lynn Seiffer, Ref.Libn.; Cecilia Salber, Ref.Libn.; Stephen Gencarello, Ref.Libn.; Marilyn Souders, Dir. of Tech.Serv.; Aidan Mooney, Chf. Index er; Judith Hausler, Chf. of Acq.

★11786★
Newsweek, Inc. - Washington Bureau Library (Publ)
1750 Pennsylvania Ave., Suite 1220   Phone: (202)626-2040
Washington, DC 20006   Sandra R. Fine, Bur.Libn.
Founded: 1967. **Staff:** Prof 1; Other 2. **Subjects:** Current events. **Special Collections:** Original reporting by bureau reporters, 1960s to present (140 linear feet of VF drawers). **Holdings:** 1400 books; 600 bound periodical volumes; 273 linear feet of clipping files. **Subscriptions:** 200 journals and other serials; 14 newspapers. **Services:** Interlibrary loan; library open to the public. **Computerized Information Services:** Online systems.

Newsweek Video Archive
See: **Arizona State University - Special Collections (1019)**

★11787★
Newton City Museum: The Jackson Homestead - Library & Manuscript Collection (Hist)
527 Washington St.   Phone: (617)552-7238
Newton, MA 02158   Duscha S. Weisskopf, Dir.
Founded: 1950. **Staff:** Prof 2. **Subjects:** Newton, Massachusetts history, architecture. **Special Collections:** Document collection of manuscript material from 17th century to present (includes family papers, papers of organizations, maps, plans and architectural drawings, records of the Newton Historic Properties Survey, photographs and slides, Newton ephemera). **Holdings:** 500 volumes. **Services:** Copying; library open to the public by appointment. **Publications:** The Older Houses of Newton (exhibit catalog and series), irregular. **Staff:** Malinda Blustain, Cur.

★11788★
Newton Public Schools - Teachers' Professional Library (Educ)
100 Walnut St.   Phone: (617)552-7630
Newtonville, MA 02160   Barbara Feldstein, Coord., Lib./Media
Staff: Prof 1; Other 1. **Subjects:** Children's literature, education. **Special Collections:** Sample trade books, K-10. **Holdings:** 5500 books; ERIC resources in education; 400 AV programs. **Subscriptions:** 30 journals and other serials. **Services:** Library not open to the public.

Sir Isaac Newton Collection
See: **Babson College (1396)**

★11789★
Newton-Wellesley Hospital - Paul Talbot Babson Memorial Library (Med)
2014 Washington St.   Phone: (617)243-6279
Newton Lower Falls, MA 02162   Christine L. Bell, Dir., Lib.Serv.
Founded: 1945. **Staff:** Prof 1; Other 3. **Subjects:** Medicine, surgery, nursing, health care administration, psychiatry, allied health sciences. **Special Collections:** Newton-Wellesley Hospital Archives. **Holdings:** 3500 books; 6000 bound periodical volumes; 7 VF drawers of pamphlets. **Subscriptions:** 317 journals and other serials; 7 newspapers. **Services:** Interlibrary loan; copying; library open to the public for reference use only. **Automated Operations:** Computerized cataloging. **Computerized Information Services:** MEDLARS, BRS Information Technologies; DOCLINE (electronic mail service). **Networks/Consortia:** Member of Consortium for Information Resources (CIR), Boston Biomedical Library Consortium, WELEXACOL. **Remarks:** FAX: (617)243-6630.

★11790★
Newtown Historic Association, Inc. - Research Center of Newtown Area History (Hist)
Box 303   Phone: (215)968-4004
Newtown, PA 18940   Frances T. Cronin, Libn.
Founded: 1983. **Staff:** Prof 2; Other 5. **Subjects:** History and residents of Newtown Borough and Township, 17th century to present. **Special Collections:** Edward Hicks and family reference collection; Hicks family genealogy; postmark collection; Reliance Company (caught horse thieves); Newtown Library Company papers; original deeds of local properties; maps; photographs; postcards; business account books; diaries; early newspapers (encapsulated); slide collection of house interiors and exteriors. **Holdings:** 790 books; pamphlets; business and social reports; patents for agricultural machines; 19th century letters; 47 oral history tapes; reports; manuscripts; archives; minute books. **Subscriptions:** 5 journals and other serials; 2 newspapers. **Services:** Interlibrary loan; copying; center open to the public. **Special Indexes:** Indexes to Local History Publications (book); Index to Historical Collection of Persons, Land, Business & Events in Newtown (book); Index to Surveys Newtown , 1850-1907; Index to Real Estate Survey, (4 vols.) 1831-1907. **Staff:** Doris Soden; Alberta Lewis.

★11791★
Elisabet Ney Museum and Archives (Art)
305 E. 44th   Phone: (512)458-2255
Austin, TX 78751   Mary Collins Blackmon, Cur.
Staff: 4. **Subjects:** 19th century sculpture, Elisabet Ney. **Holdings:** 300 books; 3000 letters and photographs; 5 VF drawers. **Services:** Library open to the public for reference use only. **Remarks:** Maintained by the Austin City Parks & Recreation Department.

★11792★
Nez Perce County Law Library (Law)
Court House
1230 Main
Box 896   Phone: (208)799-3040
Lewiston, ID 83501   Ron Schilling, District Judge
Subjects: Law. **Holdings:** 10,000 volumes. **Services:** Library not open to the public. **Remarks:** Alternate telephone number(s): 799-3057. FAX: (208)799-3058.

Nez Perce Music Archives
See: **Washington State University - Manuscripts, Archives, & Special Collections (20045)**

Nez Perce National Historical Park
See: **U.S. Natl. Park Service (17759)**

★11793★
NGK Metals Corporation - Library (Sci-Engr)
Box 13367
Reading, PA 19612-3367   Phone: (215)921-5000
Staff: Prof 1. **Subjects:** Copper-beryllium alloys, metallurgy. **Holdings:** 2000 volumes; 2000 patents, reports, documents. **Subscriptions:** 37 journals and other serials. **Services:** Interlibrary loan; library not open to the public. **Computerized Information Services:** DIALOG Information Services. **Remarks:** FAX: (215)921-5358. Telex: 628 34582.

★11794★
Niagara College of Applied Arts and Technology - Learning Resource Centre (Educ)
Woodlawn Rd.
Box 1005   Phone: (416)735-2211
Welland, ON, Canada L3B 5S2   P. Labonte, Libn.
Founded: 1967. **Staff:** Prof 1; Other 7. **Subjects:** Applied arts, business, technology, health. **Holdings:** 35,000 books; 3000 AV programs. **Subscriptions:** 440 journals and other serials; 13 newspapers. **Services:** Interlibrary loan; copying; center open to the public. **Networks/Consortia:** Member of The Bibliocentre. **Remarks:** FAX: (416)735-5365.

★ 11795 ★
Niagara College of Applied Arts and Technology - Mack Nursing Education Centre - Learning Resource Centre (Educ)
178 Queenston St.   Phone: (416)688-5310
St. Catharines, ON, Canada L2R 2Z7   Maria Edelman, Libn.
Founded: 1973. **Staff:** Prof 1.5. **Subjects:** Nursing, medicine, anatomy and physiology, biological sciences. **Holdings:** 1800 books; 465 bound periodical volumes; 370 AV programs. **Subscriptions:** 65 journals and other serials. **Services:** Interlibrary loan; copying; center open to persons affiliated with an outside college, university, or hospital. **Automated Operations:** Computerized cataloging and acquisitions. **Networks/Consortia:** Member of The Bibliocentre. **Staff:** Charlotte Boyd, Lib.Techn.

★ 11796 ★
Niagara County Historical Society - Library (Hist)
215 Niagara St.
Lockport, NY 14094   Phone: (716)434-7433
Founded: 1954. **Staff:** 1. **Subjects:** Local and state history, Indians, antiques. **Holdings:** 200 volumes; 25 VF drawers of clippings, pamphlets, ephemera. **Services:** Copying; library open to the public. **Publications:** NCHS Publications.

★ 11797 ★
Niagara Gazette Publishing Corporation - Library (Publ)
310 Niagara St.   Phone: (716)282-2311
Niagara Falls, NY 14303   Alan Johnson, Libn.
Staff: Prof 1. **Subjects:** Newspaper reference topics. **Special Collections:** Love Canal clippings. **Holdings:** 100 VF drawers; 52 lateral file drawers; 240,000 clippings and photographs. **Subscriptions:** 6 newspapers. **Services:** Interlibrary loan; library open to the public by appointment. **Remarks:** FAX: (716)282-2311, ext. 302.

Niagara Grape and Wine Festival Archives
See: **St. Catharines Historical Museum - Library/Archives** (14253)

★ 11798 ★
Niagara Parks Commission - School of Horticulture - Horticultural Library (Biol Sci)
P.O. Box 150   Phone: (416)356-8554
Niagara Falls, ON, Canada L2E 6T2   Ruth Stoner, Lib.Techn.
Founded: 1936. **Staff:** Prof 1. **Subjects:** Horticulture. **Holdings:** 3120 volumes; 12 VF drawers of clippings, theses, reports, pamphlets. **Subscriptions:** 65 journals and other serials. **Services:** Library not open to the public. **Computerized Information Services:** Internal databases.

★ 11799 ★
Niagara University - Space Settlement Studies Program - Library (Sci-Engr)
Niagara University, NY 14109   Phone: (716)285-1212
    Leslie Morris
Founded: 1974. **Staff:** Prof 1. **Subjects:** Space colonization - social aspects. **Holdings:** 600 books; 7 bound periodical volumes; 4 AV programs; 350 manuscripts. **Services:** Library open to the public.

★ 11800 ★
(Niamey) Centre Culturel Americain - USIS Library (Educ)
Ave. de la Liberte
Post Box 11201
Niamey, Niger
Remarks: Maintained or supported by the U.S. Information Agency. Focus is on materials that will assist peoples outside the United States to learn about the United States, its people, history, culture, political processes, and social milieux.

★ 11801 ★
Nichols College - Conant Library (Bus-Fin)
Center Rd.   Phone: (508)943-1560
Dudley, MA 01571   Kay Lee, Lib.Dir.
Founded: 1962. **Staff:** Prof 2; Other 4. **Subjects:** Management, advertising, finance and accounting, small business, marketing, taxation, economics, international trade, humanities. **Holdings:** 65,000 volumes; 300 nonprint titles; 110 Princeton files of pamphlets; conference proceedings. **Subscriptions:** 450 journals and other serials. **Services:** Interlibrary loan; copying; library open to Dudley and Webster residents. **Publications:** Acquisitions list, 4/year - for internal distribution only. **Staff:** Michael Kubic, AV/Ref.Libn.

★ 11802 ★
Nichols House Museum, Inc. - Library (Art)
55 Mt. Vernon
Boston, MA 02108   Phone: (617)227-6993
Founded: 1961. **Subjects:** Gardening, art history. **Holdings:** Uncataloged books, documents, nonbook items. **Services:** Library open by arrangement for special research only.

Nichols Professional Library
See: **Alexandria City Public Schools - Educational Media Center** (342)

★ 11803 ★
Nicollet County Historical Society - Nicollet County Museum (Hist)
Central Community Center, 2nd Fl.
301 S. Washington
Box 153   Phone: (507)931-2160
St. Peter, MN 56082   John W. Hans, Dir.
Founded: 1928. **Staff:** Prof 2; Other 1. **Subjects:** County and town history, genealogy. **Special Collections:** Daughters of the American Revolution (DAR) lineage books (Volumes 24-83); early maps of Nicollet and LeSueur Counties (1 case); newspapers, 1855-1920 (25 reels of microfilm); Traverse des Sioux (local history and treaty site). **Holdings:** 500 books; 30 bound periodical volumes; 300 manuscripts; 2500 photographs; 50 other cataloged items; dissertations. **Subscriptions:** 4 journals and other serials. **Services:** Interlibrary loan; copying; museum open to the public. **Networks/Consortia:** Member of Southcentral Minnesota Inter-Library Exchange (SMILE). **Publications:** Early History of Nicollet County; Nicollet County Bicentennial Historical Markers.

★ 11804 ★
(Nicosia) American Center - USIS Library (Educ)
33B Homer Ave.
Nicosia, Cyprus
Remarks: Maintained or supported by the U.S. Information Agency. Focus is on materials that will assist peoples outside the United States to learn about the United States, its people, history, culture, political processes, and social milieux.

NICTAS
See: **Ahmedabad Textile Industry's Research Association** (142)

NIDA Addiction Research Center
See: **National Institute on Drug Abuse - Addiction Research Center Library** (11209)

★ 11805 ★
Niedersachsisches Ministerium fur Ernahrung - Landwirtschaft und Forsten - Bibliothek (Agri, Biol Sci)
Calenberger Str 2   Phone: 511 1106602
W-3000 Hannover 1, Germany   Stefan Goetz
Founded: 1948. **Staff:** Prof 2. **Subjects:** Agriculture, forestry, nutrition, law. **Holdings:** 27,000 books. **Subscriptions:** 260 journals and other serials. **Services:** Interlibrary loan. **Remarks:** FAX: 511 1202060.

★ 11806 ★
Niedersachsisches Oberverwaltungsgericht - Bibliothek (Law)
Uelzener Str 40
Postfach 2371
W-2120 Luneburg, Germany   Phone: 4131 718145
    Jang Kampf
Founded: 1949. **Staff:** Prof 2.5. **Subjects:** Law - administrative, civil, international. **Holdings:** 32,600 books and bound periodical volumes; 2000 microfiche; 140 maps. **Subscriptions:** 174 journals and other serials. **Services:** Interlibrary loan; copying; library open to the public for reference use only. **Remarks:** FAX: 4131 718208.

★11807★
Nielsen Engineering & Research, Inc. - NEAR Technical Library (Sci-Engr)
510 Clyde Ave.
Mountain View, CA 94043-2287
Phone: (415)968-9457
Judy A. Faltz, Mgr.
Founded: 1966. **Staff:** Prof 1. **Subjects:** Aerodynamics, fluid and structural mechanics. **Holdings:** 1200 volumes; 43,000 technical reports; 2650 microfiche. **Subscriptions:** 60 journals and other serials. **Services:** Interlibrary loan; library not open to the public. **Automated Operations:** Computerized cataloging. **Computerized Information Services:** DIALOG Information Services, NASA/RECON, DTIC. Performs searches on fee basis. **Networks/Consortia:** Member of SOUTHNET. **Publications:** In the Library, semimonthly - for internal distribution only. **Remarks:** FAX: (415)968-1410.

Glenn and Olive Nielson Library
See: Brigham Young University - Glenn and Olive Nielson Library (20802)

Nieman-Grant Journalism Reading Room
See: University of Wisconsin--Madison (19611)

★11808★
Nigeria - National Library of Nigeria (Area-Ethnic)
4 Wesley St.
Private Mail Bag 12626
Lagos, Nigeria
Phone: 1 634704
Mr. Muazu H. Wali
Founded: 1964. **Staff:** Prof 89; Other 512. **Subjects:** Social sciences, political science, education, library science, agriculture, science, technology. **Special Collections:** Nigeriana (monographs, documents); United Nations Collection; Africana (Economic Community of West African States publications; AOU publications). **Holdings:** 346,486 books; 248,774 bound periodical volumes; 65,410 microfiche; 4581 reels of microfilm; 17,830 other cataloged items. **Subscriptions:** 7620 journals and other serials. **Services:** Interlibrary loan; copying; library open to adults only. **Publications:** Nigerian file for ISSN; ISSN Brochure; ISBN Users Manual; National Bibligraphy of Nigeria (NBN); National Union List of Serials (NULOS). **Remarks:** Alternate telephone number(s): 1 630053. Telex: 20117 NET TDS NG.

★11809★
Nigerian Institute of International Affairs - Library (Soc Sci)
13-15 Kofo Abayomi Rd.
Victoria Island
Lagos, Lagos State, Nigeria
Phone: 1 615608
Mr. A.O. Banjo, Dir., Lib. & Doc.Serv.
Founded: 1965. **Staff:** 52. **Subjects:** Development of foreign policy, international politics, strategic studies, international economic relations, international law and organization. **Special Collections:** Press clippings collection (266,174). **Holdings:** 58,780 volumes; 17,452 pamphlets. **Subscriptions:** 1482 journals and other serials; 61 newspapers. **Services:** Interlibrary loan; copying; library open to the public for reference use only on application. **Computerized Information Services:** NIIALOC, TREATIES (internal databases). **Publications:** INFODOC; NIAA Information Bulletin; NIAA Library bibliography series. **Remarks:** Telex: 22638. **Staff:** Mr. R.O. Okotore; Mrs. Q.F. Coker; Mrs. A.S. Dada; Ms. D. Irele; Mr. J.A. Oni; Mr. A.O. Yakubu; Miss P. Ogwuazor.

Nihon Iyaku Joho Center
See: Japan Pharmaceutical Information Center (8340)

★11810★
Niles, Barton & Wilmer - Law Library (Law)
111 S. Calvert St., Suite 1400
Baltimore, MD 21202
Phone: (410)783-6300
Nancy K. Holden, Libn.
Staff: Prof 1. **Subjects:** Federal and Maryland law. **Holdings:** 7500 books; 150 bound periodical volumes. **Subscriptions:** 265 journals and other serials. **Services:** Interlibrary loan; library not open to the public. **Computerized Information Services:** LEXIS, WESTLAW. **Remarks:** FAX: (410)783-6363.

★11811★
Niles Township Jewish Congregation - Hillman Library (Rel-Phil)
4500 Dempster
Skokie, IL 60076
Phone: (708)675-4141
Lenore Kantor Segal-Allen, Libn.
Staff: Prof 1. **Subjects:** Jewish children's literature, Judaica, Israel, Jewish history, American Jewish history. **Holdings:** 5300 books; 8 bound periodical volumes; unbound periodicals. **Subscriptions:** 10 journals and other serials. **Services:** Interlibrary loan (limited); copying; library open to the public. **Networks/Consortia:** Member of North Suburban Library System (NSLS), Judaica Library Network of Chicago.

Nimitz Library
See: U.S. Navy - Naval Academy (17808)

★11812★
Nine Lives Associates - Library (Law)
North Mountain Pines Training Center
Executive Protection Institute
Arcadia Manor
Rte. 2, Box 3645
Berryville, VA 22611
Phone: (703)955-1128
Dr. Richard W. Kobetz, Exec.Sec.
Founded: 1978. **Subjects:** Law enforcement, security. **Special Collections:** Executive and personal protection. **Holdings:** 1200 volumes. **Subscriptions:** 26 journals and other serials; 5 newspapers. **Services:** Library not open to the public. **Remarks:** Affiliated with Academy of Security Educators and Trainers.

★11813★
Ninety-Nines, Inc. - Library (Trans)
Will Rogers Airport
Box 59965
Oklahoma City, OK 73159
Phone: (405)685-7969
Dorothy Niekamp, Libn.
Founded: 1929. **Staff:** Prof 1; Other 2. **Subjects:** Aviation, women in aviation. **Special Collections:** Archives of the Ninety-Nines; records from the Powder Puff Derby. **Holdings:** 900 books. **Services:** Copying; library open to researchers on request. **Publications:** 99 News. **Remarks:** FAX: (405)685-7985. **Also Known As:** International Women Pilots Association. **Staff:** Loretta Jean Gragg, Exec.Dir.; Terri Gwin, Archv.

★11814★
92nd Street Young Men's and Young Women's Hebrew Association - Archives (Area-Ethnic)
1395 Lexington Ave.
New York, NY 10128
Phone: (212)415-5542
Steven W. Siegel, Dir.
Founded: 1979. **Staff:** Prof 1. **Subjects:** American Jewish history, Jewish social welfare, performing arts history, amateur athletics, poetry and literature, philanthropy. **Special Collections:** Records of Young Men's Hebrew Association, Young Women's Hebrew Association, Clara de Hirsch Home for Working Girls, Surprise Lake Camp, 92nd Street Young Men's and Young Women's Hebrew Association. **Holdings:** 1000 cubic feet of records; 2000 sound recordings. **Services:** Copying; archives open to the public for reference use only. **Networks/Consortia:** Member of Council of Archives and Research Libraries in Jewish Studies (CARLJS). **Special Indexes:** Finding aids for archival holdings. **Remarks:** FAX: (212)415-5575.

★11815★
92nd Street Young Men's and Young Women's Hebrew Association - Buttenwieser Library (Area-Ethnic)
1395 Lexington Ave.
New York, NY 10128
Phone: (212)415-5542
Steven W. Siegel, Dir.
Founded: 1874. **Staff:** Prof 2; Other 8. **Subjects:** Judaica, literature, history, art. **Special Collections:** Moses Crystal Judaica Collection (6000 volumes); Poetry Collection (2500 volumes); Frederick William Greenfield Young People's Library (3500 volumes); young adult, large print book, and parent-child collections; foreign language collection (Hebrew, German, Yiddish, Russian). **Holdings:** 30,000 volumes. **Subscriptions:** 80 journals and other serials; 10 newspapers. **Services:** Copying; library open to the public for reference use only. **Remarks:** FAX: (212)415-5575. **Staff:** Sylvia Avner, Libn.

Nipissing University - Library
See: **North Bay College Education Centre - Library (11873)**

★11816★
Nissan Motor Corporation - Corporate Library (Bus-Fin)
18510 S. Figueroa St.
Box 191
Carson, CA 90248   Phone: (213)532-3111
Founded: 1972. **Staff:** Prof 1; Other 1. **Subjects:** Automobiles, automobile industry, business management, economics, international relations, Japan. **Special Collections:** Complete set of service and owners' manuals for all makes of Nissan. **Holdings:** 4000 books; 238 bound periodical volumes; 300 catalogs; 150 pamphlets; monthly automotive press clippings; 80 audio cassettes; video cassettes. **Subscriptions:** 250 journals and other serials. **Services:** Library not open to the public. **Publications:** Library Angle, monthly - for internal distribution only; NMC-USA Weekly News Digest. **Remarks:** FAX: (213)719-3343. Library serves employees across the U.S.

★11817★
Nitrogen Fixation by Tropical Agricultural Legumes - NIFTAL Information Center (Agri)
1000 Holomua Rd.   Phone: (808)579-9568
Paia, HI 96779-9744   Ann Coopersmith
Founded: 1976. **Staff:** Prof 2; Other 1. **Subjects:** Rhizobium, legumes, soil conditions, nitrogen-fixing trees. **Special Collections:** Legume-Rhizobium Symbiosis (12,000 documents). **Holdings:** 500 books. **Subscriptions:** 20 journals and other serials. **Services:** Interlibrary loan; copying; center open to the public with restrictions. **Automated Operations:** Computerized cataloging. **Computerized Information Services:** National Center for Standards and Certification Information (NCSCI); internal database; BITNET, Dialcom, Inc. (electronic mail services). **Remarks:** Jointly maintained by University of Hawaii and U.S. Agency for International Development. **Remarks:** FAX: (808)579-8516. Telex: 7430315. Electronic mail address(es): NIFTAL@UHCCUX (BITNET).

★11818★
Nixon Family Association - Clearinghouse (Hist)
5817 144 St. E.
Puyallup, WA 98373   Phone: (206)537-8288
Subjects: Nixon family genealogy. **Holdings:** 850 volumes. **Services:** Copying.

★11819★
Nixon, Hargrave, Devans & Doyle - Law Library (Law)
One Thomas Circle, N.W., Suite 800   Phone: (202)457-7200
Washington, DC 20005   Sara G. Eakes, Hd.
Staff: 2. **Subjects:** Law. **Holdings:** 5000 volumes. **Subscriptions:** 125 journals and other serials; 5 newspapers. **Services:** Library not open to the public.

★11820★
Nixon, Hargrave, Devans & Doyle - Law Library (Law)
30 Rockefeller Plaza
New York, NY 10112   Phone: (212)603-3132
Founded: 1985. **Staff:** 2. **Subjects:** Law. **Holdings:** 7000 volumes. **Subscriptions:** 120 journals and other serials; 7 newspapers. **Services:** Library not open to the public. **Computerized Information Services:** LEXIS, WESTLAW, Dow Jones News/Retrieval, VU/TEXT Information Services, DIALOG Information Services, Dun & Bradstreet Business Credit Services; BASIS (internal database). **Remarks:** FAX: (212)603-3111. **Staff:** Gregory F. Tague, Libn.; Maria L. Schillaci, Asst.Libn.

★11821★
Nixon, Hargrave, Devans & Doyle - Law Library (Law)
Clinton Square
200 E. Broad St.
Box 20364
Rochester, NY 14602   Phone: (716)263-1000
     Sharon A. Hayden, Mgr., Info.Serv.
Staff: Prof 7; Other 6. **Subjects:** Law - corporate, tax, estates, international, real estate, labor, environmental; litigation. **Holdings:** 30,000 books; 1000 other cataloged items. **Services:** Library open to clients. **Automated Operations:** Computerized public access catalog, cataloging, acquisitions, serials, and circulation. **Computerized Information Services:** LEXIS, NEXIS, WESTLAW, Dun & Bradstreet Business Credit Services, Dow Jones News/Retrieval, VU/TEXT Information Services, DIALOG Information Services, Current USC, Reuters, Congressional Quarterly, New York Legislative Retrieval System. **Networks/Consortia:** Member of SUNY/OCLC Library Network. **Remarks:** FAX: (716)263-1600. **Staff:** Linda C. Dean, Hd., Ref.Serv.; Marie G. Calvaruso, Acq.Libn.; Janis L. Croft, Hd. of Media Serv.; Janice L. Bowers, Hd., Tech.Serv.; Keith J. Diamond, Work Product Spec.; Tanya C. Cmunt, Work Product Spec.

Nixon Presidential Materials Staff
See: **National Archives & Records Administration (11044)**

★11822★
NKF Engineering, Inc. - Library (Sci-Engr)
4200 Wilson Blvd., Suite 900   Phone: (703)358-8600
Arlington, VA 22203   Nannette M. Bell, Libn.
Founded: 1980. **Staff:** Prof 1. **Subjects:** Shock and vibration, logistics, acoustics, naval architecture. **Special Collections:** Military specifications and standards. **Holdings:** 3000 books; 3500 government documents; 220 linear feet of microfiche. **Subscriptions:** 180 journals and other serials. **Services:** Interlibrary loan; library not open to the public. **Automated Operations:** Computerized cataloging. **Computerized Information Services:** DIALOG Information Services, PFDS Online, Commerce Business Daily, DTIC. Performs searches on fee basis. **Remarks:** FAX: (703)358-8795.

NL Baroid Library
See: **Sperry-Sun Drilling Services (15583)**

NLM
See: **U.S. National Library of Medicine (17629)**

No Man's Land Historical Museum
See: **Panhandle State University (12727)**

NOAA
See: **U.S. Natl. Oceanic & Atmospheric Administration (17650)**

Noble Army Hospital
See: **U.S. Army Hospitals (17051)**

Daniel E. Noble Science and Engineering Library
See: **Arizona State University (1013)**

★11823★
Samuel Roberts Noble Foundation, Inc. - Biomedical Division Library (Med)
2510 Hwy. 199 E.
Box 2180   Phone: (405)223-5810
Ardmore, OK 73402   Jeanine Phipps, Biomed. & Plant Biol.Libn.
Founded: 1951. **Staff:** Prof 1. **Subjects:** Cancer research, biochemistry, plant biology, medicine, immunology, nutrition, cell biology, plant cell biology, biochemical pharmacology, science, chemistry, molecular plant pathology, applied molecular biology, molecular analysis and synthesis, virology, plant transformation. **Holdings:** 1525 books; 5500 bound periodical volumes; 1150 annual publications; 2710 reels of microfilm of journals. **Subscriptions:** 153 journals and other serials. **Services:** Interlibrary loan; library open to the public for reference use only. **Computerized Information Services:** MEDLINE, Institute for Scientific Information (ISI), BRS Information Technologies, NLM. **Remarks:** FAX: (405)221-7380.

★11824★
Nobleboro Historical Society - Historical Center (Hist)
P.O. Box 122   Phone: (207)563-5874
Nobleboro, ME 04555   Dr. George F. Dow, Cur.
Founded: 1980. **Subjects:** Genealogy, local history. **Special Collections:** Genealogies. **Holdings:** 100 books; 50 bound periodical volumes; 2000 documents; war, cemetery, and town records. **Services:** Copying; center open to the public by appointment. **Publications:** History of Nobleboro.

★11825★
Bernhard Nocht Institute for Tropical Medicine - Library (Med)
Bernhard-Nocht-Strasse 74   Phone: 40 31182404
W-2000 Hamburg 36, Germany   Martina-Christine Koschwitz, Libn.
Founded: 1900. **Staff:** 2.5. **Subjects:** Tropical diseases, medicine, infectious diseases, virology, helminthology, protozoology, biochemistry, entomology, pathology, immune diagnosis. **Holdings:** 85,000 volumes. **Subscriptions:** 206 journals and other serials. **Services:** Interlibrary loan; copying; library open to the public. **Remarks:** FAX: 40 31182400. **Also Known As:** Bernhard-Nocht-Institut fuer Tropenmedizin.

★ 11826 ★
Nodaway County Genealogical Society - Library (Hist)
P.O. Box 214   Phone: (816)562-3556
Maryville, MO 64468   Letha Marie Mowry, Files Sec.
Subjects: Genealogy. **Holdings:** 100,000 file cards. **Services:** Library not open to the public. **Remarks:** Contains the holdings of the Graham Historical Society.

Judith Nogrady Library
See: **Canada - Transport Canada - Transportation Development Centre - Judith Nogrady Library (2879)**

Nogyo Kankyo Gijutsu Kenkyojo - Toshoka
See: **Japan (8335)**

★ 11827 ★
Lloyd Noland Hospital - David Knox McKamy Medical Library (Med)
701 Lloyd Noland Pkwy.   Phone: (205)783-5121
Fairfield, AL 35064   Barbara Estep, Dir., Med.Rec.
Founded: 1957. **Staff:** 2. **Subjects:** Medicine, allied health sciences. **Holdings:** 1500 volumes. **Subscriptions:** 147 journals and other serials. **Services:** Interlibrary loan; library not open to the public.

★ 11828 ★
Nolte & Associates - Library (Sci-Engr)
24741 Chrisanta Dr.   Phone: (714)837-5001
Mission Viejo, CA 92691   Donna Jacques, Libn.
Staff: Prof 1. **Subjects:** Soil engineering, civil engineering, water resources, public works, transportation, laws and codes. **Special Collections:** Environmental Impact Reports; Advance and Community Planning; geotechnical documents. **Holdings:** 7000 books; 5000 periodical volumes; 7000 engineering drawings; 8 VF drawers of newspaper clippings; 5 trays of microfiche; 6000 plans; 2000 photographs and slides. **Subscriptions:** 253 journals and other serials. **Services:** Library not open to the public. **Automated Operations:** Computerized cataloging, acquisitions, serials, and circulation. **Remarks:** FAX: (714)380-1207.

★ 11829 ★
Nome Library/Kegoayah Kozga Public Library (Hist)
Front St.
Box 1168   Phone: (907)443-5133
Nome, AK 99762   Dee J. McKenna, Libn.
Founded: 1905. **Staff:** 4. **Subjects:** Alaska, Eskimo and Gold Rush artifacts. **Special Collections:** Alaskana (75 rare volumes). **Holdings:** 14,000 books; 3000 cassette tapes; 1200 AV programs; old photographs; bilingual and oral history materials. **Subscriptions:** 70 journals and other serials. **Services:** Interlibrary loan; copying; library open to the public.

Nondestructive Testing Information Analysis Center
See: **Texas Research Institute, Inc. - Nondestructive Testing Information Analysis Center (16226)**

★ 11830 ★
Nonprescription Drug Manufacturers Association - Library (Med)
1150 Connecticut Ave., N.W., Suite 1200   Phone: (202)429-9260
Washington, DC 20036   Phyllis M. Taylor, Libn.
Founded: 1977. **Staff:** 1. **Subjects:** Medicines - nonprescription, limited prescription, allied-type groups; regulations affecting over-the-counter medicine. **Holdings:** 1000 volumes; U.S. Food and Drug Administration monographs and reports; AV programs. **Subscriptions:** 90 journals and other serials. **Services:** Interlibrary loan; copying; library open to the public with restrictions. **Remarks:** FAX: (202)223-6835.

★ 11831 ★
Nonviolence Resource Centre - Library (Soc Sci)
Argenta, BC, Canada V0G 1B0   Phone: (604)366-4307
                                                  Jack Ross
Subjects: Nonviolence. **Holdings:** 75 books; 15 AV programs. **Services:** Copying; centre open to the public with restrictions. **Publications:** Active Nonviolence (group study kit).

★ 11832 ★
Nooter Corporation - Technical Library (Sci-Engr)
Box 451   Phone: (314)621-6000
St. Louis, MO 63166   Barry S. Heuer, Welding Engr.
Subjects: Metals properties and fabrication methods. **Holdings:** 500 volumes. **Subscriptions:** 20 journals and other serials. **Services:** Library not open to the public. **Remarks:** Alternate telephone number(s): 421-7463. FAX: (314)421-7583.

NORAD - Informasjons - og dokumentasjons - senter
See: **Norwegian Agency for Development Cooperation - Information and Documentation Center (12107)**

★ 11833 ★
Noranda, Inc. - Information Services - Resource Centre (Comp Sci)
33 Yonge St., Suite 300   Phone: (416)982-6961
Toronto, ON, Canada M5E 1G4   Anna Takashiba, Sys.Libn.
Staff: Prof 1. **Subjects:** Computer science, programming application, systems documentation, microcomputer hardware and software. **Holdings:** 700 books; computer manuals. **Subscriptions:** 90 journals and other serials. **Services:** Center not open to the public. **Computerized Information Services:** DIALOG Information Services; CD-ROMs; internal database. **Special Indexes:** Indexes to computer manuals and microcomputer software packages. **Remarks:** FAX: (416)982-6963.

★ 11834 ★
Noranda Minerals Inc. - CCR Division - Technical Development Library (Sci-Engr)
220 Durocher St.   Phone: (514)645-2311
Montreal East, PQ, Canada H1B 5H6   Leslie Acs, Mgr., Tech.Dev.
Founded: 1940. **Staff:** Prof 2. **Subjects:** Chemical engineering, metallurgy, extractive and physical metallurgy, environmental control, health, safety and toxicology. **Holdings:** 1500 books; 200 reports and patents. **Subscriptions:** 20 journals and other serials. **Services:** Interlibrary loan; copying; library open to members of Noranda Group only. **Automated Operations:** Computerized cataloging. **Computerized Information Services:** Internal database. **Remarks:** FAX: (514)640-2088. **Staff:** Denise Perron, Sec., Tech.Dev.

★ 11835 ★
Noranda Minerals Inc. - Information Centre (Bus-Fin)
1 Adelaide St. E., Suite 2700   Phone: (416)982-7238
Toronto, ON, Canada M5C 2Z6   Sally A. Goodings, Libn.
Founded: 1973. **Staff:** Prof 1; Other 1. **Subjects:** Nonferrous metals, statistics, management, economics, human relations. **Special Collections:** Statistics for industrial minerals, lead and zinc, metals, and nonferrous metals; Queens University Centre for Resource Studies publications; Conference Boards. **Holdings:** 1000 books; 600 annual reports. **Subscriptions:** 250 journals and other serials; 7 newspapers. **Services:** Interlibrary loan; copying; center open to the public by appointment. **Automated Operations:** Computerized acquisitions and serials. **Computerized Information Services:** DIALOG Information Services, Info Globe, Infomart Online. **Publications:** Library Information Brochure; acquisitions list, quarterly - internal distribution and to others upon request. **Remarks:** FAX: (416)982-7021.

★ 11836 ★
Noranda Technology Centre - Library (Sci-Engr)
240 Hymus Blvd.   Phone: (514)630-9524
Pointe Claire, PQ, Canada H9R 1G5   Nathalie De Brouwer, Libn.
Founded: 1963. **Staff:** Prof 2; Other 1. **Subjects:** Metallurgy, mining, environment, forestry and energy management. **Holdings:** 15,000 books. **Subscriptions:** 400 journals and other serials. **Services:** Interlibrary loan; copying; library open with limited access. **Computerized Information Services:** DIALOG Information Services, CAN/OLE, STN International, QL Systems. **Remarks:** FAX: (514)630-9379. **Also Known As:** Bibliotheque Centre de Technolgie Noranda. **Staff:** Fleurette Gregoire, Asst.Libn.

★ 11837 ★
Norcen Energy Resources Limited - Library (Energy)
715 5th Ave., S.W.   Phone: (403)231-0886
Calgary, AB, Canada T2P 2X7   B. Zinter
Founded: 1975. **Staff:** 1. **Subjects:** Petroleum exploration, geology, coal.
Holdings: 2000 books; 3000 government documents. **Subscriptions:** 350
journals and other serials; 20 newspapers. **Services:** Interlibrary loan
(limited); library not open to the public. **Automated Operations:**
Computerized cataloging and circulation. **Computerized Information
Services:** DIALOG Information Services, ORBIT Search Service, Info
Globe. **Publications:** Library bulletin - for internal distribution only.
Remarks: FAX: (403)231-0187.

Nord Library
See: **American Swedish Historical Museum** (772)

★ 11838 ★
Norden Systems, Inc. - Information Services (Sci-Engr)
75 Maxess Rd.   Phone: (516)845-2463
Melville, NY 11747   Carol L. Sloan, Info.Spec.
Founded: 1983. **Staff:** Prof 1. **Subjects:** Radar, sonar, electronics, software
engineering. **Holdings:** 2200 books; 500 reports. **Subscriptions:** 140 journals
and other serials. **Services:** Interlibrary loan; services not open to the public.
Automated Operations: Computerized cataloging and circulation.
Computerized Information Services: DIALOG Information Services,
NEXIS, VU/TEXT Information Services, Aviation Online, Aerospace
Online, STN International, NewsNet, Inc., Dow Jones News/Retrieval,
WILSONLINE; United Technologies Online Catalog (internal database).
Remarks: A branch of United Technologies Library & Information Services.

★ 11839 ★
Norden Systems, Inc. - Library and Information Services (Sci-Engr)
Norden Place
P.O. Box 5300
Norwalk, CT 06856   Phone: (203)852-5886
                                               Vicky Spitalniak, Sr.Libn.
Founded: 1943. **Staff:** Prof 1; Other 1. **Subjects:** Electronics, electrical
engineering, physics, mathematics, business management, computers,
metallurgy. **Holdings:** 3600 books; 1400 documents; reprints, photostats.
Subscriptions: 111 journals and other serials. **Services:** Interlibrary loan;
library not open to the public. **Automated Operations:** Computerized
circulation. **Computerized Information Services:** DIALOG Information
Services, NEXIS, Aerospace Online, Aviation Online, DTIC, Dow Jones
News/Retrieval, Reuter TEXTLINE. **Remarks:** FAX: (203)852-4579. A
subsidiary of United Technologies Corporation.

★ 11840 ★
Nordens Folkliga Akademi - Biblioteket (Educ)
Box 12024
S-402 41 Goteborg, Sweden   Phone: 31 691030
                                               Monica Olsson, Chf.Libn.
Founded: 1968. **Staff:** Prof 1; Other 1.5. **Subjects:** Adult education. **Special
Collections:** Nordic aspects of adult education; fiction in the original nordic
languages. **Holdings:** 20,000 books; bound periodical volumes; reports.
Subscriptions: 200 journals and other serials. **Services:** Interlibrary loan;
copying; library open to the public and institutions in Scandanavia who deal
with adult education. **Computerized Information Services:** FOVU (internal
database). **Publications:** Newsletter; journal; literature lists on several
topics. **Remarks:** Alternate telephone number(s): 31 694315. FAX: 31
690950.

★ 11841 ★
Nordic Heritage Museum - Walter Johnson Library (Area-Ethnic)
3014 N.W. 67th St.   Phone: (206)789-5707
Seattle, WA 98117   Marianne Forssblad, Dir.
Founded: 1981. **Staff:** Prof 1; Other 2. **Subjects:** Nordic immigrant history,
history, literature, cookery, topography, folk art. **Holdings:** 10,000 books;
200 bound periodical volumes; 350 Nordic historical magazines; 275 Bibles
and religious books; musical recordings; language tapes. **Subscriptions:** 25
journals and other serials; 5 newspapers. **Services:** Library open to the public
for reference use only. **Remarks:** FAX: (206)789-3271.

Nordisk Forskningsinstitut for Maling og Trykfarver
See: **Scandinavian Paint and Printing Ink Research Institute - Library**
(14892)

Nordiska Afrikainstitutet
See: **Scandinavian Institute of African Studies** (14891)

Nordrhein Westfalisches Staatsarchiv Detmold und Nordrhein -
   Westfalisches Personenstandsarchiv Westfalen Lippe - Bibliothek
See: **North Rhine-Westphalian Public Record Office - Detmold and**
   North Rhine-Westphalian Archive of Vital Statistics - Westphalia-
   Lippe (11945)

★ 11842 ★
Nordson Corporation - Information Resource Center (Sci-Engr)
28601 Clemens Rd.   Phone: (216)892-1580
Westlake, OH 44145   Rosemary B. Davidson, Mgr., Info.Rsrcs.
Founded: 1974. **Staff:** Prof 2; Other 1. **Subjects:** Adhesives, electronics,
international business, coatings, mechanical engineering. **Holdings:** 3000
books. **Subscriptions:** 300 journals and other serials. **Services:** Department
not open to the public. **Computerized Information Services:** Dow Jones
News/Retrieval, Data-Star, DataTimes, STN International, InvesText,
VU/TEXT Information Services, DRI/McGraw-Hill, ESA/IRS,
Pergamon Financial Data Services (PFDS), ORBIT Search Service,
DIALOG Information Services, WILSONLINE, OCLC, BRS Information
Technologies, NewsNet, Inc.; Catalog of library material (internal
database). **Networks/Consortia:** Member of OHIONET. **Publications:**
Information Research Reports on various topics. **Remarks:** FAX: (216)892-
2018.

★ 11843 ★
Norex U.S.A. Inc. - Library (Sci-Engr)
Canal Square, Suite 120
1054 31st St., N.W.   Phone: (202)337-6912
Washington, DC 20007   Henry Cuschineri, Dept.Mgr.
Founded: 1985. **Staff:** 7. **Subjects:** Technical standards in: metallurgy;
chemical, mechanical, building, and civil engineering; packaging and
transport; allied subjects. **Holdings:** 5000 French standards translated into
English; complete set of AFNOR standards. **Services:** Library not open to
the public. **Computerized Information Services:** CD-ROMs (Normes et
Reglements Informations Accessible en Ligne (NORIANE), BSI
STANDARDLINE, DITR Database). **Remarks:** FAX: (202)337-3709.
Telex: 494 3650 NORUSA. Maintained by Association Francaise de
Normalisation - French National Standards Institute (AFNOR).

★ 11844 ★
Norfolk Botanical Garden Society - Frederic Heutte Memorial Library
   (Biol Sci)
Airport Rd.   Phone: (804)441-5386
Norfolk, VA 23518   Lois V. Leach, Libn.
Founded: 1962. **Staff:** 1. **Subjects:** Horticulture and allied subjects.
Holdings: 2350 books. **Services:** Library open to the public for reference use
only.

Norfolk Island Historical Society & Museum Trust
See: **H.M.S. Bounty Society, International** (6819)

★ 11845 ★
Norfolk Law Library (Law)
Superior Courthouse
650 High St.
Dedham, MA 02026   Phone: (617)329-1856
Founded: 1815. **Staff:** Prof 1; Other 1. **Subjects:** Massachusettes and
criminal law. **Holdings:** 12,000 books; 250 bound periodical volumes; 4
drawers of microfiche. **Subscriptions:** 22 journals and other serials. **Services:**
Interlibrary loan; copying; library open to the public. **Computerized
Information Services:** WESTLAW, LEXIS, OCLC. **Remarks:** Part of the
Massachusetts State Trial Court; Marnie Warner, Law Library Coordinator.
Staff: Carol M. Ewing, Libn.; Agnes M. Leathe, Libn.

★ 11846 ★
Norfolk Law Library (Law)
1300 Dominion Tower
Norfolk, VA 23510   Phone: (804)622-2910
    Jean M. Holcomb, Law Libn.
Founded: 1900. **Staff:** Prof 1; Other 1. **Subjects:** Law. **Holdings:** 24,000 books; 500 bound periodical volumes; 21 linear feet of legal periodicals. **Subscriptions:** 15 journals and other serials. **Services:** Copying; faxing; library open to the public. **Automated Operations:** Computerized cataloging. **Computerized Information Services:** WESTLAW, LEXIS. Performs searches on fee basis. **Remarks:** FAX: (804)622-4406.

★ 11847 ★
Norfolk Public Library - Sargeant Memorial Room (Hist)
301 E. City Hall Ave.   Phone: (804)441-2503
Norfolk, VA 23507   Peggy Haile
Founded: 1927. **Staff:** Prof 1; Other 1. **Subjects:** Norfolk and Virginia history and genealogy. **Special Collections:** Borjes Collection (42,000 negatives of Norfolk, 1921-1955); Mays Collection (10,500 negatives of Norfolk, 1948-1956); Walker Collection (30,000 negatives of Norfolk, 1940-1990); Norfolk newspapers, 1800 to present; complete U.S. census records, 1800-1910, for Virginia, North Carolina, Maryland, West Virginia, Washington, D.C., Kentucky, South Carolina. **Holdings:** 15,975 books; 1036 bound periodical volumes; 63 drawers of newspaper articles, original manuscripts, 19th century local business ledgers, letters, autographs, rare pamphlets; 3215 reels of microfilm of local newspapers, census records, cemetery and church records; 1280 postcards; 19,000 photographs; 1698 topographic and historic maps. **Subscriptions:** 42 journals and other serials; 7 newspapers. **Services:** Copying; room open to the public. **Remarks:** FAX: (804)441-1450. **Staff:** John Parker, Hd., Gen.Ref.

★ 11848 ★
Norfolk Regional Center - Staff Library (Med)
Box 1209
1700 N. Victory Rd.   Phone: (402)370-3400
Norfolk, NE 68702   Dolores E. Hartman, Libn. I
Founded: 1954. **Staff:** 1. **Subjects:** Clinical psychology, psychiatry, medicine, social work. **Holdings:** 1500 books. **Subscriptions:** 20 journals and other serials. **Services:** Interlibrary loan; copying; library open to students and health science professionals in community. **Networks/Consortia:** Member of Northeast Library System. **Remarks:** FAX: (402)644-3194, ext. 290.

★ 11849 ★
Norfolk State University - Lyman Beecher Brooks Library (Soc Sci)
2401 Corprew Avenue   Phone: (804)683-8517
Norfolk, VA 23504   Mrs. Mattie H. Roane
Founded: 1935. **Staff:** Prof 8; Other 21. **Subjects:** Social sciences, technology, business, education. **Special Collections:** Black Collection (7062 items); Juvenile Collection (6000 items); Theses Collection (307). **Holdings:** 307,890 books; 60,000 bound periodical volumes; 21,249 microfiche; 42,498 reels of microfilm. **Subscriptions:** 2642 journals and other serials; 9 newspapers. **Services:** Interlibrary loan; reference materials and periodicals may be used by the public in-house only. **Computerized Information Services:** DIALOG Information Services, OCLC, BRS Information Technologies, NewsBank, ProQuest. Performs searches. Contact Person: Henry Albritton, Hd. of Tech.Serv. **Publications:** Online Searching; For Your Information; Library Handbook; subject bibliographies.

Norfolk & Western Railway Archive
See: Virginia Polytechnic Institute and State University - University Libraries (19875)

Norges Byggforskningsinstitutt
See: Norwegian Building Research Institute (12112)

★ 11850 ★
Norman County Historical Society - Memorial Museum Library (Hist)
12 1st St., E.   Phone: (218)784-4989
Ada, MN 56510   Myrtle Rector, Cur.
Founded: 1957. **Staff:** Prof 2. **Subjects:** State and local history and biography. **Special Collections:** Norwegian, Swedish, French, German rare books; rare textbooks used in rural schools; county and state publications; family histories (25); government publications, 1890-1970; photograph collections (5400 items). **Holdings:** 3460 books; 56 bound periodical volumes; 80 boxes of newspapers, documents, local records, music texts; county cemetery books. **Subscriptions:** 18 journals and other serials. **Services:** Copying; library open to the public. **Networks/Consortia:** Member of Northern Lights Library Network (NLLN).

★ 11851 ★
Norman Engineering Company - Library (Sci-Engr)
5899 Venice Blvd.
Los Angeles, CA 90019   Phone: (213)937-5400
Founded: 1982. **Staff:** Prof 1. **Subjects:** Engineering - mechanical, electrical, structural, civil; architecture. **Holdings:** 350 books; 7000 manufacturers' catalogs; 300 U.S. military standards and specifications; 2000 U.S. industrial standards. **Subscriptions:** 70 journals and other serials. **Services:** Library not open to the public. **Automated Operations:** Computerized cataloging, circulation, and indexing. **Special Indexes:** Index by product to manufacturers catalogs (book).

★ 11852 ★
Norman Regional Hospital - Health Sciences Library (Med)
901 N. Porter
Box 1308   Phone: (405)360-8385
Norman, OK 73070   Michelynn McKnight, Dir.
Founded: 1973. **Staff:** 1. **Subjects:** Medicine, nursing, and allied health sciences. **Holdings:** 1000 books; 300 reels of microfilm. **Subscriptions:** 150 journals and other serials. **Services:** Interlibrary loan; copying; SDI; library open to local health personnel for reference use only. **Automated Operations:** Computerized serials. **Computerized Information Services:** DIALOG Information Services, MEDLARS, WILSONLINE, BRS Information Technologies; CompuServe Information Service, InterNet (electronic mail services). **Networks/Consortia:** Member of Greater Oklahoma City Area Health Sciences Library Consortium (GOAL), Metronet. **Remarks:** FAX: (405)321-6576. Electronic mail address(es): 72456,3532 (CompuServe Information Service); MMCKNIGHT@AARDVARK.UCS.UOKNOR.EDU (InterNet).

Kenneth T. Norris, Jr. Visual Science Library
See: Estelle Doheny Eye Institute (4944)

★ 11853 ★
Norris, McLaughlin & Marcus - Library (Law)
721 Rte. 202-206 N.
P.O. Box 1018   Phone: (908)722-0700
Somerville, NJ 08876   Janice Lustiger
Subjects: Law. **Holdings:** Figures not available. **Services:** Library not open to the public.

Norris Medical Library
See: University of Southern California - Health Sciences Campus (19330)

Norris Memorial Library
See: National Rural Electric Cooperative Association (11278)

Norristown State Hospital
See: Pennsylvania (State) Department of Public Welfare (12863)

Norsk Astronautisk Forening
See: Norwegian Astronautical Society (12110)

Norsk Polarinstitutt
See: Norwegian Polar Research Institute (12115)

Norsk Rikskringkasting - Biblioteket
See: Norwegian Broadcasting Corporation (12111)

★ 11854 ★
North Adams State College - Eugene L. Freel Library - Special Collections (Educ)
P.O. Box 9250   Phone: (413)664-4511
North Adams, MA 01247   Ann B. Terryberry, Act.Dir.
Founded: 1894. **Special Collections:** Teacher Resources Center (3380 items); Hoosac Valley Collection for Local History (400 items); College Archives (110 cubic feet); McFarlin Printing Collection (375 items). **Holdings:** 145,771 books. **Subscriptions:** 510 journals and other serials. **Services:** Interlibrary loan; copying; collections open to the public. **Automated Operations:** Computerized cataloging and circulation. **Computerized Information Services:** OCLC, DIALOG Information Services; internal database; InterNet (electronic mail service). Performs searches on fee basis. **Networks/Consortia:** Member of C/W MARS, Inc., NELINET, Inc. **Remarks:** FAX: (413)663-3033. Electronic mail address(es): aterryberry@ecn.mass.edu (InterNet).

★ 11855 ★
North America Center for Responsible Tourism - Library (Rec)
PO Box 827
San Anselmo, CA 94979   Phone: (415)258-6594
Founded: 1986. **Subjects:** Global education, travel, geography, culture. **Holdings:** 350 volumes. **Subscriptions:** 1400 newsletters. **Services:** Library open to the public by appointment. **Remarks:** FAX: (415)454-2493. Center seeks to educate Americans about the negative effects of mass Third World travel and tourism, and provides information on responsible and/or alternate travel practices.

★ 11856 ★
North American Baptist College and Divinity School - Library (Rel-Phil)
11525 23rd Ave.   Phone: (403)437-1960
Edmonton, AB, Canada T6J 4T3   Arnold Rapske, Libn.
Founded: 1940. **Staff:** Prof 2; Other 2. **Subjects:** Theology, Christianity. **Special Collections:** North American Baptist Historical Collection. **Holdings:** 46,000 volumes; 500 sound recordings; microforms. **Subscriptions:** 300 journals and other serials. **Services:** Library not open to the public. **Automated Operations:** Computerized cataloging and acquisitions. **Remarks:** FAX: (403)433-8694. **Staff:** Deborah Penner, Ref.Libn.

★ 11857 ★
North American Baptist Seminary - Kaiser-Ramaker Library (Rel-Phil)
1321 W. 22nd St.   Phone: (605)336-6588
Sioux Falls, SD 57105-1599   George W. Lang, Lib.Adm.
Founded: 1875. **Staff:** Prof 2; Other 2. **Subjects:** Theology, church history, Baptist history and doctrine, pastoral administration and counseling, Biblical studies, Christian education, homiletics, evangelism and missions. **Special Collections:** North American Baptist Conference Archives; Harris Homiletics Collection. **Holdings:** 61,273 volumes; 700 filmstrips; 261 boxes of archival materials; 2 VF drawers of pamphlets; 9526 slides; 722 microforms; 920 phonograph records; 30 reels of tape; 178 maps and charts; 646 flat pictures; 1795 audio cassettes; 108 video cassettes. **Subscriptions:** 335 journals and other serials. **Services:** Interlibrary loan; copying; library open to the public. **Computerized Information Services:** OCLC. **Networks/Consortia:** Member of MINITEX Library Information Network, South Dakota Library Network (SDLN). **Remarks:** FAX: (605)335-9090. **Staff:** Vicki Biggerstaff, Asst.Libn.

★ 11858 ★
North American Die Casting Association - H.L. "Red" Harvill Memorial Library (Sci-Engr)
9701 W. Higgins Rd., Suite 880   Phone: (708)292-3600
Rosemont, IL 60018   Jeffry W. Raynes, Found.Sec.
Founded: 1986. **Staff:** 18. **Subjects:** Die casting and allied aspects of metal casting, mechanics, engineering, and other arts and sciences. **Holdings:** 560 volumes. **Services:** Library open to members only. **Computerized Information Services:** The Harvill Information System (internal database). **Remarks:** FAX: (708)292-3620. **Formerly:** Located in River Grove, IL.

★ 11859 ★
North American Jewish Students' Network - Library
501 Madison Ave., 17th Fl.
New York, NY 10022
Defunct.

★ 11860 ★
North American Life Assurance Company - Staff Library (Bus-Fin)
5650 Yonge St.   Phone: (416)229-4515
North York, ON, Canada M2M 4G4   Lora Ruscica, Recruitment/Dev.
Staff: 1. **Subjects:** Life insurance, management, math, business, economics, taxes. **Holdings:** 8000 books; 5 VF drawers. **Subscriptions:** 27 journals and other serials. **Services:** Interlibrary loan; library not open to the public. **Remarks:** Telex: 06-22400. FAX: (416)229-6594.

★ 11861 ★
North American Native Fishes Association - Library (Biol Sci)
381 County Rd., 1300 E.   Phone: (217)867-2290
Tolono, IL 61880   Philip L. Nixon, Libn.
Subjects: Fish species native to North America. **Holdings:** Figures not available. **Services:** Copying; library open to the public. **Remarks:** Library is currently in the process of formation.

★ 11862 ★
North American Opel GT Club - Library (Rec)
15 Valewood Dr.   Phone: (708)231-4938
West Chicago, IL 60185   Richard Cooke
Founded: 1984. **Staff:** 5. **Subjects:** Opel automotive history and restoration information. **Holdings:** 28 volumes; 44 magazine articles; 13 parts catalogs; 18 technical manuals; 143 Opel club newsletters; 250 photographs; sales literature. **Subscriptions:** 91 newspapers. **Services:** Copying; library open to the public by appointment. **Publications:** Club Library Listing, annual - on request to members. **Formerly:** Located in Joliet, IL.

★ 11863 ★
North American Philips Corporation - Philips Laboratories Research Library (Sci-Engr)
345 Scarborough Rd.   Phone: (914)945-6195
Briarcliff Manor, NY 10510   Betsy McIlvaine, Hd.Libn.
Founded: 1945. **Staff:** Prof 1; Other 2. **Subjects:** Electron optics, material sciences, optical physics, physics, computer sciences. **Holdings:** 6000 books; 5000 bound periodical volumes; microfiche. **Subscriptions:** 300 journals and other serials. **Services:** Interlibrary loan; library not open to the public. **Automated Operations:** Computerized public access catalog and circulation. **Computerized Information Services:** DIALOG Information Services, BRS Information Technologies, Dow Jones News/Retrieval; internal database; electronic mail service. **Remarks:** FAX: (914)945-6375. Telex: 646326 PHILAB BFRF.

★ 11864 ★
North American Radio Archives (NARA) - Library (Info Sci)
5291 Jacks Creek Pike   Phone: (606)272-7341
Lexington, KY 40515   Janis DeMoss, Exec. Officer
Founded: 1973. **Staff:** 12. **Subjects:** Radio - drama, comedy, entertainment, news, documentary; radio programming. **Holdings:** 200 books; 25,000 radio programs, 1926-1965, on tape; slides of radio personalities; radio scripts and magazines; reproduced articles on radio. **Services:** Library open to members of NARA who may borrow its material. **Publications:** NARA News (journal), quarterly.

★ 11865 ★
North American Radio Archives (NARA) - Tape and Printed Materials Libraries (Info Sci)
Northern Arizona University
Box 15300   Phone: (602)523-6548
Flagstaff, AZ 86011   Dr. Hal Widdison, Reel-to-Reel Libn.
Staff: 9. **Subjects:** Radio - history, programming, broadcasting, scripts, publications; television broadcasting. **Holdings:** 500 books; 2500 reel-to-reel tapes; 175 scripts; 300 slides; 300 magazines; 150 reprints of articles; 9000 cassettes; 6000 television shows. **Services:** Libraries open to members only. **Publications:** The NARA News (Magazine), quarterly - to members. **Remarks:** Printed Materials Library located at 35533 Hwy. 41, Coarsegold, CA 93614. Cassette Library located at 2055 Elmwood Ave., Lakewood, OH 44107. **Staff:** James Watson, Printed Mtls.Libn.; Thomas Monroe, Cassette Libn.

★ 11866 ★
North American Students of Cooperation - Library (Soc Sci)
Box 7715   Phone: (313)663-0889
Ann Arbor, MI 48107   Robert Cox, Exec.Dir.
Founded: 1968. **Staff:** 5. **Subjects:** Cooperatives, communities. **Special Collections:** Files on North American student and consumer co-ops; cooperative collections of Art Danforth, Rose Kleinman, Luther Buchele, and Fred and Virginia Thornthwaite. **Holdings:** 2000 books. **Subscriptions:** 15 journals and other serials. **Services:** Copying; technical and operational assistance; library open to the public with advance reservation. **Publications:** Finding Co-ops: A Resource Guide and Directory, 1983; Directory of Campus-Based Co-ops (book); Directory of Cooperative Careers. **Remarks:** Library located at 1522 Hill St., Ann Arbor, MI.

★ 11867 ★
North American Tiddlywinks Association - Archives (Rec)
5505 Seminary Rd., No. 1206N   Phone: (703)671-7098
Falls Church, VA 22041-3915   Richard W. Tucker, Archv.
Founded: 1978. **Staff:** 2. **Subjects:** Tiddlywinks - origins, history, tournaments. **Holdings:** 150 journals; 2200 clippings and citations; 70 patents; statistics on 170 tournaments; 75 antique tiddlywinks sets. **Services:** Archives open to the public by appointment. **Computerized Information Services:** Internal databases. **Publications:** Tiddlywinks Bibliography (pamphlet); Newswink (periodical). **Also Known As:** NATwA.

★11868★
North American Truffling Society - Library (Biol Sci)
34197 N.E. Colorado Lake Dr. Phone: (503)752-2243
Corvallis, OR 97333 Pat Rawlinson, Libn.
Founded: 1980. **Subjects:** Truffles, mycology. **Subjects:** Books; nonbook items. **Services:** Library not open to the public. **Staff:** John Rawlinson, Libn.

★11869★
North American Weather Consultants - Technical Library (Sci-Engr)
3761 S. 700 East, Suite 200 Phone: (801)263-3500
Salt Lake City, UT 84106 Leona Blackbird, Libn.
Founded: 1955. **Staff:** 1. **Subjects:** Meteorology, climatology, weather modification, air pollution meteorology, hydrology, synoptic meteorology. **Special Collections:** Northern Hemisphere synoptic maps, 1899 to present. **Holdings:** 2500 books; 700 bound periodical volumes; 2100 volumes of historical synoptic charts and climate data; 800 volumes of historical hydrologic data on surface water and snow surveys; 6000 technical reports; 7000 technical reports on microfiche; 100 reels of microfilm; 2 motion pictures. **Subscriptions:** 100 journals and other serials. **Services:** Interlibrary loan; copying; library open to the public. **Automated Operations:** Computerized cataloging. **Computerized Information Services:** DIALOG Information Services. **Publications:** Quarterly Report; Recent Acquisitions, monthly; serials holdings list, annual; occasional memoranda.

★11870★
North American Wildlife Park Foundation - WOLF PARK - Institute of Ethology - Library (Biol Sci)
Battle Ground, IN 47920 Phone: (317)567-2265
Erich Klinghammer, Ph.D., Dir.
Subjects: Wolves - behavior, ecology, hybrids. **Holdings:** Books; scientific papers; clippings. **Subscriptions:** 2 newspapers. **Services:** Library open to the public by appointment to members. **Computerized Information Services:** Internal database. Contact Person: Monty Sloan. **Publications:** Wolf Literature References - for sale. **Remarks:** Offers Wolf Literature Reference Service, which provides information on wolves from over 2000 sources, including those from Eastern Europe and the Soviet Union.

★11871★
North American Youth Sport Institute - Information Center (Rec)
4985 Oak Garden Dr., Suite 92 Phone: (919)784-4926
Kernersville, NC 27284 Jack Hutslar, Ph.D., Dir.
Founded: 1979. **Staff:** Prof 1. **Subjects:** Coaching, teaching, youth, sports, sport sociology and psychology, education, physical education, fitness, health, recreation and leisure, models, management. **Special Collections:** Youth sport education. **Holdings:** 1000 books, manuscripts, clippings, reports, journals, newsletters, publications, and youth agency literature. **Services:** Copying; center open to the public by appointment; consultant services available for youth groups. **Computerized Information Services:** Internal database. **Publications:** Beyond X's and O's (reference manual); Jack's Weekly News; Munchkin Tennis; Sport Scene - all for sale; NAYSI Resource List - free upon request.

★11872★
North Andover Historical Society - Library (Hist)
153 Academy Rd.
North Andover, MA 01845 Phone: (508)686-4035
Founded: 1913. **Staff:** Prof 1. **Subjects:** Local history and architecture, genealogy. **Holdings:** 1200 books; manuscripts; prints; photographs. **Services:** Copying; library open to the public for reference use only.

North Atlantic Treaty Organization
See: **NATO** (11339)

★11873★
North Bay College Education Centre - Library (Educ)
100 College Dr.
Box 5002 Phone: (705)474-3450
North Bay, ON, Canada P1B 8L7 B.A. Nettlefold, Dir. of Lib.Serv.
Founded: 1972. **Staff:** Prof 2; Other 13. **Subjects:** Education, nursing, arts, commerce, science, social work, technology, statistics. **Holdings:** 130,000 volumes; VF drawers; government documents; pictures. **Subscriptions:** 800 journals and other serials; 10 newspapers. **Services:** Interlibrary loan; copying; library open to the public for reference use only. **Automated Operations:** Computerized public access catalog, acquisitions, and cataloging. **Computerized Information Services:** DIALOG Information Services, BRS Information Technologies, Info Globe, CAN/OLE; CD-ROMs; Envoy 100 (electronic mail service). Performs searches on fee basis. **Remarks:** FAX: (705)474-1947. Electronic mail address(es): ILL.ONBNU; ILL.ONBCC (both Envoy 100). Includes the holdings of the libraries of Canadore College and Nipissing University. **Staff:** B. Lee, Pub.Serv.Libn.

★11874★
North Bay College Education Centre - Statistics Canada Library
100 College Dr.
North Bay, ON, Canada P1B 8L7
Defunct. Holdings absorbed by North Bay College Education Centre - Library.

★11875★
North Bay Psychiatric Hospital - Library (Med)
Hwy. 11 North
P.O. Box 3010 Phone: (705)474-1200
North Bay, ON, Canada P1B 8L1 Judy Elston, Libn.
Remarks: No further information was supplied by respondent.

★11876★
North Carolina A&T State University - F.D. Bluford Library (Sci-Engr)
Greensboro, NC 27411 Phone: (919)334-7782
Alene C. Young, Dir., Lib.Serv.
Founded: 1894. **Staff:** Prof 17; Other 28. **Subjects:** Agriculture, business, nursing, engineering, education. **Special Collections:** Collections of Black Studies; Film Collection; Chemistry Library. **Holdings:** 365,288 volumes; 496,544 microforms; archival materials; government documents; theses; pictures; maps; modules. **Subscriptions:** 1804 journals and other serials. **Services:** Interlibrary loan; copying; cooperative lending; library open to the public. **Automated Operations:** Computerized cataloging and circulation. **Computerized Information Services:** OCLC, DIALOG Information Services, LS/2000. Performs searches on fee basis. Contact Person: Evelyn Blount, 334-7159. **Networks/Consortia:** Member of SOLINET. **Publications:** Newsletter. **Special Indexes:** Local newspaper index (online). **Remarks:** FAX: (919)334-7783. **Staff:** Waltrene Canada, Hd., Pub.Serv.; Euthena Newman, Hd., Tech.Serv.; John Akonful, Hd., Adm.Serv.; Clifton Sawyerr, Libn., Chem.Lib.

★11877★
North Carolina Central University - NCCU Law School Library (Law)
Durham, NC 27707 Phone: (919)560-6244
Deborah Mayo-Jefferies, Law Libn.
Founded: 1941. **Staff:** Prof 5; Other 5. **Subjects:** Law. **Holdings:** 28,698 books; 16,316 bound periodical volumes; 324,816 microfiche; 2303 reels of microfilm. **Subscriptions:** 1090 journals and other serials; 10 newspapers. **Services:** Interlibrary loan; copying; library open to the public. **Automated Operations:** Computerized cataloging. **Computerized Information Services:** WESTLAW, LEXIS. **Remarks:** FAX: (919)560-6339. **Staff:** Hazel C. Lumpkin, Acq.Libn.; Eurydice Smith, Cat.Libn.; Sheila Bourne, Circ.Libn.; Regina Smith, Assoc. Law Libn.

★11878★
North Carolina Central University - School of Library and Information Sciences - Library (Info Sci)
J.E. Shepard Library Phone: (919)560-5212
Durham, NC 27707 Alice S. Richmond, Libn.
Staff: Prof 2; Other 1. **Subjects:** Librarianship, children's literature. **Special Collections:** William Tucker Collection (materials for children by black authors and illustrators; 302 items; 190 volumes); Black Librarians' Collection (1200 items). **Holdings:** 24,530 books; 4650 bound periodical volumes; 455 reels of microfilm; 15,500 microfiche; 15 VF drawers. **Subscriptions:** 400 journals and other serials. **Services:** Interlibrary loan; library open to the public with restrictions. **Automated Operations:** Computerized public access catalog and cataloging. **Computerized Information Services:** DIALOG Information Services, WILSONLINE. **Networks/Consortia:** Member of SOLINET. **Publications:** Acquisitions list, irregular - for internal distribution only. **Remarks:** FAX: (919)560-6402. **Staff:** Virginia Purefoy Jones, Asst.Libn.

North Carolina Foreign Language Center
See: **Cumberland County Public Library** (4478)

★11879★
North Carolina Maritime Museum - Library (Trans)
315 Front St. Phone: (919)728-7317
Beaufort, NC 28516 Rodney Barfield, Libn.
Founded: 1975. **Staff:** 1. **Subjects:** Current and historical boat building and design, natural history, navigation, voyages. **Holdings:** 2500 books; building plans for vessels. **Subscriptions:** 14 journals and other serials. **Services:** Copying; library open to the public for reference use only.

★ 11880 ★
North Carolina Museum of Art - Art Reference Library (Art)
2110 Blue Ridge Blvd.   Phone: (919)833-1935
Raleigh, NC 27607   Dr. Anna Dvorak, Libn.
Founded: 1956. **Staff:** Prof 1; Other 1. **Subjects:** Painting, sculpture, architecture, drawing, prints, decorative arts, graphics, pre-Columbian and African art. **Holdings:** 26,600 volumes; 20,000 slides of museum's holdings; 68 VF drawers of artist clippings; 30 VF drawers of museum and subject files. **Subscriptions:** 66 journals. **Services:** Interlibrary loan; copying; library open to the public. **Remarks:** FAX: (919)733-8034.

★ 11881 ★
North Carolina Museum of Life and Science - Library (Sci-Engr)
433 Murray Ave.
Box 15190   Phone: (919)220-5429
Durham, NC 27704   Leonard J. Sherwin, Libn.
Founded: 1980. **Subjects:** Animals, science education, space science, science in medicine. **Holdings:** 1800 books; 4 filing drawers of pamphlets; hands-on exhibits. **Subscriptions:** 10 journals and other serials. **Services:** Library not open to the public. **Remarks:** FAX: (919)220-5575.

North Carolina State Data Center
See: North Carolina (State) Office of the Governor - Budget Office - Management & Information Services Library (11896)

North Carolina (State) Department of Administration - Office of Marine Affairs - NC Aquarium/Roanoke Island
See: NC Aquarium/Roanoke Island (11361)

★ 11882 ★
North Carolina (State) Department of Community Colleges - Curriculum Information Center (Educ)
200 W. Jones St.   Phone: (919)733-7051
Raleigh, NC 27603   Allen McNeely, Info./Res.Spec.
Founded: 1963. **Staff:** Prof 1. **Subjects:** North Carolina community college system, curriculum development. **Holdings:** 700 books; 200 dissertations; curriculum manuals, studies, reports, and papers. **Subscriptions:** 70 journals and other serials. **Services:** Center open to the public. **Remarks:** FAX: (919)733-0680.

★ 11883 ★
North Carolina (State) Department of Cultural Resources - Division of Archives and History - Archives & Records Section (Hist)
109 E. Jones St.   Phone: (919)733-3952
Raleigh, NC 27601   David J. Olson, State Archv.
Founded: 1903. **Staff:** Prof 38; Other 39. **Subjects:** Official records, especially county records, of the state of North Carolina and its subdivisions. **Special Collections:** Manuscript collections, colonial times to present; maps; photographs; microfilm. **Services:** Copying; search room and archives open to the public. **Computerized Information Services:** MARS (Manuscript and Archives Reference System; internal database). **Remarks:** FAX: (919)733-1354. **Staff:** Jesse R. Lankford, Jr., Hd., Archv.Serv.; Frank D. Gatton, Hd., Rec.Serv.; Catherine J. Morris, Hd., Tech.Serv.Br.

★ 11884 ★
North Carolina (State) Department of Cultural Resources - Division of Archives and History - Outer Banks History Center (Hist)
Box 250   Phone: (919)473-2655
Manteo, NC 27954   Wynne Dough, Cur.
Founded: 1988. **Staff:** 3.5. **Subjects:** History, culture, genealogy, and natural history of North Carolina, especially Outer Banks area. **Special Collections:** David Stick Collection (175,000 manuscripts; 325 paintings; 3091 photographs); Aycock Brown photographs (20,000 items); documents of the U.S. Life-Saving Service, 1892-1926 (3714 reports, crew rosters, records, contracts); annual reports and charts of the U.S. Coast Survey; Cape Hateras National Seashore Library (1500 books; various serials); Cape Lookout National Seashore Oral History Collection. **Holdings:** 15,000 books; 1100 periodicals; 600 maps (51 published before the Revolutionary War); U.S. Coast Guard documents; large collection of ephemera. **Subscriptions:** 135 journals and other serials. **Services:** Library open to the public for reference use only. **Automated Operations:** Computerized cataloging. **Computerized Information Services:** North Carolina Shipwreck Index (internal database). **Remarks:** Is said to have the second largest collection of North Caroliniana in the state. FAX: (919)473-1483.

★ 11885 ★
North Carolina (State) Department of Cultural Resources - Division of the State Library (Info Sci)
109 E. Jones St.   Phone: (919)733-2570
Raleigh, NC 27601-2807   Howard F. McGinn, Dir./State Libn.
Founded: 1812. **Staff:** Prof 33; Other 81. **Subjects:** Public policy, Southern history, library science. **Special Collections:** Genealogy; Books for the Blind and Physically Handicapped (24,123 braille books; 18,057 large-type books; 147,017 talking books, both disc and audiotape); North Carolina state documents (123,441). **Holdings:** 200,000 volumes; 600,000 state and federal documents; 33,126 reels of microfilm; 35 titles on microfiche; 166,000 containers of talking books; 7177 16mm films; 2644 videocassettes. **Subscriptions:** 646 journals and other serials; 119 newspapers. **Services:** Interlibrary loan; copying; library open to the public with circulation of materials limited to state employees. **Automated Operations:** Computerized public access catalog, cataloging, acquisitions, and serials. **Computerized Information Services:** DIALOG Information Services, BRS Information Technologies, OCLC, LC Direct, U.S. Bureau of the Census, LINC (Legislative Information Network Corporation); BITNET, InterNet (electronic mail services). Performs searches for state employees and libraries. Contact Person: David Bevan, Chf., Info.Serv.Sect., 733-3683. **Networks/Consortia:** Member of SOLINET, North Carolina Information Network (NCIN). **Publications:** Tar Heel Libraries, bimonthly; News Flash, monthly - to public libraries; Selected Acquisitions; Checklist of Official North Carolina State Publications, bimonthly. **Special Catalogs:** North Carolina Union Catalog (microfilm); North Carolina Online Union Catalog; North Carolina Online Union List of Serials. **Remarks:** FAX: (919)733-8748. **Also Known As:** State Library of North Carolina. **Staff:** John Welch, Asst. State Libn.; Diana Young, Network Coord.; Gary Harden, Sys.Libn.; Sue Farr, Asst.Chf., Info.Serv.Sect.; Lee Albright, Geneal.Ref.Libn.; Angie Suhr, AV Spec.; Denise Sigmon, Chf., Tech.Serv.; Charles Fox, Chf., Spec.Serv.; Jane Moore, Chf., Lib.Dev.; Sally Ensor, N.C. State Pubns. Clearinghouse Coord.; Penny Hornsby, Grants Adm.

★ 11886 ★
North Carolina (State) Department of Cultural Resources - Library for the Blind and Physically Handicapped (Aud-Vis)
1811 Capital Blvd.   Phone: (919)733-4376
Raleigh, NC 27635   Charles H. Fox, Reg.Libn.
Founded: 1958. **Staff:** Prof 3; Other 31. **Holdings:** 180,000 books, including talking books on phonograph records and cassettes, braille books, large type books. **Services:** Library open to the public for reference use only. **Automated Operations:** Computerized cataloging, serials, and circulation. **Publications:** Patron newsletter, 4/year; volunteer newsletter, 4/year. **Special Catalogs:** North Carolina titles in special formats. **Remarks:** FAX: (919)733-6910. Maintained by Division of State Library. **Staff:** Francine Martin, Patron Serv.Libn.; John Stein, Lib.Serv.Libn.

★ 11887 ★
North Carolina (State) Department of Cultural Resources - Tryon Palace Restoration - Gertrude S. Carraway Library (Hist)
610 Pollock St.
Box 1007   Phone: (919)638-1560
New Bern, NC 28560   John R. Barden, Hist./Libn.
Founded: 1945. **Staff:** Prof 1; Other 1. **Subjects:** Tryon Palace, William Tryon, New Bern and North Carolina history, American and English decorative arts. **Special Collections:** Archives and minutes of Tryon Palace Commission. **Holdings:** 2150 books; 320 bound periodical volumes. **Subscriptions:** 25 journals and other serials. **Services:** Interlibrary loan; copying; library open to the public by appointment. **Remarks:** FAX: (919)638-9031.

★ 11888 ★
North Carolina (State) Department of Economic and Community Development - Science and Technology Research Center
2 Davis Dr.
P.O. Box 12235
Research Triangle Park, NC 27709-2235
Defunct.

★11889★
North Carolina State (Department) of Environment, Health, and Natural
  Resources - EHNR Library (Env-Cons)
512 N. Salisbury St., Rm. 719
Box 27687   Phone: (919)733-4984
Raleigh, NC 27611   Jane Basnight, Libn.
Founded: 1987. **Staff:** Prof 1; Other 1. **Subjects:** Resources - water, air, land,
forest; hazardous waste; public health. **Special Collections:** North Carolina
Groundwater and Geology/Mineral Resources Bulletins; North Carolina
Water Quality Studies; North Carolina soil surveys; U.S. Geological Survey
and U.S. EPA series. **Holdings:** 15,000 books. **Subscriptions:** 100 journals
and other serials. **Services:** Interlibrary loan; library open to the public for
reference use only. **Automated Operations:** Computerized cataloging.
Computerized Information Services: DIALOG Information Services,
Instructional Resources Information System (IRIS), OCLC, MEDLARS.
Networks/Consortia: Member of North Carolina Information Network
(NCIN), Resources for Health Information (REHI), SOLINET. **Remarks:**
FAX: (919)733-2622. **Formerly:** Its Environmental Resources Library.

★11890★
North Carolina (State) Department of Environment, Health, and Natural
  Resources - Public Health Pest Management Section - Environmental
  Health Division - Library (Med)
Box 27687   Phone: (919)733-6407
Raleigh, NC 27611-7687   Dr. N.H. Newton, Chf.
Founded: 1979. **Subjects:** Vector-borne disease detection and control,
integrated management for mosquito control, medical entomology, coastal
ecology. **Holdings:** 200 volumes. **Subscriptions:** 4 journals and other serials.
Services: Library open to the public by appointment. **Remarks:** FAX:
(919)733-0488.

★11891★
North Carolina (State) Department of Labor - Charles H. Livengood, Jr.
  Memorial Labor Law Library (Law)
4 W. Edenton St.   Phone: (919)733-2799
Raleigh, NC 27601   Catherine Rubin, Libn.
Founded: 1975. **Staff:** Prof 1. **Subjects:** Labor law and history, occupational
safety and health. **Special Collections:** Charles H. Livengood, Jr. Collection
(legalities of labor law; 200 volumes). **Holdings:** 4500 books; 60 bound
periodical volumes; 2 vertical file cabinets; 1 box of microfiche; state
government documents. **Subscriptions:** 45 journals and other serials.
Services: Interlibrary loan; copying; SDI. **Automated Operations:**
Computerized public access catalog. **Computerized Information Services:**
DIALOG Information Services; CD-ROM (OSH-ROM). **Networks/**
Consortia: Member of Resources for Health Information (REHI). **Remarks:**
FAX: (919)733-6197.

★11892★
North Carolina (State) Department of Public Instruction - Education
  Information Center (Educ)
Education Bldg.   Phone: (919)733-7904
Raleigh, NC 27603-1712   Gloria Bowman, Coord.
Founded: 1960. **Staff:** Prof 1; Other 2. **Subjects:** Elementary and secondary
education. **Special Collections:** Department of Public Instruction
publications, 1854 to present. **Holdings:** 4500 books; 1000 reels of microfilm
of periodicals; 1000 topics in information files; 300,000 ERIC microfiche.
Subscriptions: 255 journals and other serials; 8 newspapers. **Services:**
Interlibrary loan; copying; microfiche copying; center open to the public for
reference use only. **Automated Operations:** Computerized circulation.
Computerized Information Services: Current Awareness (internal
database); CD-ROM (ERIC). Performs searches free of charge.
Publications: Annotated bibliographies. **Remarks:** FAX: (919)733-4762.

★11893★
North Carolina (State) Justice Academy - Learning Resource Center
  (Law)
Drawer 99   Phone: (919)525-4151
Salemburg, NC 28385   Donald K. Stacy, Libn.
Founded: 1973. **Staff:** Prof 2; Other 4. **Subjects:** Law enforcement,
corrections, juvenile delinquency, management, training and development,
courts. **Special Collections:** Archives of the North Carolina Criminal Justice
Association (2 VF drawers; notebooks of academy courses). **Holdings:**
20,000 books; 4000 microfiche; 1800 AV programs. **Subscriptions:** 120
journals and other serials; 12 newspapers. **Services:** Interlibrary loan;
copying; center open to the public with restrictions. **Computerized**
Information Services: DIALOG Information Services; CD-ROM; Juvenile
Justice Clearinghouse, Policies and Procedures Clearinghouse (internal
databases). **Publications:** Acquisitions list, monthly. **Special Catalogs:** AV
catalog, annual. **Remarks:** FAX: (919)525-4491.

★11894★
North Carolina (State) Legislative Library (Law)
Legislative Office Bldg.   Phone: (919)733-9390
Raleigh, NC 27603   Cathy L. Martin, Leg.Libn.
Staff: Prof 1; Other 5. **Subjects:** Legislative law. **Holdings:** 13,000 books;
legislative bills and other source materials. **Subscriptions:** 37 journals and
other serials. **Services:** Library open to the public for reference use only.
Computerized Information Services: LEXIS, LEGISNET, Bill Status
System; internal database. **Remarks:** FAX: (919)733-3113. Maintained by
General Assembly of North Carolina.

(North Carolina) State Library of North Carolina
See: **North Carolina (State) Department of Cultural Resources - Division**
  of the State Library (11885)

★11895★
North Carolina State Museum of Natural Sciences - H.H. Brimley
  Memorial Library (Biol Sci)
102 N. Salisbury St.
Box 27647   Phone: (919)733-7450
Raleigh, NC 27611   Dr. Robert G. Wolk, Dir. of Prog.
Founded: 1877. **Staff:** Prof 2. **Subjects:** Natural history, emphasis on North
Carolina and Eastern United States. **Holdings:** 6000 volumes; 12,000
pamphlets and other unbound materials. **Subscriptions:** 119 journals and
other serials. **Services:** Interlibrary loan; copying; library open to the public
for reference use only. **Publications:** Scientific and Popular Works on North
Carolina Natural History; Brimleyana, irregular - by subscription. **Remarks:**
FAX: (919)733-1048. **Staff:** Margaret Cotrufo, Educ.Asst., Lib.

★11896★
North Carolina (State) Office of the Governor - Budget Office -
  Management & Information Services Library (Info Sci)
116 W. Jones St.   Phone: (919)733-7061
Raleigh, NC 27603-8005   Francine Stephenson, Dir., Stat.Sec.
Founded: 1975. **Subjects:** State and Federal statistical publications.
Holdings: 1000 volumes. **Services:** library not open to the public.
Computerized Information Services: log into North Carolina (internal
database). Performs searches on fee basis. **Remarks:** Serves as the North
Carolina State Data Center.

★11897★
North Carolina State Supreme Court Library (Law)
Box 28006   Phone: (919)733-3425
Raleigh, NC 27611-8006   Louise H. Stafford, Libn.
Founded: 1812. **Staff:** Prof 2; Other 4. **Subjects:** Law. **Special Collections:**
North Carolina legal materials; U.S. Government publications depository.
Holdings: 112,606 volumes; 62,227 microfiche. **Subscriptions:** 2861 journals
and other serials. **Services:** Copying; library open to the public. **Remarks:**
Library located at 500 Justice Bldg., 2 E. Morgan St., Raleigh, NC 27601.
Staff: Sylvia A. Selmer, Asst.Libn.

★11898★
North Carolina State University - Burlington Textiles Library (Sci-Engr)
Campus Box 8301   Phone: (919)515-6602
Raleigh, NC 27695-8301   Paul L. Garwig, Hd.
Founded: 1944. **Staff:** Prof 2; Other 2. **Subjects:** Textiles - technology (fiber
and yarn), chemistry, engineering, management; polymer chemistry; fabric
design. **Special Collections:** Spiezman Hosiery Collection (420 items);
Harriss Fabric Collection (4000 items). **Holdings:** 13,724 books; 11,614
bound periodical volumes; 846 reels of microfilm; 80 film loops; 19 VF
drawers of pamphlets and clippings; 7 VF drawers of textile machinery trade
catalogs; 335 video cassettes. **Subscriptions:** 250 journals and other serials;
12 newspapers. **Services:** Interlibrary loan; copying; library open to the
public with restrictions. **Computerized Information Services:** DIALOG
Information Services, STN International; InterNet (electronic mail service).
Performs searches on fee basis. **Networks/Consortia:** Member of SOLINET,
Triangle Research Libraries Network (TRLN). **Publications:** Textile
Pathfinders, irregular. **Remarks:** FAX: (919)515-3926. Electronic mail
address(es): Paul-Garwig@NCSU.edu (InterNet). **Staff:** Cynthia A.
Ruffin, Asst.Libn.

★ 11899 ★
North Carolina State University - D.H. Hill Library - Documents Department (Agri, Sci-Engr)
Campus Box 7111　　　　　　　　Phone: (919)515-3280
Raleigh, NC 27695-7111　　　　　　　Jean Porter, Hd.
Founded: 1923. **Staff:** Prof 3; Other 7. **Subjects:** Agriculture, science and technology, health, aerospace. **Special Collections:** U.S. Patents (complete set); National Technical Information Service (NTIS) reports (724,720 microfiche); Department of Energy (DOE) reports (706,605 microfiche); NASA reports (131,012 microfiche and hardcopy reports); maps (topographic, geographic, outline, road; 26,228); depository for North Carolina government publication, January 1992 to present. **Holdings:** 792,147 U.S. Government publications. **Services:** Interlibrary loan; copying; department open to the public. **Computerized Information Services:** Automated Patent Searching; CD-ROMs (Marcive, 1990 Census, CASSIS/CD-ROM, National Trade Data Base, Japanese Patent Abstracts, Trademark Access, U.S. Exports of Merchandise, U.S. Imports of Merchandise); InterNet (electronic mail service). Performs searches on fee basis. **Networks/Consortia:** Member of SOLINET. **Publications:** List of Committee Hearings, Committee Prints, and Publications of the United States Senate, 99th Congress, 1985-1986, plus later Congresses. **Remarks:** FAX: (919)515-7098. Electronic mail address(es): Jean–Porter@ncsu.edu (InterNet). **Staff:** Juedi Kleindienst, Docs.Libn.; John A. McGeachy, Docs.Libn.; Sandra Lovely, Supv., Microforms Rd.Rm.

★ 11900 ★
North Carolina State University - D.H. Hill Library - Natural Resources Library (Biol Sci, Sci-Engr)
Campus Box 7114
1102 Jordan Hall　　　　　　　Phone: (919)515-2306
Raleigh, NC 27695-7114　　Carolyn Argentati, Hd., Natural Rsrc.Lib.
Founded: 1970. **Staff:** Prof 1; Other 2. **Subjects:** Forest science, wood and paper science, recreation administration, geology, atmospheric science, marine science. **Special Collections:** Remote sensing; U.S. Forest Service reports (12,100). **Holdings:** 15,351 books; 7745 bound periodical volumes; 35 AV programs. **Subscriptions:** 1045 journals and other serials. **Services:** Library open to the public with restrictions. **Automated Operations:** Computerized public access catalog. **Computerized Information Services:** DIALOG Information Services, BRS Information Technologies, NISC; CD-ROMs; InterNet (electronic mail service). Performs searches on fee basis. **Networks/Consortia:** Member of SOLINET. **Remarks:** FAX: (919)515-7231. Electronic mail address(es): CDADHHL@NCSUVM.CC (InterNet).

★ 11901 ★
North Carolina State University - D.H. Hill Library - Technical Information Center (Sci-Engr)
Campus Box 7111　　　　　　　Phone: (919)515-2830
Raleigh, NC 27695-7111　　　　　M. Ronald Simpson, Hd.
Staff: Prof 1; Other 1. **Subjects:** Science, technology, business, management, marketing. **Special Collections:** North Carolina business and industrial firms (newspaper and magazine clipping file). **Holdings:** Figures not available. **Services:** Interlibrary loan; copying; center open to the public. **Computerized Information Services:** DIALOG Information Services; InterNet (electronic mail service). **Publications:** Subject bibliographies; Japanese Serials in the DH Hill Library (1984; book); Guide to Standards in the North Carolina State University Libraries (1989); Networking (1988; technical brief); Setup Reduction (1988; technical brief); Neural Networks (1989; technical brief); A Guide to Basic Sources of Information for Exporters (1990); Simultaneous Engineering (1990); World Class Manufacturing (1990); Design for Assembly (1991); Fixturing for Modern Manufacturing (1991). **Remarks:** The Technical Information Center provides reference and literature searching services to business and industrial firms in North Carolina. FAX: (919)515-7098. Electronic mail address(es): Ron–Simpson@ncsu.edu (InterNet).

★ 11902 ★
North Carolina State University - Harrye B. Lyons Design Library (Plan)
Campus Box 7701　　　　　　　Phone: (919)515-2207
Raleigh, NC 27695-7701　　　　　Caroline S. Carlton, Libn.
Founded: 1942. **Staff:** Prof 1; Other 3. **Subjects:** Architecture, landscape architecture, visual design, product design, urban design. **Special Collections:** Art and architectural history slide collection (59,923 slides). **Holdings:** 27,454 books; 7025 bound periodical volumes; 2500 vertical file materials; 578 pieces of manufacturers' trade literature; 467 maps and plans;

22 films; 48 recordings; 178 student theses. **Subscriptions:** 195 journals and other serials. **Services:** Interlibrary loan; copying; library open to the public with restrictions. **Computerized Information Services:** CD-ROM (Art Index). **Networks/Consortia:** Member of SOLINET. **Special Catalogs:** Slide catalog. **Special Indexes:** Index to the Student Publication of the School of Design. **Remarks:** FAX: (919)515-7330.

★ 11903 ★
North Carolina State University - Herbarium - Library (Biol Sci)
Box 7612　　　　　　　　Phone: (919)515-2700
Raleigh, NC 27695　　　　　　　J.W. Hardin
Founded: 1946. **Staff:** Prof 1. **Subjects:** Plant systematics. **Holdings:** 175 books; 25 reports; 6 microfiche. **Services:** Library open to the public for reference use only. **Remarks:** FAX: (919)515-3436.

★ 11904 ★
North Carolina State University - Learning Resources Library (Educ)
400 Poe Hall
Campus Box 7801　　　　　　　Phone: (919)515-3191
Raleigh, NC 27695　　　　　　Margaret Ann Link, Coord.
Founded: 1964. **Staff:** Prof 2; Other 1. **Subjects:** Education, psychology. **Holdings:** 11,066 volumes; 2872 microfiche; 2890 AV items. **Subscriptions:** 164 journals and other serials; 2 newspapers. **Services:** Copying; library open to the public. **Computerized Information Services:** CD-ROM (ERIC). **Networks/Consortia:** Member of SOLINET. **Remarks:** FAX: (919)515-7634. **Staff:** Chrys Ann Cranford.

★ 11905 ★
North Carolina State University - Libraries (Agri, Sci-Engr, Biol Sci)
Campus Box 7111　　　　　　　Phone: (919)515-2843
Raleigh, NC 27695-7111　　　　　Susan K. Nutter, Dir.
Founded: 1889. **Staff:** Prof 51; Other 168. **Subjects:** Engineering, agriculture, forestry, textiles, architecture, biological sciences, genetics, statistics, economics, social sciences, humanities. **Special Collections:** Tippmann Collection (entomology); forestry; textiles; visual design; veterinary medicine. **Holdings:** 1.4 million volumes; 28,265 maps and plans; 3.29 million microforms. **Subscriptions:** 16,860 journals and other serials. **Services:** Interlibrary loan; copying; library open to the public for reference use only. **Automated Operations:** Computerized public access catalog, cataloging, and circulation. **Computerized Information Services:** OCLC, DIALOG Information Services, STN International, BRS Information Technologies; InfoTrac; CD-ROMs (Disclosure Incorporated, ERIC, AGRICOLA, Applied Science & Technology Index, GOVERNMENT PUBLICATIONS INDEX, Selected Water Resources Abstracts (SWRA), U.S. Patent Classification System, CAB Abstracts, COMPENDEX PLUS, County and City Statistics, Dissertation Abstracts Online, Marcive, NTIS Bibliographic Data Base, Trade Names, Art Index, CASSIS/CD-ROM, INSPEC Ondisc, MEDLINE, MLA International Bibliography, Natural Resources Metabase, Predicasts F&S Indexes, PsycLIT, Textile Technology Digest, Trademark Access, U.S. Exports of Merchandise, U.S. Imports of Merchandise, Census of Population & Housing); InterNet (electronic mail service). **Networks/Consortia:** Member of SOLINET, Triangle Research Libraries Network (TRLN). **Publications:** FOCUS, quarterly - free upon request. **Special Catalogs:** Serials catalog (microfiche). **Remarks:** Figures include holdings for several other North Carolina State University libraries. FAX: (919)515-3628. **Staff:** Donald S. Keener, Adm.; Suzanne Striedieck, Assoc.Dir, Tech.Serv. & Coll.Mgmt.; Charles Gilreath, Assoc.Dir., Pub.Serv.; John Ulmschneider, Asst.Dir., Lib.Sys.; Jinnie Y. Davis, Asst.Dir., Plan. & Res.; Wendy Scott, Prof.Dev. & Educ.Libn.; Walter M. High, Cat.Dept.; Linda P. Fuller, Access Serv.Libn.; Marta Lange, Hd., Ref.Dept.; Jean M. Porter, Hd., Doc.Dept.; M. Ronald Simpson, Hd., Tech.Info.Ctr.; Ann Baker Ward, Hd., ILL Ctr.; Margaret R. Hunt, Hd., Coll.Mgt.; Kathleen Brown, Hd., Acq.Dept.; Maurice Toler, Hd., Archv.

★ 11906 ★
North Carolina State University - Tobacco Literature Service (Agri)
2314 D.H. Hill Library
Campus Box 8009　　　　　　　Phone: (919)515-2836
Raleigh, NC 27695-8009　　　　　Pamela E. Puryear, Dir.
Founded: 1956. **Staff:** Prof 1; Other 2. **Subjects:** Tobacco. **Special Collections:** Tobacco Abstracts (Volume 1 to present, complete). **Holdings:** Figures not available. **Services:** Library open to the public by appointment. **Publications:** Tobacco Abstracts, bimonthly - by subscription or on exchange; Tobacco Literature, a Bibliography, 1979; Recent Advances in Tobacco Science, Proceedings of the Tobacco Chemists' Research Conference; Blue Mold Disease of Tobacco (book). **Remarks:** Alternate telephone number(s): (919)515-2836.

★ 11907 ★
North Carolina State University - Veterinary Medical Library (Med)
College of Veterinary Medicine
4700 Hillsborough St.
Campus Box 8401   Phone: (919)829-4218
Raleigh, NC 27606-1428   Dora Zia, Hd., Vet.Med.Lib.
Founded: 1981. **Staff:** Prof 1; Other 4. **Subjects:** Veterinary medicine, medicine, biology, biochemistry, pharmacology, toxicology, immunology. **Holdings:** 13,500 books; 17,000 bound periodical volumes; 250 autotutorial programs. **Subscriptions:** 1100 journals and other serials. **Services:** Interlibrary loan; copying; SDI; library open to the public. **Automated Operations:** Computerized cataloging. **Computerized Information Services:** DIALOG Information Services, MEDLARS, STN International, OCLC; CD-ROM (MEDLINE, CAB Abstracts, CD PLUS/MEDfive); InterNet (electronic mail service). **Networks/Consortia:** Member of SOLINET. **Remarks:** FAX: (919)829-4400. Electronic mail address(es): Dora–Zia@ncsu.edu (InterNet).

★ 11908 ★
North Central Alabama Regional Council of Governments - Library (Plan)
City Hall Tower, 5th Fl.
Box C
Decatur, AL 35602   Phone: (205)355-4515
Founded: 1966. **Staff:** Prof 10; Other 9. **Subjects:** Planning, education, housing, transportation, finance, drainage, parks, advertisements. **Holdings:** 2000 books; 1000 bound periodical volumes; 1000 other cataloged items. **Subscriptions:** 20 journals and other serials. **Services:** Library open to tri-county area citizens.

★ 11909 ★
North Central Baptist Church - Media Library (Rel-Phil)
518 N.W. 14th Ave.   Phone: (904)373-3341
Gainesville, FL 32601   Lena M. Bush, Media Lib.Dir.
Staff: 10. **Subjects:** Religion, Christian life, children's literature, biography, fiction, crafts, family. **Holdings:** 10,000 books; 100 vertical files; 350 filmstrips; 75 recordings. **Subscriptions:** 10 journals and other serials. **Services:** Interlibrary loan; copying; library open to the public with restrictions.

★ 11910 ★
North Central Bible College - T.J. Jones Memorial Library (Rel-Phil)
910 Elliot Ave., S.   Phone: (612)332-3491
Minneapolis, MN 55404   Dr. John Shirk, Lib.Dir.
Founded: 1930. **Staff:** Prof 3; Other 6. **Subjects:** Bible, theology, missions, sacred music, sign languages and the deaf, liberal arts. **Special Collections:** Archives of Assemblies of God movement (includes materials on the Holy Spirit and Divine Healing). **Holdings:** 60,241 books; 1123 bound periodical volumes; 3874 microforms; pamphlets; filmstrips; recordings; cassettes; videocassettes. **Subscriptions:** 436 journals and other serials; 7 newspapers. **Services:** Interlibrary loan; copying; library open to the public for research only. **Automated Operations:** Computerized cataloging and serials. **Computerized Information Services:** OCLC. **Networks/Consortia:** Member of MINITEX Library Information Network. **Remarks:** FAX: (612)343-4778. **Staff:** Connie Sylvester, Libn.; LaDonna Johnson, Libn.

★ 11911 ★
North Central Bronx Hospital - J.L. Amster Health Sciences Library
3424 Kossuth Ave., Rm. 14A-04
Bronx, NY 10467
Defunct. Holdings absorbed by Montefiore Medical Center - Health Sciences Library.

★ 11912 ★
North Central College - Oesterle Library - Special Collections (Hum)
320 E. School Ave.   Phone: (708)420-3425
Naperville, IL 60540   Carolyn A. Sheehy
Founded: 1861. **Staff:** 10. **Special Collections:** Lincoln Collection (711 titles); Haven Hubbard Collection of English Literature (889 titles); Sang Jazz Collection (249 titles); Sang Limited Editions (88 titles). **Services:** Interlibrary loan; copying; SDI; collections open to the public for reference use only. **Automated Operations:** Computerized cataloging, circulation, and ILL. **Computerized Information Services:** DIALOG Information Services. **Networks/Consortia:** Member of LIBRAS Inc., ILLINET, DuPage Library System. **Publications:** EX LIBRIS (newsletter). **Remarks:** FAX: (708)357-8393. **Staff:** Belinda Cheek, Tech.Serv.Libn., Monographs; Kelly Collins, Pub.Serv.Libn., ILL; Jacklyn Egolf, Pub.Serv.Libn., Circ.; Laura Johnson, Tech.Serv.Libn., Ser.: Sharon Takacs, Sys.Libn.

★ 11913 ★
North Central Minnesota Historical Center - Library (Hist)
Bemidji State University   Phone: (218)755-3349
Bemidji, MN 56601   Carol Eberhardt, Hist.Ctr.Supv.
Staff: Prof 1. **Subjects:** Minnesota politics and government, forestry, local and regional public records, local histories and biographies, school district records, Ojibwe Tribal history. **Special Collections:** Ah-Gwah-Ching State Sanitorium; Minnesota State Senator Gerald L. Willet Papers; Beltrami County records; J. Neils Lumber Company; U.S. Representative Coya Knutson papers; Kenfield Lumber Company; Star Island Cass Lake Oral Interview Project. **Holdings:** 58 books; 28 bound periodical volumes; 404 boxes of manuscripts, documents, papers; 296 volumes of public records; 217 audiotapes; 34 reels of microfilm. **Services:** Copying; library open to the public. **Remarks:** Maintained by Bemidji State University.

★ 11914 ★
North Central Nevada Historical Society - Humboldt Museum - Research Department (Hist)
P.O. Box 819
Maple Ave. & Jungo Rd.   Phone: (702)623-2912
Winnemucca, NV 89445   Pansilee Larson, Cur./Res.
Subjects: History, genealogy. **Special Collections:** Bound newspaper volumes (1900-1983); early family genealogical file and photo collection. **Holdings:** Figures not available.

★ 11915 ★
North Central Regional Educational Laboratory - Resource Center (Educ)
1900 Spring Rd.   Phone: (708)571-4700
Oak Brook, IL 60521   Jan Bakker, Rsrc.Ctr.Adm.
Founded: 1985. **Staff:** 3. **Subjects:** Curriculum and instruction, restructuring schools, education professions, school partnerships, drug-free schools and communities. **Holdings:** 2500 books and reports. **Subscriptions:** 70 journals and other serials; 2 newspapers. **Services:** Library not open to the public; information services can be requested by telephone or mail from persons in Illinois, Indiana, Iowa, Michigan, Minnesota, and Wisconsin. **Special Catalogs:** Product catalog. **Remarks:** FAX: (708)571-4716. **Staff:** Arlene Hough Res.Ctr.Asst.

★ 11916 ★
North Conway Institute - Resource Center - Alcohol and Drugs (Med)
14 Beacon St.   Phone: (617)742-0424
Boston, MA 02106   Rev. David A. Works, Pres.
Founded: 1951. **Staff:** Prof 2. **Subjects:** Alcohol, drugs. **Holdings:** Figures not available. **Subscriptions:** 50 journals and other serials. **Services:** Center open to the public. **Remarks:** Alternate telephone number(s): (617)628-2828.

★ 11917 ★
North Country Hospital & Health Center, Inc. - Medical Library (Med)
Prouty Dr.   Phone: (802)334-7331
Newport, VT 05855   Marika Szabo, Libn.
Founded: 1971. **Staff:** Prof 1. **Subjects:** Medicine, nursing. **Holdings:** 400 books. **Subscriptions:** 75 journals and other serials. **Services:** Interlibrary loan; copying; SDI; library open to hospital health personnel, students, and agencies affiliated with the hospital. **Automated Operations:** Computerized ILL (DOCLINE). **Computerized Information Services:** MEDLINE. Performs searches on fee basis. **Networks/Consortia:** Member of North Country Consortium (NCC), Health Science Libraries of New Hampshire & Vermont (HSL-NH/VT), North Atlantic Health Science Libraries (NAHSL). **Remarks:** FAX: (802) 334-8874.

★ 11918 ★
North Country Reference & Research Resources Council - Library (Info Sci)
P.O. Box 568   Phone: (315)386-4569
Canton, NY 13617   John Hammond, Exec.Dir.
Founded: 1965. **Staff:** Prof 3; Other 4. **Subjects:** Library networking, bibliographic access. **Special Collections:** Specialized bibliographic tools for interlibrary loan. **Holdings:** 500 books; library catalogs on 500 microfiche. **Subscriptions:** 15 journals and other serials. **Services:** Interlibrary loan; copying; library service to hospital libraries. **Automated Operations:** Computerized acquisitions and serials. **Computerized Information Services:** BRS Information Technologies; electronic mail service. **Publications:** Points

North (newsletter), monthly. **Special Catalogs:** Union List of Serials; catalogs of regional holdings; North Country Historical Materials; regional book and serials catalog (CD-ROM). **Remarks:** FAX: (315)379-9553. Council is one of 9 New York state systems improving reference and research services to New York state libraries and their patrons. It is supported by funds from New York State Department of Education and member libraries. **Staff:** Thomas Blauvelt, Hd., Ref.Serv.; Bridget Doyle, Reg.Serv.Coord.

★ 11919 ★
North Dakota Farmers Union - Lulu Evanson Resource Library (Agri)
1415 12th Ave., S.E.
Box 2136   Phone: (701)252-2340
Jamestown, ND 58401   Karl Limvere, State Sec.
Founded: 1927. **Staff:** Prof 1. **Subjects:** Agricultural and land use policy, cooperatives, North Dakota Legislature, transportation, social concerns. **Special Collections:** Farmers Union historical materials. **Holdings:** 3100 volumes; 25 slide programs. **Subscriptions:** 30 journals and other serials; 25 newspapers. **Services:** Interlibrary loan; library open to the public with restrictions. **Remarks:** FAX: (701)252-0404.

North Dakota Institute for Regional Studies
See: **North Dakota State University** (11929)

★ 11920 ★
North Dakota State College of Science - Mildred Johnson Library
(Educ)
Wahpeton, ND 58076   Phone: (701)671-2298
                                              Jerald Stewart, Lib.Dir.
Founded: 1903. **Staff:** Prof 4; Other 5. **Subjects:** Vocational education and technology, auto mechanics, electronics, dental hygiene, business, nursing, computers. **Holdings:** 74,000 books; 3500 bound periodical volumes; 5 drawers of major U.S. corporation reports and information; 32 VF drawers of pamphlets; 600 videotapes; 10 file drawers of microfiche; 920 nonprint kits; 1200 cassettes and recordings. **Subscriptions:** 925 journals and other serials; 35 newspapers. **Services:** Interlibrary loan; library open to the public with restrictions. **Computerized Information Services:** OCLC, ERIC, Applied Science & Technology Index, DIALOG Information Services, WILSONLINE; CD-ROM (The Serials Directory/EBSCO CD-ROM); InfoTrac. **Networks/Consortia:** Member of MINITEX Library Information Network. **Remarks:** Library is the National Library of the American Technical Education Association (ATEA). FAX: (701)671-2148. **Staff:** Mary Kroshus, Tech.Serv.; Gloria Dohman, Ref.; Dan Koper, Circ.

★ 11921 ★
North Dakota State Department of Health - Division of Health
   Promotion & Education (Med)
600 E. Boulevard Ave.   Phone: (701)224-2368
Bismarck, ND 58505-0200   Lynette Pitzer, Film Libn.
Staff: Prof 1. **Subjects:** Health. **Holdings:** 1025 16mm films and videotapes; 800 pamphlet titles. **Subscriptions:** 25 journals and other serials. **Services:** Film and pamphlet distribution throughout state; division open to health professionals. **Special Catalogs:** Health Films and Materials Catalog; Behavioral Health Risks of North Dakotans; Tobacco, Health and the Bottom Line; Cancer in North Dakota: The Need for Change.

★ 11922 ★
North Dakota (State) Department of Public Instruction - North Dakota
   State Film Library (Aud-Vis)
State University Sta., Box 5036   Phone: (701)239-7285
Fargo, ND 58105-5036   Lillian M. Wadnizak, Lib.Mgr.
Staff: Prof 1; Other 6. **Holdings:** 8000 16mm films; 4500 video cassettes. **Services:** Library open to the public. **Special Catalogs:** Film catalog, biennial. **Remarks:** FAX: (701)239-7288. Located at North Dakota State University - Division of Independent Study.

North Dakota State Film Library
See: **North Dakota (State) Department of Public Instruction - North Dakota State Film Library** (11922)

★ 11923 ★
North Dakota State Hospital - Health Science Library (Med)
Box 476   Phone: (701)253-3679
Jamestown, ND 58402-0476   Denise K. Pahl, Act.Hd.
Founded: 1959. **Staff:** Prof 1; Other 1. **Subjects:** Psychiatry, psychology, psychiatric rehabilitation, nursing, medicine, social work, alcoholism and addiction. **Special Collections:** Biennial Reports, 1890 to present; employee magazine, 1953-1986. **Holdings:** 3800 books; 3563 bound periodical volumes; 600 cassettes; 35 videocassettes; 44 biennial reports; 35 cases of pamphlets and miscellanea; 26 therapy films; 47 AV programs. **Subscriptions:** 103 journals and other serials. **Services:** Interlibrary loan; copying; library open to college students. **Automated Operations:** Computerized public access catalog (ODIN). **Computerized Information Services:** MEDLINE. Performs searches on fee basis. **Networks/Consortia:** Member of Valley Medical Network (VMN). **Special Catalogs:** Periodical Catalog (card). **Remarks:** FAX: (701)253-3999.

★ 11924 ★
North Dakota State Library (Info Sci)
Liberty Memorial Bldg.
Capitol Grounds
604 E. Boulevard Ave.   Phone: (701)224-2492
Bismarck, ND 58505-0800   Patricia Harris, State Libn.
Founded: 1907. **Staff:** Prof 7; Other 18. **Subjects:** North Dakota, state government, library science, music, education. **Holdings:** 110,000 books; 20,000 tape cassettes; state documents, 1904 to present. **Subscriptions:** 100 journals and other serials; 15 newspapers. **Services:** Interlibrary loan; copying; library open to the public. **Automated Operations:** Computerized cataloging and circulation. **Computerized Information Services:** DIALOG Information Services; ALANET, EasyLink (electronic mail services). **Networks/Consortia:** Member of North Dakota Network for Knowledge, MINITEX Library Information Network. **Publications:** Flickertale Newsletter, bimonthly. **Remarks:** FAX: (701)224-2040. Electronic mail address(es): 0711 (ALANET); 62755117 (EasyLink). **Staff:** Doris Daugherty, Dir., Info.Serv.; Susan Pahlmeyer, Hd., Ref.; Shirley Flood, Hd., ILL; Mark Bowman, Hd., Cat.; Betty Day, Hd., Circ.; Brian Erickson, Automation; Sue Clark, Cont.Educ.Coord.; Eric Halvorson, Pub.Lib.Cons.; Mike Jaugstetter, Pub.Lib.Cons.; Nancy Maxwell, Pub.Libn.Cons.

★ 11925 ★
North Dakota State Supreme Court Law Library (Law)
2nd Fl. Judicial Wing
600 E. Boulevard Ave.   Phone: (701)224-2229
Bismarck, ND 58505-0530   Marcella Kramer, Law Libn.
Founded: 1889. **Staff:** Prof 2; Other 1. **Subjects:** Law. **Special Collections:** U.S. Government depository. **Holdings:** 66,374 volumes. **Subscriptions:** 44 journals and other serials. **Services:** Interlibrary loan; copying; library open to the public for reference use only. **Staff:** Sheryl Stradinger, Cat.Libn.; Rosemary Sperle, Tech.Serv.

★ 11926 ★
North Dakota State University - Architecture and Landscape
   Architecture Library (Plan)
University Sta.
Fargo, ND 58105-5599   Phone: (701)237-8616
Staff: 1. **Subjects:** Architecture. **Special Collections:** Slide collection (26,000). **Holdings:** 7500 books; 1880 bound periodical volumes. **Subscriptions:** 112 journals and other serials. **Services:** Interlibrary loan; copying; library open to the public with restrictions. **Automated Operations:** Computerized public access catalog, cataloging, and circulation. **Remarks:** FAX: (701)237-7138.

★ 11927 ★
North Dakota State University - Bottineau Library (Biol Sci)
First & Simrall Blvd.   Phone: (701)228-2277
Bottineau, ND 58318   Jan Wysocki, Lib.Dir.
Founded: 1907. **Staff:** Prof 1. **Subjects:** Forestry, botany, horticulture. **Special Collections:** Fossum Foundation Collection (horticulture; 500 volumes). **Holdings:** 26,000 books. **Subscriptions:** 225 journals and other serials; 50 newspapers. **Services:** Interlibrary loan; copying; library open to the public. **Computerized Information Services:** FYI News. Performs searches on fee basis. **Networks/Consortia:** Member of MINITEX Library Information Network. **Remarks:** FAX: (701)228-2277, ext. 233.

★ 11928 ★

North Dakota State University - H.J. Klosterman Chemistry Library
(Sci-Engr)
Ladd Hall
University Sta.   Phone: (701)237-8293
Fargo, ND 58105-5599   Mary Markland, Libn.
Staff: 2. **Subjects:** Chemistry, biochemistry, polymers and coatings.
Holdings: 8298 books. **Subscriptions:** 198 journals and other serials.
Services: Interlibrary loan; copying; center open to the public with
restrictions. **Automated Operations:** Computerized public access catalog,
cataloging, and circulation. **Computerized Information Services:** DIALOG
Information Services, STN International, MEDLINE; BITNET (electronic
mail service). Performs searches on fee basis. **Remarks:** FAX: (701)237-
7138; Electronic mail address(es): NU157027@NDSUVM1 (BITNET).

★ 11929 ★

North Dakota State University - North Dakota Institute for Regional
Studies (Hist)
University Sta., Box 5599   Phone: (701)237-8914
Fargo, ND 58105-5599   John E. Bye, Archv.
Founded: 1950. **Staff:** Prof 1. **Subjects:** North Dakota - history, literature,
writers; bonanza farming; pioneer reminiscences; land development. **Special**
Collections: Hultstrand History in Pictures Collection (500 photographs of
sod houses and pioneer life in North Dakota); Germans from Russia
Heritage Collection (500 volumes); F.A. Pazandak Collection (175 prints
and negatives of early farm mechanization in North Dakota); Fargo city
records; women's organizations. **Holdings:** 5000 books; 550 bound
periodical volumes; 1100 linear feet of manuscripts; 35,000 photographs; 200
linear feet of university archives; 500 maps. **Subscriptions:** 42 journals and
other serials. **Services:** Copying; library open to the public. **Automated**
Operations: Computerized public access catalog and cataloging.
Computerized Information Services: Internal database; BITNET (electronic
mail service). **Publications:** North Dakota Institute for Regional Studies
Guide to Manuscripts and Archives (1985); Researching the Germans from
Russia: Annotated Bibliography of the Germans from Russia Heritage
Collection (1987); From the Northern Prairies (laser videodisc) and
accompanying guide (1991). **Special Catalogs:** Union List of North Dakota
Newspapers, 1864-1976. **Special Indexes:** North Dakota Biography Index
(card); Spectrum (North Dakota State University student newspaper) index,
1940-1980; Photograph Collection Index (card). **Remarks:** (701)237-7138.
Electronic mail address(es): NUO23101@NDSUVM1 (BITNET).

★ 11930 ★

North Dakota State University - Pharmacy Library (Med)
Sudro Hall
University Sta.   Phone: (701)237-7748
Fargo, ND 58105-5599   Linda Schultz, Supv.
Staff: 2. **Subjects:** Pharmacy, nursing. **Holdings:** 6130 books. **Subscriptions:**
265 journals and other serials. **Services:** Interlibrary loan; copying; center
open to the public with restrictions. **Automated Operations:** Computerized
public access catalog, cataloging, and circulation. **Computerized**
Information Services: DIALOG Information Services, MEDLINE, STN
International; CD-ROM (MEDLINE); BITNET (electronic mail service).
Performs searches on fee basis. **Networks/Consortia:** Member of Valley
Medical Network (VMN). **Remarks:** FAX: (701)237-7138. Electronic mail
address(es): NU019970@NDSUVM1 (BITNET).

★ 11931 ★

North Detroit General Hospital - Medical Library (Med)
3105 Carpenter
Detroit, MI 48212   Phone: (313)369-3000
Staff: Prof 1. **Subjects:** Clinical medicine, surgery, nursing, allied health
sciences. **Holdings:** 400 books; 100 bound periodical volumes. **Subscriptions:**
65 journals and other serials. **Services:** Interlibrary loan; library not open
to the public. **Computerized Information Services:** MEDLARS.

★ 11932 ★

North East Multi Regional Training (NEMRT) - Library (Law)
1 Smoke Tree Plaza, Suite 111   Phone: (708)896-8860
North Aurora, IL 60542   Sarah Cole
Founded: 1988. **Staff:** Prof 1. **Subjects:** Law enforcement. **Holdings:** 1500
books; 300 reports. **Subscriptions:** 30 journals and other serials. **Services:**
Interlibrary loan; library not open to the public.

★ 11933 ★

North General Hospital - Medical Library (Med)
1919 Madison Ave.   Phone: (212)650-4475
New York, NY 10035   Robert Feinstein, Hd.Libn.
Staff: Prof 1; Other 1. **Subjects:** Medicine. **Holdings:** 2500 books; 5400
bound periodical volumes; 3 VF drawers of clippings. **Subscriptions:** 125
journals and other serials. **Services:** Interlibrary loan; copying; library open
to health science professionals and health science students by appointment.
Automated Operations: Computerized ILL. **Computerized Information**
Services: DOCLINE (electronic mail service). **Networks/Consortia:**
Member of Medical Library Center of New York (MLCNY), Manhattan-
Bronx Health Sciences Library Consortia, New York Metropolitan
Reference and Research Library Agency, National Network of Libraries of
Medicine (NN/LM).

★ 11934 ★

North Hills Passavant Hospital - Medical Library (Med)
9100 Babcock Blvd.   Phone: (412)367-6320
Pittsburgh, PA 15237   Margaret U. Trevanion, Dir., Lib.Serv.
Founded: 1971. **Staff:** Prof 1; Other 6. **Subjects:** Medicine, nursing.
Holdings: 2419 books; 4428 bound periodical volumes; 7 VF drawers of
pamphlets. **Subscriptions:** 192 journals and other serials. **Services:**
Interlibrary loan; copying; SDI; library open to the public for reference use
only. **Automated Operations:** Computerized cataloging, serials, and ILL.
Computerized Information Services: BRS Information Technologies, NLM;
internal databases; DOCLINE (electronic mail service). Performs searches
on fee basis. **Networks/Consortia:** Member of National Network of
Libraries of Medicine - Middle Atlantic Region, Pittsburgh-East Hospital
Library Cooperative. **Publications:** NHPH Library News, monthly;
bibliographies. **Remarks:** FAX: (412)367-4776.

★ 11935 ★

North Kansas City Hospital - Medical Library (Med)
2800 Clay Edwards Dr.   Phone: (816)691-1692
North Kansas City, MO 64116   Anne Butler, Med.Libn.
Founded: 1976. **Staff:** Prof 1. **Subjects:** Clinical medicine, nursing,
pharmacy, allied health sciences, mental health. **Holdings:** 2200 books; 1700
reels of microfilm. **Subscriptions:** 220 journals and other serials. **Services:**
Interlibrary loan; copying; SDI; library open to the public for reference use
only. **Automated Operations:** Computerized serials and ILL. **Computerized**
Information Services: BRS Information Technologies, NLM; DOCLINE
(electronic mail service). Performs searches on fee basis. **Networks/**
Consortia: Member of Kansas City Library Network, Inc. (KCLN).
Remarks: FAX: (816)691-1082.

★ 11936 ★

North Memorial Medical Center - Medical Library (Med)
3300 Oakdale, N.   Phone: (612)520-5673
Robbinsdale, MN 55422   Donna Barbour-Talley, Mgr., Med.Lib.
Founded: 1968. **Staff:** Prof 2; Other 2. **Subjects:** Medicine, nursing,
dentistry, paramedical sciences. **Special Collections:** Health Information
Collection (850 books; 15 magazine titles; 1000 pamphlets). **Holdings:** 2300
books; 5100 bound periodical volumes; 700 audiotape cassettes; 350
pamphlets; 500 journal volumes on microfiche. **Subscriptions:** 525 journals
and other serials; 5 newspapers. **Services:** Interlibrary loan; copying; SDI;
library is open for professional reference use by permission. **Automated**
Operations: Computerized acquisitions and serials. **Computerized**
Information Services: DIALOG Information Services, WILSONLINE,
BRS Information Technologies, MEDLARS, Human Resource
Information Network (HRIN), BIOSIS. Performs searches on fee basis.
Contact Person: Patrick Costigan, Libn., 520-5678. **Networks/Consortia:**
Member of Twin Cities Biomedical Consortium (TCBC), Metronet,
National Network of Libraries of Medicine - Greater Midwest Region.
Remarks: Alternate telephone number(s): 520-5675. FAX: (612)520-1453.

★ 11937 ★

North Mississippi Medical Center - Resource Center (Med)
830 S. Gloster St.   Phone: (601)841-4399
Tupelo, MS 38801   Mary Lillian Randle, Educ.Res.Coord.
Founded: 1975. **Staff:** Prof 2; Other 2. **Subjects:** Medicine, nursing, health
care administration. **Holdings:** 1150 books; 1000 periodical volumes.
Subscriptions: 111 journals and other serials. **Services:** Interlibrary loan;
copying; center open to staff and health care students only. **Computerized**
Information Services: MEDLARS; DOCLINE (electronic mail service).
Networks/Consortia: Member of Mississippi Biomedical Library
Consortium (MBLC). **Staff:** Marty Davis, Media Spec.

★ 11938 ★
North Oakland Genealogical Society - Library (Hist)
Orion Township Public Library
825 Joslyn Rd.   Phone: (313)693-3000
Lake Orion, MI 48362   Linda Sickles, Dir.
Founded: 1977. **Staff:** 1. **Subjects:** Local history, genealogy. **Special Collections:** Original abstracts of land from Oakland and Wayne Counties, Michigan; family histories. **Holdings:** 1200 books; microfiche; members' ancestral charts; census records; tax records; cemetery documentation. **Subscriptions:** 100 journals and other serials. **Services:** Copying; library open to the public; special collections open to the public by appointment. **Publications:** Heir-Lines, quarterly - to members or by subscription; Oxford Township Cemetery Books. **Special Indexes:** Surname card file. **Remarks:** Housed at Orion Township Public Library.

★ 11939 ★
North Oakland Medical Center - Library/Media Department (Med)
Seminole & W. Huron   Phone: (313)857-7412
Pontiac, MI 48053   Naim K. Sahyoun, Dir., Media Serv./Lib./AV
Staff: Prof 2; Other 2. **Subjects:** Medicine, health care administration, nursing. **Holdings:** 3000 books; 10,000 bound periodical volumes; Audio-Digest tapes. **Subscriptions:** 400 journals and other serials. **Services:** Interlibrary loan; copying; SDI; library open to nursing and allied health students and physicians. **Computerized Information Services:** NLM, DIALOG Information Services, BRS Information Technologies. Performs searches on fee basis. **Publications:** For Your Information. **Formerly:** Pontiac General Hospital.

★ 11940 ★
North Olympic Library System - Port Angeles Branch - Pacific Northwest Room (Hist)
207 S. Lincoln St.   Phone: (206)452-9253
Port Angeles, WA 98362   Leslie Spotkov, Br.Mgr.
Founded: 1969. **Staff:** Prof 2; Other 3. **Subjects:** Local history. **Special Collections:** Kellogg Photo Collection (5263 negatives; 8252 prints); oral history tapes on Clallam County people and industries (55 tapes). **Holdings:** 80 books; 960 bound newspaper volumes, 1916 to present; 366 reels of microfilm. **Subscriptions:** 4 journals and other serials; 3 newspapers. **Services:** Northwest Room open to the public. **Networks/Consortia:** Member of Western Library Network (WLN). **Special Indexes:** Index to Peninsula Daily News, 1971 to present. **Staff:** Peggy M. Brady, Ref.Coord.; Beth Witters, Libn.

★ 11941 ★
North Park Baptist Church - Library (Rel-Phil)
2605 Rex Cruse Dr.   Phone: (903)892-8429
Sherman, TX 75090   Mrs. Jack Raidt, Dir. of Lib.Serv.
Founded: 1958. **Staff:** 5. **Subjects:** Bible, Baptist doctrine, Christian life, missions, history, recreation. **Holdings:** 4500 books; recordings; filmstrips; slides; VF materials; 8 8mm and 16mm movies; 40 cassette tapes; 18 videotapes. **Subscriptions:** 15 journals and other serials. **Services:** Interlibrary loan; copying; library open to the public.

★ 11942 ★
North Park College and Theological Seminary - Consolidated Libraries (Rel-Phil)
3225 W. Foster   Phone: (312)583-2700
Chicago, IL 60625   Dorothy-Ellen Gross, Assoc. Dean
Founded: 1891. **Staff:** Prof 7; Other 3. **Subjects:** Theology, Evangelical Covenant Church, Scandinavian studies, music, nursing, Swedish studies. **Special Collections:** Jenny Lind Collection (24 linear feet of books, manuscripts and memorabilia); Walter Johnson Collection in Scandinavian studies (600 volumes); Paul L. Holmer Collection (5000 volumes); G. Anderson Lincoln Collection (700 volumes); Harald Jacobson China Studies Collection (3000 volumes); Nils William Olsson Collection (3500 volumes). **Holdings:** 210,000 books and bound periodical volumes; 16,000 AV titles; 50 linear feet of vertical file materials; 8000 microforms. **Subscriptions:** 975 journals and other serials; 24 newspapers. **Services:** Interlibrary loan; copying; SDI; library open to the public with restrictions. **Automated Operations:** Computerized cataloging, acquisitions, serials, and ILL. **Computerized Information Services:** DIALOG Information Services, OCLC; InfoTrac Expanded Academic Index; CD-ROMs (ERIC, Religion Index, Religious and Theological Abstracts, General BusinessFile, CINAHL). **Networks/Consortia:** Member of ILLINET, Association of Chicago Theological Schools Library Council, National Network of

Libraries of Medicine - Greater Midwest Region, LIBRAS Inc., Chicago Library System, Metropolitan Consortium of Chicago. **Publications:** Library guide; Library Instruction for Freshmen; Traditions of the West; Authors' Festival (bibliography). **Remarks:** FAX: (312)463-0570. **Staff:** Norma S. Goertzen, Seminary Libn.; Eileen S. Karsten, Hd., Tech.Serv.; Sonia Bodi, Hd.Ref.Libn.; Sarah Anderson, Ref. & Ser. Libn.; Ann Briody, Circ.Libn.; Steven Forbes, Dir., Instr. Media; Coleen O'Connor, Cat. & Sys.Libn.

★ 11943 ★
North Princeton Developmental Center - Health Services Library (Med)
Gerry Bldg.
Box 1000   Phone: (609)466-0400
Princeton, NJ 08543-1000   W.R. Thompson, MD, Med.Dir.
Founded: 1955. **Staff:** 1. **Subjects:** Psychiatry, psychology, mental retardation, medicine. **Holdings:** 945 books. **Subscriptions:** 30 journals and other serials. **Services:** Library open to specialists in library's fields of interest. **Special Catalogs:** National Library of Medicine Classification. **Staff:** R. Brinckerhoff.

★ 11944 ★
North Rhine-Westphalia State Agency for Air Pollution and Noise Abatement - Library (Env-Cons)
Wallneyer Str. 6   Phone: 201 7995456
W-4300 Essen 1, Germany   Dietrich Plass, Reg.Dir.
Founded: 1972. **Staff:** Prof 3. **Subjects:** Air pollution - emission sources, control methods, measurement methods, atmospheric interactions, air quality measurements, effects on plants and materials; noise pollution - vibration, noise control planning. **Holdings:** 30,000 bound volumes. **Subscriptions:** 260 journals and other serials. **Services:** SDI; library open to the public. **Computerized Information Services:** Literature Information System (LISDOK, internal database). Performs searches. **Remarks:** FAX: 201 7995446. **Also Known As:** Landesanstalt fur Immissionsschutz Nordrhein- Westfalen. **Staff:** C. Olbrich; A. Gartner.

★ 11945 ★
North Rhine-Westphalian Public Record Office - Detmold and North Rhine-Westphalian Archive of Vital Statistics - Westphalia-Lippe (Hist)
Willi-Hofmann-Str 2   Phone: 5231 7660
W-4930 Detmold, Germany   Dr. Klaus Scholz, Mng.Dir.
Staff: Prof 1. **Subjects:** East Westphalia-Lippe - local history, geography. **Holdings:** 57,000 books. **Subscriptions:** 180 journals and other serials; 5 newspapers. **Services:** Copying; library open to the public for reference use only. **Special Catalogs:** Subject catalog; catalog of geographic names. **Remarks:** FAX: 5231 766114. **Also Known As:** Nordrhein Westfalisches Staatsarchiv Detmold und Nordrhein - Westfalisches Personenstandsarchiv Westfalen Lippe - Bibliothek.

★ 11946 ★
North St. Paul Historical Society - Museum Library (Hist)
2666 E. 7th Ave.   Phone: (612)770-2579
North St. Paul, MN 55109   Betty Lyon, Cur.
Subjects: North St. Paul - history, residents and families, businesses, homes, schools, churches. **Holdings:** Figures not available. **Services:** Library open to the public.

★ 11947 ★
North Shore Congregation Israel - Romanek Cultural Center - Oscar Hillel Plotkin Adult Library (Rel-Phil)
1185 Sheridan Rd.   Phone: (708)835-0724
Glencoe, IL 60022   Manuel Silver, Ph.D.
Founded: 1952. **Staff:** Prof 1. **Subjects:** Religions, philosophy and ethics, the Bible, Apocrypha, sociology, rabbinic literature, music, history of the Jews, Yiddish and Hebrew languages, Jewish biography, Jewish fiction, Zionism and Israel. **Special Collections:** Archeology; Jewish genealogy; Jewish art books. **Holdings:** 17,850 books; 150 bound periodical volumes; tapes; film; scripts; pamphlets; clippings; archives; video cassettes. **Subscriptions:** 85 journals and other serials; 10 newspapers. **Services:** Library open to the public. **Networks/Consortia:** Member of Judaica Library Network of Chicago, North Suburban Library System (NSLS). **Remarks:** FAX: (708)835-5613. Maintains the Barbara and Eli Fink Memorial Children's Library.

★ 11948 ★

North Shore Medical Center - Medical Library (Med)
1100 N.W. 95th St.   Phone: (305)835-6000
Miami, FL 33150   Stephanie Thomas, Supr.
Subjects: Surgery, pathology, thoracic medicine, cancer, dermatology, pharmacology. **Holdings:** 250 books; 44 bound periodical volumes; 30 pamphlets; 47 films. **Subscriptions:** 26 journals and other serials. **Services:** Library not open to the public.

★ 11949 ★

North Shore Synagogue - Charles Cohn Memorial Library (Rel-Phil)
83 Muttontown Rd.   Phone: (516)921-2282
Syosset, NY 11791   Ester Blumen, Libn.
Staff: Prof 1. **Subjects:** Jewish history, religion, and culture. **Special Collections:** Juvenile books. **Holdings:** 4000 volumes; phonograph records; 100 sound filmstrips; 150 silent filmstrips; VF drawers. **Subscriptions:** 20 journals and other serials. **Services:** Library not open to the public.

★ 11950 ★

North Shore University Hospital - Daniel Carroll Payson Medical Library (Med)
300 Community Dr.   Phone: (516)562-4324
Manhasset, NY 11030   Debra Eisenberg, Dir.
Founded: 1953. **Staff:** Prof 4; Other 1. **Subjects:** Clinical medicine, nursing, psychiatry, allied health sciences. **Holdings:** 5359 books; 13,622 bound periodical volumes; 2418 AV programs. **Subscriptions:** 806 journals and other serials. **Services:** Interlibrary loan; library not open to the public. **Computerized Information Services:** Mead Data Central, BRS Information Technologies, NLM, DIALOG Information Services; CD-ROM (MEDLINE Knowledge Finder). **Networks/Consortia:** Member of Long Island Library Resources Council, Medical Library Center of New York (MLCNY). **Publications:** Book lists. **Remarks:** FAX: (516)562-2865. Maintains a branch library in Glen Cove, NY. **Staff:** Ellen Rothbaum, Assoc.Libn.; Katherine Zippert, Asst.Libn.; James Redman, Libn., Glen Cove.

★ 11951 ★

North Slope Borough School District - Media Center - Library (Hum)
Pouch 8950   Phone: (907)852-8950
Barrow, AK 99723   Christina S. Barron
Staff: Prof 1; Other 1. **Special Collections:** Inupiaq language and culture collection (300 items). **Holdings:** 8000 books; 3500 AV items. **Subscriptions:** 75 journals and other serials; 2 newspapers. **Services:** Interlibrary loan; copying; library open to the public. **Remarks:** FAX: (907)852-8969.

North Star Library
See: Sons of Norway International (15375)

★ 11952 ★

North Suburban Library System - Professional Information Center (Info Sci)
200 W. Dundee   Phone: (708)459-1300
Wheeling, IL 60090   Dr. Elliott E. Kanner, Rsrcs.Coord.
Founded: 1969. **Staff:** Prof 1; Other 1. **Subjects:** Library science, information science, adult and continuing education. **Holdings:** 5490 volumes; 75 annual and technical reports; policy and procedure manuals; microfiche; kits; cassettes; videotapes. **Subscriptions:** 200 journals and other serials. **Services:** Interlibrary loan; copying; center open to the public by appointment. **Automated Operations:** Computerized cataloging and circulation. **Computerized Information Services:** OCLC. Performs searches free of charge. **Networks/Consortia:** Member of North Suburban Library System (NSLS), ILLINET. **Publications:** Nor'easter, monthly; Bulletin Board, weekly; special reports and bibliographies prepared on request. **Remarks:** FAX: (708)459-0380.

★ 11953 ★

North Suburban Library System & Suburban Library System - Suburban AV Service (Aud-Vis)
920 Barnsdale Rd.   Phone: (708)352-7671
La Grange Park, IL 60525   Ron MacIntyre, Dir.
Founded: 1970. **Staff:** Prof 2; Other 30. **Subjects:** Motion picture history and industry; AV technology; consumer electronics: video and home computers.

Holdings: 1000 books; film bibliographies; files of media distributors and producers; 16,000 video cassettes; videocassettes captioned for the deaf; 4800 16mm films; 16,000 audio recordings. **Subscriptions:** 160 journals and other serials. **Services:** Interlibrary loan; copying; SDI; tape duplication; service open to the public with restrictions. **Automated Operations:** Computerized cataloging and circulation. **Computerized Information Services:** SAVS Database (internal database). **Networks/Consortia:** Member of ILLINET. **Publications:** SAVS Short Subjects, monthly - for internal distribution only. **Remarks:** SAVS is a support service for libraries providing AV materials and reference service. FAX: (708)352-7528. **Staff:** Dennis Huslig, AV Cons.

★ 11954 ★

North Suburban Synagogue Beth El - Joseph and Mae Gray Cultural Learning Center - Maxwell Abbell Library (Rel-Phil)
1175 Sheridan Rd.   Phone: (708)432-8900
Highland Park, IL 60035   Cheryl Banks, Dir.
Founded: 1987. **Staff:** Prof 1; Other 2. **Subjects:** Judaica. **Special Collections:** Holocaust; Yiddish. **Holdings:** 10,000 books; 100 bound periodical volumes; 350 phonograph records; 3 VF drawers of pamphlets; 150 filmstrips; 225 videotapes; 50 audiotapes. **Subscriptions:** 50 journals and other serials. **Services:** Interlibrary loan; library open to the public.

★ 11955 ★

North Texas Medical Center - Library (Med)
1800 N. Graves St.   Phone: (214)548-3000
McKinney, TX 75069   Patricia Gidney, Med. Staff Coord.
Founded: 1958. **Subjects:** Medicine. **Holdings:** 150 volumes. **Services:** Library not open to the public. **Remarks:** FAX: (214)548-1425.

★ 11956 ★

North United Presbyterian Church - Library (Rel-Phil)
3410 W. Silver Spring Dr.
Milwaukee, WI 53209-4092   Phone: (414)466-1870
Founded: 1960. **Staff:** 1. **Subjects:** Religion, Bible, children's books, biographies. **Holdings:** 1000 books. **Services:** Library not open to the public.

★ 11957 ★

North West Frontier Province Agricultural University - Library (Agri)
Peshawar, Pakistan   Phone: 512 4023039
Founded: 1962. **Staff:** Prof 6; Other 9. **Subjects:** Agriculture. **Holdings:** 66,800 books; 3000 bound periodical volumes; 200 reports; 1300 microfiche. **Subscriptions:** 164 journals and other serials; 7 newspapers. **Services:** Copying; SDI; library open to the public for reference use only. **Automated Operations:** Computerized serials (INMAGIC). **Computerized Information Services:** CD-ROMs (AGRICOLA, CAB). **Publications:** AULIB Database Manual; Directory of Serials in the NWFP Agriculture University Library.

★ 11958 ★

North York Board of Education - The F.W. Minkler Library (Educ)
Education Administration Centre
5050 Yonge St.   Phone: (416)225-4661
North York, ON, Canada M2N 5N8   L. Lyons, Sr.Libn.
Founded: 1957. **Staff:** Prof 3; Other 4. **Subjects:** Education, psychology, sociology. **Special Collections:** Board Archives (24 drawers); F.W. Minkler Historical Text Collection (1000 volumes). **Holdings:** 22,000 books; ERIC microfiche, 1971 to present; 40 drawers of clippings and pamphlets. **Subscriptions:** 500 journals and other serials; 5 newspapers. **Services:** Interlibrary loan; copying; SDI; library open to the public for reference use only. **Automated Operations:** Computerized public access catalog. **Computerized Information Services:** BRS Information Technologies, DIALOG Information Services, CAN/OLE, Info Globe, WILSONLINE, Infomart Online; CD-ROMs (Books in Print Plus, Ulrich's Plus, DIALOG OnDisc, ERIC, Canadian Business and Current Affairs (CBCA), Education Index, Readers' Guide to Periodical Literature, CD:Education). Performs searches on fee basis to outside users with contracts. **Networks/Consortia:** Member of Education Libraries Sharing of Resources Network (ELSOR). **Publications:** Inside the Journals, monthly; Bound to Interest, monthly; newsletters and bibliographies, irregular. **Special Indexes:** Where to look for VF material (card). **Remarks:** FAX: (416)229-5542.

★ 11959 ★
North York Central Library - Business and Urban Affairs Department - Urban Affairs Section (Plan)
5120 Yonge St., 4th Fl.   Phone: (416)395-5699
North York, ON, Canada M2N 5N9   Harry McLeod, Dept.Mgr.
Founded: 1977. **Staff:** Prof 1; Other 1. **Subjects:** Urban and regional planning; municipal housing, government, finance, and services; urban transportation; waste management; zoning and land use, emphasizing North York and the metropolitan Toronto area. **Special Collections:** North York aerial photographs; North York Council, Committee, Board, and Department agendas, reports, and minutes; North York Municipal Voters' Lists; North York Assessment and Numbering Sheets. **Holdings:** 6000 items; 20 VF drawers; 2500 microfiche; 200 scrapbooks; 200 maps. **Subscriptions:** 45 journals and other serials. **Services:** Interlibrary loan; copying; section open to the public. **Automated Operations:** Computerized public access catalog, cataloging, and circulation. **Publications:** Acquisitions list, irregular - free upon request. **Remarks:** FAX: (416)395-5699. **Staff:** Diana Fink, Sr.Libn. for Urban Affairs.

★ 11960 ★
North York General Hospital - W. Keith Welsh Library (Med)
4001 Leslie St.   Phone: (416)756-6142
Willowdale, ON, Canada M2K 1E1 Marjory L. Morphy, Mgr., Lib.Serv.
Founded: 1968. **Staff:** Prof 1; Other 1. **Subjects:** Medicine, nursing, administration. **Holdings:** 2400 books; 100 audio cassettes; 1 file drawer of government documents. **Subscriptions:** 300 journals and other serials. **Services:** Interlibrary loan (limited); library not open to the public. **Computerized Information Services:** MEDLARS.

★ 11961 ★
North York Public Library - Canadiana Department (Area-Ethnic)
5120 Yonge St.   Phone: (416)395-5623
North York, ON, Canada M2N 5N9   Ruth Kingma, Mgr.
Founded: 1961. **Staff:** Prof 6; Other 4. **Subjects:** History - Canada, Ontario, North York; Canadian literature and culture; genealogy; Canadian art; histories of local Canadian communities. **Special Collections:** Canadian Institute for Historical Microreproductions (70,000 monographs and serials published before 1901); Ontario Genealogical Society Library; Canadian Society for Mayflower Descendants Library; Newton MacTavish Collection (150 books; 2 linear feet of manuscripts); Star Weekly Papers (3 linear feet of manuscripts); John A. Cooper Papers (12 linear feet of manuscripts and photographs). **Holdings:** 100,000 volumes; 700 bound periodical volumes; 36 VF drawers; North York Public Library Archives; 220 drawers of microfilm; 180 drawers of microfiche. **Subscriptions:** 325 journals and other serials. **Services:** Copying; collection open to the public. **Automated Operations:** Computerized cataloging. **Publications:** Newton MacTavish Collection Finding Aid; John A. Cooper Collection Finding Aid. **Special Catalogs:** Native Peoples Checklist. **Remarks:** FAX: (416)395-5668. **Staff:** Philip Singer, Sr.Libn.; Patricia Stone, Libn.Supv.; David Bain, Libn./ Archv.; Andrea Aitken, Libn.; John Jakobson, Libn.

★ 11962 ★
Northampton Community College - Learning Resources Center - Special Collections (Med)
3835 Green Pond Rd.   Phone: (215)861-5360
Bethlehem, PA 18017-7599   Sarah B. Jubinski, Dean, Lrng.Rsrcs.
Founded: 1967. **Staff:** Prof 3.5; Other 6. **Subjects:** Nursing, dental auxiliaries, funeral service. **Holdings:** 69,500 books; 78 microfilm titles. **Subscriptions:** 400 journals and other serials; 10 newspapers. **Services:** Interlibrary loan; copying; center open to the public. **Computerized Information Services:** BRS Information Technologies, OCLC; ACCESS PA (internal database). Performs searches. Contact Person: Ann Marie Janders, Coord. of Info.Serv. **Networks/Consortia:** Member of PALINET. **Publications:** Guide to Use of Learning Resources. **Remarks:** FAX: (215)861-5373. **Staff:** Patricia Renninger, Cat./Bibliog.; Pamela Sabatine, Acq.

★ 11963 ★
Northampton County Historical and Genealogical Society - Mary Illick Memorial Library (Hist)
107 S. Fourth St.   Phone: (215)253-1222
Easton, PA 18042   Dale Eden, Pres.
Founded: 1937. **Staff:** Prof 1; Other 4. **Subjects:** Local history and genealogy. **Special Collections:** Genealogical file; postal card collection; local history file. **Holdings:** 5000 books, manuscripts, deeds, letters, maps, pictures. **Subscriptions:** 18 journals and other serials. **Services:** Copying; genealogical research (fee); library open to the public on limited schedule for reference use only. **Publications:** List of books and Northampton Notes, quarterly; pamphlets - for sale. **Staff:** Jane Moyer, Libn.

★ 11964 ★
Northampton County Law Library (Law)
7th & Washington Sts.   Phone: (215)559-3076
Easton, PA 18042-7468   Anita L. DeBona, Law Libn.
Founded: 1860. **Staff:** Prof 1. **Subjects:** Law - general, tax, labor, business. **Holdings:** 23,000 volumes. **Subscriptions:** 25 journals and other serials. **Services:** Copying; library open to the public with restrictions. **Remarks:** FAX: (215)559-3047.

★ 11965 ★
Northborough Historical Society, Inc. - Library (Hist)
52 Main St.
Box 661
Northborough, MA 01532   Phone: (508)393-6298
Subjects: Local history. **Holdings:** 300 diaries, deeds, genealogical records, records of town organizations. **Services:** Library open to the public by appointment.

★ 11966 ★
Northeast Alabama Regional Medical Center - Medical Library (Med)
400 E. 10th St.
Box 2208   Phone: (205)235-5877
Anniston, AL 36202   Kathy Phillips, Libn.
Founded: 1961. **Staff:** Prof 1. **Subjects:** Medicine, allied health sciences. **Holdings:** 360 books; 850 bound periodical volumes. **Subscriptions:** 77 journals and other serials. **Services:** Interlibrary loan; copying; library open to the public for reference use only. **Automated Operations:** Computerized cataloging, serials, and circulation. **Computerized Information Services:** The Source Information Network, Dow Jones News/Retrieval, MEDLINE. **Networks/Consortia:** Member of Alabama Library Exchange, Inc. (ALEX). **Remarks:** FAX: (205)235-5094.

Northeast Archives of Folklore and Oral History
See: **University of Maine** (18778)

★ 11967 ★
Northeast Baptist Hospital - Bates Library (Med)
8811 Village Dr.   Phone: (512)653-2330
San Antonio, TX 78217   Carolyn Mueller, Libn.
Subjects: Medicine, nursing, and allied health sciences. **Holdings:** 100 books. **Subscriptions:** 4 journals and other serials. **Services:** Interlibrary loan. **Computerized Information Services:** MEDLINE. **Remarks:** FAX: (512)646-5810.

★ 11968 ★
Northeast Georgia Medical Center & Hall School of Nursing/Brenau College - Library (Med)
741 Spring St.   Phone: (404)534-6219
Gainesville, GA 30505   Caroline E. Alday, Libn.
Founded: 1963. **Staff:** Prof 2. **Subjects:** Nursing, medicine. **Holdings:** 5900 books; 2500 bound periodical volumes; 4 VF drawers; 170 videotapes; 448 filmstrip/tape sets. **Subscriptions:** 112 journals and other serials. **Services:** Interlibrary loan; copying; library open to the public for reference use only. **Automated Operations:** Computerized cataloging. **Computerized Information Services:** MEDLINE. **Remarks:** FAX: (404)535-3590. **Staff:** Mary J. Keith, Libn.

★ 11969 ★
Northeast Georgia Regional Education Service Agency - Northeast Georgia Learning Resource System (Educ)
375 Winter St.   Phone: (404)742-8292
Winterville, GA 30683   Gloria E. Frankum, Spec.Educ.Dir.
Founded: 1975. **Staff:** Prof 2; Other 2. **Subjects:** Handicapped education and training, handicapped children. **Holdings:** 2000 books. **Services:** Interlibrary loan; system not open to the public. **Computerized Information Services:** SpecialNet. **Staff:** Lynda Hale, Ch.Serv.Coord.; Barbara Elrod, Libn.

★ 11970 ★

Northeast Louisiana University - Center for Business & Economic Research - Library (Bus-Fin)
Administration Bldg. 2-104   Phone: (318)342-1215
Monroe, LA 71209   Jerry L. Wall, Dir.
Founded: 1970. **Staff:** Prof 5; Other 11. **Subjects:** Census; small business development; real estate; state, regional, and general business statistics. **Special Collections:** Small Business Development Collection (Small Business Administration publications; books; periodicals; films); income-producing property listings of Ouachita and Rapides parishes. **Holdings:** 2000 books; 500 other cataloged items; 1980 census tapes, microfiche, and disks; BEA disks. **Subscriptions:** 60 journals and other serials. **Services:** Library open to the public. **Computerized Information Services:** Online systems (through main library). Performs searches on fee basis. **Publications:** Delta Business Review, semiannual. **Remarks:** FAX: (318)342-1209. Operates the Louisiana Electronic Assistance Program (LEAP), an online statewide economic and business information bulletin board service; (800)331-3664 (Louisiana); (318)342-5576 (outside Louisiana). Operates Behavioral Risk Factor Surveillance Survey, a statewide service providing self report health-related data. Coordinating Center within the State Data Center Network.

★ 11971 ★

Northeast Minnesota Historical Center - Archives (Hist)
Library 375
University of Minnesota, Duluth   Phone: (218)726-8526
Duluth, MN 55812   Pat Maus, Adm.
Founded: 1976. **Staff:** Prof 1. **Subjects:** Regional history, transportation, iron mining technology, environmental issues, social service and civic agencies and organizations, business and industry, women. **Special Collections:** Great Lakes-St. Lawrence Tidewater Association Records (39 linear feet); Fitger's Brewery Company Records, 1904-1972; Julius Barnes papers (13 linear feet); Save Lake Superior Association Records (11 linear feet); Duluth Transit Authority Records (180 linear feet); Oliver Iron Mining Company Records; Merritt Family papers; Duluth Board of Trade Records; Seaway Port Authority of Duluth Records; Anderson Hilding papers; Reserve Mining Company Legal Case References. **Holdings:** 2500 books; 2000 linear feet of manuscripts; clippings; oral history tapes; 53,000 photographs; blueprints; maps. **Subscriptions:** 379 journals and other serials. **Services:** Copying; library open to the public. **Publications:** Guide to Manuscript Collections (1988); Genealogical Resources Available at the Northeast Minnesota Historical Center (1980); A Bibliography of Books and Pamphlets Held in the Northeast Minnesota Historical Center (1981). **Remarks:** jointly maintained by University of Minnesota, Duluth and St. Louis County Historical Society.

★ 11972 ★

Northeast Missouri State University - Pickler Memorial Library - Special Collections (Hum)
Kirksville, MO 63501-0828   Phone: (816)785-4038
                                             George N. Hartje, Lib.Dir.
Founded: 1867. **Staff:** Prof 1; Other 1. **Subjects:** Missouri history; Abraham Lincoln. **Special Collections:** Missouriana (7279 volumes); Fred and Ethel Schwengel Lincoln Collection (1133 books; 808 paintings and artifacts); Glenn Frank (60 cubic feet); Harry Laughlin Collection (22 cubic feet); Central Wesleyan College Archives (18.5 linear feet; 12 cubic feet); Hartje History of Books and Printing collection (631 volumes). **Holdings:** 12,372 books; 1210 bound periodical volumes; 518 bound newspapers; government documents. **Subscriptions:** 40 journals and other serials. **Services:** Interlibrary loan; copying; collections open to the public with restrictions. **Automated Operations:** Computerized public access catalog, cataloging, serials, and circulation (NOTIS). **Computerized Information Services:** BRS Information Technologies, DIALOG Information Services, OCLC; BITNET, InterNet (electronic mail services). **Networks/Consortia:** Member of Missouri Library Network Corp. (MLNC), Center for Research Libraries (CRL). **Remarks:** Alternate telephone number(s): (816)785-4537. FAX: (816)785-4536. Electronic mail address(es): LMO6@NEMOMUS (BITNET); LMO6%NEMOMUS@ACADEMIC.NEMOSTATE.EDU (InterNet). **Staff:** Odessa Ofstad, Spec.Coll.Libn./Archv.

★ 11973 ★

Northeast Ohio Areawide Coordinating Agency - Information Resource Center (Plan)
Atrium Office Plaza
668 Euclid Ave.   Phone: (216)241-2414
Cleveland, OH 44114-3000   Kenneth Goldberg, Info.Spec.
Founded: 1963. **Staff:** 2. **Subjects:** Transportation; land use; regional planning; health planning; housing; demographics; water quality; environmental planning; community involvement; architectural preservation; local history. **Special Collections:** Local population studies; regional planning archival materials for Northeast Ohio; Transportation Research Board series; grantsmanship. **Holdings:** 9000 volumes; 1000 unbound reports and specialized studies; subject files; monographs; 700 microfiche; dissertations; video cassettes; films; maps. **Subscriptions:** 120 journals and other serials. **Services:** Copying; center open to the public for reference use only. **Automated Operations:** Integrated library system (CLEVNET). **Computerized Information Services:** Cleveland Free-Net, Easy Access Catalog, InfoTrac. **Networks/Consortia:** Member of Cleveland Area Metropolitan Library System (CAMLS). **Remarks:** FAX: (216)621-3024.

★ 11974 ★

Northeast Ohio Four County Regional Planning & Development Organization - Library (Plan)
969 Copley Rd.
Akron, OH 44320   Phone: (216)836-5731
Founded: 1956. **Staff:** 5. **Subjects:** Urban planning, land use, community facilities, housing, environmental planning, economic development. **Special Collections:** American Society of Planning Officials; census depository for reports (bound and microfiche); Ohio Data Users Center affiliate. **Holdings:** 3500 volumes; pamphlet supplements to library. **Subscriptions:** 10 journals and other serials; 10 newspapers. **Services:** Copying; center open to the public. **Also Known As:** NEFCO.

Northeast Solar Energy Association.
See: **Northeast Sustainable Energy Association** (11975)

★ 11975 ★

Northeast Sustainable Energy Association - Library (Energy)
23 Ames St.   Phone: (413)774-6051
Greenfield, MA 01301   Nancy Hazard
Founded: 1976. **Staff:** 2. **Subjects:** Solar energy, alternative energy sources, solar electric vehicles. **Holdings:** Figures not available. **Subscriptions:** 30 journals and other serials. **Services:** Copying; library open to the public for reference use only. **Publications:** Magazine, bimonthly - to members. **Remarks:** FAX: (413)774-6053. **Formerly:** Northeast Solar Energy Association.

★ 11976 ★

Northeast Utilities Service Company - Library (Energy)
107 Selden St.   Phone: (203)665-5141
Berlin, CT 06037   Joan N. Terry, Libn.
Staff: Prof 1. **Subjects:** Public utilities, electric engineering, utility economics. **Holdings:** 1594 books; 610 bound periodical volumes; 600 volumes of transactions and proceedings of technical and engineering societies; 6 shelves of standards; 6 drawers of subject material. **Subscriptions:** 160 journals and other serials. **Services:** Interlibrary loan; copying; library open to the public for reference use only.

★ 11977 ★

Northeast Utilities Service Company - Research Information Center (Energy)
P.O. Box 270   Phone: (203)665-5890
Hartford, CT 06141   Doris E. Johnson, Info.Spec.
Founded: 1984. **Staff:** Prof 1. **Subjects:** Electric utilities, engineering, environment, economics. **Special Collections:** Electric Power Research Institute Reports. **Holdings:** 8000 volumes; 7000 microfiche; 165 videotapes. **Subscriptions:** 44 journals and other serials. **Services:** Center open to the public for reference use only. **Automated Operations:** Computerized cataloging and circulation. **Computerized Information Services:** DIALOG Information Services; MCI Mail (electronic mail service). **Publications:** Northeast Utilities Research Reports, irregular. **Remarks:** FAX: (203)665-5884; 665-5885.

★ 11978 ★
Northeast Wisconsin Technical College - Learning Resource Center
  (Educ)
2740 W. Mason
Box 19042   Phone: (414)498-5490
Green Bay, WI 54307-9042   Mary Parrott, Libn.
Founded: 1966. **Staff:** Prof 4; Other 6. **Subjects:** Health occupations, trade and industry, business and marketing, education, police science, agriculture, home economics, fire science. **Holdings:** 24,000 books; 5230 AV programs; 5400 reels of microfilm; 170 microfiche; 2730 video cassettes. **Subscriptions:** 630 journals and other serials; 50 newspapers. **Services:** Interlibrary loan; copying; center open to the public. **Automated Operations:** Computerized cataloging and circulation. **Computerized Information Services:** DIALOG Information Services, WISCAT; InfoTrac. **Networks/Consortia:** Member of Fox River Valley Area Library Consortium (FRVALC), Northeast Wisconsin Intertype Libraries (NEWIL). **Publications:** Yearly Student & Staff Handbooks; yearly update of computerized union list of periodicals for FRVALC. **Special Catalogs:** Videotape catalog; program catalogs (AV materials) - available upon request. **Remarks:** FAX: (414)498-5490. **Staff:** D.W. Rowling, LRC Spec.; John Siemering, Media Techn.

★ 11979 ★
Northeastern Bible College - Lincoln Memorial Library
12 Oak Ln.
Essex Fells, NJ 07021
Founded: 1952. **Subjects:** Bible, religion, general and elementary education. **Special Collections:** Cleaveland Collection (Judaism and Jewish evangelism; 3010 volumes). **Holdings:** 48,800 volumes; 1000 bound periodical volumes; 3100 pamphlets; 617 phonograph records; 200 filmstrips; 2500 cassette tapes; 40 reels of microfilm. **Remarks:** Currently inactive.

★ 11980 ★
Northeastern Hospital - School of Nursing Library (Med)
2301 E. Allegheny Ave.   Phone: (215)291-3168
Philadelphia, PA 19134-4499   Rae Greenberg, Libn.
Founded: 1924. **Staff:** Prof 1. **Subjects:** Nursing, medicine, natural sciences, psychology, sociology. **Holdings:** 2024 books; 160 bound periodical volumes; filmstrips; videotapes; cassettes; software programs; 6 VF boxes. **Subscriptions:** 75 journals and other serials. **Services:** Interlibrary loan; library not open to the public. **Computerized Information Services:** CD-ROMs (MEDLINE, CINAHL). **Networks/Consortia:** Member of Delaware Valley Information Consortium (DEVIC). **Remarks:** FAX: (215)291-3159.

★ 11981 ★
Northeastern Illinois Planning Commission - Library (Plan)
400 W. Madison St., Rm. 200   Phone: (312)454-0400
Chicago, IL 60606   Mary Cele Smith, Assoc.Plan.
Founded: 1958. **Staff:** 1. **Subjects:** Planning, census, transportation, ecology. **Special Collections:** Chicago area census summaries (microfilm; tapes); Northeastern Illinois Planning Commission publications and databases (forecasts, population, housing monitoring, employment estimates); municipal plans and ordinances. **Holdings:** 1000 books; 15 periodical titles; 15 VF drawers of planning materials; government documents; newsletters. **Subscriptions:** 50 journals and other serials. **Services:** Interlibrary loan; copying; library open to the public for reference use only by appointment. **Remarks:** FAX: (312)454-0411.

★ 11982 ★
Northeastern Illinois University - Ronald Williams Library (Educ, Bus-Fin)
5500 N. St. Louis Ave.   Phone: (312)794-2615
Chicago, IL 60625-4699   Bradley F. Baker, Univ.Libn.
Founded: 1961. **Staff:** Prof 21; Other 53. **Subjects:** Education, business and management, social sciences, literature and languages. **Special Collections:** U.S. and Illinois document depositories; Illinois Regional Archive Depository (IRAD) for Chicago and Cook County; African-American literature; William Gray Reading Collection; curriculum guides; textbooks. **Holdings:** 530,720 books; 65,179 bound periodical volumes; 1939 linear feet of archival materials; 28,279 reels of microfilm; 30,223 pamphlets; 823,946 microfiche. **Subscriptions:** 4481 journals and other serials; 42 newspapers. **Services:** Interlibrary loan; copying; library open to the public. **Automated Operations:** Computerized public access catalog, acquisitions, and serials. **Computerized Information Services:** DIALOG Information Services, OCLC, BRS Information Technologies, WILSONLINE, EPIC, CARL

UnCover; InfoTrac; CD-ROM (ERIC, PAIS on CD-ROM, CIRR on Disc, MLA International Bibliography, SPORT Discus, General Science Index, Disclosure Incorporated, PsycLIT, Computer Library); BITNET (electronic mail service). Performs searches on fee basis. **Contact Person:** Mary Jane Hilburger, Hd.Ref.Libn., 794-2614. **Networks/Consortia:** Member of ILLINET. **Publications:** Annual Report; departmental bibliographies and handouts. **Special Catalogs:** Library shelf lists for special collections, documents, and curriculum materials. **Special Indexes:** Periodicals holding list. **Remarks:** FAX: (312)794-2550. Electronic mail address(es): PROFS (BITNET). **Staff:** Darlene Patrick, Acq.; Sharon Scott, Inner City Stud.Libn.; Georgine Brabec, Hd., Cat.; Nell Thomas, Hd., Circ.; Patrice Stearley, Doc.Libn.; Jill Althage, Curriculum Materials Libn.; Virginia Reed, Per.Serv.Libn.; Sara Schwarz, Archv.Libn.; Richard Higginbotham, Inst. & Ext.Serv.Libn.; Sophie K. Black, Assoc.Univ.Libn.; Warren Haushalter, Coord., Media Serv.; Glen Kistner, Per./Docs.Ref.Libn.; Joe Accardi, Assoc.Univ.Libn.; Jane Jurgens, Ref./IRAD Libn.

★ 11983 ★
Northeastern Nevada Museum - Library (Hist)
1515 Idaho St.
Box 2550   Phone: (702)738-3418
Elko, NV 89801   Howard Hickson, Dir.
Founded: 1968. **Staff:** Prof 2; Other 6. **Subjects:** Northeastern Nevada, Nevada, pioneers, antiques. **Special Collections:** Area newspapers, 1869 to present (250 bound volumes). **Holdings:** 2100 books; 6000 photographs and negatives; 350 unpublished manuscripts; area newspapers on microfilm. **Subscriptions:** 6 journals and other serials; 3 newspapers. **Services:** Copying; library open to the public. **Automated Operations:** Computerized public access catalog and cataloging. **Publications:** Northeastern Nevada Historical Society Quarterly. **Special Indexes:** Area newspapers index, 1869-1978 (card). **Remarks:** FAX: (702)753-9863. Maintained by Northeastern Nevada Historical Society.

★ 11984 ★
Northeastern Ohio Universities College of Medicine - Oliver Ocasek
  Regional Medical Information Center (Med, Biol Sci)
4209 State Rte. 44
Box 95
Rootstown, OH 44272   Phone: (216)325-2511
Founded: 1976. **Staff:** Prof 8.5; Other 9.5. **Subjects:** Basic life sciences, medicine. **Holdings:** 41,171 books; 33,642 bound periodical volumes; 3087 AV programs; 270 linear feet of archival material and manuscripts. **Subscriptions:** 1109 journals and other serials. **Services:** Interlibrary loan; SDI; center open to the public for reference use only. **Automated Operations:** Computerized public access catalog, circulation, and serials. **Computerized Information Services:** DIALOG Information Services, BRS Information Technologies, MEDLINE. **Networks/Consortia:** Member of NEOMARL, OHIONET, National Network of Libraries of Medicine - Greater Midwest Region. **Publications:** Medical Periodicals in Northeastern Ohio, annual; Medical Audiovisuals in Northeast Ohio, irregular; NEOU-Communique, quarterly. **Remarks:** FAX: (216)325-0522. **Staff:** Jean Williams Sayre, Dir.; C. Jean Jarosz, Hd., Pub.Serv.; Monica A. Unger, Sys.; David Blankenship, AV/Microcomputer Libn.; Lisa Plymale, Hd., Tech.Serv.; G. Thomas Osterfield, Archv./Spec.Libn.; Josephine Poda, Ref./Reg.Serv.Libn.

★ 11985 ★
Northeastern Oklahoma State University - John Vaughan Library/LRC
  - Special Collections and Archives (Hum)
Tahlequah, OK 74464   Phone: (918)456-5511
                            Bela Foltin, Dean
Founded: 1909. **Special Collections:** Cherokee Indian Collection (589 volumes); E. Edmondson Papers (240 boxes); Government Document Depository (332,000). **Holdings:** 9565 books; 480 bound periodical volumes; 5172 microfiche; 1752 reels of microfilm. **Subscriptions:** 26 journals and other serials; 31 newspapers. **Services:** Copying; archives open to the public. **Automated Operations:** Computerized public access catalog, cataloging, acquisitions, serials, and circulation. **Computerized Information Services:** OCLC, DIALOG Information Services, BRS Information Technologies; CD-ROM (ERIC). **Networks/Consortia:** Member of AMIGOS Bibliographic Council, Inc. **Remarks:** FAX: (918)458-2197. **Staff:** Delores Sumner, Spec.Coll.Libn.; Victoria Sheffler, Univ.Archv.

★ 11986 ★
Northeastern University - Law School Library (Law)
400 Huntington Ave.   Phone: (617)437-3332
Boston, MA 02115   Rajinder S. Walia, Law Libn./Prof. of Law
Founded: 1967. **Staff:** Prof 7; Other 5. **Subjects:** Law. **Special Collections:** Sara Ehrmann Collection on Capital Punishment (250 files); international law. **Holdings:** 110,000 bound volumes; 42,650 volumes in microform. **Subscriptions:** 2400 journals and other serials. **Services:** Interlibrary loan; copying; library open to the public with written request. **Automated Operations:** Computerized cataloging. **Computerized Information Services:** OCLC, LEXIS, WESTLAW. **Networks/Consortia:** Member of New England Law Library Consortium (NELLCO). **Publications:** Acquisitions lists; research bibliographies. **Remarks:** FAX: (617)247-9264. **Staff:** Charles L. Field, Asst. Law Libn.; Filippa Anzalone, Dir. of Access & Info.Serv.; Margaret Cianfarini, Asst.Libn., Tech.Serv.; Jeanette MacAdam, Tech.Proc.Asst.; George Lucke, Pub.Serv.Asst.; Joy Plunket, Ref.Libn.

★ 11987 ★
Northeastern University - Libraries - Special Collections (Sci-Engr, Hum, Area-Ethnic)
360 Huntington Ave.   Phone: (617)437-2351
Boston, MA 02115   Alan R. Benenfeld, Dean
Staff: Prof 39; Other 36. **Special Collections:** History of Northeastern University; Northeastern University theses and faculty publications; Glen Grey-Casa Loma Orchestra Collection. **Services:** Interlibrary loan; copying; library open to the public. **Automated Operations:** Computerized public access catalog, circulation, acquisitions, and serials. **Computerized Information Services:** DIALOG Information Services, BRS Information Technologies, OCLC, Chemical Abstracts Service (CAS); internal database; electronic mail. **Networks/Consortia:** Member of Boston Library Consortium (BLC), NELINET, Inc. **Remarks:** FAX: (617)437-5409. **Staff:** Lynda Leahy, Assoc.Dean; MaryLee Xanco, Coll.Dev.Off.; John Schalow, Act.Hd., Archv./Spec.Coll.

★ 11988 ★
Northeastern University - Marine Science Center (Biol Sci)
East Point
Nahant, MA 01908
                                       Phone: (617)581-7370
Founded: 1967. **Staff:** 3. **Subjects:** Marine biology, ocean chemistry and ecology. **Holdings:** 1650 books; 325 bound periodical volumes; 12,000 reprints. **Subscriptions:** 20 journals and other serials. **Services:** Interlibrary loan; copying; center open to the public for reference use only. **Remarks:** FAX: (617)581-6076.

★ 11989 ★
Northeastern Vermont Regional Hospital - Library (Med)
Hospital Dr.
PO Box 905   Phone: (802)748-8141
St. Johnsbury, VT 05819   Eleanor B. Simons, Libn.
Founded: 1972. **Staff:** Prof 1; Other 5. **Subjects:** Medicine, nursing, allied health sciences. **Holdings:** 1232 books; 4 filing drawers of pamphlets. **Subscriptions:** 111 journals and other serials. **Services:** Interlibrary loan; copying; SDI; library open to the public with restrictions. **Computerized Information Services:** MEDLINE; DOCLINE (electronic mail service). Performs searches free of charge. **Networks/Consortia:** Member of North Country Consortium (NCC). **Remarks:** FAX: (802)748-5227. Electronic mail address(es): 05819A (DOCLINE).

★ 11990 ★
Northern Alberta Institute of Technology - McNally Library (Educ)
11762 106th St.   Phone: (403)471-8844
Edmonton, AB, Canada T5G 2R1   Helga Kinnaird, Chf.Libn.
Founded: 1963. **Staff:** Prof 6; Other 20. **Subjects:** Business, applied sciences, medical sciences, vocational education. **Special Collections:** Automotive manuals. **Holdings:** 50,000 books, pamphlets, documents. **Subscriptions:** 610 journals. **Services:** Interlibrary loan; copying; center open to the public for reference use only. **Automated Operations:** Computerized acquisitions. **Computerized Information Services:** DIALOG Information Services, UTLAS, SPIRES, BRS Information Technologies; CD-ROM; Envoy 100 (electronic mail service). **Remarks:** FAX: (403)471-8813. Electronic mail address(es): NAIT.LIB (Envoy 100). **Formerly:** Its Learning Resource Centre. **Staff:** Peggy White, Hd., Pub.Serv.; Patricia Waterton, Hd., Tech.Serv.

★ 11991 ★
Northern Arizona University - Cline Library (Educ)
Box 6022   Phone: (602)523-2171
Flagstaff, AZ 86011   Jean D. Collins, Univ.Libn.
Staff: Prof 25.5; Other 48. **Subjects:** Education, business, Arizoniana. **Special Collections:** Forestry; selective depository for federal documents and maps (393,617 documents). **Holdings:** 467,127 books; 120,708 bound periodical volumes; 29,389 maps; 18,954 reels of microfilm; 295,010 volumes on microfiche; 2702 films and videotapes; 13,358 sound recordings; 1013 AV programs. **Subscriptions:** 5253 journals and other serials; 51 newspapers. **Services:** Interlibrary loan; copying; library open to the public with restrictions. **Automated Operations:** Computerized public access catalog, cataloging, acquisitions, serials, and circulation. **Computerized Information Services:** BRS Information Technologies, DIALOG Information Services, RLIN, WILSONLINE, OCLC; Reserves (internal database); ALANET (electronic mail service). Performs searches on fee basis. Contact Person: Cynthia Childrey, Online Serv., 523-6808. **Networks/Consortia:** Member of AMIGOS Bibliographic Council, Inc., Consortium of College and University Media Centers (CCUMC). **Publications:** Discovery Series (guides to special subjects). **Remarks:** Alternate telephone number(s): 523-6805. FAX: (602)523-3770. **Staff:** James Armour, Coll.Dev.Off.; Claudia Bakula, Sys. & Plan.Coord.; Tom Carpenter, Access Serv.Coord.; Brian Forney, Ref.Coord.; Karen Jaggers, Field Serv.Coord.; Emily Hill, Media Coord.; Randall Butler, Spec.Coll.Coord.; Linda Williams, Bib.Serv.Coord.

★ 11992 ★
Northern Arizona University - Cline Library - Special Collections and Archives Department (Hist)
Box 6022   Phone: (602)523-5551
Flagstaff, AZ 86011   Randall R. Butler, Spec.Coll. & Archv.Coord.
Founded: 1966. **Staff:** Prof 4; Other 2. **Subjects:** Arizona, Southwestern U.S., Colorado River and Plateau, Grand Canyon, Elbert Hubbard (Roycroft Press), Navajo and Hopi Indians. **Special Collections:** Emery Kolb's early motion picture film and photographs of the Grand Canyon, 1911-1924 (75 reels, primarily 35mm; videotapes; 250,000 prints); Pioneer Museum, Arizona Historical Society Archives and photograph repository; United Verde (Jerome) Mining Collection; Alexander and Dorothea Leighton Collection, 1940 (Navajo field materials in anthropology); Arizona Woolgrowers Association Archives; Arizona Lumber and Timber Company Archives; Arizona AFL-CIO Labor Union Archives; First National Bank of Arizona Archives; Apachean Language Collection, including Chiricahua dialects (over 300 cassettes); Northern Arizona University Archives; Fred Harvey Collection (hotels and restaurants of the Southwest); Colorado River Collection; Stuart Young Collection (early archeologist in four corners area, 1908-1909; photographs); Malcolm (Byron) Cummings Collection (Rainbow Bridge); Gladwell (Toney) Richardson Collection (western pulp fiction writer; photographs; research files); Zane Grey book and manuscript collection; Georgie White Clark Colorado River Runner Collection. **Holdings:** 31,000 books; 1900 bound periodical volumes; 2334 linear feet of manuscripts, records, and archival materials; 3500 pamphlets; 551 oral history tapes; 1 million photographs; 4344 reels of microfilm; 3545 regional historical maps. **Subscriptions:** 300 journals and other serials; 26 newspapers. **Services:** Copying; collections open to the public with restrictions. **Automated Operations:** Computerized cataloging and indexing. **Computerized Information Services:** OCLC, VU/TEXT Information Services; internal database. **Networks/Consortia:** Member of AMIGOS Bibliographic Council, Inc., Colorado Alliance of Research Libraries (CARL). **Publications:** Emery Kolb, A Guide to the Kolb Collection in the NAU Libraries, 1980; Northern Arizona's Historical Economy, Manuscript Materials Available at NAU Special Collections, 1986; Guide to Native American Literature; Northern Arizona's Political Economy, 1986; Guide to the Special Collections Library; Steps You Can Take to Preserve Your Family's Heritage Beyond Tomorrow! **Special Indexes:** Historical Index to the Arizona Champion-Coconino Sun Newspaper of Flagstaff, 1883-1894; Spanish Southwest 1519-1776 and after. **Remarks:** FAX: (602)523-3770. **Staff:** Lois A. Leman, Lib.Spec.; Robert A. Coody, Lib.Spec.; William H. Mullane, Spec.Coll.Libn.; Karen Underhill, Archv. & Mss.Cur.; Laine Sutherland, Cur. of Photo.

Northern California Health Center
See: **California Pacific Medical Center - California Campus (2497)**

1275

★ 11993 ★
Northern Cumberland Memorial Hospital - Frederick W. Skillin Health Sciences Library (Med)
Box 230   Phone: (207)647-8841
Bridgton, ME 04009   Sally M. MacAuslan, Hea.Sci.Libn.
Founded: 1972. **Staff:** Prof 1. **Subjects:** Medicine, nursing, hospital administration, patient education, health sciences. **Holdings:** 274 books; 140 videotapes; 8 slide/tape sets; 18 audiocassettes. **Subscriptions:** 51 journals and other serials. **Services:** Interlibrary loan; copying; library open to the public for reference use only. **Computerized Information Services:** MEDLINE. **Networks/Consortia:** Member of Health Science Library and Information Cooperative of Maine (HSLIC). **Remarks:** FAX: (207)647-8703.

Northern Engineering & Testing, Inc.
See: Chen-Northern, Inc. (3476)

★ 11994 ★
Northern Illinois University - Donn V. Hart Southeast Asian Collection (Area-Ethnic)
Founders Memorial Library
DeKalb, IL 60115   Phone: (815)753-1819
Founded: 1963. **Staff:** Prof 3; Other 1. **Subjects:** Southeast Asia, including history, art history, business, economics, geography, politics, sociology, anthropology, and linguistics of Thailand, Philippines, Indonesia, Malaysia, Burma, Singapore, Indochina. **Special Collections:** Thai Collection (10,004 volumes in Thai); Burma Collection (7722 uncataloged monographs; rare and contemporary books); Philippine American Collection; modern Indonesia microfiche collection; Southeast Asia Children's Book Collection; N.P.A.C. holdings for Malaysia, Singapore, Brunei, Indonesia. **Holdings:** 52,429 volumes; 9973 pamphlets and reports; Southeast Asian newspapers on 2937 reels of microfilm; 692 maps and atlases. **Subscriptions:** 1101 journals and other serials; 16 newspapers. **Services:** Interlibrary loan; copying; collection open to the public with restrictions. **Automated Operations:** Computerized cataloging, acquisitions, serials, and circulation. **Computerized Information Services:** OCLC, BRS Information Technologies, DIALOG Information Services, WILSONLINE. **Networks/Consortia:** Member of Center for Research Libraries (CRL), Oakland Wayne Interlibrary Network (OWIN), ILLINET. **Publications:** A Guide to the Southeast Asia Collection, 1972; Newspapers in the Southeast Asia Collection, 1976; Southeast Asia Collection Bibliographic Notes, irregular. **Special Catalogs:** Card catalog of Southeast Asia holdings. **Remarks:** FAX: (815)753-2003. **Staff:** Lee Dutton, Bibliog.; May Kyi Win, Cur.

★ 11995 ★
Northern Illinois University - Earl W. Hayter Regional History Center (Hist)
155 Swen Parson Hall   Phone: (815)753-1779
DeKalb, IL 60115   Glen A. Gildemeister, Dir.
Founded: 1978. **Staff:** Prof 2; Other 3. **Subjects:** Northern Illinois history, agricultural history. **Holdings:** 1521 linear feet of manuscripts; 1408 linear feet of local government records; 2920 reels of microfilm; 1735 maps, posters, and broadsides; 486,816 photographs/negatives; 3146 vertical file materials. **Subscriptions:** 7 journals and other serials. **Services:** Copying; center open to the public. **Remarks:** FAX: (815)753-2003. **Staff:** Eva Schooley, Micrographics; Cindy Ditzler, Cur.

★ 11996 ★
Northern Illinois University - Faraday Library (Sci-Engr)
Faraday Hall, Rm. 212   Phone: (815)753-1257
DeKalb, IL 60115   Ruth Koerner, Supv.
Founded: 1964. **Staff:** 1. **Subjects:** Chemistry, physics. **Holdings:** 21,540 books; 21,290 bound periodical volumes. **Subscriptions:** 445 journals and other serials. **Services:** Interlibrary loan; copying; library open to the public with restrictions. **Automated Operations:** Computerized cataloging and circulation. **Computerized Information Services:** DIALOG Information Services, PFDS Online, OCLC, Statewide Library Computer System (LCS). Performs searches on fee basis. **Networks/Consortia:** Member of Center for Research Libraries (CRL). **Remarks:** FAX: (815)753-2003.

★ 11997 ★
Northern Illinois University - Film Library
Founders' Memorial Library
DeKalb, IL 60115-2854
Defunct. Holdings absorbed by Northern Illinois University - Founders' Memorial Library.

★ 11998 ★
Northern Illinois University - Map Library (Geog-Map)
Davis Hall 222   Phone: (815)753-1813
DeKalb, IL 60115   Elaine Blowers, Libn.
Founded: 1965. **Staff:** 1. **Subjects:** Maps - northern Illinois, United States, Southeast Asia, Latin America, census, weather, hydrology, soil, land use planning. **Holdings:** 2219 books; 12,190 map titles; 212,616 map units; 655 aerial photographs; 8636 vertical files; 66,883 government documents. **Services:** Interlibrary loan; copying; library open to the public. **Automated Operations:** Computerized cataloging. **Publications:** Acquisitions list, quarterly. **Remarks:** FAX: (815)753-2003.

★ 11999 ★
Northern Illinois University - Music Library (Mus)
175 Music Bldg.   Phone: (815)753-1426
DeKalb, IL 60115   Stephen Wright, Mus.Libn.
Founded: 1974. **Staff:** Prof 1; Other 1. **Subjects:** Music. **Holdings:** 33,055 books and scores; 2380 bound periodical volumes; 21,530 sound recordings; 85 masters' theses. **Subscriptions:** 200 journals and other serials. **Services:** Interlibrary loan; copying; library open with full service to Illinois residents; open to others for reference use only. **Automated Operations:** Computerized public access catalog, cataloging, and circulation. **Computerized Information Services:** OCLC. **Remarks:** FAX: (815)753-2003.

★ 12000 ★
Northern Illinois University - Program for Biosocial Research - Library (Sci-Engr)
DeKalb, IL 60115   Phone: (815)753-9675
     Carolyn Cradduck, Dir.
Founded: 1980. **Subjects:** Evolutionary theory, biology of behavior/ethology, biotechnology, bioethics, biopolicy, philosophy of science, biomedicine. **Holdings:** 1500 books. **Subscriptions:** 20 journals and other serials. **Services:** Library open to the public by permission. **Remarks:** FAX: (815)753-2305.

★ 12001 ★
Northern Illinois University - Regional History Center (Hist)
DeKalb, IL 60115   Phone: (815)753-1779
     Glen A. Gildemeister, Dir.
Founded: 1978. **Staff:** 4. **Subjects:** Local history - Northern Illinois University, religion, business, rural; agriculture. **Holdings:** 2384 books; 4782 microforms; 4657 linear feet of manuscripts; government records (naturalization, civil war, election, school, tax, court). **Subscriptions:** 11 journals and other serials. **Services:** Copying; center open to the public. **Computerized Information Services:** Internal databases. Performs searches free of charge. **Publications:** Guide to Regional Collections; University Archives Guide; Shelflist to Monograph Collections.

★ 12002 ★
Northern Illinois University - Taft Field Campus - Library (Educ)
P.O. Box 299   Phone: (815)753-0205
Oregon, IL 61061   Marcia Bradley, Supv.
Founded: 1952. **Staff:** 1. **Subjects:** Natural sciences; education - outdoor, environmental, experiential; ecology; arts. **Special Collections:** Camping Archives (376 archival materials); sculptor Lorado Taft Archives (515 archival materials). **Holdings:** 5540 books; 533 bound periodical volumes; 1650 other cataloged items; 1050 dissertations. **Subscriptions:** 68 journals and other serials. **Services:** Interlibrary loan; copying; center open to the public. **Automated Operations:** Computerized cataloging and circulation. **Computerized Information Services:** OCLC, Statewide Library Computer System (LCS). **Remarks:** FAX: (815)753-2003.

★12003★
Northern Illinois University - University Archives (Hist)
DeKalb, IL 60115   Phone: (815)753-1779
                        Glen A. Gildemeister, Archv.
Founded: 1964. Staff: Prof 1; Other 1. Special Collections: Charles Alexander McMurry Papers (3 linear feet; 40 volumes); John W. Cook Papers (8 linear feet). Holdings: 2000 linear feet of university records; 2800 cubic feet of state and local records; 2920 reels of microfilm; 637 reels of phonotapes; 486,816 photographs and negatives; faculty and alumni records. Services: Copying; archives open to the public. Remarks: FAX: (815)753-2003.

★12004★
Northern Indiana Historical Society - Frederick Elbel Library (Hist)
808 W. Washington   Phone: (219)284-9664
South Bend, IN 46601   Kathleen Stiso Mullins, Exec.Musm.Dir.
Founded: 1867. Staff: 26. Subjects: Native American history and language; Indiana history; French, Indian, English, and American occupations of Saint Joseph River Valley region; pioneer life; Schuyler Colfax. Special Collections: Oliver Chilled Plow Co. Records; Oliver Family personal papers, diaries, photographs. Holdings: 7500 books; 1500 pamphlets; 20,000 photographs; bound newspapers, 1831-1964; 300 boxes of archival manuscripts, dissertations, documents; clipping files; oral history tapes; videotapes. Subscriptions: 25 journals and other serials. Services: Copying; genealogy assistance; library open to the public by appointment for reference use only. Publications: Joseph Valley Record, biannual; Historic Calendar, monthly; reprints of specific books in collection, annual; books and pamphlets on area history. Remarks: FAX: (219)284-9059.

★12005★
Northern Ireland - Department of Agriculture - Library (Agri)
Dundonald House
Upper Newtownards Rd   Phone: 232 650111
Belfast DT4 3SB, Northern Ireland   Noel Menary
Founded: 1921. Staff: Prof 2; Other 4. Subjects: Agricultural science, public administration. Holdings: 50,000 books; 4000 bound periodical volumes; 3000 microfiche; 50 videotapes. Subscriptions: 450 journals and other serials; 40 newspapers. Services: Interlibrary loan; copying; library open to the public by appointment. Automated Operations: Computerized cataloging (Soutron Library System). Computerized Information Services: DIALOG Information Services, ESA/IRS, AGRA EUROPE. Remarks: FAX: 232 673433. Telex: 232 74578.

★12006★
Northern Kentucky University - Salmon P. Chase College of Law - Library (Law)
Nunn Dr.   Phone: (606)572-5394
Highland Heights, KY 41099-6110   Carol B. Allred, Law Lib.Dir.
Founded: 1893. Staff: Prof 6; Other 10. Subjects: Law. Holdings: 123,490 volumes; 101,514 volumes in microform. Subscriptions: 2478 journals and other serials; 6 newspapers. Services: Interlibrary loan; copying; library open to the public. Computerized Information Services: LEXIS, OCLC, WESTLAW. Networks/Consortia: Member of SOLINET. Remarks: FAX: (606)572-6529. Staff: Donna Bennett, Assoc.Dir./Hd., Tech.Serv.; Claudia Zaher, Ref.Libn.; Carol Bredemeyer, Hd., Pub.Serv.; Carol Furnish, Ref.Libn.; Tom Heard, Cat.

★12007★
Northern Maine Technical College - Library (Educ)
33 Edgemont Dr.   Phone: (207)769-2461
Presque Isle, ME 04769   Margaret H. Coffin, Dir.
Founded: 1968. Staff: Prof 1; Other 1. Subjects: Computer technology, business, building trades, electronics, electrical and automotive engineering, nursing. Special Collections: Federal aviation publications. Holdings: 14,000 books. Subscriptions: 206 journals and other serials. Services: Interlibrary loan; copying; library open to the public. Automated Operations: Computerized cataloging and statistics. Computerized Information Services: MAGAZINE INDEX; InfoTrac; CD-ROMs (Grolier Electronic Encyclopedia, ERIC, Nursing & Allied Health Database, MAINECAT, MEDLINE, PC Globe, Compton's MultiMedia Encyclopedia). Remarks: FAX: (207)764-8465.

Northern Michigan Hospitals, Inc.
See: The Dean C. Burns Health Sciences Library (2385)

Northern Ohio Medical History Archives
See: Cleveland Health Sciences Library - Medical History Division (3807)

Northern Pigment
See: Harcros Pigments Canada (6901)

★12008★
Northern Plains Resource Council - Library (Energy)
419 Stapleton Bldg.   Phone: (406)248-1154
Billings, MT 59101   Dennis Olson, Res.Coord.
Staff: 10. Subjects: Western coal development, Montana energy development, environmental/socioeconomic impacts, federal coal leasing, hard rock mining, agricultural credit, air quality, water, hazardous waste. Holdings: 1500 books; 1000 other cataloged items. Subscriptions: 40 journals and other serials; 12 newspapers. Services: Library open to those with approval of and supervision by NPRC. Computerized Information Services: Montana Hard Rock Mining Data Base (internal database). Publications: Plains Truth (newsletter). Remarks: FAX: (406)252-1092. Information requests will be filled as staff time permits.

★12009★
Northern Research & Engineering Corporation - Library (Sci-Engr)
39 Olympia Ave.   Phone: (617)935-9050
Woburn, MA 01801-2073   Jane Brewster Waks, Libn.
Staff: Prof 1. Subjects: Mechanical engineering, aeronautics, computer software for automation. Special Collections: National Advisory Committee for Aeronautics (NACA) and NASA documents and indexes. Holdings: 400 books; technical reports; conference proceedings; military and government documents. Subscriptions: 150 journals and other serials. Services: Telephone reference service. Computerized Information Services: DIALOG Information Services. Special Indexes: Serials holdings list. Remarks: FAX: (617)935-9052.

★12010★
Northern States Power Company - Communications Department - "Ask NSP" Tape Library
414 Nicollet Mall
Minneapolis, MN 55401
Subjects: Alternative energy, customer information, appliances, electricity, fuels, government, heating and cooling, natural gas, safety, weatherization. Holdings: 172 tapes. Remarks: Currently inactive.

★12011★
Northern States Power Company - Communications Department - Library & Record Center (Energy)
414 Nicollet Mall   Phone: (612)330-6936
Minneapolis, MN 55401   Gwenn M. Solseth, Info.Serv.Coord.
Founded: 1980. Staff: Prof 1. Subjects: Energy, environment, business, energy history, utility industry, electricity, gas. Special Collections: St. Anthony Falls, Minnesota Special Collection (photographs and journals documenting its water power); history of NSP and ancestor companies. Holdings: 300 books; 30 bound periodical volumes; 300 technical reports; 16,000 slides and photographs; 66 boxes of archival material. Subscriptions: 30 journals and other serials. Services: Interlibrary loan; copying; SDI; library open to the public by appointment. Computerized Information Services: DIALOG Information Services, WILSONLINE, NEXIS, Dow Jones News/Retrieval, VU/TEXT Information Services, Knight-Ridder Unicom, DataTimes, Utility Data Institute, OCLC EPIC, EcoNet, NewsNet, Inc., GasNet; internal databases; DIALMAIL, Knight-Ridder Unicom (electronic mail services). Special Catalogs: Catalog of NSP Energy Information publications, films, speakers, and education materials. Remarks: FAX: (612)330-6947.

★ 12012 ★
Northern Telecom, Inc. - Business Information Center (Info Sci)
2221 Lakeside
Mail Stop 0305   Phone: (214)684-8444
Richardson, TX 75082   Susan H. Rainey, Libn.
Founded: 1982. **Staff:** Prof 2; Other 2. **Subjects:** Telecommunications, networks, computers, office automation. **Holdings:** 50 books; 500 market research reports; 30 VF drawers of archival material; 15 VF drawers of competitive information files. **Subscriptions:** 90 journals and other serials; 20 newspapers. **Automated Operations:** Computerized cataloging and circulation. **Computerized Information Services:** DIALOG Information Services, Mead Data Central, BRS Information Technologies, PFDS Online, Dow Jones News/Retrieval; BIC (marketing information system; internal database). **Publications:** New Reports in the BIC, quarterly - for internal distribution only.

★ 12013 ★
Northern Telecom, Inc. - Learning Resource Center (Info Sci)
685A E. Middlefield Rd.
Box 7277   Phone: (415)940-2181
Mountain View, CA 94039-7277   Ann Recktenwald, Supv.
Founded: 1978. **Staff:** Prof 2; Other 1. **Subjects:** Telecommunications, communications, computers, office automation, management. **Holdings:** 2500 books. **Subscriptions:** 300 journals and other serials. **Services:** Interlibrary loan; center not open to the public. **Automated Operations:** Computerized acquisitions and circulation. **Computerized Information Services:** DIALOG Information Services, RLIN, NewsNet, Inc.; internal database; OnTyme Electronic Message Network Service (electronic mail service). **Networks/Consortia:** Member of CLASS. **Publications:** Info Edge (online newsletter), bimonthly. **Remarks:** FAX: (415)966-1067; (415)966-1098. Electronic mail address(es): CLASS.NTI (OnTyme Electronic Message Network Service). **Staff:** Susan Boyd, Info.Spec.; Kathy Deason, LTA.

★ 12014 ★
Northern Telecom Ltd. - Information Resource Center (Info Sci)
3 Robert Speck Pkwy.   Phone: (416)897-9000
Mississauga, ON, Canada L4Z 3C8   JoAnne Yamada, Libn.
Founded: 1928. **Staff:** Prof 3; Other 4. **Subjects:** Telecommunications, data processing, electronics, business and finance, management, human resources. **Holdings:** 5000 books; 2000 bound periodical volumes. **Subscriptions:** 386 journals and other serials. **Services:** Interlibrary loan; center not open to the public. **Automated Operations:** Computerized cataloging and journal routing. **Computerized Information Services:** DIALOG Information Services, Infomart Online, Info Globe, DOBIS Canadian Online Library System, NEXIS, CAN/OLE, Reuters Information Services (Canada), Telecommunications Information System, NewsNet, Inc., The Financial Post Information Service; DIALMAIL, Envoy 100 (electronic mail services). **Publications:** INFOTEL, monthly. **Remarks:** FAX: (416)566-3332. **Staff:** Janet Moore, Info.Spec.; Glenda Schultz, Info.Spec.; Judy Rice, ILL.

★ 12015 ★
Northern Telecom Ltd. - Information Resource Centre
522 University Ave., 14th Fl.
Toronto, ON, Canada M5G 1W7
Founded: 1976. **Subjects:** Computer science, information systems, office of the future, software development, information management, telecommunications. **Holdings:** 500 books; 500 bound periodical volumes; 100 technical reports. **Remarks:** Currently inactive.

Northern Territory - State Library of the Northern Territory
See: **State Library of the Northern Territory - Northern Australia Collection (15690)**

★ 12016 ★
Northern Trust Company - Library (Bus-Fin)
50 S. LaSalle St.   Phone: (312)630-6000
Chicago, IL 60675   Cathy A. Porter, Libn.
Founded: 1950. **Staff:** Prof 1. **Subjects:** Banking, finance, investments, accounting, management. **Special Collections:** Moody's Manuals, 1930 to present; Commercial & Financial Chronicle, 1947-1987. **Holdings:** 3500 books; 25 VF drawers of pamphlets; 35 VF drawers of annual reports. **Subscriptions:** 400 journals and other serials; 30 newspapers. **Services:** Interlibrary loan; library open to bank's customers on request through banking or trust officer. **Computerized Information Services:** DIALOG Information Services, Dow Jones News/Retrieval. **Remarks:** FAX: (312)630-0710.

★ 12017 ★
Northern Virginia Association of Realtors Inc. - Barbara Fewell
   Memorial Library (Bus-Fin)
8411 Arlington Blvd.   Phone: (703)207-3236
Fairfax, VA 22031   Resi Strickler, Dir., Lib.Serv.
Founded: 1972. **Staff:** Prof 1; Other 1. **Subjects:** Real estate - sales, management, investment, taxation, rental property, construction. **Special Collections:** Tax assessment information for Northern Virginia (microfiche). **Holdings:** 2266 books; 527 cassette tapes and tape albums; 255 videotapes. **Subscriptions:** 185 journals and other serials; 8 newspapers. **Services:** Copying; SDI; library open to the public on fee basis. **Automated Operations:** Computerized cataloging and circulation. **Publications:** Northern Virginia Association of Realtors Update, monthly - for internal distribution only. **Remarks:** FAX: (703)560-8239. **Formerly:** Northern Virginia Board of Realtors Inc.

Northern Virginia Board of Realtors Inc.
See: **Northern Virginia Association of Realtors Inc. (12017)**

★ 12018 ★
Northern Westchester Hospital Center - Health Sciences Library (Med)
400 Main St.   Phone: (914)666-1259
Mount Kisco, NY 10549   Nona C. Willoughby, Dir.
Founded: 1960. **Staff:** Prof 1; Other 1. **Subjects:** Clinical medicine, nursing, nutrition, laboratory sciences, obstetrics and gynecology, hospital management. **Holdings:** 1900 books; 3500 bound periodical volumes; 300 audio cassettes; 3 VF cabinets of pamphlets and clippings. **Subscriptions:** 142 journals and other serials. **Services:** Interlibrary loan; copying; library open to the public. **Computerized Information Services:** MEDLARS. **Networks/Consortia:** Member of Health Information Libraries of Westchester (HILOW), New York Metropolitan Reference and Research Library Agency, BHSL. **Publications:** New acquisitions, quarterly - for internal distribution only; Journal Holdings, annual; guide of library availability, resources, and services, annual update.

★ 12019 ★
Northminster Presbyterian Church - Library (Rel-Phil)
Alaska & Kalmia Rds., N.W.   Phone: (202)829-5311
Washington, DC 20012   Gloria B. Pendleton
Subjects: Bible, church history, music, children's literature. **Holdings:** 600 books; 20 reports. **Subscriptions:** 3 journals and other serials. **Services:** Library not open to the public.

★ 12020 ★
Northminster Presbyterian Church - Library (Rel-Phil)
703 Compton Rd.
Cincinnati, OH 45231   Phone: (513)931-0243
Staff: 3. **Subjects:** Bible, religion, family life, children's literature. **Holdings:** 500 books. **Services:** Library open to the public. **Staff:** Joan P. Reul, Adult Libn.; Marilyn Spreen, Children's Libn.

★ 12021 ★
Northminster Presbyterian Church - Library (Rel-Phil)
2434 Wilmington Rd.   Phone: (412)658-9051
New Castle, PA 16105   Helen Sloat, Church Libn.
Founded: 1957. **Subjects:** Religion. **Holdings:** 4200 books. **Services:** Library open to the public with restrictions.

★ 12022 ★
Northport-East Northport School District - Teachers' Professional
   Library (Educ)
110 Elwood Rd.
P.O. Box 210
Northport, NY 11768   Phone: (516)261-9000
Staff: Prof 1; Other 1. **Subjects:** Education. **Holdings:** 3000 books. **Subscriptions:** 80 journals and other serials. **Services:** Library not open to the public. **Remarks:** Maintained by Union Free School District 4.

★ 12023 ★

Northport Historical Society Museum - Library (Hist)
215 Main St.
Box 545   Phone: (516)757-9859
Northport, NY 11768   Mary Engelmann, Libn.
Founded: 1962. **Staff:** 3. **Subjects:** Northport history. **Holdings:** 300 books;
100 reports. **Subscriptions:** 4 journals and other serials; 3 newspapers.
Services: Library open to the public. **Staff:** Donald Schluter, Dir.; Mimi
Kail, Asst.Dir.

★ 12024 ★

Northridge Hospital Medical Center - Atcherley Medical Library (Med)
18300 Roscoe Blvd.   Phone: (818)885-8500
Northridge, CA 91328   Theresa Sase, M.L.S
Staff: 2. **Subjects:** Medicine, health sciences. **Special Collections:** Bioethics
books for lay people. **Holdings:** 3000 books; 7 VF drawers; pamphlet file.
Subscriptions: 376 journals and other serials. **Services:** Interlibrary loan;
copying; library open to the public with a fee for some services.
Computerized Information Services: MEDLARS.

★ 12025 ★

Northrop Corporation - Aircraft Division - Library Services, 1370/MA
(Sci-Engr)
One Northrop Ave.   Phone: (310)332-4146
Hawthorne, CA 90250   John E. Reynolds, Mgr., Lib.Serv.
Founded: 1942. **Staff:** Prof 5; Other 1. **Subjects:** Aerospace sciences,
materials, aeronautical engineering. **Holdings:** 15,000 books; 1000 bound
periodical volumes; 50,000 reports; 9000 military specifications and
standards; 15,000 military manuals, regulations, handbooks; 400,000 reports
on microfiche. **Subscriptions:** 500 journals and other serials. **Services:**
Interlibrary loan; library not open to the public. **Automated Operations:**
Computerized public access catalog, cataloging, acquisitions, serials, and
circulation. **Computerized Information Services:** DIALOG Information
Services, DTIC, NASA/RECON, NEXIS. **Publications:** Accessions List -
for internal distribution only; Library Guide. **Remarks:** FAX: (213)332-
5853. **Staff:** Marilyn Greenbaum, Mil.Pubn.; Carrol Speich, Acq.Libn.;
Renee Soiffer, Ref.Libn.

★ 12026 ★

Northrop Corporation - B-2 Division - Information Research Center (Sci-
Engr)
Dept. A450/UA
8900 E. Washington Blvd.   Phone: (213)942-6054
Pico Rivera, CA 90660-3737   Kay E. Salm, Mgr.
Founded: 1983. **Staff:** Prof 5; Other 4. **Subjects:** Aerospace, management.
Special Collections: NASA reports (5000). **Holdings:** 7000 books; 3500
reports; 3500 U.S. Air Force Technical Orders; 1700 military specifications
and standards. **Subscriptions:** 445 journals and other serials. **Services:**
Interlibrary loan; center not open to the public. **Automated Operations:**
Computerized cataloging, acquisitions, and circulation. **Computerized
Information Services:** DIALOG Information Services, BRS Information
Technologies, PFDS Online, WILSONLINE, NASA/RECON, DTIC,
Washington Alert Service, LEXIS, NEXIS, VU/TEXT Information
Services, Dow Jones News/Retrieval, DataTimes, Aerospace Online,
NewsNet, Inc., Orion, RLIN; IRCBASIS (internal database). **Remarks:**
FAX: (213)942-6478. **Staff:** Eleanor Skaggs, Res./Ref.; Marilyn Durkin,
Res./Ref.; Diane Guerrero, Mil.Docs.; Linda Long, Acq. & ILL; Sue
Colasurdo, Tech. Orders.

★ 12027 ★

Northrop Corporation - Corporate Research Library (Bus-Fin)
1840 Century Park, E.   Phone: (310)201-3132
Los Angeles, CA 90067-2199   Naomi Printz, Mgr.
Staff: Prof 2; Other 2. **Subjects:** Business, marketing, aerospace, politics,
government, management. **Holdings:** 3000 books; 150 bound periodical
volumes; 20,000 other cataloged items; newspaper clippings. **Subscriptions:**
300 journals and other serials; 3 newspapers. **Services:** Interlibrary loan;
library not open to the public. **Automated Operations:** Computerized public
access catalog, cataloging, acquisitions, serials, and circulation.
Computerized Information Services: DIALOG Information Services, Dow
Jones News/Retrieval, NEXIS, LEXIS, LEGI-SLATE, Washington Alert
Service, ORBIT Search Service, CompuServe Information Service, Orion,
OCLC, VU/TEXT Information Services, DataTimes, INVESTEXT,
Aerospace Online, DRI/McGraw-Hill, NewsNet, Inc., PERISCOPE, State
Net; BASIS, PROFS (internal databases). **Publications:** Daily news
abstracts; quarterly bibliographies. **Remarks:** Alternate telephone
number(s): 553-6262. FAX: (310)553-2076. **Staff:** Rosalyn Jackson,
Acq.Asst.; Veronis Forte-Murray, Ref.Asst.; Christine Lincoln, Res.Libn.

★ 12028 ★

Northrop Corporation - Information Resources Center (Sci-Engr)
2301 W. 120th St.
P.O. Box 5032   Phone: (213)600-3000
Hawthorne, CA 90251-5032   Joyce Farris, Adm., Lib.Serv.
Founded: 1952. **Staff:** 3. **Subjects:** Automatic test equipment; machinery
noise monitoring; command control and communications; laser systems;
guidance and control; operations systems analysis. **Holdings:** 4900 books;
4600 bound periodical volumes; 26,000 reports; vendor catalogs on
microfilm. **Subscriptions:** 300 journals and other serials. **Services:**
Interlibrary loan (limited); center not open to the public. **Computerized
Information Services:** DIALOG Information Services. **Publications:**
Accessions List, quarterly; Periodical Holdings List, annual.

★ 12029 ★

Northrop Corporation - Research and Technology Center - Library, 321/
T20
One Research Park
Palos Verdes Peninsula, CA 90274-5471
Defunct.

★ 12030 ★

Northrop University - Alumni Library - American Hall of Aviation
History
5800 W. Arbor Vitae St.
Los Angeles, CA 90045-4770
Founded: 1942. **Subjects:** Aviation history. **Holdings:** 148,000 items.
Remarks: Currently inactive.

Preston B. Northrup Memorial Library
See: **Southwest Foundation for Biomedical Research** (15529)

★ 12031 ★

Northside United Methodist Church - McDonald Memorial Library
(Rel-Phil)
2799 Northside Dr., N.W.   Phone: (404)355-6475
Atlanta, GA 30305   Lorenna R. Brown, Libn.
Founded: 1957. **Staff:** Prof 1; Other 5. **Subjects:** Religion, Bible, Methodism.
Special Collections: Bound volumes of National Geographic, 1913 to
present. **Holdings:** 3000 books; 200 bound periodical volumes.
Subscriptions: 9 journals and other serials. **Services:** Library open to the
public with restrictions.

★ 12032 ★

Northumberland County Law Library (Law)
Court House   Phone: (717)988-4162
Sunbury, PA 17801   Catherine L. Kroh, Law Libn.
Founded: 1901. **Staff:** Prof 1. **Subjects:** Law. **Holdings:** 10,480 volumes.
Subscriptions: 8 journals and other serials. **Services:** Interlibrary loan;
copying; library open to the public.

★ 12033 ★

Northville Historical Society - Library (Hist)
215 W. Main St.
Northville, MI 48167   Phone: (313)348-1845
Subjects: Architecture, historic preservation. **Holdings:** 300 books; archival
materials. **Remarks:** Library housed at Northville Public Library. Alternate
telephone number(s): 349-3020.

★ 12034 ★

Northville Public Library - Special Collections (Hist, Hum)
215 W. Main St.   Phone: (313)349-3020
Northville, MI 48167   Patricia Orr, Dir.
Staff: Prof 5; Other 8. **Special Collections:** Contemporary American plays,
local history. **Holdings:** 38,450 books. **Subscriptions:** 120 journals and other
serials; 7 newspapers. **Services:** Interlibrary loan; copying; library open to
the public. **Automated Operations:** Computerized circulation. **Networks/**
Consortia: Member of Wayne Oakland Library Federation (WOLF). **Staff:**
S. Mazzaro, Asst.Dir.; J. Dewey, Children's Serv.; A. Smitley, Ref.Libn.; M.
Louie, Ref.Libn.

★ 12035 ★
Northville Regional Psychiatric Hospital - Staff Library (Med)
41001 W. 7 Mile Rd.   Phone: (313)349-1800
Northville, MI 48167   Bonnie A. Gasperini, Hosp.Libn.
Founded: 1953. **Subjects:** Medicine, psychiatry, psychology, social service, nursing. **Holdings:** 3057 volumes; 100 reprints. **Subscriptions:** 66 journals and other serials. **Services:** Interlibrary loan; library not open to the public. **Networks/Consortia:** Member of National Network of Libraries of Medicine - Greater Midwest Region. **Remarks:** FAX: (313)349-9022. **Formerly:** Its Professional Library.

★ 12036 ★
Northwest/ACTS Library (Rel-Phil)
7600 Glover Rd.   Phone: (604)888-7511
Langley, BC, Canada V3A 4R9   W.B. Badke, Libn.
Staff: Prof 1; Other 1. **Subjects:** Theology. **Holdings:** 30,000 books. **Subscriptions:** 225 journals and other serials. **Services:** Copying; library open to the public at librarian's discretion. **Automated Operations:** Computerized cataloging.

★ 12037 ★
Northwest Alabama Council of Local Governments - Library (Soc Sci)
Box 2603   Phone: (205)383-3861
Muscle Shoals, AL 35662   Sam Minor, Exec.Dir.
Founded: 1967. **Staff:** Prof 1; Other 1. **Subjects:** Transportation, energy. **Special Collections:** Regional Data Center for Alabama State Data System (Census Bureau). **Holdings:** 1500 volumes; 500 pamphlets; 4 VF drawers of clippings; 1 VF drawer of documents; 500 maps. **Subscriptions:** 6 newspapers. **Services:** Copying; library open to the public. **Automated Operations:** Computerized cataloging. **Remarks:** Library located at 807 E. Avalon Ave., Muscle Shoals, AL 35662.

★ 12038 ★
Northwest Area Health Education Center - Library (Med)
Rowan Memorial Hospital
612 Mocksville Ave.   Phone: (704)638-1069
Salisbury, NC 28144   Connie Schardt, AHEC Lib.Dir.
Staff: Prof 2; Other 3. **Subjects:** Medicine, nursing, allied health sciences. **Holdings:** 1100 books; 1974 bound periodical volumes. **Subscriptions:** 145 journals and other serials. **Services:** Interlibrary loan; copying; SDI; library open to the public for reference use only. **Computerized Information Services:** BRS Information Technologies, MEDLINE; CD-ROM (MEDLINE, CINAHL). Performs searches on fee basis. **Networks/Consortia:** Member of Northwest AHEC Library Information Network, Yadkin Valley Consortium. **Remarks:** FAX: (704)636-5050.

★ 12039 ★
Northwest Area Health Education Center - NW AHEC Library (Med)
Watauga County Hospital
Deerfield Rd.   Phone: (704)262-4101
Boone, NC 28607   Ann McGregor, Asst.Lib.Dir.
Staff: Prof 2; Other 3. **Subjects:** Medicine, nursing, allied health sciences. **Holdings:** 910 books; 1058 unbound periodicals; 150 clippings; 80 special bibliographies. **Subscriptions:** 155 journals and other serials. **Services:** Interlibrary loan; copying; SDI; library open to the public for reference use only. **Computerized Information Services:** MEDLARS, BRS Information Technologies. **Publications:** AHEC News, monthly. **Remarks:** FAX (704)262-1102.

★ 12040 ★
Northwest Area Health Education Center - NW AHEC Library (Med)
Catawba Memorial Hospital   Phone: (704)326-3662
Hickory, NC 28602-9643   Phyllis C. Gillikin, Dir.
Founded: 1978. **Staff:** Prof 3; Other 6. **Subjects:** Medicine, nursing, health care administration, allied health sciences. **Holdings:** 2264 books. **Subscriptions:** 223 journals and other serials. **Services:** Interlibrary loan; copying; SDI; library open to the public. **Automated Operations:** Computerized cataloging. **Computerized Information Services:** BRS Information Technologies, NLM; CD-ROMs (MEDLINE, CINAHL-CD). **Networks/Consortia:** Member of Northwest AHEC Library Information Network. **Publications:** Hickory AHEC Announcements, semimonthly; LINK Newsletter, 6/year. **Special Catalogs:** Union list of serials, annual. **Remarks:** FAX: (704)322-2921. **Staff:** Karen Lee Martinez, Asst.Dir.; Judy Wojcik, Assoc.Dir.

★ 12041 ★
Northwest Atlantic Fisheries Organization - Library (Biol Sci)
P.O. Box 638   Phone: (902)469-9105
Dartmouth, NS, Canada B2Y 3Y9   Ferne Perry, Doc.Ck.
Subjects: Fisheries - management, science, conservation, statistics; fishing vessels and gears; Northwest Atlantic hydrography; international enforcement. **Holdings:** Figures not available. **Services:** Library not open to the public. **Remarks:** FAX: (902)469-5729. Telex: 019-31475.

★ 12042 ★
Northwest Bible College - J.C. Cooke Library (Rel-Phil)
11617 106th Ave.   Phone: (403)452-0808
Edmonton, AB, Canada T5H 0S1   Braden S. Fawcett, Libn.
Founded: 1979. **Staff:** Prof 1; Other 1. **Subjects:** Theology, religion, Christian education, homiletics, church history, pastoral counseling. **Holdings:** 14,000 books; clippings; archival material; microfilm. **Subscriptions:** 90 journals and other serials. **Services:** Library not open to the public. **Remarks:** Includes the faculty library known as Hillerud Memorial Library. FAX: (403)452-5803.

★ 12043 ★
Northwest Christian College - Learning Resource Center (Rel-Phil)
828 E. 11th   Phone: (503)343-1641
Eugene, OR 97401   Margaret Sue Rhee, Dir.
Founded: 1895. **Staff:** Prof 2; Other 3. **Subjects:** The Bible, religion and theology, Church Growth Movement, Brazil. **Special Collections:** Rare books and Bibles; Discipliana representing Christian Church (Disciples of Christ) Northwest; African and American Indian artifacts; hymnals; archives; missionary papers. **Holdings:** 60,000 volumes; 3120 bound periodical volumes; 250 cubic feet of manuscripts and unlisted serials; 500 reels of microfilm; 3922 AV programs. **Subscriptions:** 390 journals and other serials; 6 newspapers. **Services:** Interlibrary loan; copying; center open to public with restrictions on use of special collections. **Computerized Information Services:** OCLC, DIALOG Information Services. **Publications:** Friends of the Library Newsletter, biennial. **Remarks:** FAX: (503)343-9159. **Staff:** James R. Stoltz, Tech.Serv.; Patricia K. Harley, ILL/Circ.Supv.; Lenard Cory Lemke, AV Supv.

★ 12044 ★
Northwest College of the Assemblies of God - Hurst Library (Rel-Phil)
5520 108th Ave., N.E.
Box 579   Phone: (206)822-8266
Kirkland, WA 98083-0579   Ann D. Rosett, Libn.
Founded: 1949. **Staff:** Prof 2; Other 3. **Subjects:** Religion, elementary education, behavioral sciences, literature. **Special Collections:** Ness Bible Translations Reference Collection; Pentecostal Movement Collection; Kenneth Schlosser Near East Collection. **Holdings:** 62,465 books; 1294 graphic materials; 20,814 microfiche; 213 cartographic materials; 4326 AV programs; 2889 other cataloged items. **Subscriptions:** 541 journals and other serials; 7 newspapers. **Services:** Interlibrary loan; copying; library open to the public with nonresident fee and card. **Automated Operations:** Computerized cataloging. **Computerized Information Services:** OCLC; OCLC EPIC; InfoTrac; CD-ROMs (Academic Abstracts, Religious and Theological Abstracts, CDWord); EasyNet (electronic mail service). **Networks/Consortia:** Member of Northwest Association of Private Colleges & Universities (NAPCU). **Publications:** Faculty and student manuals. **Special Catalogs:** Catalog to the sermons of Dr. Charles S. Price. **Remarks:** FAX: (206)827-0148 (campus fax). **Also Known As:** Assemblies of God Northwest College. **Staff:** Margaret Frye, Cat.

★ 12045 ★
Northwest Community Hospital - Medical Library (Med)
800 West Central Rd.   Phone: (708)259-1000
Arlington Heights, IL 60005   Ching-Ching Liang, Hosp.Libn.
Staff: Prof 1. **Subjects:** Medicine, nursing. **Holdings:** 2100 books; 4 VF drawers of pamphlets; AV programs; journal backfiles on microfiche, 1985-1989. **Subscriptions:** 250 journals and other serials. **Services:** Interlibrary loan; copying; library open to the public for reference use only. **Computerized Information Services:** MEDLINE, BRS Information Technologies. **Networks/Consortia:** Member of North Suburban Library System (NSLS).

Northwest Educational Cooperative - Library
See: **Illinois Resource Center/Adult Resource Center Library - Library** (7679)

★ 12046 ★
Northwest Florida Water Management District - Library and Information Center (Env-Cons)
P.O. Box 3100, Rt. 1   Phone: (904)539-5999
Havana, FL 32333   Carter Belvin
Founded: 1973. **Staff:** 1. **Subjects:** Water resources, growth management, local and regional planning, environment, economic development, engineering and geology. **Special Collections:** Local history; developments of regional impacts; local government plans. **Holdings:** 1500 books; 30 bound periodical volumes; 200 reports and dissertations; projects; policies; plans. **Subscriptions:** 119 journals and other serials; 20 newspapers. **Services:** Interlibrary loan; copying; library open to the public with restrictions and for reference use only. **Remarks:** FAX: (904)539-5999, ext. 210 (must ask operator to receive FAX).

★ 12047 ★
Northwest General Hospital - Medical Library (Med)
5310 W. Capitol Dr.
Milwaukee, WI 53216   Phone: (414)447-8600
Staff: Prof 2. **Subjects:** Medicine, nursing. **Holdings:** 925 books; 300 bound periodical volumes. **Subscriptions:** 187 journals and other serials. **Services:** Interlibrary loan; library not open to the public. **Automated Operations:** Computerized ILL. **Computerized Information Services:** DOCLINE (electronic mail service). **Networks/Consortia:** Member of Southeastern Wisconsin Health Science Library Consortium (SWHSL), National Network of Libraries of Medicine (NN/LM). **Remarks:** Alternate telephone number(s): (414)447-8543.

★ 12048 ★
Northwest Geophysical Associates, Inc. - Library (Sci-Engr)
850 N.W. 15th St., Suite H   Phone: (503)757-7231
Corvallis, OR 97333   Kathy Wilkins, Libn.
Subjects: Geological exploration, gravity, magnetics, magnetotellurics, seismology, thermal energy, resistivity. **Holdings:** 2000 volumes.

★ 12049 ★
Northwest Georgia Regional Hospital at Rome - Medical Library (Med)
1305 Redmond Rd.   Phone: (404)295-6060
Rome, GA 30161   James R. Fletcher, Lib.Ck.
Founded: 1946. **Staff:** 1. **Subjects:** Chest, tuberculosis, psychiatry, psychology, mental retardation, alcoholism. **Holdings:** 916 books; 1003 bound periodical volumes; 659 audiotapes; 4 VF drawers; 13 videotapes. **Subscriptions:** 64 journals and other serials. **Services:** Interlibrary loan; copying; library open to the public with legitimate need for medical information. **Publications:** Library Handbook - for internal distribution only.

★ 12050 ★
Northwest Geriatric Education Center - Clearinghouse Resource Center (Med)
University of Washington HL-23   Phone: (206)685-7478
Seattle, WA 98195   Judith Bezy, Clghse.Mgr.
Founded: 1985. **Staff:** Prof 1. **Subjects:** Geriatrics. **Holdings:** Books, newsletters, curriculum guides, videotapes. **Services:** Center open to health professionals, educators, and practitioners in the field of aging. **Publications:** Model Curriculum Series; Viewpoint (newsletter), 3/year. **Remarks:** FAX: (206)685-3436.

★ 12051 ★
Northwest Hospital - Effie M. Storey Learning Center (Med)
1550 N. 115th   Phone: (206)368-1642
Seattle, WA 98133   Edith Sutton, Libn.
Founded: 1975. **Staff:** Prof 1. **Subjects:** Medicine, nursing, management. **Holdings:** 700 books; 100 videotapes. **Subscriptions:** 88 journals and other serials. **Services:** Interlibrary loan; center not open to the public. **Computerized Information Services:** MEDLINE; OnTyme Electronic Message Network Service (electronic mail service). **Networks/Consortia:** Member of Seattle Area Hospital Library Consortium (SAHLC).

★ 12052 ★
Northwest Industries Ltd. - Technical Data Control Centre (Sci-Engr)
Edmonton Intl. Airport
P.O. Box 9864   Phone: (403)890-6333
Edmonton, AB, Canada T5J 2T2   A.W. Young, Supv.
Staff: 6. **Subjects:** Aircraft maintenance, engineering, military specifications and standards, electronics. **Holdings:** 300 books; 500 bound periodical volumes; 40,000 military technical manuals; 55,000 specifications on microfiche; 100,000 blueprints and specifications on aperture cards; 25,000 blueprints and masters. **Subscriptions:** 150 journals and other serials; 5 newspapers. **Services:** Interlibrary loan; center open to the public with restrictions on classified materials. **Remarks:** FAX: (403)890-2351.

★ 12053 ★
Northwest Institute of Research - Library (Soc Sci)
652 W. 17th St.   Phone: (814)459-8347
Erie, PA 16502   Dr. Mark Iutcovich, Dir.
Founded: 1975. **Staff:** 7. **Subjects:** Social and behavioral sciences, mathematics, anthropology, archeology, methodology. **Holdings:** 5000 volumes. **Services:** Library not open to the public. **Remarks:** Affiliated with Keystone University Research Corporation; FAX: (814)453-4714.

★ 12054 ★
Northwest Iowa Technical College - Library (Soc Sci)
Hwy. 18 W.   Phone: (712)324-5061
Sheldon, IA 51201   Vera H. Osland
Founded: 1974. **Staff:** Prof 1. **Subjects:** Arts, sciences, technical materials, nursing, auto shop manuals. **Holdings:** 7491 books; 35 bound periodical volumes; 1400 microfiche. **Subscriptions:** 243 journals and other serials; 41 newspapers. **Services:** Interlibrary loan; copying; library open to the public with restrictions. **Remarks:** FAX: (712)324-4136.

★ 12055 ★
Northwest Minnesota Historical Center - Library (Hist, Area-Ethnic)
Moorhead State University Library   Phone: (218)236-2343
Moorhead, MN 56563   Terry L. Shoptaugh, Dir.
Founded: 1972. **Staff:** Prof 1; Other 3. **Subjects:** Ethnicity in Northwest Minnesota, social welfare, American Indians, politics, government, business, church history, oral history, women's organizations. **Special Collections:** Sugarbeet agriculture in Red River Valley; Scandinavian ethnic retention; World War II on the Homefront in the Red River Valley of the North; The Depressions in the Red River Valley of the North; oral history of Moorhead, Minnesota, and Fargo, North Dakota. **Holdings:** 546 linear feet of local history materials; photographs; microfilm; slides. **Services:** Copying; research aid; library open to the public. **Publications:** Guide to the Northwest Minnesota Historical Center Collections (1988). **Remarks:** Maintained by Moorhead State University.

★ 12056 ★
Northwest Missouri State University - Owens Library - Horace Mann Library/Learning Center (Hum)
Brown Hall, Rm. 142   Phone: (816)562-1271
Maryville, MO 64468   Nancy Thomas, Lib.Dir.
Staff: Prof 1. **Subjects:** Children's literature; library science. **Holdings:** 15,690 books; 50 multimedia kits; 3800 filmstrips; 740 records; 260 tapes; 2500 slides; 1200 pictures and art prints; 1000 transparencies; 500 software titles; 150 videocassettes; professional collection; curriculum materials. **Subscriptions:** 85 journals and other serials. **Services:** ESN satellite downlink; center open to the public. **Automated Operations:** Computerized circulation. **Remarks:** Serves as the research and resource center for the Elementary Education and the Library Science departments of the university.

★ 12057 ★
Northwest Missouri State University - Owens Library - Special Collections (Hist)
Maryville, MO 64468   Phone: (816)562-1590
                                        Georgene Timko, Lib.Dir.
Founded: 1905. **Staff:** Prof 11; Other 15. **Special Collections:** Missouriana (2500 volumes); Laboratory School Library; university archives (55 drawers). **Holdings:** 271,059 books; 39,002 bound periodical volumes; 96,081 government documents; 555,417 microfiche. **Subscriptions:** 1420 journals and other serials; 43 newspapers. **Services:** Interlibrary loan; copying; collections open to the public with restrictions. **Automated Operations:** Computerized cataloging and circulation. **Computerized Information Services:** OCLC, DIALOG Information Services; internal database; CD-ROMs (ABI/INFORM, ERIC). Performs searches on fee basis. **Networks/Consortia:** Member of Missouri Library Network Corp. (MLNC). **Remarks:** FAX: (816)562-2153; 562-1192. **Staff:** Tom Carneal, Archv.

★ 12058 ★

Northwest Municipal Conference - Government Information Center (Soc Sci)

1616 E. Golf Rd.   Phone: (708)296-9206
Des Plaines, IL 60016   William Kahles, Lib.Serv.Dir.
Staff: Prof 2. **Subjects:** Municipal government, public administration, Illinois rules and regulations. **Holdings:** 7900 books; 600 pamphlets. **Subscriptions:** 20 journals and other serials. **Services:** Interlibrary loan; copying; center open to the public. **Networks/Consortia:** Member of Iowa Computer Assisted Network (ICAN). **Remarks:** Center is a partial federal depository. FAX: (708)253-6330. **Staff:** Brian C. Nigbor, Adm.Asst.; Bill Duggan, Adm.Asst.

★ 12059 ★

Northwest Power Planning Council - Library/Public Reading Room (Energy)

851 S.W. Sixth, Suite 1100   Phone: (503)222-5161
Portland, OR 97204   Janie Pearcy, Rec.Mgr.
Founded: 1981. **Staff:** 45. **Subjects:** Energy policies and resources; fish and wildlife of the Columbia River Basin. **Special Collections:** Administrative records of the Fish and Wildlife Program, the Northwest Conservation and Electric Power Plan; Pacific Northwest energy and fisheries. **Holdings:** 900 books; 7 VF drawers; 30 feet of documents and reports. **Subscriptions:** 125 journals and other serials. **Services:** Interlibrary loan; copying; SDI; library open to the public. **Automated Operations:** Computerized cataloging and document indexing. **Computerized Information Services:** DIALOG Information Services. **Special Indexes:** Administrative Record Indexes. **Remarks:** The council is a regional interstate compact agency made up of eight members appointed by the governors of Idaho, Montana, Oregon, and Washington. It is charged with planning to meet the Northwest's electrical energy needs, and with protecting, mitigating, and enhancing the fish and wildlife resources damaged by hydroelectric development. FAX: (503)795-3370.

★ 12060 ★

Northwest Pulp and Paper Association - Technical Information Center

1300 114th Ave., S.E., Suite 110
Bellevue, WA 98004-6928   Phone: (206)455-1323
Founded: 1957. **Staff:** 5. **Subjects:** Environmental regulations, emissions, effluents, pollution expenditures. **Holdings:** 450 volumes; 200 NCASI reports. **Remarks:** FAX: (206)451-1349.

★ 12061 ★

Northwest Regional Educational Laboratory - Information Center/ Library (Educ)

One Main Place
101 S.W. Main, Suite 500   Phone: (503)275-9555
Portland, OR 97204   M. Margaret Rogers, Info.Ctr.Dir.
Founded: 1966. **Staff:** Prof 1; Other 1. **Subjects:** Educational research, psychology, evaluation, career education, computer applications in education. **Special Collections:** Loan collection of psychological/ educational tests and instruments; collection of educational materials on substance abuse education, drugs, alcohol education. **Holdings:** 4250 volumes; 56 VF drawers of pamphlets; 6 shelves of ERIC Clearinghouse Publications; ERIC microfiche collection and special indexes. **Subscriptions:** 300 journals and other serials; 10 newspapers. **Services:** Interlibrary loan; copying; SDI; center open to the public. **Computerized Information Services:** DIALOG Information Services. Performs searches on fee basis.

Northwest Territories Archives
See: **Prince of Wales Northern Heritage Centre** (13363)

★ 12062 ★

Northwest Territories Audit Bureau - Library (Bus-Fin)

Box 1320
Yellowknife, NT, Canada X1A 2L9   Phone: (403)873-7595
Founded: 1982. **Staff:** Prof 19; Other 2. **Subjects:** Auditing, accounting, management, tax. **Holdings:** 600 books; 100 bound periodical volumes. **Subscriptions:** 27 journals and other serials. **Services:** Interlibrary loan; library open to the public by appointment. **Automated Operations:** Computerized cataloging. **Computerized Information Services:** Internal database. **Publications:** List of publications - available on request.

★ 12063 ★

Northwest Territories Department of Health - Dr. Otto Schaefer Health Resource Centre (Med)

The Centre Square Tower, 2nd Fl.   Phone: (403)873-7713
Yellowknife, NT, Canada X1A 2L9   Florrie Cook, Libn.
Founded: 1981. **Staff:** Prof 1; Other 2. **Subjects:** Public health, nursing, health care administration, Northern health care, hospital operations. **Special Collections:** Dr. Otto Schaefer papers. **Holdings:** 4000 books. **Subscriptions:** 160 journals and other serials. **Services:** Interlibrary loan; copying; center open to the public. **Computerized Information Services:** DIALOG Information Services, MEDLARS, CAN/OLE. **Remarks:** FAX: (403)873-7706.

★ 12064 ★

Northwest Territories Department of Justice - Court Library (Law)

Court House
4903 49th St., 1st Fl.
Box 1320   Phone: (403)873-7618
Yellowknife, NT, Canada X1A 2L9   Susan Baer, Libn.
Founded: 1955. **Staff:** Prof 1; Other 2. **Subjects:** Law. **Holdings:** 30,000 books; 5000 bound periodical volumes; 1200 unreported cases. **Subscriptions:** 123 journals and other serials. **Services:** Interlibrary loan; copying; library open to the public for reference use only. **Computerized Information Services:** QL Systems, CAN/LAW, WESTLAW, LEXIS, DIALOG Information Services, Info Globe, Infomart Online; Envoy 100 (electronic mail service). Performs searches. **Publications:** Contents Page Bulletin; Acquisitions List. **Remarks:** FAX: (403)873-0368. Electronic mail address(es): NWT.COURT.LIB (Envoy 100).

★ 12065 ★

Northwest Territories Government - Department of Culture and Communications - Government Library (Info Sci)

Laing No. 1
P.O. Box 1320   Phone: (403)873-7628
Yellowknife, NT, Canada X1A 2L9   Vera Raschke, Govt.Libn.
Founded: 1973. **Staff:** Prof 1; Other 1. **Subjects:** Political science, northern Canada, administration, public policy. **Special Collections:** Full depository for Northwest Territories and federal government documents. **Holdings:** 20,100 books; 5000 microfiche. **Subscriptions:** 200 journals and other serials; 25 newspapers. **Services:** Interlibrary loan; copying; library open to the public with restrictions. **Computerized Information Services:** DIALOG Information Services, DOBIS Canadian Online Library System, CAN/ OLE; Envoy 100 (electronic mail service). **Remarks:** FAX: (403)873-0107. Electronic mail address(es): NWT.GOVTLIB (Envoy 100).

★ 12066 ★

Northwest Territories Renewable Resources Library (Env-Cons)

P.O. Box 1320   Phone: (403)920-8606
Yellowknife, NT, Canada X1A 2L9   Alison Welch, Libn.
Founded: 1980. **Staff:** Prof 1. **Subjects:** Wildlife, northern environment. **Holdings:** 7000 books; 3000 unpublished reports and manuscripts; 300 microfiche. **Subscriptions:** 76 journals and other serials. **Services:** Interlibrary loan; copying; library open to the public for reference use only. **Automated Operations:** Computerized cataloging. **Computerized Information Services:** DIALOG Information Services, CAN/OLE, RESORS (Remote Sensing On-Line Retrieval System); Envoy 100 (electronic mail service). **Remarks:** FAX: (403)873-0293. Electronic mail address(es): ALISON.WELCH (Envoy 100).

★ 12067 ★

Northwest Territories Safety Division - Department of Safety & Public Services - Safety Resource Centre (Med)

Yellowknife, NT, Canada X1A 2L9   Phone: (403)873-7470
      Rita Denneron, Lib.Techn.
Founded: 1983. **Staff:** Prof 1; Other 1. **Subjects:** Safety, industrial hygiene, law, legislation, occupational health and safety regulations. **Special Collections:** GE Material Safety Data Sheets; Canada Safety Council Material Data Sheets; National Safety Council Data Sheets; Special Information Package. **Holdings:** 348 volumes; 97 microfiche; 4 topic files; 6 file cabinets; 120 reports on microfiche; 6 lateral file drawers of reports and clippings; 190 manufacture equipment catalogs; 290 films and videos; 120 posters; 97 pamphlets. **Subscriptions:** 22 journals and other serials; 53 newsletters. **Services:** Interlibrary loan; copying; center open to the public. **Computerized Information Services:** Canadian Centre for Occupational Health & Safety DataScope System. Performs searches free of charge. **Publications:** Safety Resource Centre. **Special Catalogs:** Safety books; film catalog; manufacture catalog. **Remarks:** FAX: (403)873-0117. **Formerly:** Its Safety/Education Resource Centre. **Staff:** Al Shriener, Mgr., Occupational Hea./Safety.

★12068★

Northwest Territory Canadian & French Heritage Center - Minnesota Genealogical Society Library (Hist)
1650 Carol Ave.   Phone: (612)645-3671
St. Paul, MN 55102   Ozzie Thompson, Libn.
Subjects: Quebec, Canada, Canadians in the U.S., Metis Indians. **Holdings:** 2000 books; 100 bound periodical volumes; 1600 microforms; 10 manuscripts; 3 AV programs. **Services:** Library open to the public. **Publications:** Cousins et Cousines. **Staff:** Al Dahlquist, Canada Libn.; Dorothy Chandler, Res.

★12069★

Northwestern College of Chiropractic - Library (Med)
2501 W. 84th St.   Phone: (612)885-5419
Bloomington, MN 55431   Marcia Stephens, Dir., Lib.Serv.
Founded: 1966. **Staff:** Prof 2; Other 4. **Subjects:** Chiropractic, neurology, roentgenology, orthopedics, nutrition, allied medical and basic sciences. **Special Collections:** Diagnostic Radiologic Health Sciences Learning Laboratory (3300 X-rays); archives of chiropractic literature (260 items). **Holdings:** 8304 books; 1497 bound periodical volumes; 16 VF drawers of clippings, reprints, pamphlets; 1276 audiotapes; 70 models; 126 video cassettes; 351 slide sets; 1300 microfiche of chiropractic journals. **Subscriptions:** 256 journals and other serials. **Services:** Interlibrary loan; copying; SDI; cassette duplication; library open to the public with restrictions. **Computerized Information Services:** NLM, BRS Information Technologies, DIALOG Information Services. Performs searches on fee basis. **Networks/Consortia:** Member of Twin Cities Biomedical Consortium (TCBC), Chiropractic Library Consortium (CLIBCON). **Special Indexes:** Index to Chiropractic Literature, 1979 to present; index of Archives from the Canadian Memorial Chiropractic College. **Remarks:** FAX: (612)888-6713. **Staff:** Carol Y. Jones, Libn.

★12070★

Northwestern Connecticut Community College - Library (Educ)
Park Place East   Phone: (203)738-6480
Winsted, CT 06098   Anne Gifford, Dir. of Lib.Serv.
Founded: 1965. **Staff:** Prof 4; Other 2. **Subjects:** Deaf education, art. **Special Collections:** Matzke Collection (plant morphology; 500 titles); World War I (200 titles); Jazz compact discs (300 titles). **Holdings:** 50,333 books; 2000 phonograph records; 2171 microforms. **Subscriptions:** 243 journals and other serials; 12 newspapers. **Services:** Interlibrary loan; copying; library open to the public. **Computerized Information Services:** DIALOG Information Services, InfoTrac; CD-ROMs (Academic Index, National Newspaper Index). Performs searches on fee basis. **Networks/Consortia:** Member of NELINET, Inc. **Publications:** Library Handbook, annual; Periodical List, annual. **Remarks:** FAX: (203)379-4995. **Staff:** Andrea Dombrowski, Lib.Asst., ILL; Pamela Bellows, Ref./Pub.Serv.Libn.; Diane Hagymasi, Lib.Asst., Tech.Serv.

★12071★

Northwestern Medical Center - Information Center (Med)
Fairfield St.   Phone: (802)524-5911
St. Albans, VT 05478   DiAnne Bedard, Info.Ctr.Dir.
Staff: 1. **Subjects:** Medicine, nursing, behavioral science. **Holdings:** 400 books; tapes. **Subscriptions:** 20 journals and other serials. **Services:** Interlibrary loan; copying; center open to the public for reference use only.

★12072★

Northwestern Memorial Hospital - Health Learning Center (Med)
333 E. Superior St., Rm. 467   Phone: (312)908-9971
Chicago, IL 60611   Melinda Noonan, R.N.
Founded: 1980. **Staff:** Prof 1. **Subjects:** Health - general, women's. **Holdings:** 1400 books; 180 videotapes; 525 pamphlets. **Subscriptions:** 6 newsletters. **Services:** Copying; center open to the public. **Publications:** Bibliographies of popular health topics.

★12073★

Northwestern Mutual Life Insurance Company - Corporate Information Center (Bus-Fin)
720 E. Wisconsin Ave.   Phone: (414)299-2492
Milwaukee, WI 53202   Deborah A. Hall, Adm.
Founded: 1951. **Staff:** 6. **Subjects:** Management, business, life insurance. **Special Collections:** Medical Library (300 books). **Holdings:** 4000 books; 250 bound periodical volumes. **Subscriptions:** 375 journals and other serials; 21 newspapers. **Services:** Interlibrary loan; center open to the public by appointment. **Automated Operations:** Computerized cataloging and serials. **Computerized Information Services:** DIALOG Information Services, BRS Information Technologies, LEXIS, NEXIS, VU/TEXT Information Services, NewsNet, Inc., DataTimes, BestLink Market Advisor, NLM, Oil & Gas Journal, OCLC; CD-ROMs (ProQuest, Computer Select, Dun & Bradstreet Business Credit Services). **Networks/Consortia:** Member of Wisconsin Interlibrary Services (WILS), Library Council of Metropolitan Milwaukee, Inc. (LCOMM). **Publications:** Soundings, 4/year; electronic newsletters, daily and weekly. **Remarks:** FAX: (414)299-7022. Contains the holdings of its former Corporate Information Center/Medical Library. **Staff:** Joyce A. Madsen; Carolyn J. Barloga.

★12074★

Northwestern Mutual Life Insurance Company - Corporate Information Center/Medical Library
720 E. Wisconsin Ave.
Milwaukee, WI 53202
Defunct. Holdings absorbed by Northwestern Mutual Life Insurance Company - Corporate Information Center.

★12075★

Northwestern Mutual Life Insurance Company - Law Library (Law)
720 E. Wisconsin Ave.   Phone: (414)299-2422
Milwaukee, WI 53202   Patricia A. Ellingson, Law Libn.
Staff: Prof 1; Other 2. **Subjects:** Law - general, tax, insurance, investment. **Special Collections:** All state statutes and tax reports; U.S. and state case law; all state insurance regulations. **Holdings:** 18,600 books. **Subscriptions:** 600 journals and other serials. **Services:** Copying; library open to the public for reference use only. **Computerized Information Services:** DIALOG Information Services, LEXIS, NEXIS, WESTLAW, DataTimes, Comerce Clearing House, Inc. (CCH). **Networks/Consortia:** Member of Library Council of Metropolitan Milwaukee, Inc. (LCOMM). **Remarks:** FAX: (414)299-2584.

★12076★

Northwestern Oklahoma State University - Library (Educ)
Alva, OK 73717   Phone: (405)327-1700
                                        Ray D. Lau, Lib.Dir.
Founded: 1897. **Staff:** Prof 5; Other 4. **Subjects:** Education, arts and sciences, Oklahoma and local history, library science. **Special Collections:** William J. Mellor Collection of Indian artifacts, paintings, sculpture, stereoptican and slides, rare books (1000 items); Children's Literature Collection. **Holdings:** 125,000 volumes; 110,000 government publications; 300,000 items on microfiche. **Subscriptions:** 1487 journals and other serials; 20 newspapers. **Services:** Interlibrary loan; copying; library open to the public for reference use only with borrowing permitted for Alva residents. **Computerized Information Services:** DIALOG Information Services, NewsBank, OCLC; InfoTrac; CD-ROMs (ERIC, Magazine Article Summaries, NewsBank, Academic Index, GPO Monthly Catalog). **Networks/Consortia:** Member of AMIGOS Bibliographic Council, Inc. **Staff:** Bea LeValley, Cat.; Shirley Thorne, Ref.; Cindy Gottsch, Govt.Doc.; Carrie Spriggs, Circ.; Kathy Koch, Tech.Serv.Asst.; Jill Rooker, Instr. Media Dir.

Northwestern School of Law
See: Lewis and Clark Law School - Northwestern School of Law (9076)

★12077★

Northwestern State University of Louisiana - Eugene P. Watson Library - Shreveport Division (Med)
1800 Line Ave.   Phone: (318)677-3007
Shreveport, LA 71101   Dorcas M.C. McCormick, Hd.
Founded: 1949. **Staff:** Prof 1; Other 1. **Subjects:** Nursing, education. **Special Collections:** Archive collection of nursing history (3700 items). **Holdings:** 7200 books; 7200 bound periodical volumes; 186 reports and theses; 4000 microfiche; 1075 reels of microfilm; pamphlets; 1 VF drawer; 98 titles on microfilm. **Subscriptions:** 137 journals and other serials. **Services:** Interlibrary loan; copying; division open to the public. **Computerized Information Services:** BRS Information Technologies. **Remarks:** FAX: (318)226-7087.

★ 12078 ★
Northwestern University - Annenberg Washington Program in Communications Policy Studies - Library (Info Sci)
1455 Pennsylvania Ave., N.W., Suite 200
Washington, DC 20004
Founded: 1983. **Subjects:** Communications. **Holdings:** 100 books; 10 bound periodical volumes; 50 audio cassettes. **Services:** Library is accessible on a restricted basis.

★ 12079 ★
Northwestern University - Archives (Hist)
University Library   Phone: (708)491-3354
Evanston, IL 60208-2300   Patrick M. Quinn, Univ.Archv.
Staff: Prof 4. **Subjects:** Northwestern University and local history. **Holdings:** 10,000 linear feet of records and papers. **Subscriptions:** 1200 university published journals and other serials. **Services:** Copying; archives open to the public. **Computerized Information Services:** OCLC; InterNet (electronic mail service). **Networks/Consortia:** Member of ILLINET, Center for Research Libraries (CRL), Research Libraries Information Network (RLIN), North Suburban Library System (NSLS). **Remarks:** FAX: (708)491-8306. Electronic mail address(es): PQUINN@NUACUM.NWU.EDU (InterNet). **Staff:** Sheila K. O'Neill, Asst.Univ.Archv.; Tyler O. Walters, Asst.Univ.Archv.; William K. Beatty, Archv.Assoc.

★ 12080 ★
Northwestern University - Dental School Library (Med)
311 E. Chicago Ave.   Phone: (312)503-6896
Chicago, IL 60611-3008   Mary Kreinbring, Hd.Libn.
Founded: 1896. **Staff:** Prof 2; Other 4. **Subjects:** Oral hygiene, operative dentistry, prosthetics, orthodontics, endodontics, dental ethics and jurisprudence, dental office practice, oral surgery, pedodontics, periodontics, cleft palate, forensic dentistry, history of dentistry. **Special Collections:** Rare books on dentistry (all languages; 1391); catalogs of all dental schools in the United States; early anesthesia collection; dental supply catalogs; G.V. Black manuscripts; Eugene W. Skinner manuscripts. **Holdings:** 68,899 volumes; 14,589 pamphlets; 63 manuscripts; 433 reels of microfilm; 67 moving pictures; 2425 photographs and prints; 7 discs; 497 tapes; 4627 slides. **Subscriptions:** 557 journals and other serials. **Services:** Interlibrary loan; copying; library open to the public. **Automated Operations:** Computerized public access catalog and cataloging. **Computerized Information Services:** MEDLINE. **Networks/Consortia:** Member of National Network of Libraries of Medicine - Greater Midwest Region. **Special Catalogs:** Rare Books Catalog. **Remarks:** FAX: (312)503-3831. Considered the most comprehensive dental collection in the world. **Staff:** Ron Sims, Asst.Dental Sch.Libn.

★ 12081 ★
Northwestern University - Galter Health Sciences Library (Med)
303 E. Chicago Ave.   Phone: (312)503-8133
Chicago, IL 60611   James Shedlock, Act.Dir.
Founded: 1927. **Staff:** Prof 12; Other 20. **Subjects:** All basic and clinical medical sciences, nursing, behavioral sciences, allied health sciences. **Special Collections:** History of medicine; medical portraits and illustrations. **Holdings:** 249,000 volumes; slide sets; videotapes; 16mm films; audiotapes; models. **Subscriptions:** 2589 journals and other serials. **Services:** Interlibrary loan (fee); library not open to the public (corporate memberships are available). **Automated Operations:** Computerized cataloging, acquisitions, and circulation. **Computerized Information Services:** DIALOG Information Services, BRS Information Technologies, NLM, OCLC; CD-ROMs; InterNet (electronic mail service). **Networks/Consortia:** Member of National Network of Libraries of Medicine - Greater Midwest Region. **Publications:** Library Guide; brochures; Library Notes. **Remarks:** FAX: (312)503-8028. Electronic mail address(es): SHEDLOCK@CASBAH.ACNS.NWU.EDU (InterNet). **Staff:** Ramune Kubilius, Hd., Pub.Serv.; Anton Olson, Hd., Tech.Serv.; Susan Wishnetsky, Hd., Acq.Sect.; Pat Anderson, Media Libn.; Steve Harp, Hd., Media Prod.

★ 12082 ★
Northwestern University - Geology Library (Sci-Engr)
Locy Hall, Rm. 101   Phone: (708)491-5525
Evanston, IL 60208-2300   Janet Ayers, Geol.Libn.
Staff: 1. **Subjects:** Geology, geophysics, geochemistry, crystallography, paleontology, oceanography, seismology. **Special Collections:** United States Geological Survey publications. **Holdings:** 24,500 books; 2000 pamphlets;

7100 maps. **Subscriptions:** 450 journals and other serials. **Services:** Copying. **Automated Operations:** Computerized cataloging, acquisitions, and serials (NOTIS). **Computerized Information Services:** DIALOG Information Services, Chemical Abstracts Service (CAS), OCLC. **Networks/Consortia:** Member of Center for Research Libraries (CRL), ILLINET, North Suburban Library System (NSLS), Research Libraries Information Network (RLIN). **Remarks:** FAX: (708)491-4655.

★ 12083 ★
Northwestern University - Map Collection (Geog-Map)
University Library   Phone: (708)491-7603
Evanston, IL 60208-2300   Mary Fortney, Map Libn.
Founded: 1948. **Staff:** Prof 1; Other 1. **Subjects:** Maps and charts (primarily contemporary) covering all regions and countries of the world. **Special Collections:** Depository for U.S. Geological Survey topographic and special maps; Defense Mapping Agency maps and charts; National Ocean Survey aeronautical and nautical charts; Government Printing Office map depository (selected maps). **Holdings:** 2484 books and atlases; 194,548 map sheets; 1540 aerial photographs; 10 microfiche. **Subscriptions:** 22 journals and other serials. **Services:** Interlibrary loan; copying. **Computerized Information Services:** DIALOG Information Services, PFDS Online, BRS Information Technologies, Mead Data Central, OCLC. **Networks/Consortia:** Member of Center for Research Libraries (CRL), ILLINET, North Suburban Library System (NSLS), Research Libraries Information Network (RLIN). **Remarks:** FAX: (708)491-8306.

★ 12084 ★
Northwestern University - Mathematics Library (Sci-Engr)
Lunt Bldg., Rm. 111   Phone: (708)491-7627
Evanston, IL 60208-2300   Zita Hayward, Lib.Asst.
Staff: 1. **Subjects:** Pure mathematics, statistics. **Holdings:** 29,500 volumes. **Subscriptions:** 645 journals and other serials. **Services:** Copying. **Automated Operations:** Computerized cataloging, acquisitions, and serials. **Computerized Information Services:** Northwestern Online Total Integrated System (NOTIS). **Networks/Consortia:** Member of Center for Research Libraries (CRL), ILLINET, Research Libraries Information Network (RLIN), North Suburban Library System (NSLS). **Publications:** Accessions lists. **Remarks:** FAX: (708)491-4655.

★ 12085 ★
Northwestern University - Melville J. Herskovits Library of African Studies (Area-Ethnic)
University Library   Phone: (708)491-7684
Evanston, IL 60208-2300   David Easterbrook, Cur. of Africana
Founded: 1955. **Staff:** Prof 4.5; Other 2. **Subjects:** Africa - anthropology, exploration and travel, history, linguistics, literature, bibliography, statistics, geography, sociology, political science, economics. **Special Collections:** African language publications (9000); Dennis Brutus papers (3 feet); Arabic/Hausa Manuscripts from Kano (3000); G.M. Carter/T. Karis Collection on South African Politics (80 feet); African Studies Association (100 feet); African Literature Association (35 feet); Economic Survey of Liberia papers (3 feet); Vernon McKay papers (50 feet); Claude Barnett clipping files (18 feet); A. Abdurahman and Z. Gool papers (2 feet); Leo Kuper papers (8 feet); Alex Hepple (5 feet). **Holdings:** 226,000 volumes; 3900 feet of vertical files; 11,750 pamphlets; 1700 posters; 1050 phonograph records; 1.3 million feet of tape recordings; 10,211 map sheets. **Subscriptions:** 4400 journals and other serials; 110 African newspapers. **Services:** Interlibrary loan; copying; library open to the public with restrictions. **Automated Operations:** Computerized public access catalog, cataloging, acquisitions, serials, and circulation (NOTIS). **Computerized Information Services:** OCLC; LTAP (internal database). **Networks/Consortia:** Member of Center for Research Libraries (CRL), ILLINET, Research Libraries Information Network (RLIN), North Suburban Library System (NSLS). **Publications:** Joint Acquisitions List of Africana (JALA), 6/year - by subscription; Cumulation of JALA on microfiche, 1978-1988. **Special Catalogs:** Catalog of the Melville J. Herskovits Library of African Studies, Northwestern University Library and Africana in selected libraries (1972; 8 volumes); Supplement (1978; 6 volumes); Censuses in the Melville J. Herskovits Library (1991); Development Plans in the Melville J. Herskovits Library of African Studies (1991); Africana Archives on Microform at Northwestern University Library (1982). **Special Indexes:** The Africana Conference Paper Index (1982; 2 volumes). **Remarks:** FAX: (708)491-8306. **Staff:** Daniel A. Britz, Bibliog. of Africana; Mette Shayne, Francophone Africa; Patricia Ogedengbe, Libn.

★12086★
Northwestern University - Music Library (Mus)
Evanston, IL 60208-2300   Phone: (708)491-3434
    Don L. Roberts, Hd.
Founded: 1945. **Staff:** Prof 4; Other 6. **Subjects:** Music for solo and chamber performance, musicology, music theory, church music, music education, 20th century music, ethnomusicology. **Special Collections:** John Cage "Notations" Collection (manuscript); Fritz Reiner Library; John Cage Archive; Rare Book, Score, and Manuscript Collection; a portion of the Moldenhauer Archive (1000 manuscripts, correspondence, documents, photographs); Ben Johnston Archive; Ricordi Collection. **Holdings:** 35,931 volumes; 89,126 scores; 35 VF drawers of pamphlets, catalogs, brochures; 65 VF drawers of sheet music; 4179 microforms; 6297 audiotapes; 37,843 LP records; 3339 compact discs. **Subscriptions:** 426 journals. **Services:** Interlibrary loan; copying; library open to the public with restrictions. **Automated Operations:** Computerized cataloging, acquisitions, serials, and circulation (NOTIS). **Computerized Information Services:** DIALOG Information Services, PFDS Online, BRS Information Technologies, Mead Data Central, OCLC. **Networks/Consortia:** Member of Center for Research Libraries (CRL), ILLINET, Research Libraries Information Network (RLIN), North Suburban Library System (NSLS). **Publications:** NU Quarter Notes (newsletter). **Special Indexes:** WPA Music Periodical Index. **Remarks:** FAX: (708)491-8306. **Staff:** Deborah Campana, Pub.Serv.Libn.; Joan Schuitema, Tech.Serv.Libn.; Shirlene Ward, Recorded Sound Serv.Libn.

Northwestern University - Rehabilitation Institute of Chicago
See: **Rehabilitation Institute of Chicago** (13802)

★12087★
Northwestern University - School of Law - Library (Law)
357 E. Chicago Ave.   Phone: (312)503-8451
Chicago, IL 60611   George S. Grossman, Dir.
Founded: 1859. **Staff:** Prof 13; Other 20. **Subjects:** Law - Anglo-American, comparative, foreign, international, criminal; criminology. **Special Collections:** Rare Book Collection. **Holdings:** 473,000 books. **Services:** Interlibrary loan. **Computerized Information Services:** LEXIS, WESTLAW, DIALOG Information Services, EPIC. **Publications:** Selected Recent Acquisitions; The Rare Book Collection; The Collections of Foreign and International Law. **Remarks:** FAX: (312)503-9230. **Staff:** Barbara J. Hycnar, Assoc.Dir., Tech.Serv.; Chris Simoni, Assoc.Dir., Pub.Serv.; Carol J. Perkins, Acq.Libn.; Eloise Vondruska, Cat.Libn.; Pegeen Bassett, Docs.Libn.; Irene Berkey, Foreign/Intl Law Libn.; Marcia Lehr, Ref.Libn.; Terence O'Connell, Proj.Cat.; Krystyna Mrozek, Cat.; Sean LaRoque-Doherty, Evening and Weekend Ref.Libn.; Andrea Yelin, Comp.Serv.Libn.

★12088★
Northwestern University - Seeley G. Mudd Library for Science and Engineering (Sci-Engr)
2233 Sheridan Rd.   Phone: (708)491-3362
Evanston, IL 60208-2300   Robert Michaelson, Hd.Libn.
Founded: 1977. **Staff:** Prof 4; Other 5. **Subjects:** Engineering, life sciences, chemistry, computer science, physics, astronomy, applied mathematics. **Holdings:** 220,000 volumes; 25,034 Atomic Energy Commission (AEC) and NASA reports in hardcopy, 81,091 on microcard, 115,545 on microfiche. **Subscriptions:** 1950 journals and other serials; 1000 monographic series. **Services:** Interlibrary loan; copying; library open to the public with restrictions. **Automated Operations:** Computerized cataloging, acquisitions, serials, and circulation (NOTIS). **Computerized Information Services:** DIALOG Information Services, Chemical Abstracts Service (CAS), OCLC. **Networks/Consortia:** Member of Center for Research Libraries (CRL), ILLINET, Research Libraries Information Network (RLIN), North Suburban Library System (NSLS). **Publications:** Acquisitions List, monthly. **Remarks:** FAX: (708)491-4655. **Staff:** Janet Ayers, Physical Sci. & Engr.Libn.; Lloyd Davidson, Life Sci.Libn.

★12089★
Northwestern University - Special Collections - Women's Collection (Soc Sci)
University Library
1935 Sheridan Rd.   Phone: (708)491-3635
Evanston, IL 60208-2300   Russell Maylone, Cur. of Spec.Coll.
Founded: 1970. **Staff:** Prof 1. **Subjects:** Domestic and international Women's Liberation Movement, Equal Rights Amendment (ERA), women in society. **Special Collections:** Domestic and foreign feminist periodicals, 1960 to present; feminist position papers; ephmeral materials covering over 100 major subject areas. **Holdings:** 1000 books; 4000 periodicals titles; 6000 VF folders of conference papers, notices, syllabi, bibliographies, clippings; 300 posters. **Subscriptions:** 350 journals and other serials. **Services:** Copying; collection open to the public. **Automated Operations:** Computerized cataloging, acquisitions, and serials (NOTIS). **Computerized Information Services:** OCLC. **Networks/Consortia:** Member of Research Libraries Information Network (RLIN), ILLINET, Center for Research Libraries (CRL), North Suburban Library System (NSLS). **Publications:** Women's Collection Newsletter, semiannual - free upon request. **Special Catalogs:** W.E.F. Register of Inventoried Collections; W.E.F. Cards, a shelflist of folders in the topical collections; Topical Guide to Women's Serials in Special Collections; Notebook of Special Periodical Issues by Topic; Guide to LUIS Subject Headings Related to Women's Issues. **Remarks:** FAX: (708)491-8306.

★12090★
Northwestern University - Transportation Library (Trans)
Evanston, IL 60208-2300   Phone: (708)491-5273
    Jo A. Cates, Hd.Libn.
Founded: 1956. **Staff:** Prof 4; Other 2. **Subjects:** Transportation - general, modal, intermodal focusing on socioeconomic aspects; physical distribution; law enforcement; police; traffic; environmental impact. **Special Collections:** Environmental impact statements (35,000 volumes). **Holdings:** 206,000 books and reports; 18,000 pamphlets; 110,000 microforms. **Subscriptions:** 1900 journals and other serials. **Services:** Interlibrary loan; copying; library open to the public with restrictions. **Automated Operations:** Computerized cataloging, acquisitions, serials, and indexing (NOTIS). **Computerized Information Services:** DIALOG Information Services, OCLC; BITNET (electronic mail service). **Networks/Consortia:** Member of ILLINET, Center for Research Libraries (CRL), Research Libraries Information Network (RLIN), North Suburban Library System (NSLS). **Publications:** Current Literature in Traffic and Transportation, quarterly - for sale. **Special Indexes:** Index to EIS Collection. **Remarks:** FAX: (708)491-5685. Electronic mail address(es): TRAN@NUACVM (BITNET). **Staff:** Mary McCreadie, Asst.Hd./Hd., Tech.Serv.; Renee McHenry, Hd., Pub.Serv.; Dorothy Ramm, Hd., Indexing & Anl.Oper.

Northwood Institute - Margaret Chase Smith Library Center
See: **Margaret Chase Smith Library Center** (15249)

★12091★
Northwood Institute - Strosacker Library (Educ)
3225 Cook Rd.   Phone: (517)631-1600
Midland, MI 48640   Catherine Chen, Dir.
Staff: Prof 3; Other 5. **Subjects:** Business management, automotive marketing and replacement, accounting, executive secretarial science, advertising, marketing, hotel and restaurant management, fashion, liberal arts. **Special Collections:** Magill Collection; Leland I. Doan Memorial. **Holdings:** 41,000 books; 530 periodical titles; 24 VF drawers; 100 Princeton files; pamphlets. **Subscriptions:** 519 journals; 10 newspapers. **Services:** Interlibrary loan; copying; library open to the public with restrictions. **Automated Operations:** Computerized cataloging and serials. **Networks/Consortia:** Member of White Pine Library Cooperative, Michigan Library Consortium (MLC). **Remarks:** FAX: (517)832-5031. **Staff:** Connie Armstrong, Ref.Libn.; Carolyn Wolf, Ref./Per.Libn.

★12092★
Northwood Institute of Texas - Library (Educ)
Box 58   Phone: (214)291-1541
Cedar Hill, TX 75104   Jane K. Elkins, Lib.Dir.
Founded: 1968. **Staff:** Prof 1. **Subjects:** Automotive marketing, economics, fashion merchandising, hotel restaurant management, business management. **Holdings:** 18,000 books; 1100 bound periodical volumes; 26 VF drawers of pamphlets and clippings. **Subscriptions:** 150 journals and other serials; 9 newspapers. **Services:** Interlibrary loan; copying; library open to the public. **Remarks:** FAX: (214)291-3824.

★12093★
Norton Advanced Ceramics of Canada Inc. - Library (Sci-Engr)
8001 Daly St.   Phone: (416)295-4311
Niagara Falls, ON, Canada L2G 6S2   Sherry DeCloux, Libn.
Founded: 1930. **Staff:** 1. **Subjects:** Technology, abrasives, refractories, high temperature, crystallography, history of the abrasive industry. **Holdings:** 2700 books; 1600 bound periodical volumes; 6800 pamphlets; 1700 government publications; 300 vendors' catalogs; 150 reels of microfilm; 5600 patents; 400 slides. **Subscriptions:** 25 journals and other serials. **Services:** Interlibrary loan; copying; library open to the public for reference use only by request. **Remarks:** FAX: (416)295-3309.

★ 12094 ★
Norton Chemical Process Products Corporation - Technical Library (Sci-Engr)
Box 350   Phone: (216)673-5860
Akron, OH 44309   Linda Hashlamoun, Libn.
Staff: Prof 1. **Subjects:** Engineering - chemical, mechanical, ceramic; environmental research. **Holdings:** 4000 books; 460 bound periodical volumes; 6500 U.S. and foreign patents. **Subscriptions:** 130 journals and other serials. **Services:** Interlibrary loan; library not open to the public. **Computerized Information Services:** DIALOG Information Services. **Remarks:** Located at 3840 Fishcreek Rd., Stow, OH 44224. FAX: (216)677-3610. **Formerly:** Norton Company - Chamberlain Laboratories.

Norton Company - Advanced Ceramics - Loring Coes, Jr. Library
See: Norton Company - Northborough Research Center (12097)

Norton Company - Chamberlain Laboratories
See: Norton Chemical Process Products Corporation (12094)

★ 12095 ★
Norton Company - Coated Abrasive Division - Technical Library (Sci-Engr)
Box 808   Phone: (518)266-2741
Troy, NY 12181-0808   Rebecca A. Rector, Info.Spec./Hd.Libn.
Founded: 1946. **Staff:** Prof 1. **Subjects:** Organic chemistry, resins, abrasives, polymers, radiation curing, management. **Holdings:** 2800 books; 1500 bound periodical volumes; 77 VF drawers of company reports; 12 VF drawers of reprints; 7 VF drawers of pamphlets; 45 VF drawers of archival materials. **Subscriptions:** 101 journals and other serials. **Services:** Interlibrary loan; copying; library open to the public by appointment and special permission. **Automated Operations:** Computerized public access catalog and ILL. **Computerized Information Services:** DIALOG Information Services, BRS Information Technologies, STN International; internal database. **Networks/Consortia:** Member of Capital District Library Council for Reference & Research Resources (CDLC). **Remarks:** FAX: (518)266-2299.

★ 12096 ★
Norton Company - Library (Sci-Engr)
1 New Bond St.
P.O. Box 15008   Phone: (508)795-2278
Worcester, MA 01615-0008   Carol Cooper, Asst.Tech.Info.Spec.
Founded: 1909. **Staff:** Prof 1. **Subjects:** Abrasives, ceramics, refractories, chemistry, metallurgy, mineralogy. **Holdings:** 2500 books; 3600 bound periodical volumes; 40 VF drawers of pamphlets, unbound reports, documents; 16 microfiche; 100 reels of microfilm. **Subscriptions:** 80 journals and other serials. **Services:** Interlibrary loan; copying; library open to the public by permission only. **Computerized Information Services:** DIALOG Information Services, NERAC, Inc., PFDS Online, STN International, OCLC, NEXIS, Dow Jones News/Retrieval, Data-Star; internal database; DIALMAIL (electronic mail service). **Publications:** Acquisitions listing, bimonthly; user's guide. **Remarks:** FAX: (508)795-2688.

★ 12097 ★
Norton Company - Northborough Research Center - Loring Coes, Jr. Library (Sci-Engr)
Goddard Rd.   Phone: (508)351-7810
Northborough, MA 01532   Mary E. Silverberg, Supv., Lib.Serv.
Founded: 1986. **Staff:** Prof 1; Other 1. **Subjects:** Advanced ceramics, engineered materials. **Holdings:** 850 books; 40 bound periodical volumes; 500 other cataloged items; 700 microfiche. **Subscriptions:** 80 journals and other serials. **Services:** Interlibrary loan; library not open to the public. **Automated Operations:** Computerized cataloging, acquisitions, and serials. **Computerized Information Services:** DIALOG Information Services, PFDS Online, STN International, NEXIS, Dow Jones News/Retrieval, InvesText, OCLC, Data-Star; internal databases; DIALMAIL (electronic mail service). **Networks/Consortia:** Member of Worcester Area Cooperating Libraries (WACL). **Publications:** Newsletter, quarterly - for internal distribution only; acquisitions lists. **Special Catalogs:** Catalog of research reports (online); catalog of technical reports (online). **Remarks:** FAX: (508)351-7700. Electronic mail address(es): Mary Silverberg (DIALMAIL). **Formerly:** Norton Company - Advanced Ceramics - Loring Coes, Jr. Library.

★ 12098 ★
Norton Gallery and School of Art - Library (Art)
1451 S. Olive Ave.
West Palm Beach, FL 33401   Phone: (407)832-5194
Staff: 1. **Subjects:** Art history, painting, sculpture, artists. **Holdings:** 4000 books; 2000 museum pamphlets; 500 art slides. **Subscriptions:** 15 journals and other serials. **Services:** Interlibrary loan; library open to members only, with restrictions on borrowing. **Remarks:** FAX: (407)659-4689.

Mary and Edward Norton Library of Ophthalmology
See: University of Miami - School of Medicine - Bascom Palmer Eye Institute (18848)

Paul Norton Medical Library
See: Massachusetts Hospital School (9794)

★ 12099 ★
R.W. Norton Art Gallery - Reference-Research Library (Art, Hist)
4747 Creswell Ave.   Phone: (318)865-4201
Shreveport, LA 71106   Jerry M. Bloomer, Libn.
Founded: 1970. **Staff:** 2. **Subjects:** Fine arts, American history, Louisiana and Virginia history, literature, ornithology, bibliography, world history. **Special Collections:** James M. Owens Memorial Collection of Virginiana (500 volumes); rare books, including 15th-18th century atlases; J.J. Audubon's double-elephant folio edition of The Birds of America; ornithological works of James Gould (43 volumes); Charles M. Russell and Frederic Remington Collection (books; catalogs; pamphlets). **Holdings:** 7000 volumes. **Subscriptions:** 100 journals and other serials. **Services:** Copying; library open to the public for reference use only. **Remarks:** Maintained by R.W. Norton Art Foundation. FAX: (318)869-0435. **Staff:** Eva W. Moses, Asst.Libn.

★ 12100 ★
Norwalk Community College/Norwalk State Technical College - Learning Resources Center (Sci-Engr)
188 Richards Ave.   Phone: (203)857-7207
Norwalk, CT 06854   Carmen Bayles, Dir.
Founded: 1962. **Staff:** Prof 1; Other 1. **Subjects:** Engineering - electrical, chemical, mechanical; computer technology; metallurgy; architectural drafting. **Holdings:** 17,000 volumes; 200 bound periodical volumes; 8 VF drawers of pamphlets. **Subscriptions:** 129 journals and other serials; 5 newspapers. **Services:** Interlibrary loan; copying; library open to the public. **Networks/Consortia:** Member of Southwestern Connecticut Library Council (SWLC). **Publications:** Newsletter, monthly. **Formed by the merger of:** Norwalk State Technical College and Norwalk Community College.

★ 12101 ★
Norwalk Hospital - Wiggans Health Sciences Library (Med)
Maple St.   Phone: (203)852-2793
Norwalk, CT 06856   Jill Golrick, Dir.
Staff: Prof 1; Other 1. **Subjects:** Medicine, allied health sciences. **Holdings:** 1300 books; 6500 bound periodical volumes; 6 indices; 6 VF drawers. **Subscriptions:** 165 journals and other serials. **Services:** Interlibrary loan; copying; SDI; library open to the public. **Computerized Information Services:** MEDLARS, BRS Information Technologies. **Remarks:** FAX: (203)855-3575.

Norwalk State Technical College
See: Norwalk Community College/Norwalk State Technical College (12100)

★ 12102 ★
Norway - Central Bureau of Statistics - Library (Sci-Engr, Soc Sci)
Skippergt 15   Phone: 2 864643
N-0033 Oslo, Norway   Hilde Rodland, Hd.Libn.
Founded: 1917. **Staff:** Prof 7; Other 4. **Subjects:** Economics, demography, official statistics, statistics, sociology, international statistics. **Special Collections:** Official statistics from Norway and other countries; statistical publications from international organizations. **Holdings:** 172,000 books. **Subscriptions:** 4000 journals and other serials; 5 newspapers. **Services:** Interlibrary loan; copying; library open to the public. **Automated Operations:** DOBIS-LIBIS. **Computerized Information Services:** DIALOG Information Services, BLAISE LINK, UBO, LOU, SSB Data; electronic mail service. **Publications:** Accession list, monthly; list of periodicals, annual. **Remarks:** FAX: 2 864504.

★ 12103 ★
Norway - Ministry of Justice - Library (Law)
P.O. Box 8005 Dep   Phone: 2 345199
N-0033 Oslo 1, Norway   Ann Hanssen, Hd.Libn.
Staff: Prof 1. **Subjects:** Law. **Special Collections:** Common Market law.
Holdings: 20,000 books. **Subscriptions:** 150 journals and other serials.
Services: Copying; library open to the public at librarian's discretion.
Computerized Information Services: CELEX; internal database. **Remarks:**
FAX: 2 342725.

★ 12104 ★
Norway - National Archives of Norway - Library (Area-Ethnic, Hist)
Folke Bernadottes vei 21   Phone: 2 23 74 80
N-0862 Oslo 8, Norway   Turid Askjem, Hd.Libn.
Subjects: Scandinavian and Norwegian history, Norwegian biography and
family history. **Holdings:** 60,000 volumes; 500 serials. **Services:** Interlibrary
loan; library open to the public for reference use only. **Publications:**
Riksarkivets Bibliotek Tilvekst (accession list). **Remarks:** FAX: 2 23 74 89.
Also Known As: Norway - Riksarkivet - Biblioteket.

★ 12105 ★
Norway - National College of Art and Design - Library (Art)
Ullevalsveien 5   Phone: 2 201407
N-0165 Oslo, Norway   Astrid Skjerven, Chf.Libn.
Founded: 1818. **Staff:** 3.5. **Subjects:** Crafts, design, art. **Holdings:** 50,000
books; 3000 microfiche; 5000 slides. **Subscriptions:** 350 journals and other
serials. **Services:** Interlibrary loan; copying; library open to
the public with restrictions. **Automated Operations:** Computerized public
access catalog. **Remarks:** FAX: 2 111496. **Also Known As:** Statens
handverks - og kunstindustriskole - Biblioteket.

★ 12106 ★
Norway - Norwegian Parliament - Library
Stortinget   Phone: 2 313690
N-0026 Oslo 1, Norway   Brit Floistad, Parliamentary Libn.
Founded: 1871. **Staff:** Prof 8; Other 4. **Subjects:** Political science, modern
history, law, economics. **Special Collections:** Political brochures (1906);
Programme of Political Norwegian Parties (1885 to present); radio and
television recordings. **Holdings:** 163,000 books; 20,440 microfiche; 3408
reels of microfilm. **Subscriptions:** 651 journals and other serials; 181
newspapers. **Services:** Interlibrary loan; copying; library open to the public
with restrictions. **Computerized Information Services:** FT PROFILE,
Reuters. Performs searches. **Remarks:** FAX: 2 313859.

Norway - Riksarkivet - Biblioteket
See: Norway - National Archives of Norway (12104)

Norway - The Technical University Library of Norway
See: The Technical University Library of Norway (16033)

★ 12107 ★
Norwegian Agency for Development Cooperation - Information and
  Documentation Center (Soc Sci)
P.O. Box 8034 Dep.   Phone: 2 314453
N-0030 Oslo, Norway   Kirsten Brekke, Hd. of Off.
Founded: 1970. **Staff:** Prof 5; Other 2. **Subjects:** Development aid,
developing countries, international relations. **Special Collections:** NORAD
project documents (7000 titles). **Holdings:** 25,000 books. **Subscriptions:** 400
journals and other serials. **Services:** Interlibrary loan; copying; center open
to the public. **Automated Operations:** Computerized public access catalog.
Remarks: FAX: 2 314402. **Also Known As:** NORAD - Informasjons - og
dokumentasjons - senter.

★ 12108 ★
Norwegian-American Historical Association - Archives (Area-Ethnic,
  Hist)
St. Olaf College   Phone: (507)663-3221
Northfield, MN 55057   Forrest E. Brown, Cur. of Archv.
Founded: 1925. **Staff:** Prof 2. **Subjects:** Norwegian-American history and
genealogy. **Holdings:** 8000 books; 1500 bound periodical volumes; 500 other
volumes; newspapers; scrapbooks; correspondence; clippings; diaries;
records; manuscripts. **Subscriptions:** 15 journals and other serials. **Services:**
Interlibrary loan (through St. Olaf College Library; PALS); archives open
to the public. **Remarks:** FAX: (507)663-3549. **Staff:** Lloyd Hustvedt,
Exec.Sec.

★ 12109 ★
Norwegian-American Hospital, Inc. - Seufert Memorial Library (Med)
1044 N. Francisco Ave.
Chicago, IL 60622   Phone: (312)278-8800
Founded: 1921. **Staff:** 1. **Subjects:** Medicine, surgery, obstetrics, pediatrics.
Special Collections: Collection of medical illustrations (loose-leaf).
Holdings: 811 books; 173 bound periodical volumes; 200 Audio-Digest
tapes. **Subscriptions:** 65 journals and other serials. **Services:** Interlibrary
loan; library open to retired NAH doctors and medical personnel.
Networks/Consortia: Member of National Network of Libraries of
Medicine - Greater Midwest Region.

Norwegian-American Museum
See: Vesterheim Genealogical Center/Norwegian-American Museum
  (19816)

★ 12110 ★
Norwegian Astronautical Society - Library (Sci-Engr)
Postboks 52
Blindern
N-0315 Oslo, Norway
Subjects: Space science, astronomy. **Holdings:** 1000 volumes. **Also Known
As:** Norsk Astronautisk Forening.

★ 12111 ★
Norwegian Broadcasting Corporation - NRK Library (Soc Sci, Art,
  Hum)
Bjornstijerne Bjornsons plass 1   Phone: 2 458612
N-0340 Oslo, Norway   Carita Kylander Rossevik, Hd. of Lib.
Founded: 1936. **Staff:** Prof 7; Other 3. **Subjects:** Social science, art, music,
mass media, local history. **Special Collections:** World War II collection;
Press Archives; children's books collection. **Holdings:** 108,000 books;
microfilm. **Subscriptions:** 539 journals and other serials; 34 newspapers.
Services: Interlibrary loan; copying; library open to the public with
restrictions. **Computerized Information Services:** DIALOG Information
Services, FT PROFILE, BLAISE, Bibsys; CD-ROMs; Bibliofil (internal
database). Performs searches. Contact Person: Tordis Ustvedt, Libn.
Publications: List of new books, quarterly; List of dates and events, annual;
Annual report. **Remarks:** FAX: 2 458613. **Also Known As:** Norsk
Rikskringkasting - Biblioteket.

★ 12112 ★
Norwegian Building Research Institute - Library (Plan)
P.O. Box 123
Blindern   Phone: 2 965591
N-0314 Oslo 3, Norway   Anne Rogstad
Founded: 1952. **Staff:** 3. **Subjects:** Building, construction, building
management. **Holdings:** 25,000 volumes. **Subscriptions:** 300 journals and
other serials. **Services:** Library open to the public. **Computerized
Information Services:** DIALOG Information Services, ESA/IRS, STN
International, BODIL. **Remarks:** FAX: 2 965542. **Also Known As:** Norges
Byggforskningsinstitutt.

★ 12113 ★
Norwegian Computing Center for the Humanities - Library (Hum)
Harald Harfagresgate 31
P.O. Box 53 - Universitetet   Phone: 5 212954
N-5027 Bergen, Norway   Eli Schilbred, Info.Off.
Founded: 1972. **Staff:** 1. **Subjects:** Humanities, literary and linguistic
computing. **Special Collections:** Norwegian Text Archive; ICAME
(International Computer Archive of Modern English). **Holdings:** 1500
bound volumes. **Subscriptions:** 158 journals and other serials. **Services:**
Library open to researchers, educators, academic departments, archives,
museums, cultural institutions, and other institutions of advanced learning
and research related to the field of humanities. **Computerized Information
Services:** Electronic mail. **Publications:** Humanistiske Data, 3/year - free
upon request; ICAME Journal. **Remarks:** Alternate telephone number(s):
5 212955; 5 212956. FAX: 5 322656. **Also Known As:** NAVFs edb - senter
for humanistik forskning.

Norwegian DIANE Centre
See: The Technical University Library of Norway (16033)

Norwegian Institute of Technology
See: The Technical University Library of Norway (16033)

★ 12114 ★
Norwegian National Gallery - Library (Art)
Universitetsgt 13
Postboks 8157 Dep   Phone: 2 200404
N-0033 Oslo 1, Norway   Anne Lise Rabben, Libn.
Founded: 1883. **Staff:** Prof 2. **Subjects:** Art history. **Holdings:** 57,000 books; 25,000 slides. **Subscriptions:** 100 journals and other serials. **Services:** Interlibrary loan; library open to the public. **Remarks:** FAX: 2 361132. **Also Known As:** Nasjonalgalleriets Bibliotek.

Norwegian Parliament - Library
See: Norway - Norwegian Parliament - Library (12106)

★ 12115 ★
Norwegian Polar Research Institute - Library (Sci-Engr)
P.O. Box 158
Rolfstangveien 12   Phone: 2 123650
N-1330 Oslo Lufthavn, Norway   Reidunn Lund, Libn.
Staff: 1. **Subjects:** Norwegian Arctic and Antarctic - geology, geophysics, biology, expeditions. **Special Collections:** Trappers' diaries, Svalbard and Greenland. **Holdings:** 19,000 volumes. **Subscriptions:** 70 journals and other serials. **Services:** Interlibrary loan; copying; library open to the public. **Computerized Information Services:** Internal databases. **Remarks:** FAX: 2 123854. Telex: 74 745 polar n. **Also Known As:** Norsk Polarinstitutt.

★ 12116 ★
Norwegian Save the Children - Library (Soc Sci)
Postboks 6200
Etterstad
N-0602 Oslo 6, Norway   Phone: 2 570080
                                Sidsel Karin Moe, Libn.
Founded: 1984. **Staff:** 1. **Subjects:** Underprivileged children in developing countries, child welfare, community development, children's rights. **Holdings:** 3000 volumes. **Subscriptions:** 260 journals and other serials; 8 newspapers. **Services:** Library open to the public by appointment. **Remarks:** FAX: 2 674884. Telex: 19143 REDDB N. **Also Known As:** Redd Barna.

★ 12117 ★
Norwegian Telecom - Library (Info Sci)
Postboks 6701
St Olavs Pl   Phone: 2 488054
N-0130 Oslo, Norway   Else M. Skarheim, Hd. of Lib.
Founded: 1924. **Staff:** Prof 4; Other 2. **Subjects:** Telecommunications. **Holdings:** 20,000 books; 30,000 bound periodical volumes; 10,000 reports. **Services:** Interlibrary loan; copying; SDI; library open to the public with restrictions. **Computerized Information Services:** Internal database. **Publications:** New acquisitions. **Remarks:** FAX: 2 110365.

★ 12118 ★
Norwich Bulletin - Library (Publ)
66 Franklin St.
Norwich, CT 06360   Phone: (203)887-9211
                                Kathleen A. Smith
Founded: 1791. **Staff:** Prof 1; Other 2. **Subjects:** Newspaper reference topics. **Special Collections:** Norwich Bulletin volumes (1791 to present). **Services:** Library open to the public by appointment on a limited schedule. **Remarks:** FAX: (203)886-2231.

★ 12119 ★
Norwich Eaton - Film Library (Aud-Vis)
P.O. Box 819
210 Sheldon Dr.
Cambridge, ON, Canada N1R 5W6   Phone: (519)622-3000
                                Maureen Chesney, Prof.Serv.Adm.
Subjects: Urology, nutrition, neurology, spasticity, plastic and reconstructive burn therapy, gynecology. **Holdings:** 45 films. **Services:** Library open to professionals in the medical field. **Publications:** Directory of Medical Films, Audio Visual & Medical Educational Resources (book). **Remarks:** FAX: (519)622-0168.

★ 12120 ★
Norwich Eaton Pharmaceuticals, Inc. - Research Library (Med)
P.O BOX 191
Norwich, NY 13815-1709   Phone: (607)335-2678
                                Lucy Wrightington, Act.Libn.
Founded: 1947. **Staff:** Prof 6; Other 2. **Subjects:** Pharmacy, medicine, chemistry, pharmacology, basic sciences. **Holdings:** 10,000 books; periodicals and patents on microfilm. **Subscriptions:** 510 journals and other serials. **Services:** Interlibrary loan; SDI. **Computerized Information Services:** DIALOG Information Services, PFDS Online, NLM, BRS Information Technologies, Questel, Chemical Abstracts Service (CAS), DARC Pluridata System (DPDS), VU/TEXT Information Services. **Networks/Consortia:** Member of South Central Research Library Council (SCRLC). **Remarks:** Division of Procter & Gamble Company. FAX: (607)335-2098.

★ 12121 ★
Norwich Hospital - Health Sciences Library (Med)
Box 508   Phone: (203)823-5697
Norwich, CT 06360   Julia M. Traver, Libn. II
Founded: 1940. **Staff:** Prof 1; Other 1. **Subjects:** Psychiatry, neurology, psychology, general medicine, nursing, occupational therapy, social service. **Holdings:** 4000 books; 5750 bound periodical volumes. **Subscriptions:** 125 journals and other serials. **Services:** Interlibrary loan; library open to the public for reference use only. **Computerized Information Services:** MEDLINE. **Networks/Consortia:** Member of Connecticut Association of Health Science Libraries (CAHSL), Southeastern Connecticut Library Association (SECLA), BHSL.

★ 12122 ★
Norwich University - Chaplin Memorial Library - Special Collections (Hist)
South Main St.   Phone: (802)485-2168
Northfield, VT 05663   Paul C. Heller, Dir.
Founded: 1819. **Staff:** 10. **Subjects:** Military history. **Special Collections:** Papers of Captain Alden Partridge, 1785-1854 (university founder); papers of General I.D. White; Southard Military History Collection; Joel E. Fisher Mountaineering Collection. **Holdings:** 2186 books; 594 linear feet of archives and manuscripts. **Services:** Interlibrary loan; copying; collections open to the public. **Automated Operations:** Computerized public access catalog and cataloging. **Computerized Information Services:** WILSONLINE, DIALOG Information Services, BRS Information Technologies, OCLC; CD-ROMs; BITNET (electronic mail service). Performs searches on fee basis. Contact Person: Paula Arnold, Ref.Libn. **Networks/Consortia:** Member of NELINET, Inc. **Publications:** Norwich University Library Occasional Papers, irregular. **Remarks:** FAX: (802)485-2173. Electronic mail address(es): PAULA@NORWICH (BITNET). **Staff:** Catherine Swenson, Tech.Serv.Libn.; Jacqueline S. Painter, Docs.Libn. and Univ.Archv.

★ 12123 ★
Notre Dame Bay Memorial Hospital - Library (Med)
Twillingate, NF, Canada A0G 4M0   Phone: (709)884-2131
                                Barbara Hamlyn, Libn.
Remarks: No further information was supplied by respondent.

Notre Dame College
See: Athol Murray College of Notre Dame (10870)

★ 12124 ★
Notre Dame De Lafayette University - Library (Rel-Phil)
941 S. Havana   Phone: (303)341-0082
Aurora, CO 80012   Karen Degenhart, Libn.
Founded: 1988. **Staff:** 1. **Subjects:** Pastoral concerns, scripture, holistic psychology, theology, comparative religion. **Special Collections:** History of the Catholic Church to 1901. **Holdings:** 2000 books; 25 AV programs; 7 manuscripts. **Subscriptions:** 2 journals and other serials; 4 newspapers. **Services:** Library open to the public with restrictions. **Formerly:** Lafayette University - Library.

Notre Dame Hospital
See: Hopital Notre Dame (7395)

★ 12125 ★
Notre Dame Hospital - Library (Med)
1405 Edward St.
P.O. Box 8000   Phone: (705)362-4291
Hearst, ON, Canada P0L 1N0   Suzanne Allaire, Med.Rec.Supv.
Founded: 1960. **Staff:** Prof 1. **Subjects:** Medicine, nursing, paramedical
sciences, hospital administration. **Holdings:** 1000 books; 675 bound
periodical volumes. **Subscriptions:** 109 journals and other serials. **Services:**
Interlibrary loan; copying; library open to the public with permission for
reference use only. **Remarks:** FAX: (705)372-1957.

★ 12126 ★
Notre Dame de la Paix University Faculties - Informatics Institute -
   Library (Info Sci)
Rue Grandgagnage 21   Phone: 81 229065
B-5000 Namur, Belgium   Monique Noirhomme-Fraiture, Libn.
Founded: 1970. **Subjects:** Computer science, information systems. **Holdings:**
10,000 volumes. **Subscriptions:** 110 journals and other serials. **Computerized
Information Services:** UUCP (electronic mail service). **Publications:**
Travaux de l'Institut d'Informatique; Journal de Reflexion sur
l'Informatique, quarterly. **Remarks:** FAX: 81 230391. Telex: 59 222 FAC
NAM B. Electronic mail address(es): avl@fun.cs. (UUCP).

★ 12127 ★
Nova - Business Information Center (Energy)
P.O. Box 2535   Phone: (403)290-6718
Calgary, AB, Canada T2P 2N6   Rosemary Bussi, Corp.Libn.
Staff: Prof 12; Other 2. **Subjects:** Petrochemicals, energy, business
administration, engineering, environment. **Special Collections:** Regulatory
material; photo library. **Holdings:** 5000 books. **Subscriptions:** 725 journals
and other serials; 25 newspapers. **Services:** Interlibrary loan; SDI; library
access is restricted. **Automated Operations:** Computerized cataloging,
acquisitions, and circulation. **Computerized Information Services:**
DIALOG Information Services, PFDS Online, CAN/OLE, Info Globe, QL
Systems, Dow Jones News/Retrieval; NOLA (internal database). **Special
Indexes:** Indexes to major Canadian regulatory transcripts. **Remarks:** FAX:
(403)290-8940. **Staff:** Carol Weaver, Rsrcs.Supv.; Cathy Watson,
Res.Coord.

★ 12128 ★
NOVA Husky Research Corporation - Technical Information Centre
   (Energy)
2928 16 St., N.E.   Phone: (403)250-0675
Calgary, AB, Canada T2E 7K7   Shirley Veness, Supv., Tech.Info.Serv.
Founded: 1983. **Staff:** Prof 5; Other 4. **Subjects:** Chemistry, oil, gas,
electronics, engineering, asphalt, plastics, petrochemicals. **Holdings:** 4900
books; 2500 patents; NTIS reports. **Subscriptions:** 185 journals and other
serials. **Services:** Interlibrary loan; copying; SDI; library open to the public
by appointment. **Automated Operations:** Computerized public access
catalog, cataloging and serials. **Computerized Information Services:**
DIALOG Information Services, STN International, Data-Star, PFDS
Online, CAN/OLE, CAN/SND, WILSONLINE, Mead Data Central,
DOBIS Canadian Online Library System, OCLC, iNET 2000, The Financial
Post DataGroup, Info Globe, Infomart Online; NHIB (internal database);
Envoy 100, CAN/OLE (electronic mail services). Performs searches on fee
basis. **Publications:** Information Update, monthly - for internal distribution
only. **Remarks:** FAX: (403)291-3208. **Staff:** Brooke Clibbon, Sr.Lib.Anl.;
Donna Samcoe, Lib.Anl.; Merle Bumstead, Lib.Anl.; Diana Ringstrom,
Lib.Anl.

★ 12129 ★
Nova Scotia Agricultural College - MacRae Library (Agri)
P.O. Box 550   Phone: (902)893-6668
Truro, NS, Canada B2N 5E3   Bonnie R. Waddell, Chf.Libn.
Founded: 1905. **Staff:** Prof 2; Other 5. **Subjects:** Agriculture. **Special
Collections:** AGRICOLA collection. **Holdings:** 22,100 books; 12,398 bound
periodical volumes. **Subscriptions:** 817 journals and other serials. **Services:**
Interlibrary loan; copying; library open to the public. **Automated
Operations:** Computerized cataloging. **Computerized Information Services:**
DIALOG Information Services, STN International, CAN/OLE, UTLAS;
Envoy 100 (electronic mail service). Performs searches on fee basis.
Publications: Library Handbook; Serials Holdings List; subject
bibliographies. **Remarks:** FAX: (902)895-7693. Electronic mail address(es):
ILL.NSTA (Envoy 100). **Staff:** Bhagat Sodhi.

★ 12130 ★
Nova Scotia Attorney General's Library (Law)
P.O. Box 7   Phone: (902)424-7699
Halifax, NS, Canada B3J 2L6   Marie DeYoung
Founded: 1920. **Staff:** Prof 1; Other 1. **Subjects:** Law. **Holdings:** 7000
volumes. **Subscriptions:** 60 journals and other serials. **Services:** Interlibrary
loan; library not open to the public. **Automated Operations:** Computerized
cataloging. **Computerized Information Services:** QL Systems, CAN/LAW,
WESTLAW. **Special Indexes:** Opinion File; Memorandum File; Charter of
Rights & Freedom Index. **Remarks:** FAX: (902)424-4556.

★ 12131 ★
Nova Scotia Barristers' Library (Law)
Law Courts
1815 Upper Water St.   Phone: (902)425-2665
Halifax, NS, Canada B3J 1S7   Barbara Campbell, Dir.,Lib.Serv.
Founded: 1858. **Staff:** Prof 1; Other 2. **Subjects:** Canadian and British law.
Holdings: 15,000 volumes; 300 volumes of Nova Scotia Supreme Court
unreported decisions; 30 volumes of Nova Scotia County Court unreported
decisions. **Subscriptions:** 240 journals and other serials. **Services:**
Interlibrary loan; copying; library open to the public at librarian's discretion.
Computerized Information Services: QL Systems, CAN/LAW;
QUICKMAIL (electronic mail service). **Remarks:** FAX: (902)422-1697.
Electronic mail address(es): Box 47 (QUICKMAIL). Maintained by the
Nova Scotia Barristers' Society.

★ 12132 ★
Nova Scotia College of Art and Design - Library (Art)
5163 Duke St.   Phone: (902)422-7381
Halifax, NS, Canada B3J 3J6   Ilga Leja, Dir.
Founded: 1887. **Staff:** Prof 2; Other 4. **Subjects:** Art history, contemporary
art, Canadian art, Oriental art, crafts, photography, graphic and
environmental design. **Holdings:** 26,000 books; 250 bound periodical
volumes; 125,000 slides. **Subscriptions:** 304 journals and other serials.
Services: Interlibrary loan; copying; library open to the public with
restrictions. **Automated Operations:** Computerized cataloging, acquisitions,
and circulation. **Computerized Information Services:** DIALOG
Information Services, UTLAS; Envoy 100 (electronic mail service).
Remarks: FAX: (902)425-2420. Electronic mail address(es): NSCAD
(Envoy 100). **Staff:** Mary Snyder, Nonprint Libn.; Kit Clarke, Cat.; Linda
Potvin-Jones, Circ.

★ 12133 ★
Nova Scotia Commission on Drug Dependency - Library (Med)
Lord Nelson Bldg., 5th Fl.
5675 Spring Garden Rd.   Phone: (902)424-4270
Halifax, NS, Canada B3J 1H1   Ruth Vaughan, Libn.
Founded: 1973. **Staff:** Prof 1. **Subjects:** Drug and alcohol use, sociology,
social problems, psychology and psychiatry, highway safety, women's
treatment issues. **Holdings:** 3000 books and documents; 150 video tapes.
Subscriptions: 87 journals and other serials. **Services:** Interlibrary loan;
library open to the public. **Automated Operations:** Computerized cataloging.
Computerized Information Services: DIALOG Information Services, BRS
Information Technologies. **Publications:** Acquisition list; Annual Report;
Treatment Services Available, annual. **Special Catalogs:** Audio-Visual
Catalogue.

★ 12134 ★
Nova Scotia Department of Advanced Education and Job Training -
   College of Geographic Sciences - J.B. Hall Memorial Library (Comp
   Sci, Geog-Map)
50 Elliott Rd., R.R.
1   Phone: (902)584-2226
Lawrencetown, NS, Canada B0S 1M0   Donna M. Eisner, Libn.
Founded: 1977. **Staff:** 1. **Subjects:** Surveying, computer programming,
geographic information systems, cartography, community planning, remote
sensing, computer graphics. **Special Collections:** A.H. Church County maps
(8), the Canadian Abridgement. **Holdings:** 12,350 books; 450 bound
periodical volumes; 325 theses; 1800 maps; 900 microfiche. **Subscriptions:**
75 journals and other serials. **Services:** Interlibrary loan; copying; library
open to the public. **Remarks:** FAX: (902)584-7211.

★12135★
Nova Scotia Department of Community Services - Library (Soc Sci)
P.O. Box 696   Phone: (902)424-4454
Halifax, NS, Canada B3J 2T7   Jane Phillips, Libn.
Founded: 1950. **Staff:** Prof 1. **Subjects:** Social services, income security.
Special Collections: Historical collection on the development of social
services in Nova Scotia. **Holdings:** 2500 books; 317 bound periodical
volumes. **Subscriptions:** 100 journals and other serials. **Services:** Interlibrary
loan; library open to the public. **Automated Operations:** INMAGIC.
Remarks: FAX: (902)424-0502.

★12136★
Nova Scotia Department of Economic Development - Library (Plan)
1800 Argyle St., 6th Fl.
P.O. Box 519   Phone: (902)424-6178
Halifax, NS, Canada B3J 2R7   Donald Purcell, Libn.
Founded: 1971. **Staff:** Prof 1. **Subjects:** Economic and industrial
development, business, economics, trade, technology. **Holdings:** 1800 books;
2500 annual reports; 75 manufacturing and trade directories; Statistics
Canada reports (complete set). **Subscriptions:** 200 journals and other serials.
Services: Interlibrary loan; copying; library open to the public with
restrictions on borrowing. **Automated Operations:** Computerized
cataloging. **Computerized Information Services:** DIALOG Information
Services, Info Globe, CAN/OLE, Mead Data Central, Infomart Online.
Publications: Acquisitions list, irregular. **Remarks:** FAX: (902)424-5739.
Formed by the merger of: Nova Scotia Department of Industry, Trade and
Technology and Nova Scotia Department of Small Business Development.

**Nova Scotia Department of Education - Nova Scotia Museum -
  Maritime Museum of the Atlantic**
See: **Maritime Museum of the Atlantic** (9691)

★12137★
Nova Scotia Department of the Environment - Library (Env-Cons)
5151 Terminal Rd.
P.O. Box 2107   Phone: (902)424-2372
Halifax, NS, Canada B3J 3B7   Janice Laufer, Libn.
Subjects: Environment. **Holdings:** 8000 books and reports; unbound
periodical volumes. **Subscriptions:** 125 journals and other serials; 5
newspapers. **Services:** Interlibrary loan; copying; library open to the public.
Remarks: FAX: (902)424-0503.

★12138★
**Nova Scotia Department of Fisheries and Oceans - Scotia Fundy
  Regional Library - Bedford Institute of Oceanography - Library** (Biol
  Sci)
Box 1006   Phone: (902)426-3675
Dartmouth, NS, Canada B2Y 4A2   Anna Flander, Chf., Lib.Serv.
Founded: 1962. **Staff:** Prof 2; Other 4. **Subjects:** Physical and chemical
oceanography; marine biology, ecology, geology, geophysics; fisheries
research; ocean engineering; hydrographic surveys and charting. **Special
Collections:** Atlantic and Arctic Canada environmental assessment
documents. **Holdings:** 17,000 books; 3000 reports; 25,000 reports on
microfiche; 25,000 maps and charts. **Subscriptions:** 1450 journals and other
serials. **Services:** Interlibrary loan; copying; SDI; library open to the public.
Automated Operations: Computerized serials. **Computerized Information
Services:** CAN/OLE, QL Systems, DIALOG Information Services, PFDS
Online, Info Globe; WAVES (internal database); Envoy 100 (electronic mail
service). **Special Indexes:** KWIC indexes to map/chart collections.
Remarks: FAX: (902)426-7827. Electronic mail address(es): DFO.LIB.BIO
(Envoy 100). **Staff:** A. Mazerall, Lib.Info.Off.; Diane Stewart, Supv.,
Tech.Serv.; C. MacDonald, Info.Serv.Libn.; Rhonda Flynn, ILL; M.
Martin, Kardex; A. Kavanagh, Acq.

Nova Scotia Department of Industry, Trade and Technology
See: **Nova Scotia Department of Economic Development** (12136)

★12139★
Nova Scotia Department of Labour - Library (Bus-Fin)
Box 697   Phone: (902)424-8474
Halifax, NS, Canada B3J 2T8   JoAnn Richling, Libn.
Founded: 1970. **Staff:** Prof 1. **Subjects:** Labor, labor law, industrial relations,
labor economics, occupational health and safety. **Special Collections:** Nova

Scotia grievance arbitration awards. **Holdings:** 5000 books; Conference
Board in Canada publications; government documents. **Subscriptions:** 350
journals and other serials. **Services:** Interlibrary loan; copying; library open
to the public. **Computerized Information Services:** CANSIM; Envoy 100
(electronic mail service). **Publications:** Acquisitions list, quarterly - free
upon request. **Remarks:** FAX: (902)424-3239. Electronic mail address(es):
ILL.NSHDOL (Envoy 100). Library located at 5151 Terminal Rd., 6th Fl.,
Halifax, NS.

Nova Scotia Department of Mines & Energy
See: **Nova Scotia Department of Natural Resources** (12141)

★12140★
Nova Scotia Department of Municipal Affairs - Library (Soc Sci)
P.O. Box 216   Phone: (902)424-5965
Halifax, NS, Canada B3J 2M4   Audrey Manzer, Libn.
Founded: 1978. **Staff:** Prof 1. **Subjects:** Municipal government, assessment,
community planning, infrastructure. **Holdings:** Figures not available.
Subscriptions: 100 journals and other serials; 35 Nova Scotia newspapers.
Services: Interlibrary loan; library open to the public. **Remarks:** FAX:
(902)424-0531.

★12141★
Nova Scotia Department of Natural Resources - Library (Sci-Engr,
  Energy)
P.O. Box 698   Phone: (902)424-8633
Halifax, NS, Canada B3J 2T9   Valerie Brisco, Hd., Lib.Serv.
Founded: 1960. **Staff:** Prof 2. **Subjects:** Geoscience, mining, energy,
engineering, petroleum, mining engineering, forestry, parks and recreation,
wildlife. **Special Collections:** Company assessment reports (5000). **Holdings:**
1000 books; 1000 bound periodical volumes; 1003 open file maps; 868 open
file reports; 1500 reprints; 6000 maps; 6000 microfiche of technical reports;
1500 government documents; 700 theses. **Subscriptions:** 250 journals and
other serials; 11 newspapers. **Services:** Interlibrary loan; copying; library
open to the public. **Automated Operations:** Computerized cataloging.
Computerized Information Services: GEOSCAN Database. **Publications:**
Acquisitions list, irregular - free upon request; publication list, irregular -
free upon request. **Special Indexes:** Indexes to open file reports, company
assessment reports, departmental publications, and theses (all online).
Remarks: FAX: (902)424-7735. **Formerly:** Nova Scotia Department of
Mines & Energy. **Staff:** Barbara Delorey; Libn.

★12142★
**Nova Scotia Department of Tourism and Culture - Cultural Affairs
  Library** (Rec)
P.O. Box 456   Phone: (902)424-7734
Halifax, NS, Canada B3J 2R5   Gillian Webster, Libn.
Founded: 1978. **Staff:** Prof 1. **Subjects:** Theater, crafts, music, art, built
heritage, film, multiculturalism. **Special Collections:** Reading Room -
Playwrights' Union of Canada. **Holdings:** 10,000 books. **Subscriptions:** 130
journals and other serials. **Services:** Interlibrary loan; copying; library open
to the public. **Publications:** Bibliography for each subject area. **Remarks:**
FAX: (902)424-2668.

★12143★
**Nova Scotia Department of Transportation and Communications - Head
  Office Library** (Trans)
P.O. Box 186   Phone: (902)424-6720
Halifax, NS, Canada B3J 2N2   Margaret E. Reid, Libn.
Founded: 1979. **Staff:** Prof 1. **Subjects:** Highway design, transportation
planning, traffic management, social and economic aspects of highway
transportation. **Special Collections:** All publications of Transportation
Research Board, National Research Council, Washington, DC. **Holdings:**
500 books; 3000 technical reports. **Subscriptions:** Interlibrary loan; copying;
open to the public with restrictions. **Computerized Information Services:**
CAN/SND, DIALOG Information Services. **Networks/Consortia:**
Member of Nova Scotia Government Libraries Council.

★ 12144 ★
Nova Scotia Department of Transportation and Communications -
Materials Laboratory Library (Trans)
Site no. 37, R.R. no. 1   Phone: (902)861-1911
Windsor Junction, NS, Canada B0N 2V0   Margaret E. Reid, Libn.
Founded: 1979. **Staff:** Prof 1. **Subjects:** Materials testing and pavement
evaluation. **Holdings:** 500 books; 4000 technical reports. **Subscriptions:** 40
journals and other serials. **Services:** Interlibrary loan; copying; library open
to the public with restrictions. **Computerized Information Services:** CAN/
OLE, DIALOG Information Services. **Networks/Consortia:** Member of
Nova Scotia Government Libraries Council. **Special Indexes:** Trade
Literature Index.

★ 12145 ★
Nova Scotia Education Communications Agency - Education Media
Services (Aud-Vis, Educ)
3770 Kempt Rd.   Phone: (902)424-2462
Halifax, NS, Canada B3K 4X8   Bernard Hart, Asst.Dir.
Founded: 1937. **Staff:** 22. **Subjects:** Education, teacher training. **Holdings:**
7800 films; 3000 videotapes. **Services:** Video- and audiotape copying;
systems design for media-related curriculum materials; educational
television production, small format (filmstrip, slide/tape); graphic design;
photography; maintenance and repair service for schools; film library
service. **Automated Operations:** Computerized cataloging and circulation.
Remarks: FAX: (902)424-0633. Affiliated with the Educational Resources
Branch of the Department of Education. **Staff:** Nancy MacDonald, Coord.,
Media Lib.

★ 12146 ★
Nova Scotia Hospital - Health Sciences Library (Med)
P.O. Box 1004
Dartmouth, NS, Canada B2Y 3Z9   Phone: (902)464-3111
Staff: 2. **Subjects:** Psychiatry, medicine, psychology, neurology, pre-clinical
science. **Special Collections:** Nova Scotia government reports, 1856 to
present. **Holdings:** 5500 books; 400 bound periodical volumes; 8000
psychiatric and medical reprints; 450 slides and cassettes; hospital archives.
Subscriptions: 276 journals and other serials. **Services:** Interlibrary loan;
copying; library open to staff and students. **Special Indexes:** Index to
psychiatric reports and papers published by hospital staff; index to journal
articles on special psychiatric and medical subjects. **Remarks:** FAX:
(902)464-3460.

Nova Scotia House of Assembly - Office of the Speaker - Nova Scotia
Legislative Library
See: **Nova Scotia Legislative Library** (12148)

★ 12147 ★
Nova Scotia Human Rights Commission - Library (Soc Sci)
P.O. Box 2221   Phone: (902)424-4111
Halifax, NS, Canada B3J 3C4   May Lui, Pub.Educ.Off.
Founded: 1970. **Staff:** 2. **Subjects:** Civil rights. **Special Collections:**
Multiculturalism; women; aboriginal people, and other visible minorities;
disability; racism; human rights. **Holdings:** 3244 books; 26 bound periodical
volumes; 1261 reports; case decisions in braille and on audio cassette.
Subscriptions: 104 journals and other serials. **Services:** Copying; SDI;
library open to the public for reference use only. **Computerized Information**
Services: Government Documents (internal database). **Remarks:** FAX:
(902)424-0596. Telex: 01922734. **Staff:** David Eagles, lib.Techn.

★ 12148 ★
Nova Scotia Legislative Library (Soc Sci, Law)
Province House   Phone: (902)424-5932
Halifax, NS, Canada B3J 2P8   Margaret Murphy, Leg.Libn.
Founded: 1862. **Staff:** Prof 3; Other 3. **Subjects:** Legislation - federal,
provincial, U.S., Great Britain; political science; history; economics;
biography. **Special Collections:** Novascotiana (15,000 volumes). **Holdings:**
73,000 books; 4000 reels of microfilm; 40,000 microfiche. **Subscriptions:** 650
journals and other serials; 35 newspapers. **Services:** Interlibrary loan;
copying; library open to the public. **Computerized Information Services:**
Info Globe, QL Systems, The Financial Post DataGroup, DIALOG
Information Services, STM Systems Corporation, Infomart Online; Envoy
100 (electronic mail service). **Publications:** Publications of the Province of
Nova Scotia, monthly and annual - available on request; Nova Scotia Royal
Commissions and Commissions of Inquiry appointed by the Province of
Nova Scotia; Nova Scotia Book of Days, a calendar of the province's history.
Special Indexes: Index of pictorial material relating to Nova Scotia; index
to regulations of the province of Nova Scotia. **Remarks:** FAX: (902)424-
0574. Electronic mail address(es): NSHL.ILL (Envoy 100). Maintained by
the Nova Scotia House of Assembly - Office of the Speaker. **Staff:** Jean
Sawyer, Asst.Libn.; Sandy Scott, Libn.

★ 12149 ★
Nova Scotia Museum - Library (Biol Sci, Hist)
1747 Summer St.   Phone: (902)429-4610
Halifax, NS, Canada B3H 3A6   M. Susan Whiteside, Libn.
Founded: 1885. **Staff:** Prof 1; Other 1. **Subjects:** Natural history, social
history of Nova Scotia, decorative arts, museology. **Holdings:** 20,000 titles;
pamphlets; slides; slide/tape sets. **Subscriptions:** 140 journals and other
serials. **Services:** Interlibrary loan; library open to the public for reference
use only.

Nova Scotia Museum - Maritime Museum of the Atlantic
See: **Maritime Museum of the Atlantic** (9691)

★ 12150 ★
Nova Scotia Power Corporation - Corporate Research and Information
Centre (Energy)
Box 910   Phone: (902)428-6928
Halifax, NS, Canada B3J 2W5   Barbara N. MacKenzie, Hd.
Founded: 1972. **Staff:** Prof 2; Other 1. **Subjects:** Engineering, business, data
processing. **Holdings:** 24,000 documents; 450 periodical titles.
Subscriptions: 520 journals and other serials; 11 newspapers. **Services:**
Interlibrary loan; SDI; center open to the public by appointment. **Automated**
Operations: Computerized public access catalog, cataloging, acquisitions,
and serials. **Computerized Information Services:** PFDS Online, CAN/OLE,
QL Systems, DIALOG Information Services, WESTLAW, Info Globe,
Reuters Information Services (Canada) Limited, BRS Information
Technologies, WILSONLINE, Canadian Centre for Occupational Health &
Safety, The Financial Post DataGroup, American Society of Civil Engineers
(ASCE), International Energy Agency, VU/TEXT Information Services,
STM Systems Corporation. **Publications:** Library Acquisitions, irregular -
for internal distribution only. **Remarks:** FAX: (902)428-6102. **Staff:** Marged
Dewar.

★ 12151 ★
Nova Scotia Provincial Library (Info Sci)
6955 Bayers Rd.   Phone: (902)453-2810
Halifax, NS, Canada B3L 4S4   Marion L. Pape, Prov.Libn.
Founded: 1952. **Staff:** Prof 9; Other 22. **Subjects:** Bibliography, library and
information science, talking books. **Holdings:** 15,000 books; 1000 bound
periodical volumes. **Subscriptions:** 412 journals and other serials. **Services:**
Interlibrary loan; library not open to the public. **Automated Operations:**
Computerized cataloging. **Computerized Information Services:** DIALOG
Information Services, WILSONLINE, Infomart Online, QL Systems,
CAN/OLE, Info Globe, BRS Information Technologies, The Financial Post
DataGroup; Envoy 100 (electronic mail service). **Publications:** Nova Scotia
Regional Public Library Statistics, annual; Directory of Nova Scotia
Libraries, irregular; - both free upon request; Directory of Interlibrary Loan
Policies and Duplicating Services in Nova Scotia Libraries, irregular; Novia
Scotia Library Interlibrary Loan Procedures (manual). **Special Catalogs:**
Nova Scotia Talking Books Catalogue, annual. **Remarks:** Library provides
reference service to regional public and government departmental libraries.
Remarks: FAX: (902)453-0549. Electronic mail address(es): ADMIN/
NSPROV.LIBRARY (Envoy 100). **Staff:** JoAnne Irwin, Act.Coord.,
Tech.Serv.; Frank Oram, Act.Coord., Ref.Serv.; Elizabeth Armstrong,
Coord., Pub.Lib.Serv.; Elaine Rillie, Coord., Sch.Lib.Serv.

★ 12152 ★
(Nova Scotia) Public Archives of Nova Scotia (Hist)
6016 University Ave.   Phone: (902)424-6060
Halifax, NS, Canada B3H 1W4   Carman Carroll, Prov.Archv.
Founded: 1857. **Staff:** Prof 14; Other 14. **Subjects:** Novascotiana. **Special**
Collections: Akins Library (colonial history, Canadian history, and
Maritime Provinces). **Holdings:** 65,000 books; 2000 bound periodical
volumes; large collection of government records and historical documents;
200,000 photographs; 17,000 reels of microfilm; film, television, and sound
archives. **Subscriptions:** 65 journals and other serials. **Services:** Copying;
archives open to the public. **Publications:** Library acquisitions list,
bimonthly. **Special Catalogs:** Akins Library Catalog. **Remarks:** FAX:
(902)424-0516. **Staff:** Gwen Whitford, Libn.; Lois Kernaghan, Mss.; Kent
Haworth, Pub.Rec.; Garry Shutlak, Maps; Margaret Campbell, Photo.;
JoAnn Watson, Film/Sound.

★ 12153 ★
(Nova Scotia) Public Archives of Nova Scotia - Map/Architecture Division (Geog-Map)
6016 University Ave.   Phone: (902)424-6060
Halifax, NS, Canada B3H 1W4   Garry D. Shutlak, Map/Arch. Archv.
Founded: 1972. **Staff:** Prof 1.5. **Subjects:** Nova Scotia and maritime provinces - maps, plans, architecture, geology, topography, navigation. **Special Collections:** City of Halifax Engineering and Works Department and Building Inspection Department plans and drawings. **Holdings:** 650,000 maps and plans. **Subscriptions:** 6 journals and other serials. **Services:** Copying; archives open to the public. **Special Catalogs:** A Catalogue of Maps, Plans, and Charts in the Public Archives of Nova Scotia (1938). **Special Indexes:** Index to architects, architectural firms, and/or donors (binder). **Remarks:** FAX: (902)424-0516.

★ 12154 ★
Nova Scotia Research Foundation - Library (Sci-Engr)
101 Research Dr.
Woodside Industrial Park
P.O. Box 790   Phone: (902)424-8670
Dartmouth, NS, Canada B2Y 3Z7   Helen I. Hendry, Libn.
Founded: 1947. **Staff:** Prof 1; Other 2. **Subjects:** Technology, chemistry, geosciences, production management, aquaculture, energy, construction, materials science, food science, microbiology. **Holdings:** 7000 books; 6000 periodical volumes; 6500 government documents, reports, pamphlets. **Subscriptions:** 300 journals and other serials; 6 newspapers. **Services:** Interlibrary loan; copying; library open to serious inquirers. **Computerized Information Services:** DIALOG Information Services, ORBIT Search Service, CAN/OLE, QL Systems, STN International, WILSONLINE, Info Globe. **Remarks:** FAX: (902)424-4679.

★ 12155 ★
Nova Scotia Teachers College - Learning Resources Centre (Educ)
P.O. Box 810   Phone: (902)895-5347
Truro, NS, Canada B2N 5G5   Dr. Larry Burt, Dir.
Staff: Prof 3; Other 5. **Subjects:** Education. **Special Collections:** Canadiana; children's library; curriculum material. **Holdings:** 113,000 books; 340,000 microfiche; 350 magnetic tapes; 500 phonograph records; 60 videotapes; 250 filmstrips; 75 slides; 70 overhead transparencies. **Subscriptions:** 304 journals and other serials; 9 newspapers. **Services:** Interlibrary loan; copying; library open to the public. **Automated Operations:** Computerized public access catalog, cataloging, acquisitions, and circulation. **Computerized Information Services:** UTLAS; CD-ROMs (Books in Print Plus, Laser-Quest, ERIC, Microsoft Bookshelf, PC-SIG Library); Envoy 100 (electronic mail service). **Publications:** Library guide. **Special Catalogs:** Periodical holdings; acquisitions list; computer software list. **Remarks:** FAX: (902)893-5610. Electronic mail address(es): ILL.NSTT (Envoy 100). **Staff:** Tom Acker, Cat.Libn.; Jagpal S. Tiwana, Acq. & Ser.Libn.; Sheila Pearl, Circ. & Ref.Libn.

★ 12156 ★
Nova University - Law Library (Law)
3100 S.W. 9th Ave.   Phone: (305)760-5763
Fort Lauderdale, FL 33315   Carol Roehrenbeck, Dir.
Staff: Prof 7; Other 11. **Subjects:** Law - state, federal, international, patent, tax, corporate; legal history. **Special Collections:** Government document depository; United Nations document depository; AIDS Depository for the state of Florida. **Holdings:** 116,020 books; 9,923 bound periodical volumes; 3490 volumes of unbound materials; 91,074 volumes on microfiche; 16,175 volumes on microfilm; 4 phonograph records; 5 reel to reel tapes; 593 audio cassettes; 282 videocassettes; 333 machine-readable data files. **Subscriptions:** 3533 journals and other serials; 20 newspapers. **Services:** Interlibrary loan; copying; library open to the public for research only. **Automated Operations:** Computerized public access catalog, cataloging, serials, and ILL. **Computerized Information Services:** DIALOG Information Services, LEXIS, OCLC, ELSS (Electronic Legislative Search System), Maxwell Macmillan Taxes Online, NEXIS, WESTLAW; internal database; ALANET (electronic mail service). Performs searches on fee basis. Contact Person: C. Richard Gibson, Assoc. Law Libn., telephone 760-5764. **Networks/Consortia:** Member of SOLINET. **Remarks:** FAX: (305)522-7025. **Staff:** Ronald D. Stroud, Asst.Libn. for Coll.Dev.; Iris Caldwell, Ref.Libn.; Billie Jo Kaufman, Hd. of Pub.Serv.; Frank Novak, Comp.Spec.; Suzan Herskowitz, Ref.Libn.

★ 12157 ★
Nova University - Oceanographic Center Library (Biol Sci)
8000 N. Ocean Dr.   Phone: (305)920-1909
Dania, FL 33004   Kathleen Maxson, Libn.
Staff: 1. **Subjects:** Physical oceanography, marine biology. **Holdings:** 2125 books; 2500 bound periodical volumes; charts and maps; reprints. **Subscriptions:** 110 journals and other serials. **Services:** Interlibrary loan; copying; library open to the public. **Computerized Information Services:** DIALOG Information Services; internal database.

★ 12158 ★
Novato Unified School District - Instructional Materials Center (Educ)
1015 7th St.   Phone: (415)897-4247
Novato, CA 94945   Pat May, Coord.
Founded: 1965. **Staff:** Prof 1; Other 2. **Subjects:** Education, educational psychology, art. **Special Collections:** Collection of early 20th century California textbooks (150). **Holdings:** 4000 books; 100 resource guides; 650 art prints; 200 sculpture reproductions; 200 microfiche; 25 sound filmstrips; 6 VF drawers of pamphlets; 200 software programs. **Subscriptions:** 50 journals and other serials. **Services:** Interlibrary loan; copying; center open to the public with restrictions.

★ 12159 ★
Novo Nordisk Bioindustrials, Inc. - Information Services (Biol Sci)
33 Turner Rd.   Phone: (203)790-2600
Danbury, CT 06813-1907   James W. Fleagle, Mgr., Info. & Off.Serv.
Staff: Prof 2. **Subjects:** Biotechnology, industrial microbiology, enzymology, food science. **Holdings:** 3000 books; 1200 bound periodical volumes; CD-ROM. **Subscriptions:** 250 journals and other serials; 10 newspapers. **Services:** Interlibrary loan; library not open to the public. **Automated Operations:** Computerized cataloging and serials. **Computerized Information Services:** DIALOG Information Services, PFDS Online, Chemical Abstracts Service (CAS), Dow Jones News/Retrieval, Dun & Bradstreet Business Credit Services, BRS Information Technologies. **Networks/Consortia:** Member of Southwestern Connecticut Library Council (SWLC). **Remarks:** FAX: (203)790-2748. **Staff:** Maureen Coan, Asst.Libn.

Novotny Library of Economic History
See: **Syracuse University - George Arents Research Library for Special Collections** (15961)

NPR
See: **National Public Radio** (11256)

NRA
See: **National Rifle Association of America** (11275)

★ 12160 ★
NSCC Institute of Technology - Library (Educ)
5685 Leeds St.
P.O. Box 2210   Phone: (902)424-4224
Halifax, NS, Canada B3J 3C4   Nola D. Brennan, Libn.
Founded: 1972. **Staff:** Prof 1; Other 1. **Subjects:** Engineering, medical laboratory, dental, construction administration, and other resources technologies; automated manufacturing; computer technology; food services; nuclear medicine; dental assisting; business computer programming; mini/microcomputer systems; plant apprenticeship and trades. **Holdings:** 12,100 books; 1300 bound periodical volumes; 550 student reports; 35 school calendars. **Subscriptions:** 200 journals and other serials. **Services:** Interlibrary loan; copying; center open to the public with restrictions. **Remarks:** FAX: (902)424-0534.

NTIS
See: **U.S. Dept. of Commerce - National Technical Information Service** (17220)

★ 12161 ★
Nuclear Age Resource Center - Library (Soc Sci)
East 1
Cuyahoga Community College
4250 Richmond Rd.   Phone: (216)987-2224
Cleveland, OH 44122   Margie Bergstrom, Libn.
Founded: 1985. **Staff:** Prof 6. **Subjects:** Nuclear arms race, arms control, weapons systems, international relations, consequences of nuclear war, conflict resolution. **Holdings:** 1000 books; 2000 pamphlets, briefing papers, vertical file materials; 225 films, videotapes, filmstrips; 30 audio cassettes. **Subscriptions:** 107 journals and other serials. **Services:** Library open to the public. **Special Catalogs:** Catalog of AV holdings (printout); Annotated list of periodicals. **Remarks:** FAX: (216)987-2053.

★ 12162 ★
Nuclear Assurance Corporation - Information Center (Energy)
6251 Crooked Creek Rd., Suite 200   Phone: (404)447-1144
Norcross, GA 30092   H. Kim Lee, Info.Ctr.Mgr.
Founded: 1971. **Staff:** Prof 1; Other 1. **Subjects:** Nuclear fuel cycle, electric utility management, energy analysis, spent-fuel storage casks and transportation, geotechnical consulting, information management development. **Special Collections:** Nuclear science and industry book collection. **Holdings:** 6053 books; 600 archival reports; 1714 subject files; 5350 microfiche; 1788 slides and photographs. **Subscriptions:** 124 journals and other serials. **Services:** Interlibrary loan; center not open to the public. **Computerized Information Services:** DIALOG Information Services. **Networks/Consortia:** Member of SOLINET. **Publications:** Headlines, monthly; NAC Employee Bibliography, annual - both for internal distribution only. **Special Indexes:** Index to company reports (book); index to subject files (card). **Remarks:** FAX: (404)447-1797. Telex: 321 6827020.

★ 12163 ★
Nuclear Consulting Services, Inc. - Library (Sci-Engr)
7000 Huntley Rd.
Columbus, OH 43229   Phone: (614)846-5710
Subjects: Nuclear filtration systems, adsorption chemistry, chemical engineering, air purification, vapor recovery, air pollution, solvent recovery. **Holdings:** 500 volumes. **Remarks:** FAX: (614)431-0858. Telex: 6974415 NUCN WGN.

★ 12164 ★
Nuclear Free America - Library (Soc Sci)
325 E. 25th St.   Phone: (410)235-3575
Baltimore, MD 21218   Charles K. Johnson, Exec.Dir.
Founded: 1982. **Staff:** 2. **Subjects:** Nuclear free zones, nuclear weapons contracting. **Holdings:** 250 books; 12 AV programs; files on nuclear free zones in over 27 countries. **Subscriptions:** 28 journals and other serials. **Services:** Library open to the public. **Computerized Information Services:** All military and nuclear weapons contractor database, government contracts database (internal databases); PeaceNet (electronic mail service). Performs searches on fee basis. **Remarks:** FAX: (410)235-5457. **Staff:** Charlene Knott.

Nuclear Free Press Archives
See: **Ontario Public Interest Research Group (OPIRG) - Peterborough Library (12496)**

Nuclear Regulatory Commission
See: **U.S. Nuclear Regulatory Commission (17912)**

Nukewatch Library
See: **Progressive Foundation (13412)**

★ 12165 ★
Numismatics International - Library (Rec)
30 Pleasant St.   Phone: (603)237-4039
Colebrook, NH 03576   Granvyl Hulse, Libn.
Founded: 1964. **Staff:** 1. **Subjects:** Coins, currency. **Holdings:** 3000 books; slide sets. **Services:** Interlibrary loan (fee); library open to members and other numismatic organizations. **Remarks:** Maintains a branch library of numismatic catalogs and price lists in Dallas, TX and a branch library of numismatic periodicals and newspapers in St. Johnsbury, VT.

★ 12166 ★
(Nuremberg) German-American Institute - USIS Collection (Educ)
Gleisbuhlstrasse, 13   Phone: 911 203328
W-8500 Nuremberg, Germany   Xenia Klepikov
Founded: 1946. **Staff:** Prof 2. **Subjects:** United States. **Holdings:** 12,400 books; 2155 microfiche; 590 audiocassettes and videocassettes. **Subscriptions:** 71 journals and other serials; 10 newspapers. **Services:** Interlibrary loan; copying; library open to the public. **Remarks:** FAX: 911 208767. Maintained or supported by the U.S. Information Agency. Focus is on materials that will assist peoples outside the United States to learn about the United States, its people, history, culture, political processes, and social milieux. **Staff:** Gudrun Schindler.

★ 12167 ★
Nurses Association of New Brunswick - Library (Med)
165 Regent St.   Phone: (506)458-8731
Fredericton, NB, Canada E3B 3W5   Barbara Thompson, Libn.
Founded: 1959. **Staff:** Prof 1. **Subjects:** Nursing - education, research, manpower, management; medicine; allied health sciences. **Special Collections:** Archival Collection of Nurses Association of New Brunswick (publications, briefs, and reports). **Holdings:** 900 books; 300 bound periodical volumes; 9 VF drawers; 2 drawers of bulletins; clinical textbooks. **Subscriptions:** 35 journals and other serials; 4 newspapers. **Services:** Interlibrary loan; library not open to the public. **Publications:** Info-Newsletter, 5/year - for internal distribution only. **Remarks:** FAX: (506)459-2857.

NUS Corporation
See: **Halliburton NUS Environmental Corporation (6851)**

★ 12168 ★
Nutley Historical Society Museum - Alice J. Bickers Library (Hist)
65 Church St.   Phone: (201)667-1528
Nutley, NJ 07110   Peter Balma, Pres.
Founded: 1945. **Subjects:** New Jersey and local history. **Special Collections:** Nutley authors; old account books of Nutley merchants; old costumes; Annie Oakley Collection. **Holdings:** 200 volumes. **Services:** Interlibrary loan; library open to the public by appointment. **Publications:** Annual report; quarterly bulletins. **Remarks:** An alternate telephone number is 667-5239. **Staff:** Jeanne Van Steen, Musm.Coord.

★ 12169 ★
Nutra-Sweet Company - Information Services (Food-Bev)
P.O. Box 730   Phone: (708)405-6726
Deerfield, IL 60015   Cynthia Altgilbers Lesky
Founded: 1987. **Staff:** Prof 3; Other 3. **Subjects:** Food business, nutrition, fat substitutes, lifestyle, additives. **Holdings:** 900 books; 200 reports. **Subscriptions:** 300 journals and other serials; 5 newspapers. **Services:** Interlibrary loan; library not open to the public. **Computerized Information Services:** DIALOG Information Services, NEXIS, Comtex Scientific Corporation, Burrelle's Broadcast Database. **Remarks:** FAX: (708)405-7809. **Staff:** Erika Schroederus, Bus.Res.Spec.

Nutting Memorial Library
See: **Maine Maritime Academy (9553)**

★ 12170 ★
NWNL Companies, Inc. - Library (Bus-Fin)
20 Washington Ave., S.   Phone: (612)372-5606
Minneapolis, MN 55401   Laurinda C. Dahl, Libn.
Founded: 1947. **Staff:** Prof 1; Other 2. **Subjects:** Medical care, alternative health delivery systems, individual and group life and health insurance, law, taxes, business management, health statistics. **Special Collections:** Company archives. **Holdings:** 10,000 books; 200 bound periodical volumes; 20 VF drawers. **Subscriptions:** 250 journals and other serials; 7 newspapers. **Services:** Interlibrary loan; library open to the public for reference use only. **Computerized Information Services:** DIALOG Information Services, NEXIS, Dow Jones News/Retrieval, WESTLAW, VU/TEXT Information Services, DataTimes. **Remarks:** FAX: (612)342-7531.

★ 12171 ★
Nyack College and Alliance Theological Seminary - Library (Rel-Phil)
Nyack, NY 10960   Phone: (914)358-1710
     Donald E. Keeney, Dir.
Founded: 1882. **Staff:** Prof 2; Other 3. **Subjects:** Protestant missions, Bible, theology, cultural anthropology, church history, education. **Holdings:** 82,260 volumes; 40 VF drawers of pamphlets; 1000 sound recordings; 721 cassette tapes; 231 filmstrips; 929 reels of microfilm; 8909 microfiche. **Subscriptions:** 480 journals. **Services:** Interlibrary loan; copying; SDI; library open to the public for reference use only. **Automated Operations:** Computerized ILL. **Computerized Information Services:** DIALOG Information Services, OCLC. **Networks/Consortia:** Member of Southeastern New York Library Resources Council (SENYLRC). **Publications:** Acquisition list, bimonthly - to faculty; bibliographies, bimonthly; library manual - both to students. **Staff:** Randall Dick, Asst.Libn./Rd.Serv.; Kathryn Wood, Acq.

★ 12172 ★
Nyack Hospital - Memorial Library (Med)
N. Midland Ave.   Phone: (914)358-6200
Nyack, NY 10960   Christine M. Giuricin, Mgr., Lib.Serv.
Staff: Prof 1; Other 1. **Subjects:** Medicine, nursing, pediatrics. **Holdings:** 2250 books; 2500 bound periodical volumes; 50 videocassettes. **Subscriptions:** 175 journals and other serials. **Services:** Interlibrary loan; copying; document delivery; library open to the public by appointment. **Computerized Information Services:** MEDLARS, BRS Information Technologies; CD-ROM (SilverPlatter Information, Inc.). **Networks/Consortia:** Member of New York State Interlibrary Loan Network (NYSILL), Health Information Libraries of Westchester (HILOW), Southeastern New York Library Resources Council (SENYLRC), BHSL.

★ 12173 ★
Nye County Law Library (Law)
Box 393   Phone: (702)482-8141
Tonopah, NV 89049   Brenda Goodman, Exec.Sec.
Founded: 1905. **Subjects:** Law. **Holdings:** 11,000 volumes. **Services:** Library open to the public. **Computerized Information Services:** WESTLAW. **Remarks:** FAX: (702)482-8133.

Russel B. Nye Popular Culture Collections
See: **Michigan State University - Special Collections Library - Russel B. Nye Popular Culture Collections** (10337)

Norman E. Nygaard Library
See: **Woodland Hills Presbyterian Church** (20572)

★ 12174 ★
Nylander Museum - Archives (Sci-Engr)
393 Main St.   Phone: (207)493-4474
Caribou, ME 04736-1062   Gege Schawb, Dir.
Founded: 1938. **Staff:** Prof 1. **Subjects:** Geology, anthropology, botany, conchology, Native American ethnology, paleontology, butterflies and moths. **Special Collections:** Papers, correspondence, and publications of Olof Nylander (scientist and geologist of Northern Maine, 1864-1943). **Holdings:** Books; pamphlets; clippings; photographs; documents. **Services:** Archives open to the public by appointment. **Remarks:** Alternate telephone number(s): (207)493-4209.

★ 12175 ★
NYNEX Corporation - Information Access Center (Info Sci)
1111 Westchester Ave.   Phone: (914)644-6270
White Plains, NY 10604-3509   Maureen A. Roche, Staff Dir.
Founded: 1984. **Staff:** 4. **Subjects:** Telecommunications, business, computers. **Holdings:** 2000 books; 1000 consultants' reports. **Subscriptions:** 700 journals and other serials; 29 newspapers. **Services:** Interlibrary loan; center not open to the public. **Automated Operations:** TECHLIBplus. **Computerized Information Services:** DIALOG Information Services, NEXIS, Dow Jones News/Retrieval, NewsNet, Inc., VU/TEXT Information Services, ADP Network Services, DunsPrint, Telescope, OCLC. **Networks/Consortia:** Member of New York Metropolitan Reference and Research Library Agency. **Publications:** Alerting services - for internal distribution only. **Remarks:** FAX: (914)694-6280. **Staff:** Anna Green, Info.Spec.; Ellen McDermott, Info.Spec.; Teresa Wilkins, Info.Spec.; Kerry McDonald, Archv.; Suzanne Lamadore, Lib.Oper.

O

Anita O.'K. & Robert R. Young Science Library
See: Smith College (15232)

★ 12176 ★
Oak Forest Hospital - Professional Library (Med)
15900 S. Cicero Ave.   Phone: (708)928-4200
Oak Forest, IL 60452   Delores I. Quinn, Libn.
Founded: 1973. **Staff:** Prof 1; Other 2. **Subjects:** Medicine, nursing, paramedical sciences. **Holdings:** 2000 books. **Subscriptions:** 250 journals and other serials. **Services:** Library not open to the public.

★ 12177 ★
Oak Grove Lutheran Church - Memorial Library (Rel-Phil)
7045 Lyndale Ave., S.   Phone: (612)869-4917
Richfield, MN 55423   Juanita Carpenter, Libn.
Founded: 1959. **Staff:** Prof 1; Other 5. **Subjects:** Bible reference, devotional and inspirational reading, church history, religious education, family life, children's literature, biography, social concerns, world religions. **Holdings:** 4425 books; tape cassettes; religious periodicals; videotapes. **Services:** Library open to the public.

★ 12178 ★
Oak Hills Bible College - Library (Rel-Phil)
1600 Oak Hills Rd.   Phone: (218)751-8670
Bemidji, MN 56601   John T. Salley, Libn.
Founded: 1946. **Staff:** Prof 1; Other 1. **Subjects:** Biblical, philosophical, and theological studies; religious education. **Holdings:** 18,000 books; 625 bound periodical volumes; 150 files of mission material; 550 AV programs. **Subscriptions:** 107 journals and other serials. **Services:** Interlibrary loan; copying; library open to the public. **Networks/Consortia:** Member of Northern Lights Library Network (NLLN).

★ 12179 ★
Oak Lawn Public Library - Local History Area (Hist)
9427 S. Raymond Ave.   Phone: (708)422-4990
Oak Lawn, IL 60453-2434   Barbara Wolfe, Ref.Serv./Local Hist.
Staff: Prof 1. **Subjects:** Oak Lawn, IL; local history. **Special Collections:** Southtown Economist newspapers (microfilm); Oral History Collection; Village Board Meeting minutes, 1969 to present (microfilm); Village Ordinances & Resolutions, 1969 to present (microfilm). **Holdings:** 400 books; 1600 photographs; 75 files of clippings; 20 boxes of local government records. **Services:** library open to the public. **Automated Operations:** Computerized public access catalog, circulation, and indexing. **Computerized Information Services:** DIALOG Information Services, BRS Information Technologies. **Networks/Consortia:** Member of Suburban Library System (SLS). **Special Indexes:** Oak Lawn Public Library Newspaper Index (printed and online).

★ 12180 ★
Oak Park Public Library - Local Author and Local History Collections (Hist)
834 Lake St.   Phone: (708)383-8200
Oak Park, IL 60301   Carol A. Gibson, Dir.
Founded: 1903. **Subjects:** Local history, architecture, and authors. **Special Collections:** Local history collection (856 volumes; 9 VF drawers); Ernest Hemingway (323 volumes); Frank Lloyd Wright (401 volumes); Edgar Rice Burroughs (55 volumes); Grant Manson photographs of Wright buildings (350); Gilman Lane photographs of Wright buildings (700). **Holdings:** 1538 books; 5 VF drawers of Oak Park Landmarks Commission files. **Services:** Interlibrary loan; copying; collections open to the public for reference use only. **Automated Operations:** Computerized cataloging and circulation. **Computerized Information Services:** OCLC. **Networks/Consortia:** Member of Suburban Library System (SLS). **Publications:** Frank Lloyd Wright, Prairie School of Architecture (1974; bibliography). **Special Indexes:** Local newspaper index (1883-1987 on card, 1988 to present online). **Remarks:** FAX: (708)383-6384. **Staff:** William Jerousek, Libn.

★ 12181 ★
Oak Ridge Associated Universities - EES Division - Information Center (Info Sci)
Institute for Energy and Environmental Analysis
Scarboro Main Lab. Bldg.
1299 Bethel Valley Rd.   Phone: (615)576-3292
Oak Ridge, TN 37831-0117   Harry T. Burn, Libn.
Founded: 1977. **Staff:** Prof 1; Other 1. **Subjects:** Libraries, education, employment, manpower, energy, environment. **Holdings:** 400 volumes; 1000 reports. **Subscriptions:** 70 journals and other serials. **Services:** Interlibrary loan; center open to the public with restrictions. **Computerized Information Services:** OCLC, DIALOG Information Services, DTIC, CompuServe Information Service; EES Software Systems (internal database); DIALMAIL, BITNET (electronic mail services). **Networks/Consortia:** Member of FEDLINK. **Remarks:** FTS number(s): 626-3292. **FAX:** (615)576-9384. Electronic mail address(es): 12454 (DIALMAIL); BURNH@ORAU (BITNET). **Also Known As:** Energy/Environment Systems Division.

★ 12182 ★
Oak Ridge Associated Universities - Medical Library (Med)
Box 117   Phone: (615)576-3490
Oak Ridge, TN 37831-0117   Rana Yalcintas, Dir.
Founded: 1974. **Staff:** Prof 1; Other 1.5. **Subjects:** Biochemistry, occupational medicine, cytogenetics, epidemiology, radiation accidents. **Holdings:** 2300 books; 2849 bound periodical volumes; 9500 reports in microform; 1777 reels of microfilm. **Subscriptions:** 101 journals and other serials. **Services:** Interlibrary loan; copying; SDI; library open to the public for reference use only. **Automated Operations:** Computerized cataloging, circulation, and ILL. **Computerized Information Services:** DIALOG Information Services, OCLC, Integrated Technical Information System (ITIS), MEDLINE, WILSONLINE, OCLC EPIC, PRISM. **Networks/Consortia:** Member of Knoxville Area Health Sciences Library Consortium (KAHSLC), FEDLINK. **Publications:** Annual report. **Remarks:** FAX: (615)576-3194. Alternate telephone number(s): FTS 626-3490.

★ 12183 ★
Oak Ridge Associated Universities - Radiopharmaceutical Internal Dose Information Center (Sci-Engr)
Box 117   Phone: (615)576-3450
Oak Ridge, TN 37831-0117   Evelyn E. Watson, Prog.Mgr.
Founded: 1971. **Staff:** Prof 4; Other 1. **Subjects:** Internal dosimetry, radiation absorbed dose, radionuclide kinetics, nuclear medicine, health and medical physics, radiation protection. **Holdings:** Books; reports; manuscripts. **Subscriptions:** 6 journals and other serials. **Services:** Center not open to the public. **Computerized Information Services:** RIDIC (internal database). Performs limited searches free of charge. Contact Person: Audrey Schlafke-Stelson, Res.Assoc. **Publications:** Proceedings of the 4th International Radiopharmaceutical Dosimetry Symposium, 1985. **Remarks:** FAX: (615)576-3194. **Staff:** Michael G. Stabin, Int. Dosimetry Spec.; James Stubbs, Int. Dosimetry Spec.

★ 12184 ★
Oak Ridge National Laboratory - Biomedical and Environmental Information Analysis Section - Library (Med)
P.O. Box 2008, MS-6050   Phone: (615)574-7803
Oak Ridge, TN 37831-6050   Dr. Po-Yung Lu, Sect.Hd.
Subjects: Information systems, health, energy, environmental research. **Holdings:** 1200 bound volumes; 18,000 reports. **Subscriptions:** 125 journals and other serials. **Services:** Copying; library open to federal government agencies and their contractors, research and educational institutions, and industry. **Computerized Information Services:** Commercially available databases; Environmental Plutonium Data Base, Data Base on the Life History of Biofouling Organisms, Data Base on the Environmental Aspects of Transmission Lines (internal databases). Performs searches on fee basis. **Publications:** Reports; bibliographies; list of publications - available on request. **Remarks:** FAX: (615)574-9888. The Oak Ridge National Laboratory is operated by Martin Marietta Energy Systems, Inc. under contract to the U.S. Department of Energy.

★ 12185 ★
Oak Ridge National Laboratory - Carbon Dioxide Information Analysis Center (Sci-Engr)
P.O. Box 2008 (MS-6335)   Phone: (615)574-0390
Oak Ridge, TN 37831-6335   Robert M. Cushman, Dp.Dir.
Founded: 1982. **Staff:** 12.8. **Subjects:** Carbon dioxide-climate research, including atmospheric carbon dioxide measurements, fossil fuel use, forest

conversion, ocean properties characterization, historical records from ice cores, tree rings, global warming, greenhouse effect, information management, information analysis. **Holdings:** 134 reports; 34 numeric data packages, 3 computer model packages. **Subscriptions:** 12 journals and other serials. **Services:** Copying; document delivery. **Computerized Information Services:** BITNET, InterNet, SCIENCEnet (electronic mail services). **Publications:** CDIAC Communications (newsletter), 3/year; TRENDS '91: A Compendium of Data on Global Change; Glossary: Carbon Dioxide and Climate; DOE Research Summary (series), 6/year. **Special Catalogs:** Catalog of Databases and Reports. **Remarks:** FAX: (615)574-2322. Electronic mail address(es): CDP@ORNLSTC (BITNET); CDP@STC.CTD.ORNL.GOV (InterNet); CDIAC (SCIENCEnet). **Staff:** Frederick W. Stoss, Task Ldr.

★12186★

Oak Ridge National Laboratory - Controlled Fusion Atomic Data Center (Sci-Engr)
Bldg. 6003, Box 2008   Phone: (615)574-4707
Oak Ridge, TN 37831-6372   R.A. Phaneuf, Dir.
Founded: 1959. **Staff:** 1.5. **Subjects:** Atomic collision processes related to fusion energy research; heavy particle collisions; particle interactions with electrons, photons, particle penetration into matter; particle interactions with surfaces. **Holdings:** 300 books; 200 bound periodical volumes; 150 reports. **Services:** Collects, stores, evaluates, recommends, and disseminates atomic and molecular processes information and data. **Computerized Information Services:** Internal database; BITNET (electronic mail service). Performs searches free of charge. **Publications:** Atomic Data for Fusion (compilations of recommended data); Annual Bibliography of Atomic and Molecular Collision Processes (online); topical reports. **Remarks:** FAX: (615)574-1268. Electronic mail address(es): RPF@ORNLSTC (BITNET). The Oak Ridge National Laboratory operates under contract to the U.S. Department of Energy. **Staff:** M. Imogene Kirkpatrick.

★12187★

Oak Ridge National Laboratory - Environmental Teratology Information Center (ETIC)
Bldg. 2001
Box 2008
Oak Ridge, TN 37831-6050
Founded: 1975. **Subjects:** Evaluation of chemicals, biological agents, and physical agents for teratogenic activity. **Holdings:** 53,000 records. **Remarks:** Center is a branch of the Human Genome and Toxicology Information Program. The Oak Ridge National Laboratory is managed by Martin Marietta Energy Systems, Inc., under contract to the U.S. Department of Energy. Currently inactive.

★12188★

Oak Ridge National Laboratory - Health and Safety Research Division - Environmental Mutagen Information Center (Sci-Engr)
Bldg. 2001
Box 2008   Phone: (615)574-7871
Oak Ridge, TN 37831-6050   John S. Wassom, Dir.
Founded: 1969. **Staff:** Prof 4; Other 1. **Subjects:** Genetic toxicology, chemical mutagenesis. **Holdings:** 78,000 references on the genotoxicity of chemicals. **Services:** Answers information requests on time-available basis. **Computerized Information Services:** TOXLINE and TOXNET (Toxicology Data Network). **Remarks:** The Oak Ridge National Laboratory is managed by Martin Marietta Energy Systems, Inc. under contract to the U.S. Department of Energy. EMIC Is supported by the National Toxicology Program/National Institute of Environmental Health Sciences, and the Environmental Protection Agency through the National Library of Medicine. **Staff:** E.S. Von Halle; B.L. Whitfield; E.T. Owens; J.L. Couch; W.J. Barnard.

★12189★

Oak Ridge National Laboratory - Nuclear Data Project (Sci-Engr)
Box 2008   Phone: (615)574-4699
Oak Ridge, TN 37831-6371   M.J. Martin, Dir.
Founded: 1948. **Staff:** Prof 3; Other 1. **Subjects:** Nuclear physics, nuclear levels, nuclear transitions, nuclear structure, radioactivity, isotopes, nuclear reactions. **Special Collections:** Nuclear data tables (400 compilations of measured or calculated quantities). **Holdings:** 200 books; 180 shelf feet of unbound journals; 9 VF drawers of technical reports. **Subscriptions:** 32 journals and other serials. **Services:** Collection, evaluation, and publication of data on nuclear level structure; answers specific requests for nuclear

structure references or data; open to the public with special approval. **Computerized Information Services:** Evaluated Nuclear Structure Data File (ENSDF), Nuclear Structure Reference File; BITNET (electronic mail service). **Remarks:** FAX: (615)574-1268. Telex: 854468. Electronic mail address(es): MARTINM@ORPHOI (BITNET). Maintains computerized bibliographic and keyword files for over 50,000 published references and 30,000 unpublished references in expe rimental nuclear physics. From these files are produced reference lists for various selectors such as isotope, half-life, specific type of nuclear reaction. The Oak Ridge National Laboratory operates under contract to the U.S. Department of Energy. **Staff:** Y. Akovali, Res.; M.R. Schmorak, Res.; M.R. Lay, Techn.

★12190★

Oak Ridge National Laboratory - Nuclear Operations Analysis Center (Energy)
PO Box 2009   Phone: (615)574-0394
Oak Ridge, TN 37831-8065   G.T. Mays, Dir.
Founded: 1963. **Staff:** Prof 12; Other 9. **Subjects:** Nuclear facility operation and experience; electrical power systems; general safety considerations; heat transfer and thermal hydraulics; nuclear instrumentation, controls, safety systems; reactor transients, kinetics, stability; risk and reliability. **Special Collections:** Nuclear reactor safety analysis and environmental reports; nuclear facility licensing documents. **Holdings:** 500 books; 200 reports. **Subscriptions:** 10 journals and other serials. **Services:** Questions answered; consultation, free to sponsors and their designees, to others on fee basis. **Computerized Information Services:** Sequence Code and Search System (SCSS); internal databases. **Publications:** DOE Nuclear Safety Journal; periodic bibliographies; Licensee Event Report (LER) Monthly Report. **Special Catalogs:** Computer file of LERs from various utilities describing any unusual event occurring at a nuclear plant. **Remarks:** The Oak Ridge National Laboratory is operated by Martin Marietta Energy Systems Inc. under contract to the U.S. Department of Energy.

★12191★

Oak Ridge National Laboratory - Radiation Shielding Information Center (Sci-Engr)
Box 2008   Phone: (615)574-6176
Oak Ridge, TN 37831-6362   Robert W. Roussin, Dir.
Founded: 1962. **Staff:** Prof 9; Other 5. **Subjects:** Radiation protection, transport, and shielding. **Special Collections:** Digital computer code packages to perform shielding calculations; computer-readable data libraries of nuclear cross-sections and data from intranuclear cascade calculations. **Holdings:** 18,000 micronegative cards; 900 computer code packages; 160 nuclear data packages. **Subscriptions:** 1905 newspapers. **Services:** Dissemination of code/data packages; problem-solving; center open to the public. **Automated Operations:** Computerized circulation. **Computerized Information Services:** EasyLink, BITNET (electronic mail services). Contact Person: Nancy A. Hatmaker, Mgr. **Publications:** Bibliographies, irregular; newsletter, monthly; topical reports, irregular; abstracts of code/data packages, annual. **Remarks:** FAX: (615)574-9619. Telex: 854467. Electronic mail address(es): 62813374 (EasyLink); PDC@ORNLSTC (BITNET). The Oak Ridge National Laboratory is operated by Martin Marietta Energy Systems Inc. under contract to the U.S. Department of Energy. **Staff:** J.E. White; S.N. Cramer; B.L. Kirk; B.L. McGill; J.L. Bartley.

★12192★

Oak Ridge National Laboratory - Toxicology Information Response Center (Med, Biol Sci)
Bldg. 2001, MS 6050
Box 2008   Phone: (615)576-1746
Oak Ridge, TN 37831-6050   Kim Slusher, Dir.
Founded: 1971. **Staff:** 10. **Subjects:** Toxicology, pharmacology, veterinary toxicology, heavy metals, pesticides, chemistry, biology, medicine, industrial hygiene. **Holdings:** 7700 search files; 250 microfiche of published bibliographies. **Subscriptions:** 50 journals and other serials. **Services:** SDI; center open to the public. **Computerized Information Services:** DIALOG Information Services, MEDLARS, CIS, STN International, U.S. Department of Defense, U.S. Department of Energy. **Publications:** State-of-the-art reviews; specialized bibliographies; list of publications for sale - available on request. **Remarks:** FAX: (615)574-9888. Sponsored by the Toxicology Information Program/National Library of Medicine. The Oak Ridge National Laboratory is operated by Martin Marietta Energy Systems Inc. under contract to the U.S. Department of Energy.

★12193★
Oakdale Regional Center - Staff Library (Med)
2995 W. Genesee St.
Lapeer, MI 48446
Phone: (313)664-2951
Rollin Hill, Lib.Coord.
Staff: 1. **Subjects:** Mental retardation, medicine, education, management, nursing, psychiatry. **Holdings:** 2700 books; 1 vertical file collection. **Subscriptions:** 80 journals and other serials. **Services:** Interlibrary loan; copying; library open to the public with restrictions. **Networks/Consortia:** Member of Flint Area Health Science Library Network (FAHSLN). **Remarks:** Maintained by Lapeer County Library System. **Formerly:** Oakdale Regional Center for Developmental Disabilities.

★12194★
Oakite Products Inc. - Technical Library (Sci-Engr)
50 Valley Rd.
Berkeley Heights, NJ 07922
Phone: (908)464-6900
Staff: 1. **Subjects:** Chemistry. **Holdings:** 1000 books; 1250 bound periodical volumes; 90 reports. **Subscriptions:** 80 journals and other serials. **Services:** Interlibrary loan; library open to the public with approval of management.

★12195★
Oakland City Planning Department - Library (Plan)
1330 Broadway, No. 310
Oakland, CA 94612
Phone: (510)273-3941
Donna Liu, Libn.
Founded: 1952. **Subjects:** Urban and regional planning. **Holdings:** 1600 books. **Subscriptions:** 7 journals and other serials. **Services:** Library open to the public by appointment. **Remarks:** FAX: (510)287-6538.

★12196★
Oakland Community College - Highland Lakes Campus - Learning Resource Center - Special Collections (Med)
7350 Cooley Lake Rd.
Union Lake, MI 48387
Phone: (313)360-3080
Laura Kolehmainen, Libn.
Founded: 1965. **Staff:** Prof 2; Other 2. **Special Collections:** Allied health collection (nursing, dental; 3000 titles); aviation collection (200 titles). **Services:** Interlibrary loan; copying; library open to the public. **Automated Operations:** Computerized public access catalog. **Computerized Information Services:** BRS Information Technologies, DIALOG Information Services, WILSONLINE. **Special Indexes:** Index to Nursing Literature. **Remarks:** FAX: (313)360-3202.

★12197★
Oakland County Library - Adams-Pratt Law Library Division (Law)
1200 N. Telegraph Rd.
Pontiac, MI 48341-1043
Phone: (313)858-0012
Richard L. Beer, Dir.
Founded: 1925. **Staff:** Prof 5. **Subjects:** U.S. law, criminal justice, legal medicine. **Special Collections:** Michigan Supreme Court Records and Briefs, 1927-1929 and 1933 to present; House and Senate Bills of Michigan legislature, 1973 to present. **Holdings:** 49,500 books; Michigan Attorney General Reports, 1838 to present; Michigan House and Senate Journals, 1929 to present. **Subscriptions:** 1077 journals and other serials; 10 newspapers. **Services:** Interlibrary loan; copying; library open to the public for reference use only. **Automated Operations:** Computerized cataloging. **Computerized Information Services:** WESTLAW, OCLC, LEXIS, DIALOG Information Services, BRS Information Technologies, Hannah Information Systems, WILSONLINE, VU/TEXT Information Services. **Networks/Consortia:** Member of Michigan Library Consortium (MLC). **Remarks:** FAX: (313)858-2927. **Staff:** Charlotte Liner, Libn.

★12198★
Oakland County Library for the Blind & Physically Handicapped (Aud-Vis)
32737 W. 12 Mile Rd.
Farmington Hills, MI 48334
Phone: (313)553-0300
Carole Hund, Hd.Libn.
Founded: 1974. **Staff:** Prof 1; Other 3. **Subjects:** General collection of braille, large print, and recorded books. **Holdings:** Figures not available. **Services:** Interlibrary loan; library open to the public with restrictions. **Remarks:** FAX: (313)553-4037.

★12199★
Oakland County Pioneer and Historical Society - Library & Archives (Hist)
405 Oakland Ave.
Pontiac, MI 48342
Phone: (313)338-6732
Charles Martinez, Oper.Mgr.
Founded: 1874. **Staff:** 3. **Subjects:** Local, state, family histories; early Oakland County medical history; genealogy; archeology; architecture. **Special Collections:** Howlett Collection of local history on specific families (20 document boxes; 7000 items); Avery Collection of marriages, births, deaths of Oakland County families (7000 cards). **Holdings:** 2500 books; 1500 bound periodical volumes; 20 volumes of carbons of historical material; 5 VF drawers of photographs; oral histories; clippings; manuscripts; diaries; scrapbooks; maps; newspapers; slides. **Subscriptions:** 26 newspapers. **Services:** Copying; library open to the public for reference use only by appointment. **Publications:** Oakland Gazette, 4/year - mailed to members, available free at library. **Staff:** Lillian Paull, Libn.

★12200★
Oakland County Reference Library (Plan)
1200 N. Telegraph Rd.
Pontiac, MI 48341
Phone: (313)858-0738
Phyllis Jose, Dir.
Founded: 1972. **Staff:** Prof 1; Other 3. **Subjects:** Planning, solid waste management, transportation, behavioral sciences, census, architecture, municipal government. **Special Collections:** National Research Council publications; Urban Land Institute publications; American Planning Association publications; Southeastern Michigan Council of Government publications; local documents. **Holdings:** 14,200 books. **Subscriptions:** 320 journals and other serials. **Services:** Interlibrary loan; copying; library open to the public. **Automated Operations:** Computerized circulation. **Networks/Consortia:** Member of Wayne Oakland Library Federation (WOLF), Michigan Library Consortium (MLC). **Publications:** New book list, bibliographies. **Special Catalogs:** Oakland County Union List of Serials, annual. **Remarks:** FAX: (313)858-1080.

★12201★
Oakland General Hospital - Medical Library (Med)
27351 Dequindre
Madison Heights, MI 48071
Phone: (313)967-7575
Geraldine A. Bard, Libn.
Founded: 1965. **Staff:** Prof 1; Other 1. **Subjects:** Medicine. **Holdings:** 4000 books; 5500 bound periodical volumes. **Subscriptions:** 300 journals and other serials. **Services:** Interlibrary loan; library not open to the public. **Computerized Information Services:** MEDLINE; CDPlus (CD-ROM).

★12202★
Oakland Public Library - American Indian Library Project (Area-Ethnic)
Dimond Branch Library
3565 Fruitvale Ave.
Oakland, CA 94602
Phone: (510)530-3881
Founded: 1979. **Staff:** Prof 1; Other 1. **Subjects:** Native Americans - literature, culture, history. **Holdings:** 1500 books. **Subscriptions:** 20 journals and other serials. **Services:** Interlibrary loan; library open to the public. **Automated Operations:** Computerized public access catalog (DYNIX) and circulation. **Networks/Consortia:** Member of Bay Area Library and Information System (BALIS). **Remarks:** FAX: (510)530-1623.

★12203★
Oakland Public Library - Art, Music, Recreation (Art, Mus, Rec)
125 14th St.
Oakland, CA 94612
Phone: (510)273-3178
Jean Blinn, Sr.Libn.
Staff: Prof 3; Other 2. **Subjects:** History of art, architecture, painting, sculpture, decorative and graphic arts, furniture, interior decoration, photography, costume, music, sports and recreation, theater, cinema, dance. **Holdings:** 20,923 books; 2159 bound periodical volumes; 10,000 scores; 30,000 choral music copies; 9000 phonograph records, cassettes, and compact discs. **Services:** Interlibrary loan; copying; open to the public. **Networks/Consortia:** Member of Bay Area Library and Information System (BALIS). **Special Indexes:** Indexes of local events and personalities in music, art, and architecture (on cards). **Staff:** Clinton Arndt, Libn.; David Segall, Libn.

★ 12204 ★
Oakland Public Library - Asian Branch Library (Area-Ethnic)
449 9th St.   Phone: (510)273-3400
Oakland, CA 94607   Suzanne Lo, Br.Libn.
Founded: 1975. **Staff:** Prof 3. **Subjects:** Asian-American experience; East and Southeast Asian studies in English; adult and juvenile literature in Asian languages - Chinese, Tagalog, Japanese, Korean, Vietnamese, Thai, Cambodian. **Holdings:** 35,000 books; 8 VF drawers of clippings; 150 historical pictures; 2000 Asian language phonograph records and cassettes; 125 16mm films; 60 sets of filmstrips. **Subscriptions:** 100 journals and other serials; 23 newspapers. **Services:** Interlibrary loan; bilingual staff in all five Asian languages; library tours by bilingual staff; I & R services to Asian Community in East Bay area; library open to the public. **Networks/Consortia:** Member of Bay Area Library and Information System (BALIS). **Remarks:** FAX: (510)273-3400. **Staff:** Vera Yip, Ref.Libn.

★ 12205 ★
Oakland Public Library - Cityline Information Service (Soc Sci)
Oakland City Hall
1 City Hall Plaza   Phone: (510)444-2489
Oakland, CA 94612   Mary R. Weinstein, Libn.
Founded: 1977. **Staff:** Prof 1; Other 20. **Subjects:** Local services, community organizations. **Services:** Telephone inquiries answered. **Automated Operations:** Computerized cataloging. **Networks/Consortia:** Member of Bay Area Library and Information System (BALIS). **Special Catalogs:** Cityline Resource File. **Remarks:** Library located at 475 14th St. Lobby, Oakland, CA 94612.

★ 12206 ★
Oakland Public Library - History/Literature Division (Hist, Hum)
125 14th St.   Phone: (510)273-3136
Oakland, CA 94612   Lorrita Ford, Sr.Libn.
Staff: Prof 4; Other 3. **Subjects:** History, travel, biography, English and foreign languages and literature, genealogy, maps. **Special Collections:** Jack London collection (autographed first editions; signed letters; photographs, letters from literary friends; artifacts); logbooks of the cutter BEAR; Ina Coolbrith materials; U.S. Geological Survey Topographical Maps; Schomberg Collection of Black Literature and History (in microform); Negroes of New York, 1939 (Writers Program; in microform); Library of American Civilization (in microform); Sutro Library Family History and Local History Subject Catalogs (in microform); Index to Biographies in State and Local Histories in the Library of Congress (in microform). **Holdings:** 100,663 books; genealogy microfilms. **Subscriptions:** 114 journals and other serials. **Services:** Interlibrary loan; copying; division open to the public. **Networks/Consortia:** Member of Bay Area Library and Information System (BALIS). **Publications:** New Releases. **Special Indexes:** Indexes for Drama, Short Story, Poetry, Literary Criticism (on cards); local newspapers, 1978 to present; Local History. **Staff:** Christine Saed, Libn.; William Sturm, Libn.

★ 12207 ★
Oakland Public Library - Latin American Library (Area-Ethnic)
1900 Fruitvale Ave., Suite 1-A   Phone: (510)532-7882
Oakland, CA 94601   Elissa Miller, Libn.
Founded: 1966. **Staff:** Prof 3; Other 6. **Subjects:** Spanish-speaking culture and history, Hispanic literature, Chicano history and culture. **Special Collections:** La Raza/Chicano Reference Collection; juvenile and adult materials in Spanish and English (books; magazines; records; cassettes; newspapers). **Holdings:** 22,000 books; 115 study print sets; 200 slide sets; 190 tapes; 4 VF drawers of Chicano serials; 2 VF drawers of Latin American folklore and customs information. **Subscriptions:** 70 journals and other serials; 10 newspapers. **Services:** Interlibrary loan; library open to the public. **Automated Operations:** Computerized public access catalog. **Networks/Consortia:** Member of Bay Area Library and Information System (BALIS). **Remarks:** FAX: (510)532-4323. **Also Known As:** LAL. **Staff:** Saadia Sanchez, Co-Ch.Libn.

★ 12208 ★
Oakland Public Library - Science/Business/Sociology Division (Sci-Engr, Soc Sci, Bus-Fin)
125 14th St.   Phone: (510)273-3138
Oakland, CA 94612   Marilyn Rowan, Sr.Libn.
Staff: Prof 6; Other 4. **Subjects:** Business, technology, natural sciences, useful arts, sociology, government, psychology, law, religion. **Special Collections:** Pacific Rim Trade Collection; "Business" Collection; annual

reports (hardcopy); college catalogs (microfiche); Dun & Bradstreet Market Identifiers (microfiche); Oakland and Alameda County municipal documents; federal documents (5000). **Holdings:** 65,000 books; 2000 science pamphlets; 384,648 local, state, and federal government documents. **Subscriptions:** 625 journals and other serials. **Services:** Interlibrary loan; copying; division open to the public. **Automated Operations:** Computerized cataloging. **Computerized Information Services:** DIALOG Information Services, University of California On-Line Union Catalog (MELVYL), InfoTrac; BAIRS, CITYLINK (internal databases). Performs searches on fee basis. **Networks/Consortia:** Member of Bay Area Library and Information System (BALIS). **Special Catalogs:** Government documents catalog (online). **Special Indexes:** City and County municipal documents shelf list (card). **Staff:** Patricia Coffey, Docs.Libn.; Joseph Ouyang, Libn.; Barbara Bibel, Libn.; Douglas Smith, Libn.

★ 12209 ★
Oakland Schools - Library Services (Educ)
2100 Pontiac Lake Rd.   Phone: (313)858-1969
Waterford, MI 48328-2735   Jennie B. Cross, Dir., Lib.Serv.
Founded: 1955. **Staff:** Prof 3; Other 3. **Subjects:** Education. **Holdings:** 35,000 books; complete ERIC microfiche collection; state documents depository. **Subscriptions:** 550 journals and other serials. **Services:** Interlibrary loan; copying; services open to the public for reference use only. **Computerized Information Services:** DIALOG Information Services. **Remarks:** FAX: (313)858-1881. **Staff:** Judith Brooks, Libn.; Robert Kramp, Libn.; Rosemary Fenlon, Per.; Becky Mitton, Proc.; Judy Hauser, ILL.

★ 12210 ★
Oakland Tribune - Library (Publ)
Box 24424   Phone: (510)645-2743
Oakland, CA 94623   Yae Shinomiya, Libn.
Founded: 1912. **Staff:** Prof 2; Other 1.25. **Subjects:** Newspaper reference topics. **Special Collections:** Local history. **Holdings:** 96 cabinets of newspaper clippings; 117 cabinets of photographs. **Subscriptions:** 30 journals and other serials; 4 newspapers. **Services:** Library not open to the public. **Computerized Information Services:** NEXIS, DataTimes. **Networks/Consortia:** Member of Bay Area Library and Information Network. **Remarks:** FAX: (510)645-2771. **Staff:** Steven LaVoie, Asst.Libn.

★ 12211 ★
Oakland University - Library - Special Collections and Archives (Hist)
Kresge Library Building, Rm 100   Phone: (313)370-2481
Rochester Hills, MI 48309-4401   Robert G. Gaylor, Cur. of Archv./Spec.Coll.
Founded: 1959. **Staff:** Prof 1. **Holdings:** James Collection (folklore); Hicks Collection (women in literature, 17th and 18th centuries); Springer Collection (Lincolniana); Underground Press Collection; university archives. **Services:** Interlibrary loan; copying; collections open to the public with restrictions. **Automated Operations:** Computerized cataloging and circulation. **Computerized Information Services:** DIALOG Information Services, BRS Information Technologies, Dow Jones News/Retrieval, PFDS Online, OCLC, CAB Abstracts. Performs searches on fee basis. **Networks/Consortia:** Member of Michigan Library Consortium (MLC), Wayne Oakland Library Federation (WOLF), CLASS. **Publications:** Library Guide Series; Instructional Guide Series, both irregular - for campus distribution and by request. **Remarks:** FAX: (313)370-2458.

★ 12212 ★
Oakland University - School of Education and Human Services - Educational Resources Laboratory (Educ)
216 O'Dowd Hall   Phone: (313)370-2485
Rochester Hills, MI 48309-4401   Jane Bingham, Faculty Dir.
Founded: 1957. **Staff:** Prof 2. **Subjects:** Education - general, pre-school-12th grade, multi-cultural, career; aerospace; children's literature. **Special Collections:** Children's Literature Collection; Children's Trade Book Examination Center Collection (7000 books); NASA Aerospace and Aviation Center (NASA videotapes). **Holdings:** 30,000 books; 160 bound periodical volumes; kits; filmstrips; videotapes; reference materials. **Subscriptions:** 100 journals and other serials. **Services:** Teacher Explorer Center (interactive video system); new children's books and NASA Aerospace and Aviation Center open to the public. **Remarks:** FAX: (313)370-2485, ext. 4426. **Formerly:** Its School of Human and Educational Services - Resource Center. **Staff:** Karen Conrad, ERL Coord.

★ 12213 ★
Oaklawn Psychiatric Center - Staff Library (Med)
2600 Oakland Ave.   Phone: (219)533-1234
Elkhart, IN 46507   Nancy P. Price, Libn.
Founded: 1968. **Staff:** Prof 1. **Subjects:** Psychiatry, mental health, psychology, social work, addictions, pastoral counseling. **Holdings:** 2156 books; 1400 unbound periodical volumes; 24 VF drawers; 687 cassettes. **Subscriptions:** 98 journals and other serials. **Services:** Interlibrary loan; copying; library open to the public with restrictions. **Computerized Information Services:** BRS Information Technologies. **Networks/Consortia:** Member of Area 2 Library Services Authority (ALSA 2). **Remarks:** FAX: (219)522-5783.

Oakwood Forensic Center
See: Lima State Hospital (9168)

★ 12214 ★
Oakwood Hospital - Health Science Library (Med)
18101 Oakwood Blvd.
Box 2500   Phone: (313)593-7685
Dearborn, MI 48123-2500   Sharon A. Phillips, Dir.
Staff: Prof 2; Other 3. **Subjects:** Medicine, allied health sciences. **Holdings:** 13,000 volumes; AV programs. **Subscriptions:** 615 journals and other serials; 8 newspapers. **Services:** Interlibrary loan; library not open to the public. **Computerized Information Services:** MEDLINE, DIALOG Information Services, OCLC, BRS Information Technologies. **Networks/Consortia:** Member of National Network of Libraries of Medicine - Greater Midwest Region. **Remarks:** FAX: (313)441-2155. **Staff:** Peggy Zorn, Libn.

★ 12215 ★
Ober, Kaler, Grimes & Shriver - Library (Law)
120 E. Baltimore St., Suite 1000   Phone: (301)685-1120
Baltimore, MD 21202   Ginger G. Hendershot, Libn.
Staff: Prof 1; Other 3. **Subjects:** Law - admiralty, hospital/health care, corporate, tax; litigation; estates and trusts. **Holdings:** 15,000 books. **Services:** Library not open to the public. **Computerized Information Services:** DIALOG Information Services, LEXIS, NEXIS, Dow Jones News/Retrieval, WESTLAW.

★ 12216 ★
Oberlin College - Clarence Ward Art Library (Art)
Allen Art Bldg.   Phone: (216)775-8635
Oberlin, OH 44074   Jeffrey Weidman, Art Libn.
Founded: 1917. **Staff:** 2. **Subjects:** Art, architecture, archeology. **Special Collections:** Artists' books; rare books including duplication of Thomas Jefferson's architectural library. **Holdings:** 57,000 books, exhibition catalogs, bound periodical volumes; 6500 uncataloged exhibition catalogs; 10,000 art sales catalogs. **Subscriptions:** 250 journals and other serials. **Services:** Interlibrary loan; copying; library open to the public for reference use only; open to cooperating Great Lakes Colleges Association (GLCA) and NOEMARL libraries with restrictions. **Automated Operations:** Computerized public access catalog, and circulation. **Computerized Information Services:** DIALOG Information Services, RLIN, WILSONLINE; CD-ROM (Art Index); BITNET, InterNet (electronic mail services). **Networks/Consortia:** Member of NEOMARL, OHIONET. **Remarks:** Electronic mail address(es): PWEIDMAN@OBERLIN (BITNET); PWEIDMAN@OBERLIN.EDU (INTERNET).

★ 12217 ★
Oberlin College - Class of 1904 Science Library (Sci-Engr, Biol Sci)
Kettering Hall   Phone: (216)775-8310
Oberlin, OH 44074   Alison Scott Ricker, Sci.Libn.
Founded: 1961. **Staff:** Prof 1; Other 2.75. **Subjects:** Biology, chemistry, earth sciences, medicine, technology. **Holdings:** 53,500 volumes; 100 loose-leaf binders of Thermodynamics Research Center Spectral and Thermodynamics Data; 1090 reels of microfilm. **Subscriptions:** 300 journals and other serials. **Services:** Interlibrary loan; copying; library open to the public. **Automated Operations:** Computerized public access catalog, cataloging, acquisitions, serials, and circulation. **Computerized Information Services:** DIALOG Information Services, STN International; CD-ROM (General Science Index); BITNET, InterNet (electronic mail services). Performs searches on fee basis. **Networks/Consortia:** Member of NEOMARL, OHIONET. **Remarks:** FAX: (216)775-8739. Electronic mail address(es): PASRICKER@OBERLIN (BITNET); PASRICKER@OCVAXA.CC.OBERLIN.EDU (InterNet).

★ 12218 ★
Oberlin College - Conservatory of Music Library (Mus)
Oberlin, OH 44074   Phone: (216)775-8280
                               Daniel Zager, Libn.
Staff: Prof 3; Other 7. **Subjects:** Music - chamber, keyboard, vocal, education, history, theory. **Special Collections:** Violin Society of America - Herbert K. Goodkind Collection; Oberlin Conservatory recital tape archives; Mr. and Mrs. C.W. Best Collection of Autographs; George W. Andrews Collection. **Holdings:** 105,600 books and scores; 4 VF drawers; 33,500 phonograph records; 4800 compact discs; 4100 microcards; 4200 magnetic tapes; 2700 reels of microfilm; 350 microfiche. **Subscriptions:** 433 journals and other serials. **Services:** Interlibrary loan; copying; library open to the public for reference use only; open to cooperating NEOMARL libraries with restrictions. **Automated Operations:** Computerized cataloging, acquisitions, circulation, and ILL. **Computerized Information Services:** OCLC; BITNET (electronic mail service). **Networks/Consortia:** Member of OHIONET, NEOMARL. **Special Catalogs:** Catalog of the Mr. and Mrs. C.W. Best Collection of Autographs; catalog of the George W. Andrews Collection. **Remarks:** FAX: (216)775-8739. Electronic mail address(es): PZAGER@OBERLIN; PRABSON@OBERLIN (BITNET). **Staff:** Carolyn Rabson, Libn., Pub.Serv.; David Knapp, Libn., Tech.Serv.

★ 12219 ★
Oberlin College - Library - Archives (Hist)
420 Mudd Center   Phone: (216)775-8014
Oberlin, OH 44074-1532   Roland M. Baumann, Coll.Archv.
Founded: 1966. **Staff:** Prof 2; Other 1. **Subjects:** Higher education, 19th century reform, temperance, women's history, black education, architecture, Ohio history. **Special Collections:** Missions, the antislavery movement, and temperance in Oberlin; papers of Oberlin College faculty and graduates; Congressman Charles Mosher papers; Congressman Don J. Pease papers; Oberlin municipal government records; photographs of Oberlin College and Oberlin. **Holdings:** 4400 linear feet of manuscripts and archival materials. **Subscriptions:** 6 journals and other serials. **Services:** Copying; archives open to the public. **Automated Operations:** Computerized public access catalog, cataloging, acquisitions, serials, and circulation. **Computerized Information Services:** DIALOG Information Services, BRS Information Technologies; BITNET (electronic mail service). Performs searches free of charge. Contact Person: Cynthia Comer, Assoc.Hd., Ref. **Networks/Consortia:** Member of NEOMARL, OHIONET. **Publications:** Library of Congress Rule Interpretation for AACR2; Guide to the Women's History Sources in the Oberlin College Archives (1990); Current Scholarship in Women's Studies (1987). **Special Catalogs:** Catalog of the Antislavery Collection. **Remarks:** FAX: (216)775-8739. Electronic mail address(es): PBAUMANN@OBERLIN (BITNET). **Staff:** Brian A. Williams, Asst.Archv.; Valerie S. Komor, Proj.Archv.

★ 12220 ★
Oberlin College - Library - East Asian Collection (Area-Ethnic)
Mudd Center   Phone: (216)775-8285
Oberlin, OH 44074-1532   Mr. Jiann I. Lin, East Asian Spec.
Founded: 1965. **Staff:** 1. **Subjects:** Chinese and Japanese studies - literature, language, history, art, religion, political economy. **Holdings:** 20,000 volumes. **Subscriptions:** 100 journals and other serials; 6 newspapers. **Services:** Interlibrary loan; library open to the public. **Computerized Information Services:** OCLC. **Networks/Consortia:** Member of NEOMARL. **Remarks:** FAX: (216)775-8739.

★ 12221 ★
Oberlin College - Library - Special Collections Department (Hum)
Oberlin, OH 44074-1532   Phone: (216)775-8285
                               Dina Schoonmaker, Spec.Coll.Cur.
Founded: 1833. **Staff:** Prof 1. **Special Collections:** Antislavery (2500 abolitionist books and pamphlets published prior to the Emancipation Proclamation); Oberliniana (materials written by and about Oberlin and Oberlinians); Spanish Drama (8000 Spanish-language plays, late 17th century to 1924); history of the book (fine printing and binding, including manuscripts, incunabula, and limited and private press editions); early imprints (American titles published prior to 1821; English and European titles published prior to 1801); women's concerns (pamphlets); American Communist Party pamphlets; travel and exploration; American dime novel collections; popular sheet music; War of 1812; Edwin Arlington Robinson (books); Jack Schaefer (books); VSA/Goodkind collection on string instruments (books, pamphlets, journals, ephemera). **Holdings:** 28,000 books; 2500 bound periodical volumes; 1000 manuscripts. **Subscriptions:** 8 journals and other serials. **Services:** Department open to the public on a

limited schedule. **Computerized Information Services:** Internal database; BITNET InterNet (electronic mail service). **Special Catalogs:** Catalog of Spanish Drama Collection; catalog of Anti-Slavery Collection. **Special Indexes:** Index to Historical Science Books. **Remarks:** FAX: (216)775-8739. Electronic mail address(es): PSCHOONMAKER@OBERLIN; PSCHOONMAKER@OCVAXA.CC.OBERLIN.EDU.

★ 12222 ★
Oberlin College - Physics Reading Room (Sci-Engr)
Wright Physics Hall   Phone: (216)775-8310
Oberlin, OH 44074   Alison Scott Ricker, Sci.Libn.
Founded: 1937. **Subjects:** Physics, astronomy. **Holdings:** 11,200 volumes. **Subscriptions:** 60 journals and other serials. **Services:** Interlibrary loan; room open to the public with restrictions. **Automated Operations:** Computerized public access catalog. **Computerized Information Services:** STN International, DIALOG Information Services (all available through Oberlin College - Science Library); BITNET, InterNet (electronic mail services). **Networks/Consortia:** Member of NEOMARL, OHIONET. **Remarks:** FAX: (216)775-8739. Electronic mail address(es): PASRICKER@OBERLIN   (BITNET); PASRICKER@OCVAXA.CC.OBERLIN.EDU (InterNet).

★ 12223 ★
Oberoesterreichisches Landesarchiv (Hist)
Anzengruberstr. 19
A-4020 Linz, Austria   Phone: 732 55523
Founded: 1896. **Staff:** Prof 2. **Subjects:** History - Upper Austria, Austria, Germany. **Holdings:** 53,000 books; 7300 bound periodical volumes. **Subscriptions:** 300 journals and other serials; 5 newspapers. **Services:** Interlibrary loan; copying; archives open to the public. **Remarks:** Alternate telephone number(s): 732 55524. FAX: 732 55523, ext. 4619. **Staff:** Dr. Siegfried Haider; Margarita Pertlwieser; Silvia Penninger.

★ 12224 ★
Oberoesterreichisches Landesmuseum - Bibliothek (Hist)
Museumstrasse 14
A-4020 Linz, Austria   Phone: 732 774482
      Margarete Ploch
Founded: 1836. **Staff:** 3.5. **Subjects:** Art, archeology, prehistory, botany, zoology, entomology, geology, numismatics, folklore. **Holdings:** 110,000 books; bound periodical volumes; 293 manuscripts. **Subscriptions:** 898 journals and other serials; 6 newspapers. **Services:** Interlibrary loan; copying; library open to the public. **Remarks:** FAX: 732 774482, ext. 66. **Staff:** Franz Walzer; Karin Wurzinger; Waltraud Faissner.

★ 12225 ★
Louise Obici Memorial Hospital - Library (Med)
1900 N. Main   Phone: (804)934-4865
Suffolk, VA 23434   Janet B. Daum, Libn.
Founded: 1951. **Staff:** Prof 1. **Subjects:** Medicine, allied health. **Special Collections:** Nursing. **Holdings:** 1000 books. **Subscriptions:** 190 journals and other serials. **Services:** Interlibrary loan; library open to the public for reference use only. **Computerized Information Services:** MEDLARS, GRATEFUL MED. **Remarks:** FAX: (804)934-4896.

★ 12226 ★
Obispo Colombres Agro-Industrial Experiment Station - Library (Agri)
Casilla de Correo 71
Obispo Colombres   Phone: 16561
4000 San Miguel de Tucuman, Argentina   Rolando Juarez, Libn.
Subjects: Sugarcane, citrus fruits, soybeans, cereals, dry beans, potatoes, beef and dairy production, bioenergy, gasohol. **Holdings:** 58,000 volumes. **Remarks:** Maintained by Argentina - Ministry of the Economy. **Also Known As:** Estacion Experimental Agro-Industrial Obispo Colombres.

★ 12227 ★
Oblate Fathers - Bibliotheque Deschatelets (Rel-Phil)
175 Main St.   Phone: (613)237-0580
Ottawa, ON, Canada K1S 1C3   Leo Laberge, Dir.
Founded: 1885. **Staff:** Prof 1; Other 1. **Subjects:** Theology, spirituality, philosophy, church history, Canadiana, history, literature. **Holdings:** 65,000 books; 15,000 bound periodical volumes. **Subscriptions:** 100 journals and other serials. **Services:** Library open to the public with restrictions. **Staff:** Gerard Juneau, Libn.

Oblate Fathers - Universite St-Paul
See: **Universite St-Paul** (18128)

★ 12228 ★
Oblate School of Theology - Library (Rel-Phil)
285 Oblate Dr.   Phone: (512)341-1366
San Antonio, TX 78216-6693   Clifford G. Dawdy, Dir.
Founded: 1903. **Staff:** Prof 1; Other 1. **Subjects:** Theology. **Special Collections:** Oblate faculty publications. **Holdings:** 28,000 books; 11,000 bound periodical volumes; 520 pamphlets; 252 AV programs. **Subscriptions:** 282 journals and other serials; 10 newspapers. **Services:** Interlibrary loan; copying; library open to the public for reference use only. **Automated Operations:** Computerized cataloging. **Networks/Consortia:** Member of Council of Research & Academic Libraries (CORAL), AMIGOS Bibliographic Council, Inc. **Publications:** Library Report, monthly - for internal distribution only. **Remarks:** FAX: (512)341-4519.

Oblates of Mary Immaculate Archives
See: **Oblates Theology Library** (12229)

★ 12229 ★
Oblates Theology Library (Rel-Phil)
391 Michigan Ave., N.E.   Phone: (202)529-5244
Washington, DC 20017   Ward E. Gongoll, Hd.Libn.
Staff: Prof 4. **Subjects:** Theology, Sacred Scripture. **Special Collections:** Oblates of Mary Immaculate Archives; Oblates of St. Francis De Sales Collection; Special Ministries. **Holdings:** 58,500 volumes. **Subscriptions:** 105 journals and other serials; 9 newspapers. **Services:** Interlibrary loan; copying; library open to the public with restrictions. **Networks/Consortia:** Member of Washington Theological Consortium. **Remarks:** Figures include the holdings of the De Sales Hall School of Theology - Library. **Staff:** Rosabelle Kelp; Alei Bautista.

★ 12230 ★
O'Brien & Gere Engineers, Inc. - Resource Center (Sci-Engr)
5000 Brittonfield Pkwy.
P.O. Box 4873   Phone: (315)437-6100
Syracuse, NY 13221   Susan Thompson, Rsrc. & Rec.Adm.
Staff: 1. **Holdings:** 25,000 books; 75 bound periodical volumes; 2000 reports. **Subscriptions:** 200 journals and other serials. **Services:** Interlibrary loan; copying. **Computerized Information Services:** DIALOG Information Services. **Remarks:** FAX: (315)463-7554. **Staff:** Cheryl Bellucci

Kevin F. O'Brien Health Sciences Library
See: **Marquette General Hospital, Inc.** (9708)

Observatoire Royal de Belgique
See: **Royal Observatory of Belgium** (14127)

The Observatories of the Carnegie Institution of Washington
See: **Carnegie Institution of Washington - Observatories - Library** (3074)

Observatorio Astronomico di Trieste - Biblioteca
See: **Trieste Astronomical Observatory** (16498)

Observatorio Interamericano de Cerro Tololo
See: **Cerro Tololo Inter-American Observatory** (3396)

O'Callahan Science Library
See: **College of the Holy Cross - O'Callahan Science Library** (3895)

Oliver Ocasek Regional Medical Information Center
See: **Northeastern Ohio Universities College of Medicine** (11984)

★ 12231 ★
Occidental Chemical Corporation - Technical Information Center (Sci-Engr)
2801 Long Rd.   Phone: (716)773-8531
Grand Island, NY 14072   Jane Pattison, Mgr.
Founded: 1916. **Staff:** Prof 4; Other 2. **Subjects:** Chemistry - organic, inorganic, polymer, physical; analytical business. **Holdings:** 20,000 books; 20,000 bound periodical volumes; 90 VF drawers of technical reports; 10 cabinets of microforms. **Subscriptions:** 500 journals and other serials. **Services:** Center open to the public on request. **Automated Operations:** Integrated library system (CUADRA STAR). **Computerized Information Services:** DIALOG Information Services, ORBIT Search Service, NLM, STN International, VU/TEXT Information Services, Data-Star, WILSONLINE, Questel, BRS Information Technologies, Dow Jones News/Retrieval, Info Globe, Human Resource Information Network (HRIN), Mead Data Central. **Networks/Consortia:** Member of Western New York Library Resources Council (WNYLRC). **Remarks:** FAX: (716)773-8487. **Staff:** Ben Wagner, Assoc.Info.Sci.; Michael Burke, Supv.; Linda Wieland, Res.Info.Anl.; Maryanne Delpriore, Res.Info.Anl.

★ 12232 ★
Occidental College - Mary Norton Clapp Library (Hum)
1600 Campus Rd.   Phone: (213)259-2852
Los Angeles, CA 90041   Michael C. Sutherland, Spec.Coll.Libn.
Staff: Prof 1. **Subjects:** Western Americana, mystery and detective fiction, romantic literature, railroad history, fine printing, aviation, Lincoln and the Civil War. **Special Collections:** William Jennings Bryan Collection; William Henry Collection; Upton Sinclair Collection; Ward Ritchie Press Collection; Robinson Jeffers Collection; Doheny Foundation papers. **Holdings:** 100,000 volumes. **Services:** Copying; library open to the public. **Automated Operations:** Computerized cataloging. **Computerized Information Services:** OCLC. **Special Indexes:** Index to William Henry Letters; Inventory to Guymon Mystery and Detective Fiction Collection. **Remarks:** FAX: (213)341-4991.

★ 12233 ★
Occidental International Exploration & Production Company - Library (Energy)
1200 Discovery Way
P.O. Box 12021   Phone: (805)321-6565
Bakersfield, CA 93389-2021   Fred Stair, Libn.
Founded: 1968. **Staff:** Prof 1; Other 2. **Subjects:** Geology, petroleum, engineering, energy resources, environment, law. **Holdings:** 6000 volumes; 10,000 maps. **Subscriptions:** 500 journals and other serials. **Services:** Interlibrary loan; library not open to the public. **Automated Operations:** Computerized cataloging, serials, and circulation. **Computerized Information Services:** DIALOG Information Services, OCLC, PFDS Online, Reuter TEXTLINE, WILSONLINE, STN International, DRI, Global Scan. **Remarks:** FAX: (805)322-7457. Contains a portion of the holdings of the former OXY USA Inc. - Exploration & Production Library. **Staff:** Michele Hoffman; Kim Connelly.

★ 12234 ★
Occidental Society of Metempiric Analysis - Library and Research Center (Rel-Phil)
P.O. Box 203
Simla, CO 80835   Robert J. Everhart, Exec.Chm.
Founded: 1977. **Subjects:** Metempirical, occult, and UFO topics. **Special Collections:** Folklore of Americas. **Holdings:** 1500 volumes; biographical archives; research and data tapes. **Services:** Interlibrary loan; copying; answers mail enquiries (must include a No. 10 self-addressed stamped envelope). **Staff:** James Martin Stone.

★ 12235 ★
Ocean Alliance - Library (Biol Sci)
Fort Mason, Bldg. E
San Francisco, CA 94123   Phone: (415)433-3163
                                            Anthony J. Pettinato, Hd.Libn.
Staff: Prof 1. **Subjects:** Whales and whaling - commercial and aboriginal; International Whaling Commission; marine sanctuaries; whale habitat; outer-continental shelf (OCS) lease sales. **Special Collections:** International Whaling Commission documents and reports. **Holdings:** 550 books; 100 bound periodical volumes; 16 VF drawers. **Services:** Copying; library open to the public. **Publications:** Newsletters; action alerts; special publications on whaling; ethics; research.

★ 12236 ★
Ocean City Historical Museum - Library (Hist)
1735 Simpson
P.O. Box 1284   Phone: (609)399-1801
Ocean City, NJ 08226   Alberta E. Lamphear, Libn.
Subjects: History of Ocean City. **Holdings:** 200 books; photographs; deeds; documents; periodicals. **Services:** Library open to the public for reference use only.

★ 12237 ★
Ocean and Coastal Law Center - Library (Biol Sci)
School of Law
University of Oregon   Phone: (503)346-1567
Eugene, OR 97403-1221   Andrea G. Coffman, Libn.
Founded: 1968. **Staff:** Prof 1; Other 1. **Subjects:** International law of the sea, coastal zone management, ocean management and policy, fisheries, aquaculture, offshore drilling and mining, marine pollution. **Holdings:** 4900 books; 325 bound periodical volumes; 214 reprints; 200 maps; 100 fishery management plans; 7 VF drawers of documents. **Subscriptions:** 141 journals and other serials. **Services:** Interlibrary loan; copying (limited); library open to the public. **Computerized Information Services:** SCIENCEnet (electronic mail service). **Publications:** Recent Acquisitions List, monthly; Periodical Holdings List, annual; Recent Articles in Marine Legal Affairs, quarterly - all available on request. **Remarks:** FAX: (503)346-3985. Electronic mail address(es): J.Jacobson (SCIENCEnet).

★ 12238 ★
Ocean County Historical Society - Richard Lee Strickler Center (Hist)
26 Hadley Ave.   Phone: (908)341-1880
Toms River, NJ 08753   Richard L. Strickler, Libn.
Staff: 1. **Subjects:** Ocean County history and genealogy, New Jersey history, United States antiques. **Special Collections:** Family histories; Ocean County cemeteries. **Holdings:** 2000 books; 100 bound periodical volumes; 100 documents; 5 AV programs; 100 manuscripts; 100 nonbook items. **Services:** Copying; center open on a fee basis, by appointment and for reference use only. **Networks/Consortia:** Member of Central Jersey Regional Library Cooperative.

★ 12239 ★
Ocean County Law Library (Law)
Justice Complex
120 Hooper Ave.   Phone: (908)506-5026
Toms River, NJ 08753   Kathleen Galya, Sr.Libn.
Founded: 1930. **Staff:** Prof 1; Other 3. **Subjects:** Law. **Special Collections:** Family Law. **Holdings:** 15,000 books. **Subscriptions:** 15 journals and other serials. **Services:** Copying; library open to the public. **Remarks:** FAX: (908)341-6698. Maintained by Ocean County Library.

★ 12240 ★
Oceanic Institute - Working Library (Biol Sci)
Makapuu Point
Box 25280   Phone: (808)259-7951
Honolulu, HI 96825   Betty Pickart, Libn.
Founded: 1964. **Staff:** Prof 1; Other 1. **Subjects:** Aquaculture, oceanography, general science, marine biology. **Holdings:** Figures not available. **Subscriptions:** 15 journals and other serials. **Services:** Library not open to the public. **Remarks:** FAX: (808)259-5971.

★ 12241 ★
Oceanroutes, Inc. - Library (Sci-Engr)
680 W. Maude Ave., Suite 3   Phone: (408)245-3600
Sunnyvale, CA 94086   Lisa Grandstaff
Staff: Prof 1. **Subjects:** Weather, shipping, cargo. **Special Collections:** Historical weather data. **Holdings:** 2500 volumes; 500 technical reports. **Subscriptions:** 78 journals and other serials. **Services:** Interlibrary loan; copying. **Automated Operations:** Computerized cataloging. **Computerized Information Services:** DIALOG Information Services. **Special Catalogs:** Technical paper file.

Oceans Intitute of Canada
See: **Dalhousie University - Oceans Institute of Canada** (4533)

★ 12242 ★
Alton Ochsner Medical Foundation - Medical Library (Med)
1516 Jefferson Hwy.   Phone: (504)838-3760
New Orleans, LA 70121   Carol M. Liardon, Dir./Med.Libn.
Founded: 1942. **Staff:** Prof 2; Other 4. **Subjects:** Medicine, nursing, allied health sciences, research. **Special Collections:** Rare books. **Holdings:** 3000 books; 22,500 bound periodical volumes. **Subscriptions:** 565 journals and other serials. **Services:** Interlibrary loan; library not open to the public. **Computerized Information Services:** BRS Information Technologies, DIALOG Information Services, MEDLARS. **Networks/Consortia:** Member of National Network of Libraries of Medicine - South Central Region, South Central Academic Medical Libraries Consortium (SCAMEL).

★ 12243 ★
OCLC, Inc. - OCLC Library (Info Sci)
Box 7777   Phone: (614)764-6000
Dublin, OH 43017   Ann T. Dodson, Mgr.
Founded: 1977. **Staff:** Prof 7; Other 5. **Subjects:** Library and information science, computer science and engineering, telecommunications, management and business. **Special Collections:** Library Network Newsletters; state library newsletters. **Holdings:** 12,695 books; 570 bound periodical volumes; 1872 microfiche; 459 cassettes; 1424 slides; 24,568 serial microfiche; 66 maps; 3038 microcomputer software packages; 19,996 OCLC and system manuals; 650 vertical file folders. **Subscriptions:** 1178 journals and other serials. **Services:** Interlibrary loan; copying; SDI; current awareness; reference and research services; library open to the public with restrictions. **Automated Operations:** Computerized public access catalog, cataloging, acquisitions, serials, circulation, and ILL. **Computerized Information Services:** OCLC, DIALOG Information Services, BRS Information Technologies, Dun & Bradstreet Business Credit Services, CompuServe Information Service, Dow Jones News/Retrieval, Library Control System (LCS), LS/2000; CD-ROM. Performs searches on fee basis. **Networks/Consortia:** Member of Columbus Area Libraries Information Council of Ohio (CALICO). **Publications:** OCC Libline; accessions lists; bibliographies; list of periodicals (online). **Remarks:** FAX: (614)764-6096. **Also Known As:** Online Computer Library Center, Inc. **Staff:** Lawrence J. Olszewski, Mgr., Pub.Serv.Sect.; Elizabeth A. St. Pierre, Ref.Serv.Spec.; Linda Newman, Mgr., Tech.Serv.Sect.; Margaret Smith, Acq.Libn.; Teel C. Slike, Archv./Rec.Mgt.Spec.; Robert Baker, Doc.Libn.

O'Connor & Associates
See: **SBC/OC Services L.P.** (14890)

Catherine B. O'Connor Library
See: **Boston College** (1979)

★ 12244 ★
O'Connor, Cavanagh, Anderson, Westover, Killingsworth & Beshears, P.A. - Law Library (Law)
1 E. Camelback Rd., Suite 900   Phone: (602)263-2488
Phoenix, AZ 85012-1656   Kathy Shimpock-Vieweg, Dir., Lib.Serv.
Staff: Prof 1.5; Other 4. **Subjects:** Law - medical, insurance, corporate, tax, labor, real estate, bond, employment practice, workers compensation. **Holdings:** 25,000 books. **Subscriptions:** 500 journals and other serials; 20 newspapers. **Services:** Interlibrary loan; copying; library open to attorneys and clients only. **Automated Operations:** Computerized cataloging and acquisitions. **Computerized Information Services:** LEXIS, NEXIS, WESTLAW, DIALOG Information Services, Dow Jones News/Retrieval, DataTimes, LEGI-SLATE, VU/TEXT Information Services, OCLC; electronic mail. **Networks/Consortia:** Member of AMIGOS Bibliographic Council, Inc. **Publications:** Liblink. **Remarks:** FAX: (602)263-2900.

★ 12245 ★
O'Connor Hospital - Library Media Center (Med)
2105 Forest Ave.   Phone: (408)947-2950
San Jose, CA 95128   Linda Hayes, Med.Libn.
Founded: 1985. **Staff:** Prof 1. **Subjects:** Medicine, nursing, administration. **Holdings:** 800 books; 234 bound periodical volumes; 200 audio cassettes; 40 filmstrips; 15 films; 77 slide cassettes; 260 video cassettes. **Subscriptions:** 140 journals and other serials. **Services:** Interlibrary loan; center not open to the public. **Computerized Information Services:** DIALOG Information Services, MEDLARS; OnTyme Electronic Message Network Service (electronic mail service). **Special Catalogs:** Audiovisual catalog (book). **Remarks:** FAX: (408)947-2819. Electronic mail address(es): CLASS.OCON (OnTyme Electronic Message Network Service).

★ 12246 ★
Lindsay A. & Olive B. O'Connor Hospital - Library (Med)
Andes Road, Rte. 28
Box 205A   Phone: (607)746-2371
Delhi, NY 13753   Barbara Green, Lib.Serv.
Founded: 1968. **Subjects:** Medicine, nursing. **Holdings:** 200 books. **Subscriptions:** 30 journals and other serials. **Services:** Copying; library open to the public on request. **Networks/Consortia:** Member of South Central Research Library Council (SCRLC).

★ 12247 ★
Octameron Associates, Inc. - Research Library (Educ)
1900 Mount Vernon Ave.   Phone: (703)836-5480
Alexandria, VA 22301   Karen Stokstad, Libn.
Founded: 1975. **Staff:** Prof 1; Other 1. **Subjects:** College admissions and financial aid, career information, higher education. **Holdings:** 2100 books; 500 bound periodical volumes; 20 VF drawers of scholarship information; 20 linear feet of pamphlets. **Subscriptions:** 25 journals and other serials. **Services:** Library not open to the public. **Computerized Information Services:** College financial aid file (internal database). **Publications:** Annual directories of scholarship information - for sale; internal reports. **Special Indexes:** Financial aid data.

Hamilton Odell Library
See: **New York State Supreme Court - 3rd Judicial District** (11689)

★ 12248 ★
(Odessa) American - Editorial Library (Publ)
222 E. 4th
Box 2952   Phone: (915)337-4661
Odessa, TX 79760   Ms. Ronnie Raynosa
Founded: 1940. **Staff:** 1. **Holdings:** Newspaper clippings; editorial files. **Subscriptions:** 15 journals and other serials; 35 newspapers. **Services:** Library not open to the public. **Remarks:** FAX: (915)334-8641. Toll-free telephone number(s): (800)530-4554. Published by Freedom Newspapers chain.

Mayo Hayes O'Donnell Library
See: **Monterey History & Art Association, Ltd.** (10669)

O'Donoghue Medical Library
See: **St. Anthony Hospital** (14235)

★ 12249 ★
Odyssey-Eastern Puma Research Network Library (Biol Sci)
Box 3562   Phone: (301)254-2517
Baltimore, MD 21214   Linda A. Sec.
Founded: 1983. **Staff:** Prof 2. **Subjects:** Eastern cougar, mountain lion, panther, and puma - research, study, education, field investigation, nature, characteristics, statistics, habits, different species, publications, maps. **Special Collections:** Eastern Puma Network Newsletter (complete). **Holdings:** 150 books; 175 bound periodical volumes; 5000 other cataloged items. **Subscriptions:** 20 journals and other serials; 10 newspapers. **Services:** Copying; library open on weekends only. **Publications:** Eastern Puma Network News, 3/year - by subscription; statistical yearly reviews: characteristics of different pumas/dogs, maps of alleged felis concolor sightings, study/research information. **Remarks:** FAX: (301)837-2943. Alternate telephone number(s): 396-3035.

★ 12250 ★
Oelwein Register - Library (Publ)
25 1st St., S.E.
Oelwein, IA 50662   Phone: (319)283-2144
Subjects: Newspaper reference topics. **Holdings:** Microfilm of Oelwein Register.

Oesper Chemistry-Biology Library
See: **University of Cincinnati** (18479)

Oesterle Library
See: **North Central College** (11912)

Oesterreichische Nationalbibliothek
See: **Austria - Oesterreichische Nationalbibliothek - Special Collections** (1354)

Oesterreichisches Ost- und Sudosteuropa-Institut
See: **Austrian Institute of East and Southeast European Studies** (1359)

Office of the Auditor General
See: **Canada - Office of the Auditor General** (2831)

Office of Economic Information and Forecasting
See: **BIPE Conseil - Library** (1848)

Office National des Transports du Canada
See: **Canada - National Transportation Agency of Canada** (2829)

★ 12251 ★
Office of Personnel Management - Library (Soc Sci, Bus-Fin)
1900 E St., N.W.   Phone: (202)606-1381
Washington, DC 20415   Catherine Tashjean, Hd.Libn.
Founded: 1940. **Staff:** Prof 2; Other 3. **Subjects:** Personnel administration, public administration, civil service, law, legislative reference, social science, political science, management. **Special Collections:** Baruch Collection (personal papers of Ismar Baruch, expert in position classification and salary administration); civil service history. **Holdings:** 120,000 volumes. **Subscriptions:** 525 journals and other serials. **Services:** Interlibrary loan; library open to the public for reference use only. **Computerized Information Services:** DIALOG Information Services, BRS Information Technologies. **Publications:** Personnel Literature, monthly with annual index - for sale through U.S. Government Printing Office. **Remarks:** FAX: (202)606-0909. **Staff:** Leon Brody, Sr.Ref.Spec.; Linda Van Den Akker-Landrum, Ref.Libn., ILL Libn.

Office on Smoking and Health
See: **U.S. Centers for Disease Control** (17128)

Office of Thrift Supervision
See: **U.S. Office of Thrift Supervision** (17915)

Office of the United Nations Disaster Relief Coordinator
See: **United Nations - Office of the United Nations Disaster Relief Coordinator - UNDRO Reference Library** (16754)

Offshore Engineering Information Service
See: **Heriot-Watt University** (7154)

★ 12252 ★
Ogden Standard-Examiner - Library (Publ)
455-23rd St.   Phone: (801)394-7711
Ogden, UT 84401   Donna Bingham, Libn.
Founded: 1985. **Staff:** Prof 1; Other 1. **Subjects:** Newspaper reference topics. **Holdings:** 200 books; 200 reports; 150 reels of microfilm; photographs. **Subscriptions:** 10 journals and other serials; 3 newspapers. **Services:** Library not open to the public. **Computerized Information Services:** Internal database. **Remarks:** FAX: (801)625-4299.

★ 12253 ★
Ogilvie Mills Ltd. - Research & Development Library (Food-Bev)
995 Mill St.   Phone: (514)866-7961
Montreal, PQ, Canada H3C 1Y5   Muriel E. Henri, Libn.
Founded: 1970. **Staff:** 1. **Subjects:** Cereal chemistry, wheat starch, analytical chemistry. **Holdings:** 2586 books; 2779 bound periodical volumes; 821 patents. **Subscriptions:** 59 journals and other serials. **Services:** Interlibrary loan; copying; library open to the public by appointment. **Computerized Information Services:** DIALOG Information Services, CAN/OLE. **Remarks:** FAX: (514)937-9578.

★ 12254 ★
Ogilvy Adams & Rinehart - Information Center (Bus-Fin)
708 3rd Ave.   Phone: (212)557-0100
New York, NY 10017   Jennifer Farrar, Dir., Info.Serv.
Founded: 1953. **Staff:** Prof 2; Other 4. **Subjects:** Business, finance, public relations, marketing, healthcare. **Holdings:** 1600 books; 1200 annual reports. **Subscriptions:** 200 journals and other serials; 12 newspapers. **Services:** Interlibrary loan; center not open to the public. **Computerized Information Services:** DIALOG Information Services, Dow Jones News/Retrieval, NEXIS, CDA Investment Technologies, Inc., InvesText, VU/TEXT Information Services, DataTimes, NewsNet, Inc., Burrelle's Broadcast Database. **Remarks:** FAX: (212)972-6974. **Formerly:** Adams & Rinehart Inc.

★ 12255 ★
Ogilvy & Mather - Information Center (Bus-Fin)
676 St. Clair   Phone: (312)988-2766
Chicago, IL 60611   Eric Halvorson, Mgr.
Founded: 1977. **Staff:** Prof 1; Other 1. **Subjects:** Advertising, marketing, business, communications. **Holdings:** 1500 volumes; 150 corporate/industry files; Ogilvy & Mather publications, studies, and reports; annual reports of Fortune 500 corporations. **Subscriptions:** 300 journals and other serials; 5 newspapers. **Services:** Interlibrary loan; center not open to the public. **Computerized Information Services:** DIALOG Information Services, NEXIS, Dow Jones News/Retrieval, ProductScan, VU/TEXT Information Services, DataTimes. **Networks/Consortia:** Member of Chicago Library System. **Remarks:** FAX: (312)988-2691.

★ 12256 ★
Ogilvy & Mather - Research Library (Bus-Fin)
Worldwide Plaza
309 W. 49th St.   Phone: (212)237-5502
New York, NY 10019-7399   Catherine Altobello, Sr.Libn.
Founded: 1955. **Staff:** Prof 2; Other 1. **Subjects:** Advertising, marketing, drugs, cosmetics, food market segments. **Holdings:** 6000 books; 60 periodicals on microfilm; 230 VF drawers of subject files. **Subscriptions:** 400 journals and other serials; 7 newspapers. **Services:** Interlibrary loan; library not open to the public. **Computerized Information Services:** NEXIS, DIALOG Information Services, Dow Jones News/Retrieval, WILSONLINE, Reuter TEXTLINE, Marketing Analysis and Information Database (MAID), DataTimes, InvesText. **Remarks:** FAX: (212)237-5211. **Staff:** Linda Goldstein, Libn.; Harriet Causbie, Lib.Spec.

★ 12257 ★
Ogilvy, Renault - Library (Law)
1981 McGill College Ave., Suite 1100
Montreal, PQ, Canada H3A 3C1   Phone: (514)847-4701
                                    Carole Mehu, Hd.Libn.
Founded: 1879. **Staff:** Prof 1; Other 6. **Subjects:** Law - Quebec, Canada, Great Britain. **Holdings:** 17,000 volumes. **Services:** Library not open to the public. **Automated Operations:** Computerized cataloging. **Computerized Information Services:** DIALOG Information Services.

★ 12258 ★
Oglebay Institute - Mansion Museum Library (Hist)
Oglebay Park   Phone: (304)242-7272
Wheeling, WV 26003   John A. Artzberger, Dir.
Founded: 1930. **Staff:** Prof 4. **Subjects:** History of local and tri-state area; glass, china, and other decorative arts. **Holdings:** 750 books; 250 archival materials. **Services:** Interlibrary loan; copying; library open to the public for reference use and loan on request. **Staff:** Holly Hoover, Cur. of Educ.

★ 12259 ★
Oglesby Historical Society - Library (Hist)
Oglesby Public Library
128 W. Walnut   Phone: (815)883-3619
Oglesby, IL 61348   Albert Moyle, Pres.
Founded: 1919. **Subjects:** Local history. **Holdings:** Figures not available.
Services: Library open to the public.

★ 12260 ★
Oglethorpe University - Library - Archives (Hist)
4484 Peachtree Rd., N.E.   Phone: (404)261-1441
Atlanta, GA 30319   John Ryland, Libn.
Subjects: Oglethorpe University, 1835 to present. **Special Collections:**
Records of the "Crypt of Civilization" at Oglethorpe; papers and drawings
of the original Oglethorpe University buildings in Atlanta, 1913-1930;
minutes of the board of trustees, 1835-1871. **Holdings:** 1 file cabinet and 14
boxes of manuscripts and photographs; the Oglethorpe University
"Founder's Book," 1916. **Services:** Copying; archives open to the public for
research only. **Networks/Consortia:** Member of University Center in
Georgia, Inc.

★ 12261 ★
Ohev Shalom Synagogue - Ray Doblitz Memorial Library (Rel-Phil)
2 Chester Rd.   Phone: (215)874-1465
Wallingford, PA 19086   Evelyn Schott, Libn.
Founded: 1955. **Staff:** Prof 1. **Subjects:** Judaica. **Holdings:** 5500 books; 120
recordings; pamphlets; 235 video cassettes on Jewish subjects. **Subscriptions:**
12 journals and other serials. **Services:** Library open to the public with
references.

★ 12262 ★
Ohio Bell - Corporate Information Resource Center (Bus-Fin)
45 Erieview Plaza, Rm. 820   Phone: (216)822-2740
Cleveland, OH 44114-1813   Terry Szilagyi, Asst.Mgr.
Founded: 1951. **Staff:** Prof 1; Other 2. **Subjects:** Business, management,
telecommunications, personnel, computers, marketing, Ohio Bell and Bell
System history. **Special Collections:** Corporate historical photograph
collection (30,000 photographs). **Holdings:** 5000 books. **Subscriptions:** 150
journals and other serials; 10 newspapers. **Services:** Interlibrary loan;
copying; library open to the public at librarian's discretion. **Computerized
Information Services:** DIALOG Information Services; internal databases.
Publications: New Book List, quarterly - for internal distribution only.
Special Indexes: Reference File. **Remarks:** Subsidiary of Ameritech Corp.

★ 12263 ★
Ohio Brass Company - Library
8711 Wadsworth Rd.
Box 1001   Phone: (216)335-2361
Wadsworth, OH 44281-0902   Georgia Zentner, Libn.
Holdings: 200 volumes. **Remarks:** FAX: (216)336-9252. No further
information was supplied by respondent.

★ 12264 ★
Ohio College of Podiatric Medicine - Library/Media Center (Med)
10515 Carnegie Ave.   Phone: (216)231-3300
Cleveland, OH 44106   Judy Mehl Cowell, Dir.
Founded: 1916. **Staff:** Prof 1; Other 2. **Subjects:** Podiatric medicine,
orthopedics, dermatology, biomechanics, sports medicine. **Special
Collections:** Archives; podiatric medicine. **Holdings:** 12,000 books; 2500
bound periodical volumes; 350 AV programs; VF drawers of pamphlet
material; 800 reprints; School Papers File; state file. **Subscriptions:** 220
journals and other serials. **Services:** Interlibrary loan; copying; library open
to the public with restrictions. **Automated Operations:** Computerized
cataloging. **Computerized Information Services:** DIALOG Information
Services, MEDLINE. Performs searches on fee basis. **Remarks:** FAX:
(216)231-0453.

Ohio Cooperative Fish and Wildlife Research Unit
See: **Ohio State University** (12321)

★ 12265 ★
Ohio County Court - 1st Judicial District - Law Library (Law)
County Courthouse
1500 Chapline St.   Phone: (304)234-3780
Wheeling, WV 26003   Nancy L. Coughlan, Law Libn.
Founded: 1919. **Staff:** Prof 1. **Subjects:** Law. **Holdings:** 38,000 volumes.
Services: Copying; library open to the public for reference use only.
Remarks: Maintained by State of West Virginia.

★ 12266 ★
Ohio Dominican College - Spangler Library (Rel-Phil, Soc Sci)
1216 Sunbury Rd.   Phone: (614)251-4750
Columbus, OH 43219   Gabriella Petrovics-Netting, Dir.
Founded: 1911. **Staff:** Prof 5; Other 3. **Subjects:** Social sciences, theology,
philosophy. **Holdings:** 131,900 books; 12,153 bound periodical volumes;
5100 reels of microfilm; 3000 AV programs. **Subscriptions:** 595 journals and
other serials; 15 newspapers. **Services:** Interlibrary loan; copying; faxing;
library open to the public. **Automated Operations:** Computerized cataloging.
Computerized Information Services: OCLC, DIALOG Information
Services; CD-ROMs. Performs searches on fee basis. **Networks/Consortia:**
Member of OHIONET. **Remarks:** FAX: (614)252-2650. **Staff:** Larry Cepek,
Dir., Media Ctr.; Karen Pavone; Sr. Mary McElroy; Zhiwei Bi; Antoinette
Koontz; Suzanne Hoover.

★ 12267 ★
Ohio Edison Company - Corporate Library (Energy)
76 S. Main St.   Phone: (216)384-5367
Akron, OH 44308-1890   Sharon M. Malumphy, Corp.Libn.
Founded: 1981. **Staff:** Prof 2; Other 1. **Subjects:** Engineering, energy,
management. **Special Collections:** Electric Power Research Institute reports
(8000); Edison Electric Institute reports (625). **Holdings:** 7600 books; 270
bound periodical volumes; 18 shelves of company references and documents;
20 VF drawers of annual reports; 10 VF drawers of newsletters and college
catalogs; 1100 standards. **Subscriptions:** 150 journals and other serials.
Services: Interlibrary loan; SDI; library open to the public with permission.
Automated Operations: Computerized cataloging and acquisitions.
Computerized Information Services: DIALOG Information Services,
LEXIS, NEXIS, Dow Jones News/Retrieval, VU/TEXT Information
Services, OCLC EPIC, WILSONLINE, DataTimes; CompuServe
Information Service (electronic mail service). **Networks/Consortia:** Member
of Cleveland Area Metropolitan Library System (CAMLS). **Publications:**
Library Update, irregular - for internal distribution only. **Special Indexes:**
Index to standards. **Remarks:** FAX: (216)384-5014 (Attn: library).
Electronic mail address(es): EEI040 (CompuServe Information Service).
Staff: Susan R. Lloyd, Asst.Libn.

★ 12268 ★
Ohio Environmental Protection Agency - Library (Env-Cons)
1800 Watermark Dr.   Phone: (614)644-3024
Columbus, OH 43215   Ruth Ann Evans, Libn.
Founded: 1976. **Staff:** Prof 1; Other 1. **Subjects:** Pollution control,
environmental law, Ohio water quality reports. **Holdings:** 5699 books; 329
microfiche. **Subscriptions:** 121 journals and other serials. **Services:**
Interlibrary loan; copying; library open to the public for reference use only.
Automated Operations: Computerized cataloging. **Computerized
Information Services:** DIALOG Information Services, Chemical
Information Systems, Inc. (CIS), Congressional Quarterly, Hannah
Information Systems, OCLC. **Networks/Consortia:** Member of OHIONET.
Remarks: FAX: (614)644-2329.

★ 12269 ★
Ohio Genealogical Society - Library (Hist)
34 Sturges Ave.
Box 2625   Phone: (419)522-9077
Mansfield, OH 44906   Kay Hudson, Libn.
Founded: 1959. **Staff:** Prof 2. **Subjects:** History and genealogy. **Special
Collections:** Ancestor file (200,000 cards). **Holdings:** 15,000 books; census
for all Ohio counties, 1820-1910, on microfilm; original Ohio 1880 census
volumes; 24 file drawers of "First Families of Ohio" applications; 46 drawers
of unpublished family history manuscripts; 1988 I.G.I. World.
Subscriptions: 150 journals and other serials. **Services:** Copying; library
open to the public for a fee. **Publications:** The Report, quarterly; Ohio
Records & Pioneer Families, quarterly; OGS Newsletter, monthly. **Special
Indexes:** 1812 Ohio tax list (card); Ohio Bible Records. **Staff:** Thomas
Stephen Neel, Mgr.

★ 12270 ★
Ohio Genealogical Society - Muskingum County Genealogical Society - Library (Hist)
Box 3066   Phone: (614)454-0944
Zanesville, OH 43701   Rose Ellen Jenkins, Lib.Comm.Chm.
Founded: 1977. **Staff:** 9. **Subjects:** Genealogy, history. **Holdings:** 2000 books; 400 bound periodical volumes; township, county, and church registers; tombstone inscriptions; Bible records; atlases; genealogical lessons, lectures, and guides on tape; directories; court records and local newspapers on microfilm; family histories. **Subscriptions:** 12 journals and other serials. **Services:** Copying; library open to the public. **Remarks:** Alternate telephone number(s): 452-1445. **Staff:** Marion Davies, Libn.

★ 12271 ★
Ohio Historical Society - Campus Martius Museum - Library (Hist)
601 Second St.   Phone: (614)373-3750
Marietta, OH 45750   John B. Briley, Mgr.
Founded: 1920. **Subjects:** Area history and genealogy prior to 1830, river history. **Holdings:** 1000 books. **Subscriptions:** 3 journals and other serials. **Services:** Copying; library open to the public by appointment on a fee basis.

Ohio Historical Society - Rutherford B. Hayes Presidential Center
See: **Rutherford B. Hayes Presidential Center** (7060)

★ 12272 ★
Ohio Northern University - College of Law - Jay P. Taggart Memorial Law Library (Law)
Ada, OH 45810   Phone: (419)772-2250
                                         James Leonard, Dir./Hd.Libn.
Founded: 1885. **Staff:** Prof 4; Other 6. **Subjects:** Law, international law. **Special Collections:** Papers of Congressman McCullough. **Holdings:** 168,827 volumes; U.S. Government documents depository; 35,505 volumes in microform. **Subscriptions:** 3000 journals and other serials; 14 newspapers. **Services:** Interlibrary loan; copying; library open to the public. **Automated Operations:** Computerized cataloging. **Computerized Information Services:** LEXIS, NEXIS, WESTLAW, VU/TEXT Information Services, Hannah Information Systems. Performs searches on fee basis. Contact Person: Larry S. Porter, Ser.Libn., 772-2255. **Networks/Consortia:** Member of OHIONET, Ohio Regional Consortium of Law Libraries (ORCLL). **Remarks:** FAX: (419)772-1875. **Staff:** Marcia Siebesma, Assoc. Law Libn.; Andrew Rowden, Circ./Ref.Libn.; Pam Johnson, Acq.; Eleonor Courtney, Govt.Doc.; Lonnie Bell, Circ.; Lora Smith, Tech.Proc.; Madeline Hawkins, Govt.Doc./Tech.Proc.

★ 12273 ★
Ohio Poetry Therapy Center and Library (Soc Sci)
Pudding House
60 N. Main St.   Phone: (614)967-6060
Johnstown, OH 43031   Jennifer Bosveld, Dir.
Founded: 1981. **Staff:** Prof 2. **Subjects:** Poetry, creative arts in therapy, psychology, self-help and motivation, creative writing, social work, popular culture, applied poetry. **Holdings:** 3000 books; 50 dissertations and reports; 200 cassette tapes; multi-media productions. **Subscriptions:** 40 journals and other serials. **Services:** Library open to members; annual fee for membership. **Computerized Information Services:** Internal database. **Publications:** Pudding Magazine; poetry and educational books.

★ 12274 ★
Ohio Power Company - Library (Energy)
Box 24400   Phone: (216)438-7235
Canton, OH 44701-4400   James M. Beck, Libn.
Founded: 1956. **Staff:** 1. **Subjects:** Public utility regulations, engineering, law and government, statistics, management development. **Holdings:** 1100 volumes; 8 VF drawers. **Subscriptions:** 150 journals and other serials. **Services:** Library open to the public for reference use only upon request. **Remarks:** FAX: (216)438-7330.

★ 12275 ★
Ohio School for the Deaf - Library (Med)
500 Morse Rd.   Phone: (614)888-3221
Columbus, OH 43214   Ada G. Kent, Libn., Media Spec.
Staff: Prof 1. **Subjects:** General collection, deafness, professional education. **Special Collections:** Parent Collection (deafness). **Holdings:** 14,000 books; archival materials. **Subscriptions:** 42 journals and other serials. **Services:** Interlibrary loan; copying; library open to the public by appointment. **Publications:** Bibliographies.

★ 12276 ★
Ohio (State) Agricultural Research and Development Center - Library (Agri)
1680 Madison Ave.   Phone: (216)263-3773
Wooster, OH 44691-4096   Constance J. Britton, Libn.
Founded: 1892. **Staff:** Prof 1; Other 1. **Subjects:** Agricultural research. **Special Collections:** Virus diseases of corn - Maize Virus Information Service (MAVIS). **Holdings:** 57,000 volumes; microforms. **Subscriptions:** 1000 journals and other serials. **Services:** Interlibrary loan; copying; library open to the public. **Automated Operations:** Computerized cataloging and ILL. **Computerized Information Services:** OCLC, DIALOG Information Services; BITNET (electronic mail service). **Networks/Consortia:** Member of OHIONET. **Publications:** Serials in the Library - to bio-agricultural libraries. **Special Indexes:** Subject indexes to agricultural documents owned by library, monthly; index to publications of this organization. **Remarks:** FAX: (216)263-3689. Electronic mail address(es): BRITTON.4@OSU.EDU (BITNET). Maintained by Ohio State University.

★ 12277 ★
Ohio (State) Attorney General's Office - Law Library (Law)
30 E. Broad St., 17th Fl.   Phone: (614)466-2465
Columbus, OH 43215   Shelley McLane, Law Libn.
Founded: 1846. **Staff:** Prof 1; Other 1. **Subjects:** Federal and state law. **Holdings:** 36,000 books. **Subscriptions:** 25 journals and other serials; 6 newspapers. **Services:** Library not open to the public. **Automated Operations:** Computerized acquisitions (LCS). **Computerized Information Services:** LEXIS, NEXIS, Hannah Information Systems. **Special Indexes:** Tax, securities, newspaper, and magazine indexes. **Remarks:** FAX: (614)644-6135.

★ 12278 ★
Ohio (State) Bureau of Workers' Compensation - Rehabilitation Division Library (Med)
2050 Kenny Rd.   Phone: (614)421-1150
Columbus, OH 43221   Melissa Heilman
Founded: 1980. **Staff:** Prof 1. **Subjects:** Rehabilitation of the injured worker; back pain treatment; therapy - physical, psychological, occupational, vocational. **Holdings:** 1000 books. **Subscriptions:** 80 journals and other serials; 2 newspapers. **Services:** Library not open to the public. **Computerized Information Services:** DIALOG Information Services. **Remarks:** FAX: (614)421-4001.

★ 12279 ★
Ohio (State) Bureau of Workers' Compensation - Resource Center (Med)
30 W. Spring St.   Phone: (614)466-7388
Columbus, OH 43266-0581   Rosemary Larkins, Mgr.
Founded: 1974. **Staff:** Prof 3; Other 2. **Subjects:** Occupational safety, industrial hygiene, workers' compensation. **Holdings:** 4000 books; 850 standards; 200 microfiche; 20 VF drawers of pamphlets; 650 subject headings; 2 VF drawers of clippings. **Subscriptions:** 280 journals and other serials. **Services:** Interlibrary loan; copying; center open to the public. **Computerized Information Services:** DIALOG Information Services, NLM, Occupational Health Services, Inc. (OHS). **Networks/Consortia:** Member of Columbus Area Libraries Information Council of Ohio (CALICO). **Publications:** Acquisitions, quarterly. **Remarks:** FAX: (614)644-9634. **Formerly:** Ohio (State) Division of Safety and Hygiene.

★ 12280 ★
Ohio (State) Department of Aging - Resource Center (Soc Sci)
50 W. Broad St.
Columbus, OH 43266-0501   Phone: (614)466-9086
Founded: 1973. **Staff:** Prof 1; Other 1. **Subjects:** Aged and aging, social services, demographics. **Holdings:** 300 AV programs; government reports and other monographs; VF drawers. **Subscriptions:** 100 serials. **Services:** Interlibrary loan (limited); center open to the public for reference use only. **Special Catalogs:** 1991 Resource Center catalog of audio-visual titles. **Remarks:** FAX: (614)466-5741.

★ 12281 ★
Ohio (State) Department of Development - Research Library (Soc Sci)
Box 1001   Phone: (614)466-2115
Columbus, OH 43266-0101   Geraldine Waller, Libn.
Staff: Prof 1; Other 1. **Subjects:** Census, business, statistics, demography, economics. **Special Collections:** Ohio economic data. **Holdings:** 1000 books;

5000 reports; 12 drawers of microfiche. **Subscriptions:** 438 journals and other serials; 12 newspapers. **Services:** Interlibrary loan; copying; library open to the public for reference use only. **Automated Operations:** Computerized cataloging. **Publications:** New Acquisitions List, quarterly; List of Periodicals, annual; Publications Available from ODOD, annual - all for internal distribution and to government, public, and private agencies.

★ 12282 ★
Ohio (State) Department of Drug and Alcohol Addiction Services - Regional Alcohol and Drug Awareness - Resource Center (Med)
170 N. High St., 3rd Fl.   Phone: (614)466-7893
Columbus, OH 43215   Deborah Chambers, Prevention Spec.
Subjects: Drug abuse, alcohol, AIDS. **Holdings:** 1000 books. **Subscriptions:** 17 journals and other serials. **Services:** Interlibrary loan; library open to the public. **Remarks:** FAX: (614)644-5169. TDY: (614)644-9140.

★ 12283 ★
Ohio (State) Department of Mental Health - Educational Media Center (Med)
2401 W. Walnut St.
Columbus, OH 43223   Phone: (614)466-6013
Founded: 1970. **Staff:** Prof 1; Other 1. **Subjects:** Mental health, prevention of mental illness, social issues, clinical issues. **Holdings:** 250 films; 150 videotapes. **Services:** Center open to the public. **Special Catalogs:** Media Catalog. **Staff:** Charlene Pulmer; Herbert Doherty.

Ohio State Department of Mental Health - Portsmouth Receiving Hospital
See: Portsmouth Receiving Hospital (13258)

★ 12284 ★
Ohio (State) Department of Taxation - Tax Analysis and Local Government Distributions - Library (Bus-Fin)
State Office Tower
Box 530   Phone: (614)466-3960
Columbus, OH 43266-0030   Shelley J. Burger
Founded: 1956. **Subjects:** Taxation, public finance, general statistics. **Holdings:** 1400 books; 120 feet of vertical files. **Subscriptions:** 16 journals and other serials; 6 newspapers. **Services:** Library open to the public.

★ 12285 ★
Ohio (State) Department of Transportation - Library (Trans)
25 S. Front St.
Box 899   Phone: (614)466-7680
Columbus, OH 43216   Ellen Haider, Libn.
Founded: 1976. **Staff:** Prof 1; Other 2. **Subjects:** Road transportation. **Special Collections:** Ohio Department of Transportation publications; Transportation Research Board publications. **Holdings:** 14,000 books and reports; 60 bound periodical volumes. **Subscriptions:** 105 journals and other serials. **Services:** Interlibrary loan; copying; SDI; library open to the public. **Automated Operations:** Computerized public access catalog. **Computerized Information Services:** DIALOG Information Services. **Publications:** New Acquisitions, irregular - internal distribution and on request.

★ 12286 ★
Ohio (State) Division of Geological Survey - Library (Sci-Engr)
4383 Fountain Square Dr.   Phone: (614)245-6576
Columbus, OH 43224-1362   Merrianne Hackathorn, Geol./Ed.
Staff: 1. **Subjects:** Geology, mineralogy, hydrology, paleontology, petrology, mineral resources. **Holdings:** 3200 books. **Services:** Copying; library open to the public for reference use only. **Remarks:** FAX: (614)447-1918.

Ohio (State) Division of Safety and Hygiene
See: Ohio (State) Bureau of Workers' Compensation (12279)

★ 12287 ★
Ohio State Highway Patrol Training Academy - Library (Law)
740 E. 17th Ave.   Phone: (614)466-4896
Columbus, OH 43112   Maj. Gilbert Jones, Supv.
Remarks: No further information was supplied by respondent.

★ 12288 ★
Ohio State Legislative Service Commission - Research Library (Soc Sci)
Vern Riffe Center
77 S. High St., 9th Fl.   Phone: (614)466-5312
Columbus, OH 43266-0432   Barbara J. Laughon, Adm.
Founded: 1953. **Staff:** Prof 3; Other 2. **Subjects:** Social sciences, Ohio law. **Special Collections:** Laws of Ohio, 1803 to present; Laws of the Northwest Territory, 1787-1796; Codes for Northwest Territory and State of Ohio; Debates of the Ohio Constitutional Conventions. **Holdings:** 9000 books; 1000 bound volumes; 20 VF drawers of pamphlets, clippings, unbound and uncataloged documents; 350 reels of microfilm; 120 audiotape cassettes. **Subscriptions:** 262 journals and other serials. **Services:** Library not open to the public. **Automated Operations:** Computerized cataloging. **Computerized Information Services:** DIALOG Information Services, WILSONLINE, LEGISNET. **Networks/Consortia:** Member of Columbus Area Libraries Information Council of Ohio (CALICO), OHIONET.

(Ohio) State Library of Ohio
See: State Library of Ohio (15691)

★ 12289 ★
Ohio State Office of the Consumers' Counsel - Library (Energy)
77 S. High St., 15th Fl.   Phone: (614)466-9601
Columbus, OH 43266-0550   Carolyn Vensel, Libn.
Founded: 1977. **Staff:** Prof 1; Other 1. **Subjects:** Utility regulation, energy resources, Federal Energy Regulation Commission and Federal Communications Commission regulations, Ohio law, accounting. **Special Collections:** National Energy Strategy resources; acid rain; long-term forecasts of investor-owned utilities; OCC residential ratepayers reports; nuclear plant information; Department of Energy, National Regulatory Research Institute, and National Association of Regulatory Utility Commissions reports. **Holdings:** 3000 books; 2500 bound periodical volumes; 30 reports by consultants for the OCC; 900 closed cases on microfilm; utility-related newsclip files dating from 1980. **Subscriptions:** 92 journals and other serials; 12 newspapers. **Services:** Interlibrary loan; copying; library open to the public with restrictions. **Publications:** Bibliographies on least-cost planning; National Energy Strategy bibliography. **Special Indexes:** Acid rain case file index. **Remarks:** FAX: (614)466-9475.

★ 12290 ★
Ohio State School for the Blind - Library (Educ)
5220 N. High St.   Phone: (614)888-4616
Columbus, OH 43214   Beverly Kessler, Libn.
Staff: Prof 1. **Subjects:** Special education with emphasis on blindness. **Special Collections:** Children and young adults collection. **Holdings:** 10,471 books; 1673 AV programs; 150 models. **Subscriptions:** 120 journals and other serials. **Services:** Library not open to the public.

★ 12291 ★
Ohio State Supreme Court Law Library (Law)
30 E. Broad St., 4th Fl.   Phone: (614)466-2044
Columbus, OH 43266-0419   Paul S. Fu, Law Libn.
Founded: 1858. **Staff:** Prof 8; Other 10. **Subjects:** Law. **Special Collections:** Early laws of Ohio; old legal treatises. **Holdings:** 325,000 volumes. **Subscriptions:** 1179 journals and other serials; 26 newspapers. **Services:** Copying; library open to the public. **Automated Operations:** Computerized cataloging, serials, acquisitions, and circulation (NOTIS). **Computerized Information Services:** WESTLAW, OCLC. **Networks/Consortia:** Member of OHIONET. **Publications:** Monthly List of Acquisitions; Law Library Handbook. **Remarks:** FAX: (614)466-1559. **Staff:** Niann Lao, Asst.Libn. & Cat.; Kaye Floom, Ref.Libn.; Patsy Duncan, Acq.Libn.; Scott Litty, Doc.Libn.; Donna Bedford, Circ.Libn.; Diane Kier, Hd., Pub.Serv.; John Farnlacher, Sys.Libn.; Karen Plummer, Tech.Serv.

★12292★

Ohio State University - Agricultural Technical Institute - Library (Agri)
1328 Dover Rd.   Phone: (216)264-3911
Wooster, OH 44691   Ella G. Copeland, Dir., Lib. LRC
Founded: 1972. **Staff:** Prof 1; Other 10. **Subjects:** Floriculture, landscape, nursery, turf, crops, food marketing, greenhouse production, agricultural engineering and mechanics, agronomic industries, soil and water management, dairy, horse, livestock, laboratory and research science, wood science, beekeeping, construction. **Special Collections:** Beekeeping journals. **Holdings:** 15,000 books; 1700 bound periodical volumes; 23 VF drawers of pamphlets; journals in microform; 5 VF drawers of Ohio soil surveys; 21,312 microforms. **Subscriptions:** 552 journals and other serials; 12 newspapers. **Services:** Interlibrary loan; library open to the public with restrictions on borrowing. **Automated Operations:** Computerized cataloging. **Computerized Information Services:** DIALOG Information Services, WILSONLINE, Equine Line. **Special Indexes:** Table of contents indexes for various technologies. **Remarks:** FAX: (216)262-0859. **Staff:** Thai Hoang, Supv., Acq. & AV Depts.; Judy Taylor, Supv., Circ. & Per. Depts.

★12293★

Ohio State University - Agriculture Library (Agri)
45 Agriculture Bldg.
2120 Fyffe Rd.   Phone: (614)292-6125
Columbus, OH 43210   Mary P. Key, Hd.Libn.
Founded: 1956. **Staff:** Prof 1; Other 2. **Subjects:** Animal science, agriculture and allied subjects, food science and nutrition, forestry, dairy science, plant pathology, rural sociology, horticulture, natural resources, poultry science. **Special Collections:** Arnold Library of Agricultural Credit. **Holdings:** 81,589 volumes; 2827 pamphlets; CD-ROM. **Subscriptions:** 1192 journals and other serials. **Services:** Interlibrary loan; copying; library open to the public. **Automated Operations:** Computerized public access catalog, cataloging, acquisitions, serials, and circulation. **Computerized Information Services:** Online systems; BITNET (electronic mail service). **Networks/Consortia:** Member of OHIONET, Center for Research Libraries (CRL), Columbus Area Libraries Information Council of Ohio (CALICO). **Remarks:** FAX: (614)292-0590. Electronic mail address(es): MARYREY@OHSTMAIL (BITNET).

★12294★

Ohio State University - Archives (Hist)
2121 Tuttle Park Place   Phone: (614)292-2409
Columbus, OH 43210   Dr. Raimund E. Goerler, Univ.Archv.
Founded: 1963. **Staff:** Prof 2; Other 5. **Subjects:** Ohio State University history. **Special Collections:** Photographic history of OSU (800,000 images); Midwest Universities Consortium for International Activities; Byrd Polar Research Center Archival Program collection of polar explorers and scientist, including the papers of Admiral Richard Byrd and Sir Hubert Wilkins. **Holdings:** 8000 cubic feet of records; 850,000 photographs. **Services:** Copying; archives open to the public. **Computerized Information Services:** Internal database; BITNET (electronic mail service). **Special Catalogs:** Inventories of archival collections. **Remarks:** FAX: (614)292-7859. Electronic mail address(es): TS0708ATOMSTMVSA (BITNET). **Staff:** Kenneth Grossi, Asst.Archv.

★12295★

Ohio State University - Biological Sciences Library (Biol Sci)
200 B & Z Bldg.
1735 Neil Ave.   Phone: (614)292-1744
Columbus, OH 43210   Bruce Leach, Hd.Libn.
Founded: 1916. **Staff:** Prof 1; Other 3. **Subjects:** Zoology, botany, biology, entomology, microbiology, genetics, biochemistry, biophysics, biotechnology. **Holdings:** 98,095 volumes; CD-ROM. **Subscriptions:** 1039 journals and other serials. **Services:** Interlibrary loan; copying; library open to the public. **Automated Operations:** Computerized public access catalog, cataloging, acquisitions, serials, and circulation. **Computerized Information Services:** Online systems; BITNET (electronic mail service). **Networks/Consortia:** Member of OHIONET, Center for Research Libraries (CRL), Columbus Area Libraries Information Council of Ohio (CALICO). **Publications:** Quarterly lists of acquisitions. **Remarks:** FAX: (614)292-7859. Electronic mail address(es): BALEACH@OHSTMAIL (BITNET).

★12296★

Ohio State University - Black Studies Library (Area-Ethnic)
1858 Neil Ave. Mall   Phone: (614)292-2393
Columbus, OH 43210-1286   Eleanor M. Daniel, Hd.Libn.
Founded: 1971. **Staff:** Prof 1; Other 1. **Subjects:** African-American studies, African studies. **Special Collections:** Schomburg Collection; Atlanta University Black Culture Collection; Black Newspaper Collection (Bell & Howell); Tuskegee Institute News Clipping File; Martin Luther King, Jr. Assassination File; W.E.B. DuBois papers; Black Biographical Dictionaries; papers of the National Association for the Advancement of Colored People (NAACP), parts 1-8; papers of the Congress of Racial Equality, 1941-1967. **Holdings:** 30,000 books; 13,000 microforms; 70 major black U.S. newspapers. **Subscriptions:** 173 journals and other serials; 16 newspapers. **Services:** Interlibrary loan; collection open to the public. **Automated Operations:** Computerized cataloging, serials, and circulation. **Computerized Information Services:** Online systems; BITNET (electronic mail service). **Publications:** Selected List of Titles Received by the Black Studies Library, monthly. **Remarks:** FAX: (614)292-7859. Electronic mail address(es): EDANIEL@OHSTMVSA.ACS.OHIO.STATE.EDU (BITNET).

★12297★

Ohio State University - Business Library (Bus-Fin)
110 Page Hall
1810 College Rd.   Phone: (614)292-2136
Columbus, OH 43210   Charles Popovich, Hd.Libn.
Founded: 1925. **Staff:** Prof 3; Other 5. **Subjects:** Accounting, business administration, economics, marketing, public administration, geography, finance. **Special Collections:** Annual reports of corporations (84,000 microforms). **Holdings:** 177,779 volumes; 2000 theses and dissertations; 80 loose-leaf services. **Subscriptions:** 1953 journals and other serials; 10 newspapers. **Services:** Interlibrary loan; copying; library open to the public. **Automated Operations:** Computerized public access catalog, cataloging, acquisitions, serials, and circulation. **Computerized Information Services:** Online systems; BITNET (electronic mail service). **Networks/Consortia:** Member of OHIONET, Center for Research Libraries (CRL), Columbus Area Libraries Information Council of Ohio (CALICO). **Remarks:** FAX: (614)292-7859. Electronic mail address(es): CJP@OHSTMAIL (BITNET).

★12298★

Ohio State University - Byrd Polar Research Center - Goldthwait Polar Library (Sci-Engr)
125 S. Oval Mall   Phone: (614)292-6715
Columbus, OH 43210-1308   Lynn B. Lay, Libn.
Founded: 1960. **Staff:** Prof 1. **Subjects:** Antarctic, Arctic, and Alpine regions - glaciology, geology, paleoclimatology and climatology, permafrost and soil science, paleontology and palynology, biological sciences; history of polar exploration. **Holdings:** 1600 books; 70 bound periodical volumes; 500 unbound periodical volumes; 19,500 reprints; 1000 maps. **Subscriptions:** 370 journals and other serials. **Services:** Interlibrary loan; copying; library open to qualified researchers. **Computerized Information Services:** SCIENCEnet (electronic mail service). **Publications:** Accessions list, irregular. **Remarks:** FAX: (614)292-4697. Telex: 4945696 OSUPOLAR. Electronic mail address(es): BYRD.POLAR (SCIENCEnet).

★12299★

Ohio State University - Cartoon, Graphic, and Photographic Arts Research Library (Art)
Wexner Ctr., Rm. 023L
27 W. 17th Ave. Mall   Phone: (614)292-0538
Columbus, OH 43210-1393   Lucy S. Caswell, Cur. & Assoc.Prof.
Founded: 1977. **Staff:** Prof 1; Other 1. **Subjects:** Comic strips, editorial cartoons, magazine cartoons, illustrations, movie posters and stills, photographs. **Special Collections:** Milton Caniff Collection of original comic strips and related materials (500,000 items); Jon Whitcomb Collection of magazine illustrations, photographs, tear sheets, correspondence (44 paintings; 33 boxes); Philip Sills Collection of movie posters and stills (110,000); Richard Teichert Collection of silent film advertising materials (10,000 items); Ray Osrin Collection of original editorial cartoons (3100); Eugene Craig Collection of original comic strips and editorial cartoons (4000); Will Rannells Collection of illustrations (80 paintings; 6 boxes); Richard Samuel West Collection (14 boxes); Toni Mendez Collection of business files relating to licensing of comic strip and cartoon feature products (200 boxes); Ron Wolin Memorial Archive of the Cartoonist Guild Papers (90 boxes); Shel Dorf Collection of historic comic strip materials (30,000 items); Woody Gelman Collection (71 original cartoons and more than 500 newspaper tearsheets by Winsor McCay); Will Eisner Collection (5000 items); comic books and underground comics (10,000 items); Ned White Collection (editorial cartoons by White and 90 other cartoonists including Herblock, Darling, Kirby); Rinhart Collection of historic photographs, 1840-1920 (12,000); Mathew Brady photographs; Lewis Hine photographs; Farm Security Administration photographs; dye transfer prints of Harry

Callahan; photographic work by Berenice Abbott, Fratelli Alinari, Harold Edgerton, Man Ray, Anne Noggle, Weegee (Arthur Fellig); papers of Walt Kelly (45 boxes); Noel Sickles Collection (800 items); Ohio News Photographers Association Collection (10,000 items); original cartoons of Ed Ashley, Jim Baker, Brian Basset, Tom Batiuk, Ned Beard, Jim Borgman, Brian Campbell, Milton Caniff, Eugene Craig, Bill Crawford, Edwina Dumm, Will Eisner, Eddie Germano, Leo Egli, John Fischetti, Dudley T. Fisher, Jr., Creig Flessel, Larry Harris, Irwin Hasen, John E. Hazlett, Harry Herschfield, Bill Holman, Karl Hubenthal, William A. (Billy) Ireland, Lynn Johnston, Walt Kelly, Ed Kuekes, Charles Kuhn, Jim Larrick, George Levine, Paule Loring, G.T. Maxwell, Winsor McCay, John T. McCutcheon, Jim MacDonald, Dick Moores, Ray Osrin, Paul Palnik, Eugene Payne, Lute Pease, Mike Peters, Art Poinier, Milt Priggee, Bill Roberts, Jim Scancarelli, Noel Sickles, Jeff Stahler, Mark Szorady, Bert Thomas, Leslie Turner, Morrie Turner, Dow Walling, Mort Walker, L.D. Warren, Harry Westerman, Charles Werner, Ned White, Bert Whitman, Scott Willis, Al Wiseman, Elmer Woggon. **Holdings:** 6000 books on cartoon art; representative holdings of original art from editorial cartoonists and comic strip artists; comic strip clippings; Association of American Editorial Cartoonists and National Cartoonists Society Archives. **Subscriptions:** 4900 journals and other serials. **Services:** Copying; library open to the public upon registration. **Automated Operations:** Computerized cataloging. **Special Catalogs:** Exhibition catalogues. **Remarks:** FAX: (614)292-7859.

★ 12300 ★
Ohio State University - Center for Human Resource Research - Library (Bus-Fin)
921 Chatham Lane, Suite 200
Columbus, OH 43221-2418   Phone: (614)442-7300
Founded: 1965. **Subjects:** Manpower, labor market, education, economics, women, youths, blacks. **Holdings:** 200 books; 4 VF drawers of seminar and NLS (National Longitudinal Surveys) -based research papers. **Subscriptions:** 30 journals and other serials. **Services:** Copying; library open to the public with restrictions. **Computerized Information Services:** BITNET (electronic mail service). **Publications:** NLS Newsletter, quarterly; NLS Handbook, annual; NLS Bibliography Update, annual - all available on request. **Remarks:** FAX: (614)442-7FAX. Electronic mail address(es): USERSVC@OHSTHR (BITNET).

★ 12301 ★
Ohio State University - Chemistry Library (Sci-Engr)
310 McPherson Lab
140 W. 18th Ave.   Phone: (614)292-1118
Columbus, OH 43210   Arlieda Ries, Hd.Libn.
Founded: 1925. **Staff:** Prof 1; Other 2. **Subjects:** Chemistry, chemical technology and engineering. **Holdings:** 54,363 volumes. **Subscriptions:** 458 journals and other serials. **Services:** Interlibrary loan; copying. **Automated Operations:** Computerized public access catalog, cataloging, acquisitions, serials, and circulation. **Computerized Information Services:** Online systems; BITNET (electronic mail service). **Networks/Consortia:** Member of OHIONET, Center for Research Libraries (CRL), Columbus Area Libraries Information Council of Ohio (CALICO). **Publications:** Classified List of Serial Holdings in Chemistry Library. **Remarks:** FAX: (614)292-7859. Electronic mail address(es): ARIES@OHSTMAIL (BITNET). **Also Known As:** Charles Cutler Sharp Library.

★ 12302 ★
Ohio State University - Chinese Collection (Area-Ethnic)
Main Library, Rm. 310
1858 Neil Ave.   Phone: (614)292-3502
Columbus, OH 43210-1286   Daphne C. Hsueh, Chinese Stud.Libn.
Founded: 1962. **Staff:** 1.5. **Subjects:** China - history and culture. **Holdings:** 83,318 volumes; 9283 microforms. **Subscriptions:** 539 journals and other serials; 20 newspapers. **Services:** Interlibrary loan; copying; library open to the public. **Computerized Information Services:** OCLC; internal database; BITNET (electronic mail service). **Networks/Consortia:** Member of OHIONET. **Remarks:** FAX: (614)292-7859. Electronic mail address(es): DAPHNE@OHSTMUSA (BITNET).

★ 12303 ★
Ohio State University - Cole Memorial Library of the Physics and Astronomy Departments (Sci-Engr)
1011 Smith Lab
174 W. 18th Ave.   Phone: (614)292-7894
Columbus, OH 43210   Bernard Bayer, Hd.Libn.
Founded: 1930. **Staff:** Prof 1; Other 2. **Subjects:** Physics - solid state, theoretical, mathematical, low temperature, nuclear; astronomy;

astrophysics; infrared spectroscopy; condensed matter. **Holdings:** 55,923 books. **Subscriptions:** 330 journals and other serials. **Services:** Interlibrary loan. **Automated Operations:** Computerized public access catalog, cataloging, acquisitions, serials, and circulation. **Computerized Information Services:** Online systems; BITNET (electronic mail service). **Networks/Consortia:** Member of OHIONET, Center for Research Libraries (CRL), Columbus Area Libraries Information Council of Ohio (CALICO). **Remarks:** FAX: (614)292-7859. Electronic mail address(es): BBAYER@OHSTMAIL (BITNET).

★ 12304 ★
Ohio State University - Counseling and Consultation Service - Personal And Career Exploration (PACE) Resource Center (Educ)
Ohio Union, 4th Fl.
1739 N. High St.   Phone: (614)292-5766
Columbus, OH 43210-1392   Jenny Finnell
Staff: Prof 1. **Subjects:** Personal and career self-assessment, career exploration, training opportunities, job search resources. **Holdings:** 600 books. **Subscriptions:** 21 journals and other serials. **Services:** Copying; center open to the public for reference use only. **Computerized Information Services:** SIGI PLUS, DISCOVER (internal databases).

★ 12305 ★
Ohio State University - Edgar Dale Educational Media & Instructional Materials Laboratory (Educ)
260 Ramseyer Hall
29 W. Woodruff Ave.   Phone: (614)292-1177
Columbus, OH 43210-1177   Dr. Betty P. Cleaver, Dir.
Founded: 1979. **Staff:** Prof 2; Other 16. **Subjects:** Children's literature; K-12 textbooks and curriculum; classroom management and methods; library/ media center management. **Special Collections:** Historical collection of children's literature and textbooks (1000 volumes). **Holdings:** 31,000 items; 21,000 volumes children's literature; 3600 AV kits; 5500 curriculum guides (microforms); 2050 textbook series; 190 folders of pamphlets; 100 curriculum guides (bound); 4 VF drawers of transparency originals; 350 microcomputer programs. **Subscriptions:** 11 journals and other serials. **Services:** Copying; copystand and media production laboratory. **Automated Operations:** Computerized public access catalog, cataloging, and circulation. **Computerized Information Services:** OCLC, ERIC, Books in Print Plus, Electronic Encyclopedia, A-V Online, Science Helper K-8. **Networks/Consortia:** Member of OHIONET. **Special Indexes:** Subject mediagraphy file, K-12. **Staff:** Shirley V. Morrison, Asst.Dir.; Tyrone Castellarin, Lib. Media Tech.Asst.

★ 12306 ★
Ohio State University - Education/Psychology Library (Educ)
060 Arps Hall
1945 N. High St.   Phone: (614)292-6275
Columbus, OH 43210   Laura Blomquist, Hd.Libn.
Founded: 1926. **Staff:** Prof 4; Other 6. **Subjects:** Education, psychology, physical education and recreation. **Holdings:** 175,047 volumes; 289,957 ERIC microfiche. **Subscriptions:** 1199 journals and other serials. **Services:** Interlibrary loan; copying; library open to the public for reference use only. **Automated Operations:** Computerized public access catalog, cataloging, acquisitions, serials, and circulation. **Computerized Information Services:** Online systems; BITNET (electronic mail service). **Networks/Consortia:** Member of OHIONET, Center for Research Libraries (CRL), Columbus Area Libraries Information Council of Ohio (CALICO). **Special Indexes:** Supplement to Educational Index, 1919-1961 (card). **Remarks:** FAX: (614)292-7859. Electronic mail address(es): LAURA@OHSTMAIL (BITNET). **Staff:** Helena Clark-Von Ville, Ref./Automated Serv.; Mary Gouke, Ref.; Martin Jamison, Ref./Circ.

★ 12307 ★
Ohio State University - Engineering Library (Sci-Engr, Plan, Info Sci)
112 Caldwell Lab.
2024 Neil Ave.   Phone: (614)292-2852
Columbus, OH 43210   Mary Jo Arnold, Hd.Libn.
Founded: 1969. **Staff:** Prof 2; Other 4. **Subjects:** Computer and information science; engineering - industrial, mechanical, aeronautical, civil, electrical; architecture; city and regional planning; welding; landscape architecture. **Holdings:** 158,776 volumes. **Subscriptions:** 1049 journals and other serials. **Services:** Interlibrary loan; copying; library open to the public. **Automated Operations:** Computerized public access catalog, cataloging, acquisitions, serials, and circulation. **Computerized Information Services:** Online

systems; BITNET (electronic mail service). **Networks/Consortia:** Member of OHIONET, Center for Research Libraries (CRL), Columbus Area Libraries Information Council of Ohio (CALICO). **Publications:** Book List, biweekly - to campus personnel. **Remarks:** FAX: (614)292-7859. Electronic mail address(es): MJA@OHSTMAIL (BITNET). **Staff:** Jane McMaster, Ref.Libn.

★12308★
Ohio State University - Fine Arts Library (Art)
035L Wexner Center
27 W. 17th Mall   Phone: (614)292-6184
Columbus, OH 43210   Susan Wyngaard, Hd.Libn.
Founded: 1948. **Staff:** Prof 1; Other 1. **Subjects:** Visual arts; photography; history of art; archeology; art - Western and Eastern European, East Asian, American. **Holdings:** 88,414 books. **Subscriptions:** 376 journals and other serials. **Services:** Interlibrary loan; copying; library open to the public for reference use only. **Automated Operations:** Computerized public access catalog, cataloging, acquisitions, serials, and circulation. **Computerized Information Services:** Online systems; BITNET (electronic mail service). **Networks/Consortia:** Member of OHIONET, Center for Research Libraries (CRL), Columbus Area Libraries Information Council of Ohio (CALICO). **Remarks:** FAX: (614)292-7859. Electronic mail address(es): SUSANW@OHSTMAIL (BITNET).

★12309★
Ohio State University - Franz Theodore Stone Laboratory - Library (Biol Sci)
Box 119
Put-In-Bay, OH 43456   Phone: (419)285-2341
Founded: 1896. **Subjects:** Great Lakes hydrobiology and limnology, field biology, botany, zoology. **Special Collections:** Theses and dissertations (completed at the laboratory or in several departments on the main campus; 80). **Holdings:** 3000 books; 3500 bound periodical volumes; 300 boxes of reprints. **Subscriptions:** 50 journals and other serials. **Services:** Library open to the public during the summer only. **Publications:** Contributions from the Franz Theodore Stone Laboratory. **Remarks:** Part of the Biological Sciences Library of The Ohio State University.

★12310★
Ohio State University - Hilandar Research Library (Area-Ethnic)
227 Main Library, Rm. 227
1858 Neil Ave. Mall   Phone: (614)292-0634
Columbus, OH 43210-1286   Dr. Predrag Matejic, Cur.
Founded: 1978. **Staff:** Prof 1; Other 1. **Subjects:** Medieval Slavic literature, Slavic paleography, history of Slavic languages, Eastern Orthodox Church. **Special Collections:** Microfilm collection of the manuscripts and rare books of the Hilandar Monastery, Mount Athos, Greece; microfilm of Slavic manuscripts obtained through exchanges or field expeditions. **Holdings:** 2000 volumes; 800,000 pages of Slavic Cyrillic Manuscripts in microform; 4 manuscripts. **Subscriptions:** 6 journals and other serials. **Services:** Copying (limited); library open to the public with restrictions. **Automated Operations:** Computerized acquisitions, serials, and circulation. **Computerized Information Services:** OCLC. **Publications:** Mateja Matejic, Hilandar Slavic Codices; Predrag Matejic, Watermarks of the Hilandar Slavic Codices, A Descriptive Catalog; Mateja Matejic and Predrag Matejic, Hilandar Slavic Codices, Supplement Number 1. **Remarks:** FAX: (614)292-7859.

★12311★
Ohio State University - Human Ecology Library (Soc Sci, Food-Bev)
325 Campbell Hall
1787 Neil Ave.   Phone: (614)292-4220
Columbus, OH 43210   Leta Hendricks, Hd.Libn.
Founded: 1962. **Staff:** Prof 1; Other 2. **Subjects:** Family and child development, foods and nutrition, home economics education, home management and family economics, housing and furnishings, textiles and clothing, institution and hospitality management. **Special Collections:** Costume History. **Holdings:** 22,839 books; 4300 pamphlets. **Subscriptions:** 208 journals and other serials. **Services:** Interlibrary loan; copying; library open to the public for reference use only. **Automated Operations:** Computerized public access catalog, cataloging, acquisitions, serials, and circulation. **Computerized Information Services:** Online systems; BITNET (electronic mail service). **Networks/Consortia:** Member of OHIONET, Center for Research Libraries (CRL), Columbus Area Libraries Information Council of Ohio (CALICO). **Remarks:** FAX: (614)292-7859. Electronic mail address(es): HEND@OHSTMAIL (BITNET).

★12312★
Ohio State University - Japanese Collection (Area-Ethnic)
Main Library, Rm. 310
1858 Neil Ave.   Phone: (614)292-3502
Columbus, OH 43210-1286 Maureen H. Donovan, Japanese Stud.Libn.
Founded: 1962. **Staff:** 4.5. **Subjects:** Japan - history and culture. **Holdings:** 50,000 volumes; 4500 microforms. **Subscriptions:** 447 journals and other serials. **Services:** Interlibrary loan; copying; library open to the public. **Computerized Information Services:** OCLC; internal database; InterNet (electronic mail service). **Networks/Consortia:** Member of OHIONET. **Remarks:** FAX: (614)292-7859. Electronic mail address(es): donovan.1@osu.edu (InterNet)

★12313★
Ohio State University - Jerome Lawrence & Robert E. Lee Theatre Research Institute - Library (Theater)
1410 Lincoln Tower
1800 Cannon Dr.   Phone: (614)292-6614
Columbus, OH 43210   Nena Couch, Cur.
Founded: 1951. **Staff:** Prof 2; Other 5. **Subjects:** Theater and theater research. **Special Collections:** McDowell Microfilm Archives (450,000 frames of microfilm of historical theatrical documents); Lawrence & Lee Collection (100 linear feet of manuscripts, books, original cartoons, playbills, photographs); Harmount Uncle Tom's Collection (20 cubic feet of scripts, business records, photographs, scenic drops); Scrapbook Collection (125 scrapbooks); Armbruster Scenic Design Collection (200 renderings); Eileen Heckart Collection (21 linear feet of playscripts, correspondence); Earl Wilson Collection (50 linear feet of manuscripts, photographs, drafts, clippings of Wilson's newspaper column); Robert Breen Collection (200 linear feet of scripts, correspondence, photographs, theater ground plans, posters, clippings, films of 1952-1956 tour of Porgy & Bess and Breen's other activities); Robert A. Wachsman Collection (1 linear feet of photographs, clippings, programs of Porgy & Bess, 1935-1938); Los Angeles Theatre Center Archives (60 linear feet of promptscripts, publicity material, correspondence); Hartman Theatre Collection (16 linear feet of programs, scrapbooks, production files); Horse Cave (KY) Theatre Archives (12 linear feet of promptscripts, business records, correspondence); Ensemble Theatre of Cincinnati (4 linear feet of business records); Contemporary American Theatre Company of Columbus, OH (7 linear feet of business records, designs); Players Theatre Columbus (20 linear feet of business records); original scene and costume designs by Boris Anisfeld, Alexandra Exter, Mordecai Gorelik, Simon Lissim, Susan Benson, Rob ert Edmond Jones, Nancy Adzima, Raoul Pene Dubois, and others. **Holdings:** 2500 books; 330 dissertations; 40 VF drawers of playbills; 28 VF drawers of photographs, correspondence, offprints, publicity material; 8450 original documents (posters; scrapbooks; clippings); 3000 photographs. **Subscriptions:** 15 journals and other serials. **Services:** Copying; library open to the public. **Automated Operations:** Computerized public access catalog, cataloging, acquisitions, and serials. **Computerized Information Services:** OCLC; internal database; BITNET (electronic mail service). **Publications:** Theatre Studies, annual - by subscription. FAX: (614)292-7859. Electronic mail address(es): COUCH@OHSTMVSA.IRCC.OHIO.STATE.EDU (BITNET).

★12314★
Ohio State University - John A. Prior Health Sciences Library (Med)
376 W. 10th Ave.   Phone: (614)292-4861
Columbus, OH 43210   Susan Kroll, Dir.
Founded: 1849. **Staff:** Prof 8.5; Other 27.5. **Subjects:** Clinical medicine, dentistry, nursing, allied health sciences, experimental medicine, optometry. **Holdings:** 196,527 volumes; 4362 government documents. **Subscriptions:** 2169 journals and other serials. **Services:** Interlibrary loan; copying; SDI; library open to the public. **Automated Operations:** Computerized public access catalog, cataloging, acquisitions, serials, and circulation. **Computerized Information Services:** MEDLINE; BITNET (electronic mail service). **Networks/Consortia:** Member of National Network of Libraries of Medicine - Greater Midwest Region, OHIONET. **Publications:** Health Sciences Library Services Bulletin, monthly - to health sciences and library community. **Remarks:** FAX: (614)292-5717. Electronic mail address(es): SKROLL@OHSTMAIL (BITNET). **Staff:** Barbara Van Brimmer, Coll.Dev.Coord.; Pamela Bradigan, Asst.Dir.; Carol Mularski, Online Coord./User. Ed.; Debra Schneider, MHI Coord./Ref.Libn.; Mary Sprague, Ref.Libn.; Marguerite Weibel, Int.Med.

★ 12315 ★
Ohio State University - Journalism Library (Info Sci)
100 Journalism Bldg.
242 W. 18th Ave.   Phone: (614)292-8747
Columbus, OH 43210   Eleanor Block, Hd.Libn.
Founded: 1967. **Staff:** Prof 1; Other 1. **Subjects:** Journalism - newspaper, magazine, radio, television, advertising, public relations, mass communications, cinema. **Holdings:** 27,606 volumes. **Subscriptions:** 190 journals and other serials; 83 newspapers. **Services:** Interlibrary loan; copying; library open to the public for reference use only. **Automated Operations:** Computerized public access catalog, cataloging, acquisitions, serials, and circulation. **Computerized Information Services:** Online systems; BITNET (electronic mail service). **Networks/Consortia:** Member of OHIONET, Center for Research Libraries (CRL), Columbus Area Libraries Information Council of Ohio (CALICO). **Remarks:** FAX: (614)292-7859. Electronic mail address(es): EBLOCK@OHSTMAIL (BITNET).

★ 12316 ★
Ohio State University - Lake Erie Programs Library (Env-Cons)
1314 Kinnear Rd.
Columbus, OH 43212   Phone: (614)292-8949
Subjects: Great Lakes limnology, Lake Erie science and technology, Great Lakes Wetlands, oceanography, water quality and treatment, coastal engineering, hydrology. **Special Collections:** Great Lakes topographic maps and lake survey charts; early 1900s Lake Erie Survey Charts. **Holdings:** Figures not available. **Services:** Library open to the public for reference use only. **Computerized Information Services:** SCIENCEnet (electronic mail service).

★ 12317 ★
Ohio State University - Law Library (Law)
College of Law
1659 N. High St.   Phone: (614)292-6691
Columbus, OH 43210-1391   Bruce Johnson, Dir.
Founded: 1885. **Staff:** Prof 9; Other 12. **Subjects:** Anglo-American law. **Special Collections:** Ohio legal materials. **Holdings:** 449,437 volumes; 570,140 microforms. **Subscriptions:** 7544 journals and other serials. **Services:** Interlibrary loan; copying; library open to the public for legal research. **Automated Operations:** Computerized cataloging. **Computerized Information Services:** WILSONLINE, Hannah Information Systems, WESTLAW, DIALOG Information Services, NEXIS, Dow Jones News/Retrieval, VU/TEXT Information Services, LEXIS; InterNet, BITNET (electronic mail services). **Networks/Consortia:** Member of OHIONET, Ohio Regional Consortium of Law Libraries (ORCLL). **Remarks:** FAX: (614)292-3202. **Staff:** Melanie Putnam, Ref.; Val Bolen, Foreign & Intl. Law Libn.; Carole Hinchcliff, Hd., Acq.Dept.; Thomas G. Spaith, Assoc.Dir.; Nanette Moegerle, Cat.; Helen Horton, Retro.Con.Cat.; Cory Skurdal, Ref.; Christopher Noble, Circ.

★ 12318 ★
Ohio State University - Materials Engineering Library (Sci-Engr)
197 Watts Hall
2041 N. College Rd.   Phone: (614)292-9614
Columbus, OH 43210   Mary Jo Arnold, Hd.Libn.
Founded: 1925. **Staff:** Prof 1; Other 1. **Subjects:** Metallurgic and ceramic engineering; materials science. **Holdings:** 19,374 volumes. **Subscriptions:** 194 journals and other serials. **Services:** Interlibrary loan; copying; library open to the public. **Automated Operations:** Computerized public access catalog, cataloging, acquisitions, serials, and circulation. **Computerized Information Services:** Online systems; BITNET (electronic mail service). **Networks/Consortia:** Member of OHIONET, Center for Research Libraries (CRL), Columbus Area Libraries Information Council of Ohio (CALICO). **Remarks:** FAX: (614)292-7859. Electronic mail address(es): MJA@OHSTMAIL (BITNET).

★ 12319 ★
Ohio State University - Mathematics Library (Sci-Engr)
010 Mathematics Bldg.
231 W. 18th Ave.   Phone: (614)292-2009
Columbus, OH 43210   Mary Scott, Hd.Libn.
Founded: 1962. **Staff:** Prof 1; Other 2. **Subjects:** Advanced mathematics, mathematical statistics, geodetic sciences. **Holdings:** 49,363 volumes; 4750 pamphlets. **Subscriptions:** 570 journals and other serials. **Services:** Interlibrary loan; copying; library open to the public for reference use only.

Automated Operations: Computerized public access catalog, cataloging, acquisitions, serials, and circulation. **Computerized Information Services:** DIALOG Information Services; BITNET (electronic mail service). Performs searches on fee basis. **Networks/Consortia:** Member of OHIONET, Center for Research Libraries (CRL), Columbus Area Libraries Information Council of Ohio (CALICO). **Remarks:** FAX: (614)292-7859. Electronic mail address(es): MSCOTT@OHSTMAIL (BITNET).

★ 12320 ★
Ohio State University - Music/Dance Library (Mus)
186 Sullivant Hall
1813 N. High St.   Phone: (614)292-2319
Columbus, OH 43210   Thomas Heck, Hd.Libn.
Founded: 1946. **Staff:** Prof 2; Other 4. **Subjects:** Music - history, education, theory/composition, performance; dance. **Special Collections:** ABC Radio Collection; Deutsches Musikgeschichtliches Archiv (microfilm collection representing primary source material of German composers published both in Germany and foreign countries and foreign composers living in Germany, 16th and 17th centuries). **Holdings:** 93,308 volumes of music literature and scores; 1224 pamphlets; 1390 microforms; 43,175 phonograph records. **Subscriptions:** 609 journals and other serials. **Services:** Interlibrary loan; library open to the public for reference use only. **Automated Operations:** Computerized public access catalog, cataloging, acquisitions, serials, and circulation. **Computerized Information Services:** Online systems; BITNET (electronic mail service). **Networks/Consortia:** Member of OHIONET, Center for Research Libraries (CRL), Columbus Area Libraries Information Council of Ohio (CALICO). **Remarks:** FAX: (614)292-7859. Electronic mail address(es): TOMHECK@OHSTMAIL (BITNET).

★ 12321 ★
Ohio State University - Ohio Cooperative Fish and Wildlife Research Unit - Library (Biol Sci)
1735 Neil Ave.   Phone: (614)292-6112
Columbus, OH 43210   Dr. Theodore A. Bookhout, Unit Leader
Founded: 1936. **Subjects:** Wildlife and fishery research and management, animal ecology, pesticide-wildlife/fishery relationships. **Holdings:** 300 volumes; 160 theses; 300 unit reprints and releases; 30 VF drawers of other reprints; 2500 35mm color transparencies. **Services:** Interlibrary loan; library open to the public with restrictions.

Ohio State University - Ohio (State) Agricultural Research and Development Center
See: **Ohio (State) Agricultural Research and Development Center - Library (12276)**

★ 12322 ★
Ohio State University - Orton Memorial Library of Geology (Sci-Engr, Geog-Map)
180 Orton Hall
155 S. Oval Mall Dr.   Phone: (614)292-2428
Columbus, OH 43210   Regina Brown, Hd.Libn.
Founded: 1917. **Staff:** Prof 1; Other 1. **Subjects:** Geology, mineralogy, paleontology. **Special Collections:** Geologic maps; U.S. Geological Survey topographic maps (85,000 maps). **Holdings:** 66,635 volumes. **Subscriptions:** 664 journals and other serials. **Services:** Interlibrary loan; copying; collection open to the public for reference use only. **Automated Operations:** Computerized public access catalog, cataloging, acquisitions, serials, and circulation. **Computerized Information Services:** Online systems; BITNET (electronic mail service). **Networks/Consortia:** Member of OHIONET, Center for Research Libraries (CRL), Columbus Area Libraries Information Council of Ohio (CALICO). **Remarks:** FAX: (614)292-7859. Electronic mail address(es): RABROWN@OHSTMAIL (BITNET).

★ 12323 ★
Ohio State University - Perkins Collections at Smith Laboratory and Perkins Observatory (Sci-Engr)
5076 Smith Laboratory
174 W. 18th Ave.   Phone: (614)292-7894
Columbus, OH 43210-1106   Bernard Bayer, Assoc.Prof.
Subjects: Astronomy. **Special Collections:** Sky Charts. **Holdings:** 11,429 books. **Subscriptions:** 75 journals and other serials. **Services:** Interlibrary loan; library open to the public. **Computerized Information Services:** INSPEC, COMPENDEX, DISSERTATION ABSTRACTS ONLINE. **Formerly:** Its Perkins Observatory Library.

★ 12324 ★
Ohio State University - Pharmacy Library (Med)
207 Parks Hall
500 W. 12th Ave.   Phone: (614)292-8026
Columbus, OH 43210   Hazel Benson, Hd.Libn.
Founded: 1930. **Staff:** Prof 1; Other 1. **Subjects:** Pharmacy, pharmaceutical chemistry, pharmacology, pharmacognosy, pharmacy administration. **Holdings:** 33,759 volumes; 2100 pamphlets. **Subscriptions:** 443 journals and other serials. **Services:** Interlibrary loan; library open to the public for reference use only. **Automated Operations:** Computerized public access catalog, cataloging, acquisitions, serials, and circulation. **Computerized Information Services:** Online systems; BITNET (electronic mail service). **Networks/Consortia:** Member of OHIONET, Center for Research Libraries (CRL), Columbus Area Libraries Information Council of Ohio (CALICO). **Remarks:** FAX: (614)292-7859. Electronic mail address(es): HBENSON@OHSTMAIL (BITNET). **Also Known As:** Virginia B. Hall Pharmacy Library.

★ 12325 ★
Ohio State University - Social Work Library (Soc Sci)
400 Stillman Hall
1947 College Rd.   Phone: (614)292-6627
Columbus, OH 43210   Jennifer Kuehn, Hd.Libn.
Founded: 1938. **Staff:** Prof 1; Other 1. **Subjects:** Social work education, criminology, social group work, family, social casework, mental health. **Holdings:** 41,315 volumes; 700 pamphlets. **Subscriptions:** 271 journals and other serials. **Services:** Interlibrary loan; copying; library open to the public. **Automated Operations:** Computerized public access catalog, cataloging, acquisitions, serials, and circulation. **Computerized Information Services:** BRS Information Technologies; BITNET (electronic mail service). **Networks/Consortia:** Member of OHIONET, Center for Research Libraries (CRL), Columbus Area Libraries Information Council of Ohio (CALICO). **Remarks:** FAX: (614)292-7859. Electronic mail address(es): KUEHN@OHSTMAIL (BITNET).

★ 12326 ★
Ohio State University - Veterinary Medicine Library (Med)
229 Sisson Hall
1900 Coffey Rd.   Phone: (614)292-6107
Columbus, OH 43210   Norma Bruce, Hd.Libn.
Founded: 1929. **Staff:** Prof 1; Other 1. **Subjects:** Veterinary medicine, medicine, pharmacology, biochemistry, comparative medicine. **Holdings:** 41,344 volumes. **Subscriptions:** 549 journals and other serials. **Services:** Interlibrary loan; copying; library open to the public for reference use only. **Automated Operations:** Computerized public access catalog, cataloging, acquisitions, serials, and circulation. **Computerized Information Services:** Online systems; BITNET (electronic mail service). **Networks/Consortia:** Member of OHIONET, Center for Research Libraries (CRL), Columbus Area Libraries Information Council of Ohio (CALICO). **Remarks:** FAX: (614)292-7859. Electronic mail address(es): NBRUCE@OHSTMAIL (BITNET).

★ 12327 ★
Ohio State University - Women's Studies Collection (Soc Sci)
220 Main Library
1858 Neil Ave. Mall   Phone: (614)292-3035
Columbus, OH 43210   Linda Krikos, Hd., Women's Stud.Lib.
Founded: 1977. **Staff:** Prof 1; Other 1. **Subjects:** Women's studies. **Holdings:** 15,000 volumes; 2500 pamphlets and newsletters; 50 microform collections. **Subscriptions:** 100 journals and other serials. **Services:** Interlibrary loan; copying; SDI; collection open to the public for reference use only. **Automated Operations:** Computerized cataloging, serials, and circulation. **Computerized Information Services:** Online systems. **Publications:** Feminisms, (in conjunction with the Center for Women's Studies). **Remarks:** FAX: (614)292-7859.

★ 12328 ★
Ohio University - Department of Archives and Special Collections - Alden Library (Rare Book, Hist)
Park Place   Phone: (614)593-2710
Athens, OH 45701-2978   George W. Bain, Hd.
Founded: 1963. **Staff:** Prof 3; Other 1. **Subjects:** History of Ohio University and Southeastern Ohio; rare books and manuscripts; English literature, 1760-1830 and 1880-1930; 18th century English drama. **Special Collections:** Ohio University Archives (5800 linear feet); Morgan Collection of the History of Chemistry and Science (1650 volumes); Ohioana Collection (1700 volumes); Osteopathic Medicine Collection; Edmund Blunden Collection of Romantic and Georgian Literature (10,000 volumes); author collections including: Arnold Bennett, Thomas Campbell, William Combe, William Cowper, George Crabbe, Charles Dickens, Samuel Foote, John Galsworthy, Lafcadio Hearn, Maurice Hewlett, Thomas Hood, Leigh Hunt, Rudyard Kipling, Arthur Machen, George Moore, Samuel Rogers, John Ruskin, Alfred Tennyson, H.G. Wells, Henry Miller; Cornelius Ryan Memorial Collection of World War II Papers (90 cubic feet); United Mine Workers - District 6 (35 cubic feet); E.W. Scripps papers (60 cubic feet); Sammy Kaye papers (90 cubic feet); Columbus & Hocking Coal & Iron Co. (80 cubic feet); Tri-County Community Action Agency (25 cubic feet). **Holdings:** 49,000 volumes; 2400 linear feet of local government records; 1500 linear feet of private papers; 30,500 photographs and slides; 960 maps. **Subscriptions:** 115 journals and other serials. **Services:** Interlibrary loan; copying; archives open to the public. **Automated Operations:** Computerized cataloging and circulation. **Computerized Information Services:** OCLC. **Networks/Consortia:** Member of Ohio Network of American History Research Centers (ONARCH). **Publications:** Guide to Local Government Records at Ohio University Library; brochures. **Special Catalogs:** Manuscript inventories and card catalog; rare book card catalog. **Remarks:** FAX: (614)593-2959. **Staff:** Sheppard Black, Spec.Coll.Libn.; William M. Rhinehart, Rec.Mgr.

★ 12329 ★
Ohio University - Fine Arts Collection (Art)
Alden Library   Phone: (614)593-2663
Athens, OH 45701   Anne Braxton, Fine Arts Libn.
Founded: 1962. **Staff:** Prof 1; Other 1. **Subjects:** Art, architecture, photography, film. **Holdings:** 52,000 volumes; 24,000 microfiche; 7000 study plates. **Subscriptions:** 300 journals and other serials. **Services:** Interlibrary loan; copying; collection open to the public. **Automated Operations:** Computerized cataloging. **Computerized Information Services:** OCLC. **Networks/Consortia:** Member of OHIONET. **Remarks:** FAX: (614)593-2959.

★ 12330 ★
Ohio University - Health Sciences Library (Med)
Athens, OH 45701   Phone: (614)593-2680
                                   Anne S. Goss, Dir.
Founded: 1977. **Staff:** Prof 3; Other 30. **Subjects:** Medicine, nursing, psychology, basic sciences, allied health fields. **Special Collections:** Osteopathic medicine (350 books). **Holdings:** 37,244 books; 36,818 bound periodical volumes; 22,526 government documents; 14,291 microfiche. **Subscriptions:** 1679 journals and other serials. **Services:** Interlibrary loan; copying; SDI; library open to the public. **Automated Operations:** Computerized cataloging, acquisitions, circulation, and ILL. **Computerized Information Services:** DIALOG Information Services, MEDLARS; CD-ROMs; internal database; BITNET (electronic mail service). Performs searches on fee basis. **Networks/Consortia:** Member of National Network of Libraries of Medicine - Greater Midwest Region. **Publications:** Shelf Life. **Special Indexes:** Printout of journal holdings. **Remarks:** FAX: (614)593-4693. **Staff:** Jeff Ferrier, Asst.Libn.; Barbara J. Wilkus, Ref.Libn.; Cheryl Ewing, Sr.Lib.Assoc.

★ 12331 ★
Ohio University - Map Collection (Geog-Map)
Alden Library   Phone: (614)593-2659
Athens, OH 45701   Theodore Foster, Map Libn.
Founded: 1960. **Staff:** Prof 1; Other 1. **Subjects:** Maps - U.S. Geological Survey, Defense Mapping Agency, Army Mapping Service, Federal Depository Library Program, Indonesia. **Holdings:** 153,808 maps. **Services:** Interlibrary loan; copying; collection open to the public. **Computerized Information Services:** OCLC, DIALOG Information Services, BRS Information Technologies, WILSONLINE, MEDLARS. Performs searches on fee basis. Contact Person: Nancy Rue, 593-2696. **Networks/Consortia:** Member of OHIONET. **Remarks:** FAX: (614)593-2959.

★ 12332 ★
Ohio University - Music/Dance Library (Mus)
Music Bldg.   Phone: (614)594-4255
Athens, OH 45701   Dr. Holly Oberle, Libn.
Founded: 1963. **Staff:** Prof 1; Other 1.5. **Subjects:** Music, dance. **Special Collections:** Collection of Early American Sheet Music. **Holdings:** 34,000 books and scores; 600 bound periodical volumes; 26,000 recordings; college

catalogs; microforms; video cassettes; Catalog of Copyright Entries (Music) and Revision Studies. **Subscriptions:** 125 journals and other serials. **Services:** Interlibrary loan; copying; SDI; listening and microcomputer facilities; library open to residents within Athens County. **Automated Operations:** Computerized cataloging and circulation. **Computerized Information Services:** DIALOG Information Services, BRS Information Technologies, WILSONLINE, OCLC; CD-ROMs. Performs searches on fee basis. **Remarks:** FAX: (614)593-2959. **Staff:** Martha Vickers, Sr.Lib.Assoc.; Rebecca Lanning, Sr.Lib.Asst.

★ 12333 ★
Ohio University - Southeast Asia Collection (Area-Ethnic)
Alden Library   Phone: (614)593-2658
Athens, OH 45701   Lian The-Mulliner, Hd.
Founded: 1967. **Staff:** Prof 5; Other 3. **Subjects:** Southeast Asia, with emphasis on Malaysia, Brunei, Singapore, Indonesia, and other members of the Association of Southeast Asian Nations (ASEAN). **Holdings:** 66,000 books; 7800 bound periodical volumes; 8 VF drawers of clippings on Malaysia and Singapore; 6 VF drawers of pamphlets on Southeast Asia; 39,158 titles in microform. **Subscriptions:** 5236 journals and other serials; 12 newspapers. **Services:** Interlibrary loan; copying; collection open to the public. **Automated Operations:** Computerized public access catalog, cataloging, and circulation. **Computerized Information Services:** DIALOG Information Services, BRS Information Technologies, OCLC; CD-ROMs; internal database. **Networks/Consortia:** Member of OHIONET. **Publications:** Malaysia/Singapore/Brunei/Asean Bibliography, quarterly. **Remarks:** FAX: (614)593-2959. **Staff:** Swee-Lan Quah, Cat.; Lindsey Reber, Res.Bibliog.; Siew-Ben Chin, Cat.; Cheng-Yen Khoo, Cat.; David Miller, Cat.Assoc.; Kiersten Cox, Acq.Asst.; Lucy Conn, Ref.Assoc.

★ 12334 ★
Ohio Valley General Hospital - Professional Library (Med)
Heckel Rd.   Phone: (412)777-6159
McKee's Rock, PA 15136   Heidi Marshall, Libn.
Staff: Prof 1. **Subjects:** Nursing, medicine. **Holdings:** 1925 volumes. **Subscriptions:** 135 journals and other serials. **Services:** Interlibrary loan; copying; SDI; library open to the public. **Computerized Information Services:** MEDLINE. **Networks/Consortia:** Member of Pittsburgh-East Hospital Library Cooperative. **Publications:** Library Bulletin, monthly; Library News, bimonthly. **Remarks:** FAX: (412)777-6363.

★ 12335 ★
Ohio Valley Hospital - Health Sciences Library (Med)
One Ross Park
Steubenville, OH 43952   Phone: (614)283-7400
Staff: Prof 1; Other 5. **Subjects:** Medicine, nursing. **Special Collections:** Pre-1900 Rare medical books. **Holdings:** 1968 books; 2731 bound periodical volumes; 4 theses; 4 VF drawers of pamphlets; 277 filmstrip/tape sets and slide/tape sets; 35 slide sets; 16 overhead transparencies; 276 videotapes; 5 films; 14 charts; 29 audio cassettes; 45 models. **Subscriptions:** 68 journals and other serials. **Services:** Interlibrary loan; copying; library open to the public for reference use only when librarian is present. **Computerized Information Services:** MEDLINE. **Networks/Consortia:** Member of National Network of Libraries of Medicine - Greater Midwest Region, NEOUCOM Council Associated Hospital Librarians. **Publications:** Library Line, quarterly - for internal distribution only. **Special Catalogs:** Resources and Facilities Handbook, annual; Hospital Library Manual.

★ 12336 ★
Ohio Valley Medical Center - Hupp Medical Library (Med)
2000 Eoff St.   Phone: (304)234-8771
Wheeling, WV 26003   Janis Quinlisk, Med.Libn.
Founded: 1915. **Staff:** Prof 2. **Subjects:** Surgery, internal medicine, obstetrics, gynecology, radiology, hospital administration, pediatrics. **Special Collections:** History of Medicine; Osterman Collection (psychiatry). **Holdings:** 3580 books; 4038 bound periodical volumes; 2293 unbound journals; 830 audio cassettes; 66 video cassettes. **Subscriptions:** 289 journals and other serials. **Services:** Interlibrary loan; copying; library open to the public for reference use only. **Automated Operations:** Computerized ILL (DOCLINE). **Computerized Information Services:** MEDLINE. Performs searches on fee basis. **Publications:** Access. **Special Catalogs:** Audiovisual catalog. **Staff:** Erin Phillips, Asst.Libn.

★ 12337 ★
Ohioana Library Association - Ohioana Library (Hum)
1105 Ohio Departments Bldg.
65 S. Front St.   Phone: (614)466-3831
Columbus, OH 43215   Linda R. Hengst, Dir.
Founded: 1929. **Staff:** Prof 1. **Subjects:** Ohio history, literature and music by or about Ohioans. **Special Collections:** Complete works of William Dean Howells, Sherwood Anderson, Louis Bromfield, and other prominent Ohio authors; "grass roots" poetry; county histories and atlases. **Holdings:** 30,000 books; 200 bound periodical volumes; 10,000 musical compositions; 13 VF drawers of clippings about current Ohio subjects; 28 VF drawers of pamphlets; 69 linear feet of scrapbooks containing biographical information about Ohio authors, artists, composers; manuscripts. **Subscriptions:** 30 journals and other serials. **Services:** Copying; reference by mail; library open to the public for reference use only. **Networks/Consortia:** Member of Columbus Area Libraries Information Council of Ohio (CALICO). **Publications:** Ohioana Quarterly. Each issue of the Ohioana Quarterly includes a bibliography of books and music by or about Ohioans. **Staff:** Barbara Maslekoff, Libn./Ed.

★ 12338 ★
Ohr Kodesh Congregation - Sisterhood Library (Area-Ethnic)
8402 Freyman Dr.   Phone: (301)589-3880
Chevy Chase, MD 20015-3897   Rebecca Mazur, Libn.
Founded: 1965. **Staff:** Prof 1. **Subjects:** Judaica. **Holdings:** 3700 books. **Subscriptions:** 3 journals and other serials. **Services:** Library open to the public for reference use only.

Elizabeth J. Ohrstrom Library
See: **University of Virginia - Medical Center - Department of Neurology** (19506)

★ 12339 ★
Oil Information Library of Wichita Falls (Sci-Engr)
100 Energy Center
710 Lamar   Phone: (817)322-4241
Wichita Falls, TX 76301   Gail Baldon Phillips, Libn.
Founded: 1966. **Staff:** 3. **Subjects:** Oil and gas records, geological information, exploration and development material, well data. **Special Collections:** Original Bess Mason Log File (500,000); Independent Operators and Major Oil Companies electric log files (115,000); Texas Railroad Commission electric logs from Districts 9 and 7B (20,000; microfilm). **Holdings:** 450 books; 150 boxes of microfilm of scout information; 280 miscellaneous county maps; 14 boxes of microfilm of logs; 175 miscellaneous geology maps and plats; 400 VF drawers of miscellaneous oil information. **Services:** Copying; library open to the public with restrictions. **Computerized Information Services:** Petroleum Information. **Remarks:** FAX: (817)322-8695.

Oil Spill Information Center Archives
See: **University of California, Santa Barbara - Sciences-Engineering Library** (18434)

★ 12340 ★
Oil Spill Public Information Center - Library (Env-Cons)
645 G St.   Phone: (907)278-8008
Anchorage, AK 99501   Mary McGee
Founded: 1990. **Staff:** Prof 3; Other 2. **Subjects:** Exxon Valdez oil spill; oil spills in a marine environment. **Special Collections:** Scientific data from Exxon Valdez oil spill damage. **Holdings:** 1500 books; 600 reports; 6 archival collections; 209 microfiche; 12 reels of microfilm; 350 videotapes. **Subscriptions:** 78 journals and other serials. **Services:** Interlibrary loan; copying; library open to the public. **Computerized Information Services:** WLN, DIALOG Information Services, VU/TEXT Information Services, LEXIS, NEXIS; internal database. Contact Person: Peg Thompson, Tech.Serv.Libn. **Remarks:** FAX: (907)276-7178. Toll-free telephone number(s): (800)283-7745 (Alaska only); (800)478-7745 (outside Alaska).

C.G. O'Kelly Library
See: **Winston-Salem State University** (20496)

★12341★

Oklahoma City - Metropolitan Library System - Children's Literature Collection (Hum)
131 Dean A. McGee Ave.   Phone: (405)235-0571
Oklahoma City, OK 73102   Lee B. Brawner
Founded: 1966. **Special Collections:** Collection of early editions of children's books containing illustrations by famous illustrators (822 volumes). **Services:** Interlibrary loan; copying; library open to the public for reference use only. **Automated Operations:** Computerized public access catalog. **Computerized Information Services:** EasyNet, DataTimes.

★12342★

Oklahoma City Art Museum - Library (Art)
3113 Pershing Blvd.   Phone: (405)946-4477
Oklahoma City, OK 73107   Chris Young, Musm.Dir.
Subjects: 17th-20th century American art; 14th-20th century European art. **Holdings:** 7000 volumes. **Services:** Library open to the public on a limited schedule with restrictions. **Remarks:** FAX: (405)946-7671.

★12343★

Oklahoma City University - Law Library (Law)
2501 N. Blackwelder   Phone: (405)521-5271
Oklahoma City, OK 73106   Judith Morgan, Law Libn.
Founded: 1956. **Staff:** Prof 4; Other 5. **Subjects:** Law. **Holdings:** 197,486 books. **Subscriptions:** 2658 journals and other serials. **Services:** Interlibrary loan; library open to the public. **Computerized Information Services:** WESTLAW, LEXIS, OCLC, DIALOG Information Services. **Networks/Consortia:** Member of AMIGOS Bibliographic Council, Inc., Mid-America Law School Library Consortium. **Remarks:** FAX: (405)521-5172. **Staff:** Nancy Smith, Hd., Tech.Serv.; Patricia Monk, Hd., Pub.Serv.; Frances Deathe, Ref.

★12344★

Oklahoma City Zoo - Florence O. Wilson Zoological Library (Biol Sci)
2101 N.E. 50th   Phone: (405)424-3344
Oklahoma City, OK 73111   Joyce Donham, Educ.Cur.
Subjects: Zoology, natural history. **Holdings:** 4400 books. **Subscriptions:** 40 journals and other serials. **Services:** Library not open to the public.

Oklahoma College of Osteopathic Medicine & Surgery - Library
See: Oklahoma State University - College of Osteopathic Medicine - Medical Library (12364)

★12345★

Oklahoma County Law Library (Law)
County Courthouse, Rm. 247
321 Park Ave.   Phone: (405)236-2727
Oklahoma City, OK 73102   Ursula Merhib, Adm.
Staff: Prof 1; Other 2. **Subjects:** Law. **Holdings:** 28,983 books; 21,682 microfiche. **Subscriptions:** 38 journals and other serials. **Services:** Copying; library open to the public. **Remarks:** Alternate telephone number(s): 278-1355.

★12346★

Oklahoma Gas and Electric Company - Library (Energy, Sci-Engr)
P.O. Box 321   Phone: (405)272-3100
Oklahoma City, OK 73101   Pam Lee, Libn.
Founded: 1928. **Staff:** 1. **Subjects:** Engineering, electronics, mathematics, management, communication, environment, accident prevention, chemistry, physics, private and public power. **Special Collections:** Oklahoma history; the free enterprise system; world power resources; electrical engineering (185 volumes); American Society of Testing and Materials standards. **Holdings:** 5000 volumes. **Subscriptions:** 124 journals and other serials. **Services:** Interlibrary loan; library open to the public for reference use only. **Automated Operations:** Computerized circulation. **Remarks:** Library located at 321 N. Harvey Ave., Oklahoma City, OK, 73102-3499.

★12347★

Oklahoma Geological Survey - Oklahoma Geophysical Observatory Library (Sci-Engr)
Box 8   Phone: (918)366-4152
Leonard, OK 74043-0008   Charles J. Mankin, Dir.
Founded: 1960. **Staff:** Prof 1; Other 4. **Subjects:** Seismology, nuclear test ban treaty verification by seismic methods, geomagnetism, aeronomy, meteorology, solar radiation. **Special Collections:** 50 geophysical records are currently recorded on a continuous (24 hour, 7 day) basis (250,000 record days in archives); seismic data (20 gigabytes, currently increasing 1 gigabyte per week). **Holdings:** 300 books; 1500 other cataloged items. **Subscriptions:** 30 data bulletins. **Services:** Interlibrary loan; library open to the public if advance arrangements are made with the chief geophysicist. **Computerized Information Services:** Oklahoma and regional earthquakes, geomagnetic database (internal databases); electronic mail service. Contact Person: J.E. Lawson, Jr., Chf. Geophysicist. **Publications:** P/PKP Arrival Bulletin, biweekly; Phase Amplitude Bulletin, biweekly. **Remarks:** FAX: (918)366-4152. Observatory was previously operated as Leonard Earth Sciences Observatory by the Jersey Production Corporation until 1965, when it was donated to the University of Oklahoma. In 1978 it was transferred to the Oklahoma Geological Survey.

★12348★

Oklahoma Historical Society - Archives and Manuscript Division (Hist)
Historical Bldg.   Phone: (405)521-2491
Oklahoma City, OK 73105   William D. Welge, Dir.
Founded: 1893. **Staff:** Prof 5; Other 8. **Subjects:** Oklahoma and Indian territories, Indian tribes of Oklahoma, pioneer life, missionaries, territorial court records, explorers. **Special Collections:** Records from all state Indian agencies, except Osage Agency (3.5 million document pages; 6000 volumes); Dawes Commission Records (48 cubic feet; 242 bound volumes); Indian-Pioneer History (interviews; 112 volumes); Whipple Collection (8 cubic feet); Joseph Thoburn Collection (20 cubic feet). **Holdings:** 2900 reels of microfilm of Indian and Oklahoma affairs; 125,000 historical photographs; 28,000 reels of microfilm of newspapers; 4500 oral history tapes. **Subscriptions:** 10 journals and other serials. **Services:** Copying; archives open to the public. **Publications:** Microfilm of original materials for sale. **Special Catalogs:** Catalog listing films for sale. **Special Indexes:** Inventories of Five Civilized Tribes documents; card index of Indian-Pioneer History. **Remarks:** FAX: (405)525-3272. **Staff:** Sandi Smith, Indian Rec.Archv.; Joe Todd, Ms.Archv.; Chester Cowen, Photo.Archv.; Rodger Harris, Oral Hist.; Judith Michener, Archv.

★12349★

Oklahoma Historical Society - Chickasaw Council House Library (Hist)
Court House Square
Box 717   Phone: (405)371-3351
Tishomingo, OK 73460   Faye Orr, Historic Property Mgr.
Founded: 1970. **Staff:** 2. **Subjects:** Chickasaw Indian history, biographies, and statistics. **Special Collections:** Oklahoma Chronicles - Chickasaw Constitution and law books. **Holdings:** 1200 books; 150 maps; county and Chickasaw Nation records; 70 reels of microfilm; pamphlets. **Services:** Library open to the public. **Staff:** Vickie Luster.

★12350★

Oklahoma Historical Society - Division of Library Resources (Hist)
Wiley Post Historical Bldg.   Phone: (405)521-2491
Oklahoma City, OK 73105   Edward Connie Shoemaker, Lib.Dir.
Founded: 1929. **Staff:** Prof 2; Other 8. **Subjects:** Oklahoma and American Indian history, American west, Oklahoma genealogy. **Holdings:** 59,500 books; 10,600 reels of microfilm of U.S. Census, 1790-1910; 25,000 reels of microfilm of Oklahoma newspapers, 1893 to present. **Subscriptions:** 300 journals and other serials; 280 newspapers. **Services:** Copying; library open to the public for research use only. **Automated Operations:** Computerized cataloging. **Computerized Information Services:** OCLC. **Remarks:** FAX: (405)525-3272. **Staff:** Mary Huffman, Supv., Pub.Serv.

★12351★

Oklahoma Historical Society - Museum of the Western Prairie - Bernice Ford Price Reference Library (Hist)
1100 N. Hightower
Box 574   Phone: (405)482-1044
Altus, OK 73522   Frances Herron, Libn.
Founded: 1982. **Staff:** 1. **Subjects:** History of southwest Oklahoma, pioneer families, Plains Indians, cowboys, early settlers. **Special Collections:** Long

Collection (Indians of southwest); Dr. E.E. Dale History Collection; first editions of Oklahoma University Press. **Holdings:** 1500 books; 100 bound periodical volumes; documents; oral history tapes; archival collections; photographs. **Subscriptions:** 18 journals and other serials. **Services:** Copying; SDI; library open to the public for reference use only. **Publications:** Mistletoe Leaves (newsletter), monthly - to the public.

★ 12352 ★
Oklahoma Junior College - Learning Resource Center (Bus-Fin)
7370 E. 71st St.   Phone: (918)459-0200
Tulsa, OK 74133   Jan Riggs, Dir. of Lrng.Rsrcs.
Founded: 1916. **Staff:** Prof 2. **Subjects:** Business, accounting, business law, secretarial science, computer science, medical assistance, travel and airlines, electronic technology, paralegal professions, graphic arts. **Holdings:** 13,000 books; 6 VF drawers of pamphlets; 150 cassettes; 3 boxes of microfiche. **Subscriptions:** 198 journals and other serials. **Services:** Interlibrary loan; copying; center open to the public with circulation limited to associate members. **Networks/Consortia:** Member of Tulsa Area Library Cooperative (TALC). **Remarks:** FAX: (918)250-4526.

★ 12353 ★
Oklahoma Regional Library for the Blind and Physically Handicapped (Aud-Vis)
300 N.E. 18th St.   Phone: (405)521-3514
Oklahoma City, OK 73105   Geraldine Adams, Lib.Dir.
Founded: 1933. **Staff:** Prof 5; Other 21. **Subjects:** Recreational and informational reading materials in special media collections. **Special Collections:** Locally recorded books on cassette (1400 titles); large print books (1000 titles); LP textbooks (580). **Holdings:** 165,000 books; magnetic tapes; microfiche. **Subscriptions:** 56 journals and other serials. **Services:** Interlibrary loan; recording and brailling of textbooks; library not open to the public. **Automated Operations:** Computerized circulation. **Networks/Consortia:** Member of National Library Service for the Blind & Physically Handicapped (NLS). **Publications:** Bright Future; newsletter, quarterly. **Special Catalogs:** Catalog for locally produced cassette books (card); braille catalog for braille books other than those produced by the Library of Congress; LP catalog. **Remarks:** Maintained by the Oklahoma State Department of Human Services. **Staff:** Joan Shelton, Libn.; David Slemmons, Libn. ; Linda Boyd, Libn.; Gerri Beeson, Volunteer Coord.; James Gillespie, Automation Supv.; Paul Adams, Machine Lending Agency.

★ 12354 ★
Oklahoma School for the Blind - Parkview Library (Aud-Vis)
3300 Gibson St.   Phone: (918)682-6641
Muskogee, OK 74402-0309   Shonda Konemann, Lib.-Media Spec.
Founded: 1913. **Staff:** 1. **Subjects:** Books in braille and talking books; large print books; braille and large print magazines. **Special Collections:** Education of the blind. **Holdings:** 8013 titles; 840 talking books; cassettes and disks. **Subscriptions:** 81 journals and other serials. **Services:** Interlibrary loan; library open to blind, partially-sighted, and multi-handicapped persons. **Computerized Information Services:** Special Net (internal database). **Remarks:** Maintained by Oklahoma State Department of Human Services.

★ 12355 ★
Oklahoma School for the Deaf - Library (Educ)
E. 10th. and Tahlequah   Phone: (405)622-3186
Sulphur, OK 73086   Steve Whitchey, Libn.
Remarks: No further information was supplied by respondent.

★ 12356 ★
Oklahoma (State) Department of Commerce - Energy Conservation Services Division - Technical Information Center (Energy)
P.O. Box 26980   Phone: (405)841-9365
Oklahoma City, OK 73126-0980   Deborah Keith
Staff: Prof 1; Other 1. **Subjects:** Energy conservation, renewable energy. **Holdings:** 1000 books. **Services:** Center open to the public with restrictions. **Publications:** Winter Survival; Cold Weather Spells Danger; Heat Stress: what you should know about heat disorders; Hot Weather Spells Danger; Keep Your Peach Out of the Pits - Winter Car Care; Choosing & Using Your Gas Space Heater - all brochures.

★ 12357 ★
Oklahoma (State) Department of Corrections - Planning and Research Unit - Library (Law)
3400 Martin Luther King Ave.   Phone: (405)425-2590
Oklahoma City, OK 73111   Ruthie Steele, Exec.Sec.
Subjects: Criminal justice. **Holdings:** 2000 books. **Services:** Interlibrary loan; copying; library open to the public. **Automated Operations:** Computerized cataloging. **Remarks:** FAX: (405)425-2064.

★ 12358 ★
Oklahoma (State) Department of Health - Information & Referral Healthline (Med)
1000 N.E. 10th St.
Box 53551   Phone: (405)271-5600
Oklahoma City, OK 73152   Janet Smith, Dir.
Founded: 1938. **Staff:** 1. **Subjects:** Medicine, nursing, psychology, personal health, epidemiology, venereal disease. **Holdings:** 2500 volumes; 90,000 general health pamphlets covering approximately 300 areas. **Subscriptions:** 30 journals and other serials. **Services:** Department open to the public with restrictions.

Oklahoma State Department of Human Services - Oklahoma School for the Blind
See: Oklahoma School for the Blind (12354)

Oklahoma State Department of Human Services - Regional Library for the Blind and Physically Handicapped
See: Oklahoma Regional Library for the Blind and Physically Handicapped (12353)

★ 12359 ★
Oklahoma (State) Department of Libraries (Hist, Law, Info Sci)
200 N.E. 18th St.   Phone: (405)521-2502
Oklahoma City, OK 73105   Robert L. Clark, Jr., Dir.
Founded: 1890. **Staff:** Prof 40; Other 45. **Subjects:** Law; legislative reference materials; Oklahoma government, history, authors; librarianship; juvenile evaluation collection. **Special Collections:** Oklahoma Collection (11,500 titles). **Holdings:** 309,757 books; 27,323 cubic feet of state archives and manuscript collections; 28,000 cubic feet of state records; 841,508 linear feet of U.S. Government documents (regional depository); 34,095 Oklahoma document titles; 2195 films; 140,000 reels of microfilm; 273 videotapes; 150,000 microfiche titles; 257 file drawers of pamphlets and clippings. **Subscriptions:** 2604 journals and other serials; 25 newspapers. **Services:** Interlibrary loan; legislative and law reference; archival and state research assistance; department open to the public for reference use only; loans made to state agency personnel only. **Automated Operations:** Computerized cataloging, acquisitions, and circulation. **Computerized Information Services:** OCLC, DIALOG Information Services, LEXIS, Mead Data Central, BRS Information Technologies, DataTimes, AgriData Network; legislature's index to statutes, attorney general's opinions (internal databases); ALANET (electronic mail service). **Networks/Consortia:** Member of AMIGOS Bibliographic Council, Inc., Western Council of State Libraries. **Publications:** Who Is Who in the Oklahoma Legislature; Annual Report of Oklahoma Libraries; Oklahoma Register (administrative rules and regulations); Annual Directory of Oklahoma Libraries; Biographies of Governors of Oklahoma; ODL Record; ODL Archives, quarterly; Directory of Oklahoma, biennial; Lawdocs, quarterly; GPO: Government Publications for Oklahoma, bimonthly; Oklahoma State Agencies, Boards, Commissions, Courts, Institutions, Legislature and Officers; ODL Source (newsletter), monthly; Oklahoma Government Publications (checklist), quarterly; Informacion; Healthdocs; Biodex. **Remarks:** FAX: (405)525-7804. Electronic mail address(es): ALA1849 (ALANET). **Staff:** Denny Stephens, Dp.Dir.; Linda Ables, State Rec.; Steve Beleu, U.S.Govt.Docs.; Chris Bittle, State Rec.; Jan Blakely, Spec.Proj.; Mike Bruno, Inst.Cons.; Freda Chen, Cat.; Chi Ching-Yu, Cat.; Judith Clarke, Law Libn.; Donna Denniston, State Agencies Liaison; Ginny Dietrich, Pub.Lib.Cons.; Dean Doerr, Constr.Cons.; Sandy Ellison, Pub.Lib.Cons.; Karen Fite, Ref.Libn.; Leslie Gelders, Literacy; Susan Gilley, Leg.Ref.; Allan Goode, Law Libn.; Carol Guilliams, Archv.; Mary Hardick, Law Libn.; Mary Hardin, OTIS ILL/Ref.; Gary Harrington, Archv.; Beverly Jones, Network/TeleCommun.; Tom Kremm, Archv. & Rec.; Susan McVey, Law & Leg.Ref.; Vicki Mohr, Pub.Lib.Cons.; Marian Patmon, Pub.Serv.; Kitty Pittman, Ref.Libn.; Donna Skvarla, Lib.Dev.; Vicki Sullivan, OK Docs.; Marilyn Vesely, Pub.Info.; Ann Hamilton, OK Ctr. for the Bk.; Cathy Wade, Law Libn.; Bob Rankin, State Rec.; Linda Raulston, State Rec.; W.C. Boone, Archv.; Peter Dowds, State Rec.; Gary Phillips, Lib.Cons.

★12360★

Oklahoma (State) Department of Vocational and Technical Education - Resource Center (Educ)
1500 W. 7th Ave.   Phone: (405)743-5161
Stillwater, OK 74074   Denise Dow, Rsrc.Ctr.Mgr.
Founded: 1970. **Staff:** Prof 2; Other 2. **Subjects:** Vocational-technical materials, philosophy of vocational education, curriculum development, career education materials. **Special Collections:** History of Vocational Education in Oklahoma; bilingual vocational education materials. **Holdings:** 10,000 books; 1200 pamphlets; 876 videotapes. **Subscriptions:** 140 journals and other serials. **Services:** Copying; SDI and ERIC search service (to state staff and Oklahoma vocational teachers); video cassettes circulated free of charge to Oklahoma state vocational teachers on a reservation basis; center open to the public. **Automated Operations:** Computerized public access catalog, cataloging, and circulation. **Computerized Information Services:** BRS Information Technologies; Adult and Vocational Educational Electronic Mail Network (ADVOCNET; electronic mail service). **Publications:** Bibliographies. **Remarks:** Main purpose is to maintain collection of current materials in subject areas in which vocational instruction or support is offered. FAX: (405)743-5142. Electronic mail address(es): AVO 4602 (ADVOCNET).

★12361★

Oklahoma State University - Architecture Branch (Art)
University Library   Phone: (405)744-6047
Stillwater, OK 74078-0375   Teresa Fehlig, Arch.Libn.
Founded: 1978. **Staff:** Prof 1; Other 1. **Subjects:** Architecture, landscape architecture. **Holdings:** 9923 books; 2155 bound periodical volumes. **Subscriptions:** 47 journals and other serials. **Services:** Interlibrary loan; copying; branch open to the public with restrictions. **Computerized Information Services:** DIALOG Information Services, OCLC. **Remarks:** FAX: (405)744-5183.

★12362★

Oklahoma State University - Audio-Visual Center (Aud-Vis)
Stillwater, OK 74078-0383   Phone: (405)744-7212
    Dr. Ron G. Payne, Dir.
Staff: Prof 1; Other 47. **Holdings:** 4700 16mm films; 300 audiotape masters; 517 video cassettes. **Services:** Copying; SDI; audio recording and duplication; rental and repair; consultations and workshops in various areas of AV communications and operations; films and video cassettes available on rental basis; center open to the public. **Automated Operations:** Computerized cataloging and circulation. **Networks/Consortia:** Member of Consortium of College and University Media Centers (CCUMC). **Special Catalogs:** Film Rental Catalog (regional); Locator III Catalog, both every 3 years; special catalogs by subject and grade level. **Remarks:** FAX: (405)744-8445.

★12363★

Oklahoma State University - College of Arts and Sciences - Oklahoma Data Archive (Soc Sci)
Stillwater, OK 74078   Phone: (405)744-5569
    Prof. Robert Darcy
Founded: 1977. **Staff:** 1. **Subjects:** Social sciences. **Holdings:** 200 bound volumes; 200 data sets on magnetic tape. **Services:** Archive open to faculty and student researchers at Oklahoma State University. **Computerized Information Services:** BITNET (electronic mail service). **Special Catalogs:** Oklahoma Data Archive Catalog, annual. **Remarks:** FAX: (405)744-7074. Electronic mail address(es): POSCRED@OSUCC (BITNET).

★12364★

Oklahoma State University - College of Osteopathic Medicine - Medical Library (Med)
1111 W. 17th St.   Phone: (918)582-1972
Tulsa, OK 74107-1898   Linda L. Roberts, Coll.Libn.
Founded: 1974. **Staff:** Prof 3; Other 4. **Subjects:** Medicine. **Special Collections:** Osteopathy collection. **Holdings:** 22,566 books; 1611 bound periodical volumes; 3717 AV programs; 28,909 microfiche; 1099 reels of microfilm. **Subscriptions:** 514 journals; 91 serials; 4 newspapers. **Services:** Interlibrary loan; copying; library open to the public for reference use only. **Automated Operations:** Computerized cataloging, acquisitions, serials, and circulation. **Computerized Information Services:** MEDLARS, DIALOG Information Services. **Networks/Consortia:** Member of South Central Academic Medical Libraries Consortium (SCAMEL). **Publications:** Library Newsletter, quarterly - to faculty and affiliated hospitals and clinics. **Remarks:** FAX: (918)582-6316. **Staff:** Anita Sutrick, Asst.Libn.; David Money, Asst.Libn.

★12365★

Oklahoma State University - Curriculum Materials Laboratory (Educ)
University Library   Phone: (405)744-6310
Stillwater, OK 74078-0375   Donna Schwarz, Hd.
Founded: 1957. **Staff:** Prof 1; Other 2. **Subjects:** Materials for preschool-grade 12. **Special Collections:** Preschool-grade 12 fiction and nonfiction; textbooks (6023); curriculum guides (5370); professional materials for teachers and librarians; foreign language books. **Holdings:** 37,800 books; 2568 AV programs. **Subscriptions:** 112 journals and other serials. **Services:** Interlibrary loan; laboratory open to the public with restrictions. **Remarks:** FAX: (405)744-5183.

★12366★

Oklahoma State University - Documents Department (Info Sci)
University Library   Phone: (405)744-6546
Stillwater, OK 74078-0375   John B. Phillips, Hd.
Founded: 1907. **Staff:** Prof 5; Other 8. **Special Collections:** U.S. Government Regional Depository; NASA depository; Oklahoma documents depository. **Holdings:** 1.1 million items; 1,579,912 microforms. **Subscriptions:** 6275 journals and other serials. **Services:** Interlibrary loan; copying; department open to the public with restrictions. **Remarks:** FAX: (405)744-5183. **Staff:** Connie Kirby, Asst.Hd.; JoAnn Bierman, Asst.Doc.Libn.; Suzanne Latour, Asst.Doc.Libn.

★12367★

Oklahoma State University - Humanities Division (Hum)
University Library   Phone: (405)744-6544
Stillwater, OK 74078-0375   Terry Basford, Hd.
Founded: 1953. **Staff:** Prof 3; Other 1.5. **Subjects:** Literature, language, religion, computer science, library and information science, journalism, film, theater, fine arts, performing arts, philosophy, interior design, sports, recreation. **Holdings:** 125,960 books; 28,067 bound periodical volumes; 87,263 microforms. **Subscriptions:** 1597 journals and other serials. **Services:** Interlibrary loan; copying; division open to the public with restrictions. **Computerized Information Services:** DIALOG Information Services, BRS Information Technologies, OCLC; CD-ROMs. **Remarks:** FAX: (405)744-5183. **Staff:** Ella Melik, Asst.Hum.Libn.; Darcy Rankin, Asst.Hum.Libn.

★12368★

Oklahoma State University - Map Collection (Geog-Map)
University Library   Phone: (405)744-9731
Stillwater, OK 74078-0375   Greg Hines
Staff: 1.5. **Subjects:** Agriculture, geology, sociology. **Special Collections:** U.S. Geological Survey maps (regional depository); Defense Mapping Agency (DMA) maps; aerial photographs of Oklahoma, 1930s to present; aerial photograph collection presently covering more than 100 urban areas worldwide. **Holdings:** 130,000 maps; 80,000 aerial photographs. **Subscriptions:** 2 journals and other serials. **Services:** Copying; collection open to the public with restrictions. **Computerized Information Services:** DIALOG Information Services, BRS Information Technologies, OCLC; BITNET (electronic mail service). **Remarks:** FAX: (405)744-5183. Electronic mail address(es): LibrGAH@OSUCC (BITNET).

★12369★

Oklahoma State University - Oklahoma City Branch - OSU-OKC Library (Educ)
900 N. Portland   Phone: (405)945-3251
Oklahoma City, OK 73107   Vicki Buettner, Hd.Libn.
Founded: 1963. **Staff:** Prof 2; Other 3. **Subjects:** Computer science, nursing, electronics, police science, horticulture, fire protection. **Holdings:** 15,000 books. **Subscriptions:** 250 journals and other serials. **Services:** Interlibrary loan; copying; library open to the public with restrictions. **Automated Operations:** Computerized cataloging and circulation. **Computerized Information Services:** OCLC, DIALOG Information Services, WILSONLINE. Performs searches on fee basis. **Networks/Consortia:** Member of AMIGOS Bibliographic Council, Inc., Metropolitan Libraries Network of Central Oklahoma Inc. (MetroNet). **Publications:** New Book List, 4/year - for internal distribution only; Periodicals Holdings List, annual. **Remarks:** FAX: (405)945-3289. **Formerly:** Its Technical Branch Library. **Staff:** Elaine Warner, Asst.Libn.

★ 12370 ★
Oklahoma State University - Patent and Economic Development Department (Sci-Engr)
University Library   Phone: (405)744-7086
Stillwater, OK 74078-0375   Jennifer Paustenbaugh
Founded: 1989. **Staff:** Prof 1; Other 1. **Subjects:** U.S. Patents (patent and trademark depository library). **Special Collections:** Copies of all utility patents, 1790 to present. **Holdings:** 2000 volumes; 10,000 reels of microfilm. **Subscriptions:** 10 journals and other serials. **Services:** Copying; department open to the public; search assistance by appointment. **Computerized Information Services:** Japio, Federal Trademarks; CD-ROM (CASSIS); internal databases; BITNET (electronic mail service). **Remarks:** FAX: (405)744-5183. Electronic mail address(es): librjfp@OSUCC (BITNET).

★ 12371 ★
Oklahoma State University - Science and Engineering Division (Sci-Engr)
University Library   Phone: (405)744-6309
Stillwater, OK 74078-0375   Vicki W. Phillips, Hd.
Founded: 1928. **Staff:** Prof 6; Other 3. **Subjects:** Agriculture; anthropology; architecture; bacteriology; botany; entomology; medicine; home economics; zoology; chemistry; physics; mathematics; geology; engineering - chemical, aeronautical, civil, electrical, mechanical. **Holdings:** 170,900 books; 207,950 bound periodical volumes; 93,300 microforms. **Subscriptions:** 4686 journals and other serials. **Services:** Interlibrary loan; division open to the public with restrictions. **Computerized Information Services:** DIALOG Information Services, OCLC; CD-ROMs. **Remarks:** FAX: (405)744-5183. **Staff:** Dan Burgard, Asst.Sci. & Eng.Libn.; Patsy Stafford, Asst.Sci. & Eng.Libn.; Johnny Johnson, Asst.Sci. & Engr.Libn.; Maryann Seaver, Asst.Sci. & Eng.Libn.

★ 12372 ★
Oklahoma State University - Social Science Division (Soc Sci)
University Library   Phone: (405)744-6540
Stillwater, OK 74078-0375   Richard Paustenbaugh, Hd.
Founded: 1953. **Staff:** Prof 5; Other 3. **Subjects:** Business, economics, history, political science, sociology, management, anthropology, geography, education, psychology, philosophy. **Holdings:** 250,000 books; 67,500 bound periodical volumes; 5 VF drawers of serials; 39 VF drawers of pamphlets; 297,650 microforms. **Subscriptions:** 2057 journals and other serials; 16 newspapers. **Services:** Interlibrary loan; copying; division open to the public with restrictions. **Computerized Information Services:** DIALOG Information Services, BRS Information Technologies, OCLC, DataTimes; CD-ROMs; BITNET (electronic mail service). **Remarks:** Includes holdings of its Education Division. FAX: (405)744-5183. Electronic mail address(es): LIBRRT@OSUCC (BITNET). **Staff:** Jill Holmes, Educ.Libn.; Bill Cunningham, Asst.Soc.Sci.Libn.; Nancy Jurney, Asst.Soc.Sci.Libn.; Bonnie King, Assoc.Soc.Sci.Libn.

★ 12373 ★
Oklahoma State University - Special Collections and University Archives (Hist)
University Library   Phone: (405)744-6311
Stillwater, OK 74078-0375   Heather M. Lloyd, Hd.
Founded: 1950. **Staff:** Prof 3; Other 2. **Subjects:** Oklahoma State University; Oklahoma - agriculture, politics, water resources; journalism; politics; agricultural history of state and region. **Special Collections:** OSU archives; papers of Henry Bellmon, H.H. Finnell, Henry S. Johnston, Paul Miller, Angie Debo, and Claude L. Fly. **Services:** Copying; collections open to the public for reference use only. **Special Indexes:** Index to student newspapers; index to Paul Miller papers (both on microcomputers). **Remarks:** FAX: (405)744-5183. **Staff:** Susan F. Walker, Asst.Spec.Coll.Libn.;

★ 12374 ★
Oklahoma State University - Technical Branch, Okmulgee - Learning Resource Center (Sci-Engr)
1801 E. 4th   Phone: (918)756-6211
Okmulgee, OK 74447-0088   Becky Kirkbride, Libn.
Founded: 1946. **Staff:** Prof 2; Other 3. **Subjects:** Automotive technology; electrical-electronics technology; diesel technology; air conditioning and refrigeration; business occupations; construction technology; engineering graphics technology; hospitality services; manufacturing technology; visual communications; jewelry technology; upholstery; repair - shoe, boot, saddle, watch, microinstrument. **Holdings:** 8000 books; 344 reels of microfilm; 11,999 microfiche. **Subscriptions:** 357 journals and other serials; 7 newspapers. **Services:** Interlibrary loan; copying; center open to the public with restrictions. **Networks/Consortia:** Member of AMIGOS Bibliographic Council, Inc.

★ 12375 ★
Oklahoma State University - Veterinary Medicine Library (Med)
University Library   Phone: (405)744-6655
Stillwater, OK 74078-0375   Patricia Mullen, Hd.
Founded: 1948. **Staff:** Prof 1; Other 2. **Subjects:** Veterinary medicine, health sciences, laboratory animal medicine. **Holdings:** 9085 books; 9892 bound periodical volumes; 793 tapes; 694 slides; 30 study guides; 25 films. **Subscriptions:** 343 journals and other serials. **Services:** Interlibrary loan; copying; library open to the public with restrictions. **Computerized Information Services:** DIALOG Information Services, BRS Information Technologies, NLM, OCLC; BITNET (electronic mail service). **Remarks:** FAX: (405)744-5183. Electronic mail address(es): VETMPJM@OSUCC (BITNET).

★ 12376 ★
Oklahoma Water Resources Board - Library (Env-Cons)
600 N. Harvey
P.O. Box 150   Phone: (405)231-2500
Oklahoma City, OK 73101   Susan E. Lutz, Libn.
Staff: Prof 1. **Subjects:** Water, water quality and planning, safety of dams, weather modification, stream water and groundwater use. **Holdings:** 9000 volumes. **Subscriptions:** 90 journals and other serials. **Services:** Interlibrary loan; copying; library open to the public. **Remarks:** FAX: (405)231-2600.

★ 12377 ★
Oklahoma Well Log Library, Inc. (Energy)
1100 Philtower Bldg.   Phone: (918)582-6188
Tulsa, OK 74103   Janice R. Jennings, Mgr.
Founded: 1960. **Staff:** Prof 1; Other 5. **Subjects:** Geology, oil and gas. **Special Collections:** Electrical logs (450,000); scout tickets (875,000). **Holdings:** 1000 volumes; 560 reels of microfilm. **Services:** Copying; library open to the public with restrictions. **Staff:** Billie R. Weaver, Asst.Mgr.

★ 12378 ★
Olana State Historic Site - Archives (Hist)
R.D. 2   Phone: (518)828-0135
Hudson, NY 12534   Laura Kline, Archv.
Staff: Prof 3; Other 2. **Subjects:** Local history; 19th century history, literature, science. **Special Collections:** Correspondence and paintings of Frederic Edwin Church (19th century American landscape painter); 19th century photographs. **Holdings:** 3000 books; 34 bound periodical volumes; theses. **Services:** Library open to the public with restrictions. **Computerized Information Services:** Internal databases. **Publications:** The Crayon, 3/year - to members. **Staff:** Karen Zukowski, Cur.; James Ryan, Site Mgr.

Olcott Library & Research Center
See: Theosophical Society in America (16299)

Old Academy Museum Library
See: Wethersfield Historical Society - Old Academy Museum Library (20354)

★ 12379 ★
Old Brutus Historical Society, Inc. - Library (Hist)
516 N. Seneca St.   Phone: (315)834-6779
Weedsport, NY 13166   Howard J. Finley, Hist.
Staff: 1. **Subjects:** Genealogy, local history. **Special Collections:** Stanley Guppy books on history of Cayuga County (50). **Holdings:** 2000 books; 2000 photographs; 50,000 genealogy sheets; 2000 agricultural and household artifacts. **Services:** Library and museum open to the public on limited schedule. Genealogy open to the public by appointment. **Staff:** Jean H. Woodcock, Dir.

★ 12380 ★
Old Cathedral Parish Church - Brute Library (Rel-Phil)
205 Church St.
Vincennes, IN 47591   Phone: (812)882-5638
Staff: Prof 2. **Subjects:** Rare books, religion. **Special Collections:** Two hand-printed and illuminated documents from the Middle Ages; letter of St. Vincent de Paul dated 1660. **Holdings:** 11,000 books. **Services:** Library open to the public for reference use only.

★ 12381 ★
Old Charles Town Library, Inc. (Hist)
200 E. Washington St.   Phone: (304)725-2208
Charles Town, WV 25414   Anita M. Trout, Libn.
Founded: 1928. **Staff:** Prof 4; Other 1. **Subjects:** Local history, genealogy, West Virginia history. **Special Collections:** Collection of Jefferson County Historical Society; Thornton T. Perry Room (history, genealogy). **Holdings:** 50,000 books; 1034 bound periodical volumes. **Subscriptions:** 127 journals and other serials. **Services:** Interlibrary loan; copying; library open to the public.

★ 12382 ★
Old Colony Historical Society - Museum & Library (Hist)
66 Church Green   Phone: (508)822-1622
Taunton, MA 02780   June M. Strojny, Libn.
Founded: 1853. **Staff:** Prof 3; Other 3. **Subjects:** Local and military history, decorative arts, genealogy. **Special Collections:** Manuscripts of Francis Baylies. **Holdings:** 6000 books; other cataloged items. **Subscriptions:** 10 journals and other serials. **Services:** Copying; museum and library open to the public for reference use only. **Staff:** Lisa A. Compton, Dir.

★ 12383 ★
Old Dartmouth Historical Society - Whaling Museum Library (Hist)
18 Johnny Cake Hill   Phone: (508)997-0046
New Bedford, MA 02740   Virginia M. Adams, Libn.
Founded: 1903. **Staff:** Prof 2. **Subjects:** History - American whaling, New Bedford area, maritime. **Special Collections:** Ship logbooks (1130); Charles F. Batchelder Collection (whaling); Charles A. Goodwin Collection (maritime history); International Marine Archives (whaling and maritime records on microfilm). **Holdings:** 15,000 books; 500 bound periodical volumes; 875 linear feet of manuscripts; 600 maps and charts; 1800 reels of microfilm. **Subscriptions:** 30 journals and other serials. **Services:** Interlibrary loan (microfilm only); copying; library open to the public. **Publications:** Whaling Logbooks and Journals, 1613-1927: An Inventory of Manuscript Records in Public Collections (1986). **Remarks:** FAX: (508)997-0018. **Staff:** Judith M. Downey, Mss.

★ 12384 ★
Old Dominion University - Library Archive (Hist)
Norfolk, VA 23529-0256   Phone: (804)683-4485
                                         Linda Farynk, Interim Univ.Libn.
Founded: 1974. **Staff:** 1.5. **Subjects:** Old Dominion University, history of Norfolk and Tidewater cities. **Special Collections:** Papers of Henry E. Howell, Jr., Thomas R. McNamara, Joseph D. Wood, and Robert M. Hughes (500 linear feet); records of the Office of the University President. **Holdings:** 403 linear feet of correspondence; legislative and mayoral files; scrapbooks; business papers; political and legal files. **Services:** Interlibrary loan; copying; archive open to the public for reference use only. **Automated Operations:** Computerized public access catalog, cataloging, and circulation. **Computerized Information Services:** CD-ROMs. **Special Indexes:** Internal finding aids. **Remarks:** FAX: (804)683-5035.

Old Economy Village
See: **Pennsylvania (State) Historical & Museum Commission - Old Economy Village** (12880)

★ 12385 ★
Old Fort Niagara Association - Library (Hist)
Box 169   Phone: (716)745-7611
Youngstown, NY 14174-0169   Brian Leigh Dunnigan, Exec.Dir.
Founded: 1927. **Staff:** Prof 1. **Subjects:** Local and military history. **Special Collections:** Old Fort Niagara Collection (original diaries, orderly books, post records, 1813-1912). **Holdings:** 2200 books; 100 reels of microfilm. **Subscriptions:** 10 journals and other serials. **Services:** Copying; library open to serious researchers by prior arrangement. **Publications:** Old Fort Niagara - Now and Then (newsletter), monthly - to members.

Old Fort William
See: **Ontario Ministry of Tourism and Recreation** (12486)

The Old Guardhouse Museum
See: **Fort Clark Historical Society** (5994)

Old Jail Museum Library
See: **Historical Society of Porter County** (7283)

★ 12386 ★
The Old Manse Library (Hist)
100 Fountain Head Ln.   Phone: (506)622-6710
Newcastle, NB, Canada E1V 1Z3   Catherine Reid, Libn.
Founded: 1953. **Staff:** Other 3. **Subjects:** Local history and genealogy. **Special Collections:** Lord Beaverbrook Collection; Miramichi Historical Society Records. **Holdings:** 40,000 books. **Subscriptions:** 10 journals and other serials. **Services:** Interlibrary loan; copying; library open to the public. **Publications:** Newcastle on the Miramichi; The Old Manse Library, Newcastle, N.B.

Old Market House State Historic Site
See: **Illinois (State) Historic Preservation Agency - Galena State Historic Sites** (7697)

★ 12387 ★
Old St. Mary's Church - Paulist Library
614 Grant Ave.
San Francisco, CA 94108
Defunct.

★ 12388 ★
Old Salem, Inc. - Library (Hist)
Drawer F, Salem Sta.   Phone: (919)721-7348
Winston-Salem, NC 27108   Paula Locklair, Dir., Dept. of Coll.
Staff: Prof 1; Other 2. **Subjects:** Moravians in North Carolina, North Carolina history, traditional American crafts, historic preservation. **Holdings:** 2265 books; 4 VF drawers of Moraviana, preservation, crafts, interpretation clippings; 26 VF drawers of material on life in early Salem, NC and the restoration of Old Salem. **Subscriptions:** 25 journals and other serials. **Services:** Library open to the public with restrictions.

★ 12389 ★
Old Salem, Inc. - Museum of Early Southern Decorative Arts - Library (Art)
Box 10310   Phone: (919)721-7366
Winston-Salem, NC 27108   Bradford L. Rauschenberg, Dir. of Res.
Founded: 1965. **Staff:** Prof 1. **Subjects:** Decorative arts of southern United States. **Holdings:** 5500 books; 1000 bound periodical volumes; data file of 330,000 cards based on source material; 64 VF drawers of photographs and southern decorative art material; 2140 reels of microfilm of newspapers, pre-1821; court records. **Services:** Interlibrary loan; copying; library open to the public upon application.

★ 12390 ★
Old Slave Mart Library
Box 446
Sullivan's Island, SC 29482
Founded: 1924. **Subjects:** Slavery, black history, Civil War, Charleston, South Carolina. **Special Collections:** Miriam B. Wilson Collection; Chase/Graves Collection. **Holdings:** 1100 volumes; 1800 photographs; 850 slides; 130 photocopies of documents and 80 original documents; 800 realia; 300 paintings, flatwork, prints; 40 feet of uncataloged record boxes; 35 VF drawers; 10 map case drawers; 500 slides, records, tapes; 65 years of archival records; manuscripts of founder. **Remarks:** Currently inactive.

Old Songs Library
See: **Society for the Preservation and Encouragement of Barber Shop Quartet Singing in America** (15337)

Old Spanish Missions Historical Research Library
See: **Our Lady of the Lake University** (12612)

★ 12391 ★
Old Stone House - Library (Hist)
3051 M St., N.W.   Phone: (202)426-6851
Washington, DC 20007   Cathy Ingram, Pk. Ranger
Founded: 1960. **Staff:** 3. **Subjects:** American history; Georgetown; Washington, DC; domestic life. **Holdings:** 205 volumes; AV program. **Services:** Library not open to the public. **Remarks:** Above telephone number also provides TDD access.

★ 12392 ★
Old Sturbridge Village - Research Library (Hist)
1 Old Sturbridge Village Rd.   Phone: (508)347-3362
Sturbridge, MA 01566-0200   Theresa Rini Percy, Dir.
Founded: 1946. **Staff:** Prof 5; Other 2. **Subjects:** New England rural life, 1790-1840 - state and local history, agriculture, architecture, fine arts, decorative arts (ceramics, furniture, glass, silver), crafts (blacksmithing, cabinet work, pottery), costume and fabrics, politics, economics, education, law, religion; technology and industry. **Special Collections:** Charles W. Eddy Collection of glass plate negatives (turn of the century central Massachusetts townscapes); Powell Collection of printed works on agriculture (1000 volumes); Merino/Dudley Wool Company Records, Dudley, Massachusetts, 1811-1845 (35 linear feet); Bullard Family papers, Holliston, Massachusetts, 1700-1900; Town of Sturbridge, Massachusetts papers, 1738-1915 (13 boxes). **Holdings:** 32,300 volumes; 400 shelf feet of manuscripts; 1184 microforms; 165,000 images, antique photographs, modern prints, transparencies, and negatives; archives. **Subscriptions:** 125 journals and other serials. **Services:** Copying (at librarian's discretion); library open to the public for reference use only. **Automated Operations:** Computerized cataloging. **Computerized Information Services:** RLIN. **Remarks:** Prints and transparencies are available through Photographic Services Department. Fee schedule is available. FAX: (508)347-5375. **Staff:** Joan Allen, Asst.Libn.; Penny Holewa, Archv./Rec.Mgr.; Kathleen Pratt Frew, Cons.Techn.

★ 12393 ★
Old Swedes Foundation, Inc. - Hendrickson House (Hist)
606 Church St.   Phone: (302)652-5629
Wilmington, DE 19801   Barbara Ashmead, Off.Mgr.
Staff: Prof 1. **Subjects:** Church and local history, genealogy. **Special Collections:** Church books, 1697 to present; baptismal, marriage, and burial records, 1713 to present. **Holdings:** 250 books; 20 bound periodical volumes; 12 map drawers, 6 VF drawers, 4 boxes of archival materials; 5 reels of microfilm. **Services:** Requests for information by mail only. **Special Indexes:** Index to church records (book).

Old West Museum
See: **Sunset Trading Post-Old West Museum** (15879)

★ 12394 ★
Old Woodbury Historical Society - Library (Hist)
P.O. Box 705, Hurd House
Main St.   Phone: (203)263-2696
Woodbury, CT 06798   Vera T. Elsenboss
Subjects: History of Woodbury. **Holdings:** Figures not available.

★ 12395 ★
Old York Historical Society - Library (Hist)
George Marshall Store
140 Lindsay Rd.
P.O. Box 312   Phone: (207)363-4974
York, ME 03909   Virginia S. Spiller, Libn./Geneal.
Founded: 1984. **Staff:** 8. **Subjects:** Local history, decorative arts, genealogy, Maine history, architecture. **Special Collections:** Rare books (600); local manuscripts (3000); local historic photographs (2000); local genealogies (300); Mormon genealogical records (3000 microfiche). **Holdings:** 3000 books; 200 bound periodical volumes; 55 feet of manuscripts and archives; 3000 microfiche; 50 reels of microfilm; 4 VF drawers. **Subscriptions:** 12 journals and other serials. **Services:** Copying; library open to the public for reference use only. **Publications:** York Maine Then and Now; The Old Gaol Museum; Enchanted Ground; New England Miniature; Reprint of Charles Banks History of York, Maine - all items for sale.

★ 12396 ★
Old York Road Historical Society - Archives (Hist)
Jenkintown Library
York and Vista Rds.   Phone: (215)884-0593
Jenkintown, PA 19046   Warren Hilton, Libn.
Founded: 1936. **Subjects:** Local history and genealogy. **Holdings:** Books; newspapers; pamphlets; clippings; photographs; maps; deeds. **Services:** Archives open to the public for reference use on request. **Publications:** Bulletin, annual - to members and local libraries.

★ 12397 ★
Old York Road Temple Beth Am - Library (Rel-Phil)
971 Old York Rd.   Phone: (215)886-8000
Abington, PA 19001   Candace L. Berlin, Lib.Dir.
Subjects: Religion, Judaica. **Holdings:** 5000 books. **Subscriptions:** 10 journals and other serials. **Services:** Library not open to the public.

Earl K. Oldham Library
See: **Arlington Baptist College** (1038)

★ 12398 ★
Olds College - Library (Agri)
Postal Bag 1   Phone: (403)556-4600
Olds, AB, Canada T0M 1P0   Garry M. Grisak, Lib.Hd.
Staff: 8. **Holdings:** Agricultural Collection; government documents; Agdex (agricultural documents and other pamphlets). **Subscriptions:** 375 journals and other serials, 25 newspapers. **Services:** Interlibrary loan; copying; collections open to the public. **Automated Operations:** Computerized public access catalog, cataloging, acquisitions, and circulation. **Computerized Information Services:** DIALOG Information Services, Grassroots. **Remarks:** FAX: (403)556-4625. **Staff:** Barbara J. E. Smith, Asst.Mgr.

Victor Olgyay Archives
See: **Arizona State University - Architecture and Environmental Design Library** (1009)

★ 12399 ★
Olin Corporation - Business Information Center (Bus-Fin)
120 Long Ridge Rd.   Phone: (203)356-2498
Stamford, CT 06904   Kelly Stanyon, Mgr., Bus.Info.
Founded: 1973. **Staff:** Prof 2. **Subjects:** Business, marketing, chemicals, management. **Holdings:** 1500 books. **Subscriptions:** 750 journals and other serials. **Services:** Center not open to the public. **Computerized Information Services:** DIALOG Information Services, PFDS Online, Business International Corporation, Mead Data Central, InvesText, VU/TEXT Information Services, Dow Jones News/Retrieval. **Staff:** Tina Malloy, Libn.

★ 12400 ★
Olin Corporation - Research Center - Technical Information Services (Sci-Engr)
350 Knotter Dr.
Box 586   Phone: (203)271-4237
Cheshire, CT 06410-0586   Lynn D. Campo, Supv.
Founded: 1941. **Staff:** Prof 3; Other 2. **Subjects:** Chemistry, metallurgy, physics. **Holdings:** 13,000 books; 15,000 bound periodical volumes; 40,000 internal reports; 35 drawers of patents on microfilm; 10 drawers of journals on microfilm. **Subscriptions:** 300 journals and other serials; 10 newspapers. **Services:** Interlibrary loan; services not open to the public. **Automated Operations:** Computerized public access catalog and cataloging. **Computerized Information Services:** DIALOG Information Services, STN International, ORBIT Search Service, NLM. **Publications:** TIS Bulletin - for internal distribution only. **Staff:** J.J. Pitts, Sr.Res.Info.Assoc.; R.A. Nehrkorn, Info.Sci.

★ 12401 ★
Olin Corporation - Technical Information Center (Sci-Engr)
Charleston, TN 37310   Phone: (615)336-4347
                      Connie J. Upton, Supv.
Founded: 1976. **Staff:** Prof 1; Other 1. **Subjects:** Chemistry, chemical engineering, electrochemistry, engineering. **Special Collections:** IHS/VSMF Vendor Catalogs (microfilm) and material safety data sheets (CD-ROM); industry standards (NFPA, ASTM, API, TAPPI; microfilm); U.S. patent abstracts (CD-ROM). **Holdings:** 4000 books; 1000 bound periodical volumes; 5 VF drawers of translated articles and patents; American Chemical Society Journals on microfilm. **Subscriptions:** 100 journals and other serials; 6 newspapers. **Services:** Interlibrary loan; center not open to the public. **Computerized Information Services:** DIALOG Information Services, PFDS Online, STN International, Chemical Information Systems, Inc. (CIS). **Remarks:** FAX: (615)336-4554.

F.W. Olin Library
See: **Mills College** (10409)

★ 12402 ★
Olin Metals Research Laboratory - Metals Information Center (Sci-Engr)
91 Shelton Ave.   Phone: (203)781-5563
New Haven, CT 06511   Mary McCowen
Founded: 1961. **Staff:** Prof 1; Other 1. **Subjects:** Metallurgy, corrosion, aluminum, copper and brass. **Holdings:** 1800 books; 700 bound periodical volumes; 5000 internal and external reports; 5000 patents; 3500 translations. **Subscriptions:** 185 journals and other serials. **Services:** Copying; SDI; center open to the public on request. **Computerized Information Services:** DIALOG Information Services, PFDS Online, Copper Data Center (CDC). **Remarks:** FAX: (203)356-3595.

Jacob T. Oliphant Library
See: **Indiana (State) Board of Health** (7763)

Olive View Medical Health Center
See: **LAC/Olive View Medical Health Center** (8866)

Monsignor Fremiot Torres Oliver Law Library
See: **Catholic University of Puerto Rico** (3168)

Wrenshall A. Oliver Professional Library
See: **Napa State Hospital** (10971)

★ 12403 ★
Olivet Nazarene University - Benner Library and Resource Center (Rel-Phil)
P.O. Box 592   Phone: (815)939-5354
Kankakee, IL 60901   Allan L. Wiens, Dir.
Founded: 1909. **Staff:** Prof 5; Other 5. **Subjects:** Religion, education, literature, business, nursing. **Special Collections:** John Wesley; James Arminius, Archives of Olivet University; geological maps. **Holdings:** 148,000 books; 5408 bound periodical volumes; 3870 reels of microfilm; 39,435 microfiche; 10,075 maps; 4509 phonograph records. **Subscriptions:** 921 journals and other serials; 22 newspapers. **Services:** Interlibrary loan; library open to the public with courtesy card. **Automated Operations:** Computerized public access catalog, cataloging, and acquisitions. **Computerized Information Services:** DIALOG Information Services, OCLC. Performs searches on fee basis. Contact Person: Craighton Hippenhammer, Ref., 939-5355. **Networks/Consortia:** Member of ILLINET. **Remarks:** FAX: (815)939-0153. **Staff:** Kathy VanFossan, Hd., Tech.Serv.; Mary Ada Dillinger, Ref./Cat.

★ 12404 ★
Olmsted County Historical Society - Archives (Hist)
1195 County Road 22, S.W.
Box 6411   Phone: (507)282-9447
Rochester, MN 55903   Beverly Hermes, Archv.
Founded: 1926. **Staff:** Prof 3. **Subjects:** Olmsted County history, Minnesota history, genealogy, 19th century farming. **Special Collections:** Cutshall photo collection (70,000). **Holdings:** 5700 books; 400 bound periodical volumes; 800 reels of microfilm of Olmsted County newspapers, 1859 to present; 100 VF drawers of documents, pamphlets, photographs; Minnesota census records through 1920. **Subscriptions:** 21 journals and other serials. **Services:** Copying; photo reproduction; archives open to the public; fees charged for staff research. **Computerized Information Services:** Internal database. **Special Indexes:** Index to newspapers (1859-1912). **Staff:** Marilyn Burbank, Asst.Archv.; Sherry Sweetman, Asst.Archv.

Frederick Law Olmsted National Historic Site
See: **U.S. Natl. Park Service** (17717)

Charles Olson Archives
See: **University of Connecticut - Homer Babbidge Library - Special Collections** (18519)

Otto Olson Memorial Library
See: **Lutheran Theological Seminary** (9466)

★ 12405 ★
Olver Incorporated - Library (Env-Cons)
1116 S. Main St.   Phone: (703)552-5548
Blacksburg, VA 24060   Karen Veilleux
Founded: 1989. **Staff:** Prof 1. **Subjects:** Environment, sewage, wastewater. **Holdings:** 2000 books; 50 bound periodical volumes; 1000 reports; 1500 catalogs. **Subscriptions:** 25 journals and other serials; 3 newspapers. **Services:** Library not open to the public. **Remarks:** FAX: (703)552-5577.

★ 12406 ★
Olwine, Connelly, Chase, O'Donnell & Weyher - Law Library (Law)
750 7th Ave.
New York, NY 10019   Mary Crosby, Libn.
Staff: Prof 1; Other 2. **Subjects:** Law - corporate, taxation, trial practice materials. **Holdings:** 14,000 books; 550 bound periodical volumes. **Subscriptions:** 90 serial subscriptions; 5 newspapers. **Services:** Interlibrary loan; library not open to the public. **Computerized Information Services:** LEXIS, NEXIS, WESTLAW.

Olympia Fields Osteopathic Medical Center Library
See: **Chicago College of Osteopathic Medicine** (3519)

Olympic National Park
See: **U.S. Natl. Park Service - Olympic Natl. Park** (17760)

Olympic Resource & Information Center
See: **U.S. Olympic Committee** (17917)

★ 12407 ★
Omaha-Council Bluffs Metropolitan Area Planning Agency (MAPA) - Library (Plan)
2222 Cuming St.   Phone: (402)444-6866
Omaha, NE 68102-4328   Pat Jesse, Info.Spec.
Staff: Prof 1. **Subjects:** Planning and community development, transportation, housing, environment, census, employment, local and regional data. **Holdings:** 3000 volumes and documents; 75 periodicals and newsletters; 1990 Iowa and Nebraska census tapes; local data; maps; aerial photographs; area newspaper clippings. **Subscriptions:** 75 journals and other serials. **Services:** Copying; library open to the public by appointment. **Computerized Information Services:** CD-ROMs; Traffic Counts, TIP, Land Use, Employment, 1990 Census, Area Building Permits (internal databases). **Publications:** Traffic Flow Maps; publications containing five-county, 1990 census data.

★ 12408 ★
Omaha Public Library - Business, Science & Technology Department (Bus-Fin, Sci-Engr, Biol Sci)
215 S. 15th St.   Phone: (402)444-4817
Omaha, NE 68102   Janet Davenport, Hd.
Founded: 1952. **Staff:** Prof 3; Other 3. **Subjects:** Economics, insurance, mathematics, physics, investments, chemistry, engineering, agriculture, medicine, health, biology, botany. **Special Collections:** Telephone, city, and trade directories; trade catalogs; Public Document Room Collection of Nuclear Regulatory Commission reports. **Holdings:** 39,212 books; 6358 bound periodical volumes; 75 VF drawers of pamphlets, clippings, house organs, corporate annual reports; 350,603 U.S. Government documents; 56,240 topographic maps; microfilm. **Subscriptions:** 525 journals and other serials. **Services:** Interlibrary loan; copying; department open to the public. **Automated Operations:** Computerized cataloging and acquisitions. **Computerized Information Services:** DIALOG Information Services. **Publications:** Information Bulletin, monthly - to businesses, corporations, and libraries on request. **Remarks:** FAX: (402)444-4504. **Staff:** Bill Carter, Libn.; Linda Trout, Libn.; Patrick Esser Lib.Spec.; Margaret Blackstone, Lib.Spec.

★ 12409 ★
Omaha Public Power District - Information Systems Services - Library
(Comp Sci)
444 S. 16th St. Mall   Phone: (402)636-3441
Omaha, NE 68102-2247   Mary Louise Mally, Libn.
Founded: 1982. **Staff:** Prof 2. **Subjects:** Data processing, energy, business, nuclear power. **Holdings:** 500 books; 3000 EPRI reports; 1500 other catalogued items. **Subscriptions:** 450 journals and other serials. **Services:** Interlibrary loan; library not open to the public. **Computerized Information Services:** DIALOG Information Services. **Remarks:** FAX: (402)536-4002. **Staff:** Janet E. Carlson

★ 12410 ★
Omaha World-Herald - Library (Publ)
World Herald Sq.
1334 Dodge St.   Phone: (402)444-1000
Omaha, NE 68102   Jeanne Donohoe, Lib.Mgr.
Staff: Prof 1; Other 6. **Subjects:** Newspaper reference topics. **Holdings:** 4.5 million newspaper clippings; 400 drawers of photographs. **Services:** Library not open to the public. **Computerized Information Services:** DataTimes; Omaha World-Herald Data Bank (internal database). **Remarks:** FAX: (402)345-0183.

Oman Studies Association
See: **Oman Studies Centre for Documentation and Research on Oman and the Arabian Gulf - Library (12411)**

★ 12411 ★
Oman Studies Centre for Documentation and Research on Oman and the Arabian Gulf - Library (Area-Ethnic)
Dieselstr. 4   Phone: 7231 22387
W-7530 Pforzheim, Germany   Joachim Duester, Dir.Gen.
Founded: 1975. **Staff:** Prof 1. **Subjects:** Sultanate of Oman - economy, history, current affairs, law, language, culture, geology, climatology, natural history, political affairs, geography, socioeconomic development. **Holdings:** 3000 bound volumes; 1200 slides; 6000 press cuttings; 180 maps. **Subscriptions:** 20 journals and other serials. **Services:** Document delivery; center open to the public. **Publications:** Oman Studies Bibliographic Info (newsletter), 2/year; Bibliographie uber das Sultanat Oman; Oman Treaty Index; Oman Historical Index. **Remarks:** Telex: 7 262 736 TTEC D. **Formerly:** Oman Studies Association.

★ 12412 ★
O'Melveny and Myers - Library (Law)
400 S. Hope St., Suite 1300   Phone: (213)669-6018
Los Angeles, CA 90071-2899   Teresa G. White, Law Lib.Mgr.
Founded: 1885. **Staff:** Prof 6; Other 8. **Subjects:** Law - general, labor, tax. **Holdings:** 50,000 volumes; 12,000 research reports and legal memoranda. **Subscriptions:** 100 journals and other serials. **Services:** Library not open to the public. **Automated Operations:** Computerized cataloging. **Computerized Information Services:** LEXIS, DIALOG Information Services, WILSONLINE, RLIN, WESTLAW, BRS Information Technologies. **Networks/Consortia:** Member of CLASS. **Special Catalogs:** Computerized catalog/index of internal research reports. **Remarks:** FAX: (213)669-6407. Telex: 674122. **Staff:** Margaret La France, Pub.Serv.Libn.; Kathleen Smith, Hd. of Lib.Sys.; Valerie Green, Ref.Libn.; Suzanne Plessinger, Ref.Libn.; Barbara Stern, Cat.Libn.

★ 12413 ★
O'Melveny and Myers - Library (Law)
153 E. 53rd St.   Phone: (212)326-2020
New York, NY 10022   Jo Ellen Cooper, Libn.
Staff: 3. **Subjects:** Law. **Holdings:** 17,500 books. **Services:** Library not open to the public. **Computerized Information Services:** LEXIS, NEXIS, DIALOG Information Services, Dow Jones News/Retrieval, DataTimes, WESTLAW, LEGI-SLATE, Dun & Bradstreet Business Credit Services, Information America. **Remarks:** FAX: (212)326-2061. **Staff:** Gregory McNulty, Asst.Libn.

OMI College of Applied Science
See: **University of Cincinnati - OMI College of Applied Science (18480)**

★ 12414 ★
Omnigraphics, Inc. - Library (Bus-Fin)
Penobscot Bldg.   Phone: (313)961-1340
Detroit, MI 48226   Annie Brewer, Libn.
Founded: 1987. **Staff:** Prof 1. **Subjects:** Business reference. **Holdings:** 3500 volumes. **Subscriptions:** 250 journals and other serials. **Services:** Library not open to the public. **Computerized Information Services:** Access to DIALOG Information Services, CompuServe Information Service, OCLC, CBI, BookQuest; InfoTrac; CD-ROMs (WILSONDISC, PAIS, British Books in Print, Books in Print, Ulrich's Plus).

★ 12415 ★
Omniplex Science Museum - Library (Biol Sci)
2100 N.E. 52nd St.   Phone: (405)424-5545
Oklahoma City, OK 73111   Beth Bussey, Educ.Dir.
Founded: 1978. **Subjects:** Life and physical sciences, curriculum aids. **Holdings:** 500 books. **Services:** Copying; library open to the public with restrictions.

★ 12416 ★
OmniSys Corporation - Microform Library (Hum)
211 Second Ave.   Phone: (617)684-1234
Waltham, MA 02154   Randall K. Toth, Dir., Micropubn.
Staff: Prof 2; Other 5. **Subjects:** Literature - European, Russian, Victorian; folklore; library literature; drama. **Special Collections:** Public papers of Louis Dembitz Brandeis. **Holdings:** 600,000 titles. **Services:** Library not open to the public. **Remarks:** FAX: (617)684-1245. **Formerly:** General Microfilm Company located in Watertown, MA.

★ 12417 ★
On-Line Software International - Library (Comp Sci)
Fort Lee Executive Park
2 Executive Dr.   Phone: (201)592-0009
Fort Lee, NJ 07024   Christine Eckerson, Libn.
Staff: Prof 1. **Subjects:** Software, computers. **Holdings:** 250 books; 200 tapes; periodicals; guides; directories; meetings reports; IBM training manuals. **Subscriptions:** 120 journals and other serials; 30 newspapers. **Services:** Library open to guests of the company. **Automated Operations:** Computerized cataloging. **Publications:** OSI News Bits (newsletter) - for internal distribution only.

★ 12418 ★
Onan Corporation - Library Information Service (Sci-Engr)
1400 73rd Ave., N.E.   Phone: (612)574-5423
Minneapolis, MN 55432   Catherine Glick Nelson, Lib.Mgr.
Founded: 1978. **Staff:** Prof 1; Other 1. **Subjects:** Electric generators, gasoline engines, switchgear, control systems, business. **Holdings:** 2000 books; 15,000 technical reports; 8000 standards. **Subscriptions:** 300 journals and other serials. **Services:** Library not open to the public. **Computerized Information Services:** DIALOG Information Services, Teltech Expert Network. **Networks/Consortia:** Member of Metronet, Twin Cities Standards Cooperators. **Remarks:** FAX: (612)574-8209.

★ 12419 ★
ONE, Inc. - Blanche M. Baker Memorial Library (Soc Sci)
3340 Country Club Dr.   Phone: (213)735-5252
Los Angeles, CA 90019   Luis Balmaseda, Libn.
Founded: 1953. **Subjects:** Homosexuality, homophile movement, gay liberation movement, gay and lesbian literature, women's and lesbian studies. **Holdings:** 20,000 titles; 60 VF drawers of other cataloged items; archival collections of many organizations; personal papers; foreign language periodicals. **Subscriptions:** 200 journals; 46 newspapers. **Services:** Library open to qualified scholars by appointment only.

★ 12420 ★
One Sky, The Saskatchewan Cross Cultural Centre - Library (Soc Sci)
136 Ave. F
Saskatoon, SK, Canada S7M 1S8   Phone: (306)652-1571
Founded: 1973. **Staff:** 3. **Subjects:** International issues, native peoples, women and labor. **Holdings:** AV materials. **Subscriptions:** 132 journals and other serials. **Services:** Resource Centre open to the public for reference use only. **Publications:** One Sky Report. **Remarks:** FAX: (306)652-8377.

Oneida County Comprehensive Planning Program
See: **Herkimer-Oneida Counties Comprehensive Planning Program (7159)**

★12421★
Oneida County Historical Society - Colonel Tharratt Gilbert Best
  Library (Hist)
1608 Genesee St. Phone: (315)735-3642
Utica, NY 13502-5425 Douglas M. Preston, Dir.
Founded: 1876. **Staff:** Prof 3; Other 1. **Subjects:** History - Oneida County, Utica, Mohawk Valley. **Holdings:** 1500 volumes; 2500 pamphlets; 250,000 manuscript pieces. **Subscriptions:** 10 journals and other serials. **Services:** Copying; library open to the public. **Publications:** ONIOTA (newsletter), 10/year - to members, contributors, and local news media. **Special Catalogs:** Catalog of manuscripts (book). **Staff:** Betty Carpenter, Libn.

Eugene O'Neill Collection
See: **Museum of the City of New York - Theatre Collection (10892)**

★12422★
Eugene O'Neill Theater Center - Monte Cristo Cottage Library
  (Theater)
325 Pequot Ave.
New London, CT 06385 Phone: (203)443-5378
Founded: 1967. **Staff:** Prof 2. **Subjects:** Drama, dramatic literature, costume design, theater memorabilia. **Special Collections:** Johnson Briscoe Drama Collection; Virginia Dean Collection; Harold Friedlander Playbill Collection; Eugene O'Neill letters to Edward R. Keefe and Charles O'Brien Kennedy; O'Neill Theater Center National Playwrights Conference Scripts, 1966-1989; original letters; Pulitzer Prizes and Drama Circle Awards of Tennessee Williams and William Inge; original manuscript material from playwrights Frank Gagliano, Ron Cowen, Paul Foster, Israel Horovitz; Frederick Adler Collection of color movie window cards; Audrey Wood-William Liebling Collection of theater memorabilia. **Holdings:** 5000 books; playbills; theater scrapbooks; photographic stills; manuscripts; letters; set and costume designs; television manuscripts; clipping files; periodicals. **Services:** Copying; library open to the public. **Remarks:** FAX: (203)443-9653. Alternate telephone number(s): (203)443-0051. **Formerly:** Located in Waterford, CT. **Staff:** Sally Thomas Pavetti, Cur.; Lois Erickson McDonald, Assoc.Cur.

★12423★
Ongwanada Hospital - Library (Med)
191 Portsmouth Ave. Phone: (613)544-9611
Kingston, ON, Canada K7L 1J9 Rhoda McFarlane, Supv., Clin.Rec.
Founded: 1977. **Staff:** Prof 1; Other 1. **Subjects:** Mental retardation. **Holdings:** 750 books; 1 VF drawer of reprints; 95 AV programs; 1 film; 5 pieces of training equipment. **Subscriptions:** 23 journals and other serials. **Services:** Interlibrary loan; copying; library open to the public. **Remarks:** Library is located at 752 King St., W., Kingston, ON, CA K7M 8A6. **Staff:** Laura A. Kropp.

Online Computer Library Center, Inc.
See: **OCLC, Inc. (12243)**

★12424★
Onondaga County Public Library - Local History and Special
  Collections (Hist)
Galleries of Syracuse
447 S. Salina St. Phone: (315)448-INFO
Syracuse, NY 13202-2494 Patricia F. Finley, Dept.Hd.
Founded: 1852. **Staff:** Prof 4.5; Other 2.5. **Subjects:** Genealogy; history - Syracuse, Onondaga County, northeastern U.S. **Special Collections:** WPA file (19th century local newspaper extracts in subject arrangement, 200 file boxes). **Holdings:** 37,000 volumes; 40 VF drawers of clippings; 17 VF drawers of genealogical notes; 360 maps; 15,000 reels of microfilm; 26 drawers of microfiche. **Subscriptions:** 600 journals and other serials. **Services:** Copying; collections open to the public. **Automated Operations:** Computerized cataloging, acquisitions, and serials. **Computerized Information Services:** Business List, LOCNEWS (internal databases). **Publications:** Selected Obituaries - 19th century to present. **Special Indexes:** Onondaga County Pioneer Index (8 catalog drawers); Obituary Index (online); WPA file. **Staff:** Joan B. Palmer; Mark E. Allnatt; Renate C. Dunsmore; Susan D. Spence.

★12425★
Onondaga Historical Association - Library (Hist)
311 Montgomery St.
Syracuse, NY 13202 Phone: (315)428-1862
Founded: 1862. **Staff:** Prof 3. **Subjects:** Local and regional history, New York State canals. **Holdings:** 10,000 books; 100,000 photographs; 1000 cubic feet of archival materials. **Services:** Library open to the public. **Computerized Information Services:** RLIN. **Staff:** Edward Lyon, Libn.

Ontario Agricultural Museum
See: **Ontario Ministry of Agriculture and Food - Ontario Agricultural Museum - Library/Archives (12452)**

★12426★
The Ontario Archaeological Society - Library (Soc Sci)
126 Willowdale Ave. Phone: (416)730-0797
Willowdale, ON, Canada M2N 4Y2 Charles Garrad, Soc.Adm.
Staff: 1. **Subjects:** Archeology of Ontario, anthropology. **Holdings:** Reports; manuscripts. **Subscriptions:** 10 journals and other serials. **Services:** Copying; library open to the public with restrictions. **Special Indexes:** Indexes of society publications. **Remarks:** FAX: (416)730-0797.

★12427★
(Ontario) Archives of Ontario - Library (Hist)
Ministry of Culture & Communications
77 Grenville St. Phone: (416)327-1553
Toronto, ON, Canada M7A 2R9 Frank van Kalmthout, Libn.
Founded: 1903. **Staff:** Prof 1; Other 1. **Subjects:** Ontario social, political, military history; archival methodology; government records management. **Special Collections:** County and municipal directories; published minutes of Ontario municipalities; British Army Lists (60 volumes); Imperial Blue Books; Railroad and Navigation Pamphlets. **Holdings:** 6200 volumes; 13,000 pamphlets; 400 reels of microfilm; 3500 microfiche; Ontario government publications; municipal documents. **Subscriptions:** 85 journals and other serials. **Services:** Copying; library open to the public with restrictions. **Special Catalogs:** Separate author, title, and subject card file for pamphlets received prior to 1968. **Remarks:** FAX: (416)324-3600. **Staff:** Susan Watt, Lib.Techn.

★12428★
Ontario Bible College/Ontario Theological Seminary - J. William
  Horsey Library (Rel-Phil)
25 Ballyconnor Court Phone: (416)226-6380
Willowdale, ON, Canada M2M 4B3 Mr. Sandy Finlayson, Lib.Dir.
Founded: 1895. **Staff:** Prof 3; Other 3. **Subjects:** Biblical studies, theology, pastoral studies, Christian education, missions. **Special Collections:** Percival J. Baldwin Puritan Collection (53,756 books). **Holdings:** 4998 bound periodical volumes; 3316 volumes in microform; 5283 AV programs. **Subscriptions:** 570 journals and other serials. **Services:** Interlibrary loan; copying; SDI; library open to the public. **Automated Operations:** Computerized cataloging and ordering. **Computerized Information Services:** UTLAS, Books in Print Plus; internal database. **Remarks:** FAX: (416)226-6746. **Staff:** Chris Beldan, Tech.Serv./Sys.Libn.; Emma Penner, Supv., Acq.; Hugh Rendle, Pub.Serv.Libn.; Charlotte Church, Tech.Serv.Asst.; Iona Beagan, Circ.Asst.

★12429★
Ontario Cancer Foundation - Hamilton Regional Centre - Library (Med)
711 Concession St. Phone: (416)387-9495
Hamilton, ON, Canada L8V 1C3 Michael Fraumeni, Libn.
Staff: Prof 1. **Subjects:** Cancer, medical physics. **Holdings:** 1000 books; 1000 bound periodical volumes. **Subscriptions:** 58 journals and other serials. **Services:** Interlibrary loan; copying. **Computerized Information Services:** MEDLARS. **Networks/Consortia:** Member of Hamilton/Wentworth District Health Library Network. **Remarks:** FAX: (416)575-6316.

★12430★
Ontario Cancer Institute - Library (Med)
500 Sherbourne St. Phone: (416)926-4482
Toronto, ON, Canada M4X 1K9 Carol A. Morrison, Libn.
Founded: 1957. **Staff:** Prof 2; Other 3. **Subjects:** Cancer, radiotherapy, biophysics. **Holdings:** 7000 books; 10,000 bound periodical volumes;

pamphlets. **Subscriptions:** 450 journals and other serials. **Services:** Interlibrary loan; library not open to the public. **Automated Operations:** Computerized cataloging. **Computerized Information Services:** MEDLARS, DIALOG Information Services, CAN/OLE, BRS/ COLLEAGUE, DOBIS Canadian Online Library System, UTLAS, Infohealth; Infomart Online; Information Navigator (internal database); CD-ROM (MEDLINE); Envoy 100 (electronic mail service). **Remarks:** FAX: (416)926-6566. Electronic mail address(es): OTOC.LIBRARY (Envoy 100). **Staff:** Carole Tullis, Ref.Libn.

★ 12431 ★
Ontario Choral Federation - Library (Mus)
Maison Chalmers House
20 St. Joseph St.   Phone: (416)925-5525
Toronto, ON, Canada M4Y 1J9   Bev Jahnke, Exec.Adm.
Staff: 3. **Subjects:** Choral music. **Holdings:** Figures not available. **Services:** Library open to members. **Publications:** Newsletter, quarterly. **Remarks:** FAX: (416)961-7198. Alternate telephone number(s): 925-5525.

★ 12432 ★
Ontario College of Art - Dorothy H. Hoover Library (Art)
100 McCaul St.   Phone: (416)977-5311
Toronto, ON, Canada M5T 1W1   Jill Patrick, Dir.
Founded: 1930. **Staff:** Prof 5; Other 7. **Subjects:** Visual arts, design. **Special Collections:** Archives and Art Collection. **Holdings:** 20,000 books; 200 bound periodical volumes; 74,000 slides; 500 videotapes; 40,000 items in picture file; 32 VF drawers of information file. **Subscriptions:** 225 journals and other serials. **Services:** Interlibrary loan; copying; media booking; AV equipment loans; library open to the public with restrictions on borrowing. **Computerized Information Services:** Envoy 100 (electronic mail service). **Remarks:** FAX: (416)977-0235. Electronic mail address(es): J.PATRICK; ILL.OCA (Envoy 100). **Staff:** Richard Milburn, Hd., Pub.Serv.; James Forrester, Hd., Tech.Serv.; Angelo Rao, Hd., AV Serv.; Tom Ready, Media Libn.

★ 12433 ★
Ontario County Historical Society - Archives (Hist)
55 N. Main St.   Phone: (716)394-4975
Canandaigua, NY 14424   Thomas D. Mackie, Jr., Dir.
Founded: 1902. **Staff:** Prof 5; Other 4. **Subjects:** New York early land dealings, Civil War, history of Ontario County and western New York. **Special Collections:** Oliver Phelps; Oliver L. Phelps; Granger family papers (collection on western New York landholding); Hyland Kirk Collection; Jasper Parrish; Judge Smith papers; John J. Handrahan plans and drawings (landscape architecture, civil engineering). **Holdings:** 4000 books; bound Ontario County newspapers, 1803-1968; 500 maps; 40,000 manuscripts; 250 volumes in Manchester Library Collection; 6500 pieces of ephemera; 25,000 photographs and negatives; censuses on microfilm. **Services:** Copying; archives open to the public for use on premises with staff assistance.

★ 12434 ★
(Ontario) Court of Appeal for Ontario/Ontario Court of Justice - Judges' Library (Law)
Osgoode Hall
130 Queen St., W.   Phone: (416)327-5000
Toronto, ON, Canada M5H 2N5   Anne Brown, Libn.
Staff: Prof 1. **Subjects:** Law. **Holdings:** 20,000 volumes. **Subscriptions:** 20 journals and other serials. **Services:** Interlibrary loan; library not open to the public. **Remarks:** FAX: (416)327-5080. **Formerly:** (Ontario) Supreme Court of Ontario.

Ontario Court of Justice
See: **(Ontario) Court of Appeal for Ontario/Ontario Court of Justice** (12434)

★ 12435 ★
Ontario Crafts Council - Craft Resource Centre (Art)
Chalmers Bldg.
35 McCaul St.   Phone: (416)977-3551
Toronto, ON, Canada M5T 1V7   Sandra Dunn, Mgr.
Founded: 1975. **Staff:** 2. **Subjects:** All aspects of craft media. **Special Collections:** Archives (provincial, local craft guilds, prominent individuals;

vertical file); health hazards in arts and crafts (files; books; videotapes). **Holdings:** 3000 books; 300 bound periodical volumes; 500 portfolios of practicing Canadian craftspeople; 1100 exhibition catalogs; slide/videotape rental/sales programs. **Subscriptions:** 320 journals and other serials. **Services:** Consulting; center open to the public. **Computerized Information Services:** Internal databases. **Publications:** Annual Craft Shows in Ontario; Ontario Craft; CraftNews; Photography of Crafts; Trials of Jurying; Craft Shops and Galleries in Ontario; Starting Your Own Business; Business Bibliography; The Craftsperson's Guide to Good Business. **Special Catalogs:** Craft at Hand: slides and video catalog. **Special Indexes:** Indexes to publications of the Ontario Crafts Council; Ontario craftspeople (online). **Remarks:** FAX: (416)977-3552.

★ 12436 ★
Ontario Energy Board - Library (Energy)
Maple Leaf Mills Tower
2300 Yonge St., Suite 2601
P.O. Box 2319   Phone: (416)440-7655
Toronto, ON, Canada M4P 1E4   Lina Buccilli, Libn.
Founded: 1983. **Staff:** Prof 1. **Subjects:** Energy regulation, natural gas, electricity, gas pipelines, energy rates and pricing, energy economics, environmental impacts. **Special Collections:** Ontario Energy Board Reports and Decisions; National Energy Board Reports and Decisions; United States Public Utility Reports, 1932 to present; Public Utilities Fortnightly, 1962 to present. **Holdings:** 3000 books; decisions and reports. **Subscriptions:** 180 journals and other serials. **Services:** Interlibrary loan; copying; library open to the public by appointment for reference use only. **Computerized Information Services:** DIALOG Information Services, Info Globe, QL Systems, Infomart Online, CAN/OLE, WESTLAW, Dow Jones News/ Retrieval, FT PROFILE, The Financial Post DataGroup. **Remarks:** FAX: (416)440-7656.

★ 12437 ★
Ontario Federation of Labour - Resource Centre (Bus-Fin)
15 Gervais Dr., Suite 202   Phone: (416)441-2731
Don Mills, ON, Canada M3C 1Y8   Chris Schenk, Res.Dir.
Founded: 1969. **Staff:** Prof 1. **Subjects:** Labor relations, economic development, labor in politics, labor history. **Special Collections:** OFL Archives. **Holdings:** 800 books; 500 bound periodical volumes. **Subscriptions:** 50 journals and other serials. **Services:** Copying; center open to the public by appointment **Computerized Information Services:** CANSIM. **Publications:** Focus (newsletter), biweekly. **Remarks:** FAX: (416)441-0722. **Staff:** Judy Robins.

Ontario Film Institute - Library & Information Centre
See: **Cinematheque Ontario** (3712)

★ 12438 ★
Ontario Food Technology Centre - Information Services (Agri)
330 Richmond St., Suite 205   Phone: (519)351-8266
Chatham, ON, Canada N7M 1P7   Harry Oehlrich, Info.Mgr.
Founded: 1984. **Staff:** Prof 1. **Subjects:** Food processing and engineering, agricultural engineering. **Holdings:** 2000 books; 5000 microfiche; 50 videotapes. **Subscriptions:** 351 journals and other serials. **Services:** Interlibrary loan; library not open to the public. **Automated Operations:** Computerized cataloging, acquisitions, serials, and circulation. **Computerized Information Services:** DIALOG Information Services, BRS Information Technologies, CAN/OLE, QL Systems; internal databases; Envoy 100 (electronic mail service). Performs searches on fee basis. **Publications:** Newsletter - limited distribution.

Ontario Genealogical Society - Library
See: **North York Public Library - Canadiana Department** (11961)

★ 12439 ★
Ontario Genealogical Society - Library (Hist)
c/o Canadiana Collection, North York Public Library
North York Centre, 6th Fl.
5120 Yonge St.   Phone: (416)395-5623
Toronto, ON, Canada M2M 5N9   Jean Armstrong, Chm.
Founded: 1963. **Staff:** 2. **Subjects:** Genealogy and family history, heraldry, local history, biography. **Special Collections:** Cemetery Inscriptions Collection; Family Chart Collection; British County Record Offices Collection. **Holdings:** 4000 books; 45 bound periodical volumes; 1000 family histories. **Subscriptions:** 50 journals and other serials. **Services:** Interlibrary loan (limited); copying; library open to the public for reference use only. **Special Indexes:** Family Chart Collection List (printout); Inventory of Ontario Cemeteries (1987).

★ 12440 ★
**Ontario Genealogical Society, Kingston Branch - Kingston Public
Library** (Hist)
Box 1394
Kingston, ON, Canada K7L 5C6   Barbara Aitken, Br.Libn.
SFounded: 1973. **Subjects:** Genealogy, genealogical research, local history.
Holdings: 700 books; 200 bound periodical volumes; 2 VF drawers of
genealogical information; transcribed cemetery stones; transcribed census;
bibliographies. **Subscriptions:** 60 newsletters. **Services:** Copying; library
open to the public. **Publications:** OGS Kingston Branch Newsletter, 5 per
year - for internal distribution only. **Special Indexes:** Church records index
(card).

Ontario Geological Survey
See: **Ontario Ministry of Northern Development & Mines (12482)**

★ 12441 ★
Ontario Hospital Association - Library (Bus-Fin)
150 Ferrand Dr.   Phone: (416)429-2661
Don Mills, ON, Canada M3C 1H6   John Tagg, Mgr.
Founded: 1979. **Staff:** Prof 1; Other 1. **Subjects:** Hospital administration,
health economics, health insurance, management. **Holdings:** 1500 books.
Subscriptions: 102 journals and other serials. **Services:** Interlibrary loan;
copying; library open to the public for reference use only. **Computerized
Information Services:** DIALOG Information Services, MEDLARS, Info
Globe, Infomart Online, QL Systems, CAN/LAW. Performs searches on fee
basis. **Special Catalogs:** Audiovisuals Catalogue, annual. **Remarks:** FAX:
(416)429-1363.

★ 12442 ★
Ontario Hydro - Library (Energy, Sci-Engr)
700 University Ave., Mezzanine   Phone: (416)592-2719
Toronto, ON, Canada M5G 1X6   Bob Warren
Founded: 1916. **Staff:** Prof 15; Other 18. **Subjects:** Electrical engineering,
nuclear engineering, electric utilities, management. **Special Collections:**
Company reports and documents. **Holdings:** 95,000 volumes; 500,000
reports; microfiche. **Subscriptions:** 1100 journals and other serials. **Services:**
Interlibrary loan; copying; SDI; library open to the public in Public
Reference Center. **Automated Operations:** Computerized cataloging,
acquisitions, circulation, and serials routing. **Computerized Information
Services:** DIALOG Information Services, PFDS Online, QL Systems,
CAN/OLE, UTLAS, BRS Information Technologies, MEDLARS,
WESTLAW, Info Globe, Questel, STN International; internal databases;
UTLAS, CAN/OLE (electronic mail services). **Publications:** Library
bulletin; acquisitions list, monthly; brochure. **Remarks:** Holdings include
the Research Division Branch Library, the Place Nouveau Branch Library,
the College Park Branch Library, and the Public Reference Center
Consulting Services. **Remarks:** FAX: (416)978-0043. Telex: 06 217662.
Staff: Sylvia Ernesaks, Sr.Libn.; Kim Cornell, Tran Dam Info.Rsrcs.Supv.;
Chris Robinson, Info.Rsrcs.Supv.; Nancy Fish, Sr.Libn.; Carol Elder,
Sr.Libn.; Jiun Lee, Libn.; Ingrid Kalnins, Libn.; Martha Ghent, Libn.;
Karen McClymont, Libn.; Donna Gardner, Sr.Libn.; Erica Ewen, Libn.;
Myra Binstock, Libn.; Mary Wagner, Jr.Libn.; Mark Merryweather,
Jr.Libn.

★ 12443 ★
**Ontario Institute for Studies in Education (OISE) - Modern Language
Centre - Language Teaching Library** (Hum)
252 Bloor St., W.   Phone: (416)923-6641
Toronto, ON, Canada M5S 1V6   Alice Weinrib, Res.Assoc./Libn.
Founded: 1970. **Staff:** Prof 1; Other 1. **Subjects:** French as a second
langauge, English as a second language, theory and methodology of second
language teaching, Spanish, German, Italian, and Chinese. **Special
Collections:** Language curricula resources for the classroom. **Holdings:**
15,000 books; 200 bound periodical volumes; 2750 tapes; 60 language tests;
3500 documents; 110 charts and visuals; 70 filmstrip and slide programs.
Subscriptions: 50 journals and other serials. **Services:** Copying; library open
to the public with restrictions. **Computerized Information Services:** Internal
database. **Publications:** Bibliographies.

★ 12444 ★
**Ontario Institute for Studies in Education (OISE) - R.W.B. Jackson
Library** (Educ)
252 Bloor St., W.   Phone: (416)923-6641
Toronto, ON, Canada M5S 1V6   Grace F. Bulaong, Chf.Libn.
Founded: 1965. **Staff:** Prof 18; Other 25. **Subjects:** Education, psychology,
sociology, statistical methodology, linguistics, history, philosophy,
computer applications, economics, demography. **Special Collections:**
Ontario History of Education Collection (20,000 volumes); Paulo Freire
Resource Collection (books and reprints). **Holdings:** 242,031 books; 28,052
bound periodical volumes; 481,266 microforms; 16,571 films, audio- and
videotapes, kits, games, and other multimedia resources; 79 linear feet of
curriculum guides, curriculum publisher and AV distributor catalogs; 1412
computer disks and tapes. **Subscriptions:** 2301 journals and other serials.
Services: Interlibrary loan; copying; library open to the public. **Automated
Operations:** Computerized public access catalog, cataloging, circulation and
acquisitions. **Computerized Information Services:** BRS Information
Technologies, DIALOG Information Services; CD-ROM (ERIC); Envoy
100 (electronic mail service). Performs searches on fee basis. **Publications:**
J.R. Kidd: A Bibliography of His Writings. **Special Catalogs:** Ontario
Textbook Collection catalog (microfiche); theses catalog (microfiche).
Special Indexes: Index to the Paulo Freire Resource Collection (list);
periodicals (list). **Remarks:** FAX: (416)926-4725. Telex: NR062 17720.
Electronic mail address(es): GF.BULAONG (administration, Envoy 100);
ILL.OTER (ILL, Envoy 100). **Staff:** Ann Neveu, Adm.Off.; Ilze Bregzis,
Libn., Tech.Serv.; Jan Schmidt, Libn., Pub.Serv.; Carol Calder, AV Libn.;
Mary Campbell, Automation Libn.; Ruth Marks, Curric.Rsrcs.Libn.;
Valerie Downs, Acq.Libn.; Kamlesh Sharma, Supv., Circ.; Marian Press,
Ref. & Info.Serv.Libn.

★ 12445 ★
**Ontario Institute for Studies in Education (OISE) - Women's
Educational Resources Centre** (Soc Sci)
252 Bloor St., W., Rm. 11-199   Phone: (416)923-6641
Toronto, ON, Canada M5S 1V6   Frieda Forman, Coord.
Founded: 1976. **Staff:** Prof 3. **Subjects:** Women's studies and issues. **Special
Collections:** Works of Canadian women authors. **Holdings:** 7000 books;
newspaper clipping file; curriculum materials; photographs; AV programs;
archival material; vertical files; government reports. **Subscriptions:** 200
journals and 400 other serials. **Services:** Copying; center open to the public.
Special Indexes: Index of periodical articles. **Remarks:** FAX: (416)926-
4725. **Staff:** Peggy Bristow, Res.Off.; Ilda Januario, Res.Off., French
Holdings.

Ontario Labour Relations Board
See: **Ontario Ministry of Labour (12475)**

★ 12446 ★
Ontario Legislative Assembly - Legislative Library (Law, Hist)
Legislative Bldg., Queen's Park   Phone: (416)325-3900
Toronto, ON, Canada M7A 1A9   R. Brian Land, Exec.Dir.
Founded: 1867. **Staff:** Prof 44; Other 49. **Subjects:** Political science,
especially parliamentary systems; law; public administration and policy;
economics; Ontario and Canadian history. **Special Collections:** Full
depository for Ontario, Quebec, and Canadian government publications;
government publications from other provinces, British Parliament, and U.S.
Congress; U.S. Congressional Information Service, 1970 to present, on
microfiche; Microlog and CanCorps Documents Services on microfiche
from Micromedia Limited; Ontario current daily and weekly newspapers;
Canadian and British statutes and law reports. **Holdings:** 88,901 books; 7758
bound periodical volumes; 966,617 microfiche; 9127 reels of microfilm; 2955
current data files; 1366 videotapes; 209 audio cassettes. **Subscriptions:** 2842
journals and other serials; 315 newspapers. **Services:** Interlibrary loan;
copying; library open to the public with restrictions. **Automated Operations:**
Computerized cataloging, acquisitions, and serials. **Computerized
Information Services:** DIALOG Information Services, ORBIT Search
Service, QL Systems, Maxwell Online, Inc., Info Globe, CAN/LAW,
Infomart Online, The Financial Post Information Service, MEDLINE,
CAN/OLE, WESTLAW, Mead Data Central, Dow Jones News/Retrieval,
NewsNet, Inc., ELSS (Electronic Legislative Search System), FT
PROFILE, VU/TEXT Information Services, Conference Board of Canada,
BRS Information Technologies, Newstex, Yorkline; internal database;
Envoy 100 (electronic mail service). **Publications:** Annual Report of the
Executive Director; Memo to Members, irregular; Periodical Contents,
weekly during session; Periodical Selections, monthly; Selected New Titles,
monthly; Press Highlights, irregular; Services to the Legislature;

Automation Alert, biweekly; Status of Bills Report, weekly during session; Toronto Press Today, daily; Provincial Press, weekly; Current Issue Papers and Information Kits. **Special Catalogs:** Ontario Government Publications Monthly Checklist (book); Ontario Government Publications Annual Catalogue (book). **Remarks:** FAX: (416)325-3925. Electronic mail address(es): ONT.LEG.LIB (Envoy 100). **Staff:** Mary Dickerson, Dp.Exec.Dir./Dir., Info. and Ref.Serv.; Pamela Stoksik, Dir., Tech.Serv. & Sys.; Donna Burton, Act.Mgr., Press Clipping Serv.; Linda L. Reid, Mgr., Checklist & Cat.Serv.; Cynthia S. Smith, Dir., Leg.Res.Serv.; Brian Tobin, Hd., Coll.Dev.: Wyley L. Powell, Exec.Asst.

★ 12447 ★
Ontario Lottery Corporation - Library
70 Foster Dr., Suite 800
Sault Ste. Marie, ON, Canada P6A 6V2   Phone: (705)946-6464
Founded: 1978. **Subjects:** Lotteries, casinos, off-track betting, gaming and gambling, compulsive gambling, public relations, draws, community relations. **Holdings:** 100 books; draw cassettes; gaming reports; casino studies; marketing assessments; rules and regulations for social gaming; news clippings. **Remarks:** Currently inactive.

★ 12448 ★
Ontario March of Dimes - Information Service (Soc Sci)
60 Overlea Blvd.   Phone: (416)425-0501
Toronto, ON, Canada M4H 1B6   Shirley Teolis, Info.Serv.Coord.
Holdings: Figures not available. **Services:** Library open to the public. **Remarks:** FAX: (416)425-0488.

★ 12449 ★
Ontario Medical Association - Corporate Records & Library Services (Med)
525 University Ave., Suite 300   Phone: (416)599-2580
Toronto, ON, Canada M5G 2K7   Jan Greenwood, Assoc.Dir.
Founded: 1972. **Staff:** Prof 2; Other 4. **Subjects:** Canadian medical economics, medico-legal practices and sociomedical affairs, health library service. **Special Collections:** Medical office management; reference collection for health library consulting service. **Holdings:** 2000 books. **Subscriptions:** 250 journals and other serials. **Services:** Interlibrary loan; copying; library open to the public by appointment. **Automated Operations:** Computerized cataloging and serials. **Computerized Information Services:** MEDLARS; internal database; Envoy 100 (electronic mail service). **Networks/Consortia:** Member of Ontario Hospital Libraries Association (OHLA). **Publications:** Health Sciences Library Manual, 1982; Medical Office Management Bibliography, annual. **Special Indexes:** Ontario Medical Review Index. **Remarks:** Operating under a grant from the PSI Foundation for its collection in Canadian medical economics, the library also provides a consulting service for Ontario hospital libraries. **Remarks:** FAX: (416)599-9309. Electronic mail address(es): J.GREENWOOD (Envoy 100).

★ 12450 ★
Ontario Ministry of Agriculture and Food - Horticultural Research Institute of Ontario - Library (Agri)
Vineland Station, ON, Canada L0R 2E0   Phone: (416)562-4141
     Judith Wanner, Libn.
Founded: 1970. **Staff:** Prof 1. **Subjects:** Fruit and vegetable crops, ornamental plants, botany, food science, winemaking, viticulture. **Holdings:** 4000 books; 1500 bound periodical volumes; 2000 pamphlets; annual reports; documents; agricultural statistics. **Subscriptions:** 254 journals and other serials; 7 newspapers. **Services:** Interlibrary loan; copying; library open to the public for reference use only. **Computerized Information Services:** CAN/OLE, DIALOG Information Services. **Publications:** Annual Book Acquisitions List - for internal distribution only. **Remarks:** FAX: (416)562-3413.

★ 12451 ★
Ontario Ministry of Agriculture and Food - Library (Agri)
801 Bay St., 3rd Fl.   Phone: (416)326-3138
Toronto, ON, Canada M7A 2B2   Sharon Brown, Mgr., Lib.Serv.
Founded: 1969. **Staff:** Prof 2; Other 3. **Subjects:** Agricultural economics, land use, rural agricultural statistics, Ontario and Canadian agriculture, food industry and trade, agriculture and energy, animal husbandry, agricultural marketing and trade, economics, management. **Holdings:** 12,000 books; 2500 microfiche; 100 reels of microfilm. **Subscriptions:** 700

journals and other serials. **Services:** Interlibrary loan; copying; library open to the public for reference use only. **Automated Operations:** Computerized cataloging, acquisitions, serials, and circulation. **Computerized Information Services:** DIALOG Information Services, Info Globe, CAN/OLE, Infomart Online, WILSONLINE, The Financial Post DataGroup, QL Systems; CD-ROM; SYDNEY (internal database). **Publications:** New Publications, monthly - to staff and other interested libraries; bibliographies on agricultural topics. **Remarks:** FAX: (416)325-1152.

Ontario Ministry of Agriculture and Food - New Liskeard College of Agricultural Technology
See: New Liskeard College of Agricultural Technology (11518)

★ 12452 ★
Ontario Ministry of Agriculture and Food - Ontario Agricultural Museum - Library/Archives (Agri)
Box 38   Phone: (416)878-8151
Milton, ON, Canada L9T 2Y3   Susan Bennett, Res. & Ref.Libn.
Founded: 1974. **Staff:** Prof 2. **Subjects:** Ontario history - agricultural, local, social, political, economic; poultry and animal husbandry; horticulture; botany. **Special Collections:** Agricultural Implement Catalogue Collection (20,000); Agricultural history subject headings; Massey-Ferguson Archives; IHC (Canada) Archives. **Holdings:** 15,000 books; 250 films; 300 reels of microfilm; 60 videotapes; 5000 historical agricultural periodicals; 200 maps and charts; 2000 government publications; 40,000 photographs and negatives; 2000 U.S. patent records. **Subscriptions:** 45 journals and other serials. **Services:** Interlibrary loan; copying; library open to the public for reference use only. **Automated Operations:** Computerized cataloging. **Computerized Information Services:** SYDNEY, Photographic Database (internal databases). **Publications:** Occasional Papers, biennial. **Special Indexes:** Subject Index to Government Documents, Monographs, and Periodical Collection; Implement/Manufacturer Index to Agricultural Machinery Collection; Index to photographic collection (on line). **Remarks:** FAX: (416)876-4530. **Staff:** Lynn Campbell, Hist.Res.

Ontario Ministry of Agriculture and Food - Ridgetown College of Agricultural Technology
See: Ridgetown College of Agricultural Technology (13917)

★ 12453 ★
Ontario Ministry of Agriculture and Food - Veterinary Services Laboratory Library (Med)
P.O. Box 2005   Phone: (613)258-8320
Kemptville, ON, Canada K0G 1J0   Vivian Martineau, Libn.
Founded: 1948. **Staff:** 1. **Subjects:** Veterinary medicine, pathology, animal science. **Holdings:** 100 books; 250 bound periodical volumes. Figures not available. **Subscriptions:** 31 journals and other serials. **Services:** Interlibrary loan; copying; library open to veterinarians only.

★ 12454 ★
Ontario Ministry of Agriculture and Food - Veterinary Services Laboratory Library (Med)
Box 790   Phone: (705)647-6719
New Liskeard, ON, Canada P0J 1P0   Dr. S.D. Copeland, Lab.Hd.
Founded: 1961. **Staff:** Prof 3. **Subjects:** Veterinary medicine and pathology. **Holdings:** 200 books; 340 bound periodical volumes. **Subscriptions:** 25 journals and other serials; 10 newspapers. **Services:** Library open to veterinarians. **Remarks:** FAX: (705)647-6297.

★ 12455 ★
Ontario Ministry of the Attorney General - Library (Law)
720 Bay St., 9th Fl.
Toronto, ON, Canada M5G 2K1   Phone: (416)326-4566
Staff: Prof 2; Other 4. **Subjects:** Law - criminal, civil, constitutional. **Special Collections:** English reports (178 volumes); Law Reports (including Appeal Cases, Chancery Division, Probate Division, Queen's Bench, King's Bench: 1000 volumes); All England Law Reports (1500 volumes). **Holdings:** 1500 books; 12,000 bound periodical volumes. **Subscriptions:** 100 journals and other serials. **Services:** Interlibrary loan; library open to the public by appointment. **Computerized Information Services:** QL Systems, WESTLAW, CAN/LAW, LEXIS, DIALOG Information Services, Info Globe, SOQUIJ. **Remarks:** FAX: (416)326-4562. **Staff:** Maria Cece, Ref.Libn.

Ontario Ministry of Community and Social Services - Huronia Regional Centre
See: **Huronia Regional Centre (7588)**

★ 12456 ★
Ontario Ministry of Community and Social Services - Library and Learning Resources (Soc Sci)
880 Bay St., 4th Fl.   Phone: (416)326-6442
Toronto, ON, Canada M7A 1E9   Dolly E. Lyn, Mgr., Lib. & LRC
Founded: 1968. **Staff:** Prof 2.5; Other 3. **Subjects:** Adolescence, adoption, aged, public welfare, developmentally disabled, child abuse, child welfare, physically handicapped, rehabilitation, social problems, social work, juvenile delinquency, personnel management, career development. **Holdings:** 35,000 books; 1000 bound periodical volumes; 500 reels of microfilm; 18,000 microfiche; 300 audio cassettes; 200 video cassettes; 1500 reprints. **Subscriptions:** 450 journals and newsletters. **Services:** Interlibrary loan; copying; SDI; library open to the public for reference use only. **Automated Operations:** Computerized public access catalog, cataloging, acquisitions, serials, and circulation. **Computerized Information Services:** DIALOG Information Services, BRS Information Technologies, QL Systems, LEXIS, NEXIS, Info Globe, Infomart Online, UTLAS; Envoy 100 (electronic mail service). **Publications:** New Resources: Books, Audiovisuals (acquisitions list), bimonthly; New Resources: Journal Articles, bimonthly - both to ministry personnel, affiliated agencies, and government libraries. **Special Catalogs:** Audiovisual resources catalog, annual. **Remarks:** Alternate telephone number(s): 326-6448 (reference). FAX: (416)326-6453. Electronic mail address(es): ILL.OTPW (Envoy 100). **Staff:** Elizabeth Sharp, Coord., Lib.Serv.; Patricia Fortin, Ref.Libn.

Ontario Ministry of Community and Social Services - Prince Edward Heights - Resident Records Library
See: **Prince Edward Heights - Resident Records Library (13348)**

★ 12457 ★
Ontario Ministry of Community and Social Services - Resource Library (Med)
Hwy. 59 N.
P.O. Box 310   Phone: (519)539-1251
Woodstock, ON, Canada N4S 7X9   Rita Thompson, Libn.
Staff: Prof 1. **Subjects:** Mental retardation, epilepsy, tuberculosis. **Holdings:** 800 books; tapes, cassettes. **Subscriptions:** 69 journals and other serials. **Services:** Interlibrary loan; copying; library open to the public with restrictions. **Publications:** Bibliotheca Medica Canadiana, quarterly - to members.

★ 12458 ★
Ontario Ministry of Community and Social Services - Rideau Regional Centre - Staff Library & Information Centre (Med)
P.O. Box 2000   Phone: (613)284-0123
Smiths Falls, ON, Canada K7A 4T7   Pat Kiteley, Lib.Techn.
Founded: 1977. **Staff:** Prof 1. **Subjects:** Mental retardation, psychology, social work, medicine. **Holdings:** 4000 books. **Subscriptions:** 127 journals and other serials. **Services:** Interlibrary loan; library open to the public with restrictions. **Publications:** VOX and RefeRenCe (newsletter) - for internal distribution only.

Ontario Ministry of Community and Social Services - Thistletown Regional Centre
See: **Thistletown Regional Centre (16310)**

★ 12459 ★
Ontario Ministry of Consumer and Commercial Relations - Consumer Information Centre (Bus-Fin)
555 Yonge St., 1st Fl.   Phone: (416)326-8556
Toronto, ON, Canada M7A 2H6   Brenda Darby, Mgr.
Founded: 1978. **Staff:** 11. **Subjects:** Law; business; securities regulation; consumer information, education, and protection; insurance; financial institutions. **Holdings:** 7000 books. **Subscriptions:** 150 journals and other serials. **Services:** Interlibrary loan; public inquiry in person, by phone, and by mail; development of educational material; center open to the public for reference use only. **Remarks:** In Ontario, the toll-free number is (800)268-1142. Telephone for Speech/Hearing Impaired: (416)326-8566. FAX: (416)326-8543.

★ 12460 ★
Ontario Ministry of Correctional Services - Staff Library (Law)
200 1st Ave., W
P.O. Box 4100   Phone: (705)494-3397
North Bay, ON, Canada P1B 9M3   Mrs. Silva Minassian, Chf.Libn.
Founded: 1958. **Staff:** Prof 2; Other 2. **Subjects:** Penology, criminology, social work, psychology, substance abuse. **Holdings:** 5000 books; 50 feet of pamphlets and reports. **Subscriptions:** 150 journals and other serials. **Services:** Interlibrary loan; SDI. **Automated Operations:** Computerized cataloging and serials. **Computerized Information Services:** DIALOG Information Services, CAN/OLE, DOBIS Canadian Online Library System. Performs searches. **Publications:** New Acquisitions List, 4/year - for internal distribution only; periodical holdings list, annual. **Remarks:** FAX: (705)494-3398. **Staff:** Caroline Sewards, Staff Libn.

★ 12461 ★
Ontario Ministry of Culture and Communications - Libraries and Community Information Branch (Info Sci)
77 Bloor St., W., 3rd Fl.   Phone: (416)965-2696
Toronto, ON, Canada M7A 2R9   Barbara Clubb, Dir.
Staff: 23. **Subjects:** Professional development in librarianship, public library statistics. **Services:** Branch not open to the public. **Remarks:** Administers Public Libraries Act, promotes public library and community information services, coordinates library services, and provides financial aid to public libraries and information centers. Also administers Ontario Library Service. FAX: (416)965-5883. **Staff:** Maureen Cubberley, Mgr., Ontario Lib.Serv.; Brian Beattie, Mgr., Plan./Evaluation/Grants Adm. Unit; Stan Squires, Mgr., Tech.Dev.

★ 12462 ★
Ontario Ministry of Education - Information Services (Educ)
Mowat Block, 13th Fl.
Queen's Park   Phone: (416)325-2630
Toronto, ON, Canada M7A 1L2   Hilary Roy, Coord.
Founded: 1979. **Staff:** Prof 6; Other 6. **Subjects:** Education theory and practice at all levels, literacy, business/management. **Special Collections:** Ministry of Education; Ministry of Colleges and Universities; Ministry of Skills Development publications; Ontario college and university calendars; briefs of Ontario Education Commissions. **Holdings:** 30,000 books; 25 drawers of microfiche; 45 VF drawers; federal and Ontario sessional papers. **Subscriptions:** 1000 journals and other serials; 7 newspapers. **Services:** Interlibrary loan; center open to the public for reference use only. **Automated Operations:** Computerized cataloging and serials. **Computerized Information Services:** DIALOG Information Services, QL Systems, Info Globe, CAN/OLE, Questel, UTLAS, WILSONLINE, Infomart Online; CD-ROMs (ERIC, CD:Education). **Publications:** Daily, Weekly Newsclipping Service: What's New, monthly; Routing Journals, irregular; Acronyms List, annual. **Remarks:** FAX: (416)325-4235. **Staff:** Simon Loban, Supv., Info.Serv.; Edna Nickie, Supv., Tech.Serv.

★ 12463 ★
Ontario Ministry of Education - Midnorthern Regional Office - Education Center Library (Educ)
199 Larch St., 7th Fl.   Phone: (705)675-4401
Sudbury, ON, Canada P3E 5P9   Marie Wright, Lib.Techn.
Founded: 1967. **Staff:** Prof 1. **Subjects:** Education, psychology. **Holdings:** 25,000 books; 5000 unbound periodicals; 2000 microfiche. **Subscriptions:** 100 journals and other serials; 5 newspapers. **Services:** Interlibrary loan; copying. **Publications:** Additions to the Library Catalog/Additions au Catalogue de la Bibliotheque. **Remarks:** FAX: (705)675-4186.

★ 12464 ★
Ontario Ministry of Education - Northwestern Ontario Region - Reference Library (Educ)
435 James St., S.
P.O. Box 5000   Phone: (807)475-1543
Thunder Bay, ON, Canada P7C 5G6   Fay Nagy, Libn.
Founded: 1975. **Staff:** 1. **Subjects:** Education. **Holdings:** 200 books; 300 reports; 100 archival items; 5000 microfiche. **Subscriptions:** 60 journals and other serials; 3 newspapers. **Services:** Interlibrary loan; library not open to the public. **Formerly:** Its Teachers' Resource Library.

★ 12465 ★
Ontario Ministry of Energy - Information Resource Centre (Energy)
56 Wellesley St., W., 10th Fl.   Phone: (416)327-1247
Toronto, ON, Canada M7A 2B7   Marusia Borodacz, Coord.
Founded: 1974. **Staff:** Prof 2; Other 2. **Subjects:** Energy policy, programs,
and technologies. **Special Collections:** Statistics Canada catalogs on
microfiche. **Holdings:** 15,000 books. **Subscriptions:** 500 journals and other
serials; 10 newspapers. **Services:** Interlibrary loan; copying; center open to
the public by appointment. **Automated Operations:** Computerized
cataloging, acquisitions, and circulation. **Computerized Information
Services:** DIALOG Information Services, PFDS Online, QL Systems, Info
Globe, Infomart Online, The Financial Post Information Service, CAN/
OLE, STN International; internal databases; Envoy 100, UTLAS (electronic
mail services). **Remarks:** FAX: (416)327-1510. **Staff:** Susanne Baker,
Tech.Info.Anl.; Heather Ara, Info.Spec.; Tana Chirita, Acq.Ser. &
Cir.Tech.

★ 12466 ★
Ontario Ministry of the Environment - Air Resources Branch Library
  (Env-Cons)
880 Bay St., 4th Fl.   Phone: (416)326-1633
Toronto, ON, Canada M5S 1Z8   David Reynolds, Libn.
Subjects: Air pollution, emission technology, phytotoxicology. **Special
Collections:** Ministry Technical Reports. **Holdings:** 1200 books; 1700
reports. **Subscriptions:** 95 journals and other serials. **Services:** Interlibrary
loan; copying; library open to the public by appointment. **Remarks:** FAX:
(416)326-1733.

★ 12467 ★
Ontario Ministry of the Environment - Laboratory Library (Env-Cons,
  Sci-Engr)
125 Resource Rd.
P.O. Box 213   Phone: (416)235-5751
Rexdale, ON, Canada M9W 5L1   Norville McIlroy, Lab.Libn.
Founded: 1960. **Staff:** Prof 2. **Subjects:** Water pollution, water supply, solid
waste, air, noise, biology, chemistry. **Special Collections:** Ministry of the
Environment technical publications. **Holdings:** 35,000 books; 2000 bound
periodical volumes; 40 VF drawers of reprints, government reports,
documents; 60,000 microfiche. **Subscriptions:** 150 journals and other serials.
Services: Interlibrary loan; library open to the public for reference use only.
Computerized Information Services: QL Systems, CAN/OLE, DIALOG
Information Services, MEDLINE. **Publications:** Acquisitions list,
bimonthly. **Remarks:** FAX: (416)235-0189. Telex: 06-23496. Includes
holdings of the Ministry of the Environment - Laboratory and Research
Library.

★ 12468 ★
**Ontario Ministry of Government Services - C.T.S. Information Resource
  Centre** (Comp Sci)
155 University Ave., 8th Fl.   Phone: (416)327-3329
Toronto, ON, Canada M5H 3B7   Jin Lei, Libn.
Founded: 1975. **Staff:** Prof 1. **Subjects:** Electronic data processing (EDP)
technical and product reference. **Holdings:** 250 books; 70 government
documents; 25 video reference journals. **Subscriptions:** 65 journals and other
serials. **Services:** Library open to government personnel. **Computerized
Information Services:** Info Globe, Infomart Online, DIALOG Information
Services. **Publications:** IRC Informer, bimonthly - to selected government
offices. **Remarks:** FAX: (416)327-3348.

★ 12469 ★
**Ontario Ministry of Government Services - Library & Information
  Services** (Info Sci)
Ferguson Block, 4th Fl.   Phone: (416)327-2533
77 Wellesley St. W.   Marilyn MacKellar, Coord., Lib.
Toronto, ON, Canada M7A 1N3   and Info.Serv.
Founded: 1987. **Staff:** Prof 1. **Subjects:** Government documents,
information processing and systems, personnel, property management.
Special Collections: Ministry publications. **Holdings:** 2000 books and
government documents; 5 videotapes; 10 audiotapes. **Subscriptions:** 50
journals and other serials. **Services:** Library open to Ministry personnel.
Computerized Information Services: DIALOG Information Services,
Infomart Online, Info Globe, QL Systems, LEXIS, NEXIS, CAN/OLE,
UTLAS; internal database; CD-ROMs. **Remarks:** FAX: (416)326-2533;
327-2530.

★ 12470 ★
Ontario Ministry of Health - Library (Med)
15 Overlea Blvd., 1st Fl.   Phone: (416)965-7881
Toronto, ON, Canada M4H 1A9   Veronica Brunka, Lib.Supv.
Founded: 1933. **Staff:** Prof 1; Other 4. **Subjects:** Public health, preventive
medicine, health care services, hospital administration. **Holdings:** 9000
books; 25 VF drawers; 400 microfiche. **Subscriptions:** 1100 journals and
other serials. **Services:** Interlibrary loan; library open to the public with
restrictions. **Computerized Information Services:** MEDLARS, DIALOG
Information Services, Infomart Online, Info Globe. **Publications:** Library
Bulletin, quarterly - to ministry personnel.

**Ontario Ministry of Health - Mental Health Division - Hamilton
  Psychiatric Hospital**
See: **Hamilton Psychiatric Hospital** (6865)

**Ontario Ministry of Health - Mental Health Division - Kingston
  Psychiatric Hospital**
See: **Kingston Psychiatric Hospital** (8732)

**Ontario Ministry of Health - Mental Health Division - St. Thomas
  Psychiatric Hospital**
See: **St. Thomas Psychiatric Hospital** (14599)

★ 12471 ★
Ontario Ministry of Health - Public Health Laboratories - Library
  (Med)
Box 9000, Postal Terminal A   Phone: (416)235-5935
Toronto, ON, Canada M5W 1R5   Doris A. Standing, Libn.
Founded: 1963. **Staff:** Prof 1; Other 1. **Subjects:** Medical microbiology,
medical laboratory technology. **Holdings:** 3500 volumes; 3 VF drawers of
pamphlets. **Subscriptions:** 135 journals and other serials. **Services:**
Interlibrary loan (limited); copying (to medical and Ontario government
libraries only); library open to the public by special permission for reference
use only. **Computerized Information Services:** MEDLARS.

★ 12472 ★
Ontario Ministry of Housing - Library (Plan)
2-777 Bay St.   Phone: (416)585-6527
Toronto, ON, Canada M5G 2E5   Frank Szucs, Libn.
Founded: 1965. **Staff:** Prof 2; Other 2. **Subjects:** Housing, community
planning, urban renewal, city planning, municipal government and finance.
Holdings: 25,000 books; 20,000 microfiche. **Subscriptions:** 340 journals and
other serials. **Services:** Interlibrary loan; copying; library open to the public
for reference use only. **Computerized Information Services:** QL Systems,
CAN/OLE, DIALOG Information Services, Info Globe, Infomart Online,
DOBIS Canadian Online Library System, UTLAS. **Publications:** Library
Bulletin, irregular - to ministry staff. **Special Indexes:** List of periodical
literature. **Remarks:** FAX: (416)585-7300. **Staff:** Annette Dignan,
Asst.Libn.

★ 12473 ★
**Ontario Ministry of Industry, Trade and Technology - Information
  Centre** (Bus-Fin)
Hearst Block, 3rd Fl.
Queen's Park
900 Bay St.   Phone: (416)325-6625
Toronto, ON, Canada M7A 2E1   Muin Hasan, Mgr.
Founded: 1946. **Staff:** Prof 2; Other 2. **Subjects:** Trade, industrial
development, small business, technology, management. **Holdings:** 15,000
books. **Subscriptions:** 300 journals and other serials; 7 newspapers. **Services:**
Interlibrary loan; copying; center open to the public for reference use only.
Automated Operations: Computerized cataloging and serials. **Computerized
Information Services:** Info Globe, DIALOG Information Services, CAN/
OLE, QL Systems, Infomart Online, The Financial Post Information
Service, UTLAS, BOSS, STM Systems Corporation. **Publications:**
Information Center News, monthly; Current Contents, monthly - limited
distribution. **Remarks:** FAX: (416)324-3511. **Staff:** Nazlin Chagpar, Ref./
Info.Spec.; Dragana Martinovic, Cat.Spec.

★ 12474 ★

Ontario Ministry of Labour - Library and Information Services (Bus-Fin)
400 University Ave., 10th Fl.   Phone: (416)326-7840
Toronto, ON, Canada M7A 1T7   Sandra A. Walsh, Mgr.
Founded: 1949. **Staff:** Prof 6; Other 10. **Subjects:** Labor relations, occupational health and safety, pay equity, employment, women, industrial relations, manpower. **Special Collections:** International Labor Organization materials. **Holdings:** 73,000 books; 1000 bound periodical volumes; 14,000 pamphlets; 412,500 microforms. **Subscriptions:** 1200 serials. **Services:** Interlibrary loan; copying; SDI; library open to the public. **Automated Operations:** Computerized cataloging, acquisitions, and serials. **Computerized Information Services:** Questel, BRS Information Technologies, Canadian Financial Database (C.F.D.), DIALOG Information Services, PFDS Online, QL Systems, Infomart Online, MEDLINE, Info Globe, Occupational Health Services, Inc., CAN/OLE, UTLAS, TOMES, SkillsLink; internal databases; Envoy 100 (electronic mail service). **Publications:** Info Link: Occupational Health and Safety; Info Link: Labour Relations and Employment; Library Bulletin: Occupational Health and Safety; Library Bulletin: Labour Topics. **Remarks:** FAX: (416)326-7844. Electronic mail address(es): ILL.OTDL (Envoy 100). **Staff:** Janet Tyrell, Hd., Tech.Serv.; Sandra Gold, Hd., Info.Serv.; Brian Morrison, Occupational Hea. & Safety Libn.; Rohini Tiwari, Cat.

★ 12475 ★

Ontario Ministry of Labour - Ontario Labour Relations Board - Library (Law)
400 University Ave., 4th Fl.   Phone: (416)326-7468
Toronto, ON, Canada M7A 1V4   Kevin Jenkins, Lib.Hd.
Founded: 1975. **Staff:** Prof 1; Other 2. **Subjects:** Labor law. **Holdings:** 1000 books; 4000 bound periodical volumes; Ontario Labour Relations Board reports, 1944 to present; National Labour Relations Board publications, volume 1 to volume 272; unreported OLRB decisions. **Subscriptions:** 160 journals and other serials. **Services:** Interlibrary loan; copying; library open to the public. **Automated Operations:** Computerized cataloging. **Computerized Information Services:** QL Systems, CAN/LAW, WESTLAW, LEXIS, Infomart Online; internal database; QUICKMAIL. **Publications:** Library newsletter, monthly; bibliographies, monthly - both for internal distribution only. **Special Indexes:** Index to Ontario Labour Relations Board reports (on microfiche). **Remarks:** FAX: (416)326-7531.

★ 12476 ★

Ontario Ministry of Labour - Resource Centre for Occupational Health & Safety (Med)
Lakehead University
Oliver Rd.   Phone: (807)343-8128
Thunder Bay, ON, Canada P7B 5E1   Shann Brown, Info/Educ.Off.
Founded: 1979. **Staff:** 2. **Subjects:** Hazardous substances, occupational health, toxicology, radiation, noise, health services. **Holdings:** 850 books; 2200 reprints in 4 VF drawers; 30 videotapes; 4 slide programs. **Subscriptions:** 51 journals and other serials. **Services:** Interlibrary loan; copying; center open to the public. **Computerized Information Services:** DIALOG Information Services, CAN/OLE, Canadian Centre for Occupational Health & Safety Database; internal database. Performs searches on fee basis. Telephone 343-8197. **Publications:** Northern Ontario Occupational Hygiene Monitor, 3/year - to mailing list. **Remarks:** FAX: (807)343-8616.

Ontario Ministry of Natural Resources - Algonquin Park Museum
See: **Algonquin Park Museum (354)**

★ 12477 ★

Ontario Ministry of Natural Resources - Centre for Northern Forest Ecosystem Research - Ontario Forest Research Institute - Library (Env-Cons)
c/o Lakehead Univ.
955 Oliver Rd.   Phone: (807)343-4014
Thunder Bay, ON, Canada P7B 5E1 Colette Hanmore, Forest Res.Libn.
Founded: 1948. **Subjects:** Forestry, silviculture, boreal forests, ecosystem management, Northern Ontario. **Special Collections:** Lakehead University forestry theses (18); U.S.D.A. Forest Service publications; Canadian Forestry Service publications. **Holdings:** 356 books; 255 bound periodical volumes; 15,000 reprints, reports, and unpublished papers. **Services:** Copying; library open to the public by appointment for reference use only. **Computerized Information Services:** Internal database. Performs searches. **Remarks:** FAX: (807)343-4001.

★ 12478 ★

Ontario Ministry of Natural Resources - Glenora Fisheries Station - Library
Box 50
Maple, ON, Canada L6A 1S9
Founded: 1958. **Subjects:** Fisheries and aquatic sciences. **Holdings:** 600 volumes. **Remarks:** Currently inactive.

★ 12479 ★

Ontario Ministry of Natural Resources - Natural Resources Library (Rec, Biol Sci)
ICI Bldg., 5th Fl.
90 Sheppard Ave., E.   Phone: (416)314-1208
North York, ON, Canada M2N 3A1   Sandra Louet, Mgr.
Founded: 1972. **Staff:** Prof 3; Other 3. **Subjects:** Forestry, ecology, parks and recreation, land use planning, fish and wildlife. **Holdings:** 80,000 books; 500 bound periodical volumes; 60,000 reprints and unpublished papers; 100 microforms. **Subscriptions:** 252 journals and other serials. **Services:** Interlibrary loan; library open to the public by appointment. **Automated Operations:** Computerized cataloging. **Computerized Information Services:** DIALOG Information Services, BASIS, QL Systems, Info Globe, CAN/OLE, Infomart Online, CAN/LAW, ORBIT Search Service; Envoy 100 (electronic mail service). **Remarks:** FAX: (416)314-1210. Telex: 06-219701. **Formerly:** Located in Toronto, ON. **Staff:** Margaret Wells, Ref.Libn.

★ 12480 ★

Ontario Ministry of Natural Resources - Research Library, Maple (Biol Sci)
P.O. Box 5000   Phone: (416)832-7145
Maple, ON, Canada L6A 1S9   Helle Arro, Lib.Supv.
Founded: 1942. **Staff:** Prof 2; Other 2. **Subjects:** Forestry, fisheries, wildlife. **Special Collections:** U.S. Forest Service and the U.S. Fish and Wildlife Service publications. **Holdings:** Figures not available. **Subscriptions:** 250 journals and other serials. **Services:** Interlibrary loan; copying; SDI; literature searches; library open to the public with restrictions. **Automated Operations:** Computerized cataloging. **Computerized Information Services:** DIALOG Information Services, CAN/OLE; Envoy 100 (electronic mail service). **Publications:** New Materials List, monthly - for internal distribution only. **Remarks:** FAX: (416)832-7149. Electronic mail address(es): OMAPFW (Envoy 100). **Staff:** Ginnie Galloway.

★ 12481 ★

Ontario Ministry of Northern Development & Mines - Library, Records and Services (Area-Ethnic)
159 Cedar St.   Phone: (705)670-7130
Sudbury, ON, Canada P3E 6A5   Linda Davis
Founded: 1978. **Staff:** 1. **Subjects:** Northern Ontario - socioeconomic development, natural resources, community and regional planning, history, culture. **Special Collections:** Ministry Reading Room; Northern Ontario newspapers; college and university calendars for Northern Ontario. **Holdings:** 3000 books and reports; 1 VF drawers of Northern Ontario materials; 2 VF drawers of annual reports. **Subscriptions:** 60 journals and other serials; 30 newspapers. **Services:** Interlibrary loan; library open to the public with restrictions. **Publications:** What's New in the Library (list of periodical contents pages and cataloged material), bimonthly. **Remarks:** Telex: 065-24131; FAX: (705)670-7108.

★ 12482 ★

Ontario Ministry of Northern Development & Mines - Ontario Geological Survey - Geoscience Information Services (Sci-Engr)
77 Grenville St., Rm. 812   Phone: (416)965-1352
Toronto, ON, Canada M7A 1W4   Nancy Thurston, Mgr., Geoscience Info.Serv.
Founded: 1945. **Staff:** 9. **Subjects:** Geology of Ontario, mining, Precambrian geology, metallurgy, mineralogy, environmental geology. **Special Collections:** Geological and aeromagnetic maps (20,000); assessment files; annual reports of mining companies. **Holdings:** 15,000 texts and reference books; 25,000 government reports. **Subscriptions:** 400 journals and other serials. **Services:** Interlibrary loan; copying; library open to the public for reference use only. **Automated Operations:** Computerized cataloging. **Computerized Information Services:** CAN/OLE, PFDS Online. **Publications:** Accessions list, monthly - to other libraries on request. **Remarks:** FAX: (416)963-3278.

★ 12483 ★
Ontario Ministry of Revenue - Library (Bus-Fin)
33 King St., W.
P.O. Box 627   Phone: (416)433-6135
Oshawa, ON, Canada L1H 8H5   Wendy Craig, Mgr., Lib.Serv.
Founded: 1973. **Staff:** Prof 1; Other 3. **Subjects:** Economics, public finance, taxation, property assessment, computer science. **Special Collections:** Technology Collection. **Holdings:** 13,000 books; 390 bound periodical volumes; Statistics Canada, July 1985 to present, on microfiche. **Subscriptions:** 300 journals and other serials. **Services:** Interlibrary loan; copying; library open to the public for reference use only. **Computerized Information Services:** DIALOG Information Services, Info Globe, QL Systems, Infomart Online. **Publications:** Library Link, irregular; What's New, irregular - both for internal distribution only. **Remarks:** FAX: (416)433-6037.

★ 12484 ★
Ontario Ministry of the Solicitor General - Centre of Forensic Sciences - H. Ward Smith Library (Law, Sci-Engr)
25 Grosvenor St., 2nd Fl.   Phone: (416)965-2561
Toronto, ON, Canada M7A 2G8   Eva Gulbinowicz, Libn.
Founded: 1967. **Staff:** Prof 1; Other 2. **Subjects:** Forensic science, toxicology, biology, chemistry, engineering, firearms, photography, questioned documents. **Special Collections:** Home Office Central Research Establishment (England) reports; Metropolitan Police Forensic Science Laboratory Reports (London, England), 1981 to present. **Holdings:** 15,000 books; 6000 bound periodical volumes; 1500 reports; 13,000 reprints; 2500 government documents and pamphlets; 14,000 slides. **Subscriptions:** 308 journals and other serials. **Services:** Interlibrary loan; copying (limited); library open to criminal justice and medical professionals by telephone appointment. **Automated Operations:** Computerized cataloging, acquisitions, serials, and circulation. **Computerized Information Services:** MEDLARS, BRS Information Technologies, DIALOG Information Services, CAN/OLE, UTLAS, Data-Star, CCINFOdisc; MESSAGES (electronic mail service). **Special Catalogs:** Slide catalog (online). **Remarks:** FAX: (416)324-3434.

★ 12485 ★
Ontario Ministry of the Solicitor General - Office of the Fire Marshal - Fire Sciences Library (Sci-Engr)
7 Overlea Blvd., 3rd Fl.   Phone: (416)325-3235
Toronto, ON, Canada M4H 1A8   Jean Chong, Libn.
Founded: 1961. **Staff:** Prof 1; Other 1. **Subjects:** Fire - prevention, protection, science; fire protection engineering; fire investigation and litigation; firefighting service. **Special Collections:** National Fire Protection Association Fire Codes; Canadian Standards Association (CSA) and Underwriters Laboratories of Canada (ULC) standards (525). **Holdings:** 6000 books; 200 bound periodical volumes; 900 technical reports; 1000 standards; 500 catalogs and pamphlets; 40 AV items. **Subscriptions:** 145 journals and other serials. **Services:** Interlibrary loan; copying; SDI; library open to the public for reference use only. **Automated Operations:** Computerized cataloging and acquisitions. **Computerized Information Services:** CAN/OLE, DIALOG Information Services, QL Systems; ONFIRE (internal database). **Publications:** Recent Accessions, monthly; bibliographies of library material, irregular - both free upon request. **Remarks:** FAX: (416)325-3213.

Ontario Ministry of Tourism and Recreation - Huronia Historical Parks
See: **Huronia Historical Parks (7587)**

★ 12486 ★
Ontario Ministry of Tourism and Recreation - Old Fort William - Resource Library (Hist)
Vicker's Heights Post Office   Phone: (807)577-8461
Thunder Bay, ON, Canada P0T 2Z0   Shawn J. Allaire, Lib.Techn.
Founded: 1975. **Staff:** Prof 1. **Subjects:** North American fur trade history and society, North West Company, Ojibway Indians, early 19th century trades and technology, material culture. **Special Collections:** National Heritage Limited (200 transfer cases of primary, secondary, pictorial data); Fort William Archaeological Project (400 files; 20 boxes of subject cards); interpreted buildings (41 kits of specialized data). **Holdings:** 4000 books; 700 documents; 20 VF drawers; 100 reels of microfilm. **Subscriptions:** 75 journals and other serials. **Services:** Interlibrary loan; copying; library open to the public daily in summer; open to the public by appointment in winter. **Publications:** Acquisitions lists; bibliographies, irregular. **Special Indexes:** Indexes to textiles, voyageurs, tools, material culture, fur trade history, posts, personnel. **Remarks:** FAX: (807)473-2327.

★ 12487 ★
Ontario Ministry of Transportation - Library and Information Centre (Trans)
Central Bldg., Rm. 129
1201 Wilson Ave.   Phone: (416)235-4546
Downsview, ON, Canada M3M 1J8   Stefanie A. Pavlin, Mgr.Lib.Serv.
Founded: 1956. **Staff:** Prof 3; Other 5. **Subjects:** Highway and bridge design, engineering, maintenance; materials testing; transportation economics; photogrammetry; highway safety and accident statistics; personnel management and supervision; traffic engineering; energy conservation; Ontario statutes and regulations; computer technology and programming. **Special Collections:** Publications and reports of the Transportation Research Board, the Ministry of Transportation, and the American Association of State Highway and Transportation Officials. **Holdings:** 81,000 books; 1200 bound periodical volumes; 30,000 microforms. **Subscriptions:** 500 journals and other serials. **Services:** Interlibrary loan; copying; SDI; library open to qualified users. **Automated Operations:** Computerized cataloging, circulation, and serials. **Computerized Information Services:** ESA/IRS, DIALOG Information Services, UTLAS, Infomart Online, CAN/OLE, Info Globe. **Publications:** Library News, monthly; Journal Contents, weekly. **Remarks:** FAX: (416)235-4846. **Staff:** Laila Zvejnieks, Tech. Serv.; Ian Mann, ILL; Noreen Searson, Ref.Serv.

★ 12488 ★
Ontario Ministry of Treasury and Economics - Library Services (Bus-Fin, Soc Sci)
Frost Bldg. North, 1st Fl.
Queen's Park   Phone: (416)325-1200
Toronto, ON, Canada M7A 1Y8   Helen Katz, Coord.
Founded: 1944. **Staff:** Prof 4; Other 7. **Subjects:** Economics, finance, statistics, all levels of government, management, business. **Special Collections:** Budgets, estimates, and public accounts for Canadian federal, all provincial, U.S. federal and some state governments; Stastics Canada (complete collection). **Holdings:** 120,000 books; 32 VF drawers. **Subscriptions:** 500 journals and other serials; 6 newspapers. **Services:** Interlibrary loan; library not open to the public. **Automated Operations:** Computerized cataloging and ILL. **Computerized Information Services:** Mead Data Central, DIALOG Information Services, BRS Information Technologies, Infomart Online, QL Systems, Info Globe, CAN/OLE, UTLAS, Reuters; iNET 2000, Envoy 100 (electronic mail services). **Publications:** Library Update, weekly - for internal distribution only. **Special Indexes:** Ontario regulations and Ontario debates, both indexed weekly; private acts in Ontario. **Remarks:** FAX: (416)325-1212. Electronic mail address(es): TNE.LIB (Envoy 100). **Staff:** P. Dunn, Chf.Cat.; Ann Martin, Libn.

★ 12489 ★
Ontario Municipal Board - Library (Plan)
180 Dundas St., W.   Phone: (416)598-2266
Toronto, ON, Canada M5G 1E5   B.C. Alty, Mgr., Fin. and Adm.
Subjects: Appraisal and assessment, land use and values, planning and zoning. **Holdings:** Figures not available. **Services:** Library not open to the public. **Remarks:** FAX: (416)979-8808.

★ 12490 ★
Ontario Nurses Association - ONA Library (Med)
85 Grenville St., Suite 600   Phone: (416)964-8833
Toronto, ON, Canada M5S 3A2   Victoria While, Lib.Techn.
Founded: 1977. **Staff:** Prof 2; Other 1. **Subjects:** Industrial relations, nursing, occupational health and safety, medical and health care. **Holdings:** 3000 books; 200 bound periodical volumes; 4 drawers of ONA archives; 15 VF drawers of nursing and industrial relations materials; 1 drawer of news clippings. **Subscriptions:** 204 journals and other serials. **Services:** Interlibrary loan; copying (limited); library open to the public by appointment for material that is not widely available. **Automated Operations:** Computerized cataloging **Publications:** ONA Library: Acquisitions, monthly - for internal distribution only. **Special Indexes:** Card index of nursing materials. **Remarks:** FAX: (416)964-8864. **Staff:** Jean Buchanan, Lib.Asst.

★ 12491 ★
Ontario Police College - Library (Law)
Box 1190   Phone: (519)773-5361
Aylmer West, ON, Canada N5H 2T2   Mr. Yen-pin Chao, Libn.
Staff: Prof 1; Other 2. **Subjects:** Police science, criminal law, criminology, sociology. **Holdings:** 10,000 volumes. **Subscriptions:** 330 journals and other

serials; 8 newspapers. **Services:** Interlibrary loan; copying (limited); library open to the public at librarian's discretion. **Automated Operations:** Computerized cataloging. **Computerized Information Services:** DIALOG Information Services, QL Systems, CAN/LAW; Police Resources Online (internal database). **Publications:** Acquisitions list. **Remarks:** FAX: (519)773-5762.

★ 12492 ★

Ontario Police Commission - Library (Law)
25 Grosvenor St., 10th Fl.   Phone: (416)965-3281
Toronto, ON, Canada M7A 2H3   Bill Ambrose, Libn.
Founded: 1981. **Staff:** Prof 1. **Subjects:** Police studies, computer and radio systems, police technology and management, justice. **Holdings:** 6000 books. **Subscriptions:** 69 journals and other serials. **Services:** Interlibrary loan; copying; library open to the public with restrictions. **Automated Operations:** Computerized cataloging. **Computerized Information Services:** DIALOG Information Services.

★ 12493 ★

Ontario Provincial Police - General Headquarters Library (Law)
90 Harbour St.   Phone: (416)965-1372
Toronto, ON, Canada M7A 2S1   Lorna E. Brown, Libn.
Founded: 1979. **Staff:** Prof 1; Other 2. **Subjects:** Criminology, computer science, law enforcement, management, laws and regulations of Ontario and Canada. **Holdings:** 11,000 books; 500 bound periodical volumes; 250 AV programs. **Subscriptions:** 260 journals and other serials. **Services:** Interlibrary loan; copying; library open to the public by appointment for reference use only. **Computerized Information Services:** DIALOG Information Services, Infomart Online, Info Globe, QL Systems, CAN/LAW. **Publications:** List of new acquisitions, bimonthly - for internal distribution only.

★ 12494 ★

Ontario Provincial Police Academy - Library (Law)
15 McLaughlin Rd.
Box 266   Phone: (416)459-4193
Brampton, ON, Canada L6V 2L1   Catherine Dowd, Libn.
Founded: 1983. **Staff:** Prof 1. **Subjects:** Criminal law, federal and Ontario legislation, law enforcement, administration and management. **Holdings:** 3000 books; 2000 bound periodical volumes; 50 audiotapes; 1 drawer of microfiche. **Subscriptions:** 22 journals and other serials. **Services:** Interlibrary loan; copying; SDI; library open to the public with restrictions. **Publications:** In-service training manual, annual; Police Beat, 10/year (both distributed to all provincial police detachments). **Remarks:** FAX: (416)874-4032.

★ 12495 ★

Ontario Public Interest Research Group (OPIRG) - Guelph Library (Soc Sci)
University of Guelph
Trent Lane   Phone: (519)824-2091
Guelph, ON, Canada N1G 2W1   Karen Farbridge, Lib.Hd.
Founded: 1973. **Staff:** 2. **Subjects:** Environment, women's issues, nuclear power, energy from waste, native rights, transportation, other social issues. **Holdings:** 2000 volumes. **Subscriptions:** 70 journals and other serials; 10 newspapers. **Services:** Interlibrary loan; copying; library open to the public. **Computerized Information Services:** CCINFOdisc.

★ 12496 ★

Ontario Public Interest Research Group (OPIRG) - Peterborough Library (Soc Sci)
Trent University   Phone: (705)748-1767
Peterborough, ON, Canada K9J 7B8   Keith Stewart, Coord.
Founded: 1976. **Staff:** Prof 1; Other 10. **Subjects:** Energy, nuclear power, peace/militarism, environment, civil liberties, Third World development, native issues, food and agriculture, occupational health and safety, politics and government. **Special Collections:** Nuclear Free Press Archives. **Holdings:** 1000 books; 300 vertical files. **Subscriptions:** 40 journals and other serials; 15 newspapers. **Services:** Copying; library open to the public. **Remarks:** FAX: (705)748-1795.

★ 12497 ★

Ontario Puppetry Association Puppet Centre - Resource Library (Theater)
171 Avondale Ave.   Phone: (416)222-9029
Willowdale, ON, Canada M2N 2V4   Julia von Flotow, Musm.Dir.
Founded: 1980. **Staff:** 4. **Subjects:** Puppetry, education and puppetry, museum exhibitions. **Holdings:** 300 books; 200 magazines and journals; 5 VF drawers of research folders. **Services:** Library not open to the public. **Publications:** OPAL, bimonthly. **Remarks:** FAX: (416)222-9182. **Also Known As:** The Puppet Centre.

Ontario St. Lawrence Parks Commission
See: St. Lawrence Parks Commission (14431)

★ 12498 ★

Ontario Science Centre - Library (Sci-Engr)
770 Don Mills Rd.   Phone: (416)696-3149
Don Mills, ON, Canada M3C 1T3   Valerie Hatten
Founded: 1965. **Staff:** Prof 2. **Subjects:** Chemistry, physics, biology, astronomy, mathematics, zoology, botany, technology, engineering, graphic arts, museum studies. **Holdings:** 9000 books; 35,000 slides; 11,500 prints and negatives; 600 films; 150 videotapes. **Subscriptions:** 230 journals and other serials. **Services:** Interlibrary loan; copying; library open to the public by appointment. **Computerized Information Services:** DIALOG Information Services. **Remarks:** FAX: (416)696-3189. **Staff:** Jessy Mathew, Lib.Techn.

★ 12499 ★

Ontario Secondary School Teachers' Federation - Library and Information Centre (Educ)
60 Mobile Dr.   Phone: (416)751-8300
Toronto, ON, Canada M4A 2P3   Christopher Ball, Res.Libn.
Founded: 1972. **Staff:** Prof 2; Other 3. **Subjects:** Education, labor relations, collective bargaining, education legislation, occupational stress. **Special Collections:** Archives of OSSTF publications. **Holdings:** 5375 books; 6250 bound periodical volumes; 820 reports; 128 videotapes. **Subscriptions:** 249 journals and other serials; 13 newspapers. **Services:** Library open to members only. **Automated Operations:** Computerized cataloging. **Computerized Information Services:** UTLAS, Info Globe, DIALOG Information Services, ERIC; internal databases; Envoy 100 (electronic mail service). **Networks/Consortia:** Member of Education Libraries Sharing of Resources Network (ELSOR). **Publications:** New in the Library, quarterly; Education Legislation: An Annotated Listing, quarterly; Education Conference Calendar, annual. **Special Indexes:** Vertical file index; video index (both online and printouts). **Remarks:** FAX: (416)751-3394. Electronic mail address(es): LIBRARY.OSSTF (Envoy 100).

★ 12500 ★

Ontario Securities Commission - Library (Law)
20 Queen St., W., 8th Fl.   Phone: (416)593-8268
Toronto, ON, Canada M5H 3S8   Donna Sinclair, Libn.
Founded: 1984. **Staff:** Prof 1. **Subjects:** Law, accounting, investment. **Special Collections:** Commission Bulletins and Weekly Summaries, 1949 to present. **Holdings:** 5000 books; 300 bound periodical volumes; 4 drawers of pamphlets. **Subscriptions:** 200 journals and other serials; 6 newspapers. **Services:** Interlibrary loan; library not open to the public. **Computerized Information Services:** QL Systems, LEXIS, NEXIS, Info Globe, Infomart Online. **Special Indexes:** Index to Ontario Securites Commission Bulletins. **Remarks:** FAX: (416)593-8241. Telex: 06217548.

(Ontario) Supreme Court of Ontario
See: (Ontario) Court of Appeal for Ontario/Ontario Court of Justice (12434)

Ontario Theological Seminary
See: Ontario Bible College/Ontario Theological Seminary (12428)

★ 12501 ★

Ontario Women's Directorate - Resource Centre (Soc Sci)
480 University Ave., 2nd Fl.   Phone: (416)597-4591
Toronto, ON, Canada M5G 1V2   J. Huie, Libn.
Founded: 1983. **Staff:** Prof 2. **Subjects:** Women's issues. **Holdings:** 3000 books; 4000 journal articles; AV materials. **Subscriptions:** 100 journals and other serials; 5 newspapers. **Services:** Copying; SDI; library open to the public. **Automated Operations:** Computerized acquisitions and circulation. **Computerized Information Services:** Internal databases.

★ 12502 ★
OPERA America Information Service (Mus)
777 14th St., N.W., Suite 520   Phone: (202)347-9262
Washington, DC 20005   Nancy Roberts-Lea, Info.Serv.Dir.
Staff: 2. **Subjects:** Opera, musical theater. **Special Collections:** Performance histories of 30,000 operas. **Holdings:** 500 books; 15 VF drawers of programs and reviews. **Subscriptions:** 40 journals and other serials. **Services:** library open to the public with restrictions. **Computerized Information Services:** Performance information from 1991 (internal database). **Publications:** Directory of Operas and Music Theater Works for Young People, 1985; list of special publications - available upon request. **Remarks:** FAX: (202)393-0735. Telex: 650-3159369 MCI UW. Contains holdings of the former Central Opera Service - Information Center and Library.

★ 12503 ★
Oppenheimer & Co., Inc. - Information Center (Bus-Fin)
Oppenheimer Tower
World Financial Center
200 Liberty St.   Phone: (212)667-7890
New York, NY 10281   Marilyn H. Adamo, V.P.
Staff: Prof 3; Other 9. **Subjects:** Corporations, investment, government statistics, stock price sources. **Holdings:** 4200 books; 1500 subject files on various industries; corporation files of annual reports, proxy statements, prospectuses. **Subscriptions:** 1000 journals and other serials. **Services:** Interlibrary loan; center not open to the public. **Automated Operations:** Computerized cataloging, serials, and circulation. **Computerized Information Services:** DIALOG Information Services, LEXIS, NEXIS, Dow Jones News/Retrieval, TEXTLINE, Dun & Bradstreet Business Credit Services, Disclosure Information Group, Spectrum Ownership Profiles Online, FactSet Data Systems. **Remarks:** FAX: (212)667-5792. **Staff:** Linda Rolufs, Asst.Mgr.; Helen Hamilton, Ref.Libn.; Donna Blundo, Files Supv.; Wei-Nee Sung, Tech.Serv.Libn.

★ 12504 ★
Oppenheimer Wolff & Donnelly - Library (Law)
1700 First Bank Bldg.   Phone: (612)223-2500
St. Paul, MN 55101   Gretchen Haase, Dir.
Staff: Prof 4; Other 3. **Subjects:** Business law. **Holdings:** 30,000 books; 800 bound periodical volumes. **Subscriptions:** 400 journals and other serials; 20 newspapers. **Services:** Interlibrary loan; library not open to the public. **Automated Operations:** Computerized public access catalog, serials, and routing. **Computerized Information Services:** DIALOG Information Services, WESTLAW, LEXIS, LEGI-SLATE, Dow Jones News/Retrieval, DataTimes, VU/TEXT Information Services; internal database. **Networks/Consortia:** Member of Metronet. **Remarks:** FAX: (612)224-7504. **Staff:** Gail McCain, Mpls.Libn.; Trudi Busch, St. Paul Libn.; Barb Minor, Sys.Libn.

★ 12505 ★
Optikon Research Laboratories - Library (Sci-Engr)
P.O. Box 259   Phone: (203)672-6614
West Cornwall, CT 06796   William Covington, Libn.
Founded: 1960. **Staff:** Prof 1; Other 3. **Subjects:** Polymer sciences, optics. **Special Collections:** Dioptric materials. **Holdings:** 10,000 books; 700 bound periodical volumes. **Services:** Interlibrary loan; library open to the public by appointment upon written request.

Oral History Project in Labor History
See: **Roosevelt University** (14059)

Orange Agricultural College
See: **University of New England** (19028)

★ 12506 ★
Orange County Department of Education - Library (Educ)
200 Kalmus Dr.
Box 9050
Costa Mesa, CA 92628-9050   Phone: (714)966-4466
Staff: 1. **Subjects:** Educational administration, teaching and teachers, philosophy and psychology of education, school buildings, early childhood education, special education. **Special Collections:** Curriculum guides (300). **Holdings:** 500 books; 20 VF drawers of pamphlets. **Subscriptions:** 100 journals and other serials. **Services:** Interlibrary loan; copying (limited); library open to the public for reference use only. **Remarks:** FAX: (714)662-3570.

★ 12507 ★
Orange County Environmental Management Agency - EMA Library (Env-Cons, Plan)
400 Civic Center Dr., W.
Box 4048   Phone: (714)834-3497
Santa Ana, CA 92702   Janet Hilford, Libn.
Founded: 1963. **Staff:** Prof 1. **Subjects:** Environmental management, water resources, hydrology, flood control, transportation engineering, recreational design, urban planning, land use and zoning, public administration, housing/community development. **Holdings:** 7500 books; 20,000 technical reports. **Subscriptions:** 50 journals and other serials. **Services:** Library not open to the public. **Automated Operations:** Computerized public access catalog (Data Trek).

★ 12508 ★
Orange County Historical Museum - Library (Hist)
812 E. Rollins Ave.
Loch Haven Park   Phone: (407)898-8320
Orlando, FL 32803   Frank Mendola, Libn.
Founded: 1942. **Staff:** Prof 1. **Subjects:** Local and state history, Seminole Indians. **Holdings:** 1550 volumes; 900 directories and yearbooks; 400 scrapbooks and ledgers; 57 photograph albums; 10,000 pictures; 350 maps; 17 linear feet of vertical file materials; 19 reels of microfilm and 131 sheets of microfiche of newspapers; 1 million feet of television news film (1950s and 1960s); 50 oral history audio tapes. **Subscriptions:** 11 journals and other serials. **Services:** Copying; library open to the public when librarian is on duty. **Publications:** Orange County Historical Quarterly - to members and visitors. **Remarks:** FAX: (407)896-2661.

★ 12509 ★
Orange County Law Library (Law)
515 N. Flower St.   Phone: (714)834-3397
Santa Ana, CA 92703   Maryruth Storer, Dir.
Founded: 1891. **Staff:** Prof 5; Other 19. **Subjects:** Law. **Special Collections:** Up-to-date codes for the law of all the states, federal government, and U.S. territories as well as case reports and some administrative regulations and rulings; CIS microfiche service. **Holdings:** 144,977 bound volumes; 6345 tapes; 600,754 microfiche; 8360 ultrafiche; depository for California and U.S. Government documents. **Subscriptions:** 1505 journals and other serials; 8 newspapers. **Services:** Interlibrary loan; copying; library open to the public. **Computerized Information Services:** WESTLAW, DataTimes, Prentice Hall Online. **Networks/Consortia:** Member of CLASS, Research Libraries Information Network (RLIN). **Remarks:** FAX: (714)834-4375. **Staff:** Richard Ayotte, Pub.Serv.Libn.; Michele Finerty, Tech.Serv.Libn.; Michael Bryant, Ref.Libn.; Hugh Treacy, Ref.Libn.

★ 12510 ★
Orange County Library System - Genealogy Department (Hist)
101 E. Central Blvd.   Phone: (407)425-4694
Orlando, FL 32801   Eleanor B. Crawford, Dept.Hd.
Founded: 1923. **Staff:** Prof 4; Other 2. **Subjects:** Genealogy, family history, heraldry, surnames. **Special Collections:** Barbour Collection of Connecticut Vital Records (97 reels of microfilm); vital records of 190 Massachusetts towns to 1850 (216 volumes); Florida State Society, Daughters of the American Revolution Collection, 1929 to present; lectures on genealogy (125 cassette tapes); federal populations census returns, 1790-1910 (complete); Emigration-Immigration Book collection. **Holdings:** 11,000 books; 2400 bound periodical volumes; 8 VF drawers of the papers of Beatrice Brown Commander; 14 VF drawers of miscellaneous family papers; 100 exchange periodicals. **Subscriptions:** 80 journals and other serials. **Services:** Interlibrary loan; copying; department open to the public. **Automated Operations:** Computerized cataloging, acquisitions, and circulation. **Computerized Information Services:** OCLC. Performs searches free of charge for service area patrons. **Publications:** Obituaries from local newspaper, 1949 to present.

★ 12511 ★
Orange County Planning & Local Government Department - Library (Law)
Orange County Library System
101 E. Central Blvd.   Phone: (407)425-4694
Orlando, FL 32801   Eleanor Gentry, Hd.
Founded: 1980. **Staff:** Prof 5; Other 3. **Subjects:** Law, public policy research. **Special Collections:** Land use planning; local documents. **Holdings:** 42,000 books; 4500 other cataloged items. **Subscriptions:** 230 journals and other

serials. **Services:** SDI; library open to the public with referral from another library department or local government staff member. **Automated Operations:** Computerized cataloging and acquisitions. **Computerized Information Services:** OCLC, LOGIN. **Networks/Consortia:** Member of Florida Library Network (FLN), SOLINET. **Remarks:** Includes holdings of Orange County Law Library.

★12512★
Orange County Register - News Research Center (Publ)
625 N. Grand Ave.　　　　　　　　Phone: (714)953-4936
Santa Ana, CA 92701　　　　Sharon Ostmann, Dir., News Res.
Founded: 1962. **Staff:** Prof 5; Other 4. **Subjects:** Newspaper reference topics. **Subscriptions:** 30 journals and other serials; 6 newspapers. **Services:** Library not open to the public. **Computerized Information Services:** DIALOG Information Services, DataTimes, Legi-Tech, NEXIS, VU/TEXT Information Services, LEXIS, DataQuick, Prentice Hall Online; Orange County Register (internal database). **Staff:** Walter Johnston, Res.; Penny Signorelli, Res.; Pamla Eisenberg, Res.

★12513★
Orange County Sheriff/Coroner - Forensic Science Services Library (Med)
550 N. Flower St.
Box 449　　　　　　　　　　　Phone: (714)834-4540
Santa Ana, CA 92702　　　　Mr. Frank Fitzpatrick, Lab.Dir.
Founded: 1948. **Staff:** Prof 1. **Subjects:** Chemistry, criminalistics, toxicology, forensic medicine, investigation. **Holdings:** 2600 books; 4 VF drawers of catalogs and brochures; 2 VF drawers of lab equipment manuals; 3200 reprints; 22 videotapes; 3 boxes of microfiche and microfilm. **Subscriptions:** 71 journals and other serials. **Services:** Interlibrary loan; library not open to the public. **Remarks:** FAX: (714)834-4519. **Staff:** Monika Stopniewicz.

Orange County Transit District
See: **Orange County Transportation Authority (12514)**

★12514★
Orange County Transportation Authority - Resource Center (Trans)
11222 Acacia Pkwy.　　　　　　Phone: (714)638-9250
Garden Grove, CA 92642　　Catherine Wilson-Smith, Rec.Mgt.Supv.
Founded: 1974. **Staff:** 5. **Subjects:** Transportation, employee relations, urban mass transit, rail, multi-modal transportation, high occupancy vehicles. **Special Collections:** History of transit in Orange County (20 years of documents and pictures). **Holdings:** 15,000 books; 500 reports on microfiche; 6515 slides and cassettes. **Services:** Copying; center open to the public by appointment. **Automated Operations:** Computerized cataloging and serials. **Computerized Information Services:** DIALOG Information Services; RMS (internal database). **Remarks:** FAX: (714)638-9250, ext. 4555. **Formerly:** Orange County Transit District. **Staff:** Mary Justus, Libn.Techn.; Antonio Del Rosario, Micrographics Spec.; Gina Marie Bowen, Micrographics Spec.

★12515★
Orange and Rockland Utilities, Inc. - Library (Energy)
1 Blue Hill Plaza　　　　　　　Phone: (914)577-2680
Pearl River, NY 10965　　　　　　Ann G. Sheer, Libn.
Founded: 1968. **Staff:** Prof 1; Other 1. **Subjects:** Electric power, gas industry, energy, environment, management, engineering. **Holdings:** 6000 books; 1200 technical reports and pamphlets; EPRI Collection on microfiche; 25 VF drawers of annual reports; special events clippings, 1970 to present. **Subscriptions:** 200 journals and other serials. **Services:** Interlibrary loan; library not open to the public. **Computerized Information Services:** DIALOG Information Services; LAN. **Remarks:** FAX: (914)577-2730.

★12516★
Orangeburg-Calhoun Technical College - Gressette Learning Resource Center (Educ)
3250 Matthews Rd.　　　　　　Phone: (803)536-0311
Orangeburg, SC 29115　　　Mary Anne Braithwaite, Dean, LRC
Founded: 1969. **Staff:** Prof 3; Other 6. **Subjects:** Science and technology, business, allied health sciences, college transfer program. **Holdings:** 28,600

books; 19,700 microforms; 517 video cassettes; 2040 filmstrips. **Subscriptions:** 388 journals and other serials; 13 newspapers. **Services:** Interlibrary loan; copying; center open to the public. **Automated Operations:** Computerized public access catalog, cataloging, and circulation. **Computerized Information Services:** DIALOG Information Services; CD-ROM (CINAHL-CD, UMI Periodical Abstracts Ondisc). Performs searches on fee basis. **Networks/Consortia:** Member of SOLINET. **Publications:** LRC Handbook, irregular - to students; Faculty LRC Handbook, irregular; Monthly Acquisitions List; Special Bibliographies. **Remarks:** FAX: (803)531-4364. **Staff:** Christopher Murray, Tech.Serv.Libn.; Larry Freeman, Rd.Serv.Libn.; Julie Sohm, Media Rsrcs.Coord.

★12517★
Oratoire St-Joseph - Centre de Documentation (Rel-Phil)
3800 Queen Mary Rd.　　　　　Phone: (514)733-8211
Montreal, PQ, Canada H3V 1H6　　　Mariette Bedard, Libn.
Founded: 1950. **Staff:** Prof 3; Other 3. **Subjects:** Saint Joseph and his cult, patrology, Canadiana, iconography, theology, spirituality, religious history. **Special Collections:** St. Joseph and the Holy Family collection (8000 books). **Holdings:** 70,000 books; 72 VF drawers of archival materials; 1200 reels of microfilm; 400 titles on microcards. **Subscriptions:** 192 journals and other serials. **Services:** Interlibrary loan; copying; center open to the public for reference use only. **Publications:** Cahiers de Josephologie, semiannual - by subscription. **Remarks:** FAX: (514)733-9735. **Also Known As:** St. Joseph's Shrine. **Staff:** Roland Gauthier, Dir.

Orde der Augustijnen - Bibliotheek
See: **Augustinian Historical Institute - Library (1301)**

Order of St. Benedict - Abbey of Regina Laudis
See: **Abbey of Regina Laudis, Order of St. Benedict (11)**

★12518★
Order of Servants of Mary - Eastern Province Library - Morini Memorial Collection (Rel-Phil)
3121 W. Jackson Blvd.　　　　　Phone: (312)533-0360
Chicago, IL 60612　　Rev. Conrad Borntrager, O.S.M., Archv.
Staff: 1. **Subjects:** Provincial archives. **Holdings:** 4500 books and pamplets; 250 bound periodical volumes; 330 linear feet of archival materials; 900 clippings; 60 albums and 4 filing drawers of photographs; 100 blueprints. **Services:** Library open to the public with restrictions. **Also Known As:** Servites.

★12519★
Ordre des Infirmieres et des Infirmiers du Quebec - Centre de Documentation (Med)
4200 Dorchester, W.
Montreal, PQ, Canada H3Z 1V4　　Phone: (514)935-2501
　　　　　　　　　　　　　　　Maryse Dumas, Libn.
Founded: 1964. **Staff:** 3. **Subjects:** Nursing. **Holdings:** 10,000 books; 150 bound periodical volumes; 12 films; 8 slide programs; 25 videotapes. **Subscriptions:** 325 journals and other serials. **Services:** Center open to members only. **Publications:** Nursing Quebec, 6/year. **Remarks:** Toll-free telephone number(s): (800)363-6048. FAX: (514)935-1799.

Oregon Art Institute - Portland Art Museum
See: **Portland Art Museum (13236)**

★12520★
Oregon Electric Railway Historical Society, Inc. - Trolley Park - Library (Hist)
HCR 71
Box 1318-A　　　　　　　　　　Phone: (503)357-3574
Forest Grove, OR 97116　　　　　William Hayes, Hist.
Staff: 1. **Subjects:** Electric railways, tram and trolley history. **Special Collections:** Tram and trolley business records and employment files from street railway companies. **Holdings:** 200 books; 150 unbound periodicals; 2500 photographs, slides, and negatives. **Services:** Copying; library open to the public by appointment for reference use only. **Publications:** Trolley Park News, quarterly - to members and by exchange.

★ 12521 ★
Oregon Graduate Institute of Science & Technology - Library (Sci-Engr)
19600 N.W. Von Neumann Dr.   Phone: (503)690-1060
Beaverton, OR 97006-1999   Maureen G. Sloan, Lib.Dir.
Staff: Prof 3; Other 2. **Subjects:** Chemistry, biochemistry, laser physics, solid state and surface physics, computer science and engineering, materials science, welding, environmental science. **Holdings:** 22,000 books; 1500 bound periodical volumes; 600 reels of microfilm; 6000 government reports on microfiche. **Subscriptions:** 500 journals and other serials. **Services:** Interlibrary loan; copying; library open to the public. **Computerized Information Services:** OCLC, STN International, DIALOG Information Services. Performs searches on fee basis. **Networks/Consortia:** Member of Washington County Cooperative Library Services (WCCLS). **Special Catalogs:** OGI Catalog, annual - available on request. **Remarks:** FAX: (503)690-1029. **Staff:** Rosemary Burris, Libn.; Julianne Williams, Libn.

★ 12522 ★
Oregon Health Sciences University - Library (Med)
3181 S.W. Sam Jackson Park Rd.
Box 573   Phone: (503)494-8026
Portland, OR 97207   James E. Morgan, Dir. of Libs.
Founded: 1939. **Staff:** Prof 7.8; Other 16.10. **Subjects:** Medicine, dentistry, nursing, allied health sciences. **Special Collections:** Pacific Northwest Collection (medical history); History of Medicine Collection; History of Dentistry. **Holdings:** 200,771 volumes; 2089 AV programs. **Subscriptions:** 2723 journals and other serials. **Services:** Interlibrary loan; copying; SDI; library open to the public for reference use only. **Automated Operations:** Computerized ILL (DOCLINE). **Computerized Information Services:** NLM, BRS Information Technologies, DIALOG Information Services, OCLC, Chemical Abstracts Service (CAS), Occupational Health Services, Inc. (OHS), MEDLINE, ORHION; DOCLINE, OnTyme Electronic Message Network Service (electronic mail service). **Networks/Consortia:** Member of Oregon Health Information Online (ORHION), National Network of Libraries of Medicine - Pacific Northwest Region. **Publications:** Accessions list; Eye on ORHION; INFORM (library newsletter). **Remarks:** FAX: (503)494-5241. Electronic mail address(es): OHSU (OnTyme Electronic Message Network Service). Figures include holdings of Dental Branch Library and the CDRC Branch Library. A telephone number for the CDRC Branch Library is (503)494-8356. A telephone number for the Dental Branch Library is (503)494-8822. **Staff:** Carrie Willman, Asst.Dir., Lib.Oper.; Dan Kniesner, Chf.Cat.; Leslie Wykoff, Hd.Ref.Libn.; Patrice O'Donovan, Info.Rsrcs.Libn.; Heather Rosenwinkel, Monographic Acq. & HOM Libn.; Patty Davies, Ref.Libn.; Leslie Cable, Ref.Libn.; Cynthia Cunningham, ILL/Cir.Libn.; Steve Teich, Coord., Outreach Serv.; Dolores Judkins, Ref.Libn.

★ 12523 ★
Oregon Health Sciences University - Oregon Hearing Research Center - Library (Med)
3181 S.W. Sam Jackson Park Rd.   Phone: (503)494-8032
Portland, OR 97201   Jill Lilly
Founded: 1967. **Subjects:** Auditory science, hearing. **Holdings:** 200 books; 500 bound periodical volumes. **Subscriptions:** 10 journals and other serials. **Services:** Library open to members of Academic community only. **Remarks:** FAX: (503)494-5656.

★ 12524 ★
Oregon Historical Society - Library (Hist)
1230 S.W. Park Ave.   Phone: (503)222-1741
Portland, OR 97205   Louis Flannery, Chf.Libn.
Founded: 1898. **Staff:** Prof 12; Other 8. **Subjects:** The Pacific Northwest and the Oregon Country; Northwest explorations and voyages; cartography of Northwest; missionaries; overland migration; politics and government; business - fur trade, lumbering, fishing, agriculture, transportation, mining; arts; women; ethnic groups; labor movement. **Special Collections:** Oregon Provisional Government Papers (microfilm); state and regional architecture; ship and vehicle plans; Oregon Trail diaries; Oregon Imprints by Belknap; Russian-American studies; Pacific Rim; papers of Jesse Applegate, James Nesmith, Matthew Deady, Eva Emery Dye, Thompson Elliott, Seth Pope, Marcus Whitman and others; Malaspina Collection; M.M. Hazeltine Collection; Benjamin Gifford Collection; Carlton E. Watkins Collection. **Holdings:** 100,000 volumes; 8500 linear feet of manuscript material; 22,000 reels of microfilm; 2.5 million photographs; 20,000 maps; 15,000 reels of film. **Subscriptions:** 720 journals and other serials; 80 newspapers. **Services:** Interlibrary loan; copying; library open to the public for reference use only. **Computerized Information Services:** OCLC. **Special Catalogs:** Catalog of Microfilm Collections (book); Union Catalog of Photograph Collections in Pacific Northwest. **Staff:** Sieglinde Smith, Asst.Libn.

Oregon Institute of Marine Biology
See: **University of Oregon** (19156)

★ 12525 ★
Oregon Institute of Technology - Learning Resources Center (Sci-Engr)
3201 Campus Dr.   Phone: (503)885-1772
Klamath Falls, OR 97601-1276   Leonard Freiser, Dir.
Founded: 1950. **Staff:** Prof 8; Other 8. **Subjects:** History of science and technology, engineering, electronics, health sciences, computer science, industrial processes, paramedical sciences, business. **Holdings:** 105,000 books; 18,000 bound periodical volumes; microfilm. **Subscriptions:** 2000 journals and other serials. **Services:** Interlibrary loan; copying; media services; center open to the public. **Automated Operations:** Computerized public access catalog, cataloging, and acquisitions. **Computerized Information Services:** OCLC, DIALOG Information Services. **Networks/Consortia:** Member of CLASS, Southern Oregon Library Federation (SOLF). **Remarks:** FAX: (503)885-1777. **Staff:** Charlotte Pierce, Mgt.Asst.; Steven Prouty, ASC Coord.; Karen Chase, Tech.Serv.Libn.; Robert Freese, Circ.Libn.; Cecil Chase, Ref.Libn.; Ann du Pont, Acq./Ser.Libn.; Joan Willis, Doc.Libn.; Sharon Hanson, Media Supv.

★ 12526 ★
Oregon Institute of Technology - Shaw Historical Library (Hist)
Learning Resources Center
3201 Campus Dr.   Phone: (503)885-1770
Klamath Falls, OR 97601-8801   Leonard H. Freiser, LRC Dir.
Founded: 1983. **Staff:** Prof 7. **Subjects:** Klamath County and Oregon history, Pacific Northwest, including High Desert Area and Land of the Lakes. **Holdings:** 5000 volumes; 20,000 manuscripts and photographs. **Services:** Interlibrary loan; copying; SDI; library open to the public for reference use only. **Automated Operations:** Computerized acquisitions. **Computerized Information Services:** DIALOG Information Services, OCLC. **Networks/Consortia:** Member of CLASS, Southern Oregon Library Federation (SOLF). **Publications:** The Journal of the Shaw Historical Library, semiannual - for sale. **Remarks:** FAX: (503)885-1777. **Staff:** Karen Chase.

★ 12527 ★
Oregon Regional Primate Research Center - Isabel McDonald Library (Biol Sci)
505 N.W. 185th Ave.   Phone: (503)690-5311
Beaverton, OR 97006-3499   Dorrie Towne, Libn.
Founded: 1961. **Staff:** 2. **Subjects:** Biomedicine, zoology. **Special Collections:** Primatology. **Holdings:** 19,650 volumes; 35 films; 196 reels of microfilm. **Subscriptions:** 200 journals and other serials. **Services:** Interlibrary loan; copying; SDI; library open to visiting scientists and others on request. **Automated Operations:** Computerized cataloging. **Computerized Information Services:** MEDLARS, OCLC; internal database; OnTyme Electronic Message Network Service DOCLINE (electronic mail services). **Networks/Consortia:** Member of Western Library Network (WLN), Washington County Cooperative Library Services (WCCLS), Oregon Health Information Online (ORHION). **Special Catalogs:** Files on center's publications; card files and computer files on primate articles, films, and theses. **Remarks:** Electronic mail address(es): CLASS.ORPRCL (OnTyme Electronic Message Network Service); 97005B (DOCLINE).

★ 12528 ★
Oregon Research Institute - Library (Soc Sci)
1899 Willamette   Phone: (503)484-2123
Eugene, OR 97401   Amy Greenwold, Lib.Mgr.
Founded: 1960. **Staff:** 2. **Subjects:** Psychology, behavioral sciences, behavioral medicine, health psychology, depression, tobacco cessation, AIDS prevention, personality. **Holdings:** 1500 volumes; 6000 reprints of journal articles. **Subscriptions:** 150 journals and other serials. **Services:** Library not open to the public. **Computerized Information Services:** DIALOG Information Services, OCLC; BITNET (electronic mail service). **Networks/Consortia:** Member of OCLC Pacific Network. **Remarks:** FAX: (503)484-1108. Electronic mail address(es): AMY@ORI.ORG (BITNET).

★ 12529 ★
Oregon School of Arts and Crafts - Library (Art)
8245 S.W. Barnes Rd.   Phone: (503)297-5544
Portland, OR 97225   Lorrie Perkins, Libn.
Founded: 1979. **Staff:** Prof 1. **Subjects:** Textiles, ceramics, woodworking, drawing and design, metals, book arts, photography, calligraphy, painting, sculpture, art history, art criticism. **Special Collections:** Rare book collection. **Holdings:** 3400 books; 10,000 slides; 4 VF drawers of archival materials. **Subscriptions:** 72 journals and other serials. **Services:** Interlibrary loan; library open to the public for reference use only. **Networks/Consortia:** Member of Washington County Inter-Library Information Network.

★12530★
Oregon (State) Department of Education - Resource/Dissemination Center (Educ)
700 Pringle Parkway, S.E.
Salem, OR 97310
Phone: (503)378-8471
Juanita Maloney, Libn.
Founded: 1970. **Staff:** Prof 1; Other 1. **Subjects:** General education. **Special Collections:** Career and vocational education; school standards documents; summarized information packets on selected priority topics; collection of files on cost cutting ideas. **Holdings:** 2200 books; 16 VF drawers; 4000 unbound periodicals and newsletters; 360,000 documents on microfiche; complete set of ERIC microfiche. **Subscriptions:** 200 journals and other serials; 6 newspapers. **Services:** Interlibrary loan; copying; SDI; center open to the public with restrictions. **Computerized Information Services:** DIALOG Information Services, BRS Information Technologies, The Source Information Network; SpecialNet, OreNet (electronic mail services). Performs searches free of charge.

★12531★
Oregon (State) Department of Environmental Quality - Library (Env-Cons)
811 S.W. 6th Ave.
Portland, OR 97204
Phone: (503)229-6854
Linda J. Rober, Mgr.
Founded: 1988. **Staff:** Prof 1. **Subjects:** Environment. **Holdings:** 4000 books; 36,000 reports. **Subscriptions:** 300 journals and other serials. **Services:** Interlibrary loan; copying; SDI; library open to the public. **Computerized Information Services:** DIALOG Information Services. **Remarks:** FAX: (503)229-6124.

★12532★
Oregon (State) Department of Fish and Wildlife - Library
17330 S.E. Evelyn St.
Clackamas, OR 97015-9514
Founded: 1957. **Subjects:** Fisheries and fisheries statistics, wildlife. **Holdings:** Figures not available. **Remarks:** Currently inactive.

Oregon (State) Department of Fish and Wildlife - Newport Laboratory Library
See: **Oregon State University - Hatfield Marine Science Center - Library** (12551)

★12533★
Oregon (State) Department of Geology and Mineral Industries - Library (Sci-Engr, Energy)
800 N.E. Oregon St., No. 28, Suite 965
Portland, OR 97232
Phone: (503)731-4100
Klaus Neuendorf, Ed./Libn.
Founded: 1937. **Staff:** 1. **Subjects:** Oregon geology, energy. **Special Collections:** Publications of the U.S. Geological Survey, the U.S. Bureau of Mines, other state geological surveys, and some foreign governments; theses and dissertation on the geology of Oregon. **Holdings:** 23,000 volumes; 20 linear yards of maps; 800 unpublished theses and dissertations on Oregon geology; unpublished open-file reports issued by U.S. Geological Survey and other federal and state agencies. **Subscriptions:** 20 journals and other serials. **Services:** Interlibrary loan (through Oregon State Library); copying (limited); library open to the public with restrictions. **Publications:** Oregon Geology, bimonthly; Bulletins; Special Papers; Oil and Gas Investigations; Geologic Map Series; open-file reports; bibliography of the geology and mineral resources of Oregon; bibliography of theses and dissertations on the geology of Oregon; bibliography of Oregon paleontology. **Special Indexes:** Index to Ore Bin/Oregon Geology, cumulative, 1939-19 82, annual; list of available well records. **Remarks:** FAX: (503)731-4066. Public access to much of the material in this collection is more readily obtained through Portland State University Science Library or the Oregon State Library in Salem, OR.

★12534★
Oregon (State) Department of Human Resources - Senior and Disabled Services Division - Library (Soc Sci)
313 Public Service Bldg.
Salem, OR 97310
Phone: (503)378-4728
Subjects: Aging and the elderly - abuse and crime, long term care and housing, health; management. **Holdings:** Figures not available. **Remarks:** FAX: (503)373-7823.

★12535★
Oregon (State) Department of Land Conservation and Development - Library
1175 Court St., N.E.
Salem, OR 97310
Defunct.

Oregon (State) Department of Transportation - State Parks and Recreation Division - Collier State Park Logging Museum
See: **Collier State Park Logging Museum** (3921)

★12536★
Oregon (State) Department of Transportation - TranSearch Library (Trans)
522 Transportation Bldg.
Salem, OR 97310
Phone: (503)378-6268
Garnet K. Elliott, Libn.
Founded: 1937. **Staff:** Prof 1. **Subjects:** Transportation, highway engineering, planning, economics, environment, aeronautics, motor vehicles, traffic safety. **Holdings:** 10,900 books and reports; 45 audio titles; 120 video titles. **Subscriptions:** 85 journals. **Services:** Interlibrary loan; copying; library open to the public with restrictions. **Automated Operations:** Computerized cataloging (Data Trek). **Computerized Information Services:** DIALOG Information Services, OCLC; internal database. Performs searches. **Publications:** Recent TranSearch Acquisitions, quarterly. **Remarks:** FAX: (503)373-7376.

★12537★
Oregon (State) Economic Development Department - Library (Bus-Fin)
775 Summer St., N.E.
Salem, OR 97310
Phone: (503)373-1200
Arthur Ayre, Res.Econ.
Founded: 1980. **Subjects:** Economic development and statistics, industrial development. **Holdings:** 1500 books. **Subscriptions:** 2 journals and other serials. **Services:** Library not open to the public. **Publications:** International Trade Directory; Directory of Oregon Manufacturers; Directory of Oregon Wood Products Manufacturers; Economic Profile of Oregon; Oregon County Economic Indicators. **Remarks:** FAX: (503)581-5115.

★12538★
Oregon (State) Environmental Council - Library (Energy)
027 S.W. Arthur St.
Portland, OR 97201
Phone: (503)222-1963
Char O'Mohundro, Fiscal Mgr.
Founded: 1940. **Staff:** 4. **Holdings:** Figures not available. **Services:** Library open to the public. **Publications:** Earthwatch Oregon.

★12539★
Oregon State Hospital - Staff Library (Med)
2600 Center St., N.E.
Salem, OR 97310-1319
Phone: (503)378-4375
Carol Snyder, Libn.
Founded: 1950. **Staff:** 1. **Subjects:** Psychiatry, psychology. **Special Collections:** Complete Psychological Works of Sigmund Freud (24 volumes). **Holdings:** 1500 books; 250 videotapes. **Subscriptions:** 40 journals and other serials. **Services:** Library not open to the public. **Remarks:** FAX: (503)378-2023.

★12540★
Oregon (State) Legislative Library (Law)
S-427 State Capitol
Salem, OR 97310
Phone: (503)378-8871
Marcia E. Hoak, Leg.Libn.
Founded: 1979. **Staff:** 2. **Subjects:** Oregon legislation. **Holdings:** 8000 reports. **Subscriptions:** 200 journals and other serials. **Services:** Library open to the public by appointment. **Automated Operations:** Computerized public access catalog. **Computerized Information Services:** DIALOG Information Services, WESTLAW, VU/TEXT Information Services, LEGISNET, State Net, ISIS. **Remarks:** FAX: (503)378-3289.

★12541★
Oregon State Library (Info Sci)
State Library Bldg.
Summer and Court Sts.
Salem, OR 97310
Phone: (503)378-4274
Jim Scheppke, Act. State Libn.
Founded: 1848. **Staff:** Prof 22; Other 32. **Subjects:** Oregon history and government, business, librarianship, social sciences, humanities, science and

technology. **Special Collections:** Oregoniana; materials for the blind and physically handicapped; history of Oregon library development; Oregon library statistics; Patent Depository Library; Foundation Center collection. **Holdings:** 1.5 million books and government documents; 1349 video cassettes; 20 videodiscs; 21,648 maps; clippings; pamphlets. **Subscriptions:** 1250 journals and other serials; 51 newspapers. **Services:** Interlibrary loan; copying; SDI; library open to the public. **Automated Operations:** Computerized public access catalog, cataloging, and circulation. **Computerized Information Services:** DIALOG Information Services, LEGISNET, BRS Information Technologies, NLM, EROS Data Center, OCLC; ALANET OnTyme Electronic Message Network Service (electronic mail services). **Publications:** Letter to Libraries (online). Directory and Statistics of Oregon Libraries, annual - to all Oregon libraries. **Special Indexes:** ORULS; Oregon index; Subject and biography index to Salem daily newspaper and other publications. **Remarks:** FAX: (503)588-7119. Electronic mail address(es): ALA0212 (ALANET); CLASS.OSL (OnTyme Electronic Message Network Service). **Staff:** John Webb, Dp. State Libn.; Merrialyce Kasner, Hd., Tech.Serv.; Craig Smith, Ref.Supv.; Sharon Walbridge, Adm., Access Serv.

★ 12542 ★
Oregon State Library - Talking Book & Braille Services (Aud-Vis)
State Library Bldg.   Phone: (503)378-3849
Salem, OR 97310-0645   Nancy Stewart, Adm.
Founded: 1932. **Staff:** Prof 2; Other 7.5. **Subjects:** General collection. **Special Collections:** Recorded books about Oregon (377 volumes); collection of textbooks on cassette (493 titles). **Holdings:** 171,784 volumes, including 38,100 volumes on records; 9075 braille volumes, 117,436 book volumes on cassette tapes; 7173 large print titles. **Services:** Interlibrary loan; adaptive computer equipment for blind or visually impaired. **Automated Operations:** Computerized circulation. **Computerized Information Services:** DRANET. **Networks/Consortia:** Member of National Library Service for the Blind & Physically Handicapped (NLS). **Publications:** Newsletter, quarterly - to registered patrons, other regional libraries, and by request. **Remarks:** Alternate telephone number(s): 378-3635. The telephone number for Portland residents is 224-0610. Other state residents may call (800)452-0292. **Staff:** Mary Mohr, Asst.Adm.

★ 12543 ★
Oregon State Penitentiary - Staff Library (Law)
2605 State St.   Phone: (503)378-2453
Salem, OR 97310   Mary Handie, Libn.
Holdings: 8000 books. **Services:** Library not open to the public.

★ 12544 ★
Oregon State School for the Blind - Media Center (Aud-Vis)
700 Church St., S.E.   Phone: (503)378-8025
Salem, OR 97310   Margie C. Jordan, Media Spec.
Staff: Prof 1. **Subjects:** Visual and hearing impairment; multihandicapped. **Special Collections:** World Book Recorded Encyclopedia Collection. **Holdings:** 3000 books; 250 talking books. **Subscriptions:** 18 journals and other serials. **Services:** Center open to the public. **Computerized Information Services:** APH-CARL; Special Net (electronic mail service).

★ 12545 ★
Oregon State School for the Deaf - Library (Educ, Aud-Vis)
999 Locust St., N.E.   Phone: (503)378-6252
Salem, OR 97310   Adoracion A. Alvarez, Curric.Dir.
Staff: Prof 2; Other 1. **Subjects:** Education of deaf children, lipreading, audiology, audio-visual education, vocational education, arts and crafts, science. **Special Collections:** American Annals of the Deaf, 1848 to present; Volta, 1900 to present; Proceedings of Convention of American Instructors of the Deaf, 1870 to present. **Holdings:** 9800 books; 340 bound periodical volumes; 2405 filmstrips. **Subscriptions:** 49 journals and other serials. **Services:** Interlibrary loan; library open to the public with restrictions. **Remarks:** Serves the school's students, teachers and staff members, parents of deaf students, and students in the Education of the Deaf training programs. **Staff:** Robert Bontrager, Media Spec.

★ 12546 ★
Oregon (State) Secretary of State - State Archives Division (Hist)
800 Summer St., N.E.   Phone: (503)378-4240
Salem, OR 97310   Timothy Backer, Supv.Ref.Archv.
Founded: 1946. **Staff:** Prof 3. **Subjects:** Oregon government - provisional, territorial, state, county, municipal, special districts. **Special Collections:**

Records of the Legislative Assembly; the Governor; the Secretary of State; the departments of Forestry, Corrections, Mental Health, and Public Welfare; and many Oregon counties, dating to the territorial period. **Holdings:** 25,000 cubic feet of records. **Services:** Copying; archives open to the public for reference use only. **Automated Operations:** Computerized public access catalog. **Computerized Information Services:** RLIN; internal database. **Networks/Consortia:** Member of Research Libraries Information Network (RLIN). **Remarks:** FAX: (503)371-6680.

★ 12547 ★
Oregon State Supreme Court Library (Law)
1163 State St.   Phone: (503)378-6030
Salem, OR 97310-0260   Roger Andrus, Law Libn.
Staff: Prof 2; Other 1. **Subjects:** Law. **Holdings:** 159,500 volumes. **Subscriptions:** 553 journals and other serials. **Services:** Library open to the public. **Computerized Information Services:** OCLC. **Remarks:** FAX: (503)373-7536.

★ 12548 ★
Oregon State Traffic Safety Division - Library (Trans)
State Library Bldg., 4th Fl.
Salem, OR 97310   Phone: (503)378-3669
Subjects: Traffic safety. **Holdings:** 2000 books. **Services:** Library open to the public for reference use only. **Remarks:** FAX: (503)378-8445. **Formerly:** Oregon State Traffic Safety Commission.

★ 12549 ★
Oregon State University - Archives (Hist)
Administrative Services, BO94   Phone: (503)737-2165
Corvallis, OR 97331-2103   Michael E. Holland
Founded: 1961. **Staff:** Prof 4; Other 1. **Subjects:** University archives. **Holdings:** 200 record groups; 2300 cubic feet of archival material; 4000 reels of microfilm; 140,000 photographs; 95 manuscripts; 375 cubic feet of manuscript material. **Services:** Copying; archives open to the public during office hours. **Computerized Information Services:** Internal databases; InterNet (electronic mail service). **Remarks:** FAX: (503)754-2400. Electronic mail address(es): hollandm@cc mail.orst.edu(InterNet). **Staff:** Larry A. Landis, Asst.Archv.; Colene H. Voll, Archv.Spec.; Elizabeth A. Nielson, Archv.Spec.

★ 12550 ★
Oregon State University - Department of Forest Products - Library (Sci-Engr)
Forest Research Laboratory 206   Phone: (503)737-4258
Corvallis, OR 97331-5709   Mary B. Scroggins, Libn.
Founded: 1947. **Staff:** Prof 1. **Subjects:** Forest products. **Holdings:** 3000 books; 300 bound periodical volumes; 200 dissertations; 3 VF drawers of patents; 60 VF drawers of pamphlets. **Subscriptions:** 80 journals and other serials. **Services:** Copying; library open to the public for reference use only. **Computerized Information Services:** DIALOG Information Services. **Publications:** Research Notes; Research Bulletins; Recent Publications; Special Bulletin; Biennial Report; Research Papers; Special Publications - all available on request. **Remarks:** FAX: (503)737-3385.

★ 12551 ★
Oregon State University - Hatfield Marine Science Center - Library (Biol Sci)
2030 S. Marine Science Dr.   Phone: (503)867-0249
Newport, OR 97365   Janet Webster, Libn.
Founded: 1966. **Staff:** Prof 1; Other 2. **Subjects:** Marine biology and fisheries, aquaculture, marine pollution. **Holdings:** 12,000 books; 14,000 bound periodical volumes; 5000 reprints; microforms. **Subscriptions:** 310 journals and other serials. **Services:** Interlibrary loan; copying; library open to the public. **Automated Operations:** Computerized public access catalog, cataloging, and ILL. **Computerized Information Services:** BRS Information Technologies, DIALOG Information Services, OCLC; CD-ROMs (ASFA, MEDLINE, Science Citation Index, WLN); Omnet, InterNet (electronic mail services). Performs searches on fee basis. **Remarks:** Contains the holdings of Oregon State Department of Fish and Wildlife - Marine Regional Laboratory Library. FAX: (503)867-0105. Electronic mail address(es):   HATFIELD.OSU.LIBRARY   (Omnet); WEBSTERU@CCMAIL.ORST.EDU (InterNet).

★ 12552 ★
Oregon State University - Herbarium - Library (Biol Sci)
Corvallis, OR 97331-2910   Phone: (503)737-4106
                                            Aaron Liston
Staff: Prof 2. **Subjects:** Herbaria. **Holdings:** Figures not available.

★ 12553 ★
Oregon State University - William Jasper Kerr Library (Agri, Sci-Engr, Biol Sci)
Corvallis, OR 97331   Phone: (503)737-3411
                                            Melvin R. George, Univ.Libn.
Founded: 1887. **Staff:** Prof 52; Other 62. **Subjects:** Engineering, agriculture, marine science, forestry. **Special Collections:** Ava Helen and Linus Pauling Papers; Atomic Energy Collection. **Holdings:** 1.2 million volumes; 175,200 maps; 10,249 photographs, pictures, and prints; 324,938 U.N. and U.S. Government documents; 35,965 reels of microfilm; 1.7 million microforms. **Subscriptions:** 19,125 journals and other serials; 99 newspapers. **Services:** Interlibrary loan; copying; library open to the public with restrictions. **Automated Operations:** Computerized cataloging, acquisitions, and serials. **Computerized Information Services:** DIALOG Information Services, BRS Information Technologies, MEDLARS, STN International, OCLC, RLIN, WILSONLINE, SPIN. Performs searches on fee basis. Contact Person: Robert Lawrence, Lib.Info.Ret.Coord., 737-3260. **Publications:** Bibliography of forestry theses, annual. **Special Catalogs:** Oregon Union List of Serials. **Special Indexes:** Newspaper index to the Gazette Times; Oregon Index. **Remarks:** FAX: (503)737-3453. **Staff:** Karyle Butcher, Asst.Univ.Libn., Res. & Ref.Serv.; Craig Wilson, Asst.Univ.Libn., Coll.Dev. Fin.Mgt; Michael Kinch, Hd., Ref.Serv.; Shirley Scott, Hd., Res.Serv.; Rodney Goins, Hd., Acq.; Clifford Mead, Hd., Spec.Coll.; Debra Hackleman, Hd., Cat.; Janet Webster, Hd., Marine Sci.; Patrick Grace, Hd., Spec.Ref.Serv.; Richard Griffin, Automation Coord.

★ 12554 ★
Oregon (State) Water Resources Department - Library & Information Center (Sci-Engr)
3850 Portland Rd., N.E.
Salem, OR 97310   Phone: (503)378-3671
Founded: 1956. **Subjects:** Water, water supply statistics, dams and reservoirs, water rights, ground water, land and water management plans. **Holdings:** 2500 books. **Services:** Interlibrary loan (within state only); library open to the public by advance arrangement only. **Computerized Information Services:** Water Rights Information System (WRIS; internal database). **Remarks:** (503)378-8130.

★ 12555 ★
Oregonian Publishing Co. - The Oregonian Library (Publ)
1320 S.W. Broadway   Phone: (503)221-5375
Portland, OR 97201   Sandra Macomber, Hd.Libn.
Founded: 1936. **Staff:** Prof 9. **Subjects:** Newspaper reference topics. **Special Collections:** Portland and Oregon history. **Holdings:** 5500 books; microfilm and microfiche of the Oregonian from 1850; microfilm of the Oregon Journal from 1902-1982; indexes; maps; pamphlets, photographs. **Subscriptions:** 55 newspapers. **Services:** Library open to the public for reference use only on a limited basis; telephone inquiries. **Computerized Information Services:** VU/TEXT Information Services, DIALOG Information Services, DataTimes, CompuServe Information Service, NEXIS, LEXIS, POLL; internal databases. **Special Catalogs:** Catalog to reference collection. **Special Indexes:** Indexes to the Oregonian and Oregon Journal. **Remarks:** FAX: (503)227-5306. **Staff:** Gail Hulden, Asst.Libn.

Organ Historical Society - Boston Organ Club
See: **Boston Organ Club** (1989)

Organ Historical Society Archives
See: **Westminster Choir College - Talbott Library** (20327)

Organ Pipe Cactus National Monument
See: **U.S. Natl. Park Service** (17761)

★ 12556 ★
Organisation of Eastern Caribbean States, Economic Affairs Secretariat - Documentation Centre (Bus-Fin)
P.O. Box 822   Phone: (809)462-1530
St. Johns, Antigua-Barbuda   Sue Evan-Wong, Info.Spec.
Founded: 1981. **Staff:** 2.5. **Subjects:** Economic integration within the Eastern Caribbean in the areas of trade and commercial policies, agriculture, industry, energy, tourism, and manpower development. **Holdings:** 12,000 volumes; 450 journal and serial titles. **Subscriptions:** 17 journals and other serials; 20 newspapers. **Services:** Interlibrary loan; copying; SDI; library open to the public for reference use only. **Computerized Information Services:** INFONET (electronic mail service). **Publications:** Current Awareness Bulletin, quarterly; Select Bibliograpy, semiannual. **Remarks:** FAX: (809)462-1537. Telex: 2157 ECON SEC AK. **Staff:** Claudette deFreitas, Doc.

Organisation Internationale du Cafe
See: **International Coffee Organization** (8084)

Organisation Mondiale de la Propriete Intellectuelle
See: **World Intellectual Property Organization - Library** (20621)

Organisation Mondiale de la Sante
See: **World Health Organization** (20619)

Organisation Regionale Africaine de Normalisation
See: **African Regional Organization for Standardization** (128)

Organisation Universitaire Interamericaine
See: **Inter-American Organization for Higher Education - Library** (8030)

Organisme National sur la Recherche Scientifique - Centre d'Etudes et de Recherches en Economie Apliquee
See: **Algeria - National Organization of Scientific Research - Applied Economics Studies and Research Center for Development** (350)

Organizacion de los Estados Americanos - Instituto Indigenista Interamericano
See: **Organization of American States - Inter-American Indian Institute** (12559)

Organizacion Internacional de Proteccion Civil
See: **International Civil Defence Organization** (8083)

Organizacion Mundial de la Propiedad Intelectual
See: **World Intellectual Property Organization - Library** (20621)

★ 12557 ★
Organization of African Unity - Library (Soc Sci)
P.O. Box 3243
Addis Ababa, Ethiopia   Phone: 1 517700
Subjects: Africa - unity, sovereignty, territorial integrity, independence, colonialism. **Holdings:** 10,000 volumes. **Remarks:** Telex: OAU 21046. Cable: OAU ADDIS ABABA.

★ 12558 ★
Organization of American States - Columbus Memorial Library (Area-Ethnic)
19th St. & Constitution Ave., N.W.   Phone: (202)458-6037
Washington, DC 20006   Thomas L. Welch, Dir.
Founded: 1890. **Staff:** Prof 12; Other 12. **Subjects:** Inter-American system, member states, laws, regional development. **Special Collections:** OAS offical documents and technical and informational publications; publications of the specialized agencies; documents and publications of other international organizations; official gazettes of member states. **Holdings:** 721,000 books; 181,000 bound periodical volumes; 329,000 documents and publications of OAS, its predecessors and specialized agencies; 1 million microforms. **Subscriptions:** 3412 journals and other serials; 61 newspapers. **Services:** Interlibrary loan; copying; library open to the public for reference use only. **Automated Operations:** Computerized cataloging and ILL. **Computerized Information Services:** DIALOG Information Services; internal database. **Networks/Consortia:** Member of CAPCON Library Network. **Publications:** List of Recent Acquisitions; CML Documentation and Information Services; Hipolito Unanue Bibliographic Series. **Special Indexes:** Index to OAS documents; index to Latin American periodical literature. **Remarks:** FAX: (202)458-3914. **Also Known As:** OAS. **Staff:** Nora Fernandez, Hd., Cat.; Lucilla Harrington, Hd., Rd.Serv.; Beverly Wharton-Lake, Archv.; Jean Craigwell, Acq.; Rene L. Gutirrez, Doc.Libn.; Gladys Ingram, Ser.Libn.

★ 12559 ★
Organization of American States - Inter-American Indian Institute - Library (Area-Ethnic)
Insurgentes Sur, 1690   Phone: 6600007
01030 Mexico City, DF, Mexico   Hilda Obregon, Libn.
Founded: 1940. **Staff:** 2. **Subjects:** Indians of the Americas, anthropology. **Holdings:** 30,000 books. **Subscriptions:** 11 journals and other serials. **Services:** Interlibrary loan; copying; SDI; library open to the public. **Computerized Information Services:** Internal database. **Remarks:** FAX: 5348090. **Also Known As:** Organizacion de los Estados Americanos - Instituto Indigenista Interamericano. **Staff:** Adalberto Vajda, Asst.

★ 12560 ★
Organization Development Institute - Library (Soc Sci)
11234 Walnut Ridge Rd.   Phone: (216)461-4333
Chesterland, OH 44026   Dr. Donald W. Cole, RODC, Pres.
Founded: 1968. **Subjects:** Organization and management development, conflict management. **Holdings:** 100 volumes. **Services:** Library not open to the public. **Computerized Information Services:** FreeNet (electronic mail service). **Publications:** Organizations and Change, monthly; The Organization Development Journal, quarterly; The International Registry of Organization Development Professionals, annual. **Remarks:** FAX: (216)729-9319. Electronic mail address(es): aa 563 (FreeNet).

★ 12561 ★
Organization for Economic Cooperation and Development - Publications and Information Center (Soc Sci)
2001 L St., N.W., Suite 700   Phone: (202)785-6323
Washington, DC 20036   Kerstin Segerstrom, Hd.
Founded: 1961. **Staff:** Prof 3; Other 7. **Subjects:** International economic development, comparative statistics, agriculture, energy, educational research, environment, finance, transportation. **Holdings:** 1000 books; 500 bound periodical volumes. **Subscriptions:** 20 journals and other serials. **Services:** Copying; center open to the public. **Publications:** Recent OECD Publications, 4/year. **Remarks:** FAX: (202)785-0350.

★ 12562 ★
Organization of Egyptian Antiquities - Greco-Romain Museum - Library (Art)
5, rue du Musee   Phone: 482-5820
Alexandria, Egypt   Mme. Lalla Halim, Lib.Dir.
Subjects: Terra-cotta, Greek sculpture, coins, history of fine arts, Coptic and Islamic art. **Special Collections:** Discription de l'Egypt; Atlas of Youssef Kamal; Omar Tousson Collection (4000 items). **Holdings:** 15,500 volumes; periodicals. **Services:** Library open to students and researchers only.

★ 12563 ★
Organization for Equal Education of the Sexes, Inc. - Library (Educ)
P.O. Box 438   Phone: (207)374-2489
Blue Hill, ME 04614   Lucy Simpson, Pres.
Founded: 1978. **Staff:** 2. **Subjects:** Nonsexist curricula, women's history, sexism in education. **Holdings:** 1000 volumes. **Services:** Library open to the public by appointment for reference use only. **Formerly:** Located in Brooklyn, NY.

Organization Internacional del Trabajo - Centro Interamericano de Investigacion y Documentacion sobre Formacion Profesional
See: Inter-American Center for Research and Documentation on Vocational Training (8024)

★ 12564 ★
Organization of the Islamic Conference - Research Center for Islamic History, Art and Culture - IRCICA Library (Rel-Phil)
Barbaros Bulvari
Yildiz Sarayi
Besiktas 80700   Phone: 1 1605989
Istanbul, Turkey   Mr. Halit Eren, Libn.
Founded: 1980. **Staff:** 6. **Subjects:** Islamic history, art, culture, history of science. **Special Collections:** Necmeddin Bammatte; Zaki Ali; Ahmet Ates; Oktay Aslanapa; Vedat Eldem; Salih Saban; Mehmet Ferit Ayiter. **Holdings:** 25,000 volumes. **Subscriptions:** 1038 journals and other serials. **Services:** Copying; library open to scholars and researchers. **Computerized Information Services:** Internal database. **Remarks:** Alternate telephone number(s): 1 1605988. FAX: 1584365. Telex: 26484 ISAM TR. **Staff:** Mihin Eren Lugal; Abdullah Topaloglu.

Organization of News Ombudsmen - Archives
See: Poynter Institute for Media Studies - Eugene Patterson Library (13283)

★ 12565 ★
Organization Resources Counselors, Inc. - Information Center (Bus-Fin)
1211 Ave. of the Americas   Phone: (212)719-3400
New York, NY 10036   Mary J. DuVal, Libn.
Founded: 1953. **Staff:** Prof 1; Other 1. **Subjects:** Human resources management, collective bargaining, labor law, organization development, compensation administration. **Holdings:** 2000 books; 100 VF drawers. **Subscriptions:** 200 journals and other serials. **Services:** Interlibrary loan; center not open to the public. **Computerized Information Services:** DIALOG Information Services, Human Resource Information Network (HRIN). **Remarks:** FAX: (212)398-1358.

★ 12566 ★
Organization for Tropical Studies, Inc. - Library (Biol Sci)
P.O. Box DM, Duke Sta.   Phone: (919)684-5774
Durham, NC 27706   Beverly Stone, Admin.Asst.
Founded: 1963. **Subjects:** Tropical biology and conservation, Costa Rica, Latin America. **Holdings:** Books; reports; reprints. **Subscriptions:** 7 journals and other serials; 2 newspapers. **Services:** Copying; library open to the public upon permission only. **Computerized Information Services:** La Selva Bibliography, Costa Rican holdings (internal databases); MCI Mail (electronic mail service). **Publications:** La Selva Bibliography; Costa Rican titles; OTS course books. **Remarks:** Library maintains three locations: North American Office (Durham, NC), Costa Rican Office, and La Selva Biology Station (Costa Rica). **Remarks:** FAX: (919)684-5661. Electronic mail address(es): 380-1983 (MCI Mail).

Oriental Healing Arts Institute - Brion Research Institute of Taiwan
See: Brion Research Institute of Taiwan (2126)

★ 12567 ★
Oriental University - Department of Asian Studies - Library (Hum, Area-Ethnic)
Piazza San Domenico Maggiore, 12   Phone: 81 5526178
I-80134 Naples, Italy   Prof. Aldo Gallotta
Founded: 1977. **Staff:** Prof 9. **Subjects:** Chinese literature, Indian philosophy, ancient Middle East, Oriental archeology, Japanese history and literature, Iranian studies. **Holdings:** 160,000 books; 750 microfilm. **Subscriptions:** 350 journals and other serials; 50 newspapers. **Services:** Library open to the public with restrictions. **Automated Operations:** Computerized public access catalog. **Remarks:** FAX: 81 5517852. **Also Known As:** Instituto Universitario Orientale - Dipartimento di Studi Asiatici - Biblioteca.

★ 12568 ★
Origins Research Foundation - Library Center (Rel-Phil)
321 Iuka   Phone: (419)485-3602
Montpelier, OH 43543   Jerry Bergman, Ph.D.
Founded: 1971. **Staff:** Prof 1. **Subjects:** Origins - creation and evolution theories, religious and scientific views, myths. **Holdings:** 3800 volumes; 2300 other cataloged items. **Subscriptions:** 37 journals and other serials. **Services:** Interlibrary loan; copying; library open to the public by written request. **Automated Operations:** Computerized cataloging. **Publications:** Origins Research Foundation Newsletter.

★ 12569 ★
Orlando Municipal Reference Service (Soc Sci)
City Hall
400 S. Orange Ave.   Phone: (407)246-2371
Orlando, FL 32801   Annette Main, Libn.
Founded: 1973. **Staff:** Prof 1; Other 1. **Subjects:** City of Orlando, public administration, other local governments. **Special Collections:** City publications (800 volumes). **Holdings:** 3000 documents; 11 VF drawers; Orlando reports and studies. **Subscriptions:** 150 journals and other serials. **Services:** Interlibrary loan; copying; library open to the public for reference use only. **Computerized Information Services:** LOGIN, DIALOG Information Services, VU/TEXT Information Services. **Networks/Consortia:** Member of Central Florida Library Consortium (CFLC). **Publications:** Municipal Reference Service newsletter, 3/year. **Remarks:** FAX: (407)246-3010.

★12570★
Orlando Museum of Art, Inc. - Library (Art)
2416 N. Mills Ave.   Phone: (407)896-4231
Orlando, FL 32803   R. Goldman
Founded: 1960. **Subjects:** Fine arts, 19th-20th century American art, Pre-Columbian and African art. **Holdings:** 1500 books; 1650 catalogs and brochures on artists, museums, collections, exhibitions, and galleries. **Subscriptions:** 10 journals and other serials. **Services:** Interlibrary loan; copying; library open to the public on a limited schedule. **Remarks:** FAX: (407)894-4314.

★12571★
Orlando Regional Medical Center - Medical Library (Med)
1414 S. Kuhl Ave.   Phone: (407)841-5111
Orlando, FL 32806   Naomi F. Elia, Lib.Mgr.
Founded: 1950. **Staff:** Prof 2; Other 1.5. **Subjects:** Medicine, nursing, and allied health sciences. **Holdings:** 2500 books; 15,985 bound periodical volumes. **Subscriptions:** 327 journals and other serials. **Services:** Interlibrary loan; copying; library open to authorized personnel only. **Automated Operations:** LUIS. **Computerized Information Services:** MEDLARS, BRS Information Technologies, CD-Plus; DOCLINE (electronic mail service). **Remarks:** FAX: (407)237-6349. **Staff:** Rose S. Lear, Libn.

★12572★
Orlando Sentinel Newspaper - Library (Publ)
633 N. Orange Ave., Mail Point 9   Phone: (407)420-5510
Orlando, FL 32801   Judy L. Grimsley, Info.Rsrcs.Mgr.
Founded: 1945. **Staff:** Prof 10. **Subjects:** Newspaper reference topics, biography. **Holdings:** 1200 books; 600 bound periodical volumes; 3650 reels of microfilm of newspapers, 1911 to present; 3 million clippings; 1 million photographs; pamphlets. **Subscriptions:** 50 journals and other serials. **Services:** Library open to journalists by special permission. **Computerized Information Services:** DataTimes, NEXIS, VU/TEXT Information Services, LEXIS, CompuServe Information Service, DIALOG Information Services. **Remarks:** Alternate telephone number(s): 420-5511. FAX: (407)420-5042. **Staff:** Susan Thompson, Res.Libn.; Janice Paiano, Info.Sys.Spec.; Jill Simser, Ref.Libn.; Carolyn McClendon, Weekend Supv.

Orleans-Niagara Educational Communications Center
See: **BOCES** (1929)

★12573★
Oroville Hospital - Goddard Memorial Library (Med)
2767 Olive Hwy.   Phone: (916)533-8500
Oroville, CA 95966   Roger E. Brudno, Dir.
Staff: Prof 1. **Subjects:** Medicine. **Holdings:** 200 books. **Subscriptions:** 60 journals and other serials. **Services:** Interlibrary loan; library not open to the public. **Computerized Information Services:** MEDLARS. **Networks/Consortia:** Member of National Network of Libraries of Medicine - Pacific Southwest Region, Northern California and Nevada Medical Library Group (NCNMLG). **Remarks:** FAX: (916)532-8519.

★12574★
Orphan Voyage - Kammandale Library (Hist)
57 N. Dale   Phone: (612)224-5160
St. Paul, MN 55102   Jeanette G. Kamman, Dir.
Founded: 1975. **Staff:** Prof 4. **Subjects:** Local history, genealogy, graphology. **Special Collections:** Local school yearbooks (500); books on books; authors; nationalities (countries); cartoon scrapbooks (450); genealogies (300); city directories. **Holdings:** 25,000 books; 5000 bound periodical volumes; pamphlets; maps; obituaries; newspaper clippings. **Services:** Library open to the public by appointment. **Staff:** Clark Bradley Hansen, Libn., Bookdealer; Robert Olson, Geneal.

★12575★
Orphan Voyage - Museum of Orphanhood - Library (Soc Sci)
2141 Road 2300   Phone: (303)856-3937
Cedaredge, CO 81413   Jean Paton, Coord.
Staff: 1. **Subjects:** Orphans as explorers and discoverers, philosophers and religious, fantasy writers, scholars and scientists, painters and poets; fiction by orphans; biographies of orphans in public affairs. **Special Collections:** Americana on orphans; Heritage Press Collection of orphan writers; legislative hearings about adoption. **Holdings:** 850 books; unbound reports; manuscripts; clippings; magnetic tapes; paperbound books. **Services:** Copying (limited); library open to the public by appointment for reference use. **Publications:** The Adoption Series.

★12576★
Orr and Reno - Law Library (Law)
1 Eagle Square
Box 709   Phone: (603)224-2381
Concord, NH 03302-0709   David E. Selden, Libn.
Staff: 1. **Subjects:** Law - corporate, estate, medical malpractice, tort. **Holdings:** 1000 volumes. **Subscriptions:** 36 journals and other serials. **Services:** Interlibrary loan; library not open to the public. **Computerized Information Services:** DIALOG Information Services, WESTLAW, LEGISLATE, Jury Verdict Research, New Hampshire Automated Information System, Current USC, State Net, BRS/COLLEAGUE; internal databases. Performs searches on fee basis. **Remarks:** FAX: (603)224-2301; 224-2318.

★12577★
Orrick, Herrington & Sutcliffe - Library (Law)
400 Sansome St.   Phone: (415)392-1122
San Francisco, CA 94111   Cynthia Papermaster, Libn.
Founded: 1863. **Staff:** Prof 2; Other 6. **Subjects:** Law. **Holdings:** 42,000 volumes; 6 drawers of cassettes; microfiche. **Subscriptions:** 573 journals and other serials. **Services:** Interlibrary loan; library open by arrangement to members of the Special Libraries Association and the American Association of Law Libraries. **Automated Operations:** Computerized public access catalog, cataloging, acquisitions, and serials. **Computerized Information Services:** LEXIS, DIALOG Information Services, WESTLAW, RLIN, Dow Jones News/Retrieval, VU/TEXT Information Services, DataTimes, Information America, Dun & Bradstreet Business Credit Services, LEGISLATE, Legi-Tech, Data Quick, TRW Information Services. **Publications:** OH&S Library News (newsletter) - for internal distribution only. **Special Indexes:** Index to Memoranda of Law (online); index to company prospectuses (online, book). **Remarks:** FAX: (415)773-5759. **Staff:** Debi Mazor.

Orszagos Erdeszeti Egyesulet
See: **Forest Association of Hungary** (5976)

Orszagos Muszaki Informacios Kozpont es Konyvtar
See: **Hungary - National Technical Information Centre and Library** (7558)

Orszagos Orvostudomanyi Informacios Intezet Es Konyvtar
See: **Hungary - National Institute for Medical Information and Library of Medicine** (7556)

Orszagos Pedagogiai Konyvtar es Muzeum
See: **Hungary - National Educational Library and Museum** (7555)

Orszagos Szechenyi Konyvtar - Konyvtartudomanyi es Modszertani Kozpont
See: **Hungary - National Szechenyi Library - Centre for Library Science and Methodology** (7557)

Lewis J. Ort Library
See: **Frostburg State University** (6185)

★12578★
Ortho-McNeil Inc. - Scientific Information Resources (Med)
19 Green Belt Dr.   Phone: (416)442-2500
Don Mills, ON, Canada M3C 1L9   Mr. M. Papadimitropoulos
Founded: 1967. **Staff:** 2. **Subjects:** Contraception, family planning, immunology, biotechnology, business management. **Holdings:** 1565 books; 580 bound periodical volumes; microfiche. **Subscriptions:** 285 journals and other serials. **Services:** Interlibrary loan; library open to the public by appointment. **Automated Operations:** Computerized circulation. **Computerized Information Services:** MEDLINE, TOXLINE, DIALOG Information Services, Infomart Online, Info Globe, Data-Star, INSIGHT, PFDS Online, The Financial Post Information Service; internal database; CD-ROM; Envoy 100 (electronic mail service). **Publications:** Book List, semiannual; Journal Distribution List, semiannual. **Remarks:** FAX: (416)442-2520. Electronic mail address(es): PRI.SIR (Envoy 100). **Formed by the merger of:** Ortho Pharmaceutical (Canada), Ltd. - R.W. Johnson Pharmaceutical Research Institute, and McNeil Pharmaceutical (Canada) Ltd. **Staff:** Marta Bodnar, Libn.; Irene Meiklejohn, Libn.

Ortho Pharmaceutical (Canada), Ltd. - R.W. Johnson Pharmaceutical
   Research Institute
See: **Ortho-McNeil Inc.** (12578)

★ 12579 ★
Orthodox Church in America - Department of History and Archives
   (Rel-Phil, Hist)
Rte. 25A, Box 675   Phone: (516)922-0550
Syosset, NY 11791   Alexis Liberovsky, Archv.
Founded: 1845. **Staff:** Prof 2. **Subjects:** American Orthodox Church history
- Carpatho-Russian, Greek; immigration history - Russian, Syrian,
Albanian. **Holdings:** 270 linear feet of administrative archival materials; 240
linear feet of personal papers and collections; 200 linear feet of books,
periodicals, photos, and other cataloged items. **Subscriptions:** 30 journals
and other serials; 20 newspapers. **Services:** Copying; archives open to the
public at librarian's discretion. **Publications:** Orthodox America 1794-1976
(A History for the Bicentennial); Orthodoxy and Native Americans: The
Alaskan Mission (1980). **Special Catalogs:** Comprehensive guides and
catalogs are under preparation. **Remarks:** FAX: (516)922-0954.

★ 12580 ★
Orthopaedic and Arthritic Hospital - Health Sciences Library (Med)
43 Wellesley St., E.   Phone: (416)967-8545
Toronto, ON, Canada M4Y 1H1   Susan Baillie, Libn.
Founded: 1966. **Staff:** Prof 2. **Subjects:** Orthopedics, arthritis, physical and
occupational therapy. **Holdings:** 1000 books; 550 bound periodical volumes.
Subscriptions: 80 journals and other serials. **Services:** Interlibrary loan;
library not open to the public. **Computerized Information Services:**
DIALOG Information Services. **Remarks:** FAX: (416)967-8593.

★ 12581 ★
Orthopaedic Hospital - Rubel Memorial Library (Med)
2400 S. Flower St.
Box 60132, Terminal Annex   Phone: (213)742-1530
Los Angeles, CA 90060-0132   Mina R. Mandal, Dir., Med.Lib.
Founded: 1944. **Staff:** Prof 1. **Subjects:** Orthopedics. **Holdings:** 3030 books;
3290 bound periodical volumes. **Subscriptions:** 143 journals and other
serials. **Services:** Interlibrary loan; library not open to the public. **Automated
Operations:** Computerized ILL (DOCLINE). **Computerized Information
Services:** MEDLINE. **Networks/Consortia:** Member of National Network
of Libraries of Medicine - Pacific Southwest Region. **Publications:** New
Book List; Serials List. **Remarks:** Alternate telephone number(s): 742-1531.

★ 12582 ★
Orthopaedics Indianapolis, Inc. - Library (Med)
1801 Senate Blvd., No. 200   Phone: (317)923-5352
Indianapolis, IN 46202   Jean Bonner
Founded: 1984. **Subjects:** Clinical orthopaedics. **Holdings:** 400 books.
Subscriptions: 21 journals and other serials. **Services:** Interlibrary loan;
copying; SDI; library open to the public by appointment. **Computerized
Information Services:** BRS Information Technologies. **Remarks:** FAX:
(317)924-0115.

★ 12583 ★
Orthopedic Foundation for Animals - OFA Hip Dysplasia Registry
   (Med)
2300 Nifong Blvd.   Phone: (314)442-0418
Columbia, MO 65201   Dr. E. A. Corley, Proj.Dir.
Staff: 5. **Subjects:** Veterinary medicine. **Holdings:** 120,000 radiographs - Hip
Registry X-Ray, evaluated for canine hip dysplasia in purebred dogs.
Remarks: Sponsored by the Orthopedic Foundation for Animals at the
University of Missouri, Columbia - College of Veterinary Medicine.

★ 12584 ★
Orthotics and Prosthetics National Office - Library (Med)
1650 King St., 5th Fl.   Phone: (703)836-7116
Alexandria, VA 22314   Dr. Ian R. Horen, Exec.Dir.
Subjects: Prosthetics and orthotics. **Holdings:** 200 books. **Subscriptions:** 10
journals and other serials. **Services:** Library not open to the public.

Arnold E. Ortmann Library
See: **Carnegie Museum of Natural History - Library** (3085)

Orton Memorial Library of Geology
See: **Ohio State University - Orton Memorial Library of Geology**
   (12322)

Orwig Music Library
See: **Brown University** (2279)

★ 12585 ★
Oryx Technology Center - Library
P.O. Box 830936
Richardson, TX 75083-0936
Defunct.

★ 12586 ★
Osaka American Center - USIS Library (Educ)
Sankei Bldg., 6th Fl.
2-4-9 Umeda, Kita-ku
Osaka 530, Japan
Remarks: Maintained or supported by the U.S. Information Agency. Focus
is on materials that will assist peoples outside the United States to learn
about the United States, its people, history, culture, political processes, and
social milieux.

★ 12587 ★
**Osawatomie State Hospital - Rapaport Professional Library - Mental
   Health Library** (Med)
Osawatomie, KS 66064   Phone: (913)755-3151
                 Connie Park, Dir., Lib.Serv.
Founded: 1949. **Staff:** Prof 1; Other 2. **Subjects:** Psychiatry, psychology,
social sciences, medicine, nursing, special education. **Holdings:** 6045 books;
1704 bound periodical volumes; 624 audiotapes; 120 videotapes; 30 VF
drawers of dissertations, reprints, pamphlets, documents. **Subscriptions:** 50
journals and other serials. **Services:** Interlibrary loan; copying; library open
to the public at librarian's discretion. **Networks/Consortia:** Member of
National Network of Libraries of Medicine - Midcontinental Region.

★ 12588 ★
Osborn Laboratories of Marine Sciences - New York Aquarium Library
   (Biol Sci)
W. 8th St. & Surf Ave.   Phone: (718)265-3415
Brooklyn, NY 11224   Louis E. Garibaldi, Dir.
Founded: 1902. **Subjects:** Ichthyology, aquariology, diseases of fish,
invertebrates, amphibians and reptiles, marine biochemistry, invertebrate
zoology, physiology of fish, marine mammalogy. **Special Collections:**
Diseases of aquatic organisms; complete card file of animals of Bay of
Naples. **Holdings:** 3000 books; 100 bound periodical volumes; photographs,
films, and slides of aquatic organisms. **Services:** Library open to the public
by special permission. **Remarks:** FAX: (718)265-3420. **Also Known As:** New
York Zoological Society - New York Aquarium Library. **Staff:** Mildred
Montalbano, Libn.

Osborn Library of Vertebrate Paleontology
See: **American Museum of Natural History** (689)

Stanley H. Osborn Medical Library
See: **Connecticut (State) Department of Health Services** (4189)

Osborne Collection of Early Children's Books
See: **Toronto Public Library** (16418)

Osborne Library
See: **Connecticut Agricultural Experiment Station** (4176)

Richard E. Osgood, M.D. Medical Library
See: LAC/High Desert Medical Center (8865)

OSHA
See: U.S. Dept. of Labor - OSHA (17277)

O'Shaughnessy Library
See: College of St. Thomas (3912)

★ 12589 ★
Oshawa General Hospital - Education Resource Centre (Med)
24 Alma St.   Phone: (416)576-8711
Oshawa, ON, Canada L1G 2B9   Susan Hendricks, Med.Libn.
Founded: 1973. **Staff:** Prof 1; Other 1. **Subjects:** Medicine, nursing, allied health sciences. **Special Collections:** Genetics. **Holdings:** 1000 books; 3000 bound periodical volumes; VF drawers. **Subscriptions:** 155 journals and other serials. **Services:** Interlibrary loan; copying; SDI; center open to the public by appointment to adults for reference use only . **Computerized Information Services:** MEDLARS, MEDLINE, DIALOG Information Services; Envoy 100 (electronic mail service). Performs searches on fee basis. **Networks/Consortia:** Member of Ontario Hospital Libraries Association (OHLA). **Remarks:** FAX: (416)433-2794. Electronic mail address(es): OGH.LIB (Envoy 100).

★ 12590 ★
Oshawa Historical Society - Oshawa Community Archives (Hist)
7 Henry St.
P.O. Box 2303   Phone: (416)436-7624
Oshawa, ON, Canada L1H 7V5   Norah Herd, Archv.
Founded: 1957. **Staff:** 1. **Subjects:** Oshawa history, industry. **Special Collections:** Pedlar manuscripts on microfilm. **Holdings:** Family histories; manuscripts; microfilm. **Services:** Copying; archives open to the public for reference use only. **Remarks:** Alternate telephone number(s): 436-7625.

★ 12591 ★
Oshkosh Public Museum - Library & Archives (Hist)
1331 Algoma Blvd.   Phone: (414)236-5150
Oshkosh, WI 54901   Kitty A. Hobson, Archv.
Founded: 1924. **Staff:** Prof 1. **Subjects:** Local and state history, anthropology and archeology, arts and crafts, botany and zoology. **Special Collections:** River Steamboat History (3 VF drawers of photographs, clippings, narratives); Lumbering and Logging (3 VF drawers of photographs, clippings, narratives); Inland Lakes Yachting Association minutes, 1899 to 1916. **Holdings:** 8000 clippings and manuscripts; 200 bound periodical volumes; 68 VF drawers of historical photographs and pamphlets; 400 maps. **Subscriptions:** 25 journals and other serials. **Services:** Interlibrary loan; copying; library open to the public for reference use only.

Osler Library
See: McGill University - Osler Library (9908)

★ 12592 ★
Oslo School of Architecture - Library (Plan)
St. Olavsgt 4
Postboks 6768, St. Olavs plass   Phone: 2 208316
N-0130 Oslo 1, Norway   Anne Frivoll, Univ.Libn.
Founded: 1968. **Staff:** Prof 2; Other 1. **Subjects:** Architecture, planning, building technology. **Holdings:** 32,000 books; 2500 bound periodical volumes; slides. **Subscriptions:** 150 journals and other serials. **Services:** Interlibrary loan; library not open to the public. **Computerized Information Services:** Bibliofil (internal database). **Remarks:** FAX: 2 111970. **Also Known As:** Arkitekthogskolen - Biblioteket.

★ 12593 ★
(Oslo) U.S. Reference Center - USIS Library (Educ)
Drammensveien 18   Phone: 2 448550
N-0244 Oslo 2, Norway   Petter Naess, Lib.Dir.
Founded: 1945. **Staff:** 2. **Subjects:** United States government and foreign policy. **Holdings:** 5000 books; 3000 reports; government documents.

Subscriptions: 120 journals and other serials; 2 newspapers. **Services:** Interlibrary loan; copying; library open to the public by appointment. **Automated Operations:** Computerized public access catalog. **Computerized Information Services:** DIALOG Information Services, LEGI-SLATE; InterNet, DIALMAIL (electronic mail services). **Publications:** Aquisition lists. **Special Catalogs:** Periodical catalog. **Remarks:** FAX: 2 440436. Electronic mail address(es): z–naess–p kari.uio.no (InterNet); 9511 (DIALMAIL). Maintained or supported by the Maintained or supported by the U.S. Information Agency. Focus is on materials that will assist peoples outside the United States to learn about the United States, its people, history, culture, political processes, and social milieux. Provides reference and documentation services to host country journalist, government officials, researchers, teachers, students, and others who need accurate and current U.S. information in a professional or educational capacity. Particular emphasis on U.S. government information. **Staff:** Tove Modahl, Ref.Libn.

★ 12594 ★
Osseo Area Municipal Hospital & Nursing Home - Medical Library (Med)
P.O. Box 70   Phone: (715)597-3121
Osseo, WI 54758   Mary Gunderson, Libn.
Remarks: FAX: (715)597-3121. No further information was supplied by respondent.

★ 12595 ★
Ossining Historical Society Museum - Library (Hist)
196 Croton Ave.   Phone: (914)941-0001
Ossining, NY 10562   Roberta Y. Arminio, Info.Dir.
Founded: 1931. **Staff:** Prof 2; Other 3. **Subjects:** Local history and genealogy. **Special Collections:** Video Cassette Library (local history, 175th anniversary interviews, Village of Ossining incorporation); oral history; local interviews (30 audiocassettes); newspapers from 1830. **Holdings:** 1100 books; 122 bound periodical volumes; 390 volumes of newspapers; 10 VF drawers of manuscripts, pamphlets, clippings, documents, and reports; 300 maps; 1000 photographs. **Subscriptions:** 10 journals and other serials; 2 newspapers. **Services:** Interlibrary loan; copying; library open to the public. **Staff:** Marion Custons; Greta Cornell.

Osterreichische Bundesbahnen - Bibliothek
See: Austrian Federal Railways - Library (1358)

★ 12596 ★
Osterreichische Gesellschaft fur Filmwissenschaft - Kommunikations und Medienforschung - Osterreichisches Filmarchiv Bibliothek (Art)
Rauhensteingasse 5
Postfach 253
A-1015 Vienna, Austria   Phone: 222 5129936
Founded: 1955. **Subjects:** Biography, reference, film history, film scripts, technical books. **Holdings:** Books; bound periodical volumes; reports. **Services:** Copying; library open to the public for reference use only. **Staff:** Dr. Walter Fritz; Elisabeth Streit.

Osterreichisches Patentamt - Bibliothek
See: Austrian Patent Office - Library (1360)

Osteuropa-Institut Munchen
See: East European Institute, Munich (5119)

Ostrobothnian Archives of Traditional Culture in Vasa
See: Svenska Litteratursallskapet I Finland - Folk kultur-arkivet (15898)

Donald F. and Mildred Topp Othmer Library of Chemical History - National Foundation for History of Chemistry
See: University of Pennsylvania - National Foundation for History of Chemistry - Library (19190)

Otis Art Institute
See: **Parsons School of Design (12769)**

★ 12597 ★
Ottawa Board of Education - Library Service Centre (Educ)
330 Gilmour   Phone: (613)596-4853
Ottawa, ON, Canada K2P 0P9   Barbara Lance, Mgr.
Founded: 1966. **Staff:** Prof 5; Other 15. **Subjects:** Education, librarianship. **Special Collections:** Primary novel sets (1000 titles); Junior novel sets (450 titles); Intermediate novel sets (450 titles); enriched novel sets (215 titles); ESL (2400 titles). **Holdings:** 3705 books; 189 reports. **Subscriptions:** 273 journals and other serials. **Services:** Interlibrary loan; copying; library open to the public with restrictions (no reference services to outside users). **Computerized Information Services:** BRS Information Technologies, CAN/OLE, DIALOG Information Services, UTLAS. **Remarks:** FAX: (613)596-9010. **Staff:** Laura Baxter.

★ 12598 ★
Ottawa Citizen - Library (Publ)
1101 Baxter Rd.
Box 5020   Phone: (613)596-3746
Ottawa, ON, Canada K2C 3M4   James Van Der Mark, Act.Chf.Libn.
Founded: 1970. **Staff:** Prof 5; Other 2. **Subjects:** Biography - local, national, international; newspaper reference topics. **Holdings:** 400 volumes; 20,000 subject clipping files; 15,000 biographical clipping files. **Subscriptions:** 100 journals and other serials. **Services:** Library open to the media only. **Computerized Information Services:** Info Globe, QL Systems, NEXIS, Infomart Online, The Financial Post DataGroup, DataTimes, FT PROFILE, VU/TEXT Information Services; internal database. **Remarks:** FAX: (613)726-1198. **Staff:** Ronald P. Tysick, Photo.Libn.; Charlene Ruberry, Ref. and Graphics; James Van Der Mark, Sys.Libn.; Lois Kirkup, Database Enhancement; Liisa Tuominen, Photo.Libn.

★ 12599 ★
Ottawa Civic Hospital - Dr. George S. Williamson Health Sciences Library (Med)
1053 Carling Ave.   Phone: (613)761-4450
Ottawa, ON, Canada K1Y 4E9   Mabel C. Brown, Dir., Lib.Serv.
Founded: 1957. **Staff:** Prof 3; Other 7. **Subjects:** Medicine, nursing, allied health sciences. **Holdings:** 3000 books; 5000 bound periodical volumes. **Subscriptions:** 300 journals and other serials. **Services:** Interlibrary loan; copying; SDI; Clinical Librarian Service; Regional Library Service; Current Awareness Service; library open to the public with restrictions. **Automated Operations:** Computerized public access catalog, cataloging, acquisitions, serials, and circulation. **Computerized Information Services:** Info Globe, CAN/OLE, DIALOG Information Services, BRS Information Technologies, CD-ROMs (MEDLINE, CINAHL, Health Planning and Administrative Data Base); Envoy 100 (electronic mail service). **Networks/Consortia:** Member of O.H.A. Region 9 Hospital Libraries. **Publications:** Acquisition lists, irregular; bibliographies; newsletter. **Remarks:** FAX: (613)725-1692. Electronic mail address(es): OTT.CIV.HOS.LIB. (Envoy 100). **Staff:** Kyungja Shin, Mgr.; Ursula Riendeau, Reg. & Clin.Libn.

★ 12600 ★
Ottawa General Hospital - Medical Library (Med)
501 Smyth Rd.   Phone: (613)737-8530
Ottawa, ON, Canada K1H 8L6   Francine Ryan, Mgr.
Founded: 1936. **Staff:** Prof 2.5. **Subjects:** Medicine, nursing, and allied health sciences. **Holdings:** 994 books; 3000 bound periodical volumes. **Subscriptions:** 245 journals and other serials. **Services:** Interlibrary loan; library not open to the public. **Computerized Information Services:** DIALOG Information Services, MEDLARS; Envoy 100 (electronic mail service). **Remarks:** FAX: (613)737-8470. Electronic mail address(es): ILL.OGH (Envoy 100). **Also Known As:** Hopital General d'Ottawa.

★ 12601 ★
Ottawa Public Library - Ottawa Room (Hist)
120 Metcalfe St., 3rd Fl.   Phone: (613)236-0301
Ottawa, ON, Canada K1P 5M2   Thomas Rooney, Libn.
Founded: 1955. **Staff:** Prof 1. **Subjects:** Ottawa - history, municipal affairs, authors, genealogy, imprints; Ottawa Valley. **Special Collections:** Graphic Publishers Ltd. imprints. **Holdings:** 16,903 books; 92 boxes of archival records; 95 boxes of annual reports; 351 periodicals and city and telephone directories; 23 cassettes; 63 microfiche; 12 reels of microfilm; 257 vertical files; 13 volumes of Ottawa history scrapbooks; 2 volumes of Ottawa schools' scrapbooks; 54 linear feet of uncataloged municipal documents; 224 rare books; 931 maps. **Subscriptions:** 53 journals and other serials; 8 newspapers. **Services:** Copying; room open to the public for reference use only. **Automated Operations:** Computerized cataloging. **Computerized Information Services:** UTLAS, ATLAS, Infomart Online; Envoy 100 (electronic mail service). Performs searches free of charge. **Publications:** Ottawa History Bibliography (in preparation). **Special Indexes:** Ottawa Where-To-Look Index; Ottawa Journal Vital Records Index, 1885-1922; City of Ottawa Bylaws Index (online); Associations (online); Ottawa Public Library, 1990 to present (online). **Remarks:** FAX: (613)567-4013. Electronic mail address(es): ILL.OOC (Envoy 100).

★ 12602 ★
Ottawa Regional Cancer Centre - Education Services - Beattie Library (Med)
190 Melrose Ave.   Phone: (613)725-6277
Ottawa, ON, Canada K1Y 4K7   Anne LeBrun, Libn.
Staff: 3. **Subjects:** Cancer. **Special Collections:** Consumer Health Information. **Holdings:** 950 books; 1500 bound periodical volumes. **Subscriptions:** 165 journals and other serials. **Services:** Interlibrary loan; copying; library open to the public. **Computerized Information Services:** MEDLARS, CANCERLIT, DIALOG Information Services, Infomart Online; Envoy 100 (electronic mail service). **Remarks:** FAX: (613)725-6320. Electronic mail address(es): OOOCF (Envoy 100).

★ 12603 ★
Ottawa Research Corporation - Irene Holm Memorial Library (Hist)
1465 Osborn Dr.   Phone: (614)486-5028
Columbus, OH 43221   Ms. Bobbi Wilson, Libn.
Founded: 1976. **Staff:** Prof 2; Other 1. **Subjects:** Historic recordings, archives of Ottawa Institute, religious music. **Special Collections:** Edwardian music (400 cassette tapes); Arthur Lindner Memorial Collection of Historic Radio Broadcasts (3000 cassette tapes). **Holdings:** 600 books; 6200 audio cassettes; 40 VF drawers of institute archival materials; 200 compact discs; 100 open reel tapes; 1000 discs. **Services:** Interlibrary loan; copying (limited); library open to the public with restrictions. **Publications:** Research reports, irregular - by request. **Staff:** Scott-Eric Lindner, Audio Techn.; Timur Lenk, Audio Engr.

★ 12604 ★
Ottawa Sun - Library (Publ)
Station T, PO Box 9729
380 Hunt Club Rd.   Phone: (613)739-7000
Ottawa, ON, Canada K1G 5H7   Catherine Flegg
Founded: 1988. **Staff:** Prof 1; Other 1. **Subjects:** Newspaper reference topics. **Holdings:** 100 books; 200 reports; microfilm (1988 to present); photographs. **Subscriptions:** 15 journals and other serials; 6 newspapers. **Services:** Library not open to the public. **Computerized Information Services:** Info Globe, Infomart Online; Symphony (internal database). **Remarks:** FAX: (613)739-8041.

★ 12605 ★
Otter Tail County Historical Society - E.T. Barnad Library (Hist)
1110 Lincoln Ave., W.
Fergus Falls, MN 56537   Phone: (218)736-6038
Founded: 1927. **Staff:** Prof 1; Other 2. **Subjects:** Local history. **Special Collections:** County newspapers, 1871 to present; Thirties Project Papers: New Deal Programs in Otter Tail County. **Holdings:** 300 books; 100 bound periodical volumes; manuscripts; business records; oral histories; records and newspapers on microfilm; slides; dissertations; maps; photographs. **Subscriptions:** 18 journals and other serials; 7 newspapers. **Services:** Library open to the public with restrictions. **Computerized Information Services:** Internal database. **Networks/Consortia:** Member of Northern Lights Library Network (NLLN).

★ 12606 ★
Otter Tail Power Company - Library (Energy)
215 S. Cascade   Phone: (218)739-8213
Fergus Falls, MN 56537   Janet Johnson, Lib.
Staff: 1. **Subjects:** Business management, engineering. **Holdings:** 200 books; 250 Electric Power Research reports; 45 films; 15 videotapes; 11 slide presentations; Federal Registers on microfiche. **Subscriptions:** 145 journals and other serials; 20 newspapers. **Services:** Copying; library open to the public with restrictions. **Publications:** Library Notes, quarterly. **Special Catalogs:** Film catalog, annual. **Remarks:** FAX: (218)739-8218.

★ 12607 ★
Herman Otto Museum - Library (Hist)
Felszabaditok u. 28   Phone: 46 361411
H-3529 Miskolc, Hungary   Dr. Csak Leventene
Founded: 1899. **Staff:** Prof 2. **Subjects:** History, fine art, natural history, ethnography, archeology, history of literature. **Holdings:** 40,148 books; 57,759 bound periodical volumes. **Subscriptions:** 292 journals and other serials; 6 newspapers. **Services:** Interlibrary loan; copying; library open to the public for reference use only. **Automated Operations:** Computerized public access catalog. **Remarks:** FAX: 46 367975. **Also Known As:** Herman Otto Muzeum - Konyvtar.

★ 12608 ★
Ottumwa Regional Health Center - Library (Med)
1001 Pennsylvania Ave.   Phone: (515)682-7511
Ottumwa, IA 52501   Bette Pope, Libn.
Founded: 1951. **Staff:** Prof 1. **Subjects:** Nursing, medicine, allied health sciences, management. **Holdings:** 1520 books; 700 bound periodical volumes; 1712 pamphlets; 155 maps. **Subscriptions:** 93 journals and other serials. **Services:** Interlibrary loan; copying. **Automated Operations:** Computerized public access catalog. **Computerized Information Services:** MEDLINE, BRS Information Technologies. **Networks/Consortia:** Member of National Network of Libraries of Medicine - Greater Midwest Region. **Publications:** Medical Library Newsletter - for internal distribution only. **Remarks:** FAX: (515)682-4137.

★ 12609 ★
Ouachita Baptist University - Riley-Hickingbotham Library (Mus, Hist)
Arkadelphia, AR 71923   Phone: (501)246-4531
                                                               Ray Granade, Dir.
Founded: 1886. **Staff:** Prof 5; Other 4. **Subjects:** Liberal arts, music. **Special Collections:** Francis McBeth Collection (original manuscripts of music compositions, primarily for band and orchestra); U.S. Senator John L. McClellan Papers, 1942-1978; Baptist history collection; Arkansas history; university archives. **Holdings:** 115,181 books; 16,333 bound periodical volumes; 226,323 microforms including ERIC; 7557 AV programs including 2990 scores, 3161 recordings, 904 tapes; 60,571 documents. **Subscriptions:** 1034 journals and other serials; 8 newspapers. **Services:** Interlibrary loan; copying; library open to the public by request. **Automated Operations:** Computerized public access catalog, cataloging, circulation, acquisitions, and ILL (CLSI). **Computerized Information Services:** OCLC. **Networks/Consortia:** Member of AMIGOS Bibliographic Council, Inc. **Staff:** Jenny Petty, Per.Libn.; Dorothy Blevens, Circ.Libn.; Kim Patterson, AV Supv.; Janice Cockerham, Govt.Docs.; Allison Malone, Circ.Libn.

★ 12610 ★
(Ouagadougou) Centre Culturel Americain - USIS Library (Educ)
Ave. Binger
B.P. 539
Ouagadougou, Burkina Faso
Remarks: Maintained or supported by the U.S. Information Agency. Focus is on materials that will assist peoples outside the United States to learn about the United States, its people, history, culture, political processes, and social milieux.

★ 12611 ★
Our Lady of the Lake Regional Medical Center - Health Sciences Library (Med)
5000 Hennessy Blvd.   Phone: (504)765-8756
Baton Rouge, LA 70808   Ivy L. Prewitt, Libn.
Founded: 1923. **Staff:** Prof 1. **Subjects:** Medicine, nursing. **Holdings:** 5000 volumes. **Subscriptions:** 175 journals and other serials. **Services:** Interlibrary loan; library not open to the public. **Computerized Information Services:** DIALOG Information Services, MEDLARS; DOCLINE (electronic mail service). **Networks/Consortia:** Member of National Network of Libraries of Medicine - South Central Region, Baton Rouge Hospital Library Consortium. **Remarks:** FAX: (504)769-8201.

★ 12612 ★
Our Lady of the Lake University - Old Spanish Missions Historical Research Library (Hist)
411 S.W. 24th St.   Phone: (512)434-6711
San Antonio, TX 78207-4666   Maria Carolina Flores, C.D.P., Archv.
Founded: 1971. **Subjects:** Franciscan missions in Texas, 1682-1834; Spanish shipwrecks off the coast of Texas; Texas Colonial history; Spanish Colonial

period in Texas; missions in northern Mexico. **Special Collections:** Archival materials from Mexico, Spain, and other European countries (100 reels of microfilm). **Holdings:** 105 books; 50 maps; 20 photographs; 2000 slides. **Services:** Copying; library open to the public with restrictions. **Computerized Information Services:** DIALOG Information Services. Performs searches on fee basis. Contact Person: Antoinette Garza, Dir. of Lib.Serv., 434-6711, ext. 325. **Publications:** Documentary series, numbers 1-7. **Staff:** Margaret Rose Warburton, C.D.P., Cur.

★ 12613 ★
Our Lady of the Lake University - Worden School of Social Service - Library (Soc Sci)
411 S.W. 24th St.   Phone: (512)434-6711
San Antonio, TX 78285   Sr. Julianna Kozuch, Libn.
Founded: 1942. **Staff:** Prof 1. **Subjects:** Social work. **Holdings:** 16,752 books; 2484 bound periodical volumes; 325 case records; 259 theses. **Subscriptions:** 88 journals and other serials. **Services:** Interlibrary loan; copying; library open to the public. **Computerized Information Services:** DIALOG Information Services. Performs searches on fee basis. Contact Person: Judy Larson, Ref.Libn. **Networks/Consortia:** Member of Council of Research & Academic Libraries (CORAL).

★ 12614 ★
Our Lady of Light Library
Box 91529
Santa Barbara, CA 93190-1529
Founded: 1949. **Subjects:** Spiritual reading, biography, fiction, church history, philosophy, psychology. **Holdings:** 5500 books. **Remarks:** Currently inactive.

★ 12615 ★
Our Lady of Lourdes Medical Center - Medical Library (Med)
1600 Haddon Ave.   Phone: (609)757-3548
Camden, NJ 08103   Fred Kafes, Dir.
Staff: Prof 1. **Subjects:** Medicine, nursing, allied health sciences, hospital administration. **Holdings:** 900 books; 873 audio cassettes; 109 video cassettes; 5 slide/sound sets. **Subscriptions:** 293 journals and other serials. **Services:** Interlibrary loan; copying; SDI; library open to the public for reference use only. **Automated Operations:** Computerized cataloging and serials. **Computerized Information Services:** MEDLARS. Performs searches. **Networks/Consortia:** Member of Southwest New Jersey Consortium for Health Information Services, Health Sciences Library Association of New Jersey (HSLANJ), South Jersey Regional Library Cooperative. **Remarks:** FAX: (609)757-3215.

★ 12616 ★
Our Lady of Lourdes Regional Medical Center - Learning Resource Center (Med)
P.O. Box 4027C   Phone: (318)231-2141
Lafayette, LA 70502   Annette Tremie, Med.Libn.
Staff: Prof 1; Other 1. **Subjects:** Medicine, nursing, pastoral care. **Holdings:** 2500 books; unbound periodicals. **Subscriptions:** 128 journals and other serials. **Services:** Interlibrary loan; copying; center not open to the public. **Computerized Information Services:** BRS Information Technologies. **Networks/Consortia:** Member of National Network of Libraries of Medicine - South Central Region. **Remarks:** Library located at 611 St. Landry St., Lafayette, LA.

★ 12617 ★
Our Lady of Lourdes School of Nursing - Library (Med)
1565 Vesper Blvd.   Phone: (609)757-3722
Camden, NJ 08103   Eleanor M. Kelly, Libn.
Founded: 1961. **Staff:** Prof 1. **Subjects:** Medicine, nursing, allied health sciences. **Holdings:** 2446 books; 74 bound periodical volumes; 322 AV programs; 4 VF drawers of clippings, reports, pamphlets. **Subscriptions:** 79 journals and other serials. **Services:** Interlibrary loan; copying; library use restricted to nursing students. **Automated Operations:** Computerized ILL (DOCLINE). **Networks/Consortia:** Member of Southwest New Jersey Consortium for Health Information Services, Health Sciences Library Association of New Jersey (HSLANJ), BHSL, South Jersey Regional Library Cooperative.

★ 12618 ★
Our Lady of Mercy Medical Center - Medical Library (Med)
600 E. 233rd St., Rm. B-11   Phone: (212)920-9869
Bronx, NY 10466   Sr. Jeanne Atkinson, Dir./Med.Libn.
Staff: Prof 1; Other 1. **Subjects:** Medicine. **Holdings:** 2185 books; 7840
bound periodical volumes; 64 volumes of microforms. **Subscriptions:** 350
journals and other serials. **Services:** Interlibrary loan; copying; library open
to health care personnel. **Computerized Information Services:** BRS
Information Technologies, NLM. **Networks/Consortia:** Member of Medical
Library Center of New York (MLCNY), Manhattan-Bronx Health Sciences
Library Consortia, New York Metropolitan Reference and Research
Library Agency.

★ 12619 ★
Our Lady of Peace Hospital - Medical Library (Med)
P.O. Box 32690   Phone: (502)451-3330
Louisville, KY 40232   Irene Satory, S.C.N., Dir.
Founded: 1951. **Staff:** Prof 1. **Subjects:** Psychiatry, alcoholism and
substance abuse, nursing, pediatrics. **Holdings:** 1244 books; 688 bound
periodical volumes; 500 cassettes (psychiatric series); 10 VF drawers of
pamphlets, clippings, archives. **Subscriptions:** 62 journals and other serials.
Services: Interlibrary loan; library not open to the public. **Networks/**
Consortia: Member of Kentucky Health Sciences Library Consortium.
Remarks: Library located at 2020 Newburg Rd., Louisville, KY.

★ 12620 ★
Our Lady Queen of Martyrs - St. Lucian Library (Rel-Phil)
32340 Pierce   Phone: (313)644-8620
Birmingham, MI 48025   Eleanor M. Benkert, Lib.Chm.
Founded: 1957. **Staff:** Prof 3; Other 7. **Subjects:** Religion, philosophy,
biography, geography, history, travel. **Holdings:** 4500 books. **Services:**
Library open to church congregation.

Our Lady of the Rock
See: **Abbey of Regina Laudis, Order of St. Benedict** (12)

★ 12621 ★
Our Lady of the Resurrection Medical Center - Medical Library (Med)
5645 W. Addison St.   Phone: (312)282-7000
Chicago, IL 60634   Sr. Joan McGovern, SSND, Med.Libn.
Founded: 1973. **Staff:** Prof 1. **Subjects:** Medicine, nursing, hospital
administration, allied health sciences. **Holdings:** 1000 books; 5000 bound
periodical volumes; 5 drawers of patient education pamphlets.
Subscriptions: 150 journals and other serials. **Services:** Interlibrary loan;
copying; SDI; library open to staff and employees. **Networks/Consortia:**
Member of ILLINET, National Network of Libraries of Medicine - Greater
Midwest Region, Metropolitan Consortium of Chicago. **Publications:**
Quarterly book lists; brochures.

Our Lady of the Rock
★ 12622 ★
Our Lady of Sorrows Basilica - Archives (Rel-Phil)
3121 W. Jackson Blvd.   Phone: (312)638-5800
Chicago, IL 60612   Rev. Conrad Borntrager, O.S.M., Archv.
Staff: 1. **Subjects:** Parish archives. **Holdings:** 66 bound periodical volumes;
78 linear feet of archives; 2 filing drawers of photographs; 56 blueprints.
Services: Archives open to the public with restrictions.

★ 12623 ★
Our Lady of Victory Hospital - Hospital Library (Med)
55 Melroy at Ridge Rd.   Phone: (716)825-8000
Lackawanna, NY 14218   Judy Pacholec, Lib.Mgr.
Founded: 1960. **Staff:** 1. **Subjects:** Medicine, surgery, head trauma
rehabilitation, allied health sciences. **Holdings:** 650 books. **Subscriptions:** 70
journals and other serials. **Services:** Interlibrary loan; library not open to the
public. **Remarks:** FAX: (716)825-7271.

★ 12624 ★
Our Lady of the Way Hospital - Medical Library (Med)
Box 910   Phone: (606)285-5181
Martin, KY 41649   Sonya Bergman, Act.Libn.
Staff: Prof 1. **Subjects:** Medicine, nursing. **Holdings:** 100 books.
Subscriptions: 25 journals and other serials. **Services:** Interlibrary loan;
library not open to the public. **Automated Operations:** Computerized
cataloging. **Networks/Consortia:** Member of Eastern Kentucky Health
Science Information Network (EKHSIN).

★ 12625 ★
Our Redeemers Lutheran Church - Library (Rel-Phil)
10th St., S. & Oakwood Ave.   Phone: (612)843-3151
Benson, MN 56215   Marlene Skold, Libn.
Founded: 1958. **Staff:** 1. **Subjects:** Theology, devotional material. **Holdings:**
2000 books; pamphlets; filmstrips. **Services:** Library open to the public with
restrictions.

★ 12626 ★
Our Savior's Lutheran Church - Library (Rel-Phil)
3300 Rural St.   Phone: (815)399-0531
Rockford, IL 61107   Steven Thompson, Chm., Lib.Comm.
Subjects: Christian life, biblical teachings, Lutheran faith. **Special**
Collections: Continuing education for ministry and laity (audiocassettes;
1973 to present). **Holdings:** 2000 books; 1 shelf of archival materials.
Subscriptions: 6 journals and other serials. **Services:** Library not open to the
public.

★ 12627 ★
Our Savior's Lutheran Church - Library (Rel-Phil)
3022 W. Wisconsin Ave.   Phone: (414)342-5252
Milwaukee, WI 53208   Karen Roe, Libn.
Founded: 1955. **Subjects:** Religion. **Special Collections:** Cassette tapes
recorded by staff members and members of congregation (concerts; sermons;
lectures). **Holdings:** 6000 books; 2000 pictures; 400 filmstrips; 200
phonograph records. **Subscriptions:** 35 journals and other serials. **Services:**
Library open to the public with restrictions.

★ 12628 ★
Outagamie County Law Library (Law)
410 S. Walnut St., Rm. C304
Appleton, WI 54911   Phone: (414)832-5131
Staff: 1. **Subjects:** Law. **Holdings:** 10,000 volumes. **Services:** Library open
to the public.

★ 12629 ★
Outboard Marine Corporation - Research Center Library
1700 Rockwood Dr., W238 N.
Waukesha, WI 53188-1133
Subjects: Mechanical and electrical engineering, mechanics, internal
combustion engines, mathematics, metallurgy. **Holdings:** 1900 volumes;
6000 technical reports; 2000 vendors' catalogs; 200 reels of microfilm; 3000
corporation reports; 9000 technical society papers. **Remarks:** Currently
inactive.

Outdoor Education Resource Library
See: **National Outdoor Leadership School** (11248)

Outer Banks History Center
See: **North Carolina (State) Department of Cultural Resources - Division**
of Archives and History (11884)

Jean Outland Chrysler Library
See: **Chrysler Museum** (3645)

★ 12630 ★
W.H. Over State Museum - Library (Hist)
414 E. Clark   Phone: (605)677-5228
Vermillion, SD 57069   Cleo Kosters, Cur.
Founded: 1883. **Staff:** Prof 4. **Subjects:** Archeology, anthropology, natural
history, history, museology, decorative arts, photography. **Special**
Collections: Papers of William H. Over; Morrow Photographic Collection
(600). **Holdings:** 1200 books; 36 bound periodical volumes; 22 museum
notebooks of clippings; 50 manuscripts. **Subscriptions:** 15 journals and other
serials. **Services:** Copying; library open to the public for reference use only.
Special Indexes: Morrow Photograph Collection. **Remarks:** Maintained by
South Dakota State Department of Education and Cultural Affairs.

★ 12631 ★
Overbrook School for the Blind - Library (Aud-Vis)
6333 Malvern Ave.   Phone: (215)877-0313
Philadelphia, PA 19151   Julia A. Flinchbaugh, Libn.
Founded: 1832. **Staff:** Prof 1. **Subjects:** Standard, large print, and braille books for kindergarten through high school; general library of braille, talking book, tape, and print titles for primary, elementary, and high school; library of print for faculty members. **Special Collections:** Historical material on education of the blind and other aspects of blindness; deafness. **Holdings:** 12,500 braille books; 5000 printed books; 600 large print books; 3000 talking books, tapes, cassettes. **Subscriptions:** 75 journals and other serials in print and braille. **Services:** Library open to the public for reference use only by request.

★ 12632 ★
Overlook Hospital - Health Sciences Library (Med)
99 Beauvoir Ave.   Phone: (201)522-2119
Summit, NJ 07902-0220   Kathleen A. Moeller, Dir.
Founded: 1946. **Staff:** Prof 1; Other 3. **Subjects:** Medicine, surgery, nursing, radiology, emergency medicine, psychiatry, pediatrics, orthopedics. **Special Collections:** Consumer Health Information Collection (2000 books; 50 journals; free pamphlets). **Holdings:** 6000 books; 12,000 bound periodical volumes; 2000 subject files for LATCH Program; 600 AV programs. **Subscriptions:** 550 journals and other serials. **Services:** Interlibrary loan; copying; library open to the public. **Automated Operations:** Computerized public access catalog, serials, circulation, and acquisitions. **Computerized Information Services:** MEDLARS, DIALOG Information Services, BRS Information Technologies. **Networks/Consortia:** Member of Cosmopolitan Biomedical Library Consortium (CBLC), Health Sciences Library Association of New Jersey (HSLANJ), Medical Library Center of New York (MLCNY). **Remarks:** FAX: (201)522-2274. **Staff:** Victoria Sciuk.

★ 12633 ★
Overseas Development Council - Library (Soc Sci)
1717 Massachusetts Ave., N.W., Suite 501   Phone: (202)234-8701
Washington, DC 20036   Katherine Bowen, Libn.
Founded: 1970. **Staff:** Prof 1; Other 1. **Subjects:** International trade and industrial policy, international finance and investment, development strategies and development assistance, U.S. foreign policy toward developing countries. **Holdings:** 1300 books. **Subscriptions:** 50 journals and other serials; 6 newspapers. **Services:** Interlibrary loan; copying; library open to the public by appointment. **Remarks:** FAX: (202)745-0067.

★ 12634 ★
Overseas Private Investment Corporation - Library (Bus-Fin)
1615 M St., N.W.
Washington, DC 20527   Phone: (202)457-7123
Founded: 1974. **Staff:** Prof 2; Other 1. **Subjects:** Multinational business, foreign investment, international law, economics of developing countries, foreign relations. **Special Collections:** Legislative histories on foreign assistance and international development (300 volumes); country file (54 linear feet). **Holdings:** 6000 books; 8 linear feet of VF drawers. **Subscriptions:** 150 journals and other serials; 10 newspapers. **Services:** Interlibrary loan; copying; SDI; library open to the public by appointment. **Automated Operations:** Computerized cataloging, acquisitions, and circulation. **Computerized Information Services:** DIALOG Information Services, NEXIS, LEXIS, Dow Jones News/Retrieval, TEXTLINE, OCLC. **Networks/Consortia:** Member of FEDLINK. **Publications:** User's Guide to Information Services. **Remarks:** OPIC is an independent U.S. Government agency which provides financing and political risk insurance to U.S. businesses to encourage investment in developing countries. **Remarks:** FAX: (202)223-3514.

Oviatt Library
See: **California State University, Northridge (2572)**

★ 12635 ★
Owatonna Public Library - Toy Library (Educ)
105 N. Elm
Box 387   Phone: (507)451-4660
Owatonna, MN 55060   Graham Benoit, Hd., Ch.Serv.
Staff: Prof 1; Other 2. **Subjects:** Manipulative toys, reading readiness, math and science, parenting. **Holdings:** 300 toys; 50 pamphlets. **Services:** Library open to the public with restrictions. **Automated Operations:** Computerized cataloging, acquisitions, and circulation. **Computerized Information Services:** ATLAS (internal database). **Special Catalogs:** Illustrated toy catalog (loose-leaf). **Remarks:** FAX: (507)451-3909.

Owen Science and Engineering Library
See: **Washington State University (20047)**

★ 12636 ★
Owens-Corning Fiberglass Corporation - Technical Data Center (Sci-Engr)
Technical Center
2790 Columbus Rd., Rte. 16   Phone: (614)587-7265
Granville, OH 43023-0415   Nancy Lemon, Supv., Res.Lib.
Staff: Prof 1; Other 2. **Subjects:** Glass, ceramics, polymers, reinforced plastics, glass textiles, mathematics, chemistry, management, safety engineering, science. **Holdings:** 10,000 books; 20,000 bound periodical volumes; 2500 translations; 500 annual reports. **Subscriptions:** 200 journals and other serials. **Services:** Interlibrary loan; SDI; Current Awareness Service; center open to the public by appointment. **Automated Operations:** Computerized cataloging and acquisitions. **Computerized Information Services:** OCLC, DIALOG Information Services, STN International, BRS Information Technologies, CompuServe Information Service, PFDS Online. **Networks/Consortia:** Member of OHIONET. **Remarks:** FAX: (614)587-7255.

Owens Library
See: **Northwest Missouri State University - Owens Library (12056)**

★ 12637 ★
Owensboro Area Museum - Library (Sci-Engr)
2829 S. Griffith Ave.   Phone: (502)683-0296
Owensboro, KY 42301   Donald M. Boarman, Dir.
Founded: 1966. **Staff:** Prof 8. **Subjects:** Archeology, geology, botany, antiques, astronomy, ornithology. **Holdings:** 300 books; 400 bound periodical volumes; 50 filmstrips; 100 movies; 500 slides; 50 reels of microfilm. **Services:** Interlibrary loan; copying; Library open to the public with restrictions. **Staff:** Kathy Olson, Reg.

★ 12638 ★
Owensboro-Daviess County Public Library - Kentucky Room (Hist)
450 Griffith Ave.   Phone: (502)684-0211
Owensboro, KY 42301   Shelia E. Heflin, Supv.
Staff: 3. **Subjects:** Kentucky history, local history, genealogy. **Special Collections:** Photograph collection; Rotary Club records (4 VF drawers); oral history. **Holdings:** 3000 volumes; 5 VF drawers of family files; 30 VF drawers of clippings and pamphlets; local newspapers and state census on microfilm; Kentucky county tax lists through 1875 on microfilm (limited); Ohio County, Kentucky circuit court equity records, 1800-1900, on microfilm; various Daviess County courthouse records, 1815-1985, on microfilm; various McLean County court records, 1854-1911. **Subscriptions:** 130 journals and other serials. **Services:** Copying; limited research; room open to the public with restrictions. **Special Indexes:** Obituary index to Owensboro Messenger and Inquirer, 1910 to present; local newspaper index, 1977 to present.

★ 12639 ★
Owensboro Messenger-Inquirer - Library (Publ)
1401 Frederica St.   Phone: (502)926-0123
Owensboro, KY 42301   Sherri Evans Heckel, Libn.
Founded: 1973. **Staff:** Prof 1; Other 1. **Subjects:** Newspaper reference topics. **Holdings:** 2500 books; 50 bound periodical volumes; 127,000 clippings; 21,000 photographs; 1500 pamphlets; Messenger-Inquirer, 1862 to present, on microfilm. **Subscriptions:** 10 journals and other serials; 15 newspapers. **Services:** Library not open to the public. **Computerized Information Services:** Info-Ky & Personal Librarian full-text retrieval system (internal database). Performs searches on fee basis. **Special Indexes:** Index to microfiche clippings, photographs, books, pamphlets, maps, graphics (online). **Remarks:** FAX: (502)685-3446.

Marion Ownbey Herbarium - Library
See: **Washington State University (20046)**

★ 12640 ★
Owyhee County Historical Complex - Helen Nettleton Library (Hist)
Box 67   Phone: (208)495-2319
Murphy, ID 83650   Glenda R. Bean, Cur.
Founded: 1961. **Staff:** Prof 1; Other 3. **Subjects:** Owyhee County history, mining, agriculture, Indians, ranching, transportation. **Special Collections:** 4500 historic photographs documenting Owyhee County history. **Holdings:** 1100 books; 10 boxes of reports and manuscripts; 8 VF drawers of clippings and pictures; 20 boxes of archival materials; 1 drawer of microfilm; 50 oral history tapes. **Subscriptions:** 13 journals and other serials; 5 newspapers. **Services:** Copying; library open to the public with restrictions. **Automated Operations:** Computerized cataloging. **Publications:** Owyhee Outpost, annual. **Special Indexes:** Biographical index (online). **Remarks:** Maintained by the Owyhee County Historical Society.

★ 12641 ★
Oxfam - Overseas Division Library (Soc Sci)
274 Banbury Rd.   Phone: 865 312284
Oxford OX2 7DZ, England   June Stephen, Libn.
Founded: 1982. **Staff:** 1. **Subjects:** World poverty, economic self-sufficiency, health, agriculture, gender, technology, social development. **Holdings:** 9000 volumes. **Subscriptions:** 50 journals and other serials. **Services:** Interlibrary loan; copying; library open to university researchers. **Computerized Information Services:** Internal databases; electronic mail. **Remarks:** FAX: 865 312600. Telex: 83610.

Oxford Free Public Library
See: **Oxford Museum - Library** (12643)

★ 12642 ★
Oxford Gerontology Center - Library (Med)
New York State Veterans' Home   Phone: (607)843-6991
Oxford, NY 13830   Raymond Vickers, M.D.
Founded: 1982. **Subjects:** Long-term care, gerontology. **Holdings:** 450 books; 130 bound periodical volumes; 112 reports. **Services:** Library open to accredited students and others with prior written permission. **Remarks:** FAX: (607)843-6991, ext. 300.

★ 12643 ★
Oxford Museum - Library (Hist)
339 Main St.   Phone: (508)987-2882
Oxford, MA 01540   Timothy A. Kelley, Hd.Libn.
Founded: 1978. **Staff:** Prof 1. **Subjects:** Local history, genealogy, Huguenots. **Special Collections:** Town records; local newspapers; books by and about Clara Barton and Dr. Elliott P. Joslin. **Holdings:** 1000 volumes. **Services:** Interlibrary loan; copying; library open to the public for reference use only. **Remarks:** Maintained by the Oxford Free Public Library.

★ 12644 ★
Oxford United Methodist Church - Oscar G. Cook Memorial Library (Rel-Phil)
465 Main St.   Phone: (508)987-5378
Oxford, MA 01540   Sandy Brennan, Sec.
Founded: 1965. **Staff:** 2. **Subjects:** Religion and Bible, family living, theology, history, biography. **Holdings:** 450 books; AV programs. **Services:** Library open to the public.

★ 12645 ★
Oxford University Press, Inc. - Library (Publ)
200 Madison Ave.   Phone: (212)679-7300
New York, NY 10016   Elizabeth Moleti, Libn.
Staff: Prof 1; Other 1. **Subjects:** Humanities; sciences - social, biological, physical. **Holdings:** 8000 books; 42 periodical volumes; publications of the press. **Subscriptions:** 16 journals and other serials. **Services:** Library not open to the public. **Special Catalogs:** Catalog of all titles in print; spring and fall catalog of new publications. **Remarks:** FAX: (212)725-2972.

John Oxley Library
See: **State Library of Queensland** (15692)

★ 12646 ★
OXY USA Inc. - Legal Division Library (Law, Energy)
Box 300   Phone: (918)561-2272
Tulsa, OK 74102   Jo C. Cherry, Libn.
Founded: 1917. **Staff:** Prof 1. **Subjects:** Oil and gas production; law - environmental, labor, computer. **Special Collections:** Indian affairs; laws and treaties (50 volumes). **Holdings:** 10,000 books; 100 shelves of miscellaneous reports, 30 videocassettes. **Subscriptions:** 100 journals and other serials; 5 newspapers. **Services:** Interlibrary loan (limited); library not open to the public. **Computerized Information Services:** LEXIS. **Remarks:** FAX: (918)561-4364.

Oy Keskuslaboratorio - Centrallaboratorium Ab
See: **Finnish Pulp and Paper Research Institute** (5720)

Oy Yleisradio Ab: n Kirjastotietopalvelu
See: **Finnish Broadcasting Company** (5715)

Oyer Memorial Library
See: **Washington Bible College/Capital Bible Seminary** (19991)

★ 12647 ★
Oyster Bay Historical Society - Research Library (Hist)
20 Summit St.
Box 297   Phone: (516)922-5032
Oyster Bay, NY 11771-0297   Julia Clark, Libn./Archv.
Founded: 1960. **Staff:** Prof 2. **Subjects:** Long Island - revolutionary, colonial, 18th-19th century history and genealogy; Oyster Bay history. **Special Collections:** Theodore Roosevelt Collection. **Holdings:** 750 books; 20 bound periodical volumes; 30 filing boxes of letters and manuscripts; 200 photographs; 25 maps and atlases; original deeds, letters, documents. **Services:** Copying; library open to the public for reference use only.

★ 12648 ★
Oysterponds Historical Society, Inc. - OHS Research Library (Hist)
Village Lane
Box 844   Phone: (516)323-2480
Orient, NY 11957   Donald Boerum, Hd.Libn.
Founded: 1944. **Staff:** Prof 1; Other 10. **Subjects:** Genealogy, local history. **Special Collections:** Photographs of Eastern Long Island, 1860-1920 (2000 photographs). **Holdings:** 1350 volumes; 3000 documents and records; 12 VF drawers; 3500 glass plates; 19th century diaries and recipe books; whaling logs, 1848-1852; postcards; local wills and papers. **Services:** Copying; library open to the public by appointment.

★ 12649 ★
Ozark Christian College - Seth Wilson Library (Rel-Phil)
1111 N. Main St.   Phone: (417)624-2518
Joplin, MO 64801-1188   William F. Abernathy, Dir., Lib.Serv.
Founded: 1942. **Staff:** Prof 1; Other 6. **Subjects:** Religion, Christian Restoration Movement, archaeology, Bible. **Holdings:** 40,495 books; 2453 bound periodical volumes; 2271 AV programs; 5320 audio cassettes; 12 VF drawers of missions files; 9 VF drawers of essay files. **Subscriptions:** 302 journals and other serials. **Services:** Interlibrary loan; copying; library open to the public. **Automated Operations:** Computerized cataloging and acquisitions. **Computerized Information Services:** EasyNet, BiblioFile. Performs searches on fee basis. **Special Catalogs:** Audiovisuals Catalog, annual; Audio Cassette Catalog, annual. **Staff:** Mark Sloneker, Cat.

★ 12650 ★
Ozark Folk Center - Library (Area-Ethnic)
Mt. View, AR 72560   Phone: (501)269-3851
     W.K. McNeil, Folklorist
Founded: 1976. **Staff:** Prof 1; Other 1. **Subjects:** Ozark folklore, crafts, and music. **Holdings:** 3000 books; 50 bound periodical volumes; 100 unbound periodicals; 250 pieces of ephemera; sheet music; phonograph records. **Subscriptions:** 40 journals and other serials. **Services:** Interlibrary loan; copying; library open to the public.

P

★12651★
P.T. Boats, Inc. - Library, Archives & Technical Information Center
(Mil)
U.S.S. Massachusetts
Battleship Cove   Phone: (508)678-1100
Fall River, MA 02721   Frank J. Szczepaniak, P.T. Boat Coord.
Founded: 1975. **Staff:** 1. **Subjects:** Patrol Torpedo (P.T.) boats, naval
history. **Special Collections:** Personal photo albums of 43 World War II
operating squadrons. **Holdings:** 400 books; 300 bound periodical volumes;
150 manuals; 200 P.T. boat blueprints; 100 designs; 5000 photographs; 15
reels of microfilm; 60 reels of P.T. movies. **Services:** Copying; center open
to the public by appointment. **Publications:** Newspaper, semiannual; 3
books on P.T. boats of World War II. **Remarks:** Claims to be the only P.T.
Boat Museum and Library in the world. All mail should be sent to P.T.
Boats, Inc., Box 109, Memphis, TN 38101. Telephone (901)272-9980.

★12652★
**P.T. Boats, Inc. - Library, Archives & Technical Information Center -
National Headquarters** (Mil)
Box 38070   Phone: (901)755-8440
Memphis, TN 38183-070   Alyce N. Guthrie, Exec. V.P.
Founded: 1946. **Staff:** 4. **Subjects:** Patrol Torpedo (P.T.) boats - World War
II operations, squadrons, tenders, bases, training center, P.T. boat builders.
Special Collections: Photographs (10,000); 78 foot Higgins P.T. Boat; 80
foot Elco P.T. Boat; artifacts, memorabilia, uniforms, and weapons.
Holdings: 500 books; 75 bound periodical volumes; 20 charts; 50 operation
action reports; 5000 clippings; 2000 feet of microfilm; 20,000 feet of World
War II film; 20 VF drawers of letters, citations, orders, and records of P.T.
boaters. **Services:** Copying; library open to the public by appointment.
Publications: The P.T. Boater Newspaper, 2/year; technical manuals on the
history of P.T. Boat squadrons. **Special Catalogs:** Rosters of P.T. Boaters
(online). **Staff:** Jake Oswalt, Res.

William Paca Garden Conservation Center
See: **Historic Annapolis, Inc.** (7238)

★12653★
**PACCAR Inc. - Technical Center Library and Quality Technology
Center** (Sci-Engr)
1261 Hwy. 237   Phone: (206)757-5234
Mount Vernon, WA 98273   Maryanne Ward, Tech.Pubns.Mgr.
Founded: 1985. **Staff:** Prof 2; Other 1. **Subjects:** Automotive and mechanical
engineering, computer science, trucking industry. **Holdings:** Figures not
available. **Computerized Information Services:** DIALOG Information
Services, OCLC; internal databases. **Remarks:** FAX: (206)757-5370.

PACE Resource Center
See: **Ohio State University - Counseling and Consultation Service**
(12304)

★12654★
Pace University - Edward and Doris Mortola Library (Bus-Fin)
861 Bedford Rd.   Phone: (914)773-3382
Pleasantville, NY 10570   William J. Murdock, Lib.Dir.
Founded: 1963. **Staff:** Prof 8; Other 9. **Subjects:** Business administration,
period histories, accounting, nursing, 19th century English literature,
computer science. **Special Collections:** St. Joan of Arc. **Holdings:** 190,400
volumes; 7172 pamphlets; 1641 corporation reports; 251 college bulletins;
14,962 reels of microfilm. **Subscriptions:** 1300 journals and other serials.
Services: Interlibrary loan; copying; library open to the public for reference
use only. **Automated Operations:** Computerized cataloging and serials
(INNOPAC/INNOVACQ, PALS). **Computerized Information Services:**
DIALOG Information Services, Dow Jones News/Retrieval, BRS
Information Technologies, OCLC. Performs searches on fee basis. Contact
Person: R. Loomis, Ref.Libn., 773-3505. **Networks/Consortia:** Member of
Westchester Library System (WLS), New York Metropolitan Reference and
Research Library Agency. **Remarks:** FAX: (914)773-3508. **Staff:** L.
Jackson, Tech.Serv.; N. McGuire, Ref.Libn.; E. Reiman, Ref.Libn.; J. Lee,
Ref.Libn.; M. Boyd, Ref.Libn.

★12655★
Pace University - Henry Birnbaum Library (Bus-Fin)
Pace Plaza   Phone: (212)346-1331
New York, NY 10038   Melvin S. Isaacson, Lib.Dir.
Founded: 1936. **Staff:** Prof 10; Other 25. **Subjects:** Liberal arts and sciences,
accounting, finance, management, marketing, real estate, taxation.
Holdings: 382,500 volumes; domestic and foreign corporation annual
reports; 7200 pamphlets; 20,200 reels of microfilm. **Subscriptions:** 1900
journals and other serials; 6 newspapers. **Services:** Interlibrary loan; library
not open to the public. **Automated Operations:** Computerized public access
catalog and cataloging. **Computerized Information Services:** BRS
Information Technologies, DIALOG Information Services, OCLC; CD-
ROMs (ABI/INFORM, Periodical Abstracts Ondisc, PsycLIT, Compact
Disclosure, Investext, National Trade Data Base). **Networks/Consortia:**
Member of New York Metropolitan Reference and Research Library
Agency. **Remarks:** FAX: (212)346-1615. **Staff:** Adele Jann,
Tech.Serv.Libn.; Michelle Fanelli, Rd.Serv.Libn.; Elizabeth Birnbaum, ILL
Libn.; Maria Ptakowski, Per.Libn.; Arthe Kelly, Circ.Coord.

★12656★
Pace University - School of Law Library (Law)
78 N. Broadway   Phone: (914)422-4273
White Plains, NY 10603   Nicholas Triffin, Dir.
Founded: 1976. **Staff:** Prof 8; Other 8. **Subjects:** U.S. and international law,
jurisprudence. **Special Collections:** Selective U.S. Government documents
depository; environmental law (2800 titles). **Holdings:** 51,574 titles; 253,950
volumes. **Subscriptions:** 3362 journals and other serials. **Services:**
Interlibrary loan; copying; library open to the public. **Automated
Operations:** Computerized cataloging. **Computerized Information Services:**
LEXIS, DIALOG Information Services, WESTLAW, OCLC, RLIN.
Performs searches on fee basis. **Networks/Consortia:** Member of New York
Metropolitan Reference and Research Library Agency, SUNY/OCLC
Library Network. **Publications:** Acquisitions list; bibliographies; reference
aids. **Remarks:** FAX: (914)422-4139. **Staff:** Martha W. Keister, Hd.,
Pub.Serv.; Anne Sauter, Ref./Doc.Libn.; Susan Nosseir, Ref./ILL Libn.;
Alice Pidgeon, Acq.Libn.; David Williams, Database/Ref.Libn.; Xia Lin,
Sys.Libn.

★12657★
Pacific Asia Museum - Library (Area-Ethnic)
46 N. Los Robles   Phone: (818)449-2742
Pasadena, CA 91101   Sarah McKay, Libn.
Founded: 1976. **Subjects:** Asia and the Pacific - art, applied art, history,
culture. **Special Collections:** Paul Sherbert Collection (India; 1560 volumes).
Holdings: 2500 volumes. **Subscriptions:** 10 journals and other serials.
Services: Copying; library open to the public by appointment. **Remarks:**
FAX: (818)449-2754.

★12658★
Pacific Asia Travel Association - Library (Bus-Fin)
Telesis Tower, Suite 1750
1 Montgomery St.   Phone: (415)986-4646
San Francisco, CA 94104   Jordan G. Yee
Founded: 1975. **Staff:** 1. **Subjects:** Travel and tourism in the countries and
isles of the Greater Pacific region. **Holdings:** 2000 publications, films, and
videos. **Subscriptions:** 120 journals and other serials; 3 newspapers. **Services:**
Interlibrary loan; copying; library open to non-members for a fee.
Computerized Information Services: DIALOG Information Services,
DataTimes, Reuters; internal databases. **Remarks:** FAX: (415)986-3458.
Telex: 170685. Cable: PATA.

Pacific Basin Rehabilitation Research & Training Center
See: **University of Hawaii - John A. Burns School of Medicine** (18619)

★12659★
Pacific Bell - Corporate Information Center (Info Sci)
2600 Camino Ramon, Rm. 1CS95   Phone: (510)823-8000
San Ramon, CA 94583   Harry Allen, Mgr.
Founded: 1982. **Staff:** Prof 4; Other 3. **Subjects:** Telecommunications,
management, business. **Holdings:** 5500 books; 500 bound periodical
volumes; Pacific Bell & AT & T annual reports; Bell System publications.
Subscriptions: 500 journals and other serials; 11 newspapers. **Services:**
Interlibrary loan; copying; SDI; center open to the public by appointment.
Automated Operations: Computerized cataloging, acquisitions, and serials.
Computerized Information Services: DIALOG Information Services, PFDS
Online, NewsNet, Inc., Dow Jones News/Retrieval, NEXIS, DataTimes,
VU/TEXT Information Services, RLIN; internal databases. **Publications:**
CIC Bulletin, quarterly - for internal distribution only. **Staff:** Anna Mancini,
Info.Res.Anl.; Jensa Woo, Info.Res.Anl.; Helen Suomela-Tyrrell,
Info.Res.Anl.

★ 12660 ★
Pacific Bio-Marine Laboratories, Inc. - Research Library
124 N. Ash Ave.
Inglewood, CA 90301
Founded: 1961. **Staff:** 1. **Subjects:** Marine biology, water quality, marine resources. **Special Collections:** Marine resources of southern California. **Holdings:** 2000 books; 500 reports; 2000 reprints. **Remarks:** Currently inactive.

Pacific Bio-Medical Research Center
See: **University of Hawaii (18620)**

★ 12661 ★
Pacific Christian College - Hurst Memorial Library (Rel-Phil)
2500 E. Nutwood Ave.   Phone: (714)879-3901
Fullerton, CA 92631   Jeffrey L. Wilson, Lib.Dir.
Founded: 1929. **Staff:** Prof 2; Other 2. **Subjects:** Theology, Christian education, church history, Bible, missions, sociology, psychology, philosophy, world history. **Holdings:** 56,000 books; 300 bound periodical volumes; 1000 other cataloged items; 6 VF drawers Christian Church mission papers; 2200 tapes; 100 reels of microfilm; 1000 microfiche. **Subscriptions:** 381 journals and other serials. **Services:** Interlibrary loan; copying; library open to the public with restrictions. **Automated Operations:** Computerized cataloging and ILL. **Computerized Information Services:** DIALOG Information Services, OCLC. Performs searches on fee basis.

★ 12662 ★
Pacific Coast Banking School - Library (Bus-Fin)
1601 5th Ave., Suite 1402   Phone: (206)447-4141
Seattle, WA 98101   Susanne Phillips, Libn.
Founded: 1950. **Staff:** 5. **Subjects:** Bank capital, bank deposits, marketing and personnel operations, economic studies, international banking, regulatory studies, bank investments, loans, trust department studies. **Holdings:** 450 unbound theses; 1 drawer of microfilm. **Services:** Interlibrary loan; library open to the public by appointment. **Remarks:** FAX: (206)447-4144. Telex:: 350601.

★ 12663 ★
Pacific Cultural Foundation - Library (Area-Ethnic)
Palace Office Bldg., Suite 807
346 Nanking E. Rd., Sect. 3
Taipei, Taiwan   Phone: 2 7527424
Subjects: China - culture, history, contemporary problems. **Holdings:** 2000 volumes. **Remarks:** FAX: 2 7527429. Telex: 12849 PCFROC.

★ 12664 ★
Pacific Energy & Resources Center - Library (Energy)
Bldg. 1055, Fort Cronkhite
Sausalito, CA 94965   Phone: (415)332-8200
Staff: Prof 1. **Subjects:** Energy, energy management, renewable energy technologies. **Special Collections:** Energy products and services directories and materials; California State Office of Appropriate Technology's Collection (energy issues, technologies, research; 3000 items). **Holdings:** 400 books; 300 bound periodical volumes; 800 other cataloged items. **Services:** Library open to the public by appointment.

★ 12665 ★
Pacific Enterprises - Law Library (Law)
633 W. 5th St.   Phone: (213)895-5195
Los Angeles, CA 90071   Kathryn Lee, Law Libn.
Staff: Prof 2; Other 1. **Subjects:** Law - corporate, utility, oil and gas, energy, environmental. **Holdings:** 25,000 volumes. **Subscriptions:** 350 journals and other serials; 5 newspapers. **Services:** Interlibrary loan; library not open to the public. **Automated Operations:** Computerized cataloging and acquisitions. **Computerized Information Services:** LEXIS, NEXIS, WESTLAW, DIALOG Information Services. **Remarks:** FAX: (213)629-9620. **Staff:** Richard Mogg, Asst. Law Libn.

★ 12666 ★
Pacific Fleet Submarine Memorial Association - USS Bowfin Submarine Museum & Park - Library (Mil)
11 Arizona Memorial Dr.   Phone: (808)423-1341
Honolulu, HI 96818   B.J. Dorman, Dir.
Founded: 1979. **Subjects:** Submarine history and warfare, World Wars I and II, post war salvage and rescue. **Special Collections:** World War II patrol reports for U.S. submarines; special files on all U.S. submarines and related vessels. **Holdings:** 1000 books; 500 bound periodical volumes; reports; manuscripts and investigations; film; microfilm. **Subscriptions:** 5 journals and other serials; 25 newspapers. **Services:** Library open to the public by appointment for reference use only. **Computerized Information Services:** Internal database. **Publications:** On Eternal Patrol, 1991 (lists U.S. submarines lost during WWII and their crews). **Remarks:** FAX: (808)422-5201. **Staff:** Mary Jo Yaldes, Musm.Coll.Mgr.; Aldona Sendzikas, Exhibit Spec.

★ 12667 ★
Pacific Gas and Electric Company - Corporate Library (Bus-Fin, Energy)
77 Beale St.   Phone: (415)973-2573
San Francisco, CA 94106   Michele F. Sullivan, Dir./Corp.Libn.
Founded: 1913. **Staff:** Prof 3; Other 3. **Subjects:** Engineering, energy, business, finance. **Special Collections:** Company history. **Holdings:** 7500 volumes; 53 VF drawers. **Subscriptions:** 570 journals and other serials. **Services:** Interlibrary loan; copying; SDI; library open to the public by appointment. **Automated Operations:** Computerized cataloging, acquisitions, serials, circulation, and ILL. **Computerized Information Services:** DIALOG Information Services, PFDS Online, OCLC, LEXIS, NEXIS; OnTyme Electronic Message Network Service (electronic mail service). **Networks/Consortia:** Member of CLASS. **Remarks:** FAX: (415)973-9331. Electronic mail address(es): EEI039 (OnTyme Electronic Message Network Service).

★ 12668 ★
Pacific Gas and Electric Company - Law Library (Law)
Box 7442   Phone: (415)973-4293
San Francisco, CA 94120   Gary L. Stromme, Law Libn.
Founded: 1906. **Staff:** Prof 2; Other 2. **Subjects:** Law. **Holdings:** 35,000 volumes. **Services:** Library not open to the public. **Remarks:** FAX: (415)973-9274. **Staff:** Betty A. Merritt, Asst. Law Libn.

★ 12669 ★
Pacific Graduate School of Psychology - Research Library (Med, Soc Sci)
935 East Meadow Dr.   Phone: (415)494-7477
Palo Alto, CA 94303-4233   Christine Dassoff, Res.Libn.
Founded: 1975. **Staff:** Prof 1; Other 2. **Subjects:** Clinical psychology, psychological assessment, psychopathology, psychotherapy, neuropsychology, developmental psychology, child psychiatry, research methodology and statistics. **Special Collections:** Faculty reprint file. **Holdings:** 5200 books; 2500 bound periodical volumes; 100 psychological tests; 100 dissertations; 350 audio cassettes; 100 videocassettes. **Subscriptions:** 175 journals and other serials. **Services:** Interlibrary loan; copying; center open to students, faculy and alumni. **Automated Operations:** Computerized public access catalog (SOCRATES) and ILL (DOCLINE). **Computerized Information Services:** BRS Information Technologies, NLM, MELVYL, RLIN. **Networks/Consortia:** Member of CLASS, Northern California Medical Library Group, National Network of Libraries of Medicine - Pacific Southwest Region, Northern California Consortium of Psychology Libraries (NCCPL). **Remarks:** FAX: (415)856-6734.

★ 12670 ★
Pacific Grove Museum of Natural History - Library (Biol Sci)
165 Forest Ave.   Phone: (408)648-3116
Pacific Grove, CA 93950   Vernal L. Yadon, Musm.Dir.
Subjects: Natural history of Monterey County. **Holdings:** 1000 books. **Services:** Library open to the public for reference use only.

★ 12671 ★
Pacific Grove Public Library - Alvin Seale South Seas Collection (Area-Ethnic)
550 Central Ave.   Phone: (408)648-3160
Pacific Grove, CA 93950   Barbara Morrison, Lib.Dir.
Founded: 1896. **Staff:** Prof 4; Other 12.5. **Subjects:** Pacific Islands, voyages. **Holdings:** 1200 volumes. **Services:** Interlibrary loan (limited); copying;

collection open to the public with restrictions. **Computerized Information Services:** OnTyme Electronic Message Network Service (electronic mail service). **Networks/Consortia:** Member of Monterey Bay Area Cooperative Library System (MOBAC). **Special Indexes:** Index to Seale Collection. **Remarks:** FAX: (408)373-3268. Electronic mail address(es): CLASS.PGRV (OnTyme Electronic Message Network Service). **Staff:** Polly Archer, Adult Serv.Libn.; Lisa Maddalena, Children's Libn.

★ 12672 ★
Pacific Hospital of Long Beach - Medical Staff Library (Med)
2776 Pacific Ave.
Box 1268   Phone: (213)595-1911
Long Beach, CA 90801   Lois E. Harris, Dir., Lib.Serv.
Founded: 1964. **Staff:** Prof 1. **Subjects:** General medicine, surgery, osteopathy, nursing. **Special Collections:** Acupuncture. **Holdings:** 2000 volumes. **Subscriptions:** 200 journals and other serials. **Services:** Interlibrary loan; SDI; library open to the public for reference use only when user is sponsored by physician. **Computerized Information Services:** MEDLARS, BRS Information Technologies. Performs searches on fee basis. **Remarks:** FAX: (213)492-1363.

Pacific Lighting Corporation - Law Library
See: **Pacific Enterprises (12665)**

Pacific Lutheran Theological Seminary
See: **Graduate Theological Union (6613)**

★ 12673 ★
Pacific Medical Center - Ellen Griep Memorial Library (Med)
1200 12th Ave., S.   Phone: (206)326-4085
Seattle, WA 98144   Seungja Song, Mgr., Med.Lib.
Founded: 1969. **Staff:** Prof 1; Other 1. **Subjects:** Ambulatory care medicine, medicine, dentistry, hospital administration. **Holdings:** 1300 books; 5000 bound periodical volumes. **Subscriptions:** 154 journals and other serials. **Services:** Interlibrary loan; library not open to the public. **Automated Operations:** Computerized ILL. **Computerized Information Services:** WLN, MEDLARS, BRS Information Technologies, DIALOG Information Services; OnTyme Electronic Message Network Service EMA. **Networks/Consortia:** Member of Seattle Area Hospital Library Consortium (SAHLC). **Publications:** Library News, 3/month. **Remarks:** FAX: (206)326-4073. Electronic mail address(es): PACMC (OnTyme Electronic Message Network Service).

Pacific Northwest Agricultural History Archives
See: **Washington State University - Manuscripts, Archives, & Special Collections (20045)**

Pacific Northwest Anthropological Archives
See: **University of Idaho (18653)**

Pacific Northwest National Parks Association - Fort Vancouver National Historic Site
See: **U.S. Natl. Park Service - Fort Vancouver Natl. Historic Site - Library (17715)**

Pacific Northwest Publishers' Archives
See: **Washington State University - Manuscripts, Archives, & Special Collections (20045)**

Pacific Northwest River Basin Commission Library
See: **Washington State Water Research Center - Library (20051)**

★ 12674 ★
Pacific Power and Light Company - Library
920 S.W. Sixth Ave.
Portland, OR 97204
Defunct.

Pacific Presbyterian Medical Center
See: **California Pacific Medical Center/University of the Pacific School of Dentistry (2498)**

★ 12675 ★
Pacific Press, Ltd. - Press Library (Publ)
2250 Granville St.   Phone: (604)732-2519
Vancouver, BC, Canada V6H 3G2   Jan Wallace, Chf.Libn.
Founded: 1966. **Staff:** Prof 4; Other 17. **Subjects:** Newspaper reference topics. **Holdings:** 1000 volumes; 260 VF drawers of newspaper clipping files; 325,000 microjackets of clipping files; 200 VF drawers of pictures; 250 VF drawers of biographical files; 360 boxes of pamphlets; photographic negatives. **Subscriptions:** 37 journals and other serials. **Services:** Copying; library open to the public with restrictions. **Computerized Information Services:** Infomart Online. Performs searches on fee basis. Contact Person: Debra Millward, Database Mgr., Libn., 732-2653. **Remarks:** FAX: (604)732-2323. **Staff:** Steve Proulx, Mgr., Ed.Serv.; Kate Abbott, Graphics Libn.

★ 12676 ★
Pacific Salmon Commission - Library (Biol Sci)
1155 Robson St., Suite 600   Phone: (604)684-8081
Vancouver, BC, Canada V6E 1B5   Teri Tarita, Libn.
Founded: 1947. **Staff:** Prof 1. **Subjects:** Fisheries management, salmon research and biology. **Special Collections:** Commission field notes and data records; history of fisheries in British Columbia. **Holdings:** 600 books; 600 bound periodical volumes; 8000 reports and reprints; 75 meters of archival material; 800 reprints; 1 box of microfiche; 50 dissertations; 17 file drawers of data sheets; 400 maps. **Subscriptions:** 32 journals and other serials. **Services:** Interlibrary loan; copying; library open to the public for reference use only. **Automated Operations:** Computerized cataloging. **Computerized Information Services:** InmagicInc. (internal database). **Publications:** Annual Report; Technical Report; handbook. **Remarks:** FAX: (604)666-8707.

Pacific School of Religion
See: **Graduate Theological Union (6613)**

★ 12677 ★
Pacific-Sierra Research Corporation - Library (Sci-Engr)
12340 Santa Monica Blvd.   Phone: (213)820-2200
Los Angeles, CA 90025   Karin F. Sehlmeyer, Res.Libn.
Founded: 1971. **Staff:** Prof 1; Other 1. **Subjects:** Laser optics, nuclear physics, geophysics, foreign policy, computer science. **Special Collections:** Technical reports on atmospheric nuclear testing (150). **Holdings:** 1000 books; 100 maps; 9000 technical reports. **Subscriptions:** 140 journals and other serials. **Services:** Library not open to the public. **Computerized Information Services:** DIALOG Information Services, DTIC, PFDS Online, Aerospace Online, STN International; CompuServe Information Service (electronic mail service). **Remarks:** FAX: (213)820-4141.

★ 12678 ★
Pacific Studies Center - Library (Bus-Fin)
222B View St.   Phone: (415)969-1545
Mountain View, CA 94041   Leonard M. Siegel, Dir.
Founded: 1969. **Staff:** Prof 2. **Subjects:** Multinational corporations, high technology industry, defense industry, Southeast Asia, U.S. military and foreign policy, military toxics. **Holdings:** 7000 books; 165 drawers of working research files arranged by geographical area, country, industry, corporation. **Subscriptions:** 150 periodicals. **Services:** Copying; library open to the public. **Computerized Information Services:** PeaceNet (electronic mail service). **Publications:** Global Electronics (newsletter), monthly. **Remarks:** FAX: (415)968-1126. Electronic mail address(es): LSIEGEL (PeaceNet).

★ 12679 ★
Pacific-Union Club - Library (Hist)
1000 California St.   Phone: (415)775-1234
San Francisco, CA 94108   T. Sample Connelly, Libn.
Founded: 1900. **Staff:** Prof 1. **Special Collections:** Californiana. **Services:** Library open to members only. **Publications:** Annotated acquisitions lists, monthly - for internal distribution only. **Remarks:** FAX: (415)673-0104.

★ 12680 ★
Pacific Union College - Pitcairn Islands Study Center - Library (Area-Ethnic)
Angwin, CA 94508-9705   Phone: (707)965-6675
                                          Gary Shearer, Cur.
Founded: 1977. **Staff:** Prof 1; Other 1. **Subjects:** Pitcairn Islands. **Holdings:** 160 books; 700 indexed articles; 300 other indexed materials; pamphlets; articles; clippings; stamp collection, including first day covers; films; 700 slides; photographs; cassettes; island artifacts and curios; correspondence of Pitcairn Islanders; complete file of Pitcairn Miscellany; partial file of Pitcairn Pilhi; obituary file. **Subscriptions:** 3 journals and other serials. **Services:** Copying; library open to the public for reference use only.

★ 12681 ★
Pacific University - Harvey Scott Memorial Library - Music Library (Mus)
2043 College Way   Phone: (503)357-6151
Forest Grove, OR 97116   Santha Zaik
Founded: 1849. **Staff:** Prof 1; Other 1. **Subjects:** Music. **Holdings:** 6523 books and scores; 5249 phonograph records, tapes, and compact discs; 22 videotapes. **Subscriptions:** 8 journals and other serials. **Services:** Interlibrary loan; library open to the public with restrictions. **Computerized Information Services:** OCLC. **Remarks:** FAX: (503)359-2242. **Staff:** Tracy Boucher, Hum.Libn.

★ 12682 ★
Pacific Whale Foundation - Library (Biol Sci)
101 N. Kihei Rd.   Phone: (808)879-8860
Kihei, HI 96753   Dr. Paul Forestell, Dir., Res. & Educ.
Founded: 1980. **Subjects:** Marine mammals, human impacts on marine mammals. **Special Collections:** Color images of humpback whales and other marine mammals in Hawaii, Alaska, Australia, and Japan (10,000). **Holdings:** 300 books; 1500 journal articles. **Subscriptions:** 5 journals and other serials; 2 newspapers. **Services:** Interlibrary loan; library open to the public with restrictions. **Publications:** Fin & Fluke, Soundings. **Remarks:** FAX: (808)879-2615. **Staff:** Sue Kelley, Info.Serv.

★ 12683 ★
Pacifica Foundation - Pacifica Program Service - Pacifica Radio Archive (Aud-Vis)
3729 Cahuenga Blvd. W.   Phone: (818)506-1077
North Hollywood, CA 91604-3584   Bill Thomas, Dir.
Founded: 1968. **Staff:** Prof 9. **Subjects:** Politics and government, social sciences, Third World, minorities, women's studies, philosophy. **Special Collections:** Noncommercial radio programs, 1950 to present. **Holdings:** 28,000 magnetic audiotapes. **Services:** Offers audiocassettes for sale; archive open to the public by appointment. **Automated Operations:** Computerized cataloging and acquisitions. **Special Catalogs:** Collection catalog (microfiche); cassette tape catalog.

★ 12684 ★
Packaged Facts - Library (Bus-Fin)
581 Avenue of the Americas
New York, NY 10011   Phone: (212)627-3228
Founded: 1963. **Staff:** 6. **Subjects:** Trademarks, advertising, market studies. **Holdings:** 10,000 consumer and trade magazines; marketing data. **Services:** Library open by appointment only. **Computerized Information Services:** DIALOG Information Services, NEXIS, PRODUCTSCAN. **Remarks:** FAX: (212)627-9312.

★ 12685 ★
Packaging Corporation of America - Information Services Department (Sci-Engr)
5401 Old Orchard Rd.   Phone: (708)470-2303
Skokie, IL 60077   Jacqueline J. True, Mgr.Info.Serv.
Staff: Prof 1; Other .5. **Subjects:** Paper chemistry; packaging; manufacture of paper, pulpboard, aluminum foil, plastics. **Holdings:** 1000 books; 2500 bound periodical volumes; 150 VF drawers of Institute of Paper Chemistry, Technical Association of Pulp & Paper Industry, and Boxboard Research & Development Association publications. **Subscriptions:** 184 journals and other serials. **Services:** Interlibrary loan; copying; department open to the public with restrictions. **Computerized Information Services:** DIALOG Information Services, STN International, PFDS Online, Dow Jones News/Retrieval, VU/TEXT Information Services, LEXIS, NEXIS. **Networks/Consortia:** Member of North Suburban Library System (NSLS). **Remarks:** Alternate telephone number(s): 470-2305. FAX: (708)470-2325.

★ 12686 ★
Packanack Community Church of Wayne - Library (Rel-Phil)
120 Lake Dr., E.   Phone: (201)694-0608
Wayne, NJ 07470   Sandra Hulse
Staff: 1. **Subjects:** Religion, Bible study, counseling. **Holdings:** 2300 books; church history notebooks; church newsletters; AV programs. **Services:** Library open to the public with restrictions.

Packard Library
See: **Columbus College of Art and Design** (4032)

★ 12687 ★
Packard Truck Organization - Library (Trans)
1196 Mountain Rd.   Phone: (717)528-4920
York Springs, PA 17372   David B. Lockard, Founder
Founded: 1981. **Subjects:** Packard trucks, 1905-1923. **Holdings:** Truck manuals; advertisements; general information. **Services:** Copying; written inquiries only.

Robert Packer Hospital Health Sciences Library
See: **Guthrie Medical Center** (6816)

Paddock Music Library
See: **Dartmouth College** (4613)

Archivo Jose Leon Pagano
See: **(Buenos Aires) Museo de Arte Moderno** (2324)

Inman E. Page Library
See: **Lincoln University** (9189)

Percy Page Resource Centre
See: **Alberta Recreation & Parks** (301)

★ 12688 ★
Paier College of Art, Inc. - Library (Art)
44 Circular Ave.   Phone: (203)287-1585
Hamden, CT 06514   Gail J. Nachin, Lib.Dir.
Staff: Prof 2; Other 8. **Subjects:** Fine arts, graphic design, interior design, photography, illustration, general academics. **Special Collections:** Picture Reference. **Holdings:** 13,000 books; 90 periodical titles; 40,000 pictures; 35,000 slides. **Subscriptions:** 100 journals and other serials. **Services:** Interlibrary loan; copying; library open to the public for research only. **Networks/Consortia:** Member of Southern Connecticut Library Council (SCLC). **Staff:** Olga Majewski, Asst.Libn.

Ralph M. Paiewonsky Library
See: **University of the Virgin Islands** (19494)

Dr. Harry Paikin Library
See: **Hamilton Board of Education (6859)**

★ 12689 ★
Paine Art Center and Arboretum - George P. Nevitt Library (Art)
1410 Algoma Blvd.   Phone: (414)235-4530
Oshkosh, WI 54901   Corinne H. Spoo, Libn.
Staff: Prof 2; Other 2. **Subjects:** Art, interior decoration, English houses, gardening. **Holdings:** 3933 volumes. **Subscriptions:** 10 journals and other serials. **Services:** Library open to the public for reference use only. **Special Catalogs:** Exhibition catalogs, irregular - available on request. **Staff:** Ardyce Zillges, Slide Libn., Arboretum.

★ 12690 ★
Thomas Paine National Historical Association (of New Rochelle) -
   Hufeland Library (Hist)
983 North Ave.   Phone: (914)632-5376
New Rochelle, NY 10804   Ed Temkin, Chm., Lib.Comm.
Staff: Prof 1. **Subjects:** Local history. **Special Collections:** Early Americana with emphasis on lower Westchester County and upper Bronx. **Holdings:** 5000 books; maps; manuscripts. **Services:** Library open to scholars by appointment. **Remarks:** Included in the Hufeland Library are the book collections of the Huguenot and Historical Association and the New Rochelle Historical Society. **Staff:** Catherine T. Goulding, Libn.

★ 12691 ★
Paine Webber Inc. - Library (Bus-Fin)
1285 Ave. of the Americas   Phone: (212)713-3671
New York, NY 10019   Barbara A. Fody, V.P.
Staff: Prof 5; Other 15. **Subjects:** Finance, investments, money and banking, economic and business conditions. **Special Collections:** Corporation records. **Holdings:** 3000 books; 700 industry subject files; 500 shelves of corporation records; 300 reels of microfilm; microfiche. **Subscriptions:** 700 journals and other serials; 15 newspapers. **Services:** Interlibrary loan; library open to members of Special Libraries Association. **Computerized Information Services:** DIALOG Information Services, Dow Jones News/Retrieval, TEXTLINE, BRS Information Technologies, NEXIS, DunsPrint, Vickers Institutional Stock System, LEXIS, VU/TEXT Information Services, DataTimes, Investment Dealers Digest. **Publications:** Paine Webber Library Bulletin, monthly - for internal distribution only. **Remarks:** FAX: (212)713-3078. **Staff:** Penny Cagan, Asst.Mgr.; Cindy Furlinger, Ref.Libn.; Christopher Lezenby, Ref.Libn.; Andrea Crone, Corp.Docs.Supv.

★ 12692 ★
Pajaro Valley Historical Association - William H. Volck Museum -
   Archives/Library (Hist)
261 E. Beach St.
Watsonville, CA 95076   Phone: (408)722-0305
Founded: 1965. **Staff:** 1. **Subjects:** History of the Pajaro Valley, 1865 to present. **Holdings:** 102 linear feet of letters, literary manuscripts, genealogical source materials, account books, business and financial records, noncurrent records of schools, city and county government agencies, community groups and associations, architectural drawings, aerial photographs, oral history tapes and transcripts, and photographs. **Services:** Museum open to the public; archives open to the public by appointment. **Publications:** Newsletter - to members. **Staff:** Karen Lopez, Adm.; Jane Borg, Libn.; Alzora Snyder, Archv.

★ 12693 ★
Pakistan - Ministry of Food, Agriculture and Cooperatives - Department
   of Plant Protection - Library (Biol Sci)
Jinnah Ave., Malir Halt   Phone: 21 480111
Karachi 27, Pakistan   Miss Nuzhat Mustafa, Libn.
Subjects: Entomology, mycology, plant pathology. **Holdings:** 14,000 volumes.

★ 12694 ★
Pakistan - National Archives of Pakistan (Hist)
Administrative Block Area
N Block   Phone: 51 812044
Islamabad, Pakistan   Mr. Ashraf Ali, Deputy Dir.
Founded: 1951. **Staff:** Prof 1; Other 2. **Subjects:** Pakistan - history, culture, geography, literature. **Special Collections:** Collection of rare manuscripts in

Persian and Arabic (200 items); Quaid-e-Azam Papers; Mohtarma Fatima Jinnah Collection; Lakha Collection on Quaid-e-Azam; Correspondence of Nowab Viqar-ul-Malik; Muslim Freedom Archives; Lal Khan Collection; K.R. Dawoodi Collection. **Holdings:** 16,000 books; bound periodical volumes; reports; archival materials; microfiche; microfilm; audiocassettes. **Subscriptions:** 3 journals and other serials; 4 newspapers. **Services:** Copying; archives open to the public with restrictions. **Publications:** Pakistan Archives (journal), biannual; Archives News (newsletter), quarterly. **Remarks:** Alternate telephone number(s): 51 813531.

★ 12695 ★
Pakistan - Planning and Development Division - Pakistan Institute of
   Development Economics - Library (Bus-Fin, Soc Sci)
Quaid-I-Azam Univ. Campus
P.O. Box 1091   Phone: 51 826911 14
Islamabad, Pakistan   Mr. Zafar Javed Naqvi, Chf.Libn./Doc.
Founded: 1957. **Staff:** 104. **Subjects:** Economics, Islamic economics, demography, agricultural and rural development, industrial growth, international trade, fiscal and monetary policy, health, education, housing. **Holdings:** 27,226 volumes; 6200 microfiche; 11,500 research documents. **Subscriptions:** 370 journals and other serials; 9 newspapers. **Services:** Interlibrary loan; library not open to the public. **Computerized Information Services:** CDS/ISIS (internal database). **Publications:** List of publications - available on request. **Remarks:** FAX: 51 811186. Alternate telephone number(s): 51 812440. Telex: 5602 PIDE PK. **Staff:** Aziz Khan, Sr.Doc.Off.; Abida Almashadi, Doc.Off.; Naurin Ehsan, Doc.Off.; Khawaja Mahmoad, Joint Libn.; M. Tahir Hasan Bult, Asst.Libn.

★ 12696 ★
Pakistan Council of Appropriate Technology - Library (Sci-Engr)
1-B, St. 47, F-7/1
P.O. Box 1306
Islamabad, Pakistan   Phone: 51 824483
Subjects: Technological development - food and water, energy, housing, health and hygiene; rural development. **Holdings:** 1274 volumes.

★ 12697 ★
Pakistan Institute of Cotton Research and Technology - Library (Sci-Engr)
Moulvi Tamizuddin Khan Rd.   Phone: 21 512238
Karachi 1, Pakistan   Miss Rafia Sultana, Libn.
Subjects: Textile technology. **Holdings:** 15,000 volumes. **Remarks:** Telex: 25992. Affiliated with Pakistan Central Cotton Committee.

Pakistan Institute of Development Economics
See: **Pakistan - Planning and Development Division - Pakistan Institute of Development Economics - Library (12695)**

★ 12698 ★
Paleontological Research Institution - Library (Biol Sci)
1259 Trumansburg Rd.   Phone: (607)273-6623
Ithaca, NY 14850-1398   Peter R. Hoover, Dir.
Founded: 1932. **Staff:** Prof 1. **Subjects:** Paleontology, geology, conchology, fossils, mollusca. **Holdings:** 50,000 volumes; 48 VF cabinets; 6000 reprints and papers; microfilm; maps; photographs. **Subscriptions:** 400 journals and other serials. **Services:** Interlibrary loan (fee); library open to specialists by appointment. **Publications:** Library Serials List, 1979.

★ 12699 ★
PALINET (Info Sci)
3401 Market St., Suite 262   Phone: (215)382-7031
Philadelphia, PA 19104   James E. Rush, Exec.Dir.
Founded: 1935. **Staff:** Prof 14; Other 4. **Computerized Information Services:** Computer Access Linking Libraries (CALL) (electronic mail service). **Publications:** PALINET News (newsletter), monthly - to members and for sale; PALINET Annual Report; PALINET Tech Memo (newsletter), monthly - to members. **Remarks:** Card file closed in 1975; microfilm available since 1976. Provides full OCLC and microcomputer support services for more than 300 member libraries in Pennsylvania, New Jersey, Delaware, Maryland, and Washington, D.C. Brokers CD-ROM products and reference database services and provides archive tape management services. FAX: (215)382-0022. **Staff:** Meryl Cinnamon, Mgr., OCLC Serv.Div.; Donna Wright, Mgr., Adm.Serv.Div.; Jean Dorrian, Info.Off.

★ 12700 ★
Pall Corporation - Library (Sci-Engr)
30 Sea Cliff Ave.   Phone: (516)671-4000
Glen Cove, NY 11542   Susanne Silverman, Corp.Libn.
Staff: Prof 1; Other 1. **Subjects:** Filtration, chemistry, technology, medicine.
Holdings: 3000 books; 350 periodical titles; industrial market directories.
Subscriptions: 400 journals and other serials. **Services:** Library not open to the public. **Computerized Information Services:** DIALOG Information Services, DunsPrint. **Networks/Consortia:** Member of Long Island Library Resources Council. **Publications:** Acquisitions Report. **Remarks:** FAX: (516)671-4066; (516)671-4072. Telex: 126329. **Staff:** Nancy Reed-Schatzle, ILL.

★ 12701 ★
Pallottine Provincialate Library (Rel-Phil)
5424 W. Blue Mound Rd.   Phone: (414)258-0653
Milwaukee, WI 53208   Rev. Jerome Kuskowski, S.A.C., Libn.
Founded: 1923. **Staff:** Prof 1. **Subjects:** Theology, philosophy, hagiography. **Special Collections:** St. Vincent Pallotti Collection (29 items). **Holdings:** 3273 books. **Subscriptions:** 20 journals and other serials; 7 newspapers. **Services:** Interlibrary loan; copying; library open to the public. **Remarks:** Maintained by the Society of the Catholic Apostolate.

★ 12702 ★
Palm Beach County Law Library (Law)
County Courthouse, Rm. 339
300 N. Dixie Hwy.   Phone: (407)355-2928
West Palm Beach, FL 33401   Linda Sims, Law Lib.Mgr.
Staff: Prof 1; Other 3. **Subjects:** Law. **Holdings:** 27,000 volumes; 1950 microfiche. **Services:** Interlibrary loan; copying; library open to the public for reference use only. **Computerized Information Services:** WESTLAW. Performs searches on fee basis.

★ 12703 ★
The Palm Beach Post - Library (Publ)
2751 S. Dixie Hwy.   Phone: (407)820-4495
West Palm Beach, FL 33405   Mary Kate Leming, Lib.Dir.
Staff: Prof 2; Other 5. **Subjects:** Newspaper reference topics. **Special Collections:** Miami News microfilm, clipping, and photograph files. **Holdings:** 500 books; clippings; microfiche; microfilm; pamphlet files. **Subscriptions:** 73 journals and other serials; 14 newspapers. **Services:** Interlibrary loan; copying; library open to other non-competing media and special libraries. **Computerized Information Services:** DIALOG Information Services, VU/TEXT Information Services, CompuServe Information Service.

★ 12704 ★
Palm Springs Desert Museum - Toor Library & Hoover Natural Science Library (Hist)
101 Museum Dr.
P.O. Box 2288   Phone: (619)325-7186
Palm Springs, CA 92263   Janice Lyle, Ph.D., Educ.Dir.
Founded: 1943. **Staff:** 1. **Subjects:** Art, natural science, local history, state history. **Special Collections:** Art slide collection (11,433). **Holdings:** 6700 books; 20 bound periodical volumes. **Subscriptions:** 90 journals and other serials; 3 newspapers. **Services:** Libraries not open to the public. **Computerized Information Services:** Internal database. **Remarks:** FAX: (619)327-5069. **Staff:** Mary Fahr, Libn.

Roland Palmedo National Ski Library
See: **National Ski Hall of Fame and Museum** (11286)

★ 12705 ★
Palmer, Biezup & Henderson - Library
Public Ledger Bldg., Suite 956
620 Chestnut St.   Phone: (215)625-9900
Philadelphia, PA 19106-3409   Wendy Glazer, Lib.Dir.
Remarks: No further information was supplied by respondent.

★ 12706 ★
Palmer College of Chiropractic - David D. Palmer Health Sciences Library (Med)
1000 Brady St.   Phone: (319)326-9641
Davenport, IA 52803   Dennis Peterson, Dir.
Founded: 1895. **Staff:** Prof 7; Other 13. **Subjects:** Chiropractic, health sciences. **Special Collections:** B.J. Palmer papers; chiropractic history and research; conservative health care; Lyndon Lee papers; Kenneth Cronk papers. **Holdings:** 26,062 books; 15,679 bound periodical volumes; 9145 microfiche; 1138 reels of microfilm; 1465 audiotapes; 1066 videotapes; 19,800 slides; 910 biological specimens and models; 1534 x-ray sets. **Subscriptions:** 900 journals and other serials; 14 newspapers. **Services:** Interlibrary loan; copying; SDI; library open to the public with restrictions. **Automated Operations:** Computerized cataloging and serials. **Computerized Information Services:** MEDLARS, DIALOG Information Services, BRS Information Technologies; internal database; DIALMAIL (electronic mail service). Performs searches on fee basis. Contact Person: Robert Stout, Pub.Serv.Libn., 326-9890. **Networks/Consortia:** Member of National Network of Libraries of Medicine - Greater Midwest Region, Quad Cities Libraries in Cooperation (Quad-LINC), Chiropractic Library Consortium (CLIBCON), Quad City Area Biomedical Consortium, Bi-State Academic Libraries (BI-SAL). **Publications:** NEXUS, biweekly - campus distribution and by subscription; Chiropractic Contents, biweekly - campus distribution. **Special Indexes:** Chiropractic Literature Index, 1970-1979 (online). **Remarks:** FAX: (319)326-9897. **Staff:** Glenda Wiese, Archv.; Susan Burns, Tech.Serv.Libn.; Ruth Hall, Tech.Serv.Libn.; Phyliss Harvey, Tech.Serv.Libn.; Barbara Schmiechen Pub.Serv.Libn.; Jim Bandes, Instr. Media Serv.

★ 12707 ★
Palmer College of Chiropractic - West - Library (Med)
1095 Dunford Way   Phone: (408)983-4142
Sunnyvale, CA 94087   Patricia McGrew, Dir.
Founded: 1981. **Staff:** Prof 3; Other 1. **Subjects:** Chiropractic, health sciences, medicine, basic sciences, education. **Special Collections:** Chiropractic history (400 volumes); Chiropractic Research Archives collection. **Holdings:** 6300 books; 2750 bound periodical volumes; 600 AV programs; 30,000 microfiche; periodicals. **Subscriptions:** 200 journals and other serials. **Services:** Interlibrary loan (fee); library open to the public for reference use only. **Automated Operations:** Computerized cataloging, serials, and audiovisuals. **Computerized Information Services:** Internal database; OnTyme Electronic Message Network Service (electronic mail service). **Networks/Consortia:** Member of National Network of Libraries of Medicine - Pacific Southwest Region, Northern California and Nevada Medical Library Group (NCNMLG), Chiropractic Library Consortium (CLIBCON). **Publications:** New in the Library, bimonthly - for internal distribution only. **Special Indexes:** Historical books (online); index to chiropractic literature. **Remarks:** FAX: (408)983-4017. Electronic mail address(es): CLASS.CWBCONO13 (OnTyme Electronic Message Network Service). **Staff:** Jeanette Defayette, Asst.Libn.; Merilyn Nelson, Asst.Libn.

David D. Palmer Health Sciences Library
See: **Palmer College of Chiropractic** (12706)

★ 12708 ★
Palmer, O'Connell, Leger, Roderick, Glennie - Law Library (Law)
One Brunswick Square, Suite 1600
P.O. Box 1324
Saint John, NB, Canada E2L 4H8   Phone: (506)632-8900
Staff: Prof 1; Other 1. **Subjects:** Law. **Special Collections:** Canadian and English common law. **Holdings:** 2000 books; 5000 bound periodical volumes. **Subscriptions:** 20 journals and other serials; 10 newspapers. **Services:** Library open to the public with restrictions. **Remarks:** FAX: (506)632-8809.

Sophia F. Palmer Library
See: **American Journal of Nursing Company** (658)

★ 12709 ★
Palmerton Hospital - Library (Med)
135 Lafayette Ave.   Phone: (215)826-3141
Palmerton, PA 18071   Marie T. Krepicz, Lib.Dir.
Remarks: No further information was supplied by respondent.

★12710★
Palo Alto Medical Foundation - Barnett-Hall Library (Med)
860 Bryant St.　　　　　　　　　　Phone: (415)321-4121
Palo Alto, CA 94301　　　　　Judith M. Cummings, Hd.Libn.
Founded: 1950. **Staff:** Prof 2. **Subjects:** Medicine, medical research, basic sciences, nursing, pharmacology. **Holdings:** 11,631 volumes; 13 VF drawers of pamphlets. **Subscriptions:** 330 journals and other serials. **Services:** Interlibrary loan; copying; library open to physicians and technological researchers of the county. **Computerized Information Services:** MEDLARS. **Networks/Consortia:** Member of National Network of Libraries of Medicine - Pacific Southwest Region, Northern California and Nevada Medical Library Group (NCNMLG). **Publications:** Annual Report. **Special Indexes:** Periodical holdings visible file index. **Staff:** Natalie Hazen, Ser.Libn.

★12711★
Palo Alto Unified School District - Instructional Materials Center
750 N. California　　　　　　　　Phone: (415)858-0980
Palo Alto, CA 94303　　　　Jack Gibbany, Adm., K-12 Curric.Serv.
Founded: 1950. **Staff:** Prof 14; Other 7. **Subjects:** Curriculum materials, children's fiction. **Holdings:** 200,000 books. **Subscriptions:** 15 journals and other serials; 8 newspapers. **Services:** Interlibrary loan; copying; center open to the public for reference use only. **Automated Operations:** Computerized cataloging. **Computerized Information Services:** Picodyne (internal database). **Staff:** Virginia Hartman, Dist.Libn.

★12712★
Palomar Community College - Library - Special Collections (Hum)
1140 Mission Rd.　　　　　　　　Phone: (619)744-1150
San Marcos, CA 92069　　　　Judy J. Carter, Dir., Lib./Media Ctr.
Founded: 1946. **Holdings:** Fine arts (15,500 volumes); American Indian (3400 volumes); Iceland (200 volumes); World War I poster collection. **Services:** Interlibrary loan; copying; collections open to the public with restrictions. **Automated Operations:** Computerized cataloging and serials. **Computerized Information Services:** BRS Information Technologies, DIALOG Information Services, OCLC. **Networks/Consortia:** Member of CLASS. **Remarks:** FAX: (619)744-1150, ext. 2766. **Staff:** Daniel C. Arnsan, Media Serv.Libn.; Alexis K. Ciurczak, Pub.Serv.Libn.; Byung Kang, Cat.Libn.; Carolyn Wood, Acq.Libn.

Palomar Observatory Sky Survey
See: **Cornell University - Arecibo Observatory** (4303)

★12713★
Palomino Horse Breeders of America - Library (Rec)
15253 E. Skelly Dr.　　　　　　Phone: (918)438-1234
Tulsa, OK 74116-2620　　　　Cindy Chilton, Gen.Mgr.
Founded: 1941. **Staff:** 6. **Subjects:** Horses and equine-related activities, the Palomino horse. **Special Collections:** Palomino Horse Breeders of America Stud Book Listings. **Holdings:** Figures not available. **Services:** Library not open to the public. **Remarks:** FAX: (918)438-1232.

★12714★
Palos Community Hospital - Medical Library (Med)
80th Ave. & McCarthy Rd.　　　Phone: (708)361-4500
Palos Heights, IL 60463　　　Gail Lahti, Libn.
Founded: 1983. **Staff:** Prof 1. **Subjects:** Medicine, allied health sciences. **Holdings:** 1000 books. **Subscriptions:** 100 journals and other serials. **Services:** Interlibrary loan; library not open to the public. **Computerized Information Services:** DIALOG Information Services. **Networks/Consortia:** Member of Chicago and South Consortium.

★12715★
Pan-African Resource Center - Library (Area-Ethnic)
P.O. Box 3307
Washington, DC 20010
Subjects: Africa - reunification, history, resources; world hunger. **Special Collections:** Biographical archives. **Holdings:** 43,000 volumes.

Pan-American Association of Forensic Sciences - Secretariat
See: **International Reference Organization in Forensic Medicine & Sciences - Library and Reference Center** (8180)

Pan American Center for Sanitary Engineering & Environmental Sciences
See: **Pan American Health Organization - Pan American Center for Sanitary Engineering & Environmental Sciences - REPIDISCA Network** (12719)

★12716★
Pan American Health Organization - Caribbean Food and Nutrition Institute - Library (Med, Food-Bev)
Univ. of the West Indies, Mona Campus
P.O. Box 140　　　　　　　　　Phone: (809)927-1540
Kingston 7, Jamaica　　　　Enett Noble, Libn.
Staff: Prof 1; Other 1. **Subjects:** Caribbean area - nutrition, food issues, public health. **Special Collections:** Community nutrition theses. **Holdings:** 6000 books; 1071 bound periodical volumes; 1803 documents; 164 AV programs; theses. **Subscriptions:** 100 journals and other serials. **Services:** Interlibrary loan; copying; SDI; library open to the public for reference use only. **Computerized Information Services:** CNFI, PAHO (internal databases). **Remarks:** Maintains a branch library at the University of West Indies campus in Trinidad. Telex: 3705 Cajanus.

★12717★
Pan American Health Organization - Institute of Nutrition of Central America and Panama - Library (Med)
Carretera Roosevelt
Apdo. Postal 1188, Zona 11　　　Phone: 723765
Guatemala City, Guatemala　　　Lidia Lopez, Libn.
Subjects: Human and animal nutrition, public health, food technology. **Holdings:** 35,000 volumes. **Subscriptions:** 700 journals and other serials. **Services:** Interlibrary loan; copying; library open to the public for reference use only. **Computerized Information Services:** DIALOG Information Services, MEDLINE; internal database. **Remarks:** FAX: 736529. Telex: 5696 INCAP. **Also Known As:** Instituto de Nutricion de Centro America y Panama.

★12718★
Pan American Health Organization - Library (Med)
525 23rd St., N.W.
Mail Code HBL　　　　　　　　Phone: (202)861-3305
Washington, DC 20037　　　　Maria Teresa Astroza, Hd.
Founded: 1945. **Staff:** Prof 3; Other 4. **Subjects:** Scientific and technical health literature. **Special Collections:** Documents of the World Health Organization, Pan American Health Organization, and Latin American and Caribbean Ministries of Health. **Holdings:** 30,000 books; 1500 periodical titles; 25 file drawers of microfilm. **Subscriptions:** 150 journals and other serials. **Services:** Interlibrary loan; document delivery; SDI; extramural educational programs; center open to the public. **Automated Operations:** Computerized cataloging, acquisitions, and serials. **Computerized Information Services:** MEDLINE, DIALOG Information Services; PAHO/INFO (internal database). **Publications:** Acquisitions Bulletin; TABCONT. **Remarks:** FAX: (202)223-5971. Telex: 440057. A regional office of the World Health Organization. **Staff:** Madga Ziver, Ref.Libn.; Ernesto Spinak, Info.Sys.Spec.; Ms. Carmen Chand, ILL; Amanda Ellauri, Indexer; Olga Rojo, Indexer.

★12719★
Pan American Health Organization - Pan American Center for Sanitary Engineering & Environmental Sciences - REPIDISCA Network (Env-Cons, Sci-Engr)
Los Pinos 259
Urbanizacion Camacho　　　　Phone: 14 354135
Lima 12, Peru　　　　Marta Bryce, REPIDISCA Coord.
Founded: 1968. **Staff:** 8. **Subjects:** Sanitation, water supply, sanitary and environmental engineering, environmental pollution, solid and hazardous wastes. **Holdings:** 32,000 volumes; documents. **Subscriptions:** 369 journals and other serials. **Services:** SDI; network open to the public. **Computerized Information Services:** AIDS, CCINFOline, CITIS, ECO, LEYES, LILACS, MEDLINE, PAHO, POPLINE, SeCS, TOXLINE, Water Resources Abstracts; CD-ROM (Women, Water and Sanitation); produces REPINDEX. Performs searches on fee basis. **Publications:** List of publications - available on request. **Remarks:** Telex: 21052. **Also Known As:** Centro Panamericano de Ingenieria Sanitaria y Ciencias del Ambiente. **Staff:** Monica Bonifaz; Julia Garcia; Claudia Hilbck; Rosa Siles.

★ 12720 ★
Pan American Institute of Geography and History - Library (Geog-Map)
Ex-Arzobispado 29
Col. Observatorio
11860 Mexico City 18, DF, Mexico   Phone: 905 2775888
Subjects: Cartography, geography, history, geophysics, anthropology, archeology, folklore. **Holdings:** 150,000 volumes. **Services:** Library open to the public. **Computerized Information Services:** Internal database. **Remarks:** FAX: 271 61 72.

★ 12721 ★
PAN North America Regional Center - International Information Links Program (Agri)
965 Mission St., No. 514   Phone: (415)541-9140
San Francisco, CA 94103   Andrea J. Davis, Prog.Dir.
Founded: 1988. **Staff:** 2. **Subjects:** Pesticides - worldwide issues, concerns, alternatives; agriculture; international development; consumer protection; worker welfare; public health, regulation and policy; household pest management; toxic substances; activism. **Holdings:** 12,000 books, reports, articles, slides, and other materials. **Subscriptions:** 500 journals and other serials. **Services:** Copying; open to the public by appointment on fee basis. **Computerized Information Services:** Internal database; EcoNet (electronic mail service). **Remarks:** FAX: (415)541-9253. Telex: 156283472 PANNA. Electronic mail address(es): PANNA (EcoNet). Parent organization acts as a network for pesticide action groups at the local, state, national, and international levels. **Formerly:** Pesticide Action Network North America Regional Center - Information Services.

★ 12722 ★
Panama Canal Commission - Community Services Division - Technical Resources Center (Area-Ethnic)
Unit 2300
APO AA   Phone: 507 524920
Miami, FL 34011   Mania Nita, Adm.Libn.
Founded: 1914. **Staff:** Prof 4; Other 18. **Subjects:** Panama Canal, shipping, engineering, personnel management. **Special Collections:** Panama Collection (35,700 items, including 6 VF drawers of newspaper clippings; 5410 photographs; manuscripts). **Holdings:** 67,000 books; 288 bound periodical volumes; 122 manuscripts; 841 maps and prints; 4657 reels of microfilm; 3403 microfiche; 10,641 microforms. **Subscriptions:** 360 journals and other serials; 11 newspapers. **Services:** Copying; mail reference service; library open to researchers and university students referred by other libraries. **Automated Operations:** Computerized public access catalog, cataloging, acquisitions, serials, and circulation. **Computerized Information Services:** DIALOG Information Services, OCLC; PROFS (electronic mail service). **Publications:** A History of the Panama Canal (1984); bibliographies, irregular; Library Resources Up-date, monthly; Conference Calendar, irregular - all for internal distribution only. **Remarks:** FAX: 507 523131. Telex: 3034 PCCAMRM PG. **Formerly:** Its Technical Library. **Staff:** Roberto Sarmiento, Rsrcs.Libn.; Nan S. Chong, Libn., Panama Canal Coll.; Aleyda Aguilar, Tech.Serv.Libn.

(Panama City) USIS Library
See: **Biblioteca Amador-Washington** (1817)

★ 12723 ★
PanCanadian Petroleum Ltd. - Corporate Library (Energy)
P.O. Box 2850   Phone: (403)290-2386
Calgary, AB, Canada T2P 2S5   Marcia G. Kennedy, Corp.Libn.
Founded: 1981. **Staff:** Prof 2; Other 6. **Subjects:** Petroleum, natural gas, geology. **Holdings:** 20,000 books. **Subscriptions:** 575 journals and other serials; 10 newspapers. **Services:** Interlibrary loan; library not open to the public. **Automated Operations:** Computerized cataloging, acquisitions, serials, and circulation. **Computerized Information Services:** Online systems; DIALMAIL (electronic mail service). **Publications:** Current Awareness, monthly - for internal distribution only. **Remarks:** FAX: (403)290-2950. **Staff:** J. Nixon, Cat.Libn.

★ 12724 ★
Panel Displays, Inc. - Technical Library (Sci-Engr)
211 S. Hindry Ave.   Phone: (213)641-6661
Inglewood, CA 90301   Ken O. Fugate, Pres. & Libn.
Staff: Prof 1. **Subjects:** Electronics, electro-acoustics and electro-optics, radar, solid state physics, computers, mathematics, oceanography, ultrasonics. **Holdings:** 2100 books; 5200 bound periodical volumes; 1000 product catalogs; 3000 special subject technical papers. **Subscriptions:** 102 journals and other serials. **Services:** Interlibrary loan; library not open to the public.

★ 12725 ★
Panhandle Eastern Corporation - Corporate Library (Bus-Fin)
P.O. Box 1642   Phone: (713)627-5588
Houston, TX 77251-1642   Bob Kirtner
Founded: 1991. **Staff:** Prof 1. **Subjects:** Business, petroleum, natural gas pipeline. **Holdings:** 750 books; 100 bound periodical volumes; 250 archival items; 100 files; annual reports; government filings. **Subscriptions:** 100 journals and other serials; 12 newspapers. **Services:** Library open to the public with restrictions. **Publications:** Serials holdings list. **Remarks:** FAX: (713)627-4091. **Formed by the merger of:** Texas Eastern - Library, and Trunkline Gas - Library.

★ 12726 ★
Panhandle-Plains Historical Museum - Research Center (Hist)
Box 967, WT. Sta.   Phone: (806)656-2260
Canyon, TX 79016   Claire R. Kuehn, Archv./Libn.
Founded: 1932. **Staff:** Prof 2; Other 2. **Subjects:** Texas and Southwest history; ranching; Indians of the Great Plains; archeology of Texas Panhandle; ethnology; clothing and textiles; fine arts; antiques; museum science. **Special Collections:** Interviews with early settlers collected over a period of 63 years; Bob Wills Memorial Archive of Popular Music, 1915 to present (5000 phonograph records); Southwest regional architectural drawings, 1978 to present (microfilm). **Holdings:** 15,000 books; 12,000 cubic feet of manuscripts; 20 VF drawers of pamphlets; 800 maps; 1600 reels of microfilm; 45 cubic feet of manufacturers' trade literature; 250,000 historic photographs. **Subscriptions:** 250 journals and other serials; 12 newspapers. **Services:** Copying; center open to the public. **Special Indexes:** Index to the Panhandle-Plains Historical Review (card); Index to the Canyon (Texas) News. **Remarks:** FAX: (806)656-2250. Center is the Regional Historical Resource Depository for noncurrent county documents for 24 Texas Panhandle counties (a Texas State Library program). **Staff:** Betty L. Bustos, Asst.Archv./Libn.

★ 12727 ★
Panhandle State University - No Man's Land Historical Museum - Library (Hist)
Sewel St.
Box 278   Phone: (405)349-2670
Goodwell, OK 73939   Dr. Harold S. Kachel, Cur.
Founded: 1934. **Staff:** 1. **Subjects:** Western history, No Man's Land, Dust Bowl, genealogy. **Holdings:** 3000 books; 2000 bound periodical volumes; 2000 other cataloged items. **Services:** Copying; library open to the public with restrictions.

★ 12728 ★
Pannell Kerr Forster - Library (Bus-Fin)
420 Lexington Ave.   Phone: (212)867-8000
New York, NY 10170   Leslie Slocum, Libn.
Founded: 1945. **Staff:** Prof 1. **Subjects:** Research on hospitality, tourism, accounting, auditing, real estate. **Holdings:** 2000 volumes; pamphlets; clippings. **Subscriptions:** 300 journals and other serials. **Services:** Interlibrary loan; library not open to the public. **Computerized Information Services:** DIALOG Information Services, LEXIS, NEXIS, Dun & Bradstreet Business Credit Services, Dow Jones News/Retrieval, National Planning Data Corporation (NPDC).

★ 12729 ★
Pannell Kerr Forster - Library (Bus-Fin)
262 N. Belt Dr., E., Suite 300
Houston, TX 77060-2012   Phone: (713)999-5134
Staff: 2. **Subjects:** Hotel operations, travel, tourism. **Holdings:** 5015 volumes; 5000 manuscripts and studies. **Subscriptions:** 25 journals and other serials; 10 newspapers. **Services:** Library not open to the public. **Computerized Information Services:** DIALOG Information Services, Data-Star; INFOSTAR (internal database). **Publications:** Monthly Trends in the Hotel Industry (for Texas, Houston, Dallas/Fort Worth, San Antonio, Austin); Trends in the Hotel Industry - U.S. Edition, annual; Trends in the Hotel Industry - International Edition, annual. **Remarks:** FAX: (713)820-6727.

★12730★
Pannell Kerr Forster - Management Advisory Services - Library (Bus-Fin)
510 Lake Cook Rd., Ste. 350
Deerfield, IL 60015 Phone: (708)945-5061
Staff: Prof 1; Other 1. **Subjects:** Hotels and motels, food service and restaurants, travel and tourism, economics and demographics, commercial real estate. **Holdings:** 350 books; 25 hotel/motel and foodservice operation manuals; statistics and trends of the hotel industry. **Subscriptions:** 129 journals and other serials; 12 newspapers. **Services:** Library not open to the public. **Publications:** Newsletter - for internal distribution only; Annual trends in the Hotel Industry-US Edition-International; Chicago Hotel Market Overview, annual; Monthly Trends in the Hotel Industry; Hospitality Investment Survey; Clubs in Town & Country, annual. **Special Indexes:** Index of market demand and economic feasibility studies for hotels, motels, condominiums; food and beverage operation studies; economic valuations and data processing studies. **Remarks:** FAX: (312)715-1866.

Panstwowe Zbiory Sztuki na Wawelu - Biblioteka
See: **The Wawel State Collection - Library** (20107)

★12731★
Paoli Memorial Hospital - Robert M. White Memorial Library (Med)
Lancaster Pike Phone: (215)648-1570
Paoli, PA 19301 Frances G. DeMillion, Hea.Sci.Libn.
Staff: Prof 1. **Subjects:** Clinical and pre-clinical medicine. **Holdings:** 800 books; 110 publications of medical staff members; 4 VF drawers of pamphlets. **Subscriptions:** 159 journals and other serials. **Services:** Interlibrary loan; copying; library open to the public for reference use only. **Computerized Information Services:** BRS Information Technologies, MEDLARS. **Networks/Consortia:** Member of Consortium for Health Information & Library Services (CHI). **Remarks:** FAX: (215)648-1551.

★12732★
Papeterie Reed Ltd. - Development Library
P.O. Box 1487
Quebec, PQ, Canada G1K 7H9
Founded: 1965. **Subjects:** Pulp and paper, science and engineering. **Holdings:** 3000 books; 700 bound periodical volumes. **Remarks:** Currently inactive.

Pappas Law Library
See: **Boston University** (2016)

★12733★
Papua New Guinea - Department of Culture and Tourism - Institute of Papua New Guinea Studies - Library (Area-Ethnic)
P.O. Box 1432
Boroko, Papua New Guinea Phone: 25-4644
Dr. John Kolia, Libn.
Subjects: Papua New Guinea - music, oral history, ethnology, literature, film. **Holdings:** 5000 volumes.

★12734★
Parade Publications, Inc. - Library (Publ)
750 Third Ave., 6th Fl. Phone: (212)573-7189
New York, NY 10017 Roberta J. Gardner, Lib.Dir.
Founded: 1980. **Staff:** Prof 5. **Subjects:** Editorial research materials. **Special Collections:** Parade Magazine, 1941 to present (bound and on microfiche). **Holdings:** 1200 volumes; internal research material; pamphlets; clippings. **Subscriptions:** 125 journals and other serials; 6 newspapers. **Services:** Library not open to the public. **Computerized Information Services:** NEXIS, BASELINE, DataTimes, VU/TEXT Information Services, DIALOG Information Services. **Publications:** Parade Magazine; Sunday News Magazine. **Remarks:** Alternate telephone number(s): 573-7188; FAX: (212)573-7087. **Staff:** Anita B. Goss, Sr.Res.Libn.; Louis C. Leventhal, Sr.Res.Libn.; Caryn Friedman, Sr.Libn.

★12735★
Paradise Valley Hospital - Medical Library (Med)
2400 E. 4th St. Phone: (619)470-4155
National City, CA 92050 Valeria Bouchard, CMSC, Libn.
Founded: 1974. **Staff:** Prof 1; Other 1. **Subjects:** Medicine, nursing, hospital administration. **Holdings:** 600 books; 50 other cataloged items. **Subscriptions:** 60 journals and other serials. **Services:** Library not open to the public.

★12736★
Paraguay - Biblioteca Nacional del Paraguay (Area-Ethnic)
Calle De La Residenta 820
P.O. Box 2931 Phone: 21 204670
Asuncion, Paraguay Carlos Fernandez-Caballero, Dir.
Founded: 1887. **Staff:** Prof 5; Other 9. **Subjects:** Paraguay - general, history, culture. **Holdings:** 35,000 books; 300 bound periodical volumes. **Subscriptions:** 60 journals and other serials; 5 newspapers. **Services:** Library open to the public.

Paramax Systems Corporation
See: **UNISYS Corporation - Paramax Systems Corporation** (16678)

Paramount Collection
See: **Academy of Motion Picture Arts and Sciences - Margaret Herrick Library** (35)

Paramount Studios Research Library
See: **Lucasfilm Ltd. - Research Library** (9432)

★12737★
Parapsychology Foundation Inc. - Eileen J. Garrett Library (Rel-Phil)
228 E. 71st St. Phone: (212)628-1550
New York, NY 10021-5136 Joanne D.S. McMahon, Ph.D., Libn.
Founded: 1951. **Staff:** 1. **Subjects:** Experimental parapsychology and allied sciences, altered states of consciousness, extrasensory perception, psychokinesis. **Special Collections:** Rare books dealing with psychical research and spiritualism. **Holdings:** 10,000 books; 1030 bound periodical volumes; 11 VF drawers of pamphlets, clippings, reprints. **Subscriptions:** 100 journals and other serials. **Services:** Copying (limited); library open to the public for reference use only. **Publications:** Guide to Sources of Information on Parapsychology, annual - for sale. **Special Indexes:** Index to periodical literature in parapsychology, 1966 to present (card). **Remarks:** FAX: (212)628-1559.

★12738★
Parapsychology Sources of Information Center (Rel-Phil)
2 Plane Tree Ln. Phone: (516)271-1243
Dix Hills, NY 11746 Rhea A. White, Dir.
Staff: Prof 1; Other 6. **Subjects:** Experimental parapsychology, psychical research, consciousness studies, mysticism, transpersonal psychology, analytical psychology/Jung. **Special Collections:** Sports and mysticism (4000 items); parapsychology from a nonparapsychological viewpoint (12,000 articles); parapsychology and transpersonal psychology organizations (files on 100 organizations); biographies of parapsychologists (350 files). **Holdings:** 5200 books; 40 bound periodical volumes; 150 manuscripts; 25 dissertations; 70 cassette tapes. **Subscriptions:** 122 journals and other serials. **Services:** Interlibrary loan; copying; SDI; center open to the public by appointment. **Computerized Information Services:** PsiLine Database System (internal database). Performs searches on fee basis. **Publications:** PSI Center bibliographies; Parapsychology: A Reading and Buying Guide to the Best Books in English; On Being Psychic: A Reading Guide; Psychology in Print: Author List to the Best Books in English, annual - all for sale; Exceptional Human Experience, semiannual. List of publications - available on request. **Special Indexes:** Index to reviews of parapsychology books; parapsychology index; index to biographical information on parapsychologists; index to sports and mysticism collection (all on cards). **Remarks:** FAX: (516)271-1243.

S.C. Pardee Medical Library
See: **Adventist Health Systems Sunbelt - Walker Memorial Hospital** (95)

★ 12739 ★
Parents Helping Parents - Special Children's Resource Center (Soc Sci)
535 Race St., Suite 140   Phone: (408)288-5010
San Jose, CA 95126   June Wright, Libn.
Founded: 1977. **Staff:** 1. **Subjects:** The welfare of children with physical, mental, emotional, or learning disabilities. **Holdings:** 800 volumes. **Subscriptions:** 80 journals and other serials. **Services:** Library open to the public.

(Paris) USIS Library
See: Centre de Documentation Benjamin Franklin (3232)

★ 12740 ★
Parish & Weiner, Inc. - Library (Plan)
560 White Plains Rd.
Tarrytown, NY 10591   Phone: (914)631-9003
Staff: Prof 1. **Subjects:** Land and park planning, environmental studies, traffic and transportation, urban design, zoning and comprehensive planning, economic and market analyses. **Holdings:** 550 books; 175 bound periodical volumes; 12,990 documents; 10 VF drawers of pamphlets. **Subscriptions:** 100 journals and other serials. **Services:** Interlibrary loan; library open to the public with restrictions. **Publications:** Current contents, monthly; acquisitions lists, monthly - both for internal distribution only. **Staff:** Nathaniel Parish, Co-Dir.; Michael Weiner, Co-Dir.

William J. Parish Memorial Library
See: University of New Mexico (19050)

★ 12741 ★
Park Avenue Synagogue - Edmond de Rothschild Library (Rel-Phil)
50 E. 87th St.   Phone: (212)369-2600
New York, NY 10128   Susan Vogelstein, Libn.
Founded: 1956. **Staff:** Prof 3. **Subjects:** Judaica - adult, juvenile. **Special Collections:** Holocaust; Jewish biographies; early childhood Judaica; Jewish history; Israel; Jewish cookbooks; Jewish holidays; Bible; Customs and Ethics; Jewish art and music. **Holdings:** 8000 books. **Subscriptions:** 12 journals and other serials. **Services:** Library open to the public with special permission only. **Staff:** Rose Rudich, Sunday Libn.; Grace Weil, Asst.Libn.

★ 12742 ★
Park City Hospital - Carlson Foundation Memorial Library (Med)
695 Park Ave.
Bridgeport, CT 06604   Phone: (203)579-5097
Staff: Prof 1. **Subjects:** Medicine, nursing, dentistry, allied health sciences. **Holdings:** 2013 books; 2850 bound periodical volumes; 350 videotapes; 2 VF drawers. **Subscriptions:** 177 journals and other serials. **Services:** Interlibrary loan; copying; library open to the public for reference use only. **Computerized Information Services:** BRS Information Technologies, MEDLINE. Performs searches on fee basis. **Networks/Consortia:** Member of Southwestern Connecticut Library Council (SWLC), Connecticut Association of Health Science Libraries (CAHSL), North Atlantic Health Science Libraries (NAHSL). **Special Catalogs:** Catalog of the Videotape Collection, updated periodically - for internal distribution only. **Remarks:** FAX: (203)334-4946.

★ 12743 ★
Park College - McAfee Memorial Library - Special Collections (Hist)
8700 Riverpark Dr.   Phone: (816)741-2000
Parkville, MO 64152-3795   Tom Peterman, Dir. of Lib.Sys.
Founded: 1908. **Staff:** Prof 2.5; Other 4.5. **Subjects:** Park College history. **Special Collections:** John A. McAfee Personal Papers (10 boxes of archival materials); George S. Park Personal Papers (20 boxes of archival materials); Park College Photographic Archive. **Services:** Interlibrary loan; copying; library open to the public. **Automated Operations:** Computerized public access catalog and indexing. **Computerized Information Services:** DIALOG Information Services, WILSONLINE. Performs searches. Contact Person: Ann Schultes, Ref.Libn. **Remarks:** FAX: (816)741-4911.

★ 12744 ★
Park County Bar Association - Law Library (Law)
Court House
1002 Sheridan Ave.
Cody, WY 82414   Phone: (307)587-2204
Staff: 2. **Subjects:** Law. **Holdings:** 10,600 volumes. **Services:** Library open to the public with restrictions. **Computerized Information Services:** WESTLAW. Performs searches on fee basis.

★ 12745 ★
Park County Museum Association - Museum Library (Hist)
118 W. Chinook   Phone: (406)222-3506
Livingston, MT 59047   Diana Whithorn, Caretaker
Founded: 1976. **Staff:** 5. **Subjects:** State and local history, railroads. **Holdings:** 1400 books; 1000 bound periodical volumes; 32,000 newspapers; 140 cassettes; 1120 family history reports; association scrapbooks and minutes. **Services:** Library open to the public with restrictions.

★ 12746 ★
Park Forest Public Library - Park Forest Local History Collection (Hist)
400 Lakewood Blvd.   Phone: (708)748-3731
Park Forest, IL 60466   Jane Nicoll, Ref.Libn.
Founded: 1980. **Staff:** 1. **Subjects:** Park Forest - history (1946 to present), architecture, shopping centers, government. **Special Collections:** Oral History of Park Forest (102 audiotapes; 72 transcripts of audiotapes; 5 videotapes). **Holdings:** 45 boxes of archival materials; 26 boxes and 103 reels of microfilm of Park Forest newspapers, 1949 to present; 127 videocassettes; 231 mounted photographs; 2274 photographs; 491 slides; 16 audiotapes; scrapbooks; 7 VF drawers of local government documents; 3 VF drawers of local history materials; 2 oversize packets; 1 document box for oversize materials. **Services:** Interlibrary loan (limited); copying; collection open to the public. **Computerized Information Services:** DIALOG Information Services. **Networks/Consortia:** Member of Suburban Library System (SLS). **Publications:** Oral History Park Forest (booklet) - for sale. **Special Indexes:** Index to the Oral History transcripts (card); index of oversize photographs (card); VF local history material (card). **Remarks:** FAX: (708)748-8829.

★ 12747 ★
Park-Nicollet Medical Foundation - Arneson Library (Med)
5000 W. 39th St.   Phone: (612)927-3097
Minneapolis, MN 55416   Barbara K. Latta, Dir.
Founded: 1954. **Staff:** Prof 2; Other 1. **Subjects:** Medicine, nursing, allied health sciences. **Holdings:** 1212 books; 4206 bound periodical volumes; 5 boxes of pamphlets and reprints; 4 drawers of microfiche. **Subscriptions:** 159 journals and other serials. **Services:** Interlibrary loan (limited); library not open to the public. **Computerized Information Services:** DIALOG Information Services, BRS Information Technologies, MEDLARS. Performs searches on fee basis. **Networks/Consortia:** Member of Twin Cities Biomedical Consortium (TCBC). **Publications:** Bulletin, quarterly. **Remarks:** FAX: (612)927-3741.

Philip M. Park Memorial Library
See: Jesse Besser Museum (1761)

★ 12748 ★
Park Place Church of God - Carl Kardatzke Memorial Library (Rel-Phil)
501 College Dr.   Phone: (317)642-0216
Anderson, IN 46012   Trish B. Janutolo, Chm., Lib.Comm.
Subjects: Bibles, religion, Christian education, doctrinal theology, family ethics, biography, missions, children's books. **Holdings:** 2000 books. **Services:** Library open to the public with restrictions.

★ 12749 ★
Park Ridge Hospital - Nathaniel J. Hurst Library (Med)
1555 Long Pond Rd.   Phone: (716)723-7755
Rochester, NY 14626   Kathleen A. Martin, Libn.
Founded: 1975. **Staff:** Prof 1. **Subjects:** Medicine, nursing, surgery, hospital administration, alcoholism and drug abuse. **Holdings:** 1500 books; 2840 bound periodical volumes; 880 audio cassettes; 430 videotapes. **Subscriptions:** 140 journals and other serials. **Services:** Interlibrary loan; copying; library open to health professionals upon request. **Automated Operations:** Computerized ILL. **Computerized Information Services:** MEDLARS, OCLC; DOCLINE (electronic mail service). **Networks/Consortia:** Member of Rochester Regional Library Council (RRLC). **Remarks:** FAX: (716)723-7078.

★12750★
Park Synagogue Library - Kravitz Memorial Library (Rel-Phil)
3300 Mayfield Rd.   Phone: (216)371-2244
Cleveland Heights, OH 44118   Susan W. Traub, Libn.
Staff: Prof 1. **Subjects:** Judaica, Jewish history. **Holdings:** 15,000 books; 100 bound periodical volumes. **Subscriptions:** 70 journals and other serials; 10 newspapers. **Services:** Interlibrary loan; library open to the public for reference use only.

William Hallock Park Memorial Library
See: New York City Public Health Laboratories (11566)

Parke-Davis
See: Warner-Lambert/Parke-Davis (19970)

★12751★
PARKER & AMCHEM - Technical Library (Sci-Engr)
32100 Stephenson Hwy.   Phone: (313)583-9300
Madison Heights, MI 48071   Martha Hart, H.R. Sec.
Subjects: Chemical research. **Holdings:** 1500 books. **Subscriptions:** 30 journals and other serials. **Services:** Interlibrary loan; library not open to the public. **Remarks:** FAX: (313)583-2976. Telex: 211 872 PSTP UR. A division of Henkel Corporation.

★12752★
Parker Chapin Flattau and Klimpl - Library (Law)
1211 Ave. of the Americas   Phone: (212)704-6330
New York, NY 10036   Kathy Lefco, Libn.
Founded: 1940. **Staff:** Prof 2; Other 3. **Subjects:** Law - litigation, antitrust, tax, labor, trusts and estates, corporations, banking, securities, real estate. **Holdings:** 15,500 books; 150 bound periodical volumes; 600 pamphlets. **Subscriptions:** 200 journals and other serials. **Services:** Interlibrary loan; library not open to the public. **Computerized Information Services:** LEXIS, DIALOG Information Services, WESTLAW, Dow Jones News/Retrieval, Spectrum Ownership Profiles Online, Dun & Bradstreet Business Credit Services, VU/TEXT Information Services, LEGI-SLATE, DataTimes. **Special Catalogs:** Catalog of memoranda and briefs (card); corporate forms catalog (card). **Staff:** Suki Scott, Asst.Libn.

★12753★
Parker Memorial Baptist Church - Library (Rel-Phil)
1205 Quintard Ave.
Box 2104
Anniston, AL 36201   Phone: (205)236-5628
                                     Mrs. Logene Griffin, Libn.
Founded: 1932. **Staff:** Prof 1; Other 6. **Subjects:** Religion, fiction, biography, history, geography. **Holdings:** 5653 books. **Services:** Library open to the public.

J.H. Parkin Branch - Library
See: Canada - National Research Council - CISTI - J.H. Parkin Branch - Library (2822)

Robert L. Parkinson Library & Research Center
See: Circus World Museum (3716)

★12754★
Parkland College - Library (Educ)
2400 W. Bradley Ave.   Phone: (217)351-2223
Champaign, IL 61820   Raymond Bial, Dir.
Founded: 1967. **Staff:** Prof 5; Other 20. **Subjects:** Education. **Holdings:** 100,000 books; 15,000 other cataloged items. **Subscriptions:** 700 journals and other serials; 38 newspapers. **Services:** Interlibrary loan; copying; center open to students and faculty. **Automated Operations:** Computerized public access catalog, cataloging, and acquisitions. **Computerized Information Services:** DIALOG Information Services, OCLC. **Networks/Consortia:** Member of ILLINET, Lincoln Trail Libraries System (LTLS). **Remarks:** FAX: (217)351-2581. **Staff:** William C. Gaines, Ref.Libn.; Ann Neely, Ref.Libn.; Ken Strickler, Tech.Serv.Libn.; Julia Hough, Ref.Libn.

Parkland Hospital - Information Center/Library
See: Parkland Medical Center - Library (12755)

★12755★
Parkland Medical Center - Library (Med)
1 Parkland Dr.   Phone: (603)432-1500
Derry, NH 03038   Holly Eddy, Libn.
Founded: 1984. **Subjects:** Medicine. **Subscriptions:** 79 journals and other serials. **Services:** Interlibrary loan; library not open to the public. **Automated Operations:** Computerized ILL (DOCLINE). **Computerized Information Services:** MEDLARS. **Networks/Consortia:** Member of BHSL, Health Science Libraries of New Hampshire & Vermont (HSL-NH/VT), Merrimack Valley/Lakes Region Health Science Librarians, North Atlantic Health Science Libraries (NAHSL). **Remarks:** FAX: (603)432-1500, ext. 375. **Formerly:** Parkland Hospital - Information Center/Library.

Parklawn Health Library
See: U.S. Public Health Service (17932)

Timothy Parkman Memorial Library
See: Newman Catholic Student Center (11770)

★12756★
Parkridge Centre - Staff Library (Med)
110 Gropper Crescent   Phone: (306)978-2333
Saskatoon, SK, Canada S7M 5N9   Kristine Goulding, Dir. of Hea.Rec.
Founded: 1987. **Staff:** Prof 1. **Subjects:** Medicine, nursing, gerontology, psychosocial, rehabilitation, therapies, support services, pharmacology. **Holdings:** 566 volumes. **Subscriptions:** 33 journals and other serials. **Services:** Copying; library open to the public with restrictions. **Computerized Information Services:** Internal database. **Remarks:** FAX: (306)978-2232.

Parks College
See: St. Louis University (14467)

★12757★
Parkview - Osteopathic Medical Center of Philadelphia - Medical Library (Med)
1331 E. Wyoming Ave.   Phone: (215)537-7449
Philadelphia, PA 19124   Eileen Smith, Med.Lib.Coord.
Founded: 1967. **Staff:** Prof 1. **Subjects:** Osteopathic medicine, orthopedics, medicine, nursing. **Holdings:** 1220 books; 357 bound periodical volumes; 335 cassettes. **Subscriptions:** 45 journals and other serials. **Services:** Interlibrary loan; copying; library open to the public with permission of hospital administrator. **Computerized Information Services:** NLM. **Networks/Consortia:** Member of Delaware Valley Information Consortium (DEVIC), National Network of Libraries of Medicine - Middle Atlantic Region. **Remarks:** FAX: (215)537-7723. **Formerly:** Philadelphia - College of Osteopathic Medicine, Parkview - Hospital.

★12758★
Parkview Episcopal Medical Center - Medical Library (Med)
400 W. 16th St.   Phone: (719)584-4582
Pueblo, CO 81003   Alma Williams, Lib.Coord.
Founded: 1959. **Staff:** Prof 1. **Subjects:** Medicine, nursing, surgery, hospital administration, allied health sciences. **Holdings:** 2119 books; 200 bound periodical volumes; pamphlet file. **Subscriptions:** 120 journals and other serials. **Services:** Interlibrary loan; copying; SDI; library open to the public for reference use only. **Computerized Information Services:** MEDLARS, BRS Information Technologies, OCLC; TenTime (electronic mail service). Performs searches on fee basis. **Networks/Consortia:** Member of Colorado Council of Medical Librarians.

Parkview Library
See: Oklahoma School for the Blind (12354)

★ 12759 ★
Parkview Memorial Hospital - Health Science Library (Med)
2200 Randallia Dr.   Phone: (219)484-6636
Fort Wayne, IN 46805   Shannon Clever, Lib.Mgr.
Founded: 1975. **Staff:** Prof 2; Other 1. **Subjects:** Medicine, nursing, and allied health sciences, hospital administration. **Special Collections:** Patient Education. **Holdings:** 3500 books. **Subscriptions:** 180 journals and other serials. **Services:** Interlibrary loan (fee); copying; library open to staff and health science students. **Automated Operations:** Computerized cataloging, circulation, and ILL (DOCLINE). **Computerized Information Services:** MEDLARS, BRS Information Technologies, DIALOG Information Services; CD-ROMs (MEDLINE, CINAHL-CD). **Networks/Consortia:** Member of Northeast Indiana Health Sciences Libraries, Tri-ALSA, National Network of Libraries of Medicine - Greater Midwest Region. **Remarks:** FAX: (219)480-5961. **Staff:** Nancy Meyer, Asst.Libn.; Betty Schell, Lib.Techn.

★ 12760 ★
Parkview Osteopathic Hospital - Library (Med)
1920 Parkwood Ave.   Phone: (419)242-8471
Toledo, OH 43624   Cynthia Jones, Libn.
Staff: 1. **Subjects:** Osteopathy, orthopedics, radiology, surgery, anesthesiology, pediatrics, clinical and family medicine. **Special Collections:** Osteopathic Collection (including rare books by the founder of the osteopathic medical profession). **Holdings:** 1050 books; 1450 bound periodical volumes; Audio-Digest tapes. **Subscriptions:** 74 journals and other serials. **Services:** Interlibrary loan; library not open to the public. **Computerized Information Services:** MEDLINE. **Remarks:** FAX: (419)242-0512.

★ 12761 ★
ParkView Regional Medical Center - Medical Library (Med)
100 McAuley Dr.
P.O. Box 509
Vicksburg, MS 39180   Phone: (601)631-2131
Founded: 1900. **Staff:** Prof 2; Other 1. **Subjects:** Medicine, surgery, obstetrics, gynecology, allied health sciences. **Special Collections:** Rare medical books. **Holdings:** 2400 books; 3532 unbound and bound periodical volumes. **Subscriptions:** 66 journals and other serials. **Services:** Interlibrary loan; copying; library open to the public with restrictions. **Networks/Consortia:** Member of Central Mississippi Consortium of Medical Libraries. **Remarks:** FAX: (601)631-2124. **Formerly:** Mercy Regional Medical Center.

★ 12762 ★
Parlee, McLaws Barristers & Solicitors - Library (Law)
10180 101st, No. 1500   Phone: (403)423-8594
Edmonton, AB, Canada T5J 4K1   Priscilla Kennedy, Dir. of Legal Res.
Founded: 1889. **Staff:** Prof 2; Other 5. **Subjects:** Law, government. **Holdings:** 35,000 books. **Services:** Copying; library open to the public with permission. **Automated Operations:** Computerized cataloging. **Computerized Information Services:** QL Systems, WESTLAW, Info Globe, CAN/LAW, LEXIS, CT-ONLINE; Memo Bank (internal database) . Performs searches on fee basis. **Remarks:** FAX: (403)423-2870. A branch library is maintained at 3400 707-Eighth Ave., S.W., Calgary, AB T2P 1H5. **Staff:** Laura Lemmens, Libn.; Phyllis Thornton, Libn.

Parliament of Zimbabwe
See: Zimbabwe - Parliament of Zimbabwe (20842)

Parlin-Ingersoll Library
See: Fulton County Historical and Genealogical Society (6205)

A.F. Parlow Library of the Health Sciences
See: Los Angeles County/Harbor-UCLA Medical Center (9330)

Parma Technical Center
See: UCAR Carbon Company, Inc. (16609)

★ 12763 ★
Parmly Billings Library - Montana Room (Hist)
510 N. Broadway   Phone: (406)657-8290
Billings, MT 59101   James E. Curry, Ref.Libn.
Staff: Prof 1. **Subjects:** Western U.S. and Montana history, Battle of Little Bighorn, Crow Indians, other Montana Indian tribes. **Special Collections:** Local histories (100); city archives (75 archival materials). **Holdings:** 7000 books; 100 bound periodical volumes; 120 filing drawers. **Subscriptions:** 12 journals and other serials; 6 newspapers. **Services:** Copying; library open to the public for reference use only and on a limited scedule. **Remarks:** Alternate telephone number(s): 657-8257.

Parral Archives
See: Amerind Foundation, Inc. - Fulton-Hayden Memorial Library (800)

★ 12764 ★
Parrish Art Museum - Library
25 Job's Lane
Southampton, NY 11968
Founded: 1954. **Subjects:** American and European art, architecture, crafts. **Special Collections:** William Merritt Chase Archives; Fairfield Porter Archives; Aline B. Saarinen Library; Moses and Ida Soyer Library; Samuel Parrish Library. **Holdings:** 5700 books; 3900 catalogs. **Remarks:** Currently inactive.

June Austin Parrish Memorial Library
See: Employers Reinsurance Corporation (5344)

Samuel Parrish Library
See: Parrish Art Museum - Library (12764)

Parrot Health Sciences Library
See: Eastern Maine Medical Center (5152)

Dr. Victor Parsonnet Memorial Library
See: Newark Beth Israel Medical Center (11741)

★ 12765 ★
Parsons Brinckerhoff - Corporate Library (Sci-Engr)
One Penn Plaza
250 W. 34th St.   Phone: (212)465-5474
New York, NY 10119   Marsha Herman, Libn.
Founded: 1976. **Staff:** 1. **Subjects:** Transportation, civil and structural engineering, electrical and mechanical engineering, urban and environmental planning, water resources, geotechnical. **Special Collections:** Parsons Brinckerhoff qualifications, proposals, reports, and videos. **Holdings:** 5500 books; 4500 technical reports. **Subscriptions:** 250 journals and other serials. **Services:** Interlibrary loan; copying. **Automated Operations:** Computerized periodicals routing. **Computerized Information Services:** DIALOG Information Services, American Society of Civil Engineers (ASCE). **Remarks:** FAX: (212)465-5096. **Formerly:** Parsons, Brinckerhoff, Quade & Douglas, Inc. - Library.

★ 12766 ★
Elbert H. Parsons Public Law Library (Law)
205 East Side Square   Phone: (205)532-1585
Huntsville, AL 35801   Jim Porter, Libn.
Staff: Prof 1. **Subjects:** Law. **Holdings:** 15,500 books; 1100 bound periodical volumes; videotapes. **Subscriptions:** 45 journals and other serials. **Services:** Copying; library open to the public. **Remarks:** Maintained by Madison County. **Remarks:** FAX: (205)533-5881.

★ 12767 ★
Ralph M. Parsons Company Inc. - Central Library (Sci-Engr)
100 W. Walnut St.   Phone: (818)440-3998
Pasadena, CA 91124-0001   Claire Hammond, Libn.
Staff: Prof 1; Other 1. **Subjects:** Engineering, mining, nuclear engineering, power. **Holdings:** 6000 books; 1000 bound periodical volumes; 7000 reports; 3500 vendor equipment catalogs. **Subscriptions:** 200 journals and other serials; 5 newspapers. **Services:** Interlibrary loan; library not open to the public.

Ralph M. Parsons Laboratory
See: Massachusetts Institute of Technology - Civil Engineering Department (9798)

★ 12768 ★
Parsons School of Design - Adam and Sophie Gimbel Design Library (Art)
2 W. 13th St., 2nd Fl.
New York, NY 10011   Phone: (212)229-8914
Founded: 1896. **Staff:** Prof 3; Other 6.5. **Subjects:** Fine arts, architecture, costume, crafts, design, environmental design, fashion, graphic arts, photography, typography. **Special Collections:** Sketchbooks by American fashion designer Claire McCardell (125 volumes). **Holdings:** 37,000 books; 35,000 mounted picture plates; 60,000 slides. **Subscriptions:** 230 journals and other serials. **Services:** Interlibrary loan; library open to the public by appointment. **Automated Operations:** Computerized cataloging and circulation. **Networks/Consortia:** Member of New York Metropolitan Reference and Research Library Agency, Research Library Association of South Manhattan, Research Libraries Information Network (RLIN). **Remarks:** Affiliated with New School for Social Research. **Remarks:** FAX: (212)929-2456. **Staff:** Claire Petrie, Ref./Tech.Serv.Libn.

★ 12769 ★
Parsons School of Design - Otis Art Institute - Library (Art)
2401 Wilshire Blvd.
Los Angeles, CA 90057   Phone: (213)251-0560
Founded: 1947. **Staff:** Prof 3; Other 1. **Subjects:** Fine arts, communication design, architecture, fashion, ceramics, photography. **Special Collections:** Artists' books (670 titles); fine prints and artists' realia (54 titles). **Holdings:** 27,000 books; 2900 bound periodical volumes; 60,000 slides; 54 VF drawers of artists' ephemera files; 16 VF drawers of clipping files; 9 VF drawers of art reproduction files; 267 audio cassettes; 123 films; 87 videotapes and cassettes. **Subscriptions:** 218 journals and other serials. **Services:** Copying; library open to the public by appointment only. **Automated Operations:** Computerized cataloging. **Staff:** Barbara Furbush, Slide/Media Cur.

★ 12770 ★
Parsons State Hospital and Training Center - Medical Library (Med)
2601 Gabriel
Box 738
Parsons, KS 67357-0738   Phone: (316)421-6550
                            Linda Lee Stahlman, Staff Libn.
Founded: 1953. **Staff:** Prof 1. **Subjects:** Mental retardation, developmental disabilities, psychology, speech pathology, audiology, behavioral science. **Holdings:** 5200 books; 4 VF drawers of pamphlets; 282 working papers. **Subscriptions:** 75 journals and other serials. **Services:** Interlibrary loan; copying; library open to the public. **Computerized Information Services:** Online systems. Performs searches on fee basis. **Special Indexes:** Index to Parsons Sun articles concerning the hospital (in preparation). **Remarks:** Maintained by the Kansas State Department of Social & Rehabilitation Services. Center maintains an active library for mentally retarded and emotionally disturbed children and young people, aged 6 to adult. FAX: (316)421-3623 (Attn.: Library).

★ 12771 ★
Partners for Livable Places - National Resource Center (Plan, Art)
1429 21st St., N.W.   Phone: (202)887-5990
Washington, DC 20036   Daniel McCahan, Dir.
Founded: 1977. **Subjects:** Livability, public art, urban design, historic preservation, public/private partnerships. **Holdings:** 15,000 books; 350 bound periodical volumes; 50 AV programs. **Services:** Copying; library open to the public. **Computerized Information Services:** Design Arts Program and Visual Arts Program Grant Award Databases (internal databases). **Publications:** Amenities; Place. **Remarks:** FAX: (202)466-4845. **Formerly:** Its Livability Clearinghouse. **Staff:** Ben Silverstein, Info.Spec.

★ 12772 ★
Pasadena Historical Society - Library & Archives (Hist)
470 W. Walnut St.   Phone: (818)577-1660
Pasadena, CA 91103-3594   Susan E. Coffman, Archv./Libn.
Founded: 1924. **Staff:** Prof 1; Other 12. **Subjects:** History of the Pasadena area. **Special Collections:** Photographs and slides of early Pasadena (500,000). **Holdings:** 1500 books; pamphlets; clippings; albums; diaries; maps; documents; magazines; manuscript materials. **Services:** Copying; library and archives open to the public for research only.

★ 12773 ★
Pasadena Presbyterian Church - Library (Rel-Phil)
100 Pasadena Ave., N.   Phone: (813)345-0148
St. Petersburg, FL 33710-8315 Patricia B. McLeod, Libn.
Founded: 1960. **Staff:** Prof 2; Other 2. **Subjects:** Religion, religious education. **Holdings:** 5000 books; 75 filmstrips; 24 videotapes; Presbyterian curriculum materials. **Subscriptions:** 10 journals and other serials. **Services:** Copying; library open to the public for reference use only. **Staff:** Maxine Perry, Cat.Libn.; Richard Howe, AV Libn.

★ 12774 ★
Pasadena Public Library - Business-Technology Room (Bus-Fin, Sci-Engr)
285 E. Walnut St.   Phone: (818)405-4052
Pasadena, CA 91101   Victoria Johnson, Prin.Libn.
Founded: 1970. **Staff:** Prof 1. **Subjects:** Investments, finance, business management, real estate, taxation, industrial technology, engineering. **Special Collections:** Pasadena industries; trade and industrial directories; tax and investment services. **Holdings:** 20,485 books; 520 trade and professional directories; 1670 corporate annual reports; 45 investment services. **Subscriptions:** 162 journals and other serials; 17 newspapers. **Services:** Interlibrary loan; division open to the public. **Automated Operations:** Computerized cataloging, acquisitions, and circulation. **Computerized Information Services:** OCLC, DIALOG Information Services, VU/TEXT Information Services, RLIN, Mead Data Central, OCLC EPIC, WILSONLINE, BRS Information Technologies, Dow Jones News/Retrieval. Customized searches on fee basis. Contact Person: Elaine Zorbas, 405-4052. **Networks/Consortia:** Member of Metropolitan Cooperative Library System (MCLS). **Special Indexes:** Subject index to directory collection. **Remarks:** FAX: (818)449-2165. **Staff:** Millicent Sharma, Libn.

★ 12775 ★
Pasadena Public Library - Pasadena Centennial Room (Hist)
285 E. Walnut St.   Phone: (818)405-4052
Pasadena, CA 91101   Victoria Johnson, Prin.Libn.
Founded: 1989. **Staff:** Prof 1. **Subjects:** California and Pasadena local history, genealogy. **Holdings:** 5000 books; 183 periodicals and newsletters; 4000 Pasadena photographs; 230 Pasadena scrapbooks; 1700 Pasadena documents; 54 linear feet of Pasadena ephemera and clippings; 10 linear feet of pamphlets; 75 16mm films; 165 videocassettes; 1325 reels of microfilm of Pasadena newspapers; 200 architectural drawings. **Subscriptions:** 50 journals and other serials; 3 newspapers. **Services:** Interlibrary loan, copying, division open to the public. **Automated Operations:** Computerized cataloging and acquisitions. **Computerized Information Services:** OCLC, DIALOG Information Services, VU/TEXT Information Services, RLIN, Mead Data Central, WILSONLINE, BRS Information Technologies, Dow Jones News/Retrieval, OCLC EPIC; InfoTrac; CD-ROM (WILSONDISC). Customized searches on fee basis. Contact Person: Elaine Zorbas, 405-4052. **Networks/Consortia:** Member of Metropolitan Cooperative Library System (MCLS). **Remarks:** FAX: (818)449-2165. **Staff:** Carolyn Garner.

★ 12776 ★
Pascack Valley Hospital - David Goldberg Memorial Medical Library (Med)
Old Hook Rd.   Phone: (201)358-3240
Westwood, NJ 07675   Debbra Michaels, Dir.
Founded: 1968. **Staff:** Prof 1; Other 1. **Subjects:** Medicine, surgery, nursing, allied health sciences, management. **Special Collections:** Sports medicine. **Holdings:** 2000 books; 25 bound periodical volumes; 4 indexes; 9 audiotape subscriptions; 100 videotapes; pamphlets. **Subscriptions:** 216 journals and other serials. **Services:** Interlibrary loan; copying; SDI; library open to the public with restrictions. **Computerized Information Services:** NLM, DIALOG Information Services, BRS Information Technologies; MESSAGES (electronic mail service). Performs searches on fee basis. **Networks/Consortia:** Member of Bergen Passaic Regional Library Cooperative, Health Sciences Library Association of New Jersey (HSLANJ), New Jersey Multitype Library Network. **Remarks:** FAX: (201)358-6215.

★ 12777 ★
Pasqua Hospital - Health Sciences Library (Med)
4101 Dewdney Ave.   Phone: (306)527-9641
Regina, SK, Canada S4T 1A5   Leona Lang, Dir.
Founded: 1953. **Staff:** 1. **Subjects:** Medicine, nursing, administration. **Holdings:** 1200 books; 2800 bound periodical volumes; Audio-Digest tapes; videotapes. **Subscriptions:** 72 journals and other serials. **Services:** Library not open to the public.

Malca Pass Library
See: Agudath Israel Congregation (139)

★ 12778 ★
**Passaic County Historical Society - Local History and Genealogy
    Library** (Hist)
Lambert Castle
Valley Rd.   Phone: (201)881-2761
Paterson, NJ 07503   Susan Pumilia, Dir.
Founded: 1926. **Subjects:** Genealogy, local history. **Special Collections:**
Society for the Establishment of Useful Manufactures papers; Abraham
Hewitt papers (iron industry); Family Group Sheets Collection (3 filing
cabinets). **Holdings:** 2000 books. **Services:** Copying; library open to the
public by appointment. **Publications:** A Guide to the Collections - for sale.
Special Catalogs: Researchers Card File.

★ 12779 ★
Passaic River Coalition - Environmental Library (Env-Cons)
246 Madisonville Rd.   Phone: (201)766-7550
Basking Ridge, NJ 07920   Alfred J. Porro, Jr., Chm.
Founded: 1971. **Staff:** 1. **Subjects:** Environmental quality in the Passaic
River Watershed, urban river systems, water pollution, water quality and
supply, flood control, sewage and garbage disposal, urban decay, land use,
wildlife and vegetation, historic preservation, solid waste, environmental
education. **Holdings:** 8000 volumes; special interest collections.
Subscriptions: 15 journals and other serials; 5 newspapers. **Services:**
Copying; library open to the public. **Publications:** Vibes from the Libe,
quarterly. **Remarks:** FAX: (201)766-7550. **Staff:** Francis Tucker; Betty
Deans.

★ 12780 ★
Passavant Area Hospital - Sibert Library (Med)
1600 W. Walnut St.   Phone: (217)245-9541
Jacksonville, IL 62650   Dorothy H. Knight, Libn.
Founded: 1902. **Staff:** Prof 1. **Subjects:** Nursing, medicine. **Holdings:** 3040
books; 140 bound periodical volumes; AV programs. **Subscriptions:** 361
journals and other serials. **Services:** Interlibrary loan; copying; library open
to the public. **Automated Operations:** Computerized public access catalog
(ILLINET). **Computerized Information Services:** Data-Star;
MICROMEDIX (internal database). **Networks/Consortia:** Member of
National Network of Libraries of Medicine - Greater Midwest Region,
Capital Area Consortium (CAC), Great River Library System (GRLS).
Remarks: FAX: (217)245-9331; (217)245-9341. Maintains Community
Health Information Center.

★ 12781 ★
Passionist Academic Institute - Library (Rel-Phil)
5700 N. Harlem Ave.   Phone: (312)631-1686
Chicago, IL 60631   Irene Horst
Staff: Prof 1. **Subjects:** Theology, philosophy. **Special Collections:** Cardinal
Newman Collection (200 books). **Holdings:** 20,000 books; 1320 bound
periodical volumes. **Subscriptions:** 70 journals and other serials; 10
newspapers. **Services:** Interlibrary loan; library open to the public.
Computerized Information Services: OCLC. **Remarks:** FAX: (312)631-
8059.

★ 12782 ★
Passionist Monastic Seminary - Library (Rel-Phil)
86-45 178th St.   Phone: (718)739-6502
Jamaica, NY 11432   Br. James G. Johnson, C.P., Libn.
Founded: 1934. **Staff:** Prof 1. **Subjects:** Theology, spirituality, preaching,
philosophy, Passion of Christ, adult education. **Holdings:** 53,648 books; 142
bound periodical volumes. **Subscriptions:** 125 journals and other serials.
Services: Copying; library open to the public by appointment. **Remarks:**
FAX: (718)657-0578. Maintained by the Passionist Community.

★ 12783 ★
Passive Solar Industries Council - Library (Energy)
1090 Vermont Ave., N.W., Suite 1200   Phone: (202)371-0357
Washington, DC 20005   Helen English, Dir.
Subjects: Passive solar energy - design, construction, technology, industry.
Holdings: Documents from national laboratories, government contractors
and agencies, and private programs. **Publications:** Passive Solar Sourcebook
(annotated bibliography).

★ 12784 ★
Pasteur Institute - Library (Biol Sci, Med)
25, rue du Docteur Roux   Phone: 45 68 82 80
F-25724 Paris Cedex 15, France   Mrs. Verry, Chf.Libn.
Subjects: Microbiology, virology, immunology, biochemistry, cell and
molecular biology, pharmacology, developmental biology, mycology,
protozoology, medicine. **Holdings:** 120,000 volumes. **Subscriptions:** 600
journals and other serials. **Services:** Interlibrary loan; copying; library open
to biological sciences specialists. **Remarks:** Telex: PASTEUR 250609. **Also
Known As:** Institut Pasteur.

★ 12785 ★
Pasteur Institute of Algeria - Library (Biol Sci)
Rue du Dr. Laveran
Algiers, Algeria   Jamila Arib, Libn.
Subjects: Microbiology, immunology, life sciences. **Holdings:** 55,000
volumes. **Remarks:** Telex: 53715. Sponsored by the Pasteur Institute in
Paris. Also affiliated with Algeria - Ministry of Public Health. **Also Known
As:** Institut Pasteur d'Algerie.

Sherman Pastor Memorial Library
See: Congregation Shalom (4167)

Pastore Library
See: Philadelphia College of Textiles and Science (12981)

Chancellor Paterson Library
See: Lakehead University (8902)

★ 12786 ★
(Paterson) Herald & News - Library/Newspaper Morgue (Publ)
988 Main Ave.
Passaic, NJ 07055   Phone: (201)365-3000
Founded: 1890. **Staff:** 1. **Subjects:** Newspaper reference topics. **Special
Collections:** New Jersey Legislative Directory, 1879 to present; Passaic
County Freeholders Reports, 1975 to present; Paterson Morning Call and
News, 1889 to present (microfilm). **Holdings:** Photographs; reference books;
local sports material. **Subscriptions:** 16 journals and other serials. **Services:**
Library not open to the public.

Norman Paterson School of International Affairs
See: Carleton University (3056)

★ 12787 ★
**William Paterson College of New Jersey - Sarah Byrd Askew Library -
    Special Collections** (Hist)
300 Pompton Rd.   Phone: (201)595-2116
Wayne, NJ 07470   Robert Wolk, Spec.Coll.Libn.
Founded: 1924. **Special Collections:** New Jerseyana (1500 volumes); first
and limited editions of American and English authors (525); professional
papers of William Paterson (senator, governor, Supreme Court Justice).
Holdings: 1595 books; 55 bound periodical volumes; 250 archival materials.
Services: Interlibrary loan; copying; collections open to the public for
reference use only. **Automated Operations:** Computerized cataloging,
acquisitions, and circulation. **Computerized Information Services:**
WILSONLINE, BRS Information Technologies, DIALOG Information
Services, OCLC. **Networks/Consortia:** Member of PALINET.

Pathfinders Memorial Resource Library
See: Chapelwood United Methodist Church (3431)

★ 12788 ★
Patient Care - Library
690 Kinderkamack Rd.
Oradell, NJ 07649-1506
Defunct. Holdings absorbed by Medical Economics Publishing.

Patmos/Jones Memorial Library
See: **Emma L. Bixby Hospital (1871)**

★12789★
James Paton Memorial Hospital - Staff Library (Med)
Trans Canada Hwy.   Phone: (709)256-5527
Gander, NF, Canada A1V 1P7   Teresita Hearn, Libn.
Staff: Prof 1. **Subjects:** Medicine, orthopedics, ophthalmology, pediatrics, obstetrics, gynecology, allied health sciences. **Holdings:** 700 books. **Subscriptions:** 130 journals and other serials. **Services:** Interlibrary loan; copying; library open to the public. **Automated Operations:** Computerized cataloging, acquisitions, serials, and circulation.

★12790★
Patricof & Co. - Information Center (Bus-Fin)
445 Park Ave., 11th Fl.   Phone: (212)753-6300
New York, NY 10022   Paul Patterson, Res.Info.Spec.
Founded: 1984. **Staff:** Prof 1; Other 1. **Subjects:** Venture capital. **Holdings:** 200 books. **Subscriptions:** 118 journals and other serials. **Services:** Interlibrary loan; copying; SDI; library open to the public with restrictions. **Automated Operations:** Computerized cataloging, acquisitions, and serials. **Computerized Information Services:** DIALOG Information Services, Dow Jones News/Retrieval, LEXIS, NEXIS, Vickers Stock Research Corporation, Dun & Bradstreet Business Credit Services, InvesText, COMPUSTAT, CORIS, SDC, Global Scan, Lotus OneSource, IDD Information Services. **Special Indexes:** Index to conference material (online). **Remarks:** FAX: (212)319-6155. **Formerly:** Alan Patricof Associates. **Staff:** Patricia Rappa.

★12791★
Patriot News Company - Library (Publ)
812 Market St.
Box 2265   Phone: (717)255-8402
Harrisburg, PA 17105   Deanna Mills, Libn.
Staff: Prof 2; Other 2. **Subjects:** Newspaper reference topics. **Holdings:** 200 books; newspapers clipping files on microfiche; photographs; local paper, 1911 to present, on microfilm. **Services:** Library not open to the public. **Computerized Information Services:** DataTimes. **Special Indexes:** Clippings index; graphics index; photo index. **Remarks:** FAX: (717)255-8456.

PATSCAN
See: **University of British Columbia - Patent Search Service (18278)**

A.B. Patterson Professional Library
See: **Scarborough Board of Education (14893)**

★12792★
Patterson, Belknap, Webb & Tyler - Library (Law)
30 Rockefeller Plaza   Phone: (212)698-2103
New York, NY 10112   Christina M. Senezak, Chf.Libn.
Staff: Prof 2; Other 4. **Subjects:** Law - litigation, corporate, tax, patent/copyright, media/communication, environment, insurance, product liability. **Holdings:** 30,000 volumes; 6000 current annual reports; 15 VF drawers; 150 audio cassettes. **Subscriptions:** 370 journals and other serials; 12 newspapers. **Services:** Interlibrary loan; library not open to the public. **Computerized Information Services:** WESTLAW, DIALOG Information Services, Dow Jones News/Retrieval, NewsNet, Inc., Mead Data Central, Maxwell Macmillan Taxes Online, Legi-Tech, Congressional Quarterly, Inc. (CQ), VU/TEXT Information Services, Dun's Marketing Services (DMS), CCH Access. **Special Catalogs:** Cataloging Manual (online, printout). **Special Indexes:** Tax Club Memoranda Index; List of On-Line Databases; Annual Reports List; Periodicals List (all online and printout). **Remarks:** FAX: (212)956-3153. **Staff:** Betty Hunter-Beatty, Asst.Libn.

Eugene Patterson Library
See: **Poynter Institute for Media Studies - Eugene Patterson Library (13283)**

Patterson Reference Library and Economics Reference Center
See: **Midwest Research Institute (10378)**

★12793★
Patton Boggs and Blow - Law Library (Law)
2550 M St., N.W., 8th Fl.   Phone: (202)457-6000
Washington, DC 20037   Kevin McCall, Libn.
Staff: Prof 1. **Subjects:** Law. **Holdings:** 7000 books. **Subscriptions:** 36 journals and other serials. **Services:** Interlibrary loan. **Computerized Information Services:** WESTLAW, DIALOG Information Services, LEXIS.

★12794★
George S. Patton, Jr. Historical Society - Library (Hist)
3116 Thorn St.   Phone: (619)271-6517
San Diego, CA 92104-4618   Charles M. Province, Pres.
Founded: 1970. **Staff:** Prof 1; Other 1. **Subjects:** George S. Patton, Jr., Third U.S. Army, military science and history. **Holdings:** 300 books; 500 bound periodical volumes; videotapes; films. **Services:** Copying; library open to the public. **Automated Operations:** Computerized cataloging, acquisitions, and serials.

Patton Museums of Calvary & Armor
See: **U.S. Army - TRADOC - Patton Museum of Cavalry & Armor (17020)**

★12795★
Patton State Hospital - Staff Library (Med)
3102 E. Highland Ave.   Phone: (714)862-8121
Patton, CA 92369   Laurie Piccolotti, Sr.Libn.
Founded: 1947. **Staff:** Prof 1. **Subjects:** Psychiatry, psychology, psychiatric nursing, forensic psychiatry. **Holdings:** 3600 books; 2025 bound periodical volumes; 1100 unbound periodical volumes; 2 VF drawers of unbound reports; 2 VF drawers of documents. **Subscriptions:** 101 journals and other serials. **Services:** Interlibrary loan; copying; library open to mental health professionals. **Computerized Information Services:** MEDLARS; DOCLINE (electronic mail service). **Networks/Consortia:** Member of National Network of Libraries of Medicine - Pacific Southwest Region, San Bernardino, Inyo, Riverside Counties United Library Services (SIRCULS). **Remarks:** Maintained by California State Department of Mental Health.

Patuxent Wildlife Research Center
See: **U.S. Fish & Wildlife Service (17505)**

★12796★
Paul, Hastings, Janofsky and Walker - Law Library (Law)
555 S. Flower, 26th Fl.   Phone: (213)683-6000
Los Angeles, CA 90071   Susan Streiker, Law Libn.
Founded: 1972. **Staff:** Prof 2; Other 4. **Subjects:** Federal and state law. **Special Collections:** Labor law. **Holdings:** 30,000 volumes. **Subscriptions:** 185 journals and other serials. **Services:** Interlibrary loan. **Automated Operations:** Computerized cataloging. **Computerized Information Services:** DIALOG Information Services, LEXIS, WESTLAW, Dow Jones News/Retrieval, Information America, VU/TEXT Information Services, Prentice Hall Online Services, RLIN, Data-Star, DAMAR. **Remarks:** FAX: (213)627-0705. **Staff:** Shih-Mei Lin, Assoc. Law Libn.

★12797★
Paul Smith's College of Arts and Sciences - Frank L. Cubley Library (Educ)
Paul Smiths, NY 12970   Phone: (518)327-6313
                                   Theodore D. Mack, Libn.
Founded: 1946. **Staff:** Prof 2; Other 4. **Subjects:** Hotel and restaurant management, chef training, cookery, forestry, urban tree management, environmental science, forest recreation, surveying. **Holdings:** 48,000 books; 28,000 forestry pamphlets; 6342 forestry and surveying slides. **Subscriptions:** 504 journals and other serials; 8 newspapers. **Services:** Interlibrary loan; copying; library open to the public with restrictions. **Automated Operations:** Computerized ILL and cataloging. **Computerized Information Services:** OCLC. **Networks/Consortia:** Member of North Country Reference and Research Resources Council (NCRRRC). **Remarks:** FAX: (518)327-3634. **Staff:** Susan Grimm, Asst.Libn.

★ 12798 ★
Paul, Weiss, Rifkind, Wharton & Garrison - Library (Law)
1285 Avenue of the Americas   Phone: (212)729-2416
New York, NY 10019-6064   Deborah S. Panella, Mng.Libn.
Founded: 1927. **Staff:** Prof 13; Other 27. **Subjects:** Law. **Holdings:** 75,000 books; 1000 bound periodical volumes; 7500 reels of microfilm. **Subscriptions:** 600 journals and other serials; 25 newspapers. **Services:** Interlibrary loan; library not open to the public. **Automated Operations:** Computerized cataloging, acquisitions, and serials. **Computerized Information Services:** LEXIS, WESTLAW, DIALOG Information Services, PFDS Online, RLIN, BRS Information Technologies, Reuters Information Services (Canada) Limited, VU/TEXT Information Services, Dow Jones News/Retrieval, LEGI-SLATE, ELSS (Electronic Legislative Search System), DataTimes, Information America. **Remarks:** FAX: (212)373-2268. **Staff:** Michele Falkow, Asst.Libn.; Karen Botkin, Hd., Tech.Serv.; Maureen McMahon, Hd. of Ref.; Diane Rosenberg, Corp.Libn.; Maria Giaimo, Ref.Libn.; Paula Moskowitz, Ref.Libn.; Kathleen McCartin, Ref.Libn.; Darika Chonachote, Ref.Libn.; Joanne Scala, Ref.Libn.; Theresa A. O'Leary, Tax Libn.; Armando Gonzalez, ILL Libn.; Fanny L. Tibay, Cat.Libn.

Pavements & Soil Trafficability Information Analysis Center
See: **U.S. Army - Engineer Waterways Experiment Station** (16969)

Pavillon Albert-Prevost
See: **Hopital du Sacre Coeur de Montreal** (7398)

Pawtucket Memorial Hospital
See: **Memorial Hospital of Rhode Island** (10041)

★ 12799 ★
Payette Associates, Inc. - Library (Plan)
40 Isabella St.   Phone: (617)423-0070
Boston, MA 02116   Ann Collins
Founded: 1979. **Staff:** Prof 2; Other 1. **Subjects:** Architecture, interior design, landscape architecture, graphics. **Special Collections:** Healthcare Facilities; Research Laboratories. **Holdings:** 1000 books; 2000 catalogs; 500 samples; 10 VF drawers of reports and clippings; 5 drawers of prints and plans; 17,000 slides. **Subscriptions:** 80 journals and other serials. **Services:** Interlibrary loan; library open to the public upon request to librarian. **Computerized Information Services:** DIALOG Information Services, VU/ TEXT Information Services. **Remarks:** FAX: (617)482-1284. **Staff:** Bob Drake, Archv.

Bishop Payne Library
See: **Virginia Theological Seminary** (19897)

★ 12800 ★
Payne Theological Seminary - R.C. Ransom Memorial Library (Rel-Phil, Area-Ethnic)
P.O. Box 474   Phone: (513)376-2946
Wilberforce, OH 45384   J. Dale Balsbaugh, Dir. of the Lib.
Founded: 1844. **Staff:** Prof 1; Other 1. **Subjects:** Philosophy, Biblical studies, pastoral theology, doctrinal theology, black studies, African Methodist Episcopal Church history. **Special Collections:** Arno Press Black Studies Program - The American Negro, His History and Literature (150 volumes). **Holdings:** 20,000 books; 500 archival materials. **Subscriptions:** 2 journals and other serials; 2 newspapers. **Services:** Interlibrary loan; copying; library open to the public. **Special Catalogs:** Union Serials List of Seminaries, every 4 years.

★ 12801 ★
Payne Whitney Psychiatric Clinic Library (Med)
New York Hospital-Cornell University Medical College
525 E. 68th St.   Phone: (212)746-3795
New York, NY 10021   Patricia Tomasulo, Dept.Libn.
Staff: Prof 1; Other 2. **Subjects:** Psychiatry, psychology, behavioral sciences. **Special Collections:** History of psychiatry; Archives of Psychiatry. **Holdings:** 21,000 volumes; 125 video cassettes; 50 audio cassettes. **Subscriptions:** 140 journals and other serials. **Services:** Interlibrary loan. **Automated Operations:** Computerized public access catalog, cataloging, acquisitions, serials, and circulation. **Computerized Information Services:** miniMEDLINE; CD-ROM (MEDLINE, Excerpta Medica: Psychiatry). **Networks/Consortia:** Member of Medical Library Center of New York (MLCNY), New York Metropolitan Reference and Research Library Agency. **Publications:** Acquisitions List, bimonthly; Department Bibliography, annual. **Special Catalogs:** Media Catalog. **Remarks:** FAX: (212)746-8934.

Daniel Carroll Payson Medical Library
See: **North Shore University Hospital** (11950)

★ 12802 ★
PCL-Braun-Simons Ltd. - PBS Library
400-401 9th Ave., S.W.
Golf Canada Sq. W. Tower, 4th Fl.
Calgary, AB, Canada T2P 3C5
Subjects: Engineering, project management, construction, procurement. **Special Collections:** Engineering standards (2000). **Holdings:** 500 books; 200 periodical volumes. **Remarks:** Currently inactive.

Pea Ridge National Military Park
See: **U.S. Natl. Park Service** (17762)

Peabody Conservatory of Music
See: **Johns Hopkins University** (8424)

Frances W. Peabody Research Library
See: **Greater Portland Landmarks, Inc.** (6709)

George Peabody Collection
See: **Johns Hopkins University - Milton S. Eisenhower Library** (8420)

★ 12803 ★
George Peabody College for Teachers - Kennedy Center - Materials Center
Box 62
Nashville, TN 37203
Defunct.

★ 12804 ★
Peabody Institute Library - Danvers Archival Center (Hist)
15 Sylvan St.   Phone: (508)774-0554
Danvers, MA 01923   Richard B. Trask, Town Archv.
Founded: 1972. **Staff:** Prof 1; Other 1. **Subjects:** History and development of Danvers and Salem Village, New England witchcraft. **Special Collections:** Ellerton J. Brehaut Witchcraft Collection (1000 items); Parker Pillsbury Anti-Slavery Collection (179 volumes). **Holdings:** 5000 books; 300 bound periodical volumes; 250,000 manuscript materials; 300 reels of microfilm; 500 maps; 10,000 photographs; 250 audiotapes; 50 magnetic tapes. **Subscriptions:** 10 journals and other serials. **Services:** Center open to the public. **Special Catalogs:** Catalogs of witchcraft, manuscripts, history.

Peabody Library
See: **Miami University** (10269)

★ 12805 ★
Peabody Museum of Salem - Phillips Library (Hist)
East India Square   Phone: (508)745-1876
Salem, MA 01970-1682   John Koza
Founded: 1799. **Staff:** Prof 1; Other 13. **Subjects:** Maritime history, ethnology of non-European peoples, natural history of Essex County, Asian export art. **Holdings:** 80,000 volumes; 1100 linear feet of logbooks, account books, shipping papers. **Subscriptions:** 200 journals and other serials. **Services:** Copying; library open to the public.

★ 12806 ★
Robert S. Peabody Museum for Archeology - Library (Soc Sci)
Phillips Academy   Phone: (508)749-4490
Andover, MA 01810   James W. Bradley, Dir.
Staff: Prof 1; Other 1. **Subjects:** North American archeology and ethnography, especially Eastern North America; general anthropology. **Holdings:** 4400 books; 100 bound periodical volumes; 5000 reprints and pamphlets. **Services:** Library open to the public. **Publications:** Papers of the Robert S. Peabody Foundation for Archeology, irregular; first annual report of the Coxcatlan Project; Prehistory of the Ayacucho Basin, Peru series; First Annual Report of the Belize Archaic Archaeological Reconnaissance.

Peace Corps
See: **U.S. Peace Corps** (17919)

★ 12807 ★
Peace River Centennial Museum - Archives (Hist)
10302 99 St.   Phone: (403)624-4261
Peace River, AB, Canada T8S 1K1   Kirstin Clausen, Dir./Cur.
Founded: 1967. **Staff:** Prof 1; Other 2. **Subjects:** Pioneers, fur trade, river and rail transportation, petroleum industry, native culture. **Special Collections:** Local area histories (25); local photograph negatives (300); pre-1930 fictional monographs. **Holdings:** 200 books; 20 bound periodical volumes; 8 VF drawers of manuscripts and documents; 42 reels of microfilm; 500 photograph negatives; 3 reels of 16mm film; 52 audio cassettes; 1476 slides. **Subscriptions:** 10 journals and other serials. **Services:** Copying; archives open to the public with restrictions. **Publications:** Programme calendar, monthly - to special mailing list. **Special Catalogs:** Artifacts catalog. **Remarks:** FAX: (403)624-4664. Maintained by the Town of Peace River and Sir Alexander Mackenzie Historical Society.

★ 12808 ★
PeaceSmiths Social Change Library (Soc Sci)
90 Pennsylvania Ave.   Phone: (516)798-0778
Massapequa, NY 11758   David Hacker, Libn.
Remarks: No further information was supplied by respondent.

Peale Museum
See: **Baltimore City Life Museums** (1445)

Pearce Memorial Library and Media Center
See: **Monte Vista Christian Church** (10660)

★ 12809 ★
Pearl Harbor Survivors Association - Archives (Hist)
1106 Maplewood Ave.   Phone: (603)436-5835
Portsmouth, NH 03801   Mr. W.M. Cleveland, Hist.
Founded: 1972. **Staff:** 1. **Subjects:** Japanese attack on Pearl Harbor. **Special Collections:** Nameplate from plane shot down December 7, 1941; pieces from planes; expended ammunition. **Holdings:** Books; 5 cubic feet of records, reports, artifacts; 10 photograph albums; administrative and historical records, 1962-1986. **Services:** Copying; archives open to the public with restrictions. **Publications:** Pearl Harbor Gram, quarterly; newsletter.

Milton A. Pearl Environmental Law Library
See: **Lewis and Clark Law School - Northwestern School of Law** (9076)

A.S. Pearse Memorial Library
See: **Duke University - Marine Laboratory** (5044)

George Pearson Centre
See: **British Columbia Rehabilitation Society - G.F. Strong Centre** (2172)

★ 12810 ★
Lester B. Pearson College of the Pacific - Norman McKee Lang Library (Hist)
RR 1   Phone: (604)478-5591
Victoria, BC, Canada V9B 5T7   Margaret McAvity, Libn.
Founded: 1974. **Staff:** Prof 1; Other 1. **Special Collections:** Personal library of the late Lester B. Pearson (history and international affairs; 1000 titles); videotape collection of lectures by Dr. Giovanni Costigan, professor emeritus at University of Washington (history and international relations; 50 videotapes). **Holdings:** 14,000 books; 1000 phonograph records; 50 cassettes; 900 slides; 2500 microfiche; 150 video cassettes; 50 compact discs. **Subscriptions:** 100 journals and other serials; 10 newspapers. **Services:** Interlibrary loan; copying; SDI; library open to the public by appointment. **Computerized Information Services:** Electronic mail. **Remarks:** Affiliated with the United World Colleges. FAX: (604)478-6421. Telex: 049 7488.

Pearson Library
See: **California Lutheran University** (2493)

★ 12811 ★
Peckar & Abramson - Library (Law)
70 Grand Ave.   Phone: (201)343-3434
River Edge, NJ 07661   Edmund Dabkowski, Libn.
Founded: 1978. **Staff:** Prof 1. **Subjects:** Law - construction, contract. **Holdings:** 5500 books; 200 bound periodical volumes; 900 microfiche. **Subscriptions:** 65 journals and other serials; 4 newspapers. **Services:** Interlibrary loan; library not open to the public. **Computerized Information Services:** LEXIS. **Remarks:** FAX: (201)343-6306.

★ 12812 ★
Pee Dee AHEC Health Sciences Library (Med)
McLeod Regional Medical Center
555 E. Cheves St.   Phone: (803)667-2275
Florence, SC 29501   Lillian Fisher, Reg.Libn.
Founded: 1975. **Staff:** Prof 1; Other 1. **Subjects:** Clinical medicine, nursing, allied health sciences, competency-based nursing orientation, management. **Holdings:** 1565 books; 1587 bound periodical volumes; 1181 AV programs. **Subscriptions:** 317 journals and other serials. **Services:** Interlibrary loan; copying; SDI; library open to professional health personnel, students, and community members. **Automated Operations:** Computerized cataloging. **Computerized Information Services:** MEDLARS, BRS Information Technologies; SCHIN. Performs searches on fee basis. **Networks/Consortia:** Member of South Carolina Health Information Network (SCHIN). **Publications:** Serials List; Media Holdings. **Special Indexes:** Subject index to periodicals. **Remarks:** FAX: (803)667-2272. **Formerly:** Pee Dee Area Health Education Center Library.

★ 12813 ★
Peel Board of Education - J.A. Turner Professional Library (Educ)
5650 Hurontario St.   Phone: (416)890-1099
Mississauga, ON, Canada L5R 1C6   Catherine Wilkins, Prof.Libn.
Founded: 1969. **Staff:** Prof 1; Other 3. **Subjects:** Education, child psychology, sociology, educational research, educational administration. **Special Collections:** Peel curriculum collection; Ontario Ministry of Education documents. **Holdings:** 2000 books; 1000 other cataloged items. **Subscriptions:** 470 journals and other serials. **Services:** Interlibrary loan; library open to the public for reference use only. **Automated Operations:** Computerized public access catalog, cataloging, serials, and circulation. **Computerized Information Services:** BRS Information Technologies, DIALOG Information Services, CAN/OLE, Infomart Online, The Financial Post Information Service, WILSONLINE, Info Globe, UTLAS, Mead Data Central; CD-ROMs; Envoy 100 (electronic mail service). **Networks/Consortia:** Member of Education Libraries Sharing of Resources Network (ELSOR). **Publications:** Research Bulletin, monthly - for internal distribution only. **Remarks:** FAX: (416)890-4780. **Staff:** Shelley Andrews, Lib.Res.Sup.Spec.; Marsha Hunt, Info.Res.Techn.

Bruce Peel Special Collections Library
See: **University of Alberta - Humanities and Social Sciences Library - Bruce Peel Special Collections Library** (18196)

★ 12814 ★
Peel Regional Police Force - Library (Law)
7750 Hurontario St.   Phone: (416)453-3311
Brampton, ON, Canada L6V 3W6   Lorna Mays, Lib.Techn.
Founded: 1974. **Staff:** Prof 1. **Subjects:** Police science, Canadian law, behavioral sciences, management. **Holdings:** 2000 books; 280 bound periodical volumes. **Subscriptions:** 80 journals and other serials. **Services:** Interlibrary loan; copying; library not open to the public.

PEI Associates, Inc.
See: **International Technology Corporation** (8195)

★ 12815 ★
Peirce Junior College - Library - Special Collections (Bus-Fin)
1420 Pine St.   Phone: (215)545-6400
Philadelphia, PA 19102   Debra S. Schrammel, Dir.
Founded: 1963. **Staff:** 5. **Subjects:** Business, law. **Special Collections:** Pre-1900 business textbooks; legal collection (3400 volumes). **Holdings:** 38,000 books; 400 videotapes. **Subscriptions:** 178 journals and other serials; 6 newspapers. **Services:** Interlibrary loan; copying; collections open to local college students. **Computerized Information Services:** CD-ROM (Moody Company Data). **Staff:** Dorothy Iams, AV Libn.; Gary Shecter, Ref.

Peirce Memorial Library
See: **First Presbyterian Church of Flint** (5801)

Peking Union Medical College - Library
See: **Chinese Academy of Medical Sciences and Peking Union Medical College** (3609)

Pell Marine Science Library
See: **University of Rhode Island** (19266)

Olin Sewall Pellingill Library
See: **Vermont Institute of Natural Sciences - Library** (19804)

★ 12816 ★
Pellissippi State Technical Community College - Educational Resource Center (Educ)
Box 22990   Phone: (615)694-6517
Knoxville, TN 37933-0990   Nina McPherson, Dean, Educ.Rsrc.Ctr.
Founded: 1975. **Staff:** Prof 3; Other 4. **Subjects:** Business data processing; electronics; engineering - mechanical, electrical, construction; management; humanities; transfer programs. **Holdings:** 28,000 books; 531 bound periodical volumes; 1064 reels of microfilm; 83,121 cubic feet of microfiche. **Subscriptions:** 576 journals and other serials. **Services:** Copying; library open to the public for reference use only. **Computerized Information Services:** DIALOG Information Services, OCLC; CD-ROMs (Academic Abstracts, Applied Science & Technology Index, Wilson Business Abstracts). **Networks/Consortia:** Member of SOLINET. **Special Catalogs:** Serials Holdings List (notebook). **Remarks:** FAX: (615)694-6625; library located at 100915 Hardin Valley Rd., Knoxville, TN. **Staff:** Jane Cameron, Libn., Cat.; Peter Nerzak, Automation/Acq.

Paul Peltason Library
See: **Temple Israel** (16113)

★ 12817 ★
Pemaquid Historical Association - Harrington Meeting House - Museum (Hist)
Box 44   Phone: (207)529-5578
Round Pond, ME 04564   C. Weston Dash, Pres.
Founded: 1965. **Subjects:** Local history. **Holdings:** 100 volumes; genealogical records; pamphlets; local records and maps; hymnals; ledgers; early school books; newspapers; historical documents. **Services:** Museum open to the public on a limited schedule. **Remarks:** Museum is located at Old Harrington Rd., Pemaquid, ME, 04558.

★ 12818 ★
Pemco Aeroplex Inc. - Engineering Technical Library (Sci-Engr)
Municipal Airport
Box 2287   Phone: (205)592-0011
Birmingham, AL 35201   Melinda Holloway, Libn.
Remarks: No further information was supplied by respondent.

★ 12819 ★
Pen and Brush Inc. - Library (Hum)
16 E. Tenth St.   Phone: (212)475-3669
New York, NY 10003   Marion Andrews, Pres.
Founded: 1893. **Staff:** 2. **Subjects:** Literature, art. **Holdings:** 1200 books.

Pena Library
See: **CRSS, Inc. - Pena Library** (4451)

★ 12820 ★
Pendle Hill - Library (Rel-Phil)
Wallingford, PA 19086   Phone: (215)566-4507
                                       Yuki T. Brinton, Libn.
Founded: 1930. **Staff:** Prof 1. **Subjects:** Religion, Quakers. **Special Collections:** Quaker Collection. **Holdings:** 14,000 volumes. **Subscriptions:** 35 journals and other serials. **Services:** Interlibrary loan; library open to the public.

★ 12821 ★
Pendleton District Historical and Recreational Commission - Reference Library (Hist)
125 E. Queen St.
Box 565   Phone: (803)646-3782
Pendleton, SC 29670   Hurley Badders, Commn.Dir.
Founded: 1974. **Staff:** Prof 2; Other 1. **Subjects:** History - Pendleton district, South Carolina, U.S.; genealogy; church history; travel, tourism, and recreation; antiques and historic preservation; archeology. **Special Collections:** Anderson Cotton Mill Records (71 ledgers, 1890-1950s); Speaking of History (interviews with citizens of Anderson, Oconee, and Pickens counties; 35 oral history tapes). **Holdings:** 800 books; 200 boxes of clippings, unbound reports, other cataloged items; 90 books and documents on microfilm; 10 drawers of photographs; 2 drawers of family histories; 75 maps; 90 ledgers. **Subscriptions:** 19 journals and other serials. **Services:** Copying; library open to the public for reference use only. **Special Indexes:** Index to names mentioned in library materials (card). **Remarks:** FAX: (803)646-2506. **Staff:** Donna Roper, Asst.Dir.

Charlotte and Paul Penfield Library
See: **Polk Museum of Art - Charlotte and Paul Penfield Library** (13191)

Penfield Library
See: **State University College at Oswego** (15711)

★ 12822 ★
Peninsula Community Foundation - Funding Information Library (Bus-Fin)
1700 S. El Camino Real, No.301   Phone: (415)358-9392
San Mateo, CA 94402   Georgia W. McDaniel, Libn.
Staff: Prof 1. **Subjects:** Funding sources and management assistance for nonprofit organizations; fundraising activities; proposal writing; nonprofit careers. **Holdings:** 600 books; 460 foundation annual reports; 9 fundraising videotapes. **Subscriptions:** 50 journals and other serials; 10 newspapers. **Services:** Library open to the public. **Publications:** Newsletter, quarterly - to organizations upon request. **Remarks:** FAX: (415)358-9817.

★ 12823 ★
Peninsula Conservation Foundation - Library of the Environment (Env-Cons)
2448 Watson Ct.   Phone: (415)494-9301
Palo Alto, CA 94303   Connie S. Sutton, Libn.
Founded: 1971. **Staff:** Prof 1. **Subjects:** Conservation, ecology, energy, wildlife and endangered species, backpacking and trails, pollution control. **Special Collections:** Environmental Volunteers Collection; Audubon Collection (250); Conservation Collection (2000); Trails Collection (300 books; 4 VF drawers). **Holdings:** 6000 books; 636 bound periodical volumes; 50 VF drawers; 2000 maps. **Subscriptions:** 35 journals and other serials; 5 newspapers. **Services:** Interlibrary loan; copying; library open to the public. **Networks/Consortia:** Member of Energy Librarians of the Bay Area, South Bay Cooperative Library System (SBCLS). **Publications:** The Center View, quarterly - to members or on exchange. **Special Indexes:** The Harbinger File.

★ 12824 ★
Peninsula Daily News - Library (Publ)
305 W. First
P.O. Box 1330   Phone: (206)452-2345
Port Angeles, WA 98362   Geri Zanon
Subjects: Newspaper reference topics. **Holdings:** 75 years of microfilm.

★ 12825 ★
Peninsula Hospital Center - Medical Library (Med)
51-15 Beach Channel Dr.   Phone: (718)945-7100
Far Rockaway, NY 11691   Pauila Green, Dir.
Founded: 1970. **Staff:** Prof 1; Other 1. **Subjects:** Medicine, surgery, nursing, dentistry, podiatry, orthopedics. **Holdings:** 1182 books; 2150 bound periodical volumes; 100 videocassettes; 228 audiocassettes. **Subscriptions:** 105 journals and other serials. **Services:** Interlibrary loan; copying; library open to the public for reference use only. **Computerized Information Services:** MEDLARS; DOCLINE (electronic mail service). **Networks/Consortia:** Member of Brooklyn-Queens-Staten Island Health Sciences Librarians (BQSI), Medical & Scientific Libraries of Long Island (MEDLI), BHSL.

★ 12826 ★
Peninsula Library and Historical Society (Hist)
6105 Riverview Rd.
P.O. Box 236   Phone: (216)657-2291
Peninsula, OH 44264   Edith M. Minns, Libn.
Founded: 1943. **Staff:** Prof 3; Other 5. **Subjects:** History, biography, literature, arts. **Special Collections:** Local history (2000 volumes; manuscripts; clippings; maps; pictures; cemetery records). **Holdings:** 35,000 books; 162 bound periodical volumes; 1050 AV programs; depository for U.S. Army Corps of Engineer reports; 24 VF drawers of pamphlets and clippings; 150 maps. **Subscriptions:** 103 journals and other serials; 5 newspapers. **Services:** Interlibrary loan; copying; library open to the public. **Publications:** Newsletter, monthly - local distribution. **Special Indexes:** Index to Local History (card). **Remarks:** FAX: (216)657-2311. **Staff:** Randolph Bergdorf, Archv.; Judy Ertel, Ch.Libn./Prog.

★ 12827 ★
Peninsula Temple Beth El - Library (Rel-Phil)
1700 Alameda de Las Pulgas   Phone: (415)341-7701
San Mateo, CA 94403   Elayne L. Kane, Lib.Chm.
Founded: 1961. **Staff:** Prof 2; Other 7. **Subjects:** Philosophy of Judaism; history of Judaism and the Jewish religion; fiction of Jewish content or by Jewish authors; Israel - description and travel; history of the Jews in the U.S. **Special Collections:** Biographies of Jewish leaders; children and young adult collection. **Holdings:** 5000 books; periodicals; cassettes; records. **Subscriptions:** 3 journals and other serials, 3 newspapers. **Services:** Library open to the public.

★ 12828 ★
Annie Penn Memorial Hospital - Medical Library (Med)
618 S. Main St.   Phone: (919)349-8461
Reidsville, NC 27320   Sandra King, Libn.
Staff: Prof 1. **Subjects:** Medicine, nursing, allied health sciences. **Holdings:** 500 books. **Subscriptions:** 43 journals and other serials. **Services:** Interlibrary loan; library not open to the public.

★ 12829 ★
Penn Kem, Inc. - Library
341 Adams St.   Phone: (914)241-4777
Bedford Hills, NY 10507   Janet Tretsch, Libn.
Remarks: FAX: (914)241-4842. No further information was supplied by respondent.

★ 12830 ★
Penn Mutual Life Insurance Company - Law Library (Law, Bus-Fin)
119 Rock Rd.   Phone: (215)956-7752
Horsham, PA 19044   Wouter Keesing, Assoc.Gen.Couns.
Founded: 1940. **Staff:** 1. **Subjects:** Insurance, law. **Holdings:** 15,000 books; 30 bound periodical volumes. **Subscriptions:** 38 journals and other serials; 3 newspapers. **Services:** Library not open to the public. **Computerized Information Services:** LEXIS, NEXIS. **Remarks:** FAX: (215)956-7750.

★ 12831 ★
Penn Mutual Life Insurance Company - Shared Resource Center (Comp Sci)
Penn Mutual Independence Place
600 Dresher Rd.   Phone: (215)956-8178
Horsham, PA 19044   Sheri C. Reinhart, Supv./Libn.
Founded: 1984. **Staff:** Prof 1; Other 1. **Subjects:** Microcomputers, mainframes, management training and development, insurance, business. **Holdings:** 300 books; 350 manuals; 75 computer programs; 120 video cassettes; 100 telephone books. **Subscriptions:** 45 journals and other serials. **Services:** Center not open to the public. **Automated Operations:** Computerized cataloging and circulation. **Computerized Information Services:** Internal database; Ethernet (electronic mail service). **Publications:** Micro News (newsletter), monthly.

★ 12832 ★
William Penn College - Wilcox Library - Special Collections (Rel-Phil)
Oskaloosa, IA 52577   Phone: (515)673-1096
                                           Julie Hansen, Dir.
Staff: Prof 2.5; Other 3. **Subjects:** Quakers - history, biography, genealogy. **Holdings:** 2038 books; 350 bound periodical volumes; cemetery records on microfilm; clippings; scrapbooks; pictures. **Subscriptions:** 22 journals and other serials. **Services:** Interlibrary loan; copying; collections open to the public. **Automated Operations:** Computerized public access catalog, circulation, and indexing. **Computerized Information Services:** OCLC. **Networks/Consortia:** Member of Bibliographical Center for Research, Rocky Mountain Region, Inc. (BCR). **Publications:** William Penn College: A Product and a Producer, 1973. **Remarks:** FAX: (515)673-1098. **Staff:** Jeff Beck, Ref.; Marion Rains, Libn. Emeritus; Jim Krutson, Tech.Serv.

George Pennal Library
See: St. Joseph's Health Centre (14396)

★ 12833 ★
J.C. Penney Company, Inc. - Law Library (Law, Bus-Fin)
Box 659000   Phone: (214)591-1284
Dallas, TX 75265-9000   Kaethryn Luetkemeyer, Law Libn.
Staff: Prof 1; Other 2. **Subjects:** Law, business. **Holdings:** 20,000 books; 400 bound periodical volumes; 2800 volumes of West's reporters on ultrafiche. **Subscriptions:** 200 journals and other serials; 16 newspapers. **Services:** Interlibrary loan; library not open to the public. **Computerized Information Services:** WESTLAW, LEXIS, DIALOG Information Services.

★ 12834 ★
Pennie & Edmonds - Law Library (Law)
1155 Ave. of the Americas   Phone: (212)790-9090
New York, NY 10036   Mary Gilligan, Libn.
Founded: 1884. **Staff:** Prof 2; Other 2. **Subjects:** Law - patent, copyright, trademark; biotechnology; chemistry; electronics. **Special Collections:** Foreign Collection (intellectual property). **Holdings:** 20,000 books; 100 bound periodical volumes; videotapes. **Subscriptions:** 135 serials; 10 newspapers. **Services:** Interlibrary loan (limited); library not open to the public. **Computerized Information Services:** DIALOG Information Services, WESTLAW, LEXIS, PFDS Online, VU/TEXT Information Services, Questel, IMSMARQ, CompuMark, Information America, STN International, DataTimes. **Publications:** Library Acquisitions Bulletin, quarterly - for internal distribution only; newsletter, irregular. **Remarks:** FAX: (212)869-8864; 869-9741. Telex: 66141 PENNIE. **Staff:** Daniel J. Doran, Asst.Libn.

Rev. Dr. George Penniman Genealogical Library
See: Braintree Historical Society - Library (2066)

★ 12835 ★
Pennock Hospital - Medical Library (Med)
1009 W. Green St.   Phone: (616)945-3451
Hastings, MI 49058   Pam Nail, Info.Spec.
Staff: 1. **Subjects:** Medicine, nursing, pharmacy, allied health sciences. **Holdings:** 750 books. **Subscriptions:** 125 journals and other serials. **Services:** Interlibrary loan; copying; library open to the public by appointment. **Computerized Information Services:** MEDLARS, DIALOG Information Services. Performs searches on fee basis. **Networks/Consortia:** Member of Capital Area Library Network (Calnet), Michigan Library Consortium (MLC), Michigan Health Sciences Libraries Association (MHSLA). **Remarks:** FAX: (616)945-3035.

★ 12836 ★
Pennsylvania Academy of the Fine Arts - Library (Art)
1301 Cherry St.   Phone: (215)972-7600
Philadelphia, PA 19107   Marietta P. Boyer, Libn.
Founded: 1805. **Staff:** Prof 1. **Subjects:** Art history, painting, sculpture, graphics, with concentration on American art. **Holdings:** 12,000 books; 60 VF drawers of artists clippings; 20 VF drawers of subject-idea clippings. **Subscriptions:** 70 journals and other serials. **Services:** Interlibrary loan; copying; library open to the public for reference use only. **Remarks:** FAX: (215)569-0153.

★ 12837 ★
Pennsylvania Board of Probation and Parole - Library (Law)
3101 N. Front St.
P.O. Box 1661   Phone: (717)787-6297
Harrisburg, PA 17105-1661   David Withers, Lib.Dir.
Holdings: 285 books. **Services:** Library not open to the public.

★ 12838 ★
Pennsylvania College of Optometry - Albert Fitch Memorial Library (Med)
1200 W. Godfrey Ave.   Phone: (215)276-6270
Philadelphia, PA 19141   Marita J. Krivda, Lib.Dir.
Staff: Prof 1; Other 3. **Subjects:** Optometry, ophthalmology, optics theory, ophthalmic optics, contact lenses, low vision rehabilitation. **Special Collections:** Visual Science Rare Book Collection, 17th-19th centuries (250 books); eye spectacles, turn of the century ophthalmic instruments, and ophthalmoscopes. **Holdings:** 6112 books; 6500 bound periodical volumes; 2 VF drawers of old instruments pamphlets; 50 video cassettes; 800 audio cassettes; 6640 slides. **Subscriptions:** 320 journals and other serials. **Services:** Interlibrary loan; copying; library open to the public with restrictions. **Computerized Information Services:** MEDLARS, OCLC, BRS Information Technologies. Performs searches on fee basis. **Networks/Consortia:** Member of National Network of Libraries of Medicine - Middle Atlantic Region, PALINET, Association of Visual Science Librarians (AVSL). **Publications:** Acquisitions list. **Special Indexes:** Ophthalmic Literature. **Remarks:** FAX: (215)276-6081.

★ 12839 ★
Pennsylvania College of Podiatric Medicine - Center for the History of Foot Care and Footwear (Med)
Eighth St. & Race   Phone: (215)629-0300
Philadelphia, PA 19107   Lisabeth M. Holloway, Dir.
Staff: Prof 2. **Subjects:** Podiatric medicine, anatomy and diseases of the foot, podiatry/chiropody as a profession, ethnic footwear. **Holdings:** 1800 books; 200 bound periodical volumes; 130 linear feet of archival materials; 700 other cataloged items; 750-item footwear collection. **Services:** Copying; center open to the public for reference use only. **Publications:** The ClioPedic Items (newsletter), irregular - to members; A Fast Pace Forward: Chronicles of American Podiatry (1987); Index of early practitioners in U.S. (prior to 1907).

★ 12840 ★
Pennsylvania College of Podiatric Medicine - Charles E. Krausz Library (Med)
Eighth St. & Race   Phone: (215)629-0300
Philadelphia, PA 19107   Linda C. Stanley, Coll.Libn.
Founded: 1962. **Staff:** Prof 2; Other 2. **Subjects:** Podiatry, foot diseases, orthopedics, sports medicine, dermatology, medicine. **Holdings:** 11,000 books; 10,500 bound periodical volumes; 16 VF drawers of reprints of articles pertaining to the foot; 2500 pamphlets on medical subjects; 1000 video cassettes; 101 films; 4 microfiche drawers; 2000 slides. **Subscriptions:** 375 journals and other serials. **Services:** Interlibrary loan; copying; SDI; library open to the public for reference use only. **Automated Operations:** DataTrek. **Computerized Information Services:** BRS Information Technologies, DIALOG Information Services; CD-ROM (MEDLINE); DOCLINE (electronic mail service). Performs searches on fee basis. **Networks/Consortia:** Member of National Network of Libraries of Medicine - Middle Atlantic Region, Delaware Valley Information Consortium (DEVIC), BHSL, Health Sciences Libraries Consortium (HSLC). **Publications:** Foot Notes (newsletter); list of new acquisitions, bimonthly; periodical holdings list. **Remarks:** FAX: (215)629-1622. **Staff:** Frances E. Peters, Ser.Libn.

★ 12841 ★
Pennsylvania Dutch Folk Culture Society, Inc. - Baver Memorial Library (Hist)
Lenhartsville, PA 19534   Phone: (215)562-4803
                     Florence Baver, Pres.
Founded: 1965. **Staff:** Prof 1. **Subjects:** Genealogy, folklore, local history. **Holdings:** 1000 books; 200 bound periodical volumes; pamphlets; photographs; diaries; tape recordings; clippings; postcards; church records. **Services:** Copying; library open to the public. **Publications:** Pennsylvania Dutch News & Views, semiannual. **Remarks:** FAX: (215)682-7432.

★ 12842 ★
Pennsylvania Economy League - Eastern Division - Library (Soc Sci, Bus-Fin)
1211 Chestnut St., Suite 600   Phone: (215)864-9562
Philadelphia, PA 19107-4116   Ellen Brennan, Libn.
Founded: 1932. **Staff:** Prof 1. **Subjects:** Public administration, charters and constitutions, city government, municipal finance. **Holdings:** 16,000 volumes. **Services:** Interlibrary loan; copying; library open to the public for reference use only. **Remarks:** FAX: (215)864-9921.

★ 12843 ★
Pennsylvania Economy League - Western Division - Library (Soc Sci)
Two Gateway Center   Phone: (412)471-1477
Pittsburgh, PA 15222   Judith A. Eves, Libn.
Founded: 1936. **Staff:** Prof 1. **Subjects:** State and local government, finance, taxation, public personnel. **Holdings:** 1025 volumes; 2500 pamphlets; 24 VF drawers of financial reports and news clippings. **Subscriptions:** 160 journals and other serials; 3 newspapers. **Services:** Copying; library open to the public with restrictions. **Computerized Information Services:** Internal database. **Remarks:** FAX: (412)471-7080.

★ 12844 ★
Pennsylvania Electric Company - Technical Libraries (Energy)
1001 Broad St.   Phone: (814)533-8101
Johnstown, PA 15906-2437   Joseph J. Richnavsky, Libn.
Founded: 1988. **Staff:** Prof 1; Other 2. **Subjects:** Fossil fuel generation, electric transmission and distribution, environmental affairs, utility-based engineering, electric utility business. **Holdings:** 5289 books; Electric Power Research Institute (EPRI) microfiche. **Subscriptions:** 87 journals and other serials. **Services:** Copying; libraries open to public utility companies only. **Computerized Information Services:** CARIRS (internal database). **Publications:** Newsletter - for internal distribution only. **Remarks:** FAX: (814)533-8591.

★ 12845 ★
Pennsylvania Environmental Council - Library (Env-Cons)
1211 Chestnut St., Suite 900   Phone: (215)563-0250
Philadelphia, PA 19107   Lori Greenberg, Res.Assoc.
Founded: 1970. **Subjects:** Solid waste and recycling, energy issues, water issues, hazardous waste, air pollution. **Holdings:** 100 books; 50 reports. **Subscriptions:** 10 journals and other serials; 2 newspapers. **Services:** Copying; library open to the public by appointment. **Remarks:** FAX: (215)563-0528. Toll-free telephone number(s): (800)322-9214 (Pennsylvania only).

★ 12846 ★
Pennsylvania Horticultural Society - Library (Biol Sci, Agri)
325 Walnut St.   Phone: (215)625-8261
Philadelphia, PA 19106-2777   Janet Evans, Libn.
Founded: 1827. **Staff:** Prof 2; Other 3. **Subjects:** Ornamental horticulture, botany, landscape design, garden history. **Special Collections:** Rare herbals and gardening books; 19th century horticulture; Pennsylvania horticulture. **Holdings:** 14,000 books; 4000 bound periodical volumes; 16 VF drawers of horticultural information; 1000 slides; 100 videotapes on gardening. **Subscriptions:** 200 journals and other serials. **Services:** Interlibrary loan; copying; slide sets available for rent; Horticulture Hotline (telephone plant information service); library open to the public for reference use only. **Computerized Information Services:** OCLC. **Networks/Consortia:** Member of PALINET. **Special Catalogs:** Early and contemporary seed and nursery catalogs (card). **Remarks:** FAX: (215)625-8288. **Staff:** Sandra K. Myers, Cat.; Peggy D. Grady, Asst.Libn.; Lillian Greenberg, Cons.

★12847★

Pennsylvania Hospital - Department for Sick and Injured - Historical Library (Med)
Eighth & Spruce Sts.   Phone: (215)829-3998
Philadelphia, PA 19107   Caroline Morris, Dir. of Libs.
Founded: 1761. **Staff:** 1. **Subjects:** Pre-1800 chemistry, physics, botany, zoology, natural history, materia medica; medicine and surgery prior to 1940. **Special Collections:** Hospital archives and case reports; early M.D. dissertations. **Holdings:** 8500 books; 4464 bound periodical volumes. **Services:** Library open to the public by appointment requested in writing. **Remarks:** FAX: (215)829-7155.

★12848★

Pennsylvania Hospital - Department for Sick and Injured - Medical Library (Med)
Eighth & Spruce Sts.   Phone: (215)829-3998
Philadelphia, PA 19107   Caroline Morris, Dir. of Libs.
Founded: 1940. **Staff:** Prof 3; Other 2. **Subjects:** Medicine, nursing, allied health sciences. **Holdings:** 2367 books; 16,615 bound periodical volumes; 3700 other cataloged items; 2 VF drawers. **Subscriptions:** 595 journals and other serials. **Services:** Interlibrary loan; copying (limited); library open to the public for reference use only. **Computerized Information Services:** BRS Information Technologies. **Networks/Consortia:** Member of Health Sciences Libraries Consortium (HSLC), Medical Library Center of New York (MLCNY). **Remarks:** Includes holdings of School of Nursing - Lydia Jane Clark Library. FAX: (215)829-3291. **Also Known As:** Nemser-Scarf Reading Room. **Staff:** Barbara Bernoff Cavanaugh; Margaret Halvey Gingle.

Pennsylvania Industrial Arts Association Archives
See: **Millersville University (10403)**

★12849★

Pennsylvania Institute of Technology - Library (Sci-Engr)
800 Manchester Ave.   Phone: (215)565-7900
Media, PA 19063   Ms. Lenore Bushlin, Libn.
Staff: Prof 1; Other 1. **Subjects:** Electronics, computers, architecture, civil and mechanical engineering, office technology. **Holdings:** 10,900 books; 10 boxes of pamphlets. **Subscriptions:** 148 journals and other serials. **Services:** Interlibrary loan; copying; library open to the public for reference use only. **Publications:** List of Recently Processed Books, quarterly - to faculty, staff, and students. **Remarks:** FAX: (215)565-7909.

★12850★

Pennsylvania Intergovernmental Council - Library (Soc Sci)
Box 11880   Phone: (717)783-3700
Harrisburg, PA 17108   Karen L. Gingrich
Holdings: 1200 books; intergovernmental publications; reports; other materials. **Services:** Library not open to the public. **Computerized Information Services:** Internal database. **Remarks:** FAX: (717)772-3694.

★12851★

Pennsylvania Legal Services Center - Library (Law)
118 Locust St.
Harrisburg, PA 17101   Phone: (717)236-9486
Subjects: Law. **Remarks:** No further information was supplied by respondent.

Pennsylvania Lumber Museum
See: **Pennsylvania (State) Historical & Museum Commission (12881)**

★12852★

Pennsylvania Public Utility Commission - Library (Energy)
Box 3265   Phone: (717)787-4466
Harrisburg, PA 17120   William M. Smith, Libn.
Staff: Prof 1. **Subjects:** Public utility law, energy conservation, economics, transportation, coal, oil, gas technology. **Holdings:** 6500 books; 204 bound periodical volumes; 3100 unbound reports; 4 VF drawers; 16 sets of loose-leaf reporters. **Subscriptions:** 118 journals and other serials. **Services:** Interlibrary loan; copying; library open to the public for reference use only. **Computerized Information Services:** LEXIS, DIALOG Information Services. **Remarks:** FAX: (717)787-4193.

★12853★

Pennsylvania Resources and Information Center for Special Education (Educ)
200 Anderson Rd.   Phone: (215)265-7321
King of Prussia, PA 19406   Dr. James B. Duffey, Dir.
Staff: Prof 6; Other 2. **Subjects:** Education of exceptional students. **Special Collections:** Publishers and supply catalogs (12 VF drawers). **Holdings:** 9000 books; tests; curriculum guides; special education dissertations on microfiche; ERIC indexes and microfiche. **Subscriptions:** 425 journals and other serials; 200 newsletters. **Services:** Center open to the public for reference use only. **Computerized Information Services:** DIALOG Information Services, BRS Information Technologies. **Publications:** PRISE, 5/year. **Remarks:** Toll-free telephone number(s): (800)441-3215 (in Pennsylvania). Holdings are shared with Eastern Instructional Support Center.

★12854★

Pennsylvania School for the Deaf - Library (Educ)
100 W. School House Lane   Phone: (215)951-4743
Philadelphia, PA 19144   Judith Finestone, Libn.
Staff: Prof 1; Other 2. **Subjects:** Deafness, children's literature. **Holdings:** 13,000 books; 90 bound periodical volumes. **Subscriptions:** 50 journals and other serials; 5 newspapers. **Services:** Interlibrary loan; library open to the public for reference use only. **Automated Operations:** Computerized cataloging.

Pennsylvania Sociological Association Archives
See: **Millersville University (10403)**

★12855★

Pennsylvania State Auditor General - Law Library (Law)
Finance Bldg., Rm. 224   Phone: (717)787-4546
Harrisburg, PA 17120   Paul Yatron, Lib.Dir.
Subjects: Law. **Remarks:** No further information was supplied by respondent.

★12856★

(Pennsylvania State) Commonwealth Court of Pennsylvania - Law Library (Law)
South Office Bldg., Rm. 603   Phone: (717)787-1940
Harrisburg, PA 17120   Mary Rinesmith, Lib.Dir.
Subjects: Law. **Services:** Library not open to the public. **Remarks:** FAX: (717)787-7427.

★12857★

Pennsylvania (State) Community Affairs Department - Office of Legal Services - Law Library (Law)
334 Forum Bldg.   Phone: (717)783-8027
Harrisburg, PA 17120   Patricia Steele, Libn.
Subjects: Law. **Holdings:** Figures not available. **Services:** Library not open to the public.

★12858★

Pennsylvania (State) Department of Education - State Library of Pennsylvania (Info Sci)
Box 1601   Phone: (717)787-2646
Harrisburg, PA 17105   Sara Parker, Commnr. of Libs.
Founded: 1745. **Staff:** Prof 35; Other 43. **Subjects:** Government, law, education, public welfare and administration, Pennsylvania history and biography, Central Pennsylvania genealogy, social and behavioral science, economics, library science. **Special Collections:** Early Pennsylvania Imprints; Colonial Assembly Collection. **Holdings:** 985,338 books; 900,000 federal and Pennsylvania government publications; 2.4 million microforms, including Congressional Information Service and American Statistics Index microfiche series; Newsbank, 1977 to present; ERIC microfiche. **Subscriptions:** 4097 journals and other serials; 171 newspapers. **Services:** Interlibrary loan; copying; library open to the public. **Automated Operations:** Computerized public access catalog, cataloging, acquisitions, serials, and circulation (NOTIS). **Computerized Information Services:** DIALOG Information Services, BRS Information Technologies, LEXIS, VU/TEXT Information Services, DataTimes, WILSONLINE; ALANET,

BITNET (electronic mail services). Performs LEXIS searches on a fee basis. Contact Person: Susan Payne, Online Ref.Libn., 783-5950. **Networks/ Consortia:** Member of PALINET, Interlibrary Delivery Service of Pennsylvania (IDS), Associated College Libraries of Central Pennsylvania (ACLCP). **Publications:** Directory-Pennsylvania Libraries, annual; Pennsylvania Public Library Statistics, annual. **Special Catalogs:** Pennsylvania Imprints, 1689-1789. **Remarks:** FAX: (717)783-2070 (library); 783-5420 (resource center). Electronic mail address(es): ALA0806 (ALANET); 00LIBRARY@PSUPEN (BITNET). **Staff:** David R. Hoffman, Dir., Lib.Serv.Div.; Ruth Coble, Asst.Dir., Tech.Coll.Serv.; Alice L. Lubrecht, Asst.Dir., Pub.Serv.; Gary Wolfe, Dir., Lib.Dev.Div.; Elizabeth Ann Funk, Asst.Dir., Advisory Serv.; Barbara Cole, Adm., Subsidies & Grants; Doris M. Epler, Dir., Sch.Lib. Media Serv.Div.; Evelyn Werner, Asst.Dir., Rsrc.Ctr.; Margaret Goodlin, Asst.Dir., Sch.Lib. & Network Serv.

★ 12859 ★

Pennsylvania (State) Department of Environmental Resources - Bureau of Topographic & Geologic Survey Library (Geog-Map)
916 Executive House Apts.
Second & Chestnut Sts.　　　　　Phone: (717)783-8077
Harrisburg, PA 17120　　　　　　Sandra Blust, Libn.
Founded: 1854. **Staff:** Prof 1; Other 1. **Subjects:** Geology, geography. **Special Collections:** Maps Collection; aerial photographs of Pennsylvania. **Holdings:** 5500 books; 7800 bound periodical volumes; 5000 government publications; 150 unpublished manuscripts; 200 dissertations on Pennsylvania geology, hardcopy and microfilm. **Subscriptions:** 83 journals and other serials. **Services:** Interlibrary loan; copying; library open to the public for reference use only. **Computerized Information Services:** GeoRef (Geological Reference File), DIALOG Information Services.

★ 12860 ★

Pennsylvania (State) Department of Environmental Resources - Environmental Protection Technical Reference Library (Env-Cons)
Fulton Bldg., Basement
Box 2063
Harrisburg, PA 17105-2063　　　　Phone: (717)787-9647
Founded: 1971. **Staff:** 1. **Subjects:** Water quality, sewerage, industrial waste, mining and reclamation, air quality, surface mines, solid waste, radiation protection, community environmental control. **Special Collections:** Pennsylvania State University Special Research Report on Coal (90 volumes); U.S. and Pennsylvania Geological Surveys (700 items); IARC monographs. **Holdings:** 2400 books; 600 bound periodical volumes; Pennsylvania phone book collection; vertical files containing material on 200 environmental subjects. **Subscriptions:** 250 journals and other serials. **Services:** Interlibrary loan; copying; library open to the public by appointment. **Automated Operations:** Computerized public access catalog, cataloging, circulation, and serials control. **Computerized Information Services:** DIALOG Information Services, OCLC. **Publications:** EPI Center newsletter, quarterly - for internal distribution only and upon request. **Special Catalogs:** Serials catalog. **Remarks:** FAX: (717)783-2802.

★ 12861 ★

Pennsylvania (State) Department of Health - Bureau of Laboratories - Herbert Fox Memorial Library (Biol Sci)
Pickering Way & Welsh Pool Rd.　　Phone: (215)363-8500
Lionville, PA 19353　　　　M. Jeffery Shoemaker, Ph.D., Libn.
Staff: Prof 1; Other 1. **Subjects:** Clinical chemistry, microbiology and virology, toxicology, hematology, laboratory legislation. **Holdings:** 500 books. **Subscriptions:** 50 journals and other serials. **Services:** Interlibrary loan; copying; library open to the public by appointment. **Remarks:** FAX: (215)436-3346. **Staff:** Andrea O'Leary, Asst.Libn.

Pennsylvania (State) Department of Public Welfare - Hamburg Center for the Mentally Retarded
See: **Hamburg Center for the Mentally Retarded** (6857)

Pennsylvania (State) Department of Public Welfare - Haverford State Hospital
See: **Haverford State Hospital** (7016)

★ 12862 ★

Pennsylvania (State) Department of Public Welfare - Mayview State Hospital - Mental Health and Medical Library (Med)
1601 Mayview Rd.　　　　　　Phone: (412)257-6496
Bridgeville, PA 15017-1599　　William A. Suvak, Jr., Libn.Supv. I
Founded: 1966. **Staff:** Prof 1. **Subjects:** Psychiatry, psychoanalysis, psychiatric nursing, psychology, hospital administration, psychiatric social work, psychopharmacology. **Holdings:** 4500 books; 1400 bound periodical volumes. **Subscriptions:** 78 journals and other serials. **Services:** Interlibrary loan; copying; library open to community mental health professionals. **Networks/Consortia:** Member of National Network of Libraries of Medicine - Middle Atlantic Region. **Publications:** Newsletter, quarterly. **Remarks:** FAX: (412)257-6320. **Staff:** Elaine Gruber, Libn.

★ 12863 ★

Pennsylvania (State) Department of Public Welfare - Norristown State Hospital - Professional/Staff Library (Med)
Bldg. 11　　　　　　　　　Phone: (215)270-1369
Norristown, PA 19401-5399　　　Frieda Liem, Libn.
Staff: Prof 1; Other 1. **Subjects:** Psychiatry and neurology; clinical psychology; psychiatric nursing; psychiatric and clinical social work; activities therapy - recreational, music, occupational, vocational; aging; geriatrics; gerontology. **Holdings:** 8450 books; 2 VF drawers; pamphlets. **Subscriptions:** 100 journals and other serials. **Services:** Interlibrary loan; library open to the public with restrictions. **Automated Operations:** Computerized cataloging. **Computerized Information Services:** OCLC. **Networks/Consortia:** Member of Health Sciences Libraries Consortium (HSLC), National Network of Libraries of Medicine - Middle Atlantic Region, Health Sciences Libraries Consortium (HSLC), Pennsylvania State Institutional Libraries. **Remarks:** FAX: (215)270-1370.

★ 12864 ★

Pennsylvania (State) Department of Public Welfare - Office of Children, Youth & Families - Research Center (Soc Sci)
Harrisburg State Hospital
Lanco Lodge Bldg.
Box 2675　　　　　　　　　Phone: (717)257-7291
Harrisburg, PA 17105-2675　　Richard Fiene, Ph.D, Res.Dir.
Founded: 1979. **Staff:** Prof 6; Other 4. **Subjects:** Day care, program evaluation, child care research, child welfare, child abuse, youth services. **Special Collections:** Compliance Theory Data Base and Library. **Holdings:** 5000 books; 500 bound periodical volumes; 2000 other cataloged items. **Subscriptions:** 10 journals and other serials. **Services:** Interlibrary loan; copying; SDI; center open to the public. **Automated Operations:** Computerized public access catalog. **Computerized Information Services:** Internal databases. **Remarks:** FAX: (717)948-6432. **Staff:** Lawrence Woods, Info.Chf.; Vickie Harle, Trng.Coord.

★ 12865 ★

Pennsylvania (State) Department of Public Welfare - Philadelphia State Hospital - Staff Library
Stanbridge Sterigere St.
Norristown, PA 19401-5315
Defunct.

★ 12866 ★

Pennsylvania (State) Department of Public Welfare - Philipsburg State General Hospital - Library
Loch Lomond Rd.
Philipsburg, PA 16866
Defunct.

★ 12867 ★

Pennsylvania (State) Department of Public Welfare - Somerset State Hospital - Library (Med)
Box 631　　　　　　　　　Phone: (814)443-0231
Somerset, PA 15501　　　　Eve Kline, Dir., Lib.Serv.
Founded: 1968. **Staff:** Prof 2; Other 1. **Subjects:** Psychiatry, psychology, mental retardation. **Holdings:** 9300 books; 500 filmstrips; 650 cassettes; 125 videotapes. **Subscriptions:** 150 journals and other serials; 7 newspapers. **Services:** Interlibrary loan; copying; SDI. **Automated Operations:** Computerized acquisitions. **Computerized Information Services:** OCLC, DIALOG Information Services, VU/TEXT Information Services, BRS Information Technologies. Performs searches on fee basis. **Networks/Consortia:** Member of Health Information Resources Consortium (HIRESCU), State System of Higher Education Libraries Council (SSHELCO), National Network of Libraries of Medicine - Middle Atlantic Region, Health Sciences Libraries Consortium (HSLC). **Publications:** Newsletter, weekly. **Remarks:** FAX: (814)443-0217. Alternate telephone number(s): 443-0319. **Staff:** Kathy Plaso, Libn.

★ 12868 ★

Pennsylvania (State) Department of Public Welfare - Western Center - Library Services (Med)
333 Curry Hill Rd.
Canonsburg, PA 15317   Nicholas L. Liguori, Libn.
Phone: (412)873-3200
Founded: 1962. **Staff:** Prof 1. **Subjects:** Medicine, psychology, special education. **Holdings:** 1080 volumes. **Subscriptions:** 41 journals and other serials. **Services:** Interlibrary loan; copying; library open to the public with restrictions.

★ 12869 ★

Pennsylvania (State) Department of Revenue - Law Library (Law)
Strawberry Square, 10th Fl.
Harrisburg, PA 17128-1061   Phone: (717)787-1382
Subjects: Law. **Services:** Library not open to the public. **Remarks:** No further information was supplied by respondent.

★ 12870 ★

Pennsylvania (State) Department of Transportation - Office of Chief Counsel - Library (Law)
Transport & Safety Bldg., Rm. 521   Phone: (717)787-2830
Harrisburg, PA 17120   Elizabeth S. Howe, Libn.
Subjects: Law. **Holdings:** Figures not available. **Remarks:** No further information was supplied by respondent.

★ 12871 ★

Pennsylvania (State) Department of Transportation - Transportation Employees Library (Trans)
903 Transportation & Safety Bldg.   Phone: (717)787-6527
Harrisburg, PA 17120   Judy H. Gutshall, Libn.
Founded: 1979. **Staff:** Prof 1; Other 1. **Subjects:** Transportation and allied subjects, management, microcomputer use, customer service, communications, engineering. **Special Collections:** TRB Publications; U.S. and Pennsylvania Department of Transportation documents; audiovisual collection (1400 programs). **Holdings:** 20,000 publications. **Subscriptions:** 300 journals and other serials. **Services:** Interlibrary loan; copying; library open to the public for research purposes. **Automated Operations:** Computerized cataloging, serials, and circulation. **Computerized Information Services:** DIALOG Information Services, DataTimes; AASHTO (electronic mail service). **Publications:** Look It Up. **Special Catalogs:** Audio/Visual Catalog; Internal Reports Catalog. **Remarks:** FAX: (717)783-8217 (include center phone number and librarian name). Electronic mail address(es): HTO10039 (AASHTO).

★ 12872 ★

Pennsylvania State Fish Commission Library - Benner Spring Fish Research Station (Biol Sci)
1225 Shiloh Rd.   Phone: (814)355-4837
State College, PA 16801-8495   Thomas R. Bender, Jr., Biol.
Staff: 1. **Subjects:** Freshwater fisheries, fish culture, fish disease. **Holdings:** 450 books; 3500 reprints of manuscripts. **Subscriptions:** 50 journals and other serials. **Services:** Library not open to the public.

★ 12873 ★

Pennsylvania (State) Game Commission - Headquarters Library (Env-Cons)
2001 Elmerton Ave.   Phone: (717)787-9229
Harrisburg, PA 17110-9797   Cheryl Bodan, Libn.
Founded: 1988. **Staff:** Prof 1. **Subjects:** Wildlife management, hunting and trapping, conservation, land management, arms and ammunition, hunter education. **Holdings:** 3000 books; 100 bound periodical volumes; 1500 other cataloged items. **Subscriptions:** 200 journals and other serials. **Services:** Interlibrary loan; copying; library open to the public for reference use only. **Remarks:** FAX: (717)772-2411.

★ 12874 ★

Pennsylvania (State) Governor's Office of Budget - Library
Strawberry Square, Rm. 734
Harrisburg, PA 17120   Phone: (717)787-5442
Subjects: Finance. No further information was supplied by respondent.

★ 12875 ★

Pennsylvania (State) Historical & Museum Commission - Division of Archives and Manuscripts (Hist)
William Penn Memorial Museum & Archives Bldg.
Box 1026   Phone: (717)787-2701
Harrisburg, PA 17108-1026   Harry E. Whipkey, State Archv.
Founded: 1903. **Staff:** Prof 14; Other 6. **Subjects:** Archives of Pennsylvania and historical manuscripts. **Special Collections:** Record groups of the holdings of state agencies and political subdivisions (57); manuscript collections (425). **Holdings:** 17,500 books; 27,000 cubic feet of archival materials; 20,000 cubic feet of personal papers; 14,770 reels of microfilm; 4500 maps. **Subscriptions:** 180 journals and other serials. **Services:** Interlibrary loan (limited); division not open to the public. **Automated Operations:** Computerized cataloging. **Computerized Information Services:** OCLC, RLIN; internal databases. **Networks/Consortia:** Member of Research Libraries Information Network (RLIN). **Publications:** List of publications - available on request; Finding Aids. **Staff:** Carol Tallman, Libn., Bur. of Archv. & Hist.

★ 12876 ★

Pennsylvania (State) Historical & Museum Commission - Drake Well Museum - Library (Hist)
R.D. 3   Phone: (814)827-2797
Titusville, PA 16354   Emma Stewart
Founded: 1934. **Staff:** 1. **Subjects:** Petroleum industry, local area history, geological surveys. **Special Collections:** Brewer Papers (50 letters and papers of Dr. Francis B. Brewer); Mather Photographic Collection, 1860-1890 (2500 prints, 2761 identified negatives, 1061 unidentified negatives of the oil region). **Holdings:** 1500 books; 900 bound periodical volumes; 1500 other cataloged items; 115 cubic feet of Roberts Torpedo Company papers, 1865-1881; 8 cubic feet of John H. Scheide Papers, 1860-1890; 5 cubic feet of Ida M. Tarbell Papers; early maps, atlas, ledgers, scrapbooks. **Subscriptions:** 1300 oil company periodicals and early newspapers of the region. **Services:** Interlibrary loan; copying; library open to the public by appointment.

★ 12877 ★

Pennsylvania (State) Historical & Museum Commission - Ephrata Cloister - Library (Hist)
632 W. Main St.   Phone: (717)733-6600
Ephrata, PA 17522   Nadine A. Steinmetz, Dir.
Subjects: History of Ephrata Cloister, Pennsylvania German culture. **Special Collections:** Eighteenth and nineteenth century imprints printed at Ephrata Cloister. **Holdings:** 250 books. **Services:** Copying; library open to the public by appointment.

★ 12878 ★

Pennsylvania (State) Historical & Museum Commission - Fort Pitt Museum - Library (Hist)
Point State Park   Phone: (412)281-9284
Pittsburgh, PA 15222   Robert J. Trombetta, Dir.
Founded: 1967. **Staff:** 5. **Subjects:** French and Indian War, Western Pennsylvania to 1800, 18th century forts and artillery, regimental histories. **Holdings:** 450 volumes; unbound periodicals; 10 French and Indian War letters and documents. **Services:** Library not open to the public.

★ 12879 ★

Pennsylvania (State) Historical & Museum Commission - Library (Hist)
Box 1026   Phone: (717)783-9898
Harrisburg, PA 17108-1026   Carol W. Tallman, Libn.
Founded: 1947. **Staff:** Prof 1. **Subjects:** Pennsylvania history, museum technology. **Holdings:** 20,000 volumes; 15 VF drawers of pamphlets and clippings. **Subscriptions:** 180 journals and other serials. **Services:** Interlibrary loan (limited); library open to the public by appointment. **Automated Operations:** Computerized cataloging. **Computerized Information Services:** OCLC; internal databases. **Publications:** Finding aids.

★ 12880 ★

Pennsylvania (State) Historical & Museum Commission - Old Economy Village - Harmony Society Library (Hist)
14th & Church Sts.   Phone: (412)266-4500
Ambridge, PA 15003   Raymond V. Shepherd, Jr., Dir.
Founded: 1919. **Staff:** Prof 2; Other 10. **Subjects:** History of Harmony Society, communitarian and social experiments in U.S., industrial and

economic history, religion, German language, natural science. **Special Collections:** Music of Harmony Society (5000 manuscripts). **Holdings:** 5000 original books; 325,000 pages of manuscripts on microfilm. **Services:** Library open to the public by appointment. **Remarks:** Historic correspondence, pamphlets, and documents have been transferred to the Pennsylvania State Historical & Museum Commission - Division of Archives and Manuscripts, Harrisburg, PA. Site contains 17 historic buildings, 1824-1830.

★ 12881 ★
Pennsylvania (State) Historical & Museum Commission - Pennsylvania Lumber Museum - Library (Hist)
Box K   Phone: (814)435-2652
Galeton, PA 16922   Dolores M. Buchsen, Adm.
Founded: 1972. **Staff:** 1. **Subjects:** History of logging, antique tools, logging railroads. **Special Collections:** Disston Crucible (113 copies on milling, 1912-1926). **Holdings:** 1500 books; 650 bound periodical volumes. **Subscriptions:** 3 journals and other serials. **Services:** Interlibrary loan; copying (limited); library open to the public for reference use only. **Staff:** Carol Tallman, PHMC Lib., State Musm. of Pennsylvania

★ 12882 ★
Pennsylvania (State) Human Relations Commission - Library (Soc Sci)
Executive House, 3rd Fl.
101 S. 2nd St.
Harrisburg, PA 17105-3145   Phone: (717)783-8266
Remarks: No further information was supplied by respondent.

★ 12883 ★
Pennsylvania (State) Joint State Government Commission - Library (Soc Sci)
G-16 Finance Bldg.   Phone: (717)787-6803
Harrisburg, PA 17120   Yoga Adhola, Libn.
Founded: 1937. **Staff:** Prof 1. **Subjects:** Education, state legislation, finance, taxes. **Holdings:** 3000 books; 500 bound periodical volumes; 5000 reports and pamphlets; 12 VF drawers of federal and state releases. **Subscriptions:** 30 journals and other serials; 10 newspapers. **Services:** Research on Pennsylvania laws for other states' agencies; library open to members of legislature and authorized visitors. **Publications:** Studies prepared by the staff - limited distribution. **Remarks:** FAX: (717)787-7020.

★ 12884 ★
Pennsylvania (State) Legislative Budget & Finance Committee - Library (Bus-Fin)
Finance Bldg., Rm. 400
Box 8737
Harrisburg, PA 17105-8737   Phone: (717)783-1600
Subjects: State government programs. **Holdings:** 100 reports. **Services:** Library not open to the public. **Remarks:** FAX: (717)787-5487.

★ 12885 ★
(Pennsylvania State) Legislative Reference Bureau Library (Law)
Main Capitol Bldg., Rm. 641   Phone: (717)787-4816
Harrisburg, PA 17120-0033   Susan K. Zavacky, Libn.
Founded: 1909. **Staff:** Prof 1. **Subjects:** State legislation, law, bill drafting, state court cases, federal case and statutory law. **Special Collections:** Laws of Pennsylvania; Senate and House journals, 1911 to present; Senate and House bills, 1826 to present. **Holdings:** 9000 volumes; 75 pamphlet files of state documents; 16 VF cases of pamphlets and newspaper clippings; 5 drawers of microfilm; 5 boxes of microfiche. **Subscriptions:** 50 journals and other serials. **Services:** Copying (limited); library open to the public for reference use only. **Computerized Information Services:** Internal databases. **Remarks:** (717)783-2396.

Pennsylvania State Modern Language Association Archives
See: **Millersville University (10403)**

★ 12886 ★
Pennsylvania State Office of Attorney General - Law Library (Law)
1525 Strawberry Square   Phone: (717)787-3176
Harrisburg, PA 17120   Ellen R. Chack, Chf., Law Lib.Sect.
Founded: 1873. **Staff:** Prof 1; Other 2. **Subjects:** Law. **Holdings:** 30,000 books; 500 bound periodical volumes. **Subscriptions:** 50 journals and other serials; 5 newspapers. **Services:** Library not open to the public. **Computerized Information Services:** LEXIS, NEXIS. **Special Indexes:** Pennsylvania Official Opinions of the Attorney General (card).

★ 12887 ★
Pennsylvania (State) Office of Chief Counsel - Law Library (Law)
City Towers Bldg., 3rd Fl.
301 Chestnut St.   Phone: (717)783-8440
Harrisburg, PA 17101-2702   Brenda Houck, Libn.
Subjects: Law. **Services:** Library not open to the public. **Remarks:** Alternate telephone number(s): 787-4449.

★ 12888 ★
Pennsylvania (State) Senate Library (Law)
Main Capitol Bldg., Rm. 157   Phone: (717)787-6120
Harrisburg, PA 17120   Evelyn F. Andrews, Lib.Dir.
Subjects: Pennsylvania legislation. **Holdings:** 10,000 books. **Subscriptions:** 50 journals and other serials. **Services:** Copying; library open to the public. **Remarks:** FAX: (717)783-5021; (717)772-2683.

★ 12889 ★
Pennsylvania State Superior Court - Appellate Courts Library (Law)
530 Walnut St., Ste. 311
Philadelphia, PA 19106   Phone: (215)560-5840
Staff: Prof 1. **Subjects:** Law, court administration. **Holdings:** 12,200 volumes; 2500 microfiche. **Subscriptions:** 123 journals and other serials. **Services:** Interlibrary loan; library not open to the public. **Automated Operations:** Computerized cataloging. **Computerized Information Services:** LEXIS, NEXIS, OCLC. Performs searches free of charge. **Networks/Consortia:** Member of PALINET. **Publications:** Library Bulletin, quarterly; book catalog, annual. **Remarks:** FAX: (215)560-5841.

★ 12890 ★
Pennsylvania (State) Supreme Court - Library (Law)
468 City Hall   Phone: (215)560-6370
Philadelphia, PA 19107   Charles John, Chf.Ck.
Subjects: Law. **Holdings:** Figures not available.

★ 12891 ★
Pennsylvania (State) Supreme & Superior Courts - Library (Law)
434 Main Capital   Phone: (717)787-6199
Harrisburg, PA 17120   Mildred Williamson, Lib.Dir.
Subjects: Law. **Remarks:** No further information was supplied by respondent.

★ 12892 ★
Pennsylvania State University - Applied Research Laboratory - Library (Sci-Engr)
P.O. Box 30   Phone: (814)865-6621
State College, PA 16804   Patricia G. Hayes, Supv. of Lib.Serv.
Founded: 1945. **Staff:** Prof 1; Other 1. **Subjects:** Electronics, engineering, acoustics, physics, applied mathematics, hydrodynamics, oceanography, materials engineering, manufacturing technology. **Holdings:** 3500 books; 1300 bound periodical volumes; 5000 technical reports. **Subscriptions:** 300 journals and other serials. **Services:** Library not open to the public. **Automated Operations:** Computerized cataloging, acquisitions, serials, and circulation (INMAGIC). **Computerized Information Services:** DIALOG Information Services, DTIC; Library Information Access System (LIAS) (internal database); BITNET, InterNet (electronic mail services). **Publications:** Accessions Listing, monthly - to ARL personnel. **Remarks:** FAX: (814)865-1615. Electronic mail address(es): PGH@PSUARL (BITNET); PGH@ARLVAX.PSU.EDU (InterNet).

★ 12893 ★
Pennsylvania State University - Architecture Library (Plan)
207 Engineering Unit C
University Park, PA 16802   Phone: (814)863-0511
Staff: Prof 1; Other 2. **Subjects:** Architecture, history of architecture, landscape architecture, building construction, architectural engineering. **Holdings:** 19,500 volumes. **Subscriptions:** 125 journals. **Services:** Interlibrary loan; copying; room open to the public. **Automated Operations:** Computerized cataloging, serials, and circulation. **Computerized Information Services:** DIALOG Information Services, BRS Information Technologies. **Staff:** Linda Zimmers, Arch. Lib.Supv.

★ 12894 ★
Pennsylvania State University - Arts Library (Art, Mus)
University Library, Rm. E405
University Park, PA 16802   Phone: (814)865-6481
Founded: 1964. **Staff:** Prof 2; Other 4. **Subjects:** History of art and architecture; painting; sculpture; drawing; graphic arts; decorative arts; music - history and literature, theory and composition. **Special Collections:** Warren Mack Memorial Collection (550 original prints); Charles Wakefield Cadman Collection; music performance scores and parts; collected sets and monuments of music. **Holdings:** 100,000 books, including 22,000 scores and parts; 1100 spoken word phonograph records; 27,000 music sound recordings in all formats. **Subscriptions:** 610 journals and other serials. **Services:** Interlibrary loan; copying; listening room for music; library open to the public. **Automated Operations:** Computerized cataloging, serials, and circulation. **Computerized Information Services:** DIALOG Information Services, BRS Information Technologies. **Remarks:** FAX: (814)865-3665. **Staff:** Kathleen Haefliger, Mus.Libn.; Gwen Catchen, Mus.Spec.

★ 12895 ★
Pennsylvania State University - Audiovisual Services (Aud-Vis)
Special Services Bldg.
1127 Fox Hill Rd.   Phone: (814)865-6314
University Park, PA 16803-1824   Robert L. Allen, Dir.
Founded: 1942. **Subjects:** Anthropology, psychology, life sciences, sociology, arts, humanities. **Special Collections:** Psychological Cinema Register (350 film titles); American Archive of Encyclopaedia Cinematographica (2000 film titles). **Holdings:** 26,000 motion picture films and videotapes. **Services:** Film and video rental and sales; materials available to public with some restrictions. **Automated Operations:** Computerized circulation. **Computerized Information Services:** Medianet (internal database); BITNET (electronic mail service). **Networks/Consortia:** Member of Consortium of College and University Media Centers (CCUMC). **Publications:** 12 catalogs in series organized along lines of recognized interest areas; alphabetical listing by title only of 16mm films and video cassettes; reference publication. **Remarks:** Toll-free telephone number(s): is (800)826-0132; FAX: (814)863-2574.

★ 12896 ★
Pennsylvania State University - Berks Campus - Memorial Library (Sci-Engr)
Tulpehocken Rd.
Box 7009   Phone: (215)320-4822
Reading, PA 19610-6009   Deena J. Morganti, Hd.Libn.
Founded: 1958. **Staff:** Prof 2; Other 5. **Subjects:** Engineering, business, liberal arts, food service, science. **Holdings:** 35,000 books; 3100 bound periodical volumes; 24 VF drawers of pamphlets; 2000 microforms; 700 phonograph records; 70 maps; 287 film loops; 34 art reproductions; 25 videotapes; 17 media kits. **Subscriptions:** 375 journals and other serials; 6 newspapers. **Services:** Interlibrary loan; copying; library open to the public with restrictions. **Automated Operations:** Computerized public access catalog. **Computerized Information Services:** Library Information Access System (LIAS; internal database). Performs searches on fee basis. **Publications:** Library Handbook. **Remarks:** FAX: (215)320-4914.

★ 12897 ★
Pennsylvania State University - Biomechanics Laboratory - Library (Sci-Engr)
200 Biomechanics Laboratory   Phone: (814)865-3445
University Park, PA 16802   Richard C. Nelson, Ph.D., Dir.
Founded: 1987. **Subjects:** Exercise science, biomechanics, sport biomechanics. **Special Collections:** M.S. Theses (75); Ph.D. Dissertations (45). **Holdings:** 300 books; 450 periodical volumes. **Subscriptions:** 22 journals and other serials. **Services:** Library open to the public for reference use only. **Remarks:** FAX: (814)865-2440.

★ 12898 ★
Pennsylvania State University - Biotechnology Institute - Library (Biol Sci)
519 Wartik Laboratory   Phone: (814)863-3650
University Park, PA 16802   Patricia Corbett
Founded: 1984. **Staff:** 1. **Subjects:** Science, genetics, biotechnology. **Holdings:** 100 books. **Subscriptions:** 15 journals and other serials; 2 newspapers. **Computerized Information Services:** DIALOG Information Services; internal database. Contact Person: Gina Zang. **Remarks:** FAX: (814)863-1357.

★ 12899 ★
Pennsylvania State University - College of Business Administration - Center for Research - Research Support Center (Bus-Fin)
104 Beam Business Adm. Bldg.   Phone: (814)863-0598
University Park, PA 16802   Margaret E. Smith, Libn.
Staff: Prof 1; Other 7. **Subjects:** Accounting and management information systems, business logistics, finance, international business and business law, insurance and real estate, marketing, management science and operations management, organizational behavior. **Holdings:** Doctoral dissertations, masters theses, MBA professional papers; Pennsylvania State University publications; Association for University Business and Economic Research publications; trade association and accounting firm publications; Financial Accounting Standards Board publications; Bureau of National Affairs Tax Management Portfolios; Pennsylvania state and federal government documents. **Subscriptions:** 650 journals and other serials. **Services:** SDI; center open to the public with special permission. **Automated Operations:** Computerized acquisitions and serials. **Computerized Information Services:** DIALOG Information Services. **Special Catalogs:** Journal Holdings List (printout). **Remarks:** FAX: (814)863-2753.

★ 12900 ★
Pennsylvania State University - College of Medicine - George T. Harrell Library (Med)
Milton S. Hershey Medical Center   Phone: (717)531-8629
Hershey, PA 17033   Lois J. Lehman, Libn./Dir.
Founded: 1965. **Staff:** Prof 6; Other 8. **Subjects:** Medicine. **Special Collections:** Rare medical books (1022 volumes). **Holdings:** 23,641 books; 86,910 bound periodical volumes; 271 motion pictures, videotapes, video discs, and cassettes; 950 phonograph records, audiotapes, and audio cassettes; 72 slide programs; 6 filmstrips. **Subscriptions:** 1837 journals and other serials. **Services:** Interlibrary loan; copying; SDI; library open to the public for reference use only. **Computerized Information Services:** Online systems. **Networks/Consortia:** Member of National Network of Libraries of Medicine - Middle Atlantic Region, Health Sciences Libraries Consortium (HSLC). **Publications:** Library Bulletin, irregular - to state medical school libraries and Hershey Medical Center. **Special Catalogs:** Library Serials Title Catalog. **Remarks:** Alternate telephone number(s): 531-8626. FAX: (717)531-8635. **Staff:** M. Sandra Wood, Libn./Ref.; Barbara E. Nwoke, Sr.Asst.Libn./Hd.Cat.; Virginia A. Lingle, Sr.Asst.Libn./Ref.; Franceen Wilson, Lib.Asst./Hd., Circ.; Esther Y. Dell, Sr.Asst.Libn./Ref./ILL; Eric Delozier, Asst.Libn./Ref.

★ 12901 ★
Pennsylvania State University - Documents/Maps Section (Geog-Map)
Pattee Library   Phone: (814)863-0094
University Park, PA 16802   Debora Cheney, Act.Hd., Docs. & Maps
Staff: Prof 1; Other 2. **Subjects:** Topography, city planning, place names, map reading and interpretation. **Special Collections:** Pennsylvania County boundary maps, 1790-1876; Pennsylvania Land Ownership Maps (microfiche); Pennsylvania Warrentee Maps. **Holdings:** 1200 books; 86 bound periodical volumes; 350,000 maps; 200 raised relief maps; 1740 aerial photographs; 133 reels of microfilm; 464 microfiche; 3000 atlases; 8 globes; 5 VF drawers of map interpretation files. **Subscriptions:** 36 journals and other serials. **Services:** Interlibrary loan; copying; library open to the public. **Automated Operations:** Computerized public access catalog, cataloging, and serials. **Computerized Information Services:** DIALOG Information Services, RLIN; SuperMap, PC USA, PC-GLOBE (internal databases); BITNET (electronic mail service). **Special Indexes:** Atlas Index File (card). **Remarks:** FAX: (814)863-2653. Electronic mail address(es): KHP@PSULIAS; DLC@PSULIAS (BITNET). **Staff:** Karl Proehl, Map Libn.; Patricia Scott, Maps Spec.

★ 12902 ★
Pennsylvania State University - Earth and Mineral Sciences Library
(Sci-Engr, Energy)
105 Deike Bldg.   Phone: (814)865-9517
University Park, PA 16802   Linda Musser, Hd.
Founded: 1931. **Staff:** Prof 2; Other 4. **Subjects:** Geosciences, materials science, meteorology, mineral economics and mineral engineering. **Special Collections:** Coal mining and processing as a fuel (1300 items). **Holdings:** 90,000 books; 22,000 geologic and topographic maps; 10,000 microfiche. **Subscriptions:** 1500 journals and other serials. **Services:** Interlibrary loan; copying; library open to the public. **Automated Operations:** Computerized circulation. **Computerized Information Services:** DIALOG Information Services, PFDS Online, BRS Information Technologies, OCLC; BITNET (electronic mail service). Performs searches on fee basis. **Networks/Consortia:** Member of Research Libraries Information Network (RLIN). **Remarks:** Electronic mail address(es): EMS@PSULIAS (BITNET). **Staff:** Elaine Clement.

★ 12903 ★
Pennsylvania State University - Engineering Library (Sci-Engr)
325 Hammond Bldg.   Phone: (814)865-3451
University Park, PA 16802   Thomas W. Conkling, Hd.
Founded: 1950. **Staff:** Prof 2; Other 5. **Subjects:** Engineering. **Special Collections:** Schweitzer, diesel engines and diesel research. **Holdings:** 87,000 volumes; 300,000 technical reports and papers from NASA, DOE, DOD, American Institute of Aeronautics and Astronautics, Society of Automotive Engineers, Society of Manufacturing Engineers, American Society of Mechanical Engineers. **Subscriptions:** 1200 journals and other serials. **Services:** Interlibrary loan; copying; library open to the public. **Automated Operations:** Computerized public access catalog, cataloging, and circulation. **Computerized Information Services:** DIALOG Information Services, BRS Information Technologies, Integrated Technical Information System (ITIS), WILSONLINE, PFDS Online, NASA/RECON; BITNET (electronic mail service). **Remarks:** Electronic mail address(es): TWC@PSULIAS (BITNET).

Pennsylvania State University - Environmental Resources Research - Center for Environment Studies - CAES Information Services
See: Pennsylvania State University - Environmental Resources Research Institute (12904)

★ 12904 ★
Pennsylvania State University - Environmental Resources Research Institute - Library (Env-Cons)
Land & Water Research Bldg.   Phone: (814)863-1386
University Park, PA 16802   Eva Brownawell, Info.Spec.
Founded: 1963. **Staff:** Prof 2. **Subjects:** Air pollution - monitoring, control, effects; environmental health; acid precipitation; water quality and conservation; hazardous waste; land reclamation; remote sensing. **Special Collections:** Water Center Reports (listed by state); ERRI reports; air environment reprint collection; historic Bay Area microfilm collection (air quality). **Holdings:** 1500 books; 55,000 reprints and microfiche; 15,000 technical reports, pamphlets, maps. **Subscriptions:** 70 journals and other serials; 100 newsletters. **Services:** Interlibrary loan; library open to the public. **Computerized Information Services:** DIALOG Information Services; CD-ROM; internal databases. **Publications:** Air Pollution Titles - available by subscription; ERRI-Reports and Newsletters; list of publications - available upon request. **Remarks:** Alternate telephone number(s): 863-0140. FAX: (814)863-1696; 865-3378. Holdings reflect the recent merger of the Institutes' Library and its Center for Air Environment Studies - CAES Information Services.

★ 12905 ★
Pennsylvania State University - Frost Entomological Museum - Taxonomic Research Library (Biol Sci)
Head House 3   Phone: (814)863-2865
University Park, PA 16802   Ke Chung Kim, Cur.
Founded: 1972. **Staff:** Prof 2; Other 2. **Subjects:** Taxonomy, entomology, insect identification and information. **Special Collections:** Anoplura, Odonata, Aphid collections. **Holdings:** 1000 books; bound volumes; taxonomic references and reprints. **Subscriptions:** 5 journals and other serials. **Services:** Library open for research use by appointment. **Computerized Information Services:** BITNET (electronic mail service). **Remarks:** FAX: (814)865-3048; Electronic mail address(es): KCK@PSUVM (BITNET).

★ 12906 ★
Pennsylvania State University - Fruit Research Laboratory - Library
(Agri)
290 Univ. Dr.
PO Box 309   Phone: (717)677-6116
Biglerville, PA 17307-0309   Kenneth D. Hickey
Founded: 1972. **Subjects:** Tree fruit - culture, pest management. **Holdings:** 250 books; 300 bound periodical volumes; 200 reports. **Services:** Library open to the public. **Remarks:** FAX: (717)677-4112.

★ 12907 ★
Pennsylvania State University - Gerontology Center - Human Development Collection (Soc Sci)
S109 Henderson Human Development Bldg.   Phone: (814)863-0776
University Park, PA 16802   Faye Wohlwill, Coll.Dir.
Staff: Prof 1; Other 2. **Subjects:** Gerontology, adolescent and child psychology, marriage and family. **Holdings:** 3500 volumes. **Subscriptions:** 25 journals and other serials. **Services:** Copying; collection open to the public.

★ 12908 ★
Pennsylvania State University - Great Valley - Library (Sci-Engr, Educ)
30 E. Swedesford Rd.   Phone: (215)648-3215
Malvern, PA 19355   Adele F. Bane, Ph.D., Hd.Libn.
Founded: 1964. **Staff:** Prof 1; Other 3. **Subjects:** Engineering, business management, training design and development, elementary and special education. **Holdings:** 18,000 books; 2200 bound periodical volumes. **Subscriptions:** 338 journals and other serials. **Services:** Interlibrary loan; copying; library open to the public. **Automated Operations:** Computerized public access catalog, cataloging, and acquisitions. **Computerized Information Services:** BRS/After Dark, DIALOG Information Services, OCLC, RLIN, UnCover; CD-ROMs (ABI/INFORM, ERIC, Business Dateline); internal database. Performs searches on fee basis. **Publications:** Know News (newsletter), quarterly. **Remarks:** FAX: (215)889-1334.

★ 12909 ★
Pennsylvania State University - Laboratory for Human Performance Research - Library (Med)
Noll Laboratory Bldg.
University Park, PA 16802   Phone: (814)865-3453
Founded: 1963. **Subjects:** Applied physiology. **Holdings:** 300 books; 500 bound periodical volumes; 100 reports. **Subscriptions:** 6 journals and other serials. **Services:** Library open to the public. **Remarks:** FAX: (814)865-4602. **Staff:** E.R. Buskirk; B. Maurer.

★ 12910 ★
Pennsylvania State University - Life Sciences Library (Biol Sci, Med, Agri)
E205 Pattee Library   Phone: (814)865-7056
University Park, PA 16802   Katharine Clark, Hd.
Founded: 1888. **Staff:** Prof 5; Other 3. **Subjects:** Agriculture, biology, forestry, microbiology, biophysics, biochemistry, veterinary science, health planning and administration, nursing, food science, nutrition. **Special Collections:** Mycology and mushrooms; early American agricultural journals; Lumbering in Pennsylvania Collection (manuscripts; films; slides). **Holdings:** 275,000 books. **Subscriptions:** 4000 journals and other serials. **Services:** Interlibrary loan; library open to the public. **Automated Operations:** Computerized cataloging and circulation. **Computerized Information Services:** PFDS Online, RLIN, DIALOG Information Services, BRS Information Technologies, The Faxon Company, OCLC; Library Information Access System (LIAS) (internal database); CD-ROMs; BITNET (electronic mail service). **Publications:** Acquisitions List, monthly. **Remarks:** FAX: (814)865-3665. **Staff:** Frederick Sepp, Sr.Asst.Libn.; Amy Paster, Sr.Asst.Libn.; Helen Smith, Sr.Asst.Libn.; Nancy Henry, Asst.Libn.

★ 12911 ★
Pennsylvania State University - Mathematics Library (Sci-Engr, Comp Sci)
109 McAllister Bldg.   Phone: (814)865-6822
University Park, PA 16802   Robert S. Seeds, Hd.
Founded: 1966. **Staff:** Prof 1; Other 2.5. **Subjects:** Mathematics, statistics, computer science. **Holdings:** 47,500 volumes. **Subscriptions:** 600 journals and other serials. **Services:** Interlibrary loan; copying; library open to the

public. **Automated Operations:** Computerized public access catalog, cataloging, serials, and circulation. **Computerized Information Services:** BRS Information Technologies, DIALOG Information Services, PFDS Online, WILSONLINE, OCLC, RLIN; CD-ROMs; Library Information Access System (LIAS; internal database); BITNET (electronic mail service). **Networks/Consortia:** Member of Research Libraries Information Network (RLIN), Pittsburgh Regional Library Center (PRLC). **Remarks:** Electronic mail address(es): MATW@PSULIAS (BITNET).

★12912★
Pennsylvania State University - Physical Sciences Library (Sci-Engr)
230 Davey Laboratory   Phone: (814)865-7617
University Park, PA 16802   Nancy J. Butkovich, Hd.
Founded: 1889. **Staff:** Prof 2; Other 4. **Subjects:** Chemistry, physics, chemical engineering, astronomy, biophysics, biochemistry. **Special Collections:** PSU dissertations in chemistry, physics, astronomy and chemical engineering. **Holdings:** 91,200 volumes. **Subscriptions:** 1192 journals and other serials. **Services:** Interlibrary loan; copying. **Automated Operations:** Computerized cataloging, acquisitions, serials, and circulation. **Computerized Information Services:** DIALOG Information Services, STN International, Chemical Abstracts Service (CAS), BRS Information Technologies; Library Information Access System (LIAS; internal database). Performs searches on fee basis. **Networks/Consortia:** Member of Research Libraries Information Network (RLIN). **Staff:** C.J. McKown, Libn.

★12913★
Pennsylvania State University - Slavic and Soviet Language and Area Center - Library (Area-Ethnic)
306 Burrowes Bldg.   Phone: (814)865-0436
University Park, PA 16802   Emagene M. Fitzgerald, Libn.
Founded: 1965. **Subjects:** Eastern Europe - history, politics, foreign policy, society, economics, geography, language, literature. **Holdings:** 1050 books. **Subscriptions:** 62 journals and other serials; 16 newspapers. **Services:** Library open to the public. **Remarks:** FAX: (814)863-7084.

★12914★
Pennsylvania State University - Transportation Institute Working Collection (Trans)
227 Research Office Bldg.   Phone: (814)863-3953
University Park, PA 16802   Gina Giansante, Lib. Aide
Founded: 1968. **Staff:** Prof 1. **Subjects:** Transportation engineering and materials, automotive research, public transportation, transportation planning, policy analysis. **Special Collections:** Tire-Pavement Interaction Collection (2600 items); Bureau of Highway Traffic theses. **Holdings:** 3200 books; 700 bound periodical volumes; 8700 reports. **Subscriptions:** 170 journals and other serials. **Services:** Interlibrary loan; copying; collection open to the public. **Computerized Information Services:** DIALOG Information Services. **Remarks:** FAX: (814)865-3039.

★12915★
Pennzoil Company - Technical Information Services (Sci-Engr)
700 Milam
Box 2967   Phone: (713)546-6481
Houston, TX 77252-2967   Barbara F. West, Libn.
Founded: 1981. **Staff:** Prof 1. **Subjects:** Geology, geophysics, reservoir engineering, enhanced recovery. **Holdings:** 7000 books; 2000 bound periodical volumes; 1500 technical reports; 2000 maps. **Subscriptions:** 125 journals and other serials. **Services:** Interlibrary loan; services not open to the public. **Automated Operations:** Computerized cataloging and circulation. **Computerized Information Services:** DIALOG Information Services, PFDS Online, BRS Information Technologies, WILSONLINE, OCLC; DIALMAIL (electronic mail service). **Networks/Consortia:** Member of AMIGOS Bibliographic Council, Inc. **Publications:** Journals Received, weekly; Books Cataloged, monthly - both for internal distribution only. **Formerly:** Pennzoil Exploration and Production Company.

★12916★
Penobscot County Law Library (Law)
Penobscot County Court House
97 Hammond St.   Phone: (207)947-0751
Bangor, ME 04401   Judith Lancaster, Libn.
Subjects: Law. **Holdings:** 14,000 volumes. **Services:** Library open to the public.

★12917★
Penobscot Marine Museum - Stephen Phillips Memorial Library (Hist)
Church St.
Box 498   Phone: (207)548-2529
Searsport, ME 04974   Paige S. Lilly, Libn./Archv.
Founded: 1936. **Staff:** Prof 1; Other 1. **Subjects:** Maritime history, biography of mariners. **Special Collections:** Local history and genealogy (83 linear feet); ships' registers; logbooks and journals. **Holdings:** 6000 volumes; archival materials; clippings; 1900 navigational charts; manuscripts; photographs; vital records and census data of Knox, Waldo, Hancock counties on microfilm. **Subscriptions:** 40 journals and other serials. **Services:** Copying; library open to the public. **Publications:** Searsport Sea Captains. **Remarks:** FAX: (207)548-2520.

★12918★
Penrose Hospital - Webb Memorial Library (Med)
2215 N. Cascade Ave.
Box 7021   Phone: (719)630-5288
Colorado Springs, CO 80933   Nina Janes, Dir.
Founded: 1959. **Staff:** Prof 2. **Subjects:** Medicine, hospital administration. **Special Collections:** Penrose Cancer Hospital Collection; partial depository for government documents on cancer; history of medicine/historical medical texts (100 volumes); rare medical books. **Holdings:** 1000 books; 12,000 bound periodical volumes. **Subscriptions:** 500 journals and other serials. **Services:** Interlibrary loan; copying; SDI; library open to persons employed in medical fields and students of local colleges. **Automated Operations:** Computerized public access catalog, acquisitions, serials, and circulation. **Computerized Information Services:** DIALOG Information Services, MEDLARS, MEDLINE, BRS Information Technologies; ABACUS (electronic mail service). **Networks/Consortia:** Member of Colorado Council of Medical Librarians. **Remarks:** Alternate telephone number(s): 630-5289. FAX: (719)630-5603. **Staff:** Dick Maxwell.

Penrose Library
See: **University of Denver** (18548)

★12919★
Pensacola Historical Society - Lelia Abercrombie Historical Library (Hist)
405 S. Adams St.   Phone: (904)433-1559
Pensacola, FL 32501   Sandra L. Johnson, Cur.
Founded: 1960. **Staff:** Prof 3. **Subjects:** Pensacola, Escambia County, and West Florida history. **Special Collections:** Stephen R. Mallory letters, 1861-1870; Brosnaham Collection (land transfers, 1821; letters, deeds, documents, ledgers, 1782-1935); manuscripts (80 Hollinger manuscript boxes). **Holdings:** 2500 books; 700 maps, charts, architectural drawings; 30 hours of oral history recordings by local citizens; 3600 genealogical family data sheets; VF drawers; 140 reels of microfilm; 25,000 photographs; 20,000 glass negatives. **Services:** Copying; library open to the public.

★12920★
Pensacola Museum of Art - Harry Thornton Memorial Library (Art)
407 S. Jefferson St.   Phone: (904)432-6247
Pensacola, FL 32501   Carol Malt, Ph.D.
Founded: 1964. **Subjects:** Fine arts. **Holdings:** 1500 books; catalogs; AV programs. **Services:** Interlibrary loan; library open to the public for reference use only.

★12921★
Pension Benefit Guaranty Corporation - Office of the General Counsel - Library (Law)
2020 K St., N.W., Suite 7200   Phone: (202)778-8820
Washington, DC 20006-1806   Lillian H. Fry, Libn.
Founded: 1976. **Staff:** Prof 1. **Subjects:** Pension law, pensions. **Holdings:** 12,000 volumes. **Subscriptions:** 125 journals and other serials. **Services:** Interlibrary loan. **Computerized Information Services:** LEXIS. **Special Indexes:** Indexes to PBGC regulations and notices in the Federal Register. **Remarks:** Pension Benefit Guaranty Corporation is a government corporation that insures private pension plans. FAX: (202)778-8877.

Pentagon Library
See: **U.S. Army - Headquarters Services - Washington - Pentagon Library (16974)**

★ 12922 ★
Penton Publishing - Information Services (Publ)
1100 Superior Ave.   Phone: (216)696-7000
Cleveland, OH 44114-2543   Kenneth Long, Dir.
Founded: 1960. **Staff:** Prof 4; Other 2. **Subjects:** Industrial and consumer markets, advertising, marketing. **Special Collections:** Penton market studies. **Holdings:** 3400 books; 3100 government documents; 190 VF drawers of market data, articles, annual reports, company catalogs, government reports. **Subscriptions:** 220 journals and other serials. **Services:** Interlibrary loan; copying; SDI; center open to advertisers and potential advertisers by staff referral. **Computerized Information Services:** DIALOG Information Services, NEXIS, DataTimes. **Publications:** Market Profiles (computation of product sales to consuming industries), annual; Penton Research Overview Reports (summaries of business-to-business marketplace research); industry analyses for Penton magazines. **Remarks:** FAX: (216)696-4135. **Staff:** Michael Keating, Sr. Market Anl.; Mary Zielinsky, Market Anl.; Bryan Havighurst, Market Anl.

★ 12923 ★
Peoples Gas Light and Coke Company - Library (Energy)
122 S. Michigan Ave., Rm. 727   Phone: (312)431-4677
Chicago, IL 60603   Anne C. Roess, Chf.Libn.
Founded: 1911. **Staff:** Prof 1; Other 2. **Subjects:** Gas industry for manufactured and natural gas; public utilities; accounting; engineering; energy; management. **Holdings:** 6314 books; 1200 reports. **Subscriptions:** 350 journals; 10 newspapers. **Services:** Interlibrary loan; library not open to the public. **Automated Operations:** Computerized public access catalog and cataloging. **Computerized Information Services:** DIALOG Information Services, ORBIT Search Service, WILSONLINE, OCLC, Dow Jones News/Retrieval, NEXIS; A.G.A. GasNet (electronic mail service). **Networks/Consortia:** Member of ILLINET, Chicago Library System. **Publications:** Newsclips, daily; Info-line, monthly. **Remarks:** FAX: (312)431-4847.

People's Music Weekend Archive
See: **New Song Library (11549)**

★ 12924 ★
Peoples Natural Gas Company - Law Library (Law, Energy)
625 Liberty Ave.   Phone: (412)471-5100
Pittsburgh, PA 15222   Kimberly W. Prelich
Staff: 1. **Subjects:** Law - general, oil and gas, public utilities. **Holdings:** 7500 books; 185 bound periodical volumes. **Subscriptions:** 10 journals and other serials. **Services:** Library not open to the public. **Remarks:** FAX: (412)497-6630. **Staff:** Carol A. Miller.

★ 12925 ★
People's Republic of China - Institute of Scientific and Technical Information of China - Library (Sci-Engr)
15 Fuxinglu
P.O. Box 3827
Beijing 100038, People's Republic of China   Phone: 1 464746
Subjects: Science and technology. **Holdings:** 1.5 million research reports, proceedings, scientific and technical publications; 1.3 million microfiche; 4000 films. **Subscriptions:** 19,500 journals and other serials. **Services:** Library open to the public. **Computerized Information Services:** Chinese Pharmacy Abstracts data base (internal database). Performs searches on fee basis. **Remarks:** FAX: 8014025. Telex: 20079 ISTIC CN.

★ 12926 ★
People's Republic of China - Ministry of Communications - Shanghai Ship and Shipping Research Institute - Library (Trans)
200 Minsheng Rd.
Shanghai, People's Republic of China   Phone: 21 840438
Subjects: Shipping economics; ship evaluation, performance, structure, automation; marine engineering; marine navigation; navigation instruments and equipment; anti-corrosion and anti-fouling techniques for ships; computers. **Holdings:** 47,000 volumes; 1700 periodicals; 3800 technical reports. **Services:** Interlibrary loan; copying. **Publications:** Journal of Shanghai Ship and Shipping Research Institute; Navigation Science and Technology Information, monthly; The Journal of Navigation of China, semiannual (all have contents and summaries in English) - all on exchange.

★ 12927 ★
People's Republic of China - Ministry of Light Industry - Salt Industry Research Institute - Scientific and Technical Library (Sci-Engr)
15 Yingkoudao
Tanggu District
Tianjin, People's Republic of China   Ge Wenming, Libn.
Founded: 1955. **Staff:** 2. **Subjects:** Salt manufacturing technology, machinery, equipment; salt analysis; comprehensive utilization of sea water. **Holdings:** 5660 volumes; 634 periodicals; 7721 technical reports; 1900 AV programs and microforms. **Services:** Interlibrary loan (limited); copying. **Computerized Information Services:** Internal database.

★ 12928 ★
People's Republic of China - National Geological Library (Sci-Engr)
277 Ganjiakou
Fuchengmenwai   Phone: 89 2637
Beijing 100037, People's Republic of China   Li Yuwei
Founded: 1922. **Staff:** 55. **Subjects:** Geology, structure, stratigraphy, paleontology, rocks, minerals, mineral deposits, geophysics, geochemistry, hydrographic geology, engineering geology, analysis and identification of rocks and minerals, geological reconnaissance survey methods. **Special Collections:** Worldwide geological survey publications (emphasis on paleontology). **Holdings:** 300,000 volumes; 7600 periodicals; 800 AV programs and microforms. **Services:** Interlibrary loan; copying. **Computerized Information Services:** Internal database. **Special Catalogs:** Catalog of Chinese Scientific and Technical Literatures--Geology, bimonthly; Catalog of Foreign Scientific and Technical Literatures--Geology, bimonthly.

★ 12929 ★
People's Republic of China - The National Library of China (Info Sci, Area-Ethnic)
39 Baishigiao Rd.   Phone: 1 831-5566
Beijing 100081, People's Republic of   Ken Jiyu, Prof. of Chinese
China   Philosophy
Founded: 1910. **Subjects:** General collection. **Special Collections:** Wenyuange Collection (imperial library of Ming Dynasty); Wenjinge Collection (depository library of Four Vaults of Emperor Qianlong); Iron Lute and Copper Sword Mansion of Qu's Family Collection (total of 2.5 million rare books). **Holdings:** 6.4 million volumes; 65,000 periodicals; 260,000 technical reports; 933,000 AV programs and microforms; Chinese publications in 24 minority languages; hand copies, blockprint, and monograph editions of famous writers; inscribed tortoise shells and bones; books of rubbings; atlases. **Subscriptions:** 22,841 journals and other serials; 637 newspapers. **Services:** Interlibrary loan; copying; library open to the public. **Remarks:** Telex: 222211 NLC CN.

★ 12930 ★
People's Republic of China - National Vaccine & Serum Institute - Library (Biol Sci, Med)
Sanjianfang, Chaoyang District   Phone: 1 571161-1665
Beijing, People's Republic of China   Yang Xichang, Libn.
Founded: 1919. **Staff:** 7. **Subjects:** Natural sciences, cytology, genetics, biochemistry, molecular biology, microbiology, preventive medicine, public health, medicine, clinical diagnosis, infectious diseases, oncology, experimental zoology. **Special Collections:** Medical biological products. **Holdings:** 21,109 volumes; 172 technical reports; 20 microforms and AV programs. **Subscriptions:** 1342 journals and other serials. **Services:** Copying. **Publications:** Annual Review, irregular.

People's Republic of China - People's University of China
See: **The People's University of China (12932)**

★ 12931 ★
People's Republic of China - State Administration of Publications - Archives Library of Chinese Publications (Info Sci)
32 Bei Zhongbu Hutong
Dongcheng District   Phone: 1 553694
Beijing, People's Republic of China   Song Zhicheng, Libn.
Founded: 1950. **Staff:** 60. **Subjects:** Chinese Government documents. **Holdings:** 1 million volumes; 5000 periodicals; reproductions of paintings; picture-story books; textbooks; braille books; facsimiles of Chinese ancient and rare books. **Services:** Archives open to publishers only. **Special Catalogs:** National Catalogue of New Books, monthly; National General Catalogue, annual; Catalogue of Chinese Ancient Books, irregular; Catalogue of Translations of Foreign Classics, irregular; National General Catalogue of Juvenile Books, irregular.

(People's Republic of) China Nationality Library
See: **China Nationality Library** (3606)

★12932★
The People's University of China - Library - Special Collections (Soc Sci)
39 Hai Dian Lu Rd.   Phone: 1 283985
Beijing 100872, People's Republic of China   Prof. Dai Yi
Founded: 1937. **Staff:** 154. **Subjects:** Philosophy, social science, politics, economics, law, culture, education, science, arts, language, literature, history, geography, comprehensive science. **Special Collections:** Collection of books published during War of Resistance against Japan and the War of Liberation (4000 books); Rare Book Collection (31,600 books published in different dynasties); Local Chronicle Collection (36,000 books); Ancient Poetry Anthology Collection (51,570 books); Ancient Genealogy Collection (2680 books); Academic Monographs Collection (2600 books). **Holdings:** 227,000 books; 300,000 bound periodical volumes; 3180 microfiche; 719 microfilm. **Subscriptions:** 2300 journals and other serials; 120 newspapers. **Services:** Interlibrary loan. **Publications:** Classification of the Library of People's University of China. **Special Catalogs:** Book catalog of the base of liberated area; catalog of ancient rare book collection. **Special Indexes:** Subject index to works of Marx and Engels; index to complete works of Lenin. **Remarks:** FAX: 1 2566380. Telex: 0086. **Staff:** Prof. Yang Dong-Liang, Dp.Libn.

Peoria Bahai Assembly - Baha'i Faith Library & Archives
See: **Baha'i Faith Library & Archives** (1406)

★12933★
Peoria County Law Library (Law)
Peoria County Court House, Rm. 211   Phone: (309)672-6084
Peoria, IL 61602   Vicky L. Mundwiler, Law Libn.
Staff: 1. **Subjects:** Law. **Holdings:** 12,000 volumes. **Subscriptions:** 17 journals and other serials. **Services:** Copying; library open to the public. **Computerized Information Services:** WESTLAW. **Networks/Consortia:** Member of Illinois Valley Library System.

★12934★
Peoria Historical Society - Library (Hist)
Bradley University Library   Phone: (309)677-2822
Peoria, IL 61625   Charles Frey, Spec.Coll.Libn.
Founded: 1962. **Staff:** Prof 1; Other 3. **Subjects:** Peoria - pictures, biographies, churches, schools, business and industry, authors. **Special Collections:** Ernest E. East Collection; A. Wilson Oakford Collection of Peoria history and pictures (34 loose-leaf binders); Journal of Illinois State Historical Society, complete with index, 1909 to present; Peoria and Peoria County Atlas; historical encyclopedias; Works Progress Administration (WPA) file. **Holdings:** 1700 books; 96 LF VF drawers; 14,000 photographic images. **Services:** Interlibrary loan (limited); copying; library open to the public. **Automated Operations:** Computerized cataloging, acquisitions, serials, and circulation. **Computerized Information Services:** DIALOG Information Services, BRS Information Technologies, OCLC, DataTimes. **Networks/Consortia:** Member of Illinois Valley Library System, Resource Sharing Alliance of West Central Illinois, Inc., ILLINET. **Remarks:** Alternate telephone number(s): 677-2823.

Anthony Pepe Memorial Law Library
See: **Hamilton Law Association** (6863)

★12935★
Pepper, Hamilton and Scheetz - Law Library (Law)
3000 Two Logan Square
18th & Arch Sts.   Phone: (215)981-4100
Philadelphia, PA 19103-2799   Robyn L. Beyer, Dir., Lib.Serv.
Staff: Prof 3; Other 6. **Subjects:** Law. **Holdings:** 35,000 volumes. **Subscriptions:** 250 journals and other serials; 5 newspapers. **Services:** Interlibrary loan; SDI; library open to other law libraries and those connected with the firm. **Computerized Information Services:** LEXIS, NEXIS, DIALOG Information Services, VU/TEXT Information Services, WESTLAW, Dun & Bradstreet Business Credit Services, Dow Jones News/Retrieval. **Remarks:** An alternate telephone number is 981-4000. Telex: 710-670-0777. FAX: (215)981-4750. **Staff:** Lynn Stram, Assoc.Libn.; Janis Lee, Ref.Libn.

★12936★
Pepperdine University - Law Library (Law)
24255 Pacific Coast Hwy.   Phone: (310)456-4647
Malibu, CA 90263   Daniel W. Martin, Dir.
Founded: 1969. **Staff:** Prof 5; Other 5. **Subjects:** Law. **Holdings:** 113,827 volumes; 101,710 other cataloged items. **Subscriptions:** 3209 journals and other serials; 20 newspapers. **Services:** Interlibrary loan; copying; library open to the public for reference use only. **Automated Operations:** Computerized public access catalog, cataloging, acquisitions, serials, and circulation. **Computerized Information Services:** LEXIS, WESTLAW, OCLC. **Remarks:** FAX: (310)456-4266. **Staff:** Nancy Kitchen, Assoc.Dir.; Bernard Segel, Hd., Tech.Serv.; Ramona Stahl, Circ.; Susan Phillips, Ref.

★12937★
Pepperdine University - Library - Special Collections (Hum, Hist)
24255 Pacific Coast Hwy.   Phone: (310)456-4434
Malibu, CA 90265   Herbert Gore, Coord., Coll.Dev.
Subjects: California history, early children's literature, Churches of Christ, T.E. Lawrence, 19th century Paris. **Holdings:** Figures not available. **Services:** Interlibrary loan; copying; collections open to the public. **Automated Operations:** Computerized public access catalog, cataloging, circulation, serials, and acquisitions. **Computerized Information Services:** DIALOG Information Services, OCLC. **Remarks:** FAX: (310)456-4117.

★12938★
Pepperdine University - National School Safety Center - Library (Educ)
4165 Thousand Oaks Blvd., Suite 290   Phone: (805)373-9977
Westlake Village, CA 91362   Jane Grady, Exec.Asst.
Subjects: School safety, discipline, and social climate. **Holdings:** 500 volumes; 100,000 clippings. **Services:** Library open to school safety practitioners, school administrators, law enforcers, legislators, journalists. **Remarks:** FAX: (805)373-9277. **Formerly:** Located in Encino, CA.

★12939★
Pepsi-Cola International - Information Access Center (Food-Bev)
100 Stevens Ave.   Phone: (914)742-4882
Valhalla, NY 10595   Myron E. Menewitch, Mgr.
Founded: 1950. **Staff:** Prof 3; Other 3. **Subjects:** Beverages, food science, technology, chemistry, nutrition, engineering. **Holdings:** 3500 books. **Subscriptions:** 450 journals and other serials. **Services:** Center not open to the public. **Automated Operations:** Computerized public access catalog, cataloging, acquisitions, serials, and circulation. **Computerized Information Services:** DIALOG Information Services, STN International, NEXIS, PIERS (Port Import/Export Reporting Services), Dow Jones News/Retrieval, NewsNet, Inc., Reuters, DataTimes; internal database; DIALMAIL (electronic mail service). **Publications:** Information Access Center News, 10/year; Industry & Technical Alert, semimonthly - both for internal distribution only. **Remarks:** FAX: (914)742-4501. **Staff:** Mykel Lockwood, Tech.Serv.Info.Sci.

Pepsico - Information Access Center
See: **Pepsi-Cola International - Information Access Center** (12939)

★12940★
(Pereira) Biblioteca Colombo-Americano - USIS Collection (Educ)
Carrera 6, No. 22-26   Phone: 963 354291
Pereira, Colombia   Juliana B. Parra, Libn.
Founded: 1971. **Staff:** 2. **Holdings:** 2500 books; 21 bound periodical volumes; archival materials. **Subscriptions:** 21 journals and other serials; 3 newspapers. **Services:** Library open to the public. **Remarks:** Maintained or supported by the U.S. Information Agency. Focus is on materials that will assist peoples outside the United States to learn about the United States, its people, history, culture, political processes, and social milieux.

Peres Oblat
See: **Oblate Fathers - Bibliotheque Deschatelets** (12227)

Performing Arts Collection of South Australia
See: **Adelaide Festival Centre Trust** (72)

★ 12941 ★
Periodicals Institute - Library (Publ)
Box 899   Phone: (201)882-1130
West Caldwell, NJ 07007   John E. Fitzmaurice, Jr., Pres.
Founded: 1979. **Subjects:** Marketing for the publishing industry. **Holdings:** 2000 volumes. **Remarks:** FAX: (201)227-7475.

Perkes Library
See: **Canada - National Defence** (2790)

★ 12942 ★
Perkin-Elmer Corporation - Applied Science Division - Library
2771 N. Garey Ave.
Pomona, CA 91767
Founded: 1981. **Subjects:** Mass spectrometry, electronics, atmospheric monitors, analytical instrumentation, optics. **Holdings:** 659 books; 374 government documents, reports, patents. **Remarks:** Currently inactive.

★ 12943 ★
Perkin-Elmer Corporation - Corporate Library & Information Service (Sci-Engr)
761 Main Ave.   Phone: (203)834-4798
Norwalk, CT 06859-0249   Debra Kaufman, Mgr.
Founded: 1958. **Staff:** Prof 3; Other 3. **Subjects:** Analytical instruments, chemistry, optics, physics, mathematics, computer science, management. **Holdings:** 15,000 volumes; 20,000 documents; 40 VF drawers of reprints. **Subscriptions:** 450 journals and other serials. **Services:** Interlibrary loan; copying; library open to the public by appointment. **Automated Operations:** Computerized acquisitions, serials, and circulation. **Computerized Information Services:** DIALOG Information Services, STN International, NEXIS, Dow Jones News/Retrieval, InvesText. **Networks/Consortia:** Member of Southwestern Connecticut Library Council (SWLC). **Special Catalogs:** Catalog of internal and external engineering reports (book). **Remarks:** FAX: (203)834-4976. **Staff:** Bonnie Russ, Ref.Libn.; Karen Lanigan, Tech.Serv.Libn; Jude Boccuzzi, Lib.Sys.Admin.; Catherine Gardiner, Adm.; Theresa Napoletano.

★ 12944 ★
Perkin-Elmer Corporation - Metco Division - Engineering Library (Sci-Engr)
1101 Prospect Ave.
P.O. Box 1006   Phone: (516)334-1300
Westbury, NY 11590-0201   Joanne Festa, Adm.
Founded: 1964. **Staff:** 3. **Subjects:** Engineering - chemical, ceramic, electrical, mechanical, metallurgical. **Holdings:** 640 volumes; standards; handbooks; technical research and development reports. **Subscriptions:** 150 journals and other serials. **Services:** Interlibrary loan; library not open to the public. **Remarks:** FAX: (516)338-2488.

Richard S. Perkin Library
See: **American Museum of Natural History - Hayden Planetarium** (688)

★ 12945 ★
Perkins Coie - Library (Law)
1201 3rd Ave., 40th Fl.   Phone: (206)583-8888
Seattle, WA 98101-3099   Carol I. Warner, Mgr.
Staff: Prof 5; Other 6. **Subjects:** Law. **Holdings:** 40,000 volumes. **Subscriptions:** 1000 journals and other serials. **Services:** Interlibrary loan; library not open to the public. **Computerized Information Services:** LEXIS, WESTLAW, VU/TEXT Information Services, DataTimes, DIALOG Information Services, LEGI-SLATE, Dow Jones News/Retrieval, Dun & Bradstreet Business Credit Services, Reuters. **Networks/Consortia:** Member of Western Library Network (WLN). **Remarks:** FAX: (206)583-8500. **Staff:** Mark W. Munson, Libn.; Barbara Rothwell, Libn.; Catherine Horan, Libn.; Karen Braucht, Libn.

Perkins Observatory Library
See: **Ohio State University - Perkins Collections at Smith Laboratory and Perkins Observatory** (12323)

Ralph Perkins Memorial Library
See: **John D. Archbold Memorial Hospital** (940)

★ 12946 ★
Perkins School for the Blind - Samuel P. Hayes Research Library (Educ)
175 N. Beacon St.   Phone: (617)924-3434
Watertown, MA 02172   Kenneth A. Stuckey, Res.Libn.
Founded: 1880. **Staff:** Prof 1; Other 1. **Subjects:** Nonmedical aspects of blindness and deaf-blindness, including education, rehabilitation, welfare. **Special Collections:** Historical collection of embossed books printed for the blind; pictures of blind people; books by blind and deaf-blind; postage stamps which honor and aid the blind. **Holdings:** 18,000 volumes; bound newspaper clippings; Helen Keller material. **Subscriptions:** 125 journals and other serials. **Services:** Interlibrary loan; copying (articles and pamphlets only); library open to the public for reference use only. **Publications:** Accessions List, biennial - free upon request. **Remarks:** Collection includes a museum showing the history of education of the blind and aids and appliances for the blind.

Perkins School of Theology
See: **Southern Methodist University - Perkins School of Theology - The Bridwell Library** (15503)

★ 12947 ★
Perkins and Will Architects, Inc. - Resource Center (Plan)
123 N. Wacker Dr.   Phone: (312)977-1100
Chicago, IL 60606   Diane Johnson, Libn.
Staff: 1. **Subjects:** Building technology and products, architecture, design, planning, interior decorating, engineering. **Holdings:** 1000 books; 124 bound periodical volumes; 9 drawers and 750 linear feet of product literature; 100 linear feet of code files. **Subscriptions:** 130 journals and other serials. **Services:** Interlibrary loan; center not open to the public. **Remarks:** FAX: (312)977-0060.

★ 12948 ★
Permian Basin Petroleum Museum, Library and Hall of Fame - Archives Center (Energy)
1500 Interstate 20 W.   Phone: (915)683-4403
Midland, TX 79701   Betty Orbeck, Archv.
Staff: Prof 1; Other 1. **Subjects:** Petroleum industry and company history; biographies and autobiographies of oil personnel; oil well exploration, drilling, production, refining, marketing, transportation, service, supply; Permian Basin of West Texas and Southeastern New Mexico. **Holdings:** 1000 books; 600 bound periodical volumes; 500 taped oral history interviews with typed transcripts; 6000 photographic prints and negatives; equipment and tool catalogs, 1884, 1891-1982; oil company internal journals, 1918-1936; motion picture films, 1926-1951 and 1985; newspapers, 1911-1963; maps. **Subscriptions:** 20 journals and other serials. **Services:** Interlibrary loan; copying; center open to the public. **Publications:** Museum Memo, bimonthly.

★ 12949 ★
Perry County Law Library (Law)
Court House   Phone: (717)582-2131
New Bloomfield, PA 17068   Jeffrey Sotland, Libn.
Founded: 1856. **Staff:** 1. **Subjects:** Law. **Holdings:** 3000 books. **Subscriptions:** 3 journals and other serials. **Services:** Copying; library open to the public. **Publications:** Perry and Juniata Reporter.

★ 12950 ★
Perry Historians - Library (Hist)
P.O. Box 73
Newport, PA 17074   Jean Bonham
Founded: 1976. **Staff:** 3. **Subjects:** Genealogy, local history. **Special Collections:** Taufschein Collection (60 items). **Holdings:** 3000 books; 400 reels of microfilm; 1000 land drafts; 4500 family surname files; 500,000 index cards. **Subscriptions:** 9 journals and other serials. **Services:** Copying; library open to the public on a limited schedule; provides research services. **Computerized Information Services:** Internal database (under development). Contact Person: Fae Cupp. **Publications:** The Perry Review, annual; The Airy View (newsletter with inquiry section), 6/year.

★ 12951 ★
Perry Memorial Hospital - Dr. Kenneth O. Nelson Library of the Health Sciences (Med)
530 Park Ave., E.   Phone: (815)875-2811
Princeton, IL 61356   Linda Litherland, Dir.Med.Rec.
Staff: Prof 1. **Subjects:** Medicine. **Holdings:** 750 books. **Subscriptions:** 31 journals and other serials. **Services:** Interlibrary loan; copying; library open to the public with restrictions. **Automated Operations:** Computerized cataloging, acquisitions, serials, and circulation. **Networks/Consortia:** Member of National Network of Libraries of Medicine - Greater Midwest Region, Heart of Illinois Library Consortium (HILC), ILLINET.

Merle G. Perry Archives
See: **Alfred P. Sloan, Jr. Museum** (15222)

Perry's Victory & International Peace Memorial
See: **U.S. Natl. Park Service** (17763)

★ 12952 ★
Pershing & Company Inc. - Research Library (Bus-Fin)
1 Pershing Plaza   Phone: (201)413-2205
Jersey City, NJ 07399   Rose M. Acevedo, Res.Asst.
Founded: 1969. **Staff:** Prof 1; Other 2. **Subjects:** Business and finance. **Special Collections:** Publications of Arthur D. Little, Inc. **Holdings:** 900 books; 60 bound periodical volumes; 3000 corporate files; 5000 institutional studies; 80 Conference Board publications. **Subscriptions:** 147 journals and other serials; 25 newspapers. **Services:** Interlibrary loan; copying; library open to correspondents, staff, and other libraries. **Remarks:** FAX: (212)413-5299. Pershing & Company Inc. is a division of Donaldson, Lufkin & Jenrette, Inc.

★ 12953 ★
Personal Products Company - Research & Development Library (Sci-Engr)
Van Liew Ave.   Phone: (908)524-0225
Milltown, NJ 08850   P. Otani, Sr.Info.Sci.
Founded: 1954. **Staff:** Prof 1. **Subjects:** Chemistry, paper, textiles, microbiology. **Holdings:** 3150 books; 2550 bound periodical volumes; 2 VF drawers and 21 reels of microfilm of patents; 35 VF drawers and 700 microfiche of company reports. **Subscriptions:** 140 journals and other serials. **Services:** Interlibrary loan; library not open to the public. **Automated Operations:** Computerized patent files, circulation, and indexing of research reports. **Computerized Information Services:** DIALOG Information Services. **Remarks:** FAX: (908)524-0201. A subsidiary of Johnson & Johnson.

Perth Amboy General Hospital
See: **Raritan Bay Medical Center** (13717)

★ 12954 ★
(Perth) American Center - USIS Library (Educ)
Scottish Amicable House, 9th Fl.
246 St. George's Terrace
Perth, WA 6000, Australia
Remarks: Maintained or supported by the U.S. Information Agency. Focus is on materials that will assist peoples outside the United States to learn about the United States, its people, history, culture, political processes, and social milieux.

W.T. Peryam Library
See: **Grand Encampment Museum, Inc. - Library** (6621)

★ 12955 ★
(Peshawar) American Center - USIS Library (Educ)
17 Chinar Rd.
University Town
Peshawar, Pakistan
Remarks: Maintained or supported by the U.S. Information Agency. Focus is on materials that will assist peoples outside the United States to learn about the United States, its people, history, culture, political processes, and social milieux.

Pesticide Action Network North America Regional Center
See: **PAN North America Regional Center - International Information Links Program** (12721)

★ 12956 ★
Pet Incorporated - Corporate Information Center (Food-Bev)
400 S. 4th St.   Phone: (314)622-6134
St. Louis, MO 63102   Laurence R. Walton, Mgr.
Founded: 1960. **Staff:** Prof 2; Other 1. **Subjects:** Food science and technology, nutrition, microbiology, cookery, dairy science, food business, food economics, marketing. **Special Collections:** Cookbook Collection (2500 volumes; 400 pre-1900 volumes). **Holdings:** 25,000 books; 2000 bound periodical volumes; microfiche; government research reports on food. **Subscriptions:** 650 journals and other serials; 12 newspapers. **Services:** Interlibrary loan; copying; center open to the public by appointment. **Automated Operations:** Computerized cataloging and serials. **Computerized Information Services:** DIALOG Information Services, Dow Jones News/ Retrieval, PFDS Online, NEXIS, The Financial Post DataGroup, MEDLINE, STN International, DataTimes. **Networks/Consortia:** Member of St. Louis Regional Library Network. **Publications:** PET News Notes, weekly. **Remarks:** FAX: (314)622-6525. **Staff:** Roseann Huddleston, Asst.Libn.

Petawawa National Forestry Institute
See: **Canada - Forestry Canada** (2744)

Peter Memorial Library
See: **Moravian Music Foundation, Inc.** (10722)

Peterborough Cathedral Library
See: **University of Cambridge - Library** (18441)

★ 12957 ★
Peterborough Historical Society - Library (Hist)
Grove St.
Box 58   Phone: (603)924-3235
Peterborough, NH 03458   Ellen Derby, Exec.Dir.
Founded: 1902. **Staff:** Prof 1; Other 2. **Subjects:** History of Peterborough and New Hampshire, antiques. **Special Collections:** 19th century photographs of local people and scenes; early school books; antiques (books; pamphlets). **Holdings:** 1000 books; tax records; clippings; early mill account books; maps; letters; early deeds; scrapbooks. **Services:** Library open to the public.

Peters Health Sciences Library
See: **Rhode Island Hospital** (13870)

Petersburg National Battlefield
See: **U.S. Natl. Park Service** (17764)

★ 12958 ★
Petersham Historical Society, Inc. - Library (Hist)
Main St.   Phone: (508)724-3380
Petersham, MA 01366   Delight Gale Haines, Libn./Cur.
Founded: 1912. **Staff:** Prof 1. **Subjects:** Petersham history and genealogy. **Special Collections:** Shays' Rebellion; Howe/Negus/Willard papers, 1786-1892. **Holdings:** 800 books; 600 pamphlets and reports; 15 VF drawers of documents, diaries, pictures; 8 VF drawers of clippings and manuscripts; 20 maps. **Services:** Library open to the public with restrictions.

★ 12959 ★
Peterson & Ross - Library (Law)
200 E. Randolph Dr., Suite 7300   Phone: (312)861-1400
Chicago, IL 60601-6969   Linda DeVaun
Staff: Prof 1; Other 1.5. **Subjects:** American law. **Holdings:** 18,000 books. **Subscriptions:** 150 journals and other serials; 3 newspapers. **Services:** Interlibrary loan; library not open to the public. **Computerized Information Services:** DIALOG Information Services, BRS Information Technologies, VU/TEXT Information Services, DataTimes, Dow Jones News/Retrieval, NewsNet, Inc., Data-Star, OCLC EPIC, LEGI-SLATE, Hannah Information Systems. **Publications:** Newsletter. **Remarks:** FAX: (312)861-9538. **Formerly:** Peterson, Ross, Schloerb, & Seidel - Library.

★ 12960 ★
Symon Petlura Institute - Archives (Area-Ethnic)
381 Concord Ave.   Phone: (416)533-8205
Toronto, ON, Canada M6H 2P9   Dr. Oleh S. Pidhainy, Pres./Archv.Dir.
Founded: 1977. **Staff:** Prof 1. **Subjects:** Ukraine. **Special Collections:**
Ukrainian and East European scholarship in North America and the world;
The Great Artificial Famine in Ukraine, 1932-1933; Christianization of the
Ukraine, 988 A.D.; Symon Petlura, 1879-1926; 20th century Ukraine.
Holdings: Figures not available.

★ 12961 ★
Petoskey News-Review - Library (Publ)
319 State St.   Phone: (616)347-2544
Petoskey, MI 49770   Babette Stenuis
Founded: 1960. **Subjects:** Newspaper reference topics. **Holdings:** Newspaper
clippings; microfilm. **Remarks:** FAX: (616)347-6833.

Petrified Forest National Park
See: **U.S. Natl. Park Service** (17765)

★ 12962 ★
Petro-Canada - Law Library (Law)
150 6th Ave., S.W.
P.O. Box 2844
Calgary, AB, Canada T2P 3E3   Phone: (403)296-8592
                                          Susan Beugin, Law Libn.
Founded: 1984. **Staff:** Prof 1. **Subjects:** Law. **Holdings:** 5000 volumes.
Subscriptions: 171 journals and other serials. **Services:** Interlibrary loan;
library not open to the public. **Automated Operations:** Computerized
cataloging, acquisitions, and serials. **Computerized Information Services:**
QL Systems, Canada Systems Group (CSG), Info Globe; internal database.
Remarks: FAX: (403)296-4990.

★ 12963 ★
Petro-Canada - Library Services (Energy)
150 6th Ave., S.W.
P.O. Box 2844
Calgary, AB, Canada T2P 3E3   Phone: (403)296-8955
Staff: Prof 4; Other 5. **Subjects:** Petroleum geology and engineering,
environment, energy economics, marketing. **Holdings:** 15,000 books; 600
company reports. **Subscriptions:** 500 journals and other serials; 10
newspapers. **Services:** Interlibrary loan; library not open to the public.
Automated Operations: Computerized cataloging, acquisitions, serials,
circulation, and ILL. **Computerized Information Services:** Online systems;
CD-ROM; Envoy 100 (electronic mail service). **Remarks:** FAX: (403)296-
3030. Electronic mail address(es): ILL.ACPC (Envoy 100). **Staff:** Joyce
Johnston; Buffy Knill; Cecilia Harel; Jean Peterson.

★ 12964 ★
Petro-Canada Products - Technical Library (Energy)
2489 N. Sheridan Way   Phone: (416)822-6770
Mississauga, ON, Canada L5K 1A8   W.A. Davis, Supv.
Founded: 1965. **Staff:** Prof 1. **Subjects:** Petroleum chemistry and
technology. **Special Collections:** Society of Automotive Engineers
Transactions, 1965 to present; Canadian Patents, 1977-1985; U.S. Chemical
Patents, 1952 to present. **Holdings:** 9000 books; 1600 bound periodical
volumes. **Subscriptions:** 275 journals and other serials; 5 newspapers.
Services: Interlibrary loan; copying; SDI; library open to the public by
appointment. **Automated Operations:** Computerized cataloging and serials.
Computerized Information Services: CAN/OLE, DIALOG Information
Services, Info Globe, STN International, ORBIT Search Service. **Networks/**
Consortia: Member of Sheridan Park Association. **Remarks:** FAX:
(416)896-6740.

Petroleo Brasileiro, S.A. - Leopoldo A. Miguez de Mello Research and
   Development Center
See: **Leopoldo A. Miguez de Mello Research and Development Center**
   (10384)

Petroleum Recovery Institute - I.N. McKinnon Memorial Library
See: **I.N. McKinnon Memorial Library** (9933)

★ 12965 ★
Petrolite Corporation - Information Center (Sci-Engr)
369 Marshall Ave.   Phone: (314)968-6008
St. Louis, MO 63119   Yvonne Ali, Mgr.
Founded: 1959. **Staff:** Prof 2; Other 2. **Subjects:** Chemistry - organic,
petroleum, corrosion; water treatment; wax. **Holdings:** 7500 books; 8900
bound periodical volumes; 99,100 patents; 36,000 microfiche; 10 VF drawers
of trade literature. **Subscriptions:** 250 journals and other serials. **Services:**
Interlibrary loan; copying; center open to the public by appointment.
Automated Operations: Computerized circulation and periodical routing.
Computerized Information Services: DIALOG Information Services,
ORBIT Search Service, Chemical Information Systems, Inc. (CIS), STN
International, NLM, OCLC; internal database; DIALMAIL (electronic
mail service). **Networks/Consortia:** Member of St. Louis Regional Library
Network, Missouri Library Network Corp. (MLNC). **Publications:**
Acquisitions, quarterly. **Remarks:** FAX: (314)968-6290. Telex 193164.

★ 12966 ★
Pettaquamscutt Historical Society - Library (Hist)
2636 Kingstown Rd.   Phone: (401)783-1328
Kingston, RI 02881   Elizabeth R. Albro, Cur.
Founded: 1958. **Staff:** 1. **Subjects:** Local history and genealogy, Rhode
Island history. **Holdings:** 1000 books; manuscripts. **Services:** Library open
to the public on a limited schedule or by appointment. **Publications:**
Pettaquamscutt Reporter, 5/year - to members.

James Pettinger Memorial Library
See: **Economic Development Council of Northeastern Pennsylvania**
   (5215)

★ 12967 ★
Pettit & Martin - Library (Law)
101 California, 35th Fl.   Phone: (415)434-4000
San Francisco, CA 94111   Lynn Brazil, Hd.Libn.
Staff: Prof 2; Other 2. **Subjects:** Law. **Holdings:** 28,000 books; 1100 bound
periodical volumes. **Subscriptions:** 400 journals and other serials. **Services:**
Interlibrary loan; copying; library open to the public by permission only.
Computerized Information Services: LEXIS, NEXIS, DIALOG
Information Services, Dow Jones News/Retrieval, RLIN, DataTimes,
Information America, VU/TEXT Information Services, InvesText, LEGI-
SLATE, Dun & Bradstreet Business Credit Services, CCH. **Networks/**
Consortia: Member of CLASS. **Staff:** Nancy Adams, Asst.Libn.

Almeda May Castle Petzinger Library
See: **The Haggin Museum - Almeda May Castle Petzinger Library** (6827)

John G. Pew Memorial Library
See: **Delaware County Historical Society** (4717)

Joseph N. Pew, Jr. Medical Library
See: **Bryn Mawr Hospital** (2306)

Annie Merner Pfeiffer Library
See: **West Virginia Wesleyan College** (20226)

Henry Pfeiffer Library
See: **MacMurray College** (9504)

Pfeiffer Physics Library
See: **Washington University** (20066)

Richard C. Pfeiffer Library
See: **Tiffin University** (16351)

★12968★
Pfizer Canada Inc. - Medical Library (Med)
P.O. Box 800
Pointe Claire-Dorval, PQ, Canada   Phone: (514)426-7060
H9R 4V2   Miriam Hayward, Sci.Info.Off.
Founded: 1980. **Staff:** Prof 1. **Subjects:** Pharmacology, drug therapy, rheumatology, cardiovasology, psychotherapy, microbiology, allergies, dermatology. **Holdings:** 900 books; 100 bound periodical volumes; 50 audiocassettes; 9000 reprints; 125 meeting and symposia proceedings; 90 pieces of product information; journals on microfilm; 80 other cataloged items. **Subscriptions:** 130 journals and other serials. **Services:** SDI; library open to health professionals, sales representatives, and students. **Computerized Information Services:** MEDLARS, DIALOG Information Services, Data-Star, Lithium Library; Envoy 100 (electronic mail service). **Publications:** Bibliographies; Current Awareness - both for internal distribution only. **Remarks:** FAX: (514)426-7065. Electronic mail address(es): HAYWARD.M (Envoy 100).

★12969★
Pfizer, Inc. - Central Research - Research Library (Med, Sci-Engr)
Eastern Point Rd.   Phone: (203)441-3687
Groton, CT 06340   Dr. Roger P. Nelson, Dir.
Founded: 1960. **Staff:** Prof 8; Other 6. **Subjects:** Organic and pharmaceutical chemistry, pharmacology, antibiotics. **Holdings:** 7000 books; 30,000 bound periodical volumes; 2500 reels of microfilm of patent specifications. **Subscriptions:** 1000 journals and other serials. **Services:** Library open on request to students and researchers. **Automated Operations:** Computerized cataloging, acquisitions, and serials. **Computerized Information Services:** DIALOG Information Services, PFDS Online, NLM, Chemical Abstracts Service (CAS). **Networks/Consortia:** Member of Southeastern Connecticut Library Association (SECLA), NELINET, Inc. **Publications:** Infosource. **Special Indexes:** Central Patents Index - Sections A, B, D, and E; Unlisted Drugs (card). **Remarks:** FAX: (203)441-5729. **Staff:** John B. Hare, Info.Sci.; Roberta Lewis Morton, Libn.; E. Shoop, Info.Sci.; Dr. David Larson, Info.Sci.; Chih-Wu Chang, Info.Sci.; Georgia Rodeffer, Hd., Lib.Serv.; Candace Way, Ser.Libn.

★12970★
Pfizer, Inc. - N.Y.O. Library 235-5-16 (Med)
235 E. 42nd St.   Phone: (212)573-2966
New York, NY 10017   Veronica Plucinski, Mgr., Lib.Serv.
Staff: Prof 3; Other 1. **Subjects:** Pharmaceuticals, pharmacology, clinical medicine. **Holdings:** 15,000 volumes; 1500 reels of microfilm. **Subscriptions:** 630 journals and other serials. **Services:** Interlibrary loan; SDI; library open to students and researchers by appointment. **Automated Operations:** Computerized serials. **Computerized Information Services:** DIALOG Information Services, PFDS Online, BRS Information Technologies, Data-Star, MEDLARS. **Networks/Consortia:** Member of Medical Library Center of New York (MLCNY). **Publications:** Periodical Subscription List, annual; Periodical Subject List, annual - free upon request. **Remarks:** FAX: (212)573-7851. **Staff:** Karen Erani, Assoc.Libn.; Clara Henson, Lib.Asst.

★12971★
Pfizer, Inc. - Technical Center Library (Law)
640 N. 13th St.   Phone: (215)250-3284
Easton, PA 18042-1497   Vicky Schafer, Libn.
Staff: 1. **Holdings:** Patents. **Services:** Library not open to the public. **Remarks:** FAX: (215)250-3352.

Anthony C. Pfohl Health Science Library
See: **Mercy Health Center** (10129)

Carl & Lily Pforzheimer Foundation, Inc. - Carl H. Pforzheimer Library
See: **New York Public Library - Carl H. Pforzheimer Shelley and His Circle Collection** (11599)

Pforzheimer Library of English Literature
See: **University of Texas at Austin - Harry Ransom Humanities Research Center** (19392)

Pharmacia Ophthalmics - Library
See: **KABI Pharmacia Ophthalmics - Library** (8502)

★12972★
Pharmacia P-L Biochemicals, Inc. - Library (Biol Sci)
2202 N. Bartlett Ave.
Milwaukee, WI 53202   Phone: (414)227-3663
Founded: 1944. **Staff:** Prof 1. **Subjects:** Microbiology, biochemistry, chemistry. **Holdings:** 2786 books; 1482 bound periodical volumes. **Subscriptions:** 90 journals and other serials. **Services:** Interlibrary loan; SDI; library open to the public by appointment. **Computerized Information Services:** DIALOG Information Services, NLM, STN International. **Networks/Consortia:** Member of Library Council of Metropolitan Milwaukee, Inc. (LCOMM). **Publications:** P-L Library News - for internal distribution only. **Remarks:** FAX: (414)227-3759. Telex: 260101.

★12973★
Pharmaco-Medical Documentation Inc. - Library (Med)
P.O. Box 429   Phone: (201)822-9200
Chatham, NJ 07928   Rajka B. Anzlowar, Tech.Dir.
Staff: Prof 4. **Subjects:** Pharmaceuticals, pharmacology, drug marketing. **Holdings:** 3500 volumes; machine-readable tapes; and other cataloged items. **Subscriptions:** 400 journals and other serials. **Services:** Library not open to the public. **Publications:** Pharm-AID; Unlisted Drugs, monthly, semiannual indexes; Unlisted Drugs Index-Guide; Unlisted Drugs on Cards, monthly; World Pharmaceuticals Directory. **Remarks:** FAX: (201)765-0722.

Phase Diagrams for Ceramists
See: **U.S. Natl. Institute of Standards and Technology - Phase Diagrams for Ceramists** (17622)

Gerald B. Phelan Archives
See: **University of Toronto - Pontifical Institute of Mediaeval Studies - Library** (19458)

Hal C. Phelps Archives
See: **Miami County Museum** (10248)

Philadelphia - College of Osteopathic Medicine, Parkview - Hospital
See: **Parkview - Osteopathic Medical Center of Philadelphia** (12757)

★12974★
Philadelphia Association for Psychoanalysis - Louis Kaplan Memorial Library (Med)
15 St. Asaph's Rd., P.O. Box 36   Phone: (215)839-3966
Bala Cynwyd, PA 19004   June M. Strickland, Libn.
Founded: 1950. **Staff:** Prof 1. **Subjects:** Psychoanalysis. **Holdings:** 2500 books; 2400 bound periodical volumes. **Subscriptions:** 10 journals and other serials. **Services:** Library not open to the public.

Philadelphia Baptists - Audio-Visual Resource Library
See: **Audio-Visual Resource Library** (1288)

★12975★
Philadelphia City Archives (Hist)
Dept. of Records
Rm. 942
401 N. Broad St.   Phone: (215)686-1580
Philadelphia, PA 19108   Ward J. Childs, C.A., City Archv.
Founded: 1952. **Staff:** Prof 5; Other 5. **Subjects:** Archives of the City and County of Philadelphia, 1683 to present. **Special Collections:** Official records of the 1876 Centennial Exhibition, 1926 Sesquicentennial Exposition, and 1976 Bicentennial celebration of the city of Philadelphia. **Holdings:** 20,000 cubic feet of archives; 100,000 cubic feet of Records Center holdings. **Services:** Copying; archives open to the public with restrictions. **Publications:** City Archives Newsletter; list of other publications - available on request. **Special Catalogs:** Descriptive Inventory of the Archives of the City and County of Philadelphia (book). **Special Indexes:** Subject Index to the Photograph Collection of the Philadelphia City Archives (book); Warrants and Surveys of the Province of Pennsylvania including the Three Lower Counties, 1759. **Remarks:** Maintained by the Records Department, City of Philadelphia. **Staff:** Jefferson M. Moak, Archv. II; Lee Stanley, C.A., Archv. II; John Di Crosta, Act.Rec. Storage Ctr. Supv.; Marjorie Van Note, Cons.

★ 12976 ★
Philadelphia City Planning Commission - Library
1515 Market St., 17th Fl.
Philadelphia, PA 19103
Founded: 1944. **Subjects:** City and regional planning, housing, transportation, government, architecture, engineering, business and industry, sociology, statistics. **Special Collections:** Archives of the commission (2 VF drawers); Philadelphia renewal areas (4000 35mm slides). **Holdings:** 22,000 books and pamphlets; 1000 bound periodical volumes. **Remarks:** Currently inactive.

★ 12977 ★
(Philadelphia City) Water Department - Library (Biol Sci, Env-Cons)
ARA Tower, 3rd Fl.
1101 Market St.   Phone: (215)592-6232
Philadelphia, PA 19107   Raymond F. Roedell, Jr., Libn. II
Founded: 1988. **Staff:** 3. **Subjects:** Water - all aspects; civil engineering; public utility management; hazardous waste; water pollution; sludge/wastewater. **Holdings:** 3000 books; bound periodical volumes; documents; AV programs; nonbook items. **Subscriptions:** 100 journals and other serials; 7 newspapers. **Services:** Interlibrary loan; copying; SDI; library open to the public with restrictions. **Computerized Information Services:** DIALOG Information Services, BRS Information Technologies, VU/TEXT Information Services, MEDLARS, MEDLINE, LEXIS, NEXIS, WILSONLINE, OCLC, EPIC. **Networks/Consortia:** Member of Delaware Valley Information Consortium (DEVIC), Philadelphia Regional Interlibrary Loan Group (PRILL), BHSL, Delaware Library Consortium (DLC). **Remarks:** Alternate telephone number(s): 592-6370. FAX: (215)592-6154.

★ 12978 ★
Philadelphia College of Bible - Learning Resource Center (Rel-Phil)
200 Manor Ave.   Phone: (215)752-5800
Langhorne, PA 19047-2992   Julius C. Bosco, Dir.
Founded: 1913. **Staff:** Prof 2; Other 1. **Subjects:** Theology and Bible study, music, Christian education, elementary education, social work, missions. **Special Collections:** Hymnals; C.I. Scofield Library of Biblical Studies. **Holdings:** 60,576 books, bound periodical volumes, scores; 5623 slides; 1112 reels of microfilm; 17,164 microfiche; 3737 phonograph records; 317 filmstrips; 36 films; 926 cassettes; 2798 curriculum materials. **Subscriptions:** 479 journals and other serials; 8 newspapers. **Services:** Interlibrary loan; library open to the public with restrictions. **Automated Operations:** Computerized cataloging. **Computerized Information Services:** OCLC. **Remarks:** FAX: (215)752-5812. **Formerly:** Its Library. **Staff:** Dorothy M. Black, Asst.Libn.

★ 12979 ★
Philadelphia College of Osteopathic Medicine - O.J. Snyder Memorial Medical Library (Med)
4150 City Ave.   Phone: (215)871-2821
Philadelphia, PA 19131   Dr. Shanker H. Vyas, Prof./Dir. of Libs.
Founded: 1898. **Staff:** Prof 3; Other 7. **Subjects:** Osteopathy, medicine, surgery. **Special Collections:** First editions of works on osteopathy, many autographed; archives of osteopathy. **Holdings:** 65,406 volumes; 5239 audiotapes; 1608 videotapes; 112 reels of 35mm microfilm; 6255 slides; 323 view master reels; 946 filmstrips; 16 anatomy study wheels. **Subscriptions:** 671 journals; 97 osteopathic serials. **Services:** Interlibrary loan; copying; microfilming; library open to the public for reference use only with permission. **Computerized Information Services:** MEDLINE. **Networks/Consortia:** Member of National Network of Libraries of Medicine - Middle Atlantic Region, Health Sciences Libraries Consortium (HSLC). **Publications:** List of publications - available upon request. **Special Indexes:** Major medical indices; Union List of Osteopathic Literature. **Remarks:** FAX: (215)871-2824. **Staff:** Prof. Hansa S. Vyas, Assoc.Dir./Search Anl./Ref.Libn.; Kathryn Picardo, Asst.Prof./Cat.Libn.

★ 12980 ★
Philadelphia College of Pharmacy and Science - Joseph W. England Library (Med)
42nd St. & Woodland Ave.   Phone: (215)596-8960
Philadelphia, PA 19104-4491   Mignon Adams, Dir., Lib.Serv.
Founded: 1822. **Staff:** Prof 7; Other 10. **Subjects:** Pharmacy, pharmacology, biological sciences, chemistry, pharmacognosy, toxicology. **Special Collections:** History of pharmacy. **Holdings:** 62,361 volumes; 5000 reels of microfilm; 18,000 microfiche; 150 audio cassettes; 24 VF drawers of

pamphlets; AV programs. **Subscriptions:** 751 journals and other serials. **Services:** Interlibrary loan; copying; library open to the public for reference use only. **Automated Operations:** Integrated automated system. **Computerized Information Services:** DIALOG Information Services, BRS Information Technologies, NLM, Chemical Information Systems, Inc. (CIS), OCLC, STN International, WILSONLINE; InterNet (electronic mail service). Performs searches on fee basis. Contact Person: Sue Brizuela, Hd., Pub.Serv., 596-8963. **Networks/Consortia:** Member of National Network of Libraries of Medicine - Middle Atlantic Region, PALINET, Interlibrary Delivery Service of Pennsylvania (IDS), Health Sciences Libraries Consortium (HSLC), Tri-State College Library Cooperative (TCLC). **Remarks:** Fax: (215)222-5060. Electronic mail address(es): ADAMS@SHRSYS.HSLS.ORG (InterNet). **Staff:** Leslie Bowman, Hd., Tech.Serv./Cat.; Kathleen Smith, ILL/Ser.; Jacqueline Smith, Hd., Lrng.Rsrcs.

★ 12981 ★
Philadelphia College of Textiles and Science - Pastore Library (Sci-Engr)
School House Lane & Henry Ave.   Phone: (215)951-2840
Philadelphia, PA 19144   Evelyn Minick, Dir. of Lib.Serv.
Founded: 1949. **Staff:** Prof 5; Other 7. **Subjects:** Textiles, textile manufacturing, apparel, fashion, architecture, design, business. **Special Collections:** Textile history. **Holdings:** 75,000 books; 12,000 bound periodical volumes; 6000 reels of microfilm. **Subscriptions:** 1542 journals and other serials; 20 newspapers. **Services:** Interlibrary loan; copying; library open to the public for reference use only. **Automated Operations:** Computerized cataloging, acquisitions and serials. **Computerized Information Services:** DIALOG Information Services, OCLC EPIC, WILSONLINE, DunsPrint, Textile Technology Digest, BPI; Infotrack. Performs searches on fee basis. Contact Person: Stan Gorski, Hd., Pub.Serv./Access Serv., 951-2841. **Networks/Consortia:** Member of Tri-State College Library Cooperative (TCLC), PALINET. **Remarks:** FAX: (215)848-1144. **Staff:** J. Thomas Vogel, Coll.Dev.; Barbara Lowry, Hd., Tech.Serv.; Wilfred Frisby, Ref.Libn.; Barry Cohen, Audiovisual Serv.

★ 12982 ★
Philadelphia Common Pleas & Municipal Court - Law Library (Law)
City Hall, Rm. 600   Phone: (215)686-3799
Philadelphia, PA 19107   James M. Clark, Law Libn.
Founded: 1970. **Staff:** Prof 1; Other 4. **Subjects:** U.S. and Pennsylvania law. **Holdings:** 34,000 books; 500 bound periodical volumes; 3 VF drawers of Pennsylvania House and Senate bills; 3 VF drawers of Pennsylvania Appellate Court Slip opinions; 50 audio cassettes; 20 videocassettes. **Subscriptions:** 125 journals and other serials; 10 newspapers. **Services:** Interlibrary loan; library not open to the public. **Automated Operations:** Computerized cataloging. **Computerized Information Services:** LEXIS, NEXIS, OCLC. **Special Indexes:** Subject index to Pennsylvania Appellate Court Slip Opinions. **Remarks:** FAX: (215)686-2215. **Staff:** Francis F. Klock, Dir., Spec.Proj.

(Philadelphia) Community Legal Services, Inc.
See: Community Legal Services, Inc. (4085)

★ 12983 ★
Philadelphia Corporation for Aging - Library (Soc Sci)
642 N. Broad St.   Phone: (215)765-9000
Philadelphia, PA 19130   Maureen Neville, Ref.Libn.
Founded: 1978. **Staff:** Prof 1; Other 1. **Subjects:** Gerontology, gerontological literature, programs for the aging. **Special Collections:** Service Center for Aging Information Microfiche Repository Collection (SCAN; 3000 gerontology-related research documents on microfiche). **Holdings:** 2000 books; 127 periodical volumes on microfiche; 400 government publications; 6540 documents; 16 VF drawers of pamphlets and reports. **Subscriptions:** 70 journals and other serials; 5 newspapers. **Services:** Interlibrary loan; copying; library open to the public for reference use only by appointment. **Computerized Information Services:** BRS Information Technologies. **Networks/Consortia:** Member of National Network of Libraries of Medicine - Middle Atlantic Region. **Publications:** Quarterly Acquisitions List. **Remarks:** Corporation is an Area Agency on Aging. FAX: (215)765-9066.

★12984★
Philadelphia District Attorney's Office - Library (Law)
1421 Arch St. Phone: (215)686-5768
Philadelphia, PA 19102 Carol Sue Steinbach, Lib.Dir.
Subjects: Law. **Remarks:** No further information was supplied by respondent.

★12985★
Philadelphia Electric Company - Library (Energy)
2301 Market St. Phone: (215)841-4358
Philadelphia, PA 19101 Sabina D. Tannenbaum, Libn.
Founded: 1909. **Staff:** Prof 2; Other 2. **Subjects:** Engineering - civil, electrical, mechanical, chemical; generating stations - hydro, nuclear, steam; nuclear energy; public utilities. **Special Collections:** Electric Power Research Institute reports. **Holdings:** 8000 volumes; 10,000 pamphlets and reports. **Subscriptions:** 250 journals and other serials. **Services:** Interlibrary loan; library open to the public by appointment. **Computerized Information Services:** DIALOG Information Services, ORBIT Search Service, VU/TEXT Information Services, Dow Jones News/Retrieval, WESTLAW; Knight-Ridder Unicom/GASNET; DIALMAIL (electronic mail services). **Networks/Consortia:** Member of Philadelphia Regional Interlibrary Loan Group (PRILL). **Remarks:** FAX: (215)841-4088. Electronic mail address(es): EEI058 (Knight-Ridder Unicom/GASNET). **Staff:** Christian C. Braig, Assoc.Libn.

★12986★
Philadelphia Geriatric Center - Library (Soc Sci, Med)
5301 Old York Rd. Phone: (215)456-2971
Philadelphia, PA 19141 Joyce A. Post, Libn.
Founded: 1959. **Staff:** Prof 1; Other 1. **Subjects:** Gerontology, geriatrics, psychology, sociology, housing, long-term care administration, anthropology, research methods, death and dying. **Holdings:** 1100 books; 450 bound periodical volumes. **Subscriptions:** 200 journals and other serials. **Services:** Interlibrary loan; copying; library open to the public by appointment. **Automated Operations:** Computerized cataloging and acquisitions. **Computerized Information Services:** MEDLINE, DIALOG Information Services, BRS Information Technologies, EPIC; DOCLINE (electronic mail service). Performs searches on fee basis. **Networks/Consortia:** Member of Delaware Valley Information Consortium (DEVIC), BHSL, Philadelphia Regional Interlibrary Loan Group (PRILL). **Publications:** Library Newsletter and Acquisitions list, bimonthly. **Remarks:** FAX: (215)456-2017.

★12987★
Philadelphia Historical Commission - Library (Hist)
1401 Arch St., Suite 1301 Phone: (215)686-4543
Philadelphia, PA 19102 Dr. Richard Tyler, Hist.
Founded: 1955. **Staff:** Prof 4. **Subjects:** Philadelphia - architectural history, architecture, history. **Holdings:** 1500 books; 25 cabinets of manuscript records including insurance surveys, briefs of titles, photostats of old prints, photographs of buildings in Philadelphia. **Subscriptions:** 10 journals and other serials. **Services:** Library open to the public by appointment. **Staff:** Daniel W. Simox; Randal Baron.

★12988★
Philadelphia Jewish Archives Center at the Balch Institute (Area-Ethnic)
18 S. 7th St. Phone: (215)925-8090
Philadelphia, PA 19106 Lily G. Schwartz, Archv.
Founded: 1972. **Staff:** Prof 2. **Subjects:** Jewish community of Philadelphia - social welfare agencies, synagogues, fraternal organizations. **Holdings:** 2000 books; 2400 cubic feet of archival materials; 3000 photographs; 270 reels of microfilm. **Services:** Interlibrary loan; copying; center open to the public for reference use only. **Publications:** PJAC News, biennial; Guide to the Holdings of the Philadelphia Jewish Archives Center (1977). **Remarks:** Maintained by the Jewish Federation of Greater Philadelphia. **Staff:** Franklin C. Muse, Asst.Archv.

★12989★
Philadelphia Maritime Museum - Library (Hist)
321 Chestnut St. Phone: (215)925-5439
Philadelphia, PA 19106 E. Ann Wilcox, Libn.
Founded: 1974. **Staff:** Prof 1. **Subjects:** Philadelphia port and general maritime history. **Special Collections:** Vessel registers (1500 volumes); Port Records, 1798 to present; Boat Plans (9000). **Holdings:** 12,000 books; 12 VF drawers of photographs; manuscripts; oral history tapes; microfilm; pamphlets; charts; maps. **Subscriptions:** 200 journals and other serials. **Services:** Copying; library open to the public by appointment. **Automated Operations:** Computerized cataloging. **Computerized Information Services:** OCLC. **Networks/Consortia:** Member of PALINET.

★12990★
Philadelphia Museum of Art - Library (Art)
Box 7646 Phone: (215)763-8100
Philadelphia, PA 19101 Anita Gilden, Libn.
Founded: 1876. **Staff:** Prof 3; Other 3. **Subjects:** Fine arts. **Special Collections:** Kienbusch Library of Arms and Armour (2500 volumes); museum archives; medieval and renaissance art; decorative art; Italian and Dutch painting; Americian art; 20th century art. **Holdings:** 130,000 books, periodicals, pamphlets; auction catalogs. **Subscriptions:** 450 journals and other serials. **Services:** Copying; library open to the public for reference use only on limited schedule. **Automated Operations:** Computerized cataloging. **Computerized Information Services:** RLIN, DIALOG Information Services. **Networks/Consortia:** Member of Research Libraries Information Network (RLIN), PALINET. **Special Indexes:** Index to Philadelphia Museum of Art Bulletin (card). **Remarks:** Alternate telephone number(s): 787-5494. **FAX:** (215)236-4465. **Staff:** Gina Erdreich, Res. & Ref.Libn.; Robin Miller, Slide Libn.

★12991★
Philadelphia Museum of Art - Slide Library (Aud-Vis, Art)
Parkway at 26th St.
Box 7646 Phone: (215)763-8100
Philadelphia, PA 19101 Mr. Robin Miller, Slide Libn.
Founded: 1939. **Staff:** 1. **Subjects:** History of art and architecture. **Holdings:** 130,000 slides (noncirculating). **Services:** Department not open to the public. **Remarks:** FAX: (215)236-4465. Figures include slides of works in the Rodin Museum and John G. Johnson Collection. Sales requests should be referred to Rosenthal Art Slides, 5456 S. Ridgewood Court, Chicago, IL 60615.

★12992★
Philadelphia Newspapers, Inc. - Inquirer and Daily News Library (Publ)
400 N. Broad St.
Box 8263 Phone: (215)854-4665
Philadelphia, PA 19101 Mary Jo Crowley, Mgr.
Founded: 1925. **Staff:** 15. **Subjects:** Newspaper reference topics. **Holdings:** 6000 volumes; 600 pamphlets; clippings and photographs from Inquirer, Daily News, and selected papers and periodicals; Philadelphia Inquirer, 1926 to present, Daily News, 1960 to present, and New York Times, 1958 to present, on microfilm. **Subscriptions:** 32 journals and other serials; 40 newspapers. **Services:** Library not open to the public. **Computerized Information Services:** NEXIS, DIALOG Information Services, VU/TEXT Information Services, DataTimes, Dow Jones News/Retrieval; electronic retrieval system for Daily News and Inquirer (internal database). **Special Indexes:** Philadelphia Inquirer index, 1926-1954 (card); selective index, 1955-1979. **Remarks:** Toll-free telephone number(s): (800)848-0200. FAX: (215)854-5884. **Staff:** Teresa Banik; Denise Boal; Joe Daley; Frank Donahue; Steve Elliott; Jennifer Ewing; Joe Gradel; Virginia Graham; Gene Loielo; Michael Panzer; Jeri Scott; Ron Taylor; Ed Voves.

★12993★
Philadelphia Orchestra Association - Library (Mus)
Academy of Music
Broad and Locust Sts. Phone: (215)893-1929
Philadelphia, PA 19102 Clinton F. Nieweg, Prin.Libn.
Founded: 1900. **Staff:** Prof 4. **Subjects:** Symphony orchestra music. **Holdings:** 4200 orchestrations with complete scores and parts; 15,200 choral parts (150 titles); 1500 scores. **Services:** Library open for research on premises only. **Remarks:** Alternate telephone number(s): 893-1954; 893-1960. FAX: (215)893-1948. Telex: 7106701048 PHA. **Staff:** Nancy M. Bradburd, Asst.Libn.; Robert M. Grossman, Asst.Libn.; Mark Laycock, Staff Asst.

★12994★
Philadelphia Psychiatric Center - Professional Library (Med)
Ford Rd. & Monument Ave. Phone: (215)877-2000
Philadelphia, PA 19131 Ann Vosburgh, Libn.
Staff: Prof 1. **Subjects:** Psychiatry, psychology, psychoanalysis, family therapy. **Holdings:** 7500 volumes. **Subscriptions:** 90 journals and other serials. **Services:** Interlibrary loan; copying (limited); library open to the public with restrictions. **Networks/Consortia:** Member of National Network of Libraries of Medicine - Middle Atlantic Region, PALINET.

★ 12995 ★
(Philadelphia) School District of Philadelphia - Pedagogical Library (Educ)
Adm. Bldg., Rm. 301
21st St. & Parkway   Phone: (215)299-2544
Philadelphia, PA 19103   Doreen Velnich, Hd.Libn.
Founded: 1883. **Staff:** Prof 2; Other 2. **Subjects:** Elementary and secondary education, psychology and testing, intercultural human relations, special education, reading. **Holdings:** 48,000 books and bound periodical volumes; ERIC microfiche; VF drawers of Philadelphia courses of study, pictures, teaching units, bibliographies, pamphlets; 300,000 documents on microfiche. **Subscriptions:** 425 journals and other serials; 6 newspapers. **Services:** Interlibrary loan; copying; library open to the public for reference use only. **Computerized Information Services:** BRS Information Technologies, OCLC. **Publications:** New book lists and flyers, monthly; current list of periodicals, annual. **Staff:** Dorothy L. Williams, Dir.

★ 12996 ★
Philatelic Foundation - Archives and Library (Rec)
21 E. 40th St.   Phone: (212)889-6483
New York, NY 10016   William Crowe
Founded: 1945. **Staff:** 3. **Subjects:** Philately. **Special Collections:** Luff Reference Collection; Ashbrook Correspondence and Special Service. **Holdings:** 1500 books; 600 bound periodical volumes; 5000 documents and archival materials. **Subscriptions:** 25 journals and other serials; 10 newspapers. **Services:** Copying; library open to contributors, by appointment. **Remarks:** FAX: (212)447-5258.

Philbrick Library of Dramatic Literature and Theater History
See: The Claremont Colleges - Honnold/Mudd Library (3753)

★ 12997 ★
Philbrook Museum of Art - Chapman Library (Art)
Box 52510   Phone: (918)748-5306
Tulsa, OK 74152   Thomas E. Young, Libn.
Founded: 1939. **Staff:** Prof 1. **Subjects:** Art. **Special Collections:** Roberta Campbell Lawson Indian Library (1105 volumes). **Holdings:** 10,000 books; 7000 bound periodical volumes; 196 VF drawers; 450 linear feet of archival materials. **Subscriptions:** 143 journals and other serials. **Services:** Interlibrary loan; copying; library open to the public by appointment. **Remarks:** Located at 2727 South Rockford Road, Tulsa, OK 74114. FAX: (918)743-4230.

★ 12998 ★
Philhaven Hospital - Library (Med)
283 S. Butler Rd.   Phone: (717)270-2419
Mt. Gretna, PA 17064   Kenneth Yoder, Coord.Ed.
Founded: 1965. **Staff:** Prof 1. **Subjects:** Psychology, psychiatry, pastoral care. **Holdings:** 1900 books. **Subscriptions:** 83 journals and other serials. **Services:** Library open to the public. **Remarks:** FAX: (717)270-2455.

★ 12999 ★
Philip Morris, U.S.A. - Research Center Library (Biol Sci)
Box 26583   Phone: (804)274-2877
Richmond, VA 23261   Marian Z. DeBardeleben, Assoc.Sr.Sci.
Founded: 1959. **Staff:** Prof 7; Other 3. **Subjects:** Tobacco, chemistry, biochemistry, botany, physics, plant physiology. **Holdings:** 40,000 books; 10,000 bound periodical volumes; 350 AV programs; 5000 microfiche; 40 VF drawers of clippings; 7500 reels of microfilm of periodicals. **Subscriptions:** 750 journals and other serials; 6 newspapers. **Services:** Interlibrary loan. **Automated Operations:** Computerized cataloging, acquisitions, serials, and circulation. **Computerized Information Services:** DIALOG Information Services, ORBIT, NLM, Mead Data Central, RLIN, STN International, Dow Jones News/Retrieval, International Patent Documentation Center (INPADOC); Philip Morris Information Network (internal database). **Publications:** Dictionary of Tobacco Terminology (book). **Special Catalogs:** Published Papers and Journal Holdings, annual (both printouts). **Staff:** Charity McDonald, Assoc.Libn.; Carla Gregory, Asst.Libn.

Isidore Philipp Archive
See: University of Louisville - Dwight Anderson Memorial Music Library (18769)

★ 13000 ★
Philippine Invention Development Institute - PIDI Library (Sci-Engr)
General Santos Ave.
Bicutan   Phone: 2 822-09-61
Taguig, Metro Manila, Philippines   Mrs. Levita Portugal, Libn.
Subjects: Local and foreign patents, science, technology, inventions. **Holdings:** 10,000 volumes. **Remarks:** Maintained by Philippines - Ministry of Science and Technology. Telex: 23312 RHPA.

★ 13001 ★
Philippine Resource Center - PRC Library/Databank (Area-Ethnic)
2288 Fulton St., Suite 103   Phone: (510)548-2546
Berkeley, CA 94704   Ramon Abad
Founded: 1984. **Staff:** 2. **Subjects:** Philippines - economy, politics, culture; Philippine support movements in U.S., Canada, and Europe. **Special Collections:** Philippine newsclips, newsletters, and magazines; sectoral issues amd special interest. **Holdings:** 200 books; 75 bound periodical volumes; 400 other cataloged items; uncataloged manuscripts; films, slides, photographs, VCR, and other AV materials; reports. **Subscriptions:** 25 journals and other serials; 8 newspapers. **Services:** Copying; library open to the public by appointment. **Publications:** Philippine Resource Center Monitor, irregular - to the public.

Philippines - Ministry of Science and Technology - Philippine Invention Development Institute
See: Philippine Invention Development Institute (13000)

★ 13002 ★
Philippines - National Library - Special Collections (Rare Book)
T.M. Kalaw St.   Phone: 2 505143
Manila, Philippines   Narcissa V. Munasque, Dir.
Founded: 1900. **Subjects:** Social sciences, humanities, applied sciences, technology. **Special Collections:** Rare books and manuscripts of the Philippines; Presidential papers. **Holdings:** 400,000 books; 100,000 bound periodical volumes; 100,000 reports; 10,000 microfiche; 50,000 reels of microfilm. **Subscriptions:** 300 journals and other serials; 25 newspapers. **Services:** Interlibrary loan; copying; library open to the public. **Publications:** Philippine National Bibliography; Union Catalog of Philippine Materials. **Remarks:** FAX: 2 502329. Telex: 40726. **Also Known As:** Ang Pambansang Aklatan.

Philips Autograph Library
See: West Chester University - Francis Harvey Green Library (20186)

Philips Laboratories Research Library
See: North American Philips Corporation (11863)

★ 13003 ★
Phillips 66 Natural Gas Company - Library (Energy)
910 Plaza Office Bldg.
Bartlesville, OK 74004   Phone: (918)661-5803
     E. Jane Nichols, Supv., Rec.Mgt. & Lib.
Founded: 1951. **Staff:** 5. **Subjects:** Natural gas industry, natural gas liquids, energy industries. **Holdings:** 215 books; 262 paperback books. **Subscriptions:** 17 journals and other serials. **Services:** Library not open to the public.

★ 13004 ★
Phillips Academy - Addison Gallery of American Art - Library (Art)
Chapel Ave.
Andover, MA 01810   Phone: (508)749-4015
Subjects: American art. **Holdings:** Reference books; paintings; prints; drawings; photographs; sculpture; AV materials. **Services:** Library open to the public by appointment for reference use only. **Remarks:** Art books shelved at Oliver Wendell Holmes Library on campus of Phillips Academy, with exception of those books dealing with specific American artists in the Addison Collection of American Art. **Remarks:** FAX: (508)749-4025.

★ 13005 ★
Phillips Academy - Oliver Wendell Holmes Library - Special Collections
(Hum)
Andover, MA 01810   Phone: (508)749-4230
                                          Susan Ezell Noble, Dir.
Founded: 1796. **Staff:** Prof 8; Other 10. **Special Collections:** Oliver Wendell
Holmes Collection; Charles H. Forbes Collection of Vergiliana and Bancroft
Collection of Vergil Translations (1000 volumes and 450 pamphlets);
Audobon Collection; Thomas Y. Cooper Collection of American Humor;
Americana Collection. **Holdings:** 102,000 books. **Subscriptions:** 275 journals
and other serials; 10 newspapers. **Services:** Collections accessed in-house
upon request. **Automated Operations:** Unicorn Collection Management
System. **Computerized Information Services:** OCLC, DIALOG
Information Services. **Networks/Consortia:** Member of NELINET, Inc.
Special Catalogs: Catalog of the Charles H. Forbes Collection of Vergiliana
in the Oliver Wendell Holmes Library. **Remarks:** FAX: (508)749-4233.
Staff: Ruth Quattlebaum, Archv.; Rachal Penner, Hd., Ref.; Jo Wang,
Automation Coord.; Muriel Casper, Hd., Circ.; M. Frances Gallagher, Ref.;
Timothy Sprattler, Ref.; Roberta McDonnell, Ref.

★ 13006 ★
The Phillips Collection - Library (Art)
1600 21st St., N.W.   Phone: (202)387-2151
Washington, DC 20009   Karen Schneider, Libn.
Founded: 1976. **Staff:** 1. **Subjects:** 19th and 20th century European and
American painting and sculpture. **Special Collections:** Phillips Collection
exhibition catalogs; monographs on artists represented in the Phillips
Collection. **Holdings:** 5000 books; 65 reels of microfilm of the Phillips
Collection correspondence, 1920-1960; 20 VF drawers of exhibition
catalogs, clippings, articles. **Subscriptions:** 30 journals and other serials.
Services: Copying; library open to researchers by appointment. **Remarks:**
FAX: (202)387-2436.

★ 13007 ★
Frank Phillips Foundation, Inc. - Woolaroc Museum - Library (Area-
Ethnic)
Rte. 3   Phone: (918)336-0307
Bartlesville, OK 74003   Linda Stone Laws, Cur. of Art
Founded: 1929. **Subjects:** Native American culture, art, early Americana,
weaponry, natural history, history. **Holdings:** 800 books. **Subscriptions:** 15
journals and other serials. **Services:** Library open to the public with
director's permission.

★ 13008 ★
Phillips Graduate Seminary - Library (Rel-Phil)
University Sta., Box 2218   Phone: (405)237-4433
Enid, OK 73702   Roberta Hamburger, Dir.
Founded: 1950. **Staff:** Prof 2; Other 3. **Subjects:** Religion. **Special
Collections:** Discipliana. **Holdings:** 94,203 books; 12,176 bound periodical
volumes; 22 VF drawers of pamphlets; 8756 books of microfiche; 465 books
of microfilm; 155 books of microcards; 1457 journals on microfiche; 106
journals on microfilm; 2910 journals on microcards. **Subscriptions:** 455
journals and other serials. **Services:** Interlibrary loan; copying; library open
to the public. **Automated Operations:** Computerized cataloging and
acquisitions. **Computerized Information Services:** OCLC, BRS Information
Technologies. **Networks/Consortia:** Member of AMIGOS Bibliographic
Council, Inc. **Staff:** Logan S. Wright, Theol.Libn.; Ruth Ann Hammond,
Adm.Asst./Supv., Acq.; Marilee Pralle, Pub.Serv.Supv.; Barbara Cook,
Circ.Asst.

James Duncan Phillips Library
See: **Essex Institute** (5448)

Phillips Laboratory Geophysics Research Library
See: **U.S. Air Force - Air Force Materiel Command - Phillips Laboratory
Geophysical Research Library** (16801)

Phillips Laboratory Technical Library
See: **U.S. Air Force - Air Force Materiel Command - Phillips Laboratory
Technical Library** (16802)

Phillips Library
See: **Harvard University - Harvard-Smithsonian Center for Astrophysics
(CFA) - Library** (6971)

Phillips Library
See: **Peabody Museum of Salem** (12805)

★ 13009 ★
Phillips, Lytle, Hitchcock, Blaine and Huber - Library (Law)
3400 Maine Midland Ctr.   Phone: (716)847-8400
Buffalo, NY 14203   Jeanne M. Kern, Hd.Libn.
Staff: Prof 2; Other 3. **Subjects:** New York law, federal law, taxation.
Holdings: 24,000 books; 500 bound periodical volumes; 75 audio- and
videotapes. **Subscriptions:** 430 journals and other serials; 7 newspapers.
Services: Interlibrary loan; copying; SDI; library open to the public at
librarian's discretion. **Automated Operations:** Computerized serials.
Computerized Information Services: LEXIS, DIALOG Information
Services, WESTLAW, Legislative Retrieval System (LRS), VU/TEXT
Information Services. **Publications:** Library Newsletter, monthly;
Bibliographies, irregular - both for internal distribution only. **Special
Catalogs:** Internal catalogs. **Remarks:** FAX: (716)852-6100. **Staff:** Mary
Ellen O'Hara, Libn.

Phillips Memorial Library
See: **Providence College** (13442)

★ 13010 ★
Phillips Petroleum Company - N.A. E & P Technical Library (Energy)
P.O. Box 1967   Phone: (713)669-3596
Houston, TX 77251-1967   Frances Parker, Tech.Libn.
Founded: 1980. **Staff:** 1. **Subjects:** Petroleum. **Remarks:** FAX: (713)669-
3541. **Formerly:** Its Houston Region - Technical Library.

★ 13011 ★
Phillips Petroleum Company - R&D Library (Energy, Sci-Engr)
122 PLB   Phone: (918)661-3433
Bartlesville, OK 74004   Annabeth Robin, Lib.Supv.
Founded: 1945. **Staff:** Prof 2; Other 3. **Subjects:** Chemistry, petroleum
science and technology, polymer science and technology, biotechnology,
geosciences, plastics, physics. **Holdings:** 30,000 books; 30,000 bound
periodical volumes; 2 million U.S. and foreign patents; 5500 microfilm
cartridges. **Subscriptions:** 522 journals and other serials. **Services:** Library
not open to the public. **Automated Operations:** Computerized public access
catalog, cataloging, acquisitions, serials, and circulation (VTLS).
Computerized Information Services: OCLC, DIALOG Information
Services, ORBIT Search Service, WILSONLINE. **Networks/Consortia:**
Member of AMIGOS Bibliographic Council, Inc. **Publications:** Library
Services Newsletter - for internal distribution only. **Remarks:** FAX:
(918)662-2171. **Staff:** Myrtle Ingerson, Cat.; Tanya Corle, ILL; Janet Elias,
Ser.

Seymour J. Phillips Health Sciences Library
See: **Beth Israel Medical Center** (1771)

Stephen Phillips Memorial Library
See: **Penobscot Marine Museum** (12917)

★ 13012 ★
Philosophical Research Society, Inc. - PRS Library (Rel-Phil)
3910 Los Feliz Blvd.   Phone: (213)663-2167
Los Angeles, CA 90027   Alice M. Buse, Libn.
Founded: 1934. **Staff:** Prof 1; Other 8. **Subjects:** Alchemy; astrology;
Baconiana; ancient and modern philosophy; metaphysics; theosophy;
rosicrucianism; orientalia - philosophy, culture, customs; freemasonry.
Special Collections: Reiser; Parker; Manly P. Hall (founder); Le Plongeon
(Yucatan; books; slides). **Holdings:** 50,000 books. **Services:** Interlibrary
loan; copying; library open to the public. **Publications:** Library Bulletin,
irregular; Art Bulletin, quarterly; bibliography of alchemy and rosicrucian
holdings. **Special Indexes:** Quarterly journal index; titles of holdings, special
collections, and lecture notes by Manly P. Hall, founder (all on cards).

★ 13013 ★
Ford Philpot Evangelistic Association - Library (Rel-Phil)
Box 3000   Phone: (606)276-1479
Lexington, KY 40533   Dr. Ford Philpot, Pres.
Subjects: Christianity. **Holdings:** 500 volumes. **Remarks:** Library located at
1815 Nicholasville Rd., Lexington, KY 40503.

★ 13014 ★
Phippard & Associates Strategic & Technological Consulting, Inc. -
    Research Library (Info Sci)
35 Dartmoor Dr.
Kanata, ON, Canada K2M 1S6   Phone: (613)591-3800
Founded: 1983. **Subjects:** Microcomputers, office automation, videotex,
teletext, business graphics, technology marketing, related new information
technologies, and their opportunities in the business market. **Holdings:** 200
bound volumes; 500 research items. **Subscriptions:** 30 journals and other
serials. **Services:** Library not open to the public.

★ 13015 ★
Phoenix Art Museum - Library (Art)
1625 N. Central Ave.   Phone: (602)257-1880
Phoenix, AZ 85004   Clayton C. Kirking, Dir. of Lib.
Founded: 1959. **Staff:** Prof 1; Other 1. **Subjects:** Painters and sculptors,
history of painting and art, Egyptology, prints, museums and galleries
(collections and exhibitions); 19th and 20th century American painting; 20th
century Mexican art. **Special Collections:** Ambrose Lansing Collection of
Egyptology (208 volumes); exhibition catalogs for one-man shows (10,000);
international auction records; museum bulletins (100 boxes); Orme Lewis
Collection of Rembrandt Etching Catalogs; Art Libraries Society Archives
of Arizona Artists; Arizona Costume Institute Library (1000 volumes);
P.A.M. Slide Collection (50,000 images). **Holdings:** 40,000 books; 560
bound periodical volumes; 152 file drawers of gallery catalogs, museum
publications, artistic biographies, archives. **Subscriptions:** 109 journals and
other serials. **Services:** Interlibrary loan; copying; library open to the public
for reference use only. **Automated Operations:** Computerized public access
catalog. **Special Indexes:** Index of artists and subjects in exhibition and
museum catalogs (card). **Remarks:** FAX: (602)253-8662.

★ 13016 ★
Phoenix Children's Hospital - Family Learning Center - Library (Med)
909 E. Brill St.   Phone: (602)239-2567
Phoenix, AZ 85006   Kathy Werner, Dir.
Founded: 1989. **Subjects:** Medicine, health, abuse, family life issues,
parenting, safety. **Holdings:** 719 books; 19 audiotapes; 39 videotapes;
pamphlets. **Subscriptions:** 51 journals and other serials. **Services:**
Interlibrary loan; copying; library open to the public. **Publications:**
Bibliography.

★ 13017 ★
Phoenix Day School for the Deaf - Library/Media Center (Educ)
1935 W. Hayward Ave.   Phone: (602)255-3448
Phoenix, AZ 85021   Donna L. Farman, Libn.
Founded: 1966. **Staff:** Prof 2. **Subjects:** Juvenile fiction, signed English.
Special Collections: Parent Lending Library; captioned filmstrips; captioned
and signed videotapes. **Holdings:** 8000 books. **Subscriptions:** 28 journals and
other serials. **Services:** Library not open to the public. **Automated
Operations:** Mac Library System (MLS). **Staff:** Lori Elliott, Media Coord.

★ 13018 ★
Phoenix Elementary School District No. 1 - Curriculum Library (Educ)
2301 N. 3rd St.   Phone: (602)257-3774
Phoenix, AZ 85004   Tom Lind, Instr.Sup.Rsrc.Spec.
Founded: 1956. **Staff:** Prof 2; Other 8. **Subjects:** Elementary education,
Arizona history. **Special Collections:** Juvenile Trade Book Examination
Center; 16mm film library (2500 films); Arizona Collection (800 volumes).
Holdings: 10,000 books; 200 bound periodical volumes; 140 cassettes.
Subscriptions: 60 journals and other serials. **Services:** Library not open to
the public. **Automated Operations:** Computerized public access catalog,
cataloging, and circulation. **Computerized Information Services:** VU/
TEXT Information Services, EDLINK. **Staff:** Mary Brewer, Lib.Cat.

Phoenix Gazette
See: **Phoenix Newspapers, Inc.** (13022)

★ 13019 ★
Phoenix General Hospital - Chapman Memorial Medical Library
19829 N. 27th Ave.
Phoenix, AZ 85027
Founded: 1958. **Subjects:** Family practice, internal medicine, surgery,
pediatrics, orthopedics, obstetrics/gynecology. **Holdings:** 500 books; 20
bound periodical volumes. **Remarks:** Currently inactive.

★ 13020 ★
Phoenix Indian Medical Center - Library (Med)
4212 N. 16th St.   Phone: (602)263-1200
Phoenix, AZ 85016   Jean Crosier, Adm.Libn.
Founded: 1965. **Staff:** Prof 1; Other 1. **Subjects:** Medicine, nursing,
dentistry. **Special Collections:** Indian history; Indian health. **Holdings:** 1800
books; 2000 bound periodical volumes; 524 medical tapes; 3000 unbound
journals; 5 VF drawers of pamphlets and reprints. **Subscriptions:** 180
journals and other serials. **Services:** Interlibrary loan; copying (both
limited); SDI; library open to the public for reference use only. **Automated
Operations:** Computerized cataloging, serials, and ILL. **Computerized
Information Services:** MEDLINE; Indian Health (internal database);
DOCLINE (electronic mail service). **Networks/Consortia:** Member of
Central Arizona Biomedical Libraries (CABL). **Publications:** List of
acquisitions - for internal distribution only. **Remarks:** FAX: (602)263-1669.

★ 13021 ★
Phoenix Mutual Life Insurance Company - Library (Bus-Fin)
100 Bright Meadow Blvd.   Phone: (203)253-2325
Enfield, CT 06082   Elaine Loehr
Founded: 1915. **Staff:** 1. **Subjects:** Insurance, business, management.
Holdings: 17,500 volumes. **Subscriptions:** 200 journals and other serials; 5
newspapers. **Services:** Interlibrary loan; copying; library open to the public
by appointment. **Remarks:** FAX: (203)253-1478.

★ 13022 ★
Phoenix Newspapers, Inc. - Library (Publ)
Box 1950   Phone: (602)271-8115
Phoenix, AZ 85001   Paula Stevens, Lib.Mgr.
Founded: 1948. **Staff:** Prof 6; Other 13. **Subjects:** General reference topics.
Special Collections: Subject file of Arizona Republic and Phoenix Gazette
clippings, 1948-1986 (7 million). **Holdings:** 2000 books; Arizona Republic
and Phoenix Gazette, 1880 to present, on microfilm; 150,000 photographs;
pamphlets; maps. **Subscriptions:** 75 journals and other serials; 30
newspapers. **Services:** Library not open to the public; provides limited
service to other libraries. **Computerized Information Services:** DIALOG
Information Services, NEXIS, LEXIS, VU/TEXT Information Services,
DataTimes, DataQuick, Burrelle's, NewsNet, Inc., TOXNET; produces the
Phoenix Gazette, Arizona Business Gazette, and Arizona Republic.
Remarks: Publishes the Arizona Republic, Phoenix Gazette, and Arizona
Business Gazette. FAX: (602)271-8914. **Staff:** Cheryl Thomas, Database
Supv.; Joanne Dawson, Ref.Libn.; Heather Goebel, Ref.Libn.; Donna
Colletta, Ref.Libn.; Mary Soza, Photo Libn.

★ 13023 ★
Phoenix Planning Department - Library (Plan)
125 E. Washington St., 3rd Fl.   Phone: (602)261-8590
Phoenix, AZ 85004-2342   Fred J. Osgood
Founded: 1960. **Staff:** 1. **Subjects:** General urban development, land use,
economics, population, community facilities, public utilities, urban renewal,
central business district, transportation. **Holdings:** 3200 books; 70 bound
periodical volumes. **Subscriptions:** 65 journals and other serials. **Services:**
Library open to the public. **Computerized Information Services:** Internal
databases. **Remarks:** FAX: (602)495-3793. **Staff:** Carolyn E. Stremple, Plan.
I.

★ 13024 ★
Phoenix Public Library - Arizona Room (Area-Ethnic)
12 E. McDowell Rd.
Phoenix, AZ 85004   Phone: (602)262-4636
Staff: Prof 1; Other 1. **Subjects:** Phoenix and Arizona history, Southwestern
Indians, Southwestern water and land use, Mexican Americans,
Southwestern art. **Special Collections:** James Harvey McClintock papers,
1864-1934. **Holdings:** 17,500 books; 225 bound periodical volumes; Phoenix
municipal records; Arizona Republic clipping file, 1977-1990.
Subscriptions: 45 journals and other serials. **Services:** Copying; room open
to the public. **Staff:** Fay Freed, Libn. II.

★13025★
Phoenix Public Library - Art of the Book Room (Rare Book)
12 E. McDowell Rd.   Phone: (602)262-6110
Phoenix, AZ 85004   Gladys S. Mahoney, Rare Bk.Libn.
Staff: Prof 1. **Subjects:** Shakespeare, Napoleon, book arts, rare books, fine editions, small presses. **Special Collections:** Alfred Knight Collection (Shakespeare, Napoleon, first editions, incunabula, Bibles; 2900 volumes). **Holdings:** 4000 volumes; incunabula; cuneiform tablets; scrolls; manuscripts. **Services:** Copying; room open to the public with restrictions. **Automated Operations:** Computerized cataloging, acquisitions, serials, and circulation. **Computerized Information Services:** OCLC, LIBRIS; internal database. Performs searches on fee basis. Contact Person: Liz Laurent, 262-4794. **Networks/Consortia:** Member of AMIGOS Bibliographic Council, Inc. **Publications:** Newsletter - for internal distribution only. **Remarks:** FAX: (602)495-5841.

★13026★
Phoenix Public Library - Arts & Humanities Unit (Hum)
12 E. McDowell Rd.   Phone: (602)262-4602
Phoenix, AZ 85004   Sarah McGarry, Libn.
Staff: Prof 11; Other 12. **Subjects:** History, literature, art, languages, biography, music, religion, fiction, performing arts. **Special Collections:** Arizona history; art of the book. **Holdings:** 400,000 books. **Subscriptions:** 400 journals and other serials. **Services:** Interlibrary loan; copying; open to the public. **Automated Operations:** Computerized circulation. **Computerized Information Services:** Internal database. **Special Indexes:** Plan Index; Song Index. **Staff:** Brenda Tevis, Libn.; Jan Buckwalter, Libn.; Gerald Giordano, Libn.; Cathy Chung, Libn.; Stephanie Moritz, Libn.; Fay Freed, Libn.; Gladys Mahoney, Libn.; Yvonne Murphey, Libn.

★13027★
Phoenix Public Library - Business & Sciences Department (Bus-Fin, Sci-Engr)
12 E. McDowell Rd.   Phone: (602)262-4636
Phoenix, AZ 85004   Teresa Landas, Hd.
Staff: Prof 12; Other 6. **Subjects:** Business and economics, technology, social sciences, sciences, medicine, psychology. **Special Collections:** Arizona business; Arizona law; Career Center; Foundations and Grants. **Holdings:** 200,000 books; government documents. **Subscriptions:** 900 journals and other serials. **Services:** Interlibrary loan; department open to the public. **Automated Operations:** Computerized public access catalog, cataloging, acquisitions, and serials. **Computerized Information Services:** DIALOG Information Services, VU/TEXT Information Services, OCLC. Contact Person: Liz Laurent, Comp.Serv.Ref.Coord., 261-8667. **Networks/Consortia:** Member of AMIGOS Bibliographic Council, Inc.

★13028★
Phoenix Public Library - Foreign Languages - Library (Hum)
12 E. McDowell Rd.   Phone: (602)262-4732
Phoenix, AZ 85004   Catherine Chung, Libn.
Staff: Prof 1. **Subjects:** Foreign language books in 34 languages - fiction, nonfiction, biography, literature, language, history, English as a second language. **Holdings:** 20,000 books. **Subscriptions:** 28 journals and other serials; 13 newspapers. **Services:** Interlibrary loan; copying; open to the public. **Computerized Information Services:** DIALOG Information Services. Performs searches on fee basis. **Remarks:** FAX: (602)495-5841.

★13029★
Phoenix Public Library - Motor and Appliance Repair Collection (Sci-Engr)
12 E. McDowell Rd.   Phone: (602)262-4636
Phoenix, AZ 85004   Donald W. Guy, Lib.Asst.
Staff: Prof 1. **Subjects:** Vehicle and motor repair - performance, flat rate, interchange, body repair, paint and upholstery; collecting and investing in custom cars; electronic data and schematics for computers, appliances, transistor and ham radios. **Special Collections:** Wiring diagrams; vacuum diagrams; Rider electronic manuals. **Holdings:** 3050 books; 10,000 schematics and 284 volumes of SAMS photofact publications as well as peripheral publications. **Subscriptions:** 17 journals and other serials. **Services:** Interlibrary loan; collection open to the public. **Computerized Information Services:** DIALOG Information Services, Mitchell On-Demand.

★13030★
Phoenix Public Library - Special Needs Center (Aud-Vis)
12 E. McDowell Rd.   Phone: (602)261-8690
Phoenix, AZ 85004   Cynthia R. Holt, Supv.
Founded: 1983. **Staff:** Prof 3; Other 4. **Subjects:** Special education, rehabilitation, blindness and visual impairment, deafness and speech impairment, physical disability, mental disability. **Special Collections:** Technology for People with Disabilities; manual communication; basic adult collection. **Holdings:** 5800 books; 6000 large type books; 105 videotapes; 200 toys in toybrary. **Subscriptions:** 180 journals and other serials. **Services:** Center open to the public; computer workplace for people with diabilities. **Publications:** Technology and the Handicapped (bibliography), annual; Manual Communications (bibliography), annual. **Special Catalogs:** Toybrary Catalog (large type).

John Phoschek Memorial Bus Transportation Library
See: **Motor Bus Society, Inc.** (10775)

★13031★
Photo Researchers, Inc. - Library (Aud-Vis)
60 E. 56th St.   Phone: (212)758-3420
New York, NY 10022   Bug Sutton, Creative Dir.
Founded: 1956. **Staff:** 24. **Subjects:** Color and black/white photographic prints in the fields of natural history, travel, social studies, industry, technology, anthropology, biology, botany, medicine, education. **Special Collections:** Edited files of 1200 photographers; Science Library; National Audubon Society Collection. **Holdings:** 1 million original color transparencies and custom black/white prints. **Subscriptions:** 27 journals and other serials. **Services:** Photographs available for reproduction; library open to the public on fee basis. **Special Catalogs:** Promotional photo catalog. **Remarks:** FAX: (212)355-0731. **Staff:** Terry Cordasci, Gen.Lib.; Steve Gerard, Sci.Libn.; John Kaprielian, Nat.Hist.Libn.

Photon and Charged Particle Data Center
See: **U.S. Natl. Institute of Standards and Technology** (17623)

★13032★
Photophile - Library (Aud-Vis)
6150 Lusk Blvd., Suite B203   Phone: (619)453-3050
San Diego, CA 92121   Kelly Nelson
Founded: 1968. **Staff:** Prof 1. **Subjects:** Industry, business, scenic photography, Southern California, recreation, people. **Holdings:** 150,000 color transparencies. **Services:** Copying; library open to the public. **Remarks:** Photophile is a stock photograph agency. Usage is for publications and advertising only. FAX: (619)452-5528. **Staff:** Sergio Damasceno.

★13033★
Physics International Company - Library (Sci-Engr)
2700 Merced St.   Phone: (510)577-7278
San Leandro, CA 94577   M. Misegades, Libn.
Staff: Prof 1. **Subjects:** Physics, nuclear physics, electronics, mechanical engineering, computer software. **Holdings:** 3000 books; 8000 technical reports. **Subscriptions:** 292 journals and other serials. **Services:** Interlibrary loan; library not open to the public. **Computerized Information Services:** DIALOG Information Services. **Networks/Consortia:** Member of Bay Area Library and Information System (BALIS). **Remarks:** FAX: (510)577-7283.

★13034★
Jean Piaget Society - Library (Soc Sci)
c/o Kurt Fischer, Dept. of Human Development
Graduate School of Education
Larsen Hall
Harvard University
Cambridge, MA 02138
Founded: 1971. **Staff:** Prof 1; Other 1. **Subjects:** Psychology, child development, education, language development, cognition. **Special Collections:** Catalog of the archives of Jean Piaget. **Holdings:** 400 books; 150 cataloged articles; 10 shelves of dissertations; journal articles; original manuscripts; speeches; films; cassette tapes. **Services:** Copying; library open to the public for reference use only. **Publications:** Journal, quarterly; proceedings of the Jean Piaget Society. **Remarks:** Library located at Paley Library, Temple University, Philadelphia, PA.

★ 13035 ★
Piarist Central Library (Rel-Phil)
Mikszath Kalman ter 1   Phone: 1 330-701
H-1444 Budapest 8, Hungary   Somogyvary Gyula, Libn.
Subjects: Piarist authors. **Holdings:** 100,000 books; 8000 bound periodical volumes. **Remarks:** Maintained by Magyarorszagi Kegyestanitorend/ Piaristak. **Also Known As:** Kegyesrendi Kozponti Konyvtar.

★ 13036 ★
Piatt County Historical & Genealogical Society - Resource Center (Hist)
P.O. Box 111   Phone: (217)762-2442
Monticello, IL 61856   Linda Redmond, Libn.
Founded: 1979. **Subjects:** Genealogy. **Holdings:** 500 books. **Subscriptions:** 25 journals and other serials. **Services:** Copying; center open on a limited schedule and by appointment. **Publications:** Cemetery Records (all known in county); census records (1850-1910); marriage records (1841-1910); atlases (1876-1920); members' ancestor charts - all for sale. **Remarks:** Resource center located at Courthouse Annex, Marion St., Monticello, IL.

Picatinny Arsenal Archive
See: **U.S. Army - Armament, Munitions & Chemical Command - Armament Research, Development & Engineering Center - Scientific & Tech.Info. Branch - Information Center** (16918)

Albert Pick Music Library
See: **University of Miami - School of Music - Albert Pick Music Library** (18850)

Lawrence Mercer Pick Memorial Library
See: **LaRabida Children's Hospital and Research Center** (8952)

★ 13037 ★
Pickaway County Law Library (Law)
Courthouse
Box 727   Phone: (614)474-6026
Circleville, OH 43113   William Ammer, Treas.
Subjects: Law. **Holdings:** 19,000 volumes. **Services:** Interlibrary loan; library not open to the public.

Timothy Pickering Library
See: **Wenham Museum** (20166)

Pickett Library
See: **Alderson-Broaddus College** (336)

Ralph E. Pickett Medical Library
See: **Licking Memorial Hospital** (9149)

Pickler Memorial Library
See: **Northeast Missouri State University** (11972)

Pictorial Parade
See: **Archive Photos - Library** (957)

★ 13038 ★
Piedmont Bible College - George M. Manuel Memorial Library (Rel-Phil)
716 Franklin St.   Phone: (919)725-8344
Winston-Salem, NC 27107   William P. Thompson, Hd.Libn.
Founded: 1947. **Staff:** Prof 3. **Subjects:** Theology, religious education, education, philosophy, history, music. **Holdings:** 47,251 books; 1310 bound periodical volumes; 3600 other cataloged items. **Subscriptions:** 214 journals and other serials. **Services:** Interlibrary loan; copying; library open to the public. **Automated Operations:** Computerized cataloging. **Computerized Information Services:** Bibliofile (internal database). **Staff:** Cathie L. Chatmon, Asst.Libn./Ref.; June Delnay, Asst.Libn./Tech.Serv.

★ 13039 ★
Piedmont Hospital - Sauls Memorial Library (Med)
1968 Peachtree Rd., N.W.   Phone: (404)605-3641
Atlanta, GA 30309   Mark Barbaree, Act.Dir.
Staff: Prof 2; Other 1. **Subjects:** Clinical medicine, nursing. **Special Collections:** Patient education (1184 items). **Holdings:** 4010 books; 4081 bound periodical volumes; 769 videocassettes. **Subscriptions:** 322 journals and other serials. **Services:** Interlibrary loan. **Computerized Information Services:** MEDLARS, BRS Information Technologies, DIALOG Information Services, Silver Platter, Loansome Doc, Micromedix, Inc.,; CD-ROMs. **Networks/Consortia:** Member of Atlanta Health Science Libraries Consortium (AHSLC). **Remarks:** FAX: (404)350-9217. **Staff:** Suzanne Byrne Sen.

Piedmont Publishing Company - Winston-Salem Journal
See: **Winston-Salem Journal** (20495)

★ 13040 ★
Piedmont Technical College - Library (Educ)
Emerald Rd.
P.O. Drawer 1467   Phone: (803)223-8357
Greenwood, SC 29648   Ruth Nicholson, Lib.Coord.
Staff: Prof 2; Other 2. **Subjects:** Economics, technology, allied health, small business. **Holdings:** 26,000 books; 400 bound periodical volumes; 36 drawers of microfilm; 2000 AV programs. **Subscriptions:** 336 journals and other serials; 10 newspapers. **Services:** Interlibrary loan; copying; library open to the public. **Automated Operations:** Computerized public access catalog, cataloging, and circulation. **Computerized Information Services:** DIALOG Information Services, OCLC. Performs searches on fee basis. Contact Person: Nancy Dulniak, Tech.Serv.Libn. **Networks/Consortia:** Member of SOLINET. **Remarks:** FAX: (803)223-1405.

★ 13041 ★
Pierce County Law Library (Law)
930 Tacoma Ave., S., Rm. 1A-105   Phone: (206)591-7494
Tacoma, WA 98402   Janet Gildenhar, Law Libn.
Founded: 1933. **Staff:** Prof 2; Other 2. **Subjects:** Primary and secondary law. **Holdings:** 30,000 books. **Subscriptions:** 30 journals and other serials. **Services:** Copying; library open to the public for reference use only. **Automated Operations:** Computerized cataloging. **Computerized Information Services:** WESTLAW; internal database. Performs searches on fee basis for local bar association members. **Staff:** Tina Aure, Asst. Law Libn.

Franklin Pierce Collection
See: **Bowdoin College - Library - Special Collections** (2033)

★ 13042 ★
Franklin Pierce Law Center - Library (Law)
2 White St.   Phone: (603)228-1541
Concord, NH 03301   Judith A. Gire, Law Libn./Prof.
Founded: 1973. **Staff:** Prof 4; Other 4. **Subjects:** Law. **Special Collections:** Intellectual property. **Holdings:** 121,736 volumes; 282,723 microfiche. **Subscriptions:** 2000 journals and other serials. **Services:** Interlibrary loan; copying; SDI; library open to government depository users and attorney members. **Computerized Information Services:** WESTLAW, LEXIS, NEXIS, DIALOG Information Services, EPIC. **Networks/Consortia:** Member of New England Law Library Consortium (NELLCO). **Remarks:** FAX: (603)228-0388. **Staff:** Cynthia Landau, Asst. Law Libn.; Melanie Barton, Tech.Serv.Libn.

★ 13043 ★
Pierce/Goodwin/Alexander - Library/Resource Center (Plan)
800 Bering Dr.
Box 130319   Phone: (713)977-5777
Houston, TX 77219-0319   Jane Cominsk, Act.Libn.
Founded: 1980. **Staff:** Prof 1. **Subjects:** Architecture, interiors. **Holdings:** 690 books; 79 bound periodical volumes; 1600 vendor catalogs; vendor samples; 100 maps. **Subscriptions:** 72 journals and other serials. **Services:** Library not open to the public. **Special Indexes:** Index to product literature (card). **Remarks:** FAX: (713)977-6584.

Lawrence J. Pierce Rhododendron Library
See: Rhododendron Species Foundation (13885)

Dean Pierose Memorial Health Sciences Library
See: Moritz Community Hospital (10742)

William Pierson Medical Library
See: Hospital Center at Orange (7418)

★ 13044 ★
Pigeon District Library - Special Collections (Hist)
7236 Nitz St.   Phone: (517)453-2341
Pigeon, MI 48755   Naomi R. Jantzi, Dir.
Founded: 1913. Staff: 2. Special Collections: Michigan Collection; toys (300); Adult Literacy Collection; audio books (71). Holdings: 24,051 books; 45 microfiche; 50 reels of microfilm. Subscriptions: 42 journals and other serials; 3 newspapers. Services: Interlibrary loan; copying; SDI; collections open to the public. Automated Operations: Computerized cataloging, serials, and circulation. Computerized Information Services: OCLC. Performs searches free of charge. Remarks: FAX: (517)453-2266. Staff: Jane Himmel, Asst.Libn.

★ 13045 ★
Pike County Law Library (Law)
Courthouse
Broad St.   Phone: (717)296-6216
Milford, PA 18337   Jan Lokuta, Law Clerk
Subjects: Law. Remarks: FAX: (717)296-6054. No further information was supplied by respondent.

★ 13046 ★
Pikes Peak Library District - Local History Collection (Hist, Aud-Vis)
P.O. Box 1579   Phone: (719)531-6333
Colorado Springs, CO 80901   Ree Mobley, Local Hist.Libn.
Staff: Prof 4; Other 4. Subjects: History - Pikes Peak, Colorado High Plains, local gold mining towns. Special Collections: Myron Wood photograph collection (5000 photographs documenting the Southwest); Mathews Collection (100 glass negatives, circa 1890); Payne Collection (52,000 negatives from Colorado Springs Gazette, 1950-1975); Stewart Collection (3000 photographs and negatives of Colorado Springs/Pikes Peak area, 1896-1970). Holdings: 23,000 books; 2000 bound periodical volumes; 5000 pamphlets; 1000 maps; 27,000 clippings; 100 cubic feet of manuscript material from League of Women Voters of Pikes Peak Region; 30 cubic feet of manuscript material from Mental Health Association; 30 cubic feet of Chase Stone papers; 50 cubic feet of Cliff House papers; 50 Gordon Sweet blueprints; 30 cubic feet of Ghost Town papers; 2 reels of microfilm of Pike National Forest History file. Subscriptions: 110 journals and other serials; 16 newspapers. Services: Interlibrary loan; copying; collection open to the public. Automated Operations: Computerized cataloging, acquisitions, and circulation. Computerized Information Services: Local Authors, Local Documents Data Base (internal databases). Networks/Consortia: Member of Colorado Alliance of Research Libraries (CARL). Publications: Potpourri, monthly - for internal distribution and to mailing list. Special Indexes: Indexes to Gazette Telegraph (book), Free Press (card), Colorado City Iris (book), and Pike National Forest (book). Remarks: Collection located at 20 N. Cascade, Colorado Springs, CO 80903. FAX: (719)632-5744. Staff: Nancy Thaler, Mss.Libn.; Steve Gregory, Local Docs.Libn.

★ 13047 ★
Pilgrim Congregational Church - Library (Rel-Phil)
2310 E. 4th St.   Phone: (218)724-8503
Duluth, MN 55812   Judy Casserberg, Libn.
Staff: 3. Subjects: Bible, liberal theology, church and social action, United Church of Christ and Congregational history, social issues, meditation and prayer. Holdings: 1800 books. Subscriptions: 6 journals and other serials. Services: Library open to church members. Publications: Newsletter - for internal distribution only.

★ 13048 ★
Pilgrim Psychiatric Center - Health Sciences Library (Med)
Bldg. 23
Box A   Phone: (516)434-5775
West Brentwood, NY 11717   Irving Tredwell, Jr., Sr.Libn.
Founded: 1932. Staff: Prof 2; Other 2. Subjects: Psychiatry, social sciences, psychology, medicine, nursing. Holdings: 6000 books; 120 bound periodical volumes; 8 VF drawers of pamphlets and clippings; 3 VF drawers of reports and manuscripts; 1 VF drawer of documents; 145 reels of microfilm; 260 cassette tapes. Subscriptions: 120 journals and other serials; 7 newspapers. Services: Interlibrary loan; copying; library open to the public. Computerized Information Services: MEDLINE, SPIRS.

★ 13049 ★
Pilgrim Society - Pilgrim Hall Library (Hist)
75 Court St.   Phone: (508)746-1620
Plymouth, MA 02360-3891   Laurence R. Pizer, Dir.
Founded: 1820. Staff: 1. Subjects: Pilgrim history, Plymouth, Massachusetts and Plymouth Colony, 1620-1692. Special Collections: William Brewster imprints; books that belonged to the Pilgrims; rare book collection (300 volumes). Holdings: 10,000 books; 1000 bound periodical volumes; 4000 photographs; 12,000 manuscripts, maps, prints, charts, ephemera. Services: Copying; library open to researchers by appointment. Publications: The Pilgrim Journal; A Brief Guide to the Pilgrim Society Library Collections; Guide to the Manuscript Collections; Rare Book Collection Checklist. Special Catalogs: Catalog of artifacts. Special Indexes: Index to manuscripts, Rare Book Inventory. Staff: Peggy M. Timlin, Cur., Mss. & Bks.

★ 13050 ★
Pillsbury Company - Business Information Center (Bus-Fin)
Pillsbury Ctr.
200 S. 6th St.
Minneapolis, MN 55402-1464   Phone: (612)330-7232
Founded: 1959. Staff: Prof 3; Other 2. Subjects: Consumer products marketing, marketing research, food industry, foodservice industry, supermarket industry, advertising research, management training. Special Collections: Pillsbury primary market research projects (15,000 documents). Holdings: 700 books; 790 reference titles; 3500 subject documents; 5000 microfiche. Subscriptions: 300 journals and other serials. Services: Library not open to the public. Computerized Information Services: Online systems. Publications: New Products Bulletin, biweekly - for internal distribution only. Special Indexes: New Products Index, classed by company and food category; Company Index; internally generated subject index; internal materials indexed via library-developed thesaurus. Remarks: Maintains a Consumer Service Library specializing in cookbooks and recipe development materials. FAX: (612)330-5200. Staff: Barbara Rostad, Res.Libn.; Sandra Date, Mgr.

★ 13051 ★
Pillsbury Company - Technical Information Center (Food-Bev)
330 University Ave., S.E.   Phone: (612)330-4750
Minneapolis, MN 55414   James B. Tchobanoff, Mgr.
Founded: 1941. Staff: Prof 2; Other 3. Subjects: Food science and technology, cereal chemistry, microbiology, mathematics, statistics, agriculture, plant science. Holdings: 7000 books; 9000 bound periodical volumes; 40,000 patents; 35,000 internal reports. Subscriptions: 350 journals and other serials. Services: Interlibrary loan; SDI; center open to the public by appointment on limited schedule. Automated Operations: Computerized cataloging and circulation of journals. Computerized Information Services: DIALOG Information Services, MEDLINE, Chemical Abstracts Service (CAS), ORBIT, OCLC; internal database; OnTyme Electronic Message Network Service, DIALMAIL (electronic mail services). Networks/Consortia: Member of Metronet. Publications: Food Patent Digest, monthly; Current Literature, monthly - all for internal distribution only. Special Indexes: KWIC index to research notebooks and internal reports. Remarks: FAX: (612)330-4099. Staff: Dennis Pedersen, Sr.Tech.Info.Sci.

★ 13052 ★
Pillsbury Madison & Sutro - Law Library (Law)
725 S. Figueroa St., 13th Fl.   Phone: (213)488-7100
Los Angeles, CA 90071-2513   Hui-Chuan Chen, Dir., Info.Rsrcs.
Staff: Prof 3; Other 2. Subjects: Law - maritime, banking, real estate, corporate, tax; litigation. Special Collections: Maritime law (900 items). Holdings: 20,000 books; 250 bound periodical volumes. Subscriptions: 240 journals and other serials; 9 newspapers. Services: Interlibrary loan; library not open to the public. Computerized Information Services: DIALOG Information Services, WESTLAW, LEXIS, NEXIS. Remarks: FAX: (213)629-1033. Formerly: Lillick & McHose. Staff: Valerie Green, Assoc.Libn.; Rebecca Lu, Asst.Libn.

★ 13053 ★
Pillsbury Madison & Sutro - Library (Law)
Box 7880   Phone: (415)983-1130
San Francisco, CA 94120-7880   Kenneth Johnson, Lib.Mgr.
Founded: 1874. **Staff:** Prof 5; Other 9. **Subjects:** Law. **Holdings:** Figures not available. **Services:** Interlibrary loan; library not open to the public. **Automated Operations:** Computerized cataloging (BiblioTech). **Computerized Information Services:** DIALOG Information Services, DataTimes, VU/TEXT Information Services, Information America, Dun & Bradstreet Business Credit Services, Dow Jones News/Retrieval, RLIN, Legi-Tech, LEGI-SLATE, Reuters. **Remarks:** Library located at 225 Bush St., San Francisco, CA 94104-4278. FAX: (415)477-4966. **Staff:** Betty Howell; Cindy Beck Weller; Marilyn Willats; Leslie Mahtani; Margaret Shediac.

★ 13054 ★
Pilots International Association - Library (Sci-Engr)
Box 907   Phone: (612)588-5175
Minneapolis, MN 55440   Dale Brideau, Libn.
Staff: Prof 1; Other 1. **Subjects:** Aviation. **Holdings:** 105 books; 2 VF drawers of aviation clippings; 3 VF drawers of information on aviation organizations. **Subscriptions:** 22 journals and other serials. **Services:** Interlibrary loan; copying; library open to the public with restrictions.

Pilsudski Archives
See: Yale University - Slavic & East European Collection (20730)

★ 13055 ★
Jozef Pilsudski Institute of America - Library and Archives (Hist, Area-Ethnic)
381 Park Ave., S., Suite 701   Phone: (212)683-4342
New York, NY 10016   Mr. Jan Weiss, Chf.Libn.
Founded: 1943. **Staff:** Prof 2. **Subjects:** Polish history and politics, 1863 to present; United States history. **Special Collections:** Diplomatic and military documents of Polish Chief of State Jozef Pilsudski's Military Chancellery (45,000). **Holdings:** 16,000 books; 260 linear feet of bound periodical volumes; 399 linear feet of archival documents; 30,000 clippings; 1900 titles of cataloged pamphlets; 19,600 pictures; 800 maps; 498 reels of microfilm. **Subscriptions:** 21 journals and other serials; 19 newspapers. **Services:** Interlibrary loan; copying; SDI; library open to the public. **Computerized Information Services:** Internal database. **Publications:** Niepodleglosc (in Polish with English summaries); Bulletin (in Polish with English summaries). **Remarks:** FAX: (212)683-4514.

★ 13056 ★
Pima Air Museum - Library (Hist)
6000 E. Valencia Rd.   Phone: (602)574-0462
Tucson, AZ 85706   Cynthia J. Coan, Libn.
Founded: 1988. **Staff:** 1. **Subjects:** Aviation history, current aviation, military and civil aircraft, military history, aeronautics, astronautics. **Special Collections:** Rhodes Arnold Collection (430 folders); Colonel Schirmer Collection (archival materials, 70 notebooks). **Holdings:** 1800 books; 620 serial titles; 1000 government documents; 2400 technical aircraft manuals; 5 audiocassettes; 13 videotapes; 24 microfiche; 4 boxes of reels of microfilm; 50 manuscripts; maps; lithographs. **Subscriptions:** 5 journals and other serials; 10 newspapers. **Services:** Copying; library open to the public by appointment. **Computerized Information Services:** Internal databases. **Remarks:** FAX: (602)574-9238.

★ 13057 ★
Pima Council on Aging - Library (Soc Sci)
2919 E. Broadway   Phone: (602)795-5800
Tucson, AZ 85716-5311   Mary C. Guilbert, Libn.
Founded: 1979. **Staff:** Prof 1; Other 1. **Subjects:** Aging programs and services, gerontology, longterm care. **Holdings:** 500 books; 24 VF drawers; 20,000 other cataloged items. **Subscriptions:** 30 journals and other serials; 350 newsletters; 6 newspapers. **Services:** Interlibrary loan; copying; SDI; library open to the public by appointment. **Automated Operations:** Computerized cataloging and acquisitions. **Computerized Information Services:** BRS Information Technologies. **Remarks:** FAX: (602)323-3099.

★ 13058 ★
Pima County Juvenile Court Center - Library (Law)
2225 E. Ajo Way   Phone: (602)740-2082
Tucson, AZ 85713   Gwen Reid, Ct.Libn.
Founded: 1978. **Staff:** Prof 1. **Subjects:** Juvenile crime, penal institutions, adolescent problems, drug addiction, status offenses, sexual and child abuse. **Holdings:** 800 books. **Subscriptions:** 30 journals and other serials. **Services:** Copying; library open to judicial staff only. **Remarks:** FAX: (602)798-1942.

★ 13059 ★
Pima County Law Library (Law)
New Courts Bldg.
110 W. Congress   Phone: (602)740-8456
Tucson, AZ 85701-1317   Cecilia Torres-Zawada
Founded: 1915. **Staff:** Prof 1; Other 3. **Subjects:** Law. **Special Collections:** Conciliation Court - Family, Marriage, and Woman; Court Clinic Social Pathology and Criminology. **Holdings:** 52,000 volumes. **Subscriptions:** 80 journals and other serials. **Services:** Library open to the public.

★ 13060 ★
Pima County Planning and Development Services Department - Library (Plan)
130 W. Congress St.   Phone: (602)740-8361
Tucson, AZ 85701-1317   Paul Matty, Libn.
Founded: 1975. **Staff:** Prof 1. **Subjects:** Land use planning, demography, natural features. **Holdings:** 4000 books; 300 maps. **Subscriptions:** 50 journals and other serials. **Services:** Interlibrary loan; copying; SDI; library open to the public by appointment. **Remarks:** FAX: (602)884-1152.

★ 13061 ★
Pimeria Alta Historical Society - Museum/Archives (Hist)
223 Grand Ave.
Box 2281   Phone: (602)287-4621
Nogales, AZ 85628-2281   Anne Wheeler, Reg.
Founded: 1948. **Subjects:** Prehistory and history of Southern Arizona and Northern Sonora, 1000 to present; border history; mining; ranching; archeology. **Special Collections:** City of Nogales archives; oral history tapes of local history, business activities, ranching, women's history. **Holdings:** 2000 books; 115 periodicals. **Services:** Copying; museum and archives open to the public for reference use only. **Remarks:** FAX: (602)281-4087.

Douglas Pimlot Memorial Library
See: Canadian Arctic Resources Committee (2893)

★ 13062 ★
Pinal County Historical Society, Inc. - Library (Hist)
715 S. Main St.
Box 851   Phone: (602)868-4382
Florence, AZ 85232   Mary A. Faul, Libn.
Staff: Prof 1. **Subjects:** Arizona and Southwest history, Pinal County. **Holdings:** 625 books; 75 bound periodical volumes; clippings and pictures of local history. **Services:** Library open to researchers on a limited schedule.

★ 13063 ★
Pine Rest Christian Hospital - West Michigan Mental Health Information Center (Med)
P.O. Box 165   Phone: (616)455-5000
Grand Rapids, MI 49501-0165   Thomas Van Dam, Libn.
Founded: 1962. **Staff:** Prof 1. **Subjects:** Psychiatry, psychiatric nursing, psychiatric social work, clinical psychology. **Holdings:** 4000 books; cassette tapes. **Subscriptions:** 140 journals and other serials. **Services:** Interlibrary loan (fee); copying; library open to mental health professionals. **Computerized Information Services:** CD-ROM (MEDLINE).

★ 13064 ★
Pine Ridge Hospital - Library (Med)
150 Wyoming St.   Phone: (307)332-5700
Lander, WY 82520   Jane Heuer, Libn.
Founded: 1986. **Staff:** 1. **Subjects:** Alcohol and drug abuse, psychiatry, anorexia and bulemia. **Holdings:** 100 books. **Subscriptions:** 19 journals and other serials. **Services:** Interlibrary loan; copying; library open to the public at librarian's discretion. **Computerized Information Services:** MEDLARS. Performs searches on fee basis. **Formerly:** Psychiatric Institute of Wyoming - Library.

★ 13065 ★
Pineland Center - Library (Med)
Box E
Pownal, ME 04069-0902   Phone: (207)688-4811
Margaret Greenlaw, SDS III, Staff Dev.
Founded: 1958. **Staff:** 3. **Subjects:** Developmental disabilities, mental retardation, epilepsy, autism, cerebral palsy, medicine. **Holdings:** 1200 books; 80 videotapes. **Subscriptions:** 40 journals and other serials. **Services:** Interlibrary loan; copying; library open to the public. **Computerized Information Services:** BRS Information Technologies, MEDLINE. **Networks/Consortia:** Member of Health Science Library and Information Cooperative of Maine (HSLIC).

Pinellas County Historical Museum
See: **Heritage Park** (7156)

★ 13066 ★
Pinellas County Juvenile Welfare Board - Mailande W. Holland Library
(Soc Sci)
4140 49th St., N.   Phone: (813)521-1853
St. Petersburg, FL 33709   Alison R. Birmingham, Libn.
Founded: 1976. **Staff:** Prof 1; Other 1. **Subjects:** Child welfare, marriage and family therapy, juvenile delinquency, substance abuse, child abuse and neglect, day care and early childhood education, primary prevention, adolescent health, mental health, advocacy for economically disadvantaged, legislation, administration, funding and grant writing, community planning and development, community education. **Special Collections:** Intergenerational relations; funding collection (20 volumes). **Holdings:** 2000 books; 300 government documents; 300 AV programs. **Subscriptions:** 120 journals and other serials. **Services:** Interlibrary loan; library open to Pinellas County residents and child-serving nonprofit agencies. **Computerized Information Services:** DIALOG Information Services. **Networks/Consortia:** Member of Tampa Bay Library Consortium, Inc. (TBLC). **Publications:** Bulletin, quarterly. **Special Catalogs:** Media Catalogue, annual. **Remarks:** FAX: (813)528-0803.

★ 13067 ★
Pinellas County Law Library - Clearwater Branch (Law)
315 Court St.   Phone: (813)462-3411
Clearwater, FL 34616-5165   Patricia E. Spaulding
Founded: 1966. **Staff:** 3. **Subjects:** Law, taxes. **Holdings:** 30,000 books. **Subscriptions:** 43 journals and other serials. **Services:** Copying; library open to the public for reference use only. **Staff:** Patricia E. Spaulding, Libn.; Margaret Shewell, Libn.

★ 13068 ★
Pinellas County Law Library - St. Petersburg Branch - Allen C.
Anderson Memorial Law Library (Law)
Judicial Bldg., Rm. 500
545 1st Ave., N.   Phone: (813)892-7875
St. Petersburg, FL 33701   Martha F. Otting, Libn.
Founded: 1949. **Staff:** 2. **Subjects:** Law. **Holdings:** 30,000 volumes. **Subscriptions:** 100 journals and other serials. **Services:** Copying; library open to the public for reference use only. **Computerized Information Services:** WESTLAW. Performs searches on fee basis. **Staff:** Alice J. Snyder, Asst.Libn.

★ 13069 ★
Pinellas County School Board - Tomlinson Adult Learning Center -
Library/Media Center (Educ)
296 Mirror Lake Dr.   Phone: (813)821-4593
St. Petersburg, FL 33701   Helen G. Campbell, Media Spec.
Founded: 1969. **Staff:** Prof 1 ; Other 1. **Subjects:** Adult education - Adult Basic Education (ABE), high school credit, General Equivalency Diploma (GED); English as a Second Language (ESL); art; painting; data processing, typing, and practical business skills; foreign languages; music; piano/organ; reupholstery; slipcovers; sewing; custom dressmaking; creative writing; wood carving; sign language. **Holdings:** 8778 books; 1127 filmstrips; 350 phonograph records; 1960 slides; 5 16mm films; 1214 tape recordings; 20 microfiche; 49 videotapes; 431 diskettes. **Subscriptions:** 94 journals and other serials. **Services:** Interlibrary loan; copying; center open to the public for reference use only. **Publications:** Media Alert. **Staff:** Margaret Crawford.

★ 13070 ★
Pioneer Hi-Bred International, Inc. - Corporate Library (Agri)
400 Locust
700 Capital Sq.   Phone: (515)245-3518
Des Moines, IA 50309   Cynthia K. Via, Corp.Libn.
Founded: 1983. **Staff:** Prof 2; Other .5. **Subjects:** Agriculture, agribusiness, law, taxation, business. **Holdings:** 1430 books. **Subscriptions:** 363 journals and other serials. **Services:** Interlibrary loan; library not open to the public. **Automated Operations:** Computerized cataloging, serials, and circulation. **Computerized Information Services:** DIALOG Information Services, PFDS Online, BRS Information Technologies, LEXIS, NEXIS, OCLC, On-Line Research, Inc., Questel, Dow Jones News/Retrieval; BASIS (internal database). Performs searches on fee basis. **Remarks:** FAX: (515)245-3650.

★ 13071 ★
Pioneer Hi-Bred International, Inc. - Plant Breeding Research Library
(Agri)
7301 N.W. 62nd Ave.   Phone: (515)270-3147
Johnston, IA 50131   Helen Hoeven, Res.Lib.Coord.
Founded: 1982. **Staff:** Prof 1; Other 3. **Subjects:** Plant breeding, crop science, plant genetics, agriculture, biotechnology, microbial genetics. **Holdings:** 3000 books; 500 bound periodical volumes. **Subscriptions:** 600 journals and other serials. **Services:** Interlibrary loan; copying; SDI; library open to the public with restrictions. **Automated Operations:** Computerized cataloging, acquisitions, and serials. **Computerized Information Services:** DIALOG Information Services, PFDS Online, BRS Information Technologies, AGNET, National Pesticide Information Retrieval System (NPIRS), AgriData Network, Germplasm Resources Information Network (GRIN); internal database. **Networks/Consortia:** Member of Bibliographical Center for Research, Rocky Mountain Region, Inc. (BCR). **Publications:** Electronic Newsletter - for internal distribution only. **Remarks:** FAX: (515)253-2125.

★ 13072 ★
Pioneer Historical Society - Library (Hist)
P.O. Box 421   Phone: (814)623-2011
Bedford, PA 15522   Kay Williams, Libn.
FO 1975. **Staff:** 1. **Subjects:** Bedford County history, genealogy. **Holdings:** 1570 items. **Services:** Copying; library open to the public. **Special Indexes:** Obituary index (card).

Pioneer Memorial Museum
See: **U.S. Natl. Park Service - Olympic Natl. Park** (17760)

Pioneer Museum, Arizona Historical Society Archives
See: **Northern Arizona University - Cline Library - Special Collections**
and Archives Department (11992)

Pioneer Valley Resource Center
See: **Greenfield Community College** (6730)

Pioneers' Museum
See: **Colorado Springs Pioneers Museum** (3951)

★ 13073 ★
Piper & Marbury - Law Library (Law)
1100 Charles Center S.
36 S. Charles St.   Phone: (301)576-1617
Baltimore, MD 21201   Katherine E. Hobner, Libn.
Staff: 5. **Subjects:** Law. **Holdings:** 30,000 volumes. **Subscriptions:** 418 journals and other serials; 16 newspapers. **Services:** Interlibrary loan; library not open to the public. **Automated Operations:** Computerized cataloging. **Computerized Information Services:** LEXIS, DIALOG Information Services, WESTLAW. **Remarks:** (301)539-0489.

★ 13074 ★
Pipestone County Historical Society - Research Library (Hist)
113 S. Hiawatha   Phone: (507)825-2563
Pipestone, MN 56164   David Rambow, Musm.Dir.
Subjects: Local, county, and state history. **Special Collections:** Rose
biographies (unpublished). **Holdings:** 500 books; 150 bound periodical
volumes; 212 reels of microfilm; oral history transcripts; county newspapers.
Services: Copying; library open to the public with restrictions. **Special
Indexes:** Obituary index (card); biography index (card); business directory
index. **Staff:** Joe Ager, Asst.Musm.Dir.

Pipestone National Monument
See: **U.S. Natl. Park Service** (17766)

Chesley A. Pippy, Jr. Medical Library
See: **Salvation Army Grace General Hospital** (14653)

**Pira: Research Association for the Paper and Board, Printing and
   Packaging Industries**
See: **Pira International** (13075)

★ 13075 ★
Pira International - Information Services (Bus-Fin)
Randalls Rd.
Leatherhead, Surrey KT22 7RU,   Phone: 372 376161
   England   Marie Rushton, Mgr., Info.Serv.
Subjects: Paper - board making, nonwovens, printing, packaging,
management, marketing, publishing, legislation, technical and business
developments. **Holdings:** 6000 bound volumes; 30,000 reports, standards,
translations, pamphlets, and other cataloged items. **Subscriptions:** 1000
journals and other serials. **Services:** SDI. **Computerized Information
Services:** Produces Pira Abstracts, EPUBS (available through ORBIT
Search Service); MMA (available through Pergamon Financial Data
Services). **Remarks:** FAX: 372 377526. Telex: 929810. **Formerly:** Pira:
Research Association for the Paper and Board, Printing and Packaging
Industries.

Pirate House Library
See: **Cumberland County Historical Society** (4474)

★ 13076 ★
Malcolm Pirnie, Inc. - Technical Library (Env-Cons, Sci-Engr)
2 Corporate Park Dr.
Box 751   Phone: (914)641-2954
White Plains, NY 10602   Marianne Gregg
Staff: Prof 1; Other 2. **Subjects:** Environmental engineering, water, waste
water, air pollution, hazardous waste and solid waste management.
Holdings: 15,000 volumes; 1000 U.S. Environmental Protection Agency
reports. **Subscriptions:** 150 journals and other serials. **Services:** Interlibrary
loan; copying; library open to the public by appointment. **Computerized
Information Services:** DIALOG Information Services, Chemical
Information Systems, Inc. (CIS), Dow Jones News/Retrieval, MEDLARS,
U.S. Environmental Protection databases. **Publications:** Acquisitions - for
internal distribution only. **Remarks:** FAX: (914)694-9286.

George W. Pirtle Geological Sciences Library
See: **University of Kentucky** (18749)

★ 13077 ★
Piscataquis County Law Library (Law)
Court House Annex   Phone: (207)564-2161
Dover-Foxcroft, ME 04426   Julia Knight, Treas.
Staff: 1. **Subjects:** Law. **Holdings:** 5500 volumes. **Services:** Library open to
the public.

Pitcairn Island Museum and Library.
See: **H.M.S. Bounty Society, International** (6819)

Pitcairn Islands Study Center
See: **Pacific Union College** (12680)

★ 13078 ★
Pitman-Moore, Inc. - Research & Development Library (Sci-Engr)
1331 S. 1st St.
Box 207   Phone: (812)232-0121
Terre Haute, IN 47808   Lori E. Wahl, Lib.Supv.
Founded: 1927. **Staff:** Prof 3; Other 4. **Subjects:** Chemistry, biochemistry,
biological sciences, microbiology, animal health and nutrition, veterinary
science, agriculture. **Holdings:** 8000 books; 20,000 bound periodical
volumes; 40,000 internal reports; chemical patents in microform; microfilm;
audiotapes. **Subscriptions:** 250 journals and other serials. **Services:**
Interlibrary loan; SDI; translation; library open to the public by
appointment. **Automated Operations:** Computerized cataloging, serials, and
circulation. **Computerized Information Services:** DIALOG Information
Services, STN International, Chemical Information Systems, Inc. (CIS),
NLM, Mead Data Central, OCLC; internal databases. **Networks/Consortia:**
Member of INCOLSA. **Remarks:** FAX: (812)238-1077. **Staff:** Kurt O.
Baumgartner, Sr.Assoc.Info.Sci.; Penny R. Kyker, Assoc.Info.Sci.

★ 13079 ★
Pitney Bowes - Business and Technical Information Center (Info Sci)
35 Waterview Dr., 26-33   Phone: (203)924-3235
Shelton, CT 06484-8000   Mary Jane Miller, Mgr.
Founded: 1953. **Staff:** Prof 2; Other 3. **Subjects:** Telecommunications,
electronics, optics, chemistry, printing technology, physics,
electrophotography, computers, postal service. **Holdings:** 3500 books; 700
reels of microfilm. **Subscriptions:** 350 journals and other serials. **Services:**
Interlibrary loan; center not open to the public. **Automated Operations:**
Computerized cataloging, serials, and circulation. **Computerized
Information Services:** DIALOG Information Services, OCLC, NEXIS,
LEXIS. **Networks/Consortia:** Member of Southwestern Connecticut
Library Council (SWLC). **Publications:** New From the Conference Board
(New Materials Bulletin). **Special Catalogs:** Technical report file. **Remarks:**
FAX: (203)924-3406 (Attn: Business and Technical Information Center).
Staff: Jack F. Stevens, Info.Spec.

★ 13080 ★
Pitney, Hardin, Kipp & Szuch - Law Library (Law)
Park Ave. at Morris County
P.O. Box 1945   Phone: (201)966-8120
Morristown, NJ 07962   Julie L. von Schrader, Libn.
Staff: Prof 2; Other 4. **Subjects:** Law. **Special Collections:** New Jersey
Statutes, 1680 to present (200 publications). **Holdings:** 30,000 books; 1000
bound periodical volumes; 100 video cassettes. **Subscriptions:** 75 journals
and other serials; 7 newspapers. **Services:** Interlibrary loan; copying; library
open to attorneys for reference use only on request. **Computerized
Information Services:** LEXIS, DIALOG Information Services,
WESTLAW, DataTimes, LEGI-SLATE. **Remarks:** FAX: (201)966-1550.
Telex: 642014. **Staff:** Susan M. DeBare.

★ 13081 ★
Pitt-Des Moines, Inc. - Engineering Library (Sci-Engr)
3400 Grand Ave.   Phone: (412)331-3000
Pittsburgh, PA 15225-1508   Louise Franz, Libn.
Staff: Prof 1. **Subjects:** Engineering. **Holdings:** 800 books; 200 bound
periodical volumes; 24 VF drawers of technical reports; 500 binders of
clippings. **Subscriptions:** 50 journals and other serials. **Services:** Interlibrary
loan; library not open to the public. **Computerized Information Services:**
DIALOG Information Services. **Remarks:** FAX: (412)331-6807.

Pitts Memorial Library
See: **Baptist Medical Center** (1509)

Pitts Theology Library
See: **Emory University - Pitts Theology Library** (5334)

★ 13082 ★
Pittsburg State University - Leonard H. Axe Library - Special Collections (Hist)
S. Joplin
Pittsburg, KS 66762
Phone: (316)231-7000
Eugene H. DeGruson, Spec.Coll.Libn.
Founded: 1903. **Special Collections:** Haldeman-Julius Collection (45,000 items); Southeast Kansas Collection (110,500 items); Kansas and U.S. documents (161,000); college and community archives (21,300 archival materials). **Services:** Interlibrary loan; copying; collections open to the public. **Automated Operations:** Computerized cataloging, serials, circulation, and ILL. **Computerized Information Services:** DIALOG Information Services, PFDS Online, BRS Information Technologies, MEDLARS. **Networks/Consortia:** Member of Bibliographical Center for Research, Rocky Mountain Region, Inc. (BCR).

★ 13083 ★
Pittsburgh Board of Education - Professional Library (Educ)
635 Ridge Ave.
Pittsburgh, PA 15212
Phone: (412)323-4146
Dorothy Hopkins, Libn.
Founded: 1928. **Staff:** Prof 1; Other 1. **Subjects:** Education, early childhood through high school. **Special Collections:** Depository for Pittsburgh Public School textbooks; courses of study and Board of Education minutes. **Holdings:** 15,000 books; 20 drawers of pamphlets, clippings, reports, articles; 12 VF drawers of archival material. **Subscriptions:** 200 journals, newsletters, and other serials; 5 newspapers. **Services:** Interlibrary loan; copying; library open to the public for research only. **Computerized Information Services:** BRS Information Technologies, OCLC. **Networks/Consortia:** Member of Pittsburgh Regional Library Center (PRLC). **Remarks:** FAX: (412)323-4148. **Staff:** Judy G. Westerman, Dir., Lib.Serv.

★ 13084 ★
Pittsburgh Corning Corporation - Technical Library (Sci-Engr)
800 Presque Isle Dr.
Pittsburgh, PA 15239
Phone: (412)327-6100
Susan Funk, Libn.
Founded: 1962. **Subjects:** Glass, ceramics, chemistry, physics, materials engineering. **Holdings:** 2000 books; 2600 bound periodical volumes; 3500 patents. **Remarks:** FAX: (412)733-4815.

★ 13085 ★
Pittsburgh History & Landmarks Foundation - James D. Van Trump Library (Hist)
450 Landmarks Bldg.
Station Square
Pittsburgh, PA 15219
Phone: (412)471-5808
Albert M Tannler, Archv.
Founded: 1964. **Staff:** Prof 1. **Subjects:** History of Pittsburgh and Western Pennsylvania, architecture, architectural history, historic preservation, landscaping, transportation. **Special Collections:** Architectural drawings, maps, sketches, prints; articles of James D. Van Trump (manuscripts; recordings; notes); articles of Walter C. Kidney. **Holdings:** 3000 books; 20 bound periodical volumes; 20 VF drawers of Pittsburgh clippings and brochures; 40 drawers of slides; 50 audiotapes; 20 drawers of architectural and engineering drawings and maps; 32 shelves of plat books; 50 loose-leaf manuscripts; 20 unbound periodical titles. **Subscriptions:** 12 journals and other serials. **Services:** Copying; library open to the public with restrictions. **Automated Operations:** Computerized acquisitions. **Remarks:** FAX: (412)471-1633.

★ 13086 ★
Pittsburgh Post-Gazette Publishing Company - Library (Publ)
50 Boulevard of the Allies
Pittsburgh, PA 15222
Phone: (412)263-1397
Angelika R. Kane, Libn.
Founded: 1939. **Staff:** Prof 5. **Subjects:** Newspaper reference topics. **Special Collections:** Movie stills. **Holdings:** 500 books; 40 bound periodical volumes; 500 VF drawers of clippings; 6 VF drawers of subject files; 160,000 picture files; 15 drawers of microfilm. **Subscriptions:** 32 journals and other serials; 24 newspapers. **Services:** Copying (limited); library open to the public. **Automated Operations:** Computerized circulation. **Computerized Information Services:** NEXIS. **Special Catalogs:** Photograph catalog (card). **Special Indexes:** Index to newspaper clippings files (notebooks). **Remarks:** FAX: (412)263-0908.

★ 13087 ★
Pittsburgh Press - Library (Publ)
Boulevard of the Allies
Pittsburgh, PA 15230
Phone: (412)263-1480
Eileen E. Finster, Hd.Libn.
Founded: 1884. **Staff:** Prof 1; Other 5. **Subjects:** Newspaper reference topics. **Holdings:** 250 books; clippings; photographs; Pittsburgh Press, 1884 to present, on microfilm. **Services:** Library not open to the public. **Computerized Information Services:** VU/TEXT Information Services.

★ 13088 ★
Pittsburgh Theological Seminary - Clifford E. Barbour Library (Rel-Phil)
616 N. Highland Ave.
Pittsburgh, PA 15206
Phone: (412)362-5610
Stephen D. Crocco, Libn.
Founded: 1794. **Staff:** Prof 4; Other 2. **Subjects:** Theology, philosophy. **Special Collections:** Newburgh Collection (17th and 18th century theological works); James Warrington Collection of hymnology. **Holdings:** 225,300 volumes; 10,028 microforms; 820 phonograph records; 994 theses; 1508 tapes; 6200 archival materials. **Subscriptions:** 903 journals and other serials. **Services:** Interlibrary loan; library open to undergraduate students with special permission from their institutions. **Automated Operations:** Computerized cataloging and serials. **Networks/Consortia:** Member of Pittsburgh Regional Library Center (PRLC). **Publications:** Bibliographia Tripotamopolitana, irregular. **Staff:** Andrew Sopko; Cassandra Brush; Jayne Schneider.

★ 13089 ★
Pittsburgh Toy Lending Library, Inc. (Educ)
5410 Baum Blvd.
Pittsburgh, PA 15232
Phone: (412)682-4430
Founded: 1974. **Subjects:** Toys - imaginative play, cognitive development, infant; parenting; children's books. **Holdings:** 300 books; 1000 toys. **Subscriptions:** 4 journals and other serials. **Services:** Play area; toy lending; library open to members.

★ 13090 ★
Pittsburgh Zoo - Pittsburgh Aqua Zoo Library (Biol Sci)
Highland Park
Box 5250
Pittsburgh, PA 15206
Phone: (412)665-3768
Randolph Goodlett, Cur.
Founded: 1982. **Staff:** Prof 1. **Subjects:** Freshwater fish, marine biology, freshwater dolphins, microcosm exhibits, freshwater and marine plankton. **Special Collections:** Papers published on the Amazon River Dolphins; papers published on the new "microcosm" exhibits designed by Smithsonian Institution; papers on Ciquatera Poisoning in fish. **Holdings:** 1000 books; 15 bound periodical volumes; 2500 research papers. **Subscriptions:** 45 journals and other serials; 5 newspapers. **Services:** Library open to the public by written request. **Automated Operations:** Computerized cataloging. **Publications:** Pittsburgh Zoo Newsletter - for internal distribution only; Animal Talk (magazine), quarterly. **Remarks:** FAX: (412)665-3661.

★ 13091 ★
Placer County Law Library (Law)
350 Nevada St.
Auburn, CA 95603
Phone: (916)889-4115
Tanemi Klahn, Law Libn.
Staff: Prof 1. **Subjects:** Law. **Holdings:** 5579 volumes; 26 cassettes. **Services:** Interlibrary loan; library open to the public. **Computerized Information Services:** LEXIS. **Remarks:** FAX: (916)889-4112.

★ 13092 ★
Placer Dome Inc. - Library (Sci-Engr)
Bentall Postal Sta., P.O. Box 49330
Vancouver, BC, Canada V7X 1P1
Phone: (604)682-7082
Rachele Oriente, Libn.
Founded: 1952. **Staff:** 1. **Subjects:** Geology, mining, metallurgy, business and economics. **Holdings:** 15,000 books. **Subscriptions:** 350 journals and other serials; 20 newspapers. **Services:** Interlibrary loan; library not open to the public. **Automated Operations:** Computerized serials and acquisitions. **Computerized Information Services:** DIALOG Information Services, QL Systems, Info Globe, Infomart Online, CAN/OLE, Reuters; Envoy 100 (electronic mail service). **Remarks:** FAX: (604)682-7092. Electronic mail address(es): PLACER.LIB (Envoy 100).

★ 13093 ★
Plain Dealer Publishing Company - Library (Publ)
1801 Superior Ave.   Phone: (216)344-4195
Cleveland, OH 44114   Patti A. Graziano, Lib.Dir.
Founded: 1908. **Staff:** Prof 4; Other 7. **Subjects:** Newspaper reference topics.
Special Collections: Great Lakes; Ohio and Cleveland history. **Holdings:**
3970 books; 500,000 pictures; 4.8 million clippings; 4811 reels of microfilm;
38 VF drawers of pamphlets. **Subscriptions:** 200 journals and other serials;
65 newspapers. **Services:** Interlibrary loan; library not open to the public.
Computerized Information Services: DIALOG Information Services, VU/
TEXT Information Services, DataTimes. **Special Catalogs:** Subject
Authority File (printout). **Remarks:** FAX: (216)694-6363. **Staff:** Mary Ann
Cofta, Asst.Hd.Libn.

★ 13094 ★
Plainfield Public Library - Guilford Township Historical Collection
(Hist)
1120 Stafford Rd.   Phone: (317)839-6602
Plainfield, IN 46168   Susan Miller Carter, Dept.Hd.
Founded: 1967. **Staff:** Prof 1; Other 2. **Subjects:** History and genealogy -
Plainfield, Hendricks, Morgan, Montgomery, Putnam, and Boone counties;
Society of Friends Western Yearly Meeting; local authors; Indianapolis city
directories 1880-1940. **Holdings:** 6379 books; 170 bound periodical volumes;
120 bound newapaper volumes; 24 oral history tapes and transcripts; 2 file
drawers of photographs; 27 file drawers of clippings and pamphlets; 84 boxes
of manuscripts; obituary file; 422 reels of microfilm of local newspapers; 75
reels of microfilm of census data; 142 reels of microfilm of local history
materials. **Subscriptions:** 25 journals and other serials; 7 newspapers.
Services: Copying; collection open to the public, (call for hours and
information). **Special Indexes:** Indexes for Hendricks County authors,
biographies, 50th wedding anniversaries, place-names, obituaries, local
newspapers, Maple Hill cemetery (cards); name indexes for books of local
interest (book).**Remarks:** FAX: (317)839-4044.

★ 13095 ★
Plains Art Museum - Library (Art)
219 S. 7th St.
Box 2338
Fargo, ND 58108-2338   Phone: (701)293-0903
                                      Marla Green, Cur., Educ.
Staff: 1. **Subjects:** Art history, museology, Native American art. **Holdings:**
240 books; 200 unbound periodicals; 200 videotapes; 100 slide programs.
Subscriptions: 12 journals and other serials. **Services:** Library not open to
the public. **Publications:** Film, Video, and Slides Catalog, annual - available
to educators within five-state region. **Remarks:** Library serves as the film,
video and slide lending institution for the National Gallery of Art and the
private collection of the museum. FAX: (701)237-0336. **Staff:** David
Wooley, Cur.; Elizabeth Hannaher, Dir.

★ 13096 ★
Plains Health Centre - Dr. W.A. Riddell Health Sciences Library (Med)
4500 Wascana Pkwy.   Phone: (306)584-6426
Regina, SK, Canada S4S 5W9   Beth Silzer, Dir.
Founded: 1974. **Staff:** Prof 1; Other 3. **Subjects:** Medicine, nursing,
pharmacy, physiotherapy. **Holdings:** 4764 books; 4500 bound periodical
volumes; 800 AV programs. **Subscriptions:** 294 journals and other serials.
Services: Interlibrary loan; SDI; library open to health sciences personnel.
Automated Operations: Computerized cataloging (NOTIS). **Computerized
Information Services:** DIALOG Information Services; CD-ROM
(MEDLINE); Envoy 100 (electronic mail service). **Remarks:** FAX:
(306)584-6334.

★ 13097 ★
PLAN International - U.S.A. - Library (Soc Sci)
155 Plan Way, Dept. KO24   Phone: (401)738-5600
Warwick, RI 02886   Jaya Sarkar
Founded: 1984. **Subjects:** Development - theory, practice, education;
intercultural communication; hunger and poverty in Third World; multicultural educational materials. **Special Collections:** Country and Culture
Collection (materials on countries participating in PLAN International-
USA program). **Holdings:** 300 books. **Subscriptions:** 15 journals and other
serials; 5 newspapers. **Services:** Library open to the public. **Remarks:** FAX:
(401)738-5608.

★ 13098 ★
Max Planck Institute - Bibliotheca Hertziana (Art)
Palazzo Zuccari
Via Gregoriana 28   Phone: 6 6841198
I-00187 Rome, Italy   Dr. Ernst Guldan
Founded: 1913. **Staff:** Prof 13; Other 7. **Subjects:** Italian art history. **Special
Collections:** Rome guides (1100 volumes); Travels in Italy (1200 volumes).
Holdings: 146,000 books; 31,000 bound periodical volumes; 7000
microfiche. **Subscriptions:** 980 journals and other serials. **Services:** Copying;
library open to art historians only. **Special Catalogs:** Kataloge der
Bibliotheca Hertziana in Rome, Section 1-111, 1985. **Remarks:** FAX: 6
6790740.

★ 13099 ★
Max Planck Institute for Biophysical Chemistry - Otto Hahn Library
(Biol Sci, Sci-Engr)
Am Fassberg 2
Postfach 2841   Phone: 551 201349
W-3400 Goettingen, Germany   Bernhard Reuse, Hd.Libn.
Founded: 1947. **Staff:** Prof 3; Other 3. **Subjects:** Biochemistry, physics,
neurobiology, spectroscopy, laser physics, molocular biology, biochemical
kinetics, membrane physics, cell physiology, molecular genetics. **Holdings:**
33,000 books; 60,000 bound periodical volumes. **Subscriptions:** 755 journals
and other serials; 22 newspapers. **Services:** Copying; library open to the
public for reference use only. **Remarks:** FAX: 551 201222. Telex: 96 786
mpibpc d. **Also Known As:** Max-Planck-Institut fuer Biophysikalische
Chemie - Otto-Hahn-Bibliothek.

★ 13100 ★
Max Planck Institute for Brain Research - Library (Med)
Deutschordenstrasse 46
Postfach 71 0667   Phone: 69 670 41
W-6000 Frankfurt 71, Germany   Inge Schroter, Libn.
Subjects: Brain research. **Holdings:** 18,000 volumes. **Remarks:** FAX: 69 670
4433. **Also Known As:** Max-Planck-Institut fuer Hirnforschung.

★ 13101 ★
Max Planck Institute for Breeding Research - Library (Biol Sci)
Carl-von-Linne-Weg 10
W-5000 Cologne 30, Germany   Phone: 221 50621
Subjects: Plant genetics, plant breeding, plant biochemistry. **Holdings:**
19,000 volumes. **Subscriptions:** 200 journals and other serials. **Services:**
Library not open to the public. **Remarks:** FAX: 221 5062513. Telex: 8 881
028 mpiz d. **Also Known As:** Max-Planck-Institut fuer Zuechtungforschung.

★ 13102 ★
**Max Planck Institute for Comparative Public Law and International
Law - Library** (Law)
Berliner Strasse 48   Phone: 6221 4821
D-6900 Heidelberg, Germany   Joachim Schwietzke, Libn.
Founded: 1924. **Staff:** 17. **Subjects:** Public law - foreign, international,
comparative; international organizations. **Holdings:** 375,000 volumes;
United Nations (UN) documents; European Economic Community (EEC)
documents. **Subscriptions:** 4500 journals and other serials; 30 newspapers.
Services: Library open to scholars; UN and EEC documents open to the
public. **Computerized Information Services:** LEXIS, DIALOG Information
Services, Questel, CED, CELEX, BELINDIS, JURIS, DBI (Deutsches
Bibliotheksinstitut). **Publications:** List of acquisitions, bimonthly; Public
International Law, a current bibliography of books and articles, 2/year.
Remarks: FAX: 6221 482288. **Also Known As:** Max-Planck-Institut fuer
Auslaendisches Oeffentliches Recht und Voelkerrecht.

★ 13103 ★
Max Planck Institute for Developmental Biology - Library
Spemannstrasse 35
W-7400 Tubingen, Germany
Defunct.

★ 13104 ★
Max Planck Institute for Foreign and International Patent, Copyright, and Competition Law - Library (Law)
Siebertstrasse 3   Phone: 89 9246256
W-8000 Munich 80, Germany   Dr. J. Straus, Prof.
Founded: 1966. **Staff:** Prof 7; Other 13. **Subjects:** Law - industrial property, copyright, competition, antitrust. **Holdings:** 87,877 books; 23,942 bound periodical volumes; microfiche. **Subscriptions:** 672 journals and other serials; 7 newspapers. **Services:** Copying; library open to the public by appointment. **Computerized Information Services:** JURIS. **Remarks:** FAX: 89 9246247. Alternate telephone number(s): 89 9246257. **Also Known As:** Max-Planck-Institut fuer Auslaendisches und Internationales Patent-, Urheber-, und Wettbewerbsrecht. **Staff:** Ines Saler, Supv.Libn.; Susanne Von Brescius, Libn.; Mrs. Anke Rohrbacher, Libn.; Elke List, Libn.

★ 13105 ★
Max Planck Institute for Foreign and International Private Law - Library (Law)
Mittelweg 187
W-2000 Hamburg 13, Germany   Phone: 40 41271
Founded: 1926. **Staff:** Prof 12; Other 6. **Subjects:** Law - private international, private, economic, comparative; unification of law. **Holdings:** 300,000 volumes; 9000 other cataloged items. **Subscriptions:** 2000 journals and other serials; 12 newspapers. **Services:** Copying; library open to the public with restrictions. **Automated Operations:** Computerized serials. **Computerized Information Services:** LEXIS, JURIS GmbH, CELEX. **Publications:** The Library of the Max Planck Institute for Foreign and International Private Law, Hamburg; Information and Regulations for Visitors on the Use of the Library (with bibliography, 1987). **Remarks:** FAX: 40 4127288. Telex: 212893 mpipd. **Also Known As:** Max-Planck-Institut fuer Auslaendisches und Internationales Privatrecht. **Staff:** Dr. Juergen C. Godan, Dir.; Dr. Ralph Lansky, Dir.; Dr. Holger Knudsen; Jutta Voss; Ruediger Baatz; Vera Klemp.

★ 13106 ★
Max Planck Institute for Foreign and International Social Law - Library (Law)
Leopold Strasse 24
Postfach 440109
W-8000 Munich 40, Germany   Phone: 89 386021
                                          Mrs. I. Deltaglia, Libn.
Founded: 1975. **Staff:** 4.5. **Subjects:** Law - international, social, welfare, social security. **Holdings:** 48,000 volumes; 220 loose-leaf items. **Subscriptions:** 310 journals; 11 newspapers. **Services:** Interlibrary loan; copying; SDI; library open to the public. **Computerized Information Services:** JURIS. **Remarks:** FAX: 89 342473. **Also Known As:** Max-Planck-Institut fur Auslaendisches und Internationales Sozialrecht.

★ 13107 ★
Max Planck Institute of History - Library (Hist)
Hermann-Foege-Weg 11   Phone: 495644
W-3400 Goettingen, Germany   Heidemarie Oltmann, Libn.
Founded: 1956. **Subjects:** History - social, institutional, intellectual, economic, legal, educational. **Holdings:** 71,000 volumes. **Subscriptions:** 419 journals and other serials. **Services:** Copying; library open to the public with restrictions. **Remarks:** FAX: 055 495670. **Also Known As:** Max-Planck-Institut fuer Geschichte.

★ 13108 ★
Max Planck Institute of Limnology - Library (Biol Sci)
August-Thienemann-Strasse 2
Postfach 165
W-2320 Plon, Germany   Phone: 4522 802 263
                                          Brigitte Lechner, Libn.
Founded: 1891. **Staff:** 1.5. **Subjects:** Limnology, tropical ecology, plankton. **Holdings:** 11,000 volumes. **Subscriptions:** 435 journals and other serials. **Services:** Interlibrary loan; copying; library open to the public. **Computerized Information Services:** Electronic mail. **Remarks:** FAX: 4522 802318. **Also Known As:** Max-Planck-Institut fuer Limnologie.

★ 13109 ★
Max Planck Institute for Metals Research - Library (Sci-Engr)
Heisenbergstrasse 1   Phone: 6860-229
W-7000 Stuttgart 80, Germany   Ingeborg Jaiser, Libn.
Staff: Prof 3. **Subjects:** Solid state physics, semiconductors, electron microscopy, magnetism, superconductivity. **Holdings:** 10,000 books; 13,000 bound periodical volumes. **Subscriptions:** 299 journals and other serials. **Services:** Library not open to the public. **Remarks:** Telex: Nr. 7-255 555. **Also Known As:** Max-Planck-Institut fuer Metallforschung. **Staff:** Ute Muller, Libn.; Daniela Kabinova, Libn.

★ 13110 ★
Max Planck Institute for Nutrition Physiology - Library (Biol Sci, Med)
Rheinlanddamm 201   Phone: 1 20 61
W-4600 Dortmund 1, Germany   Ute Graesiek, Libn.
Subjects: Biochemistry, physiology, metabolic processes. **Holdings:** 16,600 volumes. **Also Known As:** Max-Planck-Institut fuer Ernahrungsphysiologie.

★ 13111 ★
Max Planck Institute for Physics - Werner Heisenberg Institute - Library (Sci-Engr)
Fohringer Ring 6
Postfach 401212   Phone: 89 32308278
W-8000 Munich 40, Germany   Uwe Kollmorgan, Dipl.-Bibl.
Staff: Prof 1; Other 1.5. **Subjects:** High energy physics, general physics, mathematics. **Special Collections:** Preprints and reports collection. **Holdings:** 11,192 books; 16,046 bound periodical volumes. **Subscriptions:** 173 journals and other serials. **Services:** Interlibrary loan; library not open to the public. **Computerized Information Services:** SLAC (internal database). **Publications:** Weekly acquisitions list. **Remarks:** FAX: 89 3226704. Telex: 52 15 619.

★ 13112 ★
Max Planck Institute of Plasma Physics - Library (Sci-Engr)
Boltzmannstrasse 2   Phone: 89 329901
W-8046 Garching, Germany   Angelika Hohaus, Libn.
Staff: 4. **Subjects:** Controlled nuclear fusion, plasma physics in the development of a fusion reactor. **Holdings:** 47,000 books; 25,000 bound periodical volumes; 55,000 reports. **Subscriptions:** 600 journals and other serials. **Services:** Library not open to the public. **Automated Operations:** Computerized cataloging. **Computerized Information Services:** STN International; LIBRIS (internal database). **Remarks:** FAX: 89 32992200. Telex: 5215808. **Remarks:** FAX: 089 3299-2200. **Also Known As:** Max-Planck-Institut fuer Plasmaphysik.

★ 13113 ★
Max Planck Institute for Psychiatry - Library (Med)
Kraepelinstrasse 2 and 10   Phone: 30 622333
W-8000 Munich 40, Germany   Angelika Kaufmann, Libn.
Subjects: Clinical research: neurology and neuroradiology, neuropsychology, clinical chemistry, clinical neurophysiology, and experimental, social, and clinical psychology. **Special Collections:** Laehrjammling. **Holdings:** 33,000 volumes. **Subscriptions:** 200 journals and other serials. **Services:** Copying; library open to the public for reference use only. **Computerized Information Services:** MEDLINE; CD-ROM (Current Contents). **Also Known As:** Max-Planck-Institut fuer Psychiatrie.

★ 13114 ★
Max Planck Institute for Psychiatry - Theoretical Institute - Library (Med)
Am Klopferspitz 18 a   Phone: 89 85783529
W-8033 Planegg-Martinsried, Germany   Ingrid Holzinger, Libn.
Staff: 1.5. **Subjects:** Normal/abnormal functions of the nervous system, neuromorphology, neurochemistry, neuroanatomy, neuropharmacology, neuroimmunology, neurophysiology, neurobiochemistry. **Holdings:** 10,000 volumes. **Subscriptions:** 100 journals and other serials. **Services:** Library open to the public for reference use only during institute hours. **Remarks:** FAX: 89 85783777. **Also Known As:** Max-Planck-Institut fur Psychiatrie. **Staff:** Sigrid Oertel, Libn.

★ 13115 ★
Max Planck Institute for Radio Astronomy - Library (Sci-Engr)
Auf dem Huegel 69
W-5300 Bonn 1, Germany   Phone: 228 52 51
Subjects: Radio astronomy, radio spectroscopy. **Holdings:** 12,000 volumes. **Remarks:** Telex: 868440. **Also Known As:** Max-Planck-Institut fuer Radioastronomie. **Staff:** Karina Kaulins, Libn.; Silke Niehaus-Weingartner, Libn.

★ 13116 ★
Max Planck Institute for System Physiology - Library (Med)
Rheinlanddamm 201   Phone: 120 640 80
W-4600 Dortmund 1, Germany   Mrs. Ute Grzesiek, Libn.
Subjects: System physiology, solute transport in epithelia, differentiation of epithelial cells. **Holdings:** 16,000 volumes. **Also Known As:** Max-Planck-Institut fuer System- und Ernahrungsphysiologie.

★ 13117 ★
Planetary Association for Clean Energy, Inc. (PACE) - Clean Energy Centre (Energy)
100 Bronson, No. 1001   Phone: (613)236-6265
Ottawa, ON, Canada K1R 6G8   Andrew Michrowski, Pres.
Founded: 1984. **Staff:** Prof 4; Other 3. **Subjects:** Biological effects of electromagnetic radiation, clean energy systems, emerging energy sciences; problems associated with video display systems. **Special Collections:** Nikola Tesla Collection. **Holdings:** 10,000 books; 500 bound periodical volumes; emerging energy science and technology manuscripts. **Subscriptions:** 160 journals and other serials. **Services:** Interlibrary loan; copying; center open to the public. **Remarks:** FAX: (613)232-0495. **Formerly:** Located in Hull, PQ. **Staff:** Monique Michaud.

★ 13118 ★
Planetree - Health Resource Center (Med)
2040 Webster St.   Phone: (415)923-3680
San Francisco, CA 94115   Tracey Cosgrove, Med.Libn.
Founded: 1981. **Staff:** Prof 1; Other 5. **Subjects:** Consumer health information, preventive medicine, self-care, holistic health, body systems and diseases, nutrition, fitness, pharmeceutical drugs. **Special Collections:** Complementary therapies; codependency. **Holdings:** 2000 books; 24 VF drawers of clippings; 2000 entries in Information and Reference System. **Subscriptions:** 58 journals and other serials. **Services:** Copying; center open to the public. **Computerized Information Services:** DIALOG Information Services, NLM. **Networks/Consortia:** Member of San Francisco Biomedical Library Network, Northern California and Nevada Medical Library Group (NCNMLG). **Publications:** Planetalk Newsletter, 2/year. **Remarks:** FAX: (415)441-5742.

★ 13119 ★
Planetree - Health Resource Center (Med)
San Jose Medical Center
98 N. 17th St.   Phone: (408)977-4549
San Jose, CA 95112   Candace Ford, Med.Dir./Libn.
Founded: 1988. **Staff:** Prof 2; Other 2. **Subjects:** Consumer health information. **Special Collections:** Material on health and medical topics in Spanish and in Vietnamese (limited); audio-visual tape library; current medical textbooks. **Holdings:** 2000 books; 18 VF drawers of clippings. **Subscriptions:** 40 journals and other serials. **Services:** Center open to the public. **Automated Operations:** Computerized public access catalog. **Computerized Information Services:** DIALOG Information Services, BRS Information Technologies, NLM. Performs searches on fee basis. **Networks/Consortia:** Member of Northern California and Nevada Medical Library Group (NCNMLG). **Publications:** Planetalk Newsletter, 2/year. **Remarks:** Maintained by the San Jose Medical Center. **Staff:** Carole Clark.

★ 13120 ★
Planned Parenthood of Arizona - Library (Soc Sci)
5651 N. 7th St.   Phone: (602)265-2495
Phoenix, AZ 85014   Mauryne Young
Founded: 1937. **Staff:** Prof 1. **Subjects:** Family planning, sexuality education, sexually transmitted diseases, abortion, teen pregnancy, world population. **Special Collections:** Pregnancy/childbirth collection (50 items); Sexuality Information for Children and Teens (100 items); Sexuality Education Curricula and Guides (150). **Holdings:** 1800 books; 100 bound periodical volumes; 100 reports; 300 videotapes. **Subscriptions:** 25 journals and other serials; 2 newspapers. **Services:** Interlibrary loan; library open to the public. **Automated Operations:** Computerized cataloging. **Publications:** Educational Resource Guide. **Remarks:** FAX: (602)277-5243.

★ 13121 ★
Planned Parenthood of Central Indiana - Resource Center (Med)
3209 N. Meridian St.   Phone: (317)925-3644
Indianapolis, IN 46208   Betsy Lambie, Libn.
Founded: 1980. **Staff:** Prof 1; Other 1. **Subjects:** Birth control, human sexuality, teen pregnancy, human reproduction, abortion, sex education,

women's health, STDs, AIDS. **Holdings:** 1200 books; 130 films and videotapes; vertical files; poster collection. **Subscriptions:** 55 journals and other serials. **Services:** Copying; center open to the public. **Automated Operations:** Computerized cataloging (INMAGIC). **Networks/Consortia:** Member of Central Indiana Area Library Services Authority (CIALSA). **Remarks:** FAX: (317)927-3663.

★ 13122 ★
Planned Parenthood of Cleveland, Inc. - Library (Med)
3135 Euclid Ave., No. 101   Phone: (216)881-7742
Cleveland, OH 44115   Betsey C. Kaufman, Exec.Dir.
Founded: 1928. **Staff:** 1. **Subjects:** Birth control and contraceptives, family planning, population, sexuality, family life education. **Special Collections:** Historical information on the birth control movement. **Holdings:** 900 books; 10 films; 103 videotapes. **Subscriptions:** 10 journals and other serials. **Services:** Copying; library open to health, social, and medical professionals, students, educators, and parents. **Publications:** The Source, a directory of services and holdings. **Remarks:** FAX: (216)881-1834. **Staff:** Dori Stupp, Rsrc.Coord.

★ 13123 ★
Planned Parenthood of Connecticut - Library (Med)
129 Whitney Ave.   Phone: (203)865-5158
New Haven, CT 06510   Susan Killheffer
Founded: 1979. **Staff:** Prof 1. **Subjects:** Reproductive health, sexuality curricula, teen sexuality and pregnancy, contraception, abortion, pregnancy, childbirth, rape, sexual abuse. **Special Collections:** Curricular materials in the area of sexuality education from across the United States and the state of Connecticut (350 titles). **Holdings:** 2500 books; 300 videotapes. **Subscriptions:** 55 journals and other serials. **Services:** Copying; library open to the public. **Automated Operations:** Computerized cataloging. **Remarks:** FAX: (203)624-1333. Maintains branch libraries in Bridgeport, Hartford, New London, Norwalk, Willimantic, Waterbury, and Danielson, CT.

★ 13124 ★
Planned Parenthood Federation of America, Inc. - Katharine Dexter McCormick Library (Med)
810 Seventh Ave.   Phone: (212)261-4637
New York, NY 10019   Gloria A. Roberts, Hd.Libn.
Founded: 1964. **Staff:** Prof 2; Other 1. **Subjects:** Family planning in the U.S., contraceptives, abortion and sterilization, history of birth control, population, sexuality, sexuality education, reproductive rights, teen sexuality. **Holdings:** 4000 books; 35 VF drawers of journal articles, reprints, unpublished mimeographs. **Subscriptions:** 125 journals and other serials. **Services:** Interlibrary loan (articles only); copying; library open to the public for reference use only. **Computerized Information Services:** DIALOG Information Services, VU/TEXT Information Services, LEXIS, POPLINE; LINK (Library and Information Network; internal database). Performs searches on fee basis. **Networks/Consortia:** Member of APLIC International Census Network, New York Metropolitan Reference and Research Library Agency, Manhattan-Bronx Health Sciences Library Consortia. **Publications:** A Family Planning Library Manual; A Small Library in Family Planning; Current Literature in Family Planning (review of books and journal articles in the field, annotated and classified), monthly; Directory of Population Research and Family Planning Training Centers in the U.S.A., 1980-1981; LINK Line (newsletter) - for sexuality educators and other professionals. **Remarks:** FAX: (212)247-6269. **Staff:** Harriet P. Schick, Assoc.Libn.

★ 13125 ★
Planned Parenthood of Houston & Southeast Texas, Inc. - Mary Elizabeth Hudson Library (Med)
3601 Fannin St.   Phone: (713)522-6363
Houston, TX 77004   Natalie H. Thrall, Volunteer Libn.
Founded: 1970. **Staff:** 3. **Subjects:** Sexuality education, family planning, parenting, reproductive health, reproductive rights, population, women's issues. **Holdings:** 2500 books; 100 bound periodical volumes; 400 file folders of reprints and newspaper clippings. **Subscriptions:** 23 journals and other serials. **Services:** Copying; library open to the public with restrictions.

★ 13126 ★
Planned Parenthood of Minnesota - Phyllis Cooksey Resource Center (Med)
1965 Ford Pkwy.
St. Paul, MN 55116
Phone: (612)698-2401
Debra Bauer, Rsrc.Ctr.Coord.
Founded: 1972. **Staff:** Prof 2. **Subjects:** Family planning, population growth, human sexuality, abortion, sex education. **Special Collections:** Works of Margaret Sanger (8 volumes). **Holdings:** 1500 books; 12 VF drawers of pamphlets and ephemera; 100 films, video- and audio cassettes. **Subscriptions:** 100 journals and other serials. **Services:** Interlibrary loan; copying; center open to the public. **Computerized Information Services:** Internal database. **Networks/Consortia:** Member of APLIC International Census Network, Metronet. **Publications:** Acquisitions lists, newsnotes, semiannual - free upon request; educational brochure catalog; AV catalog - both available upon request; list of other publications - available upon request. **Remarks:** FAX: (612)698-2401. Telex: 612 698-1183. **Staff:** Darcy Kjome, Rsrc.Libn.

Planned Parenthood New York City
See: Margaret Sanger Center-Planned Parenthood New York City (14794)

★ 13127 ★
Planned Parenthood of Northern New England - PPNNE Resource Center (Med)
23 Mansfield Ave.
Burlington, VT 05401
Phone: (802)862-9638
Tracy Fisk, Res.Coord.
Founded: 1967. **Staff:** Prof 1. **Subjects:** Family life education, sexual development, parenting and child care, women's health, infertility. **Special Collections:** Agency history; sex education. **Holdings:** 2300 books; 4 VF drawers of articles. **Subscriptions:** 17 journals and other serials; 30 newsletters. **Services:** Interlibrary loan; copying; center open to the public. **Computerized Information Services:** Internal database. **Publications:** Edsource, 3/year - to area educators; K-12 Family Life Curriculum - for sale. **Remarks:** FAX: (802)863-5284.

★ 13128 ★
Planned Parenthood of the St. Louis Region - Education Department - Library (Med)
7415 Manchester Rd.
St. Louis, MO 63143
Phone: (314)781-3800
Karen Omzig, Dir. of Pub.Educ.
Founded: 1972. **Staff:** Prof 2. **Subjects:** Family planning, human reproduction, sexually transmitted diseases, pregnancy, homosexuality, human sexuality, abortion, parenting. **Special Collections:** Birth Control Review, 1922-1927 (complete); Social Welfare Forum, 1948-1965. **Holdings:** 500 books; 20 bound periodical volumes; clippings and articles. **Subscriptions:** 11 journals and other serials. **Services:** Copying; library open to the public by appointment for reference use.

★ 13129 ★
Planned Parenthood of San Antonio and South Central Texas - Library (Med)
104 Babcock Rd.
San Antonio, TX 78201
Phone: (512)736-2244
Patricia Sidebottom, Exec.Dir.
Founded: 1939. **Staff:** Prof 2. **Subjects:** Birth control, population, human sexuality, sex education, family planning, AIDS, women's health, teenage pregnancy. **Holdings:** 1500 books; 500 periodicals; pamphlets; vertical files; 100 films, filmstrips, slide sets. **Subscriptions:** 35 journals and other serials. **Services:** Interlibrary loan; copying; library open to the public with restrictions. **Networks/Consortia:** Member of Planned Parenthood Federation of America, Inc. **Publications:** Pamphlets on venereal disease and birth control. **Special Catalogs:** Interregional Library Loan Catalog; PPCSA Media Catalog. **Remarks:** FAX: (512)736-0011. **Staff:** Kathy Van Reusen, Educ.Dir.

★ 13130 ★
Planned Parenthood Southeastern Pennsylvania - Resource Center (Med)
1144 Locust St.
Philadelphia, PA 19107-5740
Phone: (215)351-5590
Wanda Mial, Rsrc.Ctr.Coord.
Founded: 1975. **Staff:** Prof 1. **Subjects:** Family planning, reproductive health, venereal diseases, childbearing and pregnancy options, sex education. **Holdings:** 2500 books; 40 bound periodical volumes; 12 VF drawers; 100 slides, videotapes, films, filmstrips. **Subscriptions:** 65 journals and other serials. **Services:** Copying; SDI; center open to the public for reference use only. **Networks/Consortia:** Member of National Network of Libraries of Medicine - Middle Atlantic Region. **Publications:** List of publications - available on request. **Remarks:** FAX: (215)351-5595. **Staff:** Lisa DeVuono, Educ.Rsrcs.Coord.

★ 13131 ★
Planned Parenthood of Southwestern Indiana, Inc. - Resource Center (Med)
Hebron Plaza
971 Kenmore Dr.
Evansville, IN 47714
Phone: (812)473-8800
Toni Godeke, Dir. of Educ.
Founded: 1986. **Staff:** 1. **Subjects:** Contraceptives, sexuality, family life education curriculum, women's health, infertility, population. **Holdings:** 300 books; 5 VF drawers. **Subscriptions:** 6 journals and other serials. **Services:** Interlibrary loan; copying; center open to the public by appointment for reference use. **Networks/Consortia:** Member of Evansville Area Libraries Consortium, Planned Parenthood Federation of America, Inc. **Remarks:** FAX: (812)473-8818.

★ 13132 ★
Planned Parenthood of Wisconsin - Maurice Ritz Resource Library and Bookstore (Med)
302 N. Jackson St.
Milwaukee, WI 53202
Phone: (414)271-7930
Ann H. McIntyre, Libn.
Founded: 1972. **Staff:** Prof 1; Other 1. **Subjects:** Family planning, reproductive health, sexuality education, contraception, obstetrics/gynecology nursing education, population. **Holdings:** 1500 books; 12 VF drawers of clippings and reports; 100 pamphlets, booklets, reprints; 80 films, slides, tapes, videotapes. **Subscriptions:** 55 journals and other serials. **Services:** Interlibrary loan; copying; library open to the public by appointment. **Computerized Information Services:** MEDLINE; PPXNET (internal database). **Networks/Consortia:** Member of Library Council of Metropolitan Milwaukee, Inc. (LCOMM), APLIC International Census Network, Southeastern Wisconsin Health Science Library Consortium (SWHSL). **Publications:** Audiovisual list; pamphlets list; material available for rent or purchase; subject bibliographies. **Remarks:** FAX: (414)271-1935.

★ 13133 ★
Planning and Development Collaborative International - Library (Plan)
1012 N St., N.W.
Washington, DC 20001
Phone: (202)789-1140
Subjects: Urban, regional, and rural development and management; housing; disaster relief planning. **Holdings:** 500 volumes. **Remarks:** Telex: 248529.

★ 13134 ★
Planning and Forecasting Consultants - Library (Bus-Fin)
Box 820228
Houston, TX 77282-0228
Phone: (713)467-4732
Dale Steffes
Founded: 1973. **Subjects:** Forecasting - technological, social, political, economic, ecological, geographical, natural resources. **Holdings:** 1000 volumes. **Services:** Library open to clients only. **Computerized Information Services:** Internal databases.

★ 13135 ★
Planning Forum - Library (Bus-Fin)
5500 College Corner Pike
Oxford, OH 45056
Phone: (513)523-4185
Amanda Lewis, Libn.
Founded: 1985. **Subjects:** Strategic management and planning. **Holdings:** 1300 volumes. **Services:** Library open to members only. **Computerized Information Services:** Internal database. **Special Catalogs:** 1990 Library Catalog. **Remarks:** FAX: (513)523-7539.

Planning Research Corporation
See: PRC Inc. - Technical Library (13308)

★ 13136 ★
Morton Plant Hospital - Medical Library (Med)
323 Jeffords St.
Box 210
Clearwater, FL 34617
Phone: (813)462-7889
Cynthia Kisby, Med.Libn.
Founded: 1955. **Staff:** Prof 1. **Subjects:** Medicine, nursing, hospital administration. **Holdings:** 1200 books; 925 bound periodical volumes; 600 volumes on microfiche. **Subscriptions:** 200 journals and other serials. **Services:** Interlibrary loan; copying; SDI; library open to the public by appointment. **Automated Operations:** Computerized serials. **Computerized Information Services:** MEDLARS, DIALOG Information Services; DOCLINE (electronic mail service). Performs searches on fee basis. **Networks/Consortia:** Member of Tampa Bay Medical Library Network. **Remarks:** FAX: (813)461-8858.

★13137★
Planting Fields Arboretum - Horticultural Library (Biol Sci)
Planting Fields Rd.   Phone: (516)922-9024
Oyster Bay, NY 11771   Elizabeth K. Reilley, Dir.
Founded: 1975. **Staff:** Prof 4; Other 3. **Subjects:** Horticulture, botany.
Holdings: 5800 books. **Subscriptions:** 50 journals and other serials. **Services:**
Copying; library open to the public for reference use only. **Staff:** Helen S.
Moskowitz, Asst. to Dir.

★13138★
Plastics Institute of America - Library (Sci-Engr)
277 Fairfield Rd., Suite 100   Phone: (201)808-5950
Fairfield, NJ 07004-1932   Irene Sacks, Prog.Coord.
Staff: 1. **Subjects:** Polymer science and engineering. **Holdings:** Figures not
available. **Services:** Library not open to the public. **Publications:** Polymer
Science and Engineering Programs, biennial; Foodplas Proceedings, annual;
Recyclingplas Proceedings, annual; Secondary Reclamation of Plastics
Waste - all for sale. **Remarks:** Alternate telephone number(s): (201)808-
5951. FAX: (201)808-5953.

★13139★
Platt Saco Lowell Corporation - Engineering Library (Sci-Engr)
Drawer 2327   Phone: (803)859-3211
Greenville, SC 29602   Alice K. Dill, Patent Techn.
Founded: 1850. **Staff:** Prof 1. **Subjects:** Engineering, textile machinery and
manufacture, patent and trademark law. **Special Collections:** U.S., British,
and foreign patents on textile machinery. **Holdings:** 3000 books; 1500 bound
periodical volumes; 350,000 patent copies; 2200 microfiche cards of
abstracts and patents; 3000 paper copies of abstracts and patents.
Subscriptions: 85 journals and other serials. **Services:** Library not open to
the public except with prior permission. **Computerized Information
Services:** MicroPatent; CD-ROM (CASSIS). **Remarks:** FAX: (803)859-
2908.

★13140★
Platte County Historical Society - Ben Ferrel Platte County Museum/
Library - Library (Hist)
3rd and Ferrel St.
P.O. Box 103   Phone: (816)431-5121
Platte City, MO 64079   Fran Bohachick, Hd.Libn.
Founded: 1985. **Subjects:** Platte County, genealogy, county history, county
architecture. **Special Collections:** Archives Room; Duncan Family history
(2 file cabinets of family group sheets and documents); early Platte County
newspapers (35 reels of microfilm). **Holdings:** 300 books; 200 bound
periodical volumes; 2 file cabinets of family group sheets; 2000 nonbook
items. **Subscriptions:** 200 journals and other serials. **Services:** Library open
to the public on a limited schedule or by appointment. **Publications:** List of
publications - available on request.

★13141★
Platte River Power Authority - Library (Energy)
2000 E. Horsetooth Rd.   Phone: (303)229-5230
Fort Collins, CO 80525-2942   Rosalie Feldman, Libn.
Founded: 1977. **Staff:** Prof 1; Other 1. **Subjects:** Electric energy. **Holdings:**
2000 books; 300 reports; clippings. **Subscriptions:** 240 journals and other
serials; 25 newspapers. **Services:** Interlibrary loan; copying; library open to
the public with restrictions. **Automated Operations:** Computerized
cataloging, serials, and routing. **Computerized Information Services:**
DIALOG Information Services. **Networks/Consortia:** Member of High
Plains Regional Library Service System. **Publications:** Additions to the
Library, quarterly. **Remarks:** FAX: (303)229-5244.

★13142★
Playboy Enterprises, Inc. - Photo Library (Aud-Vis)
680 N. Lakeshore Dr.   Phone: (312)751-8000
Chicago, IL 60611   Tim Hawkins, Photo.Libn.
Founded: 1953. **Staff:** 4. **Holdings:** 11 million photographs. **Services:**
Library open for research by special arrangement. **Computerized
Information Services:** Internal database. **Remarks:** FAX: (312)751-2818.
Staff: Elizabeth Georgiou, Res.

Playwrights Union of Canada
See: **Manitoba Association of Playwrights - Library/Archive** (9597)

Mariam J. Pleak Memorial Library and Archive
See: **Hobart Historical Society, Inc.** (7298)

Plenty - U.S.A.
See: **Natural Rights Center - Library** (11344)

★13143★
Milton Plesur Memorial Library (Rel-Phil)
2640 N. Forest Rd.   Phone: (716)689-8844
Getzville, NY 14068   Lora Keister, Libn.
Founded: 1928. **Staff:** Prof 1. **Subjects:** Religion, philosophy, Bible, Jewish
history, Hebraica, Jewish music, educational programs. **Special Collections:**
Judaica video cassettes. **Holdings:** 13,000 books; 2000 pamphlets; AV
programs. **Subscriptions:** 20 journals and other serials. **Services:** Interlibrary
loan; copying; library open to the public. **Computerized Information
Services:** Online systems. **Special Catalogs:** Video Catalog with Index.
Remarks: FAX: (716)689-8862.

★13144★
Plimoth Plantation, Inc. - William Bradford Library (Hist)
Warren Ave.
Box 1620   Phone: (508)746-1622
Plymouth, MA 02362   Carolyn Freeman Travers, Hd. of Res.
Founded: 1949. **Staff:** Prof 1; Other 2. **Subjects:** New England history, 16th
and 17th century social history, early travel and exploration, crafts,
antiques, colonial archeology. **Holdings:** 4500 books; 3200 pamphlets; 4
volumes of Plymouth Colony wills (photocopies). **Subscriptions:** 80 journals
and other serials. **Services:** Library open to the public for reference use only.
Remarks: FAX: (508)746-4978.

Plimpton Library
See: **Columbia University - Rare Book and Manuscript Library** (4023)

Oscar Hillel Plotkin Library
See: **North Shore Congregation Israel - Romanek Cultural Center -**
Oscar Hillel Plotkin Adult Library (11947)

★13145★
Plumas County Law Library (Law)
Court House
Box 10686   Phone: (916)283-6325
Quincy, CA 95971   Tom van Rossem
Founded: 1905. **Staff:** Prof 1. **Subjects:** State and federal law. **Holdings:** 6000
volumes. **Services:** Interlibrary loan; copying; library open to the public for
reference use only. **Remarks:** FAX: (916)283-6340.

★13146★
Plumas County Museum - Library (Hist)
500 Jackson St.
P.O. Box 10776   Phone: (916)283-6320
Quincy, CA 95971   Linda Brennan, Cur.
Founded: 1924. **Staff:** 2. **Subjects:** Plumas county history, agricultural
history, Maidu Indians, mining history, logging and lumber. **Special
Collections:** Local residents' diaries, journals, and daybooks (25); Plumas
County newspapers (1857-1972); unpublished manuscripts; genealogies;
local maps, 1850-1955 (2000). **Holdings:** 3000 books; 30 taped interviews;
100 manuscripts; bound periodical volumes; letters; government documents;
other cataloged items. **Services:** Copying (limited); library open to the
public. **Computerized Information Services:** Internal databases. **Remarks:**
FAX: (916)283-0946. **Staff:** Scott Lawson, Asst.Cur.

Plumbing and Heating Wholesalers of New England
See: **New England Wholesalers Assn. - Lending Library** (11479)

★ 13147 ★
Plummer Memorial Public Hospital - Library (Med)
969 Queen St., E.   Phone: (705)759-3434
Sault Ste. Marie, ON, Canada P6A 2C4   Kathy You, Dir., Lib.Serv.
Founded: 1979. **Staff:** 1. **Subjects:** Medicine, nursing, allied health sciences, management, psychiatry, social work, sexual assault treatment, psychogeriatrics. **Holdings:** 1000 books. **Subscriptions:** 120 journals and other serials. **Services:** Interlibrary loan; copying; SDI; library open to the public for reference use only. **Computerized Information Services:** MEDLARS, DOBIS Canadian Online Library System. Performs searches on fee basis. **Remarks:** FAX: (705)254-5353 (LAB).

★ 13148 ★
Plunkett & Cooney - Law Library (Law)
900 Marquette Bldg.   Phone: (313)983-4877
Detroit, MI 48226   Melanie J. Dunshee, Hd.Libn.
Founded: 1913. **Staff:** Prof 2; Other 2. **Subjects:** Medical liability; products liability; insurance; municipal liability; corporate law. **Holdings:** 13,000 volumes. **Services:** Copying; library open with restrictions to librarians. **Computerized Information Services:** WESTLAW, LEXIS, DIALOG Information Services, VU/TEXT Information Services, Dun & Bradstreet Business Credit Services, LEGI-SLATE, OCLC. **Networks/Consortia:** Member of Michigan Library Consortium (MLC). **Remarks:** FAX: (313)961-0029. **Staff:** Jill Davidson, Asst.Libn.

★ 13149 ★
Plymouth Congregational Church - Library (Rel-Phil)
1900 Nicollet Ave., S.   Phone: (612)871-7400
Minneapolis, MN 55403   Joanne Lee, Libn.
Staff: Prof 1. **Subjects:** Religion and theology, global concerns, social and women's issues, art, children's literature. **Special Collections:** Free to Be collection (women's issues; 40 books); Global Concerns collection (60 books and pamphlets); art lending library (35 framed pictures). **Holdings:** 2000 books; 100 tapes. **Subscriptions:** 12 journals and other serials. **Services:** Library open to the public.

★ 13150 ★
Plymouth Congregational Church - Vida B. Varey Library (Rel-Phil)
1217 6th Ave.   Phone: (206)622-4865
Seattle, WA 98101   Jessie Attri, Lib.Coord.
Subjects: Religion. **Holdings:** 2000 books. **Services:** Library open to the public.

★ 13151 ★
Plymouth Historical Society Museum - Library & Archives (Hist)
155 S. Main St.   Phone: (313)455-8940
Plymouth, MI 48170   Beth A. Stewart, Dir.
Subjects: Plymouth history, genealogy, Michigan history, Michigan in the Civil War, Civil War history. **Special Collections:** War & Rebellion - Official History/Records of Union and Confederate Armies (Series I and II; 60 volumes); Michigan Pioneer & Historical Collection, 1874-1921. **Holdings:** 500 books; 1000 documents; 1000 photographs; Plymouth newspapers, 1878-1956 on microfilm; census records; marriage and cemetery records, 1840-1950. **Subscriptions:** 10 journals and other serials. **Services:** Interlibrary loan; copying; library open to the public for reference use only. **Staff:** Helen Kerstens, Archv.; Elaine Pierce, Archv.

★ 13152 ★
Plymouth Marine Laboratory and Marine Biological Association of the United Kingdom - Library and Information Services (Biol Sci)
Citadel Hill   Phone: 752 222772
Plymouth PL1 2PB, England   Allen Varley, Hd.
Founded: 1888. **Staff:** 7. **Subjects:** Marine biology, pollution, and chemistry; oceanography; fisheries; marine and estuarine ecology. **Special Collections:** Marine pollution (50,000 documents). **Holdings:** 15,000 books; 50,000 bound periodical volumes; 60,000 pamphlets and reprints. **Subscriptions:** 1250 journals and other serials. **Services:** Interlibrary loan; copying; SDI; library open to the public by appointment. **Computerized Information Services:** CDS/ISIS, ECDIN (Environmental Chemicals Data and Information Network), IRPTC (International Register of Potentially Toxic Chemicals); cooperates in producing ASFA (Aquatic Sciences and Fisheries Abstracts); SCIENCEnet (electronic mail service). Performs searches on fee basis. Contact Person: Mr. D.S. Moulder. **Publications:** Marine Pollution Research Titles (bulletin), monthly; Estuaries and Coastal Waters of the British Isles (bibliography), annual. **Remarks:** FAX: 752 226865. Electronic mail address(es): MBA.LIBRARY (SCIENCEnet). **Formed by the merger of:** Marine Biological Association of the United Kingdom and Institute for Marine Environmental Research.

★ 13153 ★
Plymouth State College - Geographers on Film Collection (Geog-Map)
Dept. of Social Sciences   Phone: (603)535-2213
Plymouth, NH 03264   Prof. Maynard Weston Dow, Dir.
Staff: Prof 1; Other 1. **Subjects:** Geographers, geography, oral history. **Holdings:** 260 film and television interviews; tapes of special conferences, paper sessions, longer interviews. **Services:** Library open to the public for film rental by request. **Publications:** Geographers on Film (brochure; 1987) - available on request. **Remarks:** FAX: (603)535-2654. Electronic mail address(es): WESD@PSC.PLYMOUTH.EDU.

★ 13154 ★
Plymouth State College - Herbert H. Lamson Library - Special Collections (Educ, Hist)
Plymouth, NH 03264   Phone: (603)535-2258
                                     Philip C. Wei, Dir.
Founded: 1871. **Staff:** Prof 9; Other 11. **Subjects:** Education, New Hampshire and Plymouth (town) history. **Special Collections:** Robert Frost Collection (200 books; 25 films and recordings; 30 letters from Frost, 1915-1922; 10 typescripts of poems, 1915-1922; 15 photographs, 1915-1920; 200 clippings, memorabilia, pamphlets, lecture notes; 1 drawer of archival material). **Services:** Interlibrary loan; copying; collections open to the public on fee basis. **Automated Operations:** Computerized public access catalog, cataloging, acquisitions, serials, and circulation. **Computerized Information Services:** DIALOG Information Services, BRS Information Technologies, OCLC; EPIC; CD-ROM. Performs searches on fee basis. Contact Person: Elaine Stano. **Networks/Consortia:** Member of NELINET, Inc., New Hampshire College & University Council Library Policy Committee (NHCUC). **Publications:** Handbook; Newsletter, semimonthly. **Remarks:** FAX: (603)536-1896. **Staff:** Lissa A. Pearson, Archv.

PMS Access - Library
See: **Madison Pharmacy Associates** (9526)

★ 13155 ★
Pocono Medical Center - Marshall R. Metzgar Medical Library (Med)
206 E. Brown St.   Phone: (717)476-3515
East Stroudsburg, PA 18301   Ellen P. Woodhead, Lib.Dir.
Founded: 1977. **Staff:** Prof 1. **Subjects:** Medicine, nursing. **Holdings:** 780 books; 1450 periodical volumes; 16 VF drawers and 1270 pamphlets of patient education materials and AV programs. **Subscriptions:** 138 journals and other serials. **Services:** Interlibrary loan; copying; library open to the public by appointment. **Computerized Information Services:** BRS Information Technologies, NLM. **Networks/Consortia:** Member of Cooperating Hospital Libraries of the Lehigh Valley Area, Health Information Library Network of Northeastern Pennsylvania (HILNNEP), BHSL, Laurel Highlands Health Sciences Library Consortium (LHHSLC). **Publications:** QUEST (library newsletter) - for internal distribution only. **Remarks:** FAX: (717)476-3472.

Pocumtuck Valley Memorial Association - Library
See: **Historic Deerfield, Inc./Pocumtuck Valley Memorial Association - Memorial Libraries** (7242)

★ 13156 ★
Poetry Society of America - Van Voorhis Library (Hum)
15 Gramercy Park   Phone: (212)254-9628
New York, NY 10003   Cynthia Atkins, Asst.Dir.
Founded: 1910. **Staff:** Prof 1; Other 1. **Subjects:** American poetry and poetics, biography. **Special Collections:** Turn of the century and contemporary American poetry. **Holdings:** 8000 books. **Services:** Library open to researchers by appointment. **Remarks:** Large holograph collection and memorabilia of the Poetry Society of America are included in the Rare Book Division of the New York Public Library.

★ 13157 ★
Point Loma Nazarene College - Ryan Library (Rel-Phil)
3900 Lomaland Dr.   Phone: (619)221-2355
San Diego, CA 92106   James D. Newburg, Dir.
Staff: Prof 6; Other 8. **Subjects:** Religion. **Special Collections:** Arminianism and Wesleyana Collection; 19th and 20th century Christian Holiness movement; Pasadena and Point Loma College authors; college archives (170 linear feet). **Holdings:** 155,000 books; 23,790 bound periodical volumes; 4929 microforms. **Subscriptions:** 621 journals and other serials; 6 newspapers. **Services:** Interlibrary loan; copying; library open to the public. **Automated Operations:** Computerized cataloging. **Computerized Information Services:** DIALOG Information Services, OCLC. Performs searches on fee basis. **Networks/Consortia:** Member of CLASS. **Staff:** Clem Guthro, Cat.Libn.; Sharon Bull, Instr.Serv.Libn.; William K. Harmaning, Hd. of Media Serv.; Ann Ruppert, Instr.Serv.Libn.

★ 13158 ★
Point Pelee National Park - Library (Biol Sci)
R.R. 1   Phone: (519)322-2365
Leamington, ON, Canada N8H 3V4   Rob A. Watt, Chf.Pk.Interp.
Founded: 1968. **Staff:** 5. **Subjects:** Ornithology, botany, biology, natural history, history, geology. **Special Collections:** Herbarium (1000 specimens); live mounts; study skins; insects (300 specimens). **Holdings:** 4000 books; 40,000 35mm slides; 1500 reprints and manuscripts; 1500 black/white prints; 30 16mm film titles; 14 videotapes. **Subscriptions:** 10 journals and other serials. **Services:** Library not open to the public. **Remarks:** FAX (519)322-1277; (519)322-2372. Maintained by Canadian Parks Service.

★ 13159 ★
Point of Purchase Advertising Institute - Information Center (Bus-Fin)
66 N. Van Brunt St.   Phone: (201)894-8899
Englewood, NJ 07631-2707   John Kawula, Pres.
Founded: 1936. **Staff:** 15. **Subjects:** Point of purchase information, slide and videotape presentation. **Holdings:** 162 volumes; 15 VF drawers; reports; surveys. **Subscriptions:** 90 journals and other serials; 10 newspapers. **Services:** Interlibrary loan; copying; center open to those involved with point of purchase. **Remarks:** FAX: (201)894-0529. **Also Known As:** POPAI Information Center.

★ 13160 ★
Point Reyes Bird Observatory - Library (Biol Sci)
4990 Shoreline Hwy.   Phone: (415)868-1221
Stinson Beach, CA 94970   Karen Hamilton
Founded: 1973. **Staff:** 1. **Subjects:** Ornithology, environment. **Holdings:** 2600 books; 700 bound periodical volumes; 300 reports; archival items; slide sets. **Subscriptions:** 175 journals and newsletters. **Services:** Interlibrary loan; copying; library open to members only. **Remarks:** FAX: (415) 868-1946.

Point Reyes National Seashore
See: **U.S. Natl. Park Service** (17767)

★ 13161 ★
Poland - Biblioteka Narodowa (Soc Sci, Hist)
Al. Niepodleglosci 213
skr.poczt. 36   Phone: 22 259270
PL-00-973 Warsaw 22, Poland   Dr. Stanislaw Czajka, Dir.
Founded: 1928. **Staff:** Prof 380; Other 430. **Subjects:** Poland, social sciences, humanities. **Special Collections:** Polonica collection; The November Uprising (1830) collection; Polish Emigration (1830-1870); rare pamphlets (1848; World War I). **Holdings:** 1.7 million books; 557,500 bound periodical volumes; 1.5 million print items, posters, leaflets. **Subscriptions:** 7800 journals and other serials. **Services:** Interlibrary loan; copying; library open to the public. **Computerized Information Services:** National Bibliography, Union Catalogues of Foreign Publications (internal databases); BITNET (electronic mail service). Performs searches. Contact Person: Czeslaw Wrzesien. **Publications:** Rocznik Biblioteki Narodowej (National Library Year Book); Biuletyn Informacyjny Biblioteki Narodowej (National Library Information Bulletin), quarterly; Przewodnik Bibliograficzny (Bibliographical Guide), weekly; Polonica Zagraniczne (Foreign Polonica), annual; Polska Bibliografia Bibliologiczna (Polish Bibliography Of Library Science), annual; Ruch Wydawniczy w Liczbach (Polish Publishing in Figures), annual; Polish Libraries Today (in English), irregular. **Special Indexes:** Bibliografia Zawartosci Czasopism (Index to Periodicals), monthly. **Remarks:** FAX: 22 255251. Telex: 816761 BNPL. Electronic mail address(es): biblnar@plearn (BITNET).

★ 13162 ★
Poland - Biblioteka Narodowa - Dzial Zbiorow Specjalnych - Special Collections (Hist, Geog-Map)
Pl. Krasinskich 3/5   Phone: 22 313241
PL-00-207 Warsaw, Poland   Mr. Maciej Dabrowski
Founded: 1928. **Staff:** Prof 72; Other 8. **Subjects:** Polish and Polish-related rare books (pre 1800), music, literature, graphic art. **Special Collections:** Wilanow Library; Zamoyski's Estate Library; Zaluski Library; Krasinski's Estate Library. **Holdings:** 149,672 books; 148,441 reels of microfilm; 67,513 maps and atlases; 357,613 graphic art items; 13,766 manuscripts; 95,740 scores; 27,728 sound recordings. **Services:** Interlibrary loan; copying; library open to the public with restrictions. **Publications:** Zbiory Rekopisow w Bibliotekach i Muzeach w Polsce (Manuscript Collections in Libraries and Museums in Poland). **Special Catalogs:** Katalog Rekopisow (Catalog of Manuscripts); Katalog Mikrofilmow (Catalog of Microfilms). **Remarks:** FAX: 22 6355567.

★ 13163 ★
Poland - Biblioteka Narodowa - Zaklad Documentacji Ksiegoznawczej - Bibliological Documentation Division (Info Sci)
ul. Hankiewicza 1   Phone: 22 223542
PL-00-973 Warsaw, Poland   Ewa Mahrburg
Founded: 1952. **Staff:** Prof 7; Other 1. **Subjects:** Library science, information science, archive science, book trade and publishing. **Holdings:** 60,000 books; 52,000 bound periodical volumes; 82 microfiche; 50,000 booksellers' and publishers' catalogs; 100,000 clippings; 76,000 unpublished materials. **Subscriptions:** 142 journals and other serials. **Services:** Interlibrary loan; copying; library open to the public. **Remarks:** FAX: 22 223541.

★ 13164 ★
Poland - Centralna Biblioteka Rolnicza (Agri)
ul. Krakowskie Przedmiescie 66
skrytka pocztowa 360   Phone: 22 266041
PL-00-950 Warsaw, Poland   Dr. Jerzy Rasinski
Founded: 1955. **Staff:** Prof 70; Other 18. **Subjects:** Agriculture, forestry, hunting, food industry, and allied subjects. **Special Collections:** Old print collection (428 volumes). **Holdings:** 260,700 volumes; 140,244 bound periodical volumes. **Subscriptions:** 1989 journals and other serials; 44 newspapers. **Services:** Interlibrary loan; copying; SDI; library open to the public. **Computerized Information Services:** National Information System on Food Economy (internal database). **Publications:** Bibliography of Polish agricultural writings; information publications. **Remarks:** Branch libraries are maintained in Pulawy, Poland and Bydgoszcz, Poland.

★ 13165 ★
Poland - Centrum Mechanizacji Gornictwa - KOMAG - Jednostka Badawczo-Rozwojowa (Sci-Engr)
ul. Pszczynska 37   Phone: 310841
PL-44-101 Gliwice, Poland   Wieslawa Pasnik
Staff: Prof 2. **Subjects:** Mining machines. **Special Collections:** Reports on research works. **Holdings:** 17,621 books; 2344 reports; 7246 catalogs. **Subscriptions:** 158 journals and other serials; 18 newspapers. **Services:** SDI; library open to the public. **Publications:** News From the Mining World. **Remarks:** Alternate telephone number(s): 310847.

★ 13166 ★
Poland - Ministry of Health and Social Welfare - National Research Institute of Mother and Child - Library (Med)
Kasprzaka 17   Phone: 22 32-68-58
PL-01-211 Warsaw, Poland   Wanda Foltyn, Libn.
Subjects: Reproduction, child growth and development. **Holdings:** 17,000 volumes. **Also Known As:** Instytut Matki i Dziecka.

★ 13167 ★
Poland - Polish Academy of Sciences - Center for Studies on Non-European Countries - Library (Area-Ethnic)
ulica Nowy Swiat 72   Phone: 22 265231
PL-00-330 Warsaw, Poland   Irena Wojsz, Libn.
Founded: 1962. **Subjects:** Social and cultural problems of Asia, Africa, Latin America. **Holdings:** 50,000 volumes. **Subscriptions:** 204 journals and other serials. **Services:** Interlibrary loan (through National Library); copying; library open to the public for reference use only. **Also Known As:** Polska Akademia Nauk - Zaklad Krajow Pozaeuropejskich - Biblioteka. **Staff:** Barbara Wierzbicka.

★ 13168 ★
Poland - Polish Academy of Sciences - Gdansk Library (Hum, Soc Sci, Area-Ethnic)
Walowa 15   Phone: 58 315523
PL-80-858 Gdansk, Poland   Zbigniew Nowak, Dir.
Founded: 1596. **Staff:** 73. **Subjects:** Humanities, social sciences, maritime studies, Pomeranian and Gdansk affairs. **Holdings:** 487,057 books; 65,339 bound periodical volumes; 17,414 documents; 3147 AV programs; 4726 manuscripts; 15th-20th century material; 54,995 old prints; 7231 graphics; 7092 maps; 12,435 exlibrises/bookplates; 2950 numismatic materials. **Services:** Interlibrary loan; copying; library open to the public for reference use only. **Publications:** Libri Gedanenses, 1967-1975; Rocznik Gdanski, semiannual. **Special Catalogs:** Catalogs of manuscripts, old books, incunabula, graphics, maps, numismatics, exlibrises, photographs to 1945, books, 1800 to present. **Remarks:** Alternate telephone number(s): 58 313086; 58 313087. **Also Known As:** Polska Akademia Nauk - Biblioteka Gdanska. **Staff:** Dr. Jadwiga Wroblewska.

★ 13169 ★

Poland - Polish Academy of Sciences - Institute of Anthropology - Library (Soc Sci, Hist, Biol Sci)
ul. Kuznicza 35
PL-50951 Wroclaw, Poland   Phone: 38675
Founded: 1954. **Staff:** 1.5. **Subjects:** Physical and cultural anthropology, human biology. **Holdings:** 9590 books; 6450 bound periodical volumes. **Subscriptions:** 16 journals and other serials. **Services:** Interlibrary loan; copying; library open to the public for reference use only. **Remarks:** Telex: 071-5555. **Also Known As:** Zaklad Antropologii PAN - Biblioteka.

★ 13170 ★

Poland - Polish Academy of Sciences - Institute of Art - Library (Art, Mus, Theater)
ulica Dluga 26/28
Skrytka Pocztowa 994   Phone: 22 313149
PL-00-950 Warsaw, Poland   Jolanta Ewa Jankowska, Hd.Libn.
Founded: 1949. **Staff:** 12. **Subjects:** History and theory of fine arts, music, theater, film, and folklore. **Holdings:** 110,000 volumes. **Subscriptions:** 85 journals and other serials; 7 newspapers. **Services:** Interlibrary loan; copying; library not open to the public. **Publications:** Biuletyn Nowych Nabytkow Zagranicznych. **Remarks:** FAX: 22 313149. **Also Known As:** Polska Akademia Nauk - Instytut Sztuki. **Staff:** Bozena Bockowska; Malgorzata Chocianowska; Zenon Chojecki; Krzysztof Koziejowski; Beata Lubawska; Alina Manowiecka; Ewa Staszewska; Joanna Sosnowska; Marzena Kuras; Anna Zasada.

Poland - Polish Academy of Sciences - Institute of Fundamental Technological Research
See: **Institute of Fundamental Technological Research** (7940)

★ 13171 ★

Poland - Polish Academy of Sciences - Institute of the History of Material Culture - Library (Area-Ethnic, Soc Sci)
Swierczewskiego 105   Phone: 22 20 28 81
PL-00-140 Warsaw, Poland   Piotr Podgorski, Libn.
Founded: 1954. **Staff:** 6. **Subjects:** Prehistoric and medieval archeology of Poland and Europe; classical archeology; etnography and ethnology of Poland and Slavonic peoples in general; Mesoamerica; history of material culture of medieval and modern Poland; numismatics. **Holdings:** 65,000 volumes. **Subscriptions:** 1730 journals and other serials. **Services:** Interlibrary loan; library open to the public for reference use only. **Special Indexes:** Acquisition Index, quarterly. **Remarks:** FAX: 22 240100. **Also Known As:** Polska Akademia Nauk. **Staff:** Beata Kolodziejska; Joanna Kozminska; Marzena Kubacz; Beata Malarz; Maria Pawlowska.

★ 13172 ★

Poland - Polish Academy of Sciences - L. Hirszfeld Institute of Immunology and Experimental Therapy - Library (Med, Biol Sci)
ulica Czerska 12   Phone: 67 90 81
PL-53-114 Wroclaw, Poland   Helena Kopec, M.A., Lib.Hd.
Subjects: Immunology, microbiology, biochemistry, experimental therapy. **Holdings:** 11,500 books. **Subscriptions:** 10,000 journals and other serials. **Services:** Interlibrary loan; copying; library open to the public for reference use only. **Remarks:** Telex: 0715121 imtpl. **Also Known As:** Polska Akademia Nauk - Instytut Immunologii i Terapii Doswiadczalnej im. Ludwika Hirszfelda.

★ 13173 ★

Poland - Polish Academy of Sciences - Literary Research Institute - Library (Hum)
ulica Nowy Swiat 72   Phone: 26 68 63
PL-00-330 Warsaw, Poland   Edward Ruziewicz, Libn.
Staff: Prof 17; Other 5. **Subjects:** Literary theory, Polish literature and culture. **Holdings:** 175,000 books; 37,500 bound periodical volumes; 84,100 other cataloged items. **Subscriptions:** 500 journals and other serials. **Services:** Interlibrary loan; copying; library open to the public. **Also Known As:** Polska Akademia Nauk - Instytut Badan Literackich.

Polar Information Center
See: **American Polar Society** (717)

★ 13174 ★

Polaroid Corporation - Research Library (Sci-Engr)
549 Technology Sq.   Phone: (617)577-2000
Cambridge, MA 02139   Jean M. Vnenchak, Dept.Mgr.
Staff: Prof 3; Other 3. **Subjects:** Photography, chemistry, physics, engineering, mathematics, social sciences, general business. **Special Collections:** Photography and polarized light; Polaroid issued patents; photographs. **Holdings:** 30,000 books; 9000 bound periodical volumes; 60 drawers of annual reports, standards, government documents, translations, scientific papers, technical reports. **Subscriptions:** 900 journals and other serials; 5 newspapers. **Services:** Interlibrary loan; copying; library open to the public for reference use only with approval of the department manager or the library administrator. **Automated Operations:** Computerized cataloging, acquisitions, serials, and circulation. **Computerized Information Services:** DIALOG Information Services, STN International, PFDS Online, BRS Information Technologies, Image Technology Patent Information System (ITPAIS). **Publications:** Library Bulletin, monthly; Journal and Periodical Listings, semiannual - both for internal distribution only. **Remarks:** FAX: (617)577-4879. **Staff:** Richard Gurner, Lib.Adm.; Rebecca Kenney, Assoc.Tech.Libn.

★ 13175 ★

Policy Innovations Inc. - Library (Soc Sci)
1566 Tiffany Dr.   Phone: (412)221-9280
Pittsburgh, PA 15241   Paul Y. Hammond, Libn.
Subjects: National security. **Holdings:** 1200 books. **Services:** Library not open to the public.

★ 13176 ★

Policy Management Systems Corporation - Library
P.O. Box 10   Phone: (803)735-4000
Columbia, SC 29202   Gina Latham, Lib.Supv.
Remarks: Library located at 21 N. I-77 Hwy., Wilson Rd., Blythewood, SC 29016. No further information was supplied by respondent.

Shad Polier Memorial Library
See: **American Jewish Congress - Commission on Law and Social Action** (654)

Polish Academy of Sciences
See: **Poland - Polish Academy of Sciences** (13167)

Polish Academy of Sciences - Gdansk Library
See: **Poland - Polish Academy of Sciences - Gdansk Library** (13168)

★ 13177 ★

Polish Amateur Astronomical Society - Library (Sci-Engr)
Ulica Solskiego 30/8
PL-31-027 Cracow, Poland   Phone: 12 223892
Subjects: Astronomy, Polish space exploration. **Holdings:** 5000 volumes. **Also Known As:** Polskie Towarzystwo Milosnikow Astronomii.

★ 13178 ★

Polish American Congress, Inc. - Southern California-Arizona Division - Poland's Millenium Library (Area-Ethnic)
3424 W. Adams Blvd.   Phone: (213)734-5249
Los Angeles, CA 90018   Frances Tuszynski, Ph.D.
Founded: 1966. **Staff:** Prof 2; Other 3. **Subjects:** Poland - literature, history; Polish culture. **Holdings:** 9000 books; 12 magazines. **Subscriptions:** 3 journals and other serials. **Services:** Library open to the public. **Staff:** Martin G. Henzel, Pres.; Mrs. Wanda Jazwinski, V.P.

★ 13179 ★

Polish Institute of Arts and Sciences of America, Inc. - Alfred Jurzykawski Memorial Library (Area-Ethnic)
208 E. 30th St.   Phone: (212)686-4164
New York, NY 10016   Krystyna Baron, Chf.Libn.
Founded: 1950. **Staff:** Prof 2; Other 1. **Subjects:** Poland - humanities, social sciences, ethnicity. **Special Collections:** Polish art collection; Polish history, 1918-1945 (pamphlets); Bohdan and Leszek Pawtowicz Collection; translator's workshop (3000 books). **Holdings:** 25,000 books; 500 periodical titles; newspapers on microfilm; maps. **Subscriptions:** 40 journals and other serials. **Services:** Copying; library open to the public on a limited schedule. **Publications:** Guide to the archives (book). **Staff:** Krystyna Swierbutowicz, Asst.Libn.

★ 13180 ★
Polish Institute of Arts and Sciences in Canada - Polish Library (Area-Ethnic)
McGill University
3479 Peel St.   Phone: (514)398-6978
Montreal, PQ, Canada H3A 1W7   Dr. Hanna Pappius, Dir.
Founded: 1943. **Staff:** Prof 3; Other 2. **Subjects:** Polish literature, history, social science, political science, art, folklore; East European problems. **Special Collections:** Wartime publications in English and Polish. **Holdings:** 35,000 books; 5000 periodicals; reports; videotapes; manuscripts; clippings; documents; files; 200 engravings; 30 paintings; 700 slides; 15 atlases; 40 maps; 300 photographs. **Subscriptions:** 85 journals and other serials; 15 newspapers. **Services:** Interlibrary loan; copying; library open to the public. **Computerized Information Services:** Electronic mail. **Publications:** Biuletyn Informacyjny P.I.N.u (bulletin), annual. **Special Indexes:** Index to "Tygodnik Powszechny"; "Kultura," Paris; "Polish Review," New York; "News," London; Abstracts of articles in library periodical holdings in English, French, and Polish (4000 cards). **Staff:** Wanda Stachiewicz, Hon.Cur.; Stefan Wladysiuk, Libn.; Sophie Bogdanski, Cat.Libn.

★ 13181 ★
Polish Institute of International Affairs - Department for Scientific Information - Library (Soc Sci)
ulica Warecka 1a
Skrytka Pocztowa 1000   Phone: 22 272826
PL-00-950 Warsaw, Poland   Leszek Cyrzyk, Libn.
Founded: 1947. **Staff:** 15. **Subjects:** Contemporary international relations, international law, politics, military affairs, economics, social affairs. **Special Collections:** United Nations depository library; European Documentation Center of the European Economic Community; League of Nations publications. **Holdings:** 85,000 books; 35,000 bound periodical volumes; 5000 microforms. **Subscriptions:** 350 journals and other serials; 15 newspapers. **Services:** Interlibrary loan; library open to academic users only. **Publications:** List of Acquisitions, bimonthly; selected bibliographies, irregular. **Remarks:** FAX: 22 274738. **Staff:** Tadeusz Bartkowski; Anna Bozyk; Maria Goralska; Aleksandra Jasik; Anna Lukasik-Herman; Lucja Klos; Zofia Kosowska; Karolina Krajewska; Malgorzata Lawacz; Elzbieta Nurkiewicz; Krystyna Rozek; Maria Safianowska; Zuzanna Wojciechowska.

★ 13182 ★
The Polish Library (Area-Ethnic)
238/246 King St.   Phone: 81 7410474
London W6 0RF, England   Zdzislaw K. Jagodzinski, Ph.D.
Founded: 1942. **Staff:** 7. **Subjects:** Poland - culture, history, language, arts, geography, economy, law, literature, folklore, sociology; World War II. **Special Collections:** Anglo-Polonica; Conradiana; Polish underground publications; bookplates; photographs; manuscripts; maps. **Holdings:** 115,000 volumes; 28,000 bound periodical volumes. **Services:** Interlibrary loan; copying; library open to the public with borrowing privileges for members only. **Publications:** List of publications - available on request. **Remarks:** Library is the seat of the Joseph Conrad Society/U.K. and is owned by the Polish Social and Cultural Association.

★ 13183 ★
Polish Museum of America - Archives & Library (Area-Ethnic)
984 Milwaukee Ave.   Phone: (312)384-3352
Chicago, IL 60622   Dr. Christoph Kamyszew, Dir. & Cur.
Founded: 1935. **Staff:** Prof 3; Other 3. **Subjects:** Polonica. **Special Collections:** 16th and 17th century original Polish works; 16th-18th century royal Polish manuscripts; original manuscripts of Kosciuszko, Pulaski, Tyssowski, Paderewski, and others; Polish American newspapers and magazines; Polish-American publishers; Archives of Modern History. **Holdings:** 60,000 books; 6000 periodical titles and reels of microfilm; 1000 art pieces, reports, clippings, booklets, museum and archival materials. **Subscriptions:** 35 journals and other serials; 20 newspapers. **Services:** Interlibrary loan; copying; rental of Polish movie videotapes; library open to the public. **Remarks:** FAX: (312)384-3799. **Staff:** Anna Czerwinska, Libn.; Maria Karpowicz, Cat.

★ 13184 ★
Polish Nobility Association - Villa Anneslie Archives (Area-Ethnic)
218A N. Henry St.
Brooklyn, NY 11222   Leonard Suligowski, Dir. of Heraldry
Founded: 1955. **Staff:** Prof 2. **Subjects:** Polish history, heraldry, nobility. **Special Collections:** Heraldry of Eastern Europe; nobility-family archives. **Holdings:** 500 books; 100 other cataloged items. **Subscriptions:** 10 journals and other serials. **Services:** Archives not open to the public. **Staff:** Thomas Hollowak, Res. Herald.

★ 13185 ★
Polish Singers Alliance of America - Library (Mus)
Seven Norwood Court   Phone: (212)720-6089
Staten Island, NY 10304   Walter Witkowicki, Libn.
Subjects: Choral and orchestral music. **Holdings:** 200,000 sheets of music for male, female, mixed choruses, and orchestra. **Services:** Library not open to the public; music available to member choruses at librarian's discretion.

Polish Social and Cultural Association
See: **The Polish Library** (13182)

Politechnika Wroclawska - Biblioteka Glowna i Osrodek Informacji Naukowo-Technicznej
See: **Technical University of Wroclaw - Main Library and Scientific Information Center** (16035)

★ 13186 ★
Politecnico di Milano - Dipartimento di Matematica - Biblioteca (Sci-Engr)
Piazza Leonardo da Vinci 32   Phone: 2 23994500
I-20133 Milan, Italy   Prof. Laura Gotusso
Founded: 1925. **Staff:** Prof 2. **Subjects:** Mathematics, mathematical analysis, geometry, algebra, mechanics, statistics, probability, numerical analysis. **Holdings:** 45,000 books and bound periodical volumes. **Subscriptions:** 222 journals and other serials. **Services:** Copying; library open to the public. **Computerized Information Services:** BOMAS (internal database). **Remarks:** FAX: 2 23994568. **Staff:** Elda Baio, Libn.

★ 13187 ★
Polk County Department of Social Services - Child Care Resource Center (Educ)
1200 University
City View Plaza, Suite F   Phone: (515)286-3536
Des Moines, IA 50314   Karen King, Hd., Res.Ctr.
Staff: Prof 1; Other 1. **Subjects:** Child development. **Holdings:** 500 books; 1500 toys and equipment; musical instruments; children's books; craft items. **Subscriptions:** 10 journals and other serials. **Services:** Center not open to the public. **Publications:** Local newsletter - to childcare givers, parents, trainers, and patrons.

★ 13188 ★
Polk County Historical and Genealogical Library (Hist)
100 E. Main St.   Phone: (813)534-4380
Bartow, FL 33830   Wendy K. Davies, Lib.Serv.Supv.
Founded: 1937. **Staff:** Prof 3. **Subjects:** History - Polk County, Florida, Southeastern United States; genealogies of Southeastern United States families. **Special Collections:** Florida history. **Holdings:** 13,000 books; 610 bound periodical volumes; 800 family histories; 6000 reels of microfilm of census reports; 600 reels of microfilm including census reports, newspapers, county records. **Subscriptions:** 100 journals and other serials; 8 newspapers. **Services:** Copying; library open to the public. **Remarks:** Maintained by Polk County Historical Commission and the Board of County Commissioners. **Staff:** Joseph E. Spanz, Jr.; Virginia A. Schnarre.

★ 13189 ★
Polk County Law Library (Law)
Courthouse, Rm. 3076
255 N. Broadway   Phone: (813)534-4013
Bartow, FL 33830   Hope L. Shaw, Libn.
Founded: 1955. **Staff:** Prof 1; Other 2. **Subjects:** Law. **Holdings:** 16,000 volumes. **Subscriptions:** 75 journals and other serials. **Services:** Copying; library open to the public for reference use only. **Automated Operations:** Computerized circulation. **Computerized Information Services:** WESTLAW. Performs searches on fee basis. **Remarks:** Maintained by Polk County Board of County Commissioners.

★ 13190 ★
James K. Polk Ancestral Home - Library (Hist)
Box 741   Phone: (615)388-2354
Columbia, TN 38402   John C. Holtzapple, Dir.
Founded: 1929. **Staff:** 2. **Subjects:** James K. Polk. **Holdings:** 300 books; 1500 artifacts. **Services:** Library open to the public by written permission. **Remarks:** Maintained by James K. Polk Memorial Association. Personal letters and memorabilia are on deposit at the Tennessee State Archives.

★ 13191 ★
Polk Museum of Art - Charlotte and Paul Penfield Library (Hum)
800 E. Palmetto   Phone: (813)688-7743
Lakeland, FL 33801   Ken Rollins, Exec.Dir.
Staff: Prof 3. **Subjects:** Art, antiques. **Special Collections:** Catalogs on Florida artists. **Holdings:** 1000 books. **Subscriptions:** 40 journals and other serials. **Services:** Library open to the public for reference use only. **Staff:** Corinne Sherwood, Libn.; Mary Kay Smith, Libn.; Martha Bier, Libn.

Pollack Library
See: Maimonides Hospital Geriatric Centre (9546)

Pollack Library
See: Yeshiva University - Pollack Library (20758)

Calvin E. Pollins Memorial Library
See: Westmoreland County Historical Society (20337)

Channing Pollock Theatre Collection
See: Howard University (7474)

★ 13192 ★
Pollution Probe Foundation - Ecology House Library
12 Madison Ave.
Toronto, ON, Canada M5R 2S1
Defunct.

Polska Akademia Nauk - Biblioteka Gdanska
See: Poland - Polish Academy of Sciences - Gdansk Library (13168)

Polska Akademia Nauk - Instytut Sztuki
See: Poland - Polish Academy of Sciences - Institute of Art - Library (13170)

Polska Akademia Nauk - Zaklad Krajow Pozaeuropejskich - Biblioteka
See: Poland - Polish Academy of Sciences (13167)

★ 13193 ★
Polska Akademia Nauk w Warszawie - Instytut Matematyczny - Biblioteka (Sci-Engr)
Sniadeckich 8   Phone: 22 282471
PL-00-950 Warsaw, Poland   Maria Mostowska
Founded: 1948. **Staff:** Prof 7; Other 1. **Subjects:** Mathematics. **Holdings:** 62,000 books; 45,000 bound periodical volumes; 4000 preprints. **Subscriptions:** 546 journals and other serials. **Services:** Interlibrary loan; copying; library open to the public. **Computerized Information Services:** BITNET (electronic mail service). **Publications:** List of new acquisitions. **Remarks:** FAX: 22 293997. Telex 816112 PANIM PL. Electronic mail address(es): IMPANW@PLWATU21 (BITNET).

Polskie Towarzystwo Milosnikow Astronomii
See: Polish Amateur Astronomical Society (13177)

Brian Polsley Memorial Audio/Video Library
See: ALS and Neuromuscular Research Foundation (416)

★ 13194 ★
Polychrome Corporation - Research & Development Library (Art)
631 Central Ave.
Carlstadt, NJ 07072   Phone: (201)346-8800
Staff: Prof 1. **Subjects:** Graphic arts, chemistry, business management. **Holdings:** 1500 books; 100 unbound periodicals; 4 drawers of U.S. patents; 1 drawer of foreign patents. **Subscriptions:** 100 journals and other serials. **Services:** Copying; library open to the public for reference use only on request. **Formerly:** Located in Yonkers, NY.

★ 13195 ★
Polyclinic Medical Center - Medical Library (Med)
2601 N. 3rd St.   Phone: (717)782-4292
Harrisburg, PA 17110   Suzanne M. Shultz, Libn.
Founded: 1925. **Staff:** 1. **Subjects:** Medicine, medical specialities. **Holdings:** 2000 books; 8000 bound periodical volumes. **Subscriptions:** 200 journals and other serials. **Services:** Interlibrary loan; copying; library open to students and medical professionals. **Computerized Information Services:** MEDLARS, WILSONLINE; CD-ROMs (MEDLINE, CINAHL). Performs searches on fee basis. **Networks/Consortia:** Member of Central Pennsylvania Health Sciences Library Association (CPHSLA), National Network of Libraries of Medicine - Middle Atlantic Region. **Remarks:** FAX: (717)782-4293.

★ 13196 ★
Polymer Corporation - Library
2120 Farmont Ave.
P.O. Box 14235
Reading, PA 19612
Founded: 1966. **Subjects:** Polymer science, polymer technology, engineering, chemistry, physics, management, mathematics. **Holdings:** 2500 volumes; 1275 laboratory notebooks. **Remarks:** Currently inactive.

★ 13197 ★
Polypure, Inc. - Syracuse Research Laboratory - Library (Sci-Engr)
Box 500   Phone: (315)487-4151
Solvay, NY 13209-0006   Linda Griffo, Libn.
Founded: 1900. **Staff:** 1. **Subjects:** Applied technology, inorganic chemistry, chemical engineering. **Holdings:** 6000 books; 6000 bound periodical volumes; 19 VF drawers of U.S. patents; 15 VF drawers of foreign patents. **Subscriptions:** 35 journals and other serials. **Services:** Interlibrary loan (local only); copying; library open to the public for reference use by appointment only. **Computerized Information Services:** DIALOG Information Services, Chemical Abstracts Service (CAS). Performs searches on fee basis. **Networks/Consortia:** Member of Central New York Library Resources Council (CENTRO). **Publications:** Information Briefs, irregular - for internal distribution only.

★ 13198 ★
Polysar - Information Centre (Sci-Engr)
1265 Vidal St.
P.O. Box 3001   Phone: (519)337-8251
Sarnia, ON, Canada N7T 7M2   Rosemary O'Donnell, Supv.
Founded: 1944. **Staff:** Prof 4; Other 5. **Subjects:** Rubber, latexes, chemicals, polymer science, organic chemistry. **Holdings:** 13,000 books; 6000 bound periodical volumes; 1900 reels of microfilm; 10,500 microfiche; 35,000 internal reports. **Subscriptions:** 400 journals and other serials; 30 newspapers. **Services:** Interlibrary loan; copying; SDI; center open to the public by advance request. **Automated Operations:** Computerized public access catalog, cataloging, serials, and circulation. **Computerized Information Services:** DIALOG Information Services, PFDS Online, Info Globe, Mead Data Central, Dun & Bradstreet Business Credit Services, STN International, CAN/OLE, Infomart Online, NewsNet, Inc., STM Systems Corporation; internal databases. **Publications:** Polysar Information Bulletin. **Special Indexes:** Index to internal reports (book). **Remarks:** FAX: (519)339-7748. Telex: 06476158. **Staff:** Sharon Freeman, Info.Spec.; Tina DeMars, Info.Spec.; Mary Mahoney, Info.Spec.

★ 13199 ★
Polysciences Incorporated - Library (Sci-Engr)
Paul Valley Industrial Park   Phone: (215)343-6484
Warrington, PA 18976   Joy R. Myers, Adm.Asst.
Founded: 1961. **Subjects:** Plastics, polymers in dentistry and medicine. **Holdings:** Figures not available. **Remarks:** FAX: (215)343-0214.

★ 13200 ★
Polytechnic of East London - Greengate House Annexe - Library (Art)
89 Greengate St.   Phone: 81 5907722
London E13 0BG, England   Judith Preece
Founded: 1977. **Staff:** Prof 2; Other 1. **Subjects:** Art history, textiles, film, design history, graphics, photography. **Special Collections:** William Morris Collection (90 volumes). **Holdings:** 16,000 books; 50,000 slides. **Subscriptions:** 108 journals and other serials; 4 newspapers. **Services:** Library open to the public for reference use only. **Special Indexes:** Colour Supplement Index. **Remarks:** FAX: 81 8493694.

★ 13201 ★
Polytechnic of East London - Science Fiction Foundation Research Library (Hum)
Longbridge Rd.
Dagenham, Essex RM8 2AS, England   Phone: 81 5907722
Staff: 1. **Subjects:** Science fiction, fantasy. **Special Collections:** Pulp magazines, 1920s to present; critical works; Russian science fiction; Flat Earth Society papers; fanzines. **Holdings:** 12,750 books; 100 microforms; 100 manuscripts. **Services:** Copying; library open to the public by appointment. **Staff:** Joyce Day, Sec.; Pat Green, Sec.

★ 13202 ★
Polytechnic, Inc. - Library (Sci-Engr)
3740 Morse Ave.   Phone: (708)677-0450
Lincolnwood, IL 60645   Ruby Warso
Founded: 1961. **Staff:** Prof 1. **Subjects:** Engineering, vehicle engineering, product evaluation and safety, fire/explosion, guarding and labeling, zoning, pollution. **Special Collections:** Historical collections of standards and codes. **Services:** Interlibrary loan; library not open to the public. **Computerized Information Services:** ORBIT Search Service. **Remarks:** FAX: (708)677-0480.

★ 13203 ★
Polytechnic University - Library (Sci-Engr)
5 Metro Tech Center, 3rd Fl.   Phone: (718)260-3109
Brooklyn, NY 11201   Richard T. Sweeney, Dean of Libs.
Staff: Prof 8; Other 8. **Subjects:** Aerospace technology; engineering - civil, industrial, electrical; electrophysics; chemistry; industrial management; mathematics; physics. **Special Collections:** Joseph Mattiello Collection of works of interest to the paint, varnish, and lacquer industries; history of science and technology collection. **Holdings:** 219,673 volumes; 31,966 microtexts. **Subscriptions:** 1233 journals and other serials. **Services:** Interlibrary loan; copying; library open to the public with letter from parent organization. **Automated Operations:** Computerized cataloging, acquisitions, serials, and interlibrary loans. **Computerized Information Services:** DIALOG Information Services, OCLC. Performs searches on fee basis. Contact Person: Aline Locascio, Hd., Info.Serv.Div. **Publications:** Serials 1991, irregular. **Remarks:** FAX: (718)260-3756. **Staff:** James Jarman, Asst. Dean of Libs.

★ 13204 ★
Polytechnic University - Long Island Campus Library (Sci-Engr)
Rte. 110   Phone: (516)755-4320
Farmingdale, NY 11735   Lorraine Schein, Lib.Mgr.
Founded: 1960. **Staff:** Prof 3; Other 2. **Subjects:** Electrical engineering, electrophysics, aeronautics, fluid mechanics, physics, mathematics. **Holdings:** 30,000 books; 10,000 bound periodical volumes; NASA depository library; 20 VF drawers of pamphlets; 1 file drawer of cassettes. **Subscriptions:** 250 journals and other serials. **Services:** Interlibrary loan; copying; library open to the public with restrictions. **Automated Operations:** Computerized public access catalog. **Networks/Consortia:** Member of Long Island Library Resources Council. **Remarks:** FAX: (516)755-4379.

★ 13205 ★
Pomona Public Library - Special Collections Department (Hist)
625 S. Garey Ave.
Box 2271
Pomona, CA 91766   Phone: (714)620-2033
                                          David Streeter, Supv.
Founded: 1887. **Special Collections:** Californiana (3000 items); philately (1200 items); genealogy (3000 items); Citrus Company Records (28 companies); citrus box labels (4200); water company records (16 companies); Frasher photographs (60,000); Cooper photographs (4000); historical photographs (10,000); Tatum photographs (150); post card collection (35,000); glass plate negatives and prints (2500); California Wine Labels (10,000); non-California wine labels (1500); Laura Ingalls Wilder Collection (Little House on the Prairie holograph manuscripts; letters; photographs); Clara Webber Collection of Historic Children's Books; Padua Theater Collection (Mexican Players); 15 linear feet of uncataloged manuscripts and photographs). **Services:** Interlibrary loan; copying; department open to the public. **Automated Operations:** Computerized cataloging, acquisitions, and circulation. **Computerized Information Services:** OCLC. **Networks/Consortia:** Member of Metropolitan Cooperative Library System (MCLS), State of California Answering Network (SCAN). **Special Indexes:** Pomona Progress Bulletin Index (card); CULP; CATALIST. **Remarks:** FAX: (714)623-0850.

★ 13206 ★
Pomona Valley Community Hospital - Medical Library (Med)
1798 N. Garey Ave.   Phone: (714)865-9878
Pomona, CA 91767   Deborah Klein, Libn.
Staff: Prof 1. **Subjects:** Clinical medicine, nursing, bioethics. **Holdings:** 1400 books; 5000 bound periodical volumes; 600 audiotapes. **Subscriptions:** 180 journals and other serials; 10 audiotape subscriptions. **Services:** Interlibrary loan; library open to the public for reference use only. **Computerized Information Services:** DIALOG Information Services, MEDLARS. **Remarks:** Alternate telephone number(s): 865-9500.

★ 13207 ★
Pomorski Muzej - Biblioteka (Hist)
Kotor, Yugoslavia   Phone: 82 11216
                                     Nebojsa Bulatovic, Libn.
Founded: 1950. **Staff:** Prof 1; Other 3. **Subjects:** Naval studies; archeology. **Special Collections:** Collection of regional newspaper, Boka, 1935-1941. **Holdings:** 7650 books; 854 bound periodical volumes; 578 reports; 11 microfiche; 47 nautical maps. **Subscriptions:** 32 journals and other serials; 5 newspapers. **Services:** Interlibrary loan; copying; SDI; library open only to students and museum staff. **Publications:** Godisnjak (Maritime Museum yearbook). **Also Known As:** Maritime Museum Kotor.

★ 13208 ★
Ponca City Cultural Center & Museums - Library (Area-Ethnic)
1000 E. Grand Ave.   Phone: (405)765-5268
Ponca City, OK 74601   LaWanda French, Supv.
Founded: 1938. **Staff:** 1. **Subjects:** American Indian, anthropology, archeology, American cowboy, museology. **Special Collections:** Personal letters and photographs of Bryant Baker, sculptor of the Pioneer Woman; Ponca Indian music (tape recordings). **Holdings:** 200 books; 15 bound periodical volumes; VF drawers of unbound reports, clippings, pamphlets, dissertations, documents. **Subscriptions:** 15 journals and other serials. **Services:** Copying (limited); library open to the public. **Publications:** Museum Brochure. **Special Catalogs:** Classification, Source, Tribe, Location, and Documents Catalogs (card file).

★ 13209 ★
Ponce School of Medicine Foundation - Medical Library (Med)
University Ave. No. 1
Box 7004   Phone: (809)840-2549
Ponce, PR 00731   Carmen G. Malavet, Lib.Dir.
Founded: 1977. **Staff:** Prof 2; Other 6. **Subjects:** Clinical and basic sciences, anatomy, microbiology. **Special Collections:** Puerto Rican medical authors; hispanic medical journals. **Holdings:** 9786 books; 7546 bound periodical volumes; 17,332 uncataloged items. **Subscriptions:** 486 journals and other serials. **Services:** Interlibrary loan; copying; library open to the public. **Computerized Information Services:** BRS Information Technologies, MEDLINE, PaperChase; CD-ROM (MEDLINE); internal database. Performs searches on fee basis. Contact Person: Gerardo Caraballo, Res.Techn. **Publications:** User's guide; library newsletter with acquisitions list, quarterly; library procedures; subject bibliographies. **Special Indexes:** Index to the Journal: Asociacion Medica de Puerto Rico Boletin. **Remarks:** FAX: (809)844-3685. **Staff:** Milagros de Jesus.

Pontiac General Hospital
See: **North Oakland Medical Center** (11939)

★ 13210 ★
Pontiac Osteopathic Hospital - Medical Library (Med)
50 N. Perry St.
Pontiac, MI 48342   Phone: (313)338-5000
Founded: 1963. **Staff:** 2. **Subjects:** Medicine. **Holdings:** 2586 books; 3100 bound periodical volumes; AV programs; Audio-Digest tapes; slide/tape sets. **Subscriptions:** 149 journals and other serials. **Services:** Interlibrary loan; library not open to the public.

★ 13211 ★
Pontifical College Josephinum - A.T. Wehrle Memorial Library (Rel-Phil)
7625 N. High St.   Phone: (614)885-5585
Columbus, OH 43235-1498   Peter G. Veracka, Dir.
Founded: 1889. **Staff:** Prof 2; Other 3. **Subjects:** Patristics, scholastic philosophy, Catholic theology and liturgy. **Special Collections:** Dissertations on the work and thought of Bernard Lonergan (53); books on the catacombs. **Holdings:** 92,425 books; 14,134 bound periodical volumes; 112 reels of microfilm; 1270 microfiche; 1984 cassettes. **Subscriptions:** 514 journals and other serials; 51 newspapers. **Services:** Interlibrary loan; copying; library open to the public on request. **Automated Operations:** Computerized cataloging. **Computerized Information Services:** OCLC, BRS Information Technologies. **Networks/Consortia:** Member of OHIONET. **Remarks:** (614)885-2307. **Staff:** Beverly Lane, Asst.Libn.

Pontifical Institute of Mediaeval Studies
See: **University of Toronto - Pontifical Institute of Mediaeval Studies - Library** (19458)

★ 13212 ★
Pontifical Institute of Spirituality of the Teresianum - Library (Rel-Phil)
Piazza San Pancrazio 5/a   Phone: 6 58 23 62
I-00152 Rome, Italy   Fr. Faustino Macchiella, Libn.
Subjects: Spiritual theology. **Holdings:** 150,000 volumes. **Publications:** Bibliographia Internationalis Spiritualitatis. **Also Known As:** Pontificio Instituto di Spiritualita del Teresianum.

★ 13213 ★
Pontificia Universidad Catolica de Chile - Facultad de Medicina y Ciencias Biologicas - Biblioteca Biomedica (Med, Biol Sci)
Av Bernardo O'Higgins 340
Casilla 114-D   Phone: 2 2224516
Santiago, Chile   Sonia Vaisman Abramson
Founded: 1932. **Staff:** Prof 3; Other 12. **Subjects:** Medicine, biological sciences. **Holdings:** 21,000 books; 9000 bound periodical volumes; 150,000 unbound volumes; 900 reports. **Subscriptions:** 600 journals and other serials; 2 newspapers. **Services:** Library open to the public on a limited schedule. **Automated Operations:** Computerized public access catalog. **Computerized Information Services:** DIALOG Information Services; CD-ROMs (MEDLINE, LILACS, POPLINE). **Publications:** New Acquisitions - Novedades. **Remarks:** FAX: 2 2224516, ext. 2678.

★ 13214 ★
Pontificia Universidad Catolica del Peru - Biblioteca Central (Hum, Law, Hist)
Avenida Universitaria Cuadra 18 s/n   Phone: 14 622540
Lima 32, Peru   Carmen Villanueva, Hd.
Founded: 1917. **Staff:** Prof 23; Other 63. **Subjects:** Literature, linguistics, history, law, pure sciences and engineering, social sciences, theology, arts. **Special Collections:** Coleccion Sabroso (political party documents); Coleccion Majluf; Coleccion Martin Adan (manuscripts of poems); Coleccion Universidades (original documents and publications from universities). **Holdings:** 330,000 volumes; 30,000 documents; 35,000 slides; 1450 periodical titles. **Subscriptions:** 870 journals and other serials; 30 newspapers. **Services:** Interlibrary loan; copying; SDI; library open to the public with letter of presentation. **Automated Operations:** Computerized serials. **Computerized Information Services:** BIB-SOC, Cendoc, UNIVER (internal databases). **Publications:** Current awareness bulletins in all humanities areas; current awareness bulletins in management sciences, law, engineering, pure sciences, social sciences. **Remarks:** Maintains 8 campus libraries and two additional information centers (Electronic Engineering and Chemistry). FAX: 611785. **Staff:** Ana Maria Talavera, Hd., Tech.Serv.

★ 13215 ★
Pontificia Universidad Catolica del Peru - Riva-Aguero Institute - Library (Area-Ethnic)
Jiron Camana 459   Phone: 14 277-678
Lima 1, Peru   Angela Portocarrero, Libn.
Founded: 1947. **Subjects:** Peruvian history; hispanic literature, arts, and philosophy. **Special Collections:** El Comercio, from 1839 (daily newspaper). **Holdings:** 60,000 volumes. **Services:** Library open to scholars. **Remarks:** FAX: 14 61 17 85. **Also Known As:** Instituto Riva-Aguero.

POPAI Information Center
See: **Point of Purchase Advertising Institute - Information Center** (13159)

★ 13216 ★
Pope, Ballard, Shepard and Fowle - Library (Law)
69 W. Washington St., Suite 3200   Phone: (312)214-4200
Chicago, IL 60602   Ronald E. Feret, Libn.
Staff: Prof 1; Other 1. **Subjects:** Law. **Holdings:** 25,950 books; 200 bound periodical volumes. **Subscriptions:** 18 journals and other serials. **Services:** Library not open to the public.

★ 13217 ★
Pope County Historical Society & Museum - Library (Hist)
809 S. Lakeshore Dr.   Phone: (612)634-3293
Glenwood, MN 56334   Merlin Berglin, Cur.
Founded: 1932. **Staff:** Prof 2. **Subjects:** History - local, business, personal; genealogy. **Special Collections:** Bound newspapers, 1891 to present; Pope County Census, 1880-1910 (microfiche); Immigration for Pope County (microfiche). **Holdings:** 1343 volumes. **Subscriptions:** 2 newspapers. **Services:** Copying; library open to the public for reference use only. **Automated Operations:** Computerized cataloging and acquisitions.

★ 13218 ★
Pope John XXIII National Seminary - Library (Rel-Phil)
558 South Ave.   Phone: (617)899-5500
Weston, MA 02193   Rev. James L. Fahey, Libn.
Founded: 1964. **Staff:** Prof 2; Other 4. **Subjects:** Theology, philosophy, scripture, humanities, social sciences. **Holdings:** 45,376 books; 7269 bound periodical volumes; 2 vertical files. **Subscriptions:** 282 journals and other serials. **Services:** Interlibrary loan; copying; library open to the public for reference use only. **Remarks:** Maintained by the Archdiocese of Boston. **Staff:** Ann Kidney, Asst.Libn.

Poplar Bluff Library
See: **Genealogical Society of Butler County** (6288)

★ 13219 ★
Population Council - Library (Soc Sci)
1 Dag Hammarskjold Plaza   Phone: (212)339-0532
New York, NY 10017   Hugh Neil Zimmerman, Libn.
Founded: 1953. **Staff:** Prof 1; Other 1. **Subjects:** Population; demography; family planning; contraception; statistics; public health; development - economic, social, agricultural. **Holdings:** 20,000 books; 6,000 pamphlets, mimeographs, reprints, other cataloged items. **Subscriptions:** 350 journals and other serials. **Services:** Interlibrary loan; library open to researchers by appointment. **Automated Operations:** Computerized serials. **Computerized Information Services:** POPLINE. **Networks/Consortia:** Member of Consortium of Foundation Libraries (CFL), APLIC International Census Network, New York Metropolitan Reference and Research Library Agency. **Publications:** Acquisitions List, irregular. **Remarks:** FAX: (212)755-6052.

★ 13220 ★
Population Crisis Committee/Draper Fund - Library (Soc Sci)
1120 19th St., N.W., Suite 550   Phone: (202)659-1833
Washington, DC 20036   Anne Marie B. Amantia, Sr.Libn./Info.Mgr.
Staff: Prof 1; Other 1. **Subjects:** Family planning, demography, contraceptive technology, status of women, food, environment. **Special Collections:** Female circumcision; history of population legislation. **Holdings:** 5000 books; 65 VF drawers. **Subscriptions:** 500 journals and other serials. **Services:** Interlibrary loan; copying; SDI; library open to the public by appointment only. **Computerized Information Services:** Internal database. **Networks/Consortia:** Member of APLIC International Census Network. **Publications:** Serials holdings list, - free upon request. **Remarks:** Telex: 440450.

★ **13221** ★
Population and Development Program Research - Library (Soc Sci)
Cornell University
218 Warren Hall   Phone: (607)255-4924
Ithaca, NY 14853-7801   Beatrix Johnson, Libn.
Subjects: Population, social science. **Special Collections:** Data archive
(international fertility surveys, other surveys; samples of Latin American
and Asian censuses). **Holdings:** 8000 books. **Services:** Library not open to
the public. **Remarks:** FAX: (607)255-9984. Telex: 6713054 WUI.

★ **13222** ★
Population Reference Bureau, Inc. - Library/Information Service (Soc
Sci)
1875 Connecticut Ave., N.W., Suite 520   Phone: (202)483-1100
Washington, DC 20009   Nazy Roudi
Founded: 1929. **Staff:** Prof 2. **Subjects:** Demography, U.S. census, family
planning, migration, environment, population policy. **Special Collections:**
Historical U.S. census collection, including selected 1930-1960 census
volumes and complete set of 1970-1990 census volumes; U.S. Vital and
Health Statistics, 1939 to present; Census Bureau's U.S. Current Population
Reports (P-Series); United Nations Statistical Publications. **Holdings:**
12,000 books; 2500 reprints and papers; 15 VF drawers of pamphlets,
clippings, reprints. **Subscriptions:** 450 journals and other serials. **Services:**
Interlibrary loan; copying; library open to the public. **Computerized
Information Services:** POPLINE. **Networks/Consortia:** Member of APLIC
International Census Network. **Publications:** List of publications - available
on request. **Remarks:** FAX: (202)328-3937. Telex: 4900010456 (PRB UI).
Staff: Zuali Malsawma.

(Port-au-Prince) Institut Haitiano-Americain
See: **Bibliotheque Martin Luther King, Jr.** (1828)

★ **13223** ★
Port Authority of Allegheny County - Transit Research Library (Trans)
Beaver & Island Aves.   Phone: (412)237-7336
Pittsburgh, PA 15233   Richard Feder, Mgr.Plan.
Founded: 1974. **Staff:** Prof 1. **Subjects:** Rapid transit, paratransit, urban
mass transit. **Holdings:** 3500 books; 200 reels of microfilm; Federal Register.
Subscriptions: 81 journals and other serials. **Services:** Interlibrary loan;
copying; library open to the public. **Remarks:** FAX: (412)237-7101.

★ **13224** ★
Port Authority of New York and New Jersey - Library (Trans, Bus-Fin)
55 N., One World Trade Center   Phone: (212)435-3550
New York, NY 10048   Jane M. Janiak, Chf.Libn.
Founded: 1946. **Staff:** Prof 7; Other 6. **Subjects:** Transportation, public
administration, international trade, business, management, engineering,
aviation. **Holdings:** 25,000 books; 25,000 documents; 150 titles on microfilm;
Urban Mass Transportation Administration Depository. **Subscriptions:**
1200 journals; 500 serials. **Services:** Interlibrary loan; SDI; library open to
students and librarians by appointment. **Automated Operations:**
Computerized cataloging and circulation. **Computerized Information
Services:** NEXIS, DIALOG Information Services, VU/TEXT Information
Services, Washington Alert Service, WILSONLINE, Reuter TEXTLINE,
RLIN, OCLC, LEGI-SLATE. **Networks/Consortia:** Member of SUNY/
OCLC Library Network. **Publications:** Library Bulletin. **Remarks:** FAX:
(212)435-3565. **Staff:** Lewis R. Borress, Asst.Chf.Libn., Cat.; Diane
Sciattara, Ref.Libn.; Patricia Cose, Asst.Chf.Libn., Ref.; Margaret Russell
Ling, Ref.Libn.; Barbara LaFave, Cat.; Dolores Rescigno, Cat.

★ **13225** ★
(Port Huron) Times Herald - Library (Publ)
911 Military
P.O. Box 5009
Port Huron, MI 48061-5009   Phone: (313)985-7171
                                     Michael Patterson, Lib.Ck.
Staff: 1. **Subjects:** Newspaper reference topics. **Holdings:** 10,000 files of
clippings and photographs; 670 reels of microfilm. **Services:** Library open
to the public with permission.

★ **13226** ★
**Port Jefferson Hospital - John T. Mather Memorial Hospital - Medical
Library** (Med)
North Country Rd.   Phone: (516)473-1320
Port Jefferson, NY 11777   Margaret Corrigan, Lib.Ck.
Remarks: No further information was supplied by respondent.

★ **13227** ★
Port Moody Station Museum - Library and Archives (Hist)
2734 Murray St.   Phone: (604)939-1648
Port Moody, BC, Canada V3H 1X2   A. McNeil, Pres.
Founded: 1967. **Subjects:** Museum training materials, Canadian Pacific
Railway history, local history, Salish art and culture. **Special Collections:**
Archives (100 linear feet of archival materials, including Port Moody City
records, newspapers, and local business records, Canadian Pacific Railway
papers, film and cassette recordings). **Holdings:** 500 books. **Subscriptions:**
10 journals and other serials. **Services:** Copying; library open to the public
with restrictions. **Publications:** Original Inhabitants. (1983); History of Port
Moody 1880's; museum notes series; Heritage Express (newsletter), monthly
- for internal distribution and upon request. **Remarks:** Maintained by Port
Moody Heritage Society.

★ **13228** ★
Port of Portland - Library and Information Services (Bus-Fin, Trans)
P.O. Box 3529   Phone: (503)731-7582
Portland, OR 97208   Lynn Shannon, Info.Spec.
Staff: Prof 1. **Subjects:** Maritime and waterborne commerce, aviation.
Special Collections: Port of Portland studies (Port-run airports, ship repair
yard, marine terminals). **Holdings:** 3500 books. **Subscriptions:** 950 journals
and other serials; 20 newspapers. **Services:** Interlibrary loan; library open
to the public. **Computerized Information Services:** DIALOG Information
Services, Reuter TEXTLINE, Dun's Marketing Services (DMS). **Special
Indexes:** Index to Port Studies. **Remarks:** Toll-free telephone number(s):
(800)547-8441. FAX: (503)731-7626. Telex: 474 2039 PORT-PTL.

★ **13229** ★
(Port of Spain) American Center - USIS Library (Educ)
21 Marli St.
P.O. Box 752
Port of Spain, Trinidad and Tobago
Remarks: Maintained or supported by the U.S. Information Agency. Focus
is on materials that will assist peoples outside the United States to learn
about the United States, its people, history, culture, political processes, and
social milieux.

★ **13230** ★
Portage County Historical Society - Library and Museum (Hist)
6549 N. Chestnut St.   Phone: (216)296-3523
Ravenna, OH 44266   Thomas E. Cadwallader, Pres.
Founded: 1951. **Subjects:** County history - families, industries,
organizations, genealogy. **Special Collections:** Frederick J. Loudin
Collection; Alford photograph collection. **Holdings:** 500 books; 40 family
histories; early tax records; county records, documents, atlas; cemetery
records. **Services:** Copying; library open to the public for reference use only
on a limited schedule. **Staff:** Bonita S. Lock, Libn.; Betty Walters,
Genealogist.

Portage County Historical Society Collection
See: **University of Wisconsin--Stevens Point - University Archives**
(19649)

Dana Porter Library
See: **University of Waterloo - Dana Porter Library** (19543)

Fairfield Porter Archives
See: **Parrish Art Museum - Library** (12764)

Katherine Anne Porter Library
See: University of Maryland, College Park Libraries - McKeldin Library (18819)

★ 13231 ★
Langley Porter Psychiatric Institute - Reading Room (Med)
University of California
401 Parnassus Ave.
Box 13-B/C
San Francisco, CA 94143-0984   Phone: (415)476-7380
                                      Lisa M. Dunkel, Libn.
Founded: 1943. Staff: Prof 1; Other 2. Subjects: Psychiatry, psychoanalysis, clinical psychology, allied mental health sciences. Holdings: 6575 books; 4145 bound periodical volumes; pamphlets. Subscriptions: 160 journals and other serials. Services: Interlibrary loan; library not open to the public. Computerized Information Services: MEDLARS, BRS Information Technologies. Performs searches on fee basis. Remarks: Alternate telephone number(s): 476-7203. Formerly: Its Professional Library.

★ 13232 ★
Porter Medical Center - Medical Library (Med)
South St.
Middlebury, VT 05753   Phone: (802)388-7901
                                   Rebecca Mueller, Libn.
Founded: 1974. Staff: Prof 1. Subjects: Medicine, nursing. Holdings: 1000 books; 500 videocassettes. Subscriptions: 95 journals and other serials. Services: Interlibrary loan; library open to the public with restrictions. Automated Operations: Computerized public access catalog. Computerized Information Services: NLM. Networks/Consortia: Member of Health Science Libraries of New Hampshire & Vermont (HSL-NH/VT), North Country Consortium (NCC). Remarks: FAX: (802)388-4903.

★ 13233 ★
Porter Memorial Hospital - Harley E. Rice Memorial Library (Med)
2525 S. Downing St.
Denver, CO 80210   Phone: (303)778-5656
                                   W. Robin Waters, Mgr.
Staff: Prof 1. Subjects: Medicine. Holdings: 2250 books; 6500 bound periodical volumes; 125 audiotapes. Subscriptions: 350 journals and other serials. Services: Interlibrary loan; copying; SDI; library open to the public for reference use only. Automated Operations: Computerized cataloging. Computerized Information Services: BRS Information Technologies, MEDLARS; TenTime (electronic mail service). Performs searches on fee basis. Networks/Consortia: Member of Colorado Council of Medical Librarians, Bibliographical Center for Research, Rocky Mountain Region, Inc. (BCR), National Network of Libraries of Medicine - Midcontinental Region. Staff: Patricia Perry, Libn.; Donna Greer, Libn.; Earl Pugh, Libn.

Sister Esther Porter Medical-Nursing Library
See: Bethesda Lutheran Hospital - Library (1789)

★ 13234 ★
Porter, Wright, Morris & Arthur - Library (Law)
41 S. High St.
Columbus, OH 43215   Phone: (614)227-2090
                                   Susan M. Schaefgen, Lib.Mgr.
Founded: 1852. Staff: Prof 1; Other 4. Subjects: Law, Ohio law. Holdings: 25,000 books; 1500 bound periodical volumes. Subscriptions: 1000 journals and other serials; 10 newspapers. Services: Library not open to the public. Automated Operations: Computerized cataloging and serials. Computerized Information Services: LEXIS, NEXIS, WESTLAW, DIALOG Information Services, VU/TEXT Information Services, Dow Jones News/Retrieval, Haystack; ZyIndex (internal database); MCI Mail (electronic mail service). Networks/Consortia: Member of OHIONET. Special Indexes: Periodicals; videotapes; memo, prospectus, expert witness, and lawyer referral files. Remarks: FAX: (614)227-2100. Telex: 650 321 3584. Electronic mail address(es): 321-3584 (MCI Mail).

★ 13235 ★
Porterville Developmental Center - Professional Library (Med)
Box 2000
Porterville, CA 93258   Phone: (209)782-2609
                                   Mary Jane Berry, Libn.
Staff: Prof 1. Subjects: Mental retardation - psychology, medical aspects, education, social welfare. Holdings: 6000 books; 3800 bound periodical volumes. Subscriptions: 125 journals and other serials. Services: Interlibrary loan; copying; library open to the public for reference use only on request. Computerized Information Services: MEDLINE, DIALOG Information Services. Remarks: FAX: (209)784-5630.

★ 13236 ★
Portland Art Museum - Rex Arragon Library (Art)
1219 S.W. Park
Portland, OR 97205   Phone: (503)226-2811
                                   Daniel G. Lucas, Libn.
Founded: 1892. Staff: Prof 1. Subjects: Art. Special Collections: Art of Indian tribes of the Pacific Northwest; Oriental art, especially Japanese prints; English silver books. Holdings: 22,442 books; 1100 bound periodical volumes; 365 pamphlet cases of catalogs relating to artists, movements, and exhibitions; 175 pamphlet cases of museum reports and bulletins; 71,500 slides. Subscriptions: 84 journals and other serials. Services: Interlibrary loan; library open to the public for reference use only. Remarks: FAX: (503)226-4842. Maintained by the Oregon Art Institute.

★ 13237 ★
Portland Cement Association - Library Services (Sci-Engr)
5420 Old Orchard Rd.
Skokie, IL 60077   Phone: (708)966-6200
                                   Cynthia Spigelman, Libn.
Founded: 1950. Staff: Prof 1. Subjects: Concrete technology, cement chemistry, steel and wood, structural engineering, civil engineering, construction. Special Collections: Collection of Portland Cement Association publications; U.S. Patent file, 1890 to present; Foreign Literature Studies (500 translations); bibliographies (450). Holdings: 9000 books; 13,500 bound periodical volumes; 50,000 serials; 100,000 abstracts; microfiche; pamphlet file. Subscriptions: 300 journals and other serials. Services: Interlibrary loan; copying; services open to the public on fee basis. Networks/Consortia: Member of ILLINET, North Suburban Library System (NSLS). Publications: List of Publications Received, monthly. Remarks: FAX: (708)965-6541; (708)966-9781. Telex: 9102407163.

★ 13238 ★
Portland City Bureau of Planning - Research Room (Plan)
1120 S.W. 5th Ave., 10th Fl.
Portland, OR 97204-1966   Phone: (503)796-7700
Founded: 1975. Subjects: City planning, historic and urban design, housing and land use policy, development and administration. Special Collections: Planning Commission minutes. Holdings: 6000 books, reports, bound periodical volumes. Services: Research room not open to the public.

★ 13239 ★
Portland General Electric - Corporate Library (Energy)
121 S.W. Salmon St. 3WTC-5
Portland, OR 97204   Phone: (503)464-8700
                                   Robert F. Weber, Corp.Libn.
Founded: 1914. Staff: Prof 2; Other 2. Subjects: Electrical engineering, management, alternative energy sources, environmental sciences. Holdings: 16,000 books; 48,000 technical reports, hardcopy and microfiche; 1500 standards. Subscriptions: 1300 journals and other serials; 25 newspapers. Services: Interlibrary loan; copying (limited); library open to the public with restrictions. Automated Operations: Computerized public access catalog, cataloging, acquisitions, serials, and ILL. Computerized Information Services: DIALOG Information Services, VU/TEXT Information Services, Dow Jones News/Retrieval, DataTimes, NewsNet, Inc., OCLC; LINX Courier, Knight-Ridder Unicom (electronic mail services). Remarks: FAX: (503)464-8706. Staff: Barb Buckley, Tech.Serv.Libn.

★ 13240 ★
Portland General Electric - Energy Resource Center - Technical Library (Energy)
7895 S.W. Mohawk St.
Tualatin, OR 97062   Phone: (503)691-3965
                                   Bette L. Stewart, Info.Spec.
Founded: 1986. Staff: Prof 1; Other 1. Subjects: Heating, ventilation, and air conditioning; electrical applications; commercial food facilities; lighting; industrial processes; energy efficiency; electrotechnologies. Holdings: 800 books; 1100 technical reports; standards; videotapes. Subscriptions: 75 journals and other serials. Services: Library open to the public with restrictions. Automated Operations: Computerized cataloging and acquisitions. Computerized Information Services: DIALOG Information Services. Remarks: FAX: (503)691-3999.

★ 13241 ★
Portland General Electric - Trojan Technical Library (Energy)
71760 Columbia River Hwy.
Rainier, OR 97048   Phone: (503)556-5673
                                   Mary O'Brien, Libn.
Founded: 1989. Staff: 5. Subjects: Nuclear power and engineering. Holdings: Figures not available. Services: Library not open to the public. Computerized Information Services: DIALOG Information Services, EPRINET. Remarks: FAX: (503)556-5405.

★ 13242 ★
Portland Museum of Art - Library (Art)
7 Congress Sq.   Phone: (207)775-6148
Portland, ME 04101   Elizabeth DeWolf, Act.Cur of Educ.
Subjects: Art. **Holdings:** 3000 volumes; slides. **Services:** Library not open to the public. **Remarks:** FAX: (207)773-7324.

Portland Press Herald-Maine Sunday Telegram
See: Guy Gannett Publishing Company (6245)

★ 13243 ★
Portland Public Library - Art Department (Art, Mus)
5 Monument Sq.   Phone: (207)871-1710
Portland, ME 04101-4072   Sally Regan, Art Libn.
Founded: 1867. **Staff:** Prof 1; Other 4. **Subjects:** Visual and performing arts, music, costume. **Special Collections:** Picture file (21 drawers); Maine composers, artists, musicians; choral music; art school catalogs. **Holdings:** 16,815 books; 21 drawers of sheet music. **Subscriptions:** 96 journals and other serials. **Services:** Interlibrary loan; copying; SDI; department open to the public. **Automated Operations:** Computerized cataloging, acquisitions, and circulation. **Computerized Information Services:** DIALOG Information Services. Performs searches on fee basis. Contact Person: Suzanne Thompson, Ref.Libn. **Remarks:** FAX: (207)871-1756.

★ 13244 ★
Portland Public Schools - Professional Library (Educ)
501 N. Dixon St.
Box 3107
Portland, OR 97208   Phone: (503)249-2000
      Connie Stanton, Libn.
Staff: Prof 1; Other 2. **Subjects:** Education. **Holdings:** 17,000 books. **Subscriptions:** 170 journals and other serials; 7 newspapers. **Services:** Interlibrary loan; copying; SDI; library open to the public with restrictions. **Computerized Information Services:** DIALOG Information Services, OCLC, ED-LINE, WILSONLINE, Books in Print (BIP). **Remarks:** FAX: (503)280-7800.

★ 13245 ★
Portland School of Art - Library (Art)
619 Congress St.   Phone: (207)775-5153
Portland, ME 04101   Edna Keyes, Libn.
Founded: 1973. **Staff:** Prof 2; Other 12. **Subjects:** Art and art history, graphic design, printmaking, metalsmithing, jewelry, sculpture, ceramics, liberal arts, photography. **Holdings:** 18,000 books; 45,000 slides. **Subscriptions:** 115 journals and other serials. **Services:** Interlibrary loan; copying; library open to the public with restrictions. **Staff:** Jeffory Clough, Asst.Libn.

★ 13246 ★
Portland State University - Audio-Visual Services (Aud-Vis)
Box 1151   Phone: (503)725-3495
Portland, OR 97207   Frank F. Kuo, Dir.
Founded: 1953. **Staff:** Prof 2; Other 9. **Subjects:** General AV collection to support university curriculum. **Holdings:** 625 guides and indexes to media materials; media catalogs; 410 media kits; 2060 16mm films; 100 8mm films; 500 35mm filmstrips; 50,000 35mm slides; 12,000 phonograph records; 1700 audiotapes; 5000 scores; 3100 cassettes; 2500 compact discs; 10 laser discs; 50 microcomputer programs. **Subscriptions:** 20 journals and other serials. **Services:** Copying (limited); production of AV materials; services open to the public for campus use only. **Networks/Consortia:** Member of Western Library Network (WLN). **Special Catalogs:** Film catalog; compact disc catalog; Media Kits Catalog; Foreign Languages (26) Audiotape Catalog - all for internal distribution only. **Special Indexes:** Slide index; cassette tape index - both for internal distribution only. **Staff:** Stan Nuffer, Asst.Dir., Lrng./Comp.Labs.; Susan Jackson, AV Lib.Tech.

★ 13247 ★
Portland State University - Continuing Education Film and Video Library (Aud-Vis)
1633 S.W. Park Ave.
P.O. Box 1383
Portland, OR 97207   Phone: (503)725-4890
      Anthony J. Midson, Dir.
Founded: 1932. **Staff:** Prof 1; Other 4. **Subjects:** General subjects. **Holdings:** 7000 16mm films; 3000 videotapes. **Services:** Rental collection available to public. **Publications:** Collection catalog - free upon request. **Remarks:** FAX: (503)725-4882. Contains the holdings of the Oregon Art Institute - Northwest Film and Video Center - Circulating Film Library.

★ 13248 ★
Portland State University - Middle East Studies Center (Area-Ethnic, Soc Sci)
Box 751
Portland, OR 97207   Phone: (503)725-4074
Founded: 1962. **Staff:** 2.25. **Subjects:** Arabic, Hebrew, Persian, and Turkish languages. **Holdings:** 34,000 volumes in vernacular languages; additional volumes in Western languages to supplement area studies. **Subscriptions:** 12 newspapers. **Services:** Interlibrary loan; copying; center open to the public with restrictions. **Computerized Information Services:** OCLC; SIRSI (internal database). **Networks/Consortia:** Member of Western Library Network (WLN). **Remarks:** Holdings housed at Portland State University - Millar Library. Alternate telephone number(s): (503)725-4617. FAX: (503)725-4882. **Staff:** William Abrams, Coord.; Janet K. Wright, Humanities Libn.

★ 13249 ★
John Portman & Associates - Library (Plan)
231 Peachtree St., N.E., Suite 200   Phone: (404)614-5010
Atlanta, GA 30303   Alice Stevens, Rsrc.Coord.
Founded: 1972. **Staff:** 1. **Subjects:** Architecture, civil engineering, construction industry, real estate, art, interior design. **Special Collections:** Archives of John Portman. **Holdings:** 2750 books; 259 bound periodical volumes; 1000 tubes of drawings, reports, clippings; 21,000 sheets of microfilm; 10,000 photographs and slides; drawings. **Subscriptions:** 114 journals and other serials; 7 newspapers. **Services:** Interlibrary loan; library not open to the public. **Remarks:** FAX: (404)614-5400.

★ 13250 ★
(Porto Alegre) Instituto Cultural Brasileiro Norteamericano - USIS Collection (Educ)
Rua Riachuelo, 1257, 3rd Andar   Phone: 512 252255
90000 Porto Alegre, RS, Brazil   Tania Morandi Ayub, Libn.
Founded: 1938. **Staff:** 5. **Holdings:** 19,000 books; 4000 audio recordings; 132 video recordings. **Subscriptions:** 68 journals and other serials; 5 newspapers. **Services:** Interlibrary loan; copying; SDI; library open to the public. **Computerized Information Services:** Internal database. **Remarks:** Maintained or supported by the U.S. Information Agency. Focus is on materials that will assist peoples outside the United States to learn about the United States, its people, history, culture, political processes, and social milieux.

★ 13251 ★
Portsmouth Athenaeum - Library and Museum (Hist)
9 Market Sq.
Box 848
Portsmouth, NH 03801-0848   Phone: (603)431-2538
      Ronan Donohoe, Pres.
Founded: 1817. **Staff:** 3. **Subjects:** Local history, genealogy, 19th century travel and description, biography. **Special Collections:** Local and New England Maritime/Naval History; New Hampshire Fire & Marine Insurance Company records, 1801-1822; local history, politics, and military affairs, 1700-1900 (450 manuscripts); Green's Drug Store records (83 volumes; 7 boxes); Portsmouth Fire Societies and Companies (5 volumes); Arthur D. Hill Collection (17 boxes); Peirce and Haven family manuscripts (3 boxes); 18th and 19th century English and American magazines; Wendell family papers, 1738-1982 (44 linear feet); Pepperrell papers (1 box); North Church deposit; photograph collection (9 linear feet); Frost Family Papers (2 linear feet); William Badger Papers (1 linear foot); Kittery Point Congregational Church Library (300 volumes); St. John's Church records (3 linear feet); South Church records. **Holdings:** 32,000 books; 350 bound volumes of New Hampshire newspapers; charts; maps. **Subscriptions:** 25 journals and other serials. **Services:** Library open to the public three days a week or by appointment. **Staff:** Jane M. Porter, Kpr.; F. Jeanette Mitchell, Libn.; Carolyn Eastman, Spec.Coll.

★ 13252 ★
Portsmouth Bar and Law Library (Law)
Scioto County Court House, 3rd Fl.   Phone: (614)353-8259
Portsmouth, OH 45662   Charles L. Smith, Libn.
Staff: 1. **Subjects:** Law. **Holdings:** 25,000 volumes. **Services:** Library not open to the public.

★ 13253 ★
Portsmouth General Hospital - Medical Library (Med)
850 Crawford Pkwy.   Phone: (804)398-4217
Portsmouth, VA 23704   Sallie B. Dellinger, Libn.
Staff: Prof 1. **Subjects:** Medicine, allied health sciences. **Special Collections:**
Continuing Medical Education Video Cassette Tapes. **Holdings:** 985 books;
2150 bound periodical volumes; 60 other cataloged items. **Subscriptions:** 30
journals and other serials. **Services:** Interlibrary loan; library not open to the
public. **Remarks:** FAX: (804)398-4130.

★ 13254 ★
**Portsmouth Military Museum and Library - Military Aviation Archives
    and Library** (Mil)
1106 Maplewood Ave.   Phone: (603)436-5835
Portsmouth, NH 03801   Mr. W.M. Cleveland, Hist.
Founded: 1973. **Staff:** Prof 1. **Subjects:** World War II; air war in the Pacific,
Korea, Vietnam; U.S. military aviation history and military history.
Holdings: 75 books; 11 cubic feet of reports and archival materials; 200 reels
of microfilm; 6 VF drawers; 20 boxes. **Services:** Copying; library open to the
public by appointment.

★ 13255 ★
Portsmouth Naval Shipyard Museum - Marshall W. Butt Library (Mil)
2 High St.
Box 248
Portsmouth, VA 23705   Phone: (804)393-8591
                                      Alice C. Hanes, Cur.
Founded: 1962. **Staff:** 3. **Subjects:** Naval history and ordnance, local history,
Norfolk naval shipyard. **Special Collections:** Early naval ordnance books
and engineer journals. **Holdings:** 4000 books. **Subscriptions:** 10 journals and
other serials. **Services:** Copying; library open to the public by appointment.

★ 13256 ★
Portsmouth Psychiatric Center - Medical Library
301 Fort Ln.
Portsmouth, VA 23704
Defunct.

★ 13257 ★
Portsmouth Public Library - Local History Room (Hist)
601 Court St.   Phone: (804)393-8501
Portsmouth, VA 23704   Mrs. Brooke Maupin, Lib.Asst.
Staff: 1. **Subjects:** Local history, lighthouses and lightships, genealogy.
Special Collections: Judge White Collection; Lee Rogers Collection
(photographs of Portsmouth's Black community, 1920s-1960s; 6
scrapbooks). **Holdings:** 4000 books; 200 bound periodical volumes; 70 maps;
350 documents; 21,400 photographs; Norfolk County and Portsmouth wills
and deeds, 1637-1820. **Services:** Interlibrary loan; copying; room open to the
public. **Automated Operations:** Computerized public access catalog,
cataloging, acquisitions, and circulation. **Special Indexes:** Portsmouth and
Norfolk County Documents; Emmerson Papers (abstracts of local
newspapers, 1700-1880); Butt papers (17th century land holdings in Norfolk
county; all on cards). **Remarks:** FAX: (804)393-5107. **Staff:** Susan H.
Burton, Hd., Ref.

★ 13258 ★
Portsmouth Receiving Hospital - Medical Library (Med)
25th St. & Elmwood Dr.
Box 561
Portsmouth, OH 45662   Phone: (614)354-2804
                                      Marilyn Stafford, Educ.Dir.
Founded: 1966. **Staff:** Prof 1. **Subjects:** Psychiatry, psychology, allied health
sciences. **Holdings:** 1509 books; 26 bound periodical volumes. **Subscriptions:**
24 journals and other serials. **Services:** Interlibrary loan; library open to
college students for reference use only. **Networks/Consortia:** Member of
Ohio Valley Area Libraries (OVAL). **Remarks:** Maintained by Ohio State
Department of Mental Health.

★ 13259 ★
**Portugal - Directorate General of Shipping - Information and
    Documentation - Library** (Trans)
Praca Luis de Camoes 22   Phone: 1 3473821
P-1200 Lisbon, Portugal   Maria Leonor Oliveira, Dir.
Founded: 1940. **Staff:** Prof 3; Other 3. **Subjects:** Maritime transport,
shipbuilding, maritime law, shipping, ports, maritime policy. **Special
Collections:** Reference manuals (50 volumes); Portuguese shipping
collection (500 volumes). **Holdings:** 5000 books; 3000 bound periodical
volumes; 800 reports. **Subscriptions:** 180 journals and other serials; 13
newspapers. **Services:** Interlibrary loan; copying; SDI; library open to the
public. **Computerized Information Services:** Bibliographic internal
database. **Publications:** Boletim - DGNTM; Publicacoes Recedidas;
Legislacas. **Remarks:** FAX: 1 3476423. Telex: 16753.

Portugal - Laboratorio Nacional de Engenharia Civil
See: Portugal - Ministerio das Obras Publicas Transportes e
Communicacoes (13260)

Portugal - Ministerio de Habitadao e Obras Publicas
See: Portugal - Ministerio das Obras Publicas Transportes e
Communicacoes (13260)

★ 13260 ★
**Portugal - Ministerio das Obras Publicas Transportes e Communicacoes
    - Laboratorio Nacional de Engenharia Civil - Library** (Sci-Engr)
Avenida do Brasil, 101   Phone: 8482131
P-1799 Lisbon Codex, Portugal   Eduardo Sampaio Franco, Res.Off.
Subjects: Building, construction and materials, structures, geotechnics,
hydraulics, roads, airfields, dams. **Holdings:** 105,000 books; 1500 bound
periodical volumes. **Services:** Copying; SDI; library open to the public.
Computerized Information Services: Questel, DIALOG Information
Services, ESA/IRS. Performs searches on fee basis. **Publications:** Technical
papers, standards, specifications, handbooks. **Remarks:** Telex: 16760.
Formerly: Portugal - Ministerio de Habitadao e Obras Publicas.

★ 13261 ★
Portugal - Ministry of Education - Institute of Anthropology - Library
    (Soc Sci, Biol Sci)
University of Coimbra   Phone: 39 29051
P-3000 Coimbra, Portugal   Maria Isilda Figueiras, Libn.
Founded: 1885. **Staff:** 5. **Subjects:** Sociocultural and physical anthropology,
social biology, human genetics, paleoanthropology. **Holdings:** 14,000 books;
13,700 bound periodical volumes. **Subscriptions:** 435 journals and other
serials. **Services:** Interlibrary loan; copying; library open to the public.
Publications: Boletine Informativo, bimonthly - on exchange. **Remarks:**
FAX: 39 23491. Affiliated with University of Coimbra. **Staff:** Maria Isabel
da Costa Lourenco Simoes; Maria Margarida Santana Henriques; Maria
Aldina Campos da Paz; Adelina da Conceicao Santos.

★ 13262 ★
**Portugal - National Institute for Scientific Research - Scientific and
    Technical Documentation Center** (Info Sci)
Ave. Prof. Gama Pinto 2   Phone: 1 762891
P-1699 Lisbon Codex, Portugal Gabriela Lopes da Silva, Hd., Info.Dept.
Founded: 1946. **Staff:** 15. **Subjects:** Information science, librarianship.
Holdings: 300 bound volumes. **Subscriptions:** 200 journals and other serials.
Services: SDI; center open to government agencies and private businesses.
Computerized Information Services: ESA/IRS, STN International,
DIALOG Information Services, Questel, BLAISE; Data-Mail (electronic
mail service). Performs searches. **Publications:** Union List of Periodicals
existing in Portuguese Libraries. **Remarks:** FAX: 1 765622. Telex: 62593
IIFM P. Electronic mail address(es): G. Lopes da Silva (Data-Mail). **Also
Known As:** Instituto Nacional de Investigacao Cientifica. **Staff:** Lusa
Barreira; Teresa Amaro; Antonieta Vigario; Rosario Costa; Mrs. M. Jose
Campos.

★ 13263 ★
Portugal - Portuguese Navy - Naval Central Library (Mil, Hist, Trans)
Praca do Imperio   Phone: 1 3620029
P-1400 Lisbon, Portugal   Victor Crespo, Rear Admiral
Founded: 1835. **Staff:** Prof 13; Other 15. **Subjects:** Naval sciences, naval
history, Portuguese discoveries, travelling literature, colonial history,
marine sciences. **Special Collections:** 16th century book collection (300);
17th century book collection (700); manuscripts and several bequeathed
libraries; geographical maps and atlases; 18th and 19th century navigation
charts (2000). **Holdings:** 40,000 book titles; 1200 bound periodical titles; 414
manuscripts; 4 incunabulas. **Services:** Copying; library open to the public;
rare books available to researchers with credentials only. **Automated
Operations:** Computerized cataloging. **Computerized Information Services:**
CDS/ISIS, Mini-Micro Systems. Contact Person: Dr. Alice Santos, First
Libn. **Special Indexes:** NCL XV, XVI Century Books Index; Teixeira Da
Mota and Nunes Ribeiro Bequeathed Libraries Index. **Remarks:** FAX: 1
3620028.

★ 13264 ★
Portuguese Continental Union of the U.S.A. - Library (Area-Ethnic)
899 Boylston St.   Phone: (617)536-2916
Boston, MA 02115   Francisco T. Mendonca, Supreme Sec.
Founded: 1955. **Staff:** 2. **Subjects:** Portugal and overseas provinces - history, geography, statistics, literature. **Holdings:** 2200 volumes. **Services:** Library open to members for reference and research work on request.

★ 13265 ★
Portuguese Foundry Association - Technical Library (Energy)
Rua do Campo Alegre 672-2E
P-4100 Porto, Portugal   Phone: 2 6090675
Founded: 1964. **Staff:** 5. **Subjects:** Portuguese foundry industry. **Holdings:** 12,000 volumes. **Subscriptions:** 30 journals and other serials. **Services:** Interlibrary loan; library not open to the public. **Publications:** Fundiegao (magazine); Portuguese Foundry Directory. **Remarks:** FAX: 2 6000764. Telex: 27180 APF P. **Also Known As:** Asociacao Portuguesa de Fundicao.

Portuguese Navy - Naval Central Library
See: Portugal - Portuguese Navy - Naval Central Library (13263)

★ 13266 ★
POS Pilot Plant Corporation - Library (Food-Bev)
118 Veterinary Rd.   Phone: (306)975-7066
Saskatoon, SK, Canada S7N 2R4   Betty Vankoughnett, Mgr., Info. Serv.
Founded: 1977. **Staff:** Prof 1; Other 4. **Subjects:** Oilseeds, chemistry, food science and technology. **Special Collections:** Corporate archives; slide and photograph collection (3000). **Holdings:** 4000 books; 380 bound periodical volumes; 2 VF drawer of patents; 1 VF drawer of reports; 7000 reprints. **Subscriptions:** 270 journals and other serials; 9 newspapers. **Services:** Interlibrary loan; copying; library open to the public for reference use only. **Computerized Information Services:** DIALOG Information Services, CAN/OLE, UTLAS, CCINFO, Infomart Online; internal database. Performs searches on fee basis. **Publications:** exPOSure, quarterly. **Remarks:** FAX: (306)975-3766.

C.W. Post Campus
See: Long Island University (9296)

★ 13267 ★
Post-Tribune - Library (Publ)
1065 Broadway   Phone: (219)881-3134
Gary, IN 46402   Louise K. Tucker, Chf.Libn.
Founded: 1936. **Staff:** Prof 1; Other 2. **Subjects:** Newspaper reference topics. **Special Collections:** Gary history; anniversary and special editions. **Holdings:** 300 books; 55 VF drawers of biographical clippings; 80 VF drawers of subject clipping files; 40 VF drawers of local and national photographs; microfilm, 1909 to present. **Services:** Library not open to the public. **Computerized Information Services:** VU/TEXT Information Services; internal database. Performs searches on fee basis. **Remarks:** FAX: (219)881-3232.

★ 13268 ★
Winfred L. and Elizabeth C. Post Foundation - Post Memorial Art Reference Library (Art)
300 Main St.   Phone: (417)782-5419
Joplin, MO 64801-2384   Leslie Simpson, Libn./Dir.
Founded: 1981. **Staff:** Prof 1; Other 1. **Subjects:** Visual arts, antiques, architecture, photography, historic preservation, heraldry. **Special Collections:** Picture file (reproductions of works of art; 4000 pictures); 16th and 17th century furniture; sculpture and paintings, 13th century to present; Joplin's historic buildings and homes (slides; photographs). **Holdings:** 2500 books; 228 bound periodical volumes; 16 VF drawers of pictures, articles, pamphlets; 1000 slides. **Subscriptions:** 31 journals and other serials. **Services:** Copying; library open to the public.

★ 13269 ★
Rubin Postaer and Associates - Marketing Information Center (Bus-Fin)
11601 Wilshire Blvd.   Phone: (213)208-5000
Los Angeles, CA 90025   Maria Hinds, Mgr., Info.Serv.
Founded: 1981. **Staff:** Prof 1. **Subjects:** Advertising, marketing. **Holdings:** 300 books; 350 subject and company files. **Subscriptions:** 200 journals and other serials. **Services:** Center not open to the public. **Computerized Information Services:** DIALOG Information Services, NEXIS, DataTimes. **Remarks:** FAX: (213)478-3106.

Postal History Society Library
See: American Philatelic Research Library (711)

★ 13270 ★
Postgraduate Center for Mental Health - Emil & Lilly Gutheil Memorial Library (Med)
124 E. 28th St.   Phone: (212)689-7700
New York, NY 10016   Leona Mackler, Dir.
Founded: 1947. **Staff:** Prof 1; Other 2. **Subjects:** Psychiatry, psychology, psychoanalysis, psychotherapy, clinical social work, pastoral counseling. **Holdings:** 10,000 books; 150 bound periodical volumes; 7000 unbound journals; 2 VF cabinets of pamphlets. **Subscriptions:** 100 journals and other serials. **Services:** Interlibrary loan; copying; SDI; library open to nonaffiliated professionals on fee basis. **Computerized Information Services:** BRS Information Technologies, DIALOG Information Services, MEDLINE. Performs searches on fee basis. **Networks/Consortia:** Member of National Network of Libraries of Medicine - Middle Atlantic Region, Manhattan-Bronx Health Sciences Library Consortia, New York Metropolitan Reference and Research Library Agency. **Publications:** Acquisitions list, quarterly - to staff and fellows. **Remarks:** FAX: (212)889-7276.

★ 13271 ★
Potash Corporation of Saskatchewan - Library Services (Agri)
122 1st Ave., S., Suite 500   Phone: (306)933-8501
Saskatoon, SK, Canada S7K 7G3   Marybelle Peet, Lib.Techn.
Founded: 1979. **Staff:** Prof 1. **Subjects:** Fertilizers, agriculture, engineering, chemicals, computers, business. **Holdings:** 4000 books. **Subscriptions:** 230 journals and other serials; 20 newspapers. **Services:** Library open to students with restrictions. **Automated Operations:** Computerized cataloging. **Computerized Information Services:** DIALOG Information Services. **Remarks:** Alternate telephone number(s): 933-8500. FAX: (306)652-2699. Telex: 074 2699.

★ 13272 ★
Potomac Electric Power Company - Corporate Library - 601 (Sci-Engr)
1900 Pennsylvania Ave., N.W.   Phone: (202)872-2361
Washington, DC 20068   Mary J. Meyers, Mgr.Fin. & Employee Pubns.
Founded: 1932. **Subjects:** Electrical and mechanical engineering, energy, finance, accounting, personnel management, computers, data processing, Washingtoniana. **Holdings:** 8000 volumes; Electric Power Research Institute (EPRI) research reports on microfilm. **Subscriptions:** 215 journals and other serials; 7 newspapers. **Services:** Interlibrary loan; library not open to the public. **Automated Operations:** Computerized acquisitions and circulation. **Computerized Information Services:** DIALOG Information Services, Dow Jones News/Retrieval. **Publications:** Accessions list of new books.

★ 13273 ★
Potomac Hospital - Richard P. Immerman Memorial Library (Med)
2300 Opitz Blvd.   Phone: (703)670-1331
Woodbridge, VA 22191   Debra G. Scarborough, Hea.Sci.Libn.
Founded: 1972. **Staff:** Prof .5. **Subjects:** Medicine, hospital administration, nursing. **Holdings:** 450 books; 1000 microfiche. **Subscriptions:** 200 journals and other serials; 2 newspapers. **Services:** Interlibrary loan; library open to the public for reference use only. **Computerized Information Services:** MEDLARS; OCLC. **Networks/Consortia:** Member of Northern Virginia Health Sciences Libraries.

William Potoroka Memorial Library
See: Alcoholism Foundation of Manitoba (329)

★ 13274 ★
Potter County Law Library (Law)
Court House   Phone: (814)274-9720
Coudersport, PA 16915   Patricia Fluty, Ct.Adm.
Subjects: Law. **Holdings:** 300 books; 25 bound periodical volumes; 10 reports. **Subscriptions:** 50 journals and other serials. **Services:** Copying; library open to the public for reference use only. **Remarks:** FAX: (814)274-0584.

★ 13275 ★
Potter County Law Library (Law)
501 S. Fillmore, Suite 2B   Phone: (806)379-2347
Amarillo, TX 79101   Charlotte Eaton, Libn.
Founded: 1911. **Staff:** Prof 1; Other 1. **Subjects:** Law. **Special Collections:** State reporters, 1800-1900. **Holdings:** 17,000 books; 3000 bound periodical volumes. **Subscriptions:** 14 journals and other serials. **Services:** Copying; library open to the public. **Remarks:** Also serves the Amarillo Bar Association. Alternate telephone number(s): 379-2400. FAX: (806)379-2928.

★ 13276 ★
Pottstown Memorial Medical Center - Medical Staff Library (Med)
1600 E. High St.   Phone: (215)327-7468
Pottstown, PA 19464   Marilyn D. Chapis, Med. Staff Libn.
Staff: 1. **Subjects:** Medical and surgical specialties. **Holdings:** 300 books; 1000 bound periodical volumes. **Subscriptions:** 50 journals and other serials. **Services:** Interlibrary loan; library not open to the public. **Computerized Information Services:** BRS Information Technologies, MEDLARS. **Networks/Consortia:** Member of Delaware Valley Information Consortium (DEVIC), BHSL. **Remarks:** FAX: (215)327-7432.

★ 13277 ★
Pottsville Hospital and Warne Clinic - Medical Library (Med)
420 S. Jackson St.   Phone: (717)621-5033
Pottsville, PA 17901   Diane Leinheiser, Libn.
Founded: 1955. **Staff:** Prof 1. **Subjects:** Medicine, surgery. **Holdings:** 255 books; 1750 bound periodical volumes. **Subscriptions:** 21 journals and other serials. **Services:** Interlibrary loan; copying; will answer brief inquiries and make referrals. **Networks/Consortia:** Member of Central Pennsylvania Health Sciences Library Association (CPHSLA), National Network of Libraries of Medicine - Middle Atlantic Region. **Remarks:** FAX: (717)622-8221.

★ 13278 ★
Poudre Valley Hospital - Medical Library (Med)
1024 Lemay Ave.   Phone: (303)490-4155
Fort Collins, CO 80524   Jerry Carlson, Med.Libn.
Founded: 1969. **Staff:** Prof 1. **Subjects:** Medicine, nursing. **Special Collections:** Ethics; management. **Holdings:** 3000 books; 3500 bound periodical volumes. **Subscriptions:** 225 journals and other serials. **Services:** Interlibrary loan; copying; library open to the public for reference use only. **Computerized Information Services:** MEDLINE, OCLC; internal database. Performs searches on fee basis. **Networks/Consortia:** Member of Colorado Council of Medical Librarians, National Network of Libraries of Medicine - Midcontinental Region, High Plains Regional Library Service System **Publications:** Library DATABANK (newsletter), monthly. **Remarks:** FAX: (303)490-4294.

Ezra Pound Institute of Civilization
See: **Bankers Research Institute (1490)**

★ 13279 ★
Roscoe Pound Foundation - Library (Law)
1050 31st St., N.W.   Phone: (202)965-3500
Washington, DC 20007   Jack Marshall, Exec.Dir.
Founded: 1956. **Staff:** Prof 1. **Subjects:** Jurisprudence, philosophy, social sciences, history, literature, botany. **Special Collections:** Personal library of Dean Roscoe Pound. **Holdings:** 8700 volumes. **Services:** Interlibrary loan; copying; library open to scholars and students with appropriate credentials. **Special Catalogs:** Catalog of publications listed by author (card). **Remarks:** FAX: (202)965-0355.

★ 13280 ★
Powell, Goldstein, Frazer & Murphy - Library (Law)
141 Peachtree St, N.E., 16th Fl.   Phone: (404)572-6600
Atlanta, GA 30303   Barbara Geier, Dir.
Staff: Prof 4; Other 6. **Subjects:** Law - corporation, banking, securities, tax, labor, real estate, health care. **Holdings:** 30,000 books; 1000 bound periodical volumes. **Subscriptions:** 441 journals and other serials. **Services:** Interlibrary loan; library not open to the public. **Automated Operations:** Computerized cataloging, acquisitions, serials, and routing. **Computerized Information Services:** LEGI-SLATE, LEXIS, DIALOG Information Services, WESTLAW, Information America, VU/TEXT Information Services, Dow Jones News/Retrieval; internal databases. **Remarks:** FAX: (404)572-6669. **Staff:** Ruth Fuller, Ref.; Julie Schein, Hd.Libn.; Pattie Johnson, Oper.Libn.

★ 13281 ★
John Wesley Powell Memorial Museum - Library (Hist)
6 N. Lake Powell Blvd.
Box 547
Page, AZ 86040   Phone: (602)645-9496
Founded: 1969. **Staff:** 1. **Subjects:** John Wesley Powell (1834-1902) and his explorations of the Colorado Plateau areas of Utah and Arizona; Dominguez-Escalante expedition of 1776; Lake Powell Country and the Colorado River, 1776-1909; history of the City of Page, 1957 to present. **Holdings:** 4 file drawers of manuscripts and photographs. **Services:** Library open to the public with restrictions from February to November.

Robert L. Powell Memorial Library
See: **Master's College and Seminary - Robert L. Powell Library (9841)**

F.B. Power Pharmaceutical Library
See: **University of Wisconsin--Madison (19597)**

Howard Anderson Power Memorial Library
See: **Magee-Womens Hospital (9534)**

Patrick Power Library
See: **St. Mary's University (14540)**

★ 13282 ★
Powertech Labs Inc. - Library (Sci-Engr)
12388 88th Ave.   Phone: (604)590-7456
Surrey, BC, Canada V3W 7R7   J. Kibblewhite, Libn.
Founded: 1980. **Staff:** Prof 1. **Subjects:** Electrical research, materials testing, polymers and plastics. **Special Collections:** Canadian Electrical Association Research Reports. **Holdings:** 1000 books; 1500 reports; government documents; standards. **Subscriptions:** 200 journals and other serials. **Services:** Interlibrary loan; copying; SDI. **Computerized Information Services:** DIALOG Information Services, PFDS Online, InfoLine, Info Globe, Infomart Online; internal database; Envoy 100 (electronic mail service). **Remarks:** FAX: (604)590-5347. Electronic mail address(es): POWERTECH (Envoy 100). Powertech Labs Inc. is a wholly-owned subsidiary of B.C. Hydro.

David R. Poynter Legislative Research Library
See: **Louisiana State House of Representatives Legislative Services (9369)**

★ 13283 ★
Poynter Institute for Media Studies - Eugene Patterson Library (Info Sci)
801 3rd St., S.   Phone: (813)821-9494
St. Petersburg, FL 33701   Nora Paul, Lib.Dir.
Founded: 1985. **Staff:** Prof 4; Other 1. **Subjects:** Journalism, mass communications, newspaper design and graphics, journalistic ethics, media management, writing and composition. **Special Collections:** Newsleaders videotape series; Organization of News Ombudsmen Archives. **Holdings:** 6000 books; 400 videotapes; vertical files; microfiche. **Subscriptions:** 275 journals and other serials; 40 newspapers. **Services:** Interlibrary loan; library not open to the public. **Computerized Information Services:** DIALOG Information Services, VU/TEXT Information Services, LEXIS, NEXIS, WILSONLINE, DataTimes. Performs searches on fee basis. **Publications:** Bibliographies on newspaper design, media management, ethics, writing (printout), AIDS and the media, and other subjects. **Staff:** Nelida Miranda, Asst.Libn.; David Shedden, Media Libn.

★ 13284 ★
(Poznan) Biblioteka Amerykanska - USIS Library (Educ)
Konsulat Stanow Zjednoczonych Ameryki
Ulica Chopina 4
Poznan, Poland
Remarks: Maintained or supported by the U.S. Information Agency. Focus is on materials that will assist peoples outside the United States to learn about the United States, its people, history, culture, political processes, and social milieux.

★ 13285 ★
Dr. Joseph Pozsonyi Memorial Library (Med)
CPRI
600 Sanatorium Rd.   Phone: (519)471-2540
London, ON, Canada N6H 3W7   Alexander Lyubechansky, Lib.Supv.
Founded: 1960. **Staff:** Prof 1; Other 1. **Subjects:** Administration; audiology;
behavior modification; biochemistry; clinical chemistry; cytogenetics;
electroencephalography; therapy - music, physical, occupational, speech;
neurology; nursing; pathology; nutrition; pediatrics; psychiatry; psychology;
public health; recreation; social work; sociology; special education.
Holdings: 4000 books; 3800 bound periodical volumes; 400 staff papers;
6000 reprints; 60 government directories and acts. **Subscriptions:** 125
journals and other serials. **Services:** Interlibrary loan; copying; library open
to professionals, university and community college faculty, and students.
Computerized Information Services: CD-ROM (MEDLINE). **Publications:**
CPRI Annual Symposium Monographs. **Formerly:** University of Western
Ontario - Dr. Joseph Pozsonyi Memorial Library. **Also Known As:**
Children's Psychiatric Research Institute.

★ 13286 ★
PPG Industries, Inc. - C & R Group - Technical Information Center
(Sci-Engr)
Rosanna Dr.
Box 1009   Phone: (412)492-5443
Allison Park, PA 15101   William J. Birkmeyer, Supv., Info.Serv.
Founded: 1924. **Staff:** Prof 2; Other 3. **Subjects:** Chemistry - paint, polymer,
organic; plastics; resins. **Holdings:** 5000 books; 7000 bound periodical
volumes; 200 linear feet of patents; 142 linear feet of pamphlets, government
documents. **Subscriptions:** 500 journals and other serials. **Services:**
Interlibrary loan; copying; center open to the public with restrictions.
Computerized Information Services: STN International, OCLC, DIALOG
Information Services, PFDS Online. **Networks/Consortia:** Member of
Pittsburgh Regional Library Center (PRLC). **Publications:** Research
Review, monthly - for internal distribution only. **Remarks:** FAX: (412)492-
5509. **Staff:** Mary Lee Richner.

★ 13287 ★
PPG Industries, Inc. - Chemicals Group Technical Center - Technical
Information Center (Sci-Engr)
440 College Park Dr.   Phone: (412)325-5221
Monroeville, PA 15146   Tina B. Ross, Libn.
Founded: 1940. **Staff:** Prof 1; Other 2. **Subjects:** Analytical chemistry,
ophthalmic materials, industrial and specialty chemicals, pigments.
Holdings: 12,000 books; 5000 bound periodical volumes; 30,000 internal
research reports on microfilm; 5 VF drawers of translations; Chemical
Abstracts; U.S. Chemical Patents in microform. **Subscriptions:** 300 journals
and other serials. **Services:** Interlibrary loan; center open to the public with
restrictions. **Automated Operations:** Computerized cataloging, acquisitions,
serials, and circulation. **Computerized Information Services:** DIALOG
Information Services, PFDS Online, NLM, OCLC, STN International;
internal database. **Networks/Consortia:** Member of Pittsburgh Regional
Library Center (PRLC). **Publications:** Technical Reports Abstract Bulletin,
monthly - for internal distribution only. **Remarks:** FAX: (412)325-5105.

★ 13288 ★
PPG Industries, Inc. - Fiber Glass Research Center - Library (Sci-Engr)
Box 2844   Phone: (412)782-5130
Pittsburgh, PA 15230   Cheryl Edwards, Lib.Asst.
Staff: 1. **Subjects:** Fiber glass, glass, plastics, rubber, polymer science.
Special Collections: Foreign and domestic patents on fiber glass science and
technology. **Holdings:** 1500 books; 310 technical reports; 100 translations;
50 college catalogs; internal documents control. **Subscriptions:** 150 journals
and other serials. **Services:** Interlibrary loan; copying; SDI. **Automated
Operations:** Computerized cataloging. **Computerized Information Services:**
STN International, DIALOG Information Services. **Networks/Consortia:**
Member of Pittsburgh Regional Library Center (PRLC). **Publications:**
Patent Bulletin, semimonthly; Current Contents, biweekly. **Special Indexes:**
Index of internal documents (card).

★ 13289 ★
PPG Industries, Inc. - Glass Research Center - Information Services
(Sci-Engr)
Box 11472   Phone: (412)665-8566
Pittsburgh, PA 15238   Patricia C. Edge, Supv.
Founded: 1912. **Staff:** Prof 2; Other 1. **Subjects:** Glass technology, physics,
mathematics, chemistry, engineering. **Special Collections:** U.S. patents on

microfilm. **Holdings:** 25,000 books; 18,000 translations and technical
reports; 1000 16mm cartridges of microfilm of journals; 2000 microfiche of
technical reports. **Subscriptions:** 300 journals and other serials. **Services:**
Interlibrary loan; services not open to the public. **Automated Operations:**
Computerized cataloging and serials. **Computerized Information Services:**
DIALOG Information Services, BRS Information Technologies, OCLC,
PFDS Online. **Networks/Consortia:** Member of Pittsburgh Regional
Library Center (PRLC). **Publications:** Technical Information Bulletin,
monthly - for internal distribution only. **Special Catalogs:** Catalog of
internal research reports (card). **Remarks:** FAX: (412)665-8512. **Staff:**
Hazel Green, Tech.Serv.Libn.

★ 13290 ★
PQ Corporation - Business Library (Bus-Fin)
Box 840   Phone: (215)293-7255
Valley Forge, PA 19482   Barbara S. Mattscheck, Bus.Libn.
Staff: Prof 1; Other 1. **Subjects:** Business, marketing, chemistry,
engineering. **Holdings:** 1500 books. **Subscriptions:** 150 journals and other
serials. **Services:** SDI; library open by personal invitation. **Automated
Operations:** Computerized cataloging, acquisitions, serials, and circulation.
Computerized Information Services: DIALOG Information Services, Dun
& Bradstreet Business Credit Services, Piers (Port Import/Export Reporting
Service), Dow Jones News/Retrieval. **Publications:** Business Page,
bimonthly - for internal distribution only.

★ 13291 ★
PQ Corporation - Technical Information Center (Sci-Engr)
280 Cedar Grove Rd.   Phone: (215)941-2029
Conshohocken, PA 19428-2240 Dolores A. Whitehurst, Mgr., Tech.Info.
Founded: 1927. **Staff:** Prof 1. **Subjects:** Inorganic chemistry, specializing in
soluble silicates and silica. **Holdings:** 2500 books; 550 bound periodical
volumes; 42 VF drawers of reports and patents. **Subscriptions:** 165 journals
and other serials. **Services:** Interlibrary loan; copying; SDI; library open to
the public with approval. **Automated Operations:** Computerized public
access catalog, cataloging, acquisitions, and serials. **Computerized
Information Services:** DIALOG Information Services, ORBIT Search
Service, Dow Jones News/Retrieval, WILSONLINE, STN International,
Data-Star, Questel; OCLC; DIALMAIL, CompuServe Information Service
(electronic mail services). **Networks/Consortia:** Member of PALINET.
Publications: Newsletter, bimonthly. **Remarks:** FAX: (215)825-1421.
Electronic mail address(es): 76675,721 (CompuServe Information Service).

★ 13292 ★
Practising Law Institute - Library (Law)
810 Seventh Ave.   Phone: (212)765-5700
New York, NY 10019   Henry W. Enberg, Sr. Legal Ed.
Founded: 1933. **Staff:** Prof 1. **Subjects:** Law. **Holdings:** 3000 books.
Subscriptions: 50 journals and other serials. **Services:** Library not open to
the public.

★ 13293 ★
Pragmatica Corp. - Library (Sci-Engr)
301 W. Maple Ave., Suite 100   Phone: (703)938-9239
Vienna, VA 22180   Dr. T.K. Gardenier, Libn.
Founded: 1990. **Subjects:** Quantitative literacy, statistics procedure,
optimization, math with music, biostatistics, business statistics, operation
research . **Special Collections:** Garden-ear Math/Stat Series Collection;
Data Efficiency Proceedings Symposium Collection. **Holdings:** 1200 books;
3000 bound periodical volumes; 1000 reports. **Subscriptions:** 12 journals and
other serials; 3 newspapers. **Services:** Library not open to the public.
Computerized Information Services: NLM, MEDLINE, TOXLINE.
Remarks: FAX: (703)938-7134.

★ 13294 ★
Prague - Information and Advisory Centre for Local Culture - Library
(Art, Educ)
Blanicka 4   Phone: 2 251200
CS 120 00 Prague, Czechoslovakia   Hana Kolmanova, Mgr.
Founded: 1991. **Staff:** Prof 3. **Subjects:** Cultural studies, adult education,
amateur art, aesthetic education, music, theatre, dance, graphic art, plastic
art. **Special Collections:** Historical literature from the end of 19th century.
Holdings: 23,000 books; 3000 bound periodical volumes; 6 videotapes; 6
audiocassettes, archival materials. **Services:** Copying; library open to the
public. **Computerized Information Services:** Internal databases.
Publications: Mistni kultura, bulletin; Tvoriva dramtika; Vykricnik;
D'Artaman; Poeticke forum. **Remarks:** FAX: 2 258434. Alternate telephone
number(s): 2 250161.

★ 13295 ★
Prairie Agricultural Machinery Institute - Library (Agri)
Box 1900   Phone: (306)682-2555
Humboldt, SK, Canada S0K 2A0   Sharon Doepker, Libn.
Staff: Prof 1. **Subjects:** Agriculture, farm machinery testing, electronics, business management, photography. **Holdings:** 2283 books; 80 bound periodical volumes; 14,000 technical papers. **Subscriptions:** 100 journals and other serials; 5 newspapers. **Services:** Interlibrary loan; copying; SDI; library open to the public. **Automated Operations:** Computerized cataloging. **Publications:** Evaluation reports - by subscription; master bibliography and updates to technical papers. **Remarks:** FAX: (306)682-5080.

★ 13296 ★
Prairie Bible Institute - Library (Rel-Phil)
Box 4020   Phone: (403)443-5511
Three Hills, AB, Canada T0M 2A0   Ron Jordahl, Lib.Dir.
Staff: Prof 3; Other 4. **Subjects:** Biblical studies, Christian missions, Christian biography, Christian education. **Holdings:** 41,000 books; 715 bound periodical volumes; 40 VF drawers of clippings; 692 reels of microfilm; 98,100 volumes on microfiche; 4500 cassettes. **Subscriptions:** 400 journals and other serials. **Services:** Interlibrary loan; copying; library open to the public. **Automated Operations:** Computerized public access catalog, cataloging, and acquisitions. **Computerized Information Services:** CD-ROM (ERIC). **Remarks:** FAX: (403)443-5540. **Staff:** Dr. Fred Youngs, Pub.Serv.Libn.; Jacob Geddert, Tech.Serv.Libn.; Colleen Charter, Acq.Libn.

Prairie Farm Rehabilitation Administration
See: Canada - Prairie Farm Rehabilitation Administration (2834)

Prairie Migratory Bird Research Centre
See: Canada - Environment Canada, Conservation & Protection - Canadian Wildlife Service (2717)

★ 13297 ★
Prairie View A & M University - Special Collections/University Archives (Hum, Area-Ethnic)
John B. Coleman Library, Rm. 505   Phone: (409)857-3119
Prairie View, TX 77446   Joyce K. Thornton, Interim Lib.Dir.
Founded: 1912. **Staff:** 2. **Special Collections:** T.K. Lawless Collection; Black Heritage of the West Collection; university archives; rare books collection; Blacks in the Military Collection. **Holdings:** 2059 books; 74 bound periodical volumes; 761 reels of microfilm; VF drawers; 1254 folders, pictures, memorabilia; 164 cubic feet of official records; 114 cubic feet of papers; 44 cubic feet of university publications; 19 cubic feet of clippings and pamphlets. **Services:** Interlibrary loan; copying; collections open to the public. **Automated Operations:** Computerized public access catalog (NOTIS) and cataloging. **Computerized Information Services:** DIALOG Information Services, OCLC; internal databases. Performs searches on fee basis. **Networks/Consortia:** Member of Houston Area Research Library Consortium (HARLIC), AMIGOS Bibliographic Council, Inc. **Publications:** Annual report. **Special Catalogs:** Record series control (card). **Remarks:** FAX: (409)857-2755. **Staff:** Eric Key.

Prang-Mark Society
See: American Life Foundation (669)

Gordon W. Prange Collection & Archive
See: University of Maryland, College Park Libraries (18817)

Edward L. Pratt Library
See: Children's Hospital Research Foundation (3584)

★ 13298 ★
Enoch Pratt Free Library - Audio-Visual Department (Aud-Vis)
400 Cathedral St.   Phone: (301)396-4616
Baltimore, MD 21201   Marc Sober
Founded: 1949. **Staff:** Prof 2; Other 13. **Subjects:** History of film, experimental film, music, art, social sciences, other arts and crafts, religion, black history/culture, children's films. **Special Collections:** Maryland and Baltimore history. **Holdings:** 5194 16mm films; 161 super and standard 8mm films; 486 filmstrips; 36,805 slides; 926 videotapes; 120 videodiscs; 412 audiotape cassettes. **Subscriptions:** 14 journals and other serials. **Services:** Interlibrary loan (within Maryland only); department open to the public. **Special Catalogs:** Audio-visual catalog. **Remarks:** FAX: (301)396-5837. **Staff:** FAX: Robert Burke.

★ 13299 ★
Enoch Pratt Free Library - Business, Science and Technology Department (Bus-Fin, Sci-Engr)
400 Cathedral St.   Phone: (301)396-5316
Baltimore, MD 21201   Sherry Ledbetter, Dept.Hd.
Founded: 1916. **Staff:** Prof 8; Other 2. **Subjects:** Science, business, economics, technology, census material, medicine, consumerism. **Special Collections:** Directories (14 shelves); auto repair (40 VF drawers). **Holdings:** 122,769 books; 3750 bound periodical volumes; 128 VF drawers of pamphlets; 2176 shelves of U.S. documents; 360 periodical titles on microfiche; 34 drawers of U.S. documents on microfiche. **Subscriptions:** 1002 journals and other serials. **Services:** Interlibrary loan; copying; department open to the public. **Computerized Information Services:** Mead Data Central. **Networks/Consortia:** Member of Maryland Interlibrary Organization (MILO). **Remarks:** FAX: (301)396-5837. **Staff:** Marcia Dysart, Asst.Hd.

★ 13300 ★
Enoch Pratt Free Library - Fine Arts and Recreation Department (Art, Mus)
400 Cathedral St.   Phone: (301)396-5491
Baltimore, MD 21201   Ellen Luchinsky, Hd.
Staff: Prof 3; Other 3. **Subjects:** Art, music, architecture, sports and recreation, antiques, dance, prints. **Special Collections:** Holme Collection (a chronological record of illustrated books). **Holdings:** 41,000 volumes; 18,865 musical recordings; 64 VF drawers; 196 VF drawers of pictures; 35,000 libretti; 11,800 pieces of sheet music. **Subscriptions:** 172 journals and other serials. **Services:** Interlibrary loan; copying; department open to the public. **Computerized Information Services:** Mead Data Central. **Networks/Consortia:** Member of Maryland Interlibrary Organization (MILO). **Special Indexes:** Song index; analytical index; popular sheet music index; dance index; games index (all on cards). **Remarks:** FAX: (301)396-5837. **Staff:** Ruth Sundermeyer, Prof.Asst.; Paul McCutcheon.

★ 13301 ★
Enoch Pratt Free Library - Job and Career Information Center (Soc Sci)
400 Cathedral St.   Phone: (301)396-5394
Baltimore, MD 21201   Patricia Dougherty, Libn./Couns.
Founded: 1981. **Subjects:** Vocational guidance, job/person matching, trades. **Holdings:** 270 reference titles; 16 VF drawers. **Subscriptions:** 22 journals and other serials. **Services:** Center open to the public. **Remarks:** Center located in Business, Science and Technology Department. FAX: (301)396-5837.

★ 13302 ★
Enoch Pratt Free Library - Maryland Department (Hist)
400 Cathedral St.   Phone: (301)396-5468
Baltimore, MD 21201   John Sandheim, Dept.Hd.
Founded: 1934. **Staff:** Prof 4; Other 3. **Subjects:** State of Maryland - persons, places, subjects. **Holdings:** 40,000 volumes; 7000 uncataloged documents; 2100 maps; 24,000 photographs; 1272 fine prints; 4000 postcards; clippings; pamphlets. **Subscriptions:** 40 journals and other serials. **Services:** Interlibrary loan; copying; department open to the public. **Special Indexes:** Biography file, query file, documents file (all card). **Remarks:** FAX: (301)396-9537. **Staff:** Eva Slezak, Spec.; Jeffrey Korman, Asst.Hd.

★ 13303 ★
Enoch Pratt Free Library - Social Science and History Department (Soc Sci, Hist)
400 Cathedral St.   Phone: (301)396-5430
Baltimore, MD 21201   Harriet Jenkins, Act.Hd.
Staff: Prof 8; Other 2. **Subjects:** Sociology, biography, travel, anthropology, political science, law, history, education. **Special Collections:** Foundation Center Collection; college catalogs (4225). **Holdings:** 250,000 volumes; 161 VF drawers; 250 recordings; depository library for government documents. **Subscriptions:** 625 journals and other serials. **Services:** Interlibrary loan; copying; department open to the public. **Computerized Information Services:** Mead Data Central. **Networks/Consortia:** Member of Maryland Interlibrary Organization (MILO). **Remarks:** FAX: (301)396-5837.

★ 13304 ★
Pratt Institute - Library (Art, Sci-Engr)
200 Willoughby Ave.   Phone: (718)636-3684
Brooklyn, NY 11205   F. William Chickering, Dean of Libs.
Founded: 1887. **Staff:** Prof 11; Other 13. **Subjects:** Fine arts, architecture, library science, science and technology. **Special Collections:** History of printing (2000 volumes). **Holdings:** 201,000 books; 35,000 bound periodical volumes; 11,000 government documents; 198,000 prints; 56,000 art slides; 52,000 microforms. **Subscriptions:** 823 journals. **Services:** Interlibrary loan; copying; library open to the public with restrictions. **Automated Operations:** Computerized public access catalog, cataloging, acquisitions, serials, and circulation. **Computerized Information Services:** DIALOG Information Services, OCLC; CD-ROMs. **Networks/Consortia:** Member of New York Metropolitan Reference and Research Library Agency. **Special Catalogs:** Periodicals in the Library. **Remarks:** FAX: (718)622-6174. **Staff:** Sydney Keaveney, Asst. Dean of Libs.; Josephine McSweeney, Ref.Libn.; Margot Karp, Ref.Libn.; Jean Hines, Art & Arch.Libn.; Dohery Dorszynski, Art & Arch.Libn.; Roger Cartmill, Tech.Serv.Libn.; Steven Cohen, Cat.; Mary L. Vincent, Dir., Multimedia Serv.; Cynthia Johnson, Pub.Serv.Libn.

★ 13305 ★
Pratt Institute - Pratt Manhattan Library (Art)
295 Lafayette St.   Phone: (212)925-8481
New York, NY 10012   F. William Chickering, Dean of Libs.
Founded: 1974. **Staff:** Prof 1. **Subjects:** Decoration and ornament; interiors; furnishings; fashion illustration; portrait, figure, still life, landscape painting; advertising design and illustration; magazine and book illustration; photography and film; furniture design; airbrush technique. **Holdings:** 1500 books; 8 VF drawers; 10,000 pictures; photograph file. **Subscriptions:** 11 journals and other serials. **Services:** Library not open to the public. **Networks/Consortia:** Member of New York Metropolitan Reference and Research Library Agency. **Remarks:** FAX: (212)941-6397. A branch of the Pratt Institute Library, Brooklyn, NY 11205. **Staff:** Debra Leigh Shenkman, Pratt Manhattan Lib.Coord.

★ 13306 ★
Pratt & Lambert, Inc. - Paint Division Laboratory Library
75 Tonawanda St.
Box 22   Phone: (716)873-6000
Buffalo, NY 14207   Maggie Giordano, Libn.
Remarks: FAX: (716)877-9646. No further information was supplied by respondent.

★ 13307 ★
Pratt and Whitney Canada Inc. - Library (Sci-Engr)
1000 Marie Victorin   Phone: (514)647-7341
Longueuil, PQ, Canada J4G 1A1   Elizabeth Reader, Chf.Libn.
Founded: 1958. **Staff:** Prof 3; Other 3. **Subjects:** Aeronautics, mechanical and materials engineering, gas turbine engines, industrial management. **Holdings:** 15,000 books; 2500 periodical volumes; 50,000 reports, patents, standards; 13,000 reports on microfiche. **Subscriptions:** 1200 journals and other serials. **Services:** Interlibrary loan; library not open to the public. **Automated Operations:** Computerized cataloging and serials routing. **Computerized Information Services:** CAN/OLE, WILSONLINE, DIALOG Information Services, InvesText, Infomart Online, Information/Documentation (INFO/DOC); internal database. **Publications:** Periodical Articles bulletin, biweekly - for internal distribution only; Periodicals in the Library, annual; Library Bulletin, Technical Reports Bulletin, both bimonthly - for internal distribution only. **Remarks:** A subsidiary of United Technologies Corporation. FAX: (514)647-7652. **Staff:** Lysane St. Amour, Ref.Libn.

Pratt & Whitney Information Services
See: **United Technologies Corporation** (17962)

★ 13308 ★
PRC Inc. - Technical Library (Comp Sci, Info Sci)
1500 Planning Research Dr.
Mail Stop 1N3   Phone: (703)556-1163
McLean, VA 22102   Pat Garman, Act.Mgr.
Founded: 1961. **Staff:** Prof 4; Other 1. **Subjects:** Computer software, engineering, information science, computer science. **Special Collections:** Data Pro reports. **Holdings:** 12,000 books; 10,000 company reports; 3000

documents; 250 cassettes. **Subscriptions:** 250 journals and other serials; 4 newspapers. **Services:** Interlibrary loan; library not open to the public. **Automated Operations:** Computerized cataloging and circulation. **Computerized Information Services:** DIALOG Information Services, LEXIS, NEXIS, Aerospace Online, OCLC; DUNSNET (electronic mail services). **Networks/Consortia:** Member of Interlibrary Users Association (IUA), CAPCON Library Network. **Publications:** Journal Holdings list; library brochure. **Remarks:** Alternate telephone number(s): 556-1165; 556-1164; 556-1166. FAX: (703)556-1174. **Formerly:** Planning Research Corporation. **Staff:** Alice Hill-Murray, Ref.Libn.; Barbara Kopp, ILL; Patricia Wolf, Acq./Cat.

★ 13309 ★
Precision Castparts Corporation - Technical Information Center (Sci-Engr)
4600 S.E. Harney Dr.   Phone: (503)777-3881
Portland, OR 97206-0898   Andrea J Drury, Tech.Info.Spec.
Staff: Prof 1; Other 1. **Subjects:** Materials, metals, ceramics, physical sciences, robotics and automation, statistics, process control, investment casting, superalloys, titanium, stainless steels, nickel alloys, cobalt alloys. **Holdings:** 1600 books; 2500 unbound reports; 900 patents; 1000 government reports; 1200 reprints. **Subscriptions:** 175 journals and other serials. **Services:** Interlibrary loan; copying; SDI; center open to the public by appointment. **Automated Operations:** Computerized cataloging and serials. **Computerized Information Services:** DIALOG Information Services, OCLC, PFDS Online. **Remarks:** Alternate telephone number(s): (503)652-4544. FAX: (503)652-4532.

★ 13310 ★
Predicasts Library (Publ)
11001 Cedar Ave.   Phone: (216)795-3000
Cleveland, OH 44106   Diane Oberbeck, Mgr.
Founded: 1960. **Staff:** Prof 4; Other 5. **Subjects:** Business, industries, economics, statistics. **Holdings:** 250 books. **Subscriptions:** 1300 journals and other serials; 200 newspapers. **Services:** Library not open to the public. **Automated Operations:** Computerized serials. **Publications:** Predicasts Company Thesaurus; The Source Directory of Predicasts. **Remarks:** FAX: (216)229-9944. Telex 985-604. **Staff:** Cary McCullough, Thesauri Ed.; Lisette Sabbach, Thesauri/Cat.; Christopher Grierson, Ser.Acq.

★ 13311 ★
Preformed Line Products - Research & Engineering Library (Sci-Engr)
660 Beta Dr.
Box 91129   Phone: (216)461-5200
Cleveland, OH 44143   Edwina T. Barron, Libn.
Founded: 1956. **Staff:** Prof 1. **Subjects:** Vibration, fatigue, strains and stresses, fiber optics, pole line hardware, underground distribution, electric power lines. **Special Collections:** CIGRE (International Conference on Large Electric Systems); American Institute of Electrical Engineers. **Holdings:** 5010 books; 195 bound periodical volumes; 65 VF drawers of technical papers (indexed); internal reports on microfiche (indexed); 125 16mm films; 175 videotapes. **Subscriptions:** 200 journals and other serials. **Services:** Interlibrary loan; copying; library open by permission. **Remarks:** FAX: (216)442-8816. Telex: 196195.

★ 13312 ★
Pregnancy and Infant Loss Center - Lending Library (Med)
1415 E. Wayzata Blvd., No. 105   Phone: (612)473-9372
Wayzata, MN 55391   Sherokee Ilse, Pres.
Founded: 1983. **Staff:** Prof 2. **Subjects:** Perinatal bereavement, coping with grief, children and death. **Holdings:** 100 books. **Subscriptions:** 30 newspapers. **Services:** Library open to the public with restrictions. **Automated Operations:** Computerized public access catalog.

★ 13313 ★
Premark International - Business Information Center
1717 Deerfield Rd.
Deerfield, IL 60015
Defunct.

Prentis Memorial Library
See: **Temple Beth El** (16084)

★13314★
Presbyterian Church of the Atonement - Library (Rel-Phil)
10613 Georgia Ave.
Silver Spring, MD 20902   Phone: (301)649-4131
Staff: 1. **Subjects:** Christian doctrine, life and character, missions, biography, education; Bible. **Holdings:** 5500 books; pictures; 500 AV programs; 80 filmstrips; 900 cassette tapes; 250 music tapes; 235 videotapes; 28 maps. **Subscriptions:** 25 journals and other serials. **Services:** Library open to the public.

★13315★
Presbyterian Church (U.S.A.) - Department of History (Montreat) - Library and Archives (Rel-Phil)
Box 849   Phone: (704)669-7061
Montreat, NC 28757   Michelle A. Francis, Dp.Dir.
Founded: 1927. **Staff:** Prof 4; Other 5. **Subjects:** Presbyterianism in the South, Reformed Churches of the world. **Special Collections:** History of churches and women's work in the Presbyterian Church, U.S.A. (6000 volumes); records and minutes of Presbyterian and Reformed Churches of the world (7500 volumes). **Holdings:** 40,000 books; 25,000 bound periodical volumes; 75,000 other cataloged items; 6500 linear feet of archival materials and manuscripts; 3000 reels of microfilm. **Subscriptions:** 150 journals and other serials. **Services:** Interlibrary loan; copying; library open to the public. **Automated Operations:** Computerized cataloging. **Computerized Information Services:** OCLC; internal database (archives and manuscripts). **Networks/Consortia:** Member of SOLINET. **Publications:** Presbyterian Heritage, 3/yr.; Survey of Records and Minutes in the Historical Foundation; The Historical Foundation and its Treasures; Guide to the Manuscript Collection of the Presbyterian Church, U.S.; Eighteenth-Century American Publications; Conservation of Church Records. **Special Catalogs:** Catalogs of Presbyterian and Reformed institutions (printed). **Special Indexes:** Individuals, local churches, photographs (card). **Remarks:** FAX: (704)669-5369. **Staff:** William G. Bynum, Res.Hist.; John M. Walker, III, Cat.Libn.; Diana R. Sanderson, Asst.Res.Hist.

Presbyterian Church (U.S.A.) - Ghost Ranch Conference Center
See: **Ghost Ranch Conference Center** (6463)

★13316★
Presbyterian College - Library (Rel-Phil)
3495 University St.   Phone: (514)288-5257
Montreal, PQ, Canada H3A 2A8   Rev. Daniel Shute, Libn.
Founded: 1867. **Staff:** Prof 1; Other 2. **Subjects:** Reformed theology and history, philosophy. **Special Collections:** Patrologia Graeco-Latina (Migne; 382 volumes). **Holdings:** 22,200 volumes. **Subscriptions:** 50 journals and other serials. **Services:** Interlibrary loan; library open to the public during academic year. **Computerized Information Services:** UTLAS.

★13317★
Presbyterian Healthcare System - Green Learning Center - Library (Med)
8200 Walnut Hill Ln.   Phone: (214)891-2310
Dallas, TX 75231   Barbara D. Pace, Dir., Lib.Serv.
Founded: 1966. **Staff:** 3. **Subjects:** Medicine, nursing, psychiatry. **Holdings:** 2450 books; 3465 bound periodical volumes. **Subscriptions:** 366 journals and other serials. **Services:** Interlibrary loan; copying; library open to the public for medical and nursing research only. **Computerized Information Services:** BRS Information Technologies, MEDLARS; CD-ROM (MEDLINE, CD Plus, CINAHL). **Networks/Consortia:** Member of Health Libraries Information Network (HealthLINE). **Remarks:** FAX: (214)891-2350. **Staff:** Janet Kovatch; Nancy Taylor.

★13318★
Presbyterian Historical Society - Library (Hist, Rel-Phil)
425 Lombard St.   Phone: (215)627-1852
Philadelphia, PA 19147   Frederick J. Heuser, Jr., Dir.
Founded: 1852. **Staff:** Prof 10; Other 7. **Subjects:** Presbyterian Church history, history of Protestantism, hymnology, slavery. **Special Collections:** Sheldon Jackson Collection (Alaska, circa 1870-1905); Westminster Assembly of Divines Collection (300 17th century pamphlets dealing with British church history); Westminster Press Depository Collection (2800 volumes); Religious News Services archives; American Sunday-school Union archives; National Council of Churches archives. **Holdings:** 250,000 books; 1875 reels of microfilm; 9000 pictures of churches and ministers; 5000 communion tokens; 21 million arranged archival materials. **Subscriptions:** 407 journals and other serials. **Services:** Copying; library open to the public. **Publications:** Journal of Presbyterian History, quarterly - to members and by subscription. **Remarks:** FAX: (215)627-0509. **Staff:** Gerald W. Gillette, Mgr., Res. & Lib.Serv.; Barbara Schnur, Tech.Serv.; Kristin Gleeson, Archv.; Boyd Reese, Ref.Serv.

★13319★
Presbyterian Hospital - Learning Resource Center (Med)
Box 33549   Phone: (704)384-4258
Charlotte, NC 28233-3549   Mary Wallace Berry, Libn.
Staff: Prof 2; Other 2. **Subjects:** Nursing, medicine, allied health education. **Holdings:** 6000 books; 3 VF drawers; AV programs. **Subscriptions:** 200 journals and other serials. **Services:** Interlibrary loan; center not open to the public. **Computerized Information Services:** MEDLINE. **Networks/Consortia:** Member of North Carolina Area Health Education Centers Program Library and Information Services Network. **Remarks:** FAX: (704)384-5058.

★13320★
Presbyterian Hospital - Medical Library (Med)
N.E. 13th and Lincoln Blvd.   Phone: (405)271-4266
Oklahoma City, OK 73104   Mary Lou Tremblay, Lib.Dir.
Founded: 1919. **Staff:** Prof 1; Other 1. **Subjects:** Medicine, nursing, surgery, cardiology. **Holdings:** 4000 books; 6000 bound periodical volumes; 24 boxes of pamphlets; 175 file boxes of unbound periodicals; 2 VF drawers; 800 cassettes. **Subscriptions:** 257 journals and other serials. **Services:** Interlibrary loan; library open to medical and health personnel for reference use only. **Computerized Information Services:** MEDLINE. **Networks/Consortia:** Member of Greater Oklahoma City Area Health Sciences Library Consortium (GOAL), Metronet.

★13321★
Presbyterian Hospital - Robert Shafer Memorial Library (Med)
Box 26666   Phone: (505)841-1516
Albuquerque, NM 87125-6666   Revathi A. Davidson, Dir.
Founded: 1962. **Staff:** Prof 3; Other 2. **Subjects:** Medicine. **Holdings:** 1500 books; 460 journal titles; AV collection. **Subscriptions:** 140 journals. **Services:** Interlibrary loan; copying; library open to the public by permission. **Computerized Information Services:** DIALOG Information Services, MEDLARS. **Networks/Consortia:** Member of New Mexico Consortium of Biomedical and Hospital Libraries, National Network of Libraries of Medicine - South Central Region. **Remarks:** Library located at 1100 Central Ave., S.E., Albuquerque, NM 87106. **Staff:** Janet Williams, Libn.; Mary Ellen Kenreich, Libn.

★13322★
Presbyterian Medical Center of Philadelphia - Health Sciences Library (Med)
39TH & Market Sts.   Phone: (215)662-9181
Philadelphia, PA 19104   Julia Urwin, Lib.Dir.
Staff: Prof 1; Other 2. **Subjects:** Clinical medicine, nursing, management. **Holdings:** 2500 books; 3500 bound periodical volumes; 300 archival materials; 70 AV programs; 3 VF drawers. **Subscriptions:** 246 journals and other serials. **Services:** Interlibrary loan; copying; library open to the public with restrictions. **Computerized Information Services:** MEDLARS, BRS Information Technologies, DIALOG Information Services, OCLC; CD-ROMs (Medline, CINAHL). **Networks/Consortia:** Member of Delaware Valley Information Consortium (DEVIC), National Network of Libraries of Medicine - Middle Atlantic Region, BHSL, Philadelphia Regional Interlibrary Loan Group (PRILL), Association of Visual Science Librarians (AVSL). **Remarks:** FAX: (215)662-8453.

Presbyterian-University Hospital
See: **University of Pittsburgh** (19221)

★ 13323 ★
Presbytery of Long Island - Resource Center (Rel-Phil)
50 Hauppauge Rd.   Phone: (516)499-7171
Commack, NY 11725   Rev. R. Scott Sheldon, Assoc.Exec.
Founded: 1983. **Staff:** 1. **Subjects:** Christian education, worship, social issues, women's studies. **Holdings:** 1000 books; 300 videotapes. **Subscriptions:** 35 journals and other serials; 12 newspapers. **Services:** Copying; center open to the public. **Automated Operations:** Computerized cataloging, acquisitions, and circulation. **Computerized Information Services:** Internal database.

★ 13324 ★
Presbytery of Western North Carolina - Resource Center (Rel-Phil)
123 Kenilworth Rd.   Phone: (704)258-8143
Asheville, NC 28803   Sara Dixon, Coord.
Founded: 1984. **Subjects:** Church, theology, Christian living, Bible, Christian education, community services. **Holdings:** 1000 books; 125 videocassettes; 150 filmstrips; 25 audiocassettes; reports. **Services:** Interlibrary loan; library open to the religious community. **Special Catalogs:** Catalog of Resources (in process).

Prescott Historical Society
See: **Sharlot Hall/Prescott Historical Societies** (15081)

Presel Memorial Library
See: **The Providence Center** (13441)

★ 13325 ★
Presentation College - Library (Med, Rel-Phil)
1500 N. Main   Phone: (605)229-8468
Aberdeen, SD 57401   Arvyce Burns, Lib.Dir.
Founded: 1950. **Staff:** Prof 2.5; Other 1. **Subjects:** Nursing, theology, allied health. **Holdings:** 33,797 books; 2317 bound periodical volumes; 2577 recordings, filmstrips, reels of microfilm, cassettes; 8 VF drawers of pamphlets. **Subscriptions:** 210 journals and other serials; 9 newspapers. **Services:** Interlibrary loan; copying; library open to the public with restrictions. **Automated Operations:** Computerized public access catalog, cataloging, and circulation. **Computerized Information Services:** OCLC; CD-ROMs (CINAHL, Magazine Index Select). **Networks/Consortia:** Member of MINITEX Library Information Network, South Dakota Library Network (SDLN). **Remarks:** FAX: (605)229-8489. **Staff:** Anita Bertsch, Asst.Libn.; Sr. Judith O'Brien, Cat.

Presidential Studies Archive
See: **University of California, Davis - Institute of Governmental Affairs - Library** (18352)

President's Committee on Employment of the Handicapped Archives
See: **Marquette University - Department of Special Collections and University Archives - Manuscript Collections Memorial Library** (9709)

★ 13326 ★
Preston Gates Ellis & Rouvelas Meeds - Library (Law)
1735 New York Ave., N.W., Suite 500   Phone: (202)662-8415
Washington, DC 20006   Gretchen W. Asmuth, Libn.
Founded: 1982. **Staff:** Prof 1; Other 1. **Subjects:** Law - federal, maritime, insurance, personal injury litigation, transportation, antitrust, trade, cable communications; lobbying; federal administrative practice. **Special Collections:** Washington state legal materials. **Holdings:** 6000 books. **Subscriptions:** 200 journals and other serials; 15 newspapers. **Services:** Interlibrary loan; copying; library open to the public by appointment. **Computerized Information Services:** LEXIS, NEXIS, LEGI-SLATE, DIALOG Information Services, WESTLAW, DataTimes; internal database. Performs searches on fee basis. **Remarks:** FAX: (202)331-1024.

Halina Wind Preston Holocaust Education Resource Center
See: **Jewish Federation of Delaware & Jewish Community Center** (8389)

Preston Library
See: **Virginia Military Institute** (19867)

Preston Medical Library
See: **University of Tennessee at Knoxville - Medical Center** (19369)

★ 13327 ★
Preston Thorgrimson Shidler Gates & Ellis - Library (Law)
5400 Columbia Center
701 5th Ave.   Phone: (206)623-7580
Seattle, WA 98104   Barbara Cornwell Holt, Lib.Mgr.
Staff: Prof 3; Other 3. **Subjects:** Law. **Holdings:** 30,000 books. **Subscriptions:** 300 journals and other serials; 9 newspapers. **Services:** Interlibrary loan; copying; SDI; library open to the public with permission. **Computerized Information Services:** LEXIS, WESTLAW, DIALOG Information Services, DataTimes, VU/TEXT Information Services. **Publications:** New Acquisitions List, irregular. **Remarks:** FAX: (206)623-7022. **Staff:** Crystal Robinson, Asst.Libn.; Sue Sorensen, Assoc.Libn.

Preus Library
See: **Luther College** (9440)

★ 13328 ★
Prevention & Intervention Center of Alcohol & Other Drug Abuse - Library (Med)
2000 Fordham Ave.   Phone: (608)246-7606
Madison, WI 53704   Martha Nicholson, Libn.
Remarks: No further information was supplied by respondent.

★ 13329 ★
Prevention Research Center - Library (Med)
2532 Durant Ave.   Phone: (510)486-1111
Berkeley, CA 94704   Christina Miller
Founded: 1984. **Staff:** Prof 1. **Subjects:** Alcohol and drug abuse prevention research. **Holdings:** 700 books; 4000 reprints. **Subscriptions:** 35 journals and other serials. **Services:** Library not open to the public. **Automated Operations:** Computerized cataloging. **Computerized Information Services:** DIALOG Information Services, BRS Information Technologies. **Networks/Consortia:** Member of Substance Abuse Librarians and Information Specialists (SALIS).

Bernice Ford Price Reference Library
See: **Oklahoma Historical Society** (12351)

Isser and Rae Price Library of Judaica
See: **University of Florida** (18573)

★ 13330 ★
Price-Pottenger Nutrition Foundation - Library (Food-Bev, Biol Sci)
5871 El Cajon Blvd.   Phone: (619)582-4168
San Diego, CA 92115   Marion Patricia Connolly, Exec.Dir.
Founded: 1975. **Staff:** 3. **Subjects:** Nutrition research, preventative medicine, health, agrobiology, gardening, pesticides. **Special Collections:** Complete works of Dr. Weston A. Price and Dr. Francis M. Pottenger; Linda Clark Library; pesticide research of Dr. G.F. Knight; papers of Dr. William A. Albrecht; scientific studies. **Holdings:** Scientific reprints; tapes; videotapes. **Services:** Library open to the public for reference use only. **Publications:** PPNF Journal, quarterly.

★ 13331 ★
Price Waterhouse - Information Center (Bus-Fin)
400 S. Hope St.   Phone: (213)236-3515
Los Angeles, CA 90071-2889   Mignon Veasley, Hd.Libn.
Staff: Prof 2; Other 1. **Subjects:** Accounting, business, management, investment, auditing, taxation. **Holdings:** 550 books; 385 bound periodical volumes; 1050 microfiche; 312 reels of microfilm. **Subscriptions:** 400 journals and other serials. **Services:** Interlibrary loan; center not open to the public. **Computerized Information Services:** LEXIS, NEXIS, DIALOG Information Services, DataTimes, WILSONLINE, VU/TEXT Information Services, InvesText, Dow Jones News/Retrieval, UMI Article Clearinghouse (UMAC), Interactive Data Services, Information America, Prentice Hall Online. **Publications:** Periodical list, annual; acquisitions list, bimonthly; Authoritative Sources Update, quarterly. **Remarks:** FAX: (213)622-9062. Telex: 6831270. **Staff:** Dorothy Royse, Asst.Libn.

★ 13332 ★
Price Waterhouse - Information Center (Bus-Fin)
200 S. Biscayne Blvd., Suite 3000   Phone: (305)381-9400
Miami, FL 33131   Christine Molineri, Info.Spec.
Staff: Prof 1; Other 2. **Subjects:** Accounting and auditing, taxation, business. **Holdings:** 1500 books; 600 annual reports; Price Waterhouse external publications; 55 loose-leaf services. **Subscriptions:** 80 journals and other serials; 6 newspapers. **Services:** Interlibrary loan; center open to the public by appointment. **Computerized Information Services:** DIALOG Information Services, LEXIS, NEXIS, VU/TEXT Information Services, DataTimes. **Remarks:** FAX: (305)381-7696.

★ 13333 ★
Price Waterhouse - Information Center (Bus-Fin)
160 Federal St.   Phone: (617)439-7412
Boston, MA 02110   Jean M. Scanlan, Dir.
Founded: 1976. **Staff:** Prof 2. **Subjects:** Accounting, taxation, management, finance. **Holdings:** 2500 books; microfiche. **Subscriptions:** 300 journals and other serials. **Services:** Interlibrary loan; copying; SDI; center open to the public by appointment. **Automated Operations:** Computerized cataloging. **Computerized Information Services:** DunsPrint, DIALOG Information Services, PFDS Online, DataTimes, Dow Jones News/Retrieval, LEXIS, NewsNet, Inc., VU/TEXT Information Services; DIALMAIL (electronic mail service). Performs searches on fee basis. **Publications:** What's New in the Price Waterhouse Information Center, monthly - for internal distribution only. **Remarks:** FAX: (617)439-7393. **Staff:** Nic Cooper, Asst to Dir.

★ 13334 ★
Price Waterhouse - Information Center (Bus-Fin)
200 Renaissance Ctr., Suite 3900   Phone: (313)259-0500
Detroit, MI 48243   Jerrie Calloway, Info.Spec.
Founded: 1976. **Staff:** Prof 1. **Subjects:** Accounting, taxation. **Holdings:** 5500 books; 8 boxes of microfiche; Price Waterhouse publications. **Subscriptions:** 180 journals and other serials; 18 newspapers. **Services:** Center not open to the public. **Automated Operations:** Computerized cataloging. **Computerized Information Services:** DIALOG Information Services, VU/TEXT Information Services, LEXIS, NEXIS, Dun & Bradstreet Business Credit Services. **Remarks:** FAX: (313)568-5265.

★ 13335 ★
Price Waterhouse - Information Center (Bus-Fin)
1001 Fourth Avenue Plaza, Suite 4200   Phone: (206)622-1505
Seattle, WA 98154   Michael R. McPherson, Info.Spec.
Founded: 1972. **Staff:** Prof 1; Other 1. **Subjects:** Accounting, taxation, auditing, management, data processing, litigation. **Holdings:** 3540 books; 50 state tax services; loose-leaf tax services. **Subscriptions:** 360 journals and other serials; 22 newspapers. **Services:** Center not open to the public. **Automated Operations:** Computerized cataloging. **Computerized Information Services:** CCH Access, DIALOG Information Services, Dun & Bradstreet Business Credit Services, Dow Jones News/Retrieval, LEXIS, NEXIS, National Automated Accounting Research System (NAARS), DataTimes; internal databases. Performs searches on fee basis. **Publications:** Acquisitions list, monthly - for internal distribution only.

★ 13336 ★
Price Waterhouse - Library (Bus-Fin)
200 E. Randolph Dr.   Phone: (312)565-1500
Chicago, IL 60601   Ann Raup, Libn.
Founded: 1970. **Staff:** 2. **Subjects:** Accounting, auditing, management. **Holdings:** 1000 books; 120 bound periodical volumes; 49 VF drawers of corporate annual reports. **Subscriptions:** 133 journals and other serials. **Services:** Interlibrary loan (local only); library open to the public by appointment.

★ 13337 ★
Price Waterhouse - Library (Bus-Fin)
121 S.W. Morrison, Suite 1800   Phone: (503)224-9040
Portland, OR 97204   Beckie Kennedy, Libn.
Founded: 1979. **Staff:** Prof 1. **Subjects:** Tax law, accounting, auditing, management consulting. **Holdings:** Figures not available. **Subscriptions:** 80 journals and other serials; 7 newspapers. **Services:** Interlibrary loan; copying; SDI; library open to the public by appointment. **Publications:** New books list, bimonthly. **Special Catalogs:** Management proposals and reports; brochures (both online).

★ 13338 ★
Price Waterhouse - Library (Bus-Fin)
601 W. Hastings St.   Phone: (604)682-4711
Vancouver, BC, Canada V6B 5A5   Janet A. Parkinson, Supv., Lib. and Res.
Founded: 1980. **Staff:** Prof 1. **Subjects:** Accounting, auditing, taxation, management consulting. **Holdings:** 2000 volumes; newspaper financial pages; Price Waterhouse external publications; company annual reports for 500 Canadian companies. **Subscriptions:** 50 journals and other serials; 7 newspapers. **Services:** Interlibrary loan; library not open to the public. **Computerized Information Services:** DIALOG Information Services, Infomart Online. Performs searches on fee basis (clients only). **Remarks:** FAX: (604)662-5300.

★ 13339 ★
Price Waterhouse - Library (Bus-Fin)
20 Queen St., W., Suite 200
Box 75   Phone: (416)977-2555
Toronto, ON, Canada M5H 3V7   Margaret Ashton, Libn.
Staff: Prof 1. **Subjects:** Hospitality, real estate, taxation, accounting. **Special Collections:** Leisure time industries; lodging; taxation. **Holdings:** Figures not available. **Subscriptions:** 65 journals and other serials; 7 newspapers. **Services:** Interlibrary loan; copying; SDI; library open to the public with restrictions. **Automated Operations:** INMAGIC. **Computerized Information Services:** Info Globe, Infomart Online, QL Systems, DIALOG Information Services, Canadian Tax Online. **Remarks:** FAX: (416)977-3538.

★ 13340 ★
Price Waterhouse - Library
1100, blvd. Rene Levesque W.
Montreal, PQ, Canada H3B 2G4
Founded: 1945. **Subjects:** Accounting, auditing, management, consulting, taxation. **Holdings:** 600 books; 100 bound periodical volumes. **Remarks:** Currently inactive.

★ 13341 ★
Price Waterhouse - National Information Center (Bus-Fin)
1251 Ave. of the Americas   Phone: (212)819-5000
New York, NY 10020   Masha Zipper, Dir., Info.Serv.
Founded: 1902. **Staff:** Prof 9; Other 10. **Subjects:** Accounting, auditing, business, management consulting, United States and international taxation. **Holdings:** 15,000 books. **Subscriptions:** 500 journals and other serials. **Services:** Interlibrary loan (to staff, clients and SLA members). **Automated Operations:** Computerized cataloging and routing system. **Computerized Information Services:** DIALOG Information Services, Dow Jones News/Retrieval, LEXIS, NEXIS, National Automated Accounting Research System (NAARS), ORBIT Search Service, WILSONLINE, VU/TEXT Information Services, NewsNet, Inc.; CD-ROMs. **Publications:** National Information Center Acquisitions. **Special Indexes:** Price Waterhouse Review Twenty-Five Year Index, 1955-1980. **Remarks:** FAX: (212)790-6641. **Staff:** Terry Bennett, Info.Serv.Mgr.; Jane Axelrod, U.S. Tax Spec.; Dennis Dilno, Tech.Serv.Mgr.; Chung Lee, Info.Spec.; Rita Van Buren, Intl. Tax Spec.; Denise Whitmire, Tech.Serv.Spec.; Deborah Yaffe, Info.Spec.

★ 13342 ★
Price Waterhouse - National/Toronto Office Library (Bus-Fin)
1 First Canadian Place, Suite 3300   Phone: (416)863-1133
Box 190   Dorothy L. Sedgwick, Mgr., Info./
Toronto, ON, Canada M5X 1H7   Lib.Serv.
Founded: 1976. **Staff:** Prof 2; Other 2. **Subjects:** Accounting, auditing, business, finance, management. **Holdings:** 5000 volumes; annual reports for 1200 Canadian, U.S., and other corporations; Conference Board publications; financial statements for Canadian federally incorporated companies on CD-ROM. **Subscriptions:** 400 journals and other serials; 6 newspapers. **Services:** Interlibrary loan; library not open to the public. **Automated Operations:** Computerized cataloging. **Computerized Information Services:** PFDS Online, Info Globe, QL Systems, DIALOG Information Services, Dun & Bradstreet Business Credit Services, The Financial Post DataGroup, Mead Data Central; internal database. **Remarks:** FAX: (416)947-8998. **Staff:** Nancy Wells, Asst.Libn.; Elizabeth Gibbon, Techn.

★ 13343 ★
Price Waterhouse - New York Office Information Center (Bus-Fin)
153 E. 53rd St.   Phone: (212)371-2000
New York, NY 10022   Patricia R. Pauth, Mgr.
Founded: 1972. **Staff:** Prof 4; Other 4. **Subjects:** Accounting, auditing, business, finance. **Holdings:** 5000 books; 90 bound periodical volumes; corporation reports for 2000 companies; securities prices in microform. **Subscriptions:** 350 journals and other serials. **Services:** Interlibrary loan; center open to the public by appointment. **Automated Operations:** Computerized cataloging. **Computerized Information Services:** DIALOG Information Services, Dow Jones News/Retrieval, LEXIS, NEXIS, Dun & Bradstreet Business Credit Services; internal database. **Remarks:** FAX: (212)685-5460; (212)355-0688. **Staff:** Elizabeth Croft, Asst.; Barbara Posner, Info.Spec.; Jessica McBride, Info.Spec.

★ 13344 ★
Price Waterhouse - Tax Library (Law)
153 E. 53rd St.   Phone: (212)371-2000
New York, NY 10022   Ann Hayes, Tax Libn.
Staff: 1. **Subjects:** Taxation law, international tax law. **Holdings:** 500 books; 280 bound periodical volumes. **Subscriptions:** 22 journals and other serials. **Services:** Interlibrary loan; library open to clients and SLA members. **Computerized Information Services:** LEXIS. **Remarks:** FAX: (212)688-5460.

Cleveland Prichard Memorial Library
See: **Bienville Historical Society** (1835)

★ 13345 ★
Prickett, Jones, Elliott, Kristol, Schnee Law Offices - Law Library
   (Law)
1310 King St.
Box 1328   Phone: (302)888-6500
Wilmington, DE 19899   Loretta Yaller, Libn.
Staff: 1.5. **Subjects:** Law. **Holdings:** 11,000 books. **Services:** Interlibrary loan; library not open to the public. **Computerized Information Services:** LEXIS, WESTLAW, DIALOG Information Services, VU/TEXT Information Services, LEGI-SLATE, Dow Jones News/Retrieval, Dun's Legal Search. **Remarks:** FAX: (302)658-8111.

PRIDE
See: **National Parents' Resource Institute for Drug Education, Inc.**
   (11249)

Bill J. Priest Institute for Economic Development
See: **Dallas County Community College District** (4547)

Joseph Priestley Collection
See: **Bowdoin College - Library - Special Collections** (2033)

Diana M. Priestly Law Library
See: **University of Victoria - Diana M. Priestly Law Library** (19487)

Primate Information Center
See: **University of Washington - Regional Primate Research Center**
   (19541)

★ 13346 ★
Prime Computer, Inc. - Information Center (Comp Sci)
500 Old Connecticut Path   Phone: (508)620-2800
Framingham, MA 01701   Sally Keith, Mgr.
Founded: 1978. **Subjects:** Computer science, business, management, library science. **Holdings:** 4500 books; 6000 technical reports, patents, dissertations; 80 journal titles on microfiche. **Subscriptions:** 250 journals and other serials; 10 newspapers. **Services:** Library not open to the public. **Automated Operations:** Computerized cataloging, serials, and circulation. **Computerized Information Services:** OCLC, DIALOG Information Services; internal database. **Networks/Consortia:** Member of NELINET, Inc. **Publications:** Newsletter, monthly - for internal distribution only.

Primerica Corp. - American Capital Co.
See: **American Capital Asset Management, Inc.** (514)

Primrose International Viola Archive
See: **Brigham Young University** (20805)

★ 13347 ★
Prince County Hospital - Medical Library (Med)
259 Beattie Ave.   Phone: (902)436-9131
Summerside, PE, Canada C1N 2A9   Dr. J.P. Schaefer, Dir.
Subjects: Medicine. **Holdings:** 2000 books; 200 bound periodical volumes. **Subscriptions:** 20 journals and other serials. **Services:** Interlibrary loan; library open to the public with restrictions.

★ 13348 ★
Prince Edward Heights - Resident Records Library (Med)
Box 440   Phone: (613)476-2104
Picton, ON, Canada K0K 2T0   Cindy Renaud, Libn.
Founded: 1971. **Staff:** 1. **Subjects:** Mental retardation, psychology, medicine, pharmacy, social work, management. **Special Collections:** Sign language programs; developmental disabilities files. **Holdings:** 730 volumes; 93 files of reference material; 2 educational kits. **Subscriptions:** 34 journals and other serials. **Services:** Interlibrary loan; copying; library open to the public. **Remarks:** FAX: (613)476-6857. Maintained by Ontario Ministry of Community and Social Services.

★ 13349 ★
Prince Edward Island Department of Education - Media Centre (Aud-Vis)
202 Richmond St.   Phone: (902)368-4639
Charlottetown, PE, Canada C1A 1J2   Bill Ledwell, Chf., Educ. Media
Founded: 1974. **Staff:** Prof 1; Other 5. **Subjects:** General collection. **Special Collections:** National Film Board of Canada Collection (614 English and 451 French videotapes). **Holdings:** 3839 16mm films; 2650 videotapes; 200 multimedia kits. **Subscriptions:** 10 journals and other serials. **Services:** Center open to the public. **Special Catalogs:** Film and video catalogs - annual. **Remarks:** FAX: (902)368-4663. Media centre serves as distribution outlet for National Film Board of Canada in Prince Edward Island.

★ 13350 ★
Prince Edward Island Government Services Library (Plan)
Box 2000   Phone: (902)368-4653
Charlottetown, PE, Canada C1A 7N8   Nichola Cleaveland, Libn.
Founded: 1968. **Staff:** Prof 1. **Subjects:** Planning and development, economics, education, social services, recreation and tourism, health services administration. **Holdings:** 8000 books; 1080 linear feet of Canadian federal government publications (depository); 150 linear feet of provincial government publications. **Subscriptions:** 165 journals and other serials. **Services:** Interlibrary loan; copying; library open to the public. **Computerized Information Services:** DIALOG Information Services, DOBIS Canadian Online Library System, UTLAS; Envoy 100 (electronic mail service). Performs searches. **Remarks:** FAX: (902)368-5544. Electronic mail address(es): ILL.PCPL (Envoy 100).

★ 13351 ★
Prince Edward Island Museum and Heritage Foundation - Genealogical Collection (Hist)
2 Kent St.   Phone: (902)892-9127
Charlottetown, PE, Canada C1A 1M6   Douglas Fraser, Geneal.Coord.
Founded: 1975. **Staff:** Prof 2. **Subjects:** Genealogy. **Holdings:** 250 books; 140 bound periodical volumes; 16 drawers of manuscript genealogies; 150 bound genealogies; 2 VF drawers of manuscript transcriptions of local cemetery records. **Subscriptions:** 35 journals and other serials. **Services:** Copying (limited); collection open to the public on a fee basis. **Special Indexes:** Master Name Index to Prince Edward Island newspapers, census, marriage, cemetery transcriptions (550,000 cards); baptismal records (110,000 cards); burial records (20,000 cards). **Remarks:** FAX: (902)368-5544. **Staff:** Charlotte Stewart, Asst.Geneal.

★ 13352 ★
Prince Edward Island Public Archives and Records Office (Hist)
P.O. Box 1000
Charlottetown, PE, Canada C1A 7M4   H.T. Holman, Prov.Archv.
Founded: 1964. **Staff:** Prof 3; Other 2. **Subjects:** History and government of Prince Edward Island. **Holdings:** 600 books; 40 linear meters of bound periodical volumes; 3800 linear meters of archival materials; microfilm. **Subscriptions:** 15 journals and other serials. **Services:** Copying; archives open to the public.

★ 13353 ★
Prince George Citizen - Newspaper Library (Publ)
150 Brunswick St.
P.O. Box 5700
Prince George, BC, Canada V2L 5K9   Sharon Grams, Libn.
Staff: Prof 1. **Subjects:** Newspaper reference topics. **Holdings:** 100 books; 2000 files of clippings; 420 files of photographs; 365 reels of microfilm; 200 documents and pamphlets. **Subscriptions:** 16 journals and other serials. **Services:** Library open to the public with restrictions. **Special Indexes:** Editorial index (card). **Remarks:** FAX: (604)562-7453.

★ 13354 ★
Prince George City Planning Division - Planning Library (Plan)
1100 Patricia Blvd.
Phone: (604)561-7618
Prince George, BC, Canada V2L 3V9   Kent Sedgwick, Libn.
Subjects: Planning, policy, environmental studies, economic development, design, housing, zoning bylaws. **Holdings:** 1000 books. **Subscriptions:** 25 journals and other serials. **Services:** Library open to the public with prior permission of librarian. **Computerized Information Services:** Internal database. **Remarks:** FAX: (604)563-8775.

★ 13355 ★
Prince George's County Circuit Court - Law Library (Law)
Courthouse
Box 580
Phone: (301)952-3438
Upper Marlboro, MD 20772-0580   Pamela J. Gregory, Law Libn.
Staff: Prof 2; Other 2. **Subjects:** Law, Maryland law and history. **Special Collections:** Maryland State documents depository. **Holdings:** 40,000 books; 500 bound periodical volumes; 3 VF drawers of state agency regulations and materials; 20 years of county local legislation. **Subscriptions:** 300 journals and other serials. **Services:** Interlibrary loan; copying; library open to the public. **Computerized Information Services:** WESTLAW, LEXIS, DIALOG Information Services, OCLC. **Networks/Consortia:** Member of CAPCON Library Network. **Publications:** Selected List of Acquisitions. **Special Indexes:** Index to County Charter; Index to Prince George's County Legislation. **Remarks:** FAX: (301)952-4465. **Staff:** Tora Williamson-Berry.

★ 13356 ★
Prince George's County Health Department - Public Health Resource Center (Med)
3003 Hospital Dr.
Phone: (301)386-0264
Cheverly, MD 20785   Janet Swann, Mgr.
Staff: Prof 1; Other 1. **Subjects:** Public health, health education, nursing, mental health, administration, geriatrics. **Holdings:** 1500 books; educational pamphlets. **Subscriptions:** 100 journals and other serials. **Services:** Interlibrary loan; copying; center open to the public. **Publications:** Resource Center Register, quarterly - for internal distribution only.

★ 13357 ★
Prince George's County Memorial Library System - Parent Child Collection (Soc Sci)
6530 Adelphi Rd.
Phone: (301)779-9330
Hyattsville, MD 20782-2098   Clara MacFarland, Ch.Libn.
Founded: 1984. **Staff:** Prof 1. **Subjects:** Parenting. **Holdings:** 400 books. **Subscriptions:** 6 journals and other serials. **Services:** Interlibrary loan; copying; room open to the public.

★ 13358 ★
Prince George's County Memorial Library System - Public Documents Reference Library (Plan)
County Adm. Bldg., Rm. 2198
Phone: (301)952-3904
Upper Marlboro, MD 20772   Ellen Lodwick, Docs.Libn.
Founded: 1977. **Staff:** Prof 1; Other 1. **Subjects:** County government, regional planning, zoning. **Special Collections:** Published county documents; documents from bi-county and regional agencies, municipalities (3000). **Holdings:** 800 books; 3000 documents; 250 microfilm cartridges; 63 feet of bill files; 192 feet of zoning files. **Subscriptions:** 50 journals and other serials; 8 newspapers. **Services:** Copying; library open to the public for reference use only. **Computerized Information Services:** DIALOG Information Services; LOGIN (electronic mail service). **Publications:** Newsletter, bimonthly - to county departments and selected libraries. **Special Catalogs:** Catalog of county publications. **Special Indexes:** Subject index to county council bills and resolutions (card). **Remarks:** FAX: (301)952-3238.

★ 13359 ★
Prince George's County Memorial Library System - Sojourner Truth Room (Area-Ethnic)
6200 Oxon Hill Rd.
Phone: (301)839-2400
Oxon Hill, MD 20745   Teresa M. Stakem, Libn. II
Founded: 1968. **Staff:** Prof 2. **Subjects:** African American history - women, family, slavery, civil rights; literary criticism; military. **Special Collections:** Slave narratives (30). **Holdings:** 4500 books; 130 bound periodical volumes; 12 VF drawers of clippings, pamphlets, government documents; 100 reels of microfilm and 35 microfiche of periodicals. **Subscriptions:** 28 journals and other serials. **Services:** Copying; room open to the public with restrictions. **Automated Operations:** Computerized circulation. **Computerized Information Services:** CLSI (internal database).

Prince George's County Public Schools - Multicultural Resource Center
See: **Prince George's County Public Schools - Professional Library** (13360)

★ 13360 ★
Prince George's County Public Schools - Professional Library (Educ)
8437 Landover Rd.
Phone: (301)386-1595
Landover, MD 20785-3599   Esther Hardin, Supv.
Founded: 1960. **Staff:** Prof 3; Other 2. **Subjects:** Education. **Special Collections:** Multicultural Resource Center. **Holdings:** 14,500 books; 800 AV programs; 750 public school curriculum guides; 295 journals in microform. **Subscriptions:** 349 journals and other serials. **Services:** Interlibrary loan; copying; library open to the public for reference use only. **Automated Operations:** Computerized cataloging, acquisitions, serials, circulation, and card printing. **Computerized Information Services:** Online systems; CD-ROM (ERIC). **Networks/Consortia:** Member of Maryland Interlibrary Organization (MILO). **Publications:** Bits and Pieces (newsletter), 4/academic year - for internal distribution only. **Remarks:** Alternate telephone number(s): 386-1596; 386-1597. **Staff:** Joyce E. Meucci, Lib.Assoc.; Gloria Cobbs, Libn.; Cristina Jimenez, Asst.

★ 13361 ★
Prince George's Hospital Center - Saul Schwartzbach Memorial Library (Med)
Cheverly, MD 20785
Phone: (301)618-2490
Penny Martin, Med.Libn.
Staff: Prof 1. **Subjects:** Medicine. **Holdings:** 1000 books; 2500 bound periodical volumes; 2350 AV programs. **Subscriptions:** 100 journals and other serials. **Services:** Interlibrary loan; copying; library open to the public for reference use only. **Computerized Information Services:** MEDLINE. **Networks/Consortia:** Member of Maryland and D.C. Consortium of Resource Sharing (MADCORS), Maryland Association of Health Science Librarians (MAHSL).

★ 13362 ★
Prince of Peace Lutheran Church - Library (Rel-Phil)
4419 S. Howell Ave.
Phone: (414)483-3828
Milwaukee, WI 53207   Mrs. Robert Heinritz, Hd.Libn.
Founded: 1963. **Staff:** 6. **Subjects:** Religion, missions, children's literature. **Special Collections:** Works of Martin Luther. **Holdings:** 3085 books; archival materials; VF drawers; cassette tapes; maps. **Services:** Library not open to the public.

★ 13363 ★
Prince of Wales Northern Heritage Centre - Library (Hist)
Yellowknife, NT, Canada X1A 2L9   Phone: (403)873-7177
                                         Carolynn Kobelka, Libn.
Founded: 1982. **Staff:** Prof 1; Other 1. **Subjects:** History of the Northwest
Territories, archeology, Arctic exploration, heritage resource management,
native cultures of the Northwest Territories. **Special Collections:** Admiral
Sir Leopold M'Clintock and Rear Admiral Noel Wright Collections (600
19th century imprints of Arctic exploration). **Holdings:** 7000 books; federal
and provincial government publications; microfilm; microfiche; reprints.
Subscriptions: 150 journals and other serials; 15 newspapers. **Services:**
Copying; library open to the public for reference use only. **Computerized
Information Services:** Internal database; Envoy 100 (electronic mail
service). **Remarks:** FAX: (403)873-0205. Electronic mail address(es):
PWNHC.L (Envoy 100). **Formerly:** Its Northwest Territories Archives.

★ 13364 ★
Prince William County Schools - Staff Library (Educ)
Box 389   Phone: (703)791-7334
Manassas, VA 22110   Dr. Bobbie Bowyer, Libn.
Founded: 1962. **Staff:** Prof 1; Other 2. **Subjects:** Education, psychology,
management, library science. **Holdings:** 8383 books; 2765 pamphlets,
monographs, special reports; educational material files; unbound
periodicals; newsletters. **Subscriptions:** 232 journals and other serials.
Services: SDI; library open to the public. **Computerized Information
Services:** DIALOG Information Services; CD-ROM (Education Index).
Staff: Fanchon Fischer; Connie Murphy.

★ 13365 ★
Princeton Antiques Bookfinders - Art Marketing Reference Library
  (Art, Sci-Engr)
2915-17-31 Atlantic Ave.   Phone: (609)344-1943
Atlantic City, NJ 08401   Robert Eugene, Cur.
Founded: 1974. **Staff:** Prof 1. **Subjects:** Science and technology, living arts,
fiction, collectibles, art, gambling. **Special Collections:** Postcard Photo
Library (250,000). **Holdings:** 175,000 books. **Subscriptions:** 25 journals and
other serials. **Services:** Library open to the public by appointment.

★ 13366 ★
Princeton Library in New York (Hist)
15 W. 43rd St., Fifth Fl.   Phone: (212)840-1565
New York, NY 10036   Constance Clark, Libn.
Founded: 1962. **Staff:** 2. **Subjects:** General liberal arts. **Special Collections:**
Princetoniana; History of New York. **Holdings:** 10,000 books.
Subscriptions: 90 journals and other serials. **Services:** Library open to
Princeton Club members, alumni, visiting scholars, and accredited members
of historical, literary, or comparable organizations. **Staff:** Betty Dornheim,
Lib.Asst.

★ 13367 ★
Princeton Theological Seminary - Speer Library (Rel-Phil)
Mercer St. & Library Pl.
Box 111   Phone: (609)497-7930
Princeton, NJ 08542   James Armstrong, Libn.
Founded: 1812. **Staff:** Prof 9; Other 16. **Subjects:** Theology,
Presbyterianism, Semitic philology, Biblical studies, church history. **Special
Collections:** Benson Collection of Hymnology; collection of Puritan and
English theological literature; Agnew Collection on the Baptism
Controversy; Sprague Collection of Early American Pamphlets. **Holdings:**
360,863 volumes; 61,608 bound pamphlets; 100,000 manuscripts; 17,484
titles in microform; 3000 cuneiform tablets. **Subscriptions:** 2200 journals
and other serials. **Services:** Interlibrary loan; copying; library open to the
public with restrictions. **Automated Operations:** Computerized public access
catalog, cataloging, acquisitions, and serials. **Computerized Information
Services:** DIALOG Information Services, RLIN, OCLC. **Networks/
Consortia:** Member of Research Libraries Information Network (RLIN).
Remarks: FAX: (609)497-1826. **Staff:** Dr. James S. Irvine, Assoc.Libn.,
Tech.Serv.; Paul Powell, Cat.Libn.; Donna Schleifer, Cat.Libn.; Julie
Dawson, Ser.Libn.; Donald Vorp, Coll.Dev.Libn.; William Harris, Archv.;
Dan McKeon, Cat.Libn.; Kate Skrebutenas, Ref.Libn.; Sarita Ravinder,
Asst.Ser.Libn.

Princeton University - American Civil Liberties Union - Archives
See: American Civil Liberties Union - Library/Archives (526)

★ 13368 ★
Princeton University - Astrophysics Library (Sci-Engr)
Peyton Hall   Phone: (609)258-3820
Princeton, NJ 08544   Jane Holmquist, Libn.
Staff: 1.5. **Subjects:** Astronomy, astrophysics. **Special Collections:**
European Southern Observatory (ESO) Atlas of the Southern Sky; Mount
Palomar Sky Atlas. **Holdings:** 17,693 books; 537 slides; preprints.
Subscriptions: 301 journals and other serials. **Services:** Interlibrary loan;
copying; library open to the public for reference use only. **Automated
Operations:** Computerized public access catalog, cataloging, acquisitions,
and serials. **Computerized Information Services:** RLIN, DIALOG
Information Services, SIMBAD; BITNET (electronic mail service).
Performs searches on fee basis. **Remarks:** FAX: (609)258-1020. Electronic
mail address(es): jane@pucc.princeton.edu (BITNET). **Formerly:** Its
Astronomy Library.

★ 13369 ★
Princeton University - Biology Library (Biol Sci)
Guyot Hall   Phone: (609)258-3235
Princeton, NJ 08544   Dr. David Goodman, Libn.
Staff: Prof 2; Other 3. **Subjects:** Biology, biochemistry, microbiology,
zoology, botany, molecular biology, genetics, ecology, population biology.
Holdings: 23,000 books; 27,000 bound periodical volumes. **Subscriptions:**
1050 journals and other serials. **Services:** Interlibrary loan; copying; library
open to the public for reference use only. **Automated Operations:**
Computerized public access catalog, acquisitions, and circulation.
Computerized Information Services: DIALOG Information Services; CD-
ROMs (MEDLINE, Biological Abstracts). Performs searches on fee basis.
Networks/Consortia: Member of Research Libraries Information Network
(RLIN). **Publications:** Acquisitions List. **Staff:** Jane Holmquist,
Asst.Biol.Libn.

★ 13370 ★
Princeton University - Chemistry Library (Sci-Engr, Biol Sci)
Frick Chemical Laboratory   Phone: (609)258-3238
Princeton, NJ 08544   Lois Nase, Libn.
Staff: Prof 1; Other 2. **Subjects:** Chemistry - general, physical, organic,
inorganic, biochemistry. **Holdings:** 20,500 books; 25,000 bound periodical
volumes; 1200 departmental dissertations. **Subscriptions:** 550 journals and
other serials. **Services:** Interlibrary loan (through main library); copying;
library open to the public for reference use only. **Computerized Information
Services:** DIALOG Information Services, Chemical Abstracts Service
(CAS), BRS Information Technologies. **Networks/Consortia:** Member of
Research Libraries Information Network (RLIN). **Publications:** New Books
and News. **Remarks:** FAX: (609)258-6746. **Staff:** Jayashri Nagaraja,
Chem.Libn.

★ 13371 ★
**Princeton University - Department of Art & Archaeology - Index of
  Christian Art** (Art)
McCormick Hall   Phone: (609)258-3773
Princeton, NJ 08544   Brendan Cassidy, Dir.
Founded: 1917. **Staff:** Prof 4; Other 2. **Subjects:** Christian art before 1400.
Holdings: Iconographic index of 700,000 cards; 200,000 photographs.
Services: Reference for visiting scholars, mainly in history of art. **Staff:** A.L.
Bennett Hagens; R. Melzak; L. Drewer.

★ 13372 ★
Princeton University - Engineering Library (Sci-Engr)
Engineering Quadrangle   Phone: (609)258-3200
Princeton, NJ 08544   Dolores M. Hoelle, Libn.
Staff: Prof 4; Other 6. **Subjects:** Engineering - chemical, civil, electrical,
mechanical, nuclear, aeronautical; solid state physics; polymers; computer
science; transportation; environmental studies; water resources. **Special
Collections:** DOE and NASA reports (microfiche); Society of Automotive
Engineers (SAE) and American Institute of Aeronautics and Astronautics
(AIAA) conference papers (microfiche). **Holdings:** 90,000 books; 90,000
bound periodical volumes; 600,000 technical reports and government
documents, including 52 file cabinets of microfiche. **Subscriptions:** 1500
journals and other serials. **Services:** Interlibrary loan; copying; library open

to the public for reference use only. **Automated Operations:** Computerized public access catalog, cataloging, acquisitions, and circulation. **Computerized Information Services:** DIALOG Information Services, WILSONLINE, BRS Information Technologies, STN International, NASA/RECON, DTIC; InterNet, BITNET (electronic mail services). Performs searches on fee basis. **Networks/Consortia:** Member of Research Libraries Information Network (RLIN), PALINET. **Special Catalogs:** Serials list (print and online). **Remarks:** Alternate telephone number(s): 258-3201. FAX: (609)258-6744. Electronic mail address(es): DMHOELLE@PUCC (BITNET); DMHOELLE@PUCC.PRINCETON.EDU (InterNet). **Staff:** Ann C. Doyle, Asst.Libn.; Leilani Hall, Asst.Libn.; Louise Deis, Asst.Libn.

★13373★
Princeton University - Geology Library (Sci-Engr)
Guyot Hall   Phone: (609)258-3267
Princeton, NJ 08544 Patricia A. Gaspari-Bridges, Geol.Libn./Map Libn.
Founded: 1909. **Staff:** Prof 1; Other 6. **Subjects:** Geology - crystallography, geochemistry, geomorphology, geophysics, mineralogy, oceanography, paleontology, petrology, sedimentation, stratigraphy, structural geology. **Holdings:** 60,000 volumes; 900 theses; 276,000 maps; 450 technical reports. **Subscriptions:** 1200 journals and other serials. **Services:** Interlibrary loan; copying; library open to the public. **Computerized Information Services:** DIALOG Information Services, RLIN; GEOMAP (internal database); BITNET (electronic mail service). Performs searches on fee basis. **Remarks:** Alternate telephone number(s): 258-5483. Electronic mail address(es): 0522037@PUCC (BITNET).

★13374★
Princeton University - Gest Oriental Library and East Asian Collections (Area-Ethnic)
317 Palmer Hall   Phone: (609)258-3182
Princeton, NJ 08544   Antony Marr, Cur.
Founded: 1926. **Staff:** Prof 7; Other 15. **Subjects:** China, Japan, Korea. **Special Collections:** Buddhist sutras, Sung and Yuan editions (2864 volumes); Ming editions (24,000 volumes); Hishi copies, Ming works reproduced in Japan (2100 volumes); Chinese medicine and materia medica (1700 volumes); "Go" collection (500 volumes); rare books including Mongolian, Tibetan, and Manchurian titles (1300). **Holdings:** 445,000 books; 3000 manuscripts; 19,000 microforms. **Subscriptions:** 2400 journals and other serials; 29 newspapers. **Services:** Interlibrary loan; copying; information service for outside inquirers on questions relating to China, Japan, and Korea. **Automated Operations:** Computerized public access catalog, cataloging, and ILL. **Computerized Information Services:** SPIRES; RLIN catalog (internal database); BITNET (electronic mail service). Contact Person: Charmian Cheng, Hd., Pub.Serv.Sect., 258-3259. **Networks/Consortia:** Member of Research Libraries Information Network (RLIN). **Special Catalogs:** A Catalogue of the Chinese Rare Books in the Gest Collection of the Princeton University Library (book); Union List of Current Japanese Periodicals in the East Asian Libraries of Columbia, Harvard, Princeton, and Yale (book), 1985. **Special Indexes:** List of Periodicals in Japanese in the Gest Oriental Library and East Asian Collections (book), 1980. **Remarks:** FAX: (609)258-4105. Electronic mail address(es): gest@pucc.princeton.edu (BITNET). **Staff:** Iping K. Wei, Hd., Tech.Serv.Sect.; Soowon Y. Kim, Japanese/Korean Bibliog.; Mariko Shimomura, Asst.Hd., Tech.Serv.; Shu-Sheng Wang, Chinese/Japanese Cat.; Martin Heijdra, Chinese/Western Bibliog.

★13375★
Princeton University - Industrial Relations Library (Bus-Fin)
Firestone Library   Phone: (609)258-4936
Princeton, NJ 08544   Kevin P. Barry, Libn.
Founded: 1922. **Staff:** Prof 1; Other 1. **Subjects:** Industrial relations, labor legislation, labor unions, human resource planning, labor economics, social insurance, benefit plans, personnel administration. **Holdings:** 8000 volumes; 105 VF drawers; 100,000 pamphlets, labor union publications; International Labor Organization (ILO) documents. **Subscriptions:** 650 journals and other serials. **Services:** Library open for a fee. **Computerized Information Services:** DIALOG Information Services, LEXIS, BRS Information Technologies, WILSONLINE, HRIN. **Networks/Consortia:** Member of Research Libraries Information Network (RLIN). **Publications:** Selected References, 5/year - by subscription.

★13376★
Princeton University - Marquand Library (Art)
McCormick Hall   Phone: (609)258-3783
Princeton, NJ 08544   Janice J. Powell, Libn.
Founded: 1908. **Staff:** Prof 2; Other 9. **Subjects:** History of art, history of architecture, archeology. **Special Collections:** Barr Ferree Collection (architecture); Friend Collection (early Christian and manuscript illumination); sales catalogs; exhibition catalogs. **Holdings:** 170,000 volumes. **Subscriptions:** 1000 journals and other serials. **Services:** Library not open to the public. **Networks/Consortia:** Member of Research Libraries Information Network (RLIN).

★13377★
Princeton University - Mathematics, Physics and Statistics Library (Sci-Engr)
Princeton, NJ 08544   Phone: (609)258-3188
                                               Peter Cziffra, Libn.
Staff: Prof 1; Other 4. **Subjects:** Mathematics, physics, statistics - history, development, philosophy. **Holdings:** 44,000 books; 35,000 bound periodical volumes; 5000 pamphlets; 10 VF drawers of Princeton theses; 250 VF drawers of uncataloged pamphlets; 16 VF drawers of undergraduate theses. **Subscriptions:** 805 journals and other serials. **Services:** Interlibrary loan; copying; library open to qualified readers for reference use only. **Automated Operations:** Computerized public access catalog, cataloging, acquisitions, and circulation. **Computerized Information Services:** DIALOG Information Services, RLIN. Performs searches on fee basis.

★13378★
Princeton University - Music Collection (Mus)
Firestone Library, Floor C   Phone: (609)258-3230
Princeton, NJ 08544-2098   Paula Morgan, Mus.Libn.
Staff: Prof 1; Other 1. **Subjects:** Music. **Holdings:** 18,000 books; 3000 bound periodical volumes; 19,000 volumes of music; 2500 microforms. **Subscriptions:** 150 journals and other serials. **Services:** Interlibrary loan; copying; collection open to the public for reference use only.

★13379★
Princeton University - Music Listening Library (Mus)
Woolworth Center of Musical Studies   Phone: (609)258-4251
Princeton, NJ 08544   Thomson Moore, Recordings Libn.
Staff: Prof 1; Other 1. **Subjects:** Music - western classical, nonwestern, jazz. **Holdings:** 1200 score titles in multiple copies; 25,000 phonograph records; 2000 tapes; 2000 compact discs. **Subscriptions:** 30 journals and other serials. **Services:** Library not open to the public. **Computerized Information Services:** BITNET (electronic mail service). **Remarks:** FAX: (609)258-6793. Electronic mail address(es): STMOORE@PUCC (BITNET).

★13380★
Princeton University - Near East Collections (Area-Ethnic)
Jones Hall
Firestone Library   Phone: (609)258-3279
Princeton, NJ 08540   James Weinberger, Cur.
Staff: Prof 4; Other 3. **Subjects:** Arabic, Persian, Turkish, and Hebrew languages and literature. **Special Collections:** Garrett Collection of Near Eastern Manuscripts. **Holdings:** 130,000 volumes; 12,000 volumes of manuscripts. **Services:** Interlibrary loan; copying; collections open to the public on fee basis. **Networks/Consortia:** Member of Research Libraries Information Network (RLIN), Center for Research Libraries (CRL). **Staff:** Joan Biella, Ldr., Cat. Team; Mr. Kambiz Eslami; David Hirsch; Kathy Van der Vate.

★13381★
Princeton University - Office of Population Research - Library (Soc Sci)
21 Prospect Ave.   Phone: (609)258-4874
Princeton, NJ 08544   Thomas Holzmann, Libn.
Founded: 1936. **Staff:** Prof 2; Other 1. **Subjects:** Population studies, demography (emphasis on methodology), fertility, mortality, census, vital statistics. **Holdings:** 30,000 volumes; 5500 reprints; 10,000 manuscripts and pamphlets; 1100 reels of microfilm. **Subscriptions:** 400 journals and other serials. **Services:** Interlibrary loan; copying; library open to the public for reference use only. **Automated Operations:** Computerized cataloging, acquisitions, and circulation. **Computerized Information Services:** POPLINE. **Networks/Consortia:** Member of APLIC International Census Network. **Publications:** Acquisitions list - for local distribution. **Special Indexes:** Population Index (quarterly index of the demographic field). **Remarks:** FAX:(609)258-1039. **Staff:** Maryann Belanger, Asst.Libn.

★ 13382 ★
Princeton University - Plasma Physics Library (Sci-Engr)
Box 451   Phone: (609)243-3567
Princeton, NJ 08543   Judith Frazer, Libn.
Founded: 1961. **Staff:** Prof 2; Other 2. **Subjects:** Fusion reactor technology, plasma physics. **Holdings:** 6000 books; 7000 bound periodical volumes; 3000 project reports; 20,000 technical reports and reprints; 38,000 microfiche. **Subscriptions:** 130 journals and other serials. **Services:** Interlibrary loan; library open to the public for reference use only. **Computerized Information Services:** DIALOG Information Services, STN International; BITNET (electronic mail service). **Publications:** Monthly Bulletin and Acquisitions List - for internal distribution only. **Remarks:** FAX: (609)243-2160. Electronic mail address(es): JHFRAZER@PUCC.PRINCETON.EDU (BITNET). **Staff:** Rhoda Stasiak, Asst.Libn.

★ 13383 ★
Princeton University - Pliny Fisk Library of Economics and Finance (Bus-Fin)
1 Washington Rd.   Phone: (609)258-3211
Princeton, NJ 08544   Louise Tompkins, Libn.
Founded: 1915. **Staff:** Prof 1; Other 2. **Subjects:** Economics, finance, international economics. **Special Collections:** Pliny Fisk Collection of Railroad and Corporation Finance (annual reports and other financial documents, 1830-1900). **Holdings:** 5575 books; current annual reports of 800 corporations; 21 VF drawers of pamphlets; selected economics working papers. **Subscriptions:** 942 journals and other serials. **Services:** Interlibrary loan.

★ 13384 ★
Princeton University - Psychology Library (Soc Sci)
Green Hall   Phone: (609)258-3239
Princeton, NJ 08544   Mary C. Chaikin, Psych.Libn.
Staff: Prof 1; Other 2. **Subjects:** Psychology - cognitive, developmental, social, experimental, health, physiological; neuropsychology; perception; personality; psychotherapy; psycholinguistics; artificial intelligence. **Holdings:** 19,200 books; 14,800 bound periodical volumes; 5300 microfiche. **Subscriptions:** 420 journals and other serials. **Services:** Interlibrary loan; copying; library open to the public for reference use only. **Automated Operations:** Computerized cataloging and circulation. **Computerized Information Services:** DIALOG Information Services, RLIN; CD-ROMs (PsycLIT, MEDLINE). **Networks/Consortia:** Member of Research Libraries Information Network (RLIN). **Publications:** Acquisition list and bibliographies - local distribution.

★ 13385 ★
Princeton University - Public Administration Collection (Soc Sci)
Princeton University Library
1 Washington Rd.   Phone: (609)258-3209
Princeton, NJ 08544   Rosemary Allen Little, Libn.
Founded: 1930. **Staff:** Prof 1; Other 4. **Subjects:** Public administration; government on the national, state, county, and municipal levels; law; politics; planning. **Special Collections:** Recent U.S. censuses in housing and population; depository for New Jersey state government documents; official depository for United Nations publications. **Holdings:** 5000 books; 2000 bound periodical volumes; 18,000 pamphlets; 28 VF drawers of clippings. **Subscriptions:** 1600 journals and other serials. **Services:** Interlibrary loan; collection open to the public. **Networks/Consortia:** Member of Research Libraries Information Network (RLIN).

★ 13386 ★
Princeton University - Rare Books and Special Collections (Rare Book)
Firestone Library   Phone: (609)258-3184
Princeton, NJ 08544   William L. Joyce, Assoc.Libn.
Founded: 1746. **Staff:** 45. **Subjects:** Papyri; Babylonian clay tablets; Medieval, Renaissance, Ethiopian, Batak, and Arabic manuscripts; early printing; English, French, German, and American literature and history of the 16th to 20th centuries; theater history; dramatic literature; New Jerseyana; emblem books; Western Americana; American Indians; Mormons; history and examples of bookmaking, printmaking, fine printing, binding, photography; motion picture history; private press books. **Special Collections:** Behrman American Literature; Sylvia Beach Collection; Carton Hunting Collection; Grover Cleveland Library; Cook Chess Collection; College of One Collection of Sheilah Graham; Meirs Collection of George Cruikshank; de Coppet Collection of American Historical Manuscripts; Derrydale Press Collection and The Sporting Books of Eugene V. Connett;

general rare books collection; Jonathan Edwards Library; J. Harlin O'Connell Collection of English Literature of the 1890's; Kenneth McKenzie Fable Collection; Hall Handel Collection; Sinclair Hamilton Collection of American Illustrated Books; incunabula; Otto von Kienbusch Angling Collection; Charles Scribner Collection of Charles Lamb; James McCosh Library; Robert F. Metzdorf Collection of Victorian Bookbindings; Harry B. Vandeventer Poetry Collection; Orlando F. Weber Collection of Economic History; Goertz Collection; Gryphius Imprints Collection; Laurence Hutton Collection; Miriam Y. Holden Collection on the History of Women (Rare Books Section); Grenville Kane Collection of Americana; Stanley Lieberman Memorial Collection of Hero Fiction; Cyrus McCormick Collection of Americana; William Nelson Collection of New Jerseyana; New Jersey Imprints; Morris L. Parrish Collection of Victorian Novelists; Princeton Borough Collection; Princeton Borough Agricultural Association Records; Pitney Collection on International Law and Diplomacy (Rare Books Section); Robert Patterson Collection of Horace; Kenneth H. Rockey Angling Collection (Rare Books Section); Richard Sheridan Collection; Robert H. Taylor Library; Junius Spencer Morgan Collection of Virgil; John Shaw Pierson Civil War Collection; John Witherspoon Library; Woodrow Wilson Collection; Scribner papers; papers of: F. Scott Fitzgerald, Ernest Hemingway, Allen Tate, Caroline Gordon, Anthony Trollope, the Rosetti family, Thomas Mann, John Day (publisher), Henry Holt (publisher), Luigi Pirandello (playwright), John Foster Dulles, Allen Dulles, James Forrestal, Bernard Baruch, George F. Kennan, David Lilienthal, Adlai Stevenson, American Civil Liberties Union (ACLU), Committee to Aid America by Defending the Allies, America First Committee, other 20th century literary and historical papers. **Holdings:** 250,000 books; 1000 manuscript collections; 40,000 maps and charts; 25,000 prints and drawings. **Services:** Interlibrary loan; copying; collections open to the public with identification. **Computerized Information Services:** LITMSS (internal database); BITNET (electronic mail service). **Special Indexes:** Guide to Modern Manuscripts in the Princeton University Library, 2 vol. (Boston: G.K. Hall and Co., 1989). **Remarks:** Electronic mail address(es): WLJOYCE@PUCC (BITNET). **Staff:** Stephen Ferguson, Cur. of Rare Bks.; Dan C. Skemer, Cur. of Mss.; Alfred L. Bush, Cur., W. Americana/Historic Maps; Brooks Levy, Cur. of Coins; Ben Primer, Univ.Archv./Cur., Pub.Aff. Papers; Dale Roylance, Cur., Graphic Arts; Alexander D. Wainwright, Cur., Parrish Coll.; Mary Ann Jensen, Cur. of Theatre Coll.; Mark R. Farrell, Cur. of Taylor Lib.

★ 13387 ★
Princeton University - School of Architecture Library (Plan)
Princeton, NJ 08544   Phone: (609)258-3256
                                           Frances Chen, Libn.
Founded: 1967. **Staff:** Prof 1; Other 3. **Subjects:** Current architectural practice, urban affairs, physical planning, transportation, sociology. **Special Collections:** Library of the former Bureau of Urban Research. **Holdings:** 27,000 books; 5000 pamphlets. **Subscriptions:** 450 journals and other serials. **Services:** Interlibrary loan; copying; library open to the public for reference use only. **Automated Operations:** Computerized public access catalog and circulation. **Computerized Information Services:** DIALOG Information Services, RLIN. **Networks/Consortia:** Member of Research Libraries Information Network (RLIN).

★ 13388 ★
Princeton University - William Seymour Theatre Collection (Theater)
Firestone Library
1 Washington Rd.   Phone: (609)258-3223
Princeton, NJ 08544   Mary Ann Jensen, Cur.
Founded: 1936. **Staff:** Prof 1; Other 5. **Subjects:** Performing arts - theater, musical theater, popular music, dance, circus, film. **Special Collections:** Papers of: William Seymour, Fanny Davenport, Mathews family, Otto Kahn, E.L. Davenport, George Crouse Tyler, Alan S. Downer, Sarah Enright, Woody Allen; collections of: Ashton Sly, Lulu Glaser, Max Gordon, Joseph McCaddon, Bretaigne Windust, Clinton Wilder, Sam H. Harris; archives of: Warner Bros. Inc., Tams-Witmark, Theatre Intime, Triangle Club, McCarter Theatre; A.M. Friend Collection of 18th century theatre drawings. **Holdings:** 15,200 books; 3300 VF drawers of programs, pictures, pamphlets; 50 map drawers of posters; 500 scrapbooks; 1400 paperbound playbooks. **Subscriptions:** 150 journals and other serials. **Services:** Copying (limited); collection open to qualified scholars. **Automated Operations:** Computerized public access catalog and circulation. **Computerized Information Services:** LTMSS (internal database). **Networks/Consortia:** Member of Research Libraries Information Network (RLIN).

★ 13389 ★
Princeton University - Woodrow Wilson School of Public and International Affairs - Library (Soc Sci)
Robertson Hall   Phone: (609)258-5455
Princeton, NJ 08540   Laird Klingler, Libn.
Founded: 1964. **Staff:** Prof 1; Other 4. **Subjects:** Political science, economics, international affairs. **Holdings:** 18,000 books; 1361 bound periodical volumes. **Subscriptions:** 284 journals and other serials; 7 newspapers. **Services:** Interlibrary loan; library open to the public for reference use only. **Automated Operations:** Computerized circulation and reserves. **Computerized Information Services:** DIALOG Information Services, LEXIS, NEXIS, RLIN, DataTimes, Dow Jones News/Retrieval, InfoTrac, Congressional Information Service, Inc. (CIS), SCAD, PAIS; internal database; BITNET (electronic mail service). Performs searches on fee basis. **Remarks:** FAX: (609)258-2809.

Pringle Herbarium
See: **University of Vermont** (19483)

★ 13390 ★
Printing Brokerage Association - Library
15050 N.E. 20th Ave.
North Miami, FL 33181
Defunct.

John A. Prior Health Sciences Library
See: **Ohio State University** (12314)

Walter F. Prior Medical Library
See: **Frederick Memorial Hospital** (6108)

★ 13391 ★
Prison Fellowship - Information Center (Soc Sci)
Box 17500   Phone: (703)478-0100
Washington, DC 20041-0500   Kim I. Robbins, Info.Ctr.Supv.
Staff: Prof 1; Other 2. **Subjects:** Criminal justice and criminal justice reform, corrections, Christian theology and life. **Holdings:** 7 VF drawers of clippings; 5 VF drawers of archival materials; 20 VF drawers. **Services:** Copying; center open to the public with prior approval of coordinator. **Computerized Information Services:** NEXIS, EPIC; internal database. **Remarks:** FAX: (703)478-0452. **Formerly:** Prison Fellowship Ministries.

H. Wayne Pritchard Library
See: **Soil and Water Conservation Society** (15349)

Pritzker Institute of Medical Engineering
See: **Illinois Institute of Technology** (7676)

★ 13392 ★
Pro Football Hall of Fame - Library/Research Center (Rec)
2121 George Halas Dr., N.W.   Phone: (216)456-8207
Canton, OH 44708   Sandi Self, Libn.
Founded: 1963. **Staff:** Prof 3; Other 1. **Subjects:** Professional football. **Special Collections:** Spalding football guides, 1892-1940; Scrapbooks of Commissioner Bert Bell (19); other football scrapbooks (140); pre-NFL rare documents (player contracts). **Holdings:** 2436 volumes; 4207 periodical volumes; 66,000 photographs of players, teams, officials, coaches; 800 slides of player and game action; 65 audiotapes; 1156 16mm films; 29 team media guides; 11,800 microforms; 80 VF drawers of present, defunct league, and semi-pro team files. **Subscriptions:** 25 journals and other serials; 5 newspapers. **Services:** Interlibrary loan; copying; library open to researchers and writers by appointment. **Remarks:** FAX: (216)456-8175. **Also Known As:** National Football Museum. **Staff:**; Joe Horrigan, Cur.Res.; Pete Fierle, Asst.Res.; Saleem Choudry, Microfilmer.

★ 13393 ★
Pro-Life Action League - Library (Soc Sci)
6160 N. Cicero, No. 600
Chicago, IL 60646   Phone: (312)777-2900
Subjects: Abortion - pro-life perspective, legal aspects, proposed constitutional amendment, public protests and demonstrations, sidewalk counseling, statistics. **Special Collections:** Biographical archives. **Holdings:** 1000 volumes, tapes, videocassettes, and vertical files. **Remarks:** Alternate telephone number(s): (312)777-2525 (24-hour Action Line).

Pro-Life Library
See: **Diocese of Allentown** (4875)

★ 13394 ★
Probe Economics, Inc. - Library (Sci-Engr)
Millwood Business Ctr., Rte. 100
Postal Drawer M
Millwood, NY 10546-0909   Phone: (914)923-4505
Subjects: Raw materials markets. **Holdings:** 500 volumes; 22 periodicals. **Remarks:** FAX: (914)923-4508. Telex: (TWX) 710-110-2304.

Probus Club Resource Center
See: **Connecticut State Department of Mental Retardation, Region 2** (4191)

★ 13395 ★
Procter & Gamble Cellulose - Cellulose & Specialties Division Technical Information Services (Sci-Engr)
1001 Tillman Ave.   Phone: (901)320-8311
Memphis, TN 38112   Sandra Sharp, Lib.Ck.
Founded: 1953. **Staff:** Prof 1; Other 1. **Subjects:** Chemistry - cellulose, physical, organic, analytical; polymer sciences; colloid science; textiles. **Holdings:** 5000 books; 5000 bound periodical volumes; 10,000 technical reports; 8 VF drawers of government documents; 10,000 U.S. and foreign patents; 500 reels of microfilm. **Subscriptions:** 354 journals and other serials. **Services:** Interlibrary loan. **Computerized Information Services:** PFDS Online, NLM, DIALOG Information Services.

★ 13396 ★
Procter & Gamble Company - Ivorydale Technical Center - Library (Sci-Engr)
5299 Spring Grove Ave.
Cincinnati, OH 45217   Phone: (513)983-1100
Holdings: Figures not available. **Services:** Library not open to the public. **Computerized Information Services:** DIALOG Information Services. **Remarks:** Library is one of several units comprising the Procter & Gamble Company Information Management Group.

★ 13397 ★
Procter & Gamble Company - Library (Bus-Fin)
Box 599   Phone: (513)983-1100
Cincinnati, OH 45201   Shirley Caldwell, Libn.
Subjects: Detergents, advertising, business. **Holdings:** Figures not available. **Services:** Library not open to the public.

★ 13398 ★
Procter & Gamble Company - Miami Valley Laboratories - Technical Library (Sci-Engr)
Box 398707   Phone: (513)245-2557
Cincinnati, OH 45239-8707   Emelyn L. Hiland, Lib.Mgr.
Staff: Prof 1; Other 4. **Subjects:** Chemistry, surface and colloid sciences, life sciences. **Holdings:** 8000 books; 12,000 bound periodical volumes. **Subscriptions:** 600 journals and other serials. **Services:** Library not open to the public. **Computerized Information Services:** DIALOG Information Services, PFDS Online, OCLC, Chemical Abstracts Service (CAS), Chemical Information Systems, Inc. (CIS); internal database.

Procter & Gamble Company - Norwich Eaton Pharmaceuticals, Inc.
See: **Norwich Eaton Pharmaceuticals, Inc. (12120)**

★ 13399 ★
Procter & Gamble Company - Sharon Woods Technical Center - HB Library (Sci-Engr)
11511 Reed Hartman   Phone: (513)626-3595
Cincinnati, OH 45241   Sue Kues, Lib.Mgr.
Founded: 1982. **Holdings:** Figures not available. **Subscriptions:** 100 journals and other serials. **Services:** Library not open to the public. **Remarks:** Library is one of several units comprising the Procter & Gamble Company Information Management Group. FAX: (513)562-4500.

★ 13400 ★
Procter & Gamble Company - Winton Hill Technical Center - Library (Sci-Engr)
Administration Bldg.
6090 Center Hill Rd.   Phone: (513)634-7257
Cincinnati, OH 45224   Victoria L. Houlihan
Holdings: Figures not available. **Services:** Library not open to the public. **Remarks:** FAX: (513)634-3724. Library is one of five units comprising the Procter & Gamble Company Technical Information Service with combined holdings of 35,000 volumes.

★ 13401 ★
Proctor Community Hospital - Medical Library (Med)
5409 N. Knoxville Ave.   Phone: (309)691-1000
Peoria, IL 61614   Starr Jones
Founded: 1972. **Staff:** Prof 1. **Subjects:** Medicine, nursing, allied health sciences. **Holdings:** 500 books; 210 bound periodical volumes; 550 unbound journal volumes. **Subscriptions:** 120 journals and other serials. **Services:** Interlibrary loan; copying; SDI; library open to qualified patrons. **Computerized Information Services:** MEDLINE. **Networks/Consortia:** Member of Heart of Illinois Library Consortium (HILC), Illinois Valley Library System, National Network of Libraries of Medicine - Greater Midwest Region, ILLINET. **Publications:** Internal pamphlets. **Remarks:** FAX: (309)691-4543.

★ 13402 ★
Proctor & Redfern, Consulting Engineers - Library (Sci-Engr, Plan)
45 Green Belt Dr.   Phone: (416)445-3600
Don Mills, ON, Canada M3C 3K3   Catherine Spark, Hd.Libn.
Staff: Prof 1; Other 2. **Subjects:** Civil and environmental engineering, urban and regional planning, hydrology, transportation, waste management. **Holdings:** 18,000 books; 600 bound periodical volumes. **Subscriptions:** 160 journals and other serials; 20 newspapers. **Services:** Interlibrary loan; copying; library open to the public with restrictions. **Automated Operations:** Computerized cataloging. **Computerized Information Services:** DIALOG Information Services, CAN/OLE, QL Systems. **Publications:** Information Update, bimonthly; FYI, irregular - both for internal distribution only.

★ 13403 ★
Procurement Associates - Library (Bus-Fin)
733 N. Dodsworth Ave.   Phone: (818)966-4576
Covina, CA 91724   Marie Sirney, Libn.
Staff: Prof 1; Other 2. **Subjects:** Government contracts, business administration. **Holdings:** 4000 books; 6500 government and industry reports; government courses in the field of government contracts. **Subscriptions:** 91 journals and other serials. **Services:** Interlibrary loan; copying; library open to the public.

★ 13404 ★
Prodinform Technical Consulting Co. - Library (Bus-Fin)
P.O. Box 453
H-1372 Budapest, Hungary   Phone: 1 112 870
Subjects: Industry. **Holdings:** 40,000 bound volumes; 100,000 trade catalogs; 5000 conference proceedings. **Subscriptions:** 300 journals and other serials. **Remarks:** Telex: H 227750 PROD H.

★ 13405 ★
Produce Marketing Association - PMA Information Center (Food-Bev)
1500 Casho Mill Rd.
Box 6036   Phone: (302)738-7100
Newark, DE 19714-6036   Julie Stewart, Mgr., Info.Ctr.
Founded: 1949. **Staff:** 4. **Subjects:** Fresh fruit and vegetables, floral products, packaging, marketing, consumer information. **Special Collections:** Microfilm Library (100,000 pages). **Holdings:** 22,000 volumes. **Subscriptions:** 40 journals and other serials; 15 newspapers. **Services:** Interlibrary loan (to other association libraries); library open to the public by appointment. **Computerized Information Services:** Internal database. Performs searches on fee basis for nonmembers. **Publications:** Industry listings of promotional organizations; industry calendar of events. **Remarks:** FAX: (302)731-2409. **Staff:** Leigh Ann Betters; Ginger Pierce; Chris Murray.

★ 13406 ★
Production Engineering Research Association of Great Britain - Information Centre - Library (Sci-Engr)
Melton Mowbray, Leicestershire, England   Phone: 664 501501
       R.J. Willars, Hd. of Info.Ctr.
Subjects: Manufacturing technology - robotics, automation, metal machining, metal forming, castings, inspection, materials, management, finishing, fabrication, materials handling, packaging, safety, and allied subjects. **Holdings:** 15,000 bound volumes. **Subscriptions:** 600 journals and other serials. **Services:** Library not open to the public. **Computerized Information Services:** DIALOG Information Services, ESA/IRS, BLAISE, Data-Star, Infocheck, Ltd.; produces OTISLINE. **Remarks:** FAX: 664 501264. Telex: 34684 PERAMM G.

Proescher Pathology Library
See: **Santa Clara Valley Medical Center - Milton J. Chatton Medical Library (14811)**

Professional Corporation of Physicians of Quebec
See: **Corporation Professionnelle des Medecins du Quebec (4338)**

★ 13407 ★
Professional Educators Resource Center - Cunningham Center (Educ)
9659 E. Mississippi Ave.   Phone: (303)341-6477
Denver, CO 80231   Dawn P. Vaughn, Mgr.
Founded: 1991. **Staff:** Prof 1; Other 3. **Subjects:** Education - elementary, secondary, early childhood, special. **Holdings:** 3000 books; preview books; textbooks. **Subscriptions:** 300 journals and other serials. **Services:** Interlibrary loan; copying; fax service. **Automated Operations:** Computerized cataloging. **Computerized Information Services:** BRS Information Technologies; CD-ROMs (ERIC, BIP-PLUS, Education Index (EDI), Granger's Index to Poetry). **Networks/Consortia:** Member of Bibliographical Center for Research, Rocky Mountain Region, Inc. (BCR), Central Colorado Library System (CCLS). **Remarks:** FAX: (303)341-9347. **Formerly:** Southeast Metropolitan Board of Cooperative Services - Professional Information Center located in Aurora, CO. **Staff:** Nancy Conklin; Barbara Crosby; Laurel McFarland.

★ 13408 ★
Professional Insurance Agents - Library (Bus-Fin)
400 N. Washington St.   Phone: (703)836-9340
Alexandria, VA 22314   J. Welter
Staff: 1. **Subjects:** Insurance. **Holdings:** 10,000 volumes. **Subscriptions:** 300 journals and other serials; 9 newspapers. **Services:** Library not open to the public. **Computerized Information Services:** LEXIS, NEXIS. **Remarks:** FAX: (703)836-1279.

★ 13409 ★
Professional Psychics United - Library (Rel-Phil)
1839 S. Elmwood
Berwyn, IL 60402   Phyllis Allen
Founded: 1977. **Subjects:** Extrasensory perception. **Holdings:** 203 volumes; biographical archives. **Services:** Library open to the public.

★ 13410 ★
Professional School of Psychology - Library (Med)
2190 Sutter   Phone: (415)563-9289
San Francisco, CA 94115   Alan Schut, Libn.
Founded: 1978. **Staff:** Prof 1. **Subjects:** Psychology - general, clinical, organizational. **Holdings:** 2800 books; dissertations. **Subscriptions:** 55 journals and other serials. **Services:** Interlibrary loan; copying; library open to the public with restrictions. **Automated Operations:** Computerized cataloging. **Computerized Information Services:** BRS Information Technologies. Performs searches on fee basis. **Networks/Consortia:** Member of CLASS, Bay Area Library and Information Network. **Remarks:** FAX: (415)563-9267.

★ 13411 ★
Program Planners, Inc. - Library/Information Center (Bus-Fin)
230 W. 41st St., 19th Fl.   Phone: (212)840-2600
New York, NY 10036   Doreen Lilore, Info.Off.
Founded: 1970. **Staff:** Prof 1; Other 2. **Subjects:** Collective bargaining, education, public employee pensions/retirement systems, local government, urban affairs, health care, insurance, sanitation. **Special Collections:** Annual budgets and financial reports for major U.S. cities and school districts; fire, police, sanitation, and transportation departments annual reports; retirement system annual reports; reports of the New York City Special Deputy Comptroller and the New York Financial Control Board, 1976 to present. **Holdings:** 10,000 books and reports; 26 VF drawers of clippings. **Subscriptions:** 110 journals and other serials. **Services:** Interlibrary loan; library open to the public by appointment only. **Computerized Information Services:** Internal databases. **Publications:** Monthly New York City Economic Report.

Programa de las Naciones Unidas para el Medio Ambiente
See: United Nations Environment Programme (16771)

★ 13412 ★
Progressive Foundation - Nukewatch Library (Soc Sci)
P.O. Box 2658
Madison, WI 53701   Phone: (608)256-4146
Founded: 1979. **Staff:** 3. **Subjects:** Nuclear weapons; civil disobedience, non-violence. **Holdings:** 70 books; films; slides. **Services:** Center open to the public. **Publications:** Pathfinder (newsletter). **Staff:** Linda Urfer, Co-Dir.; Bonnie Urfer, Co-Dir.; Alistair Cairns, Co-Dir.

★ 13413 ★
Project Group for Technical Development Cooperation - Library (Soc Sci)
Groot-Brittannienlaan 43
B-9000 Ghent, Belgium   Phone: 91 252793
Staff: 2. **Subjects:** Third World development, agriculture, energy. **Holdings:** 500 volumes. **Services:** Interlibrary loan; copying; library open to the public. **Computerized Information Services:** Internal database. **Remarks:** FAX: 91 256607.

★ 13414 ★
Project for Public Spaces - Library (Plan)
153 Waverly Place   Phone: (212)620-5660
New York, NY 10014   Alexa Berlow, Media Spec.
Founded: 1978. **Staff:** 13. **Subjects:** Urban design and planning, public space design, downtown management, transportation planning, environmental psychology, public markets. **Special Collections:** Slide collection of public spaces, amenities, and issues (100,000 items). **Holdings:** 400 books; 300 research reports and articles. **Services:** Library open to the public by appointment. **Computerized Information Services:** Internal database. PU List of publications, videotapes, and audiotapes - available on request. **Remarks:** FAX: (212)620-3821.

★ 13415 ★
Project SAVE, Inc. - Archive (Area-Ethnic)
46 Elton Ave.   Phone: (617)923-4563
Watertown, MA 02172   Ruth Thomasian
Founded: 1975. **Staff:** Prof 1. **Subjects:** Armenia. **Holdings:** 1000 books; 11,000 photographs; oral histories. **Services:** Archive open to the public by appointment. **Publications:** Photograph calendar, annual.

★ 13416 ★
Project Starlight International - Library (Sci-Engr)
Box 599
College Park, MD 20740
Founded: 1964. **Subjects:** UFOs - physical effects, optical images, locations. **Holdings:** 470 volumes; films emphasizing physics of UFOs and UFO events. **Services:** Library open to qualified researchers only.

Project TALENT Data Bank
See: American Institutes for Research (645)

★ 13417 ★
Promus Companies - Corporate Resource Center (Bus-Fin)
1023 Cherry Rd.   Phone: (901)762-8788
Memphis, TN 38117   Shirley Money, Lib.Res.
Founded: 1979. **Staff:** 1. **Subjects:** Lodging, leisure, gaming, business, management, planning, forecasting. **Holdings:** 900 books; 3000 annual, quarterly, 10K, and proxy reports of major American companies in hardcopy; 2500 internal reports on microfilm. **Subscriptions:** 80 journals and other serials. **Services:** Center not open to the public. **Automated Operations:** Computerized public access catalog, cataloging, acquisitions, serials, and circulation. **Computerized Information Services:** NEXIS, DIALOG Information Services, Dow Jones News/Retrieval.

★ 13418 ★
ProRodeo Hall of Fame - Library (Hist)
101 ProRodeo Dr.   Phone: (719)593-8840
Colorado Springs, CO 80919   Patricia Florence, Asst.Dir./Cur.
Founded: 1979. **Staff:** 1. **Subjects:** Rodeo history, cowboys. **Special Collections:** Everett Bowman Collection. **Holdings:** 500 books; 100 bound periodical volumes; 1000 unbound periodicals. **Services:** Copying; library open to the public by appointment. **Remarks:** FAX: (719)593-9315.

★ 13419 ★
Proskauer, Rose, Goetz & Mendelsohn - Library (Law)
1585 Broadway   Phone: (212)969-5010
New York, NY 10036   Marsha Pront, Dir., Lib.Serv.
Staff: Prof 8; Other 5. **Subjects:** Law. **Holdings:** 50,000 books; 1000 bound periodical volumes. **Subscriptions:** 400 journals and other serials; 35 newspapers. **Services:** Interlibrary loan; copying; library open to the public with permission. **Computerized Information Services:** LEXIS, NEXIS, WESTLAW, Dun & Bradstreet Business Credit Services, BRS Information Technologies, Dow Jones News/Retrieval, Information America, LEGI-SLATE, VU/TEXT Information Services, DataTimes, NewsNet, Inc., RLIN. **Publications:** Library Bulletin, quarterly - internal distribution and to selected libraries. **Remarks:** FAX: (212)969-2900. Maintains 5 branch libraries at: 2121 Avenue of the Stars, Los Angeles, CA 90067, telephone (213)557-2900; 2001 L St., N.W., Washington, DC 20036, telephone (202)466-7300; 150 E. Palmetto Park Rd., Boca Raton, FL 33432, telephone (407)391-9700; 600 Montgomery St., San Francisco, CA 94111, telephone (415)956-2218; 1373 Broad St., Clifton, NJ 07013, telephone (201)779-6300. **Staff:** Nathan Rosen, Assoc.Dir.; David Johnson, Hd. of Ref.; James O'Meara, Ref.Libn.; Linda Hauck, Ref.Libn.; Sadako Oracca, Tech.Serv.Libn.; Dennis Lynch, ILL.

★ 13420 ★
Prospect Congregational Church - U.C.C. Library (Rel-Phil)
On the Green   Phone: (203)758-4872
Prospect, CT 06712   Mary M. Hinman, Libn.
Founded: 1988. **Staff:** 1. **Subjects:** Religion, Bible, missionary works. **Special Collections:** Bereaved Parents collection. **Holdings:** 500 books; 10 videotapes; 10 audiocassettes. **Subscriptions:** 4 journals and other serials. **Services:** Library open with request in writing.

★ 13421 ★
Prosperos - Server's Center (Rel-Phil)
Box 4969
Culver City, CA 90231-4969   Phone: (213)287-1663
Founded: 1956. **Staff:** 1. **Subjects:** Metaphysics, psychology, philosophy, sociology, astrology, religion. **Special Collections:** Thane of Hawaii; C.G. Jung; Emma Curtis Hopkins; Lillian DeWaters. **Holdings:** 4500 volumes. **Services:** Center open to the public by appointment for reference use only. **Publications:** Newsletter of the Prosperos. **Remarks:** Located at 4234 Overland Ave., Culver City, CA 90230.

★ 13422 ★
Protape, Inc. - Library (Bus-Fin, Law)
370 7th Ave., 2nd Fl.   Phone: (212)244-0500
New York, NY 10001   Richard Sobelsohn
Founded: 1970. **Staff:** Prof 3; Other 7. **Subjects:** Accounting, law, real estate, English, math, insurance, travel. **Holdings:** 25,000 books; 250 bound periodical volumes. **Subscriptions:** 75 journals and other serials; 20 newspapers. **Services:** Library not open to the public. **Remarks:** Firm specializes in educational training.

★ 13423 ★
Protestant Episcopal Church - Archives (Rel-Phil)
Box 2247   Phone: (512)472-6816
Austin, TX 78768   Dr. Virginia Nelle Bellamy, Archv.
Staff: Prof 3; Other 1. **Subjects:** History of the Protestant Episcopal Church in America. **Special Collections:** Correspondence of the Domestic and Foreign Missionary Society; archives of the General Convention. **Holdings:** 10,000 volumes; manuscripts; documents. **Services:** Copying; archives open to the public.

★ 13424 ★
Protestant Episcopal Church - Diocese of Indianapolis, Indiana - Archives (Rel-Phil)
Indiana State Library
1100 W. 42nd St.   Phone: (317)926-5454
Indianapolis, IN 46208   Dr. Wendell Calkins, Historiographer
Subjects: Church history. **Special Collections:** Diocesan manuscripts, 1833 to present (85 file boxes). **Holdings:** 40 books; bishop's correspondence; church records; personnel jackets. **Services:** Interlibrary loan; copying; archives open to the public with restrictions. **Special Catalogs:** Archive inventory; catalog of bishop's correspondence (card). **Remarks:** Correspondence and requests for permission to work in the archives should be sent to Bishop Edward W. Jones, Episcopal Diocesan Headquarters, 1100 W. 42nd St., Indianapolis, IN 46208.

★ 13425 ★
Protestant Episcopal Church - Diocese of Pennsylvania - Information Center (Rel-Phil)
240 S. 4th St.
Philadelphia, PA 19106   Phone: (215)627-6434
Staff: 1. **Subjects:** Episcopal Church, Diocese of Pennsylvania, Anglicanism. **Holdings:** 300 books; parish records; diocesan journals; confirmation records; archives. **Services:** Center open to public.

★ 13426 ★
Protestant Episcopal Church - Episcopal Diocese of Connecticut - Diocesan Library and Archives (Rel-Phil)
1335 Asylum Ave.   Phone: (203)233-4481
Hartford, CT 06105   Rev. Dr. Robert G. Carroon, Archv.
Founded: 1850. **Staff:** Prof 1; Other 2. **Subjects:** History of the Episcopal Church in Connecticut. **Special Collections:** Papers of the Bishops of Connecticut, 1784-1955 (6000 pieces); letters and historical documents of the Episcopal Church in Connecticut, 1786-1885 (6000 pieces); early sermons (Colonial period); cathedral and parochial historical materials; parish registers and records of diocesan organizations, 1790 to present; papers of the Standing Committee, 1796 to present; papers of the Society for the Increase of the Ministry (12,000 pieces); films of reports of the missionaries under the Society for the Propagation of the Gospel in Foreign Parts, 1700-1776; records of the Episcopal Academy of Connecticut at Cheshire. **Holdings:** 100,000 manuscripts and films; 400 reference books; 3000 bound pamphlets. **Subscriptions:** 51 journals and other serials; 6 newspapers. **Services:** Copying; library open to the public by appointment. **Computerized Information Services:** Internal database. **Remarks:** FAX: (203)523-1410.

★ 13427 ★
Protestant Episcopal Church - Episcopal Diocese of Massachusetts - Diocesan Library and Archives (Rel-Phil)
138 Tremont St.   Phone: (617)482-5800
Boston, MA 02111   Mary Eleanor Murphy, Archv.
Founded: 1884. **Staff:** 2. **Subjects:** History of churches in the diocese and published work of the clergy. **Special Collections:** Americana (Colonial sermons); published records of the Society for the Propagation for the Gospel, 1701-1892. **Holdings:** Offical papers of the diocese, its bishops and affiliated agencies; historical manuscripts and pre-1905 vital records of its parishes; 50 linear feet of 19th and 20th century pamphlets. **Subscriptions:** 2 journals and other serials; 2 newspapers. **Services:** Archives open to the public for reference use only. **Publications:** Guide for Parish Historians (1961); brochures on history of the Diocese of Massachusetts; Guide to the Parochial Archives of the Episcopal Church in Boston (1981). **Remarks:** A description of the manuscript collection was published by Works Progress Administration, Boston, 1939. FAX: (617)482-8431. **Staff:** Ruth S. Leonard, Lib.Cons.

Protestant Episcopal Church - Episcopal Diocese of New Jersey - Audio-Visual Resource Library
See: **Audio-Visual Resource Library** (1288)

★ 13428 ★
Protestant Episcopal Church - Episcopal Diocese of Oregon - Archives (Rel-Phil)
Box 467   Phone: (503)636-5613
Lake Oswego, OR 97034   Rev. Chandler Jackson
Founded: 1912. **Staff:** Prof 1. **Subjects:** Diocese history. **Holdings:** 100 books; 200 bound periodical volumes; manuscripts; correspondence; archival materials; pictures; statistics. **Subscriptions:** 3 journals and other serials. **Services:** Interlibrary loan; archives open to the public. **Publications:** Journal of Convention of the Diocese of Oregon, annual. **Remarks:** FAX: (503)636-5616.

Protestant Episcopal Church - Episcopal Diocese of Pennsylvania - Audio-Visual Resource Library
See: **Audio-Visual Resource Library** (1288)

★ 13429 ★
Protestant Episcopal Church - Episcopal Diocese of South Dakota - Archives (Rel-Phil)
Center for Western Studies
Augustana College
Box 727   Phone: (605)336-4007
Sioux Falls, SD 57197   Harry F. Thompson, Cur.
Staff: Prof 1; Other 2. **Subjects:** History - Episcopal church, South Dakota, Great Plains, United States; missionary work; Indian culture. **Special Collections:** Bishop William H. Hare papers (10 cubic feet); Rev. Joseph W. Cook journals (28 volumes); Bishop Hugh L. Burleson papers (4 cubic feet); Bishop W. Blair Roberts papers (25 cubic feet); Bishop Conrad H. Gesner papers (25 cubic feet). **Holdings:** 40 volumes of church registers. **Services:** Copying; archives open to the public with restrictions.

★ 13430 ★
Protestant Episcopal Church - Episcopal Diocese of Southwest Florida - Brown Memorial Library (Rel-Phil)
P.O. Box 661
Ellenton, FL 34222   Phone: (813)776-1018
Founded: 1984. **Subjects:** Religion. **Holdings:** 2000 books. **Subscriptions:** 3 journals and other serials. **Services:** library open to the public. **Remarks:** Library is located at DaySpring Conference Center of the Episcopal Diocese of Southwest Florida.

★ 13431 ★
Protestant Episcopal Church - Episcopal Diocese of Springfield, Illinois - Diocesan Center Library (Hist)
821 S. 2nd St.   Phone: (217)525-1876
Springfield, IL 62704   Philip L. Shutt, Reg./Historiographer
Staff: Prof 2. **Subjects:** Diocesan archives. **Special Collections:** Journals of Diocese of Illinois, 1835-1877; journals of Diocese of Springfield, 1878 to present; journals of the General Convention of the Episcopal Church, 1823 to present. **Holdings:** 187 volumes; manuscripts; reports; diocesan records; defunct parish records; maps; photographs. **Services:** Interlibrary loan; library open to the public. **Staff:** Betty Howard Leinicke, Asst.Hist.

★13432★

Protestant Episcopal Church - Episcopal Diocese of Utah - Archives
(Rel-Phil)
Box 3090
Salt Lake City, UT 84110-3090   Phone: (801)322-3400
Subjects: History of the Episcopal Diocese of Utah, 1867 to present.
Holdings: 65 cubic feet of diocesan records, journals of annual conventions,
confirmation records, financial records, parish statistical reports, diaries and
registers of the clergy. **Services:** Archives open to the public by appointment.
Remarks: FAX: (801)322-5096.

★13433★

Protestant Episcopal Church - Episcopal Diocese of West Texas -
Cathedral House Archives (Rel-Phil)
111 Torcido Dr.
Box 6885   Phone: (512)824-5387
San Antonio, TX 78209   Ms. Winifred Toon, Hist.
Subjects: Religion, history, education. **Special Collections:** History of the
Episcopal Diocese of West Texas and its institutions, including St. Philip's
College, St. Mary's Hall, and Texas Military Institute, 1874 to present.
Holdings: 5000 books; 50 linear feet of letters, minutes, diaries, records,
scrapbooks, and manuscripts. **Services:** Copying; archives open to other
churches. **Automated Operations:** Computerized cataloging and
acquisitions.

★13434★

Protestant Episcopal Church - Episcopal Diocese of Western North
Carolina - Library & Archives (Rel-Phil)
Bishop Henry Center
In-the-Oaks
Vance Ave.
Box 368
Black Mountain, NC 28711   Phone: (704)669-2921
Founded: 1975. **Staff:** Prof 2. **Subjects:** Theology, religion, Christian
education, church history, Bible study, handicrafts, music, drama,
biography. **Special Collections:** Diocese and congregational papers, 1800 to
present. **Holdings:** 6000 books; AV programs; hymn and prayer books;
handicrafts; archival material. **Subscriptions:** 90 journals and other serials.
Services: Interlibrary loan; copying; library open to the public with
restrictions. **Computerized Information Services:** Internal database.
Remarks: FAX: (704)669-2756. **Also Known As:** Episcopal Church in the
U.S.A. **Staff:** Carolyn Hughes, Libn.; Dr. Philip Walker, Archv.

★13435★

Protestant Episcopal Church - Missouri Diocese - Diocesan Archives
(Rel-Phil)
1210 Locust St.   Phone: (314)231-1220
St. Louis, MO 63103-2390   Charles F. Rehkopf, Archv./Reg.
Founded: 1840. **Staff:** Prof 1; Other 2. **Subjects:** History - diocesan, parish,
Anglican Church, Missouri, St. Louis. **Special Collections:** Journals of the
General Convention, 1784 to present (71 volumes); Journals of the Diocese
of Missouri, 1841 to present (151 volumes); The Spirit of Missions Forth,
the Episcopalian and Episcopal Life, 1835 to present (158 volumes);
Historical Magazine of the Episcopal Church, 1932 to present; Episcopal
Church Almanacs and Annuals, 1830 to present (104 volumes); Episcopal
Clerical Directories, 1785 to present (24 volumes). **Holdings:** 572 books; 223
bound periodical volumes; 83.5 linear feet of diocesan archives; 40 linear feet
of parish files. **Subscriptions:** 13 journals and other serials. **Services:**
Interlibrary loan; copying; archives open to the public by appointment.
Special Indexes: Index of diocesan publications and official records (card);
finding aids for diocesan historical collections.

★13436★

Protestant Episcopal Church of Western Washington - Diocese of
Olympia - Archives (Rel-Phil)
1551 10th Ave., E.
Box 12126   Phone: (206)325-4200
Seattle, WA 98102   Peggy Ann Hansen, Archv.
Founded: 1976. **Staff:** Prof 1. **Subjects:** Diocesan archives. **Special**
Collections: Bishop Stephen Fielding Bayne, Jr. Collection; Bishop Simeon
Arthur Huston Collection. **Holdings:** 1000 books; bishop's office and
diocesan records; journals; newspapers; pictures; tapes; early Washington
and Oregon Episcopal territory newspapers; Olympia Churman, 1923-1986;
Evergreen Messenger, 1986 to present; complete set of Findings magazine;
complete set of Episcopalian, on microfilm; incomplete sets of Living

Church and Spirit of Missions; complete set of Forth, on microfilm;
confirmation records, 1894-1988 (online); Journals of the Missionary
District, 1851-1910; Diocese of Olympia, 1911-1989 (microfiche);
confirmation records, 1894-1989 (online). **Subscriptions:** 5 journals and
other serials. **Services:** Copying; genealogical search (fee); archives open to
the public with restrictions. **Computerized Information Services:** Internal
databases. **Remarks:** FAX: (206)325-4631.

★13437★

Protestant Episcopal Church of Western Washington - Diocese of
Olympia - Diocesan Resource Center (Rel-Phil)
1551 10th Ave., E.
Box 12126   Phone: (206)325-4200
Seattle, WA 98102   Janice Matsumoto, Libn.
Founded: 1965. **Staff:** Prof 1; Other 1. **Subjects:** Religion, theology, religious
education, leadership training. **Holdings:** 4000 volumes; 46 films; 30
filmstrips; 350 video cassettes; 75 cassette tapes. **Subscriptions:** 18 journals
and other serials. **Services:** Interlibrary loan; center open to the public.
Special Catalogs: Audio-visual catalog. **Remarks:** FAX: (206)325-4631.

★13438★

Protestant School Board of Greater Montreal - Sarah Maxwell Library
(Educ)
6000 Fielding Ave.   Phone: (514)483-7200
Montreal, PQ, Canada H3X 1T4   I. Gammon, Libn.
Founded: 1963. **Staff:** Prof 1. **Subjects:** Education, child psychology, school
administration, curriculum, special education. **Holdings:** 8000 books; 452
bound periodical volumes; unbound materials. **Subscriptions:** 100 journals
and other serials. **Services:** Interlibrary loan; copying; library open to the
public for reference use only. **Publications:** Copycat, semiannual.

Prouty-Chew Museum and Library
See: **Geneva Historical Society** (6358)

★13439★

Proverbs Heritage Organization - John Freeman Walls Historic Site &
Underground Railroad Museum - Library (Hist)
1307 Pelissier St.   Phone: (519)977-1588
Windsor, ON, Canada N8X 1M4   Allen E. Walls, Hd.Libn. &
                                      Asst.Musm.Cur.
Subjects: Underground Railroad history, black Canadian and American
history, Walls family history, Essex County and Maidstone Township
history, American and Canadian history. **Holdings:** 100 books; 75 AV
programs; 4 manuscripts. **Services:** Copying; library open to the public by
appointment. **Remarks:** Historic site is said to be located where the
underground railroad had its end. **Remarks:** FAX: (519)258-5499.

★13440★

Providence Athenaeum - Library (Hum)
251 Benefit St.   Phone: (401)421-6970
Providence, RI 02903   Michael Price, Dir./Libn.
Founded: 1753. **Staff:** Prof 2; Other 15. **Subjects:** History, literature,
biography, art, voyage and travel, natural history. **Special Collections:**
Audubon Collection; Bowen Collection; Robert Burns Collection;
collections in 19th century fiction and juvenile literature; rare books.
Holdings: 151,486 books; 304 bound periodical titles. **Subscriptions:** 155
journals and other serials. **Services:** Interlibrary loan; copying; research
facilities; library open to the public. **Networks/Consortia:** Member of Rhode
Island Library Network (RHILINET). **Publications:** Providence
Athenaeum Bulletin; Annual Report. **Special Catalogs:** Travel and
Exploration: Catalogue of the Providence Athenaeum Collection, 1988.
Remarks: FAX: (401)421-2860. **Staff:** Juliet T. Saunders, Asst.Dir.; Risa
Gilpin, Hd. of Pub.Serv.; Dolly Borts, Hd., Tech.Serv.; Mary Iacobba,
Ch.Libn.; Mary Moore, Ch.Libn.; Susan Newkirk, Cons.Mgr.

★13441★

The Providence Center - Presel Memorial Library (Med)
520 Hope St.   Phone: (401)274-2500
Providence, RI 02906   Patricia M. Vigorito
Founded: 1985. **Subjects:** Psychiatry, psychology, social work. **Holdings:**
600 books. **Subscriptions:** 40 journals and other serials. **Services:**
Interlibrary loan; copying; library open to the public by appointment.

★ 13442 ★
Providence College - Phillips Memorial Library (Rel-Phil, Soc Sci)
River Ave. at Eaton St.   Phone: (401)865-2377
Providence, RI 02918   Jane Jackson, Dir. of Archv.
Founded: 1917. **Staff:** Prof 7; Other 35. **Subjects:** Works of St. Thomas Aquinas, Thomistic philosophy and theology, Dominican Order. **Special Collections:** John E. Fogarty Papers (500,000 pieces); Dennis J. Roberts Papers (3000 pieces); William Henry Chamberlin Papers (120 pieces and 40 diaries on microfilm); Louis Francis Budenz Papers (9500 pamphlets and periodicals); Rhode Island Constitutional Convention Collection, 1964-1968 (1000 pieces); Cornelius Moore Papers (250 pieces); J. Lyons Moore Collection (3000 pieces); Robert E. Quinn Papers and Oral History Project; Rhode Island Urban League Papers (200,000 items); Nazi Bund Collection (300 pieces); John J. Fawcett Collection (3000 drawings); Limited Constitutional Convention, 1973 (500 pieces); Quonset Point Collection (9500 pieces); Blackfriars' Guild Collection (2500 pieces); Joseph A. Doorley, Jr. Collection (60,000 pieces); Black Regiment Collection (600 pieces); Bonniwell Liturgical Collection (2100 books); Coutu Genealogy; Aime J. Forand Collection (4500 pieces); Irish Literature Collection (100 pieces); John O. Pastore Collection (100,000 pieces); Social Justice Collection, 1936-1942 (325 pieces); Walsh Civil War Diary (30 pages); Black Newspapers, 1932-1957 (8 reels of microfilm); Confederation Period in Rhode Island Newspapers Collection (48 pieces); Reunification of Ireland Clippings (7 pieces); National Association for the Advancement of Colored People Collection (pending); English and Colonial 18th Century Trade Statistics Collection (500,000 I.B.M. cards); Alice Lafond Altieri Collection (925 pieces); J. Howard McGrath Collection (62,100 pieces); Thomas Matthew McGlynn, O.P. Collection (5000 pieces and art objects); Edward J. Higgins Collection; Edward P. Beard Collection (75,100 pieces); Patrick T. Conley Photograph Collection (460 reprints); Rhode Island Football Officials' Association Collection (900 pieces); Rhode Island Constitutional Convention Collection, 1986 (2300 pieces); Frank Lanning Collection (57 drawings). **Holdings:** 247,852 books; 51,007 bound periodical volumes; 118,830 government documents; 26,609 microforms; 1113 AV items. **Subscriptions:** 1877 journals. **Services:** Interlibrary loan (books only); copying; library open to the public for reference use only. **Automated Operations:** Computerized cataloging, acquisitions, and ILL. **Computerized Information Services:** DIALOG Information Services, BRS Information Technologies, OCLC; CD-ROM. **Networks/Consortia:** Member of Consortium of Rhode Island Academic and Research Libraries, Inc. (CRIARL), NELINET, Inc. **Remarks:** FAX: (401)865-2057. **Staff:** Edgar C. Bailey, Jr., Dir. of Lib.; Elaine Shanley, Hd.Cat.; Norman Desmarais, Acq.Libn.; Janice Schuster, Hd. of Pub.Serv.; Julia Tryon, Ref.Libn.

★ 13443 ★
Providence College & Seminary - Library (Rel-Phil)
Otterburne, MB, Canada R0A 1G0   Phone: (204)433-7488
      Larry Wild, Hd.Libn.
Founded: 1925. **Staff:** Prof 3; Other 11. **Subjects:** Theology, Old and New Testament. **Holdings:** 41,114 books; 1991 bound periodical volumes; 1932 book titles in microform; 149 periodical titles in microform; 44 VF drawers; 360 scores; 620 sound recordings; 1643 cassette tapes; 580 choral music items; 104 media kits. **Subscriptions:** 372 journals and other serials. **Services:** Interlibrary loan; copying; library open to the public. **Automated Operations:** Computerized cataloging and ILL. **Computerized Information Services:** OCLC; internal databases. **Remarks:** FAX: (204)433-7158. **Formerly:** Winnipeg Bible College - Reimer Library. **Staff:** Jennifer Kroeker, Pub.Serv.Libn.; Martha Loeppky, Tech.Serv.Libn.

★ 13444 ★
Providence Hospital - Health Science Library (Med)
Box 850724   Phone: (205)633-1373
Mobile, AL 36685   Mary Ann Donnell, Libn.
Founded: 1980. **Staff:** Prof 1. **Subjects:** Nursing, medicine, hospital administration, allied health sciences. **Holdings:** 1800 books; bound periodical volumes. **Subscriptions:** 111 journals and other serials. **Services:** Interlibrary loan; copying; library open to the public at librarian's discretion. **Computerized Information Services:** MEDLARS, BRS Information Technologies. Performs searches on fee basis. **Networks/Consortia:** Member of National Network of Libraries of Medicine (NN/LM), Alabama Health Libraries Association (ALHELA). **Remarks:** Library located at 6801 Airport Blvd., Mobile, AL 36608.

★ 13445 ★
Providence Hospital - Health Sciences Library (Med)
1150 Varnum St., N.E.   Phone: (202)269-7144
Washington, DC 20017   RoseMarie G. Leone, Dir.
Founded: 1968. **Staff:** Prof 1; Other 3. **Subjects:** Medicine, nursing, hospital administration, allied health sciences. **Holdings:** 1905 books; 5040 bound periodical volumes. **Subscriptions:** 200 journals and other serials. **Services:** Interlibrary loan; library not open to the public. **Computerized Information Services:** MEDLARS, DIALOG Information Services. **Networks/Consortia:** Member of National Network of Libraries of Medicine - Southeastern/Atlantic Region.

★ 13446 ★
Providence Hospital - Helen L. DeRoy Medical Library (Med)
16001 W. 9 Mile Rd.
Box 2043   Phone: (313)424-3294
Southfield, MI 48037   Carole M. Gilbert, Dir., Lib.Serv.
Founded: 1988. **Staff:** Prof 3; Other 2. **Subjects:** Medicine, nursing, allied health sciences, hospitals. **Holdings:** 3000 books; 8500 bound periodical volumes; 700 audio-visuals and computer-assisted instruction programs. **Subscriptions:** 550 journals and other serials. **Services:** Interlibrary loan; library not open to the public. **Automated Operations:** Computerized cataloging, acquisitions, serials, and circulation. **Computerized Information Services:** DIALOG Information Services, BRS Information Technologies, MEDLARS, WILSONLINE, VU/TEXT Information Services. **Networks/Consortia:** Member of Oakland Wayne Interlibrary Network (OWIN). **Remarks:** FAX: (313)424-3201. **Staff:** Karen Tubolino, Libn.; Robin Terebelo, Libn.

★ 13447 ★
Providence Hospital - Medical Library (Med)
2446 Kipling Ave.   Phone: (513)853-5806
Cincinnati, OH 45239   Carol Mayor
Founded: 1978. **Staff:** Prof 1. **Subjects:** Medicine, nursing, and allied health sciences. **Holdings:** 300 books; 4000 bound periodical volumes. **Subscriptions:** 179 journals and other serials. **Services:** Interlibrary loan; library not open to the public. **Computerized Information Services:** BRS Information Technologies; DOCLINE (electronic mail service). **Networks/Consortia:** Member of National Network of Libraries of Medicine - Greater Midwest Region. **Remarks:** FAX: (513)853-9510.

★ 13448 ★
Providence Hospital - School of Nursing Library (Med)
1912 Hayes Ave.   Phone: (419)625-8450
Sandusky, OH 44870   Marie L. Paulson, Libn.
Founded: 1905. **Staff:** Prof 1. **Subjects:** Nurses and nursing, medicine, social sciences, natural science, philosophy, religion. **Holdings:** 3160 books; 600 bound periodical volumes; 12 VF drawers of pamphlets, leaflets, pictures, articles. **Subscriptions:** 81 journals and other serials. **Services:** Interlibrary loan; copying; library open to the public with restrictions. **Computerized Information Services:** DIALOG Information Services.

Providence Hospital, Everett - Health Information Network Services
See: **Health Information Network Services (7077)**

★ 13449 ★
Providence Journal Company - News Library (Publ)
75 Fountain St.   Phone: (401)277-7390
Providence, RI 02902   Linda L. Henderson, Libn.
Founded: 1920. **Staff:** Prof 2; Other 5. **Subjects:** Newspaper reference topics. **Special Collections:** Journal Bulletin Almanacs, 1892 to present. **Holdings:** 2500 books; clippings; picture collection; microforms; pamphlets. **Subscriptions:** 40 journals and other serials; 18 newspapers. **Services:** Library open to the public by appointment. **Computerized Information Services:** DIALOG Information Services, Dow Jones News/Retrieval, VU/TEXT Information Services, NEXIS, DataTimes; J/TEXT (internal database). **Publications:** Journal Bulletin Almanac.

★ 13450 ★
Providence Medical Center - Horton Health Sciences Library (Med)
500 17th Ave., C-34008   Phone: (206)320-2423
Seattle, WA 98124   Kathleen Murray, Dir., Lib.Serv.
Founded: 1950. **Staff:** 5. **Subjects:** Clinical medicine, surgery, cardiology, nursing, psychiatry. **Holdings:** 9000 volumes; 1 VF drawer. **Subscriptions:** 650 journals and other serials. **Services:** Interlibrary loan; copying; SDI; library open to patients and family members. **Automated Operations:** Computerized public access catalog, cataloging, acquisitions, serials, and circulation. **Computerized Information Services:** Western Library Network (WLN), MEDLINE, BRS Information Technologies, DIALOG Information Services; InterNet, OnTyme Electronic Message Network Service (electronic mail services). Performs searches on fee basis. **Networks/Consortia:** Member of Seattle Area Hospital Library Consortium (SAHLC). **Remarks:** FAX: (206)324-5871. Electronic mail address(es): kmurray@u.washington.edu (InterNet); PMC (OnTyme Electronic Message Network Service). **Staff:** Val Schultheiss, Outreach Libn.; Susan Bott, ILL/Ser.Techn.

★ 13451 ★
Providence Medical Center - Medical Library (Med)
4805 N.E. Glisan   Phone: (503)230-6075
Portland, OR 97213   Peggy R. Burrell, Med.Lib.Dir.
Staff: Prof 1; Other .5. **Subjects:** Nursing, medicine, administration. **Holdings:** 600 books. **Subscriptions:** 214 journals and other serials. **Services:** Interlibrary loan; library open to the public with restrictions. **Computerized Information Services:** MEDLARS, DIALOG Information Services, BRS/COLLEAGUE; OnTyme Electronic Message Network Service (electronic mail service). Performs searches. **Networks/Consortia:** Member of Oregon Health Sciences Libraries Association (OHSLA). **Remarks:** FAX: (503)232-4298.

★ 13452 ★
Providence Presbyterian Church - Library (Rel-Phil)
Box 64033
Virginia Beach, VA 23464   Phone: (804)420-6159
Founded: 1985. **Staff:** Prof 1; Other 6. **Subjects:** Presbyterian Church, Bible. **Holdings:** 350 books. **Services:** Library open to the public for reference use only.

★ 13453 ★
Providence Public Library - Reference Services Department - Business Collection (Bus-Fin, Sci-Engr)
225 Washington St.
Providence, RI 02903   Phone: (401)455-8000
Founded: 1923. **Staff:** Prof 4. **Subjects:** Pure and applied sciences, technology, business. **Special Collections:** Historical textiles collection. **Holdings:** 20,000 books; 18,500 bound periodical volumes; 20 VF drawers of federal and military specifications; 3400 annual reports; U.S. patents, 1790 to present, on microfilm; indexes to U.S. patents, 1790 to present; official gazettes, 1872 to present, on microfilm; pamphlets. **Subscriptions:** 306 journals and other serials. **Services:** Interlibrary loan; copying; department open to the public. **Automated Operations:** Computerized acquisitions and circulation. **Computerized Information Services:** DIALOG Information Services, OCLC. Performs searches on fee basis. **Networks/Consortia:** Member of Consortium of Rhode Island Academic and Research Libraries, Inc. (CRIARL), Rhode Island Library Network (RHILINET). **Publications:** Annual report - available upon request. **Special Indexes:** Index to Rhode Island Inventors and Inventions. **Remarks:** FAX: (401)455-8080. **Formerly:** Its Business-Industry-Science Collection. **Staff:** Peter Holscher, Ref.Libn.; William Keach, Ref.Libn.; Ann Poulos, Ref.Libn./Patent Libn.

★ 13454 ★
Providence Public Library - Special Collections Department (Soc Sci)
225 Washington St.
Providence, RI 02903   Phone: (401)455-8021
                    Ms. Dale Thompson
Founded: 1878. **Staff:** Prof 1. **Special Collections:** Daniel Berkeley Updike Printing Collection (7000 volumes; 500 letters; engraved portraits; ephemera; 3 presses); C. Fiske Harris Collection on the Civil War and Slavery (6000 pamphlets; 1500 books; 100 volumes of newspaper clippings; 107 volumes of bound newspapers; boxes and albums of songs and ballads; prints; manuscripts; photographs; broadsides); Potter/Williams Collection on Irish Culture (2000 volumes; 450 pamphlets; 1000 broadside ballads); Wetmore Collection of Children's Books (2000 volumes; drawings; manuscripts); Nicholson Whaling Collection (750 manuscript logbooks that

record over 1000 voyages; books; boxes of manuscripts and photographs); Percival Collection on Magic (1200 volumes and pamphlets; periodicals; manuscripts); William H. Edwards Collection on Legal History and the U.S. Supreme Court (1050 volumes); rare books collection (1000 books); Updike Pamphlet Collection (17th-19th century British and American books and pamphlets on law and Rhode Island history; 665 volumes); Edward B. Hanes Collection on Checkers (542 volumes); Barney Collection on Whist (500 volumes); Wetmore Collection of Illustrated Books (400 volumes); Alfred E. Brownwell Collection on Maritime History (320 volumes; 550 blueprints and technical drawings; prints; photographs; 11 ship models); Rhode Island Soldiers' and Sailors' Historical Society Collection (Civil War; 300 volumes); World War I and World War II posters (200); Reeves Collection of Band Music (65 cartons of music; 2 cartons of wax cylinders); Archives of the Providence Public Library (12 shelves of archival material); prints and broadsides relating to Rhode Island (2 map case drawers); Updike/Arnold Collection of Autographs (1500 letters and manuscripts). **Holdings:** 24,500 books; 1000 bound periodical volumes; 42 linear feet of archival materials. **Services:** Copying; collections open to the public. **Publications:** The Voice of the Whaleman, With an Account of the Nicholson Whaling Collection, 1965. **Remarks:** FAX: (401)455-8080. **Staff:** Philip J. Weimerskirch, Spec.Coll.Libn.

★ 13455 ★
Providence-St. Margaret Health Center - Library (Med)
8929 Parallel Pkwy.   Phone: (913)596-4795
Kansas City, KS 66112   Paul Nixon, Med.Libn.
Staff: Prof 1; Other 1. **Subjects:** Medicine, surgery, nursing, health sciences. **Holdings:** 1300 books; 773 bound periodical volumes; AV programs; videocassettes; cassette tapes; 4 VF drawers. **Subscriptions:** 115 journals and other serials. **Services:** Interlibrary loan; copying; library open to hospital staff and students. **Computerized Information Services:** MEDLINE, DIALOG Information Services. **Networks/Consortia:** Member of Kansas City Library Network, Inc. (KCLN).

Provincial Archives of Alberta - Library
See: **Alberta Culture and Multiculturalism** (259)

Provincial Archives of New Brunswick
See: **(New Brunswick) Provincial Archives of New Brunswick** (11453)

★ 13456 ★
Prowers County Historical Society - Big Timbers Museum - Library (Hist)
North Santa Fe Trail
Box 362   Phone: (719)336-2472
Lamar, CO 81052   Edith Birchler, Cur.
Subjects: Local history. **Holdings:** 200 books; Prowers County newspapers. **Services:** Library open to the public for reference use only.

★ 13457 ★
Prudential Insurance Company of America - Business Library (Bus-Fin)
24 Greenway Plaza, Suite 1900   Phone: (713)993-3526
Houston, TX 77046   W.T. Shelton, Jr.
Founded: 1952. **Subjects:** Group life insurance, group accident and health insurance, sales promotion, business and business methods, statistics, economics. **Holdings:** 150 volumes. **Subscriptions:** 15 journals and other serials. **Services:** Library not open to the public. **Remarks:** FAX: (713)965-8202.

★ 13458 ★
Prudential Insurance Company of America - Corporate Finance Group - Financial Research Center (Bus-Fin)
Gateway Center IV, 7th Fl.
100 Mulberry St.   Phone: (201)802-4967
Newark, NJ 07102   Marilyn Lukas, Mgr.
Staff: Prof 3; Other 2. **Subjects:** Finance, business, industry. **Holdings:** 1000 books. **Subscriptions:** 350 journals and other serials; 25 newspapers. **Services:** Center not open to the public. **Automated Operations:** Computerized cataloging, acquisitions, serials, and circulation (INMAGIC). **Computerized Information Services:** Dow Jones News/Retrieval, TEXTLINE, DIALOG Information Services, The Globe and Mail Online, VU/TEXT Information Services, DataTimes, IDD Mergers & Acquisitions Database, IDD Information Services, Inc. (IDDIS), MAID; CD-ROM (Lotus One Source); READMORE (internal database). **Publications:** Acquisitions list, bimonthly. **Remarks:** FAX: (201)802-2237. **Staff:** Lynn Reiff, Fin.Res.Cons.; Anna Shallenberger, Fin.Res.Cons.

★ 13459 ★
Prudential Insurance Company of America - Corporate Law Library
(Law, Bus-Fin)
22 Plaza
751 Broad St.   Phone: (201)802-2360
Newark, NJ 07102-3777   Bill Fellers, Mgr., Corp. Law Lib.
Staff: Prof 2; Other 4. **Subjects:** Law, securities, real estate, tax, insurance. **Special Collections:** International securities. **Holdings:** 50,000 volumes. **Subscriptions:** 203 journals and other serials. **Services:** Interlibrary loan; copying; SDI; library open to the public with permission of director. **Computerized Information Services:** DIALOG Information Services, WESTLAW, ELSS (Electronic Legislative Search System), LEXIS, DataTimes; PROFS (electronic mail service) **Remarks:** FAX: (201)802-2298. **Formerly:** Its Law Library. **Staff:** Henry Hoyt, Jr.

★ 13460 ★
Prudential Insurance Company of America - Dryden Business Library
(Bus-Fin)
751 Broad St.   Phone: (201)802-7583
Newark, NJ 07102-3777   Barbara Ciccone, Mktg.Res.Cons.
Founded: 1941. **Staff:** Prof 3; Other 1. **Subjects:** Insurance, personnel management, office management, census statistics. **Special Collections:** Actuarial proceedings. **Holdings:** 5600 books; 95 VF drawers. **Subscriptions:** 150 journals and other serials. **Services:** Interlibrary loan; library not open to the public. **Computerized Information Services:** DIALOG Information Services, BRS Information Technologies, NEXIS, The Source Information Network, Washington Alert Service, NewsNet, Inc., VU/TEXT Information Services, DataTimes, Reuter TEXTLINE, Global Report; internal database.

Prussian Cultural Foundation
See: Stiftung Preussischer Kulturbesitz (15795)

★ 13461 ★
Pryor, Carney and Johnson - Library (Law)
6200 S. Syracuse, Suite 400
P.O. Box 6559   Phone: (303)771-6200
Englewood, CO 80155-6559   Terry Wilkens, Libn.
Staff: Prof 2. **Subjects:** Law. **Holdings:** 5000 books. **Subscriptions:** 225 journals and other serials. **Services:** Library not open to the public. **Computerized Information Services:** WESTLAW; internal database. **Special Indexes:** Document file (online, card).

★ 13462 ★
Psi Epsilon Delta - Library (Rel-Phil)
c/o Rev. Lawrence Kohlman, SCM
Notre Dame de Lafayette University
941 S. Havana St.   Phone: (303)341-0084
Aurora, CO 80012   Karen Degenhart
Founded: 1988. **Staff:** 18. **Subjects:** Pastoral wellness, holistic healthcare, prayer, meditation, theology, psychotherapy, chiropathy. **Holdings:** 2000 volumes. **Services:** Library open to persons with a Lafayette University library card or other local college ID. **Computerized Information Services:** Internal database. **Publications:** NDLU Spotlight; Alumni News. **Staff:** Rev. Michael Mason, SCM; Brother David Wilson, SCM, Ed.

★ 13463 ★
PSI Research - Library (Rel-Phil)
216 Power Ln.   Phone: (918)456-6213
Tahlequah, OK 74464   Larissa Vilenskaya, Dir.
Founded: 1982. **Staff:** 1. **Subjects:** Parapsychological studies in the USSR, Eastern Europe, and China. **Holdings:** 250 books; 6 filing drawers and 20 boxes of bound and unbound periodicals, manuscripts, archival materials. **Services:** Interlibrary loan; copying; library open to the public by appointment. **Remarks:** FAX: (918)458-5501. **Formerly:** Located in Monterey, CA.

★ 13464 ★
Psoriasis Research Association - Library (Med)
107 Vista del Grande
San Carlos, CA 94070   Phone: (415)593-1394
Subjects: Psoriasis - cause, cure, related subspecialties. **Holdings:** 1500 volumes.

★ 13465 ★
PSP: Human Resource Development - Library (Soc Sci)
2 Mellon Bank Center, Suite 470   Phone: (412)261-1333
Pittsburgh, PA 15219   Dina J. Fulmer, Libn.
Founded: 1946. **Staff:** Prof 1. **Subjects:** Industrial psychology; counseling - educational, career, personal; mental health; organization development; psychological testing; work attitudes and motivation; personnel selection; research techniques and statistical methods. **Holdings:** 500 volumes; 16 VF drawers of reports, pamphlets, reprints, clippings. **Subscriptions:** 40 journals and other serials. **Services:** Interlibrary loan; copying; SDI; library open to qualified persons by appointment. **Computerized Information Services:** DIALOG Information Services. **Remarks:** FAX: (412)261-5014.

Psychiatric Institute of Wyoming - Library
See: Pine Ridge Hospital (13064)

★ 13466 ★
Psychic Science Institute - Haunt Hunters - Library (Rel-Phil)
2188 Sycamore Hill Ct.
Chesterfield, MO 63017   Phone: (314)831-1379
Subjects: Psychic phenomenon, ghosts and hauntings, psychic abilities, witchcraft, voodoo, and allied subjects. **Holdings:** 10,000 books; 5000 manuscripts. **Services:** Library responds to telephone inquiries.

★ 13467 ★
Psychic Science International Special Interest Group - Library (Rel-Phil)
7514 Belleplain Dr.   Phone: (513)236-0361
Huber Heights, OH 45424-3229   Richard Allen Strong, Pres.
Founded: 1976. **Subjects:** Psychic studies, allied research and education. **Holdings:** 200 volumes; biographical archives. **Subscriptions:** 200 journals and other serials. **Services:** Library not open to the public. **Computerized Information Services:** CompuServe Information Service (electronic mail service); internal database. **Remarks:** Electronic mail address(es): 71446,1462 (CompuServe Information Service).

★ 13468 ★
Psychical Research Foundation - David Wayne Hooks Memorial Library
(Rel-Phil)
Psychology Department
West Georgia College
Carrollton, GA 30118   Phone: (404)836-8696
Founded: 1961. **Subjects:** Parapsychology, death, meditation and religion, mediumship, hauntings and poltergeists, states of consciousness, physics and biophysics, psychology, anthropology. **Special Collections:** Journals and Proceedings of the British Society for Psychical Research, 1882 to present; American Society for Psychical Research Journal, 1941 to present; Journal of Parapsychology, 1937 to present; Proceedings of Parapsychology Association (complete series); Proceedings of American Society for Psychical Research, 1886 to present. **Holdings:** 1500 books; 300 bound periodical volumes; 200 journals; 4 VF drawers of manuscripts, reprints, articles. **Subscriptions:** 35 journals and other serials. **Services:** Library open to students and faculty. **Publications:** THETA, quarterly - international distribution.

Psychoanalytic Foundation of Minnesota Library
See: Ramsey County Medical Society - Boeckmann Library (13702)

Psychoanalytic Society of Seattle
See: Seattle Institute for Psychoanalysis - Edith Buxbaum Library (14994)

★ 13469 ★
Psynetics Foundation - Library (Rel-Phil)
1212 E. Lincoln Ave.   Phone: (714)533-2311
Anaheim, CA 92805   Marilyn Livingston, Oper.Mgr.
Staff: 3. **Subjects:** Metaphysics, philosophy, parapsychology. **Holdings:** Figures not available. **Services:** Library not open to the public.

★ 13470 ★
Public Affairs Research Council of Louisiana - Research Library (Soc Sci)
Box 14776   Phone: (504)926-8414
Baton Rouge, LA 70898-4776   Jan Carlock, Res.Libn.
Founded: 1951. **Staff:** Prof 1. **Subjects:** State and local government and finance; education; statistics; public administration; elections and voting; Louisiana law. **Holdings:** 4000 books; 20 pamphlet boxes of state agency reports. **Subscriptions:** 44 journals and other serials. **Services:** Copying; library open to the public for reference use only. **Publications:** PAR List of Publications: Selective Subject Index to PAR Research, annual - to members, press, libraries; PAR Analysis, irregular; Legislative Bulletin, weekly during Louisiana legislative session. **Remarks:** Library located at 4664 Jamestown Ave., No. 300, Baton Rouge, LA 70808. FAX: (504)926-8417.

Public Archives of Nova Scotia
See: (Nova Scotia) Public Archives of Nova Scotia (12153)

★ 13471 ★
Public Broadcasting Service - PTV Archives (Info Sci)
1320 Braddock Pl.   Phone: (703)739-5014
Alexandria, VA 22314-1698   Glenn Clatworthy, Assoc.Dir.
Staff: Prof 3. **Subjects:** Fine arts, public affairs, science, history, natural history. **Special Collections:** National Educational Television (NET) Film and Videotape Collection; Public Broadcasting Service (PBS) Videotape Collection; NET and PBS program files. **Holdings:** 38,000 pieces on videotape and 16mm film. **Services:** Archives not open to the public. **Computerized Information Services:** PBS Program Database (PDB; internal database). **Special Catalogs:** Biographical Catalog, 1953-1973 (printout). **Remarks:** Archives handle all requests for information or copies of PBS and NET programs for which all PBS broadcast rights have expired. Provides videotapes copies on a fee basis after receiving clearance from the copyright holder. Alternate telephone number(s): 739-5230. FAX: (703)739-0775. Telex: 910 350 1854.

★ 13472 ★
Public Citizen - Congress Watch Library (Law, Soc Sci)
215 Pennsylvania Ave., S.E.
Washington, DC 20003   Phone: (202)546-4996
Founded: 1973. **Staff:** Prof 1. **Subjects:** Congressional, consumer, and environmental issues. **Special Collections:** Complete collection of Public Citizen reports, studies, voting indices; publications of other Ralph Nader groups (books; reports; articles). **Holdings:** 3000 books; 200 bound periodical volumes; congressional hearings and reports. **Subscriptions:** 10 journals and other serials; 6 newspapers. **Services:** Interlibrary loan; copying; library open to the public by appointment. **Remarks:** FAX: (202)547-7392.

★ 13473 ★
Public Citizen - Critical Mass Energy Project - Library (Energy)
215 Pennsylvania Ave., S.E.
Washington, DC 20003   Phone: (202)546-4996
                                                       Ken Bossong, Dir.
Founded: 1974. **Staff:** Prof 6. **Subjects:** Nuclear power, least-cost energy planning, energy conservation, global warming, solar energy. **Special Collections:** Collection of antinuclear materials (500 books). **Holdings:** 2000 books. **Subscriptions:** 153 journals and other serials. **Services:** Library open to the public by appointment. **Computerized Information Services:** Internal database. **Remarks:** FAX: (202)547-7392.

★ 13474 ★
Public Education Association - Library and Archives (Educ)
39 W. 32nd St., 15th Fl.   Phone: (212)868-1640
New York, NY 10018   Judith Baum, Dir., Info.Serv.
Founded: 1940. **Staff:** Prof 1. **Subjects:** Education, New York City. **Special Collections:** Integration; decentralization; P.E.A. Archives; collective bargaining; special education (handicapped); alternative education; school finance reform. **Holdings:** 5060 volumes and documents; 28 VF drawers; 40 drawers of archival materials. **Subscriptions:** 25 journals and other serials. **Services:** Interlibrary loan; copying; library open to the public by appointment. **Computerized Information Services:** Internal database. **Publications:** Public Education Alert, 6/year; internal subject bibliography. **Remarks:** FAX: (212)268-7344.

★ 13475 ★
Public Law Education Institute - Library (Law)
1601 Connecticut Ave., N.W., Suite 450   Phone: (202)232-1400
Washington, DC 20009   William J. Straub, Circ.Mgr.
Founded: 1968. **Staff:** 5. **Subjects:** Military civil and criminal law; allied federal law; government torts; selective service law and administration; veterans law. **Special Collections:** Principal U.S. archive of selective service court opinions, 1968-1988; Defense Department regulations on manpower/military justice. **Holdings:** 1100 volumes; 35 VF drawers of federal court opinions. **Subscriptions:** 50 journals and other serials. **Services:** Interlibrary loan; copying; facsimile service and selective service document locator; library open to the public. **Publications:** Military Law Reporter, 1973-1990 (18 volumes). **Special Catalogs:** Catalog of Selected Litigation - Selective Service, 1980-1983. **Remarks:** FAX: (202)234-9501.

★ 13476 ★
Public Library of Anniston & Calhoun County - Alabama Room (Hist)
108 E. 10th St.
Box 308   Phone: (205)237-8501
Anniston, AL 36202   Janice Y. Earnest, Dept.Hd.
Founded: 1918. **Staff:** Prof 1; Other 1. **Subjects:** History - Anniston, Calhoun County, Alabama, and southeastern states; genealogy. **Special Collections:** Leonardo Andrea collection; Alabama records by Gandrud; Bessie Coleman Robinson Collection; Calhoun County cemetery and funeral home records. **Holdings:** 9000 books; 400 bound periodical volumes; 9500 microfilms/microfiche; manuscripts. **Subscriptions:** 45 journals and other serials; 5 newspapers. **Services:** Copying; room open to the public. **Publications:** AlaBenton Genealogical Quarterly (newsletter) - available on request. **Special Catalogs:** Genealogical holdings of the Alabama Room (book). **Remarks:** Alabama Room is affiliated with the AlaBenton Genealogical Society.

★ 13477 ★
Public Library of Cincinnati and Hamilton County - Art and Music Department (Art, Mus)
800 Vine St.   Phone: (513)369-6955
Cincinnati, OH 45202   Charles E. Ishee, Hd.
Founded: 1872. **Staff:** Prof 7; Other 2. **Subjects:** Art, music, architecture, antiques, numismatics, theater arts, photography, crafts, dance, cinema, costume. **Special Collections:** Choral Music (208,752 copies of 1840 titles); Delta Omicron Music Composers Library (1221 items); Valentines, 1835-1920s (225); Theodore Langstroth Collection of Lithographs (1000 volumes); Jacob Plaut Collection (limited editions of artists' illustrated books; 61 volumes); Emma Roedter Collection (music scores; 531 titles); A.J. Valerio Collection (Italian art). **Holdings:** 152,504 books and cataloged scores; 16,845 bound periodical volumes; 31,156 pieces of sheet music; 779,996 clippings; 21,799 theater, dance, music programs; 6827 exhibition catalogs; 2480 librettos; 1035 Strobridge circus posters; 1632 reels of microfilm; 19,503 microfiche. **Subscriptions:** 712 journals and other serials. **Services:** Interlibrary loan; copying; department open to the public. **Computerized Information Services:** OCLC. **Networks/Consortia:** Member of Art Research Libraries of Ohio (ARLO), Greater Cincinnati Library Consortium (GCLC). **Special Indexes:** 26 Symphony Orchestra program notes; Cincinnati Summer Opera Index by season, opera, artist, character; Index to Langstroth Reference Lithographs Collection; Matinee Musicale Recital Series; Analytic Index of Published Songs and Music Collections; Cincinnati Composers Manuscript Collection. **Remarks:** Alternate telephone number(s): 369-6954. FAX: (513)369-6063. **Staff:** Anna J. Horton, First Asst.

★ 13478 ★
Public Library of Cincinnati and Hamilton County - Children's Department (Educ)
800 Vine St.
Library Square   Phone: (513)369-6922
Cincinnati, OH 45202-2071   Consuelo W. Harris, Hd.
Founded: 1900. **Staff:** Prof 4; Other 3. **Subjects:** Children's literature, children's literature reference materials. **Special Collections:** Jean Alva Goldsmith Memorial Collection (juvenile titles - fiction, easy, nonfiction, foreign language, toy books; 5200 books); Historical Collection (examples of late 19th and early 20th century children's books; 1000 books). **Holdings:** 89,208 books; 262 bound periodical volumes; 3 VF drawers; 20 notebooks on authors and illustrators; 5 bibliography notebooks; 2000 other uncataloged items. **Subscriptions:** 99 journals and other serials. **Services:** Interlibrary loan; copying; department open to the public. **Networks/Consortia:** Member of Greater Cincinnati Library Consortium (GCLC). **Staff:** Susan Hansel, First Asst.

★ 13479 ★
Public Library of Cincinnati and Hamilton County - Department of Rare Books & Special Collections (Rare Book, Hum)
800 Vine St.   Phone: (513)369-6957
Cincinnati, OH 45202   Alfred Kleine-Kreutzmann, Cur.
Founded: 1955. **Staff:** Prof 2; Other 1. **Special Collections:** Discovery and exploration of America (200 volumes); Ohio Valley; Cincinnatiana (20,000 volumes; 5000 pamphlets); Reece C. Vidler Collection of American and European Bibles (500 volumes); Author Collections (rare and/or first editions): Edgar Rice Burroughs (110 volumes), Sir Winston Churchill (150 volumes), Charles Dickens (100 volumes), William Faulkner (150 volumes), Lafcadio Hearn (400 volumes), Ernest Hemingway (200 volumes), W. Somerset Maugham (85 volumes), Christopher Morley (150 volumes), A. Edward Newton (130 volumes), John Steinbeck (140 volumes), Mark Twain (120 volumes), Hugh Walpole (70 volumes); Louis E. Kahn English Language Dictionary Collection (from 1511; 459 volumes); books about books and fine printing; George Cruikshank; Milestone Books; Mormons and Shakers; Inland Rivers Library (commercial transportation on the Ohio and Mississippi Rivers and their navigable tributaries; 3100 books, 22,000 photographs, 200 oral history tapes); Illustrator Collections: Robert and George Cruikshank (300 volumes), Rockwell Kent (60 volumes), Loeb Collection of Great Artists and the Book (150 rare signed limited editions by 19th and 20th century artists); Simon Lazarus, Jr. Collection of Johnsoniana; Nora May Nolan Collection of Irish Literature (100 volumes); Nobel Prize Collection. **Holdings:** 39,085 books; 1400 bound periodical volumes; 22,473 photographs of steamboats; 40 VF drawers of pamphlets; 157 boxes; 5 drawers of manuscripts; 15 map case drawers of maps, blueprints, broadsides, prints of steamboats. **Subscriptions:** 40 journals and other serials. **Services:** Copying; department open to the public. **Networks/Consortia:** Member of Greater Cincinnati Library Consortium (GCLC). **Publications:** Occasional checklists and brochures describing holdings. **Special Catalogs:** Printed catalog of Inland Rivers Library and 1989 Supplement; Catalog of Kahn English Language Dictionary Collection - all for sale. **Staff:** Claire Pancero, First Asst. & Cat.

★ 13480 ★
Public Library of Cincinnati and Hamilton County - Education and Religion Department (Educ, Rel-Phil)
800 Vine St.   Phone: (513)369-6940
Cincinnati, OH 45202   Susan F. Hettinger, Hd.
Founded: 1952. **Staff:** Prof 7; Other 1. **Subjects:** Education, library science, religion, grantsmanship, sports and recreation, philosophy, psychology, sociology. **Special Collections:** Theological and Religious Collection (church history and 19th-20th century Protestant theological writings; 20,000 volumes); Foundation Center Regional Collection (250 volumes). **Holdings:** 182,417 books; 22,136 bound periodical volumes; 43,400 microfiche of Internal Revenue Service (IRS) 990 forms for foundations in Kentucky, Indiana, Ohio; 65 VF drawers of pamphlets and vocational literature; 25 VF drawers of government documents; college catalogs of 2400 institutions on microfiche; ERIC microfiche, 1976 to present. **Subscriptions:** 900 journals and other serials. **Services:** Interlibrary loan; copying. **Computerized Information Services:** BRS Information Technologies, DIALOG Information Services, NEXIS, VU/TEXT Information Services, InfoTrac. **Networks/Consortia:** Member of Greater Cincinnati Library Consortium (GCLC). **Remarks:** FAX: (513)369-6063. **Staff:** Joan Hamilton, First Asst.

★ 13481 ★
Public Library of Cincinnati and Hamilton County - Exceptional Children's Division (Educ)
800 Vine St.   Phone: (513)369-6065
Cincinnati, OH 45202   Coy Kate Hunsucker, Hd.
Founded: 1966. **Staff:** Prof 3; Other 2. **Subjects:** Programs and materials for deaf and hearing impaired, visually impaired, mentally handicapped, learning disabled, physically handicapped, socially maladjusted, emotionally disturbed, severely behaviorally disordered, and gifted and talented children and young adults in schools, hospitals, and institutions. **Holdings:** 22,151 volumes. **Subscriptions:** 23 journals and other serials. **Services:** Story hours; book talks and puppet shows for children; talks for parent groups, teachers, and workers with special needs children; special summer programs for gifted and talented children. **Networks/Consortia:** Member of Greater Cincinnati Library Consortium (GCLC). **Publications:** Feelings and Emotions for Younger Children; Books for Visually Handicapped Children: Intermediate Grades; Books for Developmentally Handicapped Children; Books for Severe and Profoundly Handicapped Children; High Interest/Low Vocabulary Books for Intermediate Grades. **Staff:** Mark A. Kelso, First Asst.

★ 13482 ★
Public Library of Cincinnati and Hamilton County - Films and Recordings Center (Aud-Vis)
800 Vine St.   Phone: (513)369-6924
Cincinnati, OH 45202   Robert Hudzik, Hd.
Founded: 1947. **Staff:** Prof 5; Other 10. **Subjects:** Audiovisual advisory service in all subjects. **Special Collections:** Slides on the history of Cincinnati (1750); The Fountain Speaks (26 radio programs of local history on 78rpm records); Reference Collection of Cincinnati Symphony recordings (40); American International Music Fund Tapes (reel-to-reel tapes of contemporary music unavailable on records). **Holdings:** 3447 reels of 16mm sound film (2629 titles); 1040 35mm filmstrips; 32,715 slides; 46,716 sound recordings; 29,677 tape cassettes; 6501 videocassettes; 15,717 compact discs. **Services:** 16mm films and video cassettes loaned to individuals, organizations, schools in Hamilton County and surrounding counties for a fee; circulation of other holdings free to card holders; center open to the public. **Networks/Consortia:** Member of Greater Cincinnati Library Consortium (GCLC). **Special Catalogs:** 16mm Film Catalog; 35mm Filmstrip Catalog; Slide Catalog; Tape Cassette Catalog; Video Cassette Catalog. **Staff:** Kent Newlon, First Asst.

★ 13483 ★
Public Library of Cincinnati and Hamilton County - Government and Business Department (Bus-Fin, Soc Sci)
800 Vine St.   Phone: (513)369-6932
Cincinnati, OH 45202   Carl G. Marquette, Jr., Hd.
Founded: 1952. **Staff:** Prof 9; Other 7. **Subjects:** Economics, business, labor, accounting, statistics, finance, government, law, insurance, international relations, military science. **Special Collections:** Telephone directories (1025; Phonefiche); Murray Seasongood Collection of Government, Law and Public Administration (5000 items); Lenke Insurance Library (1000 items). **Holdings:** 172,379 books; 36,225 bound periodical volumes; complete U.S. Government depository, 1884 to present; 40 VF drawers of pamphlets; 80 VF drawers of documents; 148 drawers of microfilm and microfiche. **Subscriptions:** 1757 journals and other serials. **Services:** Interlibrary loan; copying. **Computerized Information Services:** BRS Information Technologies, DIALOG Information Services, NEXIS, Dow Jones News/Retrieval, WILSONLINE, VU/TEXT Information Services, Hannah Information Systems, LEXIS, DataTimes. Performs searches on fee basis. **Networks/Consortia:** Member of Greater Cincinnati Library Consortium (GCLC). **Special Indexes:** Indexes for Cincinnati Enquirer, Cincinnati Post, Ohio Business, Greater Cincinnati Business Record, Cincinnati Business Courier, Cincinnati Magazine. **Staff:** John Graham, First Asst.

★ 13484 ★
Public Library of Cincinnati and Hamilton County - History Department (Hist, Geog-Map)
800 Vine St.   Phone: (513)369-6905
Cincinnati, OH 45202   J. Richard Abell, Hd.
Founded: 1854. **Staff:** Prof 7; Other 5. **Subjects:** History, genealogy, maps, bibliography, geography, travel. **Special Collections:** Travel files (U.S. and foreign); genealogy and family history collection (U.S. census population schedules, 1790-1910, on microfilm; state census indexes); town, county, and state histories (U.S. and foreign); military unit histories rosters, indexes; local history collection (local history index; local newspaper index). **Holdings:** 232,949 books; 40,782 bound periodical volumes; 9949 bound newspaper volumes; 95,613 reels of microfilm; 165,242 microfiche. **Subscriptions:** 1735 journals and other serials; 50 newspapers. **Services:** Interlibrary loan; copying. **Computerized Information Services:** NEWSDEX (internal database). **Networks/Consortia:** Member of Greater Cincinnati Library Consortium (GCLC). **Staff:** Patricia Van Skaik, First Asst.

★ 13485 ★
Public Library of Cincinnati and Hamilton County - History Department - Map Unit (Geog-Map)
800 Vine St.   Phone: (513)369-6909
Cincinnati, OH 45202   Douglas S. Magee, Map Libn.
Founded: 1955. **Staff:** Prof 1; Other 1. **Subjects:** Maps, atlases, cartography, place name studies, gazetteers. **Special Collections:** Ohio county cadastral atlases; maps of Cincinnati; U.S. county cadastral atlases (1085); current street maps of U.S. cities with populations of 20,000 and over. **Holdings:** 156,333 maps; 1888 atlases; 451 gazetteers; 235 carto-bibliographies; 421 reels of microfilm; 6505 microfiche; 14 globes; 1095 bound periodical volumes. **Subscriptions:** 43 journals and other serials. **Services:** Copying; unit open to the public. **Networks/Consortia:** Member of Greater Cincinnati Library Consortium (GCLC).

★13486★
Public Library of Cincinnati and Hamilton County - Institutions/Books by Mail/Bookmobile (Info Sci)
Library Square
800 Vine St.   Phone: (513)369-6070
Cincinnati, OH 45202   Keith C. Kuhn, Hd.
Founded: 1969. **Staff:** Prof 3; Other 12. **Subjects:** Fiction and nonfiction. **Special Collections:** Large-print materials (35,116 volumes). **Holdings:** 149,713 volumes; 914 sound recordings; 670 cassettes. **Subscriptions:** 83 journals and other serials. **Services:** Interlibrary loan; books-by-mail for the homebound; specialized services for the institutionalized; deposit collections for hospitals, senior centers, schools, correctional facilities; bookmobile service to schools and centers for the handicapped; Special Services Area in main library. **Networks/Consortia:** Member of Greater Cincinnati Library Consortium (GCLC). **Special Catalogs:** Large-print catalog of holdings, annual; Books-by-Mail catalog, annual; large print juvenile and young adult catalog, annual. **Staff:** Tonia H. Moorman, First Asst.

★13487★
Public Library of Cincinnati and Hamilton County - Library for the Blind and Physically Handicapped (Aud-Vis)
Library Square
800 Vine St.   Phone: (513)369-6075
Cincinnati, OH 45202   Donna Foust, Reg.Libn.
Founded: 1901. **Staff:** Prof 2; Other 13. **Subjects:** Books for the blind and physically handicapped in braille, on records and cassettes. **Holdings:** 20,061 volumes in braille; 74,797 recorded disc containers; 196,110 cassette containers. **Subscriptions:** 45 on talking books; 40 in braille; 29 on cassettes. **Services:** Interlibrary loan; library open to residents of 33 Ohio counties who are certified as eligible for services. **Automated Operations:** Computerized circulation; automatic subject selection by reader interest categories. **Publications:** Newsletter, monthly. **Remarks:** Toll-free telephone number(s): for Ohio residents is (800)582-0335.

★13488★
Public Library of Cincinnati and Hamilton County - Literature Department (Hum)
800 Vine St.   Phone: (513)369-6991
Cincinnati, OH 45202   Donna S. Monnig, Hd.
Founded: 1983. **Staff:** Prof 6; Other 2. **Subjects:** Literature, foreign fiction, folklore, journalism, linguistics. **Special Collections:** Ohio author bibliographies; Valerio Collection of Italian Literature. **Holdings:** 191,278 books; 14,273 bound periodical volumes; 15,567 reels of microfilm; dictionaries. **Subscriptions:** 468 journals and other serials. **Services:** Interlibrary loan; copying; department open to the public. **Networks/Consortia:** Member of Greater Cincinnati Library Consortium (GCLC). **Special Indexes:** Ohioana Hamilton County Authors Bibliography (pamphlet), annual. **Staff:** Georganne F. Bradford, First Asst.

★13489★
Public Library of Cincinnati and Hamilton County - Municipal Reference Library (Soc Sci)
801 Plum St.   Phone: (513)369-6076
Cincinnati, OH 45202   Cindy Chermely, Libn.
Founded: 1913. **Staff:** Prof 1. **Subjects:** Municipal administration, waste collection and management, public health and safety. **Special Collections:** Cincinnati city government. **Holdings:** 8100 books; 42,000 other cataloged items. **Subscriptions:** 65 journals and other serials. **Services:** Library open to the public. **Computerized Information Services:** BRS Information Technologies, DIALOG Information Services, NEXIS. **Networks/Consortia:** Member of Greater Cincinnati Library Consortium (GCLC).

★13490★
Public Library of Cincinnati and Hamilton County - Science and Technology Department (Sci-Engr)
800 Vine St.   Phone: (513)369-6936
Cincinnati, OH 45202-2071   Rosemary Dahmann, Hd.
Founded: 1902. **Staff:** Prof 7; Other 6. **Subjects:** Pure and applied science, especially chemistry. **Special Collections:** U.S. Depository Library, including U.S. patents, 1790 to present, and Official Gazette, 1872 to present; U.S. military and federal, ASTM, and ANSI standards and specifications; trade directories; Rand Corporation documents. **Holdings:** 220,518 books; 66,362 bound periodical volumes; 54,350 pamphlets; 364,484 microforms. **Subscriptions:** 1266 journals and other serials. **Services:** Interlibrary loan; copying; faxing. **Computerized Information Services:** DIALOG Information Services, WILSONLINE, BRS Information Technologies, NEXIS. Performs searches on fee basis. **Networks/Consortia:** Member of Greater Cincinnati Library Consortium (GCLC). **Remarks:** FAX: (513)369-6063. **Staff:** Mary Beth Brestel, First Asst.

Public Library of the High Seas
See: United Seaman's Service - American Merchant Marine Library Association (16780)

★13491★
Public Library of Nashville and Davidson County - Business Information Division (Bus-Fin)
8th and Union   Phone: (615)862-5842
Nashville, TN 37203   Caroline Stark
Founded: 1931. **Staff:** Prof 2; Other 3. **Subjects:** Business. **Special Collections:** Foundation Center. **Holdings:** 8700 books; 5000 bound periodical volumes; 95,000 government documents. **Subscriptions:** 454 journals and other serials. **Services:** Interlibrary loan. **Computerized Information Services:** DIALOG Information Services; InfoTrac; CD-ROM (Government Documents Index). **Publications:** Newsletter Quarterly: Information For Profit. **Staff:** Janet Batchelor; Bob Russell; Robin Knox; Saundra Peterson; Ron Perry, Dept.Hd.

★13492★
Public Library of Nashville and Davidson County - The Nashville Room (Hist)
8th Ave., N. & Union   Phone: (615)259-6125
Nashville, TN 37203-3585   Mary Glenn Hearne, Dir., Nashville Rm.
Staff: Prof 1; Other 2. **Subjects:** History and genealogy of Nashville and its residents, 1779 to present. **Special Collections:** Jeter-Smith Dance Collection; Naff Collection of performing artists; Weil Ornithological Collection; Stahlman Collection of Southern Books. **Holdings:** 10,000 books; scrapbooks; school diaries of the 1890s; 5 file drawers of census microfilm; manuscripts of local authors; interviews with local authors; Nashville obituaries (online); Nashville movies; photographs; slides; oral history tapes. **Services:** Copying; room open to the public. **Special Indexes:** Index to photographs (cards); index to Naff Collection; index to scrapbooks and maps (cards); index to Jeter-Smith Collection (cards).

★13493★
Public Library of Youngstown and Mahoning County - Science and Industry Collection (Bus-Fin, Sci-Engr)
305 Wick Ave.   Phone: (216)744-8636
Youngstown, OH 44503   Janet K. Moy, Hd.
Founded: 1949. **Holdings:** 52,151 books; 4883 bound periodical volumes; 55 VF drawers of pamphlets, documents, house organs, clippings; 1384 reels of microfilm; 17 periodicals on microfiche, 1985 to present. **Subscriptions:** 234 journals and other serials. **Services:** Interlibrary loan; copying; collection open to the public. **Networks/Consortia:** Member of NOLA Regional Library System. **Remarks:** FAX: (216)744-3355.

★13494★
Public Policy Forum - Library (Soc Sci)
633 W. Wisconsin Ave., Suite 406   Phone: (414)276-8240
Milwaukee, WI 53203-1918   Jean B. Tyler, Exec.Dir.
Founded: 1913. **Subjects:** Local government, urban concerns of state government, municipal administration, local school districts. **Special Collections:** Data about local governments and school districts in 5-county Milwaukee metropolitan area. **Holdings:** 3000 books; clippings files; unbound reports, manuscripts, archives, documents. **Subscriptions:** 45 journals and other serials; 25 newspapers. **Services:** Interlibrary loan; copying (both limited); library open to the public with permission. **Computerized Information Services:** Internal database. **Publications:** Bulletin, 8-12/year - to mailing list of public officials and other opinion leaders, citizen activists, civic organizations across the U.S. **Remarks:** FAX: (414)276-9964.

★13495★
Public/Private Ventures - Resource Center (Bus-Fin)
399 Market St.   Phone: (215)592-9099
Philadelphia, PA 19106   Victoria K. Evalds, Libn.
Staff: Prof 1. **Subjects:** Employment, youth unemployment, labor market information, training programs, economic development, supported work, vocational and remedial education, foundations, disadvantaged populations. **Holdings:** 3000 books; brochures; clippings; annual reports. **Subscriptions:** 71 journals and other serials. **Services:** Copying; center open to the public by appointment. **Computerized Information Services:** DIALOG Information Services, BRS Information Technologies. **Publications:** List of publications - available on request. **Remarks:** FAX: (215)592-0099.

★ 13496 ★
Public Record Office of Northern Ireland - Library (Bus-Fin)
66 Balmoral Ave.
Belfast BT9 6NY, Northern Ireland   Phone: 232 661621
Founded: 1923. **Staff:** Prof 13; Other 42. **Subjects:** Records - departmental, nondepartmental, private, business, church. **Holdings:** 100,000 cubic feet of archival materials. **Services:** Copying; library open to the public with restrictions. **Publications:** Reports of the Deputy Keeper of the Records. **Remarks:** FAX: 232 665718. **Staff:** Dr. G.J. Slater, Dep.Dir.

★ 13497 ★
Public Relations Society of America - PRSA Information Center (Bus-Fin)
33 Irving Place, 3rd Fl.   Phone: (212)995-2230
New York, NY 10003-2376   Amy Goldfarb Zerman, Mgr.
Founded: 1955. **Staff:** Prof 1; Other 2. **Subjects:** Public relations. **Special Collections:** Public relations plans and proposals; examples of employee communications. **Holdings:** 1000 books; 90 VF drawers. **Subscriptions:** 87 journals and other serials. **Services:** Interlibrary loan; center open to the public on fee basis. **Automated Operations:** Computerized public access catalog. **Computerized Information Services:** NEXIS, DIALOG Information Services, CompuServe Information Service. **Publications:** Bibliography of PR Materials, annual - for sale. **Remarks:** FAX: (212)995-0757.

★ 13498 ★
Public Service Company of Colorado - Library (Energy)
1225 17th St. Plaza Bldg.
Box 840   Phone: (303)571-7084
Denver, CO 80202   Mary Ann Hamm, Libn.
Founded: 1956. **Staff:** Prof 1; Other 1. **Subjects:** Business management, public utilities, economics, electrical engineering. **Special Collections:** Electric Power Research Institute reports; Conference Board publications. **Holdings:** 3500 books; 500 government documents. **Subscriptions:** 300 journals and other serials; 6 newspapers. **Services:** Interlibrary loan; library not open to the public. **Computerized Information Services:** DIALOG Information Services, Utility Data Institute, A.G.A. GasNet, Evans Economics, Inc., Knight-Ridder Unicom, DataTimes, Human Resource Information Network (HRIN). **Publications:** Library bulletin, monthly - for internal distribution only; bibliographies - available on request. **Remarks:** FAX: (303)571-8640.

★ 13499 ★
Public Service Co. of Oklahoma - Corporate Procedures & Reference Services (Energy)
212 E. 6th St.
Box 201   Phone: (918)599-2499
Tulsa, OK 74119   Jean Thompson, Ref. Lead
Founded: 1967. **Staff:** Prof 1. **Subjects:** Electric utilities, electrical engineering, business. **Holdings:** 10,000 volumes; 6200 technical and conference papers. **Subscriptions:** 451 journals and other serials. **Services:** Interlibrary loan; services not open to the public. **Automated Operations:** Computerized serials. **Computerized Information Services:** DIALOG Information Services. **Networks/Consortia:** Member of Tulsa Area Library Cooperative (TALC).

★ 13500 ★
Public Service Electric and Gas Company - Corporate Library (Energy, Sci-Engr)
80 Park Plaza, P3C
Box 570   Phone: (201)430-7332
Newark, NJ 07101   Dona McDermott, Corp.Libn.
Founded: 1911. **Staff:** Prof 3; Other 2. **Subjects:** Public utilities, electric industry, electrical engineering, gas industry, mechanical engineering, business, management, nuclear power. **Holdings:** 26,500 books; 4000 bound periodical volumes; 800 directories; 165 VF drawers of pamphlets, reports, separates; 60 shelves of government documents; 5 shelves of annual reports and prospectuses of public utility companies; 100,000 microfiche of U.S. Government energy-related reports. **Subscriptions:** 765 journals and other serials. **Services:** Interlibrary loan; copying; limited service to public by appointment only. **Automated Operations:** Computerized cataloging and serials. **Computerized Information Services:** DIALOG Information Services, OCLC, ORBIT Search Service, LEXIS, NEXIS, Dun & Bradstreet Business Credit Services, NLM, TOXNET, Dow Jones News/Retrieval, BRS Information Technologies, WILSONLINE, VU/TEXT Information Services; Corporate Information System (internal database). **Networks/Consortia:** Member of PALINET, Essex Hudson Regional Library Cooperative. **Publications:** InfoConnection, bimonthly. **Remarks:** FAX: (201)802-1054. **Staff:** Harriet Mayer, Libn., Ref.; Robert Nelson, Assoc.Libn.

★ 13501 ★
Public Service Electric and Gas Company - Nuclear Library, N02 (Energy)
P.O. Box 236   Phone: (609)339-1135
Hancocks Bridge, NJ 08308   Virginia L. Swichel, Libn.
Founded: 1983. **Staff:** Prof 2; Other 2. **Subjects:** Nuclear power and engineering. **Holdings:** 19,112 books and reports; 85,000 vendor catalogs on microfilm; 218 reels of microfilm of current and Retrospective Industry Standards; 600 reels of microfilm of Military Standards; 1134 hardcopy Industry Standards; 16 drawers of microfiche; 2980 reels of microfilm; 5 VF drawers of pamphlets; 3 VF drawers of clippings. **Subscriptions:** 186 journals and other serials; 7 newspapers. **Services:** Interlibrary loan; library not open to the public. **Automated Operations:** Computerized cataloging, acquisitions, and serials. **Computerized Information Services:** DIALOG Information Services, BRS Information Technologies, ORBIT Search Service, LEXIS, NEXIS, WILSONLINE, WESTLAW; Corporate Information System (internal database). **Networks/Consortia:** Member of South Jersey Regional Library Cooperative. **Publications:** InfoConnection-Nuclear Library Update, 6/year - for internal distribution only. **Remarks:** FAX: (609)339-1136. **Staff:** Kathleen Piperato, Asst.Libn.

★ 13502 ★
Public Service Electric and Gas Company - Nuclear Training Center Library (Energy)
244 Chestnut St.   Phone: (609)339-3773
Salem, NJ 08079   Richard E. Bater, Info.Coord.
Founded: 1983. **Staff:** Prof 1; Other 2. **Subjects:** Nuclear reactor operations - training, engineering, management. **Holdings:** 8300 books; plant documents. **Subscriptions:** 60 journals and other serials. **Services:** Copying; SDI. **Automated Operations:** Computerized cataloging. **Computerized Information Services:** DIALOG Information Services, SOJOURN, Institute of Nuclear Power Operations (INPO); internal database. **Networks/Consortia:** Member of South Jersey Regional Library Cooperative. **Publications:** Acquisition list, monthly; holdings list, semiannual. **Remarks:** FAX: (609)339-3997.

Public Technology Inc. - Information Center
See: **National League of Cities - Municipal Reference Service** (11226)

★ 13503 ★
Public Utilities Commission of Ohio (PUCO) - PUCO Library (Law, Energy)
180 E. Broad St. 7th Fl.   Phone: (614)466-5082
Columbus, OH 43266-0573   Ms. Riek A. Oldenquist, Libn.
Founded: 1975. **Staff:** Prof 3. **Subjects:** Law, public utilities, economics, forecasting, accounting, engineering, management, transportation. **Special Collections:** PUCO annual reports, 1867 to present; official copies of session and administrative orders, 1913 to present; National Association of Regulatory Utility Commissioners (NARUC) publications, 1922 to present; Public Utilities Fortnightly, 1945 to present; long-term forecasts of the Ohio Utility companies, 1976 to present. **Holdings:** 18,167 books; 2829 government documents; 547 staff reports of investigations; 490 technical reports. **Subscriptions:** 197 journals and other serials; 8 newspapers. **Services:** Interlibrary loan; copying; library open to the public with restrictions. **Computerized Information Services:** LEXIS, NEXIS, WESTLAW, Dow Jones News/Retrieval; internal databases. **Publications:** PUCO Code of Rules and Regulations, volumes 1, 2, and 3 and revisions. **Special Catalogs:** PUCO Recent Acquisitions, quarterly. **Remarks:** FAX: (614)644-9546. **Staff:** Ina Walker, Asst.Libn.; Edna Newkirk, Acq.Libn.

★ 13504 ★
Public Utility Commission of Texas - Library (Energy, Law)
7800 Shoal Creek Blvd.   Phone: (512)458-0254
Austin, TX 78757   Marsha W. McGuire, Libn.
Founded: 1976. **Staff:** Prof 2; Other 2. **Subjects:** Public utilities, law, telecommunications, electric utilities, economics, energy. **Special Collections:** Electric Power Research Institute Reports (500 items); National Regulatory Research Institute Reports (100 items). **Holdings:** 16,000 books; 1000 unbound periodical volumes; 12 VF drawers; 2000 microfiche; 100 videotapes. **Subscriptions:** 357 journals and other serials; 7 newspapers. **Services:** Copying; SDI; library open to the public. **Automated Operations:** Computerized public access catalog, cataloging, acquisitions, and circulation. **Computerized Information Services:** LEXIS, DIALOG Information Services; internal database; AUTOMAIL (electronic mail service). **Publications:** PUC Library Bulletin, monthly - for internal distribution only. **Special Indexes:** Citation index to PUC Bulletin. **Remarks:** FAX: (512)458-8340. **Staff:** Helen Clements, Ref.Libn.

Public Works Canada
See: Canada - Public Works Canada (2838)

Publicacoes Tecnicas Internacionais
See: International Technical Publications, Ltd. (8194)

Newbell Niles Puckett Memorial Archives
See: Cleveland Public Library - Fine Arts and Special Collections Department - Special Collections Section - John G. White Collection and Rare Books (3823)

★ 13505 ★
Pueblo Chieftain - Library (Publ)
Box 4040   Phone: (719)544-3520
Pueblo, CO 81003   Helene M. Spitzer, Libn.
Staff: Prof 1. **Subjects:** Newspaper reference topics. **Special Collections:** Bound volumes of the Pueblo Daily Chieftain, 1868-1947, microfilm volumes, 1947 to present; bound volumes of the Pueblo Star-Journal, 1901 to 1947, microfilm volumes, 1947 to present. **Holdings:** 300 books; 6000 filing envelopes of clippings; 10,000 personal files; 1000 historical files. **Services:** Copying; library open to the public.

★ 13506 ★
Pueblo City Planning Department - Library (Soc Sci)
211 E. D St.   Phone: (719)543-6006
Pueblo, CO 81002   Donald R. Vest, Libn.
Founded: 1960. **Staff:** 1. **Subjects:** Municipal government, urban and regional planning, environmental quality, census documents, human services planning, zoning. **Special Collections:** Municipal reports. **Holdings:** 2400 volumes; 8 VF drawers; 1000 maps; planning reports. **Subscriptions:** 36 journals and other serials; 6 newspapers. **Services:** Copying; library open to the public with restrictions. **Computerized Information Services:** LOGIN; Colorado County Profiles (internal database); LINUS (electronic mail service). **Publications:** Municipal Reports, 6-10/year; Pueblo Economic Statistics Retrieval System (economic report), quarterly; City of Pueblo Data Book, annual.

★ 13507 ★
Pueblo Grande Museum - Research Library (Soc Sci)
4619 E. Washington St.   Phone: (602)495-0901
Phoenix, AZ 85034   Cathy F. Reigle
Founded: 1935. **Subjects:** Archeology, anthropology, ethnology. **Special Collections:** Odd Halseth. **Holdings:** 2000 books; reports; manuscripts; archives; microfilm; photo archives. **Subscriptions:** 35 journals and other serials. **Services:** Library open to public for reference use on request. **Remarks:** FAX: (602)495-5645.

John G. Puente Library
See: Capitol College (3035)

★ 13508 ★
Puerto Rican Culture Institute - Luis Munoz Rivera Library and Museum (Area-Ethnic)
Munoz Rivera St. 10   Phone: (809)857-0230
Barranquitas, PR 00794   Maria L. Valencia, Libn.
Founded: 1959. **Staff:** Prof 1; Other 4. **Subjects:** History, literature, language, art, folklore. **Special Collections:** Puerto Rican authors; information about Luis Munoz Rivera and Barranquitas; children's collection. **Holdings:** 2500 books; 500 pamphlets and journals; 3 VF drawers of clippings and documents. **Subscriptions:** 3 journals and other serials. **Services:** Interlibrary loan; library open to the public for reference use only. **Publications:** Boletin Cultural, quarterly. **Remarks:** Library affiliated with the General Library of Puerto Rico.

★ 13509 ★
Puerto Rico - Junta de Calidad Ambiental - Biblioteca (Env-Cons)
Apartado 11488   Phone: (809)767-7712
Santurce, PR 00910   Oneida Delgado de Diaz, Lib.Dir.
Founded: 1920. **Subjects:** Pollution - water, solid waste, air, noise; impact statements; environmental sciences. **Holdings:** 500 books; 15 bound periodical volumes; 500 reports; 500 microfiche. **Subscriptions:** 10 journals and other serials; 5 newspapers. **Services:** Interlibrary loan; copying; library open to the public. **Computerized Information Services:** Microisis (internal database). **Publications:** Library Catalogs; Library Thematic Index. **Remarks:** FAX: (809)766-2483.

★ 13510 ★
Puerto Rico Central Office of Personnel Administration - Institute of Personnel Development - Library (Bus-Fin)
Ponce de Leon Ave., Stop 22
Fernandez Juncos Sta., Box 8476   Phone: (809)721-4300
Santurce, PR 00910   Jacqueline Rivera, Libn.
Founded: 1979. **Staff:** Prof 1. **Subjects:** Public and personnel administration, Puerto Rico history. **Holdings:** 2008 volumes; 576 pamphlets; 203 reports; 56 scrapbooks of clippings. **Subscriptions:** 14 journals and other serials. **Services:** Interlibrary loan; library open to the public. **Automated Operations:** Computerized cataloging and circulation. **Publications:** Boletin Informativo, quarterly. **Special Indexes:** Public Administration (card). **Also Known As:** Puerto Rico Oficina Central Administracion Personal - Biblioteca Instituto Desarrollo Personal.

★ 13511 ★
Puerto Rico Department of Health - Medical Library (Med)
Ant. Hospital de Psiquiatria - Bo. Monacillos
Call Box 70184   Phone: (809)766-1616
San Juan, PR 00936   Jose Sorer, Libn.
Founded: 1952. **Staff:** Prof 1; Other 2. **Subjects:** Public health, emergency and ambulatory services, mental health services, planning and evaluation of hospital development, health services administration, continuing medical education, allied health professions. **Holdings:** 3500 books; 180 bound periodical volumes; 1110 monographs and pamphlets; 600 bound reports and documents; 260 state reports; 558 unbound periodical volumes; 14 VF drawers of leaflets. **Subscriptions:** 563 journals and other serials. **Services:** Interlibrary loan; copying; library open to the public for reference use only. **Publications:** Lista de revistas y series recibidas en la biblioteca, annual; bibliographies of publications edited by department, irregular. **Special Catalogs:** Catalog of Puerto Rican agencies publications.

★ 13512 ★
Puerto Rico Department of Health - Mental Health Library (Med)
Asst. Secretariat for Mental Health
Box G.P.O. 61   Phone: (809)781-5660
San Juan, PR 00936   Dr. Gomez, Libn.
Founded: 1957. **Staff:** Prof 1; Other 1. **Subjects:** Psychiatry, drugs, neurology, psychotherapy, alcoholism, psychology, psychoanalysis, hypnosis, T-groups. **Special Collections:** Collection of Dr. Luis Morales in psychiatry and psychoanalysis (2000 items); Dr. Jose Rafael Mayme Collection (200 items). **Holdings:** 5665 books; 300 bound periodical volumes; 100 special theme materials; 200 annual reports of the Mental Health Program; 50 publications of the Division of Human Resources. **Services:** Interlibrary loan; copying; library open to the public for reference use only. **Automated Operations:** Computerized cataloging. **Special Indexes:** Index to magazine articles (card).

★ 13513 ★
Puerto Rico Department of Health - Ramon E. Betances Library (Med)
Bo. Sabalos Ave., Carr. No. 2
Box 1868   Phone: (809)834-8686
Mayaguez, PR 00708   Myrna Y. Ramirez, Libn.
Founded: 1971. **Staff:** Prof 2. **Subjects:** Medicine, surgery, pediatrics, obstetrics and gynecology, laboratory medicine, dentistry. **Special Collections:** CIBA Collection. **Holdings:** 2244 books; 1258 bound periodical volumes; 13 reports. **Subscriptions:** 74 journals and other serials. **Services:** Interlibrary loan; copying; library open to the public with restrictions on circulation. **Automated Operations:** Computerized cataloging and circulation. **Computerized Information Services:** MEDLINE. Performs searches on fee basis. **Networks/Consortia:** Member of Consorcio Educativo Del Oeste - Recinto Ciencias Medicas. **Formerly:** Its Ramon Emeterio Betances Medical Center Library.

★ 13514 ★
Puerto Rico Department of Justice - Library (Law)
Box 192   Phone: (809)724-6869
San Juan, PR 00902   Carmen M. Cruz, Dir.
Founded: 1936. **Staff:** Prof 3; Other 4. **Subjects:** Common and civil law. **Special Collections:** Puerto Rican law. **Holdings:** 85,000 volumes; 25 VF drawers. **Subscriptions:** 315 journals and other serials; 30 newspapers. **Services:** Interlibrary loan; library open to the public with restrictions. **Computerized Information Services:** LEXIS. **Publications:** Opiniones del Secretario Justicia, annual; Informe anual del Secretario de Justicia, Anuario Estadistico. **Remarks:** Alternate telephone number(s): (809)721-2900 ext.237. **Staff:** Ivette Lopez Jusino; Nelly Gonzalez.

★ 13515 ★
Puerto Rico Department of Natural Resources - Library (Env-Cons)
Munoz Rivera Ave., Stop 3
Box 5887   Phone: (809)724-8774
San Juan, PR 00906   Jaime Maldonado Villafane, Libn.
Subjects: Natural resources. **Special Collections:** Encyclopedic Compendium of Natural Resources. **Holdings:** 7000 books. **Subscriptions:** 12 journals and other serials; 7 newspapers. **Services:** Interlibrary loan; copying; library open to the public.

★ 13516 ★
Puerto Rico Department of Social Services - Library (Soc Sci)
Box 11398, Fernandez Juncos Sta.   Phone: (809)722-7400
San Juan, PR 00910   Lillian Valcarcel, Libn.
Staff: Prof 1. **Subjects:** Social services to families, child welfare, social and vocational rehabilitation, child abuse and delinquency, juvenile delinquency, public assistance, training and staff development, nutrition, adult affairs, budget, federal resources. **Special Collections:** U.S. Department of Health and Human Services collection; Commonwealth of Puerto Rico collection. **Holdings:** 987 books; 9092 pamphlets. **Subscriptions:** 41 journals and other serials; 28 newspapers. **Services:** Interlibrary loan; library open to the public for reference use only. **Publications:** List of news publications. **Special Indexes:** Index to periodicals.

★ 13517 ★
Puerto Rico Economic Development Administration - Puerto Rico
Industrial Development Company - Biblioteca de Fomento (Bus-Fin)
G.P.O. Box 2350   Phone: (809)758-4747
San Juan, PR 00936   Isabel Lopez, Libn.
Founded: 1946. **Staff:** Prof 2. **Subjects:** Economy, industry, statistics, economic planning, finance. **Special Collections:** Unpublished studies of the economic and industrial development of Puerto Rico. **Holdings:** 15,300 books. **Subscriptions:** 90 journals and other serials; 7 newspapers. **Services:** Interlibrary loan; library open to the public. **Publications:** Bibliografia del desarrollo economico e industrial de Puerto Rico - suplementos, irregular. **Remarks:** Library located at Fomento Bldg., 355 Franklin D. Roosevelt Ave. & Lamar Guerra St., Hato Rey, PR 00918. **Staff:** Nimia Tosca, Ref.Libn.

★ 13518 ★
Puerto Rico General Court of Justice - Office of Court Administration -
Library Service Division (Law)
Box 917, Hato Rey Sta.   Phone: (809)751-8670
Hato Rey, PR 00919   Manuela O. Martinez, Dir.
Staff: Prof 3; Other 29. **Subjects:** Law - civil, criminal, labor; management; judicial administration. **Special Collections:** Spain's civil law. **Holdings:** 220,100 books; 3300 bound periodical volumes; 7500 pamphlets; 4200 reports; 100 dissertations; 350 Judicial & Criminal Statistics. **Subscriptions:** 570 journals and other serials; 8 newspapers. **Services:** Interlibrary loan; copying; division open to the public. **Computerized Information Services:** LEXIS, PRONLINX, MICROJURIS, COMPUCLERK. **Publications:** List of Recent Acquisitions. **Special Catalogs:** Puerto Rico Court Libraries Collective Catalogue (title, subject, author). **Remarks:** FAX: (809)767-7757. Library Services Division organizes and supervises the Superior Court libraries. **Staff:** German Nogueras, Tech.Serv.Supv.; Miriam L. Del Valle, S.J. Judicial Ctr.Lib.

(Puerto Rico) Institute of Puerto Rican Culture
See: **(Puerto Rico) La Casa del Libro** (13520)

★ 13519 ★
(Puerto Rico) Institute of Puerto Rican Culture - Archivo General de
Puerto Rico (Hist)
Ponce de Leon 500, Apartado 4184
San Juan, PR 00905   Phone: (809)722-2113
Staff: Prof 8; Other 16. **Subjects:** Public works, municipal records, legislation, notarial protocols, treasury, court records, health. **Holdings:** 40,000 cubic feet of documents; 5000 pieces of music; 600 cubic feet of private collections. **Subscriptions:** 15 journals and other serials. **Services:** Copying; archives open to the public. **Publications:** Guia Al Archivo General De Puerto Rico; Loa Archivos Historicos De Puerto Rico. **Remarks:** FAX: (809)724-8393. **Staff:** Carmen Alicia Davila, Archv.; Luis De La Rosa, Archv.; Jose Flores, Archv.; Milagros Pepin, Archv.; Hilda Chicon, Archv.

★ 13520 ★
(Puerto Rico) La Casa del Libro (Publ)
Calle del Cristo 255   Phone: (809)723-0354
San Juan, PR 00901   R. John Blackley, Dir.
Founded: 1956. **Staff:** 3. **Subjects:** Typography, history and art of the book, early printed books (especially Spanish), fine editions of modern press books, exhibition of books and Puerto Rican graphics. **Special Collections:** Medieval music library, humanities library. **Holdings:** 365 incunabula; 5000 rare books; 1000 bibliographic books. **Services:** Open to public. **Formerly:** (Puerto Rico) Institute of Puerto Rican Culture. **Staff:** Barbara Lachman, Assoc.Dir.; Mary McHale Wood, Gen.Mgr.

★ 13521 ★
Puerto Rico Municipal Services Administration - Library (Law)
306 Barbosa Ave.   Phone: (809)754-1600
Hato Rey, PR 00936   Mr. Duncan Renaldo Maldonado,
       Dir., Commun.Off.
Subjects: Municipal corporations, federal rules and regulations, urban plannings. **Special Collections:** McQuillin's Municipal Corporations, Federal Register, United States Code Anotated, laws of Puerto Rico, Puerto Rico decisions, Puerto Rico Digest. **Holdings:** 920 books. **Subscriptions:** 100 journals and other serials. **Services:** Library open to the public with restrictions.

★ 13522 ★
Puerto Rico Office of Budget & Management - Library Resources and
Information Center (Bus-Fin)
254 Tetuan & Cruz Sts.   Phone: (809)725-9420
San Juan, PR 00904   Edwin R. Reyes, Hd.Libn.
Founded: 1942. **Staff:** Prof 1; Other 2. **Subjects:** Public administration, budget management, economics, auditing, computers. **Special Collections:** Puerto Rico and U.S. Law; budget documents of the states and the federal government. **Holdings:** 5252 books; 520 bound periodical volumes; 18,500 clippings; 5833 pamphlets; 12,590 public documents. **Subscriptions:** 177 journals and other serials. **Services:** Interlibrary loan; library open to the public for reference use only. **Automated Operations:** Computerized public access catalog. **Computerized Information Services:** DIALOG Information Services; internal databases. **Publications:** New acquisitions, quarterly. **Special Indexes:** Index of professional magazines (card); Indice tematico de la Revista Presupuesto y Gerencia 1952-1983. **Remarks:** FAX: (809)721-8100. **Staff:** Miriam Melendez, Libn.

★ 13523 ★
Puerto Rico State Department of Consumer Affairs - Library (Law)
Minillas Sta., Box 41059
San Juan, PR 00940   Phone: (809)722-7555
Staff: Prof 1. **Subjects:** Law, economics. **Holdings:** 1717 books; 200 bound periodical volumes. **Subscriptions:** 11 journals and other serials. **Services:** Interlibrary loan; library open to the public with restrictions.

★ 13524 ★
Puerto Rico Supreme Court - Law Library (Law)
Box 2392   Phone: (809)723-3863
San Juan, PR 00902   Ivette Torres-Alvarez, Hd.Libn.
Founded: 1842. **Staff:** Prof 3; Other 12. **Subjects:** Law. **Special Collections:** Puerto Rican and Spanish civil law collections. **Holdings:** 100,811 volumes; 24 VF drawers; 53 drawers of microforms. **Subscriptions:** 497 journals and other serials; 7 newspapers. **Services:** Interlibrary loan; copying; library open to the public with restrictions. **Automated Operations:** Computerized public access catalog, cataloging, acquisitions, serials, and circulation. **Computerized Information Services:** LEXIS, WESTLAW, Escrutinio Legislativo. **Publications:** Nuevas Adquisiciones, monthly. **Special Indexes:** Index to articles in Spanish and to South American legal periodicals received in the library; list of magazines and law reviews received (organized by title, country, subject). **Remarks:** FAX: (809)725-4910. **Staff:** Ada N. Perez Jimenez, Cat.Libn.; Carmen Rivera-Faneytt, Ref.Libn.

Puget Sound Council of Governments
See: **Puget Sound Regional Council - Information Center** (13526)

Puget Sound Maritime Historical Society
See: **Historical Society of Seattle & King County - Sophie Frye Bass Library of Northwest Americana** (7288)

★13525★
Puget Sound Power and Light Company Library (Bus-Fin, Energy)
Box 97034   Phone: (206)454-6363
Bellevue, WA 98009-9734   Susan Campbell Ball, Libn.
Founded: 1968. **Staff:** Prof 2; Other 2. **Subjects:** Electric utility operations, economics, management, energy conservation. **Holdings:** 3000 books; 10,000 documents and technical reports; 300 videotapes; 200 audio cassettes. **Subscriptions:** 600 journals and other serials. **Services:** Interlibrary loan; copying; SDI; library open to the public by appointment. **Automated Operations:** Computerized public access catalog, routing, cataloging, and acquisitions. **Computerized Information Services:** DIALOG Information Services, DataTimes, LEXIS, URAP, EPRI; OnTyme Electronic Message Network Service (electronic mail service). **Networks/Consortia:** Member of Western Library Network (WLN). **Remarks:** FAX: (206)462-3301. Electronic mail address(es): CLASS.PSPL (OnTyme Electronic Message Network Service).

★13526★
Puget Sound Regional Council - Information Center (Plan)
216 1st Ave., S.   Phone: (206)464-7532
Seattle, WA 98104   Deana Dryden, Libn.
Founded: 1967. **Staff:** Prof 1. **Subjects:** Regional planning, transportation, population, land use. **Special Collections:** Small area regional forecasts including population, households, employment; 1990 census tape files. **Holdings:** 1500 books. **Subscriptions:** 150 journals and other serials; 10 newspapers. **Services:** Center open to the public by appointment. **Computerized Information Services:** DIALOG Information Services, OCLC. **Publications:** List of Agency Publications. **Remarks:** FAX: (206)587-4825. **Formerly:** Puget Sound Council of Governments.

Delia Biddle Pugh Library
See: **Burlington County Historical Society** (2373)

★13527★
Pulaski County Historical Society - Library (Hist)
Public Library Bldg.   Phone: (606)678-8401
Somerset, KY 42501   William J. Moore, Pres.
Subjects: Genealogy; history - local, regional, state. **Holdings:** Genealogical books and family files; census, marriage, and cemetery records. **Services:** Copying; library open to the public. **Publications:** Pulaski Revisited. **Special Indexes:** Cemetery Records, Vol. I and II; Census Records, 1850, 1860, 1870, 1900 (2 vols.); Index to Wills, 1800-1950; Marriage Records, 1799-1850, 1851-1863, 1864-1886, 1887-1900 - all for sale.

Pulaski County Law Library
See: **University of Arkansas, Little Rock** (18238)

Pulling Law Library
See: **Villanova University - School of Law** (19847)

★13528★
Pulp and Paper Research Institute of Canada - Library (Sci-Engr)
570 St. John's Blvd.   Phone: (514)630-4100
Pointe Claire, PQ, Canada H9R 3J9   Hella Stahl, Mgr.
Founded: 1929. **Staff:** Prof 3; Other 3. **Subjects:** Paper, pulp, forestry, mechanical engineering, chemistry, chemical engineering, environmental biology, physics, metallurgy, economics, mathematics. **Holdings:** 8000 books; 10,000 bound periodical volumes; pamphlets; reports; translations; technical papers; patents. **Subscriptions:** 400 journals and other serials. **Services:** Interlibrary loan. **Automated Operations:** Computerized public access catalog and cataloging. **Computerized Information Services:** DIALOG Information Services, PFDS Online, CISTI, Chemical Abstracts Service (CAS), Info Globe, STN International; PAPRICAN (internal database). **Remarks:** FAX: (514)630-4137. **Also Known As:** Institut Canadien de Recherches sur les Pates et Papiers. **Staff:** Marilyn McNamee, Lib.Supv.

The Puppet Centre
See: **Ontario Puppetry Association Puppet Centre** (12497)

★13529★
Purdue Frederick Company - Corporate Library (Med)
100 Connecticut Ave.   Phone: (203)853-0123
Norwalk, CT 06856   Kathryn Walsh, Mgr., Lib.Serv.
Founded: 1970. **Staff:** Prof 2; Other 2. **Subjects:** Pharmacology, chemistry, medicine, business. **Holdings:** 2500 books; 7000 bound periodical volumes; patent file. **Subscriptions:** 450 journals and other serials. **Services:** Interlibrary loan; library open to the public by appointment. **Computerized Information Services:** DIALOG Information Services, BRS Information Technologies, NLM, LEXIS, Dow Jones News/Retrieval, Data-Star; internal database. **Remarks:** FAX: (203)838-1576.

★13530★
Purdue University - Aviation Technology Library (Sci-Engr)
Purdue University Airport   Phone: (317)494-7640
West Lafayette, IN 47907   Edwin D. Posey, Libn.
Founded: 1960. **Staff:** Prof .5; Other 1. **Subjects:** Aviation technology, flight, aerospace education. **Special Collections:** General Aviation Manufacturers Association designated Aviation Education Resource Center (over 500 educators materials). **Holdings:** 3238 volumes. **Subscriptions:** 108 journals and other serials. **Services:** Interlibrary loan; copying; library open to the public. **Remarks:** FAX: (317)494-9007.

★13531★
Purdue University - Biochemistry Library (Sci-Engr)
Biochemistry Bldg.   Phone: (317)494-1621
West Lafayette, IN 47907   Martha J. Bailey, Life Sci.Libn.
Founded: 1952. **Staff:** Prof 5; Other 1. **Subjects:** Biochemistry, carbohydrate chemistry. **Holdings:** 12,738 volumes; 630 theses. **Subscriptions:** 127 journals and other serials. **Services:** Interlibrary loan; copying; library open to the public. **Publications:** Acquisitions list, quarterly. **Remarks:** FAX: (317)494-9007.

★13532★
Purdue University - Calumet - The Library (Sci-Engr, Hum, Soc Sci)
Hammond, IN 46323-2094   Phone: (219)989-2224
                              Bernard H. Holicky, Dir., Lib.Serv.
Founded: 1947. **Staff:** Prof 5; Other 12. **Subjects:** Science and technology, humanities, social science. **Holdings:** 226,400 volumes; 8307 reels of microfilm; 492,649 microforms. **Subscriptions:** 1775 journals and other serials. **Services:** Interlibrary loan; copying; library open to the public with limited circulation. **Automated Operations:** Computerized cataloging, acquisitions, circulation, and ILL. **Computerized Information Services:** BRS Information Technologies, DIALOG Information Services, MEDLARS, PFDS Online, OCLC, STN International, VU/TEXT Information Services, WILSONLINE. **Networks/Consortia:** Member of INCOLSA, Northwest Indiana Area Library Services Authority (NIALSA). **Publications:** Electronic new book list, monthly - to faculty. **Staff:** Peter P. Chojenski, Ref.Libn.; Karen M. Corey, Rd.Serv.Libn.; Sheila A. Rezak, Teacher Educ.Rsrcs. & ILL; Rebecca H. Stankowski, Tech.Serv.Libn.

★13533★
Purdue University - Chemistry Library (Sci-Engr)
BRWN   Phone: (317)494-2862
West Lafayette, IN 47907   John Pinzelik, Chem.Libn.
Founded: 1874. **Staff:** Prof 2; Other 2. **Subjects:** Chemistry - inorganic, organic, biological, analytical. **Special Collections:** Archives of Herbert C. Brown, 1979 Nobel Laureate in chemistry. **Holdings:** 42,247 volumes; 9769 microforms; patents. **Subscriptions:** 507 journals and other serials. **Services:** Interlibrary loan; copying; library open to the public. **Computerized Information Services:** DIALOG Information Services, Chemical Abstracts Service (CAS). **Publications:** Biweekly Acquisitions List. **Remarks:** FAX: (317)494-9007. **Also Known As:** M.G. Mellon Library of Chemistry. **Staff:** Bill Hedrick, Prof.Libn.

★ 13534 ★
Purdue University - CINDAS - Ceramics Information Analysis Center
(Sci-Engr)
2595 Yeager Rd.   Phone: (317)494-9393
West Lafayette, IN 47906-1398   Dr. C.Y. Ho, Dir.
Subjects: Material properties - monolithic ceramics, ceramic composites, hybrids, laminates, coatings utilized in defense systems and hardware. **Holdings:** Figures not available. **Remarks:** FAX: (317)496-1175. Serves as the U.S. Department of Defense's central source of engineering and technical data and research and development information on ceramics, laminates, and coatings. **Staff:** Dr. Said K. El-Rahaiby, Asst.Dir.; James F. Chaney, Asst.Dir., Inquiry/User Sup.Serv.

★ 13535 ★
**Purdue University - CINDAS - High Temperature Materials -
Mechanical, Electronic and Thermophysical Properties Information
Analysis Center** (Sci-Engr)
2595 Yeager Rd.   Phone: (317)494-9393
West Lafayette, IN 47906-1398   Dr. C.Y. Ho, Dir.
Subjects: Materials; thermophysical, thermoradiative, optical, and electronic properties; mechanical properties. **Holdings:** Figures not available. **Remarks:** FAX: (317)496-1175. Serves as the Department of Defense's central source of engineering data and technical information on high temperature materials properties, especially the properties of aerospace structural composites and metals and infrared detector/sensor materials. **Staff:** Dr. Ronald H. Bogaard, Asst.Dir.; James F. Chaney, Asst.Dir., Inquiry/User Sup.Serv.

★ 13536 ★
**Purdue University - CINDAS - High Temperature Materials
Information Analysis Center** (Sci-Engr)
2595 Yeager Rd.   Phone: (317)494-9393
West Lafayette, IN 47906   C.Y. Ho, Dir.
Founded: 1957. **Subjects:** Thermophysical properties of matter - theoretical, experimental, numerical data; thermal conductivity; accommodation coefficient; thermal contact conductance; thermal diffusivity; specific heat; viscosity; emittance; reflectance; absorptance; transmittance; solar radiation to emittance ratio; Prandtl number; thermal linear expansion coefficient; thermal volumetric expansion coefficient. **Holdings:** 98,000 indexed abstracts; 97,000 complete papers on microfiche. **Services:** Reproductions; research; special searches; center may be visited by appointment. **Publications:** Thermophysical Properties Research Literature - Retrieval Guide, Basic Edition (7 volumes; 1981); Masters Theses in the Pure and Applied Sciences, volumes 1-26, annual; Thermophysical Properties of Matter, 14 volumes; McGraw-Hill/CINDAS Data Series on Material Properties, 2-4 handbooks/year. **Remarks:** Contains the holdings of its Underground Excavation and Rock Properties Information Center. CINDAS is the acronym for Center for Information and Numerical Data Analysis and Synthesis.

★ 13537 ★
Purdue University - CINDAS - Metals Information Analysis Center (Sci-Engr)
2695 Yeager Rd.   Phone: (317)494-9393
West Lafayette, IN 47906-1398   Dr. C.Y. Ho, Dir.
Subjects: Material properties - monolithic metals, metal alloys, intermetallic compound, coatings utilized in defense systems and hardware. **Holdings:** Figures not available. **Remarks:** FAX: (317)496-1175. Serves as the U.S. Department of Defense's central source of engineering and technical data and research and development on metals. **Staff:** Dr. Pramod D. Desai, Asst.Dir.; James F. Chaney, Asst.Dir., Inquiry/User Sup.Serv.

★ 13538 ★
Purdue University - Consumer and Family Sciences Library (Bus-Fin, Soc Sci)
Stone Hall   Phone: (317)494-2914
West Lafayette, IN 47907   Judith Nixon, Libn.
Founded: 1957. **Staff:** Prof 1; Other 2. **Subjects:** Retail management; apparel design and technology; textile science; consumer affairs; financial counseling and planning; early childhood education; child development and family studies; interior design; nutrition science; dietetics; food science; food and nutrition business; restaurant, hotel, and institutional management; tourism; home economics. **Holdings:** 17,104 volumes and theses; 7 file drawers of pamphlets and clippings. **Subscriptions:** 405 journals and other serials. **Services:** Interlibrary loan; copying; library open to the public. **Computerized Information Services:** DIALOG Information Services, BRS Information Technologies, WILSONLINE, Dow Jones News/Retrieval. Performs searches on fee basis. **Special Indexes:** Lodging and Restaurant Index (print and online). **Remarks:** FAX: (317)494-9007.

★ 13539 ★
Purdue University - Earth & Atmospheric Sciences Library (Sci-Engr, Biol Sci)
Civil Engineering Bldg.   Phone: (317)494-3264
West Lafayette, IN 47907   R. Allen
Founded: 1970. **Staff:** Prof 1.5; Other 1. **Subjects:** Geology, oceanography, earth science, engineering, remote sensing, stratigraphy, meteorology, paleontology, tectonophysics, astronomy, climatology, mineralogy, sedimentology, geochemistry, biogeography, petrology, geoastrophysical geomorphology, geophysical geography. **Holdings:** 22,146 volumes and theses; 120,000 maps; 10,000 aerial photos; 17,285 microforms. **Subscriptions:** 337 journals and other serials. **Services:** Interlibrary loan; copying; library open to the public. **Computerized Information Services:** DIALOG Information Services. **Remarks:** FAX: (317)494-9007. **Staff:** C.L. Laffoon, Prof.Libn.

★ 13540 ★
Purdue University - Engineering Library (Sci-Engr)
Potter Bldg.   Phone: (317)494-2867
West Lafayette, IN 47907   Edwin D. Posey, Engr.Libn.
Founded: 1977. **Staff:** Prof 3; Other 11. **Subjects:** Engineering - aeronautical, chemical, civil, electrical, industrial, materials, mechanical, nuclear. **Special Collections:** Goss History of Engineering Library, with focus on railways and transportation. **Holdings:** 302,513 volumes, technical reports, theses; 824,747 microforms. **Subscriptions:** 2226 journals and other serials. **Services:** Interlibrary loan; copying; library open to the public. **Automated Operations:** Computerized cataloging and serials. **Computerized Information Services:** Online systems. **Special Catalogs:** New books (online). **Remarks:** FAX: (317)494-9007. **Staff:** Charlotte Erdmann, Asst.Engr.Libn.; Jean Poland, Asst.Engr.Libn.

★ 13541 ★
Purdue University - Film Library (Aud-Vis)
Stewart Center   Phone: (317)494-6742
West Lafayette, IN 47907   Carl E. Snow, Film Libn.
Founded: 1948. **Staff:** Prof 1; Other 5. **Subjects:** Agriculture, electrical engineering, aviation technology, home economics, horticulture, psychology. **Special Collections:** Medieval Archives (10,000 35mm slides of Medieval illuminations in 500 sets). **Holdings:** 2676 films; 512 filmstrip sets; 4604 tape recordings; 283 media kits; 2434 videotapes; 1289 slide sets; 59 phonograph records. **Services:** Interlibrary loan; library open to organized groups. **Special Catalogs:** Film Catalog - to library users; special subject catalogs (printout). **Remarks:** FAX: (317)494-9007.

★ 13542 ★
Purdue University - Humanities, Social Science and Education Library
(Educ, Soc Sci, Hum)
West Lafayette, IN 47907   Phone: (317)494-2831
                                               J. Mark Tucker
Staff: Prof 13; Other 24. **Subjects:** English and American literature, U.S. history, education, audiology and speech science, political science, sociology. **Holdings:** 666,746 volumes; 450,069 government documents; 772,006 microforms; United Nations documents; ERIC documents. **Subscriptions:** 3925 journals and other serials. **Services:** Interlibrary loan; copying; SDI; library open to state residents. **Automated Operations:** Computerized cataloging. **Computerized Information Services:** OCLC. **Networks/Consortia:** Member of INCOLSA. **Remarks:** Alternate telephone number(s): 494-2826. FAX: (317)494-9007. **Staff:** Barbara Pinzelik, Assoc.Hum.Libn.; Stewart Saunders, Hum.Sr.Bibliog.; Pam Baxter, Ref.Libn., Psych./Soc.Sci.; Mary E. Collins, Educ.Bibliog./Ref.Libn.; J.P. Herubel, Polit.Sci./Phil. Bibliog./Ref.; Larry Murdock, Govt.Docs.; K. Anderson, Hum.Bibliog./Ref.; D. Hovde, Hum.Bibliog./Ref.; J. Garrett, Foreign Lit.Bibliog./Ref.; E. Goedeken, Ref.; P. Greer, Prof .Libn.

★ 13543 ★
Purdue University - Library - Special Collections Unit (Hist)
West Lafayette, IN 47907   Phone: (317)494-2904
                                               Helen Q. Schroyer, Libn.
Founded: 1978. **Staff:** Prof 1; Other 1.5. **Subjects:** History of Purdue University (higher education), 1873 to present; book design and printing; time and motion studies; flight charts and maps; glass technology; cartoons; early 20th century literature. **Special Collections:** Papers of George Ade; Billerback Collection of Limited Edition Club Books; Amelia Earhart; Frank B. and Lillian M. Gilbreth; Indiana Collection; Charles Major; Bruce Rogers; A.A. Potter; R.B. Stewart; B.F. Miessner; faculty publications.

Holdings: 9500 books; 58,830 volumes; 860 bound periodical volumes; 47,385 microforms; 700 cubic feet and 4300 linear feet of archival material; 25 vertical file drawers; 38,500 other cataloged items. **Subscriptions:** 35 journals and other serials; 5 newspapers. **Services:** Copying; unit open to the public during business hours. **Automated Operations:** Computerized cataloging. **Computerized Information Services:** OCLC; internal database. Performs searches on fee basis. Contact Person: Katherine M. Markee, 494-2808. **Publications:** Access, irregular - to patrons, donors, and friends. **Special Catalogs:** Finding aids. **Special Indexes:** Index to Purdue Exponent, 1889 to present. **Remarks:** FAX: (317)494-9007.

★ 13544 ★
Purdue University - Life Sciences Library (Agri, Biol Sci)
Lilly Hall of Life Sciences
West Lafayette, IN 47907
Phone: (317)494-2910
Martha J. Bailey, Life Sci.Libn.
Founded: 1959. **Staff:** Prof 3; Other 7. **Subjects:** Biological sciences, entomology, forestry, horticulture, agronomy, botany, animal science, plant pathology, soil science. **Holdings:** 72,737 volumes; 16,498 microforms. **Subscriptions:** 1067 journals and other serials. **Services:** Interlibrary loan; copying; SDI; library open to the public. **Computerized Information Services:** DIALOG Information Services, BRS Information Technologies, WILSONLINE, PFDS Online, MEDLARS; CD-ROM (AGRICOLA). **Publications:** Acquisitions list, monthly. **Remarks:** FAX: (317)494-9007. **Staff:** Sarah A. Kelly, Asst. Life Sci.Libn.; Nancy S. Hewison, Asst. Life Sci.Libn.

★ 13545 ★
Purdue University - Management and Economics Library (Bus-Fin)
Krannert Graduate School of Management
West Lafayette, IN 47907
Phone: (317)494-2920
Gordon Law, Libn.
Founded: 1959. **Staff:** Prof 3; Other 8. **Subjects:** Business organization and management; economics - applied, history, principles, theory, systems; industrial relations; agricultural economics; statistics and mathematics; marketing; taxation; real estate; finance; accounting. **Special Collections:** Estey Collection (business cycles); rare books in economics and business history, 16th-19th century (7500 volumes). **Holdings:** 160,641 volumes and theses; 4000 bound annual reports; 1482 reels of microfilm; 24,833 microforms; newspaper clippings. **Subscriptions:** 1224 journals and other serials. **Services:** Interlibrary loan; copying; library open to the public. **Automated Operations:** Computerized serials. **Computerized Information Services:** DIALOG Information Services, PFDS Online, BRS Information Technologies, OCLC, Dow Jones News/Retrieval, NEXIS, Reuters Information Services (Canada) Limited, Human Resource Information Network (HRIN). **Networks/Consortia:** Member of INCOLSA. **Publications:** Monthly Acquisitions List; occasional publications - available on request. **Special Catalogs:** Catalog of rare books (book). **Remarks:** FAX: (317)494-9007. **Staff:** Priscilla C. Geahigan, Asst.Libn.; Anne Buchanan, Asst.Libn.

★ 13546 ★
Purdue University - Mathematical Sciences Library (Sci-Engr, Comp Sci)
Mathematical Sciences
West Lafayette, IN 47907
Phone: (317)494-2855
Richard L. Funkhouser, Sci.Libn.
Founded: 1910. **Staff:** Prof 2; Other 2. **Subjects:** Mathematics, statistics, computer sciences. **Holdings:** 48,624 volumes and theses; 160 reels of microfilm; 3800 technical reports. **Subscriptions:** 1176 journals and other serials. **Services:** Interlibrary loan; copying; library open to the public. **Remarks:** FAX: (317)494-9007.

★ 13547 ★
Purdue University - Pharmacy, Nursing and Health Sciences Library (Med)
Pharmacy Bldg.
West Lafayette, IN 47907
Phone: (317)494-1416
Vicki Killion, Libn.
Founded: 1982. **Staff:** Prof 2; Other 2. **Subjects:** Pharmaceutical sciences, pharmacy, clinical medicine, nursing, bionucleonics, environmental sciences. **Special Collections:** Drug abuse collection (1275 volumes); herbal medicine (350 volumes). **Holdings:** 40,220 volumes; 24 VF drawers of pamphlets; 150 audio cassettes; 105,026 microforms. **Subscriptions:** 649 journals and other serials. **Services:** Interlibrary loan; copying; SDI; library open to the public. **Automated Operations:** Computerized cataloging and serials (through General Library). **Computerized Information Services:** Online systems. **Networks/Consortia:** Member of National Network of Libraries of Medicine - Greater Midwest Region. **Publications:** Purdue University Pharmacy, Nursing and Health Sciences Library Notes, quarterly - to faculty, graduate students, pharmacy libraries, and mailing list. **Remarks:** FAX: (317)494-9007.

★ 13548 ★
Purdue University - Physics Library (Sci-Engr)
Physics Bldg.
West Lafayette, IN 47907
Phone: (317)494-2858
Robert Allen, Libn.
Founded: 1905. **Staff:** Prof 1; Other 3. **Subjects:** Physics - classical, mathematical, modern, solid state, nuclear; pure and applied mathematics; astronomy. **Holdings:** 49,660 volumes and theses. **Subscriptions:** 360 journals and other serials. **Services:** Interlibrary loan; copying; library open to the public. **Computerized Information Services:** DIALOG Information Services. **Publications:** New Acquisitions List, monthly; Library Handbook - both available on request. **Remarks:** FAX: (317)494-9007.

★ 13549 ★
Purdue University - Psychological Sciences Library (Soc Sci)
Peirce Hall
West Lafayette, IN 47907
Phone: (317)494-2968
Pam Baxter, Psych.Libn.
Founded: 1966. **Staff:** Prof 1; Other 2. **Subjects:** Psychology. **Holdings:** 26,693 volumes and theses. **Subscriptions:** 347 journals and other serials. **Services:** Interlibrary loan; copying; library open to the public. **Computerized Information Services:** DIALOG Information Services, BRS Information Technologies; BITNET (electronic mail service). **Remarks:** FAX: (317)494-9007.

★ 13550 ★
Purdue University - Veterinary Medical Library (Med)
C.V. Lynn Hall, Rm. 108
West Lafayette, IN 47907
Phone: (317)494-2852
Gretchen Stephens, Libn.
Founded: 1960. **Staff:** Prof 2; Other 2. **Subjects:** Comparative and veterinary medicine, animal behavior, comparative anatomy, neuroanatomy, pathology, laboratory animal medicine. **Holdings:** 26,268 volumes. **Subscriptions:** 793 journals and other serials. **Services:** Interlibrary loan; copying; SDI; library open to the public. **Automated Operations:** Computerized cataloging. **Computerized Information Services:** OCLC, MEDLINE, DIALOG Information Services, BRS Information Technologies. Performs searches on fee basis. **Networks/Consortia:** Member of INCOLSA. **Publications:** New & Notable (acquisitions list), quarterly - by request. **Remarks:** FAX: (317)494-9007.

Purdue University at Indianapolis
See: **Indiana University-Purdue University at Indianapolis** (7812)

Purdy/Kresge Library
See: **Wayne State University** (20122)

Purdy Memorial Library
See: **Canton Art Institute** (3016)

Ross Coffin Purdy Museum of Ceramics
See: **American Ceramic Society - James I. Mueller Ceramic Library** (519)

★ 13551 ★
Pure Carbon Co., Inc. - Engineering Library (Sci-Engr)
441 Hall Ave.
St. Marys, PA 15857
Phone: (814)781-1573
Founded: 1966. **Staff:** 1. **Subjects:** Carbon. **Holdings:** 1272 books; 3003 technical brochures; 2020 U.S. and foreign patents. **Services:** Library not open to the public.

★ 13552 ★
Purvin & Gertz, Inc. - Library
1201 Main St., Suite 2600
Dallas, TX 75202
Phone: (214)742-7201
Camillus Kerwin, Info.Serv.Mgr.
Remarks: No further information was supplied by respondent.

Purvis Library
See: **Kemptville College of Agricultural Technology** (8612)

Pusa Library
See: **Indian Agricultural Research Institute (7747)**

★ 13553 ★
(Pusan) American Cultural Center - USIS Library (Educ)
No. 24, 2-ka Dae Chung Dong
Chung-ku
Pusan 600, Republic of Korea
Remarks: Maintained or supported by the U.S. Information Agency. Focus is on materials that will assist peoples outside the United States to learn about the United States, its people, history, culture, political processes, and social milieux.

★ 13554 ★
Putnam Companies - Investment Research Library (Bus-Fin)
1 Post Office Square   Phone: (617)292-1335
Boston, MA 02109   Jill M. Hayes, Mgr., Lib.Serv./V.P.
Founded: 1968. **Staff:** Prof 3; Other 4. **Subjects:** Investment, financial and economic data. **Holdings:** Books; files on major U.S. and foreign companies including financial filings. **Subscriptions:** 200 journals and other serials; 10 newspapers. **Services:** Interlibrary loan; library not open to the public. **Computerized Information Services:** DIALOG Information Services, LEXIS, NEXIS, Dow Jones News/Retrieval; internal database. **Remarks:** A subsidiary of Marsh and McLennan, Inc. FAX: (617)292-8545. **Staff:** Ellen Callahan; Karin Gravina.

★ 13555 ★
Putnam County Historical Society - Archives (Hist)
Roy O. West Library
DePauw University   Phone: (317)658-4406
Greencastle, IN 46135   Wesley W. Wilson, Coord., Archv. & Spec.Coll.
Founded: 1950. **Staff:** Prof 1; Other 4. **Subjects:** County history and genealogy. **Special Collections:** County records; Greencastle City Records. **Holdings:** 126 linear feet including of clippings, letters, diaries, scrapbooks; microfilm; tape recordings; movies. **Services:** Copying; genealogical research on fee basis; archives open to the public. **Computerized Information Services:** BITNET (electronic mail service). **Publications:** Newsletter; annual report of Archives and Special Collections. **Remarks:** Maintains collection of 500 photographs, 1850-1980, at Putnam County Public Library. FAX: (317)658-4445. Electronic mail address(es): WWWILSON@DEPAUW (BITNET).

★ 13556 ★
Putnam County Historical Society - Foundry School Museum - Reference Library (Hist)
63 Chestnut St.   Phone: (914)265-4010
Cold Spring, NY 10516   Elaine Baldwin, Libn.
Founded: 1908. **Staff:** 1. **Subjects:** Genealogy; Putnam, Westchester, and Dutchess County history; West Point; American Revolution; Hudson River; West Point Foundry. **Special Collections:** Works of Susan and Anna Warner (24 volumes). **Holdings:** 1200 volumes; 2 VF drawers of clippings and newspapers; 30 boxes of archival materials and letters; 2 VF drawers of maps; manuscripts. **Services:** Library open to the public on a limited schedule.

★ 13557 ★
Putnam Museum - Library (Hist)
1717 W. 12th St.   Phone: (319)324-1933
Davenport, IA 52804   Michael J. Smith, Dir.
Founded: 1867. **Staff:** 14. **Subjects:** Local and regional history, natural history, anthropology, geology, steamboat history. **Special Collections:** Upper Mississippi River steamboat history; photographs; Civil War; early settlers; newspapers. **Holdings:** 5,000 volumes; 50 VF drawers of documents, pamphlets, maps, broadsides, handbills; 12 VF drawers of Black Store papers. **Subscriptions:** 15 journals and other serials. **Services:** Library open to the public by appointment with research fee. **Staff:** Scott Roller, Cur., Hist.Coll.

Putnam/Northern Westchester - BOCES Professional Library
See: **BOCES (1930)**

★ 13558 ★
Putney, Twombly, Hall & Hirson - Law Library (Law)
36 W. 44th St., 6th Fl.   Phone: (212)704-0300
New York, NY 10036-8102   Mary Young, Libn.
Staff: Prof 1. **Subjects:** Law - labor, corporate, trust, estate, tax. **Holdings:** 8000 books. **Subscriptions:** 12 journals and other serials. **Services:** Library not open to the public.

Pu'uhonua o Honaunau National Historical Park
See: **U.S. Natl. Park Service (17768)**

★ 13559 ★
PW Communications International - Corporate Library (Med)
400 Plaza Dr.   Phone: (201)865-7500
Secaucus, NJ 07096   Leila M. Hover, Corp.Libn.
Staff: Prof 1. **Subjects:** Medicine, pharmaceuticals. **Holdings:** 900 books; 919 bound periodical volumes. **Subscriptions:** 100 journals and other serials. **Services:** Interlibrary loan; library not open to the public. **Computerized Information Services:** DIALOG Information Services, BRS Information Technologies, NLM, Data-Star. **Networks/Consortia:** Member of BHSL. **Remarks:** FAX: (201)865-9247.

Howard Pyle Library
See: **Delaware Art Museum - Helen Farr Sloan Library (4715)**

Pymatuning Laboratory of Ecology
See: **University of Pittsburgh - Pymatuning Laboratory of Ecology (19222)**

Q

★ 13560 ★
Q.I.T. - Fer et Titane Inc. - Bibliotheque (Sci-Engr)
B.P. 560   Phone: (514)746-3000
Sorel, PQ, Canada J3P 5P6   C. Stroemgren, Libn.
Founded: 1950. **Subjects:** Chemistry, engineering, business. **Holdings:** Figures not available. **Services:** Interlibrary loan; copying; library open to the public by appointment. **Also Known As:** Fer et Titane du Quebec, Inc.; Quebec Iron and Titanium Corporation.

★ 13561 ★
Q & R Medcenter One - Health Sciences Library (Med)
622 Ave. A East   Phone: (701)222-5390
Bismarck, ND 58501   Leeila Bina, Med.Libn.
Founded: 1920. **Staff:** Prof 1; Other 3. **Subjects:** Clinical medicine, nursing, hospital administration. **Holdings:** 8000 books; 10,000 bound periodical volumes; 4 VF drawers of pamphlets and reprints; 2000 AV items. **Subscriptions:** 300 journals and other serials. **Services:** Interlibrary loan; copying; SDI; library open to the public with permission. **Computerized Information Services:** MEDLINE; EasyLink, DOCLINE (electronic mail services). **Networks/Consortia:** Member of National Network of Libraries of Medicine - Greater Midwest Region. **Publications:** Childhood Gastroenterology Registry.

★ 13562 ★
Quaco Historical Society - Library (Hist)
St. Martins, NB, Canada E0G 2Z0   Phone: (506)833-4740
                                         Elizabeth Thibodeau, Libn.
Founded: 1974. **Subjects:** Atlantic maritime history, wooden shipbuilding, local history. **Holdings:** 5000 books. **Services:** Copying; library open to the public. **Remarks:** Maintains archives in conjunction with Quaco Museum.

★ 13563 ★
Quail Botanical Gardens Foundation Inc. - Library (Biol Sci)
P.O. Box 230005   Phone: (619)436-3036
Encinitas, CA 92023-0005   Druscilla C. Luers, Libn.
Founded: 1970. **Subjects:** Plants, allied subjects. **Special Collections:** Old botanical books. **Holdings:** 1300 books; periodical volumes. **Subscriptions:** 5 journals and other serials. **Services:** Library open to the public for reference use only; borrowing privileges to members. **Remarks:** FAX: (619)436-9516.

★ 13564 ★
Quaker Chemical Corporation - Information Center (Sci-Engr)
Conshohocken, PA 19428-0873   Phone: (215)832-4000
                                         Joseph R. Bowen, Mgr.
Founded: 1952. **Staff:** Prof 1; Other 5. **Subjects:** Chemical technology for the metals and paper specialty fields. **Holdings:** 6100 volumes; 7000 pamphlets; 18 VF drawers of vendor literature; 85 VF drawers of documents and miscellanea; chemical patents, 1966 to present, on microfilm; 475 reels of microfilm of journals; 450 reels of microfilm of documents; 4 VF drawers of government reports on microfiche; 45 audio cassettes. **Subscriptions:** 275 journals and other serials. **Services:** Interlibrary loan; copying; SDI; center open to the public by appointment. **Automated Operations:** Computerized circulation. **Computerized Information Services:** DIALOG Information Services, STN International, WILSONLINE, U.S. Patents Files; internal databases. **Publications:** Current awareness lists; Current Contents Alert. **Remarks:** FAX: (215)832-4498. **Staff:** Jane L. Williams, Info.Rsrcs.Coord.

★ 13565 ★
Quaker Oats Company - John Stuart Research Laboratories - Research Library (Food-Bev, Sci-Engr)
617 W. Main St.   Phone: (708)381-1980
Barrington, IL 60010   Geraldine R. Horton, Mgr., Lib.
Founded: 1956. **Staff:** Prof 3; Other 2. **Subjects:** Food, biochemistry, nutrition, exercise physiology. **Holdings:** 7,000 books; 1000 bound periodical volumes; 50 VF drawers of reprints and pamphlets; internal reports. **Subscriptions:** 400 journals and other serials. **Services:** Interlibrary loan; copying (limited); library open to the public with permission. **Automated Operations:** Computerized cataloging and serials. **Computerized Information Services:** DIALOG Information Services, ORBIT Search Service, STN International, PRODUCTSCAN. **Remarks:** FAX: (708)304-2062. Alternate telephone number(s): (708)304-2058. **Staff:** Jeanne M. Head, Acq.Libn.; Adrienne Jasnich, Sr.Info.Sci.; Dawn Le Duc, Tech.Serv.Libn.

★ 13566 ★
Quaker Oats Company - Marketing Information Center (Food-Bev)
Suite 15-8
P.O. Box 049001   Phone: (312)222-7029
Chicago, IL 60604-9001   Duncan J. McKenzie, Mgr. of Mktg.
Founded: 1976. **Subjects:** Food, demography, marketing. **Holdings:** Figures not available. **Services:** Center not open to the public. **Computerized Information Services:** DIALOG Information Services, Mead Data Central, PRODUCTSCAN, VU/TEXT Information Services, DataTimes, Market Analysis and Information Database (MAID); Proprietary Research (internal database). **Publications:** Monday Morning; Monthly Information Developments. **Remarks:** FAX: (312)222-2732.

★ 13567 ★
Quakertown Community Hospital - Health Sciences Library (Med)
1021 Park Ave.
P.O. Box 9003
Quakertown, PA 18951-9003   Phone: (215)538-4563
Staff: Prof 1; Other 1. **Subjects:** Internal medicine, surgery, geriatrics, psychiatry. **Holdings:** 400 books. **Subscriptions:** 137 journals and other serials. **Services:** Interlibrary loan; copying; SDI; library open to the public. **Computerized Information Services:** BRS/COLLEAGUE, MEDLINE, MEDLARS. Performs searches on fee basis. **Networks/Consortia:** Member of Cooperating Hospital Libraries of the Lehigh Valley Area, BHSL. **Remarks:** FAX: (215)538-9102. **Staff:** Kerry L. Dennigan, Libn.

★ 13568 ★
Quantum Chemical Corporation - USI Division - Allen Research Center Library (Sci-Engr)
11530 N. Lake Dr.   Phone: (513)530-6599
Cincinnati, OH 45249   Susan Bellas, Hd.Libn.
Staff: Prof 1. **Subjects:** Organometallic chemistry, catalysis, polymer science, business. **Holdings:** 10,000 books; U.S. chemical patents, 1966 to present in microform. **Subscriptions:** 400 journals and other serials. **Automated Operations:** Data Trek. **Computerized Information Services:** STN International, Dow Jones News/Retrieval, DRI/McGraw-Hill, OCLC; CD-ROMs. **Publications:** Newsletter, quarterly. **Remarks:** Contains the holdings of its former USI Division - Library located in Rolling Meadows, IL.

★ 13569 ★
Quantum Chemical Corporation - USI Division - Library
3100 Golf Rd.
Rolling Meadows, IL 60008
Defunct. Holdings absorbed by Quantum Chemical Corporation - USI Division - Allen Research Center Library.

★ 13570 ★
Quantum Chemical Corporation - USI Division - Process Research Center - Library (Sci-Engr)
8935 N. Tabler Rd.   Phone: (815)942-7558
Morris, IL 60450-9988   Ingrid M. Voss, Info.Spec.
Founded: 1970. **Staff:** Prof 1; Other 2. **Subjects:** Plastics, chemistry, physics, chemical engineering, packaging. **Holdings:** 3078 books; 2080 bound periodical volumes; 8 VF drawers of company archives; 4 shelves of conference material; 4 drawers of competitor notes; 3 drawers of AV programs and microfilm; 8 VF drawers; 4 drawers of specifications; 8 drawers of central files; patents on microfilm. **Subscriptions:** 178 journals and other serials. **Services:** Interlibrary loan; copying; SDI; library open to the public for reference use only. **Automated Operations:** Computerized cataloging, acquisitions, serials, and circulation. **Computerized Information Services:** Chemical Abstracts Service (CAS), NERAC, Inc., ORBIT Search Service; CD-ROM; internal database. **Networks/Consortia:** Member of ILLINET, Bur Oak Library System. **Publications:** Slide/Sound Library Orientation Program; newsletters. **Remarks:** FAX: (815)942-7440.

★ 13571 ★
Quarles & Brady - Library (Law)
411 E. Wisconsin Ave.   Phone: (414)277-5880
Milwaukee, WI 53202-4497   Susan H. Jankowski, Libn.
Founded: 1910. **Staff:** Prof 2; Other 4. **Subjects:** Law - litigation, labor, tax, patent, environmental, health care, immigration, securities, pension, banking. **Special Collections:** Wisconsin Statutes, 1898 to present; Federal Register, 1970 to present. **Holdings:** 44,000 volumes. **Subscriptions:** 125 journals and other serials; 18 newspapers. **Services:** Library not open to the public. **Computerized Information Services:** LEXIS, DIALOG Information Services. **Networks/Consortia:** Member of Library Council of Metropolitan Milwaukee, Inc. (LCOMM), Private Downtown Law Librarians. **Remarks:** FAX: (414)277-5252. **Staff:** Linda Marifke, Sr.Asst.Libn.; Kay Christiansen, Asst.Libn.; Jacquelyn Ignatowski, Asst.Libn.

★ 13572 ★
Quatrefoil Library (Soc Sci)
1619 Dayton Ave., Suite 105
St. Paul, MN 55104-6208   Phone: (612)641-0969
Founded: 1983. **Subjects:** Gay and lesbian materials, sexual minorities. **Holdings:** 5000 books; 30 bound periodical volumes; unbound newspapers and magazines, 1946 to present; 125 videotapes; 120 audiotapes; 65 sound recordings; 6 file cabinets of clippings; button collection; clothing; art work; Out and About Theater archives; posters. **Subscriptions:** 40 journals and other serials. **Services:** Copying; library open to the public. **Publications:** Newsletter.

Quayle Rare Bible Collection
See: Baker University (1426)

Quebec Association for Hearing-Impaired Children - Information Center for Deafness
See: Association Quebecoise pour Enfants avec Problemes Auditifs - Centre de Documentation en Deficience Auditive (1167)

Quebec Iron and Titanium Corporation
See: Q.I.T. - Fer et Titane Inc. (13560)

★ 13573 ★
Quebec and Ontario Paper Company - Library (Sci-Engr)
Allanburg Rd.   Phone: (416)227-1121
Thorold, ON, Canada L2V 3Z5   Isabelle Ridgway, Libn.
Founded: 1949. **Staff:** 1. **Subjects:** Pulp and paper (newsprint); chemical engineering; business. **Special Collections:** Patents concerning all phases of pulp and paper manufacture. **Holdings:** 2650 books; 2282 bound periodical volumes; 1800 pamphlets; 1750 unbound company reports; 125 filing boxes of other reports. **Subscriptions:** 300 journals and other serials; 5 newspapers. **Services:** Interlibrary loan; copying; library open to the public for reference use only on request. **Automated Operations:** Computerized cataloging and circulation. **Computerized Information Services:** Info Globe, The Financial Post DataGroup, Infomart Online, DIALOG Information Services. **Publications:** Recycling Review; Newsclips, monthly - both for internal distribution only. **Remarks:** FAX: (416)227-2353. Telex: 061 5110.

Quebec Pension Board
See: Quebec Province Regie des Rentes (13617)

★ 13574 ★
(Quebec Province) Archives Nationales du Quebec - Bibliotheque (Hist)
C.P. 10450   Phone: (418)644-4797
Ste. Foy, PQ, Canada G1V 4N1   Gilles Heon, Archv.
Founded: 1920. **Staff:** Prof 1; Other 2. **Subjects:** Genealogy; government institutions; archives management and the administration of documents; history of French America. **Holdings:** 39,800 books; 1802 bound periodical volumes; 7000 other cataloged items; 306 reels of microfilm of journals; 482 reels of microfilm; 1096 serials on microfiche. **Subscriptions:** 54 serials. **Services:** Interlibrary loan; copying; library open to the public. **Publications:** Rapport des Archives Nationales du Quebec; inventaires; guides. **Remarks:** FAX: (418)646-0868.

★ 13575 ★
(Quebec Province) Bibliotheque de l'Assemblee Nationale (Law, Soc Sci)
Edifice Pamphile-Le May   Phone: (418)646-2534
Quebec, PQ, Canada G1A 1A5   Jacques Premont, Exec.Dir.
Founded: 1802. **Staff:** Prof 23; Other 45. **Subjects:** Law - Canadian, French, English, American; political science; economics; legislation; legislative bodies; Canadiana. **Special Collections:** British Parliamentary Papers. **Holdings:** 268,000 books; 41,000 bound periodical volumes; 19,000 Canadian pamphlets and other cataloged items; 23,000 reels of microfilm journals and newspapers; 360,000 microfiche of government publications. **Subscriptions:** 487 journals and other serials; 249 newspapers. **Services:** Interlibrary loan; copying; library open to the public with restrictions. **Automated Operations:** Computerized cataloging. **Computerized Information Services:** DIALOG Information Services, PFDS Online, Prima Telematic Inc., UTLAS, Infomart Online, Societe Quebecoise d'Information Juridique (SOQUIJ), QL Systems, OLF, SDM; Envoy 100 (electronic mail service). **Publications:** Bulletin; Bibliographie et Documentation (series); Biblio eclair (series); Bibliographie (series). **Special Indexes:** Index du Journal des debats, sessional; index of Laurentian collective works (1960-1982; microforms); newspapers index (1956-1966; cards). **Remarks:** FAX: (418)646-3207. Electronic mail address(es): PEB.QQL (Envoy 100). **Staff:** Gaston Bernier, Adj.Dir.; J.L. Fortin, Chf., Ref.; G. Deschenes, Chf., Res.

★ 13576 ★
(Quebec Province) Bibliotheque Nationale du Quebec (Info Sci)
125, rue Sherbrooke W.   Phone: (514)873-1100
Montreal, PQ, Canada H2X 1X4   M. Philippe Sauvageau, Pres.-Dir.
Founded: 1967. **Staff:** Prof 44; Other 75. **Subjects:** Quebec. **Special Collections:** Books printed before 1821. **Holdings:** 308,803 titles; 25,234 reels of microfilm; 6663 monographic map titles; 43,010 serial maps; 1471 linear meters of manuscripts; 103,534 pieces of sheet music. **Subscriptions:** 10,051 journals and other serials; 686 newspapers. **Services:** Interlibrary loan; copying; library open to the public. **Automated Operations:** Computerized cataloging. **Computerized Information Services:** UTLAS, DOBIS Canadian Online Library System, SDM, BADADUQ. Performs searches. Contact Person: Gilles-Mathieu Boivin, Diffusion, (514)873-1100, ext. 421. **Publications:** Bibliographies; list of additional publications - available on request. **Remarks:** FAX: (514)873-4310. **Staff:** Marcel Fontaine, Dir., Adm.; Pierre Deslauriers, Dir., Acq.

★ 13577 ★
(Quebec Province) Bibliotheque Nationale du Quebec - Secteur des Archives Privees (Hum)
125, rue Sherbrooke ouest   Phone: (514)873-1100
Montreal, PQ, Canada H2X 1X4   Michel Biron, Mss.Libn.
Founded: 1967. **Staff:** Prof 2; Other 2. **Subjects:** Literary manuscripts of Quebec. **Holdings:** 1471 linear meters of manuscripts. **Services:** Copying; section open to the public. **Remarks:** FAX: (514)873-4310.

★ 13578 ★
(Quebec Province) Bibliotheque Nationale du Quebec - Secteur des Collections Speciales - Section des Cartes et Plans (Geog-Map)
125, rue Sherbrooke ouest   Phone: (514)873-1100
Montreal, PQ, Canada H2X 1X4   Pierre Lepine, Map Libn.
Founded: 1968. **Staff:** Prof 1. **Subjects:** Quebec maps. **Holdings:** 10,000 map titles; 50,000 sheets in maps series. **Services:** Copying; section open to the public. **Automated Operations:** Computerized cataloging. **Computerized Information Services:** UTLAS, REFCATSS; Envoy 100 (electronic mail service). Performs searches free of charge. **Special Catalogs:** Documents cartographiques depuis la decouverte de l'Amerique jusqu'a 1820: inventaire sommaire, 1985 - for sale. **Remarks:** FAX: (514)873-4310.

★ 13579 ★
(Quebec Province) Bibliotheque Nationale du Quebec - Secteur des Collections Speciales - Section de la Musique (Mus)
125 Sherbrook W.   Phone: (514)873-1100
Montreal, PQ, Canada H2X 1X4   Denis Rivest, Hd.
Staff: Prof 1. **Subjects:** Music from Quebec, Canada, and other countries. **Holdings:** 75,000 pieces of sheet music; 400 boxes of clippings; 20,000 phonograph records. **Services:** Copying; section open to the public for reference use only. **Remarks:** Books and periodicals relating to music are included in the general collection of the library.

★ 13580 ★
(Quebec Province) Bibliotheque Nationale du Quebec - Secteur des Collections Speciales - Section de la Reserve (Hist)
125, rue Sherbrook, O.   Phone: (514)873-1100
Montreal, PQ, Canada H2X 1X4   Milada Vlach, Rare Bks.Libn.
Staff: Prof 1. **Subjects:** Quebec history and society, voyages and exploration, European history and philosophy, artists' books. **Holdings:** 10,000 books; 200 reels of microfilm; Quebec imprints, 1764-1820; Quebec artists' books; incunabula. **Services:** Interlibrary loan; copying; section open to the public. **Special Catalogs:** Laurentiana Parus Avant 1821 (book); Catalogue Collectif des Impressions Quebecoises, 1764-1820 (book); Repertoire des Livres d'Artistes au Quebec, 1900-1980 (book). **Remarks:** FAX: (514)873-4310.

★ 13581 ★
(Quebec Province) Bureau de la Statistique du Quebec - Centre d'Information et de Documentation (Soc Sci, Bus-Fin)
117, rue St. Andre   Phone: (418)691-2401
Quebec, PQ, Canada G1K 3Y3   Romuald Asselin, Coord., Commun.
Founded: 1978. **Staff:** 9. **Subjects:** Economics, agriculture, census information, demographics, social science, the environment. **Special Collections:** Publications of Statistics Canada. **Holdings:** 10,000 books; 340 bound periodical volumes. **Subscriptions:** 200 journals and other serials; 12 newspapers. **Services:** Interlibrary loan; copying; center open to the public. **Computerized Information Services:** DOBIS Canadian Online Library System. **Remarks:** FAX: (418)643-4129.

★ 13582 ★
(Quebec Province) Commission de la Construction du Quebec -
  Ressources Documentaires (Plan)
3530, rue Jean-Talon W.   Phone: (514)341-7740
Montreal, PQ, Canada H3R 2G3   Nicole Cote, Chf.
Founded: 1979. Staff: Prof 4. Subjects: Construction industry, collective
agreements, fringe benefits; vocational education. Holdings: 6100 books; 500
judgments; 120 subject files. Subscriptions: 350 journals and other serials.
Services: Interlibrary loan; copying; open to the public. Computerized
Information Services: Quebec Society for Legal Information, DIALOG
Information Services. Publications: Liste des acquisitions, bimonthly;
Repertoire des periodiques, annual. Remarks: FAX: (514)341-6354. Staff:
Ghislaine Jette, Lib.Techn.; Rachel Gauthier, Lib.Techn.; Simon Flament,
Lib.Techn.

★ 13583 ★
Quebec Province Commission des Droits de la Personne - Library (Law,
  Soc Sci)
360, rue Saint-Jacques, W.   Phone: (514)873-5146
Montreal, PQ, Canada H2Y 1P5   Madeleine Beaudoin, Libn.
Founded: 1976. Staff: Prof 1; Other 2. Subjects: Human rights, law,
sociology, economics, social sciences. Special Collections: Decisions of the
Human Rights Commission. Holdings: 8191 books; 14,297 bound periodical
volumes; 415 reports and files. Subscriptions: 377 journals and other serials.
Services: Interlibrary loan; copying; library open to the public for reference
use only. Automated Operations: Computerized cataloging. Computerized
Information Services: UTLAS. Publications: New Books List; Periodicals,
monthly. Special Catalogs: Catalogue Collectif, 3/year (on microfiche).
Remarks: FAX: (514)873-6032.

★ 13584 ★
Quebec Province Commission des Normes du Travail - Centre de
  Documentation (Bus-Fin)
400 Boul. Jean-Lesage   Phone: (418)646-8713
Quebec, PQ, Canada G1K 8W1   Mireille Barriere
Founded: 1978. Staff: 2. Subjects: Labor standards. Holdings: 1675 books.
Subscriptions: 100 journals and other serials; 10 newspapers. Services:
Interlibrary loan; copying; center open to the public. Publications: Liste des
nouveautes, quarterly. Remarks: FAX: (418)643-5132.

★ 13585 ★
Quebec Province Commission de la Sante et de la Securite du Travail -
  Centre de Documentation (Med, Sci-Engr)
1199 de Bleury, 4th Fl.
C.P. 6067, Succ. A
Montreal, PQ, Canada H3C 4E1   Phone: (514)873-3160
                                           Marc Fournier, Chef de Serv.
Founded: 1980. Staff: Prof 6; Other 16. Subjects: Occupational health and
safety. Holdings: 39,300 books; 700 bound periodical volumes; 500 AV
programs; 35,000 other cataloged items. Subscriptions: 500 journals and
other serials; 6 newspapers. Services: Interlibrary loan; copying; center open
to the public. Automated Operations: Computerized cataloging,
acquisitions, circulation, and ILL. Computerized Information Services:
DIALOG Information Services, PFDS Online, MEDLARS, Prima
Telematic Inc.; internal databases. Publications: Sommaire des Periodiques,
25/year; liste des nouvelles acquisitions, 12/year; ISST: Titres Selectionnes,
12/year. Remarks: FAX: (514)873-6593. Staff: Rosedany Enea; Pierre
Vincent; Germain Roy; Johanne Lauzon; Sylvie Lacerte; Ginette Vadnais.

★ 13586 ★
Quebec (Province) Commission des Services Juridiques - Library (Law)
2 Complexe Desjardins, Suite 1404   Phone: (514)873-3562
Montreal, PQ, Canada H5B 1B3   Francine Godin, Doc.
Staff: Prof 1; Other 1. Subjects: Law, legal aid. Holdings: 3000 books; 220
bound periodical volumes; reports. Subscriptions: 245 journals and other
serials. Services: Library not open to the public. Computerized Information
Services: Judicial Cases Abstracts; specific legal question opinions (internal
databases). Remarks: FAX: (514)873-9263.

★ 13587 ★
Quebec Province Conseil Superieur de l'Education - Centre de
  Documentation (Educ)
2050 St-Cyrille Blvd., W.   Phone: (418)643-3850
Ste. Foy, PQ, Canada G1V 2K8   Bernard Audet, Dir.
Founded: 1975. Staff: Prof 1; Other 1. Subjects: Education. Special
Collections: Ministere de l'Education publications. Holdings: 10,000 books;
40 bound periodical volumes. Subscriptions: 90 journals and other serials;
5 newspapers. Services: Interlibrary loan; copying; center open to the public.
Automated Operations: Computerized cataloging and acquisitions.
Remarks: FAX: (418)644-2530. Staff: Patricia Rehel, Asst.Libn.

★ 13588 ★
Quebec Province l'Inspecteur General des Institutions Financieres -
  Bibliotheque (Bus-Fin)
800, place d'Youville   Phone: (418)643-5236
Quebec, PQ, Canada G1R 4Y5   Sylvie Nadeau, Biblio.
Founded: 1979. Staff: Prof 1; Other 1. Subjects: Financial institutions,
finance, insurance, law. Holdings: 5000 books; 175 bound periodical
volumes; 200 annual reports. Subscriptions: 110 journals and other serials;
5 newspapers. Services: Interlibrary loan; copying; library open to the public
with restrictions. Publications: Bibliotheque Documentation, monthly.
Remarks: Telex: 643-3336.

★ 13589 ★
Quebec Province Ministere des Affaires Culturelles - Conservatoire
  d'Art Dramatique - Centre de Documentation (Theater)
100 Notre-Dame St., E.   Phone: (514)873-3002
Montreal, PQ, Canada H2Y 1C1   Manon Ouimet, Doc.Techn.
Founded: 1967. Staff: 1. Subjects: Theater, film, literature, biography.
Holdings: 8000 books; slides; reel-to-reel tapes; video and audio cassettes;
phonograph records. Subscriptions: 50 journals and other serials. Services:
Interlibrary loan; library open to the public. Remarks: FAX: (514)873-7943.

Quebec Province Ministere des Affaires Culturelles - Musee du Quebec
See: Musee du Quebec (10880)

★ 13590 ★
Quebec Province Ministere des Affaires Municipales - Centre de
  Documentation (Plan)
20, rue Chauveau
Secteur B, 2nd Fl.   Phone: (418)691-2018
Quebec, PQ, Canada G1R 4J3   Ernest Bertrand Roy, Resp.
Founded: 1976. Staff: Prof 1; Other 2. Subjects: Municipal administration,
urban affairs, planning, urbanization, real estate. Holdings: 9000 books; 130
bound periodical volumes; maps. Subscriptions: 180 journals and other
serials. Services: Interlibrary loan; copying (limited); center open to the
public with restrictions. Automated Operations: Computerized cataloging
and acquisitions. Computerized Information Services: UTLAS.
Publications: Monthly Bulletin for Acquisitions. Special Indexes: Index of
authors, titles, subjects, regions (online). Remarks: FAX: (418)646-9266.

★ 13591 ★
Quebec Province Ministere de l'Agriculture, des Pecheries et de
  l'Alimentation - Bibliotheque (Agri)
200-A, chemin Ste-Foy, 1st Fl.   Phone: (418)643-2428
Quebec, PQ, Canada G1R 4X6   Sylvie Belanger, Chf.Libn.
Founded: 1942. Staff: Prof 1; Other 5. Subjects: Agriculture, food,
veterinary medicine. Special Collections: Ministry publications. Holdings:
15,000 books; 1200 bound periodical volumes. Subscriptions: 360 journals
and other serials. Services: Interlibrary loan; library open to the public.
Computerized Information Services: DIALOG Information Services,
CAN/OLE, Questel, SDM. Publications: Sommaire des periodiques.
Remarks: FAX: (418)643-8344. Telex: 0513378.

★ 13592 ★
Quebec Province Ministere des Communautes Culturelles et de
  l'Immigration - Centre de Documentation (Soc Sci)
360, rue McGill   Phone: (514)873-3255
Montreal, PQ, Canada H2Y 2E9   Denis Robichaud, Chf.
Founded: 1968. Staff: Prof 1; Other 6. Subjects: Immigration, demography,
population, ethnicity, minorities, refugees. Holdings: 7000 books; 150 bound
periodical volumes; 75,000 newspaper clippings on immigration.
Subscriptions: 200 journals and other serials; 30 newspapers. Services:
Interlibrary loan; copying; center open to the public. Computerized
Information Services: CAN/SDI. Publications: Revue de Presse, monthly;
En Revue, weekly; A La Fiche, monthly; Revue de Presse Internationale,
monthly. Remarks: FAX: (514)864-2468.

★ 13593 ★
Quebec Province Ministere des Communications - Bibliotheque
Administrative (Bus-Fin, Soc Sci)
1056, rue Conroy, rez-de-chaussee   Phone: (418)643-1515
Quebec, PQ, Canada G1R 5E6   Jean-Pierre Gagnon, Dir.
Founded: 1972. **Staff:** Prof 6; Other 31. **Subjects:** Public administration, management, education, communications, labor and manpower, law, data processing, international and interprovincial relations, economics. **Holdings:** 140,000 volumes; 200,000 microforms. **Subscriptions:** 600 journals and other serials. **Services:** Interlibrary loan; copying; SDI; library open to the public for reference use only. **Automated Operations:** Computerized cataloging. **Computerized Information Services:** DIALOG Information Services, PFDS Online, CAN/OLE, QL Systems, UTLAS, Questel, Info Globe, SDM. **Publications:** Nouveautes de la Bibliotheque Administrative; Le Depositaire; Liste Bimestrielle des Publications du Gouvernement du Quebec; Apercu de la Documentation Courante; Economie et Politique. **Special Catalogs:** Union catalog of periodicals in Quebec government libraries; CDM union catalog. **Remarks:** The Bibliotheque Administrative includes two libraries which jointly serve sixteen Quebec government departments. FAX: (418)646-8132. Telex: 051 3542. Electronic mail address(es): PEB.QQMCG (Envoy 100). **Staff:** Lise Villeneuve, Network; Marie Jose Pean, Acq.; Sylvie Belanger, Online Serv.; Gilbert Plaisance, Ref.; Lucien Levesque, Ref., Edifice H; Elaine Wait, Coll.Dev.

★ 13594 ★
Quebec Province Ministere des Communications - Centre de
Documentation des Technologies de l'Information (Comp Sci)
1500 blvd. Charest, W., RC-92   Phone: (418)644-7006
Ste. Foy, PQ, Canada G1N 2E5   Pierre Drolet, Dir.
Founded: 1977. **Staff:** 2. **Subjects:** Computers, information technology, expert systems, artificial intelligence, videodisks, software. **Special Collections:** Gardner Group reports; Auerbach Library; Databook reports. **Holdings:** 2700 books. **Subscriptions:** 235 journals and other serials; 15 newspapers. **Services:** Interlibrary loan; copying; library open to the public. **Automated Operations:** Computerized cataloging, acquisitions, and serials. **Computerized Information Services:** VOLUMES (internal database). **Publications:** Parutions Recentes, monthly - to Quebec Province government computer community. **Remarks:** FAX: (418)643-5402. Telex: 418 646 3571. **Staff:** Isabelle Poulin, Asst.

★ 13595 ★
Quebec Province Ministere de l'Energie et des Ressources - Bureau de
l'Efficacite Energetique - Centre de Documentation (Energy)
425 Viger Ave., W.
Bureau 600   Phone: (514)873-5463
Montreal, PQ, Canada H2Z 1W9   Ginette Comtois, Libn.
Founded: 1980. **Staff:** Prof 1. **Subjects:** Energy conservation in industry, commerce, housing, urban planning, transportation. **Special Collections:** Provincial and federal publications on energy conservation. **Holdings:** 5000 books; slide sets; video cassettes. **Subscriptions:** 143 journals and other serials. **Services:** Interlibrary loan; SDI; center open to the public for reference use only. **Computerized Information Services:** CAN/OLE, DIALOG Information Services. **Remarks:** FAX: (514)873-6946.

★ 13596 ★
Quebec Province Ministere de l'Energie et des Ressources - Centre de
Documentation (Sci-Engr, Agri)
Edifice de l'Atrium
5700 4th Ave. W., L.B-200   Phone: (418)643-4624
Charlesbourg, PQ, Canada G1H 6R1   Reine Tremblay, MBSI
Founded: 1979. **Staff:** Prof 1; Other 12. **Subjects:** Forests and forestry, forest economics, mines and mining, geology, mineral chemistry, energy, surveying, geodesy, pollution, metallurgy, law, conservation, entomology. **Special Collections:** U.S. Bureau of Mines; USDA; CGC; departmental records. **Holdings:** 80,000 books; 40,000 bound periodical volumes; 350 patents; 1600 reels of microfilm; 1250 microfiche. **Subscriptions:** 700 journals and other serials. **Services:** Interlibrary loan (fee); copying; SDI; center open to the public with restrictions. **Automated Operations:** Computerized cataloging and serials. **Computerized Information Services:** DIALOG Information Services, QL Systems, PFDS Online, CAN/OLE, CAN/SDI, Prima Telematic Inc., Questel, Infomart Online. **Publications:** List of Periodicals; Info-Mer-Mines, monthly; Info-Mer-Terres et Forets, monthly; Info-Mer-Energie, monthly - all available to the public with restrictions. **Remarks:** FAX: (418)644-3814.

★ 13597 ★
Quebec Province Ministere de l'Enseignement Superieur et de la Science
- Centre de Documentation (Educ)
1033, rue de la Chevrotiere, 20th Fl.   Phone: (418)643-1572
Quebec, PQ, Canada G1R 5K9   Claudine Tremblay, Techn.
Founded: 1981. **Staff:** 1. **Subjects:** Higher education, research, university finances, teacher education. **Special Collections:** Commission d'etude sur les universites archives; university publications concerning continuing education for teachers in vocational education. **Holdings:** 9200 books. **Subscriptions:** 60 journals and other serials; 10 newspapers. **Services:** Interlibrary loan; copying; center open to the public with restrictions. **Automated Operations:** Computerized cataloging. **Computerized Information Services:** EDiBASE; UNIV (internal database). Performs searches free of charge. **Publications:** Guide du Centre de documentation; Bulletin de nouveautes, monthly - for internal distribution only. **Remarks:** FAX: (418)646-8462.

★ 13598 ★
Quebec Province Ministere de l'Enseignement Superieur et de la Science
- Centre de Documentation - Secteur Science (Sci-Engr)
1000, route de l'Eglise, 5e etage   Phone: (418)643-0667
Ste. Foy, PQ, Canada G1V 3V9   Francine Breton, Lib.Techn.
Founded: 1981. **Staff:** 2. **Subjects:** Science, research and development, science and technology. **Holdings:** 4000 books. **Subscriptions:** 178 journals and other serials. **Services:** Interlibrary loan; copying; library open to the public for reference use only. **Publications:** Sommaire des nouveautes (newsletter), weekly - for internal distribution only. **Remarks:** FAX: (418)643-6947. **Staff:** Lina Cantin, Lib.Techn.

★ 13599 ★
Quebec Province Ministere de l'Environnement - Library (Env-Cons)
3900, rue Marly, 3e etage   Phone: (418)643-5363
Ste. Foy, PQ, Canada G1X 4E4   Gerard Nobrega, Chf.Libn.
Founded: 1980. **Staff:** Prof 6; Other 8. **Subjects:** Pollution control, acid rain, Quebec environmental issues. **Holdings:** 30,000 books; 10,000 bound periodical volumes; 10,000 maps; 6000 government documents. **Subscriptions:** 200 journals and other serials. **Services:** Interlibrary loan; library open to the public. **Automated Operations:** Computerized public access catalog, cataloging, acquisitions, serials, and circulation. **Computerized Information Services:** Questel, DIALOG Information Services, CAN/OLE, QL Systems, MEDLARS; internal databases; Envoy 100 (electronic mail service). **Networks/Consortia:** Member of Quebec Province Government Library Network. **Publications:** List of acquisitions, monthly - for internal distribution only. **Special Indexes:** Indexes to materials on acid precipitation and Quebec environment (online). **Remarks:** FAX: (418)643-3358. Electronic mail address(es): PEB.QQEN (Envoy 100). **Staff:** Alain Aubin, Ref.; Veronique Pare, Cat.; Carole Robitzilb.

★ 13600 ★
Quebec Province Ministere de l'Industrie, du Commerce et de la
Technologie - Bibliotheque et Gestion Documentaire (Bus-Fin)
710, place d'Youville, local 203   Phone: (418)691-5972
Quebec, PQ, Canada G1R 4Y4   Jacques Fournier, Chf.Libn.
Founded: 1957. **Staff:** Prof 1; Other 7. **Subjects:** Economics, industrial development, commerce, statistics, finance, cooperative societies and technology. **Special Collections:** Statistics Canada (10,000 documents); Financial Post Corporation Service Cards (complete set); Stanford Research Institute publications (500). **Holdings:** 16,000 books; 100 bound periodical volumes; 30,000 unbound periodicals. **Subscriptions:** 450 journals and other serials; 25 newspapers. **Services:** Interlibrary loan (limited); copying; library open to the public with restrictions. **Automated Operations:** Computerized cataloging. **Computerized Information Services:** DIALOG Information Services, Questel. **Publications:** Bulletin mensuel de la documentation courante, monthly - for internal distribution only. **Remarks:** FAX: (418)643-9719.

★ 13601 ★
Quebec Province Ministere de la Justice - Bibliotheque (Law)
1200, route de l'Eglise
Edifice Delta, 4th Fl.   Phone: (418)643-8409
Ste. Foy, PQ, Canada G1V 4M1   Michel Ricard, Responsable
Founded: 1965. **Staff:** Prof 1; Other 4. **Subjects:** Law. **Special Collections:** Statutes. **Holdings:** 17,500 books; 225 bound periodical volumes; 250 reports and government documents; 450 unbound periodicals; 14,000 microfiche. **Subscriptions:** 170 journals and other serials. **Services:** Copying; SDI; library open to the public. **Computerized Information Services:** QL Systems, CAN/LAW, WESTLAW. **Publications:** New acquisitions list. **Remarks:** FAX: (418)643-9749. **Staff:** Solange Tardif, Biblio.; Martine Boivin, Biblio.; Paulette Landry, Biblio.

★ 13602 ★

Quebec Province Ministere du Loisir, de la Chasse et de la Peche -
Bibliotheque (Env-Cons, Biol Sci)
6255 13th Ave.   Phone: (514)374-5840
Montreal, PQ, Canada H1X 3E6   Richard Mathieu, Chf.Libn.
Founded: 1945. **Staff:** Prof 1; Other 2. **Subjects:** Aquatic fauna, limnology, mammology, ecology, North American birds, environmental pollution. **Special Collections:** 16th-18th century natural history; 17th-19th century works of French, American, English naturalists. **Holdings:** 8500 books; 160,000 periodical volumes; 3000 reprints. **Subscriptions:** 65 journals and other serials. **Services:** Interlibrary loan; copying; library open to qualified users only. **Publications:** Monthly recent books list.

★ 13603 ★

Quebec Province Ministere du Loisir, de la Chasse et de la Peche -
Bibliotheque (Env-Cons, Biol Sci)
150 est, blvd. St-Cyrille, Main Fl.   Phone: (418)643-5300
Quebec, PQ, Canada G1R 4Y1   Peter Lavalliere, Hd.Libn.
Founded: 1967. **Staff:** 4. **Subjects:** Wildlife management, conservation, ecology, zoology, ornithology, fish culture, game, hunting, sport fishing, recreation. **Holdings:** 20,000 books; 1500 bound periodical volumes; 44 VF drawers of reprints and pamphlets; 6000 research reports and manuscripts. **Subscriptions:** 250 journals and other serials. **Services:** Interlibrary loan; copying; library open to the public with restrictions. **Computerized Information Services:** DIALOG Information Services. **Remarks:** FAX: (418)643-3330.

★ 13604 ★

Quebec Province Ministere du Revenu - Bibliotheque (Bus-Fin)
3800, rue Marly   Phone: (418)652-6835
Ste. Foy, PQ, Canada G1X 4A5   Pierre-Paul Blais, Dir.
Founded: 1966. **Staff:** 2. **Subjects:** Tax law and administration, management. **Holdings:** 8000 books; 450 bound periodical volumes. **Subscriptions:** 50 journals and other serials; 5 newspapers. **Services:** Interlibrary loan; library open to government employees. **Remarks:** FAX: (418)643-4962.

★ 13605 ★

Quebec Province Ministere de la Sante et des Services Sociaux - Service
de la Documentation (Soc Sci, Med)
1005, chemin Ste-Foy, R.C.   Phone: (418)643-6392
Quebec, PQ, Canada G1S 4N4   Yvon Papillon, Hd.Libn.
Staff: Prof 4; Other 15. **Subjects:** Health and social services, medical economics, aging, occupational and environmental health, family. **Special Collections:** World Health Organization publications. **Holdings:** 30,000 books. **Subscriptions:** 325 journals and other serials. **Services:** Interlibrary loan; service not open to the public. **Automated Operations:** Computerized cataloging. **Computerized Information Services:** DIALOG Information Services, Prima Telematic Inc. **Publications:** Informations Documentaires, 10/year. **Remarks:** Alternate telephone number(s): 643-5572. FAX: (418)643-3177. **Staff:** Francois Allard, Ref. & Coll.Dev.Libn.; Jacqueline Vallee, Ref.Techn.; Louise Boulanger, Ref.Techn.; Michele Lefebvre, Ref.Techn.; Michel Dupuis, Cat. & Rec.Mgr.Libn.; Gerard Darlington, Br.Libn.; Lise Lefrancois, Cat.Techn.; Carol Murphy, Rec.Mgt.Mgr.

★ 13606 ★

Quebec Province Ministere de la Securite Publique - Direction de la
Prevention - Bibliotheque (Law)
2525, boul. Laurier, 11e etage   Phone: (418)646-6620
Ste. Foy, PQ, Canada G1V 2L2   Francine Vallee, Lib.Techn.
Founded: 1990. **Staff:** Prof 1; Other 1. **Subjects:** Police science, sociology, criminology. **Holdings:** 4000 volumes. **Subscriptions:** 100 journals and other serials. **Services:** Interlibrary loan; copying; library open to the public. **Remarks:** FAX: (418)646-3564.

★ 13607 ★

Quebec Province Ministere des Transports - Centre de Documentation
(Trans)
35 Port-Royal E., 3rd Fl.   Phone: (514)864-1666
Montreal, PQ, Canada H3L 3T1   Mr. Vy-Khanh Nguyen, Libn.
Founded: 1979. **Staff:** Prof 1; Other 2. **Subjects:** Transportation - urban, school, design and construction; local transit; subways; transportation of the physically handicapped; environment; road construction. **Special**

Collections: Ministry working papers and studies (600); annual reports and studies from Canadian Transit Commissions; studies and reports from other transportation agencies. **Holdings:** 8000 books; 240 subject and organization files; 35 microfiche; 25 videotapes. **Subscriptions:** 200 journals and other serials. **Services:** Interlibrary loan; copying; center open to the public. **Automated Operations:** Computerized cataloging and circulation (INMAGIC). **Computerized Information Services:** DIALOG Information Services, CAN/OLE, Questel, Banque de Terminologie du Quebec, DOBIS Canadian Online Library System, ESA/IRS, QL Systems, SDM, Infomart Online, CAN/OLE; Best-seller (internal database); Envoy 100 (electronic mail service). Performs searches free of charge. **Publications:** Acquisitions Recentes, bimonthly; Sommaire des Periodiques, bimonthly - to ministry services and concerned libraries and organizations. **Remarks:** FAX: (514)873-7389.

★ 13608 ★

Quebec Province Ministere des Transports - Centre de Documentation
(Trans)
700, blvd. St. Cyrille E., 22nd Fl.   Phone: (418)643-3578
Quebec, PQ, Canada G1R 5H1   Donald Blais, Dir.
Founded: 1978. **Staff:** Prof 4; Other 13. **Subjects:** Transportation - air, road, maritime, railroad, urban. **Special Collections:** Annual reports of the ministry, 1907 to present; Transportation Research Board publications; Transport and Road Research Laboratory publications; Laboratoire Central des Ports et Chaussees publications. **Holdings:** 7000 books; 35,000 reports. **Subscriptions:** 800 journals and other serials; 15 newspapers. **Services:** Interlibrary loan; copying; SDI; center open to the public. **Computerized Information Services:** DIALOG Information Services, QL Systems, DOBIS Canadian Online Library System, CAN/OLE, ESA/IRS; Envoy 100 (electronic mail service). **Publications:** Sommaire des Periodiques, bimonthly; Acquisitions Recentes, bimonthly - both free upon request. **Remarks:** FAX: (418)643-1269. Telex: 051 3733. Electronic mail address(es): QQTR (Envoy 100). **Staff:** Marya Bradicich, Ref.Libn.; Vy-Khanh Nguyen, Ref.Libn.; Sylvia Ray, Ref.Libn.

★ 13609 ★

Quebec Province Ministere du Travail - Centre de Documentation (Bus-Fin)
675 St-Amable, 4th Fl.   Phone: (418)643-7587
Quebec, PQ, Canada G1R 2G5   Lise Laprise, Biblio.
Founded: 1962. **Staff:** 2. **Subjects:** Labor, industrial relations, employment, statistics, industry, finances. **Holdings:** 10,000 books. **Subscriptions:** 175 journals and other serials. **Services:** Interlibrary loan; copying; center open to the public with restrictions. **Remarks:** Telex: 051-3847.

★ 13610 ★

Quebec Province Office des Communications Sociales - Bibliotheque et
Centre de Documentation (Info Sci)
4005, rue de Bellechasse   Phone: (514)729-6391
Montreal, PQ, Canada H1X 1J6   Lucien Labelle, Gen.Dir.
Founded: 1957. **Staff:** Prof 1; Other 3. **Subjects:** Cinema, radio, television, cablevision, videotex, the press. **Holdings:** 6000 books; 400 bound periodical volumes; microfilm; unbound documents. **Subscriptions:** 60 journals and other serials; 10 newspapers. **Services:** Copying; library open to the public with restrictions. **Computerized Information Services:** Computerized information and evaluation on 30,000 feature films. **Publications:** List of publications for sale - available on request. **Special Indexes:** Index to film documentation. **Remarks:** FAX: (514)729-7375. Provides facilities for Centre de Documentation Cinematographique.

★ 13611 ★

Quebec Province Office de la Langue Francaise - Bibliotheque (Hum, Sci-Engr)
800, place Victoria, 15th Fl.   Phone: (514)873-2997
Montreal, PQ, Canada H4Z 1G8 Chantal Robinson, Chf., Lib./Pub.Serv.
Founded: 1970. **Staff:** Prof 1; Other 5. **Subjects:** Terminology, technology, French language. **Special Collections:** Association Francaise de Normalisation (AFNOR) standards; Bureau de Normalisation de Quebec (BNQ) standards; Techniques de Ingenieur. **Holdings:** 21,000 books; internal publications. **Subscriptions:** 175 journals and other serials; 5 newspapers. **Services:** Interlibrary loan; copying; library open to the public. **Automated Operations:** Computerized cataloging. **Computerized Information Services:** DIALOG Information Services, CAN/OLE, Questel, Banque de Terminologie du Quebec (BTQ), SDM; Envoy 100 (electronic mail service). **Publications:** Parutions Recentes, bimonthly; selective bibliographies. **Remarks:** FAX: (514)873-2884. Electronic mail address(es): OLF.BIBLMTL (Envoy 100).

★13612★
Quebec Province Office de la Langue Francaise - Bibliotheque - Quebec
(Hum, Sci-Engr)
700, boul St. Cyrille E.
Quebec, PQ, Canada G1R 5G7   Micheline Gagnon, Resp.
Founded: 1964. **Staff:** Prof 1; Other 2. **Subjects:** French terminology and linguistics. **Special Collections:** Publications de l'Office; techniques de l'ingenieur. **Holdings:** 16,000 books; 300 catalogs; 800 documents of sources and inventories. **Subscriptions:** 98 journals and other serials. **Services:** Interlibrary loan; copying; library open to the public at librarian's discretion. **Automated Operations:** Computerized cataloging. **Computerized Information Services:** SDM, DIALOG Information Services, CAN/OLE, Questel, Banque de Terminologie du Quebec (BTQ); Envoy 100 (electronic mail service). **Publications:** Parutions Recentes, monthly; selective bibliographies; Revue de presse; Hebdo Express - all for internal distribution only. **Remarks:** FAX: (418)643-3210. Electronic mail address(es): OLF.BIBLQUE (Envoy 100).

★13613★
Quebec Province Office des Personnes Handicapees du Quebec - Centre de Documentation (Soc Sci)
C.P. 820   Phone: (819)477-7100
Drummondville, PQ, Canada J2B 6X1   Sophie Janik, Doc.
Founded: 1979. **Staff:** Prof 1; Other 2. **Subjects:** Handicapped persons - social and vocational integration, adaptation and rehabilitation, deinstitutionalization, impairment, disabilities. **Holdings:** 3500 books; 15 bound periodical volumes; 500 audio cassettes; 4000 other documents; ministry reports; AV programs. **Subscriptions:** 200 journals and other serials; 10 newspapers. **Services:** Interlibrary loan; copying; center open to the public. **Computerized Information Services:** DIALOG Information Services; EDIBASE (internal database); Arctel, (electronic mail service). **Publications:** Liste d'acquisition, quarterly; Thesaurus: Personne handicapee; Bibliographies thematiques; Bibliographie quebecoise. **Special Indexes:** Repertoires audiovisuels. **Remarks:** FAX: (819)477-8493. Telex: 4778493. **Staff:** Francois Malouin, Biblio.

★13614★
Quebec Province Office de la Protection du Consommateur - Centre de Documentation
400, boul. Jean-Lesage
Bureau 450
Quebec, PQ, Canada G1K 8W4
Defunct.

★13615★
(Quebec Province) Regie de l'Assurance-Maladie - Bibliotheque (Bus-Fin)
C.P. 6600   Phone: (418)682-5118
Quebec, PQ, Canada G1K 7T3   Yvan Richard
Founded: 1970. **Staff:** Prof 1; Other 1. **Subjects:** Health insurance - law, management, medicine, psychology. **Special Collections:** Documents of the Regie de l'Assurance-Maladie. **Holdings:** 4200 books; 300 bound periodical volumes; telephone directories; government publications. **Subscriptions:** 6 newspapers. **Services:** Interlibrary loan; copying; library open to the public. **Publications:** Le Bibliothequoi, monthly; L'ABC de la Bibliotheque; Accessibilite a la Bibliotheque et a la Collection. **Remarks:** Library located at 1125 chemin St. Louis, Sillery, Quebec, PQ, Canada G15 1E7.

★13616★
Quebec Province Regie de l'Electricite et du Gaz - Bibliotheque
2100, rue Drummond, Rm. 200
Montreal, PQ, Canada H3G 1X1
Defunct.

★13617★
Quebec Province Regie des Rentes - Centre de Documentation (Bus-Fin)
C.P. 5200   Phone: (418)643-8250
Quebec, PQ, Canada G1K 7S9   Nicole Paquin, Asst.Libn.
Founded: 1965. **Staff:** Prof 1; Other 3. **Subjects:** Social security, private pension plans. **Holdings:** 18,000 volumes; 5500 microfiche; 430 pamphlets and reprints. **Subscriptions:** 305 journals and other serials. **Services:** Interlibrary loan; copying; SDI; center open to the public with permission. **Automated Operations:** Computerized cataloging. **Computerized Information Services:** DOBIS Canadian Online Library System, UTLAS. **Publications:** Nouvelles acquisitions, bimonthly - for exchange; Periodiques recus, annual with supplements - for internal distribution only; Repertoire des periodiques, 1987 - limited distribution. **Also Known As:** Quebec Pension Board.

(Quebec Province) Societe de Radio-Television du Quebec - Radio Quebec
See: **Radio Quebec** (13688)

★13618★
Quebec Safety League - Information Center (Sci-Engr)
2536, rue Lapierre   Phone: (514)595-9110
Ville Lasalle, PQ, Canada H8N 2W9   Jacques Ratthe, Lib.Techn.
Founded: 1986. **Staff:** Prof 1. **Subjects:** Road and work safety, safety at home, safety in sports and leisure. **Holdings:** 2000 books. **Subscriptions:** 31 journals and other serials. **Services:** Copying; center open to the public. **Automated Operations:** Computerized cataloging. **Remarks:** FAX: (514)595-3398. **Also Known As:** Ligue de Securite du Quebec.

★13619★
Quebec Young Farmers Provincial Federation - Library (Agri)
Box 80   Phone: (514)457-2010
Ste. Anne de Bellevue, PQ, Canada H9X 3L4   Janet Parker, Prov.Coord.
Staff: 8. **Subjects:** Rural youth, agriculture. **Holdings:** Figures not available. **Services:** Library not open to the public.

Quebec Zoological Garden
See: **Jardin Zoologique du Quebec** (8344)

★13620★
Queen of Angels - Hollywood Presbyterian Medical Center - Health Sciences Library (Med)
1300 N. Vermont Ave.   Phone: (213)413-3000
Los Angeles, CA 90027   Pacita Estepa, Hea.Sci.Libn.
Founded: 1924. **Staff:** Prof 1. **Subjects:** Medicine, nursing, allied health sciences, patient education, hospital administration, health care. **Holdings:** 5700 books; 3000 bound periodical volumes; 900 AV programs. **Subscriptions:** 182 journals and other serials. **Services:** Interlibrary loan; copying; SDI; library open to the public for reference use only on request. **Computerized Information Services:** NLM. **Networks/Consortia:** Member of National Network of Libraries of Medicine - Pacific Southwest Region.

★13621★
Queen Anne's County Law Library (Law)
Court House
P.O. Drawer 659
Centreville, MD 21617   Phone: (301)758-0216
Staff: 1. **Subjects:** U.S. and Maryland law. **Holdings:** 2800 books; 52 bound periodical volumes. **Services:** Library open to the public with restrictions.

★13622★
Queen Elizabeth Hospital - Frank J. MacDonald Library (Med)
P.O. Box 6600   Phone: (902)566-6371
Charlottetown, PE, Canada C1A 8T5   Marion K. MacArthur, Libn.
Founded: 1982. **Staff:** Prof 1; Other 1. **Subjects:** Medicine, nursing, allied health sciences, hospital administration. **Holdings:** 500 books; 500 bound periodical volumes. **Subscriptions:** 119 journals and other serials. **Services:** Interlibrary loan; copying; library open to health science workers. **Computerized Information Services:** MEDLARS; Envoy 100 (electronic mail service). **Remarks:** FAX: (902)566-6385. Electronic mail address(es): QEH.LIBRARY (Envoy 100).

★13623★
Queen Elizabeth II Hospital - Staff Library (Med)
10409 98th St.
Postal Bag 2600
Grande Prairie, AB, Canada T8V 2E8   Phone: (403)538-7186
     Phyllis Brazeau, Lib.Techn.
Founded: 1984. **Staff:** 1. **Subjects:** Medicine. **Holdings:** 4000 books; 220 bound periodical volumes; 385 videotapes. **Subscriptions:** 211 journals and other serials. **Services:** Interlibrary loan; copying; library open to the public for reference use only. **Remarks:** FAX: (403)539-9930.

Queen Elizabeth II Library
See: **Memorial University of Newfoundland - Queen Elizabeth II Library** (10055)

★13624★

Queen Street Mental Health Centre - Health Sciences Library (Med)
1001 Queen St., W.   Phone: (416)535-8501
Toronto, ON, Canada M6J 1H4   Mary Ann Georges, Staff Libn.
Founded: 1965. **Staff:** Prof 1. **Subjects:** Psychiatry, psychology, nursing, psychopharmacology, sociology, administration, rehabilitation. **Special Collections:** Hospital History File (history of Queen Street Mental Health Centre); Griffin-Greenland History of Canadian Psychiatry Collection. **Holdings:** 3000 books; 3000 bound periodical volumes; 50 theses; 150 AV cassettes; 4 VF drawers. **Subscriptions:** 185 journals and other serials. **Services:** Interlibrary loan; copying; library open to the public for reference use only. **Publications:** Acquisitions list, 2/year; journals list, annual. **Remarks:** FAX: (416)583-4307.

★13625★

Queen's Bench - Judges' Library (Law)
Law Courts Bldg.
1A Churchill Square   Phone: (403)422-2345
Edmonton, AB, Canada T5J 0R2   Shih-Sheng Hu, Chf.Prov. Law Libn.
Subjects: Law. **Holdings:** 6300 volumes. **Services:** Library not open to the public. **Remarks:** Housed with Law Society of Alberta - Edmonton Library.

Queens Borough Public Library - Art and Music Division
See: **Queens Borough Public Library - Fine Arts & Recreation Division** (13627)

★13626★

Queens Borough Public Library - Film Division (Art, Theater)
89-11 Merrick Blvd.   Phone: (718)990-0766
Jamaica, NY 11432   Fred Fishel, Div.Hd.
Founded: 1965. **Staff:** Prof 3; Other 4. **Subjects:** Feature films, documentaries, instructional films, children's films, foreign films, Hindi language films, Chinese language films, Korean language films. **Holdings:** 8500 videotapes; 3200 16mm films. **Services:** Division open to the public. **Automated Operations:** Computerized circulation. **Computerized Information Services:** Bowker's Video Directory Plus; GEnie (electronic mail service). **Remarks:** FAX: (718)658-8312. Electronic mail address(es): F.Fishel1 (GEnie). **Staff:** Norma B. Mar, Asst.Div.Hd.

★13627★

Queens Borough Public Library - Fine Arts & Recreation Division (Art, Mus)
89-11 Merrick Blvd.   Phone: (718)990-0755
Jamaica, NY 11432   Claire Kach, Div.Hd.
Founded: 1933. **Staff:** Prof 6; Other 3. **Subjects:** Art, music, theater, dance, games, sports. **Special Collections:** Picture collection (1 million reproductions, photographs, postcards, clippings). **Holdings:** 120,738 books; 4500 bound periodical volumes; 10,000 phonograph records; 10,000 cassettes; 3000 compact discs; 230 unabridged books on tape; 4000 reels of microfilm; 46 VF drawers of pamphlets; 500 libretto titles. **Subscriptions:** 405 periodical titles. **Services:** Interlibrary loan; copying; division open to the public. **Automated Operations:** Computerized cataloging and circulation. **Special Indexes:** Subject Index to Picture Collection; Song Index; Index of exhibition catalogs. **Remarks:** FAX: (718)658-8312. **Formerly:** Its Art and Music Division. **Staff:** Heidi Gottman; Sharon Kugler; Jane Montalto; Diane Irving; Richard Asaro.

★13628★

Queens Borough Public Library - History, Travel & Biography Division (Hist, Geog-Map)
89-11 Merrick Blvd.   Phone: (718)990-0762
Jamaica, NY 11432   Deborah Hammer, Hd.
Founded: 1930. **Staff:** Prof 6; Other 3. **Subjects:** History, Indians of North America, biography, geography, travel, exploration. **Special Collections:** Carter G. Woodson Collection of Afro-American Culture and Life; Schomburg microfilm collection; U.S. Geographic Survey topographic maps (10,300); physical/thematic maps of countries of the world (126); nautical

charts (8 kits); jet/ocean/world navigation charts (520); national forest maps (75); Latin American topographic maps (97); New York State planimetric maps (968); New York state, county, road maps (78); railroad transportation zone maps (82); historic/city maps (442). **Holdings:** 143,000 books; 3550 bound periodical volumes; 6800 microforms; 1 drawer of microfiche; 36 VF drawers of pamphlets; New York Daily News, 1950 to present; newspapers on microfilm. **Subscriptions:** 71 journals and other serials; 32 newspapers. **Services:** Interlibrary loan; copying; division open to the public. **Automated Operations:** Computerized cataloging and circulation. **Computerized Information Services:** ALANET (electronic mail service). **Special Indexes:** Collective biography analytics (card). **Remarks:** FAX: (718)658-8312; (718)658-8342. **Staff:** John Moran, Asst.Div.Hd.; Roy Berg, Ref.Libn.

★13629★

Queens Borough Public Library - Information Services Division (Info Sci)
89-11 Merrick Blvd.   Phone: (718)990-0714
Jamaica, NY 11432   Phyllis Poses, Div.Mgr.
Founded: 1991. **Staff:** Prof 13; Other 7. **Subjects:** Interloan/interlibrary loan; telephone reference; online information; periodicals, indexes, and government documents. **Holdings:** 5000 volumes; 1158 bound periodical volumes; 30 drawers of microfiche; 4557 reels of microfilm; partial depository for federal government documents; state and city documents. **Subscriptions:** 115 journals and other serials. **Services:** Interlibrary loan; copying; faxing to NYS residents; magazines and documents room open to the public. **Automated Operations:** Computerized public access catalog and ILL. **Computerized Information Services:** NEXIS, DIALOG Information Services, BRS Information Technologies, VU/TEXT Information Services, OCLC, New York Legislative Retrieval System, LIONS; CD-ROMs (Books in Print Plus, Books Out of Print, ABI/Inform, InfoTrac, Periodicals Abstracts Ondisc, Newspaper Abstracts Ondisc, GODIG). **Networks/Consortia:** Member of New York Metropolitan Reference and Research Library Agency. **Special Indexes:** Community information. **Remarks:** FAX: (718)658-8342; (718)658-8312. Alternate telephone number(s): (718)990-0720, (718)990-0826 (interloans); (718)990-0769 (magazines and documents). Contains holdings of the former Information/Telephone Reference, Magazines and Documents, and Interloan and Reference Divisions (previously listed separately). **Staff:** Rosemarie Riechel; Carol Shoengold; Rozeta Logore; Edward Weiss; David Alperstein; Ilham Al-Basri; Steven Sachar; Jacqueline Neus; Avis Jones; Karen Venturella; Paul Tallarico.

Queens Borough Public Library - Information/Telephone Reference Division
See: **Queens Borough Public Library** (13629)

Queens Borough Public Library - Interloan and Reference Division
See: **Queens Borough Public Library** (13629)

★13630★

Queens Borough Public Library - Library Action Committee of Corona-East Elmhurst, Inc. - Langston Hughes Community Library and Cultural Center (Soc Sci)
102-09 Northern Blvd.   Phone: (718)651-1100
Corona, NY 11368   Andrew P. Jackson, Exec.Dir.
Founded: 1969. **Staff:** Prof 6; Other 17. **Subjects:** Third World, children's literature. **Special Collections:** Langston Hughes Collection (books by and about the author); Black Heritage Reference Collection; Langston Hughes Music Collection; Langston Hughes Video Club; Langston Hughes Art Collection. **Holdings:** 110,000 books; 150 documents, manuscripts, reels of microfilm. **Subscriptions:** 105 journals and other serials; 15 newspapers. **Services:** Copying; library open to the public. **Publications:** Library Center Brochure. **Remarks:** FAX: (718)651-6258. **Staff:** Joan Whittaker, Cur., Black Heritage Ctr.; Dr. Ruby Sprott, Dir., Homework Assist.Prog.; Charlyne Gadsden, Asst. Branch Lib.Mgr.; Una Grant, Coord., Info. & Referral Serv.

★13631★

Queens Borough Public Library - Literature & Languages Division (Hum)
89-11 Merrick Blvd.   Phone: (718)990-0763
Jamaica, NY 11432   Inge M. Judd, Div.Hd.
Founded: 1928. **Staff:** Prof 11; Other 6. **Subjects:** Literature, linguistics, fiction and nonfiction in 75 languages, English fiction. **Special Collections:**

Black Literature Reference Collection. **Holdings:** 329,574 books; 7381 bound periodical volumes; 20 VF drawers of plays; 1 VF drawer of microfiche; 4243 reels of microfilm. **Subscriptions:** 326 journals and other serials. **Services:** Interlibrary loan; copying; division open to the public. **Automated Operations:** Computerized cataloging and circulation. **Special Indexes:** Play Index (card). **Remarks:** FAX: (718)658-8312; (718)658-8342. **Formerly:** Its Language & Literature Division. **Staff:** Sylvia Babb, Asst.Div.Hd.; Celia Lischner, Ref.Libn.; Anca Costea, Foreign Lang.Libn.; Casper Morsello, Foreign Lang.Libn.; James McShane, Foreign Lang.Libn.; Desiree Lee, Foreign Lang.Libn.; Michael Summers, Gen.Asst.; Ron Alvarez, Gen.Asst.

★ 13632 ★
Queens Borough Public Library - Long Island Division (Hist)
89-11 Merrick Blvd.   Phone: (718)990-0770
Jamaica, NY 11432   C.F.J. Young, Div.Hd.
Founded: 1912. **Staff:** Prof 3; Other 2. **Subjects:** Long Island local history, genealogy, and memorabilia. **Special Collections:** Books published at Marion Press (private press in Jamaica, NY); publications of Christopher Morley; Lewis Howard Latimer Collection. **Holdings:** 30,750 books; 1993 bound periodical volumes; 197 VF drawers of clippings; 5300 maps; 40,000 manuscripts; 8607 reels of microfilm; 50,000 pictures, prints, photographs, postcards, glass plate negatives. **Subscriptions:** 55 journals and other serials; 23 newspapers. **Services:** Interlibrary loan; copying; division open to the public. **Automated Operations:** Computerized cataloging and circulation. **Special Indexes:** Catalogs and indexes of manuscript, map, and photograph collections. **Remarks:** FAX: (718)658-8312; (718)658-8342. **Staff:** William Asadorian, Asst.Div.Hd.; Robert Friedrich, Ref.Libn.

Queens Borough Public Library - Magazines and Documents Division
See: **Queens Borough Public Library** (13629)

★ 13633 ★
Queens Borough Public Library - Science & Technology Division (Sci-Engr, Bus-Fin)
89-11 Merrick Blvd.
Jamaica, NY 11432   Phone: (718)990-0760
Founded: 1930. **Staff:** Prof 7; Other 4. **Subjects:** Mathematics, engineering, accounting, chemistry, biological sciences, advertising, nursing, physics, business administration, aeronautics, patents, health, fitness, home economics. **Special Collections:** Telephone directories for many major U.S. and foreign cities; automobile shop manuals; Sams Photofacts and Computerfacts. **Holdings:** 264,789 books; 44,307 bound periodical volumes; 14,267 reels of microfilm of back issue periodicals; 236 VF drawers. **Subscriptions:** 1151 journals and other serials. **Services:** Interlibrary loan; copying; division open to the public. **Automated Operations:** Computerized cataloging and circulation. **Computerized Information Services:** InfoTrac; CD-ROM (Health Reference Center). **Remarks:** FAX: (718)658-8312. **Staff:** Linda Scavetti, Asst.Div.Hd.; Joseph R. Morris; Stephen Somerdin; Shirley Evans; Dana Aylor; Judith Box; Alice Overton.

★ 13634 ★
Queens Borough Public Library - Social Sciences Division (Soc Sci, Bus-Fin, Rel-Phil)
89-11 Merrick Blvd.   Phone: (718)990-0761
Jamaica, NY 11432   Nathan Shoengold, Div.Hd.
Founded: 1930. **Staff:** Prof 6; Oth er 4. **Subjects:** Philosophy, psychology, religion, sociology, economics and investments, political scie nce, government, law, education, costumes, folklore. **Special Collections:** Investment, law, and tax services; colle ge catalogs; civil service study guides; corporate reports; curriculum-related pamphlets; Hiler Costu me Collection. **Holdings:** 251,027 books; 20,108 bound periodical volumes; 116 VF drawers; 325 drawers of microfiche; 12,590 reels of microfilm ; 154 microcards; 773,007 ERIC microfiche. **Subscriptions:** 1236 journals and other serials; 30 newspapers. **Services:** Interlibrary loan; copying; division open to the public. **Automated Operations:** Computerized cataloging and circulation. **Computerized Information Services:** CD-ROM (General BusinessFile). **Remarks:** FAX: (718)658-8312. **Staff:** Lucille Vener, Asst.Div.Hd.; Muriel Marcus, Ref.Libn.; Scott Campbell; Susan James; Lisa Errico-Cox.

★ 13635 ★
Queens Children's Psychiatric Center - Lauretta Bender Staff Library (Med)
74-03 Commonwealth Blvd.   Phone: (718)464-2900
Bellerose, NY 11426   Naomi Leiten, MD
Staff: Prof 1. **Subjects:** Psychiatry, psychology, social work. **Special Collections:** Collection of reprints from psychiatric journals (300); Lauretta Bender series (books on Bender-gestalt; reprints and limited works of Dr. Paul Ferdinand Schilder). **Holdings:** 5000 books; 300 bound periodical volumes; 650 reprints and pamphlets; 300 reels of tape; Audio-Digest tapes on psychiatry. **Subscriptions:** 80 journals and other serials. **Services:** Library open to other health facilities.

★ 13636 ★
Queens College of City University of New York - Benjamin S. Rosenthal Library - Art Library (Art)
65-30 Kissena Blvd.   Phone: (718)997-3770
Flushing, NY 11367-0904   Suzanna B. Simor, Hd.
Founded: 1937. **Staff:** Prof 2; Other 5. **Subjects:** Art, architecture, archeology, design, photography. **Holdings:** 52,000 books; 4400 bound periodical volumes; 36,000 pamphlets; 46,000 mounted reproductions; 2000 microfiche; 13,000 slides. **Subscriptions:** 200 journals and other serials. **Services:** Interlibrary loan; copying; library open to the public for reference use only. **Automated Operations:** Computerized public access catalog, cataloging, acquisitions, serials, and circulation. **Computerized Information Services:** OCLC, NOTIS. **Networks/Consortia:** Member of SUNY/OCLC Library Network. **Publications:** Serials Available, annual; Union List of Serials, annual; Collection Development Policy (2nd edition; 1985) - all for internal distribution only and available upon request. **Special Catalogs:** Art exhibition catalogs. **Remarks:** FAX: (718)793-8049. **Staff:** Alexandra de Luise.

★ 13637 ★
Queens College of City University of New York - Benjamin S. Rosenthal Library - Historical Documents Collection (Hist)
65-30 Kissena Blvd.
Flushing, NY 11367-0904   Phone: (718)997-5000
Founded: 1964. **Subjects:** State and local history, 1660-1860. **Holdings:** 18,000 cubic feet of legal records, wills, inventories, administrative papers, assessment lists, criminal court records. **Remarks:** Maintained by the university's History Department, telephone (718)520-7366.

★ 13638 ★
Queens College of City University of New York - Benjamin S. Rosenthal Library - Reference Department - Science Collection (Sci-Engr, Med)
65-30 Kissena Blvd.   Phone: (718)997-3700
Flushing, NY 11367   Matthew J. Simon, Chf.Libn.
Founded: 1937. **Staff:** Prof 2; Other 2. **Subjects:** Biology, psychology, chemistry, mathematics, physics, geology, computer science, home economics, speech pathology, audiology, sports physiology and medicine. **Holdings:** 68,000 books; 34,000 bound periodical volumes; microfilm. **Subscriptions:** 1850 journals and other serials. **Services:** Interlibrary loan; copying; library open to the public for reference use only. **Automated Operations:** Computerized cataloging, serials, and circulation. **Computerized Information Services:** DIALOG Information Services, BRS Information Technologies. **Networks/Consortia:** Member of New York Metropolitan Reference and Research Library Agency. **Publications:** Science Library Reference Guide series, irregular - to library users; Science Fair Research in a College Library - for sale. **Staff:** Jackson B. Cohen, Sci.Bibliog./Ref.Libn; Gail Ronnermann, Sci.Bibliog./Ref.Libn.

★ 13639 ★
Queens College of City University of New York - Center for Byzantine & Modern Greek Studies - Library (Hum)
65-30 Kissena Blvd.   Phone: (718)997-5000
Flushing, NY 11367   E. Lekas, Libn.
Staff: Prof 1; Other 2. **Subjects:** Modern Greek language, literature, history; Greek American community; Cyprus. **Holdings:** 2000 books; 100 other cataloged items. **Subscriptions:** 10 journals and other serials. **Services:** Library open to the public.

★ 13640 ★
Queens College of City University of New York - Ethnic Materials Information Exchange (Area-Ethnic)
Graduate School of Lib. & Info. Studies
NSF 300
65-30 Kissena Blvd.   Phone: (718)997-3790
Flushing, NY 11367   David Cohen, Prog.Dir.
Founded: 1980. **Staff:** Prof 1; Other 1. **Subjects:** Ethnic studies resources, minority groups in America, multicultural librarianship. **Holdings:** 2000 volumes; 40 filmstrips; 10 tapes; 250 pamphlets; curriculum materials; vertical file of clippings for each group and information area. **Subscriptions:** 6 journals and other serials. **Services:** Center open to the public. **Remarks:** Alternate telephone number(s): 997-3626. FAX: (718)793-8049.

★ 13641 ★
Queens College of City University of New York - Ethnic Studies Project - Rabbi Simon Hevesi Jewish Heritage Library (Rel-Phil)
67-09 108th St.
Forest Hills, NY 11375   Phone: (718)268-5011
Founded: 1982. **Staff:** 2. **Subjects:** Judaica, Hebraica, Yiddish materials. **Holdings:** 7000 books; AV materials, including cassettes and phonograph records. **Subscriptions:** 20 journals and other serials; 7 newspapers. **Services:** Interlibrary loan; copying; library open to the public with restrictions.

Queens Hospital Center
See: Long Island Jewish Medical Center (9291)

★ 13642 ★
Queen's University at Kingston - Art Library (Art)
Ontario Hall   Phone: (613)545-2841
Kingston, ON, Canada K7L 5C4   R. van Weringh, Art Libn.
Founded: 1957. **Staff:** Prof 1; Other 2. **Subjects:** Art history, art education, art conservation. **Holdings:** 32,000 volumes; 600 microfiche; 300 reels of microfilm; 10,000 exhibition catalogs; 100,000 35mm slides; 50,000 photographs; 6500 vertical file items. **Subscriptions:** 130 journals and other serials. **Services:** Interlibrary loan; library open to the public with restrictions. **Automated Operations:** Computerized public access catalog. **Computerized Information Services:** Internal databases. **Remarks:** FAX: (613)545-6810. Slides and photographs are owned and administered by the Department of Art. They are inaccessible to the public.

★ 13643 ★
Queen's University at Kingston - Biology Library (Biol Sci)
Earl Hall
Barrie St.   Phone: (613)545-2834
Kingston, ON, Canada K7L 5C4   Linda Allen, Lib.Asst.
Staff: 2. **Subjects:** Biology. **Holdings:** 22,641 volumes. **Subscriptions:** 396 journals and other serials. **Services:** Interlibrary loan; copying; SDI; library open to teachers and technical staff of local institutions. **Computerized Information Services:** CAN/OLE, QL Systems, BRS Information Technologies, DIALOG Information Services, STN International.

★ 13644 ★
Queen's University at Kingston - Bracken Library (Med)
Kingston, ON, Canada K7L 3N6   Phone: (613)545-2510
                                       Mrs. V. Ludwin, Libn.
Staff: Prof 6; Other 10. **Subjects:** Medicine, nursing, rehabilitation, life sciences. **Holdings:** 111,935 volumes. **Subscriptions:** 1411 journals and other serials. **Services:** Interlibrary loan; copying; library open to health sciences personnel. **Automated Operations:** Computerized public access catalog, cataloging, acquisitions, serials, and circulation. **Computerized Information Services:** MEDLINE, BRS Information Technologies, DIALOG Information Services, CAN/OLE; Envoy 100; BITNET (electronic mail services). **Publications:** Bracken Library Newsletter. **Staff:** Monica Webster, Pub.Serv.Libn.; Jane Law, Pub.Serv.Libn.; Janny Eikelboom, Tech.Serv. & Ser.Libn.; Suzanne Maranda, Pub.Serv.Libn.; Nancy Lemon, Pub.Serv.Libn.

★ 13645 ★
Queen's University at Kingston - Chemistry Library (Sci-Engr)
Frost Wing, Gordon Hall   Phone: (613)545-2610
Kingston, ON, Canada K7L 5C4   Ainslie Thomson, Lib.Asst.
Staff: 2. **Subjects:** Chemistry. **Holdings:** 25,078 volumes. **Subscriptions:** 384 journals and other serials. **Services:** Interlibrary loan; copying; SDI; open to teachers and technical staff of local industries. **Computerized Information Services:** CAN/OLE, QL Systems, BRS Information Technologies, STN International.

★ 13646 ★
Queen's University at Kingston - Civil Engineering Library (Sci-Engr)
Ellis Hall   Phone: (613)545-2835
Kingston, ON, Canada K7L 5C4   Jane Walker, Lib.Techn.
Staff: 1. **Subjects:** Civil engineering. **Holdings:** 22,868 volumes. **Subscriptions:** 243 journals and other serials. **Services:** Interlibrary loan; SDI; library open to the public with restrictions. **Automated Operations:** Computerized circulation. **Computerized Information Services:** DIALOG Information Services, CAN/OLE, BRS Information Technologies, QL Systems, STN International. Performs searches on fee basis.

★ 13647 ★
Queen's University at Kingston - Documents Library (Info Sci)
Mackintosh-Corry Hall   Phone: (613)545-6313
Kingston, ON, Canada K7L 3N6   Peter Girard, Hd.Doc.Lib.
Founded: 1960. **Staff:** Prof 4; Other 12. **Subjects:** Economics and business, sociology, political science, urban affairs, planning, history, geography, public administration, ecology. **Special Collections:** Royal Commissions of Canada (federal and provincial); pre-Confederation official publications (1500 volumes); federal and provincial Parliamentary publications for Canada; United Nations, EEC and OECD, and other international organizations; Canadian Personal Census records (to 1891); Statistics Canada publications, including censuses (complete set). **Holdings:** 240,000 volumes; 1 million microfiche; 324,160 microcards; 5567 reels of microfilm. **Services:** Interlibrary loan; copying; library open to the public. **Automated Operations:** Computerized public access catalog and circulation. **Computerized Information Services:** CANSIM, International Financial Statistics (IFS), CITIBASE; Eastern Ontario 1981 and 1986 censuses (internal databases). **Remarks:** Alternate telephone number(s): 545-6312. **Staff:** John Wright, Libn.; Jeffrey Moon, Ref. & Data Libn.; John Offenbeck, Pub.Serv.Libn.

★ 13648 ★
Queen's University at Kingston - Dupuis Hall Library (Sci-Engr)
Division & Clergy Sts.   Phone: (613)545-2833
Kingston, ON, Canada K7L 5C4   Ms. M.L. Ranger, Lib.Asst.
Staff: 2. **Subjects:** Engineering - chemical, mining, metallurgical. **Holdings:** 32,575 volumes. **Subscriptions:** 585 journals and other serials. **Services:** Interlibrary loan; SDI; library open to teachers and technical staff of local industries. **Computerized Information Services:** QL Systems, BRS Information Technologies, CAN/OLE, STN International.

★ 13649 ★
Queen's University at Kingston - Education Library (Educ)
Duncan McArthur Hall   Phone: (613)545-2191
Kingston, ON, Canada K7L 3N6   Sandra Casey, Educ.Libn.
Founded: 1966. **Staff:** Prof 3; Other 8. **Subjects:** Education, psychology. **Holdings:** 105,000 volumes; 700,000 microfiche titles; 9000 AV items. **Subscriptions:** 929 journals and other serials. **Services:** Interlibrary loan; copying; library open to the public. **Computerized Information Services:** CD-ROMs (ERIC, PsychLIT, CD:Education). **Publications:** Periodicals List, annual. **Remarks:** FAX: (613)545-6819. **Staff:** Judith Fraser, Pub.Serv.Libn.; Corinne Laverty, Curric.Serv.Libn.

★ 13650 ★
Queen's University at Kingston - Geological Sciences Library (Sci-Engr)
Miller Hall, Bruce Wing   Phone: (613)545-2840
Kingston, ON, Canada K7L 5C4   Mary Mayson, Sr.Lib.Techn.
Founded: 1932. **Staff:** 2. **Subjects:** Geological sciences. **Holdings:** 52,314 volumes; 52,939 maps; microfiche; microfilm. **Subscriptions:** 600 journals and other serials. **Services:** Interlibrary loan; SDI; library open to the public. **Automated Operations:** Computerized circulation. **Computerized Information Services:** CAN/OLE, BRS Information Technologies, QL Systems. **Special Indexes:** Index to maps.

★13651★
Queen's University at Kingston - John Reid Bain Library (Sci-Engr)
Technology Centre   Phone: (613)545-2836
Kingston, ON, Canada K7L 5C4   Angela Madden, Lib.Techn.
Staff: 1. **Subjects:** Electrical engineering, computing science. **Holdings:** 16,498 volumes; 12,000 technical reports. **Subscriptions:** 328 journals and other serials. **Services:** Interlibrary loan; SDI; library open to technical staff of local industries and institutions. **Computerized Information Services:** CAN/OLE, BRS Information Technologies, QL Systems, STN International.

★13652★
Queen's University at Kingston - Law Library (Law)
Sir John A. Macdonald Hall   Phone: (613)545-2842
Kingston, ON, Canada K7L 3N6   Denis S. Marshall, Prof. & Law Libn.
Founded: 1957. **Staff:** Prof 4; Other 8. **Subjects:** Law. **Special Collections:** Law - international, Quebec, labor, criminal, public, Chinese (in English translation). **Holdings:** 150,000 volumes. **Subscriptions:** 3140 journals and other serials. **Services:** Interlibrary loan; copying; library open to the public. **Computerized Information Services:** QL Systems, CAN/LAW, Info Globe, WESTLAW, DIALOG Information Services, LEXIS, VU/TEXT Information Services; NETNORTH, QUICKMAIL (electronic mail services). **Remarks:** FAX: (613)545-6611. **Staff:** Mai Chen, Coll.Dev./Coord., Tech.Serv.; Elizabeth Fox, Pub.Serv./Ref.Libn., Robert Thomson, Cat./Ref.Libn.

★13653★
Queen's University at Kingston - Map and Air Photo Library (Geog-Map)
Mackintosh-Corry Hall   Phone: (613)545-6314
Kingston, ON, Canada K7L 5C4   Shirley Harmer, Map Cur.
Staff: 1.5. **Subjects:** Cartography, aerial photography, photogrammetry, remote sensing, GIS. **Special Collections:** Historical cartography collection. **Holdings:** 2950 books; 1100 atlases; 74,000 maps; 30,500 aerial photographs; theses; soil surveys; microforms; slides. **Subscriptions:** 50 journals and other serials. **Services:** Interlibrary loan; library open to the public with restrictions. **Remarks:** FAX: (613)545-6819.

★13654★
Queen's University at Kingston - Mathematics and Statistics Library (Sci-Engr)
Jeffery Hall   Phone: (613)545-2838
Kingston, ON, Canada K7L 5C4   Janet Burgess, Lib.Asst.
Staff: 2. **Subjects:** Mathematics, statistics. **Holdings:** 33,916 volumes. **Subscriptions:** 391 journals and other serials. **Services:** Library open to the public. **Computerized Information Services:** QL Systems, DIALOG Information Services, CAN/OLE, BRS Information Technologies, STN International.

★13655★
Queen's University at Kingston - May Ball Library - Industrial Relations Collection (Bus-Fin)
Kingston, ON, Canada K7L 3N6   Phone: (613)545-6623
                   Carol Williams, Lib.Coord.
Founded: 1937. **Staff:** Prof 2; Other 2. **Subjects:** Industrial relations, labor economics, personnel administration. **Special Collections:** Canadian Government documents (20,000); United States Government documents (5000); International Labor Organization documents (5000); Canadian labor documents. **Holdings:** 5000 books; 2000 bound periodical volumes; 200 VF drawers of pamphlets, reports, dissertations; 616 reels of microfilm. **Subscriptions:** 500 journals and other serials. **Services:** Library open to the public for reference use only, by request. **Computerized Information Services:** LIBNET (electronic mail service). **Publications:** Bibliographies. **Remarks:** Electronic mail address(es): QUCDN (LIBNET). **Staff:** Wendy Gower, Libn.

★13656★
Queen's University at Kingston - Mechanical Engineering Library (Sci-Engr)
McLaughlin Hall
Stuart St.   Phone: (613)545-2584
Kingston, ON, Canada K7L 3N6   Hilary Richardson, Lib.Asst.
Staff: 1. **Subjects:** Mechanical engineering. **Holdings:** 8999 volumes. **Subscriptions:** 180 journals and other serials. **Services:** Interlibrary loan; copying; SDI; library open to technical staff of local firms. **Computerized Information Services:** CAN/OLE, QL Systems, BRS Information Technologies, DIALOG Information Services, STN International.

★13657★
Queen's University at Kingston - Music Library (Mus)
Harrison-LeCaine Hall   Phone: (613)545-2839
Kingston, ON, Canada K7L 3N6   P.A. Allen, Mus.Libn.
Staff: Prof 1; Other 2. **Subjects:** Musicology, music education, ethnomusicology. **Holdings:** 12,164 volumes; 13,322 scores; 472 cassettes; 250 open reel tapes; 100 videotapes; 340 reels of microfilm; 10,246 phonograph records and compact discs. **Subscriptions:** 120 journals and other serials. **Services:** Interlibrary loan; library open to the public with restrictions. **Remarks:** Maintains a Performance Library of choral, band, orchestral, and chamber music.

★13658★
Queen's University at Kingston - Occupational Health and Safety Resource Centre - Library (Med)
Abramsky Hall, 2nd Fl.   Phone: (613)545-2909
Kingston, ON, Canada K7L 3N6   Gloria Hetherington
Founded: 1978. **Staff:** Prof 4; Other 2. **Subjects:** Occupational health, environmental health, occupational medicine, occupational safety, epidemiology, indoor air quality, ventilation. **Holdings:** 833 books; 39 reports. **Subscriptions:** 12 journals and other serials. **Services:** Copying; library open to the public for reference use only. **Computerized Information Services:** CCINFOline, CHEMINFO/INFOCHIM, Chemical Information Systems, Inc. (CIS), CIS Abstracts, IRPTC, U.S. National Institute for Occupational Safety and Health Technical Information Center Database (NIOSHTIC), Registry of Toxic Effects of Chemical Substances (RTECS). **Remarks:** FAX: (613) 545-6686.

★13659★
Queen's University at Kingston - Physics Library (Sci-Engr)
Stirling Hall
Queen's Crescent   Phone: (613)545-2722
Kingston, ON, Canada K7L 5C4   Diane Nuttall, Lib.Asst.
Staff: 2. **Subjects:** Physics, astronomy. **Holdings:** 18,194 volumes. **Subscriptions:** 245 journals and other serials. **Services:** Interlibrary loan; SDI; library open to teachers and technical staff of local industries. **Automated Operations:** Computerized circulation. **Computerized Information Services:** CAN/OLE, BRS Information Technologies, QL Systems, STN International.

★13660★
Queen's University at Kingston - Psychology Library (Soc Sci)
Humphrey Hall   Phone: (613)545-2837
Kingston, ON, Canada K7L 5C4   Wanda Parkes, Lib.Techn.
Staff: 2. **Subjects:** Psychology. **Holdings:** 17,088 volumes. **Subscriptions:** 221 journals and other serials. **Services:** Interlibrary loan. **Computerized Information Services:** CAN/OLE, QL Systems, BRS Information Technologies.

★13661★
Queen's University at Kingston - Special Collections (Hum)
Douglas Library   Phone: (613)545-2528
Kingston, ON, Canada K7L 5C4   Pamela Thayer, Hd., Spec.Coll.
Founded: 1965. **Staff:** Prof 1; Other 4. **Subjects:** Canadiana, British history, Anglo-Irish literature. **Special Collections:** Edith and Lorne Pierce Collection of Canadiana (47,250 items); John Buchan Collection (Scotland; 4800 volumes); 18th century British pamphlets (2160); McNicol Collection on Telegraphy, Telephony, and Radio (1750 volumes); Riche-Covington Collection (astrophysics and radio astronomy; 1180 volumes); Victor Hugo (150 volumes); dated, rare books, published prior to 1700 (900 volumes); Bible collection (1450 volumes); Non-Canadian Children's Book Collection (2560 volumes); F.R. Scott Collection (little magazines; 900); Dickens British and American first and early editions (1070 volumes); Galsworthy (230 volumes); Masefield (240 volumes); sample Canadian journals (27 boxes). **Holdings:** 120,160 volumes; 14,500 Canadian pamphlets; 2100 non-Canadian pamphlets; 600 volumes in Canadian School Text collection; 95 atlases; 179,000 microforms; 440 files of information materials; 7000 Canadian programmes; 1100 pieces of Canadian sheet music; 2200 maps and plans; 5500 broadsides and posters; 2450 postcards; 8 boxes of greeting cards; 690 ephemera files; 13,000 items in papers collections. **Services:** Interlibrary loan; copying; collections open to the public. **Automated Operations:** Computerized cataloging. **Publications:** Douglas Library Occasional Papers, irregular - to Canadian libraries and others on request. **Special Indexes:** Card indexes - publisher, printer, date, provenance, Canadian imprints in English and French, 18th century British political pamphlets, maps, private presses, broadsides, sheet music, sample journals. Book indexes - Galsworthy, Masefield, sheet music, F.R. Scott, McNicol, Bible, Dickens, Riche-Covington, Victor Hugo, Canadian School Text, 18th Century British Pamphlets, Bishop Macdonell, Cartwright Kingston, and Children's Collections. **Remarks:** FAX: (613)545-6819.

Queensbury Historical Association, Inc.
See: Chapman Historical Museum (3433)

★ 13662 ★
Queensland Art Gallery - Library (Art)
Queensland Cultural Centre
P.O. Box 3686   Phone: 7 8407281
South Brisbane, QLD 4101, Australia   Judy Gunning, Libn.-In-Charge
Founded: 1975. Staff: 3. Subjects: Visual arts, museum science, arts administration. Special Collections: Ephemera collection (press-cuttings relating to artists and organizations; 37 filing cabinets); photographic archives (15,000 items); Asian and Pacific contemporary art. Holdings: 12,595 volumes; 300 serial titles; 250 videotapes; 16,000 slides. Services: Interlibrary loan; copying; library open to the public by appointment. Computerized Information Services: DIALOG Information Services, BRS Information Technologies, Conservation Information Network. Performs searches. Remarks: Library located at Queensland Cultural Center. FAX: 7 8448865. Staff: Matthew Kassay, Doc.Libn.; Catherine Pemble-Smith, Lib.Techn.

(Queensland) State Library of Queensland
See: State Library of Queensland (15692)

★ 13663 ★
Queenswood House - Library (Rel-Phil)
2494 Arbutus Rd.   Phone: (604)477-3822
Victoria, BC, Canada V8N 1V8   Patricia Dickinson, SSA, Libn.
Founded: 1963. Staff: 2. Subjects: Spirituality, dogma, theology, liturgy, church history, English literature, history, geography, psychology, art, music. Holdings: 7000 books; 2000 audiotapes. Subscriptions: 10 journals and other serials. Services: Library open to the public on fee basis. Remarks: Maintained by The Sisters of Saint Ann. Staff: Patricia Dickinson; Monica Greenall.

★ 13664 ★
Questar Service Corporation - Corporate Library (Energy)
180 E. 100 S.
P.O. Box 11150   Phone: (801)534-5705
Salt Lake City, UT 84147   Marty Weed, Corp.Lib.
Founded: 1980. Staff: Prof 1; Other 1. Subjects: Energy, oil and gas, business and industry, utilities, telecommunications, data processing. Holdings: 500 books; 2500 other cataloged items. Subscriptions: 250 journals and other serials; 5 newspapers. Services: Library not open to the public. Automated Operations: Computerized cataloging, acquisitions, serials, and circulation. Computerized Information Services: DIALOG Information Services, Dow Jones News/Retrieval, Dun & Bradstreet Business Credit Services, A.G.A. GasNet; internal database; DIALMAIL, A.G.A. GasNet (electronic mail services). Networks/Consortia: Member of American Gas Association - Library Services (AGA-LSC). Remarks: FAX: (801)534-5166.

★ 13665 ★
QuesTech - Technical Library (Sci-Engr)
7600-A Leesburg Pike
Falls Church, VA 22043   Phone: (703)760-1024
Founded: 1968. Staff: Prof 1. Subjects: Electrical engineering, electronics, radar, optics, microwave technology, military-related subjects. Holdings: 3000 books; bound periodical volumes; NTIS/DDC documents; documents on microfiche; volumes of data descriptions; volumes of military regulations, standards, specifications. Subscriptions: 50 journals and other serials. Services: Interlibrary loan; library not open to the public. Computerized Information Services: DIALOG Information Services. Remarks: FAX: (703)760-1062.

★ 13666 ★
Quidlibet Research, Inc. - Library (Law)
3 First National Plaza, Suite 1400   Phone: (312)781-9635
Chicago, IL 60690   Nina Cunningham, Pres.
Founded: 1983. Staff: Prof 1. Subjects: Law, business. Holdings: 1500 volumes; conference proceedings. Subscriptions: 12 journals and other serials. Services: Library not open to the public. Computerized Information Services: CLEER Reports (internal database). Remarks: FAX: (312)435-7578. Formerly: Located in Oak Park, IL.

May G. Quigley Collection
See: Grand Rapids Public Library (6639)

Quigley Photographic Archive
See: Georgetown University - Special Collections Division - Lauinger Memorial Library (6379)

James H. Quillen College of Medicine - Holston Valley Hospital and Medical Center
See: Holston Valley Hospital and Medical Center - The Robert D. Doty Health Sciences Library (7341)

Ellen Schulz Quillin Memorial Library
See: San Antonio Museum Association (14669)

★ 13667 ★
Quincy College - Brenner Library - Special Collections (Hist, Rare Book)
18th & College   Phone: (217)228-5345
Quincy, IL 62301   Victor Kingery, O.F.M.
Founded: 1860. Staff: Prof 4; Other 4. Special Collections: Rare Books Collection (4000 items); Patristic and Middle Ages Collection in Bonaventure Library (3000 items); Local History Collection in Fraborese Library (4000 items); Spanish American History Collection in Fraborese Library (5000 items); 19th Century English Literature Collection (2000 items); Far East Collection (3000 items); Early Americana Collection (12,000 volumes on microfiche and microcard); Vietnamese Conflict Collection (1961-1973; on microfiche). Holdings: 19,000 books; 2000 bound periodical volumes. Subscriptions: 800 journals and other serials; 12 newspapers. Services: Interlibrary loan (limited); copying; library open to the public. Computerized Information Services: OCLC, UTLAS. Contact Person: Lily Wee, Asst.Libn. Networks/Consortia: Member of Resource Sharing Alliance of West Central Illinois, Inc. Publications: Quincy College Rare Book Collection; Incunabula in Quincy College Library; Fraborese Collection. Remarks: FAX: (217)228-5354. Staff: Lily Wee, Hd., Tech.Serv.; Patricia Tomczak, Hd., Pub.Serv. & Acq.; Jeffrey Ellair.

★ 13668 ★
Quincy Historical Society - Wirtanen Library (Hist)
Adams Academy Bldg.
8 Adams St.   Phone: (617)773-1144
Quincy, MA 02169   Dr. Elliott W. Hoffman, Dir.
Founded: 1893. Staff: 10. Subjects: Quincy area history and genealogy. Holdings: 4000 books; 5000 pamphlets; 4000 photographs; 100 cubic feet of manuscripts. Services: Copying; library open to the public with restrictions.

★ 13669 ★
Quincy Museum of Natural History and Art - Research Library (Biol Sci)
1601 Maine St.   Phone: (217)224-7669
Quincy, IL 62301   Ray Shubinski, Exec.Dir.
Staff: 1. Subjects: Anthropology, ornithology, paleobotany, paleozoology, American Indian, fossils, mollusks, shells, minerals. Holdings: 350 books; 600 bound periodical volumes. Services: Library not open to the public.

Quincy Research Center - Information Services
See: Clinical Research Foundation (3835)

(Quito) USIS Library
See: Lincoln Library (9181)

★ 13670 ★
Quoddy Tides Foundation - Marine Library (Biol Sci)
123 Water St.   Phone: (207)853-4806
Eastport, ME 04631   Serena A. Wilson, Libn.
Founded: 1974. Staff: 2. Subjects: Marine sciences, local literature. Special Collections: Tidal power studies of Cobscook and Passamaquoddy Bays; environmental impact studies of proposed Pittston Company Project; government reports on commercial fishing in U.S. and Canadian waters. Holdings: 784 books; 650 bound periodical volumes; reports; manuscripts. Subscriptions: 10 journals and other serials; 14 newspapers. Services: Copying; library open to the public with restrictions. Remarks: FAX: (207)853-4095. Staff: John Pike, Cons.

★13671★
Quorum Health Resources - Corporate Information Center
1 Park Plaza
Box 24347
Nashville, TN 37203
Defunct.

R

R & D Associates
See: **Logicon R & D Associates - Information Services (9253)**

★ **13672** ★
Racal Datacom, Inc . - Information Resources (Info Sci)
Box 407044   Phone: (305)846-6100
Fort Lauderdale, FL 33340   Jan Stern, Mgr.
Founded: 1963. **Staff:** Prof 1; Other 2. **Subjects:** Telecommunications, computer science, electronics, business. **Holdings:** Figures not available. **Services:** Interlibrary loan; resources open to the public by appointment. **Computerized Information Services:** Online systems; CD-ROMs; internal database. **Remarks:** FAX: (305)846-4942. **Formerly:** Racal-Milgo, Inc.

Racal-Milgo, Inc.
See: **Racal Datacom, Inc (13672)**

★ **13673** ★
Racine County Historical Society and Museum, Inc. - Local History and Genealogical Reference Archives (Hist)
S. 701 Main St.   Phone: (414)636-3926
Racine, WI 53403   Dr. Mary Ellen Conaway, Dir.
Founded: 1969. **Staff:** 2. **Subjects:** Local history, Racine County, military history, genealogy. **Special Collections:** Pictorial Collection of Prints, portraits, Billings' Glass Plates; Century Family files; surname card index to early County residents; DAR lineage books (166); New England Register (first 50 volumes; 84 items). **Holdings:** 1500 books; 12 four-drawer vertical files of clippings and pamphlets. **Services:** Copying; library open to the public on a limited schedule. **Special Indexes:** Surname indexes for early marriages, histories, cemetery inscriptions, veterans, 1858 landowners, Declaration of Intent or Naturalization, and censuses for Racine County for years 1840, 1850, 1860, 1870, and 1880.

★ **13674** ★
Racine County Law Library (Law)
730 Wisconsin Ave.   Phone: (414)636-3773
Racine, WI 53403   Lawrence E. Flynn, Ck. of Courts
Founded: 1850. **Subjects:** Law. **Holdings:** 10,500 books; Wisconsin Briefs on microfiche. **Services:** Copying; library open to the public.

★ **13675** ★
Racine Journal Times - Library (Publ)
212 4th St.   Phone: (414)634-3322
Racine, WI 53403   Steve Lovejoy, News Ed.
Founded: 1958. **Staff:** 1. **Subjects:** Newspaper reference topics. **Holdings:** 300 books; 940 reels of microfilm of the Journal Times, through 1888; miscellaneous pamphlets; 10,900 obituaries; 10,000 biographical files. **Subscriptions:** 18 journals and other serials. **Services:** Library not open to the public. **Special Indexes:** Clippings, mostly of local stories; biographical files, editorials; business and industry activities (card). **Remarks:** FAX: (414)631-1702. **Staff:** Peggy Anderson.

★ **13676** ★
Racquet and Tennis Club - Library (Rec)
370 Park Ave.   Phone: (212)753-9700
New York, NY 10022   Gerard J. Belliveau, Jr., Libn.
Founded: 1916. **Staff:** Prof 2. **Subjects:** Sports, court and lawn tennis, early American sport. **Holdings:** 18,500 books. **Subscriptions:** 45 journals and other serials. **Services:** Mail queries answered; copying; library open to researchers by appointment. **Publications:** Annual Report - to members. **Special Catalogs:** A Dictionary Catalog of the Library of Sports in the Racquet and Tennis Club (1970). **Staff:** Todd M. Thompson, Asst.Libn.

Pal Racz Memorial Library
See: **Institute for East-West Security Studies (7931)**

★ **13677** ★
Radcliffe College - Arthur and Elizabeth Schlesinger Library on the History of Women in America (Soc Sci, Hist)
10 Garden St.   Phone: (617)495-8647
Cambridge, MA 02138   Dr. Patricia M. King, Dir.
Founded: 1943. **Staff:** Prof 10; Other 6. **Subjects:** Women - suffrage, medicine, education, law, social service, labor, family, organizations; history of American women in all phases of public and private life. **Special Collections:** Beecher-Stowe; Woman's Rights; Blackwell Family; Charlotte Perkins Gilman; Emma Goldman; Somerville-Howorth; Dr. Martha May Eliot; Jeannette Rankin; National Organization for Women; National Women's Political Caucus; Black Women Oral History Project; Culinary Collection (9000 volumes); etiquette books; picture collection (50,000). **Holdings:** 35,000 volumes; 3000 bound periodical volumes; 850 major collections of papers on individual American women, families, women's organizations; 9500 reels of microfilm; 2250 magnetic tapes; 70 VF drawers; 2500 reels of audio- and videotapes; 6500 linear feet of manuscripts; 50,000 photographs. **Subscriptions:** 495 journals and other serials. **Services:** Interlibrary loan; copying; library open to the public. **Automated Operations:** Computerized public access catalog, cataloging and serials. **Publications:** Occasional Reports, sent on request. **Special Catalogs:** Manuscript Inventories; Catalogs of the Manuscripts, Books and Periodicals, 1984 (10 volumes); Women of Courage exhibition catalog, 1984. **Remarks:** Library located at 3 James St., Cambridge, MA, 02138. **Staff:** Eva Moseley, Cur., Mss.; Barbara Haber, Cur., Printed Bks.; Ruth E. Hill, AV Coord.; Jane S. Knowles, Archv.

★ **13678** ★
Radcliffe College - Henry A. Murray Research Center (Soc Sci)
10 Garden St.   Phone: (617)495-8140
Cambridge, MA 02138   Anne Colby, Dir.
Founded: 1976. **Staff:** Prof 5; Other 12. **Subjects:** Human development and social change; women - work, careers, education, mental health, political participation, family life, widowhood, aging. **Special Collections:** Archival materials dealing with data sets of raw and computer-accessible social science research studies. **Holdings:** 190 data sets; 150 books; 500 boxes of raw data; 50 dissertations; 300 unpublished reports; 150 computer magnetic tapes. **Services:** Center open to the public. **Automated Operations:** Computerized acquisitions. **Publications:** Murray Center News, semiannual - free upon request. **Special Indexes:** Guide to the Data Resources of the Henry A. Murray Research Center. **Remarks:** FAX: (617)495-8422. **Staff:** Jacquelyn James, Res.Assoc.; Erin Phelps, Sr., Res.Assoc.; Beth Paul, Res.Assoc.

Radcliffe College - Morse Music Library
See: **Harvard University - Radcliffe College - Morse Music Library (6988)**

★ **13679** ★
Radford University - Department of Geography - Map Collection (Geog-Map)
Box 5811   Phone: (703)831-5558
Radford, VA 24142   Dr. Bernd H. Kuennecke, Cur.
Founded: 1977. **Staff:** 2. **Subjects:** Maps - Virginia, topographic, land use. **Holdings:** 20,000 maps. **Services:** Copying; collection open to the public with restrictions.

★ **13680** ★
Radford University - McConnell Library - Special Collections (Hist)
Radford, VA 24142   Phone: (703)831-5471
Subjects: Southwestern Virginia - institutions, people, culture; Civil War; folklore. **Holdings:** Manuscripts; photographs; tapes. **Services:** Copying; collection open to the public. **Automated Operations:** Computerized public access catalog, cataloging, and circulation. **Staff:** Robert L. Turner, Jr.

★ **13681** ★
Radian Corporation - Library (Env-Cons)
10395 Old Placerville Rd.   Phone: (916)362-5332
Sacramento, CA 95824   Jerry McGovern, Libn.
Founded: 1986. **Staff:** Prof 1; Other 1. **Subjects:** Environment, air quality, hazardous waste. **Holdings:** 5000 books; technical and government reports; government agency rules and regulations. **Subscriptions:** 75 journals and other serials. **Services:** Interlibrary loan; library not open to the public. **Computerized Information Services:** DIALOG Information Services, NLM, National Ground Water Information Center Data Base, Legi-Tech, ORBIT Search Service; U.S. Environmental Protection Agency. **Remarks:** FAX: (916)362-2318.

★ 13682 ★
Radian Corporation - Library (Energy)
8501 MoPac Blvd.
Box 201088   Phone: (512)454-4797
Austin, TX 78720   Barbara J. Maxey, Mgr., Lib.Serv.
Staff: Prof 3; Other 4.5. **Subjects:** Coal conversion processes, air and water pollution control, petroleum refining emissions, ambient air monitoring, artificial intelligence. **Special Collections:** Gasification and liquefaction (20,000 items); sulphur dioxide control (3250 items). **Holdings:** 1950 volumes; 2500 microforms; 21,000 articles, patents, maps; 21,000 technical reports. **Subscriptions:** 380 journals and other serials. **Services:** Interlibrary loan; copying; library open to the public by appointment. **Automated Operations:** Computerized cataloging and circulation. **Computerized Information Services:** Online systems. **Publications:** Library Briefs, irregular; Biweekly List of Books and Reports - both for internal distribution only. **Remarks:** FAX: (512)345-9684.

★ 13683 ★
Radiation Effects Research Foundation - Library (Med)
5-2, Hijiyama Park
Minami-ku
Hiroshima 732, Japan   Phone: 82 2613131
Subjects: Health effects of radiation exposure, atomic bomb radiation, Hiroshima and Nagasaki. **Holdings:** 26,000 volumes; 260 journals and other serials. **Remarks:** FAX: 82 2637279.

Radiation Research Archives
See: **University of Tennessee at Knoxville - Special Collections (19370)**

★ 13684 ★
Radio Advertising Bureau - Marketing Information Center (Bus-Fin)
304 Park Ave., S., 7th Fl.   Phone: (212)254-4800
New York, NY 10010-4302   Kenneth J. Costa, V.P., Mktng.Info.
Founded: 1951. **Staff:** Prof 1; Other 1. **Subjects:** Radio, advertising and marketing, consumer markets, demographics, competitive media, leading advertisers, retailing. **Special Collections:** Tape Library (30,000 commercials; separate department); company and radio industry archives; Broadcasting Yearbook, 1935 to present. **Holdings:** 600 volumes; 70 VF drawers of clippings. **Subscriptions:** 152 journals and other serials. **Services:** Interlibrary loan (limited); copying; center open to the public by special permission. **Computerized Information Services:** Internal database. **Remarks:** FAX: (212)254-8713. **Staff:** Steven O'Rourke, Asst.

★ 13685 ★
Radio Free Europe/Radio Liberty - Research Institute - Information Resources Department (Info Sci, Soc Sci)
W-8000 Munich 22, Germany   Phone: 89 21022538
                                  Jeffrey Gardner, Dir.
Staff: 80. **Subjects:** East European, Soviet, and world affairs. **Special Collections:** Radio Liberty Samizdat Archive ("self-published writing" from the USSR); East European Archives; Soviet Archives (4000 items). **Holdings:** 102,000 volumes - 35,000 in 6 East European languages, 29,000 in Russian and Soviet languages, 38,000 in western languages. **Subscriptions:** 600 Soviet, Western, and emigre newspapers and periodicals. **Services:** Interlibrary loan; library open to the public by appointment to scholars. **Computerized Information Services:** Internal database. **Remarks:** FAX: 89 21022539. Telex: 523228. **Formerly:** Its Radio Liberty Research - REE/RL Library. **Staff:** Mario Corti, Dp.; Iwanka Rebet, Chf.Libn.; Dawn Mann, Hd., Soviet Archv.; Anna Pomian, Hd., E. European Archv.; Jan Trapans, Chf., Ext. Affairs.

★ 13686 ★
Radio Free Europe/Radio Liberty Inc. - Reference Library (Area-Ethnic)
1775 Broadway   Phone: (212)397-5343
New York, NY 10019   Irene V. Dutikow, Chf.Libn.
Founded: 1958. **Staff:** Prof 1; Other 3. **Subjects:** Soviet Union and Eastern European cultural, economic, and political life. **Special Collections:** Soviet magazines and newspapers (184); biographical file on Soviet personalities; Samizdat materials depository (underground documents; 12 drawers and bound volumes); RFE research papers, 1973 to present; RL Research Bulletin, 1964 to present. **Holdings:** 20,000 books; 150 VF drawers; 3500 reels of microfilm and microfiche. **Subscriptions:** 260 journals and other serials; 70 newspapers. **Services:** Interlibrary loan; copying; library open to the public by appointment. **Automated Operations:** Computerized public access catalog, cataloging, acquisitions, serials, and circulation. **Computerized Information Services:** Internal database. **Remarks:** FAX: (212)397-5374.

★ 13687 ★
Radio New Zealand - Reference Library (Info Sci)
Bowen State Bldg., 2nd Fl.
P.O. Box 1770   Phone: 4 4741408
Wellington, New Zealand   Ms. E.M. Herring
Staff: Prof 2.5; Other 3. **Subjects:** News and current affairs, biography, broadcasting, music, film, entertainment, sports. **Special Collections:** Newspaper clipping files (approximately 25,000 items). **Holdings:** 20,000 books; 100 reports. **Subscriptions:** 100 journals and other serials; 16 newspapers. **Services:** Interlibrary loan; copying; SDI; library open to the public for a fee. **Computerized Information Services:** Kiwinet; NewsSource (internal database). Contact Person: Marketing Manager, RNZ News. **Publications:** Subject headings list for clipping files. **Remarks:** FAX: 4 4741406. **Staff:** Donna Beattie, Act.Hd.Libn.

★ 13688 ★
Radio Quebec - Centre des Ressources Documentaires (Info Sci)
800, rue Fullum   Phone: (514)521-2424
Montreal, PQ, Canada H2K 3L7   Nicole Charest, Dir.
Founded: 1969. **Staff:** Prof 4; Other 9. **Subjects:** Canadian and Quebec history, communications, television, graphic arts. **Holdings:** 18,000 books; 20,000 phonograph records; 2200 clipping files; 1800 biographical files. **Subscriptions:** 220 journals and other serials. **Services:** Interlibrary loan; center not open to the public. **Automated Operations:** Computerized cataloging. **Computerized Information Services:** DOBIS Canadian Online Library System, Infomart Online, SDM; Edibase (internal database). **Publications:** List of serials, annual. **Remarks:** Maintained by (Quebec Province) Societe de Radio-Television du Quebec. FAX: (514)525-5511. Telex: 05-25808.

★ 13689 ★
Radio-Television Belge de la Communaute Francaise - Bibliotheque Generale (Info Sci)
Boulevard A
Reyers 52 local 1 M 57   Phone: 2 7374013
B-1044 Brussels, Belgium   Dominique Dewelssemaker
Founded: 1945. **Staff:** Prof 1; Other 2. **Subjects:** Broadcasting and allied subjects. **Holdings:** 30,000 books. **Subscriptions:** 7 journals and other serials. **Services:** Interlibrary loan; copying; library open to the public by appointment.

Radio Writers Guild Archives
See: **New York Public Library for the Performing Arts (11634)**

★ 13690 ★
Radiological Society of North America, Inc. - Library (Med)
2021 Spring Rd., Suite 600
Oak Brook, IL 60521   Phone: (708)571-2670
Subjects: Clinical radiology, allied health sciences. **Holdings:** 800 volumes; records of manuscripts received annually. **Subscriptions:** 120 journals and other serials. **Services:** Library not open to the public. **Publications:** RSNA Today; Video Journal, bimonthly; Radiology, monthly; Radio Graphics, bimonthly. **Special Indexes:** Indexes of selected radiological journals. **Remarks:** FAX: (708)571-7837. Telex: 333956.

Radiopharmaceutical Internal Dose Information Center
See: **Oak Ridge Associated Universities (12183)**

★ 13691 ★
Radnor Historical Society - Research Library and Museum (Hist)
Finley House
113 W. Beech Tree Lane   Phone: (215)688-2668
Wayne, PA 19087   George W. Smith, Pres.
Founded: 1948. **Subjects:** Local and Pennsylvania history. **Holdings:** 300 volumes; 4 boxes of genealogical papers; 4 drawers of maps; 4 boxes of photographs, 1880 to present. **Services:** Library open to the public. **Publications:** Bulletin of the Radnor Historical Society, annual - to members and for sale. **Special Indexes:** Index to articles on local history (card).

Morris P. Radov Library
See: Congregation Brith Shalom - Jewish Center (4156)

RAE Collection on Architecture
See: Monterey Public Library (10673)

Bernard B. Raginsky Research Library
See: Institute for Research in Hypnosis (7972)

★ 13692 ★
Rahr-West Art Museum - Library
Park St. at N. 8th
Manitowoc, WI 54220
Subjects: Art, county and state history. **Holdings:** 1000 volumes. **Remarks:** Currently inactive.

Railroad Commission of Texas
See: (Texas State) Railroad Commission of Texas (16266)

★ 13693 ★
Railroad and Pioneer Museum - Library (Hist)
710 Jack Baskin St.
Box 5126   Phone: (817)778-6873
Temple, TX 76505   Mary L. Irving, Libn. & Dir.
Founded: 1977. **Staff:** Prof 1. **Subjects:** Railroads, local and pioneer history. **Special Collections:** Original manuscripts. **Holdings:** 400 books. **Subscriptions:** 19 journals and other serials. **Services:** Copying; library open to the public for reference use only. **Remarks:** Maintained by the City of Temple, Texas.

Railroad Retirement Board
See: U.S. Railroad Retirement Board (17935)

★ 13694 ★
Railway Mail Service Library (Hist)
12 E. Rosemont Ave.   Phone: (703)549-4095
Alexandria, VA 22301-2325   Dr. Frank R. Scheer, Cur.
Founded: 1950. **Staff:** Prof 1. **Subjects:** Post office mail transportation, postal markings, postal labor unions and fraternal organizations. **Special Collections:** E.B. Bergman Schedule of Mail Routes Collection (2100 postal schedules); H.E. Rankin General Scheme Collection (1500 post office distribution schemes). **Holdings:** 986 books; 77 bound periodical volumes; 380,000 documents; 662 copies of rare publications; 2170 unbound periodicals; 85 oral history audiocassettes; 13 videocassettes; 5 16mm films. **Subscriptions:** 18 journals and other serials. **Services:** Interlibrary loan; copying; library open to the public by appointment.

★ 13695 ★
Railways Library (Trans, Sci-Engr)
Daliushu North Stop
Xizhimenwai
Beijing, People's Republic of China   Gao Wen, Dp.Libn.
Founded: 1950. **Staff:** 25. **Subjects:** Railroads, electric engineering, electronics, machinery, metallurgy, construction, chemical engineering. **Holdings:** 168,223 volumes; 116,594 other cataloged items. **Subscriptions:** 2200 journals and other serials. **Services:** Interlibrary loan; copying. **Special Catalogs:** Catalog of Foreign Periodicals for Subscription; Catalog of Foreign Books.

★ 13696 ★
Railways to Yesterday, Inc. - Lehigh Valley Transportation Research Center (Trans)
12th and Cumberland Sts.
General Office, 2nd Fl.   Phone: (215)797-3242
Allentown, PA 18103   Douglas E. Peters, Hist./Libn.
Founded: 1965. **Staff:** 1. **Subjects:** Electric and steam railways. **Special Collections:** Company records of the Lehigh Valley Transit Company; Howard Sell Collection (photographs and negatives of Lehigh Valley area railways and trolley lines); trolley artifacts; James MacDonald Collection (railway photographs and negatives); Tom Ruddell Collection (railway negatives). **Holdings:** 150 volumes; 10 VF cabinets and 15 boxes of railway material, including railway maps and timetables; newspaper clippings. **Subscriptions:** 10 journals and other serials. **Services:** Center open to the public by appointment. **Publications:** Trolley Museum Reporter, 6/year.

★ 13697 ★
Rainbow Fleet, Inc. - Library (Educ)
3016 Paseo   Phone: (405)521-1426
Oklahoma City, OK 73103   Marti Nicholson, Exec.Dir.
Founded: 1972. **Staff:** Prof 5. **Subjects:** Child development; infant stimulation; preschool enhancement, including language and sensorial development, pre-math skills, and practical life skills. **Special Collections:** Toys and learning materials for pre-school children. **Holdings:** 2500 books; 3000 toys and games. **Services:** Library open to licensed daycare centers and homes, preschools, other programs providing group care for children, and parents.

★ 13698 ★
Rainforest Action Network - Library (Env-Cons)
450 Sansome St., Suite 700   Phone: (415)398-4404
San Francisco, CA 94111   Victor A. Menotti, Info.Off.
Subjects: Tropical rain forests, indigenous people, biodiversity, banking. **Holdings:** VF drawers. **Subscriptions:** 51 journals and other serials. **Services:** Copying; library open to the public at librarian's discretion. **Computerized Information Services:** EcoNet (electronic mail service). **Publications:** Action alert, monthly; World Rainforest Report, quarterly. **Remarks:** Telex: 15127-6475. FAX: (415)398-2732. Electronic mail address(es): RAINFOREST (EcoNet).

Rainier School Branch Library
See: Washington State Library (20038)

William M. Rains Library
See: Loyola Marymount University - School of Law (9419)

The Leonard S. and Juliette K. Rakow Library
See: Corning Museum of Glass (4336)

★ 13699 ★
Ralston Purina Company - Information Center (Food-Bev, Med)
Checkerboard Square   Phone: (314)982-2150
St. Louis, MO 63164-0001   Linda S. Lincks, Mgr.
Founded: 1929. **Staff:** Prof 3; Other 2. **Subjects:** Animal and human nutrition, veterinary medicine, food processing, food science, business. **Special Collections:** Food and Agricultural Organization of the United Nations (FAO) Publications (20 VF drawers). **Holdings:** 13,000 volumes; 20 VF drawers of proceedings; 69 VF drawers of government reports. **Subscriptions:** 500 journals and other serials. **Services:** Interlibrary loan; copying; SDI; center open to the public by appointment. **Automated Operations:** Computerized cataloging, acquisitions, and ILL. **Computerized Information Services:** DIALOG Information Services, NLM, Dow Jones News/Retrieval, Mead Data Central, OCLC, Reuters Information Services (Canada) Limited, Chemical Abstracts Service (CAS). **Networks/Consortia:** Member of St. Louis Regional Library Network. **Remarks:** FAX: (314)982-1078. **Staff:** Sharon Rhodes, Libn.; Ann Young, Coord., Search Serv.

Willo Ralston Memorial Library for Historical Research
See: Mondak Heritage Center (10606)

Ramsayer Research Library
See: McKinley Museum of History, Science, and Industry (9930)

★ 13700 ★
Ramsey County Historical Society - Research Center - Library (Hist)
75 W. 5th St., Rm. 323   Phone: (612)222-0701
St. Paul, MN 55102   Daniel J. Hoisington, Exec.Dir.
Staff: Prof 5. **Subjects:** Local history. **Special Collections:** Heman Gibbs papers. **Holdings:** 300 books; maps; pamphlets; documents; pictures. **Services:** Library open to the public for reference use only. **Formerly:** Its Joseph E. Karth Research Center.

★ 13701 ★
Ramsey County Law Library (Law)
1815 Court House
St. Paul, MN 55102
Phone: (612)298-5208
Carol C. Florin, Lib.Dir.
Founded: 1935. **Staff:** Prof 1; Other 1. **Subjects:** Law - Minnesota, tax, real property, criminal, corporate; practice. **Special Collections:** Minnesota Supreme Court Briefs and Paperbooks, 1950 to present (1400 volumes). **Holdings:** 20,000 books; 300 bound periodical volumes. **Subscriptions:** 15 journals and other serials. **Services:** Interlibrary loan; copying; library open to the public with restrictions. **Networks/Consortia:** Member of Metronet.

★ 13702 ★
Ramsey County Medical Society - Boeckmann Library (Med)
345 N. Smith Ave.
St. Paul, MN 55102
Phone: (612)224-3346
Mary Sandra Tarman, Libn.
Founded: 1897. **Staff:** Prof 3; Other 4. **Subjects:** Medicine, nursing, hospital administration. **Special Collections:** Psychoanalytic Foundation of Minnesota Library (300 books; 7 periodicals). **Holdings:** 15,000 books; 28,500 bound periodical volumes; 6500 unbound periodical volumes; 18 VF drawers of pamphlets and clippings; 800 medical instruments and memorabilia. **Subscriptions:** 650 journals and other serials; 8 newspapers. **Services:** Interlibrary loan; copying; library open to the public with restrictions. **Computerized Information Services:** DIALOG Information Services, MEDLINE. **Networks/Consortia:** Member of Twin Cities Biomedical Consortium (TCBC), National Network of Libraries of Medicine - Greater Midwest Region. **Remarks:** FAX: (612)220-5186.

Ramsey Library
See: U.S. Army - TRADOC - Military Police School - Ramsey Library (17017)

★ 13703 ★
Rancho Los Amigos Medical Center - Health Sciences Library (Med)
7601 E. Imperial Hwy.
Downey, CA 90242-3456
Phone: (213)940-7696
Staff: Prof 1; Other 3. **Subjects:** Rehabilitation medicine, orthopedics, nursing, diabetes, pulmonary disease, rheumatology. **Holdings:** 6500 books; 15,000 bound periodical volumes; 250 Rancho resident papers; 650 audio cassettes. **Subscriptions:** 634 journals and other serials. **Services:** Interlibrary loan; copying; SDI; library open to the public. **Computerized Information Services:** MEDLINE, PFDS Online. **Networks/Consortia:** Member of Los Angeles County Health Sciences Library Consortium, National Network of Libraries of Medicine - Pacific Southwest Region. **Publications:** New Book List, quarterly.

Rancho Los Cerritos Historic Site
See: Long Beach Public Library (9282)

★ 13704 ★
Rancho Santa Ana Botanic Garden - Library (Biol Sci)
1500 N. College Ave.
Claremont, CA 91711
Phone: (714)625-8767
Beatrice M. Beck, Libn.
Founded: 1927. **Staff:** Prof 1; Other 1. **Subjects:** Botany, horticulture, drought tolerant plants, ethnobotany of California Indians, evolutionary biology. **Special Collections:** Floras of the world. **Holdings:** 40,000 items; 28,360 reprints; 2000 maps; nursery catalogs. **Subscriptions:** 1000 serials. **Services:** Interlibrary loan (limited); copying; library open to qualified users. **Automated Operations:** Computerized cataloging. **Computerized Information Services:** OCLC. **Publications:** Drought Tolerant Planting Bibliography, 1990; A California Indian Ethnobotanical Bibliography, 1992.

★ 13705 ★
Rancocas Hospital - Health Sciences Library (Med)
218A Sunset Rd.
Willingboro, NJ 08046
Phone: (609)835-2900
Gary J. Christopher, Libn.
Founded: 1969. **Staff:** Prof 1; Other 1. **Subjects:** Medicine, nursing, hospital administration. **Holdings:** 600 books; 2800 bound periodical volumes; 190 videotapes. **Subscriptions:** 101 journals and other serials; 2 newspapers. **Services:** Interlibrary loan; copying; library open to the public by appointment. **Computerized Information Services:** BRS/COLLEAGUE; DOCLINE (electronic mail service). Performs searches. **Networks/Consortia:** Member of BHSL, Health Sciences Library Association of New Jersey (HSLANJ), Pinelands Consortium for Health Information. **Remarks:** FAX: (609)835-3061.

Anne Rand Research Library
See: International Longshoremen's and Warehousemen's Union (8149)

★ 13706 ★
Rand Corporation - Library (Soc Sci)
1700 Main St.
Box 2138
Santa Monica, CA 90407-2138
Phone: (310)393-0411
Elizabeth D. Gill, Lib.Dir.
Founded: 1948. **Staff:** Prof 11; Other 24. **Subjects:** Policy analysis, decision-making, military strategy, international affairs, urban development, education, economics of medical care services, criminal and civil justice, regulatory policy, labor, population. **Special Collections:** Russian language collection in economics, political science, and military science. **Holdings:** 51,000 books; 143,200 documents and reports; 3000 maps. **Subscriptions:** 3200 journals and other serials. **Services:** Interlibrary loan; library not open to the public. **Automated Operations:** Computerized cataloging and serials. **Computerized Information Services:** BRS Information Technologies, DataTimes, DIALOG Information Services, DTIC, ELSS (Electronic Legislative Search System), LEXIS, MEDLARS, NASA/RECON, NewsNet, Inc., NEXIS, ORBIT Search Service, Reuters, Reuter TEXTLINE, RLIN, Reuters Information Services (Canada), USNI Military Database, VU/TEXT Information Services, WILSONLINE; OnTyme Electronic Message Network Service (electronic mail service). Performs searches on fee basis. Contact Person: Roberta Shanman, Hd., Ref.Serv. **Networks/Consortia:** Member of CLASS. **Publications:** Accessions List, monthly; Interest List, irregular; periodicals listing, monthly. **Special Catalogs:** Microfiche catalog, monthly. **Remarks:** FAX: (213)393-4818. **Staff:** Andrea Burkenroad, Ser. & Acq.Serv.; Doris Helfer, Hd., Bibliog. Access/Control Serv.; Joan Schlimgen, Hd., User Serv.; Marge Behrens, Slavic/Oriental Libn.; Walter Nelson, Hd., Class.Info.Serv.; Barbara Neff, Hd., ILL; Susan Baksh, Lib.Adm.; Mary Lou Kravetz, User Serv.Libn.; David Acheson, Cat.Libn.

★ 13707 ★
Rand Corporation - Library (Soc Sci, Mil)
2100 M St., N.W.
Washington, DC 20037-1270
Phone: (202)296-5000
Deborah Peetz, Libn.
Staff: 2. **Subjects:** Social studies, military studies, education. **Holdings:** 10,000 books; 2000 Congressional hearings. **Subscriptions:** 250 journals and other serials; 6 newspapers. **Services:** Interlibrary loan; library not open to the public. **Automated Operations:** Computerized serials. **Networks/Consortia:** Member of Interlibrary Users Association (IUA). **Remarks:** FAX: (202)296-7960.

★ 13708 ★
Rand McNally and Company - Map Library (Geog-Map, Publ)
8255 Central Park Ave.
Skokie, IL 60076
Phone: (708)673-9100
Debs A. Otis, Map Libn.
Founded: 1949. **Staff:** Prof 2. **Subjects:** U.S. and world history, geography, cartography, census, place names, railroads. **Special Collections:** Toponymy (place names); county maps; aeronautical charts; topographic, political, transportation, mineral resources maps. **Holdings:** 8000 volumes; 2400 atlases; 250,000 sheet maps; 725 gazetteers; 15 globes; 30 relief models. **Subscriptions:** 85 journals. **Services:** Interlibrary loan (to libraries and specialized research institutions); geographical reference service to librarians; library open to graduate researchers for reference use. **Automated Operations:** Computerized cataloging. **Publications:** Accession list, quarterly. **Remarks:** FAX: (708)673-1944. Telex: 210041.

Helen Randal Library
See: Registered Nurses' Association of British Columbia - Helen Randal Library (13799)

Ollie A. Randall Library
See: The National Council on the Aging, Inc. (11137)

William Madison Randall Library
See: University of North Carolina at Wilmington - William Madison Randall Library (19093)

★ 13709 ★
Randolph Circuit Court - Law Library (Law)
Courthouse, Rm. 307
Winchester, IN 47394
Phone: (317)584-7070
Joan Benson, Sec.
Subjects: Law. **Holdings:** 15,000 volumes. **Services:** Library open to the public with restrictions.

★ 13710 ★
Randolph County Genealogical Society - Library (Hist)
Asheboro Public Library
201 Worth St.
Asheboro, NC 27203
Phone: (919)629-3329
Marsha F. Haithcock, Libn., Randolph Rm.
Staff: 1. **Subjects:** Genealogy. **Holdings:** 2000 books; 82 reels of microfilm; photographs; VF drawers of memorabilia; historical maps. **Services:** Copying; library open to the public with restrictions. **Publications:** The Genealogical Journal, quarterly - to members only.

Jeannette Rankin Library Program
See: **U.S. Institute of Peace** (17559)

Lydia Rankin Technical Library
See: **Boeing Helicopters** (1939)

Edward Warder Rannells Art Library
See: **University of Kentucky - Edward Warder Rannells Art Library** (18748)

★ 13711 ★
Rannsoknastofnun Landbunadarins - Bokasafn (Agri)
Keldnaholt
IS-110 Reykjavik, Iceland
Phone: 1 812230
Gudrun Palsdottir, Libn.
Founded: 1965. **Staff:** Prof 45; Other 35. **Subjects:** Soils and fertilizers, plant production, grassland utilization, animal production, food science, farm technology. **Holdings:** 3000 books; 750 bound periodical volumes and reports. **Subscriptions:** 500 journals and other serials. **Services:** Interlibrary loan; copying; SDI; library open to the public. **Computerized Information Services:** DIALOG Information Services; internal database. **Publications:** Inhouse acquisitions lists. **Remarks:** FAX: 91 814604.

Harry Ransom Humanities Research Center
See: **University of Texas at Austin - Harry Ransom Humanities Research Center** (19392)

R.C. Ransom Memorial Library
See: **Payne Theological Seminary** (12800)

Rapaport Professional Library
See: **Osawatomie State Hospital** (12587)

★ 13712 ★
Rapid City Journal - Library (Publ)
507 Main St.
Rapid City, SD 57701
Phone: (605)394-8409
Sheri Sponder
Subjects: Newspaper reference topics. **Holdings:** News clippings; photographs. **Services:** Library not open to the public. **Remarks:** FAX: (605)342-4610.

★ 13713 ★
Rapid City Regional Hospital - Health Sciences Library (Med)
353 Fairmont Blvd.
Rapid City, SD 57701-6000
Phone: (605)341-7101
Patricia J. Hamilton, Dept.Mgr./Lib.Serv.
Founded: 1927. **Staff:** Prof 2; Other 1. **Subjects:** Medicine, nursing. **Holdings:** 8695 books; 4480 unbound periodicals; 2300 government documents. **Subscriptions:** 500 journals and other serials. **Services:** Interlibrary loan; copying; library open to the public with restrictions. **Computerized Information Services:** OCLC, MEDLARS, BRS Information Technologies; DOCLINE (electronic mail service). Performs searches. **Networks/Consortia:** Member of National Network of Libraries of Medicine - Greater Midwest Region, South Dakota Library Network (SDLN). **Remarks:** FAX: (605)348-1578. **Staff:** Carol Davis, Ref.Libn.

★ 13714 ★
Rapides General Hospital - Medical Library (Med)
Box 30101
Alexandria, LA 71301
Phone: (318)473-3563
Janet Dawkins, Libn.
Founded: 1963. **Staff:** Prof 1. **Subjects:** Medicine. **Holdings:** 1800 books; 1112 bound periodical volumes. **Subscriptions:** 65 journals and other serials. **Services:** Interlibrary loan; library open to the public at librarian's discretion.

★ 13715 ★
Rappahannock Community College - Library (Med, Bus-Fin)
Glenns Campus Library
Box 287
Glenns, VA 23149
Phone: (804)758-5324
Carol L. Jones
Founded: 1970. **Staff:** Prof 1. Other 3. **Subjects:** Nursing, business management, drafting, design, history, art. **Special Collections:** Kearns Collection (Japanese). **Holdings:** 20,000 books; 500 microfiche; 1450 reels of microfilm. **Subscriptions:** 170 journals and other serials; 15 newspapers. **Services:** Interlibrary loan; copying; library open to the public. **Computerized Information Services:** OCLC. **Remarks:** FAX: (804)758-0213.

★ 13716 ★
RAPRA Technology - Library (Sci-Engr)
Shawbury
Shrewsbury, Shropshire SY4 4NR, England
Phone: 939 250383
Pamela Roberts, Libn.
Subjects: Rubber, plastics, polymer synthesis. **Holdings:** 45,000 volumes, pieces of trade literature, standards, specifications, government reports. **Services:** Library not open to the public. **Computerized Information Services:** Produces RAPRA Abstracts. **Remarks:** FAX: 939 251118. Telex: 35134.

★ 13717 ★
Raritan Bay Medical Center - Health Science Library (Med)
530 New Brunswick Ave.
Perth Amboy, NJ 08861
Phone: (201)442-3700
Catherine A. Hilman, Hea.Sci.Libn.
Staff: Prof 1; Other 1. **Subjects:** Medicine, nursing, allied health sciences. **Special Collections:** Administrative collection (200 volumes). **Holdings:** 1800 books; 770 bound periodical volumes. **Subscriptions:** 140 journals and other serials. **Services:** Library not open to the public. **Formerly:** Perth Amboy General Hospital.

Rasche Memorial Library
See: **Milwaukee Area Technical College** (10417)

Raspet Flight Research Laboratory
See: **Mississippi State University** (10528)

Rat fuer Formgebung
See: **German Design Council** (6424)

★ 13718 ★
Ratcliff Architects - Library (Art, Plan)
Box 1022
Berkeley, CA 94701
Phone: (510)652-1972
Founded: 1986. **Staff:** Prof 1. **Subjects:** Architecture. **Holdings:** 1000 books. **Subscriptions:** 77 journals and other serials. **Services:** Library not open to the public. **Computerized Information Services:** DIALOG Information Services. **Publications:** Newsletter - for internal distribution only. **Remarks:** FAX: (510)655-6654.

Erich Rath Music Library & Listening Center
See: **Hollins College - Music Department** (7332)

Rauh Memorial Library
See: **Children's Museum of Indianapolis** (3591)

Ravalli County Museum
See: Bitter Root Valley Historical Society - Ravalli County Museum - Miles Romney Memorial Library (1870)

★ 13719 ★
Ravenswood Hospital Medical Center - Medical-Nursing Library (Med)
4550 N. Winchester at Wilson   Phone: (312)878-4300
Chicago, IL 60640   Mr. Zia Solomon Gilliana, Med.Libn.
Founded: 1908. **Staff:** Prof 1; Other 2. **Subjects:** Medicine, nursing. **Special Collections:** History of medicine; history of nursing. **Holdings:** 4588 books; 6300 bound periodical volumes. **Subscriptions:** 252 journals and other serials. **Services:** Interlibrary loan; copying; SDI; library open to the public with restrictions. **Computerized Information Services:** MEDLARS. **Publications:** Guide to the Library. **Remarks:** FAX: (312)878-7924.

Marguerite Rawalt Resource Center
See: Business and Professional Women's Foundation (2403)

★ 13720 ★
Rawle and Henderson - Law Library (Law)
Widener Bldg.
1 S. Penn Square   Phone: (215)575-4480
Philadelphia, PA 19107   Christine Harvan, Libn.
Founded: 1783. **Staff:** Prof 1; Other 2. **Subjects:** Law - ships and shipping, medical malpractice, insurance defense, general practice. **Holdings:** 11,000 books; 505 Paper Books. **Subscriptions:** 203 journals and other serials. **Services:** Interlibrary loan; library not open to the public. **Computerized Information Services:** LEXIS, DIALOG Information Services, WESTLAW, Information America, Dun & Bradstreet Business Credit Services. **Publications:** Paper Books (firm's important cases). **Remarks:** This is said to be the oldest established law firm and law library in Philadelphia. FAX: (215)563-2583. Telex: 83-4286.

★ 13721 ★
Ray College of Design - Library (Art)
1051 Perimeter Dr.   Phone: (708)619-3450
Schaumburg, IL 60173   Juliet Teipel
Founded: 1985. **Staff:** 1.75. **Subjects:** Graphic design; merchandising - fashion, visual; interior design; photography; fashion history; furniture history. **Holdings:** 2000 books; photographs. **Subscriptions:** 48 journals and other serials. **Services:** Interlibrary loan; library open to the public with restrictions. **Remarks:** FAX: (708)619-3064.

★ 13722 ★
Ray County Historical Society and Museum - Museum Library (Hist)
911 W. Royle St.   Phone: (816)776-2305
Richmond, MO 64085   Sandra McKemy, Libn.
Subjects: Genealogy, history. **Special Collections:** Kentucky Collection; William Jeremiah Burke Collection (manuscripts). **Holdings:** 1248 books; 55 bound periodical volumes; 371 nonbook items; manuscripts; newspapers on microfilm. **Services:** Copying; library open to the public. **Publications:** 1881 Ray County Historical Reprint; genealogical books. **Special Indexes:** Quarterly indexes. **Remarks:** Co-sponsored by the Ray County Genealogical Society.

Isaac Ray Medical Library
See: Butler Hospital (2413)

Otto Ernest Rayburn Library of Folklore
See: University of Arkansas, Fayetteville - Special Collections Division (18236)

Sam Rayburn Foundation - Library
See: University of Texas at Austin - Sam Rayburn Foundation - Library (19404)

Sam Rayburn Memorial Veterans Center
See: U.S. Dept. of Veterans Affairs (TX-Bonham) (17422)

★ 13723 ★
Raychem Corporation - Corporate Library (Sci-Engr)
300 Constitution Dr.   Phone: (415)361-3282
Menlo Park, CA 94025-1164   Phyllis Oda, Mgr.
Founded: 1967. **Staff:** Prof 3; Other 4. **Subjects:** Chemistry, polymer science, electronics. **Holdings:** 6000 books; 8000 bound periodical volumes. **Subscriptions:** 450 journals and other serials. **Services:** Interlibrary loan; library not open to the public. **Computerized Information Services:** PFDS Online, DIALOG Information Services, BRS Information Technologies; BASIS (internal database). **Remarks:** FAX: (415)361-2655.

★ 13724 ★
Raymond, Chabot, Martin, Pare - Library/Bibliotheque (Bus-Fin)
600, de la Gauchetiere, W., No. 1900   Phone: (514)878-2691
Montreal, PQ, Canada H3B 4L8   Isabelle Boudreau-Gaudet, Dir.
Founded: 1979. **Staff:** Prof 1. **Subjects:** Accounting, management, business, computer science. **Holdings:** 4500 books; 125 bound periodical volumes. **Services:** Interlibrary loan; library not open to the public. **Automated Operations:** Computerized cataloging. **Computerized Information Services:** Dun & Bradstreet Business Credit Services, DIALOG Information Services. **Remarks:** FAX: (514)878-2127.

John Raymond Memorial Library
See: Waukegan Historical Society (20099)

★ 13725 ★
Rayovac Corp. - Technology Center Library (Sci-Engr)
601 Rayovac Dr.   Phone: (608)275-4714
Madison, WI 53711-2497   Sandra Plisch, Libn.
Founded: 1967. **Staff:** Prof 1. **Subjects:** Electrochemistry, primary and secondary batteries, chemical engineering, plastics, business and management. **Special Collections:** U.S. Government and internal reports. **Holdings:** 2200 books; 300 bound periodical volumes; 3000 patents; 7000 technical reports. **Subscriptions:** 100 journals and other serials. **Services:** Interlibrary loan; copying; library open to the public by appointment. **Computerized Information Services:** DIALOG Information Services, NERAC, Inc.; IZE (internal database). **Networks/Consortia:** Member of Multitype Advisory Library Committee (MALC). **Publications:** Acquisition List, monthly. **Special Indexes:** Uniterm Index to documents collection. **Remarks:** FAX: (608)275-4992.

★ 13726 ★
Raytheon Company - Badger Engineers, Inc. - Library (Sci-Engr)
1 Broadway   Phone: (617)494-7565
Cambridge, MA 02142   Jacqueline Bassett, Libn.
Staff: Prof 1; Other 1. **Subjects:** Chemical engineering, energy, petroleum refining, environmental engineering. **Holdings:** 4500 books; 1500 bound periodical volumes; 8 VF drawers of patents; 16 VF drawers of codes and specifications; 20 VF drawers of process data files; 41 VF drawers of pamphlets, reprints, special services. **Subscriptions:** 100 journals and other serials. **Services:** Interlibrary loan; library not open to the public. **Computerized Information Services:** DIALOG Information Services.

★ 13727 ★
Raytheon Company - Business Information Center (Bus-Fin)
141 Spring St.   Phone: (617)860-2579
Lexington, MA 02173   Jerry O'Connor, Mgr.
Founded: 1960. **Staff:** Prof 1. **Subjects:** Business, marketing, economics, finance. **Special Collections:** Annual reports; Conference Board reports. **Holdings:** 1000 books; 10,000 archival materials and back copies of journals; 20 VF drawers; 2 cabinets of microfilm; government documents. **Subscriptions:** 400 journals and other serials; 5 newspapers. **Services:** Interlibrary loan; center not open to the public. **Computerized Information Services:** DIALOG Information Services, LEXIS, NEXIS, Dow Jones News/Retrieval, Reuters. **Publications:** Periodical holdings, annual. **Remarks:** FAX: (617)860-2172.

★ 13728 ★
Raytheon Company - Electromagnetic Systems Division - Engineering Library (Sci-Engr)
6380 Hollister Ave.   Phone: (805)967-5511
Goleta, CA 93117   Sheila Anderson, Libn.
Founded: 1957. **Staff:** Prof 2. **Subjects:** Electrical and electronic engineering; communications; radar technology; navigation and guidance systems and equipment; materials science. **Holdings:** 3000 volumes; 2 drawers of microfiche of government documents; 2400 microfilm cartridges of specifications, standards, military documents, vendor information; 88 VF drawers of hardcopy specifications and standards. **Subscriptions:** 126 journals and other serials. **Computerized Information Services:** DTIC, NEXIS. **Remarks:** FAX: (805)964-0470.

★ 13729 ★
Raytheon Company - Equipment Division - Technical Information Center (Info Sci)
1001 Boston Post Rd.   Phone: (508)490-2288
Marlborough, MA 01752   Ray Niro, Mgr.
Founded: 1988. **Staff:** Prof 3. **Subjects:** Communications, electronics, computer science. **Special Collections:** IEEE Conference proceedings. **Holdings:** 10,000 books and reports. **Subscriptions:** 200 journals and other serials. **Services:** Interlibrary loan; center not open to the public. **Automated Operations:** Computerized cataloging and circulation. **Computerized Information Services:** DIALOG Information Services, DataTimes, EPIC, Global Scan, PERISCOPE. **Networks/Consortia:** Member of NELINET, Inc. **Remarks:** FAX: (508)490-2562. **Staff:** Jim Cornacchia, Sr.Libn.; Maureen Dolan, Asst.

★ 13730 ★
Raytheon Company - Equipment Division - Technical Information Center (Sci-Engr)
528 Boston Post Rd.   Phone: (508)440-2282
Sudbury, MA 01776   Filomena Didiano, Libn.
Founded: 1963. **Staff:** Prof 1; Other 3. **Subjects:** Electronics, computers, communications. **Holdings:** 7000 books; 30 bound periodical volumes; 300 other cataloged items; 330,000 microfiche of NASA reports; 350 tape cassettes; 2 files of reports on microfiche. **Subscriptions:** 160 journals and other serials. **Services:** Interlibrary loan; center not open to the public. **Computerized Information Services:** DIALOG Information Services, DTIC, OCLC. **Networks/Consortia:** Member of NELINET, Inc. **Publications:** Technical Information Center Bulletin, monthly - for internal distribution only. **Special Catalogs:** Raytheon Libraries Union List of Books; Raytheon Libraries Union List of Serials. **Remarks:** FAX: (508)440-4412.

★ 13731 ★
Raytheon Company - Equipment Division - Technical Information Center (Sci-Engr)
430 Boston Post Rd.   Phone: (508)440-8067
Wayland, MA 01778   Margaret Pappas, Sr.Libn.
Founded: 1955. **Staff:** Prof 1. **Subjects:** Electronics, electrical engineering, physics, radar, mathematics. **Holdings:** 7000 books; 2 files of reports on microfiche. **Subscriptions:** 350 journals and other serials. **Services:** Interlibrary loan; center not open to the public. **Automated Operations:** Computerized cataloging, circulation, acquisitions, and periodical control. **Computerized Information Services:** DIALOG Information Services, OCLC. **Publications:** TIC Bulletin, monthly - for internal distribution only. **Special Catalogs:** Raytheon Libraries Union List of Serials, monthly (printout); Raytheon Libraries Union List of Books, quarterly (printout). **Special Indexes:** Technical Information Center Index to internal memos and reports, annual (printout). **Remarks:** FAX: (508)440-8556.

★ 13732 ★
Raytheon Company - Law Library (Law)
Office of the General Counsel
141 Spring St.   Phone: (617)860-4829
Lexington, MA 02173   Joan Cook, Libn.
Founded: 1930. **Subjects:** Law. **Holdings:** 2600 volumes. **Subscriptions:** 10 journals and other serials. **Services:** Library not open to the public.

★ 13733 ★
Raytheon Company - Missile Systems Laboratories - Technical Information Center (Sci-Engr)
50 Apple Hill Dr.   Phone: (508)858-4700
Tewksbury, MA 01876   Lorraine K. Gregoire, Mgr.
Founded: 1954. **Staff:** Prof 3; Other 2. **Subjects:** Guided missiles, electronics, aerodynamics, physics, mathematics, management techniques. **Holdings:** 40,000 books; 100,000 research reports. **Subscriptions:** 225 journals and other serials. **Services:** Interlibrary loan; center not open to the public. **Computerized Information Services:** DIALOG Information Services, DTIC, NASA/RECON, OCLC; LIBCAR (internal database). **Publications:** Technical Abstract Bulletin, monthly - for internal distribution only; Library Scanner. **Staff:** Patricia Healey, Sr.Libn.; Michael Hedrich, Sr.Libn.; Roberta McMillan, ILL; Linda Tarbox, Acq.

★ 13734 ★
Raytheon Company - Research Division - Library (Sci-Engr)
131 Spring St.   Phone: (617)860-3192
Lexington, MA 02173   Vicary Maxant, Mgr., Tech.Info.Serv.
Founded: 1952. **Staff:** Prof 3. **Subjects:** Applied physics, advanced materials, semiconductor physics, physical chemistry. **Holdings:** 6000 books; 5000 bound periodical volumes; 15,000 technical reports; 9000 archival materials. **Subscriptions:** 350 journals and other serials. **Services:** Interlibrary loan; library open to the public with approval of security officer. **Automated Operations:** Computerized cataloging, serials, circulation, and ILL. **Computerized Information Services:** DIALOG Information Services, OCLC, DTIC, Chemical Abstracts Service (CAS). **Networks/Consortia:** Member of NELINET, Inc. **Publications:** Accessions Bulletin, monthly; special bibliographies; Update, monthly. **Remarks:** FAX: (617)860-3196. **Staff:** Johanna Grenda, Tech.Info.Spec.

★ 13735 ★
Raytheon Company - Submarine Signal Division - Technical Information Center (Sci-Engr)
1847 W. Main Rd.   Phone: (401)847-8000
Portsmouth, RI 02871   Mark F. Baldwin, Mgr.
Founded: 1960. **Staff:** Prof 2; Other 2. **Subjects:** Electronics, acoustics, oceanography, antisubmarine warfare. **Holdings:** 13,000 books; 1200 bound periodical volumes; 30,000 reports and documents. **Subscriptions:** 220 journals and other serials; 5 newspapers. **Services:** Interlibrary loan; center not open to the public. **Automated Operations:** Computerized cataloging, acquisitions, and circulation. **Computerized Information Services:** DIALOG Information Services, DTIC, OCLC, NEXIS, Dow Jones News/Retrieval, U.S.N.I. Military Database; internal database. **Publications:** Accession Bulletin, monthly; News & Views, weekly; TIC Bulletin, monthly. **Staff:** Bea Digovanni, Class.Docs.

Raytheon Company - United Engineers & Constructors Inc.
See: **United Engineers & Constructors Inc.** (16709)

★ 13736 ★
Raytheon Service Company - Information Center (Bus-Fin)
Spencer Laboratory
2 Wayside Rd.   Phone: (617)272-9300
Burlington, MA 01803   Jean Cameron, Info.Spec.
Founded: 1970. **Staff:** Prof 1; Other 1. **Subjects:** Business, marketing. **Holdings:** 2000 books; 3000 reports. **Subscriptions:** 100 journals and other serials. **Services:** Interlibrary loan; copying; center open to the public by arrangement. **Computerized Information Services:** DIALOG Information Services, Dun & Bradstreet Business Credit Services, OCLC. **Publications:** Accessions bulletin, bimonthly; Current Contents, monthly - both for internal distribution only. **Remarks:** FAX: (617)272-0580.

Raza Unida Party Archive
See: **University of Texas at Austin - Benson Latin American Collection** (19380)

★ 13737 ★
RBC Securities Pitfield - Library
Commerce Court S.
Box 21
Toronto, ON, Canada M5L 1A7
Defunct.

★ 13738 ★
RCA Service Company - Keystone Job Corps Center - Research Library
Foothill Drive   Phone: (717)788-1164
Drums, PA 18222   David Stout, Dir.
Remarks: No further information was supplied by respondent.

★ 13739 ★
RCM Capital Management - Research Library (Bus-Fin)
4 Embarcadero Center, Suite 2900   Phone: (415)954-5474
San Francisco, CA 94111   Maggie O'Brien, Dir.
Founded: 1976. **Staff:** Prof 2; Other 3. **Subjects:** Investment. **Holdings:** 50
books; 5000 company reports; 4000 broker reports; 20,000 company reports
on microfiche. **Subscriptions:** 400 journals and other serials; 10 newspapers.
Services: Interlibrary loan; library not open to the public. **Computerized
Information Services:** DIALOG Information Services, Dow Jones News/
Retrieval, NewsNet, Inc., VU/TEXT Information Services, Reuters;
DIALMAIL (electronic mail service). **Remarks:** FAX: (415)954-5304.
Staff: Lizabeth O'Meara, Res.Libn.

Sir Herbert Read Archives
See: University of Victoria - McPherson Library - Special Collections
(19489)

★ 13740 ★
Reader's Digest - Marketing Information Center (Publ)
261 Madison Ave.   Phone: (212)907-6898
New York, NY 10016   Helen Fledderus, Libn.
Staff: 2. **Subjects:** Advertising, marketing, media research. **Holdings:** 800
volumes; 40 lateral file drawers of commodity and industry data; 4 lateral
file drawers of media information. **Subscriptions:** 150 journals and other
serials. **Services:** Interlibrary loan. **Computerized Information Services:**
NEXIS, DIALOG Information Services, VU/TEXT Information Services.
Remarks: FAX: (212)907-6605.

★ 13741 ★
Reader's Digest Association - Editorial and Research Libraries (Info Sci)
1 Roaring Brook Rd.   Phone: (914)241-5289
Pleasantville, NY 10570   Joanne Frasene, Hd.Libn.
Founded: 1938. **Staff:** Prof 3; Other 4. **Subjects:** General reference, current
news, Reader's Digest. **Holdings:** 12,000 books; archival materials.
Subscriptions: 500 journals and other serials; 20 newspapers. **Services:**
Interlibrary loan (limited); libraries not open to the public. **Computerized
Information Services:** BRS Information Technologies, DataTimes,
DIALOG Information Services, NEXIS, VU/TEXT Information Services,
WILSONLINE, Reuter Textline, Burrelle's Information Search Service.
Remarks: FAX: (914)238-0534. **Staff:** Cindy Rubino, Assoc.Libn.; Rosanne
Fleury, Assoc.Libn.

★ 13742 ★
Reader's Digest Association - General Books Library (Publ)
260 Madison Ave., 6th Fl.   Phone: (212)850-7044
New York, NY 10016   Jo Manning, Libn./Hd.
Founded: 1975. **Staff:** Prof 2; Other 1. **Subjects:** Bible, arts and crafts,
American history, nature, occult. **Special Collections:** Reader's Digest, 1922
to present; Reader's Digest international books (microfiche). **Holdings:**
40,000 books; New York Times, 1851 to present, on microfilm.
Subscriptions: 250 journals and other serials. **Services:** Interlibrary loan;
library not open to the public. **Computerized Information Services:**
DIALOG Information Services, NEXIS, CATNYP, LIONS. **Publications:**
Books! (acquisition list), monthly. **Remarks:** FAX: (212)850-7079. Alternate
telephone number(s): (212)850-7043. **Staff:** Nettie Seaberry, Assoc.Libn.

★ 13743 ★
Reader's Digest Association - Index (Publ)
Pleasantville, NY 10570   Phone: (914)238-1000
                                        Laura Giangrande, Ed.
Founded: 1922. **Staff:** 4. **Holdings:** Articles and book condensations;
anecdotes in the magazine, 1950 to present. **Services:** Index area not open
to the public; staff will answer inquiries. **Computerized Information
Services:** STAIRS, RAMIS (internal databases).

★ 13744 ★
Reader's Digest Magazines Limited - Editorial Library (Publ)
215 Redfern Ave.   Phone: (514)934-0751
Montreal, PQ, Canada H3Z 2V9   Penelope Body, Libn.
Founded: 1973. **Staff:** Prof 1; Other 1. **Subjects:** Canadiana. **Holdings:** 6000
books; 22 VF drawers of newspaper clippings. **Subscriptions:** 200 journals
and other serials; 6 newspapers. **Services:** Interlibrary loan; library not open
to the public. **Automated Operations:** Computerized cataloging.
Computerized Information Services: Info Globe, Infomart Online, The
Financial Post DataGroup; internal database. **Special Indexes:** Index to
Canadian Reader's Digest. **Remarks:** FAX: (514)935-4463. Telex: 05 25800.

★ 13745 ★
Reading Eagle Company - Eagle-Times Library (Publ)
345 Penn St.   Phone: (215)371-5077
Reading, PA 19601   Gordon Boltz, Libn.
Subjects: Newspaper reference topics. **Holdings:** General reporter reference
materials; Reading Eagle, 1868 to present (microfilm); Reading Times, 1941
to present (microfilm). **Services:** Library not open to the public.
Computerized Information Services: DataTimes, Dow Jones News/
Retrieval; internal database (local and regional news since 1987). **Remarks:**
FAX: (215)371-5089.

★ 13746 ★
Reading Hospital & Medical Center - Medical Library (Med)
P.O. Box 16052   Phone: (215)378-6418
Reading, PA 19612-6052   Margaret Hsieh, Med.Libn.
Founded: 1940. **Staff:** Prof 1. **Subjects:** Medicine, medical specialties,
medical ethics, consumer health education. **Special Collections:** Elaine G.
Dunitz Hospice Library. **Holdings:** 1500 books; 18,000 bound periodical
volumes; 300 audiotapes. **Subscriptions:** 150 journals and other serials.
Services: Interlibrary loan; copying; SDI; library open to the public by
appointment for research and reference. **Computerized Information
Services:** BRS Information Technologies; CD-ROM (MEDLINE,
MICROMEDEX). **Networks/Consortia:** Member of National Network of
Libraries of Medicine - Middle Atlantic Region, Central Pennsylvania
Health Sciences Library Association (CPHSLA), Berks County Library
Association (BCLA), BHSL. **Publications:** Newsletter - for internal
distribution only.

★ 13747 ★
**Reading Hospital & Medical Center - Reading Hospital School of
  Nursing Library** (Med)
P.O. Box 16052   Phone: (215)378-6359
Reading, PA 19612-6052   Cynthia J. Spayd, Libn.
Founded: 1935. **Staff:** Prof 1; Other 1. **Subjects:** Nursing, psychiatry,
psychology. **Special Collections:** History of nursing. **Holdings:** 8590
volumes. **Subscriptions:** 36 journals and other serials. **Services:** Interlibrary
loan; copying; SDI; library open to the public by appointment. **Networks/
Consortia:** Member of Berks County Library Association (BCLA), Central
Pennsylvania Health Sciences Library Association (CPHSLA), Cooperating
Hospital Libraries of the Lehigh Valley Area, BHSL. **Publications:** RHSN
Library News, quarterly.

★ 13748 ★
Reading Public Museum and Art Gallery - Reference Library (Art, Sci-
  Engr)
500 Museum Rd.   Phone: (215)371-5850
Reading, PA 19611-1425   Bruce L. Dietrich, Dir.
Founded: 1904. **Staff:** Prof 1; Other 1. **Subjects:** Art, natural science,
anthropology. **Special Collections:** Unger Geology Collection; American
Bureau of Ethnology Collection. **Holdings:** 3000 books; 2000 bound
periodical volumes; 4 VF drawers of museum catalogs; 4 VF drawers of
artist catalogs; 4 VF drawers of art catalogs; 3000 unbound periodicals.
Subscriptions: 30 journals and other serials. **Services:** Interlibrary loan;
library open to the public for reference use only with advance written
permission. **Publications:** List of publications - available upon request.
Remarks: FAX: (215)371-5979.

★ 13749 ★
Reading Rehabilitation Hospital - Medical Library (Med)
Rte. 1, Box 250   Phone: (215)775-8297
Reading, PA 19607-9727   Frances A. Mozloom, Libn.
Founded: 1977. **Staff:** Prof 1. **Subjects:** Rehabilitation, physical medicine, neurology, diabetes, spinal cord and head injuries, communication disorders. **Holdings:** 765 books; 700 bound periodical volumes; 170 videotapes; 70 audio cassettes; 56 slide programs. **Subscriptions:** 144 journals and other serials. **Services:** Interlibrary loan; copying; library open to the public by appointment. **Computerized Information Services:** BRS Information Technologies, DIALOG Information Services, EPIC. Performs searches on fee basis. **Networks/Consortia:** Member of Central Pennsylvania Health Sciences Library Association (CPHSLA), Cooperative Hospital Libraries, Berks County Library Association (BCLA), BHSL. **Publications:** Rehab. Scanner, quarterly - for internal distribution only. **Remarks:** FAX: (215)775-8353.

★ 13750 ★
Reading School District Planetarium - Library (Sci-Engr)
1211 Parkside Dr., S.   Phone: (215)371-5854
Reading, PA 19611-1441   Bruce L. Dietrich, Dir. of Planetarium
Founded: 1969. **Staff:** 1. **Subjects:** Astronomy. **Holdings:** 900 books; 100 bound periodical volumes; 7000 35mm slides; 1 VF drawer of manuscripts; 700 magnetic tapes; 2 VF drawers of clippings and pamphlets; 25 film loops; 20 movies; 15 videodiscs. **Services:** Library open to the public with written permission. **Remarks:** FAX: (215)371-5844.

William Ready Division of Archives and Research Collections
See: **McMaster University - The William Ready Division of Archives and Research Collections** (9954)

Lindley B. Reagan Health Sciences Library
See: **Memorial Hospital of Burlington County** (10037)

Ronald Reagan Library
See: **U.S. Presidential Libraries** (17929)

★ 13751 ★
Real Estate Board of New York - Library (Plan)
12 E. 41st St.   Phone: (212)532-3100
New York, NY 10017   Marie Hill
Subjects: Manhattan real estate. **Holdings:** 200 volumes. **Subscriptions:** 70 journals and other serials. **Services:** Library open to member trade associations only.

★ 13752 ★
Real Estate Research Corporation - Library (Bus-Fin)
2 N. LaSalle St., Suite 400   Phone: (312)346-5885
Chicago, IL 60602   Kent Picha, Libn.
Staff: Prof 2; Other 2. **Subjects:** Real estate management, urban planning, appraisal, land use, housing. **Holdings:** 1100 books; 100 bound periodical volumes; 20,000 internal reports on microfiche; 40 VF drawers. **Subscriptions:** 300 journals and other serials; 6 newspapers. **Services:** Interlibrary loan; library open to the public with permission of librarian.

Real Estate, Shopping Center & Urban Development Information Center
See: **The Vineyard** (19852)

Lauren Taylor Reardon Family Library
See: **Children's Medical Center of Dallas** (3587)

★ 13753 ★
Rebound, Inc. - Corporate Library (Med)
P.O. Box 2159   Phone: (615)822-8430
Hendersonville, TN 37077   Virginia Collier, Libn.
Founded: 1987. **Staff:** Prof 1; Other 1. **Subjects:** Head injuries, rehabilitation, medical management, administration. **Special Collections:** Brain injury (periodicals). **Holdings:** 150 books; 85 audiotapes; 100 videotapes. **Subscriptions:** 40 journals and other serials. **Services:** Interlibrary loan; copying; library open to the public for reference use only. **Automated Operations:** Computerized cataloging. **Computerized Information Services:** DIALOG Information Services. **Remarks:** Library located at 103 Hazel Path, Hendersonville, TN, 37075.

Recon/Optical, Inc. - CAI
See: **CAI** (2443)

★ 13754 ★
Reconstructionist Rabbinical College - Mordecai M. Kaplan Library (Rel-Phil)
Church Rd. & Greenwood Ave.   Phone: (215)576-0800
Wyncote, PA 19095   Eliezer Wise, Lib.Dir.
Founded: 1968. **Staff:** Prof 1; Other 3. **Subjects:** Biblical studies, Rabbinics, Jewish history, Hasidism, Hebrew language, Jewish liturgy, Jewish mysticism, Judaism, Jewish philosophy, ethics, comparative religion, Middle East politics, Israel. **Special Collections:** Mordecai M. Kaplan Archives and Personal Library; Creative Liturgy File. **Holdings:** 35,560 books; 1500 bound periodical volumes. **Subscriptions:** 149 journals and other serials; 20 newspapers. **Services:** Interlibrary loan; library open to the public with restrictions. **Computerized Information Services:** OCLC. **Networks/Consortia:** Member of Southeastern Pennsylvania Theological Library Association (SEPTLA), Council of Archives and Research Libraries in Jewish Studies (CARLJS), PALINET. **Publications:** Ha-Sefer - recent acquisitions of the Kaplan Library.

★ 13755 ★
The Record - Library (Publ)
501 Broadway   Phone: (518)272-2000
Troy, NY 12180   Susan B. Chasney, Libn.
Staff: Prof 1. **Subjects:** Newspaper reference topics. **Holdings:** 100 books; newspapers, 1884 to present, on microfilm; clippings. **Services:** Library not open to the public. **Special Indexes:** Index of clippings, 1977 to present. **Remarks:** FAX: (518)272-1190.

★ 13756 ★
Recording for the Blind, Inc. - Library and Borrower Services Departments (Aud-Vis)
20 Roszel Rd.   Phone: (609)452-0606
Princeton, NJ 08540   John Kelly, Dir., Lib. & Borrower Serv.
Founded: 1948. **Staff:** Prof 6; Other 11. **Subjects:** Collection consists of recorded educational materials. **Holdings:** 77,000 titles on master tapes. **Subscriptions:** 5 journals and other serials. **Services:** Library and recording service available to qualified print-handicapped students who are registered with RFB. **Automated Operations:** Computerized cataloging and circulation; MINISIS public access catalog. **Computerized Information Services:** BRS Information Technologies, OCLC, APH-CARL; SpecialNet (electronic mail service). Performs searches free of charge to registered borrowers. **Networks/Consortia:** Member of FEDLINK, National Library Service for the Blind & Physically Handicapped (NLS). **Special Catalogs:** Catalog of recorded books. **Remarks:** FAX: (609)987-8116. **Staff:** Elizabeth McElroy; Laura Coope; Marjorie White; Pam Johnson; Julia Hullar.

★ 13757 ★
Recording Industry Association of America - Reference Library (Art)
1020 19th St., N.W., Suite 200   Phone: (202)775-0101
Washington, DC 20036   Cheryl Gibbs, Coord.
Subjects: Audio and video recording industry. **Holdings:** Books; magazines; clippings; other cataloged materials. **Services:** Library not open to the public.

★ 13758 ★
Recycling Council of Ontario - Library (Env-Cons)
489 College St., Ste. 504   Phone: (416)960-1025
Toronto, ON, Canada M6G 1A5   Irene Fedun
Staff: 1. **Subjects:** Waste management. **Holdings:** 1300 books, reports, and documents. **Subscriptions:** 80 journals and other serials. **Services:** Library open to the public on a limited schedule. **Computerized Information Services:** Internal database. **Special Indexes:** Index to Ontario Recycling Update (newsletter), monthly. **Remarks:** FAX: (416)960-8053.

★ 13759 ★
Red Cross of Constantine - United Grand Imperial Council - Edward A. Glad Memorial Library (Rec)
500 E. Monroe St., Suite 700   Phone: (217)523-3838
Springfield, IL 62705   G. Wilbur Bell, Grand Recorder
Founded: 1974. **Staff:** 2. **Subjects:** Freemasonry, American history. **Holdings:** 1700 books; 50 periodical volumes; 200 tapes. **Subscriptions:** 20 journals and other serials. **Services:** Library open to Masonic researchers. **Remarks:** FAX: (217)523-0013.

★ 13760 ★
(Red Deer) Advocate - Newspaper Library (Publ)
2950 Bremner Ave.
Box 5200　　　　　　　　　　　Phone: (403)343-2400
Red Deer, AB, Canada T4N 5G3　　Patricia J. Goulet, Libn.
Staff: Prof 1. **Subjects:** Newspaper reference topics. **Special Collections:**
Biography files (240). **Holdings:** 100 books; 300 bound periodical volumes;
136 VF drawers of newspaper clippings; 312 reels of microfilm; 15,000
photographs. **Subscriptions:** 10 journals and other serials; 10 newspapers.
Services: Copying; library open to the public. **Remarks:** FAX: (403)341-6560.

★ 13761 ★
Red Deer Regional Hospital Centre - Learning Resource Centre (Med)
3942 50A Ave.　　　　　　　　Phone: (403)343-4557
Red Deer, AB, Canada T4N 4E7　　Elizabeth Kavanagh, Libn.
Founded: 1981. **Staff:** Prof 1. **Subjects:** Medicine, nursing, allied health
sciences, hospital administration. **Holdings:** 850 books; 520 bound periodical
volumes; 110 videotapes; 350 audiotapes; 120 filmstrips. **Subscriptions:** 115
journals and other serials. **Services:** Interlibrary loan; copying; center open
to the public for reference use only.

★ 13762 ★
Red Notes Italy Bulletin - Library (Area-Ethnic)
BP 15
2A St. Paul's Rd.
London N1, England　　　　　　　　　　Phil Saunders
Founded: 1976. **Subjects:** Italian social, communist, revolutionary
movements; Italian culture. **Holdings:** 200 volumes; newspapers; pamphlets.
Services: Copying; library open by advance written notification.

Redd Barna
See: **Norwegian Save the Children** (12116)

★ 13763 ★
Redding Museum & Art Center - Research Library (Hist)
P.O. Box 427　　　　　　　　Phone: (916)225-4155
Redding, CA 96099　　　　　　Hazel McKim, Libn.
Subjects: Local history, pioneer genealogy, anthropology. **Special
Collections:** James Dotta Anthropology Library. **Holdings:** 2000 books; 6
bound periodical volumes. **Subscriptions:** 10 journals and other serials.
Services: Copying; library open to the public. **Computerized Information
Services:** Internal databases. **Staff:** Milton Black. Cat.

★ 13764 ★
Reddy Communications, Inc. - Information/Research Services (Energy)
5801 Osuna Rd., N.E.　　　　　　Phone: (505)884-7500
Albuquerque, NM 87109　　　　　Ann M. Klos, Mgr.
Staff: Prof 2; Other 2.5. **Subjects:** Public utilities, energy, communication
techniques, public relations, management. **Holdings:** 1000 books and
technical reports; 55 VF drawers of clippings, publications, reports,
speeches. **Subscriptions:** 200 journals and other serials. **Services:** Services
not open to the public. **Computerized Information Services:** DIALOG
Information Services; internal database. **Remarks:** FAX: (505)883-1753.
Staff: Gail Gerstner Miller.

★ 13765 ★
Redeemer College - Library - Special Collections (Rel-Phil, Hum)
777 Hwy. 53, E.
P.O. Box 7349　　　　　　　　Phone: (416)648-2131
Ancaster, ON, Canada L9G 3N6　　Daniel A. Savage, Chf.Libn.
Founded: 1982. **Staff:** 11. **Subjects:** Liberal Arts. **Special Collections:** Dutch
Reformed theology (in Dutch; 5000 volumes); Arthur C. Custance Natural
Sciences and Christian Faith Collection (4000 volumes). **Services:**
Interlibrary loan; copying; SDI; library open to the public. **Computerized
Information Services:** CAN/OLE, DIALOG Information Services, BRS
Information Technologies; internal database; Envoy 100 (electronic mail
service). **Publications:** Annual reports; strategic plan; Library Mission,
Goals and Objectives; library handbook. **Remarks:** FAX: (416)648-2134.
Electronic mail address(es): DAN.SAVAGE (Envoy 100). **Staff:** Margaret
Grift, Hd., Pub.Serv.

Redington Museum
See: **Waterville Historical Society - Library and Archives** (20093)

Jules Redish Memorial Medical Library
See: **South Nassau Communities Hospital** (15432)

Redstone Scientific Information Center
See: **U.S. Army - Missile Command & Marshall Space Flight Center**
(16996)

★ 13766 ★
**Redwood Community Action Agency - Energy Demonstration Center -
Appropriate Technology Library** (Env-Cons)
904 G Street　　　　　　　　Phone: (707)444-3831
Eureka, CA 95501　　　　　　Lorna Montoya, Sec.
Subjects: Passive solar energy, energy conservation, weatherization, solar
retrofits, wind energy, wood stoves. **Holdings:** 1000 books; 18 bound
periodical volumes; 2 shelves of energy policy and planning documents; 2
shelves of California Energy Commission reports; 1 shelf of energy
curriculum; 3 VF drawers of general information files; 1 VF drawer of
organization and agency files. **Services:** Library open to the public and by
appointment.

★ 13767 ★
Redwood Empire Association - Information Center (Aud-Vis)
785 Market St., 15th Fl.　　　　　Phone: (415)543-8334
San Francisco, CA 94103　　　　　Jim Steenbakkers, Exec.Dir.
Founded: 1925. **Staff:** Prof 3. **Subjects:** Scenic, recreational, and travel
photos of nine counties in Northwestern California and Southwestern
Oregon. **Holdings:** 100 reference books; news releases and fact sheets; 5000
black/white photographic negatives; 500 color transparencies and slides.
Services: Interlibrary loan; copying; photographs and news releases
available without charge; special stories on this area prepared to order;
center open to the public by appointment. **Publications:** Redwood Empire,
Visitors Guide to California's North Coast, San Francisco and southern
Oregon; calendar of events, both irregular. **Remarks:** FAX: (415)543-8337.

★ 13768 ★
Reebie Associates - Library (Trans)
411 W. Putnam Ave., Suite 111
Box 1436　　　　　　　　　Phone: (203)661-8661
Greenwich, CT 06836　　　　　J.R. Thomson, Res.Assoc.
Founded: 1968. **Staff:** Prof 1. **Subjects:** Transportation - freight, rail, water,
trucking; statistics. **Holdings:** 2500 books and reports; 460 subject and
statistics files; annual reports; maps. **Subscriptions:** 50 journals and other
serials. **Services:** Library not open to the public. **Remarks:** FAX: (203)661-8886.

★ 13769 ★
Reed College - Eric V. Hauser Memorial Library - Special Collections
(Hist)
Portland, OR 97202-8199　　　　　Phone: (503)777-7702
　　　　　　　　　　　　　　Victoria Hanawalt, Coll.Libn.
Founded: 1911. **Staff:** 14. **Subjects:** College and Oregon history. **Special
Collections:** Simeon Gannett Reed papers (19th century Oregon business);
papers of Indian scout Edouard Chambreau, Thomas Lamb Eliot, poet
Philip Whalen. **Holdings:** 81.5 linear feet of archival material. **Services:**
Interlibrary loan; copying; collections open to the public with restrictions.
Automated Operations: Computerized public access catalog, cataloging, and
acquisitions. **Computerized Information Services:** DIALOG Information
Services, BRS Information Technologies, MEDLARS, Chemical Abstracts
Service (CAS), WILSONLINE; InterNet (electronic mail service).
Remarks: FAX: (503)777-7786. Telex: 4947538 REED LIB PTL.
Electronic mail address(es): HANAWALT@REED.EDU (InterNet).
Staff: Marilyn Kierstead, Rd.Serv.Libn.; Jennie McKee, Tech.Serv.Libn.;
Jack Levine, Acq.Libn.; Victoria Mitchell, Sci.Libn.

★13770★
Reed Smith Shaw and McClay - Law Library (Law)
1200 18th St., N.W., Suite 1000   Phone: (202)457-8970
Washington, DC 20036   Elizabeth C. Kossmann, Libn.
Staff: Prof 3; Other 2. **Subjects:** Law - communications, labor, taxation, health care; government contracts. **Holdings:** 20,000 books; 300 bound periodical volumes. **Subscriptions:** 175 journals and other serials; 10 newspapers. **Services:** Interlibrary loan; copying; library open to the public with restrictions. **Automated Operations:** Computerized cataloging and serials. **Computerized Information Services:** LEXIS, NEXIS, DIALOG Information Services, Dun & Bradstreet Business Credit Services, LEGISLATE, NewsNet, Inc., Dow Jones News/Retrieval, VU/TEXT Information Services, OCLC, DataTimes, Compu-Mark U.S. On-Line. **Remarks:** FAX: (202)457-6113. Telex: 64711. **Staff:** Lorraine DeSouza, Asst.Libn.; Allyn Dady, Ref.Libn.

★13771★
Reed Smith Shaw and McClay - Main Library (Law)
435 Sixth Ave.   Phone: (412)288-3084
Pittsburgh, PA 15219   Ronda W. Fisch, Hd.Libn.
Staff: Prof 4; Other 6. **Subjects:** Law, business. **Holdings:** 32,000 volumes. **Subscriptions:** 130 journals and other serials . **Services:** Library not open to the public. **Computerized Information Services:** WESTLAW, STN International, WILSONLINE, Dun & Bradstreet Business Credit Services, LEXIS, NEXIS, Compu-Mark U.S., Dow Jones News/Retrieval, DIALOG Information Services, VU/TEXT Information Services, DataTimes, LEGISLATE, ORBIT. **Publications:** Library Bulletin. **Remarks:** FAX: (412)288-3063. **Staff:** Maggie Moffett, Tech.Serv.Libn.; Louise Weimer, Ref.Coord.; Robert J. Sullivan, Ref.Libn.

★13772★
Reed Stenhouse, Ltd. - Research Department Library (Bus-Fin)
20 Bay St., 20th Fl.   Phone: (416)868-5520
Toronto, ON, Canada M5J 2N9   Olga Gil, Mgr., Res.
Founded: 1957. **Staff:** 2. **Subjects:** Insurance, risk management. **Holdings:** 300 volumes; clippings. **Subscriptions:** 80 journals and other serials. **Services:** Library not open to the public. **Computerized Information Services:** Info Globe, The Financial Post DataGroup, Infomart Online, LEXIS, NEXIS, QL Systems; internal database. **Remarks:** FAX: (416)868-5580. Telex: 06 219611.

Thomas F. Reed Memorial Library
See: **Davenport College - Kalamazoo Branch (4633)**

★13773★
Reed Travel Group - Travel Weekly Library (Publ, Rec)
500 Plaza Dr.   Phone: (201)902-1636
Secaucus, NJ 07094   Rose Lynn Boddie, Lib.Mgr.
Founded: 1972. **Staff:** Prof 1. **Subjects:** Travel and tourism. **Holdings:** 3500 books; 178 bound periodical volumes; VF drawers; 11,000 microjackets. **Subscriptions:** 95 journals and other serials. **Services:** Reader-printer retrieval of Travel Weekly articles; library open to the public by appointment. **Computerized Information Services:** CompuServe Information Service, InfoTrac, DIALOG Information Services, NEXIS. **Remarks:** FAX: (201)319-1755.

Walter Reed Archives
See: **University of Virginia - Health Sciences Center - Claude Moore Health Sciences Library (19504)**

Walter Reed Army Institute of Research
See: **U.S. Army - Medical Research & Development Command - Walter Reed Army Institute of Research (16992)**

Walter Reed Army Medical Center
See: **U.S. Army Hospitals - Walter Reed Army Medical Center - WRAMC Medical Library (17054)**

Lloyd Reeds Map Library/Urban Documentation Centre
See: **McMaster University (9952)**

William Marion Reedy Library
See: **St. Louis Public Library - Rare Book & Special Collections Department (14457)**

Mina Rees Library
See: **Graduate School and University Center of the City University of New York (6612)**

Michael Reese Hospital & Medical Center
See: **Humana Hospital-Michael Reese (7534)**

David L. Reeves Medical Library
See: **Cottage Hospital (4351)**

Reeves Library
See: **Moravian College (10721)**

Reeves Memorial Library
See: **Bridgeport Hospital (2115)**

★13774★
The Reference Center - (London) USIS Library (Educ)
55/56 Upper Brook St.
London W1A, England
Remarks: Maintained or supported by the U.S. Information Agency. Focus is on materials that will assist peoples outside the United States to learn about the United States, its people, history, culture, political processes, and social milieux.

★13775★
Reference Pictures - Library (Aud-Vis)
900 Broadway   Phone: (212)254-0008
New York, NY 10003   Doris Denhil, Pres.
Founded: 1950. **Holdings:** 7 million reference pictures covering a wide variety of subjects. **Services:** Library open to the public.

★13776★
Reflectone, Inc. - Library (Sci-Engr)
4908 Tampa W. Blvd.   Phone: (813)885-7481
Tampa, FL 33634   Betsy King, Libn.
Staff: Prof 1. **Subjects:** Flight simulation, aeronautics, engineering. **Special Collections:** Military standards; aircraft manuals. **Holdings:** 600 books; 800 technical reports. **Subscriptions:** 100 journals and other serials. **Services:** Interlibrary loan; library not open to the public. **Computerized Information Services:** DIALOG Information Services. **Remarks:** FAX: (813)885-1177.

★13777★
Reform Congregation Keneseth Israel - Meyers Library (Rel-Phil)
York Rd. & Township Line   Phone: (215)887-8700
Elkins Park, PA 19117   Sidney August, Libn.
Founded: 1870. **Staff:** Prof 1; Other 1. **Subjects:** Judaica. **Holdings:** 10,200 books; 200 bound periodical volumes. **Subscriptions:** 30 journals and other serials. **Services:** Interlibrary loan; library open to the public with permission.

★13778★
Reformed Bible College - Library (Rel-Phil)
3333 E. Beltline Ave., N.E.   Phone: (616)363-2050
Grand Rapids, MI 49505-9749   Dianne Zandbergen, Libn.
Staff: Prof 1; Other 8. **Subjects:** Reformed theology, religious education, missions, Bible study, cults. **Holdings:** 47,150 books; 3235 bound periodical volumes; 20 VF drawers; 3092 tapes; 994 volumes in microform; 706 filmstrips. **Subscriptions:** 271 journals and other serials. **Services:** Interlibrary loan; copying; library open to the public. **Automated Operations:** Computerized cataloging and acquisitions. **Networks/Consortia:** Member of Lakeland Area Library Network (LAKENET). **Publications:** Library handbook.

★ 13779 ★
Reformed Episcopal Church - Philadelphia Theological Seminary -
   Kuehner Memorial Library (Rel-Phil)
4225 Chestnut St.   Phone: (215)222-5158
Philadelphia, PA 19104-2998   Walter G. Truesdell, Libn.
Founded: 1886. **Staff:** 3. **Subjects:** Theology, church history, Oxford
Movement, English Reformation. **Holdings:** 35,000 volumes. **Subscriptions:**
85 journals and other serials. **Services:** Interlibrary loan; library open to the
public for reference use only. **Automated Operations:** Computerized public
access catalog and cataloging. **Networks/Consortia:** Member of
Southeastern Pennsylvania Theological Library Association (SEPTLA).
Remarks: FAX: (215)222-5164.

★ 13780 ★
Reformed Presbyterian Theological Seminary - Library (Rel-Phil)
7418 Penn Ave.   Phone: (412)731-8690
Pittsburgh, PA 15208   Rachel George, Libn.
Founded: 1810. **Staff:** Prof 1; Other 1. **Subjects:** Biblical studies, systematic
and pastoral theology, church history, devotional works, sermons. **Special
Collections:** Covenanter history and testimony; Psalms and psalmody.
Holdings: 29,913 books; 3859 bound periodical volumes; 131 boxes of
pamphlets; 1463 tapes; 58 reels of microfilm; 2504 microfiche. **Subscriptions:**
214 journals and other serials. **Services:** Interlibrary loan; copying; library
open to the public by appointment with fee for borrowing. **Automated
Operations:** Computerized cataloging and ILL. **Computerized Information
Services:** DIALOG Information Services, OCLC, WILSONLINE, EPIC;
CD-ROMs (WILSONDISC, REX). **Networks/Consortia:** Member of
Pittsburgh Regional Library Center (PRLC).

★ 13781 ★
Reformed Theological Seminary - Library (Rel-Phil)
5422 Clinton Blvd.   Phone: (601)922-4988
Jackson, MS 39209   Rev. Thomas G. Reid, Jr., Dir.
Founded: 1966. **Staff:** Prof 2; Other 4. **Subjects:** Theology, religion, Biblical
studies, Southern Presbyterianism, Christian education, marriage and family
therapy. **Special Collections:** George C. Blackburn Memorial Library
(Southern Presbyterian history and theology; 1100 volumes; pamphlets;
periodicals; church minutes; manuscripts); Southern Presbyterian
Collection. **Holdings:** 82,000 books; 11,000 bound periodical volumes; 7700
tapes; 30,000 microfiche; 2400 reels of microfilm. **Subscriptions:** 620
journals and other serials. **Services:** Interlibrary loan; copying; library open
to the public. **Automated Operations:** Computerized cataloging, ILL, public
access catalog. **Computerized Information Services:** BRS Information
Technologies. **Networks/Consortia:** Member of SOLINET. **Remarks:** FAX:
(601)922-1153. **Staff:** Chris Cullnane, Tech.Serv.Libn.

★ 13782 ★
The Refrigeration Research Foundation - Library (Sci-Engr)
7315 Wisconsin Ave., Suite 1200N   Phone: (301)652-5674
Bethesda, MD 20814   J. William Hudson, Exec.Dir.
Founded: 1944. **Subjects:** Handling of perishable commodities. **Holdings:**
500 volumes. **Subscriptions:** 50 journals and other serials. **Services:** Library
open to the public. **Remarks:** FAX: (301)652-7269.

★ 13783 ★
Refrigeration Service Engineers Society - Library (Sci-Engr)
1666 Rand Rd.   Phone: (708)297-6464
Des Plaines, IL 60016-3552   Mr. Nari Sethna, Exec. V.P.
Subjects: Refrigeration and air conditioning. **Holdings:** Figures not
available.

★ 13784 ★
Regent University - Law Library (Law)
Virginia Beach, VA 23464-9881
                    Phone: (804)523-7463
                    Richard A. Leiter, Dir.
Founded: 1979. **Staff:** Prof 4; Other 3. **Subjects:** Law. **Holdings:** 101,949
volumes; 633,969 microforms. **Subscriptions:** 1883 journals and other serials.
Services: Interlibrary loan; copying; library open to the public with
restrictions. **Automated Operations:** Computerized cataloging, acquisitions,
and circulation. **Computerized Information Services:** LEXIS, WESTLAW.
Remarks: FAX: (804)434-7051. **Staff:** Eric Welsh; Jack Kotvas; Donna
Bousch.

★ 13785 ★
Regina City Police Service - Planning Research - Library (Law)
1717 Osler St.   Phone: (306)777-9799
Regina, SK, Canada S4P 3W3   Lois Wallace, Plan.Res.Anl.
Founded: 1980. **Subjects:** Police science, criminology. **Holdings:** 1500 books;
150 reports. **Subscriptions:** 40 journals and other serials; 3 newspapers.
Services: Library not open to the public.

Regina Cleri Resource Library
See: **Diocese of Tucson** (4886)

Regina Coeli Seminary - American Catholic Union - Library
See: **American Catholic Union - Library** (517)

★ 13786 ★
Regina General Hospital - Health Sciences Library (Med)
1440 14th Ave.   Phone: (306)359-4314
Regina, SK, Canada S4P 0W5   Ms. Terry Bouchard, Hea.Sci.Libn.
Founded: 1942. **Staff:** Prof 1; Other 2. **Subjects:** Pediatrics, perinatology,
neonatology, obstetrics/gynecology, surgery, medicine, family practice,
radiology, psychiatry, nursing, allied health sciences. **Holdings:** 8000 books;
bound periodical volumes; VF drawers; AV programs. **Subscriptions:** 425
journals and other serials; 5 newspapers. **Services:** Interlibrary loan;
copying; library open to the public by appointment. **Automated Operations:**
Computerized acquisitions; public access catalog. **Computerized
Information Services:** BRS Information Technologies, MEDLINE; CD-
ROM (MEDLINE); Envoy 100 (electronic mail service). **Networks/
Consortia:** Member of Health Sciences Library Council. **Remarks:** Alternate
telephone number(s): 359-4514. FAX: (306)359-4723.

★ 13787 ★
(Regina) Leader Post - Library (Publ)
1964 Park St.   Phone: (306)565-8234
Regina, SK, Canada S4P 3G4   E. Jenkins
Staff: Prof 1; Other 3. **Subjects:** Newspaper reference topics. **Holdings:**
Newspaper clippings; photographs; government documents. **Services:**
Library not open to the public. **Remarks:** FAX: (306)565-2588. **Staff:** Susan
Sandery, Hd.Libn.

Regina Library
See: **Rivier College** (13958)

★ 13788 ★
Regina Urban Planning Department - Research & Library Section (Plan)
P.O. Box 1790   Phone: (306)777-7758
Regina, SK, Canada S4P 3C8   D.G. Mercer, A/Sr.Res.Plan.
Founded: 1976. **Subjects:** Urban planning, zoning, housing, heritage
conservation, land use and controls. **Holdings:** 5000 books. **Subscriptions:**
50 journals and other serials. **Services:** Interlibrary loan (limited); copying.
Special Catalogs: Publications lists, annual. **Remarks:** FAX: (306)525-1801.

★ 13789 ★
Region V Educational Service Agency - Library (Educ)
1210 13th St.   Phone: (304)485-6513
Parkersburg, WV 26101   Harold Hendricks
Staff: 1. **Subjects:** Education. **Holdings:** 2400 16mm films; 555 videotapes;
1300 other cataloged items. **Services:** Library open to civic organizations in
the 8 county region.

★ 13790 ★
Region West Research Consultants, Inc. - Library (Plan)
620 S.W. 5th Ave., Suite 1200   Phone: (503)222-9029
Portland, OR 97204-1426   Vikki Phloumer
Founded: 1968. **Staff:** 1. **Subjects:** Urban development and land economics,
land use regulation, demography, market research, finance. **Holdings:** 1500
items. **Subscriptions:** 20 journals and other serials; 5 newspapers. **Services:**
Library open to clients only. **Computerized Information Services:** Internal
databases (economics, financial development, and government issues).
Publications: TrendsWest.

Regional Arab Bureau of Education - Gulf Arab States Educational Research Center
See: **Gulf Arab States Educational Research Center (6806)**

Regional Conference on International Voluntary Service
See: **European FORUM on Development Service (5485)**

★13791★
Regional Educational Media Center 7 (Allegan and Ottawa Counties) (Educ)
13565 Port Sheldon Rd. Phone: (616)399-6940
Holland, MI 49424 Cynthia Kleinheksel, Media Spec.
Staff: Prof 1. **Subjects:** Education. **Holdings:** 2000 books. **Subscriptions:** 50 journals and other serials. **Services:** Center open primarily to educators in Allegan and Ottawa counties, Michigan. **Computerized Information Services:** DIALOG Information Services; CD-ROM (ERIC). **Remarks:** FAX: (616)399-8263.

★13792★
Regional Medical Center - Medical Library (Med)
900 Hospital Dr. Phone: (502)825-5252
Madisonville, KY 42431-1694 Melanie J. Holles, Med.Libn.
Founded: 1969. **Staff:** Prof 1. **Subjects:** Medicine, surgery. **Holdings:** 1200 books; 1765 bound periodical volumes; 840 audio cassettes; 4000 unbound journals. **Subscriptions:** 173 journals and other serials. **Services:** Interlibrary loan; copying; library open to the public with restrictions. **Computerized Information Services:** DIALOG Information Services, BRS Information Technologies; CD-ROM (CORE MEDLINE). **Remarks:** Alternate telephone number(s): 825-5253. FAX: (502)825-3411.

★13793★
Regional Medical Center of Orangeburg and Calhoun Countries - Library (Med)
3000 St. Matthews Rd. Phone: (803)533-2293
Orangeburg, SC 29115 Barbara Sifly, Dir., Med. Staff Serv.
Staff: 1. **Holdings:** 175 books. **Subscriptions:** 14 journals and other serials. **Services:** Copying; library open to the public with restrictions. **Remarks:** FAX: (803)533-2557. **Staff:** E. Sue Davis.

★13794★
Regional Memorial Hospital - Health Sciences Library (Med)
58 Baribeau Dr. Phone: (207)729-0181
Brunswick, ME 04011 Joan M. Barnes, Libn.
Founded: 1972. **Staff:** Prof 1. **Subjects:** Internal medicine, orthopedics, surgery, pediatrics, psychiatry, nursing. **Holdings:** 800 books; 2000 bound periodical volumes; 100 audio cassettes; 50 videotapes. **Subscriptions:** 146 journals and other serials. **Services:** Interlibrary loan; copying; SDI; library open to the public with restrictions. **Computerized Information Services:** DIALOG Information Services, MEDLINE. Performs searches on fee basis. **Networks/Consortia:** Member of Health Science Library and Information Cooperative of Maine (HSLIC).

★13795★
Regional Plan Association, Inc. - Library (Plan)
1211 Avenue of the Americas Phone: (212)398-1140
New York, NY 10018 Peter Haskel, Libn.
Founded: 1929. **Staff:** Prof 1. **Subjects:** Urban and regional planning, housing, transportation, land use, public administration, environment. **Special Collections:** Municipal and county planning reports. **Holdings:** 2000 books; 8000 research and technical reports; 8 file drawers of newspaper clippings; 8 VF drawers. **Subscriptions:** 302 journals and other serials. **Services:** Interlibrary loan; copying; library open to members. **Publications:** Accessions list, biennial - to members.

★13796★
Regional Transportation District - Research & Records Services (Trans)
1600 Blake St. Phone: (303)299-2120
Denver, CO 80202 Lou Gattoni, Mgr. of Int.Serv.
Founded: 1975. **Staff:** Prof 1; Other 2. **Subjects:** Public transportation, land use, urban planning, civil engineering. **Holdings:** 6275 books; 3000 reports; 2394 microfiche; 4 films; 38 videotapes; 8000 slides. **Subscriptions:** 250 journals and other serials; 11 newspapers. **Services:** Interlibrary loan; services open to the public by appointment. **Automated Operations:** Computerized cataloging and serials. **Computerized Information Services:** DIALOG Information Services; SYDNEY (internal database); DIALMAIL (electronic mail service). **Networks/Consortia:** Member of Central Colorado Library System (CCLS), Bibliographic Center for Research, Rocky Mountain Region, Inc. (BCR).

★13797★
Regis College - Library (Rel-Phil)
15 Saint Mary St. Phone: (416)922-0536
Toronto, ON, Canada M4Y 2R5 Richard Tetreau, Chf.Libn.
Founded: 1931. **Staff:** Prof 1; Other 4. **Subjects:** Theology, religion, allied subjects. **Special Collections:** Lonergan Centre (manuscripts; books; tapes; off-prints). **Holdings:** 98,000 books; 20,000 bound periodical volumes. **Subscriptions:** 445 journals and other serials; 5 newspapers. **Services:** Interlibrary loan (fee); copying; library open to University of Toronto and Toronto School of Theology students, and outside readers with approval of chief librarian. **Automated Operations:** Computerized cataloging.

★13798★
Register-Guard - Library (Publ)
975 High St.
Box 10188 Phone: (503)485-1234
Eugene, OR 97440 Suzanne Boyd, Lib.Mgr.
Founded: 1950. **Staff:** Prof 1; Other 1. **Subjects:** Newspaper reference topics. **Holdings:** 1500 books; newspaper clippings. **Subscriptions:** 25 journals and other serials; 10 newspapers. **Services:** Library open to the public with restrictions. **Remarks:** FAX: (503)683-7631.

★13799★
Registered Nurses' Association of British Columbia - Helen Randal Library (Med)
2855 Arbutus St. Phone: (604)736-7331
Vancouver, BC, Canada V6J 3Y8 Joan I. Andrews, Lib.Mgr.
Founded: 1969. **Staff:** Prof 2; Other 3. **Subjects:** Nursing and allied health. **Holdings:** 3000 books; 450 bound periodical volumes; 30 shelves of pamphlets; 400 audiotapes; 150 videotapes. **Subscriptions:** 125 journals and other serials. **Services:** Interlibrary loan; copying; library open to RNABC members and holders of temporary library cards. **Computerized Information Services:** MEDLINE, DIALOG Information Services; Envoy 100 (electronic mail service). **Remarks:** FAX: (604)738-2272. Electronic mail address(es): RNABCLIB (Envoy 100). **Staff:** Carol MacFarlane, Ref.Libn.

★13800★
Registered Nurses' Association of Ontario - Resource Centre (Med)
33 Price St.
Toronto, ON, Canada M4W 1Z2 Phone: (416)923-3523
Staff: Prof 1. **Subjects:** Nursing, health. **Special Collections:** RNAO Archives. **Holdings:** 2000 books; 258 bound periodical volumes; 8 VF drawers of reports. **Subscriptions:** 50 journals and other serials. **Services:** Centre open for staff use only. **Remarks:** FAX: (416)923-4494. **Staff:** Moira Lynch.

Regner Health Sciences Library
See: **St. Michael Hospital - Regner Health Sciences Library (14544)**

★13801★
The Rehabilitation Institute - Library & Learning Resources (Med)
6301 Northumberland St. Phone: (412)521-9000
Pittsburgh, PA 15217 Nancy J. Sakino-Spears, Dir.
Founded: 1981. **Staff:** 4. **Subjects:** Head injuries, pediatrics, diabetes, asthma, rehabilitation, spina bifida, Prader-Willi Syndrome. **Special Collections:** Hospital archives, 1902 to present. **Holdings:** 256 bound periodical volumes; 25 titles on microfiche. **Subscriptions:** 155 journals and other serials. **Services:** Interlibrary loan; copying; SDI; library open to the public. **Computerized Information Services:** BRS Information Technologies, NLM, Data-Star, OCLC, Human Resource Information Network (HRIN). **Networks/Consortia:** Member of BHSL. **Remarks:** FAX: (412)521-0570. **Staff:** Colleen Lako, Lrng.Rsrc.Spec.; Jennifer Cousins, Sch. Media Spec.; Belinda Doles, Tech.Asst.

★13802★
Rehabilitation Institute of Chicago - Learning Resources Center (Med)
345 E. Superior, Rm. 1671 Phone: (312)908-2859
Chicago, IL 60611 Ellie Wydeven, Med.Libn.
Staff: Prof 1. **Subjects:** Physical rehabilitation, spinal cord injury, stroke, vocational rehabilitation, brain trauma. **Holdings:** 1400 books; 20 bound periodical volumes; 200 films and videotapes; 50 slide/sound sets and filmstrips; 7 VF drawers. **Subscriptions:** 145 journals and other serials. **Services:** Interlibrary loan; copying; center open to the public by appointment. **Computerized Information Services:** BRS Information Technologies, DIALOG Information Services, NLM, OCLC; DOCLINE (electronic mail service). **Networks/Consortia:** Member of National Network of Libraries of Medicine - Greater Midwest Region, Chicago Library System, ILLINET, Metropolitan Consortium of Chicago. **Publications:** Recent Acquisitions, irregular - to staff. **Remarks:** Affiliated with Northwestern University.

★ 13803 ★
Rehabilitation Institute of Michigan - Learning Resources Center (Med)
261 Mack Blvd.   Phone: (313)745-9860
Detroit, MI 48201   Daria Shackelford, Med.Libn./Dir.
Founded: 1958. **Staff:** Prof 2; Other 1. **Subjects:** Physical medicine, rehabilitation, general medicine, physical therapy, occupational therapy, social service, patient education. **Holdings:** 3200 books; 3200 bound periodical volumes; 6 VF drawers of pamphlets; 5 boxes of reports; 1 VF drawer of reprints; 15 16mm films; 1000 35mm slides; 400 videotapes. **Subscriptions:** 125 journals and other serials. **Services:** Interlibrary loan; copying; center open to the public with permission. **Computerized Information Services:** BRS Information Technologies, NLM; CD-ROM. **Networks/Consortia:** Member of National Network of Libraries of Medicine - Greater Midwest Region. **Remarks:** FAX: (313)745-9863. **Formerly:** Rehabilitation Institute, Inc.

Rehabilitation International
See: **International Society for Rehabilitation of the Disabled/ Rehabilitation International** (8190)

★ 13804 ★
Rehabilitation and Research Center for Torture Victims - Library (Med)
Juliane Maries vej 34   Phone: 31394694
DK-2100 Copenhagen 0, Denmark   Svend B. Christensen, Hd., Doc.Ctr.
Founded: 1987. **Staff:** 3.2. **Subjects:** Torture victims - treatment and rehabilitation. **Holdings:** 13,000 books, serials, articles, reports, seminar papers, slides, videos. **Subscriptions:** 148 journals and other serials; 3 newspapers. **Services:** Interlibrary loan; copying; SDI; library open with written request. **Computerized Information Services:** Internal databases. **Publications:** Torture (journal on rehabilitation for torture victims and prevention of torture), quarterly. **Remarks:** FAX: 31395020. **Formerly:** International Rehabilition and Research Center for Torture Victims. **Also Known As:** Rehabiliterings-og Forskningscenter for Torturofre. **Staff:** Johanne Cummings; Kirsti Sparrevohn.

Rehabiliterings-og Forskningscenter for Torturofre
See: **Rehabilitation and Research Center for Torture Victims** (13804)

Rehn Gallery Archive
See: **State University College at Buffalo - Burchfield Art Center - Research Library** (15703)

★ 13805 ★
Reichhold Chemicals, Inc. - Library
407 S. Pace Blvd.
Box 1433
Pensacola, FL 32596
Defunct. Merged with Reichhold Chemicals, Inc. - Research Center Library to form Reichhold Chemicals, Inc. - Technical Library.

★ 13806 ★
Reichhold Chemicals, Inc. - Research Center Library
4201 Genesee St.
Box 210
Buffalo, NY 14225
Defunct. Merged with Reichhold Chemicals, Inc. - Information Resources Center to form Reichhold Chemicals, Inc. - Technical Library.

★ 13807 ★
Reichhold Chemicals, Inc. - Technical Library (Sci-Engr)
2400 Ellis Rd.
Research Triangle Park, NC 27709   Phone: (919)990-7500
Founded: 1950. **Staff:** Prof 1. **Subjects:** Chemistry - coatings, polymers, resins. **Holdings:** 1000 books; 1500 bound periodical volumes; 6 VF drawers of U.S. and foreign patents; U.S. chemical patents, 1987 to present, on microfilm. **Subscriptions:** 60 journals and other serials. **Services:** Interlibrary loan; center open to qualified persons by appointment. **Computerized Information Services:** DIALOG Information Services, STN International. **Formed by the merger of:** Its Information Resources Center and Research Center Library. **Staff:** T.O. Burrill, Info.Spec.

★ 13808 ★
Reid & Priest - Law Library (Law)
40 W. 57th St.   Phone: (212)603-2265
New York, NY 10019   Ruth Ulferts, Dir., Lib.Serv.
Founded: 1935. **Staff:** Prof 2; Other 4. **Subjects:** Law - securities, public utilities, international, tax. **Special Collections:** Securities and Exchange Commission (SEC) releases; state tax. **Holdings:** 20,000 books. **Services:** Interlibrary loan; library not open to the public. **Automated Operations:** Computerized cataloging and serials. **Computerized Information Services:** DIALOG Information Services, VU/TEXT Information Services, DataTimes, NewsNet, Inc., WESTLAW, LEXIS, Dow Jones News/ Retrieval, Information America, Dun's Legal Search, Prentice Hall Online. **Remarks:** FAX: (212)603-2298. **Staff:** Cassandra Morrow, Ref.Libn.

Reigner Medical Library
See: **Liberty Medical Center, Inc.** (9097)

Reimer Library
See: **Providence College & Seminary - Library** (13443)

Fritz Reiner Library
See: **Northwestern University - Music Library** (12086)

Reinert/Alumni Memorial Library
See: **Creighton University** (4427)

Max Reinhardt Archive and Library
See: **State University of New York at Binghamton - Special Collections** (15731)

★ 13809 ★
Reinhart, Boerner, Van Deuren, Norris & Rieselbach - Information Resource Center (Law)
111 E. Wisconsin Ave., Suite 1800   Phone: (414)283-8253
Milwaukee, WI 53202   Carol Bannen, Libn.
Founded: 1975. **Staff:** Prof 3; Other 2. **Subjects:** Law - taxation, real estate, labor, employee benefits, banking, corporate, securities. **Holdings:** 12,000 books; 200 cassette tapes; 40 reels of microfilm; 6 boxes of microfiche; 80 videocassettes. **Subscriptions:** 250 journals and other serials. **Services:** Interlibrary loan; copying; SDI; center open to the public with restrictions. **Computerized Information Services:** DIALOG Information Services, WESTLAW, LEXIS, VU/TEXT Information Services, Dow Jones News/ Retrieval; Work Producer Database (internal database). Performs searches on fee basis. **Networks/Consortia:** Member of Library Council of Metropolitan Milwaukee, Inc. (LCOMM), Private Downtown Law Librarians. **Publications:** New Book List, monthly; Current Education Opportunities in Law, monthly - for internal distribution only. **Remarks:** FAX: (414)283-8097. **Staff:** Cathy Loomis, Asst.Libn.

Reis Law Library
See: **Western State University - College of Law** (20300)

★ 13810 ★
Joy Reisinger Research Library (Hist)
1020 Central Ave.   Phone: (608)269-6361
Sparta, WI 54656   Joy Reisinger, Owner
Founded: 1975. **Subjects:** Genealogy, Canadian history, Quebec and Ontario history. **Special Collections:** Rapports de l'Archiviste du Quebec (complete collection); inventories of notaries; published marriage repertories of Quebec (complete collection); Ontario county and local histories; Repertoire des Actes de Bapteme, Mariage, Sepulture et des Recensements du Quebec Ancien (complete set) Wisconsin Historical Collections (complete collection); International Genealogical Index; locality, subject, and author/ title catalogs of the FHL; Loiselle index; Archives Nationales du Quebec parish records; index to Wisconsin vital records (pre-1907). **Holdings:** 270 linear feet of shelves. **Subscriptions:** 80 journals and other serials. **Services:** Copying; library open to subscribers by appointment. **Publications:** Lost in Canada Canadian-American Genealogical Journal; Shelf List of Lost in Canada Library. List of publications - available on request.

★13811★
Reiss-Davis Child Study Center - Research Library (Soc Sci)
3200 Motor Ave.   Phone: (310)204-1666
Los Angeles, CA 90034   Leonore W. Freehling, Libn.
Founded: 1950. **Staff:** Prof 1. **Subjects:** Child psychology, child psychiatry, child development, psychiatric social work, educational psychology, child analysis, psychoanalysis. **Special Collections:** Freud Collection. **Holdings:** 12,500 books; 3500 bound periodical volumes; 10 VF drawers of information files; 25 films; 500 audiotapes; 25 videotapes. **Subscriptions:** 125 journals and other serials. **Services:** Interlibrary loan; copying; SDI; library open to the public on payment of membership fee. **Computerized Information Services:** MEDLINE. Performs searches on fee basis. **Networks/Consortia:** Member of National Network of Libraries of Medicine - Pacific Southwest Region. **Publications:** Acquisitions list, quarterly. **Special Indexes:** Index to contributions by authors in collections (pre-1977). **Remarks:** FAX: (310)204-1405.

Click Relander Collection
See: **Yakima Valley Regional Library - Reference Department (20694)**

★13812★
Reliability Engineering & Management Institute - Technical Information Center (Sci-Engr)
7340 N. La Oesta Ave.   Phone: (602)621-2495
Tucson, AZ 85704   Dr. Dimitri Kececioglu, Prof./Cons.
Founded: 1963. **Staff:** 3. **Subjects:** Reliability; maintainability; availability; testing - life, accelerated, Bayesian. **Special Collections:** Mechanical reliability. **Holdings:** 3350 books; reports. **Services:** Copying; library not open to the public. **Remarks:** FAX: (602)621-8191.

★13813★
Reliance Group Holdings, Inc. - Corporate Library (Bus-Fin)
Park Ave. Plaza   Phone: (212)909-1888
New York, NY 10055   Laurie Meyers, Corp.Libn.
Founded: 1980. **Staff:** Prof 1; Other 1. **Subjects:** Investment, business, insurance, management. **Special Collections:** Investment and Insurance Reference Collection. **Holdings:** 400 books; 150 unbound periodicals. **Subscriptions:** 200 journals and other serials; 10 newspapers. **Services:** Interlibrary loan; library not open to the public. **Computerized Information Services:** DIALOG Information Services, Dun & Bradstreet Business Credit Services, Info Globe, Dow Jones News/Retrieval, LEXIS, NEXIS, VU/TEXT Information Services, Spectrum Ownership Profiles Online, Vickers Stock Research Corporation, TEXTLINE, NewsNet, Inc., DataTimes, InvesText, Invest/Net, Infomart Online, Securities Data. **Remarks:** FAX: (212)909-1864.

★13814★
Religious News Service - Library and Morgue (Publ)
Radio City Sta., Box 1015   Phone: (212)315-0870
New York, NY 10101   Jerry O'Guinn, Off.Mgr.
Founded: 1933. **Staff:** 1. **Subjects:** News stories of the world's religions. **Holdings:** Figures not available. **Services:** Library open on limited basis for research by authorized personnel. **Computerized Information Services:** NewsNet, Inc. **Remarks:** FAX: (212)315-5850. Library carries stories from the past 3-4 years only. Older files are available through the United Presbyterian Church in the U.S.A. - Presbyterian Historical Society in Philadelphia, PA.

★13815★
Religious News Service - Photograph Library (Aud-Vis)
Radio City Sta., Box 1015   Phone: (212)315-0870
New York, NY 10101   Sean B. Murray, Photo Ed.
Founded: 1945. **Staff:** Prof 1. **Subjects:** Religion, current events, social concerns. **Holdings:** 200,000 black/white photographs. **Services:** Library not open to the public.

Religious Society of Friends
See: **Society of Friends (15323)**

Rembert-Stokes Learning Center
See: **Wilberforce University (20424)**

Renaissance: Gender Identity Services - J2CP Information Services
See: **J2CP Information Services (8299)**

★13816★
Renew America - Library (Sci-Engr)
1400 16th St., N.W., Suite 710   Phone: (202)232-2252
Washington, DC 20036   Tina Hobson, Exec.Dir.
Founded: 1979. **Staff:** 12. **Subjects:** Environment, natural resources. **Holdings:** 300 books; 500 bound periodical volumes; 100 reports. **Services:** Library not open to the public. **Computerized Information Services:** Internal database. **Publications:** List of publications - available on request. **Special Indexes:** 1991 Environmental Success Index. **Remarks:** FAX: (202)232-2617. Renew America is an education and networking forum dedicated to the efficient use of all natural resources.

Renewable Energy Information Center
See: **Eco-Inventors & Eco-Entrepeneurs Chapter - Renewable Energy Information Center (5202)**

C.G. Renfro and Associates
See: **Acphanutics Corporation (54)**

Frederic G. Renner Memorial Library
See: **Charles M. Russell Museum (14151)**

★13817★
Rensselaer County Historical Society - Library (Hist)
59 Second St.   Phone: (518)272-7232
Troy, NY 12180   Stacy P. Draper, Cur.
Founded: 1927. **Staff:** Prof 1; Other 2. **Subjects:** Rensselaer County history. **Special Collections:** City directories; collection of photographs of Troy and Rensselaer County; Tibbitts Collection. **Holdings:** 2500 books; letters; local business daybooks; pamphlets. **Subscriptions:** 3 journals and other serials. **Services:** Copying; library open to the public for reference use only.

★13818★
Rensselaer Polytechnic Institute - Architecture Library (Art, Plan)
Greene Bldg.   Phone: (518)276-6465
Troy, NY 12180-3590   Virginia S. Bailey, Arch.Libn.
Founded: 1930. **Staff:** Prof 2; Other 2. **Subjects:** Architecture, art, city and regional planning, landscaping. **Special Collections:** Vance Architecture Bibliography Series; Historic American Building Survey (microfiche); Armenian Architecture (a documented photo-archival collection on microfiche); Garland Architectural Archives: Le Corbusier collection; Frank Lloyd Wright collection; Louis Kahn collection; Miles van der Rohe; Walter Gropius collection; Holabird & Roche and Holabird & Root collection; R. Bockminster collection; Global Architecture Series (documents, houses, architects, details, interiors, villages and towns). **Holdings:** 34,300 books; 6100 bound periodical volumes; 8 VF drawers of manufacturers' literature; 75,600 slides; 1900 maps; 37 architectural drawing sets. **Subscriptions:** 275 journals and other serials. **Services:** Interlibrary loan; copying; library open to the public. **Automated Operations:** Computerized cataloging, acquisitions, serials, and circulation. **Computerized Information Services:** InfoTrax (internal database); CD-ROMs (Art Index, Sweet's Catalog Files). **Staff:** Jeanne Keefe, Graphics Cur.

★13819★
Rensselaer Polytechnic Institute - Center for Manufacturing Productivity and Technology Transfer - Library (Comp Sci)
110 Eighth St.   Phone: (518)276-6000
Troy, NY 12180   Katherine N. Miller, Info.Mgr.
Founded: 1979. **Subjects:** Robotics, sensor technologies, computer-aided design and manufacturing, artificial intelligence, advanced powder processing. **Holdings:** 250 books; technical reports; theses; dissertations. **Services:** Library open to the public with restrictions on circulation. **Remarks:** FAX: (518)276-2990.

★ 13820 ★
Rensselaer Polytechnic Institute - RPI Libraries (Sci-Engr, Soc Sci)
Troy, NY 12180-3590   Phone: (518)276-8300
                                            Barbara A. Lockett, Dir. of Lib.
Founded: 1824. **Staff:** Prof 23; Other 28. **Subjects:** Science, engineering,
management, social sciences, architecture, humanities. **Special Collections:**
History of Science and Technology; technical reports; Geological Survey
Quadrangle Maps. **Holdings:** 251,119 books; 143,835 bound periodical
volumes; 541,219 microforms; 3620 recordings; 78,151 slides; 493,811
reports; 63,951 documents; 57,438 maps; government documents.
Subscriptions: 3484 journals and other serials; 40 newspapers. **Services:**
Interlibrary loan; copying; libraries open to the public. **Automated
Operations:** Computerized cataloging, acquisitions, serials, and circulation.
Computerized Information Services: BRS Information Technologies,
DIALOG Information Services, Dow Jones News/Retrieval, New York
State Education and Research Network (NYSERNet). **Networks/
Consortia:** Member of Capital District Library Council for Reference &
Research Resources (CDLC), SUNY/OCLC Library Network.
Publications: Library Guide; library use manuals; Guide to the Roebling
Collections; Guide to the George M. Low Papers. **Remarks:** FAX: (518)276-
8559. Telex: 6716050 RPITROU. **Staff:** Pat Molholt, Assoc.Dir.; Irving E.
Stephens, Hd., Bldg.Serv.; Richard Kaplan, Hd., Ref.; Marilyn K. Moody,
Hd., Tech.Serv.; Alice R. Wilson, Sci.Libn.; Colette Holmes, Inst.Libn.;
Polly-Alida Farrington, Info.Sys.Libn.; Elizabeth Christie, Ref.Libn.;
Kathleen Forsythe, Cat.Libn.; Kristina MacCormick, Cat.Libn.; John
Dojka, Archv.; Sheldon Wein, Mgt.Libn.; Susan Zappen, Acq.Libn.;
Virginia Bailey, Arch.Libn.

★ 13821 ★
Rentaw Foundation, Inc. - Library (Soc Sci)
Box 1275   Phone: (803)472-2750
Gramling, SC 29348   Carl Watner, Libn.
Founded: 1981. **Staff:** Prof 1; Other 1. **Subjects:** Libertarianism,
voluntaryism, anarchism, pacifism, Austrian and free market economics.
Special Collections: Rentaw Collection on voluntaryism. **Holdings:** 1500
books; 10 reels of microfilm; microfiche. **Subscriptions:** 16 journals and
other serials. **Services:** Interlibrary loan; copying; library open to the public
at librarian's discretion. **Publications:** The Voluntaryist Newsletter, 6 per
year - for sale.

★ 13822 ★
**Reorganized Church of Jesus Christ of Latter Day Saints - Library &
    Archives** (Rel-Phil)
RLDS Auditorium
Box 1059   Phone: (816)833-1000
Independence, MO 64051   Patricia Struble, Libn.
Founded: 1865. **Staff:** Prof 2; Other 1. **Subjects:** Mormon history,
Reorganized Latter Day Saint thought and doctrine, religion and theology.
Special Collections: Herald House publications; state histories related to
Latter Day Saint movement; Latter Day Saints pamphlets; archival
collection (500 linear feet of unpublished records, journals, manuscripts,
photographs). **Holdings:** 15,000 books; 2700 bound periodical volumes; 900
reels of microfilm; 250 cassettes. **Subscriptions:** 100 journals and other
serials. **Services:** Interlibrary loan; copying; library open to the public.
Networks/Consortia: Member of Kansas City Metropolitan Library
Network (KCMLN). **Special Indexes:** Index to current periodical
publications of the Reorganized Church of Jesus Christ of Latter Day Saints.
Staff: Ron Romig, Archv.; Kathleen Mosgrove, Asst.Libn.

★ 13823 ★
**Reorganized Church of Jesus Christ of Latter Day Saints - Services to
    the Blind** (Rel-Phil, Aud-Vis)
1001 Walnut
Box 1059   Phone: (816)833-1000
Independence, MO 64051   Carol White, Supv.
Staff: 2. **Subjects:** Religion. **Holdings:** 200 books on cassette; 1200 volumes
in braille; 30 large print pamphlets; brochures; instruction manuals; braille
calendars. **Services:** Braille transcription instruction and service;
thermoform and computer duplication of braille materials; services open to
the public.

★ 13824 ★
**Repertoire International d'Iconographie Musicale - Research Center for
    Music Iconography - Information Center** (Mus)
Ph.D. Program in Music
CUNY - Graduate Center
33 W. 42nd St.   Phone: (212)642-2709
New York, NY 10036   Dr. Barry S. Brook, Dir.
Founded: 1975. **Staff:** Prof 1. **Subjects:** Music iconography, portraits of
musicians, paintings with musical subjects. **Special Collections:** Martin
Bernstein Slide Collection; Viennese Classical Period Collection (Haydn,
Mozart, Beethoven, Schubert iconography - slides and transparencies);
Vienna Gesellschaft der Musikfreunde Portrait Collection (transparencies).
Holdings: 800 volumes; 1500 documents and pictures with accompanying
catalog card; 2000 slides; 8000 pictures. **Subscriptions:** 5 journals and other
serials. **Services:** Copying; center open to the public. **Automated Operations:**
Computerized cataloging. **Computerized Information Services:** Internal
database; BITNET (electronic mail service). Performs searches on fee basis.
Contact Person: Zdravko Blazekovic, Assoc.Dir. **Publications:** RIdIM/
RCMI Newsletter, semiannual; RIdIM/RCMI Inventories of Music
Iconography, irregular. **Special Catalogs:** The Musical Ensemble, circa
1730-1830 (exhibition catalog; 1978); Autour de la viole de gambe
(exhibition catalog; 1979); catalogs and indexes of artwork with musical
subject matter in individual museums (card); inventories of the music
iconography in the National Gallery (Washington) and the Art Museum of
Chicago; Pierpont Morgan Library manuscripts; Frick Collection (New
York); Cleveland Museum of Art. **Special Indexes:** Indexes to pictures
housed at the center and at other national RIdIM centers. **Remarks:** FAX:
(212)642-2642. Electronic mail address(es): 2DR@CUNYVMS1
(BITNET).

★ 13825 ★
Reptile Breeding Foundation - Library
R.R. 3, Box 1450
Picton, ON, Canada K0K 2T0
Defunct.

★ 13826 ★
Republic of China - Ministry of Education - National Central Library
    (Hum, Info Sci)
20 ChungShan S. Rd.   Phone: 2 3619132
Taipei 10040, Taiwan   Chung-sen Yang, Dir.
Founded: 1933. **Staff:** 360. **Subjects:** Chinese literature, library history and
science, history, art, humanities, social sciences. **Special Collections:**
Chinese rare books; maps; law books; official gazettes; Japanese-language
books; older materials on Taiwan and Southeast Asia; braille materials.
Holdings: 1.6 million books; 196,260 bound periodical volumes; 135,147
patents and documents; 307,040 microforms; 186,111 volumes of
manuscripts. **Subscriptions:** 4118 journals and other serials; 120 newspapers.
Services: Interlibrary loan; copying; SDI; children's services; blind readers'
services; library open to the public with restrictions. **Computerized
Information Services:** DIALOG Information Services, LEXIS, NEXIS;
CD-ROM. Performs searches on fee basis. Contact Person: Chia-ning
Chiang. **Publications:** National Bibliography of the Republic of China;
Directory of the Cultural Organizations of the Republic of China; News
Bulletin of the National Central Library; Bulletin of the National Central
Library; additional publications available. **Special Indexes:** Index to Chinese
Periodical Literature; Index to Chinese Official Gazettes; additional indexes
available. **Remarks:** FAX: 2 3110155.

★ 13827 ★
**Republic of Ireland - Department of the Taoiseach - National Library of
    Ireland** (Area-Ethnic, Info Sci)
Kildare St.   Phone: 1 618811
Dublin 2, Ireland   Patricia Donlon, Dir.
Founded: 1877. **Staff:** Prof 13; Other 42. **Subjects:** Irish studies; official
publications of Ireland, Great Britain, and Europe. **Special Collections:** Dix
Collection (early Irish printings; circa 5000 items); Thom Collection (Irish
and general literature, history, topography; circa 2000 items); Joly
Collection (Irish history and topography, French history; 23,000 volumes).
Holdings: 500,000 books; 15,000 reels of microfilm; 40,000 manuscripts;
5000 newspapers and periodicals; 3000 prints and drawings; 60,000
photographic negatives. **Subscriptions:** 1000 journals and other serials; 700
newspapers. **Services:** Copying; library open to the public with restrictions.
Publications: Irish Publishing Record, annual; Annual Report of Council
of Trustees; Sources for the history of Irish Civilisation. **Special Indexes:**
Clar Litridheacht na Nua-Ghaeilge 1850-1936 (Index to literature in Irish).
Remarks: Serves as a copyright library for Republic of Ireland. FAX: 1
766690.

★13828★

Republic of Ireland - National Archives (Law)
Bishop St.   Phone: 1 783711
Dublin 8, Ireland   Dr. David Craig, Dir.
Founded: 1988. **Staff:** Prof 6.5; Other 19. **Subjects:** Government departments, courts, private entities, individuals. **Holdings:** 85,000 cubic feet of archival materials. **Subscriptions:** 25 journals and other serials. **Services:** Copying; archives open to the public. **Publications:** Annual Report of Director. **Remarks:** FAX: 1 783650. National Archives is an amalgamation of The Public Record Office of Ireland (founded in 1867) and The State Paper Office (founded in 1702). **Staff:** Ken Hannigan, Sr.Archv.

★13829★

Republic of Korea - Rural Development Administration - RDA Library (Agri)
250 Seodoon-dong   Phone: 2101
Suweon 170, Republic of Korea   Heu Noon, Lib.Dir.
Subjects: Agriculture, rural sociology. **Holdings:** 56,000 volumes. **Remarks:** Maintained by Korea - Ministry of Agriculture and Fisheries.

★13830★

Republican Associates of Los Angeles County - Research Library (Soc Sci)
850 Colorado Blvd., Suite 103   Phone: (213)244-3602
Los Angeles, CA 90041   John H. Harriman, Pres.
Founded: 1951. **Staff:** Prof 2; Other 3. **Subjects:** Current issues; state and federal administrations; political officeholders; assembly, senate, and congressional districts. **Special Collections:** Richard Nixon Collection (120 items); campaign materials (100 items); Governor Jerry Brown clipping file; Governor George Deukmejian clipping file; President Reagan and Reagan Administration clipping file. **Holdings:** 170 VF drawers of newspaper clippings; Governor Ronald Reagan Press releases, 1966-1974 (complete and inclusive); Congressional Quarterly Weekly Reports, 1956 to present. **Subscriptions:** 29 journals and other serials; 11 newspapers. **Services:** Copying; library open to the public with restrictions (no Democratic candidates or officeholders). **Networks/Consortia:** Member of State of California Answering Network (SCAN). **Publications:** Newsletter, monthly - to members and Republican officeholders; campaign material - on request. **Special Catalogs:** Catalog of judicial appointments. **Special Indexes:** List of speeches by Governor Reagan, 1966-1974; list of appointments by Governor Reagan, 1966-1974; index of past and present political figures; index of current federal and California issues. **Formerly:** Located in Glendale, CA. **Staff:** Gene Wiberg, Exec.Dir.; William Graham, Res.Dir.

★13831★

Republican National Committee - Library (Soc Sci)
310 First St., S.E.   Phone: (202)863-8626
Washington, DC 20003   Doug Campbell, Lib.Dir.
Founded: 1936. **Staff:** Prof 1. **Subjects:** Government, legislation, politics, election results, demographic material, voting statistics, political history, presidential documents. **Special Collections:** Collection of Republican National Committee Proceedings of Nominating Conventions, 1856 to present. **Holdings:** 5000 books; microfilm. **Subscriptions:** 180 journals and other serials; 25 newspapers. **Services:** Library open to the public by special arrangement. **Computerized Information Services:** Mead Data Central, NEXIS.

Dr. Antonio Requena Library
See: **Lisandro Alvarado Foundation - Biblioteca Dr. Antonio Requena** (435)

★13832★

Research for Better Schools - Resource Center (Educ)
444 N. Third St.   Phone: (215)574-9300
Philadelphia, PA 19123   Peter J. Donahoe, Dir., Info.Serv.
Founded: 1978. **Staff:** Prof 1. **Subjects:** Elementary and secondary education. **Special Collections:** School restructuring (700 documents); Basic Skills (1200 documents); educational technology (600 items); Research for Better Schools (1400 documents); school improvement (1000 documents); training materials (150 documents); rural education (200 documents); educating at-risk youth (200 documents). **Holdings:** 1000 books; complete ERIC microfiche collection. **Subscriptions:** 92 journals and other serials. **Services:** Center open to the public by appointment. **Computerized Information Services:** DIALOG Information Services, BRS Information Technologies, ERIC; internal database; GTE (electronic mail service). **Special Indexes:** Indexes to special collections (online). **Remarks:** FAX: (215)574-0133. Electronic mail address(es): RBS.LAB (GTE).

Research Center of Islamic History, Art and Culture
See: **Organization of the Islamic Conference - Research Center for Islamic History, Art and Culture** (12564)

Research Centre for Management of Advanced Technology/Operations
See: **Wilfrid Laurier University - Research Centre for Management of Advanced Technology/Operations** (8980)

Research Center for Musical Iconography
See: **Repertoire International d'Iconographie Musicale** (13824)

★13833★

Research Center for Religion & Human Rights in Closed Societies - Information Center (Rel-Phil)
475 Riverside Dr., Suite 448   Phone: (212)870-2481
New York, NY 10115   Olga S. Hruby, Dir.
Founded: 1962. **Staff:** 4. **Subjects:** Religion and human rights in Communist and post-Communist countries; religious and atheistic literature published in Communist countries. **Holdings:** Periodicals; clippings; reports; occasional papers; underground publications from Communist countries. **Subscriptions:** 100 journals and other serials. **Services:** Center open to members and scholars by special arrangement only. **Publications:** RCDA, quarterly. **Special Indexes:** Index to RCDA, annual.

★13834★

Research and Development Associates for Military Food & Packaging Systems - Library (Food-Bev)
16607 Blanco Rd., No. 305   Phone: (512)493-8024
San Antonio, TX 78232-1940   David D. Dee, Exec.Dir.
Founded: 1947. **Staff:** 3. **Subjects:** Food and container developments. **Holdings:** 600 volumes. **Subscriptions:** 2 journals and other serials. **Remarks:** FAX: (512)493-8036.

Research and Development Center of the Caribbean
See: **University of Puerto Rico - Mayaguez Campus Library - Research and Development Center of the Caribbean** (19254)

★13835★

Research & Education Association - Library (Sci-Engr)
61 Ethel Rd., W.   Phone: (908)819-8880
Piscataway, NJ 08854   Carl Fuchs, Libn.
Staff: Prof 2. **Subjects:** Science and technology, mathematics, physics, chemistry. **Holdings:** 2000 books. **Services:** Library not open to the public. **Staff:** P. Weston.

★13836★

Research Foundation for Jewish Immigration, Inc. - Archives (Area-Ethnic)
570 7th Ave., 3rd Fl.   Phone: (212)921-3871
New York, NY 10018   Dennis E. Rohrbaugh, Archv.
Subjects: Biography, bibliography, oral history. **Special Collections:** International Biographical Archive of Central European Emigres, 1933-1945 (data on 25,000 emigres from German-speaking Central Europe). **Holdings:** 300 transcriptions of oral history interviews with German-Jewish emigres in the United States. **Services:** Archives open to the public by appointment; telephone and written inquiries accepted. **Publications:** Jewish Immigrants of the Nazi Period in the U.S.A. (series); International Biographical Dictionary of Central European Emigres 1933-1945. **Remarks:** Affiliated with the American Federation of Jews from Central Europe, Inc. **Staff:** Dr. Herbert A. Strauss, Sec. & Coord. of Res.

★13837★

Research & Information Services for Education - Montgomery County Intermediate Unit Library (Educ)
725 Caley Rd.   Phone: (215)265-6056
King of Prussia, PA 19406   Richard R. Brickley, Dir.
Founded: 1966. **Staff:** Prof 1. **Subjects:** Education, curriculum design, educational research, administration, methodology and evaluation, program dissemination. **Holdings:** 1000 volumes; 450 literature searches; 4 vertical files of newsletters; ERIC microfiche collection. **Subscriptions:** 100 journals and other serials; 50 newspapers. **Services:** Copying; library open to the public. **Computerized Information Services:** BRS Information Technologies, DIALOG Information Services; internal database. Performs searches on fee basis. Contact Person: Lois Perkins, Info.Spec. **Publications:** RISE Newsletter, 4/year. **Special Catalogs:** Search catalog (book). **Remarks:** FAX: (215)265-6562.

★ 13838 ★
Research Institute on Alcoholism - Library (Med)
1021 Main St.   Phone: (716)887-2511
Buffalo, NY 14203   Diane Augustino, Res.Sci. I
Founded: 1974. **Staff:** Prof 1.5; Other 1.5. **Subjects:** Alcoholism, drug dependence, and alcohol and drug abuse - physiological, psychological, sociological, biochemical, pharmacological aspects. **Holdings:** 6600 books; 1600 bound periodical volumes; 8 VF drawers. **Subscriptions:** 120 journals and other serials. **Services:** Copying; library open to the public for reference use only. **Computerized Information Services:** BRS Information Technologies, DIALOG Information Services, MEDLARS; BITNET (electronic mail service). **Networks/Consortia:** Member of Western New York Library Resources Council (WNYLRC), Library Consortium of Health Institutions in Buffalo (LCHIB), BHSL. **Publications:** RIA Publications List, annual; List of Serials, annual; Library Acquisitions List, bimonthly. **Remarks:** FAX: (716)882-6350. Electronic mail address(es): LIBRARY%RIAVAX@UBVMS (BITNET).

Research Institute of the Friedrich Ebert Foundation - Library of Social Democracy
See: **Friedrich Ebert Foundation (5198)**

Research Institute for Inner Asian Studies
See: **Indiana University (7799)**

★ 13839 ★
Research Institute for International Politics and Security - Library (Soc Sci)
Haus Eggenberg   Phone: 8178 700
W-8026 Ebenhausen, Germany   Dr. Gerhard Weiher, Libn.
Staff: Prof 30; Other 3. **Subjects:** International relations, security, economics; worldwide area studies. **Holdings:** 90,000 volumes; 10,000 clippings files. **Subscriptions:** 1400 journals and other serials; 100 newspapers. **Services:** Library open to the public with restrictions. **Automated Operations:** Computerized cataloging, acquisitions, serials, and circulation. **Computerized Information Services:** IRIS (International Relations Information System; internal database). Performs searches on fee basis. Contact Person: Volker Steidle, 70271. **Remarks:** FAX: 8178 70-216. **Also Known As:** Forschungsinstitut fuer Internationale Politik und Sicherheit. **Staff:** Peter Bottger; Matthias Bauermeister; Joachim Held.

★ 13840 ★
Research Institute for the Study of Man - Library (Area-Ethnic)
162 E. 78th St.   Phone: (212)535-8448
New York, NY 10021   Judith Selakoff, Libn.
Founded: 1955. **Staff:** Prof 1; Other 1. **Subjects:** Social sciences of the Caribbean and non-Hispanic West Indies. **Special Collections:** Caribbeana (pamphlets; dissertations; manuscripts; government publications). **Holdings:** 16,500 books. **Subscriptions:** 120 journals and other serials. **Services:** Interlibrary loan (limited); copying; library open to the public for reference use only. **Special Indexes:** Index to West Indian Periodical Literature at RISM; periodical holdings; Listing of RISM Associated Publications (punched card).

★ 13841 ★
Research Library for Edward Woodward (Theater)
P.O. Box 180412   Phone: (303)759-4828
Brooklyn, NY 11218   E.H. Pearson
Founded: 1986. **Subjects:** Edward Woodward - television and theater career, personal background. **Holdings:** 300 items (books, scripts, video- and audiotapes, record albums, books on audiotape, photographs). **Services:** Slide and video presentations on request; library open to the public with restrictions on borrowing. **Publications:** Archive newsletter, quarterly. **Special Catalogs:** 25 Research/Finders Books and Indexes. **Remarks:** Maintains three international library branches.

Research Library for Solid Waste
See: **U.S. Environmental Protection Agency (17473)**

★ 13842 ★
Research Medical Center - Carl R. Ferris, M.D. Medical Library (Med)
2316 E. Meyer Blvd.   Phone: (816)276-4310
Kansas City, MO 64132-1199   Richard Dalton, Lib.Dir.
Founded: 1963. **Staff:** Prof 1; Other 4. **Subjects:** Medicine, nursing. **Holdings:** 8500 books; 10,000 bound periodical volumes. **Subscriptions:** 404 journals and other serials. **Services:** Interlibrary loan; copying; SDI; library open to the public for reference use only. **Computerized Information Services:** MEDLARS, DIALOG Information Services. **Networks/Consortia:** Member of Kansas City Library Network, Inc. (KCLN).

★ 13843 ★
Research Planning, Inc. - Library (Env-Cons, Biol Sci)
1200 Park St.
P.O. Box 328
Columbia, SC 29201   Phone: (803)256-7322
Subjects: Environment and natural resource problems, coastal dynamics, aquaculture, biology, geochemistry, geology, hydrogeology, energy development, oil spills, hazardous materials, environmental mapping. **Special Collections:** Map collection. **Holdings:** 25,000 items. **Services:** Library not open to the public. **Remarks:** FAX: (803)254-6445.

★ 13844 ★
Research Publications, Inc. - Rapid Patent Service - Library (Bus-Fin)
1921 Jefferson Davis Hwy., Suite 1821-D   Phone: (703)413-5050
Arlington, VA 22202   Robert L. Genua, V.P., Gen.Mgr.
Founded: 1975. **Staff:** 40. **Subjects:** Patents - United States, international, documentation. **Holdings:** United States patents (microfilm; 1908 to present); international patents (microfilm; 1970 to present). **Services:** Copying; translations; document delivery; library not open to the public. **Computerized Information Services:** Produces Patent Status File and LitAlert databases (available online through ORBIT Search Service); DIALMAIL, ORBIT Mail (electronic mail services). Performs searches. **Publications:** Patentview (full text patents with drawings on CD-ROM). **Remarks:** Toll-free telephone number(s): 800-336-5010. FAX: (703)413-0127. Telex: 892362. Electronic mail address(es): RPIPAT (DIALMAIL, ORBIT Mail). **Staff:** Eleanor Roberts; Mark Hornick; John Sylvester; Cyndy Seegren.

★ 13845 ★
Research Technique, International - Library (Agri)
3111 Victoria Dr.   Phone: (619)445-6645
Alpine, CA 92001-2194   Dwight L. Roberts
Founded: 1967. **Staff:** 2. **Subjects:** Agricultural chemistry relating to fruit, with emphasis on soil, water, air, and wastes; agricultural science history; propagation. **Holdings:** 15,000 volumes. **Subscriptions:** 25 journals and other serials; 6 newspapers. **Services:** Library not open to the public.

★ 13846 ★
Research and Training Center on Independent Living - Library (Soc Sci)
BCR/4089 Dole
University of Kansas   Phone: (913)864-4095
Lawrence, KS 66045   Deanna Reinhard
Subjects: Independent living skills and technical assistance for disabled individuals; U.S. independent living centers (ILC's). **Holdings:** 220 volumes. **Services:** Lirary not open to the public. **Remarks:** FAX: (913)864-5323. Above telephone number also serves the deaf.

★ 13847 ★
Research Triangle Institute - Technical Information Center (Sci-Engr, Biol Sci)
Box 12194   Phone: (919)541-6455
Research Triangle Park, NC 27709-2194   Lois Melton, Libn.
Founded: 1960. **Staff:** Prof 5; Other 2. **Subjects:** Organic and inorganic chemistry, life sciences, health research, engineering, social sciences, environmental sciences, statistics, industrial processes, meteorology, pharmaceuticals and pharmacology, economics, toxicology, computer science. **Holdings:** 50,000 books. **Subscriptions:** 1125 journals and other serials. **Services:** Library not open to the public. **Automated Operations:** Computerized serials. **Computerized Information Services:** DIALOG Information Services, PFDS Online, BRS Information Technologies, STN International, MEDLARS. **Remarks:** FAX: (919)541-5985.

Reseau d'Innovations Educatives pour le Developpement en Afrique
See: Network of Educational Innovation for Development in Africa
(11415)

★ 13848 ★
**Resource Center for Nonviolence - Roy C. Kepler Library for
Nonviolence and Social Change** (Soc Sci)
515 Broadway   Phone: (408)423-1626
Santa Cruz, CA 95060-4621   Rosalie Pizzo-Strain, Off.Coord.
Founded: 1977. **Staff:** 1. **Subjects:** Theory and practice of nonviolence, peace education, draft resistance. **Special Collections:** Gandhi (300 volumes); Garland Library of War and Peace (300 volumes). **Holdings:** 4000 books. **Subscriptions:** 20 journals and other serials. **Services:** Library open to the public. **Remarks:** FAX: (408)423-8716.

★ 13849 ★
Resource & Research Center for Beaver County & Local History (Hist)
Carnegie Free Library
1301 7th Ave.   Phone: (412)846-4340
Beaver Falls, PA 15010   Vivian C. McLaughlin, Dir.
Founded: 1974. **Staff:** Prof 2. **Subjects:** Local history, genealogy. **Special Collections:** Beaver County newspapers, 1830 to present, on microfilm; obituaries, 1971 to present. **Holdings:** 3000 books; marriage and death notices; cemetery listings; census microfilm; Pennsylvania archives; Daughters of the American Revolution lineage materials. **Subscriptions:** 65 journals and other serials. **Services:** Interlibrary loan; copying; center open to the public for reference use only. **Publications:** Gleanings (genealogical journal), quarterly; The Beaver Countian, quarterly - by subscription; cemetery listings - for sale. **Special Indexes:** Index to census; index to deeds and articles; index to taxables through 1840, early marriages, early deaths, probate records; index to New Beaver County history through 1985. **Remarks:** FAX: (412)846-0370.

★ 13850 ★
Resources and Counseling for the Arts - Library (Bus-Fin)
75 W. 5th St., Rm. 429   Phone: (612)292-4381
St. Paul, MN 55102   Barbara Davis, Dir.
Founded: 1979. **Staff:** 5. **Subjects:** Arts management, business skills for artists, nonprofit management. **Holdings:** 500 books; 5 VF drawers of clippings, pamphlets, ephemera. **Subscriptions:** 20 journals and other serials. **Services:** Copying; library open to the public for reference use only by appointment. **Automated Operations:** Computerized cataloging. **Formerly:** United Arts - Resources & Counseling Division.

★ 13851 ★
Resources for the Future - Library (Env-Cons)
1616 P St., N.W.   Phone: (202)328-5089
Washington, DC 20036   Chris Clotworthy, Libn.
Founded: 1985. **Staff:** Prof 1; Other 1. **Subjects:** Economics, energy, natural resources, environment, agriculture. **Special Collections:** Complete RFF publications collection. **Holdings:** 6500 books; 350 periodical titles. **Subscriptions:** 88 journals and other serials. **Services:** Interlibrary loan; copying; library open to the public by appointment. **Computerized Information Services:** BRS Information Technologies, DIALOG Information Services, OCLC. **Publications:** Resources (newsletter), quarterly - available upon request; acquisitions list. **Remarks:** FAX: (202)265-8069.

★ 13852 ★
Response Analysis Corporation - Library (Soc Sci)
377 Wall St.
Box 158
Princeton, NJ 08542   Phone: (609)921-3333
                                     Anne R. Frihart, Libn.
Founded: 1979. **Staff:** Prof 1. **Subjects:** Survey research methodology, energy consumption and conservation, marketing and market research, advertising and advertising research, communications and media, employee relations. **Holdings:** 1200 books; 1 VF drawer of clippings; 56 reels of microfilm; 1400 internal company reports; 500 corporate annual reports. **Subscriptions:** 80 journals and other serials. **Services:** Interlibrary loan; copying; library open to the public with restrictions. **Automated Operations:** Computerized public access catalog and serials. **Computerized Information Services:** DIALOG Information Services; internal databases. Performs searches on fee basis for clients only. **Networks/Consortia:** Member of New Jersey Library Network, Northwest Regional Library Cooperative. **Publications:** BookRAC, monthly - for internal distribution only. **Special Catalogs:** Catalog of master records for company reports (book). **Remarks:** FAX: (609)921-2611.

★ 13853 ★
Resurrection Medical Center - Medical Library (Med)
7435 W. Talcott Rd.   Phone: (312)774-8000
Chicago, IL 60631   Laura M. Wimmer, Med.Libn.
Founded: 1953. **Staff:** Prof 1. **Subjects:** Medicine, administration. **Holdings:** 1307 books; 3671 bound periodical volumes; 624 cassettes. **Subscriptions:** 120 journals and other serials. **Services:** Interlibrary loan; library not open to the public. **Automated Operations:** Computerized cataloging and ILL. **Computerized Information Services:** MEDLINE, OCLC; DOCLINE (electronic mail service). Performs searches on fee basis. **Networks/Consortia:** Member of National Network of Libraries of Medicine - Greater Midwest Region, Metropolitan Consortium of Chicago, Chicago Library System, ILLINET. **Remarks:** FAX: (312)792-7900.

Retina Foundation
See: Eye Research Institute/Boston Biomedical Research Institute - Library (5539)

★ 13854 ★
Reveille United Methodist Church - Reveille Memorial Library (Rel-Phil)
4200 Cary Street Rd.   Phone: (804)359-6041
Richmond, VA 23221   Janet P. Sigman, Adult Libn.
Staff: Prof 5; Other 6. **Subjects:** Bible studies, devotions, travel, art, philosophy, psychology, fiction. **Holdings:** 11,062 books; 10 bound periodical volumes; tapes; pictures; slides; films; 4 VF drawers. **Subscriptions:** 18 journals and other serials. **Services:** Interlibrary loan; library open to the public. **Publications:** In-church book reviews, monthly; reading lists for United Methodist Women's Circles, annual. **Staff:** Mrs. William Guthrie, Cat.; Martha Kurtz, AV Rm. 33.

Revenue Canada
See: Canada - Revenue Canada (2841)

★ 13855 ★
Review & Herald Publishing Association - Library (Rel-Phil, Publ)
55 W. Oak Ridge Dr.   Phone: (301)791-7000
Hagerstown, MD 21740   Bruce Pierce, Libn.
Staff: Prof 1. **Subjects:** Seventh-Day Adventism, church history. **Special Collections:** Early Seventh-Day Adventist publications; William Miller Collection. **Holdings:** 40,000 books; 3000 bound periodical volumes; 2500 pamphlets; 18 VF drawers; Review & Herald, 1850-1971, on microcard. **Subscriptions:** 143 journals and other serials. **Services:** Copying (limited); library open for research on written request to chairman of library committee. **Special Indexes:** Index and catalogs to church periodicals (Adventist Review; Insight). **Remarks:** FAX: (301)791-7012. Telex: 705600 R&HPA MD UD.

★ 13856 ★
Revlon Group, Inc. - Revlon Research Center - Information Services (Sci-Engr)
2121 Rte. 27   Phone: (201)287-7650
Edison, NJ 08818   Lee J. Tanen, Mgr., Lib./Info.Serv.
Founded: 1955. **Staff:** Prof 1; Other 1. **Subjects:** Cosmetics, soaps, chemistry, perfumery, dermatology, pharmacology, microbiology, aerosols. **Holdings:** 11,000 books; 4000 bound periodical volumes; central files; research notebooks. **Subscriptions:** 300 journals and other serials. **Services:** Interlibrary loan; copying; SDI; library open to the public by appointment. **Automated Operations:** Computerized acquisitions, serials, and circulation. **Computerized Information Services:** DIALOG Information Services, STN International, NLM; internal database. **Publications:** RRC Abstracts, biweekly; Cosmetics Patents Abstracts, monthly - both for internal distribution only. **Special Indexes:** Index to research notebooks. **Remarks:** FAX: (201)248-2230.

★ 13857 ★
Rex Hospital - Library (Med)
4420 Lake Boone Trail   Phone: (919)783-3032
Raleigh, NC 27607   Barbara Zimmerman, Libn.
Founded: 1937. **Staff:** Prof 1. **Subjects:** Medicine, nursing. **Holdings:** 1650 books; 2000 bound periodical volumes; 4 VF drawers of pamphlets, brochures, clippings. **Subscriptions:** 100 journals and other serials. **Services:** Interlibrary loan; copying; library open to the public with restrictions. **Computerized Information Services:** MEDLARS; EasyLink (electronic mail service). **Remarks:** FAX: (919)783-9088. Electronic mail address(es): 62853836 (EasyLink).

★ 13858 ★
Rexene Products Company - Research and Development Library (Sci-Engr)
Box 3986
Odessa, TX 79760   Phone: (915)333-8470
Founded: 1957. **Staff:** 1. **Subjects:** Chemistry, chemical engineering, polyolefin polymers. **Holdings:** 4500 books; 5000 bound periodical volumes; 1000 pamphlets; 24 VF drawers of reports; 9 VF drawers of patents; 350 reels of microfilm of patents. **Subscriptions:** 30 journals and other serials. **Services:** Library not open to the public. **Computerized Information Services:** DIALOG Information Services, PFDS Online, STN International. **Remarks:** FAX: (915)333-8440.

★ 13859 ★
REXFOR - Centre de Documentation (Sci-Engr)
1195 de Lavigerie   Phone: (418)659-4530
Ste. Foy, PQ, Canada G1V 4N3   Danielle Dussault, Dir.
Founded: 1978. **Staff:** 2. **Subjects:** Forestry, lumber, wood panelling, medium-density fiberboard, pulp and paper. **Holdings:** 1900 books. **Subscriptions:** 46 journals and other serials; 20 newspapers. **Services:** Interlibrary loan; center not open to the public. **Automated Operations:** Computerized cataloging and circulation. **Computerized Information Services:** Internal database. **Remarks:** FAX: (418)643-4037. **Staff:** Rejeanne Fournier.

★ 13860 ★
(Reykjavik) American Library - USIS Library (Educ)
American Cultural Center
Neshagi 16
IS-107 Reykjavik, Iceland
Remarks: Maintained or supported by the U.S. Information Agency. Focus is on materials that will assist peoples outside the United States to learn about the United States, its people, history, culture, political processes, and social milieux.

★ 13861 ★
Reynolda House, Inc. - Library (Art)
Reynolda Rd.
Box 11765   Phone: (919)725-5325
Winston-Salem, NC 27106   Ruth Mullen, Libn.
Staff: Prof 1; Other 2. **Subjects:** American art and literature, art appreciation for children and adults. **Holdings:** 1850 books; 370 museum, gallery, special art collection catalogs; clippings and other items about American artists and American life; 3000 slides; musical recordings; compact discs. **Subscriptions:** 23 journals and other serials. **Services:** Copying; library open to the public with restrictions.

Reynolds-Alberta Museum
See: Alberta Culture and Multiculturalism (260)

Reynolds Audio-Visual Department
See: Rochester Public Library (13994)

★ 13862 ★
Reynolds Electrical and Engineering Company, Inc. - Coordination and Information Center (Sci-Engr, Energy)
3084 S. Highland   Phone: (702)295-0731
Las Vegas, NV 89109   Bernardo Maza, Supv.
Founded: 1979. **Staff:** Prof 8; Other 9. **Subjects:** Radioactive fallout, radiation monitoring, nuclear weapons testing, biological effects of radiation. **Special Collections:** U.S. Public Health Service Archive (effects of nuclear weapons testing on health; 76 reels of microfilm; 12,000 documents); U.S. Environmental Protection Agency's Las Vegas files 1955-1972 (30,302 documents); U.S. Department of Energy Historian Archives Office (102,443 documents); Los Alamos National Laboratory (12,014 documents); other agencies (48,071 documents). **Holdings:** 783 books; 43,336 reports; 95,462 letters and memos; 7772 data documents; 1548 Atomic Energy Commission staff papers; 3229 articles; 2277 listings; 2308 meeting minutes; 8527 clippings; 13,540 press releases; 3825 field and monitoring logs; 22,223 other cataloged items. **Services:** Copying; center open to the public. **Automated Operations:** Computerized cataloging. **Special Indexes:** KWIC author or and document indexes (microfiche). **Remarks:** FAX: (702)295-1808. Operates under contract to the U.S. Department of Energy. **Staff:** Martha E. DeMarre, Proj.Mgr.

Fred J. Reynolds Historical Genealogy Collection
See: Allen County Public Library (376)

Reynolds Historical Library
See: University of Alabama at Birmingham - Lister Hill Library of the Health Sciences (18171)

★ 13863 ★
Reynolds Metals Company - Alumina Division Technology - Technical Information Center (Sci-Engr)
Box 9911   Phone: (512)777-2676
Corpus Christi, TX 78469   Dolores J. Mancias Phegan, Div.Tech.Libn.
Founded: 1979. **Staff:** 1. **Subjects:** Aluminum industry, engineering. **Holdings:** 755 volumes; 75 file cabinets of internal documents; 2 VF drawers of patents; 6 VF drawers of journal articles; 20 VF drawers of drawings. **Subscriptions:** 115 journals and other serials; 7 newspapers. **Services:** Interlibrary loan; copying; center open to the public with restrictions. **Automated Operations:** Computerized cataloging and acquisitions. **Computerized Information Services:** DIALOG Information Services, BRS Information Technologies; INQUIRE (internal database). **Remarks:** FAX: (512)777-2218.

★ 13864 ★
Reynolds Metals Company - Manufacturing Technology Laboratory Library (Sci-Engr)
3326 E. 2nd St.   Phone: (205)386-9574
Muscle Shoals, AL 35661-1258   Mary Lou Screeton, Libn.
Founded: 1956. **Staff:** Prof 1. **Subjects:** Engineering, electrochemistry, aluminum production, material science, extraction metallurgy of aluminum physics, physical chemistry. **Holdings:** 1900 books; 700 bound periodical volumes; 11 VF drawers of patents. **Subscriptions:** 125 journals and other serials. **Services:** Interlibrary loan; library not open to the public. **Automated Operations:** Computerized cataloging and acquisitions. **Computerized Information Services:** DIALOG Information Services; INQUIRE (internal database); electronic mail service. **Remarks:** Alternate telephone number(s): 386-9574. FAX: (205)386-9612. Telex: 827 448 LRED. **Formerly:** Located in Sheffield, AL.

★ 13865 ★
Reynolds Metals Company - Technical Information Services Library (Sci-Engr)
401 E. Canal St.   Phone: (804)788-7409
Richmond, VA 23219   Jane Hockaday, Libn.
Founded: 1958. **Subjects:** Aluminum industry, metals and materials processes. **Holdings:** 500 books. **Subscriptions:** 20 journals and other serials. **Services:** Interlibrary loan. **Computerized Information Services:** DIALOG Information Services. **Remarks:** FAX: (804)788-7557. **Formerly:** Its Business and Technical Information Center.

★ 13866 ★
Reynolds Metals Company - Technical Information Services Library (Sci-Engr)
4th & Canal Sts.
Box 27003   Phone: (804)788-7409
Richmond, VA 23261   W. Jane Hockaday, Lib.Spec.
Founded: 1965. **Staff:** Prof 1. **Subjects:** Metallurgy, materials science, applied sciences, engineering, chemistry, physics. **Holdings:** 15,000 books; 4600 bound periodical volumes; 6200 microfiche; 300 microfilm cartridges; 2200 internal technical reports. **Subscriptions:** 200 journals and other serials. **Services:** Interlibrary loan; copying; library open to the public by appointment. **Computerized Information Services:** DIALOG Information Services. **Remarks:** FAX: (804)788-7557.

★ 13867 ★
R.J. Reynolds Tobacco Company - R&D Scientific Information Services Library (Sci-Engr, Agri)
Bowman Gray Technical Ctr., 611-12, 205C   Phone: (919)741-4360
Winston-Salem, NC 27102   Kenneth L. Rush, Mgr.
Founded: 1951. **Staff:** Prof 4; Other 7. **Subjects:** Tobacco, chemistry, biochemistry, agriculture, chemical engineering. **Holdings:** 28,000 books; 26,000 bound periodical volumes; 1769 unbound periodicals; 7460 internal reports; 1.5 million patents on microfilm. **Subscriptions:** 1340 journals and other serials; 6 newspapers. **Services:** Interlibrary loan; copying; SDI; library open to the public with permission. **Automated Operations:** Computerized cataloging, acquisitions, serials, and circulation. **Publications:** Current awareness bulletin. **Remarks:** FAX: (919)741-4682. **Staff:** Helen Chung, Sr. R&D Lit.Sci.; Nellie W. Sizemore, R&D Lit.Sci.; Richard W. Williams, R&D Lit.Sci.; Randy D. Ralph, Master R&D Lit.Sci.

Reynolds Research Center
See: **Hall County Museum - Stuhr Museum (6844)**

★ 13868 ★

Russell Reynolds Associates, Inc. - Library (Bus-Fin)
200 S. Wacker Dr., Suite 3600   Phone: (312)993-9696
Chicago, IL 60606-4958   Gerri Hilt, Dir. of Res.
Staff: Prof 7; Other 3. **Subjects:** Business, financial services, banking. **Holdings:** 1000 books; company annual reports; subject files. **Subscriptions:** 50 journals and other serials. **Services:** Interlibrary loan; copying; library open to the public by appointment. **Automated Operations:** Computerized cataloging. **Computerized Information Services:** DIALOG Information Services, Dow Jones News/Retrieval, Dun & Bradstreet Business Credit Services, NEXIS, VU/TEXT Information Services; Compulog (internal database). **Remarks:** FAX: (312)876-1919. **Staff:** Patricia Mortensen, Sr.Res.Assoc.; Kim Agriesti, Anl.; Brenda Stenger, Res.Assoc.; Linda Feldman, Anl.; Rob Tillman, Anl.

Z. Smith Reynolds Library
See: **Wake Forest University - Z. Smith Reynolds Library (19942)**

Rheinische Landesbibliothek
See: **Germany - Rhenish Regional Library (6452)**

Rhenish Regional Library
See: **Germany - Rhenish Regional Library (6452)**

J.B. and L.E. Rhine Archives
See: **Foundation for Research on the Nature of Man - Library/Archives (6047)**

★ 13869 ★

Rhode Island Historical Society - Library (Hist)
121 Hope St.   Phone: (401)331-8575
Providence, RI 02906   Madeleine B. Telfeyan, Lib.Dir.
Founded: 1822. **Staff:** Prof 5. **Subjects:** Rhode Island history, New England genealogy, local history. **Special Collections:** Film Archives (feature films, newsreels, TV footage on Rhode Island); Rhode Island newspapers; Rhode Island imprints; business history. **Holdings:** 150,000 volumes; 1500 linear feet of manuscripts; 12,000 reels of microfilm of newspapers. **Subscriptions:** 1000 journals and other serials; 1000 newspapers. **Services:** Interlibrary loan; copying; library open to the public for reference use only on a seasonally variable scedule. **Automated Operations:** Computerized cataloging. **Networks/Consortia:** Member of Consortium of Rhode Island Academic and Research Libraries, Inc. (CRIARL), Rhode Island Library Network (RHILINET), NELINET, Inc. **Publications:** Rhode Island History, quarterly - to members, by subscription to institutions. **Special Indexes:** Indexes to the Rhode Island Census for 1850, 1860 and 1865 (card). **Remarks:** FAX: (401)751-7930. **Staff:** Cynthia J. Bendroth, Mss.Cur.; Denise Bastien, Graphics Cur.; Charlene S. Baer, Asst. Graphics Cur.; Revathi Narsu, Tech.Serv.Libn.; Patricia Redfearn, Tech.Serv.Libn.; Marilyn I. Glantz, Asst.Tech.Serv.Libn.; Maureen Taylor, Ref.Libn.

★ 13870 ★

Rhode Island Hospital - Peters Health Sciences Library (Med)
593 Eddy St.   Phone: (401)277-4671
Providence, RI 02902   Irene M. Lathrop, Dir., Lib.Serv.
Founded: 1931. **Staff:** Prof 5; Other 7. **Subjects:** Medicine, medical specialities, nursing, hospital administration. **Special Collections:** Pratt Collection in Hospital Administration. **Holdings:** 9000 books; 11,000 bound periodical volumes. **Subscriptions:** 602 journals and other serials. **Services:** Interlibrary loan; copying; AV facilities; library open to the public with restrictions. **Automated Operations:** Computerized cataloging. **Computerized Information Services:** MEDLINE, OCLC. **Networks/Consortia:** Member of Consortium of Rhode Island Academic and Research Libraries, Inc. (CRIARL), NELINET, Inc. **Publications:** Library Access (newsletter); Peters Library Guides. **Remarks:** FAX: (401)277-8260.

★ 13871 ★

Rhode Island Jewish Historical Association - Library (Area-Ethnic)
130 Sessions St.   Phone: (401)331-1360
Providence, RI 02906   Eleanor F. Horvitz, Libn./Archv.
Founded: 1951. **Staff:** Prof 1; Other 1. **Subjects:** History of Rhode Island Jews, Jews in the United States. **Special Collections:** Family papers; papers and pictures of organizations and institutions; oral history tapes. **Holdings:** 114 square feet of books. **Subscriptions:** 13 journals and other serials. **Services:** Library open to the public in presence of librarian. **Computerized Information Services:** Membership lists (internal database). **Publications:** Rhode Island Jewish Historical Notes, annual - to members and by subscription; newsletter. **Special Indexes:** Rhode Island Jewish Historical Notes Cumulative Index, 1954-1978 (volumes 1-7); Volume 10, 1989, No. 3, part A (annotated bibliograph of materials on history of Rhode Island Jews in Rhode Island depositories, 1967-1989); Volume 10, 1989, No. 3, part B; Volume 10, 1990, No. 4 (includes index for Volume 10).

Rhode Island Oral History Project
See: **University of Rhode Island (19267)**

★ 13872 ★

Rhode Island Public Expenditure Council - Library (Soc Sci)
300 Richmond St.   Phone: (401)521-6320
Providence, RI 02903-4214   Gary S. Sasse, Exec.Dir.
Founded: 1932. **Staff:** Prof 3; Other 2. **Subjects:** State and local government administration and finance. **Holdings:** 200 books; 500 research reports and government documents. **Subscriptions:** 100 journals and other serials. **Services:** Copying; library open to the public for reference use only on request. **Publications:** RIPEC Comments on Your Government, irregular - to members and government officials; Budget Watch; Reform Watch.

★ 13873 ★

Rhode Island School for the Deaf - Library (Educ)
Corliss Park   Phone: (401)277-3525
Providence, RI 02908   Gerry Dunn, Libn.
Remarks: No further information was supplied by respondent.

★ 13874 ★

Rhode Island School of Design - Library (Art)
2 College St.   Phone: (401)454-6225
Providence, RI 02903   Carol S. Terry, Dir.
Founded: 1878. **Staff:** Prof 5; Other 10. **Subjects:** Fine arts, architecture, applied arts. **Special Collections:** Lowthorpe Collection of Landscape Architecture (1200 volumes); artists' books (400 volumes). **Holdings:** 71,591 books; 8670 bound periodical volumes; 121,628 slides; 390,625 clippings; 18,946 mounted photographs; 1700 posters and color reproductions; 780 phonograph records; 241 videotapes. **Subscriptions:** 377 journals and other serials. **Services:** Interlibrary loan; copying; library open to the public for reference use only. **Computerized Information Services:** OCLC. **Networks/Consortia:** Member of Consortium of Rhode Island Academic and Research Libraries, Inc. (CRIARL), NELINET, Inc. **Remarks:** FAX: (401)831-7106. **Staff:** Robert Garzillo, Tech.Serv.Libn.; Laurie Whitehill, Rd.Serv.Libn.; Debra Kruse, Vis.Res.Libn.; Elinor Nacheman, Cat./Ref.Libn.

★ 13875 ★

Rhode Island State Archives (Hist)
337 Westminster St.   Phone: (401)277-2353
Providence, RI 02903-3302   Timothy A. Slavin, State Arch.
Staff: 1. **Subjects:** Rhode Island history. **Special Collections:** Private letters of Ellery and Huntington. **Holdings:** Acts and resolves of the General Assembly; colony records; Revolutionary War records; petitions and reports to the General Assembly; military and maritime charters. **Services:** Copying; archives open to the public with restrictions.

★ 13876 ★

Rhode Island (State) Department of Administration - Planning - Office of Municipal Affairs - Reference Library (Plan, Soc Sci)
1 Capitol Hill   Phone: (401)277-3975
Providence, RI 02908-5893   Patricia Chorney, Hd.Libn.
Founded: 1969. **Staff:** Prof 1. **Subjects:** Planning, U.S. census, public administration and finance, transportation, economics, human services, land use, zoning. **Holdings:** 4000 volumes. **Subscriptions:** 50 journals and other serials; 6 newspapers. **Services:** Library open to the public by appointment. **Staff:** Paul Egan, Census Libn.

★13877★
Rhode Island (State) Department of Economic Development - Research
  Division Library (Bus-Fin)
7 Jackson Walkway   Phone: (401)277-2601
Providence, RI 02903   Vincent K. Harrington, Res.Dir.
Subjects: Economic statistics. **Holdings:** Figures not available.
Computerized Information Services: Economic Statistics on Rhode Island
(internal database); CD-ROM. **Remarks:** Telex: WUI 6814132. **Remarks:**
FAX: (401)277-2102.

★13878★
Rhode Island (State) Department of Elderly Affairs - Eve M. Goldberg
  Library and Resource Center
160 Pine St.
Providence, RI 02903
Founded: 1958. **Subjects:** Gerontology, geriatrics, retirement. **Special
Collections:** Legislation and programs relating to aging. **Holdings:** 600
volumes; 50 state studies on aging; 100 pamphlets; 10 films; 40 video
cassettes. **Remarks:** Currently inactive.

★13879★
Rhode Island (State) Department of Health - Gertrude E. Sturges
  Memorial Library (Med)
3 Capitol Hill, Rm. 407   Phone: (401)277-2506
Providence, RI 02908   Barry J. Levin, Libn.
Founded: 1939. **Staff:** Prof 1; Other 1. **Subjects:** Public health, preventive
medicine, nursing. **Holdings:** 9400 books and pamphlets; 1200 bound
periodical volumes; 4 drawers of newsletters; 2 cabinets of vertical files.
Subscriptions: 200 journals and other serials; 5 newspapers. **Services:**
Interlibrary loan; copying; library open to the public. **Automated
Operations:** Computerized ILL (DOCLINE). **Computerized Information
Services:** MEDLARS, BRS/COLLEAGUE. **Networks/Consortia:**
Member of Association of Rhode Island Health Sciences Librarians
(ARIHSL). **Remarks:** FAX: (401)277-6548.

★13880★
Rhode Island (State) Department of State Library Services (Info Sci)
300 Richmond St.   Phone: (401)277-2726
Providence, RI 02903-4222   Barbara F. Weaver, Dir.
Founded: 1964. **Staff:** Prof 20; Other 11. **Special Collections:** Regional
Library for the Blind and Physically Handicapped; Professional Library
Science Collection (3300 volumes); books on handicaps (350 volumes).
Holdings: 15,000 books; 410 bound periodical volumes; pamphlet files.
Subscriptions: 180 journals and other serials. **Services:** Interlibrary loan;
copying; library open to librarians, library school students, trustees, and the
blind and handicapped. **Automated Operations:** Computerized cataloging
and circulation. **Computerized Information Services:** DIALOG
Information Services, OCLC, WILSONLINE; electronic mail service.
Networks/Consortia: Member of NELINET, Inc., Rhode Island Library
Network (RHILINET). **Publications:** Newsletter, bimonthly - to libraries.
Special Catalogs: Books about Handicaps (book); Non-print Media:
Accession List (book). **Remarks:** Administers grants-in-aid to public
libraries, serves as the Regional Library for the Blind and Handicapped, and
gives professional leadership and consultant services for the development of
improved library service. **Remarks:** FAX: (401)351-1311. **Staff:** Beth Perry,
Chf., Reg.Lib. for Blind; Howard Boksenbaum, Chf., Lib.Plan./Dev./
Info.Serv.; Dorothy Frechette, Dp.Dir.

★13881★
Rhode Island (State) Department of Transportation - Planning Division -
  Library (Trans)
State Office Bldg.
2 Capitol Hill   Phone: (401)277-2694
Providence, RI 02903   Brenda Myette, Sr.Plan.
Staff: Prof 1. **Subjects:** Transportation. **Holdings:** 7500 volumes.
Subscriptions: 12 journals and other serials. **Services:** Library open to the
public by appointment. **Remarks:** FAX: (401)277-6038.

★13882★
Rhode Island (State) Governor's Office of Housing & Energy - Library
  (Energy)
275 Westminster St.   Phone: (401)277-3370
Providence, RI 02903-3393   Julie Capabianco, Assoc.Exec.Asst.
Founded: 1979. **Staff:** 1. **Subjects:** Energy conservation, oil, gas, renewables.
Special Collections: Appropriate technology. **Holdings:** 2000 books.
Services: Copying; library open to the public. **Remarks:** FAX: (401)277-
1260.

★13883★
Rhode Island (State) Law Library (Law)
Providence County Court House
250 Benefit St.   Phone: (401)277-3275
Providence, RI 02903   Kendall F. Svengalis, State Law Libn.
Founded: 1827. **Staff:** Prof 5; Other 2. **Subjects:** Law. **Special Collections:**
Rare law books. **Holdings:** 110,000 volumes. **Subscriptions:** 363 journals and
other serials; 9 newspapers. **Services:** Interlibrary loan; copying; library
open to the public. **Automated Operations:** Computerized cataloging.
Computerized Information Services: WESTLAW, NEXIS, OCLC.
Networks/Consortia: Member of New England Law Library Consortium
(NELLCO). **Remarks:** Maintained by Rhode Island State Supreme Court.
FAX: (401)277-3865. **Staff:** Sondra L. Giles, Dp. Law Libn.; Karen Quinn,
Hd. of Res.Serv.; Marcia LaKomski, Ref.Libn.; Colleen McConaghy, Hd.
of Govt.Docs.

★13884★
Rhode Island (State) Library (Info Sci, Law)
State House, Rm. 208   Phone: (401)277-2473
Providence, RI 02903   Thomas R. Evans, State Libn.
Founded: 1851. **Staff:** Prof 3; Other 2. **Subjects:** Legislative law; reference
and research. **Special Collections:** Rhode Island history and law. **Holdings:**
155,000 books; 260,000 U.S. Government documents. **Subscriptions:** 86
journals and other serials; 50 newspapers. **Services:** Interlibrary loan;
copying; library open to the public with restrictions. **Automated Operations:**
Computerized cataloging. **Computerized Information Services:** J-text.
Networks/Consortia: Member of NELINET, Inc. **Publications:** Checklist
of Rhode Island State Documents, quarterly. **Special Catalogs:** Reports filed
for all state agencies with special emphasis on governor's office and
legislative materials. **Staff:** Margot McLaren, Tech.Serv.Libn.; Civia A.
White, Gov.Docs.Prof.

Rhode Island State Supreme Court - Rhode Island State Law Library
See: **Rhode Island (State) Law Library** (13883)

★13885★
Rhododendron Species Foundation - Lawrence J. Pierce Rhododendron
  Library (Biol Sci)
2525 S. 336th St.
Box 3798   Phone: (206)927-6960
Federal Way, WA 98063-3798   Frances P. Harrison, Chm., Lib.Comm.
Staff: Prof 2; Other 3. **Subjects:** Rhododendrons, azaleas, companion plants,
trees and shrubs, general horticulture, plant explorers. **Special Collections:**
Collections of field notes, photographs, and personal memorabilia of recent
plant collectors. **Holdings:** 1000 books; 60 bound periodical volumes; 1500
files of other cataloged items. **Subscriptions:** 20 journals and other serials;
28 newsletters. **Services:** Copying; library open to the public. **Automated
Operations:** Computerized cataloging. **Computerized Information Services:**
Internal database. Performs searches on fee basis. **Networks/Consortia:**
Member of Council on Botanical Horticultural Libraries. **Publications:**
Selected Rhododendron Bibliography.

★13886★
Rhone-Poulenc Ag Company - Library Services Group (Sci-Engr, Agri)
2 T.W. Alexander Dr.
Box 12014   Phone: (919)549-2649
Research Triangle Park, NC 27709-2014   Valerie Eslyn Wolford, Mgr.
Founded: 1981. **Staff:** Prof 1; Other 3. **Subjects:** Biochemistry,
biotechnology, agricultural marketing, plant growth regulators, weed
identification and control, insect identification and control, organic
chemistry. **Holdings:** 13,000 books; 5200 bound periodical volumes; 700
volumes of Agricultural Market Reports; 100 VF drawers of statistics,
product information; crop reports; 2000 reels of microfilm; 21,000
microfiche. **Subscriptions:** 250 journals and other serials. **Services:**
Interlibrary loan; library open to the public by appointment for reference use
only. **Computerized Information Services:** DIALOG Information Services,
PFDS Online, Chemical Abstracts Service (CAS), National Pesticide
Information Retrieval System (NPIRS), OCLC, InvesText, Dow Jones
News/Retrieval, Data-Star. **Networks/Consortia:** Member of SOLINET.
Remarks: FAX: (919)549-4168. **Staff:** Deborah K. Doerr; Susan C. Elliott;
Kathryn L. Flynn.

★ 13887 ★
Rhone-Poulenc, Inc. - Information Center (Sci-Engr)
9800 Bluegrass Pkwy.   Phone: (502)499-4020
Jeffersontown, KY 40299   John J. Vaccaro, Sr.Info.Spec.
Founded: 1947. **Staff:** Prof 2. **Subjects:** Polymer chemistry, organic chemistry, general physics, mathematics, paper technology. **Holdings:** 2500 books; 4500 bound periodical volumes; U.S. chemical patents, 1968 to present, on microfilm. **Subscriptions:** 180 journals and other serials. **Services:** Center open to the public by appointment. **Computerized Information Services:** DIALOG Information Services, PFDS Online, Chemical Information Systems, Inc. (CIS), VU/TEXT Information Services, Chemical Abstracts Service (CAS), Occupational Health Services, Inc. (OHS), MEDLARS; InterNet (electronic mail service). **Remarks:** FAX: (502)499-4141. Electronic mail address(es): johnu@info.uucp (InterNet). **Formerly:** Hi-Tek Polymers, Inc. - Technical Information Center.

★ 13888 ★
Rhone-Poulenc, Inc. - Research Library (Sci-Engr)
CN 7500   Phone: (609)860-4465
Cranbery, NJ 08512-7500   V. Vukov, Mgr.
Founded: 1990. **Staff:** Prof 2. **Subjects:** Chemistry - monomers, polymers, surfactants, specialty chemicals. **Special Collections:** Company documents. **Holdings:** 4500 books. **Subscriptions:** 180 journals. **Services:** Interlibrary loan; copying; SDI. **Automated Operations:** INMAGIC. **Computerized Information Services:** DIALOG Information Services, STN International, NLM. Performs searches on fee basis. **Remarks:** FAX: (609)860-4522. **Staff:** D. Bentivenga.

★ 13889 ★
Rhone-Poulenc Rorer - Armour Pharmaceutical Company - Library (Med)
Box 511   Phone: (815)932-6771
Kankakee, IL 60901   Mary Blunk, Libn.
Staff: 1. **Subjects:** Chemistry, biology, medicine, pharmacy. **Holdings:** 1000 books; 2000 bound periodical volumes. **Subscriptions:** 200 journals and other serials. **Services:** Interlibrary loan; library not open to the public. **Networks/Consortia:** Member of Chicago and South Consortium.

★ 13890 ★
Rhone-Poulenc Rorer Central Research - Library (Med)
640 Allendale Rd.   Phone: (215)962-3937
King of Prussia, PA 19406   Cynthia Supeau, Mgr.
Staff: Prof 5; Other 3. **Subjects:** Organic chemistry, biochemistry, pharmacology, medicine, pharmacy, biotechnology. **Holdings:** 10,000 books; 45,000 bound periodical volumes; 1500 reels of microfilm. **Subscriptions:** 800 journals and other serials. **Services:** Interlibrary loan; library not open to the public. **Computerized Information Services:** DIALOG Information Services, ORBIT Search Service, STN International, NLM, Questel, BRS Information Technologies, Data-Star, IMSBASE. **Remarks:** FAX: (215)265-1705. **Staff:** Veronique Michaud Weinstein, Info.Spec.; Mary Kay Ludovicy, Supv., Tech.Serv.; Mary Arrison, ILL; Elaine Spykee, Lib. Automation Spec.; Geraldine Klumpp, Info.Spec.

Rice County Historical Society - Archives
See: **Rice County Museum & Library** (13891)

★ 13891 ★
Rice County Museum & Library (Hist)
1814 2nd Ave., N.W.
Box 5   Phone: (507)332-2121
Faribault, MN 55021   Mark Lemenager, Dir.
Founded: 1926. **Staff:** Prof 1. **Subjects:** Rice County, Minnesota. **Special Collections:** Rice County directories, 1895 to present. **Holdings:** 800 books; 500 manuscripts; 250 magazines and scrapbooks. **Subscriptions:** 14 journals and other serials; 3 newspapers. **Services:** Copying; archives open to the public with restrictions. **Publications:** Rice County Families - Their History, Our Heritage (1981); Portraits and Memoirs of Rice County, Minnesota (1987); 60 Years of Good Cooking in Rice County (1986). **Formerly:** Rice County Historical Society - Archives. **Staff:** John Dalby, Archv.

Harley E. Rice Memorial Library
See: **Porter Memorial Hospital** (13233)

James E. Rice Poultry Library
See: **Cornell University - Albert R. Mann Library** (4302)

Rice Library
See: **U.S. Natl. Marine Fisheries Service - Southeast Fisheries Center** (17642)

★ 13892 ★
Rice Memorial Hospital - Health Science Library (Med)
301 Becker Ave., S.W.   Phone: (612)235-4543
Willmar, MN 56201   Carol Conradi, Libn.
Founded: 1978. **Staff:** Prof 1. **Subjects:** Clinical medicine. **Holdings:** 1400 books; 925 bound periodical volumes. **Subscriptions:** 120 journals and other serials. **Services:** Interlibrary loan; copying; library open to the public with restrictions. **Computerized Information Services:** DIALOG Information Services.

Rice Millers Association Archives
See: **University of Southwestern Louisiana - Jefferson Caffery Louisiana Room** (19356)

★ 13893 ★
Rice University - Alice Pratt Brown Library (Art, Mus)
Fondren Library
Box 1892
Houston, TX 77251-1892   Phone: (713)527-4832
Founded: 1986. **Staff:** Prof 2; Other 1. **Subjects:** Art history, architecture, music performance, music composition and theory, conducting. **Special Collections:** American music imprints, 1850-1950 (5100 titles); Halford Collection (Renaissance and Baroque keyboard; 200 titles); Richard Lert Library (conductor and student of Strauss; 250 books; 260 scores); Sylvester Collection (607 titles of stone lithographed music; 400 acoustical recordings). **Holdings:** 67,980 books and bound periodical volumes; 18,238 sound recordings; 18,846 scores; art exhibition catalogs. **Subscriptions:** 460 journals and other serials. **Services:** Interlibrary loan; copying; SDI; library open to the public. **Automated Operations:** Computerized cataloging and circulation. **Computerized Information Services:** DIALOG Information Services, PFDS Online, BRS Information Technologies, Knowledge Index, VU/TEXT Information Services, DataTimes; LIBRIS (internal database). Performs searches on fee basis. **Networks/Consortia:** Member of AMIGOS Bibliographic Council, Inc., Houston Area Research Library Consortium (HARLIC), Houston Music Librarians' Consort (HMLC). **Publications:** Rice Notes (newsletter), irregular. **Staff:** Jet Prendeville, Art & Arch.Libn.; Robert Follett, Mus.Libn.

★ 13894 ★
Rice University - Division of Government Publications & Special Resources (Info Sci)
Fondren Library
Box 1892   Phone: (713)285-5483
Houston, TX 77251-1892   Barbara Kile, Dir.
Founded: 1971. **Staff:** Prof 2; Other 5. **Holdings:** 500,000 government documents; 600,000 technical reports; 2 million microforms; U.S. patents: utility, 1960 to present; design, 1842 to present; reissues, 1838 to present; plant, 1978 to present; 900 videotapes; 25 software packages. **Services:** Interlibrary loan; copying; department open to the public. **Computerized Information Services:** U.S. Patent Classification System; BITNET (electronic mail service). **Publications:** Guides to the collections, irregular - free upon request. **Remarks:** FAX: (713)285-5258. Electronic mail address(es): Kilebar@Ricelibr (BITNET). **Staff:** Kerry Keck, Libn.

★ 13895 ★
Rice University - Jones Graduate School of Administration - Business Information Center (Bus-Fin)
Herring Hall   Phone: (713)527-6062
Houston, TX 77251   Peggy Shaw, Bus.Libn.
Founded: 1984. **Staff:** Prof 1; Other 1. **Subjects:** Accounting, finance, public administration, management, marketing. **Holdings:** 5268 books; New York Stock Exchange companies' annual and 10K reports, 1980 to present, on microfiche. **Subscriptions:** 245 journals and other serials. **Services:** Interlibrary loan; copying; center open to the public. **Automated Operations:** Computerized cataloging. **Computerized Information Services:** DIALOG Information Services, BRS Information Technologies, PFDS Online, Knowledge Index, VU/TEXT Information Services, DataTimes, BRS/AfterDark; CD-ROMs (DIALOG OnDisc, ABI/INFORM, Business Dateline, DISCLOSURE, Predicasts). Performs searches on fee basis. **Remarks:** FAX: (713)285-5251.

★ 13896 ★
Rice University - Office of Computing and Information Services -
  Computing Reference Area (Comp Sci)
Box 1892   Phone: (713)527-4076
Houston, TX 77251-1892   Martin Halbert, Ref.Libn.
Founded: 1988. **Staff:** 3. **Subjects:** Computer science, microcomputers, software. **Holdings:** 2000 books; 500 nonbook items; 200 software programs; documentation for IBM Systems, Apple Computers, and Sun Microsystems. **Subscriptions:** 230 journals and other serials. **Services:** Interlibrary loan; reference area open to the public. **Computerized Information Services:** CD-ROM (Computer Library); InterNet (electronic mail service). **Remarks:** FAX: (713)527-6099. Electronic mail address(es): HALBERT@RICEVM1.RICE.EDU (InterNet).

★ 13897 ★
Rice University - Woodson Research Center (Hist, Hum)
Fondren Library   Phone: (713)527-8101
Houston, TX 77251-1892   Nancy L. Boothe, Dir.
Founded: 1968. **Staff:** Prof 2; Other 2. **Subjects:** Texas history and entrepreneurship, Civil War, Rice University history, history of U.S. spaceflight, 20th century American literature, history of aeronautics and science. **Special Collections:** Masterson Texana (1700 volumes); Julian S. Huxley (92 cubic feet of papers; 1400 volumes); Johnson Space Center History Archive (965 cubic feet); James A. Baker, III Political Archive (153 cubic feet); Anderson History of Aeronautics (3800 volumes); Axson 18th Century British Drama (4800 volumes); Confederate imprints (1000); Carlota and Maximilian manuscript collection (4 cubic feet). **Holdings:** 27,000 books and bound periodical volumes; 1410 cubic feet of university archives; 2690 cubic feet of literary, historical, political, scientific, business, and artistic manuscript collections; 3000 cubic feet of faculty papers. **Services:** Copying (limited); center open to the public. **Computerized Information Services:** InterNet (electronic mail service). **Publications:** Bibliography of cataloged archival publications in the Fondren Library (book); library guides. **Special Catalogs:** Manuscript collection guides: Julian Sorell Huxley papers; Johnson Space Center History Archive, 1952-1980; William Ward Watkin papers; Walter Benona and Estelle Sharp Collection, 1868-1978; Thomas Moore letters; Walter Gardner Hall papers; James Lockhart Autry papers; Masterson Texana Collection catalog; other in-house finding aids. **Remarks:** ADD BOOTHE@LIBRARY.RICE.EDU (InterNet).

★ 13898 ★
Ricerca Information Services (Bus-Fin, Sci-Engr)
7528 Auburn Rd.
Box 1000
Painesville, OH 44077   Phone: (216)357-3475
                       Carol Duane, Mgr.Info.Serv.
Founded: 1980. **Staff:** Prof 3; Other 4. **Subjects:** Chemistry, agriculture, business, biotechnology, engineering, management, marketing research, finance. **Holdings:** 10,000 books; 4500 bound periodical volumes; 8800 reels of microfilm; 300,000 patents; 550 dissertations. **Subscriptions:** 205 journals and other serials. **Services:** Interlibrary loan; copying; SDI; consulting; fee-based information services; services open to companies and persons under contract. **Automated Operations:** Computerized public access catalog, acquisitions, and circulation. **Computerized Information Services:** DIALOG Information Services, ORBIT Search Service, PFDS Online, BRS Information Technologies, WILSONLINE, STN International, NewsNet, Inc., Questel, Data-Star, Reuters, NLM, Dow Jones News/Retrieval; MACCS (chemical registry database), Central Files Index database (internal databases). Performs searches on fee basis. **Publications:** Quarterly newsletter. **Remarks:** Alternate telephone number(s): 357-3471. FAX: (216)354-4415. Telex: 196212 RICERCA UT. **Staff:** Elizabeth Wainio, Supv. of Rec., Tech.Info.Serv.; Susan Branchick, Supv., Corp.Lib., Ref.Serv.

★ 13899 ★
Buddy Rich Fan Club - Library (Mus)
Box 2014
Warminster, PA 18974   Charles Braun, Pres.
Founded: 1984. **Staff:** 5. **Subjects:** Buddy Rich. **Holdings:** Recordings; videotapes; paper memorabilia; photographs; access to 2000 hours of taped concerts. **Services:** Library open to the public.

★ 13900 ★
Richards and Associates - Library (Trans)
P.O. Box 10350
College Station, TX 77842   Phone: (409)690-1408
Subjects: Railroad and highway safety. **Holdings:** 500 volumes. **Remarks:** FAX: (409)690-1408.

★ 13901 ★
Richards, Layton & Finger - Law Library (Law)
1 Rodney Sq., 10th Fl.
Box 551   Phone: (302)651-7782
Wilmington, DE 19899   Jean D. Winstead, Law Libn.
Founded: 1929. **Staff:** 2. **Subjects:** Law - corporate, commercial, labor, tax, real estate. **Holdings:** 8400 books; 100 bound periodical volumes; 9 VF drawers of unreported Chancery, Supreme, and District Court opinions; 7 VF drawers of current and past Delaware legislation. **Subscriptions:** 115 journals and other serials. **Services:** Interlibrary loan; copying; library open to the public by referral only. **Computerized Information Services:** LEXIS, WESTLAW, Dow Jones News/Retrieval, DELCAT, Information America. **Special Indexes:** Indexes to unreported Chancery Court opinions, reference file, and state legislation. **Remarks:** FAX: (302)658-6548. Alternate telephone number(s): 658-6541.

Richardson Archives
See: **University of South Dakota - I.D. Weeks Library** (19317)

★ 13902 ★
Richardson Greenshields of Canada, Ltd. - Research Library (Bus-Fin)
130 Adelaide St., W., Suite 1400
Toronto, ON, Canada M5H 1T8   Phone: (416)860-3432
                             Alison Ritchie
Founded: 1921. **Staff:** Prof 1; Other 3. **Subjects:** Securities industry, economics, business, finance. **Holdings:** 1200 books and bound periodical volumes; 4800 classified files. **Subscriptions:** 140 journals and other serials. **Services:** Library open to university students and associate firms. **Publications:** Research publications. **Remarks:** FAX: (416)368-2481.

Richardson Memorial Library
See: **St. Louis Art Museum** (14434)

Richardson Public Library - Dallas County Law Library Branch
See: **Dallas County Law Library - Richardson Branch** (4551)

★ 13903 ★
Richardson Vicks U.S.A. Research Center - Library (Biol Sci, Med)
One Far Mill Crossing
Shelton, CT 06484   Phone: (203)929-2500
                       Mary Lou Wells, Libn.
Founded: 1942. **Staff:** Prof 1; Other 1. **Subjects:** Drugs and pharmaceuticals, medicine, cosmetics and cosmetic science, analytical and physical chemistry, microbiology, biochemistry, biology, nutrition. **Holdings:** 6500 books; 7000 bound periodical volumes. **Subscriptions:** 275 journals and other serials. **Services:** Interlibrary loan; library not open to the public. **Automated Operations:** Computerized serials. **Networks/Consortia:** Member of Southwestern Connecticut Library Council (SWLC), Connecticut Association of Health Science Libraries (CAHSL), BHSL.

William S. Richardson School of Law Library
See: **University of Hawaii** (18631)

★ 13904 ★
Richland College - Adult Resource Center (Educ)
12800 Abrams Rd.
Dallas, TX 75243-2199   Phone: (214)238-6034
                       Elaine Sullivan, Dir.
Staff: 6. **Subjects:** Personal growth, career development, women's issues. **Holdings:** 105 volumes. **Services:** Center open to clients and community.

★ 13905 ★
Richland County Law Library (Law)
Court House
50 Park Ave., E.
Mansfield, OH 44902   Phone: (419)524-9944
                       Libby Kaup, Libn.
Founded: 1896. **Staff:** Prof 2. **Subjects:** Law and allied subjects. **Holdings:** 20,000 books. **Services:** Library open to students on introduction.

★ 13906 ★
Richland Memorial Hospital - Josey Memorial Health Sciences Library
(Med)
5 Richland Medical Park   Phone: (803)765-6312
Columbia, SC 29203   Kay F. Harwood, Dir.
Founded: 1940. **Staff:** Prof 1; Other 3. **Subjects:** Medicine, medical specialities, nursing, hospital administration. **Holdings:** 3000 books; 5000 bound periodical volumes; 600 videotapes; 1000 audiotapes; 5400 slides. **Subscriptions:** 450 journals and other serials. **Services:** Interlibrary loan; copying; SDI; library open to the public. **Computerized Information Services:** MEDLARS, BRS Information Technologies, DIALOG Information Services. Performs searches on fee basis. **Networks/Consortia:** Member of Columbia Area Medical Librarians' Association (CAMLA), South Carolina Health Information Network (SCHIN). **Remarks:** FAX: (803)253-4372.

★ 13907 ★
Richland Memorial Hospital - Staff Library (Med)
800 East Locust   Phone: (618)395-2131
Olney, IL 62450   Beverly Keyth, Dir., Med.Rec.
Staff: 1. **Subjects:** Internal medicine, surgery, oncology, hematology, orthopedics, obstetrics-gynecology. **Holdings:** 448 books. **Subscriptions:** 12 journals and other serials. **Services:** Library not open to the public.

Richmond Area Development Archives
See: **Virginia Commonwealth University - James Branch Cabell Library** (19861)

Mary Richmond Archives
See: **Columbia University - Whitney M. Young, Jr. Memorial Library of Social Work** (4028)

★ 13908 ★
Richmond Memorial Hospital - Medical and Nursing School Libraries (Med)
1300 Westwood Ave.   Phone: (804)254-6008
Richmond, VA 23227   Merle L. Colglazier, Libn.
Founded: 1960. **Staff:** Prof 1; Other 1. **Subjects:** Medicine, nursing, health sciences. **Holdings:** 8000 books and bound periodical volumes; nursing AV programs. **Subscriptions:** 149 journals and other serials. **Services:** Interlibrary loan; copying; libraries open to qualified users for reference use only. **Computerized Information Services:** MEDLARS, DIALOG Information Services. **Networks/Consortia:** Member of Richmond Health Information Group.

★ 13909 ★
Richmond Museum - Library (Hist)
400 Nevin Ave.
P.O. Box 1267   Phone: (510)235-7387
Richmond, CA 94801   Lois Boyle, Pres., Musm.Assoc.
Founded: 1954. **Staff:** 2. **Subjects:** Richmond history. **Holdings:** 640 volumes; 1500 photographs; archival material. **Services:** Interlibrary loan; library open to the public for reference use only by appointment. **Remarks:** Jointly maintained by the City of Richmond and the Richmond Museum Association. **Staff:** Kathleen Rupley, Adm./Cur.

Richmond National Battlefield Park
See: **U.S. Natl. Park Service** (17769)

★ 13910 ★
Richmond Newspapers - Library (Publ)
Box C-32333   Phone: (804)649-6286
Richmond, VA 23293   Charles D. Saunders, Libn.
Staff: 8. **Subjects:** Newspaper reference topics. **Holdings:** 2000 books; 56 file cases of clippings; 59 file cases of pictures; newspapers on microfilm. **Services:** Copying; library open to the public.

★ 13911 ★
Richmond Public Library - Art and Music Department (Art, Mus)
101 E. Franklin St.   Phone: (804)780-4740
Richmond, VA 23219   Helen M. Ogden, Sr.Libn.
Staff: Prof 3; Other 2. **Subjects:** Fine arts, crafts, decoration, antiques, music, dance. **Special Collections:** Scott Fund Orchestral Scores (280). **Holdings:** 23,500 books; 2132 bound periodical volumes; 12,400 scores; 271 large print reproductions; 13 VF drawers of art and music clippings; 15 VF drawers of pamphlets; 38 VF drawers of sheet music; 10,900 recordings; 32 VF drawers of pictures. **Subscriptions:** 90 journals and other serials. **Services:** Interlibrary loan; copying (limited); department open to the public. **Staff:** Margaret Harter, Libn.Asst.; Therese Wagenknecht, Libn.; Ellen Anderson, Libn.

★ 13912 ★
Richmond Public Library - Business, Science & Technology Department (Bus-Fin, Sci-Engr)
101 E. Franklin St.   Phone: (804)780-8223
Richmond, VA 23219   Robert Costa, Libn.
Founded: 1972. **Staff:** Prof 4; Other 1. **Subjects:** Social sciences, business, pure sciences, applied sciences. **Holdings:** Books; Foundation Center Regional Collection; 1100 annual reports of business corporations; government publications; city documents. **Subscriptions:** 415 journals and other serials; 8 newspapers. **Services:** Interlibrary loan; copying (limited); department open to the public. **Publications:** Miscellaneous book lists. **Remarks:** FAX: (804)643-1516. **Staff:** Carol Callahan, Libn.; Isabell Singh, Libn.; Fenton Shugrhe, Libn.; Diane Heil, Libn.; Beverly Mitchell, Libn.Asst.

★ 13913 ★
Richmond Public Library - Special Collections (Educ)
325 Civic Center Plaza   Phone: (510)620-6561
Richmond, CA 94804   Adelia Lines, Dir.
Founded: 1905. **Special Collections:** Local history; job information center; AV collection (film; video cassettes); motor manuals; art prints; Afro-American history; LEAP (literacy program). **Services:** Interlibrary loan; collections open to the public. **Automated Operations:** Computerized cataloging and circulation. **Computerized Information Services:** DIALOG Information Services, WILSONLINE; CLSI (internal database); OnTyme Electronic Message Network Service (electronic mail service). Performs searches on fee basis. Contact Person: Douglas Holtzman. **Networks/Consortia:** Member of Bay Area Library and Information Network, Bay Area Library and Information System (BALIS). **Staff:** Emma J. Clark, Supv.Ref.Libn.; Lynnea Kleinschmidt, Supv.Tech.Serv.Libn.; Janet Hellerick, Supv. Children's Libn.

★ 13914 ★
Richmond Public Schools - Curriculum Materials Center (Educ)
301 N. 9th St., 11th Fl.   Phone: (804)780-7692
Richmond, VA 23219   Dr. Delores Z. Pretlow, Dept. of Media & Tech.
Founded: 1964. **Staff:** Prof 1; Other 3. **Subjects:** Education. **Holdings:** 6500 books; 300 pamphlets; multimedia kits for grades K-12. **Subscriptions:** 150 journals and other serials. **Services:** Center open to school and city employees. **Automated Operations:** Computerized cataloging, acquisitions, and circulation. **Computerized Information Services:** DIALOG Information Services. **Remarks:** FAX: (804)644-8120. **Staff:** Linda Bendall, Televised Instr.; Connie Moore, Coord., Lib. Automation.

Richter Library
See: **Desert Botanical Garden** (4796)

Otto G. Richter Library
See: **University of Miami** (18846)

Ricker Library of Architecture and Art
See: **University of Illinois** (18690)

Helen Rickson Library
See: **Taylor Business Institute** (16017)

Dr. W.A. Riddell Health Sciences Library
See: **Plains Health Centre** (13096)

Rideau Regional Centre
See: **Ontario Ministry of Community and Social Services** (12458)

★ 13915 ★
Rider, Bennett, Egan & Arundel - Library (Law)
2000 Lincoln Ctr.
333 S. 7th St.   Phone: (612)335-3825
Minneapolis, MN 55402   Marillyn Soulen, Hd.Libn.
Staff: Prof 2. **Subjects:** Law. **Holdings:** 5500 books. **Subscriptions:** 50 journals and other serials. **Services:** Library not open to the public. **Computerized Information Services:** LEXIS, WESTLAW. **Remarks:** FAX: (612)375-0701. **Staff:** Marillyn Soulen, Hd.Libn.; Kathy McGuire, Libn.

★ 13916 ★
Rider College - Franklin F. Moore Library (Bus-Fin)
2083 Lawrenceville Rd.   Phone: (609)896-5111
Lawrenceville, NJ 08648-0399   Dr. Ross Stephen, Dir., Lib.Serv.
Founded: 1934. **Staff:** Prof 14; Other 13. **Subjects:** Business. **Special Collections:** Kendric C. Hill Shorthand Collection; Riderana. **Holdings:** 325,000 books; 40,000 bound periodical volumes; Delaware Valley newspapers. **Subscriptions:** 1800 journals and other serials. **Services:** Interlibrary loan; copying; library open to the public. **Automated Operations:** Computerized public access catalog, cataloging, acquisitions, and circulation. **Computerized Information Services:** DIALOG Information Services, Dow Jones News/Retrieval, ABI/INFORM, OCLC. Performs searches on fee basis. Telephone 896-5115. **Networks/Consortia:** Member of PALINET, New Jersey Library Network.

Rider College - Westminster Choir College - Talbott Library
See: **Westminster Choir College - Talbott Library** (20327)

★ 13917 ★
Ridgetown College of Agricultural Technology - Library (Agri)
Ridgetown, ON, Canada N0P 2C0   Phone: (519)674-5456
                                       Mrs. I.R. Roadhouse, Libn.
Founded: 1951. **Staff:** Prof 2; Other 3. **Subjects:** Agriculture, soils, crop production, horticulture, biology, agricultural engineering and chemistry, livestock production, farm economics, ornamental horticulture, fruit and vegetable production, food microbiology. **Holdings:** 12,000 books and bound periodical volumes; 2000 pamphlets and clippings, 100 video recordings. **Subscriptions:** 150 journals and other serials; 15 newspapers. **Services:** Interlibrary loan; copying; library open to the public. **Computerized Information Services:** Online systems. **Publications:** Bibliographies. **Remarks:** FAX: (519)674-3042. College is a branch of the Ontario Ministry of Agriculture and Food. **Staff:** M. Hill.

Riecker Memorial Library
See: **Catherine McAuley Health System** (9868)

Riemenschneider Bach Institute
See: **Baldwin-Wallace College - Riemenschneider Bach Institute** (1432)

★ 13918 ★
Rifkind Center for German Expressionist Studies - Art Library and Graphics Collection (Art)
Los Angeles County Museum of Art
5905 Wilshire Blvd.   Phone: (213)857-6165
Los Angeles, CA 90036   Susan Trauger, Art Libn.
Founded: 1979. **Staff:** Prof 1. **Subjects:** German Expressionist art. **Special Collections:** German Expressionist art exhibition catalogs, monographs, illustrated books, and portfolios; Expressionist periodicals; German Expressionist graphics collection. **Holdings:** 5000 volumes. **Services:** Copying (limited); library open to graduate students and art historians. **Automated Operations:** INMAGIC. **Publications:** German Expressionist Prints and Drawings: The Robert Gore Rifkind Center for German Expressionist Studies: Essays, vol. 1; German Expressionist Prints and Drawings: Catalogue of the Collection, vol. 2; Bibliography of the Library: the Robert Gore Rifkind Center for German Expressionist Studies; German Expressionist Art - the Robert Gore Rifkind Collection: Prints, Drawings, Illustrated Books, Periodicals, Posters. **Remarks:** FAX: (213)931-7347.

★ 13919 ★
Austen Riggs Center, Inc. - Austen Fox Riggs Library (Med)
Main St.   Phone: (413)298-5511
Stockbridge, MA 01262   Helen Linton, Libn.
Founded: 1919. **Staff:** Prof 1. **Subjects:** Psychoanalysis, psychiatry, psychology. **Holdings:** 9821 books; 2064 bound periodical volumes; 74 cassettes. **Subscriptions:** 142 journals and other serials. **Services:** Interlibrary loan; library open to the public upon recommendation of staff member or librarian. **Computerized Information Services:** DIALOG Information Services. Performs searches on fee basis. **Remarks:** FAX: (413)298-4020.

★ 13920 ★
Right to Life League of Southern California - Library (Soc Sci)
50 N. Hill Ave., Suite 306   Phone: (818)449-8408
Pasadena, CA 91106   Lori Hougens, Dir., Educ.
Founded: 1969. **Staff:** Prof 25; Other 10. **Subjects:** Abortion, pre-natal development, euthanasia, genetic engineering, infanticide, human experimentation. **Special Collections:** The Human Life Review, 1975-1986. **Holdings:** Books; periodicals; clippings; pamphlets; cassettes; videotapes. **Services:** Library open to the public with restrictions. **Publications:** Life Issues Report (newsletter) - free upon request. **Special Catalogs:** Catalog of pro-life materials; catalog of audiovisual aids. **Remarks:** FAX: (818)449-4822. **Staff:** Elaine Stevens.

★ 13921 ★
Right to Life of Michigan - Downriver Resource Center (Soc Sci)
1638 Eureka   Phone: (313)282-6100
Wyandotte, MI 48192-6104   Betty Pevovar, Region 4 Dir. & Off.Mgr.
Subjects: Abortion, euthanasia, infanticide, legislation. **Holdings:** Books; videotapes; 16mm films; audiocassettes; slides; VF files; booklets; newspaper clippings; pamphlets. **Services:** Center open to the public. **Formerly:** Located in Lincoln Park, MI.

★ 13922 ★
Right to Life of Michigan - Macomb County Education/Resource Center (Soc Sci)
27417 Harper   Phone: (313)774-6050
St. Clair Shores, MI 48081   Andrea Treall
Subjects: Abortion, euthanasia, infanticide, legislation. **Holdings:** 60 books; 50 videotapes; 12 16mm films; 150 audiocassettes; slides; booklets; pamphlets. **Services:** Center open to the public. **Staff:** Margaret Moleck, Exec.Sec.

★ 13923 ★
Right to Life of Michigan - Resource Center (Soc Sci)
Knapp's Centre, Suite 588
300 S. Washington Sq.   Phone: (517)487-3376
Lansing, MI 48933   Karen Davis
Subjects: Abortion, euthanasia, infanticide, legislation. **Holdings:** Books; videotapes; 16mm films; audiocassettes; slides; VF files; booklets; newspaper clippings; pamphlets. **Services:** Center open to the public.

★ 13924 ★
Right to Life of Michigan - Resource Center (Soc Sci)
43000 9 Mile Rd., Suite 213   Phone: (313)347-1601
Novi, MI 48375   Barbara Lowman
Subjects: Abortion, euthanasia, infanticide, legislation. **Holdings:** Books; videotapes; 16mm films; audiocassettes; slides; VF files; booklets; newspaper clippings; pamphlets. **Services:** Center open to the public.

★ 13925 ★
Right to Life of Michigan - State Central Resource Center (Soc Sci)
920 Cherry, S.E.   Phone: (616)451-0225
Grand Rapids, MI 49506   Sheri Hicks, Dir.
Subjects: Abortion, euthanasia, infanticide, legislation. **Holdings:** Books; videotapes; 16mm films; audiocassettes; slides; VF files; booklets; newspaper clippings; pamphlets. **Services:** Center open to the public.

★ 13926 ★
RII-Triton - Library
1010 Wayne Ave., Suite 300
Silver Spring, MD 20910
Subjects: Health promotion, disease prevention. **Holdings:** 400 books; 1000 bound periodical volumes. **Remarks:** Sponsored by the U.S. Department of Health and Human Services. Currently inactive.

Erling Riis Research Laboratory
See: **International Paper Company** (8171)

Rijksherbarium
See: **Netherlands - National Herbarium of the Netherlands** (11409)

Rijksmuseum - Bibliotheek
See: **Netherlands - State Museum - Library** (11411)

★ 13927 ★
Rijksuniversiteit te Groningen - Bibliotheek Sociale Wetenschappen (Soc Sci)
Grote Kruisstraat 2/7   Phone: 50 636368
NL-9712 TS Groningen, Netherlands   Mr. H.J.D. Oude Lenferink
Founded: 1990. **Subjects:** Social sciences, psychology, sociology, pedagogy, education. **Holdings:** 90,000 books. **Subscriptions:** 800 journals and other serials. **Services:** Interlibrary loan; copying; library open to the public at librarian's discretion. **Computerized Information Services:** InterNet (electronic mail service). **Remarks:** FAX: 50 636304. Electronic mail address(es): H.E.E.Blaauw@PPSW.rug.nl (InterNet).

★ 13928 ★
Rijksuniversiteit te Leiden Sinologisch Instituut - Documentatiecentrum voor het Huidige China - Bibliotheek (Hum)
Postbus 9515   Phone: 71 272533
NL-2300 RA Leiden, Netherlands   Joyce Yung-tzu Wu
Founded: 1930. **Staff:** Prof 1; Other 4. **Subjects:** Chinese studies - ancient and modern; Chinese and Japanese language, literature, history, and philosophy. **Special Collections:** Van Gulik Collection; rare book collection; Go Collection. **Holdings:** 228,000 books; 4000 microfiche; 5500 reels of microfilm. **Subscriptions:** 1000 journals and other serials; 45 newspapers. **Services:** Interlibrary loan; copying; library open to the public with permission from the University Library. **Remarks:** FAX: 71 272615. Holdings are in Western languages, Chinese, and Japanese.

★ 13929 ★
Riker, Danzig, Scherer, Hyland & Perretti - Library (Law)
Headquarters Plaza
1 Speedwell Ave.   Phone: (201)538-0800
Morristown, NJ 07962-1981   Karen B. Brunner
Staff: Prof 1; Other 4. **Subjects:** Law. **Holdings:** 12,000 books; 1000 bound periodical volumes. **Subscriptions:** 285 journals and other serials; 9 newspapers. **Services:** Interlibrary loan; library not open to the public. **Computerized Information Services:** LEXIS, NEXIS, WESTLAW, DIALOG Information Services, DataTimes. **Remarks:** FAX: (201)538-1984.

★ 13930 ★
Riley Consolidated, Inc. - Library (Sci-Engr, Energy)
5 Neponset St.   Phone: (508)852-7100
Worcester, MA 01606   Jane M. Milligan, Info.Spec.
Staff: Prof 1. **Subjects:** Steam generation, fuel burning equipment, power generation, boilers and pressure vessels, petroleum chemicals, coal gasification, municipal solid waste incineration. **Special Collections:** American Society of Mechanical Engineers (ASME) Boiler and Pressure Vessel Codes; Environmental Protection Agency, U.S. Dept. of Energy, and Electric Power Research Institute reports. **Holdings:** 1700 books; 18 VF drawers of reports and papers; 625 patents. **Subscriptions:** 80 journals and other serials. **Services:** Interlibrary loan; copying; SDI; library open to the public by appointment. **Automated Operations:** Computerized cataloging. **Computerized Information Services:** DIALOG Information Services; VAX (internal database). Performs searches on fee basis. **Networks/Consortia:** Member of Worcester Area Cooperating Libraries (WACL). **Publications:** Monthly Bulletin.

★ 13931 ★
Riley County Genealogical Society - Library (Hist)
2005 Claflin Rd.   Phone: (913)537-2205
Manhattan, KS 66502   Miriam B. Field, Pres.
Founded: 1963. **Staff:** Prof 3. **Subjects:** Genealogy, state and local history. **Holdings:** 3800 books; 600 bound periodical volumes; 3 VF drawers of original biographies; 1 VF drawer and 15 card file drawers of genealogical charts of society members' ancestors; 250 reels of microfilm of census materials; 6 card drawers of microfiche of genealogical and land records. **Subscriptions:** 125 journals and other serials. **Services:** Copying; SDI; library open to the public. **Special Indexes:** Indexes to censuses of Riley County and 1880 census of surrounding counties; index to cemetery records. **Staff:** Mildred Loeffler, Res.; Helen R. Long, Cat./Acq.Libn.; Sherry Butler, Lib.Chm.

★ 13932 ★
Riley County Historical Society - Seaton Memorial Library - Taylor and Charlson Archives (Hist)
2309 Claflin Rd.   Phone: (913)537-2210
Manhattan, KS 66502   Jeanne C. Mithen, Libn./Archv.
Founded: 1914. **Staff:** Prof 1; Other 2. **Subjects:** History of Manhattan City and Riley County, Kansas; Kansas State University. **Special Collections:** Photograph collection of Riley County towns and cities; Riley County tax records, 1862-1920; Riley County marriage records; Riley County and Manhattan maps; Riley County club and church records. **Holdings:** 4500 books; 100 bound periodical volumes; 200 scrapbooks; 6000 local photographs; 2 architect's filing cabinets of maps, documents, newspaper tear sheets and special issues; 2230 cubic feet of manuscripts and archival records; 20 oral history tapes; 20 videocassettes. **Subscriptions:** 5 journals and other serials. **Services:** Copying; library open to the public for reference use only. **Special Indexes:** Indexes to Riley County marriage records; MHK city clerk scrapbooks. **Staff:** Helen Long, Asst.Libn.

Riley-Hickingbotham Library
See: **Ouachita Baptist University** (12609)

★ 13933 ★
John and Mable Ringling Museum of Art - Art Research Library (Art, Rare Book)
Box 1838   Phone: (813)355-5101
Sarasota, FL 34230   Lynell A. Morr, Art Libn.
Founded: 1930. **Staff:** Prof 2; Other 1. **Subjects:** Baroque art; 16th, 17th, and 18th century European art; contemporary art; Rubens. **Special Collections:** Rare books (16th, 17th, and 18th century art history sources); Emblem books; Iconography; Gluck (Gustav) collection of offprints of materials on early Flemish and Dutch painters; museum archives. **Holdings:** 16,500 books; 3003 bound periodical volumes; 38,000 art catalogs; 100 VF drawers of art auction sale catalogs; 4 VF drawers of clippings; 16 VF drawers of Phototeca files. **Subscriptions:** 100 journals and other serials. **Services:** Interlibrary loan; copying; library open to the public. **Computerized Information Services:** OCLC, DIALOG Information Services, EPIC. **Networks/Consortia:** Member of SOLINET. **Special Catalogs:** Exhibition Catalogs: Rare Books of the 16th, 17th, and 18th centuries from the Library of the Ringling Museum of Art, Sarasota, FL, November 3-23, 1969. **Remarks:** FAX: (813)351-7959. **Staff:** Deborah Walk, Archv.

★ 13934 ★
Ringling School of Art and Design - Library (Art)
2700 N. Tamiami Trail   Phone: (813)351-4614
Sarasota, FL 34234   Yvonne Morse, Lib.Dir.
Founded: 1928. **Staff:** Prof 2; Other 5. **Subjects:** Art history, interior design, advertising design, computer design, photography, architecture, graphics, painting. **Special Collections:** Print Collection of Japanese Art (Robert M. Jackson Collection; 800 items); European prints of 17th and 18th century (500 items). **Holdings:** 14,100 books; 1600 bound periodical volumes; 800 museum catalogs; 40,000 art slides; 34 16mm films; 320 videocassettes. **Subscriptions:** 295 journals and other serials. **Services:** Interlibrary loan; copying; library open to artists and researchers. **Computerized Information Services:** CASTLE (internal database). **Networks/Consortia:** Member of Florida Library Network (FLN), West Coast Library Consortium (WELCO). **Remarks:** FAX: (813)359-7517. **Staff:** Allen R. Novak, AV Libn.

★ 13935 ★
Rio Algom, Ltd. - Information Centre (Sci-Engr)
120 Adelaide St., W.   Phone: (416)365-6800
Toronto, ON, Canada M5H 1W5   Penny Lipman, Mgr., Info.Serv.
Founded: 1966. **Staff:** Prof 1; Other 1. **Subjects:** Mining, uranium, copper, tin, potash, coal. **Holdings:** 4000 books; 1000 bound periodical volumes; annual reports for 1000 companies; 1000 Canadian and U.S. federal and provincial geological reports. **Subscriptions:** 200 journals and other serials; 15 newspapers. **Services:** Interlibrary loan; copying; library open to librarians. **Automated Operations:** INMAGIC. **Computerized Information Services:** DIALOG Information Services, Info Globe, QL Systems, Dow Jones News/Retrieval, Reuter TEXTLINE, WILSONLINE, Infomart Online, CAN/LAW, NewsNet, Inc., The Financial Post DataGroup. **Publications:** The Blue Pages (acquisitions list). **Remarks:** FAX: (416)365-6870. Telex: 065 24134. **Staff:** Lynn Sinclair.

★ 13936 ★
(Rio de Janeiro) Instituto Brasil-Estados Unidos - Library (Educ)
Ave. N. Sra. de Copacabana
690, 3rd Andar   Phone: 21 2558332
22050 Rio de Janeiro, RJ, Brazil   Dr. Adroaldo de Alencar
Founded: 1937. **Staff:** Prof 6. **Holdings:** 24,232 books; musical and non-musical recordings. **Subscriptions:** 81 journals and other serials; 10 newspapers. **Services:** Library open to members only. **Remarks:** FAX: 21 2558332. Maintained or supported by the U.S. Information Agency. Focus is on materials that will assist peoples outside the United States to learn about the United States, its people, history, culture, political processes, and social milieux. **Staff:** Liana Wolff, Hd.Libn.; Almerita De Sousa, Libn.; Regina Silva, Libn.

★ 13937 ★
(Rio de Janeiro) USIS Reference Library (Educ)
Ave. Pres. Wilson, 147, Mezzanine   Phone: 21 2927117
20030 Rio de Janeiro, RJ, Brazil   Daniel Yett, Dir.
Staff: 9. **Subjects:** United States - history, society, art. **Holdings:** 4000 books; reports; microfiche; microfilm. **Subscriptions:** 320 journals and other serials. **Services:** Interlibrary loan; copying; SDI; library open to the public. **Remarks:** FAX: 21 5333455. Maintained or supported by the U.S. Information Agency. Focus is on materials that will assist peoples outside the United States to learn about the United States, its people, history, culture, political processes, and social milieux.

★ 13938 ★
Riso National Laboratory - Riso Library (Energy)
PO Box 49   Phone: 2 371212
DK-4000 Roskilde, Denmark   Birgit Pedersen, Chf.Libn.
Founded: 1957. **Staff:** Prof 11; Other 9. **Subjects:** Energy - biomass, coal, wind, geothermal, nuclear, solar; oil, uranium, and other energy sources; air pollution and environmental issues; heating and power generation; reactors and thermal plants; waste heat utilization. **Holdings:** 60,000 volumes; 500,000 reports. **Subscriptions:** 1545 journals and other serials. **Services:** Interlibrary loan; copying; SDI; library open to the public. **Automated Operations:** Computerized cataloging, acquisitions, and circulation. **Computerized Information Services:** INIS (International Nuclear Information System), IEA Energy Data Base (EDB), ESA/IRS, DIALOG Information Services, PFDS Online; produces Nordic Energy Index (NEI). Performs searches on fee basis. **Publications:** Acquisitions List, 2/week; Periodical Holdings, annual. **Remarks:** FAX: 46755627. Telex: 43 116 RISO DK.

Maurice Ritz Resource Library and Bookstore
See: **Planned Parenthood of Wisconsin (13132)**

Riva-Aguero Institute
See: **Pontificia Universidad Catolica del Peru - Riva-Aguero Institute (13215)**

Luis Munoz Rivera Library and Museum
See: **Puerto Rican Culture Institute (13508)**

★ 13939 ★
Riverside County Historical Commission - Library (Hist)
4600 Crestmore Rd.
Box 3507   Phone: (714)275-4310
Rubidoux, CA 92509   Diana Seider, Dir.
Founded: 1974. **Staff:** Prof 5. **Subjects:** Local and California history, Indian history, museum science. **Special Collections:** History of Riverside County. **Holdings:** 500 volumes; manuscripts and ephemera relating to Riverside County history; 90 oral history tapes. **Subscriptions:** 17 journals and other serials. **Services:** Copying; library open to the public for reference use only. **Publications:** Historical Commission Press, annual. **Remarks:** FAX: (714)684-7044.

★ 13940 ★
Riverside County Law Library (Law)
3535 10th St., Suite 100   Phone: (714)275-6390
Riverside, CA 92501   Gayle Webb, Law Libn.
Staff: Prof 2; Other 5. **Subjects:** Law. **Holdings:** 47,236 books and bound periodical volumes; 3808 microforms; 128 cassettes; county ordinances and codes; state and federal statutes; treatises. **Subscriptions:** 62 journals and other serials. **Services:** Copying; SDI; library open to the public. **Computerized Information Services:** WESTLAW, OCLC, LEXIS, NEXIS, DIALOG Information Services, VU/TEXT Information Services. **Remarks:** FAX: (714)787-2966. **Staff:** Laura Stockton.

★ 13941 ★
Riverside County Law Library - Indio Law Library (Law)
46-209 Oasis St.   Phone: (619)863-8316
Indio, CA 92201   Patricia Stewart, Lib.Asst.
Staff: 1. **Subjects:** Law. **Special Collections:** Local municipal ordinances. **Holdings:** 17,215 volumes. **Subscriptions:** 4 newspapers. **Services:** copying; open to the public. **Computerized Information Services:** OCLC, WESTLAW. **Remarks:** FAX: (619)342-2581.

★ 13942 ★
Riverside General Hospital - Medical Library (Med)
9851 Magnolia Ave.   Phone: (714)358-7066
Riverside, CA 92503   Rosalie Reed, Med.Lib.Coord.
Staff: Prof 1; Other 1. **Subjects:** Medicine, surgery, nursing, allied health sciences. **Holdings:** 1189 books; 5616 bound periodical volumes. **Subscriptions:** 216 journals and other serials. **Services:** Interlibrary loan; copying; SDI; library open to the public with permission. **Computerized Information Services:** NLM. **Networks/Consortia:** Member of Inland Empire Medical Library Cooperative (IEMLC).

★ 13943 ★
Riverside Hospital - Medical Library (Med)
Box 845   Phone: (302)764-6120
Wilmington, DE 19899   Roxanne Walston, Libn.
Founded: 1967. **Staff:** 1. **Subjects:** Osteopathic medicine, internal medicine, nursing. **Holdings:** 500 books. **Subscriptions:** 60 journals and other serials. **Services:** Interlibrary loan; library open to the public by appointment. **Networks/Consortia:** Member of Wilmington Area Biomedical Library Consortium (WABLC), Libraries in the New Castle County System (LINCS). **Remarks:** FAX: (302)764-2863.

★ 13944 ★
Riverside Hospital - Sarah and Julius Steinberg Memorial Library (Med)
1600 N. Superior St.   Phone: (419)729-6198
Toledo, OH 43604   Kathryn Maluchnik, Lib.Spec.
Staff: Prof 1. **Subjects:** Medicine, nursing, podiatry, sports medicine, health promotion, hospital management. **Holdings:** 1000 books; 850 bound periodical volumes. **Subscriptions:** 55 journals and other serials. **Services:** Interlibrary loan; copying; SDI; library open to qualified users by request. **Computerized Information Services:** MEDLINE, BRS Information Technologies, MEDLARS. **Networks/Consortia:** Member of National Network of Libraries of Medicine - Greater Midwest Region. **Remarks:** FAX: (419)729-6031.

★ 13945 ★
Riverside Hospital - Scobie Health Sciences Library (Med)
1967 Riverside Dr.   Phone: (613)738-8230
Ottawa, ON, Canada K1H 7W9   Jean E. White, Libn.
Founded: 1968. **Staff:** Prof 1; Other 5. **Subjects:** Medicine, nursing, hospital administration. **Holdings:** 1000 books; 500 bound periodical volumes; 200 videotapes and cassettes. **Subscriptions:** 175 journals and other serials. **Services:** Interlibrary loan; copying; library open to the public. **Automated Operations:** Computerized public access catalog. **Remarks:** FAX: (613)738-8521.

★ 13946 ★
Riverside Medical Center - Health Science Library (Med)
800 Riverside Dr.   Phone: (715)258-1065
Waupaca, WI 54981   Andrea Crane, Libn.
Founded: 1978. **Staff:** Prof 1. **Subjects:** Medicine, nursing, health care administration, pathology. **Holdings:** 630 books. **Subscriptions:** 90 journals and other serials. **Services:** Interlibrary loan; copying; library open to the public. **Automated Operations:** Computerized cataloging, acquisitions, serials, and circulation. **Computerized Information Services:** MEDLARS. **Networks/Consortia:** Member of Fox River Valley Area Library Consortium (FRVALC). **Remarks:** FAX: (715)258-1202.

★ 13947 ★
Riverside Medical Center - Health Sciences Library (Med)
Riverside at 25th Ave., S.   Phone: (612)371-6545
Minneapolis, MN 55454   Mary Finnegan, Lib.Mgr.
Founded: 1971. **Staff:** Prof 1; Other 4. **Subjects:** Medicine, orthopedics, nursing. **Holdings:** 3067 books; 4500 bound periodical volumes; 233 audiotapes. **Subscriptions:** 300 journals and other serials. **Services:** Library not open to the public. **Computerized Information Services:** BRS Information Technologies, MEDLINE, DIALOG Information Services, DataTimes. **Networks/Consortia:** Member of Twin Cities Biomedical Consortium (TCBC).

★ 13948 ★
Riverside Medical Center - Medical Library (Med)
350 N. Wall St.   Phone: (815)933-1671
Kankakee, IL 60901   Brenda Brower, Libn.
Founded: 1977. **Staff:** Prof 1; Other 6. **Subjects:** Medicine, nursing, hospital administration, mental health, substance abuse. **Holdings:** 300 books; 200 bound periodical volumes; 110 cassettes; 120 slide/cassette sets. **Subscriptions:** 230 journals and other serials; 10 newspapers. **Services:** Interlibrary loan; library open to the public with physician referral. **Automated Operations:** Computerized acquisitions. **Computerized Information Services:** MEDLINE. **Networks/Consortia:** Member of Chicago and South Consortium, Bur Oak Library System, National Network of Libraries of Medicine - Greater Midwest Region.

★ 13949 ★
Riverside Methodist Hospital - D.J. Vincent Medical Library (Med)
3535 Olentangy River Rd.   Phone: (614)566-5230
Columbus, OH 43214   Josephine W. Yeoh, Dir.
Staff: Prof 3; Other 7. **Subjects:** Clinical medicine, nursing, hospital administration, microcomputers, management, patient education, fiction. **Special Collections:** Complete collection of American Journal of Nursing, 1901 to present; historical medical books; Health Education Library. **Holdings:** 24,000 books; 15,000 bound periodical volumes; 4 Audio-Digest tapes; NCME video cassettes; books, videotapes, and pamphlet files for patient education; professional reprints file; 500 archives of papers published by professionals connected with the hospital. **Subscriptions:** 450 journals and other serials. **Services:** Interlibrary loan; copying; faxing; SDI; library open to the public. **Automated Operations:** Computerized cataloging and circulation. **Computerized Information Services:** MEDLINE, DIALOG Information Services, OCLC, BRS/COLLEAGUE; CD-ROMs (MEDLINE, CINAHL-CD, Hospital Literature Index). Performs searches on fee basis. **Networks/Consortia:** Member of OHIONET, Columbus Area Libraries Information Council of Ohio (CALICO), Central Ohio Hospital Library Consortium. **Publications:** Newsletter, bimonthly - for internal distribution only; bibliographies - by request. **Remarks:** FAX: (614)265-2437. **Staff:** Lynn Cooper, Med.Libn.; Jo Clark, Supv.

★ 13950 ★
Riverside Municipal Museum - Library (Hist)
3720 Orange St.   Phone: (714)782-5273
Riverside, CA 92501   William G. Dougall, Dir.
Founded: 1924. **Subjects:** History, anthropology, decorative arts, geology and paleontology, botany, zoology. **Holdings:** 1600 books; 400 bound periodical volumes; 250 feet of archival material; 2200 unbound periodicals. **Subscriptions:** 15 journals and other serials. **Services:** Library open to the public for reference use only and with restrictions.

★ 13951 ★
Riverside Osteopathic Hospital - Medical Library (Med)
150 Truax St.   Phone: (313)676-4200
Trenton, MI 48183   Susan E. Skoglund, Dir. of Lib.Serv.
Staff: Prof 1; Other 1. **Subjects:** Medicine, nursing. **Holdings:** 1360 books; 1566 bound periodical volumes; 4 VF drawers of pamphlets; 576 Audio-Digest tapes. **Subscriptions:** 125 journals and other serials. **Services:** Interlibrary loan; library open to the public with restrictions. **Computerized Information Services:** MEDLINE, DIALOG Information Services, BRS Information Technologies, WILSONLINE. **Remarks:** FAX: (313)676-7399.

★ 13952 ★
Riverside Presbyterian Church - Jean Miller Library (Rel-Phil)
849 Park St.   Phone: (904)355-4585
Jacksonville, FL 32204   Evelyn Parker, Libn.
Staff: Prof 2. **Subjects:** Religion, general subjects. **Holdings:** 1500 books. **Subscriptions:** 5 journals and other serials. **Staff:** Blaine Walker, Minister of Educ.

★ 13953 ★
Riverside Press-Enterprise Company - Editorial Library (Publ)
3512 14th St.   Phone: (714)782-7578
Riverside, CA 92501   Joan K. Douglas, Lib.Dir.
Founded: 1968. **Staff:** Prof 1; Other 6. **Subjects:** Newspaper reference topics. **Holdings:** 350 books; clippings; microfilm. **Subscriptions:** 10 journals and other serials. **Services:** Copying; library open to the public on a limited schedule. **Computerized Information Services:** NEXIS, Dow Jones News/Retrieval. **Special Indexes:** Index of newspapers (notebooks and microfiche). **Remarks:** FAX: (714)782-7572.

★ 13954 ★
Riverside Regional Medical Center - Health Sciences Library (Med)
J. Clyde Morris Blvd.
Newport News, VA 23601   Phone: (804)599-2175
Staff: Prof 2; Other 5. **Subjects:** Family practice, medicine, pediatrics, obstetrics-gynecology, nursing, allied health sciences. **Holdings:** 4038 books; 6742 bound periodical volumes. **Subscriptions:** 203 journals and other serials. **Services:** Interlibrary loan; copying; library open to the public for reference use only. **Computerized Information Services:** MEDLINE. **Remarks:** Alternate telephone number(s): 599-2682. FAX: (804)599-2986. **Staff:** Joan Taylor, Nurs.Libn.; Linda Chelmow, Med.Libn.

★ 13955 ★
Riverside Research Institute - Library (Sci-Engr)
330 W. 42 St.   Phone: (212)563-4545
New York, NY 10036   Noreen Reilly, Libn.
Founded: 1967. **Subjects:** Biomedical engineering, radar, military systems, electro-optics. **Holdings:** 12,000 volumes. **Subscriptions:** 50 journals and other serials; 2 newspapers. **Services:** Library not open to the public. **Remarks:** FAX: (212)502-1629.

Riverton Memorial Hospital
See: Healthtrust (7084)

★ 13956 ★
Riverview Hospital - Library Services (Med)
500 Lougheed Hwy.   Phone: (604)524-7018
Port Coquitlam, BC, Canada V3C 4J2   Min-Ja Laubental, Libn.
Founded: 1949. **Staff:** Prof 1; Other 3. **Subjects:** Psychiatry, psychology, psychiatric nursing, social sciences, medicine, hospital administration,

forensic psychiatry. **Special Collections:** Audiovisual collection (125 tapes; 100 filmstrips). **Holdings:** 10,000 books; 1510 bound periodical volumes; 160 staff publications; 50 annual reports; 580 pamphlets. **Subscriptions:** 150 journals and other serials. **Services:** Interlibrary loan; copying; library open to the public for reference use only on request. **Automated Operations:** Computerized cataloging. **Computerized Information Services:** MEDLINE; Envoy 100 (electronic mail service). **Publications:** In the Journals, monthly; acquisitions list - both for internal distribution only. **Remarks:** FAX: (604)660-9718. Electronic mail address(es): RIV.LIB (Envoy 100). Maintains a Patients' Library of 5000 volumes.

★ 13957 ★
Riverview Medical Center - Clinical Library (Med)
1 Riverview Plaza   Phone: (908)530-2275
Red Bank, NJ 07701   Cheryl Newman, Dir.
Founded: 1968. **Staff:** Prof 1; Other 1. **Subjects:** Clinical medicine. **Holdings:** 2500 books; 900 audio cassettes; microfilm. **Subscriptions:** 250 journals and other serials. **Services:** Interlibrary loan; copying; library open to health professionals only. **Computerized Information Services:** MEDLARS, BRS Information Technologies; MESSAGES (electronic mail service). Performs searches on fee basis. **Networks/Consortia:** Member of Monmouth-Ocean Biomedical Information Consortium (MOBIC), Central Jersey Regional Library Cooperative, BHSL. **Remarks:** FAX: (908)530-2394.

★ 13958 ★
Rivier College - Regina Library (Area-Ethnic, Hum)
429 Main St.   Phone: (603)888-1311
Nashua, NH 03060   Sr. Arlene Callahan, Lib.Dir.
Founded: 1933. **Staff:** Prof 8; Other 7. **Subjects:** French-Canadians, education, business, law. **Holdings:** 122,018 volumes; 48,925 nonprint items. **Subscriptions:** 795 journals and other serials; 15 newspapers. **Services:** Interlibrary loan; copying; library open to the public for reference use only. **Automated Operations:** Integrated library system (MULTILIS). **Networks/Consortia:** Member of New Hampshire College & University Council Library Policy Committee (NHCUC). **Publications:** Now and New (acquisitions list), biweekly - for internal distribution only. **Special Catalogs:** Regina Library Union List of Serials (printout). **Remarks:** FAX: (603)888-6447. **Staff:** Elaine Bean, Hd., Info.Serv.; Jane Williams, Hd., Tech.Serv.

★ 13959 ★
RJR Nabisco - Nabisco Brands, Inc. - Technology Center Library
(Food-Bev)
200 Deforest Ave.
P.O. Box 1944   Phone: (201)503-3467
East Hanover, NJ 07936-1944   Sonia D. Meurer, Supv., Lib.
Founded: 1952. **Staff:** Prof 3; Other 3. **Subjects:** Food science. **Holdings:** 6000 books; 3000 bound periodical volumes. **Subscriptions:** 402 journals and other serials. **Services:** Interlibrary loan; copying; SDI; library open to the public. **Automated Operations:** Computerized cataloging, circulation, and serials. **Computerized Information Services:** DIALOG Information Services, PFDS Online, LEXIS, NEXIS, Dun & Bradstreet Business Credit Services, Dow Jones News/Retrieval, PRODUCTSCAN, BRS Information Technologies, Chemical Abstracts Service (CAS). **Publications:** Guide to Current Literature, weekly; Library Bulletin, monthly; Technical Meetings List, annual. **Remarks:** Alternate telephone numbers are 503-3539 and 503-3479. FAX: (201)428-8950. **Staff:** Carol Butler, Libn.

RKO Collection
See: **Academy of Motion Picture Arts and Sciences - Margaret Herrick Library** (35)

RKO Pictures Archive
See: **University of California, Los Angeles - Arts, Architecture and Urban Planning Library** (18370)

★ 13960 ★
RMI Titanium Company - Research & Development Department Library
1000 Warren Ave.   Phone: (216)544-7643
Niles, OH 44446   Carol Muszik, Chf.Libn.
Remarks: No further information was supplied by respondent.

★ 13961 ★
RMT, Inc. - Library (Sci-Engr)
744 Heartland Trail
P.O. Box 8923   Phone: (608)831-4444
Madison, WI 53708-8923   Kathy Horton, Mgr.Corp.Info.Servs.
Founded: 1977. **Staff:** Prof 2. **Subjects:** Solid and hazardous waste management, environmental engineering, industrial hygiene, regulatory compliance, hydrogeology, consulting engineering. **Holdings:** Figures not available. **Subscriptions:** 300 journals and other serials. **Services:** Interlibrary loan; copying; SDI; library open to the public for reference use only by appointment. **Computerized Information Services:** DIALOG Information Services, Chemical Information Systems, Inc. (CIS), STN International, LEXIS, NEXIS, NLM, Ground Water On-Line. Performs searches on fee basis. **Networks/Consortia:** Member of Multitype Advisory Library Committee (MALC). **Remarks:** FAX: (608)831-3334. **Staff:** Eva Cry, Corp.Libn.

★ 13962 ★
Roanoke Law Library (Law)
315 Church Ave., S.W.   Phone: (703)981-2268
Roanoke, VA 24016   Clayne Calhoun, Law Libn.
Founded: 1925. **Staff:** Prof 1; Other 1. **Subjects:** State and federal law, federal taxation. **Holdings:** 20,000 volumes; 39,000 microfiche. **Subscriptions:** 170 journals and other serials. **Services:** Interlibrary loan; copying; library open to the public. **Computerized Information Services:** WESTLAW, Veralex 2, DIALOG Information Services, LEXIS, Virginia Legislative Information System. Performs searches on fee basis. **Publications:** Virginia 23rd Circuit Reports. **Remarks:** FAX: (703)342-8664.

★ 13963 ★
Roanoke Memorial Hospitals - Health Sciences Library (Med)
Box 13367   Phone: (703)981-7371
Roanoke, VA 24033   Lucy D. Glenn, Dir.
Founded: 1959. **Staff:** Prof 2; Other 3. **Subjects:** Medicine, nursing, allied health sciences, management. **Holdings:** 3147 books; 4299 bound periodical volumes. **Subscriptions:** 288 journals and other serials. **Services:** Interlibrary loan; copying; SDI; library open to medical and health agencies staff. **Computerized Information Services:** MEDLINE; DOCLINE (electronic mail service). Performs searches. **Networks/Consortia:** Member of Southwestern Virginia Health Information Librarians (SWVAHILI). **Remarks:** FAX: (703)981-8666. **Formerly:** Its Medical Library.

Roanoke Times & World-News
See: **Times-World Corporation** (16360)

★ 13964 ★
Roanoke Valley Historical Society - Library (Hist)
Box 1904   Phone: (703)342-5770
Roanoke, VA 24008   Clare White, Hd.Libn.
Founded: 1957. **Staff:** 4. **Subjects:** Roanoke and Southwest Virginia history. **Special Collections:** James Breckinridge and William Preston family letters and papers (1030 items); Dr. W.C. Campbell papers. **Holdings:** 500 books. **Subscriptions:** 600 journals and other serials. **Services:** Library open to researchers by appointment.

★ 13965 ★
Roaring Fork Energy Center - Library (Energy)
242 Main St.   Phone: (303)963-0311
Carbondale, CO 81623   Steve Standiford, Dir.
Founded: 1974. **Staff:** 3. **Subjects:** Solar energy, alternative energy, solar greenhouses, energy planning and conservation, renewable resources, wind and water power. **Holdings:** 1200 books; films; videotapes; slides; computer software programs. **Subscriptions:** 12 journals and other serials. **Services:** Interlibrary loan; copying; library open to the public.

Jerome Robbins Archive
See: **New York Public Library for the Performing Arts - Dance Collection** (11636)

John E. Robbins Library
See: **Brandon University** (2078)

Robbins Library
See: **Harvard University** (6990)

Robbins Museum
See: **Massachusetts Archaeological Society - Robbins Museum** (9786)

Rossell Hope Robbins Library
See: **University of Rochester** (19285)

Warren M. Robbins Library - National Museum of African Art
See: **Smithsonian Institution Libraries** (15286)

Roberson Center for the Arts and Sciences - Broome County Historical Society
See: **Broome County Historical Society - Josiah T. Newcomb Library** (2251)

A. Webb Roberts Library
See: **Southwestern Baptist Theological Seminary** (15538)

★ 13966 ★
H. Armstrong Roberts, Inc. - Stock Photography Library (Aud-Vis)
4203 Locust St.   Phone: (215)386-6300
Philadelphia, PA 19104   H. Armstrong Roberts, III, Pres.
Founded: 1920. **Subjects:** Photography of H. Armstrong Roberts and select contributing photographers. **Special Collections:** Charles Phelps Cushing Collection of historical engravings and photographs. **Holdings:** 1 million black/white original contemporary photographs and color transparencies. **Remarks:** FAX: (215)386-3521. Also maintains offices or representatives in New York City, Chicago, Los Angeles, and Toronto, Canada.

★ 13967 ★
Oral Roberts University - Graduate Theology Library - John Messick Learning Resource Center (Rel-Phil)
7777 S. Lewis   Phone: (918)495-6894
Tulsa, OK 74171   Oon-Chor Khoo, Libn.
Founded: 1962. **Staff:** Prof 2; Other 8. **Subjects:** Biblical literature, historical and theological studies, Christianity and culture, practices of ministry. **Special Collections:** Holy Spirit Research Center (Charismatic and Pentecostal Movement, Gifts of the Holy Spirit, Divine Healing). **Holdings:** 106,507 books; 6432 bound periodical volumes; 23,861 microforms; 11,661 AV programs; 48 VF drawers of pamphlets; 141 tracts; 133 scores and kits. **Subscriptions:** 1784 journals and other serials. **Services:** Interlibrary loan; center open to the public with special written permission. **Automated Operations:** Computerized public access catalog, cataloging, acquisitions, serials, and circulation. **Computerized Information Services:** DIALOG Information Services, MEDLINE, OCLC, DYNIX. Performs searches on fee basis. **Networks/Consortia:** Member of AMIGOS Bibliographic Council, Inc. **Special Indexes:** Subject index of periodical articles on Pentecostal and Charismatic studies (1977 to present; vertical files). **Remarks:** FAX: (918)495-6033. **Staff:** Jim Zeigler.

★ 13968 ★
Oral Roberts University - Library - Holy Spirit Research Center (Rel-Phil)
7777 S. Lewis   Phone: (918)495-6899
Tulsa, OK 74171   Jim Zeigler, Dir.
Founded: 1962. **Staff:** Prof 1; Other 1. **Subjects:** Glossolalia, divine healing, history of Pentecostalism, Charismatic movement, Pentecostal denominations and organizations, gifts and manifestations of the Holy Spirit. **Special Collections:** Divine healing; William Braham Sermons and Photograph Collection (printed material and audio cassettes). **Holdings:** 12,000 books; 1800 bound periodical volumes; 1800 tapes and cassettes; 40 VF drawers of pamphlets; 37 reels of microfilm; 54 records; 90 video cassettes; theses and dissertations. **Subscriptions:** 500 journals and other serials. **Services:** Interlibrary loan; photocopying; center open to the public for reference use only with advanced notice. **Automated Operations:** Computerized public access catalog, cataloging and acquisitions. **Computerized Information Services:** Internal databases. **Publications:** Bibliographies on Pentecostal and charismatic materials, the Holy Spirit and divine healing; Microfilm Holdings in HSRC; Annotated Bibliography of Catholic Charismatic Materials in HSRC; General Works on the Baptism in the Holy Spirit as Taught by Pentecostals - for sale; Oral Roberts books - for sale. **Special Indexes:** Periodicals index for articles on Pentecostal & Charismatic studies, 1979 to present.

★ 13969 ★
Roberts Wesleyan College - Kenneth B. Keating Library - Archives (Hist, Rel-Phil)
2301 Westside Dr.   Phone: (716)594-9471
Rochester, NY 14624   Charles H. Canon, III, Archv.
Founded: 1976. **Staff:** Prof 1. **Subjects:** History of the college and the Free Methodist Church. **Special Collections:** Papers of Benjamin Titus Roberts, founder of the college (manuscripts; photographs; diaries; ephemera). **Holdings:** 4196 archival items. **Services:** Copying; archives open to the public by appointment. **Computerized Information Services:** DIALOG Information Services. Performs searches on fee basis. **Networks/Consortia:** Member of Rochester Regional Library Council (RRLC). **Remarks:** FAX: (716)594-4383.

J.C. Robertson Memorial Library
See: **Indian River Memorial Hospital** (7750)

Robertson Library, Archives and Special Collections
See: **University of Prince Edward Island** (19232)

Paul Robeson Library
See: **State University of New York - Syracuse Educational Opportunity Center - Paul Robeson Library** (15725)

John P. Robin Library
See: **Carnegie Museum of Natural History - Library** (3085)

E. Claiborne Robins School of Business
See: **University of Richmond** (19269)

Arthur H. Robinson Map Library
See: **University of Wisconsin--Madison** (19580)

★ 13970 ★
Robinson, Bradshaw & Hinson, P.A. - Guardian Building Law Library (Law)
PO Drawer 12070   Phone: (803)325-2900
Rock Hill, SC 29730-2070   Dawn A. Bartholic, Libn.
Founded: 1984. **Staff:** Prof 1. **Subjects:** Law. **Holdings:** 5000 books. **Subscriptions:** 200 journals and other serials; 14 newspapers. **Services:** Copying; library open to area attorneys by membership. **Computerized Information Services:** WESTLAW, DIALOG Information Services. **Special Indexes:** Reffile (reference file index; online). **Remarks:** Library located at One Law Place, Suite 600, Rock Hill, SC 29730. FAX: (803)325-2929. **Formerly:** Roddey, Carpenter, and White, P.A.

★ 13971 ★
Robinson & Cole - Library (Law)
One Commercial Plaza   Phone: (203)275-8200
Hartford, CT 06103-3597   David S. Matthewson, Dir. of Lib.Oper.
Staff: Prof 1; Other 2. **Subjects:** Law, business. **Holdings:** 20,000 books. **Subscriptions:** 300 journals and other serials; 6 newspapers. **Services:** Interlibrary loan; library not open to the public. **Computerized Information Services:** WESTLAW, LEXIS, NEXIS, Information America. **Remarks:** FAX: (203)275-8299.

Elwyn B. Robinson Department of Special Collections
See: **University of North Dakota** (19095)

Robinson-Lehane Library
See: **Dorchester Historical Society** (4962)

Robinson Library
See: **Hartford Hospital - Health Science Libraries** (6934)

Mary & Louis Robinson Library
See: Jewish Board of Family & Children Services (8377)

★ 13972 ★
Rowland E. Robinson Memorial Association - Rokeby Museum - Library (Hist)
RD 1   Phone: (802)877-3406
Ferrisburg, VT 05456   Karen E. Petersen, Musm.Dir.
Founded: 1963. **Subjects:** Family history, abolition, reform, agriculture, Quakerism. **Special Collections:** Robinson/Stevens Family Papers Collection (30 cubic feet). **Holdings:** 2000 books; 30 cubic feet of archival materials; 60 reels of microfilm; 1000 unbound periodicals. **Services:** Library open to the public by appointment.

★ 13973 ★
Robinson, Sheppard, Borenstein, Shapiro - Law Library (Law)
800 Place Victoria, Suite 4700
Box 322, Succ. Tour de la Bourse   Phone: (514)878-2631
Montreal, PQ, Canada H4Z 1H6   Angela Belle Tietolman, Law Libn.
Staff: Prof 2; Other 1. **Subjects:** Law - civil, insurance, corporate, commercial, family and divorce, taxation, labor, environment. **Holdings:** Figures not available. **Services:** Interlibrary loan; library not open to the public. **Computerized Information Services:** QL Systems, WESTLAW, SOQUIJ, CAN/LAW. **Remarks:** FAX:(514)878-1865.

★ 13974 ★
Robinson, Silverman, Pearce, Aronsohn, & Berman - Library & Information Center (Law)
1290 Avenue of the Americas   Phone: (212)541-2166
New York, NY 10104   Christine Wierzba, Law Libn.
Founded: 1950. **Staff:** Prof 2. **Subjects:** Law. **Holdings:** 12,000 books; New York Law Journal, 1979 to present, on microfiche. **Subscriptions:** 95 journals and other serials; 8 newspapers. **Services:** Interlibrary loan; library not open to the public. **Automated Operations:** Computerized cataloging, acquisitions, and serials. **Computerized Information Services:** LEXIS, DIALOG Information Services, Dow Jones News/Retrieval, Information America, WESTLAW, Spectrum Ownership Profiles Online, Dun & Bradstreet Business Credit Services, VU/TEXT Information Services, RLIN; internal databases; EasyLink (electronic mail service). **Publications:** Robinson, Silverman, et al Library Bulletin, quarterly. **Remarks:** FAX: (212)541-4630. Telex: 237392 RSPABUR. Electronic mail address(es): 62948172 (EasyLink). **Staff:** Michael Popolino, Asst.Libn.

Robotics International of the Society of Manufacturing Engineers Collection
See: Society of Manufacturing Engineers - SME Library (15334)

★ 13975 ★
Rochester Academy of Medicine - Library (Med)
1441 East Ave.   Phone: (716)271-1313
Rochester, NY 14610   Mrs. Stockweather, Libn.
Founded: 1900. **Staff:** 1. **Subjects:** Medicine and allied health sciences. **Holdings:** 31,300 volumes. **Subscriptions:** 90 journals. **Services:** Interlibrary loan; copying; library open to the public. **Networks/Consortia:** Member of Rochester Area Libraries in Healthcare.

★ 13976 ★
Rochester Business Institute - Betty Cronk Memorial Library (Bus-Fin)
1850 E. Ridge Rd.   Phone: (716)266-0430
Rochester, NY 14622   Lois Klonick, Libn.
Founded: 1925. **Staff:** Prof 1. **Subjects:** Business and allied subjects. **Special Collections:** Computer books; annual reports; college brochures; accounting books; Career Corner. **Holdings:** 2600 volumes. **Subscriptions:** 110 journals and other serials. **Services:** Interlibrary loan; copying; library open to the public by appointment for research. **Computerized Information Services:** Internal database. **Networks/Consortia:** Member of Rochester Regional Library Council (RRLC). **Remarks:** FAX: (716)325-7297.

Rochester Democrat & Chronicle
See: Rochester Times-Union and Rochester Democrat & Chronicle (13996)

★ 13977 ★
Rochester Gas and Electric Corporation - Technical Information Center (Sci-Engr, Energy)
89 East Ave.   Phone: (716)724-8125
Rochester, NY 14649   Sharon M. Paprocki, Tech.Info.Coord.
Staff: Prof 1; Other 1. **Subjects:** Electrical power generation, nuclear power, energy, engineering, environment, management. **Special Collections:** Electric Power Research Institute (EPRI) reports (9500). **Holdings:** 7000 books and reports; 6500 items on nuclear power, including codes, standards, and regulations; 2600 power plant documents; 500 internal reports; 8 drawers of pamphlets and company historical information. **Subscriptions:** 125 journals and other serials. **Services:** Interlibrary loan; copying; center open to the public by appointment and with escort. **Automated Operations:** Computerized cataloging, circulation, and indexing. **Computerized Information Services:** DIALOG Information Services. **Networks/Consortia:** Member of Rochester Regional Library Council (RRLC). **Publications:** RG & E News, bimonthly; book review columns and acquisitions lists. **Special Indexes:** Industry codes & standards; technical manuals for power plant systems & components; technical reports (all online). **Remarks:** FAX: (716)724-8405.

★ 13978 ★
Rochester General Hospital - Lillie B. Werner Health Sciences Library (Med)
1425 Portland Ave.   Phone: (716)338-4743
Rochester, NY 14621   Bernie Todd Smith, Lib.Dir.
Founded: 1883. **Staff:** Prof 4; Other 5. **Subjects:** Medicine, psychiatry, nursing. **Special Collections:** History of Medicine Collection (200 books). **Holdings:** 6000 books; 6000 bound periodical volumes; 1500 AV programs. **Subscriptions:** 400 journals and other serials. **Services:** Interlibrary loan; library not open to the public. **Computerized Information Services:** MEDLINE, DIALOG Information Services, BRS Information Technologies; CD-ROM (MEDLINE, HEALTH, Nursing & Allied Health Database, CONSULT). **Networks/Consortia:** Member of Rochester Regional Library Council (RRLC). **Publications:** Information Alert, quarterly; Circuit Librarian Program brochure; Werner Lite, monthly; Circuit Connection, monthly. **Special Catalogs:** Catalog of AV materials, quarterly (computer-generated book). **Remarks:** FAX: (716)461-5440. **Staff:** Edward Lewek, Asst.Lib.Dir.; Tami Hartzell, Circuit Libn.; Lana Rudy, Circuit Libn.; Patricia Doring, Acq. & AV Libn.

★ 13979 ★
Rochester Historical Society - Library (Hist)
485 East Ave.   Phone: (716)271-2705
Rochester, NY 14607   Christina Oddleifson, Lib.Cons.
Founded: 1861. **Staff:** 2. **Subjects:** Local history. **Holdings:** 6000 titles; 200 periodical titles; 25 volumes of RHS publications; manuscript and archival material; photographs; maps; genealogical material; complete file of Rochester directories, 1827 to present. **Subscriptions:** 10 journals and other serials. **Services:** Library open to the public with restrictions. **Staff:** Elizabeth Yonkers, Archv.

★ 13980 ★
Rochester Institute of Technology - Chemistry Graduate Research Library
One Lomb Memorial Dr.
Rochester, NY 14623
Defunct. Holdings absorbed Rochester Institute of Technology - Wallace Memorial Library.

★ 13981 ★
Rochester Institute of Technology - Melbert B. Cary, Jr. Graphic Arts Collection (Art, Publ)
Wallace Memorial Library   Phone: (716)475-2408
Rochester, NY 14623   David Pankow, Cur.
Founded: 1969. **Staff:** Prof 2. **Subjects:** Printing history, typography, book arts, press books, calligraphy, papermaking, graphic arts. **Special Collections:** Rudolf Koch; Fritz Kredel; Officina Bodoni; Grabhorn Press; Spiral Press; W.A. Dwiggins; T.M. Cleland; Press of the Woolly Whale;

Laboratory Press; Bruce Rogers; Frederic W. Goudy; Bernard Middleton Collection (books on book binding); Hermann Zapf Collection; Type Specimen books; broadsides and posters; fore edge paintings; Paul Standard archive on calligraphy and bookmaking; Patricia England Collection of American Fine Printing. **Holdings:** 18,000 books; 16 VF drawers of clippings; ephemera; pamphlets; 12 boxes of posters, broadsides, drawings. **Subscriptions:** 20 journals and other serials. **Services:** Copying (limited); collection open to the public. **Computerized Information Services:** InterNet (electronic mail service). **Remarks:** FAX: (716)475-6900. Electronic mail address(es): IN%"DPPWML@RITVAX.ISC.RIT.EDU (InterNet).

★ 13982 ★
Rochester Institute of Technology - National Technical Institute for the Deaf - Staff Resource Center (Med)
Lyndon Baines Johnson Bldg., Rm. 2490
1 Lomb Memorial Dr. Phone: (716)475-6823
Rochester, NY 14623 Gail Kovalik, Res.Spec.
Founded: 1978. **Staff:** Prof 1; Other 1. **Subjects:** Deafness. **Special Collections:** National Center on Employment of the Deaf information collection (4 VF drawers). **Holdings:** 800 books; 1100 videotapes; 300 AV programs; 3000 pamphlets. **Subscriptions:** 30 journals and other serials. **Services:** Interlibrary loan; copying; center open to the public by appointment. **Networks/Consortia:** Member of Rochester Regional Library Council (RRLC). **Publications:** A Deafness Collection: Selected and Annotated, ASCLA/ALA, 1985.

★ 13983 ★
Rochester Institute of Technology - Wallace Memorial Library (Art, Sci-Engr, Soc Sci, Comp Sci)
P.O. Box 9887 Phone: (716)475-2565
Rochester, NY 14623 Patricia A. Pitkin, Dir.
Staff: Prof 28; Other 17. **Subjects:** Art, business, criminal justice, printing, micro-optics, computer science, imaging science, photography, social work, engineering, science. **Special Collections:** The deaf and deafness. **Holdings:** 285,000 books and bound periodical volumes; 1824 theses; 140 VF drawers of archives; 70,000 slides; 400 films; 22,231 reels of microfilm; 250,000 microfiche. **Subscriptions:** 6334 journals and other serials; 35 newspapers. **Services:** Interlibrary loan; library open to the public. **Automated Operations:** Computerized cataloging, acquisitions, and circulation. **Computerized Information Services:** OCLC; internal databases. Performs searches on fee basis. **Networks/Consortia:** Member of Rochester Regional Library Council (RRLC). **Publications:** Faculty Writings and Achievements, 1951 to present; Yet Another Newsletter; bibliographies. **Staff:** Joan Green, Dir., Instr. Media Serv.; Lois Goodman, Archv.; Chandra Mckenzie, Asst.Dir., Access.Serv.; Margaret Fallon, Hd., Acq.

★ 13984 ★
Rochester Methodist Hospital - Methodist Kahler Library (Med)
Rochester, MN 55902 Phone: (507)286-7425
Karen Larsen, Supv.
Staff: Prof 2; Other 2. **Subjects:** Nursing services and education, hospital administration and management. **Special Collections:** History of Nursing. **Holdings:** 11,500 books; 500 bound periodical volumes; 1000 AV programs; 12 VF drawers of newspaper clippings and pamphlets. **Subscriptions:** 350 journals and other serials. **Services:** Interlibrary loan; copying; library open to the public with limited outside circulation. **Computerized Information Services:** DIALOG Information Services. Performs searches on fee basis. **Networks/Consortia:** Member of National Network of Libraries of Medicine - Greater Midwest Region. **Remarks:** A branch library of the Mayo Foundation - Section of Mayo Medical Center Libraries. **Staff:** Ruth Hadley Hoover, Asst.Libn.; Mary Ellen Smith, Libn., Patients' Lib.

★ 13985 ★
Rochester Museum and Science Center - Library (Hist, Sci-Engr, Soc Sci)
657 East Ave.
Box 1480
Rochester, NY 14603-1480 Phone: (716)271-4320
Leatrice M. Kemp, Libn.
Founded: 1914. **Staff:** Prof 1. **Subjects:** Natural sciences, anthropology, local history, American Indians, antiques, archeology, costume, technology, museology. **Special Collections:** Albert Stone Collection of local photographs, 1904-1934 (15,000); slide library. **Holdings:** 26,000 volumes; museum bulletins; archival material and ephemera. **Subscriptions:** 60 journals and other serials. **Services:** Copying; library open to the public. **Automated Operations:** Computerized cataloging. **Networks/Consortia:** Member of Rochester Regional Library Council (RRLC).

★ 13986 ★
Rochester Museum and Science Center - Strasenburgh Planetarium - Todd Library (Sci-Engr)
657 East Ave. Phone: (716)271-4320
Rochester, NY 14607 Grace Matthews, Libn.
Staff: Prof 1. **Subjects:** Astronomy, space science. **Holdings:** 1500 books; 500 bound periodical volumes. **Subscriptions:** 21 journals and other serials. **Services:** Library open to the public for reference use only. **Remarks:** FAX: (716)271-5935.

★ 13987 ★
Rochester Post-Bulletin - Library (Publ)
18 1st Ave., S.E. Phone: (507)285-7737
Rochester, MN 55903 Gretchen Meredith
Staff: Prof 1; Other 1. **Subjects:** Newspaper reference topics, Mayo Clinic, IBM. **Holdings:** 260 books; 2 drawers of microfilm of Rochester Post-Bulletin, 1977 to present; Agri News, 1976 to present, on microfilm. **Subscriptions:** 19 journals and other serials; 17 newspapers. **Services:** Interlibrary loan; library not open to the public. **Computerized Information Services:** DIALOG Information Services. **Networks/Consortia:** Member of Southeastern Libraries Cooperating (SELCO).

Rochester Psychiatric Center
See: **New York (State) Office of Mental Health** (11676)

★ 13988 ★
Rochester Public Library - Art Division (Art, Mus)
115 South Ave. Phone: (716)428-7332
Rochester, NY 14604 Mary Lee Miller, Hd.
Staff: Prof 4; Other 5. **Subjects:** Fine arts, music, photography, film history, antiques, ornamental gardening, architecture, urban planning, crafts. **Special Collections:** Picture file (84 VF drawers). **Holdings:** 48,000 books; 12,000 slides; 20,000 sound recordings; choir music; framed prints. **Subscriptions:** 216 journals and other serials. **Services:** Interlibrary loan; copying. **Networks/Consortia:** Member of Rochester Regional Library Council (RRLC). **Remarks:** FAX: (716)428-7313. **Staff:** Shirley Iversen; Robert Scheffel; Martin Steinhauser.

★ 13989 ★
Rochester Public Library - Business, Economics and Law Division (Bus-Fin, Soc Sci, Law)
115 South Ave. Phone: (716)428-7328
Rochester, NY 14604 Carolyn Johnson, Hd.
Staff: Prof 7; Other 2. **Subjects:** Business, economics, labor, employment, political science, law. **Special Collections:** Industrial directories; financial services; corporation annual reports; Foundation Center Collection. **Holdings:** 72,000 books; 15 VF drawers of pamphlets and clippings; federal, state, and local documents; microfilm; recordings. **Subscriptions:** 700 journals and other serials. **Services:** Interlibrary loan; copying. **Computerized Information Services:** DIALOG Information Services. **Networks/Consortia:** Member of Rochester Regional Library Council (RRLC). **Remarks:** FAX: (716)428-7313. **Staff:** Patricia Genberg; Ilena Montana; Larry Dunsker; Maria Stein; Diane Kozlowski; Alla Levi.

★ 13990 ★
Rochester Public Library - Education, Sociology and Religion Division (Educ, Rel-Phil, Soc Sci)
115 South Ave. Phone: (716)428-7330
Rochester, NY 14604 Judith Prevratil, Hd.
Staff: Prof 3; Other 2. **Subjects:** Education, religion, philosophy, psychology, psychiatry, ethics, sociology, folklore, etiquette. **Special Collections:** College catalog collection (paperback and microfiche); Education/Job Information Center. **Holdings:** 53,000 books; 300 pamphlets. **Subscriptions:** 234 journals and other serials. **Services:** Interlibrary loan; copying; Regents External Degree Advisory Service. **Computerized Information Services:** DIALOG Information Services. **Networks/Consortia:** Member of Rochester Regional Library Council (RRLC). **Publications:** New Books for Teachers - distributed to city and county school districts for duplication and distribution to teachers. **Remarks:** FAX: (716)428-7313. **Staff:** Nanci Rosenberg-Nugent; Joan Kelly; Mary Keenan.

★ 13991 ★
Rochester Public Library - History, Government and Travel Division
(Hist, Soc Sci)
115 South Ave.   Phone: (716)428-7323
Rochester, NY 14604   Sheila O'Donnell, Hd.
Staff: Prof 3; Other 1. **Subjects:** History, government, travel, international law and relations, archeology, the military. **Special Collections:** Map collection including topographic maps for New York State. **Holdings:** 68,000 volumes; 26 VF drawers of pamphlets and travel brochures; slides; recordings. **Subscriptions:** 216 journals and other serials. **Services:** Interlibrary loan; copying. **Networks/Consortia:** Member of Rochester Regional Library Council (RRLC). **Publications:** Booklists, irregular. **Remarks:** FAX: (716)428-7313. **Staff:** Jeanne Mino; Thomas Bolkan.

★ 13992 ★
Rochester Public Library - Literature, Biography and Sports Division
(Hum, Rec)
115 South Ave.
Rochester, NY 14604   Phone: (716)428-7315
Staff: Prof 5; Other 3. **Subjects:** Literature, fiction, biography, language, speech, journalism, sports and games. **Special Collections:** Talking books; books in French, Spanish, German, Italian, Hungarian. **Holdings:** 147,000 books; 3000 large print books; 12 VF drawers of pamphlets and clippings; 3500 phonograph records; 3500 cassettes. **Subscriptions:** 160 journals and other serials. **Services:** Interlibrary loan; copying. **Networks/Consortia:** Member of Rochester Regional Library Council (RRLC). **Remarks:** FAX: (716)428-7313. **Staff:** Lucie B. Miller; Jill Kidder; Ernestine Hebert; Shelley Karlsons.

★ 13993 ★
Rochester Public Library - Local History and Genealogy Division (Hist)
115 South Ave.   Phone: (716)428-7338
Rochester, NY 14604   Wayne Arnold, Hd.
Staff: Prof 3; Other 1. **Subjects:** History of Rochester and Genesee area, genealogy (primarily New York and New England). **Special Collections:** Local newspapers. **Holdings:** 25,000 books; 15 cases and 400 volumes of manuscripts; 1800 maps; 500 scrapbooks; 145 VF drawers of newspaper clippings; 80 VF drawers of pamphlets and ephemera; 20 VF drawers of pictures; 12 drawers of postcards; 638 reels of microfilm; 120 films. **Subscriptions:** 200 journals and other serials; 78 newspapers. **Services:** Copying (limited). **Networks/Consortia:** Member of Rochester Regional Library Council (RRLC). **Remarks:** FAX: (716)428-7313. The majority of the holdings of the Rochester Historical Society are on permanent loan to the Local History Division. **Staff:** Pamela Scheffel; Deborah Jop.

★ 13994 ★
Rochester Public Library - Reynolds Audio-Visual Department (Aud-Vis)
115 South Ave.   Phone: (716)428-7335
Rochester, NY 14604   Marvin Andrews, Hd.
Staff: Prof 2; Other 7. **Holdings:** 1500 books; 5900 16mm films; 937 filmstrips; 4700 video cassettes. **Subscriptions:** 50 journals and other serials. **Services:** Interlibrary loan; media preview facilities; equipment loans. **Networks/Consortia:** Member of Rochester Regional Library Council (RRLC). **Special Catalogs:** Catalogs of 16mm films and video cassette tapes. **Remarks:** FAX: (716)428-7313. **Staff:** Elizabeth Gilbert; Bonnie Vaccarella.

★ 13995 ★
Rochester Public Library - Science and Technology Division (Sci-Engr, Biol Sci)
115 South Ave.   Phone: (716)428-7327
Rochester, NY 14604   Jeffrey Levine, Hd.
Staff: Prof 4; Other 2. **Subjects:** Physical and natural sciences, applied science and technology, health sciences, environmental sciences, agriculture, home economics. **Special Collections:** Trade catalogs of national firms; automobile shop manuals; Sam's Photofacts Service; Official Gazette of U.S. Patent Office, 1846 to present. **Holdings:** 59,600 books; 15 VF drawers of pamphlets; 130 slide sets; 85 phonograph records; 140 cassettes. **Subscriptions:** 425 journals and other serials. **Services:** Interlibrary loan; copying. **Computerized Information Services:** DIALOG Information Services. **Networks/Consortia:** Member of Rochester Regional Library Council (RRLC). **Publications:** Booklists, irregular. **Remarks:** FAX: (716)428-7313. **Staff:** Carolyn Van Ness; Jackie Katz; Sue Shippey.

★ 13996 ★
Rochester Times-Union and Rochester Democrat & Chronicle - Library
(Publ)
55 Exchange St.   Phone: (716)232-7100
Rochester, NY 14614   Peter Ford, Lib.Mgr.
Founded: 1929. **Staff:** Prof 3; Other 3. **Subjects:** Newspaper reference topics. **Holdings:** 1500 books; clippings; photographs; microfilm. **Subscriptions:** 70 journals and other serials. **Services:** Library not open to the public. **Computerized Information Services:** NEXIS, DataTimes, VU/TEXT Information Services. **Remarks:** FAX: (716)258-2691.

★ 13997 ★
Rock County Health Care Center - Staff Library (Med)
Box 351   Phone: (608)755-2590
Janesville, WI 53547   Ruth Beyer, Inserv.Dir.
Founded: 1971. **Staff:** Prof 1. **Subjects:** Psychiatry, psychiatric social work, geriatrics, nursing. **Holdings:** 1052 books; 29 bound periodical volumes; AV programs. **Subscriptions:** 63 journals and other serials. **Services:** Interlibrary loan; copying; library open to the public. **Networks/Consortia:** Member of South Central Wisconsin Health Science Libraries Consortium. **Remarks:** FAX: (608)755-2553.

★ 13998 ★
Rock County Historical Society - Archives of Rock County History
(Hist)
10 S. High
Box 896   Phone: (608)756-4509
Janesville, WI 53545   Maurice J. Montgomery, Archv.
Founded: 1948. **Staff:** Prof 1. **Subjects:** Rock County local history; land speculation. **Special Collections:** Tallman Family papers (3000 items dealing with land speculation, railroad matters, building construction, 1830-1880). **Holdings:** 1500 books; 40 VF drawers of manuscripts and photocopies of clippings; 500 volumes of school records, business records, diaries; 4 boxes and 15 cubic feet of maps; 50 drawers of cataloged photographs and other miscellaneous items; 4000 abstracts of title of Rock County Lands; 17,000 probate records, 1839-1930. **Subscriptions:** 15 journals and other serials; 5 newspapers. **Services:** Copying; archives open to the public on a limited schedule. **Publications:** Recorder, bimonthly. **Special Catalogs:** Iconographic catalog; artifact catalog (both card). **Special Indexes:** Biographical index to Rock County (card); cemetery records (card); index to published and nonpublished materials (book).

★ 13999 ★
Rock County Law Library (Law)
Courthouse
P.O. Box 425
Bassett, NE 68714
Subjects: Law. **Subscriptions:** 2 journals and other serials. **Services:** Library open to the public. **Remarks:** No further information was supplied by respondent.

Rock Creek Nature Center Library
See: **U.S. Natl. Park Service - National Capital Region** (17758)

Rock Island Argus
See: **(Moline) Daily Dispatch/Rock Island Argus** (10596)

Rock Island Public Library - Blackhawk Genealogical Society
See: **Blackhawk Genealogical Society** (1882)

Rockbridge Historical Society Collection
See: **Washington & Lee University - Special Collections Department** (20013)

Rockdale Temple
See: **K.K. Bene Israel/Rockdale Temple** (8500)

Abby Aldrich Rockefeller Folk Art Center
See: **Colonial Williamsburg Foundation Library** (3931)

★ 14000 ★
Rockefeller Foundation - Library (Soc Sci, Bus-Fin)
1133 Avenue of the Americas　　　　Phone: (212)869-8500
New York, NY 10036　　　　　　Meredith S. Averill, Mgr.
Founded: 1915. **Staff:** Prof 2.5; Other 1. **Subjects:** Philanthropy, social sciences, biography. **Special Collections:** Annual reports of philanthropic institutions; Rockefeller Foundation reports and publications. **Holdings:** 7500 volumes. **Subscriptions:** 580 journals and other serials. **Services:** Interlibrary loan; copying; current awareness; library open to the public by appointment. **Automated Operations:** Computerized cataloging and serials. **Computerized Information Services:** DIALOG, OCLC, NEXIS, DataTimes, VU/TEXT Information Services, MEDLINE, WILSONLINE. **Networks/Consortia:** Member of Consortium of Foundation Libraries (CFL), New York Metropolitan Reference and Research Library Agency, Medical Library Center of New York (MLCNY). **Publications:** Acquisitions list, quarterly - to members of the Consortium of Foundation Libraries and available upon request; periodicals list, annual. **Remarks:** FAX: (212)764-3468. Telex: 224862 ROCKFEL. **Staff:** Laura Covino, Libn.; Maureen Manning, Asst.Libn.

★ 14001 ★
Rockefeller University - Library (Biol Sci, Med, Sci-Engr)
1230 York Ave.
RU Box 263　　　　　　　　　Phone: (212)570-8914
New York, NY 10021-6399　　　　Patricia E. Mackey, Libn.
Founded: 1906. **Staff:** Prof 1; Other 14. **Subjects:** Biological sciences, medicine, chemistry, physics, mathematics. **Holdings:** 185,772 volumes. **Subscriptions:** 499 journals and other serials. **Services:** Interlibrary loan; library not open to the public. **Automated Operations:** Computerized cataloging, acquisitions, serials, and circulation. **Computerized Information Services:** DIALOG Information Services, BRS Information Technologies, NLM, WILSONLINE, NEXIS; BITNET (electronic mail service). **Networks/Consortia:** Member of Medical Library Center of New York (MLCNY), National Network of Libraries of Medicine - Middle Atlantic Region. **Remarks:** FAX: (212)570-7840. Telex: 710 581 4164. Electronic mail address(es): ILL@ROCKVAX.; ILL@ROCKVAX.ROCKEFELLER.EDU (both BITNET).

★ 14002 ★
Rockefeller University - Rockefeller Archive Center (Hist, Soc Sci)
15 Dayton Ave.
Pocantico Hills　　　　　　　Phone: (914)631-4505
North Tarrytown, NY 10591　　　Dr. Darwin H. Stapleton, Dir.
Founded: 1975. **Staff:** Prof 10; Other 6. **Subjects:** American philanthropy; Rockefeller family; education; medicine; physical, natural, and social sciences; public health; arts; humanities; agriculture; Black history; international relations and economic development; labor; politics; population; religion; social welfare; women's history. **Special Collections:** Rockefeller Foundation (6120 cubic feet); General Education Board (350 cubic feet); Laura Spelman Rockefeller Memorial (58 cubic feet); Bureau of Social Hygiene (32 cubic feet); Sealantic Fund (48 cubic feet); John D. Rockefeller (550 cubic feet); Nelson A. Rockefeller papers; John and Mary R. Markle Foundation records (47 cubic feet); Office of the Messrs. Rockefeller (580 cubic feet); International Education Board (37 cubic feet); Spelman Fund of New York (42 cubic feet); Rockefeller University (2400 cubic feet); The Commonwealth Fund (400 cubic feet); International Basic Economy Corporation (94 cubic feet; microforms); Russell Sage Foundation (43 cubic feet); Products of Asia (27 cubic feet); Asia Society (264 cubic feet); China Medical Board (82 cubic feet); Rockefeller Brothers Fund (520 cubic feet); Agricultural Development Council (225 cubic feet); American International Association for Economic and Social Development (143 cubic feet); Population Council (657 cubic feet); Arts, Education and Americans Panel (21 cubic feet); Davison Fund, Inc. (16 cubic feet); JDR 3rd Fund (143 cubic feet); Memorial Sloan-Kettering Cancer Center (582 cubic feet); Martha B. Rockefeller Fund for Music (118 cubic feet); Rockefeller Sanitary Commission for the Eradication of Hookworm Disease (6.5 cubic feet); Union Tank Car Company (6 cubic feet); Lawrence B. Dunham (2 cubic feet); Frederick T. Gates (2 cubic feet); Lewis W. Hackett (20 cubic feet); J. George Harrar (15 cubic feet); John H. Knowles (23 cubic feet); William Rockefeller (12 cubic feet). **Holdings:** 23,000 cubic feet of archival and manuscript collections; 250,000 photographs; 4000 microfiche; 1600 films. **Services:** Copying; center open to scholars by appointment. **Computerized Information Services:** RLIN. **Networks/Consortia:** Member of Research Libraries Information Network (RLIN). **Publications:** Newsletter, annual; occasional papers; Research Reports from the Rockefeller Archive Center. **Special Catalogs:** A Guide to Archives and Manuscripts at the Rockefeller Archive Center, 1989 (pamphlet); Photograph Collections in the Rockefeller Archive Center, 1986. **Remarks:** FAX: (914)631-6017. **Staff:** Lee Hiltzik, Univ.Archv.; Erwin Levold, Archv.; Thomas Rosenbaum, Archv.; Emily Oakhill, Archv.; Harold Oakhill, Archv.; Kenneth W. Rose, Asst. to the Dir.; Melissa Smith, Archv.; Gretchen Koerpel, Archv.; Renee Mastrocco, Archv.; Chris Gratzel, Asst.Archv.; Michele Hiltzik, Asst.Archv.

★ 14003 ★
Rockford College - Howard Colman Library - Special Collections (Soc Sci)
5050 E. State St.　　　　　　Phone: (815)226-4035
Rockford, IL 61108-2393　　　　James T. Michna, Libn.
Founded: 1847. **Staff:** Prof 3; Other 3.5. **Special Collections:** Jane Addams Papers; Julia Lathrop Papers; Holbrook ABC Collection (children's literature; 1000 items); World War I Posters. **Holdings:** 142,786 books; 16,132 bound periodical volumes; 3301 microfilm. **Subscriptions:** 800 journals and other serials; 16 newspapers. **Services:** Interlibrary loan; copying; SDI; special collections open to the public by appointment for reference use only. **Computerized Information Services:** DIALOG Information Services, BRS Information Technologies, WILSONLINE, OCLC; internal database. **Networks/Consortia:** Member of ILLINET. **Publications:** List of Journals, annual. **Staff:** Joan B. Surrey, Pub.Serv.Libn.

★ 14004 ★
Rockford Memorial Hospital - Health Science Library (Med)
2400 N. Rockton Ave.　　　　Phone: (815)968-6861
Rockford, IL 61101　　　Phyllis Nathan, Coord., Lib.Serv.
Staff: Prof 2; Other 1. **Subjects:** Clinical medicine, nursing, health care administration. **Special Collections:** Hunter Memorial Pediatric Library (300 volumes); School of Nursing (3000 volumes). **Holdings:** 2000 books; 2000 bound periodical volumes; 2 VF drawers; 100 nonprint items. **Subscriptions:** 240 journals and other serials. **Services:** Interlibrary loan; copying; library open to the public by arrangement. **Computerized Information Services:** DIALOG Information Services, MEDLARS. **Networks/Consortia:** Member of National Network of Libraries of Medicine - Greater Midwest Region, Northern Illinois Library System (NILS), Upstate Illinois Consortium. **Remarks:** FAX: (815)968-7007.

★ 14005 ★
Rockingham Memorial Hospital - Health Sciences Library (Med)
235 Cantrell Ave.　　　　　Phone: (703)433-4166
Harrisonburg, VA 22801-3293　　　Ilene N. Smith, Lib.Dir.
Founded: 1912. **Staff:** Prof 1. **Subjects:** Clinical medicine, nursing, allied health subjects. **Holdings:** 6000 books and bound periodical volumes; 337 AV programs. **Subscriptions:** 280 journals and other serials. **Services:** Interlibrary loan; SDI; library open to the public with restrictions. **Computerized Information Services:** BRS Information Technologies, MEDLINE, ASTD; DOCLINE (electronic mail service). **Networks/Consortia:** Member of Southwestern Virginia Health Information Librarians (SWVAHILI), SOLINET. **Publications:** Library newsletter, quarterly - for internal distribution only. **Remarks:** FAX: (703)433-3106.

★ 14006 ★
Rockingham Society of Genealogists - Library (Hist)
Exeter Public Library
Box 81　　　　　　　　　Phone: (603)382-5034
Exeter, NH 03833　　　　　　Martha Healey, Libn.
Founded: 1978. **Staff:** 1. **Subjects:** Genealogy, biography, history. **Special Collections:** Rockingham County cemetery records **Holdings:** 20 books. **Services:** Library open to the public. **Special Indexes:** Cemetery surname list (card). **Remarks:** Library is located in Special Collections, Exeter Public Library.

★ 14007 ★
Rockland County Career Information Center (Educ)
83 Main St.　　　　　　　Phone: (914)358-9390
Nyack, NY 10960　　　　　　Dr. Rita Lieberman, Dir.
Founded: 1966. **Staff:** Prof 1; Other 3. **Subjects:** Career information, employment, education, financial aid, personal development. **Holdings:** 500 books; 16 VF drawers of pamphlets; college catalogs for New York, New Jersey, and Connecticut; 480 audiotapes; 10 videotapes. **Subscriptions:** 12 journals and other serials. **Services:** Copying; center open to the public. **Automated Operations:** Computerized public access catalog. **Computerized Information Services:** Internal database (career counseling). **Publications:** Newsletter, semiannual. **Staff:** Esther Cember, Career Info.Asst.

★ 14008 ★
Rockville General Hospital - Medical Library/Resource Room (Med)
31 Union St.   Phone: (203)872-0501
Rockville, CT 06066   Laurie S. Fornes, Dir., Lib.Serv.
Founded: 1960. **Staff:** Prof 1. **Subjects:** Medicine. **Holdings:** 600 books; 300 bound periodical volumes; Audio-Digest tapes, 1960 to present. **Subscriptions:** 118 journals and other serials. **Services:** Interlibrary loan; copying; library open to the public by appointment. **Computerized Information Services:** MEDLINE, Grateful MED; DOCLINE (electronic mail service). **Networks/Consortia:** Member of Connecticut Association of Health Science Libraries (CAHSL), BHSL. **Remarks:** FAX: (203)872-0656.

Rockwell Chemistry Library
See: Tufts University (16554)

Rockwell International
See: Allen-Bradley Company (370)

★ 14009 ★
Rockwell International - Automotive Businesses - Reference Center (Sci-Engr)
2135 W. Maple Rd.   Phone: (313)435-1668
Troy, MI 48084   Cheryl Varga, Libn.
Founded: 1960. **Staff:** Prof 1; Other 1. **Subjects:** Automotive engineering, marketing, technical sciences. **Special Collections:** Society of Automotive Engineers technical papers; American Society for Testing and Materials (ASTM) standards. **Holdings:** 2600 books; 33 bound periodical volumes; 750 annual reports; 300 laboratory reports. **Subscriptions:** 732 journals and other serials; 5 newspapers. **Services:** Interlibrary loan; center not open to the public. **Computerized Information Services:** DIALOG Information Services, PFDS Online, Dow Jones News/Retrieval, NEXIS, Dun & Bradstreet Business Credit Services, InvesText; internal database; OnTyme Electronic Message Network Service (electronic mail service). **Publications:** Reference Center Notes, monthly - for internal distribution only. **Remarks:** FAX: (313)435-8205. Telex: 4997691 Rockwell TRMI. Electronic mail address(es): ROCKWELL15 (OnTyme Electronic Message Network Service).

★ 14010 ★
Rockwell International - Business Research Center (Bus-Fin)
625 Liberty Ave.   Phone: (412)565-5880
Pittsburgh, PA 15222   Lee Whiteman, Supv., Info.Rsrcs.
Founded: 1967. **Staff:** Prof 1. **Subjects:** Business, economic, and financial information for the aerospace, automotive, electronic, and industrial automation businesses. **Holdings:** 1000 books; 800 pamphlets and reports; 5000 Securities and Exchange Commission reports. **Subscriptions:** 350 journals and other serials; 12 newspapers. **Services:** Interlibrary loan; center not open to the public. **Computerized Information Services:** DIALOG Information Services, Dow Jones News/Retrieval, Dun & Bradstreet Business Credit Services, NEXIS, LEXIS, InvesText; CLASS OnTyme Electronic Message Network Service (electronic mail service). **Publications:** Annotated Checklist of Acquisitions, monthly - for internal distribution only; annual list of periodicals and services; Companies of Interest, annual. **Remarks:** FAX: (412)565-2075. Electronic mail address(es): CLASS.ROCKWELL1 (OnTyme Electronic Message Network Service).

★ 14011 ★
Rockwell International - Collins Divisions - Information Center (Sci-Engr)
400 Collins Rd., N.E.   Phone: (319)395-3070
Cedar Rapids, IA 52498   Judith A. Leavitt, Supv.
Founded: 1942. **Staff:** Prof 1; Other 6. **Subjects:** Electronics, management, space, navigation, mathematics, aeronautics, communication equipment, computers, physics. **Holdings:** 7000 books and bound periodical volumes; military, federal, and industrial specifications. **Subscriptions:** 400 journals and other serials. **Services:** Center not open to the public. **Automated Operations:** Computerized public access catalog, cataloging, acquisitions, serials, and circulation. **Computerized Information Services:** DIALOG Information Services, NewsNet, Inc., VU/TEXT Information Services, PFDS Online, WILSONLINE, DTIC, Dow Jones News/Retrieval, Dun & Bradstreet Business Credit Services, NEXIS, DataTimes, LEXIS; Rockwell Technical Information System (RTIS; internal database); OnTyme Electronic Message Network Service (electronic mail service). **Networks/Consortia:** Member of Linn County Library Consortium (LCLC). **Publications:** Acquisition list, biweekly; Communique (newsletter), bimonthly - both for internal distribution only. **Remarks:** FAX: (319)395-5429.

Rockwell International - Electronics Operations - Dallas Information Center
See: Alcatel Network Systems, Inc. - Information Center (326)

★ 14012 ★
Rockwell International - North American Aircraft - Technical Information Center (Sci-Engr)
P.O. Box 92098
Los Angeles, CA 90009   Phone: (213)414-2608
Founded: 1940. **Staff:** 9. **Subjects:** Aeronautics, materials, mathematics and computer sciences, electronics and electrical engineering. **Holdings:** 11,500 books; 5400 bound periodical volumes; 282,000 technical reports; microfiche. **Subscriptions:** 230 journals and other serials. **Services:** Interlibrary loan; center not open to the public. **Automated Operations:** Computerized cataloging. **Computerized Information Services:** DTIC, NASA/RECON, DIALOG Information Services, Rockwell Technical Information System (RTIS; internal database); OnTyme Electronic Message Network Service (electronic mail service). **Remarks:** Center located at 201 N. Douglas St., El Segundo, CA 90245. FAX: (213)414-2170.

★ 14013 ★
Rockwell International - Rocketdyne Division - Technical Information Center (Sci-Engr)
6633 Canoga Ave.   Phone: (818)710-2575
Canoga Park, CA 91303   Julia Keim, Mgr.
Founded: 1955. **Staff:** Prof 4; Other 4. **Subjects:** Engineering, chemistry, physics, nuclear engineering, directed energy, materials science. **Holdings:** 38,000 books; 8709 bound periodical volumes; 6000 reels of microfilm of periodicals; 145,000 technical reports. **Subscriptions:** 635 journals and other serials. **Services:** Interlibrary loan; center not open to the public. **Automated Operations:** Computerized public access catalog, cataloging, acquisitions, and circulation. **Computerized Information Services:** DIALOG Information Services, BRS Information Technologies, Integrated Technical Information System (ITIS), NASA/RECON, DTIC, LEXIS, NEXIS; Rockwell Technical Information System (RTIS; internal database); OnTyme Electronic Message Network Service (electronic mail service). **Networks/Consortia:** Member of CLASS. **Publications:** Current Technical Information; demand bibliographies. **Special Catalogs:** Catalog of microcomputer software programs. **Remarks:** FAX: (818)710-4667. Electronic mail address(es): ROCKWELL2 (OnTyme Electronic Message Network Service). **Staff:** Haroldeane Snell, Br.Supv.; Marie Sigari, Cat.; Scott Peters, Lit. Search; Lyn Ligerman, Acq.

★ 14014 ★
Rockwell International - Rockwell Graphic Systems, Inc. - Technical Information Center (Sci-Engr)
700 Oakmont Ln.   Phone: (708)850-6452
Westmont, IL 60559   Helen Dibler, Adm.
Founded: 1987. **Staff:** Prof 1. **Subjects:** Engineering, graphic arts, electronics. **Holdings:** 3000 books. **Subscriptions:** 100 journals and other serials. **Services:** Interlibrary loan; center not open to the public. **Automated Operations:** Computerized serials. **Computerized Information Services:** DIALOG Information Services, STN International, PFDS Online, NIKKEI TELECOM - Japan News & Retrieval.

★ 14015 ★
Rockwell International - Space Systems Division (SSD) - Technical Information Center (Sci-Engr, Comp Sci)
12214 Lakewood Blvd.   Phone: (213)922-4648
Downey, CA 90241   Nan H. Paik, Mgr.
Founded: 1947. **Staff:** Prof 5; Other 4. **Subjects:** Aerospace technology, information systems, electronics, astronautics, mathematics, engineering, computer sciences. **Holdings:** 48,000 books; 7000 bound periodical volumes; 75,000 technical reports; 650,000 microfiche. **Subscriptions:** 600 journals and other serials. **Services:** Interlibrary loan; copying; SDI and retrospective search; center open to the public by appointment for reference use only. **Automated Operations:** Computerized public access catalog, cataloging, serials, and circulation. **Computerized Information Services:** DIALOG Information Services, Aerospace Online, Dow Jones News/Retrieval, NASA/RECON, DTIC, DataTimes; Rockwell Technical Information System (RTIS; internal database). **Publications:** Custom bibliographies; Monhtly Update; Conference Alert. **Remarks:** FAX: (213)922-0273. **Staff:** Deborah Hull, Lib.Res.Anl.; Charlotte Baughman, Lib.Res.Anl.; Douglas Kelly, Lib.Res.Anl.; Alice Hamilton, Lib.Res.Anl.

★ 14016 ★

Rockwell International - Switching Systems Division - Technical Library
(Comp Sci)
1431 Opus Place   Phone: (708)960-8019
Downers Grove, IL 60515   Patricia A. Ulery, Tech.Libn.
Founded: 1984. **Staff:** Prof 1. **Subjects:** Telecommunications, switching systems, electronics, computers. **Holdings:** 2515 books; 135 NTIS and government reports; 4375 marketing and business reports; 3737 standards and recommendations. **Subscriptions:** 185 journals and other serials. **Services:** Interlibrary loan; library not open to the public. **Computerized Information Services:** DIALOG Information Services, Dun & Bradstreet Business Credit Services, Dow Jones News/Retrieval; OnTyme Electronic Message Network Service, ALANET (electronic mail services). **Networks/Consortia:** Member of Suburban Library System (SLS). **Publications:** Current Literature Accession List, semimonthly - for internal distribution only. **Remarks:** FAX: (708)960-8165.

★ 14017 ★

Rockwell International - Technical Information Center (Sci-Engr)
3370 Miraloma Ave.   Phone: (714)762-2089
Anaheim, CA 92803   Carol Pryor, Mgr.
Founded: 1955. **Staff:** Prof 2; Other 5. **Subjects:** Electronics, chemistry, physics, solid state electronics, microelectronics, inertial navigation, computers, radar, lasers. **Special Collections:** Management Development. **Holdings:** 68,000 books; 5500 bound periodical volumes; 130,000 technical reports; 80,000 technical reports on microfiche. **Subscriptions:** 519 journals and other serials. **Services:** Interlibrary loan; center not open to the public. **Computerized Information Services:** DIALOG Information Services. **Publications:** Weekly Accession Bulletin.

★ 14018 ★

Rockwell International - Technical Information Center (Sci-Engr)
2000 N. Memorial Dr.
Box 582808   Phone: (918)835-3111
Tulsa, OK 74158   Jim Sanders, Mgr.
Founded: 1962. **Staff:** Prof 2. **Subjects:** Aerospace, aircraft, manufacturing and industrial engineering, management. **Holdings:** 2445 books; 6000 military and federal specifications on microfilm; 3000 NASA and DOD reports; 3175 industry technical reports. **Subscriptions:** 92 journals and other serials; 4 newspapers. **Services:** Interlibrary loan (limited); copying; center open to the public with restrictions. **Computerized Information Services:** NASA/RECON, DTIC, DIALOG Information Services; Rockwell Technical Information System (RTIS; internal database); OnTyme Electronic Message Network Service (electronic mail service). **Publications:** Technical Documents - Rockwell Briefings & Reports. **Special Indexes:** Indexes of Engineering Specifications. **Remarks:** FAX: (918)835-3111. Telex: 463 7057. **Staff:** Wenona Hurd, Libn.

★ 14019 ★

Rockwell International Canada Ltd. - Collins Canada Division - TIC Library
150 Bartley Dr.
Toronto, ON, Canada M4A 1C7
Defunct.

★ 14020 ★

Rockwell International Corp. - Digital Communications Division - Library (Sci-Engr, Comp Sci)
4311 Jamboree Rd.
P.O. Box C   Phone: (714)833-4600
Newport Beach, CA 92658-8902   C.A. Blackwell, Mgr.
Staff: Prof 1. **Subjects:** Electronics; communications; data systems/materials; automatic navigation; sensing, monitoring, and reporting; computers; manufacturing research and development. **Special Collections:** Transactions and proceedings of electronics and communications conferences and societies. **Holdings:** 8200 books; 550 bound periodical volumes; 20 VF drawers of working papers (last 5 years, earlier ones on microfilm); 10 VF drawers of engineers' notebooks; 5 VF drawers of procedures. **Subscriptions:** 300 journals and other serials. **Services:** Interlibrary loan; center not open to the public. **Computerized Information Services:** DIALOG Information Services, DTIC.

★ 14021 ★

Rockwell International Corp. - Science Center - Technical Information Center (Sci-Engr)
PO Box 1085   Phone: (805)373-4721
Thousand Oaks, CA 91358   Yolanda O. Fackler, Mgr.
Founded: 1962. **Staff:** Prof 2; Other 1. **Subjects:** Electronics, physics and chemistry, fracture and metal physics, structural materials, semiconductor devices, fluid mechanics, physical metallurgy, computer science, artificial intelligence, robotics, optics. **Holdings:** 9000 books; 6500 bound periodical volumes; 5500 technical reports; 6000 microfiche. **Subscriptions:** 220 journals and other serials. **Services:** Interlibrary loan; copying; SDI; library open to the public by appointment. **Automated Operations:** Computerized cataloging and circulation. **Computerized Information Services:** DIALOG Information Services, NASA/RECON, DTIC, BRS Information Technologies, Dow Jones News/Retrieval, PFDS Online; CD-ROMS (Rockwell Technical Information System - RTIS, DIALOG Information Services, COMPENDEX PLUS, NTIS, Powder Diffraction File, Sigma-Aldrich Meterial Safety Data Sheets). **Networks/Consortia:** Member of Total Interlibrary Exchange (TIE). **Publications:** Library Announcements - for internal distribution only. **Remarks:** FAX: (805)373-4296. Library located at 1049 Camino Dos Rios, Thousand Oaks, CA 91360-2362. **Staff:** Florina Carvalho, ILL; Michele Brown, Cat.

★ 14022 ★

Norman Rockwell Museum at Stockbridge - Reference Department (Art)
Main St.   Phone: (413)298-3539
Stockbridge, MA 01262   Maureen Hart Hennessey, Cur.
Staff: Prof 4. **Subjects:** Norman Rockwell. **Holdings:** 4000 photographic images of Rockwell art work; 100,000 photographic prints and negatives of artist's models and sketches; archive of 4000 original publications; 100 books with Rockwell images; 100,000 item archive which includes clippings file; business and fan letters. **Services:** Department not open to the public. **Remarks:** FAX: (413)298-4253. **Staff:** Linda Szekely, Asst.Cur.

Solomon Rockwell House
See: **Winchester Historical Society** (20473)

★ 14023 ★

Rocky Hill Historical Society - Academy Hall Museum - Library (Hist)
785 Old Main St.
Box 185   Phone: (203)563-6704
Rocky Hill, CT 06067   Ethel M. Cooke, Libn.
Founded: 1962. **Staff:** 1. **Subjects:** Local history. **Special Collections:** 19th century general reading matter; antiques; costumes; accessories; farm implements; tools; handmade quilts; local Indian artifacts; Treat & Davis Melodeon; Ruth Wilcox Collection (antique salts; 500 items); manuscript collection; picture collection. **Holdings:** 1000 books; 20 magnetic tapes (some oral history); local news scrapbooks; 18th and 19th century school texts; local Indian artifacts. **Services:** Library open to the public by appointment.

★ 14024 ★

Rocky Mount Historical Association - Library (Hist)
200 Hyder Hill Rd.
Rocky Mount Parkway   Phone: (615)538-7396
Piney Flats, TN 37686   E. Alvin Gerhardt, Jr., Exec.Dir.
Founded: 1961. **Staff:** Prof 3. **Subjects:** Local history, Southwest Territory history, genealogy, technology, biography. **Holdings:** 1000 books; 1000 bound periodical volumes; 7 VF drawers of clippings; 2 VF drawers and 2 boxes of manuscripts; photographs. **Subscriptions:** 10 journals and other serials. **Services:** Copying; library open to the public for reference use only. **Staff:** Norman O. Burns II, Asst.Dir.

★ 14025 ★

Rocky Mountain Jewish Historical Society - Ira M. Beck Memorial Archives (Rel-Phil)
Center for Judaic Studies
University of Denver   Phone: (303)871-3020
Denver, CO 80208   Dr. Jeanne Abrams, Archv.
Founded: 1975. **Staff:** Prof 1. **Subjects:** Jewish history of region. **Holdings:** Figures not available. **Services:** Copying; library open to the public. **Publications:** Rocky Mountain Jewish Historical Notes, quarterly; Rocky Mountain Chai newsletter, quarterly.

Rocky Mountain National Park
See: U.S. Natl. Park Service (17770)

★ 14026 ★
Rocky Mountain News - Library (Publ)
400 W. Colfax Ave.
Denver, CO 80204
Phone: (303)892-2746
Diane Spooner, Libn.
Founded: 1859. **Staff:** Prof 3; Other 5. **Subjects:** Newspaper reference topics.
Special Collections: Index to historic houses of Denver. **Holdings:** 500 books; 5 million newspaper clippings; 8000 filing inches of photographs. **Subscriptions:** 4 newspapers. **Services:** Library not open to the public. **Computerized Information Services:** VU/TEXT Information Services, DIALOG Information Services. **Publications:** Rocky Mountain Library News (newsletter). **Remarks:** FAX: (303)892-5123. **Staff:** Janet Boss; Carol Fabry.

Rod Library
See: University of Northern Iowa (19108)

Roddey, Carpenter, and White, P.A.
See: Robinson, Bradshaw & Hinson, P.A. (13970)

Billie Davis Rodenberg Memorial Library
See: Temple Beth El (16081)

★ 14027 ★
Rodey, Dickason, Sloan, Akin & Robb, P.A. - Library (Law)
201 3rd St., N.W., Suite 2200
Box 1888
Albuquerque, NM 87102
Phone: (505)768-7348
Pamela M. Dempsey, Libn.
Staff: Prof 2; Other 1. **Subjects:** Law - antitrust, labor, tax. **Holdings:** 15,000 books. **Subscriptions:** 250 journals and other serials; 5 newspapers. **Services:** Interlibrary loan; library not open to the public. **Computerized Information Services:** LEXIS, WESTLAW, DIALOG Information Services; internal database. Performs searches on fee basis. **Remarks:** FAX: (505)768-7395. **Staff:** Mary A. Jebsen, Asst.Libn.

Eric and Sarah Rodgers Library for Science and Engineering
See: University of Alabama - Eric and Sarah Rodgers Library for Science and Engineering (18163)

Rodgers & Hammerstein Archives of Recorded Sound
See: New York Public Library for the Performing Arts (11638)

★ 14028 ★
Rodman Hall Arts Centre/National Exhibition Centre - Office Reference Library (Art)
109 St. Paul Crescent
St. Catharines, ON, Canada L2S 1M3
Phone: (416)684-2925
Debra Attenborough, Cur., Educ.
Founded: 1960. **Staff:** Prof 1. **Subjects:** Canadian art history, 15th-19th century European masters, contemporary international artists. **Special Collections:** Exhibition catalogs (6000 items). **Holdings:** 500 books; 2000 bound periodical volumes; 6000 other cataloged items. **Subscriptions:** 8 journals and other serials. **Services:** Copying; library open to the public for reference use only. **Automated Operations:** Computerized public access catalog. **Computerized Information Services:** Internal database. **Special Catalogs:** Exhibition catalogs.

Roebling Building Library
See: New Jersey (State) - Roebling Building Library (11505)

★ 14029 ★
G. Allan Roeher Institute - Library (Med)
Kinsmen Bldg., York University
4700 Keele St.
Downsview, ON, Canada M3J 1P3
Phone: (416)661-9611
Miriam Ticoll, Libn.
Founded: 1964. **Staff:** Prof 2; Other 2. **Subjects:** Mental handicaps, developmental disabilities, deinstitutionalization, special education, community organization. **Holdings:** 10,000 books; 12 VF drawers of pamphlets and reprints; 75 films. **Subscriptions:** 100 journals and other serials. **Services:** Interlibrary loan; copying; network open to the public. **Automated Operations:** Computerized cataloging. **Computerized Information Services:** Althea (internal database). **Publications:** Specialized bibliographies. **Special Catalogs:** Film and videotape catalog; publications catalog. **Remarks:** FAX: (416)661-5701. Institute is sponsored by the Canadian Association for Community Living.

Winona Roehl Library
See: First Christian Church (Disciples of Christ) (5763)

Roemisch-Germanische Kommission des Deutschen Archaeologischen Instituts
See: Roman-Germanic Commission of German Archaeological Institute (14046)

Roesch Library
See: University of Dayton (18534)

★ 14030 ★
Rogers Corporation - Electronics Library (Sci-Engr)
2400 S. Roosevelt St.
Tempe, AZ 85282
Phone: (602)967-0624
Mary McPherson, Tech.Libn.
Founded: 1984. **Staff:** Prof 1; Other 1. **Subjects:** Electronics, computers, chemistry, engineering, technology, business. **Holdings:** 700 books; internal documents. **Subscriptions:** 75 journals and other serials. **Services:** Interlibrary loan; library not open to the public. **Automated Operations:** Computerized public access catalog, cataloging, acquisitions, serials, and circulation. **Computerized Information Services:** DIALOG Information Services, PFDS Online, STN International, OCLC; Bibliotech - Comstow Inc. (internal database). **Networks/Consortia:** Member of AMIGOS Bibliographic Council, Inc., NELINET, Inc. **Remarks:** FAX: (602)967-9385.

★ 14031 ★
Rogers Corporation - Lurie Library (Sci-Engr)
1 Technology Dr.
Rogers, CT 06263
Phone: (203)774-9605
Myrna D. Riquier
Founded: 1970. **Staff:** Prof 3; Other 1. **Subjects:** Polymeric materials, electronics, management. **Holdings:** 4500 books; 200 bound periodical volumes; 6000 reports. **Subscriptions:** 300 journals and other serials. **Services:** Interlibrary loan; copying; SDI; library open to the public for reference use only and by appointment. **Computerized Information Services:** DIALOG Information Services, OCLC EPIC, STN International; Bibliotech Library Management, Information Navigator (internal databases). Contact Persons: Mary K. Van Ullen Tech.Spec.; Emily A. Westbrook, Libn. **Remarks:** FAX: (203)774-2278.

Edith Nourse Rogers Memorial Veterans Hospital
See: U.S. Dept. of Veterans Affairs (MA-Bedford) (17342)

Rogers, Golden and Halpern, Inc.
See: CH2M Hill, Inc. - Information Resource Center (3403)

★ 14032 ★
Lauren Rogers Museum of Art - Library (Art, Hist)
Box 1108
Laurel, MS 39441
Phone: (601)649-6374
Tammy D. Atkinson, Libn.
Founded: 1922. **Staff:** Prof 1; Other 3. **Subjects:** Fine arts, local history, Mississippiana. **Special Collections:** Museum archives; bookplate collection; historic photographs collection; rare Mississippiana and southern history; postcards; artist's files. **Holdings:** 20,000 books; 1185 bound periodical volumes; museum archives; microforms; videotapes. **Subscriptions:** 110 journals and other serials. **Services:** Interlibrary loan; copying; library open to the public. **Computerized Information Services:** Internal databases. **Remarks:** Maintained by the Eastman Memorial Foundation. Library located at 5th Ave. at 7th St., Laurel, MS 39440. FAX: (601)649-6379.

Rogers Library
See: **Maryknoll Sisters of St. Dominic (9746)**

★ 14033 ★
Millicent Rogers Museum - Library (Area-Ethnic)
Box A   Phone: (505)758-2462
Taos, NM 87571   Ann Lamont McVicar, Libn.
Founded: 1953. **Staff:** 1. **Subjects:** Indians of North America, local history, fine arts, museology, anthropology. **Special Collections:** Registry of Hispanic artists in New Mexico. **Holdings:** 3000 books; 81 subject classification files. **Subscriptions:** 36 journals. **Services:** Library open to the public by appointment for reference use only. **Remarks:** FAX: (505)758-5751.

Mr. Roger's Neighborhood Archives
See: **University of Pittsburgh - School of Library & Information Science - Library (19223)**

★ 14034 ★
Rogers & Wells - Library (Law)
201 N. Figueroa St., 15th Fl.   Phone: (213)580-1000
Los Angeles, CA 90012-2638   Shirley Frost, Libn.
Staff: Prof 1; Other 1. **Subjects:** Taxation, real property, securities, corporations, litigation, finance, bankruptcy, labor, insurance. **Holdings:** 8000 books. **Services:** Library not open to the public. **Automated Operations:** Computerized cataloging. **Computerized Information Services:** LEXIS, NEXIS, DIALOG Information Services, WESTLAW, Information America, Dow Jones News/Retrieval. **Remarks:** FAX: (213)580-1234.

★ 14035 ★
Rogers & Wells - Library (Law)
1737 H St., N.W.   Phone: (202)331-7760
Washington, DC 20006   Beverly R. Miller, Libn.
Staff: Prof 1. **Subjects:** Law. **Holdings:** 5700 volumes; 4.5 shelves of U.S. International Trade Commission publications; U.S. Bureau of the Census statistics and Custom Service decisions and rulings on microfiche. **Subscriptions:** 41 journals and other serials. **Services:** Interlibrary loan; library open to the public by appointment. **Computerized Information Services:** LEXIS, NEXIS, WESTLAW. **Remarks:** FAX: (202)331-0463.

★ 14036 ★
Rogers & Wells - Library (Law)
200 Park Ave., 52nd Fl.   Phone: (212)878-8210
New York, NY 10166   Daniel J. Pelletier, Dir., Lib.Serv.
Staff: Prof 4; Other 4. **Subjects:** Law - tax, antitrust, securities, labor, trusts and estates. **Holdings:** 25,000 volumes; 15,000 volumes in microformat. **Subscriptions:** 150 journals and other serials; 10 newspapers. **Services:** Interlibrary loan; library not open to the public. **Computerized Information Services:** DIALOG Information Services, Dow Jones News/Retrieval, VU/TEXT Information Services, NewsNet, Inc., LEXIS, WESTLAW, RLIN, OCLC, LEGI-SLATE, Data-Star, DataTimes, EPIC, Prentice Hall Online, Information America, Securities Data Municipal New Issues, Current USC. **Publications:** Information Bulletin, monthly - for internal distribution only. **Remarks:** FAX: (212)878-8375. **Staff:** D. Mark Strandberg, ILL.

★ 14037 ★
Will Rogers Library (Hist)
121 N. Weenonah   Phone: (918)341-1564
Claremore, OK 74017   Margaret L. Guffey, Libn.
Founded: 1936. **Staff:** 5. **Subjects:** Will Rogers, American Indians, Oklahoma and regional history. **Holdings:** 50,000 books; 265 bound periodical volumes; 1 VF drawer of clippings and pamphlets. **Subscriptions:** 73 journals and other serials; 8 newspapers. **Services:** Interlibrary loan; copying; library open to the public. **Automated Operations:** Computerized circulation. **Remarks:** Maintained by the City of Claremore. **Staff:** Vera Baker, Asst.Libn.

★ 14038 ★
Rohm & Haas Company - Home Office Library (Bus-Fin, Law)
Independence Mall, W.   Phone: (215)592-3631
Philadelphia, PA 19105   Ellen Wallace, Libn.
Founded: 1965. **Staff:** Prof 1; Other 1. **Subjects:** Law, management, finance, marketing, employee relations. **Holdings:** 5500 books and bound periodical volumes; 500 pamphlets; microfiche; annual reports. **Subscriptions:** 250 journals and other serials. **Services:** Interlibrary loan; library open to the public by appointment. **Automated Operations:** Computerized serials and circulation. **Computerized Information Services:** DIALOG Information Services, Dow Jones News/Retrieval, NewsNet, Inc., VU/TEXT Information Services, PIERS (Port Import/Export Reporting Services), OCLC, LEXIS, NEXIS. **Networks/Consortia:** Member of PALINET. **Publications:** Library Bulletin, bimonthly - for internal distribution only.

★ 14039 ★
Rohm & Haas Company - Research Division - Information Services Department (Sci-Engr)
727 Norristown Rd.   Phone: (215)641-7816
Spring House, PA 19477   Dr. Frederick H. Owens, Mgr., Info.Serv.
Founded: 1936. **Staff:** Prof 10; Other 12. **Subjects:** Agricultural chemistry, coatings, plastics, textiles and fibers, petroleum chemicals. **Holdings:** 50,000 volumes; 10,000 reels of microfilm; 5000 microfiche; 20 VF drawers of pamphlets, government reports, patents, trade literature. **Subscriptions:** 900 journals and other serials. **Services:** Interlibrary loan; copying; library open to the public by appointment. **Automated Operations:** Computerized cataloging, serials, and circulation. **Computerized Information Services:** DIALOG Information Services, Chemical Information Systems, Inc. (CIS), Chemical Abstracts Service (CAS), OCLC, ORBIT Search Service, DARC Pluridata System (DPDS) Data Base, PFDS Online, BRS Information Technologies, NLM. **Networks/Consortia:** Member of PALINET. **Publications:** Bimonthly library bulletin - for internal distribution only. **Remarks:** FAX: (215)641-7857. **Staff:** Patricia A. Rock, Libn.; Ellen C. Dotterrer, Acq.; Dominic R. Falgiatore, Info.Sci.; Margot B. Licitis, Transl.; Jacalyn L. Martin, Info.Sci.; Dr. Virginia Piccolini, Info.Sci.; Susan Jones, Info.Sci.; Joanne L. Witiak, Sr.Info.Sci.; Sandra F. Hostetter, Libn.

★ 14040 ★
Rohm & Haas Company - Research Division - Information Services Department - Library (Sci-Engr)
Box 718   Phone: (215)781-4092
Bristol, PA 19007   Sandra F. Hostetter, Libn.
Founded: 1932. **Staff:** Prof 2; Other 5. **Subjects:** Polymer chemistry, chemical engineering, chemistry. **Holdings:** 23,000 volumes; government reports. **Subscriptions:** 1000 journals and other serials. **Services:** Interlibrary loan; copying; SDI; library open to the public by appointment. **Automated Operations:** Computerized serials, circulation, and ILL. **Automated Operations:** Computerized public access catalog (CD-ROM). **Computerized Information Services:** DIALOG Information Services, Maxwell Online, Inc., NLM, BRS Information Technologies, STN International; CD-ROM (Books In Print). **Networks/Consortia:** Member of PALINET, National Network of Libraries of Medicine - Middle Atlantic Region. **Remarks:** FAX: (215)785-8999. **Staff:** Susan E. Jones, Info.Chem.

★ 14041 ★
Rohr Industries, Inc. - Corporate Library (Trans)
Foot of H St.
Box 1516   Phone: (619)691-2150
Chula Vista, CA 91912   Richard J. Tommey, Sr.Tech.Libn.
Staff: Prof 1; Other 2. **Subjects:** Aerospace, materials, metallurgy, manufacturing. **Special Collections:** Advanced composites. **Holdings:** 5000 books; 35,000 reports. **Subscriptions:** 400 journals and other serials. **Services:** Interlibrary loan; library not open to the public. **Computerized Information Services:** DIALOG Information Services, NASA/RECON, DTIC. **Networks/Consortia:** Member of Serra Cooperative Network. **Remarks:** FAX: (619)691-3550.

Rohrbach Library
See: **Kutztown University (8832)**

★ 14042 ★
Rohss Museum of Arts and Crafts - Library (Art)
Vasagt 37-39
Box 53178
S-400 15 Goteborg, Sweden   Phone: 31 200605
                                           Bisse Evers, Cur.
Founded: 1916. **Staff:** Prof 1.5. **Subjects:** Textiles, architecture, ceramics, furniture, glass. **Special Collections:** Book bindings; exhibition catalogs from Europe and the United States. **Holdings:** 30,000 books. **Subscriptions:** 27 journals and other serials; 4 newspapers. **Services:** Interlibrary loan; copying; library open to the public by appointment. **Remarks:** FAX: 31 184692. **Also Known As:** Rohsska Konstslojdmuseet - Biblioteket.

Rohsska Konstslojdmuseet - Biblioteket
See: **Rohss Museum of Arts and Crafts** (14042)

Rokeby Museum
See: **Rowland E. Robinson Memorial Association** (13972)

Rolfing Memorial Library
See: **Trinity Evangelical Divinity School** (16508)

★ 14043 ★
C.A. Rolloff Tri-County Law Library (Law)
Chippewa County Courthouse
11th St. & Hwy. 7   Phone: (612)269-7733
Montevideo, MN 56265   Nancy Johnson, Sec./Libn.
Staff: 1. **Subjects:** Law. **Holdings:** 5000 volumes; Briefs from the Minnesota Supreme Court, 1943-1980. **Services:** Interlibrary loan; library open to the public.

★ 14044 ★
Rolls-Royce Inc. - Information Center (Sci-Engr)
2849 Paces Ferry Rd.   Phone: (404)436-7900
Atlanta, GA 30339-3769   Marlene Sue Heroux, Mgr., Info.Ctr.
Staff: Prof 1; Other 1. **Subjects:** Jet engine technology, thermodynamics, metallurgy, aeronautics, contract management, advanced materials. **Holdings:** 3000 books; 1000 government documents; 4000 conference papers; 150 videotapes. **Subscriptions:** 225 journals and other serials. **Services:** Center not open to the public. **Automated Operations:** INMAGIC. **Computerized Information Services:** DIALOG Information Services, Aerospace Online; QUIKSERV (internal database); DIALMAIL (electronic mail service). **Networks/Consortia:** Member of Georgia Online Database (GOLD). **Remarks:** FAX: (404)436-8570.

★ 14045 ★
Roman Catholic Archdiocese of Los Angeles - Archival Center Library and Historical Museum (Rel-Phil, Hist)
15151 San Fernando Mission Blvd.   Phone: (818)365-1501
Mission Hills, CA 91345   Msgr. Francis J. Weber, A.C.A. Archv.
Founded: 1962. **Staff:** Prof 3. **Subjects:** American Catholicism, Californiana, western American bibliography, early Western travels, Los Angeles, the Gold Rush. **Special Collections:** Robert G. Cowan Collection; Estelle Doheny Collection of Californiana. **Holdings:** 8500 books; 1200 bound periodical volumes; 350,000 manuscripts, documents, memorabilia. **Subscriptions:** 30 journals and other serials; 7 newspapers. **Services:** Copying; archives open to the public by appointment to qualified users. **Computerized Information Services:** Internal database. **Publications:** Newsletter, quarterly - to Friends of the Archival Center. **Special Indexes:** Finding index (online). **Staff:** Kevin Feeney, A.C.A., Adjunct Archv.

Roman Catholic Diocese of Brooklyn - Francis X. McDermott Library
See: **Francis X. McDermott Library** (9880)

★ 14046 ★
Roman-Germanic Commission of German Archaeological Institute - Library (Soc Sci)
Palmengartenstrasse 10-12   Phone: 69 752025
W-6000 Frankfurt am Main 1, Germany   Dr. E. Schubert, Prehist.
Founded: 1902. **Staff:** Prof 4. **Subjects:** European archeology, Stone Age through Middle Ages, ancient history, epigraphy, numismatics. **Holdings:** 73,000 volumes. **Subscriptions:** 1250 journals. **Services:** Library open to researchers and other qualified individuals. **Publications:** Neuzugange der Bibliothek der RGK (in periodical Germania), 2/year. **Remarks:** Alternate telephone number(s): 69 752026. FAX: 69 745668. **Also Known As:** Roemisch-Germanische Kommission des Deutschen Archaeologischen Instituts.

Romanek Cultural Center
See: **North Shore Congregation Israel - Romanek Cultural Center - Oscar Hillel Plotkin Adult Library** (11947)

★ 14047 ★
Romania - Administratia Rezervatiei Biosferei Delta Dunarii - Institutul de Cercetari si Projectari Delta Dunarii (Agri)
str. Babadag nr.165   Phone: 15 24242
Tulcea 8800, Romania   Adina Gradea
Founded: 1970. **Staff:** Prof 1. **Subjects:** Agriculture, ichthyology, genetics, biology, fishery, ecology, topography. **Holdings:** 7000 books; 100 bound periodical volumes; 300 reports. **Subscriptions:** 11 journals and other serials. **Services:** Library open to the public. **Remarks:** Alternate telephone number(s): 15 24550. FAX: 15 24547.

★ 14048 ★
Romania - Ministry of Health - Cantacuzino Institute - Library (Biol Sci)
Splaiul Independentei 103
C.P. 1-525   Phone: 13 97 20
70100 Bucharest, Romania   Maria Lucia Sandu, Libn.
Subjects: Bacteriology, virology, parasitology, immunology, biochemistry. **Holdings:** 101,071 volumes. **Services:** Interlibrary loan; library open to the public. **Remarks:** Telex: C 712 Canta B Romania. **Also Known As:** Institutul Cantacuzino.

Romania - National Committee for Science and Technology
See: **Romania - National Institute for Information and Documentation - Library** (14049)

★ 14049 ★
Romania - National Institute for Information and Documentation - Library (Sci-Engr, Info Sci)
Str. George Enescu, no. 27-29
Sector 1   Phone: 0 90134010
70141 Bucharest, Romania   Mr. Gheorghe Anghel, Gen.Dir.
Founded: 1949. **Staff:** 126. **Subjects:** Science, technology, information science. **Holdings:** 700,000 volumes; 100,000 periodicals; microforms. **Subscriptions:** 1250 journals and other serials. **Services:** Copying (microform and hard copy); SDI. **Computerized Information Services:** Internal database. Performs searches. **Publications:** Abstracts of Romanian Scientific and Technical Literature, 2/year; Information and Documentation Problems, quarterly. **Remarks:** Telex: 11 247 INID. Coordinates a national network of information and documentation centers and other scientific and technical units. **Formerly:** Its National Committee for Science and Technology - National Institute for Information and Documentation - Library. **Staff:** Claudia Cerkez.

★ 14050 ★
Romania - National Institute of Metrology - Library (Sci-Engr)
Sos. Vitan-Birzesti 11   Phone: 0 83 35 20
75669 Bucharest, Romania   Anca Dragan, Libn.
Subjects: Metrology; standards for physical quantities; calibration and measurement techniques; development of high precision instruments. **Holdings:** 50,000 volumes. **Also Known As:** Institutul National de Metrologie.

★ 14051 ★
Romanian Library (Area-Ethnic)
200 E. 38th St.
New York, NY 10016   Phone: (212)687-0180
Founded: 1971. **Staff:** 2. **Subjects:** Romania - literature, history, arts, science, economy. **Special Collections:** Constantin Brancusi (30 volumes); minorities in Romania (50 volumes); Romania's present day domestic policy; Romania's foreign policy (50 volumes). **Holdings:** 15,000 books; 500 bound periodical volumes; 500 phonograph records; 1000 slides; 500 photographs; films. **Subscriptions:** 100 journals and other serials; 10 newspapers. **Services:** Interlibrary loan; annual Romanian language courses; library open to the public. **Publications:** Romanian Library monthly program - free upon request; bibliographies on Romanian topics. **Remarks:** Maintained by the Ministry of Foreign Affairs, Central State Library at Bucharest. Alternate telephone number(s): (212)687-0181.

★ 14052 ★
(Rome) American Library - USIS Library (Educ)
Via Veneto 119a
I-00187 Rome, Italy
Remarks: Maintained or supported by the U.S. Information Agency. Focus is on materials that will assist peoples outside the United States to learn about the United States, its people, history, culture, political processes, and social milieux.

★ 14053 ★
Rome Historical Society - William E. Scripture Memorial Library (Hist)
200 Church St.   Phone: (315)336-5870
Rome, NY 13440   Jon N. Austin, Exec.Dir.
Founded: 1936. **Staff:** Prof 1; Other 3. **Subjects:** Rome and Oneida County, genealogy, Civil War, American Revolution, social history, industrial history. **Holdings:** 2500 books; 500 bound periodical volumes; 3000 archival documents; La Vita (Italian language newspaper), 1918-1945, on microfilm; historical documents on microfilm. **Subscriptions:** 11 journals and other serials. **Services:** Copying; library open to the public.

Miles Romney Memorial Library
See: **Bitter Root Valley Historical Society - Ravalli County Museum - Miles Romney Memorial Library** (1870)

★ 14054 ★
Rooks Pitts & Poust - Library (Law)
55 W. Monroe, Suite 1500
Chicago, IL 60603   Phone: (312)372-5600
                                         Mary E. Williamson, Hd.Libn.
Staff: Prof 1; Other 2. **Subjects:** Law - corporate, medical, securities, tax. **Holdings:** 16,000 books. **Subscriptions:** 644 journals and other serials. **Services:** Interlibrary loan; copying. **Computerized Information Services:** LEXIS, WESTLAW, DIALOG Information Services, Information America, Hannah Information Systems, DataTimes. **Networks/Consortia:** Member of Chicago Library System, ILLINET. **Remarks:** FAX: (312)372-9239.

Franklin D. Roosevelt Library
See: **U.S. Presidential Libraries - Franklin D. Roosevelt Library** (17922)

★ 14055 ★
Roosevelt Hospital - Health Science Library (Med)
Box 151   Phone: (201)321-6800
Metuchen, NJ 08840   Karen Rubin, Libn.
Staff: 1. **Subjects:** Medicine, nursing. **Holdings:** 1000 books. **Subscriptions:** 45 journals and other serials. **Services:** Library open to the public for reference use only. **Networks/Consortia:** Member of BHSL, Cosmopolitan Biomedical Library Consortium (CBLC).

★ 14056 ★
Roosevelt Hospital - Medical Library (Med)
428 W. 59th St.   Phone: (212)523-6100
New York, NY 10019   Paul E. Barth, Libn.
Founded: 1955. **Staff:** Prof 1; Other 1. **Subjects:** Medicine, surgery, gerontology, geriatrics, hospital administration, pediatrics, anesthesia. **Holdings:** 20,000 books and bound periodical volumes. **Subscriptions:** 500 journals and other serials. **Services:** Interlibrary loan; copying; library open to the public for reference use only by appointment. **Computerized Information Services:** NLM, BRS Information Technologies. **Networks/Consortia:** Member of Medical Library Center of New York (MLCNY), New York Metropolitan Reference and Research Library Agency. **Remarks:** FAX: (212)523-6108.

Theodore Roosevelt Collection
See: **Bridgewater State College** (2122)

Theodore Roosevelt Collection
See: **Dickinson State University** (4855)

Theodore Roosevelt Hunting Library
See: **Library of Congress - Rare Book & Special Collections Division** (9135)

Theodore Roosevelt National Park
See: **U.S. Natl. Park Service** (17784)

★ 14057 ★
Roosevelt University - Murray-Green Library - Archives (Hist)
430 S. Michigan Ave.   Phone: (312)341-3643
Chicago, IL 60605   Lucinda J. Angell, Hd. of Ref.
Founded: 1945. **Staff:** Prof 3; Other 2. **Subjects:** University and Chicago history. **Special Collections:** Auditorium Theater records and broadsides (30 boxes; 30 volumes; 80 broadsides); Labor Oral History Collection. **Holdings:** 30 books; 100 boxes of university records. **Services:** Copying; collections open to the public for reference use only. **Computerized Information Services:** DIALOG Information Services, OCLC. **Networks/Consortia:** Member of ILLINET. **Publications:** General guide; Portraits (photograph collection). **Special Indexes:** The Early Years: An Index to the Scrapbook Collection. **Staff:** Rebecca Jeffords; Charles Laurier.

★ 14058 ★
Roosevelt University - Music Library (Mus)
430 S. Michigan Ave.   Phone: (312)341-3651
Chicago, IL 60605   Donald Draganski, Libn.
Founded: 1945. **Staff:** Prof 1; Other 3. **Subjects:** Music, music education. **Special Collections:** Archives of Chicago Musical College. **Holdings:** 35,000 volumes; 10,000 phonograph records; 100 reels of microfilm; 200 dissertations; 400 magnetic tapes. **Subscriptions:** 105 journals and other serials. **Services:** Interlibrary loan; copying; library open to the public for reference use only. **Computerized Information Services:** OCLC. **Networks/Consortia:** Member of ILLINET. **Remarks:** FAX: (312)341-3655.

★ 14059 ★
Roosevelt University - Oral History Project in Labor History (Hist)
430 S. Michigan Ave.   Phone: (219)931-9791
Chicago, IL 60605   Elizabeth Balanoff, Prof. of Hist.
Subjects: Oral histories in labor history. **Holdings:** 246 hours of taped interviews. **Services:** Copying. **Remarks:** The oral history transcripts are held in the Roosevelt University library where they may be read but not checked out. People who wish to read a transcript for scholarly research but are unable to come to Roosevelt University may order the transcript they need through their own university library. Orders should be sent to Director of Oral History Project.

★ 14060 ★
Roosevelt Warm Springs Institute for Rehabilitation (Med)
Professional Library   Phone: (404)655-2707
Warm Springs, GA 31830-0268   Michael D. Shadix
Staff: Prof 1. **Subjects:** Medical rehabilitation, physical therapy, occupational therapy, nursing, medicine, speech rehabilitation. **Holdings:** 2000 books. **Subscriptions:** 140 journals and other serials. **Services:** Interlibrary loan; copying; library open to the public. **Computerized Information Services:** BRS/COLLEAGUE, MEDLINE. **Remarks:** FAX: (404)655-2827.

Roper Center Archives
See: **Yale University - Social Science Library** (20731)

Roper Center for Public Opinion Research
See: **University of Connecticut** (18528)

★ 14061 ★
Ropes & Gray - Central Library (Law)
1 International Place   Phone: (617)951-7000
Boston, MA 02110-2624   Cornelia Trubey, Dir., Lib.Serv.
Staff: Prof 3; Other 4. **Subjects:** Law. **Holdings:** 30,000 books; 1000 bound periodical volumes. **Subscriptions:** 600 journals and other serials; 10 newspapers. **Services:** Interlibrary loan; library not open to the public. **Computerized Information Services:** LEXIS, NEXIS, DIALOG Information Services, WESTLAW, Dow Jones News/Retrieval, VU/TEXT Information Services, LEGI-SLATE, Dialcom Inc., RLIN, NewsNet, Inc., Spectrum Ownership Profiles Online.

Rosario National University - Faculty of Exact Sciences and Engineering - Ing. Juan C. Van Wyck Center for Research and Development
See: Ing. Juan C. Van Wyck Center for Research and Development (19751)

Carl G. Rosberg International Studies Library
See: University of California, Berkeley - Institute of International Studies Library (18328)

★ 14062 ★
Benjamin Rose Institute - Library (Med)
12200 Fairhill Rd.   Phone: (216)231-7230
Cleveland, OH 44120   Karen McNally Bensing, Libn.
Staff: Prof 1; Other 1. **Subjects:** Aged - research, home care, long-term care, nursing homes, social work, nursing. **Special Collections:** Margaret Blenkner Research Collection. **Holdings:** 3600 books; 116 bound periodical volumes; 7 lateral file drawers and 4 VF drawers of reports, papers, manuscripts. **Subscriptions:** 80 journals and other serials. **Services:** Interlibrary loan; copying; library open to the public by appointment on a limited schedule. **Computerized Information Services:** DIALOG Information Services, BRS Information Technologies. **Remarks:** FAX: (216)231-7323.

Billy Rose Theatre Collection
See: New York Public Library for the Performing Arts (11634)

David J. Rose Library
See: Massachusetts Institute of Technology - Plasma Fusion Center (9813)

★ 14063 ★
Rose-Hulman Institute of Technology - John A. Logan Library (Sci-Engr)
5500 E. Wabash Ave.   Phone: (812)877-8200
Terre Haute, IN 47803-3999   John M. Robson, Dir.
Founded: 1874. **Staff:** Prof 1; Other 2. **Subjects:** Engineering and science. **Holdings:** 41,000 books; 18,000 bound periodical volumes; 1200 records; 6000 documents; 675 reels of microfilm; 800 archival volumes. **Subscriptions:** 500 journals and other serials; 10 newspapers. **Services:** Interlibrary loan; copying; library open to the public. **Automated Operations:** Computerized public access catalog, cataloging, and circulation. **Computerized Information Services:** OCLC, STN International, DIALOG Information Services, EPIC; CD-ROMs. **Networks/Consortia:** Member of INCOLSA, Wabash Valley Health Science Library Consortium, Stone Hills Area Library Services Authority. **Remarks:** FAX: (812)877-3198.

★ 14064 ★
Rose Medical Center - Library (Med)
4567 E. 9th Ave.   Phone: (303)320-2160
Denver, CO 80220   Nancy Simon, Med.Libn.
Founded: 1949. **Staff:** Prof 1. **Subjects:** Medicine. **Holdings:** 1000 books; 2989 bound periodical volumes; 257 Audio-Digest tapes. **Subscriptions:** 197 journals and other serials. **Services:** Interlibrary loan; library not open to the public. **Computerized Information Services:** MEDLARS, DIALOG Information Services. **Networks/Consortia:** Member of Colorado Council of Medical Librarians. **Publications:** Annual Report; procedure manual.

Rose Memorial Library
See: Biola University - Rose Memorial Library (1845)

★ 14065 ★
Rose, Schmidt, Hasley & DiSalle - Library
900 Oliver Bldg.
Pittsburgh, PA 15222   Phone: (412)434-8600
Remarks: FAX: (412)263-2829. No further information was supplied by respondent. **Formerly:** Rose, Schmidt, Dixon, Hasley.

Sidney G. Rose Memorial Library
See: K.K. Bene Israel/Rockdale Temple (8500)

★ 14066 ★
Roseland Community Hospital - Health Science Library (Med)
45 W. 111th St.   Phone: (312)995-3191
Chicago, IL 60628   Mary T. Hanlon, Libn.
Staff: Prof 1. **Subjects:** Medicine and nursing. **Holdings:** 900 books; 2 VF drawers of pamphlets. **Subscriptions:** 39 journals and other serials. **Services:** Interlibrary loan; copying. **Networks/Consortia:** Member of National Network of Libraries of Medicine - Greater Midwest Region, ILLINET, Chicago and South Consortium. **Remarks:** FAX: (312)995-5863.

Rosemead Graduate School of Professional Psychology - Library
See: Biola University - Rose Memorial Library (1845)

★ 14067 ★
Rosemont College - Gertrude Kistler Memorial Library - Special Collections (Educ)
Rosemont, PA 19010-1699   Phone: (215)527-0200
    C. Danial Elliott, Dir., Lib.Serv.
Founded: 1922. **Staff:** Prof 3; Other 7. **Special Collections:** Rosemont Collection. **Services:** Interlibrary loan; copying; library open to persons with academic credentials. **Automated Operations:** Computerized cataloging and ILL. **Computerized Information Services:** DIALOG Information Services, OCLC; CD-ROMs (ERIC, PAIS, Religious and Theological Abstracts, Access Pennsylvania). Performs searches on fee basis. **Networks/Consortia:** Member of Tri-State College Library Cooperative (TCLC), PALINET, Interlibrary Delivery Service of Pennsylvania (IDS). **Remarks:** FAX: (215)525-2930. **Staff:** April Nelson, Tech.Proc.Serv.Libn.; Sr. Frances Gopsill, S.H.C.J., Rd.Serv.Libn.

★ 14068 ★
Rosenbach Museum & Library (Hist, Hum)
2010 DeLancey Pl.   Phone: (215)732-1600
Philadelphia, PA 19103   Ellen S. Dunlap, Dir.
Founded: 1954. **Staff:** Prof 6; Other 8. **Subjects:** Americana, English literature, incunabula, Judaica, book illustration. **Special Collections:** Marianne Moore Archive; Maurice Sendak original drawings; Latin-American historical manuscripts. **Holdings:** 30,000 books; 270,000 manuscripts. **Services:** Copying; museum open for tours and exhibitions; library open to scholars by appointment. **Automated Operations:** Computerized cataloging. **Networks/Consortia:** Member of Research Libraries Information Network (RLIN), Philadelphia Area Consortium of Special Collections Libraries (PACSCL). **Publications:** Recent Acquisitions, irregular; fine press and facsimile editions of important rare books and manuscripts; collection guides; Rosenbach Newsletter. **Special Catalogs:** Exhibition catalogs on aspects of collection. **Staff:** Leslie A. Morris, Asst.Cur., Bks. & Mss.; Natalia Rosenfeld, Asst.Cur., Bks.& Mss.

Joseph H. Rosenberg American Jewish Archives
See: Hebrew Union College - Jewish Institute of Religion - Frances-Henry Library (7097)

★ 14069 ★
Rosenberg Library - Special Collections (Hist)
2310 Sealy Ave.   Phone: (409)763-8854
Galveston, TX 77550   Lisa Shippee Lambert, Hd./Archv.
Founded: 1904. **Staff:** Prof 3; Other 2. **Subjects:** State and local history, Civil War, historic preservation, Texas Republic, Galveston, TX. **Holdings:** 13,000 books; 1000 bound periodical volumes; 2000 linear feet of manuscripts; 20,000 photographs; 1500 maps; microfilm; architectural drawings; newspapers; vertical files. **Subscriptions:** 75 journals and other serials. **Services:** Copying; collections open to the public. **Computerized Information Services:** Marcon (internal database). **Networks/Consortia:** Member of Houston Area Library System (HALS). **Publications:** Manuscript Sources in the Rosenberg Library: A Selective Guide; Cartographic Sources in the Rosenberg Library. **Special Catalogs:** Book and manuscript catalogs. **Special Indexes:** News article index; biographical index; map index; photograph subject index; lists of newspaper holdings; architectural and engineering drawings and films. **Staff:** Casey Greene, Asst.Archv.; Lise Darst, Cur.; Margaret Schlankey, Rare Bks./Archv.Asst.

★14070★
Paul Rosenberg Associates - Library (Sci-Engr)
Box 729   Phone: (914)834-3939
Larchmont, NY 10538   Miss M. Hill, Libn.
Founded: 1945. **Staff:** Prof 1; Other 1. **Subjects:** Applied physics, engineering, aerospace, photogrammetry, remote sensing, energy, navigation, lasers, electro-optics, ultrasonics, radon. **Holdings:** 1000 books; 500 bound periodical volumes; 2000 reports and reprints. **Subscriptions:** 40 journals and other serials. **Services:** Library not open to the public.

★14071★
M. Rosenblatt & Son, Inc. - Technical Exchange (Sci-Engr)
350 Broadway   Phone: (212)431-6900
New York, NY 10013   Edward Hoover, Libn.
Founded: 1947. **Staff:** Prof 1. **Subjects:** Naval architecture; engineering - marine, ocean, civil; naval science; offshore structures. **Special Collections:** Mandell Rosenblatt Collection of sports vessels and yachts, 1910-1959. **Holdings:** 2400 books; 1650 bound periodical volumes; 2400 reports; 3000 reels of microfilm; 2000 microfiche; 9000 ships plans. **Subscriptions:** 25 journals and other serials; 10 newspapers. **Services:** Interlibrary loan; not open to the public. **Computerized Information Services:** DIALOG Information Services, MCAUTO (McDonnell Douglas Automation Company); INFO MFD 2: Ships Maneuvering, Vibration, Stability Programs (internal database). **Publications:** Library List (newsletter), irregular - for internal distribution only. **Remarks:** FAX: (212)334-0837.

Sol Rosenbloom Library
See: Jewish Education Institute (8388)

Blanche and Ira Rosenblum Memorial Library
See: Beth Shalom Congregation (1773)

★14072★
Rosenman & Colin - Library (Law)
575 Madison Ave.   Phone: (212)940-8598
New York, NY 10022   Rochelle C. Cheifetz, Hd.Libn.
Staff: Prof 3; Other 4. **Subjects:** Law. **Holdings:** 35,000 books and bound periodical volumes; New York Law Journal, 1964 to present, on microfilm. **Subscriptions:** 300 journals and other serials; 8 newspapers. **Services:** Interlibrary loan; library open to clients and library community by appointment. **Computerized Information Services:** LEXIS, NEXIS, WESTLAW, DIALOG Information Services. **Remarks:** FAX: (212)940-8776. **Staff:** Henry Skillman; Megan Taylor.

★14073★
Rosenn, Jenkins & Greenwald, Attorneys at Law - Library (Law)
15 S. Franklin St.   Phone: (717)821-4709
Wilkes-Barre, PA 18711-0075   Sarah P. Carr, Libn.
Staff: Prof 1. **Subjects:** State and federal law. **Holdings:** 8000 books; 200 bound periodical volumes. **Subscriptions:** 350 journals and other serials. **Services:** Interlibrary loan; library not open to the public. **Computerized Information Services:** LEXIS. **Remarks:** FAX: (717)826-5640.

Dorothy & Lewis Rosenstiel School of Marine & Atmospheric Sciences
See: University of Miami (18842)

Benjamin S. Rosenthal Library
See: Queens College of City University of New York - Benjamin S. Rosenthal Library (13636)

Samuel Rosenthal Memorial Library
See: St. Joseph's Hospital (14408)

Edward Rosenthall Mathematics & Statistics Library
See: McGill University - Edward Rosenthall Mathematics & Statistics Library (9897)

Rosenzweig Health Sciences Library
See: St. Luke's Medical Center (14488)

★14074★
Roseville Early Childhood Family Education Program - Parent Resource Center & Toy Library (Educ)
Parkview Center
701 W. County Rd. B   Phone: (612)487-4378
Roseville, MN 55113   Kristin Ferguson, Libn.
Founded: 1979. **Staff:** Prof 1; Other 2. **Subjects:** Educational toys, children's literature, parenting, birth through adolescence. **Holdings:** 900 children's books; 3000 toys; activity kits for children up to 5 years of age; 500 parenting books. **Services:** Library open to the public on fee basis. **Computerized Information Services:** Internal database.

★14075★
Roseville Hospital - Medical Library (Med)
333 Sunrise Ave.   Phone: (916)781-1580
Roseville, CA 95661   Shirley Lyon, Med.Libn.
Founded: 1976. **Staff:** Prof 1. **Subjects:** Medicine, nursing, surgery. **Holdings:** 1560 books; 8 VF drawers of pamphlets; audiocassettes; videocassettes. **Subscriptions:** 175 journals and other serials. **Services:** Interlibrary loan; copying. **Computerized Information Services:** NLM. Performs searches. **Networks/Consortia:** Member of Northern California and Nevada Medical Library Group (NCNMLG), National Network of Libraries of Medicine - Pacific Southwest Region, Sacramento Area Health Sciences Librarians (SAHSL). **Remarks:** FAX: (916)773-0692.

★14076★
Rosewood Center - Miriam Lodge Professional Library
Owings Mills, MD 21117
Founded: 1955. **Subjects:** Mental retardation, special education, social work, learning disorders, pediatrics, psychology. **Holdings:** 3000 books; 1000 bound periodical volumes; 6 VF drawers of pamphlets; 7 VF drawers of staff papers; 30 manuscripts. **Remarks:** Currently inactive.

★14077★
Rosicrucian Fellowship - Library (Rel-Phil)
2222 Mission Ave.
Box 713   Phone: (619)757-6600
Oceanside, CA 92054   Helen Schroeder, Libn.
Staff: Prof 1. **Subjects:** Christian mysticism, Bible study, spiritual astrology, health and healing. **Holdings:** 1500 books. **Services:** Library open to members for reference use only.

★14078★
Rosicrucian Fraternity - Library (Rel-Phil)
Beverly Hall Corp.
5966 Clymer Rd.
Box 220   Phone: (215)536-7048
Quakertown, PA 18951   Gerald E. Poesnecker, Libn.
Founded: 1906. **Staff:** 1. **Subjects:** Religion, philosophy. **Holdings:** 4000 books; 200 manuscripts; 25 patents. **Services:** Library not open to the public. **Remarks:** Library serves as the archive for the fraternity and as study reference center for students enrolled in the fraternity.

★14079★
Rosicrucian Order, AMORC - Rosicrucian Research Library (Rel-Phil)
Rosicrucian Park
Park & Naglee Aves.   Phone: (408)287-9176
San Jose, CA 95191   Myra Marsh, Hd.Res.Libn.
Founded: 1939. **Staff:** Prof 1; Other 1. **Subjects:** Egyptology, Rosicrucianism, parapsychology, mysticism, Baconiana. **Holdings:** 14,000 books; 260 bound periodical volumes; 6 VF drawers of pamphlets and manuscripts. **Subscriptions:** 25 journals and other serials. **Services:** Library open to the public on a fee basis. **Computerized Information Services:** Internal databases. **Publications:** Rosicrucian Digest, quarterly - to members and by subscription. **Special Indexes:** Rosicrucian Digest index; Rosicrucian Forum index (card); Index to Rosicrucian books (book); Rosicrucian Lessons (book). **Remarks:** FAX: (408)286-4038.

★ 14080 ★
Annie Halenbake Ross Library - Special Collections (Hist)
232 W. Main St.   Phone: (717)748-3321
Lock Haven, PA 17745   Diane L. Whitaker
Founded: 1910. **Staff:** Prof 1; Other 12. **Subjects:** Pennsylvania, genealogy.
Special Collections: John Sloan Memorial Room (paintings, books, and memorabilia of John Sloan); Pennsylvania Historic Photo File. **Holdings:** 110,000 books; 85 bound periodical volumes; 825 reels of microfilm. **Subscriptions:** 115 journals and other serials; 6 newspapers. **Services:** Interlibrary loan; copying; library open to the public. **Publications:** Mountain Folks; Old Town; A Peek at the Past; Another Peek at the Past; A Third Peek at the Past; Indians of Clinton County - all books on local history.

★ 14081 ★
Ross County Law Library (Law)
28 N. Paint St.   Phone: (614)773-1075
Chillicothe, OH 45601-3108   Rita Fuchsman, Libn.
Staff: 1. **Subjects:** Law. **Holdings:** 17,700 books; 337 bound periodical volumes; 4300 microfiche. **Subscriptions:** 60 journals and other serials. **Services:** Copying; library open to the public with restrictions. **Remarks:** Maintained by Ross County Law Library Association.

★ 14082 ★
Ross & Hardies - Library (Law)
150 N. Michigan Ave., Suite 2500   Phone: (312)558-1000
Chicago, IL 60601   Monice M. Kaczorowski, Dir. of Libs.
Founded: 1902. **Staff:** Prof 3; Other 2. **Subjects:** Law, health. **Holdings:** 26,196 volumes. **Subscriptions:** 200 journals and other serials. **Services:** Interlibrary loan; library not open to the public. **Computerized Information Services:** DIALOG Information Services, Dow Jones News/Retrieval, LEXIS, WESTLAW, OCLC. **Remarks:** FAX: (312)750-8600; (312)750-8689. **Staff:** Jean Sanders; Tom Champagne.

Howard Ross Library of Management
See: McGill University (9900)

★ 14083 ★
Ross Laboratories - Library (Food-Bev)
625 Cleveland Ave.   Phone: (614)624-3503
Columbus, OH 43215   Linda Mitro Hopkins, Mgr.
Staff: Prof 2; Other 2. **Subjects:** Nutrition, food technology, business, analytical chemistry. **Holdings:** 3500 books; 6000 bound periodical volumes. **Subscriptions:** 550 journals and other serials. **Services:** Interlibrary loan; copying; SDI; library open to the public with restrictions. **Automated Operations:** Computerized cataloging, serials, and circulation. **Computerized Information Services:** DIALOG Information Services, OCLC, NLM, MEDLINE, ORBIT Search Service, CompuServe Information Service, Dow Jones News/Retrieval; internal databases. **Networks/Consortia:** Member of OHIONET. **Publications:** Internal newsletter and journal holdings list. **Remarks:** FAX: (614)624-3868.

Ross Library
See: U.S. Dept. of Energy - Bonneville Power Administration (17231)

★ 14084 ★
Ross Roy Group - Information Resource Center (Bus-Fin)
100 Bloomfield Pkwy.   Phone: (313)433-6117
Bloomfield Hills, MI 48304-3100   April Vossberg, Mgr.
Founded: 1920. **Staff:** Prof 1; Other 1. **Subjects:** Marketing, sales promotion, automobile data, advertising, retail. **Holdings:** 800 books. **Subscriptions:** 600 journals and other serials; 8 newspapers. **Services:** Library open to the public at librarian's discretion. **Automated Operations:** Computerized cataloging and budget. **Computerized Information Services:** DIALOG Information Services, VU/TEXT Information Services, NEXIS, Dun & Bradstreet Business Credit Services, DataTimes. **Special Indexes:** Periodicals list.

★ 14085 ★
Rossland Historical Museum Association - Archives (Hist)
Box 26   Phone: (604)362-7722
Rossland, BC, Canada V0G 1Y0   Joyce Tadevic, Archv.
Founded: 1955. **Staff:** 1. **Subjects:** Rossland history including mining, biography, business, entertainment, sports. **Holdings:** 400 books; 50 bound periodical volumes; 50 items of city records; 48 drawers of indexed documents, clippings, reports, letters; 2700 photographs of Rossland area. **Services:** Copying (limited); archives open to the public for reference use only. **Remarks:** FAX: (604)362-5379.

Rostad Library
See: Evangelical School of Theology (5504)

★ 14086 ★
Roswell Museum and Art Center - Research Library (Art)
100 W. 11th St.   Phone: (505)624-6744
Roswell, NM 88201   William Ebie, Dir.
Founded: 1950. **Subjects:** Art - contemporary, Native American, Spanish Colonial, Western United States; rocketry; archeology. **Holdings:** 2500 books; 3600 bound periodical volumes; 3500 color slides. **Subscriptions:** 75 journals and other serials. **Services:** Copying; library open to scholars.

★ 14087 ★
Roswell Park Cancer Institute - Medical and Scientific Library (Med)
Carlton & Elm Sts.   Phone: (716)845-5966
Buffalo, NY 14263   Ann P. Hutchinson, Lib.Dir.
Founded: 1898. **Staff:** Prof 4; Other 6. **Subjects:** Cancer and allied diseases. **Holdings:** 74,000 books and bound periodical volumes; 400 AV programs. **Subscriptions:** 1000 journals and other serials. **Services:** Interlibrary loan; copying; SDI; library open to the public. **Automated Operations:** Computerized cataloging, acquisitions, and serials. **Computerized Information Services:** DIALOG Information Services, BRS Information Technologies, OCLC, MEDLINE; CD-ROM (MEDLINE); DOCLINE (electronic mail service). Performs searches on fee basis. Contact Person: Gayle Ablove, Ref. & ILL Libn. **Networks/Consortia:** Member of Western New York Library Resources Council (WNYLRC), Medical Library Center of New York (MLCNY), National Network of Libraries of Medicine - Middle Atlantic Region. **Remarks:** Maintained by New York State Department of Health. FAX: (716)845-8699. **Formerly:** Roswell Park Memorial Institute. **Staff:** Gail Franke, Ser.Libn.; Suzanne Zajac, Acq. & Cat. Libn.

Roswell Park Memorial Institute
See: Roswell Park Cancer Institute (14087)

Rotch Library of Architecture and Planning
See: Massachusetts Institute of Technology (9816)

Rothschild Medical Library
See: Jewish Hospital at Washington University Medical Center (8398)

★ 14088 ★
Rounce and Coffin Club, Los Angeles - Library (Hum)
Occidental College Library
1600 Campus Rd.   Phone: (213)259-2852
Los Angeles, CA 90041   Michael C. Sutherland, Sec./Treas.
Founded: 1938. **Staff:** Prof 1. **Subjects:** Western printing, 1938 to present. **Holdings:** 1400 books. **Services:** Library not open to the public. **Special Catalogs:** Western Books Catalog, annual.

Pere Rouquette Library
See: St. Joseph Seminary College (14392)

★ 14089 ★
Rowan Public Library - Edith M. Clark History Room (Hist)
201 W. Fisher St.
P.O. Box 4039   Phone: (704)638-3020
Salisbury, NC 28144-0101   Evelyn T. Stallings, Local Hist., Geneal.Libn.
Founded: 1955. **Staff:** Prof 1; Other 1. **Subjects:** Local and regional history and genealogy. **Special Collections:** McCubbins Collection (Rowan County families; 150,000 documents relating to history and genealogy of families who settled in North Carolina); Smith Collection (papers and correspondence of families who migrated to Kentucky and westward); Archibald Henderson Collection (rare volumes and pamphlets); James Brawley Collection (papers and indexes to early Rowan County newspapers; 8 cubic feet); letters from George Washington and Dwight D. Eisenhower; historic maps. **Holdings:** 6000 books; 226 bound periodical volumes; 1200 reels of microfilm; 700 microfiche; 70 linear feet of documents; 300 maps. **Subscriptions:** 45 journals and other serials. **Services:** Copying; room open to the public. **Remarks:** FAX: (704)638-3013. **Staff:** Shirley Hoffman.

Dr. Hugh Grant Rowell Circus Library Collection
See: Somers Historical Society (15361)

Nellie Langford Rowell Library
See: York University (20792)

Earl Rowland Art Library
See: San Joaquin Pioneer and Historical Society (14751)

Rowland Medical Library
See: University of Mississippi - Medical Center (18953)

Rownd Historical Library
See: Cedar Falls Historical Society (3184)

Gradie R. Rowntree Medical Library
See: Humana Hospital University (7536)

★ 14090 ★
Roxborough Memorial Hospital - School of Nursing and Medical Staff Libraries (Med)
5800 Ridge Ave.   Phone: (215)487-4345
Philadelphia, PA 19128   Marvin Thornton, Libn.
Founded: 1948. **Staff:** Prof 2. **Subjects:** Nursing, medicine, psychology, sociology, history of nursing, nursing education. **Holdings:** 2500 books; 1575 bound periodical volumes; 6 VF drawers of pamphlets and newsletters; 3 VF drawers of National League of Nursing publications; 371 AV programs; 23 computer programs. **Subscriptions:** 203 journals and other serials. **Services:** Interlibrary loan; copying; library open to the public for reference use only. **Computerized Information Services:** BRS Information Technologies; CD-ROM (CINAHL-CD). Performs searches on fee basis. **Networks/Consortia:** Member of National Network of Libraries of Medicine - Middle Atlantic Region, Delaware Valley Information Consortium (DEVIC). **Remarks:** FAX: (215)487-4591. **Staff:** Walter Silver, Instr. Media Spec.

★ 14091 ★
Royal Academy of Arts (of London) - Library (Art, Hist)
Piccadilly Burlington House   Phone: 71 4945737
London W1V 0DS, England   Maryanne Stevens, Libn./Hd. of Educ.
Founded: 1768. **Staff:** Prof 2; Other 3. **Subjects:** British art (18th to 20th century), history of Royal Academy, graphic/applied art in Great Britain (18th to 20th century). **Special Collections:** Artists' papers; Royal Academy Archives; architectural drawings; history book collections (pre-1870 imprints; 15,000 volumes). **Holdings:** 30,000 books; archival materials. **Subscriptions:** 10 journals and other serials. **Services:** Copying; library open to the public at librarian's discretion. **Remarks:** FAX: 71 4340837.

★ 14092 ★
Royal Academy of Sciences - Netherlands Institute for Developmental Biology - Hubrecht Laboratory Library (Biol Sci)
Uppsalalaan 8   Phone: 30 510211
NL-3584 CT Utrecht, Netherlands   Mrs. Oeke Kruythof, Hd. of Lib.
Staff: Prof 1. **Subjects:** Developmental biology of animals and man; embryology - descriptive, experimental, molecular; recombinant DNA research; developmental genetics; regeneration; asexual reproduction and development; pattern formation. **Holdings:** 3240 books; 4250 bound periodical volumes; 143,000 reprints. **Subscriptions:** 77 journals and other serials. **Services:** Interlibrary loan; copying; library open to biologists and embryologists. **Automated Operations:** Computerized cataloging. **Computerized Information Services:** Current Contents on Diskette; internal database; CD-ROM (Cambridge Scientific Abstracts Life Sciences Collection). **Remarks:** FAX: 30 516464.

★ 14093 ★
Royal Aeronautical Society - Library (Sci-Engr)
4 Hamilton Place   Phone: 71 499-3515
London W1V 0BQ, England   A.W.L. Nayler, Libn.
Founded: 1866. **Subjects:** Aerospace engineering and technology. **Special Collections:** Hodgson Collection (700 titles; 600 lithographs); Poynton Collection (100 titles). **Holdings:** 25,000 books; 1000 periodical titles; 75,000 documents; technical reports; photographs. **Subscriptions:** 300 journals and other serials. **Services:** Interlibrary loan; copying; library open to the public on fee basis. **Special Indexes:** Publications index, 1897-1977. **Remarks:** Telex: 262826 RAESOC. FAX: 1 499-6230.

★ 14094 ★
Royal Agricultural College - Hosier Library (Agri)
Stroud Rd   Phone: 285 652531
Cirencester, Gloucestershire GL7 6JS, England   Rachel M. Rowe
Staff: Prof 3; Other 2.75. **Subjects:** Agriculture, rural estate management, forestry, agribusiness, management. **Special Collections:** Historical farming book collection (2000). **Holdings:** 7000 books; 300 videotapes. **Subscriptions:** 600 journals and other serials; 10 newspapers. **Services:** Interlibrary loan; copying; library open to the public for reference use only. **Computerized Information Services:** ESA/IRS. Contact Person: Tessa Holloway. **Special Indexes:** Update Overseas (index to periodical literature on non-temperate agriculture). **Remarks:** FAX: 285 650219.

★ 14095 ★
Royal Alexandra Hospital - Library Services (Med)
10240 Kingsway Ave.   Phone: (403)477-4135
Edmonton, AB, Canada T5H 3V9   Donna M. Dryden, Dir., Lib. & AV Serv.
Founded: 1963. **Staff:** Prof 1; Other 1. **Subjects:** Medicine, allied health sciences. **Holdings:** 1600 books. **Subscriptions:** 180 journals and other serials. **Services:** Interlibrary loan; copying; SDI; services open to hospital personnel. **Computerized Information Services:** MEDLINE, DIALOG Information Services; Envoy 100 (electronic mail service). **Remarks:** Electronic mail address(es): ILL.AERA (Envoy 100).

★ 14096 ★
Royal Alexandra Hospital - School of Nursing Library (Med)
10415 111th Ave.   Phone: (403)477-4939
Edmonton, AB, Canada T5G 0B8   Kay B. Walker, Libn.
Founded: 1960. **Staff:** Prof 1; Other 2. **Subjects:** Nursing, medicine, social and behavioral sciences. **Holdings:** 13,073 books; 250 videotapes, 200 filmstrips, 30 models. **Subscriptions:** 120 journals and other serials. **Services:** Interlibrary loan; copying; library open to nursing students, faculty, and hospital personnel. **Computerized Information Services:** Internal database; CD-ROM (CINAHL). **Remarks:** FAX: (403)477-4048.

★ 14097 ★
Royal Astronomical Society of Canada - National Library (Sci-Engr)
136 Dupont St.   Phone: (416)924-7973
Toronto, ON, Canada M5R 1V2   Kathy Cresswell, Libn.
Founded: 1904. **Subjects:** Astronomy and allied sciences. **Holdings:** 2000 volumes; 600 35mm slides; 11 16mm films. **Subscriptions:** 50 journals and other serials. **Services:** Library open to members only. **Computerized Information Services:** BITNET (electronic mail service). **Remarks:** FAX: (416)968-6687. Electronic mail address(es): RASC@VELA.ASTRO.UTORONTO.CA (BITNET).

★ 14098 ★
Royal Australian Naval College - Library (Mil)
HMAS Creswell   Phone: 44 421001
Jervis Bay, NSW 2540, Australia   Virginia Costello, Libn.
Founded: 1915. **Staff:** Prof 1; Other 2. **Subjects:** Naval history, maritime strategy, naval forces and warfare, military art and science. **Special Collections:** Rare books on naval history (300). **Holdings:** 15,000 books. **Subscriptions:** 98 journals and other serials; 2 newspapers. **Services:** Interlibrary loan; copying; SDI; library open to the public with written permission from the captain of the establishment. **Computerized Information Services:** DIALOG Information Services, AUSINET, ABN. **Remarks:** FAX: 44 421175.

★ 14099 ★
Royal Bank of Canada - Information Resources (Bus-Fin)
Royal Bank Plaza, 4th Fl., S. Tower   Phone: (416)974-2780
Toronto, ON, Canada M5J 2J5   Jane Dysart, Mgr.
Founded: 1972. **Staff:** Prof 8; Other 3. **Subjects:** Banking, finance, Canadian industry, business, world economic conditions, economics, management. **Holdings:** 10,000 books; 250 subject files; 200 association files; 200 country files; 300 industry files; 15 drawers of microfiche of financial statements of Canadian companies. **Subscriptions:** 2000 journals and other serials; 50 newspapers. **Services:** Interlibrary loan; resources open to the public on a fee basis. **Automated Operations:** Computerized cataloging, acquisitions, serials, and circulation. **Computerized Information Services:** DIALOG Information Services, Reuters, Info Globe, LEXIS, Dow Jones News/Retrieval, Canada Systems Group (CSG), Questel, QL Systems, NewsNet, Inc., CompuServe Information Service, Data-Star, iNET 2000, Infomart Online, The Financial Post DataGroup, STM Systems Corporation, InvesText, Nihon Keizai Shimbun, Inc. (NIKKEI), VU/TEXT Information Services, WILSONLINE; Envoy 100 (electronic mail service). **Publications:** On the Shelf (current awareness bulletin), bimonthly - for internal distribution only. **Remarks:** FAX: (416)974-0135. **Staff:** Pat Williams, Sys.Coord.; Deborah Nicholas, Info.Rsrcs.Coord.

★ 14100 ★
Royal Bank of Canada - Information Resources (Bus-Fin)
P.O. Box 6001   Phone: (514)874-2452
Montreal, PQ, Canada H3C 3A9   John O'Shaughnessy, Coord.
Founded: 1913. **Staff:** Prof 2; Other 2. **Subjects:** Banks and banking; finance and international finance; economics and business; Canadian and world economic conditions; management. **Holdings:** 17,000 volumes; pamphlets; speeches; archives. **Subscriptions:** 1000 journals and other serials; 15 newspapers. **Services:** Interlibrary loan; copying; open to the public on fee basis. **Automated Operations:** Computerized cataloging, acquisitions, serials, and circulation. **Computerized Information Services:** PFDS Online, DIALOG Information Services, Info Globe, Dow Jones News/Retrieval, QL Systems, LEXIS, NEXIS, TEXTLINE; ROBIN (internal database). **Publications:** On the Shelf, bimonthly. **Remarks:** FAX: (514)874-2445. **Also Known As:** Banque Royale du Canada - Informatheque. **Staff:** Janis Wheatley, Sr.Info.Serv.Off.; Karen Lawlor, Info.Serv.Techn.

★ 14101 ★
Royal BC Museum - Library (Biol Sci, Soc Sci)
675 Belleville St.   Phone: (604)387-2916
Victoria, BC, Canada V8V 1X4   Frederike Verspoor, Chf.Libn.
Founded: 1886. **Staff:** 2. **Subjects:** Museology, natural history, human history. **Special Collections:** British Columbia ornithology and herpetology bibliographies. **Holdings:** 20,000 books; bound periodical volumes; unbound periodicals. **Subscriptions:** 201 journals and other serials. **Services:** Interlibrary loan, copying, library open to the public. **Computerized Information Services:** DIALOG Information Services, CAN/OLE; Envoy 100 (electronic mail service). **Remarks:** FAX: (604)387-5360. Electronic mail address(es): ROYAL.BC.MUS (Envoy 100).

★ 14102 ★
Royal Botanic Garden , Edinburgh - Library (Biol Sci)
Edinburgh EH3 5LR, Scotland   Phone: 31 5527171
                   Dr. C.D. Will, Libn.
Founded: 1670. **Staff:** 6. **Subjects:** Botany, horticulture, early medicine and agriculture. **Special Collections:** Pre-Linnean literature; herbals; prints, paintings, and clippings collection; archival collection. **Holdings:** 60,000 books; 120,000 bound periodical volumes; 90 linear feet of microforms; 150,000 manuscripts. **Subscriptions:** 1774 journals and other serials. **Services:** Interlibrary loan; copying; library open to the public with restrictions. **Computerized Information Services:** Internal database. **Publications:** History of the Royal Botanic Garden Library, Edinburgh; Ericales bibliography. **Special Indexes:** Periodicals holding list. **Remarks:** FAX: 31 5520382. **Staff:** A. Welsh; L. Taylor.

★ 14103 ★
Royal Botanic Gardens , Kew - Library & Archives (Biol Sci)
Richmond, Surrey TW9 3AE,   Phone: 81 9401171
  England   Miss S.M.D. FitzGerald, Chf.Libn.
                              & Archv.
Founded: 1852. **Staff:** Prof 7; Other 7. **Subjects:** Plants - taxonomy, distribution, conservation, anatomy, genetics, biochemistry; economic botany; horticulture; seed storage; micropropagation. **Special Collections:** Pre-Linnean and Linnean collections; botanical illustrations; archives. **Holdings:** 120,000 books; 37,000 bound periodical volumes; 20,000 microforms; 250,000 manuscripts. **Subscriptions:** 2000 journals and other serials. **Services:** Copying; library open to bona fide researchers by appointment with written application. **Computerized Information Services:** DIALOG Information Services, DIALTECH. **Publications:** Selective bibliographies. **Special Catalogs:** Author and Classified Catalogue (9 volumes; 1974). **Remarks:** FAX: 81 9481197. Telex: 296694. **Staff:** John P. Flanagan, Dp.Libn.; C.M. Edmondson, Sr. Paper Cons.

★ 14104 ★
Royal Botanic Gardens & National Herbarium - Library (Biol Sci)
Dept. of Conservation, Forests and Lands
Birdwood Ave.   Phone: 3 6552320
South Yarra, VIC 3141, Australia   H.M. Cohn, Libn.
Founded: 1853. **Staff:** 1. **Subjects:** Botany - taxonomic, economic, history; horticulture; landscape architecture. **Holdings:** 36,000 books; 15,000 bound periodical volumes; 8500 microforms; 100 manuscripts. **Subscriptions:** 250 journals and other serials. **Services:** Interlibrary loan; copying; library open to the public by appointment. **Special Indexes:** Indexes to Australian taxonomic literature, registered cultivars, botanical collectors and artists, and botanists. **Remarks:** FAX: 3 6552350. Maintained by Victoria Department of Conservation and Environment.

★ 14105 ★
Royal Botanical Gardens - Library (Biol Sci)
Box 399   Phone: (416)527-1158
Hamilton, ON, Canada L8N 3H8   Ina Vrugtman, Libn./Cur.
Founded: 1947. **Staff:** Prof 1; Other 2. **Subjects:** Botany, ornamental horticulture, natural history and conservation, ornithology. **Special Collections:** Centre for Canadian Historical Horticulture Studies (CCHHS). **Holdings:** 12,000 books; 1500 bound periodical volumes; 2500 pamphlets and reprints; 15,000 nursery and seed trade catalogs. **Subscriptions:** 450 journals and other serials. **Services:** Interlibrary loan; copying; library open to the public for reference use only. **Publications:** Canadian Horticultural History/Histoire de l'Horticulture au Canada, irregular - available by subscription. **Special Indexes:** Gray Herbarium card index. **Remarks:** FAX: (416)577-0375.

★ 14106 ★
Royal Canadian Artillery Museum - Library (Mil)
Canadian Forces Base   Phone: (204)765-3534
Shilo, MB, Canada R0K 2A0   Mr. W.M. Lunan, Cur.
Founded: 1956. **Staff:** Prof 1. **Subjects:** Military history; artillery - ordnance, carriages, ammunition, technical data, small arms, vehicles. **Special Collections:** War diaries of the Canadian Artillery from World War II and the Korean Conflict (640 boxes). **Holdings:** 13,000 books; 13,000 bound periodical volumes; 428 maps; 81 boxes of documents; 118 videotapes; pamphlets. **Subscriptions:** 14 journals and other serials; 5 newspapers. **Services:** Copying; library open to the public by appointment for research. **Remarks:** Library is maintained by Royal Regiment of Canadian Artillery. **Also Known As:** RCA Museum.

★ 14107 ★
Royal Canadian Military Institute - Library (Mil)
426 University Ave.   Phone: (416)597-0286
Toronto, ON, Canada M5G 1S9   Ann Melvin, Libn.
Founded: 1890. **Staff:** Prof 1; Other 1. **Subjects:** Military science; military, naval, and air force history; army, navy, and air force technical topics; Canadiana. **Special Collections:** Denison Collection (500 volumes); Frost Collection (200 volumes); War of the Rebellion: compilation of official records of Union and Confederate Armies. **Holdings:** 25,000 books; 2000 bound periodical volumes; 1000 antique volumes; 2500 photographs (World War I). **Subscriptions:** 40 journals and other serials. **Services:** Interlibrary loan; library open to the public for reference use by appointment only.

★ **14108** ★

Royal Canadian Mounted Police - Canadian Police College - Law Enforcement Reference Centre (Law)
St. Laurent Blvd. & Sandridge Rd.
Box 8900   Phone: (613)993-3225
Ottawa, ON, Canada K1G 3J2   Nancy Park, Mgr.
Founded: 1936. **Staff:** Prof 3; Other 12. **Subjects:** Police science, criminal justice, management, criminology, sociology, physical fitness. **Holdings:** 43,000 books; 40,000 microforms; 950 motion pictures; 20 VF drawers; 1300 AV materials. **Subscriptions:** 1500 journals and other serials; 10 newspapers. **Services:** Interlibrary loan; copying; SDI; center open to the public with permission of RCMP Commissioner. **Automated Operations:** Computerized public access catalog, cataloging, acquisitions, and serials (Library Automated System). **Computerized Information Services:** The Financial Post DataGroup, DIALOG Information Services, CAN/OLE, CAN/LAW, Info Globe, DOBIS, Infomart Online, CBANET; Envoy 100 (electronic mail service). **Publications:** Bibliographies, irregular; Acquisitions List, monthly - available to libraries upon request; list of periodicals. **Special Catalogs:** Listing of AV material. **Remarks:** FAX: (613)990-9738. Electronic mail address(es): RCMP.LERC (Envoy 100). Telex: 053-3305. **Also Known As:** Gendarmerie Royale du Canada - College Canadien de Police - Centre du Documentation Policiere (CDP). **Staff:** Margaret Brignell, Hd. , Tech.Serv.; Emmett Will, Hd., Pub.Serv.; Terry Thibert, Lib.Techn.

★ **14109** ★

Royal Canadian Mounted Police - Centennial Museum Research Room (Mil, Hist)
P.O. Box 6500   Phone: (306)780-5838
Regina, SK, Canada S4P 3J7   Malcolm J.H. Wake, Musm.Dir.
Founded: 1933. **Staff:** 4. **Subjects:** Royal Canadian Mounted Police, military, Saskatchewan and Canadian history. **Special Collections:** History of the Royal Canadian Mounted Police (500 volumes). **Holdings:** 800 books; 200 bound periodical volumes; historical photographs; 8 VF drawers of R.C.M.P. archives. **Subscriptions:** 10 journals and other serials. **Services:** Copying; room open to the public by appointment for reference use only. **Remarks:** FAX: (306)780-6337.

★ **14110** ★

(Royal Canadian) Ordnance Corps Museum - Library (Mil)
6560 Hochelaga St.
P.O. Box 4000, Succursale K   Phone: (514)252-2241
Montreal, PQ, Canada H1N 3R9   Philias Sippley, Asst.Cur.
Founded: 1962. **Staff:** 1. **Subjects:** Military history and equipment, weapons, ammunition and explosives. **Holdings:** 3000 volumes. **Subscriptions:** 5 journals and other serials. **Services:** Library open to the public. **Remarks:** Maintained by Canada - National Defence.

★ **14111** ★

Royal College of Nursing - Library (Med)
20 Cavendish Sq.   Phone: 71 4093333
London W1M 0AB, England   Mr. A. Shepherd, Hd.
Founded: 1921. **Staff:** 13.5. **Subjects:** Nursing, health service, education, psychology, management. **Special Collections:** Steinberg Collection of Nursing Research (515 thesis titles); historical collection (320 linear feet); Nursing Archive. **Holdings:** 50,000 books; 400 manuscripts. **Subscriptions:** 365 journals and other serials. **Services:** Interlibrary loan; copying; SDI. **Computerized Information Services:** Data-Star, DIALOG Information Services; RCN Library data base (internal database). **Publications:** Nursing bibliography. **Special Catalogs:** Catalog to Steinberg Collection. **Remarks:** FAX: 71 3551379.

★ **14112** ★

Royal College of Physicians of Edinburgh - Library (Med)
9 Queen St.   Phone: 31 225 7324
Edinburgh EH2 1JQ, Scotland   Joan P.S. Ferguson, Libn.
Founded: 1681. **Staff:** Prof 2; Other 2. **Subjects:** History of medicine and Scottish medicine. **Special Collections:** Simpson Collection (obstetrics and gynecology); J.W. Ballantyne Collection (fetal pathology). **Holdings:** 300,000 volumes; 1000 volumes of manuscripts. **Subscriptions:** 100 journals and other serials. **Services:** Interlibrary loan; copying; library open to the public. **Computerized Information Services:** Data-Star, BLAISE LINK, BRS Information Technologies. **Publications:** Annual Report. **Special Catalogs:** A Catalogue of Sixteenth-Century Medical Books in Edinburgh Libraries - for sale. **Remarks:** FAX: 31 220 3939. **Staff:** Iain Milne, Asst.Libn.

★ **14113** ★

Royal College of Physicians of London - Library (Med)
11 St. Andrew's Pl.   Phone: 71 9351174
London NW1 4LE, England   Geoffrey Davenport, Libn.
Founded: 1518. **Staff:** 6. **Subjects:** Medical history and biography. **Special Collections:** Library of Marquis of Dorchester, 1606-1680 (3000 volumes); Evan Bedford Library of Cardiology (history of cardiology; 1112 books and pamphlets; 215 bound periodical volumes); Heberden Library of British Association of Rheumatology (history of rheumatology; 1200 items); Willan Library of British Association of Dermatologists (history of dermatology; 500 books and pamphlets; 113 bound periodical volumes). **Holdings:** 50,000 volumes; 100 AV programs; 184 microforms; 18,000 manuscripts. **Subscriptions:** 102 journals and other serials. **Services:** Interlibrary loan; copying; library open to bona fide researchers. **Special Catalogs:** Catalog of Evan Bedford Library of Cardiology; catalog of engraved portraits in the Royal College of Physicians of London. **Remarks:** FAX: 71 4875218. **Staff:** Julie Ann Allum, BA ALA; Terry Maria Parker, BA DAA.

★ **14114** ★

Royal College of Surgeons of England - Library (Med)
35-43 Lincoln's Inn Fields   Phone: 71 4053474
London WC2A 3PN, England   Ian F. Lyle, Libn.
Founded: 1800. **Staff:** 6. **Subjects:** Surgery, pathology, anatomy, anesthesia, physiology, history of medicine. **Special Collections:** Hunter-Baillie Collection (1500 autograph letters and manuscripts); John Hunter and his pupils and contemporaries (1100 books, manuscripts, and autograph letters); engraved portraits (3000); medical bookplates (2000). **Holdings:** 60,000 books; 115,000 bound periodical volumes; 50 AV programs; 5000 manuscripts and autograph letters. **Subscriptions:** 600 journals and other serials. **Services:** Interlibrary loan; copying; library open to the public with restrictions. **Computerized Information Services:** MEDLINE. Performs searches on fee basis. **Special Catalogs:** English books before 1701 in the Library of the Royal College of Surgeons. **Remarks:** FAX: 71 8319438. Telex: 936573 RCSEN G. **Staff:** F.K. Sherwood; C.M. Craig.

★ **14115** ★

Royal College of Veterinary Surgeons - Wellcome Library (Med)
32 Belgrave Sq.   Phone: 71 2356568
London SW1X 8QP, England   Benita Horder, Libn.
Founded: 1850. **Staff:** Prof 5.5. **Subjects:** Veterinary science, animal husbandry, comparative medicine. **Special Collections:** Historical collection (2500 volumes); Henry Gray Collection (ornithology; 250 volumes). **Holdings:** 25,000 books. **Subscriptions:** 500 journals and other serials. **Services:** Interlibrary loan; copying; SDI; library open to the public with restrictions. **Automated Operations:** Computerized public access catalog and circulation. **Computerized Information Services:** DIALOG Information Services, BLAISE Online Services, IRS-DIALTECH, Data-Star, PFDS Online; CD-ROMs (CABI Abstracts, JUSTIS). **Remarks:** FAX: 71 2456100. Maintained by Royal College of Veterinary Surgeons' Trust Fund. **Staff:** Jenny Harris, Asst.Libn.; Vivia Carbines, Asst.Libn.

★ **14116** ★

Royal Columbian Hospital - Library (Med)
330 E. Columbia St.   Phone: (604)520-4255
New Westminster, BC, Canada V3L 3W7   Ms. S. Abzinger, Mgr.
Founded: 1978. **Staff:** Prof 1; Other 1. **Subjects:** Medicine, allied health sciences. **Holdings:** 2300 books; 2200 bound periodical volumes. **Subscriptions:** 172 journals and other serials. **Services:** Interlibrary loan; library not open to the public. **Automated Operations:** Computerized acquisitions. **Computerized Information Services:** MEDLARS, DIALOG Information Services. **Remarks:** Maintained by the Fraser-Burrard Hospital Society. Affiliated with Eagle Ridge Hospital Library.

Royal Danish Navy
See: Denmark - Royal Danish Navy - Library (4769)

★ **14117** ★

Royal Dublin Society - Library (Area-Ethnic)
Ballsbridge   Phone: 1 680645
Dublin 4, Ireland   Mary Kelleher, Libn.
Founded: 1731. **Staff:** 5. **Subjects:** Ireland, agriculture, fine arts, biography, literature. **Special Collections:** Ireland (80 volumes of pamphlets); Dante Collection (120 volumes). **Holdings:** 120,000 books; 80,000 bound periodical volumes; 20 microforms; 50 manuscripts. **Services:** Interlibrary loan; copying; SDI; library open to bona fide researchers. **Publications:** Annual List of Accessions. **Remarks:** FAX: 1 604014.

★ 14118 ★
Royal Geographical Society of Australasia, Inc. - South Australian
   Branch - Library (Geog-Map, Area-Ethnic)
c/o State Lib. of S. Australia
N. Terrace
G.P.O. Box 419   Phone: 8 2077266
Adelaide, SA 5001, Australia   Roslyn Blandy, Libn.
Founded: 1885. **Staff:** Prof 1. **Subjects:** Australia - discovery, exploration, description, travel; voyages and travels; geography; Australian aborigines; biography. **Special Collections:** The York Gate Geographical and Colonial Library (9300 volumes). **Holdings:** 15,000 books; 5500 bound periodical volumes; 15 reels of microfilm; 2200 pictorial records; 800 maps; 200 manuscripts. **Subscriptions:** 148 journals and other serials. **Services:** Interlibrary loan; copying; library open to the public for reference use only. **Computerized Information Services:** ABN (Australian Bibliographic Network). **Publications:** Subject bibliographies. **Special Catalogs:** Catalogue of the York Gate Library; Catalogue of the Manuscripts in the Library of the RGSASA. **Special Indexes:** Index to Society's Proceedings, volumes 1-40 - for sale. **Remarks:** FAX: 8 2233390. Telex: 82074.

★ 14119 ★
Royal Greenwich Observatory - Library (Sci-Engr)
Madingley Rd.   Phone: 223 374000
Cambridge CB3 0EZ, England   Ingrid Howard, Libn.
Founded: 1675. **Staff:** Prof 1. **Subjects:** Astronomy, geodesy, physics, history of science, science policy, chronometry and time. **Special Collections:** Airy Collection (astronomy, mathematics, voyages of discovery, science, chronometry; 1000 rare and pre-1830 books); archives of Astronomers Royal (150,000 manuscripts). **Holdings:** 50,000 books; 60,000 bound periodical volumes; 100 microforms; 3500 slides. **Subscriptions:** 300 journals and other serials; 4 newspapers. **Services:** Interlibrary loan; copying; library open to the public with written application. **Computerized Information Services:** DIALOG Information Services, SIMBAD; internal database. **Remarks:** FAX: 223 374700. Telex: 817235 RGOSTR. **Remarks:** Observatory's parent organization is the Science Engineering Research Council. **Formerly:** Located in Hailsham, East Sussex, England.

Royal Greenwich Observatory Archives
See: **University of Cambridge - Library** (18441)

★ 14120 ★
Royal Institute of British Architects - British Architectural Library
   (Plan)
66 Portland Pl.   Phone: 71 5805533
London W1N 4AD, England   Ruth Kamen, Dir. of Lib.
Founded: 1834. **Staff:** 24. **Subjects:** Architecture, construction technology, design and environmental studies, landscaping, urban planning, allied subjects. **Holdings:** 140,000 books; 2000 periodical titles; 700 meters of manuscripts and documents; 85,000 photographs; 20,000 negatives; 10,000 postcards; 18,000 slides; 400,000 drawings and architectural renderings; microforms; vertical files. **Subscriptions:** 400 journals and other serials. **Services:** Copying; library open to the public. **Computerized Information Services:** Produces Architectural Periodicals Index database (available online through DIALOG Information Services). **Publications:** Architectural Keywords (print, microform) - available by subscription. **Special Indexes:** Architecture Periodicals Index, quarterly with annual cumulation - available by subscription. **Remarks:** FAX: 71 6311802. Telex: 24224 MONREF G.

★ 14121 ★
Royal Institute for Cultural Heritage of Belgium - Library (Art)
parc du Cinquantenaire 1   Phone: 2 7396711
B-1040 Brussels, Belgium   Robert Didier, Chf.Libn.
Founded: 1962. **Staff:** 8. **Subjects:** Art, conservation of works of art. **Holdings:** 30,500 books; 50,000 bound periodical volumes. **Subscriptions:** 500 journals and other serials. **Services:** Interlibrary loan; copying; library open to the public. **Publications:** New acquisitions list. **Remarks:** FAX: 2 7396868.

★ 14122 ★
Royal Institute of International Affairs - Library (Soc Sci)
Chatham House
10 St. James's Sq.   Phone: 71 9575700
London SW1Y 4LE, England   Susan J. Boyde, Libn.
Founded: 1921. **Staff:** Prof 13. **Subjects:** International affairs, end of World War II to present. **Special Collections:** International press clippings library. **Holdings:** 160,000 books and pamphlets. **Subscriptions:** 640 journals and other serials. **Services:** Interlibrary loan; copying; library open to bona fide postgraduate researchers by appointment on a fee basis. **Automated Operations:** Computerized cataloging. **Computerized Information Services:** FT PROFILE. **Publications:** List of articles indexed in periodicals, monthly; list of books and pamphlets added to the library, monthly. **Special Catalogs:** The Classified Catalogue of the Library of the RIIA. **Special Indexes:** Index to periodical articles in the library of the RIIA (2 volumes, 3 supplements; 1950-1990). **Remarks:** FAX: 71 9575710. **Staff:** Mary Bone, Dp.Libn.; Margaret Julian, Ser.Libn.

Royal Institute of Technology (of Sweden)
See: **Sweden - Royal Institute of Technology** (15910)

Royal Library (of Denmark)
See: **Denmark - Royal Library** (4770)

Royal Meteorological Institute of Belgium
See: **Royal Observatory of Belgium** (14127)

★ 14123 ★
Royal Military College of Canada - Massey Library & Science/
   Engineering Library (Mil)
Kingston, ON, Canada K7K 5L0   Phone: (613)541-6004
                         Samuel O. Alexander
Founded: 1876. **Staff:** Prof 5. **Subjects:** Engineering; military history, arts, and science. **Special Collections:** Military Studies (30,524 volumes). **Holdings:** 211,353 volumes; 57,946 documents; 17,710 technical reports; 12,685 microforms; 2353 artifacts, manuscripts, prints, photographs. **Subscriptions:** 1100 journals. **Services:** Interlibrary loan; copying; library open to the public for consultation. **Automated Operations:** Computerized public access catalog, acquisitions, and cataloging. **Computerized Information Services:** DIALOG Information Services, CAN/OLE, MARC Records Distribution Service (MRDS), UTLAS, DOBIS Canadian Online Library System; Envoy 100 (electronic mail service). **Networks/Consortia:** Member of Ontario Council of University Libraries (OCUL). **Remarks:** FAX: (613)542-5055. Electronic mail address(es): ILL.OKR; ILL.OKRS (Envoy 100). Maintained by Canada - National Defence. **Staff:** Ms. S.J. Toomey, Act.Hd., Tech.Serv. & Sys.; Mrs. N. Turkington, Hd., Sci./ Engr.Div.; Mr. B. Cameron, Act.Hd., Massey Lib.Div.; Ms. S. Burt, Act.Hd./Ref.Lib.; Ms. F. Giberson, Act.Hd., Cat.

★ 14124 ★
Royal Museum of Fine Arts (of Denmark) - Department of Paintings -
   Library (Art)
Solvgade 48-50   Phone: 1112126
DK-1307 Copenhagen K, Denmark   Maria A. Barolini, Libn.
Founded: 1847. **Staff:** Prof 1. **Subjects:** Paintings, sculptures. **Holdings:** 71,000 books. **Subscriptions:** 300 journals and other serials. **Services:** Interlibrary loan; copying; library open to the public. **Computerized Information Services:** ALBA. **Also Known As:** Statens Museum for Kunst - Den Kongelige Malerisamlings - Bibliotek.

★ 14125 ★
Royal Museum of Fine Arts (of Denmark) - Department of Prints and
   Drawings - Library (Art)
Solvgade 48-50   Phone: 3 3912126
DK-1307 Copenhagen K, Denmark   Susanne Hansen, Libn.
Founded: 1843. **Staff:** Prof 1. **Subjects:** Drawings, prints, photography. **Special Collections:** Artists' books. **Holdings:** 55,000 books. **Subscriptions:** 60 journals and other serials. **Services:** Interlibrary loan; copying; SDI; library open to the public with restrictions. **Computerized Information Services:** ALBA. **Remarks:** FAX: 3 3142326. **Also Known As:** Statens Museum for Kunst - Den Kongelige Kobberstiksamlings - Bibliotek.

Royal Naval Observatory and Institute
See: **Spain - Royal Naval Observatory and Institute - Library** (15567)

★ 14126 ★
Royal Netherlands Academy of Arts and Sciences - Library (Med, Sci-Engr)
Joan Muyskenweg 25
P.O. Box 41950
NL-1009 DD Amsterdam, Netherlands   Phone: 20 6685511
                                           Dr. W.J. van Gils, Dir.
Founded: 1808. **Staff:** 62. **Subjects:** Medicine, biology, chemistry, physics, pharmacy, astronomy. **Holdings:** 350,000 volumes; 2.4 million microfiche. **Subscriptions:** 12,500 journals and other serials. **Services:** Interlibrary loan; copying; SDI; library open to the public. **Automated Operations:** Computerized cataloging, acquisitions, and serials. **Computerized Information Services:** INIS (International Nuclear Information System), BIOREP, Current Research Information System. Performs searches on fee basis. **Remarks:** FAX: 20 6685079. **Also Known As:** Bibliotheek Koninklijke Nederlandse Akademie van Wetenschappen. **Staff:** Th.W.J. Pieters; A.T. Hogenaar; R. Brandsma; J.A. Dijkman; H. Lalieu; B. ten Tusscher; R. Boer.

★ 14127 ★
Royal Observatory of Belgium - Library (Sci-Engr)
3, ave. Circulaire   Phone: 2 3730274
B-1180 Brussels, Belgium   P.H. Dale, First Asst.
     Founded: 1833. **Subjects:** Astronomy, astrophysics, geophysics, meteorology. **Holdings:** 150,000 volumes. **Subscriptions:** 4468 journals and other serials. **Services:** Interlibrary loan; copying; library open to the public for reference use only. **Computerized Information Services:** DP CI (internal databases). **Remarks:** FAX 2 3749822. Telex: 21565 OBSBEL. Maintained by Belgium - Ministry of the Interior. Also serves the Royal Meteorological Institute of Belgium. **Also Known As:** Observatoire Royal de Belgique; Institut Royal Meteorologique de Belgique.

★ 14128 ★
Royal Observatory, Hong Kong - Library (Sci-Engr)
134A Nathan Rd.   Phone: 3 7329200
Kowloon, Hong Kong   Patrick P. Sham, Dir.
Founded: 1883. **Special Collections:** Climatic data of Hong Kong. **Holdings:** 39,400 volumes. **Subscriptions:** 71 journals and other serials; 8 newspapers. **Services:** Interlibrary loan; copying; library not open to the public. **Publications:** Royal Observatory Almanac; Royal Observatory Calandar; Hong Kong Tide Tables, annual; Marine Climatological Summary Charts for the South China Sea, annual - on exchange; Daily Weather Charts; Monthly Weather Summaries; Surface Observations, annual - on exchange; A Summary of Radiosonde-Radiowind Ascents made at King's Park, Hong Kong, annual - on exchange; Tropical Cyclone Summaries, annual - on exchange; Occasional Papers, irregular; Technical Notes, irregular - on exchange; Technical Notes (Local), irregular - on exchange. **Remarks:** FAX: 3 3119448; 3 7215034. Telex: 54777GEOPHHX. Cable: OBSERVAHKG. Observatory is a department of the Hong Kong government. It operates weather forecasting, tropical cyclone warning, and various other meteorological and geophysical services to meet the needs of the public, shipping, aviation, industry, and engineering.

★ 14129 ★
Royal Ontario Museum - Canadian Decorative Arts Library
14 Queen's Park Crescent, W.
Toronto, ON, Canada M5S 2C6
Defunct. Holdings absorbed by Royal Ontario Museum - Main Library.

★ 14130 ★
Royal Ontario Museum - H.H. Mu Library (Area-Ethnic, Art)
100 Queen's Park   Phone: (416)586-5718
Toronto, ON, Canada M5S 2C6   Jack Howard, Libn.
Founded: 1933. **Staff:** Prof 1. **Subjects:** Art and archeology of the Far East including China, Japan, India, and Southeast Asia. **Special Collections:** Stone inscriptions and carvings from monuments in China; Chinese and Japanese rare books. **Holdings:** 30,000 books and bound periodical volumes; 12 VF drawers. **Subscriptions:** 650 journals and other serials. **Services:** Interlibrary loan; copying; library open to the public with restrictions. **Automated Operations:** Computerized cataloging. **Computerized Information Services:** UTLAS; Envoy 100 (electronic mail service). **Remarks:** FAX: (416)586-8093. Electronic mail address(es): OTRM.ILL (Envoy 100). **Also Known As:** Far Eastern Library.

★ 14131 ★
Royal Ontario Museum - Main Library (Art, Sci-Engr, Biol Sci)
100 Queen's Park   Phone: (416)586-5595
Toronto, ON, Canada M5S 2C6   Julia Matthews
Founded: 1961. **Staff:** Prof 4; Other 6. **Subjects:** Anthropology, archeology, botany, geology, mineralogy, museology, paleontology, zoology, decorative arts, ethnology, textiles, contemporary culture. **Holdings:** 140,000 books and bound periodical volumes. **Subscriptions:** 800 journals and other serials. **Services:** Interlibrary loan; copying; library open to the public for reference use only. **Automated Operations:** Computerized cataloging, acquisitions, and circulation. **Computerized Information Services:** UTLAS, DIALOG Information Services, Questel. **Publications:** Accessions list, monthly - internal distribution and by request; Current Contents, monthly; newsletter, irregular - both for internal distribution only. **Remarks:** FAX: (416)586-5863. Electronic mail address(es): ILL.OTRM (Envoy 100). **Staff:** Isabella Guthrie-McNaughton, Libn.; Mrs. Champa Ramjass, ILL; Sharon Hick, Libn.; Arthur Smith, Assoc.Libn.

★ 14132 ★
Royal Roads Military College - Coronel Memorial Library (Mil, Hist)
Fleet Mail Office   Phone: (604)363-4540
Victoria, BC, Canada V0S 1B0   Susan E. Day, Chf.Libn.
Founded: 1952. **Staff:** Prof 3; Other 3. **Subjects:** Academic topics, military science and history. **Holdings:** 84,000 books; 23,360 bound periodical volumes. **Subscriptions:** 437 journals and other serials; 25 newspapers. **Services:** Interlibrary loan; copying; library open to the public by permission only. **Automated Operations:** Computerized public access catalog, cataloging, acquisitions, and serials. **Computerized Information Services:** CAN/OLE, DIALOG Information Services, Info Globe; Envoy 100, BITNET (electronic mail services). **Publications:** Library handbook, annual - for internal distribution only. **Special Catalogs:** Periodical list (printout). **Remarks:** Maintained by Canada - National Defence. FAX: (604)380-4513. Electronic mail address(es): ILL.BRC (Envoy 100); ROYALROADS.CA (BITNET). **Staff:** J.C. Inkster, User Serv.; L.B. Jensen, Tech.Serv.

★ 14133 ★
Royal School of Librarianship - Library (Info Sci)
Birketinget 6   Phone: 3 1586066
DK-2300 Copenhagen S, Denmark   Ivar A.L. Hoel, Lib.Dir.
Founded: 1956. **Staff:** Prof 8. **Subjects:** Library science, documentation, information. **Holdings:** 127,000 books; 4000 AV documents; 6500 microforms; 158 electronic documents; 7400 pamphlets; 6500 graphic documents. **Subscriptions:** 1589 journals and other serials. **Services:** Interlibrary loan; copying; SDI; library open to the public. **Computerized Information Services:** Library and Information Science Abstracts (LISA), Library Literature. Performs searches free of charge. **Special Indexes:** Nordisk BDI-Index (index of Nordic library and information literature). **Remarks:** FAX: 3 2840201. **Also Known As:** Danmarks Biblioteksskoles Bibliotek.

★ 14134 ★
Royal Scientific Society - Library (Sci-Engr)
P.O. Box 925819   Phone: 844700
Amman, Jordan   Ghazwa Malhas
Founded: 1970. **Subjects:** Applied engineering, economics, computer science, industrial chemistry. **Special Collections:** Standards - BS (British Standard); DIN (Deutsch Institut fuer Normung/German Institute for Standardization); ISO (International Organization for Standardization; United Nations); Japanese; Australian; Indian. **Holdings:** 46,000 volumes; 1390 foreign periodical titles, primarily English; 350 Arabic periodical titles; microforms. **Subscriptions:** 600 journals and other serials; 12 newspapers. **Services:** Interlibrary loan; copying; SDI; library open to the public. **Computerized Information Services:** BRS Information Technologies, DIALOG Information Services, ORBIT Search Service; CD-ROM. **Publications:** Monthly Accession List; Bibliography of Jordan; Current List of Periodical Holdings. **Remarks:** Society objective is to promote research and provide scientific and technological consultation relating to economic and social development in Jordan. FAX: 9626 844 806. Telex: 21276 RAMAH JO.

Royal Scottish Museum - Library
See: **Scotland - National Museums of Scotland - Library** (14955)

Royal Shakespeare Theatre Library
See: Shakespeare Birthplace Trust - Shakespeare Centre Library (15070)

★ 14135 ★
Royal Society of Canada - Library (Sci-Engr, Hum, Biol Sci)
P.O. Box 9734   Phone: (613)991-6990
Ottawa, ON, Canada K1G 5J4   Michael R. Dence, Exec.Dir.
Founded: 1882. **Staff:** 23. **Subjects:** Humanities, social sciences, mathematics, chemistry, physics, earth sciences, animal and plant biology, microbiology and biochemistry, applied science, medical science, interdisciplinary studies. **Special Collections:** Proceedings and Transactions, annually, 1882 to present; Presentation, annually, 1942 to present. **Holdings:** Proceedings of symposiums. **Subscriptions:** 6 newspapers. **Services:** Copying (limited); library open to members only. **Publications:** List of publications - available on request. **Remarks:** FAX: (613)991-6996. Society's collections are stored in the Canada Institute for Scientific and Technical Information (CISTI) and the National Library of Canada. **Also Known As:** Societe royale du Canada.

★ 14136 ★
Royal Society of Medicine - Library (Med)
1 Wimpole St.   Phone: 71 408 2119
London W1M 8AE, England   David W.C. Stewart, Libn.
Founded: 1805. **Staff:** 27. **Subjects:** Medicine, history of medicine. **Special Collections:** Alex Comfort Gerontology Collection. **Holdings:** 100,000 books; 400,000 bound periodical volumes; 500 microforms; 500 manuscripts. **Subscriptions:** 2000 journals and other serials. **Services:** Interlibrary loan; copying; SDI; library open to the public with restrictions. **Computerized Information Services:** DIALOG Information Services, Data-Star, BLAISE Online Services; British Telecom GOLD (electronic mail service). Performs searches on fee basis. Contact Person: Linda Griffiths. **Publications:** Current periodicals list. **Remarks:** FAX: 71 4080062. Telex: 298902 ROYMED G. Electronic mail address(es): 78:MFL001 (British Telecom GOLD).

★ 14137 ★
Royal Trust Corporation of Canada - Research & Information Services (Bus-Fin)
246 Bloor St., W., 3rd Fl.   Phone: (416)864-6170
Toronto, ON, Canada M5S 1V4   Vicki Whitmell, Act.Mgr.
Founded: 1988. **Staff:** Prof 4; Other 4. **Subjects:** Business, finance, marketing, information systems, telecommunications, computers, office automation, law, investment, technology, management. **Holdings:** 4000 books; 25,000 microforms; 320 monographs; software guides; annual reports. **Subscriptions:** 250 journals and other serials; 8 newspapers. **Services:** Interlibrary loan; center not open to the public. **Automated Operations:** Computerized public access catalog, cataloging, acquisitions, and serials. **Computerized Information Services:** DIALOG Information Services, Info Globe, Infomart Online, The Financial Post DataGroup, Dow Jones News/Retrieval, LEXIS, NEXIS, PROFILE, Reuters, STM Systems Corporation, CAN/LAW, QL Systems. **Publications:** Holdings list; library newsletter; acquisitions bulletin. **Remarks:** Telex: 06524306. FAX: (416)367-1054. **Staff:** Irene Kowalski, Ref.Libn.; Parin Daya, Tech.Sys.Libn.

★ 14138 ★
Royal Tyrrell Museum of Palaeontology - Library (Biol Sci, Sci-Engr)
Box 7500
Drumheller, AB, Canada T0J 0Y0   Phone: (403)823-7707
Founded: 1982. **Staff:** 2. **Subjects:** Paleontology, geology, palynology, comparative anatomy, museums. **Special Collections:** Vertebrate paleontology (2650 Ph.D. dissertations; 9500 reprints; 10,000 maps; 100 field notes; monographs; serials; periodicals). **Holdings:** 30,000 books; 2000 bound periodical volumes; 22 periodical titles on microform; 200 reels of microfilm; 100 monographic serial titles. **Subscriptions:** 500 journals and other serials. **Services:** Interlibrary loan; copying; library open to the public for reference use only. **Automated Operations:** Computerized cataloging, serials, and document indexing. **Computerized Information Services:** DIALOG Information Services, CAN/OLE, UTLAS, STN International; internal database; BITNET, Envoy 100 (electronic mail services). **Publications:** Bibliosaurus (accession/current awareness newsletter), biweekly - for internal distribution only. **Remarks:** FAX: (403)823-7131. Electronic mail address(es): TMP/IUS.E8053 (Envoy 100). Maintained by Alberta Culture and Multiculturalism. **Staff:** Lorna Johnston Hodge, Lib.Techn.; Del Frey, Lib.Techn.

★ 14139 ★
The Royal Veterinary and Agricultural University - The Danish Veterinary and Agricultural Library (Med, Agri)
Bulowsvej 13   Phone: 35282145
DK-1870 Frederiksberg C, Denmark   Inger Mathiesen, Hd.
Founded: 1783. **Staff:** 29. **Subjects:** Veterinary science, agriculture, food science. **Holdings:** 420,000 volumes. **Subscriptions:** 4000 journals and other serials. **Services:** Interlibrary loan; copying; SDI; library open to the public. **Computerized Information Services:** DIALOG Information Services, DIMDI. Performs searches on fee basis. **Remarks:** FAX: 35282138.

★ 14140 ★
Royal Victoria Hospital - Allan Memorial Institute - Eric D. Wittkower Library (Med)
1025 Pine Ave., W.   Phone: (514)842-1231
Montreal, PQ, Canada H3A 1A1   Barbara Gartner, Libn.
Founded: 1946. **Staff:** Prof 1. **Subjects:** Psychiatry, psychology, child psychiatry. **Special Collections:** Works of Sigmund Freud. **Holdings:** 3000 books; 2500 bound periodical volumes; 120 unbound journals. **Subscriptions:** 46 journals and other serials. **Services:** Interlibrary loan; copying; library open to hospital staff and McGill University medical students. **Computerized Information Services:** MEDLARS; Envoy 100 (electronic mail service). **Networks/Consortia:** Member of McGill Medical and Health Libraries Association (MMHLA).

★ 14141 ★
Royal Victoria Hospital - Medical Library (Med)
687 Pine Ave., W., Rm. H4.01   Phone: (514)842-1231
Montreal, PQ, Canada H3A 1A1   Sandra R. Duchow, Chf.Med.Libn.
Founded: 1935. **Staff:** Prof 2; Other 4. **Subjects:** Medicine, surgery, anesthesia, nursing. **Holdings:** 2000 books; 10,000 bound periodical volumes. **Subscriptions:** 300 journals and other serials. **Services:** Interlibrary loan; library not open to the public. **Computerized Information Services:** MEDLARS, BRS Information Technologies. **Networks/Consortia:** Member of McGill Medical and Health Libraries Association (MMHLA). **Staff:** Elizabeth Lamont, Asst.Med.Libn.

★ 14142 ★
Royal Victoria Hospital - Women's Pavilion Library (Med)
687 Pine Ave., W.   Phone: (514)842-1231
Montreal, PQ, Canada H3A 1A1   Lynda Dickson, Libn.
Founded: 1957. **Staff:** Prof 1. **Subjects:** Gynecology, obstetrics, newborn physiology, neuroendocrinology. **Holdings:** 500 books; 1000 bound periodical volumes; 4 drawers of reprints. **Subscriptions:** 30 journals and other serials. **Services:** Interlibrary loan; audiovisual lectures (cassette tapes, slides, and prints) on obstetrics and gynecology available to medical students and other interested personnel for use on the premises only; telephone reference service; library open to members of medical and paramedical professions. **Computerized Information Services:** MEDLINE; Envoy 100 (electronic mail service). **Remarks:** FAX: (514)843-1678. Electronic mail address(es): ILL.QMRVW (Envoy 100).

Willis Royle Library
See: Connecticut Valley Hospital - Willis Royle Library (4208)

★ 14143 ★
RSA Corporation - Library
Box 607   Phone: (914)693-1818
Ardsley, NY 10502-0607   Stephanie Weber, Libn.
Services: Library not open to the public. **Remarks:** FAX: (914)693-3446. Telex: 131 148. No further information was supplied by respondent.

Rubber Research Institute of Malaysia
See: Malaysian Rubber Research and Development Board (9570)

Rubel Asiatic Research Collection
See: Harvard University - Fine Arts Library (6965)

Rubel Memorial Library
See: **Orthopaedic Hospital** (12581)

Ruben Library
See: **Temple Adath Israel** (16079)

Rubenianum
See: **Kunsthistorische Musea** (8826)

Bernard Rubinstein Library
See: **Congregation Agudas Achim** (4146)

★ 14144 ★
Rudnick & Wolfe Library (Law)
203 N. LaSalle St., Suite 1800   Phone: (312)368-4000
Chicago, IL 60601-1293   Annette J. Cade, Hd.Libn.
Founded: 1936. **Staff:** Prof 2; Other 2. **Subjects:** Law. **Holdings:** 14,000
books; 5000 microfiche. **Subscriptions:** 300 journals and other serials; 3
newspapers. **Services:** Interlibrary loan; copying; library open to the public
at librarian's discretion. **Computerized Information Services:** WESTLAW,
LEXIS, DIALOG Information Services, LEGI-SLATE, Information
America, Hannah Information Systems, VU/TEXT Information Services,
DataTimes. **Remarks:** FAX: (312)984-6798. **Staff:** Sue Umbdenstock.

Rudnyc'ki Archives
See: **Concordia University - Loyola Campus - Georges P. Vanier Library**
(4121)

Ida and Matthew Rudofker Library
See: **Har Zion Temple** (6895)

Richard C. Rudolph East Asian Library
See: **University of California, Los Angeles** (18397)

George C. Ruhle Library
See: **U.S. Natl. Park Service - Glacier Natl. Park** (17722)

**Ruhr-University - Institute for Development Research and Development
Policy**
See: **Institute for Development Research and Development Policy** (7926)

★ 14145 ★
Rumrill-Hoyt, Inc. - Library
60 Corporate Woods   Phone: (716)272-6100
Rochester, NY 14623   Christine Giovanniello, Libn.
Staff: 1. **Holdings:** 50 books; 15 bound periodical volumes. **Subscriptions:**
100 journals and other serials; 4 newspapers. **Services:** Interlibrary loan;
library not open to the public.

Harry Ruppel Memorial Library
See: **Vandercook College of Music** (19779)

★ 14146 ★
**Rural Advancement Fund of the National Sharecroppers Fund Inc. -
Library** (Agri)
2128 Commonwealth Ave.   Phone: (704)334-3051
Charlotte, NC 28205   Georgia Good, Interim Exec.Dir.
Founded: 1979. **Staff:** Prof 1; Other 1. **Subjects:** Agriculture/farming,
gardening, rural political movements, agricultural political economy.
Special Collections: Organic agriculture; agricultural materials for new
readers. **Holdings:** 4000 books; 8 VF drawers of subject files and clippings;
75 instructional tape recordings. **Subscriptions:** 53 journals and other serials.
Services: Copying (limited); center open to the public with advance notice
and approval. **Publications:** Rural Advance; RAFI Report; Farm Survival
News - all to the public. **Special Indexes:** Indexes to subject files and AV
programs. **Remarks:** Affiliated with the Farm Survival Project.

Rural Development Administration (of the Republic of Korea)
See: **Republic of Korea - Rural Development Administration** (13829)

★ 14147 ★
Rural Enterprises, Inc. - Central Industrial Applications Center (Sci-
Engr)
422 Cessna
P.O. Box 1335   Phone: (405)924-5094
Durant, OK 74702   Dr. Dickie Deel, CIAC Dir.
Founded: 1964. **Staff:** Prof 6; Other 3. **Subjects:** Aviation, astronautics,
science, electronics, instrumentation, photography, mathematics, physics,
computer science, space sciences. **Special Collections:** NASA-sponsored
research documents. **Holdings:** 275,000 microfiche of reports. **Services:**
Interlibrary loan; document delivery; copying; center open to the public with
restrictions. **Computerized Information Services:** NASA/RECON,
DIALOG Information Services, PFDS Online. **Publications:** Quarterly and
annual reports. **Remarks:** FAX: (405)920-2745. CIAC is a NASA Industrial
Applications Center serving the states of Oklahoma, Texas, Kansas,
Nebraska, North Dakota, and South Dakota. **Staff:** Alice Craig,
Bus.Info.Spec.; Jim Berish, Mktg.Assoc.; Jim Vercelli, Res.Asst.

Charles Andrew Rush Learning Center/Library
See: **Birmingham Southern College** (1862)

★ 14148 ★
**Rush-Presbyterian-St. Luke's Medical Center - Library of Rush
University** (Med)
600 S. Paulina St.   Phone: (312)942-5950
Chicago, IL 60612-3874   Trudy A. Gardner, Ph.D., Dir.
Founded: 1898. **Staff:** Prof 11; Other 15. **Subjects:** Biomedical sciences,
nursing, hospital administration, allied health fields, health care delivery.
Special Collections: Rare medical books (10,000). **Holdings:** 50,912 books;
54,420 bound periodical volumes; 112 microforms; 6898 AV programs.
Subscriptions: 2271 journals and other serials; 6 newspapers. **Services:**
Interlibrary loan; copying; SDI; library open to the public for reference use
only. **Automated Operations:** Computerized public access catalog,
cataloging, acquisitions, serials, and circulation. **Computerized Information
Services:** MEDLINE, DIALOG Information Services, BRS Information
Technologies, OCLC, FAXON; internal databases. Performs searches on fee
basis. **Contact Person:** Gerald Perry, Hd., Ref.Libn., 942-5952. **Networks/
Consortia:** Member of National Network of Libraries of Medicine - Greater
Midwest Region, ILLINET. **Special Catalogs:** Serials list. **Remarks:** FAX:
(312)942-3143. **Staff:** Christine Frank, Assoc.Dir., Info.Serv; Maggie
Marshall, Coord., Access Serv.; Marianne Doherty, Ref.Libn.; Minna
Sellers, Ref.Libn.; Philip Adrian, Ser.Spec.; David Prochazka, Cat.Libn.;
Eric Schnell, LRC Mgr.; Johnnie Jones, ILL Spec.; Jean Demas, Ref.Libn.

★ 14149 ★
Rush University - Center for Health Management Studies (Med)
202 Academic Facility
600 S. Paulina   Phone: (312)942-5402
Chicago, IL 60612   Dr. Michael Counte, Assoc.Dir.
Founded: 1982. **Subjects:** Health care organizations and management.
Holdings: 1000 books and professional journals. **Services:** Library not open
to the public.

Rusk State Hospital - Staff Library
See: **Texas (State) Department of Mental Health & Mental Retardation**
(16247)

★ 14150 ★
Bertrand Russell Society, Inc. - Library (Hum)
29 Gillette St.
Box 434   Phone: (802)295-9058
Wilder, VT 05088   Thomas Stanley, Libn.
Founded: 1975. **Staff:** 1. **Subjects:** Bertrand Russell. **Holdings:** 100 books;
8 films; 6 video cassettes; 25 audio cassettes; archives of the Bertrand Russell
Society. **Services:** Library open to the public with restrictions. **Special
Indexes:** Index of newsletters of the Bertrand Russell Society, 1974-1989.

Russell Cave National Monument
See: U.S. Natl. Park Service (17772)

★ 14151 ★
Charles M. Russell Museum - Frederic G. Renner Memorial Library
(Art)
400 13th St., N.　　　　　　　　　Phone: (406)727-8787
Great Falls, MT 59401　　　　　Janet W. Postler, Reg./Libn.
Founded: 1952. **Staff:** Prof 1; Other 4. **Subjects:** Artist Charles M. Russell,
Western art and artists, history of the West. **Special Collections:** Richard
Flood Collection of art and archives related to Charles M. Russell and Joe
DeYong; Karl Yost Archives. **Holdings:** 1200 books; 1000 periodical
volumes; 600 manuscripts and letters. **Subscriptions:** 4 journals and other
serials. **Services:** Copying; library open to the public by appointment for
reference use only. **Automated Operations:** Computerized cataloging and
acquisitions. **Special Catalogs:** Museum Permanent Collections Catalog.
Remarks: FAX: (406)727-2402.

★ 14152 ★
Russell and Dumoulin - Library (Law)
1500-1075 W. Georgia St.　　　　　Phone: (604)631-3131
Vancouver, BC, Canada V6E 3G2　　Johanne A.C. Blenkin, Libn.
Staff: Prof 3; Other 3. **Subjects:** Law, labor law. **Holdings:** 24,000 volumes.
Services: Library not open to the public. **Automated Operations:**
Computerized cataloging, acquisitions, and serials. **Computerized
Information Services:** QL Systems, WESTLAW, Info Globe, Infomart
Online, CAN/LAW, The Financial Post Information Service, DIALOG
Information Services, LEXIS, NEXIS; Labour Index (internal database).
Remarks: FAX: (604)631-3232.

Helen Crocker Russell Library of Horticulture
See: Strybing Arboretum Society - Helen Crocker Russell Library of
Horticulture (15833)

Ina Dillard Russell Library
See: Georgia College (6382)

Richard B. Russell Agricultural Research Center Library
See: U.S.D.A. - Agricultural Research Service - South Atlantic Area
(17193)

Richard B. Russell Memorial Library
See: University of Georgia (18602)

Susan V. Russell Tape Library
See: Wittenberg University - Thomas Library (20546)

Russell Vermontiana Collection
See: Canfield Memorial Library (3010)

Russian Orthodox Diocese of Alaska - Archives
See: St. Herman's Theological Seminary - St. Innocent Veniaminov
Research Institute - Library (14321)

★ 14153 ★
Rust International Corporation - Library (Sci-Engr)
P.O. Box 101　　　　　　　　　　Phone: (205)995-6540
Birmingham, AL 35201-0101　　Calberta O. Atkinson, Libn.
Founded: 1957. **Staff:** Prof 1; Other 1. **Subjects:** Engineering -
environmental, civil, chemical, electrical, mechanical; pulp and paper.
Holdings: 7500 books; 330 bound periodical volumes; 5200 technical
reports; 81 microfiche; 180 videocassettes; 124 audiocassettes; 34 slides.
Subscriptions: 200 journals and other serials. **Services:** Interlibrary loan;
SDI; library open to the public for reference use only. **Computerized
Information Services:** DIALOG Information Services, OCLC. **Networks/
Consortia:** Member of SOLINET. **Publications:** This is Your Library
(brochure). **Remarks:** Corporation is a subsidiary of Wheelabrator
Technologies, Inc. Library located at Meadow Brook Corporate Park, 500
Corporate Pkwy, Birmingham, AL 35243. FAX: (205)995-6090.

★ 14154 ★
Rust-Oleum Corporation - R & D Library (Sci-Engr)
8105 Fergusson Dr.
P.O. Box 70　　　　　　　　　　　Phone: (414)947-7220
Pleasant Prairie, WI 53158　　Lorraine Fernandez, Libn.
Founded: 1972. **Staff:** Prof 1; Other 1. **Subjects:** Coatings, resins, corrosion,
environment. **Holdings:** 430 books; 100 bound periodical volumes; 100
patents; 100 suppliers' catalogs. **Subscriptions:** 122 journals and other
serials. **Services:** Library not open to the public. **Publications:** Technical
Newsletter, quarterly; Book List, Periodical List - annual.

★ 14155 ★
Rutan and Tucker - Library (Law)
611 Anton, Suite 1400　　　　　Phone: (714)641-3460
Costa Mesa, CA 92626　　　　Cecelia Harner, Libn.
Subjects: Law. **Holdings:** 33,000 volumes. **Services:** Library not open to the
public.

Rutgers Center of Alcohol Studies
See: Rutgers University - Rutgers Center of Alcohol Studies (14172)

★ 14156 ★
Rutgers University - Art Library (Art)
Voorhees Hall　　　　　　　　　　Phone: (908)932-7739
New Brunswick, NJ 08903　　　Halina Rusak, Hd.
Staff: Prof 2; Other 1. **Subjects:** Art, architecture. **Special Collections:** Louis
E. Stern Collection of Modern Art; Bartlett Cowdrey Collection of
American Art; Howard Hibbard Collection of Italian Renaissance and
Baroque Art. **Holdings:** 46,500 books; 6077 bound periodical volumes;
17,000 items in microform; 24 VF drawers of exhibition catalogs, museum
guides, reports, ephemeral materials. **Subscriptions:** 142 journals and other
serials. **Services:** Copying; library open to the public. **Automated
Operations:** Computerized cataloging and acquisitions. **Computerized
Information Services:** DIALOG Information Services, BRS Information
Technologies, WILSONLINE; internal database. Performs searches on fee
basis. **Networks/Consortia:** Member of Research Libraries Information
Network (RLIN). **Remarks:** FAX: (908)932-6743. **Staff:** Beryl Smith,
Asst.Libn.

★ 14157 ★
Rutgers University - Blanche and Irving Laurie Music Library (Mus)
Box 270　　　　　　　　　　　　Phone: (908)932-9783
New Brunswick, NJ 08903-0270　Roger M. Tarman, Hd., Pub.Serv.
　　　　　　　　　　　　　　　　　　　& Chf.Bib.
Founded: 1982. **Staff:** Prof 2; Other 5. **Subjects:** Music. **Holdings:** 42,238
books; 3134 bound periodical volumes; 24,333 sound recordings and
videotapes. **Subscriptions:** 212 journals and other serials. **Services:**
Interlibrary loan; library open to the public. **Automated Operations:**
Computerized cataloging, acquisitions, and circulation. **Computerized
Information Services:** DIALOG Information Services, OCLC, RLIN;
internal database. Performs searches on fee basis. Contact Person: Lil
Maman, 932-9407. **Networks/Consortia:** Member of Research Libraries
Information Network (RLIN). **Remarks:** FAX: (908)932-6777. **Staff:**
Harriette Hemmesi, Hd., Tech.Serv.; Ines Gessner, Cat.Asst.; Arlene
Pelayo, Acq.Assoc.; Glenn Sandberg, Media Supv.; Bruce Roter, Night
Supv.

★ 14158 ★
**Rutgers University - Center for Plastics Recycling Research -
Information Services** (Sci-Engr)
Livingston Campus, Bldg. 4109
New Brunswick, NJ 08903-5062　Raymond J. Saba, Dir.
Founded: 1986. **Staff:** Prof 1. **Subjects:** Plastics recycling, solid waste
management. **Holdings:** Periodicals; monographs; pamphlets; government
publications. **Subscriptions:** 30 journals and other serials. **Services:** Copying;
center open to the public. **Computerized Information Services:** Internal
database. **Publications:** Listing of CPPR Technical Reports/Papers.
Remarks: FAX: (908)932-5636. **Formerly:** Located in Piscataway, NJ.
Staff: Catherine M. Kasziba, Lib.Assoc.

★ 14159 ★
Rutgers University - Center for Urban Policy Research Library (Soc Sci, Plan)
Bldg. 4161, Kilmer Campus
New Brunswick, NJ 08903
Phone: (908)932-3136
Edward E. Duensing, Jr., Dir.
Founded: 1962. **Staff:** Prof 2; Other 1. **Subjects:** Urban/regional planning, environmental planning, municipal finance, intergovernmental relations, housing. **Holdings:** 3263 books; 182 bound periodical volumes; 4486 other cataloged items; 263 microfiche of research papers, manuscripts, government documents. **Subscriptions:** 174 journals and other serials. **Services:** Interlibrary loan; library open to the public. **Automated Operations:** Computerized cataloging and acquisitions. **Computerized Information Services:** RLIN, DIALOG Information Services. **Networks/Consortia:** Member of Research Libraries Information Network (RLIN). **Publications:** New Acquisitions List. **Remarks:** FAX: (908)932-2363. **Staff:** Azar Aryanpour.

★ 14160 ★
Rutgers University - Chemistry Library (Sci-Engr)
Busch Campus
P.O. Box 939
Wright-Riemann Laboratories
Piscataway, NJ 08855-0939
Phone: (908)932-2625
Dr. Howard M. Dess, Physical Sci.Rsrc.Libn.
Staff: Prof 1; Other 2. **Subjects:** Chemistry. **Holdings:** 9649 books; 17,692 bound periodical volumes. **Subscriptions:** 307 journals and other serials. **Services:** Interlibrary loan; copying; library open to the public. **Automated Operations:** Computerized circulation. **Computerized Information Services:** DIALOG Information Services, BRS Information Technologies, STN International, Beilstein Online, NLM, RLIN. **Networks/Consortia:** Member of Research Libraries Information Network (RLIN). **Publications:** Additions to the Chemistry Library, monthly. **Remarks:** FAX: (908)932-3255. **Staff:** Mary Roussos, Supv.

★ 14161 ★
Rutgers University - Computing Services (Comp Sci)
Computer Reference Ctr.
Busch Campus
Box 879 Hill Ctr.
Piscataway, NJ 08854
Phone: (908)932-2296
Christopher P. Jarocha-Ernst, Coord.
Founded: 1964. **Staff:** Prof 1; Other 2. **Subjects:** Computers, data archives, U.S. Census, electronics. **Special Collections:** University newsletters (200 serials); IBM manuals (1000 volumes); Digital Equipment Corporation (DEC) manuals (200 volumes); U.S. Census tapes and documents; Inter-University Consortium for Political and Social Research (ICPSR) Archives. **Holdings:** 1500 books; 500 vendor manuals. **Subscriptions:** 350 journals and other serials. **Services:** Center open to the public for reference use only. **Automated Operations:** Computerized cataloging, acquisitions, and serials. **Computerized Information Services:** Internal database; InterNet, BITNET (electronic mail services). **Publications:** CCIS Newsletter, bimonthly; CCIS Education Series, monthly - by subscription. **Special Catalogs:** CCIS Technical Documents catalog; data archives catalog; ICPSR and census material catalog; CCIS Software Catalog (all online). **Remarks:** Electronic mail address(es): cje@elbereth.rutgers.edu (InterNet); CRC@ZODIAC (BITNET).

★ 14162 ★
Rutgers University - Criminal Justice/NCCD Collection (Law)
S.I. Newhouse Center for Law and Justice
15 Washington St., 4th Fl.
Newark, NJ 07102
Phone: (201)648-5522
Phyllis A. Schultze, Libn.
Founded: 1921. **Staff:** Prof 1. **Subjects:** Crime and juvenile delinquency - prevention, control, and treatment; criminology and correction. **Holdings:** 11,000 books; 900 bound periodical volumes; 10,000 documents on microfiche; 50,000 unpublished and published reports, studies, monographs, letters, clippings, pictures. **Subscriptions:** 275 journals and other serials. **Services:** Interlibrary loan (to organizations only); copying; telephone information service; collection open to the public. **Computerized Information Services:** WESTLAW; Criminal Justice Abstracts (internal database). **Publications:** Accessions list. **Remarks:** FAX: (201)648-1275.

★ 14163 ★
Rutgers University - East Asian Library (Area-Ethnic)
Alexander Library
College Ave.
New Brunswick, NJ 08903
Phone: (908)932-7161
Dr. Nelson Ling-Sun Chou, Libn.
Founded: 1970. **Staff:** Prof 1; Other 1. **Subjects:** China - language, literature, history, philosophy, religion, children's literature, arts and sciences;

Japanese history, language, literature; Korean history. **Special Collections:** Complete microfilm collection of the rare books in the National Central Library, Taiwan (up to Series 7); Pamphlet Collection of Tiao-yu-t'ai Problems; Complete Set of Ssu k'u ch'uan shu (chi pu). **Holdings:** 100,000 volumes; 4000 reels of microfilm; 5000 pamphlets. **Subscriptions:** 360 journals and other serials; 12 newspapers. **Services:** Interlibrary loan; SDI (limited); library open to the public. **Automated Operations:** Computerized cataloging and acquisitions. **Computerized Information Services:** BITNET (electronic mail service). **Networks/Consortia:** Member of Research Libraries Information Network (RLIN). **Publications:** Serial Holding List, irregular - available on request. **Remarks:** FAX: (908)932-6808. Electronic mail address(es): NCHOU@ZODIAC (BITNET).

★ 14164 ★
Rutgers University - Gottscho Packaging Information Center (Sci-Engr)
Busch Campus, Bldg. 3529
Piscataway, NJ 08855
Phone: (908)932-3044
James D. Idol, Dir.
Staff: Prof 3; Other 2. **Subjects:** Packaging. **Holdings:** Periodicals; monographs; pamphlets; government publications. **Subscriptions:** 200 journals and other serials. **Services:** Copying; center open to the public. **Publications:** Current Packaging Abstracts, semimonthly - by subscription.

★ 14165 ★
Rutgers University - Hill Center for the Mathematical Sciences - Mathematical Sciences Library (Comp Sci, Sci-Engr)
Piscataway, NJ 08855
Phone: (908)932-3735
Sylvia Walsh, Libn.
Founded: 1971. **Staff:** Prof 1; Other 2. **Subjects:** Pure and applied mathematics, computer science, statistics, artificial intelligence, operations research. **Holdings:** 28,514 books; 17,500 bound periodical volumes; 4832 items on microform; 3994 technical reports. **Subscriptions:** 757 journals and other serials. **Services:** Copying; library open to the public. **Automated Operations:** Computerized circulation. **Computerized Information Services:** BRS Information Technologies, RLIN. **Networks/Consortia:** Member of Research Libraries Information Network (RLIN). **Publications:** Daily Acquisitions List (hardcopy and online). **Special Indexes:** Index to technical reports. **Remarks:** FAX: (908)932-3064.

★ 14166 ★
Rutgers University - Institute of Jazz Studies (Mus)
135 Bradley Hall
Warren St. and Martin Luther King Blvd.
Newark, NJ 07102
Phone: (201)648-5595
Dan Morgenstern, Dir.
Founded: 1952. **Staff:** Prof 4; Other 1. **Subjects:** Jazz, blues, popular music. **Special Collections:** National Endowment for the Arts (NEA) Jazz Oral History Project Repository (135 taped interviews and transcriptions). **Holdings:** 6000 books; 650 bound periodical volumes; 75,000 records and transcriptions; 2000 audiotapes; cylinders; 30 VF drawers of clippings; manuscripts; piano rolls; jazz periodicals; sheet music; instruments; dissertations; works of art; photographs; memorabilia. **Subscriptions:** 100 journals and other serials. **Services:** Copying; institute open to the public by appointment. **Automated Operations:** Computerized cataloging. **Computerized Information Services:** RLIN; IJS Jazz Register (register of recorded jazz performances; internal database). Performs searches free of charge. Contact Person: Vincent Pelote, Libn. **Networks/Consortia:** Member of Research Libraries Information Network (RLIN). **Publications:** Annual Review of Jazz Studies - by subscription; Studies in Jazz (monograph series): Benny Carter, 1982; Art Tatum, 1982; Erroll Garner, 1984; James P. Johnson, 1986; Pee Wee Erwin, 1987; Benny Goodman, 1988; Ellingtonia, 1988 . **Special Indexes:** Index to IJS Jazz Register (microfiche). **Staff:** Edward Berger, Asst.Dir.; Vincent Pelote, Libn.; Don Luck, Spec.Proj.Libn.

★ 14167 ★
Rutgers University - Institute of Management/Labor Relations Library (Soc Sci)
Ryders Ln. & Clifton Ave.
New Brunswick, NJ 08903
Phone: (201)932-9513
George Kanzler, Dir.
Founded: 1947. **Staff:** Prof 2; Other 2. **Subjects:** Industrial relations, labor education, human resources, collective bargaining, labor-management cooperation. **Holdings:** 3400 books; 820 bound periodical volumes; 78 VF drawers of pamphlets; state and federal documents; 38 VF drawers of union and company reports. **Subscriptions:** 673 journals and other serials. **Services:** Interlibrary loan; copying; library open to the public. **Automated Operations:** Computerized public access catalog. **Computerized Information**

Services: DIALOG Information Services, Human Resource Information Network (HRIN), LEXIS, NEXIS. **Networks/Consortia:** Member of Research Libraries Information Network (RLIN), New Jersey Library Network. **Publications:** Selected Acquisitions List, irregular. **Remarks:** Alternate telephone number(s): 932-9608. **FAX:** (201)932-8677. **Staff:** Jeffrey Katz, Assoc.Libn.; Eugene McElroy, Lib.Assoc.

★ 14168 ★
Rutgers University - Justice Henry Ackerson Law Library (Law)
S.I. Newhouse Center for Law & Justice
15 Washington St.   Phone: (201)648-5675
Newark, NJ 07102-3192   Charlie H. Woods, Law Libn.
Founded: 1946. **Staff:** Prof 9; Other 14. **Subjects:** Law. **Special Collections:** Justice Bradley Law Library (1000 volumes). **Holdings:** 215,000 books and bound periodical volumes; 3510 linear feet of New Jersey and other state documents, records, and briefs; 4307 linear feet of U.S. Government documents; 134,000 volumes in microform. **Subscriptions:** 3548 journals and other serials; 6 newspapers. **Services:** Interlibrary loan; copying; library open to the public. **Automated Operations:** Computerized cataloging. **Computerized Information Services:** LEXIS, NEXIS, WESTLAW, QL Systems, VU/TEXT Information Services, DIALOG Information Services, WILSONLINE. **Networks/Consortia:** Member of Research Libraries Information Network (RLIN). **Publications:** Selected New Acquisitions, monthly - by exchange. **Special Catalogs:** Shelf lists of Federal and New Jersey documents. **Staff:** Brenda Adams, Hd., Tech.Serv.; Barbara Sanders-Harris, Hd., User Serv.; Ernest Nardone, Ref.; Paul Axel-Lute, Coll.Dev.; Glen Bencivengo, Ref.; Hugh Breyer, Ref.; Robert Schriek, Ref.; Ronnie Joan Mark, Ser./Acq.; Marjorie Crawford, ILL/Circ.

★ 14169 ★
Rutgers University - Library of Science & Medicine (Med, Sci-Engr, Biol Sci)
Box 1029   Phone: (908)932-3850
Piscataway, NJ 08855-1029   Jeanne E. Boyle, Dir.
Founded: 1963. **Staff:** Prof 14; Other 29. **Subjects:** Medicine, agriculture, biology and biochemistry, engineering, geology, pharmacy, pharmacology, psychology. **Holdings:** 197,228 books; 180,957 bound periodical volumes; 455,677 government documents; 508,898 microforms; 14,552 maps. **Subscriptions:** 5432 periodicals. **Services:** Interlibrary loan; copying; library open to the public. **Automated Operations:** Computerized public access catalog and circulation. **Computerized Information Services:** DIALOG Information Services, BRS Information Technologies, STN International, PFDS Online, UnCover, RLIN. **Networks/Consortia:** Member of Research Libraries Information Network (RLIN). **Remarks:** FAX: (908)932-3208. **Staff:** Ellen Calhoun; Howard Dess; Susan Goodman; Helen Hoffman; Richard Hoover; Marty Kesselman; Jackie Mardikian; Mary Page; Pat Piermatti; Addie Tallau; Irwin Weintraub; Connie Wu.

★ 14170 ★
Rutgers University - Microbiology Library (Biol Sci)
Waksman Institute
Box 759   Phone: (908)932-2906
Piscataway, NJ 08855-0759   Helen Hoffman, Libn.
Founded: 1954. **Staff:** Prof 1; Other 1. **Subjects:** Microbiology. **Holdings:** 8182 books; 8741 bound periodical volumes. **Subscriptions:** 107 journals and other serials. **Services:** Interlibrary loan; copying; library open to the public for reference use only. **Automated Operations:** Computerized cataloging and acquisitions. **Computerized Information Services:** DIALOG Information Services, BRS Information Technologies, NLM, RLIN. **Networks/Consortia:** Member of Research Libraries Information Network (RLIN). **Staff:** Libby Herman, Supv.

★ 14171 ★
Rutgers University - Physics Library (Sci-Engr)
Busch Campus
P.O. Box 849
Serin Physics Laboratory   Phone: (908)932-2500
Piscataway, NJ 08855-0849 Dr. Howard M. Dess, Physical Sci.Rsrc.Libn.
Staff: Prof 1; Other 2. **Subjects:** Physics, astronomy. **Holdings:** 11,560 books; 12,384 bound periodical volumes; 61,896 preprints. **Subscriptions:** 275 journals and other serials. **Services:** Interlibrary loan; copying; library open to the public. **Automated Operations:** Computerized circulation. **Computerized Information Services:** DIALOG Information Services, STN International, NLM, BRS Information Technologies, RLIN. **Networks/Consortia:** Member of Research Libraries Information Network (RLIN). **Remarks:** FAX: (908)932-4964. **Staff:** Pathmosothy Padmanathan, Lib.Assoc.

★ 14172 ★
Rutgers University - Rutgers Center of Alcohol Studies - Library (Soc Sci)
Busch Campus
Smithers Hall   Phone: (908)932-4442
Piscataway, NJ 08855-0969   Penny B. Page, Hd.Libn.
Founded: 1940. **Staff:** Prof 2; Other 3. **Subjects:** Alcohol, drinking, alcoholism. **Special Collections:** McCarthy Memorial Collection (50,000 documents). **Holdings:** 8600 books; 2800 bound periodical volumes; 150 boxes of archival materials; 20,000 abstracts on 6x7 edge notched cards (Classified Abstract Archive of the Alcohol Literature); 1750 doctoral dissertations on microfilm; 120 alcohol-related bibliographies; 500 questionnaires, interview schedules, survey forms. **Subscriptions:** 200 journals and other serials. **Services:** Interlibrary loan; copying; reference service for researchers and students; library open to the public. **Computerized Information Services:** BRS Information Technologies, DIALOG Information Services, NLM; Alchohol Database (internal database); BITNET (electronic mail service). **Networks/Consortia:** Member of Substance Abuse Librarians and Information Specialists (SALIS), Regional Alcohol and Drug Abuse Resource Network (RADAR). **Publications:** Bibliographies. **Remarks:** FAX: (908)932-5944. Electronic mail address(es): PAGE@ZOCIAC. Contains the holdings of the former National Council on Alcoholism, Inc. - Yvelin Gardner Alcoholism Library. **Staff:** Catherine Weglarz, Libn.

★ 14173 ★
Rutgers University - Rutgers Center of Alcohol Studies - New Jersey Alcohol/Drug Resource Center and Clearinghouse (Soc Sci)
Box 518   Phone: (201)932-5528
Piscataway, NJ 08855-0518   Penny B. Page, Dir.
Founded: 1988. **Staff:** Prof 2; Other 1. **Subjects:** Alcohol and drug use, alcohol and drug education, substance abuse prevention. **Special Collections:** Video Collection; Curricula. **Holdings:** 2000 books and pamphlets. **Subscriptions:** 220 journals and other serials. **Services:** Interlibrary loan; copying; center and clearinghouse open to the public with restrictions. **Computerized Information Services:** BRS Information Technologies; internal database. Performs searches on fee basis. Contact Person: Valerie Mead, Rsrc.Ctr Libn. **Networks/Consortia:** Member of Substance Abuse Librarians and Information Specialists (SALIS), New Jersey Library Network, Regional Alcohol and Drug Abuse Resource Network (RADAR). **Publications:** Annotated media list; select resource lists for specialized audiences; booklists; College Funding Guide; School Drug Curricula Evaluation Guide; fact sheets. **Staff:** Pat Bellanca.

★ 14174 ★
Rutgers University - School of Law Library (Law)
5th & Penn Sts.   Phone: (609)757-6172
Camden, NJ 08102   Arno Liivak, Law Libn.
Founded: 1926. **Staff:** Prof 8; Other 14. **Subjects:** Law. **Special Collections:** Collection of Soviet Legal Materials, 1945 to present (28,468 volumes). **Holdings:** 362,552 volumes; 164,564 government documents; 3769 reels of microfilm; 415,924 microfiche. **Subscriptions:** 2821 journals and other serials. **Services:** Interlibrary loan; copying; library open to the public with restrictions. **Automated Operations:** Computerized cataloging, acquisitions, and serials. **Computerized Information Services:** LEXIS, WESTLAW, RLIN; RLG (electronic mail service). **Networks/Consortia:** Member of Research Libraries Information Network (RLIN), Center for Research Libraries (CRL). **Remarks:** FAX: (609)757-6488. **Staff:** Gloria Chao, Assoc. Law Libn./Tech.Serv.; Anne Dalesandro, Assoc. Law Libn./Pub.Serv.; David Batista; Linda Bove; Lucy Cox; Jessie Matthews; Marion Townend.

★ 14175 ★
Rutgers University - Special Collections and Archives (Hist, Hum)
Alexander Library
College Ave. & Huntington St.   Phone: (908)932-7006
New Brunswick, NJ 08903   Ronald L. Becker, Dir.
Founded: 1946. **Staff:** Prof 6; Other 4. **Subjects:** History of education, social policy and social welfare, labor, exploration and travel, Puritanism, genealogy, Latin America, history of science and technology. **Special Collections:** New Jersey Collections; Rutgers University Archives (6500 cubic feet of archival material); Women's Archives (including the records of SIGNS and the Womens Caucus for Art); literary collection (including Philip Freneau, Daniel DeFoe, William Cobbett, and the J. Alexander Symington Collection of 19th and early 20th century British authors); political papers collection (including the papers of Robert Morris, William Paterson, Clifford Case, Harrison Williams, Millicent Fenwick); westerners

in Japan collections (including the William Elliot Griffis Collection); consumer movement collections; Roebling Family Collections; social policy collections (records of the American Council of Voluntary Agencies for Foreign Services, World Policy Institute, World Hunger Year); Edward J. Bloustein Dictionary Collection; early American newspapers; rare books (65,000). **Holdings:** 152,000 volumes; 1000 newspaper titles; 2000 manuscript collections (6500 cubic feet); 200,000 pictures; 5500 almanacs; 4400 maps; 12,500 broadsides; 500 reels of microfilm; genealogical materials; ephemera; museum objects. **Subscriptions:** 842 journals and other serials. **Services:** Interlibrary loan (limited); copying; collections open to the public for reference use only. **Automated Operations:** Computerized cataloging. **Computerized Information Services:** IRIS (internal database); BITNET (electronic mail service). **Networks/Consortia:** Member of Research Libraries Information Network (RLIN), Center for Research Libraries (CRL). **Publications:** Acquisitions reports; user guides. **Special Catalogs:** Checklist of New Jersey Periodicals in Special Collections, Rutgers University Libraries, 1982 (book); Guide to the Manuscript Collections, 1964; Guide to Manuscript Diaries and Journals, 1980; A Guide to the Women's History Archives at Rutgers, 1990; Labor History Resources at the Rutgers University Libraries, 1990. **Remarks:** FAX: (908)932-7637. Electronic mail address(es): BECKER@ZODIAC.RUTGERS.EDU (BITNET). **Staff:** Thomas Frusciano, Univ.Archv.; Bonita Grant, NJ Bibliog.; Albert King, Mss.Libn./Archv.; Janet Riemer, Presrv.; Ruth Simmons, Senior Archv. & Cur., Griffis Collection.

★ 14176 ★
Rutgers University, the State University of New Jersey - Media Services Department (Aud-Vis)
Kilmer Area Library
Piscataway, NJ 08855
Phone: (908)932-4685
Nancy Putnam
Founded: 1972. **Staff:** Prof 1; Other 12. **Subjects:** Cinema studies, anthropology, history, women's studies. **Holdings:** 1100 16mm films; 1000 videocassettes. **Services:** Library open to the public with restrictions. **Remarks:** FAX: (908)932-3472.

★ 14177 ★
Rutland Regional Medical Center - Health Sciences Library (Med)
160 Allen St.
Rutland, VT 05701
Phone: (802)747-3777
Daphne S. Pringle, Dir.
Founded: 1970. **Staff:** Prof 1. **Subjects:** Medicine, nursing, and allied health sciences, hospital administration. **Holdings:** 1000 books; unbound reports, clippings; journal reprints. **Subscriptions:** 94 journals and other serials. **Services:** Interlibrary loan; copying; literature searches; library open to the public with restrictions. **Automated Operations:** Computerized public access catalog. **Computerized Information Services:** BRS Information Technologies, MEDLARS, NLM. **Networks/Consortia:** Member of Health Science Libraries of New Hampshire & Vermont (HSL-NH/VT).

Ruusbroecgenootschap Centrum voor Spiritualiteit
See: **Universiteit Antwerpen - Universitaire Faculteiten Sint-Ignatius Antwerpen** (18131)

★ 14178 ★
Ryan-Biggs Associates, P.C. - Library (Plan)
291 River St.
Troy, NY 12180
Phone: (518)272-6266
Susan Benjamin, Libn.
Founded: 1977. **Staff:** Prof 1; Other 1. **Subjects:** Building codes and specifications; construction - concrete, steel, masonry, wood; structural engineering. **Holdings:** 1000 books; 130 bound periodical volumes; 160 technical reports. **Subscriptions:** 42 journals and other serials. **Services:** SDI; library open to local companies. **Remarks:** FAX: (518)272-4467.

The C. Ryan Library
See: **San Diego Aero-Space Museum - N. Paul Whittier Historical Aviation Library** (14686)

Calvin T. Ryan Library
See: **University of Nebraska at Kearney** (19008)

Ryan Library
See: **Point Loma Nazarene College** (13157)

Ryan Memorial Library
See: **St. Charles Borromeo Seminary** (14256)

★ 14179 ★
Rye Historical Society - Library (Hist)
One Purchase St.
Rye, NY 10580
Phone: (914)967-7588
Jan Kelsey, Libn./Archv.
Founded: 1964. **Staff:** Prof 1. **Subjects:** Local history, local family genealogy. **Special Collections:** Slater papers (1500 pages of 18th century documents); Parsons papers (15 linear feet; 150 years of one family in Rye; 1830s-1980s). **Holdings:** 1500 books; 20 bound periodical volumes; 30 linear feet of manuscripts; 750 maps; 100 oral history audiotapes; 105 almanacs. **Subscriptions:** 5 journals and other serials. **Services:** Copying; library open to the public. **Publications:** Finding aids for manuscript collection.

Ryerson Library
See: **Art Institute of Chicago - Ryerson and Burnham Libraries** (1082)

Ryerson Nature Library
See: **Lake County Forest Preserve District** (8884)

★ 14180 ★
Ryerson Polytechnical Institute - Library (Sci-Engr, Bus-Fin, Soc Sci)
350 Victoria St.
Toronto, ON, Canada M5B 2K3
Phone: (416)979-5031
Richard Malinski, Chf.Libn.
Founded: 1948. **Staff:** Prof 14; Other 75. **Subjects:** Business, nursing, engineering, mathematics, technology, architecture, urban planning, interior design, journalism, broadcasting, environmental health, public administration, photography, nutrition, family studies. **Special Collections:** Resource Center for Developing Studies(6943 volumes); Rare books (835); Urban Planning Collection (5082 volumes). **Holdings:** 301,158 books; 24,332 bound periodical volumes; 7847 AV materials; 5482 reels of microfilm; 80,596 microfiche; 16,459 maps. **Subscriptions:** 2113 journals and other serials; 35 newspapers. **Services:** Interlibrary loan (fee); copying; library open to the public for reference use only. **Automated Operations:** Computerized public access catalog, cataloging, acquisitions, and circulation. **Computerized Information Services:** DIALOG Information Services, Info Globe, International Development Research Centre (IDRC), DOBIS Canadian Online Library System, CCINFO; CD-ROMs (ERIC, MEDLINE, Canadian Business and Current Affairs, Compact Disclosure Canada); Envoy 100, Net North, BITNET, PROFS (electronic mail services). Performs searches on fee basis. **Networks/Consortia:** Member of The Bibliocentre. **Publications:** Periodicals holdings list, annual. **Special Catalogs:** Reserve list; urban planning keyword index; map index; current information file list, Ryerson theses, index to NGOs, AIDSCAN. **Remarks:** FAX: (416)979-5341. **Staff:** Sue Giles, Hd., Info.Serv.; Diane Granfield, Soc. & Political Sci.Libn.; Lucia Martin, Supv., Circ.; Eva Friesen, Tech.Serv.Libn.; Joan Parsons, AV Libn.; Olive King, Bus.Mgt.Libn.; Elizabeth Bishop, Assoc.Libn., Pub.Serv.; Robert Jackson, Assoc.Libn., Tech.Sup.; Zita Murphy, Comp. Search Libn.; Ophelia Kam, Econ. & Adm.Stud.Libn.; Daniel Phelan, Hd., Distance Sup.; Don Kinder, Engr. & Hea.Sci.Libn.; Diane Smith, Lit. & Design Libn.; Claude Doucet, Archv.

★ 14181 ★
Ryerson Polytechnical Institute - Resource Centre for Development Studies (Sci-Engr, Soc Sci)
350 Victoria St., 7th Fl.
Toronto, ON, Canada M5B 2K3
Phone: (416)979-5000
Olive King, Bus.Mgt.Libn.
Founded: 1977. **Staff:** 1. **Subjects:** Economic and social development, technology transfer, development education, communications, environment, primary health care, women, developing regions and countries. **Special Collections:** Annual reports of 380 international development organizations; development broadcasting with special reference to Asia (400 documents); collection of briefing documents by the Canadian International Development Agency on countries in Africa, Asia, Latin America, Caribbean. **Holdings:** 3000 volumes; 24 VF drawers of uncataloged documents. **Subscriptions:** 240 journals and other serials. **Services:** Copying; library open to the public for reference use only. **Automated Operations:** Computerized cataloging and acquisitions. **Computerized Information Services:** DIALOG Information Services, BRS Information Technologies, Developmental Databases Service (International Development Research Centre); CD-ROMs; Envoy 100 (electronic mail service). **Publications:** List of Acquisitions, 3/year - by exchange and to other institutions. **Remarks:** FAX: (416)979-5341. **Formerly:** Its Third World Resource Centre.

★14182★
Robert W. Ryerss Library & Museum
Burholme Park
Central & Cottman Aves.   Phone: (215)745-3061
Philadelphia, PA 19111-3055   Mary L. Campbell, Libn.
Remarks: No further information was supplied by respondent.

S

S.A.T.H.
See: **Society for the Advancement of Travel for the Handicapped (15308)**

★ 14183 ★
S-Cubed - Technical Library (Sci-Engr)
Box 1620   Phone: (619)453-0060
La Jolla, CA 92038-1620   LaDonna L. Rowe, Libn.
Staff: Prof 1; Other 1. **Subjects:** Physics, geophysics, seismology, energy technology, nuclear technology, environmental sciences. **Holdings:** 2500 books; 1000 bound periodical volumes. **Subscriptions:** 115 journals and other serials. **Services:** Library open to the public by appointment. **Computerized Information Services:** DIALOG Information Services, MELVYL. **Remarks:** FAX: (619)755-0474. S-Cubed is a division of Maxwell Laboratories, Inc.

★ 14184 ★
S.D. Warren Co. - Research Library (Sci-Engr)
Box 5000   Phone: (207)856-3538
Westbrook, ME 04098   Deborah G. Chandler, Info.Spec.
Staff: Prof 1; Other 2. **Subjects:** Papermaking, printing, chemistry, physics, engineering. **Holdings:** 4000 books; 1300 bound periodical volumes. **Subscriptions:** 162 journals and other serials. **Services:** Interlibrary loan; library not open to the public. **Computerized Information Services:** DIALOG Information Services. **Remarks:** S.D. Warren Co. is a subsidiary of Scott Paper Co.

★ 14185 ★
S.E.A., Inc. - Library (Sci-Engr)
7349 Worthington-Galena Rd.   Phone: (614)888-4160
Columbus, OH 43085   Michael J. Sens, Info.Res.
Founded: 1982. **Staff:** 1. **Subjects:** Vehicles and industrial products - accident investigation, failure analysis. **Holdings:** 3500 volumes. **Subscriptions:** 27 journals and other serials. **Services:** Library not open to the public. **Computerized Information Services:** DIALOG Information Services, STN International. **Remarks:** FAX: (614)885-8014. **Also Known As:** Systems Engineering Associates, Inc.

★ 14186 ★
S.E.A. Rescue Foundation - Reference Collection (Soc Sci)
Hangar 6, Taxiway Lindy Loop
Spruce Creek Airport   Phone: (904)760-5295
Daytona Beach, FL 32124   Theodore G. Schweitzer, III, Pres.
Founded: 1982. **Staff:** Prof 1; Other 2. **Subjects:** Vietnamese boat refugees, refugee experiences vis-a-vis pirates; U.S. POW/MIAs in Vietnam and Laos. **Special Collections:** Firsthand accounts, manuscripts, scripts, and photographs of actual pirates and victims; Vietnamese documents on POWs. **Holdings:** 1000 books; 100 bound periodical volumes; 2000 photographs. **Subscriptions:** 12 journals and other serials. **Services:** Library open to the public at librarian's discretion. **Remarks:** FAX: (904)760-6050. **Formerly:** Located in Palm Coast, FL. **Also Known As:** Southeast Asia Rescue Foundation, Inc.

S.I.A.S.T.
See: **Saskatchewan Institute of Applied Science and Technology (14857)**

★ 14187 ★
S.N.C. Lavalin Inc. - Library (Sci-Engr, Env-Cons)
2235 Sheppard Ave., E.   Phone: (416)756-2300
Willowdale, ON, Canada M2J 5A6   Agnes M. Croxford, Chf.Libn.
Staff: Prof 3. **Subjects:** Engineering, hydrology, nuclear science, pollution control, waste management, urban and regional planning, transportation. **Holdings:** 20,000 books; 650 bound periodical volumes; 1500 maps; 1500 Transportation Research Board publications. **Subscriptions:** 200 journals and other serials; 10 newspapers. **Services:** Interlibrary loan; copying; library open to the public with restrictions. **Automated Operations:** Computerized cataloging and serials. **Computerized Information Services:** PFDS Online, DIALOG Information Services, CAN/OLE, Chemical Information Systems, Inc. (CIS), MEDLARS, Technical Database Services, Inc. (TDS), STN International, NewsNet, Inc., iNET 2000, STN International; ADLIB (internal database). **Publications:** Library Bulletin, bimonthly - for internal distribution only. **Remarks:** FAX: (416)756-4998. Telex: 06 986781. **Formerly:** Lavalin Engineers, Inc. **Staff:** Patricia Miller, Asst.Libn.

★ 14188 ★
(Saarbrucken) German-American Institute - USIS Collection (Educ)
Berliner Promenade 15
Postfach 484
W-6600 Saarbrucken, Germany
Remarks: Maintained or supported by the U.S. Information Agency. Focus is on materials that will assist peoples outside the United States to learn about the United States, its people, history, culture, political processes, and social milieux.

Aline B. Saarinen Library
See: **Parrish Art Museum - Library (12764)**

★ 14189 ★
Saarlandischer Rundfunk - Bibliothek (Info Sci)
SchloB Halberg
Postfach 1050   Phone: 681 6022465
W-6600 Saarbrucken, Germany   Frank Rainer Huck
Founded: 1948. **Staff:** Prof 2. **Subjects:** Reference, biography, art, music. **Special Collections:** Media and communication studies; history of the Saarland collection. **Holdings:** 20,000 books; 1000 bound periodical volumes; 1200 reels of microfilm. **Subscriptions:** 215 journals and other serials; 80 newspapers. **Services:** Interlibrary loan; library not open to the public. **Publications:** List of new acquisitions, quarterly. **Remarks:** FAX: 681 6022469.

Saatchi & Saatchi - Yankelovich Clancy Schulman - Information Center
See: **Yankelovich Clancy Schulman - Information Center (20743)**

★ 14190 ★
Saatchi & Saatchi Advertising Inc. - Information Centre (Bus-Fin)
145 King St. E.   Phone: (416)359-9595
Toronto, ON, Canada M5C 2Y8   J. Marcotte, Media Supv.
Founded: 1959. **Staff:** Prof 1. **Subjects:** Advertising, media, marketing. **Holdings:** 230 books; 2600 magazines and periodicals; 16 drawers of clippings; 12 drawers of Statistics Canada material. **Subscriptions:** 20 journals and other serials. **Services:** Library not open to the public. **Publications:** Media Research Bulletin, semimonthly - to company personnel and agency clients. **Remarks:** FAX: (416)866-8485. **Formerly:** Saatchi & Saatchi Compton Hayhurst Ltd.

★ 14191 ★
Saatchi & Saatchi Advertising, Inc. - Research Library (Bus-Fin)
375 Hudson St.   Phone: (212)463-2300
New York, NY 10014   Shirley Damon, Hd.Libn.
Staff: Prof 2; Other 1. **Subjects:** Advertising, marketing, business. **Holdings:** 7000 books. **Subscriptions:** 200 journals and other serials; 7 newspapers. **Services:** Interlibrary loan; library not open to the public. **Computerized Information Services:** DIALOG Information Services, Mead Data Central. **Publications:** Acquisitions bulletin, irregular. **Remarks:** FAX: (212)463-9855. **Staff:** Joyce Melito, Ref.Libn.

Saatchi & Saatchi Compton Hayhurst Ltd.
See: **Saatchi & Saatchi Advertising Inc. (14190)**

Albert B. Sabin, M.D. Archives
See: **University of Cincinnati - Medical Center Information and Communications - Cincinnati Medical Heritage Center (18475)**

C.B. Sacher Medical Library
See: **St. Paul Medical Center (14559)**

Arthur M. Sackler Gallery Library
See: **Freer Gallery of Art (6137)**

Saclay Research Center
See: France - Atomic Energy Commission - Saclay Research Center - MIST (6060)

Sacramento Archives & Museum Collection Center
See: (City of) Sacramento History & Science Division (3744)

★ 14192 ★
Sacramento Area Council of Governments - Library (Plan)
3000 S St., Suite 300   Phone: (916)457-2264
Sacramento, CA 95816   Rhonda R. Egan, Libn.
Founded: 1974. **Staff:** Prof 1; Other 1. **Subjects:** Planning, census. **Special Collections:** Census data for SACOG region and Northern California. **Holdings:** 3000 cataloged items; Federal census materials. **Subscriptions:** 24 journals and other serials. **Services:** Interlibrary loan; copying; library open to the public for reference use only. **Automated Operations:** Computerized public access catalog and cataloging. **Remarks:** Library located at 106 K St., Suite 200, Sacramento, CA 95814. FAX: (916)457-3299.

★ 14193 ★
Sacramento Bee - Editorial Library (Publ)
PO Box 15779   Phone: (916)321-1108
Sacramento, CA 95852   George Schlukbier, Libn.
Founded: 1930. **Staff:** 10. **Subjects:** Newspaper reference topics. **Special Collections:** Sacramento city history. **Holdings:** 2950 books; 24,000 microfiche; 3750 reels of microfilm; 7500 photo files; 57,000 clipping files. **Subscriptions:** 17 journals and other serials; 10 newspapers. **Services:** Library not open to the public. **Computerized Information Services:** DIALOG Information Services, DataTimes, NEXIS, LEXIS, VU/TEXT Information Services; internal database. **Remarks:** FAX: (916)321-1109. Library located at 21st & Q Sts., Sacramento, CA 95814. **Staff:** Pete Basofin; Rebecca Boyd.

★ 14194 ★
Sacramento County Law Library (Law)
Sacramento County Courthouse
720 9th St.   Phone: (916)440-6011
Sacramento, CA 95814-1397   Shirley H. David, Dir.
Founded: 1905. **Staff:** Prof 3; Other 4. **Subjects:** Law, taxes, California and federal documents. **Holdings:** 46,688 volumes; 4825 bound periodical volumes; 2743 audiotapes; 612 volumes on microfiche; 15 videotapes; 9 interactive videotapes. **Subscriptions:** 245 journals and other serials; 11 newspapers. **Services:** Interlibrary loan; copying; faxing; library open to the public. **Automated Operations:** Computerized cataloging, acquisitions, and serials. **Computerized Information Services:** LEXIS. Performs searches on fee basis. **Networks/Consortia:** Member of CLASS. **Remarks:** FAX: (916)440-5691. **Staff:** Tana S. Smith, Tech.Serv.Libn.; Ruth Nunez-Schaldach, Pub.Serv.Libn.

★ 14195 ★
Sacramento-El Dorado Medical Society - Guttman Library and Information Center (Med)
5380 Elvas Ave.   Phone: (916)456-2687
Sacramento, CA 95819   Dorothy Thurmond, Libn.
Founded: 1949. **Staff:** 1. **Subjects:** Clinical medicine. **Special Collections:** California Medical History. **Holdings:** 1500 books; 1500 bound periodical volumes. **Subscriptions:** 130 journals and other serials. **Services:** Interlibrary loan; copying; library open to the public for reference use only. **Computerized Information Services:** MEDLARS, DIALOG Information Services, BiblioMed. Performs searches on fee basis. **Networks/Consortia:** Member of Sacramento Area Health Sciences Librarians (SAHSL), Northern California and Nevada Medical Library Group (NCNMLG). **Remarks:** FAX: (916)456-2904.

★ 14196 ★
Sacramento Union - Editorial Library (Publ)
301 Capitol Mall   Phone: (916)442-7811
Sacramento, CA 95812   Denise Kreutzberg, Libn.
Staff: Prof 1. **Subjects:** Newspaper reference topics. **Special Collections:** Sacramento Union, 1846 to present (bound volumes). **Holdings:** 300 books; 180,000 newspaper clipping files. **Services:** Interlibrary loan; library not open to the public.

★ 14197 ★
Sacred Heart General Hospital - Professional Library Services (Med)
1255 Hilyard St.
PO Box 10905   Phone: (503)686-6837
Eugene, OR 97440   Kim E. Tyler, Dir.
Founded: 1971. **Staff:** Prof 3.5; Other 3. **Subjects:** Medicine, nursing, paramedicine, hospital administration, patient education. **Special Collections:** School of Nursing archives, 1942-1970 (2 boxes). **Holdings:** 4000 books; 7000 bound periodical volumes; 1000 video recordings. **Subscriptions:** 450 journals and other serials. **Services:** Interlibrary loan (fee); copying; SDI. **Automated Operations:** Computerized cataloging and ILL (DOCLINE). **Computerized Information Services:** CompuServe Information Service, MEDLARS, DIALOG Information Services, BRS Information Technologies; OnTyme Electronic Message Network Service, CompuServe Information Service (electronic mail services). Performs searches on fee basis. **Networks/Consortia:** Member of Western Library Network (WLN). **Remarks:** FAX: (503)686-7391. Electronic mail address(es): SHGH (OnTyme Electronic Message Network Service, CompuServe Information Service). **Staff:** Beverly Schriver, Ref.Libn.; Bonne Starks, Ref.Libn.

★ 14198 ★
Sacred Heart Hospital - Medical Library (Med)
5151 N. 9th Ave.   Phone: (904)474-7110
Pensacola, FL 32504   Florence V. Ruby, Hosp.Libn.
Founded: 1959. **Staff:** 2. **Subjects:** Medicine, pediatrics, nursing, management. **Special Collections:** Pediatrics library. **Holdings:** 942 books; 4269 bound periodical volumes. **Subscriptions:** 161 journals and other serials. **Services:** Interlibrary loan; copying; library open to the public by appointment. **Computerized Information Services:** MEDLARS.

★ 14199 ★
Sacred Heart Hospital - Medical Library (Med)
501 Summit   Phone: (605)665-9371
Yankton, SD 57078   Roxie Olson, Med.Libn.
Founded: 1975. **Staff:** Prof 1. **Subjects:** Life and health sciences, nursing, hospital administration. **Holdings:** 2700 volumes; 300 AV programs; 5 VF drawers. **Subscriptions:** 200 journals and other serials. **Services:** Interlibrary loan; copying; library open to the public with restrictions. **Computerized Information Services:** MEDLARS, NLM. Performs searches on fee basis. **Remarks:** FAX: (605)665-8840.

★ 14200 ★
Sacred Heart Hospital - Medical Library (Med)
900 W. Clairemont Ave.   Phone: (715)839-4330
Eau Claire, WI 54701   Bruno Warner, Libn.
Founded: 1964. **Staff:** Prof 1. **Subjects:** Medicine, nursing, dentistry, hospital administration, patient teaching. **Special Collections:** Neurology. **Holdings:** 5000 books; 1000 bound periodical volumes; 2000 unbound periodicals; 4 VF drawers of pamphlets. **Subscriptions:** 286 journals and other serials. **Services:** Interlibrary loan; copying; library open to the public. **Networks/Consortia:** Member of National Network of Libraries of Medicine - Greater Midwest Region. **Remarks:** FAX: (715)839-8417.

★ 14201 ★
Sacred Heart Hospital - Sister Martha Malloy Medical Library (Med)
900 Seton Dr.   Phone: (301)759-5229
Cumberland, MD 21502   Betty Ramsey, Libn.
Founded: 1967. **Staff:** 1. **Subjects:** Medicine, nursing, allied health sciences. **Holdings:** 2100 books; 50 bound periodical volumes. **Subscriptions:** 63 journals and other serials. **Services:** Interlibrary loan; copying; library open to the public with restrictions. **Computerized Information Services:** MEDLINE. **Remarks:** FAX: (301)759-5583.

★ 14202 ★
Sacred Heart Hospital - William A. Hausman Medical Library (Med)
4th & Chew Sts.   Phone: (215)776-4747
Allentown, PA 18102   Diane M. Horvath, Libn.
Founded: 1928. **Staff:** Prof 1. **Subjects:** Nursing, medicine. **Holdings:** 1438 books; 5290 bound periodical volumes; 804 Audio-Digest tapes; clippings of Sacred Heart Hospital and School of Nursing history. **Subscriptions:** 77 journals and other serials. **Services:** Interlibrary loan; copying; library open to medical, nursing, and allied health personnel and students for reference use. **Computerized Information Services:** MEDLARS.

Sacred Heart Jesuit Center - Jesuit Center Library
See: California Province of the Society of Jesus - Jesuit Center Library (2501)

★14203★
Sacred Heart Major Seminary - Ward Memorial Library (Rel-Phil)
2701 W. Chicago Blvd.   Phone: (313)883-8500
Detroit, MI 48206   Arnold M. Rzepecki, Libn.
Founded: 1919. **Staff:** Prof 1; Other 1.5. **Subjects:** Scholastic philosophy, modern philosophy, church history. **Special Collections:** Cardinal Mooney Collection (church and social problems); Michigan Historical Collection (church history in Michigan); Gabriel Richard Collection. **Holdings:** 70,000 books; 15,000 bound periodical volumes; 500 reels of microfilm. **Subscriptions:** 250 journals and other serials; 25 newspapers. **Services:** Interlibrary loan; copying; library open to the public at librarian's discretion. **Automated Operations:** Computerized cataloging. **Remarks:** FAX: (313)868-6440.

★14204★
Sacred Heart Medical Center - Health Sciences Library (Med)
9th & Wilson Sts.   Phone: (215)494-0700
Chester, PA 19013   Wesley Sollenberger, Hea.Sci.Libn.
Staff: Prof 1. **Subjects:** Medicine, nursing, and allied health sciences. **Holdings:** 900 books. **Subscriptions:** 125 journals and other serials. **Services:** Interlibrary loan; copying; library not open to the public. **Networks/Consortia:** Member of Consortium for Health Information & Library Services (CHI), BHSL. **Remarks:** FAX: (215)494-1918.

★14205★
Sacred Heart Medical Center - Health Sciences Library (Med)
W. 101 8th Ave.
TAF-C9
Spokane, WA 99220-4045   Phone: (509)455-3094
  Sandra L. Keno, Libn.
Staff: 3. **Subjects:** Medicine and surgery, nursing, dietetics, psychiatry, administration and management, clinical laboratory. **Holdings:** 2500 books; 3000 bound periodical volumes; 16 VF drawers of clippings, pamphlets, pictures; slides; videotapes; cassettes; filmstrips. **Subscriptions:** 300 journals and other serials. **Services:** Interlibrary loan; copying (limited); library open to the public with restrictions. **Automated Operations:** Computerized cataloging. **Computerized Information Services:** MEDLINE, DIALOG Information Services; OnTyme Electronic Message Network Service, CLASS (electronic mail services). Performs searches on fee basis. **Networks/Consortia:** Member of Inland Northwest Health Sciences Libraries (INWHSL). **Remarks:** Electronic mail address(es): SHMC (CLASS). **Staff:** Agnes D. Wright, Ref.Libn.; Gail Leong, Lib.Techn.

Sacred Heart Monastery
See: Sacred Heart School of Theology (14207)

★14206★
Sacred Heart Rehabilitation Hospital - Staff Library (Med)
1545 S. Layton Blvd.   Phone: (414)383-4490
Milwaukee, WI 53215   Patti Malmberg, Libn.
Remarks: No further information was supplied by respondent.

★14207★
Sacred Heart School of Theology - Leo Dehon Library (Rel-Phil)
7335 S. Lovers Lane Rd.
Box 429   Phone: (414)425-8300
Hales Corners, WI 53130-0429   Sr. Agnese Jasko, P.H.J.C., Libn.
Founded: 1932. **Staff:** Prof 2; Other 2. **Subjects:** Dogmatic theology, ascetical theology, canon law, church history, scripture, liturgy, moral theology, comparative religion, philosophy. **Special Collections:** Sacred Heart Collection (612 titles). **Holdings:** 75,177 books; 6637 bound periodical volumes; 1000 pamphlets; 323 reels of microfilm; 41 volumes on microfiche; 1873 cassette tapes; 10,893 phonograph records. **Subscriptions:** 409 journals and other serials. **Services:** Interlibrary loan; copying; library open to the public. **Networks/Consortia:** Member of Library Council of Metropolitan Milwaukee, Inc. (LCOMM), Southeastern Wisconsin Information Technology Exchange (SWITCH). **Remarks:** FAX: (414)529-6999. **Staff:** Rev. Charles Yost, S.C.J., Cons.; Kathy Jastrab, Assoc.Libn.

★14208★
Sacred Heart University - Library (Rel-Phil)
5151 Park Ave.   Phone: (203)371-7700
Fairfield, CT 06432   Dorothy Kijanka, Dir.
Founded: 1963. **Staff:** Prof 6; Other 11. **Subjects:** Religious studies, business administration. **Special Collections:** International Children's Literature Collection; Heywood Hale Broun Collection; Msgr. Ronald Knox Collection. **Holdings:** 158,000 books; 62,000 AV programs. **Subscriptions:** 731 journals and other serials. **Services:** Interlibrary loan; copying; library open to the public. **Automated Operations:** Computerized cataloging, circulation, and ILL. **Computerized Information Services:** OCLC, DIALOG Information Services, OCLC EPIC, BRS Information Technologies, WESTLAW, BIBLIOMATION. **Networks/Consortia:** Member of Southwestern Connecticut Library Council (SWLC), NELINET, Inc. **Publications:** Acquisitions List, monthly - for internal distribution only. **Remarks:** FAX: (203)374-9968. **Staff:** Mary Rogers, Asst.Univ.Libn.; Bing Li, Hd.Ref.Libn.; John Maroney, Ref.Libn.; Roch DiLisio, Bibliog.Instr.Libn.; Constance Fraser, Ref.Libn.

Sadtler Research Laboratories
See: Bio-Rad Laboratories (1843)

★14209★
SAE International - Library (Sci-Engr)
400 Commonwealth Dr.   Phone: (412)776-4841
Warrendale, PA 15096-0001   Janet M. Jedlicka, Libn./Res.
Founded: 1974. **Staff:** Prof 1; Other 1. **Subjects:** Automotive and aerospace engineering, including trucks, buses, and farm machinery; design and development; fuels and lubricants; fuel economy. **Special Collections:** SAE publications, 1905 to present. **Holdings:** 1700 books; 160 bound periodical volumes; 42,000 technical papers; 5000 aerospace material specifications; 1700 automotive standards. **Subscriptions:** 203 journals and other serials. **Services:** Copying; library open to the public by appointment. **Computerized Information Services:** PFDS Online; produces SAE Global Mobility Database; SDC (electronic mail service). Performs searches on fee basis. Contact Person: Mary Hodder, Customer Serv.Supv. **Remarks:** FAX: (412)776-5760. Telex: 866 355 SAE IN WNDE. **Also Known As:** Society of Automotive Engineers, Inc.

★14210★
Safeco Insurance Company - Library (Bus-Fin)
Safeco Plaza   Phone: (206)545-5505
Seattle, WA 98185   Kimberly S. Anicker, Libn.
Founded: 1958. **Staff:** 2. **Subjects:** Insurance, finance, management, business. **Holdings:** 9000 books; 1 VF drawer of unbound materials; 160 16mm films; 20 shelves of archives; 1 VF drawers of pamphlets, brochures; 175 video cassettes; AV programs. **Subscriptions:** 210 journals and other serials; 10 newspapers. **Services:** Interlibrary loan; copying; library open to the public with restrictions. **Automated Operations:** Computerized serials, cataloging, and circulation (Data Trek). **Computerized Information Services:** OCLC. **Remarks:** FAX: (206)545-5995. **Staff:** Teresa White, Asst.Libn.

★14211★
Safeway, Inc. - Library (Food-Bev, Bus-Fin)
201 4th St.   Phone: (510)891-3236
Oakland, CA 94660   Catherine Ghent, Lib.Mgr.
Founded: 1938. **Staff:** Prof 1; Other 1.5. **Subjects:** Food, retail food chains, business. **Holdings:** 15,000 books; clippings; corporate reports. **Subscriptions:** 160 journals and other serials. **Services:** Interlibrary loan; library not open to the public. **Automated Operations:** Computerized cataloging, acquisitions, and serials. **Computerized Information Services:** DIALOG Information Services, DataTimes, VU/TEXT Information Services, LEXIS, Dun & Bradstreet Business Credit Services, Dow Jones News/Retrieval.

★14212★
Sag Harbor Whaling and Historical Museum - Library (Hist)
Main St.   Phone: (516)725-0770
Sag Harbor, NY 11963   George A. Finckenor, Sr., Cur.
Founded: 1979. **Staff:** Prof 1; Other 3. **Subjects:** Whaling, fishing, antiques, shipping, Indians. **Special Collections:** Log books of whaling ships; scrimshaw (on sperm whale teeth, walrus tusks, and narwhal tusks); model ships - merchant, yachting, naval, whalers; 1943 WPA report, drawings of wooden ships of the east and west coasts, and survey with line drawings of the Great Lakes and the Mississippi River (7 volumes). **Holdings:** 300 books; memorabilia. **Services:** Library open to the public for reference use only on application.

★ 14213 ★
Sagadahoc County Law Library (Law)
County Court House
752 High St.
Bath, ME 04530   Phone: (207)443-9734
Subjects: Law. **Holdings:** 5500 books. **Services:** Library open to the public.

Elliot L. and Annette Y. Sagall Library
See: **American Society of Law & Medicine** (751)

★ 14214 ★
Sagamore Hills Children's Psychiatric Hospital - Staff Medical Library (Med)
11910 Dunham Rd.
Northfield, OH 44067   Phone: (614)467-7955
Subjects: Child psychology, institutional care, nursing, activity and educational therapy, psychiatry. **Holdings:** 950 books; tapes. **Subscriptions:** 15 journals and other serials. **Services:** Library not open to the public.

Gardner A. Sage Library
See: **New Brunswick Theological Seminary** (11455)

★ 14215 ★
Russell Sage Foundation - Library (Soc Sci)
112 E. 64th St.   Phone: (212)750-6008
New York, NY 10021   Pauline M. Rothstein, Dir., Info.Serv.
Staff: Prof 1; Other 2. **Subjects:** Social science. **Special Collections:** Foundation publications. **Holdings:** 1500 books. **Subscriptions:** 100 journals and other serials; 5 newspapers. **Services:** Interlibrary loan; copying; library open to the public by appointment. **Computerized Information Services:** DIALOG Information Services, OCLC, NEXIS; CD-ROMs (Social Sciences Citation Index (SSCI), Books in Print, Ulrich's Plus). **Networks/Consortia:** Member of Consortium of Foundation Libraries (CFL), New York Metropolitan Reference and Research Library Agency. **Remarks:** FAX: (212)371-4761. Foundation archives are held at Rockefeller Archive Center, Pocantico Hills, North Tarrytown, NY 10591-1598.

★ 14216 ★
Saginaw County Law Library (Law)
Courthouse, Rm. 215
111 S. Michigan Ave.   Phone: (517)790-5490
Saginaw, MI 48602   Jannis Corley, Law Libn.
Founded: 1945. **Staff:** Prof 4. **Subjects:** Law. **Holdings:** 20,000 volumes. **Services:** Copying; library open to the public with restrictions.

★ 14217 ★
Saginaw Health Sciences Library (Med)
1000 Houghton St., Suite 2000   Phone: (517)771-6846
Saginaw, MI 48602   Stephanie John, Dir.
Founded: 1978. **Staff:** Prof 3; Other 7. **Subjects:** Medicine, nursing, allied health sciences, dentistry, health care administration, behavioral health. **Holdings:** 10,500 books; 14,750 bound periodical volumes; 1448 AV programs; 6 VF drawers of pamphlets. **Subscriptions:** 494 journals and other serials. **Services:** Interlibrary loan; copying; SDI; library open to the public by referral only. **Automated Operations:** Computerized cataloging. **Computerized Information Services:** OCLC, CompuServe Information Service, PaperChase, NLM, BRS Information Technologies, MEDLINE, DIALOG Information Services, VU/TEXT Information Services, WILSONLINE; CD-ROMs (CINAHL, MEDLINE). Performs searches on fee basis. Contact Person: June Cronenberger, Assoc.Dir., 771-6869. **Networks/Consortia:** Member of Michigan Library Consortium (MLC). **Remarks:** Library maintained by Saginaw Cooperative Hospitals, Inc. which serves 4 area hospitals. Library serves more than 100 individuals and institutions in a 32-county area via membership programs. FAX: (517)753-3439. **Staff:** Cheryl Putnam.

★ 14218 ★
Saginaw News - Library (Publ)
203 S. Washington Ave.   Phone: (517)776-9672
Saginaw, MI 48607-1283   Lorri D. Lea, Hd.Libn.
Founded: 1946. **Staff:** Prof 1; Other 1. **Subjects:** Newspaper reference topics. **Holdings:** 1000 books; 5.5 million clippings; area newspapers, 1840 to present, on microfilm. **Subscriptions:** 25 journals and other serials; 12 newspapers. **Services:** Library not open to the public, accepts telephone queries. **Remarks:** FAX: (517)752-3115. **Staff:** Suzanne J. Grant, Asst.Libn.

Saguenay Region Historical Society
See: **Societe Historique du Saguenay** (15304)

Sahatdjan Library
See: **California State University, Fresno - Armenian Studies Program** (2560)

★ 14219 ★
SAIC Corporate Technical Resource Acquisition Center (CTRAC) (Sci-Engr)
1710 Goodridge Dr.
Mail Stop 1-14-6   Phone: (703)749-8701
McLean, VA 22102-3799   Madeleine Hahn, Libn./Mgr.
Founded: 1975. **Staff:** 12. **Subjects:** Engineering, energy, health. **Holdings:** Military and federal specifications and standards on microfiche. **Services:** Interlibrary loan; center not open to the public. **Automated Operations:** Computerized acquisitions. **Computerized Information Services:** DIALOG Information Services, NEXIS, DataTimes. Performs searches on fee basis. Contact Person: Kathy Pitt, Asst.Dir., 749-8703. **Networks/Consortia:** Member of Interlibrary Users Association (IUA). **Remarks:** FAX: (703)821-3071. **Also Known As:** SAIC/CTRAC. **Staff:** M. Kamaluddin, ILL Spec.

SAIC/CTRAC
See: **SAIC Corporate Technical Resource Acquisition Center (CTRAC)** (14219)

★ 14220 ★
St. Agnes Hospital - Health Sciences Library (Med)
430 E. Division St.   Phone: (414)929-1559
Fond du Lac, WI 54935-4597   Sr. Sharon McEnery, C.S.A., Libn.
Founded: 1918. **Staff:** Prof 1. **Subjects:** Medicine, nursing, allied health, hospital management. **Holdings:** 1575 books; 4061 bound periodical volumes. **Subscriptions:** 115 journals and other serials. **Services:** Interlibrary loan open to the public to students and area residents. **Automated Operations:** Computerized serials and ILL. **Computerized Information Services:** MEDLARS, GRATEFUL MED; DOCLINE (electronic mail service). **Networks/Consortia:** Member of Fox River Valley Area Library Consortium (FRVALC), National Network of Libraries of Medicine - Greater Midwest Region, Fox Valley Library Council. **Remarks:** FAX: (414)929-1306.

★ 14221 ★
St. Agnes Hospital - L.P. Gundry Health Sciences Library (Med)
900 S. Caton Ave.   Phone: (301)368-3123
Baltimore, MD 21229   Joanne Sullivan, Dir.
Founded: 1959. **Staff:** Prof 1; Other 2.5. **Subjects:** Medicine, surgery, pediatrics, obstetrics, gynecology, pathology, nursing, psychiatry, management, health care careers. **Holdings:** 2500 books; 6000 bound periodical volumes. **Subscriptions:** 275 journals and other serials. **Services:** Interlibrary loan; copying; library open to the public with restrictions. **Automated Operations:** Computerized cataloging and serials. **Computerized Information Services:** BRS Information Technologies, MEDLARS; CD-ROMs (MEDLINE, CINAHL, Health Care and Administration). **Remarks:** FAX: (301)368-3298.

★ 14222 ★
St. Agnes Medical Center - Health Science Library (Med)
1900 S. Broad St.   Phone: (215)339-4448
Philadelphia, PA 19145   Marian Schaner, Dir.
Founded: 1975. **Staff:** Prof 1; Other 1. **Subjects:** Medicine, nursing, and allied health sciences. **Holdings:** 4000 books; 2000 bound periodical volumes; 8 VF drawers. **Subscriptions:** 200 journals and other serials. **Services:** Interlibrary loan; library not open to the public. **Computerized Information Services:** BRS Information Technologies, DIALOG Information Services. **Networks/Consortia:** Member of Delaware Valley Information Consortium (DEVIC), BHSL. **Remarks:** FAX: (215)755-1295.

★ 14223 ★
St. Agnes Medical Center - Medical Library (Med)
1303 E. Herndon Ave.   Phone: (209)449-3322
Fresno, CA 93720   Sr. Louise Lovely, Mgr., Med.Lib.
Founded: 1956. **Staff:** 1.5. **Subjects:** Nursing, cardiovascular system, medicine, oncology, surgery, pharmocology. **Holdings:** 1034 books; 4000 bound periodical volumes; 4200 reports; 14,077 microfiche. **Subscriptions:** 160 journals and other serials. **Services:** Interlibrary loan; copying; library open to health services personnel and students. **Computerized Information Services:** DIALOG Information Services, MEDLARS. **Networks/ Consortia:** Member of Northern California and Nevada Medical Library Group (NCNMLG), Area Wide Library Network (AWLNET). **Remarks:** FAX: (209)449-3315.

★ 14224 ★
St. Alexis Hospital - Health Sciences Library (Med)
5163 Broadway Ave.   Phone: (216)429-8245
Cleveland, OH 44127   Verne Zach
Staff: Prof 1; Other 1. **Subjects:** Medicine, allied health sciences, hospitals, nursing. **Holdings:** 2000 books; 1500 bound periodical volumes; 400 AV programs; pamphlets; reprints. **Subscriptions:** 175 journals and other serials. **Services:** Interlibrary loan; library not open to the public. **Automated Operations:** Computerized cataloging. **Computerized Information Services:** MEDLINE, DIALOG Information Services. **Remarks:** FAX: (216)641-9184.

★ 14225 ★
St. Alphonsus Regional Medical Center - Health Sciences Library (Med)
1055 N. Curtis Rd.   Phone: (208)378-2271
Boise, ID 83706   Judy A. Balcerzak, Libn.
Founded: 1970. **Staff:** Prof 1; Other 1.25. **Subjects:** Medicine, nursing, and allied health sciences. **Holdings:** 1000 books. **Subscriptions:** 224 journals and other serials. **Services:** Interlibrary loan; copying; library open to the public for reference use only. **Computerized Information Services:** MEDLINE, BRS Information Technologies, WLN; OnTyme Electronic Message Network Service, DOCLINE (electronic mail services). **Networks/ Consortia:** Member of Boise Valley Health Sciences Library Consortium, Idaho Health Information Association. **Remarks:** FAX: (208)378-2702. Electronic mail address(es): ST/ALPHONSUS (OnTyme Electronic Message Network Service).

★ 14226 ★
St. Amant Centre Inc. - Medical Library (Med)
440 River Rd.   Phone: (204)256-4301
Winnipeg, MB, Canada R2M 3Z9   Pauline Dufresne, Techn.
Staff: Prof 1. **Subjects:** Mental retardation, genetics. **Holdings:** 450 books. **Subscriptions:** 20 journals and other serials. **Services:** Copying; library open to the public with restrictions.

★ 14227 ★
St. Ambrose University - McMullen Library - Special Collections (Rel-Phil)
518 W. Locust St.   Phone: (319)383-8795
Davenport, IA 52803   Corinne J. Potter
Founded: 1892. **Staff:** Prof 5; Other 5. **Special Collections:** Davenport and Scott County Collection (25 items); Catholic Messenger (newspaper on microfilm, 1883 to present); imprints collection (1000 items, pre-1850); St. Ambrose University historic materials collection (500 items). **Services:** Interlibrary loan; copying; library open to the public; archives open to the public by appointment for reference use only. **Automated Operations:** Computerized public access catalog. **Computerized Information Services:** DIALOG Information Services, OCLC; CD-ROM (ERIC). Contact Person: Marylaine Block, Assoc.Dir. **Remarks:** FAX: (319)383-8791.

★ 14228 ★
St. Andrew's College - Library (Rel-Phil)
1121 College Dr.   Phone: (306)966-8983
Saskatoon, SK, Canada S7N 0W3   June Sinclair Smith, Libn.
Founded: 1912. **Staff:** Prof 1; Other 2. **Subjects:** Religion and theology. **Holdings:** 29,900 books; 3815 bound periodical volumes; 400 microfiche; 260 cassettes; 25 reels of microfilm; dissertations. **Subscriptions:** 158 journals and other serials. **Services:** Interlibrary loan; copying; library open to the public. **Automated Operations:** Computerized cataloging (CD-ROM); public access catalog. **Remarks:** College is an autonomous affiliate of the University of Saskatchewan.

★ 14229 ★
St. Andrews Hospital - Medical Library (Med)
3 St. Andrews Ln.
PO Box 417   Phone: (207)633-2121
Boothbay Harbor, ME 04538-0417   Margaret Pinkham, R.N., Educ.Dir.
Staff: 1. **Subjects:** Medicine, surgery, orthopedics, obstetrics/gynecology, pediatrics, urology, ophthalmology. **Holdings:** 100 books. **Services:** Interlibrary loan; library open for general hospital use. **Remarks:** FAX: (207)633-4209.

★ 14230 ★
St. Andrews Presbyterian College - Music Library (Mus)
Vardell Bldg.   Phone: (919)277-5266
Laurinburg, NC 28352   Prof. David Fish, Supv.
Founded: 1961. **Staff:** 1. **Subjects:** Music. **Special Collections:** Amos Abrams collection of musical theater recordings; ethnomusicology/world music recordings. **Holdings:** 18,000 scores; 4 VF drawers of unbound scores; 2000 phonograph records. **Services:** Library open to students. **Computerized Information Services:** OCLC. **Remarks:** FAX: (919)277-5020.

★ 14231 ★
St. Anne's Hospital - Sullivan Medical Library (Med)
795 Middle St.   Phone: (508)674-5741
Fall River, MA 02721   Elaine M. Crites, Med.Libn.
Founded: 1956. **Staff:** Prof 2. **Subjects:** Oncology, medicine, surgery, allied health sciences, pediatrics. **Holdings:** 100 books; 4000 bound periodical volumes. **Subscriptions:** 80 journals and other serials. **Services:** Interlibrary loan; copying; library open to the public with restrictions. **Networks/ Consortia:** Member of Southeastern Massachusetts Consortium of Health Science Libraries (SEMCO), Massachusetts Health Sciences Libraries Network (MaHSLiN). **Publications:** Hospital Newsletter - local distribution. **Remarks:** FAX: (508)675-5606. **Staff:** Sr. Therese Joseph Hazera.

★ 14232 ★
St. Anselm College - Geisel Library (Rel-Phil)
87 St. Anselm Dr.   Phone: (603)641-7300
Manchester, NH 03102-1310   Joseph W. Constance, Jr., Libn.
Founded: 1929. **Staff:** Prof 7; Other 20. **Subjects:** Church history, theology, medieval history, nursing. **Special Collections:** New England Collection (3000 volumes). **Holdings:** 175,000 books; 18,000 bound periodical volumes; 17,500 reels of microfilm; 36,000 microfiche; 6700 phonograph records and tapes. **Subscriptions:** 1859 journals and other serials; 50 newspapers. **Services:** Interlibrary loan; copying; library open to the public for reference use only. **Automated Operations:** Computerized circulation. **Computerized Information Services:** DIALOG Information Services. Performs searches on fee basis. Contact Person: Nancy S. Urtz, Pub.Serv. **Networks/ Consortia:** Member of NELINET, Inc., New Hampshire College & University Council Library Policy Committee (NHCUC). **Publications:** Accession list, monthly; subject bibliographies. **Remarks:** FAX: (603)641-7116. **Staff:** Eunice Wang, Tech.Serv.; Jeanne Welch, ILL; Scott Stangroom, Per.; Karen S. Metz, Coll.Dev.

★ 14233 ★
St. Anthony College of Nursing - Bishop Lane Library (Med)
5658 E. State St.   Phone: (815)395-5091
Rockford, IL 61108-2468   Sr. Mary Linus, OSF, M.S.N.E.
Staff: Prof 1. **Subjects:** Nursing. **Holdings:** 4000 books; 600 bound periodical volumes. **Subscriptions:** 43 journals and 100 other serials. **Services:** Interlibrary loan; library not open to the public. **Networks/ Consortia:** Member of Upstate Consortium of Medical Libraries in Northern Illinois. **Special Indexes:** Cumulative index to nursing and allied health literature.

St. Anthony Falls Hydraulic Laboratory
See: **University of Minnesota - St. Anthony Falls Hydraulic Laboratory** (18927)

★ 14234 ★
St. Anthony Hospital - Medical Library (Med)
2875 W. 19th St.
Chicago, IL 60623   Phone: (312)521-1710
Founded: 1945. **Staff:** 2. **Subjects:** Medicine, nursing, administration. **Holdings:** Figures not available. **Services:** Interlibrary loan; library open to the public with restrictions. **Networks/Consortia:** Member of National Network of Libraries of Medicine - Greater Midwest Region, Chicago and South Consortium, Chicago Library System. **Publications:** Bibliographies.

★ 14235 ★
St. Anthony Hospital - O'Donoghue Medical Library (Med)
1000 N. Lee St.
Box 205   Phone: (405)272-6284
Oklahoma City, OK 73102   Sharon Jorski, Dir.
Founded: 1950. **Staff:** Prof 1; Other 1. **Subjects:** Cardiovascular medicine, neurosurgery and neurology, general medicine, nursing, community health, allied health sciences, dentistry. **Holdings:** 4000 books; 3800 bound periodical volumes. **Subscriptions:** 185 journals and other serials. **Services:** Interlibrary loan; copying. **Computerized Information Services:** MEDLINE, TOXLINE, DIALOG Information Services, WILSONLINE, LONESOME DOC. **Networks/Consortia:** Member of Greater Oklahoma City Area Health Sciences Library Consortium (GOAL), Metropolitan Libraries Network of Central Oklahoma Inc. (MetroNet), National Network of Libraries of Medicine - South Central Region. **Remarks:** FAX: (405)272-7075.

★ 14236 ★
St. Anthony Hospital - Sister M. Francis Medical Library (Med)
1313 St. Anthony Pl.   Phone: (502)587-1161
Louisville, KY 40204   Alma Hall Berry, Libn.
Subjects: Medicine. **Holdings:** 500 books; 100 bound periodical volumes. **Subscriptions:** 25 journals and other serials. **Services:** Interlibrary loan; library not open to the public. **Remarks:** Alternate telephone number(s): 627-1756. FAX: (502)627-1770.

★ 14237 ★
St. Anthony Hospital Systems - Memorial Medical Library (Med)
4231 W. 16th Ave.   Phone: (303)629-3790
Denver, CO 80204   Christine Yolanda Crespin, Supv.Libn.
Founded: 1948. **Staff:** Prof 1; Other 1. **Subjects:** Emergency medicine, trauma, critical care, allied health sciences. **Special Collections:** Emergency Medicine. **Holdings:** 1000 books; 3500 bound periodical volumes; 50 pamphlets. **Subscriptions:** 254 journals and other serials. **Services:** Interlibrary loan; library not open to the public. **Automated Operations:** Computerized cataloging and serials. **Computerized Information Services:** DIALOG Information Services, MEDLINE, NLM. **Publications:** Current Awareness Service, monthly.

★ 14238 ★
St. Anthony Medical Center - Health Information Resource Center (Med)
5666 E. State St.   Phone: (815)395-5191
Rockford, IL 61108   Nancy Dale, Med.Libn.
Staff: Prof 1. **Subjects:** Clinical medicine, nursing, hospital management. **Holdings:** 800 books; 2000 bound periodical volumes. **Subscriptions:** 200 journals and other serials. **Services:** Interlibrary loan; copying; SDI; library open to the public by prior arrangement. **Computerized Information Services:** MEDLARS, DIALOG Information Services, NLM. **Networks/Consortia:** Member of National Network of Libraries of Medicine - Greater Midwest Region, Northern Illinois Library System (NILS), Upstate Consortium of Medical Libraries in Northern Illinois. **Remarks:** FAX: (815)395-5551.

★ 14239 ★
St. Anthony Medical Center - Philip B. Hardymon Library (Med)
1492 E. Broad St.   Phone: (614)251-3248
Columbus, OH 43205   Pamela L. Caruzzi, Chf.Med.Libn.
Founded: 1956. **Staff:** Prof 1; Other 1. **Subjects:** Medicine, medical specialties. **Holdings:** 2800 books; 3500 bound periodical volumes; 92 pamphlets; 392 audio cassettes; holdings in various hospital departments. **Subscriptions:** 200 journals and other serials. **Services:** Interlibrary loan; copying; SDI. **Automated Operations:** Computerized ILL. **Computerized Information Services:** DIALOG Information Services, NLM. **Networks/Consortia:** Member of National Network of Libraries of Medicine - Greater Midwest Region, Central Ohio Hospital Library Consortium. **Publications:** Bibliographies - to doctors, nursing personnel, and administration. **Remarks:** FAX: (614)251-3864.

★ 14240 ★
St. Anthony-on-Hudson Theological Library (Rel-Phil)
St. Anthony-on-Hudson
517 Washington Ave.
Rensselaer, NY 12144   Phone: (518)463-2261
Founded: 1912. **Staff:** Prof 1. **Subjects:** Theology. **Special Collections:** Franciscana (4000 volumes); Newmaniana (300 volumes); patristic-monastic-medieval theology (10,000 items). **Holdings:** 110,000 books; 15,000 bound periodical volumes; 60 incunabula and post-incunabula; 3 medieval codices; 60 manuscripts; 400 pamphlets; 260 volumes on microfilm; 75 boxes of archival material; 1000 phonograph records. **Subscriptions:** 300 journals and other serials. **Services:** Copying; library open to scholars by appointment.

★ 14241 ★
St. Anthony's Health Center - St. Anthony's Hospital - Medical Library (Med)
Saint Anthony's Way
PO Box 340   Phone: (618)463-5645
Alton, IL 62002   Darla Ann Reif, Libn.Asst.
Staff: Prof 1. **Subjects:** Medicine, nursing. **Holdings:** 1179 books. **Subscriptions:** 125 journals and other serials. **Services:** Interlibrary loan; copying; library open to health personnel. **Networks/Consortia:** Member of Areawide Hospital Library Consortium of Southwestern Illinois (AHLC), Saint Louis Medical Librarians Consortia, ILLINET, Lewis & Clark Library System. **Publications:** Current Journal Contents, weekly - for internal distribution only; bibliographies. **Remarks:** FAX: (618)463-5640.

★ 14242 ★
St. Anthony's Health Center - St. Clare's Hospital - Medical Library (Med)
915 E. 5th St.
PO Box 340   Phone: (618)463-5645
Alton, IL 62002   Darla Ann Reif, Libn.Asst.
Staff: Prof 1. **Subjects:** Medicine, nursing. **Holdings:** 1179 volumes. **Subscriptions:** 125 journals and other serials. **Services:** Interlibrary loan; copying; library open to health personnel. **Networks/Consortia:** Member of Areawide Hospital Library Consortium of Southwestern Illinois (AHLC), ILLINET, Saint Louis Medical Librarians Consortia, Lewis & Clark Library System. **Publications:** Current Journal Contents, weekly - to department heads and doctors; bibliographies. **Remarks:** FAX: (618)463-5640.

★ 14243 ★
St. Anthony's Hospital, Inc. - Medical Library (Med)
1200 7th Ave. N.   Phone: (813)825-1286
St. Petersburg, FL 33705   Grace DeWald, Med.Libn.
Founded: 1958. **Staff:** Prof 1. **Subjects:** Internal medicine, surgery, radiology, psychiatry, oncology, nursing. **Special Collections:** Wellness. **Holdings:** 2248 books; 4412 bound periodical volumes; 240 unbound reports; 33 archival materials. **Subscriptions:** 141 journals and other serials; 6 newspapers. **Services:** Interlibrary loan; copying; library open to professionals only. **Automated Operations:** Computerized cataloging, acquisitions, and serials. **Computerized Information Services:** NLM, internal database; DOCLINE (electronic mail service). Performs searches on fee basis. **Networks/Consortia:** Member of Tampa Bay Medical Library Network. **Publications:** Library Users Guide; current acquisitions. **Remarks:** FAX: (813)823-0655. **Staff:** Susan Steele, Dir., Educ.

★ 14244 ★
St. Anthony's Memorial Hospital - Health Science Library (Med)
503 N. Maple St.   Phone: (217)342-2121
Effingham, IL 62401   Sr. M. Angelus Gardiner, Libn.
Founded: 1977. **Staff:** 2. **Subjects:** Health, medicine, nursing. **Holdings:** 1444 books; 636 tapes; 73 video cassettes; archives; 12 VF drawers of other cataloged items. **Subscriptions:** 191 journals and other serials. **Services:** Interlibrary loan; copying; library open to the public with restrictions. **Networks/Consortia:** Member of ILLINET, Rolling Prairie Library System (RPLS).

★14245★
St. Augustine Historical Society - Library (Hist)
271 Charlotte St. Phone: (904)824-2872
St. Augustine, FL 32084 Jean Trapido-Rosenthal, Lib.Dir.
Founded: 1883. **Staff:** 7. **Subjects:** History of St. Augustine and environs, history of Florida, genealogy. **Special Collections:** Cathedral Parish records, St. Augustine, 1594-1763 and 1784-1882 (marriages, baptisms, burials); archives (manuscripts; city papers; St. Johns County court records). **Holdings:** 8000 books; photocopies; manuscripts; documents; microfilm; photographs; maps; pictures; card calendar of Spanish documents, 1512-1764; card index of St. Augustine people, 1821 to present. **Subscriptions:** 12 journals and other serials. **Services:** Interlibrary loan; copying; library open to the public for reference use only. **Publications:** El Escribano, annual - by subscription; East Florida Gazette, quarterly.

St. Augustine Retreat Center - Library
See: Divine Word Seminary of St. Augustine - Library (4924)

★14246★
St. Augustine's Seminary - Library (Rel-Phil)
2661 Kingston Rd. Phone: (416)261-7207
Scarborough, ON, Canada M1M 1M3 Sr. Jean Harris, Libn.
Founded: 1913. **Staff:** Prof 1; Other 2. **Subjects:** Theology, scripture, canon law, church history. **Holdings:** 28,000 books; 3750 bound periodical volumes. **Subscriptions:** 190 journals and other serials; 9 newspapers. **Services:** Interlibrary loan; copying; library open to Toronto School of Theology students, St. Augustine's alumni, and to religious education students with permission.

★14247★
St. Barnabas Medical Center - Medical Library (Med)
Old Short Hills Rd. Phone: (201)533-5050
Livingston, NJ 07039 A. Christine Connor, Lib.Dir.
Staff: Prof 1; Other 3. **Subjects:** Medicine, nursing. **Special Collections:** Plastic surgery (225 books). **Holdings:** 5000 books; 15,000 bound periodical volumes. **Subscriptions:** 365 journals and other serials. **Services:** Interlibrary loan (fee); copying; library open to qualified researchers and members of the community with restrictions. **Computerized Information Services:** MEDLINE. **Networks/Consortia:** Member of Medical Library Center of New York (MLCNY), Cosmopolitan Biomedical Library Consortium (CBLC), Health Sciences Library Association of New Jersey (HSLANJ). **Remarks:** FAX: (201)533-5279.

★14248★
St. Benedict's Abbey - Benet Library (Rel-Phil)
12605 224th Ave. Phone: (414)396-4311
Benet Lake, WI 53102 Bro. Vincent Wedig, O.S.B., Libn.
Founded: 1945. **Staff:** Prof 2. **Subjects:** Theology, scripture, psychosocial sciences, history, literature. **Holdings:** 20,000 books; 1000 bound periodical volumes; 200 unbound periodicals. **Subscriptions:** 35 journals and other serials; 10 newspapers. **Services:** Interlibrary loan; copying; library open to the public for reference use only. **Staff:** Sr. Mary Benedict, O.S.B., Asst.Libn.

★14249★
St. Benedicts Family Medical Center - Library (Med)
709 N. Lincoln Phone: (208)324-4301
Jerome, ID 83338 Karen Field, Libn.
Staff: Prof 1. **Subjects:** Medicine, nursing. **Holdings:** 100 books. **Subscriptions:** 25 journals and other serials. **Services:** Interlibrary loan; copying; library open to the public with restrictions. **Networks/Consortia:** Member of Southeast Idaho Health Information Consortium. **Remarks:** FAX: (208)324-3878.

★14250★
St. Benedict's Hospital - Health Sciences Library (Med)
5475 S. 500 East Phone: (801)479-2055
Ogden, UT 84405-6978 Sandy Eckersley, Info.Spec.
Founded: 1947. **Staff:** Prof 1. **Subjects:** Medicine, nursing, and allied health sciences. **Holdings:** 600 books; 50 videotapes. **Subscriptions:** 141 journals and other serials. **Services:** Interlibrary loan; copying; library open to the public. **Computerized Information Services:** MEDLARS, MEDLINE, DIALOG Information Services. **Networks/Consortia:** Member of National Network of Libraries of Medicine - Midcontinental Region, Utah Health Sciences Library Consortium (UHSLC).

★14251★
St. Bernardine Medical Center - Norman F. Feldheym Library (Med)
2101 N. Waterman Ave. Phone: (714)883-8711
San Bernardino, CA 92404 Kathy Crumpacker, Lib.Asst.
Founded: 1981. **Staff:** 1. **Subjects:** Medicine, paramedical fields, nursing, surgery. **Special Collections:** Hospital Satellite Network (videocassette); AREN; American Hospital Association teleconferences; AID SATELLITE programming; NCME; MEDICOM. **Holdings:** 1500 books. **Subscriptions:** 155 journals and other serials. **Services:** Interlibrary loan; copying; library open to the public. **Computerized Information Services:** MEDLINE, BRS Information Technologies. **Networks/Consortia:** Member of Inland Empire Medical Library Cooperative (IEMLC), San Bernardino, Inyo, Riverside Counties United Library Services (SIRCULS).

St. Bernard's Institute - Ambrose Swasey Library
See: Ambrose Swasey Library (15904)

★14252★
St. Catharines General Hospital - Health Sciences Library (Med)
142 Queenston St. Phone: (416)684-7271
St. Catharines, ON, Canada L2R 7C6 Susan P. Armbrust, Libn.
Founded: 1978. **Staff:** Prof 1; Other 2. **Subjects:** Medicine, nursing, laboratory and business administration. **Holdings:** 1400 books; audiotapes; vertical files. **Subscriptions:** 152 journals and other serials. **Services:** Interlibrary loan; copying; SDI; library open to the public. **Computerized Information Services:** MEDLINE, CAN/OLE. Performs searches on fee basis. **Networks/Consortia:** Member of Niagara Peninsula Hospital Libraries.

★14253★
St. Catharines Historical Museum - Library/Archives (Hist)
1932 Government Rd.
PO Box 3012
St. Catharines, ON, Canada L2R 7C2 Phone: (416)984-8880
Founded: 1965. **Staff:** 7. **Subjects:** History - St. Catharines, Welland Canal, shipping; museology principles; artifact reference. **Special Collections:** St. Lawrence Seaway Authority Collection (121 maps); Norris Papers (mid-19th century shipping business; 60.95 centimeters); Ingersoll Papers (19th century business and household accounts; 25.4 centimeters); Niagara Grape and Wine Festival Archives; DeCew Falls Waterworks Collection; James Kidd Marine Photographs Collection; Alan Howard Photographs Collection. **Holdings:** 1600 books; 2000 maps and plans; 350 pamphlets and leaflets; 210 unbound periodicals; 187 reels of microfilm; 79 street directories; 5 drawers of documents; 3400 historical photographs. **Subscriptions:** 11 journals and other serials. **Services:** Copying; library open to the public. **Publications:** A Guide to the Grand River Canal (1982); Recollections of St. Catharines, 1837-1902 (1982); Glimpses Into Our Past, Volumes 1 and 2 (1984), Volume 3 (1986); A Canadian Enterprise - The Welland Canals (1984). **Special Catalogs:** Port of St. Catharines Shipping Register (card); Catalog of the Niagara Heritage Collection. **Special Indexes:** Index the ship names appearing in the St. Catharines Standard Newspaper column "Ships That Ply the Lakes" (booklet). **Remarks:** FAX: (416)984-6910. Library includes the St. Catharines and Lincoln Historical Society Collection.

★14254★
St. Catherine Hospital - Regional Educational Services - McGuire Memorial Library (Med)
4321 Fir St. Phone: (219)392-7230
East Chicago, IN 46312 Madeline E. Downen, Coord., Lib.Serv.
Founded: 1935. **Staff:** 1. **Subjects:** Medicine and allied health sciences. **Holdings:** 3447 volumes. **Subscriptions:** 154 journals and other serials. **Services:** Interlibrary loan; copying; library open to the public at librarian's discretion. **Computerized Information Services:** BRS Information Technologies, MEDLARS. **Networks/Consortia:** Member of Northwest Indiana Health Science Library Consortium. **Publications:** AV Software, annual update - free upon request. **Remarks:** FAX: (219)392-7184.

★14255★
St. Catherine's Hospital - Medical Library (Med)
3556 7th Ave. Phone: (414)656-3230
Kenosha, WI 53140 Pat Campbell, Asst.
Founded: 1962. **Staff:** Prof 1. **Subjects:** Medicine, family practice. **Holdings:** 1500 volumes; 300 videocassettes. **Subscriptions:** 120 journals and other serials. **Services:** Interlibrary loan; copying. **Computerized Information Services:** MEDLINE, DIALOG Information Services. **Networks/Consortia:** Member of Southeastern Wisconsin Health Science Library Consortium (SWHSL), National Network of Libraries of Medicine - Greater Midwest Region. **Remarks:** FAX: (414)656-3443.

★ 14256 ★
St. Charles Borromeo Seminary - Ryan Memorial Library (Rel-Phil)
1000 East Wynnewood Rd.   Phone: (215)667-3394
Overbrook, PA 19096-3012   Lorena Filosa Boylan, Dir. of Lib. Serv.
Founded: 1832. **Staff:** Prof 4; Other 6. **Subjects:** Theology, philosophy, patristics, scripture, church history. **Special Collections:** Ryan Library Archives; historical collections of American Catholic Historical Society of Philadelphia; Pre-1850 Book Collection (incunabula, 16th, 17th, and 18th century books in sacred sciences; 15,000 volumes). **Holdings:** 116,500 books and bound periodical volumes; 7800 AV programs and microforms; 567 paintings and prints. **Subscriptions:** 605 journals and other serials; 19 newspapers. **Services:** Interlibrary loan; copying; library open to the public with registration. **Automated Operations:** Computerized cataloging, acquisitions, and ILL. **Computerized Information Services:** OCLC, DIALOG Information Services; CD-ROMs (Religion Index, Philosopher's Index). Contact Person: Noel McFerran, Ref.Libn. **Networks/Consortia:** Member of PALINET, Tri-State College Library Cooperative (TCLC), Southeastern Pennsylvania Theological Library Association (SEPTLA). **Publications:** Acquisitions bibliography, monthly. **Special Catalogs:** Holdings of periodicals and newspapers (card); art collections (book). **Remarks:** FAX: (215)664-7913. **Staff:** Christine Schone, Cat.Libn.; Ruth Hughes, Rare Bk.Libn.

★ 14257 ★
St. Charles County Historical Society - Archives (Hist)
101 S. Main St.   Phone: (314)946-9828
St. Charles, MO 63301   Carol Wilkins, Archv.
Staff: Prof 1; Other 6. **Subjects:** St. Charles County and Missouri history; genealogy. **Special Collections:** Mrs. Edna McElhiney Olson's Collection (genealogy and local history; 24 VF drawers); St. Charles Banner-News collection of newspapers, 1870-1978 (140 reels of microfilm). **Holdings:** Figures not available for books; 12 VF drawers of court records; 7 VF drawers of miscellanea; 4 VF drawers of photographs; 161 reels of microfilm; deeds; cemetery records; school records. **Services:** Copying; archives open to the public on fee basis. **Special Indexes:** Index of cemetery, church, and land records for St. Charles County; card indexes to Mrs. Olson's Collection, court records, and genealogy.

★ 14258 ★
St. Charles Seminary - Library
Carthagena, OH 45822
Founded: 1861. **Subjects:** Scholastic philosophy, Catholic theology, hagiography. **Holdings:** 28,000 books; 6000 bound periodical volumes. **Remarks:** Currently inactive.

★ 14259 ★
St. Christopher's Episcopal Church - Library (Rel-Phil)
93 N. Kainalu Dr.
Box 456
Kailua, HI 96734   Phone: (808)262-8176
Staff: 3. **Subjects:** Religion. **Holdings:** 700 books; tapes; filmstrips. **Subscriptions:** 20 journals and other serials. **Services:** Library open to the public.

★ 14260 ★
St. Christopher's Hospital for Children - Margery H. Nelson Medical Library (Med)
3601 A St.   Phone: (215)427-5374
Philadelphia, PA 19134   Frances B. Pinnel, Med.Libn.
Staff: Prof 1; Other 1. **Subjects:** Pediatrics. **Holdings:** 3790 books; 2284 bound periodical volumes. **Subscriptions:** 150 journals and other serials. **Services:** Interlibrary loan; library open to parents and guardians of patients. **Networks/Consortia:** Member of Delaware Valley Information Consortium (DEVIC), BHSL. **Publications:** Literature List, monthly; Periodical List, annual. **Remarks:** FAX: (215)427-5598.

★ 14261 ★
St. Clair County Mental Health Service - Medical/Staff Library (Med)
1011 Military   Phone: (313)985-8900
Port Huron, MI 48060   John O'Dell
Founded: 1980. **Subjects:** Mental illness, developmental disabilities, mental health treatment. **Holdings:** 346 books; 199 videotapes. **Subscriptions:** 5 journals and other serials. **Services:** Library open to the public. **Remarks:** FAX: (313)985-7620.

★ 14262 ★
St. Claire Medical Center - Medical Library (Med)
222 Medical Circle   Phone: (606)784-6661
Morehead, KY 40351   Betty Ison, Med.Libn.
Founded: 1963. **Staff:** Prof 1. **Subjects:** Medicine, nursing, pharmacy, allied health sciences, health administration. **Holdings:** 2115 books; 910 bound periodical volumes; 300 videotapes; filmstrips; audiocassettes. **Subscriptions:** 160 journals and other serials; 12 newspapers. **Services:** Interlibrary loan; copying; library open to the public. **Computerized Information Services:** MEDLARS, BRS Information Technologies. Performs searches. **Networks/Consortia:** Member of Eastern Kentucky Health Science Information Network (EKHSIN), Kentucky Library Network, Inc. (KLN). **Remarks:** FAX: (606)784-2178.

★ 14263 ★
St. Clare Hospital - Medical Library (Med)
515 22nd Ave.   Phone: (608)328-0244
Monroe, WI 53566   Carol Hasse, Libn.
Founded: 1972. **Staff:** 1. **Subjects:** Health science. **Holdings:** 700 books. **Subscriptions:** 150 journals and other serials. **Services:** Interlibrary loan, copying, library open to the public for reference use only. **Computerized Information Services:** MEDLINE.

★ 14264 ★
St. Clare's Hospital & Health Center - Medical Library (Med)
415 W. 51st St.   Phone: (212)459-8221
New York, NY 10019   Mitchell A. Bogen, Med.Libn.
Founded: 1934. **Staff:** Prof 1; Other 1. **Subjects:** Medicine, surgery. **Holdings:** 1500 books; 6000 bound periodical volumes; tapes. **Subscriptions:** 81 journals and other serials. **Services:** Interlibrary loan; library not open to the public. **Networks/Consortia:** Member of Manhattan-Bronx Health Sciences Library Consortia.

★ 14265 ★
St. Clare's Mercy Hospital - Library (Med)
St. Clare Ave.   Phone: (709)778-3414
St. John's, NF, Canada A1C 5B8   Catherine Lawton, Libn.
Founded: 1974. **Staff:** 1. **Subjects:** Medicine, nursing, hospital administration, allied health sciences. **Holdings:** 500 books; 100 AV tapes. **Subscriptions:** 121 journals and other serials. **Services:** Interlibrary loan; copying; center open to visiting doctors for reference use. **Computerized Information Services:** CD-ROM (MEDLINE). **Remarks:** FAX: (709)738-0080.

★ 14266 ★
St. Clare's Mercy Hospital - School of Nursing Library (Med)
250 Waterford Bridge Rd.   Phone: (709)778-3577
St. John's, NF, Canada A1E 1E3   Dora M. Braffet, Instr.Mtls.Spec.Libn.
Founded: 1958. **Staff:** Prof 1; Other 4. **Subjects:** Nursing. **Holdings:** 3000 books; 236 AV programs. **Subscriptions:** 31 journals and other serials. **Services:** Interlibrary loan; copying; library open to the public with restrictions. **Automated Operations:** Computerized cataloging and acquisitions. **Special Catalogs:** AV Catalog. **Remarks:** FAX: (709)754-4160.

★ 14267 ★
St. Clares-Riverside Medical Center - American Self-Help Clearinghouse (Soc Sci)
Denville, NJ 07834   Phone: (201)625-7101
     Edward J. Madara, Dir.
Founded: 1981. **Staff:** Prof 8; Other 5. **Subjects:** Self-help organizations. **Special Collections:** Collection of how-to materials for starting and maintaining self-help groups. **Holdings:** Self-help literature; directories of state and national self-help groups; conference proceedings. **Services:** Library open to the public by appointment. **Computerized Information Services:** MASHnet (internal database); CompuServe Information Service (electronic mail service). **Publications:** The Self-Help Sourcebook, biennial. **Remarks:** Toll-free telephone number(s): (800)367-6274 (in New Jersey). FAX: (201)625-8848. Electronic mail address(es): 70275,1003 (CompuServe Information Service).

★14268★
St. Clares-Riverside Medical Center - Health Sciences Library (Med)
Pocono Rd.　　　　　　　　　Phone: (201)625-6547
Denville, NJ 07834　　　　　　Mildred E. Schaeffer, Libn.
Staff: 1. **Subjects:** Medicine, surgery, dentistry, mental health, allied health sciences. **Holdings:** 300 books; 300 unbound periodicals; microfiche. **Subscriptions:** 81 journals and other serials. **Services:** Interlibrary loan; library not open to the public. **Computerized Information Services:** MEDLARS; DOCLINE (electronic mail service). **Networks/Consortia:** Member of Cosmopolitan Biomedical Library Consortium (CBLC).

★14269★
St. Cloud Hospital - Health Sciences Library (Med)
1406 6th Ave., N.　　　　　　Phone: (612)251-2700
St. Cloud, MN 56301　　　　　Judith Heeter, Libn.
Staff: Prof 1. **Subjects:** Medicine, nursing, hospital management. **Holdings:** 1000 books; 800 bound periodical volumes; 120 videotapes; 25 16mm films; 50 audio cassettes; 20 AV programs. **Subscriptions:** 100 journals and other serials. **Services:** Interlibrary loan; library not open to the public. **Computerized Information Services:** MEDLARS. Performs searches on fee basis.

St. Cloud State University - Central Minnesota Historical Center
See: **Central Minnesota Historical Center** (3349)

St. Croix Collection
See: **Stillwater Public Library** (15797)

St. Cyril and St. Methodius National Library
See: **Bulgaria - Committee of Culture - St. Cyril and St. Methodius National Library** (2345)

★14270★
St. David Episcopal Church - Library (Rel-Phil)
Gales Ferry, CT 06335　　　　Phone: (203)464-6516
　　　　　　　　　　　　　　Charlotte S. Sanford
Staff: 1. **Subjects:** Religion, the Episcopal Church, the Bible. **Holdings:** 2700 books. **Services:** Library open to the public.

★14271★
St. David's United Church - Library (Rel-Phil)
3303 Capitol Hill Crescent, N.W.
Calgary, AB, Canada T2M 2R2　　Phone: (403)284-2276
Founded: 1968. **Subjects:** Religion, theology, Bible. **Holdings:** 480 books; 210 filmstrips and slides; 30 transparencies; 5 tapes. **Services:** Copying; library open to the public with restrictions.

★14272★
St. Deiniol's Residential - Library (Hist, Rel-Phil, Hum)
Hawarden　　　　　　　　　Phone: 244 532350
Deeside, Clwyd CH5 3DF, Wales　Peter J. Jagger, Rev.Dr.
Founded: 1896. **Staff:** Prof 2; Other 2. **Subjects:** 19th century studies, Gladstoniana, theology, history, social history, English literature, philosophy. **Special Collections:** Pre-1800 Collection; Glynne Library (16th-19th centuries); Benson Judaica Collection; French Spirituality Collection (17th-20th centuries); Bishop Moorman Franciscan Library; Glynne-Gladstone Manuscripts; Sir Stephen Glynne's Church Notes. **Holdings:** 200,000 books; 1000 bound periodical volumes; 250,000 archival items; 400 reels of microfilm. **Subscriptions:** 150 journals and other serials. **Services:** Interlibrary loan; copying; library open to resident users and to external users on annual subscription. **Publications:** Bibliographies of special collections and subjects within main collection. **Remarks:** FAX: 244 520643.

★14273★
St. Dominic-Jackson Memorial Hospital - Luther Manship Medical Library (Med)
969 Lakeland Drive　　　　　Phone: (601)982-0121
Jackson, MS 39216　　　　　Nyla Stevens, Libn.
Founded: 1973. **Staff:** Prof 1. **Subjects:** Medicine, nursing, mental health. **Holdings:** 1911 books; 439 bound periodical volumes. **Subscriptions:** 127 journals and other serials. **Services:** Interlibrary loan; library not open to the public. **Computerized Information Services:** MEDLARS. **Networks/Consortia:** Member of Central Mississippi Library Council, Central Mississippi Consortium of Medical Libraries.

★14274★
St. Elias Orthodox Church - Library (Rel-Phil)
408 E. 11th St.　　　　　　　Phone: (512)476-2314
Austin, TX 78701　　　　　　Rev. James D. Kenna
Founded: 1949. **Staff:** 1. **Subjects:** Orthodox theology, church history, liturgics. **Special Collections:** Greek and Arabic liturgical texts. **Holdings:** 750 books; 800 unbound periodicals. **Services:** Copying; library open to the public. **Staff:** David Stier.

★14275★
St. Elizabeth Community Health Center - Medical Library (Med)
555 S. 70th St.　　　　　　　Phone: (402)486-7306
Lincoln, NE 68510　　　　　　Beth Goble, Med.Libn.
Founded: 1970. **Staff:** Prof 1; Other 1. **Subjects:** Medicine, nursing. **Holdings:** 2000 books; 1400 bound periodical volumes; 500 AV programs; 2524 unbound journals; 12 file drawers of pamphlets. **Subscriptions:** 130 journals and other serials. **Services:** Interlibrary loan; copying; library open to the public with restrictions. **Computerized Information Services:** MEDLINE, BRS Information Technologies. Performs searches free of charge. **Networks/Consortia:** Member of Lincoln Health Science Library Group (LHSLG), National Network of Libraries of Medicine - Midcontinental Region. **Special Catalogs:** AV catalog.

★14276★
St. Elizabeth Hospital - Health Science Library (Med)
1506 S. Oneida St.　　　　　Phone: (414)738-2324
Appleton, WI 54915　　　　　Mary M. Bayorgeon, Dir., Lib.Serv.
Founded: 1973. **Staff:** Prof 1; Other 1. **Subjects:** Medicine, nursing, hospital administration. **Special Collections:** Consumer health collection. **Holdings:** 3000 books; 3875 bound periodical volumes; 1550 audiotapes; 630 videotapes. **Subscriptions:** 350 journals and other serials. **Services:** Interlibrary loan; copying; library open to the public with restrictions. **Computerized Information Services:** DIALOG Information Services, MEDLINE; CD-ROM (CINAHL). **Networks/Consortia:** Member of National Network of Libraries of Medicine - Greater Midwest Region, Fox Valley Library Council, Fox River Valley Area Library Consortium (FRVALC). **Remarks:** FAX: (414)738-0949.

★14277★
St. Elizabeth Hospital - Health Sciences Library (Med)
225 Williamson St.　　　　　Phone: (201)527-5371
Elizabeth, NJ 07207　　　　　Sally Holdorf, Libn.
Staff: Prof 1; Other 3. **Subjects:** Medicine, nursing, and allied health fields. **Holdings:** 1000 books; 1200 bound periodical volumes. **Subscriptions:** 117 journals and other serials. **Services:** Interlibrary loan; copying. **Computerized Information Services:** NLM. **Networks/Consortia:** Member of Cosmopolitan Biomedical Library Consortium (CBLC), Health Sciences Library Association of New Jersey (HSLANJ), BHSL.

★14278★
St. Elizabeth Hospital - Health Sciences Library (Med)
2830 Calder Ave.
Box 5405
Beaumont, TX 77702　　　　　Phone: (409)899-7189
　　　　　　　　　　　　　　Sue Martin, Libn.
Founded: 1958. **Staff:** Prof 1; Other 1. **Subjects:** Medicine, dentistry, allied health sciences. **Holdings:** 900 books; 5400 bound periodical volumes; AV programs. **Subscriptions:** 307 journals and other serials. **Services:** Interlibrary loan; copying; SDI. **Computerized Information Services:** NLM, DIALOG Information Services, BRS Information Technologies.

★14279★
St. Elizabeth Hospital Medical Center - Bannon Health Science Library (Med)
1501 Hartford St.
Box 7501
Lafayette, IN 47903-7501　　Ruth Pestalozzi Pape, Dir., Prof.Lib.Serv.
　　　　　　　　　　　　　　Phone: (317)423-6143
Founded: 1919. **Staff:** 2. **Subjects:** Medicine, health care management, allied subjects, computer applications. **Special Collections:** Bioethics. **Holdings:** 1600 books; 6200 bound periodical volumes; 700 audiocassettes; 350 videocassettes. **Subscriptions:** 300 journals and other serials. **Services:** Interlibrary loan; copying; faxing; library open to medical staff, hospital personnel, and health care students of formally affiliated programs. **Computerized Information Services:** BRS Information Technologies, MEDLARS, OCLC. **Networks/Consortia:** Member of National Network of Libraries of Medicine - Greater Midwest Region. **Publications:** Bibliography of Bioethics Material in this Library. **Remarks:** FAX: (317)742-5764. **Staff:** Gregory J. Rothenberger, Asst.Libn.

★14280★
St. Elizabeth Hospital Medical Center - Medical Library (Med)
1044 Belmont Ave.   Phone: (216)746-7211
Youngstown, OH 44501   Barbara G. Rosenthal, Med.Libn.
Founded: 1929. **Staff:** 5. **Subjects:** Medicine and related subjects. **Holdings:** 4305 books; 8814 bound periodical volumes; 720 reels of microfilm. **Subscriptions:** 305 journals and other serials. **Services:** Interlibrary loan; copying; library open to the public at librarian's discretion. **Computerized Information Services:** MEDLINE, DIALOG Information Services; Freenet Network (electronic mail service). **Publications:** Bibliographies. **Remarks:** Alternate telephone number(s): 746-2255. FAX: (216)744-5926.

★14281★
St. Elizabeth Hospital Medical Center - School of Nursing - Library (Med)
1044 Belmont Ave.   Phone: (216)746-7211
Youngstown, OH 44501   Doris L. Crawford, Lib./AV Mgr.
Founded: 1911. **Staff:** Prof 1; Other 2. **Subjects:** Nursing, health education, medicine, allied health. **Special Collections:** Historical Collection (nursing). **Holdings:** 9286 books; 2294 bound periodical volumes; 20 lateral file drawers of pamphlets; 10 drawers of microfiche; 1104 AV programs; 200 computer programs. **Subscriptions:** 350 journals and other serials. **Services:** Interlibrary loan; copying; SDI; library open to the public for reference use only. **Automated Operations:** Computerized cataloging. **Computerized Information Services:** DIALOG Information Services, MEDLINE; CD-ROM (CINAHL, HealthPLAN-CD). **Networks/Consortia:** Member of NEOUCOM Council Associated Hospital Librarians. **Publications:** Library News, bimonthly - to faculty, students, and hospital departments; Library Information: Guide Series - to faculty, students, and library users; bibliographies - to library users. **Special Catalogs:** Audiovisual catalog (card and book). **Special Indexes:** Subject Index to New Acquisitions (book and audiovisuals); Serials List (book); TIC/TOC Service. **Remarks:** FAX: (216)746-2255.

★14282★
St. Elizabeth Medical Center - Allnutt Health Sciences Library (Med)
20 Medical Village Dr., Suite No. 261   Phone: (606)344-2248
Edgewood, KY 41017   Donald R. Smith, Libn.
Founded: 1978. **Staff:** Prof 2. **Subjects:** Health sciences. **Holdings:** 2450 books; 4000 bound periodical volumes. **Subscriptions:** 200 journals and other serials; 5 newspapers. **Services:** Interlibrary loan; copying; library open to health professionals. **Computerized Information Services:** BRS Information Technologies. **Staff:** Donald R. Smith; Mary Ann Hausfeld.

★14283★
St. Elizabeth Medical Center - Health Sciences Library (Med)
601 Edwin Moses Blvd., W.   Phone: (513)229-6061
Dayton, OH 45408   Ann L. Lewis, Med.Libn.
Staff: 4. **Subjects:** Medicine, sports medicine, rehabilitation, physical medicine, family practice, gastroenterology. **Special Collections:** Archives of St. Elizabeth Medical Center. **Holdings:** 7239 books; 6752 bound periodical volumes; AV programs. **Subscriptions:** 450 journals and other serials. **Services:** Interlibrary loan; copying; SDI; library open to the public for reference use only. **Computerized Information Services:** MEDLINE, OCLC, BRS Information Technologies.

★14284★
St. Elizabeth Medical Center - Health Sciences Library (Med)
110 S. 9th Ave.   Phone: (509)575-5073
Yakima, WA 98902   Marilyn Jardine, Med.Libn.
Founded: 1969. **Staff:** Prof 1; Other 1. **Subjects:** Medicine, nursing, health sciences, hospital administration. **Holdings:** Figures not available. **Subscriptions:** 95 journals and other serials. **Services:** Interlibrary loan; copying; library open to the public. **Computerized Information Services:** MEDLARS, DIALOG Information Services; OnTyme Electronic Message Network Service, DOCLINE (electronic mail service). Performs searches on fee basis. **Networks/Consortia:** Member of National Network of Libraries of Medicine - Pacific Northwest Region. **Remarks:** FAX: (509)454-6127.

★14285★
St. Elizabeth Medical Center - St. Elizabeth Hospital School of Nursing - Library (Med)
1508 Tippecanoe St.   Phone: (317)423-6125
Lafayette, IN 47904   Lorraine Rund, Libn.
Staff: Prof 1. **Subjects:** Nursing, medicine, psychiatry. **Holdings:** 4000 books; 302 filmstrips; 6 16mm films; 50 charts; 300 videotapes. **Subscriptions:** 160 journals and other serials; 10 newspapers. **Services:** Interlibrary loan; copying; library open to the public. **Publications:** Annual report; bibliographies of various fields in nursing.

★14286★
St. Elizabeth's Hospital - Health Science Library (Med)
211 S. Third St.   Phone: (618)234-2120
Belleville, IL 62221   Michael A. Campese, Lib.Dir.
Staff: Prof 1; Other 2. **Subjects:** Medicine, nursing, hospital administration. **Special Collections:** Medical books, 1879-1890. **Holdings:** 2000 books; 1200 bound periodical volumes. **Subscriptions:** 323 journals and other serials. **Services:** Interlibrary loan; copying; library open to the public on a limited schedule. **Computerized Information Services:** MEDLARS. **Networks/Consortia:** Member of National Network of Libraries of Medicine - Greater Midwest Region, Kaskaskia Library System (KLS), Areawide Hospital Library Consortium of Southwestern Illinois (AHLC).

★14287★
St. Elizabeth's Hospital - Luken Health Sciences Library (Med)
1431 N. Claremont Ave.
Chicago, IL 60622   Phone: (312)278-2000
Founded: 1955. **Staff:** Prof 1; Other 1. **Subjects:** Medicine, nursing and allied health sciences. **Holdings:** 1500 books; 722 bound periodical volumes; 309 volumes of unbound medical journals; 160 cassette tapes; 81 filmstrips. **Subscriptions:** 101 journals and other serials. **Services:** Interlibrary loan; library not open to the public. **Networks/Consortia:** Member of Metropolitan Consortium of Chicago.

★14288★
St. Elizabeth's Hospital - Nursing School Library (Med)
2215 Genesee St.   Phone: (315)798-8209
Utica, NY 13501   Ann M. Kelly, Libn.
Staff: Prof 1; Other 2. **Subjects:** Nursing, medicine, sociology, psychology. **Holdings:** 4868 books; 711 bound periodical volumes; 9 VF drawers; 220 phonograph records; 209 videotapes; 293 AV programs. **Subscriptions:** 75 journals and other serials. **Services:** Interlibrary loan; copying; library open to the public for reference use only with permission from librarian. **Publications:** Library manual.

★14289★
St. Elizabeth's Hospital - School of Nursing - Library (Med)
159 Washington St.   Phone: (617)789-2304
Brighton, MA 02135   Robert L. Loud, Libn.
Staff: 1. **Subjects:** Nursing, medicine. **Holdings:** 2260 books; 1163 bound periodical volumes. **Subscriptions:** 89 journals and other serials. **Services:** Interlibrary loan; library not open to the public. **Networks/Consortia:** Member of Libraries and Information for Nursing Consortium (LINC).

★14290★
St. Elizabeth's Hospital - Stohlman Library (Med)
736 Cambridge St.   Phone: (617)789-2177
Brighton, MA 02135   Robin E. Braun, Dir.
Staff: Prof 1; Other 1. **Subjects:** Medicine. **Holdings:** 1500 books; 5135 bound periodical volumes. **Subscriptions:** 172 journals and other serials. **Services:** Interlibrary loan; copying; library open to the public with restrictions. **Computerized Information Services:** MEDLARS, BRS Information Technologies; MEDLINK (electronic mail service). **Networks/Consortia:** Member of Boston Biomedical Library Consortium, Massachusetts Health Sciences Libraries Network (MaHSLiN). **Remarks:** FAX: (617)789-2573.

St. Faith Episcopal Church - Audio-Visual Resource Library
See: **Audio-Visual Resource Library (1288)**

★ 14291 ★
St. Frances Cabrini Hospital - Medical Library (Med)
3330 Masonic Dr.   Phone: (318)487-1122
Alexandria, LA 71301   Carol Holloway, Act.Libn.
Founded: 1957. Staff: Prof 1; Other 1. Subjects: Medicine, nursing, and allied health sciences. Holdings: 3471 books and bound periodical volumes; 900 tapes; 157 unbound journals. Subscriptions: 60 journals and other serials. Services: Interlibrary loan; copying; SDI; library open to the public with restrictions. Computerized Information Services: AIDSLINE, AVLINE, CANCERLIT, CATLINE, CHEMLINE, DIRLINE, HEALTH, SDILINE, TOXLINE, TOXLINE65, TOXLIT, TOXLIT65, PDQ, MEDLINE. Remarks: FAX: (318)443-0927.

St. Francis Chapel Information Center & Free-Lending Library
See: St. Francis Monastery and Chapel (14310)

St. Francis Hospital
See: Miami Beach Community Hospital (10246)

★ 14292 ★
St. Francis Hospital - Health Science Library (Med)
North Rd.   Phone: (914)431-8132
Poughkeepsie, NY 12601   Linda Lee Paquin, Med.Libn.
Founded: 1983. Staff: Prof 1. Subjects: Internal medicine, surgery, health care administration. Holdings: 1200 books; 130 unbound journals. Subscriptions: 130 journals and other serials. Services: Interlibrary loan; copying; library open to the public. Computerized Information Services: BRS Information Technologies, NLM, MEDLINE. Networks/Consortia: Member of Southeastern New York Library Resources Council (SENYLRC), Health Information Libraries of Westchester (HILOW).

★ 14293 ★
St. Francis Hospital - Health Sciences Library (Med)
6161 S. Yale Ave.   Phone: (918)494-1210
Tulsa, OK 74316   Elizabeth Richards, Med.Libn.
Founded: 1966. Staff: Prof 1. Subjects: Health sciences, nursing, hospital management. Holdings: 2002 books; 4904 bound periodical volumes; 278 government documents. Subscriptions: 250 journals and other serials. Services: Interlibrary loan; library not open to the public. Computerized Information Services: CD-ROM. Remarks: FAX: (918)494-1893.

★ 14294 ★
St. Francis Hospital - Library/AV Center (Med)
3237 S. 16th St.   Phone: (414)647-5156
Milwaukee, WI 53215   Joy Shong, Dir.
Founded: 1974. Staff: 4. Subjects: Medicine, nursing, paramedicine. Special Collections: Materials relating to and serving patient education. Holdings: 2000 books; 3200 bound periodical volumes; 1000 AV programs. Subscriptions: 245 journals and other serials. Services: Interlibrary loan; copying; SDI; center open to the public. Automated Operations: Computerized serials. Computerized Information Services: MEDLINE, BRS Information Technologies. Networks/Consortia: Member of Southeastern Wisconsin Health Science Library Consortium (SWHSL), Library Council of Metropolitan Milwaukee, Inc. (LCOMM). Remarks: FAX: (414)647-5195. Formerly: Its Health Science Learning Center.

★ 14295 ★
St. Francis Hospital - Medical Library (Med)
601 E. Micheltorena   Phone: (805)962-7661
Santa Barbara, CA 93103   Marilyn Shearer, Dir.
Staff: 2. Subjects: Medicine and medical specialties. Holdings: 1020 books; 469 bound periodical volumes; videotapes; cassettes. Subscriptions: 38 journals and other serials. Services: Library not open to the public.

★ 14296 ★
St. Francis Hospital - Medical Library (Med)
250 W. 63rd St.   Phone: (305)868-5000
Miami Beach, FL 33141   Wilma S. Grover, Libn.
Founded: 1927. Staff: Prof 1. Subjects: Medicine and allied health sciences. Holdings: 700 books; 2750 bound periodical volumes; 856 audiotapes; 12 phonograph records; 576 slides; videotapes. Subscriptions: 100 journals and other serials. Services: Interlibrary loan; library not open to the public; bioethics collection and services open to Bioethics Institute members. Computerized Information Services: BRS Information Technologies. Networks/Consortia: Member of National Network of Libraries of Medicine - Southeastern/Atlantic Region, Miami Health Sciences Library Consortium (MHSLC).

★ 14297 ★
St. Francis Hospital - Medical Library (Med)
2230 Liliha St.   Phone: (808)547-6481
Honolulu, HI 96817   Julie J. Sirois, Libn.
Founded: 1955. Staff: Prof 1; Other 2. Subjects: Nursing, medicine, hospital administration, sociology, psychology, pre-clinical sciences. Holdings: 5000 books; 1600 bound periodical volumes; 500 slides and tapes; 6 VF drawers of pamphlets. Subscriptions: 394 journals and other serials. Services: Interlibrary loan; copying; SDI; library open to the public. Computerized Information Services: MEDLARS. Performs searches on fee basis. Networks/Consortia: Member of National Network of Libraries of Medicine - Pacific Southwest Region. Publications: Brochure, annual - to library users; Library Acquisition List, monthly - for internal distribution only. Remarks: FAX: (808)545-5818.

★ 14298 ★
St. Francis Hospital - Medical Library (Med)
100 Port Washington Blvd.   Phone: (516)562-6673
Roslyn, NY 11576   Judith Weinstein, Med.Libn.
Staff: Prof 1; Other 1. Subjects: Cardiology, pulmonary diseases, biomedical sciences, hospitals, management. Special Collections: Thoracic and cardiovascular surgery. Holdings: 2000 books; 1000 bound periodical volumes; 200 audio cassettes; pamphlets. Subscriptions: 70 journals and other serials. Services: Interlibrary loan; library not open to the public. Computerized Information Services: MEDLINE, BRS Information Technologies; DOCLINE (electronic mail service). Networks/Consortia: Member of Medical & Scientific Libraries of Long Island (MEDLI), BHSL. Publications: Semi-annual acquisitions list. Remarks: FAX: (516)562-6695.

★ 14299 ★
St. Francis Hospital - School of Nursing Library (Med)
319 Ridge Ave.   Phone: (708)492-6268
Evanston, IL 60202   Patricia Gibson, Libn.
Staff: Prof 1; Other 1. Subjects: Medicine, nursing, allied health sciences. Holdings: 3000 books; 420 bound periodical volumes; 6 VF drawers of clippings and pamphlets; 234 filmstrip programs; 160 film loops; 60 audio cassettes; 150 video cassettes; 6 16mm films. Subscriptions: 60 journals and other serials. Services: Interlibrary loan; copying; library open to medical and nursing personnel. Networks/Consortia: Member of Metropolitan Consortium of Chicago, North Suburban Library System (NSLS).

★ 14300 ★
St. Francis Hospital, Inc. - Medical Library (Med)
7th & Clayton Sts.   Phone: (302)421-4834
Wilmington, DE 19805   Marga Hirsch, Libn.
Founded: 1936. Staff: Prof 1; Other 1. Subjects: Medicine, nursing. Holdings: 1400 books; 123 bound periodical volumes; 12 VF drawers of reprints, original articles, ephemera. Subscriptions: 150 journals and other serials. Services: Interlibrary loan. Computerized Information Services: MEDLARS. Networks/Consortia: Member of Wilmington Area Biomedical Library Consortium (WABLC). Remarks: Alternate telephone number(s): 421-4835. FAX: (302)421-4167. Staff: Bridget Scheing, Asst.Libn.

★ 14301 ★
St. Francis Hospital and Medical Center - School of Nursing Library
338 Asylum St.
Hartford, CT 06103
Defunct. Holdings absorbed by its Wilson C. Jainsen Library.

★ 14302 ★
St. Francis Hospital and Medical Center - Wilson C. Jainsen Library (Med)
114 Woodland St.   Phone: (203)548-4746
Hartford, CT 06105   Ruth Carroll, Dir. of Libs.
Staff: Prof 6; Other 9. Subjects: Medicine, nursing, management, psychiatry, psychology. Holdings: 20,000 books; 450 periodical titles on microfilm; 1800 AV programs. Subscriptions: 850 journals and other serials. Services: Interlibrary loan; copying; SDI; library open to the public. Automated Operations: Computerized ILL (DOCLINE). Computerized Information Services: BRS Information Technologies, NLM, DIALOG Information Services. Networks/Consortia: Member of Connecticut Association of Health Science Libraries (CAHSL), North Atlantic Health Science Libraries (NAHSL). Publications: Library Notes. Remarks: FAX: (203)548-4947. Staff: Carolyn Wilcox, Asst.Dir.; Teal Friedmann, Clin.Libn.; Tania Wilson, Clin.Libn.; Mark Gentry, Sys.Coord.; Florence Hidalgo, Clin.Libn.

★ 14303 ★
St. Francis Medical Center - Community Health Science Library (Med)
415 Oak St.
Breckenridge, MN 56520   Geralyn Matejcek
Founded: 1975. **Staff:** Prof 1; Other 1. **Subjects:** Medicine, nursing, and allied health sciences. **Holdings:** 310 books; 4 VF drawers of pamphlets; 23 AV programs. **Subscriptions:** 88 journals and other serials. **Services:** Interlibrary loan; SDI; library open to health care professionals. **Networks/Consortia:** Member of Valley Medical Network (VMN), National Network of Libraries of Medicine - Greater Midwest Region.

★ 14304 ★
St. Francis Medical Center - Health Sciences Library (Med)
601 Hamilton Ave.   Phone: (609)599-5068
Trenton, NJ 08629   Donna Barlow, Dir.
Founded: 1930. **Staff:** Prof 2; Other 1. **Subjects:** Medicine, nursing, allied health sciences. **Holdings:** 5000 books. **Subscriptions:** 300 journals and other serials. **Services:** Interlibrary loan; SDI; library open to the public. **Computerized Information Services:** BRS Information Technologies, NLM; MESSAGES (electronic mail service). Performs searches on fee basis. **Networks/Consortia:** Member of Central Jersey Health Science Libraries Association (CJHSLA), Health Sciences Library Association of New Jersey (HSLANJ). **Publications:** Library Bulletin, quarterly. **Remarks:** FAX: (609)599-5773. **Staff:** Eileen Monroe, Tech.Info.Spec.

★ 14305 ★
St. Francis Medical Center - Health Sciences Library (Med)
615 S. 10th St.   Phone: (608)785-0940
La Crosse, WI 54601   Sr. Louise Therese Lotze, Lib.Supv.
Founded: 1972. **Staff:** Prof 1. **Subjects:** Medicine, dentistry, nursing, allied health sciences. **Special Collections:** History of medicine. **Holdings:** 3500 books; 5400 bound periodical volumes; 12 VF drawers of clippings and articles. **Subscriptions:** 300 journals and other serials. **Services:** Interlibrary loan; library open to the public. **Computerized Information Services:** MEDLINE. **Publications:** Library Bulletin, quarterly - for internal distribution only.

★ 14306 ★
St. Francis Medical Center - Medical Library (Med)
530 N.E. Glen Oak Ave.   Phone: (309)655-2210
Peoria, IL 61637   Carol Galganski, Med.Libn.
Founded: 1942. **Staff:** Prof 2; Other 4. **Subjects:** Surgery, internal medicine, neurology, orthopedics, family practice, pediatrics. **Holdings:** 3169 books; 8833 bound periodical volumes; 133 AV units; 550 videocassettes. **Subscriptions:** 541 journals and other serials. **Services:** Interlibrary loan; copying. **Computerized Information Services:** MEDLINE, DIALOG Information Services, BRS Information Technologies. **Networks/Consortia:** Member of Heart of Illinois Library Consortium (HILC), National Network of Libraries of Medicine - Greater Midwest Region. **Publications:** Newsletter, monthly; acquisitions list, monthly. **Remarks:** FAX: (309)655-6997.

★ 14307 ★
St. Francis Medical Center - Medical Library (Med)
211 St. Francis Dr.   Phone: (314)339-6859
Cape Girardeau, MO 63701   Kilja Israel, Libn.
Founded: 1950. **Staff:** Prof 1; Other 2. **Subjects:** Medicine, nursing, health care administration. **Holdings:** 1000 books; 325 bound periodical volumes; 85 volumes on microfilm. **Subscriptions:** 30 journals and other serials; 3 newspapers. **Services:** Interlibrary loan; copying; library open to medical, nursing, and allied health care personnel only. **Computerized Information Services:** NLM, MEDLARS. **Networks/Consortia:** Member of National Network of Libraries of Medicine - Midcontinental Region. **Remarks:** FAX: (314)339-6920.

★ 14308 ★
St. Francis Medical Center - Mother Macaria Health Science Library (Med)
3630 E. Imperial Hwy.   Phone: (213)603-6045
Lynwood, CA 90262   Eva Kratz, Dir. of Lib.Serv.
Founded: 1971. **Staff:** Prof 1; Other 1. **Subjects:** Medicine, nursing, hospital administration, paramedical sciences. **Holdings:** 3000 books; 4000 bound periodical volumes; 120 other cataloged items; 800 audiotapes; 90 boxes of peripheral material; 175 archival materials; 48 videotapes. **Subscriptions:** 300 journals and other serials. **Services:** Interlibrary loan; copying; SDI; library open to health professionals. **Computerized Information Services:** Online systems. **Publications:** Annual report; Monthly Acquisitions List.

★ 14309 ★
St. Francis Memorial Hospital - Walter F. Schaller Memorial Library (Med)
Box 7726   Phone: (415)202-6320
San Francisco, CA 94120   Maryann Zaremska, Dir., Lib.Serv.
Staff: Prof 1; Other 1. **Subjects:** Medicine, nursing. **Special Collections:** Plastic and reconstructive surgery; burns. **Holdings:** 6300 volumes; 650 audiotapes. **Subscriptions:** 145 journals and other serials and newspapers. **Services:** Interlibrary loan; SDI; library open to affiliated personnel only. **Automated Operations:** Computerized ILL (DOCLINE). **Computerized Information Services:** MEDLARS, BRS Information Technologies, DIALOG Information Services; OnTyme Electronic Message Network Service (electronic mail service). **Networks/Consortia:** Member of San Francisco Biomedical Library Network, National Network of Libraries of Medicine - Pacific Southwest Region. **Remarks:** FAX: (415)202-6323. Electronic mail address(es): STFMH (OnTyme Electronic Message Network Service).

★ 14310 ★
St. Francis Monastery and Chapel - St. Francis Chapel Information Center & Free-Lending Library (Rel-Phil)
20 Page St.   Phone: (401)331-6510
Providence, RI 02903   Fr. John Bosco Valente, O.F.M. Libn.
Founded: 1959. **Staff:** Prof 2; Other 25. **Subjects:** Religion. **Special Collections:** Franciscana. **Holdings:** 12,000 books; pamphlets; picture files. **Subscriptions:** 20 journals and other serials. **Services:** Interlibrary loan; copying; library open to the public. **Staff:** Regina Cross.

★ 14311 ★
St. Francis Regional Medical Center - Marcus Health Education Center (Med)
929 N. St. Francis   Phone: (316)268-6080
Wichita, KS 67214   Betty B. Wood, Libn.
Founded: 1988. **Subjects:** Patient education, consumer education, wellness, prevention. **Holdings:** 190 books; pamphlet collection; videotapes. **Subscriptions:** 5 journals and other serials. **Services:** Copying; library open to the public. **Computerized Information Services:** MEDLARS, BRS Information Technologies, DIALOG Information Services. Performs searches on fee basis. **Remarks:** FAX: (316)268-8694. **Staff:** Carolyn Herl, Patient Educ.

★ 14312 ★
St. Francis Regional Medical Center - Professional Library (Med)
929 N. St. Francis   Phone: (316)268-5979
Wichita, KS 67214   Betty B. Wood, Libn.
Founded: 1945. **Staff:** Prof 2; Other 3. **Subjects:** Medicine, nursing, surgery, orthopedics, management. **Holdings:** 6000 books; 10,000 bound periodical volumes. **Subscriptions:** 550 journals and other serials. **Services:** Interlibrary loan; copying. **Automated Operations:** Computerized ILL (DOCLINE). **Computerized Information Services:** MEDLINE, BRS Information Technologies, DIALOG Information Services, OCLC. **Publications:** Journal Holdings, annual - to hospital staff and local special libraries. **Remarks:** FAX: (316)268-8694. **Staff:** Rosemary Mattox.

★ 14313 ★
St. Francis-St. George Hospital - Health Sciences Library (Med)
3131 Queen City Ave.   Phone: (513)389-5118
Cincinnati, OH 45238   Carol Mayor, Libn.
Staff: Prof 1. **Subjects:** Medicine, nursing, hospital administration. **Holdings:** 830 books; 365 periodicals. **Subscriptions:** 143 journals and other serials. **Services:** Interlibrary loan; copying; library open to the public with special permission. **Computerized Information Services:** Online systems.

★ 14314 ★
St. Francis Seminary - Salzmann Library (Rel-Phil)
3257 S. Lake Dr.   Phone: (414)747-6477
St. Francis, WI 53235   Colette Zirbes, O.S.F., Lib.Dir.
Founded: 1908. **Staff:** Prof 3. **Subjects:** Theology, church history, canon law, scripture, philosophy, patristics and related subjects. **Special Collections:** Wisconsin Catholic Church History, hagiology, liturgy (2000 items); Catholic Americana. **Holdings:** 70,000 books; 4000 bound periodical volumes; 1380 dissertations; 10 VF drawers of pamphlets, documents; 350 reels of microfilm; 2800 AV programs. **Subscriptions:** 366 journals and other serials; 16 newspapers. **Services:** Interlibrary loan; copying; library open to the public. **Automated Operations:** Computerized cataloging. **Computerized Information Services:** DIALOG Information Services; CD-ROMs. **Networks/Consortia:** Member of Wisconsin Interlibrary Services (WILS). **Remarks:** Alternate telephone number(s): 747-6479. FAX: (414)747-6442. **Staff:** Colleen Deignan Koll, Assoc.Libn.

★ 14315 ★
St. Francis of the Woods - St. Francis Library (Rel-Phil)
P.O. Box 400   Phone: (405)466-3774
Coyle, OK 73027-0400   Kay E. Adair, Lib.Mgr.
Founded: 1983. Staff: 2. Subjects: Eastern Orthodox theology, patristics, Biblical theology, liturgics, Byzantine music, philosophy, psychology, homiletics, Roman Catholic theology, Anglican theology. Special Collections: Monumentae Musicae Byzantinae (11th-17th century Byzantine music manuscripts on microfilm; 100); Carl G. Jung; sustainable agriculture; St. Francis of Asissi (books; journals). Holdings: 18,000 books; 5000 bound periodical volumes; 300 reels of microfilm; 3000 unbound periodicals; 1000 leaflets, pamphlets; 500 phonograph recordings. Subscriptions: 12 journals and other serials. Services: Library open to the public with restrictions. Staff: Diane Lamecker, Libn.

★ 14316 ★
St. Francis Xavier University - Angus L. MacDonald Library - Special Collections (Area-Ethnic)
Antigonish, NS, Canada B2G 1C0   Phone: (902)867-2267
                                             Maureen Williams, Cur.
Founded: 1964. Staff: Prof 7; Other 33. Subjects: Celtic studies. Holdings: Celtic Collection (includes writings in Gaelic); 6150 books; pamphlets; family trees; private correspondence; Scottish works. Subscriptions: 25 journals and other serials. Services: Copying; collections open to alumni and open to the public at librarian's discretion. Automated Operations: Computerized cataloging. Computerized Information Services: DIALOG Information Services; Envoy 100 (electronic mail service). Remarks: FAX: (902)867-5153. Electronic mail address(es): ILL.NSAS (Envoy 100). Staff: Lillian Beltaos, Univ.Libn.; Susan Cameron, Per.; Rita Campbell, Comp.Serv.; Barb Phillips, Ref.

★ 14317 ★
St. Francis Xavier University - Coady International Institute - Marie Michael Library (Bus-Fin, Educ)
Antigonish, NS, Canada B2G 1C0   Phone: (902)867-3964
                                             Sue Adams, Libn.
Founded: 1974. Staff: Prof 1. Subjects: Cooperatives, community development, adult education, health education, labor economics, appropriate technology, management, women in development, small business. Holdings: 4700 volumes; 1600 microfiche; 110 videotapes; seminar reports. Subscriptions: 55 journals and other serials; 5 newspapers. Services: Interlibrary loan; library open to the public. Publications: Seminar reports; Coady Newsletter. Remarks: FAX: (902)867-5153.

★ 14318 ★
St. Gabriel's Hospital - Library (Med)
815 S.E. 2nd St.   Phone: (612)632-5441
Little Falls, MN 56345   Peggy Martin, Dir., Educ.
Founded: 1942. Staff: Prof 1. Subjects: Nursing, medicine, science. Holdings: Figures not available. Services: Interlibrary loan; copying; library open to the public at librarian's discretion.

★ 14319 ★
St. Gallen Graduate School of Economics, Law, Business, and Public Administration - Swiss Research Institute of Small Business - Library (Bus-Fin)
Dufourstrasse 48   Phone: (071)30 23 30
CH-9000 St. Gallen, Switzerland   Mrs. M. Habersaat, Libn.
Subjects: Small and medium-sized businesses. Holdings: 12,000 volumes. Also Known As: Schweizerisches Institut fuer Gewerbliche Wirtschaft.

St. George Hospital
See: St. Francis-St. George Hospital (14313)

★ 14320 ★
St. George's Episcopal Mission - Library (Rel-Phil)
First & Arizona Sts.
Box V
Holbrook, AZ 86025   Phone: (602)524-2361
                                       Rev. Allen P. Rothlisberg, Libn.
Founded: 1975. Staff: Prof 1. Subjects: Theology. Special Collections: Clyde Smallwood Theology Collection. Holdings: 1000 books. Services: Interlibrary loan; copying; library open to the public. Networks/Consortia: Member of Channelled Arizona Information Network (CHAIN).

St. Helena Public Library - Napa Valley Wine Library Association
See: Napa Valley Wine Library Association (10973)

★ 14321 ★
St. Herman's Theological Seminary - St. Innocent Veniaminov Research Institute - Library (Rel-Phil, Area-Ethnic)
414 Mission Rd.   Phone: (907)486-3524
Kodiak, AK 99615   Jeffrey MacDonald, Act.Dir.
Subjects: Alaskan history, Native American culture, Alaskan Church History, Russian and Siberian studies. Special Collections: Archives of the Russian Orthodox Diocese of Alaska, 1823-1940 (10 cubic meters); Ilvani File (tapes of interviews with Kodiak senior citizens). Holdings: 100 cassette tapes; 10,000 ethnographic photographs. Services: Copying; institute open to the public by appointment.

St. Innocent Veniaminov Research Institute
See: St. Herman's Theological Seminary - St. Innocent Veniaminov Research Institute - Library (14321)

★ 14322 ★
St. James Community Hospital - Health Sciences Library (Med)
400 S. Clark   Phone: (406)782-8361
Butte, MT 59702   Carole Ann Clark, Med.Libn.
Founded: 1981. Staff: Prof 1. Subjects: Oncology, nursing, medicine, ethics, pediatrics, obstetrics, gynecology. Holdings: 750 books; 600 bound periodical volumes; 400 video cassettes. Subscriptions: 159 journals and other serials. Services: Interlibrary loan; copying; library open to the public. Computerized Information Services: MEDLINE; OnTyme Electronic Message Network Service (electronic mail service). Publications: Monthly Report - for internal distribution only. Special Catalogs: Audiovisual Catalog. Special Indexes: Health Sciences Serial List.

★ 14323 ★
St. James Hospital - Medical Library (Med)
610 E. Water St.   Phone: (815)842-2828
Pontiac, IL 61764   Patty Wolf, Lib.Ck.
Founded: 1978. Staff: 1. Subjects: Medicine and allied health sciences. Holdings: 120 volumes; 16 video cassettes; 9 videotapes. Subscriptions: 21 journals and other serials. Services: Interlibrary loan; library not open to the public. Networks/Consortia: Member of National Network of Libraries of Medicine - Greater Midwest Region, Heart of Illinois Library Consortium (HILC). Remarks: FAX: (815)842-2423.

★ 14324 ★
St. James Hospital and Health Centers - Dr. Hugo Long Library (Med)
Chicago Rd. at Lincoln Hwy.   Phone: (708)756-1000
Chicago Heights, IL 60411   Margaret A. Lindstrand, Libn.
Founded: 1956. Staff: 1. Subjects: Medicine and related subjects. Holdings: 800 books; 800 bound periodical volumes. Subscriptions: 61 journals and other serials. Services: Interlibrary loan; library open to the public with restrictions. Networks/Consortia: Member of Chicago and South Consortium. Formerly: St. James Hospital and Medical Centers.

★ 14325 ★
St. James Mercy Hospital - Medical & School of Nursing Library (Med)
440 Monroe Ave.   Phone: (607)324-0841
Hornell, NY 14843   Brian Smith, Libn.
Staff: Prof 1. Subjects: Nursing. Holdings: 3500 books; 475 bound periodical volumes; 300 AV programs. Subscriptions: 65 journals and other serials. Services: Interlibrary loan; copying; SDI; library open to the public. Automated Operations: Computerized acquisitions and serials. Computerized Information Services: MEDLARS, OCLC; DOCLINE (electronic mail service). Performs searches on fee basis. Networks/Consortia: Member of South Central Research Library Council (SCRLC). Remarks: FAX: (607)324-5122.

★ 14326 ★
Saint Jerome Hospital - Medical Library (Med)
16 Bank St.   Phone: (716)343-3131
Batavia, NY 14020   Eleanor Randall, Libn.
Staff: 1. Subjects: Medicine, nursing, and allied health sciences. Holdings: Figures not available. Services: Library not open to the public. Computerized Information Services: MEDLARS.

★ 14327 ★
St. John Hospital - Macomb Center - Medical Library (Med)
26755 Ballard Rd.   Phone: (313)465-5501
Mt. Clemens, MI 48045   Deborah R. Cicchini, Libn.
Subjects: Podiatry, orthopedics, physical and emergency medicine, neurotrauma, alcoholism. **Holdings:** 427 books; 879 bound periodical volumes. **Subscriptions:** 104 journals and other serials. **Services:** Interlibrary loan; copying; library open to the public for reference use only. **Computerized Information Services:** MEDLARS. **Networks/Consortia:** Member of Macomb Region of Cooperation, Michigan Library Consortium (MLC), Michigan Health Sciences Libraries Association (MHSLA). **Remarks:** FAX: (313)465-5510.

★ 14328 ★
St. John Hospital - Medical Library (Med)
22101 Moross Rd.   Phone: (313)343-3733
Detroit, MI 48236   Ellen E. O'Donnell, Dir.
Founded: 1952. **Staff:** Prof 2; Other 3. **Subjects:** Medicine, nursing, allied health sciences, health care administration and management. **Holdings:** 5000 books; 5900 bound periodical volumes; 600 AV programs; 10 VF drawers of pamphlets, documents; 7 series of medical audiotapes; 245 journal titles on microfiche. **Subscriptions:** 425 journals and other serials. **Services:** Interlibrary loan; copying; library open to the public with permission of the director. **Automated Operations:** Computerized cataloging, serials, and circulation. **Computerized Information Services:** MEDLINE, DIALOG Information Services, BRS Information Technologies. **Remarks:** FAX: (313)343-7598. **Staff:** Barbara Burson, Ref.Libn.

★ 14329 ★
St. John Medical Center - Health Sciences Library (Med)
1923 S. Utica   Phone: (918)744-2970
Tulsa, OK 74104   James M. Donovan, Libn.
Founded: 1946. **Staff:** Prof 1; Other 1. **Subjects:** Medicine, nursing, and allied health sciences, management. **Special Collections:** Catholic bioethics. **Holdings:** 3200 books; 8000 bound periodical volumes; Audio-Digest tapes. **Subscriptions:** 160 journals and other serials. **Services:** Interlibrary loan; copying; library open to the public by appointment. **Computerized Information Services:** MEDLINE, miniMEDLINE. **Networks/Consortia:** Member of National Network of Libraries of Medicine - South Central Region, Tulsa Area Library Cooperative (TALC).

★ 14330 ★
Saint John Regional Hospital - Dr. Carl R. Trask Health Sciences Library (Med)
Box 2100   Phone: (506)648-6763
Saint John, NB, Canada E2L 4L2   Anne Kilfoil, Mgr.
Staff: Prof 1; Other 2. **Subjects:** Medicine, nursing, and allied health sciences. **Holdings:** 6000 books; 300 bound periodical volumes; 1000 AV items. **Subscriptions:** 402 journals and other serials. **Services:** Interlibrary loan; copying; library open to health professionals in the community. **Computerized Information Services:** MEDLINE, DIALOG Information Services, CAN/OLE; Envoy 100, DATAPAC (electronic mail services). **Remarks:** Electronic mail address(es): SJRH.LIB (Envoy 100).

St. John del Rey Mining Company Archives
See: **University of Texas at Austin - Benson Latin American Collection** (19380)

St. John Seminary - Library
See: **Assumption - St. John Seminary - Library** (1175)

★ 14331 ★
St. John United Church of Christ - Library (Rel-Phil)
307 W. Clay St.   Phone: (618)344-2526
Collinsville, IL 62234   Shere Pinter, Libn.
Founded: 1959. **Staff:** Prof 1; Other 7. **Subjects:** Bible, life and teachings of Jesus, prayer and devotions, faith and theology, religions, worship and music. **Holdings:** 7075 books; 35 phonograph records; 35 cassettes; 6 videotapes.

★ 14332 ★
St. John Vianney College Seminary - Mary Louise Maytag Memorial Library (Rel-Phil)
2900 S.W. 87th Ave.   Phone: (305)223-4561
Miami, FL 33165   Maria M. Rodriguez, Dir.
Founded: 1960. **Staff:** Prof 1; Other 1. **Subjects:** Religion, philosophy, psychology. **Special Collections:** Paintings by Jehan Georges Vibert (17). **Holdings:** 48,336 books; 4086 bound periodical volumes. **Subscriptions:** 155 journals and other serials; 11 newspapers. **Services:** Copying; library open to the public. **Publications:** Library handbook (available in English and Spanish). **Special Catalogs:** Periodical directory (booklet); AV catalog.

★ 14333 ★
St. John and West Shore Hospital - Media Center (Med)
29000 Center Ridge Rd.   Phone: (216)835-6000
Westlake, OH 44145   Jennifer Jung Gallant, Dir.
Founded: 1981. **Staff:** Prof 1. Other 2. **Subjects:** Medicine, nursing, allied health sciences. **Special Collections:** Osteopathic historical collections (35 items). **Holdings:** 2300 books; 2 drawers of pamphlets. **Subscriptions:** 130 journals and other serials. **Services:** Interlibrary loan; copying; center open to the public with restrictions. **Computerized Information Services:** MEDLARS, DIALOG Information Services. **Remarks:** Alternate telephone number(s): 835-6020. FAX: (216)835-6115.

★ 14334 ★
St. John's Abbey and University - Hill Monastic Manuscript Library - Bush Center (Rel-Phil, Hist)
Collegeville, MN 56321   Phone: (612)363-3514
      Dr. Julian G. Plante, Exec.Dir.
Founded: 1965. **Staff:** Prof 9; Other 1. **Subjects:** Medieval theology, science, literature, philosophy, medicine, church history, codicology, papyrology, monasticism, paleography, calligraphy, art, liturgy. **Special Collections:** Pre-1600 manuscripts of 76 Austrian libraries; manuscripts from Spain, Ethiopia, Malta, England, Germany, Portugal, Italy, and Hungary (75,000 total manuscript books); 130,000 papyri totalling 23 million pages of documentation (microfilm). **Services:** Copying; research assistance; center open to the public. **Computerized Information Services:** InterNet, BITNET (electronic mail services). **Publications:** Progress Reports; Festschrift. **Special Catalogs:** Checklists of manuscripts, occasional; Descriptive Inventories of Manuscripts, occasional. **Remarks:** FAX: (612)363-2504. Electronic mail address(es): JPLANTE%55862@MSUS1.MSUS.EDU (InterNet); JPLANTE@CSBSJU (BITNET). **Staff:** Dr. Getatchew Haile, Mss.Cat.; Fr. Aelred Tegels, O.S.B., Field Dir.; Dr. Diane Warne Anderson, Mss.Cat.; Dr. Gregory Sebastian, O.S. B., Mss.Cat.

St. John's College
See: **University of Manitoba** (18793)

★ 14335 ★
St. John's and District Health Unit - Public Health Services - Library (Med)
Forest Rd.
P.O. Box 8700   Phone: (709)729-3440
St. John's, NF, Canada A1B 4J6   Linda Carter, Hea.Educ.
Founded: 1985. **Subjects:** Health. **Holdings:** 500 books. **Subscriptions:** 30 journals and other serials. **Services:** Library not open to the public. **Remarks:** FAX: (709)729-2165. **Formerly:** Newfoundland Department of Health - Public Health Nursing Division.

St. John's Episcopal Hospital
See: **Episcopal Health Services, Inc.** (5387)

St. John's Episcopal Hospital
See: **Interfaith Medical Center** (8040)

St. John's Episcopal Hospital (South Shore Division)
See: **Episcopal Health Services of Long Island - St. John's Episcopal Hospital (South Shore Division)** (5388)

★ 14336 ★
St. John's Health Care Corporation - Health Sciences Library (Med)
2015 Jackson St.   Phone: (317)646-8262
Anderson, IN 46016   Scott S. Loman, Hea.Sci.Libn.
Staff: Prof 1. **Subjects:** Medicine, nursing, allied health sciences, health administration, marketing. **Holdings:** 2000 books; 4000 bound periodical volumes; 150 audio cassettes; 400 video cassettes. **Subscriptions:** 200 journals and other serials; 7 newspapers. **Services:** Interlibrary loan; copying; SDI; library open to the public at librarian's discretion. **Computerized Information Services:** BRS Information Technologies. Performs searches on fee basis. **Networks/Consortia:** Member of National Network of Libraries of Medicine - Greater Midwest Region. **Remarks:** FAX: (317)646-8264.

★ 14337 ★
St. John's Hospital - Health Science Library (Med)
800 E. Carpenter   Phone: (217)544-6464
Springfield, IL 62769   Kathryn Wrigley, Dir.
Founded: 1931. **Staff:** Prof 2; Other 2. **Subjects:** Cardiovascular system, surgery, pediatrics, emergency medicine, nursing, pathology, psychiatry. **Holdings:** 5400 books; 555 AV programs; pamphlets. **Subscriptions:** 367 journals and other serials. **Services:** Interlibrary loan; copying; SDI; library open to the public for reference use only on request. **Computerized Information Services:** NLM, DIALOG Information Services, OCLC; CD-ROM. **Networks/Consortia:** Member of Capital Area Consortium (CAC), ILLINET, National Network of Libraries of Medicine - Greater Midwest Region. **Publications:** Libri (acquisitions list). **Special Catalogs:** Periodical holdings; media holdings. **Remarks:** FAX: (217)525-2895. **Staff:** Roger Swartzbaugh, Ref.Libn.

★ 14338 ★
St. John's Hospital - Health Science Library (Med)
P.O. Box 30   Phone: (508)458-1411
Lowell, MA 01853   Gale Cogan, Dir.
Founded: 1970. **Staff:** Prof 2. **Subjects:** Medicine and allied health sciences, hospital administration. **Holdings:** 1500 books. **Subscriptions:** 400 journals and other serials. **Services:** Interlibrary loan; copying; library open to the public. **Computerized Information Services:** MEDLARS, BRS Information Technologies; CD-ROM. **Networks/Consortia:** Member of Northeastern Consortium for Health Information (NECHI), Massachusetts Health Sciences Libraries Network (MaHSLiN), Boston Biomedical Library Consortium. **Remarks:** FAX: (508)934-8241.

★ 14339 ★
St. John's Hospital and Health Center - Hospital Library (Med)
1328 22nd St.   Phone: (213)829-8494
Santa Monica, CA 90404   Cathey L. Pinckney, Libn.
Founded: 1952. **Staff:** Prof 1; Other 1. **Subjects:** Medicine, nursing, and hospital administration. **Holdings:** 5878 books; 2706 bound periodical volumes; 3142 unbound journal volumes. **Subscriptions:** 321 journals and other serials. **Services:** Interlibrary loan; copying; library open to qualified users.

★ 14340 ★
St. John's Lutheran Church - Library (Rel-Phil)
5th and Wilhelm   Phone: (316)564-2044
Ellinwood, KS 67526   Paula Knop, Libn.
Founded: 1980. **Staff:** Prof 1. **Subjects:** Children's literature, Biblical fiction, Christian biographies, Christian life, bibliotherapy, reference. **Special Collections:** Dr. James Dobson Collection (212 cassettes); Christian Living cassettes (158); children's cassettes and records (266). **Holdings:** 3790 books; 306 music cassettes and records; 355 videotapes; 15 filmstrips; 2 computer Bible games. **Services:** Interlibrary loan; copying; library open to the public. **Automated Operations:** Computerized cataloging and acquisitions. **Computerized Information Services:** Internal databases.

★ 14341 ★
St. John's Medical Center - Herbert H. Minthorn Memorial Library (Med)
1614 E. Kessler Blvd.
Box 3002
Longview, WA 98632   Phone: (206)423-1530
          Barbara Sherry, Med.Libn.
Founded: 1987. **Staff:** Prof 1. **Subjects:** Medicine, nursing, and allied health sciences. **Holdings:** 1200 books. **Subscriptions:** 200 journals and other

serials. **Services:** Interlibrary loan; copying. **Automated Operations:** Computerized cataloging and acquisitions. **Computerized Information Services:** MEDLINE, HEALTH, Cumulative Index to Nursing & Allied Health Literature (CINAHL); internal database; OnTyme Electronic Message Network Service (electronic mail service). Performs searches free of charge. **Remarks:** FAX: (206)636-4955. Electronic mail address(es): SJHLV (OnTyme Electronic Message Network Service).

★ 14342 ★
St. John's Mercy Medical Center - Medical Center Library (Med)
621 S. New Ballas Rd.   Phone: (314)569-6340
St. Louis, MO 63141-8221   Saundra H. Brenner, Dir.
Founded: 1912. **Staff:** Prof 3; Other 2. **Subjects:** Medicine, nursing. **Holdings:** 1391 books; 10,000 bound periodical volumes. **Subscriptions:** 600 journals and other serials. **Services:** Interlibrary loan; library not open to the public. **Automated Operations:** Computerized public access catalog, cataloging, acquisitions, serials, circulation, and ILL (DOCLINE). **Computerized Information Services:** MEDLARS, OCLC, BRS Information Technologies, DIALOG Information Services; CD-ROMs (MEDLINE, MICROMEDEX, CANCER-CD, CINAHL, Health Planning and Administrative Data Base); Philnet (electronic mail service). Performs searches free of charge. **Networks/Consortia:** Member of St. Louis Regional Library Network, Saint Louis Medical Librarians Consortia. **Special Indexes:** Res Medica Index. **Remarks:** FAX: (314)569-6910. **Formerly:** Its John Young Brown Memorial Library. **Staff:** Jennifer Nakeff-Plaat, Asst.Dir.

★ 14343 ★
St. John's Northeast Hospital - Medical Library (Med)
1575 Beam Ave.   Phone: (612)779-4276
Maplewood, MN 55109   Sherry Oleson, Lib.Serv.Dir.
Staff: Prof 1. **Subjects:** Medicine, nursing, allied health sciences. **Holdings:** 500 books. **Subscriptions:** 135 journals and other serials. **Services:** Interlibrary loan; copying; library open to students and health professionals by appointment only. **Computerized Information Services:** BRS Information Technologies. **Networks/Consortia:** Member of Twin Cities Biomedical Consortium (TCBC), MINITEX Library Information Network, National Network of Libraries of Medicine - Greater Midwest Region, Metronet. **Publications:** Library newsletter, 9/year - for internal distribution only. **Remarks:** Maintained by HealthEast.

★ 14344 ★
St. John's Regional Health Center - Medical Library (Med)
1235 E. Cherokee   Phone: (417)885-2795
Springfield, MO 65804-2263   Anna Beth Crabtree, Dir., Med.Lib.Serv.
Founded: 1904. **Staff:** Prof 2; Other 3. **Subjects:** Medicine, nursing, and allied health sciences, management. **Holdings:** 2500 books; 6500 bound periodical volumes; 240 videotapes; 200 audiotapes; 125 microforms. **Subscriptions:** 430 journals and other serials; 20 newspapers. **Services:** Interlibrary loan; copying; SDI; library open to health care professionals and students with permission. **Automated Operations:** Computerized cataloging, serials, and ILL. **Computerized Information Services:** MEDLARS, WILSONLINE, BRS Information Technologies, OCLC, DOCLINE, Philnet; CD-ROM; BRS Information Technologies (electronic mail service). **Networks/Consortia:** Member of Missouri Library Network Corp. (MLNC), Saint Louis Medical Librarians Consortia. **Publications:** Medical Library Express (newsletter), quarterly - for internal distribution and to physicians in Southwest Missouri. **Special Catalogs:** Journal holdings list. **Remarks:** FAX: (417)885-2795. Electronic mail address(es): TAER (BRS).

★ 14345 ★
St. John's Regional Medical Center - Health Science Library (Med)
333 N. F St.   Phone: (805)988-2820
Oxnard, CA 93030   Joanne Kennedy, Libn.
Founded: 1973. **Staff:** Prof 1. **Subjects:** Clinical medicine, nursing, health management. **Holdings:** 3200 volumes. **Subscriptions:** 200 journals and other serials. **Services:** Interlibrary loan; copying; library not open to the public. **Computerized Information Services:** MEDLINE, BRS Information Technologies; DOCLINE (electronic mail service). Performs searches free of charge. **Remarks:** FAX: (805)385-7298.

★14346★
St. Johns River Water Management District - Library (Sci-Engr, Env-Cons)
Hwy. 100, W.
Box 1429   Phone: (904)329-4132
Palatka, FL 32178-1429   Judith G. Hunter, Libn.
Founded: 1975. **Staff:** Prof 1; Other 1. **Subjects:** Hydrology, water management, engineering, ecology, botany, geology. **Holdings:** 13,000 books. **Subscriptions:** 263 journals and other serials. **Services:** Interlibrary loan; copying; library open to the public for reference use only. **Automated Operations:** Library Users' Information Service (LUIS). **Computerized Information Services:** Current Contents, Ground Water On-Line, Florida Water Resources Bibliography. **Publications:** Monthly Bibliography of recent acquisitions - for internal distribution only. **Remarks:** FAX: (904)329-4508.

★14347★
St. John's Riverside Hospital - Library (Med)
967 N. Broadway   Phone: (914)964-4281
Yonkers, NY 10701   Margaret Haag, Lib.Hd.
Staff: 1.5. **Subjects:** Nursing, medicine. **Holdings:** 2738 books. **Subscriptions:** 97 journals and other serials. **Services:** Interlibrary loan; copying; library open to the public by appointment. **Computerized Information Services:** MEDLARS. **Networks/Consortia:** Member of Health Information Libraries of Westchester (HILOW). **Remarks:** FAX: (914)964-4971.

★14348★
St. John's School of Nursing - Library (Med)
4431 S. Fremont   Phone: (417)885-2104
Springfield, MO 65804   Sandy J. Anderson, Libn.
Founded: 1909. **Staff:** Prof 1; Other 4. **Subjects:** Nursing, medicine, and allied health sciences. **Special Collections:** Nursing Archives. **Holdings:** 5000 books; 155 reels of microfilm; 8 VF drawers of pamphlets; charts; models; pictures; cassette tapes; video tapes; filmstrips. **Subscriptions:** 70 journals and other serials. **Services:** Library open to the public for reference use only. **Computerized Information Services:** CD-ROM (CINAHL); internal databases. **Publications:** Book Acquisitions List, monthly.

★14349★
St. John's Seminary - Edward Laurence Doheny Memorial Library (Rel-Phil)
5012 Seminary Rd.   Phone: (805)482-2755
Camarillo, CA 93012   Mark Lager, Dir.
Founded: 1940. **Staff:** Prof 2; Other 4. **Subjects:** Theology, philosophy, church history. **Holdings:** 50,000 books; 10,000 bound periodical volumes. **Subscriptions:** 300 journals and other serials; 10 newspapers. **Services:** Interlibrary loan copying; library open to the public. **Automated Operations:** Computerized public access catalog and cataloging. **Computerized Information Services:** DIALOG Information Services, OCLC; CD-ROMs. Performs searches free of charge. **Remarks:** FAX: (805)987-0885. **Staff:** Patricia Fessier.

★14350★
St. John's Seminary - Library (Rel-Phil)
99 Lake St.   Phone: (617)254-2610
Brighton, MA 02135   Rev. L.W. McGrath, Hd.
Founded: 1884. **Staff:** Prof 1; Other 3. **Subjects:** Ecclesiastical sciences. **Holdings:** 138,000 books; 7600 bound periodical volumes. **Subscriptions:** 451 journals and other serials. **Services:** Interlibrary loan; copying; library open to accredited scholars. **Automated Operations:** Computerized cataloging. **Computerized Information Services:** OCLC. **Networks/Consortia:** Member of NELINET, Inc., Boston Theological Institute Libraries.

★14351★
St. John's University - Archives (Hist)
Grand Central & Utopia Pkwys.   Phone: (718)990-6201
Jamaica, NY 11439   Rev. George E. Krock, C.M., Archv.
Founded: 1972. **Staff:** Prof 1. **Special Collections:** Vincentian Papers (Archives of the Eastern Province of the Congregation of the Mission); university archives; autograph collection. **Holdings:** 1750 books and bound periodical volumes. **Subscriptions:** 24 journals and other serials; 2 newspapers. **Services:** Copying; archives open to the public by appointment. **Remarks:** Alternate telephone number(s): 990-6734. FAX: (718)380-0353.

★14352★
St. John's University - Asian Collection - Library (Area-Ethnic)
Grand Central & Utopia Pkwys.   Phone: (718)990-6201
Jamaica, NY 11439   Mr. Hou Ran Ferng, Hd.Libn.
Founded: 1966. **Staff:** Prof 1; Other 3. **Subjects:** Chinese and Japanese literature, religions, history, arts, philosophy, social sciences. **Special Collections:** Taoism (7000 volumes); Buddhism (9000 volumes); Oriental Art Books Collection (1200 volumes); Serial Collections (22,500 volumes). **Holdings:** 62,000 books; 745 bound periodical volumes; survey of China mainland press, 1958-1978; selections from China mainland magazines, 1960-1978; Mainichi Daily News (Japanese daily newspaper), 1960 to present, on microfilm; current background, 1958-1978; The Asian Wall Street Journal, 1982 to present. **Subscriptions:** 167 journals and other serials; 14 newspapers. **Services:** Interlibrary loan; copying; library open to the public with restrictions. **Remarks:** FAX: (718)380-0353.

★14353★
St. John's University - College of Pharmacy & Allied Health Professions - Health Education Resource Center (Med)
Grand Central & Utopia Pkwys.   Phone: (718)990-6685
Jamaica, NY 11439   Mary A. Grant, Dir.
Founded: 1974. **Staff:** Prof 3; Other 1. **Subjects:** Clinical pharmacy, pharmacology, pharmacy administration, toxicology, pharmacokinetics, industrial pharmacy, allied health. **Holdings:** 1863 volumes; 12 newsletters; 346 video cassettes; 120 audio slide programs; 116 audiocassettes; 16 drawers of article and pamphlet files; 279 transparencies; 41 Computer Assisted Learning programs; 106 slide programs; 8 16mm films. **Subscriptions:** 85 journals and other serials. **Services:** Center open to students, faculty, and health care professionals with a special need. **Computerized Information Services:** MEDLARS. **Remarks:** FAX: (718)969-0753. **Staff:** Geraldine P. DiBari, Asst. to Dir.; Neil Frick, AV Asst.

★14354★
St. John's University - Government Documents Department (Soc Sci)
Grand Central & Utopia Pkwys.   Phone: (718)990-6201
Jamaica, NY 11439   Shu-fang Lin, Govt.Docs.Libn.
Founded: 1956. **Staff:** Prof 1; Other 3. **Subjects:** Politics and government, education, business and economics. **Special Collections:** U.S. Reports; Congressional Record, 1st Congress to present; Congressional Serial Set; 75th Congress to present; Presidential papers (microfilm); statutes at large. **Holdings:** 99,403 books; 4027 bound periodical volumes; 4761 reels of microfilm; 110,212 microfiche. **Subscriptions:** 173 journals. **Services:** Department open to the public for reference use only; collection open to the public for reference use only. **Automated Operations:** Computerized cataloging. **Computerized Information Services:** WESTLAW; Census Bureau CD-ROMs. **Remarks:** FAX: (718)380-0353.

★14355★
St. John's University - Hugh L. Carey Collection (Hist)
Grand Central & Utopia Parkways   Phone: (718)990-6048
Jamaica, NY 11439   Szilvia E. Szmuk, Spec.Coll.Libn.
Founded: 1984. **Staff:** Prof 1. **Subjects:** American government and legislation, 1960s-1970s; education; handicapped; New York state public policy; naval shipyards; urban planning in Park Slope, New York. **Special Collections:** Hugh L. Carey Collection, including Congressional Papers, 1960-1974, and Gubernatorial Papers, 1975-1983. **Holdings:** Elementary and Secondary Education Act (ESEA) papers; American government, campaign, and convention files. **Services:** Interlibrary loan (limited); copying; collection open to the public by appointment. **Computerized Information Services:** DIALOG Information Services, BRS Information Technologies, WILSONLINE; internal database. **Networks/Consortia:** Member of New York Metropolitan Reference and Research Library Agency, SUNY/OCLC Library Network. **Publications:** Brochure on Hugh L. Carey and collection; guide to the collection. **Remarks:** FAX: (718)380-0353.

★14356★
St. John's University - Instructional Materials Center (Educ, Aud-Vis)
Grand Central & Utopia Pkwys.   Phone: (718)990-6680
Jamaica, NY 11439   Connie Kuntz-Thorsen, Libn./Instr.
Staff: Prof 1; Other 3. **Subjects:** Education. **Special Collections:** Drug and alcohol education books and films; educational and psychological tests; educational software. **Holdings:** 12,000 books; 2500 curriculum guides; 2000 filmstrips; 1500 study prints; 1600 cassettes; 1650 slides; 100 video cassettes; 300 computer software programs; 160 records. **Subscriptions:** 28 journals and other serials. **Services:** Copying; center open to the public for reference use only. **Networks/Consortia:** Member of New York Metropolitan Reference and Research Library Agency. **Special Catalogs:** Film catalog (book). **Remarks:** FAX: (718)380-0353.

★ 14357 ★
St. John's University - Law Library (Law)
Fromkes Hall
Grand Central & Utopia Pkwys. Phone: (718)990-6161
Jamaica, NY 11439 Julius Marke, Dir.
Founded: 1925. **Staff:** Prof 9; Other 14. **Subjects:** Law - Anglo-American, international, ecclesiastical, foreign, comparative, Roman; jurisprudence. **Special Collections:** Collected works of St. Thomas More (original editions and works about); canon law. **Holdings:** 215,662 books; 9374 bound periodical volumes; 4509 reels of microfilm; 47,155 microcards; 860,402 microfiche. **Subscriptions:** 5259 journals and other serials; 10 newspapers. **Services:** Interlibrary loan; copying; library open to the public with restrictions. **Automated Operations:** Computerized cataloging and serials. **Computerized Information Services:** LEXIS, WESTLAW, NEXIS, DIALOG Information Services, OCLC. **Remarks:** FAX: (718)990-6649. **Staff:** Robert Nagy, Cat.; Karl Christensen, Circ./Ref.; Antonio Ramirez, Ref.Libn.; Patrick Rudolph, Ref.Libn.; William Manz, Assoc.Dir.; Ruth Rosner, Comp.Serv./Ref.; Marian Shulman, Media/Ref.; Aru Satcalmi, Asst.Cat.

★ 14358 ★
St. John's University - Library and Information Science Library (Info Sci)
Grand Central & Utopia Pkwys. Phone: (718)990-6024
Jamaica, NY 11439 Ross Dealy, LIS Libn.
Staff: Prof 1; Other 1. **Subjects:** Library and information science, children's/young adult literature. **Holdings:** 22,600 books; 1350 bound periodical volumes; 670 reels of microfilm. 3 cabinets of vertical files and annual reports. **Subscriptions:** 400 journals and other serials; 185 newsletters. **Services:** Interlibrary loan; copying; library open to the public with identification. **Automated Operations:** Computerized cataloging. **Computerized Information Services:** OCLC. **Remarks:** FAX: (718)380-0353.

★ 14359 ★
St. John's University - Loretto Memorial Library (Bus-Fin)
300 Howard Ave. Phone: (718)390-4545
Staten Island, NY 10301 Sr. Monica Wood, S.C., Asst. Dean
Staff: Prof 7; Other 20. **Subjects:** Education, business administration. **Holdings:** 119,520 books; 9359 bound periodical volumes; 24,508 reels of microfilm; 12 VF drawers. **Subscriptions:** 1082 journals and other serials. **Services:** Interlibrary loan; copying; SDI; library open to the public with restrictions. **Computerized Information Services:** BRS Information Technologies, DIALOG Information Services, PFDS Online, OCLC, WESTLAW; CD-ROMs (ERIC, ABI/INFORM, PsycLIT). Performs searches on fee basis. Contact Person: Lois Cherepon. **Publications:** Library handbook. **Remarks:** FAX: (718)442-3612. **Staff:** Sandra Math; Eugene Hunt; Kathleen Delaney; Mark Meng; Carole Bruce.

★ 14360 ★
St. John's University - Special Collections (Bus-Fin, Hum)
Grand Central & Utopia Pkwys. Phone: (718)990-6737
Jamaica, NY 11439 Szilvia E. Szmuk, Spec.Coll.Libn.
Founded: 1870. **Staff:** Prof 2; Other 1. **Subjects:** Lawn tennis, accounting, American literature. **Special Collections:** William M. Fischer Tennis Collection (2500 volumes); Myer Collection (accounting; 170 volumes); Baxter Collection (American literature; 350 volumes); Heller Collection; James L. Buckley Senatorial papers; Paul O'Dwyer and Cormac O'Malley Collections (Irish-American affairs); James J. Needham papers (Wall Street business affairs); American League for an Undivided Ireland Collection, 1947-1963; American Friends of Irish Neutrality Collection; Meehan Collection (ecclesiastical and civic historical clippings); Alfred Politz Papers (marketing research); Marcel Zitkus Collection of papers on Father Coughlin. **Holdings:** 6000 books; 40 papal letters. **Services:** Collections open to the public by appointment. **Automated Operations:** Computerized cataloging. **Computerized Information Services:** DIALOG Information Services, BRS Information Technologies, WILSONLINE. **Networks/Consortia:** Member of New York Metropolitan Reference and Research Library Agency, SUNY/OCLC Library Network. **Publications:** Guide to the Manuscript Collections in St. John's University Libraries; Guide to the Alfred Politz Papers; finding aid for the Marcel Zitkus collection. **Remarks:** FAX: (718)380-0353.

★ 14361 ★
St. Joseph Abbey - Library (Rel-Phil)
St. Benedict, LA 70457 Phone: (504)892-1800
Fr. Timothy J. Burnett, Libn.
Founded: 1910. **Staff:** Prof 1; Other 2. **Subjects:** Theology, scripture, patristics, monastica, church history. **Holdings:** 16,000 books; 1850 bound periodical volumes. **Subscriptions:** 65 journals and other serials. **Services:** Interlibrary loan; library not open to the public.

★ 14362 ★
St. Joseph Community Hospital - Library (Med)
600 N.E. 92nd Ave.
Box 1600 Phone: (206)256-2045
Vancouver, WA 98668 Sylvia E. MacWilliams, Lib.Coord.
Staff: Prof 1. **Subjects:** Medicine, nursing. **Holdings:** 1054 books. **Subscriptions:** 354 journals and other serials. **Services:** Interlibrary loan; library not open to the public. **Computerized Information Services:** MEDLARS. **Remarks:** Maintained by Southwest Washington Hospitals.

★ 14363 ★
St. Joseph County Law Library (Law)
Court House
101 S. Main Phone: (219)284-9657
South Bend, IN 46601 Lynda Daley, Libn.
Founded: 1973. **Staff:** 1. **Subjects:** Law. **Special Collections:** ICLEF Manuals. **Holdings:** 17,716 volumes. **Services:** Library open to the public for reference use only.

★ 14364 ★
St. Joseph Gazette - Library (Publ)
9th & Edmond Sts. Phone: (816)271-8575
St. Joseph, MO 64502 Don E. Thornton, Dir.
Staff: 1. **Subjects:** Newspaper reference topics. **Holdings:** 55,000 clippings; microfilm. **Subscriptions:** 18 newspapers. **Services:** Library open to the public with director's consent. **Formerly:** St. Joseph News-Press & Gazette.

★ 14365 ★
St. Joseph Health Center - Health Science Library (Med)
1000 Carondelet Dr. Phone: (816)943-2160
Kansas City, MO 64114 Janice Foster, Libn.
Founded: 1929. **Staff:** Prof 1; Other 1. **Subjects:** Medicine, nursing, and allied health sciences. **Holdings:** 1000 books; 1200 bound periodical volumes. **Subscriptions:** 156 journals and other serials. **Services:** Interlibrary loan; copying. **Computerized Information Services:** MEDLARS, BRS Information Technologies. **Networks/Consortia:** Member of Kansas City Library Network, Inc. (KCLN), National Network of Libraries of Medicine - Midcontinental Region. **Remarks:** Alternate telephone number(s): 943-2162.

★ 14366 ★
St. Joseph Health Center - Health Science Library (Med)
300 First Capitol Dr. Phone: (314)947-5109
St. Charles, MO 63301 Lucille Dykas, Lib.Mgr.
Staff: Prof 1. **Subjects:** Medicine. **Holdings:** 500 books; 320 bound periodical volumes. **Subscriptions:** 80 journals and other serials. **Services:** Interlibrary loan; library open to the public by appointment. **Computerized Information Services:** MEDLARS. **Networks/Consortia:** Member of Saint Louis Medical Librarians Consortia. **Remarks:** FAX: (314)947-5258.

★ 14367 ★
St. Joseph Hospital - Burlew Medical Library (Med)
1100 Stewart Dr. Phone: (714)771-8291
Orange, CA 92668 Julie Smith, Lib.Mgr.
Founded: 1929. **Staff:** Prof 2; Other 2. **Subjects:** Medicine, nursing, hospital administration. **Holdings:** 10,000 books; 4798 bound periodical volumes; 7800 AV programs. **Subscriptions:** 713 journals and other serials. **Services:** Interlibrary loan (fee); copying; library open to the public. **Automated Operations:** Computerized cataloging, serials, and circulation. **Computerized Information Services:** MEDLINE, DIALOG Information Services, BRS Information Technologies; OnTyme Electronic Message Network Service (electronic mail service). Performs searches on fee basis. **Networks/Consortia:** Member of National Network of Libraries of Medicine - Pacific Southwest Region. **Remarks:** FAX: (714)744-8533. **Staff:** Ann Ryan, Libn.

★ 14368 ★
St. Joseph Hospital - Fatima Unit - Health Science Library (Med)
200 High Service Ave.   Phone: (401)456-3036
North Providence, RI 02904   Mary Zammarelli, Dir., Lib.Serv.
Founded: 1977. **Staff:** 2. **Subjects:** Medicine, surgery, nursing, allied health sciences. **Holdings:** 945 books; 3365 bound periodical volumes; 2 VF drawers. **Subscriptions:** 105 journals and other serials. **Services:** Interlibrary loan; copying; library open to the public for reference use only by appointment. **Computerized Information Services:** MEDLINE. **Networks/Consortia:** Member of Association of Rhode Island Health Sciences Librarians (ARIHSL), BHSL, Rhode Island Library Network (RHILINET). **Remarks:** FAX: (401)456-3066. Alternate telephone number(s): (401)456-3035.

★ 14369 ★
St. Joseph Hospital - Health Reach Patient & Community Library (Med)
1835 Franklin St.   Phone: (303)837-7188
Denver, CO 80218   Margaret Bandy, Libn.
Founded: 1985. **Staff:** Prof 1; Other 3. **Subjects:** Consumer health. **Holdings:** 600 books. **Subscriptions:** 15 journals and other serials. **Services:** Interlibrary loan; library open to the public. **Remarks:** FAX: (303)837-7017.

★ 14370 ★
St. Joseph Hospital - Health Science Library (Med)
220 Overton
Box 178
Memphis, TN 38105-0178   Phone: (901)577-2828
    Patricia Irby, Libn.
Founded: 1938. **Staff:** 1. **Subjects:** Medicine, nursing, management. **Holdings:** 2735 books; 2834 bound periodical volumes. **Subscriptions:** 172 journals and other serials. **Services:** Interlibrary loan; copying; SDI; library open to the public for reference use only on request. **Computerized Information Services:** NLM, MEDLINE. Performs searches on fee basis. **Networks/Consortia:** Member of Association of Memphis Area Health Science Libraries (AMAHSL).

★ 14371 ★
St. Joseph Hospital - Health Science Library (Med)
1919 LaBranch   Phone: (713)757-1000
Houston, TX 77002   Shelley G. Mao, Dir.
Founded: 1940. **Staff:** Prof 1; Other 1. **Subjects:** Medicine, sciences, management. **Holdings:** 3817 books; 4793 bound periodical volumes; 83 titles on Network for Continuing Medical Education (NCME) tapes; 83 volumes of Audio-Digest tapes. **Subscriptions:** 200 journals and other serials. **Services:** Interlibrary loan; copying; library open to professionals by appointment. **Computerized Information Services:** NLM; internal database.

★ 14372 ★
St. Joseph Hospital - Health Sciences Library (Med)
1835 Franklin St.   Phone: (303)837-7188
Denver, CO 80218   Margaret Bandy, Libn.
Founded: 1965. **Staff:** Prof 1. **Subjects:** Medicine, nursing, hospital management. **Holdings:** 700 books. **Subscriptions:** 208 journals and other serials. **Services:** Interlibrary loan; copying. **Automated Operations:** Computerized public access catalog, cataloging, circulation, and serials (CARL). **Computerized Information Services:** MEDLINE, DIALOG Information Services, OCLC, BRS Information Technologies. **Networks/Consortia:** Member of Colorado Council of Medical Librarians, National Network of Libraries of Medicine - Midcontinental Region. **Remarks:** FAX: (303)837-7017.

★ 14373 ★
St. Joseph Hospital - Health Sciences Library (Med)
302 Kensington Ave.   Phone: (313)762-8519
Flint, MI 48503-2000   Ria Brown Lukes, Med.Libn.
Staff: Prof 1; Other 2. **Subjects:** Medicine, nursing. **Holdings:** 3000 books; 8500 bound periodical volumes; 1227 audio cassettes; 250 video cassettes. **Subscriptions:** 245 journals and other serials. **Services:** Interlibrary loan; copying; library open to the public for reference use only. **Automated Operations:** Computerized acquisitions and serials. **Computerized Information Services:** MEDLINE, DIALOG Information Services; DOCLINE (electronic mail service). **Networks/Consortia:** Member of Flint Area Health Science Library Network (FAHSLN), Michigan Health Sciences Libraries Association (MHSLA). **Publications:** New book lists. **Remarks:** FAX: (313)762-3548.

★ 14374 ★
St. Joseph Hospital - Health Sciences Library (Med)
12th & Walnut Sts.   Phone: (215)378-2389
Reading, PA 19603   Kathleen A. Izzo, Dir.
Founded: 1973. **Staff:** Prof 1; Other 1. **Subjects:** Medicine, nursing, patient education, allied health professions, hospital administration, public health. **Holdings:** 2982 books; 4526 bound periodical volumes; 4 VF drawers of pamphlets. **Subscriptions:** 214 journals and other serials. **Services:** Interlibrary loan; copying; SDI; library open to the public. **Automated Operations:** Computerized cataloging. **Computerized Information Services:** DIALOG Information Services, NLM, BRS Information Technologies. Performs searches on fee basis. **Networks/Consortia:** Member of National Network of Libraries of Medicine - Middle Atlantic Region, Berks County Library Association (BCLA), Central Pennsylvania Health Sciences Library Association (CPHSLA), Cooperating Hospital Libraries of the Lehigh Valley Area. **Publications:** Library Ledger, monthly - for internal distribution only. **Special Catalogs:** AV Catalog (notebook). **Remarks:** FAX: (215)378-2390.

★ 14375 ★
St. Joseph Hospital - Library (Med)
2605 Harlem Rd.
Cheektowaga, NY 14225   Phone: (716)891-2400
Staff: Prof 1; Other 1. **Subjects:** Medicine. **Holdings:** 750 books; 57 bound periodical volumes. **Subscriptions:** 30 journals and other serials. **Services:** Interlibrary loan; library not open to the public. **Networks/Consortia:** Member of Western New York Library Resources Council (WNYLRC). **Publications:** Library Handbook; Cataloging Handbook.

★ 14376 ★
St. Joseph Hospital - Library (Med)
2901 Squalicum Pkwy.   Phone: (206)734-5400
Bellingham, WA 98225   Bea Dickerson, Libn.
Founded: 1975. **Staff:** Prof 1. **Subjects:** Medicine, nursing, and allied health sciences. **Holdings:** 800 books. **Subscriptions:** 150 journals and other serials. **Services:** Interlibrary loan; library open to the public by appointment. **Computerized Information Services:** DIALOG Information Services, MEDLINE, BRS Information Technologies; OnTyme Electronic Message Network Service (electronic mail service). Performs searches on fee basis for persons not affiliated with hospital; telephone (206)734-5400, ext. 2438. **Remarks:** FAX: (206)733-3569. Electronic mail address(es): SJH/WABEL (OnTyme Electronic Message Network Service).

★ 14377 ★
St. Joseph Hospital - Medical Library (Med)
1 St. Joseph Dr.   Phone: (606)278-3436
Lexington, KY 40504   Jerri Trimble, Libn.
Founded: 1968. **Staff:** 1. **Subjects:** Medicine, nursing, and allied health sciences. **Holdings:** 1115 books; 2935 bound periodical volumes; 10 directories; 818 audiotapes; 55 AV programs. **Subscriptions:** 177 journals and other serials. **Services:** Interlibrary loan; library not open to the public. **Computerized Information Services:** GRATEFUL MED. **Networks/Consortia:** Member of Kentucky Health Sciences Library Consortium. **Remarks:** FAX: (606)278-2449.

★ 14378 ★
St. Joseph Hospital - Otto C. Brantigan, M.D. Medical Library (Med)
7620 York Rd.   Phone: (301)337-1210
Towson, MD 21204   Marianne Prenger, Med.Libn.
Founded: 1940. **Staff:** Prof 2; Other 2. **Subjects:** Medicine, surgery, obstetrics, gynecology, pediatrics, nursing. **Holdings:** 1445 books; 404 bound periodical volumes; Audio-Digest tapes; audio and video cassette tapes. **Subscriptions:** 151 journals and other serials. **Services:** Interlibrary loan; copying; library open to students. **Computerized Information Services:** MEDLINE, MEDLARS; DOCLINE, MedSig (electronic mail services). **Networks/Consortia:** Member of Maryland Association of Health Science Librarians (MAHSL). **Remarks:** Contains the holdings of the former Sister Mary Alvina Nursing Library.

★ 14379 ★
St. Joseph Hospital - Our Lady of Providence Unit - Health Science Library (Med)
21 Peace St. Phone: (401)456-4035
Providence, RI 02907 Mary Zammarelli, Dir., Lib.Serv.
Founded: 1940. **Staff:** Prof 1; Other 2. **Subjects:** Medicine, nursing, and allied health sciences. **Holdings:** 1500 books; 8855 bound periodical volumes; 4 VF drawers of pamphlets, reports. **Subscriptions:** 141 journals and other serials. **Services:** Interlibrary loan; copying; library open to the public by appointment with referral from another library. **Computerized Information Services:** MEDLARS, MEDLINE. Performs searches. **Networks/Consortia:** Member of BHSL, Association of Rhode Island Health Sciences Librarians (ARIHSL), Rhode Island Library Network (RHILINET), North Atlantic Health Science Libraries (NAHSL).

★ 14380 ★
St. Joseph Hospital - William O. Umiker Medical Library (Med)
250 College Ave.
Box 3509 Phone: (717)291-8119
Lancaster, PA 17604 Patricia Ruch Miller, Libn.
Founded: 1940. **Staff:** Prof 1; Other 1. **Subjects:** Medicine, nursing, and allied health sciences. **Holdings:** 4000 books; 300 AV programs. **Subscriptions:** 250 journals and other serials. **Services:** Interlibrary loan; copying; library open to the public. **Computerized Information Services:** MEDLARS. Performs searches on fee basis. **Networks/Consortia:** Member of Central Pennsylvania Health Sciences Library Association (CPHSLA), BHSL. **Remarks:** FAX: (717)291-8130.

★ 14381 ★
St. Joseph Hospital and Health Care Center - Hospital Library (Med)
1718 South I St.
Box 2197 Phone: (206)591-6778
Tacoma, WA 98401 Brynn Beals, Libn.
Staff: Prof 1. **Subjects:** Medicine, nursing, health sciences, autism. **Holdings:** 2000 books; 150 bound periodical volumes. **Subscriptions:** 100 journals and other serials. **Services:** Interlibrary loan; copying; library open to the public for reference use only. **Computerized Information Services:** DIALOG Information Services, MEDLINE; OnTyme Electronic Message Network Service (electronic mail service). **Networks/Consortia:** Member of National Network of Libraries of Medicine - Pacific Northwest Region, Western Library Network (WLN). **Remarks:** FAX: (206)591-6789. Electronic mail address(es): STJH/TAC (OnTyme Electronic Message Network Service).

★ 14382 ★
St. Joseph Hospital and Health Care Center - Library (Med)
2900 N. Lake Shore Phone: (312)975-3038
Chicago, IL 60657 Gwen Jones, Libn.
Staff: Prof 1; Other 1. **Subjects:** Medicine, nursing. **Special Collections:** Hospital archives. **Holdings:** 5500 books; 8000 bound periodical volumes; 2500 audiotapes; 48 sets of slides and filmstrips; 10 VF drawers; 200 videotapes. **Subscriptions:** 170 journals and other serials. **Services:** Interlibrary loan; library open to the public at librarian's discretion. **Computerized Information Services:** NLM. **Networks/Consortia:** Member of ILLINET, Metropolitan Consortium of Chicago, National Network of Libraries of Medicine - Greater Midwest Region. **Remarks:** FAX: (312)975-3416.

★ 14383 ★
St. Joseph Hospital and Health Center - Medical Library (Med)
205 W. 20th St. Phone: (216)233-1000
Lorain, OH 44052 John L. Reese, Libn.
Founded: 1953. **Staff:** Prof 1; Other 1. **Subjects:** Medicine, nursing. **Holdings:** 1597 books; 1650 bound periodical volumes; 386 video cassettes. **Subscriptions:** 187 journals and other serials. **Services:** Interlibrary loan; copying; SDI; library open to the public. **Computerized Information Services:** DIALOG Information Services, MEDLINE; CD-ROM. Performs searches on fee basis. **Networks/Consortia:** Member of Lake Erie Medical Librarians Association, Cleveland Area Metropolitan Library System (CAMLS). **Remarks:** FAX: (216)246-4931.

St. Joseph Library
See: Loyola Marymount University - St. Joseph Library (9418)

★ 14384 ★
St. Joseph Medical Center - Health Science Library (Med)
501 S. Buena Vista St. Phone: (818)843-5111
Burbank, CA 91505-4866 Sr. Naomi Hurd, S.P., Libn.
Founded: 1953. **Staff:** Prof 2; Other 2. **Subjects:** Medicine, nursing, hospital administration. **Special Collections:** History of Medicine; rare book collection. **Holdings:** 3258 books; 5000 bound periodical volumes; 1200 audio cassettes; 245 video cassettes; 25 16mm films; 40 filmstrips; 65 slide programs; 4 transparency programs; 36 items of miscellanea. **Subscriptions:** 623 journals and other serials. **Services:** Interlibrary loan; copying; library open to the public for reference use only. **Automated Operations:** Computerized cataloging and serials. **Computerized Information Services:** MEDLINE; DOCLINE (electronic mail service). Performs searches on fee basis. **Networks/Consortia:** Member of National Network of Libraries of Medicine - Pacific Southwest Region, San Fernando Valley Medical Library Group. **Publications:** Journal list, annual. **Remarks:** FAX: (818)843-0970; (818)841-2307. **Staff:** Ann Miller, Asst.Libn./AV Coord.

★ 14385 ★
St. Joseph Medical Center - Health Science Library (Med)
333 N. Madison St. Phone: (815)725-7133
Joliet, IL 60435 Catherine Siron, Mgr., Lib.Serv.
Founded: 1976. **Staff:** Prof 2; Other 1. **Subjects:** Clinical medicine and nursing. **Special Collections:** Nursing library (4000 volumes). **Holdings:** 2000 books; 5200 bound periodical volumes. **Subscriptions:** 300 journals and other serials. **Services:** Interlibrary loan; copying; library open to the public for reference use only. **Computerized Information Services:** NLM, DIALOG Information Services, OCLC; DOCLINE (electronic mail service). Performs searches on fee basis. **Networks/Consortia:** Member of Chicago and South Consortium, National Network of Libraries of Medicine - Greater Midwest Region, Bur Oak Library System. **Remarks:** FAX: (815)725-9459. **Staff:** Virginia Gale, Asst.Libn.

★ 14386 ★
St. Joseph Medical Center - Health Sciences Library (Med)
128 Strawberry Hill Ave.
Box 1222 Phone: (203)353-2095
Stamford, CT 06904-1222 Lucille Lieberman, Dir.
Founded: 1970. **Staff:** Prof 1; Other 1. **Subjects:** Medicine, nursing, and allied health sciences. **Holdings:** 1412 books; 160 bound periodical volumes; 106 video cassettes. **Subscriptions:** 160 journals and other serials. **Services:** Interlibrary loan; copying; SDI; library open to the public by arrangement. **Computerized Information Services:** MEDLINE. Performs searches on fee basis. **Networks/Consortia:** Member of Connecticut Association of Health Science Libraries (CAHSL), North Atlantic Health Science Libraries (NAHSL). **Publications:** A Guide to Use of the Health Sciences Library, updated annually - to new employees and the medical community. **Remarks:** FAX: (203)353-2307.

★ 14387 ★
St. Joseph Medical Center - Medical Library (Med)
601 Grand Ave., N.E. Phone: (505)848-8291
Albuquerque, NM 87102 Melba Clark, Med.Libn.
Founded: 1959. **Staff:** 1. **Subjects:** Medicine, nursing, rehabilitation, orthopedics, neurology. **Holdings:** 700 books; 800 bound periodical volumes. **Subscriptions:** 90 journals and other serials. **Services:** Interlibrary loan; copying; library open to students and workers in health professions. **Computerized Information Services:** MEDLINE. **Remarks:** FAX: (505)848-7118. Maintained by the Sisters of Charity. **Formerly:** St. Joseph Hospital.

★ 14388 ★
St. Joseph Memorial Hospital - Health Science Library (Med)
1907 W. Sycamore St. Phone: (317)452-5611
Kokomo, IN 46901 Jean Romack, Personnel Asst.
Staff: 1. **Subjects:** Medicine, nursing, hospital administration and management. **Holdings:** 1609 books; 736 bound periodical volumes; 348 AV programs; 4 VF drawers. **Subscriptions:** 129 journals and other serials. **Services:** Interlibrary loan; copying; library open to the public with limited circulation. **Networks/Consortia:** Member of National Network of Libraries of Medicine - Greater Midwest Region.

★ 14389 ★
St. Joseph Mercy Hospital - Library (Med)
900 Woodward   Phone: (313)858-3495
Pontiac, MI 48341-2985   Elaine L. Kissel, Lib.Mgr.
Staff: Prof 4. **Subjects:** Medicine, nursing, health care administration, allied health sciences. **Special Collections:** Consumer health information. **Holdings:** 5000 books; 8000 bound periodical volumes; 300 media programs. **Subscriptions:** 500 journals and other serials. **Services:** Interlibrary loan; copying; SDI; LATCH. **Automated Operations:** Computerized public access catalog, cataloging, acquisitions, serials, circulation, and ILL. **Computerized Information Services:** MEDLARS, OCLC, DIALOG Information Services; CD-ROMs (MEDLINE, Health Planning and Administration). Performs searches on fee basis. **Networks/Consortia:** Member of Oakland Wayne Interlibrary Network (OWIN). **Staff:** Jerry Stuenkel; Lora Seaboldt; Dori J. Pullan.

★ 14390 ★
St. Joseph Mercy Hospital - Medical Library (Med)
84 Beaumont Dr.   Phone: (515)424-7699
Mason City, IA 50401   Judy I. Madson, Dir.
Staff: Prof 1; Other 1. **Subjects:** Medicine, nursing, hospital administration. **Holdings:** 5300 volumes. **Subscriptions:** 250 journals and other serials. **Services:** Interlibrary loan; copying; SDI; library open to the public with restrictions. **Automated Operations:** Computerized cataloging, serials, and ILL. **Computerized Information Services:** MEDLARS, BRS Information Technologies. Performs searches on fee basis. **Networks/Consortia:** Member of National Network of Libraries of Medicine - Greater Midwest Region. **Remarks:** FAX: (515)424-7698.

★ 14391 ★
St. Joseph Museum - Library (Hist)
11th at Charles   Phone: (816)232-8471
St. Joseph, MO 64501   Richard A. Nolf, Dir.
Founded: 1927. **Staff:** 1. **Subjects:** Local and area history, Western movement, ethnology, natural history. **Special Collections:** American Indian Collection; Civil War period local history collection; Pony Express; bird, mammal, and fish exhibits. **Holdings:** 6500 volumes. **Subscriptions:** 40 journals and other serials. **Services:** Copying; library open to the public by appointment. **Publications:** Happenings of the St. Joseph and Pony Express Museums. **Remarks:** FAX: (816)232-8482. **Staff:** Bonnie Watkins, Cur., Coll.; Jackie Lewin, Cur., Hist.; Marilyn Taylor, Cur., Ethnology; David Mead, Cur., Natural Hist.; Robbie Sipes, Cur., Exhibits

St. Joseph News-Press & Gazette
See: St. Joseph Gazette (14364)

★ 14392 ★
St. Joseph Seminary College - Pere Rouquette Library (Hum, Rel-Phil)
River Rd.   Phone: (504)892-9895
St. Benedict, LA 70457   Rev. Timothy J. Burnett, O.S.B., Dir., Lib.
Founded: 1889. **Staff:** Prof 1; Other 9. **Subjects:** Literature, religion, history, social sciences, psychology, philosophy, sciences, languages, fine arts. **Holdings:** 75,000 books; 9000 bound periodical volumes. **Subscriptions:** 181 journals and other serials. **Services:** Interlibrary loan; copying; SDI; library open to the public for reference use only on request.

★ 14393 ★
St. Joseph State Hospital - Mental Health Resource Library (Med)
3400 Frederick Ave.   Phone: (816)387-2300
St. Joseph, MO 64506   Judith L. Moore, Lib.Dir.
Founded: 1966. **Staff:** Prof 1; Other 1. **Subjects:** Psychiatry, psychology, social work, nursing, alcoholism, psychotherapy, pharmacology. **Holdings:** 1500 books; 100 periodical titles; 500 Audio-Digest tapes; 200 videocassettes. **Subscriptions:** 60 journals and other serials. **Services:** Interlibrary loan; copying; SDI; library open to the public with restrictions. **Networks/Consortia:** Member of National Network of Libraries of Medicine - Midcontinental Region. **Remarks:** FAX: (816)387-2329. **Formerly:** Its Professional Library.

★ 14394 ★
St. Joseph's Abbey - Monastic Library (Rel-Phil)
Spencer, MA 01562   Phone: (508)885-3901
      Fr. Basil Byrne, Libn.
Founded: 1951. **Staff:** Prof 1. **Subjects:** Monasticism, theology, philosophy, history, psychology, art, literature. **Holdings:** 40,000 books; 1000 bound periodical volumes. **Subscriptions:** 25 journals and other serials; 5 newspapers. **Services:** Interlibrary loan; library open to the public for reference use only with restrictions.

★ 14395 ★
St. Joseph's General Hospital - Library (Med)
P.O. Box 3251   Phone: (807)343-2431
Thunder Bay, ON, Canada P7B 5G7   Ms. Wright, Libn.
Founded: 1961. **Staff:** Prof 1. **Subjects:** Medicine, nursing, management, rehabilitation, ethics. **Holdings:** 800 books. **Subscriptions:** 42 journals and other serials. **Services:** Interlibrary loan; copying. **Remarks:** FAX: (807)345-4994.

★ 14396 ★
St. Joseph's Health Centre - George Pennal Library (Med)
30 The Queensway   Phone: (416)530-6726
Toronto, ON, Canada M6R 1B5   Barbara Iwasiuk, Med.Libn.
Founded: 1963. **Staff:** Prof 1; Other 1. **Subjects:** Medicine, nursing, hospital administration, pastoral care. **Holdings:** 3500 books; 3000 bound periodical volumes. **Subscriptions:** 172 journals and other serials. **Services:** Interlibrary loan; library not open to the public. **Computerized Information Services:** MEDLARS; CD-ROM (MEDLINE). **Publications:** Health Administration Update, quarterly. **Remarks:** FAX: (416)530-6034.

★ 14397 ★
St. Joseph's Health Centre of London - Library Services (Med)
268 Grosvenor St.   Phone: (519)439-3271
London, ON, Canada N6A 4V2   Louise Lin, Mgr., Lib.Serv.
Founded: 1966. **Staff:** Prof 1; Other 2. **Subjects:** Clinical medicine, nursing, allied health sciences. **Special Collections:** World Health Organization International Histological Classification of Tumors (books and slides). **Holdings:** 4000 books; 5422 bound periodical volumes; 2000 hematology teaching slides. **Subscriptions:** 420 journals and other serials. **Services:** Interlibrary loan; copying; services open to the public for reference use only. **Computerized Information Services:** MEDLINE. Performs searches on fee basis.

★ 14398 ★
St. Joseph's Hospital - Drug Information Centre (Med)
50 Charlton Ave., E.   Phone: (416)522-4941
Hamilton, ON, Canada L8N 4A6   Miss N. Giovinazzo, Act.Dir., Pharm.Serv.
Staff: 1. **Subjects:** Drugs, pharmacology, disease, clinical pharmacy services, pharmaceutical techniques. **Holdings:** 175 volumes; 125 cassette tapes; 50 videotapes; archives and teaching files. **Subscriptions:** 32 journals and other serials. **Services:** Interlibrary loan; center open to public with approval. **Computerized Information Services:** CD-ROM (Drugdex System). **Remarks:** FAX: (416)521-6066.

★ 14399 ★
St. Joseph's Hospital - Health Science Library (Med)
220 Pawtucket St.
Lowell, MA 01854   Phone: (508)453-1761
Founded: 1971. **Staff:** Prof 1. **Subjects:** Medicine and nursing. **Holdings:** 3050 volumes. **Subscriptions:** 50 journals and other serials. **Services:** Interlibrary loan; copying; library open to the public for reference use only. **Networks/Consortia:** Member of Northeastern Consortium for Health Information (NECHI), Massachusetts Health Sciences Libraries Network (MaHSLiN). **Remarks:** FAX: (508)458-9903.

★ 14400 ★
St. Joseph's Hospital - Health Sciences Library (Med)
350 W. Thomas Rd.
Box 2071   Phone: (602)285-3299
Phoenix, AZ 85001   Kay E. Wellik, Mgr., Lib.Serv.
Founded: 1942. **Staff:** Prof 1; Other 2. **Subjects:** Medicine. **Special Collections:** Library of neurological sciences. **Holdings:** 4500 books; 8500 bound periodical volumes. **Subscriptions:** 450 journals and other serials. **Services:** Interlibrary loan; library not open to the public. **Computerized Information Services:** MEDLARS, BRS Information Technologies, DIALOG Information Services; OnTyme Electronic Message Network Service (electronic mail service). **Remarks:** FAX: (602)650-7154. Electronic mail address(es): STJH/PHX (OnTyme Electronic Message Network Service).

★14401★

St. Joseph's Hospital - Helene Fuld Learning Resource Center (Med)
555 E. Market St.
Elmira, NY 14902
Phone: (607)733-6541
Arlene C. Pien, Libn.
Founded: 1975. **Staff:** 1. **Subjects:** Medicine, nursing. **Holdings:** 5000 books; 4000 bound periodical volumes; 1500 AV programs; 10 drawers of pamphlets. **Subscriptions:** 165 journals and other serials. **Services:** Interlibrary loan; copying. **Computerized Information Services:** Online systems. Performs searches on fee basis. **Remarks:** FAX: (607)733-3946.

★14402★

St. Joseph's Hospital - Jerome Medical Library (Med)
69 W. Exchange St.
St. Paul, MN 55102
Phone: (612)291-3193
Karen Brudvig, Med.Libn.
Founded: 1949. **Staff:** Prof 1. **Subjects:** Medicine, hospital administration, nursing. **Holdings:** 2500 books; 2900 bound periodical volumes. **Subscriptions:** 200 journals and other serials. **Services:** Interlibrary loan; copying; library open to the public for reference use only. **Computerized Information Services:** BRS Information Technologies, MEDLINE. **Networks/Consortia:** Member of Twin Cities Biomedical Consortium (TCBC). **Remarks:** FAX: (612)291-3601.

★14403★

St. Joseph's Hospital - Learning Resource Center (Med)
611 St. Joseph Ave.
Marshfield, WI 54449
Phone: (715)387-7374
Ruth Wachter-Nelson, Libn.
Founded: 1914. **Staff:** Prof 1; Other 2. **Subjects:** Nursing. **Holdings:** 7800 books; 881 bound periodical volumes; 10 VF drawers of pamphlets; school archives; 1054 AV programs. **Subscriptions:** 157 journals and other serials. **Services:** Interlibrary loan; center open to the public with restrictions. **Automated Operations:** Computerized cataloging. **Computerized Information Services:** CD-ROMs (MEDLINE Professional, CINAHL, Health Plan). Performs searches on fee basis. **Special Catalogs:** Audiovisual catalog. **Remarks:** Includes a 2800 volume patient library. FAX: (715)389-2922 (Attn: LRC).

★14404★

St. Joseph's Hospital - Library Services (Med)
50 Charlton Ave., E.
Hamilton, ON, Canada L8N 1Y4   Mrs. Gayle Fitzgerald, Hd., Lib.Serv.
Phone: (416)522-4941
Founded: 1964. **Staff:** 2. **Subjects:** Medicine, nursing, hospital administration. **Holdings:** 2200 books; 7000 bound periodical volumes. **Subscriptions:** 200 journals and other serials. **Services:** Interlibrary loan; library not open to the public. **Computerized Information Services:** BRS Information Technologies, MEDLINE; CD-ROMs (CINAHL, MEDLINE). **Networks/Consortia:** Member of Hamilton/Wentworth District Health Library Network. **Remarks:** FAX: (416)521-6066. **Staff:** Mrs. Jean Maragno, Lib.Techn.

★14405★

St. Joseph's Hospital - Medical Library (Med)
3000 W. Buffalo Ave.
Box 4227
Tampa, FL 33677
Phone: (813)870-4658
Adelia P. Seglin, Dir., Med.Lib.
Staff: Prof 2; Other 1. **Subjects:** Medicine, nursing, cancer, pharmacology, management, cardiology. **Holdings:** 1500 books; 5800 bound periodical volumes. **Subscriptions:** 257 journals and other serials. **Services:** Interlibrary loan; library not open to the public. **Computerized Information Services:** MEDLARS, DIALOG Information Services, BRS Information Technologies, WILSONLINE. Performs searches on fee basis. **Networks/Consortia:** Member of Tampa Bay Medical Library Network. **Remarks:** FAX: (813)870-4479. **Staff:** Mrs. Gita Halder, Med.Libn.

★14406★

St. Joseph's Hospital - Medical Library (Med)
11705 Mercy Blvd.
Savannah, GA 31419
Phone: (912)925-4100
Judy G. Henry, Libn.
Staff: Prof 1. **Subjects:** Medicine, surgery, nursing, allied health sciences. **Holdings:** 750 books; 150 bound periodical volumes; 100 pamphlets; 80 filmstrips with records; 4 VF drawers. **Subscriptions:** 104 journals and other serials. **Services:** Interlibrary loan; copying; library open to the public with restrictions. **Computerized Information Services:** Online systems.

★14407★

St. Joseph's Hospital - Medical Library (Med)
158-40 79th Ave.
Flushing, NY 11366
Phone: (718)591-1000
Frances Taub, Libn.
Subjects: Medicine. **Holdings:** Figures not available. **Remarks:** FAX: (718)591-2707.

★14408★

St. Joseph's Hospital - Samuel Rosenthal Memorial Library (Med)
5000 W. Chambers St.
Milwaukee, WI 53210
Phone: (414)447-2194
Sunja Shaikh, Lib.Coord.
Founded: 1967. **Staff:** Prof 2. **Subjects:** Medicine, nursing, and allied health sciences, management. **Special Collections:** Human Values in Medicine. **Holdings:** 3000 books; 8000 bound periodical volumes; 150 Audio-Digest tapes. **Subscriptions:** 305 journals and other serials. **Services:** Interlibrary loan; copying; SDI; library open to the public for reference use only. **Computerized Information Services:** BRS Information Technologies, MEDLINE; CD-ROM (MEDLINE); DOCLINE (electronic mail service). Performs searches free of charge. **Networks/Consortia:** Member of Southeastern Wisconsin Health Science Library Consortium (SWHSL). **Publications:** Library Newsletter, quarterly - for internal distribution only. **Special Indexes:** Library Journal Holdings List (online). **Remarks:** FAX: (414)447-3513. **Staff:** June Regis, Med.Libn.

★14409★

St. Joseph's Hospital of Atlanta - Russell Bellman Medical Library (Med)
5665 Peachtree Dunwoody Rd., N.E.
Atlanta, GA 30342
Phone: (404)851-7040
Jo Dilbeck, Libn.
Founded: 1965. **Staff:** Prof 1; Other 1. **Subjects:** Medicine, nursing, hospital administration, allied health sciences. **Special Collections:** Medical Ethics; periodicals, 1970 to present (microfilm). **Holdings:** 2000 books; 2000 bound periodical volumes; videotapes. **Subscriptions:** 260 journals and other serials. **Services:** Interlibrary loan. **Automated Operations:** Computerized cataloging and ILL. **Computerized Information Services:** NLM, OCLC, BRS Information Technologies; CD-ROM (MEDLINE). Performs searches on fee basis for non-affiliated personnel. **Networks/Consortia:** Member of Atlanta Health Science Libraries Consortium (AHSLC), Georgia Health Sciences Library Association (GHSLA), SOLINET. **Remarks:** Alternate telephone number(s): 851-7039. FAX: (404)851-7869. **Formerly:** Its Russell Bellman Memorial Library.

★14410★

St. Joseph's Hospital & Health Center - Bruce M. Cole Memorial Library (Med)
350 N. Wilmot
Tucson, AZ 85711
Phone: (602)721-3925
Marcia Arsenault, Libn.
Staff: Prof 1; Other 5. **Subjects:** Surgery, internal medicine, infection control, ophthalmology, nursing. **Special Collections:** Alcoholism (45 books; 25 AV programs; 6 journal subscriptions). **Holdings:** 800 books; 1100 bound periodical volumes; 50 other cataloged items. **Subscriptions:** 144 journals and other serials. **Services:** Interlibrary loan; copying; SDI; library open to the public with doctor's approval. **Computerized Information Services:** MEDLARS, BRS Information Technologies; OnTyme Electronic Message Network Service (electronic mail service). **Networks/Consortia:** Member of National Network of Libraries of Medicine - Pacific Southwest Region. **Remarks:** Alternate telephone number(s): 296-3211. FAX: (602)721-3945.

★14411★

St. Joseph's Hospital and Health Center - Medical Library (Med)
30 W. 7th St.
Dickinson, ND 58601
Phone: (701)225-7515
Sr. Salome Tlusty, Lib.Ck.
Founded: 1951. **Staff:** 1. **Subjects:** Medicine, nursing, administration, life search (MHU), womankind. **Holdings:** 1575 books; 28 bound periodical volumes; microfiche. **Subscriptions:** 128 journals and other serials; 4 newspapers. **Services:** Interlibrary loan; library open to the public with restrictions. **Computerized Information Services:** MEDLINE. **Networks/Consortia:** Member of National Network of Libraries of Medicine - Greater Midwest Region, Valley Medical Network (VMN). **Publications:** National Library of Medicine Classification and Dewey Decimal. **Remarks:** FAX: (701)225-9669.

★14412★
St. Joseph's Hospital Health Center - Medical and School of Nursing Libraries (Med)
206-301 Prospect Ave.   Phone: (315)448-5053
Syracuse, NY 13203   Mr. V. Juchimek, Hd.Libn.
Founded: 1940. **Staff:** Prof 2; Other 2. **Subjects:** Nursing, medicine, psychology, social sciences, religion. **Holdings:** 10,000 books; 3000 bound periodical volumes; 30 VF drawers of pamphlets; 450 cassette programs; models; slides; filmstrips; recordings. **Subscriptions:** 195 journals and other serials. **Services:** Interlibrary loan (limited); libraries open to the public for reference use only. **Networks/Consortia:** Member of Central New York Library Resources Council (CENTRO). **Publications:** Accessions List, monthly; Exchange List.

★14413★
St. Joseph's Hospital and Medical Center - Health Sciences Library (Med)
703 Main St.   Phone: (201)977-2104
Paterson, NJ 07503   Patricia May, Lib.Serv.
Staff: Prof 4; Other 1. **Subjects:** Medicine, biological sciences, dentistry, psychology, nursing. **Holdings:** 4500 books; 4800 bound periodical volumes. **Subscriptions:** 275 journals and other serials. **Services:** Interlibrary loan; copying; library open to the public for reference use only. **Computerized Information Services:** MEDLARS, DIALOG Information Services. **Networks/Consortia:** Member of Bergen Passaic Regional Library Cooperative. **Remarks:** FAX: (201)977-2479. **Staff:** Hannah Berkley, Asst.Med.Libn.; Eleanor Cohen, Asst.Med.Libn.; David Conchado, Asst.Med.Libn.; Hsin Ling Hsiao, Asst.Med.Libn.

★14414★
St. Joseph's Medical Center - Library (Med)
1800 N. California St.   Phone: (209)467-6332
Stockton, CA 95204   Colleen Lamkin, Lib.Coord.
Staff: Prof 1; Other 1. **Subjects:** Medicine, nursing, hospital administration, human relations. **Holdings:** 400 books; 840 bound periodical volumes; 50 video cassettes. **Subscriptions:** 140 journals and other serials. **Services:** Interlibrary loan; library not open to the public. **Computerized Information Services:** MEDLARS.

★14415★
St. Joseph's Medical Center - Medical Library (Med)
700 Broadway   Phone: (219)425-3094
Fort Wayne, IN 46802   Ellen Schellhause, Med.Info.Spec.
Founded: 1945. **Staff:** Prof 1.5. **Subjects:** Medical and health sciences. **Special Collections:** Aging and Geriatric Professional Collection. **Holdings:** 850 books; 300 periodical volumes; 106,000 microfiche. **Subscriptions:** 391 journals and other serials. **Services:** Interlibrary loan; library not open to the public. **Computerized Information Services:** NLM, BRS Information Technologies, DIALOG Information Services; CD-ROM. **Networks/Consortia:** Member of Northeastern Indiana Health Science Library Consortium, Tri-ALSA. **Remarks:** FAX: (219)425-3093. **Staff:** Joy Thorp.

★14416★
St. Joseph's Medical Center - Medical Library (Med)
801 E. Lasalle
Box 1935
South Bend, IN 46634-1935   Phone: (219)237-7228
     Jennifer N. Helmen, Libn.
Founded: 1981. **Staff:** Prof 1. **Subjects:** Medicine, nursing, pharmacy, health administration, pastoral care, social work. **Holdings:** 2955 books; 13,170 unbound periodicals; 580 documents, pamphlets, brochures, and clippings; 50 video cassettes; 13 drawers of microfiche. **Subscriptions:** 280 journals and other serials. **Services:** Interlibrary loan; copying; library open to the public. **Computerized Information Services:** BRS Information Technologies, MEDLARS. Performs searches free of charge. **Networks/Consortia:** Member of Area 2 Library Services Authority (ALSA 2), INCOLSA, National Network of Libraries of Medicine - Greater Midwest Region, National Network of Libraries of Medicine (NN/LM).

★14417★
St. Joseph's Medical Center - Medical Library (Med)
127 S. Broadway   Phone: (914)738-7539
Yonkers, NY 10701   Virginia Gregory, Libn.
Staff: Prof 1; Other 1. **Subjects:** Medicine, psychiatry, geriatrics, rehabilitation, family medicine. **Holdings:** 1600 volumes; 125 bound periodical volumes. **Subscriptions:** 125 journals and other serials. **Services:** Interlibrary loan; library open to the public by appointment. **Computerized Information Services:** GRATEFUL MED; CD-ROM. **Networks/Consortia:** Member of Health Information Libraries of Westchester (HILOW), New York Metropolitan Reference and Research Library Agency, BHSL. **Remarks:** FAX: (914)378-1071.

★14418★
St. Joseph's Mercy Hospitals - Medical Library (East Site) (Med)
215 North Ave.   Phone: (313)466-9485
Mt. Clemens, MI 48043   Sandra A. Studebaker, Mgr.
Staff: Prof 1.2.; Other 1.5. **Subjects:** Medicine, nursing, allied health sciences, consumer health, healthcare management. **Holdings:** 3650 titles; 3500 bound periodical volumes. **Subscriptions:** 485 journals and other serials. **Services:** Interlibrary loan; copying; current awareness; library open to the public for reference use only. **Computerized Information Services:** NLM, BRS Information Technologies. **Publications:** Library Acquisitions List - for internal distribution only. **Remarks:** FAX: (313)466-9487. The west site library is located at 15855 19 Mile Rd., Mt. Clemens, MI 48044; the telephone number is 263-2485. **Formerly:** St. Joseph's Hospital Centers.

★14419★
St. Joseph's Seminary - Archbishop Corrigan Memorial Library (Rel-Phil)
201 Seminary Ave.   Phone: (914)968-6200
Yonkers, NY 10704   Sr. Regina A. Melican, O.P., Lib.Dir.
Founded: 1953. **Staff:** Prof 3; Other 3. **Subjects:** Sacred scripture, moral and dogmatic theology, liturgy, canon law, patristics. **Special Collections:** Archdiocesan Archives. **Holdings:** 68,927 books; 10,600 bound periodical volumes. **Subscriptions:** 260 journals and other serials; 7 newspapers. **Services:** Interlibrary loan; copying; library open to the public for reference use only. **Automated Operations:** Computerized cataloging. **Computerized Information Services:** OCLC. **Networks/Consortia:** Member of SUNY/OCLC Library Network. **Publications:** Recent Acquisitions, monthly - to faculty and students. **Staff:** Barbara Carey, Asst.Libn.; Sr. Kathleen McCann, Per.Libn.

★14420★
St. Joseph's Seminary - Library (Rel-Phil, Area-Ethnic)
1200 Varnum St., N.E.   Phone: (202)526-4231
Washington, DC 20017   Laurence A. Schmitt, Libn.
Founded: 1930. **Staff:** Prof 1; Other 1. **Subjects:** Philosophy and theology, black studies. **Holdings:** 24,000 volumes. **Subscriptions:** 75 journals and other serials. **Services:** Interlibrary loan (limited); library open to the public by appointment.

St. Joseph's Shrine
See: **Oratoire St-Joseph** (12517)

★14421★
St. Joseph's University - Academy of Food Marketing - Campbell Library (Food-Bev)
5600 City Ave.   Phone: (215)660-1196
Philadelphia, PA 19131   Anna Mae Penrose, Libn.
Founded: 1965. **Staff:** Prof 1; Other 1. **Subjects:** Food marketing, retailing, consumerism, agricultural products. **Special Collections:** Bound food trade journals; U.S. Department of Agriculture Yearbooks, 1865 to present. **Holdings:** 4025 books; 1490 bound periodical volumes; 1710 items in corporation files; 207 reels of microfilm; journals and doctoral dissertations; 535 microfiche; 4372 subject information files. **Subscriptions:** 270 journals and other serials. **Services:** Interlibrary loan; copying; library open to the public for reference use only, reciprocal privileges extended to food industry libraries and organizations. **Computerized Information Services:** DIALOG Information Services. **Publications:** Serials Holdings, annual; Selected Acquisitions; internal bibliographies. **Remarks:** FAX: (215)660-1604.

★14422★
St. Joseph's University - Xavier-Damians Christian Life Community Library (Rel-Phil)
5600 City Line Ave.   Phone: (215)660-1905
Philadelphia, PA 19131   Victoria Montavon, Libn.
Subjects: Religon and theology. **Remarks:** No further information was supplied by respondent.

★14423★
St. Jude Catholic Church - Fr. William Dowell Parish Library (Rel-Phil)
15889 E. 7 Mile Rd.
Detroit, MI 48205   Phone: (313)527-0380
Founded: 1984. **Subjects:** Catholic faith, prayer, Bible, theology, ministry, saints. **Holdings:** 4750 books; audiotapes.

★ 14424 ★

St. Jude Children's Research Hospital - Biomedical Library (Med)
332 N. Lauderdale
Box 318   Phone: (901)525-0389
Memphis, TN 38101   Mary Edith Walker, Lib.Dir.
Founded: 1962. **Staff:** Prof 2; Other 2. **Subjects:** Medicine, biological sciences. **Holdings:** 2200 books; 12,000 bound periodical volumes; 17 dissertations; 300 audio cassettes; 120 AV programs. **Subscriptions:** 275 journals and other serials. **Services:** Interlibrary loan; SDI; library open to medical professionals only for reference use. **Automated Operations:** Computerized ILL (DOCLINE). **Computerized Information Services:** DIALOG Information Services, PaperChase, MEDLINE; CD-ROMs (MEDLINE, CANCER-CD, CINAHL). **Networks/Consortia:** Member of Association of Memphis Area Health Science Libraries (AMAHSL). **Publications:** InfoLink - for internal distribution only. **Remarks:** FAX: (901)527-2770. **Staff:** Cindy Suter.

★ 14425 ★

St. Jude Medical Center - Medical Library
101 E. Valencia Mesa Dr.   Phone: (714)871-3280
Fullerton, CA 92635   Carol Bondurant, Lib.Techn.
Founded: 1974. **Staff:** 1. **Subjects:** Medicine, nursing. **Holdings:** 500 books; 20 sound-slide sets; 100 video cassettes. **Subscriptions:** 105 journals and other serials. **Services:** Interlibrary loan; copying; SDI; library open to consortia members and local librarians. **Computerized Information Services:** MEDLARS. **Remarks:** FAX: (714)738-3057.

★ 14426 ★

St. Kevork Armenian Church - Library (Hist)
3211 Synott Rd.   Phone: (713)558-2722
Houston, TX 77082   Fr. Nersess Jebejian
Founded: 1986. **Subjects:** Armenia - history, literature, genocide, art. **Holdings:** 1000 books; 10 bound periodical volumes; 5 reports; videocassettes; films. **Subscriptions:** 30 journals and other serials; 20 newspapers. **Services:** Library open to the public. **Staff:** Silva Dekmezian.

★ 14427 ★

St. Lawrence College Saint-Laurent - Learning Resource Centre (Educ)
Windmill Point   Phone: (613)933-6080
Cornwall, ON, Canada K6H 4Z1   Sherwin Raichman, Dir.
Founded: 1967. **Staff:** 6. **Subjects:** Education, psychology, social sciences, literature, art, technology, history, medicine. **Special Collections:** St. Lawrence College Saint-Laurent (Cornwall) Archives. **Holdings:** 500 volumes. **Subscriptions:** 210 journals and other serials; 9 newspapers. **Services:** Interlibrary loan; copying; center open to the public. **Computerized Information Services:** Infomart Online, Info Globe, DOBIS Canadian Online Library System; Envoy 100 (electronic mail service). **Remarks:** FAX: (613)937-1523. Electronic mail address(es): ILL.OCSL (Envoy 100). Maintains a toy lending library.

★ 14428 ★

St. Lawrence College Saint-Laurent - Learning Resource Centre (Hum, Sci-Engr)
King & Portsmouth
Box 6000   Phone: (613)544-5400
Kingston, ON, Canada K7L 5A6   Sherwin Raichman, Dir.
Founded: 1967. **Staff:** Prof 2; Other 16. **Subjects:** Humanities, technologies, nursing, arts, business. **Holdings:** 120,000 books. **Subscriptions:** 1322 journals and other serials; 32 newspapers. **Services:** Interlibrary loan; copying; personal computer user's center; center open to the public. **Automated Operations:** Computerized public access catalog, cataloging, and circulation. **Computerized Information Services:** QL Systems, Info Globe, DIALOG Information Services, Infomart Online, CAN/OLE. **Special Catalogs:** Union list of campus libraries in Brockville, Cornwall, and Kingston, Ontario; union list of medical serials in Kingston and area institutions. **Remarks:** FAX: (613)545-3920. **Staff:** Barbara Carr, Ref.Libn.; Barbara Love, Ref.Libn. - Kingston.

★ 14429 ★

St. Lawrence County Historical Association - Archives (Hist)
3 E. Main St.
Box 8   Phone: (315)386-8133
Canton, NY 13617   Shirley Tramontana, Dir.
Founded: 1947. **Staff:** Prof 3. **Subjects:** St. Lawrence County history. **Special Collections:** Silas Wright Papers (250 items); local genealogy (1000 items). **Holdings:** 1500 books; 150 bound periodical volumes; 4000 maps, clippings, pamphlets, documents. **Services:** Copying; archives open to the public. **Publications:** Local history journal, quarterly - available through membership only.

★ 14430 ★

St. Lawrence Hospital - Medical Library (Med)
1210 W. Saginaw   Phone: (515)377-0354
Lansing, MI 48915   Jane B. Claytor, Mgr.
Staff: Prof 1; Other 1. **Subjects:** Medicine, nursing, mental health, hospital management, allied health science. **Holdings:** 2900 books; 8700 bound periodical volumes. **Subscriptions:** 360 journals and other serials. **Services:** Interlibrary loan; copying; library open to health care professionals. **Computerized Information Services:** MEDLARS, BRS Information Technologies, OCLC, WILSONLINE, DIALOG Information Services. **Networks/Consortia:** Member of Capital Area Library Network (Calnet), Michigan Library Consortium (MLC), Michigan Health Sciences Libraries Association (MHSLA), Mid-Michigan Health Sciences Libraries (M-MHSL). **Remarks:** FAX: (517)377-0315.

★ 14431 ★

St. Lawrence Parks Commission - Upper Canada Village Reference Library (Hist)
Hwy. 2, R.R. 1   Phone: (613)543-3704
Morrisburg, ON, Canada K0C 1X0   Jack Schecter, Libn./Archv.
Staff: Prof 1. **Subjects:** Canadian and Eastern Ontario history; local history and genealogy; history of everyday life, especially agricultural trades and technology; practical and decorative arts; material culture; social history; museums. **Holdings:** 3000 books; 38 bound periodical volumes; 100 boxes of manuscripts, documents, photographs, maps; 242 reels of microfilm; 59 microfiche. **Subscriptions:** 46 journals and other serials. **Services:** Copying; library open to the public for reference use only. **Remarks:** FAX: (613)543-2847.

St. Lawrence Psychiatric Center
See: **New York (State) Office of Mental Health** (11677)

★ 14432 ★

St. Lawrence Seaway Authority - Information Office (Trans)
360 Albert St.   Phone: (613)598-4614
Ottawa, ON, Canada K1R 7X7   G. Hemsley, Info.Off.
Founded: 1954. **Subjects:** St. Lawrence Seaway. **Holdings:** Studies; reports; general information material. **Services:** Collection open for reference use only on request. **Remarks:** FAX: (613)598-4620.

★ 14433 ★

St. Lawrence University - Special Collections (Hist)
Owen D. Young Library   Phone: (315)379-5476
Canton, NY 13617   Lynn Ekfelt, Cur.
Staff: 2. **Subjects:** 19th century farm, village, and family life in the northern counties of New York; political, cultural, and industrial history of the area. **Special Collections:** Papers of Irving Bacheller, Frederic Remington, David Parish, Nathaniel Hawthorne, George Redington, Robert McEwen, Owen D. Young, and Rabbi Dr. Seymour Siegel; St. Lawrence Seaway Collection. **Holdings:** 1500 linear feet of manuscripts, documents, and other materials. **Services:** Interlibrary loan (limited); copying; collections open to the public. **Automated Operations:** Integrated Library System. **Computerized Information Services:** DIALOG Information Services, OCLC, BRS Information Technologies. **Networks/Consortia:** Member of New York State Interlibrary Loan Network (NYSILL), Associated Colleges of the St. Lawrence Valley, Inc. (ACSLV). **Publications:** Bulletin of the Friends of the Owen B. Young Library. **Remarks:** FAX: (315)379-5729. **Staff:** Richard J. Kuhta, Dir.

★ 14434 ★

St. Louis Art Museum - Richardson Memorial Library (Art)
Forest Park
1 Fine Arts Dr.   Phone: (314)721-0067
St. Louis, MO 63110-1380   Stephanie C. Sigala, Hd.Libn.
Founded: 1915. **Staff:** Prof 3; Other 6. **Subjects:** Art history, painting, sculpture, decorative arts, American art, graphic arts. **Special Collections:** Museum archives; clippings about St. Louis artists. **Holdings:** 52,000 books and bound periodical volumes; 35,000 pamphlets; 37,000 slides; 15,000 art auction catalogs. **Subscriptions:** 300 journals and other serials. **Services:** Interlibrary loan; copying; library open to adult public. **Automated Operations:** Computerized cataloging. **Computerized Information Services:** DIALOG Information Services, RLIN, WILSONLINE, St. Louis Public Library MULSP. **Networks/Consortia:** Member of Research Libraries Information Network (RLIN). **Special Indexes:** Bulletin of St. Louis Art Museum; St. Louis Artist Files; exhibitions of the St. Louis Art Museum (1909 to present); exhibitions of the St. Louis Museum of Fine Arts (1881-1909). **Remarks:** FAX: (314)721-6172. **Staff:** Norma Sindelar, Archv.; Marianne L. Cavanaugh, Assoc.Libn.

St. Louis Children's Hospital Library
See: Washington University Medical Center - St. Louis Children's Hospital Library (20073)

★ 14435 ★
St. Louis Christian College - Library (Rel-Phil)
1360 Grandview Dr.   Phone: (314)837-6777
Florissant, MO 63033   Christian D. Schink, Dir.
Founded: 1956. **Staff:** Prof 1; Other 1. **Subjects:** Restoration, Christian Church, Bible, church history, religions, Christian eduction. **Holdings:** 46,000 books; 60 bound periodical volumes; 14,000 volumes on microfiche; 1500 reels of microfilm of Restoration-Christian Church history and Bible commentaries. **Subscriptions:** 138 journals and other serials. **Services:** Interlibrary loan; copying; library open to the public. **Staff:** Elizabeth McCaslin, Hd. of Tech.Serv.

★ 14436 ★
St. Louis College of Pharmacy - O.J. Cloughly Alumni Library (Med)
4588 Parkview Pl.   Phone: (314)367-8700
St. Louis, MO 63110   Judith A. Longstreth, Lib.Dir.
Staff: Prof 4; Other 3. **Subjects:** Pharmacy, pharmacology, medicine, drug information, materia medica. **Holdings:** 35,000 volumes; 500 audiotapes; 12,700 microforms. **Subscriptions:** 450 journals and other serials; 8 newspapers. **Services:** Interlibrary loan; copying; library open to the public for reference use only. **Automated Operations:** Computerized cataloging, serials, and acquisitions. **Computerized Information Services:** OCLC, DIALOG Information Services, Data-Star; CD-ROMs (MEDLINE, Drugdex, Poisondex, International Pharmaceutical Abstracts); BITNET (electronic mail service). **Networks/Consortia:** Member of Missouri Library Network Corp. (MLNC), St. Louis Regional Library Network. **Publications:** Acquisition List, quarterly; library newsletter, quarterly. **Remarks:** FAX: (314)367-2784. **Staff:** R. David Weaver, Asst.Libn./Archv.; Suraya Coorey, LRC Coord./Asst.Libn.; Irwin Mitchell, AV Coord.

★ 14437 ★
St. Louis Community College at Forest Park - Instructional Resources - Special Collections (Area-Ethnic)
5600 Oakland Ave.   Phone: (314)644-9209
St. Louis, MO 63110   Carol S. Warrington
Founded: 1968. **Staff:** Prof 5.5; Other 20.5. **Subjects:** African Americans, allied health, tourism. **Services:** Interlibrary loan; collection open to the public. **Automated Operations:** Computerized cataloging (NOTIS). **Computerized Information Services:** DIALOG Information Services, BRS Information Technologies, WILSONLINE. Performs searches. Contact Person: Carol Shahriary, Ref.Libn. **Remarks:** Interlibrary loan requests should be directed to 5460 Highland Pk. Dr., St. Louis, MO 63110. FAX: (314)644-9240.

★ 14438 ★
St. Louis Comptrollers Office - Microfilm Department (Hist)
1200 Market St., Rm. 1   Phone: (314)622-4274
St. Louis, MO 63104   Edward J. Machowski, Mgr.
Founded: 1960. **Staff:** Prof 3; Other 9. **Subjects:** St. Louis, Missouri; genealogy. **Special Collections:** French, English, and Spanish documents to 1901; French and Spanish land grants; birth records, 1863-1909; death records, 1850-1909; cancelled voter affidavits, 1896-1983; building information, 1876-1977; plans, 1940-1988. **Holdings:** 60,000 reels of microfilm of fiscal records, vital statistics, building and tax records. **Services:** Copying; department open to the public. **Staff:** Ruth Brown, Asst.Mgr.; Mary Kelso, Adm.Asst.

★ 14439 ★
St. Louis Conservatory and Schools for the Arts (CASA) - Mae M. Whitaker Library (Mus)
560 Trinity Ave.   Phone: (314)863-3033
St. Louis, MO 63130   Kathleen Higgins, Libn.
Founded: 1974. **Staff:** Prof 1. **Subjects:** Music. **Special Collections:** Performance and listening libraries; Thomas B. Sherman Collection; Robert Orchard Opera Collection; Max Risch Wind Ensemble and Bassoon Music Collection. **Holdings:** 13,683 titles books and scores; 284 bound periodical volumes; 12,373 phonograph records and tapes; 20 videocassettes; 2 VF drawers of music publishers' catalogs; 1915 microfiche. **Subscriptions:** 40 journals and other serials. **Services:** Interlibrary loan; library open to the public for reference use only. **Networks/Consortia:** Member of St. Louis Regional Library Network. **Special Catalogs:** Catalog of music for performance.

St. Louis County Historical Society - Northeast Minnesota Historical Center
See: Northeast Minnesota Historical Center (11971)

★ 14440 ★
St. Louis County Law Library (Law)
100 N. 5th Ave., W., Rm. 515   Phone: (218)726-2611
Duluth, MN 55802   Michele Des Rosier, Law Libn.
Founded: 1889. **Staff:** Prof 1. **Subjects:** Law. **Holdings:** 20,000 books. **Services:** Copying; library open to the public for reference use only. **Remarks:** FAX: (218)726-2612.

★ 14441 ★
St. Louis County Law Library (Law)
Courts Bldg.
7900 Carondelet Ave., Suite 536   Phone: (314)889-2726
Clayton, MO 63105   Mary C. Dahm, Libn.
Staff: Prof 1; Other 2. **Subjects:** Law. **Holdings:** 18,600 volumes. **Subscriptions:** 17 journals and other serials. **Services:** Copying; library open to the public.

★ 14442 ★
St. Louis Genealogical Society - Library (Hist)
9011 Manchester Rd., Suite 3   Phone: (314)968-2763
St. Louis, MO 63144   Lorraine C. Cates, Libn.
Founded: 1969. **Staff:** 2. **Subjects:** Genealogy, family histories. **Special Collections:** Daughters of the American Revolution Collection (lineage books and indexes; bound volumes of DAR Magazine, 1896 to present). **Holdings:** 30,000 volumes; 500 reels of microfilm; 250 microfiche; 100 cassette tapes. **Subscriptions:** 275 journals and other serials. **Services:** Copying; limited genealogical research (fee based); library open to the public. **Publications:** List of publications - available on request. **Special Indexes:** Index to 1860 St. Louis City & County Census (book). **Remarks:** Library is located at University City Library, 6701 Delmar Blvd., University City, MO 63130.

★ 14443 ★
St. Louis Hearing and Speech Centers - Library (Med)
9526 Manchester   Phone: (314)968-4710
St. Louis, MO 63119-1313   Peggy Thompson, Exec.Dir.
Founded: 1920. **Staff:** 18. **Subjects:** Audiology, speech pathology, sign language, industrial hearing conservation, accent reduction, stutterers, preschool language. **Holdings:** 600 volumes. **Services:** Interlibrary loan; library open to the public. **Publications:** Health Information. **Remarks:** St. Louis Hearing and Speech Centers are nonprofit United Way agencies.

★ 14444 ★
St. Louis Mercantile Library Association - Library (Hum)
510 Locust St., 6th Fl.   Phone: (314)621-0670
St. Louis, MO 63101   Jeffrey E. Smith, Ph.D., Exec.Dir.
Founded: 1846. **Staff:** Prof 8; Other 10. **Subjects:** History, biography, social sciences, science, fine arts, fiction, literature, railroad, inland river transportation. **Special Collections:** Alchemy, dating to 1420; Ethan Allen Hitchcock Collection; early Western Americana; early French and German literature; early state papers; Colonial Dames of America (155 items; pamphlets); John Mason Peck Collection; Herman T. Pott National Inland Waterways Collection (10,000 volumes; pamphlets; documents); John W. Barriger, III National Railroad Collection (11,000 volumes; 50,000 photographs; papers; files); St. Louis Globe-Democrat morgue (10 million clippings; 125,000 photographs); Robert Campbell family papers; St. Louis Globe-Democrat Glass Plate Negative Collection; Isabel H. Benham Papers; Ends Bridge-Terminal Railroad Association of St. Louis Financial Papers. **Holdings:** 225,000 books; 1 million manuscript items in 2000 linear feet; 175,000 photographs; 25,000 newspapers (separate issues); 500 pieces of art, prints , maps. **Subscriptions:** 300 journals and other serials. **Services:** Interlibrary loan; copying; special tours; library open to the public with restrictions. **Automated Operations:** Computerized cataloging. **Computerized Information Services:** OCLC. **Networks/Consortia:** Member of St. Louis Regional Library Network. **Publications:** Mercantile Associations (newsletter), quarterly; New Books Bulletin, monthly; annual reports. **Special Catalogs:** Rare and Beautiful: Two Centuries of Ornithological Book Illustration; Seed for Thought: Seed Catalogues; Adventures and Suffering: The American Indian Captivity Through the

Centuries; The Early Histories of St. Louis; Stories On Stone: The Darley Lithographs for "The Legend of Sleepy Hollow" & "Rip Van Winkle"; A Century of American Railway Bridges and Building. **Special Indexes:** Guide to the Robert Campbell Family Papers; Guide to the Federal Barge Lines Collection; Guide to the Waterways Collection; Guide to the St. Louis Globe-Democrat; Guide to the Shorter Manuscript Collections; Guide to the John Mason Peck Collection; Guide to the Ethan Allen Hitchcock Collection; Inventory and Guide to the Archives. **Remarks:** FAX: (314)621-1782. **Staff:** Mark Cedeck, Barriger Lib.Cur.; David Cassens, Pott Lib.Cur.; Elaine Bell, Actuary; Charles E. Brown, Ref.Libn.; John Hoover, Assoc.Libn.; Rika Beckley, Dev.Dir.; Judy Friedrich, Cat.; Ellen Thomasson, Outreach Coord.; Geraldine Pabst, Exec.Sec.

★ 14445 ★
St. Louis Metropolitan Police Department - Library (Soc Sci, Law)
315 S. Tucker   Phone: (314)444-5581
St. Louis, MO 63102   Barbara L. Miksicek, Libn.
Founded: 1947. **Staff:** Prof 1. **Subjects:** Police science, criminology, corrections, juvenile delinquency, criminal law, narcotics. **Special Collections:** Annual Reports, 1861 to present. **Holdings:** 21,000 books; 1002 bound periodical volumes; 515 titles on microfiche; 20 VF drawers of reports, pamphlets, clippings, manuscripts; 466 pictures. **Subscriptions:** 153 journals and other serials. **Services:** Interlibrary loan; library open to the public for reference use only. **Networks/Consortia:** Member of St. Louis Regional Library Network, Criminal Justice Information Exchange Group. **Publications:** Bibliographies; Directory of Law Enforcement Agencies in Metropolitan St. Louis; newsletters, monthly; booklists. **Special Indexes:** Index of articles in eight police journals (card); index of St. Louis Police Journal, 1912 to present (card). **Remarks:** FAX: (314)444-5689.

★ 14446 ★
St. Louis Post-Dispatch - Reference Library (Publ)
900 N. Tucker Blvd.   Phone: (314)622-7148
St. Louis, MO 63101   Gerald D. Brown, Lib.Dir.
Staff: Prof 3; Other 10. **Subjects:** Newspaper reference topics. **Holdings:** 1200 books; 2500 reports and pamphlets; 10 million clippings; 3 million photographs. **Subscriptions:** 15 journals and other serials. **Services:** Copying; library open to the public with restrictions. **Computerized Information Services:** VU/TEXT Information Services, DataTimes, NEXIS, DIALOG Information Services; UNIDAS 1100/72 (internal database). Performs searches on fee basis by mail only. **Remarks:** FAX: (314)622-7093. **Staff:** Michael A. Marler, Asst.Lib.Dir.

★ 14447 ★
St. Louis Psychoanalytic Institute - Betty Golde Smith Memorial Library (Med)
4524 Forest Park Ave.   Phone: (314)361-7075
St. Louis, MO 63108   Celia D. Bouchard
Founded: 1956. **Staff:** Prof 1; Other 1. **Subjects:** Psychoanalysis and related subjects. **Holdings:** 6000 volumes. **Subscriptions:** 33 journals and other serials. **Services:** Interlibrary loan; literature searching; library open to the public. **Publications:** Newsletter, 3/year - to mailing list.

St. Louis Public library - Applied Science Department
See: **St. Louis Public Library - Business, Science & Technology Department** (14449)

★ 14448 ★
St. Louis Public Library - Adult Education Department (Educ)
1301 Olive   Phone: (314)241-2288
St. Louis, MO 63103   A. James Lyons, Mgr., Adult Educ.
Founded: 1974. **Staff:** Prof 1. **Subjects:** Careers, job searching, U.S. and foreign educational institutions, test preparation, literacy. **Holdings:** 5000 books; U.S. college catalogs on microfice. **Subscriptions:** 13 journals and other serials. **Services:** Interlibrary loan; center open to the public. **Automated Operations:** Computerized public access catalog. **Computerized Information Services:** The Guidance Information System (GIS). Performs searches free of charge. **Special Catalogs:** St. Louis Vo-Tech continuing education file. **Remarks:** FAX: (314)241-4305.

★ 14449 ★
St. Louis Public Library - Business, Science & Technology Department (Sci-Engr)
Central Library
1301 Olive St.   Phone: (314)241-2288
St. Louis, MO 63103-2389   Sara Beck, Mgr.
Founded: 1912. **Staff:** Prof 2; Other 3.5. **Subjects:** Business, engineering; electricity and electronics; materials science; manufacturing processes; home remodeling; radio, Television, and automobile repair; popular medical; cookbooks. **Special Collections:** Patent and Trademark Depository Collection. **Holdings:** 20,000 books; 45,000 bound periodical volumes; 40 VF drawers of Sams Photofacts; 2300 automobile repair manuals. **Subscriptions:** 600 journals and other serials. **Services:** Interlibrary loan; copying; department open to the public. **Computerized Information Services:** BRS Information Technologies. DIALOG Information Services. **Remarks:** FAX (314)241-4305. **Formerly:** Its Applied Science Department. **Staff:** Carol Giles.

★ 14450 ★
St. Louis Public Library - Central Youth Services, Downtown Branch (Hum)
Central Library
1301 Olive St.   Phone: (314)539-0380
St. Louis, MO 63103-2389   Julanne M. Good, Youth Serv., Central Lib.
Founded: 1912. **Staff:** Prof 1; Other 1. **Subjects:** Children's literature, emphasizing fairy tales, folklore; history and criticism of children's literature. **Special Collections:** Award-winning American children's books; Jacob Abbott (50 titles); William Taylor Adams (38 titles); Horatio Alger (60 titles); Beatrix Potter; Charles Austin Fordick (32 titles); early children's literature (2000 books); history of children's literature (500 books); folklore (2000 titles); Mother Goose (50 editions, 1878 to present); St. Nicholas (complete run); story telling; representative collection of early fantasy illustrators including Arthur Rackham, Kay Nielsen, Maxfield Parrish and others. **Holdings:** 28,500 volumes. **Subscriptions:** 20 journals and other serials. **Services:** Interlibrary loan; copying; programs for children and adults; room open to the public. **Remarks:** FAX: (314)241-4305. **Formerly:** Its Children's Literature Room.

St. Louis Public Library - Children's Literature Room
See: **St. Louis Public Library - Central Youth Services, Downtown Branch** (14450)

★ 14451 ★
St. Louis Public Library - Film Library Service (Aud-Vis)
1624 Locust St.   Phone: (314)241-0478
St. Louis, MO 63103-2389   Diane Freiermuth, Mgr., Film Serv.
Founded: 1948. **Staff:** Prof 1; Other 4. **Holdings:** 3000 16mm sound educational films; 2500 videocassettes. **Services:** Service open to the public within the City of St. Louis and St. Louis County Library Districts. **Computerized Information Services:** Media Minder (internal database). **Publications:** New additions list, annual. **Special Catalogs:** Catalog of 16mm sound films and educational video cassettes, semiannual. **Remarks:** FAX: (314)241-5052.

★ 14452 ★
St. Louis Public Library - Fine Arts Department (Art)
Central Library
1301 Olive St.   Phone: (314)539-0393
St. Louis, MO 63103-2389   Mary E. Frechette, Mgr., Fine Arts
Founded: 1912. **Staff:** Prof 2; Other 1. **Subjects:** Fine arts and related fields - music, painting, sculpture, costume, architecture, design, photography, graphics. **Special Collections:** Steedman Architectural Collection; Local Artists Clipping File. **Holdings:** 75,000 books; 135 VF drawers; 17,500 slides; 3000 phonograph records; 2000 compact discs; unframed prints. **Subscriptions:** 195 journals and other serials. **Services:** Interlibrary loan; copying; department open to the public. **Automated Operations:** Computerized public access catalog. **Computerized Information Services:** St. Louis Artists File (internal database). **Special Catalogs:** Steedman Architectural Library Catalog. **Remarks:** FAX: (314)241-4305. **Staff:** Michael Lomar, Libn.

★ 14453 ★
St. Louis Public Library - Government Information Unit (Info Sci, Geog-Map)
Central Library
1301 Olive St.   Phone: (314)241-2288
St. Louis, MO 63103-2389   Anne Watts, Downtown Br.Coord.
Founded: 1865. **Staff:** Prof 1; Other 5. **Special Collections:** Defense Mapping Agency map and chart depository; U.S. Geological Survey map depository; Missouri state document depository, 1976 to present; U.S. Government document depository, 1866 to present. **Holdings:** Missouri documents. **Services:** Interlibrary loan; copying; department open to the public. **Automated Operations:** Computerized public access catalog and cataloging. **Computerized Information Services:** DIALOG Information Services, BRS Information Technologies, U.S. Patent Classification System; CD-ROMs. Performs some searches on a fee basis. **Remarks:** FAX: (314)539-0353. **Formerly:** Its Access and Information Services.

★ 14454 ★
St. Louis Public Library - History and Genealogy Department (Hist)
Central Library
1301 Olive St.   Phone: (314)539-0385
St. Louis, MO 63103-2389   Joseph M. Winkler, Coord. of Res.Coll.
Founded: 1973. **Staff:** Prof 2. **Subjects:** U.S. history; genealogy of Missouri, Illinois, and most states east of the Mississippi River; heraldry; maps. **Special Collections:** Complete set of St. Louis city directories; early printed records of Eastern States; British learned societies publications; American Colonial and State Papers: passenger lists and indexes of the 19th century (microfilm); St. Louis newspapers; Boston Evening Transcript: Genealogical Queries (microfiche); U.S. state and county histories and genealogical materials; Missouri Union and Confederate service records and indexes (microfilm); federal population censuses (microfilm) and indexes; territorial papers of U.S.; family histories (4000). **Holdings:** 143,000 volumes; 1150 genealogy files; 8482 reels of microfilm; U.S. Geological Survey depository for topographic maps; U.S. Army maps of foreign countries; U.S. and foreign gazetteers. **Subscriptions:** 395 current journals and other serials. **Services:** Interlibrary loan; copying; department open to the public. **Computerized Information Services:** CD-ROMs (Biography Index, Place Name Index, U.S. History on CD-ROM). **Publications:** Genealogical Materials and Local Histories in the St. Louis Public Library (bibliography of holdings), 1965, 1st supplement, 1971. **Special Indexes:** Heraldry Index of the St. Louis Public Library, 1980 (4 volumes); Genealogy index (card); heraldry index supplement (card); map index; surname and locations file. **Remarks:** FAX: (314)539-0393. **Staff:** Cynthia Millar; Thomas Pearson.

★ 14455 ★
St. Louis Public Library - Humanities and Social Sciences Department (Hum, Bus-Fin)
Central Library
1301 Olive St.   Phone: (314)241-2288
St. Louis, MO 63103-2389   Barbara Murphy, Mgr.
Founded: 1973. **Staff:** Prof 3. **Subjects:** Religion, psychology, philosophy, social sciences, English and American literature, foreign languages, education, performing arts, sports, recreation. **Special Collections:** Augusta and Fred Gottlieb Collection; Missouri Statutes collection; Code of Federal Regulations, U.S. Code; Missouri regulations; federal register; IRS regulations; Supreme Court slip decisions. **Holdings:** Books; pamphlets; journals; clippings; 1200 domestic and foreign telephone directories; foreign language study tapes and videotapes. **Subscriptions:** 200 journals. **Services:** Interlibrary loan; copying; department open to the public. **Automated Operations:** Computerized public access catalog. **Computerized Information Services:** InfoTrac. **Remarks:** Alternate telephone number(s): (314)539-0316. **Staff:** Katherine Sathi. Donald Allen.

★ 14456 ★
St. Louis Public Library - Popular Library (Mus)
Central Library
1301 Olive St.   Phone: (314)241-2288
St. Louis, MO 63103-2389   Margaret Ganyard, Dept.Hd.
Founded: 1956. **Staff:** Prof 1; Other 1. **Subjects:** General collection. **Holdings:** 500 books; videotapes; books on tape; music cassettes; phonograph records; compact disks; magazines. **Remarks:** FAX: (314)241-4305. **Staff:** Anthony King.

★ 14457 ★
St. Louis Public Library - Rare Book & Special Collections Department (Rare Book)
Central Library
1301 Olive St.   Phone: (314)241-2288
St. Louis, MO 63103-2389   Jean E. Meeh Gosebrink, Mgr., Rare Bks. & Spec.Coll.
Founded: 1965. **Staff:** Prof 1; Other 1. **Subjects:** St. Louis and regional history, St. Louis authors and imprints, history of the book and printing, natural history. **Special Collections:** St. Louis Collections; Reedy's Mirror, volumes 4-29, 1894-1920; William Marion Reedy Library; Pre-1801 Imprints Collection; N.J. Werner Typographic Collection; Benjamin Franklin Shumard Library; Grolier Society Collection (history of writing and the book); St. Louis media archives; German-American Heritage Archives. **Holdings:** 14,000 books; archives of St. Louis Public Library; manuscripts. **Subscriptions:** 25 journals and other serials. **Services:** Department open to the public with restrictions. **Publications:** The Word in Print: Bibles in St. Louis Public Library's Special Collection, 1991; Guide to Collections in the St. Louis Media Archives, St. Louis Public Library: A Preliminary Finding Aid, 1990. **Remarks:** FAX: (314)241-4305.

★ 14458 ★
St. Louis Public Library - St. Louis Area Studies Center (Hist)
Central Library
1301 Olive St.
St. Louis, MO 63103-2389   Noel Holobeck, Libn.
Founded: 1991. **Staff:** Prof 1. **Subjects:** St. Louis and metropolitan area - history, culture, urban studies. **Special Collections:** St. Louis city directories (microfilm); St. Louis clippings and pamphlets (vertical file drawers). **Holdings:** 1300 volumes; maps. **Publications:** The German-American Heritage of St. Louis: A Guide, 1991; Saint Louis: An Annotated Bibliography on the City and its Area, 1991. **Special Indexes:** Reedy's Mirror Index, 1894-1914 (card); local history index (card).

★ 14459 ★
St. Louis Public Schools - Library Services Center (Educ)
1100 Farrar St.   Phone: (314)436-4664
St. Louis, MO 63107   Robert G. Nador, Dir.
Staff: Prof 5; Other 15. **Subjects:** Education. **Holdings:** Figures not available for books; ERIC microfiche, 1968 to present. **Services:** Interlibrary loan; copying; center open to the public by appointment. **Automated Operations:** Computerized cataloging and acquisitions. **Networks/Consortia:** Member of St. Louis Regional Library Network. **Remarks:** FAX: (314)436-7514. **Staff:** Howard Thomas, Coord., Fac.; Reola Boyd, Coord., Instr.; Helen Grauel, Coord., Acq.; Nancy McCullough, Coord., Ref. & Sel.; Robert Levitt, Cat.

★ 14460 ★
St. Louis Regional Medical Center - Medical Library (Med)
5535 Delmar Blvd.   Phone: (314)879-6272
St. Louis, MO 63112   Mrs. Bernie Ferrell, Med.Libn.
Founded: 1985. **Staff:** Prof 1. **Subjects:** Medicine, surgery, pediatrics, orthopedics, obstetrics and gynecology, neurology, neonatology. **Holdings:** 1000 books; 10,000 bound periodical volumes. **Subscriptions:** 125 journals and other serials. **Services:** Interlibrary loan; library not open to the public. **Computerized Information Services:** MEDLINE.

St. Louis Roman Catholic Theological Seminary
See: **Kenrick-Glennon Seminary (8640)**

★ 14461 ★
St. Louis Science Center - Library (Sci-Engr)
5050 Oakland Ave.   Phone: (314)533-8282
St. Louis, MO 63110   James Houser, Coll.Mgr.
Founded: 1984. **Staff:** 1. **Subjects:** General science, natural history, astronomy, aeronautics, technology. **Holdings:** 3200 books; 18 bound periodical volumes. **Subscriptions:** 25 journals and other serials. **Services:** Library not open to the public. **Networks/Consortia:** Member of St. Louis Regional Library Network. **Remarks:** FAX: (314)289-4420. **Staff:** Lynn C. Fendler, Libn.

★ 14462 ★
St. Louis University - Center for Urban Programs - Library (Plan)
221 N. Grand Blvd.   Phone: (314)658-3934
St. Louis, MO 63103   Kathleen Stratmann, Adm.Asst.
Subjects: Urban affairs, urban planning. **Holdings:** 7500 volumes. **Services:** Library open to the public.

★ 14463 ★
St. Louis University - Divinity Collection (Rel-Phil)
Pius XII Memorial Library
3650 Lindell Blvd.
St. Louis, MO 63108   Phone: (314)658-3103
Founded: 1848. **Subjects:** Catholic church, monasticism and religious orders, mysticism, patrology, Bible, canon law. **Holdings:** 134,805 books; 18,106 bound periodical volumes; 193 reels of microfilm; 1563 microfiche. **Subscriptions:** 1421 journals and other serials. **Services:** Collection open to the public for reference use only. **Remarks:** FAX: (314)658-3108. **Formerly:** Its Divinity Library.

★ 14464 ★
St. Louis University - Knights of Columbus Vatican Film Library (Hum)
Pius XII Memorial Library
3650 Lindell Blvd.
St. Louis, MO 63108   Phone: (314)658-3090
                          Frances Bonham, Ph.D., Univ.Libn.
Founded: 1953. **Staff:** Prof 2; Other 1. **Subjects:** Greek, Latin, Arabic, Ethiopic, and Hebrew manuscripts from Vatican Library; Jesuitica and Hispanic Americana from European and Latin American collections; rare and out-of-print books. **Holdings:** 27,554 reels of microfilm (including 40,000 volumes of manuscript material); 52,603 slides of illuminated manuscripts. **Services:** Interlibrary loan; copying (both limited); library open to the public with restrictions. **Publications:** Manuscripta, 3/year - by subscription and exchange. **Special Catalogs:** Published and unpublished catalogs of manuscripts. **Remarks:** FAX: (314)658-3108. **Staff:** Charles J. Ermatingen, Ph.D., Libn.

★ 14465 ★
St. Louis University - Law Library (Law)
3700 Lindell Blvd.   Phone: (314)658-2755
St. Louis, MO 63108   Eileen H. Searls, Law Libn.
Founded: 1842. **Staff:** Prof 8.5; Other 7. **Subjects:** Law - American, health, labor, business, Missouri, Illinois, Irish; urban legal problems; jurisprudence; constitutional law; taxation; law and ethics. **Special Collections:** U.S. Government documents, 1967 to present; Missouri government documents, 1977 to present; Congressman Leonor Sullivan papers, 1952-1976; Father Leo Brown Labor Law Archives; Smurfit Irish Law Center; Jewish Law Center. **Holdings:** 262,613 books; 3460 reels of microfilm; 447,841 microfiche. **Subscriptions:** 5249 journals and other serials; 15 newspapers. **Services:** Interlibrary loan; copying; library open to the public with restrictions. **Automated Operations:** Computerized cataloging. **Computerized Information Services:** LEXIS, WESTLAW, DIALOG Information Services, NEXIS; BITNET (electronic mail service). Contact Person: James Milles. **Networks/Consortia:** Member of Mid-America Law School Library Consortium, Missouri Library Network Corp. (MLNC). **Publications:** Faculty Bibliography, irregular; Recent Acquisitions, monthly. **Special Catalogs:** Smurfit Irish Law Center Bibliographic Guide; Leonor K. Sullivan, A Guide to the Collection. **Remarks:** FAX: (314)658-3966. Electronic mail address(es): MILLESJG@SLUVCA (BITNET). **Staff:** Richard Amelung, Hd., Tech.Serv.; James Milles, Hd., Comp.Serv.; Betsy McKenzie, Hd., Pub.Serv.; Carol Moody, Hd., Govt.Docs.

★ 14466 ★
St. Louis University - Medical Center Library (Med)
1402 S. Grand Blvd.   Phone: (314)577-8605
St. Louis, MO 63104   T. Scott Plutchak, Dir.
Founded: 1890. **Staff:** Prof 9; Other 27. **Subjects:** Medicine, nursing, allied health sciences, hospital administration. **Holdings:** 46,723 books; 76,026 bound periodical volumes; 15 VF drawers of pamphlets; 400 pictures; 500 historical volumes; 3000 microfiche; 26,000 slides; 870 video cassettes; 155 CAI titles; instrument collection. **Subscriptions:** 1628 journals and other serials; 4 newspapers. **Services:** Interlibrary loan; copying; SDI; library open to the public with restrictions. **Automated Operations:** Computerized public access catalog, cataloging, and serials. **Computerized Information Services:** NLM, BRS Information Technologies, DIALOG Information Services; CD-ROM (MEDLINE, CINAHL); BITNET (electronic mail service).

Networks/Consortia: Member of Center for Research Libraries (CRL), National Network of Libraries of Medicine - Midcontinental Region, St. Louis Regional Library Network. **Publications:** InfoLink. **Remarks:** FAX: (314)772-1307. Electronic mail address(es): PLUTCHAKTS@SLUVCA.SLU.EDU (BITNET). **Staff:** Suzanne Conway, Asst.Dir., Info.Serv.; Christine Sullivan, Ref.Libn.; Linda Hulbert, Asst.Dir., Tech.Serv.; Kathy Gallagher, Ref.Libn.; Janice Walker, Cat.; Grace Roth, Asst.Dir. Access Serv.; Susan Sunderman, Hd., Educ.Rsrcs.; George Booth, Sys.Libn.

★ 14467 ★
St. Louis University - Parks College - Library (Sci-Engr)
400 Falling Springs Rd.   Phone: (618)337-7575
Cahokia, IL 62206   Lori Calcaterra, Dir.
Founded: 1927. **Staff:** Prof 1; Other 6.5. **Subjects:** Aeronautics, aerospace, science and technology. **Special Collections:** Federal Aviation Administration, Civil Aeronautics Board, International Civil Aviation Organization, and NASA Documents Depository; Wecker and Sutorius Collections - clippings files on the history of aviation. **Holdings:** 33,808 books; 10,619 bound periodical volumes; 2501 reels of microfilm; 55,132 government documents; 24,651 microfiche; 24 drawers of archives. **Subscriptions:** 298 journals and other serials; 11 newspapers. **Services:** Interlibrary loan; copying; library open to the public for reference use only. **Automated Operations:** Computerized cataloging and ILL. **Computerized Information Services:** DIALOG Information Services, OCLC; InterNet (electronic mail service). **Networks/Consortia:** Member of Kaskaskia Library System (KLS), St. Louis Regional Library Network, ILLINET. **Remarks:** FAX: (618)332-6802.

★ 14468 ★
St. Louis Zoo - Library & Teacher Resource Center (Biol Sci)
Forest Park   Phone: (314)781-0900
St. Louis, MO 63110   Jill Gordon, Libn.
Founded: 1988. **Staff:** Prof 1. **Subjects:** Zoos, zoology, animal behavior, conservation. **Special Collections:** St. Louis Zoo history. **Holdings:** 2500 books. **Subscriptions:** 50 journals and other serials. **Services:** Library open to the public for reference use only by appointment. **Automated Operations:** Computerized public access catalog. **Computerized Information Services:** DIALOG Information Services. **Networks/Consortia:** Member of St. Louis Regional Library Network, American Association of Zoological Parks & Aquariums. **Special Indexes:** Journals and Newsletters Received by Zoo and Aquarium Libraries. **Remarks:** FAX: (314)647-7969.

St. Luc Hospital
See: **Hopital Ste-Luc** (7403)

★ 14469 ★
St. Lucia - Central Library of St. Lucia (Area-Ethnic, Hum)
P.O. Box 103   Phone: (809)452-2875
Castries, St. Lucia   Mrs. Naula Williams, Chf.Libn.
Founded: 1923. **Staff:** Prof 3; Other 28. **Subjects:** West Indies - literature, socioeconomics, history, general. **Holdings:** 106,000 books; 200 bound periodical volumes. **Subscriptions:** 75 journals and other serials. **Services:** Copying; library open to the public. **Computerized Information Services:** INFONET (electronic mail service).

St. Lucian Library
See: **Our Lady Queen of Martyrs** (12620)

★ 14470 ★
St. Lucie County Historical Museum - Library (Hist)
414 Seaway Dr.   Phone: (407)468-1795
Fort Pierce, FL 34949   Edward Swanson, Supt.
Founded: 1968. **Staff:** Prof 3; Other 3. **Subjects:** History of Indian River area; national, state, and local history; genealogy and archives of early families. **Holdings:** 235 volumes. **Services:** Library open to the public for reference use only.

★ 14471 ★
St. Lucie County Law Library (Law)
102 Courthouse Addition
218 S. 2nd St.   Phone: (407)467-2370
Fort Pierce, FL 34950   Cheryl LeBlanc, Libn.
Founded: 1991. **Staff:** 1. **Subjects:** Law. **Holdings:** 14,000 volumes. **Services:** Library open to the public by appointment. **Computerized Information Services:** WESTLAW. **Remarks:** FAX: (407)467-2145. **Staff:** Nora Everlove.

★ 14472 ★
St. Luke the Evangelist, Catholic Community - Resource Library (Rel-Phil)
11011 Hall Rd.   Phone: (713)481-2137
Houston, TX 77089   Rita M. Hubbard, Libn.
Founded: 1985. **Staff:** Prof 1; Other 17. **Subjects:** Religion, parenting and family life, self-help, biography, children's literature. **Special Collections:** Local authors (3 collections); St. Luke (4 collections). **Holdings:** 1400 books. **Services:** Library not open to the public.

★ 14473 ★
St. Luke Medical Center - William P. Long Medical Library (Med)
2632 E. Washington Blvd., Bin 7021   Phone: (818)797-1141
Pasadena, CA 91109-7021   Christine De Cicco, Cons.Libn.
Founded: 1948. **Staff:** Prof 1. **Subjects:** Clinical medicine, surgery, nursing. **Holdings:** 690 books; 87 bound periodical volumes; 2 cassettes. **Subscriptions:** 84 journals and other serials. **Services:** Interlibrary loan; copying; SDI; library open to the public for reference use only. **Computerized Information Services:** MEDLARS. **Networks/Consortia:** Member of National Network of Libraries of Medicine - Pacific Southwest Region.

★ 14474 ★
St. Luke's Episcopal & Texas Children's Hospitals - Medical Library (Med)
6621 Fannin St.   Phone: (715)791-3054
Houston, TX 77030   Robert C. Park, Dir. of Lib.Serv.
Founded: 1954. **Staff:** Prof 1; Other 1. **Subjects:** Medicine and related fields. **Holdings:** 15,000 books. **Subscriptions:** 154 journals and other serials. **Services:** Interlibrary loan; copying; library open to physicians only.

St. Luke's Hospital
See: **Metro Health St. Luke's Medical Center - Taylor Family Health Sciences Library** (10191)

★ 14475 ★
St. Luke's Hospital - Health Science Library (Med)
1026 A Ave., N.E.   Phone: (319)369-7358
Cedar Rapids, IA 52402   Donald Pohnl, Dir.
Founded: 1969. **Staff:** Prof 1; Other 2. **Subjects:** Medicine, nursing, allied health sciences, health administration, child abuse. **Holdings:** 5000 books; 11,000 bound periodical volumes; 1500 AV programs. **Subscriptions:** 500 journals and other serials. **Services:** Interlibrary loan; copying; library open to the public with restrictions. **Automated Operations:** Computerized cataloging. **Computerized Information Services:** DIALOG Information Services, MEDLARS, BRS Information Technologies; internal database. Performs searches on fee basis. Contact Person: L. Christine White, Cat. & Online Database Searcher, 369-7866. **Networks/Consortia:** Member of Linn County Library Consortium (LCLC), National Network of Libraries of Medicine - Greater Midwest Region. **Special Catalogs:** Book Catalog; Area Serials List. **Remarks:** FAX: (319)369-7489.

★ 14476 ★
St. Luke's Hospital - Health Sciences Library (Med)
601 E. 19th Ave.   Phone: (303)869-2395
Denver, CO 80203   Lisa Traditi, Dir.
Founded: 1954. **Staff:** Prof 1. **Subjects:** Medicine, nursing, oncology, geriatrics, womens' health, cardiology, pediatrics, neonatology, transplantation. **Holdings:** 2599 books; 5815 bound periodical volumes. **Subscriptions:** 140 journals and other serials. **Services:** Interlibrary loan; library not open to the public. **Computerized Information Services:** DIALOG Information Services, MEDLINE, OCLC; DOCLINE, TenTime (electronic mail services). **Networks/Consortia:** Member of National Network of Libraries of Medicine (NN/LM), Colorado Council of Medical Librarians, Health Sciences Libraries Consortium (HSLC). **Remarks:** FAX: (303)869-1633. Electronic mail address(es): SLD (TenTime).

★ 14477 ★
St. Luke's Hospital - Hilding Medical Library (Med)
915 E. 1st St.   Phone: (218)726-5320
Duluth, MN 55805   Doreen Roberts, Libn.
Founded: 1944. **Staff:** Prof 1; Other 1. **Subjects:** Clinical medicine, nursing. **Holdings:** 1100 books; 8000 bound periodical volumes; 300 videotapes. **Subscriptions:** 270 journals and other serials. **Services:** Interlibrary loan; library not open to the public. **Computerized Information Services:** MEDLINE. **Networks/Consortia:** Member of Arrowhead Professional Libraries Association (APLA). **Remarks:** FAX: (218)726-5181.

★ 14478 ★
St. Luke's Hospital - Medical Library (Med)
3555 Army St.   Phone: (415)641-6949
San Francisco, CA 94110   Laurie Bagley, Med.Libn.
Founded: 1959. **Staff:** Prof 1. **Subjects:** Medicine and nursing. **Holdings:** 2000 books; 4319 bound periodical volumes. **Subscriptions:** 115 journals and other serials. **Services:** Interlibrary loan; library not open to the public. **Computerized Information Services:** MEDLINE; DOCLINE (electronic mail service). **Networks/Consortia:** Member of San Francisco Biomedical Library Network, Northern California and Nevada Medical Library Group (NCNMLG).

★ 14479 ★
St. Luke's Hospital - MeritCare Library (Med)
720 4th St., N.   Phone: (701)234-5571
Fargo, ND 58122   Margaret Wagner, Lib.Mgr.
Founded: 1925. **Staff:** 4. **Subjects:** Medicine, paramedicine, consumer medicine, nursing, hospital administration. **Special Collections:** Consumer Health Information Section; Cancer Collection. **Holdings:** 3370 books; 3871 bound periodical volumes; 721 volumes on microfiche; 1080 AV programs. **Subscriptions:** 359 library journals and other serials; 309 hospital journals and other serials. **Services:** Interlibrary loan; copying; SDI; library open to the public. **Automated Operations:** Computerized public access catalog and ILL (DOCLINE). **Computerized Information Services:** MEDLINE, BRS Information Technologies; CD-ROM; EasyLink (electronic mail service). Performs searches on fee basis. **Networks/Consortia:** Member of Valley Medical Network (VMN). **Publications:** Recent Additions, monthly - distributed internally and to members of Valley Medical Network. **Remarks:** FAX: (701)234-5927. Electronic mail address(es): 62847922 (Western Union).

★ 14480 ★
St. Luke's Hospital Association - Medical, Nursing and Allied Help Library (Med)
4201 Belfort Rd.   Phone: (904)296-3735
Jacksonville, FL 32216   Carole Saville, Libn.
Staff: Prof 1; Other 1. **Subjects:** Medicine, nursing. **Holdings:** 1500 books; 1730 bound periodical volumes. **Subscriptions:** 148 journals and other serials. **Services:** Interlibrary loan; library not open to the public. **Computerized Information Services:** Online systems. **Remarks:** FAX: (904)296-4644.

★ 14481 ★
St. Luke's Hospital of Bethlehem, Pennsylvania - Audiovisual Library (Aud-Vis, Med)
801 Ostrum St.   Phone: (215)954-4000
Bethlehem, PA 18015   Robert R. Fields, AV Coord.
Staff: 1. **Subjects:** Medicine, nursing, allied health sciences, patient education. **Holdings:** 700 AV programs. **Services:** Interlibrary loan; library not open to the public.

★ 14482 ★
St. Luke's Hospital of Bethlehem, Pennsylvania - School of Nursing - Trexler Nurses' Library (Med)
Bishopthorpe & Ostrum Sts.   Phone: (215)954-3407
Bethlehem, PA 18015   Diane Frantz, Libn.
Staff: Prof 1; Other 2. **Subjects:** Nursing and allied health sciences. **Special Collections:** Historical Nursing Collection. **Holdings:** 4600 volumes; 15 VF drawers. **Subscriptions:** 63 journals and other serials. **Services:** Interlibrary loan; copying; library open to the public for reference use only. **Computerized Information Services:** MEDLINE, DIALOG Information Services.

★ 14483 ★
**St. Luke's Hospital of Bethlehem, Pennsylvania - W.L. Estes, Jr.
  Memorial Library** (Med)
801 Ostrum St.   Phone: (215)954-4650
Bethlehem, PA 18015   Maria D. Collette, Libn.
Founded: 1947. **Staff:** Prof 1; Other 1. **Subjects:** Medicine, medical
specialities, allied health sciences. **Special Collections:** Historical collection
(251 books). **Holdings:** 2150 books; 5250 bound periodical volumes; 164
folders of ephemeral file articles. **Subscriptions:** 465 journals and other
serials; 4 newspapers. **Services:** Interlibrary loan; copying; library open to
the public for reference use only. **Automated Operations:** Computerized
serials. **Computerized Information Services:** DIALOG Information
Services, MEDLARS, BRS Information Technologies; CD-ROM
(MEDLINE). Performs searches on fee basis. **Networks/Consortia:**
Member of National Network of Libraries of Medicine - Middle Atlantic
Region, Cooperating Hospital Libraries of the Lehigh Valley Area, BHSL.
Remarks: FAX: (215)954-4651.

★ 14484 ★
**St. Luke's Hospital Center - Richard Walker Bolling Memorial Medical
  Library** (Med)
Amsterdam Ave. & 114th St.   Phone: (212)523-4315
New York, NY 10025   Nancy Mary Panella, Libn. & Dir.
Founded: 1884. **Staff:** Prof 3; Other 2. **Subjects:** Medicine, surgery. **Special
Collections:** History of medicine; old and/or rare medical books; archives
and historical collections of St. Luke's Hospital, Women's Hospital, and
School of Nursing. **Holdings:** 10,000 books; 42,000 bound periodical
volumes; 4 VF drawers. **Subscriptions:** 475 journals and other serials.
Services: Interlibrary loan; copying; library open to the public by
appointment. **Automated Operations:** Computerized cataloging.
Computerized Information Services: MEDLINE, OCLC. Performs
searches on fee basis. **Networks/Consortia:** Member of Medical Library
Center of New York (MLCNY). **Staff:** Joan Carvajal, Archv.; C.H. Otis,
Ser.; R.J. Garrett, ILL.

★ 14485 ★
St. Luke's Hospital of Kansas City - Medical Library (Med)
Spencer Center for Education
44th & Wornall Rd.   Phone: (816)932-2333
Kansas City, MO 64111   Karen Wiederaenders, Dir. of Lib.Serv.
Founded: 1948. **Staff:** Prof 3; Other 6. **Subjects:** Cardiology, nursing, sports
medicine, medicine. **Holdings:** 2500 books; 12,000 bound periodical
volumes; 1000 other cataloged items. **Subscriptions:** 624 journals and other
serials. **Services:** Interlibrary loan; copying; library open to the public for
reference use only. **Automated Operations:** Computerized cataloging.
Computerized Information Services: NLM, DIALOG Information
Services, OCLC, BRS Information Technologies. **Networks/Consortia:**
Member of Kansas City Library Network, Inc. (KCLN), Kansas City
Metropolitan Library Network (KCMLN). **Publications:** News and Notes,
monthly - for internal distribution only. **Remarks:** FAX: (816)932-5197.
Staff: Mary Shriner, Asst.Libn.; Mary Webb, Ser.Libn.

★ 14486 ★
St. Luke's Hospital of Middleborough - Medical Staff Library (Med)
52 Oak St.   Phone: (617)947-6000
Middleboro, MA 02346   Gail Twomey, Med.Libn.
Staff: Prof 1. **Subjects:** Medicine and allied health sciences. **Holdings:** 112
volumes; 2000 unbound periodicals. **Subscriptions:** 45 journals and other
serials. **Services:** Interlibrary loan; copying; library open to the public with
permission. **Networks/Consortia:** Member of Massachusetts Health
Sciences Libraries Network (MaHSLiN), Southeastern Massachusetts
Consortium of Health Science Libraries (SEMCO).

★ 14487 ★
St. Luke's Medical Center - Medical Library (Med)
2900 W. Oklahoma Ave.
P.O. Box 2901   Phone: (414)649-7357
Milwaukee, WI 53201-2901   Midge Wos, Dir.
Founded: 1967. **Staff:** Prof 1; Other 2. **Subjects:** Medicine, nursing,
paramedicine. **Holdings:** 25,000 books; 9000 bound periodical volumes; 100
filmstrips, records, transparencies, slides, film reels; 1080 cassettes; 2000
video cassettes; 1176 volumes on microfilm. **Subscriptions:** 805 journals and
other serials; 15 newspapers. **Services:** Interlibrary loan; copying; SDI;
library open to professional staff and employees only. **Automated
Operations:** Computerized acquisitions, serials, circulation, and ILL.
Computerized Information Services: MEDLINE, BRS Information
Technologies, DIALOG Information Services. **Networks/Consortia:**
Member of Southeastern Wisconsin Health Science Library Consortium
(SWHSL). **Remarks:** FAX: (414)649-4548.

★ 14488 ★
St. Luke's Medical Center - Rosenzweig Health Sciences Library (Med)
1800 E. Van Buren St.   Phone: (602)251-8100
Phoenix, AZ 85006   Barbara Hasan, Dir.
Founded: 1983. **Staff:** Prof 1. **Subjects:** Cardiology, nursing, behavioral
health. **Holdings:** 1000 books; 2050 bound periodical volumes; 500
videotapes. **Subscriptions:** 217 journals. **Services:** Interlibrary loan; library
not open to the public. **Computerized Information Services:** DIALOG
Information Services, MEDLARS, BRS Information Technologies; CD-
ROM (MEDLINE); OnTyme Electronic Message Network Service,
DOCLINE (electronic mail services). Performs searches free of charge.
Networks/Consortia: Member of Central Arizona Biomedical Libraries
(CABL). **Publications:** Foxglove (newsletter), bimonthly - for internal
distribution only. **Remarks:** FAX: (602)251-8179. Electronic mail
address(es): CLASS.SLXPHX (OnTyme Electronic Message Network
Service).

★ 14489 ★
**St. Lukes Midland Regional Medical Center - Dr. Paul G. Bunker
  Memorial Medical Library** (Med)
305 S. State St.   Phone: (605)622-5355
Aberdeen, SD 57401   Jeanette Croft, Med.Libn.
Founded: 1972. **Staff:** Prof 1. **Subjects:** Medicine, nursing. **Holdings:** 1200
books. **Subscriptions:** 220 journals and other serials; 7 newspapers. **Services:**
Interlibrary loan; copying; library open to the public with restrictions.
Computerized Information Services: MEDLARS, DIALOG Information
Services. Performs searches on fee basis. **Networks/Consortia:** Member of
National Network of Libraries of Medicine - Greater Midwest Region.
Remarks: FAX: (605)622-5041.

★ 14490 ★
St. Luke's Regional Medical Center - Instructional Technology Center
  (Med)
2720 Stone Park Blvd.   Phone: (712)279-3156
Sioux City, IA 51104   Cathy Perley, Instr.Tech.Mgr.
Staff: Prof 2. **Subjects:** Medicine, nursing. **Holdings:** 2000 books; 200
filmstrips; 2000 video cassettes. **Subscriptions:** 125 journals and other
serials. **Services:** Interlibrary loan; copying; center open to the public.
Computerized Information Services: MEDLINE, WESTLAW.

★ 14491 ★
St. Luke's Regional Medical Center - Medical Library (Med)
190 E. Bannock   Phone: (208)386-2277
Boise, ID 83712   Pamela S. Spickelmier, Dir.
Staff: Prof 1; Other 2. **Subjects:** Medicine, nursing, administration.
Holdings: 1200 volumes. **Subscriptions:** 200 journals and other serials.
Services: Interlibrary loan; copying; SDI; library open to the public with
restrictions. **Automated Operations:** Computerized cataloging and
circulation. **Computerized Information Services:** MEDLARS, BRS
Information Technologies. **Remarks:** Library also houses the Idaho Health
Information Retrieval Center.

St. Margaret Health Center
See: **Providence-St. Margaret Health Center (13455)**

★ 14492 ★
St. Margaret Hospital - Sallie M. Tyrrell, M.D. Memorial Library
  (Med)
5454 Hohman Ave.   Phone: (219)932-2300
Hammond, IN 46320   Laurie Broadus, Lib.Coord.
Staff: Prof 1; Other 1. **Subjects:** Medicine, nursing. **Holdings:** 2000 books;
1500 bound periodical volumes; Audio-Digest tapes. **Subscriptions:** 150
journals and other serials. **Services:** Interlibrary loan; library not open to the
public. **Computerized Information Services:** BRS Information
Technologies. **Networks/Consortia:** Member of National Network of
Libraries of Medicine - Greater Midwest Region, Northwest Indiana Health
Science Library Consortium. **Remarks:** FAX: (219)933-2146.

★ 14493 ★
St. Margaret Memorial Hospital - School of Nursing Library (Med)
4631 Davison St.   Phone: (412)622-7075
Pittsburgh, PA 15201   Robert Jewell, Libn.
Staff: Prof 2; Other 2. **Subjects:** Medicine, nursing, allied health sciences. **Holdings:** 3500 books; 3100 bound periodical volumes; 8 VF drawers of pamphlets; 3 shelves of archives; videotapes; audiotapes; filmstrips; slides; AV programs. **Subscriptions:** 265 journals and other serials. **Services:** Interlibrary loan; library not open to the public. **Computerized Information Services:** MEDLINE. **Networks/Consortia:** Member of Pittsburgh-East Hospital Library Cooperative. **Remarks:** Alternate telephone number(s): 784-4239. **Formerly:** Its Paul Titus Memorial Library and School of Nursing Library. **Staff:** Sandra Arjona, Med.Libn.

★ 14494 ★
St. Maria Goretti Church Library (Rel-Phil)
5405 Flad Ave.
Madison, WI 53711
Founded: 1962. **Subjects:** Religion and allied subjects. **Holdings:** 3000 books. **Subscriptions:** 15 journals and other serials. **Services:** Library open to the public on a limited schedule.

★ 14495 ★
St. Mark's Episcopal Church - Bishop Jones Library (Rel-Phil)
315 E. Pecan St.   Phone: (512)226-2426
San Antonio, TX 78205   Dorothy B. Brown, Parish Libn.
Staff: Prof 1; Other 7. **Subjects:** Religion, children's literature. **Special Collections:** Jack Kent Collection (children's author; 56 books). **Holdings:** 4280 books; 550 AV programs. **Subscriptions:** 8 journals and other serials. **Services:** Copying; library open to the public with restrictions.

★ 14496 ★
St. Mark's Episcopal Church - Parish Library (Rel-Phil)
680 Calder   Phone: (409)832-3405
Beaumont, TX 77701   Mrs. W.E. Krueger, Libn.
Staff: Prof 1. **Subjects:** Religion, social sciences, history, arts, philosophy, literature. **Holdings:** Figures not available. **Subscriptions:** 16 journals and other serials. **Services:** Library not open to the public.

★ 14497 ★
St. Mark's Hospital - Library and Media Services (Med)
1200 East 3900 South St.   Phone: (801)268-7004
Salt Lake City, UT 84124   Jane M. Errion, Libn.
Staff: Prof 1. **Subjects:** Medicine and allied health sciences. **Holdings:** 1000 books; unbound periodicals; 300 AV programs. **Subscriptions:** 230 journals and other serials. **Services:** Interlibrary loan (fee); copying; patient education instruction; library open to the public with restrictions. **Automated Operations:** Computerized acquisitions and serials. **Computerized Information Services:** MEDLINE, BRS Information Technologies, OCLC; DOCLINE (electronic mail service). **Networks/Consortia:** Member of Utah Health Sciences Library Consortium (UHSLC). **Remarks:** FAX: (801)268-7876.

St. Mark's Library
See: General Theological Seminary (6352)

★ 14498 ★
St. Mark's Presbyterian Church - Library (Rel-Phil)
3809 E. 3rd St.   Phone: (602)325-1519
Tucson, AZ 85716   Janet M. Tower, Lib.Adm.
Founded: 1965. **Staff:** 6. **Subjects:** Theology, Bible and Bible study, devotions, church history, social problems. **Holdings:** 3000 books. **Services:** Library open to church members.

★ 14499 ★
St. Martha's Hospital - School of Nursing Library (Med)
25 Bay St.   Phone: (902)863-2830
Antigonish, NS, Canada B2G 2G5   Sr. Mary Chisholm, Libn.
Staff: Prof 1. **Subjects:** Nursing. **Holdings:** 4152 books; 158 bound periodical volumes; 50 videotapes; AV programs. **Subscriptions:** 70 journals and other serials. **Services:** Library open to the public.

★ 14500 ★
Saint Mary College - De Paul Library - Special Collections Center
(Hum, Hist)
4100 S. 4 St.   Phone: (913)682-5151
Leavenworth, KS 66048-5082   S. Therese Deplazes, Spec.Coll.Libn.
Founded: 1923. **Staff:** Prof 1. **Subjects:** Sacred scripture; Abraham Lincoln; Charles Dickens; William Shakespeare, Americana. **Special Collections:** Sir John and Mary Craig Scripture-Theology Collection (2000 titles in 100 languages: Bibles; scriptural texts and exegesis; leaves; manuscripts; scrolls; codices; incunabula; facsimiles; transcriptions; printed books, 15th century to present; memorabilia; Bernard H. Hall Abraham Lincoln Collection (1450 volumes; framed pictures and documents (including an original parchment of the 13th Amendment); unframed prints, manuscripts, and original autographs; rare pamphlets; postcards; organized tearsheets and clippings; original contemporary sheet music and song sheets; medallions; plaques; busts; periodicals; memorabilia); Americana (holographs of American personalities; manuscripts documenting United States and Kansas history: slave papers, ships papers, property deeds, contracts, territorial textbooks); Shakespeariana (rare volumes; scrapbooks of theater programs and photographs; memorabilia); Charles Dickens (rare volumes; titles in original monthly paper wrappings; first editions; facsimiles; rare print collections; memorabilia); Maurice C. Fields, 1915-1938 (letters from his mother, teachers, friends; poems about him; masters' thesis on his life and work; published works). **Holdings:** 5500 books; 75 bound periodical volumes; 35 reports; 526 manuscripts; 200 microfilm titles; memorabilia. **Subscriptions:** 2 journals and other serials. **Services:** Copying; center open to the public for viewing and research. **Networks/Consortia:** Member of Kansas City Regional Council for Higher Education (KCRCHE). **Publications:** Descriptive bibliographic listings for rare Shakespeariana, Dickensania, and Lincolniana; Kansas: General, the Church, early education; Craig Americana Manuscript Collection, 1607-1865 (calendared, with indexes). **Special Catalogs:** Complete card catalog for Scripture-Theology and Abraham Lincoln collections. **Remarks:** FAX: (913)682-2406. Maintained by the Sisters of Charity of Leavenworth.

★ 14501 ★
St. Mary-Corwin Hospital - Finney Memorial Library (Med)
1008 Minnequa Ave.   Phone: (719)560-5598
Pueblo, CO 81004-9988   Shirley Chun-Harper, Med.Libn.
Founded: 1958. **Staff:** Prof 1. **Subjects:** Internal medicine, surgery, pediatrics, pathology, allied health sciences. **Holdings:** 2568 volumes; 112 video cassettes; 1154 Audio-Digest tapes. **Subscriptions:** 116 journals and other serials. **Services:** Interlibrary loan; copying; library open to the public for reference use only. **Automated Operations:** Computerized cataloging. **Computerized Information Services:** MEDLINE, OCLC.

★ 14502 ★
St. Mary Hospital - Health Science Library (Med)
3600 Gates Blvd.   Phone: (409)985-7431
Port Arthur, TX 77643-3696   Ethel M. Granger, Libn.
Founded: 1930. **Staff:** Prof 2. **Subjects:** Allergic diseases, dermatology, radiology, pathology, genitourinary medicine, physicians and surgeons, family practice, hemodialysis, thoracic and cardiovascular surgery, internal medicine, obstetrics/gynecology, child specialists, dentistry, infection. **Special Collections:** Industrial medicine (340 items). **Holdings:** 3710 books; 839 bound periodical volumes; 400 unbound reports; 168 Audio-Digest tapes; 700 video cassettes. **Subscriptions:** 135 journals and other serials. **Services:** Interlibrary loan; library open to the public with approval of administrator. **Automated Operations:** Computerized cataloging, circulation, and ILL. **Computerized Information Services:** NLM. **Special Indexes:** Cumulated Index Medicus, annual; Index Medicus, monthly.

★ 14503 ★
St. Mary Hospital - Medical Library (Med)
36475 5 Mile Rd.   Phone: (313)464-4800
Livonia, MI 48154   Sr. Mary Sancia, MSLS
Founded: 1959. **Staff:** Prof 1; Other 2. **Subjects:** Medicine, surgery, radiology, nursing, obstetrics and gynecology, pediatrics, mental health. **Holdings:** 2185 books; 1230 bound periodical volumes; 864 tapes; 20 videotapes; 7 16mm films; 8 35mm filmstrips; Audio-Digest tapes; filmstrip/tape sets. **Subscriptions:** 40 journals and other serials. **Services:** Interlibrary loan; library not open to the public. **Networks/Consortia:** Member of Wayne Oakland Library Federation (WOLF). **Remarks:** FAX: (313)591-2949. Maintained by the Felician Sisters.

★ 14504 ★
St. Mary Hospital - Staff Library (Med)
1415 Vermont
Quincy, IL 62301
Phone: (217)223-1200
Dorcas Recks, Libn.
Founded: 1962. **Subjects:** Medicine, consumer health information. **Holdings:** 950 books; 650 bound periodical volumes. **Subscriptions:** 46 journals and other serials. **Services:** Interlibrary loan; copying; library open to the public. **Computerized Information Services:** DIALOG Information Services; DOCLINE (electronic mail service). **Networks/Consortia:** Member of ILLINET. **Remarks:** FAX: (217)223-1276.

★ 14505 ★
St. Mary Medical Center - Bellis Medical Library (Med)
1050 Linden Ave.
Box 887
Long Beach, CA 90801-0887
Phone: (213)491-9295
Lorraine B. Attarian, Mgr.
Founded: 1955. **Staff:** Prof 1; Other 2. **Subjects:** Medicine, nursing. **Holdings:** 30,000 volumes; pamphlet files; historical collection. **Subscriptions:** 500 journals and other serials. **Services:** Interlibrary loan; copying; SDI; library open to the public with restrictions. **Computerized Information Services:** MEDLARS, DIALOG Information Services; CD-ROM (MEDLINE). Performs searches on fee basis. **Remarks:** FAX: (213)491-9293.

★ 14506 ★
St. Mary of Nazareth Hospital Center - Sister Stella Louise Health Sciences Library (Med)
2233 W. Division St.
Chicago, IL 60622
Phone: (312)770-2219
Ms. Olivija Fistrovic, Med.Libn.
Founded: 1949. **Staff:** Prof 1; Other 2. **Subjects:** Medicine. **Holdings:** 1400 books; 2200 bound periodical volumes; 65 slide sets; 200 video cassettes. **Subscriptions:** 116 journals and other serials. **Services:** Interlibrary loan; SDI; library open to the public by appointment. **Automated Operations:** Computerized cataloging and serials. **Computerized Information Services:** MEDLARS. **Networks/Consortia:** Member of National Network of Libraries of Medicine - Greater Midwest Region, Metropolitan Consortium of Chicago. **Remarks:** FAX: (312)770-2221.

★ 14507 ★
St. Mary Seminary - The Bruening-Marotta Library (Rel-Phil)
28700 Euclid Ave.
Wickliffe, OH 44092-2585
Phone: (216)943-7600
Alan Rome, Libn.
Founded: 1848. **Staff:** Prof 1; Other 1. **Subjects:** Liturgy, dogmatic and moral theology, history of the Catholic Church, patristic writings, sacred scripture, ecumenism, canon law, religious education, pastoral care. **Special Collections:** Bishop Horstmann Collection (1600 books). **Holdings:** 40,000 books; 9000 bound periodical volumes; 250 drafts and reports of Vatican Council II; 5 boxes of U.S. Catholic Conference pamphlets; 759 cassettes; 293 filmstrips; 367 microfiche; 253 reels of microfilm; 281 theses. **Subscriptions:** 358 journals and other serials; 5 newspapers. **Services:** Interlibrary loan; copying; library open to the public by appointment. **Networks/Consortia:** Member of Cleveland Area Metropolitan Library System (CAMLS), Ohio Theological Librarians. **Formerly:** Its Joseph M. Bruening Library.

★ 14508 ★
St. Mary's Armenian Apostolic Church - Balian Library (Area-Ethnic)
4125 Fessenden St., N.W.
Washington, DC 20016
Phone: (202)363-1923
Elizabeth K. Garabedian, Libn.
Founded: 1988. **Staff:** 1. **Subjects:** Armenia - history, culture, literature, religious traditions, art, poetry, music, fiction, biography. **Special Collections:** Armenian Earthquake of 1988 (clipping files); Nagorno-Karabagh conflict in Azerbaijan-U.S.S.R. (clipping files). **Holdings:** 1200 books. **Subscriptions:** 3 journals and other serials; 3 newspapers. **Services:** Library not open to the public. **Remarks:** FAX: (202)537-0229.

★ 14509 ★
St. Mary's College - Cushwa-Leighton Library - Special Collections (Hum)
Notre Dame, IN 46556
Phone: (219)284-5280
Sr. Bernice Hollenhorst, C.S.C., Lib.Dir.
Holdings: Books by and about Dante Alighieri (600 titles). **Services:** Interlibrary loan; copying; collections open to the public with restrictions. **Computerized Information Services:** BRS Information Technologies, OCLC. **Networks/Consortia:** Member of INCOLSA, Area 2 Library Services Authority (ALSA 2). **Remarks:** FAX: (219)284-4716.

★ 14510 ★
St. Mary's College - Music Seminar Room (Mus)
Moreau Hall, Rm. 322
Notre Dame, IN 46556
Phone: (219)284-4638
Sr. Rita Claire Lyons, C.S.C., Dir.
Founded: 1957. **Staff:** Prof 2; Other 10. **Subjects:** Music. **Holdings:** 744 books; 3365 scores; 3584 phonograph records; 197 audiotapes and audiocassettes; 25 compact discs. **Subscriptions:** 13 journals and other serials. **Services:** Interlibrary loan; copying; room open to professors and students. **Automated Operations:** Computerized cataloging. **Staff:** Mrs. Lee Klei, Cat.

★ 14511 ★
St. Mary's College of California - Library - Special Collections (Rel-Phil)
1928 St. Mary's Rd.
Box 4290
Moraga, CA 94575
Phone: (510)631-4229
Andrew Simon, Spec.Coll.Libn.
Staff: Prof 2. **Subjects:** Cardinal John Henry Newman, Saint Jean Baptiste de la Salle, Christian Brothers, 17th and 18th century French Catholic spirituality. **Special Collections:** John Henry Newman and His Times (5000 items); Library for Lasallian Studies (5000 volumes); Saint Mary's College Archives. **Services:** Collections open to the public for reference use only by appointment. **Networks/Consortia:** Member of CLASS, Bay Area Library and Information Network. **Special Catalogs:** Book Catalog of the Library for Lasallian Studies. **Remarks:** FAX: (510)376-6097. The Library for Lasallian Studies is owned by De La Salle Institute of Napa, CA. **Staff:** Linda Seekamp, Coll.Archv.; Stephanie Bangert, Lib.Dir.

★ 14512 ★
St. Mary's Health Center - Health Sciences Library (Med)
6420 Clayton Rd.
St. Louis, MO 63117
Phone: (314)768-8112
Candace W. Thayer, Libn.
Founded: 1933. **Staff:** Prof 1; Other 3. **Subjects:** Clinical medicine, nursing, allied health sciences. **Holdings:** 1000 books; 12,000 bound periodical volumes. **Subscriptions:** 200 journals and other serials. **Services:** Interlibrary loan; library not open to the public. **Computerized Information Services:** MEDLARS. **Networks/Consortia:** Member of Sisters of St. Mary - System Wide Library Consortium, St. Louis Regional Library Network.

★ 14513 ★
St. Mary's Hospital - Finkelstein Library (Med)
56 Franklin St.
Waterbury, CT 06702
Phone: (203)574-6408
Jean Fuller, Libn.
Founded: 1970. **Staff:** Prof 1; Other 2. **Subjects:** Medicine and nursing. **Holdings:** 1200 books; 2240 bound periodical volumes. **Subscriptions:** 291 journals and other serials. **Services:** Interlibrary loan; copying; SDI; library open to the public for reference use only. **Remarks:** FAX: (203)597-3238.

★ 14514 ★
St. Mary's Hospital - Health Science Library (Med)
1800 E. Lake Shore Dr.
Decatur, IL 62525
Phone: (217)464-2182
Laura L. Brosamer, Libn.
Staff: Prof 1; Other 1. **Subjects:** Medicine, nursing, hospital administration. **Holdings:** 2200 books; 1700 bound periodical volumes; 184 slide/tape programs; 9 linear feet of vertical files; 300 video cassettes. **Subscriptions:** 300 journals and other serials. **Services:** Interlibrary loan; copying; SDI; library open to the public with librarian's permission. **Computerized Information Services:** MEDLARS, BRS Information Technologies, Data-Star; CD-ROMs (MEDLINE, CINAHL). **Networks/Consortia:** Member of Rolling Prairie Library System (RPLS), National Network of Libraries of Medicine - Greater Midwest Region, Capital Area Consortium of Health Science Libraries. **Publications:** The Appendix (new book list), quarterly. **Remarks:** FAX: (217)429-2925.

St. Mary's Hospital - Health Sciences Library
See: St. Mary's Regional Medical Center - Health Sciences Library (14534)

★ 14515 ★
St. Mary's Hospital - Health Sciences Library (Med)
901 45th St.   Phone: (407)881-2724
West Palm Beach, FL 33407   Christine M. McMahon, Libn.
Founded: 1946. **Staff:** Prof 1; Other 1. **Subjects:** Medicine, nursing, allied health sciences. **Holdings:** 464 books; 6416 bound periodical volumes. **Subscriptions:** 150 journals and other serials. **Services:** Interlibrary loan; copying. **Computerized Information Services:** DIALOG Information Services, MEDLARS. **Networks/Consortia:** Member of Palm Beach Health Sciences Library Consortium (PBHSLC). **Remarks:** FAX: (407)840-6112.

★ 14516 ★
St. Mary's Hospital - Health Sciences Library (Med)
5801 Bremo Rd.   Phone: (804)281-8247
Richmond, VA 23226   Damon Persiani, Libn.
Founded: 1966. **Staff:** Prof 1. **Subjects:** Medicine, hospital administration, nursing. **Holdings:** 600 books; 1000 bound periodical volumes. **Subscriptions:** 115 journals and other serials. **Services:** Interlibrary loan; copying; library open to the public with permission. **Computerized Information Services:** BRS Information Technologies. Performs searches on fee basis. **Remarks:** FAX: (804)285-2448.

★ 14517 ★
St. Mary's Hospital - Health Sciences Library (Med)
2323 N. Lake Dr.
Box 503   Phone: (414)225-8149
Milwaukee, WI 53201   Sharon A. Wochos, Libn.
Founded: 1959. **Staff:** Prof 1. **Subjects:** Nursing, medicine, management. **Holdings:** 2500 books; 3500 bound periodical volumes. **Subscriptions:** 260 journals and other serials. **Services:** Interlibrary loan; copying; SDI; library open to the public for reference use only. **Automated Operations:** Computerized ILL (DOCLINE). DIALOG Information Services, MEDLINE, BRS Information Technologies; CD-ROM. Performs searches on fee basis. **Networks/Consortia:** Member of Southeastern Wisconsin Health Science Library Consortium (SWHSL). **Remarks:** Alternate telephone number(s): 225-8149. FAX: (414)272-6279.

★ 14518 ★
St. Mary's Hospital - Health Sciences Library (Med)
3830 Lacombe   Phone: (514)345-3317
Montreal, PQ, Canada H3T 1M5   Jeannine Lawlor, Libn.
Founded: 1952. **Staff:** Prof 1; Other 1. **Subjects:** Medicine, nursing, obstetrics, gynecology, psychiatry, surgery. **Holdings:** 3000 books; 5600 bound periodical volumes; 1300 audio cassettes; 65 video cassettes; 5065 slides; 60 slide/tape sets. **Subscriptions:** 230 journals and other serials. **Services:** Interlibrary loan; library not open to the public. **Computerized Information Services:** MEDLARS. **Remarks:** Electronic mail address(es): ILL.QMSMA (Envoy 100). FAX: (514)345-3695.

★ 14519 ★
St. Mary's Hospital - Library (Med)
200 Jefferson, S.E.   Phone: (616)774-6243
Grand Rapids, MI 49503   Mary A. Hanson, Med.Libn.
Founded: 1927. **Staff:** Prof 2; Other 1. **Subjects:** Medicine, nursing. **Special Collections:** Historical medical collections from Kent County Medical Society, St. Mary's Hospital, and Mercy Central School of Nursing. **Holdings:** 3500 books; 8000 bound periodical volumes; 12 VF drawers. **Subscriptions:** 230 journals and other serials. **Services:** Interlibrary loan; copying; library open to the public with restrictions. **Computerized Information Services:** MEDLINE, DIALOG Information Services. Performs searches on fee basis. **Networks/Consortia:** Member of Lakeland Area Library Network (LAKENET). **Staff:** Yvonne Mathis, Asst.Libn.

★ 14520 ★
St. Mary's Hospital - Library (Med)
1216 2nd St., S.W.   Phone: (507)255-5647
Rochester, MN 55902   Mona Stevermer, Supv.
Founded: 1913. **Staff:** Prof 2; Other 6. **Subjects:** Nursing, allied health sciences, nutrition, hospital administration, medicine. **Holdings:** 5000 books. **Subscriptions:** 300 journals and other serials. **Services:** Interlibrary loan; current awareness. **Computerized Information Services:** DIALOG Information Services. **Publications:** New Books List, monthly. **Remarks:** A branch library of the Mayo Foundation - Section of Mayo Medical Center Libraries. **Staff:** Janet Behrens, Asst.Libn.; Ardis Sawyer, Libn., Patients' Lib.

★ 14521 ★
St. Mary's Hospital - Medical Allied Health Library (Med)
211 Pennington Ave.   Phone: (201)470-3055
Passaic, NJ 07055   Sr. Gertrude Doremus, S.C., Dir., Lib.Serv.
Staff: Prof 1. **Subjects:** Medicine, surgery, orthopedics, vascular surgery, psychiatry, urology, gastrointestinal diseases, cardiovascular systems, hematology, gynecology and obstetrics, plastic surgery, podiatry. **Holdings:** 450 books; 1900 bound periodical volumes. **Subscriptions:** 120 journals and other serials. **Services:** Interlibrary loan; copying; library open to the public with identification. **Automated Operations:** Computerized cataloging and circulation. **Networks/Consortia:** Member of Bergen Passaic Regional Library Cooperative.

★ 14522 ★
St. Mary's Hospital - Medical Library (Med)
305 S. Fifth St.
Box 232   Phone: (405)249-3092
Enid, OK 73701   Janet Puckett, Med.Libn.
Staff: Prof 1. **Subjects:** Medicine, nursing, hospital administration. **Holdings:** 2364 books; 2052 bound periodical volumes; 350 videotapes. **Subscriptions:** 160 journals and other serials. **Services:** Interlibrary loan; copying; library open to medical and paramedical professionals. **Computerized Information Services:** BRS Information Technologies, MEDLINE. **Remarks:** FAX: (405)249-3091.

★ 14523 ★
St. Mary's Hospital - Medical Library (Med)
803 E. Dakota Ave.   Phone: (605)224-3178
Pierre, SD 57501   DeAnn DeKay Hilmoe, Med.Libn.
Staff: Prof 1. **Subjects:** Medicine, nursing, allied health sciences. **Holdings:** 2100 books; 25 bound periodical volumes. **Subscriptions:** 195 journals and other serials. **Services:** Interlibrary loan; copying; SDI; library open to the public with restrictions. **Automated Operations:** Computerized cataloging. **Computerized Information Services:** BRS Information Technologies, MEDLARS; DOCLINE (electronic mail service). Performs searches on fee basis. **Networks/Consortia:** Member of Central South Dakota Health Science Library Consortium. **Publications:** CSDHSLC Newsletter, monthly - to members and interested professionals in the region. **Remarks:** FAX: (605)224-8339.

★ 14524 ★
St. Mary's Hospital - Medical Library (Med)
6-East   Phone: (304)526-1314
Huntington, WV 25702-1271   Kay Gibson, Med.Libn.
Founded: 1924. **Staff:** Prof 1; Other 1. **Subjects:** Medicine, surgery, allied health sciences. **Holdings:** 591 books; 2223 bound periodical volumes; 664 unbound periodicals; 104 pamphlets. **Subscriptions:** 141 journals and other serials. **Services:** Copying; SDI; library open to staff. **Computerized Information Services:** Access to MEDLARS, MEDLINE. **Networks/Consortia:** Member of Huntington Health Science Library Consortium. **Publications:** Bibliographies - to physicians. **Special Catalogs:** Huntington Health Science Library Consortium Serial Holdings; St. Mary's Hospital serial holdings by title and subject; book holdings by author and subject.

★ 14525 ★
St. Mary's Hospital - Medical Library (Med)
911 Queen St. N.   Phone: (519)744-3311
Kitchener, ON, Canada N2M 1B2   Elaine Baldwin, Libn.
Founded: 1963. **Staff:** Prof 1. **Subjects:** Medicine, nursing, hospital administration. **Holdings:** 1000 books; 900 bound periodical volumes. **Subscriptions:** 100 journals and other serials. **Services:** Library not open to the public. **Computerized Information Services:** MEDLARS. **Remarks:** FAX: (519)749-6461.

★ 14526 ★
St. Mary's Hospital - Medical Staff Library (Med)
1300 Massachusetts Ave.   Phone: (518)272-5000
Troy, NY 12180   Audna T. Clum, Libn.
Founded: 1960. **Staff:** Prof 1. **Subjects:** Medicine. **Holdings:** 450 books; 1300 bound periodical volumes; 719 other cataloged items. **Subscriptions:** 78 journals and other serials. **Services:** Interlibrary loan; library open to the public. **Networks/Consortia:** Member of Capital District Library Council for Reference & Research Resources (CDLC). **Remarks:** FAX: (518)272-0257.

★ 14527 ★
St. Mary's Hospital of Brooklyn - Medical Library (Med)
170 Buffalo Ave. Phone: (718)774-3600
Brooklyn, NY 11213 Paul Tobin, Dir.
Staff: 1. **Subjects:** Medicine, allied health sciences, nursing. **Holdings:** 1000 books; 100 administrative materials; Audio-Digest tapes. **Subscriptions:** 112 journals and other serials. **Services:** Interlibrary loan; copying; library open to paramedical personnel and others with proper identification. **Computerized Information Services:** MEDLINE; DOCLINE (electronic mail service). **Networks/Consortia:** Member of Brooklyn-Queens-Staten Island Health Sciences Librarians (BQSI), Medical & Scientific Libraries of Long Island (MEDLI), BHSL. **Publications:** CMC Newsletter, quarterly.

★ 14528 ★
St. Mary's Hospital & Health Center - Ralph Fuller Medical Library (Med)
1601 W. St. Mary's Rd.
Box 5386 Phone: (602)620-4974
Tucson, AZ 85703 Michelle C. Bureau, Libn.
Founded: 1939. **Staff:** Prof 1; Other 3. **Subjects:** Medicine, nursing, hospital administration, allied health sciences. **Holdings:** 900 books; 3000 bound periodical volumes; 166 videotapes; 4 VF drawers of pamphlets and reprints. **Subscriptions:** 133 journals and other serials. **Services:** Interlibrary loan; library not open to the public. **Automated Operations:** Computerized cataloging and acquisitions. **Computerized Information Services:** MEDLINE, DIALOG Information Services; CD-ROM (MEDLINE). Performs searches on fee basis. **Networks/Consortia:** Member of National Network of Libraries of Medicine - Pacific Southwest Region, Southeast Arizona Medical Library Consortium. **Publications:** Serials Holdings List, annual - free upon request; Audiovisual Holdings List, annual. **Remarks:** FAX: (602)792-2962. Maintained by Carondelet Health Services, Inc.

St. Mary's Hospital & Medical Center - Dr. E.H. Munro Medical Library
See: **Dr. E.H. Munro Medical Library** (10865)

★ 14529 ★
St. Mary's Hospital and Medical Center - Medical Library (Med)
450 Stanyan St. Phone: (415)750-5784
San Francisco, CA 94117 Rochelle Perrine Schmalz, Dir., Lib.Serv.
Founded: 1937. **Staff:** Prof 1; Other 2. **Subjects:** Medicine, psychiatry, nursing, orthopedics, patient information. **Holdings:** 5250 books; 7800 bound periodical volumes; surgical, psychiatry, orthopedics, patient information audio and video cassettes. **Subscriptions:** 350 journals and other serials. **Services:** Interlibrary loan; copying; library open to the public. **Computerized Information Services:** DIALOG Information Services, BRS Information Technologies, MEDLINE; internal database. Performs searches on fee basis. **Networks/Consortia:** Member of National Network of Libraries of Medicine - Pacific Southwest Region, San Francisco Biomedical Library Network. **Remarks:** FAX: (415)750-4954.

★ 14530 ★
St. Mary's of the Lake Hospital - Gibson Medical Resource Centre (Med)
Box 3600 Phone: (613)544-5220
Kingston, ON, Canada K7L 5A2 Penny G. Levi, Dir., Lib.Serv.
Founded: 1978. **Staff:** Prof 1; Other 1. **Subjects:** Geriatrics and chronic care, rehabilitation, allied health sciences. **Special Collections:** Hospital archives. **Holdings:** 2900 books; 700 bound periodical volumes. **Subscriptions:** 130 journals and other serials. **Services:** Interlibrary loan; copying; center open to the public with restrictions. **Computerized Information Services:** MEDLARS; CD-ROMs (MEDLINE, CINAHL); Envoy 100 (electronic mail service). Performs searches on fee basis. **Publications:** New Book List, bimonthly - local distribution on request; Patient/Family Resource Guides: Arthritis, Multiple Sclerosis, Stroke, Palliative Care, Alzheimer's Disease (pamphlets); Library Orientation (video); Reference Books: That's the Librarian's Job (video). **Remarks:** FAX: (613)544-6947.

★ 14531 ★
St. Mary's Medical Center - Herman M. Baker, M.D. Memorial Library (Med)
3700 Washington Ave. Phone: (812)479-4151
Evansville, IN 47750 E. Jane Saltzman, Mgr.
Founded: 1967. **Staff:** Prof 1; Other 1. **Subjects:** Medicine, nursing, health administration. **Holdings:** 1200 volumes; 800 AV programs. **Subscriptions:**

155 journals and other serials; 10 newspapers. **Services:** Interlibrary loan; copying; library open to the public with restrictions. **Computerized Information Services:** MEDLARS; CD-ROMs. Performs searches on fee basis. **Networks/Consortia:** Member of National Network of Libraries of Medicine - Greater Midwest Region, Evansville Area Libraries Consortium. **Remarks:** FAX: (812)473-7564.

★ 14532 ★
St. Mary's Medical Center - Library (Med)
3801 Spring St. Phone: (414)636-4300
Racine, WI 53405 Vicki Budzisz, Dir., Lib.Serv.
Subjects: Medicine, nursing, and allied health sciences. **Holdings:** 500 books. **Subscriptions:** 75 journals and other serials. **Services:** Library open to the public. **Remarks:** FAX: (414)636-4540.

★ 14533 ★
St. Mary's Medical Center, Inc. - Medical Library (Med)
Oak Hill Ave. Phone: (615)971-7916
Knoxville, TN 37917 Kenton O'Kane, Libn.
Staff: Prof 1. **Subjects:** Medicine, nursing, hospital administration. **Holdings:** 1500 books; 425 bound periodical volumes; 300 pamphlets. **Subscriptions:** 122 journals and other serials. **Services:** Interlibrary loan; copying; library open to the public for reference use only. **Computerized Information Services:** MEDLARS. Performs searches on fee basis. **Networks/Consortia:** Member of Knoxville Area Health Sciences Library Consortium (KAHSLC). **Remarks:** FAX: (615)971-6732.

★ 14534 ★
St. Mary's Regional Medical Center - Health Sciences Library (Med)
P.O. Box 291 Phone: (207)777-8776
Lewiston, ME 04243-0291 Debra G. Warner, Libn.
Founded: 1908. **Staff:** Prof 1. **Subjects:** Medicine, nursing, hospital administration. **Special Collections:** Crisis intervention. **Holdings:** 1112 books; 510 bound periodical volumes. **Subscriptions:** 170 journals and other serials. **Services:** Interlibrary loan; copying; SDI; library open to the public. **Computerized Information Services:** MEDLARS, DIALOG Information Services, BRS Information Technologies, WILSONLINE; DOCLINE (electronic mail service). Performs searches on fee basis. **Networks/Consortia:** Member of Health Science Library and Information Cooperative of Maine (HSLIC). **Formerly:** St. Mary's Hospital.

★ 14535 ★
St. Mary's Regional Medical Center - Max C. Fleischmann Medical Library (Med)
235 W. 6th St. Phone: (702)789-3108
Reno, NV 89520-0108 Kathleen L. Davis, Lib.Coord.
Founded: 1958. **Staff:** Prof 1. **Subjects:** Medicine, nursing, management. **Holdings:** 1564 books; 1244 bound periodical volumes. **Subscriptions:** 152 journals and other serials. **Services:** Interlibrary loan; copying. **Computerized Information Services:** MEDLINE. **Networks/Consortia:** Member of National Network of Libraries of Medicine - Pacific Southwest Region, Northern California and Nevada Medical Library Group (NCNMLG), Nevada Medical Library Group (NMLG).

★ 14536 ★
Saint Mary's Romanian Ethnic Museum - Library (Area-Ethnic)
3256 Warren Rd. Phone: (216)941-5550
Cleveland, OH 44111 Rev. Remus Grama, Priest
Founded: 1953. **Staff:** 2. **Subjects:** Romania, Romanians. **Holdings:** 4000 books. **Services:** Library open to the public with restrictions; borrowing privileges to members only. **Staff:** Mary Jane Vendel, Libn.

★ 14537 ★
St. Mary's School for the Deaf - Information Center (Educ)
2253 Main St. Phone: (716)834-7200
Buffalo, NY 14214 Jean Odien, Libn.
Staff: Prof 1. **Subjects:** Deafness, audiology, speech, special education. **Holdings:** 11,207 books; 683 bound periodical volumes; 436 microfiche. **Subscriptions:** 57 journals and other serials. **Services:** Interlibrary loan; copying; center open to the public with restrictions. **Automated Operations:** Computerized cataloging.

★ 14538 ★
St. Mary's Seminary - Cardinal Beran Library (Rel-Phil)
9845 Memorial Dr.   Phone: (713)686-4345
Houston, TX 77024   Constance Walker, Libn.
Staff: Prof 1; Other 2. **Subjects:** Philosophy, theology, canon law, church history, scripture. **Holdings:** 47,392 books; 4504 bound periodical volumes; 1952 cassette tapes; 1417 microforms. **Subscriptions:** 365 journals and other serials; 14 newspapers. **Services:** Interlibrary loan; library open to the public for reference use only. **Computerized Information Services:** Access to OCLC. **Remarks:** FAX: (713)686-7550.

★ 14539 ★
St. Mary's University - Geography Department - Map Library (Geog-Map)
Robie St.   Phone: (902)420-5742
Halifax, NS, Canada B3H 3C3   Benoit Ouellette, Cart./Map Libn.
Founded: 1975. **Staff:** 1. **Subjects:** Marine and coastal studies, urban and regional development, North America, Canadian Atlantic region, Western Europe, Asia. **Holdings:** 1000 books, pamphlets, journals, atlases; 25,000 maps. **Services:** Library open to the public for reference use only. **Computerized Information Services:** Internal database. **Remarks:** FAX: (902)420-5561. Library is depository for Canadian topographical maps from Canada Map Office.

★ 14540 ★
St. Mary's University - Patrick Power Library (Rel-Phil, Bus-Fin)
Halifax, NS, Canada B3H 3C3   Phone: (902)420-5544
      Ronald A. Lewis, Univ.Libn.
Staff: Prof 7; Other 36. **Subjects:** Religious studies, Canadiana, business administration. **Special Collections:** Eric Gill Collection (30 volumes); Santamariana Collection (575 volumes); Irish Studies Collection. **Holdings:** 300,000 volumes; ERIC microfiche, 1969 to present; 200 titles of Canadian labor newspapers on microfilm; corporate reports for 1400 companies. **Subscriptions:** 2000 journals and other serials; 33 newspapers. **Services:** Interlibrary loan; copying; library open to the public with restrictions. **Automated Operations:** Computerized public access catalog, cataloging, acquisitions, and serials. **Computerized Information Services:** CAN/OLE, DIALOG Information Services, PFDS Online, QL Systems, Mead Data Central, Info Globe, International Development Research Centre (IDRC), UTLAS. Performs searches on fee basis. Contact Person: Douglas Vaisey. **Publications:** Patrick Power Library News; The Perfect Term Paper: A Do-It-Yourself Guide; Guide to the Patrick Power Library, irregular; statistics collected by the Federal Government of Canada, irregular; The Census of Canada, irregular; statistics published by provincial governments in Canada, irregular; pamphlets on corporate reports and group study rooms - all free upon request. **Remarks:** FAX: (902)420-5561. **Staff:** Cynthia Tanner, Coll.Dev./User Educ.; Rashid Tayyeb, Hd., Tech.Serv.; Andrea John, Coord.Spec.Serv.; Margot Schenk, Hd., Pub.Serv.; Paul Rooney, Media Serv.; Sally Wood, Cat.; Ken Clare, Circ.; David Manning, Acq.; Bob Cook, Bibliog. Searching Dept.

★ 14541 ★
St. Mary's University - School of Law - Sarita Kenedy East Law Library (Law)
1 Camino Santa Maria   Phone: (512)436-3435
San Antonio, TX 78228   Robert L. Summers, Jr., Dir.
Founded: 1937. **Staff:** Prof 7; Other 50. **Subjects:** Law. **Special Collections:** Early Spanish law. **Holdings:** 129,882 books; 11,079 bound periodical volumes; 522,025 microfiche; 3547 reels of microfilm. **Subscriptions:** 3505 journals and other serials. **Services:** Interlibrary loan; copying (limited); library open to the public for reference use only. **Automated Operations:** Computerized public access catalog, cataloging, acquisitions, and ILL. **Computerized Information Services:** WESTLAW, LEXIS. **Networks/Consortia:** Member of AMIGOS Bibliographic Council, Inc. **Staff:** Lee Unterborn, Ref./Comp.Serv.; Duane Henricks, Govt.Doc.Libn.; Janetta K. Paschal, Hd.Cat.; Bea Citron, Media/Ref.; Lady Jane Hickey, Cat.; Jim Bass, Acq./Ser.

★ 14542 ★
St. Matthew's & St. Timothy's Neighborhood Center, Inc. - Tutorial Program Library (Educ)
26 W. 84th St.   Phone: (212)362-6750
New York, NY 10024   Linda Watrous, Dir., Star Lrng.Ctr.
Staff: Prof 3. **Subjects:** Remedial reading and mathematics. **Special Collections:** Remedial reading and mathematics materials and professional literature; children's literature (600 volumes). **Holdings:** 11,000 books. **Services:** Library open to Neighborhood Center participants. **Staff:** Jennifer Anderson, Asst.Dir., Tutoring Prog.; Anne Austin, Coord., Toddler & Parent Component.

St. Maur Hospitality
See: Catholic Seminary Foundation of Indianapolis - Library (3151)

★ 14543 ★
St. Meinrad Archabbey - College & School of Theology - Library (Rel-Phil)
St. Meinrad, IN 47577   Phone: (812)357-6566
      Rev. Simeon Daly, O.S.B., Libn.
Staff: Prof 2; Other 7. **Subjects:** Religion, Catholic theology. **Holdings:** 140,000 books; 15,000 bound periodical volumes. **Subscriptions:** 567 journals and other serials. **Services:** Interlibrary loan; copying; library open to the public for reference use only. **Automated Operations:** Computerized cataloging and ILL. **Computerized Information Services:** BRS Information Technologies. Performs searches on fee basis. **Networks/Consortia:** Member of INCOLSA, Four Rivers Area Library Services Authority (ALSA). **Staff:** Rev. Justin DuVall, O.S.B., Asst.Libn.

★ 14544 ★
St. Michael Hospital - Regner Health Sciences Library (Med)
2400 W. Villard Ave.   Phone: (414)527-8477
Milwaukee, WI 53209   Vicki Schluge, Med.Libn.
Founded: 1957. **Staff:** Prof 1; Other 4. **Subjects:** Medicine, nursing, allied health sciences, management. **Special Collections:** Golden Care Resource Center; women and infants resources. **Holdings:** 1700 books; 80 video cassettes. **Subscriptions:** 225 journals and other serials. **Services:** Interlibrary loan; current awareness service; copying; library open to the public for reference use only. **Automated Operations:** Computerized cataloging, serials, and ILL (DOCLINE). **Computerized Information Services:** DIALOG Information Services, BRS Information Technologies, NLM, Plus NetDirectory. Performs searches free of charge. **Networks/Consortia:** Member of Southeastern Wisconsin Health Science Library Consortium (SWHSL), National Network of Libraries of Medicine - Greater Midwest Region. **Publications:** Infoscope, quarterly. **Remarks:** FAX: (414)527-2604.

★ 14545 ★
St. Michael Medical Center - Aquinas Medical Library (Med)
268 Dr. Martin Luther King Jr. Blvd.   Phone: (201)877-5471
Newark, NJ 07102   Joann Mehalick, Dir., Med.Lib.
Staff: Prof 1; Other 1. **Subjects:** Medicine, pediatrics, obstetrics and gynecology, surgery, infectious diseases. **Special Collections:** Podiatry; hematology. **Holdings:** 1500 books; 4500 bound periodical volumes; 1 VF drawer of clippings. **Subscriptions:** 103 journals and other serials. **Services:** Interlibrary loan; library not open to the public. **Automated Operations:** Computerized ILL (DOCLINE). **Computerized Information Services:** NLM, LONESOME DOC; CD-ROM. Performs searches on fee basis. **Networks/Consortia:** Member of Cosmopolitan Biomedical Library Consortium (CBLC), Health Sciences Library Association of New Jersey (HSLANJ), BHSL. **Remarks:** FAX: (201)877-5429.

St. Michael's College
See: University of Toronto - St. Michael's College - John M. Kelly Library (19459)

★ 14546 ★
St. Michael's in the Hills Episcopal Church - Parish Library (Rel-Phil)
4718 Brittany Rd.   Phone: (419)531-1616
Toledo, OH 43615-2399   Claudia Hannaford, Libn.
Founded: 1952. **Staff:** 3. **Subjects:** Religion, devotion, inspiration, interpersonal relations, Christian social concerns. **Special Collections:** Summa Theologicae (St. Thomas Aquinas; 60 volumes). **Holdings:** 1850 books; 13 audio cassettes; 20 phonograph records; 21 games; 3 VF drawers of pictures; 12 video cassettes. **Subscriptions:** 12 periodicals and newsletters. **Services:** Library open to the public with identification, address, and telephone number. **Automated Operations:** Computerized cataloging. **Computerized Information Services:** Internal database. **Publications:** Descriptive bookmark; subject bibliographies.

★ 14547 ★
St. Michael's Hospital - Health Science Library/Archives (Med)
30 Bond St.   Phone: (416)864-5059
Toronto, ON, Canada M5B 1W8   Anita Wong, Dir.
Founded: 1956. **Staff:** Prof 3; Other 6. **Subjects:** Medicine and surgery. **Holdings:** 8300 books; 12,900 bound periodical volumes; reprints of staff publications. **Subscriptions:** 500 journals and other serials. **Services:** Interlibrary loan; library not open to the public. **Computerized Information Services:** MEDLARS, CAN/OLE, DIALOG Information Services. **Publications:** Monthly Library Bulletin; library journal holdings by title and by subject, annual. **Remarks:** FAX: (416)864-5296.

★ 14548 ★
St. Michael's Hospital - Health Sciences Library (Med)
900 Illinois Ave.   Phone: (715)346-5091
Stevens Point, WI 54481   Jan Kraus, Libn.
Founded: 1967. **Staff:** Prof 1; Other 1. **Subjects:** Medicine, nursing. **Holdings:** 900 books. **Subscriptions:** 185 journals and other serials. **Services:** Interlibrary loan; copying; library open to the public. **Automated Operations:** Computerized ILL (DOCLINE). **Computerized Information Services:** MEDLINE, MEDLARS, LONESOME DOC. **Networks/Consortia:** Member of National Network of Libraries of Medicine - Greater Midwest Region, Northwestern Wisconsin Health Science Library Consortium. **Remarks:** FAX: (715)346-5077; (715)341-7429.

★ 14549 ★
St. Monica's Church - Library (Rel-Phil)
31 Mather St.   Phone: (203)522-7761
Hartford, CT 06112   Ilene Tobey, Libn.
Founded: 1985. **Subjects:** Religion. **Special Collections:** Books by and about Blacks. **Holdings:** 100 books. **Services:** Copying; library open to the public.

★ 14550 ★
St. Nicholas Hospital - Health Sciences Library (Med)
1601 N. Taylor Dr.   Phone: (414)459-4713
Sheboygan, WI 53081   Kathleen Blaser, Coord., Lib.Serv.
Staff: Prof 1. **Subjects:** Medicine, nursing, management, philosophy. **Holdings:** 850 books. **Subscriptions:** 125 journals and other serials. **Services:** Interlibrary loan; copying; literature searches; library open to persons in health fields. **Computerized Information Services:** DOCLINE (electronic mail service). **Networks/Consortia:** Member of Fox River Valley Area Library Consortium (FRVALC), National Network of Libraries of Medicine - Greater Midwest Region.

★ 14551 ★
St. Norbert Abbey - Augustine Library (Rel-Phil)
1016 N. Broadway   Phone: (414)336-1321
De Pere, WI 54115   Steven Herro
Staff: Prof 1. **Subjects:** Theology, philosophy. **Special Collections:** Abbey Archives (1200 rare books); Premonstratensian Order history (1300 books); manuscripts and letters (90,000 items). **Holdings:** 10,000 books; 350 bound periodical volumes. **Services:** Copying; library open to the public by appointment.

★ 14552 ★
St. Olaf College - Howard and Edna Hong Kierkegaard Library (Rel-Phil, Hum)
Northfield, MN 55057   Phone: (507)663-3846
                                     Dr. C. Stephen Evans, Cur.
Founded: 1976. **Staff:** Prof 3. **Subjects:** Philosophy, theology, religion, history, literature and translation, classic literature. **Special Collections:** Kierkegaard's writings (complete set of first editions and later editions); replication of Kierkegaard's personal library; Kierkegaard's manuscripts (microfilm); critical secondary sources and background materials published after 1855. **Holdings:** 9000 volumes; doctoral dissertations; microfilm; cassette tapes. **Subscriptions:** 4 journals and other serials. **Services:** Copying; library open to the public with restrictions. **Computerized Information Services:** OCLC; internal database. **Remarks:** FAX: (507)663-3549. **Staff:** Howard V. Hong, Assoc.Cur.; Cynthia Lund, Asst.Cur.

★ 14553 ★
St. Olaf Lutheran Church - Carlsen Memorial Library (Rel-Phil)
29th & Emerson Ave., N.   Phone: (612)529-7726
Minneapolis, MN 55411   Donna Weflen, Libn.
Founded: 1962. **Staff:** 2. **Subjects:** Religion and related topics. **Special Collections:** Books in Norwegian. **Holdings:** 1457 books. **Services:** Library not open to the public.

★ 14554 ★
St. Patrick Hospital - Library (Med)
500 W. Broadway
Box 4587   Phone: (406)543-7271
Missoula, MT 59806   Kimberley M. Granath, Libn.
Staff: Prof 1; Other 1. **Subjects:** Nursing, medicine, hospital administration, patient education. **Holdings:** 1200 books; 24 VF drawers of pamphlets; 1200 videocassettes. **Subscriptions:** 250 journals and other serials. **Services:** Interlibrary loan; copying; literature searches; library open to the public. **Automated Operations:** ILL (DOCLINE). **Computerized Information Services:** DIALOG Information Services, MEDLARS; EMSCL, OnTyme Electronic Message Network Service (electronic mail services). Performs searches on fee basis. **Networks/Consortia:** Member of National Network of Libraries of Medicine - Pacific Northwest Region. **Remarks:** FAX: (406)543-8992. Electronic mail address(es): CLASS.STPATSMT (OnTyme Electronic Message Network Service).

★ 14555 ★
St. Patrick's Seminary - McKeon Memorial Library (Rel-Phil)
320 Middlefield Rd.   Phone: (415)321-5655
Menlo Park, CA 94025   Cecil R. White, Dir.
Founded: 1898. **Staff:** Prof 2. **Subjects:** Theology, philosophy, scripture, patrology. **Special Collections:** Bibliotheca Sancti Francisci Archdioceseos. **Holdings:** 72,653 books; 4800 bound periodical volumes; 1057 tapes. **Subscriptions:** 288 journals and other serials; 15 newspapers. **Services:** Interlibrary loan; copying; library open to the public for reference use only. **Networks/Consortia:** Member of OCLC Pacific Network. **Remarks:** FAX: (415)322-0997.

St. Paul Bible College
See: Crown College (4446)

★ 14556 ★
St. Paul City Council - Research Library (Plan)
539A City Hall
15 W. Kellogg Blvd.   Phone: (612)298-4163
St. Paul, MN 55102   Rosanne D'Agostino
Founded: 1973. **Staff:** 1. **Subjects:** St. Paul, urban affairs. **Special Collections:** St. Paul city documents. **Holdings:** 3200 books; 150 bound periodical volumes; 29 VF drawers; 8 drawers of microfilm; newsletters. **Subscriptions:** 150 journals and other serials. **Services:** Interlibrary loan; copying; library open to the public with restrictions. **Special Indexes:** Document index (book).

★ 14557 ★
St. Paul Fire & Marine Insurance Company - Library (Bus-Fin)
385 Washington St.   Phone: (612)221-7470
St. Paul, MN 55102   Sharon Carter, Lib.Info.Spec.
Founded: 1953. **Staff:** Prof 1; Other 2. **Subjects:** Insurance, management. **Holdings:** 12,000 volumes. **Subscriptions:** 432 journals and other serials. **Services:** Interlibrary loan; copying; library open to the public by appointment. **Computerized Information Services:** DataTimes, DIALOG Information Services, Human Resource Information Network (HRIN), Mead Data Central, Dow Jones News/Retrieval, VU/TEXT Information Services, WILSONLINE, NLM.

★ 14558 ★
St. Paul Lutheran Church and School - Parish Library (Rel-Phil)
5201 Galitz
Skokie, IL 60077   Phone: (708)967-5030
Founded: 1960. **Staff:** 1. **Subjects:** Religion. **Holdings:** 11,000 books; 40 bound periodical volumes; 9 VF drawers of pamphlets; AV programs; records; computer software; pictures; posters; filmstrips. **Subscriptions:** 25 journals and other serials. **Services:** Library not open to the public. **Publications:** Book lists, irregular - to parishioners. **Special Catalogs:** Computer software catalog.

★ 14559 ★
St. Paul Medical Center - C.B. Sacher Medical Library (Med)
5909 Harry Hines Blvd.   Phone: (214)879-2390
Dallas, TX 75235   Eva G. Osborn, Coord., Lib.Serv.
Founded: 1900. **Staff:** Prof 2; Other 2. **Subjects:** Nursing, medicine, and
allied health sciences. **Holdings:** 3000 books; 1100 bound periodical
volumes; 750 audio cassettes. **Subscriptions:** 150 journals and other serials.
Services: Interlibrary loan; copying; library open to the public with
restrictions. **Automated Operations:** Computerized cataloging.
Computerized Information Services: DIALOG Information Services, BRS
Information Technologies, NLM, Compact Cambridge; DOCLINE
(electronic mail service). **Networks/Consortia:** Member of Health Libraries
Information Network (HealthLINE). **Remarks:** Alternate telephone
number(s): 879-3790. **FAX:** (214)879-3154. **Staff:** Rachelle Howarton-
Smith, Med.Libn.

★ 14560 ★
St. Paul Pioneer Press - Library (Publ)
345 Cedar St.   Phone: (612)228-5557
St. Paul, MN 55101   Linda L. James, Hd.Libn.
Founded: 1906. **Staff:** Prof 1; Other 8. **Subjects:** Newspaper reference.
Special Collections: Historic photographs, 1900 to present; local newspaper
clipping files, 1945 to present. **Holdings:** 3000 books; 500,000 clippings; 1
million pictures. **Subscriptions:** 60 journals and other serials; 5 newspapers.
Services: Library not open to the public. **Computerized Information
Services:** VU/TEXT Information Services, DataTimes, NEXIS, LEXIS,
DIALOG Information Services, Dow Jones News/Retrieval. **Remarks:**
FAX: (612)228-5500.

★ 14561 ★
St. Paul Public Library - Art, Music & Video (Art, Mus)
90 W. 4th St.   Phone: (612)292-6189
St. Paul, MN 55102   Sue Ellingwood, Supv.
Founded: 1917. **Staff:** Prof 4; Other 5. **Subjects:** Fine and applied arts,
music, video. **Holdings:** 33,500 books; 3750 bound periodical volumes; 1,080
mounted pictures; 64,000 unmounted pictures; 1300 exhibit catalogs; 2000
art slides; 4000 phonograph records; 23,000 scores; 1700 compact discs;
2900 videotapes; 250 16mm films. **Subscriptions:** 225 journals and other
serials. **Services:** Interlibrary loan; copying; faxing; searching; library open
to the public. **Computerized Information Services:** DIALOG Information
Services. **Networks/Consortia:** Member of Metronet, Metropolitan Library
Service Agency (MELSA), Cooperating Libraries in Consortium (CLIC).
Special Indexes: Song Index; Art and Music Biography/Criticism Indexes;
Index to Public Art in St. Paul. **Remarks:** Maintains listening facilities for
sound recordings. FAX: (612)292-6141. **Staff:** Rose Ann Foreman,
Prof.Asst.

★ 14562 ★
St. Paul Public Library - Business & Science Room (Bus-Fin, Sci-Engr)
90 W. 4th St.   Phone: (612)292-6176
St. Paul, MN 55102   Virginia B. Stavn, Supv.
Staff: Prof 5; Other 4. **Subjects:** Economics, business, labor, finance, science,
technology, popular medicine. **Holdings:** 65,000 books; 7300 bound
periodical volumes; 24 VF drawers. **Subscriptions:** 442 journals and other
serials. **Services:** Interlibrary loan; copying; room open to the public.
Computerized Information Services: DIALOG Information Services,
WILSONLINE, VU/TEXT Information Services, DataTimes, DataNet;
CD-ROM (Mitchell On-Demand). **Networks/Consortia:** Member of
Metropolitan Library Service Agency (MELSA), Cooperating Libraries in
Consortium (CLIC), Metronet. **Special Indexes:** Indexes for handicraft
materials and consumer information (card). **Remarks:** FAX: (612)292-6141.
Staff: Larry Hlavsa, Prof.Asst.; Doug Guthrie, Libn.; Nancy Litin, Libn.

★ 14563 ★
St. Paul Public Library - Government Publications Office (Info Sci)
90 W. 4th St.   Phone: (612)292-6178
St. Paul, MN 55102   Rosamond T. Jacob, Libn.
Founded: 1914. **Staff:** Prof 1; Other 1. **Subjects:** Federal and state depository
publications. **Holdings:** 250,000 documents. **Services:** Interlibrary loan;
copying; office open to the public. **Computerized Information Services:**
DIALOG Information Services, DATANET. Performs searches free of
charge. **Networks/Consortia:** Member of Metropolitan Library Service
Agency (MELSA), Cooperating Libraries in Consortium (CLIC), Metronet.
Publications: Documents/Classified, semimonthly. **Remarks:** FAX:
(612)292-6141.

★ 14564 ★
St. Paul Public Library - Highland Park Branch - Perrie Jones
   Memorial Room (Rare Book)
1974 Ford Pkwy.   Phone: (612)292-6622
St. Paul, MN 55116   Kathleen Tregilgas, Supv.
Special Collections: Sumerian Clay Tablets (41); Horn Collection: classics
published in the 16th, 17th, and 18th centuries (154); Cruikshank
Collection: books illustrated and/or written by George Cruikshank and his
brother (26); Fitzgerald Collection: books by or about F. Scott Fitzgerald
and his times (38); Johnston Collection: rare books, 16th century to present
(1430); Local Collection: miscellaneous books on Twin Cities and Minnesota
(43); Perrie Jones Collection: books and other material by or related to
Perrie Jones (50). **Holdings:** 1800 books; letters; manuscripts; photographs;
autographs. **Services:** Room open to the public by appointment for reference
use only.

★ 14565 ★
St. Paul Public Library - Social Sciences & Literature (Soc Sci, Hum)
90 W. 4th St.   Phone: (612)292-6206
St. Paul, MN 55102   Elaine Wagner, Supv.
Founded: 1917. **Staff:** Prof 6; Other 5. **Subjects:** Literature, fiction, history
and travel, philosophy and religion, biography, political and social sciences,
dance, sports and games. **Special Collections:** Large print books (2000);
foreign languages (5104 titles in 15 languages); books on tape (1000).
Holdings: 220,000 volumes. **Services:** Interlibrary loan; copying; library
open to the public. **Automated Operations:** CLSI Inc. **Networks/Consortia:**
Member of Metronet, Metropolitan Library Service Agency (MELSA),
Cooperating Libraries in Consortium (CLIC). **Special Catalogs:** Large-print
book catalog. **Special Indexes:** Card indexes to biography and literary
criticism file; short story file; play file; games and sports index. **Remarks:**
TDD: (612)292-4184. FAX: (612)292-6141. **Staff:** Richard Hemming,
Prof.Asst.

★ 14566 ★
St. Paul Public Library - Social Sciences & Literature Reference Room
   (Hum, Soc Sci)
90 W. 4th St.   Phone: (612)292-6307
St. Paul, MN 55102   Kathleen Flynn, Supv.
Staff: Prof 6; Other 5. **Subjects:** Literature, philosophy, religion, history,
social science, psychology, law, biography, sports, geography, travel,
education, politics, government. **Special Collections:** St. Paul Collection
(city documents; newspapers; clippings); selected Minnesota documents;
telephone directories (35,000 U.S. cities). **Holdings:** 20,000 volumes.
Subscriptions: 231 journals; 257 serials; 22 newspapers. **Services:**
Interlibrary loan; room open to the public. **Computerized Information
Services:** DIALOG Information Services, DataTimes, DATANET,
WILSONLINE, VU/TEXT Information Services. **Networks/Consortia:**
Member of Metropolitan Library Service Agency (MELSA), Metronet.
Special Indexes: St. Paul Pioneer Press and St. Paul Dispatch Index, 1967
to present; local clubs and organization file; St. Paul Pioneer Press and
Dispatch Morgue File, 1910-1945. **Remarks:** FAX: (612)292-6141. **Staff:**
Carol Martinson, Asst. to Supv.

★ 14567 ★
St. Paul Public Schools Independent School District 625 - District
   Professional Library (Educ)
1930 Como Ave.   Phone: (612)293-8783
St. Paul, MN 55108   Walter M. Ostrem, Libn.
Staff: Prof 1. **Subjects:** Education, psychology, child development. **Special
Collections:** Archives of St. Paul School District (1000 items). **Holdings:**
7000 books; 22,000 unbound periodicals; 500 reels of microfilm of
periodicals; 900 documents; 3000 clippings. **Subscriptions:** 24 journals and
other serials. **Services:** Interlibrary loan; copying; library open to the public.
Networks/Consortia: Member of MINITEX Library Information Network,
Cooperating Libraries in Consortium (CLIC). **Remarks:** FAX: (612)293-
8990.

★ 14568 ★
St. Paul Ramsey Medical Center - Medical Library (Med)
640 Jackson St.   Phone: (612)221-3607
St. Paul, MN 55101   Mary Dwyer, Hd.Libn.
Founded: 1961. **Staff:** Prof 2; Other 2. **Subjects:** Medicine and nursing.
Holdings: 4000 books; 6000 bound periodical volumes. **Subscriptions:** 390
journals and other serials. **Services:** Interlibrary loan; library open to
professionals only. **Computerized Information Services:** MEDLARS.
Networks/Consortia: Member of Twin Cities Biomedical Consortium
(TCBC). **Staff:** Audrey Woodke, Asst.Libn.

★ 14569 ★
St. Paul School of Theology - Dana Dawson Library (Rel-Phil)
5123 Truman Rd.   Phone: (816)483-9600
Kansas City, MO 64127-2499   Dr. William S. Sparks, Libn.
Founded: 1958. Staff: Prof 1; Other 4. Subjects: Theology. Holdings: 76,000 volumes. Subscriptions: 350 journals and other serials. Services: Interlibrary loan; copying; library open to the public with restrictions. Computerized Information Services: DIALOG Information Services, EPIC. Remarks: FAX: (816)483-9605.

★ 14570 ★
St. Paul Technical College - Library (Sci-Engr)
235 Marshall Ave.   Phone: (612)221-1410
St. Paul, MN 55102   Ada Anderson, Libn.
Founded: 1967. Staff: Prof 1; Other 3. Subjects: Trades and technical occupations, business subjects, health support occupations. Holdings: 12,000 books. Subscriptions: 165 journals and other serials. Services: Interlibrary loan; copying; library open to the public for reference use only. Networks/Consortia: Member of MINITEX Library Information Network. Remarks: FAX: (612)221-1416.

★ 14571 ★
St. Paul's Church - Archives (Rel-Phil)
605 Reynolds St.   Phone: (404)724-2485
Augusta, GA 30901   Mary Henning, Parish Sec.
Staff: 1. Subjects: St. Paul's Church history, 1750 to present. Holdings: 4000 church records, meetings minutes, correspondence of church officers, church registers, and marriage, baptism, and communicant records. Services: Archives open to the public. Publications: St. Paul's 1820-1868; Marriages, Deaths, Baptisms, and Confirmations - A Listing (1989); Respect This Stone, 1976; St. Paul's Churchyard 1783-1820 (listing local and nationally known burials).

St. Paul's College
See: University of Manitoba (18794)

★ 14572 ★
St. Paul's College - Library (Rel-Phil)
3015 Fourth St., N.E.   Phone: (202)832-6262
Washington, DC 20017   Lawrence Boadt, C.S.P., Libn.
Founded: 1889. Staff: Prof 1; Other 3. Subjects: Philosophy, scripture, church history, liturgy, theology, American history, canon law. Special Collections: Paulist Fathers Archival Materials (4 filing cases). Holdings: 45,000 books; 5000 bound periodical volumes; 2500 pamphlets; 1000 recordings; 100 reels of microfilm. Subscriptions: 137 journals and other serials. Services: Copying; library open to the public with permission of librarian. Networks/Consortia: Member of Washington Theological Consortium. Staff: Dorothy E. Cattaneo, C.S.P., Asst.Libn.

★ 14573 ★
St. Paul's Episcopal Church - Library (Rel-Phil)
Rock Creek Church Rd. & Webster St., N.W.   Phone: (202)726-2080
Washington, DC 20011   Anne Greenwood
Founded: 1980. Subjects: Religion. Special Collections: 19th century family bibles; Eastern Rite liturgical books. Holdings: 500 books. Subscriptions: 10 journals and other serials. Services: Library open to the public by appointment.

★ 14574 ★
St. Paul's Episcopal Church - Library (Rel-Phil)
1066 Washington Rd.
Pittsburgh, PA 15228   Sandra W. Ludman, Libn.
Staff: Prof 3; Other 2. Subjects: Church and local history. Holdings: 2000 books; tapes. Services: Copying; library open to the public.

★ 14575 ★
St. Paul's Episcopal Church - Library (Rel-Phil)
815 E. Grace St.   Phone: (804)643-3589
Richmond, VA 23219   Carol D. Hiett, Lib.Cons.
Staff: 1. Subjects: Bible, theology, Christian art, worship, meditation, Christian education, church history, children's books. Holdings: 3500 books. Subscriptions: 12 journals and other serials. Services: Copying; library open to the public.

★ 14576 ★
St. Paul's Hospital (Grey Nuns') of Saskatoon - Medical Library (Med)
1702 20th St., W.   Phone: (306)664-5224
Saskatoon, SK, Canada S7M 0Z9   Colleen Haichert, Lib.Techn.
Founded: 1962. Staff: Prof 1. Subjects: Medicine, nursing. Holdings: 880 books. Subscriptions: 64 journals and other serials. Services: Interlibrary loan; library not open to the public.

St. Paul's Hospital Health Sciences Library
See: University of British Columbia (18279)

★ 14577 ★
St. Paul's Presbyterian Church - Library (Rel-Phil)
5225 Alhambra Dr.   Phone: (407)293-3696
Orlando, FL 32808   Beryl Mills, Chm.
Founded: 1980. Subjects: Religion - resources, literature, children's literature. Holdings: 3000 books. Services: Library not open to the public.

★ 14578 ★
St. Paul's United Methodist Church - Johnson Memorial Library (Rel-Phil)
225 W. Griggs
Box 696   Phone: (505)526-6689
Las Cruces, NM 88004   Margery Askew, Libn.
Founded: 1965. Staff: Prof 2. Subjects: Bible, philosophy, prayer, missions, psychology, history, biography, Byzantine and Medieval art, church histories. Holdings: 6300 books; tapes. Subscriptions: 3 journals and other serials. Services: Library open to church members only. Publications: History of St. Paul's Methodist Church.

★ 14579 ★
St. Paul's United Methodist Church - Library (Rel-Phil)
3334 Breton Rd., S.E.   Phone: (616)949-0880
Kentwood, MI 49512   Loni Soderfelt, Libn.
Staff: Prof 2; Other 4. Subjects: Religion. Holdings: Figures not available. Services: Library open to the public.

★ 14580 ★
St. Paul's United Methodist Church - Library (Rel-Phil)
9500 Constitution Ave., N.E.   Phone: (505)298-5596
Albuquerque, NM 87112   Nancy Hill, Libn.
Founded: 1957. Staff: Prof 1; Other 1. Subjects: Religion, children's literature, teacher training and aids, contemporary living. Holdings: 3000 books; 150 reels of microfilm; 25 tapes; 50 phonograph records. Services: Library not open to the public.

★ 14581 ★
St. Peter Hospital - Library Services (Med)
413 Lilly Rd. N.E.   Phone: (206)493-7222
Olympia, WA 98506-5166   Edean Berglund, Dir.
Staff: Prof 3. Subjects: Health care. Holdings: Figures not available. Subscriptions: 400 journals and other serials. Services: Interlibrary loan; copying; library open to the public with restrictions. Computerized Information Services: NLM, MEDLINE, BRS Information Technologies, DIALOG Information Services; DOCLINE, OnTyme Electronic Message Network Service (electronic mail services). Performs searches on fee basis. Remarks: Fax: (206)493-7924.

★ 14582 ★
St. Peter Regional Treatment Center - Burton P. Grimes Staff Library
100 Freeman Dr.
St. Peter, MN 56082
Founded: 1869. Subjects: Medicine, nursing, drug addiction, mental retardation, and allied health sciences. Holdings: 1300 books; 650 bound periodical volumes; 3 VF drawers; 400 audiotapes; 200 microfiche; clippings. Remarks: Currently inactive.

★ 14583 ★
St. Peter's Abbey & College - Library (Rel-Phil)
Box 10   Phone: (306)682-4402
Muenster, SK, Canada S0K 2Y0   Andrew M. Britz, Libn.
Founded: 1892. **Staff:** 1. **Subjects:** Arts and science, Roman Catholic theology, monasticism. **Holdings:** 40,000 volumes. **Subscriptions:** 100 journals and other serials. **Services:** Interlibrary loan; copying; library open to the public. **Remarks:** FAX: (306)682-4402.

★ 14584 ★
St. Peter's Hospital - Health Sciences Library (Med)
315 S. Manning Blvd.   Phone: (518)454-1670
Albany, NY 12208   Phyllis Miyauchi, Dir.
Founded: 1950. **Staff:** Prof 1; Other 1. **Subjects:** Medicine, surgery, nursing. **Holdings:** 1324 books; 1194 bound periodical volumes; 162 audiotapes. **Subscriptions:** 185 journals and other serials. **Services:** Interlibrary loan; copying; table of contents service; tailored bibliographies; library open to the public for reference use only. **Computerized Information Services:** BRS Information Technologies, NLM, DOCLINE (electronic mail service). **Networks/Consortia:** Member of Capital District Library Council for Reference & Research Resources (CDLC). **Staff:** Sue Rauber.

★ 14585 ★
St. Peter's Hospital - Library (Med)
88 Maplewood Ave.   Phone: (416)549-6525
Hamilton, ON, Canada L8M 1W9   Peggy Ross, Libn.
Founded: 1971. **Staff:** 1. **Subjects:** Geriatrics, nursing. **Holdings:** 1100 books. **Subscriptions:** 90 journals and other serials. **Services:** Interlibrary loan; library not open to the public. **Computerized Information Services:** CD-ROMs (MEDLINE, CINAHL).

★ 14586 ★
St. Peter's Medical Center - Library (Med)
254 Easton Ave.   Phone: (908)745-8545
New Brunswick, NJ 08903   Ellen Tanner, Mgr., Lib.Serv.
Founded: 1907. **Staff:** Prof 2; Other 5. **Subjects:** Medicine, nursing. **Special Collections:** History of medicine. **Holdings:** 10,000 books; 20,000 bound periodical volumes; 3600 AV programs. **Subscriptions:** 400 journals and other serials. **Services:** Interlibrary loan; library open to the public for reference use only. **Automated Operations:** Computerized ILL (DOCLINE). **Computerized Information Services:** NLM, DIALOG Information Services, BRS Information Technologies, Physician Data Query (PDQ); CD-ROM (MEDLINE). **Networks/Consortia:** Member of MEDCORE, Health Sciences Library Association of New Jersey (HSLANJ). **Remarks:** FAX: (908)745-7093. **Staff:** Natalie Richman, Med.Libn.

★ 14587 ★
St. Peter's Seminary - A.P. Mahoney Library (Rel-Phil)
1040 Waterloo St., N.   Phone: (519)432-1824
London, ON, Canada N6A 3Y1   Lois Cote, Libn.
Founded: 1926. **Staff:** Prof 1; Other 3. **Subjects:** Theology, philosophy. **Holdings:** 51,000 books and bound periodical volumes; 6225 AV materials, microforms, slides and other cataloged items. **Subscriptions:** 483 journals and other serials. **Services:** Interlibrary loan; copying; library open to the public. **Remarks:** Alternate telephone number(s): 439-3963. FAX: (519)672-6379.

★ 14588 ★
St. Petersburg Historical Museum - Archives (Hist)
335 Second Ave., N.E.   Phone: (813)894-1052
St. Petersburg, FL 33701   Mary Wyatt Allen, Pres.
Founded: 1920. **Staff:** 3. **Subjects:** St. Petersburg history. **Special Collections:** Newman Collection (autographs and holographs of American historical figures); books by local authors; local photograph collection. **Holdings:** 600 books, manuscripts, documents, and records. **Subscriptions:** 6 journals and other serials; 2 newspapers. **Services:** Copying; archives open to members. **Formerly:** St. Petersburg Historical Society, Inc. - Library and Archives. **Staff:** Susan Burkhart, Dir.

★ 14589 ★
St. Rita's Medical Center - Medical Library (Med)
730 W. Market St.   Phone: (419)227-3361
Lima, OH 45801   Sharon A. Bilopavlovich, Libn.
Founded: 1948. **Staff:** 1. **Subjects:** Medicine. **Holdings:** 1582 volumes. **Subscriptions:** 46 journals and other serials. **Services:** Library open to physicians, medical staff, and paramedical personnel. **Computerized Information Services:** MEDLINE. **Networks/Consortia:** Member of National Network of Libraries of Medicine - Greater Midwest Region, Health Science Librarians of Northwest Ohio (HSLNO). **Remarks:** FAX: (419)226-9779.

★ 14590 ★
St. Stephen Centre Library (Rel-Phil)
PO Box 2400   Phone: (519)439-7211
London, ON, Canada N6A 4G3   Guy Lajoie
Founded: 1966. **Subjects:** Scripture, theology, anthropology, religious education, social analysis. **Holdings:** 6000 books. **Services:** Library not open to the public. **Formerly:** Guided Study Programs/Communications Office of the Diocese of London - Library.

★ 14591 ★
St. Stephen United Church of Christ - Centennial Library (Rel-Phil)
905 E. Perkins Ave.   Phone: (419)626-1612
Sandusky, OH 44870   Linda Richards, Libn.
Founded: 1982. **Staff:** 7. **Subjects:** Religion, church history, Bible. **Special Collections:** Historical Bibles (many in German; 40). **Holdings:** 2207 books. **Services:** Copying; library open to the public. **Automated Operations:** Computerized cataloging, acquisitions, and serials.

★ 14592 ★
St. Stephen's College - Library (Rel-Phil)
University of Alberta   Phone: (403)439-7311
Edmonton, AB, Canada T6G 2J6   Sharon Costall, Libn.
Founded: 1909. **Staff:** 1. **Subjects:** Religion and theology. **Special Collections:** Liberation theology; feminist theology. **Holdings:** 10,000 books. **Subscriptions:** 70 journals and other serials. **Services:** Interlibrary loan; library open to the public with librarian's approval. **Remarks:** FAX: (403)433-8875. Maintained by the United Church of Canada, the college serves as a Centre for Continuing Education for the professional ministry and laity.

★ 14593 ★
St. Stephen's United Methodist Church - Library (Rel-Phil)
4601 Juan Tabo, N.E.   Phone: (505)293-9673
Albuquerque, NM 87111   Bea Allshouse, Libn.
Founded: 1980. **Staff:** 3. **Subjects:** Christianity. **Holdings:** 3400 books. **Subscriptions:** 3 journals and other serials. **Services:** Library open to the public by appointment.

St. Therese Library
See: Society of the Little Flower (15330)

★ 14594 ★
St. Thomas Catholic Church - Barr Memorial Library (Rel-Phil)
2210 Lincoln Way   Phone: (515)292-3810
Ames, IA 50010   Anne Recker, Libn.
Subjects: Bible, Catholic doctrine, family/ethics, saints/biography, meditations, children's literature. **Special Collections:** Concilium; John Henry Cardinal Newman; western spirituality; Fathers of the Church. **Holdings:** 5000 books. **Subscriptions:** 40 periodicals; 5 newspapers. **Services:** Library open to the public.

★ 14595 ★
St. Thomas Episcopal Church - Gardner Memorial Library (Rel-Phil)
231 Sunset Ave.   Phone: (408)736-4155
Sunnyvale, CA 94086   Carol Campbell, Parish Libn.
Founded: 1979. **Staff:** 5. **Subjects:** Christian life, prayer, parenting, psychology. **Special Collections:** Summa Theologicae (St. Thomas Aquinas). **Holdings:** 3000 books; 500 cassette tapes; 50 phonograph records; 2 VF drawers; 20 filmstrips; 100 video recordings; 150 slides. **Services:** Interlibrary loan; library open to the public with restrictions. **Automated Operations:** Computerized cataloging.

★ 14596 ★
St. Thomas Institute - Library
6714 Sperti Ln.
Burlington, KY 41005-9640
Defunct.

★ 14597 ★
St. Thomas Medical Center - Medical Library (Med)
444 N. Main St.   Phone: (216)379-5505
Akron, OH 44310   Linda E. Bunyan, Med.Libn.
Founded: 1929. **Staff:** Prof 1; Other 2. **Subjects:** Medicine, nursing, and allied health sciences. **Holdings:** 1758 books; 3381 bound periodical volumes; 400 cassette tapes; 600 slides; 1 file case of clippings and pamphlets; AV programs; computer software. **Subscriptions:** 170 journals and other serials. **Services:** Interlibrary loan; library not open to the public. **Computerized Information Services:** NLM, BRS Information Technologies. **Networks/Consortia:** Member of NEOUCOM Council Associated Hospital Librarians.

★ 14598 ★
St. Thomas More College - Shannon Library (Rel-Phil, Soc Sci)
1437 College Dr.   Phone: (306)966-8962
Saskatoon, SK, Canada S7N 0W6   Jane Morris, Libn.
Founded: 1936. **Staff:** 2. **Subjects:** Theology, women in monasticism, church history, Christian sociology, history, English, philosophy, psychology, sociology, economics, political science, Biblical literature. **Special Collections:** St. Thomas More (all books and editions); complete holdings of Chesterton, Belloc, Wells, and Christopher Dawson. **Holdings:** 50,000 volumes. **Subscriptions:** 175 journals and other serials. **Services:** Interlibrary loan; library open to the public. **Computerized Information Services:** CD-ROM. **Remarks:** FAX: (306)966-8904. College is an autonomous affiliate of the University of Saskatchewan.

★ 14599 ★
St. Thomas Psychiatric Hospital - Library Services (Med)
Box 2004   Phone: (519)631-8510
St. Thomas, ON, Canada N5P 3V9   Dr. Fred Rutherford, Libn.
Founded: 1973. **Staff:** Prof 1; Other 1. **Subjects:** Psychiatry, psychology, medicine, nursing, allied health professions. **Holdings:** 6000 books; 4000 bound periodical volumes; 250 videotapes. **Subscriptions:** 175 journals and other serials; 5 newspapers. **Services:** Interlibrary loan; copying; SDI; library open to the public with restrictions. **Computerized Information Services:** iNET 2000, BRS Information Technologies, MEDLINE; Envoy 100 (electronic mail service). **Publications:** Current Awareness, monthly - for internal distribution only; Recent Acquisitions, quarterly - distributed to health library network. **Remarks:** FAX: (519)633-0852. Electronic mail address(es): ST.THOMAS.PSYCH (Envoy 100). Maintained by Ontario Ministry of Health - Mental Health Division.

★ 14600 ★
St. Thomas Seminary - Library (Rel-Phil)
1300 S. Steele   Phone: (303)722-4687
Denver, CO 80210   Joyce L. White, Dir.
Founded: 1906. **Staff:** Prof 3; Other 1. **Subjects:** Theology, Bible, social problems. **Special Collections:** Catholic theology; Anglican theology; social problems; Minorities Collection, with emphasis on the Chicano; De Andreis Seminary Collection. **Holdings:** 145,000 volumes. **Subscriptions:** 400 journals and other serials. **Services:** Interlibrary loan; copying; library open to those with an identification card. **Staff:** Dig Chinn, Assoc.Libn.; Sharon Figlino, Circ.; Patricia Regal, Per.; Frank Germovnik, C.M., Retrospective Cat.

★ 14601 ★
St. Thomas Seminary - Library - Alumni Collection (Rel-Phil, Rare Book)
467 Bloomfield Ave.   Phone: (203)242-5573
Bloomfield, CT 06002   Lucille S. Halfpenny, Libn.
Founded: 1950. **Staff:** Prof 1. **Subjects:** Catholic Americana, 1790-1860; Catholic theology. **Special Collections:** Incunabula; Bibles, 1522 to present. **Holdings:** 13,700 books; 1500 bound periodical volumes; 600 pamphlets; 220 cassette tapes; 34 video cassettes. **Subscriptions:** 98 journals and other serials; 10 newspapers. **Services:** Interlibrary loan; copying; collection open to the public for reference use only. **Publications:** Reading Guide for Religious Studies; What Do You Think of the Priest, a bibliographic commentary on the priesthood.

★ 14602 ★
St. Tikhon's Seminary - Library (Rel-Phil)
South Canaan, PA 18459   Phone: (717)937-4411
                                             Sarah Jubinski, Hd.Libn.
Staff: Prof 2; Other 3. **Subjects:** Theology. **Special Collections:** Orthodox theology; Russian language and literature. **Holdings:** 24,000 books; 500 bound periodical volumes. **Subscriptions:** 70 journals and other serials; 10 newspapers. **Services:** Interlibrary loan; library open to the public with restrictions. **Staff:** Fr. Juvenaly, Asst.Libn., Acq./Cat.; Sergei Arhipov, Asst.Libn., Russian Coll.

St. Timothy's Neighborhood Center
See: St. Matthew's & St. Timothy's Neighborhood Center, Inc. (14542)

★ 14603 ★
St. Vincent Charity Hospital - Library (Med)
2351 E. 22nd St.   Phone: (216)861-6200
Cleveland, OH 44115   Joanne Billiar, Hd.Libn.
Founded: 1937. **Staff:** Prof 1. **Subjects:** Medicine, nursing, administration, allied health sciences. **Special Collections:** Historical ophthalmology. **Holdings:** 2500 titles; 3 audio cassette series. **Subscriptions:** 180 journals and other serials. **Services:** Interlibrary loan; copying; library open to the public for reference use only. **Computerized Information Services:** NLM. Performs searches on fee basis. **Remarks:** FAX: (216)363-3337.

★ 14604 ★
St. Vincent College and Archabbey - Libraries (Rel-Phil, Hist)
Latrobe, PA 15650-2690   Phone: (412)539-9761
                                             Rev. Chrysostom V. Schlimm,
                                             O.S.B., Dir., Libs.
Founded: 1846. **Staff:** Prof 5; Other 8. **Subjects:** Liberal arts, Benedictina, patrology, Catholic Church history, medieval studies, Pennsylvaniana, ecclesiastical history. **Special Collections:** Incunabula, Austria-Hungary, England, France, Germany, Switzerland (90 volumes; 15 leaves). **Holdings:** 207,166 books; 37,162 bound periodical volumes; 88,704 microcards; 1228 microfiche; 8299 reels of microfilm; 590 audiocassettes; 80 videocassettes. **Subscriptions:** 889 journals and other serials; 27 newspapers. **Services:** Interlibrary loan; copying; library open to the public. **Automated Operations:** Computerized cataloging. **Computerized Information Services:** OCLC, DIALOG Information Services; CD-ROMs. **Networks/Consortia:** Member of Pittsburgh Regional Library Center (PRLC). **Special Catalogs:** A Descriptive Catalogue of the Incunabula in the St. Vincent College and Archabbey Library (book). **Remarks:** FAX: (412)537-4558. **Staff:** Dr. John F. Macey, Hd., Tech.Serv.; John C. Benyo, Asst.Libn.; Pamela Reed, Cat.; Denise Hegemann, Pub.Serv.Libn.

★ 14605 ★
St. Vincent College and Archabbey - Music Library
Latrobe, PA 15650
Subjects: Music. **Special Collections:** Wimmer Music Collection, 1750-1900 (2500 items). **Holdings:** 1100 music scores. **Remarks:** Currently inactive.

★ 14606 ★
St. Vincent College and Archabbey - Physics Departmental Library
Latrobe, PA 15650
Subjects: Physics, astronomy, mathematics. **Holdings:** 1000 books; 200 bound periodical volumes; 600 unbound periodicals. **Remarks:** Currently inactive.

★ 14607 ★
St. Vincent De Paul Regional Seminary - Library (Rel-Phil)
10701 S. Military Trail   Phone: (407)732-4424
Boynton Beach, FL 33436-4811   Jose L. Romo, Lib.Dir.
Founded: 1962. **Staff:** Prof 1; Other 3. **Subjects:** Theology, philosophy, Latin American studies, philosophical and theological classics in Spanish and English. **Special Collections:** Spanish language collection. **Holdings:** 68,323 books; 9098 bound periodical volumes; 705 tapes and cassettes; 740 microforms. **Subscriptions:** 396 journals and other serials; 30 newspapers. **Services:** Interlibrary loan; library open to the public for reference use only. **Computerized Information Services:** DIALOG Information Services, BRS Information Technologies. **Remarks:** FAX: (407)737-2205.

★ 14608 ★
St. Vincent Health Center - Health Science Library (Med)
232 W. 25th St.   Phone: (814)452-5740
Erie, PA 16544   Joni M. Alex, Med.Libn.
Founded: 1894. **Staff:** Prof 1; Other 2. **Subjects:** Clinical medicine, nursing, dentistry. **Holdings:** 3500 books; 5000 bound periodical volumes; 8 filing drawers of pamphlets; 200 cassettes and slides. **Subscriptions:** 279 journals and other serials. **Services:** Interlibrary loan; copying; library open to the public for reference use only. **Computerized Information Services:** DIALOG Information Services; CD-ROM (Index Medicus). Performs searches on fee basis. **Networks/Consortia:** Member of National Network of Libraries of Medicine - Middle Atlantic Region, Erie Area Health Information Library Cooperative (EAHILC). **Remarks:** FAX: (814)454-8741.

★ 14609 ★
St. Vincent Hospital - Health Science Library (Med)
835 S. VanBuren St.
Box 13508
Green Bay, WI 54305   Phone: (414)433-8171
Founded: 1982. **Staff:** Prof 2; Other 1. **Subjects:** Medicine, allied health sciences. **Holdings:** 3100 books; 525 bound periodical volumes. **Subscriptions:** 140 journals and other serials. **Services:** Interlibrary loan; copying; SDI. **Computerized Information Services:** DIALOG Information Services, MEDLINE; NEWIL (electronic mail service). Performs searches on fee basis. Contact Person: Sue Jauquet, Libn. **Networks/Consortia:** Member of Northeast Wisconsin Intertype Libraries (NEWIL), Fox River Valley Area Library Consortium (FRVALC). **Remarks:** FAX: (414)433-8403. **Staff:** Betty Gorsegner, Libn.

★ 14610 ★
St. Vincent Hospital - John J. Dumphy Memorial Library (Med)
25 Winthrop St.   Phone: (508)798-6117
Worcester, MA 01604   Kris Benishek, Libn.
Staff: Prof 1; Other 1. **Subjects:** Medicine, allied health sciences. **Holdings:** 1500 books; 5500 bound periodical volumes. **Subscriptions:** 162 journals and other serials. **Services:** Interlibrary loan. **Computerized Information Services:** MEDLARS. Performs searches on fee basis. **Networks/Consortia:** Member of Central Massachusetts Consortium of Health Related Libraries (CMCHRL). **Remarks:** FAX: (508)798-1118.

★ 14611 ★
St. Vincent Hospital - Library (Med)
455 St. Michael's Dr.   Phone: (505)989-5218
Santa Fe, NM 87501   Jane Knowles, Libn.
Staff: Prof 1. **Subjects:** Clinical medicine, hospital problems, basic nursing. **Special Collections:** Altitude and its problems (textbooks, pamphlets, and articles). **Holdings:** 1000 books; 1600 periodical volumes. **Subscriptions:** 100 journals and other serials. **Services:** Interlibrary loan; copying; library open to the public for reference use only. **Computerized Information Services:** MEDLINE, DOCLINE. **Networks/Consortia:** Member of New Mexico Consortium of Biomedical and Hospital Libraries, National Network of Libraries of Medicine - South Central Region. **Publications:** Que Pasa (newsletter), weekly - for internal distribution only. **Remarks:** FAX: (505)989-5267.

★ 14612 ★
St. Vincent Hospital - Library/AV Services (Med)
60 Cambridge St.   Phone: (613)233-4041
Ottawa, ON, Canada K1R 7A5   Anita Beausoleil, Dir.
Staff: Prof 5; Other 1. **Subjects:** Gerontology, physiotherapy, occupational therapy, speech and hearing therapy, longterm care, rehabilitation, research, head injuries. **Holdings:** 4500 books; 50 unbound documents; 8 VF drawers; 118 video cassettes; 26 slide kits; 21 filmstrip kits; 95 audio cassettes; government documents, catalogs, and theses on microfiche. **Subscriptions:** 271 journals and other serials. **Services:** Interlibrary loan; copying; library open to interns and field practice students. **Automated Operations:** Computerized public access catalog. **Computerized Information Services:** BRS Information Technologies, DOBIS Canadian Online Library System, CAN/OLE, Canadian Centre for Occupational Health & Safety; CD-ROM (MEDLINE); Envoy 100 (electronic mail service). **Networks/Consortia:** Member of Disability Research Library Network. **Publications:** Acquisitions lists (book), monthly. **Special Catalogs:** AV Catalog (book), annual; serials catalog, annual. **Remarks:** FAX: (613)782-2751. Electronic mail address(es): ST.VINC.HOSP. (Envoy 100). **Formed by the merger of:** Its Medical Library/AV, Printing, Graphic Arts, and Forms Departments. **Staff:** Mireille Ethier-Danis, Lib.Techn.; Jonathan LaReau, AV Techn.

★ 14613 ★
St. Vincent Hospital and Medical Center - Health Sciences Library (Med)
9205 S.W. Barnes Rd.
Portland, OR 97225   Ann M. von Segen
Staff: Prof 1; Other 2. **Subjects:** Medicine, nursing, hospital administration. **Special Collections:** Patient education (400 books, pamphlets, AV programs). **Holdings:** 4200 books; 8000 bound periodical volumes. **Subscriptions:** 625 journals and other serials. **Services:** Interlibrary loan; library not open to the public. **Automated Operations:** Computerized cataloging. **Computerized Information Services:** DIALOG Information Services, MEDLINE. **Networks/Consortia:** Member of Oregon Health Information Online (ORHION), Washington County Cooperative Library Services (WCCLS). **Remarks:** FAX: (503)297-2085.

★ 14614 ★
St. Vincent Infirmary - Medical Library (Med)
2 St. Vincent Circle   Phone: (501)660-3000
Little Rock, AR 72205   Sr. Jean B. Roberts, S.C.N., Med.Libn.
Founded: 1900. **Staff:** Prof 1; Other 1. **Subjects:** Medicine, medical specialties. **Special Collections:** Hospital Archives (35 volumes). **Holdings:** 4935 books; 3500 bound periodical volumes. **Subscriptions:** 200 journals and other serials. **Services:** Interlibrary loan; copying; library open to students and interns of University of Arkansas Medical Center; open to the public with restrictions. **Networks/Consortia:** Member of National Network of Libraries of Medicine - South Central Region.

★ 14615 ★
St. Vincent Medical Center - Health Science Library (Med)
2213 Cherry St.
Toledo, OH 43608   Phone: (419)321-4329
Founded: 1970. **Staff:** Prof 2; Other 3. **Subjects:** Clinical medicine and surgery, nursing, hospital administration. **Holdings:** 10,101 books; 8000 bound periodical volumes. **Subscriptions:** 704 journals and other serials. **Services:** Interlibrary loan; library not open to the public. **Automated Operations:** Computerized cataloging and circulation. **Computerized Information Services:** MEDLARS, OCLC, BRS Information Technologies; CD-ROMs (MEDLINE, HEALTH, CINAHL). Performs searches on fee basis. **Networks/Consortia:** Member of Health Science Librarians of Northwest Ohio (HSLNO). **Remarks:** FAX: (419)321-4967. **Staff:** Claudia Grainger, Co-Dir.; Susan Schafer, Co-Dir.

★ 14616 ★
St. Vincent Medical Center - Health Sciences Library (Med)
2131 W. 3rd St.   Phone: (213)484-5530
Los Angeles, CA 90057   Marsha Gelman-Kmec, Dir., Lib.Serv.
Founded: 1938. **Staff:** Prof 1; Other 1. **Subjects:** Medicine, nursing, administration, cardiology, heart and kidney transplantation. **Holdings:** 1200 books; 400 bound periodical volumes. **Subscriptions:** 202 journals and other serials. **Services:** Interlibrary loan; copying; faxing; library open to the public with restrictions. **Automated Operations:** Computerized acquisitions. **Computerized Information Services:** MEDLINE, BRS Information Technologies. Performs searches on fee basis. **Publications:** Monthly newsletter - for internal distribution only. **Remarks:** FAX: (213)484-7092.

★ 14617 ★
St. Vincent's Hospital - Cunningham Wilson Library (Med)
Box 12407
Birmingham, AL 35202-2407   Phone: (205)320-7830
Staff: Prof 2; Other 1. **Subjects:** Medicine, nursing, hospital administration. **Special Collections:** Historical Nursing Collection. **Holdings:** 2537 books; 1316 bound periodical volumes; 335 vertical files; 20 videotapes; 240 audiotapes. **Subscriptions:** 158 journals and other serials. **Services:** Interlibrary loan; library not open to the public. **Automated Operations:** Computerized cataloging. **Computerized Information Services:** MEDLINE. Performs searches on fee basis. **Networks/Consortia:** Member of Jefferson County Hospital Librarians' Association, Alabama Health Libraries Association (ALHELA). **Remarks:** FAX: (205)930-2182. **Staff:** Priscilla Toman, Lib.Mgr.; Stephanie Pluscht, Lib.Mgr.

★ 14618 ★
St. Vincent's Hospital - Garceau Library (Med)
2001 W. 86th St.   Phone: (317)871-2095
Indianapolis, IN 46260   Virginia Durkin, Mgr., Lib.Serv.
Founded: 1927. **Staff:** Prof 2. **Subjects:** Medicine, paramedical sciences, nursing, hospital administration. **Special Collections:** Hospital archives. **Holdings:** 6980 volumes; 420 audiotapes; 4 VF drawers of pamphlets; 600 AV programs; microfiche. **Subscriptions:** 250 journals and other serials. **Services:** Interlibrary loan; copying; SDI. **Computerized Information Services:** BRS Information Technologies, MEDLINE, OCLC. **Networks/Consortia:** Member of Central Indiana Health Science Library Consortium, National Network of Libraries of Medicine - Greater Midwest Region, INCOLSA. **Publications:** Acquisitions list, biannual; library handbook. **Staff:** Louise Hass, Libn.

★ 14619 ★
St. Vincent's Hospital - School of Nursing Library (Med)
27 Christopher St.   Phone: (212)790-8486
New York, NY 10014   Clare E. Higgins, Libn.
Founded: 1892. **Staff:** Prof 1. **Subjects:** Nursing and allied professional sciences, social sciences, medicine. **Holdings:** 3000 books; 225 bound periodical volumes; 8 VF drawers of pamphlets; 825 AV programs. **Subscriptions:** 65 journals and other serials. **Services:** Copying; library open to faculty, students, hospital personnel.

★ 14620 ★
St. Vincent's Hospital and Medical Center of New York - Medical Library (Med)
153 W. 11th St.   Phone: (212)790-7811
New York, NY 10011   Agnes T. Frank, Dir.
Founded: 1934. **Staff:** Prof 2; Other 2. **Subjects:** Health sciences, psychology. **Holdings:** 8805 volumes. **Subscriptions:** 250 journals and other serials. **Services:** Interlibrary loan (fee); library not open to the public. **Computerized Information Services:** MEDLINE, BRS Information Technologies. Performs searches on fee basis. **Networks/Consortia:** Member of Medical Library Center of New York (MLCNY). **Remarks:** FAX: (212)366-6067. **Staff:** Nina Hollander, Asst.Dept.Hd.

★ 14621 ★
St. Vincent's Hospital and Medical Center of New York, Westchester Branch - Medical Library (Med)
240 North St.   Phone: (914)967-6500
Harrison, NY 10528   Ethel Eisenberg, Med.Libn.
Staff: Prof 1. **Subjects:** Psychiatry, psychology, alcoholism, drug abuse. **Holdings:** 3000 books; 2000 bound periodical volumes; cassettes. **Subscriptions:** 60 journals and other serials. **Services:** Interlibrary loan; library not open to the public. **Networks/Consortia:** Member of National Network of Libraries of Medicine - Middle Atlantic Region. **Remarks:** FAX: (914)967-1633.

★ 14622 ★
St. Vincent's Medical Center - Daniel T. Banks Health Science Library (Med)
2800 Main St.   Phone: (203)576-5336
Bridgeport, CT 06606   Janet Goerig, Dir., Lib.Serv.
Founded: 1903. **Staff:** Prof 2; Other 4. **Subjects:** Medicine, nursing, and allied health sciences. **Holdings:** 4298 books; 4058 bound periodical volumes; 40 VF drawers of reprints and pamphlets; 5988 AV programs. **Subscriptions:** 305 journals and other serials. **Services:** Interlibrary loan; library not open to the public. **Computerized Information Services:** Silver Platter.

★ 14623 ★
St. Vincent's Medical Center of Richmond - Medical Library (Med)
355 Bard Ave.   Phone: (718)876-3117
Staten Island, NY 10310   Lucy DiMatteo, Dir.
Founded: 1925. **Staff:** Prof 1; Other 1. **Subjects:** Medicine, nursing, health administration. **Holdings:** 3000 books; 3000 bound periodical volumes. **Subscriptions:** 180 journals and other serials. **Services:** Interlibrary loan; copying; library open to students. **Automated Operations:** Computerized circulation and ILL (DOCLINE). **Computerized Information Services:** MEDLARS, OCLC. **Networks/Consortia:** Member of Brooklyn-Queens-Staten Island Health Sciences Librarians (BQSI), BHSL, New York Metropolitan Reference and Research Library Agency. **Remarks:** FAX: (718)727-2456.

★ 14624 ★
St. Vladimir Institute - St. Vladimir Institute Library: A Resource Center for Ukrainian Studies (Area-Ethnic)
620 Spadina Ave.   Phone: (416)923-8266
Toronto, ON, Canada M5S 2H4   Ihor Krut
Founded: 1969. **Staff:** Prof 1; Other 1. **Subjects:** Ukrainian Canadiana; Ukrainian folk and fine arts, history, geography, archeology, politics, literature, language, and music; Ukrainian Orthodox Church. **Special Collections:** Photograph archives (2 boxes); Ukrainians in Canada 1979 Collection (clippings). **Holdings:** 20,000 books; 15 VF drawers of clippings and pamphlets; 50 AV programs; 500 phonograph records; 1000 posters; 500 cassette tapes; 3 boxes of printed archival material. **Subscriptions:** 100 journals and other serials; 17 newspapers. **Services:** Copying; library open to the public. **Computerized Information Services:** CDS/ISIS (internal database).

★ 14625 ★
St. Vladimir's Orthodox Theological Seminary - Fr. Georges Florovsky Library (Rel-Phil)
575 Scarsdale Rd.   Phone: (914)961-8313
Yonkers, NY 10707   Eleana Silk, Libn.
Founded: 1938. **Staff:** Prof 1; Other 1. **Subjects:** Eastern Orthodox Church, Russian Orthodox church history and theology, Byzantine and Balkan church history and theology, Russian church music, iconography, Orthodox Church in America church history. **Special Collections:** 19th century theological periodicals. **Holdings:** 77,000 books; 475 volumes of dissertations; 620 sound recordings; 1330 titles in microform. **Subscriptions:** 335 journals and other serials. **Services:** Interlibrary loan; copying; library open to the public for reference use only. **Automated Operations:** Computerized public access catalog, cataloging, serials, and circulation. **Computerized Information Services:** Unix (internal database), OCLC. Performs searches free of charge. **Remarks:** FAX: (914)961-4507. **Staff:** Irina Itina.

★ 14626 ★
St. Vladimir's Ukrainian Orthodox Cultural Centre - Library and Archives (Area-Ethnic)
404 Meredith Rd., N.E.   Phone: (403)264-3437
Calgary, AB, Canada T2E 5A6   Mykola Woron, Libn.
Founded: 1959. **Staff:** 3. **Subjects:** Ukraine. **Special Collections:** Programs of Ukrainian events (1 VF drawer); XXI Olympic Games in Montreal (118 items); Ukrainian Democratic Press Publications (88). **Holdings:** 8831 books; 73 bound periodical volumes; 773 unbound periodicals; 51 videocassettes; 799 cards; 19 maps; 1000 clippings; 161 photographs. **Subscriptions:** 24 journals and other serials; 6 newspapers. **Services:** Interlibrary loan; library open to the public at librarian's discretion. **Staff:** Bill Swiityk, Asst.Libn.; Orest Slypokura, Asst.Libn.; Stan Humenuk, Asst.Libn.

★ 14627 ★
St. Walburg Monastery of Benedictine Sisters of Covington, Kentucky - Archives (Rel-Phil)
2500 Amsterdam Rd.   Phone: (606)331-6324
Covington, KY 41017   Sr. Teresa Wolking, O.S.B., Archv.
Founded: 1859. **Staff:** Prof 1; Other 3. **Subjects:** History and records of the Benedictine Sisters of Covington, KY; archives of St. Scholastica Convent, Covington, LA. **Holdings:** 200 square feet of archival material, focusing on religious women. **Services:** Copying; archives open to the public with restrictions by appointment.

★ 14628 ★
Salem Athenaeum (Rare Book)
337 Essex St.   Phone: (617)744-2540
Salem, MA 01970   Cynthia Wiggin, Libn.
Founded: 1810. **Staff:** Prof 1. **Subjects:** Religion, early sciences, early children's literature, early natural history. **Special Collections:** Social Library of 1760; Philosophical Library of 1781; Dr. Edward Augustus Holyoke, M.D., Personal Library. **Holdings:** 54,000 books. **Services:** Copying; library open to the public for research. **Special Catalogs:** 18th Century Short Title Catalogue of 637 items, a complete listing of Social Library of 1760, Philosophical Library of 1781, and Personal Library of Dr. Edward Augustus Holyoke, M.D.

★ 14629 ★

Salem County Historical Society - Library (Hist)
79-83 Market St.   Phone: (609)935-5004
Salem, NJ 08079   Alice G. Boggs, Libn.-Sec.
Founded: 1884. **Staff:** Prof 2. **Subjects:** Genealogy and history of Salem County. **Special Collections:** Dolls; samplers; local Native American Lenni Lenape artifacts; H.J. Heinz Barn and Cane Collections; glass; furniture; clocks; antique fire equipment. **Holdings:** Scrapbooks; photographs; maps; Salem County newspapers, 1819-1959; family histories; real estate transactions; deeds; architectural drawings; microfilm; oral histories; documents; books. **Subscriptions:** 10 journals and other serials. **Services:** Copying; research assistance; library open to the public for reference use only during restricted hours for a fee (no charge to members). **Publications:** Place names of Salem County; Specific Family Genealogies from 1675; Fenwick's Papers; The Way We Were, 1976. **Special Indexes:** Index of all collections.

★ 14630 ★

Salem County Law Library (Law)
Salem County Court House
92 Market St.
P.O. Box 18   Phone: (609)935-7510
Salem, NJ 08079   Frank Miller, Law Libn.
Staff: Prof 1. **Subjects:** Law. **Holdings:** 4200 books; 200 bound periodical volumes. **Services:** Interlibrary loan; library open to the public at librarian's discretion. **Remarks:** FAX: (609)935-8882.

★ 14631 ★

Salem Free Public Library - Special Collections (Hist)
112 W. Broadway   Phone: (609)935-0526
Salem, NJ 08079   Elizabeth C. Fogg, Dir.
Founded: 1920. **Staff:** Prof 1; Other 1. **Subjects:** South Jersiana, especially Salem County history. **Special Collections:** Granville S. Thomas South Jersey Collection (700 items); U.S. Nuclear Regulatory Commission/Public Service Electric & Gas Company Salem I & II Nuclear Power Station document collection (316 linear feet of reports and documents). **Holdings:** 700 books; 6 reels of microfilm of Salem County census information; 200 audio cassettes; 7 cases of pamphlets, reports, and newspaper clippings. **Subscriptions:** 158 journals and other serials. **Services:** Interlibrary loan (limited); copying; collections open to the public for reference use only. **Networks/Consortia:** Member of South Jersey Regional Library Cooperative.

★ 14632 ★

Salem Hospital - Health Sciences Library (Med)
81 Highland Ave.   Phone: (508)741-1200
Salem, MA 01970   Nancy Fazzone, Dir., Lib.Serv.
Founded: 1928. **Staff:** Prof 2; Other 2. **Subjects:** Medicine, nursing, and allied health sciences. **Holdings:** 3500 books; 7000 bound periodical volumes. **Subscriptions:** 275 journals and other serials. **Services:** Interlibrary loan; current awareness; library open to the public. **Computerized Information Services:** NLM, BRS Information Technologies; CD-ROM (DIALOG OnDisc, CINAHL); internal database. **Networks/Consortia:** Member of Northeastern Consortium for Health Information (NECHI). **Publications:** Library News (newsletter) 3/year. **Remarks:** FAX: (508)744-9110. **Staff:** Janet Ohles, Assoc.Libn.

★ 14633 ★

Salem Hospital - Health Sciences Library (Med)
665 Winter St., S.E.
Box 14001
Salem, OR 97309-5014   Phone: (503)370-5377
      Carol Jones, Dir., Lib.Serv.
Founded: 1961. **Staff:** Prof 1; Other 2. **Subjects:** Clinical medicine, allied health sciences. **Holdings:** 4000 monographs. **Subscriptions:** 355 journals and other serials. **Services:** Interlibrary loan (fee); library open to the public with restrictions. **Automated Operations:** Computerized cataloging, acquisitions, serials, and ILL. **Computerized Information Services:** MEDLARS, DIALOG Information Services, OCLC; internal database; OnTyme Electronic Message Network Service (electronic mail service); CD-ROM; internal databases. **Publications:** Annual Report. **Special Indexes:** Citation Index; clinical and medical indexes. **Remarks:** Alternate telephone number(s): 370-5559. FAX: (503)370-5534. Electronic mail address(es): ORSAH (OnTyme Electronic Message Network Service).

Salem Maritime National Historic Site
See: U.S. Natl. Park Service (17773)

★ 14634 ★

Salem State College - Library - Special Collections (Soc Sci)
352 Lafayette St.   Phone: (508)741-6230
Salem, MA 01970   Neil B. Olson, Dir. of Libs.
Staff: 1. **Special Collections:** Congressmen George and William Bates Archives (140 boxes of papers and books); Congressman Michael Harrington papers (200 boxes); 19th century school materials (800 items); U.S. Geological Survey maps (71,000); Principal Joseph Pitman papers (12 boxes). **Services:** Interlibrary loan; copying; SDI; microform reproduction; collections open to the public for reference use only. **Automated Operations:** Computerized cataloging and ILL. **Computerized Information Services:** DIALOG Information Services, OCLC; internal database. **Networks/Consortia:** Member of North of Boston Library Exchange, Inc. (NOBLE), Northeast Consortium of Colleges and Universities in Massachusetts (NECCUM), Northeastern Consortium for Health Information (NECHI). **Publications:** Library Handbook. **Remarks:** FAX: (508)744-6596. **Staff:** Glenn MacNutt, Act.Archv.; Camilla M. Glynn, Asst.Dir.

★ 14635 ★

Salem State College - Library of Social Alternatives (Soc Sci)
Salem, MA 01970   Phone: (508)741-6000
      Margaret Andrews, Coord.
Founded: 1972. **Staff:** Prof 1. **Subjects:** Alternative lifestyles, Third World, social change, ecology, gays/lesbians, health care, women, hobbies, radical left. **Holdings:** 3000 books; magazine archives. **Subscriptions:** 20 journals and other serials. **Services:** Library open to the public.

★ 14636 ★

Salem State College - Professional Studies Resources Center (Educ)
Library, 352 Lafayette St.   Phone: (508)741-6000
Salem, MA 01970   Gertrude L. Fox, Libn.
Founded: 1964. **Staff:** Prof 1. **Subjects:** Education - materials, textbooks and trade books (K-12), nonprint materials, standardized tests; marine science. **Special Collections:** Resource Center for Marine Science (elementary and secondary). **Holdings:** 14,148 books; 126 bound periodical volumes; ERIC microfiche, 1968 to present; 5 filing cabinets of curriculum guides; 2 file drawers of pamphlets; 1 file drawer of pictures and maps; 7700 curriculum guides on microfiche. **Subscriptions:** 6 journals and other serials. **Services:** Interlibrary loan; copying; center open to the public. **Automated Operations:** Computerized serials. **Remarks:** FAX: (508)744-6596.

★ 14637 ★

Salinas Public Library - John Steinbeck Library (Hum)
110 W. San Luis St.   Phone: (408)758-7311
Salinas, CA 93901   Mary Gamble, Steinbeck Libn.
Founded: 1964. **Staff:** 1. **Special Collections:** John Steinbeck Collection (first and foreign language editions of Steinbeck's works). **Holdings:** 100 oral interview recordings; 2000 photographs; letters; movie posters; manuscripts; galley proofs; clipping files. **Subscriptions:** 3 journals and other serials. **Services:** Interlibrary loan; copying; library open to the public by appointment. **Networks/Consortia:** Member of Monterey Bay Area Cooperative Library System (MOBAC). **Publications:** John Steinbeck: A Guide to the Collection of the Salinas Public Library, 1979; Guide to Steinbeck Country, 1984. **Remarks:** FAX: (408)758-7336.

★ 14638 ★

The Salisbury Association - History Room (Hist)
c/o Scoville Memorial Library
Main St.   Phone: (203)435-9440
Salisbury, CT 06068   Virginia F. Moskowitz
Subjects: Iron, railroads, genealogy. **Holdings:** Figures not available. **Services:** Copying; room open to the public for reference use only. **Remarks:** FAX: (203)435-8136.

★ 14639 ★

Salisbury Historical Society - Archives (Hist)
P.O. Box 202   Phone: (603)648-2244
Salisbury, NH 03268   Anne Smith, Pres.
Founded: 1966. **Staff:** 2. **Subjects:** Local history, genealogy. **Special Collections:** Oral history tapes and transcriptions. **Holdings:** 50 books; manuscripts and original documents pertaining to Salisbury. **Services:** Genealogical research; archives open to the public on a limited schedule. **Publications:** News Letter, monthly - to members.

★ 14640 ★
Salisbury State University - Blackwell Library - Special Collections
   (Hist)
Salisbury, MD 21801   Phone: (301)543-6130
                                       James R. Thrash, Dir.
Founded: 1925. **Staff:** 21. **Special Collections:** Maryland Room (3200 volumes; 12 VF drawers of clippings); Education Resources Center; U.S. Government documents depository (selected); Leisure Studies; juvenile literature; Les Callette Memorial Civil War Collection; Maryland State documents depository. **Holdings:** 218,544 volumes; 503,697 microfiche, 12,028 reels of microfilm. **Subscriptions:** 1639 journals and other serials; 20 newspapers. **Services:** Interlibrary loan; copying; collections open to the public. **Automated Operations:** Computerized cataloging and circulation. **Computerized Information Services:** DIALOG Information Services, OCLC, ABI/INFORM, Corporate and Industry Research Reports, ERIC. Performs searches on fee basis. Contact Person: Keith R. Vail, Assoc.Dir. **Networks/Consortia:** Member of PALINET. **Remarks:** FAX: (301)543-6068.

★ 14641 ★
Salk Institute for Biological Studies - Library (Biol Sci, Sci-Engr)
Box 85800   Phone: (619)453-4100
San Diego, CA 92186-5800   June A. Gittings, Libn.
Founded: 1962. **Staff:** 4. **Subjects:** Biochemistry, molecular biology, plant biology, chemistry, genetics, neuropsychology, language studies, virology, neurobiology, philosophy of science, cancer, neuroscience, AIDS. **Holdings:** 15,200 books and serials. **Subscriptions:** 216 journals; 6 newspapers. **Services:** Interlibrary loan; copying; library open to the public for reference use only by permission. **Computerized Information Services:** MEDLINE.

★ 14642 ★
Salmagundi Club - Library (Art)
47 Fifth Ave.   Phone: (212)255-7740
New York, NY 10003   Ken Fitch
Founded: 1899. **Subjects:** Art. **Holdings:** 8000 books. **Services:** Library open to qualified persons submitting written applications and references.

★ 14643 ★
Salmon Brook Historical Society - Reference and Educational Center
   (Hist)
208 Salmon Brook St.   Phone: (203)653-3965
Granby, CT 06035   Carol Laun, Cur.
Founded: 1959. **Staff:** 1. **Subjects:** Local and area history, genealogy, religion, agriculture and industry, military history. **Special Collections:** James L. Loomis Collection (Loomis Store, 1862-1931, and Connecticut Home Guard, 1917-1918; 600 items); Richard E. Holcomb papers (Panama Canal and Civil War; 250 items). **Holdings:** 1500 books; 50 bound periodical volumes; 250 other cataloged items; 9 VF drawers of original documents; 22 VF drawers of research information and clippings; 20 boxes of pamphlets, booklets, newspapers; 300 deeds; 150 account books; 5 VF drawers of genealogy materials; 30 boxes of genealogy materials. **Services:** Center open to the public by appointment. **Publications:** Collections II, III, and IV - to members and for sale; Granby Town Records 1786-1853; Heritage of Granby; Granby, CT: A Brief History 1786-1986; Granby Bicentennial Quilt - all for sale. **Special Indexes:** Granby Soldiers in Revolutionary War & Civil War (card); Granby cemetery inscription and death records (card); Granby census records, 1790-1910 (book; indexed).

★ 14644 ★
Salomon Brothers Inc. - Library (Bus-Fin)
7 World Trade Center   Phone: (212)783-1700
New York, NY 10048   Gloria D. McDonald, Lib.Mgr.
Founded: 1976. **Staff:** Prof 6; Other 31. **Subjects:** Investment banking, corporate and international finance, securities industry. **Special Collections:** Eurobond prospectuses (7100); underwriting indentures on microfiche (7500). **Holdings:** 8300 books; 3000 international files of annual reports and prospectuses; 5000 corporate files; transaction files; 900,000 microforms. **Subscriptions:** 700 journals and other serials; 25 newspapers. **Services:** Interlibrary loan; library not open to the public. **Automated Operations:** Computerized cataloging and acquisitions. **Computerized Information Services:** DIALOG Information Services, Dow Jones News/Retrieval, Info Globe, NEXIS, OCLC. **Publications:** Business Publications, quarterly; Periodicals in the Library, quarterly - all for internal distribution only. **Remarks:** FAX: (212)783-2032. **Staff:** Elizabeth Bryant, Res.Assoc.; Louise Klusek, Res.Assoc.; Arthur Di Meglio, Res.Assoc.; Lisa Gluck, Res.Assoc.; Terrence McDonough, Assoc. Cat. & Acq.; Cecelia B. Scotti, Tech.Serv.Assoc.; Awilda Edwards-Catus, Doc.Supv.

Salomon Center for the Study of Financial Institutions
See: New York University (11730)

Sophie and Ivan Salomon Library Collection
See: Congregation Shearith Israel - Sophie and Ivan Salomon Library Collection (4168)

Salt Industry Research Institute
See: People's Republic of China - Ministry of Light Industry (12927)

★ 14645 ★
Salt Lake City Schools - District Media Center (Educ, Aud-Vis)
1430 Andrew Ave.   Phone: (801)328-7279
Salt Lake City, UT 84104   Marian Karpisek, Supv., Lib. Media Serv.
Founded: 1965. **Staff:** Prof 1; Other 8. **Subjects:** School curriculum. **Holdings:** 101 audio cassettes; 1842 16mm films; 5496 videotapes; 976 sound filmstrips; 871 kits; 32 filmstrips; 47 slides; 75 models; 122 pictures; 107 transparencies; 76 ditto masters; 90 Alcohol and Drug kits. **Subscriptions:** 19 journals and other serials. **Services:** Center open to district related organizations. **Automated Operations:** Computerized cataloging, acquisitions, and circulation. **Computerized Information Services:** WILSONLINE; internal database. **Special Catalogs:** District holdings. **Remarks:** FAX: (801)328-7272.

★ 14646 ★
Salt Lake County Law Library (Law)
240 E. 400 South, Rm. 219   Phone: (801)535-7518
Salt Lake City, UT 84111   Jeff Lund, Law Libn.
Founded: 1900. **Staff:** Prof 1. **Subjects:** Law. **Holdings:** 13,000 volumes. **Services:** Copying; library open to the public with restrictions. **Remarks:** Maintained by Third Judicial District Court.

★ 14647 ★
Salt Lake Tribune - Library (Publ)
143 S. Main St.   Phone: (801)237-2001
Salt Lake City, UT 84117   Ben Ling, Dept.Hd.
Staff: 4. **Subjects:** Newspaper reference topics. **Holdings:** 2500 books; photographs; microfilm. **Services:** Copying; library open to the public with restrictions (fee). **Computerized Information Services:** DataTimes; internal databases. **Special Indexes:** Annual Index (through 1989). **Remarks:** FAX: (801)521-9418.

★ 14648 ★
Salt River Project - Library (Energy, Bus-Fin)
Box 52025
Phoenix, AZ 85072-2025   Phone: (602)236-2259
Founded: 1975. **Staff:** Prof 2. **Subjects:** Business, management, finance, utilities, energy, water, engineering, computer science, environment, law, government, Arizona history, professional development. **Special Collections:** EPRI Reports; IBM Manuals. **Holdings:** 10,000 books and reports. **Subscriptions:** 150 journals and other serials; 8 newspapers. **Services:** Interlibrary loan; SDI; library open to the public by appointment. **Automated Operations:** Computerized cataloging, acquisitions, serials, circulation, and ILL. **Computerized Information Services:** DIALOG Information Services, RLIN, EPRINET, NGWIC, IBMLINK; internal databases. **Remarks:** FAX: (602)236-2505. **Staff:** Cathy Large, PAB; Alice N. McGarvey, ISB.

★ 14649 ★
(Saltillo) Instituto Mexicano-Norteamericano de Relaciones Culturales -
   USIS Collection (Educ)
P. Cardenas y Purceli
25000 Saltillo, Coahuila, Mexico
Remarks: Maintained or supported by the U.S. Information Agency. Focus is on materials that will assist peoples outside the United States to learn about the United States, its people, history, culture, political processes, and social milieux.

★ 14650 ★
(Salvador) Associacao Cultural Brasil-Estados Unidos - Leonard Ross Klein USIS Collection (Educ)
Ave. Sete de Setembro, 1883   Phone: 71 3364411
40120 Salvador, Bahia, Brazil   Marlene Morbeck Coelho
Founded: 1941. **Staff:** 3. **Holdings:** 8000 books; 65 bound periodical volumes. **Subscriptions:** 70 journals and other serials; 5 newspapers. **Services:** Library open to the public. **Remarks:** FAX: 71 2459233. Maintained or supported by the U.S. Information Agency. Focus is on materials that will assist peoples outside the United States to learn about the United States, its people, history, culture, political processes, and social milieux. **Staff:** Edna Dourado Silva, Asst.Libn.; Ana Maria Oliveira de Carvalho; Zaira Nascimento Franco.

★ 14651 ★
Salvation Army - Archives and Research Center (Hist, Rel-Phil)
615 Slaters Ln.   Phone: (703)684-5500
Alexandria, VA 22313   Susan M. Mitchem, Archv.
Founded: 1975. **Staff:** Prof 2. **Subjects:** Salvation Army history and records, social service, churches, religion. **Holdings:** 2600 books; 800 bound periodical volumes; 1000 cubic feet of archives; 67 cubic feet of manuscript collections; 30,000 photographs; 1600 reels of microfilm; 750 microfiche; 45 VF drawers; 300 sound recordings; 280 audiotapes; 250 slides; 500 films. **Services:** Interlibrary loan; copying; library open to the public. **Automated Operations:** Computerized cataloging, acquisitions, and serials. **Publications:** Historical Newsview, quarterly - available upon request. **Special Indexes:** Inventories of processed archives and manuscript collections; Index to Salvation Army Social Service Periodicals (card); Index to The War Cry (card). **Formerly:** Located in Verona, NJ.

Salvation Army - Catherine Booth Bible College
See: **Catherine Booth Bible College** (1961)

★ 14652 ★
Salvation Army - Education Department Library (Hist)
440 W. Nyack Rd.   Phone: (212)337-7349
West Nyack, NY 10994   Mrs. R.G. Russell
Staff: Prof 1. **Subjects:** Salvation Army - biography, history, activities. **Holdings:** 2000 books; clippings; manuscripts; pamphlets; documents. **Services:** Library open to the public by appointment. **Remarks:** FAX: (212)337-7482.

★ 14653 ★
Salvation Army Grace General Hospital - Chesley A. Pippy, Jr. Medical Library (Med)
241 Lemarchant Rd.   Phone: (709)778-6796
St. John's, NF, Canada A1E 1P9   Elizabeth Duggan, Med.Libn.
Staff: 1. **Subjects:** Medicine. **Holdings:** 950 books; 1200 bound periodical volumes. **Subscriptions:** 110 journals and other serials. **Services:** Interlibrary loan; library not open to the public. **Publications:** Newsletter and recent acquisitions, quarterly.

★ 14654 ★
Salvation Army Grace General Hospital - Library (Med)
300 Booth Dr.   Phone: (204)837-0127
Winnipeg, MB, Canada R3J 3M7   Mrs. J. Kochan, Dir.
Founded: 1974. **Staff:** 3. **Subjects:** Medicine, nursing, and allied health sciences. **Holdings:** 10,562 books; 689 AV programs; 18 linear feet of pamphlets. **Subscriptions:** 172 journals and other serials. **Services:** Interlibrary loan; copying; library open to the public with restrictions. **Remarks:** FAX: (204)885-7909.

★ 14655 ★
Salvation Army Grace Hospital - Hospital Library (Med)
1402 8th Ave., N.W.
Calgary, AB, Canada T2N 1B9   Phone: (403)284-1141
Founded: 1967. **Subjects:** Medicine, paramedicine, history and poetry of medicine. **Holdings:** 2000 books; 50 bound periodical volumes; 40 tapes. **Subscriptions:** 30 journals and other serials. **Services:** Library not open to the public.

★ 14656 ★
Salvation Army Grace Hospital - Library (Med)
339 Crawford Ave.   Phone: (519)255-2245
Windsor, ON, Canada N9A 5C6   Anna Henshaw, Libn.
Staff: Prof 1; Other 1. **Subjects:** Medicine, nursing. **Holdings:** 2000 books; 880 bound periodical volumes. **Subscriptions:** 200 journals and other serials. **Services:** Interlibrary loan; library not open to the public. **Computerized Information Services:** MEDLINE, Canadian Centre for Occupational Health & Safety, BRS Information Technologies. **Remarks:** FAX: (519)255-2458.

★ 14657 ★
Salvation Army School for Officers Training - Elftman Memorial Library (Rel-Phil, Soc Sci)
30840 Hawthorne Blvd.   Phone: (213)377-0481
Rancho Palos Verdes, CA 90274   Lavonne D. Robertson, Hd.Libn.
Staff: 3. **Subjects:** Salvation Army history and services, Bible and theology, social welfare. **Holdings:** 30,000 books; AV programs. **Subscriptions:** 206 journals and other serials. **Services:** Library open to the public by appointment. **Remarks:** FAX: (213)541-1697. **Staff:** Janet Fine.

★ 14658 ★
Salzburg Seminar in American Studies - Library (Soc Sci, Law)
Schloss Leopoldskron
Postfach 129   Phone: 662 83983
A-5010 Salzburg, Austria   Marie-Louise Ryback, Libn.
Subjects: American law, history, and literature; social sciences; political science. **Special Collections:** Tapes of faculty lectures (700). **Holdings:** 10,000 books; 120 bound periodical volumes; 22 AV programs; 500 phonograph records. **Services:** Copying; library open to the public by appointment. **Publications:** Serial Holdings, annual. **Special Catalogs:** Catalog of music and spoken recordings (card). **Special Indexes:** Index to seminar session lectures (online). **Remarks:** FAX: 662 839837. Telex: 847 633701 SASEM A.

Salzmann Library
See: **St. Francis Seminary** (14314)

★ 14659 ★
Samaritan Hospital - Medical Library (Med)
2215 Burdett Ave.   Phone: (518)271-3200
Troy, NY 12180   Annie J. Smith, Med.Libn.
Staff: Prof 1. **Subjects:** Medicine, allied health sciences. **Special Collections:** Spafford Collection (health-related books for laymen; 450 books). **Holdings:** 290 books; 1500 bound periodical volumes. **Subscriptions:** 72 journals and other serials. **Services:** Interlibrary loan; library not open to the public. **Computerized Information Services:** BRS Information Technologies, MEDLINE; internal database. **Networks/Consortia:** Member of Capital District Library Council for Reference & Research Resources (CDLC). **Publications:** Bookbag. **Remarks:** FAX: (518)271-3434.

★ 14660 ★
Samarskij Architekturno-Stroitelnoj Institut - Biblioteka (Sci-Engr, Plan)
ul. Molodogvardenskaja 194   Phone: 33666
443099 Samara, Russia   Ludmila Ivanova Korytina, Dir. of Lib.
Founded: 1930. **Staff:** 39. **Subjects:** Engineering - sanitary, sewage, heating, management, economic aspects; architecture; planning. **Holdings:** 630,245 books. **Subscriptions:** 244 journals and other serials; 38 newspapers. **Services:** Library open to the public with restrictions. **Publications:** Bibliographies.

Samford University - Baptist Medical Centers
See: **Baptist Medical Centers-Samford University - Ida V. Moffett School of Nursing** (1512)

★ 14661 ★
Samford University - Cumberland School of Law - Cordell Hull Law Library (Law)
800 Lakeshore Dr.   Phone: (205)870-2714
Birmingham, AL 35229   Laurel R. Clapp, Law Libn.
Founded: 1847. **Staff:** Prof 5; Other 7. **Subjects:** American law, common law. **Holdings:** 197,918 books; documents; microfilm. **Subscriptions:** 2829 journals and other serials. **Services:** Interlibrary loan; library open to the public. **Automated Operations:** Computerized cataloging. **Computerized Information Services:** WESTLAW, LEXIS. **Publications:** Selected List of Recent Acquisitions, monthly - to faculty. **Staff:** Linda Jones, Acq.Libn.; Rebecca Hutto, Cat.Libn.; Edward Craig, Jr., Ref.Libn.; Virginia Downes, Ser.Libn.

★ 14662 ★
Samford University - Harwell Goodwin Davis Library - Baptist Historical Collection (Rel-Phil)
800 Lakeshore Dr.   Phone: (205)870-2749
Birmingham, AL 35229   Dr. William Nelson, Cur.
Founded: 1958. **Staff:** Prof 1; Other 1. **Subjects:** Alabama Baptist history and biography. **Holdings:** 2500 books; 2200 bound periodical volumes; 10,000 Baptist Association Annuals; Baptist Church minutes and records; oral history tapes and transcripts. **Subscriptions:** 55 journals and other serials. **Services:** Interlibrary loan; copying; collection open to the public. **Computerized Information Services:** DIALOG Information Services. **Publications:** Alabama Baptist Historian. **Special Indexes:** Index to Alabama Baptist newspaper (card and computerized book form); Annuals, Alabama Baptist State Convention; Analytical Information Index. **Remarks:** Library is the official depository of the archives of the Alabama Baptist State Convention. **Staff:** Elizabeth C. Wells, Spec.Coll.Libn.

★ 14663 ★
Samford University - Harwell Goodwin Davis Library - Special Collections (Hist)
800 Lakeshore Dr.   Phone: (205)870-2749
Birmingham, AL 35229   Elizabeth C. Wells, Spec.Coll.Libn.
Founded: 1957. **Staff:** Prof 1; Other 3. **Subjects:** Alabama history, literature, and imprints; Early Southeast - Indians, travel, law; genealogical source records; Southern Reconstruction; Irish history and genealogy. **Special Collections:** William H. Brantley Collection (books; 19th and 20th century manuscripts; 18th and 19th century maps); Albert E. Casey Collection (books; manuscripts; periodicals; maps of Ireland); Douglas C. McMurtrie Collection; John Ruskin Collection; John Masefield Collection; Alfred Tennyson Collection; Lafcadio Hearn Collection. **Holdings:** 25,653 books; 2562 bound periodical volumes; 806 microcards; 349 phonograph records; 2725 maps; 1477 linear feet of manuscripts; 7739 reels of microfilm; 7828 prints and photographs; 3113 microfiche; 150 oral histories; 37 atlases; 1 globe; 60 relief models. **Subscriptions:** 330 journals and other serials. **Services:** Interlibrary loan; copying; collections open to the public. **Computerized Information Services:** DIALOG Information Services. **Special Catalogs:** Map Catalog; Catalog of the Casey Collection of Irish History and Genealogy. **Special Indexes:** Analytical Information Index; index to The Alabama Baptist (newspaper).

★ 14664 ★
Samson Belair Deloitte & Touche - Library (Bus-Fin)
One Place Ville Marie
Royal Bank Bldg.   Phone: (514)393-5066
Montreal, PQ, Canada H3B 4T9   Nancy Bouchard, Libn.
Founded: 1961. **Staff:** Prof 1; Other 1. **Subjects:** Accounting, auditing. **Holdings:** 50,000 books. **Subscriptions:** 210 journals and other serials; 11 newspapers. **Services:** Interlibrary loan; copying; library open to the public by appointment. **Computerized Information Services:** DIALOG Information Services, Info Globe, Infomart Online, The Financial Post DataGroup, Canadian Tax Online; internal database. **Special Catalogs:** Classification of business literature. **Remarks:** FAX: (514)876-4570. Telex: 05 267693 ROSSPART.

Bernard Samuels Library
See: **New York Eye and Ear Infirmary** (11576)

San Angelo Standard-Times
See: **Harte-Hanks Communications, Inc.** (6932)

★ 14665 ★
San Antonio College - Learning Resources Center - Special Collections (Hist)
1001 Howard St.   Phone: (512)733-2480
San Antonio, TX 78212   Oscar F. Metzger, Dir., Lrng.Rsrcs.
Founded: 1925. **Staff:** 46. **Subjects:** Texana. **Special Collections:** Morrison Collection of 18th century British imprints (6100 volumes); McAllister Collection of Texas and Western America (7250 volumes). **Services:** Interlibrary loan; copying; collections open to the public for reference use only. **Automated Operations:** Computerized cataloging, acquisitions, and circulation. **Computerized Information Services:** DIALOG Information Services, BRS Information Technologies, OCLC, WILSONLINE; Computer Augmented Resources System (internal database). **Networks/Consortia:** Member of AMIGOS Bibliographic Council, Inc., Council of Research & Academic Libraries (CORAL), Health Oriented Libraries of San Antonio (HOLSA). **Remarks:** FAX: (512)733-2597.

★ 14666 ★
San Antonio Community Hospital - Weber Memorial Library (Med)
999 San Bernardino Rd.   Phone: (714)920-4972
Upland, CA 91786   Francena Johnston, Med.Libn.
Founded: 1956. **Staff:** Prof 1; Other 1. **Subjects:** Medicine, health services management, allied health sciences. **Holdings:** 4800 books; 3225 bound periodical volumes; 1850 other cataloged items; 1031 audio cassettes; 720 Audio-Digest tapes; 510 videotapes; 100 filmstrip/cassette sets; 15 films. **Subscriptions:** 810 journals and other serials; 17 newspapers. **Services:** Interlibrary loan; library not open to the public. **Automated Operations:** Computerized cataloging, acquisitions, and serials. **Computerized Information Services:** DIALOG Information Services, MEDLINE; internal databases; DOCLINE (electronic mail service). Performs searches on fee basis. **Networks/Consortia:** Member of Inland Empire Medical Library Cooperative (IEMLC). **Remarks:** FAX: (714)931-0102.

★ 14667 ★
San Antonio Conservation Society - Foundation Library & Archives (Hist)
107 King William St.   Phone: (512)224-6163
San Antonio, TX 78204   Marianna C. Jones, Libn.
Founded: 1971. **Staff:** Prof 4. **Subjects:** History of San Antonio; historic preservation; architectural history. **Special Collections:** Ernst Raba Photograph Collection (250 glass negatives); Texas Heritage Resource Center (300 publications); Dorothy Matthis Postcard Collection (early San Antonio, Galveston, Houston; 767 items); John M. Sr. & Eleanor Freeborn Bennett Collection (Texana); Historic American Buildings Survey: Texas (microfiche). **Holdings:** Books; archives; documents; maps; photographs; blueprints; slides; AV programs; clippings. **Subscriptions:** 20 journals and other serials. **Services:** Interlibrary loan; copying; library open to the public on a limited schedule. **Staff:** Eva Milstead, Libn.; Barbara Santella, Libn.; Dolly Ports, Libn.; Frances George, Libn.

★ 14668 ★
San Antonio Light - Library (Publ)
420 Broadway
Box 161   Phone: (512)271-2775
San Antonio, TX 78291   Jeanette Curby, Hd.Libn.
Subjects: Newspaper reference topics. **Holdings:** Figures not available. **Services:** Newspaper research by mail for a fee. **Computerized Information Services:** DataTimes; Stauffer Gold (internal database). **Remarks:** FAX: (512)271-2770.

San Antonio Museum of Art
See: **San Antonio Museum Association** (14669)

★ 14669 ★
San Antonio Museum Association - Ellen Schulz Quillin Memorial Library (Art)
Box 2601   Phone: (512)820-2131
San Antonio, TX 78299-2601   George Anne Cormier, Libn.
Founded: 1926. **Staff:** Prof 1; **Subjects:** Texana; art - American, Indian, folk, decorative; natural history; history; antiquities; oriental anthropology. **Holdings:** 14,000 books; 4000 bound periodical volumes; 20 drawers of documents, maps, pictures; 12 VF drawers; 25 boxes of archival materials; 17,000 slides. **Subscriptions:** 78 journals and other serials. **Services:** Interlibrary loan; copying; library open to the public for reference use only by appointment. **Remarks:** FAX: (512)820-2109. The association maintains libraries for the Witte Memorial Museum and the San Antonio Museum of Art, located at 3801 Broadway, San Antonio, TX 78209.

★ 14670 ★
San Antonio Public Library and Information Center - Art, Music and Films Department (Art, Mus, Rec)
203 S. St. Mary's St.   Phone: (512)299-7795
San Antonio, TX 78205   Mary A. Wright, Hd.
Founded: 1959. Staff: Prof 3; Other 9. Subjects: Art history and criticism; painting, sculpture, and crafts; architecture - history, criticism, design; interior decoration; antiques; glass; graphics; photography; music; theater; performing arts; sports; stamp and coin collecting. Special Collections: Theater archives (3000 items); art gallery. Holdings: 105,306 books; picture file; local artists' biographical file; 4100 phonograph records; 5350 scores; 500 libretti; 12,000 videocassettes; 500 audio cassettes; 7000 compact discs; 5000 books on tape; 10,569 newspapers on microfilm. Subscriptions: 170 journals and other serials. Services: Interlibrary loan; copying; department open to the public. Publications: News releases on art gallery exhibits and special display case gallery. Remarks: FAX: (512)271-9497. Staff: Raymond Villarreall, Libn.

★ 14671 ★
San Antonio Public Library and Information Center - Business, Science and Technology Department (Bus-Fin, Sci-Engr)
203 S. St. Mary's St.   Phone: (512)299-7800
San Antonio, TX 78205   James Sosa, Hd.
Founded: 1959. Staff: Prof 6; Other 2. Subjects: Business, science, technology, economics, statistics, population demographics, useful arts, commerce, business and realty law. Special Collections: Trade directories; corporate annual reports; Texas business. Holdings: 23,399 bound periodical volumes; 17,598 hardbound U.S. Government documents; 90 VF drawers of pamphlets, clippings, and reports; 487,653 government pamphlets; 25,179 AEC reports; 65,700 AEC microcards; 303,822 U.S. Government documents on microfiche; 30,000 Texas State documents; Small Business/Entrepreneur Collection. Subscriptions: 630 journals and other serials. Services: Interlibrary loan; copying; department open to the public. Computerized Information Services: UNPLEX (electronic mail service). Remarks: FAX: (512)271-9497. Electronic mail address(es): U300sp01766 (UNIPLEX). Staff: Sam Plemmons, Libn.; Twyla Henson, Libn.; Dorothy Blow, Libn.; Sally Bauer, Libn.; Charles Gillis, Libn.

★ 14672 ★
San Antonio Public Library and Information Center - Hertzberg Circus Collection and Museum (Hist)
210 Market St.
San Antonio, TX 78205   Phone: (512)299-7810
Founded: 1942. Staff: Prof 1; Other 3. Subjects: Circus and circus history. Special Collections: Jenny Lind; P.T. Barnum; Charles S. Stratton (Tom Thumb); rare books. Holdings: 1200 volumes; 1500 lithographs; 200 circus route books; 40 19th century clown songsters; photographs; circus necrological file; archives; memorabilia; letters; documents. Subscriptions: 11 journals and other serials. Services: Copying; research collection open by appointment to historians, graduate students, publishers, and authors. Publications: A Guide to the Hertzberg Circus Collection, for sale. Remarks: FAX: (512)271-9497. Staff: Jill Blake, Archv./Presrv.Libn.

★ 14673 ★
San Antonio Public Library and Information Center - History, Social Science & General Reference Department (Soc Sci, Hist)
203 S. St. Mary's St.   Phone: (512)299-7813
San Antonio, TX 78205   Josephine Myler
Founded: 1959. Staff: Prof 4; Other 4. Subjects: History, travel, biography, social science, Texana, genealogy, education, general reference. Special Collections: Texana Collection; genealogy. Holdings: 107,680 books; 4327 bound periodical volumes; 16,850 reels of microfilm; 27,558 microfiche; 2397 ultrafiche; San Antonio and Texas vertical file. Subscriptions: 586 journals and other serials. Services: Interlibrary loan. Special Indexes: Index to San Antonio and Texas vertical file. Remarks: FAX: (512)271-9497. Staff: Frank Faulkner, Libn.; W. Conley Johnson, Libn.; James Stewart, Libn.

★ 14674 ★
San Antonio Public Library and Information Center - Literature, Philosophy and Religion Department (Hum)
203 S. St. Mary's St.   Phone: (512)299-7817
San Antonio, TX 78205   Wendy Friedman
Founded: 1959. Staff: Prof 4; Other 6. Subjects: Library science, psychology, languages, literature, philosophy, religion. Special Collections: Reading

Development Collection; Spanish Collection. Holdings: 77,138 books; 5489 bound periodical volumes; 4000 reels of microfilm; 1000 ultrafiche; 4000 large print books. Subscriptions: 226 journals and other serials; 40 newspapers. Services: Interlibrary loan; department open to the public. Computerized Information Services: WILSONDISC; internal database. Remarks: FAX: (512)271-9497. Staff: Guadalupe Negrete, Libn.; Thomas W. Massey, Libn.; L.H. Blocker, Libn.

★ 14675 ★
San Antonio State Chest Hospital - Health Science Library (Med)
Highland Hills Sta., Box 23340   Phone: (512)534-8857
San Antonio, TX 78223   Patricia Beaman, Libn.
Staff: Prof 1. Subjects: Medicine, chest diseases, nursing. Holdings: 1800 books; 1680 bound periodical volumes; 415 AV programs. Subscriptions: 120 journals and other serials. Services: Interlibrary loan; copying; library open to the public for reference use only. Automated Operations: Computerized serials. Computerized Information Services: MEDLINE. Networks/Consortia: Member of Health Oriented Libraries of San Antonio (HOLSA). Publications: Newsletter (includes recent acquisitions), bimonthly. Remarks: FAX: (512)534-8857.

★ 14676 ★
San Antonio State Hospital - Staff Library (Med)
Box 23991, Highland Hills Sta.   Phone: (512)532-8811
San Antonio, TX 78223-0991   Alma D. Guevara, Lib.Asst.
Staff: 1. Subjects: Medical sciences, psychology, psychiatric medicine, theology, mental health, mental hospitals. Holdings: 4000 books and bound periodical volumes; 12 VF drawers of reports, pamphlets, and documents; cassette tapes. Subscriptions: 130 journals and other serials. Services: Interlibrary loan; copying; library open to the public; outside users may check out materials only through ILL. Networks/Consortia: Member of Health Oriented Libraries of San Antonio (HOLSA), National Network of Libraries of Medicine - South Central Region, South Central Academic Medical Libraries Consortium (SCAMEL). Remarks: Maintained by Texas State Department of Mental Health & Mental Retardation.

★ 14677 ★
San Antonio Symphony Orchestra - Symphony Library (Mus)
109 Lexington Ave., Suite 207   Phone: (512)554-1050
San Antonio, TX 78205   Gregory Vaught, Libn.
Founded: 1939. Staff: Prof 2. Subjects: Orchestral and choral music, opera. Holdings: 1800 orchestrations with operas, full scores, and miniature scores. Services: Library open to the public for reference use only. Computerized Information Services: OLIS (internal database). Publications: Report of all performances and timings by the San Antonio Symphony, annual. Remarks: FAX: (512)554-1008. Staff: Dianne Byberg, Asst.Libn.

★ 14678 ★
San Bernardino Community Hospital - Medical Library (Med)
1805 Medical Center Dr.   Phone: (714)887-6333
San Bernardino, CA 92411   V. Neil Goodwin
Staff: Prof 1. Subjects: Medicine. Holdings: 1500 books; 5000 bound periodical volumes. Subscriptions: 126 journals and other serials. Services: Interlibrary loan; library not open to the public. Automated Operations: Computerized ILL (DOCLINE). Computerized Information Services: MEDLINE. Networks/Consortia: Member of Inland Empire Medical Library Cooperative (IEMLC). Publications: Library Notes, bimonthly.

★ 14679 ★
San Bernardino County Archives (Hist)
777 E. Rialto Ave.   Phone: (714)387-2030
San Bernardino, CA 92415-0795   James D. Hofer, Archv.
Founded: 1979. Staff: Prof 2. Subjects: County government records. Special Collections: Sullivan Collection (emphasis on San Bernardino history, 1923-1974, and southern California highway system; 25 volumes); W. Jacob Schaefer Collection (Chino, California agricultural history, 1898-1959; journals and ledgers); transcripts of Mormon diaries, journals, and life sketches (microfilm); official records for San Bernardino County, 1854-1920 (includes Board of Supervisors minutes); property and vital records; Superior Court case files. Holdings: 12,000 books; county maps; early newspapers; government documents; resident journals; scrapbooks. Services: Copying; archives open to the public by appointment.

★ 14680 ★

San Bernardino County Law Library (Law)
401 N. Arrowhead Ave.   Phone: (714)885-3020
San Bernardino, CA 92415-0015   Carolyn J. Poston, County Law Libn.
Founded: 1891. **Staff:** Prof 2; Other 9. **Subjects:** Law. **Holdings:** 71,507 books. **Subscriptions:** 392 journals and other serials; 5 newspapers. **Services:** Interlibrary loan; copying; library open to the public for reference use only. **Automated Operations:** Computerized cataloging. **Computerized Information Services:** WESTLAW, OCLC. Performs searches on fee basis. **Networks/Consortia:** Member of San Bernardino, Inyo, Riverside Counties United Library Services (SIRCULS). **Remarks:** FAX: (714)885-1869. **Formerly:** Don A. Turner County Law Library.

★ 14681 ★

San Bernardino County Law Library - West End Branch (Law)
8303 N. Haven Ave.   Phone: (714)944-5106
Rancho Cucamonga, CA 91730-   Carolyn J. Poston, County Law
3848   Libn.
Founded: 1891. **Staff:** Prof 1; Other 1. **Subjects:** Law. **Special Collections:** California Continuing Education of the Bar Collection (117 hardbound volumes). **Holdings:** 11,296 books; 491 bound periodical volumes; 397 volumes on ultrafiche; 485 titles of program materials; 725 cassette tapes. **Subscriptions:** 30 journals and other serials. **Services:** Interlibrary loan; copying; library open to the public for reference use only. **Automated Operations:** Computerized cataloging. **Computerized Information Services:** WESTLAW, OCLC, LIBS 100 System. Performs searches on fee basis. **Remarks:** FAX: (714)989-0118. **Formerly:** Don A. Turner County Law Library, West End.

★ 14682 ★

San Bernardino County Medical Center - Medical Library (Med)
780 E. Gilbert St.   Phone: (714)387-7996
San Bernardino, CA 92415-0935   Marlene E. Nourok, Med.Libn.
Staff: Prof 1; Other .5. **Subjects:** Medicine. **Holdings:** 2000 volumes; 1020 Audio-Digest tapes; 4 VF drawers of pamphlets. **Subscriptions:** 212 journals and other serials. **Services:** Interlibrary loan; copying; library open to the public for reference use only. **Automated Operations:** Computerized cataloging. **Computerized Information Services:** MEDLINE, DIALOG Information Services. **Networks/Consortia:** Member of National Network of Libraries of Medicine - Pacific Southwest Region, Inland Empire Medical Library Cooperative (IEMLC), San Bernardino, Inyo, Riverside Counties United Library Services (SIRCULS).

★ 14683 ★

San Bernardino County Museum - Wilson C. Hanna Library/Research Library (Hist, Biol Sci)
2024 Orange Tree Ln.   Phone: (714)798-8570
Redlands, CA 92373   Dr. Allan D. Griesemer, Dir.
Founded: 1963. **Subjects:** Local history, anthropology, archeology, natural history. **Special Collections:** Ornithology. **Holdings:** 6000 books; 2000 bound periodical volumes. **Subscriptions:** 20 journals and other serials. **Services:** Library open to the public by appointment. **Publications:** Technical Series; occasional papers.

★ 14684 ★

San Bernardino Sun - Editorial Library (Publ)
399 North D St.   Phone: (714)889-9666
San Bernardino, CA 92401   Anita Kaschube, Hd.Libn.
Founded: 1950. **Staff:** Prof 2; Other 1. **Subjects:** Newspaper reference topics. **Holdings:** 900 books; San Bernardino Sun, 1894 to present; 150 archival materials; 43 file cabinets; 1108 films; clippings; microfilm; photographs. **Subscriptions:** 20 journals and other serials. **Services:** Library not open to the public. **Remarks:** FAX: (714)885-8741. **Staff:** Peggy Hardy, Asst.Libn.

★ 14685 ★

San Clemente Presbyterian Church - Library (Rel-Phil)
119 Estrella Ave.   Phone: (714)492-4068
San Clemente, CA 92672   Margaret Helm, Libn.
Staff: 3. **Subjects:** Religion, christian living, Presbyterian Church, church policy. **Holdings:** 1200 books; 100 cassettes. **Services:** Library open to the public.

★ 14686 ★

San Diego Aero-Space Museum - N. Paul Whittier Historical Aviation Library (Mil, Hist)
2001 Pan America Plaza, Balboa Park   Phone: (619)234-1531
San Diego, CA 92101   Ray Wagner, Archv.
Founded: 1980. **Staff:** Prof 4; Other 2. **Subjects:** History of World Wars I and II including military aircraft, civil aircraft, personnel, early aircraft history, Lighter than Air aircraft, rotary wing, gliding, engines. **Special Collections:** L.N. Forden Collection; L.R. Hackney Collection (Air Cargo Library); T.P. Hall; W.F. Schult; E. Cooper Air Mail Pioneers; Wally Wiberg; Lou E. Gordon; Willard F. Schmitt Air Mail History; Early Birds of Aviation; U.S. Navy Helicopter Association; George E.A. Hallett; Warren S. Eaton; Frank T. Courtney; Errold G. Bahl; T.C. MacAulay; Hugh M. Rockwell; John Sloan; Admiral Mitscher; American Aviators in China; The C. Ryan Library. **Holdings:** 17,000 books; 3000 bound and unbound periodicals; 850,000 microfiche; 1200 airline insignia; 3400 aircraft drawings; 2500 aircraft and engine manuals; 45 VF drawers of photographs; 3000 negatives; 4000 slides; 150 scrapbooks; 300 aircraft brochures. **Subscriptions:** 16 journals and other serials. **Services:** Interlibrary loan; copying; library open to the public by appointment. **Remarks:** FAX: (619)233-4526. **Staff:** Marion L. Buckner, Libn.; Mary Scott, Res.Assoc.; Ron Bulinski, Asst.Archv.

★ 14687 ★

San Diego County Department of Planning and Land Use - Library (Plan)
5201 Ruffin Rd., Suite B-2   Phone: (619)694-3095
San Diego, CA 92123   Sonya M. Heiserman, Libn.
Staff: Prof 1; Other 1. **Subjects:** Urban planning, zoning, hydrology. **Holdings:** 2000 books; 1500 other cataloged items. **Subscriptions:** 50 journals and other serials; 10 newspapers. **Services:** Interlibrary loan; library open to the public for reference use only. **Automated Operations:** Computerized public access catalog. **Computerized Information Services:** DIALOG Information Services, LOGIN.

★ 14688 ★

San Diego County Law Library (Law)
1105 Front St.   Phone: (619)531-3900
San Diego, CA 92101-3999   Charles R. Dyer, Dir.
Founded: 1891. **Staff:** Prof 15; Other 16. **Subjects:** Law. **Special Collections:** California Appellate Court Briefs, 1950 to present; legal history of San Diego County. **Holdings:** 229,139 books and bound periodical volumes; 208 volumes of microcards; 36,760 volumes of microfiche; 1550 volumes of ultrafiche; 3021 audiocassettes; 1030 reels of microfilm; 135 videotapes. **Subscriptions:** 937 journals and other serials; 10 newspapers. **Services:** Interlibrary loan; copying; library open to the public; borrowing restricted to those with deposit accounts. **Automated Operations:** Computerized public access catalog, cataloging, acquisitions, serials, and circulation. **Computerized Information Services:** WESTLAW, LEXIS, OCLC, DIALOG Information Services, PFDS Online, Maxwell Macmillan Taxes Online, FYI News, Information America, WILSONLINE; SDCLL Laws (internal database). **Networks/Consortia:** Member of CLASS. **Publications:** Guide to San Diego County Law Library, irregular - to patrons and other interested persons; "Bits 'n' Writs" (newsletter); Time Table for California Courts. **Special Indexes:** Index of Current Mexican Legal Materials; Index of Opinions of Appellate Division, Superior Court, San Diego; Index to California League. **Remarks:** FAX: (619)238-7716. **Staff:** Florence Ewing, Ref.Coord.; Thomas Johnsrud, Hd.Ref.Libn; Colleen Buskirk, Acq.Libn.; Elaine Peabody, Hd.Ref.Libn.; Mewail Mebrahtu, Ref.Libn.; Saw Ch'ng, Ref.Libn.; Michael Kaye, Ref.Libn.; Martha Childers, Cat.Libn.; Ed White, Rsrcs. & Sys.; Marie Waltz, Access Serv.

★ 14689 ★

San Diego County Law Library - East County Branch (Law)
250 E. Main   Phone: (619)441-4451
El Cajon, CA 92020-3941   Charles R. Dyer, Dir.
Founded: 1983. **Staff:** Prof 2. **Subjects:** Law. **Holdings:** 9066 books and bound periodical volumes; 38 audiocassettes; 251 volumes of microfiche; 1550 volumes of ultrafiche. **Subscriptions:** 48 journals and other serials. **Services:** Copying; library open to the public for reference use only. **Automated Operations:** Computerized cataloging, acquisitions, serials, and circulation. **Computerized Information Services:** SDCLL Laws (internal database). **Remarks:** FAX: (619)441-0235. **Staff:** Carolyn Dulude, Br.Libn.

★14690★
San Diego County Law Library - North County Branch (Law)
325 S. Melrose, Suite 140   Phone: (619)940-4386
Vista, CA 92083-6627   Charles R. Dyer, Dir.
Founded: 1973. **Staff:** 2. **Subjects:** Law. **Holdings:** 17,040 books and bound periodical volumes; 76 audiocassettes; 247 volumes of microfiche. **Subscriptions:** 45 journals and other serials. **Services:** Copying; library open to the public for reference use only. **Automated Operations:** Computerized cataloging, acquisitions, serials, and circulation. **Computerized Information Services:** SDCLL Laws (internal database). **Remarks:** FAX: (619)724-7694. **Staff:** Eleanor Slade, Br.Libn.

★14691★
San Diego County Law Library - South Bay Branch (Law)
500 3rd Ave.   Phone: (619)691-4929
Chula Vista, CA 92010-5617   Charles R. Dyer, Dir.
Founded: 1982. **Staff:** 2. **Subjects:** Law. **Holdings:** 14,793 books; 38 audiocassettes; 307 volumes of microfiche. **Subscriptions:** 45 journals and other serials. **Services:** Copying; library open to the public for reference use only. **Automated Operations:** Computerized cataloging, acquisitions, serials, and circulation. **Computerized Information Services:** SDCLL Laws (internal database). **Remarks:** FAX: (619)427-7521. **Staff:** Edna Thiel, Br.Libn.

★14692★
San Diego County Library - Governmental Reference Library (Soc Sci, Bus-Fin)
602 County Administration Center
1600 Pacific Hwy.   Phone: (619)531-5787
San Diego, CA 92101   Ann Terrell, Govt.Ref.Libn.
Founded: 1946. **Staff:** Prof 1; Other 4. **Subjects:** Local government, public administration, public finance, health and welfare, public works, transportation, parks and recreation, criminal justice, personnel management. **Special Collections:** City and county documents (15,000); local surveys and studies by consultants. **Holdings:** 11,000 books; 8527 bound periodical volumes; 28,000 pamphlets, surveys, reports. **Subscriptions:** 110 journals and other serials; 7 newspapers. **Services:** Interlibrary loan; copying; library open to the public for reference use only. **Automated Operations:** Computerized cataloging, acquisitions, and ILL. **Computerized Information Services:** DIALOG Information Services, DataTimes, OCLC, LOGIN, WILSONLINE, Legi-Tech, EPIC, University of California MELVYL. **Networks/Consortia:** Member of Serra Cooperative Network. **Remarks:** FAX: (619)557-4009. **Staff:** Carol Stein, Br.Mgr.

★14693★
San Diego County Office of Education - Research and Reference Center (Educ)
6401 Linda Vista Rd.   Phone: (619)292-3556
San Diego, CA 92111   P. Marvin Barbula, Dir.
Staff: Prof 1; Other 2. **Subjects:** Education and related subjects. **Special Collections:** Software Examination Center; grant research materials. **Holdings:** 20,000 books and bound periodical volumes; 320,000 ERIC microfiche; 25,000 pamphlets, courses of study; state adopted textbooks for grades K-8; secondary textbook collection; instructional materials. **Subscriptions:** 230 journals and other serials. **Services:** Center open to public school personnel within San Diego County. **Computerized Information Services:** DIALOG Information Services. **Publications:** Curriculum Currents. **Remarks:** Alternate telephone number(s): 292-3669. FAX: (619)569-7851. **Staff:** Dorothy Smith Collins, Media Serv.Mgr.

★14694★
San Diego Daily Transcript - Library (Publ)
2131 3rd Ave.
P.O. Box 85469   Phone: (619)232-4381
San Diego, CA 92101   John F. Thomas
Founded: 1973. **Staff:** Prof 1. **Subjects:** Newspaper reference topics. **Holdings:** Clipping files (San Diego Daily Transcript, San Diego Union/Tribune, Los Angeles Times, Wall Street Journal, and San Diego Business Journal); 125 books; 106 bound periodical volumes. **Subscriptions:** 6 newspapers. **Services:** Library open to staff and suscribers only. **Remarks:** FAX: (619)236-8126.

★14695★
San Diego Historical Society - Research Archives (Hist)
Box 81825   Phone: (619)232-6203
San Diego, CA 92138   Richard W. Crawford, Archv.
Founded: 1929. **Staff:** Prof 2. **Subjects:** History - San Diego County, California, Baja California. **Special Collections:** San Diego Biography (374 notebooks); oral history (550 transcripts); Kerr Collection (California ranchos; 19 notebooks). **Holdings:** 9500 volumes; 4500 bound periodical volumes; 500 photostats of documents in the Archivo General, Cuidad de Mejico Collection, 1769-1840; 1500 feet of local public records; business ledgers and reports; census reports; maps; architectural records; newspapers on microfilm. **Subscriptions:** 21 journals and other serials. **Services:** Copying; archives open to the public with restrictions. **Special Catalogs:** Guide to the Public Records Collection. **Remarks:** FAX: (619)232-6297. Library located at Balboa Park, Casa de Balboa, 1649 El Prado, San Diego, CA 92101.

★14696★
San Diego Historical Society - Research Archives - Photograph Collection (Aud-Vis)
Box 81825   Phone: (619)232-6203
San Diego, CA 92138   Larry Booth, Cur. of Photo.
Founded: 1947. **Staff:** 54. **Subjects:** San Diego city and county, 1867-1986; Baja California and Southwestern Native American photographs. **Holdings:** 1.5 million large format professional glass plate and film negatives, vintage prints, and reference prints; slides; films. **Services:** Collection open to the public on a limited schedule; photographs available for research, display, publication, and advertising on fee basis. **Remarks:** Collection is located at Casa de Balboa, 1649 El Prado, Balboa Park, San Diego, CA 92101. Alternate telephone number(s): 297-3258.

★14697★
San Diego Maritime Museum - Jerry MacMullen Library (Hist)
1492 N. Harbor Dr.   Phone: (619)234-9153
San Diego, CA 92101   Craig Arnold, Libn.
Founded: 1977. **Staff:** 1. **Subjects:** Maritime history, especially pertaining to U.S. West Coast. **Special Collections:** Kingsbury Collection (passenger liner memorabilia, 1910-1970); MacMullen Collection (San Diego and West Coast maritime memorabilia); Brown Collection (steamboat items). **Holdings:** 9000 books; 500 bound periodical volumes; 1000 documents; 200 manuscripts; logbooks (on microfiche). **Subscriptions:** 142 journals and other serials; 25 newspapers. **Services:** Copying; library open to the public. **Computerized Information Services:** Internal database. **Publications:** Mains'l Haul, quarterly. **Remarks:** Library located on board the Berkeley, a ferryboat built in 1898.

★14698★
San Diego Model Railroad Museum - Research Library (Rec)
1649 El Prado   Phone: (619)696-0199
San Diego, CA 92101   John Rotsart, Cur.
Founded: 1983. **Staff:** 1. **Subjects:** Railroads, model railroads, railroad equipment. **Holdings:** 110 books; 213 bound periodical volumes; 800 slides; 10 videocassettes. **Services:** Library not open to the public until late 1991.

★14699★
San Diego Museum of Art - Library (Art)
Balboa Park
Box 2107   Phone: (619)232-7931
San Diego, CA 92112   Claire Eike, Libn.
Founded: 1926. **Staff:** Prof 1; Other 1. **Subjects:** Art (especially Spanish and Italian Renaissance to Baroque) American art, Asian art. **Holdings:** 20,000 books; 1100 bound periodical volumes; 3000 auction catalogs; 125 linear feet of vertical files; 15,000 slides. **Subscriptions:** 62 journals and other serials. **Services:** Copying; library open to the public by appointment. **Computerized Information Services:** OCLC, RLIN, DIALOG Information Services, ArtQuest, Gordon's Print Price Annual. **Special Catalogs:** Bibliographical card file to artists in art exhibition catalogs. **Remarks:** FAX: (619)232-9367.

★14700★
San Diego Museum of Contemporary Art - Helen Palmer Geisel Library (Art)
700 Prospect St.   Phone: (619)454-3541
La Jolla, CA 92037   Erika Torri, Libn.
Subjects: Contemporary art. **Holdings:** 4000 books; 251 bound periodical volumes; 106 file boxes of monographs on artists; 11 VF drawers of clippings; 6000 slides; 2000 file folders on contemporary artists; 400 exhibition catalogs. **Subscriptions:** 50 journals and other serials. **Services:** Copying; library open to the public by appointment.

★ 14701 ★
San Diego Museum of Man - Scientific Library (Hist)
Balboa Park
1350 El Prado   Phone: (619)239-2001
San Diego, CA 92101   Jane Bentley, Libn.
Founded: 1916. **Staff:** Prof 1. **Subjects:** Anthropology, pre-Columbian art, Indians of the Americas, archeology, ethnology, physical anthropology. **Special Collections:** North American Indians. **Holdings:** 6500 books; 5500 bound periodical volumes; 51 archival manuscripts. **Subscriptions:** 325 journals and other serials. **Services:** Interlibrary loan; copying (both limited); library open to the public by appointment. **Publications:** Ethnic Technology Notes, irregular; San Diego Museum Papers, irregular - both for sale or exchange. **Remarks:** FAX: (619)239-2749.

San Diego Natural History Museum Library
See: San Diego Society of Natural History (14712)

★ 14702 ★
San Diego Public Library - Art, Music & Recreation Section (Art, Mus, Rec)
820 E St.   Phone: (619)236-5810
San Diego, CA 92101   Kathleen M. Griffin, Supv.
Staff: Prof 4; Other 2. **Subjects:** Art and music history, architecture, sculpture, antiques, interior decoration, crafts, music theory and techniques, painting, drawing, printmaking, photography, sports, games, theater, cinema, dance. **Special Collections:** Language instruction recordings; pop songs, 1900-1970. **Holdings:** 92,370 books; 515,000 pictures; 25,000 picture postcards; 10,000 choral music pieces; 14,500 phonograph records; 14,000 scores; 1770 audio cassettes; libretti, miniature scores; 900 compact discs; 850 videocassettes; 125 videodiscs. **Subscriptions:** 339 journals and other serials. **Services:** Chamber music series. **Automated Operations:** Computerized cataloging and circulation. **Computerized Information Services:** DIALOG Information Services; InfoTrac. Performs searches free of charge. **Networks/Consortia:** Member of Serra Cooperative Network, CLASS. **Special Catalogs:** Phono-Record Catalog. **Special Indexes:** Song Title Index; Choral Music Index; Film Review File. **Remarks:** FAX: (619)236-5811. **Staff:** Eugene Fischer, Libn.; Christina Clifford, Libn.; Jacqueline Adams, Libn.

★ 14703 ★
San Diego Public Library - Children's Literature Special Collection (Hum)
820 E St.   Phone: (619)236-5838
San Diego, CA 92101-6478   William W. Sannwald, City Libn.
Founded: 1882. **Staff:** Prof 2.5; Other 1.5. **Subjects:** Children's literature - fairy tales, science, countries, social sciences, environment, classic fiction. **Special Collections:** Caldecott Collection (52 books); Newbery Collection (69 books); Dr. Seuss, His Works and Biographical Information Collection (67 books); Mother Goose Through the Ages (85 books); Oz Collection (50 books); Local History Children's Collection (170 books). **Holdings:** 34,000 books; 20 bound periodical volumes; 2000 archival items. **Subscriptions:** 48 journals and other serials. **Services:** Interlibrary loan; collection open to the public for reference use only. **Computerized Information Services:** DIALOG Information Services, DataTimes; AGILE (internal database). Contact Person: Joanne Anderson, Supv.Libn. **Publications:** Bibliograhies. **Remarks:** FAX: (619)231-0985. **Staff:** Jean Stewart, Children's Rm.Libn.; Kathy Askin, Children's Rm.Libn.

★ 14704 ★
San Diego Public Library - History & World Affairs Section (Hist)
820 E St.   Phone: (619)236-5820
San Diego, CA 92101   Carolyn Demaray, Supv.
Staff: Prof 4; Other 3. **Subjects:** World history, travel, biography, archeology, atlases and maps. **Special Collections:** World Wars I and II personal narratives. **Holdings:** 95,040 books; 1400 maps; 24 VF drawers of pamphlets and clippings; Facts on File, 1944 to present; Editorials on File. **Subscriptions:** 260 journals and other serials. **Services:** Interlibrary loan; copying; section open to the public. **Automated Operations:** Computerized cataloging and circulation. **Computerized Information Services:** DIALOG Information Services; InfoTrac; CD-ROM (WILSONDISC). Performs searches free of charge. **Networks/Consortia:** Member of Serra Cooperative Network, CLASS. **Remarks:** FAX: (619)236-5811. **Staff:** Kathleen Burns, Libn.; Catherine van Sonnenberg, Libn.

★ 14705 ★
San Diego Public Library - Information Service Section (Info Sci)
820 E St.   Phone: (619)236-5800
San Diego, CA 92101   Carolyn Demaray, Supv.
Staff: Prof 1; Other 6. **Holdings:** 1400 telephone directories; 74 reference titles. **Services:** Copying; section open to the public. **Automated Operations:** Computerized cataloging and circulation. **Computerized Information Services:** DIALOG Information Services. Performs searches free of charge. **Networks/Consortia:** Member of Serra Cooperative Network, CLASS. **Special Indexes:** Index to directories (card). **Remarks:** FAX: (619)236-5811.

★ 14706 ★
San Diego Public Library - Literature & Languages Section (Rel-Phil, Hum)
820 E St.   Phone: (619)236-5816
San Diego, CA 92101   Margaret M. Kazmer, Supv.
Staff: Prof 4; Other 2. **Subjects:** Literature, psychology, languages, philosophy, religion, information science. **Special Collections:** Occult sciences; Bacon-Shakespeare controversy; theosophy. **Holdings:** 162,750 books; 4 VF drawers of pamphlets; large print books; 12,500 foreign language books (especially Spanish). **Subscriptions:** 500 journals and other serials. **Services:** Home delivery for shut-ins; section open to the public. **Automated Operations:** Computerized cataloging and circulation. **Computerized Information Services:** DIALOG Information Services; InfoTrac. Performs searches free of charge. **Networks/Consortia:** Member of Serra Cooperative Network, CLASS. **Publications:** Booklists, irregular. **Special Catalogs:** Subject Guide to Fiction. **Remarks:** FAX: (619)236-5811. **Staff:** Linda Griffin, Libn.; Evelyn Kooperman, Libn.; Susanna Engelsman, Libn.

★ 14707 ★
San Diego Public Library - Science & Industry Section (Sci-Engr, Bus-Fin)
820 E St.   Phone: (619)236-5813
San Diego, CA 92101   Matt J. Katka, Supv.
Staff: Prof 3; Other 4. **Subjects:** Business, industry, science, cookery, automobile repair. **Special Collections:** Space and aeronautics historical collection; depository for U.S., California, and San Diego city and county government publications (over 1.4 million); American National Standards Institute (ANSI) and American Society for Testing and Materials (ASTM) standards on microfiche; U.S. Utility Patents, 1790-1871 and 1942 to present; U.S. Design Patents, 1951 to present. **Holdings:** 63,890 books; 25,500 maps; 323,000 microforms; Sams Photofacts (complete collection); Atomic Energy Commission (AEC) and NASA depository collections. **Subscriptions:** 526 journals and other serials. **Services:** Interlibrary loan; copying. **Automated Operations:** Computerized cataloging and circulation. **Computerized Information Services:** DIALOG Information Services, U.S. Patent Classification System; InfoTrac. Performs searches free of charge. **Networks/Consortia:** Member of Serra Cooperative Network, CLASS. **Special Indexes:** Subject index to government documents (card); California Mines Index (card). **Remarks:** FAX: (619)236-5811. **Staff:** Robert Taylor, Libn.; Thomas Karras, Libn.

★ 14708 ★
San Diego Public Library - Social Sciences Section (Soc Sci)
820 E St.   Phone: (619)236-5894
San Diego, CA 92101   Jean C. Hughes, Supv.
Staff: Prof 4; Other 4.5. **Subjects:** Sociology, education, political science, law, economics, finance, conservation, transportation, military service, folklore. **Special Collections:** General and specialized business directories; Business Reference Center. **Holdings:** 71,650 books; 5 VF drawers of corporation annual reports; 5 VF drawers of vocational pamphlets; 19 VF drawers of miscellaneous pamphlets; 5000 college catalogs on microfiche; corporation annual reports, 1978 to present, on microfiche; talking books and cassette tapes for the visually handicapped. **Subscriptions:** 520 journals and other serials. **Services:** Interlibrary loan; copying; section open to the public. **Automated Operations:** Computerized cataloging and circulation. **Computerized Information Services:** DIALOG Information Services, General BusinessFile; InfoTrac. Performs searches free of charge. **Networks/Consortia:** Member of Serra Cooperative Network, CLASS. **Publications:** Booklists, irregular. **Special Indexes:** Black American Firsts File (card); Women Firsts File (card). **Remarks:** FAX: (619)236-5811. **Staff:** Sharon Stevelman, Libn.; Frances Bookheim, Libn.

★ 14709 ★
San Diego Public Library - Special Collections - California Room (Hist)
820 E St.   Phone: (619)236-5834
San Diego, CA 92101   Mary Allely, Supv.
Staff: Prof 2. **Subjects:** History of California counties, especially San Diego and Imperial Counties; history and description of Baja California. **Special Collections:** Records of the Little Landers Colony, San Ysidro, California; Kelly Papers (records of a pioneer family); Hatfield (rainmaker) papers; San Diego Park Department records, including exposition material; official repository of San Diego 200th Anniversary Committee papers; San Diego Great Registers, 1866-1909; Horton House registers; local Sanborn Fire Insurance maps (film and atlases). **Holdings:** 12,930 books; 57 reels of microfilm; 300 maps; 60 VF drawers of pamphlets and clippings; 800,000 index cards covering San Diego Herald, 1851-1860, San Diego Union, 1868-1903 and 1930-1983, partially available on microfiche. **Subscriptions:** 280 journals and other serials; 7 newspapers. **Services:** Copying; room open to the public for reference use only. **Computerized Information Services:** DataTimes. **Remarks:** FAX: (619)236-5811. **Staff:** Eileen Boyle, Libn.

★ 14710 ★
San Diego Public Library - Special Collections - Genealogy Room (Hist)
820 E St.   Phone: (619)236-5834
San Diego, CA 92101-6478   Mary Allely, Supv.
Founded: 1940. **Subjects:** General genealogy. **Special Collections:** California census, 1850-1910, on microfilm; roster of California pioneers; state censuses; Boston Transcript: Obituary Scrapbooks and Index (emphasis on the 13 original colonies and the Eastern states). **Holdings:** 4000 books; 314 reels of microfilm. **Subscriptions:** 52 journals and other serials. **Services:** Copying; room open to the public for reference use only. **Remarks:** FAX: (619)236-5811.

★ 14711 ★
San Diego Public Library - Special Collections - Wangenheim Room (Rare Book)
820 E St.   Phone: (619)236-5807
San Diego, CA 92101   Eileen Boyle, Libn.
Founded: 1954. **Staff:** Prof 1. **Subjects:** History of printing and the development of the book with specimens ranging from cunieform tablets to cassettes; famous presses and modern private presses; incunabula; fine book bindings. **Special Collections:** Dime novels (769 items); bookplates (6000); fore-edge paintings (185 volumes); works of Kate Greenaway (65 volumes); works of John Ruskin (250 volumes); Curtis' North American Indians (20 volumes and 20 portfolios of photographs); Monumenta Scenica (12 portfolios); Grayson's Birds of the Pacific Slope (158 plates). **Holdings:** 9550 books; selected antiquarian book dealers' catalogs; periodicals; manuscripts; autographs; artifacts. **Services:** Room open to the public. **Special Catalogs:** Chronological card catalog arranged by date and place of publication.

★ 14712 ★
San Diego Society of Natural History - San Diego Natural History Museum Library (Biol Sci)
P.O. Box 1390   Phone: (619)232-3821
San Diego, CA 92112   Carol B. Barsi, Libn.
Founded: 1874. **Staff:** Prof 2. **Subjects:** Birds and mammals, botany, geology, paleontology, mineralogy, entomology, marine invertebrates, herpetology, biology. **Special Collections:** A.W. Vodges Library of Geology and Paleontology (20,000 volumes); L. Klauber Herpetological Library (1462 volumes; 19,000 pamphlets and reprints); photoarchives (1904-1940); Ray Gilmore Archives (marine mammals). **Holdings:** 90,000 volumes; maps; 58 boxes of microfiche; 3 boxes of microfilm; 12,000 photographs; Valentien wildflower originals. **Subscriptions:** 850 journals and other serials. **Services:** Interlibrary loan; copying; library open to the public by appointment for reference use only. **Computerized Information Services:** MELVYL (internal database). **Publications:** Proceedings and Occasional Papers of the San Diego Society of Natural History. **Remarks:** FAX: (619)232-0248. **Staff:** Ann C. Payne, Asst.Libn.

★ 14713 ★
San Diego Space & Science Foundation - Harding Library (Sci-Engr)
Box 33303   Phone: (619)238-1233
San Diego, CA 92163   Lynne Kennedy, Educ.Dir.
Founded: 1976. **Staff:** 1. **Subjects:** Astronomy, photography, scientific research. **Holdings:** 600 books; 50 bound periodical volumes. **Subscriptions:** 10 journals and other serials. **Services:** Library open to members only. **Publications:** Space Reflections, bimonthly - to members. **Remarks:** FAX: (619)231-8971.

★ 14714 ★
San Diego State University - Bureau of Business & Economic Research Library (Bus-Fin)
College of Business Administration
Love Library
5300 Campanile Dr.   Phone: (619)594-5301
San Diego, CA 92182-0511   Dr. Oliver Galbraith, Dir.
Founded: 1958. **Staff:** Prof 1; Other 2. **Subjects:** Accounting, auditing, business, business education, economics, finance, management, marketing, labor. **Special Collections:** Research studies of Bureau members; Arthur Young Tax Research Library; regional data on San Diego and southern California; national data by states. **Holdings:** Figures not available. **Subscriptions:** 27 serials. **Services:** Interlibrary loan; library open to the public. **Publications:** Monographs; Business Case Studies; Faculty Working Papers.

★ 14715 ★
San Diego State University - Center for Public Economics Library (Plan, Bus-Fin)
ACE 124-126   Phone: (619)594-6707
San Diego, CA 92182-0378   Dr. George Babilot, Dir.
Staff: Prof 9; Other 5. **Subjects:** Economics, health and welfare, land use and taxation, natural resources and environment, population and demography, poverty, public finance, urban regional studies. **Special Collections:** Fiscal studies from all 50 states; San Diego County documents. **Holdings:** 4000 books. **Subscriptions:** 80 journals and other serials. **Services:** Interlibrary loan; library open to the public. **Automated Operations:** Computerized cataloging. **Computerized Information Services:** DIALOG Information Services; Macroeconomic Data, San Diego Regional Economic (internal databases). **Publications:** Working papers in public economics. **Staff:** Joseph Drew, Cons.; Chris Marusin, Res.Coord.

★ 14716 ★
San Diego State University - European Studies Center - Library (Area-Ethnic)
San Diego, CA 92182-0511   Phone: (619)594-5200
                                           Dr. Leon Rosenstein, Dir.
Staff: Prof 12; Other 1. **Subjects:** European studies. **Holdings:** 1500 books; 200 bound periodical volumes; 18,000 slides; 1000 records and tapes. **Services:** Library not open to the public. **Remarks:** Alternate telephone number(s): (619)594-5186.

★ 14717 ★
San Diego State University - Government Publications Division (Info Sci)
San Diego, CA 92182-0511   Phone: (619)594-5832
                                           Carolyn D. Baber, Div.Hd.
Staff: Prof 4; Other 4. **Holdings:** 549,077 U.S., United Nations, and California documents; 1.5 million microforms. **Services:** Interlibrary loan; copying; division open to the public. **Computerized Information Services:** DIALOG Information Services, BRS Information Technologies, WILSONLINE. **Special Catalogs:** U.S., California, United Nations card catalogs. **Remarks:** FAX: (619)594-2700. **Staff:** Greta Marlatt, Ref.Libn.; Bruce Harley, Ref.Libn.

★ 14718 ★
San Diego State University - Malcolm A. Love Library - Special Collections (Hum, Sci-Engr)
San Diego, CA 92182-0511   Phone: (619)594-6791
                                           Martha E. McPhail, Spec.Coll.Libn.
Founded: 1897. **Staff:** 1.5. **Subjects:** History - astronomy, natural sciences, science fiction, music, English literature, women's studies. **Special Collections:** Ernst Zinner Collection of the History of Astronomy and Sciences (1500 volumes; 4200 uncataloged items); Lord Chesterfield Collection (150 volumes); Norland Collection on Entemology and the History of Biology (3500 volumes; 1000 other cataloged items); Davis Orchid Collection (2000 volumes); Chater Collection in Science Fiction; George Phillips Collection of Sweepiana; Archive of Popular American Music; H.L. Mencken Collection of Autographed First Editions; Wallace Pearce Collection on Printing, Binding and Book Collecting; Archives of San Diego State University; Henry James Collection of First Editions; Adams Postcard Collection (200,000 postcards); San Diego History Collection (3200 linear feet of archival papers). **Holdings:** 27,000 volumes; 3980 linear feet of archives and manuscripts. **Services:** Interlibrary loan; collections open to the public. **Automated Operations:** Computerized public access catalog. **Networks/Consortia:** Member of Serra Cooperative Network. **Publications:** Catalogue of the Rare Astronomical Books in the San Diego State University Library (1988). **Remarks:** FAX: (619)594-2700. **Staff:** Lyn Olsson, Arch.Asst.

★14719★
San Diego State University - Media Center (Educ, Aud-Vis)
University Library   Phone: (619)594-5691
San Diego, CA 92182-0511   Stephen D. Fitt, Ph.D., Hd., Spec.Rsrcs.Div.
Founded: 1951. **Staff:** 2. **Subjects:** Nonprint media for all educational levels. **Special Collections:** Public domain software collection. **Holdings:** 10 VF drawers of publishers' and AV producers' catalogs; 18,000 nonbook media. **Services:** Facilities for previewing and listening. **Automated Operations:** Computerized public access catalog. **Staff:** Janet Klein, Media Ctr.Supv.

★14720★
San Diego State University - Public Administration Center Library (Soc Sci)
PSFA 100   Phone: (619)594-5200
San Diego, CA 92182-0367   Elaine Wonsowicz, Mgr.
Founded: 1950. **Staff:** Prof 1; Other 3. **Subjects:** American and comparative public administration; urban affairs; public policy and planning; resource utilization; city planning; criminal justice. **Special Collections:** San Diego Region Collection. **Holdings:** 3000 books; 70,000 other cataloged items; depository of public institutional reports. **Subscriptions:** 300 journals and other serials. **Services:** Copying; library open to the public for reference use only. **Publications:** Selected monographs; reports.

★14721★
San Diego State University - Science Library (Energy)
San Diego, CA 92182-0511   Phone: (619)594-6715
                                   Robert Carande, Hd.
Staff: 5. **Subjects:** Energy systems and allied topics. **Holdings:** 250,000 volumes. **Services:** Library open to the public. **Automated Operations:** Computerized public access catalog. **Computerized Information Services:** DIALOG Information Services, BRS Information Technologies, STN International; Periodical Information Network (PIN) (internal database); InterNet (electronic mail service). **Staff:** Lillian Chan; Katalin Harkanyi; Mary Harris; Anne Turhollow.

★14722★
San Diego State University - University Library - Science Division (Sci-Engr, Biol Sci)
San Diego, CA 92182-0511   Phone: (619)594-6715
                                   Robert Carande
Founded: 1897. **Staff:** Prof 5; Other 3. **Subjects:** Biology, chemistry, mathematics, geology, physics, engineering, industrial arts, astronomy, military science, history of sciences, nursing, public health. **Special Collections:** Natural history and sciences collection (4500 volumes); Ernst Zinner Collection on the History of Astronomy and Science (1500 volumes; 4200 other cataloged items); W.M. Pearce Spider Collection (300 items). **Holdings:** 216,200 books; 137,700 bound periodical volumes; 12,040 hardcopy science reports; 158,900 microfiche of science reports; 1300 reels of microfilm and filmstrips; 277,000 microfiche; 46,668 microcards. **Subscriptions:** 3353 journals and other serials. **Services:** Interlibrary loan; copying; division open to the public with fee for borrowing. **Automated Operations:** Computerized public access catalog, cataloging, and serials. **Computerized Information Services:** DIALOG Information Services, PFDS Online, MEDLINE, STN International. **Publications:** Union List of Standards in the San Diego County Area; Literature of Time in the Ernst Zinner Collection, a checklist; Copernicus; Johann Kepler, a bibliography; Tycho Brahe, a bibliography; Geology of Baja California, a bibliography; Geology of Imperial County, a bibliography; Botany of San Diego County, guide to research materials; Guide to the Botanical Literature of Baja California in the Collections of the San Diego State University Library; Sunbeams and Solar Energy; Science and Engineering Resource Series; Guide to Special Information in Scientific and Engineering Journals. **Remarks:** FAX: (619)594-5642. **Staff:** Lillian Chan, Libn.; Katalin Harkanyi, Assoc.Sci.Libn.; Mary E. Harris, Assoc.Sci.Libn.; Anne Turhollow, Assoc.Sci.Libn.; Eric Lamb, Div.Supv.

★14723★
San Diego Unified School District - Instructional Media Center (Hum, Aud-Vis)
2441 Cardinal Ln.   Phone: (619)496-8122
San Diego, CA 92123   Larry Pierce, Coord., Educ.Services
Staff: Prof 3; Other 27. **Subjects:** Children's literature, science, social studies. **Holdings:** 1 million books; 100,000 AV items.

★14724★
San Diego Union-Tribune Publishing Company - Library (Publ)
350 Camino De La Reina
P.O. Box 191   Phone: (619)299-3131
San Diego, CA 92108   Sharon Stewart Reeves, Lib.Dir.
Staff: Prof 2; Other 15. **Subjects:** Newspaper reference topics. **Holdings:** 5000 books; 240 drawers of newspaper clippings; 4000 reels of microfilm. **Subscriptions:** 50 journals and other serials; 8 newspapers. **Services:** Library not open to the public. **Automated Operations:** Computerized cataloging. **Computerized Information Services:** DIALOG Information Services, NEXIS, VU/TEXT Information Services, DataTimes, Dow Jones News/Retrieval, Legi-Tech, DataQuick; internal databases. **Special Indexes:** Index of negatives of photographs taken by staff photographers (online); indexes to clip files and photograph files. **Staff:** Linda F. Ritter, Asst.Libn.

★14725★
San Francisco Academy of Comic Art - Library (Art, Hum)
2850 Ulloa   Phone: (415)681-1737
San Francisco, CA 94116   Bill Blackbeard, Dir.
Founded: 1968. **Staff:** 5. **Subjects:** Science fiction, crime fiction, popular literature, comic strip art in all aspects, dime novels, pulp and other popular magazines, motion picture data, critical literature. **Special Collections:** Dickensiana; Sherlockiana; Oz books; foreign popular literature; 19th century fiction and art; children's books; nationally representative bound newspaper runs, including many rare Hearst papers. **Holdings:** 59,000 books; one million comic strips; 25,000 unbound periodicals; manuscripts, original comic strips, and other graphic work; movie stills and pressbooks; newspaper and magazine ads and art; science fiction fanzines and fanzines of other areas of interest; segregated editorial pages, columns, film and auto sections, comic strips. **Subscriptions:** 100 journals and other serials; 100 newspapers. **Services:** Interlibrary loan; copying; library open to the public by appointment. **Staff:** William Loughman, Dir.; Chris Berglas, Dir.; William Murr, Dir.; Gale Paulson, Dir.; Barbara Tyger, Dir.

★14726★
San Francisco Art Institute - Anne Bremer Memorial Library (Art)
800 Chestnut St.   Phone: (415)749-4559
San Francisco, CA 94133   Jeff Gunderson, Lib.Dir.
Founded: 1871. **Staff:** Prof 3; Other 3. **Subjects:** Fine arts, photography, filmmaking, humanities, social sciences. **Special Collections:** Artists' book collection (300 volumes); manuscripts documenting Northern California Art, 1871 to present. **Holdings:** 25,000 books; 1300 bound periodical volumes; 60,000 slides; 300 films; 100 audiocassettes; prints; 6 VF drawers; 80 100mm films; 600 audiotapes; 150 videotapes. **Subscriptions:** 190 journals and other serials. **Services:** Copying; library open to the public with restrictions and by appointment only. **Staff:** Charles Stephanian, Media Dir.; Carolyn Franklin, Cat.; Claudia Marlowe, Circ.; Deborah White, Cat.Asst.; Trish Carney, Media Asst.

San Francisco Ballet Archives
See: San Francisco Performing Arts Library and Museum - Library (14737)

★14727★
San Francisco Chronicle - Library (Publ)
901 Mission St.   Phone: (415)777-1111
San Francisco, CA 94103   Richard Geiger, Lib.Dir.
Founded: 1879. **Staff:** Prof 18. **Subjects:** Newspaper reference topics. **Holdings:** 1500 books; 100 pamphlets; 7.5 million clippings; 3 million news photographs; San Francisco Chronicle Database, 1985 to present. **Subscriptions:** 50 journals and other serials; 15 newspapers. **Services:** Copying; library open to the public by telephone during limited hours. **Computerized Information Services:** DataTimes, NEXIS, DIALOG Information Services, VU/TEXT Information Services, Dow Jones News/Retrieval. **Staff:** June Dellapa, Asst.Hd.Libn.

★14728★
San Francisco City Attorney's Office - Library (Law)
206 City Hall   Phone: (415)554-4247
San Francisco, CA 94102   Marjorie O'Toole, Law Libn.
Staff: Prof 1; Other 3. **Subjects:** San Francisco municipal law and codes; city attorney opinions. **Holdings:** 25,000 volumes. **Subscriptions:** 75 journals and other serials. **Services:** Library not open to the public. **Remarks:** Maintains a branch library at 214 Van Ness Ave.

★14729★
San Francisco College of Mortuary Science - Library (Sci-Engr)
1363 Divisadero St.   Phone: (415)567-0674
San Francisco, CA 94115-3912   Jacquie Taylor, Pres.
Founded: 1930. **Staff:** 2. **Subjects:** Embalming, restorative art, anatomy, pathology, bacteriology, chemistry, funeral directing and management. **Special Collections:** Burial customs of foreign countries (16mm color films); death and dying (20 filmstrips). **Holdings:** 512 books and bound periodical volumes. **Subscriptions:** 12 journals and other serials. **Services:** Library open to the public with permission.

★14730★
San Francisco Conservatory of Music - Library (Mus)
1201 Ortega St.   Phone: (415)564-8086
San Francisco, CA 94122   Lucretia Wolfe, Hd.Libn.
Founded: 1967. **Staff:** Prof 2; Other 3. **Subjects:** Music. **Special Collections:** Performance materials. **Holdings:** 5200 books; 27,500 musical scores; 230 bound periodical volumes; 1400 tapes; 450 slides; 8100 phonograph records. **Subscriptions:** 57 journals and other serials. **Services:** Interlibrary loan; library open to the public for reference use only. **Remarks:** FAX: (415)665-4004. **Staff:** Joan O'Connor, Asst.Libn.

★14731★
San Francisco Craft & Folk Art Museum - Library (Art)
Landmark Bldg. A
Fort Mason Center
San Francisco, CA 94123-1382   Phone: (415)775-0990
     Barbara Rogers, Libn.
Founded: 1984. **Subjects:** Contemporary crafts, folk art. **Holdings:** 1000 books, vertical file. **Subscriptions:** 17 journals and other serials. **Services:** Copying; library open to the public for reference use only.

★14732★
San Francisco Examiner - Library (Publ)
110 5th St.   Phone: (415)777-7845
San Francisco, CA 94103   Judy Gerritts Canter, Chf.Libn.
Founded: 1865. **Staff:** Prof 4; Other 8. **Subjects:** Newspaper reference topics, state and local history. **Special Collections:** San Francisco Examiner, 1865 to present (microfilm); historical photographs and clippings of San Francisco and California. **Holdings:** 5000 books and pamphlets; 12 million newspaper clippings on microjackets; negatives; photographs. **Subscriptions:** 24 journals and other serials; 10 newspapers. **Services:** Interlibrary loan; library not open to the public. **Computerized Information Services:** NEXIS, DataTimes, DIALOG Information Services, VU/TEXT Information Services, DataQuick, Dun & Bradstreet Business Credit Services; internal database. **Remarks:** FAX: (415)512-9486. Published by Hearst Corporation. **Staff:** Melissa Hom; Yarka Odvarko; Michael Tuller; Lois Jermyn; C.L. Moss; Marvin Gilbreath; Rebecca David.

★14733★
San Francisco General Hospital Medical Center - Barnett-Briggs Library (Med)
1001 Potrero Ave.   Phone: (415)821-3113
San Francisco, CA 94110   Miriam Hirsch, Med.Libn.
Founded: 1950. **Staff:** Prof 1; Other 4. **Subjects:** Medicine. **Holdings:** 13,857 books; 21,568 bound periodical volumes. **Subscriptions:** 585 journals and other serials. **Services:** Interlibrary loan; copying; library open to the public. **Automated Operations:** Computerized ILL (DOCLINE). **Computerized Information Services:** NLM, BRS Information Technologies, DIALOG Information Services; OnTyme Electronic Message Network Service (electronic mail service). Performs searches on fee basis. **Networks/Consortia:** Member of National Network of Libraries of Medicine - Pacific Southwest Region, San Francisco Biomedical Library Network, CLASS. **Remarks:** Electronic mail address(es): CLASS.SFGEN (OnTyme Electronic Message Network Service). FAX: (415)695-6102.

★14734★
San Francisco Law Library (Law)
436 City Hall
400 Van Ness Ave.   Phone: (415)554-6821
San Francisco, CA 94102-4672   Marcia R. Bell, Libn.
Founded: 1870. **Subjects:** Law. **Holdings:** 360,786 volumes. **Subscriptions:** 580 journals and other serials. **Services:** Library open to the public for reference use only. **Computerized Information Services:** WESTLAW. **Remarks:** FAX: (415)554-6820. Maintains branch library at 685 Market St., Rm. 420. **Staff:** John M. Moore, Br.Libn.

San Francisco Metaphysical Library
See: **Association for Research and Enlightenment - Edgar Cayce Foundation - Library** (1168)

★14735★
San Francisco Municipal Railway - Library (Trans)
949 Presidio Ave., Rm. 204   Phone: (415)923-6100
San Francisco, CA 94115   Dr. Marc Hofstadter, Libn.
Staff: Prof 1. **Subjects:** Mass transit, transportation planning and engineering, Bay Area transportation history. **Holdings:** 4500 books; 350 Bay Area Environmental Impact Reports; 600 San Francisco transit maps; 1000 pamphlets. **Subscriptions:** 50 journals and other serials. **Services:** Interlibrary loan; library open to the public by appointment. **Remarks:** FAX: (415)923-6218.

★14736★
San Francisco Museum of Modern Art - Louise S. Ackerman Fine Arts Library (Art)
401 Van Ness Ave.   Phone: (415)252-4120
San Francisco, CA 94102   Eugenie Candau, Libn.
Founded: 1935. **Staff:** Prof 1; Other 5. **Subjects:** Modern and contemporary visual arts, history of photography. **Special Collections:** Margery Mann Collection of the Literature of Photography. **Holdings:** 15,000 books; 40,000 art exhibition catalogs; 150 VF drawers of biographical clippings; 18 files of archives. **Subscriptions:** 300 journals and other serials. **Services:** Copying; library open to the public for reference use only. **Remarks:** Alternate telephone number(s): (415)252-4121. FAX: (415)431-6590.

★14737★
San Francisco Performing Arts Library and Museum - Library (Theater, Mus)
399 Grove St.   Phone: (415)255-4800
San Francisco, CA 94102   Margaret Norton, Exec.Dir.
Staff: 4. **Subjects:** Dance, opera, theater, symphony, music, theater buildings. **Special Collections:** San Francisco Ballet Archives; San Francisco Symphony Archives; Chevron "Standard Hour" Collection; Lew Christensen Collection; Isadora Duncan Collection; Alan Farley Interview Collection; Kirsten Flagstad Collection. **Holdings:** 5000 books; 300 bound periodical volumes; 3000 libretti; 100 manuscripts; 750,000 photographs, playbills, broadsides, and other items. **Subscriptions:** 29 journals and other serials; 3 newspapers. **Services:** Copying; library open to the public for reference use only. **Automated Operations:** Computerized public access catalog. **Publications:** Journal of the San Francisco Performing Arts Library; Encore (newsletter of library and museum). **Remarks:** FAX: (415)255-1913. **Staff:** Barbara Geisler, Libn.; Laurie Ratliff, Archv.; Lottie Shustak, Tech.Serv.; Kirsten Tanaka, Ref.

★14738★
San Francisco Press Club - Will Aubrey Memorial Library (Hum)
555 Post St.
San Francisco, CA 94102   Phone: (415)775-7800
Founded: 1888. **Subjects:** Biography, Californiana, fiction, history. **Holdings:** 5000 volumes. **Services:** Library not open to the public.

★14739★
San Francisco Psychoanalytic Institute - Erik H. Erikson Library (Soc Sci)
2420 Sutter St.   Phone: (415)563-4477
San Francisco, CA 94115   Susanna Bonetti, Asst.Libn.
Founded: 1954. **Staff:** Prof 1; Other 1. **Subjects:** Psychoanalysis. **Special Collections:** Siegfried Bernfield Collection (300 books); Bernice S. Engle Memorial Collection (80 books). **Holdings:** 5000 books; 1700 bound periodical volumes; 2 VF drawers of pamphlets; 3000 reprints and manuscripts; 5 boxes of audiotapes; 150 audio cassette tapes; 3 VF drawers of archives. **Subscriptions:** 25 journals and other serials. **Services:** Interlibrary loan; copying; SDI; library open to the public. **Computerized Information Services:** JOURLIT (internal database). **Networks/Consortia:** Member of National Network of Libraries of Medicine - Pacific Southwest Region, San Francisco Biomedical Library Network, Northern California and Nevada Medical Library Group (NCNMLG). **Publications:** Journal holdings list - available on request.

San Francisco Public Library - San Francisco Archives
See: San Francisco Public Library - San Francisco History Department (14740)

★14740★
San Francisco Public Library - San Francisco History Department (Hist)
Civic Ctr.
San Francisco, CA 94102
Phone: (415)557-4567
Faun McInnis
Founded: 1963. **Staff:** Prof 1; Other 2. **Subjects:** History of San Francisco and California. **Special Collections:** California biography; California Sheet Music; History of California; History of San Francisco; Italian-American Archives; list of registered voters, 1906-1975; Mayor Joseph Alioto, 1968-1976; Robert Durden Slide Collection, 1940 to present; San Francisco districts and hills; San Francisco ephemera; San Francisco Examiner newspaper morgue, 1906-1980; San Francisco fairs (1894 Midwinter Exposition; 1915 Panama Pacific International Exposition; 1939-1940 Golden Gate International Exposition); San Francisco land records; San Francisco Manuscript Collection; San Francisco menus; San Francisco municipal records, 1850-1906; San Francisco News Call-Bulletin photo morgue, 1925-1965; San Francisco photographs; San Francisco theater, 1860-1980; San Francisco and California postcards and trade cards. **Holdings:** 20,000 books; 910 bound periodical volumes. **Subscriptions:** 17 journals and other serials; 2 newspapers. **Services:** Copying; archives open to the public. **Remarks:** FAX: (415)864-8351. **Formerly:** Its San Francisco Archives.

★14741★
San Francisco Public Library - Special Collections Department (Rare Book)
Civic Ctr.
San Francisco, CA 94102
Phone: (415)557-4560
Stanley Carroll, Spec.Coll.Libn.
Founded: 1963. **Staff:** Prof 1; Other 1. **Special Collections:** Grabhorn Collection on the history of the printed book; Harrison Collection of calligraphy and lettering; Schmulowitz Collection of wit and humor; Phelan Collection of California authors; Fox Collection of early children's books; Robert Frost Collection; Panama Canal Collection. **Holdings:** 25,000 books; 100 VF drawers of pamphlets and other ephemera. **Subscriptions:** 40 journals and other serials. **Services:** Copying; collections open to the public. **Remarks:** FAX: (415)864-8351.

★14742★
San Francisco State University - Frank V. De Bellis Collection (Area-Ethnic)
1630 Holloway Ave.
San Francisco, CA 94132
Phone: (415)338-1649
Raymond Van De Moortell, Cur.
Founded: 1963. **Staff:** Prof 1; Other 4. **Subjects:** Italian and Roman civilization, including history, literature, fine arts, music. **Holdings:** 20,000 books; 15,000 music scores; 2200 manuscripts; 25,000 sound recordings; 600 reels of microfilm; 450 prints; 356 artifacts; 1800 coins. **Subscriptions:** 48 journals. **Services:** Interlibrary loan; copying; collection open to the public. **Publications:** The Frank V. de Bellis Collection (revised edition, 1967). **Special Catalogs:** Published catalog of artifacts: Etruscan, Greek and Roman Artifacts in the Frank V. de Bellis Collection (revised edition, 1975). **Remarks:** FAX: (415)338-6199.

★14743★
San Francisco State University - J. Paul Leonard Library - Special Collections/Archives (Hist, Aud-Vis)
1630 Holloway Ave.
San Francisco, CA 94132
Phone: (415)338-1856
Helene Whitson, Spec.Coll.Libn./Archv.
Staff: Prof 1; Other 1. **Subjects:** San Francisco Bay Area, San Francisco State University history. **Special Collections:** San Francisco Bay Area Television News Archives including the KQED Film Archive (Bay Area news and events, 1967-1980: student protests; gay rights and activities; interviews with local political, social, and cultural figures; 1.8 million feet of 16mm newsfilm), KPIX Film Library (1949-1980; 6 million feet of 16mm newsfilm and selected documentaries), Local Emmy Award Winners (500 3/4" videotapes); Over Easy collection (660 3/4" half-hour programs concerning aging, produced by KQED); University archives (newspapers; catalogs; yearbooks; publications; photographs; microfiche; selected University Presidents' records; materials on San Francisco State College strike, 1968-1969). Marguerite Archer Collection of Historic Children's Books (4000 works of fiction; textbooks; toys; games; 18th century to the present). **Holdings:** 288 linear feet of printed books and records; 176 cubic feet of records; 4000 special collections. **Services:** Special Collections/Archives open to the public for reference use only and with restrictions. **Remarks:** FAX: (415)338-6199. Alternate telephone number(s): 338-6217. **Staff:** Meredith Eliassen.

San Francisco Symphony Archives
See: San Francisco Performing Arts Library and Museum - Library (14737)

San Francisco Theological Seminary
See: Graduate Theological Union (6613)

★14744★
San Francisco Theosophical Society - Library (Rel-Phil)
809 Mason St.
San Francisco, CA 94108
Phone: (415)771-8777
Richard Power, Libn.
Founded: 1892. **Staff:** 2. **Subjects:** Theosophy, religion, metaphysics, psychic research, anthropology, healing. **Special Collections:** Popular American metaphysics, circa 1880-1950. **Holdings:** 5000 books; 200 bound periodical volumes; 6 file drawers of pamphlets and clippings; 3 cases of manuscripts. **Services:** Library open to the public.

★14745★
San Francisco Unified School District - Teachers Professional Library (Educ)
2550 25th Ave.
San Francisco, CA 94116
Phone: (415)564-2985
Helen M. Boutin, Lib.Techn.
Staff: 1. **Subjects:** Educational philosophy and psychology, guidance and personnel, human relations, social work, curriculum development, educational administration, educational practices. **Special Collections:** Californiana and San Franciscana (archives files of the school district). **Holdings:** 38,375 books; 9 drawers of pamphlets; 135 feet of documents and curriculum guides. **Subscriptions:** 104 journals and other serials. **Services:** Copying; library open to the public for reference use only. **Publications:** Bibliographies of special collections and recent acquisitions (mimeographed) - to district personnel only.

★14746★
San Gorgonio Memorial Hospital - Medical Library (Med)
600 N. Highland Springs Ave.
Banning, CA 92220
Phone: (714)845-1121
Linda Rubin, Med.Lib.Cons.
Subjects: Medicine. **Holdings:** 100 volumes. **Subscriptions:** 20 journals and other serials. **Services:** Library not open to the public. **Computerized Information Services:** MEDLARS. **Remarks:** FAX: (714)845-2836.

★14747★
San Jacinto Museum of History Association - Library (Hist)
3800 Park Rd. 1836
La Porte, TX 77571
Phone: (713)479-2421
T.J. Zalar, Asst.Dir.
Founded: 1939. **Staff:** Prof 1. **Subjects:** Texas and regional history. **Special Collections:** Espinosa Hacienda Papers, 1740-1840; Duncan Papers, 1820s-1860s; Austin-Bryan-Perry Families, 1820s-1900. **Holdings:** 10,000 books; 250 linear feet of manuscripts and documents; historic maps; photographs. **Services:** Copying; library open to qualified scholars by appointment. **Publications:** The Advance, quarterly; occasional monographs. **Remarks:** FAX: (713)479-6619.

★14748★
San Joaquin College of Law - Library (Law)
3385 E. Shields Ave.
Fresno, CA 93726
Phone: (209)225-4953
Diane Johnson, Libn.
Founded: 1969. **Staff:** Prof 1; Other 5. **Subjects:** Law. **Special Collections:** Water policy, land use and public trust doctrine. **Holdings:** 20,800 books; 2500 bound periodical volumes. **Subscriptions:** 70 journals and other serials. **Services:** Library not open to the public. **Computerized Information Services:** LEXIS. **Remarks:** FAX: (209)225-4322.

★14749★
San Joaquin County Historical Museum - Library (Hist)
Micke Grove Park
Box 21
Lodi, CA 95241
Phone: (209)368-9154
Donald Walker, Libn./Archv.
Founded: 1966. **Staff:** 6. **Subjects:** Local and agricultural history. **Holdings:** 2000 books; 1000 bound periodical volumes; clippings; bound newspapers. **Subscriptions:** 11 journals and other serials. **Services:** Library open to the public by appointment for reference use with supervision. **Remarks:** FAX: (209)369-2178.

★14750★
San Joaquin County Law Library (Law)
County Court House, 4th Fl.   Phone: (209)468-3920
Stockton, CA 95202   Gertrudes J. Ladion, Law Libn.
Founded: 1984. **Staff:** 1.25. **Subjects:** Law. **Holdings:** 24,510 volumes; microfiche. **Subscriptions:** 33 journals and other serials. **Services:** Copying; library open to the public.

★14751★
San Joaquin Pioneer and Historical Society - Earl Rowland Art Library (Art)
1201 N. Pershing Ave.   Phone: (209)462-1404
Stockton, CA 95203   Tod Ruhstaller, Act.Libn.
Founded: 1963. **Staff:** Prof 1. **Subjects:** Art history and appreciation. **Holdings:** 1200 books; 500 unbound periodicals; museum catalogs. **Services:** Copying; library open to the public by appointment.

(San Jose) Centro Cultural Costarriense Norteamericano
See: **Mark Twain Biblioteca (16597)**

★14752★
San Jose Christian College - Memorial Library (Rel-Phil)
790 S. 12th St.
Box 1090   Phone: (408)293-9058
San Jose, CA 95108-1090   Camille S. Muir, Lib.Dir.
Founded: 1939. **Staff:** Prof 1; Other 1. **Subjects:** Bible, youth ministry, theology, counseling, church history, psychology, Greek, Hebrew. **Special Collections:** Restoration history. **Holdings:** 30,774 books; 121 bound periodical volumes; 644 microfiche; 252 kits; 1189 audio recordings; 43 videocassettes; 865 audiocassettes; 3044 uncataloged items; 22,328 stored journal issues. **Subscriptions:** 110 journals and other serials. **Services:** Interlibrary loan; library open to the public.

★14753★
San Jose Historical Museum - Archives (Hist)
1600 Senter Rd.   Phone: (408)287-2290
San Jose, CA 95112   Leslie Masunaga, Archv.
Founded: 1971. **Staff:** Prof 1; Other 1. **Subjects:** Santa Clara Valley and San Jose history, Victorian materials. **Special Collections:** New Almaden Mines Collection; pueblos and ranchos (original papers); Santa Clara Valley historic photographs. **Holdings:** 200 cubic feet of books, ledgers, pamphlets; 374 linear feet of manuscripts and public records; San Jose newspapers, 1880s-1947 on microfilm; Sanborn maps. **Services:** Copying (limited); archives open to the public with limited access to materials. **Remarks:** FAX: (408)277-3890.

★14754★
San Jose Medical Center - Health Sciences Library (Med)
675 E. Santa Clara St.   Phone: (408)998-3212
San Jose, CA 95114   Deloris Osby, Dir.
Founded: 1934. **Staff:** Prof 1; Other 2. **Subjects:** Medicine, nursing, health care administration, family practice, allied health sciences, wellness. **Special Collections:** Family practice; Health Care Management/Administration. **Holdings:** 41,000 books; 15,000 bound periodical volumes; 12 VF drawers of pamphlets and clippings; 150 AV programs; 80 filmstrips; 19 films; 200 archival items. **Subscriptions:** 450 journals and other serials; 6 newspapers. **Services:** Interlibrary loan; copying; SDI; library open to the public by appointment. **Automated Operations:** Computerized cataloging, acquisitions, and serials. **Computerized Information Services:** MEDLINE, BRS Information Technologies, WILSONLINE, DIALOG Information Services; OnTyme Electronic Message Network Service (electronic mail service). Performs searches on fee basis. **Networks/Consortia:** Member of Medical Library Consortium of Santa Clara Valley, Northern California and Nevada Medical Library Group (NCNMLG). **Special Catalogs:** Journal Collection Catalog. **Remarks:** FAX: (408)993-7031. Electronic mail address(es): SJH (OnTyme Electronic Message Network Service). Maintained by Health Dimensions Inc.

San Jose Medical Center - Planetree Health Resource Center
See: **Planetree - Health Resource Center (13119)**

★14755★
San Jose Mercury News - Library (Publ)
750 Ridder Park Dr.   Phone: (408)920-5345
San Jose, CA 95190   Gary L. Lance, Lib.Mgr.
Founded: 1929. **Staff:** Prof 8; Other 1. **Subjects:** Newspaper reference topics, local history. **Holdings:** 2000 volumes; 3.5 million clippings; 600,000 photographs; 7500 reels of microfilm of newspapers. **Subscriptions:** 60 journals and other serials; 30 newspapers. **Services:** Interlibrary loan; library not open to the public. **Computerized Information Services:** DIALOG Information Services, NEXIS, VU/TEXT Information Services, DataTimes. **Remarks:** FAX: (408)288-8060. **Staff:** Debbie Bolvin, Asst.Chf.Libn.; Mona Baird, Libn.; Karen Draper, Libn.; Marcia Gordon, Libn.; Lorene Laffranchi, Libn.; Jane Metz, Libn.; Diana Stickler, Libn.

★14756★
San Jose Museum of Art - Library (Art)
110 S. Market St.   Phone: (408)294-2787
San Jose, CA 95113   Jean F. Wheeler, Libn.
Founded: 1978. **Staff:** Prof 1. **Subjects:** Art. **Special Collections:** Children's art books. **Holdings:** 1925 books; 2575 exhibition catalogs; 4 VF drawers of art information files; 1850 slides. **Subscriptions:** 4 journals and other serials. **Services:** Library open only to curatorial staff and museum volunteers. **Publications:** Framework (newsletter), bimonthly. **Remarks:** FAX: (408)294-2977.

★14757★
San Jose Public Library - Silicon Valley Information Center (Hist)
180 W. San Carlos St.   Phone: (408)277-5754
San Jose, CA 95113   Wynne M. Dobyns, Sr.Libn.
Founded: 1985. **Staff:** Prof 6; Other 2.5. **Subjects:** Santa Clara County, California - high technology industries, history, environmental issues, social and cultural impact, personalities. **Special Collections:** Corporate document archives (600 companies represented). **Holdings:** 1800 books; 30 bound periodical volumes; 39,000 clippings; 110 posters; 125 videotapes. **Services:** Copying; center open to the public. **Automated Operations:** Computerized public access catalog. **Computerized Information Services:** DIALOG Information Services. Performs limited searches free of charge. **Publications:** Tomorrow, irregular - to the public. **Remarks:** Center is said to be the first centralized public facility to document the birth, development, and impact of the high technology industries in Santa Clara County, California.

★14758★
San Jose State University - Environmental Resource Center (Env-Cons)
San Jose, CA 95192-0116   Phone: (408)924-5467
    Stephen Shunk
Founded: 1972. **Staff:** 1. **Subjects:** Alternative energy, environmental education, alternative transportation, toxics and hazardous waste, solid waste, ecological restoration. **Holdings:** Figures not available. **Services:** Library open to the public. **Automated Operations:** Computerized cataloging. **Publications:** Paradisaea (newsletter). **Remarks:** FAX: (408)924-6220.

★14759★
San Jose State University - Ira F. Brilliant Center for Beethoven Studies (Mus)
1 Washington Square   Phone: (408)924-4590
San Jose, CA 95192-0171   Dr. William Meredith, Dir.
Founded: 1983. **Staff:** Prof 2; Other 1. **Subjects:** Beethoven. **Special Collections:** First and early editions of Beethoven's music; William S. Newman Beethoven Collection. **Holdings:** 1600 books; 115 bound periodical volumes; 1500 scores; 400 recordings; 2 Beethoven manuscripts; 50 reels of microfilm; 40 slides; 15 videotapes. **Subscriptions:** 10 journals and other serials. **Services:** Interlibrary loan; copying; center open to the public. **Automated Operations:** Computerized cataloging. **Computerized Information Services:** Beethoven Bibliography Database (internal database); BITNET (electronic mail service). **Publications:** Bibliography of Beethoven materials (card); The Beethoven Newsletter, 3/year - by subscription. **Remarks:** FAX: (408)924-4365. Electronic mail address(es): ELLIOTT@SJSUVM1 (BITNET). **Staff:** Patricia Elliott, Cur.

★14760★
San Jose State University - Steinbeck Research Center (Hum)
Wahlquist Library
1 Washington Square   Phone: (408)924-4588
San Jose, CA 95192-0202   Susan Shillinglaw, Dir.
Founded: 1971. **Staff:** Prof 1; Other 1. **Subjects:** John Steinbeck. **Holdings:** 6000 manuscripts, typescripts, pieces of correspondence, first editions, photographs, and memorabilia. **Services:** Copying; center open to the public. **Publications:** Steinbeck Newsletter, 2/year; The Grapes of Wrath: An Annotated Bibliography; Your Only Weapon is Your Work (Steinbeck Letter to Dennis Murphy); San Jose Studies Special Issue on The Grapes of Wrath (Winter 1990). **Special Catalogs:** The Steinbeck Research Center at San Jose State University: A Descriptive Catalog by Robert W. Woodward. **Staff:** Robert Harmon, Res.Libn.; Jack Douglas, Hd., Spec.Coll.

★14761★
San Jose State University - Wahlquist Library - Chicano Library Resource Center (Area-Ethnic)
1 Washington Sq.   Phone: (408)924-2707
San Jose, CA 95192-0028   Jeff Paul, Dir.
Founded: 1979. **Staff:** Prof 1; Other 3. **Subjects:** Chicano studies. **Special Collections:** Hispanic Link (newspaper articles and editorials on the role of the Hispanic in the United States); National Hispanic Feminist Conference Papers, 1980; United Farm Workers Resources (pictures; songs; poems; accounts of Cesar Chavez; a history of the UFW; announcements of boycotts, 1973-1975); Chicano oral history project (audiotapes, videotapes, memorabilia, news clippings as well as interviews and transcripts of individuals in the Chicano movement in San Jose, 1960-1980). **Holdings:** 2100 books; 700 unbound periodicals; 400 reels of microfilm; 1500 clippings and pamphlets; 50 posters; transcripts, corespondence, and oral histories of activists in the Chicano Movement in San Jose, 1960s-1970s. **Subscriptions:** 15 journals and other serials. **Services:** Interlibrary loan; center open to the public. **Computerized Information Services:** CD-ROM (Chicano Database); BITNET (electronic mail service). **Publications:** CLRC Bibliography. **Special Indexes:** Index to Chicano Serials (microfilm). **Remarks:** Alternate telephone number(s): (408)924-2815. FAX: (408)924-2701. Electronic mail address(es): PAUL@SJSUVM1 (BITNET).

★14762★
San Juan County Archaeological Research Center & Library (Hist)
P.O. Box 125   Phone: (505)632-2013
Bloomfield, NM 87413   Penny Whitten, Libn.
Founded: 1973. **Staff:** Prof 1. **Subjects:** Southwest archeology, history, anthropology, natural science. **Special Collections:** Slide/tape programs; historical records of San Juan Basin (3 VF drawers); Four Corners area rock art (1700 slides and photographs); archival records of excavation of Salmon Ruin Site (60 feet); Navaho Mythology Collection. **Holdings:** 2600 books and monographs; 6630 reports and pamphlets; 2250 journals and periodicals; 1 VF drawer of clippings; 1 VF drawer of photographs; 36 oral history tapes and transcriptions; 10 videotapes; 3 VF drawers of botany specimens; 5 drawers of historic maps; children's section (30 books, 4 slide shows). **Subscriptions:** 25 journals and other serials. **Services:** Copying; library open to the public for reference use only. **Publications:** Contributions to Anthropology Series, irregular; cemeteries in San Juan County, irregular. **Special Indexes:** Computer index to pioneer families in the area. **Remarks:** FAX: (505)632-1707. Library located at the upper level of the Research Center. Maintained by the San Juan County Museum Association. **Formerly:** Located in Farmington, NM.

★14763★
San Juan County Historical Society - Archive (Hist)
P.O. Box 154
Silverton, CO 81433   Allen Nossaman, Archv.Dir.
Founded: 1965. **Subjects:** San Juan County and Colorado history. **Holdings:** 40 books; 900 photographs; 36 reels of microfilm; 115 oral history tapes; 600 cubic feet of maps, slides, correspondence, records. **Services:** Archive open to the public by appointment. **Publications:** The Story of Hillside Cemetery: Burials, 1874-1988. **Special Indexes:** San Juan County Newspaper Index, 1879-1883; San Juan County Newspaper Index, 1884-1887; Index to Cataloged Collection, San Juan County Historical Society Archives.

San Juan County Museum Association
See: **San Juan County Archaeological Research Center & Library** (14762)

★14764★
San Luis Obispo County Law Library (Law)
Government Center, Rm. 125   Phone: (805)549-5855
San Luis Obispo, CA 93408   Jean Borraccino, Law Libn.
Founded: 1896. **Staff:** Prof 1; Other 3. **Subjects:** Law. **Holdings:** 24,386 volumes; 1000 pamphlets; 219 tapes; 3146 microforms. **Subscriptions:** 64 journals and other serials. **Services:** Copying; library open to the public with restrictions.

★14765★
San Luis Obispo County Planning Department - Technical Information Library (Env-Cons, Plan)
County Government Center
976 Osos St.   Phone: (805)549-5600
San Luis Obispo, CA 93408   Dolores Quezada, Libn.
Founded: 1969. **Subjects:** Conservation and natural resources, recreation, circulation, land data, social and economic analysis, public utilities and services, aesthetic and historical data, administration data, housing and building research. **Holdings:** 600 books; 1000 pamphlets and documents; 5000 maps. **Subscriptions:** 30 journals and other serials; 7 newspapers. **Services:** Interlibrary loan; library open to the public for reference use only on request.

★14766★
(San Luis Potosi) Instituto Mexicano-Norteamericano de Relaciones Culturales - USIS Collection (Educ)
Venustiano Carranza No. 766
78150 San Luis Potosi, SLP, Mexico
Remarks: Maintained or supported by the U.S. Information Agency. Focus is on materials that will assist peoples outside the United States to learn about the United States, its people, history, culture, political processes, and social milieux.

★14767★
San Martin Society of Washington, DC - Information Center (Hist)
Box 33   Phone: (703)883-0950
McLean, VA 22101-0033   Dr. Christian Garcia-Godoy, Pres.
Subjects: General Jose de San Martin; the emancipation of Argentina, Chile, and Peru. **Holdings:** 1300 volumes; microfilm; dissertations; speeches; pamphlets; documents. **Services:** Copying; center open to the public by written request.

★14768★
San Mateo County - Medical Library (Soc Sci)
225 37th Ave.   Phone: (415)573-2520
San Mateo, CA 94403   Mark Constantz, Med.Libn.
Founded: 1967. **Staff:** Prof 1. **Subjects:** Clinical medicine, public health, mental health. **Holdings:** 100 books; 500 bound periodical volumes. **Subscriptions:** 100 journals and other serials. **Services:** Interlibrary loan; copying; library open to the public for reference use only. **Automated Operations:** Computerized cataloging. **Computerized Information Services:** CD-ROMS (CD-PLUS). OnTyme Electronic Message Network Service (electronic mail service). **Remarks:** FAX: (415)573-2116. Electronic mail address(es): SMCHSD (OnTyme Electronic Message Network Service). **Formerly:** San Mateo County Department of Health Services - Library.

San Mateo County Department of Health Services - Library
See: **San Mateo County - Medical Library** (14768)

★14769★
San Mateo County Historical Association - Library (Hist)
College of San Mateo Campus
1700 W. Hillsdale Blvd.   Phone: (415)574-6441
San Mateo, CA 94402   Marion C. Holmes, Archv.
Founded: 1935. **Staff:** Prof 1. **Subjects:** San Mateo County history. **Holdings:** 1070 books; 3007 pamphlets; 26,000 photographs; 345 manuscripts; 416 student monographs; 562 documents, including assessment books, diaries, municipal and county records. **Services:** Copying; library open to the public. **Publications:** La Peninsula (journal), annual - to members. **Special Indexes:** La Peninsula index; alphabetical list of 1860 and 1870 censuses; alphabetical list of Richard N. Schellens Collection.

★14770★
San Mateo County Law Library (Law)
710 Hamilton St.   Phone: (415)363-4160
Redwood City, CA 94063   Robert D. Harrington, Dir.
Staff: 3. **Subjects:** Law. **Holdings:** 40,000 volumes. **Services:** Library open to the public.

★14771★
San Mateo County Office of Education - The SMERC Library (Educ, Comp Sci)
101 Twin Dolphin Dr.   Phone: (415)802-5655
Redwood City, CA 94065-1064   Mrs. Karol Thomas, Dir.
Founded: 1967. **Staff:** Prof 3; Other 8. **Subjects:** Education. **Holdings:** 22,000 books; 10,000 textbooks; 400,000 microfiche. **Subscriptions:** 500 education journals. **Services:** Interlibrary loan; copying; library open to the public with restrictions. **Computerized Information Services:** DIALOG Information Services, ERIC; CD-ROM. **Networks/Consortia:** Member of CLASS. **Publications:** Newsnotes, 4/year. **Remarks:** FAX: (415)802-5322. **Staff:** Mary Moray, Ref.Coord.; Linda Field, Lib.Serv.Supv.

★14772★
San Mateo Public Library - Business Section (Bus-Fin)
55 W. 3rd Ave.   Phone: (415)377-4685
San Mateo, CA 94402   Marjorie H. Johansen, Bus.Ref.Libn.
Staff: Prof 1; Other 2. **Subjects:** Small business, investment. **Holdings:** 10,000 books. **Subscriptions:** 95 journals and other serials; 10 newspapers. **Services:** Interlibrary loan; section open to the public. **Automated Operations:** Computerized cataloging and circulation. **Computerized Information Services:** DIALOG Information Services, DataTimes, OCLC EPIC, VU/TEXT Information Services, WILSONLINE, Dow Jones News/Retrieval; OnTyme Electronic Message Network Service (electronic mail service). **Networks/Consortia:** Member of Peninsula Library System (PLS). **Publications:** Business Bibliographies. **Remarks:** FAX: (415)344-0580. Electronic mail address(es): SMPL (OnTyme Electronic Message Network Service).

★14773★
(San Nicolas de Los Garza) Instituto Mexicano-Norteamericano de Relaciones Culturales Anahuac, A.C. - Benjamin Franklin Library Anahuac - USIS Collection (Educ)
Jose Santos Chocano, No. 600
Col. Anahuac 66450   Phone: 83 764879
San Nicolas de Los Garza, NL, Mexico   Maria C.G. Rivera
Staff: 1. **Holdings:** 1823 books; 2 videotapes. **Subscriptions:** 19 journals and other serials. **Services:** Copying; library open to the public. **Remarks:** FAX: 83 765187. Alternate telephone number(s): 83 767692. Maintained or supported by the U.S. Information Agency. Focus is on materials that will assist peoples outside the United States to learn about the United States, its people, history, culture, political processes, and social milieux. **Formerly:** (Monterrey) Instituto Mexicano-Norteamericano de Relaciones Culturales - USIS Collection located in Monterrey, Mexico.

★14774★
San Pedro Peninsula Hospital - John T. Burch, M.D. Memorial Library (Med)
1300 W. 7th St.   Phone: (213)832-3311
San Pedro, CA 90732-3593   James H. Harlan, Lib.Cons.
Founded: 1940. **Staff:** Prof 1; Other 2. **Subjects:** Clinical medicine, nursing. **Holdings:** 348 books; 1300 bound periodical volumes; 250 Audio-Digest tapes; 22 videotapes; 8 reels of microfilm. **Subscriptions:** 40 journals and other serials. **Services:** Interlibrary loan; copying; SDI; library open to the public by appointment. **Computerized Information Services:** MEDLINE, DIALOG Information Services; OnTyme Electronic Message Network Service (electronic mail service). Performs searches on fee basis. **Remarks:** FAX: (310)534-5323. Electronic mail address(es): SPPHOSP/CA (OnTyme Electronic Message Network Service).

Sanborn House English Library
See: **Dartmouth College** (4614)

Carl Sandburg Home National Historic Site
See: **U.S. Natl. Park Service** (17683)

Ottys Sanders Herpetological Library
See: **Baylor University** (1608)

★14775★
Sanders & Thomas, Inc. - STV Group Library (Sci-Engr)
11 Robinson St.   Phone: (215)326-4600
Pottstown, PA 19464   Carol S. Leh, Tech.Libn.
Founded: 1962. **Staff:** Prof 1. **Subjects:** Engineering, architecture, planning. **Special Collections:** Solid Waste/Energy Collection (873 titles). **Holdings:** 702 books; catalogs for 1253 companies; 8 information file boxes; 3 films; 738 specifications; 148 transportation reports. **Subscriptions:** 30 journals and other serials. **Services:** Library not open to the public. **Remarks:** FAX: (215)326-3833.

Leonard M. Sandhaus Memorial Library
See: **Temple Israel** (16107)

★14776★
Sandia Baptist Church - Media Center (Rel-Phil)
9429 Constitution, N.E.   Phone: (505)292-2713
Albuquerque, NM 87112   Margaret Haynes Mills, Media Serv.Dir.
Founded: 1960. **Staff:** 4. **Subjects:** Bible study, Christian life, family living, children's books. **Holdings:** 2500 books; 150 filmstrips; 15 AV programs; 25 audiotapes. **Subscriptions:** 10 journals and other serials. **Services:** Center open to church members.

★14777★
Sandia National Laboratories - Technical Library (Sci-Engr)
7011 East Ave., Bldg. 921   Phone: (510)294-3000
Livermore, CA 94550   Saundra Lormand, Group Ldr.
Founded: 1957. **Staff:** Prof 2; Other 6. **Subjects:** Engineering, materials, electrical and mechanical engineering, physics, chemistry, electronics, defense. **Holdings:** 8400 books; 9790 bound periodical volumes; 900 reels of microfilm of periodicals; 48,750 technical reports. **Subscriptions:** 433 journals and other serials. **Services:** Interlibrary loan; library not open to the public. **Automated Operations:** Computerized cataloging, acquisitions, serials, and circulation. **Computerized Information Services:** DIALOG Information Services, BRS Information Technologies, PFDS Online, NEXIS, Chemical Abstracts Service (CAS), WILSONLINE, DTIC. **Remarks:** FAX: (510)294-3410. The Sandia National Laboratories operate under contract to the U.S. Department of Energy. **Staff:** Hugh Keleher, Tech.Info.Spec.; Mavis Flower, ILL.

★14778★
Sandia National Laboratories - Technical Library (Sci-Engr, Energy)
Dept. 3140
Box 5800   Phone: (505)845-8195
Albuquerque, NM 87185   J.L. Negin, Mgr.
Founded: 1948. **Staff:** Prof 24; Other 38. **Subjects:** Nuclear weapons, nuclear waste management, nuclear safety and security, electronics, explosives, materials, aerodynamics, solid state physics, ordnance, energy research. **Special Collections:** Videotapes on Sandia's weekly colloquia, 1976 to present. **Holdings:** 53,000 volumes; 24,000 bound periodical volumes; 22,000 periodical volumes on microfilm; 125,000 hardcopy technical reports; 1 million technical reports on microfiche; 73,000 internal reports. **Subscriptions:** 1700 journals and other serials. **Services:** Interlibrary loan; library not open to the public. **Automated Operations:** Computerized cataloging, acquisitions, serials, and circulation. **Computerized Information Services:** DIALOG Information Services, Integrated Technical Information System (ITIS), BRS Information Technologies, DTIC, NEXIS, NASA/RECON, RLIN, STN International, WILSONLINE, NLM, United States Naval Institute (USNI), Inside N.R.C. (U.S. Nuclear Regulatory Commission), Integrated Document Control System (IDCS); internal database. **Publications:** SCAN (Sandia Laboratories Accession News), monthly. **Remarks:** FAX: (505)846-1521. The Sandia National Laboratories operate under contract to the U.S. Department of Energy. **Staff:** Sally Landenberger, Tech.Proc.Supv.; Dennis Rowley, Sys.Supv.; Susan Stinchcomb, Ref.Supv.; Nancy Pruett, Rec.Info.Mgt.Supv.; Beth Moser, Info.Anl.; Carmen Ward, Info.Anl.; Ferne Allan, Info.Spec.; Mary Compton, Info.Spec.; Judy Geitgey, Info.Spec.; Lynn Llull-Kaczor, Info.Spec.; David Mays, Info.Spec.; Cathy Pasterczyk, Info.Spec.; Gladys Sheldon, Info.Spec.; Linda Cusimano, Rec.Mgt.Anl.; Kary Ledbetter, Rec.Mgt.Anl.; Kim Denton-Hill, Info.Sys.Anl.; Ruby Hsia, Info.Sys.Anl.; Jim Hutchins, Info.Sys.Anl.; Paul Kirby, Info.Sys.Anl.; John Larson, Info.Sys.Anl.; Joe Maloney, Info.Sys.Anl.; Barbara Ortiz, Info.Sys.Anl.; Gina Bell, Info.Sys.Anl.; P.J. McKee, Info.Sys.Anl.

★ 14779 ★
Sandoz AGRO - Research Library (Biol Sci, Sci-Engr)
975 California Ave.
Box 10975 Phone: (415)354-3475
Palo Alto, CA 94303 Martha L. Manion, Supv., Lib.
Founded: 1968. **Staff:** Prof 2; Other 1. **Subjects:** Organic chemistry, invertebrate biochemistry, molecular biology, plant genetics, entomology, pest control. **Holdings:** 7000 books; 6000 bound periodical volumes; 17,000 reprints; 1000 cartridges of microfilm; 4000 microfiche. **Subscriptions:** 300 journals and other serials. **Services:** Interlibrary loan; copying; library open to the public by request. **Computerized Information Services:** DIALOG Information Services, PFDS Online, LEXIS, STN International, National Pesticide Information Retrieval System (NPIRS), OCLC, NLM. **Remarks:** FAX: (415)857-1125. **Formerly:** Sandoz Crop Protection Corporation. **Staff:** Sarah White, Info.Spec.

★ 14780 ★
Sandoz Canada Inc. - Bibliotheque/Library (Med)
385 Bouchard Blvd. Phone: (514)631-6775
Dorval, PQ, Canada H9S 1A9 Jean Charbonneau, Hd.Libn.
Founded: 1950. **Staff:** Prof 1; Other 2. **Subjects:** Pharmaceuticals, cardiology, immunology, endocrinology, neurology. **Holdings:** 3250 books; 500 bound periodical volumes; 50,000 microfiche. **Subscriptions:** 300 journals and other serials. **Services:** Interlibrary loan; services not open to the public. **Automated Operations:** Computerized cataloging and serials. **Computerized Information Services:** MEDLARS, DIALOG Information Services, Data-Star, CAN/OLE; internal database; Envoy 100 (electronic mail service). **Remarks:** FAX: (514)631-1867. Telex: 05 821 886. Electronic mail address(es): QMSAC (Envoy 100).

★ 14781 ★
Sandoz Chemical Corporation - Corporate Library (Sci-Engr)
Box 669304 Phone: (704)547-5519
Charlotte, NC 28266 Jacqueline N. Kirkman, Corp.Libn.
Founded: 1963. **Staff:** Prof 1; Other 1. **Subjects:** Dyestuffs, organic chemistry. **Holdings:** 2250 books; 2331 bound periodical volumes; 11,000 patents; 300 unbound reports; 110 reels of microfilm; 4000 microfiche. **Subscriptions:** 171 journals and other serials. **Services:** Interlibrary loan; library open to the public with restrictions. **Computerized Information Services:** DIALOG Information Services, Chemical Abstracts Service (CAS), Occupational Health Services, Inc. (OHS), PFDS Online, NLM, Chemical Information Systems, Inc. (CIS). **Remarks:** FAX: (704)547-5588.

Sandoz Crop Protection Corporation
See: **Sandoz AGRO (14779)**

★ 14782 ★
Sandoz Crop Protection Corporation - Corporate Library (Agri, Biol Sci)
1300 E. Touhy Ave. Phone: (708)390-3859
Des Plaines, IL 60018 Candy J. Ortman, Libn./Archv.
Founded: 1940. **Staff:** Prof 1; Other 1. **Subjects:** Pesticides, herbicides, organic chemistry, entomology, botany, agribusiness. **Special Collections:** Proceedings and reports of various weed society conferences from 1945 to present. **Holdings:** 7000 books; 7000 bound periodical volumes; 7000 reels of microfilm. **Subscriptions:** 201 journals and other serials. **Services:** Interlibrary loan; copying; library open to the public by appointment. **Computerized Information Services:** DIALOG Information Services, PFDS Online, Chemical Information Systems, Inc. (CIS), National Pesticide Information Retrieval System (NPIRS), NLM, Occupational Health Services, Inc., LEXIS, Environmental Technical Information Services (ETIS), Ground Water On-Line, Technical Database Service (TDS). **Networks/Consortia:** Member of ILLINET, North Suburban Library System (NSLS). **Remarks:** FAX: (708)390-3945.

★ 14783 ★
Sandoz Pharmaceuticals Corporation - Library (Biol Sci, Med)
Route 10
East Hanover, NJ 07936 Phone: (201)503-7741
Staff: Prof 10; Other 5. **Subjects:** Medicine, chemistry, pharmacology, toxicology, biochemistry, business, management. **Special Collections:** Clinical medicine. **Holdings:** 15,700 books; 26,285 bound periodical volumes; 20 drawers of microfilm; 2 drawers of annual reports. **Subscriptions:** 923 journals and other serials; 8 newspapers. **Services:** Interlibrary loan; copying; SDI; library not open to the public. **Automated Operations:** Computerized cataloging (DATALIB). **Computerized Information Services:** Current Contents Search, DIALOG Information Services, PFDS Online, MEDLINE, BRS Information Technologies, Chemical Abstracts Service (CAS); CD-ROMs. **Networks/Consortia:** Member of PALINET. **Publications:** Infoscan, quarterly - available on request. **Remarks:** FAX: (201)503-6357. **Formerly:** Sandoz, Inc. **Staff:** Veong Kwon, Mgr., Lib.Serv.; Sue Mellen, Mgr., Clin./Bus.Info.; Sigfried Wahrman, Supv., Preclinical Info.

★ 14784 ★
Sandoz Pharmaceuticals Corporation - Medical Information Services (Med, Bus-Fin)
Route 10 Phone: (201)503-8105
East Hanover, NJ 07936 Joyce G. Koelle, Assoc.Dir.
Founded: 1939. **Staff:** Prof 6; Other 4. **Subjects:** Corporation products, biomedicine, business. **Holdings:** Figures not available. **Computerized Information Services:** DIALOG Information Services, PFDS Online, INVESTEXT, IMSWorld Online Service, Data-Star, NLM; Sandoz Product Information System (internal database). **Publications:** Current Awareness Bulletin, biweekly - for internal distribution only. **Remarks:** FAX: (201)503-7925.

★ 14785 ★
Sandusky County Law Library (Law)
Courthouse, 100 N. Park Ave. Phone: (419)334-6165
Fremont, OH 43420 John T. Stahl, Res.Asst.
Staff: Prof 1. **Subjects:** Law. **Special Collections:** Historical law books (especially early Ohio legal history). **Holdings:** 11,000 books; 1100 bound periodical volumes; 600 other cataloged items. **Subscriptions:** 200 journals and other serials. **Services:** Library open to the public for reference use only on request. **Computerized Information Services:** WESTLAW, Veralex 2. **Remarks:** FAX: (419)334-6164. **Staff:** Sharon L. Hintze, Ck./Bookkeeper.

★ 14786 ★
Sandvig Collections - Library (Hist, Art)
N-2600 Lillehammer, Norway Phone: 62 50135
Guri Velure, Libn.
Founded: 1930. **Staff:** Prof 1. **Subjects:** History, cultural history, arts, crafts. **Special Collections:** Winter Olympics, 1994 (newspaper articles). **Holdings:** 18,000 books. **Subscriptions:** 85 journals and other serials; 4 newspapers. **Services:** Interlibrary loan; copying; library open to the public for reference use only. **Computerized Information Services:** Internal database. **Remarks:** FAX: 62 53959. **Also Known As:** De Sandvigske Samlinger - Biblioteket.

★ 14787 ★
Sandy Bay Historical Society and Museums - Library (Hist)
Box 63 Phone: (508)546-9533
Rockport, MA 01966-0063 Dr. Marshall W.S. Swan, Cur.
Founded: 1925. **Staff:** Prof 1. **Subjects:** History of Rockport (Sandy Bay), Cape Ann, Essex County; Rockport families. **Special Collections:** Local history. **Holdings:** 300 books; 750 manuscripts. **Services:** Interlibrary loan; copying; library open to qualified researchers. **Publications:** Bulletin, 3-4/year - to members. **Remarks:** Alternate telephone number(s): (508)546-3514.

★ 14788 ★
Sandy Corporation - Library (Bus-Fin)
1500 W. Big Beaver Rd. Phone: (313)649-0800
Troy, MI 48084 Judith Wilson, Lib.Dir.
Founded: 1971. **Staff:** Prof 1; Other 1. **Subjects:** Consulting, training, communication. **Holdings:** 3000 books; 2000 pamphlets; 32 VF drawers of automotive product information; 36 VF drawers of business and management literature; 3000 square feet of periodicals, videodiscs, cartridges, slides, filmstrips, motion pictures, scripts. **Subscriptions:** 150 journals and other serials. **Services:** Interlibrary loan; library not open to the public. **Computerized Information Services:** DIALOG Information Services, Dun & Bradstreet Business Credit Services. **Networks/Consortia:** Member of Library Cooperative of Macomb (LCM), Council on Resource Development (CORD). **Publications:** Library Bulletin, biweekly; Acquisitions Bulletin, 5/year - both for internal distribution only. **Remarks:** FAX: (313)649-3619.

★ 14789 ★
Sandy Spring Museum - Library (Hist)
P.O. Box 1484   Phone: (301)774-0022
Sandy Spring, MD 20860   Doris E. Chickering, Dir.
Founded: 1980. **Staff:** 1. **Subjects:** Local history and genealogy. **Holdings:** 1700 books; 735 documents; 2015 manuscripts. **Services:** Copying; library open to the public. **Computerized Information Services:** Internal database. **Remarks:** Library located at 2707 Rte. 108, Olney, MD 20832. **Staff:** Sylvia Nash, Hist.

★ 14790 ★
Sanford Museum & Planetarium - Library
117 E. Willow St.   Phone: (712)225-3922
Cherokee, IA 51012   Linda A. Burkhart, Dir.
Founded: 1951. **Staff:** 4. **Subjects:** Archeology, astronomy, geology, history, paleontology, museology. **Holdings:** 5000 volumes. **Subscriptions:** 30 journals and other serials. **Services:** Interlibrary loan; library open to the public.

Nevitt Sanford Archives
See: **The Wright Institute** (20643)

★ 14791 ★
Sangamon State University - Archives - Oral History Collection (Hist)
Brookens Library, Rm. 377   Phone: (217)786-6521
Springfield, IL 62794-9243   Linda S. Jett, Coord.
Founded: 1972. **Staff:** 2. **Subjects:** History - 20th century American, Illinois, ethnic and minority, coal mining, labor, agricultural; state and local politics. **Holdings:** 1000 oral history memoirs (2900 hours of taped interviews and 87,000 pages of transcripts). **Services:** Interlibrary loan; copying; office open to the public for reference use only. **Automated Operations:** Computerized public access catalog. **Publications:** History with a Tape Recorder: an Oral History Handbook; Oral History: From Tape to Type. **Special Catalogs:** Subject descriptions and inventories for Coal Mining and Union Activities, The Jewish Experience, Agricultural History, Women's History, and Sangamon County History. **Formerly:** Its Oral History Office. **Also Known As:** Illinois Oral History Clearinghouse.

★ 14792 ★
Sangamon State University - Brookens Library - Special Collections (Bus-Fin, Soc Sci)
Shepherd Rd.   Phone: (217)786-6520
Springfield, IL 62708   Brian Alley
Founded: 1970. **Staff:** 3.5. **Special Collections:** Handy Writers Colony Collection (30 cubic feet); Illinois regional archives depository (800 cubic feet); Springfield area history; Walt Whitman collection; 1893 World Columbian Exposition; Sangamon State University faculty publications; James Jones collection. **Holdings:** 500 books; 70 bound periodical volumes; 100 manuscripts; 800 archival items; 60 reels of microfilm. **Subscriptions:** 5 journals and other serials. **Services:** Interlibrary loan; library open to the public for reference use only. **Computerized Information Services:** DIALOG Information Services; BITNET (electronic mail service). Contact Person: John Holz. **Publications:** Guides to sources. **Remarks:** FAX: (217)786-6208. Electronic mail address(es): SSUBIT16@VMD.CSO.UIUC.EDU (BITNET). **Staff:** Thomas J. Wood, Univ.Archv./Hd., Spec.Coll.

★ 14793 ★
Sangamon State University - East Central Network for Curriculum Coordination - Library (Educ)
F-2   Phone: (217)786-6375
Springfield, IL 62794-9243   Susie Shackleton, Libn.
Founded: 1971. **Staff:** Prof 10; Other 9. **Subjects:** Education - vocational, career, adult; sex equity. **Holdings:** 30,000 books; 5000 AV programs; 8 VF drawers of publishers files. **Subscriptions:** 100 journals and other serials. **Services:** Interlibrary loan; copying; library open to the public. **Automated Operations:** Computerized public access catalog, cataloging, and circulation. **Computerized Information Services:** BRS Information Technologies; Task Listing File (internal database). Performs searches free of charge. Contact Person: Jeff Lake, Microcomp.Cons. **Networks/Consortia:** Member of Rolling Prairie Library System (RPLS). **Publications:** Occasional papers; subject bibliographies. **Remarks:** FAX: (217)786-6036. The network is funded by the U.S. Department of Education and maintained by the Illinois State Board of Education. **Staff:** Rebecca Douglass, Dir.; Ruth Patton, Coord.

★ 14794 ★
Margaret Sanger Center-Planned Parenthood New York City - Abraham Stone Library (Soc Sci)
380 Second Ave.
New York, NY 10010   Phone: (212)677-6474
Subjects: Abortion, adolescent sexuality, infertility, sex, family living, demography, population, sexuality of the handicapped, women's health. **Holdings:** 6000 books; 3000 bound periodical volumes; 60 VF drawers of reprints and newspaper clippings. **Subscriptions:** 85 journals and other serials. **Services:** Interlibrary loan; copying; library open by appointment to graduate students and agencies.

★ 14795 ★
Sani-Pure Food Laboratories - Library (Food-Bev)
178-182 Saddle River Rd.
Saddle Brook, NJ 07662   Phone: (201)843-2525
Founded: 1946. **Staff:** 1. **Subjects:** Food testing and analysis. **Holdings:** 500 volumes. **Subscriptions:** 21 journals and other serials. **Services:** Library not open to the public. **Remarks:** FAX: (201)843-4934.

★ 14796 ★
Santa Barbara Botanic Garden - Library (Biol Sci)
1212 Mission Canyon Rd.   Phone: (805)682-4726
Santa Barbara, CA 93105   Rebecca J. Eldridge, Libn.
Founded: 1942. **Staff:** Prof 1; Other 1. **Subjects:** Botany; floras of Western North America and Mediterranean climates; California horticulture; California offshore islands; cactus and succulents. **Special Collections:** Oral history collection (60 taped interviews). **Holdings:** 8500 books; 2500 bound periodical volumes; maps (indexed); 1 file cabinet of exchange newsletters from other gardens. **Subscriptions:** 200 journals and other serials. **Services:** Copying; library open to the public by appointment. **Computerized Information Services:** OCLC. **Networks/Consortia:** Member of Total Interlibrary Exchange (TIE). **Remarks:** FAX: (805)563-0352.

★ 14797 ★
Santa Barbara County Genealogical Society - Library (Hist)
Box 1303
Santa Barbara, CA 93116-1303   Doris Crawford, Libn.
Founded: 1974. **Staff:** Prof 1; Other 8. **Subjects:** Genealogy. **Holdings:** 1400 books; 1100 periodical volumes; 12 boxes of Earl Hazard Family history papers; family histories; ancestral charts. **Subscriptions:** 110 journals and other serials. **Services:** Library open to the public. **Publications:** Ancestors West, quarterly - to members, by subscription or exchange; TREE TIPS (newsletter), monthly - to members. **Remarks:** Library located at 711 Santa Barbara St., Santa Barbara, CA 93102.

★ 14798 ★
Santa Barbara County Law Library (Law)
County Courthouse   Phone: (805)568-2296
Santa Barbara, CA 93101   Raymond W. MacGregor, Law Libn.
Founded: 1891. **Staff:** Prof 3; Other 2. **Subjects:** Law. **Special Collections:** Historical Treatises: Collection of California Codes, 1885 to present. **Holdings:** 40,211 volumes; 3247 microfiche; 495 cassettes. **Services:** Interlibrary loan; copying; library open to the public for reference use only. **Automated Operations:** Computerized cataloging and acquisitions. **Computerized Information Services:** Internal database. **Networks/Consortia:** Member of Total Interlibrary Exchange (TIE). **Remarks:** FAX: (805)568-2299. Figures include holdings of a branch library located in Santa Maria, CA. FAX: (805)346-7692. **Staff:** Steven Zaharias, Asst.Libn.

★ 14799 ★
Santa Barbara Historical Society - Gledhill Library (Hist)
136 E. De La Guerra St.
Box 578   Phone: (805)966-1601
Santa Barbara, CA 93102-0578   Michael Redmon, Hd.Libn.
Founded: 1967. **Staff:** Prof 1; Other 8. **Subjects:** Local history and genealogy. **Holdings:** 5000 books; 20,000 photographs; 300 oral history tapes. **Subscriptions:** 20 journals and other serials. **Services:** Copying; photograph reproduction; library open to the public.

★14800★
Santa Barbara Mission Archive-Library (Hist, Rel-Phil)
Old Mission, Upper Laguna St.   Phone: (805)682-4713
Santa Barbara, CA 93105   Fr. Virgilio Biasiol, O.F.M., Dir.
Founded: 1786. **Staff:** Prof 1. **Subjects:** Early missions and missionaries in the Santa Barbara area, Californiana and Mexicana, Spain and Hispanic America. **Special Collections:** De la Guerra Collection (12,000 pages of documents on California); Wilson Collection (rare books; globes; works of art); Alexander Taylor Collection (copies of 2300 documents from the Archdiocesan Archives in San Francisco); photographs of the late mission period in California, Spain, and Mexico (4000); original mission music (1000 brochures); original mission documents (3500). **Holdings:** 15,000 books; 200 scrapbooks, newspaper clippings; 3000 pamphlets. **Services:** Library open to the public on a limited schedule. **Publications:** Newsletter, irregular - to Friends of Archive-Library; list of other publications - available on request. **Special Catalogs:** Catalog of documents and old books. **Remarks:** Maintained by the Franciscan Fathers of California. **Staff:** Rev. Francis F. Guest, O.F.M., Archv.-Hist.

★14801★
Santa Barbara Museum of Art - Museum Library and Archives (Art)
1130 State St.   Phone: (805)963-4364
Santa Barbara, CA 93101   Ron Crozier, Libn.
Founded: 1941. **Staff:** Prof 1; Other 2. **Subjects:** Art, artists. **Special Collections:** Exhibition catalogs (20,000); Single Artist File. **Holdings:** 3000 books; 500 linear feet of archives; pamphlet library consisting of museum calendars and artists' exhibition notices; museum and gallery bulletins; annual reports; newspaper clipping file; sale catalogs; slides. **Subscriptions:** 45 journals and other serials. **Services:** Interlibrary loan; copying; library open to the public with restrictions.

★14802★
Santa Barbara Museum of Natural History - Library (Biol Sci)
2559 Puesta del Sol Rd.   Phone: (805)682-4711
Santa Barbara, CA 93105   Susan G. Dixon, Libn.
Founded: 1929. **Staff:** Prof 1. **Subjects:** Natural history - anthropology, botany, geology, zoology, astronomy. **Special Collections:** Chumash Indians; Harrington California Indian Archives; Stillman Berry Malacology Collection; Channel Islands Archive; Dick Smith Archives; Pacific Voyages Collection; antique nature illustrations. **Holdings:** 30,000 volumes; 200 feet of reprints. **Subscriptions:** 400 journals and other serials. **Services:** Interlibrary loan (limited); copying; library open to the public for reference use only. **Automated Operations:** Computerized cataloging. **Computerized Information Services:** OCLC, DIALOG Information Services. **Publications:** Occasional papers on natural history - by gift and exchange. **Remarks:** FAX: (805)569-3170.

★14803★
Santa Barbara News Press - Library (Publ)
P.O. Box 1359   Phone: (805)564-5200
Santa Barbara, CA 93102-1359   Susan V. DeLapa, Libn.
Staff: Prof 1; Other 1. **Subjects:** Newspaper reference topics. **Holdings:** 1490 books; microfilm; pictures; negatives; 512 linear feet of clippings; 80 pamphlets; 100 maps. **Services:** Library not open to the public. **Remarks:** FAX: (805)966-6258.

★14804★
Santa Clara County Department of Land Use and Development - Library (Plan)
County Government Center, East Wing
70 W. Hedding St.   Phone: (408)299-2521
San Jose, CA 95110   Cheriel Jensen, Libn./Assoc.Plan.
Founded: 1955. **Subjects:** Urban planning, regional planning, housing, census, economics, water, air quality, noise, geology, transportation, energy, environmental assessment. **Special Collections:** Local general and specific plans; energy ordinances from local communities; October 17, 1989 earthquake collection. **Holdings:** 6000 volumes; 1200 environmental impact statements; 2500 maps; current historic aerial photographs; microfiche; 3 VF cabinets of pamphlets and clippings. **Subscriptions:** 40 journals and other serials. **Services:** Library open to the public by appointment for reference use only. **Computerized Information Services:** Internal databases. **Publications:** Acquisitions Lists, irregular - for internal distribution only; Santa Clara County general and specific plans, studies, maps, and photographs related to land use and strategic planning. **Special Catalogs:** Map Catalogue (online). **Remarks:** FAX: (408)279-8537.

★14805★
Santa Clara County Health Department - Library
2220 Moorpark Ave.
San Jose, CA 95128
Defunct.

★14806★
Santa Clara County Law Library (Law)
360 N. 1st St.   Phone: (408)299-3567
San Jose, CA 95113   Susan B. Kuklin, Dir.
Founded: 1874. **Staff:** Prof 2; Other 4. **Subjects:** Law. **Holdings:** 70,000 bound volumes. **Subscriptions:** 263 journals and other serials. **Services:** Copying; library open to the public. **Computerized Information Services:** WESTLAW. Performs searches on fee basis. **Remarks:** FAX: (408)286-9283. **Staff:** Elaine Taranto, Ref.Libn.

★14807★
Santa Clara County Office of Education - EMC/Professional Library (Educ)
100 Skyport Dr.
Mail Code 232   Phone: (408)453-6800
San Jose, CA 95115   Susan Choi, Lib.Serv.Mgr.
Staff: Prof 1; Other 5. **Subjects:** Education, administration, technology. **Special Collections:** Curriculum Resource Center (500 government-funded curriculum programs); MEPIC Resource Center (60 migrant education programs); state-adopted textbooks (3000 volumes); curriculum projects (450 titles). **Holdings:** 13,000 books; 18 VF drawers of newspaper clippings; 8 VF drawers of publisher and vendor catalogs. **Subscriptions:** 341 journals and other serials. **Services:** Interlibrary loan; copying; SDI; library open to residents of Santa Clara County. **Automated Operations:** Computerized circulation. **Computerized Information Services:** DIALOG Information Services. Performs limited searches free of charge. Contact Person: Donna Wheelehan, Lib.Tech.Asst. **Networks/Consortia:** Member of SOUTHNET. **Publications:** Education Bulletin (newsletter). **Remarks:** FAX: (408)453-6659.

★14808★
Santa Clara University - Archives (Hist, Rel-Phil)
Santa Clara, CA 95053   Phone: (408)554-4117
          Julia O'Keefe, Univ.Archv.
Subjects: Mission Santa Clara, Santa Clara University, Jesuits, higher education. **Special Collections:** John J. Montgomery Aviation Collection; Bernard J. Reid papers; Bernard R. Hubbard, S.J. papers and collection of Alaskan Photographs (1926-1961); Mission Santa Clara sacramental registers, 1777-1903; Jerome S. Ricard, S.J., papers (1910-1931) on weather and earthquake forecasting; George M.A. Schoener papers on horticulture. **Holdings:** 1000 books and bound periodical volumes; university archives; all Santa Clara University publications and newspapers. **Services:** Copying; archives open to the public by appointment. **Computerized Information Services:** Internal database; BITNET (electronic mail service). **Remarks:** FAX: (408)554-6827. Electronic mail address(es): JOKEEFE@SCUACC (BITNET).

★14809★
Santa Clara University - Heafey Law Library (Law)
Santa Clara University   Phone: (408)554-4452
Santa Clara, CA 95053   Dean Mary B. Emery, Dir.
Founded: 1963. **Staff:** Prof 7.5; Other 8. **Subjects:** Law. **Holdings:** 125,976 volumes; 1550 AV programs; 6046 volumes on ultrafiche; 83,272 volumes on microfiche. **Subscriptions:** 2498 journals and other serials; 17 newspapers. **Services:** Interlibrary loan; library not open to the public. **Automated Operations:** Computerized cataloging and acquisitions. **Computerized Information Services:** LEXIS, WESTLAW, DIALOG Information Services; BITNET (electronic mail service). **Networks/Consortia:** Member of CLASS, South Bay Cooperative Library System (SBCLS). **Publications:** Acquisitions List, irregular. **Remarks:** FAX: (408)554-5318. **Staff:** Mary D. Hood, Assoc.Dir.; Regina T. Wallen, Hd., Tech.Serv.; Kendra Anderson, Acq.Libn.; Barbara Friedrich, Pub.Serv.Libn.; Prano Amjadi, Cat.; Jill Stephens, Ref.; David Bridgman, Ref.

★ 14810 ★
Santa Clara University - de Saisset Museum - Library
Santa Clara, CA 95053
Subjects: Art publications. **Holdings:** Art magazines, art catalogs from the de Saisset Museum and other institutions. **Remarks:** Currently inactive.

★ 14811 ★
Santa Clara Valley Medical Center - Milton J. Chatton Medical Library (Med)
751 S. Bascom Ave.   Phone: (408)299-5650
San Jose, CA 95128   Shirley Kinoshita, Med.Libn.
Staff: Prof 2; Other 4. **Subjects:** Clinical medicine, nursing, pathology, physical medicine. **Special Collections:** Proescher Pathology Library. **Holdings:** 4000 books; 25,000 bound periodical volumes. **Subscriptions:** 450 journals and other serials. **Services:** Interlibrary loan; copying; SDI; library open to students or professionals in the health care field. **Computerized Information Services:** MEDLINE, DIALOG Information Services. Performs searches on fee basis. **Networks/Consortia:** Member of Medical Library Consortium of Santa Clara Valley. **Remarks:** FAX: (408)299-8859.

★ 14812 ★
Santa Cruz Apiaries - American Apicultural Lending Library (Agri)
Box 2280   Phone: (408)457-8952
Santa Cruz, CA 95063   James Meyer, Dir.
Founded: 1985. **Staff:** 1. **Subjects:** Beekeeping, honey, bees, social insects, beeswax, pollen, propolis. **Holdings:** 400 books. **Services:** Library open to the public by mail. **Computerized Information Services:** MCI Mail (electronic mail service). **Remarks:** FAX: (408)685-3835. Electronic mail address(es): JMEYER (MCI Mail). Telephones answered between 2 and 3 PM only.

★ 14813 ★
Santa Cruz County Historical Trust - Archives (Hist)
1543 Pacific Ave., No.220   Phone: (408)425-3499
Santa Cruz, CA 95060-3928   Rachel McKay, Exec.Dir.
Founded: 1954. **Staff:** Prof 4; Other 2. **Subjects:** Santa Cruz County history, lumbering, tourism, local historical preservation issues. **Special Collections:** Paul D. Johnston Photo Collection (mid-county history; 700 photographs); letters from the Gold Rush era; history of the town band; photographs, 1865 to present; special event programs and memorabilia; history of the Santa Cruz Mission Adobe; Evergreen Pioneer Cemetery records, from 1850; public records; local clipping files. **Holdings:** 400 books; 13 bound local newspapers; 50 reports; 100 manuscripts; 15 archival items; scrapbooks; 50 clippings and photographs. **Subscriptions:** 6 journals and other serials. **Services:** Archives open to the public by appointment for specific research requests. **Publications:** Newsletter, monthly - to members and by subscription. **Remarks:** FAX: (408)429-3499. Alternate telephone number(s): (408)438-7787. FAX: (408)429-1512.

★ 14814 ★
Santa Cruz County Law Library (Law)
55 River St.   Phone: (408)425-2211
Santa Cruz, CA 95060   Patricia J. Pfremmer, Law Libn.
Founded: 1896. **Staff:** Prof 1; Other 1. **Subjects:** Law. **Holdings:** 20,000 books; 1000 bound periodical volumes. **Services:** Interlibrary loan; copying; library open to the public. **Computerized Information Services:** WESTLAW. Performs searches on fee basis. **Remarks:** Maintains branch library of 3600 volumes in Watsonville, CA. FAX: (408)925-4110.

★ 14815 ★
Santa Cruz Sentinel - Library (Publ)
207 Church St.   Phone: (408)423-4242
Santa Cruz, CA 95061   Christine Watson
Staff: Prof 1. **Subjects:** Newspaper reference topics. **Holdings:** 250,000 files; newspaper clippings; photographs; negatives. **Services:** Copying; library open to the public on a limited basis and with restrictions. **Remarks:** FAX: (408)429-9620.

Santa Fe Trail Association Archives
See: **Fort Larned Historical Society, Inc.** (6003)

Santa Fe Trail Center Library
See: **Fort Larned Historical Society, Inc.** (6003)

★ 14816 ★
Santa Monica Hospital Medical Center - Library (Med)
1250 16th St.   Phone: (310)319-4000
Santa Monica, CA 90404   Lenore F. Orfirer, Libn.
Staff: Prof 1. **Subjects:** Medicine. **Holdings:** 1600 books; 1050 bound periodical volumes; 2300 unbound periodical volumes; 200 video cassettes. **Subscriptions:** 125 journals and other serials. **Services:** Interlibrary loan; library not open to the public. **Computerized Information Services:** MEDLARS.

★ 14817 ★
Santa Monica Public Library - California Special Collection (Hist)
1343 6th St.   Phone: (310)458-8629
Santa Monica, CA 90401   Winona Allard, City Libn.
Staff: Prof 12. **Subjects:** Local history. **Special Collections:** Photographs of the Santa Monica Bay area, 1875 to present (2000). **Holdings:** 2600 books; 300 bound periodical volumes; Santa Monica Evening Outlook, 1875 to present, on microfilm. **Subscriptions:** 10 journals and other serials. **Services:** Interlibrary loan (limited); copying; collection open to the public with restrictions. **Automated Operations:** Computerized public access catalog, cataloging, and circulation. **Networks/Consortia:** Member of Metropolitan Cooperative Library System (MCLS). **Special Indexes:** Selective indexing of Santa Monica Evening Outlook. **Remarks:** FAX: (310)458-6980. **Staff:** Nancy O'Neill, Hd. of Ref.; Cynthia Murphy, Image Archv.Libn.

★ 14818 ★
Santa Rosa Health Care - Harold S. Toy, M.D. Memorial Health Science Library (Med)
519 W. Houston St.
P.O. Box 7330, Sta. A   Phone: (512)228-2284
San Antonio, TX 78207-3108   Marjorie McFarland, Med.Libn.
Founded: 1948. **Staff:** Prof 1. **Subjects:** Medicine, nursing, pediatrics, cancer. **Special Collections:** Terminal Care (30 books). **Holdings:** 1879 books; 4451 bound periodical volumes; 193 audio cassette tapes; 4 file drawers of pamphlets. **Subscriptions:** 130 journals and other serials. **Services:** Interlibrary loan; copying; department open to health care professionals only. **Computerized Information Services:** NLM, MEDLINE; miniMEDLINE, NurseSearch. Performs searches on fee basis. **Networks/Consortia:** Member of Health Oriented Libraries of San Antonio (HOLSA). **Remarks:** FAX: (512)228-3177. **Formerly:** Santa Rosa Health Care Corporation - Health Science Library - Educational Resources Department.

★ 14819 ★
Santa Rosa Press Democrat - Editorial Library (Publ)
427 Mendocino Ave.
Box 569   Phone: (707)526-8585
Santa Rosa, CA 95402   Alison J. Head, Lib.Dir.
Staff: Prof 1; Other 5. **Subjects:** Newspaper reference topics. **Holdings:** Books; bound periodical volumes; 1.75 million clippings; 100,000 photographs; newspapers, 1857 to present, on microfilm. **Services:** Copying; SDI; telephone and mail requests only. **Computerized Information Services:** DIALOG Information Services, NEXIS, DataQuick, Legi-Tech, DataTimes. **Special Indexes:** Criminal file index; biographical file index (both on cards). **Remarks:** FAX: (707)546-7538. Published by New York Times Group.

Santa Rose Health Care Corporation - Health Science Library - Educational Resources Department
See: **Santa Rosa Health Care** (14818)

Santa Teresa Laboratory Library
See: **IBM Corporation - Programming Services Division - Santa Teresa Laboratory Library** (7628)

★ 14820 ★
Santa Ynez Valley Historical Society - Ellen Gleason Library (Hist)
Box 181   Phone: (805)688-7889
Santa Ynez, CA 93460   Phil Lockwood, Cur.
Founded: 1961. **Staff:** 1. **Subjects:** History of Santa Ynez Valley, Santa Barbara County, early California. **Special Collections:** Early land deeds. **Holdings:** 1000 books. **Services:** Library open to the public for reference use only by appointment.

Monserrate Santana de Pales Library
See: **University of Puerto Rico - Library System (19245)**

Sante et Bien-Etre Social Canada
See: **Canada - Health and Welfare Canada (2750)**

★ 14821 ★
(Santiago) Centro Cultural Domenico Americano - USIS Collection
   (Educ)
Ave. Salvador Estrella Sadala
Apdo. 767   Phone: (809)582-6627
Santiago, Dominican Republic   Annabella Cabral, Lib.Dir.
Founded: 1963. **Staff:** 3. **Holdings:** 5684 books. **Subscriptions:** 26 journals and other serials; 8 newspapers. **Services:** Interlibrary loan; SDI; library open to the public. **Remarks:** FAX: (809)587-3858. Maintained or supported by the U.S. Information Agency. Focus is on materials that will assist peoples outside the United States to learn about the United States, its people, history, culture, political processes, and social milieux. **Staff:** Florinda Luna; Betzaida Vargas.

★ 14822 ★
(Santiago) Instituto Chileno-Norteamericano de Cultura - USIS
   Collection (Educ)
Moneda 1467
P.O. Box 9286
Santiago, Chile   Maria Teresa Herrero, Lib.Dir.
Founded: 1941. **Staff:** 6. **Subjects:** United States culture. **Special Collections:** Teaching English as a second language; higher education; environment; American legislation. **Holdings:** 10,000 books; 3000 microfiche; 710 reels of microfilm. **Subscriptions:** 128 journals and other serials; 10 newspapers. **Services:** Interlibrary loan; SDI; library open to the public. **Computerized Information Services:** LEGI-SLATE. **Remarks:** Maintained or supported by the U.S. Information Agency. Focus is on materials that will assist peoples outside the United States to learn about the United States, its people, history, culture, political processes, and social milieux. Institute also services two provincial centers in Concepcion and Valparaiso, Chile. **Staff:** Magaly Rojas; Maria Teresa Dussert; Veronica Szabo.

(Santo Domingo) USIS Library
See: **Biblioteca Lincoln (1823)**

★ 14823 ★
(Santos) Centro Cultural Brasil-Estados Unidos - USIS Collection
   (Educ)
Rua Jorge Tibirica, 5   Phone: 132 349965
11100 Santos, SP, Brazil   Mirian Lopez Goncalves, Lib.Coord.
Founded: 1948. **Staff:** 5. **Holdings:** 15,000 books. **Subscriptions:** 35 journals and other serials; 3 newspapers. **Services:** Library open to the public. **Remarks:** Maintained or supported by the U.S. Information Agency. Focus is on materials that will assist peoples outside the United States to learn about the United States, its people, history, culture, political processes, and social milieux. **Staff:** Neube Estela Fumagalli Vieira, Libn.

★ 14824 ★
(Sao Luis) Instituto Cultural Brasil-Estados Unidos - USIS Collection
   (Educ)
Rua Nina Rodrigues, 247
65000 Sao Luis, Maranhao, Brazil
Remarks: Maintained or supported by the U.S. Information Agency. Focus is on materials that will assist peoples outside the United States to learn about the United States, its people, history, culture, political processes, and social milieux.

★ 14825 ★
(Sao Paulo) Uniao Cultural Brasil-Estados Unidos - USIS Collection
   (Educ)
Rua Cel. Oscar Porto, 208   Phone: 11 8851022
04003 Sao Paulo, SP, Brazil   Roseli Ferreira de Azevedo, Lib.Hd.
Founded: 1942. **Staff:** 14. **Subjects:** United States; Brazilian culture and civilization. **Special Collections:** Rare Records Collection. **Holdings:** 34,500 books; 4400 bound periodical volumes; 5000 records; 70 compact discs; 30,400 slides; 700 cassette tapes; 24,000 clippings; 800 lyrics; 1700 guides; 100 videotapes; reports; manuscripts; patents; archival material; microfiche. **Subscriptions:** 70 journals and other serials; 7 newspapers. **Services:** Interlibrary loan; copying; SDI; library open to the public. **Publications:** Inquire; Annotated Bibliography. **Remarks:** FAX: 11 8850376. Alternate telephone number(s): 11 8851233. Maintained or supported by the U.S. Information Agency. Focus is on materials that will assist peoples outside the United States to learn about the United States, its people, history, culture, political processes, and social milieux.

★ 14826 ★
(Sao Paulo) USIS Reference Library (Educ)
Rua Pe. Joao Manoel, 933   Phone: 11 641775
01411 Sao Paulo, SP, Brazil   Marisa Teixeira Pinto, Lib.Dir.
Founded: 1952. **Staff:** 3. **Subjects:** Economics and finance, environment, minorities, labor, science and technology. **Holdings:** 5000 books; 1380 reels of microfilm. **Subscriptions:** 200 journals and other serials; 6 newspapers. **Services:** Interlibrary loan; copying; SDI; library open to the public. **Remarks:** FAX: 11 8521395. Telex: 11-31574; 11-22183. Maintained or supported by the U.S. Information Agency. Focus is on materials that will assist peoples outside the United States to learn about the United States, its people, history, culture, political processes, and social milieux. **Staff:** Sonia Martingo Tulha, Tech.Libn.

Sapelo Marine Institute - Library
See: **University of Georgia - Science Library (18605)**

★ 14827 ★
Sapporo American Center - USIS Library (Educ)
Nishi 28-chome
Oodori
Chuo-ku
Sapporo 064, Japan   Phone: 11 6410211
Founded: 1948. **Staff:** 2. **Subjects:** International relations, literature, U.S. society, art, global economy. **Special Collections:** CIS Collection. **Holdings:** 4000 books; 100 bound periodical volumes; 400 reports; 30,000 microfiche; 150 videotapes. **Subscriptions:** 100 journals and other serials; 3 newspapers. **Services:** Interlibrary loan; copying; SDI; library open to the public. **Computerized Information Services:** DIALOG Information Services. **Remarks:** FAX: 11 6410911. Maintained or supported by the U.S. Information Agency. Focus is on materials that will assist peoples outside the United States to learn about the United States, its people, history, culture, political processes, and social milieux. **Staff:** Kayoko Okubo; Mayumi Abiko, Ref.Libn.

★ 14828 ★
(Sarajevo) Americki Centar - USIS Library (Educ)
Omladinska broj 1
Post Box 82
YU-71000 Sarajevo, Yugoslavia
Remarks: Maintained or supported by the U.S. Information Agency. Focus is on materials that will assist peoples outside the United States to learn about the United States, its people, history, culture, political processes, and social milieux.

Sarasota County Public Library System - Environmental Library of
   Sarasota County
See: **Environmental Library of Sarasota County (5379)**

★ 14829 ★
Sarasota Memorial Hospital - Medical Library (Med)
1700 S. Tamiami Trail   Phone: (813)953-1730
Sarasota, FL 34239-3555   Barbara C. Hartman, Med.Libn.
Founded: 1960. **Staff:** Prof 1. **Subjects:** Medicine, nursing. **Holdings:** 2000 books; 10,000 bound periodical volumes. **Subscriptions:** 200 journals. **Services:** Interlibrary loan; copying; library open to the public. **Computerized Information Services:** NLM; CD-ROM; DOCLINE (electronic mail service). **Networks/Consortia:** Member of West Coast Library Consortium (WELCO), Tampa Bay Medical Library Network. **Remarks:** FAX: (813)953-1218.

★ 14830 ★
Saratoga Community Hospital - Health Science Library (Med)
15000 Gratiot Ave.   Phone: (313)245-1200
Detroit, MI 48205   Viju Karnik, Med.Libn.
Staff: Prof 1. **Subjects:** Medicine, nursing, hospital administration.
Holdings: 1100 books; 300 bound periodical volumes. **Subscriptions:** 137
journals and other serials. **Services:** Interlibrary loan; library not open to the
public. **Computerized Information Services:** BRS Information
Technologies, MEDLINE. **Remarks:** Alternate telephone number(s): 245-
1213. FAX: (313)245-1452.

★ 14831 ★
Saratoga County Historical Society - Brookside Saratoga County
   History Center (Hist)
6 Charlton St.   Phone: (518)885-4000
Ballston Spa, NY 12020   William C. Garrison, Coll.Mgr.
Founded: 1971. **Subjects:** Saratoga County, New York. **Holdings:** 901
volumes; manuscripts; photographs; genealogy materials. **Services:**
Copying; library open to the public. **Computerized Information Services:**
Internal database. **Publications:** Local History, quarterly; Brookside
Columns, monthly. **Special Catalogs:** Catalogue of the Manuscript
Collection (1979); Genealogical Guide to Saratoga County, NY (1980).

★ 14832 ★
Saratoga Hospital - Medical Staff Library (Med)
211 Church St.   Phone: (518)583-8301
Saratoga Springs, NY 12866   Julie VanDussen, Mgr.
Staff: 4. **Subjects:** Medicine, nursing, surgery, psychiatry. **Holdings:** 340
books. **Subscriptions:** 32 journals and other serials. **Services:** Interlibrary
loan; copying; library open to the public for reference use only.
Computerized Information Services: Internal database. **Networks/
Consortia:** Member of Capital District Library Council for Reference &
Research Resources (CDLC).

Saratoga National Historical Park
See: **U.S. Natl. Park Service** (17774)

★ 14833 ★
Saratogian - Library (Publ)
20 Lake Ave.   Phone: (518)584-4242
Saratoga Springs, NY 12866   Eleanor Brower, Libn.
Founded: 1894. **Staff:** 1. **Subjects:** Newspaper reference topics. **Special
Collections:** Saratogian, 1890 to present, (microfilm). **Holdings:** Microfilm.
Services: Interlibrary loan; copying; library open to the public.

Sargeant Memorial Room
See: **Norfolk Public Library** (11847)

★ 14834 ★
Sargent & Lundy Engineers - Computer Software Library (Comp Sci)
55 E. Monroe   Phone: (312)269-2582
Chicago, IL 60603   William J. Kakish, Supv., CSL
Staff: 5. **Subjects:** Computer applications. **Holdings:** 250 books; 723
computer program manuals; 70 VF drawers of computer program
documentation; microfiche. **Subscriptions:** 27 journals and other serials.
Services: Copying; library open to the public by appointment. **Automated
Operations:** Computerized circulation. **Computerized Information Services:**
DIALOG Information Services, Telenet Telecommunications Corporation.
Networks/Consortia: Member of ILLINET. **Remarks:** FAX: (312)269-
3680; 269-3596; 269-3475; 269-3569 (to verify). Telex: 280 603.

★ 14835 ★
Sargent & Lundy Engineers - Technical Library (Sci-Engr)
55 E. Monroe St., Rm. 26U63   Phone: (312)269-3526
Chicago, IL 60603   Helen P. Heisler, Libn.
Founded: 1969. **Staff:** Prof 1. **Subjects:** Engineering - civil, mechanical,
electrical; nuclear science; public utilities; air and water pollution. **Holdings:**
1000 books; 85 bound periodical volumes; 20 drawers of standards and
specifications; 20 VF drawers. **Subscriptions:** 250 journals and other serials.
Services: Interlibrary loan; copying; library open to other libraries by
appointment.

★ 14836 ★
David Sarnoff Research Center - Library (Sci-Engr)
CN 5300   Phone: (609)734-2608
Princeton, NJ 08543-5300   Wendy Chu, Mgr., Lib.Serv.
Founded: 1941. **Staff:** Prof 1; Other 1. **Subjects:** Radio, electronics,
television, physics, chemistry, mathematics, metallurgy, acoustics,
computers, semiconducting materials, space technology. **Special
Collections:** David Sarnoff Collection (history of communications; 1000
books). **Holdings:** 30,000 books; 12,000 bound periodical volumes; 3000
reels of microfilm; 110 VF drawers of company reports; 100 VF drawers of
pamphlets. **Subscriptions:** 350 journals and other serials. **Services:**
Interlibrary loan; copying; library open to the public by appointment.
Automated Operations: Computerized public access catalog, cataloging,
acquisitions, serials, and circulation. **Computerized Information Services:**
DIALOG Information Services, ORBIT Search Service, STN International,
Dow Jones News/Retrieval, OCLC. **Publications:** Library Bulletin - for
internal distribution only. **Remarks:** FAX: (609)734-2339. David Sarnoff
Research Center is a subsidiary of SRI International. **Staff:** Larry Eubank,
Coord., Info.Serv.

★ 14837 ★
Sasaki Associates, Inc. - Library (Plan)
64 Pleasant St.   Phone: (617)926-3300
Watertown, MA 02172   Cynthia A. Fordham, Libn.
Founded: 1966. **Staff:** Prof 1. **Subjects:** Landscape architecture,
architecture, planning, environment, engineering. **Holdings:** 3500 books; 55
bound periodical volumes; 600 office publications. **Subscriptions:** 150
journals and other serials. **Services:** Library not open to the public.
Computerized Information Services: DIALOG Information Services.
Publications: DIALOGUE, biweekly - for internal distribution only.
Remarks: FAX: (617)924-2748.

★ 14838 ★
Saskatchewan Alcohol & Drug Abuse Commission - Library (Med)
1942 Hamilton St., 3rd Fl.   Phone: (306)787-4656
Regina, SK, Canada S4P 3V7   Andrew Stirling, Libn.
Founded: 1968. **Staff:** Prof 1. **Subjects:** Alcohol and alcoholism, drugs and
other dependencies, health care. **Holdings:** 5000 books; 400 bound periodical
volumes; 100 archival items; reports; pamphlets; government publications.
Subscriptions: 90 journals and other serials. **Services:** Interlibrary loan;
copying; library open to the public. **Automated Operations:** Computerized
cataloging, acquisitions, and circulation. **Computerized Information
Services:** BRS Information Technologies, DIALOG Information Services.
Performs searches free of charge. **Remarks:** FAX: (306)787-4300.

★ 14839 ★
Saskatchewan Archives Board (Hist)
University of Regina   Phone: (306)787-4068
Regina, SK, Canada S4S 0A2   Trevor J.D. Powell, Prov.Archv.
Founded: 1945. **Staff:** Prof 14; Other 15. **Subjects:** Saskatchewan history.
Holdings: 600 books; 2000 bound periodical volumes; 35,000 feet of
archives; 830,000 historical photographs; 26,000 reels of microfilm; 15,000
hours of sound recordings; 16,300 maps; 12,371 architectural drawings.
Services: Copying; archives open to the public. **Publications:** Saskatchewan
History, 3/year; Saskatchewan Archives Reference Series; irregular reports.
Special Indexes: Index to Saskatchewan History (volumes 1-30). **Remarks:**
Maintains additional office at Murray Bldg., University of Saskatchewan,
Saskatoon, SK S7N 0W0. FAX: (306)787-1975 (Regina); (306)933-7305
(Saskatoon). **Staff:** Mr. D. Hande, Dir., Saskatoon Off.; Mr. D. Herperger,
Dir., Govt.Rec.; Mr. D. Richan, Dir., Hist.Rec.; Mr. K. Gebhard, Staff
Archv.; Ms. J. Harvey, Staff Archv.; Mrs. L. McIntyre-Putz, Staff Archv.;
Mrs. M. Fox, Staff Archv.; Mr. D. Mombourquette, Staff Archv.; Mrs. N.
Small, Staff Archv.; Ms. M-L. Perron, Francophone Archv.; Mr. I.
Saunders, City of Regina Archv.

★ 14840 ★
Saskatchewan Cancer Foundation - Allan Blair Memorial Clinic -
   Library (Med)
4101 Dewdney Ave.   Phone: (306)359-2203
Regina, SK, Canada S4T 7T1   Barbara Karchewski, Libn.
Founded: 1948. **Staff:** 1. **Subjects:** Cancer, medical and radiation oncology,
physics. **Holdings:** 900 books; 500 bound periodical volumes; 1500 reprint
articles on cancer. **Subscriptions:** 100 journals and other serials. **Services:**
Interlibrary loan; copying; library open to medical professionals and some
research personnel. **Remarks:** FAX: (306)359-2688.

Saskatchewan Cross-Cultural Centre
See: One Sky, The Saskatchewan Cross-Cultural Centre (12420)

★14841★
Saskatchewan Department of Agriculture and Food - Library (Agri, Bus-Fin)
B33-3085 Albert St.
Regina, SK, Canada S4S 0B1   Phone: (306)787-5151
Founded: 1974. **Staff:** Prof 1; Other 3. **Subjects:** Agricultural economics, marketing, and statistics; extension; current Canadian agriculture; food products research and marketing. **Holdings:** 1500 books; 400 bound periodical volumes; 6000 pamphlets and technical reports; 1450 Canadian, U.S., international government annuals; 10,000 fact sheets; 4 VF drawers. **Subscriptions:** 650 journals and other serials; 10 newspapers. **Services:** Interlibrary loan; copying; library open to the public for reference use only. **Computerized Information Services:** BRS Information Technologies, DIALOG Information Services, CAN/OLE, AgriData Network, Sydney Library Systems; Envoy 100 (electronic mail service). **Publications:** Information Notes, 6/year; periodical list, annual. **Remarks:** FAX: (306)787-0216. Electronic mail address(es): SK.AG.LIB (Envoy 100). **Staff:** Olive MacDonald, Lib.Techn. II; Shirley Burns, Lib.Techn.I.

★14842★
Saskatchewan Department of Culture, Multiculturalism and Recreation - Resource Centre (Rec, Env-Cons)
1942 Hamilton St., Rm. 224   Phone: (306)787-5715
Regina, SK, Canada S4P 3V7   Randi Kelly, Libn.
Founded: 1987. **Staff:** Prof 3; Other 2. **Subjects:** Plains heritage archeology, architectural conservation, Saskatchewan history, Canadian arts and multiculturalism, recreation, sports and sports administration, parks management, fisheries, wildlife, forestry, lands management, historic parks. **Special Collections:** Saskatchewan local histories. **Holdings:** 7000 books; 200 bound periodical volumes; 500 other cataloged items. **Subscriptions:** 250 journals and other serials; 20 newspapers. **Services:** Interlibrary loan; center not open to the public. **Automated Operations:** Computerized public access catalog, cataloging, serials, and circulation. **Computerized Information Services:** DIALOG Information Services, Newswatch Media Sources, UTLAS, CAN/OLE; Envoy 100 (electronic mail service). Performs searches on fee basis. **Special Indexes:** Saskatchewan Local History Geographical Index. **Remarks:** FAX: (306)787-5742. Electronic mail address(es): SASK.SPRC (Envoy 100). **Staff:** Tanya Evancio, Ref.Serv.; Ilya Margoshes, Tech.Serv.

★14843★
Saskatchewan Department of Economic Diversification & Trade - Business Library (Soc Sci)
1870 Albert St., Main Fl.   Phone: (306)787-7460
Regina, SK, Canada S4P 3V7   Jan McDowell, Bus.Info. & Res.Off.
Founded: 1983. **Staff:** Prof 1; Other 1. **Subjects:** Tourism, business, international trade, co-operatives, economics, diversification and industrial development, science and technology, joint ventures. **Holdings:** 2000 books; 2000 reports; trade directories; government documents; files. **Subscriptions:** 300 journals and other serials; 6 newspapers. **Services:** Interlibrary loan. **Automated Operations:** Computerized cataloging. **Computerized Information Services:** DIALOG Information Services, Info Globe, CAN/OLE, INSIGHT; Envoy 100 (electronic mail service). **Remarks:** FAX: (306)787-7055; Electronic mail address(es): SRTSB (Envoy 100).

Saskatchewan Department of Education
See: Saskatchewan Education - Resource Centre (14851)

★14844★
Saskatchewan Department of Environment and Public Safety - Library (Env-Cons)
Walter Scott Bldg.
3085 Albert St.
Regina, SK, Canada S4S 0B1   Phone: (306)787-6114
                                    Janice Szuch, Lib.Supv.
Founded: 1974. **Staff:** 1. **Subjects:** Water pollution, air pollution, sustainable development, environmental protection and policy, impact assessments, hazardous wastes, wastewater treatment. **Holdings:** 1000 books; 25 bound periodical volumes; 6000 reports; 10 VF drawers of pamphlets; 32 shelves of unbound periodicals. **Subscriptions:** 129 journals and other serials. **Services:** Interlibrary loan; library open to the public. **Publications:** Acquisitions list, irregular. **Remarks:** FAX: (306)787-0197.

★14845★
Saskatchewan Department of Highways and Transportation - Planning Support Library (Trans, Plan)
1855 Victoria Ave., 7th Fl.   Phone: (306)787-4778
Regina, SK, Canada S4P 3V5   Ellen Basler, Libn.
Founded: 1957. **Staff:** Prof 1. **Subjects:** Highway and traffic engineering, transportation planning, management, traffic safety. **Holdings:** 10,000 books. **Subscriptions:** 150 journals and other serials. **Services:** Interlibrary loan; copying; SDI; library open to the public for reference use only. **Computerized Information Services:** DIALOG Information Services. **Publications:** Library acquisitions, quarterly. **Remarks:** FAX: (306)787-3963.

★14846★
Saskatchewan Department of Human Resources, Labour and Employment - Library (Bus-Fin, Soc Sci)
1870 Albert St.   Phone: (306)787-2429
Regina, SK, Canada S4P 3V7   Fraser Russell, Libn.
Founded: 1957. **Staff:** Prof 1. **Subjects:** Labor law and legislation, occupational health, women in the work force, sexism in society, changing roles of women, economic conditions of Canada, industrial relations, income security, trade unions, employment programs. **Special Collections:** Saskatchewan collective labor agreements (500). **Holdings:** 4500 books; 500 bound periodical volumes; 860 linear feet of Canada and Saskatchewan government publications and other documents. **Subscriptions:** 530 journals and other periodicals; 5 newspapers. **Services:** Interlibrary loan; copying; library open to the public on a limited basis. **Computerized Information Services:** DIALOG Information Services, CAN/OLE, WILSONLINE, CCINFO, BRS Information Technologies, MEDLARS; Envoy 100 (electronic mail service). **Publications:** Labour Bibliographies, irregular; Acquisitions List, monthly. **Remarks:** FAX: (306)787-7229. Electronic mail address(es): RAD.SAFETY (Envoy 100).

★14847★
Saskatchewan Department of Justice - Civil Law Library (Law)
1874 Scarth St., 9th Fl.   Phone: (306)787-7281
Regina, SK, Canada S4P 3V7   Cheryl Charron, Lib.Techn.
Staff: 1. **Subjects:** Law. **Holdings:** Figures not available. **Subscriptions:** 78 journals and other serials. **Services:** Library not open to the public. **Computerized Information Services:** QL Systems. **Remarks:** FAX: (306)787-9111.

★14848★
Saskatchewan Department of Justice - Court of Appeal Library (Law)
Court House, 2425 Victoria Ave.   Phone: (306)787-7399
Regina, SK, Canada S4P 3V7   Shirley A. Hurnard, Libn.
Staff: Prof 1. **Subjects:** Law - Canadian, American, English. **Holdings:** 8000 volumes. **Subscriptions:** 30 journals and other serials. **Services:** Library not open to the public. **Remarks:** FAX: (306)569-0155.

★14849★
Saskatchewan Department of Parks and Renewable Resources - Fisheries Management Library (Biol Sci)
Box 3003   Phone: (306)953-2891
Prince Albert, SK, Canada S6V   Brian Christensen, Fisheries
6G1   Ecologist
Staff: 1. **Subjects:** Fisheries management, fisheries and aquatic biology, fish enhancement, aquaculture, aquatic habitat protection, commercial and sport fishing. **Holdings:** Books; pamphlets; reports; bulletins; periodical volumes. **Subscriptions:** 11 journals and other serials. **Services:** Library open to the public. **Remarks:** FAX: (306)953-2300.

★14850★
Saskatchewan Department of Social Services - Resource Centre (Soc Sci)
1920 Broad St.   Phone: (306)787-3680
Regina, SK, Canada S4P 3V6   Muriel Griffiths, Lib.Techn.
Staff: 1. **Subjects:** Social work, child welfare, social policy and welfare, management, juvenile delinquency and corrections, social sciences. **Holdings:** 4600 books; 200 bound periodical volumes. **Subscriptions:** 80 journals and other serials. **Services:** Interlibrary loan; copying; center open to the public. **Remarks:** FAX: (306)787-0925.

★ 14851 ★
Saskatchewan Education - Resource Centre (Educ)
2220 College Ave.   Phone: (306)787-2262
Regina, SK, Canada S4P 3V7   Charlene Kramer, Libn.
Founded: 1976. **Staff:** Prof 2; Other 2. **Subjects:** Education. **Holdings:** 25,000 books; ERIC microfiche; vertical files; test collections; large print books; audiotapes; braille books. **Subscriptions:** 330 journals and other serials. **Services:** Interlibrary loan; copying; center open to the public for reference use only. **Computerized Information Services:** BRS Information Technologies, DIALOG Information Services; internal database; CD-ROMs (ERIC, Microlog, and Bibliofile); Envoy 100 (electronic mail service). **Publications:** Bibliographies - for internal distribution only. **Special Catalogs:** Special Format Catalog (for teachers of visually impaired students in Saskatchewan). **Remarks:** FAX: (306)787-2223. Alternate telephone number(s): 787-5998. Electronic mail address(es): SRED.ILL (Envoy 100). **Staff:** Wilma Olmsted, Lib.Techn.; Rebecca Landau, Spec.Mtls.Libn.

★ 14852 ★
Saskatchewan Genealogical Society - Library (Hist)
1870 Lorne St.   Phone: (306)780-9207
Regina, SK, Canada S4P 2L7   Laura M. Hanowski, Libn.
Founded: 1969. **Staff:** Prof 1. **Subjects:** Genealogy, local and family history. **Special Collections:** I.G.I. Ontario Land Records Index; 1891 census information for Northwest Territories, Manitoba, and Ontario; Index to St. Catherines House (1857-1871, 1882); Saskatchewan Cemetery Record; Loiselle Index; Ontario marriage records (microfilm); Ontario cemetery records (microfilm); Griffith Valuations for Ireland (microfiche); Old Parochical Register Index (microfiche). **Holdings:** 5000 books; 35 bound periodical volumes; 13,000 microfiche; 900 reels of microfilm; 10 videotapes. **Subscriptions:** 255 journals and other serials. **Services:** Interlibrary loan; copying; library open to the public for reference use only. **Special Indexes:** Periodical Index; Obituary Index; Cemetery Index. **Remarks:** FAX: (306)781-6021.

★ 14853 ★
Saskatchewan Health - Library (Med)
3475 Albert St.   Phone: (306)787-8699
Regina, SK, Canada S4S 6X6   Lynn Kozun, Libn.
Founded: 1940. **Staff:** 4. **Subjects:** Public health, nutrition, public health nursing, medicine. **Holdings:** 6000 books; 8000 bound periodical volumes; 2000 technical reports. **Subscriptions:** 358 journals and other serials. **Services:** Interlibrary loan; copying (limited); library open to health professionals. **Computerized Information Services:** DIALOG Information Services, CAN/OLE, BRS Information Technologies; Envoy 100 (electronic mail service). **Publications:** Library Acquisitions, monthly. **Remarks:** FAX: (306)787-0218. Electronic mail address(es): ILL.SRPH (Envoy 100).

★ 14854 ★
Saskatchewan Hospital - Department of Psychiatric Services - Staff Library (Med)
P.O. Box 39   Phone: (306)446-7913
North Battleford, SK, Canada S9A 2X8   Doris Allan, Libn.
Staff: 1. **Subjects:** Psychiatry, medicine, psychology, nursing, hospital administration. **Holdings:** 1500 books; 700 bound periodical volumes. **Subscriptions:** 35 journals and other serials; 5 newspapers. **Services:** Interlibrary loan; copying; library open to the public with special permission.

★ 14855 ★
Saskatchewan Indian Federated College - Library (Area-Ethnic)
University of Regina
118 College W.   Phone: (306)584-8333
Regina, SK, Canada S4S 0A2   Phyllis G. Lerat, Libn.
Founded: 1977. **Staff:** Prof 2; Other 9. **Subjects:** Indian studies; art; band administration; health careers; Indian education; management; economics; Indian languages, linguistics, and literature. **Special Collections:** Extension collection; RG 10 series; Eeniwuk collection. **Holdings:** 16,800 books; 533 bound periodical volumes; 20 VF drawers; 38 VF drawers of clippings, pamphlets, reports; 24 drawers of microfilm/microfiche; 250 videotapes. **Subscriptions:** 120 journals and other serials; 40 newspapers. **Services:** Interlibrary loan; copying; library open to the public with restrictions. **Automated Operations:** NOTIS. **Publications:** Acquisitions list, monthly. **Remarks:** FAX: (306)584-0955. A branch library is maintained on the Saskatoon campus, 310 20th St. E., Saskatoon, SK, CA S7K 0A7. **Staff:** Allan Groen, Libn.

★ 14856 ★
Saskatchewan Indian Federated College - Saskatoon Campus Library (Area-Ethnic)
310 20th St., E.   Phone: (306)931-1825
Saskatoon, SK, Canada S7K 0A7   Phyllis G. Lerat, Hd.Libn.
Founded: 1985. **Staff:** Prof 1; Other 2. **Subjects:** North American Indian studies, social work, and art. **Holdings:** 4782 books; 28 bound periodical volumes; 30 videotapes; 12 VF drawers. **Subscriptions:** 54 journals and other serials; 25 newspapers. **Services:** Interlibrary loan; copying; library open to the public with restrictions. **Remarks:** FAX: (306)665-0175.

★ 14857 ★
Saskatchewan Institute of Applied Science and Technology , Kelsey Campus - Learning Resources Centre (Educ)
Idylwyld Dr. & 33rd St., W.
P.O. Box 1520   Phone: (306)933-6417
Saskatoon, SK, Canada S7K 3R5   T.K. Harrison, Libn.
Founded: 1963. **Staff:** Prof 2; Other 7. **Subjects:** Applied sciences, health sciences, industrial arts, service programs. **Holdings:** 41,000 books; 9480 AV programs; 379 reels of microfilm; 100 maps. **Subscriptions:** 600 journals and other serials. **Services:** Interlibrary loan; copying; center open to the public for reference use only. **Automated Operations:** Computerized acquisitions, cataloging, circulation, and public access catalog. **Computerized Information Services:** Envoy 100 (electronic mail service). **Remarks:** Alternate telephone number(s): 933-7617. FAX: (306)933-6490. Electronic mail address(es): ILL.SSSI (Envoy 100). **Staff:** E. Crosthwaite, Hd., AV Area

★ 14858 ★
Saskatchewan Institute of Applied Science & Technology, Palliser Campus - Library (Sci-Engr, Bus-Fin)
Saskatechewan St. & 6th Ave. N.W.
P.O. Box 1420   Phone: (306)694-3255
Moose Jaw, SK, Canada S6H 4R4   A.E. Wallbridge, Libn.
Founded: 1961. **Staff:** Prof 1; Other 3. **Subjects:** Business, technology, industrial arts. **Holdings:** 16,500 books; 771 AV items (films, videotapes, kits); 1200 microforms; 100 VF drawers; Canadian Government publications. **Subscriptions:** 350 journals and other serials. **Services:** Interlibrary loan; copying; SDI; library open to the public with restrictions. **Automated Operations:** Computerized cataloging, circulation, and acquisitions. **Computerized Information Services:** DIALOG Information Services, UTLAS, CAN/OLE, CCINFO; Envoy 100 (electronic mail service). **Remarks:** Library is a selective depository for Canadian Government publications. FAX: (306)693-3321. Electronic mail address(es): SMJT (Envoy 100). **Also Known As:** SIAST. **Staff:** Beverly Brooks, Lib.Techn.; Shawna North, Lib.Techn.

★ 14859 ★
Saskatchewan Institute of Applied Science & Technology, Wascana Campus - Resource and Information Centre (Educ)
4635 Wascana Pkwy.
Box 556   Phone: (306)787-4321
Regina, SK, Canada S4P 3A3   Colleen Warren, Mgr., Lib.Serv.
Founded: 1972. **Staff:** Prof 1; Other 9. **Subjects:** Nursing, health sciences, dental nursing, agriculture, industrial arts, business, adult basic education. **Holdings:** 50,000 books and AV programs. **Subscriptions:** 450 journals and other serials; 8 newspapers. **Services:** Interlibrary loan; copying; SDI; center open to the public for reference use only. **Automated Operations:** Integrated library system (MULTILIS). **Networks/Consortia:** Member of Health Sciences Library Council. **Remarks:** Includes holdings of libraries at St. John Street Campus, Albert South Campus, Winnipeg North Campus, Maxwell Crescent Campus, and branch libraries in North Battleford, Yorkton, Moose Jaw, and Prince Albert. **Formerly:** Wascana Institute of Applied Arts and Sciences. **Also Known As:** SIAST.

★ 14860 ★
Saskatchewan Legislative Library (Hist, Law, Soc Sci)
234 Legislative Bldg.   Phone: (306)787-2276
Regina, SK, Canada S4S 0B3   Marian Powell, Leg.Libn.
Founded: 1905. **Staff:** Prof 5; Other 9. **Subjects:** Political and social sciences with emphasis on Canada; history, especially Canadian and Western Canadian. **Special Collections:** Saskatchewan, Canadian, and Ontario Government documents (176,813 volumes). **Holdings:** 33,592 books; 150,385 microforms, including 149,314 government publications. **Subscriptions:** 744 journals and other serials; 145 newspapers. **Services:**

Interlibrary loan; copying; library open to the public with restrictions on borrowing. **Automated Operations:** Integrated library system (NOTIS). **Computerized Information Services:** CODOC (Cooperative Documents Network Project), DIALOG Information Services, CAN/OLE, QL Systems, LEXIS, NEXIS, Info Globe, Infomart Online; Envoy 100 (electronic mail service). **Publications:** Selected List of Accessions, bimonthly; Checklist of Saskatchewan Government Publications, monthly; Annual Report. **Special Catalogs:** Publications of the governments of the North-West Territories, 1876-1905, and the Province of Saskatchewan, 1905-1952; **Special Indexes:** Saskatchewan Newspaper Index, 1978-1981. **Remarks:** FAX: (306)787-1772. Electronic mail address(es): SASKLEG.LIBR (Envoy 100). **Staff:** Judy Brennan, Asst.Leg.Libn.; A. Yvonne Mack, Members' Serv.Libn.; Tim Prince, Ref.Libn.; Pat Kolesar, Tech.Serv.Libn.

★14861★
Saskatchewan Museum of Natural History - Library (Biol Sci)
Family Foundation
Wascana Park   Phone: (306)787-2850
Regina, SK, Canada S4P 3V7   Donna Tanton, Cur.Sec.
Staff: Prof 3. **Subjects:** Archeology, anthropology and ethnology, paleontology and earth sciences, botany and other life sciences, conservation and wildlife, taxidermy. **Holdings:** 2000 books; 225 bound periodical volumes; 200 unbound items. **Subscriptions:** 50 journals and other serials. **Services:** Library open to researchers and students by appointment only. **Remarks:** FAX: (306)787-2645. **Staff:** M. Hanna, Archeo.Libn.; T. Tokaryk, Earth Sci.Libn.; D. Tanton, Libn.

★14862★
Saskatchewan Piping Industry - Joint Training Board - Library (Sci-Engr)
1366 Cornwall St.   Phone: (306)522-4237
Regina, SK, Canada S4R 2H5   Darlene Pellerin, Sec.
Founded: 1971. **Staff:** 1. **Subjects:** Plumbing, pipefitting, welding. **Holdings:** 500 volumes; 28 visual aids; training manuals. **Services:** Library not open to the public. **Remarks:** FAX: (306)781-7949.

★14863★
Saskatchewan Power Corporation - Technical Services & Research Library (Energy)
2025 Victoria Ave.   Phone: (306)566-3333
Regina, SK, Canada S4P 0S1   Debbie Tsakires, Lib.Ck.
Founded: 1970. **Staff:** 1. **Subjects:** Electric power engineering, economics, statistics, management. **Holdings:** 500 books; 300 unbound periodical volumes. **Subscriptions:** 125 journals and other serials. **Services:** Interlibrary loan; library not open to the public. **Remarks:** FAX: (306)566-3348.

★14864★
Saskatchewan Provincial Library
1352 Winnipeg St.   Phone: (306)787-2976
Regina, SK, Canada S4P 3V7   Gloria Materi, A/Prov.Libn.
Founded: 1953. **Staff:** Prof 15; Other 32. **Subjects:** Library science, Canada and Saskatchewan documents, general reference. **Special Collections:** Multicultural Collection (26 languages; 66,600 titles); Native Collection (4000 titles); large print and talking books (8400 titles). **Holdings:** 200,000 volumes; 5900 cassettes and tapes; 5000 phonograph records. **Subscriptions:** 870 journals and other serials. **Services:** Interlibrary loan; coordinates public library services throughout the province; centralized cataloging service to public libraries; library not open to the public. **Automated Operations:** Computerized public access catalog (UTLAS, DYNIX), cataloging, circulation, and acquisitions. **Computerized Information Services:** DIALOG Information Services, PFDS Online, BRS Information Technologies, CAN/OLE, Info Globe, QL Systems, MEDLARS, DOBIS Canadian Online Library System, REFCATSS, WILSONLINE; Envoy 100 (electronic mail service). Performs searches on fee basis. Contact Person: Marie Sakon, Hd., Ref. & Res.Serv., 787-2984. **Publications:** Focus, bimonthly; Directory of Saskatchewan Libraries; Saskatchewan Bibliography. **Special Catalogs:** Saskatchewan Union Catalog. **Remarks:** FAX: (306)787-8866. Electronic mail address(es): ILL.SRP (Envoy 100). **Staff:** Joylene Campbell, Dir., Prof.Serv.; Ved Arora, Hd., Bibliog.Serv.; Jim Oxman, Info.Serv.

★14865★
Saskatchewan Registered Nurses Association - L. Jane Knox Resource Centre (Med)
2066 Retallack St.   Phone: (306)757-4643
Regina, SK, Canada S4T 2K2   Alice M.A. Lalonde
Founded: 1979. **Staff:** 1. **Subjects:** Nursing. **Holdings:** 4000 books; 140 bound periodical volumes. **Subscriptions:** 100 journals and other serials. **Services:** Interlibrary loan; copying; center open to the public for reference use only. **Remarks:** FAX: (306)525-0849.

★14866★
Saskatchewan Research Council - Information Centre (Sci-Engr)
15 Innovation Blvd.   Phone: (306)933-5490
Saskatoon, SK, Canada S7N 2X8   Margaret Samms, Mgr.
Staff: Prof 1; Other 4. **Subjects:** Geology and engineering resources; analytical chemistry; environmental studies - land, water, air; small business assistance and technology transfer. **Holdings:** 6000 books; 25,000 government publications and technical reports. **Subscriptions:** 680 journals and other serials. **Services:** Interlibrary loan; copying; center open to the public with restrictions. **Automated Operations:** Computerized cataloging and acquisitions. **Computerized Information Services:** DIALOG Information Services, Info Globe, CAN/OLE; Envoy 100 (electronic mail service). Performs searches on fee basis. **Remarks:** FAX: (306)933-7446. Telex: 074-2484.

★14867★
Saskatchewan Research Council - Petroleum Research Technical Library (Sci-Engr)
515 Henderson Dr.   Phone: (306)787-9327
Regina, SK, Canada S4N 5X1   Doreen Sinclair, Tech.Info.Off.
Founded: 1981. **Staff:** 2. **Subjects:** Engineering - petroleum, chemical, reservoir; enhanced recovery; analytical chemistry. **Special Collections:** Heavy oil. **Holdings:** 1450 books; 1900 technical reports; 1050 patents; 20,000 reports, papers, articles on microfiche. **Subscriptions:** 100 journals and other serials. **Services:** Interlibrary loan; copying; library open to the public. **Remarks:** FAX: (306)787-8811.

★14868★
Saskatchewan Teachers' Federation - Stewart Resources Centre (Educ)
2317 Arlington Ave.   Phone: (306)373-1660
Saskatoon, SK, Canada S7J 2H8   Jean Nahachewsky, Rsrc.Ctr.Coord.
Founded: 1958. **Staff:** Prof 2; Other 3. **Subjects:** Education, educational psychology, psychology, economic and social conditions. **Special Collections:** Current elementary and secondary school textbooks. **Holdings:** 20,000 volumes; 4000 pamphlets. **Subscriptions:** 680 journals and other serials; 15 newspapers. **Services:** Interlibrary loan; copying; center open to the public with restrictions. **Publications:** Acquisition list - limited distribution; booklists in subject areas. **Remarks:** FAX: (306)374-1122. **Staff:** Joan Elliot, Teacher/Libn.; Marian Driedger, Techn.; Mark Reineke, Techn.

★14869★
Saskatchewan Telecommunications - Corporate Library (Sci-Engr)
2121 Saskatchewan Dr., 2nd Fl.   Phone: (306)777-2229
Regina, SK, Canada S4P 3Y2   Basil G. Pogue, Mgr., Info.Rsrcs.
Founded: 1980. **Staff:** Prof 2; Other 3. **Subjects:** Electronics, management, data processing, planning, telecommunications, engineering. **Holdings:** 5000 books; 50 bound periodical volumes; 2000 government documents; 4 drawers of microfiche. **Subscriptions:** 550 journals and other serials; 25 newspapers. **Services:** Interlibrary loan; library not open to the public. **Automated Operations:** Computerized cataloging, acquisitions, serials, and circulation. **Computerized Information Services:** DIALOG Information Services, Dun & Bradstreet Business Credit Services, The Financial Post DataGroup, Info Globe, CAN/OLE, QL Systems; Envoy 100 (electronic mail service). **Publications:** Library Bulletin, 12/year - for internal distribution only. **Remarks:** FAX: (306)359-9022. Electronic mail address(es): ILL.SRST (Envoy 100). **Staff:** Karen King, Corp.Libn.

★ 14870 ★
Saskatchewan Western Development Museums - George Shepherd Library (Agri, Trans)
2935 Melville St.
P.O. Box 1910   Phone: (306)934-1400
Saskatoon, SK, Canada S7K 3S5   Warren A. Clubb, Res.Coord.
Founded: 1972. **Subjects:** Technology - general, agricultural, transportation; Western Canadian history; advertising. **Special Collections:** Agricultural implement catalogs, 1880 to present (120 feet). **Holdings:** 10,000 books; 1500 catalogs and other items; 9 drawers of photographs; 1000 glass slides. **Subscriptions:** 30 journals and other serials; 5 newspapers. **Services:** Copying; library open to serious researchers by appointment. **Special Indexes:** Index to Agricultural Implement Catalog collection; Index to Automotive Catalog collection; pamphlet subject indexes. **Remarks:** FAX: (306)934-4467.

★ 14871 ★
Saskatchewan Wheat Pool - Corporate Library (Agri)
2625 Victoria Ave.   Phone: (306)569-4480
Regina, SK, Canada S4T 7T9   Diana Grodzinski, Libn.
Founded: 1925. **Staff:** 2. **Subjects:** Agriculture, economics, cooperation, agribusiness, transportation. **Special Collections:** Saskatchewan Wheat Pool history; history of co-operatives. **Holdings:** 5000 books; documents and special reports from Statistics Canada, Royal Commissions, and others. **Subscriptions:** 800 journals and other serials; 25 newspapers. **Services:** Interlibrary loan; copying; library open to the public. **Computerized Information Services:** BRS Information Technologies, CAN/OLE, Info Globe, DIALOG Information Services, GRAINBASE, AgriData Network; Envoy 100 (electronic mail service). **Publications:** Library newsletter. **Remarks:** FAX: (306)569-4885. Electronic mail address(es): DIANA.GRODZINSKI (Envoy 100).

★ 14872 ★
Saskatoon Cancer Centre - Harold E. Johns Library (Med)
University of Saskatchewan Campus
20 Campus Dr.   Phone: (306)966-2662
Saskatoon, SK, Canada S7N 4H4   Mrs. B. Piercy, Libn.
Staff: 1. **Subjects:** Treatment and diagnosis of cancer, radiation therapy, physics, nuclear medicine. **Holdings:** 600 books; 700 bound periodical volumes; 25 tapes. **Subscriptions:** 55 journals and other serials. **Services:** Library not open to the public. **Computerized Information Services:** CANCERLIT. **Remarks:** FAX: (306)966-2910.

★ 14873 ★
Saskatoon City Hospital - Medical Library (Med)
701 Queen St.   Phone: (306)934-0228
Saskatoon, SK, Canada S7K 0M7   Shirley Blanchette, Lib.Techn.
Founded: 1967. **Staff:** Prof 1. **Subjects:** Medicine. **Holdings:** 300 books; 257 bound periodical volumes. **Subscriptions:** 62 journals and other serials. **Services:** Interlibrary loan; copying; library open to hospital personnel. **Computerized Information Services:** BRS Information Technologies.

★ 14874 ★
Saskatoon Gallery and Conservatory Corporation - Mendel Art Gallery - Library (Art)
950 Spadina Crescent E.
P.O. Box 569   Phone: (306)975-7610
Saskatoon, SK, Canada S7K 3L6   Joan Steel, Libn.
Founded: 1964. **Staff:** Prof 1. **Subjects:** Art, museology. **Holdings:** 10,685 books; 610 bound periodical volumes; 16,859 slides; 64 VF drawers of clippings and exhibition announcements; 1000 photographs. **Subscriptions:** 52 journals and other serials. **Services:** Interlibrary loan; copying; library open to the public for reference use only - slides may be borrowed. **Remarks:** FAX: (306)975-7670.

★ 14875 ★
Saskatoon Public Library - Fine and Performing Arts Department (Art, Mus)
311 23rd St., E.   Phone: (306)975-7579
Saskatoon, SK, Canada S7K 0J6   Frances Bergles, Dept.Hd.
Staff: Prof 3; Other 9.5. **Subjects:** Art, music, theater, crafts, cinema. **Holdings:** 26,000 books; 23,745 sound recordings; 10,624 cassettes; 3518 videotapes; 2458 compact discs. **Subscriptions:** 120 journals and other serials. **Services:** Interlibrary loan; copying; department open to the public. **Automated Operations:** Computerized cataloging, acquisitions, and circulation. **Computerized Information Services:** Envoy 100 (electronic mail service). **Remarks:** FAX: (306)975-7542. **Staff:** Miriam Caplan; Lynda L. Gordon.

★ 14876 ★
(Saskatoon) Star-Phoenix - Library (Publ)
204 5th Ave., N.   Phone: (306)652-9200
Saskatoon, SK, Canada S7K 2P1   Miriam Clemence, Libn.
Staff: 2. **Subjects:** Newspaper reference topics, local and provincial news. **Holdings:** 520 books; 105 drawers of photographs and cuts; 30 VF drawers of clippings; 1080 reels of microfilm. **Subscriptions:** 80 journals and other serials; 21 newspapers. **Services:** Library not open to the public. **Remarks:** FAX: (306)664-0437.

Sateilyturvakeskus (STUK)
See: **Finland - Ministry of Social Affairs and Health - Finnish Center for Radiation and Nuclear Safety** (5707)

★ 14877 ★
Satellite Video Exchange Society - Video In Library (Info Sci, Aud-Vis)
1102 Homer St.   Phone: (604)688-4336
Vancouver, BC, Canada V6B 2X6   Karen Knights, Libn.
Founded: 1973. **Staff:** Prof 2. **Subjects:** Media arts, arts, national and international politics, community service. **Special Collections:** International videotapes (2000). **Holdings:** 6000 volumes; 6 VF drawers; clippings. **Subscriptions:** 3000 journals and other serials; 300 newspapers. **Services:** Interlibrary loan; copying; library open to the public for reference use only. **Automated Operations:** Computerized cataloging and circulation. **Computerized Information Services:** Online systems. Performs searches on fee basis. **Publications:** Video Guide - by subscription. **Special Catalogs:** Video Out (catalog for distribution of independently produced videotapes); Video In Video Library Catalog. **Remarks:** FAX: (604)683-1642. **Staff:** Crista Dahl, Print Libn.

★ 14878 ★
Saturday Evening Post Society - Archives (Publ, Bus-Fin)
1100 Waterway Blvd.   Phone: (317)636-8881
Indianapolis, IN 46206   Steven Cornelius Pettinga, Archv.
Founded: 1897. **Staff:** Prof 1; Other 1. **Subjects:** Advertising, marketing, general fiction. **Special Collections:** Correspondence of Cyrus H.K. Curtis, 1900-1930 (15 VF drawers); complete files of Saturday Evening Post, Jack and Jill, Country Gentleman. **Holdings:** 4500 volumes; 4 VF drawers of manuscripts; clippings; pamphlets. **Subscriptions:** 100 journals and other serials. **Services:** Archives not open to the public. **Computerized Information Services:** DIALOG Information Services. **Special Indexes:** Author, title, and subject card index of the Saturday Evening Post, 1900 to present; Saturday Evening Post cartoonists, 1971 to present, and artists, 1920 to present. **Remarks:** FAX: (317)637-4630.

Serge A. Sauer Map Library
See: **University of Western Ontario - Department of Geography** (19557)

Saugus Iron Works National Historic Site
See: **U.S. Natl. Park Service** (17775)

★ 14879 ★
Sauk County Historical Society, Inc. - Historical Museum Library (Hist)
531 4th Ave.   Phone: (608)356-1001
Baraboo, WI 53913   Eleanor Chiquoine, Cur.
Founded: 1905. **Staff:** 1. **Subjects:** State and local history, Indian ethnology. **Special Collections:** William H. Canfield writings; H.E. Cole notes and negatives. **Holdings:** 2000 books; 2000 newspaper clippings. **Services:** Copying; library open to the public by appointment. **Publications:** Old Sauk Trails.

★ 14880 ★
Saul, Ewing, Remick & Saul - Law Library (Law)
3800 Centre Square W.   Phone: (215)972-7873
Philadelphia, PA 19102   Judy Abriss, Libn.
Founded: 1921. **Staff:** 4. **Subjects:** Law. **Holdings:** 26,000 books; 775 bound periodical volumes. **Subscriptions:** 230 journals and other serials; 5 newspapers. **Services:** Interlibrary loan; library not open to the public. **Computerized Information Services:** LEXIS, NEXIS, DIALOG Information Services, Dun & Bradstreet Business Credit Services, Dow Jones News/Retrieval, Information America, VU/TEXT Information Services, WESTLAW, LEGI-SLATE. **Remarks:** FAX: (215)972-7795. **Staff:** Teresa Dembinski, Asst.Libn.

Sauls Memorial Library
See: **Piedmont Hospital** (13039)

★ **14881** ★
Sault Ste. Marie General Hospital - Health Sciences Library (Med)
941 Queen St., E. Phone: (705)759-3333
Sault Ste. Marie, ON, Canada P6A 2B8 Elizabeth Iles, Dir., Lib.Serv.
Founded: 1978. **Staff:** 1. **Subjects:** Medicine, nursing, hospital administration. **Holdings:** 1000 books; unbound journals kept for 10 years. **Subscriptions:** 100 journals and other serials. **Services:** Interlibrary loan; copying; library open to the public for reference use only. **Computerized Information Services:** MEDLARS. Performs searches on fee basis.

Rabie Saunders Library
See: **University of the Orange Free State** (19140)

John E. Savage Medical Library
See: **Greater Baltimore Medical Center** (6703)

★ **14882** ★
Savannah-Chatham County Public Schools - Instructional Media Center (Educ)
1410 Richards St. Phone: (912)651-7025
Savannah, GA 31401 Grace W. Burke, Adm.Coord.
Founded: 1975. **Staff:** Prof 2; Other 4. **Subjects:** K-12 education. **Holdings:** 4973 books; 5000 videotapes; 4000 curriculum-related materials. **Subscriptions:** 50 journals and other serials. **Services:** Copying; center open to the public for reference use only. **Automated Operations:** Computerized cataloging and circulation. **Publications:** Bibliographies of holdings (printout). **Remarks:** FAX: (912)651-7554. Maintains a Teacher Center, where teachers can make and borrow instructional materials for classroom use; open to all Savannah-Chatham County Public School personnel. **Staff:** Thomas W. Downen, Media Spec.

Savannah Evening Press
See: **Savannah Morning News-Savannah Evening Press** (14883)

★ **14883** ★
Savannah Morning News-Savannah Evening Press - Library (Publ)
111 W. Bay St.
Box 1088
Savannah, GA 31402 Phone: (912)236-9511
Julia C. Muller, Chf.Libn.
Staff: Prof 2. **Subjects:** Newspaper reference topics. **Holdings:** Newspaper clippings; local and wire pictures; microfilm. **Subscriptions:** 10 newspapers. **Services:** Library not open to the public. **Remarks:** FAX: (912)234-6522. **Staff:** Sara Wright.

★ **14884** ★
Savannah Municipal Research Library (Soc Sci)
P.O. Box 1027 Phone: (912)651-6412
Savannah, GA 31402 Glenda E. Anderson, Res.Libn.
Founded: 1974. **Staff:** Prof 2. **Subjects:** Urban administration, municipal management, public services, community development, municipal finance/budgeting, urban public works. **Special Collections:** Savannah Area Local Documents Collection (1486 items). **Holdings:** 4294 volumes; 933 periodical volumes; 1552 microfiche. **Subscriptions:** 150 journals and other serials. **Services:** Interlibrary loan; copying; SDI; library open to the public for reference use only. **Computerized Information Services:** LOGIN; LINUS, PTI-NET (electronic mail services). **Networks/Consortia:** Member of Georgia Online Database (GOLD). **Publications:** Savannah Area Local Documents, 1960-1979 (bibliography and indexes). **Staff:** Judith C. Wood, Cat.Libn.

★ **14885** ★
Savannah Science Museum - Energy Library (Energy)
4405 Paulsen St. Phone: (912)355-6705
Savannah, GA 31405 Christopher J. Schuberth, Dir.
Founded: 1981. **Staff:** Prof 1. **Subjects:** Energy - solar, wind, alternative, conservation; appropriate technology. **Holdings:** 400 books; 200 pamphlets; 150 Department of Energy publications. **Services:** Library not open to the public.

★ **14886** ★
Savannah Science Museum - Resource Center (Sci-Engr)
4405 Paulsen St.
Savannah, GA 31405 Phone: (912)355-6705
Subjects: Herpetology, general biology, ichthyology, invertebrate zoology, energy, computer technology. **Special Collections:** Copeia (all); herpetologica (all). **Holdings:** 400 books; 200 bound periodical volumes; 150 other cataloged items. **Services:** Center open to members only. **Computerized Information Services:** Internal database. **Staff:** Robert Williamson; Chris Schuberth, Dir.

★ **14887** ★
Save the Children Federation - Library (Soc Sci)
54 Wilton Rd.
Westport, CT 06880 Phone: (203)226-7271
Staff: Prof 1. **Subjects:** Community development - planning and evaluation; health and nutrition; technical foreign aid; appropriate technology; North American Indians. **Holdings:** 3200 books; 6 VF drawers of pamphlets; 6 VF drawers of information on organizations; 2 VF drawers of United Nations information. **Subscriptions:** 300 journals and other serials; 20 newspapers. **Services:** Interlibrary loan; copying; library open to the public with restrictions. **Networks/Consortia:** Member of Information Network for Materials Effecting Development (INFORMED), Southwestern Connecticut Library Council (SWLC). **Publications:** New materials list, quarterly; Core Bibliographies. **Remarks:** FAX: (203)454-3914. Telex: 671 7730.

Savery Library
See: **Talladega College - Savery Library - Historical Collections** (15992)

Ron Savey Library for Bird Conservation
See: **International Crane Foundation** (8094)

★ **14888** ★
Saving and Preserving Arts & Cultural Environments - Library (Art)
1804 N. Van Ness Phone: (213)463-1629
Los Angeles, CA 90028 Seymour Rosen, Dir.
Founded: 1978. **Staff:** 1. **Subjects:** Folk art environments worldwide. **Holdings:** Books; photographs; catalogs; videotapes; nonbook items. **Services:** Copying; library open to the public by appointment. **Also Known As:** SPACES.

Savitt Medical Library
See: **University of Nevada--Reno** (19021)

Savitz Library
See: **Glassboro State College - Savitz Library** (6489)

★ **14889** ★
Sawyer, Finn & Thatcher Advertising - Corporate Library (Publ)
645 Griswold
Detroit, MI 48226 Karen Bratton, Corp.Libn.
Subjects: Publishing - general, history, current trends. **Holdings:** 25,000 books; 1200 journals and other serials. **Services:** Library not open to the public. **Computerized Information Services:** DIALOG Information Services, BRS Information Technologies, ORBIT Search Service, Dow Jones News/Retrieval.

Mildred F. Sawyer Library
See: **Suffolk University** (15852)

Ruth Sawyer Collection
See: **College of St. Catherine - Library** (3908)

Sayers Memorial Library
See: U.S. Army Post - Fort Benning (17059)

★ 14890 ★
SBC/OC Services L.P. - Library (Bus-Fin)
141 W. Jackson Blvd.   Phone: (312)554-5352
Chicago, IL 60604   Judith J. Longman
Founded: 1985. **Staff:** Prof 2. **Subjects:** Finance, mathematics, computer science, general business, economics. **Holdings:** 2000 books; 1000 reports. **Subscriptions:** 200 journals and other serials; 4 newspapers. **Services:** Library not open to the public. **Automated Operations:** Computerized cataloging. **Computerized Information Services:** DIALOG Information Services, NEXIS. **Remarks:** FAX: (312)554-5062. **Formerly:** O'Connor & Associates. **Staff:** Matthew Robison.

Lenore Scallen Library
See: University of Minnesota - Newman Center (18926)

★ 14891 ★
Scandinavian Institute of African Studies - Library (Area-Ethnic)
Postfack 1703   Phone: 18 155480
S-751 47 Uppsala, Sweden   Ms. B. Fahlander, Libn.
Founded: 1962. **Staff:** 4. **Subjects:** Developmental problems of modern Africa. **Special Collections:** Current government documents from African countries. **Holdings:** 36,000 volumes. **Subscriptions:** 600 journals and other serials; 25 newspapers. **Services:** Interlibrary loan; copying; library open to the public. **Automated Operations:** Computerized acquisitions. **Computerized Information Services:** Access to LIBRIS, DIALOG Information Services, Questel, Ibiscus. **Publications:** AFRICANA (acquisitions list), annual. **Remarks:** Institute is supported by the governments of Sweden, Denmark, Finland, Iceland, and Norway. FAX: 18 695629. Telex: 8195077 AFRICAN. **Also Known As:** Nordiska Afrikainstitutet. **Staff:** Kristina Rylander; Barbro Norstrom Ridaeus; Hakan Gidlof; Annica van Gylswyk.

★ 14892 ★
Scandinavian Paint and Printing Ink Research Institute - Library (Sci-Engr)
Agern Alle 3
DK-2970 Horsholm, Denmark   Phone: 42 570355
Subjects: Research, development, testing, and analysis of dry and wet coatings and printing inks. **Holdings:** 6000 volumes. **Services:** Interlibrary loan; copying; library open to the public. **Remarks:** Institute serves Denmark, Sweden, Norway, and Finland. FAX: 42 571081. **Also Known As:** Nordisk Forskningsinstitut for Maling og Trykfarver.

★ 14893 ★
Scarborough Board of Education - A.B. Patterson Professional Library (Educ)
140 Borough Dr., Level 1   Phone: (416)396-7515
Scarborough, ON, Canada M1P 4N6   Rowan Amott, Supv.
Founded: 1956. **Staff:** Prof 2; Other 5. **Subjects:** Education, child study, sociology, psychology. **Holdings:** 30,000 books; 600 reels of microfilm; 86,000 microfiche; 15 VF drawers; ONTERIS microfiche. **Subscriptions:** 400 journals and other serials. **Services:** Interlibrary loan; copying; library open to the public by appointment. **Automated Operations:** Computerized public access catalog, cataloging, and acquisitions. **Computerized Information Services:** DIALOG Information Services, Infomart Online, BRS Information Technologies, UTLAS, CAN/OLE. **Networks/Consortia:** Member of Education Libraries Sharing of Resources Network (ELSOR). **Special Catalogs:** Journal listing, annual - for internal distribution only.

★ 14894 ★
Scarborough City Health Department - Health Resource Centre - Jean Crew Deeks Memorial Library (Med)
305 Milner Ave., Suite 510   Phone: (416)396-7453
Scarborough, ON, Canada M1B 3V4   Dianne Beal, Libn.
Founded: 1967. **Staff:** Prof 1. **Subjects:** Nursing; prenatal, maternal, and child care; psychology; geriatrics; nutrition. **Special Collections:** Nutrition; sexually transmitted disease; family planning; health inspection; dentistry. **Holdings:** 2000 books; 500 studies and reports; 100 posters; 700 pamphlet titles; 100 audio cassettes; 180 videotapes; 60 resource kits. **Subscriptions:** 82 journals and other serials. **Services:** Center not open to the public; pamphlet material is available to the public. **Automated Operations:** INMAGIC. **Publications:** Library Bulletin, biweekly - for internal distribution only. **Special Catalogs:** Studies and reports; resource kits and audio- and videotapes (both on cards). **Remarks:** FAX: (416)396-5299.

★ 14895 ★
Scarborough General Hospital - Health Sciences Library (Med)
3050 Lawrence Ave., E.   Phone: (416)431-8114
Scarborough, ON, Canada M1P 2V5   Helvi Thomas, Coord., Lib.Serv.
Founded: 1958. **Staff:** Prof 1. **Subjects:** Health sciences. **Holdings:** 1900 books; 85 bound periodical volumes. **Subscriptions:** 200 journals and other serials. **Services:** Interlibrary loan. **Computerized Information Services:** MEDLINE, MEDLARS; Envoy 100 (electronic mail service). Performs searches. **Remarks:** FAX: (416)438-9318. Electronic mail address(es): SGH.LIB (Envoy 100).

Scarborough Memorial Library
See: College of the Southwest (3914)

★ 14896 ★
Scarborough Resource Centre (Plan)
Scarborough Civic Centre
150 Borough Dr.   Phone: (416)396-7215
Scarborough, ON, Canada M1P 4N7   Dave Hawkins, Mgr.
Founded: 1973. **Staff:** Prof 1; Other 2. **Subjects:** Urban affairs with emphasis on Scarborough and metropolitan Toronto. **Holdings:** 2000 books; 12 VF drawers of documents. **Subscriptions:** 400 journals and other serials; 10 newspapers. **Services:** Interlibrary loan; copying; center open to the public. **Publications:** Recent Additions, bimonthly - to city staff and interested individuals. **Remarks:** FAX: (416)396-5232.

★ 14897 ★
Scarritt-Bennett Center - Virginia Davis Laskey Library (Rel-Phil)
1008 19th Ave., S.   Phone: (615)340-7479
Nashville, TN 37212-2166   Mary Lou Moore, Dir. of Lib.Serv.
Founded: 1892. **Staff:** Prof 1; Other 1. **Subjects:** Christian education, church music, spiritual formation. **Special Collections:** Bibles (297). **Holdings:** 53,200 books; 5175 bound periodical and curriculum volumes; 327 recordings; 510 tapes and AV kits. **Subscriptions:** 130 journals and other serials. **Services:** Interlibrary loan; copying; library open to the public with restrictions on borrowing. **Remarks:** Laskey Library is a specialized theological library developed to support the programs of the Scarritt-Bennett Center, a lay training center of the United Methodist Church. **Remarks:** FAX: (615)340-7463.

★ 14898 ★
Scenic General Hospital - Stanislaus County Medical Library (Med)
830 Scenic Dr.   Phone: (209)526-6926
Modesto, CA 95350   Margie A. Felt, Med.Lib.Asst.
Founded: 1956. **Staff:** Prof 1; Other 1. **Subjects:** General and family practice, orthopedics, surgery, pediatrics, radiology, nursing, psychiatry. **Holdings:** 3563 books; 4330 bound periodical volumes; 931 other cataloged items; 97 slides; Audio-Digest tapes. **Subscriptions:** 162 journals and other serials. **Services:** Interlibrary loan; copying; library open to the public with doctor's referral.

★ 14899 ★
Sceptre Resources Limited - Library (Energy)
2000, 400 3rd Ave., S.W.   Phone: (403)298-9685
Calgary, AB, Canada T2P 4H2   Terry-lyn Martin, Libn.
Founded: 1989. **Staff:** 2. **Subjects:** Petroleum, engineering. **Holdings:** 200 books; 100 bound periodical volumes. **Subscriptions:** 50 journals and other serials. **Services:** Library not open to the public. **Automated Operations:** INMAGIC. **Computerized Information Services:** DIALOG Information Services. **Remarks:** FAX: (403)290-1106. Telex: 03-822619.

Dr. Otto Schaefer Health Resource Centre
See: Northwest Territories Department of Health (12063)

Philip Schaff Library
See: Lancaster Theological Seminary of the United Church of Christ (8923)

Schaffer Law Library
See: **Union University - Albany Law School** (16669)

Schaffer Library
See: **Union College - Schaffer Library - Special Collections** (16650)

Schaffer Library of Health Sciences
See: **Albany Medical College** (229)

Walter F. Schaller Memorial Library
See: **St. Francis Memorial Hospital** (14309)

ScheideMantel House
See: **Aurora Historical Society - ScheideMantel House** (1305)

Schendel Memorial Library
See: **First Lutheran Church of the Lutheran Church in America** (5780)

Schenectady Archives of Science and Technology
See: **Union College - Schaffer Library - Special Collections** (16650)

★14900★
Schenectady Chemicals, Inc. - W. Howard Wright Research Center - Library (Sci-Engr)
2750 Balltown Rd.   Phone: (518)370-4200
Schenectady, NY 12309   Dorothy M. Kraus, Mgr., Tech.Info.Serv.
Founded: 1968. **Staff:** Prof 1; Other 1. **Subjects:** Polymer and organic chemistry. **Holdings:** 1200 books; 1300 bound periodical volumes. **Subscriptions:** 70 journals and other serials. **Services:** Interlibrary loan; copying; SDI; library open to the public with restrictions. **Computerized Information Services:** DIALOG Information Services, STN International, ORBIT Search Service. **Networks/Consortia:** Member of Capital District Library Council for Reference & Research Resources (CDLC). **Remarks:** FAX: (518)382-8129. Telex: 145 457.

★14901★
Schenectady County Historical Society - Library and Archives (Hist)
32 Washington Ave.   Phone: (518)374-0263
Schenectady, NY 12305   Scott Haefner, Act.Libn.
Founded: 1905. **Staff:** 1. **Subjects:** Schenectady County and New York State history, genealogy. **Special Collections:** Local church and cemetery records; Revolutionary War documents; family record file; 1850 census of New York State counties (microfilm); federal census of Schenectady County, 1790-1900; state census of Schenectady County, 1835, 1855; 1900 federal census of New York State counties. **Holdings:** 2500 volumes; clippings; manuscripts; pamphlets; documents; slides; pictures; maps. **Subscriptions:** 5 journals and other serials. **Services:** Copying; family research (fee); library open to the public on fee basis.

★14902★
(Schenectady) Daily Gazette - Library (Publ)
2345 Maxon Rd.   Phone: (518)374-4141
Schenectady, NY 12301-1090   Colleen J. Daze, Libn.
Founded: 1976. **Staff:** 2. **Subjects:** Newspaper reference topics. **Holdings:** 250 books; 250,000 newspaper clippings; newspaper on microfilm, 1899 to present. **Subscriptions:** 38 journals and other serials. **Services:** Library not open to the public. **Computerized Information Services:** DIALOG Information Services, DataTimes, VU/TEXT Information Services. **Special Indexes:** Index to Schenectady Gazette, 1979 to present. **Remarks:** FAX: (518)395-3089.

★14903★
Schenectady Museum and Planetarium - Library (Art, Sci-Engr)
Nott Terrace Heights   Phone: (518)382-7890
Schenectady, NY 12308   Mrs. Wini Brice, Act.Libn.
Founded: 1934. **Subjects:** Art, history, science, industry, technology, natural history. **Special Collections:** Early electricity and technology; Charles P. Steinmetz Collection. **Holdings:** 1000 books. **Subscriptions:** 11 journals and other serials. **Services:** Library open to staff and associates.

Heinrich Schenker Archive
See: **University of California, Riverside - Music Library** (18411)

Frank H. Schepler, Jr. Memorial Library
See: **Chatsworth Historical Society** (3454)

Schering Foundation Library of Health Care
See: **Harvard University - School of Medicine** (6993)

★14904★
Schering-Plough Corporation - Library Information Center (Biol Sci, Med)
60 Orange St.   Phone: (201)429-3737
Bloomfield, NJ 07003   Gerald Wagman, Mgr.
Founded: 1940. **Staff:** Prof 12; Other 7. **Subjects:** Pharmacy, biomedicine, microbiology, organic chemistry. **Holdings:** 30,000 volumes. **Subscriptions:** 1400 journals and other serials. **Services:** Interlibrary loan; copying; SDI; center open to qualified users by appointment only. **Automated Operations:** Computerized public access catalog, cataloging, acquisitions, serials, and circulation. **Computerized Information Services:** DIALOG Information Services, WILSONLINE, Questel, Chemical Abstracts Service (CAS); ICON, SCHOLAR/Inquire (internal databases). **Remarks:** FAX: (201)429-3763. **Staff:** Monica R. McKenzie, Supv., Tech.Serv.; Jean Nocka, Supv., Lit. Dissemination.

★14905★
Schering-Plough Corporation - Library Information Center (Bus-Fin)
Galloping Hill Rd.   Phone: (908)298-5121
Kenilworth, NJ 07033   Esther M. Jankovics, Supv.
Staff: Prof 3; Other 1. **Subjects:** Management, pharmaceutical marketing, business. **Holdings:** 2500 books and bound periodical volumes; 2 drawers of annual reports; 5 VF drawers. **Subscriptions:** 303 journals and other serials; 5 newspapers. **Services:** Interlibrary loan; center not open to the public. **Automated Operations:** Computerized public access catalog. **Computerized Information Services:** DIALOG Information Services, Data-Star, NEXIS, VU/TEXT Information Services. **Publications:** In the News, 2/week. **Remarks:** FAX: (201)298-2338. **Staff:** Allison Warzala, Libn.

★14906★
Schering-Plough Health Care - R & D Library (Med)
3030 Jackson Ave.
Box 377   Phone: (901)320-2702
Memphis, TN 38151   Martha Hurst, Libn.
Staff: Prof 2. **Subjects:** Pharmacology, toxicology, medicine, chemistry, pharmaceutical technology. **Holdings:** 1600 books; 1800 bound periodical volumes; 3000 reprints. **Subscriptions:** 113 journals and other serials. **Services:** Interlibrary loan; library open to the public by permission only. **Computerized Information Services:** DIALOG Information Services, NLM, Data-Star, STN International; DOCLINE (electronic mail service). **Networks/Consortia:** Member of Association of Memphis Area Health Science Libraries (AMAHSL). **Remarks:** FAX: (901)320-2954. **Staff:** Carolyn Wilhite.

Schering-Plough Library
See: **Massachusetts Institute of Technology** (9818)

Harry Scherman Library
See: **Mannes College of Music** (9636)

★14907★
Paul Scherrer Institute - Library (Energy)
CH-5232 Villigen PSI, Switzerland   Phone: 56 99 26 27
                                       Dr. S. Huwyler, Libn.
Subjects: Nuclear energy, nuclear reactors, allied sciences. **Holdings:** 30,000 books; 100,000 reports. **Subscriptions:** 800 journals and other serials. **Services:** Interlibrary loan; library open to the public. **Computerized Information Services:** Data-Star, DIALOG Information Services, ESA/IRS, STN International. **Remarks:** FAX: 56 98 23 27. Telex: 82 74 17 psi ch. **Formerly:** Swiss Federal Institutes for Technology - Swiss Federal Institute of Reactor Research/Eidgenoessisches Institut fuer Reaktorforschung.

Galka E. Scheyer Archives
See: Norton Simon Museum of Art at Pasadena - Library and Archives (15180)

★ 14908 ★

J. Schick International, Ltd. - Private Library for Clients (Bus-Fin)
1306 Montgomery St.
San Francisco, CA 94133   Phone: (415)788-4444
Founded: 1970. **Subjects:** International business in relation to Mexico, Central America, and the Caribbean. **Holdings:** 400 volumes. **Subscriptions:** 23 journals and other serials; 4 newspapers. **Services:** Library not open to the public. **Computerized Information Services:** Internal databases. **Publications:** Private reports for clients. **Remarks:** FAX: (415)788-4447.

★ 14909 ★

Schick Shadel Hospital - Medical Library
Box 48149
Seattle, WA 98148
Subjects: Medicine, smoking, alcoholism and substance abuse, behavior modification. **Holdings:** 800 books; 60 unbound periodical volumes; 15 VF drawers of reports, reprints, clippings. **Remarks:** Currently inactive.

★ 14910 ★

Schiele Museum of Natural History and Planetarium - Library (Biol Sci)
1500 E. Garrison Blvd.
Box 953   Phone: (704)866-6900
Gastonia, NC 28053-0953   M. Turney, Reg./Libn.
Staff: Prof 1; Other 17. **Subjects:** Ecology, natural history, marine biology, archeology, anthropology, land use, zoology, botany, local history. **Holdings:** 6000 books; 141 films; 15,000 slides; 89 planetarium program tapes; 5000 wildflower transparencies; 400 items in research egg collection; serial publications of the Natural History Museum of Los Angeles County; biweekly bulletins of Wildlife Management Institute, 1972 to present. **Subscriptions:** 37 journals and other serials. **Services:** Interlibrary loan; copying; library open to the public with restrictions. **Publications:** Newsletter, quarterly; annual report. **Remarks:** Library serves as an Environmental Reference Center for the State of North Carolina and also as a Regional Reference Center for the Library of Congress.

Mary R. Schiff Library
See: Cincinnati Art Museum - Mary R. Schiff Library (3698)

Rabbi Schiff Library
See: Telshe Yeshiva - Rabbi A.N. Schwartz Library (16078)

Arthur and Elizabeth Schlesinger Library on the History of Women in America
See: Radcliffe College (13677)

Charles H. Schlichter, M.D. Health Science Library
See: Elizabeth General Medical Center (5299)

★ 14911 ★

Schlumberger-Doll Research Library (Sci-Engr, Energy)
Old Quarry Rd.   Phone: (203)431-5600
Ridgefield, CT 06877-4108   Mary Ellen Banks, Supv., SDR Lib.
Founded: 1947. **Staff:** Prof 2. **Subjects:** Oil well logging, physics, nuclear science, mathematics, computer science, chemistry, geology, geoscience, petroleum exploration. **Holdings:** 12,000 books; 2500 bound periodical volumes; microforms; 10,000 articles and reprints; 2000 government reports. **Subscriptions:** 330 journals and other serials. **Services:** Interlibrary loan; copying (limited); library open to the public by appointment. **Automated Operations:** Computerized cataloging, acquisitions, and circulation (LINX, DATALIB). **Computerized Information Services:** ORBIT Search Service, STN International, DIALOG Information Services, OCLC. **Networks/Consortia:** Member of NELINET, Inc., Southwestern Connecticut Library Council (SWLC). **Remarks:** Interlibrary loan telephone number is 431-5604. **Staff:** Maureen Jones, ILL Libn.

★ 14912 ★

Schlumberger, Ltd. - EMR Photoelectric (Sci-Engr)
Box 44   Phone: (609)799-1000
Princeton, NJ 08542   Elaine Vliet, Libn.
Founded: 1954. **Staff:** 1. **Subjects:** Photomultiplier tubes, thin films, optical physics, electro-optics, vacuum technology, high voltage technology, dielectric materials, ceramic technology, nuclear instrumentation. **Holdings:** 1000 books; 1500 bound periodical volumes; 15 VF drawers of company technical reports; 2 VF drawers of patents. **Subscriptions:** 31 journals and other serials. **Services:** Interlibrary loan; center not open to the public. **Publications:** Monthly Library Acquisitions Bulletin; Current Interest Profiles, monthly. **Remarks:** FAX: (609)799-2247.

★ 14913 ★

Schlumberger Well Services - Engineering Library (Sci-Engr)
5000 Gulf Fwy.
Box 2175   Phone: (713)928-4411
Houston, TX 77252-2175   Margaret Kuo, Libn.
Founded: 1953. **Staff:** Prof 1. **Subjects:** Engineering, electronics, geology, petroleum. **Holdings:** 4990 books; 100 bound periodical volumes; 30 drawers of company reports. **Subscriptions:** 130 journals and other serials. **Services:** Interlibrary loan; library not open to the public. **Automated Operations:** Computerized cataloging, serials, and circulation. **Computerized Information Services:** ORBIT Search Service, DIALOG Information Services; internal database. **Publications:** Monthly New Acquisitions Online. **Remarks:** FAX: (713)928-4477.

Grace Schmidt Room of Local History
See: Waterloo Historical Society - Grace Schmidt Room of Local History (20087)

Schmidt Herpetology Library
See: Field Museum of Natural History - Library (5684)

Schmidt Library
See: York College of Pennsylvania (20768)

Schmidt Medical Library
See: California College of Podiatric Medicine (2474)

Dietrich Schmitz Memorial Library
See: Washington Mutual Savings Bank - Information Center & Dietrich Schmitz Memorial Library (20018)

★ 14914 ★

Schnader, Harrison, Segal & Lewis - Library (Law)
1600 Market St., Suite 3600   Phone: (215)751-2111
Philadelphia, PA 19103   Paul B. Gloeckner, Dir.
Founded: 1935. **Staff:** Prof 4; Other 3. **Subjects:** Law. **Holdings:** 30,000 volumes. **Subscriptions:** 100 journals and other serials; 10 newspapers. **Services:** Interlibrary loan; copying; library open to the public with restrictions. **Computerized Information Services:** DIALOG Information Services, LEXIS, VU/TEXT Information Services, Dow Jones News/Retrieval, Dun & Bradstreet Business Credit Services, NewsNet, Inc., WESTLAW, RLIN, OCLC, Burelle's Broadcast Database. **Remarks:** FAX: (215)751-2205. **Staff:** Katherine Cater, Hd.Ref.Libn.; Gwen Yohannan; Annemarie Lorenzer.

Schneider Services International
See: U.S. Bureau of Mines - SSI - Library (17117)

Kenneth H. Schnepp Professional Library
See: Memorial Medical Center (10045)

Arthur Schnitzler Archives
See: State University of New York at Binghamton - Special Collections (15731)

★14915★

Schocken Institute for Jewish Research - Library (Rel-Phil)
6 Balfour St.   Phone: 2 631288
92102 Jerusalem, Israel   Yehoshua Greenberg, Hd.Libn.
Subjects: Jewish mysticism, medieval Jewish poetry, Halacha, Hasidism, prayer, Jewish history. **Special Collections:** Manuscripts, early printings, and special editions; archival material. **Holdings:** 50,000 books; 1000 bound periodical volumes; 400 manuscripts. **Services:** Library open to persons with a letter of introduction from a known scholar or institution. **Computerized Information Services:** ALEPH (internal database). **Remarks:** FAX: 2 636857. Maintained by Jewish Theological Seminary of America.

★14916★

Arnold Schoenberg Institute - Archives (Mus)
University of Southern California
University Park - MC 1101   Phone: (213)740-4086
Los Angeles, CA 90089-1101   R. Wayne Shoaf, Archv.
Founded: 1975. **Staff:** Prof 2; Other 1. **Subjects:** Arnold Schoenberg, 20th century music, Los Angeles war emigres. **Holdings:** 3050 books; 6000 pages of manuscripts; 230 audiotapes; 730 phonograph records; 200 microfiche; 60 reels of microfilm; 15 boxes of concert programs, news clippings; 3300 photographs; 120 theses and dissertations; 1930 scores; 6 maps; 18 films; 500 AV programs. **Subscriptions:** 45 journals and other serials. **Services:** Copying; archives open to the public by appointment. **Automated Operations:** Computerized cataloging. **Computerized Information Services:** RLIN; BITNET (electronic mail service). **Remarks:** FAX: (213)746-4507. Electronic mail address(es): BM.X04@RLG (BITNET). Institute is maintained and supported by the University of Southern California.

★14917★

Schoharie County Historical Society - Reference Library (Hist)
Old Stone Fort Museum
N. Main St.
R.D. 2, Box 30A   Phone: (518)295-7192
Schoharie, NY 12157   Ellen McHale, Dir.
Founded: 1888. **Staff:** 7. **Subjects:** Schoharie County history and genealogy, regional and New York State history. **Special Collections:** Early Schoharie County land patents; early local newspapers, 1830s-1982 (125 reels of microfilm). **Holdings:** 2000 books; 200 bound periodical volumes; 500 pamphlets; 12,000 documents, letters, indentures, manuscripts, maps; scrapbooks; pictures. **Subscriptions:** 15 journals and other serials. **Services:** Copying; library open to the public for reference use only on a fee basis (free to Schoharie County residents and SCHS members). **Publications:** Schoharie County Historical Review, semiannual - to members.

★14918★

Scholastic Magazines & Book Services - General Library (Publ)
730 Broadway   Phone: (212)505-3000
New York, NY 10003   Lucy Evankow, Chf.Libn.
Founded: 1931. **Staff:** Prof 2; Other 3. **Subjects:** Current affairs, biography, sports, education of youth, juvenile and teenage literature, political cartoons, arts. **Holdings:** 205 VF drawers of biographical and pamphlet material; periodical volumes; syllabi; photographs. **Subscriptions:** 300 journals and other serials. **Services:** Interlibrary loan; library not open to the public.

Samuel R. Scholes Library of Ceramics
See: New York State College of Ceramics at Alfred University (11645)

★14919★

Dr. William M. Scholl College of Podiatric Medicine - Library (Med)
1001 N. Dearborn St.   Phone: (312)280-2891
Chicago, IL 60610   Richard S. Klein, Dir., Lib.Serv./Instr. Media
Staff: Prof 2; Other 2. **Subjects:** Podiatric medicine, orthopedics, dermatology, anatomy, neurology, sports medicine, biomechanics. **Special Collections:** Historical podiatric books. **Holdings:** 19,000 books and bound periodical volumes; AV programs. **Subscriptions:** 233 journals and other serials. **Services:** Interlibrary loan; copying; SDI; library open to the public

for reference use only. **Automated Operations:** Computerized cataloging, serials, acquisitions, circulation, and ILL (DOCLINE). **Computerized Information Services:** OCLC, DIALOG Information Services, MEDLINE; Sydney Micro Library System (internal database); OnTyme Electronic Message Network Service (electronic mail service). Performs searches on fee basis. Contact Person: Donald Nagolski, Assoc.Dir., 280-2493. **Networks/Consortia:** Member of National Network of Libraries of Medicine - Greater Midwest Region, Metropolitan Consortium of Chicago, Chicago Library System. **Publications:** Acquisitions List, quarterly; Library User's Manual, annual; Library Report, annual; Periodicals Holdings List, annual; MEDLINE Fact Sheet. **Remarks:** FAX: (312)280-2495. Electronic mail address(es): SCHOLL (OnTyme Electronic Message Network Service).

Schomburg Center for Research in Black Culture
See: New York Public Library (11629)

★14920★

School of American Research - Library (Sci-Engr, Area-Ethnic)
Box 2188   Phone: (505)982-3583
Santa Fe, NM 87504-2188   Jane P. Gillentine, Libn.
Staff: Prof 1. **Subjects:** Anthropology, archeology, ethnology, Southwest Indian arts. **Holdings:** 6000 books; 300 bound periodical volumes. **Subscriptions:** 40 journals and other serials. **Services:** Interlibrary loan; library not open to the public. **Publications:** Exploration, annual; monographs, irregular; advanced seminar publications, annual; Indian Arts Series books; Archaeology of the Grand Canyon series; Arroyo Hondo Archaeological series.

School of the Art Institute of Chicago
See: Art Institute of Chicago - School of the Art Institute of Chicago (1083)

★14921★

School of Fine Arts - Library (Mus, Theater)
38660 Mentor Ave.   Phone: (216)951-7500
Willoughby, OH 44094   Nancy C. Schrott, Libn.
Founded: 1978. **Staff:** Prof 1; Other 2. **Subjects:** Music, theater, art, dance. **Special Collections:** Opera collection; original scripts. **Holdings:** 3600 books; 700 phonograph records. **Services:** Library open to faculty, staff, and students.

★14922★

School of Living - Ralph Borsodi Memorial Library and Archives
R.D. 1
Box 185 A
Cochranville, PA 19330
Defunct.

★14923★

School Management Study Group - Library (Educ)
860 18th Ave.   Phone: (801)532-5340
Salt Lake City, UT 84103   Dr. Donald Thomas, Exec.Dir.
Founded: 1969. **Staff:** Prof 2; Other 1. **Subjects:** Educational administration and management. **Special Collections:** Incentive Pay; Character Education. **Holdings:** 400 books; 200 bound periodical volumes; manuscripts. **Services:** Interlibrary loan; copying; library open to the public. **Remarks:** FAX: (801)484-2089.

School of Theology at Claremont - Center for Process Studies
See: Center for Process Studies (3281)

★14924★

School of Theology at Claremont - Library (Rel-Phil)
1325 N. College Ave.   Phone: (714)626-3521
Claremont, CA 91711   Michael P. Boddy, Dir.
Founded: 1958. **Staff:** Prof 4; Other 3. **Subjects:** Bible, Ancient Near East, church history, theology, ethics, pastoral care, homiletics, hymnology. **Special Collections:** Methodistica; Kirby Page Manuscripts (8 VF drawers); Bishop James C. Baker Manuscripts; archives for the California Pacific Conference of the United Methodist Church; Robert H. Mitchell Hymnology Collection. **Holdings:** 114,438 books; 19,391 bound periodical volumes; 5654 microforms; 78 audio cassettes; dissertations; manuscripts. **Subscriptions:** 585 journals and other serials. **Services:** Interlibrary loan; copying; library open to the public with proper identification. **Automated Operations:** Computerized cataloging. **Computerized Information Services:** OCLC. **Remarks:** FAX: (714)626-7062. **Staff:** Eugene Fieg, Cat.Libn.; Elaine Walker, Circ.Libn.; K.C. Hanson, Ref.Libn.

★ 14925 ★
School of Visual Arts - Library (Art)
380 2nd Ave., 2nd Fl.
New York, NY 10010
Phone: (212)679-7350
Robert Lobe, Chf.Libn.
Founded: 1961. **Staff:** Prof 4; Other 4. **Subjects:** Fine arts, graphic design, advertising, photography, film, computer graphics, humanities. **Special Collections:** Afro-Americans in television and film; Alumni Book Collection. **Holdings:** 60,000 books and bound periodical volumes; 1000 pamphlets; 245,000 pictures; 100,000 slides. **Subscriptions:** 250 journals and other serials. **Services:** Copying; library open to students, faculty, staff, and alumni; METRO passes honored. **Networks/Consortia:** Member of New York Metropolitan Reference and Research Library Agency. **Publications:** Accessions lists, quarterly - to staff and students; library handbook. **Remarks:** FAX: (212)725-3587. **Staff:** Mary Beth Powmesamy, Cat.; Stephen Sinon, Ref.Libn.; Matthew Halberstroh, Slide Cur.; Diane Thodos, Picture Libn.

★ 14926 ★
Schoolcraft College - Women's Resource Center (Soc Sci)
18600 Haggerty Rd.
Livonia, MI 48152
Phone: (313)462-4443
Nancy K. Swanborg, Dir.
Founded: 1975. **Staff:** Prof 6. **Subjects:** Women and single parents - career information, education, employment, counseling, health. **Holdings:** 500 books; 1000 newsletters, pamphlets, government publications, research reports, reprints; 6 VF drawers. **Subscriptions:** 18 journals and other serials. **Services:** Center open to the public. **Publications:** Reprints, irregular; Newsletter, quarterly - free upon request. **Remarks:** FAX: (313)462-4506.

★ 14927 ★
Schreiber Foods, Inc. - Library (Food-Bev)
P.O. Box 19010
Green Bay, WI 54307-9010
Phone: (414)437-7601
Rob Smits, Libn.
Founded: 1977. **Staff:** Prof 1. **Subjects:** Cheese, food industry. **Holdings:** 1200 books; 200 bound periodical volumes; government documents. **Subscriptions:** 315 journals and other serials. **Services:** Library not open to the public. **Computerized Information Services:** DIALOG Information Services.

★ 14928 ★
IBJ Schroder Bank & Trust Company - Library (Bus-Fin)
One State St., 8th Fl.
New York, NY 10004
Phone: (212)858-2000
Founded: 1930. **Staff:** 2. **Subjects:** Banking, investments, international finance, economic and business conditions, international trade, corporate records. **Special Collections:** Foreign bank letters. **Holdings:** 125 books. **Subscriptions:** 100 journals and other serials. **Services:** Interlibrary loan; library not open to the public. **Staff:** Mary Montalto, Libn.; Luz Cajigas, Libn.

Walter Schroeder Library
See: **Milwaukee School of Engineering** (10432)

Andrew S. Schuler Educational Resources Center
See: **Clarkson University** (3779)

★ 14929 ★
Schumpert Medical Center - Medical Library (Med)
915 Margaret Pl.
Box 21976
Shreveport, LA 71120-1976
Phone: (318)227-4501
Marilyn Willis, Med.Libn.
Staff: Prof 1. **Subjects:** Medicine, surgery, and allied health sciences. **Holdings:** 1200 books; 3400 bound periodical volumes. **Subscriptions:** 140 journals and other serials. **Services:** Interlibrary loan; library not open to the public. **Computerized Information Services:** MEDLINE. **Remarks:** Hospital network also includes Pathology, Radiology, and Anesthesiology Libraries.

★ 14930 ★
Schuyler County Genealogical Center and Historical Museum - Genealogy Library (Hist)
200 S. Congress
Rushville, IL 62681
Phone: (217)322-6975
Judy Ward, Libn.
Subjects: Genealogy. **Holdings:** 2000 books. **Services:** Library open to the public.

★ 14931 ★
Schuyler County Historical Society Inc. - Research Library (Hist)
108 N. Catharine St.
Box 651
Montour Falls, NY 14891
Phone: (607)535-9741
Belva Dickinson, Musm.Dir.
Founded: 1960. **Staff:** 1. **Subjects:** Schuyler County history and genealogy. **Special Collections:** Lamoka and Seneca Indian artifacts (300 items); 19th century furniture, tools, household appliances, toys and clothing (800 items); 19th century private sanitarium items; paintings by Talitha Botsford (22). **Holdings:** 5000 books; 220 bound periodical volumes; 300 cemetery records; 5000 clippings; 100 manuscripts; 20 maps. **Services:** Copying; library open with staff supervision. **Special Catalogs:** Newspaper, scrapbook, and photograph catalogs. **Special Indexes:** Indexes to Schuyler County Historical Society Journal and quarterlies. **Staff:** Barbara H. Bell, Hist.

★ 14932 ★
Schuyler Technical Library (Sci-Engr)
238 Encino Vista Dr.
Thousand Oaks, CA 91362
Gilbert S. Bahn, Hd.
Founded: 1952. **Subjects:** Chemical thermodynamics, combustion processes, chemical kinetics, analysis of digital imagery. **Special Collections:** Private technical papers of Gilbert S. Bahn. **Holdings:** Figures not available. **Services:** Library not open to the public. **Remarks:** Most of the library's holdings are now located at the University of Virginia, on permanent loan.

★ 14933 ★
Schuylkill Center for Environmental Education - Library (Biol Sci, Env-Cons)
8480 Hagy's Mill Rd.
Philadelphia, PA 19128-9975
Phone: (215)482-7300
Karin James, Libn.
Founded: 1965. **Staff:** 1. **Subjects:** Natural history, zoology, ornithology, botany, ecology, geology/mineralogy, environmental concerns, astronomy, weather, gardening. **Special Collections:** Rare books on the natural sciences (150 volumes); environmental science teaching resource center (3000 books). **Holdings:** 6500 books; 8 VF drawers of clippings and leaflets; 3 VF drawers of nature center brochures; 3 VF drawers of descriptive material of environmental organizations and newsletters; environmental science software. **Subscriptions:** 42 journals and other serials. **Services:** Library open to the public for reference use only. **Publications:** The Spider's Web (calendar of events), annual - to members and for sale; The Quill (newsletter), 4/year; brochures of courses and workshops - both sent to members and others on request. **Remarks:** FAX: (215)482-8158.

★ 14934 ★
Schuylkill County Law Library (Law)
Court House
401 N. 2nd St.
Pottsville, PA 17901
Phone: (717)628-1235
Patricia G. Kellet, Law Libn.
Staff: Prof 1. **Subjects:** Law. **Holdings:** 24,000 volumes; 2500 ultrafiche. **Subscriptions:** 25 journals and other serials. **Services:** Copying; library open to the public for reference use only. **Remarks:** FAX: (717)628-1108.

Charles Schwab Library
See: **Hugh Moore Historical Park and Museums - Canal Museum - Research Library/Archives** (10711)

Arnold & Marie Schwartz College of Pharmacy & Health Sciences
See: **Long Island University** (9293)

Arnold & Marie Schwartz Library
See: **Temple Beth-El of Great Neck** (16087)

B. Davis Schwartz Memorial Library
See: Long Island University (9294)

Joseph & Elizabeth Schwartz Library
See: Beth Shalom Congregation (1774)

★14935★
Schwartz, Kelm, Warren & Rubenstein - Law Library (Law)
41 S. High St., Suite 2300   Phone: (614)222-2604
Columbus, OH 43215   Jill Bradshaw, Libn.
Staff: 3. Subjects: Securities, taxation, general litigation, bankruptcy.
Holdings: 8500 books; 7 drawers of microfiche. Subscriptions: 70 journals
and other serials; 7 newspapers. Services: Library not open to the public.
Computerized Information Services: LEXIS, NEXIS, DIALOG
Information Services, Dow Jones News/Retrieval, VU/TEXT Information
Services, WESTLAW. Remarks: FAX: (614)224-0360. Staff: Laura
Shinnick.

Marie Smith Schwartz Medical Library
See: Brookdale Hospital Medical Center (2215)

Rabbi A.N. Schwartz Library
See: Telshe Yeshiva - Rabbi A.N. Schwartz Library (16078)

Saul Schwartzbach Memorial Library
See: Prince George's Hospital Center (13361)

Ernst Schwarz Library
See: Zoological Society of San Diego - Ernst Schwarz Library (20849)

Paul Schweiker Archives
See: Arizona State University - Architecture and Environmental Design
Library (1009)

Schweizerische Botanische Gesellschaft
See: Swiss Botanical Society - Library (15936)

★14936★
Schweizerischer Bauernverband - Bibliothek (Agri)
Laurstr. 10   Phone: 56 325111
CH-5200 Brugg, Switzerland   Dr. Michel Gakuba, Agri.Engr.
Founded: 1897. Staff: 2. Subjects: Agriculture - policies, markets, trade,
economics; country planning; rural sociology; landed rights. Holdings:
70,000 books; 200 bound periodical volumes; 100 reports. Subscriptions: 500
journals and other serials; 120 newspapers. Services: Interlibrary loan;
copying; library open to the public. Remarks: FAX: 56 415348.

Schweizerisches Institut fuer Gewerbliche Wirtschaft
See: St. Gallen Graduate School of Economics, Law, Business, and
Public Administration (14319)

★14937★
Schwenkfelder Library (Rel-Phil)
Pennsburg, PA 18073   Phone: (215)679-3103
                                               Dennis K. Moyer, Dir.
Founded: 1946. Staff: Prof 1; Other 3. Subjects: Schwenkfelder Church
history, history of Perkiomen Valley, history of Protestant Reformation in
Silesia. Special Collections: Writings of Caspar von Schwenkfeld. Holdings:
30,000 volumes. Subscriptions: 10 journals and other serials. Services:
Interlibrary loan; copying; library open to the public. Staff: Dr. Peter C. Erb.

Simon Schwob Medical Library
See: Medical Center (9987)

★14938★
Science Associates/International, Inc. - Library (Publ, Info Sci)
465 West End Ave.   Phone: (212)873-0656
New York, NY 10024   Roxy Bauer, Libn.
Staff: Prof 3; Other 1. Subjects: Information science, library science,
documentation, publishing, computer science. Holdings: 2000 books; 750
library and information science reports; 100 newsletters. Subscriptions: 100
journals and other serials. Services: Library not open to the public.
Remarks: FAX: (212)873-5587.

Science Fiction Foundation Research Library
See: Polytechnic of East London (13201)

Science Institute of the Northwest Territories
See: Canada - Science Institute of the Northwest Territories (2846)

★14939★
Science Museum - Library (Sci-Engr)
S. Kensington   Phone: 71 9388234
London SW7 5NH, England   Dr. L.D. Will, Lib.Hd.
Founded: 1883. Staff: Prof 33. Subjects: History and public understanding
of science and technology. Special Collections: Pictorial and archival
collection; early books on science and technology; Comben Collection of
early books on veterinary science. Holdings: 600,000 volumes; British
patents; trade literature; microforms. Subscriptions: 2403 journals and other
serials. Services: Copying; library open to the public. Computerized
Information Services: Online systems; JANET (electronic mail service).
Performs searches on fee basis. Contact Person: Ian Carter, Hd. of Rd.Serv.
Publications: Bibliographies; additional publications available - all for sale.
Remarks: FAX: 71 9388213. Telex: 21200 SCMLIB G. Electronic mail
address(es): L.WILL@UK.AC.IC.CC.VAXA (JANET). Staff: Graeme
Fyffe, Coll.Dev.Libn.; Pauline Dingley, Tech.Serv.Libn.; Robert Sharp,
Archv.; John Singleton, Accessions; Barbara Relph, Cat.; Colin Neilson,
Cat.; Nicholas Wyatt, Cat.; Rosemary Smith, Info.Serv.Libn.; Tony Clark,
Loans & Photocopies; Wendy Sheridan, Pictorial Coll.

★14940★
Science Museum of Minnesota - Louis S. Headley Memorial Library
   (Biol Sci, Sci-Engr)
30 E. 10th St.   Phone: (612)221-9488
St. Paul, MN 55101   Mary S. Finlayson, Libn.
Founded: 1907. Staff: Prof 1. Subjects: Geology, anthropology, biology,
archeology, paleontology, botany, technology. Holdings: 20,250 books; 439
bound periodical volumes; 2687 U.S. Geological Survey publications;
International Catalog, 1903-1919; Zoological Record, 1915 to present; 9 VF
drawers of pamphlets; 208 file boxes of museum publications. Subscriptions:
150 journals and other serials. Services: Interlibrary loan; copying; library
open to the public by special request. Remarks: Alternate telephone
number(s): 221-9430. FAX: (612)221-4777.

★14941★
The Science Place - Library (Sci-Engr)
Fair Park, Box 151469
Dallas, TX 75315-1469   Phone: (214)428-5555
Founded: 1961. Subjects: Health, astronomy, medicine, earth sciences,
astronautics, sex education, natural science, physical science. Holdings:
1600 books and bound periodical volumes. Remarks: FAX: (214)428-2033.
The official name is the Southwest Museum of Science and Technology. The
Science Place is supported in part by funds from the Dallas Park and
Recreation Department - Division of Cultural Affairs.

★14942★
Science Service, Inc. - Library
1719 N St., N.W.
Washington, DC 20036
Defunct.

★ 14943 ★
Science Trends - Library (Sci-Engr)
National Press Bldg., Suite 1079
Washington, DC 20045   Arthur Kranish, Hd.
Phone: (202)393-0031
Founded: 1958. **Subjects:** Government sponsored research and development, science, energy, environment. **Holdings:** Figures not available. **Services:** Maintains information and documents relating to government sponsorship of research and development; subscription includes inquiry service without additional charge. **Publications:** Science Trends, weekly, monthly in July and August - by subscription; Energy Today, monthly; Environment Report, semimonthly. **Remarks:** FAX: (202)393-1732. **Also Known As:** Trends Publishing, Inc.

★ 14944 ★
Scientific-Atlanta, Inc. - Library (Sci-Engr)
3845 Pleasantdale Rd.   Phone: (404)449-2222
Atlanta, GA 30340   Martha Patterson, Lib.Serv.Coord.
Founded: 1965. **Subjects:** Antennas, electronic engineering, mechanical engineering, telecommunications. **Holdings:** 1200 books; 450 bound periodical volumes; 700 documents and technical reports. **Subscriptions:** 74 journals and other serials. **Services:** Interlibrary loan; library not open to the public. **Networks/Consortia:** Member of SOLINET. **Publications:** Acquisitions Bulletin, every 12 weeks - for internal distribution only.

★ 14945 ★
Scientific Library of the Academy of Arts of the USSR (Art)
Universitetskaya nab. 17   Phone: 2136529
199034 St. Petersburg, Russia   K. N. Odar-Boyarskaya, Dir.
Founded: 1757. **Staff:** Prof 30; Other 15. **Subjects:** Painting, sculpture, history of arts, drawing, architecture. **Special Collections:** Count I.I. Shuvalov collection; A.M. Romanov (architect) collection; G.G. Grimm (architect) collection; G.S. Vereyskyi (artist) collection. **Holdings:** 270,127 books; 62,550 gravures and reproductions. **Subscriptions:** 132,558 journals and other serials. **Services:** Library open to the public.

Scientific Research Council of Spain
See: **Spain - Biological Research Center** (15558)

★ 14946 ★
Scientific Resource Surveys, Inc. - Library (Soc Sci)
P.O. Box 4377   Phone: (714)891-7458
Huntington Beach, CA 92605   Nancy Desautels
Founded: 1973. **Staff:** 7. **Subjects:** Archeology, anthropology, pre-history, ethnography, history, biology, geology, paleontology, underwater cultural resources. **Special Collections:** Map Library (U.S. Geological Survey quadrangle maps for Southern California; U.S. Dept. of Agriculture aerial photographs; vegetation maps); Marine Nautical Library (submerged artifact conservation, shipwrecks). **Holdings:** 5000 books, articles, and manuscripts. **Subscriptions:** 11 journals and other serials. **Services:** Library open to trade professionals by appointment. **Remarks:** Provides evaluations and recommendations regarding archeological, historical, and paleontological sites located on land parcels that will be affected by proposed land development. FAX: (714)891-7458.

★ 14947 ★
Scientific & Technical Library of Highway & Waterway Transport (Trans)
12 West Beihuan Lu
Beijing, People's Republic of China
Founded: 1964. **Staff:** 40. **Subjects:** Bridge engineering, road construction and maintenance machinery, motor transport and maintenance, communication engineering, port and channel engineering, shipbuilding, canals and navigation, navigation, navigation marks, shipyards and docks, rescue and salvage. **Holdings:** 78,500 volumes; 3280 periodicals; 46,000 technical reports; 50 AV programs and microforms. **Services:** Interlibrary loan; copying. **Computerized Information Services:** Internal database. **Publications:** Road Transport Abstracts; Water Transport Abstracts; New Books on Communication and Transportation. **Special Catalogs:** Union Catalogue of Foreign Periodicals Held by Departments of Communication; catalogs of Chinese scientific and technical materials on land and water transport; communication science and technology product catalogs.

Scientific and Technical Research Council of Turkey
See: **Turkey - Scientific and Technical Research Council of Turkey** (16581)

★ 14948 ★
Scientists Center for Animal Welfare - Library (Soc Sci)
4805 St. Elmo Ave.   Phone: (301)654-6390
Bethesda, MD 20814   Lee Krulisch
Subjects: Science, education, animal welfare. **Holdings:** Books; microfilm. **Remarks:** FAX: (301)907-3993.

★ 14949 ★
Scituate Historical Society - Kathleen Laidlaw Historical Center - Library (Hist)
43 Cudworth Rd.   Phone: (617)545-1083
Scituate, MA 02066   Dorothy B. Wood, Libn.
Founded: 1917. **Staff:** Prof 1. **Subjects:** Local history, genealogy. **Holdings:** 600 books. **Services:** Library open to the public. **Publications:** Bulletin, semiannual - to members.

★ 14950 ★
SCM Chemicals - Library (Sci-Engr)
3901 Fort Armistead Rd.   Phone: (301)354-7779
Baltimore, MD 21226   Nancy Freeman, Libn.
Founded: 1944. **Staff:** Prof 1; Other 1. **Subjects:** Chemistry - inorganic, physical, analytical; ceramics; inorganic pigments; paint; paper; colors; rubbers; plastics; enamels. **Holdings:** 4000 books and bound periodical volumes; U.S. and foreign patents; reprints; clippings; pamphlets; reports. **Subscriptions:** 150 journals and other serials; 10 newspapers. **Services:** Interlibrary loan; library open to the public with prior approval. **Computerized Information Services:** PFDS Online, DIALOG Information Services, STN International, Dow Jones News/Retrieval, DataTimes, NewsNet, Inc. **Publications:** Resource Update, bimonthly - for internal distribution only. **Remarks:** Alternate telephone number(s): (301)354-7773. FAX: (301)354-7963. SCM Chemicals is a division of Hanson Industries.

★ 14951 ★
SCM Glidco Organics - Technical Library (Sci-Engr)
Box 389
Jacksonville, FL 32201   Phone: (904)768-5800
Founded: 1958. **Subjects:** Organic and analytical chemistry, chemical engineering, flavor and fragrance chemicals, marketing. **Special Collections:** Catalysis; terpene chemicals. **Holdings:** 5730 books; 5000 bound periodical volumes; 5500 patents; 2050 technical reports; 201,000 abstracts on cards; chemical abstracts on microfilm. **Services:** Library not open to the public.

Scobie Health Sciences Library
See: **Riverside Hospital** (13945)

C.I. Scofield Library of Biblical Studies
See: **Philadelphia College of Bible - Learning Resource Center** (12978)

Scotch-Irish Foundation Library and Archives
See: **Balch Institute for Ethnic Studies** (1430)

Scotia Fundy Regional Library
See: **Nova Scotia Department of Fisheries and Oceans - Scotia Fundy Regional Library** (12138)

★ 14952 ★
Scotia McLeod Inc. - Information Centre (Bus-Fin)
Commercial Union Tower
Toronto-Dominion Centre, Box 433   Phone: (416)863-7737
Toronto, ON, Canada M5K 1M2   Angela Devlin, Libn.
Founded: 1979. **Staff:** Prof 2; Other 3. **Subjects:** Investments, finance, security analysis, economics. **Special Collections:** Toronto Stock Exchange Monthly Review, 1960 to present; Toronto Stock Exchange Daily Record, 1973 to present; Ontario Securities Commission Bulletin, 1967 to present; Financial Post Surveys; Ontario Securities Commission Filings on microfiche. **Holdings:** 1000 books; 50,000 microfiche; 260 VF drawers. **Subscriptions:** 180 journals and other serials; 6 newspapers. **Services:** Interlibrary loan; copying. **Computerized Information Services:** Online systems. **Remarks:** FAX: (416)862-3299. **Staff:** Ann Struthers.

★ 14953 ★
Scotland - National Library of Scotland (Area-Ethnic, Info Sci)
George IV Bridge   Phone: 31 2264531
Edinburgh EH1 1EW, Scotland   I.D. McGowan, Libn.
Staff: 220. **Subjects:** Scotland, Scottish literature and history, Scots overseas.
Special Collections: Astorga Collection (Spanish); Balfour Collection (Handel); Blaikie Collection (Jacobitism); Blairs (libraries of Scottish Roman Catholic communities at home and abroad - on deposit); Bute Collection (17th-18th century English plays); Dieterichs Collection (German Reformation); Educational Institute of Scotland Library; Glen Collection (Scottish music); Graham Brown Collection (alpine and mountaineering); Gray Collection (theology and classics, 15th-17th centuries); Hopkinson Collection (Berlioz and Verdi); Inglis Collection (Scottish music); Institute of Chartered Accountants (Antiquarian Collection - on deposit); Jolly Collection (theology, pre-1801); Lauriston Castle Collection (Scottish books, pamphlets, chap-books); Lloyd Collection (alpine and mountaineering); Macadam Collection (baking and confectionery); Mason Collection (children's books); Nichol Smith Collection (French and English literature, 16th-18th centuries); Rosebery Collection (early and rare Scottish books and pamphlets); Scandinavian Collection (founded on Grimur Thorkelin's library); Hugh Sharp Collection (English and American first editions); Warden Collection (shorthand); Wordie Collection (polar exploration). **Holdings:** 5 million books; 70,000 bound manuscripts. **Subscriptions:** 18,000 journals and other serials. **Services:** Interlibrary loan; copying. **Automated Operations:** Computerized public access catalog and cataloging. **Computerized Information Services:** DIALOG Information Services, Data-Star, ORBIT Search Service, ESA/IRS; TELECOM GOLD (electronic mail services). **Publications:** Annual Report; Bibliography of Scotland, annual; catalog of publications - available upon request. **Special Catalogs:** Catalog of manuscripts; Gaelic Union Catalogue. **Special Indexes:** Current Periodicals in the National Library of Scotland; Directory of Scottish Newspapers. **Remarks:** FAX: 31 2206662. Telex: 72638 NLSEDIG. Electronic mail address(es): 79:LLA1021 (TELECOM GOLD).

★ 14954 ★
Scotland - National Library of Scotland - Scottish Science Library (Sci-Engr, Bus-Fin)
Causewayside Building
33 Salisbury Place   Phone: 31 2264531
Edinburgh EH9 1SL, Scotland   Antonia J. Bunch, Dir.
Founded: 1989. **Staff:** Prof 8; Other 5. **Subjects:** Science, business. **Services:** Interlibrary loan; copying; library open to the public. **Automated Operations:** Computerized cataloging. **Computerized Information Services:** DIALOG Information Services, Data-Star, ESA/IRS, ORBIT Search Service, DunsPrint. **Remarks:** FAX: 31 6620644. Telex: 72638 NLSEDI G.

★ 14955 ★
Scotland - National Museums of Scotland - Library (Sci-Engr, Art, Biol Sci)
Chambers St.   Phone: 31 2257534
Edinburgh EH1 1JF, Scotland   S.M. McClure, MA, ALA
Founded: 1985. **Staff:** Prof 7; Other 5. **Subjects:** Decorative arts, archeology, zoology, geology, history of science and technology. **Special Collections:** Society of Antiquaries of Scotland Library. **Holdings:** 200,000 books; 75,000 bound periodical volumes; microforms. **Subscriptions:** 2500 journals and other serials. **Services:** Interlibrary loan; copying; library open to the public by appointment. **Automated Operations:** Computerized public access catalog. **Computerized Information Services:** DIALOG Information Services, BLAISE; JANET (electronic mail service). **Publications:** Serials Finding List. **Remarks:** The National Museums of Scotland Library was formed by the amalgamation of the libraries of the Royal Scottish Museum, National Museum of Antiquities of Scotland, and Scottish United Services Museum. FAX: 31 2204819.

Scotland - Royal Botanic Garden
See: **Royal Botanic Garden** (14102)

Scotland - Royal College of Physicians of Edinburgh
See: **Royal College of Physicians of Edinburgh** (14112)

★ 14956 ★
Scott County Bar Association - Grant Law Library (Law)
416 W. 4th St.   Phone: (319)326-8741
Davenport, IA 52801   Ginger F. Wolfe, Libn.
Staff: 1. **Subjects:** Law. **Special Collections:** Iowa Supreme Court records and briefs. **Holdings:** 10,000 volumes. **Services:** Library open to lawyers and judges; open to the public on a limited schedule. **Computerized Information Services:** WESTLAW.

★ 14957 ★
Scott County Iowa Genealogical Society - Special Collection (Hist)
P.O. Box 3132   Phone: (319)326-7832
Davenport, IA 52808-3132   Patricia L. Scott, Soc.Libn.
Subjects: Scott County, genealogy. **Holdings:** Books; microfilm; microfiche; vital records. **Services:** Interlibrary loan; copying; collection open to the public. **Remarks:** Collection housed at Davenport Public Library, 321 Main St., Davenport, IA 52801. Contact Person: Amy Groskopf, Archv.

★ 14958 ★
Scott Environmental Technology, Inc. - Scott Technical Information Center Library (Env-Cons)
Rte. 611   Phone: (215)766-8861
Plumsteadville, PA 18949   Cindy Morris, Libn.
Remarks: No further information was supplied by respondent.

F.R. Scott Library
See: **McGill University - Department of Rare Books & Special Collections** (9895)

★ 14959 ★
Scott Foresman - Library (Publ, Educ)
1900 E. Lake Ave.   Phone: (708)729-3000
Glenview, IL 60025   Judith L. Besterfeldt, Hd.Libn.
Staff: Prof 1; Other 2. **Subjects:** Education, children's literature, study and teaching of reading. **Special Collections:** Company publications. **Holdings:** 35,000 trade books; 3000 reels of microfilm of periodicals. **Subscriptions:** 200 journals and other serials; 5 newspapers. **Services:** Interlibrary loan; library open to the public for reference use only. **Computerized Information Services:** BRS Information Technologies, DataTimes. **Networks/Consortia:** Member of North Suburban Library System (NSLS). **Publications:** List of Recent Additions, bimonthly. **Remarks:** FAX: (708)729-8910. **Formerly:** Scott, Foresman & Company, Inc. - Editorial Library.

Harvey Scott Memorial Library
See: **Pacific University** (12681)

★ 14960 ★
Scott, Hulse, Marshall, Feuille, Finger & Thurmond - Library (Law)
Texas Commerce Bank Bldg., 11th Fl.   Phone: (915)533-2493
El Paso, TX 79901   Richard Rosenthal, Libn.
Staff: Prof 1; Other 1. **Subjects:** Law. **Special Collections:** Firm correspondence and docket books, 1897-1946. **Holdings:** 15,000 books; 500 bound periodical volumes. **Subscriptions:** 567 journals and other serials. **Services:** Interlibrary loan (limited); copying; SDI; library open to the public by appointment. **Automated Operations:** Computerized cataloging. **Computerized Information Services:** DIALOG Information Services, Information America, LEXIS, WESTLAW. Performs searches on fee basis. **Publications:** Acquisitions list, monthly - for internal distribution only. **Special Catalogs:** Expert witness deposition file (online); brief and memorandum file (card). **Remarks:** FAX: (915)546-8333.

John W. Scott Health Sciences Library
See: **University of Alberta** (18200)

Scott Memorial Library
See: **Thomas Jefferson University** (8360)

★ 14961 ★
O.M. Scott and Sons - Information Services (Biol Sci, Sci-Engr)
Dwight G. Scott Research Center
Marysville, OH 43041
Phone: (513)644-0011
Betty Seitz, Supv., Info.Serv.
Staff: 1. **Subjects:** Horticulture, botany, chemistry, business. **Special Collections:** Lawn Care magazine (15 volumes). **Holdings:** 5100 books; 275 bound periodical volumes; 15 VF drawers of research reports. **Subscriptions:** 100 journals and other serials. **Services:** Services open to the public with prior arrangement. **Computerized Information Services:** Online systems.

★ 14962 ★
Scott Paper Company - Business Library (Bus-Fin)
Scott Plaza One
Philadelphia, PA 19113
Phone: (215)522-6262
Eva K. Butler, Mgr.
Founded: 1960. **Staff:** Prof 1. **Subjects:** Paper industry, advertising, statistics, marketing, marketing research, management. **Holdings:** 3000 books; 153 bound periodical volumes; 45 VF drawers of pamphlets; 8 drawers of microfiche; 30 VF drawers of internal research reports. **Subscriptions:** 155 journals and other serials. **Services:** Interlibrary loan; library open to the public for reference use only on request. **Computerized Information Services:** DIALOG Information Services, LEXIS, NEXIS; CD-ROM (Lotus One Source). **Publications:** Magazine article highlights, quarterly; acquisitions bulletin, quarterly - both for internal distribution only. **Remarks:** FAX: (215)522-6485.

Scott Paper Company - S.D. Warren Co.
See: S.D. Warren Co. (14184)

★ 14963 ★
Scott Paper Company - Technology Library & Technical Information Service (Sci-Engr)
Scott Plaza 3
Philadelphia, PA 19113
Phone: (215)522-6416
George Burna, Mgr.
Founded: 1958. **Staff:** Prof 2; Other 2. **Subjects:** Pulp and paper, chemistry, engineering, physics, textiles, management. **Holdings:** 10,000 volumes; 150,000 patents; internal research reports; microfilm; dissertations. **Subscriptions:** 300 journals and other serials. **Services:** Interlibrary loan; copying; library open to the public for reference use only on request. **Computerized Information Services:** DIALOG Information Services, Chemical Abstracts Service (CAS), PFDS Online. **Publications:** Biweekly bulletin listing recent acquisitions - for internal distribution only. **Remarks:** FAX: (215)522-5290. **Staff:** Cheryl R. Stickle, Libn.

★ 14964 ★
Scott & White Memorial Hospital - Richard D. Haines Medical Library (Med)
2401 S. 31st St.
Temple, TX 76508
Phone: (817)774-2228
Penny Worley, Dir.
Founded: 1897. **Staff:** Prof 4; Other 9. **Subjects:** Clinical medicine, nursing care and education, allied health sciences. **Holdings:** 9057 books; 25,458 bound periodical volumes. **Subscriptions:** 989 journals and other serials. **Services:** Interlibrary loan; copying; SDI; library open to the public with restrictions. **Automated Operations:** Computerized public access catalog, cataloging, serials, and circulation. **Computerized Information Services:** DIALOG Information Services, MEDLARS, BRS Information Technologies; internal database. Performs searches on fee basis. Contact Person: Linda Backus, Pub.Serv.Libn., 774-2379. **Networks/Consortia:** Member of National Network of Libraries of Medicine - South Central Region, TAMU Consortium of Medical Libraries, AMIGOS Bibliographic Council, Inc. **Publications:** List of Acquisitions. **Remarks:** FAX: (817)774-4229. **Staff:** Barbara Henry, Pub.Serv.Libn.; Sheila Reynolds, Lib.Tech.Coord.; Michelle Meara, Archv.; Janet Chlapek, ILL.

William A. Scott Business Library
See: University of Wisconsin--Madison (19626)

★ 14965 ★
Scottish Agricultural College - W.J. Thomson Library (Agri)
Donald Henrie Bldg.
Auchincruive
Ayr KA6 5HW, Scotland
Phone: 292 520331
Angela M. Hissett, Lib.Hd.
Founded: 1896. **Staff:** Prof 1; Other 4. **Subjects:** Agriculture, horticulture, food science, poultry science. **Special Collections:** Agricultural history collection. **Holdings:** 18,000 books; 10,000 bound periodical volumes; 5000 archival items; 20,000 pamphlets. **Subscriptions:** 350 journals and other serials. **Services:** Interlibrary loan; copying; SDI; library open to the public for reference use only. **Computerized Information Services:** DIALOG Information Services. **Publications:** Library Information Monthly. **Remarks:** FAX: 292 521119.

★ 14966 ★
Scottish Office - Agriculture & Fisheries Department - Marine Laboratory Library (Biol Sci, Sci-Engr, Rec, Food-Bev)
PO Box 101
Aberdeen AB9 8DB, Scotland
Phone: 224 876544
John Burne
Staff: Prof 2; Other 4. **Subjects:** Marine biology, oceanography, fisheries, fishing methods and gear. **Special Collections:** Ogilvie Collection on Diatomaceae (90 books, 130 pamphlets); Bremerhaven Papers on Aquatic Nematodes (35mm microfilm). **Holdings:** 40,000 books. **Subscriptions:** 1100 journals and other serials. **Services:** Library open to the public for reference use only. **Computerized Information Services:** DIALOG Information Services. **Remarks:** FAX: 224 295511.

★ 14967 ★
Scottish Office - Library (Educ, Sci-Engr, Med)
New St. Andrew's House
Edinburgh EH1 3TG, Scotland
Phone: 31 2444795
Mr. H.A. Colquhoun
Founded: 1939. **Staff:** Prof 11; Other 24. **Subjects:** Education, industry, health, agriculture, environment, engineering. **Holdings:** 150,000 books; 10,000 bound periodical volumes. **Subscriptions:** 2000 journals and other serials; 100 newspapers. **Services:** Interlibrary loan; copying; SDI; library open to the public by appointment. **Automated Operations:** Computerized public access catalog. **Computerized Information Services:** DIALOG Information Services, ESA/IRS, Data-Star, FT PROFILE, ORBIT Search Service; BT Gold (electronic mail service). Contact Person: Jean Smith, Dp.Libn. **Publications:** Scottish Office Publications List, annual. **Special Indexes:** Scottish Office Circulars Index, annual. **Remarks:** FAX: 31 2444785; 31 2444786. Telex: 727301 NSCOTO G. Electronic mail address(es): 79:SOV004 (BT Gold).

Scottish Research Library
See: American Scottish Foundation, Inc. (736)

★ 14968 ★
Scottish Rite Bodies, San Diego - Scottish Rite Masonic Library (Rec)
1895 Camino Del Rio
San Diego, CA 92108
Phone: (714)297-0395
Alfred D. Sawyer, Chm., Lib.Comm.
Founded: 1974. **Staff:** 20. **Subjects:** Masonic literature and history. **Special Collections:** The Scottish Rite Journal, 1904 to present; Quatuor Coronati Research Lodge, London, England, 1880 to present. **Holdings:** 4000 books; 200 bound periodical volumes; video and audio cassette tapes. **Subscriptions:** 20 journals and other serials. **Services:** Interlibrary loan (limited); copying; library open to the public with restrictions on borrowing. **Publications:** Library Newsletter, monthly - for internal distribution only. **Remarks:** FAX: (619)297-2751.

★ 14969 ★
Scottish Rite Supreme Council - Library (Hist, Rec)
1733 Sixteenth St., N.W.
Washington, DC 20009
Phone: (202)232-3579
Inge Baum, Libn.
Founded: 1888. **Staff:** Prof 1. **Subjects:** Freemasonry and all its aspects, American history, biography, philosophy, religion. **Special Collections:** Claudy Collection (Goethe); Louis D. Carman Collection (Lincolniana); William R. Smith Collection (Burnsiana); Albert Pike Collection; Maurice H. Thatcher Collection (Panama Canal); John Edgar Hoover Collection. **Holdings:** 175,000 books and bound periodical volumes; 50 cases of Masonic patents, documents, clippings; manuscripts; prints; photographs; microfilm. **Subscriptions:** 175 journals and other serials. **Services:** Interlibrary loan; copying; library open to the public. **Publications:** Dynamic Freedoms Series; The Scottish Rite Journal, monthly. **Remarks:** FAX: (202)387-1843.

Scottish Science Library
See: Scotland - National Library of Scotland - Scottish Science Library (14954)

Scottish United Services Museum - Library
See: Scotland - National Museums of Scotland - Library (14955)

Scotts Bluff National Monument
See: U.S. Natl. Park Service (17776)

★14970★
Scottsdale Memorial Hospital - Dr. Robert C. Foreman Health Sciences Library (Med)
7400 E. Osborn Rd.
Scottsdale, AZ 85251
Phone: (602)481-4870
Marihelen O'Connor, Med.Libn.
Founded: 1968. **Staff:** Prof 1; Other 3. **Subjects:** Family practice, medicine, surgery, pediatrics, cardiology, orthopedics, radiology, nursing. **Special Collections:** History of Medicine. **Holdings:** 2500 books; 5000 bound periodical volumes; 40 VF items; videotapes; audiotapes. **Subscriptions:** 235 journals and other serials. **Services:** Interlibrary loan; library not open to the public. **Computerized Information Services:** DIALOG Information Services, MEDLINE. **Remarks:** FAX: (602)481-4072.

★14971★
Scottsdale Memorial Hospital - North - Health Sciences Library (Med)
10450 N. 92nd St.
Scottsdale, AZ 85258-4514
Phone: (602)860-3870
Mary Lou Goldstein, Libn.
Founded: 1984. **Staff:** Prof 1; Other 1. **Subjects:** Cardiology, nursing, anesthesiology. **Holdings:** 1000 books; 150 bound periodical volumes. **Subscriptions:** 175 journals and other serials; 2 newspapers. **Services:** Interlibrary loan; library not open to the public. **Computerized Information Services:** DIALOG Information Services, BRS Information Technologies, MEDLARS. **Remarks:** FAX: (602)860-3116.

★14972★
Scranton Times-Tribune - Library (Publ)
149 Penn Ave.
Scranton, PA 18501
Phone: (717)348-9140
William P. Hines, Chf.Libn.
Founded: 1895. **Staff:** 3. **Subjects:** Newspaper reference topics. **Special Collections:** Local history; news clips; photo library. **Holdings:** Archival materials; microfilm. **Subscriptions:** 5 newspapers. **Services:** Copying; library open to the public. **Computerized Information Services:** Associated Press (AP). **Remarks:** FAX: (717)348-9145. **Formerly:** Scranton Times - Library & Reference Department. **Staff:** Jerry Moon; Paul King.

Scripps Clinic & Research Foundation
See: **Scripps Research Institute (14973)**

Scripps College Archives
See: **The Claremont Colleges - Ella Strong Denison Library (3752)**

E.W. Scripps Co. - Cincinnati Post
See: **Cincinnati Post (3707)**

Scripps Howard Publishing Company - The Commercial Appeal
See: **The Commercial Appeal (4049)**

Scripps Institution of Oceanography Library
See: **University of California, San Diego (18419)**

★14973★
Scripps Research Institute - Kresge Medical Library (Med)
10666 N. Torrey Pines Rd.
La Jolla, CA 92037
Phone: (619)554-8705
Paula K. Turley, Mgr.
Founded: 1956. **Staff:** 4. **Subjects:** Immunology, medicine, molecular and cellular biology, biochemistry, chemistry. **Holdings:** 3500 books; 40,000 bound periodical volumes. **Subscriptions:** 700 journals and other serials. **Services:** Interlibrary loan; copying. **Computerized Information Services:** MEDLARS, DIALOG Information Services, BRS Information Technologies, OCLC, OCLC EPIC, Reference Update. **Remarks:** FAX: (619)554-6044. **Formerly:** Scripps Clinic & Research Foundation. **Staff:** N. Joseph Theisen, Asst.Libn.

William E. Scripture Memorial Library
See: **Rome Historical Society (14053)**

★14974★
SCS Engineers - Library (Env-Cons)
3711 Long Beach Blvd.
Long Beach, CA 90807
Phone: (310)426-9544
Jackie Ivy, Libn.
Founded: 1970. **Staff:** 2. **Subjects:** Environmental and civil engineering, hazardous waste control, landfill gas, energy conservation, environmental protection. **Holdings:** 50,000 volumes; government reports; trade journals. **Subscriptions:** 115 journals and other serials; 3 newspapers. **Services:** Copying; library not open to the public. **Computerized Information Services:** Internal database. **Remarks:** FAX: (310)427-0805. Telex: 2134270805.

★14975★
Scudder, Stevens & Clark - Library (Bus-Fin)
175 Federal St.
Boston, MA 02110
Phone: (617)482-3990
Anita Sybertz, Libn.
Staff: Prof 1. **Subjects:** Investments. **Holdings:** 1750 volumes; 135 drawers of 10K reports, clippings, and pamphlets; microfilm. **Subscriptions:** 200 journals and other serials. **Services:** Interlibrary loan; library not open to the public. **Computerized Information Services:** COMPUSTAT Services, Inc. (C/S), Interactive Data Services, Inc., Data Resources (DRI), FactSet Data Systems, Inc., Wharton Econometric Forecasting Associates, Inc.

★14976★
Scudder, Stevens & Clark - Library (Sci-Engr)
345 Park Ave.
New York, NY 10154
Phone: (212)326-6371
Alan Blackmer, Libn.
Founded: 1926. **Staff:** Prof 1; Other 1. **Subjects:** Banking and finance, investment research, business administration. **Special Collections:** Finance; economics. **Holdings:** 500 books. **Subscriptions:** 300 journals and other serials. **Services:** Interlibrary loan; library open to clients and staff. **Computerized Information Services:** DIALOG Information Services, NEXIS, Dow Jones News/Retrieval, Reuters, FactSet Data Systems. **Remarks:** FAX: (212)326-6748.

Sea Lamprey Control Centre
See: **Canada - Fisheries & Oceans - Central & Arctic Region (2728)**

★14977★
Sea View Hospital and Home - Health Sciences Library (Med)
460 Brielle Ave.
Staten Island, NY 10314
Phone: (718)317-3231
Patricia Whitehouse, Dir. of Educ.
Founded: 1932. **Staff:** 1. **Subjects:** Medicine, nursing, geriatrics, hospital administration, social service, rehabilitation, dentistry. **Holdings:** 3000 books; 4160 bound periodical volumes. **Subscriptions:** 150 journals and other serials. **Services:** Interlibrary loan; copying; library open to the public for reference use only. **Computerized Information Services:** NLM. Performs searches on fee basis. **Networks/Consortia:** Member of Brooklyn-Queens-Staten Island Health Sciences Librarians (BQSI). **Remarks:** FAX: (718)351-7898.

★14978★
Sea World, Inc. - Education Department Library (Biol Sci)
1720 S. Shores Rd.
San Diego, CA 92109
Phone: (619)222-6363
Joy Wolf, Dir., Educ.Dept.
Founded: 1973. **Staff:** Prof 10. **Subjects:** Marine biology. **Holdings:** 2000 books; 1000 periodicals, scientific and government reports. **Subscriptions:** 15 journals and other serials. **Services:** Library not open to the public. **Publications:** Information sheets on marine mammals and curriculum guides on marine life for teachers and students - for sale (telephone (619)226-3834). **Remarks:** Maintained by Anheuser-Busch Entertainment Corp.

Seabury McCoy Library
See: **Los Angeles College of Chiropractic (9327)**

Seabury-Western Theological Seminary
See: **United Library of Garrett-Evangelical and Seabury-Western Theological Seminaries (16723)**

★14979★
Joseph E. Seagram & Sons, Inc. - Corporate Library (Food-Bev)
800 Third Ave.   Phone: (212)572-7873
New York, NY 10022   Alice Gross, Mgr., Lib.Serv.
Founded: 1973. **Staff:** Prof 2; Other 2. **Subjects:** Distilled spirits and wine, corporate finance, U.S. and international government, statistics. **Holdings:** 1000 books; 200 newsletters; microfiche. **Subscriptions:** 300 journals and other serials; 75 newspapers. **Services:** Interlibrary loan; library not open to the public. **Automated Operations:** Computerized serials. **Computerized Information Services:** DIALOG Information Services, NEXIS, Reuter TEXTLINE, InvesText, NewsNet, Inc., VU/TEXT Information Services. Performs searches on fee basis. **Special Catalogs:** Library union catalog. **Remarks:** FAX: (212)572-7395.

★14980★
Joseph E. Seagram & Sons, Ltd. - Seagram Library
225 Lafleur Ave.
LaSalle, PQ, Canada H8R 3H2   Phone: (514)366-2410
Remarks: No further information was supplied by respondent.

★14981★
Seagram Museum - Library (Food-Bev)
57 Erb St., W.   Phone: (519)885-1857
Waterloo, ON, Canada N2L 6C2   Sandra Lowman, Archv./Libn.
Founded: 1970. **Staff:** Prof 1; Other 1. **Subjects:** Beverage alcohol industry; wine, beer, and spirits; alcoholism; prohibition; cooperage; copper-smithing; cork production; glassmaking; decorative arts. **Special Collections:** Label and Advertising Collections, 1880 to present (100,000 labels; 6000 advertisements); Photograph, Slide and Film Library (industry and company activities; 25,000 items); Packaging and Bottle Library (5000 items, 1880s to present); Alfred Fromm Rare Wine Books Library; fine art collection (drawings and engravings related to the history of beverage alcohol). **Holdings:** 6000 books (in 7 languages); 100 bound periodical volumes; 1200 company reports and industry booklets. **Subscriptions:** 50 journals. **Services:** Interlibrary loan; copying; library open to the public by appointment. **Automated Operations:** Computerized cataloging. **Remarks:** FAX: (519)746-1673. **Staff:** Sean Thomas, Archv./Lib.Asst.

★14982★
SEAL Laboratories - Library (Sci-Engr)
250 N. Nash St.
El Segundo, CA 90245   Phone: (310)322-2011
Founded: 1971. **Staff:** 39. **Subjects:** Electronics, electron microscopy, electron microprobe analysis, transmission electron microscopy, X-ray flourescence spectroscopy. **Holdings:** 5000 volumes. **Subscriptions:** 6 journals and other serials. **Services:** Library not open to the public. **Remarks:** FAX: (310)322-2243.

Alvin Seale South Seas Collection
See: **Pacific Grove Public Library** (12671)

Lloyd George Sealy Library
See: **John Jay College of Criminal Justice of CUNY** (8345)

A.E. Seaman Mineralogical Museum
See: **Michigan Technological University** (10342)

★14983★
Seamen's Church Institute of New York - Center for Seafarers' Rights (Law)
241 Water St.   Phone: (212)349-9090
New York, NY 10038   Douglas Stevenson, Dir.
Subjects: Seafarers' rights, laws protecting seafarers' legal and human rights. **Holdings:** Figures not available. **Services:** Center open to the public by appointment for research. **Remarks:** FAX: (212)349-8342.

★14984★
Sear Brown Group - Information Center (Sci-Engr)
85 Metro Park   Phone: (716)475-1440
Rochester, NY 14623   Ulrich Bobitz, Info.Ctr.Rep.
Staff: Prof 1. **Subjects:** Civil and structural engineering, architecture, surveying, water and waste treatment, management, hydraulics. **Holdings:** 2800 books; 1400 manufacturers' catalogs; 4 VF drawers of planning information on local municipalities; 31 VF drawers, 27 shelves, 3 drawing files, and 320 reels of microfilm of Sear-Brown project files and drawings; 10 reels of microfilm of Land Data for Monroe and Ontario counties. **Subscriptions:** 133 journals and other serials. **Services:** Interlibrary loan; center open to the public by appointment. **Automated Operations:** Computerized records management. **Computerized Information Services:** DIALOG Information Services; internal databases. **Networks/Consortia:** Member of Rochester Regional Library Council (RRLC). **Publications:** New From the Information Center (list of new books), bimonthly - for internal distribution only.

★14985★
Search Group, Inc. - Library (Law)
7311 Greenhaven Dr., Suite 145   Phone: (916)392-2550
Sacramento, CA 95831   Twyla Cunningham, Dir., Corp.Commun.
Founded: 1969. **Staff:** 4. **Subjects:** Law enforcement, corrections, courts, identification, statistics. **Holdings:** 250 books; 30 technical reports; 85 unbound periodicals; state statutes on criminal history record information and victim/witness legislation. **Subscriptions:** 24 journals and other serials. **Services:** Library not open to the public. **Computerized Information Services:** Automated Index of Criminal Justice Information Systems Database. Searches performed free of charged to criminal justice practitioners. Contact Person: Cheryl Moore, Res.Anl. **Remarks:** FAX: (916)392-8440.

★14986★
Searle Canada Inc. - Corporate Information Research Services (Med)
400 Iroquois Shore Rd.   Phone: (416)844-1040
Oakville, ON, Canada L6H 1M5   Alison J. Ball, Corp.Libn.
Staff: 1.5. **Subjects:** Pharmacy and pharmacology, cardiology, gastroenterology, therapeutics. **Holdings:** 900 books; 8 drawers of microfiche. **Subscriptions:** 275 serials. **Services:** Library not open to the public. **Computerized Information Services:** Internal database; Envoy 100 (electronic mail service). **Remarks:** FAX: (416)844-7181. Electronic mail address(es): SEARLE.LIBRARY (Envoy 100).

★14987★
Searle Research Library (Med)
4901 Searle Pkwy.   Phone: (708)982-8285
Skokie, IL 60077   Anthony Petrone, Mgr.
Founded: 1952. **Staff:** Prof 2; Other 2. **Subjects:** Chemistry, biology, gastroenterology, gynecology and contraception, hypertension, pharmacology. **Holdings:** 6500 books. **Subscriptions:** 700 journals and other serials; 35 newsletters. **Services:** Interlibrary loan; SDI; library open to the public by appointment on a limited basis. **Automated Operations:** Computerized cataloging, acquisitions, serials, and circulation. **Computerized Information Services:** DIALOG Information Services, PFDS Online, BRS Information Technologies. **Networks/Consortia:** Member of North Suburban Library System (NSLS), Center for Research Libraries (CRL). **Publications:** Acquisitions List, monthly - for internal distribution only. **Remarks:** FAX: (708)982-4701. **Staff:** M. Louise Lasworth, Ser.Supv.; Elaine Lehmann, Info.Spec.

Searls Historical Library
See: **Nevada County Historical Society** (11418)

Charles B. Sears Law Library
See: **State University of New York at Buffalo** (15734)

★14988★
Sears, Roebuck and Co. - Archives (Bus-Fin, Hist)
Sears Tower, Dept. 703
Chicago, IL 60684   Phone: (312)875-8321
Founded: 1955. **Staff:** 1. **Subjects:** Company history, retailing. **Special Collections:** Historical material covering company development, 1886 to present; biographical collection of papers of officers, directors, key personalities, Americana; catalog collection of Sears, Roebuck and Co., 1888 to present (7500 volumes). **Holdings:** 150 VF drawers of pamphlets; 36,500 photographs; 350 reels of microfilm. **Services:** Copying; research services available; archives open to researchers only with approval.

★14989★
Sears, Roebuck and Co. - Merchandise Development and Testing Laboratory - Library, Department 817 (Sci-Engr)
Sears Tower, 23rd Fl.
Chicago, IL 60684   Phone: (312)875-8943
Founded: 1928. **Staff:** Prof 1; Other 1. **Subjects:** Textiles, electrical and electronics engineering, design. **Holdings:** 8000 books; 60 VF drawers of government and state publications, specifications and standards of standards organizations. **Subscriptions:** 377 journals and other serials. **Services:** Interlibrary loan; library open to the public with restrictions. **Automated Operations:** Computerized serials. **Computerized Information Services:** DIALOG Information Services. **Remarks:** FAX: (312)875-5991.

Murray Seasongood Library
See: University of Colorado--Denver - Auraria Library - Archives and Special Collections (18510)

Seaton Memorial Library
See: Riley County Historical Society (13932)

★14990★
Seattle Aquarium - Staff Library (Biol Sci)
Pier 59
Waterfront Park   Phone: (206)386-4300
Seattle, WA 98101   Marcia Kamin, Aquarium Biol.
Founded: 1977. **Subjects:** Marine biology, marine animal husbandry, fisheries, zoology, biology, environmental and conservation issues. **Holdings:** 665 books; 101 bound periodical volumes. **Subscriptions:** 16 journals and other serials. **Services:** Library open to the public by appointment. **Remarks:** FAX: (206)386-4328.

★14991★
Seattle Art Museum - Dorothy Stimson Bullitt Library (Art)
100 University St.   Phone: (206)654-3121
Seattle, WA 98101-2902   Elizabeth De Fato, Libn.
Founded: 1933. **Staff:** Prof 1; Other 1. **Subjects:** Art, history of art, archeology. **Holdings:** 15,000 books and exhibition catalogs; 6 drawers of Northwest artists clipping files. **Subscriptions:** 50 journals and other serials. **Services:** Copying; library open to the public on a limited schedule. **Computerized Information Services:** DIALOG Information Services. **Networks/Consortia:** Member of OCLC Pacific Network.

★14992★
Seattle-First National Bank - Library (Bus-Fin)
Box 3586   Phone: (206)358-3292
Seattle, WA 98124   Jeannette M. Privat, A.V.P. & Mgr.
Founded: 1968. **Staff:** Prof 3; Other 3. **Subjects:** Finance and financial institutions; investments and public corporations; economies of Washington state, United States, and other countries; small business operations. **Holdings:** 8700 books; 100 bound periodical volumes; 349 VF drawers of pamphlets; 4000 microfiche; 15,000 financial reports; 170 videotapes. **Subscriptions:** 2200 journals and other serials; 30 newspapers. **Services:** Interlibrary loan; copying; library open to the public with permission of librarian. **Automated Operations:** Computerized cataloging, acquisitions, circulation, and serials (Sydney Integrated Library System). **Computerized Information Services:** DIALOG Information Services, Dow Jones News/Retrieval, Reuter TEXTLINE, OCLC, VU/TEXT Information Services, DataTimes, the Faxon Company; LINX Courier (electronic mail service). **Remarks:** FAX: (206)358-7598. **Staff:** Pamela Westbrooke, Ref.Libn.; Nan. K. Holcomb, Acq.Libn.

★14993★
Seattle Genealogical Society - Genealogical Library (Hist)
P.O. Box 1708   Phone: (206)682-1410
Seattle, WA 98111   Sarah T. Little, Pres.
Founded: 1923. **Subjects:** Genealogy, family history, Washington state history. **Holdings:** 3000 books; microfilm; microfiche. **Subscriptions:** 200 journals and other serials. **Services:** Copying; library open to the public on fee basis. **Publications:** Seattle Genealogical Society Bulletin, quarterly - to members and libraries. **Remarks:** Library located at 1405 5th Ave., Suite 210, Seattle, WA.

★14994★
Seattle Institute for Psychoanalysis - Edith Buxbaum Library (Med)
4020 E. Madison St., Ste. 230   Phone: (206)328-5315
Seattle, WA 98112   Roger C. Eddy, M.D., Chm., Lib.Comm.
Staff: Prof 1. **Subjects:** Psychoanalysis, allied health sciences. **Special Collections:** Edith Buxbaum Collection. **Holdings:** 1750 volumes; 24 pamphlet boxes of journal reprints; 811 unbound journals; videotapes. **Subscriptions:** 20 journals and other serials. **Services:** Library open on a limited schedule to contributing members. **Remarks:** FAX: (206)328-5315. **Formerly:** Psychoanalytic Society of Seattle.

★14995★
(Seattle) Metro Library (Trans, Env-Cons)
821 2nd Ave.   Phone: (206)684-1132
Seattle, WA 98104   Anne McBride, Libn.
Founded: 1972. **Staff:** Prof 2.5; Other 1. **Subjects:** Public transportation, wastewater treatment, water pollution control, toxicants, hazardous waste, industrial waste. **Holdings:** 10,000 books and documents. **Subscriptions:** 298 journals and other serials; 16 newspapers. **Services:** Interlibrary loan; library open to the public for reference use only. **Automated Operations:** Computerized cataloging, serials, and circulation (Data Trek). **Computerized Information Services:** DIALOG Information Services, PFDS Online, OCLC, DataTimes, VU/TEXT Information Services. **Networks/Consortia:** Member of OCLC Pacific Network. **Remarks:** FAX: (206)684-1533. **Staff:** Douglas Ammons; Leroy Chadwick.

★14996★
Seattle Post-Intelligencer - Newspaper Library (Publ)
101 Elliott West   Phone: (206)448-8000
Seattle, WA 98119   Lytton Smith, Chf.Libn.
Founded: 1890. **Staff:** Prof 1; Other 2. **Subjects:** Newspaper reference topics. **Holdings:** 700 books; news photographs; index files; pamphlets; Post-Intelligencer, 1876 to present, on microfilm. **Services:** Library not open to the public. **Computerized Information Services:** Produces Seattle Post-Intelligencer database (available online through VU/TEXT Information Services and DataTimes); VU/TEXT Information Services; internal database.

★14997★
Seattle Public Library - Business and Technology Department (Sci-Engr, Bus-Fin)
1000 4th Ave.   Phone: (206)386-4634
Seattle, WA 98104   Anne Thatcher, Coord.
Founded: 1978. **Staff:** Prof 12; Other 9. **Subjects:** Local marketing and economics, international trade, Pacific Rim business, gardening, employment, motor vehicle repair, investments, skilled trades, domestic science, history of aviation. **Special Collections:** Aeronautics collection (12,000 books; 76 periodicals); Washington Companies File (268 drawers of cards; 2500 microfiche of clippings); Pacific Northwest historical telephone and city directory collection (1450 volumes); Ornithology Collection (500 volumes); Clock and Watch Repair Collection (107 volumes); Automotive Repair Collection (30,000 volumes); Pacific Rim Business Information Service; Small Business Collection; International Trade Collection; Orchid Collection. **Holdings:** 250,000 books; 80 VF drawers of pamphlets, directories, clippings, annual reports; 28 VF drawers of standards and specifications; federal document depository (state, local, and foreign document holdings). **Subscriptions:** 1200 journals and other serials. **Services:** Interlibrary loan; copying; department open to the public. **Automated Operations:** Computerized cataloging. **Computerized Information Services:** DIALOG Information Services, WILSONLINE, NEXIS, VU/TEXT Information Services, NewsNet, Inc., DataTimes; InfoTrac. **Networks/Consortia:** Member of Western Library Network (WLN). **Special Indexes:** Local company and organizations file; Boat file; Washington science and business subject index; Pacific Rim Business Information Service. **Remarks:** FAX: (206)386-4634. **Staff:** Betty Tonglao, Pacific Rim Libn.

★14998★
Seattle Public Library - Douglass-Truth Branch Library (Area-Ethnic)
2300 E. Yesler Way   Phone: (206)684-4704
Seattle, WA 98122   Irene Haines, Team Ldr. & Young Adult Libn.
Founded: 1914. **Staff:** Prof 3; Other 4. **Subjects:** African-American history and literature - the African-American experience in the Pacific Northwest, the portrayal of blacks in children's literature. **Special Collections:** African-American Collection; Children's Literature Research Collection. **Holdings:**

6477 books; 346 bound periodical volumes; 5 VF drawers of pictures and pamphlets; 95 sound recordings; 3 boxes of microfiche; 200 video recordings. **Subscriptions:** 17 journals and other serials; 6 newspapers. **Services:** Interlibrary loan; copying; library open to the public. **Automated Operations:** Computerized public access catalog, serials, and circulation. **Computerized Information Services:** InfoTrac. **Networks/Consortia:** Member of Western Library Network (WLN). **Special Indexes:** Afro-American History Index (card). **Remarks:** FAX: (206)684-4346. **Staff:** Barbara McKeon, Libn.; Carlene Barnett, Children's Libn.

Seattle Public Library - Education, Psychology, Sociology, Sports Department
See: Seattle Public Library - Science & Social Science Department (15003)

★ 14999 ★
Seattle Public Library - Fine and Performing Arts Department (Art, Mus)
1000 4th Ave.   Phone: (206)386-4612
Seattle, WA 98104   Charles P. Coldwell, Coord.
Founded: 1891. **Staff:** Prof 9; Other 7. **Subjects:** Art, art history, architecture, photography, costume history, antiques and collectibles, crafts, music history, music theory, music scores, dance, drama, theater, radio, motion pictures. **Special Collections:** Scrapbooks containing information on Seattle and Northwest artists, architecture, theater, and music (250 volumes); photographs of Seattle and the Northwest (35,000); original art (paintings and prints); KOMO Collection of live radio music. **Holdings:** 140,000 books; 11,000 bound periodical volumes; 19,200 mounted pictures; 45,000 pieces of sheet music and music scores; 16,000 sound recordings; 535,000 vertical file items including images by subject. **Subscriptions:** 570 journals and other serials. **Services:** Interlibrary loan; copying; photo lab copies of photographs owned by institution; department open to the public. **Automated Operations:** Computerized public access catalog, cataloging, acquisitions, and circulation (Dynix, WLN). **Computerized Information Services:** DIALOG Information Services, DataTimes, EPIC, VU/TEXT Information Services, WILSONLINE, InfoTrac; CD-ROMs. Performs searches free of charge. **Networks/Consortia:** Member of Western Library Network (WLN). **Publications:** Art in Seattle's Public Places: Five Urban Walking Tours, 5 vols., 1980. **Special Catalogs:** Compact Disc Holdings. **Special Indexes:** Artists opportunity file index, monthly; Song Titles Index (card); premieres index (card); program notes index (card); Play File Index (online). **Remarks:** FAX: (206)386-4616. Alternate telephone number(s): (206)386-4613 (Fine Arts). **Staff:** Emily Carter, Art Libn.; John Coleman, Mus.Libn.; Jo Ann Fenton, Art Libn.; Christine Firth, Art Libn.; Kathy Harvey, Theater Libn.; Marlene Jameson, Mus.Libn.; Sheila Knutsen, Dance Libn.; Stanley Shiebert, Art Libn.

Seattle Public Library - Governmental Research Assistance Library
See: Seattle Public Library - Local Government Information Center (15001)

★ 15000 ★
Seattle Public Library - Humanities Department (Hum, Hist)
1000 4th Ave.   Phone: (206)386-4625
Seattle, WA 98104   Norma Arnold, Mng.Libn.
Founded: 1891. **Staff:** Prof 13; Other 14. **Subjects:** History, politics, biography, travel, literature, languages, philosophy, religion, drama, poetry, fiction, general bibliography. **Special Collections:** Northwest history; Geneology Collection; multilingual collection (52 languages; 40,000 volumes); library literature; maps. **Holdings:** 452,000 books, and bound periodical volumes; 28 VF drawers of unbound plays and scripts; 31 volumes of Seattle Theatre scrapbooks; microrecords; newspapers. **Subscriptions:** 1657 journals and other serials; 129 newspapers. **Services:** Interlibrary loan; copying; lazer disc stations for public use; department open to the public. **Automated Operations:** Computerized cataloging, acquisitions, and circulation. **Computerized Information Services:** DIALOG Information Services, WILSONLINE, DataTimes, VU/TEXT Information Services. Performs searches free of charge. **Publications:** Where to Learn Languages in and Around Seattle. **Special Indexes:** Northwest Index (300 drawers, subject index of local newspapers). **Remarks:** Alternate telephone number(s): (206)386-4640. FAX: (206)386-4640.

★ 15001 ★
Seattle Public Library - Local Government Information Center (Soc Sci)
Municipal Bldg., Rm. 307
600 4th Ave.   Phone: (206)684-8031
Seattle, WA 98104   Sally Halverson, Mng.Libn.
Founded: 1931. **Staff:** Prof 3; Other 4. **Subjects:** Public administration, local government, police science, fire fighting, city planning, public personnel administration, municipal finance. **Special Collections:** City and county documents. **Holdings:** 18,000 volumes; 68 VF drawers. **Subscriptions:** 300 journals and other serials. **Services:** Interlibrary loan; Municipal Reference Exchange Program; library open to the public for reference use only. **Computerized Information Services:** DIALOG Information Services, NEXIS, LOGIN, LEGI-SLATE, DataTimes, VU/TEXT Information Services, WILSONLINE; governmental bulletin boards. **Publications:** Recent Additions, irregular - to city and county personnel, civic organizations, and other municipal reference libraries; RA-DOCS (new local documents list), bimonthly - free upon request. **Remarks:** FAX: (206)684-8296. **Formerly:** Its Governmental Research Assistance Library. **Staff:** Jeannette Voiland, Libn.; Sally Wermcrantz, Libn.

★ 15002 ★
Seattle Public Library - Media & Program Services
1000 4th Ave.
Seattle, WA 98104
Defunct.

★ 15003 ★
Seattle Public Library - Science & Social Science Department (Soc Sci)
1000 4th Ave.   Phone: (206)386-4620
Seattle, WA 98104   Lynn Daniel, Coord.Dir.
Staff: Prof 7; Other 6. **Subjects:** Education, psychology, sociology, human relations, recreation, sports and games, vocations, occult, etiquette, childbirth, child care, criminology, sex, marriage, family, science, medicine. **Special Collections:** Career Information Center Collection; Regional Foundation Center Collection. **Holdings:** 80,000 books; microforms; college catalogs. **Services:** Interlibrary loan; department open to the public. **Computerized Information Services:** DIALOG Information Services, NEXIS. **Special Catalogs:** Local club file; Seattle-King County social agencies file. **Remarks:** FAX: (206)386-4634. **Formerly:** Its Education, Psychology, Sociology, Sports Department.

Seattle Public Library - Washington Library for the Blind and Physically Handicapped
See: Washington Library for the Blind and Physically Handicapped (20014)

★ 15004 ★
Seattle Times - Library (Publ)
Fairview, N. & John Sts.   Phone: (206)464-2307
Seattle, WA 90109   Theresa Redderson, Lib.Mgr.
Founded: 1900. **Staff:** 11. **Subjects:** Newspaper reference topics. **Holdings:** 4000 books; 13 bound periodical volumes; 8000 pamphlets and maps; 1 million photographs; 10 million news clippings (1900-1984); 1 million photographs; 30 drawers of microfilm. **Subscriptions:** 75 journals and other serials. **Services:** Library not open to the public. **Computerized Information Services:** DIALOG Information Services, NEXIS, DataTimes, VU/TEXT Information Services; Seattle Times/Electronic Reference Version of Newspaper (1985 to present; internal database); DataTimes (electronic mail service). **Special Indexes:** Thesaurus for searching the electronic version of newspaper (online). **Remarks:** FAX: (206)464-3258.

Seaver Center for Western History Research
See: Natural History Museum of Los Angeles County (11342)

★ 15005 ★
Seaworthy Systems, Inc. - Library (Sci-Engr)
P.O. Box 965   Phone: (203)767-9061
Essex, CT 06426   Martin Toyen, Libn.
Subjects: Marine engineering, naval architecture, engine and cycle design, fuels and fuel analysis. **Holdings:** 8000 items; supplier catalogs. **Remarks:** FAX: (203)767-1263. Telex: 517391 Seaworthysys.

★15006★
Sebastian County Law Library (Law)
Stephens Bldg., Suite 418
Fort Smith, AR 72901
Phone: (501)783-4730
Rachel L. Piercy, Libn.
Founded: 1972. **Staff:** Prof 1. **Subjects:** Law. **Holdings:** 14,000 volumes. **Services:** Copying; library open to the public.

Sebring Memorial Library
See: **Chevy Chase Baptist Church** (3507)

★15007★
Second Baptist Church - Library (Rel-Phil)
2800 Silverside Rd.
Wilmington, DE 19810
Phone: (302)478-5921
Nancy P. Minnich, Libn.
Staff: Prof 1; Other 4. **Subjects:** Religion, philosophy. **Holdings:** 3000 books. **Services:** Interlibrary loan; library not open to the public. **Networks/Consortia:** Member of Libraries in the New Castle County System (LINCS).

★15008★
Second Presbyterian Church - Capen Memorial Library (Rel-Phil)
313 N. East St.
Bloomington, IL 61701
Phone: (309)828-6297
Founded: 1939. **Subjects:** Religion, religious education, missions. **Special Collections:** Local church history. **Holdings:** 2700 books; 1 VF drawer. **Services:** Library open to the public upon request to church office.

★15009★
Secretaria de Agricultura y Ganaderia - Cenid-Microbiologia Library (Agri)
PO Box 41-682
11001 Mexico City, DF, Mexico
Phone: 5 5700629
Arturo Garcia Fraustro, Lib.Hd.
Founded: 1954. **Staff:** Prof 3; Other 2. **Subjects:** Veterinary medicine, animal production, forages. **Holdings:** 8844 books. **Subscriptions:** 65 journals and other serials; 2 newspapers. **Services:** Interlibrary loan; copying; SDI; library open to the public. **Remarks:** FAX: 5 5700682.

Securities and Exchange Commission
See: **U.S. Securities and Exchange Commission** (17936)

★15010★
Security Benefit Life Insurance Company - Library (Bus-Fin)
700 Harrison St.
Topeka, KS 66636
Phone: (913)295-3000
Marsha C. Laurie, Mgr. of HRD
Subjects: Insurance, law, securities, marketing, Life Office Management Association. **Holdings:** 3000 books; company records and annual reports; case histories. **Subscriptions:** 25 journals and other serials. **Services:** Library not open to the public. **Staff:** Karen Hudson; Terri Peason.

★15011★
Security Pacific Bank of Washington - Information Center (Bus-Fin)
Box 3966
Seattle, WA 98124
Phone: (206)585-4089
Vivienne C. Burke, Asst. V.P./Mgr.
Founded: 1968. **Staff:** Prof 1; Other 1. **Subjects:** Banking and finance. **Holdings:** 3200 books; 600 annual reports. **Subscriptions:** 600 journals and other serials; 32 newspapers. **Services:** Interlibrary loan; copying; center open to the public for reference use only with permission. **Automated Operations:** Computerized cataloging, serials, and circulation. **Computerized Information Services:** DIALOG Information Services, DataTimes, OCLC. **Remarks:** FAX: (206)585-5302. **Staff:** Krishna Sharma, Res.Anl.

★15012★
SED Systems, Inc. - Library (Sci-Engr)
Box 1464
Saskatoon, SK, Canada S7K 3P7
Phone: (306)933-1672
Lynn Kennedy, Lib.Tech.
Founded: 1968. **Staff:** Prof 1. **Subjects:** Space and communications systems. **Holdings:** 1600 books; standards; manuals; 500 project documents. **Subscriptions:** 73 journals and other serials. **Services:** Interlibrary loan; copying; library open to the public. **Automated Operations:** Computerized cataloging. **Computerized Information Services:** Internal databases. **Remarks:** FAX: (306)933-1486. Telex: 074-2495.

★15013★
Sedgwick County Law Library (Law)
301 N. Main St., Suite 700
Wichita, KS 67202
Phone: (316)263-2251
Susie Barnes, Law Libn.
Founded: 1950. **Staff:** Prof 1; Other 2. **Subjects:** Case law. **Holdings:** 30,000 books; 4000 bound periodical volumes. **Subscriptions:** 30 journals and other serials; 10 newspapers. **Services:** Interlibrary loan; copying; library open to the public for reference use only. **Automated Operations:** Computerized public access catalog. **Computerized Information Services:** DIALOG Information Services, Veralex 2. **Remarks:** Maintained by the Wichita Bar Association. **Staff:** Kevin L. Hinshaw, Libn.

★15014★
Sedgwick, Detert, Moran & Arnold - Library (Law)
1 Embarcadero Ctr., 16th Fl.
San Francisco, CA 94111-3765
Phone: (415)781-7900
Stephanie Changaris, Libn.
Staff: Prof 1; Other 3. **Subjects:** Law. **Special Collections:** Insurance law. **Holdings:** 10,000 books. **Subscriptions:** 100 journals and other serials; 10 newspapers. **Services:** Interlibrary loan; library not open to the public. **Computerized Information Services:** LEXIS, WESTLAW, DIALOG Information Services, RLIN, BRS Information Technologies, MEDLARS, Information America, VU/TEXT Information Services, Dow Jones News/Retrieval, LEGI-SLATE. **Remarks:** FAX: (415)781-2635. Telex: 356455.

★15015★
Sedgwick James, Inc. - National Resource Centre (Bus-Fin)
Toronto-Dominion Center
P.O. Box 439
Toronto, ON, Canada M5K 1M3
Phone: (416)361-6976
Barbara Wilson, Mgr.
Founded: 1978. **Staff:** 4. **Subjects:** Insurance, employee benefits, risk management, pensions, insurance law, actuarial science. **Special Collections:** Client reports and presentations. **Holdings:** 3000 monographs; 10 VF drawers of annual reports; 6 VF drawers of internal reports; 3000 subject files. **Subscriptions:** 130 journals and other serials; 6 newspapers. **Services:** Interlibrary loan; copying; center open to the public by appointment. **Automated Operations:** Computerized cataloging. **Computerized Information Services:** DIALOG Information Services, PROFILE Information, Questel, NEXIS, LEXIS, Info Globe, The Financial Post DataGroup, QL Systems, Infomart Online. Performs searches on fee basis. **Publications:** National Information Bulletin; Information Update (newsletter), bimonthly - to clients; Adviser (newsletter) - to clients. **Remarks:** FAX: (416)361-6743. **Staff:** Lynn McIntyre, Res.Cons.; Michael Lowndes, Res.Cons.; Kathy Barnes, Res.Asst.

Lindon Seed Library
See: **Grant Hospital of Chicago** (6651)

Segal-Dion Family Library
See: **Congregation Beth Jacob-Beth Israel** (4153)

Jacob and Frances Seidman Educational Resource Center
See: **Central Agency for Jewish Education of Greater Philadelphia** (3322)

★15016★
Seiko Telecommunication Systems Inc. - Information Resource Center (Info Sci)
9205 S.W. Gemini Dr., Bldg 14A
Box 23339
Beaverton, OR 97005
Phone: (503)626-2299
Cheryl Cole, Doc. Control Asst.
Founded: 1984. **Staff:** 1. **Subjects:** Telecommunications, paging. **Holdings:** 400 books; 200 standards. **Subscriptions:** 300 journals and other serials; 8 newspapers. **Services:** Interlibrary loan; center not open to the public. **Automated Operations:** Computerized cataloging, acquisitions, and serials. **Networks/Consortia:** Member of Washington County Cooperative Library Services (WCCLS). **Formerly:** AT&E Laboratories, Inc.

★15017★
Seingalt Society - Library (Hist)
555 13th Ave.
Salt Lake City, UT 84103
Phone: (801)532-2204
Tom Vitelli, Pres.
Founded: 1978. **Staff:** 1. **Subjects:** Giacomo Casanova de Seingalt. **Holdings:** 1000 volumes; photographs; microfilm; manuscripts. **Services:** Interlibrary loan; copying; library open to the public by appointment. **Special Indexes:** Index to manuscripts. **Remarks:** FAX: (801)538-5702.

★15018★
Marie Selby Botanical Gardens - Library (Biol Sci)
811 S. Palm Ave.   Phone: (813)366-5730
Sarasota, FL 34236   Debbie Woolverton, Hd.Libn.
Founded: 1975. **Staff:** Prof 3. **Subjects:** Tropical plant biology, plant
taxonomy, horticulture. **Special Collections:** Epiphyte literature; 19th
century botanical illustrations. **Holdings:** 6000 books; 8000 nonbook items.
Subscriptions: 150 journals and other serials. **Services:** Copying; library
open to the public by appointment. **Computerized Information Services:**
DIALOG Information Services; Epiphyte bibliography (internal database).
Publications: Selbyana.

★15019★
Self Winding Clock Society - Bengt E. Honning Memorial Library (Rec)
3736 Atlantic Ave., Suite 4
P.O. Box 7704   Phone: (213)427-8001
Long Beach, CA 90807   Bengt E. Honning, Ph.D., Dir.
Founded: 1979. **Staff:** Prof 1; Other 2. **Subjects:** Self Winding Clock Co.,
Western Union Co., U.S. horological history (1850-1975). **Special
Collections:** Horology manuscripts (75); American Jeweler & Horologist,
1880-1910 (5 reels of microfilm). **Holdings:** 500 books; 70 unbound
periodical volumes; 75 reels of microfilm. **Subscriptions:** 10 journals and
other serials. **Services:** Library not open to the public. **Publications:** SWC
Library Newsletter, quarterly; Update Information & Library News - to
society members. **Remarks:** FAX: (213)427-8001.

★15020★
J. & W. Seligman & Co. Incorporated - Research Library (Bus-Fin)
130 Liberty St.   Phone: (212)488-0456
New York, NY 10006   Paula A. Nier, Chf.Libn.
Founded: 1931. **Staff:** Prof 1; Other 3. **Subjects:** Corporations, finance,
investment companies, general business statistics, economics. **Holdings:**
1000 books; 450 bound periodical volumes; 2000 corporate and industry
files; 2 drawers of maps; telephone directories; 240 reels of microfilm; 1500
microfiche. **Subscriptions:** 300 journals and other serials; 25 newspapers.
Services: Interlibrary loan; library not open to the public. **Computerized
Information Services:** Dow Jones News/Retrieval, FactSet Data Systems,
Inc. **Publications:** Serials List, semiannual - for internal distribution only.
Special Catalogs: Catalog of Company History. **Remarks:** FAX: (212)488-
0846.

Seligman Library
See: **Columbia University - Rare Book and Manuscript Library** (4023)

★15021★
Selkirk Mental Health Centre - Central Library (Med)
Box 9600   Phone: (204)482-3810
Selkirk, MB, Canada R1A 2B5   B. Scarsbrook, Chm., Lib.Comm.
Founded: 1976. **Staff:** Prof 1. **Subjects:** Psychiatry, psychiatric nursing,
psychology, social service, nursing, allied health sciences. **Holdings:** 4000
books; 1050 bound periodical volumes; AV programs. **Subscriptions:** 100
journals and other serials. **Services:** Interlibrary loan; library not open to the
public. **Remarks:** FAX: (204)785-8936. **Staff:** Lorna Weiss, Lib.Techn.

Sellers-Coombs Library
See: **Wentworth Military Academy** (20168)

Sellers Library
See: **Hendrick Medical Center** (7134)

David O. Selznick Film Archives
See: **University of Texas at Austin - Harry Ransom Humanities
Research Center** (19392)

★15022★
Semantodontics, Inc. - Library (Med)
3400 E. McDowell
P.O. Box 29222   Phone: (602)225-9090
Phoenix, AZ 85038   Jim Rhode, Pres.
Staff: 1. **Subjects:** Dentistry, patient care, dental staff training, psychology,
communications, transactional analysis, motivation. **Holdings:** 400 books;
50 bound periodical volumes; 200 magnetic tapes; 100 patient education
pamphlets. **Subscriptions:** 43 journals and other serials; 8 newspapers.
Services: Copying; library open to the public by appointment. **Publications:**
Practice Smart (newsletter), 11/year - to the public. **Remarks:**
"Semantodontics" means "semantics in dentistry."

Semi-Arid Tropical Crops Information Service
See: **International Crops Research Institute for the Semi-Arid Tropics**
(8095)

★15023★
Seminaire de Chicoutimi - Bibliotheque (Rel-Phil, Hum)
679, rue Chabanel   Phone: (418)549-0190
Chicoutimi, PQ, Canada G7H 1Z7   Clement-Jacques Simard, Dir.
Founded: 1873. **Staff:** Prof 2. **Subjects:** Religion, theology, science,
philosophy, philology, art, history, literature. **Special Collections:** Canadian
literature; Latin and ancient Greek literature. **Holdings:** 80,000 books;
20,000 archival materials. **Subscriptions:** 100 journals and other serials.
Services: Interlibrary loan; copying; library open to the public with
restrictions.

★15024★
Seminaire de Quebec - Archives
9, rue de l'Universite
Box 460   Phone: (418)692-2843
Quebec, PQ, Canada G1R 4R7   Rev. Laurent Tailleur, Dir.
Founded: 1941. **Staff:** Prof 1; Other 2. **Subjects:** History - local, Canadian,
American, economic, religious. **Special Collections:** Canadian public
documents, 1763-1867 (250 volumes). **Holdings:** 4545 books; 250 bound
periodical volumes; 50,000 photographs; 3500 maps; 275 reels of microfilm;
1235 linear feet of manuscripts. **Services:** Copying; archives open to the
public with restrictions. **Remarks:** (418)692-5206.

★15025★
Seminaire St-Alphonse - Bibliotheque (Hum, Rel-Phil)
10026, rue Royale   Phone: (418)827-3744
Ste. Anne de Beaupre, PQ, Canada G0A 3C0   Robert Boucher, Dir.
Staff: 3. **Subjects:** Literature, Canadian history, education, art. **Holdings:**
32,000 volumes; 10,000 slides; 2000 phonograph records. **Subscriptions:** 90
journals and other serials. **Services:** Copying; library open to the public with
restrictions.

Seminaire St-Joseph - Archives du Seminaire de Trois-Rivieres
See: **Corporation du Seminaire St-Joseph de Trois-Rivieres - Archives du
Seminaire de Trois-Rivieres** (4339)

★15026★
Seminaire St-Joseph - Bibliotheque (Rel-Phil)
858, rue Laviolette
C.P. 548   Phone: (819)376-4459
Trois-Rivieres, PQ, Canada G9A 5S3   Danielle Cossette, Libn.
Founded: 1860. **Staff:** Prof 1; Other 2. **Subjects:** Religion, French literature,
history, foreign literature, sciences. **Holdings:** 45,000 books. **Subscriptions:**
100 journals and other serials; 3 newspapers. **Services:** Library not open to
the public.

Seminario Evangelico de Puerto Rico
See: **Evangelical Seminary of Puerto Rico** (5505)

★ 15027 ★
Seminary of the Immaculate Conception - Library (Rel-Phil)
440 West Neck Rd. Phone: (516)423-0483
Huntington, NY 11743 Jiri (George) Lipa, Ph.D., Libn.
Founded: 1930. **Staff:** Prof 2; Other 2. **Subjects:** Theology, scripture, church history, patrology, canon law, liturgy, catechetics. **Holdings:** 55,000 books; 7115 bound periodical volumes. **Subscriptions:** 320 journals and other serials. **Services:** Interlibrary loan; copying; library open to the public by appointment. **Networks/Consortia:** Member of Long Island Library Resources Council. **Remarks:** FAX: (516)423-2346. **Staff:** Mrs. Frances Brophy, Assoc.Libn.

Seminex Library
See: **Christ Seminary** (3629)

★ 15028 ★
Seminole Producer - Library (Publ)
121 N. Main St. Phone: (405)382-1100
Seminole, OK 74868 Nancy Phillips
Founded: 1927. **Staff:** Prof 1. **Subjects:** Newspaper reference topics. **Holdings:** 300 bound periodical volumes; 300 reels of microfilm. **Subscriptions:** 10 newspapers. **Services:** Library not open to the public.

★ 15029 ★
Semiotic Society of America - Library (Hum)
Applied Behavioral Science
University of California
Davis, CA 95616 Phone: (916)752-6437
Dean MacConnell, Exec.Sec.
Founded: 1975. **Subjects:** Semiotics. **Holdings:** 200 volumes; offprint files.

★ 15030 ★
Semmelweis Orvostudomanyi Egyetem - Kozponti Konyvtar (Med, Biol Sci)
Ulloi ut 26 Phone: 1 1331943
H-1085 Budapest VIII, Hungary Dr. Livia Vasas
Founded: 1828. **Staff:** Prof 1. **Subjects:** Medicine, biology, chemistry, psychology. **Special Collections:** Historiae Morborum (1738-1848); Picture Collection by Magyari-Kossa; Sandor Koranyi and Tibor Gyori collections. **Holdings:** 84,352 books; 69,654 bound periodical volumes; 82,412 reports; 15 archival items; CD-ROMs. **Subscriptions:** 505 journals and other serials. **Services:** Interlibrary loan; copying; SDI; library open to the public with restrictions. **Computerized Information Services:** Internal databases; BITNET (electronic mail service). **Publications:** New Books; journals catalog. **Remarks:** FAX: 1 1335126. Electronic mail address(es): H3305VAS@ELLA.HU (BITNET).

★ 15031 ★
Semmes, Bowen & Semmes - Law Library (Law)
250 W. Pratt St., 14th Fl. Phone: (301)539-5040
Baltimore, MD 21201 Helen Y. Harris, Libn.
Staff: Prof 2; Other 2. **Subjects:** Law. **Special Collections:** Admiralty and maritime law. **Holdings:** 21,000 books; 330 bound periodical volumes; 225 volumes and 16 pamphlet boxes of memos and briefs. **Subscriptions:** 85 journals and other serials. **Services:** Library open to the public by appointment. **Automated Operations:** Computerized acquisitions. **Computerized Information Services:** DIALOG Information Services, LEXIS, WESTLAW, Maxwell Macmillan Taxes Online, DataTimes, PaperChase, Current USC; internal database. **Publications:** Semmes Library Information Publication (SLIP), monthly - for internal distribution only. **Special Indexes:** Index to firm memoranda and briefs (online). **Remarks:** FAX: (301)539-5223. **Staff:** Patricia Gudas, Ref.Libn.; Kathie Payne, Acq.Libn.

★ 15032 ★
Semmes-Murphey Clinic - Library (Med)
920 Madison Ave., Suite 201 Phone: (901)522-7700
Memphis, TN 38103 Patricia P. Irby, Libn.
Staff: Prof 1. **Subjects:** Neurosurgery, neurology. **Holdings:** 1327 books; 819 bound periodical volumes. **Subscriptions:** 38 journals and other serials. **Services:** Library not open to the public. **Networks/Consortia:** Member of Association of Memphis Area Health Science Libraries (AMAHSL).

Senate House State Historic Site
See: **New York (State) Office of Parks, Recreation and Historic Preservation** (11683)

Senckenberg Library
See: **Johann Wolfgang Goethe University** (6530)

★ 15033 ★
Seneca College of Applied Arts and Technology - Leslie Campus Library/Resource Centre (Med)
1255 Sheppard Ave., E. Phone: (416)491-5050
North York, ON, Canada M2K 1E2 Vinh P. Le, Campus Libn.
Staff: Prof 1; Other 4. **Subjects:** Nursing, dentistry. **Special Collections:** International health (420 volumes). **Holdings:** 14,565 books; 266 audiotapes; 803 videotapes; 103 films; 200 slide sets; 146 dental models. **Subscriptions:** 104 journals and other serials. **Services:** Interlibrary loan; copying; center open to the public on fee basis. **Automated Operations:** Computerized cataloging, acquisitions, and circulation. **Computerized Information Services:** DIALOG Information Services, DOBIS; CD-ROM (CINAHL, MEDLINE); internal databases; DOBIS (electronic mail service). Performs searches on fee basis. **Networks/Consortia:** Member of The Bibliocentre. **Publications:** Health Sciences Programs Required Reading Lists; Seneca Union List of Periodicals, both annual - both for internal distribution only; bibliographies. **Remarks:** FAX: (416)494-9323.

★ 15034 ★
Seneca Falls Historical Society - Jessie Beach Watkins Memorial Library (Hist)
55 Cayuga St. Phone: (315)568-8412
Seneca Falls, NY 13148 Sylvia Farrer-Bornarth, Exec.Dir.
Staff: 3.5. **Subjects:** Local and area history, Victoriana, Civil War. **Special Collections:** Women's Rights Collection (documents, 1848 to present). **Holdings:** 1500 books; 4 VF drawers; local newspaper, 1839 to present, on microfilm. **Subscriptions:** 10 journals and other serials. **Services:** Copying; library open to the public. **Staff:** Shelden King, Libn.; Jane Wood, Res.

★ 15035 ★
Seneca Zoological Society - Library (Biol Sci)
2222 St. Paul St.
Rochester, NY 14621 Phone: (716)342-2744
Founded: 1978. **Subjects:** Zoos, zoo animals, veterinary medicine, ecology, zoology, herpetology. **Holdings:** 2100 books; 7800 slides; 1900 photographs; 30 zoo guidebooks. **Subscriptions:** 55 journals and other serials. **Services:** Library open to the public by appointment. **Remarks:** FAX: (716)342-1477.

★ 15036 ★
Senegal - Direction des Archives du Senegal (Soc Sci)
Immeuble Administratif
avenue Roume Phone: 235072
Dakar, Senegal Saliou Mbaye, Dir.
Founded: 1913. **Staff:** Prof 50. **Subjects:** Social sciences, humanities, administration. **Holdings:** 25,000 books; 341 microfiche and reels of microfilm; 8500 official publications; 25,000 cubic meters of documents. **Services:** Interlibrary loan; copying; archives open to the public. **Computerized Information Services:** Internal databases. Performs searches. Contact Person: Oumar Diallo, Lib.Cur. **Publications:** Bibliographie Nationale du Senegal; Liste de Nouvelles Acquisitions; Rapport d'activite.

★ 15037 ★
Senior Alliance - Area Agency on Aging Region 1C - Library (Soc Sci)
3850 2nd St., Suite 160
Wayne, MI 48184 Phone: (313)722-2830
Founded: 1980. **Staff:** 1. **Subjects:** Senior citizens - regulations, legislation, services, demographics. **Holdings:** 300 books; 20 bound periodical volumes; 100 reports. **Subscriptions:** 20 journals and other serials. **Services:** Interlibrary loan; library open to the public with restrictions on borrowing. **Remarks:** FAX: (313)722-2836.

★ 15038 ★
Sentara Hampton General Hospital - Medical Library (Med)
3120 Victoria Blvd.   Phone: (804)727-7102
Hampton, VA 23669   Jane D. Austin ', Act.Libn.
Founded: 1892. **Staff:** Prof 1. **Subjects:** Medical sciences, hospital
administration, nursing. **Holdings:** 759 books; 2275 bound periodical
volumes. **Subscriptions:** 75 journals and other serials. **Services:** Interlibrary
loan; copying; library open to Sentara Health Systems employees.
Computerized Information Services: MEDLARS; DOCLINE (electronic
mail service). **Remarks:** FAX: (804)722-3391.

★ 15039 ★
Sentry Insurance Company - Library (Bus-Fin)
1800 N. Point Dr.
Stevens Point, WI 54481   Phone: (715)346-6787
Founded: 1930. **Staff:** 3. **Subjects:** Insurance - property/casualty and life;
pensions; law; business management. **Holdings:** 21,000 books; 6000 bound
periodical volumes; 125 VF drawers of monographs, booklets, clippings,
pamphlets, reports, pictures, and archives. **Subscriptions:** 475 journals and
other serials; 17 newspapers. **Services:** Interlibrary loan; copying; library
open to the public by permission. **Publications:** Acquisition List - for
internal distribution only. **Remarks:** FAX: (715)346-7516. **Staff:** Lynne
Chase, Lib.Coord.

★ 15040 ★
(Seoul) American Cultural Center - USIS Library (Educ)
63, 1-ka, Ulchi-ro
Chung-ku
C.P.O. 277
Seoul 100, Republic of Korea
Remarks: Maintained or supported by the U.S. Information Agency. Focus
is on materials that will assist peoples outside the United States to learn
about the United States, its people, history, culture, political processes, and
social milieux.

Sequa Corporation - Kollsman Division
See: **Kollsman, Division of Sequa Corporation** (8782)

★ 15041 ★
Sergent, Hauskins & Beckwith, Consulting Geotechnical Engineers -
  Library (Sci-Engr)
3232 W. Virginia Ave.   Phone: (602)272-6848
Phoenix, AZ 85009   Susanne M. Jerome, Libn.
Staff: Prof 2. **Subjects:** Engineering - geology, geotechnical, earthquake,
mining, environmental; hydrology; dam safety. **Special Collections:**
Geotechnical engineering problems in arid regions (1500 volumes).
Holdings: 7050 books and bound periodical volumes; 13,000 other cataloged
items; 2 VF drawers; 70 boxes of unbound periodicals; 2 drawers of
microfiche. **Subscriptions:** 94 journals and other serials. **Services:** Copying;
library open to the public with permission. **Automated Operations:**
Computerized cataloging and acquisitions. **Computerized Information
Services:** DIALOG Information Services. **Remarks:** FAX: (602)272-7239.
Staff: Diane Walden, Asst.Libn.

★ 15042 ★
Servants of the Immaculate Heart of Mary - Archives (Rel-Phil)
Villa Maria House of Studies   Phone: (215)647-2160
Immaculata, PA 19345   Sr. Genevieve Mary, Archv.
Subjects: Congregation history, 1840 to present. **Holdings:** 160 cubic feet of
correspondence, journals, financial records, architectural drawings, and
photographs. **Services:** Copying; archives open to the public on a limited
schedule.

★ 15043 ★
Service Historique de la Marine a Cherbourg - Bibliotheque (Hist, Sci-
  Engr)
57 rue de l'Abbaye
BP 31
F-50115 Cherbourg Naval, France   Phone: 33 926507
Founded: 1836. **Staff:** Prof 8; Other 1. **Subjects:** Marine voyages, naval
engineering. **Holdings:** 20,000 books. **Subscriptions:** 100 journals and other
serials. **Services:** Interlibrary loan; copying; library open to the public.
Publications: List of acquisitions, annual.

Services for Independent Living, Inc.
See: **FES Information Center - Library** (5675)

★ 15044 ★
Servico de Documentacao Geral da Marinha - Departamento de
  Bbiblioteca da Marinha (Hist)
Praca Barao de Ladario
s/n Ilha das Cobras   Phone: 21 2239211
20091 Rio de Janeiro, RJ, Brazil   Mario Vieira Raymundo
Founded: 1802. **Staff:** Prof 11; Other 2. **Subjects:** Naval history, history of
Brazil, cartography, biography. **Special Collections:** Rare books collection.
Holdings: 110,000 books; maps. **Subscriptions:** 10 journals and other serials.
Services: Interlibrary loan; copying; library open to the public for reference
use only. **Computerized Information Services:** BIBLIODATA, CALCO
(internal databases). **Special Catalogs:** Catologo da Biblioteca da Marinha.
Remarks: FAX: 21 2166716.

★ 15045 ★
Servio Corporation - Corporate Information Center (Comp Sci)
733 N.W. Everett 5A   Phone: (503)221-2022
Portland, OR 97209   Susan Thompson, Mgr.
Founded: 1983. **Staff:** Prof 1. **Subjects:** Computer science, programming,
management, electronics industry. **Holdings:** 2000 books; company and
product literature. **Subscriptions:** 163 journals and other serials. **Services:**
Interlibrary loan; copying; SDI; center open to the public at librarian's
discretion. **Automated Operations:** Computerized cataloging and ILL.
Computerized Information Services: DIALOG Information Services,
DunsPrint, OCLC. Performs searches on fee basis. **Remarks:** FAX:
(503)221-2026.

Servites
See: **Order of Servants of Mary - Eastern Province Library** (12518)

★ 15046 ★
Sessions & Fishman - Law Library (Law)
201 St. Charles Ave., Suite 3500   Phone: (504)582-1563
New Orleans, LA 70170   Julia Overstreet, Libn.
Staff: Prof 1; Other 1. **Subjects:** Law. **Holdings:** 15,000 books; 600 bound
periodical volumes. **Subscriptions:** 100 journals and other serials; 6
newspapers. **Services:** Interlibrary loan; copying; library open to the public
with restrictions. **Computerized Information Services:** WESTLAW, LEXIS,
DIALOG Information Services. **Publications:** Now Hear This (newsletter)
- for internal distribution only. **Remarks:** FAX: (504)582-1555.

Particia M. Sessions Memorial Library
See: **U.S. Navy - Naval Hospital (TX-Corpus Christi)** (17856)

★ 15047 ★
Seton Hall University - Immaculate Conception Seminary - Library
  (Rel-Phil)
400 S. Orange Ave.   Phone: (201)761-9584
South Orange, NJ 07079   Msgr. James C. Turro, Dir.
Founded: 1858. **Staff:** Prof 2; Other 2. **Subjects:** Theology, Biblical studies,
liturgy, philosophy, bioethics, Catholic church history. **Special Collections:**
Cardinal Newman Center; Sources Chretiennes; rare sacred books.
Holdings: 75,000 books; 4000 bound periodical volumes (690 periodical
titles); 492 theses dissertations; 575 microfirms; 500 sound recordings; 60
videocassettes. **Subscriptions:** 490 journals and other serials; 30 newspapers.
Services: Interlibrary loan; copying; 5 computer workstations; library open
to University students with required university library pass and to the public
upon recommendation. **Automated Operations:** Computerized cataloging.
Computerized Information Services: OCLC. **Also Known As:** Seton Hall
University - School of Theology. **Staff:** Sr. Concetta Russo, Libn.

★ 15048 ★
Seton Hall University - Library - Special Collections Center (Hist, Hum)
400 South Orange Ave.   Phone: (201)761-9126
South Orange, NJ 07079-2690 Msgr. William N. Field, Dir. of Spec.Coll.
Founded: 1856. **Staff:** 6. **Special Collections:** Gerald Murphy Civil War
Collection (1000 volumes); Asian Collection (10,000 volumes); MacManus
Collection (Irish literature, history and politics, and home rule; 4000
volumes); complete works of Liam O'Flaherty (300 autographed first
editions; periodicals and news clippings); Steciuk Collection (classical
studies). **Services:** Interlibrary loan; copying; collections open to the public
on fee basis. **Automated Operations:** Computerized cataloging and ILL.
Networks/Consortia: Member of Essex Hudson Regional Library
Cooperative, PALINET. **Remarks:** Alternate telephone number(s): 761-
9476. FAX: (201)761-9432. **Staff:** Jo Ann Cotz, Cur. of Spec.Coll.

Seton Hall University - McLaughlin Library - Special Collections
See: **Seton Hall University - Library - Special Collections Center (15048)**

★ 15049 ★
Seton Hall University - School of Law - Law Library (Law)
1111 Raymond Blvd. Phone: (201)642-8766
Newark, NJ 07102 Deborah D. Herrera, Dir.
Founded: 1950. **Staff:** Prof 10; Other 15. **Subjects:** Law. **Holdings:** 290,000 books, bound periodical volumes, and volumes in microform; 50 audiovisual programs. **Subscriptions:** 5462 journals and other serials. **Services:** Interlibrary loan; Federal and state depository. **Automated Operations:** Computerized cataloging and serials. **Computerized Information Services:** OCLC, LEXIS, WESTLAW, InfoTrac, NEXIS; CD-ROM (Auto-Graphics). **Networks/Consortia:** Member of PALINET, Essex Hudson Regional Library Cooperative. **Remarks:** FAX: (201)642-8748. **Staff:** Eileen Denner, Hd., Rd.Serv./Ref.Libn.; Kathleen McCarthy, Ref./Coll.Mgt.Libn.; Maja Basioli, Ref./Adm.Libn.; Elaine Garcia-Romero, Ref.Libn., Weekends; Alma De Jesus, Ref./Cir.Libn.; Barbara J. Meade, Hd., Tech.Serv./Cat.Libn.; Diane West, Asst.Cat.; Veronica Chris, Acq.Libn.; Phyllis Rossmann, Govt.Docs.Libn.; Dianne Oster, Ser.Libn.

Seton Hall University - School of Theology
See: **Seton Hall University - Immaculate Conception Seminary (15047)**

★ 15050 ★
Seton Hall University - University Archives - Special Collections Center
(Hist, Rel-Phil)
Duffy Hall
400 South Orange Ave. Phone: (201)761-9476
South Orange, NJ 07079 Msgr. William Field, Univ.Archv. & Presrv.Off.
Founded: 1978. **Staff:** Prof 2; Other 4. **Subjects:** Seton Hall and New Jersey Catholicism. **Special Collections:** Seton Hall University Archives (1296 cubic feet); Archives of the Archdiocese of Newark (1080 cubic feet); personal papers of Bernard Shanley, Leonard Dreyfuss, Richard Hughes, and Brendan Byrne (90 cubic feet); personal papers of the Seton-Jevons Family (21 cubic feet); personal papers of Congressman Peter W. Rodino, Jr. (750 cubic feet). **Services:** Copying; archives open to the public. **Publications:** New Jersey Catholic Records Newsletter, 3/year - for sale. **Special Catalogs:** Catholic Parish and Institutional Histories in the State of New Jersey; Guide to Northern New Jersey Catholic Parish and Institutional Records. **Remarks:** FAX: (201)761-9432. **Staff:** Jo Ann Elizabeth Cotz, Cur. of Spec.Coll.

★ 15051 ★
Seton Medical Center - Library (Med)
1900 Sullivan Ave. Phone: (415)991-6700
Daly City, CA 94015 Janice Perlman-Stites, Libn.
Staff: Prof 1. **Subjects:** Medicine, nursing, hospital administration. **Holdings:** 1000 books; 2000 bound periodical volumes; 4 shelves of audio cassettes and tapes. **Subscriptions:** 175 journals and other serials. **Services:** Interlibrary loan; copying; library open to professionals and by referral. **Computerized Information Services:** DIALOG Information Services, NLM. **Networks/Consortia:** Member of San Francisco Biomedical Library Network, San Mateo County Hospital Library Consortium. **Remarks:** FAX: (415)991-6024.

★ 15052 ★
Seton Memorial Library
Philmont Scout Ranch Phone: (505)376-2281
Cimarron, NM 87714 Stephen Zimmer
Founded: 1967. **Staff:** 2. **Subjects:** Books written by Ernest T. Seton, Boy Scouts, Southwest, natural history, Indian Art, Bureau of American Ethnology. **Special Collections:** Ernest T. Seton Collection (200 volumes; 7 VF drawers of manuscripts and correspondence). **Holdings:** 6000 books; 250 bound periodical volumes; 2000 photographs; local archeology reports (2 VF drawers). **Subscriptions:** 11 journals and other serials. **Services:** Copying; library open to the public. **Remarks:** Maintained by Boy Scouts of America-Philmont Scout Ranch.

★ 15053 ★
Settlement Music School - Blanche Wolf Kohn Library (Mus)
416 Queen St.
Box 25120 Phone: (215)336-0400
Philadelphia, PA 19147 Maura Boland, Libn.
Staff: Prof 2; Other 2. **Subjects:** Music. **Special Collections:** J. Gershon Cohen Chamber Music; William M. Kincaid Flute Music; Mischa Schneider Cello Music; Herman Busch Violin Music; woodwind music. **Holdings:** 1200 books; 10,000 scores; 100,000 pieces of classical sheet music. **Subscriptions:** 20 journals and other serials. **Services:** Copying; library open to alumni and noted musicians. **Special Catalogs:** Catalogs of special collections and woodwind music (both card).

Seufert Memorial Library
See: **Norwegian-American Hospital, Inc. (12109)**

Eric Sevareid Journalism Library
See: **University of Minnesota - Eric Sevareid Journalism Library (18908)**

★ 15054 ★
Seventh-Day Adventists General Conference - Archives (Rel-Phil)
12501 Old Columbia Pike Phone: (301)680-6000
Silver Spring, MD 20904 F. Donald Yost, Dir.
Founded: 1973 **Staff:** Prof 3; Other 1. **Subjects:** Seventh-day Adventism - history, theology, missions, institutions. **Special Collections:** Personal collections of prominent SDA leaders. **Holdings:** 50 books; 2000 bound periodical volumes; pamphlets; administrative records. **Services:** Copying; archives open to the public. **Publications:** Guide to Holdings of Archives. **Staff:** Bert Haloviak, Asst.Dir.

★ 15055 ★
Seventh Day Baptist Historical Society - Library (Rel-Phil, Hist)
3120 Kennedy Rd.
Box 1678 Phone: (608)752-5055
Janesville, WI 53547 Don A. Sanford, Hist.
Founded: 1916. **Staff:** Prof 2. **Subjects:** Seventh Day Baptist history; Sabbatarian literature, church history, religion; New England history; genealogy. **Special Collections:** Julius F. Sachse Ephrata Collection; Nyasaland-Malawi Collection, 1895-1915. **Holdings:** 2500 books; 500 bound and indexed periodical volumes; 250 society record books; tracts; reports; church records; letters; manuscripts. **Subscriptions:** 20 journals and other serials. **Services:** Interlibrary loan; copying; library open to the public (appointment suggested). **Publications:** Annual Report; occasional bulletins; demoninational histories. **Staff:** Janet Thorngate, Libn.

★ 15056 ★
73rd Bomb Wing Association - Library (Hist)
c/o Ray Ebert
706 Starcrest Phone: (512)629-7792
New Braunfels, TX 78130 Ray Ebert, Vice Chm.
Founded: 1980. **Subjects:** World War II history, with emphasis on the 73rd wing of the 20th Air Force in the Marianna Islands and Guam. **Holdings:** 500 volumes; biographical archives. **Services:** Copying; library open to the public for reference use only. **Formerly:** Located in Universal City, TX.

★ 15057 ★
Severin Wunderman Museum - Library (Hist)
3 Mason Phone: (714)472-1138
Irvine, CA 92718 Tony Clark, Exec.Dir.
Founded: 1985. **Subjects:** Jean Cocteau. **Holdings:** 400 books; 20 AV programs; 50 manuscripts; 200 nonbook items. **Subscriptions:** 6 journals and other serials. **Services:** Copying; library open to the public by appointment for reference use only. **Remarks:** FAX: (714)472-0931; 472-9348. Telex: 703685 SEVERINLSA.

Severson National Information Center
See: **Family Service America (5592)**

Seward House
See: Foundation Historical Association (6044)

★15058★
Seward & Kissel - Library (Law)
1 Battery Park Plaza   Phone: (212)574-1478
New York, NY 10004   Robert J. Davis, Libn.
Founded: 1950. Staff: Prof 2; Other 2. Subjects: Law. Holdings: 18,500
volumes; 21 VF drawers of pamphlets. Subscriptions: 175 journals and other
serials. Services: Interlibrary loan; library not open to the public.
Computerized Information Services: LEXIS, DIALOG Information
Services, Dow Jones News/Retrieval, NEXIS, WESTLAW, Maxwell
Macmillan Taxes Online. Remarks: FAX: (212)480-8421. Staff: Claudia
Picci.

★15059★
Sewell & Riggs - Library (Law)
333 Clay Ave., Suite 800   Phone: (713)652-8736
Houston, TX 77002   Tommie Lu Maulsby, Libn.
Founded: 1975. Staff: 2. Subjects: Law. Holdings: 1680 titles. Subscriptions:
60 journals and other serials; 2 newspapers. Services: Interlibrary loan (to
members of Houston Area Law Librarians); library not open to the public.
Automated Operations: INMAGIC. Computerized Information Services:
LEXIS, Information America, WESTLAW, DIALOG Information
Services. Remarks: FAX: (713)652-8808. Staff: Ann Quin Wilson.

★15060★
Sex Information & Education Council of the U.S. (SIECUS) - Mary S.
    Calderone Library (Soc Sci)
130 W. 42nd St., Suite 2500   Phone: (212)819-9770
New York, NY 10036   James L. Shortridge
Founded: 1979. Staff: Prof 1. Subjects: Sex education, behavior, and
research; human sexuality; family life education. Holdings: 4500 books; 200
curriculum items; 15 VF drawers; 750 pamphlets and booklets; 350
curricula. Subscriptions: 100 journals and other serials. Services: Copying;
library open to the public on fee basis. Computerized Information Services:
Internal databases. Performs searches on fee basis. Networks/Consortia:
Member of APLIC International Census Network. Publications: List of
bibliographies and other publications available on request. Remarks: FAX:
(212)819-9776.

★15061★
Seyfarth, Shaw, Fairweather & Geraldson - Library (Law)
2029 Century Park East, Suite 3300   Phone: (213)277-7200
Los Angeles, CA 90067   Beth Bernstein, Libn.
Staff: Prof 1. Subjects: Labor and agricultural labor law. Special
Collections: California Agricultural Labor Relations Board decisions, 1975
to present. Holdings: 12,000 books. Services: Interlibrary loan; library open
to area law firms. Automated Operations: Computerized cataloging.
Computerized Information Services: LEXIS, DIALOG Information
Services. Special Indexes: Index to Agricultural Labor Relations Board
decisions.

★15062★
Seyfarth, Shaw, Fairweather & Geraldson - Library (Law)
55 E. Monroe St.   Phone: (312)346-8000
Chicago, IL 60603   Carolyn Hayes, Libn.
Founded: 1946. Staff: Prof 3; Other 5.5. Subjects: Law - labor, corporate,
patent, environmental, securities; industrial relations; taxation. Holdings:
34,100 books; 910 bound periodical volumes; 164 lateral file drawers of
pamphlets, decisions, briefs, agreements, news clippings; 9 lateral file
drawers of audio- and videocassettes. Subscriptions: 455 journals and other
serials. Services: Interlibrary loan; library not open to the public. Automated
Operations: Computerized cataloging. Computerized Information Services:
DataTimes, DIALOG Information Services, Hannah Information Systems,
LEGI-SLATE, VU/TEXT Information Services, WESTLAW, Information
America, LEXIS, Legislative Information System (LIS), Labor Relations
Press (LRP), OCLC EPIC, Human Resource Information Network
(HRIN), Dun's Legal Search, NEXIS; CD-ROM (ASSIST, CASSIS);
internal databases. Networks/Consortia: Member of ILLINET, Chicago
Library System. Remarks: FAX: (312)269-8948. Staff: Nancy Faust,
Ref.Libn.; Cindi Anderson, Tech.Serv.Libn.

★15063★
Seyfarth, Shaw, Fairweather & Geraldson - Library (Law)
767 3rd Ave., 19th Fl.   Phone: (212)715-9037
New York, NY 10017   Grace Alviar, Libn.
Founded: 1979. Staff: Prof 1. Subjects: Law - labor, securities, corporate.
Holdings: 10,000 books; 100 bound periodical volumes. Subscriptions: 53
journals and other serials; 8 newspapers. Services: Interlibrary loan; library
not open to the public. Automated Operations: Computerized cataloging
and serials. Computerized Information Services: LEXIS, WESTLAW.
Remarks: FAX: (212)752-3116.

Henry M. Seymour Library
See: Knox College (8769)

William Seymour Theatre Collection
See: Princeton University - William Seymour Theatre Collection (13388)

★15064★
SF Camerawork - Reference Library (Art)
70 12th St.   Phone: (415)621-1001
San Francisco, CA 94103   Wendy Oberlander, Prog.Coord.
Founded: 1974. Subjects: Photography, contemporary art, art theory and
critisicm. Special Collections: Artists' books (75); exhibition catalogs (150).
Holdings: 1200 books; 700 bound periodical volumes. Subscriptions: 7
journals and other serials. Services: Copying; library open to the public.

★15065★
Shaare Zedek Medical Center - Medical Library (Med)
P.O. Box 3235   Phone: 2 555440
91031 Jerusalem, Israel   Benjamin B. Schachter, Dir., Med.Lib.
Founded: 1969. Staff: Prof 1.5. Subjects: Clinical medicine, Jewish
medicine. Holdings: 10,000 books; 75,000 bound periodical volumes.
Subscriptions: 270 journals and other serials; 2 newspapers. Services:
Interlibrary loan; copying; SDI; library open to the public for reference use
only. Computerized Information Services: MEDLINE. Contact Person:
Pamela Ben Eliezer. Publications: Accession List of New Books and
Periodicals, annual. Remarks: FAX: 2 513946.

Shadek-Fackenthal Library
See: Franklin and Marshall College (6095)

Shadelands Ranch Historical Museum
See: Walnut Creek Historical Society (19955)

★15066★
Shadyside Hospital - James Frazer Hillman Health Sciences Library
    (Med)
5230 Centre Ave.   Phone: (412)623-2415
Pittsburgh, PA 15232   Malinda Fetkovich, Dir.
Founded: 1975. Staff: Prof 1; Other 5. Subjects: Thoracic medicine,
cardiology, internal medicine, nursing. Holdings: 3000 books; 7000 bound
periodical volumes. Subscriptions: 300 journals and other serials. Services:
Interlibrary loan; copying; library open to the public with restrictions.
Computerized Information Services: MEDLARS, DIALOG Information
Services, BRS Information Technologies. Performs searches on fee basis.
Networks/Consortia: Member of Pittsburgh-East Hospital Library
Cooperative. Remarks: Alternate telephone number(s): 623-2441. FAX:
(412)683-8027.

Robert Shafer Memorial Library
See: Presbyterian Hospital (13321)

Charles E. Shain Library
See: Connecticut College - Charles E. Shain Library (4178)

The Shaker Library
See: **United Society of Believers (16782)**

Shaker Library
See: **Warren County Historical Society - Museum and Library (19975)**

★ 15067 ★
Shaker Museum and Library - Emma B. King Library (Rel-Phil)
Shake Museum Rd.   Phone: (518)794-9100
Old Chatham, NY 12136   Jerry V. Grant, Asst.Dir. for Coll. & Res.
Founded: 1950. **Staff:** Prof 1; Other 1. **Subjects:** Shakers and Shakerism - industry, economy, history, music, theology, religious practices, material culture. **Holdings:** 2000 books; 50 bound periodical volumes: 550 pamphlets; 2500 other cataloged items; 2500 slides; 120 reels of microfilm; AV programs; 2500 manuscripts; 3500 photographs; 40 maps; diaries; account books; drawings. **Subscriptions:** 20 journals and other serials. **Services:** Copying; library open to the public on fee basis. **Publications:** List of publications - available on request. **Remarks:** Library is a repository of Shaker Society manuscripts and records.

★ 15068 ★
Shakertown at Pleasant Hill - Museum Library (Hist)
3500 Lexington Rd.   Phone: (606)734-5411
Harrodsburg, KY 40330   Philip N. Dare, Libn.
Subjects: Shakers of Pleasant Hill, collective settlements. **Special Collections:** Cathcart Film Collection; Filson Historical Society collection on Shakers. **Holdings:** 900 books; 300 bound periodical volumes; 300 VF drawers; 173 reels of 35mm film; 965 microfiche. **Services:** Copying; library open to the public by appointment.

★ 15069 ★
Shakertown at South Union - South Union Shaker Museum - Library
(Rel-Phil)
Hwy. 68-80   Phone: (502)542-4167
South Union, KY 42283   Tommy Hines, Musm.Dir.
Founded: 1961. **Staff:** 1. **Subjects:** Shakers in Kentucky and the U.S., Kentucky history. **Special Collections:** South Union Shaker Colony manuscript collection (1000). **Holdings:** 350 books; 500 bound periodical volumes. **Subscriptions:** 10 journals and other serials. **Services:** Library open to the public by appointment.

★ 15070 ★
Shakespeare Birthplace Trust - Shakespeare Centre Library (Theater)
Henley St.
Stratford-upon-Avon, Warwickshire   Phone: 789 204016
CV37 6QW, England   Marian J. Pringle, Sr.Libn.
Founded: 1853. **Staff:** Prof 9. **Subjects:** Shakespeare, Warwickshire, theater, Elizabethan England. **Special Collections:** Royal Shakespeare Theatre Library, 1879 to present; Bram Stoker Collection of Henry Irving; Wheler and Saunders Collections of Warwickshire Documents. **Holdings:** 40,000 books; 1000 bound periodical volumes; 50,000 documents and manuscripts; 200 video titles; 200 phonograph records, tapes, films; 200 reels of microfilm; 100 microfiche titles; 6000 photographs; 10,000 prints and drawings. **Subscriptions:** 43 journals and other serials. **Services:** Copying; library open to the public with restrictions. **Computerized Information Services:** FESTE database of Shakespeare Memorial Theatre/Royal Shakespeare Company, 1879 to present (internal database). **Publications:** Shakespeare at Stratford-upon-Avon (microfilm), 1991. **Remarks:** FAX: 789 296083. **Staff:** Roger Pringle, Dir.; Robert Bearman, Sr.Archv.

★ 15071 ★
The Shakespeare Newsletter - The Shakespeare Data Bank (Hum)
1217 Ashland Ave.   Phone: (708)475-7550
Evanston, IL 60202   Louis Marder, Ed./Publ.
Founded: 1984. **Subjects:** Shakespeareana. **Holdings:** 8000 books and periodicals; 350 other cataloged items. **Services:** Library open to professors, teachers, students, theater personnel, Shakespeare Club members, and press service. **Computerized Information Services:** Shakespeare Data Bank, Inc. (SDB). **Publications:** Shakespeare Newsletter, quarterly. **Remarks:** The Shakespeare Data Bank Inc. is an international consortium of volunteeers compiling a Shakespeare Data Bank to enhance the scholarship, teaching, studying, directing, acting, understanding, and appreciation of the life, times, and works of Shakespeare. The SDB has access to the Shakespeare Hall of Fame, a large collection of Shakespeare memorabilia from which exhibitions and illustrated lectures can be arranged.

Shakespeare Research Collection
See: **University of Wisconsin--Milwaukee - Golda Meir Library (19638)**

★ 15072 ★
Shakespeare Society of America - New Place Rare Book Library (Hum)
1107 N. Kings Rd.   Phone: (213)654-5623
West Hollywood, CA 90069   R. Thad Taylor, Pres.
Founded: 1967. **Staff:** Prof 3; Other 2. **Subjects:** Shakespeare - all aspects of his works. **Special Collections:** Renaissance literature; early science; antique furniture; Shakespeare Stamp Collection; Shakespeare coins and medals. **Holdings:** 3000 books; 1500 bound periodical volumes; 1000 catalogs; 500 magazines and pamphlets; 450 clippings and articles; 2000 photographs and slides; 100 tapes and phonograph records. **Subscriptions:** 50 journals and other serials; 5 newspapers. **Services:** Interlibrary loan; library open to the public with written request. **Publications:** Shakespeare's Proclamation - to members, for sale to nonmembers. **Remarks:** The library is adjacent to a one-half scale replica of Shakespeare's Globe Theatre.

★ 15073 ★
Shand, Morahan & Company, Inc. - Library (Bus-Fin)
1007 Church St.   Phone: (708)866-2800
Evanston, IL 60201   Constance N. Field, Libn.
Staff: Prof 1; Other 1. **Subjects:** Property and casualty insurance, reinsurance, professional liability, management. **Holdings:** 2500 books; 200 unbound periodical titles; pamphlets and clippings. **Subscriptions:** 240 journals and other serials. **Services:** Interlibrary loan; copying; library open to the public by appointment. **Computerized Information Services:** DIALOG Information Services, WESTLAW, NEXIS, Datatimes, Veralex 2. **Networks/Consortia:** Member of ILLINET. **Publications:** Sources (bulletin), bimonthly - for internal distribution only. **Remarks:** FAX: (312)866-0796.

★ 15074 ★
Shanghai Institute of Pharmaceutical Industry - Library (Med, Biol Sci)
1320 West Beijing Lu   Phone: 2539828
Shanghai, People's Republic of China   Zhang Wenyu, Libn.
Founded: 1956. **Staff:** 14. **Subjects:** Pharmacy, medicine, microbiology, organic and analytical chemistry, biochemistry, chemical engineering. **Holdings:** 50,000 volumes; 40,000 bound periodical volumes; 36 AV programs; 7 journals on microcard. **Subscriptions:** 650 journals and other serials. **Services:** Copying. **Publications:** Collected Abstracts of Annual Meeting Papers - on exchange; Chinese Journal of Pharmaceuticals - on exchange. **Special Indexes:** Medicines (card, microfiche). **Remarks:** FAX: 21 2551779.

★ 15075 ★
Shanghai Library (Hum, Sci-Engr, Area-Ethnic)
325 West Nanjing Lu   Phone: 3273176
Shanghai 200003, People's Republic of China   Zhu Qing Zuo, Libn.
Founded: 1952. **Staff:** 557. **Subjects:** Philosophy, social sciences, natural sciences, applied sciences. **Special Collections:** Song, Yuan, Ming dynasties; The Six Dynasties, 222-589 A.D. (manuscripts); Sui and Tang dynasties; Ming and Qing writers (handwritten copies; manuscripts); early revolutionary documents. **Holdings:** 10 million volumes; technical reports; 11,250 reels of microfilm; 140,000 phonograph records; 1020 audiotapes; pre-liberation newspapers and magazines. **Subscriptions:** 14,449 journals and other serials. **Services:** Interlibrary loan; copying. **Special Catalogs:** Catalog of Shanghai Library Collection of Local Histories; Catalog of Works and Translations by Guo Moruo; Shanghai Union Catalog of New Foreign Books; additional catalogs available. **Special Indexes:** National Index of Newspapers and Periodicals: Philosophy and Social Sciences series; National Index of Newspapers and Periodicals: Science and Technology series - domestic distribution only.

★ 15076 ★
Shanghai Second Medical University - Health Sciences Library and
Information Center (Med, Biol Sci)
280 S. Chongqing Rd.   Phone: 21 3286590
Shanghai 200025, People's Republic of China   Ben-yu Quian
Founded: 1952. **Staff:** Prof 28; Other 25. **Subjects:** Medicine, biology. **Holdings:** 435,187 books; 12,085 bound periodical volumes. **Subscriptions:** 1820 journals and other serials; 63 newspapers. **Services:** Interlibrary loan; copying; SDI; library open to the public with restrictions. **Computerized Information Services:** CD-ROMs (MEDLINE, Chinese Medical Literature Database). Contact Person: Li Pei-zhu, Chf., Ref.Div. **Publications:** Scandinavian Journal of Gastroenterology (Chinese edition); Abstracts on Viral Hepatitis. **Remarks:** Telex: 30314 SSMC CN.

Shanghai Ship and Shipping Research Institute
See: **People's Republic of China - Ministry of Communications** (12926)

Shank Memorial Library
See: **Good Samaritan Hospital** (6554)

★ 15077 ★
Shanley & Fisher - Law Library (Law)
131 Madison Ave.   Phone: (201)285-1000
Morristown, NJ 07960-1979   Margaret M. Wang, Libn.
Staff: Prof 2; Other 3. **Subjects:** Law. **Holdings:** 20,000 volumes. **Services:** Library not open to the public. **Computerized Information Services:** LEXIS, WESTLAW, DIALOG Information Services, DataTimes, VU/TEXT Information Services. **Remarks:** FAX: (201)540-8819; (201)285-1625.

Shannon Library
See: **St. Thomas More College** (14598)

★ 15078 ★
Shannon & Wilson, Inc. - Technical Library (Sci-Engr)
400 N. 34th St., Suite 100
Box 300303   Phone: (206)633-6821
Seattle, WA 98103-9703   Jean Boucher, Lib./Info.Rsrcs.Mgr.
Founded: 1965. **Staff:** Prof 1; Other 1. **Subjects:** Geotechnical engineering, rock mechanics, applied geophysics, earthquake effects on soils, waste management. **Holdings:** 4000 volumes; 6000 reports, documents, and clippings; 1400 maps. **Subscriptions:** 90 journals and other serials. **Services:** Interlibrary loan; copying; library open to the public with permission of librarian. **Computerized Information Services:** DIALOG Information Services, ASCE Civil Engineering Database, STN International, EPIC, NISEE (UC-Berkeley). **Networks/Consortia:** Member of Western Library Network (WLN). **Publications:** Recent acquisitions, monthly. **Remarks:** FAX: (206)633-6777. **Staff:** Judy Davis.

Shanower Memorial Library
See: **Geauga County Historical Society** (6274)

Shapiro Library
See: **New Hampshire College** (11483)

Max Shapiro Library
See: **Beth El Synagogue** (1765)

★ 15079 ★
Samuel H. Shapiro Developmental Center - Professional Library (Med)
100 E. Jeffery St.   Phone: (815)939-8505
Kankakee, IL 60901   Juanita Licht, Br.Libn.
Founded: 1877. **Staff:** 1. **Subjects:** Developmental disabilities, mental retardation. **Holdings:** 2200 volumes; videotapes; educational games. **Subscriptions:** 62 journals and other serials. **Services:** Interlibrary loan; library open to the public by appointment.

★ 15080 ★
Shared Medical Systems (SMS) - Resource Library & Information Center (Comp Sci)
51 Valley Stream Pkwy.   Phone: (215)251-4896
Malvern, PA 19355   Deborah Sunday, Sr.Lib.Info.Spec.
Founded: 1981. **Staff:** Prof 2; Other 1. **Subjects:** Computers, health care administration. **Holdings:** 1000 books. **Subscriptions:** 225 journals and other serials; 10 newspapers. **Services:** Interlibrary loan; library not open to the public. **Automated Operations:** Computerized public access catalog and serials. **Computerized Information Services:** DIALOG Information Services, NEXIS, LEXIS, VU/TEXT Information Services, Dun & Bradstreet Business Credit Services, Dow Jones News/Retrieval. **Networks/Consortia:** Member of Consortium for Health Information & Library Services (CHI). **Remarks:** FAX: (215)251-8855. **Staff:** Cheryl Berdell.

★ 15081 ★
Sharlot Hall/Prescott Historical Societies - Library/Archives (Hist)
415 W. Gurley St.   Phone: (602)445-3122
Prescott, AZ 86301   Sue Abbey, Archv.
Founded: 1929. **Staff:** Prof 1; Other 1. **Subjects:** Anglo and Indian history of the Southwest, especially Arizona; Arizona history and mining. **Special Collections:** Sharlot Hall Collection (7 cubic feet); cowboy folklore and music collection (100 cassette tapes). **Holdings:** 9000 volumes; 200 linear feet of uncataloged items; 200 oral history/folklore tapes; photographs; manuscripts; diaries; artifacts; letters. **Subscriptions:** 13 journals and other serials. **Services:** Interlibrary loan; copying; library/archives open to the public. **Publications:** Quarterly newsletter; Prescott Union List of Periodicals, annual - to in-state libraries.

★ 15082 ★
Sharon Hospital - Health Sciences Library (Med)
W. Main St.   Phone: (203)364-4095
Sharon, CT 06069   Jackie Rorke, Libn.
Founded: 1975. **Staff:** Prof 1. **Subjects:** Medicine. **Holdings:** 400 books; 1440 bound periodical volumes. **Subscriptions:** 107 journals and other serials. **Services:** Interlibrary loan; copying; library open to the public for reference use only. **Computerized Information Services:** MEDLARS. **Networks/Consortia:** Member of Northwestern Connecticut Health Science Library Consortium (NW-CT-HSL), Connecticut Association of Health Science Libraries (CAHSL), North Atlantic Health Science Libraries (NAHSL), BHSL. **Remarks:** FAX: (203)364-4003.

★ 15083 ★
Sharon Regional Health System - Medical Staff Library (Med)
740 E. State St.   Phone: (412)983-3911
Sharon, PA 16146   Jean Burke, Sec.
Staff: 1. **Subjects:** Medicine and allied health sciences. **Holdings:** 283 books; 679 bound periodical volumes; 2422 unbound journals; 2 VF drawers of clip sheets and pamphlets. **Subscriptions:** 46 journals and other serials. **Services:** Interlibrary loan; copying; library open to community residents. **Networks/Consortia:** Member of Erie Area Health Information Library Cooperative (EAHILC). **Remarks:** FAX: (412)983-3958 (administration). **Staff:** Judy Schroeder, Libn.

★ 15084 ★
Sharon Regional Health System - School of Nursing - Library (Med)
740 E. State St.   Phone: (412)983-3911
Sharon, PA 16146   Judy Schroeder, Libn.
Staff: 1. **Subjects:** Nursing, medicine, nutrition, and allied health sciences. **Holdings:** 1500 books; 200 bound periodical volumes; 50 volumes of unbound journals; 4 VF drawers of clipsheets and pamphlets; 117 videotapes; 261 filmstrips and records; 14 slide cassette programs; 23 audio cassettes. **Subscriptions:** 25 journals and other serials. **Services:** Interlibrary loan; copying; library open to community residents. **Networks/Consortia:** Member of Erie Area Health Information Library Cooperative (EAHILC). **Remarks:** FAX: (412)983-3958 (administration).

Sharon Woods Technical Center
See: **Procter & Gamble Company** (13399)

Charles Cutler Sharp Library
See: **Ohio State University - Chemistry Library** (12301)

★ 15085 ★
Ella Sharp Museum - Research Library (Hist)
3225 4th St.   Phone: (517)787-2320
Jackson, MI 49203   Lynnea Loftus, Dir. of Coll.
Founded: 1987. **Staff:** 2. **Subjects:** Local history. **Special Collections:** Merriman-Sharp Collection (family papers, 1835-1912); Anna Berger-Lynch Papers; Withington Civil War Papers; Hurst Collection (16th to 18th century European prints); rare books. **Holdings:** 4000 reference books; 300 cubic feet of archival materials including 19th century periodicals; 5000 photographs. **Services:** Library open to the public by appointment for reference use only.

★ 15086 ★
George Sharp, Inc. - Library (Sci-Engr)
100 Church St.   Phone: (212)732-2800
New York, NY 10007   Ines White, Libn.
Subjects: Naval architecture, marine engineering. **Special Collections:** Ship design, engineering, and management information systems (1000 software programs). **Holdings:** Figures not available. **Computerized Information Services:** Internal database.

★ 15087 ★
Sharp Memorial Hospital - Health Sciences Library (Med)
7901 Frost St.   Phone: (619)541-3242
San Diego, CA 92123   A. Peri Worthington, Mgr.
Founded: 1970. **Staff:** Prof 1; Other 3. **Subjects:** Clinical medicine, nursing. **Special Collections:** Management collection. **Holdings:** 1100 books; 2957 bound periodical volumes. **Subscriptions:** 250 journals and other serials; 5 newspapers. **Services:** Interlibrary loan; copying; SDI; library open to the public by appointment. **Automated Operations:** Computerized public access catalog, acquisitions, serials, and circulation. **Computerized Information Services:** MEDLARS, DIALOG Information Services, BRS Information Technologies, Data-Star, OCLC; DOCLINE (electronic mail service). Performs searches on fee basis. **Networks/Consortia:** Member of National Network of Libraries of Medicine - Pacific Southwest Region. **Publications:** Newsletter, quarterly - for internal distribution only. **Special Catalogs:** Journal holdings list. **Remarks:** FAX: (619)541-3763. **Staff:** Laura S. Stubblefield.

Reuben L. Sharp Health Science Library
See: Cooper Hospital/University Medical Center (4275)

★ 15088 ★
Sharples Inc. - Research Laboratory - Library
955 Mearns Rd.   Phone: (215)443-4130
Warminster, PA 18974   Mary McFarland, Libn.
Remarks: No further information was supplied by respondent.

★ 15089 ★
Shasta County Law Library (Law)
Court House, Rm. 301
1500 Court St.   Phone: (916)225-5645
Redding, CA 96001   Carol Tracy, Law Libn.
Founded: 1851. **Subjects:** Law. **Holdings:** 13,500 books and bound periodical volumes. **Subscriptions:** 12 journals and other serials. **Services:** Interlibrary loan; copying; library open to the public.

★ 15090 ★
Lemuel Shattuck Hospital - Medical Library (Med)
170 Morton St.   Phone: (617)522-8110
Jamaica Plain, MA 02130   Anne Lima, Libn.
Founded: 1954. **Staff:** Prof 1. **Subjects:** Medicine and allied health sciences. **Holdings:** 940 books; 4360 bound periodical volumes; 320 audio cassettes. **Subscriptions:** 185 journals and other serials. **Services:** Interlibrary loan; library not open to the public. **Automated Operations:** Computerized ILL (DOCLINE). **Computerized Information Services:** NLM, OCLC. **Networks/Consortia:** Member of Southeastern Massachusetts Consortium of Health Science Libraries (SEMCO).

Shattuck Memorial Library
See: Bisbee Mining and Historical Museum (1864)

★ 15091 ★
Shaver Hospital - Health Sciences Library (Med)
541 Glenridge Ave.   Phone: (416)685-1381
St. Catharines, ON, Canada L2R 6S5   Ruth Servos, Dir., Hea.Rec./Lib.
Staff: 1. **Subjects:** Medicine, nursing, palliative care, geriatrics, and allied health sciences. **Special Collections:** Canadian Tuberculosis Association, 1927 to present; Tuberculosis in Industry, 1941 to present; Financial & Medical Statistics of Sanitoria of Ontario, 1930 to present; chest diseases. **Holdings:** 3000 books; 300 bound periodical volumes; manuscripts; reports and clippings. **Subscriptions:** 52 journals and other serials. **Services:** Interlibrary loan; copying; library open to medical personnel. **Remarks:** FAX: (416)685-6035.

Robert E. Shaver Library of Engineering
See: University of Kentucky (18758)

Alfred Shaw and Edward Durell Stone Library
See: Boston Architectural Center - Alfred Shaw and Edward Durell Stone Library (1975)

Charles E. Shaw Herpetological Library
See: Zoological Society of San Diego - Ernst Schwarz Library (20849)

Edwin Shaw Archives
See: Akron Art Museum - Library (167)

Shaw Historical Library
See: Oregon Institute of Technology (12526)

J. Porter Shaw Library
See: National Maritime Museum (11234)

★ 15092 ★
The Lloyd Shaw Foundation - Archives (Rec)
1620 Los Alamos Ave., S.W.   Phone: (505)247-3921
Albuquerque, NM 87104   Dr. William M. Litchman, Dir.
Founded: 1977. **Staff:** Prof 1. **Subjects:** Dancing - square, round, contra, social, folk. **Special Collections:** Dance Away Library (5000 items); Charlie Thomas Collection (square dance; 2000 items); Bob Osgood Collection (square dance recordings). **Holdings:** 1000 books; 10,000 unbound periodicals; letters; sheet music; phonograph records; audio- and videotapes; wire recordings; photographs; Square Dancing Hall of Fame portraits; clothing. **Subscriptions:** 50 journals and other serials. **Services:** Copying; archives open to the public. **Automated Operations:** Computerized cataloging. **Computerized Information Services:** Internal databases; electronic mail. **Publications:** Bibliography of American Country Dancing; Comprehensive Index of the Harry Davidson Cassette Tapes; Known Copies of Playford's "English Dancing Master" and "The Country Dancing Master"; List of Dissertations on Dance; The Plain Quadrille. **Special Catalogs:** Catalog of Dance Videotapes; Catalog of Videotapes (printout); Catalog of the Dance Away Library (printout). **Remarks:** Alternate telephone number(s): 255-2661. Library is located at 5506 Coal Ave., S.E., Albuquerque, NM 87108.

★ 15093 ★
Shaw, Pittman, Potts & Trowbridge - Library (Law)
2300 N St., N.W.   Phone: (202)663-8500
Washington, DC 20037   Carolyn P. Ahearn, Libn.
Staff: Prof 4; Other 6. **Subjects:** Law. **Holdings:** 24,000 books; 550 bound periodical volumes; 1000 congressional hearings; 8 VF drawers of pamphlets. **Subscriptions:** 200 journals and other serials. **Services:** Interlibrary loan; copying; library open to the public with restrictions. **Computerized Information Services:** LEXIS, DIALOG Information Services, WESTLAW, Dow Jones News/Retrieval, LEGI-SLATE; internal database. **Remarks:** FAX: (202)663-8007. **Staff:** Kelly A. Vinopal; F. Michael Welsh; Susan M. Trevisan.

★ 15094 ★
Shawmut Bank, N.A. - Library
1 Federal St., 8th Fl.
Boston, MA 02211
Defunct.

★ 15095 ★
Shawnee Mission Medical Center - Medical Library (Med)
9100 W. 74th
Box 2923   Phone: (913)676-2101
Shawnee Mission, KS 66201   Clifford L. Nestell, Lib.Dir.
Staff: Prof 1; Other 3. **Subjects:** Medicine. **Holdings:** 8366 books; 8691 bound periodical volumes; 2640 audiotapes; 503 videotapes; 76 software packages. **Subscriptions:** 612 journals and other serials. **Services:** Interlibrary loan; copying; SDI; library open to the public with restrictions. **Automated Operations:** Computerized cataloging, acquisitions, serials, circulation, and ILL. **Computerized Information Services:** DIALOG Information Services, NLM, OCLC. **Networks/Consortia:** Member of Kansas City Library Network, Inc. (KCLN). **Remarks:** FAX: (913)676-2106.

★ 15096 ★
SH&E, Inc. - Library (Trans)
90 Park Ave., 27th Fl.   Phone: (212)682-8455
New York, NY 10016   Beth L. Geltman, Libn.
Founded: 1963. **Staff:** Prof 1. **Subjects:** Transportation, aircraft, airport
planning, tourism, travel, economics, finance, marketing. **Holdings:** 10,000
books; 100 bound periodical volumes; 500 statistical volumes. **Subscriptions:**
100 journals and other serials. **Services:** Interlibrary loan; copying; library
open to the public by appointment. **Remarks:** FAX: (212)986-1825. Telex:
4949296.

★ 15097 ★
Shea & Gardner - Library (Law)
1800 Massachusetts Ave., N.W.   Phone: (202)828-2019
Washington, DC 20036   Sharon Kissel, Libn.
Founded: 1950. **Staff:** Prof 2; Other 3. **Subjects:** Law - labor, maritime,
transportation, environment. **Special Collections:** Legislative histories (500
volumes). **Holdings:** 30,000 books; 700 bound periodical volumes; 2000
other cataloged items. **Subscriptions:** 1100 journals and other serials.
Services: Interlibrary loan; library not open to the public. **Computerized
Information Services:** LEXIS, NEXIS, DIALOG Information Services,
WESTLAW, VU/TEXT Information Services, NewsNet, LEGI-SLATE.
Remarks: FAX: (202)828-2195. Telex: 89 2399.

★ 15098 ★
Shea & Gould - Library (Law)
1251 Avenue of the Americas   Phone: (212)827-3489
New York, NY 10020   C. Shireen Kumar, Dir., Leg.Info.Serv.
Founded: 1964. **Staff:** Prof 4; Other 5. **Subjects:** Law - real estate, corporate,
tax, trusts and estates, administrative, public utilities, bankruptcy, labor;
litigation. **Holdings:** 50,000 books. **Subscriptions:** 300 journals and other
serials; 10 newspapers. **Services:** Interlibrary loan; library not open to the
public. **Automated Operations:** Computerized cataloging. **Computerized
Information Services:** Information America, LEGI-SLATE, LEXIS,
NEXIS, DIALOG Information Services, WESTLAW, DataTimes, Dow
Jones News/Retrieval, Dun & Bradstreet Business Credit Services, VU/
TEXT Information Services, OCLC, NewsNet, Inc., InvesText, Legislative
Retrieval System (LRS), FT PROFILE, ORBIT Search Service, Brief
Touch, Superior On-line; Litigation Brief, Memo Bank (internal databases).
Publications: Library News (newsletter), monthly - for internal distribution
only. **Remarks:** FAX: (212)840-6702; 840-6703; 840-6704. **Staff:** Susan
Foster, Hd. of Ref.; Danielle Rudi, Corp.Info.Spec.; Gail Wright, Acq.;
Mansoureh Niamir, ILL Coord.

James J. Shea Memorial Library
See: **American International College** (648)

★ 15099 ★
Shearman & Sterling - Library (Law)
725 S. Figueroa St., 21st Fl.   Phone: (213)239-0358
Los Angeles, CA 90017   Jill Sidford, Libn.
Staff: Prof 1; Other 1. **Subjects:** Law. **Holdings:** 7500 volumes. **Services:**
Interlibrary loan (limited); library not open to the public. **Automated
Operations:** Computerized cataloging. **Computerized Information Services:**
LEXIS, WESTLAW, Dow Jones News/Retrieval, DIALOG Information
Services, Information America. **Remarks:** FAX: (213)239-0381.

★ 15100 ★
Shearman & Sterling - Library (Law)
555 California St.   Phone: (415)616-1100
San Francisco, CA 94104   Debbie Giahos, Libn.
Staff: Prof 1; Other 1. **Subjects:** Law. **Holdings:** 10,000 books.
Subscriptions: 80 journals and other serials; 10 newspapers. **Services:**
Interlibrary loan; library not open to the public. **Automated Operations:**
Computerized cataloging. **Computerized Information Services:** LEXIS,
WESTLAW, Dow Jones News/Retrieval, DIALOG Information Services,
Information America. **Remarks:** FAX: (415)616-1199.

★ 15101 ★
Shearman & Sterling - Library (Law)
801 Pennsylvania Ave., N.W., 9th Fl.   Phone: (202)508-8055
Washington, DC 20004   Jeanette Richmond, Libn.
Founded: 1989. **Staff:** Prof 1. **Subjects:** Law. **Holdings:** 5000 volumes.
Subscriptions: 50 journals and other serials; 10 newspapers. **Services:**
Interlibrary loan; library not open to the public. **Computerized Information
Services:** LEXIS, WESTLAW, DIALOG Information Services, LEGI-
SLATE, Dow Jones News/Retrieval, Current USC. **Remarks:** FAX:
(202)298-6750.

★ 15102 ★
Shearman & Sterling - Library (Law)
153 E. 53rd St., Rm. 3205   Phone: (212)848-4624
New York, NY 10022   Jack S. Ellenberger, Dir. of Libs.
Founded: 1873. **Staff:** Prof 4; Other 10. **Subjects:** Law. **Special Collections:**
Banking, legislative histories. **Holdings:** 70,000 volumes. **Subscriptions:** 400
journals and other serials; 50 newspapers. **Services:** Interlibrary loan; library
not open to the public. **Automated Operations:** Computerized public access
catalog and cataloging. **Computerized Information Services:** Dow Jones
News/Retrieval, LEXIS, WESTLAW, DIALOG Information Services,
NewsNet, Inc., LEGI-SLATE. **Publications:** Library Bulletin. **Remarks:**
Alternate telephone number(s): (212)848-5400 (ILL); FAX: (212)848-5229.
Staff: Nancy Rine, Hd.Ref.Libn.; John Lai, Cat. & Sys.Libn.; Katharine
Wolpe, Adm.Libn.

Paul B. Sheatsley Library
See: **University of Chicago - National Opinion Research Center (NORC)**
(18456)

★ 15103 ★
Sheboygan County Historical Research Center (Hist)
518 Water St.   Phone: (414)467-4667
Sheboygan Falls, WI 53085   Janice Hildebrand, Libn.
Founded: 1983. **Staff:** Prof 1; Other 1. **Subjects:** County history and
genealogy. **Special Collections:** Civil War; World War I. **Holdings:** 5000
books; historic photographs and negatives; 100,000 county land records.
Subscriptions: 4 newspapers. **Services:** Copying; center open to the public
for reference use only. **Remarks:** Jointly maintained by Sheboygan County
Genealogy Society, Sheboygan County Historical Society, and Sheboygan
County Landmarks, Ltd.

★ 15104 ★
Sheboygan Press Library (Publ)
632 Center Ave.   Phone: (414)457-7711
Sheboygan, WI 53081   Janice Hildebrand, Libn.
Staff: Prof 1. **Subjects:** Newspaper reference topics. **Special Collections:**
Wisconsin Blue Books; city directories; local and state histories. **Holdings:**
200 books; 600 bound periodical volumes; newspapers, 1907 to present, on
microfilm. **Subscriptions:** 10 journals and other serials; 30 newspapers.
Services: Copying; library open to the public. **Special Catalogs:** Local
obituaries, 1966 to present. **Remarks:** FAX: (414)457-0178.

★ 15105 ★
John G. Shedd Aquarium - McCormick-Tribune Reference Library (Biol
Sci)
1200 S. Lake Shore Dr.   Phone: (312)939-2426
Chicago, IL 60605   Janet E. Powers, Coord. of Lib.Serv.
Founded: 1975. **Staff:** Prof 2; Other 4. **Subjects:** Marine and freshwater
biology, marine mammals, fishes, water pollution, fisheries, Lake Michigan,
aquatic education. **Holdings:** 12,000 books; 300 file folders of clippings,
reprints, pamphlets. **Subscriptions:** 300 journals and other serials. **Services:**
Interlibrary loan (limited); copying; library open to the public by
appointment. **Automated Operations:** Computerized cataloging. **Networks/
Consortia:** Member of Chicago Library System, Consortium of Museum
Libraries in the Chicago Area. **Remarks:** FAX: (312)939-8069.

★15106★
Sheehan, Phinney, Bass & Green - Library (Law)
1000 Elm St.
P.O. Box 3701   Phone: (603)668-0300
Manchester, NH 03101   Lynne J. Spence, Libn.
Staff: Prof 1; Other 1. Subjects: Law. Holdings: Figures not available.
Services: Interlibrary loan; copying; library open to the public at librarian's discretion. Computerized Information Services: LEXIS, NEXIS, WESTLAW, DIALOG Information Services, Dow Jones News/Retrieval. Remarks: FAX: (603)627-8121.

Sheely-Lee Law Library
See: Dickinson School of Law (4854)

Fulton J. Sheen Archives
See: Ambrose Swasey Library (15904)

Sheffield Botanical Library
See: Atlanta Botanical Garden (1235)

★15107★
Sheffield City Polytechnic - Psalter Lane Site Library (Art, Hist)
Psalter Lane
Sheffield S11 8UZ, England   Phone: 0742 556101
Founded: 1843. Subjects: Art, design, film, history.Holdings: Figures not available. Services: Interlibrary loan; copying; library open to the public.

★15108★
Shelburne Museum, Inc. - Research Library (Hist, Art)
Shelburne, VT 05482   Phone: (802)985-3346
                                        Audrey Ritter, Libn.
Founded: 1947. Subjects: Antiques, art, Vermontiana, furniture, architecture, textiles, transportation. Holdings: 7000 books; 600 bound periodical volumes; 1400 pamphlets; 164 magazines on antiques; 260 manuscripts; 600 volumes of records of museum holdings. Subscriptions: 55 journals and other serials. Services: Copying; library open to the public by appointment.

★15109★
Shelby County Law Library (Law)
Courthouse   Phone: (513)498-7221
Sidney, OH 45365   Rita Miller, Libn.
Staff: 2. Subjects: Law. Holdings: 18,000 books; microfiche. Subscriptions: 75 journals and other serials. Services: Copying; library open to the public for reference use only.

★15110★
Sheldon Museum - Research Center (Hist)
1 Park St.   Phone: (802)388-2117
Middlebury, VT 05753   Polly C. Darnell, Libn.
Founded: 1882. Staff: Prof 2. Subjects: Addison County and Vermont history. Special Collections: Newspapers published in Middlebury, 1801 to present (bound). Holdings: 4000 books; pamphlets; 200 scrapbooks compiled by Henry L. Sheldon; 500 linear feet of manuscripts, account books, letters, diaries; 2500 photographs of local scenes and people; 117 maps; 57 audiotapes; 3 videotapes. Subscriptions: 3 journals and other serials. Services: Library open to the public for reference use only. Automated Operations: Computerized cataloging of manuscripts. Publications: Annual report; Addison County Heritage: Historical Studies from the Library of the Sheldon Museum, irregular - for sale. Special Catalogs: Manuscript collection (online). Staff: Phyllis B. Cunningham, Asst.Libn.

Sheldon Museum & Cultural Center
See: Chilkat Valley Historical Society (3599)

★15111★
Shell Canada Limited - Corporate Library (Energy)
400 4th Ave., S.W.
Sta. M, P.O. Box 100
Calgary, AB, Canada T2P 2H5   Phone: (403)691-4070
Founded: 1958. Staff: Prof 3; Other 8. Subjects: Geology, earth sciences, petroleum and chemical engineering, minerals, business and economics. Special Collections: Geological Survey of Canada publications. Holdings: 6500 books; 120 bound periodical volumes; 9000 government documents; 160 microfiche; 200 reels of microfilm; 625 theses. Subscriptions: 1200 journals and other serials; 12 newspapers. Services: Interlibrary loan (limited); library open to the public for reference use only. Automated Operations: Computerized cataloging, serials, and circulation. Computerized Information Services: DIALOG Information Services, PFDS Online, Compusearch Market and Social Research Ltd., CAN/OLE, Info Globe, Infomart Online, FT PROFILE; SCROLL (internal database). Publications: New Additions to the Corporate Library, monthly - for internal distribution only. Remarks: Alternate telephone number(s): 691-3249; 691-2348; 691-3281. FAX: (403)269-6760. Staff: Mila E. Carozzi, Hd.Libn., Searching and Ref.Serv.; Janet Feero, Hd.Libn., Tech.Serv.; Kris Barge, Libn.

★15112★
Shell Canada Limited - Oakville Research Centre - Library (Energy)
P.O. Box 2100   Phone: (416)825-4308
Oakville, ON, Canada L6J 5C7   Marie R. Bonfield, Libn.
Founded: 1970. Staff: 2. Subjects: Petroleum technology products and processes. Holdings: Books; 88,500 proprietary research and technical reports; pamphlets; journal articles; patents. Subscriptions: 123 journals. Services: Interlibrary loan. Automated Operations: Computerized cataloging, acquisitions, serials, circulation, and ILL. Computerized Information Services: CAN/OLE, DIALOG Information Services, NLM, ORBIT Search Service, Canadian Centre for Occupational Health & Safety, NTIS; CD-ROM (MSDS/FTSS); INFO/ORC (internal database); Envoy 100, DIALMAIL, Shell PROFS System (electronic mail services). Networks/Consortia: Member of Shell Canada Technical Information System. Publications: Monthly Accession List of Final Reports and Monographs. Special Indexes: Eight separate indexes (corporate author, title, personal author, series, project, subject, KWIC index, and shelf list or master file), produced cumulatively every month on computer tape and merged annual with previous years. Remarks: FAX: (416)827-0027. Formerly: Its Shell Research Centre Library.

★15113★
Shell Development Company - Bellaire Research Center Library
Box 481
Houston, TX 77001
Defunct. Merged with Shell Western E & P Inc. - Woodcreek Library to form Shell Oil-E&P - Technical Information Center.

★15114★
Shell Development Company - Westhollow Research Center Library (Sci-Engr, Energy)
Box 1380
Houston, TX 77251-1380   Phone: (713)493-7530
                                        Elsie Kwok, Supv.
Founded: 1975. Subjects: Corrosion, petrochemicals, petroleum refining, toxicology. Holdings: 14,000 volumes. Subscriptions: 1430 journals and other serials. Computerized Information Services: DIALOG Information Services, PFDS Online.

John N. Shell Library
See: Nassau County Medical Society - Nassau Academy of Medicine (11007)

★15115★
Shell Oil Company - Information & Library Services (Energy, Bus-Fin)
Box 587   Phone: (713)241-5433
Houston, TX 77001   Lydia Foght, Lib.Supv.
Founded: 1971. Staff: Prof 8; Other 14. Subjects: Petroleum, business, management. Special Collections: Shell Oil Archive Collection. Holdings: 15,730 volumes. Subscriptions: 1045 journals and other serials. Services: Interlibrary loan; SDI; library services open to the public. Automated Operations: Computerized cataloging, acquisitions, serials, and circulation.

Computerized Information Services: DIALOG Information Services, PFDS Online, Dow Jones News/Retrieval, NEXIS, RLIN, PIERS (Port Import/ Export Reporting Service), VU/TEXT Information Services, DRI/ McGraw-Hill, DataTimes, Oil & Gas Journal Energy Database, BRS Information Technologies, NewsNet, Inc.; OnTyme Electronic Message Network Service, DIALMAIL (electronic mail services). **Publications:** Current Awarenes Bulletin (CAB), monthly - proprietary; New Acquisition List (NAL), monthly - both available by mailing list and electronic bulletin board; Published Periodical List, quarterly; Proprietary Periodical List, quarterly - both available upon request and on electronic bulletin board. **Remarks:** FAX: (713)241-6255, Library Processing Ctr; (713)241-4068, Library Services. **Staff:** Library Services: Patricia A. Kanter, Sect.Supv.; J. Foster, Info.Anl.; C. Wehmeyer, Info.Anl.; C. Marty, Anl. Library Processing: Frances K. Bown, Supv.; N. Linden, Sr.Info.Anl.

★ 15116 ★
Shell Oil-E&P - Technical Information Center (Energy, Sci-Engr)
P.O. Box 481   Phone: (713)245-7293
Houston, TX 77001   Mimi Pappas, Supv.
Founded: 1946. **Staff:** Prof 3; Other 6. **Subjects:** Geology, production, computing, energy, mining, minerals. **Holdings:** 43,200 books; 6720 bound periodical volumes; 63,000 Shell proprietary reports. **Subscriptions:** 619 journals and other serials. **Services:** Interlibrary loan; copying; SDI; library open to the public by appointment. **Automated Operations:** Computerized cataloging, acquisitions, serials, and circulation. **Computerized Information Services:** DIALOG Information Services, RLIN, OCLC, NEXIS, PFDS Online; internal databases. **Publications:** Awareness Bulletins for books, journals, and proprietary reports. **Remarks:** FAX: (713)245-7581. Contains holdings of the former Shell Development Company - Bellaire Research Center Library and Shell Western E & P Inc. - Woodcreek Library. **Staff:** L.J. Pharis, Sr.Info.Tech.; A.H. Krum, Info.Tech.; M.L. West, Info.Tech.

★ 15117 ★
Shell Western E & P Inc. - Woodcreek Library
Box 4423
Houston, TX 77210-4423
Defunct. Merged with Shell Development Company - Bellaire Research Center Library to form Shell Oil-E&P - Technical Information Center.

Ruth M. Shellens Memorial Library
See: **English-Speaking Union of the U.S.A.** (5360)

★ 15118 ★
Shelter Island Historical Society - Havens House Museum - Archives (Hist)
P.O. Box 847   Phone: (516)749-0025
Shelter Island, NY 11964-0847   Peggy Dickerson, Chm.
Founded: 1972. **Staff:** 9. **Subjects:** Local history. **Special Collections:** Worthington journals and notebooks (ornithology); Shelter Island historic house research and photographic records. **Holdings:** 200 books; 25 bound periodical volumes; 200 postcards; 400 literary documents; 100 financial documents; 30 maps; 1600 clippings; 425 photographs; genealogical material. **Services:** Copying; archives open to the public for reference use only.

Herbert Shelton Library
See: **American Natural Hygiene Society, Inc.** (695)

Shenandoah Natl. Park
See: **U.S. Natl. Park Service** (17777)

★ 15119 ★
Shenandoah University - Howe Library - Special Collections (Rel-Phil)
Winchester, VA 22601   Phone: (703)665-4553
                                               Christopher A. Bean, Dir.
Founded: 1875. **Staff:** Prof 4; Other 5. **Special Collections:** History of Evangelical United Brethren Church; Shenandoah College & Conservatory archives; Close Collection (history of Shenandoah Valley). **Holdings:** 2800 uncataloged items. **Services:** Interlibrary loan; copying; collections open to the public. **Automated Operations:** Computerized cataloging. **Computerized Information Services:** DIALOG Information Services, OCLC. Performs searches on fee basis. Contact Person: Rosemary Green, Ref.Libn. **Networks/Consortia:** Member of SOLINET. **Remarks:** FAX: (703)665-4609. **Staff:** Michael DeLalla, Media Ctr.Dir.

★ 15120 ★
Shenango Valley Medical Center - Medical Library (Med)
2200 Memorial Dr. Extended   Phone: (412)981-3500
Farrell, PA 16121   Ethelnel Baron, Staff Sec.
Staff: 1. **Subjects:** Medicine. **Holdings:** 500 books; 200 video cassettes; 200 Audio-Digest tapes. **Subscriptions:** 40 journals and other serials. **Services:** Interlibrary loan; library not open to the public. **Networks/Consortia:** Member of National Network of Libraries of Medicine - Middle Atlantic Region.

★ 15121 ★
Shenkar College of Textile Technology and Fashion - Library (Sci-Engr, Art)
12 Anna Frank St.   Phone: 3 7521133
52526 Ramat Gan, Israel   Paula Ostfeld, Lib.Hd.
Founded: 1970. **Staff:** Prof 5. **Subjects:** Textile technology and machinery, fashion, fashion history, apparel industry, production management. **Special Collections:** History of Costumes (250 items); Pollak Collection (108 items). **Holdings:** 17,000 books; 250 periodical titles. **Subscriptions:** 250 journals and other serials. **Services:** Interlibrary loan; copying; library open to the public. **Computerized Information Services:** DIALOG Information Services. Performs searches on fee basis. **Publications:** Bibliographies. **Special Catalogs:** Catalog of New Books in the Library, annual. **Remarks:** FAX: 3 7521141. Telex: 341118 BXTV-IL, ext. 5790. **Staff:** Esther Heimer; Margot Kurzweil; Orit Mussin-Levi.

Drs. Ben and A. Jess Shenson Library
See: **Triton Museum of Art** (16524)

Carl F. Shepard Memorial Library
See: **Illinois College of Optometry** (7671)

Edward M. Shepard Memorial Room
See: **Springfield-Greene County Public Libraries** (15603)

★ 15122 ★
Shepard's/McGraw-Hill - Library (Law)
555 Middle Creek Pkwy.
P.O. Box 35300   Phone: (719)481-7548
Colorado Springs, CO 80935-3530   Gregory P. Harris, Libn.
Founded: 1873. **Staff:** Prof 4. **Subjects:** Law. **Holdings:** 100,000 books; 79,500 reports; 20,000 statutes, digests. **Subscriptions:** 500 journals and other serials. **Services:** Library not open to the public. **Computerized Information Services:** WESTLAW, LEXIS, CCH-ACCESS.

George Shepherd Library
See: **Saskatchewan Western Development Museums** (14870)

Sheppard Library
See: **Massachusetts College of Pharmacy and Allied Health Sciences** (9790)

★ 15123 ★
Sheppard, Mullin, Richter & Hampton - Law Library (Law)
333 S. Hope St., 48th Fl.   Phone: (213)620-1780
Los Angeles, CA 90071   Glen Gustafson, Libn.
Staff: Prof 2; Other 1. **Subjects:** Law. **Holdings:** 50,000 books. **Subscriptions:** 200 journals and other serials. **Services:** Interlibrary loan; library not open to the public. **Automated Operations:** Computerized cataloging, acquisitions, and circulation. **Computerized Information Services:** LEXIS, DIALOG Information Services, WESTLAW, Dow Jones News/Retrieval, VU/TEXT Information Services, DataTimes, LEGI-SLATE, Information America, Legi-Tech.

Sherbrooke Historical Society
See: **Societe d'Histoire de Sherbrooke** (15303)

★ 15124 ★
Sheridan College - Griffith Memorial Library - Special Collections (Rare Book, Hist)
Box 1500   Phone: (307)674-6446
Sheridan, WY 82801   Deborah Iverson, Lib.Dir.
Staff: Prof 1; Other 5. **Special Collections:** Reynolds Memorial Collection of Western Americana; Sheridan College history; Thorne-Rider memorabilia; Griffith Indian art collection (early reservation, Plains Indian); rare book collection. **Subscriptions:** 325 journals and other serials. **Services:** Interlibrary loan; copying; collections open to the public. **Automated Operations:** Computerized cataloging and ILL (DOCLINE). **Computerized Information Services:** BRS Information Technologies, MEDLARS; InterNet (electronic mail service). Performs searches on fee basis. **Networks/Consortia:** Member of Bibliographical Center for Research, Rocky Mountain Region, Inc. (BCR), Northeastern Wyoming Medical Library Consortium. **Remarks:** FAX: (307)672-6157.

★ 15125 ★
Sheridan County Historical Society, Inc. - Agnes & Clarence Benschoter Memorial Library (Hist)
Box 274   Phone: (308)327-2917
Rushville, NE 69360   Robert W. Buchan, Cur.
Founded: 1958. **Staff:** Prof 1; Other 1. **Subjects:** Western and Nebraska history; military; genealogy. **Special Collections:** Camp Sheridan, Nebraska archives, 1874-1881. **Holdings:** 700 books; 100 bound periodical volumes; clippings; manuscripts; albums. **Services:** Copying; library open to the public by appointment. **Publications:** Recollections of Sheridan County.

Sherman Art Library
See: **Dartmouth College** (4615)

★ 15126 ★
Sherman College of Straight Chiropractic - Tom and Mae Bahan Library (Med)
Box 1452   Phone: (803)578-8770
Spartanburg, SC 29304   David M. Bowles, Lib.Dir.
Founded: 1973. **Staff:** Prof 1; Other 4. **Subjects:** Chiropractic, clinical and basic sciences. **Special Collections:** B.J. Palmer Collection. **Holdings:** 9443 books; 1137 bound periodical volumes; 328 audiotapes; 187 videotapes; 4514 slides; 8 16mm films; 8 phonograph records; 4 VF drawers. **Subscriptions:** 83 journals and other serials. **Services:** Interlibrary loan; copying; library open to chiropractic doctors. **Automated Operations:** Computerized cataloging and ILL. **Computerized Information Services:** OCLC, MEDLINE; internal database. Performs searches on fee basis. **Networks/Consortia:** Member of Chiropractic Library Consortium (CLIBCON).

★ 15127 ★
Sherman Family Association - Clearinghouse (Hist)
626 Black Rock Rd.   Phone: (215)525-8929
Bryn Mawr, PA 19010   Robert C. Fraunberger, Pres. & Certified Geneal.
Founded: 1890. **Subjects:** Genealogy. **Special Collections:** Sherman genealogies. **Holdings:** 1000 volumes; manuscripts; charts. **Services:** Library not open to the public. Will respond to questions from Sherman descendants with SASE. **Remarks:** Maintains genealogical data on the descendants of Edmund Sherman who arrived in the Massachusetts Bay Colony in 1634.

★ 15128 ★
Sherman Research Library (Hist)
614 Dahlia Ave.   Phone: (714)673-1880
Corona Del Mar, CA 92625   Dr. William O. Hendricks, Dir.
Founded: 1966. **Staff:** Prof 2. **Subjects:** Pacific Southwest history, 1870 to present - economic development, land and water, transportation, immigration. **Special Collections:** Sherman papers; Brant papers; Colorado River Land Company documents. **Holdings:** 15,000 books; 400 bound periodical volumes; 2500 pamphlets; 375 document boxes of business papers; 1475 reels of microfilm of newspapers; 200 theses and dissertations on microfilm; 2000 maps. **Subscriptions:** 30 journals and other serials. **Services:** Interlibrary loan; library open to the public. **Special Catalogs:** Inventory catalogs to the papers. **Staff:** Judith Buckle, Res.Asst.

Henry Knox Sherrill Resource Center
See: **Episcopal Church Executive Council** (5385)

★ 15129 ★
Sherritt Gordon, Ltd. - Information Services (Sci-Engr)
Fort Saskatchewan, AB, Canada T8L 3W4   Phone: (403)992-5066
                                            Mary Lee Kennedy, Info.Sci.
Founded: 1953. **Staff:** 5. **Subjects:** Metallurgy, inorganic chemistry, physical chemistry, advanced materials. **Holdings:** 7000 books and bound periodical volumes; 1500 slides; 1000 laboratory reports, pilot plant reports, Sherritt-published papers. **Subscriptions:** 450 journals and other serials. **Services:** Interlibrary loan; library not open to the public. **Automated Operations:** Integrated Library System. **Computerized Information Services:** EBSCONET, DIALOG Information Services, CAN/OLE, STN International, Reuters, ORBIT Search Service; internal database. **Publications:** Acquisitions report, monthly; Seminars/conferences bulletin; Journal Alert - all for internal distribution only. **Remarks:** Alternate telephone number(s): (403)992-5054. FAX: (403)992-5010. Telex: 037 2290. **Staff:** Jamie Stanley.

★ 15130 ★
Sherwin-Williams Company - Information Center (Comp Sci)
13 Midland Bldg.
101 Prospect Ave., N.W.   Phone: (216)566-2993
Cleveland, OH 44115   Pamela Kuzma, Info.Ctr.Dir.
Founded: 1982. **Staff:** Prof 1; Other 1. **Subjects:** Data processing, business. **Holdings:** 300 books; 1500 computer listings; 600 technical manuals; 6 VF drawers of hardware/software product brochures; 75 education/training courses. **Subscriptions:** 100 journals and other serials; 5 newspapers. **Services:** Center not open to the public. **Automated Operations:** Computerized cataloging, serials, circulation, and routing. **Computerized Information Services:** DIALOG Information Services, The Source Information Network, LEXIS, NEXIS Human Resource Information Network (HRIN); internal database. **Publications:** Education Newsletter, monthly; Information Center Newsletter, irregular; Library Newletter, quarterly - all for internal distribution only.

K.K. Sherwood Library
See: **University of Washington - Health Sciences Library and Information Center** (19530)

Sheth Bholabhai Jeshingbhai Institute of Learning and Research
See: **Gujarat Vidya Sabha** (6804)

★ 15131 ★
Shevchenko Scientific Society, Inc. - Library and Archives (Area-Ethnic)
63 4th Ave.   Phone: (212)254-5130
New York, NY 10003   Svitlana Andrushkiw, Dir.
Founded: 1873. **Staff:** Prof 1; Other 2. **Subjects:** Ukrainian and Slavic languages, Ukrainians in the U.S. and in foreign countries, literature, history, arts, music, geography, ethnography, sciences. **Special Collections:** World Wars I and II; Displaced Person Camps archives. **Holdings:** 50,000 books; 5000 periodicals; 3000 manuscripts, archives, pamphlets; rare books. **Subscriptions:** 21 journals and other serials. **Services:** Copying; library open to serious researchers only. **Publications:** Publications catalog; pamphlets. **Staff:** G. Navrosky, Cat.; Wasyl Lev, Acq.

★ 15132 ★
Shibley Righton - Library and Information Services (Law)
401 Bay St., 18th Fl.
Box 32   Phone: (416)363-9381
Toronto, ON, Canada M5H 2Z1   Claire M. Bowman, Libn.
Staff: Prof 1; Other 1. **Subjects:** Law - corporate, commercial, labor, tax, securities; civil litigation; real estate; estates and wills. **Holdings:** 2000 books; law reports. **Subscriptions:** 22 journals and other serials. **Services:** Interlibrary loan; copying; SDI; library open to Toronto law librarians by appointment only. **Computerized Information Services:** QL Systems, WESTLAW, Info Globe, Infomart Online, The Financial Post DataGroup, DIALOG Information Services, CAN/LAW. **Publications:** Library Bulletin, weekly - for internal distribution only. **Special Indexes:** Index to internal memoranda of law. **Remarks:** FAX: (416)365-1717.

Shichting Mathematisch Centrum
See: Center for Mathematics and Computer Science (3267)

Vera Parshall Shiffman Medical Library
See: Wayne State University - Vera Parshall Shiffman Medical Library (20124)

Shikar/Safari Club Library
See: Museum of York County - Library (10924)

★ 15133 ★
Shiloh Military Trail, Inc. - Library (Hist)
Box 17507   Phone: (901)458-4696
Memphis, TN 38187-0507   Edward F. Williams, III, Res.Hist.
Founded: 1961. **Staff:** 1. **Subjects:** Civil War history and American history. **Special Collections:** Civil War manuscripts and material related to the Battle of Shiloh and Confederate General Nathan Bedford Forrest (4 VF drawers). **Holdings:** 1000 books; 20 bound periodical volumes. **Subscriptions:** 10 journals and other serials. **Services:** Library open to the public by appointment. **Remarks:** Located in Memphis Pink Palace Museum Library, 232 Tilton, Memphis, TN 38111. Alternate telephone number(s): 454-5600.

★ 15134 ★
Shiloh Museum - Library (Hist)
118 W. Johnson Ave.   Phone: (501)750-8165
Springdale, AR 72764   Bob Besom, Dir.
Founded: 1968. **Staff:** 6. **Subjects:** Northwest Arkansas - history, authors; antiques; archeology; anthropology. **Special Collections:** Poultry industry collection. **Holdings:** 600 books; 20 AV programs; 50,000 photographs; 25 VF drawers; archival material. **Subscriptions:** 25 journals and other serials. **Services:** Copying; library open to the public. **Publications:** Research papers. **Staff:** Mary Parsons, Asst.Dir.

Shiloh National Military Park
See: U.S. Natl. Park Service (17778)

Shilstone Library
See: Barbados Museum & Historical Society (1523)

★ 15135 ★
Shippensburg Historical Society - Archives (Hist)
73 W. King St.
Shippensburg, PA 17257   Phone: (717)532-4508
Subjects: History and genealogy of Shippensburg area. **Holdings:** Figures not available. **Services:** Archives open to the public by appointment.

★ 15136 ★
Shippensburg University - Ezra Lehman Memorial Library (Bus-Fin, Soc Sci)
Shippensburg, PA 17257   Phone: (717)532-1463
                  Virginia M. Crowe, Ph.D., Dean, Lib./Media Serv.
Founded: 1871. **Staff:** Prof 10; Other 18. **Subjects:** Business, education, arts and sciences, criminal justice, public administration. **Special Collections:** Media/Curricular Center; Pennsylvaniana; rare books; university archives (415 linear feet). **Holdings:** 386,263 books; 27,241 bound periodical volumes; 48,285 reels of microfilm; 1.4 million microfiche; 10,970 microprints; 7000 microcards; U.S. and Pennsylvania government documents. **Subscriptions:** 1753 journals and other serials; 24 newspapers. **Services:** Interlibrary loan; library open to the public for serious research. **Automated Operations:** Computerized public access catalog, cataloging, and acquisitions. **Computerized Information Services:** DIALOG Information Services, BRS Information Technologies. Performs searches on fee basis. Contact Person: Berkley Laite, Hd. of Ref., 532-1473. **Networks/Consortia:** Member of PALINET, State System of Higher Education Libraries Council (SSHELCO), Associated College Libraries of Central Pennsylvania (ACLCP). **Remarks:** FAX: (717)532-1389. **Staff:** Judith Culbertson, Coll.Mgt.; Linda Gatchel, Tech.Serv.; Signe Kelker, ILL/Spec.Coll.; Karen Dyson, Bibliog.Instr.; Katherine Warkentin, Govt.Docs.; Robert Gimmi, Ser. & Circ.

★ 15137 ★
Ships of the Sea Maritime Museum - Library (Hist)
503 East River St.
Savannah, GA 31401   Phone: (912)232-1511
Founded: 1966. **Subjects:** Maritime history. **Holdings:** Figures not available. **Services:** Library open to the public for reference use only.

Shoals Marine Laboratory
See: Cornell University - Shoals Marine Laboratory (4331)

★ 15138 ★
Shodair Hospital - Medical Information & Library Services (Med)
Box 5539   Phone: (406)444-7534
Helena, MT 59604   Suzy Holt, Info.Spec.
Founded: 1979. **Staff:** Prof 1; Other 1. **Subjects:** Clinical genetics, genetic disorders, prenatal diagnosis, genetic counseling, cytogenetics, child psychiatry. **Special Collections:** Family Resource Library for parents/patients with genetic disorders (250 booklets and brochures; fact sheets on 100 disorders). **Holdings:** 2000 books; 1000 bound periodical volumes. **Subscriptions:** 65 journals and other serials. **Services:** Interlibrary loan; copying; SDI; services open to the public by prior arrangement. **Automated Operations:** Computerized ILL (DOCLINE). **Computerized Information Services:** DIALOG Information Services, WLN, MEDLARS; OnTyme Electronic Message Network Service (electronic mail service). Performs searches on fee basis. **Networks/Consortia:** Member of Helena Area Health Sciences Library Consortium (HAHSLC), Western Library Network (WLN). **Remarks:** FAX: (406)444-7536. Electronic mail address(es): SHODAIR (OnTyme Electronic Message Network Service). **Formerly:** Shodair Children's Hospital.

★ 15139 ★
Shoe and Leather Research Institute - Library (Sci-Engr)
CS-762 65 Gottwaldov, Czechoslovakia   Phone: 23151
                  Jarmila Dvorakova, Libn.
Subjects: Leather and shoemaking technology, equipment and machinery, shoemaking materials, tannery effluent treatment. **Holdings:** 51,000 volumes. **Subscriptions:** 172 journals and other serials. **Services:** Interlibrary loan; copying; library open to the public. **Computerized Information Services:** Internal database (leather industry). **Remarks:** Telex: 067 337. **Also Known As:** Vyzkumny Ustav Kozedelny.

Moses Shoenberg Memorial Library
See: Jewish Hospital - School of Nursing (8396)

★ 15140 ★
Shook, Hardy & Bacon - Library (Law)
1200 Main St., 28th Fl.   Phone: (816)474-6550
Kansas City, MO 64105   Lori Hunt, Dir., Lib. & Rec.Serv.
Staff: Prof 4; Other 3. **Subjects:** Law - federal and state, products liability, antitrust, corporate, tax, labor, international commercial, banking, intellectual property, health. **Holdings:** 40,000 books; legal memoranda; 3000 ultrafiche; AV items. **Subscriptions:** 1700 journals and other serials. **Services:** Interlibrary loan; library not open to the public. **Computerized Information Services:** NEXIS, VU/TEXT Information Services, Dow Jones News/Retrieval, LEXIS, WESTLAW, DIALOG Information Services, DataTimes, OCLC, Burrelle's Broadcast Database, LEGI-SLATE, Information America, QL Systems; CD-ROMs; MCI Mail (electronic mail service). **Networks/Consortia:** Member of Kansas City Library Network, Inc. (KCLN). **Publications:** Law Review and Legal Periodical Current Awareness Services, monthly; Acquisitions List, monthly. **Special Indexes:** Index to Expert Witness File; index to Legal Memoranda File; index to Local Counsel File (all online). **Remarks:** FAX: (816)421-5547. **Staff:** Janet Peters, Ref.Libn.; Julie Parmenter, Ref.Libn.; Melody Kinnamon, Ref.Libn.

Shore Galleries Archives
See: Boston Public Library - Fine Arts Department (1992)

★15141★
Shore Village Historical Society - Museum Library (Hist)
104 Limerock St.   Phone: (207)594-0311
Rockland, ME 04841   Robert N. Davis, Cur.
Founded: 1976. **Staff:** 1. **Subjects:** Civil War, lighthouses, lightships, local history, maritime history. **Special Collections:** Civil War Collection (dating from the 1860s); documentary records; 5000 lighthouse and lightship postcards; lighthouse videos, slides, and tapes. **Holdings:** 800 books; 12 documents. **Services:** Library open to the public. **Publications:** The Shore Village Story; The Shore Village Album; The Shore Village Newsletter. **Remarks:** Is said to have the largest collection of lighthouse artifacts in the United States.

★15142★
Shorter College - Memorabilia Room (Hist)
315 Shorter Ave.   Phone: (404)291-2121
Rome, GA 30165-4298   Robert Gardner, Cur./Hist.
Founded: 1966. **Subjects:** History of Shorter College. **Holdings:** 425 books; 30 VF drawers of archives, manuscripts, documents, unbound reports, clippings; 425 artifacts. **Services:** Copying; room open to the public by appointment.

Shortt Library of Canadiana
See: University of Saskatchewan - Special Collections (19297)

★15143★
Shostal Associates, Inc. (Aud-Vis)
10 W. 20th St.   Phone: (212)633-0101
New York, NY 10011   E.E. Liu, Libn.
Founded: 1940. **Subjects:** Complete, up-to-date file of stock color transparencies of subjects of general interest with worldwide geographical coverage; special emphasis on educational projects and advertising. **Special Collections:** Large format original color transparencies representing hundreds of photographers from around the world. **Holdings:** Figures not available. **Remarks:** FAX: (212)633-0408. **Staff:** Darryl Jacobson.

Kenneth J. Shouldice Library
See: Lake Superior State University (8898)

G.H.P. Showalter Library
See: Institute for Christian Studies - Library (7915)

★15144★
The (Shreveport) Times - Library (Publ)
222 Lake St.   Phone: (318)459-3283
Shreveport, LA 71130   Johnny L. King, Libn.
Founded: 1951. **Staff:** Prof 1; Other 2. **Subjects:** Newspaper reference topics. **Special Collections:** Shreveport Times, bound and on microfilm, 1871 to present; bound issues of the Sunday Magazine with index. **Holdings:** 2300 books; 20 bound periodical volumes; 50,000 newspaper clippings; 113 reels of microfilm; 15 VF drawers of photographs; caricatures; files of art work; 300 VF drawers. **Subscriptions:** 20 journals and other serials; 20 newspapers. **Services:** Library not open to the public. **Special Indexes:** Index to Sunday Magazine; index of daily clippings; index to Shreveport Magazine. **Remarks:** Published by Gannett Newspapers. FAX: (318)459-3301.

★15145★
Shrewsbury Daily-Sunday Register - Library
766 Shrewsbury
Tinton Falls, NJ 07724
Defunct.

★15146★
Shrine to Music Museum - Library (Mus)
University of South Dakota
414 E. Clark St.   Phone: (605)677-5306
Vermillion, SD 57069-2390   Andre P. Larson, Dir.
Founded: 1966. **Staff:** Prof 5; Other 2. **Subjects:** Musical instruments, musical history including American music, sheet and wind music. **Holdings:** 2600 books; 5500 musical instruments; 15,000 musical items; 8500 photographs; 10,000 sound recordings. **Subscriptions:** 50 journals and other serials. **Services:** Copying; library open to the public with permission of director. **Publications:** Newsletter, quarterly - free upon request. **Remarks:** FAX: (605)677-5073. Maintained by Center for Study of the History of Musical Instruments of the University of South Dakota. **Staff:** Margaret D. Banks, Cur.; John Koster, Consrv.; Joseph R. Johnson, Cur. of Educ.

★15147★
Shriners' Hospital - Medical Library (Med)
2211 N. Oak Park Ave.   Phone: (312)622-5400
Chicago, IL 60635   Laura Mueller, Med.Libn.
Staff: Prof 1. **Subjects:** Orthopedics, pediatrics. **Holdings:** 1000 books. **Subscriptions:** 100 journals and other serials; 2 newspapers. **Services:** Interlibrary loan; copying; library open to the public by appointment. **Computerized Information Services:** BRS Information Technologies, NLM. **Networks/Consortia:** Member of Metropolitan Consortium of Chicago, ILLINET.

★15148★
Shriners Hospital for Crippled Children - Orthopedic Library (Med)
1402 N. MacGregor   Phone: (713)797-1616
Houston, TX 77030-1695   Jean Rasmussen, Med. Staff Coord.
Staff: Prof 2. **Subjects:** Orthopedics. **Holdings:** 200 books; 668 bound periodical volumes. **Subscriptions:** 20 journals and other serials. **Services:** Library not open to the public. **Automated Operations:** Computerized cataloging. **Computerized Information Services:** NLM, BRS Information Technologies. **Publications:** Newsletter - for internal distribution only.

★15149★
Eunice Kennedy Shriver Center for Mental Retardation, Inc. - Biochemistry Library (Med)
200 Trapelo Rd.   Phone: (617)642-0001
Waltham, MA 02154   Dr. Peter Daniel, Libn.
Founded: 1970. **Staff:** Prof 1. **Subjects:** Biochemistry, chemistry, neurochemistry, neuroscience, genetics, cell biology. **Holdings:** 200 books; 400 bound periodical volumes; 50 pamphlets. **Subscriptions:** 30 journals and other serials. **Services:** Library not open to the public. **Computerized Information Services:** DIALOG Information Services.

Max Shulman Zionist Library
See: Hebrew Theological College - Saul Silber Memorial Library (7094)

Benjamin Franklin Shumard Library
See: St. Louis Public Library - Rare Book & Special Collections Department (14457)

Sibelius Collection
See: Butler University - Irwin Library - Hugh Thomas Miller Rare Book Room (2416)

Sibert Library
See: Passavant Area Hospital (12780)

★15150★
Sibirskij Naucnoissledovatelskij Institut Selskogo Chozjajstva - Sibirskoe Otdelenie VASCHNIL Biblioteka (Agri, Sci-Engr)
Omsk 12, Russia   Phone: 29267
                                    Valentina S. Malyshera
Founded: 1928. **Staff:** Prof 4. **Subjects:** Agriculture, science and technology, and allied subjects. **Holdings:** 89,543 books. **Subscriptions:** 342 journals and other serials; 23 newspapers. **Services:** Interlibrary loan; copying; library open to the public.

★15151★
Sibley Memorial Hospital - Medical Library (Med)
5255 Loughboro Rd., N.W.   Phone: (202)537-4110
Washington, DC 20016   Annie B. Footman, Libn.
Founded: 1903. **Staff:** Prof 1. **Subjects:** Medicine. **Holdings:** 1950 books; 913 bound periodical volumes; 4 VF drawers of clippings, reports, and documents. **Subscriptions:** 152 journals and other serials. **Services:** Interlibrary loan; library not open to the public. **Computerized Information Services:** NLM, MEDLINE; DOCLINE (electronic mail service). **Networks/Consortia:** Member of National Network of Libraries of Medicine - Southeastern/Atlantic Region, Maryland and D.C. Consortium of Resource Sharing (MADCORS), District of Columbia Health Sciences Information Network (DOCHSIN).

Sibley Music Library
See: **University of Rochester - Eastman School of Music (19279)**

★ 15152 ★
Sichuan International Studies University - Library (Hum)
Lieshimu
Shapingba
Chongqing, Sichuan, People's   Phone: 661737
 Republic of China   Wang Zhonghi, Assoc.Res.
Founded: 1950. **Staff:** Prof 22; Other 24. **Subjects:** Linguistics and philology; dictionaries; literature; encyclopedias; economy and international trade; history; geography. **Special Collections:** Encyclopedic Dictionary (in Russian, 1890 edition; 84 volumes); Dictionnaire des Dictionnaires (1886 edition; 6 volumes); Handmaerterbuch der Deutschen Sprache (1912 edition); English-, French-, German-, Japanese-, and Russian-language linguistics, philology, and literature collections (15,000 volumes). **Holdings:** 514,411 books; 27,737 bound periodical volumes; 425,213 documents; 1500 AV programs. **Services:** Interlibrary loan; copying; library open to the public for academic research. **Computerized Information Services:** Internal database (under development). **Publications:** New Book Bulletin. **Special Catalogs:** Teaching Reference Book Catalog; Foreign Book Catalog; English Book Catalog. **Remarks:** Library maintains book exchange programs with libraries in the U.S. , Japan, and the Soviet Union. **Also Known As:** Sichuan Institute of Foreign Languages - Library. **Staff:** Ye Lahui.

★ 15153 ★
Sidley & Austin - Library (Law)
1722 Eye St., N.W.   Phone: (202)736-8505
Washington, DC 20006   Sabrina I. Pacifici, Dir. of Lib. & Res.Serv.
Staff: Prof 4; Other 4. **Subjects:** Law. **Holdings:** 30,000 books; 1500 bound periodical volumes; 800 reels of microfilm; 8 boxes of microfiche; legislative histories. **Subscriptions:** 270 journals and other serials; 7 newspapers. **Services:** Interlibrary loan. **Automated Operations:** Computerized cataloging, acquisitions, serials, and ILL. **Computerized Information Services:** LEXIS, NEXIS, WESTLAW, DIALOG Information Services, Dow Jones News/Retrieval, DataTimes, LEGI-SLATE, OCLC, Information America, NewsNet, Inc. **Networks/Consortia:** Member of CAPCON Library Network. **Remarks:** FAX: (202)736-8711.

★ 15154 ★
Sidley & Austin - Library (Law)
One First National Plaza, Suite 4800   Phone: (312)853-7475
Chicago, IL 60603   Allyson D. Withers, Lib.Adm.
Staff: Prof 3; Other 12. **Subjects:** Law. **Holdings:** 45,000 volumes. **Services:** Interlibrary loan; library not open to the public. **Automated Operations:** Computerized cataloging, acquisitions, serials, and circulation. **Computerized Information Services:** LEXIS, WESTLAW, DIALOG Information Services, OCLC, DataTimes, Information America, Dow Jones News/Retrieval, LEGI-SLATE, VU/TEXT Information Services, NEXIS, State Net, WILSONLINE, Hannah Information Systems; MCI Mail (electronic mail service). **Networks/Consortia:** Member of ILLINET. **Remarks:** FAX: (312)853-7312. Telex: 25-4364 (SIDLEY AUS CGO). **Staff:** Joan M. Ogden, Ref.Libn.; Laura A. Coleman, Tax Libn.

★ 15155 ★
Siecor Corporation - Library/Information Services (Sci-Engr)
489 Siecor Park
800 17th St., N.W.   Phone: (704)327-5000
Hickory, NC 28603-0489   Nola Sain
Founded: 1980. **Staff:** 1. **Subjects:** Telephone and cable industries, telecommunications, fiber optics. **Holdings:** 1000 books; 500 bound periodical volumes; 6000 reports and documents. **Subscriptions:** 130 journals and other serials. **Services:** Interlibrary loan; library not open to the public. **Automated Operations:** Computerized cataloging. **Computerized Information Services:** DIALOG Information Services, NewsNet, Inc.

★ 15156 ★
Eli Siegel Collection (Hum, Rel-Phil)
141 Greene St.   Phone: (212)777-4490
New York, NY 10012   Richita Anderson, Libn.
Founded: 1982. **Staff:** Prof 3; Other 3. **Subjects:** Poetry, world literature, philosophy, art and literary criticism, history, labor and economics, approaches to mind, the sciences. **Special Collections:** Original manuscripts

of the poetry and prose of Eli Siegel, founder of Aesthetic Realism; poems by Eli Siegel in holograph on pages of many of the books in this collection; French, German, and Spanish literature; early American history; 19th century periodical literature; British and American poetry. **Holdings:** 30,000 books; 500 bound periodical volumes; 1000 tapes of Aesthetic Realism lessons and lectures by Eli Siegel. **Services:** Collection is open by appointment to persons seriously studying the Aesthetic Realism of Eli Siegel. **Publications:** The Right of Aesthetic Realism to Be Known, weekly international periodical, edited by Ellen Reiss, Class Chairman of Aesthetic Realism, published by the Aesthetic Realism Foundation. **Special Catalogs:** Cataloging of manuscripts within books is in process. **Remarks:** FAX: (212)777-4426. The books in this collection, with original manuscripts, poetry, and annotations by Eli Siegel, were used by him in the development and teaching of the philosophy of Aesthetic Realism. **Staff:** Leila Rosen, Libn.; Meryl Simon, Libn.

★ 15157 ★
Siemens Gammasonics, Inc. - Library (Sci-Engr)
2501 N. Barrington Rd.   Phone: (708)390-1989
Hoffman Estates, IL 60195   Kay Walsh, Libn.
Founded: 1957. **Staff:** Prof 1. **Subjects:** Nuclear instrumentation, computers, engineering, electronics, gamma camera imaging, nuclear medicine, nuclear cardiology, mathematics, software, expert systems. **Holdings:** 4000 books; 800 bound periodical volumes. **Subscriptions:** 85 journals and other serials. **Services:** Interlibrary loan; copying; SDI; library open to the public by appointment. **Automated Operations:** Computerized acquisitions, serials, and circulation. **Computerized Information Services:** DIALOG Information Services. **Networks/Consortia:** Member of North Suburban Library System (NSLS), Metropolitan Consortium of Chicago. **Remarks:** FAX: (708)390-1944.

★ 15158 ★
SIEMENS Stromberg-Carlson - Engineering Library (Info Sci)
400 Rinehart Rd.   Phone: (407)942-5000
Lake Mary, FL 32746   Dianne Kimber, Libn.
Founded: 1920. **Staff:** Prof 1. **Subjects:** Telephony, engineering, computer science and language, mathematics, science. **Holdings:** 1000 books; 100 bound periodical volumes; 200 archival materials; 100 reels of microfilm; reports. **Subscriptions:** 100 journals and other serials; 5 newspapers. **Services:** Interlibrary loan; library open to the public by appointment. **Formerly:** GPT Stromberg-Carlson.

★ 15159 ★
Sierra Club - William E. Colby Memorial Library (Env-Cons)
730 Polk St.   Phone: (415)923-5566
San Francisco, CA 94109   M.L. Phoebe Adams, Hd.Libn.
Founded: 1892. **Staff:** Prof 1. **Subjects:** Environmental policy, conservation, energy policy, mountaineering, natural history, Sierra Nevada. **Special Collections:** Foreign mountaineering journals (800 bound volumes); selected Sierra Club archives and memorabilia (500 items). **Holdings:** 10,500 books; 1450 bound periodical volumes; 10,000 indexed documents and reports; 20,000 photographs and slides. **Subscriptions:** 350 journals and other serials. **Services:** Interlibrary loan; copying; library open to the public for reference use only. **Automated Operations:** Computerized public access catalog, cataloging, and ILL. **Computerized Information Services:** OCLC. **Networks/Consortia:** Member of Bay Area Library and Information System (BALIS). **Publications:** Sierra Club Periodicals Holdings List, annual. **Special Indexes:** Subject index to documents holdings. **Remarks:** FAX: (415)776-0350.

★ 15160 ★
Sierra County Law Library (Law)
Courthouse
P.O. Box 457   Phone: (916)289-3269
Downieville, CA 95936   Sheri Johnson, Admin.Asst.
Founded: 1920. **Staff:** 2. **Subjects:** Law. **Holdings:** 4000 volumes. **Services:** Library open to the public with restrictions.

★ 15161 ★
Sierra Leone Muslim Women's Association Kankaylay - Library (Soc Sci)
P.O. Box 1168
15 Blackhall Rd.
Kissy
Freetown, Sierra Leone   Phone: 50931
Subjects: Women's education in Sierra Leone. **Holdings:** 7000 volumes.

★ 15162 ★
Sierra View District Hospital - Medical Library (Med)
465 W. Putnam Ave.   Phone: (209)784-1110
Porterville, CA 93257   Marilyn R. Pankey, Dir., Med.Rec.
Staff: 1. **Subjects:** Anatomy, physiology, medicine, surgery. **Holdings:** 150 books. **Subscriptions:** 22 journals and other serials. **Services:** Library not open to the public. **Networks/Consortia:** Member of Area Wide Library Network (AWLNET).

★ 15163 ★
Sigma Alpha Epsilon Foundation - Levere Memorial Temple Library (Rec)
Box 1856   Phone: (708)475-1856
Evanston, IL 60204   Kenneth D. Tracey, Exec.Dir.
Founded: 1930. **Staff:** Prof 1. **Subjects:** Fraternities and sororities. **Special Collections:** Complete collection of all fraternity and sorority journals; Sigma Alpha Epsilon books, authors, and papers. **Holdings:** 225 books; 4000 bound periodical volumes; 407 chapter scrapbooks. **Services:** Library open to the public for reference use only. **Remarks:** Library located at 1856 Sheridan Rd., Evanston, IL 60201. FAX: (312)475-2250.

★ 15164 ★
Sigma Theta Tau International - Virginia Henderson International Nursing Library (Med)
550 W. North St.   Phone: (317)634-8171
Indianapolis, IN 46202   Judith Schreiner, Dir. of Info.Serv.
Founded: 1987. **Staff:** Prof 1; Other 2. **Subjects:** Nursing. **Holdings:** 808 books; 214 bound periodical volumes; 209 videotapes; 811 audiocassettes. **Subscriptions:** 187 journals and other serials. **Services:** Interlibrary loan; copying; library open to the public. **Computerized Information Services:** BRS Information Technologies; Directory of Nurse Researchers (internal database); InterNet (electronic mail service). **Networks/Consortia:** Member of INCOLSA, Central Indiana Health Science Library Consortium. Performs searches on fee basis. **Publications:** Reflections (newsletter), quarterly - available on request; IMAGE: Journal of Nursing Scholarship (research journal), quarterly. **Remarks:** FAX: (317)634-8188; Electronic mail address(es): IUUV700; INDYSTTI.IUPUI.EDU (InterNet). **Formerly:** Its International Nursing Library.

Walter A. Sikes Learning Resource Center
See: **Dorothea Dix Hospital** (4925)

Sikorsky Aircraft
See: **United Technologies Corporation** (17963)

Saul Silber Memorial Library
See: **Hebrew Theological College - Saul Silber Memorial Library** (7094)

Silcox Memorial Library
See: **Huron College** (7585)

Silicon Valley Information Center
See: **San Jose Public Library** (14757)

★ 15165 ★
Silk and Art Silk Mills' Research Association - SASMIRA Library (Sci-Engr, Bus-Fin)
Sasmira Marg
Worli
Bombay 400 025, Maharashtra, India   Phone: 493 5351
Founded: 1954. **Staff:** Prof 2; Other 1. **Subjects:** Textiles and allied subjects, management and marketing, pure and applied sciences, engineering, economics, social sciences. **Special Collections:** Indian Standards on Textiles; BISFA Rules; Novelty Fabric Design Samples; press clippings. **Holdings:** 9331 books; 6284 bound periodical volumes; 8056 other cataloged items. **Subscriptions:** 190 journals and other serials; 8 newspapers. **Services:** Interlibrary loan; copying; library open to the public for reference use only. **Publications:** Man-Made Textiles in India; SASMIRA Bulletin; SASMIRA Digest. **Special Catalogs:** Selected list of books; list of dissertations; list of current periodicals and ad-hoc publications. **Special Indexes:** Index of the articles published in Man-Made Textiles in India; Index of Papers presented in Technology Conferences from 1970-1985. **Remarks:** Affiliated with India - Board of Education and India - Ministry of Textiles. **Staff:** Mr. G.D. Saraf, Asst.Libn.; Mr. S.R. Deshpande, Asst.Libn.

O.P. Silliman Memorial Library
See: **Hartnell College - Library** (6942)

★ 15166 ★
Sills, Cummis, et al. - Library (Law)
The Legal Center
1 Riverfront Plaza   Phone: (201)643-6097
Newark, NJ 07102-5400   Johanna C. Bizub, Lib.Dir.
Founded: 1971. **Staff:** Prof 2; Other 4. **Subjects:** Law. **Holdings:** 10,000 books; 500 bound periodical volumes; 5 microfiche; 5 reels of microfilm. **Subscriptions:** 250 journals and other serials; 20 newspapers. **Services:** Interlibrary loan; library not open to the public. **Computerized Information Services:** VU/TEXT Information Services, DIALOG Information Services, Dow Jones News/Retrieval, WESTLAW, LEXIS, NEXIS, DataTimes. **Networks/Consortia:** Member of Essex Hudson Regional Library Cooperative, New Jersey Library Network. **Remarks:** FAX: (201)643-6500. **Staff:** Pauline Reid, Asst.Libn.

★ 15167 ★
Siloam Springs Museum - Museum Archives (Hist)
112 N. Maxwell
P.O. Box 1164   Phone: (501)524-4011
Siloam Springs, AR 72761   Don Warden, Musm.Dir.
Founded: 1969. **Staff:** 2. **Subjects:** Siloam Springs area history. **Special Collections:** Britt and Braden Family papers (1880-1930; 500 pieces each). **Holdings:** 10,000 books, periodicals, local documents, manuscripts, newspapers, photographs, and post cards. **Services:** Copying; archives open to the public at librarian's discretion.

★ 15168 ★
Silsoe Research Institute - Agricultural and Food Research Council - Library (Agri)
Wrest Park
Silsoe   Phone: 525 60000
Bedford MK45 4HS, England   Ann Cooper, Libn.
Staff: Prof 2; Other 5. **Subjects:** Agricultural engineering. **Holdings:** 8000 books; 1500 bound periodical volumes; 30,000 reports; 5000 microfiche; 100 reels of microfilm. **Subscriptions:** 400 journals and other serials; 2 newspapers. **Services:** Interlibrary loan; copying; library open to the public. **Automated Operations:** Computerized cataloging. **Computerized Information Services:** DIALOG Information Services, ESA/IRS; internal databases. Contact Person: Patricia Tillock, Asst.Libn. **Remarks:** FAX: 525 60156. Telex: 825808 SILSOE G.

Luigi Silva Collection
See: **University of North Carolina at Greensboro** (19085)

Abba Hillel Silver Archives
See: **Temple Library** (16118)

★ 15169 ★
Silver Burdett & Ginn - Editorial Library (Publ)
250 James St.   Phone: (201)285-7961
Morristown, NJ 07960   Patricia Bailis, Libn.
Staff: Prof 1. **Subjects:** General education, publishing, market research.
Special Collections: Silver Burdett publications. **Holdings:** 10,000 books.
Subscriptions: 150 journals and other serials. **Services:** Library not open to
the public. **Computerized Information Services:** LEXIS, NEXIS.
Networks/Consortia: Member of New Jersey Library Network. **Remarks:**
FAX: (201)898-0114.

★ 15170 ★
Silver Cross Hospital - Lloyd W. Jessen Health Science Library (Med)
1200 Maple Rd.   Phone: (815)740-1100
Joliet, IL 60432   Mary Ingmire, Libn.
Founded: 1956. **Staff:** Prof 1. **Subjects:** Medicine, nursing, hospital
administration, social science. **Holdings:** 750 books; 1500 bound periodical
volumes; 8 VF drawers of articles and pamphlets. **Subscriptions:** 102
journals and other serials. **Services:** Interlibrary loan; copying; library open
to the public with referrals. **Computerized Information Services:** DIALOG
Information Services. **Networks/Consortia:** Member of Chicago and South
Consortium. **Remarks:** FAX: (815)740-7024.

★ 15171 ★
Silver Institute - Library (Sci-Engr)
1112 16th St., N.W., Suite 240   Phone: (202)835-0185
Washington, DC 20036   John H. Lutley, Exec.Dir.
Staff: Prof 4; Other 6. **Subjects:** Silver. **Holdings:** 100 volumes; newsletters.
Subscriptions: 15 journals and other serials. **Services:** Library open to the
public. **Special Catalogs:** Catalog of abstracts on silver (11,000 items).
Remarks: FAX: (202)783-2127.

★ 15172 ★
Silverado Museum (Hum)
P.O. Box 409   Phone: (707)963-3757
St. Helena, CA 94574   Ellen Shaffer, Cur.
Staff: Prof 1. **Subjects:** Life and works of Robert Louis Stevenson. **Holdings:**
3500 books; 1200 original letters; 225 manuscripts; 1000 photographs; 120
paintings, prints, drawings; 8 sculptures; 2000 pieces of memorabilia.
Services: Copying; museum open to the public on a limited schedule for
reference use only. **Publications:** The Silverado Squatters; Prayers Written
at Vailima. **Remarks:** Library is located at 1490 Library Lane.

★ 15173 ★
Silvermine School of Art - Resource Library
1037 Silvermine Rd.
New Canaan, CT 06840   Michael Cosetllo
Founded: 1959. **Subjects:** Art and allied subjects. **Holdings:** 300 books.
Remarks: Maintained by Silvermine Guild of Artists, Inc. Currently
inactive.

★ 15174 ★
Simcoe County Archives (Hist)
R.R. 2   Phone: (705)726-9331
Minesing, ON, Canada L0L 1Y0   Peter P. Moran, Archv.
Founded: 1966. **Staff:** Prof 2; Other 3. **Subjects:** Simcoe County history,
business, and genealogy; cartography; lumbering history. **Special
Collections:** Jacques and Hay Papers, 1854 to 1872 (the operation of New
Lowell, Ontario; 2000 items, mainly letters); A.F. Hunter Papers (personal
notes of local historian); Clarke Collection (500 books; 200 maps; 20,000
photographs, slides, negatives; correspondence); Sports Heritage Collection;
C. Beck Manufacturing Company records (250 cubic feet); Cavana family
records, 1860-1970 (land surveying; 20 cubic feet). **Holdings:** 1500 books;
500 bound periodical volumes; 50 Women's Institute histories; 130 county
assessment rolls; 800 feet of Simcoe County municipal records; 150 magnetic
tapes; 50 feet of Georgian Bay Lumber Company papers; 400 maps; 2000
photographs; census records on microfilm. **Subscriptions:** 29 journals and
other serials. **Services:** Copying; archives open to the public. **Special
Indexes:** Index of newspaper Barrie Northern Advance, 1847-1940; index
of photographs; index of maps (all on cards). **Remarks:** FAX: (705)726-
3991. **Staff:** Bruce Beacock, Asst.Archv.; James Campbell, Hist.Res.; Chris
McBain, Microfilm Camera Techn.; Cindy Patterson, Cler.

★ 15175 ★
Simcoe County Law Association - Law Library (Law)
Court House
30 Poyntz St.   Phone: (705)739-6569
Barrie, ON, Canada L4M 1M1   Patricia Henry, Libn.
Staff: 1. **Subjects:** Law - criminal, civil, family, income tax, corporate.
Special Collections: Ontario Municipal Board Decisions; Ontario
Government Bills and Statutes (revisions). **Holdings:** 7000 books and bound
periodical volumes. **Services:** Library not open to the public.

★ 15176 ★
Simi Valley Historical Society - Archives (Hist)
R.P. Strathearn Historical Park
137 Strathearn Place
Box 351
Simi Valley, CA 93065   Phone: (805)526-6453
Subjects: Simi Valley history, 1874-1960. **Holdings:** 500 letters and archival
materials. **Services:** Archives open to the public by appointment.

Simmel-Fenichel Library
See: Los Angeles Psychoanalytic Society and Institute (9342)

★ 15177 ★
Simmons College - Archives (Soc Sci)
300 The Fenway   Phone: (617)738-3141
Boston, MA 02115   Megan Sniffin-Marinoff, Arch.Hd.
Founded: 1974. **Staff:** Prof 2. **Subjects:** Social welfare, nursing, home
economics, children's literature, library science, women's history. **Special
Collections:** Donald Moreland Collection (history of social welfare; 1500
volumes); Knapp Collection (19th and early 20th Century children's
literature); public health nursing collection (200 volumes). **Holdings:** 3200
books; 2000 linear feet of archival materials. **Services:** Copying; archives
open to the public by appointment. **Computerized Information Services:**
DIALOG Information Services, OCLC. **Publications:** Guides to archives;
guides to manuscript collections. **Remarks:** FAX: (617)738-2099.

★ 15178 ★
**Simmons College - Graduate School of Library and Information Science
- Library** (Info Sci)
300 The Fenway   Phone: (617)738-2226
Boston, MA 02115   Linda H. Watkins, Libn.
Founded: 1902. **Staff:** Prof 1; Other 12. **Subjects:** Library and information
science, publishing, media resources and study, library management.
Holdings: 24,030 books; 8881 bound periodical volumes; 4935 microfiche;
911 reels of microfilm; 34 VF drawers; School of Library Science doctoral
field studies; information files on 100 library-related subjects; doctoral
dissertations on microfilm. **Subscriptions:** 500 journals and other serials.
Services: Interlibrary loan; copying; library open to the public for reference
use only by appointment. **Automated Operations:** Computerized public
access catalog, cataloging, and circulation. **Computerized Information
Services:** OCLC, DIALOG Information Services, BRS Information
Technologies. **Networks/Consortia:** Member of NELINET, Inc., Fenway
Library Consortium (FLC).

★ 15179 ★
Simmons College - School of Social Work Library (Soc Sci)
51 Commonwealth Ave.   Phone: (617)738-2943
Boston, MA 02116   Marilyn Smith Bregoli, Libn.
Founded: 1904. **Staff:** Prof 1; Other 3. **Subjects:** Social work, public welfare,
psychiatry. **Holdings:** 21,000 books; 2600 bound periodical volumes; 1200
theses. **Subscriptions:** 208 journals and other serials. **Services:** Interlibrary
loan; library open to the public by appointment. **Automated Operations:**
Computerized cataloging. **Computerized Information Services:** DIALOG
Information Services, BRS Information Technologies. **Remarks:** Alternate
telephone number(s): 738-2944.

Simon Fraser University
See: Simon Fraser University (6105)

Simon-Lowenstein Collection
See: **The American Institute of Wine & Food (642)**

★15180★
Norton Simon Museum of Art at Pasadena - Library and Archives (Art)
411 W. Colorado Blvd.
Pasadena, CA 91105   Phone: (818)449-6840
Subjects: Art history. **Special Collections:** The Knoedler Library (auction and exhibition catalogs on microfiche, 18th century to 1970); The Galka E. Scheyer Archives (materials pertaining to the life and collections of Galka E. Scheyer and "The Blue Four" - Paul Klee, Wassily Kandinsky, Lyonel Feininger, and Alexei Jawlensky). **Holdings:** 150 books; 200 brochures and catalogs; letters of "The Blue Four"; photographs of artists and collections. **Services:** Use of archives limited to scholars. **Remarks:** FAX: (818)796-4978.

★15181★
H.A. Simons Ltd. - Corporate Library (Sci-Engr)
425 Carrall St.   Phone: (604)664-4311
Vancouver, BC, Canada V6B 2J6   David Pepper, Corp.Libn.
Founded: 1981. **Staff:** Prof 4; Other 1. **Subjects:** Pulp/paper, automation, food/beverage, applied technology. **Holdings:** 5000 books; annual reports; standards. **Subscriptions:** 500 journals and other serials; 10 newspapers. **Services:** Interlibrary loan; copying; SDI; library open to the public. **Automated Operations:** Computerized cataloging, acquisitions, serials, and circulation. **Computerized Information Services:** DIALOG Information Services, PFDS Online, Dow Jones News/Retrieval, QL Systems, Reuter TEXTLINE, Data-Star, STN International, Info Globe, CAN/OLE; Envoy 100, DIALMAIL (electronic mail services). Performs searches on fee basis. **Publications:** TREND Report; Economic Indicators, bimonthly; Daily Newsflash - all for internal distribution only. **Remarks:** Alternate telephone number(s): 664-4305. FAX: (604)669-9516. Electronic mail address(es): D.PEPPER (Envoy 100); 13871 (DIALMAIL). **Staff:** Kit Tam, Assoc.Corp.Libn.; Deborah Schachter, Ref.Libn.; Brad McGuigan, Tech.Serv.Libn.

Harry Simons Library
See: **Beth David Congregation (1763)**

Leonard N. Simons Research library
See: **Michigan Cancer Foundation (10284)**

Menno Simons Historical Library and Archives
See: **Eastern Mennonite College and Seminary (5154)**

Albert B. Simpson Historical Library & Archives
See: **Christian and Missionary Alliance (3635)**

Simpson Geographic Research Center
See: **University of Wisconsin--Eau Claire (19569)**

★15182★
Simpson Gumpertz & Heger Inc. - Library (Sci-Engr)
297 Broadway   Phone: (617)643-2000
Arlington, MA 02174   Evelyn Neuburger
Founded: 1956. **Staff:** 1. **Subjects:** Engineering, with emphasis on building materials and investigation of structural failures. **Holdings:** 6000 volumes; technical journals; manuals. **Subscriptions:** 70 journals and other serials. **Services:** Library not open to the public. **Computerized Information Services:** Internal database. **Remarks:** FAX: (617)643-2009. Telex: 940103.

Harold B. Simpson Confederate Research Center and Audie L. Murphy Gun Museum
See: **Hill College - Harold B. Simpson Confederate Research Center and Audie L. Murphy Gun Museum (7209)**

★15183★
Simpson, Thacher & Bartlett - Library (Law)
425 Lexington Ave.   Phone: (212)455-2802
New York, NY 10017   Elaine T. Sciolino, Libn.
Founded: 1884. **Staff:** Prof 6; Other 14. **Subjects:** Law - antitrust, corporate, labor, banking, trade regulations, public utilities, taxation, securities. **Holdings:** 40,000 volumes. **Subscriptions:** 3500 journals and other serials; 20 newspapers. **Services:** Interlibrary loan; library not open to the public. **Automated Operations:** Computerized cataloging, and serials. **Computerized Information Services:** LEXIS, NEXIS, WESTLAW, DIALOG Information Services, Dow Jones News/Retrieval; internal databases; MCI Mail (electronic mail service). **Remarks:** FAX: (212)455-3142. Alternate telephone number(s): 455-2802. **Staff:** Bobby Smith, Asst.Libn.; Michael Bronson, Ref.Libn.

L.A. Sims Memorial Library
See: **Southeastern Louisiana University (15450)**

★15184★
Simsbury Historical Society - Blanche C. Skoglund Memorial Library (Hist)
800 Hopmeadow St.
Box 2   Phone: (203)658-2500
Simsbury, CT 06070   Mary L. Nason, Dir.
Founded: 1975. **Subjects:** Simsbury area history and genealogy. **Holdings:** 2000 books, pamphlets, serials; 30 boxes of manuscripts; photographs; slides; maps. **Services:** Library open to the public by request. **Remarks:** Established as a bicentennial project, the library includes materials that had been in storage since 1911.

★15185★
Sinai Hospital of Baltimore, Inc. - Eisenberg Medical Staff Library (Med)
Belvedere & Greenspring   Phone: (410)578-5015
Baltimore, MD 21215   Rita Matcher, Dir., Lib.Serv.
Founded: 1890. **Staff:** Prof 1; Other 2. **Subjects:** Medicine, nursing, Jewish medicine, medical ethics, management, thanatology. **Special Collections:** Jewish book collection. **Holdings:** 2400 books; 10,000 bound periodical volumes. **Subscriptions:** 216 journals and other serials. **Services:** Interlibrary loan; library not open to the public. **Computerized Information Services:** MEDLINE, DIALOG Information Services. **Networks/Consortia:** Member of Maryland Association of Health Science Librarians (MAHSL). **Remarks:** FAX: (410)664-7432.

★15186★
Sinai Hospital of Detroit - Samuel Frank Medical Library (Med)
6767 W. Outer Dr.   Phone: (313)493-5140
Detroit, MI 48235   Barbara L. Finn, Dir., Med.Lib.
Founded: 1953. **Staff:** Prof 3; Other 5. **Subjects:** Medicine, nursing, and allied health sciences. **Special Collections:** History of Medicine (emphasis on Jewish contributions). **Holdings:** 9600 books; 15,135 bound periodical volumes; 9 VF drawers of reprints and pamphlets; cassettes; Audio-Digest tapes. **Subscriptions:** 571 journals and other serials. **Services:** Interlibrary loan; copying; SDI; library open to medical and paramedical personnel. **Computerized Information Services:** Online systems. **Publications:** Accession list of new books, monthly - for internal distribution only. **Staff:** Cathy Palmer, Lib.Supv.; Laura Grab, Asst.Dir.

★15187★
Sinai Samaritan Medical Center - Hurwitz Memorial Library (Med)
1121 W. State St.
P.O. Box 0342   Phone: (414)283-6710
Milwaukee, WI 53201-0342   Mary Jo Baertschy, Libn.
Founded: 1957. **Staff:** Prof 1. **Subjects:** Clinical medicine, surgery. **Holdings:** 1500 books; 5400 periodical volumes. **Subscriptions:** 385 journals and other serials. **Services:** Interlibrary loan; copying; library open to the public on request. **Computerized Information Services:** BRS Information Technologies, NLM, DIALOG Information Services. **Networks/Consortia:** Member of Southeastern Wisconsin Health Science Library Consortium (SWHSL). **Remarks:** FAX: (414)283-6708. Alternate telephone number(s): 283-6709. Library is operated by Aurora Health Care Libraries.

★ 15188 ★
Sinai Samaritan Medical Center - Jamron Health Science Library
(Med)
Box 342   Phone: (414)937-5412
Milwaukee, WI 53201-0342   Ann Towell, Libn.
Founded: 1940. **Staff:** Prof. 1. **Subjects:** Medicine, nursing, hospital administration. **Holdings:** 900 volumes; 4 VF drawers of professional pamphlets. **Subscriptions:** 150 periodical titles. **Services:** Copying; library open to the public with restrictions. **Computerized Information Services:** MEDLARS. **Networks/Consortia:** Member of Southeastern Wisconsin Health Science Library Consortium (SWHSL). **Publications:** Acquisitions list, irregular. **Remarks:** FAX: (414)937-5312. Library located at 2000 W. Kilbourn Ave., Milwaukee, WI 53233. Library is operated by Aurora Health Care Libraries.

Singapore - Ministry of Community Development
See: **Singapore - Ministry of Information and the Arts** (15189)

★ 15189 ★
Singapore - Ministry of Information and the Arts - National Library - Reference Services Division (Area-Ethnic, Bus-Fin)
Stamford Rd.   Phone: 65 3309665
Singapore 0617, Singapore   Miss Lim Kek Hwa, Asst.Dir.
Founded: 1958. **Staff:** Prof 11; Other 18. **Special Collections:** Southeast Asia Collection (125,922 volumes; microforms and rare books; maps; serials); Asian Collection of Children's Books (18,000 volumes); Arts Resource Centre; United Nations Collection; newspaper collection. **Holdings:** 221,341 books; 27,151 bound periodical volumes; 1191 reels of microfilm; 441 microfiche; 6120 AV items. **Subscriptions:** 4229 journals and other serials; 50 newspapers. **Services:** Interlibrary loan; copying; SDI; division open to the public. **Automated Operations:** Computerized public access catalog, cataloging, acquisitions, serials, and circulation. **Computerized Information Services:** PRECIS; NALINET (internal database). **Publications:** Guides to the special reference collection; subject bibliographies; books about Singapore, biennial; Singapore National Bibliography - for sale. **Special Catalogs:** Masterlist of Southeast Asian Microforms Supplement, 1978-1983 (on microfiche) - for sale. **Special Indexes:** Singapore Periodicals Index (SP) (book), annual - for sale. **Remarks:** FAX: 65 3309611. Telex: RS 26620 NATLIB. Alternate telephone number(s): 65 3309664. **Formerly:** Its Ministry of Community Development. **Staff:** Mrs. V. Perumbulavil, Asst.Hd., Spec.Coll.; Mr. Chan Fook Weng, Asst.Hd., Gen.Ref.Serv.; Miss Azizah Sidek, Lib. Networking and Interchange.

★ 15190 ★
Singapore - Ministry of National Development - National Parks Board - Singapore Botanic Gardens - Library (Biol Sci)
Cluny Rd.   Phone: 4741165
Singapore 1025, Singapore   Christina Soh, Lib.Techn.
Subjects: Taxonomic and floristic botany, especially in Southeast Asia. **Holdings:** 16,600 volumes. **Services:** Interlibrary loan; library not open to the public. **Remarks:** FAX: 4754295. **Formerly:** Singapore - Ministry of National Development - Parks and Recreation Department - Botanic Gardens.

Singapore - National Library
See: **Singapore - Ministry of Information and the Arts** (15189)

Singapore - National University of Singapore
See: **National University of Singapore** (11319)

★ 15191 ★
(Singapore) American Library Resource Center - USIS Library (Educ)
30 Hill St.
Singapore 0617, Singapore
Remarks: Maintained or supported by the U.S. Information Agency. Focus is on materials that will assist peoples outside the United States to learn about the United States, its people, history, culture, political processes, and social milieux.

Singapore Botanic Gardens
See: **Singapore - Ministry of National Development - National Parks Board** (15190)

★ 15192 ★
H. Douglas Singer Mental Health and Developmental Center - Library
(Med)
4402 N. Main St.   Phone: (815)987-7092
Rockford, IL 61103-1278   Pat Ellison, Lib.Assoc.
Founded: 1966. **Staff:** Prof 1. **Subjects:** Mental health, psychology, psychiatry, psychotherapy, sociology. **Holdings:** 2000 books. **Subscriptions:** 100 journals and other serials. **Services:** Interlibrary loan; library open to the public with restrictions. **Networks/Consortia:** Member of Northern Illinois Library System (NILS), Upstate Consortium of Medical Libraries in Northern Illinois. **Remarks:** FAX: (815)987-7075. Maintained by Illinois State Department of Mental Health and Developmental Disabilities.

Singewald Reading Room
See: **Johns Hopkins University - Department of Earth and Planetary Sciences** (8418)

★ 15193 ★
Singing River Hospital - Medical Library (Med)
2809 Denny Ave.   Phone: (601)938-5040
Pascagoula, MS 39567   Mary Evelyn Dowell, Dir., Med.Lib.
Founded: 1979. **Staff:** Prof 1; Other 1. **Subjects:** Medicine, nursing, allied health sciences, hospital administration, consumer health. **Holdings:** 4000 books; 10,000 bound periodical volumes. **Subscriptions:** 250 journals and other serials. **Services:** Interlibrary loan; copying; SDI; library open to Jackson County allied health students and hospital system employees and physicians. **Automated Operations:** Computerized cataloging. **Computerized Information Services:** MEDLARS, DIALOG Information Services, DOCLINE. **Networks/Consortia:** Member of Mississippi Biomedical Library Consortium (MBLC). **Publications:** Library Lifeline - for internal distribution only. **Remarks:** Maintains Community Health Information Library.

John and Marjorie Sinkankas Gemology & Mineralogy Library
See: **Gemological Institute of America - Research Library** (6281)

Sino-Soviet Information Center
See: **George Washington University - Melvin Gelman Library** (20008)

★ 15194 ★
Sint-Andriesabdij van de Benedictijnen te Brugge - Bibliotheek van de Sint-Andriesabdij (Rel-Phil)
Zevenkerken 4   Phone: 50 38 01 36
B-8200 Brugge 2, Belgium   J.D. Broekaert, Biblio.
Subjects: Theology, missiology, monasticism. **Special Collections:** Regel van Sint-Benedictus (900 volumes); Newmaniana (1100 books); Central Africa (6000 books). **Holdings:** 145,000 volumes. **Subscriptions:** 150 journals and other serials. **Services:** Interlibrary loan; library open to the public with restrictions.

★ 15195 ★
Sioux City Art Center Association - Library (Art)
513 Nebraska St.   Phone: (712)279-6272
Sioux City, IA 51101   Mary Mello-Nee, Educ.Cur.
Subjects: Art and art history. **Holdings:** 800 books; exhibition catalogs; reproduction slides. **Subscriptions:** 15 journals and other serials. **Services:** Library open to the public for reference use only. **Publications:** Artifact, quarterly. **Special Catalogs:** Exhibition catalogs.

★ 15196 ★
Sioux Falls Argus Leader - Library (Publ)
P.O. Box 5034   Phone: (605)331-2352
Sioux Falls, SD 57117-5034   Waltraut Kondert, Libn.
Staff: Prof 1. **Subjects:** Newspaper reference topics. **Holdings:** Figures not available. **Services:** Library not open to the public. **Remarks:** FAX: (605)331-2371. Library located at 200 S. Minnesota, Sioux Falls, SD 57102.

★ 15197 ★

Sioux Valley Hospital - Medical Library (Med)
1100 S. Euclid Ave.
Box 5039
Sioux Falls, SD 57117-5039
Phone: (605)333-6330
Anna Gieschen, Libn.
Founded: 1954. **Staff:** 3. **Subjects:** Medicine, nursing, allied health sciences. **Holdings:** 4195 books; 3925 unbound and bound periodical volumes; 4 VF drawers of pamphlets, reprints, articles, clippings. **Subscriptions:** 300 journals and other serials. **Services:** Interlibrary loan; copying; library open to the public for reference use only. **Computerized Information Services:** MEDLINE, BRS Information Technologies. **Remarks:** FAX: (605)333-1392.

★ 15198 ★

Siouxland Heritage Museums - Library (Hist)
200 W. 6th St.
Sioux Falls, SD 57102
Phone: (605)339-7097
William J. Hoskins, Cur. of Coll.
Founded: 1926. **Staff:** Prof 1. **Subjects:** South Dakota history; U.S. history - silver question; 19th century works on ethnology and natural science; Indians. **Special Collections:** Arthur C. Phillips Collection; Northern League Baseball records (4 linear feet); library and private papers of U.S. Senator R.F. Pettigrew (1000 volumes); South Dakota history (1500 items). **Holdings:** 9000 books; 200 bound periodical volumes; 100 maps; 150 linear feet of manuscripts; 10,000 photographs. **Subscriptions:** 10 journals and other serials. **Services:** Copying; library open to the public. **Publications:** Community Report, bimonthly - free upon request. **Remarks:** Alternate telephone number(s): 335-4210.

I. Philip Sipser Technical Library
See: **Technical Careers Institute - TCI Technical Library (16029)**

★ 15199 ★

Sirote & Permutt, P.C. - Law Library (Law)
2222 Arlington Ave., S.
Birmingham, AL 35205
Phone: (205)930-5233
Wm. Preston Peyton, Libn.
Staff: Prof 1; Other 1. **Subjects:** Law - taxation, litigation, business, collection. **Holdings:** 15,000 volumes; 100 cassettes. **Subscriptions:** 79 journals and other serials. **Services:** Interlibrary loan; copying; library open to the public with permission of member of the firm. **Computerized Information Services:** WESTLAW. **Special Indexes:** Holdings list of tax materials (card). **Remarks:** FAX: (205)930-5301.

★ 15200 ★

Siskiyou County Law Library (Law)
311 4th St., Courthouse
Yreka, CA 96097
Phone: (916)842-8330
Janet L. Whitaker, Libn.
Founded: 1939. **Staff:** 1. **Subjects:** Law. **Holdings:** 14,633 volumes; 12 bound periodical volumes; 3800 volumes on ultrafiche. **Services:** Copying; library open to the public for reference use only. **Remarks:** FAX: (916)842-8093. Maintained by Siskiyou County Law Library Association.

★ 15201 ★

Siskiyou County Museum - Library (Hist)
910 S. Main St.
Yreka, CA 96097
Phone: (916)842-3836
Michael Hendryx, Musm.Dir.
Founded: 1950. **Staff:** Prof 1; Other 1. **Subjects:** History of Siskiyou County. **Special Collections:** Bancroft Histories (set); Siskiyou Pioneer yearbooks (1947-1989). **Holdings:** 1000 books; 250 ledgers and account books; 2500 documents; 17,000 photographs; 275 bound volumes of county newspapers, 1862-1956; voter registers. **Services:** Library open to the public by appointment. **Publications:** Siskiyou Pioneer, annual; NUGGETS, 6/year; occasional papers. **Special Indexes:** Index to Siskiyou Pioneer.

Sister Formation Conference/Religious Formation Conference Archives
See: **Marquette University - Department of Special Collections and University Archives - Manuscript Collections Memorial Library (9709)**

Sisters of Charity - St. Joseph Medical Center
See: **St. Joseph Medical Center (14387)**

★ 15202 ★

Sisters of Charity Hospital - Medical Staff Library (Med)
2157 Main St.
Buffalo, NY 14214
Phone: (716)862-2846
Anne Cohen, Med.Libn.
Founded: 1948. **Staff:** Prof 1. **Subjects:** Medicine, surgery, obstetrics and gynecology, pediatrics. **Holdings:** 5974 books and bound periodical volumes. **Subscriptions:** 99 journals and other serials. **Services:** Interlibrary loan; copying; library open to medical staff only. **Remarks:** FAX: (716)833-9465.

Sisters of Charity of Leavenworth - Saint Mary College
See: **Saint Mary College - De Paul Library - Special Collections Center (14500)**

★ 15203 ★

Sisters of the Holy Family of Nazareth - Provincial Archives (Rel-Phil, Hist)
4001 Grant Ave.
Philadelphia, PA 19114-2999
Phone: (215)637-6464
Sr. Mary Frances, Info.Dir.
Founded: 1973. **Staff:** Prof 2. **Subjects:** History of the Sisters of the Holy Family of Nazareth and the Immaculate Conception Province. **Special Collections:** Autobiography and biographies of the Foundress of the Sisters of the Holy Family of Nazareth; Constitutions of the Congregation, 1887-1983; Proceedings of the General Chapters, 1895-1983; Books of Customs, 1894-1966; Reports of Provincial Superiors; Educational Conference Proceedings, 1941-1979; circular letters of the General and Provincial Superiors; Album of Fine Arts of the Sisters of the Holy Family of Nazareth (CSFN); information on various programs held in the province; Inter-Province News Letters; blueprints of all institutions of the province. **Holdings:** 1180 books; 41 bound periodical volumes; 120 doctoral and masters' dissertations; active files of convents and members; chronicles and annals of homes; necrologies of deceased sisters. **Services:** Archives not open to the public. **Publications:** Guide to Nazareth Literature 1873-1973 (1st edition).

★ 15204 ★

Sisters of Notre Dame de Namur - Ohio Province - Archives (Rel-Phil)
Provincial House
701 E. Columbia Ave.
Cincinnati, OH 45215
Phone: (513)821-7448
Sr. Mary Elaine, Dir.
Subjects: Houses, institutions, and works of the Ohio Province of the Sisters of Notre Dame de Namur, 1840 to present; work of St. Julie Billiart. **Special Collections:** Manuscripts (original and copied letters of church officials and sisters of the convent); biographies and memoirs of sisters, Catholic women, and clergy. **Holdings:** 785.3 cubic feet of church records, conference proceedings, catechisms, educational writings, academic theses, institutional histories, cemetery records, necrologies, church rules, prayers; photographs; slides. **Services:** Copying; archives open to public with permission.

★ 15205 ★

Sisters of Providence - Sacred Heart Province - Archives (Rel-Phil)
4800 37th Ave., S.W.
Seattle, WA 98126
Phone: (206)937-4600
Sr. Rita Bergamini, S.P., Archv.
Founded: 1856. **Staff:** Prof 2. **Subjects:** Sisters of Providence; history of health care, education, missions, social welfare institutions, Catholic church. **Special Collections:** Mother Joseph, a Sister of Providence (1823-1902; represents Washington State in Statuary Hall, Washington, D.C.); educational history; medical history of Sisters of Providence health care institutions, managed health care plans, and housing programs in Alaska, Washington, Oregon, and California, 1856 to present. **Holdings:** 3000 books; 2800 linear feet of archival materials; 50 file drawers of photographs, film, slides. **Services:** Copying; archives open to the public by appointment. **Computerized Information Services:** Internal database (sister personnel data, 1856 to present). **Staff:** Loretta Zwolak Greene, Asst.Archv.

★ 15206 ★

Sisters of Providence HealthCare Corporation - Corporate Library (Med)
Box C11038
Seattle, WA 98111
Phone: (206)464-3028
Keith Dahlgren, Lib.Coord.
Founded: 1985. **Staff:** 1. **Subjects:** Health care - administration, planning, law, financing. **Holdings:** 1200 books. **Subscriptions:** 350 journals and other serials; 10 newspapers. **Services:** Interlibrary loan; library not open to the public. **Computerized Information Services:** DIALOG Information Services; internal database. **Remarks:** FAX: (206)464-3038.

Sisters of Saint Ann - Queenswood House
See: **Queenswood House** (13663)

Sisters of St. Elizabeth of Hungary - J2CP Information Services
See: **J2CP Information Services** (8299)

Sisters of St. Francis - Lourdes College
See: **Lourdes College - Duns Scotus Library** (9402)

★ 15207 ★
Sisters of St. Joseph of Carondelet - St. Paul Province - Archives (Rel-Phil)
1884 Randolph Ave.   Phone: (612)690-7000
St. Paul, MN 55105   Mary E. Kraft, C.S.J., Archv.
Staff: Prof 1; Other 1. **Subjects:** Religious life, education, health care, social justice, women. **Holdings:** Archival collections. **Services:** Copying; archives open to the public with restrictions.

★ 15208 ★
Sisters of St. Mary of Namur - Mount St. Mary Research Center (Rel-Phil, Hist)
3756 Delaware Ave.   Phone: (716)875-4705
Kenmore, NY 14217   Sr. Martin Joseph Jones, Archv./Libn.
Founded: 1975. **Staff:** Prof 2. **Subjects:** History of Sisters of St. Mary, Bible, biography, church history. **Special Collections:** Slides of Dante. **Holdings:** 6210 books and bound periodical volumes; 8 boxes of slides; 500 cassettes. **Subscriptions:** 25 journals and other serials. **Services:** Interlibrary loan; copying; center open to the public. **Staff:** Sr. Mary R. Thompson, Acq.

Sitka National Historical Park
See: **U.S. Natl. Park Service** (17779)

★ 15209 ★
SJO Consulting Engineers Inc. - Engineering Library (Sci-Engr)
1500 S.W. 12th Ave.   Phone: (503)226-3921
Portland, OR 97201   Anna LaRocco, Libn.
Founded: 1978. **Staff:** 1. **Subjects:** Engineering - mechanical, structural, civil, electrical, environmental. **Special Collections:** Environmental Protection Agency materials on air/noise pollution control. **Holdings:** 810 volumes; 50 reports; 8 VF drawers of vendors' brochures. **Subscriptions:** 79 journals and other serials. **Services:** Interlibrary loan; copying; SDI; library open to the public with restrictions. **Computerized Information Services:** Online systems.

★ 15210 ★
Skadden, Arps, Slate, Meagher & Flom - Library (Law)
One Rodney Square
Box 636   Phone: (302)651-3224
Wilmington, DE 19899   Leslie Bard Corey, Libn.
Founded: 1979. **Staff:** Prof 1; Other 1. **Subjects:** Corporate and securities law, Delaware corporate law. **Holdings:** 8000 books; 160 bound periodical volumes. **Subscriptions:** 45 journals and other serials; 9 newspapers. **Services:** Interlibrary loan; library not open to the public. **Computerized Information Services:** DIALOG Information Services, VU/TEXT Information Services, Information America, LEXIS, WESTLAW, Quotron Systems, Inc. **Publications:** Library Bulletin, monthly - to attorneys. **Remarks:** FAX: (302)651-3001.

★ 15211 ★
Skadden, Arps, Slate, Meagher & Flom - Library (Law)
919 3rd Ave.   Phone: (212)735-3000
New York, NY 10022   Carrie Hirtz, Libn.
Staff: Prof 8; Other 22. **Subjects:** Law. **Holdings:** 60,000 books; 500 bound periodical volumes; 150 VF drawers. **Subscriptions:** 1000 journals and other serials; 6 newspapers. **Services:** Interlibrary loan; library not open to the public. **Automated Operations:** Computerized circulation. **Computerized Information Services:** DIALOG Information Services, WESTLAW, Dow Jones News/Retrieval, PFDS Online, LEXIS, VU/TEXT Information Services, TEXTLINE, DataTimes, Newsnet, Inc. **Remarks:** FAX: (212)735-2000.

★ 15212 ★
Skagit County Historical Museum - Historical Reference Library (Hist)
501 S. 4th St.
P.O. Box 818   Phone: (206)466-3365
La Conner, WA 98257   Mary Anderson, Archv.Mgr.
Founded: 1968. **Staff:** Prof 3; Other 2. **Subjects:** Skagit County history, pioneer family genealogies, local Indian histories, late 19th century novels. **Special Collections:** Diaries of Grant Sisson, W.J. Cornelius, Arthur Champenois, and others, 1844-1964; Darius Kinsey Photographs; personal and legal papers of Key Pittman, U.S. Senator from Nevada, 1913-1940. **Holdings:** 1500 books; 308 bound periodical volumes; 6000 photographs; 599 newspapers; 658 business documents; 109 old letters; 106 old district school accounts/records; 81 maps; 626 clippings and clipping scrapbooks; 183 old programs/announcements; 64 pioneer diaries; 220 oral history tapes with transcripts; old American popular music, 1866-1954; local newspapers, 1900 to present. **Services:** Copying; library open to the public by appointment. **Staff:** Eunice Darvill, Dir.; Margaret K. Pederson, Cur. of Educ.; Pat Doran, Reg./Coll.Mgr.

★ 15213 ★
Skagit County Law Library (Law)
County Court House   Phone: (206)336-9324
Mount Vernon, WA 98273   Cathy Pfahl
Subjects: Law, decisions of appellate courts. **Holdings:** 6500 volumes. **Services:** Library open to the public for reference use only.

Ski Hall of Fame
See: **Colorado Ski Museum** (3948)

Skidaway Institute of Oceanography
See: **University of Georgia** (18606)

Louis Skidmore Room
See: **Massachusetts Institute of Technology - Rotch Library of Architecture and Planning - Visual Collections** (9817)

★ 15214 ★
Skidmore, Owings & Merrill - Information Services Department (Plan, Art)
220 E. 42nd St.   Phone: (212)309-9500
New York, NY 10017   Frances C. Gretes, Dir., Info.Serv.
Founded: 1980. **Staff:** Prof 1. **Subjects:** Architecture, art, engineering, interior design, New York history, planning. **Special Collections:** Archives. **Holdings:** 3000 books; 170 bound periodical volumes; 200 master plans; 10,000 drawings; specifications; 300 reels of microfilm; 5000 project clippings; 5000 photographs; 1000 unbound periodicals. **Subscriptions:** 160 journals and other serials. **Services:** Interlibrary loan (limited); copying; SDI; department open to other librarians and students for reference use only. **Computerized Information Services:** PFDS Online, Civil Engineering Database, DIALOG Information Services, RLIN, NEXIS, VU/TEXT Information Services, DataTimes. **Publications:** Monthly list of new publications; bibliography on the work of the firm (published articles). **Remarks:** FAX: (212)309-9750.

★ 15215 ★
Skidmore, Owings & Merrill - Library (Plan, Art)
1201 Pennsylvania Ave., N.W., Ste. 600
Washington, DC 20004   Phone: (202)393-1400
                                        Nasim Ahmed, Libn.
Founded: 1976. **Staff:** Prof 1. **Subjects:** Architecture, interior design, urban planning and transportation, landscape architecture. **Holdings:** 2000 books; 100 bound periodical volumes; 1000 SOM reports; 500 SOM proposals; slides; maps; photographs; clippings. **Services:** Interlibrary loan; copying; library open to the public by appointment.

★ 15216 ★
Skidmore, Owings & Merrill - Library (Plan)
33 W. Monroe St.   Phone: (312)641-5959
Chicago, IL 60603   Ann Dutt-Milano, Libn.
Founded: 1973. **Staff:** Prof 1. **Subjects:** Engineering and architecture design and technology. **Holdings:** 7000 books; 60 bound periodical volumes; 25 VF drawers of photographs and pamphlets. **Subscriptions:** 50 journals and other serials. **Services:** Interlibrary loan; library not open to the public. **Computerized Information Services:** Internal databases. **Networks/Consortia:** Member of Chicago Library System.

Frederick W. Skillin Health Sciences Library
See: **Northern Cumberland Memorial Hospital** (11993)

Blanche C. Skoglund Memorial Library
See: **Simsbury Historical Society** (15184)

Skogs och Jordbruksbiblioteket
See: **Sweden - National Board of Agriculture - Library** (15908)

★ 15217 ★
(Skopje) Amerikanski Centar - USIS Library (Educ)
Grandski Zid, blok IV
P.O. Box 296
YU-91000 Skopje, Yugoslavia
Remarks: Maintained or supported by the U.S. Information Agency. Focus is on materials that will assist peoples outside the United States to learn about the United States, its people, history, culture, political processes, and social milieux.

★ 15218 ★
Skynet - Library (Sci-Engr)
257 Sycamore Glen   Phone: (213)256-8655
Pasadena, CA 91105   Ann Druffel, Proj.Coord.
Founded: 1965. **Subjects:** UFO research, psychic phenomena research, ley-line research. **Special Collections:** UFO history (Southern California sightings and reports, 1950 to present). **Holdings:** 550 books; 700 periodicals; 11 cases of magnetic tapes; 800 other cataloged items. **Subscriptions:** 30 journals and other serials. **Services:** Accepts mail inquiries (self-addressed stamped envelope required). **Computerized Information Services:** Internal database.

SLA
See: **Special Libraries Association** (15576)

SLAC High Energy Preprint Library
See: **University of California, Los Angeles - Physics Library** (18395)

Frank J. Sladen Library
See: **Henry Ford Hospital** (5963)

★ 15219 ★
Slater Mill Historic Site - Research Library (Hist)
Roosevelt Ave.
Box 727
Pawtucket, RI 02862   Phone: (401)725-8638
                                             Gail Fowler Mohanty, Cur.
Founded: 1955. **Staff:** 1. **Subjects:** Handicraft and factory textile production, machine tools, local industrial and social history. **Holdings:** 700 volumes. **Subscriptions:** 5 journals and other serials; 3 newspapers. **Services:** Library open to the public by appointment. **Publications:** The Flyer, quarterly.

★ 15220 ★
Slavia Library (Area-Ethnic)
418 W. Nittany Ave.   Phone: (814)238-5215
State College, PA 16801   Dr. W.O. Luciw, Dir.
Staff: Prof 1; Other 2. **Subjects:** Ukrainian history, literature, language, social studies, art, science. **Special Collections:** Ukrainian and Slavic archives. **Holdings:** 45,000 books; 5000 unbound periodical volumes; 17,000 other cataloged items; 40,000 items in microform; Slavic book plates; American and Slavic historical documents. **Subscriptions:** 60 journals and other serials. **Services:** Copying; SDI; library open to the public by appointment for reference use only. **Publications:** Life and School, 5/year; Free World. **Special Catalogs:** Book publications catalog.

★ 15221 ★
Slavonic Benevolent Order of the State of Texas - Library, Archives, Museum (Area-Ethnic)
520 N. Main St.   Phone: (817)773-1575
Temple, TX 76501   Dorothy Pechal, Libn./Cur.
Founded: 1968. **Staff:** 1. **Subjects:** Czech education, medicine, religion, history, music, fiction, genealogy. **Holdings:** 28,000 volumes (mostly in Czech language). **Services:** Interlibrary loan; copying; library open to the public. **Computerized Information Services:** Genealogy of Members (internal database). **Publications:** Museum brochure.

Thomas Baker Slick Memorial Library
See: **Southwest Research Institute** (15535)

★ 15222 ★
Alfred P. Sloan, Jr. Museum - Merle G. Perry Archives (Trans)
1221 E. Kearsley St.
Flint, MI 48503   Phone: (313)760-1415
Founded: 1966. **Staff:** 3. **Subjects:** Automotive history, carriage industry, local history. **Special Collections:** Automotive catalogs (300). **Holdings:** 750 volumes. **Subscriptions:** 24 journals and other serials. **Services:** Copying; archives open to the public for reference use only. **Staff:** Carol DeKalands, Reg.

Helen Farr Sloan Library
See: **Delaware Art Museum - Helen Farr Sloan Library** (4715)

John Sloan Memorial Library
See: **Delaware Art Museum - Helen Farr Sloan Library** (4715)

John Sloan Memorial Room
See: **Annie Halenbake Ross Library - Special Collections** (14080)

Sloane Art Library
See: **University of North Carolina at Chapel Hill** (19077)

Sloat Chemistry Library
See: **Gettysburg College** (6458)

Dr. Barney A. Slotkin Memorial Library
See: **Kennedy Memorial Hospitals - Cherry Hill Division** (8632)

★ 15223 ★
Slovak Academy of Science - Institute of Musicology - Library (Mus)
Dubravska cesta 9   Phone: 7 3783410
CS-813 64 Bratislava, Czechoslovakia   Juraj Potucek
Founded: 1942. **Staff:** Prof 1. **Subjects:** Music - history, ethnography, theory. **Special Collections:** Archival of songs (50,000). **Holdings:** 11,100 books; 1800 bound periodical volumes; 400 reels of microfilm; 3500 audiocassettes; 670 videotapes; 20,000 photographs. **Services:** Interlibrary loan; library not open to the public. **Computerized Information Services:** Electronic mail service. **Remarks:** FAX: 3783426. **Also Known As:** Slovenska Akademia Vied (SAV) - Ustav Hudobnej Vedy.

★ 15224 ★
Slovak Catholic Charitable Organization - Slovak Cultural Center - Library (Area-Ethnic)
5900 W. 147th St.   Phone: (708)687-2877
Oak Forest, IL 60452   Sr. M. Methodia Machalica, Dir.
Staff: Prof 1. **Subjects:** Slovakia. **Holdings:** 2030 books and bound periodical volumes; Slovak encyclopedias, periodicals, stamps; manuscripts; clippings; archival materials; documents; magnetic tapes; videotapes. **Services:** Library open to the public with restrictions.

★ 15225 ★
Slovak Writers and Artists Association - Slovak Institute - Library
(Area-Ethnic)
St. Andrew's Abbey
10510 Buckeye Rd. .   Phone: (216)721-5300
Cleveland, OH 44104   Andrew Pier, Dir.
Staff: Prof 2. **Subjects:** Slovak history, Slovak art, Slovak literature, cultural achievements of Americans of Slovak ancestry. **Holdings:** 5000 books. **Services:** Library open to the public for reference use only by special arrangement.

Slovenska Akademia Vied - Ustav Hudobnej Vedy
See: **Slovak Academy of Science - Institute of Musicology - Library**
(15223)

★ 15226 ★
Small Business Administration - Reference Library (Bus-Fin)
409 Third St., S.W., 5th floor   Phone: (202)205-7033
Washington, DC 20416   Margaret Hickey, Libn.
Founded: 1958. **Staff:** Prof 1; Other 1. **Subjects:** Small business, finance, management, venture capital. **Holdings:** 8000 volumes. **Subscriptions:** 203 journals and other serials. **Services:** Interlibrary loan; library open to the public for reference use only.

★ 15227 ★
Small Business Computer Systems, Inc. - Agri-Source Software Library
(Agri, Comp Sci)
3815 Adams St.   Phone: (402)467-3591
Lincoln, NE 68504   David McFarland, Dir.
Founded: 1983. **Staff:** Prof 3. **Subjects:** Agriculture. **Special Collections:** Public domain agricultural software. **Holdings:** 15 books; spreadsheet templates and programs. **Subscriptions:** 15 journals and other serials; 6 newspapers. **Services:** Library open to the public.

★ 15228 ★
Small, Craig & Werkenthin - Library (Law)
100 Congress Ave., Suite 1100   Phone: (512)472-8355
Austin, TX 78701-4099   Judy Hamner, Libn.
Staff: Prof 1; Other 1. **Subjects:** Law. **Holdings:** 10,700 books; 50 bound periodical volumes; 600 volumes on microfiche; 2 boxes of microfiche. **Subscriptions:** 50 journals and other serials. **Services:** Interlibrary loan; copying; library open to the public by appointment. **Computerized Information Services:** DIALOG Information Services, WESTLAW, LEXIS, NEXIS; Research Retrieval (internal database). **Remarks:** FAX: (512)320-9734.

Small Newspaper Group, Inc. - (Moline) Daily Dispatch
See: **(Moline) Daily Dispatch/Rock Island Argus** (10596)

Robert Scott Small Library
See: **College of Charleston - Robert Scott Small Library - Special Collections** (3887)

Walter M. Small Geology Library
See: **Allegheny College** (362)

A.K. Smiley Public Library - Lincoln Memorial Shrine
See: **Lincoln Memorial Shrine** (9184)

Mary Miller Smiser Heritage Library
See: **Johnson County Historical Society** (8439)

★ 15229 ★
A.O. Smith Corporation - Library (Sci-Engr)
12100 W. Park Pl.   Phone: (414)359-4200
Milwaukee, WI 53224   Judith Sayrs, Res./Info.Spec.
Subjects: Automotive and electrical engineering, chemistry, plastics. **Holdings:** 2000 volumes. **Subscriptions:** 200 journals and other serials; 4 newspapers. **Services:** Copying; SDI; library not open to the public. **Computerized Information Services:** DIALOG Information Services, NERAC, Inc., VU/TEXT Information Services, OCLC EPIC, InvesText. **Remarks:** FAX: (414)359-4248.

★ 15230 ★
Smith, Anderson, Blount, Dorsett, Mitchell & Jernigan - Library (Law)
2500 First Union Capitol Center
Box 2611   Phone: (919)821-6658
Raleigh, NC 27602-2611   Constance M. Matzen, Dir. of Lib.Serv.
Staff: Prof 1; Other 1. **Subjects:** Law. **Holdings:** 8500 volumes. **Services:** Library not open to the public. **Computerized Information Services:** LEXIS, DIALOG Information Services, WESTLAW, DataTimes, LEGI-SLATE. Performs searches on fee basis. **Publications:** Library News (newsletter), monthly - for internal distribution only. **Remarks:** FAX: (919)821-6800.

★ 15231 ★
Smith Barney, Harris Upham & Company, Inc. - Library (Bus-Fin)
1345 Avenue of the Americas   Phone: (212)698-6294
New York, NY 10105   James J. Fichter, Libn.
Founded: 1922. **Staff:** Prof 3; Other 5. **Subjects:** Investments and securities. **Special Collections:** Corporation records. **Holdings:** 1000 books and bound periodical volumes. **Subscriptions:** 450 journals and other serials. **Services:** Interlibrary loan; library open to employees only. **Computerized Information Services:** LEXIS, DIALOG Information Services, Dow Jones News/Retrieval, Vickers Stock Research Corporation. **Staff:** Caroline Marks.

Bertha Smith Library
See: **Luther Rice Seminary** (9443)

Betty Golde Smith Memorial Library
See: **St. Louis Psychoanalytic Institute** (14447)

★ 15232 ★
Smith College - Anita O.'K. & Robert R. Young Science Library (Sci-Engr, Biol Sci)
Northampton, MA 01063   Phone: (413)585-2951
              Rocco Piccinino, Jr., Sci.Libn.
Founded: 1966. **Staff:** Prof 1; Other 3. **Subjects:** Astronomy, biological sciences, chemistry, geology, mathematics, physics, psychology, computer science, exercise and sports studies, history of science, women in science. **Special Collections:** Map collection (76,000 printed, 500 manuscripts, 50 wall, 25 raised relief; 200 gazetteers; U.S. depository for U.S. Geological Survey topographic and geologic maps; U.S. Defense Mapping Agency; Geological Survey of Canada). **Holdings:** 118,342 volumes including government documents and pamphlets; 15,222 microforms; 92 audiotapes; 8 machine-readable data files. **Subscriptions:** 678 journals; 306 other serials. **Services:** Interlibrary loan. **Automated Operations:** Computerized public access catalog, cataloging, circulation, serials, and acquisitions (INNOPAC). **Computerized Information Services:** BRS Information Technologies, DIALOG Information Services, OCLC EPIC, STN International, RLIN; CD-ROMs (General Science Index, AGRICOLA, GeoRef, MathSci, MEDLINE, PsycLIT, Computing Archive: Bibliography and Reviews from ACM, McGraw-Hill CD-ROM Science & Technical Reference Set); InterNet (electronic mail service). **Remarks:** Electronic mail address(es): RPICCININO@SMITH.SMITH.EDU (InterNet). **Formerly:** Its Clark Science Library. **Staff:** Klara Dienes, Lib.Asst.; Gail Adametz, Tech.Serv.Asst.

★ 15233 ★
Smith College - Archives (Hist)
Northampton, MA 01063   Phone: (413)585-2970
              Susan Grigg, Dir.
Founded: 1922. **Staff:** Prof 1. Other 1.5. **Subjects:** Smith College - administration, faculty, students, alumnae organizations, its leading role in the separate education of women since 1875. **Special Collections:** Records of central administrative offices and academic departments; official publications; papers of faculty members; records of student organizations; letters, diaries, and memorabilia of students; records of alumnae organizations. **Holdings:** 3000 linear feet. **Services:** Copying (limited); archives open to the public with restrictions. **Staff:** Margery N. Sly, Coll.Archv.; Maida Goodwin, Archv.Spec.

Smith College - Clark Science Library
See: **Smith College** (15232)

★15234★
Smith College - Hillyer Art Library (Art)
Fine Arts Ctr.   Phone: (413)585-2941
Northampton, MA 01063   Rocco Piccinino, Unit Coord. for Branches
Staff: Prof 1; Other 4. **Subjects:** History of art, painting, design, architecture, sculpture, graphic arts, landscape architecture. **Holdings:** 60,000 books, bound periodical volumes, and exhibition catalogs; 23,000 vertical file items; 12,300 microforms. **Subscriptions:** 209 journals and other serials. **Services:** Interlibrary loan; copying; library open to the public for reference use only by special permission. **Automated Operations:** Computerized public access catalog (LS/2000). **Computerized Information Services:** CD-ROM (Art Index); electronic mail. **Remarks:** Alternate telephone number(s): (413)585-2940.

★15235★
Smith College - Nonprint Resources Center (Aud-Vis)
Library   Phone: (413)585-2954
Northampton, MA 01063   David Vikre, Dir.
Founded: 1985. **Staff:** Prof 1; Other 5. **Subjects:** Film studies, science, government, languages, history, religion. **Holdings:** 1200 videotapes; 300 audiotapes; 50 16mm films. **Services:** Center open to the public with restrictions. **Automated Operations:** Computerized cataloging. **Computerized Information Services:** DIALOG Information Services.

★15236★
Smith College - Rare Book Room (Rare Book)
Northampton, MA 01063   Phone: (413)585-2905
                                                  Ruth Mortimer, Cur.
Staff: Prof 2. **Subjects:** 18th century English literature, early science, history of printing, economics, 19th century English lithography. **Special Collections:** English and American children's books, 17th-20th centuries (525 titles); Rudyard Kipling (275 items); William Faulkner (100 items); George Bernard Shaw (264 items); Ernest Hemingway (250 items); Sylvia Plath (700 items, including 4000 pages of manuscripts); Virginia Woolf (450 items, including manuscripts); George Salter (3600 items); E. Thornton Botanical Books (89 titles). **Holdings:** 24,000 books. **Services:** Copying; room open to the public by appointment. **Special Indexes:** Chronological index (card); index of printers (card). **Staff:** Karen V. Kukil, Asst.Cur.

★15237★
Smith College - Sophia Smith Collection - Women's History Archive
  (Hist, Soc Sci)
Northampton, MA 01063   Phone: (413)585-2970
                                                  Susan Grigg, Dir.
Founded: 1942. **Staff:** Prof 2; Other .5. **Subjects:** U.S. women's history, 1820 to present, especially birth control, social work, women's suffrage and rights, journalism, medicine, international service; 19th century families. **Special Collections:** 200 major collections of personal papers and organizational records, including: Margaret Sanger; Planned Parenthood of America and Massachusetts; Hale, Ames, and Garrison families; Ellen Gates Starr; Mary van Kleeck; Pauline Frederick. **Holdings:** 3600 linear feet of manuscripts, archives, periodicals, printed ephemera, photographs, books. **Subscriptions:** 65 serials. **Services:** Copying (limited); archive open to the public with restrictions. **Special Catalogs:** Catalog of the Sophia Smith Collection (1976) - for sale; Picture Catalog of the Sophia Smith Collection - out of print; Catalogs of the Sophia Smith Collection, 7 vols. (G.K. Hall, 1984). **Staff:** Amy Hague, Asst.Cur.; Margery Sly, Rec.Archv.

★15238★
Smith College - Werner Josten Library of the Performing Arts (Mus, Theater)
Mendenhall Center   Phone: (413)585-2935
Northampton, MA 01063   Marlene M. Wong, Libn.
Founded: 1911. **Staff:** Prof 2; Other 4. **Subjects:** Music, theater, dance. **Special Collections:** Einstein Collection (music of the 16th and 17th centuries copied in score by Alfred Einstein); music and correspondence of Werner Josten. **Holdings:** 73,071 volumes; 47,931 sound recordings; 706 reels of microfilm. **Subscriptions:** 260 journals. **Services:** Interlibrary loan (circulating books and periodicals only); library open to the public for reference use only. **Automated Operations:** Computerized cataloging. **Computerized Information Services:** OCLC. **Networks/Consortia:** Member of NELINET, Inc. **Special Indexes:** Index to articles in periodicals published prior to 1949; index to American sheet music collection; index to selected song collections; index to microfilm collection of musical and dramatic criticism by Philip Hale and others. **Staff:** Kathryn E. Burnett, Assoc.Libn.

★15239★
Smith, Currie & Hancock - Law Library (Law)
233 Peachtree St., N.E., Suite 2600   Phone: (404)521-3800
Atlanta, GA 30303-1530   Kathleen Ries, Law Libn.
Founded: 1972. **Staff:** Prof 1; Other 1. **Subjects:** Law - building and construction, government contract, labor. **Holdings:** 10,000 volumes; 1500 other cataloged items; 1300 internal materials. **Subscriptions:** 80 journals and other serials. **Services:** Interlibrary loan; library open to members of the Atlanta Law Libraries Association. **Computerized Information Services:** DIALOG Information Services, LEXIS, VU/TEXT Information Services, Information America, WESTLAW. **Publications:** Library Newsletter, monthly - for internal distribution only; Construction Law; Labor Law (both annotated bibliographies). **Remarks:** FAX: (404)688-0671.

David Eugene Smith Mathematical Library
See: **Columbia University - Rare Book and Manuscript Library** (4023)

★15240★
Deaf Smith General Hospital - Library (Med)
801 E. 3rd St.   Phone: (806)364-2141
Hereford, TX 79045   Debbie Foerster, Dir., Med.Rec.
Staff: Prof 1; Other 2. **Subjects:** Medicine and allied health sciences. **Holdings:** 175 volumes. **Services:** Library not open to the public. **Remarks:** FAX: (806)364-6341.

Dick Smith Archives
See: **Santa Barbara Museum of Natural History - Library** (14802)

Dr. C.W. Smith Technical Information Center
See: **General Electric Company - Aircraft Engines** (6307)

Edgar Fahs Smith Memorial Collection in the History of Chemistry
See: **University of Pennsylvania** (19181)

Edwin Smith Historical Museum
See: **Westfield Athenaeum** (20310)

★15241★
Frederick C. Smith Clinic - Medical Library (Med)
1040 Delaware Ave.   Phone: (614)383-8098
Marion, OH 43302   Deborah Saull, Libn.
Staff: Prof 1. **Subjects:** Medicine. **Holdings:** 750 books; 2000 bound periodical volumes. **Subscriptions:** 100 journals and other serials. **Services:** Interlibrary loan; copying; library open to the public by appointment. **Networks/Consortia:** Member of Central Ohio Hospital Library Consortium. **Remarks:** FAX: (614)387-8119.

Frederick Madison Smith Library
See: **Graceland College** (6608)

Furman Smith Library
See: **Mercer University - Law School** (10111)

George F. Smith Library
See: **University of Medicine and Dentistry of New Jersey** (18837)

★15242★
George Walter Vincent Smith Art Museum - Library (Art)
222 State St.   Phone: (413)733-4214
Springfield, MA 01103   Hollister Sturges, Dir.
Founded: 1898. **Subjects:** Chinese and Japanese decorative arts, American art, arms and armor. **Holdings:** 2500 volumes. **Subscriptions:** 10 journals and other serials. **Services:** Library not open to the public. **Special Catalogs:** Exhibition catalogs. **Remarks:** Maintained by Springfield Library and Museums Association.

H. Ward Smith Library
See: Ontario Ministry of the Solicitor General - Centre of Forensic Sciences (12484)

★ 15243 ★
Smith Helms Mulliss & Moore - Law Library (Law)
300 N. Greene St.   Phone: (919)378-5272
Greensboro, NC 27401   Anne Washburn, Libn.
Staff: Prof 1; Other 1. **Subjects:** Law. **Holdings:** 20,000 books. **Subscriptions:** 175 journals and other serials. **Services:** Copying; library open to the public with restrictions. **Computerized Information Services:** DIALOG Information Services, WESTLAW, LEGI-SLATE, Information America, NewsNet, Inc., VU/TEXT Information Services, LEXIS, Veralex 2, Maxwell Macmillan Taxes Online, CompuServe Information Service. **Remarks:** Branch libraries are maintained in Charlotte and Raleigh. FAX: (919)379-9558.

★ 15244 ★
Herman Smith Associates/Coopers & Lybrand - Healthcare Library (Plan)
203 N. LaSalle St., 22nd Fl.   Phone: (312)701-6412
Chicago, IL 60601   Gail M. Langer, Mgr.
Staff: Prof 2; Other 1. **Subjects:** Hospital planning, design and construction, administration, regional health planning. **Holdings:** 1500 books; 7000 documents and reports; 55 VF drawers. **Subscriptions:** 200 journals and other serials. **Services:** Interlibrary loan. **Networks/Consortia:** Member of Chicago Library System. **Remarks:** FAX: (312)701-6540. **Staff:** Barbara A. Bauer.

Hervey Garrett Smith Research Library
See: Suffolk Marine Museum (15850)

Ian R. Smith Memorial Library and Documentation Center
See: International Center for Living Aquatic Resources Management (8072)

J.D. Smith Memorial Library
See: Akron General Medical Center (172)

★ 15245 ★
John Peter Smith Hospital - Marietta Memorial Medical Library (Med)
1500 S. Main   Phone: (817)921-3431
Fort Worth, TX 76104   M. June Bowman, Med.Libn.
Founded: 1963. **Staff:** Prof 2; Other 1. **Subjects:** Medicine, nursing, and allied health sciences. **Holdings:** 4200 books; 12,000 bound periodical volumes; 800 audiotapes. **Subscriptions:** 300 journals and other serials. **Services:** Interlibrary loan (limited); copying; complete services to the personnel of the Tarrant County Hospital District and the Tarrant County Medical Society; library open to the public but services available to health professionals only. **Computerized Information Services:** NLM, MEDLINE. **Networks/Consortia:** Member of Health Libraries Information Network (HealthLINE). **Publications:** Acquisitions List, monthly; current awareness. **Special Catalogs:** Union List of Serials, biennial - to members. **Remarks:** FAX: (817)923-0718. **Staff:** Leslie Herman, Clin.Med.Libn.

Joseph F. Smith Library
See: Brigham Young University--Hawaii Campus (20811)

Kent H. Smith Library
See: Foundation Center - Cleveland (6037)

★ 15246 ★
Smith-Kettlewell Eye Research Institute - In-House Library (Med)
2232 Webster St.   Phone: (415)561-1620
San Francisco, CA 94115   Dr. Alex Cogan, Sci.
Founded: 1959. **Subjects:** Vision research and rehabilitation engineering. **Holdings:** 2000 volumes. **Services:** Library not open to the public.

★ 15247 ★
Smith Library of Regional History (Hist)
15 S. College Ave.   Phone: (513)523-3035
Oxford, OH 45056   Valerie Edwards Elliott, Hd.
Founded: 1981. **Subjects:** Oxford, Ohio (village and township); Butler County, Ohio; Southwestern Ohio; Miami River Valleys; Old Northwest Territory; Ohio River Valley. **Special Collections:** Oxford newspapers on microfilm; Oxford Village and Township Archives (from 1830). **Holdings:** 1900 books; 110 bound periodical volumes; 180 documents; 320 microforms; 50 manuscripts; 800 photographs; Oxford cemetery burial records; county maps and atlases; county census records; county marriage, birth, death, and will records; deeds; tax lists. **Subscriptions:** 13 journals and other serials. **Services:** Copying; library open to the public. **Automated Operations:** Computerized public access catalog. **Networks/Consortia:** Member of Greater Cincinnati Library Consortium (GCLC). **Publications:** Minutes of Our Years: Oxford 1830-1981; 150-Year History of Oxford Government 1830-1980; Burial Grounds of Oxford, Ohio 1817-1987. **Special Indexes:** Oxford Names Index (card). **Remarks:** FAX: (513)523-6661. Smith Library of Regional History is a division of Lane Public Library. **Staff:** Jon E. Scharf.

Lillian H. Smith Collection of Children's Books
See: Toronto Public Library (16415)

★ 15248 ★
Smith, Lyons, Torrance, Stevenson & Mayer - Library (Law)
Scotia Plaza, Suite 6200
40 King St. W.   Phone: (416)369-7285
Toronto, ON, Canada M5H 3Z7   Yvonne MacDonald, Mgr., Lib.Serv.
Staff: Prof 1; Other 3. **Subjects:** Canadian law. **Holdings:** 14,000 volumes. **Subscriptions:** 454 journals and other serials; 6 newspapers. **Services:** Interlibrary loan; copying; SDI; library open to the public by appointment. **Computerized Information Services:** QL Systems, Info Globe, CAN/LAW, WESTLAW, Infomart Online, LEXIS, Dow Jones News/Retrieval, DIALOG Information Services, UTLAS, Canadian Tax Online. **Publications:** Library Bulletin, weekly - for internal distribution only. **Remarks:** FAX: (416)369-7250.

★ 15249 ★
Margaret Chase Smith Library Center (Hist)
Norridgewock Ave.
Box 366   Phone: (207)474-7133
Skowhegan, ME 04976   G.P. Gallant, Dir.
Founded: 1982. **Staff:** Prof 2; Other 5. **Subjects:** Senator Margaret Chase Smith's personal and professional records, American political history and biography. **Holdings:** Figures not available. **Subscriptions:** 4 newspapers. **Services:** Copying; library open to qualified scholars. **Remarks:** FAX: (207)474-8878. Maintained by Northwood Institute, Midland, Michigan. **Staff:** Margaret F. Viens, Asst.Dir.

★ 15250 ★
Smith Memorial Library - Historical Archives (Hum)
Clark & Miller Ave.   Phone: (716)357-6296
Chautauqua, NY 14722   Barbara Haug, Archv.
Founded: 1906. **Subjects:** Chautauqua. **Holdings:** Books and history of the Chautauqua Institution, 1874 to present. **Services:** Interlibrary loan; copying; collection open to the public. **Networks/Consortia:** Member of Chautauqua-Cattaraugus Library System. **Remarks:** Maintained by Chautauqua Institution. **Staff:** Helene Yurth, Libn.

Smith Museum Archives
See: Arlington Historical Society (1040)

★ 15251 ★
Smith Peterson Beckman Willson Law Firm - Smith Peterson Law Library (Law)
35 Main Place, Suite 300   Phone: (712)328-1833
Council Bluffs, IA 51502   Beverly Hobbs, Libn.
Staff: Prof 1. **Subjects:** Law. **Holdings:** 10,006 books; expert witness files. **Subscriptions:** 51 journals and other serials. **Services:** Library not open to the public. **Computerized Information Services:** WESTLAW. **Remarks:** FAX: (712)328-8320.

Ralph Smith Memorial Library
See: **American Collectors Association, Inc.** (530)

Richard Root Smith Library
See: **Blodgett Memorial Medical Center** (1899)

Richard V. Smith Art Reference Library
See: **Everson Museum of Art** (5514)

Sophia Smith Collection
See: **Smith College** (15237)

★ 15252 ★
Wilbur Smith Associates - Library (Plan)
1301 Gervais St.
Box 92
Columbia, SC 29202
Phone: (803)738-0580
Jasper Salmond, Info.Dir.
Founded: 1952. **Staff:** Prof 2. **Subjects:** Transportation, planning, architecture, civil engineering, economics, energy. **Holdings:** 40,000 books and technical reports; speeches; vertical file. **Subscriptions:** 50 journals and other serials. **Services:** Interlibrary loan; library open to the public with restrictions. **Publications:** Acquisitions list; Federal Register Report, both monthly - both for internal distribution only. **Remarks:** FAX: (803)251-2064.

William Henry Smith Memorial Library
See: **Indiana Historical Society** (7755)

★ 15253 ★
SmithKline Beecham - Consumer Brands Research and Development - Research Library (Sci-Engr)
1500 Littleton Rd.
Parsippany, NJ 07504
Phone: (201)631-8019
Kathleen Morris, Info.Serv.Spec.
Founded: 1978. **Staff:** Prof 2. **Subjects:** Cosmetics, toiletries, proprietary drugs. **Holdings:** 3000 books; 15 periodical titles on microfilm. **Subscriptions:** 190 journals and other serials. **Services:** Interlibrary loan; library not open to the public. **Computerized Information Services:** DIALOG Information Services, NLM, NERAC Inc., OCLC. **Networks/Consortia:** Member of National Network of Libraries of Medicine - Middle Atlantic Region. **Remarks:** FAX: (201)631-8795. **Staff:** Tamara Warne.

★ 15254 ★
SmithKline Beecham Clinical Laboratories - Library (Med, Biol Sci)
7600 Tyrone Ave.
Van Nuys, CA 91405
Phone: (818)376-6270
Caroline Elman, Info.Spec.
Founded: 1948. **Staff:** Prof 1. **Subjects:** Clinical chemistry, microbiology, endocrinology and immunology, toxicology. **Holdings:** 2000 books; 5000 bound periodical volumes; 200 doctors' papers written at laboratories. **Subscriptions:** 100 journals and other serials. **Services:** Interlibrary loan; copying; library open to cooperating libraries. **Computerized Information Services:** MEDLARS, DIALOG Information Services. **Publications:** Reprints of doctors' papers - free upon request. **Remarks:** FAX: (818)376-6387.

★ 15255 ★
SmithKline Beecham, Pharma Canada - Medical Library (Med)
2030 Bristle Circle
Oakville, ON, Canada L6H 5V2
Phone: (416)829-2030
Janet B. Hillis, Lib.Techn.
Founded: 1960. **Staff:** 1. **Subjects:** Medicine - antibiotics, gastrointestinal, oncology, central nervous system, cardiology; pharmacy; pharmacology; biochemistry; microbiology. **Special Collections:** Beecham product file (microfiche). **Holdings:** 500 books; 650 bound periodical volumes; 600 volumes of reprints. **Subscriptions:** 100 journals and other serials. **Services:** Library not open to the public. **Computerized Information Services:** DIALOG Information Services, CAN/OLE; INQUIRE, BEECHAMLINE (internal databases). **Remarks:** FAX: (416)829-3907.

★ 15256 ★
SmithKline Beecham Pharmaceuticals, U.S. - Marketing Library (Bus-Fin)
1 Franklin Plaza
200 N. 16th St.
PO Box 7929
Philadelphia, PA 19101-7929
Phone: (215)751-5576
Doris P. Shalley, Mktg.Libn.
Founded: 1945. **Staff:** 1. **Subjects:** Business and marketing aspects of the healthcare and pharmaceutical industries; drug therapy; disease information; general business. **Special Collections:** 500 marketing research studies. **Holdings:** 1000 books and bound periodical volumes; 10,000 internal reports; 15 shelves of clip files; 1000 government reports. **Subscriptions:** 200 journals and other serials. **Services:** Library not open to the public. **Computerized Information Services:** DIALOG Information Services, INVESTEXT, Dun & Bradstreet Business Credit Services, Pharmaprojects, NEXIS, Dow Jones News/Retrieval, NewsNet, Inc., IMSWORLD, BASIS, ExecuNet. **Publications:** MarkAlert, 4/year; CAB Bulletin - both for internal distribution only. **Remarks:** FAX: (215)751-5509.

★ 15257 ★
SmithKline Beecham Pharmaceuticals, U.S. - Product Information Library (E44) (Med)
1500 Spring Garden St.
Philadelphia, PA 19130
Phone: (215)751-6323
Augustina Yang, Mgr.
Staff: Prof 2. **Subjects:** Medicine, chemistry, biology, business, regulatory affairs. **Holdings:** 2600 books; 4765 bound periodical volumes; 2.5 VF drawers of Class 424 patents. **Subscriptions:** 300 journals and other serials. **Computerized Information Services:** DIALOG Information Services. **Remarks:** FAX: (215)751-5211. **Staff:** Sara Brower, Sr.Info.Sci.; Gary Gray, Sr.Info.Sci.

★ 15258 ★
SmithKline Beecham Pharmaceuticals, U.S. - Research and Development Information Center (L322) (Med)
709 Swedeland Rd.
Box 1539
King of Prussia, PA 19406
Phone: (215)270-6400
Jane Whittall, Info.Sci.Mgr.
Founded: 1947. **Staff:** Prof 11; Other 4. **Subjects:** Medicine, chemistry, pharmacology, pharmacy, biological sciences. **Holdings:** 15,000 books; 15,000 bound periodical volumes; 10,000 reels of microfilm. **Subscriptions:** 1100 journals and other serials. **Services:** Interlibrary loan; center not open to the public. **Automated Operations:** Computerized public access catalog, cataloging, acquisitions, serials, and circulation. **Computerized Information Services:** DIALOG Information Services, PFDS Online, BRS Information Technologies, NLM, Mead Data Central; LION, PRODOL (internal databases). **Networks/Consortia:** Member of PALINET. **Publications:** List of Acquisitions, monthly - for internal distribution only. **Remarks:** FAX: (215)270-4127. **Staff:** Alice Dempsey, Hd., Sci.Info.Serv.; Arlene Smith, Hd., Lib.Rsrc.Serv.

★ 15259 ★
Smiths Industries - Library (Sci-Engr)
4141 Eastern Ave., S.E.
Grand Rapids, MI 49518-8727
Phone: (616)241-7467
Scott Brackett, Mgr.
Founded: 1959. **Staff:** Prof 1; Other 2. **Subjects:** Electronics, electrical engineering, computer technology, aeronautics, aerospace, management. **Holdings:** 10,000 books; 2000 bound periodical volumes; 600 microforms; 1000 reels of microfilm; 100,000 specifications and standards; 6000 government technical reports; 100 compact discs. **Subscriptions:** 300 journals and other serials. **Services:** Interlibrary loan; copying; SDI; library open to the public by prior arrangement. **Automated Operations:** Computerized serials and circulation. **Computerized Information Services:** DIALOG Information Services, DTIC, NASA/RECON, Aerospace Daily, NewsNet, Inc., InvesText, CompuServe Information Service. **Publications:** Recent Acquisitions Bulletin, monthly - for internal distribution only. **Remarks:** FAX: (616)241-7533. Telex: (616)241-8301.

★ 15260 ★
Smithsonian Institution - Archives (Hist)
Arts and Industries Bldg., Rm. 2135
900 Jefferson Dr., S.W.
Washington, DC 20560
Phone: (202)357-1420
William W. Moss, Archv.
Founded: 1967. **Staff:** Prof 9; Other 11. **Subjects:** Smithsonian Institution history, history of 19th century natural science. **Special Collections:** Papers

of Joseph Henry, Spencer F. Baird, Samuel P. Langley, Charles D. Walcott, Charles G. Abbot, and Alexander Wetmore (Smithsonian Secretaries). **Holdings:** 17,000 cubic feet of records, manuscripts, private papers, and collections relating to the Smithsonian, its staff members, and other scientists. **Services:** Copying; archives open to the public. **Computerized Information Services:** SIBIS (Smithsonian Institution Bibliographic Information System, internal database). **Publications:** Guide to the Smithsonian Archives, 1983; Guides to Collections, irregular. **Remarks:** FAX: (202)357-2395.

Smithsonian Institution - Archives of American Art
See: Archives of American Art/Smithsonian Institution (959)

Smithsonian Institution - Freer Gallery of Art
See: Freer Gallery of Art (6137)

Smithsonian Institution - Harvard-Smithsonian Center For Astrophysics (CFA) - Library
See: Harvard University - Harvard-Smithsonian Center for Astrophysics (CFA) - Library (6971)

★ 15261 ★
Smithsonian Institution - Hirshhorn Museum and Sculpture Garden - Library (Art)
Independence Ave. & 8th St., S.W.   Phone: (202)357-3223
Washington, DC 20560   Anna Brooke, Libn.
Founded: 1966. **Staff:** Prof 2; Other 2. **Subjects:** Fine arts, European and American 20th century painting and sculpture, American 19th century painting. **Holdings:** 38,000 books; exhibition catalogs; 31 VF drawers of artist files. **Subscriptions:** 50 journals and other serials. **Services:** Copying; library open to scholars by appointment. **Computerized Information Services:** RLIN, DIALOG Information Services. Performs searches on fee basis. **Remarks:** Alternate telephone number(s): 357-3222. FAX: (202)786-2682. **Staff:** Maureen Turman.

★ 15262 ★
Smithsonian Institution - National Air and Space Museum - Center for Earth and Planetary Studies - Regional Planetary Image Facility (Sci-Engr)
National Air and Space Museum, Rm. 3733   Phone: (202)357-1457
Washington, DC 20560   James R. Zimbelman, Dir.
Founded: 1983. **Staff:** Prof 2. **Subjects:** Planetary sciences. **Special Collections:** Planetary images and cartographic products; spacecraft-image documentation; selected earth images. **Holdings:** 300,000 planetary images taken by manned and unmanned space probes. **Subscriptions:** 10 journals and other serials. **Services:** Facility open to the public by appointment. **Remarks:** FAX: (202)786-2566. Telex: 264729 SMTHSN UR. **Staff:** Rosemary Steingt, Photo.Libn.

★ 15263 ★
Smithsonian Institution - National Anthropological Archives (Soc Sci)
National Museum of Natural History, MRC 152
10th & Constitution Ave., N.W.   Phone: (202)357-1976
Washington, DC 20560   Mary Elizabeth Ruwell, Archv.Hd.
Founded: 1879. **Staff:** Prof 4; Other 2. **Subjects:** Anthropology, linguistics, archeology, history of anthropology, history of American Indians, history of geography. **Special Collections:** Bureau of American Ethnology manuscript collection; photographs of American Indians; Center for the Study of Man; Department of Anthropology records; Institute for Social Anthropology records; River Basin Surveys; professional papers of anthropologists; records of anthropological organizations. **Holdings:** 4000 cubic feet of archives and private papers; 350,000 photographs; 500 recordings; 100 reels of microfilm. **Services:** Copying; archives open to the public. **Computerized Information Services:** Smithsonian Institution - SIBIS System (internal database). **Special Catalogs:** Guide; manuscripts catalog (card, book); catalog of photographs (card); inventory and registers (booklets). **Staff:** James R. Glenn, Sr.Archv.; Kathleen T. Baxter, Ref.Archv.; Paula J. Fleming, Photo.Archv.

★ 15264 ★
Smithsonian Institution - National Museum of African Art - Eliot Elisofon Archives (Art)
950 Independence Ave., S.W.   Phone: (202)357-4600
Washington, DC 20560   Christraud M. Geary, Cur. of Photo.Coll.
Founded: 1973. **Staff:** Prof 3. **Subjects:** Africa, African art and culture. **Special Collections:** Eliot Elisofon Collection (1943-1973); Historic Photograph Collection (1860-1930s). **Holdings:** 220,000 color slides and prints; 80,000 black/white negatives; 70 feature films; 160,000 feet of unedited outtakes, 1860 to present; 30 video cassettes. **Services:** Copying; photo orders; archives open to the public by appointment. **Computerized Information Services:** Internal databases. **Remarks:** FAX: (202)357-4879. **Staff:** Amy Staples, Archv.; Anita Jenkins, Archv.Techn.

★ 15265 ★
Smithsonian Institution - National Museum of American Art - Inventory of American Paintings Executed Before 1914 (Art)
8th & G Sts., N.W.   Phone: (202)357-2941
Washington, DC 20560   Rachel M. Allen, Dir.
Founded: 1971. **Staff:** Prof 2; Other 1. **Subjects:** American painting. **Holdings:** Photographic study collection of over 89,000 images of American paintings; cataloged descriptions of 252,000 pre-1914 paintings. **Services:** Copying; open to the public with restrictions. **Automated Operations:** Computerized cataloging. **Computerized Information Services:** Smithsonian Institution Bibliographic Information System - Research Catalog (internal database). **Publications:** Directory to the Bicentennial Inventory of American Paintings Executed Before 1914, 1976. **Special Indexes:** Listings of approximately 252,000 pre-1914 American paintings indexed by artist, subject matter, title, and medium. **Staff:** Christine Hennessey, Coord.

★ 15266 ★
Smithsonian Institution - National Museum of American Art - Inventory of American Sculpture (Art)
8th & G Sts., N.W.   Phone: (202)786-2384
Washington, DC 20560   Rachel M. Allen, Dir.
Founded: 1985. **Staff:** Prof 2; Other 3. **Subjects:** American sculpture. **Holdings:** Cataloged descriptions of 45,000 American sculptures located in public and private collections around the United States; photographic study collection (6000 images). **Services:** Inventory open to the public. **Automated Operations:** Computerized public access catalog and cataloging. **Computerized Information Services:** Smithsonian Institution Bibliographic Information System - Research Catalog (internal database). Performs searches free of charge. Contact Person: Christine Hennessey, Coord. **Special Indexes:** Index of sculptures by artist, subject, title, and medium.

★ 15267 ★
Smithsonian Institution - National Museum of American Art - Research and Scholars Center - Slide and Photograph Archives (Art)
Washington, DC 20560   Phone: (202)357-2283
                                           Joan Stahl, Coord. Image Coll.
Founded: 1973. **Staff:** Prof 2; Other 1. **Subjects:** American art, painting, sculpture, and decorative arts; graphics. **Special Collections:** Slide Library (90,000); photographic negatives for the New York photographic firm of Peter Juley and Son (127,000); the collection documents 80 years of American artists and their works of art. **Services:** Archives open to the public with restrictions. **Automated Operations:** Computerized cataloging. **Special Indexes:** Indexes by artist, subject, source, and location (computerized). **Remarks:** FAX: (202)786-2607. **Staff:** Margaret Harman, Photo Archv.; Mark Friedl, Slide Libn.

★ 15268 ★
Smithsonian Institution - National Museum of American Art/National Portrait Gallery - Library (Art)
8th & F Sts., N.W.   Phone: (202)357-1886
Washington, DC 20560   Cecilia Chin, Chf.Libn.
Founded: 1930. **Staff:** Prof 4; Other 3. **Subjects:** American painting, sculpture, graphic arts, biography, history, photography; portraiture; contemporary art. **Special Collections:** Ferdinand Perret Collection (scrapbooks on California and West Coast art). **Holdings:** 80,000 books and bound periodical volumes; 400 VF drawers of clippings, pamphlets, correspondence, photographs. **Subscriptions:** 1000 journals and other serials. **Services:** Interlibrary loan; copying; library open to adult researchers and graduate students. **Automated Operations:** Computerized cataloging and acquisitions. **Computerized Information Services:** DIALOG Information Services, WILSONLINE, OCLC, ArtQuest, Eastman House, NEXIS, LEXIS, RLIN. **Remarks:** FAX: (202)786-2565. **Staff:** Pat Lynagh, Asst.Libn./Ref.Libn.; Kimball Clark, Cat.

★ 15269 ★

Smithsonian Institution - National Museum of American History - Archives Center (Hist)
NMAH C340
14th St. & Constitution Ave., N.W.   Phone: (202)357-3270
Washington, DC 20560   John A. Fleckner, Archv.
Founded: 1983. **Staff:** Prof 12. **Subjects:** History of advertising and technology, American history, American music. **Special Collections:** Warshaw Collection of Business Americana (800 cubic feet); Clark Radioana Collection (early history of radio; 300 cubic feet); Duke Ellington Collection (600 cubic feet). **Holdings:** 8500 cubic feet of manuscripts and other items. **Services:** Copying; center open to the public. **Computerized Information Services:** Smithsonian Institution Bibliographic Information System (internal database). **Publications:** Registers of collections, irregular. **Remarks:** FAX: (202)786-2453. **Staff:** Robert S. Harding, Dp.Archv.

★ 15270 ★

Smithsonian Institution - Office of Folklife Programs - Archives (Mus)
955 L'Enfant Plaza, S.W., Suite 2600   Phone: (202)287-3251
Washington, DC 20560   Jeff Place, Archv.
Founded: 1987. **Staff:** Prof 2. **Subjects:** Folk music, folklore, ethnomusicology. **Special Collections:** Folkways Records Archive (8000 LP phonograph records; 4000 78rpm phonograph records; 4000 disks; 40,000 reel-to-reel tapes; 2200 commercially available LPs). **Holdings:** 1000 books; 10,000 audiocassettes; 500,000 photographs; 10,000 phonograph records; 20,000 open reel tapes. **Services:** Archives open to the public by appointment. **Computerized Information Services:** Internal database. **Publications:** 2200 Commercially Available LPs on Folkways Record Label. **Remarks:** FAX: (202)287-3699. **Staff:** Lori Taylor.

★ 15271 ★

Smithsonian Institution Libraries (Sci-Engr, Hist, Art)
National Museum of Natural History
10th & Constitution Ave., N.W.   Phone: (202)357-2240
Washington, DC 20560   Barbara J. Smith, Dir.
Founded: 1846. **Staff:** Prof 54; Other 71. **Subjects:** Natural history and ethnology; ecology; history of science, technology, and flight; American history and culture; decorative and graphic arts; American and contemporary art. **Holdings:** 1.1 million volumes; photographs; clippings. **Subscriptions:** 14,383 journals and other serials. **Services:** Interlibrary loan; copying; open to qualified scholars. **Automated Operations:** Computerized public access catalog, cataloging and acquisitions. **Computerized Information Services:** DIALOG Information Services, BRS Information Technologies, Mead Data Central, RLIN, STN International. **Networks/Consortia:** Member of FEDLINK. **Remarks:** FAX: (202)786-2866. Figures given above represent combined holdings and staff for all branches. The Smithsonian Tropical Research Institute's address is P.O. Box 2072, Balboa, Republic de Panama. **Staff:** Vija Karklins, Dep.Dir.; Nancy E. Gwinn, Asst.Dir.; Bonita Perry, Asst.Dir.; Mary Augusta Rosenfeld, Asst.Dir.; Victoria Avera, Dept.Hd., Auto.Bibliog.Cont.; Sheila Riley, Dept.Hd., Cat.Rec.; Vielka Chang-Yau, Chf., STRI Lib.; Helen Nordberg, Dept.Hd., Original Cat. and Indexing; Tina Lesuik, Dept.Hd., Acq.; Tom Garnett, Dept.Hd., Sys.

★ 15272 ★

Smithsonian Institution Libraries - Botany Branch Library (Biol Sci)
Natural History Bldg., Rm. W422
10th & Constitution Ave.   Phone: (202)357-2715
Washington, DC 20560   Ruth F. Schallert, Chf.Libn.
Founded: 1894. **Staff:** 1. **Subjects:** Taxonomic botany, history of botany. **Special Collections:** Hitchcock-Chase Collection (grasses; 1500 books and reprints); Dawson Collection (algae; 1000 books and reprints). **Holdings:** 40,000 volumes; 14 shelves of collectors' field notebooks; 325 boxes of reprints; 21 herbaria on microfiche. **Subscriptions:** 400 journals and other serials. **Services:** Interlibrary loan; copying; library open to the public by appointment. **Computerized Information Services:** DIALOG Information Services. **Remarks:** FAX: (202)357-1896. **Formerly:** Its National Museum of Natural History - Botany Library.

★ 15273 ★

Smithsonian Institution Libraries - Central Reference and Loan Service, Branch Library (Info Sci)
National Museum of Natural History
10th & Constitution Ave., N.W.   Phone: (202)357-2139
Washington, DC 20560   Martin Smith, Chf.Libn.
Founded: 1982. **Staff:** Prof 4; Other 4. **Subjects:** General reference, biographical reference, bibliography, library and information sciences, management/administration, social sciences. **Special Collections:** Smithsoniana (publications by and about the Smithsonian Institution); national bibliographies. **Holdings:** 28,000 volumes. **Subscriptions:** 300 journals and other serials. **Services:** Interlibrary loan; copying; service open to the public by appointment. **Automated Operations:** Computerized public access catalog, cataloging, acquisitions, and circulation. **Computerized Information Services:** DIALOG Information Services, Mead Data Central, OCLC, RLIN, VU/TEXT Information Services, LEXIS, NEXIS. Performs searches. **Networks/Consortia:** Member of FEDLINK. **Remarks:** FAX: (202)786-2443.

★ 15274 ★

Smithsonian Institution Libraries - Cooper-Hewitt Museum of Design - Doris & Henry Dreyfuss Memorial Study Center (Art)
2 E. 91st St.   Phone: (212)860-6887
New York, NY 10128   Stephen H. Van Dyk, Chf.Libn.
Staff: Prof 1; Other 4. **Subjects:** Decorative arts, design, textiles, architecture. **Special Collections:** Rare books (4000); American and foreign auction catalogs; George W. Kubler Collection (18th and 19th century line engravings); Color Archive; Henry Dreyfuss Archive; Donald Deskey Archive; Ladislav Sutnar Archive; Therese Bonney photographs; trade catalogs. **Holdings:** 40,000 books; 4500 bound periodical volumes; 16 VF drawers; picture collection of over 40,000 items arranged by subject for designers. **Subscriptions:** 275 journals and other serials. **Services:** Interlibrary loan; copying; center open to the public by appointment. **Automated Operations:** Computerized cataloging, acquisitions, serials, and circulation. **Computerized Information Services:** OCLC, DIALOG Information Services, RLIN. **Networks/Consortia:** Member of New York Metropolitan Reference and Research Library Agency. **Remarks:** FAX: (212)860-6909.

★ 15275 ★

Smithsonian Institution Libraries - Museum Reference Center (Hum, Bus-Fin)
Arts & Industries Bldg., Rm. 2235
900 Jefferson Dr., S.W.   Phone: (202)786-2271
Washington, DC 20560   Sylvia C. Churgin, Chf.Libn.
Founded: 1974. **Staff:** 1. **Subjects:** Museology, museum programs, nonprofit organization management, fundraising and membership development, voluntarism. **Special Collections:** American Law Institute-American Bar Association annual conference proceedings, 1978 to present (legal problems of museum administration); American Association of Museums annual meeting proceedings, 1984 to present (audio cassettes). **Holdings:** 3500 books; 9000 files of documentary materials. **Subscriptions:** 1200 journals and other serials. **Services:** Interlibrary loan; copying; center open to the public by appointment. **Automated Operations:** Computerized cataloging and acquisitions. **Computerized Information Services:** DIALOG Information Services; CD-ROMs; OnTyme Electronic Message Network Service (electronic mail service). **Networks/Consortia:** Member of FEDLINK. **Publications:** List of publications - available on request. **Remarks:** The Museum Reference Center contains resources on all aspects of museum operations. It is the only central source of museological information in the United States that makes such materials available to researchers and all members of the museum community. FAX: (202)357-3346. Telex: 264729 SMTHSN.

★ 15276 ★

Smithsonian Institution Libraries - Museum Support Center Branch (Biol Sci, Sci-Engr)
Washington, DC 20560   Phone: (301)238-3666
    Earl Gilbert Taylor, Act.Hd.
Founded: 1964. **Staff:** Prof 2; Other 1. **Subjects:** Conservation of materials and museum objects; conservation science, including archeometry, study of museum environments, and analysis of materials by such means as x-ray diffraction and gas chromatography; occupational health hazards; medical entomology; taxonomic aspects of marine and estuarine fauna, molecular systematics. **Holdings:** 10,000 books; 5000 bound periodical volumes; 30,000 reprints; 200 reels of microfilm; 800 microfiche. **Subscriptions:** 120 journals and other serials. **Services:** Interlibrary loan; copying; SDI; branch open to the public by appointment only. **Automated Operations:** Computerized cataloging and acquisitions. **Computerized Information Services:** DIALOG Information Services, OCLC, STN International. **Remarks:** FAX: (301)238-3667. Electronic mail address(es): KELLEYKIM@SIMSC.

★ 15277 ★
Smithsonian Institution Libraries - National Air and Space Museum -
  Library (Sci-Engr, Trans)
National Air & Space Museum, Rm. 3100
Independence Ave. & Seventh St., S.W.   Phone: (202)357-3133
Washington, DC 20560   David Spencer, Br.Libn.
Founded: 1972. **Staff:** Prof 4; Other 2. **Subjects:** Aeronautics, astronautics, astrophysics, astronomy, earth and planetary sciences. **Special Collections:** Sherman Fairchild Photographic Collection; William A.M. Burden Collection (early ballooning works and aeronautica); Bella Landauer Aeronautical Sheet Music Collection (1500 pieces); Jerome Hunsaker papers; Samuel P. Langley aerodrome manuscripts; Harold E. Morehouse biographical files on early aircraft pioneers; Juan Trippe correspondence and papers. **Holdings:** 27,000 books; 10,800 bound periodical volumes; 125 reels of microfilm of periodicals. **Subscriptions:** 410 journals and other serials. **Services:** Interlibrary loan; copying; library open to the public by appointment. **Automated Operations:** Computerized cataloging and acquisitions. **Computerized Information Services:** DIALOG Information Services, OCLC, RLIN. **Networks/Consortia:** Member of FEDLINK. **Publications:** NASM Library Brochure. **Remarks:** FAX: (202)786-2835. **Staff:** Amy Levin, Ref.Libn.; Philip Edwards, Info.Spec.; David Spencer, Ref.Libn. Mary Pavlovich, ILL.

★ 15278 ★
Smithsonian Institution Libraries - National Museum of American
  History - Library (Sci-Engr, Hist)
Washington, DC 20560   Phone: (202)357-2414
                                                Rhoda S. Ratner, Chf.Libn.
Staff: Prof 3; Other 4. **Subjects:** American history, history of science and technology, applied science, decorative arts, domestic and community life. **Special Collections:** Exhibitions and expositions (1500 items); trade catalogs (275,000). **Holdings:** 165,000 volumes. **Subscriptions:** 600 journals and other serials. **Services:** Interlibrary loan; copying; library open to the public with restrictions. **Remarks:** FAX: (202)357-4256.

★ 15279 ★
Smithsonian Institution Libraries - National Museum of Natural History
  - Anthropology Division Library (Soc Sci)
Natural History Bldg., Rm. 330/331   Phone: (202)357-1819
Washington, DC 20560   Mary Kay Davies, Chf.Libn.
Staff: Prof 2. **Subjects:** Ethnology, physical anthropology, archeology. **Special Collections:** Bureau of American Ethnology Library Collection. **Holdings:** 68,000 volumes. **Subscriptions:** 1300 journals and other serials. **Services:** Interlibrary loan; copying; library open to the public by appointment. **Automated Operations:** Computerized acquisitions. **Computerized Information Services:** Smithsonian Institution Bibliographic Information System (internal database). **Publications:** Monthly acquisitions list. **Remarks:** FAX: (202)357-1896. **Staff:** Mayda Riopedre.

Smithsonian Institution Libraries - National Museum of Natural History
  - Botany Library
See: **Smithsonian Institution Libraries** (15272)

★ 15280 ★
Smithsonian Institution Libraries - National Museum of Natural History
  - Branch Library (Biol Sci)
Natural History Bldg., Rm. 51
10th & Constitution Ave.   Phone: (202)357-1496
Washington, DC 20560   Ann Juneau, Natural Hist.Libn.
Founded: 1881. **Staff:** Prof 4; Other 6. **Subjects:** Paleobiology, geology, oceanography, ecology, entomology, vertebrate and invertebrate zoology and paleontology, mineralogy, limnology. **Special Collections:** Cushman Collection (Foraminifera); Springer Collection (crinoids); Wilson Collection (copepoda); Remington-Kellogg Collection of Marine Mammalogy. **Holdings:** 215,000 books and bound periodical volumes. **Subscriptions:** 2000 journals and other serials. **Services:** Interlibrary loan; copying; library open to the public by appointment for reference use only. **Automated Operations:** Computerized public access catalog, cataloging, and acquisitions. **Computerized Information Services:** DIALOG Information Services, OCLC, RLIN, EPIC; SIBIS (internal database). **Networks/Consortia:** Member of FEDLINK. **Remarks:** FAX: (202)357-1896. **Staff:** David Steere, Natural Hist.Ref.Libn.; Carolyn Hahn, ILL Coord.; Robert Skarr, Ent., Min.Sci. & Pal.Ref.Libn .

★ 15281 ★
Smithsonian Institution Libraries - National Museum of Natural History
  - Entomology Branch Library (Biol Sci)
Natural History Bldg., Rm. W629C   Phone: (202)357-4696
Washington, DC 20560   Robert J. Skarr, Entomology Libn.
Founded: 1881. **Staff:** 1. **Subjects:** Taxonomic and medical entomology. **Holdings:** 28,000 volumes. **Subscriptions:** 280 journals and other serials. **Services:** Interlibrary loan; copying; library open to the public by appointment. **Automated Operations:** Computerized public access catalog. **Computerized Information Services:** DIALOG Information Services. **Remarks:** FAX: (202)357-1896.

★ 15282 ★
Smithsonian Institution Libraries - National Zoological Park - Library
  (Biol Sci)
3000 Block of Connecticut Ave., N.W.   Phone: (202)673-4771
Washington, DC 20008   Kay A. Kenyon, Br.Libn.
Founded: 1898. **Staff:** Prof 1. **Subjects:** Animal behavior, animal husbandry, wildlife conservation, animal nutrition, veterinary medicine, pathology. **Special Collections:** Zoo publications. **Holdings:** 4000 volumes. **Subscriptions:** 290 journals and other serials. **Services:** Interlibrary loan; copying; library open to the public by appointment. **Automated Operations:** Computerized public access catalog, cataloging, and acquisitions. **Computerized Information Services:** DIALOG Information Services, OCLC. **Remarks:** FAX: (202)673-4900.

★ 15283 ★
Smithsonian Institution Libraries - Office of Horticulture - Branch
  Library (Biol Sci)
Arts & Industries Bldg., Rm. 2401   Phone: (202)357-1544
Washington, DC 20560   Susan R. Gurney, Chf.Libn.
Founded: 1984. **Staff:** Prof 2. **Subjects:** History of American horticulture and landscape design. **Special Collections:** W. Atlee Burpee Seed and Nursery Company Archives (15,000 catalogs, 19th and 20th centuries). **Holdings:** 4000 books; 2000 bound periodical volumes; clipping files. **Subscriptions:** 100 journals and other serials. **Services:** Interlibrary loan; copying; library open to the public by appointment. **Automated Operations:** Computerized public access catalog, cataloging, and acquisitions. **Computerized Information Services:** DIALOG Information Services. **Staff:** Marca L. Woodhams, Asst.Libn.

★ 15284 ★
Smithsonian Institution Libraries - Smithsonian Environmental Research
  Center Library (Env-Cons)
Box 28   Phone: (301)261-4190
Edgewater, MD 21037   Angela N. Haggins, Br.Libn.
Founded: 1972. **Staff:** 1. **Subjects:** Environment, ecology, estuarine research, marine ecology, aquatic microbiology. **Holdings:** 2600 books; 3000 bound periodical volumes. **Subscriptions:** 101 journals and other serials. **Services:** Interlibrary loan; copying; library open to the public by appointment. **Automated Operations:** Computerized cataloging and acquisitions. **Computerized Information Services:** DIALOG Information Services. **Remarks:** FAX: (301)261-4174.

★ 15285 ★
Smithsonian Institution Libraries - Special Collections Department (Biol
  Sci, Sci-Engr)
MAH 5016   Phone: (202)357-1568
Washington, DC 20560   Ellen B. Wells, Hd.
Founded: 1974. **Staff:** Prof 2. **Subjects:** Physical sciences, natural history, technology, applied arts. **Special Collections:** Smithson Collection (200 books and offprints); Wetmore Bequest (ornithogy; 400 books); Burndy Library donation (science and technology; 10,000 volumes); Comegys Library (19th century Philadelphia family library; 900 volumes). **Holdings:** 25,000 books and bound periodical volumes; 2000 bound manuscript units; 300 engraved portraits; 200 science medals. **Subscriptions:** 5 journals and other serials. **Services:** Copying; library open to the public by appointment for reading room use only. **Computerized Information Services:** OCLC; SIBIS (internal database). **Publications:** Operations of the Geometric and Military Compass 1606, 1978; Heralds of Science, 1980; Manuscripts of the Dibner Collection, 1985. **Remarks:** Alternate telephone number(s): 357-1577. FAX: (202)633-9102. **Staff:** Leslie K. Overstreet, Ref.Libn.

★15286★
Smithsonian Institution Libraries - Warren M. Robbins Library -
National Museum of African Art - Branch Library (Art, Area-Ethnic)
950 Independence Ave., S.W.   Phone: (202)357-4600
Washington, DC 20560   Janet L. Stanley, Chf.Libn.
Founded: 1971. **Staff:** Prof 1; Other 1. **Subjects:** Africa - art, material
culture, anthropology, folklore history. **Holdings:** 20,000 books; 500 vertical
files. **Subscriptions:** 200 journals and other serials. **Services:** Interlibrary
loan; copying; SDI; library open to the public by appointment. **Publications:**
National Museum of African Art Library Acquisitions List, monthly; The
Arts of Africa: an annotated bibliography. **Special Catalogs:** Catalog of the
Library of the National Museum of African Art Branch of the Smithsonian
Institution Libraries, 2 vols., 1991. **Remarks:** FAX: (202)357-4879.

Smithsonian Tropical Research Institute
See: Smithsonian Institution Libraries (15271)

★15287★
Smithtown Historical Society - Library (Hist)
Box 69   Phone: (516)265-6768
Smithtown, NY 11787   Louise P. Hall, Dir.
Founded: 1955. **Staff:** 2. **Subjects:** Local history and genealogy. **Holdings:**
1000 books; 300 bound periodical volumes; 5000 deeds, ledgers, documents,
letters, surveys. **Services:** Copying; library open to the public.

★15288★
Smithtown Library - Richard H. Handley Long Island History Room
(Hist)
1 North Country Rd.   Phone: (516)265-2072
Smithtown, NY 11787   Vera Toman, L.I. Hist.Rm.
Founded: 1926. **Staff:** 2. **Subjects:** Long Island (especially Suffolk and
Smithtown) history and genealogy. **Special Collections:** Long Island History
Collection (23,075 items). **Holdings:** 4000 books; 510 bound periodical
volumes; reports, manuscripts, archives, microfiche, microfilm, V.F.
clippings and pamphlets, picture file, maps. **Services:** Copying; room open
to the public. **Networks/Consortia:** Member of Suffolk Cooperative Library
System, Long Island Library Resources Council. **Publications:** Pamphlets
on Long Island History, irregular. **Remarks:** FAX: (516)265-5945. **Staff:**
Doris Halowitch.

Smurfit Irish Law Center
See: St. Louis University - Law Library (14465)

★15289★
R.M. Smythe and Company - Obsolete and Inactive Securities Library
(Bus-Fin)
26 Broadway, Suite 271   Phone: (212)943-1880
New York, NY 10004-1701   Robert Fisher, Dir. of Res.
Staff: Prof 7; Other 6. **Subjects:** Obsolete securities, inactive U.S. securities,
foreign securities, active securities, collector's certificate reference.
Holdings: 5000 books and bound periodical volumes; 35 VF drawers of
correspondence; 20 boxes of pamphlets; 250,000 cards of company records;
50,000 cards of company reports; lost stockholder tracing reference
material; reference material for antique certificate collectors. **Services:**
Copying; library open to the public with restrictions. **Remarks:** FAX:
(212)908-4047.

★15290★
SNC Inc. - Library (Sci-Engr, Bus-Fin)
2 Place Felix-Martin   Phone: (514)866-1000
Montreal, PQ, Canada H2Z 1Z3   Lynda Thivierge, Chf.Libn.
Founded: 1911. **Staff:** Prof 1; Other 1. **Subjects:** Engineering, construction,
business, international affairs. **Holdings:** 10,000 books; 3000 standards; 100
microfiche. **Subscriptions:** 300 journals and other serials; 10 newspapers.
Services: Interlibrary loan; library not open to the public. **Computerized**
Information Services: DIALOG Information Services, Questel, CAN/OLE,
Infomart Online, QL Systems, Novell Inc.; Envoy 100 (electronic mail
service). **Publications:** New acquisitions; library news bulletin. **Remarks:**
FAX: (514)866-0795.

SNC-Lavalin Inc.
See: SNC Partec Inc. (15291)

★15291★
SNC Partec Inc. - Library
909 5th Ave., S.W.   Phone: (403)294-2785
Calgary, AB, Canada T2P 3G5   Leila Jackman, Lib.Techn.
Staff: 1. **Holdings:** Figures not available. **Subscriptions:** 71 journals and
other serials; 4 newspapers. **Services:** Interlibrary loan; library open to
employees only. **Remarks:** FAX: (403)237-8365. A Division of SNC-Lavalin
Inc. **Formed by the merger of:** Lavalin Inc. and SNC Inc.

★15292★
Snell & Wilmer - Law Library (Law)
3100 Valley Bank Center   Phone: (602)257-7316
Phoenix, AZ 85073   Arlen A. Bristol
Staff: Prof 2; Other 3. **Subjects:** Law - tax, utilities, real estate, water,
corporate, securities. **Special Collections:** Arizona archival law materials.
Holdings: 48,110 books; 911 bound periodical volumes; 700 other cataloged
items. **Subscriptions:** 771 journals and other serials; 11 newspapers.
Services: Library not open to the public. **Computerized Information**
Services: LEXIS, DIALOG Information Services, WESTLAW, VU/TEXT
Information Services, OCLC, DataTimes, Dataquick, Information America,
Dow Jones News/Retrieval. **Networks/Consortia:** Member of AMIGOS
Bibliographic Council, Inc.**Publications:** Monthly Book List of New Titles.
Special Indexes: Medical indexes of articles used in cases; memorandum
index. **Remarks:** FAX: (602)257-7864. Maintains branch offices in Tucson,
AZ, Irvine, CA, and Salt Lake City, UT. **Staff:** La Verta Anderson.

Snite Museum of Art
See: University of Notre Dame (19120)

★15293★
Snohomish County Law Library (Law)
County Court House   Phone: (206)259-5326
Everett, WA 98201   Carol A. Trapp, Libn.
Founded: 1973. **Staff:** Prof 1.5. **Subjects:** Law - federal, state, local.
Holdings: 18,000 volumes. **Subscriptions:** 6 journals and other serials.
Services: Interlibrary loan; copying; library open to the public with
restrictions on circulation. **Computerized Information Services:**
WESTLAW. **Remarks:** FAX: (206)258-3472. **Staff:** Laurie B. Miller,
Asst.Libn.

Snyder Collection of Americana
See: University of Missouri--Kansas City (18979)

★15294★
Snyder County Historical Society - Library (Hist)
30 E. Market St.
Box 276   Phone: (717)837-6191
Middleburg, PA 17842   Kathryn Gift, Libn.
Founded: 1898. **Staff:** Prof 1. **Subjects:** Local history, Pennsylvania history,
Pennsylvania military history, genealogy. **Special Collections:** Civil War
letters; Dr. Charles A. Fisher Collection. **Holdings:** 3000 volumes; 1000
historical bulletins, early land grants, warrants, deeds. **Subscriptions:** 4
journals and other serials. **Services:** Copying; library open to the public with
permission. **Publications:** Snyder County Annual Bulletin.

★15295★
H.L. Snyder Memorial Research Foundation - Library (Med)
1407 Wheat Rd.
P.O. Box 745   Phone: (316)221-4080
Winfield, KS 67156   Lisa Buffum, Libn.
Founded: 1947. **Staff:** Prof 1. **Subjects:** Biochemistry, medicine, clinical
chemistry. **Holdings:** 2000 books; 1000 bound periodical volumes.
Subscriptions: 20 journals and other serials. **Services:** Interlibrary loan;
copying; library open to the public. **Networks/Consortia:** Member of
National Network of Libraries of Medicine - Midcontinental Region.
Remarks: Includes holdings of the Snyder Clinic Library.

O.J. Snyder Memorial Medical Library
See: Philadelphia College of Osteopathic Medicine (12979)

★ 15296 ★
Soap and Detergent Association - Library (Sci-Engr)
475 Park Ave., S.   Phone: (212)725-1262
New York, NY 10016   Rose D. Api, Off.Mgr.
Staff: 1. **Subjects:** Detergents. **Holdings:** 1000 books; 200 bound periodical volumes. **Subscriptions:** 205 journals and other serials. **Services:** Copying; library open to the public by appointment. **Remarks:** FAX: (212)213-0685.

Social & Health Servies, Ltd. - National Clearinghouse of Alcohol and Drug Information
See: National Clearinghouse for Alcohol and Drug Information (11115)

★ 15297 ★
Social Law Library (Law)
1200 Court House, 12th Fl.   Phone: (617)523-0018
Boston, MA 02108   Edgar J. Bellefontaine, Libn.
Founded: 1804. **Staff:** Prof 34; Other 39. **Subjects:** Anglo-American law. **Special Collections:** Papers of the Inferior Court of Common Pleas for Suffolk County, 1692-1830; Supreme Judicial Court Records and Briefs; Papers of Lemuel Shaw. **Holdings:** 305,015 volumes; 450,000 microfiche; 2011 audio cassettes; 350 videotapes. **Subscriptions:** 3500 journals and other serials; 20 newspapers. **Services:** Interlibrary loan (limited); copying; library open to members and other authorized persons. **Computerized Information Services:** DIALOG Information Services, LEXIS, VU/TEXT Information Services, PHINet FedTax Database, WESTLAW. **Networks/Consortia:** Member of New England Law Library Consortium (NELLCO). **Publications:** Newsletter, quarterly - to members; Legal Video Review, quarterly - by subscription; Massachusetts Administrative Law Library on Compact Disc - by subscription (CD-ROM). **Remarks:** FAX: (617)523-2458.

Social Security Administration
See: U.S. Social Security Administration (17939)

Socialist Party of America Archives
See: Duke University - Special Collections Department (5049)

Sociedad Astronomica de Espana Y America
See: Hispano-American Astronomical Society (7236)

Sociedad Geografica de Lima
See: Geographic Society of Lima (6361)

★ 15298 ★
Sociedade Civil Bem Estar Familiar no Brasil - Biblioteca (Soc Sci)
Ave. Republica do Chile 230, Andar 17   Phone: 21 2102448
20031 Rio de Janeiro, RJ, Brazil   Olimpia Vale de Resende, Libn.
Founded: 1967. **Staff:** Prof 1. **Subjects:** Population, family planning, contraception, reproductive health. **Holdings:** 10,000 volumes. **Services:** Library open to the public for reference use only. **Computerized Information Services:** POPLINE, Lage e Laee; Micro-isis (internal database). **Publications:** Boletm Bibliografico. **Remarks:** FAX: 21 2204057. Telex: 21 30634.

★ 15299 ★
Societe d'Archeologie et de Numismatique de Montreal - Bibliotheque (Hist)
280 rue Notre-Dame E.   Phone: (514)861-3708
Montreal, PQ, Canada H2Y 1C5   M. Pierre Brouillard
Founded: 1895. **Staff:** 1. **Subjects:** Canadian history, numismatics. **Holdings:** 10,000 books; manuscripts; archives; documents. **Services:** Library not open to the public, but the society will consider appropriate requests by researchers. **Remarks:** Library is in process of reorganization after being inactive for over twenty years. **Also Known As:** Antiquarian and Numismatic Society of Montreal.

★ 15300 ★
Societe Asiatique - Bibliotheque (Area-Ethnic)
52, rue du Cardinal Lemoine
F-75005 Paris, France   Phone: 1 46332832
Founded: 1822. **Staff:** Prof 1.5. **Subjects:** Orientalism. **Holdings:** 90,000 books; 1800 bound periodical volumes. **Services:** Interlibrary loan; library open to members only.

Societe Canadienne d'Hypotheques et de Logement
See: Canada - Mortgage and Housing Corporation (2765)

Societe Canadienne de Psychanalyse
See: Canadian Psychoanalytic Society (2984)

★ 15301 ★
Societe Culinaire Philanthropique de New York, Inc. - Library (Food-Bev)
250 W. 57th St., Rm. 1532   Phone: (212)246-6754
New York, NY 10019   Andre Rene, Pres.
Subjects: Professional cooking. **Holdings:** Cookbooks. **Services:** Library open to members only.

★ 15302 ★
Societe de Genealogie de Quebec - Library (Hist)
C.P. 9066   Phone: (418)651-9127
Ste. Foy, PQ, Canada G1V 4A8   Rene Doucet, Libn.
Founded: 1961. **Staff:** 15. **Subjects:** Genealogy. **Holdings:** 3000 books; microfiche. **Subscriptions:** 25 journals and other serials. **Services:** Copying; library open to the public. **Publications:** L'Ancetre (newsletter), 10/year.

Societe d'Histoire des Cantons de l'Est
See: Societe d'Histoire de Sherbrooke (15303)

★ 15303 ★
Societe d'Histoire de Sherbrooke - Bibliotheque (Hist)
1304 boul. Portland   Phone: (819)562-0616
Sherbrooke, PQ, Canada J1J 1S3   Helene Liard, Archv.
Founded: 1927. **Staff:** Prof 4. **Subjects:** Local and regional history of the Eastern Townships. **Special Collections:** Newspaper collection (Le Pionnier from 1866, Le Progres de l'Est from 1885, Sherbrooke News from August 1874, La Tribune from 1910, The Record from 1897). **Holdings:** 5000 volumes; 7200 photographs; 500 maps; archives. **Services:** Bibliotheque open to the public. **Computerized Information Services:** Internal databases. **Publications:** Histoire de Sherbrooke - The Story of Sherbrooke; Sherbrooke en Images; Loyalistes ou Americains Seule l'histoire le sait; Guide Historique du Vieux Sherbrooke; La Vie Musicale a Sherbrooke; Les Deputes du Comte de Sherbrooke; Sherbrooke, Lieu de Passage Abenaquis. **Also Known As:** Sherbrooke Historical Society. **Staff:** Louise Brunelle-Lavoie, Coord.

Societe Historique-de-la-Cote-du-Sud
See: College de Ste-Anne-de-la-Pocatiere (3916)

★ 15304 ★
Societe Historique du Saguenay - Bibliotheque (Hist)
C.P. 456   Phone: (418)549-2805
Chicoutimi, PQ, Canada G7H 5C8   Roland Belanger, Archv.
Founded: 1934. **Staff:** Prof 1. **Subjects:** Regional history and geography, genealogy, oral history, folklore. **Special Collections:** Newspaper clippings, 1882 to present, concerning the Saguenay region. **Holdings:** 18,000 books; 200 bound periodical volumes; 300,000 photographs; 65,000 negatives; 1500 maps. **Subscriptions:** 50 journals and other serials; 30 newspapers. **Services:** Copying; library open to the public for reference use only. **Automated Operations:** Computerized cataloging. **Publications:** Saguenayensia, quarterly. **Also Known As:** Saguenay Region Historical Society.

Societe de Legislation Comparee
See: **Society of Comparative Legislation** (15315)

Societe des Missions-Etrangeres
See: **Foreign Missions Society of Quebec** (5974)

★ 15305 ★
Societe Quebecoise d'Exploration Miniere (SOQUEM) - Documentation
   (Sci-Engr)
Place Belle Cour
2590, blvd. Laurier, Bureau 600   Phone: (418)658-5400
Ste. Foy, PQ, Canada G1V 4M6   Bill Ledden
Founded: 1967. **Subjects:** Geology, mining. **Holdings:** 7000 books;
geological and geophysical surveys and reports. **Subscriptions:** 10 journals
and other serials; 4 newspapers. **Services:** Interlibrary loan; library not open
to the public. **Remarks:** FAX: (418)658-5459.

Societe Radio-Canada
See: **Canadian Broadcasting Corporation** (2901)

Societe Royale du Canada
See: **Royal Society of Canada** (14135)

★ 15306 ★
Society for Academic Achievement - Library (Educ)
220 WCU Bldg.
510 Maine St.   Phone: (217)224-0570
Quincy, IL 62301   C. Richard Heitholt, Exec.Dir./Libn.
Staff: 2. **Subjects:** Academic excellence, communication skills. **Holdings:**
1075 volumes. **Subscriptions:** 15 journals and other serials. **Services:** Library
not open to the public.

★ 15307 ★
Society of Actuaries - Library (Bus-Fin)
475 N. Martingale, Suite 800   Phone: (708)706-3575
Schaumburg, IL 60173-2226   Donna L. Richardson, Res.Libn.
Founded: 1949. **Staff:** Prof 1; Other 1. **Subjects:** Application of
mathematical probabilities to the design of insurance, pension, and employee
benefit programs. **Holdings:** 3000 books; 400 other cataloged items.
Subscriptions: 189 journals and other serials. **Services:** Interlibrary loan;
copying; library open to the public by appointment. **Computerized
Information Services:** DIALOG Information Services, BRS Information
Technologies. **Networks/Consortia:** Member of North Suburban Library
System (NSLS). **Remarks:** Alternate telephone number(s): (708)706-3538.
FAX: (708)706-3599.

★ 15308 ★
Society for the Advancement of Travel for the Handicapped - Library
   (Trans)
347 5th Ave., Suite 610
New York, NY 10016   Phone: (212)447-7284
Founded: 1976. **Staff:** 1. **Subjects:** Travel facilities for the handicapped.
Holdings: 300 volumes; literature provided by tourist offices, carriers, hotels,
destinations, and car rental agencies; statistics. **Services:** Library open to
members only. **Computerized Information Services:** Internal databases.
Remarks: FAX: (212)725-8253. **Also Known As:** S.A.T.H.

Society of American Archivists - Archives
See: **University of Wisconsin--Madison - Archives** (19579)

Society of American Foresters - Archives
See: **Forest History Society, Inc. - Library and Archives** (5979)

★ 15309 ★
Society of American Foresters - Information Center (Env-Cons)
5400 Grosvenor Ln.   Phone: (301)897-8720
Bethesda, MD 20814   Larry Hill, Dir., Rsrc. Policy
Founded: 1900. **Subjects:** Forestry education, forest economics, silviculture,
forest fires, forest land use, history of professional forestry. **Holdings:** 500
books; 100 bound periodical volumes; 200 reports. **Subscriptions:** 20
journals and other serials; 2 newspapers. **Services:** Center open to the public.
Remarks: FAX: (301)897-3690.

★ 15310 ★
Society of Antiquaries of Newcastle Upon Tyne - Library (Hist)
Black Gate   Phone: 91 2632793
Newcastle Upon Tyne, Tyne and Wear, England   D. Peel
Founded: 1813. **Subjects:** Local history of Northumberland and Durham.
Holdings: 15,000 books; 15,000 bound periodical volumes. **Subscriptions:** 80
journals and other serials. **Services:** Interlibrary loan; copying; library open
to the public on application.

Society of Antiquaries of Scotland - Library
See: **Scotland - National Museums of Scotland - Library** (14955)

★ 15311 ★
Society for the Application of Free Energy - Library (Energy)
1315 Apple Ave.
Silver Spring, MD 20910   Phone: (301)587-8686
Founded: 1973. **Subjects:** Research and application of natural forms of
energy, including solar, wind, metaphysical (energy of the mind), and
biocybernetic (energy of living things). **Holdings:** 2000 volumes.

Society of Arts and Crafts, Boston Archives
See: **Boston Public Library - Fine Arts Department** (1992)

Society of Automotive Engineers, Inc.
See: **SAE International** (14209)

★ 15312 ★
Society of California Pioneers - Alice Phelan Sullivan Library (Hist)
456 McAllister St.   Phone: (415)861-5278
San Francisco, CA 94102   Stanleigh Bry, Lib.Dir.
Founded: 1850. **Staff:** Prof 1. **Subjects:** California - primarily pre-1870 with
emphasis on the activities of 1849ers. **Special Collections:** Correspondence
of Thomas Starr King, Unitarian Minister, 1861-1864; letters of Jessie
Benton Fremont, writer; Jacob Rink Snyder Collection (California Battalion
documents; 295 items); handwritten diaries of forty-niners and other
pioneers (200); reminiscences of pioneers (8 volumes); photographs of the
San Francisco Bay Area and California (25,000); political scrapbooks, 1863-
1910 (18 linear feet); scrapbooks on early San Francisco history and
prominent figures (9 linear feet); Cooper-Molera Papers, 1828-1910 (10
linear feet of ship logs, account books, business papers, legal documents,
taxation and assessment papers for Monterey County, Mexican mining
deeds, household papers of Monterey adobe); Patterson Ranch papers, 1849-
1965 (ranch history; 81 linear feet); Sherman Music Collection, 1852-1923
(early theatrical posters and biographical sketches of California musicians;
rare sheet music; playbills; musical manuscripts); mining company stock
certificates and business records, 1850 to present. **Services:** Copying;
duplicate prints made of photos; library open to the public by appointment.
Automated Operations: Computerized public access catalog and cataloging.
Computerized Information Services: OCLC. **Networks/Consortia:** Member
of OCLC Pacific Network. **Publications:** The Pioneer - to members and by
mailing list.

★ 15313 ★
Society for Calligraphy - Library (Art)
Box 64174   Phone: (213)457-2968
Los Angeles, CA 90064   Andree Weinman, Libn.
Founded: 1974. **Subjects:** Calligraphy. **Holdings:** 450 volumes; slides;
movies.

Society of the Catholic Apostolate - Pallottine Provincialate Library
See: **Pallottine Provincialate Library** (12701)

★ 15314 ★
Society of the Cincinnati Library - Anderson House Museum (Hist)
2118 Massachusetts Ave., N.W.   Phone: (202)785-2040
Washington, DC 20008   Sandra L. Powers, Dir.
Founded: 1783. **Staff:** Prof 2. **Subjects:** U.S. history, American Revolution.
Special Collections: 18th century "art of war" collection. **Holdings:** 35,000
books; 25,500 items in manuscript archives and collections of the society.
Subscriptions: 52 journals and other serials. **Services:** Interlibrary loan;
copying; library and museum open to the public. **Computerized Information
Services:** OCLC. **Publications:** Annual Report of the Library and Museum;
Cincinnati 14 (newsletter), semiannual; George Rogers Clark Lectures on
the American Revolution. **Remarks:** FAX: (202)785-0729.

Society of Collectors, Inc. - Dunham Tavern Museum
See: **Dunham Tavern Museum** (5056)

★ 15315 ★
Society of Comparative Legislation - Library (Law)
28, rue Saint-Guillaume
F-75007 Paris, France   Phone: 1 4544467
Subjects: Comparative law, foreign law. **Holdings:** 100,000 volumes.
Subscriptions: 200 journals and other serials. **Services:** Interlibrary loan;
copying; library open to society members, research workers, and authorized
persons. **Remarks:** FAX: 1 45494165. **Also Known As:** Societe de Legislation
Comparee.

★ 15316 ★
**Society for Computer Applications in Engineering, Planning, and
   Architecture, Inc. - Library of Program Abstracts**
c/o Robert D. Marshall
Edwards and Kekey, Inc.
705 S. Orange Ave.
Livingston, NJ 07039
Subjects: Engineering, architecture, computers, computer software and
hardware. **Holdings:** Figures not available. **Remarks:** Currently inactive.

★ 15317 ★
Society for Coptic Archaeology - Library (Area-Ethnic)
222 Ramses Ave.
Abbassiya   Phone: 2 824252
Cairo, Egypt   Dr. Margit Toth, Libn.
Founded: 1934. **Staff:** 1. **Subjects:** Coptic language, literature, history, art,
thought, theology; papyrology. **Holdings:** 14,200 volumes. **Subscriptions:** 45
journals and other serials. **Services:** Library open to members and scholars.

Society for Ethnomusicology Archives
See: **University of Maryland, College Park Libraries - Music Library**
   (18821)

★ 15318 ★
**Society of the Founders of Norwich, Connecticut - Leffingwell Inn
   Library** (Hist)
348 Washington St.   Phone: (203)889-5990
Norwich, CT 06360   Linda Kate Edgerton, Libn.
Founded: 1901. **Staff:** Prof 1. **Subjects:** Local history and genealogy.
Holdings: 400 books; 32 bound periodical volumes; 15 linear feet of
documents and letters. **Services:** Interlibrary loan (limited); copying; library
open to the public by appointment.

★ 15319 ★
Society of the Four Arts - Library (Art)
Four Arts Plaza   Phone: (407)655-2766
Palm Beach, FL 33480   Joanne Rendon, Libn.
Founded: 1936. **Staff:** Prof 1; Other 5. **Subjects:** Painting, decorative arts,
architecture, photography. **Special Collections:** Addison Mizner Collection.
Holdings: 40,000 books and bound periodical volumes. **Subscriptions:** 98
journals and other serials; 8 newspapers. **Services:** Interlibrary loan;
copying; library open to the public. **Publications:** Library Notes and
Booklist. **Remarks:** Alternate telephone number(s): 655-2776. FAX:
(407)655-7233.

★ 15320 ★
Society of Friends - Friends House Library (Rel-Phil)
60 Lowther Ave.   Phone: (416)921-0368
Toronto, ON, Canada M5R 1C7   Jane Sweet, Lib.Coord.
Founded: 1890. **Staff:** 1. **Subjects:** History of Quakerism, peace and
nonviolence, native concerns. **Holdings:** 5900 books; 102 bound periodical
volumes; 12 boxes of pamphlets and reports. **Subscriptions:** 25 journals and
other serials. **Services:** Interlibrary loan; library open to the public.

★ 15321 ★
Society of Friends - Friends Meeting of Washington - Library (Rel-Phil)
2111 Florida Ave., N.W.   Phone: (202)483-3310
Washington, DC 20008   Martha Kenworthy, Libn.
Founded: 1932. **Staff:** 1. **Subjects:** Quaker history and beliefs. **Holdings:**
5500 books; 55 audiotapes; 25 videotapes; 50 other cataloged items.
Subscriptions: 32 journals and other serials. **Services:** Interlibrary loan;
library open by appointment to Friends doing research on Quaker subjects.
Publications: Bibliographies.

★ 15322 ★
Society of Friends - New England Yearly Meeting of Friends - Archives
   (Rel-Phil)
Rhode Island Historical Society Library
121 Hope St.   Phone: (401)331-8575
Providence, RI 02906   Cynthia Bendroth, Archv.
Founded: 1672. **Staff:** 1. **Subjects:** Archives and records of Society of Friends
in New England; Quaker historical material. **Special Collections:** Moses and
Obadiah Brown Libraries (512 volumes); Moses Brown Papers and
Pamphlets, 1774-1836 (29 file boxes). **Holdings:** 500 books; 155 bound
periodical volumes; 635 volumes of archives; 158 file boxes of pamphlets and
papers; 47 boxes of unbound periodicals; 173 reels of microfilm of archives;
1 box of newspaper clippings; 7 dissertations; 40 magnetic tapes. **Services:**
Copying; archives open to the public by appointment. **Remarks:** FAX:
(401)751-7930. Microfilm copies of records are available through the Rhode
Island Historical Society Library.

★ 15323 ★
**Society of Friends - New York Yearly Meeting - Records Committee -
   Haviland Records Room** (Rel-Phil)
15 Rutherford Pl.   Phone: (212)673-6866
New York, NY 10003   Elizabeth Haas Moger, Kpr. of the Rec.
Founded: 1900. **Staff:** 1. **Subjects:** Quaker genealogy and history in New
York and surrounding states. **Special Collections:** New York Quaker
imprints - Samuel Wood, Mahlon Day, Isaac T. Hopper (70 volumes);
papers relating to Friends and New York State Indians in the 19th century.
Holdings: 2500 books; 3000 manuscript records; photographs.
Subscriptions: 5 journals and other serials. **Services:** Room open to the
public by appointment. **Computerized Information Services:** Internal
databases. **Special Catalogs:** Catalog of manuscript records (card and
online). **Remarks:** Official depository for New York Yearly Meeting and its
subordinate meetings in New York State, western Vermont, Connecticut,
and northern New Jersey. **Also Known As:** Religious Society of Friends.

★ 15324 ★
Society of Friends - Ohio Yearly Meeting - Westgate Friends Library
   (Rel-Phil)
3750 Sullivant Ave.   Phone: (614)274-5131
Columbus, OH 43228   William T. Peters, Libn.
Founded: 1968. **Staff:** Prof 1; Other 3. **Subjects:** Quaker history and
theology. **Holdings:** 2000 books and pamphlets; 10 VF drawers.
Subscriptions: 65 journals and other serials. **Services:** Interlibrary loan;
library open to the public with restrictions. **Remarks:** Maintained by
Evangelical Friends Church, Eastern Region.

Society of Friends - Philadelphia Yearly Meeting
See: **Haverford College - Quaker and Special Collections** (7015)

★15325★
Society of Friends - Philadelphia Yearly Meeting - Library (Rel-Phil, Soc Sci)
1515 Cherry St.   Phone: (215)241-7220
Philadelphia, PA 19102   Rita I. Varley, Libn.
Founded: 1960. **Staff:** Prof 1; Other 1. **Subjects:** Quakerism; education; religious education; social concerns - religion, native Americans, criminal justice, race, service, sex, family relations, hunger, poverty, nuclear energy, peace education, nuclear weapons and disarmament. **Special Collections:** Dora Willson Collection (religion and psychology); E. Vesta Haines Collection of Christmas Literature; Jean C. Hollingshead Poetry Corner; Peace Education Resource Center; Frances Ferris Collection (books for and about children). **Holdings:** 18,000 books. **Subscriptions:** 104 journals and other serials. **Services:** Interlibrary loan; copying; library open to the public on fee basis. **Publications:** Subject reading lists; Teaching Peace: A Multimedia Catalog of Resources; Supplement to Teaching Peace. **Remarks:** FAX: (215)567-2096.

★15326★
Society for Human Resource Management - Library/Information Center (Bus-Fin)
606 N. Washington St.   Phone: (703)548-3440
Alexandria, VA 22314   Deborah A. Keary, Mgr., Info.Serv.
Founded: 1947. **Staff:** Prof 3; Other 2. **Subjects:** Personnel, human resources. **Holdings:** 3000 books; 150 newsletters; 100 journals; vertical files. **Subscriptions:** 8 newspapers. **Services:** Copying (limited); library open to the public with restrictions. **Automated Operations:** Computerized cataloging and circulation. **Computerized Information Services:** HRIN, DIALOG Information Services; HRM*Net (internal database). **Special Indexes:** Index of human resource topics. **Remarks:** FAX: (703)836-0367. **Formerly:** American Society for Personnel Administration. **Staff:** Beth Unger, Human Rsrc.Info.Spec.; David Gold, Sr. Human Rsrc.Info.Spec.

★15327★
Society for Information Display - Library (Comp Sci)
8055 W. Manchester Ave., Suite 615   Phone: (310)305-1502
Playa Del Rey, CA 90293   Deborah L. Lally, Exec.Dir.
Founded: 1962. **Staff:** 3. **Subjects:** Information display and allied arts, sciences, and effects on the human senses. **Holdings:** 4800 volumes. **Services:** Library open to the public. **Computerized Information Services:** MCI Mail (electronic mail service). **Publications:** List of publications - available on request. **Remarks:** FAX: (310)305-1433. Electronic mail address(es): 10:424-2462 (MCI Mail). **Staff:** Tony Su.

Society for Information and Documentation
See: **German National Research Center for Computer Science - GMD Information Center for Information Science and Information Work** (6431)

★15328★
Society for the Investigation of the Unexplained - Library (Sci-Engr)
Box 265   Phone: (908)842-5229
Little Silver, NJ 07739   Nancy Warth, Sec.
Founded: 1965. **Staff:** Prof 2; Other 3. **Subjects:** Forteana (works on tangible objects or events not yet accepted by orthodox science, e.g., sea monsters, abominable snowmen, poltergeists, UFOs); geology and geography; natural history; biology (all phases); cultural anthropology; astronomy; physics; chemistry; mathematics. **Special Collections:** Personal papers, original manuscripts and drawings of society's former director, the late Ivan T. Sanderson. **Holdings:** 2000 books; 105 bound periodical volumes; 95 shelf feet of unbound periodicals; 22 boxes of pamphlets; 260 ring binders of clippings, original reports, tear sheets; 300 maps; 2 map case drawers and 1 VF drawer of charts, diagrams, original drawings; 6 VF drawers of photographs, clippings, slides; 25 magnetic tapes. **Subscriptions:** 59 journals and other serials. **Services:** Library not open to the public. **Publications:** Pursuit Quarterly Journal - to members.

Society of Jesus, Maryland Province - Archives
See: **Georgetown University - Special Collections Division - Lauinger Memorial Library** (6379)

Society of Jesus, Maryland Province - Woodstock Theological Center
See: **Woodstock Theological Center - Library** (20581)

★15329★
Society of Jesus, Oregon Province - Archives (Rel-Phil, Hist)
Crosby Library, Gonzaga University
E. 502 Boone Ave.   Phone: (509)328-4220
Spokane, WA 99258   Rev. Neill R. Meany, S.J., Archv.
Founded: 1931. **Staff:** Prof 1; Other 2. **Subjects:** History - Northwest Church, Alaska Church and missions, Doukhobor, local; Alaskan and Indian languages. **Special Collections:** Joset Papers; Cataldo Papers; Crimont Papers; Neil Byrne Papers; Monaghan Papers; Cowley Papers; Prando Papers; Jesuit Mission Papers. **Holdings:** 3600 books; 800 bound periodical volumes; 123,000 manuscripts; 25,000 photographs. **Subscriptions:** 35 journals and other serials; 18 newspapers. **Services:** Copying; library open to those with scholarly credentials. **Automated Operations:** Computerized cataloging. **Publications:** Guides to Microfilm Editions of the Oregon Province Archives of the Society of Jesus Indian Language Collection: (1) The Alaska Native Languages; (2) The Pacific Northwest Tribes; The Alaska Mission Papers; Guide to Microfilm Editions of Papers on Pacific Northwest Jesuit Missions & Missionaries. **Remarks:** FAX: (509)484-2804. **Staff:** Bro. Ed Jennings, S.J., Asst.Archv.

★15330★
Society of the Little Flower - St. Therese Library (Rel-Phil)
1313 Frontage Rd.   Phone: (708)968-9400
Darien, IL 60559   Bob ColarResi, Dir.
Founded: 1985. **Staff:** Prof 2. **Subjects:** Therese of Lisieux. **Special Collections:** First editions. **Holdings:** 550 books; 20 bound periodical volumes; 100 other cataloged items. **Services:** Interlibrary loan; copying; library open to the public. Performs searches on fee basis. **Remarks:** FAX: (708)968-9542. **Staff:** Terrence Sempowski, Pres.

★15331★
Society of Malawi - Library (Hist)
P.O. Box 125
Blantyre, Malawi
Subjects: Malawi history. **Holdings:** 3000 volumes.

★15332★
Society of Management Accountants of Canada - Resource Centre
120 King St., W., Suite 850
Box 176
Hamilton, ON, Canada L8N 3C3
Founded: 1920. **Subjects:** Accounting, management, systems, communication, economics, marketing, mathematics, production, taxation. **Holdings:** 8000 books. **Remarks:** Currently inactive.

★15333★
Society for Manitobans with Disabilities Inc. - Stephen Sparling Library (Med)
825 Sherbrook St.
Winnipeg, MB, Canada R3A 1M5   Phone: (204)786-5601
Founded: 1957. **Staff:** 1. **Subjects:** Rehabilitation, social work, learning disorders, physical disabilities, therapy, psychology, special education, children's literature. **Holdings:** 2000 books and bound periodical volumes; 1000 monographs, reprints, and pamphlets. **Subscriptions:** 45 journals and other serials. **Services:** Interlibrary loan; copying; library open to the public. **Publications:** Monthly Library Additions. **Remarks:** FAX: (204)783-2919.

★15334★
Society of Manufacturing Engineers - SME Library (Comp Sci, Sci-Engr)
1 SME Dr.
Box 930   Phone: (313)271-1500
Dearborn, MI 48121   Paulette Groen, Libn.
Founded: 1932. **Staff:** 1. **Subjects:** Business, manufacturing engineering and materials, metallurgical processing, robotics, computerized automation in manufacturing. **Special Collections:** SME annual reports, minutes, papers, and other publications. **Holdings:** 7000 books; 15,000 technical reports, 1951 to present. **Subscriptions:** 450 journals and other serials. **Services:** Copying; library open to the public by appointment. **Automated Operations:** Computerized serials. **Computerized Information Services:** DIALOG Information Services; INTIME (internal database). Performs searches on fee basis. **Remarks:** FAX: (313)271-2861. Library contains the Robotics International of the Society of Manufacturing Engineers Collection.

★ **15335** ★
Society of Mary - Cincinnati Province - Archives (Rel-Phil)
Roesch Library, Rm. 313
University of Dayton
Box 0300   Phone: (513)229-2724
Dayton, OH 45469-0300   Bro. Bernard Laurinaitis, S.M., Archv.
Founded: 1938. **Staff:** Prof 1. **Subjects:** Church history, theology, and philosophy. **Special Collections:** Archives of the Society of Mary (Marianists) from its origin in U.S. in 1850 to the present. **Holdings:** 4000 storage boxes of archival material; 15 oral history tapes of the University of Dayton; collection of slides and photographs about various schools conducted by Marianists. **Services:** Copying; archives open to the public by appointment. **Special Indexes:** Indexes of Serial Publications of Marianists (card).

★ **15336** ★
Society of Naval Architects and Marine Engineers - Library (Sci-Engr)
601 Pavonia Ave.   Phone: (201)798-4800
Jersey City, NJ 07306   Francis M. Cagliari, Exec.Dir.
Founded: 1893. **Subjects:** Naval architecture, shipbuilding, marine engineering, and allied fields. **Holdings:** 1000 volumes. **Services:** Library not open to the public. **Remarks:** FAX: (201)798-4975.

★ **15337** ★
Society for the Preservation and Encouragement of Barber Shop Quartet Singing in America - Old Songs Library (Mus)
6315 3rd Ave.   Phone: (414)653-8440
Kenosha, WI 53143-5199   Ruth Marks, Harmony Found.Adm.
Staff: 1. **Subjects:** Piano-vocal sheet music, 1880s to present. **Special Collections:** Walter F. Wade Collection; Ken Grant Collection. **Holdings:** 65,000 pieces. **Services:** Library open to the public with restrictions. **Remarks:** FAX: (414)654-4048. **Also Known As:** Harmony Foundation.

★ **15338** ★
Society for the Preservation of New England Antiquities - Archives (Hist)
141 Cambridge St.   Phone: (617)227-3956
Boston, MA 02114   Lorna Condon, Cur. of Archv.
Founded: 1910. **Staff:** Prof 1; Other 1. **Subjects:** New England architecture and decorative arts, local history, transportation, history of photography. **Special Collections:** Photographic collections: N.L. Stebbins, Henry Peabody, Baldwin Coolidge, Soule Art Photo Company, Halliday Historic Photograph Company, New England News Company, George Noyes, Arthur Haskell, Wilfred French, Mary Northend, Emma Coleman, Fred Quimby, Wallace Nutting, and other regional photographers; Boston and Albany Railroad Collection; Boston Transit Collection (documenting construction/operation of Boston's subways and elevated mass transit systems from 1895-1950); Alfred W. Cutting Collection (2000 photos, 1882-1930); Elise R. Tyson collection (250 prints); Manuscript collections: Codman Family papers (100 linear feet); Rundlet-May papers (5 linear feet); Sayward Family papers (2 linear feet); Casey Family papers (40 linear feet); Harrison Gray Otis business records (1 linear foot); Papers of Sarah Orne Jewett; Papers of the Coffin Family (Newbury, MA); Papers of the Bowen Family (Woodstock, CN); Papers of the Sears Family (Weston-Wayland, MA); 16 linear feet of miscellaneous manuscripts, including Annie Fields correspondence; Lyman family papers; Architectural drawings: originals and blueprints including works of Asher Benjamin, Luther Briggs, Ogden Codman, Jr., Frank Chouteau Brown, Arthur Little, Herbert Browne, George Clough, Halfdan Hanson, and Arland Dirlam; rare architectural pattern books (18th and 19th centuries). **Holdings:** 300,000 photographs, including 10,000 stereographs, 10,000 postcards, 175 albums, 2500 cartes de visite portraits, 100,000 standard size prints, 1200 cataloged daguerreotypes and ambrotypes; 70,000 negatives including 40,000 glass plates; 2500 lithographs, wood engravings, and drawings primarily of New England architecture and landscape; 3000 advertising, trade catalogs, and other ephemera; 400 linear feet of manuscript collections; 10,000 architectural drawings; 6000 books. **Services:** Copying; photography; archives open to the public, appointment preferred. **Publications:** Guide and Checklist to Library Collections. **Special Catalogs:** Printed catalog to N.L. Stebbins marine photographs; Boston Transit Collection catalog; daguerreotype catalog; oversize photos catalog. **Special Indexes:** Typed inventories to photograph albums, prints and drawings, account books, maps, Soule Art Company photographs, and trade catalogs manuscripts; card index to rare architectural pattern books; card index to landscape architecture and design; inventories to all manuscript collections; card index to all architectural drawings (by architect, location, and building types). **Remarks:** FAX: (617)227-9204.

★ **15339** ★
Society for Promoting and Encouraging Arts & Knowledge of the Church - Howard Lane Foland Library
100 Skyline Dr.   Phone: (501)253-9701
Eureka Springs, AR 72632-9705   W.R. Swindells, Resident Mgr.
Founded: 1980. **Subjects:** Bible, eschatology, theology, pastoral relations, liturgies. **Holdings:** 7500 books. **Services:** Library open to scholars of the church.

Society for Research on Jewish Communities
See: Hebrew University of Jerusalem - Society for Research on Jewish Communities (7104)

★ **15340** ★
Society of St. Vincent de Paul - Library (Rel-Phil)
4140 Lindell Blvd.   Phone: (314)533-2223
St. Louis, MO 63108   Rita W. Porter, Dir.
Founded: 1845. **Subjects:** History and work of the Society of St. Vincent de Paul. **Holdings:** Figures not available. **Services:** Library not open to the public. **Publications:** Newsletter, quarterly. **Remarks:** FAX: (314)533-3747. **Staff:** Gabe Mattli.

★ **15341** ★
Society for the Study of Male Psychology & Physiology - Library (Med)
321 Iuka   Phone: (419)485-3602
Montpellier, OH 43543   Jerry Bergman, Ph.D., Dir.
Founded: 1971. **Staff:** 1. **Subjects:** Male psychology and physiology. **Holdings:** 1900 books; 1200 bound periodical volumes; 1000 reports, 800 manuscripts, 80 microfiche, 40 reels of microfilm. **Subscriptions:** 40 journals and other serials. **Services:** Interlibrary loan; copying; SDI; library open to the public by appointment. **Automated Operations:** Computerized cataloging, acquisitions, and serials.

Society of Swedish Literature in Finland
See: Svenska Litteratursallskapet I Finland (15897)

Society of Swedish Literature in Finland - Folk Culture Archives
See: Svenska Litteratursallskapet I Finland - Folk kulturs-arkivet (15898)

★ **15342** ★
Society for Technology and Rehabilitation - Technical Resource Centre (Med)
200, 1201-5 St., S.W.   Phone: (403)262-9445
Calgary, AB, Canada T2R 0Y6   Kathryn Dilts, Dir., Lib. & Info.Rsrcs.
Founded: 1979. **Staff:** 3. **Subjects:** Physical disabilities; rehabilitation - technology, aids, devices; barrier-free access; special education. **Holdings:** 1200 books; AV items; vertical files; software and supplier catalogs; technical aids. **Subscriptions:** 120 journals and newsletters. **Services:** Interlibrary loan; center open to the public. **Automated Operations:** Computerized public access catalog (INMAGIC). **Computerized Information Services:** CD-ROM (ABLEDATA). **Publications:** Subject bibliographies; serials union list. **Remarks:** FAX: (403)262-4539.

★ **15343** ★
Society of Wireless Pioneers, Inc. - Breniman Nautical-Wireless Library & Museum of Communications
P.O. Box 530
Santa Rosa, CA 95402
Founded: 1970. **Subjects:** Wireless telegraphy, communication, radio and television broadcasting, ships and shipping. **Special Collections:** Dickow Wireless Collection; Abernathy Radio-Telegraph Picture Collection; Brown Lighthouses of the World. **Holdings:** 2755 books; 1500 bound periodical volumes; 4500 maps and other cataloged items; 2300 historical papers and monographs. **Remarks:** Currently inactive.

★15344★
Society of Women Engineers - Information Center (Sci-Engr)
345 E. 47th St., Rm. 305   Phone: (212)705-7855
New York, NY 10017   B.J. Harrod, Act.Exec.Dir.
Founded: 1950. **Staff:** 10. **Subjects:** Women in engineering. **Holdings:**
Figures not available. **Services:** Center open to the public. **Publications:**
Career guidance brochures; article reprints; Survey of Women Engineers;
U.S. Woman Engineer (magazine) - bimonthly. **Remarks:** This is an
information center on women in engineering with emphasis on career
guidance for the younger girl and advancement of women in the engineering
profession. **Remarks:** FAX: (212)319-0947.

★15345★
Socioscope Inc. - Library (Sci-Engr)
29 Powell Ave.
Ottawa, ON, Canada K1S 1Z9   Phone: (613)235-7120
Subjects: Advanced technologies - implications, applications, human
factors, consumer and social impacts, markets, industrial opportunities,
training, systems analysis. **Holdings:** 200 bound volumes; 2000 nonbook
items. **Subscriptions:** 20 journals and other serials. **Remarks:** FAX:
(613)230-9279.

★15346★
Sockerbelaget AB - Biblioteket (Agri)
Fersens vag 9
Box 17124   Phone: 40 249000
S-200 10 Malmo, Sweden   Sven Eric Zethson
Founded: 1934. **Staff:** Prof 2; Other 1.5. **Subjects:** Sugar technology, sugar
beet growing, human nutrition, dietary fibre. **Holdings:** 10,000 books; 2000
bound periodical volumes; 1000 microfiche. **Subscriptions:** 550 journals and
other serials; 9 newspapers. **Services:** Interlibrary loan; copying; library
open to the public by appointment. **Automated Operations:** Computerized
cataloging. **Computerized Information Services:** BLAISE, DIALOG
Information Services, Data-Star, DAFA, DATAARKIV, STN
International; internal databases. **Remarks:** FAX: 40 979059. Telex: 32416
Socker S.

★15347★
Sod Town Pioneer Homestead Museum - Library (Hist)
Rte. 1, Box 225   Phone: (913)462-2021
Colby, KS 67701   Ronald E. Thiel, Dir.
Founded: 1955. **Staff:** 2. **Subjects:** Sod houses, dugouts, adobe buildings,
pioneer homestead history. **Special Collections:** Old photographs of sod
buildings in North America (500). **Holdings:** 20,000 personal letters and
family history reports from persons with sod house heritage. **Services:**
Library open to the public for reference use only. **Publications:** Sod Houses
and Dugouts in North America - for sale. **Remarks:** Maintained by Sons and
Daughters of the Soddies.

★15348★
Sodarcan, Inc. - Documentation Center (Bus-Fin)
1140, blvd. de Maisonneuve, W., Suite 305   Phone: (514)288-0100
Montreal, PQ, Canada H3A 1M8   Josee Plamondon, Mgr.
Founded: 1975. **Staff:** Prof 2; Other 1. **Subjects:** Insurance, law, business,
employment benefits, compensation. **Holdings:** 5000 books; 300 bound
periodical volumes; 1400 financial statements. **Subscriptions:** 250 journals
and other serials; 10 newspapers. **Services:** Interlibrary loan; center not open
to the public. **Automated Operations:** Computerized acquisitions, serials,
and circulation. **Computerized Information Services:** DIALOG
Information Services, QL Systems, Info Globe, Infomart Online, Questel,
Societe Quebecoise d'Information Juridique (SOQUIJ), CAN/OLE, CAN/
LAW; internal database; Envoy 100 (electronic mail service). **Publications:**
Monthly Bulletin - for internal distribution and by subscription. **Remarks:**
FAX: (514)282-1364. Telex: 055 60657. **Staff:** Lucie Pelletier, Tech.Libn.;
Odette Lavoie, Libn.

Sohn Memorial Health Services Library
See: **Fort Hamilton-Hughes Memorial Hospital Center** (5998)

Soil Mechanics Information Analysis Center
See: **U.S. Army - Engineer Waterways Experiment Station** (16971)

Soil Science Society of America - American Society of Agronomy
See: **American Society of Agronomy** (742)

★15349★
Soil and Water Conservation Society - H. Wayne Pritchard Library
(Env-Cons)
7515 N.E. Ankeny Rd.   Phone: (515)289-2331
Ankeny, IA 50021-9764   James L. Sanders, Mng.Ed.
Subjects: Soil and water conservation, land use planning, natural resources
management. **Special Collections:** Papers of leaders in soil and water
conservation. **Holdings:** 2500 books. **Services:** Copying; library open to the
public for reference use only.

★15350★
Sola/Barnes-Hind - Technical Library and Information Center (Med)
810 Kifer Rd.   Phone: (408)991-6435
Sunnyvale, CA 94086   Sidney C. Frederick, Tech.Libn.
Founded: 1962. **Staff:** Prof 2; Other 1. **Subjects:** Contact lens products,
polymer science, ophthalmology. **Special Collections:** Contact lens research.
Holdings: 1600 books; 70,000 bound periodical volumes; 1000 internal
reports; 6000 patents; 200 reels of microfilm. **Subscriptions:** 150 journals and
other serials. **Services:** Interlibrary loan (limited); library not open to the
public. **Automated Operations:** Computerized public access catalog
(VISION) and cataloging. **Computerized Information Services:** DIALOG
Information Services, BRS Information Technologies, STN International,
MEDLARS; internal databases; OnTyme Electronic Message Network
Service (electronic mail service). **Networks/Consortia:** Member of National
Network of Libraries of Medicine - Pacific Southwest Region, Northern
California and Nevada Medical Library Group (NCNMLG). **Remarks:**
FAX: (408)991-6480. Electronic mail address(es): CLASS.SOLA/B-H
(OnTyme Electronic Message Network Service).

Gerardo Selles Sola Library
See: **University of Puerto Rico - Library System - Gerardo Selles Sola
Library** (19240)

★15351★
Solano County Law Library (Law)
600 Union Ave.
Hall of Justice   Phone: (707)421-6520
Fairfield, CA 94533   Marianna Moore, Law Libn.
Founded: 1980. **Staff:** Prof 1; Other 1. **Subjects:** California and U.S. codes;
code law; California statutes. **Holdings:** 19,009 books; 900 bound periodical
volumes; microfiche. **Subscriptions:** 97 journals and other serials. **Services:**
Copying; faxing; library open to the public for reference use only. **Remarks:**
FAX: (707)421-6516.

★15352★
Solano County Library - Special Collections (Rare Book)
1150 Kentucky St.   Phone: (707)421-6510
Fairfield, CA 94533   Ed Kieczykowski, Dir.
Founded: 1914. **Special Collections:** Donovan J. McCune Collection
(printing history, rare books; 1500 volumes); U.S. and state government
documents depository (5000 volumes); local history (500 volumes). **Services:**
Interlibrary loan; copying; collections open to the public; Donovan J.
McCune Collection open to the public by appointment. **Automated
Operations:** Computerized cataloging, acquisitions, and circulation.
Computerized Information Services: DIALOG Information Services;
OnTyme Electronic Message Network Service (electronic mail service).
Performs searches free of charge. **Networks/Consortia:** Member of North
Bay Cooperative Library System (NBCLS). **Remarks:** FAX: (707)421-7474.

Solar Energy Research Institute - SERI Technical Library
See: **National Renewable Energy Laboratory - Library** (11267)

★15353★
Solar Turbines Incorporated - Library (Sci-Engr)
2200 Pacific Hwy.
P.O. Box 80966   Phone: (619)544-5000
San Diego, CA 92138   George Hall, Libn.
Founded: 1959. **Staff:** Prof 1. **Subjects:** Gas turbines, ceramics, high
temperature metals. **Holdings:** 2700 books; 700 bound periodical volumes;
5000 technical reports and society papers. **Subscriptions:** 30 journals and
other serials; 10 newspapers. **Services:** Interlibrary loan; library not open to
the public. **Computerized Information Services:** DIALOG Information
Services. **Publications:** New Material Bulletin, monthly. **Remarks:** FAX:
(619)544-5826. Solar Turbines Incorporated is a subsidiary of the Caterpillar
Company.

★ 15354 ★
Solartherm - Library (Energy)
1315 Apple Ave.   Phone: (301)587-8686
Silver Spring, MD 20910   Dr. Carl Schleicher, Pres.
Founded: 1977. **Subjects:** Solar energy; alternative energy systems - high-temperature solar, conservation, solid waste, tidal and methane systems. **Holdings:** 8000 volumes.

★ 15355 ★
Soldiers and Sailors Memorial Hospital - Health Science Library (Med)
Central Ave.   Phone: (717)724-1631
Wellsboro, PA 16901   Charlean Patterson, Libn.
Staff: 1. **Subjects:** Clinical medicine, nursing, hospital administration, allied health sciences, patient education. **Holdings:** 900 books; 10,000 unbound periodical volumes; 100 NCME videotapes. **Subscriptions:** 115 journals and other serials. **Services:** Interlibrary loan; copying; SDI; library open to the public. **Computerized Information Services:** MEDLINE. Performs searches on fee basis. **Networks/Consortia:** Member of Susquehanna Library Cooperative, Central Pennsylvania Health Sciences Library Association (CPHSLA), National Network of Libraries of Medicine - Middle Atlantic Region. **Remarks:** FAX: (717)724-7235.

★ 15356 ★
Soleil Limitee - Centre de Documentation (Publ)
390 E. St. Vallier   Phone: (418)647-3394
Quebec, PQ, Canada G1K 7J6   Berthold Landry, Adm.Asst.
Founded: 1967. **Staff:** Prof 5; Other 1. **Subjects:** Newspaper reference topics. **Holdings:** 1500 books; 50 bound periodical volumes; 1 million black/white photographs; 10,000 color photographs; 1 million clippings; 20,000 reels of microfilm; 150 VF drawers. **Subscriptions:** 25 journals and other serials; 15 newspapers. **Services:** Center not open to the public. **Remarks:** FAX: (418)647-3374. Telex: 051 3755. **Staff:** Claudine Gagnon, Coord.

Paolo Soleri Archives
See: **Arizona State University - Architecture and Environmental Design Library** (1009)

★ 15357 ★
Solid Waste Information Clearinghouse - Library (Law)
8750 Georgia Ave., Suite 140
P.O. Box 7219
Silver Spring, MD 20910   Phone: (301)585-2898
                                       Lori Swain, Proj.Mgr.
Staff: 3. **Subjects:** Solid and hazardous waste management - collection, disposal; landfills - operations, gas; resource recovery. **Holdings:** 6500 documents. **Services:** Copying; library open to the public by appointment. **Publications:** SWICH List of Literature, for sale. **Remarks:** FAX: (301)585-0297. **Formerly:** Governmental Refuse Collection and Disposal Association - Library.

★ 15358 ★
Solution Mining Research Institute - Library (Sci-Engr)
812 Muriel St.   Phone: (815)338-8579
Woodstock, IL 60098   Howard W. Fiedelman, Exec.Dir.
Founded: 1979. **Staff:** 1. **Subjects:** Solution mining industry, environmental issues pertinent to industry. **Holdings:** 120 research reports; 280 papers published by others; 200 meeting papers. **Services:** Copying. **Publications:** Copies of literature available upon request. **Remarks:** FAX: (815)338-1228.

★ 15359 ★
Sombra Township Museum - Reference Room (Hist)
3470 St. Clair Pkwy.
P.O. Box 76   Phone: (519)892-3982
Sombra, ON, Canada N0P 2H0   Wanda Barg, Dir.
Subjects: Local history. **Holdings:** Biographies; diaries; family histories. **Services:** Room open to the public for reference use only.

★ 15360 ★
Somers Historical Society - Archives (Hist)
574 Main St.   Phone: (203)749-8540
Somers, CT 06071   Jeanne K. DeBell, Cur.
Staff: 3. **Subjects:** Local and state history, genealogy. **Special Collections:** Civil War Letters; Sermons, 1750-1865; Public School Readers, 1830-1890. **Holdings:** 200 books; 1 VF drawer of local history material; 1 box of early deeds and letters, 1730-1865. **Services:** Archives open to the public with restrictions. **Publications:** Somers, Connecticut Through the Camera's Eye, 1978; Stories of Somers Connecticut, 1984 - both for sale. **Special Indexes:** Genealogical File of Somers Families. **Remarks:** Alternate telephone number(s): (203)749-8540.

★ 15361 ★
Somers Historical Society - Dr. Hugh Grant Rowell Circus Library Collection (Hist)
Elephant Hotel
Box 336   Phone: (914)277-4977
Somers, NY 10589   Emil Antonaccio, Pres.
Founded: 1965. **Subjects:** Circus, genealogy. **Holdings:** 600 books; 4 VF drawers of uncataloged pamphlets and manuscripts; 10 maps; 1000 circus-related materials. **Services:** Collection open to the public for reference use only by appointment.

★ 15362 ★
Somerset County Law Library (Law)
New Court House
Box 3000   Phone: (908)231-7612
Somerville, NJ 08876   Robert G. Gennett, Law Libn.
Staff: 1. **Subjects:** Law. **Holdings:** 22,000 volumes. **Services:** Library open to the public for reference use only. **Computerized Information Services:** WESTLAW.

★ 15363 ★
Somerset County Law Library (Law)
Court House   Phone: (814)443-9770
Somerset, PA 15501   Tom Cartwright, Law Libn.
Staff: 2. **Subjects:** Law. **Holdings:** 20,500 volumes. **Services:** Library open to the public for reference use only.

★ 15364 ★
Somerset Medical Center - Medical Library (Med)
110 Rehill Ave.   Phone: (908)685-2200
Somerville, NJ 08876   Kenneth Whitmore, Lib.Coord.
Staff: 1. **Subjects:** Medicine, nursing. **Holdings:** 2100 books; 1200 bound periodical volumes. **Subscriptions:** 155 journals and other serials. **Services:** Interlibrary loan; copying; SDI; library open to the public. **Computerized Information Services:** MEDLINE. **Remarks:** FAX: (908)685-2869.

Somerset State Hospital
See: **Pennsylvania (State) Department of Public Welfare** (12867)

★ 15365 ★
Somerville Hospital - Carr Health Sciences Library (Med)
230 Highland Ave.   Phone: (617)666-4400
Somerville, MA 02143   Celeste F. Kozlowski, Med.Libn.
Staff: Prof 2; Other 4. **Subjects:** Medicine, nursing. **Holdings:** 2678 books; 118 bound periodical volumes; 4 VF drawers pamphlets; 1 VF drawer of archives. **Subscriptions:** 142 journals and other serials. **Services:** Interlibrary loan; copying; library open to the public with permission. **Automated Operations:** Computerized ILL (DOCLINE). **Computerized Information Services:** MEDLARS. Performs searches on fee basis. **Networks/Consortia:** Member of Libraries and Information for Nursing Consortium (LINC), Massachusetts Health Sciences Libraries Network (MaHSLiN). **Publications:** New book list, bimonthly. **Remarks:** FAX: (617)625-0628. **Staff:** Arleen Frasca, Asst.Libn.

Sonahend Family Library
See: **Temple Emanu-El - Sonahend Family Library** (16101)

★ 15366 ★
Sonat Inc. - Corporate Library (Bus-Fin, Energy)
1900 5th Ave., N.
Birmingham, AL 35203   Phone: (205)325-7409
Staff: Prof 1; Other 1. **Subjects:** Energy, natural gas industry, alternative fuels, oil industry, business, corporate law. **Special Collections:** Financial data on major natural gas pipeline companies (53 VF drawers). **Holdings:** 8200 books; 8 VF drawers of clippings; 6 VF drawers of speeches. **Subscriptions:** 400 journals and other serials; 10 newspapers. **Services:** Copying; SDI; library open to the public for reference use only. **Computerized Information Services:** NEXIS, LEXIS, A.G.A. GasNet; A.G.A. GasNet (electronic mail service).

★ 15367 ★
Sonat Offshore Drilling, Inc. - Corporate Library
4 Greenway Plaza
Box 2765
Houston, TX 77252-2765
Founded: 1978. **Subjects:** Engineering, naval engineering, geology, social sciences. **Holdings:** 2200 books; 100 bound periodical volumes; 250 brochures. **Remarks:** Currently inactive.

★ 15368 ★
Sonnenschein Nath and Rosenthal - Library (Law)
1301 K St., Suite 600 E   Phone: (202)408-6452
Washington, DC 20004   William L. Katzenberger, Jr., Libn.
Founded: 1988. **Staff:** Prof 1. **Subjects:** American law. **Holdings:** 10,000 books. **Subscriptions:** 60 journals and other serials. **Services:** Interlibrary loan; library not open to the public. **Computerized Information Services:** DIALOG Information Services, LEXIS, WESTLAW. **Remarks:** FAX: (202)408-6399. **Staff:** Robert Humphreys.

★ 15369 ★
Sonnenschein Nath and Rosenthal - Library (Law)
8000 Sears Tower
233 S. Wacker Dr.   Phone: (312)876-7906
Chicago, IL 60606   Colleen L. McCarroll, Libn.
Staff: Prof 4; Other 3. **Subjects:** Law. **Special Collections:** Insurance statutes and regulations for all states. **Holdings:** 30,000 books; 240 bound periodical volumes; 500 microfiche; 1200 internal research reports. **Services:** Interlibrary loan; copying; SDI; library open to the public at librarian's discretion. **Automated Operations:** Computerized cataloging and serials. **Computerized Information Services:** DIALOG Information Services, OCLC, LEXIS, WESTLAW, PFDS Online, Dow Jones News/Retrieval, DataTimes, Information America, VU/TEXT Information Services, Reuters. **Networks/Consortia:** Member of Chicago Library System. **Special Indexes:** Internal research index (book and magnetic disk); corporate precedents file (card). **Remarks:** FAX: (312)876-7934. **Staff:** Ruth H. Martin, Ref.Libn.; Shelley J. Birkner, Tech.Serv.Libn.

Sonntag Library
See: **Manhattan College** (9593)

★ 15370 ★
Sonoma County Law Library (Law)
Hall of Justice, Rm. 213-J
600 Administration Dr.   Phone: (707)527-2668
Santa Rosa, CA 95403-2879   Charlotte S. Von Gunten, Law Lib.Dir.
Founded: 1891. **Staff:** Prof 2; Other 1. **Subjects:** Law. **Holdings:** 24,000 volumes; 675 tapes. **Services:** Library open to the public.

★ 15371 ★
Sonoma County Planning Department - Library (Plan)
575 Administration Dr., Rm. 105A   Phone: (707)527-2412
Santa Rosa, CA 95403   Ruth Lund, Exec.Sec.
Founded: 1961. **Staff:** Prof 1. **Subjects:** Planning, transportation, land use, housing, zoning and environmental impact information related to Sonoma County and surrounding areas. **Holdings:** Books; reports; special studies. **Services:** Copying; library open to the public with restrictions. **Remarks:** FAX: (707)527-1103 - must call 527-1925 to alert to transmission.

★ 15372 ★
Sonoma Developmental Center - Staff Library (Med)
Box 1493   Phone: (707)938-6244
Eldridge, CA 95431   Angela Brunton, Sr.Libn.
Founded: 1951. **Staff:** Prof 1; Other 1. **Subjects:** Mental retardation, psychology, nursing, social work, rehabilitation therapy, medicine. **Special Collections:** History of the hospital. **Holdings:** 9000 books; 8417 bound periodical volumes; 70 AV programs. **Subscriptions:** 91 journals and other serials. **Services:** Interlibrary loan; copying; library open to the public. **Computerized Information Services:** MEDLARS, DIALOG Information Services. **Networks/Consortia:** Member of Northern California and Nevada Medical Library Group (NCNMLG). **Remarks:** FAX: (707)938-3605.

★ 15373 ★
Sonoma State University - Northwest Information Center - California Archaeological Inventory (Hist)
Rohnert Park, CA 94928   Phone: (707)664-2494
       David A. Fredrickson, Ph.D.
Founded: 1975. **Staff:** Prof 11; Other 6. **Subjects:** Archeology, anthropology, history, cultural resource management. **Holdings:** 23,000 reports, records, and maps. **Services:** Copying; archival research (on a fee basis); center open to professional archeologists and educational tours. **Computerized Information Services:** Internal database. Performs searches on fee basis. **Publications:** Bibliography of holdings. **Remarks:** FAX: (707)664-3947.

★ 15374 ★
Sonoma Valley Historical Society - Depot Park Museum - Research Library (Hist)
270 1st St., W.
P.O. Box 861   Phone: (707)938-9765
Sonoma, CA 95476   Mrs. Ross Strickland, Libn.
Founded: 1979. **Subjects:** Sonoma Valley history and allied subjects. **Holdings:** 300 books. **Subscriptions:** 4 journals and other serials. **Services:** Library open by appointment for reference use only. **Publications:** The Sonoma Mission; Pioneer Sonoma; Sonoma Valley Legacy.

Sonora Desert Museum
See: **Arizona-Sonora Desert Museum** (992)

Sons of the American Revolution
See: **National Society of the Sons of the American Revolution** (11297)

Sons and Daughters of the Soddies - Sod Town Pioneer Homestead Museum
See: **Sod Town Pioneer Homestead Museum** (15347)

★ 15375 ★
Sons of Norway International - North Star Library (Area-Ethnic)
1455 W. Lake St.   Phone: (612)827-3611
Minneapolis, MN 55408   Anne Marie Taylor, Heritage Prog.Adm.
Staff: Prof 1. **Subjects:** Literature, World War II, travel, art, history, insurance, social studies. **Special Collections:** Norwegian Pictorial Review (55); Norwegian-American Studies (20); Norwegian-American Emigration Lists (15); 19th century Norwegian literary classics; Norwegian immigration to the U.S. **Holdings:** 2500 books (half in Norwegian, half in English); insurance reports; census and legal reference materials; photographs. **Services:** Library open to the public for reference use only. **Remarks:** FAX: (612)827-0658.

★ 15376 ★
Sons of the Revolution in the State of California - Library (Hist)
600 S. Central Ave.   Phone: (818)240-1775
Glendale, CA 91204   Edwin W. Coles, Lib.Dir.
Founded: 1893. **Staff:** Prof 1. **Subjects:** Genealogy, history. **Special Collections:** D.A.R. Lineage Books (166 volumes). **Holdings:** 25,000 volumes; 2000 bound periodical volumes; 2500 family genealogies. **Subscriptions:** 20 journals and other serials. **Services:** Copying; genealogical research; library open to the public with donation.

★ 15377 ★
Sons of the Revolution in the State of New York - Library (Hist)
Fraunces Tavern Museum
54 Pearl St.
New York, NY 10004   Phone: (212)425-1776
Subjects: Colonial and Revolutionary War period. **Holdings:** Figures not available. **Services:** Library not open to the public. **Remarks:** FAX: (212)509-3467.

★ 15378 ★
Sony Music Archives (Aud-Vis)
49 E. 52nd St.
New York, NY 10022
Phone: (212)445-4949
Martine Vinces, Archv.
Founded: 1964. **Staff:** Prof 1. **Holdings:** 90,000 phonograph records and compact discs; Columbia, Epic, and other companies' catalogs, 1894 to present; 350,000 recording matrix cards; company memoranda; photograph archive. **Services:** Archives open to professionals in the recording field by appointment only. **Remarks:** FAX: (212)445-2177. **Formerly:** CBS Records Inc. - Archives. **Staff:** Nathaniel Brewster, Res.Coord.

P.A. Sorokin Library
See: **University of Saskatchewan - Special Collections (19297)**

★ 15379 ★
Sotheby's Library (Art)
1334 York Ave.
New York, NY 10021
Phone: (212)606-7000
Rosalyn Narbutas, Libn.
Staff: Prof 1. **Subjects:** Fine arts, decorative arts. **Special Collections:** Auction catalogs; company archives. **Holdings:** Figures not available. **Subscriptions:** 200 journals and other serials; newspapers. **Services:** Library not open to the public. **Special Indexes:** Index to archive files. **Remarks:** FAX: (212)606-7011.

★ 15380 ★
Souris Valley Regional Care Centre - Health Sciences Library (Med)
Box 2001
Weyburn, SK, Canada S4H 2L7
Phone: (306)842-8344
Melva Cooke, Libn.
Founded: 1968. **Staff:** 1. **Subjects:** Gerontology, nursing, geriatrics, psychology, nutrition, physical and occupational therapy. **Holdings:** 800 books; 90 bound periodical volumes; 300 articles; 3 VF drawers of clippings. **Subscriptions:** 75 journals and other serials; 7 newspapers. **Services:** Interlibrary loan; copying; open to the public with permission of executive director. **Remarks:** FAX: (306)842-7710.

★ 15381 ★
Sourisseau Academy - Library (Hist)
History Department
San Jose State University
San Jose, CA 95192-0147
Phone: (408)924-6510
Edith Smith, Archv.
Founded: 1969. **Staff:** 2. **Subjects:** History - San Jose, Santa Clara County, California. **Holdings:** 28 linear feet of books; 5 linear feet of manuscripts; photographs; ephemera. **Services:** Library open to the public. **Remarks:** Alternate telephone number(s): 356-3462.

John Philip Sousa Music Library
See: **U.S. Marine Corps - Marine Band Library (17602)**

★ 15382 ★
South Africa - Council for Scientific and Industrial Research - Division of Information Services - Library (Sci-Engr)
P.O. Box 395
Pretoria 0001, Republic of South Africa
Phone: 12 8412852
Dr. B. Fouche, Dir.
Founded: 1946. **Subjects:** Physics; chemistry; engineering - chemical, materials, mechanical, electrical; water research; food technology; roads and transportation; building; construction research; timber; telecommunications; wool; textiles; oceanology; astronomy; computing sciences; management; library and information science. **Holdings:** 100,000 bound volumes. **Subscriptions:** 5500 journals and other serials. **Services:** Interlibrary loan; micrographic reproduction; document delivery; library open to the South African industrial and scientific communities. **Automated Operations:** Computerized cataloging. **Computerized Information Services:** WATERLIT; internal databases. **Publications:** Technical Information for Industry, 10/year; INFOPAK Manufacturing, weekly; INFOPAK Management, monthly; INFOPAK Konstrukt, monthly; INFOPAK Materials, monthly. **Special Catalogs:** CSIR Publications, quarterly - available free of charge. **Remarks:** FAX: 12 862869. Telex: 321287 SA. Is said to maintain the largest specialized techno-scientific collection in South Africa.

★ 15383 ★
South Africa - Department of Agricultural Development - Natal Region Headquarters - Cedara Library (Agri)
Cedara
Private Bag X 9059
Pietermaritzburg 3200, Republic of
South Africa
Phone: 331 33371
Dr. Rona V. Van Niekerk
Founded: 1906. **Staff:** Prof 2; Other 2. **Subjects:** Agriculture. **Special Collections:** Natal Regional Collection (all publications and reports published by the Department of Agricultural Development - Natal Region). **Holdings:** 7500 books; 7000 bound periodical volumes; 23,000 reports; 1000 archives; 20 microfiche; 300 other cataloged items. **Subscriptions:** 350 journals and other serials; 2 newspapers. **Services:** Interlibrary loan; copying; SDI; library open to persons who register as members and pay a refundable deposit. **Computerized Information Services:** SABINET, SADAL. **Remarks:** FAX: 331 431253. Telex: 643283.

★ 15384 ★
South Africa - Department of Agricultural Development - Soil and Irrigation Research Institute - Library (Agri)
Private Bag X79
Pretoria 0001, Republic of South Africa
Phone: 12 2062882
Miss E. Prinsloo, Libn.
Subjects: Soil and water research, agrometeorology, remote sensing, pedology, water quality. **Holdings:** 20,000 volumes. **Subscriptions:** 100 journals and other serials. **Services:** Interlibrary loan; copying; SDI; library open to the public. **Remarks:** FAX: 12 3232740.

South Africa - Department of Mineral and Energy Affairs - Geological Survey of South Africa
See: **Geological Survey of South Africa (6367)**

South Africa - Department of National Education - Africa Institute of South Africa
See: **Africa Institute of South Africa (119)**

South Africa - Geological Survey of South Africa
See: **Geological Survey of South Africa (6367)**

★ 15385 ★
South Africa - Nasionale Afrikaanse Letterkundige Museum en Navorsingsentrum - Biblioteek (Hum)
President Brand St.
Old Government Bldg.
Private Bag X20543
Bloemfontein 9300, Republic of South Africa
Phone: 51 4054019
M.M. vander Walt
Founded: 1974. **Staff:** Prof 6; Other 6. **Subjects:** Afrikaans literature, Afrikaans language, Afrikaans music, Afrikaans theatre. **Special Collections:** Nienaber Collection; Lategan Collection; F.C.L. Bosman Collection; Payne Collection; Van Schaik Collection. **Holdings:** 70,000 books; 5000 bound periodical volumes; 100,000 archival items; microfiche; sound recordings. **Subscriptions:** 157 journals and other serials; 17 newspapers. **Services:** Interlibrary loan; copying; library open to the public for reference use only. **Publications:** Bronnegids by die studie van die Afrikaanse Letterkunde en Taal, annual.

★ 15386 ★
South Africa - South African Library (Area-Ethnic, Info Sci)
P.O. Box 496
Cape Town 8000, Republic of South Africa
Phone: 21 24-6320
Mr. P.E. Westra, Dir.
Founded: 1818. **Staff:** Prof 26; Other 60. **Subjects:** Africana-Southern Africa, humanities. **Special Collections:** Grey Collection (112 medieval illuminated manuscripts); Dessinian Collection (17th-18th century); Fairbridge Collection (19th century); Pama Collection (heraldry and genealogy); Cape and South Africa newspaper collection; iconographic collection. **Holdings:** 600,000 books; 160,000 bound periodical volumes; 74,000 microforms; 35,000 manuscripts. **Subscriptions:** 7250 journals and other serials; 441 newspapers. **Services:** Interlibrary loan; copying; microfilming; library open to the public. **Automated Operations:** Computerized cataloging, acquisitions, serials, and circulation. **Computerized Information Services:** DIALOG Information Services; internal databases. **Publications:** Quarterly Bulletin; Grey Bibliographies; Reprint Series; Period Publications; Quarterly Newsletter; Newspapers on Microfilm. **Special Indexes:** Cape Town English Press Index. **Remarks:** The South African Library is a national library. FAX: 21 24-4848. Telex: 5 22604 SA. **Also Known As:** Suid-Afrikaanse Biblioteek. **Staff:** Mr. A.S. Kerkham, Dp.Dir.

★ 15387 ★
South Africa - State Library (Area-Ethnic, Soc Sci, Info Sci)
P.O. Box 397   Phone: 12 218931
Pretoria 0001, Republic of South Africa   Dr. Peter Johan Lor, Dir.
Founded: 1887. **Staff:** Prof 60; Other 116. **Subjects:** Social sciences, African studies. **Special Collections:** Legal deposit for South Africa, 1916 to present (newspapers; books; periodicals); official publications depository for U.S. Superintendent of Documents; U.N. and other official publications; bibliographies; maps (22,000); official publications of Southern African states. **Holdings:** 872,226 items, including 67,851 bound periodical volumes and 199,700 microforms. **Subscriptions:** 9682 journals and other serials; 425 newspapers. **Services:** Interlibrary loan; library open to the public for reference use only. **Automated Operations:** Computerized cataloging, acquisitions, and bibliography production. **Computerized Information Services:** South African Bibliographic and Information Network (SABINET), BLAISE, SA Archives Services, TERMBANK, Central Statistical Services; CD-ROMs. Performs searches free of charge. Contact Person: Mrs. Jo Boshoff, Chf.Libn. **Publications:** SANB - South African National Bibliography, quarterly with annual cumulation; Informat - Information Bulletin of the State Library, bimonthly - worldwide distribution; South African newspapers (microfilm). **Special Catalogs:** S.A. Joint Catalogue of Monographs; Periodicals in Southern African Libraries (PISAL). **Special Indexes:** Index to South African Periodicals; Index to Government Gazettes of Ciskei, Transkei, Venda, and Bophuthatswana. **Remarks:** Library located at 239 Vermeulen St., Pretoria. FAX: 12 3255984. Telex: 322171 SA. **Staff:** Mrs. J.F. de Beer, Dp.Dir.; Mr. A.G.C. Olivier, Asst.Dir., Supp.Serv.; Mrs. M.A. Botha, Asst.Dir., Lib.Serv.

★ 15388 ★
South Africa as the Fifty-first State Library (Area-Ethnic)
4845 S. Raymond   Phone: (206)725-7417
Seattle, WA 98118   William H. Davis, Libn.
Founded: 1986. **Staff:** Prof 1. **Subjects:** Events which will cause the "White Tribe" to favor union; cultural conditions to which blacks from South Africa would have to adjust; winter resort possibilities. **Holdings:** 40 books; 22 scrapbooks; Proceedings of South African tricameral Parliamentary sessions, 1988-1990 (32 volumes). **Services:** Interlibrary loan; copying; library open to the public. **Publications:** Leaflets, bimonthly - available on request.

★ 15389 ★
South African Institute of Race Relations - Library (Soc Sci)
Auden House
68 de Korte St.
Braamfontein   Phone: 11 4033600
Johannesburg, Republic of South Africa   E.S. Potter, Libn.
Staff: 8. **Subjects:** Race relations, human rights. **Holdings:** 5000 volumes. **Subscriptions:** 93 journals and other serials; 22 newspapers. **Services:** Copying; library open to members only. **Remarks:** FAX: 11 4033671.

South African Library
See: **South Africa - South African Library** (15386)

South African Medical Research Council - Institute for Biomedical Communication
See: **Medical Research Council Information Group - Library** (10011)

★ 15390 ★
South American Explorers Club - Library (Sci-Engr)
P.O. Box 18327   Phone: (303)320-0388
Denver, CO 80218   Don Montague, Pres.
Founded: 1977. **Staff:** 6. **Subjects:** Scientific field exploration research, recreation, and travel in South America and Central America; environmental and ecological concerns; history of South America and Central America. **Holdings:** 2500 volumes. **Services:** Copying, library open to the public. **Remarks:** Library located at 1510 York St., Suite 214, Denver, CO, 80206.

South Australia - Botanic Gardens of Adelaide and State Herbarium - Library
See: **Botanic Gardens of Adelaide and State Herbarium - Library** (2023)

(South Australia) State Library of South Australia
See: **State Library of South Australia** (15693)

★ 15391 ★
South Australian Museum - Library (Hist)
N. Terrace   Phone: 8 2238899
Adelaide, SA 5000, Australia   Marianne Anthony, Libn.
Founded: 1856. **Staff:** 2 **Subjects:** Natural history, anthropology, archeology, zoology, mineralogy, paleontology. **Holdings:** 11,000 books; 32,000 bound periodical volumes; slides; prints; photographs; maps. **Subscriptions:** 900 journals and other serials. **Services:** Interlibrary loan; copying; library open to the public for reference use only. **Remarks:** FAX: 8 2321714.

South Baltimore General Hospital
See: **Harbor Hospital Center - Medical Library** (6899)

★ 15392 ★
South Bend Art Center - Library (Art)
120 S. St. Joseph St.
South Bend, IN 46601   Phone: (219)284-9102
Founded: 1947. **Subjects:** Visual arts. **Special Collections:** Collection of Carlotta Murray Banta (306 volumes). **Holdings:** 13,000 volumes; 1700 catalogs. **Subscriptions:** 25 journals and other serials. **Services:** Library open to the public for reference use only.

★ 15393 ★
South Carolina Confederate Relic Room & Museum - Library (Hist)
World War Memorial Bldg.
920 Sumter St.
Columbia, SC 29201   Phone: (803)734-9813
Founded: 1896. **Staff:** 5. **Subjects:** South Carolina history, Southern Confederacy, Revolutionary history. **Special Collections:** Civil War era histories (225 volumes); War of the Rebellion (150 volumes). **Holdings:** 450 books; 50 bound periodical volumes; scrapbooks; diaries; Muster Rolls; 100 pamphlets; 50 newspapers. **Subscriptions:** 10 journals and other serials. **Services:** Research on request; library open to the public for reference use only.

★ 15394 ★
South Carolina Electric and Gas Company - Corporate Library (Energy, Bus-Fin)
Palmetto Center
1426 Main St.   Phone: (803)748-3942
Columbia, SC 29218   Patsy G. Moss, Coord., Res.Serv.
Founded: 1984. **Staff:** Prof 1. **Subjects:** Public utilities, business, engineering. **Holdings:** 2220 books; 150 unbound periodicals; Electric Power Research Institute reports. **Services:** Interlibrary loan; copying; library open to the public with restrictions. **Computerized Information Services:** DIALOG Information Services. **Remarks:** FAX: (803)748-3713.

★ 15395 ★
South Carolina Historical Society - Library (Hist)
Fireproof Bldg.
100 Meeting St.   Phone: (803)723-3225
Charleston, SC 29401   Dr. Mark V. Wetherington, Dir.
Founded: 1855. **Staff:** Prof 8; Other 3. **Subjects:** South Carolina history, architecture, literature, slavery, politics, economy, genealogy. **Holdings:** 30,000 books and bound periodical volumes; 9000 pamphlets; 2000 linear feet of manuscripts; microfiche; 2000 architectural drawings; 2000 photographs; ephemera. **Subscriptions:** 50 journals and other serials. **Services:** Copying; library open to the public on fee basis. **Publications:** South Carolina Historical Magazine, 4/year; Carologue, 4/year. **Staff:** Stephen Hoffius, Dir. of Pubns.; Anne Rosebruck, Libn.; Mary Giles, Asst.Dir., Coll.; Peter Wilherson, Archv.; Kathee Howard, Res.Cons.

★ 15396 ★
South Carolina Protection and Advocacy System for the Handicapped, Inc. - Library (Med)
3710 Landmark Dr., Suite 208   Phone: (803)782-0639
Columbia, SC 29204   Hazel Mengedoht
Subjects: Handicapped - issues, laws. **Holdings:** Figures not available.
Remarks: FAX: (803)790-1946.

★ 15397 ★
South Carolina School for the Deaf & Blind - Deaf Library (Educ)
Cedar Spring Sta.   Phone: (803)585-7711
Spartanburg, SC 29302   Deborah Wright, Libn.
Holdings: 9138 books; 136 bound periodical volumes; 1965 braille volumes; 1535 talking books; 52 audiocassettes; 27 phonograph records; 1027 captioned films; 1322 filmstrips; 284 videotapes; 13 computer software packages; 68 games and puzzles. **Services:** Library not open to the public.

★ 15398 ★
South Carolina State Attorney General's Office - Daniel R. McLeod Law Library (Law)
1000 Assembly St., Suite 701
Box 11549   Phone: (803)734-3769
Columbia, SC 29211   Susan Husman, Libn.
Founded: 1984. **Staff:** Prof 1; Other 1. **Subjects:** Law. **Special Collections:** South Carolina Attorney Generals' opinions (published and unpublished). **Holdings:** 17,000 books; 53 bound periodical volumes. **Subscriptions:** 15 journals and other serials. **Services:** Interlibrary loan; copying; library open to the public for reference use only. **Automated Operations:** Computerized cataloging and opinion index. **Computerized Information Services:** WESTLAW. **Publications:** Annual Report of the Attorney General of South Carolina. **Special Indexes:** Index of published and unpublished opinions, not available to the public. **Remarks:** FAX: (803)253-6283.

★ 15399 ★
South Carolina State College - South Carolina State College Historical Collection (Hist)
Miller F. Whittaker Library
300 College Ave.
Box 7491   Phone: (803)536-7045
Orangeburg, SC 29117-0001   Barbara Williams Jenkins, Ph.D.
Founded: 1913. **Staff:** 19. **Subjects:** College history, 1897 to present. **Special Collections:** Black Collection (by and about Blacks); South Carolina State College Historical Collection. **Holdings:** College records; presidential papers; photographs; blueprints; college publications; yearbooks; newspapers; oral history recordings; documents concerning the development of South Carolina State College. **Subscriptions:** 1274 journals and other serials; 47 newspapers. **Services:** Copying; collection open to the public with restrictions. **Computerized Information Services:** DIALOG Information Services, BRS Information Technologies, VU/TEXT Information Services, ALANET, OCLC. **Networks/Consortia:** Member of SOLINET. **Remarks:** FAX: (803)536-8902.

★ 15400 ★
South Carolina (State) Commission on Alcohol and Drug Abuse - THE DRUGSTORE Information Clearinghouse (Med)
3700 Forest Dr., Suite 204   Phone: (803)734-9559
Columbia, SC 29204   Elizabeth G. Peters, Adm.
Founded: 1969. **Staff:** Prof 1; Other 2. **Subjects:** Alcohol and drug abuse - education, prevention, intervention, treatment. **Special Collections:** South Carolina (State) Commission on Alcohol and Drug Abuse publications (complete set). **Holdings:** 1500 books; 150 bound periodical volumes; 16 VF drawers; 50 pamphlet titles; 220 16mm films and videocassettes. **Subscriptions:** 44 journals and other serials. **Services:** Interlibrary loan; copying; clearinghouse open to the public with restrictions. **Computerized Information Services:** SCHIN, RADAR. **Networks/Consortia:** Member of Columbia Area Medical Librarians' Association (CAMLA), Regional Alcohol and Drug Abuse Resource Network (RADAR). **Publications:** News in a Capsule (newsletter). **Special Catalogs:** AV catalog (book). **Remarks:** Toll-free telephone number(s): (800)942-DIAL (Drug Information Access Line; for South Carolina residents only). FAX: (803)734-9663.

★ 15401 ★
South Carolina (State) Commission on Higher Education - Library (Educ)
1333 Main St., Suite 300   Phone: (803)253-6260
Columbia, SC 29201   Ann Klingenhagen, Libn.
Founded: 1968. **Staff:** Prof 1. **Subjects:** Higher education, general education. **Holdings:** 1500 books; 4000 monographs and reports. **Subscriptions:** 35 journals and other serials. **Services:** Copying; library open to the public at librarian's discretion. **Publications:** Higher Education Forum, quarterly; reports, irregular. **Remarks:** FAX: (803)253-6267.

★ 15402 ★
South Carolina (State) Department of Archives & History - Archives Search Room (Hist)
Capitol Sta., Box 11669   Phone: (803)734-8577
Columbia, SC 29211   George L. Vogt, Dir.
Founded: 1905. **Staff:** 120. **Subjects:** History of South Carolina - political, constitutional, legal, economic, social, religious. **Special Collections:** Noncurrent public records of South Carolina, including: land records of the colony and state; Revolutionary War accounts; confederate service records; executive, legislative, and judicial records of the colony and state; probate records of the colony; county records (23,000 cubic feet of records; 15,000 reels of microfilm). **Holdings:** 2000 books; 250 bound periodical volumes. **Subscriptions:** 200 journals and other serials. **Services:** Copying; search room open to the public for reference use only. **Publications:** Colonial Records of South Carolina, 16 volumes; State Records of South Carolina, 10 volumes; Biographical Directory of the South Carolina House of Representatives; South Carolina Archives Microcopies, 15 series; New South Carolina State Gazette (newsletter), 3/year; Guide to Local Records in the South Carolina Archives; historical booklets; curriculum resource materials; historical and technical pamphlets and brochures; On the Record (newsletter), quarterly; News & Notes (newsletter), quarterly. **Special Catalogs:** Catalog of reference library (card). **Special Indexes:** Published Summary Guide to Archives; consolidated computer output microfilm index to documents; bound volume indexes to land plats and grants, marriage settlements and other records; map catalog (card); Revolutionary and Confederate War service records (card). **Remarks:** Library is located at 1430 Senate St., Columbia, SC 29201. **Staff:** Alexia J. Helsley, Dir., Pub.Prog.

★ 15403 ★
South Carolina (State) Department of Health & Environmental Control - Library (Med)
2600 Bull St.   Phone: (803)737-3945
Columbia, SC 29201   Jane R. Olsgaard, Dir.
Founded: 1965. **Staff:** Prof 1; Other 7. **Subjects:** Public health, medicine, nursing, epidemiology, environmental sciences, nutrition, toxicology, health education. **Holdings:** 3000 books; 3000 bound periodical volumes; 1500 films; 500 pamphlet and poster titles. **Subscriptions:** 250 journals and other serials. **Services:** Interlibrary loan; copying; SDI; library open to the public with restrictions. **Automated Operations:** Computerized cataloging. **Computerized Information Services:** DIALOG Information Services, MEDLARS, OCLC, SCHIN, BRS Information Technologies, NLM; EPAMAIL, DOCLINE, Public Health Network (electronic mail services). **Networks/Consortia:** Member of Columbia Area Medical Librarians' Association (CAMLA), SOLINET. **Remarks:** FAX: (803)737-3946.

★ 15404 ★
South Carolina (State) Department of Mental Health - Crafts-Farrow State Hospital - Library (Med)
7901 Farrow Rd.   Phone: (803)935-7721
Columbia, SC 29203   Elizabeth H. Bonniwell, Libn.
Staff: Prof 1; Other 2. **Subjects:** Geriatrics, psychiatry, religion, nursing homes. **Special Collections:** Geriatrics collection (207 volumes). **Holdings:** 2955 books; 18 bound periodical volumes; 4 VF drawers. **Subscriptions:** 26 journals; 34 periodicals; 16 newspapers. **Services:** Interlibrary loan; copying; library open to state employees. **Automated Operations:** Computerized cataloging, acquisitions, and circulation. **Networks/Consortia:** Member of Columbia Area Medical Librarians' Association (CAMLA). **Publications:** Changing Strides (newsletter), weekly - for internal distribution only.

★ 15405 ★
South Carolina (State) Department of Mental Health - Earle E. Morris, Jr. Alcohol & Drug Addiction Treatment Center - Library (Med)
610 Faison Dr.   Phone: (803)935-7791
Columbia, SC 29203   Alice Jonas, Libn.
Founded: 1975. **Staff:** Prof 1. **Subjects:** Alcoholism, drug addiction, group and family therapy. **Holdings:** 2000 books. **Subscriptions:** 31 journals and other serials. **Services:** Interlibrary loan; library not open to the public. **Networks/Consortia:** Member of Columbia Area Medical Librarians' Association (CAMLA), South Carolina Library Network.

South Carolina (State) Department of Mental Health - Greenville Mental Health Center
See: **Greenville Mental Health Center** (6745)

★15406★
South Carolina (State) Department of Mental Retardation - Midlands Center Library (Educ, Med)
8301 Farrow Rd.
Columbia, SC 29203   Phone: (803)935-7500
Staff: Prof 1; Other 1. **Subjects:** Mental retardation, special education. **Holdings:** 2500 books; 33 video cassettes; 10 16mm films; 295 slides. **Subscriptions:** 28 journals and other serials. **Services:** Interlibrary loan; copying; library open to state employees and local school districts.

★15407★
South Carolina (State) Department of Mental Retardation - Whitten Center Library & Media Resource Services (Educ, Med)
Columbia Hwy.
Box 239   Phone: (803)833-2736
Clinton, SC 29325   Mr. Hsiu Yun Keng, Dir.
Founded: 1965. **Staff:** Prof 1; Other 1. **Subjects:** Mental retardation, services for mentally retarded, special education, special media for mentally retarded, psychology. **Special Collections:** Mental retardation; low reading level/high interest books for mentally retarded; special education. **Holdings:** 6500 books; 170 bound periodical volumes; 13,500 AV programs; 650 educational toys, games, fish, birds, and other animals. **Subscriptions:** 14 journals and other serials. **Services:** Services open on a limited schedule to clients and employees of state institutions for the mentally retarded. **Publications:** Bibliography of Professional Materials on Mental Retardation, 2nd edition and annual supplements. **Special Catalogs:** Simplified card catalog for mentally retarded people; Audiovisual Materials in Teaching Mentally Retarded; Subject Headings and Classification Index in Mental Retardation; videotapes in teaching the mentally retarded. **Remarks:** Whitten Center Library & Media Resource Services offers specialized programs for the handicapped, including multimedia sensory stimulation therapeutic program for severely and profoundly retarded persons (25 hours weekly), pet tharapy and media therapy for retarded clients, 5 sets of closed circuit television systems for educating mentally handicapped children, electronic toys with adapted switches for mentally and physically disabled persons, and 7 computers.

★15408★
South Carolina (State) Legislative Council of the General Assembly - Library (Law)
Box 11489   Phone: (803)734-2145
Columbia, SC 29211   Videau K. Simons, Res.Libn.
Founded: 1971. **Staff:** Prof 1. **Subjects:** Legislation. **Holdings:** 20,000 books; 38 bound periodical volumes. **Subscriptions:** 20 journals and other serials; 5 newspapers. **Services:** Interlibrary loan; copying; library open to the public with restrictions. **Remarks:** Library located at State House, 1100 Gervais St., Columbia, SC 29201. **Remarks:** FAX: (803)734-2425.

★15409★
South Carolina State Library (Info Sci)
1500 Senate St.
Box 11469   Phone: (803)734-8666
Columbia, SC 29211   James B. Johnson, Jr., Dir.
Founded: 1943. **Staff:** Prof 21; Other 30. **Subjects:** Reference, government, business, political science, education, history, fine arts, South Caroliniana. **Special Collections:** Foundation Center Regional Depository. **Holdings:** 227,176 books; 2177 bound periodical volumes; 42,806 South Carolina state documents; 15,722 reels of microfilm of periodicals; 413,511 ERIC microfiche; 231,086 government documents; 951 videotapes; 2349 films; 9071 large print books. **Subscriptions:** 2608 journals and other serials; 27 newspapers. **Services:** Interlibrary loan; copying; library open to the public. **Automated Operations:** Computerized cataloging, circulation, periodicals list, and ILL. **Computerized Information Services:** DIALOG Information Services, OCLC, BRS Information Technologies, VU/TEXT Information Services; ALANET (electronic mail service). Performs searches on fee basis. Contact Person:: Mary Bull, Ref.Libn. **Networks/Consortia:** Member of SOLINET. **Publications:** News for South Carolina Libraries, monthly - to public, school, and academic libraries and trustees; New Resources - to state government agencies and libraries; News about library services for the blind and physically handicapped - to handicapped readers; News about adult services, quarterly - to public; News about youth services, quarterly - to

libraries; South Carolina Foundation Directory, irregular - for sale. **Remarks:** FAX: (803)734-8676. Electronic mail address(es): ALA 0276 (ALANET). **Staff:** John H. Landrum, Dp.Dir.; Margie E. Herron, Dir., Lib.Dev.; Frances Case, Dir., Dept. of Blind & Phys.Hndcp.; Marjorie Mazur, Dir., Tech.Serv.; Mark Pumphrey, Inst.Cons.; Mary Bostick, Doc.Libn.; Wesley Sparks, Cat.Libn.; JoAnn Olson, Pub.Lib.Cons.; Alice I. Nolte, Pub.Lib.Cons.; Pat Gilleland, Pub.Lib.Cons.; Anne M. Schneider, Dir., Rd.Serv.; Jane McGregor, Ch.Serv.Cons.; Ron Anderson, Adult Serv.Cons.; Guynell Williams, Asst.Dir.Hndcp.Serv.; Mary Morgan, ILL Libn.; Edna Horning, Asst.Ref.Libn.; Lea Walsh, Coord., Network Serv.; Deborah Hotchkiss, Asst.Dir.Rd.Serv.; Mary Bull, Ref.Libn.; Brenda Boyd, Circ.Libn.; Libby Law, Dir.Adm.Serv.

★15410★
South Carolina State Supreme Court - Library (Law)
Box 11330   Phone: (803)734-1080
Columbia, SC 29211   Janet F. Meyer, Libn.
Staff: Prof 1; Other 1. **Subjects:** Law. **Holdings:** 51,440 books; 1005 bound periodical volumes. **Subscriptions:** 75 journals and other serials. **Services:** Copying; library open to the public. **Computerized Information Services:** WESTLAW.

★15411★
South Carolina (State) Wildlife and Marine Resources Division - Library (Biol Sci)
Box 12559   Phone: (803)762-5026
Charleston, SC 29412   Helen Ivy, Libn.
Founded: 1972. **Staff:** Prof 1; Other 1. **Subjects:** Marine biology and ecology; fisheries; aquaculture; marine resources management. **Holdings:** 18,000 books; 7660 bound periodical volumes; 25,640 reprints; 48 reels of microfilm; 800 microfiche. **Subscriptions:** 403 journals and other serials. **Services:** Interlibrary loan; copying; library open to the public with restrictions. **Automated Operations:** Computerized public access catalog and cataloging. **Remarks:** FAX: (803)762-5001.

★15412★
South Chicago Community Hospital - Department of Library Services (Med)
2320 E. 93rd St.   Phone: (312)978-2000
Chicago, IL 60617   Ronald Rayman, Dir.
Staff: Prof 1; Other 1. **Subjects:** Clinical medicine, nursing, chemical dependency. **Holdings:** 3500 books; 3000 bound periodical volumes. **Subscriptions:** 250 journals and other serials. **Services:** Interlibrary loan; copying. **Automated Operations:** Computerized cataloging and serials. **Computerized Information Services:** DIALOG Information Services, BRS Information Technologies, WILSONLINE, NLM. Performs searches on fee basis. **Networks/Consortia:** Member of Chicago and South Consortium, National Network of Libraries of Medicine - Greater Midwest Region. **Remarks:** FAX: (312)978-7211.

★15413★
South China Academy/College of Tropical Crops - Library (Agri)
Baodaoxincun
Danxian
Hainan Island, Guangdong
Province, People's Republic of   Phone: 73214
China   Zhentang Yang, Libn.
Founded: 1958. **Staff:** 39. **Subjects:** Tropical crops, tropical economic crops, horticulture of tropical crops, protection of tropical crops, food processing, rubber processing, agricultural economics management, tropical crop mechanization, allied subjects. **Special Collections:** Planting and processing of rubber and other tropical crops. **Holdings:** 188,447 volumes. **Subscriptions:** 821 journals and other serials. **Services:** Interlibrary loan; library not open to the public. **Publications:** Chinese Journal of Tropical Crops (1980). **Remarks:** Telex: 7108.

★15414★
South Congregational Church - Ethel L. Austin Library (Rel-Phil)
242 Salmon Brook St.
Box 779   Phone: (203)653-7289
Granby, CT 06035   R. F. York, Libn.
Staff: 1. **Subjects:** Christian living, devotions, Bible study, biography. **Holdings:** 2000 books. **Services:** Library open to the congregation.

★ 15415 ★
South County Law Library (Law)
200 W. Atlantic Ave.   Phone: (407)274-1440
Delray Beach, FL 33444   Linda Sims, Law Lib.Mgr.
Founded: 1990. **Staff:** 1. **Subjects:** Law. **Holdings:** 3500 volumes.
Subscriptions: 4 newspapers. **Services:** Library open to the public for
reference use only. **Computerized Information Services:** WESTLAW. **Staff:**
Pat Judge-Herris.

★ 15416 ★
South Dakota Human Services Center - Medical Library (Med)
Box 76   Phone: (605)668-3165
Yankton, SD 57078   Mary Lou Kostel, Libn.
Staff: 1. **Subjects:** Psychiatry, psychology, psychiatric nursing, gerontology,
social work, medicine. **Special Collections:** Hospital history. **Holdings:** 3088
books; 158 bound periodical volumes; 541 audiotapes; VF drawers of
pamphlets; manuscripts; historical clippings. **Subscriptions:** 61 journals and
other serials. **Services:** Interlibrary loan; copying; library open to staff,
students, and professionals. **Automated Operations:** Computerized serials.
Computerized Information Services: DOCLINE (electronic mail service).
Remarks: FAX: (605)665-6449.

★ 15417 ★
South Dakota School of Mines and Technology - Devereaux Library
    (Sci-Engr)
501 E. St. Joseph St.   Phone: (605)394-2418
Rapid City, SD 57701-3995   Dr. Bernice C. McKibben, Lib.Dir.
Founded: 1886. **Staff:** Prof 4; Other 10. **Subjects:** Engineering, computer
science, chemistry, chemical engineering, physics, mathematics, mining
geology. **Special Collections:** Black Hills and Western South Dakota
History; Mining Histories of South Dakota and Adjacent Areas. **Holdings:**
93,000 volumes; 20,495 bound periodical volumes; 1643 theses and
dissertations; 11,077 maps; 1116 volumes of South Dakota documents; 932
VF items; 368 linear feet of archival items; 194,614 microfiche.
Subscriptions: 946 journals and other serials; 13 newspapers. **Services:** ILL
copying; library open to the public. **Automated Operations:** Computerized
public access catalog, cataloging, circulation, ILL. **Computerized
Information Services:** DIALOG Information Services, FAPRS (Federal
Assistance Programs Retrieval System), ORBIT Search Service, CAS
(Chemical Abstracts Service), WILSONLINE, EPIC; CD-ROMs;
EasyLink (electronic mail service). Performs searches on fee basis. Contact
Person: Patty Andersen, Hd., Info./Pub.Serv., 394-1255. **Networks/
Consortia:** Member of Bibliographical Center for Research, Rocky
Mountain Region, Inc. (BCR), MINITEX Library Information Network,
South Dakota Library Network (SDLN). **Publications:** Acquisitions List;
Guide Series. **Special Catalogs:** Thesis/Dissertation listing; periodical
holdings (book); Catalog of Reference Collection Materials; Catalog of
Black Hills Mines (in preparation). **Special Indexes:** Indexes to State
Geological Materials. **Remarks:** FAX: (605)394-1256. Electronic mail
address(es): 62860379 (EasyLink). **Staff:** Bruce Mehlhaff, Archv./Ref.;
Patty Anderson, Hd.Pub.Info.Serv.; Margaret Sandine, Cat.Libn.; Donna
Neal, ILL Supv.; Jo Ann Meyer, Circ.Supv.; Cindy Davies, Hd., Tech.Serv./
Sys.; Karolyn Karge, Govt.Docs.; Vicki Massingale, Per.Supv.; Janet
Taylor, Adm.Asst.

South Dakota State Archives
See: South Dakota State Historical Society - Office of History (15421)

South Dakota (State) Department of Education and Cultural Affairs -
    W.H. Over State Museum
See: W.H. Over State Museum (12630)

★ 15418 ★
South Dakota (State) Department of Game, Fish and Parks - Division of
    Wildlife - South Dakota Natural Heritage Program - Library (Energy)
523 E Capitol
Pierre, SD 57501   Phone: (605)773-4345
Staff: 3. **Subjects:** South Dakota - natural communities, rare species,
threatened species, endangered species. **Holdings:** 500 bound volumes; 2000
articles; maps; vertical files. **Subscriptions:** 5 journals and other serials.
Services: Library open to the public with written requests for information.
Computerized Information Services: South Dakota Natural Heritage
Database (internal database). Performs searches on fee basis. **Remarks:**
FAX: (605)773-6245.

★ 15419 ★
South Dakota (State) Department of Transportation - Research Library
    (Trans)
700 Broadway Ave., E.   Phone: (605)773-3292
Pierre, SD 57501-2586   Virginia Ripley, Sr.Sec.
Staff: Prof 1; Other 1. **Subjects:** Transportation, highway engineering.
Special Collections: South Dakota Research Reports. **Holdings:** 17,000
volumes. **Services:** Interlibrary loan; copying; library open to the public.
Remarks: FAX: (605)773-3921.

★ 15420 ★
South Dakota (State) Developmental Center, Redfield - Media Center
    (Med)
Box 410   Phone: (605)472-2400
Redfield, SD 57469-0410   Mr. Lynn Loveland, Libn.
Founded: 1970. **Staff:** Prof 1. **Subjects:** Mental retardation, developmentally
disabled, special education. **Holdings:** 999 books; 848 filmstrips; 28 films;
911 phonograph records; 274 cassettes; 44 compact disks; 300 games and
manipulative toys; 119 videotapes; 40 computer programs; 25 microfiche;
194 AV materials. **Services:** Interlibrary loan; center open to Redfield and
surrounding area residents. **Networks/Consortia:** Member of South Dakota
Library Network (SDLN). **Special Indexes:** Professional holdings
purchased by other areas of this institution (online, card). **Remarks:** FAX:
(605)472-0922.

★ 15421 ★
South Dakota State Historical Society - Office of History - South
    Dakota State Archives (Hist)
900 Governors Dr.   Phone: (605)773-3458
Pierre, SD 57501   Linda M. Sommer, State Archv.
Founded: 1986. **Staff:** Prof 4; Other 4. **Subjects:** South Dakota history,
culture and government; Great Plains; government administration.
Holdings: 26,000 volumes; 6000 cubic feet of records; 70 cubic feet of
photographs; 12,000 maps. **Subscriptions:** 174 journals and other serials; 140
newspapers. **Services:** Interlibrary loan; copying; office open to the public.
Automated Operations: Computerized public access catalog, cataloging, and
serials. **Computerized Information Services:** OCLC. **Networks/Consortia:**
Member of South Dakota Library Network (SDLN). **Remarks:** FAX:
(605)773-6041. **Staff:** Ann Jenks, Libn.

★ 15422 ★
South Dakota State Library (Info Sci)
800 Governors Dr.   Phone: (605)773-3131
Pierre, SD 57501-2294   Jane Kolbe, State Libn.
Founded: 1913. **Staff:** Prof 10; Other 34. **Subjects:** General collection.
Special Collections: South Dakota; large print books; South Dakota
documents. **Holdings:** 159,185 volumes; 192,961 documents; 6147 pictures;
581 maps; 11,300 films, filmstrips, videotapes, and other media; 34,000
talking book titles; 456,941 microfiche; 8243 reels of microfilm.
Subscriptions: 1236 journals and other serials; 21 newspapers. **Services:**
Interlibrary loan; copying; library open to the public. **Automated
Operations:** Computerized public access catalog, cataloging, acquisitions,
serials, circulation, ILL; READS system for the handicapped.
Computerized Information Services: DIALOG Information Services, PFDS
Online, BRS Information Technologies, ALANET, OCLC, RLIN, Western
Library Network (WLN). **Networks/Consortia:** Member of CLASS,
MINITEX Library Information Network, Western Council of State
Libraries, South Dakota Library Network (SDLN). **Publications:** Large
print bibliography; South Dakota State Government Publications. **Special
Catalogs:** Film/video catalog. **Remarks:** FAX: (605)773-4950. **Staff:**
Dorothy Liegl, Dp. State Libn./Film Serv.Libn.; Colleen Kirby,
Tech.Serv.Libn.; Michele Reid, Dir.Pub.Serv.; Ann Eichinger, Ref.Libn.;
Bellen Jacobsen, ILL/Circ.Asst.; Margaret England, Doc.Libn.; Daniel
Boyd, Dir., Hndcp.Serv.; Beth Marie Quanbeck, Dir., Lib.Dev.; Donna
Gilliland, Sch.Lib.Cons.; Jerome Wagner, Inst.Lib.Cons.

★ 15423 ★
South Dakota State Supreme Court - Library (Law)
State Capitol
500 E. Capitol Ave.
Pierre, SD 57501   Phone: (605)773-4898
Staff: Prof 1; Other 1. **Subjects:** Law. **Holdings:** 27,802 volumes.
Subscriptions: 60 journals and other serials. **Services:** Library open to the
public.

★ 15424 ★
South Dakota State University - Hilton M. Briggs Library (Biol Sci, Agri, Sci-Engr, Med)
Box 2115
Brookings, SD 57007
Phone: (605)688-5106
Dr. Leon Raney, Dean of Lib.
Founded: 1886. **Staff:** Prof 12; Other 15. **Subjects:** Agriculture; pharmacy; engineering - civil, mechanical, electrical; chemistry; entomology; plant pathology; biological sciences; nursing; home economics. **Special Collections:** South Dakota history. **Holdings:** 435,617 books and bound periodical volumes; documents; 341,500 microforms. **Subscriptions:** 3577 journals and other serials; 87 newspapers. **Services:** Interlibrary loan; library open to the public. **Automated Operations:** Computerized public access catalog, cataloging, acquisitions, circulation, and ILL. **Computerized Information Services:** OCLC, DIALOG Information Services, BRS Information Technologies. Performs searches on fee basis. Contact Person: Clark Hallman, Hd., Ref.Dept. **Networks/Consortia:** Member of South Dakota Library Network (SDLN). **Publications:** South Dakota Union List of Serials, 1979. **Special Indexes:** Sioux Falls Argus Leader Index, 1979 to present; Index to SDSU Agricultural Experiment Station and Extension Service Publications, 1986 (tape; book); South Dakota Farm and Home Research, KWIC Index, 1976 (tape; book). **Remarks:** FAX: (605)688-6133. **Staff:** B.J. Kim, Hd., Cat.Dept.; Mark Bronson, Hd., Circ.Dept.; Philip Brown, Hd., Doc.; Della Herring, Hd., Acq.Dept.; Carlene Aro, Act.Hd., Ser.Dept.

★ 15425 ★
South Dakota State University - West River Agricultural Research and Extension Center - Library (Agri)
801 San Francisco St.
Rapid City, SD 57701
Phone: (605)394-2236
F.R. Gartner, Dir.
Founded: 1969. **Staff:** Range, animal, plant, crop, and soil sciences; economics; farm and ranch management; 4-H. **Holdings:** 2000 volumes. **Services:** Library open to the public.

★ 15426 ★
South Florida Regional Planning Council - Library (Plan)
3440 Hollywood Blvd., Suite 140
Hollywood, FL 33021
Phone: (305)961-2999
K. Chang, Info.Spec.
Founded: 1971. **Staff:** Prof 1. **Subjects:** Planning - regional, transportation, housing, land use, coastal zone, energy. **Holdings:** 8000 books. **Subscriptions:** 150 journals and other serials. **Services:** Interlibrary loan; copying; library open to the public for reference use only. **Automated Operations:** Computerized cataloging. **Remarks:** FAX: (305)961-0322.

★ 15427 ★
South Florida State Hospital - Medical Library (Med)
1000 S.W. 84th Ave.
Hollywood, FL 33025
Phone: (305)983-4321
Mabel E. Randall, Med.Libn.
Staff: 1. **Subjects:** Psychiatry, neurology, psychology, nursing, social work. **Holdings:** 2650 books; 230 bound periodical volumes; cassettes; 3 masters' theses; tape cassettes. **Subscriptions:** 63 journals and other serials. **Services:** Interlibrary loan; copying; library open to the public with restrictions.

South Georgia Conference Historical Society
See: United Methodist Church - South Georgia Conference - Commission on Archives and History - Arthur J. Moore Methodist Museum - Library (16739)

★ 15428 ★
South Georgia Medical Center - Medical Library (Med)
Box 1727
Valdosta, GA 31603-1727
Phone: (912)333-1160
Susan T. Statom, Med.Libn.
Founded: 1979. **Staff:** Prof 1. **Subjects:** Medicine, nursing, and allied health sciences. **Holdings:** 200 books; 300 bound periodical volumes. **Subscriptions:** 70 journals and other serials. **Services:** Interlibrary loan; copying; SDI; current awareness; library open to the public with restrictions. **Computerized Information Services:** NLM; GaIN (electronic mail service). **Networks/Consortia:** Member of South Georgia Associated Libraries (SGAL), Southwest Georgia Health Sciences Library Consortium, Georgia Interactive Network for Medical Information (GaIN). **Remarks:** FAX: (912)333-1553. Electronic mail address(es): Statom (GaIN).

South Highlands Hospital - Medical Library.
See: HealthSouth Medical Hospital (7083)

★ 15429 ★
South Hills Health System - Behan Health Science Library (Med)
Coal Valley Rd.
Box 18119
Pittsburgh, PA 15236
Phone: (412)469-5786
Barbara Palso, Libn.
Founded: 1975. **Staff:** Prof 1. **Subjects:** Medicine, nursing, and allied health sciences. **Holdings:** 300 books. **Subscriptions:** 117 journals and other serials. **Services:** Interlibrary loan; library not open to the public. **Computerized Information Services:** MEDLARS. **Networks/Consortia:** Member of National Network of Libraries of Medicine - Middle Atlantic Region, Southeast Pittsburgh Library Consortium, BHSL. **Remarks:** FAX: (412)469-5468.

★ 15430 ★
South Jersey Hospital System - Health Sciences Library (Med)
333 Irving Ave.
Bridgeton, NJ 08302-2100
Phone: (609)451-6600
Sue Dolbow, Med.Libn.
Founded: 1975. **Staff:** Prof 1. **Subjects:** Medicine, nursing. **Holdings:** 1000 books; AV catalogs; 260 AV programs; 8 VF drawers of articles and pamphlets. **Subscriptions:** 65 journals and other serials. **Services:** Interlibrary loan; copying; library open to the public with restrictions. **Networks/Consortia:** Member of Southwest New Jersey Consortium for Health Information Services, BHSL, South Jersey Regional Library Cooperative. **Remarks:** FAX: (609)451-7903.

South Jersey Regional Film Library
See: Camden County Library - Regional Film and Video Service - Library (2609)

★ 15431 ★
South Mountain Laboratories, Inc. - Library (Med)
380 Lackawanna Pl.
South Orange, NJ 07079
Phone: (201)762-0045
David Reifsnyder, Dir.
Staff: 30. **Subjects:** Biology, chemistry, medicine, pharmaceutics. **Holdings:** 1000 books; 500 bound periodical volumes. **Subscriptions:** 14 journals and other serials. **Services:** Library not open to the public. **Remarks:** FAX: (201)762-4685.

★ 15432 ★
South Nassau Communities Hospital - Jules Redish Memorial Medical Library (Med)
Oceanside Rd.
Oceanside, NY 11572
Phone: (516)763-2030
Claire Strelzoff, Med.Libn.
Subjects: Medicine, surgery, nursing. **Holdings:** 1000 books; 6000 bound periodical volumes. **Subscriptions:** 111 journals and other serials. **Services:** Interlibrary loan; copying.

★ 15433 ★
South Pacific Commission - Library (Soc Sci)
Boite Postale D5
Noumea Cedex, New Caledonia
Phone: 262000
Rosemary Cassidy, Libn.
Subjects: South Pacific nations - rural development, community development, socio-economic statistics, demography, health, marine resources, youth, women. **Holdings:** 100,000 volumes. **Subscriptions:** 1500 journals and other serials; 20 newspapers. **Services:** Interlibrary loan; copying; SDI; library open to the public by appointment. **Automated Operations:** CDS-ISIS, Pro-Cite. **Computerized Information Services:** DIALOG Information Services, Australian Bibliographic Network (ABN). **Publications:** New additions to library. **Remarks:** FAX: 263818. Telex: 3139 NM SOPACOM. **Staff:** Ellen Watters, Asst.Libn.

★ 15434 ★
South Shore Natural Science Center - Vinal Library (Biol Sci)
Jacob's Ln.
P.O. Box 429
Norwell, MA 02061
Phone: (617)659-2559
Doris Holmes, Libn.
Founded: 1976. **Staff:** 1. **Subjects:** Natural history, conservation, cultural history, travel. **Special Collections:** William Gould Vinal Collection (209 natural history books); children's books (552). **Holdings:** 1716 books. **Subscriptions:** 4 journals and other serials. **Services:** Copying; library open to the public.

★15435★
South Street Seaport Museum - Library (Hist)
207 Front St.   Phone: (212)669-9438
New York, NY 10038   Gregory Leazer, Libn.
Founded: 1967. **Staff:** Prof 2. **Subjects:** Maritime history, technology, New York City. **Holdings:** 8500 books; 400 bound periodical volumes; 15,000 plans of ships and marine engines; 7 drawers of New York Harbor photographs and negatives; 38 drawers of archives; 21 drawers of shipping photographs and negatives. **Subscriptions:** 20 journals and other serials. **Services:** Copying; library open to the public. **Remarks:** FAX: (212)732-5168. **Staff:** Norman J. Brouwer, Hist. & Cur.

★15436★
South Suburban Genealogical & Historical Society - Library (Hist)
Box 96   Phone: (708)333-9474
South Holland, IL 60473   Alice DeBoer, Hd.Libn.
Founded: 1971. **Staff:** Prof 1; Other 10. **Subjects:** Genealogy, local history. **Special Collections:** Eddy Collection; Bishop Collection. **Holdings:** 6000 books; 450 bound periodical volumes; 150 reels of microfilm; federal census; land records; indexed wills; Bible records; obituaries; family work sheet files; local church records; local township records. **Subscriptions:** 110 journals and other serials. **Services:** Copying; library open to the public. **Publications:** Where the Trails Cross, quarterly; newsletter, monthly. **Special Indexes:** Family sheets of members, wills, Bibles, and obituary notices; surname indexes; cemetery readings and indexes.

★15437★
South Texas College of Law - Library (Law)
1303 San Jacinto   Phone: (713)659-8040
Houston, TX 77002   Ann Puckett, Dir., Law Lib.
Founded: 1923. **Staff:** Prof 9; Other 12. **Subjects:** Law. **Holdings:** 250,000 volumes. **Subscriptions:** 3500 journals and other serials; 15 newspapers. **Services:** Interlibrary loan; copying; library open to lawyers and law students; government documents section open to the public. **Automated Operations:** Computerized cataloging. **Computerized Information Services:** WESTLAW, DIALOG Information Services, VU/TEXT Information Services, LEXIS, InfoTrac; CompuServe Information Service (electronic mail service). Contact Person: Susan Spillman. **Remarks:** FAX: (713)659-2217. Electronic mail address(es): 70700, 1347 (CompuServe Information Service).

South Union Shaker Museum
See: **Shakertown at South Union** (15069)

South West Africa Scientific Society
See: **Namibia Scientific Society** (10961)

★15438★
Southam Business Communication, Inc. - Library (Publ)
1450 Don Mills Rd.   Phone: (416)445-6641
Don Mills, ON, Canada M3B 2X7   Maile Loweth, Libn.
Founded: 1957. **Staff:** Prof 1; Other 1. **Subjects:** Industrial advertising, business journalism, magazine design, business periodical publishing. **Special Collections:** Southam publications. **Holdings:** 1000 books; 300 bound periodical volumes. **Subscriptions:** 60 journals and other serials. **Services:** Copying; library open to library professionals. **Automated Operations:** Computerized cataloging, acquisitions, and serials. **Computerized Information Services:** DIALOG Information Services, Infomart Online, Info Globe, CAN/OLE; DIALMAIL, Envoy 100 (electronic mail services). **Remarks:** FAX: (416)442-2248. Telex: 06 966612. **Formerly:** Southam Business Information Communications Group, Inc.

Southam Publishing Co. - Edmonton Journal
See: **Edmonton Journal** (5245)

★15439★
Southeast Alabama Medical Center - Medical Library (Med)
Drawer 6987   Phone: (205)793-8102
Dothan, AL 36302   Pat McGee, Libn.
Founded: 1963. **Staff:** Prof 1. **Subjects:** General medicine, nursing, hospital administration. **Holdings:** 700 books; 2400 bound periodical volumes. **Subscriptions:** 112 journals and other serials. **Services:** Interlibrary loan; copying; library open to the public for reference use only. **Computerized Information Services:** MEDLARS. Performs searches on fee basis. **Remarks:** FAX: (205)793-8157.

Southeast Asia Rescue Foundation, Inc.
See: **S.E.A. Rescue Foundation - Reference Collection** (14186)

★15440★
Southeast Asian Fisheries Development Center - SEAFDEC Training Department - Library (Biol Sci)
Secretariat
Olympia Bldg.
956 Rama IV Rd.   Phone: 2 2352071
Bangkok 10500, Thailand   Pimprapai Pairoh, Libn.
Founded: 1968. **Staff:** 2.5. **Subjects:** Aquaculture, marine technology, postharvest technology, marine technology. **Holdings:** 2500 volumes; microfiche. **Subscriptions:** 25 journals and other serials; 8 newspapers. **Services:** Interlibrary loan; copying; library open to the public for reference use only. **Computerized Information Services:** CDS/ISIS. **Publications:** Regional Bibliography on Fisheries and Aquaculture in S.E.A. **Remarks:** SEAFDEC coordinates activities in Japan, Malaysia, the Philippines, Singapore, and Thailand. Alternate telephone number(s): 2 2331410. FAX: 2 2352070. Telex: 82156, 87032 COMSERVE TH.

★15441★
Southeast Asian Ministers of Education Organization - SEAMED Regional Center for Education in Science and Mathematics - Library (Educ)
11700 Glugor   Phone: 883266
Penang, Malaysia   Raja Alwibin Raja Omar, Act.Libn.
Staff: 9. **Subjects:** Science and mathematics education. **Special Collections:** RECSAM's Publications. **Holdings:** 25,800 volumes; 720 pamphlets. **Subscriptions:** 100 journals and other serials. **Services:** Interlibrary loan; library not open to the public. **Remarks:** Alternate telephone number(s): 883492. FAX: 872541.

★15442★
Southeast Human Services Center - Library (Med)
700 1st Ave., S.   Phone: (701)239-1620
Fargo, ND 58103   Diane Nordeng, Libn.
Staff: Prof 1. **Subjects:** Mental health, child growth and development, counseling. **Holdings:** 210 books. **Services:** Interlibrary loan; copying; library open to the public with restrictions. **Computerized Information Services:** MEDLINE; EasyLink, DOCLINE (electronic mail services). **Remarks:** FAX: (701)239-1639.

★15443★
Southeast Institute for Group and Family Therapy - Library (Soc Sci)
103 Edwards Ridge   Phone: (919)929-1171
Chapel Hill, NC 27514   Vann Joines, Pres.
Founded: 1969. **Staff:** 5. **Subjects:** Transactional analysis, psychotherapy, family therapy, race relations, Gestalt therapy. **Special Collections:** Audio- and videotapes on racism (not available to public). **Holdings:** 2500 volumes. **Services:** Library open only to institute students.

★15444★
Southeast Louisiana Hospital - Professional Library (Med)
Box 3850   Phone: (504)626-6326
Mandeville, LA 70448   Janet D. Landrum, Libn.
Staff: Prof 1. **Subjects:** Psychiatry, psychology, sociology, psychiatric nursing, human physiology, biochemistry, philosophy. **Holdings:** 3000 books; 2800 bound periodical volumes; 70 other cataloged items; 3 VF drawers of doctoral dissertations, pamphlets, state vital statistics reports; 10 newsletters; 216 cassette tapes. **Subscriptions:** 103 journals and other serials. **Services:** Interlibrary loan; copying; SDI; library open to the public with restrictions. **Publications:** Brochure of Professional Library Services - for internal distribution only.

Southeast Metropolitan Board of Cooperative Services - Professional Information Center
See: **Professional Educators Resource Center - Cunningham Center** (13407)

★ 15445 ★
Southeast Michigan Council of Governments - SEMCOG Library (Plan, Trans)
660 Plaza Dr., Suite 1900
Detroit, MI 48226
Phone: (313)961-4266
Pamela L. Lazar, Libn.
Founded: 1972. **Staff:** Prof 2. **Subjects:** Economic development, transportation, environmental issues, intergovernmental cooperation, regional planning, public safety. **Special Collections:** Detroit Metropolitan Area Regional Planning Commission (3 VF drawers of publications); Detroit Regional Transportation and Land Use Study (TALUS; 110 volumes). **Holdings:** 13,000 books and reports; 42 VF drawers of publications; 10 VF drawers of SEMCOG archives; 5 VF drawers of zoning ordinances; 4150 reports on microfiche. **Subscriptions:** 350 journals and other serials; 30 newspapers. **Services:** Interlibrary loan; copying; SDI; library open to the public for reference use only. **Automated Operations:** Computerized cataloging and circulation. **Computerized Information Services:** CDC. Performs searches free of charge for members. **Networks/ Consortia:** Member of Detroit Associated Libraries Region of Cooperation (DALROC). **Publications:** Bibliographic accession list, monthly; periodical master list, annual - both for internal distribution only. **Remarks:** FAX: (313)961-4869. **Staff:** Katherine Smith, Lib.Techn.

★ 15446 ★
Southeast Missouri Mental Health Center - Professional Library (Med)
1010 W. Columbia
Farmington, MO 63640
Phone: (314)756-6792
Anita Kellogg, Med.Libn.
Founded: 1965. **Staff:** 1. **Subjects:** Psychiatry, psychology, nursing. **Holdings:** 1200 books. **Subscriptions:** 38 journals and other serials. **Services:** Interlibrary loan; copying; center open to the public for reference use only. **Computerized Information Services:** ALANET (electronic mail service).

★ 15447 ★
Southeast Missourian - Library (Publ)
301 Broadway
P.O. Box 699
Cape Girardeau, MO 63701
Phone: (314)335-6611
Sharon K. Sanders, Libn.
Founded: 1965. **Staff:** Prof 1. **Subjects:** Newspaper reference topics. **Holdings:** 1000 books; 572 reels of microfilm; newspaper clippings (1965 to present); local historical notes (1790s-1890s); microfilm of Southeast Missourian newspaper (1904 to present); microfilm of Bulletin-Journal newspaper (1979-1986). **Subscriptions:** 2 journals and other serials. **Services:** Copying; library open for historical research at librarian's discretion. **Computerized Information Services:** Internal database.

Southeast Waste Exchange
See: **University of North Carolina at Charlotte** (19079)

★ 15448 ★
Southeastern Bible College - Gannett-Estes Library (Rel-Phil)
3001 Highway 280, S.
Birmingham, AL 35243
Phone: (205)969-0880
Edith Taff, Libn.
Staff: Prof 1. **Subjects:** Theology, Church education, missions, church music. **Holdings:** 30,000 books and bound periodical volumes. **Subscriptions:** 159 journals and other serials; 5 newspapers. **Services:** Interlibrary loan; copying; library open to the public with restrictions.

★ 15449 ★
Southeastern General Hospital, Inc. - Library (Med)
300 W. 27th St.
Box 1408
Lumberton, NC 28358
Phone: (919)671-5046
Ida Griffin, Libn.
Staff: Prof 1. **Subjects:** Medicine, surgery, nursing. **Holdings:** 600 books. **Subscriptions:** 120 journals and other serials. **Services:** Interlibrary loan; copying; SDI; library open to the public for reference use only. **Computerized Information Services:** MEDLINE; CD-ROMs (MEDLINE Professional, CINAHL). **Networks/Consortia:** Member of Cape Fear Health Sciences Information Consortium (CFHSIC), South Central Health Information Network of North Carolina (SCHIN of NC). **Remarks:** FAX: (919)671-5337; (919)671-5337.

Southeastern Lesbian Archives
See: **Atlanta Lesbian Feminist Alliance** (1249)

★ 15450 ★
Southeastern Louisiana University - L.A. Sims Memorial Library (Educ)
Drawer 896, Univ. Sta.
Hammond, LA 70402
Phone: (504)549-2234
F. Landon Greaves, Jr., Lib.Dir.
Founded: 1925. **Staff:** Prof 11; Other 17. **Subjects:** Education, mathematics, music, American history. **Special Collections:** Papers of Congressman James H. Morrison. **Holdings:** 277,000 books; 60,000 bound periodical volumes; 91,266 AV programs. **Subscriptions:** 1900 journals and other serials; 23 newspapers. **Services:** Interlibrary loan; copying; library open to the public for reference use only. **Computerized Information Services:** DIALOG Information Services, OCLC. **Networks/Consortia:** Member of SOLINET. **Remarks:** FAX: (504)549-3995.

Southeastern Massachusetts University
See: **University of Massachusetts at Dartmouth - Library Communications Center** (18833)

Southeastern Newspapers Corporation - Augusta Chronicle-Herald News
See: **Augusta Chronicle-Herald News** (1294)

★ 15451 ★
Southeastern Pennsylvania Transportation Authority - SEPTA Library (Trans)
841 Chestnut St., 11th Fl.
Philadelphia, PA 19107
Phone: (215)580-7387
Terence W. Cassidy, Libn.
Founded: 1966. **Staff:** Prof 1. **Subjects:** Public transportation, commuter railroads, urban planning. **Special Collections:** Urban Traffic and Transportation Board Collection (history and early planning of public transportation in Philadelphia; 300 items). **Holdings:** 7000 books and technical reports; 8 VF drawers of pamphlets; 4 VF drawers of annual reports of other agencies; 8 VF drawers of clippings. **Subscriptions:** 63 journals and other serials. **Services:** Interlibrary loan; copying; library open to the public by appointment. **Computerized Information Services:** DIALOG Information Services. **Publications:** Annual Reports of Agency, 1964 to present; News Highlight - biweekly; Acquisitions List, monthly - both for internal distribution only. **Remarks:** FAX: (215)580-7997.

Southeastern Railway Museum Library
See: **National Railway Historical Society - Atlanta Chapter** (11260)

★ 15452 ★
Southeastern Universities Research Association - Continuous Electron Beam Accelerator Facility Library (Sci-Engr)
12000 Jefferson Ave.
Newport News, VA 23606
Phone: (804)249-7525
Elois A. Morgan, Libn.
Staff: Prof 1; Other 1. **Subjects:** Physics, engineering, nuclear physics. **Special Collections:** Physics preprints. **Holdings:** 7200 books; 11,000 bound periodical volumes; 2900 government documents; 18,000 microfiche; 10,000 preprints. **Subscriptions:** 118 journals and other serials; 5 newspapers. **Services:** Interlibrary loan; copying; library open to the public. **Automated Operations:** Computerized public access catalog and cataloging. **Computerized Information Services:** Integrated Technical Information System (ITIS), SPIRES, DIALOG Information Services, STN International, OCLC; InterNet, BITNET, DECNet (electronic mail services). **Networks/Consortia:** Member of SOLINET. **Publications:** Serials in the CEBAF Library; CEBAF Library Bulletin; Library Handbook. **Remarks:** FAX: (804)249-7559. Electronic mail address(es): MORGAN@CEBAFVAX; MORGAN@cebaf.gov; BOSWELL@CEBAFVAX (BITNET).

★ 15453 ★
Southeastern University of the Health Sciences - Health Sciences Library (Med)
1750 N.E. 168th St.
North Miami Beach, FL 33162
Phone: (305)949-4000
Janice Guttlieb, Lib.Dir.
Founded: 1981. **Staff:** Prof 2; Other 10. **Subjects:** Clinical medicine, basic sciences, osteopathy, pharmacy, optometry. **Special Collections:** Osteopathic medicine, optometry, pharmacy. **Holdings:** 9000 books; 5453 bound periodical volumes; 118 state osteopathic journals and newsletters. **Subscriptions:** 555 journals and other serials. **Services:** Interlibrary loan; copying; library open to the public for reference use only. **Computerized Information Services:** BRS Information Technologies, NLM; DOCLINE (electronic mail service). **Networks/Consortia:** Member of Miami Health Sciences Library Consortium (MHSLC). **Remarks:** FAX: (305)949-4000 ext. 4404. **Staff:** Lewis Jorgenson, Assoc.Libn.

★ 15454 ★
Southeastern Wisconsin Regional Planning Commission - Library (Plan)
916 N. East Ave.
P.O. Box 1607   Phone: (414)547-6721
Waukesha, WI 53187-1607   Arno M. Klausmeier, Libn.
Founded: 1960. **Staff:** Prof 1. **Subjects:** Regional planning, land use, transportation, population, housing, sewerage, drainage and flood control, environmental quality, parks and open space. **Special Collections:** Publications of Transportation Research Board, Southeastern Wisconsin Regional Planning Commission, Urban Land Institute, American Society of Planning Officials, and American Society of Civil Engineers. **Holdings:** 8400 books; census data; weather maps; climatological data. **Subscriptions:** 150 journals and other serials. **Services:** Interlibrary loan; copying; library open to students and researchers only. **Computerized Information Services:** American Planning Association Planning Advisory Service. **Networks/Consortia:** Member of Library Council of Metropolitan Milwaukee, Inc. (LCOMM), Waukesha County Federated Library System. **Remarks:** FAX: (414)547-1103.

★ 15455 ★
Southern Alberta Art Gallery - Library (Art)
601 3rd Ave., S.   Phone: (403)327-8770
Lethbridge, AB, Canada T1J 0H4   Joan Stebbins, Dir./Cur.
Founded: 1976. **Staff:** Prof 5; Other 2. **Subjects:** Canadian and international art; fund-raising; not-for-profit management. **Special Collections:** Slide library documenting sixteen years of Southern Albert Art Gallery exhibitions. **Holdings:** 400 books; 50 unbound periodicals; 2600 small publications; 6000 artists' catalogs; 5000 slides; 50 videotapes of artist interviews; exhibition catalogs. **Subscriptions:** 13 journals and other serials. **Services:** Copying; library open to the public with restrictions. **Computerized Information Services:** Internal databases. **Publications:** Annual progress report. **Special Catalogs:** Exhibition catalogs, 10-15/year - for sale. **Remarks:** FAX: (403)328-3913. **Staff:** David Clearwater, Libn./Weekend Attendant.

★ 15456 ★
Southern Alberta Institute of Technology - Educational Resources - Library (Comp Sci, Sci-Engr)
1301 16th Ave., N.W.   Phone: (403)284-8616
Calgary, AB, Canada T2M 0L4   R.C. Thornborough, Hd., Educ.Rsrcs.
Founded: 1920. **Staff:** Prof 5; Other 21. **Subjects:** Electronics, computer technology, business, chemical technology, engineering technologies, automotives, cookery, medical science, communication arts, drafting. **Holdings:** 84,386 books; 194 bound periodical volumes; 1587 film titles; 4154 videotapes; 2012 audiotapes; 128,418 microfiche; 4639 reels of microfilm; 513 film loop and filmstrip titles; 507 data files and data files with text; 50 VF drawers of pamphlets; 6 videodiscs. **Subscriptions:** 1459 journals and newspapers. **Services:** Interlibrary loan; copying; center open to the public. **Automated Operations:** Computerized cataloging, acquisitions, serials, and public access catalog. **Computerized Information Services:** DIALOG Information Services, PFDS Online, CAN/OLE, Info Globe; CD-ROM (Applied Science & Technology Indes, Bowker's BIP Plus, Microsoft Bookshelf); Envoy 100 (electronic mail service). **Publications:** Periodicals List, annual; Pathfinders. **Remarks:** FAX: (403)284-8728; (403)284-8619. Electronic mail address(es): ILL.ACSA (Envoy 100). **Staff:** Thomas Skinner, Tech. & Sys.Serv.; Gwen Chrapko, Rsrc. Provision; Heather Green, Rsrc. Access; Joe Hill, Rsrc. Assistance; Dave Weber, Instr.Serv.

Southern Appalachian Archives
See: **Berea College - Hutchins Library - Special Collections** (1727)

★ 15457 ★
Southern Baptist Convention - Foreign Mission Board - Archives Center (Rel-Phil)
3806 Monument Ave.
Box 6767   Phone: (804)353-0151
Richmond, VA 23230   Edith M. Jeter, Archv./Anl.
Staff: Prof 1. **Subjects:** Missions, missionaries, Southern Baptist Convention. **Holdings:** Board minutes; minutes of missions; administrative correspondence; correspondence with missionaries in the field. **Services:** Copying; center open to the public with restrictions. **Computerized Information Services:** BASIS (internal database). **Remarks:** FAX: (804)358-0504.

★ 15458 ★
Southern Baptist Convention - Foreign Mission Board - Jenkins Research Library (Rel-Phil)
3806 Monument Ave.
Box 6767   Phone: (804)353-0151
Richmond, VA 23230   Kathryn K. Purks, Rsrc.Mgr.
Founded: 1960. **Staff:** Prof 4; Other 4. **Subjects:** Missions, mission history, management theory and practice, Baptists, history, anthropology, area studies, travel. **Holdings:** 12,000 books. **Subscriptions:** 700 journals and other serials; 6 newspapers. **Services:** Interlibrary loan; library open to the public by written request and appointment scheduled in advance. **Automated Operations:** Computerized cataloging and serials. **Computerized Information Services:** DIALOG Information Services, NEXIS, DataTimes; CD-ROM; EasyLink (electronic mail service). **Networks/Consortia:** Member of SOLINET. **Remarks:** FAX: (804)358-0504. Telex: 827 492 FRGN BOARD RCH. Electronic mail address(es): 62222020 (EasyLink). **Staff:** Judith F. Bernicchi, Tech.Serv.Libn.; Wayne Casey, Cat.; Nancy Michael, Ref.Libn.

★ 15459 ★
Southern Baptist Convention - Historical Commission - Southern Baptist Historical Library & Archives (Rel-Phil, Hist)
901 Commerce St., Suite 400
Nashville, TN 37203-3630   Phone: (615)244-0344
Founded: 1951. **Staff:** Prof 2; Other 1. **Subjects:** Baptist history. **Special Collections:** Archives for the Southern Baptist Convention. **Holdings:** 22,000 books; 3000 linear feet of archival material; 15,000 reels of microfilm; 3000 audio recordings; 500 films and videotapes; 7200 photographs; 4040 pamphlets. **Subscriptions:** 150 journals and other serials; 100 newspapers. **Services:** Copying; library open to the public. **Automated Operations:** Computerized cataloging. **Computerized Information Services:** OCLC. **Networks/Consortia:** Member of SOLINET. **Publications:** Baptist History and Heritage, quarterly - by subscription; Baptist Heritage Update, quarterly - to members. **Special Catalogs:** Microfilm catalog. **Remarks:** FAX: (615)242-2153. **Staff:** Pat Brown, Libn.; Bill Sumners, Archv.

Southern Baptist Convention - Sunday School Board - E.C. Dargan Research Library
See: **E.C. Dargan Research Library** (4604)

★ 15460 ★
Southern Baptist Hospital - Learning Resource Center (Med)
2700 Napoleon Ave.   Phone: (504)897-5911
New Orleans, LA 70115   Bart Reilly, Dir.
Staff: Prof 2. **Subjects:** Medicine, nursing, allied health sciences, pastoral care and counseling. **Special Collections:** Harriet L. Mather Archives. **Holdings:** 7113 books; 2785 bound periodical volumes; 714 AV programs. **Subscriptions:** 203 journals and other serials. **Services:** Interlibrary loan; center not open to the public. **Automated Operations:** Computerized public access catalog. **Computerized Information Services:** BRS Information Technologies, MEDLINE. **Publications:** Library Users' Handbook. **Remarks:** FAX: (504)897-5928. **Staff:** Marylynn Rooney, Libn.

★ 15461 ★
Southern Baptist Theological Seminary - Audiovisual Center (Aud-Vis)
2825 Lexington Rd.   Phone: (502)897-4508
Louisville, KY 40280   Andrew B. Rawls, AV Libn.
Staff: Prof 1; Other 6. **Subjects:** Sermons, religious education, theology, church history, Christian missions, pastoral counseling. **Holdings:** 1929 filmstrips; 17,097 audiotapes; 3306 videotapes; 433 16mm films; 74,433 slides; 1402 phonograph records. **Services:** Center open to the public for reference use only.

★ 15462 ★
Southern Baptist Theological Seminary - Church Music Library (Mus, Rel-Phil)
2825 Lexington Rd.   Phone: (502)897-4807
Louisville, KY 40280   Martha C. Powell, Church Music Libn.
Founded: 1944. **Staff:** Prof 1; Other 3. **Subjects:** Hymnody; music - history, education, instruments, choral, folk; musicians; voice; worship. **Special Collections:** Converse Hymnal Collection; Ingersoll Evangelistic Music Collection (3000 titles); Everett B. Helm Score Collection. **Holdings:** 20,450 books; 2173 bound periodical volumes; 9445 phonograph records; 6726 audiotapes; 2366 compact discs; 165,559 scores; 275 titles on microfilm. **Subscriptions:** 112 journals and other serials. **Services:** Interlibrary loan; copying; library open to the public. **Computerized Information Services:** OCLC. **Networks/Consortia:** Member of SOLINET.

★ 15463 ★
**Southern Baptist Theological Seminary - James P. Boyce Centennial
    Library** (Rel-Phil)
2825 Lexington Rd.   Phone: (502)897-4807
Louisville, KY 40280   Dr. Ronald F. Deering, Dir.
Founded: 1859. **Staff:** Prof 7; Other 27. **Subjects:** Bible, theology,
philosophy, psychology, religious education, church history and music,
comparative religions, sociology. **Special Collections:** Baptist Historical
Collection; Billy Graham Room (books, sermons, movies and records of
revivals around the world). **Holdings:** 332,199 volumes; 109,871 pamphlets;
59,995 microforms. **Subscriptions:** 1584 journals and other serials. **Services:**
Interlibrary loan; copying; library open to the public. **Computerized
Information Services:** SOLINET, OCLC. **Staff:** Nancy Robinson, Cat.; Elsa
A. Miller, Circ.Libn.; Paul M. Debusman, Ref./Ser.Libn.; Melody Mazuk,
Tech.Serv.Libn.

★ 15464 ★
Southern Bell Telephone and Telegraph Company - Law Library (Law)
4300 Southern Bell Center
675 W. Peachtree St., N.E.   Phone: (404)529-7937
Atlanta, GA 30375   Linda Gray, Libn.
Staff: Prof 1. **Subjects:** Law. **Holdings:** 14,000 volumes. **Services:** Library
not open to the public.

Southern California Academy of Science Library
See: **Natural History Museum of Los Angeles County - Research Library**
    (11341)

★ 15465 ★
Southern California College of Chiropractic - Library (Med)
8420 Beverly Rd.   Phone: (310)699-3650
Pico Rivera, CA 90660   Gayla K. McDowell
Staff: Prof 1; Other 1. **Subjects:** Chiropractic. **Holdings:** 9000 books; 1700
bound periodical volumes; 5000 unbound periodicals. **Subscriptions:** 70
journals and other serials. **Services:** Interlibrary loan; copying; library open
to the public for reference use only. **Networks/Consortia:** Member of
Chiropractic Library Consortium (CLIBCON). **Remarks:** FAX: (213)692-
2505. **Staff:** Yolanda Williams, Asst.Libn.

★ 15466 ★
**Southern California College of Optometry - M.B. Ketchum Memorial
    Library** (Med)
2565 Yorba Linda Blvd.   Phone: (714)449-7440
Fullerton, CA 92631-1699   Mrs. Patricia T. Carlson, Dir. of Lib.Serv.
Founded: 1948. **Staff:** Prof 1; Other 3. **Subjects:** Optometry, optics,
ophthalmology; vision. **Holdings:** 8400 books; 5700 bound periodical
volumes; 450 theses; 400 AV programs. **Subscriptions:** 350 serials. **Services:**
Interlibrary loan; copying; SDI; library open to the public with restrictions.
Computerized Information Services: DIALOG Information Services,
MEDLINE, LION; CLASS OnTyme Electronic Message Network Service
(electronic mail service). **Publications:** Recent Publications Received,
bimonthly - by request. **Remarks:** FAX: (714)879-0481.

★ 15467 ★
Southern California Edison Company - Corporate Library (Sci-Engr)
2244 Walnut Grove Ave.
Box 800   Phone: (818)302-8971
Rosemead, CA 91770   N.P. Morton, Corp.Libn.
Founded: 1905. **Staff:** Prof 3; Other 3. **Subjects:** Electric power generation,
nuclear engineering, management, computer science. **Special Collections:**
EPRI Reports, industry codes and standards. **Holdings:** 12,332 books; 1253
bound periodical volumes; 10 shelves of government documents; 14 shelves
of reports; 1600 reels of microfilm of periodicals. **Subscriptions:** 570 journals
and other serials. **Services:** Interlibrary loan; copying (limited); library open
to the public by appointment only. **Automated Operations:** Computerized
public access catalog, cataloging, acquisitions, serials, and circulation (Data
Trek). **Computerized Information Services:** DIALOG Information Services,
BRS Information Technologies, Electric Power Database (EPD),
WILSONLINE, FYI News, LEXIS, NEXIS; (internal database).
Publications: Library Bulletin, bimonthly. **Remarks:** FAX: (818)302-8015.
Staff: Steven D. Lowry, Asst.Libn.; William D. Lee, Asst.Libn.; Barbara L.
Netzley, Sys.Anl.

★ 15468 ★
**Southern California Edison Company - Nuclear Training Division
    Resource Center** (Energy)
San Onofre Nuclear Generating Station, E-50B MESA
Box 128   Phone: (714)368-8457
San Clemente, CA 92672   Yolinda C. Nino, Comp.Term.Op.
Founded: 1983. **Subjects:** Nuclear power, radiation, education, and training.
Special Collections: Electric Power Research Institute - Nuclear Power
collection; Institute of Nuclear Power Operations (INPO) collection.
Holdings: 1200 books; 75 unbound volumes; 120,000 aperture cards; 60,000
microfiche; 592 standards (392 binders); 6000 vendor manuals; 150
telephone directories; 10,000 procedures; 2000 documents; 1500 NUREGS
(NRC).

★ 15469 ★
Southern California Gas Company - Engineering Information Center
Box 3249, Terminal Annex, ML730D
Los Angeles, CA 90051
Defunct. Holdings absorbed by Southern California Gas Company -
Information Center.

★ 15470 ★
Southern California Gas Company - Information Center (Energy)
555 W. 5th St.
Los Angeles, CA 90013-1011   Phone: (213)244-5196
Staff: Prof 4; Other 3. **Subjects:** Energy; natural gas; gas supply; Southern
California Gas Company history (early 1800s to present); marketing;
engineering - civil, mechanical, structural, management, training. **Special
Collections:** Federal Energy Regulatory Commission (FERC) forms; 1000
Code S Audio/Visual Collection. **Holdings:** 12,000 books. **Subscriptions:**
500 journals and other serials. **Services:** Interlibrary loan; center open to the
public with restrictions. **Automated Operations:** Computerized cataloging,
acquisitions, and circulation. **Computerized Information Services:**
DIALOG Information Services, LEXIS, NEXIS, CompuServe Information
Service, DataTimes; internal databases; A.G.A. GasNet, EasyLink
(electronic mail services). **Publications:** Acquisitions List, monthly.
Remarks: FAX: (213)244-8020. Contains the holdings of the former
Southern California Gas Company - Engineering Information Center. **Staff:**
Gloria Edwards; Janice Young; D. Wayne Sexton; Diane Peterson; Jo Anne
Pedley; Lou Martin.

★ 15471 ★
Southern California Genealogical Society, Inc. - Library (Hist)
122 S. San Fernando Blvd.
Box 4377   Phone: (818)843-7247
Burbank, CA 91503   Mrs.Virginia Emery, Pres.
Founded: 1965. **Staff:** 50. **Subjects:** State and local history, family history.
Special Collections: Alabama county records; Massachusetts town records;
Brossman genealogical columns (16 years); Pennsylvania area keys; Texas
Robertson Colony records; North Carolina Moravian records; New England
History and Genealogy Register; Joseph Brown Turner Collection
(microfiche). **Holdings:** 6700 books; 2000 bound periodical volumes; 5 file
drawers of maps; 36 drawers of manuscripts. **Subscriptions:** 200 journals and
other serials. **Services:** Copying; library open to the public. **Publications:**
Spanish-Mexican Families of Early California, 1769-1850, 2 volumes; The
Searcher, monthly - to members. **Special Indexes:** Index to family histories,
periodicals and manuscripts (card); index to Los Angeles County marriage
records; index in process to 1852 California Census.

★ 15472 ★
**Southern California Institute of Architecture (SCI-ARC) - Architecture
    Library** (Plan)
5454 Beethoven St.   Phone: (310)574-1123
Los Angeles, CA 90066   Kevin McMahon, Lib.Mgr.
Founded: 1974. **Staff:** Prof 1; Other 1. **Subjects:** Architectural history and
theory, planning, art. **Holdings:** 7000 books; 700 bound periodical volumes.
Subscriptions: 30 journals and other serials. **Services:** Copying; library open
to the public for reference use only. **Publications:** Modern Architecture:
Mexico. **Remarks:** FAX: (213)829-7518.

★ 15473 ★
Southern California Library for Social Studies and Research (Soc Sci)
6120 S. Vermont Ave.   Phone: (213)759-6063
Los Angeles, CA 90044   Sarah Cooper, Dir.
Founded: 1963. **Staff:** Prof 3; Other 8. **Subjects:** Labor; Marxism; socialism; black, Chicano, and women's movements; Southern California grassroots organizations. **Special Collections:** Civil Rights Congress (Los Angeles area) archival records; Harry Bridges papers on deportation trials; Los Angeles Committee for the Protection of the Foreign Born records; personal manuscript collections from Charlotta A. Bass, Richard Gladstein, Robert W. Kenny, and Earl Robinson. **Holdings:** 35,000 books; 30,000 pamphlets; 3500 tapes; 500,000 news clippings; 3000 periodicals titles; files from labor, peace, and civil rights organizations, 1930s to present; 100 documentary films, 1930s-1970s. **Services:** Copying; library open to the public. **Publications:** Heritage (newsletter), quarterly. **Staff:** Mary Tyler, Assoc.Dir.

★ 15474 ★
Southern California Psychoanalytic Institute - Franz Alexander Library (Med)
9024 Olympic Blvd.   Phone: (310)276-2455
Beverly Hills, CA 90211   Lena Pincus, Libn.
Founded: 1950. **Staff:** Prof 1. **Subjects:** Psychoanalysis, psychiatry, psychology. **Holdings:** 4000 volumes; 2200 reprints. **Subscriptions:** 45 journals and other serials. **Services:** Interlibrary loan; copying; library open to the public with restrictions. **Networks/Consortia:** Member of National Network of Libraries of Medicine - Pacific Southwest Region.

★ 15475 ★
Southern California Rapid Transit District - Information Center/Library (Trans)
425 S. Main St., 5th Fl.   Phone: (213)972-4859
Los Angeles, CA 90013   Dorothy Peyton Gray, Libn.
Founded: 1971. **Staff:** Prof 2. **Subjects:** Urban transportation, local transit, urban planning, parent organization history. **Holdings:** 20,000 books and bound periodical volumes; 2000 reports on microfiche; 50 maps. **Subscriptions:** 200 journals and other serials. **Services:** Interlibrary loan; copying; library open to the public with restrictions. **Automated Operations:** Computerized cataloging, acquisitions, serials; public access catalog. **Computerized Information Services:** DIALOG Information Services, LEXIS, NEXIS, OCLC. **Remarks:** FAX: (213)972-4788.

★ 15476 ★
Southern College - Library (Sci-Engr)
5600 Lake Underhill Rd.   Phone: (407)273-1000
Orlando, FL 32807   Geraldine Mattern, Libn.
Staff: Prof 1; Other 4. **Subjects:** Interior design, dentistry, computers, data processing, electronics, business and general education, computer repair. **Holdings:** 7000 books; 1500 unbound periodicals; 1747 slides; 16 film cassettes; 8 filmstrips. **Subscriptions:** 134 journals and other serials; 6 newspapers. **Services:** Library not open to the public. **Computerized Information Services:** Internal database. **Networks/Consortia:** Member of Central Florida Library Consortium (CFLC). **Publications:** Handbook.

★ 15477 ★
Southern College of Optometry - Library (Med)
1245 Madison Ave.   Phone: (901)722-3237
Memphis, TN 38104   Nancy Gatlin, Dir.
Founded: 1938. **Staff:** Prof 2; Other 1. **Subjects:** Optometry, optics, ophthalmology, psychology, exceptional education. **Holdings:** 15,330 books; 4120 bound periodical volumes; 12,302 slides; 378 microfiche; 153 reels of microfilm; 245 video cassettes. **Subscriptions:** 175 journals and other serials. **Services:** Interlibrary loan; copying; SDI; library open to the public for reference use only. **Automated Operations:** Computerized cataloging, acquisitions, and serials. **Computerized Information Services:** DIALOG Information Services, LION (internal database). Performs searches on fee basis. **Networks/Consortia:** Member of Association of Memphis Area Health Science Libraries (AMAHSL), Association of Visual Science Librarians (AVSL). **Special Indexes:** Vision Science Index (online); ocular pathology slide index (online). **Staff:** Deborah Lawless, Asst.Dir.

★ 15478 ★
Southern College of Seventh-Day Adventists - McKee Library - Special Collections (Rel-Phil, Hist)
Box 629   Phone: (615)238-2789
Collegedale, TN 37315   Peg Bennett, Dir. of Libs.
Founded: 1892. **Staff:** Prof 3; Other 4. **Subjects:** Lincoln/Civil War; Seventh-Day Adventist Church. **Special Collections:** Dr. Vernon Thomas Memorial Civil War Collection (1400 books; 2000 letters; manuscripts; newspapers; pamphlets; pictures; maps); Dr. Vernon Thomas Memorial Abraham Lincoln Collection (2000 books, letters, manuscripts, newspapers, pamphlets, pictures, paintings, maps, artifacts); Seventh-Day Adventist Church publications (10,000 books, current periodicals, bound periodicals, microforms, archives). **Holdings:** 97,030 books; 13,321 bound periodical volumes; 94,280 microfiche; 1959 reels of microfilm; 2838 nonprint items. **Subscriptions:** 947 journals and other serials. **Services:** Interlibrary loan; copying; SDI; collections open to the public with restrictions. **Automated Operations:** Computerized cataloging, acquisitions, serials, and circulation. **Computerized Information Services:** OCLC. **Networks/Consortia:** Member of SOLINET. **Remarks:** FAX: (615)238-3009.

★ 15479 ★
Southern College of Technology - Library (Sci-Engr)
1100 S. Marietta Pkwy.   Phone: (404)528-7275
Marietta, GA 30060   Nancy Shofner, Act.Dir.
Founded: 1948. **Staff:** Prof 5; Other 4. **Subjects:** Engineering and technology - apparel, architectural, civil, computer, electrical, industrial, mechanical, textile. **Special Collections:** Surveying; architecture. **Holdings:** 77,000 books; 18,000 bound periodical volumes; 10,000 serials; 11,000 AV programs; 2000 company reports. **Subscriptions:** 1400 journals and other serials. **Services:** Interlibrary loan; copying; library open to the public with restrictions. **Automated Operations:** Computerized cataloging and serials. **Computerized Information Services:** OCLC. **Networks/Consortia:** Member of SOLINET. Dorothy Ingram, Ref.Libn.; Joyce Mills, Asst.Dir., Pub.Serv.; Julius Whitaker, Acq.Libn.; David Rife, Ref.Libn.

★ 15480 ★
Southern Company Services, Inc. - Corporate Library & Learning Center (Bus-Fin)
Box 2625   Phone: (205)870-6420
Birmingham, AL 35202   Catherine Nick, Supv.
Founded: 1971. **Staff:** Prof 1; Other 1. **Subjects:** Business, engineering, electric utilities. **Holdings:** 6000 books; 251 titles on microfiche; EPRI reports; industry standards for 21 societies (microfilm); military specifications (microfilm). **Subscriptions:** 900 journals and other serials; 9 newspapers. **Services:** Interlibrary loan; copying; SDI; library open to the public for reference use only. **Automated Operations:** Computerized cataloging, acquisitions, serials, and circulation. **Computerized Information Services:** DIALOG Information Services, Knight-Ridder Unicom. **Publications:** Inside; Southern Highlights. **Remarks:** FAX: (205)868-5083.

★ 15481 ★
Southern Connecticut Newspapers Inc. - Advocate & Greenwich Time Library (Publ)
75 Tresser Blvd.   Phone: (203)964-2297
Stamford, CT 06904-9307   Leigh Baker Michels, Hd.Libn.
Founded: 1829. **Staff:** Prof 1; Other 1. **Subjects:** Newspaper reference topics. **Special Collections:** Antique newspapers, photographs, and posters. **Holdings:** Clippings; local and state documents; microfilm; photographs. **Subscriptions:** 10 journals and other serials; 12 newspapers. **Services:** Library not open to the public. **Special Catalogs:** Catalogs of clipping file and photograph file. **Remarks:** FAX: (203)964-2345 (newsroom).

★ 15482 ★
Southern Connecticut State University - H.C. Buley Library - Special Collections (Hist, Hum)
501 Crescent St.   Phone: (203)397-4505
New Haven, CT 06515   Kenneth G. Walter, Dir.
Founded: 1893. **Special Collections:** Connecticut Room (5865 volumes; 28 VF drawers); Contemporary Juvenile Collection (15,276 volumes); Carolyn Sherwin Bailey Historical Collection of Children's Books (2302 volumes); government documents (157,772 items); archives (40 VF drawers); Hartford Times newspaper morgue (300 VF drawers). **Services:** Interlibrary loan; copying; collections open to the public with restrictions. **Automated Operations:** Computerized cataloging. **Computerized Information Services:** DIALOG Information Services, BRS Information Technologies, WILSONLINE. **Special Catalogs:** Catalog of Carolyn Sherwin Bailey Children's Collection (printed). **Special Indexes:** Magazine Index (online). **Staff:** Shirley Bickoff, Docs.; Claire Bennett, CT Rm. & Assoc.Ref.Libn.

Southern Energy/Environmental Information Center (SEEIC)
See: **Southern States Energy Board (SSEB) (15517)**

★ 15483 ★
Southern Engineering - Library (Sci-Engr)
1800 Peachtree St., N.W.
Atlanta, GA 30367-8301   Phone: (404)352-9200
Founded: 1945. **Staff:** 1. **Subjects:** Electric utilities, engineering. **Holdings:** 1000 books; 50 bound periodical volumes; 5000 reports; 10 microfiche. **Subscriptions:** 250 journals and other serials; 4 newspapers. **Services:** Interlibrary loan; SDI; library not open to the public. **Computerized Information Services:** DIALOG Information Services, Dow Jones News/Retrieval, Mead Data Central. **Remarks:** FAX: (404)351-1196. **Staff:** Paula A. Vaccariello, Libn.

★ 15484 ★
Southern Forest Products Association - Library (Bus-Fin)
P.O. Box 641700   Phone: (504)443-4464
Kenner, LA 70064-1700   Janet Doyle, Libn.
Staff: Prof 1. **Subjects:** Lumber industry economics. **Special Collections:** History of Southern Pine Association/Southern Forest Products Association. **Holdings:** Figures not available. **Subscriptions:** 80 journals and other serials. **Services:** Interlibrary loan; library not open to the public. **Publications:** List of association publications and films available for sale - free upon request. **Remarks:** FAX: (504)443-6612. Telex: 756854.

★ 15485 ★
Southern Highland Handicraft Guild - Folk Art Center Library (Art)
Box 9545   Phone: (704)298-7928
Asheville, NC 28815   Celine O'Brien, Libn.
Founded: 1930. **Staff:** Prof 1; Other 15. **Subjects:** History, traditional and contemporary crafts of the southern highlands, folk art, southern decorative arts. **Holdings:** 2572 books; historical materials. **Subscriptions:** 45 journals and other serials. **Services:** Library open to the public for reference and research use only. **Publications:** Bibliographies. **Remarks:** Library located at Milepost 382, Blue Ridge Parkway, Asheville, NC 28805. FAX: (704)298-7962.

Southern Highlands Research Center
See: **University of North Carolina at Asheville (19055)**

★ 15486 ★
Southern Illinois University - School of Medicine - Medical Library (Med)
801 N. Rutledge
Box 19231   Phone: (217)782-2658
Springfield, IL 62794   Robert Berk, Ph.D., Dir.
Founded: 1970. **Staff:** Prof 7; Other 21. **Subjects:** Medical sciences. **Special Collections:** History of medicine (4500 volumes). **Holdings:** 58,200 books; 64,250 bound periodical volumes; 1600 reels of microfilm; 3050 AV programs. **Subscriptions:** 2028 journals and other serials. **Services:** Interlibrary loan; copying; library open to the public. **Automated Operations:** Integrated library system; computerized ILL (DOCLINE). **Computerized Information Services:** MEDLINE, DIALOG Information Services, OCLC, BRS Information Technologies, Data-Star, Statewide Library Computer System (LCS). Performs searches free of charge for primary users; on fee basis for others. **Networks/Consortia:** Member of National Network of Libraries of Medicine - Greater Midwest Region, ILLINET, Sangamon Valley Academic Library Consortium (SVALC), Capital Area Consortium (CAC). **Special Catalogs:** Subject and title listings of current subscriptions; subject guide to AV collection. **Remarks:** FAX: (217)782-0988; (217)782-7503 (ILL). **Staff:** Rhona Kelley, Hd.Ref. & Educ.Serv.Libn.; Roger Guard, Hd., Automated Serv./Assoc.Dir.; Carol Thornton, Ref. & Educ.Serv.Libn.; Connie Poole, Hd./Tech.Serv.

★ 15487 ★
Southern Illinois University at Carbondale - Education and Psychology Division Library (Educ, Info Sci)
Morris Library   Phone: (618)453-2121
Carbondale, IL 62901   Dr. Ruth E. Bauner, Educ. & Psych.Libn.
Founded: 1950. **Staff:** Prof 4; Other 1. **Subjects:** Education, psychology, library science, recreation, sports, guidance. **Special Collections:** John Dewey Collection; Instructional Materials Center; historical children's book collection. **Holdings:** 143,000 books; 33,170 bound periodical volumes; 40,200 curriculum guides, children's books, textbooks in instructional materials center. **Subscriptions:** 1000 journals and other serials. **Services:** Interlibrary loan; copying; library open to the public for reference use only. **Automated Operations:** Computerized cataloging, circulation, and serials. **Computerized Information Services:** DIALOG Information Services, PFDS Online, OCLC, BRS Information Technologies, Statewide Library Computer System (IO), FBR; CD-ROMs (ERIC, PsychLit, Education Index). **Networks/Consortia:** Member of ILLINET, Center for Research Libraries (CRL). **Remarks:** FAX: (618)453-8109. **Staff:** Dr. Kathy Cook, Asst.Libn.; Paul Fehrmann, Asst.Libn.; Lorene Pixley, Asst.Libn.

★ 15488 ★
Southern Illinois University at Carbondale - Humanities Division Library (Hum)
Morris Library   Phone: (618)536-3391
Carbondale, IL 62901   Angela Battaglia Rubin, Act.Hum.Libn.
Founded: 1956. **Staff:** Prof 2.5; Other 2. **Subjects:** Literature, linguistics, music, art, philosophy, religion, speech, theater, journalism, languages. **Holdings:** 530,000 books; 87,000 bound periodical volumes; 87,000 microtexts; 17,000 phonograph records; 25,000 prints. **Subscriptions:** 3600 journals and other serials. **Services:** Interlibrary loan; copying; library open to the public for reference use only. **Automated Operations:** Computerized cataloging and circulation. **Computerized Information Services:** OCLC, DIALOG Information Services, Statewide Library Computer System (IO); CD-ROMs (MLA, Dissertation Abstracts International, Art Index). **Networks/Consortia:** Member of ILLINET, Center for Research Libraries (CRL). **Remarks:** FAX: (618)453-8109. **Staff:** Loretta P. Koch, Asst.Libn.; Marta A. Davis, Asst.Libn.

★ 15489 ★
Southern Illinois University at Carbondale - School of Law Library (Law)
Lesar Bldg.   Phone: (618)536-7711
Carbondale, IL 62901-6803   Frank G. Houdek, Law Lib.Dir.
Founded: 1973. **Staff:** Prof 7; Other 12. **Subjects:** Law. **Special Collections:** Mining law; water law (208 water quality plans); federal and state government documents depository. **Holdings:** 281,281 volumes. **Subscriptions:** 5289 journals and other serials. **Services:** Interlibrary loan; copying; library open to the public. **Automated Operations:** Computerized public access catalog, cataloging, ILL, serials, and acquisitions. **Computerized Information Services:** WESTLAW, LEXIS, NEXIS, OCLC. **Networks/Consortia:** Member of ILLINET, Mid-America Law School Library Consortium. **Publications:** Recent Acquisitions and Developments, irregular - to campus and other libraries; Law Library Publication Series. **Special Catalogs:** Rare Book Collection catalog; Loose-leaf Service Holdings (both book). **Remarks:** FAX: (618)453-8728. **Staff:** Laurel A. Wendt, Assoc. Law Lib.Dir.; R. Kathy Garner, Sr.Ref.Libn.; Elizabeth W. Matthews, Proj. & Presrv.Libn.; Heija B. Ryoo, Hd. of Tech.Serv.; James E. Duggan, Comp.Serv.Libn.; Jean McKnight, Ref.Libn.

★ 15490 ★
Southern Illinois University at Carbondale - Science Division Library (Sci-Engr, Agri, Med)
Morris Library   Phone: (618)453-2700
Carbondale, IL 62901   Kathy Fahey, Act.Sci.Libn.
Founded: 1956. **Staff:** Prof 4; Other 1. **Subjects:** Agriculture, science, medicine, engineering. **Holdings:** 212,000 books; 190,000 bound periodical volumes; 2600 theses; 249,000 maps and aerial photographs; 10,000 serial reports on microfilm; 1800 books on microfilm. **Subscriptions:** 4600 journals and other serials. **Services:** Interlibrary loan; copying; library open to the public for reference use only. **Automated Operations:** Computerized cataloging and circulation. **Computerized Information Services:** DIALOG Information Services, PFDS Online, MEDLARS, BRS Information Technologies, OCLC, WILSONLINE, Statewide Library Computer System (IO); CD-ROMs (Applied Science & Technology Index, Biological Sciences, MEDLINE). **Networks/Consortia:** Member of ILLINET. **Remarks:** FAX: (618)453-8109. **Staff:** Harry O. Davis, Asst.Sci.Libn./Map Libn.; Andrew Tax, Med.Libn.

★15491★
Southern Illinois University at Carbondale - Social Studies Division
  Library (Soc Sci)
Morris Library   Phone: (618)453-2708
Carbondale, IL 62901   James Fox, Soc.Stud.Libn.
Founded: 1956. **Staff:** Prof 4; Other 2. **Subjects:** Anthropology, business, economics, geography, history, political science, sociology, Latin American studies. **Holdings:** 365,098 books; 114,380 bound periodical volumes; 367,525 U.S. Government documents in hardcopy; 502,220 government documents on microfiche; 57 cabinets of Human Relations Area Files; British Sessional Papers, 1731 to present, and American Antiquarian Society's early American newspapers and imprints; 64,000 reels of microfilm of books, newspapers, journals, National Archives material. **Subscriptions:** 3121 journals and other serials; 75 newspapers. **Services:** Interlibrary loan; copying; library open to the public for reference use only. **Automated Operations:** Computerized cataloging and circulation. **Computerized Information Services:** DIALOG Information Services, Statewide Library Computer System (IO); CD-ROMs (Social Sciences Index, Business Periodicals Index, Government Documents Catalog Service, CIS Statistical Masterfile). **Networks/Consortia:** Member of ILLINET, Center for Research Libraries (CRL). **Remarks:** FAX: (618)453-8109. **Staff:** Catherine Martinsek, Asst.Soc.Stud.Libn.; Deborah Mesplay, Asst.Soc.Stud.Libn.; Walter Stubbs, Asst.Soc.Stud.Libn.

★15492★
Southern Illinois University at Carbondale - Special Collections (Hum)
Morris Library   Phone: (618)453-2516
Carbondale, IL 62901   David V. Koch, Cur./Archv.
Founded: 1956. **Staff:** Prof 4.5; Other 3. **Special Collections:** 20th century British and American literature; Irish Literary Renaissance, proletariat theater; modern American philosophy; private press books (Black Sun, Trovillion, Nash, Cuala); Southern Illinois history; Ulysses S. Grant; John Dewey; Paul Weiss; James K. Feibleman; Open Court Press; Christian Century Magazine; Library of Living Philosophers; Henry Nelson Wieman; Robert Graves; James Joyce; D.H. Lawrence; Richard Aldington; Lawrence Durrell; Erwin Piscator; Henry Miller; Kay Boyle; John Howard Lawson; First Amendment freedoms; university archives. **Holdings:** 100,000 books; 700,000 manuscripts and letters. **Services:** Copying; microfilming, collection open to qualified scholars. **Automated Operations:** Computerized cataloging. **Computerized Information Services:** OCLC, Statewide Library Computer System (IO); internal databases. **Networks/Consortia:** Member of ILLINET. **Publications:** Bibliographic Contributions; ICarbS (journal), irregular. **Special Catalogs:** Catalogs of special exhibits. **Remarks:** FAX: (618)453-8109. **Staff:** Shelley Cox, Rare Bks.Libn.; Sheila Ryan, Cur., Mss.; Daren Callahan, Rare Bks.Cat.; Karen Drickamer, Mss.Cat.

★15493★
Southern Illinois University at Carbondale - Undergraduate Library
  (Hum)
Morris Library   Phone: (618)453-2818
Carbondale, IL 62901   Dr. Judith Ann Harwood, Libn.
Founded: 1971. **Staff:** Prof 4; Other 3. **Subjects:** Automotive technology, thanatology, cinema and photography, women's studies, radio and television, general studies. **Holdings:** 120,000 books; 9533 bound periodical volumes; 2437 reels of microfilm. **Subscriptions:** 433 journals and other serials. **Services:** Interlibrary loan; copying; library open to the public for reference use only. **Automated Operations:** Computerized cataloging and circulation. **Computerized Information Services:** DIALOG Information Services, BRS Information Technologies, OCLC, Statewide Library Computer System (IO); InfoTrac. **Networks/Consortia:** Member of ILLINET. **Remarks:** FAX: (618)453-8109. **Staff:** Jody Foote, Asst.Libn.; Roland Person, Asst.Libn.; Willie Scott, Asst.Libn.

★15494★
Southern Illinois University at Edwardsville - Documents Collection
  (Info Sci)
Lovejoy Library   Phone: (618)692-2606
Edwardsville, IL 62026   Robert J. Fortado, Doc.Libn.
Staff: Prof 1; Other 1. **Holdings:** 500,000 U.S. Government documents. **Services:** Interlibrary loan; copying; collection open to the public. **Automated Operations:** Computerized cataloging and circulation. **Computerized Information Services:** OCLC, DIALOG Information Services, University of Illinois - Statewide Library Computer System (LCS); internal database. **Remarks:** FAX: (618)692-2381.

★15495★
Southern Illinois University at Edwardsville - Research & Projects
  Office Library (Bus-Fin)
Graduate School   Phone: (618)692-3162
Box 1046   Teresa Goettsch Wingert, Res. &
Edwardsville, IL 62026-1046   Dev.Coord.
Founded: 1970. **Staff:** Prof 3. **Subjects:** Federal, state, and private grant support; federal legislation. **Holdings:** 15 VF drawers of federal and state program guidelines and applications; education directories; foundation annual reports; directories of federal and private grant support. **Subscriptions:** 20 newsletters. **Services:** Library open to the public for reference use only. **Computerized Information Services:** IRIS (Illinois Researcher Information System; internal database). Performs searches on fee basis. **Publications:** Research Highlights, monthly - to faculty and staff; Research & Creative Activities (magazine), biennial. **Remarks:** FAX: (618)692-3523.

★15496★
Southern Maine Medical Center - Health Sciences Library (Med)
1 Medical Center Dr.
Box 626   Phone: (207)283-7000
Biddeford, ME 04005   Patricia Goodwin, Libn.
Staff: Prof 1. **Subjects:** Medicine and allied health sciences. **Holdings:** 500 books; 30 bound periodical volumes. **Subscriptions:** 90 journals and other serials. **Services:** Interlibrary loan; copying; SDI; library open to the public by appointment. **Computerized Information Services:** BRS Information Technologies, NLM. Performs searches on fee basis. **Networks/Consortia:** Member of Health Science Library and Information Cooperative of Maine (HSLIC). **Remarks:** FAX: (207)283-7020.

★15497★
Southern Maine Technical College - Library (Educ)
Fort Rd.   Phone: (207)799-7303
South Portland, ME 04106   Donald A. Bertsch, Jr., Libn.
Staff: Prof 2; Other 1. **Subjects:** Electronics, law enforcement, building technology, culinary arts, plant and soil sciences, nursing and allied health sciences, marine studies. **Holdings:** 15,000 books. **Subscriptions:** 350 journals and other serials; 10 newspapers. **Services:** Interlibrary loan; copying; SDI; library open to the public. **Computerized Information Services:** DIALOG Information Services. Performs searches on fee basis. **Networks/Consortia:** Member of Health Science Library and Information Cooperative of Maine (HSLIC). **Staff:** Debbie Cameron, Ref.

★15498★
Southern Maryland Studies Center - Library (Hist)
Mitchell Rd.
P.O. Box 910   Phone: (301)934-2251
La Plata, MD 20646-0910   Sarah L. Barley, Coord.
Founded: 1976. **Staff:** 1.7. **Subjects:** Southern Maryland - history, culture, development; genealogy. **Special Collections:** Historical Society of Charles County Collection (records, manuscripts); Harry Wright Newman Collection (genealogy); Charlotte Hall School Collection (local history); J. Richard Rivoire Collection (architectural history); Southern Maryland Today Collection (local history, folklore). **Holdings:** 2000 books; 130 bound periodical volumes; 377 reels of microfilm; 30 AV programs; 141 oral history audiotapes; 147 manuscript collections. **Subscriptions:** 8 journals and other serials; 3 newspapers. **Services:** Interlibrary loan; copying; center open to the public for reference use only. **Publications:** Homeplaces: Traditional Domestic Architecture of Charles County Maryland. **Special Indexes:** Charles County, MD, Cemetery List and Tombstone Inscription Index. **Remarks:** Alternate telephone number(s): (301)870-3008. FAX: (301)934-5260. Affiliated with Charles County Community College. **Staff:** Catherine E. Parker, Coll.Lib.Dir.

★15499★
Southern Methodist University - De Golyer Library - Fikes Hall of
  Special Collections (Hist, Trans)
Central University Libraries, SMU Sta. Phone: (214)692-3231
Dallas, TX 75275   David Farmer, Dir.
Founded: 1956. **Staff:** Prof 4; Other 5. **Subjects:** Western United States history, history of the Spanish borderlands, history of the American railroad, history and technology of transportation. **Special Collections:** SMU Archives; E.L. DeGolyer, Sr. papers; Baldwin Locomotive Works papers; S.M. Vauclain papers; John Insley Blair papers; Texas and Pacific Railway papers; Muskogee Corporation papers; Paul Horgan Collection.

Holdings: 85,000 monographs; 5000 periodical volumes; 300,000 photographs; 1500 cubic feet of manuscript and archival collections; 3000 reels of microfilm. **Subscriptions:** 400 journals and other serials. **Services:** Copying; collections open to the public. **Automated Operations:** Computerized cataloging, acquisitions, indexing, and processing of manuscripts and photographs. **Computerized Information Services:** OCLC; internal database. **Networks/Consortia:** Member of AMIGOS Bibliographic Council, Inc. **Publications:** DeGolyer Library Publication Series, irregular; De Golyer Library Keepsake Series; occasional publications, irregular. **Special Catalogs:** Exhibition catalogs; Finding aids to processed manuscript, serial, photograph, and archival collections available; chronological file to printed holdings. **Staff:** Kristin Jacobsen, Ref.Libn.; Kay Bost, Mss.Cur.; Mary O'Connor, Cat.Libn.

★ 15500 ★
Southern Methodist University - Fort Burgwin Research Center - Library & Herbarium (Biol Sci, Soc Sci)
Box 300   Phone: (505)758-8322
Ranchos de Taos, NM 87557   William B. Stallcup, Resident Dir.
Founded: 1957. **Subjects:** Anthropology, biology, ecology, geology, linguistics. **Special Collections:** Herbarium of flora of Carson National Forest; Pollen Reference Collection for modern and paleoenvironments; Taos and Llano Estacado. **Holdings:** 2500 books; 800 bound periodical volumes. **Services:** Library not open to the public.

★ 15501 ★
Southern Methodist University - Institute for the Study of Earth and Man - Library (Sci-Engr, Soc Sci)
Heroy Bldg.   Phone: (214)692-2430
Dallas, TX 75275   John Phinney
Staff: 1. **Subjects:** Anthropology, geology, Texas archeology. **Special Collections:** Reprint files in archeology, anthropology, paleobotany. **Holdings:** 5000 books; 5000 bound periodical volumes; reels of microfilm. **Subscriptions:** 145 journals and other serials. **Services:** Interlibrary loan; copying (limited); library open to the public with restrictions. **Computerized Information Services:** PONI (internal database). **Remarks:** FAX: (214)692-4289.

★ 15502 ★
Southern Methodist University - Jake and Nancy Hamon Arts Library (Art)
Meadows School of the Arts   Phone: (214)692-3813
Dallas, TX 75275-0356   Thomas P. Gates, Act.Hd.
Founded: 1990. **Staff:** Prof 3; Other 5. **Subjects:** Art, art history, arts administration, cinema, dance, music, music history, Spanish art, theater. **Special Collections:** Jerry Bywaters Collection (art of the Southwest); McCord Theater Collection (Texas theater, Dallas Little Theater, Arden Club Collection, Corsicana Opera House Collections, Harriet Bacon McDonald Collection of photographs); Paul and Viola Van Katwijk Music Collection; Charles Wakefield Cadman correspondence; Ferde Grofe Library; Rosa Bonheur correspondence. **Holdings:** 80,000 books, scores, and bound periodical volumes; 16,000 audiocassettes, phonograph records, videodiscs, and videotapes; 100 computer software programs; 100,000 additional items. **Subscriptions:** 300 journals and other serials. **Services:** Interlibrary loan; copying; library open to the public for reference use only. **Computerized Information Services:** OCLC; CD-ROM (Art Index); Hamon Arts Library Network (internal database); BITNET (electronic mail service). **Networks/Consortia:** Member of AMIGOS Bibliographic Council, Inc. **Remarks:** FAX: (214)692-3272. Electronic mail address(es): VMSV1001@SMUVM1 (BITNET); FZKR1001@SMUVM1 (BITNET). **Staff:** Larry Schwartz, Theater/Film Libn.; Tom Gates, Art Libn.; Sam Ratcliffe, Hd.,Hamm Spec.Coll.; Ellen Buie, Cur., Bywaters Coll.; Dennis Bowers, Dir., Comp.Lab.

★ 15503 ★
Southern Methodist University - Perkins School of Theology - The Bridwell Library (Rel-Phil)
6005 Bishop Blvd.   Phone: (214)692-3483
Dallas, TX 75275   Dr. Robert Maloy, Libn.
Founded: 1915. **Staff:** Prof 7; Other 13. **Subjects:** Theology; Methodist Church in Texas, the United States and England; Methodist hymnology; Wesleyana; 18th century theological literature; Judaica; biblical archeology; early and fine printing. **Special Collections:** Methodistica and Wesleyana books and manuscripts; 15th century books; 15th and 16th century illustrated books; 15th-20th century Bibles; private press books; Ashendene

Press Archives; Livres d'Artistes; Fine Bindings; Reformation collection; Savonarola collection; Hume Collection; Corey Collection (Christian Science books and archives); New Thought collection; Egyptology collection; James Joyce Collection; archives of the Perkins School of Theology; Thomas J. Harrison Bible Collection (on permanent loan); Elizabeth Perkins Prothro Bible Collection (on deposit). **Holdings:** 199,951 books; 31,853 bound periodical volumes; 3553 reels of microfilm; 88,999 microfiche. **Subscriptions:** 910 journals and other serials. **Services:** Interlibrary loan; copying; library use restricted to registered users. **Automated Operations:** Computerized public access catalog, cataloging, acquisitions, and ILL. **Computerized Information Services:** OCLC. **Networks/Consortia:** Member of AMIGOS Bibliographic Council, Inc. **Special Catalogs:** Exhibition catalogs, 3/year. **Remarks:** FAX: (214)692-4295. **Staff:** Roger L. Loyd, Assoc.Libn.; Page A. Thomas, Rare Bks.Cat.; Laura H. Randall, ILL; Russell Morton, Rare Bks.Cat.; Ellen L. Frost, Acq.; James Powell, Outler Proj.; Isaac Gewirtz, Spec.Coll.; Linda Umoh, Cat.; Jan Sobota, Cons.

★ 15504 ★
Southern Methodist University - Science/Engineering Library (Biol Sci, Sci-Engr)
Dallas, TX 75275   Phone: (214)692-2276
                                          Devertt D. Bickston, Libn.
Founded: 1961. **Staff:** Prof 6; Other 7. **Subjects:** Biology, botany, chemistry, engineering, geology, mathematics, physics, statistics. **Special Collections:** E. DeGolyer Collection (petroleum, history of geology, guide books); L. MacNaughton Earth Science Collection; Edwin Foscue Map Library; SMU Herbarium with Lloyd Shinners Collection of Taxonomic Botany. **Holdings:** 203,000 books; 91,000 bound periodical volumes; 262,000 government documents; 202,000 maps. **Subscriptions:** 1207 journals and other serials. **Services:** Interlibrary loan; copying; library open to the public. **Computerized Information Services:** DIALOG Information Services, PFDS Online, BRS Information Technologies. Performs searches on fee basis. **Networks/Consortia:** Member of Association for Higher Education of North Texas (AHE), AMIGOS Bibliographic Council, Inc. **Remarks:** FAX: (214)692-4236. Business and industrial special libraries should contact Industrial Information Services at 692-2271 for service. **Staff:** Jim Stephens, Ref.Libn.; Sandra Setnick, Ref.Libn.; Mary Ellen Batchelor, Ref.Libn.; Linda Samuels, Ref.Libn.; Susan Roosth, Ref.Libn.

★ 15505 ★
Southern Methodist University - Underwood Law Library (Law)
Dallas, TX 75275-0354   Phone: (214)692-3258
                                              Gail Daly, Dir.
Founded: 1925. **Staff:** Prof 9; Other 12. **Subjects:** International law and business, commercial transactions, corporations, securities, taxation, jurisprudence, oil and gas, air and space law. **Holdings:** 377,090 volumes. **Subscriptions:** 5212 journals and other serials. **Services:** Interlibrary loan; copying; open to the public. **Automated Operations:** Computerized cataloging. **Computerized Information Services:** LEXIS, WESTLAW, DIALOG Information Services, NEXIS, VU/TEXT Information Services, PHINet FedTax Database. **Networks/Consortia:** Member of AMIGOS Bibliographic Council, Inc. **Remarks:** FAX: (214)692-4330. **Staff:** Oragene Addis, Assoc.Dir.; L. Kurt Adamson, Assoc.Dir., Coll.Dev.; Dolores Stewart, Acq.Mgr.; Sue Wright, Sr.Tech.Serv.; Bruce Muck, Hd. of Res.Serv.; Greg Ivy, Hd. of Pub.Serv.; Ana Sinfuentes, Sr.Ref.Libn.; Winston Tubb, Coll.Mgr.

★ 15506 ★
Southern Minnesota Historical Center - Library (Hist)
Mankato State University   Phone: (507)389-1029
Mankato, MN 56002-8400   Dr. William E. Lass, Dir.
Founded: 1969. **Staff:** 1. **Subjects:** Mankato civic affairs, Minnesota politics and government, business, education in Southern Minnesota. **Special Collections:** Mankato State University archives; necrology file; H.H. King Flour Mills Company records; Mankato YWCA records. **Holdings:** 1700 linear feet of local history materials and university archives; oral history cassettes; microfilm. **Services:** Copying; library open to the public. **Remarks:** Maintained by Mankato State University.

★ 15507 ★
Southern New England Telephone Company - Information Technology - Research Center (Comp Sci)
300 George St., Rm. 9C1   Phone: (203)771-8383
New Haven, CT 06511   Kathy Umbricht Straka, MLS
Founded: 1978. **Staff:** Prof 1. **Subjects:** Computers, management, telecommunications. **Special Collections:** Vietnam Collection (100 vols., 30

videocassettes). **Holdings:** 1500 books; 300 reports. **Subscriptions:** 150 journals and other serials; 15 newspapers. **Services:** Interlibrary loan; center not open to the public. **Computerized Information Services:** DIALOG Information Services. **Remarks:** The facility includes a Guided Learning Center with facilities for IVI, CBT, and video tape technical and management training.

★ 15508 ★
Southern New England Telephone Company - Network Technology Library (Comp Sci)
555 Long Wharf Dr., 3rd Fl.   Phone: (203)553-4020
New Haven, CT 06511   Monica Denman, Libn.
Founded: 1984. **Staff:** Prof 1. **Subjects:** Electronics, computer science, telecommunications, management, fiber optics, engineering. **Special Collections:** Telecommunications documents. **Holdings:** 2400 books; 200 bound periodical volumes; 3000 unbound materials; 40,000 microcards; 2000 microfiche. **Subscriptions:** 50 journals and other serials. **Services:** Interlibrary loan; library not open to the public. **Automated Operations:** Computerized cataloging and circulation. **Computerized Information Services:** DIALOG Information Services. **Networks/Consortia:** Member of Southern Connecticut Library Council (SCLC). **Special Catalogs:** Book, document, and periodical lists. **Remarks:** Alternate telephone number(s): 553-6238. FAX: (203)553-4016.

★ 15509 ★
Southern Ohio College, Northeast Campus - Library (Educ)
2791 Mogadore Rd.   Phone: (216)733-8766
Akron, OH 44312   Lisa Weiser, Libn.
Staff: 1. **Subjects:** Business administration, economics, accounting, business law, medicine, computers, secretarial science, real estate, social sciences, liberal arts. **Holdings:** 3000 books. **Subscriptions:** 50 journals and other serials. **Services:** Library open to students only. **Networks/Consortia:** Member of North Central Library Cooperative (NCLC).

★ 15510 ★
Southern Ohio Genealogical Society - Reference Library (Hist)
Box 414
Hillsboro, OH 45133
Founded: 1978. **Staff:** Prof 1; Other 10. **Subjects:** Genealogy, local history. **Special Collections:** International Genealogical Index on microfiche (65 million names and accompanying information). **Holdings:** 1200 books; 250 bound periodical volumes; 100 family files; 85 family history files; 3700 burial records of veterans buried in Highland County, OH; 83 volumes of published family histories; 75 family history manuscripts; census maps; passenger and immigration records. **Services:** Copying. **Publications:** Roots & Shoots, quarterly. **Special Indexes:** Surname/Locality Index, annual; Surname Index (card); Family File Index (card). **Remarks:** The society acts as a clearinghouse for local and out-of-state patrons in finding and establishing their genealogical lines.

★ 15511 ★
Southern Oregon Historical Society - Library/Archives Department (Hist)
106 N. Central
Medford, OR 97501   Phone: (503)733-6536
Founded: 1950. **Staff:** 1. **Subjects:** Jackson County and southern Oregon history, historic preservation, museum techniques. **Special Collections:** Peter Britt photographic collection and work of other photographers (30,000 photographs dealing with southern Oregon subjects). **Holdings:** 4100 books; 100 bound periodical volumes; 550 manuscript collections; 240 oral histories. **Subscriptions:** 55 journals and other serials; 8 newspapers. **Services:** Interlibrary loan (limited); copying; library open to the public. **Computerized Information Services:** OPAC; SOHIP (Southern Oregon Historic Images Indexing Project; internal database). **Special Catalogs:** Preliminary Guide to Local History Materials, 1978 (booklet). **Remarks:** FAX: (503)776-7994.

★ 15512 ★
Southern Oregon State College - Library (Educ)
1250 Siskiyou Blvd.   Phone: (503)552-6445
Ashland, OR 97520   Sue A. Burkholder, Lib.Dir.
Founded: 1926. **Staff:** Prof 9; Other 11. **Subjects:** Liberal arts, education, business, local and regional studies. **Special Collections:** Margery Bailey

Renaissance Collection (6000 volumes); Southern Oregon History (1500 volumes). **Holdings:** 250,000 books and bound periodical volumes; 27,000 maps; 3200 photographs and pamphlets; 210,000 state and federal government documents; 580,000 microforms. **Subscriptions:** 2100 journals and other serials; 30 newspapers. **Services:** Interlibrary loan; copying; microcomputers available for public use; library open to the public. **Automated Operations:** Computerized acquisitions and cataloging. **Computerized Information Services:** OCLC, DIALOG Information Services, WILSONLINE, BRS Information Technologies; CD-ROM reference services. Performs searches on fee basis. Contact Person: James Rible, 482-6441. **Networks/Consortia:** Member of Southern Oregon Library Federation (SOLF). **Publications:** Bibliography series, irregular; list of serials, annual. **Special Indexes:** Index to Ashland Daily Tidings, 1958 to present. **Remarks:** FAX: (503)482-6429. **Staff:** Connie Anderson; Judy Andrews; Deborah Cook; Ruth Monical; Deborah Hollens; Teresa Montgomery; Harold Otness; David Russell.

★ 15513 ★
Southern Poverty Law Center - Klanwatch - Library (Soc Sci)
Box 2087   Phone: (205)264-0286
Montgomery, AL 36102-2087   Danny Welch, Dir.
Founded: 1980. **Staff:** 8. **Subjects:** Ku Klux Klan, neo-Nazi organizations, other right-wing extremists, anti-KKK information, hate crimes, white supremacy. **Holdings:** 150 books; 100 legal documents; 50,000 news clippings; 150 videotapes; 1000 letters. **Subscriptions:** 30 journals and other serials. **Computerized Information Services:** Internal database. **Publications:** Klanwatch Intelligence Report, bimonthly - for internal distribution only; Klanwatch Law Report; The Ku Klux Klan: A History of Racism and Violence; Decade Review. **Remarks:** FAX: (205)264-0629.

Southern Railway Predecessors Archive
See: **Virginia Polytechnic Institute and State University - University Libraries** (19875)

★ 15514 ★
Southern Regional Council, Inc. - Reference Library (Soc Sci)
134 Peachtree St., N.W., 19th Fl.   Phone: (404)522-8764
Atlanta, GA 30303-2199   Stephen T. Suitts, Exec.Dir.
Subjects: Civil rights, civil liberties, poverty, politics, suffrage. **Holdings:** 1200 books; civil rights movement newspaper collection on microfilm; newsclip collection, 1946-1975; special studies. **Services:** Copying; library open to the public with restrictions. **Computerized Information Services:** EasyLink (electronic mail service). **Publications:** Southern Changes, bimonthly - by subscription; SRC House Record, Voting Rights Review, Legislative Bulletin - all quarterly; Special Reports and Studies. **Remarks:** FAX: (404)522-8791.

★ 15515 ★
Southern Regional Education Board - Anne & Winfred Godwin Library (Educ)
592 10th St., N.W.   Phone: (404)875-9211
Atlanta, GA 30318-5790   Jennifer D. Burke, Libn.
Founded: 1949. **Staff:** Prof 1. **Subjects:** Higher education in the South, southern education, mental health, computer science, nursing, medical education. **Holdings:** 14,000 books; 4 VF drawers of pamphlets; 15 linear feet of college catalogs. **Subscriptions:** 50 journals and other serials. **Services:** Interlibrary loan; library open to the public for reference use only. **Remarks:** FAX: (404)872-1477.

★ 15516 ★
Southern Research Institute - Thomas W. Martin Memorial Library (Sci-Engr, Energy, Biol Sci)
P.O. Box 55305   Phone: (205)581-2518
Birmingham, AL 35255-5305   Mary L. Pullen, Lib.Mgr.
Founded: 1945. **Staff:** Prof 2; Other 2. **Subjects:** Chemistry, biology, biomaterials, virology, AIDS research, microbiology, mechanical and materials engineering, energy, pollution, metallurgy, physics. **Holdings:** 13,000 books; 37,000 bound periodical volumes. **Subscriptions:** 850 journals and other serials. **Services:** Interlibrary loan; copying; library open to qualified users. **Computerized Information Services:** DIALOG Information Services, STN International. **Remarks:** Library located at 2000 Ninth Ave., S., Birmingham, AL 35205. FAX: (205)581-2726. **Staff:** Mary W. White, Doc.Libn.; Richard Rcmy, Info.Sci.

★15517★
Southern States Energy Board (SSEB) - Southern Energy/ Environmental Information Center (SEEIC) (Energy)
3091 Governors Lakes Dr., Suite 400   Phone: (404)242-7712
Norcross, GA 30071-1113   Ricky S. Gibson, Mgr., Info.Serv.
Founded: 1961. **Staff:** Prof 1; Other 2. **Subjects:** Energy, environment, energy policy and development. **Holdings:** 130 books; 6125 technical reports; 1000 state publications; 30 VF drawers. **Subscriptions:** 115 journals and other serials. **Services:** Interlibrary loan; copying (limited); center open to the public by appointment. **Computerized Information Services:** Internal databases. **Publications:** Southern Sources, monthly - to state officials, legislators, association members, and by subscription; Radioactive Waste News, articles and publications, bimonthly - to state officials and agencies concerned with nuclear waste transportation issues; Southern Energy Report, quarterly (newsletter to state officials and legislators). **Remarks:** FAX: (404)242-0421.

★15518★
Southern University - Law Center - Library (Law)
Southern Branch Post Office
Box 9294   Phone: (504)771-2315
Baton Rouge, LA 70813   Alvin A. Roche, Jr., Law Libn.
Founded: 1947. **Staff:** Prof 4; Other 9. **Subjects:** Law - civil, general, medical, international; political science. **Special Collections:** Civil rights; Federal and Louisiana State documents. **Holdings:** 182,982 books; 29,500 bound periodical volumes; 115,015 volumes of microfiche; 28,990 microfilm. **Subscriptions:** 550 journals and other serials; 15 newspapers. **Services:** Interlibrary loan; copying; library open to the public on a limited schedule. **Automated Operations:** Computerized cataloging and acquisitions. **Computerized Information Services:** OCLC, WESTLAW, LEXIS. **Networks/Consortia:** Member of SOLINET. **Publications:** Periodical list, annual; acquisitions list, quarterly; subject bibliographies, monthly. **Remarks:** FAX: (504)771-2474. **Staff:** Roberta S. Cummings, Asst.Libn.; Harold Isadore, Assoc.Libn.; Valanda LeDoux, Asst.Proc.Libn.; Deloris Tetteh, Chf.Cat.; Ollie Lewis, Reserve Libn.; Constance O. Helmke, Govt.Docs.; Rose Herbert, Asst.Acq.Libn.; Christine Nappier, Asst.Ref.Libn.

★15519★
Southern Utah State College - Library - Special Collections Department (Hist, Hum)
351 W. Center St.   Phone: (801)586-7945
Cedar City, UT 84720   Blanche C. Clegg, Spec.Coll.Coord.
Founded: 1962. **Staff:** Prof 1; Other 2. **Subjects:** Southern Paiute Indians history, local history, college history, Shakespeare. **Special Collections:** William Rees Palmer Western History Collection; Document Collection (various donors); John Laurence Seymour Collection (music, theater, humanities). **Holdings:** 7000 volumes; 925 oral history tapes; 457 phonograph records; 1445 linear feet of manuscript collections; 36,500 photographs and negatives; 804 linear feet of archives; 7530 microforms; 570 maps. **Services:** Interlibrary loan; copying; department open to the public for reference use only. **Automated Operations:** Computerized cataloging. **Computerized Information Services:** DIALOG Information Services; internal database. **Networks/Consortia:** Member of Utah College Library Council (UCLC). **Special Indexes:** Document collection index; oral history index; photo collection index; index of library's holdings of Latter-Day Saints periodicals; index to Palmer Western History Collection.

★15520★
Southern Wisconsin Center for the Developmentally Disabled - Medical Staff Library (Med)
21425 Spring St.
Union Grove, WI 53182-9708   Phone: (414)878-2411
Founded: 1965. **Staff:** 1. **Subjects:** Medicine, mental retardation, medical specialties, current therapy, syndromes, malformations. **Holdings:** 124 books; 260 Audio-Digest tapes; statistical reports. **Subscriptions:** 15 journals and other serials. **Services:** Library not open to the public.

★15521★
Southern Wisconsin Center for the Developmentally Disabled - Nursing Education Library (Med)
21425 Spring St.
Union Grove, WI 53182-9708   Phone: (414)878-2411
Founded: 1919. **Subjects:** Nursing, pharmacology, nutrition, mental retardation. **Special Collections:** Videotape library on nursing care and behavorial programming issues in developmental disabilities. **Holdings:** Books; AV programs. **Subscriptions:** 27 journals and other serials. **Services:** Interlibrary loan (limited); library not open to the public. **Staff:** M. Graham Molitor, Educ.Adm.; Nora Diderrich, RRA, Med.Rec.Libn.

Southern Wisconsin History and Southern Wisconsin Area Research Center
See: **University of Wisconsin--Platteville (19645)**

Southern Women's Archives
See: **Birmingham Public and Jefferson County Free Library - Linn-Henley Library for Southern Historical Research - Department of Archives and Manuscripts (1856)**

★15522★
Southfield Public Library - Special Collections (Bus-Fin, Hum)
26000 Evergreen Rd.
Box 2055   Phone: (313)948-0460
Southfield, MI 48037-2055   Douglas A. Zyskowski, City Libn.
Founded: 1960. **Staff:** 39. **Special Collections:** Business Collection; Census Affiliate Collection; Shakespeare Collection. **Holdings:** 230,000 books. **Subscriptions:** 400 journals and other serials; 30 newspapers. **Services:** Interlibrary loan; copying; document delivery; collections open to the public for reference use only. **Automated Operations:** Computerized circulation. **Computerized Information Services:** DIALOG Information Services, Dow Jones News/Retrieval, VU/TEXT Information Services, National Planning Data Corporation (NPDC), WILSONLINE; InfoTrac. **Networks/Consortia:** Member of Wayne Oakland Library Federation (WOLF). **Remarks:** FAX: (313)354-5319. **Staff:** Ann Abdoo, Coord., Adult Pub.Serv.; Carol Mueller, Dp. City Libn.; Irene Smeyers, Coord., Youth Serv.; Ann Mannisto, Coord., Sup.Serv.

★15523★
Southold Historical Society Museum - Library (Hist)
Main Rd.   Phone: (516)765-5500
Southold, NY 11971   Cynthia B. Halsey, Dir.
Founded: 1960. **Subjects:** Local and state history, genealogy, local fishing and farming, early textbooks, decorative arts. **Special Collections:** Early and local music, photographs, diaries. **Holdings:** 3000 books; pamphlets. **Services:** Library open to the public by appointment. **Publications:** Newsletter, annual. **Staff:** Helen Prince, Archv.Coord.

★15524★
Southside Hospital - Medical Library (Med)
301 E. Main St.   Phone: (516)968-3026
Bay Shore, NY 11706-8458   Caryl Kazen, Med.Libn.
Founded: 1955. **Staff:** Prof 1. **Subjects:** Family practice, internal medicine, surgery, nursing, dentistry, psychiatry. **Special Collections:** Family practice collections. **Holdings:** 700 books; 100 bound periodical volumes. **Subscriptions:** 150 journals and other serials. **Services:** Interlibrary loan; library not open to the public. **Automated Operations:** Computerized cataloging. **Computerized Information Services:** MEDLINE, BRS Information Technologies. **Networks/Consortia:** Member of Medical & Scientific Libraries of Long Island (MEDLI), BHSL. **Remarks:** FAX: (516)968-3978.

★15525★
Southside Regional Medical Center - Medical Library Media Services (Med)
801 S. Adams St.   Phone: (804)732-7220
Petersburg, VA 23803   Joan B. Pollard, Med.Lib./Media Serv.Dir.
Founded: 1956. **Staff:** Prof 1; Other 4. **Subjects:** Medicine, nursing. **Special Collections:** Old medical books. **Holdings:** 1002 books; 5230 bound periodical volumes; 4 VF drawers of reprints; 120 video cassettes; 1260 Audio-Digest tapes. **Subscriptions:** 125 journals and other serials. **Services:** Interlibrary loan; library not open to the public. **Networks/Consortia:** Member of National Network of Libraries of Medicine - Southeastern/ Atlantic Region. **Publications:** Monthly News-Acquisitions. **Remarks:** Alternate telephone number(s): 862-5357. FAX: (804)732-3360.

★15526★
Southwest Arkansas Regional Archives (Hist)
Box 134   Phone: (501)983-2633
Washington, AR 71862   Mary Medearis, Dir.
Founded: 1978. **Staff:** Prof 1. **Subjects:** History of Southwest Arkansas, Caddo Indians. **Special Collections:** Rare books collection on Southwest Arkansas and Texas; census and court records for twelve southwest Arkansas counties; newspapers of southwest Arkansas; index and service records for Civil War soldiers who served in Arkansas units. **Holdings:** 1500 books; 3000 reels of microfilm; original court records of Hempstead County, 1819-1910; pictures; manuscripts; family histories; theses; sheet music; newspapers; maps; pamphlets; journals; genealogical records. **Services:** Copying; archives open to the public for reference use only. **Publications:** SARA Newsletter, quarterly.

★ 15527 ★
Southwest Econometrics, Inc. - Library (Bus-Fin)
1 Bridgepoint, Suite 130
6300 Bridgepoint Pkwy.
Austin, TX 78730   Phone: (512)346-2255
Subjects: Economics, demography, utilities, energy. **Holdings:** 2000
volumes. **Computerized Information Services:** Internal databases. **Remarks:**
FAX: (512)346-2371.

★ 15528 ★
Southwest Florida Water Management District - Library (Env-Cons,
   Plan)
2379 Broad St.   Phone: (904)796-7211
Brooksville, FL 34609-6899   Charles Tornabene, Jr., Libn.
Founded: 1961. **Staff:** Prof 1; Other 1. **Subjects:** Water resources, regional
planning, ecology, engineering. **Holdings:** 10,000 books. **Subscriptions:** 63
journals and other serials. **Services:** Library open to the public for reference
use only. **Automated Operations:** Computerized public access catalog.
Computerized Information Services: DIALOG Information Services,
Ground Water On-Line. **Publications:** Basin Literature Assessments.
Remarks: FAX: (904)754-6876.

★ 15529 ★
Southwest Foundation for Biomedical Research - Preston G. Northrup
   Memorial Library (Biol Sci, Med)
Box 28147   Phone: (512)674-1410
San Antonio, TX 78228-0147   Maureen D. Funnell, Libn.
Founded: 1959. **Staff:** Prof 3; Other 1. **Subjects:** Biomedicine. **Special
Collections:** Primatology. **Holdings:** 9200 books; 38,000 bound periodical
volumes. **Subscriptions:** 600 journals and other serials. **Services:** Interlibrary
loan; copying; library open to the public. **Automated Operations:**
Computerized cataloging, acquisitions, serials, and circulation.
Computerized Information Services: DIALOG Information Services, PFDS
Online, MEDLARS, Chemical Abstracts Service (CAS). **Networks/
Consortia:** Member of AMIGOS Bibliographic Council, Inc., Council of
Research & Academic Libraries (CORAL), Health Oriented Libraries of
San Antonio (HOLSA). **Staff:** Ruth H. Brooks, Asst.Libn.; Mary Ann
Smith, ILL.

★ 15530 ★
Southwest Minnesota Historical Center (Hist)
Southwest State University   Phone: (507)537-7373
Marshall, MN 56258   David Nass, Dir.
Founded: 1972. **Staff:** Prof 1; Other 2. **Subjects:** Local history, church
histories, Iceland, agricultural history, genealogy. **Special Collections:**
Minnesota Farm Holiday Association (tapes); Globe Land and Loan
Company records; Verzlunarfelag Islendinga records; regional newspapers.
Holdings: 150 books; records; 200 oral history interviews. **Services:**
Copying; center open to the public (by appointment only in July and
August). **Remarks:** Maintained by Southwest State University. **Staff:** Janice
Louwagie, Coord.

★ 15531 ★
Southwest Missouri State University - Map Library (Geog-Map)
Duane G. Meyer Library
No. 175   Phone: (417)836-4534
Springfield, MO 65804-0095   James A. Coombs, Map Libn.
Founded: 1980. **Staff:** Prof 1; Other 1. **Subjects:** Cartography, outdoor
recreation. **Special Collections:** Tourist information (6647 items); pre-1920
U.S. Geological Survey topographic quadrangles; U.S. Geological Survey
Geologic Atlas of the United States (222 volumes). **Holdings:** 431 books;
117,957 maps; 54,469 aerial photographs; 1866 atlases; 8 globes; 9 raised
relief maps; 1175 microforms; 56 gazetteers. **Subscriptions:** 19 journals and
other serials. **Services:** Interlibrary loan; copying; library open to the public.
Automated Operations: Computerized public access catalog and cataloging
(NOTIS). **Computerized Information Services:** BITNET, InterNet
(electronic mail services). **Special Indexes:** Indexes to U.S. Geological
Survey geologic atlases and to small- and medium-scale geologic maps in
U.S. **Remarks:** FAX: (417)836-4764. Electronic mail address(es):
JAC324f@SMSVMA (BITNET); JAC324f@vma.smsu.edu (InterNet).

★ 15532 ★
Southwest Museum - Braun Research Library (Hist)
P.O. Box 41558   Phone: (213)221-2164
Los Angeles, CA 90041-0558   Kim Walters, Lib.Dir.
Founded: 1907. **Staff:** Prof 3; Other 3. **Subjects:** Anthropology, Native
American studies, western history. **Special Collections:** Munk Library of
Arizoniana; Hector Alliott Memorial Library of Archaeology; Charles F.
Lummis Collection; George Wharton James Collection; papers of Frank
Hamilton Cushing, John Charles Fremont, George Bird Grinnell, Frederick
Webb Hodge, Charles F. Lummis; rare Western American imprints;
children's books. **Holdings:** 50,000 volumes; 100,000 pamphlets and
ephemera; 120,000 photographs; 700 linear feet of manuscripts; 1300 sound
recordings; government publications; ϒF drawers. **Subscriptions:** 200
journals and other serials. **Services:** Library open to the public. **Automated
Operations:** Computerized cataloging. **Computerized Information Services:**
OCLC; ARGUS (internal database). Performs searches free of charge.
Contact Person: Richard Buchen, Ref.Libn. **Remarks:** Library located at
234 Museum Dr., Los Angeles, CA 90065. FAX: (213)224-8223. **Staff:**
Craig Klyver, Photo.Archv.

Southwest Museum of Science and Technology
See: **The Science Place** (14941)

★ 15533 ★
Southwest Railroad Historical Society - Age of Steam Museum - Library
   (Hist)
P.O. Box 153259   Phone: (214)428-0101
Dallas, TX 75315-3259   Robert H. LaPrelle, Exec.Dir
Founded: 1963. **Staff:** 1. **Subjects:** Railroad history. **Holdings:** 200 books;
200 bound periodical volumes. **Services:** Library open to the public with
restrictions. **Publications:** Clearance Card (newsletter), bimonthly -
available on request. **Remarks:** Library located at Washington & Parry Ave.,
Fair Park.

★ 15534 ★
Southwest Research & Information Center (Soc Sci, Env-Cons)
Box 4524   Phone: (505)262-1862
Albuquerque, NM 87106   Don Hancock, Info.Coord.
Founded: 1971. **Staff:** Prof 2; Other 1. **Subjects:** Environmental, consumer,
and social issues. **Special Collections:** Uranium publications and clippings
(3000 items); nuclear waste management publications and clippings.
Holdings: 3000 books; 7 cabinets of clippings in 1000 categories; 100
sourcebooks. **Subscriptions:** 350 journals and other serials; 15 newspapers.
Services: Copying; center open to the public for reference use only.
Computerized Information Services: DIALOG Information Services.
Publications: The Workbook, quarterly.

★ 15535 ★
Southwest Research Institute - Thomas Baker Slick Memorial Library
   (Sci-Engr)
Drawer 28510   Phone: (512)522-2125
San Antonio, TX 78228-0510   Robert D. Armor, Libn.
Founded: 1948. **Staff:** Prof 3; Other 5. **Subjects:** Engineering - chemical,
electrical, mechanical, aeronautical; chemistry; geology; physics;
mathematics. **Holdings:** 44,894 books; 16,523 bound periodical volumes;
61,477 unbound periodicals; 86,000 reports on microfiche. **Subscriptions:**
1203 journals and other serials. **Services:** Interlibrary loan; copying; library
open to the public for reference use only. **Computerized Information
Services:** DIALOG Information Services, PFDS Online, DTIC. **Networks/
Consortia:** Member of Council of Research & Academic Libraries
(CORAL), Health Oriented Libraries of San Antonio (HOLSA). **Remarks:**
FAX: (512)522-5479. **Staff:** Oralia R. Ruiz, Assoc.Libn.; Roland Craig,
Assoc.Libn.

Southwest State University - Southwest Minnesota Historical Center
See: **Southwest Minnesota Historical Center** (15530)

Southwest Texas Methodist Hospital
See: **Methodist Hospital** (10182)

Southwest Washington Hospitals - St. Joseph Community Hospital
See: St. Joseph Community Hospital (14362)

Southwest Washington Hospitals - Vancouver Memorial Hospital
See: Vancouver Memorial Hospital (19756)

Southwest Watershed Research Center
See: U.S.D.A. - Agricultural Research Service (17195)

★ 15536 ★
Southwest Wisconsin Technical College - Library (Bus-Fin, Sci-Engr)
Bronson Blvd.
Rte. 1, Box 500
Fennimore, WI 53809
Phone: (608)822-3262
Patricia Payson, Libn.
Founded: 1971. **Staff:** Prof 1; Other 1. **Subjects:** Business education, agriculture, automotive mechanics, home economics, health occupations, technical and industrial occupations. **Holdings:** 21,353 books; 3122 AV programs; 18 drawers of pamphlets; 1147 microforms. **Subscriptions:** 250 journals and other serials and newspapers. **Services:** Interlibrary loan; copying; library open to the public. **Computerized Information Services:** DIALOG Information Services. Performs searches on fee basis. **Remarks:** FAX: (608)822-6019.

★ 15537 ★
Southwestern Assemblies of God College - P.C. Nelson Memorial Library (Rel-Phil)
1200 Sycamore
Waxahachie, TX 75165
Phone: (214)937-4010
Edna A. Roberts, Dir.
Founded: 1927. **Staff:** Prof 2; Other 2. **Subjects:** Bible, liberal arts, education. **Special Collections:** Pentecostal Materials Collection (1960 volumes); William Burton McCafferty Pentecostal Periodical Collection (8 cabinets; 56 cubic feet). **Holdings:** 76,817 books; 6318 bound periodical volumes; 9959 pamphlets; 622 flannelgraphs; 967 tapes; 1608 slides; 133 maps; 1371 phonograph records; 790 filmstrips; 885 reels of microfilm; 26,935 microfiche; 1267 directories and catalogs; 246 documents; 1649 ultrafiche; 56 puppets. **Subscriptions:** 664 journals and other serials. **Services:** Interlibrary loan; copying; library open to the public on fee basis. **Special Indexes:** Index to Pentecostal Evangel, 1920, 1924, 1926, 1927, 1930-1961 (card); index to Pentecost Magazine (card); index to Church of God Evangel (card; in preparation); index to Christ's Ambassadors Herald (card; in preparation); index to Missionary Challenge (card; in preparation); index to Pentecostal Holiness Advocate (card; in preparation). **Staff:** Pearl Ellis, Asst.Dir.

★ 15538 ★
Southwestern Baptist Theological Seminary - A. Webb Roberts Library (Rel-Phil)
Box 22000-2E
Fort Worth, TX 76122
Phone: (817)923-1921
Dr. Carl R. Wrotenbery, Dir. of Libs.
Founded: 1909. **Staff:** Prof 9; Other 42. **Subjects:** Religion and theology, Bible, music and hymnology, Baptist history, religious education. **Special Collections:** Personal items and correspondence of B.H. Carroll, L.R. Scarborough, George W. Truett, M.E. Dodd, James M. Carroll (Baptist leaders); Texas Baptist Historical Collection (63,737 items); George Fitzpatrick Oxford Library (2,250 volumes); George Stebbins Memorial Library from the National Cathedral (1200 volumes); Capuchin Fathers Monastery Library (5000 volumes). **Holdings:** 293,000 books; 70,000 bound periodical volumes; 61,166 convention and association annuals; 190,000 pieces of printed music; 42,000 tapes and discs; 3313 films and filmstrips; 1906 videotapes; 447,881 manuscripts; 13,700 microforms. **Subscriptions:** 1928 journals and other serials. **Services:** Interlibrary loan; copying; SDI; library open to the public. **Automated Operations:** Computerized cataloging, acquisitions and circulation. **Computerized Information Services:** OCLC, BRS Information Technologies, WILSONLINE. Performs searches on fee basis. Contact Person: Robert Phillips, Asst.Dir./Pub.Serv., 294-7142. **Networks/Consortia:** Member of AMIGOS Bibliographic Council, Inc. **Publications:** New Titles Added, monthly. **Special Indexes:** Baptist biography index (card). **Remarks:** FAX: (817)923-1921, ext. 2810. **Staff:** Phil Sims, Music Libn.; Carol Bastien, Acq.Libn.; Cloe Smith, Circ.Libn.; Marty Hill, AV Libn.; Steve Story, Media Coord.; Barbara Russell, Cat.Libn.; Keith C. Wills, Archv.; Myrta Garrett, Asst.Dir./Tech.Serv. and Ser.Libn.

★ 15539 ★
Southwestern Conservative Baptist Bible College - Dr. R.S. Beal, Sr. Library (Rel-Phil)
2625 E. Cactus Rd.
Phoenix, AZ 85032
Phone: (602)992-6101
Alice Eickmeyer, Libn.
Founded: 1960. **Staff:** 1.5. **Subjects:** Bible, theology, missions, Christian education, elementary education. **Holdings:** 25,631 books; 2698 bound periodical volumes; 19,725 microforms; 1292 AV programs; 39 scores; 415 teaching aids. **Subscriptions:** 117 journals and other serials. **Services:** Interlibrary loan; copying; library open to the public with restrictions on circulation. **Automated Operations:** Computerized cataloging. **Computerized Information Services:** Wilson's Religion Indexes, CD WordLibrary.

★ 15540 ★
Southwestern Illinois Metropolitan and Regional Planning Commission - Technical Library (Plan)
203 W. Main St.
Collinsville, IL 62234
Phone: (618)344-4250
Bonnie C. Moore, Info.Mgr.
Founded: 1965. **Staff:** Prof 1. **Subjects:** Urban and regional planning, census data, legislation, codes and ordinances, transportation, recreation, water and sewage. **Holdings:** 4000 volumes. **Subscriptions:** 65 journals and other serials. **Services:** Interlibrary loan; copying; library open to the public.

Southwestern Indian Polytechnic Institute
See: U.S. Bureau of Indian Affairs (17099)

★ 15541 ★
Southwestern Indiana Mental Health Center, Inc. - Library (Med)
415 Mulberry St.
Evansville, IN 47713
Phone: (812)423-7791
Ina Freeman, Libn.
Founded: 1978. **Staff:** Prof 1. **Subjects:** Psychology, psychiatry, social work, child development, sexuality, therapeutic recreation, drug abuse. **Holdings:** 1000 books; 700 pamphlets; 175 AV programs. **Subscriptions:** 80 journals and other serials. **Services:** Interlibrary loan; copying; library open to the public for reference use only. **Networks/Consortia:** Member of Evansville Area Libraries Consortium, Four Rivers Area Library Services Authority (ALSA).

★ 15542 ★
Southwestern Oklahoma State University - Al Harris Library (Educ, Med, Bus-Fin)
Weatherford, OK 73096
Phone: (405)772-6611
Sheila Wilder Hoke, Lib.Dir.
Founded: 1902. **Staff:** Prof 6; Other 9. **Subjects:** Pharmacy, education, psychology, business administration. **Holdings:** 238,651 bound books and periodicals; 16,595 reels of microfilm; 421,617 microfiche; 90,250 microcards; 34,061 government documents. **Subscriptions:** 1503 subscriptions. **Services:** Interlibrary loan; library open to the public. **Computerized Information Services:** DIALOG Information Services, MEDLARS, OCLC. **Networks/Consortia:** Member of AMIGOS Bibliographic Council, Inc. **Staff:** James Wilkerson, Ser.Libn.; Linda Pye, Acq.Libn.; George Alsbach, Cat.; Caroline Armold Torrence, Ref./ILL/Govt.Docs.; David Corbly, Pub.Serv.

★ 15543 ★
Southwestern Public Service Company - Library (Bus-Fin, Energy)
6th at Tyler
Box 1261
Amarillo, TX 79170
Phone: (806)378-2741
Beth Beasley Perry, Libn.
Founded: 1971. **Staff:** Prof 1. **Subjects:** Engineering, power transmission and distribution, business administration, finance, economics, agriculture, data processing, law. **Special Collections:** Electric Power Research Institute Reports; Texas Water Development Board Reports; ASTM standards; ANSI Standards; Career development materials. **Holdings:** 3000 books; 450 periodical titles; 400 AV items; 3 drawers of microfilm; 4 drawers of microfiche; annual reports. **Subscriptions:** 400 journals and other serials; 6 newspapers. **Services:** Interlibrary loan; library not open to the public. **Automated Operations:** Computerized cataloging, serials, and public access catalog. **Computerized Information Services:** DIALOG Information Services. **Special Catalogs:** Audio-visual catalogs - on request. **Remarks:** FAX: (806)378-2995.

★ 15544 ★
Southwestern Research Station - Library (Biol Sci)
Portal, AZ 85632   Phone: (602)558-2396
                                              Wade C. Sherbrooke, Dir.
Founded: 1955. **Subjects:** Entomology, ornithology, herpetology,
mammology, botany. **Special Collections:** Collection of research papers by
scientists working at Southwestern Research Station. **Publications:**
Bibliography of publications by researchers at SWRS, 1955-1990.

★ 15545 ★
Southwestern University - School of Law Library (Law)
675 S. Westmoreland Ave.   Phone: (213)738-6723
Los Angeles, CA 90005   Linda Whisman, Dir.
Founded: 1913. **Staff:** Prof 7; Other 11. **Subjects:** Law. **Holdings:** 198,058
books; 639,701 microforms; 1097 audio- and videotapes. **Subscriptions:** 4136
journals and other serials; 25 newspapers. **Services:** Interlibrary loan; library
not open to the public. **Automated Operations:** Computerized cataloging.
Computerized Information Services: LEXIS, RLIN, WESTLAW,
WILSONLINE. **Networks/Consortia:** Member of CLASS. **Staff:** S.
Gerlach, Ref.; C. Weiner, Pub.Serv.; D. McFadden, Ref.; T. Tsui, Cat.; K.
Romanko, Ref.; C. Deng, Cat.

★ 15546 ★
Southwestern Vermont Medical Center - Medical Library (Med)
100 Hospital Dr., E.   Phone: (802)447-5120
Bennington, VT 05201   Alexandra Heintz, Libn.Mgr.
Staff: Prof 1. **Subjects:** Medicine, surgery. **Holdings:** 1300 books; 400
volumes of bound journals; 10 titles of Audio-Digest tapes; 200
videocassettes. **Subscriptions:** 120 journals and other serials. **Services:**
Interlibrary loan; copying; library open to the public with restrictions.
Networks/Consortia: Member of National Network of Libraries of
Medicine - New England Region. **Remarks:** FAX: (802)442-8331. **Staff:**
Beverly Thane, Libn.

★ 15547 ★
Southwestern Virginia Mental Health Institute - Professional Library
  (Med)
502 E. Main St.   Phone: (703)783-1200
Marion, VA 24354   Elizabeth Kent
Founded: 1941. **Staff:** Prof 1. **Subjects:** Psychiatry. **Holdings:** 900 volumes;
479 AV programs. **Subscriptions:** 35 journals and other serials. **Services:**
Interlibrary loan; copying; library open to the public. **Networks/Consortia:**
Member of Southwestern Virginia Health Information Librarians
(SWVAHILI). **Remarks:** FAX: (703)783-1239.

★ 15548 ★
Southwestern Virginia Training Center - Research & Training Library
Rte. 1
Box 415
Hillsville, VA 24343   Phone: (703)728-3121
                                              Dan Dewey, Libn.
Remarks: No further information was supplied by respondent.

★ 15549 ★
Southwire Company - R & D Technical Library (Sci-Engr)
One Southwire Dr.
Carrollton, GA 30119   Phone: (404)832-5099
Founded: 1964. **Staff:** 1. **Subjects:** Aluminum, copper, rod, wire and cable,
metallurgy, environment, management. **Holdings:** 1000 books; 500 bound
periodical volumes; 4000 information files. **Subscriptions:** 62 journals and
other serials. **Services:** Library open to company employees only. **Remarks:**
FAX: (404)832-4929.

★ 15550 ★
Southwood Community Hospital - Medical Library (Med)
111 Dedham St.   Phone: (508)668-0385
Norfolk, MA 02056   Debbie MacDonald, Med.Libn.
Founded: 1927. **Staff:** 1. **Subjects:** Oncology, medicine, surgery, nursing,
radiology. **Special Collections:** CIBA Collection, Volumes 1-7. **Holdings:**
1896 books and bound periodical volumes. **Subscriptions:** 94 journals and
other serials. **Services:** Interlibrary loan; copying; library open to the public
with restrictions. **Automated Operations:** Computerized acquisitions,
serials, and circulation. **Computerized Information Services:** MEDLINE,
NurseSearch, NLM; DOCLINE (electronic mail service). **Networks/
Consortia:** Member of Southeastern Massachusetts Consortium of Health
Science Libraries (SEMCO), Consortium for Information Resources (CIR).
Remarks: FAX: (508)668-1481.

Charles L. Souvay Memorial Library
See: **Kenrick-Glennon Seminary (8640)**

★ 15551 ★
Sovereign Hospitaller Order of St. John - Villa Anneslie - Archives (Rel-
  Phil)
1435 Fairfax St.
Denver, CO 80220   Fra Paul, H.O.S.J.
Staff: Prof 1. **Subjects:** History of the Order of St. John. **Holdings:** 1000
books and documents. **Subscriptions:** 34 journals and other serials. **Services:**
Archives open to the public by appointment. **Formerly:** Located in
Brooklyn, NY.

★ 15552 ★
Sovran Bank/Central South - Library (Bus-Fin)
1 Commerce Pl.   Phone: (615)749-4841
Nashville, TN 37219   Lillie Taylor, Libn.
Founded: 1976. **Staff:** Prof 1. **Subjects:** Banking, economics, marketing.
Holdings: 500 books; 4 VF drawers of archives; 4 VF drawers of annual
reports; 4 VF drawers of newspaper clippings; 145 reels of microfilm.
Subscriptions: 160 journals and other serials. **Services:** Interlibrary loan;
copying; library open to the public with restrictions. **Remarks:** FAX:
(615)749-4115.

★ 15553 ★
(Soweto) USIS Reading Room (Educ)
Johannesburg Library
Soweto, Republic of South Africa
Remarks: Maintained or supported by the U.S. Information Agency. Focus
is on materials that will assist peoples outside the United States to learn
about the United States, its people, history, culture, political processes, and
social milieux. Library located at Ipelegeng Community Centre, 1860 White
City Jabavu, Soweto, Republic of South Africa.

Moses and Ida Soyer Library
See: **Parrish Art Museum - Library (12764)**

★ 15554 ★
Soyfoods Center Library and Information Center (Food-Bev)
P.O. Box 234   Phone: (510)283-9091
Lafayette, CA 94549   William R. Shurtleff
Founded: 1972. **Staff:** Prof 2; Other 1. **Subjects:** Soyfoods and the soybean
industry - history, food technology, nutrition, industrial statistics, marketing
information, all known commercial soy products. **Special Collections:**
Traditional, low technology soyfoods; East Asian soyfoods; European
soyfoods; historical collection. **Holdings:** 1175 books; 36,000 article reprints,
interviews, and letters; color slides. **Subscriptions:** 27 journals and other
serials. **Services:** Copying; library open to the public by appointment.
Automated Operations: Computerized cataloging. **Computerized
Information Services:** SoyaScan Publications (36,600 records from 1100
B.C. to the present); SoyaScan Products (8873 records); SoyaScan Directory
(13,200 records). Performs searches on fee basis. **Publications:** International
Bibliographies of Soyfoods and the Soybean Industry, (40 volumes);
Soyfoods Industry and Market: Directory and Databook, annual; list of
other publications - available on request. **Remarks:** Center located at 1021
Dolores Dr., Lafayette, CA 94549. **Remarks:** FAX: (510)283-9091. **Staff:**
Claire Wickens, Asst.Dir.

★ 15555 ★
Space Systems/Loral - Technical Library MS 250 (Sci-Engr)
3825 Fabian Way
Palo Alto, CA 94303   Phone: (415)852-6993
Founded: 1957. **Staff:** Prof 1. **Subjects:** Higher mathematics, electronics,
space sciences, physics, computer sciences. **Services:** Library not open to the
public. **Computerized Information Services:** DIALOG Information
Services, FYI News, NERAC, Inc., Teltech, Inc. **Networks/Consortia:**
Member of SOUTHNET. **Remarks:** Library no longer maintains material
holdings; all holdings are now maintained electronically. FAX: (415)852-
4201.

★15556★
Space Telescope Science Institute - Library (Sci-Engr)
3700 San Martin Dr.   Phone: (410)338-4961
Baltimore, MD 21218   Sarah Stevens-Rayburn, Libn.
Founded: 1983. **Staff:** Prof 1.5; Other 1. **Subjects:** Astrophysics, astronomy, space sciences, computers. **Special Collections:** Palomar and European Southern Observatory/Science Research Council photographic sky surveys. **Holdings:** 4000 books; 3000 bound periodical volumes; 210 linear feet of observatory publications. **Subscriptions:** 436 journals and other serials. **Services:** Interlibrary loan; copying; SDI; library open to qualified users by appointment. **Automated Operations:** Computerized cataloging and circulation. **Computerized Information Services:** DIALOG Information Services, NASA/RECON, STN International; internal database; SPAN, BITNET, InterNet (electronic mail services). **Networks/Consortia:** Member of FEDLINK. **Publications:** STEPsheet (preprint listing), biweekly; acquisitions list, monthly; duplicates list, quarterly. **Remarks:** FAX: (410)338-4767. Electronic mail address(es): library@stsci.edu (InterNet). Telex: 684 9101 STSCI. **Staff:** Barbara Snead, Asst.Libn.

Spaced Out Library
See: **Toronto Public Library** (16417)

SPACES
See: **Saving and Preserving Arts & Cultural Environments** (14888)

Spahr Engineering Library
See: **University of Kansas** (18738)

★15557★
Spain - Biblioteca de la Palacio Real (Hist, Art)
C/Bailen s/n   Phone: 1 2487404
E-28071 Madrid, Spain   Maria Luisa Lopez-Vidriero, Dir.
Staff: Prof 3. **Subjects:** History, art, heraldry, literature, military history, America. **Holdings:** 253,866 books; 2000 bound periodical volumes; 90 microfiche; 105 reels of microfilm; manuscripts; printed and manuscript music; incunabula, ancient books; maps; photography; drawings; engravings. **Subscriptions:** 20 journals and other serials. **Services:** Copying; SDI; library open for accredited research. **Publications:** Incunabula; Manuscripts of America; Maps; Engravings. **Remarks:** FAX: 1 2482691.

★15558★
Spain - Biological Research Center - Library (Biol Sci)
Velazquez 144   Phone: 1 915854298
E-28006 Madrid, Spain   Concepcion Lopez Hermida
Founded: 1946. **Staff:** 7. **Subjects:** Biology, biomedicine. **Special Collections:** Dr. Gregorio Maranon's monographs. **Holdings:** 5367 volumes (books and theses). **Subscriptions:** 425 journals and other serials. **Services:** Library open to the public. **Computerized Information Services:** MEDLINE; CD-ROMs (Biological Abstracts, Current Contents); EAN (electronic mail service). **Remarks:** FAX: 1 3415627518. Telex: 42182 CSIC E. Electronic mail address(es): Bib–biologia@bib.csic.es (EAN). **Formerly:** Spain - Council for Scientific Research. **Also Known As:** Biblioteca del Centro de Investigaciones Biologicas. **Staff:** E. Cabrero Alonso; A. Hermida Gonzalez; J. Vilela Manrique.

Spain - Centro Nacional de Condiciones de Trabajo
See: **Spain - Ministry of Labour - National Institute of Occupational Safety and Health** (15564)

★15559★
Spain - Congress of Deputies - Library (Law, Soc Sci)
Floridablanca s/n   Phone: 1 4 29 51 93
E-28014 Madrid, Spain   Alicia Martin Gonzalez, Chf.
Subjects: Law, political science, history, economics, sociology. **Special Collections:** Spanish parliamentary history before and during the constitutional period (bibliography; original documents); elections; 15th century incunabula (81); 16th-17th century rare books (257); 19th century pamphlets; parliamentary activity films and photographs. **Holdings:** 100,000 book titles; 1500 periodical titles; 5000 AV programs; 25 titles in microform. **Services:** Interlibrary loan; copying; library open to historians and researchers. **Computerized Information Services:** IBERLEX, Communitatis Europae Lex (CELEX), CRONOS Data Bank, ECHO, COMEXT Data Bank; ARGO (internal database). **Publications:** Recent acquisitions information; Congress of Deputies Library history; Library and Archives holdings publications. **Special Catalogs:** Periodical catalog. **Remarks:** Telex: 46.685 HEMIE. **Also Known As:** Congreso de los Diputados - Biblioteca. **Staff:** Manuel Gonzalo, Dir. of Res. & Doc.

★15560★
Spain - Council for Scientific Research - Institute for Information and Documentation in Science and Technology - Library (Sci-Engr)
Joaquin Costa, 22
E-28002 Madrid, Spain   Phone: 1 563 54 82
Subjects: Industrial chemistry, electrical engineering, electronics, metallurgy, farm engineering, agronomics, management, physics, life sciences, pharmacology, mathematics, astronomy, astrophysics. **Holdings:** 22,000 volumes; Spanish patents. **Subscriptions:** 2225 journals and other serials. **Services:** SDI; library open to the public. **Computerized Information Services:** Internal database. Performs searches on fee basis. **Remarks:** FAX: 1 564 26 44. Telex: 22628 cidmd e. **Also Known As:** Consejo Superior de Investigaciones Cientificas - Instituto de Informacion y Documentacion en Ciencia y Tecnologia.

★15561★
Spain - Council for Scientific Research - Mila and Fontanals Institution - Library (Hum)
Calle Egipciacas 15   Phone: 3 934423489
E-08001 Barcelona, Spain   Maria Antonia Callis, Chf.Libn.
Founded: 1968. **Subjects:** Medieval and modern history, musicology, cultural anthropology and ethnology, geography, classic and romance philology, archeology, pedagogics, philosophy and religion, art, literature. **Holdings:** 66,576 volumes. **Subscriptions:** 605 journals and other serials. **Services:** Interlibrary loan; copying; SDI; library open to the public. **Computerized Information Services:** EAN (electronic mail service). **Publications:** Butlleti Bibliografic y contribucion en: International Medieval Bibliography. **Remarks:** FAX: 3 934427424. Telex: 99560 DCCSI. Electronic mail address(es): Bib–mila@bicat.csic.es (EAN). **Also Known As:** Consejo Superior de Investigaciones Cientificas - Institucion Mila y Fontanals. **Staff:** Antonia Callis; Maite Carballo; Josefina Figuls; Rosa Mayordomo; Anna Perez; Miguel Angel Plaza.

Spain - Council for Scientific Research Center
See: **Spain - Biological Research Center** (15558)

Spain - Instituto y Observatorio de Marina - Biblioteca
See: **Spain - Royal Naval Observatory and Institute - Library** (15567)

★15562★
Spain - Ministerio de Agricultura - Pesca y Alimentacion Biblioteca (Agri, Biol Sci)
Paseo Infanta Isabel 1   Phone: 1 3475567
E-28014 Madrid, Spain   Amalia Bermejo
Founded: 1931. **Staff:** Prof 6; Other 8. **Subjects:** Agriculture, fishery, economy, rural sociology, agrarian law, food. **Holdings:** 110,000 books; 30,000 bound periodical volumes. **Subscriptions:** 550 journals and other serials. **Services:** Interlibrary loan; copying; library open to the public. **Publications:** Journal summaries; new acquisitions. **Special Catalogs:** CEE, America Catalog; Cartography Catalog.

★15563★
Spain - Ministerio de Educacion y Ciencia - Biblioteca y Archivo (Educ)
C/San Agustin, No. 5   Phone: 1 3692850
E-28014 Madrid, Spain   Ernesto Calbet, Jefe.Serv.
Founded: 1942. **Staff:** Prof 15; Other 10. **Subjects:** Education, psychology, sociology. **Holdings:** 70,000 books; 30,000 bound periodical volumes; 30,000 reports. **Subscriptions:** 650 journals and other serials. **Services:** Library open to the public with restrictions. **Publications:** Bulletin of acquisitions. **Remarks:** FAX: 1 4299436.

Spain - Ministerio de Obras Publicas y Transportes - Biblioteca
See: **Spain - Ministry of Public Works and Transports - Library** (15565)

Spain - Ministry of Finance and Economy - Institute of Fiscal Studies
See: **Institute of Fiscal Studies** (7939)

★ 15564 ★

Spain - Ministry of Labour - National Institute of Occupational Safety and Health - Centro Nacional de Condiciones de Trabajo (Med)
Calle Dulcet, 2-10
E-08034 Barcelona, Spain   Jaume Llacuna Morera
Founded: 1972. **Staff:** Prof 6; Other 5. **Subjects:** Occupational health and safety, occupational medicine, industrial hygiene, industrial toxicology, ergonomics, safety education. **Holdings:** 15,000 volumes; reports; reprints. **Subscriptions:** 200 journals and other serials. **Services:** Copying; SDI; center open to the public. **Computerized Information Services:** Seguridad e Higiene en el Trabajo Bibliog (internal database). Performs searches free of charge. **Publications:** Boletin Bibliografico (current awareness bulletin), monthly; Erga Bibliografico (1988). **Remarks:** FAX: 3 2804542.

★ 15565 ★

Spain - Ministry of Public Works and Transports - Library (Sci-Engr, Plan)
Paseo de la Castellana s/n
E-28046 Madrid, Spain   Phone: 1 5531600
Founded: 1974. **Staff:** Prof 2; Other 7. **Subjects:** Civil engineering, architecture, public administration, administrative law, housing, urbanization. **Holdings:** 33,000 books. **Subscriptions:** 100 journals and other serials. **Services:** Library open to the public for reference use only. **Computerized Information Services:** KNOSYS, Olivetti. **Also Known As:** Spain - Ministerio de Obras Publicas y Transportes.

★ 15566 ★

Spain - National Institute of Statistics - Library (Sci-Engr)
Paseo de la Castellana 183
E-28046 Madrid, Spain   Phone: 1 5839410
Founded: 1972. **Staff:** Prof 2; Other 11. **Subjects:** Statistics, economics, mathematics, demography, national polls. **Special Collections:** Publications of the National Institute of Statistics (3350 volumes). **Holdings:** 30,000 books; 800 bound periodical volumes; 6700 microfiche. **Subscriptions:** 109 journals and other serials. **Services:** Library open to the public. **Computerized Information Services:** Micro Isis (internal database). Contact Person: Jose del Val. **Remarks:** FAX: 1 5839486. Telex: 49989.

★ 15567 ★

Spain - Royal Naval Observatory and Institute - Library (Sci-Engr)
E-11100 San Fernando, Spain   Phone: 956883548
Founded: 1753. **Staff:** Prof 1; Other 2. **Subjects:** Astronomy, geophysics, geodesy, physics, mathematics, history of science. **Special Collections:** Cartographic collection (3030 maps); historical documents collection (167 boxes). **Holdings:** 24,500 books; 1200 bound periodical volumes. **Subscriptions:** 20 journals and other serials. **Services:** Copying; library open to researchers and university students only. **Automated Operations:** Computerized public access catalog and cataloging. **Computerized Information Services:** Electronic mail service. **Publications:** Inventario de Mapas; Guia e Inventario del Archivo (Documentacion Historica). **Special Catalogs:** Catalogo de Obras (ss. XV - XVIII). **Remarks:** FAX: 956899302. Telex: 76 108 IOM E. **Also Known As:** Instituto y Observatorio de Marina - Biblioteca.

★ 15568 ★

Spain-United States Chamber of Commerce - Library (Bus-Fin)
350 5th Ave., Suite 3514
New York, NY 10118   Phone: (212)967-2170
Subjects: Spanish-American relations - trade, economics, statistics. **Holdings:** 1600 volumes. **Also Known As:** Camara de Comercio Espanola en los Estados Unidos.

Spangler Library
See: **Ohio Dominican College** (12266)

★ 15569 ★

Spanish Chamber of Commerce - Library (Bus-Fin)
P.O. Box 53-187
Taipei, Taiwan   Santiago M. Ruperez
Subjects: Taiwan and Spain - investment, import-export. **Holdings:** 3000 volumes; economic data. **Remarks:** Library located at Fl. 7-1. No. 40 TUN HWA S. Rd., Sec. 2, Taipei, Taiwan. **Also Known As:** Camara de Comercio Espanola. FAX: 2 7542572. Telex: 13134 OFCOMES.

★ 15570 ★

Spar Aerospace Ltd. - Satellite & Communication Systems Division - Library/Information Resource Centre (Sci-Engr)
21025 Trans Canada Hwy.   Phone: (514)457-2150
Ste. Anne de Bellevue, PQ, Canada H9X 3R2   Margaret B. Gross, Mgr.
Staff: Prof 1; Other 1. **Subjects:** Electronics, satellite communications, radar, mechanical engineering, space research, materials science. **Holdings:** 4000 books; 10,000 reports; 5000 microfiche. **Subscriptions:** 230 journals and other serials. **Services:** Interlibrary loan; library not open to the public. **Automated Operations:** Computerized public access catalog, cataloging, and circulation. **Computerized Information Services:** DIALOG Information Services, BRS Information Technologies, CAN/OLE, PFDS Online, WILSONLINE, Infomart Online, ESA/IRS, NewsNet, Inc., DOBIS Canadian Online Library System, WISDOM Network, FP Online, BOSS (Business Opportunities Sourcing System), GIDEP (Government-Industry Data Exchange Program), STN International, CompuServe Information Service; internal databases; Envoy 100, iNET 2000 (electronic mail services). **Publications:** Library Bulletin, 9/year; Current Contents, semimonthly. **Remarks:** FAX: (514)457-2724. Telex: 05 822792. Electronic mail address(es): SPAR.LIB (Envoy 100); LIB.SPAR (iNET 2000).

★ 15571 ★

Sparks Regional Medical Center - Regional Health Sciences Library (Med)
1311 S. I St.
Box 17006   Phone: (501)441-4035
Fort Smith, AR 72917-7006   Grace Anderson, Dir.
Founded: 1971. **Staff:** Prof 1; Other 1. **Subjects:** Medicine and biological sciences. **Holdings:** 2000 books; 3000 bound periodical volumes. **Subscriptions:** 237 journals and other serials. **Services:** Interlibrary loan (fee); copying; library open to students and researchers. **Automated Operations:** Computerized cataloging. **Computerized Information Services:** MEDLINE, BRS Information Technologies; OnTyme Electronic Message Network Service, DOCLINE (electronic mail services). Performs searches on fee basis. **Remarks:** Designated as an Area Health Education Center Library. **Remarks:** FAX: (501)441-4037.

Stephen Sparling Library
See: **Society for Manitobans with Disabilities Inc.** (15333)

★ 15572 ★

Edward W. Sparrow Hospital - Medical Library (Med)
1215 E. Michigan Ave.
Box 30480   Phone: (517)483-2274
Lansing, MI 48909-7980   Doris H. Asher, Med.Libn.
Founded: 1950. **Staff:** 2. **Subjects:** Medicine, nursing. **Holdings:** 3300 books. **Subscriptions:** 310 journals and other serials. **Services:** Interlibrary loan; copying; library open to health care professionals. **Computerized Information Services:** MEDLINE, BRS Information Technologies. **Remarks:** FAX: (517)483-2273.

★ 15573 ★

Spartanburg Regional Medical Center - Health Sciences Library (Med)
101 E. Wood St.   Phone: (803)591-6220
Spartanburg, SC 29303   Mary Ann Camp, Dir., Lib.Serv.
Founded: 1961. **Staff:** Prof 1; Other 2. **Subjects:** Medicine, nursing, allied health sciences, hospital administration. **Holdings:** 4000 books; 6500 bound periodical volumes; 200 AV programs. **Subscriptions:** 230 journals and other serials. **Services:** Interlibrary loan; copying; library open to the public for reference use only. **Automated Operations:** Computerized ILL. **Computerized Information Services:** PDQ, NLM, SCHIN; DOCLINE (electronic mail service). Performs searches on fee basis. **Networks/Consortia:** Member of Health Communications Network (HCN), South Carolina Health Information Network (SCHIN), Area Health Education Consortium of South Carolina (AHEC). **Publications:** Newsletter, monthly.

Harriet M. Spaulding Library
See: **New England Conservatory of Music** (11469)

Martin Speare Memorial Library
See: **New Mexico Institute of Mining and Technology** (11521)

★ 15574 ★
Special Education Resource Center (Educ)
25 Industrial Park Rd.   Phone: (203)632-1485
Middletown, CT 06457-1520   Marianne Kirner, Center Director;
Founded: 1968. **Staff:** Prof 3; Other 12. **Subjects:** Special education, education and training of handicapped people (birth to 21 years). **Special Collections:** ERIC indexes (complete) and microfiche, 1982 to present. **Holdings:** 3540 books; 16 VF drawers of material; 380 tests; 275 inservice training materials; 45 newsletters; 3570 instructional materials; 340 literature searches; 70 computer search reprints; 220 computer software packages. **Subscriptions:** 145 journals and other serials. **Services:** Copying; center open to the public with restrictions. **Publications:** How to Do Research in Special Education; Computer Software at SERC; bibliographies of research and instructional materials. **Special Catalogs:** Books and test catalog (card); instructional materials and inservice training catalog. **Staff:** Stephen Krasner, Coord., Lib.Rsrcs. & Exhibits.

★ 15575 ★
Special Education Service Agency - Library (Educ)
2217 E. Tudor Rd., Suite 1   Phone: (907)562-7372
Anchorage, AK 99507   Anne K. Freitag
Staff: 1. **Subjects:** Special education, disabilities, early childhood, alternative communication, child rearing. **Holdings:** 1900 books; software; AV materials. **Subscriptions:** 137 journals and other serials. **Services:** Copying; library open to the public with restrictions.

★ 15576 ★
Special Libraries Association - Information Resources Center (Info Sci)
1700 18th St., N.W.   Phone: (202)234-4700
Washington, DC 20009   Kathryn Dorko, Mgr., Info.Rsrcs.
Founded: 1960. **Staff:** Prof 1. **Subjects:** Special libraries, librarianship, information science, library management. **Special Collections:** Association's Archives; Management Documents Collection. **Holdings:** 3500 volumes. **Subscriptions:** 140 journals and other serials. **Services:** Interlibrary loan; center open to the public by appointment. **Automated Operations:** Computerized cataloging and serials. **Computerized Information Services:** CONSULT, a database of SLA member consultants (internal database). **Remarks:** FAX: (202)265-9317. **Also Known As:** SLA.

★ 15577 ★
Special Metals Corporation - Technical Library/Information Center (Sci-Engr)
Middle Settlement Rd.   Phone: (315)798-2081
New Hartford, NY 13413   Marjorie Warner, Libn.
Founded: 1957. **Staff:** Prof 1. **Subjects:** Metallurgy, business management, ceramics, vacuum melting, industrial maintenance. **Holdings:** 2500 books and bound periodical volumes; 5000 technical documents; 900 technical reports; company records. **Subscriptions:** 126 journals and other serials. **Services:** Interlibrary loan; library open to the public upon request. **Computerized Information Services:** DIALOG Information Services. **Networks/Consortia:** Member of Central New York Library Resources Council (CENTRO). **Remarks:** FAX: (315)798-2001. Telex: 6854583.

John Speck Memorial Library
See: **Mountaineering Foundation of Chicago, Inc.** (10830)

★ 15578 ★
Spectra Search - Library (Sci-Engr)
761 W. Kirkham
Glendale, MO 63122   Phone: (314)962-5752
Staff: Prof 2. **Subjects:** Infrared spectroscopy. **Holdings:** 300 bound volumes; 11,000 spectra on microfilm. **Subscriptions:** 15 journals and other serials. **Services:** Library not open to the public. **Computerized Information Services:** Produces the IRGO Infrared Spectroscopic Database. Performs searches on fee basis. **Publications:** On-Line Searches by Subscription or Service by Craver Consultants. **Remarks:** FAX: (314)962-5752. Spectra Search is a subsidiary of Craver and Craver, Inc. **Staff:** Clara D. Craver, Pres.

★ 15579 ★
Spectrum Control, Inc. - Library
2185 W. 8th St.
Erie, PA 16505
Defunct.

★ 15580 ★
J.B. Speed Art Museum - Library (Art)
2035 S. 3rd St.   Phone: (502)636-2893
Louisville, KY 40208   Mary Jane Benedict, Libn.
Founded: 1927. **Staff:** Prof 1. **Subjects:** Art, decorative arts, architecture, archeology, film, photography. **Special Collections:** J.B. Speed's Lincoln Collection; Weygold Indian collection. **Holdings:** 14,285 books and bound periodical volumes; 54 VF drawers. **Subscriptions:** 73 journals and other serials. **Services:** Copying; library open to the public for reference use only. **Special Indexes:** Speed Bulletin Index; Speed Scrapbook Index; Kennedy Quarterly Index; Index of Contemporary Artists file; Index to Gallery Catalogs (all on cards). **Remarks:** FAX: (502)636-2899.

Speer Library
See: **Princeton Theological Seminary** (13367)

Speizman Jewish Library at Shalom Park
See: **The Foundation of the Charlotte Jewish Community** (6041)

★ 15581 ★
Cardinal Spellman Philatelic Museum, Inc. - Library (Rec)
235 Wellesley St.   Phone: (617)894-6735
Weston, MA 02193   Ruth Koved, Libn.
Founded: 1960. **Staff:** Prof 1; Other 2. **Subjects:** Philately, postal service. **Holdings:** 13,000 books; 2320 bound periodical volumes; 2125 pamphlets; 5500 volumes of auction catalogs; 7100 unbound periodical volumes; 2 VF drawers of pamphlets, clippings, and documents. **Subscriptions:** 90 journals and other serials. **Services:** Interlibrary loan; copying; library open to members only. **Special Catalogs:** Philatelic Literature Fair Catalog, annual (book); Philatelic Literature Auction Catalog, annual (book).

David Spence Library
See: **University of Southern California - Science & Engineering Library** (19346)

Spencer Art Reference Library
See: **Nelson-Atkins Museum of Art - Spencer Art Reference Library** (11388)

Spencer Collection
See: **New York Public Library** (11632)

Spencer Entomological Museum
See: **University of British Columbia** (18283)

Spencerian Archives
See: **Dyke College - Library Resource Center** (5078)

Albert F. Sperry Library
See: **Instrument Society of America** (8006)

★ 15582 ★
Sperry Marine Inc. - Engineering Library (Sci-Engr, Comp Sci)
1070 Seminole Trail   Phone: (804)974-2441
Charlottesville, VA 22906   Grace McKenzie, Libn.
Staff: 1. **Subjects:** Engineering - electrical, mechanical; computer technology. **Holdings:** 4000 books; 400 bound periodical volumes; 20,000 technical reports; 175 volumes of standards; 1500 patents; 1000 reels of microfilm. **Subscriptions:** 200 journals and other serials. **Services:** Library not open to the public. **Automated Operations:** Computerized cataloging. **Computerized Information Services:** DIALOG Information Services. **Publications:** Acquisitions Bulletin, bimonthly - for internal distribution only. **Remarks:** FAX: (804)974-2259. Telex: 822411/240422. Sperry Marine Inc. is a subsidiary of Tenneco, Inc. - Newport News Shipbuilding.

★15583★
Sperry-Sun Drilling Services - Technical Information Center (Sci-Engr)
3000 N. Sam Houston Pkwy. E.
Box 60070   Phone: (713)987-4544
Houston, TX 77205   Connie Bihon, Sr.Tech.Info.Supv.
Staff: Prof 1; Other 1. **Subjects:** Oil and gas drilling, engineering, chemistry, petroleum, materials science, physical sciences. **Special Collections:** Society of Petroleum Engineers papers; National Technical Institute Service (NTIS) reports; U.S. Patents, 1972 to present (complete). **Holdings:** 10,000 books; 10,000 bound periodical volumes; 2000 unbound reports; 15,000 microfiche; 3500 microfilm cartridges; vendor catalogs; industry standards. **Subscriptions:** 188 journals and other serials. **Services:** Interlibrary loan; copying; SDI; center open to the public with restrictions. **Automated Operations:** Computerized cataloging, acquisitions, and serials. **Computerized Information Services:** DIALOG Information Services, PFDS Online; internal database. **Publications:** Guide to Technical Information Center, irregular - for internal distribution only. **Special Catalogs:** Master Serials List (printout). **Remarks:** FAX: (713)987-4015. Contains the holdings of the former NL Baroid Library.

★15584★
Spertus College of Judaica - Norman and Helen Asher Library (Area-Ethnic, Rel-Phil)
618 S. Michigan Ave.   Phone: (312)922-9012
Chicago, IL 60605   Michael Terry, Dir.
Founded: 1924. **Staff:** Prof 5; Other 4. **Subjects:** Judaica, Hebraica, Rabbinics, Yiddish language and literature, Zionism, Israel, Jewish current events. **Special Collections:** Badona Spertus Art Collection; Chicago Jewish Archives; Levine Microform Collection; Targ Center for Jewish Music. **Holdings:** 90,000 books; 6500 bound periodical volumes; 1437 reels of microfilm; 260 videotapes. **Subscriptions:** 400 journals and other serials; 16 newspapers. **Services:** Interlibrary loan; copying; library open to the public. **Computerized Information Services:** RLIN. **Networks/Consortia:** Member of Chicago Library System, Judaica Library Network of Chicago. **Remarks:** FAX: (312)922-6406. **Staff:** Dan Sharon, Rd.Serv.; Robbin Katzin, Tech.Serv.; Kathleen Ladien, Adm.Serv.; Ahuva Rosenberg, Cat.

★15585★
SPIE - The International Society for Optical Engineering - Library (Sci-Engr)
Box 10   Phone: (206)676-3290
Bellingham, WA 98227-0010   Joseph Yaver, Exec.Dir.
Founded: 1955. **Subjects:** Optical and electro-optical technology - electro-optics, laser, infrared, photographic, fiber optics, bio-optics, optoelectronics. **Holdings:** 1600 books. **Services:** Document delivery; library not open to the public. **Computerized Information Services:** Optolink, In Cite (internal databases). **Publications:** SPIE Proceedings of approximately 200 conferences per year; Optical Engineering Reports (newspaper), monthly; Optical Engineering journal, monthly; Optical Engineering Press (30 monographs per year). **Remarks:** FAX: (206)647-1445. Telex: 46-7053. Library located at 1022 19th St., Bellingham, WA 98225.

★15586★
Lawrence G. Spielvogel, Inc. - Library (Energy)
203 Hughes Rd.
King of Prussia, PA 19406-3785   Phone: (215)687-5900
Founded: 1970. **Staff:** 1. **Subjects:** Energy use in buildings, building mechanical systems. **Special Collections:** Measured energy use in buildings. **Holdings:** 1000 books; 1000 bound periodical volumes; 2000 reports. **Subscriptions:** 75 journals and other serials; 20 newspapers. **Services:** Library open to the public at librarian's discretion. **Remarks:** FAX: (215)687-5370. **Formerly:** Located in Wyncote, PA.

★15587★
Spill Control Association of America - Library (Env-Cons)
400 Renaissance Ctr., Suite 1900   Phone: (313)567-0500
Detroit, MI 48243-1075   Marc K. Shaye, General Counsel
Founded: 1972. **Staff:** 4. **Subjects:** Federal and state water laws, current proposed legislation, equipment and contractor listings, government agencies, oil and hazardous substances spill statistics, industry history. **Special Collections:** Current abstracts of technical documents relating to oil and hazardous substances spill control and containment research and techniques employed in the United States, Canada, and around the world. **Holdings:** Figures not available for books; SCAA Newsletters. **Services:** Interlibrary loan; copying; library open to the public upon request. **Computerized Information Services:** LEXIS. **Remarks:** Library includes the most current information regarding laws and regulations relating to oil and hazardous materials spill control, cleanup, transport, and disposal. FAX: (313)259-8943.

★15588★
Spiritual Frontiers Fellowship International - Lending Library (Rel-Phil)
Box 7868
Philadelphia, PA 19101   Elizabeth W. Fenske, Ph.D., Exec.Dir.
Founded: 1956. **Staff:** 1. **Subjects:** Psychic research and experiences, spiritual healing and development, prayer, mysticism, meditation, astrology, numerology, ESP, telepathy, reincarnation, UFOs and related phenomena, esoteric studies, metaphysics, parapsychology, depth psychology, survival of conciousness, near-death and dying. **Special Collections:** Gertrude Tubby Collection (papers and books from the former secretary of the American Society for Psychical Research); research library (4000 books, includes rare collection books). **Holdings:** 15,000 books. **Subscriptions:** 25 journals and other serials. **Services:** Library open to members only. **Publications:** Progressive reading lists and bibliographies. **Special Catalogs:** Lending Library Catalog. **Remarks:** Academic affiliate of SFFI is Academy of Religion and Psychical Research.

Rene A. Spitz Psychiatric Library
See: University of Colorado Health Sciences Center (18512)

★15589★
Spohn Hospital - Medical Library (Med)
600 Elizabeth St.   Phone: (512)881-3261
Corpus Christi, TX 78404   Sr. Julia Delaney, Libn.
Staff: Prof 1; Other 2. **Subjects:** Medicine, nursing, medical technology, management, x-ray. **Holdings:** 3500 books; 1200 bound periodical volumes; 8 VF drawers of pamphlets; AV programs. **Subscriptions:** 50 journals and other serials. **Services:** Interlibrary loan; library open to the public for reference use only. **Networks/Consortia:** Member of Coastal Bend Health Sciences Library Consortium (CBHSLC).

★15590★
Spokane County Law Library (Law)
1020 Paulsen Bldg.   Phone: (509)456-3680
Spokane, WA 99201-0402   Emily Gordon, Law Libn.
Founded: 1909. **Staff:** Prof 1. **Subjects:** Law. **Holdings:** 22,000 volumes. **Services:** Interlibrary loan; copying; library open to the public. **Computerized Information Services:** WESTLAW. **Remarks:** FAX: (509)456-4722.

★15591★
Spokane Medical Library (Med)
University Police
MS 150   Phone: (509)458-6251
Cheney, WA 99004   Michelanne Adams, Lib.Spec. I
Founded: 1929. **Staff:** 2. **Subjects:** Clinical medicine. **Holdings:** 3000 books; 10,000 bound periodical volumes. **Subscriptions:** 126 journals and other serials. **Services:** Interlibrary loan; copying; library open to the public for reference use only. **Computerized Information Services:** MEDLINE; DOCLINE, OnTyme Electronic Message Network Service (electronic mail services). Performs searches on fee basis. **Networks/Consortia:** Member of Inland Northwest Health Sciences Libraries (INWHSL). **Remarks:** Jointly maintained by the Spokane County Medical Society and Eastern Washington University. Electronic mail address(es): SPCMSL (OnTyme Electronic Message Network Service). Alternate telephone number(s): 458-6274. **Formerly:** Located in Spokane, WA.

★15592★
(Spokane) Spokesman-Review and Spokane Chronicle - Newspaper Reference Library (Publ)
Box 2160   Phone: (509)459-5468
Spokane, WA 99210   Jane E. Walter
Founded: 1928. **Staff:** 9. **Subjects:** Newspaper reference topics. **Holdings:** 3000 books; newspapers, 1881 to present, on microfilm; newspaper clipping files; pictures. **Services:** Library not open to the public. **Remarks:** Both newspapers are published by the Cowles Publishing Company. Library located at Review Tower, W. 999 Riverside Ave., Spokane, WA 99210-1615. FAX: (509)459-5234.

★15593★
Sport Information Resource Centre (Rec)
1600 Promenade James Naismith Dr.
Gloucester, ON, Canada K1B 5N4   Phone: (613)748-5658
                                        Gilles Chiasson, Pres.
Founded: 1973. **Staff:** Prof 8; Other 5. **Subjects:** Sports, physical education, coaching, the handicapped and sports, exercise physiology, sports history, recreation, physical fitness, sports medicine. **Holdings:** 30,000 books; 3000 bound periodical volumes; 8800 microfiche; SilverPlatter CD-ROMs. **Subscriptions:** 1400 journals and other serials. **Services:** Interlibrary loan; copying; SDI; center open to the public. **Automated Operations:** Computerized cataloging and acquisitions. **Computerized Information Services:** DIALOG Information Services, BRS Information Technologies, Data-Star, Infomart Online, Info Globe, CAN/OLE; Envoy 100 (electronic mail service). Performs searches on fee basis. **Publications:** The Drug File - Bibliography on Drugs and Doping in Sport; Sport Thesaurus, 1990; Sport and Recreation for the Disabled Bibliography, 1984 - 1989; SportSearch (current awareness), monthly - by subscription; SportBiblio - series of specialized bibliographies. **Remarks:** The Resource Centre creates SPORT, an online data base containing 275,000 documents. SPORT is available on CD-ROM as the SPORT Discus. FAX: (613)748-5701. Telex: 053 36 60 SPORTREC OTT. **Also Known As:** Centre de Documentation pour le Sport. **Staff:** Richard Stark, V.P., Oper.; Christine Lalande, Hd., Tech.Serv.; Linda Wheeler, Promotion & Mktg.Coord.; Celine Gendron, Hd., Ref.Svc.

★15594★
Spotsylvania Historical Association, Inc. - Frances L.N. Waller Research Museum and Library (Hist)
Court House, Box 64   Phone: (703)582-7167
Spotsylvania, VA 22553   Sonya Harvison, Asst.Dir.
Founded: 1962. **Staff:** Prof 4; Other 2. **Subjects:** Spotsylvania County history, Civil War battlefields, colonial settlers and forts since 1671, genealogy statistics, Lafayette's campaign through Spotsylvania County 1781. **Special Collections:** Early medicine; Civil War arms; Indian artifacts; colonial farm implements; family histories and collection of old home and church histories in the county. **Holdings:** 2500 books; 100 bound periodical volumes; 800 booklets; 1 bookcase of Ohio and Virginia historical reports; 4 VF drawers of local manuscripts; maps; tapes; photostats; slides; film; reprints. **Subscriptions:** 10 journals and other serials. **Services:** Copying; library open to the public for reference use only. **Publications:** Association reports; Revolutionary Times in Spotsylvania County, 1976; Spotsylvania County Historical Map, 1978; Spotsylvania County Patriots, 1774-1786. **Staff:** Merle Strickler; John E. Pruitt, Jr.; A.N. Waller.

Harry A. Sprague Library
See: **Montclair State College (10658)**

Norman F. Sprague Memorial Library
See: **The Claremont Colleges (3754)**

Spring Creek Technical Library
See: **Texas Instruments, Inc. - Spring Creek Technical Library (16220)**

★15595★
Spring Garden College - Library (Sci-Engr)
7500 Germantown Ave.   Phone: (215)248-7900
Philadelphia, PA 19119   Mildred Glushakow, Libn.
Staff: Prof 2. **Subjects:** Engineering - electrical, electronic, civil, mechanical, computer; building construction; architecture; medical technology; business management. **Holdings:** 21,900 volumes; 8 VF drawers of catalogs and pamphlets. **Subscriptions:** 454 journals and other serials. **Services:** Interlibrary loan; copying; library open to the public. **Automated Operations:** Computerized cataloging. **Networks/Consortia:** Member of Tri-State College Library Cooperative (TCLC). **Publications:** Library Handbook; Library Research Quiz; Alphabetical and Subject Lists of Periodicals - to students and faculty. **Staff:** Ella Strattis, Asst.Libn.

★15596★
Spring Grove Hospital Center - Sulzbacher Memorial Library (Med)
Isidore Tuerk Bldg.
Wade Ave.
Catonsville, MD 21228   Phone: (301)455-7824
Founded: 1938. **Staff:** 1. **Subjects:** Psychiatry, psychology, psychotherapy, pharmacology, sociology, social work, neurology, pastoral care, nursing education, therapy. **Special Collections:** History of Spring Grove Hospital Center; Rare Book Collection. **Holdings:** 2835 books; 1000 bound periodical volumes; 954 cassettes; 10 films; 15 phonograph records; 2045 pamphlets; 13 AV programs; 20 archives; 30 dissertations; 25 reels of microfilm. **Subscriptions:** 297 journals and other serials; 10 newspapers. **Services:** Interlibrary loan; copying; library open to the public for reference use only. **Computerized Information Services:** MEDLINE, DIALOG Information Services, BRS Information Technologies. **Networks/Consortia:** Member of Maryland Association of Health Science Librarians (MAHSL). **Publications:** Bibliographies; SML Acquisitions (newsletter). **Remarks:** Maintained by Maryland State Department of Health & Mental Hygiene.

★15597★
Springer, Bush & Perry - Library
2 Gateway Center, 15th Fl.
Pittsburgh, PA 15222   Phone: (412)281-4900
Remarks: No further information was supplied by respondent.

Springfield Armory National Historic Site
See: **U.S. Natl. Park Service (17781)**

★15598★
Springfield Art Association - Michael Victor II Art Library (Art)
700 N. 4th St.   Phone: (217)523-3507
Springfield, IL 62702   Joan Ekiss, Libn.
Founded: 1979. **Staff:** Prof 1; **Subjects:** Visual and related arts. **Holdings:** 4000 books; prints; booklets; exhibition catalogs. **Subscriptions:** 17 journals and other serials. **Services:** Library open to the public.

★15599★
Springfield Art Museum - Art Reference Library (Art)
1111 E. Brookside Dr.   Phone: (417)866-2716
Springfield, MO 65807   Wanda Rudolph, Libn.
Founded: 1958. **Staff:** Prof 1. **Subjects:** Art history, painting, sculpture, graphics, decorative arts, photography. **Holdings:** 4000 books; 1000 bound periodical volumes; 1000 slides; 5000 clippings; 3000 unbound magazines; 3000 exhibition catalogs. **Subscriptions:** 30 journals and other serials. **Services:** Library open to the public. **Publications:** Several Exhibition Catalogs, annually.

★15600★
Springfield City Library - Art and Music Department (Art, Mus)
220 State St.   Phone: (413)739-3871
Springfield, MA 01103   Karen A. Dorval, Supv./Art Libn.
Founded: 1857. **Staff:** Prof 3; Other 2. **Subjects:** Art, crafts, needlework, music, photography, coins. **Special Collections:** Aston Collection of wood-engravings (2250 prints). **Holdings:** 33,250 books; 3200 bound periodical volumes; 18,000 recordings; 4000 compact discs; 3000 audio cassettes; 125,000 pictures; 8000 pamphlets. **Subscriptions:** 112 journals and other serials. **Services:** Interlibrary loan; copying; department open to the public, card required to borrow books. **Automated Operations:** Computerized circulation. **Staff:** Sylvia St. Amand, Mus.Libn.

Springfield City Library - Genealogy and Local History Department
See: **Connecticut Valley Historical Museum (4206)**

★15601★
Springfield College - Babson Library - Special Collections (Educ, Rec)
263 Alden St.   Phone: (413)788-3307
Springfield, MA 01109   Gerald F. Davis, Lib.Dir.
Founded: 1885. **Special Collections:** Physical education; recreation; dance. **Holdings:** Figures not available. **Services:** Interlibrary loan; copying; collections open to the public with permission. **Computerized Information Services:** DIALOG Information Services, BRS Information Technologies, MEDLARS; CD-ROM; DIALMAIL (electronic mail service). Performs searches on fee basis for college community. Contact Person: Andrea Taupier, Sr.Ref.Libn., 788-3315. **Networks/Consortia:** Member of Cooperating Libraries of Greater Springfield, A CCGS Agency (CLGS), C/W MARS, Inc., NELINET, Inc. **Staff:** Raymond Lin, Cat.; MaryJane Sobinski-Smith, Ref.; Lisa Pitkin, Ser.; Robert Kudlay, Ref.

★15602★
Springfield College in Illinois - Becker Library (Rel-Phil, Hum, Med, Bus-Fin)
1521 N. 6th St.   Phone: (217)525-1420
Springfield, IL 62702   Stephen Iden
Founded: 1965. **Staff:** Prof 1; Other 1. **Subjects:** Religion, humanities, medicine, business. **Holdings:** 23,000 books; 3171 bound periodical volumes; 22 microfiche titles. **Subscriptions:** 121 journals and other serials; 9 newspapers. **Services:** Interlibrary loan; library open to the public. **Computerized Information Services:** InfoTrac.

★15603★
Springfield-Greene County Public Libraries - Edward M. Shepard Memorial Room (Hist)
397 E. Central   Phone: (417)869-4621
Springfield, MO 65801   Michael D. Glenn, Ref.Libn.
Founded: 1961. **Staff:** Prof 1; Other 3. **Subjects:** Missouri, Greene County, Springfield, and the Ozarks - history, biography, genealogy, literature, Missouri authors, archeology, geology, religion, language. **Special Collections:** Edward M. Shepard Collection of Rare Missouri and Ozark books; Collection of Historical Photographs; Max Hunter Collection of Ozark Folksong (1000 songs on cassette tapes). **Holdings:** 8000 books; Federal Census, Missouri, 1830-1880, 1900, 1910, on microfilm; 1200 reels of microfilm of Springfield newspapers, 1870 to present; 54 reels of microfilm of miscellaneous genealogical material; 25 VF drawers of pictures and clippings. **Subscriptions:** 75 journals and other serials. **Services:** Copying; room open to the public. **Automated Operations:** Computerized circulation and cataloging. **Computerized Information Services:** DIALOG Information Services, OCLC; DYNIX (internal database). **Special Indexes:** Card index to Springfield newspapers (articles pertaining primarily to Springfield and Greene County, also includes Missouri and the Ozarks). **Remarks:** FAX: (417)869-0320.

★15604★
Springfield Hospital - Medical Library (Med)
190 W. Sproul Rd.   Phone: (215)328-8749
Springfield, PA 19064   June Katucki, Dir., Lib. & Info.Serv.
Founded: 1962. **Staff:** Prof 1. **Subjects:** Clinical medicine, osteopathy, nursing. **Holdings:** 1000 books; 2000 bound periodical volumes; 1 VF drawer; 900 cassette tapes; slides. **Subscriptions:** 120 journals and other serials. **Services:** Interlibrary loan; copying; SDI; library open to the public with restrictions. **Computerized Information Services:** NLM. **Networks/Consortia:** Member of Consortium for Health Information & Library Services (CHI), Delaware Valley Information Consortium (DEVIC), BHSL. **Remarks:** FAX: (215)328-8712.

★15605★
Springfield Hospital - Medical Library (Med)
25 Ridgewood Rd.   Phone: (802)885-2151
Springfield, VT 05156   Janet Constantine, Educ.Dir.
Staff: Prof 1. **Subjects:** Medicine, surgery, nursing. **Holdings:** 304 volumes. **Subscriptions:** 41 journals and other serials. **Services:** Interlibrary loan; copying; center open to the public with restrictions. **Networks/Consortia:** Member of Health Science Libraries of New Hampshire & Vermont (HSL-NH/VT), COOP Group II of Southern Vermont/New Hampshire Librarians, North Atlantic Health Science Libraries (NAHSL). **Remarks:** FAX: (802)885-3959.

★15606★
Springfield Hospital Center - Medical Library (Med)
Sykesville, MD 21784   Phone: (301)795-2100
       Elizabeth D. Mercer, Libn.
Founded: 1954. **Staff:** 1. **Subjects:** Psychiatry, neurology, clinical psychology, psychotherapy, psychiatric nursing, psychiatric social work, medicine, practical nursing. **Holdings:** 2000 books; 1000 bound periodical volumes. **Subscriptions:** 84 journals and other serials. **Services:** Interlibrary loan; library open to the public for reference use only on request. **Publications:** Acquisition lists, quarterly.

★15607★
Springfield, Illinois State Journal & Register - Editorial Library (Publ)
1 Copley Plaza   Phone: (217)788-1300
Springfield, IL 62705   Sandra Vance, Libn.
Staff: 2. **Subjects:** Newspaper reference topics. **Holdings:** 460 books; 90 bound periodical volumes; 2.9 million newspaper clippings on microfiche; newspapers on microfilm; photo negative file; photos of subjects and people; graphics file. **Services:** Library open to the public. **Computerized Information Services:** Battelle Software Products Center. Performs searches on fee basis. **Remarks:** Alternate telephone number(s): 788-1504. FAX: (217)788-1551.

Springfield Library and Museums Association - George Walter Vincent Smith Art Museum
See: **George Walter Vincent Smith Art Museum** (15242)

★15608★
Springfield Museum of Art - Library (Art)
107 Cliff Park Rd.   Phone: (513)325-4673
Springfield, OH 45501   Mary McG. Miller, Chm. of Lib.Comm.
Founded: 1970. **Subjects:** Art, art history, photography. **Special Collections:** Axel Bahnson Collection (historical photographic books and periodicals); James Roy Hopkins Archives. **Holdings:** 4300 books. **Subscriptions:** 15 journals and other serials. **Services:** Library open to the public with restrictions. **Computerized Information Services:** Internal databases. **Publications:** Newsletter - to members.

★15609★
Springfield News-Leader - Library (Publ)
651 Boonville   Phone: (417)836-1215
Springfield, MO 65801   Maudie Lawson, Libn.
Founded: 1981. **Staff:** Prof 1; Other 2. **Subjects:** Newspaper reference topics. **Special Collections:** News-Leader clipping file, 1920-1991; Missouri and the Ozarks history. **Holdings:** Microfilm, clippins. **Subscriptions:** 5 journals and other serials; 10 newspapers. **Services:** Library not open to the public. **Remarks:** FAX: (417)837-1381.

★15610★
Springfield News-Sun - Library (Publ)
202 N. Limestone   Phone: (513)328-0348
Springfield, OH 45501   Anita Beaver
Founded: 1925. **Staff:** Prof 1. **Subjects:** Newspaper reference topics. **Holdings:** 200 books; 36 bound periodical volumes; microfilm (1894 to present). **Subscriptions:** 25 journals and other serials. **Services:** Copying; library open to the public with restrictions. **Computerized Information Services:** Subject Authority File (internal database). **Remarks:** FAX: (513)328-0321.

★15611★
Springfield Newspapers - Library (Publ)
1860 Main St.   Phone: (413)788-1018
Springfield, MA 01102   Ellen Christopherson, Supv.
Staff: Prof 1; Other 5. **Subjects:** Newspaper reference topics. **Special Collections:** Springfield city directories, 1852 to present; Springfield Union Index, 1912-1941. **Holdings:** 100,000 subject headings of microfiche. **Subscriptions:** 4 journals and other serials; 10 newspapers. **Services:** Library not open to the public. **Computerized Information Services:** DataTimes. **Remarks:** FAX: (413)788-1301.

★15612★
Springfield Regional Center - Library (Med)
1515 E. Pythian
P.O. Box 5030   Phone: (417)836-0400
Springfield, MO 65801-5030   Lyle Smith, Libn.
Subjects: Persons with disabilities. **Services:** Library not open to the public. **Remarks:** No further information was supplied by respondent. **Formerly:** Springfield Regional Center for the Developmentally Disabled.

★15613★
Springhouse Corporation - Corporate Library (Med, Publ)
1111 Bethlehem Pike   Phone: (215)646-8700
Spring House, PA 19477   Nancy H. Lange, Libn.
Staff: Prof 1; Other 1. **Subjects:** Nursing, health care, education, office systems, management. **Holdings:** 6000 books; company archives. **Subscriptions:** 360 journals and other serials. **Services:** Interlibrary loan; library not open to the public. **Automated Operations:** Computerized cataloging and serials. **Computerized Information Services:** BRS Information Technologies. Performs searches free of charge for consortium members. **Networks/Consortia:** Member of Delaware Valley Information Consortium (DEVIC), Tri-State College Library Cooperative (TCLC). **Remarks:** FAX: (215)646-4399. Telex: 510 661 0050.

★15614★
Springs Industries - Design Research Library (Art)
104 W. 40th St.   Phone: (212)556-6100
New York, NY 10018   June Murray, Supv., Studio Serv.
Founded: 1934. **Staff:** Prof 1. **Subjects:** Textile design; decorative arts - design, ornament, handicrafts, tapestry; children's picture books; antiques; plantlife. **Special Collections:** Textile swatch collection, 1800-1991 (1 million swatches); wallpaper collection; French printed cottons, 1800-1830; wood block designs. **Holdings:** 2500 books; 120 map drawers of original painted designs; 15 drawers of picture collection; 500 VF drawers of textile swatch cards; 150 scrapbook volumes of fabric; fashion forecasting manuals; 9 books of computer aid designs. **Subscriptions:** 8 journals and other serials. **Services:** Library not open to the public. **Special Indexes:** Index of picture collection.

★15615★
Springs Industries, Inc. - Business Systems - Data Processing Technical Library (Comp Sci)
Box 111   Phone: (803)286-2000
Lancaster, SC 29721   Robin Cole, Libn.
Remarks: No further information was supplied by respondent.

★15616★
Sprint International - Christopher B. Newport Information Resource Center (Info Sci)
12490 Sunrise Valley Dr.   Phone: (703)689-5388
Reston, VA 22096   Judith A. Adams, Mgr.
Founded: 1981. **Staff:** 6. **Subjects:** Data communications, telecommunications, computer science, international business. **Special Collections:** F.C.C. tariff filings (100). **Holdings:** 4500 books and reports; 25 VF drawers of subject/competitive country files; 24 drawers of microforms of journals, U.S. and international standards, U.S. and international company annual reports. **Subscriptions:** 360 journals and other serials; 6 newspapers. **Services:** Interlibrary loan; SDI; center open to the public by appointment only. **Automated Operations:** Computerized cataloging, acquisitions, serials, public access catalog, and circulation. **Computerized Information Services:** DIALOG Information Services, Mead Data Central, NewsNet, Inc., CompuServe Information Service, OCLC, Dun & Bradstreet Business Credit Services, Reuters; CD-ROMs (ABI/INFORM, Disclosure Incorporated, Computer Library, Worldwide Standards Information, Perinorm); SprintMail (electronic mail service). **Networks/Consortia:** Member of CAPCON Library Network. **Publications:** New Publications Alert! **Remarks:** FAX: (703)689-5053. Alternate telephone number(s): 689-5390. Electronic mail address(es): CORP.INFO.CENTER (SprintMail). **Formerly:** Telenet Communications Corporation. **Staff:** Ines Siscoe, Ref.; Carolyn Sawicki, Acq.; Charlaine Cook, Sys. & Cat.; Patricia Huff, Rec.Mgt.; Christine Sninsky, Ser. & Rec.

★15617★
Sproule Associates, Ltd. - Library
140 4th Ave., S.W., 9th Fl.   Phone: (403)269-7951
Calgary, AB, Canada T2P 3N3   Jacquie McGowan
Remarks: FAX: (403)237-0201. No further information was supplied by respondent.

Spruance Library
See: **Bucks County Historical Society (2318)**

★15618★
SPS Technologies, Inc. - Research and Development Laboratories - Corporate Technical Library (Sci-Engr)
Highland Ave.   Phone: (215)572-3564
Jenkintown, PA 19046   Kim McNamara, Corp.Tech.Libn.
Staff: Prof 1. **Subjects:** Fastener engineering and technology, mechanical engineering, metallurgy, management. **Holdings:** 1500 books; 10,000 internal technical reports; 250 technical reports; specifications; industry standards; annual reports. **Subscriptions:** 53 journals and other serials. **Services:** Interlibrary loan; copying; SDI; library open to the public by appointment. **Computerized Information Services:** DIALOG Information Services, BRS Information Technologies; internal database. Performs searches on fee basis. **Publications:** Acquisitions List, monthly; Technical Reports Issued by the Corporation, monthly - both for internal distribution only. **Special Indexes:** Chronological, author, and subject indexes to SPS technical reports and lab notes (book), annual. **Remarks:** Alternate telephone number(s): 572-3000. FAX: (215)572-3193.

★15619★
Square D Company - Library (Sci-Engr)
Box 27446   Phone: (919)266-3671
Raleigh, NC 27611   Vickie Braswell, Libn.
Founded: 1960. **Staff:** 1. **Subjects:** Electrical engineering. **Holdings:** 3000 books. **Subscriptions:** 150 journals and other serials. **Services:** Interlibrary loan; library not open to the public. **Computerized Information Services:** DIALOG Information Services. **Remarks:** FAX: (919)266-8397.

Eleanor Squire Library
See: **Garden Center of Greater Cleveland (6247)**

★15620★
SRI International - Business Intelligence Center - Information Center (Bus-Fin)
333 Ravenswood Ave.   Phone: (415)859-5450
Menlo Park, CA 94025   Carrie L. Hollenberg, Mgr., Client Serv.
Founded: 1958. **Staff:** 25. **Subjects:** Technology monitoring; trends - business and industrial, technological, government, sociological; business planning. **Holdings:** 150,000 clippings, pamphlets, and reports indexed by subject. **Subscriptions:** 500 journals and other serials. **Services:** Center use restricted to SRI staff and subscribers to the Business Intelligence Program and Tech Monitoring service. **Computerized Information Services:** DIALOG Information Services. **Special Indexes:** Index to BIP publications (computerized), quarterly - to subscribers. **Remarks:** FAX: (415)859-4544. Alternate telephone number(s): 326-6200.

★15621★
SRI International - Chemical Marketing Research Center/Process Industries - Division Research Library (Sci-Engr)
333 Ravenswood Ave.   Phone: (415)859-5041
Menlo Park, CA 94025   Lani Ritchey, Supv., Lit.Serv.
Founded: 1950. **Staff:** Prof 1; Other 2. **Subjects:** Biotechnology; chemicals - commodity, agricultural, inorganic, specialty; minerals; metals; agriculture. **Holdings:** 8000 titles. **Subscriptions:** 921 journals and other serials. **Services:** Interlibrary loan; library not open to the public. **Remarks:** FAX: (415)326-5512.

★15622★
SRI International - Computer Science Literature Center (Comp Sci)
333 Ravenswood Ave.   Phone: (415)859-3695
Menlo Park, CA 94025   Marge Wilson, Dir.
Founded: 1975. **Staff:** Prof 1; Other 1. **Subjects:** Computer science, engineering, artificial intelligence, network telecommunications. **Holdings:** 5150 books; 300 bound periodical volumes. **Subscriptions:** 95 journals and other serials. **Services:** Center not open to the public. **Computerized Information Services:** DIALOG Information Services; InterNet (electronic mail service). **Publications:** Internet Technology Handbook. **Special Indexes:** Index to protocol literature (online). **Remarks:** FAX: (415)859-6028. Electronic mail address(es): marlyn@nisc.sri.com (InterNet). **Staff:** Marlyn Johnson, Lib.Rsrc.Coord.

SRI International - David Sarnoff Research Center
See: **David Sarnoff Research Center - Library (14836)**

★15623★
SRI International - Research Information Services (Sci-Engr, Bus-Fin)
333 Ravenswood Ave.   Phone: (415)859-5976
Menlo Park, CA 94025   Marjorie A. Wilson, Dir.
Founded: 1946. **Staff:** Prof 8; Other 15. **Subjects:** Engineering, physical sciences, life sciences, management sciences, research and development, economics. **Special Collections:** SRI records and reports. **Holdings:** 47,000 books; 18,000 U.S. and foreign company and foundation annual reports; 100,000 government documents. **Subscriptions:** 1878 journals and other serials. **Services:** Interlibrary loan; SDI; library not open to the public. **Automated Operations:** Computerized cataloging, acquisitions, and serials. **Computerized Information Services:** STN International, DunsPrint, VU/TEXT Information Services, WILSONLINE, Faxon, BRS Information Technologies, DIALOG Information Services, DTIC, ORBIT Search Service, DataTimes, Reuters, Dow Jones News/Retrieval, MEDLARS, NewsNet, Inc.; CD-ROMs (Lotus Development Corporation); Guardian SRI Reports (internal database); DIALMAIL (electronic mail service). **Networks/Consortia:** Member of SOUTHNET, CLASS. **Publications:** pRISm, 6/year; Serials List, annual - both for internal distribution only. **Remarks:** FAX: (415)859-2936. Electronic mail address(es): 11664 (DIALMAIL). Maintains two branch libraries. **Staff:** Lucille Steelman, Mgr., Res.Sup.Serv.; Lisa Jensen, Acq.Supv.; Geraldine Wong, Rec.Ctr.Mgr.; Sarah Vogel, Info.Spec.; Josh Duberman, Info.Spec.; Stella Tang, Cat.Supv.

★ 15624 ★
Sri Lanka - Department of Census and Statistics - Library (Soc Sci)
11/1 Independence Ave.   Phone: 1 598445
Colombo 7, Sri Lanka   W.S. Punyawardana, Libn.
Subjects: Statistics, mathematics, demography, computer science, economics, agriculture. **Special Collections:** Sri Lanka census reports, 1871 to present; blue books; publications of United Nations and foreign statistical organizations. **Holdings:** 1593 books; 7210 bound periodical volumes; 4410 documents. **Subscriptions:** 15 journals and other serials. **Services:** Interlibrary loan; SDI; library open to the public. **Publications:** List of Current Acquisitions and Guide to Periodical Literature; Annotated List of Departmental Publications; List of the Latest Publications of the Department.

★ 15625 ★
Sri Lanka - Department of National Archives (Area-Ethnic)
P.O. Box 1414
7 Reid Ave.   Phone: 1 694523
Colombo 7, Sri Lanka   K.D.G. Wilmalaratne, Dir.
Founded: 1947. **Staff:** 2. **Subjects:** History of Sri Lanka, archival science, records management, Sri Lankan biographies, conservation of archives. **Holdings:** 16,998 books, bound periodical volumes, and reports. **Subscriptions:** 12 journals and other serials; 3 newspapers. **Services:** Copying; library open to the public by appointment. Alternate telephone number(s): 1 696917. **Staff:** Mrs. G. Hettige.

★ 15626 ★
Sri Lanka - National Library Services Board (Area-Ethnic, Info Sci, Soc Sci, Hum)
P.O. Box 1764
Independence Ave.   Phone: 1 698847
Colombo 7, Sri Lanka   M.S.U. Amarasiri, Dir.
Founded: 1990. **Staff:** Prof 58; Other 50. **Subjects:** Social sciences, humanities, science, technology. **Special Collections:** Folk culture collection (491 books, 79 manuscripts, 56 Ola Leaf, 130 audiocassettes, 4 records, 2 videotapes); Martin Wickramasinghe Collection (4613 items); UNESCO Collection (8208 items); publication assistance project deposit copies (684 items); ISBN Deposit Copies collection (1875 items); Ola Leaf Collection (157 items). **Holdings:** 136,725 books; 488 bound periodical volumes; 5153 microfiche; 122 reels of microfilm; 113 manuscripts; 951 maps; 453 slide sets; 685 sound recordings. **Subscriptions:** 60 journals and other serials; 78 newspapers. **Services:** Interlibrary loan; copying; library open primarily for researchers. **Computerized Information Services:** Library and Information Science, ISBN Sri Lanka Publishers' Directory (internal databases). Performs searches. **Publications:** International Standard Book Numbering in Sri Lanka, 2nd edition (brochure); Sri Lanka (ISBN) Publishers Directory; Directory of Social Science Libraries, Information Centres, and Databases in Sri Lanka; Library News, quarterly; Sri Lanka National Bibliography, quarterly; Proceedings of the Third International Conference of Directors of National Libraries of Asia and Oceania, 18-23 Nov. 1985; Directory of Technical College Libraries; National Library of Sri Lanka - Commemorative Volume; National Library Past and Present; A Bibliography of Bibliographies (guide to catalogs, indexes, bibliographies, and biographies in Sri Lanka); selected bibliography on SAARC. **Special Catalogs:** Catalog of Post Graduate Theses; Book Promotion Project - catalog of books published under the sponsorship of the Sri Lanka National Library Services Board. **Special Indexes:** Periodical Articles index; Conference index 1976-1986. **Remarks:** Alternate telephone number(s): 1 685199. FAX: 1 685201. **Staff:** Miss H.N.J. Fernando, Act.Asst.Dir.

★ 15627 ★
Sri Lanka Tea Board - Tea Research Institute of Sri Lanka - Library (Food-Bev, Agri)
St. Coombs
Talawakele, Sri Lanka   Phone: Hatton 601
Subjects: Tea cultivation and processing, agriculture, agro-industrial sciences. **Holdings:** 20,000 volumes. **Subscriptions:** 250 journals and other serials. **Services:** Library not open to the public. **Remarks:** Alternate telephone number(s): 52 8385; 52 8386.

★ 15628 ★
Staatliche Kunstsammlungen - Staatliche Kunsthalle und Badisches Landesmuseum - Bibliothek (Art, Hist)
Hans-Thoma-Str 2
Postfach 6149   Phone: 721 1353358
W-7500 Karlsruhe, Germany   Sabine Muller-Wirth, Dipl.Bibl.
Founded: 1934. **Subjects:** Art history, paintings, graphics, archeology, numismatics, applied art. **Holdings:** 158,000 books; 6 bound periodical volumes. **Subscriptions:** 623 journals and other serials. **Services:** Interlibrary loan; copying; library open to the public. **Remarks:** FAX: 721 1356537. **Staff:** Sabine Furst.

Staatliche Museen Kassel - Kunstbibliothek
See: **State Museum Kassel - Library** (15698)

Joan Staats Library
See: **Jackson Laboratory** (8309)

Samuel J. Stabins, M.D. Medical Library
See: **Genesee Hospital** (6356)

★ 15629 ★
Stack's Rare Coin Company of New York - Technical Information Center (Rec)
123 W. 57th St.   Phone: (212)582-2580
New York, NY 10019   Robert A. Archer, Mgr., Tech.Oper.
Staff: Prof 7. **Subjects:** Rare coins - U.S., ancient, foreign; medals and decorations. **Special Collections:** Historical busts of famous world personalities. **Holdings:** 10,000 books; 5000 bound periodical volumes. **Services:** Center open to the public by appointment. **Remarks:** FAX: (212)245-5018.

★ 15630 ★
Stadelsches Kunstinstitut und Stadtische Galerie - Bibliothek (Art, Hist)
Durerstr 2   Phone: 69 605098
W-6000 Frankfurt 70, Germany   Busso Diekamp
Founded: 1817. **Staff:** Prof 2. **Subjects:** Classical archeology, theory of art, iconography, history of art (except architecture), photography. **Special Collections:** Auction Sales Catalogs (20,000 volumes). **Holdings:** 70,000 books. **Subscriptions:** 250 journals and other serials. **Services:** Copying; library open to the public for reference use only. **Remarks:** FAX: 69 610163.

★ 15631 ★
Stagecoach Library for Genealogical Research (Hist)
1840 S. Wolcott Ct.   Phone: (303)922-8856
Denver, CO 80219   Donna J. Porter, Owner
Staff: Prof 2; Other 1. **Subjects:** Genealogy, local history. **Holdings:** 4500 books; 400 other cataloged items. **Services:** Copying; library open to the public by mail only. **Publications:** Catalog of holdings - for sale. **Remarks:** Alternate telephone number(s): 936-0118.

Helen Stahler Library
See: **Christ United Methodist Church - Helen Stahler Library** (3630)

Ralph C. Staiger Library
See: **International Reading Association** (8178)

★ 15632 ★
A.E. Staley Manufacturing Company - Technical Information Center (Food-Bev)
2200 E. Eldorado St.   Phone: (217)421-2543
Decatur, IL 62525   Richard E. Wallace, Mgr.
Founded: 1920. **Staff:** Prof 1; Other 3. **Subjects:** Carbohydrates, sweeteners, fats-oils, polymers, starch, corn products. **Holdings:** 8000 books; 10,000 bound and microfilm periodical volumes; 3000 reprints, translations, pamphlets; 50,000 patents; 28 VF drawers. **Subscriptions:** 500 journals and other serials. **Services:** Interlibrary loan; copying; center open to the public with restrictions. **Automated Operations:** Computerized cataloging, serials, circulation, and indexing. **Computerized Information Services:** DIALOG Information Services, PFDS Online, STN International, MEDLARS, OCLC, BRS Information Technologies, Dow Jones News/Retrieval, NEXIS, VU/TEXT Information Services, DataTimes. **Networks/Consortia:** Member of Rolling Prairie Library System (RPLS). **Publications:** Abstracts, weekly; New Additions to the Library, bimonthly. **Remarks:** FAX: (217)421-2519.

Staley Library
See: Millikin University (10405)

J. Kenneth Stallman Memorial Library
See: Atlantic Salmon Federation (1263)

Herbert S. Stamats Art Library
See: Cedar Rapids Museum of Art - Herbert S. Stamats Art Library
(3186)

★15633★
Stamford Catholic Library, Inc. (Rel-Phil)
14 Peveril Rd.   Phone: (203)348-4422
Stamford, CT 06902-3019   William J. Murray, Pres.
Founded: 1948. **Staff:** Prof 1. **Subjects:** Religion, theology, American
literature, history, biography, psychology. **Holdings:** 3000 books; 25
documentary series; 200 pre-Vatican II pamphlets; 20 encyclicals; 12
scripture studies; 100 papal and episcopal documents; 24 tapes; videotapes;
large-print books. **Subscriptions:** 5 journals and other serials; 3 newspapers.
Services: Interlibrary loan; library open to the public on a fee basis.
Publications: Annual Report. **Staff:** Mary Louise Flowers, LTA.

★15634★
Stamford Historical Society - Library (Hist)
1508 High Ridge Rd.   Phone: (203)329-1183
Stamford, CT 06903-4107   Ronald Marcus, Libn.
Founded: 1901. **Staff:** 3. **Subjects:** History - Stamford, Fairfield County,
State of Connecticut. **Special Collections:** Catherine Aiken School
Collection, 1855-1913; Charles Kurz Photographic Collection on Stamford,
1868-1941; Eaton, Yale and Towne Collection on Yale and Towne
Manufacturing Company of Stamford, 1868-1949; F. Stewart Andrews
Collection on Stamford Foundry Company, 1850-1950; Anson Dickinson
Collection, 1779-1852. **Holdings:** 4300 books and pamphlets; 50 Stamford
tax lists manuscripts, 1712-1876; 136 Stamford Revolutionary War damage
claims manuscripts, 1776-1783; 300 Stamford newspapers, 1829-1925; 2000
Stamford pictures, 1870-1940; 1000 Stamford slides, 1870-1920; 25
Stamford maps, 1800-1961; 65 Stamford account books manuscripts, 1787-
1941; 12 Stamford diaries, 1850-1929; 12 VF drawers of documents and
clippings. **Services:** Copying; library open to the public on a limited
schedule. **Publications:** Stamford Revolutionary War Damage Claims;
Stamford - Pictures from the Past; Stamford - Journey through Time; Fort
Stamford; Stamford in the Gilded Age - The Political Life of a Connecticut
Town 1868-1893; Stamford from Puritan to Patriot 1641-1774; list of other
publications - available on request.

★15635★
The Stamford Hospital - Health Sciences Library (Med)
Shelburne Rd.
Box 9317   Phone: (203)325-7523
Stamford, CT 06904-7523   Lynn Sabol, Dir.
Staff: Prof 1; Other 1. **Subjects:** Clinical medicine, nursing. **Holdings:** 2376
books; 5174 bound periodical volumes; 1177 tapes; 3607 slides.
Subscriptions: 353 journals and other serials. **Services:** Interlibrary loan;
copying; library open to the public by appointment only. **Computerized
Information Services:** BRS Information Technologies, NLM. **Networks/
Consortia:** Member of Connecticut Association of Health Science Libraries
(CAHSL), Health Information Libraries of Westchester (HILOW),
Southwestern Connecticut Library Council (SWLC), BHSL.

★15636★
Standard Educational Corporation - Editorial Library (Publ)
200 W. Monroe St.   Phone: (312)346-7440
Chicago, IL 60606   David E. King, Libn.
Founded: 1958. **Staff:** Prof 1; Other 1. **Subjects:** General reference.
Holdings: 10,000 books; 400 microforms; 88 VF drawers. **Subscriptions:** 161
journals and other serials. **Services:** Interlibrary loan; copying; library open
to the public by appointment. **Computerized Information Services:** CD-
ROMs. **Networks/Consortia:** Member of ILLINET. **Publications:** New
Books List, monthly; Serials List, annual. **Remarks:** FAX: (312)580-7215.

★15637★
Standard Insurance Company - Library (Bus-Fin)
Box 711
Portland, OR 97207   Phone: (503)248-2887
Remarks: No further information was supplied by respondent.

★15638★
Standard & Poor's Compustat Services, Inc. - Data Resource Center
(Bus-Fin)
7400 S. Alton Ct.   Phone: (303)771-6510
Englewood, CO 80112   Gary Pippin, Libn.
Founded: 1968. **Staff:** Prof 1; Other 8. **Subjects:** Financial reports. **Special
Collections:** Daily Stock Price Record Books; Moody publications.
Holdings: 50 books; 12 filing cabinets of Federal Reserve publications;
500,000 microfiche of financial reports; financial reports from over 10,000
companies; Standard & Poor's publications; Canadian Stock Exchange
listings. **Subscriptions:** 30 journals and other serials; 5 newspapers. **Services:**
Center open to the public by appointment. **Automated Operations:**
Computerized cataloging. **Computerized Information Services:** Compustat
(internal database). **Publications:** Compustat; Financial Dynamics, both
weekly. **Remarks:** Alternate telephone number(s): 740-4653. FAX:
(303)740-4652.

★15639★
Standard & Poor's Corporation - Business Information Center (Bus-Fin)
25 Broadway   Phone: (212)208-8514
New York, NY 10004   Cynthia A. Gagen, Lib.Mgr.
Founded: 1917. **Staff:** Prof 4; Other 11. **Subjects:** Corporations and
industries, securities and investments, finance and banking, public utilities.
Special Collections: Annual and quarterly reports, prospectuses, documents
describing corporations and their activities (300 VF drawers); Standard &
Poor's publications, 1860 to present; disclosure reports to Securities and
Exchange Commission (SEC), 1968 to present, on microfiche (3 million
pieces). **Holdings:** 25,000 volumes; 600 reels of microfilm; 50 VF drawers
of pamphlets and newsletters. **Subscriptions:** 2000 journals and other serials;
40 newspapers. **Services:** Copying (limited); library open to the public with
restrictions. **Automated Operations:** Computerized acquisitions and serials.
Computerized Information Services: DIALOG Information Services,
LEXIS, NEXIS, DRI/McGraw-Hill, IDC (International Data
Corporation), VU/TEXT Information Services, Human Resource
Information Network (HRIN), NewsNet, Inc.; EasyLink (electronic mail
service). Performs searches on fee basis. **Remarks:** Alternate telephone
number(s): 208-1199 (Central Inquiry). (212)514-7016. Telex: 446909.
Electronic mail address(es): 6294-2129 (EasyLink). **Formerly:** McGraw Hill
Financial Services Co. **Staff:** Richard Zain Eldeen, Tech.Serv.; Douglas
Green, Info.Serv.; Carol Fitzgerald, Info.Serv.

★15640★
Standard Register Company - Corporate Library (Sci-Engr)
Box 1167
Dayton, OH 45401
Defunct.

★15641★
Standards Council of Canada - Information Division (Sci-Engr)
45 O'Connor St., Suite 1200   Phone: (613)238-3222
Ottawa, ON, Canada K1P 6N7   D. Thompson, Mgr.
Founded: 1977. **Staff:** Prof 5; Other 1. **Subjects:** Standards, specifications,
codes and related documents, technical regulations. **Holdings:** 400,000
documents. **Subscriptions:** 90 journals and other serials. **Services:** Copying
(limited); division open to the public. **Computerized Information Services:**
CAN/OLE, iNET 2000, Standards Information Service (SIS). **Special
Catalogs:** National Standards of Canada (book). **Special Indexes:** KWOC
Directory and Index of Standards and Specifications. **Remarks:** Toll-free
telephone number(s): (800)267-8220 (in Canada). FAX: (613)995-4564.
Telex: 053-4403. **Also Known As:** Conseil Canadien des Normes. **Staff:** Z.
Ignatowicz, Comp.Anl.

Stanford Archive of Recorded Sound
See: Stanford University - Music Library (15656)

★ 15642 ★
Stanford Linear Accelerator Center - Library (Sci-Engr)
Box 4349   Phone: (415)926-2411
Stanford, CA 94309   Robert C. Gex, Chf.Libn.
Founded: 1962. **Staff:** Prof 5; Other 4. **Subjects:** High energy physics, particle accelerators. **Holdings:** 12,000 books; 6000 bound periodical volumes; 98,000 technical reports and preprints; 20,000 reports on microfiche. **Subscriptions:** 1214 journals and other serials. **Services:** Interlibrary loan; copying; library open to the public. **Automated Operations:** Computerized cataloging, acquisitions, circulation, and serials (SPIRES). **Computerized Information Services:** DIALOG Information Services, RLIN, InterNet (electronic mail service). Contact Person: Louise Addis, Assoc.Hd.Libn. **Publications:** Preprints in Particles and Fields, weekly - by subscription. **Remarks:** The Stanford Linear Acceleralor Center operates under contract to the U.S. Department of Energy. Located at 2575 Sand Hill Rd., Menlo Park, CA 94025. FAX: (415)323-3626. Electronic mail address(es): ADDIS@SLACUM.SLAC.STANFORD.EDU (InterNet). **Staff:** Arsella Raman, Ser.Libn.; Shirley Livengood, Tech. Data Libn.

★ 15643 ★
Stanford University - Art and Architecture Library (Art)
Nathan Cummings Art Bldg.   Phone: (415)723-3408
Stanford, CA 94305-2018   Alexander D. Ross, Hd.Libn.
Founded: 1970. **Staff:** Prof 2; Other 3. **Subjects:** Art - 19th and 20th century, Medieval, Renaissance, Baroque, Far Eastern, ancient; architectural history. **Special Collections:** Thomas Rowlandson Collection; Paris Salon Catalogues, 1673-1952; J.D. Chen Collection (Chinese art and archeology). **Holdings:** 131,000 volumes. **Subscriptions:** 500 journals and other serials. **Services:** Copying; library use limited to library card holders. **Computerized Information Services:** DIALOG Information Services; Socrates (internal database); BITNET (electronic mail service). **Networks/Consortia:** Member of CLASS, South Bay Cooperative Library System (SBCLS), Research Libraries Information Network (RLIN). **Remarks:** FAX: (415)725-6874. Electronic mail address(es): CN.ART@STANFORD (BITNET). **Staff:** Amanda W. Bowen.

★ 15644 ★
Stanford University - Branner Earth Sciences Library (Sci-Engr)
School of Earth Sciences   Phone: (415)723-2746
Stanford, CA 94305   Charlotte R.M. Derksen, Libn./Bibliog.
Founded: 1915. **Staff:** Prof 2; Other 3.5. **Subjects:** Geology, applied earth sciences, geophysics, hydrology, petroleum engineering, micropaleontology, geochemistry. **Special Collections:** Hayden, King, and Wheeler surveys; state geological survey open-file reports; geothermal technical reports. **Holdings:** 96,000 books and bound periodical volumes; 200,000 maps; 960 Stanford dissertations; 600 Stanford student reports; 26,000 microfiche; 124 microfilm; 7500 technical reports; 200 computer discs, CD-ROMs and magnetic tapes. **Subscriptions:** 1900 journals and other serials. **Services:** Interlibrary loan; copying; library open to the public for reference use only. **Automated Operations:** Computerized cataloging. **Computerized Information Services:** DIALOG Information Services, STN International, PFDS Online, Questel, RLIN; BITNET, InterNet (electronic mail services). **Networks/Consortia:** Member of CLASS, Research Libraries Information Network (RLIN). **Special Indexes:** Technical reports/open-file reports file (online); thesis index (online). **Remarks:** FAX: (415)725-6566. Electronic mail address(es): CN.EAR@FORSYTHE.STANFORD.EDU (InterNet). **Staff:** J.K. Herro, Map Libn.

★ 15645 ★
Stanford University - Center for Aeronautics and Space Information Sciences (CASIS) - Library (Comp Sci)
CSL Lab   Phone: (415)723-1450
Stanford, CA 94305-4055   Dr. Michael Flynn, Dir.
Subjects: Computer science, systems, and applications in the space sciences. **Holdings:** Figures not available. **Remarks:** FAX: (415)725-7398.

★ 15646 ★
Stanford University - Cubberley Education Library (Educ)
Stanford, CA 94305   Phone: (415)723-2121
     Barbara Celone, Hd.Libn.
Founded: 1891. **Staff:** Prof 2; Other 5. **Subjects:** Education, allied social sciences. **Special Collections:** 19th century textbooks (2000); college catalogs (78,000). **Holdings:** 144,668 volumes; 15,000 volumes of historical curriculum materials; 12,000 domestic and foreign government documents;

2000 historical textbooks; 340,718 ERIC microfiche. **Subscriptions:** 1424 journals and other serials. **Services:** Interlibrary loan; copying; library open to the public; borrowing limited to library card holders. **Automated Operations:** Computerized cataloging and acquisitions. **Computerized Information Services:** DIALOG Information Services; Socrates (internal database); CD-ROM (ERIC); BITNET (electronic mail service). **Networks/Consortia:** Member of CLASS, South Bay Cooperative Library System (SBCLS), Research Libraries Information Network (RLIN). **Remarks:** Electronic mail address(es): CN.EDU@STANFORD (BITNET). **Staff:** Ann Latta, Asst.Hd.Libn.

★ 15647 ★
Stanford University - Engineering Library (Sci-Engr)
Terman Engineering Center   Phone: (415)723-0001
Stanford, CA 94305-4029   Steve Gass, Hd. & Bibliog.
Founded: 1942. **Staff:** Prof 2; Other 5.5. **Subjects:** Engineering - civil, electrical, industrial, mechanical; engineering-economic systems; aeronautics and astronautics; materials science. **Special Collections:** Timoshenko Collection (applied mechanics; 1800 volumes). **Holdings:** 45,000 books; 43,000 bound periodical volumes; 350,000 microfiche; 60,000 technical reports. **Subscriptions:** 1700 journals and other serials. **Services:** Copying; library open to the public. **Automated Operations:** NOTIS. **Computerized Information Services:** DIALOG Information Services, STN International, RLIN; Socrates (internal database); CD-ROMs; BITNET (electronic mail service). **Networks/Consortia:** Member of CLASS, South Bay Cooperative Library System (SBCLS), Research Libraries Information Network (RLIN). **Remarks:** FAX: (415)725-1096. Electronic mail address(es): CN.ENG@FORSYTHE.STANFORD.EDU (BITNET). **Staff:** Lois Sher, Oper.Mgr.; Karen Greig, Asst.Libn.

★ 15648 ★
Stanford University - Falconer Biology Library (Biol Sci)
Stanford, CA 94305-5020   Phone: (415)723-1528
     Joseph G. Wible, Hd.Libn.
Founded: 1926. **Staff:** Prof 1; Other 2.5. **Subjects:** Biochemistry, molecular biology, population genetics and ecology, organismal biology. **Holdings:** 90,000 volumes. **Subscriptions:** 1300 journals and other serials. **Services:** Interlibrary loan (via Green Library); copying; library open to the public for reference use only. **Automated Operations:** Computerized public access catalog. **Computerized Information Services:** DIALOG Information Services, BRS Information Technologies, NLM; Socrates (internal database); CD-ROMs (CSA (Cambridge Scientific Abstracts) Life Sciences Collection, ASFA, MEDLINE); InterNet (electronic mail service). **Networks/Consortia:** Member of CLASS, South Bay Cooperative Library System (SBCLS), Research Libraries Information Network (RLIN). **Publications:** Falconer Biology Library Serials List. **Remarks:** FAX: (415)725-7712. Electronic mail address(es): CN.BIO@FORSYTHE.STANFORD.EDU (InterNet).

★ 15649 ★
Stanford University - Food Research Institute - Library
Stanford, CA 94305
Defunct. Holdings absorbed by Stanford University - Cecil M. Green Library.

★ 15650 ★
Stanford University - Hoover Institution on War, Revolution and Peace - Library (Soc Sci)
Stanford, CA 94305   Phone: (415)723-2058
     Charles G. Palm, Dp.Dir.
Founded: 1919. **Staff:** Prof 31; Other 62. **Subjects:** 20th century economic, political, and social problems with special emphasis on World Wars I and II and the following geographical areas: Africa, China, Eastern Europe, U.S.S.R., Japan, North and Latin America, Middle East, United States, Central and Western Europe. **Special Collections:** American Relief Administration records; military journals; international organizations; communist party materials; Paris Peace Conference records; propaganda and psychological warfare; underground movements. **Holdings:** 1.6 million volumes; 66,607 reels of microfilm; 60,777 microfiche; 4016 archival collections of national and international organizations, military government, political personnel; 1105 videotapes; 165,511 photographs; 4047 slides; 71,055 posters; pamphlets; government documents; newspaper and periodical file in Slavic, Western, and East Asian languages (38,770 titles). **Subscriptions:** 3756 journals and other serials; 404 newspapers. **Services:** Interlibrary loan; copying; library open to the public. **Automated**

Operations: Computerized public access catalog and cataloging. **Computerized Information Services:** DIALOG Information Services, RLIN; Socrates (internal database); BITNET (electronic mail service). **Networks/Consortia:** Member of Research Libraries Information Network (RLIN). **Publications:** List of publications - available on request. **Special Catalogs:** The Library Catalogs of the Hoover Institution; surveys of area collections. **Remarks:** FAX: (415)723-1687. Electronic mail address(es): FORTSON@HOOVER (BITNET). **Staff:** Judith Fortson, Hd.Libn.; Paul Thomas, Hd., Cat.; Viveca Seymour, Hd., Ser./Acq.; Robert Conquest, Cur., Russia & Eastern Europe; Peter Duignan, Cur., Africa & Mid East; Ramon H. Myers, Cur., E. Asia Coll.; William Ratliff, Cur., Latin & N. Amer.Coll.; Agnes Peterson, Cur., Central & Western Europe Coll.; Anne Van Camp, Archv.

★15651★
Stanford University - Hopkins Marine Station - Harold A. Miller Library (Biol Sci)
Cabrillo Point   Phone: (408)373-6658
Pacific Grove, CA 93950   Alan Baldridge, Hd.Libn.
Founded: 1920. **Staff:** Prof 1; Other 1. **Subjects:** Marine zoology and phycology, physiology and neurobiology, cell and developmental biology, biochemistry, immunology, molecular biology, ecology and population biology, oceanography. **Special Collections:** MacFarland Opisthobranchiate Molluscan Collection (800 items); G.M. Smith Algae Reprint Collection (300 volumes). **Holdings:** 27,000 volumes; 132 maps; 1400 other cataloged items. **Subscriptions:** 400 journals and other serials. **Services:** Interlibrary loan; copying; library open to the public by appointment. **Automated Operations:** Computerized cataloging and acquisitions. **Computerized Information Services:** DIALOG Information Services; CD-ROMs. **Networks/Consortia:** Member of Research Libraries Information Network (RLIN), CLASS. **Publications:** List of faculty and student publications, annual; bibliographies of common local marine invertebrates. **Remarks:** FAX: (408)373-7859.

★15652★
Stanford University - J. Hugh Jackson Library (Bus-Fin)
Graduate School of Business   Phone: (415)723-2161
Stanford, CA 94305-5016   Bela Gallo, Dir.
Founded: 1932. **Staff:** Prof 10; Other 21. **Subjects:** Accounting, business economics, finance, international business, investment, management, marketing, quantitative analysis. **Special Collections:** Favre Collection (Pacific Northwest economics); Jackson Collection (accounting information files of former Dean of School). **Holdings:** 397,908 books and other cataloged items; government documents; pamphlets; 350,000 corporate reports; 4091 reels of microfilm; 1.14 million microfiche. **Subscriptions:** 2084 periodicals; 93 newspapers. **Services:** Interlibrary loan (limited to faculty and graduate students); library not open to the public. **Automated Operations:** Computerized serials. **Computerized Information Services:** DIALOG Information Services, RLIN; BITNET (electronic mail service). **Publications:** Selected Additions to the J. Hugh Jackson Library, bimonthly. **Special Catalogs:** Jackson Library Periodicals, annual (book); Jackson Library Annuals on Standing Order, annual (book). **Remarks:** Electronic mail address(es): SGALLO@PESO.STANFORD.EDU (BITNET). **Staff:** Evelyn Hu, Hd.Per.Libn.; Janna Leffingwell, Ref.Libn.; Karen Wilson, Asst.Dir./Hd.Tech.Serv.Libn.; Robert Mayer, Asst.Dir./Hd.Pub.Serv.Libn.; Peter Latusek, Hd.Acq.Libn.; Suzanne Sweeney, Automation Libn.; Bryan McCann, Ref.Libn.; Paul Reist, Ref.Libn.; Kent Abbott, Cat.Libn.

★15653★
Stanford University - Lane Medical Library (Med)
Stanford University Medical Center Phone: (415)723-6831
Stanford, CA 94305-5323   Peter Stangl, Dir.
Founded: 1906. **Staff:** Prof 13; Other 20. **Subjects:** Clinical medicine and its specialties, preclinical and basic sciences, public health, nursing and allied fields. **Special Collections:** History of Medicine. **Holdings:** 314,956 volumes; 28,648 pamphlets and theses; 1818 audio recordings; 735 videotapes and cassettes; 217 computer materials. **Subscriptions:** 3058 journals and other serials; 6 newspapers. **Services:** Interlibrary loan; copying; SDI; library open to the public for reference use; borrowing limited to library card holders. **Automated Operations:** Computerized public access catalog, cataloging, acquisitions, and circulation (MELVYL). **Computerized Information Services:** MEDLARS, DIALOG Information Services, BRS Information Technologies, Chemical Abstracts Service (CAS), RLIN; CD-ROMs (MEDLINE, Aries Knowledge Finder, Compact Library: AIDS); OnTyme Electronic Message Network Service, EDUNET (electronic mail services).

Performs searches on fee basis. **Networks/Consortia:** Member of National Network of Libraries of Medicine - Pacific Southwest Region, Research Libraries Information Network (RLIN), Colorado Alliance of Research Libraries (CARL). **Special Catalogs:** Serials list, annual. **Special Indexes:** Reference index. **Remarks:** FAX: (415)725-7471. Electronic mail address(es): LANEINFO@KRYPTON.STANFORD.EDU (EDUNET). **Staff:** Valerie Su, Dp.Dir./Hd., Pub.Serv.; Dick Miller, Sys.Libn./Hd., Tech.Serv.; Anne Brewer, Hd., LRC; Rosemary Jepson, Hd., Circ. & Stacks Maint.; Michael Newman, Info.Cons.; Marilyn Tinsley, Info.Cons.; Betty Vadeboncoeur, Info.Cons.; Herman Pai, Tech.Serv.Libn.; Gloria Linder, Sr.Info.Cons.; Maryse Gascard, ILL Spec.; Janet Morrison, Info.Cons.; Nancy Austin, Assoc.Hd., Tech.Serv.; Mary Buttner, Assoc.Hd., Tech.Serv.

★15654★
Stanford University - Law Library (Law)
Stanford, CA 94305   Phone: (415)497-2721
                                   Lance E. Dickson, Law Libn.
Founded: 1894. **Staff:** Prof 9; Other 22. **Subjects:** Law, with particular emphasis on Anglo-American legislative and administrative materials. **Holdings:** 340,000 volumes. **Subscriptions:** 5152 journals and other serials. **Services:** Interlibrary loan; library not open to the public. **Automated Operations:** Computerized cataloging and acquisitions (NOTIS). **Computerized Information Services:** LEXIS, WESTLAW. **Networks/Consortia:** Member of Research Libraries Information Network (RLIN). **Remarks:** FAX: (415)725-1933. **Staff:** Rosalee Long, Assoc. Law Libn.; J. Paul Lomio, Pub.Serv.Libn.; Eliska Ryznar, Hd.Cat.Libn.

★15655★
Stanford University - Mathematical and Computer Sciences Library (Sci-Engr, Comp Sci)
Bldg. 380, Sloan Mathematics Center   Phone: (415)723-4672
Stanford, CA 94305   Rebecca Lasher, Hd.Libn.
Founded: 1964. **Staff:** Prof 1; Other 5. **Subjects:** Mathematics, statistics, operations research, computer science. **Holdings:** 58,000 volumes; 50,000 technical reports. **Subscriptions:** 800 journals and other serials. **Services:** Interlibrary loan; copying; library open to the public for reference use only. **Automated Operations:** Computerized public access catalog, cataloging, and acquisitions. **Computerized Information Services:** DIALOG Information Services, RLIN, STN International, Socrates (internal database); ARPANET, BITNET (electronic mail services). **Networks/Consortia:** Member of CLASS, Research Libraries Information Network (RLIN), South Bay Cooperative Library System (SBCLS). **Publications:** New Technical Reports List, monthly. **Remarks:** Electronic mail address(es): CN.MCS@FORSYTHE.STANFORD.EDU (BITNET).

★15656★
Stanford University - Music Library (Mus)
Braun Music Center   Phone: (415)723-1211
Stanford, CA 94305   Barbara Sawka, Act.Hd.Libn.
Founded: 1948. **Staff:** Prof 5; Other 8. **Subjects:** Music. **Special Collections:** Stanford Archive of Recorded Sound (200,000 sound recordings). **Holdings:** 75,000 books and scores; 2600 reels of microfilm; 6000 microcards and microfiche; 30,000 sound recordings. **Subscriptions:** 700 journals and other serials. **Services:** Interlibrary loan; copying; listening facilities for sound recordings; library use limited to library card holders. **Automated Operations:** Integrated library system (NOTIS). **Computerized Information Services:** DIALOG Information Services, PFDS Online, BRS Information Technologies; Socrates (internal database); BITNET (electronic mail service). **Networks/Consortia:** Member of CLASS, Research Libraries Information Network (RLIN), South Bay Cooperative Library System (SBCLS). **Publications:** List of publications - available on request. **Remarks:** Electronic mail address(es): CN.MUS@STANFORD (BITNET). **Staff:** Richard Koprowski, Archv.; Mimi Tashiro, Asst.Mus.Libn.; Jeffrey Earnest, Music Cat.; Kevin Freeman, Music Cat.

★15657★
Stanford University - Physics Library (Sci-Engr)
Stanford, CA 94305-4060   Phone: (415)723-4342
                                   Rebecca Lasher, Act.Hd.Libn.
Staff: Prof 1; Other 3. **Subjects:** Physics, astronomy, astrophysics. **Holdings:** 47,000 books and bound periodical volumes; technical reports; sky atlas photographs. **Subscriptions:** 600 journals and other serials. **Services:** Interlibrary loan; copying; library use limited to library card holders. **Automated Operations:** Computerized cataloging and acquisitions (through Green Library). **Computerized Information Services:** DIALOG Information Services, STN International; Socrates (internal database); BITNET (electronic mail service). **Networks/Consortia:** Member of CLASS, Research Libraries Information Network (RLIN), South Bay Cooperative Library System (SBCLS). **Remarks:** Electronic mail address(es): CN.PHY@FORSYTHE.STANFORD.EDU (BITNET).

★ 15658 ★
Stanford University - Special Collections (Hum, Hist)
Cecil H. Green Library   Phone: (415)725-1022
Stanford, CA 94305-6004   Margaret J. Kimball, Hd. & Univ.Archv.
Staff: Prof 3; Other 7. **Subjects:** British and American literature of the 19th and 20th centuries, book arts and the history of the book, 16th-18th century continental books, history of science, music, theater, the Mexican-American experience, California history and politics, Stanford University history, children's literature, higher education, science and technology, Jewish history and culture. **Special Collections:** Charlotte Ashley Felton Memorial Library (British and American literature); Morgan A. and Aline D. Gunst Memorial Library of the Book Arts; Samuel I. and Cecile M. Barchas Collection on the History of Science and Ideas; Frederick E. Brasch Collection on Sir Isaac Newton and the History of Scientific Thought; Memorial Library of Music; Antoine Borel Collection (manuscripts pertaining to California history and politics); James A. Healy Collection of Irish Literature; John Steinbeck Collection; Ernest Hemingway Collection; Taube-Baron Collection of Jewish History and Culture. **Holdings:** 190,188 books; 20 million manuscripts; 5755 maps; 248,454 photographs and prints; administrative records of the university; personal papers of faculty, trustees, staff, students; Stanford family papers; oral histories; 300 3-dimensional objects; 950 reels of microfilm; 2952 sound recordings and films; prints; posters; ephemera. **Subscriptions:** 330 journals and other serials. **Services:** Copying. **Automated Operations:** Computerized cataloging, acquisitions, and serials. **Computerized Information Services:** RLIN; Socrates (internal database); InterNet (electronic mail service). **Publications:** List of publications - available on request. **Special Catalogs:** Exhibition catalogs; descriptive guide to manuscript/archival collections; special card catalogs for maps, photographs, posters, 3-dimensional objects, theses, and dissertations. **Remarks:** FAX: (415)725-6748. Electronic mail address(es): CN.SPC@FORSYTHE.STANFORD.EDU (InterNet). **Staff:** Linda J. Long, Pub.Serv.Libn.

★ 15659 ★
**Stanford University - Swain Library of Chemistry and Chemical
  Engineering** (Sci-Engr)
Stanford, CA 94305-5080   Phone: (415)723-9237
                                  Grace Baysinger, Hd. Libn.
Founded: 1901. **Staff:** Prof 1; Other 2.5. **Subjects:** Chemistry, chemical engineering. **Holdings:** 47,804 volumes; 6492 microfiche; 390 reels of microfilm; 87 audio recordings; 8 videocassettes; 643 dissertations. **Subscriptions:** 637 journals and other serials. **Services:** Interlibrary loan; copying; library open to the public for reference use only. **Automated Operations:** Computerized public access catalog. **Computerized Information Services:** DIALOG Information Services, RLIN, STN International; Socrates (internal database); BITNET (electronic mail service). **Networks/Consortia:** Member of CLASS, Research Libraries Information Network (RLIN), South Bay Cooperative Library System (SBCLS). **Remarks:** Electronic mail address(es): CN.CHM@STANFORD (BITNET).

★ 15660 ★
Stanford University - Tanner Memorial Philosophy Library (Rel-Phil)
Department of Philosophy   Phone: (415)723-1539
Stanford, CA 94305   Zita Zukowsky, Libn.
Founded: 1960. **Staff:** Prof 1; Other 4. **Subjects:** Symbolic logic; philosophical logic; philosophy of mathematics, language, and science; metaphysics and epistemology; ethics and philosophy of action; history of philosophy; aesthetics. **Special Collections:** Clarence Irving Lewis Memorial Collection (235 volumes). **Holdings:** 5500 books; 850 bound periodical volumes; 200 dissertations; 925 reprints and typescripts. **Subscriptions:** 75 journals and other serials. **Services:** Interlibrary loan; library open to the public with approval of Stanford University Libraries. **Automated Operations:** Computerized cataloging and acquisitions. **Computerized Information Services:** Online system; electronic mail service.

★ 15661 ★
Stanislaus County Law Library (Law)
1012 11th St., Suite 400   Phone: (209)558-7759
Modesto, CA 95354   Janice K. Milliken, Law Libn.
Founded: 1893. **Staff:** Prof 1. **Subjects:** Law. **Holdings:** 20,865 volumes. **Services:** Interlibrary loan (limited); copying; library open to the public.

Stanislaus County Medical Library
See: Scenic General Hospital (14898)

★ 15662 ★
Stanislaus County Schools - Teachers' Professional Library
801 County Center No. 3 Ct.
Modesto, CA 95355
Defunct.

★ 15663 ★
Stanley Associates Engineering, Ltd. - Library (Env-Cons, Plan)
10160 112th St.   Phone: (403)423-4777
Edmonton, AB, Canada T5K 2L6   Donna Meen, Libn.
Staff: Prof 1; Other 1. **Subjects:** Pollution control, transportation, environmental and municipal engineering, land development, water supply and distribution, urban and regional planning, structural engineering. **Holdings:** 10,000 books; 300 bound periodical volumes; 12,000 internal reports and proposals; 30,000 engineering drawings on microfilm; 6000 original drawings; 1000 topographic maps. **Subscriptions:** 200 journals and other serials; 20 newspapers. **Services:** Interlibrary loan; copying; library open to the public by request. **Computerized Information Services:** DIALOG Information Services, CAN/OLE, Ground Water Online, Info Globe. **Remarks:** FAX: (403)421-4300.

★ 15664 ★
Stanley Consultants - Technical Library (Sci-Engr, Plan)
Stanley Bldg.   Phone: (319)264-6234
Muscatine, IA 52761   Marlys A. Grete, Libn.
Staff: 1. **Subjects:** Engineering, architecture, urban and regional planning. **Holdings:** 12,500 books; 1000 bound periodical volumes; 6000 catalogs; 115 videotapes of internal seminars; 24 cassettes. **Subscriptions:** 222 journals and other serials. **Services:** Interlibrary loan; copying; library open to the public with restrictions. **Computerized Information Services:** DIALOG Information Services, Institute of Electrical and Electronics Engineers, Inc. (IEEE); CD-ROM (Construction Criteria Base). **Remarks:** FAX: (319)264-6658.

Edmund Stanley Library
See: Friends University - Edmund Stanley Library - Special Collections (6176)

Patrick J. Stapleton, Jr. Library
See: Indiana University of Pennsylvania (7811)

★ 15665 ★
Star Magazine - Library (Publ)
660 White Plains Rd.   Phone: (914)332-5000
Tarrytown, NY 10591   Christopher E. Bowen, Lib.Dir.
Founded: 1974. **Staff:** Prof 1; Other 8. **Subjects:** People, entertainment, news events. **Holdings:** 500,000 clippings; 250,000 photographs; 50,000 color slides and transparencies. **Subscriptions:** 25 journals and other serials; 25 newspapers. **Services:** Library not open to the public. **Computerized Information Services:** NEXIS, BASELINE.

★ 15666 ★
Star of the Republic Museum - Library (Hist)
Box 317   Phone: (409)878-2461
Washington, TX 77880   Houston McGaugh, Dir.
Founded: 1970. **Staff:** 6. **Subjects:** Texas history, museums and museology, artifact identification. **Special Collections:** Showers-Brown Collection (Texana). **Holdings:** 3000 books; 100 bound periodical volumes; 2000 manuscripts, documents; 300 maps; 100 newspapers, census documents, dissertations on microfilm. **Subscriptions:** 40 journals and other serials. **Services:** Copying; library open to the public. **Special Indexes:** Special Formats Index (booklet).

★ 15667 ★
Star-Spangled Banner Flag House Association - Library (Hist)
844 E. Pratt St.
Baltimore, MD 21202   Phone: (301)837-1793
Subjects: History - American, Baltimore, Maryland; War of 1812; flags; Mary Pickersgill. **Holdings:** 200 books; 100 bound periodical volumes; 1 AV program; 50 manuscripts. **Services:** Copying; library open to the public with restrictions.

★15668★
Star Throwers - Agape Library (Soc Sci)
615 Trowbridge
Franklin, LA 70538
Phone: (318)828-2375
Bernard Broussard, Dir.
Founded: 1986. **Subjects:** Peace, justice, earth stewardship, world religions, civil rights, spirituality, animals. **Holdings:** 2000 books; 150 AV programs. **Subscriptions:** 20 journals and other serials; 5 newspapers. **Services:** Interlibrary loan, library open to the public. **Publications:** Books; fliers; tapes; newsletter. **Staff:** Mark Richard.

★15669★
Star Trek: The Official Fan Club - Library (Rec)
Box 111000
Aurora, CO 80011
Phone: (303)341-1813
John S. Davis, V.P./Assoc.Ed.
Founded: 1980. **Subjects:** Star Trek - new and original television shows, movies. **Holdings:** Figures not available. **Services:** Library not open to the public.

★15670★
Starhill Forest Arboretum - Library (Biol Sci)
Rte. 1, Box 272
Petersburg, IL 62675
Founded: 1976. **Staff:** 1. **Subjects:** Horticulture, ecology, landscape architecture, forestry, natural history. **Special Collections:** Antiquarian collection (horticulture, forestry, landscape architecture, natural history; 800 volumes). **Holdings:** 2000 volumes; 10 series of periodical volumes; 15,000 slides. **Subscriptions:** 10 journals and other serials. **Services:** Library and living collections open to qualified researchers for reference use only. **Staff:** Guy Sternberg, Owner; Edith Sternberg, Owner.

Stark County Historical Sociey - Ramsayer Research Library
See: **McKinley Museum of History, Science, and Industry** (9930)

★15671★
Stark County Law Library Association - Alliance Branch Law Library (Law)
City Hall
470 E. Market
Alliance, OH 44601
Phone: (216)823-6181
Founded: 1930. **Subjects:** U.S. law. **Holdings:** 3500 volumes. **Services:** Library not open to the public.

★15672★
Stark County Law Library Association - Law Library (Law)
115 Central Plaza, N.
Canton, OH 44702
Phone: (216)456-2330
Martha M. Cox, Dir.
Founded: 1890. **Staff:** Prof 1; Other 3.5. **Subjects:** U.S. and Ohio law. **Holdings:** 44,854 books; 1498 bound periodical volumes; 112,616 microfiche; 623 reels of microfilm; 423 sound cassettes; 101 videocassettes. **Subscriptions:** 850 journals and other serials. **Services:** Library open to the public for reference use only. **Automated Operations:** Computerized public access catalog, cataloging, acquisitions, serials, and circulation. **Computerized Information Services:** WESTLAW, DIALOG Information Services, LEXIS, Veralex 2. **Publications:** Newsletter, irregular. **Remarks:** FAX: (216)456-8176.

★15673★
Stark County Law Library Association - Massillon Branch Law Library (Law)
Massillon Municipal Court
2 James Duncan Plaza
Massillon, OH 44646
Phone: (216)830-1725
Ida Pedrotty, Libn.
Founded: 1940. **Subjects:** Ohio law. **Holdings:** 2500 volumes. **Services:** Library not open to the public.

Miriam Lutcher Stark Library
See: **University of Texas at Austin - Harry Ransom Humanities Research Center** (19392)

C.V. Starr Biomedical Information Center
See: **Cornell University - Medical College - Samuel J. Wood Library** (4323)

C.V. Starr East Asian Library
See: **Columbia University - C.V. Starr East Asian Library** (4006)

Dorothy C.S. Starr Civil War Research Library
See: **Fort Ward Museum** (6015)

Starr King School for the Ministry
See: **Graduate Theological Union** (6613)

Starsmore Center for Local History
See: **Colorado Springs Pioneers Museum** (3951)

★15674★
State Bar of Michigan - Library (Law)
306 Townsend St.
Lansing, MI 48933
Phone: (517)482-6248
Douglas L. Sweet, Dir., R. & D.
Staff: 1. **Subjects:** Law. **Holdings:** 3000 books; 700 bound periodical volumes. **Subscriptions:** 10 journals and other serials; 5 newspapers. **Services:** Library open to lawyers only. **Remarks:** FAX: (517)482-2648.

★15675★
State Capital Historical Association - Library and Photo Archives (Hist)
211 W. 21st Ave.
Olympia, WA 98501
Phone: (206)753-2580
Derek R. Valley, Dir.
Founded: 1941. **Staff:** Prof 7. **Subjects:** Washington history, Victoriana, museology, art. **Special Collections:** Collection of Washington photographs, including early photos of pioneers, towns, industries, Indians, and state governments; archives of Northwest Indian art. **Holdings:** 3000 historical photographs. **Services:** Copying; archives open to the public by arrangement.

★15676★
State Committee of the USSR for Inventions and Discoveries - All-Union Patent and Technical Library (Law)
Berezhkovskaya naberezhnaya, 24
121857 Moscow G-59, Russia
Phone: 095 2406425
Vladimir A. Komarov, Dir.
Founded: 1896. **Staff:** 547. Inventions, patents, patent laws. **Special Collections:** Inventive Act and Patent Right Collection (patent documentation on 60 countries in 29 languages). **Holdings:** 200,000 books; 1.6 million microfiche; 48 million reels of microfilm; 14.4 million of state files on scientific-technical examination of inventions; 829,000 files of designs. **Subscriptions:** 1392 journals and other serials; 33 newspapers. **Services:** Interlibrary loan; copying; library open to the public. **Automated Operations:** Computerized cataloging. **Computerized Information Services:** Internal databases. **Publications:** Funds of patent documentation of All-Union Patent and Technical Library; bibliography of foreign documentation, annual; bibliography of home publications, monthly. **Special Indexes:** Index of home publications, annual. **Remarks:** Library is said to be the largest patent and technical collection in Russia. FAX: 095 2404437. Telex: 411774, BIPAT SU. **Formerly:** State Committee of the USSR for Inventions and Discoveries - All-Union Patent and Technical Library.

★15677★
State Community College - Senator Kenneth Hall Learning Resource Center - Special Collections (Hist)
601 James R. Thompson Blvd.
East St. Louis, IL 62203
Phone: (618)583-2566
Dr. W.J. Van Grunsven, Dir.
Founded: 1969. **Staff:** Prof 3; Other 4. **Subjects:** African-Americans - general, history. **Holdings:** 31,250 books; 2305 reels of microfilm; bound periodical volumes. **Subscriptions:** 112 journals and other serials; 11 newspapers. **Services:** Interlibrary loan; copying; library open to the public for reference use only. **Computerized Information Services:** CD-ROM (InfoTrac). **Networks/Consortia:** Member of ILLINET. **Remarks:** FAX: (618)583-2660. **Staff:** Dr. James J. Lin, AV-TV Libn.; Ms. Bettye Brown, Ref.Libn.

★ 15678 ★
State Farm Mutual Automobile Insurance Company - Corporate Library
(Law)
One State Farm Plaza, E-5   Phone: (309)766-2780
Bloomington, IL 61710   Laura Garrett, Corp.Libn.
Founded: 1962. **Staff:** Prof 3; Other 5. **Subjects:** Law, insurance, business, commerce, management. **Holdings:** 31,000 books; 30 bound periodical volumes. **Subscriptions:** 400 journals and other serials; 10 newspapers. **Services:** Interlibrary loan; copying; SDI; library open to the public for reference use only. **Automated Operations:** Computerized cataloging. **Computerized Information Services:** DIALOG Information Services, PFDS Online, LEXIS, NEXIS, WESTLAW, Dow Jones News/Retrieval, OCLC, OCLC EPIC. **Networks/Consortia:** Member of Corn Belt Library System. **Publications:** New Acquisitions, monthly; Resource, bimonthly - for internal distribution only. **Remarks:** FAX: (309)766-4909. **Staff:** Sylvia Justice, Asst.Corp.Libn.; Lynne Nickum, Asst.Corp.Libn.

★ 15679 ★
State Historical Society of Iowa - Library/Archives Bureau (Hist)
600 E. Locust   Phone: (515)281-5111
Des Moines, IA 50319   Nancy Kraft, Bureau Chf.
Founded: 1894. **Staff:** Prof 7; Other 7.5. **Subjects:** History - Iowa, agriculture, railroad, regional Indians; historic preservation; genealogy. **Special Collections:** State Archives (17,000 cubic feet); historical Iowa photographs (100,000 images); Aldrich Autograph Collection (4000 items); Iowa historical maps (3000); Manuscript collections - Grenville Dodge, Charles Mason, Albert Cummins, William Boyd Allison, John A. Kasson. **Holdings:** 60,000 books; 2500 linear feet of manuscripts; 25,000 reels of microfilm; 42 VF drawers of pamphlets and clippings. **Subscriptions:** 200 journals and other serials; 300 newspapers. **Services:** Interlibrary loan; copying; library open to the public. **Automated Operations:** Computerized cataloging. **Networks/Consortia:** Member of Bibliographical Center for Research, Rocky Mountain Region, Inc. (BCR). **Special Indexes:** Index to Iowa GAR file (microfilm); index to selected newspapers (microfilm). **Remarks:** FAX: (515)282-0502. **Staff:** Gordon O. Hendrickson, State Archv.; Ruth Bartels, Ref.Libn.; Beth Brannen, Archv.; Becki Peterson, Photo Archv.; Sharon Avery, Archv.; Lora Bloom, Archv.

★ 15680 ★
State Historical Society of Iowa - Library/Archives Bureau (Hist)
402 Iowa Ave.   Phone: (319)335-3916
Iowa City, IA 52240   Nancy Kraft, Bureau Chf.
Founded: 1857. **Staff:** Prof 8; Other 9. **Subjects:** History - Iowa, the frontier, agriculture, railroad, women, education in Iowa, Indians of the region; genealogy. **Special Collections:** Robert Lucas papers; Jonathan P. Dolliver papers; Gilbert Haugen papers; Cyrus Carpenter papers; Iowa industry house organs; historical Iowa photographs (265,000); historical Iowa maps (3000). **Holdings:** 130,000 books; 10,000 bound periodical volumes; 15,000 pamphlets; 17,000 reels of microfilm; 10,000 bound newspapers; 25 VF drawers of newspaper clippings; 1800 oral history interviews; 4000 linear feet of manuscripts. **Subscriptions:** 575 serials; 65 newspapers. **Services:** Interlibrary loan; copying; library open to the public. **Automated Operations:** Computerized cataloging. **Networks/Consortia:** Member of Bibliographical Center for Research, Rocky Mountain Region, Inc. (BCR). **Publications:** Bibliography of Iowa newspapers, 1836-1976; Iowa History and Culture (bibliography of materials published between 1952 and 1986); a guide to resources for the study of the recent history of the United States in the libraries of the University of Iowa, the State Historical Society of Iowa, and the Herbert Hoover Presidential Library; bibliographies on immigrant groups, women in Iowa, historic Iowa homes and architecture. **Special Catalogs:** Manuscript catalog; Fire Insurance Maps of Iowa Cities and Towns. **Special Indexes:** Indexes to selected history and genealogy serials. **Remarks:** FAX: (319)335-3924. **Staff:** Eric Austin, Mss.Archv.; Mary Bennett, Audio-Visual Libn.; Karen Laughlin, Ref.Libn.; Susan Rogers, Acq.Libn.; Jane Meggers, Cons.; Linda Brown-Link, Cat.Libn.; Renee Atcherson, Cat.Libn.

★ 15681 ★
State Historical Society of Missouri - Library (Hist)
1020 Lowry St.   Phone: (314)882-7083
Columbia, MO 65201   James W. Goodrich, Exec.Dir.
Founded: 1898. **Staff:** Prof 14; Other 5. **Subjects:** Missouri and midwestern history, works by and about Missourians. **Special Collections:** J. Christian Bay Rare Book Collection (5200 books and documents); special collection of the writings of Mark Twain and Eugene Field; Bishop William Fletcher McMurray Collection; Francis A. Sampson Collection; Alice Irene

Fitzgerald Collection of Missouri's Literary Heritage for Children and Youth (1000 volumes). **Holdings:** 440,000 volumes; 1200 bound volumes of newspapers; 2400 maps; 50,000 reels of microfilm of Missouri newspapers; 100,000 photographs; 6780 reels of microfilm of genealogical records. **Subscriptions:** 520 journals and other serials; 357 newspapers. **Services:** Interlibrary loan; copying; library open to the public. **Publications:** Historic Missouri: A Pictorial Narrative (1988); Thomas Hart Benton: Artist, Writer and Intellectual (1989); My Road to Emeritus (1989). **Special Catalogs:** Missouri Newspapers on Microfilm at the State Historical Society of Missouri, irregular; Missouri Plat Books in the State, Historical Society of Missouri, irregular; Directory of Local Historical, Museum and Genealogical Agencies in Missouri, biennial; Missouri Union Burials-Missouri Units (1989); Selected Union Burials-Missouri Units (1988) - all for sale. **Staff:** Lynn Wolf Gentzler, Assoc.Dir.; Kay Pettit; Mark Thomas; Ara Kaye; Marie Concannon; Laurel Boeckman; Liz Bailey; JoAnn Tuckwood; Peggy Platner; Ann Rogers; Leona Morris.

State Historical Society of Missouri - Manuscripts Collection
See: **Western Historical Manuscript Collection** (20250)

★ 15682 ★
State Historical Society of North Dakota - State Archives and Historical Research Library (Hist)
Heritage Center   Phone: (701)224-2668
Bismarck, ND 58505   Gerald Newborg, State Archv./Div.Dir
Founded: 1905. **Staff:** Prof 8; Other 3. **Subjects:** North Dakota and Dakota Territory; social, cultural, economic, and political history; early exploration and travel; fur trade; plains military history; Northern Plains region - archeology, prehistory, ethnology, ethnohistory; historic preservation; genealogy. **Holdings:** 100,000 volumes; 2000 cubic feet of manuscripts; 10,000 cubic feet of state and county archives; 85,000 photographs; 12,100 reels of microfilm of microfilm of newspapers; 1417 titles of North Dakota newspapers; 2100 titles of periodicals; 1200 oral history interviews; sound recordings; maps; videotapes; motion pictures. **Subscriptions:** 300 journals and other serials; 103 newspapers. **Services:** Interlibrary loan (limited); copying; library open to the public for reference use only. **Automated Operations:** Computerized cataloging. **Computerized Information Services:** OCLC. **Networks/Consortia:** Member of MINITEX Library Information Network. **Publications:** North Dakota History: Journal of the Northern Plains, quarterly; Plains Talk (newsletter), quarterly; Guide to the North Dakota State Archives, 1985; Guide to Manuscripts, 1985. **Staff:** Dolores Vyzralek, Chf.Libn.; Lotte Bailey, Dp. State Archv.; Todd Strand, Photo.Archv.

★ 15683 ★
State Historical Society of Wisconsin - Archives Division (Hist)
816 State St.   Phone: (608)264-6450
Madison, WI 53706   Peter Gottlieb, State Archv.
Founded: 1846. **Staff:** Prof 17; Other 9. **Subjects:** Wisconsin history; American frontier, 1750-1815; labor and industrial relations; socialism; mass communications; theater; agricultural history; civil rights; contemporary social action movements. **Special Collections:** Draper Collection (frontier); McCormick Collection (agriculture and agricultural manufacturing); manuscript collections of American Institute of the History of Pharmacy, Mass Communications History Center, Wisconsin Center for Film and Theatre Research, and Wisconsin Jewish Archives. **Holdings:** 45,037 cubic feet of Wisconsin state and local public records; 37,776 cubic feet of nongovernmental archives and manuscripts; 15,000 unbound maps; 2000 atlases; 500 titles on 3100 audiotapes; 110 titles on 3500 phonograph records; 1.5 million iconographic items; 50 machine-readable data files of state government records. **Services:** Copying; photo and film reproduction and dubbing of recordings for television. **Automated Operations:** Computerized cataloging. **Computerized Information Services:** RLIN. **Publications:** Accession reports in Wisconsin Magazine of History, quarterly; guides and inventories. **Remarks:** FAX: (608)264-6472. Administers the Wisconsin Area Research Center Network. **Staff:** Harry Miller, Ref.Archv.; Richard Pifer, Coll.Dev.

State Historical Society of Wisconsin - Circus World Museum
See: **Circus World Museum** (3716)

★ 15684 ★

State Historical Society of Wisconsin - Library (Hist)
816 State St.   Phone: (608)264-6534
Madison, WI 53706-1482   R. David Myers, Dir.
Founded: 1846. **Staff:** Prof 19; Other 12. **Subjects:** History - American, Canadian, state, local, labor, U.S. church; radical/reform movements and groups in the U.S. and Canada; ethnic and minority groups in North America; genealogy; women's history; military history; religious history. **Holdings:** 2.8 million items. **Subscriptions:** 8500 periodicals; 320 newspapers. **Services:** Interlibrary loan; copying; library open to the public. **Automated Operations:** Computerized public access catalog and cataloging. **Computerized Information Services:** OCLC. **Networks/Consortia:** Member of Wisconsin Interlibrary Services (WILS), Center for Research Libraries (CRL). **Publications:** Wisconsin Public Documents (checklist of state government documents) - free upon request; bibliographies; guides. **Special Indexes:** Index to names in Wisconsin federal census, 1820-1870 and 1905 state census; Wisconsin necrology index; index of names in Wisconsin county histories. **Remarks:** FAX: (608)264-6520. This library is a U.S. Federal Government regional depository, a Wisconsin State official depository, and a Canadian Federal Government selective depository for government publications. FAX: (608)264-6520. **Staff:** Gerald R. Eggleston, Acq.Libn.; Jonathan D. Cooper, Cat.Libn.; Michael J. Edmonds, Pub.Serv.Libn.; John A. Peters, Govt.Pubns.Libn.

★ 15685 ★

State Law Library of Montana (Law)
Justice Bldg.
215 N. Sanders   Phone: (406)444-3660
Helena, MT 59620-3004   Judith Meadows, Dir. & State Law Libn.
Founded: 1873. **Staff:** Prof 3; Other 4. **Subjects:** Law. **Special Collections:** Montana Legal History. **Holdings:** 110,000 volumes; selective U.S. government depository. **Subscriptions:** 500 journals and other serials. **Services:** Interlibrary loan; copying; SDI; library open to the public. **Automated Operations:** Computerized public access catalog, cataloging, and ILL. **Computerized Information Services:** WESTLAW, DIALOG Information Services, LEXIS, NEXIS, VU/TEXT Information Services. Performs searches on fee basis. **Networks/Consortia:** Member of OCLC Pacific Network, Northwest Consortium of Law Libraries. **Publications:** Library Guidebook; Historical Sketch of State Law Library of Montana. **Remarks:** Fax: (406)444-3603. **Staff:** Brenda Grasmick, Tech.Serv.Libn.; Marie Hartman, Circ.Coord.; Steve Jordan, Ref.Libn.

★ 15686 ★

State Library of Florida (Info Sci)
R.A. Gray Bldg.
500 S. Bronough St.   Phone: (904)487-2651
Tallahassee, FL 32399-0250   Barratt Wilkins, State Libn.
Founded: 1845. **Staff:** Prof 32; Other 37. **Subjects:** Florida, history, social sciences, library science. **Special Collections:** Floridana (21,809 items). **Holdings:** 261,567 books; 7543 bound periodical volumes; 108,678 Florida public documents; 129,031 U.S. documents; 16,939 reels of microfilm; 219,514 microfiche; 4534 films. **Subscriptions:** 1272 journals and other serials; 13 newspapers. **Services:** Interlibrary loan; copying; SDI; library open to the public. **Automated Operations:** Computerized cataloging, serials, circulation, acquisitions, and film booking. **Computerized Information Services:** OCLC; ALANET, LOGIN (electronic mail services). **Networks/Consortia:** Member of SOLINET, Florida Library Network (FLN). **Publications:** Orange Seed (technical bulletin) - to libraries; New Books, quarterly - to state agency personnel; Florida Library Directory with Statistics, annual - free to libraries; Florida Public Documents, monthly. **Special Indexes:** KWIC Index to Florida Public Documents, quarterly. **Remarks:** FAX: (904)488-0978 (ILL); (904)488-2746 (Adm.). Electronic mail address(es): 0139 (ALANET); SLIBFL (LOGIN). Maintained by Florida State Department of State - Division of Library and Information Services. **Staff:** Lorraine D. Summers, Asst. State Libn.; Sandra M. Cooper, Chf., Bur.Lib.Dev.; Loretta Flowers, Grants Cons.; Ruth O'Donnell, Inst.Cons.; Carole Fiore, Youth Serv.Cons.; Laura Hodges, Lib.Cons.; Betty Ann Scott, Lib.Cons.; Marian Deeney, Lib.Cons.; Charles Parker, Lib.Cons.; Linda Fuchs, Chf., Bur. Interlibrary Coop.; Marvin Mounce, ILL Coop.Cons.; Bob Gorin, ILL Coop.Cons.; Patty Paul, Lib.Prog.Adm.; Debra Sears, Ref.Libn.; Lisa Close, Doc.Libn.; Mary Ann Cleveland, Florida Libn.; Helen Morgan Moeller, Lib.Prog.Adm.; Dan Lhotka, AV Libn.; Emmett Denny, Lib.Prog.Adm.

★ 15687 ★

State Library of Iowa (Info Sci)
E. 12th & Grand   Phone: (515)281-4118
Des Moines, IA 50319   Shirley George, State Libn.
Founded: 1838. **Staff:** Prof 12; Other 22. **Subjects:** State government, law, medicine, library science. **Special Collections:** State Documents Collection; Federal Documents Depository; State Data Center; Patent Depository Library. **Holdings:** 431,218 books; 10 cabinets of vertical files about Iowa; 16,000 reels of microfilm; 630,000 microfiche. **Subscriptions:** 2224 journals and other serials. **Services:** Interlibrary loan; copying; library open to the public. **Computerized Information Services:** DIALOG Information Services, PFDS Online, BRS Information Technologies, LEXIS; ALANET (electronic mail service). **Networks/Consortia:** Member of Bibliographical Center for Research, Rocky Mountain Region, Inc. (BCR), Iowa Computer Assisted Network (ICAN). **Publications:** Iowa Locator (compact disc), quarterly; Footnotes, monthly; Joblist, monthly; Public Library Statistics, annual; In Service to Iowa: Public Library Measures of Quality; Iowa Certification Manual for Public Libraries; 1991 LSCA Handbook; Iowa Library Directory, both annual; Summer Reading Program - Manual, annual - to public and regional libraries of Iowa; Check Your Opportunities, annual. **Special Catalogs:** Audio-Visual Catalog; Iowa Documents Catalog (book). **Remarks:** FAX: (515)281-3384. A Division of the Department of Cultural Affairs. Includes the Iowa State Law Library and the Iowa State Medical Library. **Staff:** Christie Brandau, Asst. State Libn.; Nancy Haigh, Ref.Libn.; Pamela Rees, Med.Ref.Libn.; Fred Chenery, Hd., Tech.Serv.; Linda Robertson, Law Ref.Libn.; Helen Dagley, AV Libn.; Dan Cates, Networking Coord.; Sandy Dixon, Cont.Educ.Coord.; Gerry Rowland, Spec. Population Cons.; Beth Henning, Hd., State Data Ctr.; Nancy Lee, Docs. Depository Libn.; Annette Van Cleave, Dir., Mktg.

State Library of Massachusetts
See: **(Massachusetts) State Library of Massachusetts (9833)**

★ 15688 ★

State Library of New South Wales - Special Collections (Area-Ethnic, Hist)
Macquarie St.   Phone: 2 230 1414
Sydney, NSW, Australia   Alison Crook, State Libn.
Founded: 1826. **Subjects:** Australiana, Southwest Pacific, history of modern Europe, 19th century British history. **Special Collections:** Mitchell Library; Dixson Library; rare books and special collections. **Holdings:** 1.1 million books and bound periodicals; 367,472 microfiche; 37,667 reels of microfilm; 3505 videocassettes; 13,059 16mm films. **Subscriptions:** 19,931 journals and other serials. **Services:** Interlibrary loan; copying; library open to the public. **Computerized Information Services:** DIALOG Information Services, WILSONLINE, PFDS Online, AUSINET, AUSTRALIS, ESA/IRS, OZLINE; CD-ROMs; internal database; ILANET (electronic mail service). Performs searches on fee basis. Contact Person: Elizabeth Swan, Mgr., 2301533; or Ann Enderby, Rdr.Serv.Libn., 2301444. **Publications:** Annual report, Library Council of New South Wales; Journal of the Library Society; Friends Group of the State of New South Wales; Upfront, Journal of the Library Society. **Remarks:** Telex: 121150. FAX: 2 2332003. Electronic mail address(es): MLN 200003 (ILANET). **Staff:** Jo McIntyre, Dir., Info.Serv.

★ 15689 ★

State Library of New South Wales - Special Collections - Mitchell Library (Area-Ethnic)
Macquarie St.   Phone: 2 2301466
Sydney, NSW 2000, Australia   Margy Burn, Mgr.
Founded: 1910. **Subjects:** New South Wales, Australia, Southwest Pacific region, Antarctica. **Holdings:** 511,883 volumes; 63,719 microforms; 8465 linear meters of manuscripts; 727,931 photographs; 147,613 maps. **Subscriptions:** 14,930 journals, newspapers, and other serials. **Services:** Copying; library open to the public with restrictions on use of original materials. **Computerized Information Services:** AUSINET, Australian Bibliographic Network (ABN), DIALOG Information Services; ILANET (electronic mail service). **Publications:** Printed guides to selected collections. **Remarks:** FAX: 2 2332003. Electronic mail address(es): MLN 200001 (ILANET).

State Library of North Carolina
See: **North Carolina (State) Department of Cultural Resources - Division of the State Library (11885)**

★ 15690 ★
State Library of the Northern Territory - Northern Australia Collection
(Area-Ethnic)
25 Cavenagh St.
P.O. Box 42   Phone: 89 897364
Darwin, NT 0801, Australia   Michael Loos, Sr.Libn.
Founded: 1980. **Staff:** Prof 2; Other 1. **Subjects:** Northern Australia.
Holdings: 8289 books; 8025 pamphlets; 1258 maps; 1252 films and
videotapes; 40,512 photographs. **Subscriptions:** 1459 journals and other
serials; 156 newspapers. **Services:** Copying; collection open to the public for
reference use only. **Automated Operations:** Computerized public access
catalog, cataloging, and acquisitions. **Computerized Information Services:**
AUSINET, ABN (Australian Bibliographic Network), N.T. News Index.
Performs searches free of charge. **Publications:** Occasional papers. **Special
Indexes:** State Library Photograph Index (online). **Remarks:** FAX: 89
411375. **Formerly:** Northern Territory Department of Education - State
Reference Library of the Northern Territory - Northern Australia
Collection.

★ 15691 ★
State Library of Ohio (Info Sci)
65 S. Front St.   Phone: (614)644-7061
Columbus, OH 43266-0334   Richard M. Cheski, State Libn.
Founded: 1817. **Staff:** Prof 42; Other 96. **Subjects:** Management, social
sciences, education, public administration, Ohio history. **Special
Collections:** Genealogy (14,000 items); Ohio and federal documents (1.5
million). **Holdings:** 609,440 books; 437,822 microforms. **Subscriptions:** 699
journals and other serials; 18 newspapers. **Services:** Interlibrary loan;
copying; faxing; library open to the public. **Automated Operations:**
Computerized cataloging, acquisitions, serials, circulation, and ILL
(DOCLINE). **Computerized Information Services:** DIALOG Information
Services, OCLC, LIBRIS, WILSONLINE, Library Control System (LCS),
OHIONET, LC DIRECT; ALANET (electronic mail service). Performs
searches for state agencies. Contact Person: Catherine Mead, Hd., Ref., 644-
6952. **Networks/Consortia:** Member of National Network of Libraries of
Medicine - Greater Midwest Region, OHIONET, Columbus Area Libraries
Information Council of Ohio (CALICO). **Publications:** Directory of Ohio
Libraries, annual; Ohio Documents, quarterly; Statistics of Ohio Libraries,
annual; Ohio Public Library Statistics Categorized by Total Income, annual;
Recent Acquisitions, irregular; News from the State Library, monthly;
Library Opportunities, monthly; Annual Report. **Remarks:** FAX: (614)644-
7004. **Staff:** Susan Thomas, Dp. State Libn.; Sondra Vandermark, Dp. State
Libn.; Floyd Dickman, Hd., Lib.Dev.; Cynthia Mclaughlin, Hd. LSCA and
Evaluation; Timothy Elsey, Automation Coord.; Bill Crowley, Dp. State
Libn. for Lib.Serv.; John Philip, Hd., Fld.Oper.; James Buchman, Hd.,
Circ.; Clyde Hordusky, Hd., Docs.; Michael Lucas, Hd., Spec.Serv.

State Library of Pennsylvania
See: **Pennsylvania (State) Department of Education** (12858)

★ 15692 ★
State Library of Queensland (Hist, Info Sci)
Queensland Cultural Ctr.
South Bank   Phone: 7 840 7666
South Brisbane, QLD 4101, Australia   Des Stephens, State Libn.
Founded: 1896. **Staff:** 208. **Subjects:** General Collection. **Special
Collections:** John Oxley Library (600,000 photographs; early Queensland
newspapers; private manuscripts; early Australian printed material); rare
books collection; James Hardie Library of Australian Fine Arts; Cable
Collection of Hymnology and Folk Music; Eber Bunker Maritime
Collection. **Holdings:** 398,400 monographs; 36,500 music scores; 16,300 AV
items. **Subscriptions:** 10,300 journals and other serials; 158 newspapers.
Services: Interlibrary loan; library open to the public. **Computerized
Information Services:** QNIS, PRESSCOM, AAPDATA, AUSINET,
AUSTRALIS, OZLINE, KIWINET, DIALOG Information Services,
ORBIT Search Service, BRS Information Technologies, Reuter
TEXTLINE; KEYLINK; ILANET (electronic mail services).
Publications: Annual Report; Directory of State and Public Library Services
in Queensland; Public Libraries in Queensland: Statistical Bulletin;
Queensland Government Publications. **Remarks:** Maintained by the Library
Board of Queensland. **Remarks:** FAX: 7 846 2421. Electronic mail
address(es): 6009:MLN400000 (ILANET).

State Library of South Africa
See: **South Africa - State Library** (15387)

★ 15693 ★
**State Library of South Australia - Children's Literature Research
Collection** (Hum)
N. Terrace
G.P.O. Box 419   Phone: 8 2238742
Adelaide, SA 5001, Australia   Juliana Bayfield, Libn. in Charge
Founded: 1959. **Staff:** 3.5. **Subjects:** Children's literature - Australian,
English, American, European. **Holdings:** 52,000 books; 1300 microfiche; 200
toys and games; ephemera. **Subscriptions:** 39 journals and other serials.
Services: Interlibrary loan (limited); copying; SDI; collection open to the
public. **Remarks:** FAX: 8 2233390. Telex: 82074.

★ 15694 ★
**State Library of South Australia - Mortlock Library of South
Australiana** (Area-Ethnic)
N. Terrace
G.P.O. Box 419   Phone: 8 223 8760
Adelaide, SA 5001, Australia   Elizabeth Ho, Mgr.
Staff: Prof 17.5; Other 13.5. **Subjects:** South Australia from pre-white
settlement (1836) to present; Northern Territory of Australia, to 1911.
Special Collections: J.D. Somerville Oral History Collection; Sir Donald
Bradman Collection of Cricketing Memorabilia; pictorial collection;
genealogy collection. **Holdings:** 39,000 monographs and pamphlets; 11,000
serial titles; 53,000 photographs; 3200 meters of archival records; 160 meters
of ephemera. **Services:** Copying; library open to the public. **Automated
Operations:** Computerized cataloging. **Computerized Information Services:**
Australian Bibliographic Network (ABN); internal database (Aboriginal
holdings, oral history collection, genealogy collection). **Special Indexes:**
Biographic and geographic subject indexes to archival and published
collections. **Remarks:** Library is a legal deposit and archival repository for
evidence of both past and contemporary South Australian life. FAX: 8 224
0771. **Staff:** Euan M. Miller, State Libn.

★ 15695 ★
State Library of South Australia - Special Collections (Hist)
N. Terrace
G.P.O. Box 419   Phone: 8 223 8718
Adelaide, SA 5001, Australia   Valmai Hankel, Fine Bks.Libn.
Staff: 2. **Subjects:** Shipping, wine, book production and history, Australian
ethnology, jazz music. **Holdings:** Paul McGuire Maritime Library (3600
volumes); A.D. Edwardes Collection (8000 photographs, mainly of sailing
ships); Arbon-Le Maistre Collection (60,000 photographs, mainly of non-
wind-powered ships); Thomas Hardy Wine Library (1500 volumes);
Mountford-Sheard Collection (life of Australian ethnologist C.P.
Mountford; 13,000 manuscripts, photographs, slides); John Purches
Collection (jazz; 20,000 78rpm phonograph records; 4000 wax cylinders);
Adelaide Circulating Library (popular literature, 1900-1975; 40,000
volumes); private press collections; modern fine book production collections;
H.A. Godson Collection (13,000 photographs of the history and ships of the
River Murray); Cellarmaster Collection of Rare Wine Books (900 volumes);
J.C. Carbutt Collection on Lighthouses (2000 slides and photographs of
world lighthouses, emphasis on Australia); John Morley Collection of
Children's Art (100,000 drawings by Australian children). **Services:**
Copying; collections open to the public. **Computerized Information
Services:** Internal database. **Remarks:** FAX: 8 2233390. Telex: 82072.

★ 15696 ★
State Library of Tasmania (Area-Ethnic, Info Sci)
91 Murray St.   Phone: 02 307011
Hobart, TAS 7000, Australia   Ms. Robyn Collins, Dir., Lib.Serv.
Founded: 1944. **Staff:** 371.6. **Subjects:** Tasmania, maritime history,
Antarctica. **Special Collections:** Tasmaniana Library (111,000 items); W.L.
Crowther Library (20,000 items, including books, manuscripts,
photographs, works of art, objects, furniture); Allport Library and Museum
of Fine Arts (rare books, manuscripts, works of art, photographs, objets
d'art, furniture). **Holdings:** 1.2 million books; 64,000 bound periodical
volumes; 11,000 AV programs; 50,000 microforms; 60,000 musical
recordings; 11,000 maps. **Subscriptions:** 7192 journals and other serials; 94
newspapers. **Services:** Interlibrary loan; copying; SDI; library open to the
public. **Computerized Information Services:** Australian Bibliographic
Network (ABN), AUSINET, AUSTLIT, OZLINE, AUSTRALIS, BRS
Information Technologies, DIALOG Information Services, ESA/IRS,
KIWINET, MEDLINE, ORBIT, Presscom, WILSONLINE. Performs
searches free of charge (fee for printout only); ILANET (electronic mail
service). **Special Indexes:** Tasmanian Index (newspaper and periodical
items; card); Tasmanian Index of Community Organisations (TICO; online).
Remarks: FAX: 02 310927. Telex: 58222. Electronic mail address(es):
MLN700000 (ILANET). **Staff:** Tony Marshall, Asst.Mgr., Tasmaniana
Serv.; Geoffrey Stilwell, Cur. Allport Lib. and Musm. of Fine Arts.

★ 15697 ★
State Library of Victoria (Hum, Info Sci)
304-328 Swanston St.   Phone: 3 6699888
Melbourne, VIC 3000, Australia   Leah Mann, Dir.
Founded: 1856. **Staff:** 235. **Subjects:** General collection. **Special Collections:** La Trobe Collection of Australiana and Victoriana; Art, Music, and the Performing Arts Library; M.V. Anderson Chess Collection; W.G. Alma Conjuring Collection; Children's Historical Research Collection; genealogy collection. **Holdings:** 1.3 million volumes; 10,000 sound recordings; 382,000 pictures; 1800 linear meters of manuscripts; rare books; maps; newspapers. **Subscriptions:** 14,000 journals and other serials; 450 newspapers. **Services:** Interlibrary loan; copying; business information service; library open to the public. **Computerized Information Services:** Australian Bibliographic Network (ABN), AUSTRALIS, BRS Information Technologies, COOL-CAT, Data-Star, DIALOG Information Services, Reuters Information Services (Canada), MEDLINE, PFDS Online, WILSONLINE. Performs searches free of charge. **Publications:** Victorian Government Publications, 1976 to present; monographs, irregular. **Remarks:** FAX: 3 6631480. **Staff:** Douglas Down, Dir., Info.Serv.; Derek Whitehead, Dir., Coll.Mgt.; David Bugeja, Dir., Corp.Serv.

★ 15698 ★
State Museum Kassel - Library (Art)
Schloss Wilhelmshohe
W-3500 Kassel, Germany   Phone: 561 36011
                                        A. Naumer
Founded: 1931. **Staff:** Prof 2. **Subjects:** Art, classical antiquities, crafts, decorative arts, technology, archeology, folk art. **Holdings:** 78,350 books; 1160 microfiche. **Subscriptions:** 570 journals and other serials. **Services:** Copying; library open to the public. **Remarks:** FAX: 561 315873. **Also Known As:** Staatliche Museen Kassel - Kunstbibliothek.

★ 15699 ★
State Mutual Companies - Resource Center (Bus-Fin)
440 Lincoln St., G9   Phone: (508)855-2435
Worcester, MA 01605   Timothy D. Rivard, Corp.Libn.
Founded: 1957. **Staff:** 2. **Subjects:** Insurance, actuarial science, business, law. **Holdings:** 1000 books; 650 bound periodical volumes; 35 VF drawers of pamphlets and reports. **Subscriptions:** 750 journals and other serials. **Services:** Interlibrary loan; copying; library open to the public by request. **Automated Operations:** Computerized public access catalog. **Computerized Information Services:** LEXIS, NEXIS, DIALOG Information Services, FYI News, Data-Star, UMI ProQuest; CD-ROM (Business Periodicals Ondisc); EasyLink (electronic mail service). **Networks/Consortia:** Member of Worcester Area Cooperating Libraries (WACL), Central Massachusetts Consortium of Health Related Libraries (CMCHRL). **Remarks:** FAX: (508)853-6332.

★ 15700 ★
State Street Consultants, Inc. - Information Center (Bus-Fin)
31 Milk St.   Phone: (617)482-1234
Boston, MA 02109   Marcia Karr, Info.Mgr.
Staff: Prof 1. **Subjects:** Management, marketing, financial marketing, industry collections. **Special Collections:** Graphic Arts Industry. **Holdings:** 1600 books; 63 VF drawers; 100 unbound reports; 150 cases of periodicals. **Subscriptions:** 95 journals and other serials. **Services:** SDI; center open to the public with restrictions. **Remarks:** FAX: (617)482-2060.

★ 15701 ★
State Technical Institute at Memphis - George E. Freeman Library (Sci-Engr)
5983 Macon Cove   Phone: (901)377-4106
Memphis, TN 38134   Rosa S. Burnett, Dir.
Founded: 1968. **Staff:** Prof 3; Other 4. **Subjects:** Engineering - electrical, electronics, instrumentation, civil, architectural, mechanical, environmental, biomedical; chemical technology; computer technologies; business technologies. **Holdings:** 41,364 books; 5590 bound periodical volumes; 36 VF drawers; 31,506 microforms. **Subscriptions:** 361 journals and other serials; 63 newspapers. **Services:** Interlibrary loan; copying; library open to the public. **Automated Operations:** Computerized indexing. **Computerized Information Services:** NewsBank Electronic Index; CD-ROM (COMPACT DISCLOSURE COMPUTER DATABASE Plus, MAGAZINE INDEX Plus). **Publications:** Library Handbook. **Remarks:** FAX: (901)373-2503. **Staff:** Bettie W. Boyd, Assoc.Libn.; Virginia Ann Howard, Assoc.Libn.

★ 15702 ★
State University College at Brockport - Drake Memorial Library (Educ)
Brockport, NY 14420   Phone: (716)395-2141
                                        Ms. Raj Madan, Dir. of Lib.Serv.
Founded: 1860. **Staff:** Prof 15; Other 20. **Subjects:** Nursing, physical and general education, U.S. history, criminal justice. **Special Collections:** Early American Imprints, 1639-1800 (Readex); Early English Books, 1475-1700 (Readex). **Holdings:** 405,021 books; 94,000 bound periodical volumes; 22,643 reels of microfilm; 841,123 microfiche; 973,235 microcards. **Subscriptions:** 2000 journals and other serials; 20 newspapers. **Services:** Interlibrary loan; copying; library open to the public. **Automated Operations:** Computerized public access catalog, cataloging, acquisitions, circulation, and reserve. **Computerized Information Services:** OCLC, DIALOG Information Services, BRS Information Technologies; BITNET (electronic mail service). Performs searches on fee basis. Contact Person: Dr. Peter Olevnik, Hd., Info.Serv., 397-2770. **Networks/Consortia:** Member of Rochester Regional Library Council (RRLC). **Publications:** Drake Library Review. **Special Indexes:** Indexes to New York State Museum Bulletins (numerical, author, subject); Index to U.S. Government Serials, 1953-1970. **Remarks:** FAX: (716)395-5651. **Staff:** Steven F. Buckley, Assoc.Dir.; Debra Ames, Asst.Hd.Cat.; Betty Chan, Asst.Hd.Info.Serv.; Robert Gilliam, ILL Libn.; Charles Cowling, Asst.Hd., Ser.; Judith Jennejahn, Hd.Acq.Libn.; Lori Lampert, Hd., Spec. Materials; Carolyn McBride, Hd., Ser.; Stuart Milligan, Hd., Circ.; Joyce Ogden, Sr.Cat.; Nan Pollot, Ref.Libn.; Margaret Rich, Ref.Libn.; Gregory Toth, Ref.Libn.

★ 15703 ★
State University College at Buffalo - Burchfield Art Center - Research Library (Art)
Rockwell Hall
1300 Elmwood Ave.   Phone: (716)878-6011
Buffalo, NY 14222   Nancy M. Weakly, Cur./Archv.
Founded: 1966. **Staff:** Prof 2; Other 5. **Subjects:** American art, art education. **Special Collections:** Archival Collections - Charles E. Burchfield, Frank K.M. Rehn Galleries, George William Eggers, Charles Cary Rumsey, Philip C. Elliott, Martha Visser't Hooft, Harold Olmsted, J.J. Lankes, Western New York State Artists, Buffalo Society of Artists, Patteran Society. **Holdings:** 2500 books; 1 drawer of microfiche; 10,000 exhibition catalogs, slides, photographs, negatives, artist files, clippings, letters, manuscripts, original materials, films, videotapes, AV programs. **Services:** Copying; library open to the public by appointment. **Computerized Information Services:** Internal databases. **Remarks:** FAX: (716)878-6003. **Staff:** Michelle Weakly, Reg./Asst.Archv.

★ 15704 ★
State University College at Buffalo - Edward H. Butler Library (Hum)
1300 Elmwood Ave.   Phone: (716)878-6314
Buffalo, NY 14222   Dr. George C. Newman, Dir.
Founded: 1871. **Staff:** Prof 22; Other 28.5. **Subjects:** Education, sciences and humanities, fine and applied arts. **Special Collections:** Curriculum Laboratory Collection (26,000 volumes); Hertha Ganey Historical Children's Book Collection (310 volumes); Root-Kempke Historical Textbook Collection (676 volumes); Lois Lenski Collection (241 autographed first edition titles; 310 original illustrations, notes, research, and dummies); Creative Studies Library (3700 volumes; 2000 dissertations on microfilm); Independent Learning Center (14,000 AV programs, nonprint items, educational games); Francis E. Fronczak Collection (18 linear feet); college archives and special collections (6863 linear feet); Paul G. Reilly Seneca Indian Land Claims Collection (27 linear feet). **Holdings:** 443,162 books; 98,148 bound periodical volumes; 21,888 reels of microfilm; 662,855 microtexts; 491 maps. **Subscriptions:** 3889 journals and other serials; 42 newspapers. **Services:** Interlibrary loan; copying; library open to the public for reference use only. **Automated Operations:** Computerized public access catalog (INNOPAC), cataloging, circulation, acquisitions, and serials (INNOVACQ). **Computerized Information Services:** DIALOG Information Services, WILSONLINE, OCLC; CD-ROMs; BITNET (electronic mail service). Contact Person: Susan Stievater, Coord., Search Serv. **Networks/Consortia:** Member of SUNY/OCLC Library Network, Western New York Library Resources Council (WNYLRC). **Publications:** Lois Lenski Children's Collection (booklet); Francis E. Fronczak Collection Inventory (booklet). **Remarks:** FAX: (716)878-3134. Electronic mail address(es): GLOGOWMF@SNYBUFVA (BITNET). **Staff:** Maryruth Glogowski, Assoc.Dir.; Mary Karen Delmont, Coll.Dev.Off.; Paul Zadner, Hd., Circ./Per.; Shirley Posner, Hd., Acq.; Ellie Munn, Hd., Cat.; Sr. Martin Joseph Jones, Hd., Archv./Spec.Coll.; Gail Ellmann, Lrng.Sys.; Marjorie Lord, ILL; Amy Rockwell, Microforms; Carol Richard, Hd., Info.Serv.; Levirn Hill, Hd., Curric. Lab.

★ 15705 ★
State University College at Cortland - Memorial Library (Educ)
Prospect Terr.
Box 2000   Phone: (607)753-2221
Cortland, NY 13045   Selby U. Gration, Dir. of Libs.
Founded: 1869. **Staff:** Prof 12; Other 19. **Subjects:** Education, recreation, physical education, health education. **Special Collections:** Teaching Materials Center (32,324 books; 8482 AV and other materials including 17,249 pictures); Cortland College Archives (8100 items); rare book collection (800). **Holdings:** 380,066 books; 48,139 bound periodical volumes; 595,583 microforms; 9022 AV programs; 271 VF drawers; 10 files of pamphlets; 8402 government documents. **Subscriptions:** 1375 journals and other serials; 8 newspapers. **Services:** Interlibrary loan; copying; SDI; library open to the public with restrictions. **Automated Operations:** Computerized cataloging, serials, acquisitions, and ILL. **Computerized Information Services:** DIALOG Information Services, OCLC; CD-ROMs; BITNET (electronic mail service). Performs searches. Contact Person: Lauren Stiles, Hd., Ref., 753-4009. **Networks/Consortia:** Member of SUNY/OCLC Library Network, South Central Research Library Council (SCRLC). **Publications:** Facets; subject bibliographies; Setting the Book Straight on the Library; occasional publications - campus distribution. **Special Indexes:** Serials and periodicals list; lists of abstracts/indexes by subject. **Remarks:** Alternate telephone number(s): 753-2525. FAX: (607)753-5669. **Staff:** Mary Beilby, Coll.Dev.Libn.; James Chapman, Electronic Media Ctr.Supv.; Gretchen Herrmann, Soc.Sci.Ref.-Bibliog.; Michael Tillman, Tchg.Mtls.Ctr.Libn.; Ellen Paterson, Sci.Ref.-Bibliog.; Johanna Bowen, Ser./Per.Libn.; Terrence McGovern, Monographs Cat.Libn.; Mary M. McGinnis, Adm.Serv.Libn.; David Ritchie, Cat.Libn.; Lauren Stiles, Hum.Ref.-Bibliog.; David Kreh, Educ.Ref.-Bibliog.; Thomas Bonn, Pol.Sci./Phys.Educ.Ref.-Bibliog.; Janet Selby, Coll.Dev.Asst.

★ 15706 ★
State University College at Fredonia - Music Collection (Mus)
Daniel A. Reed Library   Phone: (716)673-3184
Fredonia, NY 14063   Sarah Dorsey, Mus.Libn.
Founded: 1940. **Staff:** Prof 1. **Subjects:** Music - education, performance and study, history, biography, criticism; monumenta. **Special Collections:** Fox Dance music collection. **Holdings:** 37,813 scores; 15,000 music recordings; 2080 music titles in microform; 15,000 music books; 1482 cassettes; 2000 dance band arrangements; 2000 pieces of popular sheet music, 1900-1950; 160 videocassettes; 80 kits and filmstrips. **Subscriptions:** 115 journals and other serials. **Services:** Interlibrary loan; copying; library open to the public. **Automated Operations:** Computerized public access catalog (PALS) and cataloging. **Computerized Information Services:** OCLC, DIALOG Information Services; BITNET (electronic mail service). **Networks/Consortia:** Member of SUNY/OCLC Library Network, Western New York Library Resources Council (WNYLRC). **Remarks:** FAX: (716)673-3185. Electronic mail address(es): DORSEY@FREDONIA (BITNET). **Staff:** Susan P. Besemer, Dir., Lib.Serv.

★ 15707 ★
State University College at Geneseo - College Libraries (Educ)
Milne Library & Fraser Library   Phone: (716)245-5591
Geneseo, NY 14454   Richard C. Quick, Dir. of Libs.
Founded: 1871. **Staff:** Prof 15; Other 16. **Subjects:** English and American literature, natural and physical sciences, music, computer science, education and special education, business management and accounting. **Special Collections:** Aldous Huxley (600 items); Genesee Valley Historical Collection (7500 items); Carl F. Schmidt Collection in American Architecture (5050 items); Wadsworth Family Papers, 1790-1952 (50,000 items); College Archives. **Holdings:** 421,000 books; 58,214 bound periodical volumes; 725,000 microforms, including 331,000 ERIC microfiche; 274,000 U.S. Government documents. **Subscriptions:** 3158 journals and other serials; 21 newspapers. **Services:** Interlibrary loan; copying; library open to the public with restrictions. **Automated Operations:** Computerized cataloging, acquisitions, and serials. **Computerized Information Services:** BRS Information Technologies. **Networks/Consortia:** Member of SUNY/OCLC Library Network, Rochester Regional Library Council (RRLC). **Publications:** Serials Holdings List (computer printout). **Remarks:** Figures reflect the holdings of Milne Library and Fraser Library. FAX: (716)245-5003. **Staff:** Janet A. Neese, Assoc. for Admin.; Paula M. Henry, Acq.Libn.; Adelaide L. LaVerdi, Hd.Cat.; Barbara Clarke, Libn., CRC; Paul MacLean, Govt.Docs.Libn.; Diane Johnson, Ser.Libn.; Casey Bickle, Circ.Mgr.; Harriet Sleggs, ILL Mgr.; Martha Reynolds, Mng.Libn., Fraser Lib.; Judith A. Bushnell, Hd.Ref.Libn.

★ 15708 ★
State University College at New Paltz - Sojourner Truth Library - Special Collections (Area-Ethnic, Hist)
New Paltz, NY 12561   Phone: (914)257-3676
                   William E. Connors, Dean
Founded: 1833. **Staff:** 42. **Subjects:** Sojourner Truth. **Holdings:** Africa and Asia collections; New Paltz collection; college archives; U.S. Government documents (selective); New York State documents (1989); Early American Imprints (Readex); Early English Books (Readex microprint). **Subscriptions:** 1712 journals and other serials. **Services:** Interlibrary loan; copying; collections open to the public. **Automated Operations:** Computerized public access catalog, cataloging, serials, circulation, and ILL. **Computerized Information Services:** DIALOG Information Services, BRS/After Dark; CD-ROMs; BITNET (electronic mail service). Performs searches on fee basis. Contact Person: Gerlinde Barley, 257-3702. **Networks/Consortia:** Member of SUNY/OCLC Library Network, Southeastern New York Library Resources Council (SENYLRC). **Publications:** Finding aid for archives. **Remarks:** FAX: (914)257-3670. Electronic mail address(es): CONNORSWA@SNYNEWVM. (BITNET). **Staff:** Chui-Chun Lee, Assoc.Dir.; Jean Sauer, Coord. of Tech.Serv.

★ 15709 ★
State University College at Oneonta - Biological Field Station - Library (Biol Sci)
Box 1066, RD. 2   Phone: (607)547-8778
Cooperstown, NY 13326   Prof. Willard N. Harman
Founded: 1970. **Subjects:** Ecology, limnology, field biology. **Special Collections:** Reprint collections of freshwater mollusks (1000); Chironomid Flies (1500). **Holdings:** 1000 books. **Publications:** Biological Field Station Annual Report. **Remarks:** FAX: (607)547-8926. Holdings are part of the State University College at Oneonta - James L. Milne Library.

★ 15710 ★
State University College at Oneonta - James M. Milne Library - Special Collections (Hist)
Oneonta, NY 13820   Phone: (607)431-3702
                 Diane A. Clark, Spec.Coll.Libn.
Founded: 1889. **Staff:** Prof 1; Other 1. **Special Collections:** New York State Historical Collection; 19th and Early 20th Century Popular Fiction; New York State Verse Collection; Early Textbooks and Early Educational Theory. **Holdings:** 7061 volumes; 300 masters' theses; 533 linear feet of archival material; 30 tapes. **Services:** Interlibrary loan; collections open to the public with restrictions. **Automated Operations:** Computerized cataloging, serials, and ILL. **Computerized Information Services:** OCLC, DIALOG Information Services, BRS Information Technologies, WILSONLINE. Performs searches on fee basis. Contact Person: Andrea Gerberg, 431-2726. **Networks/Consortia:** Member of South Central Research Library Council (SCRLC). **Publications:** Grist. **Remarks:** FAX: (607)431-3081.

★ 15711 ★
State University College at Oswego - Penfield Library - Special Collections (Hist)
Oswego, NY 13126   Phone: (315)341-3194
                 Michael McLane, Dir.
Founded: 1973. **Special Collections:** College archives; Oswego County history; rare books; President Millard Fillmore papers. **Holdings:** 7928 books; 630 linear feet of other cataloged items; 615 reels of microfilm; 15 microfiche; 519 audio cassettes; 7186 vertical files. **Services:** Interlibrary loan; copying; library open to the public on a limited schedule. **Automated Operations:** Computerized public access catalog (Tomus). **Computerized Information Services:** OCLC. **Networks/Consortia:** Member of North Country Reference and Research Resources Council (NCRRRC). **Remarks:** Alternate telephone number(s): 341-3110. FAX: (315)341-3194. **Staff:** Judith Wellman, Co-Coord.; Nancy Osborne, Co-Coord.

★ 15712 ★
State University College at Plattsburgh - Benjamin F. Feinberg Library - Special Collections (Hist)
Plattsburgh, NY 12901   Phone: (518)564-5206
              Joseph G. Swinyer, Spec.Coll.Libn.
Founded: 1961. **Staff:** Prof 1; Other 2. **Subjects:** History of Upstate New York and northwestern Vermont; adjacent area of Quebec; folklore of Adirondacks and Champlain Valley; recent environmental, industrial, and demographic studies of the region; Rockwell Kent; university archives.

Special Collections: History of Northern New York (4950 monographs; 17,000 ephemera and manuscripts); Marjorie Lansing Porter Folklore Collection (original discs and tapes); Kent-Delord papers; William Bailey papers; Truesdell Print Collection; Signor/Langlois Collection of architectural drawings and maps; Rockwell Kent Collection (1500 items); Feinberg Collection; 1980 Lake Placid Olympics; McLellan Collection of Northern Clinton County. **Holdings:** 4950 volumes; 65,000 manuscripts; 4000 maps and atlases; 6700 photographs; 1900 reels of microfilm; 400 recordings; 3600 pamphlets; 14,400 clippings. **Subscriptions:** 36 journals and other serials. **Services:** Interlibrary loan; copying; collections open to the public. **Computerized Information Services:** DIALOG Information Services, OCLC, RLIN; BITNET (electronic mail service). **Networks/Consortia:** Member of North Country Reference and Research Resources Council (NCRRRC). **Special Catalogs:** Manuscripts for Research: Report of the Director, 1961-1974; manuscript holdings through 1988 (online). **Remarks:** FAX: (518)564-5209. Electronic mail address(es): SWINYEJG@SNYPLAVA (BITNET).

★ 15713 ★
State University College at Potsdam - Crane Music Library (Mus)
Potsdam, NY 13676   Phone: (315)267-2451
                                         David Ossenkop, Act.Mus.Libn.
Staff: Prof 1; Other 1. **Subjects:** Music - education, performance, study, history, biography, criticism, monuments. **Special Collections:** Julia E. Crane School of Music Archives; Helen M. Hosmer Papers. **Holdings:** 13,100 books; 3800 bound periodical volumes; 23,500 scores; 16,200 sound recordings. **Subscriptions:** 130 journals and other serials. **Services:** Interlibrary loan; library open to the public. **Networks/Consortia:** Member of Associated Colleges of the St. Lawrence Valley, Inc. (ACSLV), North Country Reference and Research Resources Council (NCRRRC).

★ 15714 ★
State University College at Potsdam - Frederick W. Crumb Memorial Library (Hum)
Pierrepont Ave.   Phone: (315)267-2482
Potsdam, NY 13676   Germaine C. Linkins, Dir. of Libs.
Founded: 1880. **Staff:** Prof 14; Other 12. **Subjects:** Education and curriculum materials, art, 19th and 20th century German history, urban sociology, northern New York State history, Anglo-Irish literature. **Special Collections:** Bertrand A. Snell Collection (public and private papers); college archives. **Holdings:** 281,187 books; 63,386 bound periodical volumes; 15,494 phonograph records; 557,927 microforms; 258 linear feet of archives; 5084 maps and charts. **Subscriptions:** 1737 journals and other serials; 18 newspapers. **Services:** Interlibrary loan; copying; library open to the public. **Automated Operations:** Computerized cataloging, acquisitions, serials, and ILL. **Computerized Information Services:** BRS Information Technologies, DIALOG Information Services, OCLC; CD-ROMs. Performs searches on fee basis. Contact Person: David Trithart, Ref., 267-2486. **Networks/Consortia:** Member of Associated Colleges of the St. Lawrence Valley, Inc. (ACSLV), North Country Reference and Research Resources Council (NCRRRC), SUNY/OCLC Library Network. **Publications:** Subject bibliographies and library guides; Connections (newsletter), 3/year. **Remarks:** FAX: (315)267-2744. **Staff:** Keith Compeau, Automation Libn.; Selma V. Foster, Cat.; Kay Brown, Ref.; Marion Blauvelt, Acq./Docs.; Jane Subramanian, Ser.; Nancy Alzo, Cat.; Margaret Weitzmann, Arch./Ref.; Susan Omohundro, Cat.; Holly Chambers, Ref.; Douglas Welch, Coll.Maint./ILL; Rebecca Thompson, Cat.; David Ossenkop, Mus.Libn.; David Trithart, Bibliog.Inst.

★ 15715 ★
State University College of Technology at Alfred - Walter C. Hinkle Memorial Library (Agri, Sci-Engr)
Alfred, NY 14802-1193   Phone: (607)587-4313
                                         Ellen Ehrig, Act.Dir.
Founded: 1911. **Staff:** Prof 6; Other 5. **Subjects:** Agriculture, business, health and engineering technologies. **Special Collections:** Western New York History. **Holdings:** 59,000 books; 7900 bound periodical volumes; 75,000 pamphlets; 5200 reels of microfilm; 29,000 microfiche; 1430 AV programs; 2600 corporation reports. **Subscriptions:** 1330 journals and other serials; 20 newspapers. **Services:** Interlibrary loan; copying; library open to the public. **Automated Operations:** Computerized cataloging and serials. **Computerized Information Services:** BRS Information Technologies, WILSONLINE, OCLC; BITNET (electronic mail service). Performs searches on fee basis. **Networks/Consortia:** Member of South Central Research Library Council (SCRLC). **Publications:** Salmagundi (newsletter), 1/semester; Alfred Tech Periodicals - both for local distribution only; Film

and Video Guide. **Special Indexes:** Index to Alfred Sun newspaper, 1883 to present. **Remarks:** FAX: (607)587-4351. Electronic mail address(es): @SNYALFVA (BITNET). **Staff:** Diana Hovorka, Asst.Ref.Libn.; Suzanne Wood, Tech.Serv.Libn.; Barbara Greil, Hd., Pub.Serv.; Kenneth Maracek, Ser./Ref.Libn.; David Haggstrom, Ref./AV Libn.

★ 15716 ★
State University College of Technology at Delhi - Library - Library (Agri, Sci-Engr)
Delhi, NY 13753   Phone: (607)746-4107
                                         Herbert J. Sorgen, Libn.
Founded: 1913. **Staff:** Prof 4; Other 4. **Subjects:** Veterinary science technology, engineering technologies, management, vocational education, nontraditional studies, liberal arts. **Holdings:** 48,903 books; 457 bound periodical volumes. **Subscriptions:** 335 journals and other serials. **Services:** Interlibrary loan; library open to the public. **Automated Operations:** Computerized public access catalog, cataloging, and circulation. **Computerized Information Services:** OCLC EPIC BRS Information Technologies. Performs searches on fee basis. **Networks/Consortia:** Member of SUNY/OCLC Library Network, South Central Research Library Council (SCRLC). **Publications:** Booklist, bimonthly; Pathfinders; Library Newsletter. **Remarks:** FAX: (607)746-4327. **Staff:** Donald Young, Assoc.Libn.; Pam Merriman, Asst.Libn.; Ronald Rosenblum, Sr.Asst.Libn.

★ 15717 ★
State University Health Science Center at Brooklyn - Department of Psychiatry Library (Med)
451 Clarkson Ave.
Brooklyn, NY 11203   Phone: (718)245-3131
Founded: 1947. **Staff:** Prof 1. **Subjects:** Psychiatry, psychoanalysis, child psychiatry, psychology. **Holdings:** 2038 books; 1150 bound periodical volumes; 5 VF drawers of pamphlets and reprints. **Subscriptions:** 50 journals and other serials. **Services:** Interlibrary loan; library not open to the public. **Formerly:** SUNY - Downstate Medical Center - Department of Psychiatry Library. **Also Known As:** Kings County Hospital - Psychiatry Library.

★ 15718 ★
State University Maritime College at Bronx - Stephen B. Luce Library (Sci-Engr, Trans)
Fort Schuyler   Phone: (212)409-7231
Bronx, NY 10465   Richard H. Corson, Libn.
Founded: 1946. **Staff:** Prof 5; Other 6. **Subjects:** Marine transportation, maritime history, marine engineering, naval architecture, merchant marine. **Holdings:** 100,000 books, bound periodical volumes, and government documents; 15,000 microfiche; 7500 reels of microfilm; 270 motion picture titles. **Subscriptions:** 400 journals; 250 serials; 7 newspapers. **Services:** Interlibrary loan; copying; library open to the public with identification. **Automated Operations:** Computerized cataloging, acquisitions, and ILL. **Computerized Information Services:** OCLC, DIALOG Information Services, VU/TEXT Information Services. **Networks/Consortia:** Member of SUNY/OCLC Library Network. **Publications:** Maritima, 2/year - to faculty and students; bibliographic series, irregular. **Remarks:** FAX: (212)409-7392. **Staff:** Filomena Magavero, Libn., Rd.Serv.; Alvina Kalsch, Assoc.Libn., Tech.Serv.; John Lee, Assoc.Libn.; Liza Leschinsky, Sr.Asst.Libn.

★ 15719 ★
State University of New York - Agricultural and Technical College at Farmingdale - Thomas D. Greenley Library (Agri, Sci-Engr)
Melville Rd.   Phone: (516)420-2040
Farmingdale, NY 11735   Michael G. Knauth, Hd.Libn.
Founded: 1912. **Staff:** Prof 14; Other 16. **Subjects:** Technology, engineering, business, horticulture, dental hygiene, nursing, liberal arts. **Holdings:** 125,000 books and bound periodical volumes; 22,000 pamphlets; 110,000 government documents; 11,500 reels of microfilm; 23,000 AV programs; 15,000 microfiche. **Subscriptions:** 1510 journals and other serials. **Services:** Interlibrary loan; copying (limited); library open to the public for reference use only. **Automated Operations:** Computerized cataloging, acquisitions, and serials. **Computerized Information Services:** OCLC, EPIC, DIALOG Information Services, WILSONLINE; CD-ROM (WILSONDISC, Newspaper Abstracts, Nursing & Allied Health). Performs searches on fee basis. Contact Person: Irene Keogh, Hd., Ref., 420-2184. **Networks/Consortia:** Member of Long Island Library Resources Council, SUNY/OCLC Library Network. **Publications:** Newsletter, irregular; bibliographic guides. **Staff:** Judi Bird, Hd., Acq.; Charlotte Schart, Hd., Ser.; Carol Greenholz, Hd., Tech.Serv./Cat.; Sue Schapiro, Govt.Docs.; George LoPresti, Hd., Circ./Sys.Libn.; Helene Cerky, Ref.; Elsa Leiber, Ser./Ref.; Bellinda Wise, Ref./AV.; Estelle Quartin, Ref./Cat.

★ 15720 ★
State University of New York - Agricultural and Technical College at Morrisville - Library (Agri, Sci-Engr)
Morrisville, NY 13408   Phone: (315)684-6055
         Colleen Stella, Dir.
Founded: 1910. **Staff:** Prof 4; Other 4. **Subjects:** Food service, agriculture, wood and automotive technology, natural resources conservation, nursing, horse husbandry, journalism. **Special Collections:** New York State Historical Collection. **Holdings:** 91,920 books; 5600 bound periodical volumes; 10,000 microforms; 450 audiocassettes; 800 videocassettes. **Subscriptions:** 563 journals and other serials; 23 newspapers. **Services:** Interlibrary loan; copying; library open to the public. **Automated Operations:** Computerized cataloging and ILL. **Computerized Information Services:** OCLC. **Networks/Consortia:** Member of Central New York Library Resources Council (CENTRO). **Publications:** Periodicals Received Currently; Library Guide; Ex Libris (newsletter). **Remarks:** FAX: (315)684-6115. **Staff:** Wilfred E. Drew, Ser.Libn.; Michael Gieryic, Ref.; Marian Hildebrand, Hd., Circ. & Bibliog.Instr.; Phyllis Petersen, Hd. of Tech.Serv.

State University of New York - Central Administration Research Library
See: State University of New York at Albany - Plaza Library (15728)

★ 15721 ★
State University of New York - College of Agriculture and Technology at Cobleskill - Jared Van Wagenen, Jr. Learning Resource Center (Agri)
Cobleskill, NY 12043   Phone: (518)234-5841
         Eleanor M. Carter, Dean
Founded: 1920. **Staff:** Prof 5; Other 5. **Subjects:** Agriculture, business, education of young children, food service, applied biology, reference. **Special Collections:** Schoharie County history. **Holdings:** 85,955 books; 6541 bound periodical volumes; 5326 juvenile books; 64 VF drawers of pamphlets and documents; 5771 reels of microfilm; 20,192 AV programs. **Subscriptions:** 900 journals and other serials; 16 newspapers. **Services:** Interlibrary loan; copying; media production; instructional design; center open to the public. **Automated Operations:** Computerized cataloging, acquisitions, circulation, and ILL. **Computerized Information Services:** ABI/INFORM, InfoTrac, AGRICOLA, Biological & Agricultural Index; CD-ROM (Wildlife & Fish Worldwide). **Networks/Consortia:** Member of Capital District Library Council for Reference & Research Resources (CDLC), SUNY/OCLC Library Network. **Special Indexes:** Index to Times Journal (local newspaper; book format); slide-tape programs on library use. **Staff:** Patricia Hults, Hd., Pub.Serv.; Esther Atchinson, Supv.Ck. **Staff:** Nancy VanDeusen, Hd., Tech.Serv.; Nancy Niles, Bibliog.Instr.; Gerald B. Kirsch, ILL Libn.; Caren Agata , Ser. & Cat.Libn.

★ 15722 ★
State University of New York - College of Environmental Science & Forestry - F. Franklin Moon Library and Learning Resources Center (Env-Cons, Sci-Engr, Biol Sci)
Syracuse, NY 13210   Phone: (315)470-6716
         Donald F. Webster, Dir.
Founded: 1919. **Staff:** Prof 7; Other 5. **Subjects:** Environmental studies, landscape architecture, forests and forestry, environment, botany, zoology, polymer and cellulose chemistry, paper science, wildlife management, entomology, wood products engineering, soil science, plant pathology, economics, biochemistry, management, water resources, chemical ecology, forest chemistry, environmental design, photography. **Holdings:** 37,225 books; 34,216 bound periodical volumes; 4806 bound theses; 122,305 microforms. **Subscriptions:** 4341 journals and other serials. **Services:** Interlibrary loan; copying; library open to the public for reference use only. **Automated Operations:** Computerized cataloging (NOTIS). **Computerized Information Services:** BRS Information Technologies, OCLC; CD-ROM (AGRICOLA, Enviro/Energyline Abstracts Plus); BITNET (electronic mail service). **Publications:** User guides; newsletter. **Remarks:** FAX: (315)470-6512. Electronic mail address(es): WEBSTER@SUVM. **Staff:** Elizabeth A. Elkins, Coord., Pub.Serv; Salvacion S. De La Paz, Coord., Bibliog.Oper.; Dianne Juchimek, Coord., Coll.Dev.; Jam es L. Williamson, ILL; Constance Bobbie, Cat.; Charles M. Spuches, Coord. of Instr.Serv.

★ 15723 ★
State University of New York - College of Environmental Science & Forestry - Huntington Wildlife Forest Library (Env-Cons)
Newcomb, NY 12852   Phone: (518)582-4551
         Charlotte Demers, Dir. of Libs.
Staff: 1. **Subjects:** Wildlife, wildlife management and research, forestry, ecology. **Special Collections:** Collection of birds, mammals, insects, and plants indigenous to the area; local history (notes; photographs; maps). **Holdings:** 680 books; 290 bound periodical volumes; 200 other cataloged items. **Subscriptions:** 25 journals and other serials. **Services:** Copying; library open to the public with restrictions.

★ 15724 ★
State University of New York - College of Optometry - Harold Kohn Memorial Visual Science Library (Med, Sci-Engr)
100 E. 24th St.   Phone: (212)420-5086
New York, NY 10010-3677   Claudia Perry, Libn.
Founded: 1956. **Staff:** Prof 2; Other 2.5. **Subjects:** Physiological optics, perception, developmental psychology, theory of optometry, public health, learning disabilities, ocular pathology, orthoptics. **Holdings:** 23,500 books; 7700 bound periodical volumes; 2000 tapes; 90 phonograph records; 30,000 slides; 400 reels of microfilm; 7000 pamphlets; 1200 indexed reprints on optics. **Subscriptions:** 500 journals and other serials. **Services:** Interlibrary loan; copying; library open to the public for reference use only. **Automated Operations:** Computerized public access catalog. **Computerized Information Services:** MEDLARS, OCLC, DIALOG Information Services, BRS Information Technologies; CD-ROM (MEDLINE); BITNET (electronic mail service). **Networks/Consortia:** Member of New York Metropolitan Reference and Research Library Agency. **Special Indexes:** Visual science articles, 1900-1947 (card). **Remarks:** FAX: (212)420-5094. Electronic mail address(es): OPTOM@SNYBKSAC Attn: PERRY (BITNET). **Staff:** Katherine Diaz, Asst.Libn.; Irene Vito, ILL.

★ 15725 ★
State University of New York - Syracuse Educational Opportunity Center - Paul Robeson Library (Area-Ethnic)
100 New St.   Phone: (315)472-0130
Syracuse, NY 13202   Florence Beer, Dir.
Founded: 1969. **Staff:** Prof 2. **Subjects:** Afro-Americans, job preparation, women, African fiction, business skills, minorities. **Special Collections:** Frazier Library of Afro-American Books (500 volumes); National Archives Collection of Afro-American Artists (23 trays of slides). **Holdings:** 11,000 books and bound periodical volumes; 40 VF drawers. **Subscriptions:** 139 journals and other serials; 20 newspapers. **Services:** Interlibrary loan; copying; library open to the public. **Networks/Consortia:** Member of Central New York Library Resources Council (CENTRO). **Publications:** Periodical Holdings, annual - for internal distribution only; New Acquisitions Listings, semiannual. **Special Catalogs:** Catalog to audiovisual collection. **Remarks:** FAX: (315)472-1241. **Staff:** Grace Lai, Libn.

★ 15726 ★
State University of New York at Albany - Film & Television Documentation Center (Aud-Vis)
Richardson 390-C
1400 Washington Ave.
Albany, NY 12222   Phone: (518)442-5745
Founded: 1973. **Staff:** Prof 3. **Subjects:** Film and television. **Special Collections:** Film and television journals from 28 countries, 1973 to present (250 titles). **Holdings:** 2000 unbound periodical volumes. **Subscriptions:** 220 journals and other serials. **Services:** Interlibrary loan; copying; center open to the public. **Special Indexes:** Film literature index, quarterly - available by subscription. **Remarks:** FAX: (518)442-5232 Attn: V.Aceto. Telex: 710 441 8257 Attn: FilmIndex. **Staff:** Vincent J. Aceto, Co-Dir.; Fred Silva, Co-Dir.; Linda Provinzano, Co-Ed.; Deborah Sternklar, Co-Ed.

★ 15727 ★
State University of New York at Albany - Governor Thomas E. Dewey Graduate Library for Public Affairs and Policy (Soc Sci, Law)
135 Western Ave.   Phone: (518)442-3690
Albany, NY 12222   Dennis C. Benamati, Hd.
Founded: 1981. **Staff:** Prof 6; Other 5. **Subjects:** Public policy, criminal justice, social welfare, library and information science, law. **Holdings:** 120,000 books; microfiche; periodicals. **Subscriptions:** 600 journals and other serials; 8 newspapers. **Services:** Interlibrary loan; library open to the public. **Automated Operations:** Computerized cataloging and circulation.

Computerized Information Services: BRS Information Technologies, DIALOG Information Services, VU/TEXT Information Services, WILSONLINE, WESTLAW, RLIN, OCLC; BITNET, RLIN, (electronic mail service). Networks/Consortia: Member of Capital District Library Council for Reference & Research Resources (CDLC), Criminal Justice Information Exchange Group. Remarks: FAX: (518)442-3474. Electronic mail address(es): DB851@ALBNYVMS (BITNET). Staff: Barbara Via, Ref./Bibliog.; Richard Irving, Bibliog.; H. Mendelsohn, Bibliog.; Mary Jane Brustman, Ref./Bibliog.; Janice Newkirk, Ref.; Otis Chadley, Ref.

★ 15728 ★
State University of New York at Albany - Plaza Library (Educ)
Central Administration
State University Plaza, Rm. N114
Albany, NY 12246   Phone: (518)443-5635
Founded: 1967. Staff: 1. Subjects: Education - higher, professional, international; management; finance; statistics. Special Collections: SUNY archival collection (300 items). Holdings: 25,000 books; 150 bound periodical volumes; 1500 VF items; 2000 government documents; 1000 microforms; 200 dissertations; 3000 ERIC research reports. Subscriptions: 120 journals and other serials. Services: Interlibrary loan; copying; SDI; library open to the public with restrictions. Computerized Information Services: OCLC, BRS Information Technologies, DIALOG Information Services, VU/TEXT Information Services; CD-ROMs. Networks/Consortia: Member of SUNY/OCLC Library Network, Capital District Library Council for Reference & Research Resources (CDLC). Publications: Tables of Contents of Significant Journals; Acquisitions List, both bimonthly; annotated lists of selected books; listing of new microforms. Remarks: FAX: (518)432-4346. Formerly: Its Central Administration Research Library. Staff: Glyn T. Evans; Penny Wilson; Carol Zabielski.

★ 15729 ★
State University of New York at Binghamton - Center for Medieval and Early Renaissance Studies
P.O. Box 6000
Binghamton, NY 13902
Defunct.

★ 15730 ★
State University of New York at Binghamton - Science Library (Biol Sci, Sci-Engr)
Science Building II   Phone: (607)777-2166
Binghamton, NY 13902-6012   Keith Roe, Hd., Sci.Lib.
Founded: 1973. Staff: Prof 4.5; Other 6.5. Subjects: Biological sciences, chemistry, geological sciences, physics, psychology, engineering, general science, technology, nursing and health sciences. Holdings: 110,000 books; 76,000 bound periodical volumes; microforms. Subscriptions: 1835 journals. Services: Interlibrary loan; copying; library open to the public to local citizens with courtesy card. Computerized Information Services: DIALOG Information Services, BRS Information Technologies; CD-ROMs; BITNET (electronic mail service). Networks/Consortia: Member of South Central Research Library Council (SCRLC), Research Libraries Information Network (RLIN). Remarks: FAX: (607)777-2274. Electronic mail address(es): KROE@BINGVMB (BITNET). Staff: Thomas King, Asst.Libn.; Charlotte Skuster, Asst.Libn.

★ 15731 ★
State University of New York at Binghamton - Special Collections (Rare Book, Hist)
Glenn G. Bartle Library   Phone: (607)777-4844
PO Box 6012, Vestal Pkwy., E   Jeanne Eichelberger, Hd.,
Binghamton, NY 13902-6012   Spec.Coll./Presrv.
Staff: Prof 1.5; Other 1. Subjects: History of books and printing; literary and historical collections. Special Collections: Padraic and Mary Colum papers (750 items); Max Reinhardt Library (theater); Max Reinhardt Archive (250,000 papers, letters, documents, and original prompt books); photograph and negative collection (14,000 items); scene design materials; Loften Mitchell Papers; Tillie Losch Papers; Charles Monroe Dickinson Family Papers (2000 items relating to journalist and diplomat C.M. Dickinson, 1842-1924); Edwin Link (1904-1981) papers; Broome County Medical Society Collection; Arthur Schnitzler Archives (microfilm); Frances R. Conole Archive of Sound Recordings (54,824 phonograph records with a concentration of vocal/operatic recordings); Mary Lavin papers (250 items); Associated Colleges of Upper New York Archives (5000 items); William Klenz Library & Music Collection (primarily baroque music

and art); William J. Haggerty Collection of French Colonial History (18,000 volumes, 135 periodical titles). Holdings: 20,500 volumes; 11,000 local and regional archives; 6000 publications, photographs, and reports in university archives; 507 linear feet of archives and manuscripts; 133 films; 138 videocassettes. Services: Interlibrary loan; copying; collections open to the public during limited hours and by appointment. Automated Operations: Computerized cataloging, acquisitions, and circulation. Computerized Information Services: Internal database; BITNET (electronic mail service). Networks/Consortia: Member of Research Libraries Information Network (RLIN). Publications: Lamont Montgomery Bowers Papers (pamphlet); Max Reinhardt Archives (pamphlet). Special Catalogs: Edwin Link Papers (pamphlet); Catalogue of the Colum Collection (pamphlet); Catalogue of the Lavin Collection (pamphlet); Catalog of Reinhardt Library (card); manuscript catalog (card); supplementary rare book catalogs (card); Haggery Collection (card). Remarks: FAX: (607)777-4848. Electronic mail address(es): JEICHELB@BINGVMB (BITNET). Staff: Phil Conole, Cur., Frances R. Conole Archv.

★ 15732 ★
State University of New York at Binghamton - University Libraries - Fine Arts Library (Art, Mus, Theater)
Binghamton, NY 13902-6012   Phone: (607)777-4927
Subjects: Art, art history, music, theater, cinema, dance. Holdings: 101,200 books; 1043 periodical titles; 7288 exhibition catalogs. Subscriptions: 351 journals and other serials. Services: Interlibrary loan; copying; listening facilities; library open to the public. Automated Operations: Computerized public access catalog and circulation. Networks/Consortia: Member of Research Libraries Information Network (RLIN), South Central Research Library Council (SCRLC). Special Indexes: Wilson Art Index (online); Humanities Index (online). Remarks: FAX: (607)777-4848. Electronic mail address(es): MHANSCOM@BINGVAXC (BITNET).

★ 15733 ★
State University of New York at Buffalo - Architecture & Planning Library (Plan)
Hayes Hall
Main Street Campus   Phone: (716)831-3505
Buffalo, NY 14214   Dr. Barbara Boehnke, Subj.Spec.
Founded: 1972. Staff: Prof 1; Other 1. Subjects: Architecture, design, planning. Special Collections: Rudy Bruner Award Submissions depository (microfiche). Holdings: 21,000 volumes; product catalogs; VF drawers of pamphlets, AV materials, architectural drawings, and maps. Subscriptions: 160 journals and other serials. Services: Interlibrary loan; copying; library open to the public. Automated Operations: Computerized public access catalog and circulation. Computerized Information Services: Bison (internal database); BITNET (electronic mail service). Networks/Consortia: Member of Research Libraries Information Network (RLIN). Remarks: FAX: (716)831-2297. Electronic mail address(es): uldboehn@ubvm (BITNET). Staff: Flora Dees.

★ 15734 ★
State University of New York at Buffalo - Charles B. Sears Law Library (Law)
O'Brian Hall, Amherst Campus   Phone: (716)636-2048
Buffalo, NY 14260   Ellen M. Gibson, Dir.
Founded: 1887. Staff: Prof 9; Other 11. Subjects: Law. Special Collections: John Lord O'Brian Papers; Morris L. Cohen Rare Book Collection; United Nations collection. Holdings: 385,397 volumes. Subscriptions: 6121 journals and other serials. Services: Interlibrary loan; library open to the public for reference use only. Automated Operations: Computerized cataloging, circulation, acquisitions, and serials (NOTIS); computerized ILL. Computerized Information Services: LEXIS, NEXIS, WESTLAW, LRS, OCLC, RLIN. Networks/Consortia: Member of Research Libraries Information Network (RLIN). Remarks: FAX: (716)636-3860. Staff: Marcia Zubrow, Hd.Ref.Libn.; Susan Dow, Docs.Libn.; Mary Miller, Hd., Tech.Serv.Libn.; Terry McCormack, AV Libn.; Karen Spencer, Ref.Libn.; Nina Cascio, Intl. Law Libn.; Ellen McGrath, Hd.Cat.Libn.; Carol Gloss, Cat.Libn.

★ 15735 ★
State University of New York at Buffalo - Curriculum Center (Educ)
Graduate School of Education
17 Baldy Hall   Phone: (716)636-2488
Amherst, NY 14260   Norma Shatz, Graduate Sch. of Educ.Libn.
Founded: 1954. Staff: Prof 1; Other 2. Subjects: Education and curriculum development. Special Collections: Reavis Reading Area (Phi Delta Kappa).

Holdings: 11,500 elementary and high school textbooks; 6000 retrospective and historical textbooks; 800 activity books; 700 curriculum guides; 350 educational tests; 200 curriculum-related materials; 5 VF drawers of teaching ideas; 20 VF drawers of resource files; 5 VF drawers of publishers' catalogs; 450 teaching units. **Subscriptions:** 60 newsletters. **Services:** Copying; center open to the public. **Publications:** In the Center, 2/year - free upon request. **Remarks:** FAX: (716)636-2479. **Staff:** Dr. Thomas Shuell, Dir.

★ 15736 ★
State University of New York at Buffalo - Department of Geology - Ice Core Laboratory - Library (Sci-Engr)
4240 Ridge Lea Campus, Rm. 9   Phone: (716)831-3054
Buffalo, NY 14260   Chester C. Langway, Jr., Jr., Proj.Dir.
Subjects: Glaciology, ice research. **Holdings:** 1000 volumes. **Subscriptions:** 17 journals and other serials. **Services:** Library not open to the public. **Remarks:** Laboratory is active in ice core studies and interacts on a national basis as well as with universities in Japan, Switzerland, Denmark, the USSR, France, West Germany, and Austria. FAX: (716)831-3055.

★ 15737 ★
State University of New York at Buffalo - Health Sciences Library (Med)
South Campus   Phone: (716)831-3337
Buffalo, NY 14214   Mr. C.K. Huang, Dir.
Founded: 1846. **Staff:** Prof 18; Other 25. **Subjects:** Medicine, nursing, dentistry, pharmacy, allied health sciences, basic sciences. **Special Collections:** History of Medicine Collection (12,000 volumes). **Holdings:** 132,478 books; 152,927 bound periodical volumes; 2119 AV programs; 3000 pamphlets. **Subscriptions:** 2680 journals and other serials. **Services:** Interlibrary loan; copying; SDI; library open to the public. **Automated Operations:** Computerized public access catalog, acquisitions, serials, and circulation (NOTIS). **Computerized Information Services:** MEDLINE, BRS Information Technologies, DIALOG Information Services, miniMEDLINE, Current Contents, PDQ (Physician Data Query). Performs searches on fee basis. **Networks/Consortia:** Member of Library Consortium of Health Institutions in Buffalo (LCHIB), National Network of Libraries of Medicine - Middle Atlantic Region, Western New York Library Resources Council (WNYLRC). **Publications:** Progress Report, annual - for exchange; HSL News, quarterly - to faculty. **Special Catalogs:** Pre-Nineteenth Century Catalog of the Robert L. Brown History of Medicine Collection. **Remarks:** FAX: (716)835-4891. **Staff:** Nancy Fabrizio, Assoc.Dir.; Remedios Silva, Hd.Cat.; Sharon Keller Hd., Info.Serv.; Sharon Murphy, Info.Serv.Libn.; Amy Lyons, Asst.Dir., Circ.; Cindy Bertuca, Hd., Info. Dissemination Serv.; Linda Lohr, Asst. to Dir.; Wilson Prout, Asst. to Dir.; Cindy Hepfer, Hd., Ser.; Bradley Chase, Tech.Asst.; Lilli Sentz, Hist. of Med.Libn.; Pam Rose, Acq.; Carol Lelonek, Comp.Prog.; Neville Prendergast, Asst.Libn., IDS; Lori Widzinski, Hd., Media Rsrcs.Ctr.

★ 15738 ★
State University of New York at Buffalo - Industry/University Center for Biosurfaces - Library (Med)
110 Parker Hall   Phone: (716)831-3560
Buffalo, NY 14214   Anne E. Meyer, Prog.Mgr.
Founded: 1987. **Subjects:** Biomaterials, biofouling, artificial organs. **Holdings:** 500 volumes. **Services:** Library not open to the public. **Remarks:** FAX: (716)835-4872.

★ 15739 ★
State University of New York at Buffalo - Lockwood Memorial Library - Polish Collection (Area-Ethnic)
Buffalo, NY 14260   Phone: (716)636-2817
     Jean Dickson, Cur., Polish Coll.
Founded: 1955. **Staff:** 1. **Subjects:** Poland - humanities, social sciences, language, literature; Polish-American history and culture, emphasizing Western New York. **Holdings:** 8500 books; 250 bound periodical volumes; 35 nonbook items; 30 manuscripts. **Subscriptions:** 42 journals and other serials; 5 newspapers. **Services:** Interlibrary loan; collection open to the public for reference use only. **Computerized Information Services:** Computerized public access catalog. **Networks/Consortia:** Member of Research Libraries Information Network (RLIN). **Publications:** Polish Room Acquisitions, monthly. **Remarks:** FAX: (716)636-3859.

★ 15740 ★
State University of New York at Buffalo - Music Library (Mus)
Baird Hall   Phone: (716)636-2935
Buffalo, NY 14260   James Coover, Dir.
Founded: 1970. **Staff:** Prof 4.1; Other 2. **Subjects:** Music - history, theory, performance; jazz history; music education. **Special Collections:** Archives of the Center of the Creative and Performing Arts (10 linear meters); History of Music Librarianship in the U.S. (9 linear meters); Arnold Cornelissen and Ferdinand Praeger Manuscript Collections (6 linear meters); Buffalo Musicians Collection (8 linear meters); British Concert Programs (60 linear meters); Works of Ferdinand Paer (8 linear meters); Solo songs (185 meters); Music Antiquarian Catalogues (13 meters). **Holdings:** 39,000 books; 14,500 bound periodical volumes; 58,000 scores and parts; 26,000 sound recordings; 5800 microforms; 2100 slides and photographs. **Subscriptions:** 1400 journals and other serials. **Services:** Interlibrary loan; copying; library open to the public. **Automated Operations:** Computerized cataloging and acquisitions. **Computerized Information Services:** RLIN; BITNET (electronic mail service). **Publications:** Current Acquisitions List, irregular; Newsletter, irregular. **Special Catalogs:** Evenings for New Music: A Catalogue, 1964-1977; Supplement, 1977-1980. **Remarks:** FAX: (716)636-3824. Electronic mail address(es): bm.sml. (BITNET). **Staff:** Dr. Carol June Bradley, Assoc.Dir.; Nancy Nuzzo, Record Cat.; Gudrun Kilburn, Lit.Cat./Ref.Libn.; Richard McRae, Mus.Cat./Ref.Libn.

★ 15741 ★
State University of New York at Buffalo - Poetry/Rare Books Collection (Hum, Rare Book)
University Libraries
420 Capen Hall   Phone: (716)636-2918
Buffalo, NY 14260   Robert J. Bertholf, Cur.
Founded: 1935. **Staff:** Prof 1; Other 2. **Subjects:** Twentieth-century poetry in English and in translation; rare books. **Special Collections:** Robert Graves; James Joyce; Wyndham Lewis; Dylan Thomas; William Carlos Williams; John Logan; Robert Kelly. **Holdings:** 100,000 books and ephemera; 3600 periodical titles; 911 phonograph records; 1200 tapes; photographs; paintings; sculpture; 400,000 manuscripts; 200,000 letters; microfilm. **Subscriptions:** 1300 journals and other serials. **Services:** Interlibrary loan; copying; collection open to the public. **Automated Operations:** Computerized serials. **Computerized Information Services:** RLIN. **Publications:** Lockwood Memorial Library Christmas Broadsides, annual. **Special Catalogs:** James Joyce's Manuscripts and Letters at the University of Buffalo, 1962; The Personal Library of James Joyce; The Manuscripts and Letters of William Carlos Williams in the Poetry Collection, SUNYAB; A Descriptive Catalog of the Private Library of Thomas B. Lockwood. **Remarks:** FAX: (716)636-3844.

★ 15742 ★
State University of New York at Buffalo - Science and Engineering Library (Sci-Engr, Biol Sci, Comp Sci)
Capen Hall   Phone: (716)636-2946
Buffalo, NY 14260   Kate S. Herzog, Dir.
Founded: 1949. **Staff:** Prof 6; Other 4. **Subjects:** Engineering, chemistry, physics, mathematics, geology, statistics, computer science, biology. **Special Collections:** Rare books in chemistry and metallurgy. **Holdings:** 392,600 books; 139,000 bound periodical volumes; 133,700 technical reports; 200,200 maps; 1.5 million microforms; 64 videocassettes; 1113 audiocassettes. **Subscriptions:** 2340 journals and other serials. **Services:** Interlibrary loan; copying; library open to the public. **Automated Operations:** Computerized cataloging and circulation. **Computerized Information Services:** DIALOG Information Services, BRS Information Technologies, RLIN, STN International; BITNET (electronic mail service). Performs searches on fee basis. **Networks/Consortia:** Member of Research Libraries Information Network (RLIN), Western New York Library Resources Council (WNYLRC). **Publications:** SEL NEWS, monthly; subject bibliographies, occasional. **Remarks:** Includes the holdings of the Chemistry-Mathematics Library and Earthquake Engineering Information Center. FAX: (716)636-3719. Electronic mail address(es): UNLKH@UBVM (BITNET). **Staff:** Renee Bush, Hd., Ref.; Ernest Woodson, Hd., Map Coll.; Connie Dalrymple, Act.Hd., ILL; Maiken Naylor, Hd., Chem.-Math. Lib.; Nancy Schiller, Engr.Libn.

★ 15743 ★
State University of New York at Buffalo - University Archives (Hist)
420 Capen Hall   Phone: (716)636-2916
Buffalo, NY 14260   Shonnie Finnegan, Univ.Archv.
Founded: 1966. **Staff:** 3. **Subjects:** Archives of the State University of New York at Buffalo and its predecessor, University of Buffalo, 1846 to present.

Special Collections: Documents pertaining to the Darwin D. Martin House and other Buffalo buildings designed by Frank Lloyd Wright; records of social action and women's organizations; history of Buffalo area in the 20th century; Fran Striker Collection (early radio scripts, including The Lone Ranger, 1932-1937). **Holdings:** 7000 linear feet of manuscripts, papers, and other archival materials. **Services:** Copying; archives open to the public. **Remarks:** FAX: (716)636-3844. **Staff:** Christopher Densmore.

★ 15744 ★

**State University of New York Health Science Center at Brooklyn -
Library** (Med)
450 Clarkson Ave.
Box 14   Phone: (718)270-1038
Brooklyn, NY 11203   Dr. Richard Winant
Founded: 1860. **Staff:** 26. **Subjects:** Medicine, nursing, and allied health sciences. **Holdings:** 235,202 volumes; archives and memorabilia of various Brooklyn hospitals and medical societies. **Subscriptions:** 1463 journals and other serials. **Services:** Interlibrary loan; copying; SDI; library open to qualified scientists who need access to the collection. **Automated Operations:** Computerized cataloging, acquisitions, and serials. **Computerized Information Services:** BRS Information Technologies, MEDLINE. **Networks/Consortia:** Member of National Network of Libraries of Medicine - Middle Atlantic Region, SUNY/OCLC Library Network, Medical Library Center of New York (MLCNY). **Staff:** Julie Semkow, Assoc.Dir.of Libn.; Dennis Gaffrey,Act.Hd.of Ref.; Catherine Wigfall, Hd.of Circ.; Donald Dederick, Hd.of ILL; Ronald Coombs, Act.Hd. of Tech.Serv.; Anita Ondrusek, Hd., Lrng.Rsrc.Ctr.

★ 15745 ★

**State University of New York Health Science Center at Syracuse -
Library** (Med)
766 Irving Ave.   Phone: (315)464-4582
Syracuse, NY 13210   Suzanne H. Murray, Dir.
Founded: 1834. **Staff:** Prof 9; Other 14. **Subjects:** Medicine, nursing, and allied health sciences. **Special Collections:** Medical Americana (350 volumes); Geneva Medical College Library (300 volumes); Rare Books (1500 volumes); Medical School Archives and History of Medicine in Syracuse (3 VF cabinets). **Holdings:** 52,444 books; 108,899 bound periodical volumes; 2760 AV program titles. **Subscriptions:** 1600 journals and other serials. **Services:** Interlibrary loan; copying; SDI; library open to the public. **Automated Operations:** Computerized public access catalog, cataloging, and serials. **Computerized Information Services:** DIALOG Information Services, MEDLARS, OCLC, MEDLINE, BRS Information Technologies; CD-ROMs (MEDLINE, ERIC, Science Citation Index, CINAHL, Health Planning and Administrative Data Base); BITNET (electronic mail service). Performs searches on fee basis. Contact Person: Peter Uva, Assoc.Libn./ Hd., Pub.Serv., 464-7112. **Networks/Consortia:** Member of SUNY/OCLC Library Network, Central New York Library Resources Council (CENTRO). **Publications:** Library Bulletin, quarterly; Library Guide, biennial; Annual Report; Subject List of AV Titles, annual; Alphabetical and Subject List of Currently Received Serials, annual - all available on request. **Remarks:** FAX: (315)464-7199. Electronic mail address(es): MURRAYS@SNYSYRVI (BITNET). **Staff:** James Capodagli, Sr.Asst.Ref.Libn.; Patricia Onsi, Assoc.Dir.; Christine Kucharski, Sr.Asst.Libn., Media; Diane Hawkins, Sr.Asst.Ref.Libn.; Sharon Quist, Asst.Libn./Med. Circuit Libn.; Hannah King, Asst.Libn.Coll.Dev.; Jeffrey Martin, Cat.

★ 15746 ★

State University of New York at Stony Brook - Biology Library (Biol
Sci)
Stony Brook, NY 11794-5260   Phone: (516)632-7152
                                            Rosalind Walcott, Libn.
Founded: 1975. **Staff:** Prof 1; Other 2. **Subjects:** Zoology, botany, general biology, biochemistry, microbiology, physiology, agriculture. **Special Collections:** Raymond Pearle Reprint Collection (625 volumes). **Holdings:** 43,560 books; 40,255 bound periodical volumes. **Subscriptions:** 680 journals. **Services:** Interlibrary loan; copying; library open to the public for reference use only. **Computerized Information Services:** CD-ROM (Life Sciences Collection). **Remarks:** FAX: (516)632-8331.

★ 15747 ★

State University of New York at Stony Brook - Chemistry Library (Sci-
Engr)
215 Chemistry Bldg.   Phone: (516)632-7150
Stony Brook, NY 11794-3425   Janet Steins, Libn.
Founded: 1965. **Staff:** Prof 1; Other 1.5. **Subjects:** Chemistry - analytical, inorganic, organic, physical, theoretical, crystallography; biological chemistry; spectrum analysis; quantum theory; toxicology; plants - disease and pest resistance; chemical technology. **Holdings:** 26,600 books; 30,000 bound periodical volumes. **Subscriptions:** 350 journals and other serials. **Services:** Interlibrary loan; copying; library open to the public for reference use only. **Remarks:** FAX: (516)632-9191.

★ 15748 ★

**State University of New York at Stony Brook - Computer Science
Library** (Comp Sci)
2120 Computer Science Bldg.   Phone: (516)632-7628
Stony Brook, NY 11794-4411   Donna M. Albertus, Libn.
Founded: 1987. **Staff:** Prof 1; Other 1. **Subjects:** Computer science, logic programming, artificial intelligence, computer graphics/pattern recognition. **Holdings:** 6250 books; 2735 bound periodical volumes; 2400 reports. **Subscriptions:** 200 journals and other serials. **Services:** Interlibrary loan; copying; SDI; library open to the public for reference use only. **Computerized Information Services:** DIALOG Information Services, BRS Information Technologies; BITNET, InterNet (electronic mail services). **Publications:** Computer Science Library Acquisitions Update, monthly - distributed via electronic mail. **Remarks:** FAX: (516)632-7401.

★ 15749 ★

**State University of New York at Stony Brook - Earth and Space
Sciences Library** (Sci-Engr)
167 Earth and Space Sciences Bldg.
Stony Brook, NY 11794-2199   Phone: (516)632-7146
Founded: 1968. **Staff:** 2. **Subjects:** Geology, astronomy, oceanography, paleontology, meteorology, geomorphology. **Holdings:** 42,000 books; 17,000 bound periodical volumes; 7000 sheets of geological maps; 2500 Palomar Sky Survey and Southern Sky Survey photographic prints; film copies of seismograms from 20 stations of the National Geophysical Data Center, 1964 to present. **Subscriptions:** 635 journals and other serials. **Services:** Interlibrary loan; copying; library open to the public for reference use only. **Computerized Information Services:** Online systems.

★ 15750 ★

State University of New York at Stony Brook - Engineering Library
(Sci-Engr)
220 Engineering Bldg.   Phone: (516)632-7148
Stony Brook, NY 11794-2225   Godlind Johnson, Libn.
Founded: 1964. **Staff:** Prof 1; Other 2. **Subjects:** Engineering, electrical sciences, mechanics and mechanical engineering, materials sciences, technology, medical technology, chemical technology, applied physics, aerospace sciences. **Holdings:** 32,545 books; 28,335 bound periodical volumes. **Subscriptions:** 530 journals and other serials. **Services:** Interlibrary loan; copying; library open to the public for reference use only. **Computerized Information Services:** DIALOG Information Services, BRS Information Technologies, STN International; CD-ROMs (CASSIS/CD-ROM, Applied Science & Technology Index); BITNET (electronic mail service). **Remarks:** FAX: (516)632-9193. Electronic mail address(es): GJOHNSON@SBCCMAIL (BITNET).

★ 15751 ★

**State University of New York at Stony Brook - Environmental
Information Service** (Env-Cons)
Stony Brook, NY 11794-3331   Phone: (516)632-7161
Founded: 1970. **Staff:** Prof 1; Other 1. **Subjects:** Environment of Long Island; general environmental problems and energy issues. **Holdings:** 6350 books and pamphlets; 1500 research and technical report titles; 1655 federal, state, and local document titles; 25 drawers of newspaper clippings. **Services:** Interlibrary loan; copying; service open to the public for reference use only. **Computerized Information Services:** Online systems. **Staff:** Paul J. Cammarata, Sr.Asst.Libn.

★ 15752 ★
State University of New York at Stony Brook - Health Sciences Library
  (Med)
Box 66   Phone: (516)444-2512
East Setauket, NY 11733-0066   Ruth Marcolina, Dir.
Founded: 1969. **Staff:** Prof 8; Other 17. **Subjects:** Medicine, dentistry, nursing, allied health and basic medical sciences, social welfare. **Special Collections:** History of medicine and dentistry. **Holdings:** 259,290 books and bound periodical volumes; microfilm. **Subscriptions:** 3066 journals and other serials. **Services:** Interlibrary loan; copying; SDI; library open to those involved in Nassau and Suffolk County health care. **Computerized Information Services:** NLM, DIALOG Information Services, BRS Information Technologies; BITNET (electronic mail service). **Networks/Consortia:** Member of SUNY/OCLC Library Network, National Network of Libraries of Medicine - Middle Atlantic Region. **Publications:** Guide to Health Sciences Library, annual - to patrons. **Remarks:** FAX: (516)751-5809. Electronic mail address(es): RMARCOLINA@SBCCMAIL (BITNET). **Staff:** Antonija Prelec, Assoc. Dir./Coll.Dev.; Arlee May, Asst.Dir./Pub.Serv.; Amy Young, Cat.Libn.; Esther Wei, Hd., Ref./Coord. Automation; Julitta Jo, Ser.Libn.; Robert Williams, Circ.Libn.; Colleen Kenefick, Ref.Libn.

★ 15753 ★
State University of New York at Stony Brook - Map Library (Geog-
  Map)
Stony Brook, NY 11794-3331   Phone: (516)632-7110
                       David Y. Allen, Libn.
Founded: 1974. **Staff:** Prof 1. **Subjects:** U.S. topography, nautical information, Long Island, New York State, Western Europe, U.S. soil maps. **Special Collections:** New York State historic map collection. **Holdings:** 1750 volumes; 82,000 U.S. sheet maps; 25,000 world sheet maps. **Subscriptions:** 7 journals and other serials. **Services:** Interlibrary loan; copying; library open to the public for reference use only. **Automated Operations:** Computerized cataloging (NOTIS). **Computerized Information Services:** DIALOG Information Services, BRS Information Technologies, OCLC, RLIN; BITNET (electronic mail service). **Networks/Consortia:** Member of Research Libraries Information Network (RLIN), New York State Interlibrary Loan Network (NYSILL), Long Island Library Resources Council. **Publications:** Descriptive guide to Map Collection. **Remarks:** Electronic mail address(es): DYALLEN@SBCCMAIL (BITNET). State University of New York at Stony Brook - Map Library is a federal depository library.

★ 15754 ★
State University of New York at Stony Brook - Marine Sciences
  Research Center - Library (Sci-Engr)
Stony Brook, NY 11794-5000   Phone: (516)632-8679
                      Larry P. Herschenfeld
Founded: 1989. **Staff:** Prof 1; Other 4. **Subjects:** Oceanography, marine chemistry, waste management, marine biology, marine geology, climatology. **Special Collections:** Long Island Sound collection; Peconic Bay collection; Waste Management collection; Marine Science Research Center theses and dissertation collection. **Holdings:** 4500 books; 2500 bound periodical volumes; 1000 reports. **Subscriptions:** 45 journals and other serials; marine science newsletters. **Services:** Library open to the public for reference use only. **Automated Operations:** Computerized public access catalog. **Computerized Information Services:** DIALOG Information Services. **Publications:** List of students theses and dissertations; MSRC special reports. **Special Catalogs:** Aquatic Sciences & Fisheries Abstracts (online). **Remarks:** FAX: (516)632-8820.

★ 15755 ★
State University of New York at Stony Brook - Mathematics-Physics
  Library (Sci-Engr)
Physics Bldg., C Fl.   Phone: (516)632-7145
Stony Brook, NY 11794-3855   Sherry Chang, Libn.
Founded: 1964. **Staff:** Prof 1; Other 3. **Subjects:** Mathematics, physics, applied mathematics. **Holdings:** 44,500 books; 33,000 bound periodical volumes; 500 unbound lecture notes of academic organizations; 300 reels of microfilm of journals; 2100 unbound documents; 1000 dissertations; 1000 microfiche. **Subscriptions:** 610 journals and other serials. **Services:** Interlibrary loan; copying; library open to the public for reference use only. **Computerized Information Services:** Online systems; BITNET (electronic mail service). **Remarks:** FAX: (516)632-9192. Electronic mail address(es): SHERRYCHANG@SBCC.MAIL.SUNYSB.EDU (BITNET).

★ 15756 ★
State University of New York at Stony Brook - Music Library (Mus)
Stony Brook, NY 11794-3333   Phone: (516)632-7097
                  Joyce Clinkscales, Hd., Mus.Lib.
Founded: 1974. **Staff:** Prof 2; Other 4. **Subjects:** Music. **Holdings:** 60,000 books, scores, and periodical volumes; 20,000 sound recordings; 7000 microforms. **Subscriptions:** 360 journals and other serials. **Services:** Interlibrary loan; copying; library open to the public. **Automated Operations:** Computerized public access catalog and circulation. **Remarks:** FAX: (516)632-7116. **Staff:** Mark Pitto.

★ 15757 ★
State University of New York at Stony Brook - Special Collections
  Department and University Archives (Hist, Hum)
Stony Brook, NY 11794-3323   Phone: (516)632-7119
                       Evert Volkersz, Hd.
Founded: 1969. **Staff:** Prof 2.5. **Subjects:** Contemporary letters and literature, children's literature, Ibero-Americana, Long Island, 20th century political and social movements, printing and publishing, SUNY at Stony Brook. **Special Collections:** Conrad Potter Aiken (102 volumes; 44 periodicals); Jorge Carrera Andrade (85 volumes; manuscripts); children's literature, 1820 to present (2500 volumes); Chilean Theater Pamphlets (57 bound volumes; 570 pamphlets); Robert Creeley (130 volumes, manuscripts); Fortune Press, London (110 volumes); Oakley Calvin Johnson Papers (10 volumes; 31 linear feet of manuscripts); Latin American Pamphlets (1215 items); Pablo Neruda (175 volumes and manuscripts); Robert Payne (200 volumes and manuscripts); Perishable Press, Ltd. (100 volumes; 20 linear feet of manuscripts); Juan and Eva Peron Pamphlets (380 items); Printing and Publishing Collection (750 volumes); Spanish-American Colonial Trade (103 16th century unbound pamphlets); The Typophiles, New York (120 volumes); early 19th century Chilean newspapers and journals (41 titles); Irish political pamphlets, 1789-1829 (503 pamphlets bound in 78 volumes); Environmental Defense Fund, 1967-1975 (600 linear feet); Performing Arts Foundation Collection (80 linear feet); Jacob K. Javits Collection (1200 linear feet); Fielding Dawson (45 volumes and manuscripts); Robert E. Duncan (75 volumes and manuscripts); Emery Long Island Railroad Collection (40 volumes; 5000 photographs; 262 timetables); William Everson (45 volumes and manuscripts); Allen Ginsburg (60 volumes and manuscripts); League for Industrial Democracy (150 pamphlets); Denise Levertov (35 volumes and manuscripts); Long Island manuscript collections; Long Island fiction (250 volumes); Michael McClure (45 volumes and manuscripts); Charles Olson (65 volumes and manuscripts); Ezra Pound (125 volumes); William Butler Yeats Microfilm Manuscripts Collection (80,000 frames). **Holdings:** 25,000 volumes; 4000 linear feet of manuscripts; 10,000 pieces of ephemera and clippings; 48 linear feet of pamphlets. **Services:** Copying (limited); department open to the public by appointment for reference use only. **Automated Operations:** Computerized cataloging (NOTIS). **Computerized Information Services:** Internal databases; BITNET, InterNet (electronic mail services). **Publications:** Information leaflets; research guides. **Remarks:** FAX: (516)632-7116. Electronic mail address(es): EVOLKERS@SBCCMAIL (BITNET); EVOLKERS@CCMAIL.SUNYSB.EDU (InterNet). **Staff:** Diane Englot, Instr.Sup.Assoc.

★ 15758 ★
State University School of Pharmacy at Buffalo - Drug Information
  Service - Library (Med)
Erie County Medical Center
462 Grider St.   Phone: (716)898-3927
Buffalo, NY 14215   Dr. Susan L. Rozek, Dir.
Founded: 1966. **Staff:** Prof 1. **Subjects:** Medicinals, pharmacology, therapeutics. **Holdings:** 70 books; files; microfilm. **Subscriptions:** 25 journals and other serials. **Services:** Library not open to the public. **Computerized Information Services:** Online system. **Publications:** Therapeutic Perspectives, bimonthly - to medical staff and other drug information centers.

★ 15759 ★
Staten Island Continuum of Education - Educational Resource Center
  (Educ)
631 Howard Ave.   Phone: (718)447-2600
Staten Island, NY 10301-4495   John Gino, Prog.Dir.
Founded: 1973. **Staff:** Prof 1; Other 3. **Subjects:** Education, curriculum (K-12). **Holdings:** 9000 books; 50 bound periodical volumes; 1200 curriculum guides; 200 multimedia kits; 200 testing materials; microcomputers; 10 VHS cassettes. **Services:** Interlibrary loan; copying; videotaping and editing for students and the educational community; center open to the public. **Publications:** A/V Guide to ERC, irregular; ERC Newsletter, semiannual; SPECTRUM, triannual. **Remarks:** FAX: (718)390-3467.

★ 15760 ★
Staten Island Historical Society - Library (Hist)
441 Clarke Ave.   Phone: (718)351-1611
Staten Island, NY 10306   Maxine Friedman, Chf.Cur.
Staff: Prof 1; Other 3. **Subjects:** History of Staten Island and neighboring communities, U.S. history. **Special Collections:** Rare books. **Holdings:** 5000 books; 350 bound periodical volumes; 30 VF drawers of Staten Island history; 8 VF drawers of Staten Island genealogies; 110 reels of microfilm; 545 cubic feet of manuscripts; 9000 uncataloged items; 75 audiotapes; 30 videotapes; 320 bound volumes of newspapers. **Subscriptions:** 25 journals and other serials. **Services:** Copying; library open to the public by appointment only. **Publications:** Staten Island Historian, semiannual - to members. **Staff:** Carlotta De Fillo.

★ 15761 ★
Staten Island Institute of Arts and Sciences - Archives and Library (Sci-Engr, Hist)
75 Stuyvesant Place   Phone: (718)727-1135
Staten Island, NY 10301   John-Paul Richiuso, Archv./Hist.
Founded: 1881. **Staff:** Prof 2; Other 1. **Subjects:** Natural history, Staten Island history, archeology, black history, women's history, urban planning. **Special Collections:** Architecture; N.L. Britton; G.W. Curtis; J.P. Chapin; W.T. Davis (total of 1000 cubic feet); photographs and prints of old Staten Island; local black history; repository for U.S. Geological Survey publications; complete list of special collections available on request. **Holdings:** 12,000 books; 22,000 bound periodical volumes; 3000 maps; 1200 prints; 50,000 photographs; 1500 art museum and gallery catalogs; 1500 cubic feet of manuscripts, letters, and documents; 80 reels of microfilm of Staten Island newspapers. **Subscriptions:** 200 journals and other serials. **Services:** Copying; library open to the public by appointment. **Publications:** Proceedings, 2/year - by subscription and exchange; Guide to Special Collections, 16 volumes. **Special Indexes:** Guide to Institute Archives, 2 volumes; indexes to newspapers, iconography of Staten Island, special collections (all on cards). **Remarks:** Basic library has been divided into two sections, a Science Library and a History Library. **Remarks:** FAX: (718)273-5683.

★ 15762 ★
Staten Island Institute of Arts and Sciences - William T. Davis Education Center (Env-Cons, Biol Sci)
75 Stuyvesant Pl.   Phone: (718)987-6233
Staten Island, NY 10301   John-Paul Richiuso, Archv.
Founded: 1964. **Staff:** Prof 1. **Subjects:** Environmental education, mammalogy, salt and fresh water ecology, ornithology, botany, dendrology, geology, ichthyology, zoology, astronomy, energy, photography. **Holdings:** 2758 books; 4 boxes of Cornell Science leaflets; 2 boxes of Department of Agriculture leaflets; 2 boxes of Botanic Gardens pamphlets; 12 phonograph records of bird songs; filmstrips; AV programs; Outdoor Biology Instructional Strategies (OBIS) materials. **Subscriptions:** 15 journals and other serials. **Services:** Videotape facilities. **Remarks:** FAX: (718)273-5683.

★ 15763 ★
Staten Island University Hospital - Medical Staff Library (Med)
475 Seaview Ave.   Phone: (718)226-9545
Staten Island, NY 10305   Song Ja Oh, Dir.
Founded: 1952. **Staff:** Prof 2; Other 2. **Subjects:** Internal medicine, surgery, pediatrics, obstetrics, gynecology, dentistry, nursing, psychiatry, rehabilitation, pathology, pharmacy. **Holdings:** 2200 books; 15,000 bound periodical volumes; 1736 Audio-Digest tapes; videotapes. **Subscriptions:** 400 journals; 2207 other serials. **Services:** Interlibrary loan; copying; library open to the public with restrictions. **Computerized Information Services:** MEDLINE; DOCLINE (electronic mail service). **Formerly:** Staten Island Hospital.

★ 15764 ★
Staten Island Zoological Society - Library (Biol Sci)
614 Broadway   Phone: (718)442-3101
Staten Island, NY 10310   Joanne Sinatra, Adm.Asst.
Founded: 1936. **Staff:** 1. **Subjects:** Herpetology, environmental education, mammals, invertebrates, fish, birds. **Holdings:** 750 books; 180 bound periodical volumes. **Subscriptions:** 10 journals and other serials. **Services:** Copying; library open to the public by appointment. **Remarks:** FAX: (718)981-8711.

★ 15765 ★
Statens Forsvarshistoriska Museum - Marinmuseum - Amiralitesslatten (Mil)
S-371 30 Karlskrona, Sweden   Phone: 455 84003
                                                  Ylva Lindstom
Founded: 1761. **Staff:** Prof 1. **Subjects:** Shipbuilding; figureheads; naval war history; military - weapons, uniforms. **Holdings:** 20,000 books; photograph archives. **Subscriptions:** 70 journals and other serials. **Services:** Copying; library open to the public for reference use only. **Computerized Information Services:** CDS/ISIS (internal database). **Remarks:** FAX: 455 84071.

Statens Geotekniska Institut
See: **Swedish Geotechnical Institute** (15921)

Statens Handverks - og kunstindustriskole - Biblioteket
See: **Norway - National College of Art and Design - Library** (12105)

Statens Institut for Byggnadsforskning
See: **National Swedish Institute for Building Research** (11310)

Statens Museum for Kunst - Den Kongelige Kobberstiksamlings - Bibliotek
See: **Royal Museum of Fine Arts (of Denmark) - Department of Prints and Drawings - Library** (14125)

Statens Museum for Kunst - Den Kongelige Malerisamlings - Bibliotek
See: **Royal Museum of Fine Arts (of Denmark) - Department of Paintings - Library** (14124)

Statens Psykologisk- Pedagogiska Bibliotek
See: **Sweden - The National Library for Psychology and Education** (15909)

Statens Vag- och Trafikinstitut (VTI)
See: **Swedish Road and Traffic Research Institute** (15928)

States Information Center
See: **Council of State Governments** (4371)

Statistics Canada
See: **Canada - Statistics Canada** (2855)

Statistics Sweden
See: **Sweden - Statistics Sweden** (15912)

Statistisches Bundesamt
See: **Germany - Federal Statistical Office** (6448)

Statistiska Centralbyrans Bibliotek
See: **Sweden - Statistics Sweden** (15912)

Alice Statler Library
See: **City College of San Francisco - Hotel and Restaurant Department** (3736)

Statue of Liberty-Ellis Island Library
See: **U.S. Natl. Park Service - Statue of Liberty-Ellis Island Library** (17782)

Statue of Liberty National Monument
See: **U.S. Natl. Park Service - Statue of Liberty-Ellis Island Library** (17782)

Stauffer Health Sciences Library
See: **Stormont-Vail Regional Medical Center** (15816)

★ 15766 ★
Stazione Chimico-Agraria Sperimentale - Biblioteca (Sci-Engr)
Via Ormea 47   Phone: 11 6507026
I-10125 Turin, Italy   Prof. Augusto Marchesini
Founded: 1875. **Subjects:** Biochemistry, analytic chemistry. **Special Collections:** Chemisches collection; Central Blatt collection (1830-1968). **Holdings:** 10,000 books; 500 bound periodical volumes. **Services:** Library open to the public. **Remarks:** FAX: 11 6692995.

Steacie Science Library
See: **York University** (20794)

★ 15767 ★
Steamship Historical Society of America Collection (Hist, Trans)
University of Baltimore
1420 Maryland Ave.   Phone: (301)625-3134
Baltimore, MD 21201-5779   Douglas L. Haverly, SSHSA Libn.
Founded: 1940. **Staff:** Prof 2; Other 2. **Subjects:** Marine transportation, steamship and steamboat history, naval history. **Special Collections:** Tracey Brooks Collection; T.H. Franklin's collection of 19th century steamboats; B.M. Boyles' collection of Maine material; Hudson River Day Line Collection; R. Loren Graham marine photographs; Everett Viez ocean liner photographs; C. Bradford Mitchell Marine Collection; John L. Lochhead Marine Collection; Charles Luffbarry Collection of marine photographs. **Holdings:** 5000 books; 800 pamphlets; 30,000 ship photograph negatives; 60,000 pictures of ships; 1000 steamship company folders; 200 deck and cabin plans; 25,000 colored postcards. **Subscriptions:** 100 journals and other serials. **Services:** Copying; collection open to the public. **Automated Operations:** Computerized cataloging. **Computerized Information Services:** OCLC. **Publications:** Steamboat Bill, quarterly; list of other publications - available on request. **Staff:** Ann House, Libn.

Stearn Graduate School of Business Administration
See: **New York University** (11732)

★ 15768 ★
Stearns County Historical Society - Research Center & Archives (Hist)
235 33rd Ave., S.
P.O. Box 702   Phone: (612)253-8424
St. Cloud, MN 56302-0702   John W. Decker, Archv.
Founded: 1975. **Staff:** Prof 2. **Subjects:** Genealogy, county history, architecture, agriculture, granite industry. **Special Collections:** Glanville W. Smith papers (15 boxes); Stearns County aerial sectional photographs, 1938 (474); Byron E. Barr (Gig Young) papers (2 boxes); Frank W. Jackson Architectural Firm records (12 Hollinger boxes; 100 plans); Cold Spring Granite Company photographs (250); State Senator Ed Schrom papers (10 boxes); Russell T. Wing papers (13 boxes); A.G. Alice Wheelock Whitney Family Papers (3 boxes); maps of Stearns County and Central Minnesota, 1855 to present (165); Stearns County census reports, 1850-1910; John Clark Granite Company photographs (200); Myron Hall Photo Collection (1937-1976; 275,000 images); St. Cloud, Minnesota Photo Studio Collection; Gene's Studio Photo Collection (1968-79; 20,000 images); Ron Harry's Studio (1950-1990; 30,000 images); Lee-Douglas Studio (1959-1985; 25,000 images); Luxemburger Gazette, 1871-1918 (20 reels of microfilm); local history and local artists Gig Young and June Marlowe's movies (on videotape; 70). **Holdings:** 1700 books; 775 bound periodical volumes; 16 VF drawers of biographical and family files (11,500 names); 1800 oral history tapes, 1975-1988; 975 reels of microfilm of Stearns County newspapers; 15,000 photographs and slides; 22 reels of microfilm of Stearns County naturalization records, 1852-1954; 7 reels of microfilm of Stearns County Land Office tract index records, 1853-1910; St. Cloud city directories, 1888-1990; Stearns County birth and death records, 1946-1982, and marriage records, 1916-1982. **Subscriptions:** 16 journals and other serials. **Services:** Copying; center open to the public. **Networks/Consortia:** Member of Central Minnesota Libraries Exchange (CMLE). **Publications:** Crossings (newsletter), bimonthly - to members and the public. **Special Indexes:** Gravestone surname index for Stearns, Benton, and Sherburne Counties; St. Cloud Daily Times News index, 1928 to present; Stearns County Register of Historic Places, 1991. **Staff:** Robert Lommel, Res.

Steel Information Centre and Library
See: **German Iron and Steel Institute - Steel Information Centre and Library** (6430)

★ 15769 ★
Steele County Historical Society - Archives (Hist)
Box 144   Phone: (701)945-2394
Hope, ND 58046   Todd Parkman, Cur.
Founded: 1964. **Staff:** 1. **Subjects:** Local history. **Holdings:** 400 books; 158 bound periodical volumes; 31 oral history tapes; old catalogs and magazines; photograph collection; town and school records; church and county records. **Services:** Copying; archives open to the public with restrictions.

Steen Library
See: **Stephen F. Austin State University** (1317)

Steenbock Memorial Library
See: **University of Wisconsin--Madison** (19619)

Stein Memorial Library
See: **Agudas Achim Congregation** (137)

★ 15770 ★
Stein Roe and Farnham - Library (Bus-Fin)
One S. Wacker Dr.   Phone: (312)368-7777
Chicago, IL 60606   Celeste K. Jannusch, Libn.
Founded: 1932. **Staff:** Prof 2; Other 2. **Subjects:** Business, finance. **Holdings:** 1850 books; 110 bound periodical volumes; 111,000 microfiche. **Subscriptions:** 300 journals and other serials; 30 newspapers. **Services:** Interlibrary loan; copying; library open to the public for reference use only on request. **Computerized Information Services:** DIALOG Information Services, LEXIS, NEXIS, Dun & Bradstreet Business Credit Services, INVESTEXT, DataTimes, VU/TEXT Information Services, Dow Jones News/Retrieval. **Remarks:** FAX: (312)368-8103. **Staff:** Alison Becker, Ref.Libn.

Sam and Rose Stein Children's Center - Parent Resource Library
See: **House Ear Institute** (7440)

★ 15771 ★
Steinbach Bible College - Library (Rel-Phil)
Box 1420   Phone: (204)326-6451
Steinbach, MB, Canada R0A 2A0   Myrna Friesen, Libn.
Founded: 1936. **Staff:** Prof 1; Other 1. **Subjects:** Bible, theology, Mennonite history, music. **Holdings:** 18,000 books; 600 bound periodical volumes. **Subscriptions:** 80 journals and other serials. **Services:** Interlibrary loan; copying; library open to the public. **Remarks:** FAX: (204)326-6908.

Rabbi A. Alan Steinbach Memorial Library
See: **Temple Ahavath Sholom** (16080)

John Steinbeck Library
See: **Salinas Public Library** (14637)

Steinbeck Research Center
See: **San Jose State University** (14760)

Hedi Steinberg Library
See: **Yeshiva University** (20755)

Steinberg Information Center
See: **CIBA Corning Diagnostics Corporation** (3688)

Sarah and Julius Steinberg Memorial Library
See: **Riverside Hospital** (13944)

Rudolf Steiner Library
See: **Anthroposophical Society in America** (894)

Rudolph Steiner Library
See: **Anthroposophical Society of Canada** (895)

Walter Steiner Memorial Library
See: **Hartford Medical Society** (6936)

Steinheimer Collection of Southwestern Children's Literature
See: **Tucson Public Library** (16546)

Kate Trauman Steinitz Archives
See: **University of California, Los Angeles - Arts, Architecture and Urban Planning Library** (18370)

★ 15772 ★
Stelco Steel Information Centre (Sci-Engr)
1375 Kerns Rd.   Phone: (416)528-2511
Burlington, ON, Canada L7P 3H8 Carol A. Cernile, Res.Lib.Techn.
Founded: 1962. **Staff:** 1.5. **Subjects:** Ferrous metallurgy, engineering. **Holdings:** 2200 books; 300 bound periodical volumes; microforms; patents; internal reports. **Subscriptions:** 250 journals and other serials. **Services:** Interlibrary loan; center not open to the public. **Automated Operations:** Computerized public access catalog. **Computerized Information Services:** CAN/OLE; internal database. **Networks/Consortia:** Member of Southern Ontario Library Service, Sheridan Park Association. **Publications:** Current Awareness Bulletin, weekly. **Special Indexes:** Index of project and report files (computer printout). **Remarks:** FAX: (416)332-9067. Telex: 061-8944.

Sister Stella Louise Health Sciences Library
See: **St. Mary of Nazareth Hospital Center** (14506)

John C. Stennis Space Center - NASA Library
See: **NASA Library - John C. Stennis Space Center** (10991)

★ 15773 ★
Stepan Company - Technical Information Center (Sci-Engr)
22 W. Frontage Rd.   Phone: (708)501-2277
Northfield, IL 60093   Patricia L. Brown, Mgr.
Staff: Prof 3; Other 1. **Subjects:** Chemistry. **Holdings:** 3000 books; 6000 bound periodical volumes; 13,000 internal R&D documents; 16,700 copies of U.S. and foreign patents; 1100 microfilm cartridges of U.S. patents. **Subscriptions:** 165 journals and other serials. **Services:** Interlibrary loan; center open to the public by appointment. **Computerized Information Services:** ORBIT Search Service, Questel, Chemical Economics Handbook (CEH) Program, DIALOG Information Services, NLM, STN International, Data-Star, Chemical Information Systems, Inc. (CIS), EPIC, WILSONLINE; internal databases. **Remarks:** FAX: (708)501-2100. **Staff:** Lois A. Bey, Tech.Info. Sci. Mary M. Schultze,. Libn.

★ 15774 ★
Stepfamily Foundation, Inc. - Library (Soc Sci)
333 West End Ave.   Phone: (212)877-3244
New York, NY 10023   Jeannette Lofas, Exec.Dir.
Founded: 1976. **Staff:** Prof 1; Other 4. **Subjects:** Stepfamily, gender. **Holdings:** 1100 books; 200 audiotapes. **Services:** Library not open to the public. **Computerized Information Services:** Internal database. **Publications:** Newsletter, quarterly. **Remarks:** FAX: (212)362-7030.

Stephen Decatur Chapter D.A.R. Library
See: **Decatur Genealogical Society - Library** (4689)

Stephens Bros. Boat Works Archives
See: **The Haggin Museum - Almeda May Castle Petzinger Library** (6827)

Stephens-Burnett Memorial Library
See: **Carson-Newman College - Stephens-Burnett Memorial Library - Special Collections** (3105)

★ 15775 ★
Steptoe and Johnson - Library (Law)
1330 Connecticut Ave., N.W.   Phone: (202)429-6429
Washington, DC 20036   Allen Story, Libn.
Staff: Prof 8; Other 5. **Subjects:** Law. **Holdings:** 60,000 volumes. **Services:** Library not open to the public. **Remarks:** Alternate telephone number(s): 429-8152. FAX: (202)429-9204. **Staff:** Linda Brzostowski; Linda Fowlie; Val Holley; Merilyn Marshall; Mary Lou Ranck; Amy Waldrip.

★ 15776 ★
Margaret S. Sterck School for the Hearing Impaired - Instructional Media Center - Library (Educ)
620 E. Chestnut Hill Rd.   Phone: (302)454-2098
Newark, DE 19713   Deborah P. Gary
Founded: 1968. **Staff:** Prof 1; Other 1. **Subjects:** Deafness, the deaf, deaf culture, sign language, general. **Special Collections:** Deaf collection (1000 volumes). **Holdings:** 10,000 books; 1000 bound periodical volumes; 25 reels of microfilm; videotapes; filmstrips; photographs; tapes; educational supplies. **Subscriptions:** 74 journals and other serials; 7 newspapers. **Services:** Interlibrary loan; copying; library open to the public for reference use only.

★ 15777 ★
Stereo Club of Southern California - Library (Aud-Vis, Rec)
Box 2368   Phone: (310)837-2368
Culver City, CA 90231   David Starkman, Tech.Dir.
Founded: 1977. **Staff:** 3. **Subjects:** Stereoscopy; 3-D photography, movies, television; View-Master products and history. **Holdings:** 50 books; 6 VF drawers of articles, instructional manuals, pamphlets. **Services:** Copying (limited); library open to the public by appointment. **Publications:** 3-D News, monthly - by subscription. **Remarks:** FAX: (310)558-1653.

Victor Sterki Library
See: **Carnegie Museum of Natural History - Library** (3085)

Sterling Chemistry Library
See: **Yale University** (20733)

Sterling Drug, Inc. - Corporate Medical Library
See: **Sterling Winthrop Inc. - Corporate Library** (15780)

★ 15778 ★
Sterling Drug, Inc. - Sterling Research Group - Library (Med, Biol Sci)
81 Columbia Turnpike   Phone: (518)445-8262
Rensselaer, NY 12144-3493 Patsy L. Schulenberg, Mgr., Lib. & Info.Serv.
Founded: 1950. **Staff:** Prof 2; Other 5. **Subjects:** Biomedicine, chemistry, pharmacology, biology. **Holdings:** 20,000 books; 30,000 bound periodical volumes; 2600 reels of microfilm; 8300 microfiche. **Subscriptions:** 800 journals and other serials. **Services:** Interlibrary loan; copying; SDI; library open to the public by appointment. **Automated Operations:** Computerized cataloging, public access catalog, serials, and ILL. **Computerized Information Services:** PFDS Online, DIALOG Information Services, BRS Information Technologies, Data-Star, OCLC, Chemical Abstracts Service (CAS), MEDLINE; internal database. **Networks/Consortia:** Member of SUNY/OCLC Library Network, Capital District Library Council for Reference & Research Resources (CDLC). **Publications:** Library Bulletin, quarterly - to mailing list. **Remarks:** FAX: (518)445-8648. Sterling Drug, Inc. is a subsidiary of Eastman Kodak Company. **Staff:** Ann Marie Weis, Sr.Adm., Lib.Serv.; Patricia Carroll, ILL Libn.

★ 15779 ★
Sterling Drug, Inc. - Sterling Research Group - Library & Information Services (Med)
9 Great Valley Parkway   Phone: (215)640-8654
Malvern, PA 19355   Don Miles, Mgr.
Founded: 1987. **Staff:** Prof 3; Other 2. **Subjects:** Biomedicine, biochemistry, clinical medicine, chemistry, pharmacology, toxicology. **Holdings:** 4000 books; 300 bound periodical volumes; 3000 nonbook items. **Subscriptions:** 450 journals and other serials. **Services:** Copying; SDI. **Computerized Information Services:** DIALOG Information Services, STN International, MEDLINE, BRS Information Technologies, NEXIS, PFDS Online. **Networks/Consortia:** Member of PALINET. **Remarks:** FAX: (215)859-8800. **Staff:** Mary E. Davis, Biomed.Info.Spec.; Maryann Brennan, Site Mgr.; Jim Morris, Tech.Serv.; Cheri Beard, Ser.Mgt. and ILL

Sterling Research Group
See: **Sterling Drug, Inc.** (15778)

★ 15780 ★
Sterling Winthrop Inc. - Corporate Library (Med)
90 Park Ave.   Phone: (212)907-2504
New York, NY 10016   Lynn Siegelman, Lib.Mgr.
Founded: 1927. **Staff:** Prof 4; Other 4. **Subjects:** Pharmaceuticals, clinical medicine. **Special Collections:** Articles on drugs (abstracted and indexed). **Holdings:** 3000 books and bound periodical volumes. **Subscriptions:** 260 journals and other serials. **Services:** Interlibrary loan; library open to the public by appointment. **Computerized Information Services:** MEDLARS, DIALOG Information Services, BRS Information Technologies, InvesText, DataTimes, Data-Star. **Networks/Consortia:** Member of National Network of Libraries of Medicine - Middle Atlantic Region, Medical Library Center of New York (MLCNY). **Publications:** Current References, monthly. **Remarks:** FAX: (212)907-2877. **Formerly:** Sterling Drug, Inc. - Corporate Medical Library.

Sternberg Memorial Museum
See: **Fort Hays University** (6001)

★ 15781 ★
Stetson University - Archives (Hist)
Box 8418   Phone: (904)822-7180
De Land, FL 32720   Sims Kline, Director
Founded: 1890. **Subjects:** Stetson University, 1883 to present. **Special Collections:** Stetson correspondence; catalogs and annuals. **Holdings:** 150 linear feet (5 file cabinets) of correspondence and letters from early De Land settlers; campus photographs (including faculty, students, and athletics); biographies of all presidents and faculty members. **Services:** Interlibrary loan; copying; archives open to the public.

★ 15782 ★
Stetson University - Chemistry Library (Sci-Engr)
N. Woodland Blvd.
Box 8271   Phone: (904)822-8180
De Land, FL 32720   Peter R. Hauck
Staff: 1. **Subjects:** Chemistry. **Special Collections:** Chemical Abstracts. **Holdings:** 2200 books; 4400 bound periodical volumes; 10 drawers of microfiche. **Subscriptions:** 28 journals and other serials. **Services:** Interlibrary loan; copying; library open to the public. **Computerized Information Services:** BITNET (electronic mail service). **Remarks:** FAX: (904)822-8832. Electronic mail address(es): DELAP@STETSON (BITNET).

★ 15783 ★
Stetson University - College of Law - Charles A. Dana Law Library (Law)
1401 61st St., S.   Phone: (813)345-1121
St. Petersburg, FL 33707   J. Lamar Woodard, Libn./Prof. of Law
Founded: 1900. **Staff:** Prof 6; Other 7. **Subjects:** Law. **Holdings:** 297,000 volumes. **Subscriptions:** 800 journals and other serials. **Services:** Interlibrary loan; copying; library open to qualified persons. **Automated Operations:** Computerized public access catalog, acquisitions, serials, and circulation. **Computerized Information Services:** WESTLAW, LEXIS, OCLC. **Networks/Consortia:** Member of SOLINET, Tampa Bay Library Consortium, Inc. (TBLC). **Remarks:** FAX: (813)345-8973. **Staff:** Roman Yoder, Asst.Libn., Tech.Serv.; Earlene Kuester, Ser.Libn.; Sally Waters, Ref.Libn.; Pamela Burdett, Asst.Libn., Pub.Serv.; Dorothy Clark, Pub.Serv.

★ 15784 ★
Stetson University - Du Pont-Ball Library - Garwood Baptist Historical Collection (Hist, Rel-Phil)
Box 8247   Phone: (904)822-7175
De Land, FL 32720   Dr. E. Earl Joiner, Cur.
Staff: Prof 1. **Subjects:** History of Baptist, Southern Baptist, and Florida Baptist Churches. **Holdings:** 1300 books; 825 bound periodical volumes; 260 reels of microfilm; 155 boxes of Baptist Association records; 4 cabinets of manuscripts and papers; vertical files. **Subscriptions:** 37 journals and other serials. **Services:** Interlibrary loan; copying; collection open to the public by appointment with restrictions on circulation. **Automated Operations:** Computerized cataloging and acquisitions. **Computerized Information Services:** Internal database. **Networks/Consortia:** Member of SOLINET. **Special Indexes:** Florida Baptist Historical Collection Index; Stetson Baptist Archives Index; Index to Florida Baptist Witness (online).

★ 15785 ★
Stetson University - School of Music Library (Mus)
Woodland Blvd.   Phone: (904)822-8969
De Land, FL 32720   Janice Jenkins, Music Libn.
Founded: 1936. **Staff:** Prof 1; Other 24. **Subjects:** Music. **Special Collections:** Organ music 78 rpm recordings (370). **Holdings:** 7518 books; 1345 bound periodical volumes; 12,383 scores; 9282 phonograph records; 803 pieces of old, popular sheet music; 92 cassettes; 638 compact discs; ensemble music for brass choir, band, orchestra, and choir; collected editions and monuments. **Subscriptions:** 44 journals. **Services:** Interlibrary loan; library open to the public for reference use only. **Automated Operations:** Computerized cataloging. **Computerized Information Services:** DIALOG Information Services. Performs searches on fee basis. **Networks/Consortia:** Member of SOLINET.

Ivan M. Stettenheim Library
See: **Congregation Emanu-El** (4157)

★ 15786 ★
Charles E. Stevens American Atheist Library and Archives Inc. (Rel-Phil, Soc Sci)
Box 14505   Phone: (512)458-1244
Austin, TX 78761   R. Murray-O'Hair, Dir.
Founded: 1971. **Staff:** Prof 2; Other 4. **Subjects:** Atheism, agnosticism, free thought, humanism, objectivism, rationalism, iconoclasm, ethical culturism, separation of state and church. **Special Collections:** Atheist and Freethought magazines, pre-Civil War to present. **Holdings:** 40,000 books; 2000 bound periodical volumes; 600,000 pamphlets, booklets, throw-aways, manuscripts, documents, clippings, leaflets; 600 radio tapes; 600 videotapes. **Subscriptions:** 60 journals and other serials; 10 newspapers. **Services:** Copying; library open to scholars only by appointment. **Publications:** American Atheist Library Newsletter. **Remarks:** FAX: (512)467-9525. Library located at 7215 Cameron Rd., Suite B, Austin, TX 78756.

★ 15787 ★
Stevens Clinic Hospital - Library (Med)
U.S. 52, East   Phone: (304)436-3161
Welch, WV 24801   Karen Peery, Libn.
Staff: 2. **Subjects:** Medicine, surgery, allied health sciences. **Holdings:** 800 volumes. **Services:** Copying; library open to the public with restrictions.

Stevens-German Library
See: **Hartwick College** (6944)

★ 15788 ★
Stevens Institute of Technology - Samuel C. Williams Library (Sci-Engr)
Castle Point Sta.   Phone: (201)216-5198
Hoboken, NJ 07030   Richard P. Widdicombe, Dir.
Founded: 1890. **Staff:** Prof 5; Other 4. **Subjects:** Engineering, science, mathematics, scientific management. **Special Collections:** Lieb Library of Leonardo Da Vinci; F.W. Taylor Collection (scientific management). **Holdings:** 100,000 books and bound periodical volumes; 5847 microfiche and reels of microfilm; 8 VF drawers. **Subscriptions:** 500 journals and other serials. **Services:** Interlibrary loan; copying; library open to the public. **Automated Operations:** Computerized serials, circulation, and accounting. **Computerized Information Services:** DIALOG Information Services, PFDS Online, Dow Jones News/Retrieval, WILSONLINE, BRS Information Technologies, VU/TEXT Information Services, OCLC, RLIN. Performs searches on fee basis. Contact Person: Ellen Zamir, Info.Serv.Libn., 216-5419. **Remarks:** FAX: (201)216-8319. **Staff:** Ourida Oubraham, Dp.Dir.; Robert Freeman, Tech.Serv.Libn.; Jing Wu, Automation Libn.

George B. Stevenson Library
See: Lock Haven University (9241)

J. J. Stevenson Library
See: Carnegie Museum of Natural History - Library (3085)

Stevenson Science Library
See: Vanderbilt University - Jean and Alexander Heard Library (19774)

★ 15789 ★
David M. Stewart Museum - David M. Stewart Library (Mil, Hist)
Sta. A, PO Box 12000   Phone: (514)861-6701
Montreal, PQ, Canada H3C 3P3   Eileen Meillon, Libn.
Staff: Prof 1; Other 1. Subjects: Canadian history to 1763, including military and social history; American Revolution; War of 1812; Rebellion of 1837-1838. Special Collections: Macdonald Stewart Collection (rare books, documents, engravings, and 19th century Montreal history); pre-1764 rare books (1200); maps (500). Holdings: 8000 books; 30 bound periodical volumes. Subscriptions: 30 journals and other serials. Services: Copying; consultation; library open to qualified researchers by appointment only. Publications: 4 M's Bulletins, irregular - to members; Discovery of the World: Maps of the Earth and the Cosmos (1985); From the Hearth to the Table (1986) - all both French and English editions; Madame de Pompadour et la floraison des arts (1988; French text with English translation of the historical context). Remarks: FAX: (514)284-0123.

★ 15790 ★
Stewart McKelvey Stirling Scales, Barristers & Solicitors - Library
   (Law)
1959 Upper Water St., 9th Fl.
P.O. Box 997   Phone: (902)420-3200
Halifax, NS, Canada B3J 2X2   Cynthia Murphy, Libn.
Staff: Prof 1; Other 1. Subjects: Law, legislation. Holdings: 8000 volumes. Subscriptions: 130 journals and other serials. Services: Library not open to the public. Automated Operations: Computerized cataloging and indexing. Computerized Information Services: QL Systems, CAN/LAW, WESTLAW, Info Globe, Infomart Online, FP Online, Dun & Bradstreet Business Credit Services, Insight, Canadian Tax Online; QUICKMAIL (electronic mail service). Special Indexes: Index to Halifax City ordinances (online); Opinions index (online). Remarks: FAX: (902)420-1417. Telex: 019-22593.

Stewart Resources Centre
See: Saskatchewan Teachers' Federation - Stewart Resources Centre
   (14868)

Stewart Room
See: Glassboro State College - Savitz Library (6489)

★ 15791 ★
Stichting Coordinatie Maritiem Onderzoek - Maritiem Informatie
   Centrum (Trans)
Blaak 16
Postbus 21873   Phone: 10 4130960
NL-3011 TA Rotterdam, Netherlands Cecile Berkhout
Founded: 1974. Staff: Prof 5; Other 1. Subjects: Shipbuilding, shipping, ports and waterways, inland shipping, fishing industry. Holdings: 10,000 books and reports; 5000 bound periodical volumes. Subscriptions: 350 journals and other serials; 5 newspapers. Services: Interlibrary loan; copying; SDI; library open to the public. Computerized Information Services: ESA/IRS; Marna, Shipoles (internal databases). Contact Person: Mr. G.S. Kok. Publications: Maritime Information Review; Knipseldienst Mic; summary of conferences; Symposia and Exhibitions; list of new arrivals. Remarks: FAX: 10 4112857. Telex: 26585 cmo nl.

★ 15792 ★
Stichting Het Persinstituut - Bibliotheek (Info Sci)
Oude Hoogstraat 24   Phone: 20 5253908
NL-1012 CE Amsterdam, Netherlands   J.C.E. Huizinga
Founded: 1948. Staff: Prof 3. Subjects: Communication. Holdings: 28,000 books. Subscriptions: 200 journals and other serials; 250 newspapers. Services: Interlibrary loan; copying; SDI; library open to the public. Publications: Library acquisition list. Remarks: FAX: 20 5252179.

★ 15793 ★
Stiefel Laboratories, Inc. - Research Institute Library (Med)
Oak Hill, NY 12460   Phone: (518)239-6901
                                         Joanne Fraser, Act.Libn.
Founded: 1967. Staff: 2. Subjects: Dermatology. Holdings: 300 books; 10 bound periodical volumes. Subscriptions: 40 journals and other serials. Services: Library not open to the public. Remarks: FAX: (518)239-8402.

Stiftsbibliothek Melk
See: Benedictine Monastery Melk (1716)

★ 15794 ★
Stiftung Preussischer Kulturbesitz - Bibliothek (Area-Ethnic, Law)
Potsdamer Strasse 33
Postfach 1407   Phone: 30 266-1
D-1000 Berlin 30, Germany   Dr. Richard Landwehrmeyer, Dir.Gen.
Subjects: Jurisprudence; Oriental studies; Chinese, Japanese, Korean, and Southeast Asian studies; Eastern European studies; cartography; topography. Special Collections: Manuscripts (10,221 occidental manuscripts; 3147 incunabula; 12,006 autographs; 597 collections of personal papers; rare printing and bindings, post-1500); music collection (20,892 musical manuscripts; 233,789 music printings; 13,000 libretti; musicology literature; Mendelssohn-Archive); maps and atlases, 16th-20th centuries (441,370 maps; 30,000 volumes of cartographic literature and atlases); Eastern European literature (410,000 volumes); Oriental manuscripts (32,443 manuscripts; 104,000 films of Nepalese, Indian, and Ethiopian manuscripts); East Asian literature (260,000 volumes); official publications (federal and state documents; parliamentary and government publications of 30 foreign states; publications of 60 international organizations; 30,000 volumes of old parliamentary papers); picture archive (7 million photographs, graphics, engravings, woodcuts, lithographs; 13,000 slides). Holdings: 4 million volumes; 747,900 microforms; 63,556 manuscripts. Subscriptions: 30,388 periodicals and newspapers. Services: Interlibrary loan; copying; library open to the public. Computerized Information Services: STN International, JURIS, DIMDI, DIALOG Information Services, Data-Star, Deutsches Bibliotheksinstitut (DBI), INKADATA (Informationssystem Karlsruhe), FIZ Technik, GID-IZ, ECHO (European Commission Host Organization). Performs searches on fee basis for Berlin residents. Contact Person: Johannes Ziegler, 266-2235. Publications: Jahresbericht; Mitteilungen, 3/year; additional publications available. Special Catalogs: Katalog der Bestaende zum anglo-amerikanischen Recht (catalog of library holdings in Anglo-American Law); additional catalogs available. Remarks: FAX: 30 266-2814. Telex: 1 83 160 staab d. Also Known As: Prussian Cultural Foundation. Staff: Dr. Guenter Baron, Dp.Dir.

★ 15795 ★
Stiftung Preussischer Kulturbesitz - Ibero-Amerikanisches Institut -
   Bibliothek (Area-Ethnic)
Potsdamer Strasse 37
Postfach 1247   Phone: 30 266-5
W-1000 Berlin 30, Germany   Dr. Dietrich Briesemeister, Prof.
Founded: 1930. Staff: 95. Subjects: Hispanic, Portuguese, and Latin American studies. Holdings: 680,000 volumes; 53,800 maps; 17,000 phonograph records; 22,600 slides; 4500 photographs; 35,940 microforms; 100 manuscripts; scores. Subscriptions: 4300 journals and other serials; 30 newspapers. Services: Interlibrary loan; copying; library not open to the public. Publications: List of publications - available on request. Remarks: Alternate telephone number(s): 30 266250. FAX: 30 2662814. Telex: 183160. Also Known As: Prussian Cultural Foundation. Staff: Dr. Ulrich Menge.

A.T. Still Memorial Library
See: Kirksville College of Osteopathic Medicine (8744)

A.T. Still Osteopathic Library and Research Center
See: **American Osteopathic Association** (705)

★ 15796 ★
Still Waters Foundation, Inc. - Still Waters Centre Library (Rel-Phil)
615 Stafford Ln.   Phone: (904)455-9511
Pensacola, FL 32506   Dana Faye Cobb
Staff: Prof 1; Other 3. **Subjects:** Metaphysics, parapsychology, comparative religions, earth science, space program, planetary discoveries, unexplained UFOs, astronomy, animal rights, anti-vivisection issues, animal care, preventive medicine, holistic health care theory, herbal medicine. **Special Collections:** Blavatsky; M.P. Hall; Edgar Cayce. **Holdings:** 5000 books; 2000 bound periodical volumes; 84 other cataloged items. **Subscriptions:** 23 journals and other serials. **Services:** Copying; library open to the public on a limited basis for reference use only. **Staff:** Edward Finnell.

Stillman Library
See: **Tobey Hospital** (16382)

Stillwater District 834 - Early Childhood Family Education - Toy Lending Library
See: **Early Childhood Family Education - Toy Lending Library** (5099)

★ 15797 ★
Stillwater Public Library - St. Croix Collection (Hist)
223 N. 4th St.   Phone: (612)439-1675
Stillwater, MN 55082   Sue Collins, Hist.
Founded: 1859. **Staff:** Prof 1. **Subjects:** Local history, with emphasis on Washington County. **Special Collections:** John Runk pictures (700). **Holdings:** 800 books; newspaper clippings; manuscripts; scrapbooks; city directories, 1876 to present. **Services:** Interlibrary loan; copying; room open to the public for reference use only. **Special Indexes:** Index to scrapbooks by subject; index to pictures by subject and date.

Stimson Library
See: **U.S. Army - Health Services Command - Academy of Health Sciences** (16975)

Russell L. Stimson Ophthalmic Reference Library
See: **Canada College** (2884)

Stine Laboratory Library
See: **E.I. Du Pont de Nemours & Company, Inc.** (5027)

★ 15798 ★
Stinson, Mag and Fizzell - Library (Law)
1201 Walnut, Suite 2800   Phone: (816)842-8600
Kansas City, MO 64105   Kristy Halmstad, Hd.Libn.
Staff: Prof 1; Other 3. **Subjects:** Corporate law, litigation, tax law. **Holdings:** 17,500 books. **Subscriptions:** 1200 journals and other serials. **Services:** Library not open to the public. **Computerized Information Services:** DIALOG Information Services, WESTLAW, LEXIS, Information America, Maxwell Macmillan Taxes Online.

Stirton-Kelson Library
See: **Idaho State University - Idaho Museum of Natural History** (7654)

Edward Rhodes Stitt Library
See: **U.S. Navy - National Naval Medical Center** (17805)

Stitt Library
See: **Austin Presbyterian Theological Seminary** (1314)

Edith L. Stock Memorial Library
See: **Trinity United Church of Christ** (16518)

★ 15799 ★
Stockbridge Library Association - Historical Room (Hist)
Main & Elm Sts.   Phone: (413)298-5501
Stockbridge, MA 01262   Pauline D. Pierce, Cur.
Founded: 1938. **Subjects:** Local and area history, genealogy, books by and about Stockbridge authors, Stockbridge imprints, Stockbridge Indians. **Special Collections:** Anson Clark, Jonathan Edwards, Field family, Daniel Chester French, and Sedgwick Collections. **Holdings:** 1700 books and pamphlets; vital records and cemetery inscriptions; memorabilia and manuscripts; account books. **Services:** Interlibrary loan; copying; room open to the public. **Special Catalogs:** Stockbridge Library Historical Room: An Inventory to the Collection. **Staff:** Rosemary Schneyer, Hd.Libn.

★ 15800 ★
(Stockholm) American Reference Center - USIS Library
Strandvagen 101
S-11350 Stockholm, Sweden
Defunct.

★ 15801 ★
Stockholm International Peace Research Institute - SIPRI Library and Documentation Department (Soc Sci, Mil)
Pipers vag 28
S-171 73 Solna, Sweden   Phone: 8 6559700
Founded: 1966. **Subjects:** Disarmament and arms control; military technology and expenditure; arms trade; strategy. **Holdings:** 17,000 volumes. **Subscriptions:** 350 journals and other serials; 20 newspapers. **Services:** Interlibrary loan; library open to the public by appointment. **Computerized Information Services:** Internal database. **Remarks:** FAX: 8 6559733. **Also Known As:** SIPRI. **Staff:** Olga Hardardottir, Libn.; Olle Persson, Libn.; Gunnel Von Dobeln, Hd., Lib. & Doc.Dept.

★ 15802 ★
Stockphotos - Library (Aud-Vis)
111 5th Ave., 12th Fl.   Phone: (212)529-6700
New York, NY 10003   Marion Kotbetter, Lib.Mgr.
Founded: 1967. **Staff:** Prof 4; Other 2. **Subjects:** Photography - futuristic and abstract, life styles, geographical, industrial, sports, and nature. **Services:** Library open to the public. **Automated Operations:** Computerized cataloging. **Special Catalogs:** Catalogs, 9/year - available upon request. **Remarks:** FAX: (212)477-7908. Maintained by The Image Bank.

★ 15803 ★
Stockton Developmental Center - Staff Library (Med)
510 E. Magnolia St.   Phone: (209)948-7181
Stockton, CA 95202   Walter Greening, Sr.Libn.
Staff: Prof 1. **Subjects:** Mentally handicapped, mentally ill, behavior therapy, child psychiatry, community mental health, psychiatric nursing. **Holdings:** 6700 books; 1200 bound periodical volumes; 158 reels of microfilm of periodicals; 300 audiotapes. **Subscriptions:** 100 journals and other serials. **Services:** Interlibrary loan; copying; library open to the public. **Computerized Information Services:** DIALOG Information Services. **Networks/Consortia:** Member of National Network of Libraries of Medicine - Pacific Southwest Region, Northern California and Nevada Medical Library Group (NCNMLG), North San Joaquin Health Sciences Library Consortium. **Remarks:** FAX: (209)948-7646. Maintained by California State Department of Developmental Services.

★ 15804 ★
Stockton Newspapers Inc. - Stockton Record Library (Publ)
530 Market St.   Phone: (209)546-8290
Stockton, CA 95201   Kenneth A. Mimms, Libn.
Founded: 1952. **Staff:** Prof 2; Other 1. **Subjects:** Newspaper reference topics, local history. **Holdings:** 300 books; 468 VF drawers of newspaper clippings; 42 drawers of pictures; 875 reels of microfilm. **Services:** Library open to accredited journalists. **Computerized Information Services:** Internal database. **Remarks:** FAX: (209)546-8288. **Staff:** Richard Rodriguez, Asst.Libn.

★15805★
Stockton-San Joaquin County Public Library - Local History Room
(Hist)
605 N. El Dorado   Phone: (209)944-8221
Stockton, CA 95202   Beverly Hine, Ref.Libn.
Founded: 1880. **Subjects:** History of Stockton, San Joaquin County, and gold mining regions of California, 1850 to present. **Special Collections:** Writings of local pioneers concerning library development, theater, and government; early public documents and periodicals. **Holdings:** 3000 items. **Subscriptions:** 50 journals and other serials; 10 newspapers. **Services:** Interlibrary loan; library not open to the public. **Automated Operations:** Computerized cataloging. **Remarks:** (209)944-8547.

Stoeckel Archives
See: **Ball State University - Bracken Library - Archives & Special Collections** (1438)

★15806★
Stoel, Rives, Boley, et al - Library (Law)
900 S.W. Fifth Ave., Suite 2100   Phone: (503)294-9289
Portland, OR 97204   Kay David, Libn.
Staff: Prof 3; Other 3. **Subjects:** Law. **Holdings:** 33,000 books; 1200 bound periodical volumes. **Subscriptions:** 450 journals and other serials; 10 newspapers. **Services:** Interlibrary loan (limited); copying. **Computerized Information Services:** LEXIS, WESTLAW, DIALOG Information Services, BRS Information Technologies, Information America, LEGI-SLATE, Maxwell Macmillan Taxes Online, DataTimes. **Remarks:** FAX: (503)220-2480. **Staff:** Ann W. Van Hassel; Betty Woerner.

Stohlman Library
See: **St. Elizabeth's Hospital** (14290)

Bram Stoker Memorial Association
See: **Dracula Unlimited** (4996)

★15807★
Leopold Stokowski Society of America - Stokowski Archive (Mus)
106 E. Curtis St.   Phone: (614)392-5772
Mount Vernon, OH 43050   Robert M. Stumpf, II, Pres.
Founded: 1983. **Staff:** Prof 1. **Subjects:** Leopold Stokowski, classical music. **Holdings:** 800 recordings by Stokowski, 1917-1977. **Services:** Interlibrary loan; copying; archive open to the public with restrictions. **Publications:** Maestrino, semiannual - to mailing list. **Formerly:** Located in Columbus, OH.

Stoll Memorial Library
See: **Lancaster Bible College** (8916)

Abraham Stone Library
See: **Margaret Sanger Center-Planned Parenthood New York City** (14794)

Edward Durell Stone Library
See: **Boston Architectural Center - Alfred Shaw and Edward Durell Stone Library** (1975)

Franz Theodore Stone Laboratory
See: **Ohio State University** (12309)

George G. Stone Center for Children's Books
See: **The Claremont Graduate School** (3755)

Stone Library
See: **U.S. Dept. of the Interior - Adams National Historic Site** (17245)

★15808★
Stone, Marraccini & Patterson - Library (Plan, Med)
1 Market Plaza, Spear Street Tower, Suite 400   Phone: (415)227-0100
San Francisco, CA 94105   Judy Borthwick, Libn.
Founded: 1965. **Staff:** 1. **Subjects:** Health planning, health care facilities design, medical facility planning, architecture, population statistics, urban planning. **Holdings:** 3160 books; 2100 manufacturers' catalogs; manufacturers' samples; codes; project specifications; 36 drawers of brochures, articles, documnets, reports. **Subscriptions:** 84 journals and other serials. **Services:** Library not open to the public. **Remarks:** (415)495-5091.

Olive Clifford Stone Library
See: **Butler County Historical Society** (2410)

Stone School Museum Collections
See: **Newmarket Historical Society** (11772)

Stone Science Center Library
See: **Boston University - College of Liberal Arts** (2006)

★15809★
Tavy Stone Fashion Library (Art)
Detroit Historical Museum
5401 Woodward Ave.   Phone: (313)832-0844
Detroit, MI 48202   Carol Perecman, Dir.
Founded: 1987. **Staff:** 1. **Subjects:** Fashion (antiquity to present) - American and European fashion designers, careers, advertising, merchandising, management, textiles and fabrics, cosmetics and fragrances, historic costume, fashion retailers; the business, sociological, and psychological aspects of fashion. **Holdings:** 700 books; 40 VF drawers; 10,500 slides; 10 color swatches; 21 AV programs. **Subscriptions:** 6 journals and other serials. **Services:** Copying; library open to the public with restrictions. **Remarks:** Maintained by the Fashion Group of Detroit.

★15810★
Stone and Webster Engineering Corporation - Stone and Webster Management Consultants, Inc. - Information Center (Bus-Fin, Energy)
One Penn Plaza, 30th Fl.   Phone: (212)290-6374
New York, NY 10119   Doris Einhorn, Libn.
Staff: Prof 1. **Subjects:** Accounting; engineering - chemical, civil, electrical, mechanical, nuclear power; architecture; environment; business economics; industry; construction; water resources recovery; finance; fossil power; oil; gas; public utilities; solid waste management. **Holdings:** 8000 books; corporation records; microfiche of New York and American Stock Exchanges and selected over-the-counter stocks. **Subscriptions:** 300 journals and other serials; 15 newspapers. **Services:** Interlibrary loan; center open to special libraries. **Computerized Information Services:** DIALOG Information Services, WESTLAW. **Publications:** Union List of Serials, annual. **Remarks:** FAX: (212)290-7033.

★15811★
Stone and Webster Engineering Corporation - Technical Information Center (Sci-Engr, Energy)
P.O. Box 5406   Phone: (303)741-7514
Denver, CO 80217   Donna Webster, Libn.
Founded: 1975. **Staff:** Prof 1. **Subjects:** Engineering, energy resources, power plants. **Holdings:** 5000 books; 200 reports on microfiche; plant engineering service on microfilm; 800 computer program manuals. **Subscriptions:** 100 journals and other serials. **Services:** Interlibrary loan; center not open to the public. **Automated Operations:** Computerized cataloging. **Computerized Information Services:** DIALOG Information Services. **Publications:** Acquisition list, monthly - for internal distribution only. **Remarks:** Alternate telephone number(s): 741-7700.

★15812★
Stone and Webster Engineering Corporation - Technical Information Center (Sci-Engr, Energy)
245 Summer St.   Phone: (617)589-2103
Boston, MA 02210   Audrey H. Hosford, Mgr.
Founded: 1900. **Staff:** Prof 1; Other 3. **Subjects:** Engineering - chemical, civil, nuclear, electrical, environmental, geotechnical, mechanical,

structural; electric power transmission and generation; gas processing and transmission; pulp and paper; computer systems. **Special Collections:** Visual Search microfilm file of vendors, commercial standards; microfiche file of 600,000 U.S. Nuclear Regulatory Commission reports. **Holdings:** 14,000 books and bound periodical volumes; 25,000 reports. **Subscriptions:** 1000 journals and other serials; 20 newspapers. **Services:** Interlibrary loan; copying; library open to the public by appointment. **Automated Operations:** Computerized public access catalog. **Computerized Information Services:** WESTLAW, DIALOG Information Services, ORBIT Search Service, Integrated Technical Information System (ITIS), Occupational Health Services, Inc. (OHS), NEXIS, Mead Data Central, VU/TEXT Information Services, STN International; Nuclear Regulatory Commission (NRC) Public Document Bibliographic Retrieval System (internal database); LINX Courier (electronic mail service). **Publications:** Guide to the Technical Information Center. **Special Catalogs:** List of Stone and Webster Serial and Journal Holdings. **Remarks:** FAX: (617)589-2156.

★ 15813 ★
Stonehenge Study Group - Stonehenge Viewpoint Library (Hist)
2261 Las Positas Dr.   Phone: (805)687-9350
Santa Barbara, CA 93105-4116   Joan L. Cyr, Libn.
Founded: 1970. **Staff:** Prof 2; Other 2. **Subjects:** Archeoastronomy, astroarchaeology, canopy theory, diffusion from Europe and China, Hidden Halo hypothesis, Vailian canopy research, halo motifs, pre-Columbian Ogam epigraphy sites in America, crop circles. **Special Collections:** Unpublished manuscripts and published works of Isaac N. Vail, 1840-1912 (7000 pages). **Holdings:** 15,000 books; 5000 pages on microfilm. **Subscriptions:** 32 journals and other serials. **Services:** Copying; library open to the public by appointment. **Special Catalogs:** Stonehenge Viewpoint catalog, 2/year. **Staff:** Donald L. Cyr, Ed.

★ 15814 ★
Stonehill College - Arnold B. Tofias Industrial Archives (Bus-Fin)
Washington St.   Phone: (508)230-1396
North Easton, MA 02357   Louise M. Kenneally, Archv.
Founded: 1973. **Staff:** Prof 1. **Subjects:** Business archives. **Special Collections:** O. Ames & Co. shovel papers; Union Pacific Railroad. **Holdings:** 1500 linear feet of manuscripts. **Services:** Archives open to the public by appointment. **Remarks:** FAX: (508)230-3732.

Stones River National Battlefield
See: U.S. Natl. Park Service (17783)

★ 15815 ★
Stonington Historical Society - Whitehall Library (Hist)
Box 103   Phone: (203)535-1131
Stonington, CT 06378   Norman F. Boas, Libn.
Staff: Prof 1; Other 1. **Subjects:** Genealogy, local history, biography. **Special Collections:** Stonington Banks (1822-1910). **Holdings:** 700 books; 14 feet of manuscripts; photographs; ships' logs; biographies; maps; newspaper clippings; memorabilia. **Services:** Copying; library open to the public on a limited schedule or by appointment. **Publications:** Historical Footnotes, quarterly. **Remarks:** Alternate telephone number(s): 572-8441 (librarian); 535-1131 (Historical Society).

Emery Stoops and Joyce King-Stoops Education Library
See: University of Southern California (19327)

Effie M. Storey Learning Center
See: Northwest Hospital (12051)

★ 15816 ★
Stormont-Vail Regional Medical Center - Stauffer Health Sciences Library (Med)
1500 S.W. 10th St.   Phone: (913)354-5800
Topeka, KS 66604-1353   Shirley Borglund, Dir.
Founded: 1889. **Staff:** Prof 3; Other 7. **Subjects:** Medicine, nursing. **Holdings:** 8500 books; 15,000 unbound periodicals. **Subscriptions:** 400 journals and other serials. **Services:** Interlibrary loan; copying; research; library open to the public on a limited basis. **Computerized Information Services:** MEDLARS; DOCLINE (electronic mail service). Performs searches on fee basis. **Networks/Consortia:** Member of National Network of Libraries of Medicine - Midcontinental Region, KIC Interlibrary Loan Network. **Publications:** Journal holdings list; acquisitions list - both available on request. **Remarks:** FAX: (913)354-5059. **Staff:** Carol Wadley, Asst.Dir.

Douglas Storms Memorial Library
See: York Central Hospital (20766)

★ 15817 ★
Storrowton Village Museum - Library (Hist)
1305 Memorial Ave.   Phone: (413)787-0136
West Springfield, MA 01089   Duane Groves, Lead Interp.
Founded: 1975. **Subjects:** Early America - history, costume, needlework, iron/blacksmithing, herbs, cooking. **Special Collections:** Early American school texts; genealogy collection. **Holdings:** 650 books; 250 bound periodical volumes; 3 AV programs. **Subscriptions:** 5 journals and other serials. **Services:** Copying; library open to the public by appointment.

Stott Explorers Library
See: Martin and Osa Johnson Safari Museum (8454)

Stouffer Hotels Library
See: Cornell University - Stouffer Hotels Library (4333)

★ 15818 ★
Stowe-Day Foundation - Library (Hist, Art)
77 Forest St.   Phone: (203)728-5507
Hartford, CT 06105   Joseph S. Van Why, Dir.
Founded: 1964. **Staff:** Prof 3. **Subjects:** Art, architecture, decorative arts, history, literature, slavery, women's suffrage. **Special Collections:** William H. Gillette papers, plays, and photographs, 1853-1937; suffrage papers of Isabella Beecher Hooker; Katharine S. Day Collection; Saturday Morning Club Collection; literary manuscripts of Mark Twain and Harriet Beecher Stowe; 19th century wallpaper samples. **Holdings:** 15,000 books; 1500 bound periodical volumes; 150,000 manuscripts, especially Beecher family; 1500 pamphlets, 1850-1900; 3500 miscellaneous 19th century pamphlets; photographs. **Subscriptions:** 10 journals and other serials. **Services:** Interlibrary loan; copying; library open to the public for reference use only. **Networks/Consortia:** Member of Capital Region Library Council (CRLC). **Special Catalogs:** Catalog of Nineteenth Century Chairs; American Artist Jared Flagg; William H. Gillette; microfiche of suffrage papers of Isabella Beecher Hooker. **Remarks:** The Stowe-Day Foundation maintains an active publishing program, consisting of original and reprint works, which reflects the interests of the library. **Staff:** Diana Royce, Libn.; Suzanne Zack, Asst. Libn.; Beverly Zell, Photo Libn.

Lyman Maynard Stowe Library
See: University of Connecticut - Health Center (18518)

Stoxen Library
See: Dickinson State University (4855)

★ 15819 ★
Stradley, Ronon, Stevens & Young - Law Library (Law)
2600 One Commerce Square   Phone: (215)564-8190
Philadelphia, PA 19103   Linda-Jean Schneider, Libn.
Founded: 1972. **Staff:** Prof 1; Other 2. **Subjects:** Law - corporate, Pennsylvania, tax, labor; securities. **Special Collections:** Pennsylvania Pamphlet Laws since the 1700s (200 volumes). **Holdings:** 10,000 books; 200 bound periodical volumes. **Subscriptions:** 250 journals and other serials. **Services:** Interlibrary loan; copying; library open to the public by appointment. **Computerized Information Services:** WESTLAW, LEXIS, NEXIS, DIALOG Information Services, Dun & Bradstreet Business Credit Services, Information America, Dow Jones News/Retrieval, VU/TEXT Information Services. **Publications:** Information Items, monthly - for internal distribution only. **Remarks:** FAX: (215)564-8120.

★ 15820 ★
Strasbourg Museum - Library
5 place du Chateau   Phone: 88 324895
F-67000 Strasbourg, France   Michele Chirle, Libn.
Founded: 1890. **Staff:** Prof 2; Other 2. **Subjects:** Art, fine arts, art and history of Alsace, art history, decorative arts. **Special Collections:** 19th- and early 20th-century periodicals. **Holdings:** 60,000 books; 20,000 bound periodical volumes. **Services:** Interlibrary loan; library open to the public.

Strasenburgh Planetarium
See: Rochester Museum and Science Center - Strasenburgh Planetarium (13986)

★ **15821** ★
Stratford Hall Plantation - Jessie Ball Du Pont Memorial Library (Hist)
Stratford Post Office   Phone: (804)493-8572
Stratford, VA 22558   C. Vaughan Stanley, Libn./Hist.
Founded: 1980. **Staff:** Prof 2; Other 3. **Subjects:** Lee family history; Colonial Virginia history; Robert E. Lee. **Special Collections:** Lee Family manuscripts (1200 items); Thomas Lee Shippen 1790 Inventory and Collection (600 volumes); Ditchley Collection of 16th, 17th, and 18th century books (2400 volumes); educational materials on 18th century Virginia for elementary and secondary history teachers. **Holdings:** 8000 books; 200 bound periodical volumes; 332 cubic feet of Stratford Hall archives; 125 reels of microfilm. **Subscriptions:** 32 journals and other serials. **Services:** Copying; library open to researchers by appointment. **Publications:** Jessie Ball duPont, 1884-1970. **Remarks:** Alternate telephone number(s): 493-9162. **Staff:** Judith Hynson, Archv.; Jeanne Calhoun, Res. Scholar.

★ **15822** ★
Stratford Historical Society - Library (Hist)
Box 382
967 Academy Hill   Phone: (203)378-0630
Stratford, CT 06497   Mrs. Einar M. Larson, Libn.
Founded: 1926. **Staff:** 3. **Subjects:** Stratford history and family genealogy. **Holdings:** 800 volumes; genealogical records and documents. **Services:** Library open to the public by appointment only on a limited schedule.

★ **15823** ★
Stratford Shakespearean Festival Foundation of Canada - Stratford Festival Archives (Theater)
Box 520   Phone: (519)271-4040
Stratford, ON, Canada N5A 6V2   Lisa J. Brant, Archv.
Founded: 1967. **Staff:** Prof 2. **Subjects:** The Stratford Festival, 1952 to present. **Holdings:** 1500 linear feet of production, publicity, and administration records; 1500 AV programs; 130,000 photographs and transparencies; 400,000 press clippings; 2000 costumes and property pieces; 4000 plans and design renderings. **Services:** Copying; Archives open to the public by appointment to qualified researchers. **Computerized Information Services:** D-Base III Plus, Jaques (internal databases). Performs searches on fee basis. **Publications:** Putting it Back Together (brochure). **Remarks:** Alternate telephone number(s): (416)364-8355. FAX: (519)271-2734.

Leslie M. Stratton Nursing Library
See: Methodist Hospitals of Memphis - Educational Resources Department (10187)

★ **15824** ★
Straub Clinic & Hospital, Inc. - Arnold Library (Med)
888 S. King St.   Phone: (800)522-4471
Honolulu, HI 96813   Frances P. Smith, Hd.Libn.
Founded: 1921. **Staff:** Prof 1; Other 1. **Subjects:** Medicine - internal, nuclear, pediatric, adolescent, dermatology, surgery. **Special Collections:** Straub Clinic Proceedings; reprints of articles written and published by staff members. **Holdings:** 2500 books; 100 bound periodical volumes. **Subscriptions:** 280 journals and other serials. **Services:** Interlibrary loan; copying; SDI; library open to the public for reference use only. **Computerized Information Services:** MEDLINE, DIALOG Information Services. Performs searches on fee basis. **Networks/Consortia:** Member of Medical Library Group of Hawaii. **Publications:** Straub Clinic Proceedings, quarterly - free upon request; ALS News, quarterly. **Special Indexes:** Reprint index, 1929 to present (card). **Remarks:** FAX: (808)522-3472.

Lorenz G. Straub Memorial Library
See: University of Minnesota - St. Anthony Falls Hydraulic Laboratory (18927)

Nathan Straus Young Adult Library
See: New York Public Library - Donnell Library Center (11606)

Anna Lord Strauss Library
See: Foundation for Citizen Education (6042)

★ **15825** ★
Levi Strauss & Company - Business Environment Research - Library (Bus-Fin)
1155 Battery St., LS/3
Box 7215   Phone: (415)544-6161
San Francisco, CA 94120-6935   Michelle H. Ridgway, Mgr.
Founded: 1978. **Staff:** Prof 2. **Subjects:** Apparel industry, marketing, retailing, advertising, demographics. **Holdings:** Books; reports; periodicals; subject files. **Services:** Interlibrary loan; center not open to the public. **Computerized Information Services:** DIALOG Information Services, NEXIS, Data Resources (DRI), DataTimes, Dow Jones News/Retrieval. **Remarks:** Alternate telephone number(s): 544-6167. FAX: (415)544-1481. **Staff:** Lillian Lee, Info.Spec.

★ **15826** ★
Levi Strauss & Company - Corporate Law Library (Law)
1155 Battery St. LS/7   Phone: (415)544-7064
San Francisco, CA 94111   Tom Martin, Mgr., Law Lib.
Staff: 1. **Subjects:** Antitrust law, trademarks, copyrights. **Special Collections:** U.S. Patent Office Official Gazette (1974 to present); **Holdings:** 200 books; 30 bound periodical volumes; 10 loose-leaf services; worldwide listing of trademarks and copyrights. **Subscriptions:** 15 journals and other serials; 4 newspapers. **Services:** Interlibrary loan; copying. **Remarks:** FAX: (415)544-7650. Telex: 278435.

★ **15827** ★
Strawbery Banke Museum - Thayer Cumings Library and Archives (Hist, Art)
454 Court St.
Box 300   Phone: (603)433-1100
Portsmouth, NH 03802   Greg Colati, Libn./Archv.
Founded: 1974. **Staff:** Prof 1. **Subjects:** Portsmouth history, decorative arts, architecture, archeology, horticulture. **Special Collections:** Business and family papers of Governor Ichabod and Sarah Parker Rice Goodwin, 1790s-1890s (8 cubic feet); Lowell Boat Shop Collection, 1881-1914 (5 boxes); papers of and relating to Thomas Bailey Aldrich; papers of William and Charles Neil, Capt. John Hill, and Stephen Chase; photograph collection of late 19th to mid-20th century Portsmouth. **Holdings:** 7000 books; 45 cubic feet of manuscripts; 45 reels of microfilm. **Subscriptions:** 45 journals and other serials. **Services:** Interlibrary loan; copying; library open to the public for reference use only. **Formerly:** Its Thayer Cumings Historical Reference Library.

★ **15828** ★
Strayer College - Learning Resources Center (Educ)
3045 Columbia Pike   Phone: (703)892-5100
Arlington, VA 22204   Deborah Jackson, Mgr.
Founded: 1984. **Staff:** 4. **Subjects:** Accounting, business administration, data processing. **Holdings:** 3000 books; 4 VF drawers of pamphlets; 2000 microfiche. **Subscriptions:** 95 journals and other serials; 10 newspapers. **Services:** Interlibrary loan; copying; center open to the public. **Computerized Information Services:** DIALOG Information Services. **Publications:** Library handbook. **Remarks:** FAX: (703)769-2677. Center is an extension campus facility that is a part of the main library located at the Washington, DC, campus.

★ **15829** ★
Strayer College - Wilkes Library (Bus-Fin)
1025 15th St., N.W.   Phone: (202)408-2412
Washington, DC 20005   David A. Moulton, Libn.
Staff: Prof 1; Other 10. **Subjects:** Business administration, data processing, accounting. **Holdings:** 16,500 books; 16 drawers of pamphlets. **Subscriptions:** 300 journals and other serials; 15 newspapers. **Services:** Interlibrary loan; copying; library open to the public. **Computerized Information Services:** DIALOG Information Services. **Networks/Consortia:** Member of Virginia Library Network. **Publications:** Library Handbook, annual. **Remarks:** FAX: (202)289-1831. Figures include holdings at all satellite campus Learning Resources Centers.

Strecker Museum Library
See: **Baylor University** (1608)

★ 15830 ★
Streich Lang - Library (Law)
100 W. Washington, Suite 2100   Phone: (602)229-5325
Phoenix, AZ 85008   Winifred Edwards, Libn.
Staff: Prof 1; Other 2. **Subjects:** Law - corporate, tax, real estate, banking.
Holdings: 15,000 volumes. **Subscriptions:** 217 journals and other serials; 5
newspapers. **Services:** Library not open to the public. **Automated
Operations:** Computerized cataloging. **Computerized Information Services:**
LEXIS, WESTLAW, DIALOG Information Services, Dow Jones News/
Retrieval, VU/TEXT Information Services. **Remarks:** FAX: (602)229-5690.

Richard Lee Strickler Research Center
See: **Ocean County Historical Society** (12238)

★ 15831 ★
Stroh Brewery Company - Stroh Technical Library
100 River Place
Detroit, MI 48207
Founded: 1982. **Subjects:** Brewing, chemistry, biosciences. **Special
Collections:** Food science. **Holdings:** Figures not available. **Remarks:**
Currently inactive.

Stroke Information and Referral Center
See: **National Stroke Association** (11308)

Joseph G. Stromberg Library of the Health Sciences
See: **Swedish Covenant Hospital** (15920)

G.F. Strong Centre
See: **British Columbia Rehabilitation Society - G.F. Strong Centre** (2172)

Kate Strong Historical Library
See: **Museums at Stony Brook** (10927)

★ 15832 ★
The Strong Museum - Library (Art, Hist)
1 Manhattan Sq.   Phone: (716)263-2700
Rochester, NY 14607   Kathleen D. Lazar, Lib.Dir.
Founded: 1972. **Staff:** Prof 3; Other 1. **Subjects:** U.S. social and cultural
history; 19th and 20th centuries; 19th and 20th century American domestic
life. **Special Collections:** Children's literature from late 19th and early 20th
centuries (400 titles); 19th and 20th century publishers' bindings (600);
miniature books (680); fore-edge paintings (74); Winslow Homer's library
(20 volumes). **Holdings:** 40,000 books; 8000 trade catalogs. **Subscriptions:**
225 journals and other serials. **Services:** Interlibrary loan; copying; library
open to the public. **Automated Operations:** Computerized cataloging.
Networks/Consortia: Member of Rochester Regional Library Council
(RRLC), SUNY/OCLC Library Network. **Publications:** New Acquisitions
list, monthly - for internal distribution only. **Remarks:** FAX: (716)263-2493.
Staff: Anna K. Wang, Asst.Libn./Cat.; Carol Sandler, Asst.Libn./Ref./
Archv.

Strosacker Library
See: **Northwood Institute** (12091)

Strughold Aeromedical Library
See: **U.S. Air Force - Air Force Materiel Command - Human Systems
    Division - Armstrong Laboratory** (16798)

★ 15833 ★
**Strybing Arboretum Society - Helen Crocker Russell Library of
    Horticulture** (Biol Sci)
Golden Gate Park
9th Ave. & Lincoln Way   Phone: (415)661-1514
San Francisco, CA 94122   Barbara M. Pitschel, Hd.Libn.
Founded: 1972. **Staff:** Prof 2. **Subjects:** Horticulture, plant propagation,
landscape gardening, flora of Mediterranean climates, plant hunting, history
of gardening, children and gardens, ethnobotany, botanical illustration.
Holdings: 14,000 books, including 300 rare volumes; 1000 bound periodical
volumes; 1 shelf of William Hammond Hall Archives; 2000 slide
transparencies of plants; 21 VF drawers of brochures and pamphlets; 2000
old and current nursery catalogs. **Subscriptions:** 400 journals and other
serials. **Services:** Copying; slide duplication; library open to the public.
Computerized Information Services: OCLC. **Networks/Consortia:** Member
of Council on Botanical Horticultural Libraries. **Publications:** Bibliography
series. **Special Catalogs:** Catalog of slide collection (card); catalog of book
collection (card); catalog of old and current nursery catalog collections.
Special Indexes: Printed index to current nursery catalog; printed indexes
to periodicals and vertical file. **Remarks:** "The basic purpose of the library
is to assist the public with information about plants and their uses and to
provide information about the Strybing Arboretum and Botanical
Gardens."

★ 15834 ★
Sts. Cyril and Methodius Byzantine Catholic Seminary - Library (Rel-
    Phil)
3605 Perrysville Ave.   Phone: (412)321-8383
Pittsburgh, PA 15214-2297   Msgr. Russell A. Duker, S.E.O.D.,
                                       Seminary Rector
Founded: 1950. **Staff:** Prof 1; Other 2. **Subjects:** Theology, philosophy,
Byzantine Catholic studies, Ruthenian studies, Slavic studies, Byzantine art
and history. **Special Collections:** Byzantine and Ruthenian theological
studies; Slavonic rare books. **Holdings:** 16,710 books; 3192 bound periodical
volumes; 2 VF drawers of pamphlets. **Subscriptions:** 60 journals and other
serials. **Services:** Library open to the public with permission of rector of the
seminary or head librarian. **Special Catalogs:** Language file; rare book file.
Staff: Sr. M. Demetria Zober, O.S.B.M., Hd.Libn.

★ 15835 ★
Sts. Mary and Elizabeth Hospital - Health Sciences Library (Med)
1850 Bluegrass Ave.   Phone: (502)361-6428
Louisville, KY 40215   Wanda Polley, Libn.
Founded: 1897. **Staff:** Prof 1; Other 1. **Subjects:** Medicine and nursing.
Holdings: 1800 books; 1600 bound periodical volumes; 2 VF drawers of
clippings and pamphlets. **Subscriptions:** 200 journals and other serials.
Services: Interlibrary loan; copying; library open to hospital staff and
students from surrounding area only. **Computerized Information Services:**
MEDLINE. **Publications:** Bibliographies; Library Handbook, semiannual.

★ 15836 ★
STS Consultants Ltd. - Library (Sci-Engr)
111 Pfingsten Rd.   Phone: (708)272-6520
Northbrook, IL 60062   William J. Burns, Libn.
Founded: 1987. **Staff:** 1.5. **Subjects:** Civil engineering - geotechnical,
structural, materials, environmental; water resources; hydropower.
Holdings: 5383 volumes; 1600 other cataloged items. **Subscriptions:** 265
journals and other serials. **Services:** Interlibrary loan; copying; library open
to the public by appointment. **Automated Operations:** Computerized public
access catalog, cataloging, serials, and circulation. **Computerized
Information Services:** OCLC, DIALOG Information Services, American
Society of Civil Engineers (ASCE) Database, Ground Water On-Line,
MEDLARS, Chemical Information Systems, Inc. (CIS), STN International.
Networks/Consortia: Member of ILLINET, North Suburban Library
System (NSLS). **Remarks:** FAX: (312)498-2721.

George D. Stuart Research Library
See: **Valley News Dispatch** (19736)

John Stuart Research Laboratories
See: **Quaker Oats Company** (13565)

Stuart Library of Western Americana
See: University of the Pacific - Holt-Atherton Department of Special Collections (19172)

Lyle Stuart Library of Sexual Science
See: Institute for Advanced Study of Human Sexuality - Exodus Trust Archives of Erotology - Research Library (7896)

Stuart Memorial Library
See: Alta Bates-Herrick Hospitals (418)

Avery Stubbs Memorial Archives
See: Western Hennepin County Pioneers Association, Inc. (20248)

Stuck Medical Library
See: Mount Clemens General Hospital (10802)

★ 15837 ★
Studebaker National Museum Inc. - Research Library (Hist)
525 S. Main St.   Phone: (219)284-9714
South Bend, IN 46601   Ron Radecki, Exec.Dir.
Staff: Prof 1. **Subjects:** Studebaker corporation and vehicles, South Bend industries, automotive history. **Special Collections:** Studebaker Archives (3000 linear feet); Oliver Photographic Collection (10,000 negatives, circa 1900-1950, from Oliver Corporation, manufacturers of farm equipment). **Holdings:** 300 books; 60 reels of microfilm; 15 VF drawers of trade catalogs and advertising; 12 VF drawers of photographs. **Subscriptions:** 27 journals and other serials. **Services:** Library open to the public by appointment (researchers only).

Student Volunteer Movement - Archives
See: Yale University - Divinity School Library (20708)

Students Struggle for Soviet Jewry
See: Center for Russian & East European Jewry (3291)

★ 15838 ★
Studium Biblicum Franciscanum - Library (Rel-Phil)
Via Dolorosa
P.O. Box 19424   Phone: 2 282936
91140 Jerusalem, Israel   Fr. Tomislav Vuk, Libn.
Subjects: Biblical and Christian archeology, Judeo-Christianity, Bible. **Holdings:** 30,000 volumes. **Subscriptions:** 380 journals and other serials. **Services:** Copying; library open to the public on a limited schedule. **Publications:** Liber Annuus, annual; Collectio Maior, Collectio Minor, Analecta, Museum, irregular - distributed by Franciscan Printing Press. **Remarks:** Alternate telephone number(s): 2 280271. Sponsored by Franciscan Custody of the Holy Land. **Also Known As:** Franciscan Biblical Institute.

★ 15839 ★
Study and Social Action Center - Library (Soc Sci)
Rua Aristides Novis 101
Federation 40000
Salvador, Bahia, Brazil   Phone: 71 2471232
Subjects: Social action - economics, education, history, religion, psychology, sociology. **Holdings:** 21,000 volumes.

Stuhr Museum
See: Hall County Museum - Stuhr Museum (6844)

Richard J. Stull Memorial Learning Resources Center
See: American College of Healthcare Executives (535)

★ 15840 ★
Sturdy Memorial Hospital - Health Sciences Library (Med)
211 Park St.   Phone: (508)222-5200
Attleboro, MA 02703   Juliet I. Mansfield, Libn.
Founded: 1962. **Staff:** Prof 1; Other 2. **Subjects:** Medicine, nursing. **Special Collections:** Rare editions of medical and surgical books (82 volumes). **Holdings:** 866 books; 584 bound periodical volumes; 8 VF drawers of articles, clippings, pamphlets. **Subscriptions:** 132 journals and other serials. **Services:** Interlibrary loan; copying; library open to the public for reference use only. **Networks/Consortia:** Member of Southeastern Massachusetts Consortium of Health Science Libraries (SEMCO), Massachusetts Health Sciences Libraries Network (MaHSLiN), Association of Rhode Island Health Sciences Librarians (ARIHSL), North Atlantic Health Science Libraries (NAHSL). **Remarks:** FAX: (508)226-4383.

Sturgeon Music Library
See: Mount Union College (10821)

Gertrude Sturges Memorial Library
See: Group Health Association of America, Inc. (6766)

Gertrude E. Sturges Memorial Library
See: Rhode Island (State) Department of Health (13879)

★ 15841 ★
Sturgis Library (Hist)
Main St.
Box 606   Phone: (508)362-6636
Barnstable, MA 02630   Susan R. Klein, Chf.Libn.
Founded: 1863. **Staff:** Prof 4; Other 3. **Subjects:** Genealogy, Barnstable County history, maritime history, 19th century English and American literature. **Special Collections:** Stanley W. Smith Collection (original Cape Cod documents and land deeds); Kittredge Collection (maritime history). **Holdings:** 43,960 books; 200 bound periodical volumes; 400 sound recordings, tapes, and cassettes; 125 reels of microfilm; 60 flat pictures; 1500 land deeds; 25 maps and charts. **Subscriptions:** 105 journals and other serials. **Services:** Interlibrary loan; copying; service to homebound and institutionalized; library open to the public; special collections accessible only on fee basis. **Automated Operations:** Computerized cataloging and circulation. **Publications:** Vital Records (newsletter), quarterly; A Short History of the Sturgis Library; Cape Cod Mariner (journal of the Kittredge Maritime Research Center). **Remarks:** This library has been declared the oldest library building in the U.S.; its original structure was built in 1644. **Staff:** Diane Nielsen, Staff Libn.; Alexandra Crane, Staff Libn.; Myrna Crowley, Children's Libn.

★ 15842 ★
Mary Riley Styles Public Library - Local History Collection (Hist)
120 N. Virginia Ave.   Phone: (703)241-5140
Falls Church, VA 22046   Dagmar McGill, Local Hist.Libn.
Founded: 1899. **Staff:** Prof 1; Other 3. **Subjects:** Falls Church current events and history. **Holdings:** 1880 books and public records; 46 boxes of newspapers, newsletters, periodicals; 6000 photographs; 20,000 negatives; 270 maps; 130 oral history tapes; 53 reels of microfilm; 40 VF drawers of archival materials; 6 scrapbooks; 800 slides; 12 videotapes. **Subscriptions:** 11 journals and other serials. **Services:** Copying; collection open to the public. **Automated Operations:** Computerized indexing (in progress). **Special Indexes:** Index to Focus - City government newsletter. **Remarks:** Alternate telephone number(s): 241-5030. FAX: (703)241-5144.

Subbarow Memorial Library
See: American Cyanamid Company - Lederle Laboratories Division (559)

Submarine Force Library & Museum
See: U.S. Navy (17907)

★ 15843 ★
Suburban Hennepin Regional Park District - Lowry Nature Center -
Library (Biol Sci)
Box 270   Phone: (612)472-4911
Victoria, MN 55386   Roger Stein, Outdoor Educ.Supv.
Founded: 1970. Staff: Prof 3; Other 7. Subjects: Natural history,
ornithology, mammalogy, ichthyology, herpetology, botany and forestry,
wildlife management, ecology, entomology. Holdings: 650 books; 4 VF
drawers of natural history material, organizational material, maps,
pamphlets. Subscriptions: 12 journals and other serials. Services: Library
open to the public for reference use only.

★ 15844 ★
Suburban Temple - Gries Library (Rel-Phil)
22401 Chagrin Blvd.   Phone: (216)991-0700
Beachwood, OH 44122   Tamara M. Katz, Libn.
Staff: Prof 1. Subjects: Judaica. Holdings: 6000 books; 100 phonograph
records; 4 VF drawers. Subscriptions: 10 journals and other serials.
Services: Interlibrary loan; copying; library open to the public by
appointment. Publications: New acquisitions list, semiannual - for internal
distribution only.

★ 15845 ★
(Suceava) Casa Corpului Didactic - Biblioteca (Soc Sci, Educ, Hum)
Strada Stefan cel Mare 38   Phone: 987 15798
Suceava, Romania   Georgeta Rata, Dir.
Founded: 1970. Staff: Prof 2. Subjects: Psychology, pedagogy,
methodology, textbooks; literary criticism. Special Collections: Revista
Fundatiilor Regale (The Royal Foundation Review). Holdings: 50,000
books; 1750 bound periodical volumes. Services: Interlibrary loan; library
open to the public with restrictions. Computerized Information Services:
Internal database. Contact Person: Adriana Iuzic, Comp.Libn.

★ 15846 ★
Sudbury General Hospital - Hospital Library (Med)
700 Paris St., Station B   Phone: (705)675-4710
Sudbury, ON, Canada P3E 3B5   D.M. Hawryliuk, Libn.
Founded: 1950. Staff: Prof 1. Subjects: Clinical medicine. Special
Collections: Archival history of hospital (8 volumes of newspaper clippings).
Holdings: 1200 books; 1300 bound periodical volumes. Subscriptions: 145
journals and other serials. Services: Interlibrary loan; copying; SDI; library
open to the public with restrictions. Computerized Information Services:
NLM. Publications: Health Science Serials. Remarks: FAX: (705)675-4728.

★ 15847 ★
Suermondt-Ludwig Museum - Library (Art)
Komphausbad str.19
W-5100 Aachen, Germany   Phone: 241 4324420
Founded: 1877. Staff: Prof 1. Subjects: Medieval art, arts and crafts.
Holdings: 50,000 books; 40 bound periodical volumes; 1900 old magazines;
monographs. Subscriptions: 10 journals and other serials. Services:
Copying; library open to the public with restrictions. Remarks: FAX: 241
408709.

★ 15848 ★
Suffolk Academy of Medicine - Library (Med)
850 Veterans Memorial Hwy.   Phone: (516)724-7970
Hauppauge, NY 11788   Joyce A. Bahr, Act.Dir.
Founded: 1966. Staff: 1.5. Subjects: Medicine, dentistry, nursing, history.
Special Collections: Rare book collection. Holdings: 2500 books; 10,000
periodical volumes; 90 bulletin collections; 24 shelves of pamphlets.
Subscriptions: 350 journals and other serials. Services: Interlibrary loan;
copying; library open to the public for reference use only. Automated
Operations: Computerized cataloging. Computerized Information Services:
DIALOG Information Services, MEDLARS. Performs searches on fee
basis. Networks/Consortia: Member of Long Island Library Resources
Council, National Network of Libraries of Medicine - Middle Atlantic
Region.

★ 15849 ★
Suffolk County Historical Society - Library (Hist)
300 W. Main St.   Phone: (516)727-2881
Riverhead, NY 11901   Joanne J. Brooks, Libn.
Founded: 1886. Staff: 12. Subjects: Suffolk County and Long Island history
and genealogy. Special Collections: Revolutionary War documents of
Colonel Josiah Smith; Modern Times (Brentwood); Fullerton negatives,
circa 1900; E.T. Talmage weaving collection; Professional Resources
(Museum) Collection. Holdings: 15,000 volumes; microfilm; manuscripts;
clippings; records; documents; photographs; fiber swatch-books.
Subscriptions: 12 journals and other serials. Services: Copying; library open
to the public with restrictions. Publications: Register. Special Indexes:
Index to scrapbooks, glass negatives (card); vital statistics (card); index to
documents (card); abstracts of documents (book).

★ 15850 ★
Suffolk Marine Museum - Hervey Garrett Smith Research Library
(Hist)
P.O. Box 184   Phone: (516)567-1733
West Sayville, NY 11796   David Van Popering, Res.Libn.
Founded: 1966. Staff: Prof 1. Subjects: Boat building, yachting, racing,
shipwrecks, U.S. Life Saving Service, shellfishing, history of the America's
Cup Race, the Merchant Marine, U.S. Navy, and U.S. Coast Guard. Special
Collections: Ships' logs (4); vessel construction plans; U.S. Life Saving
Service records; historical photograph collection. Holdings: 1700 books; 50
bound periodical volumes; 2 slide programs; 40 navigational charts; glass
plate negatives. Subscriptions: 11 journals and other serials. Services:
Copying; library open to members by appointment. Computerized
Information Services: Smart System Database, Librarian's Helper (internal
databases). Staff: Ruth Dougherty.

★ 15851 ★
Suffolk University - Law Library (Law)
41 Temple St.   Phone: (617)573-8177
Boston, MA 02114   Michael Slinger, Law Libn.
Founded: 1906. Staff: Prof 7; Other 9. Subjects: Law. Holdings: 223,000
books and bound periodical volumes; 62,000 volumes on microfiche; U.S.
Government documents depository. Subscriptions: 900 journals and other
serials; 20 newspapers. Services: Interlibrary loan; copying; library open to
the public for use of government documents. Automated Operations:
Computerized cataloging and acquisitions. Computerized Information
Services: LEXIS, WESTLAW, OCLC, DIALOG Information Services.
Networks/Consortia: Member of NELINET, Inc., New England Law
Library Consortium (NELLCO). Staff: Susan Sweetgall, Dir., Pub.Serv.;
Patricia I. Brown, Assoc. Law Libn.; Madeleine Wright, Govt.Docs.Libn.;
Cecelia Tavares, Asst.Dir., Tech.Serv.

★ 15852 ★
Suffolk University - Mildred F. Sawyer Library - Collection of Afro-
American Literature (Area-Ethnic)
8 Ashburton Pl.   Phone: (617)573-8532
Boston, MA 02108   E.G. Hamann, Dir.
Founded: 1937. Staff: Prof 6; Other 6. Subjects: Afro-American literature
- bibliography, history, biography, literary criticism; New England Afro-
American writers. Holdings: 5000 books; 200 bound periodical volumes.
Subscriptions: 20 journals and other serials. Services: Interlibrary loan;
copying; collection open to the public for reference use only. Automated
Operations: Computerized cataloging and indexing. Computerized
Information Services: BRS Information Technologies, ABI/INFORM,
Academic Index. Networks/Consortia: Member of NELINET, Inc.,
Fenway Library Consortium (FLC). Publications: Black Writers in New
England, a Bibliography, 1985 - for sale; Acquisitions List, annual - free
upon request. Staff: James R. Coleman, Assoc.Dir.; Joseph Middleton,
Ref.Libn.; Kathleen Maio, Ref.Libn.; Elisa McKnight, Ref.Libn.; Roberta
Schwartz, Asst.Dir.

★ 15853 ★
The Sugar Association, Inc. - Library (Food-Bev)
1101 15th St., N.W., No. 600   Phone: (202)785-1122
Washington, DC 20005   Suzanne Arnold, Libn.
Founded: 1943. Staff: Prof 1. Subjects: Sugar, nutrition and health, food
technology. Holdings: 1500 books; 1000 bound periodical volumes; 50 VF
drawers of pamphlets, clippings, patents, miscellaneous documents.
Subscriptions: 100 journals and other serials; 7 newspapers. Services:
Interlibrary loan; copying; library open to the public. Remarks: FAX:
(202)785-5019.

Sugar Industry Research Institute
See: **Mauritius Sugar Industry Research Institute (9852)**

Suicide Information and Education Centre
See: **Canadian Mental Health Association, Alberta Division (2960)**

Suid-Afrikaanse Biblioteek
See: **South Africa - South African Library (15386)**

Alice Phelan Sullivan Library
See: **Society of California Pioneers (15312)**

★15854★
Sullivan County Law Library (Law)
Court House   Phone: (717)946-5201
Laporte, PA 18626   Lynne Stabryla, Lib.Dir.
Subjects: Law. **Holdings:** 1455 books. **Subscriptions:** 2 journals and other serials. **Services:** Copying; library open to the public upon request to the Commissioner's Office.

★15855★
Sullivan and Cromwell - Library (Law)
125 Broad St.   Phone: (212)558-4000
New York, NY 10004   Christine M. Fisher, Dir. of Lib.Serv.
Founded: 1879. **Staff:** 12. **Subjects:** Law. **Special Collections:** Corporate law; international law; early New York laws (pre-1900s). **Holdings:** 50,000 volumes. **Subscriptions:** 1500 journals and other serials; 50 newspapers. **Services:** Library not open to the public. **Computerized Information Services:** LEXIS, NEXIS, WESTLAW, Dow Jones News/Retrieval, LRS, LEGI-SLATE, Information America, IDDIS, DIALOG Information Services. **Publications:** Legislative Bulletin; Database News. **Remarks:** FAX: (212)558-3346. **Staff:** Stephanie Heacox, Asst.Libn.; Michael R. Normile, Ref.Libn.; Lucy A. Redmond, Ref.Libn.; Bruno Zovich, Cat.Libn.

★15856★
Sullivan and Cromwell - Washington D.C. Library (Law)
1701 Pennsylvania Ave., N.W.   Phone: (202)956-7538
Washington, DC 20006   Denise Noller, Libn.
Founded: 1977. **Staff:** Prof 1; Other 2. **Subjects:** Law - antitrust, securities, tax; trade regulation. **Holdings:** 9000 books; 1000 bound periodical volumes; documents; microforms. **Subscriptions:** 150 journals and other serials; 8 newspapers. **Services:** Interlibrary loan; SDI; library open to the public with permission. **Computerized Information Services:** LEXIS, NEXIS, DIALOG Information Services, Dow Jones News/Retrieval, WESTLAW.

Sullivan Medical Library
See: **St. Anne's Hospital (14231)**

★15857★
P.H. Sullivan Foundation - Museum & Genealogy Library (Hist)
225 W. Hawthorne St.
P.O. Box 182   Phone: (317)873-4900
Zionsville, IN 46077   Edie Kellar Mahaney, Exec.Dir.
Founded: 1972. **Staff:** 2. **Subjects:** Boone County, Indiana history and genealogy, U.S. genealogy. **Special Collections:** Name file of Boone County residents, 1854 to present (50,000); Boone County newspapers, 1854 to present (complete set; microfilm); antique book collection. **Holdings:** 1700 books; 375 reels of microfilm. **Services:** Copying; library open to the public for reference use only.

★15858★
Sulphur Institute - Library (Sci-Engr)
1140 Connecticut Ave., N.W., Suite 612
Washington, DC 20036   Phone: (202)331-9660
Staff: 10. **Subjects:** Sulphur in agriculture and industry. **Holdings:** 500 books; 200 bound periodical volumes; 20 VF drawers. **Services:** Interlibrary loan; library open to the public by appointment. **Remarks:** FAX: (202)293-2940.

Sulzbacher Memorial Library
See: **Spring Grove Hospital Center (15596)**

Sulzberger Journalism Library
See: **Columbia University - Sulzberger Journalism Library (4026)**

★15859★
Summer Institute of Linguistics - Dallas Library (Hum, Soc Sci)
7500 W. Camp Wisdom Rd.   Phone: (214)709-2416
Dallas, TX 75236   Claudia D. Griffith, Hd.
Founded: 1972. **Staff:** Prof 4; Other 3. **Subjects:** Linguistics, anthropology, literacy, Biblical studies. **Special Collections:** Summer Institute of Linguistics archives (9000 items on microfiche); James Redden Collection (African languages and linguistics; 700 volumes). **Holdings:** 20,000 books; 1300 bound periodical volumes; 5500 vertical files. **Subscriptions:** 160 journals and other serials. **Services:** Interlibrary loan; copying; library open to the public for reference use only. **Computerized Information Services:** DIALOG Information Services. Performs searches. **Publications:** Acquisitions list, quarterly. **Remarks:** FAX: (214)709-2433. **Staff:** Dorothy L. White, Cat.; Joyce Hooley, Cat.; Ron Pappenhaggen, Ref.

W.W. Summerville Medical Library
See: **Bethany Medical Center (1781)**

★15860★
Summit Christian College - S.A. Lehman Memorial Library (Rel-Phil)
919 W. Rudisill Blvd.   Phone: (219)456-2111
Fort Wayne, IN 46807   Wava Bueschlen, Dir.
Founded: 1905. **Staff:** Prof 3; Other 2. **Subjects:** Theology, education. **Holdings:** 58,591 books; 2391 bound periodical volumes; 6816 teaching aids. **Subscriptions:** 367 journals and other serials. **Services:** Interlibrary loan; copying; library open to the public with restrictions. **Automated Operations:** Computerized cataloging. **Computerized Information Services:** OCLC; CD-ROM. Performs searches. **Networks/Consortia:** Member of INCOLSA. **Publications:** Library Handbook. **Remarks:** FAX: (219)456-2117. **Staff:** Michael VanHuisen; Ruth Silvers.

Summit County Public Library
See: **Akron-Summit County Public Library (174)**

★15861★
Sumter Area Technical College - Library (Bus-Fin, Sci-Engr)
506 N. Guignard Dr.   Phone: (803)778-1961
Sumter, SC 29150   Chris Bruggman, Coord.
Founded: 1963. **Staff:** Prof 2; Other 2. **Subjects:** Business, civil engineering, secretarial science, marketing, machine shop technology, automotive mechanics, criminal justice, accounting, electricity, natural resources management, nursing, welding, climate control, electronics, paralegal science, fashion merchandising, environmental quality control technology, drafting, tool and dye technology, industrial maintenance. **Holdings:** 18,592 books; 618 bound periodical volumes; 74 journal titles on microfiche; 250 VF drawers; 967 AV programs. **Subscriptions:** 225 journals and other serials; 16 newspapers. **Services:** Interlibrary loan; copying; library open to the public for reference use only. **Publications:** Workstudy Handbook; Library Handbook; Policies and Procedures Manual. **Special Catalogs:** Catalog to AV programs.

★15862★
Sumter Regional Hospital - Medical Library (Med)
100 Wheatley Dr.   Phone: (912)924-6011
Americus, GA 31709   Claudia LeSueur
Staff: 1. **Subjects:** Medicine, nursing, and allied health sciences. **Holdings:** Figures not available. **Services:** Interlibrary loan; library not open to the public. **Remarks:** FAX: (912)928-2020.

★ 15863 ★

Sun Chemical Corporation - Technical Information Center (Sci-Engr)
631 Central Ave.   Phone: (201)933-4500
Carlstadt, NJ 07072   Kendal Funk, Tech.Info.Spec.
Founded: 1938. **Staff:** Prof 1; Other 1. **Subjects:** Graphic arts, polymer chemistry, photochemistry, organic chemistry. **Holdings:** 2500 books; 3000 bound periodical volumes; 48 shelf feet of unbound official gazettes; 200 boxes of unbound periodicals; 7 VF drawers of reports. **Subscriptions:** 200 journals and other serials; 6 newspapers. **Services:** Center not open to the public. **Computerized Information Services:** DIALOG Information Services, PFDS Online, STN International, Info Globe. **Publications:** Library Bulletin, weekly - for internal distribution only. **Remarks:** FAX: (201)933-5658. Telex: 201 671 1405.

★ 15864 ★

Sun Financial Group - Reference Library (Bus-Fin)
1 Sun Life Executive Park   Phone: (617)237-6030
Wellesley Hills, MA 02181   Pamela A. Mahaney, Libn.
Founded: 1973. **Staff:** Prof 2. **Subjects:** Insurance, management, data processing, law, labor, taxation, accounting, pensions, real estate, salesmanship. **Special Collections:** Life Insurance Marketing and Research Association Collection; insurance codes for all states. **Holdings:** 15,000 books; 29 VF drawers. **Subscriptions:** 850 journals and other serials; 14 newspapers. **Services:** Interlibrary loan; copying; library open to the public with restrictions. **Computerized Information Services:** DIALOG Information Services, OCLC, LEXIS, NEXIS; electronic mail. **Networks/Consortia:** Member of NELINET, Inc. **Publications:** Selected Articles of Interest, weekly; Subject Alert, irregular; Book News, monthly; LIMRA Accessions, bimonthly. **Remarks:** FAX: (617)237-0707. **Staff:** Merrill H. Walsh, Asst.Libn.

★ 15865 ★

Sun Life of Canada - Research Library (Bus-Fin)
200 University Ave.   Phone: (416)359-3341
Toronto, ON, Canada M5H 3C7   Elizabeth Gibson, Mgr.
Founded: 1980. **Staff:** Prof 2; Other 5. **Subjects:** Life insurance, management, financial services, pensions, investments, actuarial, real estate. **Holdings:** 10,000 books; annual reports. **Subscriptions:** 700 journals and other serials; 20 newspapers. **Services:** Interlibrary loan; copying; library open to the public by appointment. **Automated Operations:** Computerized cataloging, circulation, and serials. **Computerized Information Services:** DIALOG Information Services, Info Globe, BRS Information Technologies, TEXTLINE, Dow Jones News/Retrieval, The Financial Post Information Service, Canada Systems Group (CSG), Infomart Online, UTLAS, WILSONLINE, Canadian Financial Database (C.F.D.), Report on Business Corporate Database; Envoy 100 (electronic mail service). Performs searches on fee basis. **Publications:** List of new books, bimonthly - distributed internally and to selected libraries; List of Periodicals, annual. **Remarks:** FAX: (416)359-3346. **Staff:** Faye Mitchell, Libn.

★ 15866 ★

The Sun News - Library (Publ)
P.O. Box 406   Phone: (803)626-0372
Myrtle Beach, SC 29578   Barbara Horner
Staff: Prof 1. **Subjects:** Newspapers. **Holdings:** 450 books; 1500 microfiche; 350 reels of microfilm. **Subscriptions:** 5 journals and other serials; 8 newspapers. **Services:** Library open to the public. **Computerized Information Services:** VU/TEXT Information Services; Atex (internal database). **Remarks:** FAX: (803)626-0356. Toll-free telephone number(s): (800)868-6866.

Sun News Library
See: **Naperville Sun** (10974)

★ 15867 ★

Sun Refining & Marketing Co. - Library and Information Center (Energy)
Box 1135   Phone: (215)447-1722
Marcus Hook, PA 19061   Dale Rodenhaver
Staff: Prof 3; Other 5. **Subjects:** Business, economics, marketing, finance, petroleum refining, chemistry, engineering. **Holdings:** 35,000 books; 14,000 bound periodical volumes; 65 VF drawers of pamphlets; 40 VF drawers of patents; 40 VF drawers of pamphlets (uncataloged); API project reports;

14,000 government documents; microfilm; microcards. **Subscriptions:** 800 journals and other serials; 19 newspapers. **Services:** Interlibrary loan; copying; library open to scholars for research by application. **Automated Operations:** Computerized public access catalog and serials. **Computerized Information Services:** DIALOG Information Services, ORBIT Search Service, STN International, Questel, Dow Jones News/Retrieval, NEXIS, VU/TEXT Information Services, OCLC. **Publications:** Book Accession List, monthly; Pamphlet Accession List, weekly - both for internal distribution only. **Remarks:** FAX: (215)447-1645. **Staff:** Phoebe Cassidy, Res.Libn.

★ 15868 ★

Sun-Sentinel/Fort Lauderdale News - Library (Publ)
101 N. New River Drive   Phone: (305)356-4741
Fort Lauderdale, FL 33301   Bob Isaacs
Founded: 1947. **Staff:** Prof 6; Other 7. **Subjects:** Newspaper reference topics. **Holdings:** 2000 books; 125 bound periodical volumes; 636 archival items; 600 microfiche; 2135 reels of microfilm. **Subscriptions:** 50 journals and other serials; 25 newspapers. **Services:** Library not open to the public; searches may be performed through outside research service on a fee basis. **Computerized Information Services:** VU/TEXT Information Services, DIALOG Information Services, NewsBank, Inc.; ATEX (internal database). **Contact Person:** Gail Bulfin, Asst.Mgr. **Remarks:** FAX: (305)356-4748.

★ 15869 ★

Sunbury Shores Arts and Nature Centre, Inc. - Sunbury Shores Library (Art, Env-Cons)
139 Water St.
P.O. Box 100   Phone: (506)529-3386
St. Andrews, NB, Canada E0G 2X0   Margaret R. Peterson, Dir.
Founded: 1965. **Founded: Staff:** 2. **Subjects:** Art history, crafts, natural science, ecology, photography. **Special Collections:** Kroenberger Memorial Collection (fine art); Vaughan Collection (fine art and natural science). **Holdings:** 800 books; 15 sleeves of slides. **Subscriptions:** 10 journals and other serials. **Services:** Interlibrary loan; copying; library open to members and area schools.

★ 15870 ★

Suncor Inc. - Library (Sci-Engr)
112 4th Ave., S.W.
P.O. Box 38   Phone: (403)269-8128
Calgary, AB, Canada T2P 2V5   Diane King, Libn.
Founded: 1959. **Staff:** 1. **Subjects:** Petroleum industry, geology, geophysics, engineering, economics, office management, statistics. **Holdings:** 500 books; 700 government publications; 3000 geological and engineering reports; 100 annual reports of other companies. **Subscriptions:** 100 journals and other serials. **Services:** Interlibrary loan; copying; library open to the public for reference use only. **Automated Operations:** INMAGIC. **Computerized Information Services:** DIALOG Information Services, CAN/OLE; internal database. Performs searches. **Publications:** Library Newsletter, quarterly - for internal distribution only. **Remarks:** FAX: (403)269-6200.

★ 15871 ★

Sundstrand Aerospace - Information Resource Center (Sci-Engr)
4747 Harrison Ave.
Box 7002   Phone: (815)226-6752
Rockford, IL 61125   D'Ann Hamilton, Info.Spec.
Staff: Prof 1. **Subjects:** Aviation design, research, and manufacturing. **Holdings:** 3500 books; government and corporate reports; specifications and standards; vendor catalogs on microfilm. **Subscriptions:** 180 journals and other serials. **Services:** Interlibrary loan; library not open to the public. **Automated Operations:** Computerized public access catalog and indexing. **Computerized Information Services:** DIALOG Information Services, Teltech; CD-ROM. **Networks/Consortia:** Member of Northern Illinois Library System (NILS). **Remarks:** FAX: (815)226-7488. **Formerly:** Sundstrand Aviation. **Staff:** Janet Larson, Asst.Info.Spec.

★ 15872 ★

Sundstrand Data Control - Engineering Library (Sci-Engr)
15001 N.E. 36th St., MS 1
P.O. Box 97001   Phone: (206)885-8420
Redmond, WA 98073-9701   Doris M. Smart, Engr.Res.Libn.
Founded: 1957. **Staff:** Prof 1. **Subjects:** Aerospace, electronics, avionics systems, instruments, passenger entertainment systems, industrial

components. **Special Collections:** Arinc data. **Holdings:** 1500 books; military specifications and standards on CD-ROM and microfilm; vendor catalogs on microfilm; commercial standards on CD-ROM and microfilm; FAA data on microfilm. **Subscriptions:** 110 journals and other serials. **Services:** Interlibrary loan; library not open to the public. **Automated Operations:** Computerized public access catalog, cataloging, and acquisitions. **Computerized Information Services:** DIALOG Information Services, OCLC, WLN; internal database; electronic mail. Performs searches. **Networks/Consortia:** Member of Western Library Network (WLN), OCLC Pacific Network. **Publications:** Engineering Library Directory. **Special Catalogs:** Bibliographies, periodicals, holdings catalog by author, title, and subject. **Remarks:** FAX: (206)885-2061. Telex: RCA 286144.

★ 15873 ★
SunHealth Corp. - Corporate Resource Center (Med)
Box 668800   Phone: (704)529-3324
Charlotte, NC 28266-8800   T. Joan Crouze, Mgr., Corp.Res.Ctr.
Founded: 1978. **Staff:** Prof 2; Other 3. **Subjects:** Hospitals, health care, safety, marketing. **Holdings:** 4000 books; 210 bound periodical volumes; 3750 confidential reports; 30 magazine volumes on microfiche; 10 sound slide sets; 150 audiocassettes; 64 videocassettes. **Subscriptions:** 477 journals and other serials. **Services:** Interlibrary loan; copying; library open to the public at librarian's discretion. **Automated Operations:** Computerized public access catalog and serials. **Computerized Information Services:** BRS Information Technologies, ORBIT Search Service, Dow Jones News/Retrieval; internal databases. Performs searches on fee basis. **Remarks:** FAX: (704)527-3654. **Formerly:** SunHealth, Inc. - SunHealth Resource Center. **Staff:** Felicia S. Lee, Cat./Libn.

★ 15874 ★
Sunkist Growers, Inc. - Research Library
760 E. Sunkist St.
Ontario, CA 91761   Phone: (714)983-9811
Founded: 1939. **Subjects:** Citrus and citrus products technology; chemistry - organic, analytical, food. **Holdings:** 1100 books; 1230 bound periodical volumes; 2000 reprints. **Remarks:** Currently inactive.

Sunland Center at Gainseville - Tacachale Library
See: **Tacachale Library** (15977)

★ 15875 ★
Sunnybrook Health Science Centre - Health Sciences Library (Med)
2075 Bayview Ave.
North York, ON, Canada M4N   Phone: (416)480-6100
  3M5   Linda McFarlane, Dir., Hea.Sci.Lib.
Founded: 1968. **Staff:** Prof 3; Other 7. **Subjects:** Medicine and nursing, hospital administration. **Holdings:** 8000 books; 19,000 bound periodical volumes; 2500 audiotapes; 260 videotapes; 15 drawers of pamphlets. **Subscriptions:** 535 journals and other serials. **Services:** Interlibrary loan; copying; SDI; library open to area medical practitioners. **Computerized Information Services:** MEDLINE, DIALOG Information Services, BRS Information Technologies; Envoy 100 (electronic mail service). **Remarks:** FAX: (416)480-6006. Electronic mail address(es): OTSMC (Envoy 100). **Formerly:** Sunnybrook Medical Centre. **Staff:** Davida Glazer.

★ 15876 ★
Sunnyvale Patent Information Clearinghouse (Law)
1500 Partridge Ave., Bldg. 7   Phone: (408)730-7290
Sunnyvale, CA 94087   Beverley J. Simmons, Dir. of Libs.
Founded: 1965. **Staff:** Prof 2; Other 5. **Subjects:** U.S. patents, 1790 to present; patent, trademark, and copyright registration information. **Holdings:** 7800 volumes; 4.8 million patents; Federal Trademark Register; Report of the Commissioner of Patents, 1790-1835; Official Gazette, 1836 to present; list of patentees, 1870 to present. **Subscriptions:** 5 journals and other serials. **Services:** Copying; mail service for patent copies; open to the public. **Computerized Information Services:** CD-ROM (U.S. Patent Classification System). **Networks/Consortia:** Member of South Bay Cooperative Library System (SBCLS). **Publications:** Information brochures; guides for conducting a patent search and trademark search. **Remarks:** Maintained by Sunnyvale Public Library. Serves as a self-search center. FAX: (408)735-8762. **Staff:** Karen Willes, Supv.Libn.

Sunnyvale Public Library - Friends of the Western Philatelic Library
See: **Friends of the Western Philatelic Library** (6177)

★ 15877 ★
Sunrise Museums, Inc. - Library (Art, Sci-Engr)
746 Myrtle Rd.
Charleston, WV 25314   Phone: (304)344-8035
Founded: 1961. **Subjects:** Fine arts, natural sciences, anthropology. **Holdings:** 3000 volumes. **Subscriptions:** 25 journals and other serials. **Services:** Library open to the public for reference use only.

★ 15878 ★
Sunsearch, Inc. - Library (Env-Cons)
P.O. Box 590
Guilford, CT 06437   Phone: (203)453-6591
Subjects: Energy-conversion technology, especially solar and thermal conversion. **Holdings:** 500 books, journals, and reports. **Computerized Information Services:** Internal database (U.S. weather data).

★ 15879 ★
Sunset Trading Post-Old West Museum - Library (Hist)
Rte. 1   Phone: (817)872-3777
Sunset, TX 76270   Jack Glover, Owner
Founded: 1960. **Staff:** 1. **Subjects:** Barbed wire, frontier, American Indian, cowboys and cattlemen, Civil War, Western painting, county history, guns and knives. **Special Collections:** Barbed Wire. **Holdings:** 2500 books; 200 pamphlets; clippings; drawings; Indian artifacts; Bronzes of the West by Jack Glover; unpublished stories; pictures; negatives. **Subscriptions:** 25 journals and other serials. **Services:** Library open to the public with restrictions. **Publications:** Barbed Wire Bible VIII, 1991 - for sale. **Remarks:** FAX: (817)872-3777. **Staff:** Nelson Glover, Lib.Dir.

SUNY
See: **State University of New York** (15719)

SUNY - Downstate Medical Center - Department of Psychiatry Library
See: **State University Health Science Center at Brooklyn - Department of Psychiatry Library** (15717)

SUNY at Albany
See: **State University of New York at Albany** (15726)

SUNY at Binghamton
See: **State University of New York at Binghamton** (15729)

SUNY at Buffalo
See: **State University of New York at Buffalo** (15733)

SUNY at Stony Brook
See: **State University of New York at Stony Brook** (15746)

Suomen Geodeettinen Laitos
See: **Finnish Geodetic Institute** (5717)

Suomen Standardisoimisliitto SFS
See: **Finnish Standards Association SFS** (5721)

★ 15880 ★
Suomi College - Finnish-American Heritage Center (Hist, Area-Ethnic)
Hancock, MI 49930-1882   Phone: (906)487-7347
                                     E. Olaf Rankinen
Founded: 1932. **Staff:** Prof 1; Other 1. **Subjects:** Suomi Synod and Finnish-American church history; Finnish Americans, especially in the Upper Midwest; temperance; mutual benefit societies; Finns; Finland. **Holdings:** 18,000 books, periodicals, and pamphlets; 1000 cassette tapes and transcripts; 12 linear feet of photographs; 400 linear feet of manuscript collections; college records; organizational and personal papers; 186 journals; 107 newspapers. **Subscriptions:** 29 journals and other serials; 6 newspapers. **Services:** Copying; archives open to the public for reference use only. **Remarks:** Alternate telephone number(s): (906)487-7347; (906)487-7273. FAX: (906)487-7300. **Staff:** Lorraine Uitto Richards, Asst.Archv.

★ 15881 ★
Super Valu Stores, Inc. - Technical Manuals Library
11840 Valley View Rd.
Eden Prairie, MN 55344
Defunct.

★ 15882 ★
Superstock - Three Lions - Picture Library (Aud-Vis)
11 W. 19th St., 6th Fl.   Phone: (212)633-0300
New York, NY 10011-4214   Beth Hinckley, Dir.
Subjects: Fine art, religion, and general interest stock photography.
Holdings: Figures not available. **Remarks:** FAX: (212)633-0408. Toll-free
telephone number(s): (800)828-4545.

★ 15883 ★
Supplee Memorial Presbyterian Church - Library (Rel-Phil)
855 Welsh Rd.   Phone: (215)646-4123
Maple Glen, PA 19002   Suzanne P. Stahler, Libn.
Founded: 1982. **Staff:** 3. **Subjects:** Religion, social concerns, children's
books. **Holdings:** 2165 books; tapes; college and seminary catalogs; religious
periodicals. **Subscriptions:** 13 journals and other serials. **Services:** Library
open to the public. **Staff:** Sylvia Eagano, Dir. of Christian Educ.

Supply and Services Canada
See: **Canada - Supply and Services Canada** (2861)

Supreme Court of Canada
See: **Canada - Supreme Court of Canada** (2863)

Supreme Court of the United States
See: **U.S. Supreme Court** (17946)

★ 15884 ★
(Surabaya) Perhimpunan Persahabatan Indonesia-Amerika - USIS
   Collection (Educ)
Jalan Dr Sumitomo, No. 110
Surabaya, Indonesia
Remarks: Maintained or supported by the U.S. Information Agency. Focus
is on materials that will assist peoples outside the United States to learn
about the United States, its people, history, culture, political processes, and
social milieux.

★ 15885 ★
Surface Mining Research Library (Energy)
Box 5024   Phone: (304)768-0489
Charleston, WV 25361   Norman Kilpatrick, Dir.
Founded: 1971. **Staff:** Prof 1. **Subjects:** Surface coal mining, deep coal
mining, coal prices, international coal competition, utility reform, energy
policy, acid rain, credibility of green house effect. **Holdings:** 500 volumes;
200 8x10 photos, 400 3x5 photos, and 1000 slides of surface coal mining,
newspaper columns on energy issues. **Subscriptions:** 6 journals and other
serials; 3 newspapers. **Services:** Copying; consulting; expert testimony.
Publications: Slide show on modernsurface mining methods - for sale.

Surratt Museum
See: **Maryland (State) National Capital Park & Planning Commission**
   (9766)

Surrey Centennial Museum - Archives
See: **Surrey Museum & Archives** (15886)

★ 15886 ★
Surrey Museum & Archives (Hist)
6022 176th Ave.   Phone: (604)574-5744
Surrey, BC, Canada V3S 4E7   Jacqueline O'Donnell, Archv.
Founded: 1958. **Staff:** Prof 2. **Subjects:** Local history. **Special Collections:**
Historic maps and photographs. **Holdings:** 1000 books; school registers;
municipal records; maps; photographs. **Services:** Copying; archives open to
the public.

★ 15887 ★
Surveyors Historical Society - Library (Geog-Map)
P.O. Box 11154   Phone: (206)378-2300
Lansing, MI 48901   John L. Thalacker, Sec.Treas.
Founded: 1977. **Subjects:** Surveying. **Holdings:** 100 books, manuals, and
catalogs; archives. **Services:** Library not open to the public. **Computerized
Information Services:** Internal database. **Special Catalogs:** Artifact
collection catalog (online).

★ 15888 ★
Survival Research Foundation - Library (Rel-Phil)
Box 63-0026   Phone: (305)936-1408
Miami, FL 33163-0026   Arthur S. Berger, Pres.
Founded: 1971. **Subjects:** Life after death, hauntings, apparitions,
poltergeists, reincarnation, out-of-body experiences. **Holdings:** 200 volumes;
teaching programs for nurses and seriously ill patients. **Formerly:** Located
in Pembroke Pines, FL.

★ 15889 ★
Susquehanna County Historical Society and Free Library Association
   (Hist)
Monument Square   Phone: (717)278-1881
Montrose, PA 18801   Susan Stone, Dir.
Founded: 1907. **Staff:** Prof 1; Other 16. **Subjects:** Genealogy, natural
science, art, music, humanities, religion. **Holdings:** 75,105 volumes; 475
genealogical items. **Subscriptions:** 125 journals and other serials; 7
newspapers. **Services:** Interlibrary loan; copying; library open to the public
with restrictions. **Remarks:** FAX: (717) 278-9336. **Staff:** Elizabeth Smith,
Cur.Hist.Soc.; Amy LaRue, Asst.Libn.; Hilary Caws-Elwitt, Ref.Libn.

★ 15890 ★
Susquehanna County Law Library (Law)
Court House
P.O. Box 218   Phone: (717)278-4600
Montrose, PA 18801   Mary Foster, Lib.Dir.
Subjects: Law. **Services:** Library not open to the public.

★ 15891 ★
Sussex County Historical Society - Library (Hist)
82 Main St.
Box 913   Phone: (201)383-6010
Newton, NJ 07860   Barbara Lewis Waskowich, Cur./Sec.
Founded: 1904. **Subjects:** New Jersey and Sussex County history,
archeology, genealogy, antiques. **Special Collections:** Roy Papers. **Holdings:**
2000 books; 300 genealogical files. **Services:** Library open to the public on
a limited schedule.

★ 15892 ★
Sussex County Law Library (Law)
Courthouse Box 390   Phone: (302)856-5483
Georgetown, DE 19947   Mary Tylecki Dickson, Libn.
Subjects: Law. **Remarks:** No further information was supplied by
respondent.

★ 15893 ★
Sussex County Law Library (Law)
Court House
3 High St.   Phone: (201)579-0702
Newton, NJ 07860   Barbara J. Smith, Libn.
Subjects: Law. **Holdings:** 45,000 books; 5000 bound periodical volumes.
Services: Copying; library open to the public. **Remarks:** Alternate telephone
number(s): (201)579-0701; 579-0900.

★ 15894 ★
Sutherland, Asbill & Brennan - Library (Law)
1275 Pennsylvania Ave., N.W.   Phone: (202)383-0450
Washington, DC 20004   Robert S. Stivers, Mgr., Lib.Serv.
Staff: Prof 2; Other 2. **Subjects:** Law - tax, energy, insurance, securities.
Special Collections: History of tax legislation, 1921 to present. **Holdings:**
30,000 books. **Subscriptions:** 1500 journals and other serials. **Services:**
Interlibrary loan; copying; library open to the public with librarian's
permission. **Computerized Information Services:** DIALOG Information
Services, OCLC, WESTLAW, Dow Jones News/Retrieval, LEXIS.
Remarks: FAX: (202)637-3593. **Staff:** Ronald Pramberger, Leg.Libn.;
Charles Roberts, Pub.Serv.Libn.

★ 15895 ★
Sutherland, Johnston, MacLean - Library (Law)
777 Dunsmuir St., Suite 1600
P.O. Box 10425
Pacific Centre　　　　　　　　　　　Phone: (604)688-0047
Vancouver, BC, Canada V7Y 1K4　　　　Pamela Barr, Libn.
Staff: Prof 1; Other 1. **Subjects:** Law - corporate, tax, estate and trust; business; forestry. **Holdings:** 100 books; 400 bound periodical volumes; 18 loose-leaf services; corporate annual reports. **Subscriptions:** 15 journals and other serials. **Services:** Library open to clients only. **Computerized Information Services:** QL Systems. **Publications:** Accessions list, bimonthly - for internal distribution only. **Remarks:** FAX: (604)688-0094.

Ladislav Sutnar Archive
See: **Smithsonian Institution Libraries - Cooper-Hewitt Museum of Design - Doris & Henry Dreyfuss Memorial Study Center (15274)**

Adolph Sutro Archive
See: **University of San Francisco - Special Collections Department/ Donohue Rare Book Room (19290)**

Sutro Library
See: **California State Library (2547)**

★ 15896 ★
Sutter County Law Library (Law)
Court House　　　　　　　　　　　Phone: (916)741-7360
Yuba City, CA 95991　　　　Pamela J. Mastelotto, Law Libn.
Staff: 1. **Subjects:** Law. **Holdings:** 7699 volumes. **Services:** Library open to the public. **Remarks:** FAX: (916)741-7214.

William M. Suttle Medical Library
See: **Hinds General Hospital (7228)**

Svenska Institutet i Rom - Istituto Svedese di Studi Classici - Biblioteca
See: **Swedish Institute of Classical Studies - Library (15925)**

★ 15897 ★
Svenska Litteratursallskapet I Finland - Allmanna Arkivet (Hum)
Sornaisten Rantatie 25　　　　　　　Phone: 90 7731077
SF-00500 Helsinki, Finland　　　　　　　David Lee
Founded: 1974. **Subjects:** Origin and evolution of Swedish culture in Finland; cultural history; personal history. **Special Collections:** Arne Jorgensen Book Collection (Finland-Swedish fiction, Finnish professional literature, foreign books in specific fields from the 17th century to present; 7500 volumes); J.L. Runenberg Collection (originals and translations of works and articles by Runeberg and his circle; 2000 works); Society of Swedish Literature in Finland Archives; Borga Collection (collections of Johan Ludvig, Fredrika and Walter Runegerg); records from the 1660s to present. **Holdings:** 1000 books; 300 running meters of manuscripts; 750 microfiche; letters; diaries; photographs; tape files; periodical, theater, business, estate archives. **Subscriptions:** 60 journals and other serials; 10 newspapers. **Services:** Copying; archives open to the public with restrictions. **Automated Operations:** Computerized cataloging. **Special Catalogs:** Printed main catalog, 1986; detail catalog of single collections. **Remarks:** FAX: 90 7731527. The task of the Allmanna Arkivet is "to collect evidence of the origin and evolution of the Swedish culture in Finland," taking perticular account of cultural and personal history as well as literary research. The Archives' manuscripts are housed in University of Helsinki - Library. **Also Known As:** Society of Swedish Literature in Finland - General Archives.

★ 15898 ★
Svenska Litteratursallskapet I Finland - Folk kulturs-arkivet (Area-Ethnic)
Sornas Strandvag 25　　　　　　　Phone: 90 7731077
SF-00500 Helsinki, Finland　　　　　　　David Lee
Founded: 1937. **Staff:** 12. **Subjects:** Finland-Swedes - folk culture, ethnology, folkloristics, dialectology. **Special Collections:** Ostrobothnian

Archives of Traditional Culture in Vasa. **Holdings:** 250,000 pages of manuscripts, from 1870s to present; 3200 tapes; transcripts; 150,000 photographs and reproductions; 200,000 negatives; 1000 drawings; 31 ethnographic films; 1300 microfiche; 190 running meters of reference literature. **Subscriptions:** 125 journals and other serials; 14 newspapers. **Services:** Copying; archives open to the public for reference use only. **Publications:** Finlands svenska folkdiktning (Swedish Folk Poetry in Finland); Folklivsstudier (Ethnological Studies); Meddelanden fran Folkkulturarkivet (Reports of the Folk Culture Archives); Studier i nordisk filologi (Studies in Nordic Languages); SLS-Arkiv (newsletter), annual; Finlandssvensk folkmusik (Finland-Swedish folk music record series). **Special Catalogs:** Tape and photograph registers; song, folk belief, folk medicine, and folk custom registers; registers and distribution maps of dialect words and phenomena of linguistic geography. **Special Indexes:** Katalog over Folkkultursarkivets och Folkmalskommissionens samlingar, 1978 (index of the first 1000 collections). **Remarks:** FAX: 90 7731527. The goals of the Folk-kulturs-arkivet are "collecting, preparing and publishing evidence of the folk culture and language of the Finland-Swedes." The telephone number for the Ostrobothnian Archives is 116 305. **Also Known As:** Society of Swedish Literature in Finland - Folk Culture Archives.

★ 15899 ★
Sverdrup Corporation - Technical Library (Sci-Engr)
801 N. 11th Blvd.　　　　　　　Phone: (314)436-7600
St. Louis, MO 63101　　　　　　　R.A. Bodapati, Libn.
Founded: 1966. **Staff:** Prof 1. **Subjects:** Engineering - civil, structural, electrical, mechanical, environmental; architecture; urban and regional planning. **Holdings:** 8000 books. **Subscriptions:** 80 journals and other serials. **Services:** Interlibrary loan (limited); library not open to the public.

George Sverdrup Library and Media Center
See: **Augsburg College (1293)**

Sveriges Riksradio - Referensbiblioteket
See: **Swedish Broadcasting Corporation (15918)**

SVP Korea - Joong Ang Daily News
See: **Joong Ang Daily News (8480)**

Swain Hall Library
See: **Indiana University (7803)**

Swain Library of Chemistry and Chemical Engineering
See: **Stanford University (15659)**

Robert S. Swain Natural History Library
See: **Thornton W. Burgess Society, Inc. - Museum and Nature Center (2371)**

James Swann Archives
See: **Cedar Rapids Museum of Art - Herbert S. Stamats Art Library (3186)**

Gloria Swanson Archives
See: **University of Texas at Austin - Harry Ransom Humanities Research Center (19392)**

Swanson Resource Room
See: **Kansas State University - Grain Science and Industry (8566)**

★ 15900 ★

Swarthmore College - Cornell Library of Science and Engineering (Sci-Engr)
500 College Ave.   Phone: (215)328-8261
Swarthmore, PA 19081-1399   Emi K. Horikawa, Sci.Libn.
Founded: 1982. **Staff:** Prof 1; Other 2. **Subjects:** Mathematics, physics, chemistry, engineering, biology, astronomy, computer science. **Holdings:** 37,000 books; 28,400 bound periodical volumes and periodicals on microfilm. **Subscriptions:** 805 journals and other serials. **Services:** Interlibrary loan (through main library); copying; library open to the public for reference use only. **Computerized Information Services:** DIALOG Information Services, BRS Information Technologies, OCLC, Chemical Abstracts Service (CAS); CD-ROM (WILSONDISC); BITNET (electronic mail service). **Networks/Consortia:** Member of PALINET.

★ 15901 ★

Swarthmore College - Daniel Underhill Music Library (Mus)
500 College Ave.   Phone: (215)328-8231
Swarthmore, PA 19081-1399   George K. Huber, Mus.Libn.
Founded: 1973. **Staff:** Prof 1. **Subjects:** Music, dance. **Holdings:** 4800 books; 1100 bound periodical volumes; 9000 scores; 14,000 phonograph records. **Subscriptions:** 40 journals and other serials. **Services:** Interlibrary loan; library open to the public with a fee charged in some cases. **Computerized Information Services:** OCLC; InterNet (electronic mail service). **Networks/Consortia:** Member of PALINET. **Special Catalogs:** Catalog for chamber music (card). **Remarks:** Electronic mail address(es): GHUBER1@CC.SWARTHMORE.EDU (InterNet).

★ 15902 ★

Swarthmore College - Friends Historical Library (Hist, Rel-Phil)
500 College Ave.   Phone: (215)328-8496
Swarthmore, PA 19081-1399   J. William Frost, Dir.
Founded: 1871. **Staff:** Prof 5; Other 1. **Subjects:** Quaker faith, history, and genealogy; Quaker social concerns - abolition of slavery, race relations, women's rights, peace, education, prison reform, mental health, Indian rights, temperance. **Special Collections:** Friends Meeting records (4000 volumes of manuscripts); Whittier (1700 books, 900 manuscripts); Quaker manuscripts (277 collections); Lucretia Mott manuscripts (7 boxes); Samuel Janney manuscripts (7 boxes); Elias Hicks manuscripts (12 boxes); journals of Quaker ministers (18 boxes); Charles F. Jenkins Autograph Collection (6 boxes). **Holdings:** 39,192 books; 1897 bound periodical volumes; 240 boxes of pictures; 81 chart case drawers of pictures, maps, broadsides, deeds, genealogical charts, marriage certificates; 2536 reels of microfilm; 750 microfiche. **Subscriptions:** 185 journals and other serials. **Services:** Interlibrary loan; copying; library open to the public. **Computerized Information Services:** OCLC; InterNet (electronic mail service). **Networks/Consortia:** Member of PALINET, Philadelphia Area Consortium of Special Collections Libraries (PACSCL). **Publications:** Descriptive leaflet; Guide to the Manuscript Collections of Friends Historical Library of Swarthmore College, 1982; Guide to the Records of Philadelphia Yearly Meeting, 1989. **Special Indexes:** Quaker picture index (card); William Wade Hinshaw Index to Quaker Meeting Records (card); checklists for Quaker manuscript collections (loose-leaf); index to Whittier Collection (card). **Remarks:** FAX: (215)328-8673. Electronic mail address(es): MCHIJIO1@CC.SWARTHMORE.EDU (InterNet). **Staff:** Mary Ellen Chijioke, Cur.; Patricia C. O'Donnel, Archv.; Nancy P. Speers, Archv.; Claire Shetter, Cat.; Patricia A. Silva, Cat.Archv.

★ 15903 ★

Swarthmore College - Peace Collection (Soc Sci)
500 College Ave.   Phone: (215)328-8557
Swarthmore, PA 19081-1399   Dr. Wendy E. Chmielewski, Cur.
Founded: 1930. **Staff:** Prof 4; Other 1. **Subjects:** History of peace movement, nonviolence, pacifism, conscientious objection and conscription, disarmament, women and peace and justice. **Special Collections:** Jane Addams (350 books; 13,000 manuscripts; 170 document boxes of clippings and pictures); A.J. Muste (23 feet of manuscripts, correspondence, writings); Emily Greene Balch (36 feet of manuscripts, correspondence, writings); Fellowship of Reconciliation; Friends Committee on National Legislation; Clergy and Laity Concerned; Women's International League for Peace and Freedom; War Resisters League; SANE; SANE/FREEZE; National Interreligious Service Board for Conscientious Objectors; Women Strike for Peace; CCCO/An Agency for Military and Draft Counseling; World Conference on Religion and Peace; World Peace Foundation. **Holdings:** 12,000 books; 504 bound periodical volumes; 4500 peace posters and broadsides; 1500 reels of microfilm; 155 document groups. **Subscriptions:**

410 journals and other serials. **Services:** Interlibrary loan; copying; library open to the public with restrictions on some collections. **Automated Operations:** Computerized public access catalog (TRIPOD), cataloging, and serials. **Computerized Information Services:** OCLC; BITNET, InterNet (electronic mail services). **Networks/Consortia:** Member of PALINET, Philadelphia Area Consortium of Special Collections Libraries (PACSCL). **Publications:** Guide to Swarthmore College Peace Collection; Guide to Sources on Women in the Swarthmore College Peace Collection. **Special Catalogs:** Checklists for major collections (loose-leaf). **Special Indexes:** Index for Jane Addams correspondence (card); indexes for archival collections (card). **Remarks:** FAX: (215)328-8673. Electronic mail address(es): CHMIELEWSKI@SWARTHMR (BITNET); WCHMIEL/1@SWARTHMORE.EDU (InterNet). **Staff:** Barbara Addison, Cat.; Eleanor M. Barr, Archv.; Martha P. Shane, Archv.; Kate Myer, Per.Asst.

Minor Swarthout Memorial Library
See: **Glenn H. Curtiss Museum of Local History (4493)**

★ 15904 ★

Ambrose Swasey Library (Rel-Phil)
1100 S. Goodman St.   Phone: (716)271-1320
Rochester, NY 14620   Norman J. Kansfield, Libn.
Founded: 1819. **Staff:** Prof 5; Other 5. **Subjects:** World religions, Christian history, theology, worship and liturgy, marriage and family, Bible. **Special Collections:** J.A.W. Neander Library; Karpinsky Collection of Reformation materials; McQuaid Papers; Fulton J. Sheen Archives. **Holdings:** 277,500 books and bound periodical volumes; 18,240 microforms; 2690 audio recordings; 587 theses. **Subscriptions:** 889 journals and other serials. **Services:** Interlibrary loan; copying; library open to the public for reference use only. **Automated Operations:** Computerized cataloging and acquisitions. **Computerized Information Services:** OCLC, BRS Information Technologies. **Networks/Consortia:** Member of Rochester Regional Library Council (RRLC). **Publications:** Book Lists, monthly; Guide to Ambrose Swasey Library. **Remarks:** FAX: (716)271-2166. Maintained by Colgate Rochester Divinity School/Bexley Hall/Crozer Theological Seminary and St. Bernard's Institute. **Staff:** Christopher Brennan, Asst.Libn. for Tech.Serv.; Gail McClain, Cat.

★ 15905 ★

Swaziland National Library Service (Area-Ethnic, Info Sci)
P.O. Box 1461   Phone: 42633
Mbabane, Swaziland   Mr. B.J.K. Kingsley, Dir.
Founded: 1986. **Staff:** 4. **Subjects:** General collection. **Special Collections:** Swaziana; United Nations documents and government publications (20,000). **Holdings:** 140,000 books. **Subscriptions:** 200 journals and other serials. **Services:** Interlibrary loan; copying; SDI; library open to the public. **Publications:** Accessions lists; National Bibliography; SDI lists. **Special Catalogs:** Subject catalogs. **Remarks:** FAX: 43863. Telex: 2270 WD. Maintains 13 urban and branch libraries. **Staff:** Ms. Dudu C. Fakudze, Sr.Libn.; Ms. Dikeledi Kunene, Libn.; Mr. Mike Gyimah, Libn.; Ms. Nomsa V. Mkhwanazi, Libn.

Sweden - Embassy of Sweden
See: **Embassy of Sweden - Library-Information Center (5325)**

★ 15906 ★

Sweden - Karolinska Institute - Department of Stress Research - Library (Med)
P.O. Box 60205   Phone: 8 7286400
S-104 01 Stockholm, Sweden   Tuula Nikkanen, Libn.
Staff: 2. **Subjects:** Stress, psychosocial medicine. **Holdings:** 2000 volumes; 24,000 reprints, monographs, reports (online). **Subscriptions:** 50 journals and other serials. **Services:** Copying; library open to the public at librarian's discretion. **Computerized Information Services:** Internal database. **Remarks:** Sponsored by Swedish Medical Research Council and Swedish Work Environment Fund. FAX: 8 344143. Telex: 12442 FOTEX. **Also Known As:** National Institute for Psychosocial Factors and Health.

★ 15907 ★
Sweden - Karolinska Institute - Library and Information Center (Med)
c/o Arnold Johannson, Info.Spec.
Box 60201   Phone: 8 7286400
S-104 01 Stockholm, Sweden   Teodora Oker-Blom
Founded: 1810. **Staff:** Prof 57; Other 26. **Subjects:** Medicine, dentistry, nursing, occupational safety and health. **Holdings:** 550,000 volumes; 875 manuscripts. **Subscriptions:** 3600 journals and other serials. **Services:** Interlibrary loan; copying; SDI; library open to the public. **Automated Operations:** Computerized public access catalog and cataloging. **Computerized Information Services:** MEDLARS, NLM, DIALOG Information Services, ESA/IRS, MEDLINE, CANCERLIT (Cancer Literature), Drugline, SWEMED, Nordser, Riskline, MBline, Arbline, NIOSHTIC, CISILO, CATS, Spriline; produces MIC-KIBIC. Performs searches on fee basis. Contact Person: Elisabeth Kjellander, M.D., 8 7288000. **Publications:** KIBIC-rapport, irregular; MIC News, bimonthly. **Special Catalogs:** List BioMed (Nordic Union Catalogue of Serials in Biomedicine). **Remarks:** FAX: 8 348793. Telex: 17179 KIBICS. **Also Known As:** Karolinska Institutets Bibliotek och Informationscentral.

Sweden - Ministry of Education - The National Library for Psychology and Education
See: **Sweden - The National Library for Psychology and Education** (15909)

Sweden - Ministry of Transport and Communications - Swedish Geotechnical Institute
See: **Swedish Geotechnical Institute** (15921)

★ 15908 ★
Sweden - National Board of Agriculture - Library (Agri)
Vallgatan 8   Phone: 36 155000
S-551 83 Jonkoping, Sweden   Inga Hedstrom, Libn.
Founded: 1975. **Subjects:** Agriculture, forestry. **Special Collections:** Pedigree collection. **Holdings:** 27,000 books, bound periodical volumes, reports, and archival items. **Subscriptions:** 500 journals and other serials; 7 newspapers. **Services:** Interlibrary loan; copying; library open to the public for reference use only. **Remarks:** FAX: 36 190546. **Also Known As:** Skogs och Jordbruksbiblioteket.

Sweden - National Board of Education Library
See: **Sweden - Statistics Sweden** (15912)

Sweden - National Board of Health and Welfare Library
See: **Sweden - Statistics Sweden** (15912)

Sweden - National Institute for Psychosocial Factors and Health
See: **Sweden - Karolinska Institute** (15906)

★ 15909 ★
Sweden - The National Library for Psychology and Education (Soc Sci, Educ)
P.O. Box 50063   Phone: 8 151820
S-104 05 Stockholm, Sweden   Tomas Lidman, Lib.Dir.
Founded: 1885. **Staff:** 19. **Subjects:** Psychology, education, special education, adult education, educational psychology. **Special Collections:** Swedish School Book Collection; ERIC microfiche collection. **Holdings:** 300,000 books; 330,000 patents and documents. **Subscriptions:** 1150 journals and other serials. **Services:** Interlibrary loan; copying; SDI; library open to the public. **Computerized Information Services:** DIALOG Information Services, ESA/IRS, Questel, DIMDI, MEDICINDATA; PEPSY (database of educational literature in the Nordic countries; internal database); CD-ROMs (ERIC, PsycLIT). Performs searches on fee basis. Contact Person: Krister Lagerborg, Info.Spec. **Publications:** Annual Bibliographies in Psychology and Education. **Remarks:** Maintained by Sweden - Ministry of Education. **Also Known As:** Statens Psykologisk-Pedagogiska Bibliotek.

Sweden - National Library of Sweden
See: **Sweden - Royal Library - National Library of Sweden** (15911)

Sweden - National Museum of Military History
See: **Statens Forsvarshistoriska Museum** (15765)

Sweden - National Swedish Institute for Building Research
See: **National Swedish Institute for Building Research** (11310)

★ 15910 ★
Sweden - Royal Institute of Technology - Library (Sci-Engr)
Valhallavagen 81   Phone: 8 7907087
S-100 44 Stockholm, Sweden   Gunnar Lager, Lib.Dir.
Founded: 1825. **Staff:** 95. **Subjects:** Physical sciences, technology, engineering, architecture. **Special Collections:** History of Sciences and Technology. **Holdings:** 610,000 volumes. **Subscriptions:** 3500 journals and other serials. **Services:** Interlibrary loan; copying; library open to the public. **Computerized Information Services:** Online systems. Performs searches on fee basis. Contact Person: Marie Wallin, 8 7908974. **Publications:** Stockholm papers in library and information science; Stockholm papers in history and philosophy of technology. **Remarks:** FAX: 8109199. Telex: 10389 KTHB S. **Also Known As:** Kungliga Tekniska Hogskolans Bibliotek (KTHB).

★ 15911 ★
Sweden - Royal Library - National Library of Sweden (Area-Ethnic, Info Sci)
Box 5039   Phone: 8 24 10 40
S-102 41 Stockholm, Sweden   Birgit Antonsson, Natl.Libn.
Staff: 272. **Subjects:** General collection. **Special Collections:** Swedish Collection; old Swedish and Icelandic manuscripts; incunabula; elzeviers. **Holdings:** 3 million volumes. **Subscriptions:** 8058 journals and other serials; 60 newspapers. **Services:** Interlibrary loan; copying; library open to the public. **Automated Operations:** Computerized cataloging. **Computerized Information Services:** LIBRIS. **Publications:** AKB-mikro; Svensk Bokforteckning (National Bibliography); Acta. **Special Catalogs:** Accessionskatalog (foreign books acquired by Swedish research libraries), annual. **Remarks:** FAX: 8 21 69 56. Telex: 19640 KBS S. **Also Known As:** Kungl. Biblioteket.

★ 15912 ★
Sweden - Statistics Sweden - Library (Sci-Engr, Soc Sci)
S-115 81 Stockholm, Sweden   Phone: 8 783 40 00
                                             Malkon Lindmark, Chf.Libn.
Founded: 1858. **Staff:** Prof 11; Other 10. **Subjects:** Statistics, statistical methodology, demography, health and welfare, education. **Special Collections:** World Health Organization (WHO) publications. **Holdings:** 300,000 volumes. **Subscriptions:** 4500 journals and other serials. **Services:** Interlibrary loan; copying; library open to the public. **Automated Operations:** Computerized cataloging. **Computerized Information Services:** LIBRIS. **Publications:** Statistik Fran Enskilda Lander; Statistik Fran Internationella Organ (annual lists of serials in the library) - both for sale. **Remarks:** Incorporates the National Board of Health and Welfare Library and National Board of Education Library. **Also Known As:** Statistiska Centralbyrans Bibliotek.

★ 15913 ★
Swedenborg Foundation - Library (Rel-Phil)
139 E. 23rd St.   Phone: (212)673-7310
New York, NY 10010   John R. Seekamp, Vice. Pres.
Staff: 6. **Subjects:** Works by and about Emanuel Swedenborg. **Special Collections:** Rare editions; image archive (slides; photographs; drawings). **Holdings:** 3000 books; 100 bound periodical volumes; engravings and prints; 10 paintings and drawings; 5 films. **Subscriptions:** 2000 journals and other serials. **Services:** Library open to the public with restrictions. **Publications:** LOGOS (newsletter); Chrysalis (journal).

Swedenborg Library
See: **Academy of the New Church** (37)

★ 15914 ★
Swedenborg Library and Bookstore (Rel-Phil)
79 Newbury St.   Phone: (617)262-5918
Boston, MA 02116   Rafael Guiu, Mgr.
Founded: 1865. **Staff:** Prof 3. **Subjects:** Swedenborg theological works, American and English Swedenborgian Church, collateral works of Swedenborgian writers. **Special Collections:** First editions of Swedenborg's writings; photolithographic and photostatic copies of Swedenborg's manuscripts. **Holdings:** 2100 books; 210 bound periodical volumes; 1000 pamphlets. **Subscriptions:** 5 journals and other serials. **Services:** Copying; library open to the public. **Publications:** MNCU Newsletter. **Special Catalogs:** Books for Sale Catalogue - free upon request. **Remarks:** Maintained by the Massachusetts New Church Union. **Staff:** Michel Giargiari, Bk.Mgr.

Swedenborg Memorial Library
See: Urbana University (19692)

★ 15915 ★
Swedenborg School of Religion - Library (Rel-Phil)
48 Sargent St.   Phone: (617)244-0504
Newton, MA 02158   Jean S. Hilliard
Founded: 1866. **Staff:** 2. **Subjects:** Writings of Emanuel Swedenborg, theology. **Special Collections:** History and literature of the Swedenborgian Church (also known as the New Church or the Church of the New Jerusalem). **Holdings:** 33,000 books and bound periodical volumes; Swedenborgian Church archive materials including letters, manuscripts, committee reports, sermons. **Subscriptions:** 67 journals and other serials. **Services:** Interlibrary loan; copying; library open to the public by appointment. **Remarks:** Incorporated as the New Church Theological School in 1881. **Staff:** Louise Woofenden, Archv.

Swedish-American Archives of Greater Chicago
See: Swedish-American Historical Society (15916)

★ 15916 ★
Swedish-American Historical Society - Swedish-American Archives of Greater Chicago (Area-Ethnic)
5125 N. Spaulding Ave.   Phone: (312)583-5722
Chicago, IL 60625   Timothy Johnson, Archv.
Founded: 1965. **Staff:** Prof 1; Other 2. **Subjects:** Swedish settlement in the U.S., Swedish culture, Swedish-American organizations, Swedish contributions to development of the U.S., outstanding Swedish-Americans, Swedish Immigration to Chicago. **Special Collections:** Contributions of Swedes to American life and culture; Swedish music; records of Swedish organizations in the U.S.; documents and papers of outstanding Swedish Americans; Henry Bengston; Carl Hjalmar Lundquist; Selma Jacobson; Swedish Royalty and Chicago; Sweden, the Land of Our Forefathers. **Holdings:** 3000 books (largely in Swedish); 400 archive boxes of records; Swedish newspapers printed in Chicago, 1871-1981. **Subscriptions:** 50 journals and other serials; 3 newspapers. **Services:** Copying; translations; archives open to the public by appointment. **Automated Operations:** Computerized cataloging. **Publications:** Items in Swedish American Historical Quarterly.

★ 15917 ★
Swedish American Hospital - Health Care Library (Med)
1400 Charles St.   Phone: (815)961-2030
Rockford, IL 61104-2298   Sharon Montana, Mgr., Educ.Serv.
Staff: Prof 2. **Subjects:** Clinical medicine, hospital administration. **Special Collections:** Consumer's Collection. **Holdings:** 2500 books; 2000 video cassettes; 7 year backlog of periodicals. **Subscriptions:** 300 journals and other serials. **Services:** Interlibrary loan; copying; library open to the public for reference use only with the exception of material in the consumer's collection area. **Computerized Information Services:** MEDLINE, DIALOG Information Services, OCLC; DOCLINE (electronic mail service). **Networks/Consortia:** Member of Upstate Consortium of Medical Libraries in Northern Illinois, Northern Illinois Library System (NILS). **Remarks:** FAX: (815)968-3713. **Staff:** Rachel Garza, Med.Libn.

★ 15918 ★
Swedish Broadcasting Corporation - Reference Library (Info Sci)
Oxenstiernsgt 20   Phone: 8 7844130
S-105 10 Stockholm, Sweden   Rosita Busch
Staff: Prof 8. **Subjects:** Communication, mass media. **Holdings:** 70,000 books. **Subscriptions:** 375 journals and other serials; 4 newspapers. **Services:** Interlibrary loan; copying; SDI; library open to academic researchers. **Remarks:** FAX: 8 7842257. **Also Known As:** Sveriges Riksradio - Referensbiblioteket.

★ 15919 ★
Swedish Council for Information on Alcohol and Other Drugs - Library (Med)
P.O. Box 27302   Phone: 8 6679720
S-102 54 Stockholm, Sweden   Sonja Valverius, Hd., Lib. & Doc.Serv.
Founded: 1980. **Staff:** Prof 5. **Subjects:** Alcohol and drugs - dependence, abuse, traffic safety, allied subjects. **Holdings:** Books; periodicals; technical reports; conference proceedings; theses; other cataloged items. **Subscriptions:** 390 journals and other serials. **Services:** Library open to researchers and educators. **Computerized Information Services:** Produces DRUGAB (available on PC) and Alconline (available online through MEDLARS). **Remarks:** FAX: 8 6616484. **Also Known As:** Centralforbundet for Alkohol- och Narkotikaupplysning. **Staff:** Miriam Klint; Lars Ygfors; Barbro Bergstrom; Dzidra Liepins; Eva Regvard.

★ 15920 ★
Swedish Covenant Hospital - Joseph G. Stromberg Library of the Health Sciences (Med)
5145 N. California Ave.   Phone: (312)878-8200
Chicago, IL 60625   Alexander D. Trakas, Lib.Coord.
Staff: 1. **Subjects:** Family practice, medicine, nursing. **Holdings:** 2000 books; 3100 bound periodical volumes; AV programs. **Subscriptions:** 103 journals. **Services:** Interlibrary loan; library not open to the public. **Computerized Information Services:** CD-ROMs (MEDLINE, CINAHL). **Networks/Consortia:** Member of National Network of Libraries of Medicine - Greater Midwest Region, Chicago Library System. **Publications:** Acquisitions List, quarterly - to staff and other medical libraries in area. **Remarks:** FAX: (312)878-1624. **Staff:** Anne Miller.

★ 15921 ★
Swedish Geotechnical Institute - Library (Sci-Engr)
Olaus Magnus vag 35   Phone: 13 115100
S-581 01 Linkoping, Sweden
Founded: 1944. **Staff:** 4. **Subjects:** Soil mechanics, foundation engineering, environmental engineering, energy technology. **Special Collections:** Conference proceedings. **Holdings:** 85,500 titles. **Subscriptions:** 800 journals and other serials. **Services:** Interlibrary loan; copying; library open to the public. **Computerized Information Services:** SGILINE (internal database). **Publications:** SGI Accession List. **Remarks:** Maintained by Sweden - Ministry of Transport and Communications. FAX: 13 131696. Telex: 50125 VTISGI S. **Also Known As:** Statens Geotekniska Institut.

★ 15922 ★
Swedish Historical Society of Rockford - Erlander Home Museum - Library (Area-Ethnic)
404 S. 3rd St.   Phone: (815)963-5559
Rockford, IL 61104   Robert Borden
Founded: 1950. **Subjects:** Swedish language. **Special Collections:** Bound volumes - Pietisten, Ungdomsvannen, Augustana, Hemlandet. **Holdings:** 2000 books; 48 bound periodical volumes. **Services:** Library open to the public by appointment. **Publications:** History of Furniture Industry in Rockford (in progress).

★ 15923 ★
Swedish Hospital Medical Center - Reference Library (Med)
747 Summit Ave.   Phone: (206)386-2484
Seattle, WA 98104   Jean C. Anderson, Chf.Libn.
Staff: Prof 2; Other 2. **Subjects:** Surgery, medicine, nursing, hospital administration. **Special Collections:** Nursing Baccalaureate Collection (420 volumes; 12 videotapes); CIBA slides. **Holdings:** 2900 volumes; 40 videotapes; 6100 slides. **Subscriptions:** 375 journals and other serials. **Services:** Interlibrary loan; library not open to the public. **Automated Operations:** Computerized acquisitions and serials. **Computerized Information Services:** MEDLARS, DIALOG Information Services, BRS Information Technologies, DataTimes, NLM; OnTyme Electronic Message Network Service (electronic mail service). **Networks/Consortia:** Member of Seattle Area Hospital Library Consortium (SAHLC), Western Library Network (WLN). **Special Catalogs:** Catalog of serials holding (print). **Remarks:** Electronic mail address(es): SWEDEMC (OnTyme Electronic Message Network Service).

★ 15924 ★
Swedish Information Service (Area-Ethnic)
1 Dag Hammerskjold Plaza, 45th Fl.   Phone: (212)751-5900
New York, NY 10017-2201   Elisabeth Halvarsson-Stapen, Libn.
Founded: 1924. **Staff:** 2. **Subjects:** Contemporary Sweden. **Holdings:** 7000 books; brochures. **Subscriptions:** 89 journals and other serials. **Services:** Service open to the public for reference use only. **Publications:** New accessions, annual - to users. **Remarks:** FAX: (212)752-4789. Telex: 125385 INFOSWED NYK.

The Swedish Institute of Building Documentation
See: BYGGDOK/The Swedish Institute of Building Documentation (2423)

★ 15925 ★
Swedish Institute of Classical Studies - Library
Via Omero 14
I-00197 Rome, Italy   Phone: 6 3601966
Founded: 1926. **Staff:** Prof 2. **Subjects:** Archeology, art, classical philology. **Holdings:** 35,000 books; 15,000 bound periodical volumes. **Subscriptions:** 500 journals and other serials. **Services:** Interlibrary loan; library open to the public with letter of introduction. **Automated Operations:** GEAC. **Also Known As:** Svenska Institutet i Rom - Istituto Svedese di Studi Classici - Biblioteca.

★ 15926 ★
Swedish International Development Authority - SIDA Library (Soc Sci)
Birger Jarlsgate 61, 6th Fl.
S-105 25 Stockholm, Sweden   Phone: 8 728 51 00
Staff: Prof 2; Other 1. **Subjects:** Third World, especially South Asia, Southeast Asia, East and South Africa, Nicaragua; developing countries; development theories and economics; multilateral and bilateral assistance; education; health; rural development; agriculture; industry; women in development. **Holdings:** 15,000 books; maps; statistics; newspapers. **Subscriptions:** 400 journals and other serials. **Services:** Interlibrary loan; copying; library open to the public. **Computerized Information Services:** LIBRIS. **Publications:** Acquisitions list, monthly - to libraries and interested parties; SIDA-library periodicals; U-bit, monthly.

★ 15927 ★
Swedish Medical Center - Library (Med)
501 E. Hampden Ave., Dept. 8640
Box 2901   Phone: (303)788-6616
Englewood, CO 80110-0101   Sandra Parker, Dir., Lib.Serv.
Founded: 1967. **Staff:** Prof 2; Other 2. **Subjects:** Neurosciences, medicine, nursing, health administration, rehabilitation, spinal cord/head injuries. **Special Collections:** Health Information Collection. **Holdings:** 1500 books; 2500 bound periodical volumes; 1110 unbound periodicals. **Subscriptions:** 350 journals and other serials. **Services:** Interlibrary loan; library open to the public. **Automated Operations:** Computerized cataloging. **Computerized Information Services:** NLM, DIALOG Information Services, BRS Information Technologies; CD-ROMs (CD-Plus, SilverPlatter, Micromedex, PDR, SciAmerican Consult). Performs searches on fee basis. **Networks/Consortia:** Member of Colorado Council of Medical Librarians. **Remarks:** Alternate telephone number(s): 788-6617. **Staff:** Lori Harding, Info.Serv.; Wanda Weathersby, ILL.

Swedish Medical Research Council - Department of Stress Research
See: Sweden - Karolinska Institute (15906)

★ 15928 ★
Swedish Road and Traffic Research Institute - Information and Documentation Section - Library (Trans)
S-581 01 Linkoping, Sweden   Phone: 13 20 42 23
          Sigvard Tim, Hd.
Subjects: Roads, traffic, vehicles, road users, traffic safety, allied topics. **Holdings:** 45,000 volumes. **Subscriptions:** 1200 journals and other serials. **Services:** SDI; library open to the public. **Computerized Information Services:** ESA/IRS, DIALOG Information Services, PFDS Online, International Road Research Documentation (IRRD) data base; ROADLINE (internal database). Performs searches on fee basis. **Remarks:** FAX: 13 141436. Telex: 50125 VTISGI S. **Also Known As:** Statens Vag- och Trafikinstitut (VTI).

★ 15929 ★
Swedish Society of Medicine - Library (Med)
P.O. Box 558   Phone: 8 243350
S-101 27 Stockholm, Sweden   Goran Falkenberg, M.D., Hd.Libn.
Founded: 1808. **Staff:** Prof 2; Other 1. **Subjects:** Medical ethics, history of medicine. **Holdings:** 20,000 books; 30,000 bound periodical volumes; rare medical books. **Subscriptions:** 30 journals and other serials; 2 newspapers. **Services:** Interlibrary loan; library not open to the public. **Publications:** List of periodicals. **Special Catalogs:** Descriptive catalog of older books. **Remarks:** Library located at Klara Ostra Kyrkogata 10, Stockholm, Sweden. **Staff:** Gunilla Sonden, Asst.

★ 15930 ★
Swedish Standards Institution - Library (Bus-Fin)
P.O. Box 3295
S-103 66 Stockholm, Sweden   Phone: 8 6135200
Subjects: Swedish standards, nongovernmental technical regulations. **Holdings:** 10,000 standards and technical regulations. **Computerized Information Services:** REGIS (internal database). Performs searches. **Remarks:** FAX: 8 117035. Telex: 17453 SIS S.

Swedish Work Environment Fund - Department of Stress Research
See: Sweden - Karolinska Institute (15906)

★ 15931 ★
Swedlow, Inc. - Technical Library (Sci-Engr)
12122 Western Ave.   Phone: (714)893-7531
Garden Grove, CA 92641   Mary Mataisz, Info.Spec.
Staff: Prof 1. **Subjects:** Polymers, engineering, plastics. **Holdings:** 700 books; 325 bound periodical volumes; 2000 patents; 24 VF drawers; 78 VF drawers of reports; 62 cartridges of microfilm of company files **Subscriptions:** 33 journals and other serials. **Services:** Interlibrary loan; library not open to the public. **Automated Operations:** Computerized cataloging, serials, circulation, and reports. **Computerized Information Services:** DIALOG Information Services. **Remarks:** FAX: (714)895-5724.

Beatrice S. Sweeney Archive
See: Historical Society of Saratoga Springs (7287)

★ 15932 ★
Sweet Briar College - Mary Helen Cochran Library (Hist)
Sweet Briar, VA 24595   Phone: (804)381-6138
          John G. Jaffe
Founded: 1906. **Subjects:** History, art history, languages. **Special Collections:** W.H. Auden Collection; Virginia Woolf Collection; Evelyn D. Mullen T.E. Lawrence Collection; George Meredith Collection. **Services:** Interlibrary loan; copying; library open to the public for reference use only. **Computerized Information Services:** BRS Information Technologies, DIALOG Information Services, STN International, WILSONLINE. Performs searches. Contact Person: Kathleen A. Lance. **Publications:** Friends of the Library Gazette. **Remarks:** FAX: (804)381-6173.

★ 15933 ★
Sweetwater County Historical Museum - Information Center (Sci-Engr)
Courthouse
80 W. Flaming Gorge Way   Phone: (307)875-2611
Green River, WY 82935   Ruth Lauritzen, Dir.
Founded: 1967. **Staff:** Prof 2; Other 1. **Subjects:** Coal mining. **Special Collections:** Pictures of coal mining in southwestern Wyoming (4000 items); pictures of Chinese employed in coal mining industry. **Holdings:** 300 books; 25 bound periodical volumes; 8 VF drawers of clippings and reports; 4 cubic feet of archival mining materials including payroll, maps, and contracts; 200 other publications; 20,000 photographs. **Subscriptions:** 2 newspapers. **Services:** Copying; center open to the public for research. **Remarks:** FAX: (307)875-8439. **Staff:** Mark Nelson, Cur.

Earl Gregg Swem Library
See: College of William and Mary (3918)

★ 15934 ★
Swenson Swedish Immigration Research Center (Area-Ethnic)
Augustana College
Box 175   Phone: (309)794-7204
Rock Island, IL 61201   Dag Blanck, Dir.
Founded: 1981. **Staff:** Prof 3; Other 1. **Subjects:** Swedish immigration to the U.S., Swedish-American life and culture, biography of Swedes in the U.S. **Special Collections:** G.N. Swan Book Collection (6000 volumes); Oliver A. Linder Book Collection (600 volumes); Scandinaviana Book Collection (750 volumes); Swedish Topographical Map Collection (5 flat case drawers); Immigration Book Collection (2000 volumes). **Holdings:** 9000 books; 1000 bound periodical volumes; 200 uncataloged periodicals; 5.5 linear feet of Scandinavian-American Picture Collection; 200 linear feet of manuscripts; 8 linear feet of Oliver A. Linder clipping files; 1560 reels of microfilm of Swedish-American newspapers; 2000 reels of microfilm of Swedish-American church records; 412 reels of microfilm of records and papers of Swedish-American benevolent, fraternal, and cultural organizations and their institutions; 59 reels of microfilm of personal and professional papers of immigrants; 89 reels of microfilm and 6 loose-leaf volumes of name indexes to Swedish port of embarkation records: Gothenburg, 1869-1930, Malmo, 1874-1895, Gavle, 1846-1858, and Ockelbo, 1864-1894; other Swedish emigrant lists, 1817-1861; 14 reels of microfilm of name indexes to Norwegian ports of embarkation: Bergen, 1874-1924, Kristiania (Oslo), 1871-1902, and Trondheim, 1867-1890. **Subscriptions:** 30 journals and other serials. **Services:** Copying; center open to the public. **Automated Operations:** Computerized cataloging and acquisitions (through Augustana College Library). **Computerized Information Services:** OCLC (through Augustana College Library). **Publications:** Swenson Center News - free upon request; Swedish-American Newspapers: A Guide to the Microfilms held by SSIRC at Augustana College, Rock Island, Illinois, compiled by Lilly Setterdahl, 1981; Guide to Resources and Holdings; The Problem of the Third Generation Immigrant - republication of 1937 address, 1987; occasional papers - contact the Center for details on all publications. **Special Indexes:** Index to O.A. Linder clipping file; index to George M. Stephenson photostat collection; index to Scandinavian-American Picture Collection; index to personal data on first generation immigrants; index of studio names and addresses of photographers represented in general photograph collection; index to subject files (all on cards); index to Swedish-American and Swedish-Canadian church records (on microfiche). **Remarks:** FAX: (309)794-7443. **Staff:** Kermit B. Westerberg, Archv./Libn., Act.Dir.; Christina Johansson, Res.

Morris Swett Technical Library
See: **U.S. Army - TRADOC - Field Artillery School** (17010)

Swift-Eckrich, Inc.
See: **Armour Swift-Eckrich** (1055)

Sherman Swift Reference Library
See: **Canadian National Institute for the Blind - Library for the Blind** (2969)

★ 15935 ★
Swigart Museum - Library (Hist, Trans)
Museum Park, Box 214   Phone: (814)643-3000
Huntingdon, PA 16652   William E. Swigart, Jr., Exec.Dir.
Founded: 1920. **Staff:** Prof 1; Other 3. **Subjects:** Automotive history, transportation, automobiliana. **Special Collections:** Early transportation evolving into the automobile. **Holdings:** 1000 books; 612 bound periodical volumes; automobile literature; extensive uncataloged material. **Subscriptions:** 12 journals and other serials. **Services:** Copying; library open to the public with restrictions. **Remarks:** Said to have world's largest collection of license plates, emblems, and nameplates. FAX: (814)643-6634.

★ 15936 ★
Swiss Botanical Society - Library (Biol Sci)
Geobotanik ETH
Zollikerstr. 107   Phone: 1 2563853
CH-8008 Zurich, Switzerland   L. Koenig, Libn.
Staff: 1. **Subjects:** Botany. **Holdings:** 600,000 volumes. **Subscriptions:** 200 journals and other serials. **Services:** Interlibrary loan; copying; library open to the public. **Remarks:** Alternate telephone number(s): 1 2565700. FAX: 1 2529613. **Formerly:** Institute for Phytomedicine. **Also Known As:** Schweizerische Botanische Gesellschaft.

Swiss Federal Archives
See: **Switzerland - Swiss Federal Archives - Library** (15942)

★ 15937 ★
Swiss Federal Institute of Technology, Lausanne - Central Library (Sci-Engr)
EPFL-Ecublens   Phone: 21 6932153
CH-1015 Lausanne, Switzerland   Mrs. J. Noeninger-Krebs
Staff: 22. **Subjects:** Civil engineering, rural engineering and surveying, mechanical engineering, renewable energy resources, electrical engineering, physics, chemical engineering, mathematics, materials science, architecture, computer science, microtechnology. **Special Collections:** Old and rare scientific books. **Holdings:** 300,000 books. **Subscriptions:** 1900 journals and other serials. **Services:** Library open to the public. **Automated Operations:** Computerized public access catalog. **Computerized Information Services:** Data-Star, DIALOG Information Services, FIZ Technik, ECHO, ESA/IRS, PFDS Online, INKDATA, Questel, ORBIT Search Service, STN International. **Remarks:** FAX: 21 6935100. Telex: 450 456. **Also Known As:** Ecole Polytechnique Federale de Lausanne. **Staff:** Pierre Cuendet, Hd. of Online Searches; Pierre Hochstrasser, Hd. of Lending Dept.; Meletis Michalakis, Hd. of Acq.; Monique Goel, Hd. of Info.Serv.; Patricia Hatley, Hd. of Per.Dept.

★ 15938 ★
Swiss Federal Institute of Technology, Zurich - Library (Sci-Engr)
Ramistrasse 101
ETH-Zentrum   Phone: 1 2562135
CH-8092 Zurich, Switzerland   H. Hug, Dir.
Founded: 1855. **Staff:** 170. **Subjects:** Mathematics; physics; chemistry; biology; earth sciences; astronomy; computer science; materials; pharmacy; agriculture; forestry; engineering - mechanical, electrical, civil, environmental; water management, surveying; architecture; humanities; social sciences. **Holdings:** 4.6 million volumes. **Subscriptions:** 11,700 journals and other serials. **Services:** Interlibrary loan; copying; library open to the public. **Automated Operations:** Computerized public access catalog. **Remarks:** FAX: 1 2625396. Telex: 817 178 BIBL CH. **Also Known As:** Eidgenossische Technische Hochschule.

Swiss Federal Institutes of Technology - Swiss Federal Institute for Reactor Research
See: **Paul Scherrer Institute** (14907)

Swiss National Library
See: **Switzerland - Swiss National Library** (15943)

★ 15939 ★
Swiss Research Institute for Marketing and Distribution - Library (Bus-Fin)
Bodanstrasse 8   Phone: 71 302742
CH-9000 St. Gallen, Switzerland   Markus Weinhold, Libn.
Subjects: Marketing and distribution, advertising, sales management, exporting, direct marketing, electronic communication. **Holdings:** 33,000 volumes. **Remarks:** FAX: 71 232274. **Also Known As:** Forschungsinstitut fuer Absatz und Handel.

Swiss Research Institute of Small Business
See: **St. Gallen Graduate School of Economics, Law, Business, and Public Administration** (14319)

★ 15940 ★
Switzerland - Federal Research Institute for Forest, Snow and Landscape - Federal Institute for Snow and Avalanche Research - Library (Sci-Engr)
Weissfluhjoch   Phone: 81 46 32 64
CH-7620 Davos, Switzerland   Mr. F. Joerg, Libn.
Subjects: Snow, avalanches. **Holdings:** 20,000 titles. **Services:** Library not open to the public. **Remarks:** FAX: 81 46 18 97. Telex: 853 209. **Formerly:** Switzerland - Federal Forest Office. **Also Known As:** Eidgenoessisches Institut fuer Schnee- und Lawinenforschung.

★ 15941 ★
Switzerland - Social Archives - Library (Soc Sci)
Stadelhoferstr 12   Phone: 1 2517644
CH-8001 Zurich, Switzerland   Anita Ulrich
Founded: 1906. **Staff:** 11.5. **Subjects:** Social politics, social sciences, work and trade unions, socialism, culture, politics. **Special Collections:** Archives of old and new social movements. **Holdings:** 150,000 books; 200 bound periodical titles; 79 archives; 735 reels of microfilm; newspaper clippings. **Subscriptions:** 1428 journals and other serials; 133 newspapers. **Services:** Interlibrary loan; copying; library open to the public.

★ 15942 ★
Switzerland - Swiss Federal Archives - Library (Info Sci)
Archivstrasse 24   Phone: 31 618989
CH-3003 Berne, Switzerland   Christoph Graf, Dir.
Founded: 1848. **Staff:** Prof 30; Other 10. **Subjects:** Helvetic Republic, 19th and 20th century Swiss history, Period of Mediation, Period of the Diet. **Special Collections:** Swiss authorities records, (19th and 20th centuries); Confederation Archives (1848 to present); private archival fonds. **Holdings:** 500 linear meters of books; 28,000 linear meters of archives; 5000 microfiche; 4000 reels of microfilm; 1000 videotapes. **Subscriptions:** 25 journals and other serials. **Services:** Copying; library open to the public with restrictions. **Computerized Information Services:** EDIBAR (internal database). **Contact Person:** Hugo Caduff, Sektionschef. **Publications:** Inventare; Studien und Quellen; Diplomatische Dokumente der Schweiz. **Remarks:** FAX: 31 617823.

★ 15943 ★
Switzerland - Swiss National Library (Info Sci)
Hallylstrasse 15   Phone: 31 618911
CH-3003 Berne, Switzerland   Dr. Bernoulli Jauslin, Techn.
Founded: 1895. **Staff:** Prof 71; Other 16. **Subjects:** Helvetica, library science. **Special Collections:** Swiss Literary Archives; Bible collection. **Holdings:** 2.2 million books; 350,000 bound periodical volumes; 7000 microfiche; 50,000 manuscripts; photographs; maps. **Subscriptions:** 9000 journals and other serials; 400 newspapers. **Services:** Interlibrary loan; copying; library open to the public. **Publications:** National Bibliography; bibliographies on Swiss literature, history, and natural sciences. **Remarks:** FAX: 31 618463. Telex: 91 2691 slb ch. **Also Known As:** Bibliotheque Nationale Suisse.

★ 15944 ★
Sheldon Swope Art Museum - Library (Art)
25 S. 7th St.   Phone: (812)238-1676
Terre Haute, IN 47807   Alice L. Wert, Libn.
Subjects: Art history, American art. **Holdings:** 1782 books. **Subscriptions:** 8 journals and other serials. **Services:** Library open to the public for reference use only. **Networks/Consortia:** Member of INCOLSA.

Sydney Community Health Centre - Health Sciences Library
See: Cape Breton Regional Hospital - School of Nursing Library (3023)

★ 15945 ★
Sydney Hospital - Medical Library (Med)
Macquarie St.
GPOB 1614   Phone: 2 2282042
Sydney, NSW 2000, Australia   Ilona Harsanyi
Staff: Prof 1.5. **Subjects:** Medicine, nursing, and allied health sciences, hands. **Holdings:** 6000 books; 250 bound periodical volumes. **Subscriptions:** 163 journals and other serials. **Services:** Interlibrary loan; copying; SDI; library open to the public for reference use only on a fee basis. **Computerized Information Services:** DIALOG Information Services, MEDLINE; ILANET (electronic mail service). **Remarks:** FAX: 2 2231360. Electronic mail address(es): MLN209850 (ILANET).

★ 15946 ★
(Sydney) USIS Library (Educ)
Elcom Bldg.
Hyde Park Square
Park & Elizabeth Sts.   Phone: 2 2619200
Sydney, NSW 2000, Australia   Peter Gilbert, Libn.
Staff: Prof 1. **Holdings:** 1800 books; 300 reels of microfilm. **Subscriptions:** 80 journals and other serials; 3 newspapers. **Services:** Interlibrary loan; SDI; library open to the public on a limited schedule. **Computerized Information Services:** DIALOG Information Services, LEGI-SLATE. **Remarks:** Maintained or supported by the U.S. Information Agency. Focus is on contemporary U.S. domestic and foreign policy.

★ 15947 ★
Syllogistics, Inc. - Library
5514 Alma Ln., Suite 400
Springfield, VA 22151
Defunct.

★ 15948 ★
Sylvester Comprehensive Cancer Center - The Cancer Information Service (Med)
Jackson Towers, Rm. 1015   Phone: (305)548-4821
Miami, FL 33136   Jo Beth Speyer, Dir.
Founded: 1976. **Staff:** Prof 7; Other 1. **Subjects:** Cancer, nutrition. **Holdings:** Figures not available. **Services:** Interlibrary loan; open to the public. **Computerized Information Services:** Physician Data Query (PDQ). Performs searches free of charge. **Contact Person:** Arianne DeVera. **Remarks:** FAX: (305)547-6678.

★ 15949 ★
Symmers, Fish and Warner - Research Library
111 E. 50th St.
New York, NY 10022
Defunct.

Synagogue Architectural and Art Library
See: Union of American Hebrew Congregations (16634)

★ 15950 ★
Syncrude Canada, Ltd. - Operations Library
P.O. Bag 4009, Mail Drop 1140
Fort McMurray, AB, Canada T9H 3L1
Defunct.

★ 15951 ★
Syncrude Canada, Ltd. - Research and Development Library (Sci-Engr, Energy)
10120 17th St.
P.O. Box 5790, Sta. L   Phone: (403)464-8400
Edmonton, AB, Canada T6C 4G3   Peter J. Bates, Info.Spec.
Founded: 1960. **Staff:** Prof 1; Other 1. **Subjects:** Oil sands, chemistry, chemical engineering, petroleum, environment, mining, engineering. **Holdings:** 12,000 books; 750 bound periodical volumes; 5000 patents; 2500 company reports; 1500 microfiche; reprints. **Subscriptions:** 170 journals and other serials; 5 newspapers. **Services:** Interlibrary loan; library not open to the public. **Automated Operations:** Computerized public access catalog and indexing. **Computerized Information Services:** Online systems; Envoy 100 (electronic mail service). **Publications:** Current awareness bulletin, monthly - for internal distribution only. **Remarks:** FAX: (403)464-8405. Telex: 037-2302. Electronic mail address(es): AESC.ILL (Envoy 100).

★ 15952 ★
Synergy Power Institute - Library
64 Via La Cumbre
Greenbrae, CA 94904
Founded: 1968. **Subjects:** Psychology, power, political science, sociology, U.S. history. **Holdings:** 6000 books. **Remarks:** Institute founded to research and disseminate information about power and ways it can be used humanely and responsibly to change society. Currently inactive.

Synod of Evangelical Lutheran Church Archives
See: Concordia Historical Institute - Department of Archives and History (4115)

★ 15953 ★
Syntex (U.S.A.) Inc. - Corporate Library/Information Services (Med, Biol Sci)
3401 Hillview Ave.   Phone: (415)855-5431
Palo Alto, CA 94304   Pamela Jajko, Mgr.
Founded: 1961. **Staff:** Prof 6; Other 4. **Subjects:** Organic chemistry, biochemistry, pharmacology, clinical medicine, veterinary medicine,

physiology. **Holdings:** 6000 books; 16,000 bound periodical volumes; 1400 microfilm cartridges; 22 volumes of bound reprints of papers authored by Syntex personnel. **Subscriptions:** 600 journals and other serials. **Services:** Interlibrary loan; copying; SDI; library open to the public by application to librarian. **Automated Operations:** Computerized cataloging, acquisitions, serials, and circulation. **Computerized Information Services:** DIALOG Information Services, NLM, LEXIS, NEXIS, Data-Star, DataTimes, BRS Information Technologies, Chemical Abstracts Service (CAS), PFDS Online, Reuters, OCLC; SPIF (internal database). **Networks/Consortia:** Member of National Network of Libraries of Medicine - Pacific Southwest Region. **Publications:** Booklist, monthly; bibliographies; Periodicals List - all for internal distribution only. **Remarks:** FAX: (415)354-7741. **Staff:** Vicki Garlow, Info.Spec.; Ann Nishimoto, Info.Spec.; Ann Hubble, Info.Spec.; Deborah Jacobstein, Info.Spec.; Abbi Lawrance, Info.Spec.

★ 15954 ★
Synthetech, Inc. - Library (Sci-Engr)
P.O. Box 646
Albany, OR 97321   Phone: (503)967-6575
Subjects: Chemistry, chemical engineering, biotechnology. **Holdings:** 200 volumes. **Remarks:** Firm manufactures custom chemicals. Telex: 322501.

Syracuse China Center for the Study of American Ceramics - Archives of American Ceramics
See: Everson Museum of Art (5514)

★ 15955 ★
Syracuse Newspapers Library - Library (Publ)
Clinton Square
PO Box 4915   Phone: (315)470-2231
Syracuse, NY 13221   Bonnie L. Ross
Staff: Prof 2; Other 4. **Subjects:** Newspaper reference topics. **Holdings:** 1000 books; 1500 reels of microfilm. **Subscriptions:** 3 journals and other serials; 2 newspapers. **Services:** Library not open to the public. **Computerized Information Services:** DIALOG Information Services, VU/TEXT Information Services, DataTimes, LEXIS, NEXIS; SAVE (internal database).

★ 15956 ★
Syracuse Research Corporation - Library (Sci-Engr, Energy)
Merrill Lane   Phone: (315)426-3202
Syracuse, NY 13210   Nancy H. Hall, Dir.
Founded: 1957. **Staff:** Prof 1. **Subjects:** Environmental sciences, policy analysis and evaluation, electrical and electronics engineering. **Holdings:** 2000 books; 1500 archival items. **Subscriptions:** 100 journals and other serials. **Services:** Interlibrary loan; library not open to the public. **Computerized Information Services:** DIALOG Information Services, STN International, Chemical Information Systems, Inc. (CIS), MEDLARS, TOXNET, SRC (Syracuse Research Corporation) Environmental Fate Databases. **Networks/Consortia:** Member of Central New York Library Resources Council (CENTRO), SUNY/OCLC Library Network. **Remarks:** FAX: (315)425-1339 (available through the copy center).

★ 15957 ★
Syracuse University - Belfer Audio Laboratory - Audio Archives (Aud-Vis)
222 Waverly Ave.   Phone: (315)443-3477
Syracuse, NY 13244-2010   William D. Storm, Dir.
Founded: 1963. **Staff:** 4.5. **Special Collections:** One hundred years of commercial sound recordings from the earliest of the Thomas Edison cylinder recordings to the most modern audiotapes; sound recordings of political leaders, poets, actresses, singers; transcriptions of audio broadcasting, musical and theatrical performances, folk music, and contemporary compositions of the 20th century (300,000 recordings). **Holdings:** 400 books; 600 bound periodical volumes; 200 microfiche; 950 reels of microfilm; record catalogs; discographies; manufacturer publications. **Subscriptions:** 12 journals and other serials. **Services:** Archives open to the public by appointment. **Computerized Information Services:** BALABASE (internal database); InterNet (electronic mail service). **Remarks:** FAX: (315)443-9510. Electronic mail address(es): LIBSTS@SUVM.ACS.SYR.EDU (InterNet). **Staff:** Susan T. Stinson, Audiographer; David C. Wickstrom, Sr.Aud.Engr.; Arnold G. Paul, Applications Spec.

★ 15958 ★
Syracuse University - E.S. Bird Library - Fine Arts Department (Art, Mus)
Syracuse, NY 13244-2010   Phone: (315)443-2440
                                                    Barbara Opar, Dept.Hd./Arch.Libn.
Staff: Prof 4; Other 8. **Subjects:** Art, architecture, music, photography. **Special Collections:** Italian libretto collection (19th century Italian opera libretti; 1350); Liechtenstein Music Archive (microfilm collection of 17th century music preserved in Czechoslovakia); papers of Marcel Breuer and Pietro Belluschi; papers of William Lescaze; prints of working drawings of 150 contemporary buildings; papers of American artists and critics including John Canaday, Richard Florsheim, John Singer Sargent, Eastman Johnson, Elihu Vedder, Jacob Lawrence, Edwin Dickinson, George Cruikshank, and photographer Margaret Bourke-White. **Holdings:** 115,000 volumes; 24,500 recordings; 22,300 scores; 1450 tapes; 250,000 slides; clipping files of 27,000 items; 15,000 exhibition catalogs; 3685 pamphlets; 1421 microcards; 1323 microfiche. **Subscriptions:** 437 journals and other serials. **Services:** Interlibrary loan; copying; department open to the public with restrictions on circulation. **Automated Operations:** Computerized cataloging, acquisitions, and circulation. **Computerized Information Services:** OCLC; BITNET (electronic mail service). **Networks/Consortia:** Member of SUNY/OCLC Library Network. **Special Catalogs:** Catalog of art exhibition catalogs (card). **Remarks:** Alternate telephone number(s): 443-2905. FAX: (315)443-9510. Electronic mail address(es): LIBBAO@SUVM (BITNET). **Staff:** Randall Bond, Art Libn.; Johanna Prins, Slide Cur.; Donald Seibert, Music Libn.

★ 15959 ★
Syracuse University - E.S. Bird Library - Media Services Department (Aud-Vis)
B101 Bird Library   Phone: (315)443-2438
Syracuse, NY 13244-2010   George Abbott, Hd.
Staff: Prof 2; Other 10. **Subjects:** Audiovisual materials. **Special Collections:** Film Study Center (500 films); Broadcast Foundation of America audio recordings (5000 reels); Visiting Artists Video Cassette Collection (300 videocassettes). **Holdings:** 700,000 items, including AV programs and microforms. **Services:** Copying; department open to the public. **Computerized Information Services:** ALANET, BITNET (electronic mail services). **Remarks:** FAX: (315)443-9510. Electronic mail address(es): ALA1177 (ALANET). **Staff:** Meseratch Zecharias, Assoc.Libn., Ref./Media.

★ 15960 ★
Syracuse University - Geology Library (Sci-Engr)
300 Heroy Geology Lab   Phone: (315)443-3337
Syracuse, NY 13244-1070   Eileen Snyder, Libn.
Staff: 1.5. **Subjects:** Geology, economic geology, geomorphology, geophysics, geochemistry, paleontology. **Holdings:** 35,209 volumes. **Subscriptions:** 184 journals. **Services:** Interlibrary loan; copying; library open to the public with restrictions. **Automated Operations:** Computerized cataloging, acquisitions, and circulation. **Computerized Information Services:** RLIN, OCLC; SUMMIT (internal database). **Networks/Consortia:** Member of SUNY/OCLC Library Network. **Remarks:** FAX: (315)443-5549. **Staff:** Eileen Snyder, Geol.Libn.

★ 15961 ★
Syracuse University - George Arents Research Library for Special Collections (Rare Book)
E.S. Bird Library   Phone: (315)443-2697
Syracuse, NY 13244-2010   Mark F. Weimer, Cur. of Spec.Coll.
Staff: Prof 4; Other 8. **Subjects:** Rare books, manuscripts. **Holdings:** RARE BOOKS (100,000 volumes) - general collection of 15th-19th century imprints; early American imprints; finely printed and privately printed books; finely illustrated books; fine bindings; 19th and 20th century literature collections arranged by author; Spire Collection on Loyalists in the American Revolution; Novotny Library of Economic History; Stephen Crane Collection; William Hobart-Royce Balzac Collection; Joyce Carol Oates Papers; Albert Schweitzer Collection; Leopold von Ranke Library; Oneida Community Collection; Rudyard Kipling Collection. MANUSCRIPTS (27,000 linear feet) - Art (papers of artists, cartoonists, industrial designers, photographers, sculptors, architects); Business History (corporate records of various types of companies, including forest industries, public utilities, publishing, printing, transportation, banking, voluntary associations, manufacturing); Government and Public Administration (papers of federal administrators, diplomats and military officers, federal and state judicial officers, state governors, department heads and administrators,

federal legislators, and statesmen); American Literature (papers of nonfiction authors, novelists, poets, playwrights, dramatists, historians, literary critics); Science Fiction (papers of science fiction writers, anthologists, and publishers as well as documents related to societies, international meetings, science fiction art, radio and television programs, and fantasy literature); Mass Communications (news photography, periodical and newspaper administration, editing and reporting, news commentators and columnists, foreign correspondents, personalities in music, entertainment, radio, and television); Religion and Theology (papers of philosophers, missionaries, theologians, Christian church administrators, and clergy); Social Science (documents relating to American military and naval history, local history, law, education, families, philanthropy, economics, explorations); Adult Education (papers of prominent adult educators and researchers and corporate records of international adult educational organizations); Industrial Design (papers of prominent 20th century designers and records of design firms). **Subscriptions:** 15 journals and other serials. **Services:** Copying; library open to the public with restrictions. **Automated Operations:** Computerized cataloging. **Computerized Information Services:** RLIN, OCLC; BITNET (electronic mail service). **Networks/Consortia:** Member of SUNY/OCLC Library Network, Research Libraries Information Network (RLIN). **Publications:** Guide to historical resources in Onondaga County New York repositories. **Remarks:** FAX: (315)443-9510. Electronic mail address(es): LIBMFW@SUVM (BITNET). **Staff:** Carolyn A. Davis, Rd.Serv.Libn.; Terrance Keenan, Rd.Serv.Libn.

★ 15962 ★
Syracuse University - H. Douglas Barclay Law Library (Law)
College of Law   Phone: (315)443-9560
Syracuse, NY 13244-1030   M. Louise Lantzy, Dir.
Founded: 1899. **Staff:** Prof 5; Other 9. **Subjects:** Law - Anglo-American, tax, criminal, American legal history, law and technology, New York State. **Special Collections:** Depository for U.S. Government documents. **Holdings:** 164,338 volumes; 128,115 microforms. **Subscriptions:** 4778 journals and other serials; 20 newspapers. **Services:** Interlibrary loan; copying; FAX service; library open to the public. **Automated Operations:** Computerized cataloging, circulation and acquisitions (NOTIS). **Computerized Information Services:** LEXIS, WESTLAW, OCLC, RLIN, NEXIS, DIALOG Information Services; BITNET (electronic mail service). **Networks/Consortia:** Member of SUNY/OCLC Library Network. **Publications:** Library Update and Guide. **Remarks:** FAX: (315)443-9568. Electronic mail address(es): LANTZYL@SUAIS (BITNET). **Staff:** John Schuster, Assoc.Libn./Cat.; Janet Fleckenstein, Sr.Asst.Libn./Circ. and Ser.; Wendy Scott, Assoc.Libn./Ref.Coord.; Tomas A. Lipinski, Assoc.Libn./Ref.

★ 15963 ★
Syracuse University - Institute for Sensory Research - Library (Biol Sci)
Merrill Ln.   Phone: (315)443-4164
Syracuse, NY 13244-5290   Robert L. Smith, Ph.D.
Founded: 1963. **Staff:** 1.5. **Subjects:** Structure and function of human and animal sensory systems. **Holdings:** 3000 books; 10,000 bound periodical volumes; reports; archival items. **Subscriptions:** 51 journals and other serials. **Services:** Copying; library not open to the public. **Computerized Information Services:** Current Contents; QUICKMAIL (electronic mail service). **Remarks:** FAX: (315)443-1184. Electronic mail address(es): R.L.Smith@SUNRISE (QUICKMAIL).

★ 15964 ★
Syracuse University - Mathematics Library (Sci-Engr)
308 Carnegie Bldg.   Phone: (315)443-2092
Syracuse, NY 13244-2010   Mary DeCarlo, Libn.
Staff: Prof 1; Other 1. **Subjects:** Mathematics, history of mathematics, mathematical statistics, logic, algebra, numerical analysis, combinatorics, topology, mathematics education. **Special Collections:** Russian journals (translated). **Holdings:** 22,594 books; 18,773 bound periodical volumes; 1400 reports. **Subscriptions:** 350 journals. **Services:** Interlibrary loan; library open to the public with restrictions. **Automated Operations:** Computerized cataloging, acquisitions, and circulation. **Computerized Information Services:** OCLC, RLIN; SUMMIT (internal database); CD-ROM (MathSci); BITNET, InterNet (electronic mail services). **Networks/Consortia:** Member of SUNY/OCLC Library Network. **Remarks:** FAX: (315)443-5549. Electronic mail address(es): LIBMMD@SUVM (BITNET); LIBMMD@SUVM.ACS.SYR.EDU (InterNet).

★ 15965 ★
Syracuse University - Physics Library (Sci-Engr)
208 Physics Bldg.   Phone: (315)443-2692
Syracuse, NY 13244-1130   Eileen Snyder, Libn.
Staff: 1.5. **Subjects:** Physics, astronomy. **Holdings:** 27,645 volumes. **Subscriptions:** 196 journals. **Services:** Interlibrary loan; copying; library open to the public. **Automated Operations:** Computerized cataloging, acquisitions and circulation. **Computerized Information Services:** OCLC, RLIN; SUMMIT (internal database). **Networks/Consortia:** Member of SUNY/OCLC Library Network. **Remarks:** FAX: (315)443-5549.

★ 15966 ★
Syracuse University - School of Education - Educational Resource Center (Educ)
050 Huntington Hall   Phone: (315)443-3800
Syracuse, NY 13244-2340   Dr. Tom Rusk Vickery, Dir.
Staff: Prof 5; Other 10. **Subjects:** Education. **Special Collections:** Diagnostic tests for school psychologists; collection of public school textbooks; children's books. **Holdings:** 19,000 books; multimedia material; curriculum material on microfiche; AV and production equipment; complete ERIC microfiche collection. **Subscriptions:** 145 journals and other serials. **Services:** Center open to students and faculty. **Computerized Information Services:** BITNET (electronic mail service). **Remarks:** TVICKERY@SUNR (BITNET).

★ 15967 ★
Syracuse University - Science and Technology Library (Biol Sci, Sci-Engr, Med)
105 Carnegie   Phone: (315)443-2160
Syracuse, NY 13244-2010   Lee M. Murray, Hd., Sci. & Tech.Dept.
Staff: Prof 5; Other 7. **Subjects:** Engineering - chemical, civil, electrical, bio-industrial, mechanical, aerospace; computers and data processing; biology; botany; zoology; microbiology; biochemistry; chemistry; immunology; genetics; ecology; public health; general medicine; medicine and society; nursing; neuroscience; general science and technology; history and philosophy of science; nutrition; mining and metallurgy; physical geography. **Special Collections:** Reports on microform from Atomic Energy Commission (AEC), Energy Research and Development Administration (ERDA), DOE, NASA, and Society of Automotive Engineers (SAE). **Holdings:** 390,000 books and bound periodical volumes; 700,000 microforms. **Subscriptions:** 1900 journals and other serials. **Services:** Interlibrary loan; copying; microform copying; library open to the public. **Automated Operations:** Computerized cataloging, acquisitions, serials, and circulation. **Computerized Information Services:** DIALOG Information Services, BRS Information Technologies, WILSONLINE, OCLC, RLIN, STN International; SUMMIT (internal database); CD-ROM. Performs searches. **Networks/Consortia:** Member of SUNY/OCLC Library Network. **Remarks:** FAX: (315)443-5549. **Staff:** Lockhart Russell, Engr. & Comp.Sci.Libn.; Nancy Herrington, Nutrition Libn.; H. Thomas Keays, Chem.Libn.; Patricia Sulouff, Biol.Libn.

★ 15968 ★
Syracuse University - Syracuse University Archives & Records Management Program (Hist)
E.S. Bird Library   Phone: (315)443-3335
Syracuse, NY 13244-2010   Amy S. Doherty, Univ.Archv. & Rec.Mgt.
Founded: 1959. **Staff:** Prof 1; Other 1. **Subjects:** History of Syracuse University. **Holdings:** General administrative records from the offices of chancellor, vice chancellor, provost, office of academic affairs, administrative operations, student affairs, university relations, and all their constituent parts; minutes, correspondence, reports, routine records of the schools and departments; personal papers of faculty and staff; university publications including those of students, alumni groups, and societies; Syracuse University theses and dissertations; photographs; memorabilia; selected articles, books, reports, speeches, and other items by members of the faculty and administration. **Services:** Copying; archives open to the public with restrictions. **Computerized Information Services:** RLIN; BITNET (electronic mail service). **Remarks:** FAX: (315)443-9510 (Attn.: 6th Floor). Electronic mail address(es): LIBASD@SUVM (BITNET). **Formerly:** Syracuse University Archives.

★15969★
Syria - Assad National Library (Soc Sci)
Malki St.
P.O. Box 3639
Damascus, Syrian Arab Republic   Phone: 338255
                                  Ghassan Lahham, Dir.Gen.
Founded: 1984. **Staff:** Prof 10; Other 260. **Subjects:** General. **Special Collections:** Arabic manuscripts; dissertations by Syrians in Syria and foreign universities; private libraries. **Holdings:** 158,805 books; 2126 bound periodical volumes; 7592 microfiche; 1180 reels of microfilm; 1670 slides; 2581 scores. **Subscriptions:** 70 journals and other serials; 10 newspapers. **Services:** Interlibrary loan; copying; library open to the public. **Computerized Information Services:** DIALOG Information Services; Syrian Legislations database (internal database). Performs searches. **Publications:** Syrian National Bibliography; Analytical Index to Syrian Periodicals; list of dissertations. **Remarks:** Telex: 419134.

★15970★
Syria - Ministry of Culture and National Guidance - Directorate General of Antiquities and Museums - Library (Area-Ethnic, Hist)
Damascus, Syrian Arab Republic   Phone: 228566
                                  Rihab Dahood, Libn.
Subjects: Syria - material culture, archeology, art history, history. **Holdings:** 30,000 volumes. **Services:** Interlibrary loan; library open to the public with restrictions. **Remarks:** Telex: 412491. **Also Known As:** Direction Generale des Antiquites et des Musees.

★15971★
System Planning Corporation - Technical Library (Mil, Comp Sci)
1500 Wilson Blvd.   Phone: (703)351-8200
Arlington, VA 22209   Phyllis W. Moon, Mgr.
Staff: Prof 2; Other 2. **Subjects:** Military science, international relations, computer science, radar. **Holdings:** 30,000 books. **Subscriptions:** 225 journals and other serials. **Services:** Interlibrary loan; library not open to the public. **Automated Operations:** Computerized cataloging. **Computerized Information Services:** DTIC, DIALOG Information Services, DMS/ONLINE. **Remarks:** FAX: (703)527-6037. **Staff:** Barbara A. Mack, ILL Libn.; Helena Pitsvada, Libn.

★15972★
Systems Applications International - Library (Sci-Engr)
101 Lucas Valley Rd.   Phone: (415)507-7100
San Rafael, CA 94903   Janet McDonald, Libn./Info.Spec.
Founded: 1975. **Staff:** Prof 1. **Subjects:** Air quality, meteorology, computer modeling. **Holdings:** 2000 books; 8000 technical reports. **Subscriptions:** 150

journals and other serials. **Services:** Interlibrary loan; copying; SDI; library open to the public by appointment. **Automated Operations:** Computerized cataloging. **Computerized Information Services:** DIALOG Information Services, NLM; internal database. Performs searches on fee basis. **Publications:** Acquisition list, irregular - for internal distribution only. **Remarks:** FAX: (415)507-7177.

★15973★
Systems Control/Power Automation/CE - Technical Library
2550 Walsh Ave.
Santa Clara, CA 95051-1315
Subjects: Computer software, electric power. **Holdings:** Figures not available. **Services:** Interlibrary loan; library open to the public with approval of librarian. **Remarks:** Currently inactive.

Systems Engineering Associates, Inc.
See: **S.E.A., Inc.** (14185)

★15974★
Syva Company - Library/Information Center (Biol Sci, Med)
3403 Yerba Buena Rd.   Phone: (408)239-2000
San Juan, CA 95161-9013   Meaghan Wheeler, Mgr.
Founded: 1966. **Staff:** Prof 4; Other 4. **Subjects:** Organic chemistry, biochemistry, microbiology, medicine. **Holdings:** 6000 books. **Subscriptions:** 300 journals and other serials. **Services:** Interlibrary loan; library not open to the public. **Computerized Information Services:** DIALOG Information Services, PFDS Online, BRS Information Technologies, Questel, OCLC, Chemical Abstracts Service (CAS). **Networks/Consortia:** Member of CLASS. **Staff:** Paul S. Hanson, Tech.Info.Spec.; Kim Kubik, Tech.Info.Spec.

Szilikatipari Kozponti Kutato es Tervezo Intezet
See: **Hungary - Central Research and Design Institute for the Silicate Industry** (7551)

★15975★
Szovetkezeti Kutato Intezet (Agri, Soc Sci)
Alkotmany u. 25
Postafiok 398
H-1371 Budapest, Hungary   Phone: 1 1116020
                            Zsuzsa Galambos
Founded: 1958. **Staff:** 1. **Subjects:** Cooperatives, economics, sociology, agriculture. **Special Collections:** The Cooperative movement. **Holdings:** 16,320 books; 1692 bound periodical volumes; 2305 reports. **Subscriptions:** 50 journals and other serials. **Services:** Interlibrary loan; copying; library open to the public.

T

★15976★
Tabor Opera House - Library (Hist)
815 Harrison Ave.   Phone: (719)486-1147
Leadville, CO 80461   Evelyn E. Furman
Founded: 1955. **Subjects:** History of Leadville, Colorado, Tabor Opera House history, Colorado history, paintings. **Services:** Library not open to the public.

★15977★
Tacachale Library (Med)
1621 N.E. Waldo Rd.   Phone: (904)395-1650
Gainesville, FL 32609-3918   Dorothy Washington
Founded: 1954. **Staff:** Prof 1; Other 1. **Subjects:** Mental retardation, exceptional education. **Holdings:** 6800 volumes; 3500 AV programs; high interest-low vocabulary picture books; professional materials. **Subscriptions:** 25 journals and other serials. **Services:** Interlibrary loan. **Formerly:** Sunland Center at Gainesville - Tacachale Library.

★15978★
Tackapausha Museum - Library (Biol Sci)
Washington Ave.   Phone: (516)785-2802
Seaford, NY 11783   Richard D. Ryder, Cur.
Staff: 2. **Subjects:** Natural history, zoology, botany, ornithology, mammalogy, herpetology. **Holdings:** 1100 books. **Subscriptions:** 10 journals and other serials. **Services:** Library open for reference use by appointment. **Remarks:** Maintained by Nassau County Department of Recreation and Parks.

★15979★
Tacoma Art Museum - Library (Art)
12th & Pacific Ave.   Phone: (206)272-4258
Tacoma, WA 98402   Sadie Uglow, Libn.
Founded: 1971. **Staff:** 1. **Subjects:** Art. **Special Collections:** Lindberg Collection of Impressionists, Northwest artists, Japanese woodblock prints, 20th century American printmakers, American Eight (Ashcan School). **Holdings:** 2140 books; clipping files; 1400 individual artist catalogs. **Subscriptions:** 38 journals and other serials. **Services:** Copying; library open to the public for reference use only. **Remarks:** FAX: (206)627-1898.

★15980★
(Tacoma) Morning News Tribune - Library (Publ)
Box 11000   Phone: (206)597-8629
Tacoma, WA 98411   Pilaivan H. Britton, Libn.
Founded: 1955. **Staff:** Prof 1; Other 2. **Subjects:** Newspaper reference topics. **Holdings:** 500 books; newspaper clippings; 5 VF drawers of pamphlets; 250 maps; News Tribune, 1909 to present, on microfilm. **Subscriptions:** 50 journals and other serials; 20 newspapers. **Services:** Library not open to the public. **Automated Operations:** Computerized acquisitions and serials. **Computerized Information Services:** VU/TEXT Information Services, DataTimes. **Special Indexes:** Index to News Tribune Clip Files (microfiche, online); subject thesauri to files (book, online); cross-reference index of cities and towns of Washington state telephone books. **Remarks:** FAX: (206)597-8274.

★15981★
Tacoma Public Library - Special Collections (Hist)
1102 Tacoma Ave., S.   Phone: (206)591-5622
Tacoma, WA 98402   Kevin Hegarty, Dir.
Founded: 1892. **Staff:** Prof 2; Other 2. **Subjects:** Pacific Northwest and Washington state history. **Special Collections:** Genealogy and local history; John B. Kaiser Collection (World War I posters and propaganda; 2000 volumes); Richards Photo Studio Collection (825,000 photographic negatives and prints). **Holdings:** 30,000 books; 2500 bound periodical volumes; 900 linear feet of manuscripts; 750 linear feet of local government archives; 30,000 slides; 35,000 maps; 80 VF drawers of clippings; 78 drawers of microforms. **Subscriptions:** 60 journals and other serials. **Services:** Interlibrary loan; copying; collections open to the public. **Automated Operations:** Computerized cataloging, acquisitions, and circulation. **Computerized Information Services:** DIALOG Information Services, DataTimes, OCLC. **Special Indexes:** Northwest Note File (200,000 cards); Northwest Biography File (75,000 cards); Calendars of Manuscripts; Local Obituary Index (1984 to present, online); Tacoma House and Building Index. **Remarks:** FAX: (206)591-5470; (206)627-1693. **Staff:** Gary Fuller Reese, Mng.Libn.

★15982★
Tacoma Public Utilities - Reference Library (Energy)
3628 S. 35th
Box 11007   Phone: (206)591-9764
Tacoma, WA 98411-5011   Barbara Werelius, Rec.Mgr., Ref.Libn.
Founded: 1954. **Subjects:** Supervisory and managerial reference; business oriented general information; public utilities general information - electrical, water; city and state laws and legislation. **Holdings:** 300 books; 2000 reports, surveys, studies; manuals for policies and procedures; archives. **Subscriptions:** 200 journals and other serials; 5 newspapers. **Services:** Copying; library open to the public. **Remarks:** FAX: (206)383-9627.

★15983★
(Taegu) American Cultural Center - USIS Library (Educ)
No. 45, 2-Ka, Sam Duk Dong
Chung-ku
Taegu 630, Republic of Korea
Remarks: Maintained or supported by the U.S. Information Agency. Focus is on materials that will assist peoples outside the United States to learn about the United States, its people, history, culture, political processes, and social milieux.

Lorado Taft Archives
See: **Northern Illinois University - Taft Field Campus** (12002)

★15984★
Taft Museum - Library (Art)
316 Pike St.   Phone: (513)241-0343
Cincinnati, OH 45202   David T. Johnson, Asst.Dir.
Founded: 1932. **Staff:** 1. **Subjects:** Art, historical buildings, museology. **Holdings:** 1200 books; 900 bound periodical volumes; 800 slides of permanent art collections. **Subscriptions:** 10 journals and other serials. **Services:** Copying; library open to the public by appointment for reference use only. **Publications:** The Taft Museum: Collections and its History. **Special Catalogs:** Taft Art Collection handbook; special exhibition catalogs. **Remarks:** FAX: (513)241-7762. Maintained by Cincinnati Institute of Fine Arts.

★15985★
Taft, Stettinius & Hollister - Law Library (Law)
1800 Star Bank Center
425 WAlnut St.   Phone: (513)381-2838
Cincinnati, OH 45202   Barbara J. Davis, Libn.
Staff: Prof 1; Other 3. **Subjects:** Law. **Holdings:** 25,000 volumes. **Subscriptions:** 670 journals and other serials; 5 newspapers. **Services:** Library not open to the public. **Computerized Information Services:** LEXIS, WESTLAW, Hannah Information Systems, DIALOG Information Services. **Publications:** Newsletter - for internal distribution only. **Remarks:** FAX: (513)381-0205; Telex: 810-461-2623.

William Howard Taft National Historic Site
See: **U.S. Natl. Park Service** (17791)

Jay P. Taggart Memorial Law Library
See: **Ohio Northern University - College of Law** (12272)

Tahtitieteellinen Yhdistys Ursa
See: **Ursa Astronomical Association** (19694)

★15986★
Taiwan - National Science Council - Science and Technology Information Center (Sci-Engr)
No. 106 Ho-Ping E. Rd., Sec 2   Phone: 2 7377631
Taipei 10636, Taiwan   Dr. Tao-Hsing Ma, STIC Dir.
Founded: 1973. **Staff:** 130. **Subjects:** Science and technology. **Holdings:** 13,560 volumes; 166,312 titles of NTIS reports on microfiche. **Subscriptions:** 1840 journals and other serials. **Services:** SDI; current awareness; document delivery. **Computerized Information Services:** DIALOG Information Services, ORBIT Search Service, BRS Information Technologies, ECHO, STIC, JOIS; CD-ROM. **Publications:** List of publications - available on request. **Remarks:** FAX: 2 7377663. Telex: 29674 STICROC.

★15987★
Taiwan Agricultural Research Institute - Library (Agri, Biol Sci)
189 Chung-Cheng Rd.
Wu-Feng   Phone: 4 3302301
Taichung 41301, Taiwan   Mr. Muh-Ning Jeng, Libn.
Staff: Prof 1; Other 2. **Subjects:** Agronomy, applied zoology, horticulture, agricultural chemistry, plant pathology, agricultural engineering, agricultural economy. **Holdings:** 13,850 books; 10,784 bound periodical volumes. **Subscriptions:** 750 journals and other serials; 12 newspapers. **Services:** Interlibrary loan; copying; SDI; library open to the public for reference use only. **Remarks:** FAX: 4 3338162.

★15988★
Taiwan Sugar Corporation - Taiwan Sugar Research Institute - Library (Food-Bev, Agri)
54 Sheng Chan Rd.   Phone: 6 267-1911
Tainan 700, Taiwan   Miss Y.H. Ting, Libn.
Subjects: Sugar industry in Taiwan; sugarcane breeding, processing, engineering; soil science; biological control of pests. **Holdings:** 40,000 volumes. **Remarks:** Telex: 4554 TAINAN.

★15989★
Talbot Associates, Inc. - Library (Sci-Engr)
11 Cleveland Pl.   Phone: (201)376-9570
Springfield, NJ 07081   Donald Blair, Pres.
Founded: 1954. **Subjects:** Metal casting, alloys. **Holdings:** References files; cross references; specifications. **Remarks:** FAX: (201)376-7617.

★15990★
Talbot County Free Library - Maryland Room (Hum, Hist)
100 W. Dover St.   Phone: (301)822-1626
Easton, MD 21601   Miss Scotti Oliver, Cur.
Subjects: History - local and state, with emphasis on Talbot County and other locations on the eastern shore; genealogy. **Special Collections:** H.L. Mencken (80 volumes); manuscripts and notes for James Michener's Chesapeake (25 boxes); manuscript of Dickson Preston's Young Frederick Douglass (1 box); manuscripts and notes for L.G. Shreve's Tench Tilghman, the Life and Times of Washington's Aide-de-Camp (3 boxes); history of the Society of Friends, 1673 to present (50 volumes); Lloyd Family papers (41 reels of microfilm); Maryland Colonial Society papers (31 reels of microfilm); Charles Carroll papers (3 reels of microfilm); Talbot County Register of Deaths, 1930-1969 (13 reels of microfilm); Talbot County Historic Sites Survey (9 volumes). **Holdings:** 4337 books; unbound periodicals; 18 VF drawers; 63 boxes of manuscripts and ephemera; 157 boxes and bound volumes of newspapers; 96 reels of microfilm of newspapers; 32 reels of microfilm of census data; 30 reels of microfilm of church records; 6 reels of microfilm of tax lists; 2 reels of microfilm of dissertations; 900 photographs; 369 maps. **Subscriptions:** 37 journals and other serials. **Services:** Copying; room open to the public for reference use only. **Special Catalogs:** Catalog of subject headings (card); catalog to manuscript and ephemera collection (card); catalog of microfilm, newspapers, and maps.

Talbot Research Library
See: **Institute for Cancer Research** (7909)

Talbott Library
See: **Westminster Choir College - Talbott Library** (20327)

★15991★
Tall Timbers Research Station - Library (Biol Sci, Env-Cons)
Rte. 1, Box 678   Phone: (904)893-4153
Tallahassee, FL 32312   Sharri Moroshok, Libn.
Founded: 1960. **Staff:** Prof 1; Other 1. **Subjects:** Fire ecology, wildlife management, ornithology, plant and general ecology, forestry. **Special Collections:** E.V. Komarek Fire File (fire ecology; 20,000 reprints and monographs). **Holdings:** 2300 books; 2900 bound periodical volumes; 27,000 reprints; 10,000 state, federal, and international documents; 5 VF drawers of scientific research data; 150 maps. **Subscriptions:** 240 journals and other serials. **Services:** Interlibrary loan (limited); copying; library open to the public by appointment. **Automated Operations:** Computerized cataloging. **Computerized Information Services:** Internal database. Performs searches on fee basis. **Publications:** Fire ecology thesaurus. **Remarks:** FAX: (904)668-7781

★15992★
Talladega College - Savery Library - Historical Collections (Area-Ethnic, Hist)
627 W. Battle St.   Phone: (205)362-0206
Talladega, AL 35160   Frances Baker Dates, Dir.
Founded: 1939. **Staff:** 6. **Subjects:** American blacks; missions in Angola, Mozambique, Zaire, and South Africa; the black church; civil rights; education. **Special Collections:** College archives (includes the activities of Talladega alumni); Historical Collections (the black church, African missions, southern Africa, civil rights, education). **Holdings:** 120 linear feet of archival items. **Subscriptions:** 4 journals and other serials. **Services:** Interlibrary loan; copying; collections open to serious researchers and noncampus undergraduates with letter from supervising faculty. **Computerized Information Services:** NCS (internal database). **Publications:** A Guide to the Archives of Talladega College, 1981; A Guide to the Collections, 1981. **Remarks:** FAX: (205)362-2268. **Staff:** Lloyd Bardell, Archv.; Marvett Sharp, Assoc.Libn.

★15993★
Talladega County Law Library (Law)
Judicial Bldg.
Northeast St.
P.O. Box 697   Phone: (205)761-2116
Talladega, AL 35160   Barry D. Matson, Law Libn.
Founded: 1951. **Staff:** Prof 1; Other 2. **Subjects:** Law. **Special Collections:** Law Review publications (150 titles). **Holdings:** 20,000 books; 3000 bound periodical volumes; 2000 pamphlets and documents. **Subscriptions:** 100 journals and other serials. **Services:** Copying; library open to the public for research only.

★15994★
Tallmadge Historical Society - Library & Archives (Hist)
213 Tallmadge Circle
P.O. Box 25   Phone: (216)630-9760
Tallmadge, OH 44278   Richard L. Smith, Pres.
Founded: 1858. **Staff:** 1. **Subjects:** History - Tallmadge, Summit County, Ohio. **Special Collections:** Bronson papers (local history and genealogy, 1807-1886; 10 handwritten volumes). **Holdings:** Figures not available. **Services:** Library open to the public by appointment.

★15995★
Tama County Historical Society - Museum Library (Hist)
200 N. Broadway
P.O. Box 84   Phone: (515)484-6767
Toledo, IA 52342   Joan Bidwell, V.P.
Founded: 1976. **Subjects:** Genealogy, local history. **Special Collections:** Family histories, censuses, newspapers, obituary scrapbooks (all on microform). **Holdings:** Books; microforms. **Subscriptions:** 25 journals and other serials **Services:** Copying; library open to the public for reference use only. **Computerized Information Services:** Internal databases.

Tamburitzans Cultural Center
See: **Duquesne University** (5065)

★15996★
Tamil Nadu Agricultural University - Library (Agri, Biol Sci, Env-Cons, Soc Sci)
PO   Phone: 41222
Coimbatore 641 003, Tamil Nadu, India K. Balasubramanian, Univ.Libn.
Founded: 1876. **Staff:** Prof 3; Other 9. **Subjects:** Agriculture, agricultural engineering, agronomy, biochemistry, biotechnology, economics, entomology, environmental biology, forestry, genetics, horticulture, rural sociology. **Holdings:** 75,000 books; 60,000 bound periodical volumes; 50,000 reports; 3000 archival items; 3000 rare books; 3000 theses and dissertations; 1690 non-book materials; 241 topographical maps; 98 microforms; 65 microfiche; 61 atlases; 33 reels of microfilm. **Subscriptions:** 875 journals and other serials; 3 newspapers. **Services:** Interlibrary loan; copying; library for use by University community, open to visitors by permission. **Publications:** READ; List of Periodicals; Back Volumes; List of Theses; APNI. **Remarks:** FAX: 422 41672. Telex: 855-360 TNAU-IN.

★ 15997 ★
Tamil Nadu Government - Oriental Manuscripts Library (Hum)
Chepauk Phone: 44 848778
Madras 600 005, Tamil Nadu, India Thiru S. Soundarapandian, Cur.
Founded: 1869. **Staff:** Prof 27. **Subjects:** Literature, religion, philosophy, medicine, history. **Special Collections:** Colonel Colin Mackenzie Collection (literature, religion, history, manners, and customs of the prople of India, Ceylon, and Java; manuscripts; coins; inscriptions; maps); Leyden Collection (manuscripts in Tamil, Telugu, and Kannada characters); C.P. Brown Collection (manuscripts of Sanskrit and Telugu works). **Holdings:** 24,057 books; 69,514 manuscripts. **Subscriptions:** 10 journals and other serials. **Services:** Library open to the public at librarian's discretion. **Publications:** Multilingual Bulletin, annual; 349 descriptive publications. **Remarks:** Library is located in the Western Wing of the first floor of the Madras University Library. Manuscripts are in the languages Sanskrit (48,884), Tamil (14,737), Telugu (2150), Kannada (250), Marathi (956), Urdu (183), Arabic (407), Persian (1386), and other Oriental languages.

Tamiment Library
See: **New York University - Tamiment Library** (11733)

Lt. David Tamir Library and Reading Room
See: **Consulate General of Israel** (4239)

★ 15998 ★
Tampa Bay Regional Information Center (Plan)
9455 Koger Blvd., Suite 206 Phone: (813)577-5151
St. Petersburg, FL 33702-2491 Lorrie A. Paul, Dir., Pub.Info.
Founded: 1962. **Staff:** Prof 1; Other 3. **Subjects:** Urban and regional planning, land use, energy, housing, human resources, transportation, environment. **Special Collections:** Local and regional comprehensive plans; environmental impact statements; developments of regional impact; U.S. Census data; aging. **Holdings:** 6000 books and technical documents; 400 maps. **Subscriptions:** 107 journals and other serials. **Services:** Research; copying; center open to the public. **Networks/Consortia:** Member of Tampa Bay Library Consortium, Inc. (TBLC). **Publications:** Visions (newsletter), monthly; technical plans. **Remarks:** The Tampa Bay Regional Information Center is maintained by the Tampa Bay Regional Planning Council. FAX: (813)570-5118.

★ 15999 ★
Tampa Electric Company - Business Information Center (Energy)
702 N. Franklin St. Phone: (813)228-1205
Tampa, FL 33602 Patricia W. Boody, Supv., Lib.Serv.
Founded: 1982. **Staff:** Prof 1; Other 2. **Subjects:** Electric power generation, energy, environment, business and economics, management, data processing. **Holdings:** 1500 books; unbound periodicals; 2000 documents; 5000 microfiche; 680 computer manuals. **Subscriptions:** 450 journals and other serials; 15 newspapers. **Services:** Interlibrary loan; copying; SDI; center open to the public. **Automated Operations:** Computerized cataloging, serials, and circulation. **Computerized Information Services:** DIALOG Information Services, CompuServe Information Service, DataTimes, Dow Jones News/Retrieval, Dun & Bradstreet Business Credit Services, LEXIS, NEXIS, VU/TEXT Information Services; DIALMAIL, CompuServe Information Service (electronic mail services). **Networks/Consortia:** Member of Tampa Bay Library Consortium, Inc. (TBLC), Florida Library Network (FLN). **Remarks:** FAX: (813)228-1670. Electronic mail address(es): EEI033 (CompuServe Information Service). **Formerly:** Its Technical Reference Center.

★ 16000 ★
Tampa General Hospital - Medical/Corporate Information Center (Med)
Box 1289 Phone: (813)251-7328
Tampa, FL 33601 Margaret Henry Petro, MLS, Libn.
Founded: 1961. **Staff:** Prof 2.5. **Subjects:** Medicine, nursing, pharmacy, otorhinolaryngology, anesthesiology, neurology, opthalmology, orthopedics, pathology, psychiatry, radiology, urology, rehabilitation, pediatrics, obstetrics, gynecology, surgery. **Special Collections:** Audio-Digest tapes on surgery, pediatrics, internal medicine, anesthesiology, otolaryngology, emergency medicine, gastro-entriology, obstetrics/gynecology, orthopedics, urology; Network for Continuing Medical Education tapes. **Holdings:** 3100 books; 3600 bound serial volumes; 12 drawers of microfiche. **Subscriptions:** 400 journals and other serials.

Services: Interlibrary loan; copying; SDI; library open to the public for hospital staff and affiliates. **Computerized Information Services:** MEDLINE, DIALOG Information Services; CD-ROMs (SilverPlatter, MEDLINE, CINAHL); OnTyme Electronic Message Network Service (electronic mail service). Performs searches on fee basis. **Networks/Consortia:** Member of Tampa Bay Medical Library Network, Florida Health Sciences Library Association (FHSLA). **Publications:** TGH Medical Library Newsletter, quarterly - to hospital staff.

★ 16001 ★
Tampa Tribune - Library (Publ)
202 S. Parker St. Phone: (813)272-7665
Tampa, FL 33601 Thomas Banks, Lib.Dir.
Founded: 1895. **Staff:** Prof 13; Other 3. **Subjects:** Newspaper reference topics. **Special Collections:** Historical Tampa photographs. **Holdings:** 2500 volumes; clippings; pamphlets; pictures; microfilm; reference books. **Subscriptions:** 18 journals and other serials; 11 newspapers. **Services:** Library open to newspaper personnel only. **Computerized Information Services:** CompuServe Information Service, VU/TEXT Information Services; SII LASR (internal database). **Remarks:** FAX: (813)272-7676. **Staff:** Mike Meiners, Lib.Mgr.; Alyce Diamandis, Sys.Libn.

★ 16002 ★
(Tampico) Centro Cultural Mexico-Americano - USIS Collection (Educ)
Calle Colon No. 317-Norte
89000 Tampico, Tamps., Mexico
Remarks: Maintained or supported by the U.S. Information Agency. Focus is on materials that will assist peoples outside the United States to learn about the United States, its people, history, culture, political processes, and social milieux.

Tams-Witmark Archives
See: **Princeton University - William Seymour Theatre Collection** (13388)

★ 16003 ★
Tandem Computers, Inc. - Corporate Information Center (Comp Sci)
10400 N. Tantau Ave., 248-07 Phone: (408)285-3160
Cupertino, CA 95014 Selma Zinker, Mgr.
Staff: Prof 4; Other 3. **Subjects:** Computer science, data processing, computer programming, communications, marketing, business. **Holdings:** 10,000 books; 4000 research reports; 2000 microfiche; 800 technical reports. **Subscriptions:** 475 journals and other serials; 22 newspapers. **Services:** Interlibrary loan; center not open to the public. **Automated Operations:** Computerized cataloging. **Computerized Information Services:** DIALOG Information Services, RLIN, The Source Information Network, VU/TEXT Information Services, Dow Jones News/Retrieval, NEXIS, NewsNet, Inc.; OnTyme Electronic Message Network Service (electronic mail service). **Networks/Consortia:** Member of CLASS. **Remarks:** FAX: (408)285-3150. Electronic mail address(es): TAND (OnTyme Electronic Message Network Service). **Staff:** Janet David; Jane Differding; Patty Turner.

★ 16004 ★
Tandem International Inc. - Library (Bus-Fin)
3625 Dufferin St., Suite 300 Phone: (416)630-8971
Downsview, ON, Canada M3K 1Z2 Rita Donorio, Lib.Techn.
Remarks: FAX: (416)630-9211. No further information was supplied by respondent. **Formerly:** Canadian Marketing Associates.

Z.T. Tang Medical Library
See: **Westerly Hospital** (20232)

Tanner Memorial Philosophy Library
See: **Stanford University** (15660)

Tante Blanche Museum
See: **Madawaska Historical Society - Madawaska Public Library Research Center** (9512)

Tanzania - Ministry of Health and Social Welfare - National Institute for Medical Research
See: **Tanzania - National Institute for Medical Research** (16006)

★16005★
Tanzania - National Central Library - Tanzania National Documentation Centre (TANDOC) (Sci-Engr, Bus-Fin)
P.O. Box 9283
Dar es Salaam, United Republic of   Phone: 26121
Tanzania   Mrs. D.A. Sekimang'a, Sr.Libn.
Subjects: Appropriate technology, agriculture, education, public health, economic development, industry and commerce. **Holdings:** 750,000 volumes; documents; reports. **Subscriptions:** 2500 journals and other serials. **Services:** Copying; center open to the public. **Publications:** Bibliographies; Directory of Libraries in Tanzania; Periodicals in the National Central Library; Abstracting Bulletins in Agriculture, Industry & Education; additional publications available.

★16006★
Tanzania - National Institute for Medical Research - Library (Med, Biol Sci)
P.O. Box 9653   Phone: 51 30770
Dar es Salaam, United Republic of Tanzania   M.K. Franc, Libn.
Subjects: Parasitology, entomology, tropical medicine, public health. **Holdings:** 19,000 volumes. **Remarks:** Maintained by Tanzania - Ministry of Health and Social Welfare.

★16007★
Tanzania Industrial Research and Development Organization - Technical Library (Sci-Engr)
P.O. Box 23235
Dar es Salaam, United Republic of Tanzania   Phone: 51 68822
Founded: 1981. **Subjects:** Tanzanian industry - technology, research, problems. **Holdings:** 15,000 volumes. **Subscriptions:** 30 journals and other serials; 15 newspapers. **Services:** Interlibrary loan; copying; SDI; library open to the public for reference use only. **Computerized Information Services:** Internal database. **Remarks:** FAX: 51 68984. Telex: 41409. **Staff:** W.N.A. Nyony, Hd., Info.Dept.; L. Limbe, Ext.Off.; J. Malinzi, Ext.Off.

★16008★
TAPPI Information Resources Center (Sci-Engr)
Box 105113   Phone: (404)446-1400
Atlanta, GA 30348   Joanne Tobin, Info.Rsrc.Adm.
Founded: 1915. **Staff:** Prof 2; Other 2. **Subjects:** Pulp, paper, packaging, and allied subjects. **Special Collections:** TAPPI Press depository. **Holdings:** 3600 books; 2125 bound periodical volumes. **Subscriptions:** 225 journals and other serials. **Services:** Interlibrary loan; technical inquiries; center open to the public. **Automated Operations:** Computerized cataloging and serials. **Computerized Information Services:** DIALOG Information Services, ORBIT Search Service; PIRA; Consultants Data Base File (internal database); TAPPI-Net (electronic mail service). Performs searches on fee basis. **Remarks:** FAX: (404)446-6947. Telex: 810-757-0145. **Staff:** Judith Dodge.

Tarlton Law Library
See: **University of Texas at Austin - School of Law** (19405)

★16009★
Tarrant County Law Library (Law)
100 W. Weatherford, Rm. 420   Phone: (817)884-1481
Fort Worth, TX 76196   Sharon Wayland, Dir.
Founded: 1945. **Staff:** Prof 4; Other 3. **Subjects:** Law. **Holdings:** 37,000 books; 2500 bound periodical volumes; 600 cassette tapes. **Subscriptions:** 250 journals and other serials. **Services:** Interlibrary loan; copying; library open to the public for reference use only. **Automated Operations:** Computerized public access catalog. **Computerized Information Services:** DIALOG Information Services, WESTLAW, Texas Legislative Service. **Special Catalogs:** Book catalog. **Special Indexes:** Index of Texas Law Review Articles. **Remarks:** FAX: (817)884-1509. **Staff:** Peggy Martindale, Asst.Dir.; Frances Perry, Libn.; Blanche Lea, Libn.

TASC Technical Library
See: **The Analytic Sciences Corporation** (828)

(Tasmania) State Library of Tasmania
See: **State Library of Tasmania** (15696)

★16010★
Tasmanian Museum & Art Gallery - Library (Biol Sci, Soc Sci)
40 Macquarie St.
GPO Box 1164M   Phone: 2 231422
Hobart, TAS 7001, Australia   Janet Middleton, Libn.
Founded: 1970. **Subjects:** Zoology, anthropology, geology, art, history, botany, museology, numismatics. **Holdings:** 6300 books; 210 periodical titles. **Subscriptions:** 160 journals and other serials. **Services:** Interlibrary loan; copying; library open to the public. **Remarks:** FAX: 2 347139.

★16011★
Tate Gallery - Library (Art)
Millbank   Phone: 71 821 1313
London SW1P 4RG, England   Beth Houghton, Libn.
Staff: Prof 5; Other 3. **Subjects:** Modern art, 1870 to present; British art, 16th century to present; museology; conservation. **Holdings:** 35,000 books; 2000 periodical titles; 110,000 current exhibition catalogs; 2000 artists' books. **Subscriptions:** 750 journals and other serials. **Services:** Interlibrary loan; copying; library open to the public by appointment. **Computerized Information Services:** ARTQUEST. **Publications:** Bibliographies. **Remarks:** FAX: 71 931 7512. **Staff:** Meg Duff, Acq.Libn.; Elisabeth Bell, Exch.Libn.; Krzysztof Cieszkowski, Cat.; Jane Savidge, Cat.

★16012★
Tatham/RSCG - Information Center (Bus-Fin)
980 N. Michigan Ave.   Phone: (312)337-4400
Chicago, IL 60611   Marilyn Stewart
Founded: 1985. **Staff:** Prof 1; Other 1.5. **Subjects:** Advertising, marketing. **Holdings:** 1200 books. **Subscriptions:** 300 journals and other serials; 5 newspapers. **Services:** Center not open to the public. **Computerized Information Services:** DIALOG Information Services, NEXIS, Dow Jones News/Retrieval, InvesText. **Formerly:** Tatham Laird & Kudner.

★16013★
Ben Taub General Hospital - Doctor's Medical Library (Med)
1502 Taub Loop   Phone: (713)791-7441
Houston, TX 77030   Angie Ortiz, Lib.Ck.
Founded: 1958. **Staff:** 1. **Subjects:** Medicine. **Holdings:** 1100 books; 110 bound periodical volumes; 12 VF drawers. **Subscriptions:** 110 journals and other serials; 8 newspapers. **Services:** Library not open to the public. **Automated Operations:** Computerized cataloging and acquisitions.

Alfred Taubman Medical Library
See: **University of Michigan** (18852)

Joseph Taussig Memorial Library
See: **Emanuel Congregation** (5319)

Tax Court of Canada
See: **Canada - Tax Court of Canada** (2864)

★16014★
Tax Executives Institute, Inc. - Library (Bus-Fin)
1001 Pennsylvania Ave., N.W., Suite 320   Phone: (202)638-5601
Washington, DC 20004-2505   Thomas P. Kerester, Exec.Dir.
Founded: 1944. **Staff:** Prof 5; Other 7. **Subjects:** Taxation; tax - legislation, administration, management. **Holdings:** 1000 books; 500 professional memoranda. **Subscriptions:** 20 journals and other serials. **Services:** Library open to TEI members upon written request. **Remarks:** FAX: (202)638-5607.

★16015★
Tax Foundation - Library
470 L'Enfant Plaza S.W.
East Bldg., No. 7112
Washington, DC 20024
Founded: 1937. **Subjects:** Taxation, federal budget, public finance, economics. **Holdings:** 1000 books. **Remarks:** Currently inactive.

Abbot Vincent Taylor Library
See: **Belmont Abbey College** (1699)

Allyn and Betty Taylor Library
See: **University of Western Ontario** (19553)

★16016★
Bayard Taylor Memorial Library (Art, Rare Book)
216 E. State St.   Phone: (215)444-2702
Kennett Square, PA 19348   Joseph A. Lordi, Dir.
Founded: 1895. **Staff:** Prof 1; Other 5. **Subjects:** Antiques, arts, social sciences, history, gardening. **Special Collections:** Harlan R. Cole Memorial Collection (reference collection about antiques); Bayard Taylor Collection (pre-1900 rare books); Pennsylvania Collection (local history); Rare Books of the Union Library Company of Kennett Square (pre-1896); Botanica Collection of Trees, Shrubs and Wildflowers. **Holdings:** 45,000 books; 4 VF drawers of pamphlets, clippings, local history materials, and maps. **Subscriptions:** 150 journals and other serials; 8 newspapers. **Services:** Interlibrary loan; copying; library open to the public. **Computerized Information Services:** Bibliofile (internal database). **Remarks:** FAX: (215)444-1752.

★16017★
Taylor Business Institute - Helen Rickson Library (Bus-Fin)
One Penn Plaza   Phone: (212)279-0510
New York, NY 10119   Mary E. Cardwell, Libn.
Founded: 1973. **Staff:** Prof 1. **Subjects:** Business, secretarial studies, accounting, travel and tourism, electronics. **Holdings:** 2521 books; 13 VF drawers; 60 video cassettes. **Subscriptions:** 77 journals and other serials. **Services:** Library not open to the public. **Publications:** New Books in the Library - to faculty and administration.

Taylor and Charlson Archives
See: **Riley County Historical Society** (13932)

★16018★
David Taylor Research Center - Carderock Division - Naval Surface
Warfare Center (Sci-Engr)
Code 3420   Phone: (202)227-1433
Bethesda, MD 20084-5000   Margaret A. Holland, Libn.
Subjects: Naval architecture; hydromechanics; structural mechanics; acoustics and vibration; mathematics; underwater ballistics; pure and applied physics; engineering - marine, electrical, mechanical, civil; environmental protection and safety; fabrication technology; energy; aerodynamics. **Special Collections:** DTRC reports. **Holdings:** 35,000 books; 18,000 bound periodical volumes; 100,000 technical reports; 23,000 classified documents; 280,000 microfiche. **Subscriptions:** 900 journals and other serials. **Services:** Interlibrary loan (to other government agencies); copying; SDI; center is open for staff use only and for other government employees by special arrangement. **Automated Operations:** Computerized cataloging, serials, and circulation. **Computerized Information Services:** DIALOG Information Services, DTIC, NASA/RECON. **Publications:** Accession Bulletin, monthly - for internal distribution only. **Special Indexes:** DTNSRDC Report index. **Remarks:** FAX: (301)227-5307. **Formerly:** Its Technical Information Center. **Staff:** Shirley B. Lyons, Hd., Annapolis TIC.

E.P. Taylor Research Library and Archives
See: **Art Gallery of Ontario** (1077)

Elizabeth Prewitt Taylor Memorial Library
See: **Arkansas Arts Center** (1022)

Frederick W. Taylor Archives
See: **Hive Publishing Company - John Franklin Mee Memorial Library** (7294)

Helen Marie Taylor Museum of Waco
See: **United Daughters of the Confederacy** (16706)

Ira J. Taylor Library
See: **Iliff School of Theology** (7666)

Larry Taylor/Billy Matthews Musical Theater Archive
See: **University of Miami - School of Music - Albert Pick Music Library** (18850)

★16019★
Moses Taylor Hospital - Library (Med)
745 Quincy Ave.   Phone: (717)963-2145
Scranton, PA 18510   Jo-Ann M. Babish, Dir., Lib.Serv.
Founded: 1978. **Staff:** Prof 1; Other 1. **Subjects:** Medicine, health administration, nursing. **Holdings:** 2000 books; journals on microfilm. **Subscriptions:** 250 journals and other serials. **Services:** Interlibrary loan; copying; SDI; library open to the public with restrictions. **Computerized Information Services:** DIALOG Information Services, MEDLARS; DOCLINE (electronic mail service). **Networks/Consortia:** Member of Health Information Library Network of Northeastern Pennsylvania (HILNNEP), BHSL. **Remarks:** FAX: (717)963-8994.

Taylor Museum Library
See: **Colorado Springs Fine Arts Center - Reference Library and Taylor Museum Library** (3949)

Robert H. Taylor Library
See: **Princeton University - Rare Books and Special Collections** (13386)

Stanley Taylor Sociology Reading Room
See: **University of Alberta** (18204)

★16020★
Taylor University - Zondervan Library - Archives/Special Collections
(Rel-Phil)
500 W. Reade   Phone: (317)998-5520
Upland, IN 46989-1001   Dwight Mikkelson, Archv.
Staff: Prof 1. **Subjects:** Protestant theology. **Special Collections:** Hillis congressional papers; Wesley materials; African, Oriental, and rare book collections; rare historical documents. **Holdings:** 1000 books. **Services:** Copying; collections open to the public. **Automated Operations:** Computerized cataloging. **Computerized Information Services:** DIALOG Information Services. Performs searches on fee basis. Contact Person: Roger Phillips. **Networks/Consortia:** Member of INCOLSA.

★16021★
TCT - Library (Env-Cons)
1908 Innerbelt Business Center Dr.   Phone: (314)426-0880
St. Louis, MO 63114   Sue Ellis, Libn./Info.Spec.
Founded: 1975. **Staff:** Prof 1. **Subjects:** Water and air pollution, wastewater treatment, hazardous waste management, chemical analysis, environmental engineering. **Holdings:** 2050 books; 500 government documents. **Subscriptions:** 40 journals and other serials. **Services:** Interlibrary loan; copying; library open to the public by appointment. **Computerized Information Services:** DIALOG Information Services. **Remarks:** FAX: (314)426-4212.

★ 16022 ★
TDS Healthcare Systems Corporation - Technical Library (Med, Comp Sci)
160 E. Tasman Dr.   Phone: (408)943-5619
San Jose, CA 95134   Cheryl Caccialanza, Tech.Libn.
Founded: 1982. **Staff:** Prof 1; Other 1. **Subjects:** Hospital information systems, physicians and computers. **Special Collections:** Federal Information Processing Standards (FIPS) publications (complete set). **Holdings:** 1300 books; 50 other cataloged items. **Subscriptions:** 98 journals and other serials. **Services:** Interlibrary loan; copying; SDI. **Computerized Information Services:** DIALOG Information Services. **Networks/ Consortia:** Member of CLASS, South Bay Cooperative Library System (SBCLS). **Remarks:** FAX: (408)943-5700.

Tea Research Institute of Sri Lanka
See: Sri Lanka Tea Board (15627)

★ 16023 ★
Teachers College - Milbank Memorial Library (Educ)
Columbia University
525 W. 120th St.
DB, Box 307   Phone: (212)678-3494
New York, NY 10027   Jane P. Franck, Dir.
Founded: 1887. **Staff:** Prof 28; Other 16. **Subjects:** Education, psychology, health sciences, nutrition, nursing, communications, computing, technology, speech and language pathology, audiology. **Special Collections:** Darton Collection (early English children's books); Annie E. Moore Collection (illustrated children's literature); chapbook collection; U.S. and foreign elementary and secondary school textbooks; rare books on education, 15th-19th centuries; Adelaide Nutting Collection (history of nursing); Teachers College Archives (administrative records, papers of faculty members, and related materials); Archives of the Board of Education of the City of New York (printed records; manuscripts; photographs); records of the Bank Street College of Education; National Kindergarten Association; National Council for the Social Studies; New York Juvenile Asylum. **Holdings:** 522,053 monograph and serial volumes; 405,968 microforms; 14,898 nonprint materials; 4025 cubic feet of manuscript material; 79,300 photographs; 9019 titles in microform; 910 software programs. **Subscriptions:** 2529 journals and other serials. **Services:** Interlibrary loan; library open to the public with special permits. **Computerized Information Services:** DIALOG Information Services, BRS Information Technologies, WILSONLINE, RLIN, ERIC. **Networks/ Consortia:** Member of Research Libraries Information Network (RLIN), New York State Interlibrary Loan Network (NYSILL). **Publications:** Circulation and Borrowing Information; ILL Guide; Online Search Services; Special Collections; Photocopy Services; Resource Center; New Titles. **Remarks:** FAX: (212)678-4048; 678-3092. **Staff:** Jennifer Whitten, Hd., Coll.Mgt.; Maureen Horgan, Plan.Coord.; David Ment, Hd., Spec.Coll.; Kathleen Murphy, Hd., Access; Allen Foresta, Hd., Ref.Serv.; Sergio Gaitan, Hd., Ctr. for Educ.Tech.Rsrcs.; Frank Webster, Hd., Bibliog.Tech.; Cecile Hastie, Ref.Libn.; Janet Pierce, Ref.Libn.; Yodit Kebede, Hd., Bibliog./Ser.Acq.; Monique Carroll, Hd.Bibliog. Monographic Acq.;Anita Lauer, Hd., Bibliog. Control; Anca Cazimir, Ref.Libn.; Miranda Martin, Cons.; Mesfin Tesfaye, Bibliog.; Richard Gibboney, Ref. Intern; Ellen Stockdale-Wolfe, Non-Print Cat.; Sung Kim, Monograph Cat.; Dennis McClelland, Ser.Cat.

★ 16024 ★
Teachers Insurance and Annuity Association of America - Business Library (Bus-Fin)
730 Third Ave.   Phone: (212)490-9000
New York, NY 10017   Kathleen Kelleher, Asst.Res.Off.
Founded: 1959. **Staff:** Prof 5; Other 3. **Subjects:** Insurance, pensions and annuities, law, higher education. **Special Collections:** Carnegie Foundation reports. **Holdings:** 12,000 books; 452 reels of microfilm. **Subscriptions:** 650 journals and other serials; 12 newspapers. **Services:** Interlibrary loan; library open to SLA members by appointment only. **Automated Operations:** Computerized serials and acquisitions. **Computerized Information Services:** DIALOG Information Services, LEXIS, NEXIS, WESTLAW, OCLC. **Staff:** Mary-Lynne Bancone, Libn.; Lisa Koch, Asst.Libn.; Carolyn Kopp, Archv.; Krista Friedman, Asst.Libn.

Teachout-Price Memorial Library
See: Hiram College (7231)

Edwin Way Teale Archives
See: University of Connecticut - Homer Babbidge Library - Special Collections (18519)

★ 16025 ★
Team Four Inc. - Library (Plan)
14 N. Newstead Ave.
St. Louis, MO 63108   Phone: (314)533-2200
Staff: Prof 1. **Subjects:** Architecture, urban planning, master plans, planning, landscape architecture. **Holdings:** 300 books; 30 bound periodical volumes; 100 reports. **Subscriptions:** 30 journals and other serials. **Remarks:** FAX: (314)533-2203.

★ 16026 ★
Teaneck Public Library - Oral and Local History Project (Hist)
840 Teaneck Rd.   Phone: (201)837-4171
Teaneck, NJ 07666   Michael McCue, Dir.
Staff: Prof 13; Other 15. **Subjects:** Local history, early families, Jewish community, black community. **Holdings:** 100 cassettes; 4 notebooks; 1000 index cards; photographs; transcriptions; documentary film; historical exhibits; slide/tape show. **Services:** Copying; project open to the public by appointment. **Computerized Information Services:** DIALOG Information Services, DataTimes. **Remarks:** FAX: (201)837-0410.

Charlton W. Tebeau Library of Florida History
See: Historical Association of Southern Florida (7256)

★ 16027 ★
Tech-U-Fit Corporation - Library (Sci-Engr)
400 Madison St., No. 210
Alexandria, VA 22314   Phone: (703)549-0512
Subjects: Engineering, psychology, human factors engineering, ergonomics. **Holdings:** 200 volumes. **Remarks:** FAX: (703)548-0780.

★ 16028 ★
Technic Inc. - Library (Sci-Engr)
1 Spectacle St.   Phone: (401)781-6100
Cranston, RI 02910   Alfred M. Weisberg, V.P.
Founded: 1948. **Staff:** Prof 1. **Subjects:** Electrochemistry, surface finishing and electroplating, metallurgy, electronics, manufacturing, jewelry. **Special Collections:** Precious metals. **Holdings:** 500 shelves of books and bound periodical volumes. **Subscriptions:** 75 journals and other serials; 5 newspapers. **Services:** Copying; library open to the public with restrictions. **Publications:** TechnicNews (newsletter). **Remarks:** FAX: (401)781-2890.

★ 16029 ★
Technical Careers Institute - TCI Technical Library (Sci-Engr)
320 W. 31st St.   Phone: (212)594-4000
New York, NY 10001   Stanley W. Zillig, Libn.
Staff: 2. **Subjects:** Electronics, electronic technology, mathematics. **Holdings:** 4500 books; 40 videotapes; 150 films. **Subscriptions:** 50 journals and other serials. **Services:** Interlibrary loan; library open to the public with restrictions. **Computerized Information Services:** Internal database. **Networks/Consortia:** Member of New York Metropolitan Reference and Research Library Agency. **Formerly:** Its I. Philip Sipser Technical Library.

Technical Library for Tropical and Hurricane Meteorology
See: U.S. Natl. Oceanic & Atmospheric Administration - National Hurricane Center - Library (17656)

★ 16030 ★
Technical Research Centre of Finland - Information Service (Sci-Engr)
P.O. Box 42   Phone: 0 4561
SF-02151 Espoo, Finland   Sauli Laitinen, Dir.
Founded: 1947. **Staff:** Prof 23; Other 33. **Subjects:** Technology - general, energy, information, process, building and community development, manufacturing. **Holdings:** 140,000 books; 25,000 bound periodical volumes; 88,000 reports on microfiche. **Subscriptions:** 2000 journals and other serials.

Services: Interlibrary loan; copying; SDI; service open to the public. **Automated Operations:** Computerized cataloging, acquisitions, serials, circulation, and ILL. **Computerized Information Services:** BRS Information Technologies, Chemical Information Systems, Inc. (CIS), DIALOG Information Services, Dow Jones News/Retrieval, EBSCO Subscription Services, Reuters Information Services (Canada), Info Globe, LEXIS, NEXIS, NewsNet, Inc., OCLC, ORBIT Search Service, QL Systems, RLIN, STN International, VU/TEXT Information Services, WILSONLINE, BELINDIS (Belgian Information and Dissemination Service), BLAISE Online Services, British Maritime Technology Ltd., BREW-INFO, CMO/Maritime Information Centre, Data-Star, FT PROFILE, DBI (Deutsches Bibliotheksinstitut), DIMDI, ECHO, ESA/IRS, FIZ Technik, L'Europeenne de Donnees, INION, MZNT, KOMPASS ON LINE, Leatherhead Food Research Association, Questel, Thermodata, VINITI (Vsesoyuznyi Institut Nauchnoy i Teknicheskoy Informatsii), AffarsData, ALIS (Automated Library Information System), BIBSYS, BYGGDOK (Institutet for Byggdokumentation), DataArkiv AB, Datacentralen (I/S), IDC-KTHB (Information and Documentation Center of the Royal Institute of Technology Library), LIBRIS, ROADLINE, Fabritius Online, LUKAS, MIC-KIBIC, Dafa, RECODEX, KCL, Minttu, Helecon, TENTTU. Performs searches on fee basis. Contact Person: Pirkko Eskola, Hd., Res. & Info.Serv.Sect., 0 4564410. **Publications:** List of new publications acquired, 6/year - by subscription; Periodica, annual - free upon request; lists of new publications published by Technical Research Centre of Finland, 12/year - by subscription; list of new research projects at Technical Research Centre of Finland, 6/year - by subscription; Informaatiopalvelu Tiedottaa (newsletter), semiannual - free upon request. **Special Catalogs:** Research Register (online); Publications Register (online); Book Acquisitions (online). **Remarks:** FAX: 0 4564374. Telex: 125 175 vttin sf. **Staff:** Pirjo Sutela, Hd., Doc. Delivery Serv.; Kerttu Tirronen, Hd., Publ.Sect.

★ 16031 ★
Technical Services Laboratories, Inc. - Library (Sci-Engr)
1612 N. Lexington Ave.   Phone: (417)864-8924
Springfield, MO 65802   Michael W. Woods, Mgr., Serv.
Subjects: Analytical chemistry, metallurgy, lubrication, paints, environmental chemistry, industrial hygiene. **Holdings:** 1000 volumes. **Services:** Library not open to the public. **Formerly:** Transportation Services Division.

★ 16032 ★
Technical University - Library (Sci-Engr)
1156 Sofia, Bulgaria   Phone: 2 6363567
          Margarita Tsvetkova
Founded: 1960. **Staff:** 8. **Subjects:** Education and training in mechanical and electrical engineering; electronics; automation and robotics; machine building; power engineering; textiles; computer science; managment. **Holdings:** 140,000 books; 35,000 bound periodical volumes. **Subscriptions:** 211 journals and other serials; 10 newspapers. **Services:** Interlibrary loan; copying; SDI; library open to the public for reference use only. **Remarks:** Telex: 22575. Maintained by Bulgaria - Ministry of National Education. **Formerly:** V.I. Lenin Higher Institute of Mechanical and Electrical Engineering - Library. **Staff:** Svetla Zheleva; Velichka Patyova; Magdalena Rashkova; Vesselina Neikova; Maria Karamarinova; Violeta Anastasova; Violeta Bailieva.

★ 16033 ★
The Technical University Library of Norway (Sci-Engr, Art)
N-7034 Trondheim, Norway   Phone: 7 595110
          Mrs. Randi Gjersvik, Dir.
Founded: 1912. **Staff:** Prof 34; Other 29. **Subjects:** Science and technology, architecture, art, trade. **Holdings:** 1 million volumes; 200,000 standards; 3.2 million patents; 250,000 reports on microfiche. **Subscriptions:** 8000 journals and other serials; 40 newspapers. **Services:** Interlibrary loan; copying; library open to the public. **Automated Operations:** Computerized public access catalog, cataloging, acquisitions, ordering, and ILL. **Computerized Information Services:** ESA/IRS, DIALOG Information Services, PFDS Online, ORBIT Search Service, Questel, STN International, Data-Star, Epos Viva. Performs searches on fee basis. **Publications:** Research reports, irregular. **Remarks:** Serves as the central technological library of Norway, and is a National Resource Library for architecture and technology. The Norwegian DIANE Centre, a national service center for online users, is located within the library. The library is also the National Center for ESA/IRS. Services are available without restrictions. FAX: 7 595103. Telex: 55 186 nthhb n. **Staff:** Wenche N. Dahl, Hd. of Acq.Dept.; Bjorn L. Hegseth, Hd. of ILL Dept.; Aud Lamvik, Hd. of Info.Ret.Dept.; Ingar Lomheim, Hd. of Pub.Dept.; Svein-Eirik Paulsen, Hd. of Per.Dept.; Knut J. Petersen, Hd. of Cat.Dept.

★ 16034 ★
Technical University of Nova Scotia - Library (Sci-Engr)
Barrington & Bishop St.
P.O. Box 1000   Phone: (902)420-7700
Halifax, NS, Canada B3J 2X4   Mohammad Riaz Hussain, Libn.
Founded: 1949. **Staff:** Prof 4; Other 11. **Subjects:** Engineering - civil, chemical, mechanical, mineral, electrical, industrial; geology; mathematics; architecture; planning; food science; fisheries; computer science. **Special Collections:** Fletcher Memorial Collection (geology and mining); Foulis Collection (environmental sciences). **Holdings:** 90,000 volumes; 70,000 microfiche; 12,000 slides; 100 video cassettes. **Subscriptions:** 1250 journals and other serials. **Services:** Interlibrary loan; copying; SDI; microfilming; library open to the public. **Automated Operations:** Computerized cataloging. **Computerized Information Services:** DIALOG Information Services, CAN/OLE; UTLAS (electronic mail service). **Networks/Consortia:** Member of Association of Atlantic Universities Librarians Council. **Publications:** Library Holdings of Serial Publications, annual. **Remarks:** FAX: (902)420-7551; (902)429-2176. Telex: 019 21566. Electronic mail address(es): NSHT.ILL (Envoy 100). **Staff:** Tahira Hussain, Sr.Libn.; Janet Servant, Pub.Serv.; Helen Powell, Tech.Serv.

★ 16035 ★
Technical University of Wroclaw - Main Library and Scientific Information Center (Sci-Engr)
Wybrzeze Wyspianskiego 27   Phone: 202305
PL-50-370 Wroclaw, Poland   Dr. Henryk Szarski, Dir.
Founded: 1946. **Staff:** Prof 71; Other 152. **Subjects:** Mathematics; physics; chemistry; architecture; engineering - civil, chemical, electric, mechanical; biochemistry; cybernetics; materials science; earth science; systems theory; environmental sciences; computer science. **Holdings:** 850,000 bound volumes. **Subscriptions:** 2321 journals and other serials. **Services:** SDI; library open to the public. **Automated Operations:** Computerized public access catalog, circulation, and cataloging. **Computerized Information Services:** INIS (International Nuclear Information System), COMPENDEX, INSPEC, ISMEC, PASCAL; SEBAN (internal database); CD-ROMs (Science Citation Index, Enviro/Energyline Abstracts Plus, CITIS CD-ROM, INSPEC Ondisc, DIALOG OnDisc, COMPENDEX PLUS, ICONDA, NTIS); EARN (electronic mail service). Performs searches on fee basis. **Publications:** Bibliography of Wroclaw Technical University Staff Publications. **Remarks:** Alternate telephone number(s): 71 212707. FAX: 71 223664. Telex: 71-25-59 pwrpl. Electronic mail address(es): SZAR@PLWRPU11 (EARN). **Also Known As:** Politechnika Wroclawska - Biblioteka Glowna i Osodek Informacji Naukowo-Technicznej.

Technicon Instruments Corporation
See: **Miles/Technicon** (10393)

★ 16036 ★
Technion Israel Institute of Technology - Faculty of Agricultural Engineering - Lowdermilk Library (Agri)
Technion City   Phone: 4 292625
32000 Haifa, Israel   Dvora Levy
Staff: Prof 2. **Subjects:** Agriculture, irrigation, soil science, agricultural mechanization, drainage, fertilizers. **Holdings:** 20,000 books; 20,000 bound periodical volumes. **Subscriptions:** 300 journals and other serials. **Services:** Interlibrary loan; copying; library open to the public for reference use only. **Computerized Information Services:** DIALOG Information Services.

★ 16037 ★
Technion Israel Institute of Technology - Faculty of Mathematics - Library (Sci-Engr)
Technion City   Phone: 4 294283
32000 Haifa, Israel   Evelyn Stern
Founded: 1956. **Staff:** 2.5. **Subjects:** Theoretical mathematics, applied mathematics. **Special Collections:** Russian books (1400); collected works of mathematicians (108); Technion Pre-print Series of Faculty Members (911). **Holdings:** 20,000 books; 9200 bound periodical volumes; 239 theses. **Subscriptions:** 209 journals and other serials. **Services:** Interlibrary loan; copying; SDI; library open to the public. **Publications:** Technion Department of Mathematics Publications of Faculty Members. **Remarks:** FAX: 4 324654.

★ 16038 ★
Technion Israel Institute of Technology - Faculty of Mechanical Engineering - Library (Sci-Engr)
Technion City   Phone: 4 292082
32000 Haifa, Israel   Hana Oppenheimer
Founded: 1960. **Subjects:** Mechanical engineering, robotics, heating and cooling, heat transfer, fracture and fatigue, energy engineering. **Special Collections:** SAE papers, ASME papers. **Holdings:** Microfiche, microfilm, thesis. **Subscriptions:** 200 journals and other serials; 5 newspapers. **Services:** Interlibrary loan; copying; library open to the public.

★ 16039 ★
Technische Hochschule Aachen - Institut fur Anglistik - Bibliothek (Hum)
Karmanstr 17/19   Phone: 241 806161
O-5100 Aachen, Germany   Barbara Bisping-Bau, Dipl.-Bibl.
Founded: 1966. **Subjects:** English literature, modern linguistics, Commonwealth literature, American literature, historical linguistics. **Special Collections:** Early English Text Society collection; Early English Manuscripts collection. **Holdings:** 40,000 books; 2084 bound periodical volumes; 1600 microfiche; 151 reels of microfilm; tapes; cassettes; phonograph recordings. **Subscriptions:** 48 journals and other serials. **Services:** Library open to the public. **Publications:** Neuerwerbungsliste (acquisitions list), semiannual. **Remarks:** FAX: 241 407712.

★ 16040 ★
Technische Universitat Hamburg-Harburg - Universitatsbibliothek (Sci-Engr)
Denickestr. 22
Postfach 91 10 52
W-2100 Hamburg 90, Germany   Phone: 40 77182845
     Horst Schild
Founded: 1979. **Staff:** Prof 55. **Subjects:** Engineering, science. **Special Collections:** International standards. **Holdings:** 300,000 volumes. **Subscriptions:** 1532 journals and other serials; 8 newspapers. **Services:** Interlibrary loan; copying; library open to the public. **Computerized Information Services:** DIALOG Information Services, STN International, ESA/IRS, DIMDI, FIZ Technik, Questel; Hamburger Verbundkatalog (internal database). Contact Person: Thomas Hapke. **Publications:** List of periodicals; list of textbooks. **Remarks:** FAX: 40 77182248.

★ 16041 ★
Technische Universitat Munchen - Bibliothek des Vorklinikums (Med)
Biedersteinerstr 29   Phone: 89 38493387
W-8000 Munich 40, Germany   Karin Mark
Founded: 1977. **Staff:** Prof 1. **Subjects:** Medicine, nursing, and allied health sciences. **Holdings:** 2382 books; 9501 bound periodical volumes. **Subscriptions:** 100 journals and other serials. **Services:** Copying; library open to the public. **Computerized Information Services:** CD-ROM (Medline).

★ 16042 ★
Technische Universitat Munchen - Universitatsbibliothek - Zweigbibliothek Weihenstephan (Agri)
W-8050 Freising 12, Germany   Phone: 816 713241
     Christiane Heilmann, Lib.Dir.
Subjects: Agriculture, food technology, horticulture, brewing science, dairy science, home economics. **Holdings:** 108,086 books and bound periodical volumes; 439 microfiche. **Subscriptions:** 656 journals and other serials; 3 newspapers. **Services:** Interlibrary loan; copying; SDI; library open to the public. **Computerized Information Services:** STN International, DIMDI. Contact Person: Leo Matschkal, Libn.

★ 16043 ★
Technische Universiteit Delft - Faculteit Luchtvaart en Ruimtevaarttechniek - Bibliotheek (Sci-Engr)
Kluyverweg 1   Phone: 15 782071
NL-2629 HS Delft, Netherlands   Ms. P.E.C. Zwagemaker
Founded: 1940. **Staff:** Prof 2. **Subjects:** Aerodynamics, airplane design, flight mechanics, stability and control of aircraft and space vehicles, production and materials, aerospace structures, space technology. **Holdings:** 9000 books; 4600 bound periodical volumes; 85,000 reports; 1200 microfiche. **Subscriptions:** 220 journals and other serials. **Services:** Interlibrary loan; copying; library open to the public.

★ 16044 ★
Technische Universiteit Eindhoven - Faculteitsbibliotheek Wiskunde en Informatica (Sci-Engr, Comp Sci)
Postbus 513   Phone: 40 472766
NL-5600 MB Eindhoven, Netherlands   P.L.J. van Rooij
Founded: 1958. **Staff:** Prof 3. **Subjects:** Mathematics, computer science. **Holdings:** 20,000 books; 3000 bound periodical volumes; 10,000 reports; 5000 microfiche. **Subscriptions:** 300 journals and other serials. **Services:** Interlibrary loan; copying; library open to the public. **Computerized Information Services:** DIALOG Information Services, ESA/IRS, STN International. Contact Person: J. Arts. **Remarks:** FAX: 40 447015.

★ 16045 ★
Technology Applications, Inc. - Technical Library
6101 Stevenson Ave.
Alexandria, VA 22304
Founded: 1984. **Subjects:** Engineering - naval, industrial, civil, aerospace; automated information systems; facilities management. **Holdings:** 1450 books, bound reports. **Remarks:** Currently inactive.

★ 16046 ★
Technology Research Corporation - Library (Comp Sci)
Springfield Professional Park
8328-A Traford Ln.   Phone: (703)451-8830
Springfield, VA 22152   M. Alexander, Info.Spec.
Founded: 1983. **Staff:** 2. **Subjects:** Robotics; applied artificial intelligence - defense systems, manufacturing, computer-aided design and manufacturing, machine vision, Computer-Assisted Logistics Support (CALS), enterprise integration, manufacturing technology. **Holdings:** 375 volumes. **Subscriptions:** 21 journals and other serials; 3 newspapers. **Services:** Interlibrary loan; copying; library open to the public by appointment. **Computerized Information Services:** DIALOG Information Services; internal databases. **Publications:** Special Reports; Advanced Manufacturing Technology; Robots; CIM. **Staff:** Peg Alexander; Dan Scherr.

★ 16047 ★
Technology Transfer Society - Library (Sci-Engr)
611 N. Capitol   Phone: (317)262-5022
Indianapolis, IN 46204   Dr. F. Timothy Janis, Dir.
Founded: 1963. **Staff:** 2. **Subjects:** Technology transfer. **Holdings:** Journals; proceedings; newsletters; reports. **Services:** Center not open to the public. **Publications:** Journal of Technology Transfer, quarterly; T'Squared (newsletter), monthly. **Remarks:** FAX: (317)262-5044. **Formerly:** Indiana University - Aerospace Research Application Center (ARAC) - NASA Technical Information Center.

★ 16048 ★
Technology Transfer Society - Library (Sci-Engr)
611 N. Capitol Ave.   Phone: (317)262-5022
Indianapolis, IN 46204   Maureen Swinney, Off.Mgr.
Founded: 1975. **Staff:** 1. **Subjects:** Technology transfer. **Special Collections:** Proceedings of the Technology Transfer Society. **Holdings:** 200 volumes. **Services:** Copying; library open to the public. **Remarks:** FAX: (317)262-5044.

★ 16049 ★
Technomic, Inc. - Information Services (Food-Bev)
300 S. Riverside Plaza, Suite 1940 S.   Phone: (312)876-0004
Chicago, IL 60606   Christine Urban, Mgr., Info.Rsrcs.
Founded: 1976. **Staff:** Prof 1; Other 1. **Subjects:** Management, food/food service, packaging. **Special Collections:** Food Service Resource Center (500 books; 100 periodicals; 60 VF drawers). **Holdings:** 606 books; 60 VF drawers of clippings. **Subscriptions:** 150 journals and other serials. **Services:** Interlibrary loan; copying; services open to the public with approval. **Computerized Information Services:** DIALOG Information Services, Dow Jones News/Retrieval, Dun & Bradstreet Business Credit Services; Restaurant Concepts, Acquisition Database (internal databases). Performs searches on fee basis. **Networks/Consortia:** Member of Chicago Library System. **Publications:** TRA Foodservice Abstracts, monthly - by subscription; Restaurant Information Service (updates), bimonthly; Top 100 Chain Restaurants, annual. **Remarks:** FAX: (312)876-1158.

★16050★

Technomic Publishing Co., Inc. (TPC) - Business Library (Sci-Engr, Publ)
851 New Holland Ave.
Box 3535   Phone: (717)291-5609
Lancaster, PA 17604   Edward Kladky, Lib.Dir.
Staff: Prof 1. **Subjects:** Plastics, resins, composites, materials engineering, sanitary engineering, environmental science, biotechnology, packaging, pharmaceuticals, educational administration. **Holdings:** 764 books; 40 bound periodical volumes. **Subscriptions:** 17 journals and other serials. **Services:** Library not open to the public. **Remarks:** FAX: (717)295-4538. Telex: 230 753565 TECHNOMIC UD.

★16051★

Teck Corporation - Library (Sci-Engr)
200 Burrard Street   Phone: (604)687-1117
Vancouver, BC, Canada V6C 3L9   Mary-Anne Pomphrey, Libn.
Staff: Prof 1; Other 1. **Subjects:** Mining, geology. **Holdings:** 2000 books; 3000 government documents; 500 maps; annual reports. **Subscriptions:** 200 journals and other serials; 15 newspapers. **Services:** Library not open to the public. **Computerized Information Services:** CAN/OLE, DIALOG Information Services, Infomart Online, Info Globe; Envoy 100 (electronic mail service). **Remarks:** FAX: (604)687-6100. Electronic mail address(es): TECK.LIB (Envoy 100).

★16052★

TECSULT, Inc. - Library Department (Sci-Engr)
85 W. Ste. Catherine   Phone: (514)287-8546
Montreal, PQ, Canada H2X 3P4   Louise Pichet, Libn.
Founded: 1975. **Staff:** Prof 1. **Subjects:** Engineering, construction, economy, developing countries, environment. **Holdings:** 6100 books; 1500 bound periodical volumes; 100 annual reports; 4300 standards and Canadian Government specifications. **Subscriptions:** 150 journals and other serials. **Services:** Interlibrary loan; library open to the public. **Automated Operations:** Computerized public access catalog, cataloging, serials, and circulation. **Computerized Information Services:** DIALOG Information Services, CAN/OLE, Questel; Envoy 100 (electronic mail service). **Publications:** Liste des nouveautes, monthly; liste des periodiques, biennial - for internal distribution only. **Remarks:** FAX: (514)287-8643. Electronic mail address(es):TECK.LIB (ENVOY 100).

★16053★

Tectonics Productions - Library
18019 Andover
P.O. Box 135
Edmonds, WA 98020
Defunct.

Tedeschi Library and Information Center
See: Framingham Union Hospital (6058)

★16054★

(Tegucigalpa) Instituto Hondureno de Cultura Interamericana - USIS Collection (Educ)
Calle Real, No. 520
Comayaguela
P.O. Box 201
Tegucigalpa, Honduras
Remarks: Maintained or supported by the U.S. Information Agency. Focus is on materials that will assist peoples outside the United States to learn about the United States, its people, history, culture, political processes, and social milieux. Also services the center located in San Pedro Sula, Honduras.

★16055★

Tehama County Law Library (Law)
Court House, Rm. 35   Phone: (916)527-0604
Red Bluff, CA 96080   Dana King-Chapman, Lib.Ck.
Staff: 1. **Subjects:** Law. **Holdings:** 8925 books; 200 bound periodical volumes; annotated codes; reports and reporters; decennials; digests; U.S. Supreme Court reports. **Subscriptions:** 11 journals and other serials. **Services:** Library open to the public.

Curt Teich Postcard Archives
See: Lake County Museum - Library and Information Center (8890)

★16056★

Teikyo Marycrest University - Cone Library (Educ)
1607 W. 12th St.   Phone: (319)326-9254
Davenport, IA 52804   Sr. Joan Sheil, Dir.
Founded: 1939. **Staff:** Prof 3; Other 4. **Subjects:** Education, social sciences, nursing, computer science. **Holdings:** 107,000 books; 47,000 curriculum guides and textbooks, microforms, films, records, slides, tapes, transparencies, kits. **Subscriptions:** 545 journals and other serials; 7 newspapers. **Services:** Interlibrary loan; copying; library open to the public. **Automated Operations:** Computerized cataloging and circulation. **Computerized Information Services:** ABI/INFORM, OCLC EPIC, CINAHL; InfoTrack. **Networks/Consortia:** Member of Bi-State Academic Libraries (BI-SAL), Quad-City Libraries in Cooperation (Quad-LINC). **Publications:** General information sheets. **Remarks:** FAX: (319)326-9250. **Formerly:** Marycrest College - Cone Library. **Staff:** Kathryn Nelson, Cat.; Sr. Leona Mary Manning, Per.; Mary Edwards, ILL; Sr. Annette Gallagher, Ref.; Sr. Sue Sellers, Circ.; Sr. Harriett Ping, Acq.

★16057★

Tektronix, Inc. - Corporate Library (Sci-Engr, Comp Sci)
Box 500, MS 50-210   Phone: (503)627-5388
Beaverton, OR 97077   Yan Y. Soucie, Libn.
Founded: 1958. **Staff:** 4. **Subjects:** Electronics, solid state physics, analytical chemistry, management, information display, computers, instrumentation, electron optics, materials science. **Holdings:** 14,000 books. **Subscriptions:** 600 journals and other serials. **Services:** Interlibrary loan. **Computerized Information Services:** DIALOG Information Services, Reuters, DataTimes. **Networks/Consortia:** Member of Washington County Cooperative Library Services (WCCLS). **Remarks:** FAX: (503)627-5502. **Staff:** Barbara Fujimoto, Libn.

★16058★

Tektronix, Inc. - Walker Road Technical Information Center
MS 94-501
Box 4600
Beaverton, OR 97076
Defunct. Holdings absorbed by Tektronix, Inc. - Corporate Library.

★16059★

Tektronix, Inc. - Wilsonville Library (Comp Sci)
Box 1000, M/S 63-531   Phone: (503)685-3986
Wilsonville, OR 97070   Linda K. Appel, Libn.
Staff: Prof 1; Other 1. **Subjects:** Computer graphics and programming, electronics, business and management. **Holdings:** 3000 books. **Subscriptions:** 175 journals and other serials; 7 newspapers. **Services:** Interlibrary loan; copying; SDI; **Computerized Information Services:** DIALOG Information Services, STN International, DataTimes, Reuters. **Networks/Consortia:** Member of CLASS, Western Library Network (WLN), Washington County Cooperative Library Services (WCCLS). **Publications:** Wilsonville Library Bulletin, biweekly - for internal distribution only. **Remarks:** FAX: (503)682-3408.

★16060★

(Tel Aviv) American Cultural Center - USIS Library (Educ)
71 Hayarkon St.
63903 Tel Aviv, Israel
Remarks: Maintained or supported by the U.S. Information Agency. Focus is on materials that will assist peoples outside the United States to learn about the United States, its people, history, culture, political processes, and social milieux.

★16061★

Tel Aviv Sourasky Medical Center - Ichilov Hospital - Medical Library (Med)
Library 6
Weizmann St   Phone: 3 6973425
64239 Tel Aviv, Israel   Mrs. Ronit Friedmann, Lib.Dir.
Founded: 1958. **Staff:** Prof 6; Other 3. **Subjects:** Medicine. **Holdings:** 4000 books; 20,000 bound periodical volumes; 200 videocassettes. **Subscriptions:** 350 journals and other serials. **Services:** Interlibrary loan; library not open to the public. **Computerized Information Services:** BRS Information Technologies, Data-Star; CD-ROM (MEDLINE). Contact Person: Irina Opincariu. **Remarks:** FAX: 3 5469580.

★ 16062 ★
Tel Aviv University - Henry and Grete Abrahams Library of Life Sciences and Medicine (Med)
Ramat Aviv Campus
POB 39345   Phone: 3 5459753
69978 Tel Aviv, Israel   Ilana Peled
Founded: 1957. **Staff:** Prof 19; Other 1.5. **Subjects:** Medicine, life sciences. **Special Collections:** History of medicine. **Holdings:** 95,000 books; 83,000 bound periodical volumes; AV materials. **Subscriptions:** 1380 journals and other serials. **Services:** Interlibrary loan; copying; SDI; library open to the public. **Computerized Information Services:** BRS Information Technologies, DIALOG Information Services, STN International, Questel. **Remarks:** FAX: 3 6427551.

★ 16063 ★
Tele-Universite - Service de la Documentation (Educ)
2635 boul. Hochelaga   Phone: (418)657-2262
Ste. Foy, PQ, Canada G1V 4V9   Lise Roberge, Resp.
Founded: 1978. **Staff:** Prof 3; Other 4. **Subjects:** Education by correspondence, educational technology, adult education, lifelong learning, didactics, communication. **Special Collections:** Education by correspondence (2500 items). **Holdings:** 12,000 volumes; 125 reels of microfilm; 975 microfiche; 185 films; 283 videotapes; 300 audiotapes; 21 records; 1105 transparencies; 25 dioramas; 75 educational games. **Subscriptions:** 449 journals and other serials; 3 newspapers. **Services:** Interlibrary loan; copying; service open to the public with restrictions. **Automated Operations:** Computerized cataloging. **Computerized Information Services:** DIALOG Information Services, BADADUQ, DOBIS Canadian Online Library System, Questel; Envoy 100 (electronic mail service). **Publications:** Les Nouveautes (a list of new acquisitions and abstracts of periodicals), biweekly. **Remarks:** FAX: (418)657-2094. **Staff:** Reine Belanger, Doc.; Claude Tousignant, Libn.

★ 16064 ★
Telecom Canada - Information Resource Centre (Bus-Fin)
410 Laurier Ave., W.   Phone: (613)560-3953
Ottawa, ON, Canada K1P 6H5   Marion Linka, Mgr.
Founded: 1978. **Staff:** Prof 1; Other 2. **Subjects:** Telecommunications, telephone industry, business, marketing. **Holdings:** 1000 books. **Subscriptions:** 250 journals and other serials. **Services:** Interlibrary loan; center not open to the public. **Automated Operations:** Computerized acquisitions and circulation. **Computerized Information Services:** PFDS Online, DIALOG Information Services, QL Systems, CAN/OLE, BRS Information Technologies, Info Globe; internal databases; CD-ROM. **Publications:** Acquisition lists, quarterly - for internal distribution only; Periodicals, annual (both annotated). **Remarks:** FAX: (613)560-3008.

★ 16065 ★
Teledyne Brown Engineering - Technical Library (Sci-Engr)
Cummings Research Park
300 Sparkman Dr., N.W.
P.O. Box 070007   Phone: (205)726-1809
Huntsville, AL 35807   Mark Sutherland, Chf.Libn.
Founded: 1962. **Staff:** Prof 1. **Subjects:** Research and development. **Holdings:** 300 bound periodical volumes; 50,000 documents; 3000 microfiche; military specifications and standards. **Subscriptions:** 200 journals and other serials. **Services:** Interlibrary loan; library not open to the public.

★ 16066 ★
Teledyne CAE Corporation - Engineering Library (Sci-Engr)
1330 Laskey Rd.   Phone: (419)470-3827
Toledo, OH 43612   Marlene S. Dowdell, Libn.
Founded: 1970. **Staff:** Prof 1. **Subjects:** Aeronautical engineering, aircraft gas turbine engines, jet engines, aerospace, metallurgy. **Holdings:** 2900 books; 38 VF cabinets of reports; 3000 microfiche. **Subscriptions:** 85 journals and other serials. **Services:** Interlibrary loan; library not open to the public. **Automated Operations:** Computerized cataloging, acquisitions, and circulation. **Computerized Information Services:** DIALOG Information Services, Aerospace Online, NASA/RECON, DTIC. **Publications:** Acquisitions Bulletin, bimonthly - for internal distribution only. **Remarks:** FAX: (419)470-3840.

★ 16067 ★
Teledyne Electronics - Technical Information Center (Sci-Engr)
649 Lawrence Dr.   Phone: (805)498-3621
Newbury Park, CA 91320   Beverly M. Switzer, Libn.
Staff: Prof 1. **Subjects:** Radar, antennas. **Holdings:** Microfiche; Visual Search Microfilm File. **Subscriptions:** 103 journals and other serials. **Services:** Interlibrary loan; center not open to the public. **Automated Operations:** Computerized acquisitions, serials, and specific document collections within the library. **Computerized Information Services:** DIALOG Information Services; ORCHID, U.C.L.A. (electronic mail services).

★ 16068 ★
Teledyne Energy Systems - Library (Energy)
110 W. Timonium Rd.   Phone: (301)252-8220
Timonium, MD 21093   Cathy Layne, Libn.
Founded: 1976. **Staff:** Prof 1. **Subjects:** Energy conversion, aerospace engineering. **Holdings:** 2400 books; 101,000 technical reports. **Subscriptions:** 80 journals and other serials. **Services:** Interlibrary loan; copying; SDI; library open to the public with restrictions. **Computerized Information Services:** DTIC. **Remarks:** FAX: (301)22-5514. Telex: 8-7780 (TDYENER TIMO).

★ 16069 ★
Teledyne Engineering Services - Information Center (Sci-Engr)
130 2nd Ave.
Waltham, MA 02254   Phone: (617)890-3350
Staff: Prof 1. **Subjects:** Mechanical and civil engineering, materials, stress analysis. **Holdings:** 1500 books; 2000 other cataloged items. **Subscriptions:** 80 journals and other serials. **Services:** Copying; SDI; center open to the public with approval of manager. **Automated Operations:** Computerized cataloging. **Computerized Information Services:** BRS Information Technologies, OCLC, DIALOG Information Services, PFDS Online; internal database; DIALMAIL (electronic mail service). **Networks/ Consortia:** Member of NELINET, Inc. **Publications:** Recent Acquisitions, bimonthly; Reports Received, irregular; Periodical Holdings, annual. **Remarks:** FAX: (617)890-0771.

★ 16070 ★
Teledyne Geotech - Alexandria Laboratories - Library (Sci-Engr)
314 Montgomery St.   Phone: (703)739-7308
Alexandria, VA 22314   Mike Amin, Libn.
Staff: Prof 1. **Subjects:** Seismology, geophysics. **Special Collections:** Seismology. **Holdings:** Figures not available for research materials. **Services:** Interlibrary loan; library not open to the public. **Computerized Information Services:** Right on Program (internal database). **Publications:** Teledyne GeoTech Technical Report.

★ 16071 ★
Teledyne, Inc. - Geotech Library (Sci-Engr)
3401 Shiloh Rd.   Phone: (214)271-2561
Garland, TX 75041   Gail Bass, Libn.
Remarks: No further information was supplied by respondent.

★ 16072 ★
Teledyne Isotopes - Business Library (Sci-Engr)
50 Vanburen Ave.   Phone: (201)664-7070
Westwood, NJ 07675   Pat Kamfor, Res.Libn./Adm.Asst.
Founded: 1957. **Staff:** 2. **Subjects:** Oil recovery/TeleTrace, radiochemistry, health physics, waste/radon analyses disposal, thermoluminescent dosimetry, carbon, nuclear instruments, geochemistry, geology. **Holdings:** Figures not available. **Subscriptions:** 55 journals and other serials. **Services:** Interlibrary loan; library open to the public by appointment. **Automated Operations:** Computerized circulation. **Remarks:** FAX: (201)664-5586.

★ 16073 ★
Teledyne Ryan Aeronautical - Technical Information Center (Sci-Engr)
P.O. Box 85311
2701 N. Harbor Dr.   Phone: (619)260-4458
San Diego, CA 92186-5311   Roxanne J. Lamorandier, Adm.
Founded: 1943. **Staff:** Prof 2. **Subjects:** Aerodynamics, avionics, materials. **Special Collections:** NASA/NACA Reports and Documents (1928 to present). **Holdings:** 4000 books; 200 bound periodical volumes; 2400 other cataloged items; 100,000 Defense Technical Information Center Reports; 60,000 NASA Documentation items. **Subscriptions:** 150 journals and other serials. **Services:** Interlibrary loan; copying; SDI; services open to the public for reference use only by appointment. **Computerized Information Services:** DIALOG Information Services, NASA/RECON, DTIC, MELVYL. **Publications:** New Book List, quarterly - for internal distribution only. **Remarks:** FAX: (619)260-5400. **Staff:** Nicole John.

★ 16074 ★
Teledyne Systems Company - Technical Library (Comp Sci)
19601 Nordhoff St. Phone: (818)886-2211
Northridge, CA 91324 Linda Zazueta, Tech.Libn.
Founded: 1979. **Staff:** 1. **Subjects:** Communication systems, computers, microprocessors, digital signal processing. **Holdings:** 3800 books; 300 bound periodical volumes; 800 technical reports. **Subscriptions:** 113 journals and other serials. **Services:** Interlibrary loan; copying; library open to other libraries with government clearance. **Special Catalogs:** Technical reports catalog; journal catalog (card).

★ 16075 ★
Teleglobe Canada Inc. - Central Library (Sci-Engr)
1000 Lagauchetiere Phone: (514)868-7120
Montreal, PQ, Canada H3B 4X5 Helene Dumont, Chf.
Founded: 1974. **Staff:** Prof 4; Other 2. **Subjects:** Telecommunications - computer, satellite, cable, and telephony. **Special Collections:** Telecommunications International Union documents; telecommunications history. **Holdings:** 13,000 books; telecommunications society annual reports. **Subscriptions:** 600 journals and other serials; 20 newspapers. **Services:** Interlibrary loan; SDI; library open to the public by appointment. **Automated Operations:** Computerized cataloging and circulation. **Computerized Information Services:** Info Globe, IST-Informatheque Inc., Infomart Online, DIALOG Information Services, National Research Council of Canada. **Publications:** Spargo (newsletter) - for internal distribution only; recent acquisitions list, semiannual; periodicals list. **Remarks:** FAX: (514)289-7083. Telex: 21 9227. **Staff:** Roger Leblanc, Libn.; Huguette Trahan, Libn.; Suzanne Meilleur, Libn.; Carol Duclos, Ck.

Telenet Communications Corporation
See: Sprint International - Christopher B. Newport Information Resource Center (15616)

★ 16076 ★
Telfair Academy of Arts and Sciences, Inc. - Library (Art)
121 Barnard St.
Savannah, GA 31401 Phone: (912)232-1177
Founded: 1885. **Staff:** Prof 1. **Subjects:** American art and artists; writings and art of Kahlil Gibran. **Holdings:** 3000 books; auction catalogs; 20 VF drawers of material on artists, associations, and museums. **Subscriptions:** 130 journals and other serials. **Services:** Copying. **Automated Operations:** Computerized cataloging and acquisitions. **Publications:** Exhibition catalogs.

★ 16077 ★
Tellus Institute - Library (Energy)
89 Broad St., 14th Fl.
Boston, MA 02110 Phone: (617)426-5844
Founded: 1977. **Subjects:** Energy systems, public utility regulation, resource planning, solid waste management. **Holdings:** Figures not available. **Computerized Information Services:** Online systems. **Remarks:** FAX: (617)426-7692.

★ 16078 ★
Telshe Yeshiva - Rabbi A.N. Schwartz Library (Rel-Phil)
28400 Euclid Ave. Phone: (216)943-5300
Wickliffe, OH 44092 Rabbi Reuven Gerson, Hd.Libn.
Founded: 1945. **Staff:** Prof 7; Other 2. **Subjects:** Talmud, Pentateuch, Jewish ethics and philosophy, Jewish law, Jewish history, Kabala, homiletics, Midrash. **Special Collections:** Hagaon Reb Eliezer Silver Collection; rare Sephardic commentaries and Responsa; early printed volumes of Biblical commentaries (1500); Rabbi Elazari Collection; Rabbi Abramowitz Collection; Rabbi Schiff Library; Rabbi Arnst Collection; Rabbi Levitan Collection. **Holdings:** 20,000 books; 1200 separate periodicals; 500 dissertations; 50 school publications; 25 manuscripts. **Subscriptions:** 10 journals and other serials. **Services:** Interlibrary loan; copying; library open to the public but a security deposit is required. **Publications:** Kol Hayeshiva, quarterly; Pe'er Mordecai, annual; Pri Etz Chaim, annual. **Remarks:** A section of this library has been named the Rabbi Neuhaus Library.

★ 16079 ★
Temple Adath Israel - Ruben Library (Rel-Phil)
270 Highland Ave. Phone: (215)664-5150
Merion, PA 19066 Fred Kazan, Rabbi
Founded: 1955. **Staff:** Prof 1. **Subjects:** Judaica. **Holdings:** 2500 books. **Subscriptions:** 12 journals and other serials. **Services:** Interlibrary loan; library open to area college students or by member sponsorship. **Staff:** Liz Eidelson, Libn.

★ 16080 ★
Temple Ahavath Sholom - Rabbi A. Alan Steinbach Library (Rel-Phil)
1906 Ave. V Phone: (718)769-5350
Brooklyn, NY 11229-4506 Penny Klein, Libn.
Founded: 1938. **Staff:** Prof 1. **Subjects:** Jewish ethics, history, music; theology; comparative religion; biography; fiction (Jewish content). **Holdings:** 4500 books; Rabbi Steinbach's manuscripts; Jewish antiquities. **Subscriptions:** 23 journals and other serials. **Services:** Library open to the public with restrictions.

★ 16081 ★
Temple Beth El - Billie Davis Rodenberg Memorial Library (Rel-Phil)
1351 S. 14th Ave. Phone: (305)920-8225
Hollywood, FL 33020 Roslyn Kurland, Libn.
Founded: 1962. **Staff:** Prof 1; Other 4. **Subjects:** Judaica. **Holdings:** 7500 volumes. **Subscriptions:** 25 journals and other serials; 6 newspapers. **Services:** Interlibrary loan; copying; library open to the public for reference use only.

★ 16082 ★
Temple Beth El - Library (Rel-Phil)
225 E. 7th St. Phone: (201)756-2333
Plainfield, NJ 07060 Fran Dorio, Libn.
Founded: 1966. **Staff:** 3. **Subjects:** Judaica and Hebraica - juvenile and adult. **Holdings:** 3500 books. **Services:** Copying; library open to the public.

★ 16083 ★
Temple Beth El - Library (Rel-Phil)
139 Winton Rd., S. Phone: (716)473-1770
Rochester, NY 14610 Anne Kirshenbaum, Libn.
Founded: 1946. **Staff:** Prof 1; Other 1. **Subjects:** Judaica - religion, philosophy, social science, history, art, literature, language, fiction, biography for adults and juveniles. **Holdings:** 6926 books; 7 file drawers of pamphlets and clippings. **Subscriptions:** 29 journals and other serials. **Services:** Interlibrary loan; library open to the public with special permission.

★ 16084 ★
Temple Beth El - Prentis Memorial Library (Rel-Phil)
7400 Telegraph Rd. Phone: (313)851-1100
Birmingham, MI 48010 Marilyn R. Brenner, Libn.
Founded: 1878. **Staff:** Prof 1. **Subjects:** Judaica, Christianity, philosophy, the arts, sociology, archeology, Bible, Jewish history, Jewish Americana. **Special Collections:** Leonard N. Simons Collection of Rare Judaica; Irving I. Katz Collection of Jewish Americana. **Holdings:** 15,000 books; AV programs; recordings; pamphlets; large print books; talking books. **Subscriptions:** 65 journals and other serials. **Services:** Copying; library open to the public with restrictions.

★ 16085 ★
Temple Beth-El - William G. Braude Library (Rel-Phil)
70 Orchard Ave. Phone: (401)331-6070
Providence, RI 02906 Reini Silverman, Libn.
Founded: 1894. **Staff:** Prof 1. **Subjects:** Judaica, Hebraica, Yiddish, Biblical studies, Holocaust, philosophy, folklore, music, rabbinics, anti-Semitism, Latin American Jewry. **Special Collections:** Englander Collection. **Holdings:** 25,000 books; 258 bound periodical volumes; 432 pamphlets; clippings; programs of interest to Rhode Island Jews; Yiddish and Hebrew books. **Subscriptions:** 73 journals and other serials; 10 newspapers. **Services:** Interlibrary loan; library open to the public. **Automated Operations:** Computerized cataloging.

★ 16086 ★
Temple Beth-El - Ziskind Memorial Library (Rel-Phil)
385 High St.   Phone: (508)674-3529
Fall River, MA 02720   Phyllis Mechaber
Staff: 1. **Subjects:** English Judaica. **Holdings:** 6000 volumes; 200 phonograph records; 300 pamphlets and clippings. **Subscriptions:** 35 journals and other serials. **Services:** Library open to the public.

★ 16087 ★
Temple Beth-El of Great Neck - Arnold & Marie Schwartz Library (Rel-Phil)
5 Old Mill Rd.   Phone: (516)487-0900
Great Neck, NY 11023   Dorothy Zimbalist, Libn.
Founded: 1950. **Staff:** Prof 1. **Subjects:** Judaica - history, Holocaust, literature, biography; Israel. **Special Collections:** Children's collection. **Holdings:** 8000 books; records; reference books. **Subscriptions:** 25 journals and other serials. **Services:** Interlibrary loan; library open to the public with restrictions.

★ 16088 ★
Temple Beth El of Greater Buffalo - Library (Rel-Phil)
2368 Eggert Rd.   Phone: (716)836-3762
Tonawanda, NY 14150   Sandra Freed Gralnick, Libn.
Founded: 1920. **Staff:** Prof 1; Other 4. **Subjects:** Judaica. **Special Collections:** Samuel S. Luskin Memorial Music Reference Library; Cantor Gerald De Bruin Music, Tapes and Record Library; Edward Weiss Reading Center for the Visually Impaired; reference collection on Jewish art; large print books; children's collection; Holocaust collection; Janet S. Adler Special Israeli Collection. **Holdings:** 5000 books; phonograph records; tapes. **Services:** Library open to the public. **Publications:** Lists of Recent Acquisitions, annual.

★ 16089 ★
Temple Beth Israel - Library (Rel-Phil)
3310 N. 10th Ave.
Phoenix, AZ 85013
                                          Phone: (602)264-4428
Subjects: Jewish history, Bible, literature, rabbinics, biography, art, music. **Special Collections:** Judaica Music Library (245 phonograph records, tapes, and cassettes). **Holdings:** 17,541 books; 26 VF drawers of pamphlets, clippings, and maps; 6 boxes of temple archives. **Subscriptions:** 72 journals and other serials. **Services:** Interlibrary loan; copying; library open to the public.

★ 16090 ★
Temple Beth Joseph - Rose Basloe Library (Rel-Phil)
N. Prospect St.
Herkimer, NY 13350
                                          Phone: (315)866-4270
Founded: 1957. **Staff:** 1. **Subjects:** Judaica. **Holdings:** 3500 books. **Services:** Library open to the public. **Staff:** Vicki L. Socolof, Volunteer Libn.

★ 16091 ★
Temple Beth Sholom - Herbert Goldberg Memorial Library (Rel-Phil)
1901 Crescent Rd.   Phone: (609)547-6113
Cherry Hill, NJ 08003   Doris Corman, Libn.
Staff: Prof 1. **Subjects:** Judaica. **Holdings:** 3000 books. **Subscriptions:** 12 journals and other serials.

★ 16092 ★
Temple Beth Sholom - Library (Rel-Phil)
4144 Chase Ave.   Phone: (305)538-7231
Miami Beach, FL 33140   Leslie Harris, Libn. & Educ. Media Spec.
Staff: Prof 1; Other 4. **Subjects:** Judaica (adult and juvenile), rabbinics. **Holdings:** 5000 books. **Subscriptions:** 60 journals and other serials. **Services:** Interlibrary loan; copying; library open to the public with restrictions.

★ 16093 ★
Temple Beth Zion - Library (Rel-Phil)
805 Delaware Ave.   Phone: (716)886-7150
Buffalo, NY 14209   Robin Macks, Libn.
Founded: 1915. **Staff:** Prof 1. **Subjects:** Jewish religion, history, literature, art. **Special Collections:** Reform Judaism; Jewish beliefs and practices; American Jewish history. **Holdings:** 12,100 books; 250 filmstrips and slides; 180 records and cassettes; video cassettes. **Subscriptions:** 38 journals and other serials. **Services:** Interlibrary loan; library open to the public. **Publications:** Lest We Forget: A Selected Annotated List of Books on the Holocaust; American Jewish Odyssey (annotated bibliography of the Jewish experience in America, as reflected in the library holdings); Jewish Children's Literature (annotated bibliography of books on Judaism and Jewish history for children up to age 14); Books on the Holocaust (list of library's holdings); Basic List for a Jewish Home Library.

★ 16094 ★
Temple B'nai Israel - Lasker Memorial Library (Rel-Phil)
3006 Ave. O   Phone: (409)765-5796
Galveston, TX 77550   Sophie Nussenblatt, Libn.
Founded: 1956. **Staff:** 3. **Subjects:** Judaism, Jewish history, biblical history, Bible commentaries. **Holdings:** 2000 books. **Subscriptions:** 15 journals and other serials. **Services:** Library open to the public.

★ 16095 ★
Temple B'rith Kodesh - Library (Rel-Phil)
2131 Elmwood Ave.   Phone: (716)244-7060
Rochester, NY 14618   Annette Sheiman, Libn.
Staff: Prof 1; Other 1. **Subjects:** Judaica. **Holdings:** 8000 books. **Subscriptions:** 25 journals and other serials. **Services:** Library open to members of local congregations and students of local colleges and universities. **Remarks:** FAX: (716)244-0557.

★ 16096 ★
Temple Daily Telegram - Library (Publ)
10 S. Third St.
P.O. Box 6114
Temple, TX 76503-6114   Phone: (817)778-4444
Staff: 1. **Subjects:** Newspaper reference topics. **Holdings:** Microfilm; files. **Subscriptions:** 5 newspapers. **Services:** Library open to the public at librarian's discretion. **Remarks:** FAX: (817)778-4444 ext. 287. **Staff:** Bette Winegar, Libn.; Susan Oberg, Libn.

★ 16097 ★
Temple Emanu-El - Alex F. Weisberg Library (Rel-Phil)
8500 Hillcrest Rd.   Phone: (214)368-3613
Dallas, TX 75225   Maureen Reister, Libn.
Founded: 1957. **Staff:** Prof 1. **Subjects:** Judaica and related topics. **Holdings:** 6000 books. **Subscriptions:** 30 journals and other serials; 7 newspapers. **Services:** Interlibrary loan; copying; programs for interfaith and senior citizens groups; library open to the public with annual fee. **Remarks:** FAX: (214)369-2752.

★ 16098 ★
Temple Emanu-El - Congregational Library (Rel-Phil)
99 Taft Ave.   Phone: (401)331-1616
Providence, RI 02906   Lillian Schwartz, Libn.
Founded: 1953. **Staff:** Prof 1. **Subjects:** Judaica, comparative religion. **Holdings:** 8000 books. **Subscriptions:** 20 journals and other serials. **Services:** Interlibrary loan; copying; library open to the public with deposit. **Publications:** Booklists, occasional - for school use.

★ 16099 ★
Temple Emanu-El - Davis Library (Rel-Phil)
225 N. Country Club Rd.   Phone: (602)327-4501
Tucson, AZ 85716   Beverly H. Morgen, Libn.
Founded: 1947. **Staff:** Prof 1. **Subjects:** Judaica. **Holdings:** 8000 books; 150 phonograph records; 50 filmstrips; 50 videotapes; 20 audiotapes. **Subscriptions:** 12 journals and other serials. **Services:** Copying; library open to the public for reference use only.

★ 16100 ★
Temple Emanu-El - Library (Rel-Phil)
1701 Washington Ave.   Phone: (305)538-2503
Miami Beach, FL 33139   Ruth M. Abelow, Libn.
Founded: 1955. **Staff:** Prof 1; Other 1. **Subjects:** Judaica including religion, Bible, Israel, biography, literature, history, sociology, and education. **Special Collections:** Samuel Friedland Collection of Rare Books (600 volumes, mainly printed in Europe). **Holdings:** 8500 books; 55 cataloged periodicals; 270 pamphlets; 40 pamphlet boxes of uncataloged pamphlets on Israel and religion; 8 books of clippings. **Subscriptions:** 48 journals and other serials; 6 newspapers. **Services:** Library open to the public with refundable deposit. **Remarks:** FAX: (305)535-3122.

★16101★
Temple Emanu-El - Sonahend Family Library (Rel-Phil)
455 Neptune Blvd. Phone: (516)431-4060
Long Beach, NY 11561 Beth Moscowitz, Libn.
Founded: 1954. **Staff:** Prof 1. **Subjects:** Jewish religion and literature; Bible; Hebraica; current events in Israel. **Holdings:** 5000 books; 50 bound periodical volumes; 25 VF drawers; 75 videotapes; audiotapes; filmstrips; sound recordings. **Subscriptions:** 30 newspapers. **Services:** Library open to members. **Automated Operations:** Computerized cataloging and circulation.

★16102★
Temple Emanu-El - William P. Budner Library (Rel-Phil)
8500 Hillcrest Rd. Phone: (214)368-3613
Dallas, TX 75225 Maureen Reister, Lib.Dir.
Founded: 1980. **Staff:** Prof 1. **Subjects:** Juvenile Judaica. **Holdings:** 1300 books. **Subscriptions:** 3 journals and other serials. **Services:** Library open to the public on fee basis. **Remarks:** FAX: (214)369-2752.

★16103★
Temple Emanu-El - William P. Engel Library (Rel-Phil)
2100 Highland Ave. Phone: (205)933-8037
Birmingham, AL 35255 Elinor Sue, Staff Libn.
Founded: 1914. **Staff:** Prof 2; Other 1. **Subjects:** Judaica, religion. **Holdings:** 3500 books. **Subscriptions:** 5 journals and other serials. **Services:** Interlibrary loan; copying; library open to the public. **Automated Operations:** Computerized public access catalog. **Staff:** Florence Goldstein, Asst.

★16104★
Temple Emanuel - Library (Rel-Phil)
150 Derby Ave.
Box 897
Orange, CT 06477 Phone: (203)397-3000
Meryl Farber, Chm., Lib.Comm.
Subjects: Judaica. **Holdings:** 1200 books; 25 phonograph records. **Services:** Library open to the public with permission.

★16105★
Temple Emanuel - Library (Rel-Phil)
Cooper River Pkwy. at Donahue Phone: (609)665-0669
Cherry Hill, NJ 08002 Rene Batterman, Libn.
Staff: Prof 1. **Subjects:** Judaism. **Special Collections:** Holocaust. **Holdings:** 5000 books; records; tapes. **Subscriptions:** 12 journals and other serials. **Services:** Copying; library open to the public with restrictions.

★16106★
Temple de Hirsch Sinai - Library (Rel-Phil)
1511 E. Pike Phone: (206)323-8486
Seattle, WA 98122-4199 Jennifer Schwerdtfeger, Libn.
Founded: 1914. **Staff:** Prof 1. **Subjects:** Judaism, Jewish history, literature, biography, Holocaust, children's literature. **Holdings:** 5500 books. **Subscriptions:** 36 journals and other serials. **Services:** Interlibrary loan; copying (limited); library open to the public with restrictions. **Staff:** Andrea Avni.

★16107★
Temple Israel - Leonard M. Sandhaus Memorial Library (Rel-Phil)
125 Pond St. Phone: (617)784-3986
Sharon, MA 02067 E. Ruth Hunt, Libn.
Founded: 1953. **Staff:** Prof 1; Other 4. **Subjects:** Jewish religion, philosophy, history; American Jewish life; Israel and Zionism; Hebrew. **Special Collections:** Jewish literature. **Holdings:** 5900 books; 200 pamphlets; 50 tapes; videos; games. **Subscriptions:** 17 journals and other serials. **Services:** Interlibrary loan; library open to the public with restrictions.

★16108★
Temple Israel - Library (Rel-Phil)
1901 N. Flagler Dr. Phone: (407)833-8421
West Palm Beach, FL 33407 Elsie Leviton, Chm., Lib.Comm.
Founded: 1958. **Staff:** Prof 1; Other 5. **Subjects:** Judaica - history, literature, sociology, arts. **Special Collections:** Americana Judaica; Holocaust. **Holdings:** 7000 books; 12 bound periodical volumes; 1000 pamphlets, bibliographies, archives, clippings; 8 VF drawers; phonograph records; filmstrips. **Subscriptions:** 16 journals and other serials; 7 newspapers. **Services:** Library open to residents of Palm Beach County. **Staff:** Adele Sayles, Libn.

★16109★
Temple Israel - Library (Rel-Phil)
Longwood Ave. & Plymouth St. Phone: (617)566-3960
Boston, MA 02215 Ann Carol Abrams, Libn.
Staff: Prof 1; Other 1. **Subjects:** Judaica. **Holdings:** 10,000 books. **Subscriptions:** 30 journals and other serials. **Services:** Library open to the public for reference use only.

★16110★
Temple Israel - Library (Rel-Phil)
2324 Emerson Ave., S. Phone: (612)377-8680
Minneapolis, MN 55405 Georgia Kalman, Libn.
Founded: 1928. **Staff:** Prof 1. **Subjects:** Judaica, Jewish religion, philosophy. **Holdings:** 6000 books. **Subscriptions:** 20 journals and other serials; 6 newspapers. **Services:** Library open to the public. **Remarks:** FAX: (612)377-6630.

★16111★
Temple Israel - Library (Rel-Phil)
140 Central Ave. Phone: (516)239-1140
Lawrence, NY 11559 Donna Z. Lifland, Libn.
Founded: 1949. **Staff:** Prof 1; Other 6. **Subjects:** Judaica and allied subjects. **Holdings:** 5100 books; 20 bound periodical volumes; 225 filmstrips; 10 cassettes. **Subscriptions:** 19 journals and other serials. **Services:** Library open to the public with permission.

★16112★
Temple Israel - Max and Edith Weinberg Library (Rel-Phil)
5725 Walnut Lake Rd. Phone: (313)661-5700
West Bloomfield, MI 48323 Bertha Wember, Libn.
Founded: 1962. **Staff:** Prof 1. **Subjects:** Judaism - history, biography, literature, arts, children's literature; Holocaust; Bible study; Israel. **Holdings:** 9000 books; 8 VF drawers of clippings and pamphlets. **Subscriptions:** 35 journals and other serials. **Services:** Library open to the public.

★16113★
Temple Israel - Paul Peltason Library (Rel-Phil)
10675 Ladue Rd. Phone: (314)432-8050
Creve Coeur, MO 63141 Rabbi Mark L. Shook
Founded: 1930. **Staff:** 1. **Subjects:** Judaica. **Holdings:** 4000 books. **Services:** Library open to the public with restrictions.

★16114★
Temple Israel - Rabbi Louis Witt Memorial Library (Rel-Phil)
1821 Emerson Ave.
Dayton, OH 45406 Phone: (513)278-9621
Founded: 1925. **Subjects:** Judaica. **Holdings:** Figures not available. **Subscriptions:** 6 journals and other serials; 4 newspapers. **Services:** Library not open to the public. **Remarks:** Temple Israel maintains a Learning Resource Center.

★16115★
Temple Israel of Greater Miami - Library (Rel-Phil)
137 N.E. 19th St. Phone: (305)573-5900
Miami, FL 33132 Beatrice T. Muskat, Libn.
Founded: 1944. **Staff:** Prof 1; Other 1. **Subjects:** Judaica, the Bible, philosophy, Israel. **Special Collections:** Haggadot; juvenile collections. **Holdings:** 11,000 books; pamphlets; American Jewish Archives; Near East reports; records; tapes; slides. **Subscriptions:** 30 journals and other serials. **Services:** Interlibrary loan; copying; library open to the public for reference use only. **Special Indexes:** Index to Jewish periodicals; pamphlet index.

★16116★
Temple Judea - Mel Harrison Memorial Library (Rel-Phil)
5500 Granada Blvd.
Coral Gables, FL 33146 Zelda Harrison, Chf.Libn.
Founded: 1967. **Staff:** 5. **Subjects:** Judaica. **Special Collections:** Holocaust Collection. **Holdings:** 6000 books. **Services:** Library not open to the public. **Staff:** Fran Hesser; Michelle Gersten.

★ 16117 ★
Temple Judea Mizpah - Library (Rel-Phil)
8610 Niles Center Rd.   Phone: (708)676-1566
Skokie, IL 60077   Claire Alport, Lib.Chm.
Staff: Prof 3; Other 14. **Subjects:** Judaica. **Holdings:** 3900 books; 20 bound periodical volumes. **Subscriptions:** 3 journals and other serials. **Services:** Copying; library open to the public with restrictions. **Networks/Consortia:** Member of Judaica Library Network of Chicago. **Staff:** Beatrice Silver, Co-Chm.

★ 16118 ★
Temple Library (Rel-Phil)
University Circle & Silver Park   Phone: (216)791-7755
Cleveland, OH 44106   Claudia Z. Fechter, Lib.Dir.
Founded: 1896. **Staff:** Prof 2; Other 2. **Subjects:** Judaica. **Special Collections:** Abba Hillel Silver Archives. **Holdings:** 40,000 books; pamphlets; maps; filmstrips; slides. **Subscriptions:** 40 journals and other serials; 10 newspapers. **Services:** Interlibrary loan; copying; library open to the public. **Special Catalogs:** The Loom and the Cloth: an Exhibition of the Fabrics of Jewish Life. **Special Indexes:** Jewish Union List (JUL) periodic list of holdings of institutions in the Greater Cleveland area. **Remarks:** FAX: (216)791-7043. Branch library, located at 26000 Shaker Blvd., contains a children's collection, adult fiction, and holocaust material. **Staff:** Frances Tramer.

★ 16119 ★
Temple Ohabai Shalom - Library (Rel-Phil)
5015 Harding Rd.   Phone: (615)352-7620
Nashville, TN 37205   Annette Levy Ratkin, Dir.
Staff: Prof 1; Other 1. **Subjects:** Bible commentary, Jewish history, children's literature. **Holdings:** 6000 books. **Subscriptions:** 10 journals and other serials. **Services:** Interlibrary loan; copying; library open to the public.

★ 16120 ★
Temple Ohabei Shalom - Sisterhood Library (Rel-Phil)
1187 Beacon St.   Phone: (617)277-6610
Brookline, MA 02146   Mary R. Rosen, Libn.
Founded: 1938. **Staff:** 1. **Subjects:** Bible, Judaism, biography, history, Israel, religion, theology. **Holdings:** 3500 books. **Subscriptions:** 14 journals and other serials. **Services:** Library open to the public with restrictions. **Remarks:** Alternate telephone number(s): 734-9109.

★ 16121 ★
Temple Shaarey Zedek - Rabbi Isaac Klein Library (Rel-Phil)
621 Getzville Rd.   Phone: (716)838-3232
Amherst, NY 14226   Rebecca Palermo Stern, Libn.
Founded: 1959. **Staff:** Prof 1; Other 4. **Subjects:** Judaica. **Holdings:** 3300 volumes. **Subscriptions:** 13 journals and other serials. **Services:** Library open to the public.

★ 16122 ★
Temple Shalom of Broomall - Library (Rel-Phil)
55 N. Church Lane   Phone: (215)356-5165
Broomall, PA 19008   David Lefcourt, Libn.
Subjects: Judaica. **Holdings:** 2400 books. **Subscriptions:** 18 journals and other serials.

★ 16123 ★
Temple Sharey Tefilo-Israel - Edward Ehrenkrantz/Elchanan Echikson Memorial Library (Rel-Phil)
432 Scotland Rd.   Phone: (201)763-4116
South Orange, NJ 07079   Carolyn E. Shane, Adm.
Subjects: Bible; Judaism - religion, history, customs, ceremonies, holidays, practices, theology, philosophy, social sciences; fiction. **Holdings:** 4755 volumes. **Subscriptions:** 12 journals and other serials; 2 newspapers. **Services:** Library open to the public for reference use only. **Remarks:** FAX: (201)763-3941.

★ 16124 ★
Temple Sinai - Dr. Alex Morrison Library (Rel-Phil)
50 Alberta Dr.
Buffalo, NY 14226   Phone: (716)834-0708
Founded: 1972. **Staff:** Prof 1; Other 2. **Subjects:** Judaica, Holocaust. **Holdings:** 3008 volumes. **Services:** Library open to the public.

★ 16125 ★
Temple Sinai - Jack Balaban Memorial Library (Rel-Phil)
New Albany Rd.   Phone: (609)829-0658
Cinnaminson, NJ 08077   Barbara Segal, Libn.
Staff: 1. **Subjects:** Holocaust; Jewish history, religion, holidays, authors. **Special Collections:** Encyclopaedia Judaica. **Holdings:** 1500 books. **Subscriptions:** 1 newspaper. **Services:** Interlibrary loan; library open to the public with restrictions.

★ 16126 ★
Temple Sinai - Library (Rel-Phil)
3100 Military Rd., N.W.   Phone: (202)363-6394
Washington, DC 20015   Margaret Chachkin, Libn.
Founded: 1960. **Staff:** Prof 1; Other 2. **Subjects:** Judaism - philosophy, history; Bible; theology; Jews in the United States; Jewish rituals, traditions, folklore, art, literature, and music; Israeli history; Holocaust. **Special Collections:** Celia B. Friedman Collection of Hebrew Material (60 books); Selis Memorial Collection (comparative religion; 55 volumes); Bianka Zwick Memorial Collection (American-Jewish immigrant experience). **Holdings:** 4000 volumes; 2 VF drawers of clippings. **Subscriptions:** 37 journals and other serials. **Services:** Copying; library open to the public. **Publications:** Bibliographies; guides.

★ 16127 ★
Temple Sinai - Library (Rel-Phil)
50 Sewall Ave.   Phone: (617)277-5888
Brookline, MA 02146   Jane Taubenfield Cohen, Prin., Rel.Sch.
Staff: Prof 1. **Subjects:** Judaica, religion, Bible, Talmud. **Holdings:** 2200 books. **Services:** Library not open to the public.

★ 16128 ★
Temple University - Center for the Study of Federalism - Library (Soc Sci)
1616 Walnut St., Rm. 507   Phone: (215)787-1483
Philadelphia, PA 19103   Marian Macatee Wolfe
Staff: Prof 1; Other 1. **Subjects:** American federalism, comparative federal systems, federal theory, political culture, state and local governments, environmental problems, covenants. **Holdings:** 1500 books; 1200 bound periodical volumes; 5 VF drawers; 1000 uncataloged items. **Subscriptions:** 102 journals and other serials. **Services:** Copying; library open to the public with director's supervision. **Publications:** CSF Notebook; Publius: The Journal of Federalism, quarterly; special reports and books on key subject areas. **Remarks:** FAX: (215)787-7784. "The center is dedicated to the study of federal principles, institutions, and processes as a practical means of organizing political power in a free society. By initiating, sponsoring, and conducting research projects and educational programs related to them, the center seeks to increase and disseminate knowledge of federalism in general and to develop specialists in the growing field of intergovernmental relations."

★ 16129 ★
Temple University - Central Library System - Ambler Campus Library (Biol Sci, Educ)
Meetinghouse Rd.   Phone: (215)283-1383
Ambler, PA 19002   Linda Cotilla, Hd. Suburban Campus Libs.
Founded: 1958. **Staff:** Prof 2; Other 6. **Subjects:** Horticulture, education, literature, history, landscape design, science, botany, sociology, business. **Special Collections:** Horticulture and landscape design (3000 volumes); Pennsylvania Affiliate Data Center (census materials). **Holdings:** 92,000 books; 7685 bound periodical volumes; 3545 recordings; 8600 pamphlets; 3500 reels of microfilm. **Subscriptions:** 600 journals and other serials; 20 newspapers. **Services:** Interlibrary loan; copying; library open to the public for reference use only. **Computerized Information Services:** RLIN, DIALOG Information Services, BRS Information Technologies, Association of Research Libraries (ARL). **Networks/Consortia:** Member of Research Libraries Information Network (RLIN), Center for Research Libraries (CRL), PALINET. **Staff:** Sandra Thompson, Asst.Libn./Rsrcs.

★ 16130 ★

Temple University - Central Library System - Biology Library (Biol Sci)
248 Life Science Bldg.   Phone: (215)787-8878
Philadelphia, PA 19122   Carol Lang, Coord.Sci.Lib.
Staff: 1. **Subjects:** Biology - cell, molecular, developmental; biochemistry; genetics; physiology. **Holdings:** 20,000 volumes; 11 VF drawers of reprints; 50 volumes of dissertations and theses. **Services:** Interlibrary loan; copying; library open to qualified users. **Automated Operations:** Computerized public access catalog and circulation. **Computerized Information Services:** Association of Research Libraries (ARL). **Networks/Consortia:** Member of Center for Research Libraries (CRL), PALINET, Research Libraries Information Network (RLIN).

★ 16131 ★

Temple University - Central Library System - Chemistry Library (Sci-Engr)
Beury Hall, 1st Fl.   Phone: (215)787-7120
Philadelphia, PA 19122   Carol Lang, Coord.Sci.Lib.
Founded: 1968. **Staff:** 1. **Subjects:** Chemistry - organic, inorganic, physical, analytical, theoretical; biochemistry. **Special Collections:** Guy F. Allen Memorial Collection in Chemical Education (100 volumes). **Holdings:** 16,500 volumes; 2 VF of reprints; 135 volumes of theses and dissertations. **Subscriptions:** 253 journals and other serials. **Services:** Interlibrary loan; copying; library open to qualified users. **Automated Operations:** Computerized circulation. **Computerized Information Services:** Association of Research Libraries (ARL). **Networks/Consortia:** Member of Research Libraries Information Network (RLIN), Center for Research Libraries (CRL), PALINET.

★ 16132 ★

Temple University - Central Library System - College of Engineering, Computer Sciences, Architecture and Science Libraries (Plan, Sci-Engr)
12th & Norris Sts.   Phone: (215)787-7828
Philadelphia, PA 19122   Betsy Tabas, Libn.
Founded: 1921. **Staff:** Prof 1; Other 2. **Subjects:** Engineering - biomedical, civil, electrical, environmental, mechanical; architecture. **Holdings:** 25,000 volumes. **Subscriptions:** 361 journals and other serials. **Services:** Interlibrary loan; copying; library open to the public. **Automated Operations:** Computerized public access catalog and circulation. **Computerized Information Services:** DIALOG Information Services, Association of Research Libraries (ARL). Performs searches on fee basis. **Networks/Consortia:** Member of Research Libraries Information Network (RLIN), Center for Research Libraries (CRL), PALINET.

★ 16133 ★

Temple University - Central Library System - Contemporary Culture Collection (Soc Sci)
13th & Berks Sts.   Phone: (215)787-8667
Philadelphia, PA 19122   Elaine Cox Clever, Cur.
Founded: 1969. **Staff:** 1. **Subjects:** Social change, peace and disarmament, small press poetry, fringe politics, alternative life styles, animal rights, feminism, gays. **Special Collections:** Counter culture and peace movement newspapers from the Vietnam era; early second wave feminist publications and literary chapbooks; Liberation News Service Archive (160 linear feet); Youth Liberation Archive (40 linear feet); Committee of Small Press Editors and Publishers Archive (32 linear feet); small presses archives (83 linear feet); personal papers of poet Lyn Lifshin (36 linear feet). **Holdings:** 8000 books and pamphlets; 4000 periodical, newspaper, and newsletter titles; 730 reels of microfilm; 70 linear feet of ephemera. **Subscriptions:** 290 journals and other serials; 90 newspapers. **Services:** Copying; collection open to the public for reference use only. **Automated Operations:** Computerized cataloging. **Computerized Information Services:** Association of Research Libraries (ARL). **Networks/Consortia:** Member of Research Libraries Information Network (RLIN), Center for Research Libraries (CRL), PALINET. **Publications:** Periodical holdings lists, 1972, 1976; Alternative Press Periodicals: A Listing of Periodicals Microfilmed at The Collection, 1976; Exhibits with related bibliographies.

★ 16134 ★

Temple University - Central Library System - Conwellana-Templana Collection (Hist)
13th & Berks Sts.   Phone: (215)787-8240
Philadelphia, PA 19122   Thomas M. Whitehead, Hd., Spec.Coll.Dept.
Founded: 1946. **Staff:** 2 Prof; 3 Other. **Subjects:** University archives; life and activities of Russell Conwell. **Special Collections:** Faculty and alumni publications (3900 volumes); sermons, manuscripts, and publications of Russell Conwell (38 linear feet); personal library of Russell Conwell (1800 volumes); personal papers of faculty and alumni (156 linear feet); Barrows Dunham-Fred Zimring Collection (128 tapes and 66 transcriptions of oral history interviews and research materials related to dismissal of faculty members and academic freedom issues; 7 linear feet); Frank Ankenbrand papers, manuscript notebooks, and publications (3 linear feet); Frank Brookhouser papers, correspondence, manuscripts, and published columns (5 linear feet); Negley K. Teeters personal papers, correspondence, manuscripts, and related files (5 linear feet); personal papers of Melville S. Green, 1950-1979 (statistical physicist; 14 linear feet); personal papers of Daniel Swern, 1961-1982 (chemist and pioneer in plastics; 35 linear feet); personal papers of Henry Dexter Learned, 1893-1978 (linguistic scholar; 7 linear feet); Weiss-Karlen Collection (papers of novelist David Weiss and poet-playwright Stymean Karlen, 1940-1982; 20 linear feet); personal papers of William W. Tomlinson, 1950-1980 (including diaries of his travels; 50 linear feet); papers of Miriam Allen De Ford, 1903-1975 (mystery and historical writer; 2 linear feet). **Holdings:** 7000 books; 2770 bound periodical volumes; 1506 catalogs and reports; 10,000 theses and dissertations; 738 linear feet of archives and manuscripts; 18 drawers of clippings, pictures, pamphlets; 620 reels of microfilm; 630 tape recordings; 2580 slides, posters, phonograph records, and memorabilia. **Subscriptions:** 121 journals and other serials. **Services:** Interlibrary loan; copying; collection open to the public for reference use only. **Computerized Information Services:** Association of Research Libraries (ARL). **Networks/Consortia:** Member of Research Libraries Information Network (RLIN), Center for Research Libraries (CRL), PALINET. **Publications:** General Guide to Archives and Manuscripts; Russell Herman Conwell: The Individual and His Influence, compiled by M.I. Crawford, 1977; Walk 100 Years in a Hundred Feet: The Temple Centennial, An Illustrated Guide to the History of Temple University; A Descriptive Guide to the University Archives of Temple University, 1986. **Special Catalogs:** Inventories of manuscripts and archives collections; Inventories of certain Record Groups and Personal Papers (in sheet form).

★ 16135 ★

Temple University - Central Library System - Mathematical Sciences Library (Sci-Engr, Comp Sci)
407 Computer Sciences Bldg.   Phone: (215)787-8434
Philadelphia, PA 19122   Carol Lang, Coord.Sci.Lib.
Founded: 1968. **Staff:** 1. **Subjects:** Pure and applied mathematics, statistics, computer and information sciences. **Holdings:** 18,800 volumes; 9 linear feet of technical reports. **Subscriptions:** 350 journals and other serials. **Services:** Interlibrary loan; copying; library open to qualified users. **Automated Operations:** Computerized public access catalog and circulation. **Computerized Information Services:** Association of Research Libraries (ARL). **Networks/Consortia:** Member of Research Libraries Information Network (RLIN), Center for Research Libraries (CRL), PALINET.

★ 16136 ★

Temple University - Central Library System - Physics Library (Sci-Engr)
209A Barton Hall   Phone: (215)787-7649
Philadelphia, PA 19122   Carol Lang, Coord.Sci.Lib.
Founded: 1968. **Staff:** 1. **Subjects:** Physics, astronomy. **Holdings:** 21,000 volumes; 1 VF drawer of reprints; 50 volumes of theses and dissertations; 1 VF drawer of preprints; 1 VF drawer of society newsletters. **Subscriptions:** 190 journals and other serials. **Services:** Interlibrary loan; copying; library open to qualified users. **Automated Operations:** Computerized circulation. **Computerized Information Services:** Association of Research Libraries (ARL). **Networks/Consortia:** Member of Research Libraries Information Network (RLIN), Center for Research Libraries (CRL), PALINET.

★ 16137 ★

Temple University - Central Library System - Rare Book & Manuscript Collection (Rare Book)
13th & Berks St.   Phone: (215)787-8230
Philadelphia, PA 19122   Thomas M. Whitehead, Hd., Spec.Coll.Dept.
Staff: Prof 1; Other 1. **Subjects:** English, French, American, and Symbolist literature; business history; science fiction; horticulture; lithography; printing, publishing, and bookselling history. **Special Collections:** Charles Morice papers; Constable & Company correspondence collection; Cochran History of Business Collection (500 volumes); Bush-Brown Horticulture Collection (500 volumes); Nordell 17th Century England Collection (150 volumes); Richard Ellis Library and Archive; Albert Caplan Limited Editions Club Collection; Sir Richard Owen correspondence collection; Walter de la Mare Collection; Paskow/Knuf Science Fiction and Fantasy

Collection. **Holdings:** 40,000 books; 2500 bound periodical volumes; 3000 war posters; 2000 linear feet of manuscripts. **Subscriptions:** 15 journals and other serials. **Services:** Copying; collection open to the public with restrictions. **Computerized Information Services:** OCLC, DIALOG Information Services, BRS Information Technologies, PFDS Online, Association of Research Libraries (ARL). **Networks/Consortia:** Member of PALINET, Center for Research Libraries (CRL), Research Libraries Information Network (RLIN). **Special Catalogs:** Andre Girard, 1970; Lithography, 1973; Richard Aldington, 1973; 30 issued registers to manuscript collection. **Remarks:** Includes the holdings of Temple University Central Library System - Science Fiction Collection. **Staff:** Sharon Fitzpatrick, Bibliog.Asst.

★16138★
Temple University - Central Library System - Reference & Information Services Department Map Unit (Geog-Map)
Paley Library
13th & Berks Sts.   Phone: (215)787-8213
Philadelphia, PA 19122   Ida G. Ginsburgs, Map Libn.
Staff: Prof 1. **Subjects:** Topography, geography, geology, hydrology. **Holdings:** 98,300 maps; 1360 atlases and gazetteers. **Services:** Copying; collection open to the public on a limited schedule. **Computerized Information Services:** BRS Information Technologies, PFDS Online, DIALOG Information Services, Questel, VU/TEXT Information Services, WILSONLINE. Performs searches on fee basis. Contact Person: David Dillard.

★16139★
Temple University - Central Library System - Tyler School of Fine Arts - Library (Art)
Beech & Penrose Aves.   Phone: (215)782-2849
Philadelphia, PA 19126   Linda Cotilla, Hd., Suburban Campus Libs.
Founded: 1935. **Staff:** Prof 2; Other 2. **Subjects:** Fine and applied arts. **Holdings:** 34,000 volumes; 6 VF drawers of pictures; 5 periodical titles on microfilm. **Subscriptions:** 118 journals and other serials. **Services:** Interlibrary loan; copying. **Computerized Information Services:** Association of Research Libraries (ARL). **Networks/Consortia:** Member of Research Libraries Information Network (RLIN), Center for Research Libraries (CRL), PALINET.

Temple University - Central Library System - Urban Archives - Housing Association of Delaware Valley
See: **Housing Association of Delaware Valley (7444)**

★16140★
Temple University - Central Library System - Urban Archives Center (Soc Sci)
13th & Berks Sts.   Phone: (215)787-8257
Philadelphia, PA 19122   Margaret Jerrido
Founded: 1967. **Staff:** Prof 3; Other 1. **Subjects:** Post Civil War Philadelphia area - history, housing, planning, social welfare, urban renewal, civil rights, politics, settlement houses, education, labor, criminal justice, business associations, photojournalism, news photography. **Special Collections:** WPVI-TV News Film, 1947-1983; Philadelphia Inquirer Newspaper Photographic Archival Collection, 1937-1979; Philadelphia Evening Bulletin photograph and clipping files, 1847-1982. **Holdings:** 3000 books; 20,000 pamphlets; 280 manuscript collections; 750 maps; 5000 photographs; 10,000 canisters of news film; 240 filing cabinets of clippings; 550 filing cabinets of photographic prints and negatives. **Subscriptions:** 10 journals and other serials. **Services:** Copying; archives open to the public. **Computerized Information Services:** RLIN, Association of Research Libraries (ARL). **Networks/Consortia:** Member of Research Libraries Information Network (RLIN), Center for Research Libraries (CRL), PALINET. **Publications:** Urban Archives Notes, biennial; Guides to Housing and Social Services Collections. **Special Catalogs:** Folder lists of manuscripts; catalog of pamphlets and photographs (card). **Staff:** George D. Brightbill, Photojournalism Cur.; Brenda Wright-Calloway, Archv.

★16141★
Temple University - Central Library System - Zahn Library - Audio Collection
Broad & Montgomery
Philadelphia, PA 19122
Subjects: Music - classical, jazz, popular, folk; musical comedy; spoken word recordings. **Special Collections:** Paley Presents Lecture Series (257 tape recordings). **Holdings:** 18,138 phonograph records; 756 audiotapes; 351 compact discs. **Remarks:** Currently inactive.

★16142★
Temple University - Central Library System - Zahn Library - Film Collection
Samuel Paley Library
13th & Berks Mall
Philadelphia, PA 19122
Subjects: History, anthropology, film as art, filmmaking, psychology, political science, feature films. **Special Collections:** Science fiction. **Holdings:** 857 films. **Services:** Library not open to the public. **Remarks:** Currently inactive.

★16143★
Temple University - Central Library System - Zahn Library - Instructional Materials Center/School of Social Administration (Educ, Soc Sci)
Ritter Annex 139
13th & Columbia Ave.
Philadelphia, PA 19122   Phone: (215)787-8481
Staff: Prof 2; Other 3. **Subjects:** Instructional materials, education, social administration, welfare. **Holdings:** 36,600 volumes; 542 volumes of masters' projects and theses; 2489 nonprint curricular materials. **Subscriptions:** 156 journals and other serials. **Services:** Interlibrary loan; copying; library open to the public. **Computerized Information Services:** Association of Research Libraries (ARL). **Networks/Consortia:** Member of Research Libraries Information Network (RLIN), Center for Research Libraries (CRL), PALINET.

★16144★
Temple University - Charles L. Blockson Afro-American Historical Collection (Hist, Area-Ethnic)
Sullivan Hall, 1st Fl.   Phone: (215)787-6632
Philadelphia, PA 19122   Charles L. Blockson, Cur.
Founded: 1983. **Staff:** Prof 1; Other 2. **Subjects:** Afro-American history, literature, and religion; African history; blacks in sports; Caribbean; sociology; education. **Special Collections:** History of blacks in Pennsylvania; underground railroad; John Mosley Photo Collection; Paul Robeson Collection; Bishop R.R. Wright, Jr. Collection. **Holdings:** 20,000 books; 169 bound periodical volumes; 20,000 other cataloged items. **Subscriptions:** 22 journals and other serials. **Services:** Copying; collection open to the public for reference use only. **Automated Operations:** Computerized cataloging and circulation. **Computerized Information Services:** RLIN. **Publications:** Afro-Americana: An Exhibition of Selected Books, Manuscripts & Prints, 1984.

★16145★
Temple University - Department of Journalism - Blitman Reading Room (Info Sci)
303 Annenberg Hall
13th & Diamond Sts.   Phone: (215)787-7350
Philadelphia, PA 19122   Robert G. Roberts, Libn.
Founded: 1969. **Staff:** Prof 1; Other 1. **Subjects:** Reporting, newspaper industry, media law, radio and television broadcasting, telecommunications. **Holdings:** 10,200 books. **Subscriptions:** 80 journals and other serials; 25 newspapers. **Services:** Copying; library open to the public.

★16146★
Temple University - Esther Boyer College of Music - New School Institute - Alice Tully Library (Mus)
1619 Walnut St.   Phone: (215)787-5531
Philadelphia, PA 19103   Susan L. Koenig, Libn.
Staff: Prof 1; Other 4. **Subjects:** Music, music literature. **Holdings:** 2000 books; 6500 scores; 2300 phonograph records; 300 tapes. **Services:** Library not open to the public.

★16147★
Temple University - Health Sciences Center - Health Sciences Libraries (Med)
Kresge Hall
3400 N. Broad St.   Phone: (215)221-2665
Philadelphia, PA 19140   Mark-Allen Taylor, Dir.
Founded: 1901. **Staff:** Prof 10; Other 10. **Subjects:** Medicine, dentistry, pharmacy, basic sciences, nursing, allied health sciences. **Special Collections:** Medical History. **Holdings:** 96,506 volumes; audiotapes. **Subscriptions:** 1247 journals and other serials. **Services:** Interlibrary loan;

copying; library open to the public. **Automated Operations:** Computerized cataloging. **Computerized Information Services:** NLM, BRS Information Technologies, DIALOG Information Services, RLIN, OCLC; InterNet (electronic mail service). **Networks/Consortia:** Member of Research Libraries Information Network (RLIN), PALINET, Health Sciences Libraries Consortium (HSLC). **Publications:** Periodicals Holdings List. **Remarks:** The Health Sciences Center holds the Dental-Allied Health-Pharmacy Library and the Medical Library. Each is housed separately. FAX: (215)221-4135. Electronic mail address(es): taylor@shrsys.hslc.org (InterNet). **Staff:** Virginia Lampson, Ref.Libn.; Karen Burstein, Ref.Libn.; Maureen Smith, Cat.; Ron Davies, PhD, Biomedical Info.Spec.; Ann Nista, Assoc.Dir.; Lillian Brazin, Asst.Dir.Pub.Serv.; Carl A. Anderson, Asst.Dir.Tech.Serv.; Robert Rooney, Asst.Dir.Adm.Lib.Serv.

★16148★
Temple University - Law Library (Law)
N. Broad St. & Montgomery Ave.   Phone: (215)787-7892
Philadelphia, PA 19122   John M. Lindsey, Law Prof./Law Libn.
Staff: Prof 7; Other 12. **Subjects:** Law, legal history. **Special Collections:** Justice of the Peace Manuals; Hirst Free Law Library. **Holdings:** 292,393 books; 15,700 bound periodical volumes; 108,195 microforms. **Subscriptions:** 2812 journals and other serials. **Services:** Interlibrary loan; copying; library open to the public for reference use only. **Networks/Consortia:** Member of Research Libraries Information Network (RLIN). **Remarks:** FAX: (215)787-1785.

★16149★
Temple University - Tyler School of Fine Arts - Slide Library (Art, Aud-Vis)
Beech & Penrose Aves.   Phone: (215)782-2848
Elkins Park, PA 19126   Diane Sarachman, Hd. Slide Cur.
Founded: 1970. **Staff:** Prof 2; Other 2. **Subjects:** Art history - prehistoric to contemporary; decorative arts; ceramics; graphics; photography; film. **Holdings:** 335,000 slides. **Services:** Copying; library open to faculty and graduate students. **Automated Operations:** Computerized acquisitions. **Computerized Information Services:** Online systems. **Staff:** Del Ramers, Assoc.Cur.

★16150★
Temple University Hospital - Diagnostic Imaging Department - Gustavus C. Bird, III, M.D. Library of Diagnostic Imaging (Med)
3401 N. Broad St.   Phone: (215)221-4226
Philadelphia, PA 19140   Nancy G. Washburne, Libn./Dir.
Founded: 1960. **Staff:** Prof 1. **Subjects:** Diagnostic imaging, radiology, nuclear medicine. **Special Collections:** Radiological Teaching File Collection (films, ultrasound, CAT scans, MRI, urograms; 35,000 items). **Holdings:** 1000 books; 900 bound periodical volumes; 9 volumes of departmental publications; 90 videotapes; 20 slide/tape sets; 50 uncataloged items. **Subscriptions:** 50 journals and other serials. **Services:** Interlibrary loan (limited); telephone reference; library open by referral and by appointment. **Automated Operations:** Computerized cataloging and serials. **Computerized Information Services:** MEDLINE. **Special Catalogs:** Catalog of 5700 ultrasound/CT/neuroradiology films (online, printout, card). **Remarks:** FAX: (215)221-4464.

Abe and Esther Tenenbaum Library
See: Agudath Achim Synagogue (138)

James F. Tennant Teachers' Centre
See: Frontenac County Board of Education (6181)

Tenneco Canada, Inc. - Albright & Wilson Americas
See: Albright & Wilson Americas (317)

★16151★
Tenneco Inc. - Corporate & Law Library (Bus-Fin, Sci-Engr)
1010 Milam St., Suite 2519
Box 2511
Houston, TX 77252   Phone: (713)757-5507
Susan M. Yancey, Corp. and Law Libn.
Staff: Prof 1; Other 3. **Subjects:** Business, technology, energy, engineering, law. **Holdings:** 27,000 books; 1200 bound periodical volumes; government documents; corporate annual reports. **Subscriptions:** 400 journals and other serials; 8 newspapers. **Services:** Interlibrary loan; copying; library open to the public by appointment. **Automated Operations:** Computerized cataloging, acquisitions, serials, and circulation. **Computerized Information Services:** DIALOG Information Services, Information America, Dow Jones News/Retrieval, LEXIS, NEXIS, VU/TEXT Information Services, DataTimes. **Remarks:** FAX: (713)757-1567.

★16152★
Tenneco, Inc. - Newport News Shipbuilding - Library (Biol Sci, Sci-Engr)
4101 Washington Ave.   Phone: (804)380-2610
Newport News, VA 23607   Linda Sleighter, Supv., Rec.Mgt.
Founded: 1947. **Staff:** Prof 3; Other 2. **Subjects:** Oceanography, management, naval architecture, marine engineering, mathematics. **Holdings:** 35,000 books; 9000 bound periodical volumes; 10,000 research reports and documents. **Subscriptions:** 1300 journals and other serials. **Services:** Interlibrary loan; library open to the public with security clearance.

Tenneco, Inc. - Newport News Shipbuilding - Sperry Marine Inc.
See: Sperry Marine Inc. (15582)

★16153★
Tennessean Newspaper - Library (Publ)
1100 Broadway   Phone: (615)259-8000
Nashville, TN 37203   Annette Morrison, Hd.Libn.
Founded: 1940. **Staff:** Prof 2; Other 5. **Subjects:** Newspaper reference topics. **Holdings:** 1550 books; 80 bound periodical volumes; 60 VF drawers of pamphlets; 1500 VF drawers of clippings; 160 VF drawers of photographs; 100 drawers of microfilm. **Subscriptions:** 30 journals and other serials. **Services:** Copying (limited); library open to the public by appointment. **Special Indexes:** Files on people, reporter by-lines, criminals, lawsuit litigants, politicians, and businesses (card); newspaper index, March, 1989 to present (online); subject heading and authority listing (online); headline index (online). **Remarks:** FAX: (615)259-8093. **Staff:** Nancy St. Cyr, Asst.Libn.; Glenda Washam, Photo.Libn., Asst.Libn.; Chantay Steptoe, Asst.Libn.

Tennessee Botanical Gardens & Fine Arts Center - Botanical Gardens Library
See: Cheekwood Botanical Gardens - Library (3463)

★16154★
Tennessee Botanical Gardens & Fine Arts Center - Fine Arts Center Library (Art)
Forrest Park Dr.   Phone: (615)353-2140
Nashville, TN 37205   Virginia Khouri, Lib. Coord.
Founded: 1977. **Staff:** Prof 1. **Subjects:** Art, art history, decorative arts, contemporary American artists, photography. **Holdings:** 2500 volumes; 2000 slides. **Subscriptions:** 20 journals and other serials. **Services:** Interlibrary loan; copying; library open to the public for reference use only. **Remarks:** FAX: (615)353-2162. **Also Known As:** Cheekwood Museum.

★16155★
Tennessee State Commission on Aging - Library (Soc Sci)
706 Church St., Suite 201
Nashville, TN 37243-0860   Phone: (615)741-2056
Founded: 1963. **Staff:** 1. **Subjects:** Aging, geriatric psychology and sociology, retirement planning, community based health and social services. **Holdings:** 500 books; VF drawers. **Subscriptions:** 10 journals and other serials. **Services:** Copying; library open to the public for reference use only. **Staff:** Jane Young, Prog.Spec.; Mason Rowe, Prog.Spec.

★16156★
Tennessee (State) Department of Agriculture - Lou Wallace Library
Ellington Agricultural Center
Melrose Sta., Box 40627
Nashville, TN 37204
Subjects: Agriculture, statistics. **Holdings:** 1500 books. **Remarks:** Currently inactive.

★16157★
Tennessee (State) Department of Economic & Community Development - Library (Bus-Fin)
Rachel Jackson Bldg., 8th Fl.   Phone: (615)741-1995
Nashville, TN 37219   Edith Snider, Libn.
Founded: 1973. **Staff:** Prof 1. **Subjects:** Industrial development, economics, minority business enterprise. **Special Collections:** Department Archives. **Holdings:** 3000 books; 300 documents; 750 file folios of corporation annual reports from Fortune 500 companies and major Tennessee companies. **Subscriptions:** 210 journals and other serials. **Services:** Interlibrary loan; copying; library open to the public with restrictions. **Remarks:** FAX: (615)741-7306

★ 16158 ★
Tennessee (State) Department of Employment Security - Research &
Statistics Division (Bus-Fin)
500 James Robertson Pkwy., 11th Fl.   Phone: (615)741-2284
Nashville, TN 37245-1000   Joe Cummings, Dir., Res. & Stat.
Staff: 1. **Subjects:** Data - labor market, census, economic. **Holdings:**
Publications of the U.S. Bureau of Census, the U.S. Department of Labor,
and the Department of Employment Security. **Services:** Copying; section
open to the public for reference use only. **Publications:** Labor Market
Information Directory; Annual Averages-Tennessee Labor Force Estimates;
Annual Planning Information; Available Labor; Labor Force Estimates
Summary; Consumer Price Index; Minorities in Tennessee; Occupations in
Demand at Tennessee Department of Employment Security; Tennessee and
Metropolitan Statistical Area Nonagricultural Employment Estimates;
Tennessee Covered Employment and Wages by Industry Statewide and by
County; Tennessee Data for Affirmative Action Plans 1984 (main
publication); Tennessee Data for Affirmative Action Plans (current
supplement); Tennessee Employment Projections; Youth in Tennessee;
Tennessee High School Graduates; The Occupational Outlook; Veterans in
Tennessee; Women in the Labor Force. **Remarks:** FAX: (615)741-3203.

★ 16159 ★
Tennessee (State) Department of the Environment - Resource Center
Cordell Hull Bldg., Rm. 546
Nashville, TN 37247-5201
Subjects: Maternal and child health, nursing, public health, health
education. **Holdings:** 500 books. **Remarks:** Currently inactive.

★ 16160 ★
Tennessee (State) Department of Health - Health Promotion/Disease
Control Section - Media Resource Center (Aud-Vis, Med)
Cordell Hull Bldg., 5th Fl., Rm. 546   Phone: (615)741-0380
Nashville, TN 37247-5201   Nancy Heaney, Dir., Media Rsrc.Ctr.
Founded: 1950. **Staff:** Prof 1. **Subjects:** Health, safety, nutrition, drug abuse,
family life, allied health fields. **Special Collections:** Degrassi Jr. High Series.
Holdings: 450 films; 300 videocassettes; filmstrips; slide series. **Services:**
Materials available for free loan to Tennessee residents; library not open to
the public. **Special Catalogs:** The Film Catalog and supplements. **Formerly:**
Tennessee (State) Department of Health and Environment.

★ 16161 ★
Tennessee (State) Department of Health and Environment - Division of
Information Resources - Library and Resource Center (Med, Plan)
419 Cordell Hull Bldg.   Phone: (615)741-3752
Nashville, TN 37247-0360   Ann Hogan, Dir.
Founded: 1976. **Staff:** Prof 1. **Subjects:** Health and vital statistics,
population, computers and personal computers, health care costs. **Special**
Collections: Rainbow Series. **Holdings:** 1500 books. **Subscriptions:** 65
journals and other serials. **Services:** Library open to the public with
restrictions. **Computerized Information Services:** MEDLINE; internal
databases. **Publications:** List of publications - available on request. **Remarks:**
FAX: (615)741-1429.

★ 16162 ★
Tennessee (State) Department of State - Tennessee State Library and
Archives (Hist, Law, Info Sci)
403 7th Ave. N.   Phone: (615)741-7996
Nashville, TN 37243-0312   Edwin S. Gleaves, Ph.D., Libn. & Archv.
Founded: 1854. **Staff:** Prof 29; Other 47. **Subjects:** Tennesseana, U.S. and
local history, state and local government, law and public administration,
genealogy. **Special Collections:** Papers of Jacob McGavock Dickinson,
James Robertson, Andrew Jackson, George P. Buell, Henry Shelton
Sanford, Richard Ewell; land records, 1777-1903 (600 volumes); state
agency records and governors' papers, 1796 to present; legislative records
and recordings, 1796 to present; state Supreme Court records, 1815-1955;
ethics records, 1975-1976; county records on microfilm; prints and cartoons
of Tennessee subjects; popular sheet music; 19th century broadsides;
Tennessee newspapers. **Holdings:** 467,000 books; 4 million manuscript
items; 22 million archival documents; 119,000 reels of microfilm; 215,000
sheets of microfiche; 38,000 audiotapes; 93,000 photographs. **Subscriptions:**
1620 periodicals; 201 newspapers on 23,685 reels of microfilm. **Services:**
Interlibrary loan; copying; library open to the public. **Automated**
Operations: Computerized cataloging. **Computerized Information Services:**
OCLC. **Networks/Consortia:** Member of SOLINET. **Publications:** List of
Tennessee State Publications, quarterly; Writings on Tennessee Counties;

Tennessee Newspapers on Microfilm; registers of manuscript materials;
checklist of microfilm; Guide to the Processed Manuscripts of the Tennessee
Historical Society; Guide to Microfilm Holdings of the Manuscripts Section.
Special Indexes: Index to City Cemetery Records of Nashville; Index to
Questionnaires of Civil War Veterans. **Remarks:** FAX: (615)741-6471. **Staff:**
Sandra S. Nelson, Asst. State Libn. & Archv. for Plan. & Dev.; Jeanne Sugg,
Tech.Serv.; Fran Schell, Dir., Pub.Serv.; Gene Hollars, Dir. Restoration and
Repro.

★ 16163 ★
Tennessee (State) Department of Transportation - Library (Trans)
James K. Polk Bldg., Suite 300   Phone: (615)741-2330
Nashville, TN 37243-0345   Ruth S. Letson, Libn. II
Founded: 1973. **Staff:** Prof 1. **Subjects:** Transportation, Tennessee planning
data, highways, road construction. **Special Collections:** Transportation
Research Board publications. **Holdings:** 8000 books; 2000 local studies.
Subscriptions: 100 journals and other serials. **Services:** Interlibrary loan;
copying; library open to the public for reference use only. **Automated**
Operations: Computerized cataloging, acquisitions, circulation, and serials.

★ 16164 ★
Tennessee (State) Human Rights Commission - Resource Library (Soc
Sci)
Capitol Boulevard Bldg., Suite 602
226 Capitol Blvd.
Nashville, TN 37243-0745   Phone: (615)741-5825
Staff: 1. **Subjects:** Race relations; discrimination in employment, housing,
and public accommodations; legislation and decisions rendered in
discrimination cases. **Holdings:** 60 books; 500 bound periodical volumes;
commission-related materials. **Subscriptions:** 10 journals and other serials.
Services: Library open to the public with restrictions. **Publications:** Annual
Report.

★ 16165 ★
Tennessee State Law Library (Law)
Supreme Court Bldg.
401 7th Ave., N.   Phone: (615)741-2016
Nashville, TN 37219   Mary Miles Prince, Lib.Coord. & Cons.
Founded: 1937. **Staff:** Prof 2; Other 1. **Subjects:** Law, Tennessee law.
Holdings: 55,000 volumes. **Subscriptions:** 100 journals and other serials.
Services: Library open to the public. **Remarks:** FAX: (615)741-5809.
Maintains law libraries at Jackson and Knoxville. **Staff:** Donna C. Wair,
Libn.

★ 16166 ★
Tennessee (State) Legislative Library (Law)
G-16 War Memorial Bldg.   Phone: (615)741-3091
Nashville, TN 37219   Julie J. McCown, Leg.Libn.
Founded: 1977. **Staff:** Prof 1. **Subjects:** Tennessee law, legislative reference.
Holdings: 8000 volumes. **Subscriptions:** 25 journals and other serials.
Services: Interlibrary loan; library open to the public for reference use only.
Remarks: Maintained by Office of Legal Services for the Tennessee General
Assembly.

★ 16167 ★
Tennessee State Library - Library for the Blind and Physically
Handicapped (Aud-Vis)
403 7th Ave., N.   Phone: (615)741-3915
Nashville, TN 37243-0313   Miss Francis H. Ezell, Dir.
Founded: 1970. **Staff:** Prof 3; Other 12. **Subjects:** General reading material
for the blind and physically handicapped. **Holdings:** 30,000 titles of books
recorded on disc and cassette, transcribed into braille; large print books.
Subscriptions: 83 journals and other serials (45 disc, 35 braille, 3 cassette).
Services: Free service to citizens of Tennessee who cannot read, hold, or turn
the pages of a regular print book due to a visual or physical handicap.
Playback equipment is provided. **Automated Operations:** Computerized
cataloging, serials, and circulation. **Computerized Information Services:**
BRS Information Technologies. **Networks/Consortia:** Member of National
Library Service for the Blind & Physically Handicapped (NLS). **Remarks:**
Toll-free telephone number(s): in Tennessee is (800)342-3308. FAX:
(615)741-6471. **Staff:** Mary Lou Markham; Wanda Shepard.

Tennessee State Library and Archives
See: **Tennessee (State) Department of State (16162)**

★ 16168 ★
Tennessee State Museum - Library (Hist)
James K. Polk State Office Bldg. & Cultural Ctr.
505 Deaderick St. Phone: (615)741-2692
Nashville, TN 33243-1120 Evadine O. McMahan, Adm.Asst.
Founded: 1977. **Staff:** Prof 1; Other 1. **Subjects:** Tennessee history, American decorative arts, Southern U.S. history, weapons, anthropology, folklore. **Special Collections:** Official records of the War of the Rebellion (153 volumes); Weesner Collection (Indians; archeology); early Smithsonian Reports (22 volumes). **Holdings:** 1558 books; 148 bound periodical volumes; 22 videotapes; 21,000 slides. **Subscriptions:** 25 journals and other serials. **Services:** Copying; library open to the public for reference use only. **Special Catalogs:** Gallery exhibit catalogs (book).

★ 16169 ★
Tennessee State Planning Office - Library (Plan)
John Sevier Bldg., Suite 310
500 Charlotte Ave. Phone: (615)741-2363
Nashville, TN 37243-0001 Charles L. Nelson, Libn.
Founded: 1935. **Staff:** Prof 1; Other 1. **Subjects:** Planning, Tennessee, public affairs. **Special Collections:** Tennessee planning studies; state planning studies from other states; archives of planning office publications (5000 items); Tennessee state publications including departmental reports, Tennessee session laws, and the Tennessee Code. **Holdings:** 13,500 books and pamphlets; 1503 community planning color slides; 1980 Census Area Boundary Maps for Tennessee; 20 VF drawers; 10 cassettes; 1 film; 720 maps; 6100 microfiche; 30 binders of computer printouts. **Subscriptions:** 260 journals and other serials. **Services:** Interlibrary loan; copying; library open to the public. **Publications:** Acquisitions List, monthly; periodical list, irregular. **Remarks:** Reference collections of 9450 items and selected journal and newspaper subscriptions are maintained in six local planning field offices.

★ 16170 ★
Tennessee State Public Service Commission - Legal Department - Library (Law)
460 James Robertson Pkwy. Phone: (615)741-3191
Nashville, TN 37243-0505 Henry Walker, Gen.Couns.
Founded: 1897. **Subjects:** Law, utility rates and service, transportation, tax assessments, railroads, transportation rates. **Holdings:** 2500 bound periodical volumes; docket files; transcripts; orders; court files. **Services:** Copying; library open to the public.

★ 16171 ★
Tennessee State Supreme Court - Law Library (Law)
Supreme Court Bldg.
719 Locust St. Phone: (615)594-6128
Knoxville, TN 37902 Susan Delp, Law Libn.
Founded: 1937. **Staff:** Prof 1. **Subjects:** Law. **Holdings:** 81,000 volumes. **Subscriptions:** 150 journals and other serials. **Services:** Library open to the public with restrictions. **Automated Operations:** Computerized cataloging.

★ 16172 ★
Tennessee State University - Lois H. Daniel Memorial Library - Special Collections (Soc Sci)
3500 John Merritt Blvd. Phone: (615)320-3682
Nashville, TN 37209-1561 Mrs. Yildiz B. Binkley, Dir.
Founded: 1912. **Staff:** Prof 16; Other 23. **Special Collections:** Tennessee State University Archives (55.74 linear feet); Thomas Poag Manuscript Collection (1.54 linear feet); Daniel E. Owens Jazz Collection (1934 recordings); papers of prominent African-Americans. **Services:** Interlibrary loan; copying; library open to the public for reference use only. **Computerized Information Services:** DIALOG Information Services; CD-ROMs (AGRICOLA, CRIS, ERIC); InfoTrac; BITNET (electronic mail service). Performs searches. **Publications:** Bibliographies; staff and student handbooks; Library Newsletter. **Remarks:** FAX: (615)320-3364. Electronic mail address(es): TSU@LIBR (BITNET). **Staff:** Murle Kenerson, Hd., Ref.Dept.; Fletcher Moon, Ref.Libn.; Anita Etheridge, Ref.Libn.

Tennessee State University Archives
See: **Tennessee State University - Lois H. Daniel Memorial Library (16172)**

★ 16173 ★
Tennessee Technological University - University Library (Bus-Fin, Sci-Engr)
Box 5066 Phone: (615)372-3326
Cookeville, TN 38505 Dr. Winston A. Walden, Dir., Lib.Serv.
Founded: 1915. **Staff:** Prof 15; Other 19. **Subjects:** Engineering. **Special Collections:** Tennessee and Upper Cumberland Region History Collection and Archives (1997 linear feet); Congressman Joe L. Evins Papers (490 linear feet). **Holdings:** 270,815 books; 93,582 bound periodical volumes; 751,125 titles in microform; 142,970 government documents. **Subscriptions:** 3957 journals and other serials. **Services:** Interlibrary loan; copying; SDI; library open to the public. **Automated Operations:** Computerized acquisitions, circulation, and public access catalog. **Computerized Information Services:** DIALOG Information Services, STN International, CD-ROMs (ERIC, PsychLIT, ABI/INFORM, CINAHL, Disclosure Incorporated, InfoTrac, Newspaper Abstracts, Dissertation Abstracts, MARCIVE). Performs searches on fee basis. Contact Person: Deanna Nipp, Coord., Pub.Serv., 372-3326. **Networks/Consortia:** Member of SOLINET. **Remarks:** FAX: (615)372-6112. **Formerly:** Jere Whitson Memorial Library. **Staff:** Roger Jones, Coord., Coll.Mgt. & Dev.; Susan LaFever, Coord., Bibliog. Control and Automation.

★ 16174 ★
Tennessee Valley Authority - Corporate Library (Energy)
1101 Market St. Phone: (615)751-4913
Chattanooga, TN 37402 Dean Robinson, Lib.Mgr.
Founded: 1957. **Staff:** Prof 2; Other 3. **Subjects:** Electric power, public utilities, environment. **Holdings:** 16,000 books; 16,000 government documents; 36,000 microfiche. **Subscriptions:** 459 journals and other serials. **Services:** Interlibrary loan; copying; SDI; library open to the public. **Automated Operations:** Computerized cataloging, circulation, and journal routing. **Computerized Information Services:** DIALOG Information Services, OCLC; CD-ROM; internal database. **Networks/Consortia:** Member of FEDLINK. **Publications:** Power and Nuclear Power Current Awareness Lists; Utility Information Report. **Special Indexes:** Index to electric utility statistical sources. **Remarks:** FAX: (615)751-4914. TVA Corporate Library in Knoxville, Tennessee handles cataloging and acquisitions. **Formerly:** Tennessee Valley Authority - Technical Library. **Staff:** Debra D. Mills, Supv., Serv.; Rick Woodlee, Ref.Libn.

★ 16175 ★
Tennessee Valley Authority - Corporate Library (Biol Sci, Sci-Engr, Env-Cons, Agri)
400 W. Summit Hill Dr. Phone: (615)632-3464
Knoxville, TN 37902 Dean Robinson, Lib.Mgr.
Founded: 1933. **Staff:** Prof 5; Other 4. **Subjects:** Administration and finance; engineering - civil, mechanical, electrical, nuclear; environmental sciences and education; flood control and navigation; forestry and wildlife; recreation; resource development; energy research development. **Special Collections:** History and development of TVA and Tennessee River Valley; TVA publications. **Holdings:** 39,000 books; 16,000 bound periodical volumes; 6000 documents; 4500 reels of microfilm; 32,000 microfiche. **Subscriptions:** 575 journals and other serials; 6 newspapers. **Services:** Interlibrary loan; copying; SDI; library open to the public. **Automated Operations:** Computerized cataloging, circulation, and journal routing. **Computerized Information Services:** DIALOG Information Services, OCLC; internal databases; CD-ROM. **Networks/Consortia:** Member of FEDLINK. **Publications:** TVA Handbook; Environmental & Corporate Current Awareness List. **Remarks:** TVA maintains Corporate Libraries in Knoxville and Chattanooga, Tennessee. The central staff in Knoxville handles cataloging of materials and acquisitions for Knoxville and Chattanooga. FAX: (615)632-4475. **Formerly:** Tennessee Valley Authority - Technical Library. **Staff:** Colene H. Siler, Supv., Serv.; Carolyn A. Andrews, Acq.; Edwin J. Best, Jr., Ref.Libn.; Betsy H. Wheeler, Ref.Libn.

★ 16176 ★
Tennessee Valley Authority - Maps and Surveys Branch - Map Information and Records Unit (Geog-Map)
101 Haney Bldg. Phone: (615)751-MAPS
Chattanooga, TN 37402-2801 J.L. Dodd, Civil Engr.
Founded: 1933. **Staff:** Prof 6; Other 1. **Subjects:** Mapping - land acquisition, land sales, special purpose; navigation charts and maps; control data; aerial photography; topography. **Holdings:** 1.2 million maps, charts, photographs, and control data. **Services:** Copying; unit open to the public. **Special Catalogs:** Price Catalog of Selected Maps and Data (book). **Remarks:** FAX: (615)751-6740.

★ 16177 ★
Tennessee Valley Authority - National Fertilizer and Environmental Research Center - Library (Sci-Engr, Agri)
Muscle Shoals, AL 35660   Phone: (205)386-3071
                                        Shirley G. Nichols, Lib.Mgr.
Founded: 1961. **Staff:** Prof 6; Other 3. **Subjects:** Agriculture, biomass energy, chemistry, chemical engineering, fertilizer, agricultural economics, environmental sciences, waste management. **Special Collections:** Fertilizer in the United States; history of fertilizer and agriculture. **Holdings:** 27,160 volumes; 2060 reels of microfilm; 400 VF drawers of pamphlets and documents. **Subscriptions:** 1351 journals and other serials. **Services:** Interlibrary loan; copying; reference services; library open to the public. **Automated Operations:** Computerized cataloging, circulation, acquisitions, and serials. **Computerized Information Services:** DIALOG Information Services, STN International, BRS Information Technologies, Integrated Technical Information System (ITIS), Washington Alert, NLM, OCLC, WILSONLINE; CATLIRS, TVAPUB (internal databases). Performs searches on fee basis. **Networks/Consortia:** Member of FEDLINK. **Publications:** Current Awareness and New Acquisitions, weekly; Fertilizer Publications with quarterly supplements. **Remarks:** Is said to be one of the most complete collections on fertilizer in the United States. **Remarks:** FAX: (205)386-2453. Telex: 797658. **Staff:** RaNae Vaughn, Ref.Libn.; Drucilla Gambrell, Ref.Libn.; Wendolyn Clark, Ref.Libn.; Earline Pollard, Acq.Libn.; Jane Mackey, Abstractor; Janice Abernathy, ILL.

★ 16178 ★
Tennessee Valley Authority - OGC Legal Research Center (Law)
400 W. Summit Hill Dr., ET 9A-K   Phone: (615)632-6645
Knoxville, TN 37902   Deborah A. Cherry, Supv., Legal Res.Ctr.
Staff: Prof 5; Other 8. **Subjects:** Law. **Holdings:** 20,000 volumes; 1 million documents. **Subscriptions:** 200 journals and other serials. **Services:** Center not open to the public. **Automated Operations:** Computerized cataloging. **Computerized Information Services:** LEXIS, NEXIS, WESTLAW, ELSS (Electronic Legislative Search System), VU/TEXT Information Services, DIALOG Information Services. **Remarks:** FAX: (615)632-4528; (615)632-6718. **Staff:** Teresa Scarlett, Ref./Thesaurus Coord.; Bessie Madison, Ref./Indexer; Michael Hamblin, Ref./Indexer; Terry Hebb, Ref./Indexer.

Tennessee Valley Authority - Technical Library
See: **Tennessee Valley Authority - Corporate Library** (16174)

★ 16179 ★
Tennessee Western History and Folklore Society - Library (Hist)
Box 60072
Nashville, TN 37206   Phone: (615)226-1890
Founded: 1979. **Staff:** Prof 2. **Subjects:** Tennessee and the Old West, Jesse and Frank James, the Seventh Cavalry (at Nashville), Ned Buntline, Clay Allison, Ambrose Bierce, Nat Love (black cowboy), Tennesseans in Texas, J. Frank Dalton (Jesse James imposter), John Joel Glanton, John Wilkes Booth, Knights of the Golden Circle, filibusters, Western music. **Special Collections:** Jesse James, 1847-1882 (275 items); Western imposters (200 items); Manifest Destiny (30 items). **Holdings:** 200 books; 100 letters; 600 magazines; 300 miscellaneous items; articles and news clippings; photographs; affidavits; artifacts; maps. **Services:** Copying; research (both limited); library open to serious scholars by appointment. **Remarks:** The society is interested in acquiring any information about Western events or persons with Tennessee connections. It is affiliated with the James Farm (Kearney, MO), Friends of the Youngers (Los Angeles, CA), and English Westerners Society (Westerners International). The society library is located at 1501 Eastland Ave., Nashville, TN 37206. **Staff:** Steve Eng, Cur.; Ted P. Yeatman, Cur.

★ 16180 ★
Tenzer Greenblatt Fallon & Kaplan - Law Library (Law)
405 Lexington Ave.   Phone: (212)573-4300
New York, NY 10174   Geoffrey C. Trigger
Founded: 1965. **Subjects:** Law - real estate, corporate, tax; litigation; securities; trusts. **Holdings:** 15,000 books. **Services:** Interlibrary loan; library not open to the public. **Computerized Information Services:** DIALOG Information Services, Dow Jones News/Retrieval, LEXIS, NEXIS, DataTimes; internal database. Contact Person: Joan Amenn, Asst.Libn.

★ 16181 ★
Terra Museum of American Art - Library (Art)
664 N. Michigan Ave.   Phone: (312)664-3939
Chicago, IL 60611   Catherine Wilson, Libn.
Founded: 1980. **Staff:** 1. **Subjects:** American painting (19th-20th centuries), art history, general art reference. **Holdings:** 4500 books. **Subscriptions:** 9 journals and other serials. **Services:** Library not open to the public. **Remarks:** FAX: (312)664-2052.

★ 16182 ★
Terra Tek Inc. - Technical Library (Sci-Engr, Energy)
University Research Park
400 Wakara Way   Phone: (801)584-2400
Salt Lake City, UT 84108   Jan Anderson, Libn.
Founded: 1975. **Staff:** Prof 1. **Subjects:** Geothermal energy, rock mechanics, drilling, petroleum, materials testing. **Special Collections:** Technical reports. **Holdings:** Figures not available. **Services:** Interlibrary loan; copying; library open to the public.

★ 16183 ★
Terrell State Hospital - Staff Library (Med)
Brin Ave.
Box 70   Phone: (214)563-6452
Terrell, TX 75160   Josie Richardson, Libn.
Founded: 1964. **Staff:** 1. **Subjects:** Psychiatry, neurology, medicine, nursing, psychology, mental health and allied sciences. **Holdings:** 6775 books; 260 bound periodical volumes; 2145 unbound journals; 2369 pamphlets and nonbook materials. **Subscriptions:** 145 journals and other serials. **Services:** Interlibrary loan; copying; library open to the public for reference use only. **Networks/Consortia:** Member of National Network of Libraries of Medicine - South Central Region, Project TexNet Interlibrary Loan Network (TexNet). **Publications:** Staff Library Handbook - to professional staff, hospital employees, and students of affiliated schools. **Remarks:** FAX: (214)563-2863.

Robert James Terry Library
See: **Texas Southern University** (16232)

Terveystieteiden Keskuskirjasto
See: **Finland - National Library of Health Sciences** (5710)

★ 16184 ★
Tesla Memorial Society - Tesla Biographical Archives (Sci-Engr)
453 Martin Rd.   Phone: (716)822-0281
Lackawanna, NY 14218   Paul Kosanovich
Founded: 1979. **Subjects:** Science - physics, electricity, electronics, history; Serbian Academy of Arts and Sciences. **Holdings:** 1000 books; 2 reels of microfilm. **Subscriptions:** 1200 journals and other serials.

Sandor Teszler Library
See: **Wofford College** (20547)

★ 16185 ★
Teton Science School - Natural History Library (Biol Sci)
Box 68   Phone: (307)733-4765
Kelly, WY 83011   Eric Stone, Res.Dir.
Founded: 1974. **Staff:** 1. **Subjects:** Natural history, ecology, man and nature, zoology, botany, earth science. **Special Collections:** Greater Yellowstone ecosystem (articles; studies; papers). **Holdings:** 2500 books; 2000 other cataloged items. **Services:** Library open to the public for reference use only.

Teuber Library
See: **Massachusetts Institute of Technology - Department of Brain and Cognitive Sciences - Teuber Library** (9799)

★ 16186 ★
Texaco Chemical Company, Inc. - Technical Literature Section (Sci-Engr)
78752 N. Lamarr
Box 15730   Phone: (512)459-6543
Austin, TX 78761   Mary E. Reese, Sr.Res.Libn.
Founded: 1946. **Subjects:** Chemistry, chemical engineering. **Holdings:** 4000 books; 3725 bound periodical volumes; 400 other cataloged items; patents; reports. **Subscriptions:** 300 journals and other serials.

★ 16187 ★
Texaco Inc. - Archives (Bus-Fin)
2000 Westchester Ave.   Phone: (914)253-7129
White Plains, NY 10650   Marjorie Federici, Ed.Asst.
Subjects: Texaco Incorporated. **Holdings:** 200 volumes; 1500 cubic feet of records; Texaco Incorporated photographs and publications. **Services:** Copying; archives open to the public by appointment upon written request. **Remarks:** FAX: (914)253-4655.

★ 16188 ★
Texaco Inc. - Business Information Center (Energy, Bus-Fin)
2000 Westchester Ave.   Phone: (914)253-6382
White Plains, NY 10650   Holly J. Furman, Adm.
Founded: 1981. **Staff:** Prof 6.5; Other 5. **Subjects:** Business, finance, management; energy and petroleum industry; area studies. **Holdings:** 13,500 volumes; 312,500 microfiche; 2800 reels of microfilm; 420 AV items. **Subscriptions:** 530 journals. **Services:** Interlibrary loan; copying; current awareness; library open to the public with restrictions. **Automated Operations:** Computerized cataloging and acquisitions. **Computerized Information Services:** CDA Investment Technologies, Inc., Congressional Quarterly, Construction Labor Research Council, Data-Star, DataTimes, DIALOG Information Services, Dow Jones News/Retrieval, Dun & Bradstreet Business Credit Services, Global Scan, Nikkei Telecom Japan News & Retrieval, NewsNet, Inc., NEXIS, Oil and Gas Journal Energy Database, ORBIT Search Service, Reuters, VU/TEXT Information Services, WILSONLINE, OCLC, RLIN, EBSCONET. **Networks/Consortia:** Member of New York Metropolitan Reference and Research Library Agency. **Publications:** The Source, monthly - for internal distribution only; Library brochures and bibliographies. **Remarks:** FAX: (914)253-6157. **Staff:** Josephine Ndinyah, Info.Spec.; Cherie Voris, Info.Spec.; Lucille Buter, Info.Spec.; Elaine Tai-Lauria, Info.Spec.; Claire Buralay, Info.Spec.

★ 16189 ★
Texaco Inc. - Exploration & Production Technology Department - Library (Energy)
3901 Briarpark Dr.
Box 770070   Phone: (713)954-6007
Houston, TX 77215-0070   Debra J. Clay, Lib.Supv.
Founded: 1960. **Staff:** Prof 3; Other 5. **Subjects:** Petroleum engineering, chemistry, geology, technology. **Holdings:** 40,000 books; 800 bound periodical volumes; AV programs; maps; company documents. **Subscriptions:** 400 journals and other serials. **Services:** Interlibrary loan; library not open to the public. **Automated Operations:** Computerized cataloging, serials, and circulation. **Computerized Information Services:** DIALOG Information Services, OCLC, STN International, Maxwell Online, Inc. **Networks/Consortia:** Member of AMIGOS Bibliographic Council, Inc. **Publications:** Library Newsletter, quarterly; announcements of acquisitions and services, quarterly. **Remarks:** FAX: (713)954-6907. **Staff:** Margy Walsh, Sys.Libn.; Jeanne Perdue, Search Libn.; Mary Hill, Ref.Libn.

★ 16190 ★
Texarkana Historical Society & Museum - Library (Hist)
219 State Line Ave.
Box 2343   Phone: (903)793-4831
Texarkana, TX 75504   Katy Caver, Cur.
Founded: 1971. **Staff:** Prof 2; Other 2. **Subjects:** Local history. **Special Collections:** Medical books of early local physicians; early school books and newspapers; local genealogy. **Holdings:** 1800 books; 15 scrapbooks of early residents; 40 Texarkana city directories; 44 annuals of local high schools. **Subscriptions:** 14 journals and newspapers. **Services:** Interlibrary loan; copying; library open to the public by request. **Staff:** Jeanette Winters, Coll.Mgr.

Texas A & M University - Forest Pest Control Section
See: Texas (State) Forest Service - Forest Pest Control Section (16252)

Texas Accelerator Center
See: Houston Area Research Center (HARC) - Texas Accelerator Center (7446)

★ 16191 ★
Texas A&M University - Archives & Manuscripts Collections (Hist)
Sterling C. Evans Library   Phone: (409)845-1815
College Station, TX 77843-5000   Dr. Charles R. Schultz, Univ.Archv.
Founded: 1950. **Staff:** Prof 2; Other 2. **Subjects:** Texas A&M University, Texas agriculture, technology, modern politics, education. **Special Collections:** Papers of Congressmen Olin E. Teague, Robert Casey, John Young, Joe Barton, and Graham Purcell; journalist Bascom N. Timmons; nuclear physicist Paul Aebersold; educational administrators and educators Tim M. Stinnett, Alvin A. Price, George Shelton, Alton D. Ice, Worth Nowlin (including records of the Southern Oceans Studies Project), Chris Groneman, Fred Sialio, Wolfgang G. Roeseler, and Kenneth C. Brandidge; author William A. Owens; Texas legislators Susan G. McBee, Tom Creighton, Will L. Smith, Bill Presnel, John Traeger, Kent Caperton, Richard Smith, and Billy W. Clayton; Texas Governor William P. Clements, Jr.; real estate broker Owen Sherrill; animal scientist John McKinley Jones; engineer and highway administrator Thomas H. McDonald; political commentator Dan Smoot; electric utilities corporation executive J.B. Thomas; agricultural editors Eugene Butler and Charles Scruggs; oil and gas developers Michel T. Halbouty and Edgar B. Davis; political and religious activist Jonnie Mae Hackworth; maritime labor union organizer Joseph Curran; prison administrator W.J. Estelle, Jr.; military officers Brig. Gen. James F. Hollingsworth and Gen. Walter Krueger; historian E.B. Long; antiquavian bookseller Jefferson Chenoweth Dykes; photograph collection of Lt. Col. Noland Varley depicting the destruction caused by the atomic bombing of Hiroshima and Nagasaki, Japan in 1945; World War I correspondence of George and Nell Steel Armstrong and Milton Jonas Gaines; space power and propulsion reference collection of J. Preston Layton; records of the Texas Cotton Association; records of the Texas section of the American Society of Civil Engineers; records of Quartet magazine. **Holdings:** 13,318 linear feet of Texas A&M University records and historical manuscripts collections; photographs of campus, rural Texas and Texans (1930-1960), Mexican Revolution (1914-1915), Spanish-American War in Cuba (1898), and citizens of Brazos and surrounding counties (1952-1979) taken by the Aggieland studio and the University studio; 675 hours of oral history interviews on agricultural science in Texas, military history, the Mexican revolution of 1910-1920, oceanography, Texas A&M University, and urban planning in Texas. **Services:** Copying; collections open to the public. **Publications:** Inventories of individual manuscript and archival collections; guides to all holdings, both irregular. **Remarks:** FAX: (409)845-6238. All inventories available on microfiche through Chadwyck-Healy. **Staff:** David L. Chapman, Assoc.Archv.

★ 16192 ★
Texas A&M University - Center for Dredging Studies - Ocean Engineering Library (Sci-Engr)
Civil Engineering Department   Phone: (409)845-4516
College Station, TX 77843-3136   Nell Bowden, Ck. III
Staff: Prof 1. **Subjects:** Dredging, coastal and ocean engineering. **Holdings:** 300 books; 60 bound periodical volumes; 3000 unbound reports; 3 VF drawers. **Subscriptions:** 40 journals and other serials. **Services:** Interlibrary loan; copying; library open to the public. **Publications:** Newsletter, 2/year; technical reports, 15/year; abstracts of articles relating to dredging technology, 12/year - by subscription. **Remarks:** FAX: (409)845-9643. **Staff:** Dr. John B. Herbich, Dir.

★ 16193 ★
Texas A&M University - Department of English - World Shakespeare Bibliography (Hum)
College Station, TX 77843-4227   Phone: (409)845-3400
Founded: 1985. **Staff:** Prof 1; Other 3. **Subjects:** William Shakespeare. **Holdings:** 3700 books; 17,000 bound periodical volumes; 500 reports; 17,000 offprints; 8000 programs. **Subscriptions:** 100 journals and other serials. **Services:** Library open to the public by appointment. **Computerized Information Services:** World Shakespeare Bibliography (1958 to present; internal databse). Contact Person: James L. Harner. **Publications:** World Shakespeare Bibliography (issue of Shakespeare Quarterly), annual. **Staff:** Harrison T. Meserole.

★ 16194 ★
Texas A&M University - Departments of Oceanography and
Meteorology - Working Collection (Sci-Engr)
Dept. of Oceanography   Phone: (409)845-7327
College Station, TX 77843   Gloria Guffy, Rsrc.Ctr.Supv.
Founded: 1949. **Staff:** Prof 1; Other 1. **Subjects:** Oceanography,
meteorology. **Holdings:** 1250 books; 850 technical reports; 985 theses and
dissertations; 825 external reports and publications. **Subscriptions:** 30
journals and other serials. **Services:** Copying; collection open to the public
for reference use only. **Publications:** Contributions in Oceanography,
irregular - for exchange.

★ 16195 ★
Texas A&M University - Map Section (Geog-Map)
Sterling C. Evans Library   Phone: (409)845-1024
College Station, TX 77843-5000 Barbara B. Alexander, Hd., Docs./Maps
Founded: 1970. **Staff:** Prof 1; Other 2. **Subjects:** Geology, soils, topography,
energy resources, transportation. **Special Collections:** U.S. Geological
Survey topographic maps; various Texas subjects (135 map cases). **Holdings:**
1757 titles; 56 bound periodical volumes; 149,525 maps; 215 slides; 3406
microfiche. **Subscriptions:** 25 journals and other serials. **Services:**
Department open to the public. **Automated Operations:** Computerized
cataloging, acquisitions, and serials. **Computerized Information Services:**
WILSONLINE. **Remarks:** FAX: (409)845-6238.

★ 16196 ★
Texas A&M University - Medical Sciences Library (Med)
College Station, TX 77843-4462   Phone: (409)845-7427
                                                 Dottie Eakin, Dir.
Founded: 1976. **Staff:** Prof 13; Other 14. **Subjects:** Biomedical sciences,
veterinary medicine. **Special Collections:** Ethnic medicine; veterinary
medicine. **Holdings:** 31,300 books; 90,250 bound periodical volumes; 27,450
microforms. **Subscriptions:** 2150 journals and other serials. **Services:**
Interlibrary loan; copying; library open to the public. **Automated**
Operations: Computerized public access catalog, cataloging, acquisitions,
serials, and circulation. **Computerized Information Services:** BRS
Information Technologies, DIALOG Information Services, NLM,
WILSONLINE; BITNET, InterNet (electronic mail services). **Networks/**
Consortia: Member of South Central Academic Medical Libraries
Consortium (SCAMEL), TAMU Consortium of Medical Libraries,
AMIGOS Bibliographic Council, Inc. **Publications:** Medical Sciences
Library Newsletter. **Special Catalogs:** Union List of Serials (computer
printout and microfiche). **Remarks:** FAX: (409)845-7493. Electronic mail
address(es): TAMVM1 (BITNET); TAMVM1.TAMU.EDU (InterNet).
Staff: Esther Carrigan, Mgr., Tech.Serv.; Gale Hannigan, Mgr., Educ. &
Info.Serv.; Barbara Thomas, Mgr., Access & Outreach Serv.; Joe Jaros,
Mgr., Comp.Sys.

★ 16197 ★
Texas A&M University - Nautical Archaeology Library (Sci-Engr)
Dept. of Anthropology
College Station, TX 77843-4352   Phone: (409)845-6398
Staff: Prof 1. **Subjects:** Nautical archeology, maritime history, archeology,
naval architecture, artifact conservation. **Special Collections:** G. Roger
Edwards Collection (Greek, Hellenistic, Roman archeology and history; 550
volumes). **Holdings:** 2000 books; 250 bound periodical volumes; 4000
offprints and theses; 13 reels of microfilm; 13 microfiche. **Subscriptions:** 36
journals and other serials. **Services:** Library open to the public for reference
use only. **Remarks:** FAX: (409)845-6399.

★ 16198 ★
Texas A&M University - Reference Division (Sci-Engr)
Sterling C. Evans Library   Phone: (409)845-5741
College Station, TX 77843-5000   Julia M. Rholes, Hd., Ref.Div.
Founded: 1876. **Staff:** Prof 17; Other 10. **Subjects:** Agriculture, engineering
and technology, physical sciences, biology, transportation, petroleum
geology. **Holdings:** 15,000 books. **Subscriptions:** 700 indexes and abstracts.
Services: Interlibrary loan; copying; SDI; division open to the public.
Automated Operations: Computerized cataloging, acquisitions, serials, and
circulation. **Computerized Information Services:** DIALOG Information
Services, BRS Information Technologies, WESTLAW, NLM, PFDS
Online, Mead Data Central, DataTimes, VU/TEXT Information Services,
STN International, U.S. Patent Classification System, Chemical
Information Systems, Inc. (CIS). **Remarks:** FAX: (409)845-6238. **Staff:**
Jeannie Miller, Sci.Ref.Libn.; Richard Eissenger, Sci.Libn.; Amy Shannon,
Sci.Libn.; Richard Stringer-Hye, Sci.Ref.Libn.; Vicki Anders, Hd.Spec.Ref.;
Karen Wielhorski, Hd. Central Ref.

★ 16199 ★
Texas A&M University - Research and Extension Center at EL Paso -
Library (Agri)
1380 A&M Circle   Phone: (915)859-9111
El Paso, TX 79927   Lorraine Martinez
Founded: 1942. **Subjects:** Soils, plant genetics, horticulture, plant
physiology, agronomy. **Holdings:** 100 books; 400 bound periodical volumes;
30 reports. **Subscriptions:** 13 journals and other serials. **Remarks:** FAX:
(915)859-1078.

★ 16200 ★
Texas A&M University - Special Collections Division (Hum)
Sterling C. Evans Library   Phone: (409)845-1951
College Station, TX 77843-5000   Donald H. Dyal, Hd., Spec.Coll.Div.
Founded: 1968. **Staff:** Prof 2; Other 6. **Subjects:** Range livestock industry,
science fiction, Texas, J. Frank Dobie, Western illustrators, Ku Klux Klan,
W. Somerset Maugham, Matthew Arnold, P.G. Wodehouse, sea fiction,
ornithology, incunabula, 16th-18th century naval architecture, Joseph
Conrad, William Faulkner, Ford Madox Ford, W.H. Auden, Rudyard
Kipling, Henry James, E.M. Forster, military history. **Special Collections:**
Jeff Dykes Range Livestock Collection; Science Fiction Research Collection;
J. Frank Dobie Collection; Great Western Illustrators Collection;
architectural pattern books. **Holdings:** 65,000 books; 8000 bound periodical
volumes; 14,000 reprints on developmental biology. **Subscriptions:** 40
journals and other serials. **Services:** Copying (limited); collections open to
the public with restrictions. **Computerized Information Services:** OCLC.
Publications: Friends of the Sterling C. Evans Library Keepsake series.
Remarks: FAX: (409)845-6238. **Staff:** Joni Gomez.

★ 16201 ★
Texas A&M University - Texas Cooperative Wildlife Collection (Biol
Sci)
Nagle Hall, Rm. 210
Mail Stop 2258   Phone: (409)845-5777
College Station, TX 77843   David J. Schmidy
Founded: 1989. **Subjects:** Mammalian systematics, avian systematics,
reptilian systematics, mammalian natural history, avian natural history.
Special Collections: Field notes of W.B. Davis. **Holdings:** 200 books; 150
bound periodical volumes; 2000 article reprints. **Services:** Library open to
the public for reference use only.

★ 16202 ★
Texas A&M University - Thermodynamics Research Center (Sci-Engr)
Texas Engineering Experiment Station
Richardson Petroleum Bldg., Rm. 916   Phone: (409)845-4940
College Station, TX 77843-3111   Dr. Kenneth N. Marsh, Dir.
Founded: 1942. **Staff:** Prof 9; Other 4. **Subjects:** Critically evaluated tables
of physical and thermodynamic properties and spectral data in six categories
(Infrared (IR), Ultraviolet (UV), Raman, Mass, 1H Nuclear Magnetic
Resonance (NMR), C13 NMR) for hydrocarbons and related compounds,
and for other organic (non-hydrocarbon) and inorganic substances;
thermodynamic properties of organic mixtures. **Holdings:** 1200 books; 1300
bound periodical volumes; 500,000 data cards on physical and
thermodynamic properties; 200 government documents on microfiche.
Subscriptions: 10 journals and other serials. **Services:** Center open to the
public with permission. **Computerized Information Services:** Produces TRC
Thermodynamic Table (available online through STN International), TRC
Vapor Pressure Database (available for IBM PC), TRC Source Database of
Thermodynamic Data From Published Literature. **Publications:** Critically
selected scientific data (loose-leaf); TRC Thermodynamic Tables -
Hydrocarbons, semiannual; TRC Thermodynamic Tables - Non-
Hydrocarbons, semiannual; TRC Spectral Data, semiannual; 1H NMR
Data ; IR Data; C13 NMR Data; UV Data; Mass Data; Raman Data;
International DATA Series, quarterly - all by subsription. **Remarks:** FAX:
(409)847-8590. **Staff:** Dr. Randolph C. Wilhoit, Assoc.Dir.; Bruce
Gammon, Assoc.Dir.

★ 16203 ★
Texas A&M University at Galveston - Jack K. Williams Library (Biol
Sci)
200 Seawolf Pkwy.
Box 1675   Phone: (409)740-4566
Galveston, TX 77553-1675   Natalie H. Wiest, Lib.Dir.
Founded: 1972. **Staff:** Prof 3; Other 5. **Subjects:** Marine biology, ecology,
maritime systems engineering, maritime history, marine transportation and

technology, maritime resources. **Special Collections:** Galveston Bay Information Center. **Holdings:** 35,000 books; 27,000 bound periodical volumes; 50,000 titles on microfiche. **Subscriptions:** 800 journals and other serials; 9 newspapers. **Services:** Interlibrary loan; copying; library open to the public. **Automated Operations:** Computerized public access catalog, cataloging, acquisitions, circulation, and ILL. **Computerized Information Services:** DIALOG Information Services, ASFA; Galveston Bay (internal database). **Networks/Consortia:** Member of AMIGOS Bibliographic Council, Inc. **Remarks:** FAX: (409)740-4407. **Staff:** Alice Davis-Rains, Act.Dir.; Diane B. Watson, Pub.Serv.Libn.

★ 16204 ★
Texas Baptist Historical Museum - Independence Historical Library (Rel-Phil)
Rte. 5, Box 222   Phone: (409)836-5117
Brenham, TX 77833   Paul Sevar, Dir.
Staff: Prof 1. **Subjects:** Baptist history. **Special Collections:** Annuals of the Baptist General Convention of Texas (60 volumes); Southern Baptist Annuals (58 volumes); Link's Letters (bound in two volumes). **Holdings:** 502 books; 12 VF drawers of other cataloged items. **Subscriptions:** 50 journals and other serials; 25 newspapers. **Services:** Library open to the public for reference use only.

★ 16205 ★
Texas Baptist Institute/Seminary - Library (Rel-Phil)
1300 Longview Dr.
Box 570   Phone: (903)657-6543
Henderson, TX 75653   Robert A. Brock, Libn.
Staff: Prof 1. **Subjects:** Religion, Baptist theology and history. **Holdings:** 7094 books; 230 dissertations. **Subscriptions:** 50 journals and other serials. **Services:** Interlibrary loan; library open to the public at librarian's discretion.

★ 16206 ★
Texas Catholic Conference - Catholic Archives of Texas (Hist, Rel-Phil)
1600 N. Congress   Phone: (512)476-4888
Austin, TX 78711   Kinga L. Perzynska, Archv.
Founded: 1923. **Staff:** Prof 1.5; Other 3. **Subjects:** Spanish exploration and missionary period (1519-1836), Catholic Church history in Texas, immigration and emigration, colonization. **Special Collections:** Ecclesiastical records of the Catholic Church in Texas, 1836-1980; Texas Catholic Conference Papers, 1958-1987; Charles S. Taylor papers, 1829-1868 (over 2000 items); Bishop Odin papers, 1840-1870 (first Bishop of Texas; 400 letters); Texas Knights of Columbus records; Papers of Volunteers for Educational & Social Services, 1958-1987; Sam Houston Papers, 1818-1860. **Holdings:** 1000 volumes; 70,000 pages of Spanish and Mexican documents, 1519-1880; 270 document cases of ecclesiastical records; 40 document cases of private collections; 170 reels of microfilm of Catholic newspapers; 15,000 photographs. **Subscriptions:** 15 journals and other serials. **Services:** Copying; library open to the public. **Computerized Information Services:** Internal database. **Publications:** Our Catholic Heritage in Texas, 1519-1950 (7 volumes); Journal of Texas Catholic History and Culture.

Texas Children's Hospital
See: **St. Luke's Episcopal & Texas Children's Hospitals** (14474)

★ 16207 ★
Texas Chiropractic College - Mae Hilty Memorial Library (Med)
5912 Spencer Hwy.   Phone: (713)487-1170
Pasadena, TX 77505   Deedra J. Walton, Act.Dir., Lib.Serv.
Founded: 1954. **Staff:** 3. **Subjects:** Chiropractic, basic sciences, diagnosis, x-ray, public health, clinical sciences. **Special Collections:** C.S. Cooley and Carver Chiropractic College Collection; Willard Carver Collection. **Holdings:** 7000 books; 3094 bound periodical volumes; 60 titles in microform; 6 VF drawers of pamphlets; 542 AV programs. **Subscriptions:** 142 journals. **Services:** Interlibrary loan; copying; library open to the public for reference use only. **Computerized Information Services:** MEDLARS, DIALOG Information Services, OCLC. Performs searches on fee basis. **Networks/Consortia:** Member of Chiropractic Library Consortium (CLIBCON), National Network of Libraries of Medicine - South Central Region. **Remarks:** FAX: (713)487-4168. **Staff:** Irene Lovell, Circ.; Mary Lee Freeman, AV; Kathy Foulch, Acq.

★ 16208 ★
Texas Christian University - Mary Couts Burnett Library - Brite Divinity School Collection (Rel-Phil)
Fort Worth, TX 76129   Phone: (817)921-7106
                                          Robert A. Olsen, Jr., Theol.Libn.
Founded: 1927. **Staff:** Prof 3; Other 3. **Subjects:** Religion, theology, biography, bibliography, literature by and about the Disciples of Christ. **Holdings:** 103,444 volumes; 56,421 volumes in microform. **Subscriptions:** 1280 journals and other serials. **Services:** Interlibrary loan; copying. **Computerized Information Services:** OCLC, DIALOG Information Services, BRS Information Technologies, MEDLINE; BITNET (electronic mail service). **Networks/Consortia:** Member of Association for Higher Education of North Texas (AHE), AMIGOS Bibliographic Council, Inc. **Remarks:** FAX: (817)921-7110. Electronic mail address(es): OLSEN@TCUCVMS (BITNET).

★ 16209 ★
Texas Christian University - Mary Couts Burnett Library - Music Library and Audio Center (Mus)
Box 32904   Phone: (817)921-7667
Fort Worth, TX 76129   Sheila Madden, Mus.Libn.
Founded: 1945. **Staff:** Prof 1; Other 2. **Subjects:** Music. **Holdings:** 12,660 books; 20,776 scores; 8125 phonograph records; 3025 78rpm records; 135 titles on microcards; 120 reels of microfilm; 2893 reel-to-reel and cassette tapes. **Subscriptions:** 72 journals and other serials. **Services:** Interlibrary loan; copying; library open to the public with restrictions. **Automated Operations:** Computerized cataloging, serials, and circulation. **Computerized Information Services:** OCLC, Automated Information Retrieval Systems, Inc. (AIRS). **Networks/Consortia:** Member of AMIGOS Bibliographic Council, Inc., Association for Higher Education of North Texas (AHE).

★ 16210 ★
Texas College of Osteopathic Medicine - Health Sciences Library (Med)
3500 Camp Bowie Blvd.   Phone: (817)735-2464
Fort Worth, TX 76107   Bobby R. Carter, Dir., Lib.Serv.
Founded: 1970. **Staff:** Prof 10; Other 24. **Subjects:** Health sciences, clinical and osteopathic medicine. **Special Collections:** Osteopathic medicine (2023 volumes); oral history collection (41 items); William G. Sutherland Collection; archives. **Holdings:** 46,229 books; 67,032 bound periodical volumes; 4532 AV programs; 4 VF drawers of pamphlets; 92 anatomical models. **Subscriptions:** 2168 journals and other serials. **Services:** Interlibrary loan; copying; SDI; library open to the public with restrictions. **Automated Operations:** Computerized public access catalog, cataloging, acquisitions, serials, and circulation. **Computerized Information Services:** DIALOG Information Services, BRS Information Technologies, OCLC, miniMEDLINE, MEDLARS. Performs searches on fee basis. Contact Person: Ann Brooks, Coord., Pub.Serv., 735-2380. **Networks/Consortia:** Member of AMIGOS Bibliographic Council, Inc., Health Libraries Information Network (HealthLINE), South Central Academic Medical Libraries Consortium (SCAMEL), National Network of Libraries of Medicine - South Central Region. **Remarks:** FAX: (817)735-2283; (817)763-0408 (ILL). Resource library for the Texas Osteopathic Medical Association. **Staff:** Craig S. Elam, Assoc.Dir., Tech.Serv.; Dohn Martin, Sys.Libn.; Sherry Porter, Ser.Libn.; Moira McInroy-Hocevar, AV Libn.; Timothy Mason, Cat./Acq.Libn.; Sue Raymond, Ref.Libn.; Regina Lee, Ref.Libn.; Gay Taber, Ref.Libn.

Texas Confederate Museum Library
See: **United Daughters of the Confederacy** (16706)

Texas Eastern - Library
See: **Panhandle Eastern Corporation - Corporate Library** (12725)

Texas Eastman Company
See: **Eastman Kodak Company** (5186)

Texas Forest Products Laboratory
See: **Texas (State) Forest Service** (16254)

★ 16211 ★
Texas Gas Transmission Corporation - Library (Energy)
Box 1160   Phone: (502)926-8686
Owensboro, KY 42302   Frieda Rhodes, Libn.
Staff: Prof 1; Other 1. **Subjects:** Natural gas technology, finance, petroleum, geology, economics. **Holdings:** 1600 books. **Subscriptions:** 225 journals and other serials. **Services:** Library not open to the public. **Remarks:** FAX: (502)926-8686, ext. 4546.

★ 16212 ★
Texas General Land Office - Archives and Records Division - Library (Hist)
Stephen F. Austin Bldg.
1700 N. Congress Ave.   Phone: (512)463-5277
Austin, TX 78701   Michael T. Moore
Founded: 1836. **Staff:** Prof 2; Other 28. **Subjects:** Texas - public lands, colonization. **Special Collections:** Spanish Land Grant Records (73 linear feet); Republic and State of Texas Land Grant Records (2155 linear feet); Public Lands - Sales and Lease Records (4300 linear feet). **Holdings:** 242 books; 6600 linear feet of archival materials. **Services:** Copying; library open to the public. **Computerized Information Services:** Republic and State of Texas Land Grant Records Index (internal database).

Texas Heritage Resource Center
See: **San Antonio Conservation Society - Foundation Library & Archives** (14667)

★ 16213 ★
Texas Instruments, Inc. - Austin Library (Comp Sci, Bus-Fin)
P.O. Box 149149, MS/2207   Phone: (512)250-7421
Austin, TX 78714-9149   Claudia Chidester, Lib.Mgr.
Founded: 1978. **Staff:** Prof 2. **Subjects:** Computer technology, marketing, business management. **Holdings:** 1700 books; 125 marketing reports; industry standards and vendor catalogs on microfilm. **Subscriptions:** 200 journals and other serials; 10 newspapers. **Services:** Interlibrary loan; library not open to the public. **Automated Operations:** Computerized cataloging. **Computerized Information Services:** DIALOG Information Services, DataTimes; CD-ROMs; internal database. Performs searches on fee basis. **Remarks:** FAX: (512)250-6671.

★ 16214 ★
Texas Instruments, Inc. - Central Research Development and Engineering Library (Sci-Engr)
Box 655936, MS 135   Phone: (214)995-2407
Dallas, TX 75265   Olga Paradis, Libn.
Staff: Prof 2. **Subjects:** Physics, chemistry, mathematics, electronics. **Holdings:** 10,000 books; 6000 bound periodical volumes; 40 VF drawers of theses and pamphlets. **Subscriptions:** 300 journals and other serials. **Services:** Interlibrary loan; library not open to the public. **Computerized Information Services:** OCLC, DIALOG Information Services, NEXIS. **Networks/Consortia:** Member of AMIGOS Bibliographic Council, Inc. **Remarks:** FAX: (214)995-5539. **Staff:** Cheryl Helmer.

★ 16215 ★
Texas Instruments, Inc. - Forest Lane Technical Library (Sci-Engr, Comp Sci)
8505 Forest Ln., MS 3132
Box 660246   Phone: (214)480-1117
Dallas, TX 75266   Kathy L. Nordhaus, Info.Spec.
Founded: 1982. **Staff:** Prof 1. **Subjects:** Optics, imaging, pattern recognition, personal computers, military electronics. **Holdings:** 4000 books. **Subscriptions:** 250 journals and other serials. **Services:** Interlibrary loan; library not open to the public. **Automated Operations:** Computerized cataloging, acquisitions, serials, and circulation. **Computerized Information Services:** DIALOG Information Services, OCLC, NEXIS, DTIC; LIBS (internal database). **Networks/Consortia:** Member of AMIGOS Bibliographic Council, Inc. **Publications:** Biblio-Tech, monthly - for internal distribution only. **Remarks:** FAX: (214)480-1198.

★ 16216 ★
Texas Instruments, Inc. - Houston Site Library (Sci-Engr)
Box 1443, MS 695   Phone: (713)274-2981
Houston, TX 77001   Lezlie Shell, Libn.
Staff: Prof 1; Other 1. **Subjects:** Electronics, marketing, electrical engineering. **Holdings:** 2100 books. **Subscriptions:** 250 journals and other serials; 10 newspapers. **Services:** Interlibrary loan; library not open to the public. **Automated Operations:** Computerized cataloging, circulation, and serials. **Computerized Information Services:** OCLC, DIALOG Information Services; internal database. **Networks/Consortia:** Member of AMIGOS Bibliographic Council, Inc. **Publications:** New at the Library, monthly. **Remarks:** FAX: (713)274-2994.

Texas Instruments, Inc. - Information Systems & Services Library
See: **Texas Instruments, Inc. - Spring Creek Technical Library** (16220)

★ 16217 ★
Texas Instruments, Inc. - Lewisville Technical Library (Sci-Engr, Comp Sci)
Box 405, M/S 3411   Phone: (214)462-5425
Lewisville, TX 75067   Carolyn Ernst, DSEG Libs.Mgr.
Founded: 1980. **Staff:** Prof 1; Other 1. **Subjects:** Electronics, electrical and mechanical engineering, computer science, aerospace, defense industry and technology. **Special Collections:** Internal papers and memos (17,000). **Holdings:** 4500 books; 10,500 microforms. **Subscriptions:** 250 journals and other serials. **Services:** Interlibrary loan; library not open to the public. **Automated Operations:** Computerized cataloging, serials, and circulation. **Computerized Information Services:** DIALOG Information Services, OCLC, DTIC; internal databases.

★ 16218 ★
Texas Instruments, Inc. - North Building Library (Sci-Engr)
Box 655474, MS 211   Phone: (214)995-2803
Dallas, TX 75265   Margaret Carroll, Info.Spec.
Founded: 1950. **Staff:** Prof 1; Other 1. **Subjects:** Electronics, engineering, physics, mathematics, artificial intelligence, computer languages. **Special Collections:** Institute of Electrical and Electronics Engineers (IEEE) periodicals (complete set); Stanford Computer Forum reports. **Holdings:** 6500 books; 3500 bound periodical volumes. **Subscriptions:** 150 journals and other serials; 5 newspapers. **Services:** Interlibrary loan; library not open to the public. **Automated Operations:** Computerized cataloging, acquisitions, serials, and circulation. **Computerized Information Services:** DIALOG Information Services. **Networks/Consortia:** Member of AMIGOS Bibliographic Council, Inc., Association for Higher Education of North Texas (AHE). **Remarks:** FAX: (214)995-2810.

★ 16219 ★
Texas Instruments, Inc. - Semiconductor Group Library (Sci-Engr, Comp Sci)
Box 655303, MS 8240   Phone: (214)997-2135
Dallas, TX 75265   Helen Manning, Mgr.
Founded: 1957. **Staff:** Prof 1; Other 1. **Subjects:** Electronics, semiconductor technology, business management, computer science. **Holdings:** 6000 books; 3000 bound periodical volumes. **Subscriptions:** 250 journals and other serials; 9 newspapers. **Services:** Interlibrary loan; library not open to the public. **Computerized Information Services:** OCLC, DIALOG Information Services; CD-ROMs. **Networks/Consortia:** Member of AMIGOS Bibliographic Council, Inc.

★ 16220 ★
Texas Instruments, Inc. - Spring Creek Technical Library (Comp Sci, Info Sci)
Box 869305, MS 8429   Phone: (214)575-2852
Plano, TX 75086   Cecilia Tung, Libn.
Founded: 1980. **Staff:** Prof 1; Other 1. **Subjects:** Computer science and graphics, data processing, information science, engineering. **Holdings:** 2500 books; 1000 IBM hardware and software manuals; industry reports. **Subscriptions:** 250 journals and other serials. **Services:** Interlibrary loan; library not open to the public. **Automated Operations:** Computerized cataloging. **Computerized Information Services:** OCLC, DIALOG Information Services. **Networks/Consortia:** Member of AMIGOS Bibliographic Council, Inc. **Special Indexes:** Keyword Index of IBM hardware and software manuals.

Texas Jazz Archive
See: **Houston Public Library - Houston Metropolitan Research Center**
(7462)

★ 16221 ★
Texas Medical Association - Library (Med)
401 W. 15th St.   Phone: (512)370-1550
Austin, TX 78701   Susan Brock, Lib.Dir.
Founded: 1922. **Staff:** Prof 5; Other 9. **Subjects:** Clinical medicine. **Special Collections:** Patient information collection, clinical medicine for lay audience (200 books; 50 videotapes; 1000 reprints and brochures; 15 journals and newsletters); core cancer library (66 books; 18 journals). **Holdings:** 60,000 volumes; 5000 reprints; 300 motion pictures; 1300 lecture tapes; 300 slide/tape programs; 400 video cassettes. **Subscriptions:** 868 journals and other serials. **Services:** Interlibrary loan; copying; SDI; current awareness; library open to nonmembers on fee basis. **Computerized Information Services:** MEDLARS, BRS Information Technologies; MIMS (internal database); CD-ROM. Performs searches on fee basis. Contact Person: Miriam Blum, Online Serv.Libn. **Networks/Consortia:** Member of National Network of Libraries of Medicine - South Central Region. **Special Catalogs:** AV Catalog and supplements (book); list of journals; new acquisitions list; core cancer library list. **Remarks:** FAX: (512)370-1630. **Staff:** Susan Michaelson; Nancy Reynolds; Barbara Mercer.

Texas Medical Center Library
See: **Houston Academy of Medicine - Texas Medical Center Library**
(7445)

★ 16222 ★
Texas Memorial Museum - Library
2400 Trinity St.
Austin, TX 78705
Founded: 1938. **Subjects:** Anthropology, archeology, museology, natural history, Texas history, geology, paleontology, arms and armor, art and antiquities. **Special Collections:** Material on pictographs and petroglyphs. **Remarks:** Currently inactive.

★ 16223 ★
Texas Municipal League - Library (Soc Sci)
211 E. 7th St., Suite 1020   Phone: (512)478-6601
Austin, TX 78701   Frank Sturzl, Exec.Dir.
Founded: 1913. **Staff:** Prof 1. **Subjects:** Municipal government. **Holdings:** 300 books; 2000 articles. **Subscriptions:** 75 journals and other serials. **Services:** Interlibrary loan; library not open to the public.

★ 16224 ★
Texas Natural Resources Information System (TNRIS) - Library (Biol Sci, Sci-Engr)
Box 13231, Capitol Sta.   Phone: (512)463-8337
Austin, TX 78711-3231   E. Charles Palmer, Mgr.
Founded: 1970. **Staff:** Prof 7; Other 1. **Subjects:** Maps, remote sensing, census, water data, weather data. **Special Collections:** United States Geological Survey (USGS) topographic maps; Landsat coverage of Texas (printed and tape format); aerial photography coverage of Texas. **Holdings:** 510,000 air photographs (black and white); 1600 rolls of aerial film; 100,000 USGS maps. **Services:** Copying; library open to the public. **Automated Operations:** Computerized cataloging. **Computerized Information Services:** NAWDEX (National Water Data Exchange), EROS Data Center; Monitor (internal database). Performs searches on fee basis. Contact Person: LaVerne Willis. **Publications:** TNRIS Newsletter, quarterly. **Special Catalogs:** File Description Report. **Remarks:** Clearinghouse for digital Geographic Informatiion Systems (GIS) files for Texas. Maintained by Texas (State) Water Development Board. Alternate telephone number(s): 463-8402. FAX: (512)475-2053.

★ 16225 ★
Texas Oil & Gas Corporation - Corporate Library
1700 Pacific Ave., LB10
Dallas, TX 75201
Defunct.

★ 16226 ★
Texas Research Institute, Inc. - Nondestructive Testing Information Analysis Center (Sci-Engr)
415A Crystal Creek Dr.   Phone: (512)263-2106
Austin, TX 78746   Dr. George A. Matzkanin, Contact
Founded: 1974. **Staff:** Prof 2; Other 2. **Subjects:** Nondestructive testing, inspection, and evaluation; quality control; inspection using liquid penetrants; radiography; electricity and magnetism; ultrasonics; heat; optical-visual devices; audible-sonic devices. **Special Collections:** Series of abstracts devoted to nondestructive evaluation. **Holdings:** 40,000 reports and journals. **Subscriptions:** 40 journals and other serials. **Services:** Rapid response literature searching; consultation; SDI; center open to U.S. citizens. **Computerized Information Services:** DIALOG Information Services, DTIC; NTIAC (internal database). Performs searches on fee basis. Contact Person: Nan Hampton, Info.Anl., (512)263-2106. **Publications:** Quarterly newsletter; list of additional publications - available on request. **Remarks:** Center is an official DOD Information Analysis Center. Operated by TRI for the U.S. Department of Defense under technical cognizance of the Under Secretary of Defense for research and Engineering. Sponsors a biennial symposium on nondestructive evaluation. FAX: (512)263-3530.

★ 16227 ★
Texas Research League - Library (Soc Sci)
1117 Red River
P.O. Box 12456   Phone: (512)472-3127
Austin, TX 78711-2456   Sarah L. Burka, Res.Libn.
Founded: 1952. **Staff:** Prof 1. **Subjects:** Texas state and local government, government finance, demographics, transportation policy, education, health care delivery. **Special Collections:** League archives (375 volumes). **Holdings:** 2500 books. **Subscriptions:** 178 journals and other serials. **Services:** Interlibrary loan; copying; library open to the public with restrictions. **Automated Operations:** Computerized public access catalog. **Computerized Information Services:** Texas Research League Archives (internal database). **Publications:** Government at Research Association, Inc.: GRA Reporter, quarterly (cumulative bibliography). **Remarks:** FAX: (512)472-4816.

★ 16228 ★
Texas School for the Deaf - Library (Educ)
Box 3538   Phone: (512)440-5364
Austin, TX 78764   Susan A. Anderson, Libn.
Founded: 1856. **Staff:** 2. **Subjects:** Deafness. **Special Collections:** American Annals of the Deaf, 1847 to present; Volta Review, 1899 to present. **Holdings:** 12,000 books; manuscripts; archives; microfilm. **Subscriptions:** 77 journals and other serials. **Services:** Library open to the public. **Remarks:** TDD: (512)440-5365. **Staff:** Mildred Meeks.

★ 16229 ★
Texas Scottish Rite Hospital for Children - Brandon Carrell, M.D., Medical Library (Med)
2222 Welborn St.   Phone: (214)521-3168
Dallas, TX 75219-0567   Mary Peters, Med.Libn.
Founded: 1979. **Staff:** Prof 1. **Subjects:** Pediatric orthopedics and neurology. **Special Collections:** History of orthopedics. **Holdings:** 700 books; 525 bound periodical volumes. **Subscriptions:** 100 journals and other serials. **Services:** Interlibrary loan; library open to the public for reference use only. **Networks/Consortia:** Member of Health Libraries Information Network (HealthLINE).

★ 16230 ★
Texas Southern University - Law Library (Law)
3100 Cleburne St.   Phone: (713)527-7125
Houston, TX 77004   Walter T. Champion, Dir.
Founded: 1947. **Staff:** Prof 3; Other 6. **Subjects:** Law - American, English, African. **Holdings:** 80,000 books; 10,000 bound periodical volumes. **Subscriptions:** 360 journals and other serials. **Services:** Interlibrary loan; copying; library open to the public. **Computerized Information Services:** LEXIS, WESTLAW. **Staff:** Marguerite L. Butler, Assoc.Dir.; Faye Webster, Loose-leaf & Govt.Docs.Supv.

★ 16231 ★
Texas Southern University - Library - Heartman Collection (Hist, Area-Ethnic)
3100 Cleburne St.   Phone: (713)527-7149
Houston, TX 77004   Dorothy H. Chapman, Libn.
Founded: 1948. **Staff:** Prof 2; Other 2. **Subjects:** Black culture and history, slavery. **Special Collections:** Barbara Jordan Archives (24 square feet); Texas Southern University Archives (12 square feet); Jazz Archives; Traditional African Art Gallery. **Holdings:** 35,000 books; 487 bound periodical volumes; 10,000 pamphlets; 66 VF drawers of clippings; 1 VF drawer of pictures; 1 VF drawer of sheet music. **Subscriptions:** 163 journals and other serials; 26 newspapers. **Services:** Interlibrary loan; copying; collection open to the public. **Automated Operations:** Computerized cataloging and acquisitions. **Remarks:** FAX: (713)639-1875. **Staff:** Sandra M. Parham, Libn.; Ruth Bigosoe; Helen Hamilton.

★ 16232 ★
Texas Southern University - Robert James Terry Library (Med)
3201 Wheeler Ave.   Phone: (713)527-7163
Houston, TX 77004   Norma Bean, Interim Dir.
Founded: 1949. **Staff:** 1. **Subjects:** Pharmacology. **Holdings:** 4500 books; 2500 bound periodical volumes. **Subscriptions:** 177 journals and other serials. **Services:** Interlibrary loan; copying; SDI; library open to the public. **Computerized Information Services:** DIALOG Information Services. Performs searches on fee basis. **Networks/Consortia:** Member of Houston Area Research Library Consortium (HARLIC). **Remarks:** FAX: (713)639-1875.

Texas Southern University Archives
See: Texas Southern University - Library - Heartman Collection (16231)

★ 16233 ★
Texas State Air Control Board - Library (Env-Cons)
12124 Park 35 Circle   Phone: (512)451-5711
Austin, TX 78753   Kerry Williams, Libn.
Staff: 1. **Subjects:** Air pollution, engineering, chemistry, physics, meteorology, law. **Special Collections:** Microfiche of technical subjects pertaining to air pollution (50,000). **Holdings:** 9000 books; 18 bound periodical volumes; 700 reprints. **Subscriptions:** 64 journals and other serials. **Services:** Copying; library open to the public for reference use only. **Publications:** Technical reports on air pollution in Texas. **Remarks:** FAX: (512)371-0245.

★ 16234 ★
Texas (State) Bureau of Economic Geology - Core Research Center (Sci-Engr)
Box X, University Sta.   Phone: (512)471-1534
Austin, TX 78713   Allan Standen, Cur.
Founded: 1937. **Staff:** Prof 15; Other 3. **Subjects:** Well cores, cuttings, thin sections; E-logs; oil scout tickets; other geologic materials. **Special Collections:** John E. (Brick) Elliot Collection (5 VF drawers and 2 map cases of geological information, well data, maps, aerial photographs); lignite; brines; DOE/SRPO salt core; Shell "Eureka" Offshore Gulf Core; Texas Superconducting Supercollider core; Oil Field core; Minerals Industry core. **Holdings:** 7000 well cores; 58,000 well cuttings; 16,000 thin sections; 800,000 drillers logs; 400,000 scout tickets. **Services:** Library open to the public. **Automated Operations:** Computerized cataloging and acquisitions. **Computerized Information Services:** Internal database. Contact Person: Jack Bailey Jr. **Special Indexes:** Computer printout listing of cuttings, cores, and thin sections. **Remarks:** FAX: (512)471-0140. Library located at 10100 Burnet Rd., Bldg. 130, Austin, TX.

★ 16235 ★
Texas State Court of Appeals - 1st Judicial District - Law Library (Law)
1307 San Jacinto, 10th Fl.
Houston, TX 77002   Phone: (713)655-2700
Founded: 1892. **Subjects:** Law. **Holdings:** 10,000 volumes. **Services:** Library not open to the public.

★ 16236 ★
Texas State Court of Appeals - 3rd Judicial District - Law Library (Law)
Box 12547, Capitol Sta.
Austin, TX 78711   Phone: (512)463-1733
Subjects: Law. **Holdings:** Figures not available. **Services:** Library not open to the public.

★ 16237 ★
Texas State Court of Appeals - 5th Judicial District - Law Library (Law)
Dallas County Courthouse
600 Commerce St.   Phone: (214)653-7382
Dallas, TX 75202   Martha Blakely Boggess, Libn.
Staff: 1. **Subjects:** Law. **Holdings:** 21,777 volumes. **Services:** Library not open to the public. **Remarks:** Alternate telephone number(s): 653-6294. FAX: (214)745-1083.

★ 16238 ★
Texas State Court of Appeals - 6th Judicial District - Law Library (Law)
Bi-State Justice Bldg.
100 N. State Line Ave.   Phone: (903)798-3046
Texarkana, TX 75501   Tibby Thomas, Ck.
Founded: 1907. **Staff:** 15. **Subjects:** Law. **Holdings:** 15,000 volumes. **Subscriptions:** 10 journals and other serials. **Services:** Library open to the public for reference use only. **Remarks:** FAX: (903)798-3034.

Texas State Court of Civil Appeals - 10th Judicial District - Library
See: McLennan County Law Library (9947)

★ 16239 ★
Texas State Court of Appeals - 11th Judicial District - Law Library (Law)
Eastland, TX 76448   Phone: (817)629-2638
Founded: 1925. **Subjects:** Law. **Holdings:** 7000 volumes. **Services:** Library open to the public for reference use only.

★ 16240 ★
Texas (State) Department of Agriculture - Library (Agri)
Stephen F. Austin Bldg., Rm. 911
Box 12847   Phone: (512)463-7670
Austin, TX 78711   Virginia Hall, Libn.
Founded: 1975. **Staff:** Prof 1. **Subjects:** Agriculture, livestock, gardening, international trade, cooking. **Special Collections:** U.S. Department of Agriculture Yearbook of Agriculture, 1897 to present. **Holdings:** 5000 books; 1000 bound periodical volumes; 200 pamphlets. **Subscriptions:** 500 journals and other serials; 50 newspapers. **Services:** Copying; library open to the public. **Remarks:** FAX: (512)463-7643.

Texas (State) Department of Aviation
See: Texas (State) Department of Transportation - Division of Aviation (16248)

★ 16241 ★
Texas (State) Department of Commerce - Library (Bus-Fin)
Box 12728, Capitol Sta.   Phone: (512)320-9447
Austin, TX 78711   Mary Ann Reynolds, Libn.
Founded: 1976. **Staff:** 1. **Subjects:** Industrial and economic development, local demographics. **Special Collections:** Texas State Data Center; U.S. Census Collection. **Holdings:** 5000 books, periodicals, and articles. **Subscriptions:** 56 journals and other serials. **Services:** Copying (limited); library open to the public for reference use only. **Automated Operations:** Computerized cataloging. **Computerized Information Services:** DataTimes. **Publications:** Monthly Acquisitions. **Remarks:** FAX: (512)320-9475.

★ 16242 ★
Texas (State) Department of Health - Library (Med)
1100 W. 49th St.   Phone: (512)458-7559
Austin, TX 78756   John Burlinson, Libn.
Founded: 1958. **Staff:** Prof 4; Other 4. **Subjects:** Public health, infectious diseases, laboratory methods, environmental health, dental health, pediatrics, nursing, hospitals and nursing homes, heart, cancer, health promotion, health funding. **Holdings:** 10,000 volumes; 2000 unbound items; 4787 AV materials. **Subscriptions:** 505 journals and other serials. **Services:** Interlibrary loan; copying; SDI; library open to the public for reference use only. **Automated Operations:** Computerized cataloging, acquisitions, circulation, and ILL. **Computerized Information Services:** DIALOG Information Services, MEDLARS, BRS Information Technologies, Dialcom Inc., Chemical Information Systems, Inc. (CIS), LEGI-SLATE; CD-ROMs (MEDLINE, Computer Select, PC-SIG Library); Dialcom, Inc. (electronic mail service). **Publications:** HIV Finding Watch (newsletter) - by subscription in Texas only; list of new publications, quarterly. **Special Catalogs:** Health Media Catalog. **Remarks:** FAX: (512)458-7683. Electronic mail address(es): TX.SHO (Dialcom, Inc.). **Staff:** Erica McCormick, Libn.; Jane Hazelton, Film Libn.; Cindy Milam, Funding Info.Spec.

Texas (State) Department of Highways and Public Transportation
See: **Texas (State) Department of Transportation (16249)**

★ 16243 ★
Texas (State) Department of Human Services - Library & Reference Services (Soc Sci)
Box 149030
MC W-211   Phone: (512)450-3530
Austin, TX 78714-9030   Brenda Ziser, Lib.Adm./Cons.
Staff: Prof 3. **Subjects:** Social work, child welfare, management, geriatrics, health services, human services, nutrition. **Special Collections:** Nutrition Education and Training Program Collection. **Holdings:** 8000 books; 1500 AV programs. **Subscriptions:** 150 journals and other serials. **Services:** Interlibrary loan; library open to the public for reference use only. **Computerized Information Services:** DIALOG Information Services. **Remarks:** FAX: (512)450-3581. **Staff:** Nancy Phillips, Ref.Libn.; Linda Newland, Nutrition Libn.

★ 16244 ★
Texas (State) Department of Mental Health & Mental Retardation - Big Spring State Hospital - Professional Library (Med)
Box 231   Phone: (915)264-4215
Big Spring, TX 79721-0231   Anna Lou Bradberry, Libn.
Founded: 1975. **Staff:** Prof 1. **Subjects:** Medicine. **Holdings:** 5000 books. **Subscriptions:** 59 journals and other serials. **Services:** Interlibrary loan; copying; library not open to the public.

★ 16245 ★
Texas (State) Department of Mental Health & Mental Retardation - Brenham State School - Staff Library (Med)
P.O. Box 161   Phone: (409)836-4511
Brenham, TX 77833   Linda Kocian
Subjects: Special education, mental retardation. **Holdings:** 250 books. **Subscriptions:** 5 journals and other serials. **Services:** Library not open to the public.

★ 16246 ★
Texas (State) Department of Mental Health & Mental Retardation - Central Office Library (Med)
Box 12668   Phone: (512)465-4621
Austin, TX 78711   Nancy Dobson
Staff: Prof 1. **Subjects:** Mental health, mental retardation, alcoholism, drug abuse, rehabilitation. **Holdings:** 6000 books; 3000 bound periodical volumes. **Subscriptions:** 50 journals and other serials. **Services:** Interlibrary loan; copying; library open to the public for reference use only. **Computerized Information Services:** DIALOG Information Services. **Staff:** Russiene Waukechon.

★ 16247 ★
Texas (State) Department of Mental Health & Mental Retardation - Rusk State Hospital - Staff Library (Med)
Box 318   Phone: (903)683-3421
Rusk, TX 75785   Judy Vermillion, Staff Libn.
Remarks: No further information was supplied by respondent.

Texas State Department of Mental Health & Mental Retardation - San Antonio State Hospital
See: **San Antonio State Hospital (14676)**

★ 16248 ★
Texas (State) Department of Transportation - Division of Aviation - Library & Information Center (Trans, Aud-Vis)
Box 12607, Capitol Sta.   Phone: (512)476-9262
Austin, TX 78711   Lois Bittner, Libn.
Founded: 1945. **Staff:** Prof 1. **Subjects:** Aviation, aircraft, airports, planning, aviation education, flight safety. **Holdings:** 200 films and videotapes; reports; government documents; 40 feet of Federal Aviation Administration, Civil Aeronautics Board, and National Transportation Safety Board regulations and publications; 2 bound volumes of clippings. **Subscriptions:** 50 journals and other serials. **Services:** Copying (limited); library open to the public for reference use only. **Networks/Consortia:** Member of Project TexNet Interlibrary Loan Network (TexNet). **Publications:** List of agency publications. **Special Catalogs:** Aviation Film Library Catalog; Aviation Video Library Catalog (book). **Remarks:** FAX: (512)479-0294. **Formed by the merger of:** Texas (State) Department of Aviation and Texas (State) Department of Highways & Public Transportation.

★ 16249 ★
Texas (State) Department of Transportation - Research & Development Section - Library (Trans)
D10 Research
Box 5051   Phone: (512)465-7644
Austin, TX 78763-5051   Dana Herring, Res.Libn.
Subjects: Highway research, transportation planning. **Holdings:** 18,000 volumes. **Subscriptions:** 20 journals and other serials. **Computerized Information Services:** DIALOG Information Services. **Publications:** Catalog of Research Studies and Reports, annual; Technical Quarterly (newsletter). **Remarks:** Provides reference and other services to highway department and other related transportation and government agencies. Distributes research reports sponsored by state Department of Transportation. **Formerly:** Texas (State) Department of Higways and Public Transportation.

★ 16250 ★
Texas (State) Education Agency - Resource Center Library (Educ)
1701 N. Congress Ave.   Phone: (512)463-9050
Austin, TX 78701-1494   Linda Kemp, Libn.
Founded: 1968. **Staff:** Prof 2. **Subjects:** Public school education. **Special Collections:** Complete ERIC microfiche collection; Texas state-adopted textbook collection. **Holdings:** 10,000 volumes. **Subscriptions:** 355 journals and other serials. **Services:** Interlibrary loan; SDI; library open to Texas educators and state government personnel only. **Computerized Information Services:** BRS Information Technologies, DIALOG Information Services; Electric Pages (electronic mail service). **Staff:** Jan Anderson, Libn.

★ 16251 ★
Texas State Employment Commission - Resource Center (Bus-Fin)
15th & Congress, Rm. 316T   Phone: (512)463-2426
Austin, TX 78778   Evelyn C. Houston, Adm.Techn.
Staff: 1. **Subjects:** Personnel management, management, public relations, occupational health and safety, employee development, and allied subjects. **Holdings:** Books; TEC reports; AV materials. **Services:** Center not open to the public. **Remarks:** FAX: (512)463-2598.

★ 16252 ★
Texas (State) Forest Service - Forest Pest Control Section - Library (Biol Sci)
Box 310   Phone: (409)639-8170
Lufkin, TX 75902-0310   Dr. Ronald F. Billings, Prin. Entomologist
Founded: 1963. **Staff:** Prof 3. **Subjects:** Forest insects and diseases in the South. **Special Collections:** Computerized records of southern pine beetle infestations in Texas, 1973 to present. **Holdings:** 500 books; 200 bound periodical volumes; 3000 color transparencies. **Subscriptions:** 12 journals and other serials. **Services:** Library open to the public with restrictions. **Remarks:** FAX: (409)639-8185. Jointly maintained with Texas A & M University.

★ 16253 ★
Texas (State) Forest Service - Library
Texas A & M University
College Station, TX 77843
Founded: 1919. **Subjects:** Forestry. **Holdings:** 625 books; 325 bound periodical volumes; 6000 pamphlets and reports on microfiche. **Remarks:** Currently inactive.

★ 16254 ★
Texas (State) Forest Service - Texas Forest Products Laboratory -
  Library (Biol Sci)
Box 310   Phone: (409)639-8180
Lufkin, TX 75901   Susan Shockley, Libn.
Founded: 1930. **Staff:** Prof 1; Other 1. **Subjects:** Wood science, forest products technology and utilization. **Holdings:** 800 books; 400 bound periodical volumes; 124,000 notebook articles; 36,400 articles in boxes. **Subscriptions:** 25 journals and other serials. **Services:** Interlibrary loan; copying; library open to the public for reference use only. **Publications:** Directory of Forest Products Industries of Texas, biennial - for sale. **Remarks:** FAX: (409)639-8185.

★ 16255 ★
Texas State Law Library (Law)
Supreme Court Bldg.
Box 12367   Phone: (512)463-1722
Austin, TX 78711-2367   Kay Schlueter, Dir.
Founded: 1972. **Staff:** Prof 5; Other 4. **Subjects:** Law. **Holdings:** 99,760 books; 3900 bound periodical volumes. **Subscriptions:** 215 journals and other serials. **Services:** Copying; library open to the public. **Automated Operations:** Computerized public access catalog. **Computerized Information Services:** Online systems. **Staff:** Tony Estrada, Law Libn.; Sally Harlow, Law Libn.; Patricia Strebeck, Law Libn.; Judith Herring, Law Libn.; Mike Bacon, Law Libn.

★ 16256 ★
Texas State Legislative Reference Library (Soc Sci, Law)
Box 12488, Capitol Sta.   Phone: (512)463-1252
Austin, TX 78711   Sally Reynolds, Dir.
Founded: 1969. **Staff:** Prof 6; Other 5. **Subjects:** Law, Texas government and politics, legislative reference, political science, current events. **Special Collections:** Newspaper clipping file; legislative bill files, 1973 to present. **Holdings:** 43,500 volumes; 726 shelves of Texas documents; 400,000 newspaper clippings; 3126 reels of microfilm; Texas and out-of-state agency reports. **Subscriptions:** 800 journals and other serials; 30 newspapers. **Services:** Copying; library open to the public for reference use only. **Automated Operations:** Computerized public access catalog, cataloging, acquisitions, and serials. **Computerized Information Services:** LEGISNET, WESTLAW, LEXIS, NEXIS; Legislative Information System of Texas (internal database). Performs searches free of charge. **Publications:** Chief Elected & Administrative Officials, biennial; bibliographies on state documents and new trade book acquisitions, monthly; Legislative Library Resources; Texas State Agency Publications, irregular; How to Do Legislative History. **Remarks:** FAX: (512)475-4626. **Staff:** Brenda Olds, TX Docs.Libn.; Tim Whisenant, Libn.; Nancy Moreno, Libn.; Marsha Ratliff, Paralegal.

★ 16257 ★
Texas State Library (Info Sci)
1201 Brazos
Box 12927   Phone: (512)463-5460
Austin, TX 78711   William D. Gooch, State Libn.
Founded: 1839. **Staff:** Prof 80; Other 128. **Subjects:** Texas history and government, genealogy, librarianship. **Special Collections:** Texana Collection. **Holdings:** 1.2 million books and bound periodical volumes; 196,500 microforms of newspapers and tax records. **Subscriptions:** 1211 journals and other serials; 22 newspapers. **Services:** Interlibrary loan; copying; library open to the public with restrictions. **Automated Operations:** Computerized cataloging. **Computerized Information Services:** OCLC, DIALOG Information Services, BRS Information Technologies; CD-ROM. **Networks/Consortia:** Member of AMIGOS Bibliographic Council, Inc. **Publications:** Texas Libraries, quarterly; Checklist of Texas State Government Publications, monthly - all free upon request. **Special Indexes:** Index to state government publications, annual (book). **Remarks:** FAX: (512)463-5436. **Staff:** Raymond W. Hitt, Asst. State Libn.; Catherine Lee, Mgr.,Adm.; Edward Seidenberg, Mgr.,Lib.Dev.; William Dyess, Mgr.,Rec.Mgt.; Marilyn Von Kohl, Mgr.,Local Rec.; Bonnie Grobar, Mgr.,Info.Serv.; Christopher LaPlante, Mgr.,Archv.; Dale W. Propp, Mgr.,Blind & Phys. Handicapped; Charles Brown, Mgr.,Automated Info.Sys.

★ 16258 ★
Texas State Library - Division for the Blind and Physically Handicapped
  (Aud-Vis)
Box 12927   Phone: (512)463-5458
Austin, TX 78711   Dale W. Propp, Mgr.
Founded: 1909. **Staff:** Prof 12; Other 41. **Subjects:** Visual impairment, physical handicaps, Texana, Spanish language, learning disabilities. **Holdings:** 787,390 books; 135 bound periodical volumes; cassettes. **Subscriptions:** 63 journals and other serials. **Services:** Interlibrary loan; copying; library open to the public with restrictions. **Automated Operations:** Computerized acquisitions, serials, and circulation. **Computerized Information Services:** BRS Information Technologies. Contact Person: Linda Lindell. **Networks/Consortia:** Member of AMIGOS Bibliographic Council, Inc., National Library Service for the Blind & Physically Handicapped (NLS). **Publications:** In Touch (newsletter), quarterly - to registered patrons. **Special Catalogs:** Large Print Catalog (large type). **Staff:** Kay Nichols, Proj.Dev.; Mike Conway, Circ.; Carmen Keltner, Pub.Awareness; Wanda Stedman, Volunteers; Robert Helfer, Automation; Dan David, Audio Prod.; Nancy Huggins, Rd.Serv.

★ 16259 ★
Texas State Library - Information Services (Info Sci, Hist)
Box 12927   Phone: (512)463-5455
Austin, TX 78711   Bonnie Grobar, Mgr., Info.Serv.
Founded: 1962. **Staff:** Prof 11; Other 16. **Subjects:** U.S. and Texas documents, genealogy, Texas history, public affairs. **Special Collections:** Texas State Publications Clearinghouse (the designated state office for the bibliographic control and distribution of Texas state documents); regional depository for U.S. government publications. **Holdings:** 105,000 books; 1000 bound periodical volumes; 100,000 Texas state government documents; 1.3 million U.S. Government documents. **Subscriptions:** 485 journals and other serials. **Services:** Interlibrary loan; copying; division open to the public. **Automated Operations:** Computerized cataloging and government documents. **Computerized Information Services:** DIALOG Information Services, DataTimes. **Publications:** Texas State Publications, monthly; Information Services, quarterly; Genealogy Duplicates Exchange List. **Special Indexes:** Texas State Publications agency, title, and subject indexes, all annual. **Remarks:** FAX: (512)463-5436. **Staff:** Diana Houston, Hd., Ref./Docs.; Chris Fowler, Hd., State Pubns. Clearinghouse; Judy Duer, Hd., Geneal.; Rama Mathis, Acq.Supv.; Carol Winship, Hd.Cat.

★ 16260 ★
Texas State Library - Library Science Collection (Info Sci)
Box 12927   Phone: (512)463-5494
Austin, TX 78711   Anne Ramos, Libn.
Founded: 1956. **Staff:** Prof 1; Other 1. **Subjects:** Library science, librarianship, information science. **Holdings:** 7000 books; 300 bound periodical volumes; 10,000 uncataloged ephemeral documents; 300 audio and video cassettes. **Subscriptions:** 120 journals and other serials. **Services:** Interlibrary loan; collection open to the public. **Automated Operations:** Computerized cataloging. **Computerized Information Services:** DIALOG Information Services. CD-ROM (WILSONDISC). Performs searches on fee basis. **Publications:** Library Developments, bimonthly - free upon request. **Remarks:** FAX: (512)463-5436. Toll-free telephone number(s): (800)252-9386 (Texas only).

★ 16261 ★
Texas State Library - Local Records (Hist)
Box 12927   Phone: (512)463-5478
Austin, TX 78711   Marilyn von Kohl, Mgr.
Staff: Prof 7; Other 8.5. **Subjects:** Texas - vital statistics, judicial proceedings, education, economic development, politics, family history/biography. **Special Collections:** Tidelands Case Papers of Justice Price Daniel (130 cubic feet); congressional and other papers of Representative Martin Dies; early manuscripts and photographs of Sam Houston, David G. Burnet, and others (400 cubic feet); early Texas furniture; American Indian artifacts. **Holdings:** 5200 books; 13,000 cubic feet of local government records; vital statistics records of county and district clerks on microfilm. **Subscriptions:** 13 journals and other serials; 10 newspapers. **Services:** Interlibrary loan; copying; depositories and division open to the public. **Publications:** Texas County Records Manual; Texas Municipal Records Manual; The Local Record (newsletter), quarterly; technical leaflets on local government records management; County Records. **Remarks:** FAX: (512)463-5436.

★16262★

Texas State Library - Local Records Division - Sam Houston Regional Library and Research Center (Hist)
Box 310 Phone: (409)336-8821
Liberty, TX 77575 Robert L. Schaadt, Dir./Archv.
Founded: 1977. **Staff:** Prof 3; Other 5. **Subjects:** Southeast Texas history. **Special Collections:** Journal of Jean Laffite; Herbert Bolton's manuscript for Athanase de Mezieres & the Louisiana-Texas Frontier, 1768-1780; French Colony Champ D'Asile, 1819; Tidelands Papers; early Texas newspapers, 1846-1860; Congressman Martin Dies Papers, 1931-1960 (54 cubic feet); Jean Houston Baldwin Collection of Sam Houston (591 items); private executive record of President of the Republic of Texas Sam Houston, 1841-1844 (1 volume); early Texas maps; Trinity River papers (8 feet); H.O. Compton Surveyors Books; Captain William M. Logan Papers; O'Brien Papers; Hardin Papers (52 feet); Julia Duncan Welder Collection (150 feet); family photograph collections; original and microfilm material from the 10 counties of the old Atascosito District of Southeast Texas, 1826-1960; Encino Press Collection; Carl Hertzog books; many individual family papers and collections. **Holdings:** 9716 books; 780 reels of microfilm; 17,137 photographs; 16,000 cubic feet of manuscripts, government records, and archives; county records. **Subscriptions:** 17 journals and other serials; 9 newspapers. **Services:** Interlibrary loan; copying; center open to the public. **Publications:** Sam Houston Regional Library and Research Center News, 2/year. **Special Indexes:** Llerena B. Friend card index on Sam Houston; inventories of collections in books. **Staff:** Sally Rogers, Asst.Dir./Cur.; Darlene Mott, Libn.

★16263★

Texas State Library - State Archives (Hist)
1201 Brazos St.
Box 12927
Austin, TX 78711 Phone: (512)463-5480
Christopher LaPlante, Mgr.,Archv.
Founded: 1876. **Staff:** Prof 9; Other 7. **Subjects:** Texas history. **Special Collections:** Archives of the Republic and State of Texas (25,000 linear feet). **Holdings:** 38,000 books; 2700 reels of microfilm; 2350 historical manuscript collections; 6500 maps; 400,000 photographic images. **Subscriptions:** 45 journals and other serials. **Services:** Copying; division open to the public. **Publications:** Historical publications, irregular.

★16264★

Texas (State) Parks & Wildlife Department - Library (Biol Sci, Env-Cons, Rec)
4200 Smith School Rd. Phone: (512)389-4960
Austin, TX 78744 Debra E. Bunch, Libn.
Founded: 1970. **Staff:** Prof 1; Other 1. **Subjects:** Natural resources, wildlife and fishery management, recreation, parks and historic sites, game laws of Texas. **Special Collections:** Complete sets of Pittman-Robertson Federal Aid in Wildlife Restoration and Dingell-Johnson Federal Aid in Fish Restoration Acts, both for Texas, 1939 to present. **Holdings:** 14,000 books. **Subscriptions:** 120 journals and other serials. **Services:** Interlibrary loan; library open to the public for reference use only. **Special Indexes:** Index to Pittman-Robertson and Dingell-Johnson federal aid research reports.

★16265★

Texas (State) Parks & Wildlife Department - Marine Laboratory Library (Biol Sci)
100 Navigation Circle Phone: (512)729-2328
Rockport, TX 78382 T.L. Heffernan, Lab.Supv.
Staff: 1. **Subjects:** Marine biology, Texas, Gulf of Mexico. **Holdings:** 200 books; 1000 bound periodical volumes; 30 VF boxes of unbound reprints. **Subscriptions:** 20 journals and other serials. **Services:** Library open to the public for reference use only. **Remarks:** FAX: (512)729-2328 (prior voice initiation).

Texas State Publications Clearinghouse
See: Texas State Library - Information Services (16259)

★16266★

(Texas State) Railroad Commission of Texas - Library (Trans, Energy)
P.O. Drawer 12967, Capitol Sta. Phone: (512)463-7160
Austin, TX 78711-2967 Susan B. Rhyne, Libn.
Founded: 1985. **Staff:** Prof 1. **Subjects:** Oil and gas, law, transportation, gas utilities. **Holdings:** 10,000 books. **Subscriptions:** 52 journals and other serials. **Services:** Copying; library open to the public for reference use only. **Computerized Information Services:** WESTLAW.

★16267★

(Texas State) Railroad Commission of Texas - Oil and Gas Division - Records Retention (Bus-Fin, Trans)
William B. Travis Bldg.
1701 N. Congress Phone: (512)463-6882
Austin, TX 78711 Woody Ervin, Dir., Mapping & Rec. Retention
Founded: 1963. **Staff:** 33. **Subjects:** Railroad Commission - Oil and Gas Division business. **Holdings:** 24,000 reels of microfilm; plats; maps; logs; hearing files; oil and gas well potential files. **Services:** Copying; research (limited); open to the public for reference use only. **Computerized Information Services:** Wellbore History (internal database). **Remarks:** The purpose of Records Retention is to file division administrative decisions and all of the forms that the Railroad Commission requires for the drilling, operation, and maintenance of oil and gas wells in the State of Texas.

★16268★

Texas (State) Rehabilitation Commission - Library (Med)
4900 N. Lamar Phone: (512)483-4240
Austin, TX 78751 Terry Foster, Libn.
Founded: 1975. **Staff:** Prof 1; Other 1. **Subjects:** Rehabilitation, disabilities, employment skills and practices, management skills, occupational therapy. **Holdings:** 12,000 books; videotapes; audio cassettes. **Subscriptions:** 75 journals and other serials. **Services:** Copying; library open to the public. **Automated Operations:** Computerized public access catalog. **Publications:** Bookmark, monthly; AV catalog, annual. **Remarks:** FAX: (512)483-4245.

★16269★

Texas State Technical College , Amarillo - Library (Educ)
Box 11117 Phone: (806)335-2316
Amarillo, TX 79111 Cynthia Sadler, Hd.Libn.
Founded: 1970. **Staff:** Prof 1; Other 3. **Holdings:** 15,800 books; 1740 AV programs; 746 microfiche of journals. **Subscriptions:** 296 journals and other serials; 10 newspapers. **Services:** Interlibrary loan; copying; library open to the public. **Computerized Information Services:** DIALOG Information Services. **Formerly:** Texas State Technical Institute, Amarillo Campus.

★16270★

Texas State Technical College, Harlingen - Library (Sci-Engr, Educ)
2424 Boxwood Phone: (512)425-0631
Harlingen, TX 78550-3697 David J. Diehl, Dir., Lib.
Founded: 1970. **Staff:** Prof 2; Other 3. **Subjects:** Data processing, allied health, electronics, drafting, chemical technology, automotive. **Holdings:** 17,000 books; 480 bound periodical volumes. **Subscriptions:** 420 journals and other serials; 20 newspapers. **Services:** Interlibrary loan; copying; library open to the public for reference use only. **Networks/Consortia:** Member of South Texas Library System, PAISANO Consortium of Libraries. **Remarks:** FAX: (512)425-0630. **Formerly:** Texas State Technical Institute. **Staff:** C. Ross Burns, Libn.

★16271★

Texas State Technical College, Harlingen - McAllen Library (Comp Sci)
3201 W. Pecan Phone: (512)631-4922
McAllen, TX 78501-6661 Jose Alfonso Gamez, Dir.
Founded: 1984. **Staff:** Prof 1; Other 2. **Subjects:** Technical and vocational training, office skills, bookkeeping, automotive, electronics and servicing, information processing, air conditioning, refrigeration. **Holdings:** 3000 books. **Subscriptions:** 85 journals and other serials; 6 newspapers. **Services:** Interlibrary loan; library open to the public for reference use only. **Automated Operations:** Computerized cataloging and acquisitions. **Networks/Consortia:** Member of PAISANO Consortium of Libraries. **Remarks:** FAX: (512)631-4922, ext. 21. **Formerly:** Texas State Technical Institute, Harlingen Campus - McAllen Extension Library.

★16272★

Texas State Technical College, Waco - Library (Sci-Engr, Educ)
3801 Campus Dr. Phone: (817)867-4846
Waco, TX 76705 Linda S. Koepf, Dir., Lib.
Founded: 1967. **Staff:** Prof 4; Other 10. **Subjects:** Laser electro-optics, electronics, air pilot training, aviation maintenance, automotive mechanics, biomedical equipment operation. **Special Collections:** Industrial Standards Collection (309 volumes); Deaf and Sign Language Collection (500 volumes). **Holdings:** 64,975 books and bound periodical volumes; 421,215 ERIC microfiche; 6790 VF items; 2442 archival clippings. **Subscriptions:** 852 journals and other serials; 20 newspapers. **Services:** Interlibrary loan; copying; SDI; library open to the public with restrictions on circulation. **Computerized Information Services:** DIALOG Information Services, BRS Information Technologies; CD-ROM. **Publications:** What's New and Worth Reading, monthly. **Remarks:** FAX: (817)799-0501. **Formerly:** Texas State Technical Institute, Waco Campus. **Staff:** Epin Zhao, Per./Media Libn.; Stephen Beeko, Tech.Serv.Libn.; Scott Kantor, Pub.Serv.Libn.

Texas State Technical Institute
See: **Texas State Technical College** (16269)

★ **16273** ★

Texas (State) Water Commission - Library (Env-Cons)
Stephen F. Austin Bldg., Rm. B-20
Capitol Sta., Box 13087   Phone: (512)463-7834
Austin, TX 78711-3087   Sylvia Von Fange, Hd.Libn.
Founded: 1965. **Staff:** Prof 1. **Subjects:** Water resources. **Special Collections:**
Publications of the commission and its predecessor agencies. **Holdings:**
55,000 books; 1700 bound periodical volumes; 8000 U.S. Geological Survey
publications; 294 periodicals in microform; 2700 volumes of U.S.
Environmental Protection Agency materials; 600 volumes of environmental
impact statements; 3100 volumes of U.S. Army Corps of Engineers
materials. **Subscriptions:** 555 journals and other serials. **Services:**
Interlibrary loan; copying; library open to the public with restrictions.
Automated Operations: Computerized cataloging, circulation, and serials.
Publications: Library Bulletin, monthly; A Bibliography of State Agency
Water Publications, 1986 (microfiche). **Remarks:** FAX: (512)463-8317.

Texas (State) Water Development Board - Texas Natural Resources
    Information System (TNRIS)
See: **Texas Natural Resources Information System (TNRIS)** (16224)

★ **16274** ★

Texas Tech University - Health Sciences Center - Library of the Health
    Sciences (Med)
Lubbock, TX 79430-0001   Phone: (806)743-2203
                                        Richard Wood, Dir. of Libs.
Staff: Prof 15; Other 25. **Subjects:** Medicine, nursing, and allied health
sciences. **Holdings:** 190,000 volumes; 100,000 slides, videotapes, and other
AV programs. **Subscriptions:** 3000 journals and other serials. **Services:**
Interlibrary loan; copying; SDI; library open to the public with restrictions.
Computerized Information Services: LIS (internal database); BITNET
(electronic mail service). **Networks/Consortia:** Member of National
Network of Libraries of Medicine - South Central Region, South Central
Academic Medical Libraries Consortium (SCAMEL). **Publications:**
Newsbriefs, bimonthly - to all full-time faculty and selected libraries. **Special
Catalogs:** TALON Union List of Serials (microfiche); Media Catalog
(computer). **Remarks:** FAX: (806)743-2218. Electronic mail address(es):
HLDIR@TTACS (BITNET). Operates teaching and learning center and
computerized review and testing center. Maintains branch libraries in
Amarillo, Odessa, and El Paso, TX. **Staff:** Carolyn Patrick, Sr.Assoc.Dir.,
Tech.Serv.; Mary Asbell, Sr.Assoc.Dir., Extramural Serv.; Mary Moore,
Sr.Assoc.Dir.; Mike Robinson, Info.Serv.Libn.; Nancy
Cammack, Info.Serv.Libn.; Margaret Vugrin, Info.Serv.Libn.; JoAnn Van
Schaik, Asst.Dir. ; Joe Blackburn, Cat.Libn.; Teresa Knott, Assoc.Dir., El
Paso; Dana Neeley, Assoc.Dir., Amarillo; Ursula Scott, Assoc.Dir., Odessa;
Jo Klemm, Asst.Dir.; Mark McKenney, Info.Serv.Libn.; Carmen Rivera-
Roman, Info.Serv.Libn.

★ **16275** ★

Texas Tech University - Health Sciences Center - Regional Academic
    Health Center Library (Med)
4800 Alberta Ave.   Phone: (915)545-6650
El Paso, TX 79905   Teresa L. Knott, Assoc.Dir., El Paso
Staff: Prof 2; Other 3. **Subjects:** Medicine. **Holdings:** 14,178 books; 17,471
bound periodical volumes; 361 audiotapes; 65 slide/tape sets; 3 models; 2675
slides; 120 videotapes. **Subscriptions:** 402 journals and other serials.
Services: Interlibrary loan; copying; SDI; library open to the public for
reference use only. **Automated Operations:** Computerized public access
catalog, cataloging, acquisitions, serials, and circulation. **Computerized
Information Services:** NLM, DIALOG Information Services, BRS
Information Technologies. **Networks/Consortia:** Member of National
Network of Libraries of Medicine - South Central Region. **Publications:**
Newsbriefs, monthly - for internal distribution only. **Remarks:** FAX:
(915)545-6656. Library is a branch of Texas Tech University - Library of
the Health Sciences in Lubbock, TX.

★ **16276** ★

Texas Tech University - Library - U.S. Documents Department (Info
    Sci)
P.O. Box 40002   Phone: (806)742-2268
Lubbock, TX 79409-0002   Mary Ann Higdon, Hd.
Founded: 1935. **Staff:** Prof 11; Other 4. **Subjects:** U.S. Government
publications. **Holdings:** 479,888 volumes; 587,388 microforms; 110,250 CIS
serials. **Services:** Interlibrary loan; copying; library open to the public.
Automated Operations: Computerized cataloging and serials. **Networks/
Consortia:** Member of AMIGOS Bibliographic Council, Inc. **Remarks:**
FAX: (806)742-1920. This is a regional depository for U.S. Government
publications. **Staff:** Thomas Rohrig, Doc./Ref.Coord.; Theresa Trost, Doc./
Ref.Libn.; Rozanne Veeser, Doc./Ref.Libn.; Jack Becker, Doc./Ref.Libn.;
Elma Fennell, Doc./Ref.Libn.; David Proctor, Maps-Docs./Ref.Libn.;
Susan Mushel, Doc./Ref.Libn.; Susan Norrisey, Doc./Ref.Libn.

★ **16277** ★

Texas Tech University - School of Law Library (Law)
Lubbock, TX 79409   Phone: (806)742-3794
                                        J. Wesley Cochran, Lib.Hd.
Founded: 1966. **Staff:** Prof 5; Other 11. **Subjects:** Law. **Holdings:** 220,000
books and bound periodical volumes; 150,000 microfiche. **Subscriptions:**
3140 journals and other serials; 16 newspapers. **Services:** Interlibrary loan;
copying; library open to the public for reference use only. **Automated
Operations:** Computerized cataloging. **Computerized Information Services:**
OCLC, LEXIS, WESTLAW. **Networks/Consortia:** Member of AMIGOS
Bibliographic Council, Inc. **Remarks:** FAX: (806)742-1629. **Staff:** Sharon
Blackburn, Automated Res.Coord./Govt.Docs.; Caroline Mullan,
Ref.Libn.; Janetta Paschal, Automation Coord.; Elizabeth Schneider,
Assoc.Dir.

★ **16278** ★

Texas Tech University - Southwest Collection (Hist)
Box 4090   Phone: (806)742-3749
Lubbock, TX 79409   Dr. David Murrah, Dir.
Founded: 1955. **Staff:** Prof 6; Other 10. **Subjects:** Texas and Southwestern
history and literature; history of Texas Tech University; social, economic,
and religious affairs of West Texas; sociohistorical data pertaining to the area
and its indigenous institutions; man-land confrontation in the arid and semi-
arid Southwest including the struggle of the pioneer settlers, especially
women; cattle industry; land colonization; mining; mechanized agriculture
and the water problem. **Special Collections:** Ranching: Matador Land and
Cattle Company, Spur Ranch, Pitchfork Land and Cattle Company, Bar S
Ranch, Swenson Land and Cattle Company; Business: Itasca Cotton
Manufacturing Company and Weavers Guild, Renfro Drug Company,
Weatherby Motor Company, Cosden Petroleum Corporation, E.S. Graham
Company, Higginbotham Brothers Company, John E. Morrison Company,
records of the Quanah, Acme and Pacific, Fort Worth and Denver, Santa
Fe railroads; Land Companies: Lone Star Land Company, Ripley Townsite
Company, Yellow House Company, Texas Land and Development
Company; Texas and Pacific Coal Company; Organizations: West Texas
Chamber of Commerce, Texas Sheep and Goat Raisers Association, League
of Women Voters; Individuals: R. Wright Armstrong, Clifford B. Jones,
Carl Coke Rister, Ross Malone, William P. Soash, Preston Smith, Marvin
Jones, George Mahon, Gordon McLendon. **Holdings:** 40,000 books; 18
million leaves of business and personal documents and university archives;
1500 maps; 3000 tape recordings; 6000 reels of microfilm; 300,000
photographs; 1200 reels of movie film. **Subscriptions:** 424 journals and other
serials. **Services:** Interlibrary loan; copying; collection open to the public for
reference use only. **Computerized Information Services:** OCLC. **Remarks:**
FAX: (806) 742-0496. **Staff:** Cindy Martin, Asst.Dir.; Janet Neugebauer,
Asst.Archv.

★ **16279** ★

Texas Woman's University - Blagg-Huey Library - Special Collections
    (Soc Sci)
TWU Sta., Box 23715   Phone: (817)898-3751
Denton, TX 76204-1715   Dawn Weston, Hd., Spec.Coll.
Founded: 1932. **Staff:** 4.5. **Subjects:** Women's biography, history, and
literature; suffrage; cookery. **Special Collections:** Woman's Collection
(45,467 books and bound periodical volumes, including the Madeleine
Henrey Collection and the LaVerne Harrell Clark Collection); Sarah
Weddington Collection; Claire Myers Owens Collection; Texas Women: A
Celebration of History collection; Texas Federation of Women's Clubs
papers; Delta Kappa Gamma - Texas papers; Cookbook and Menu
Collection (8817 books and bound periodical volumes; 2000 menus, 1844

cookbooklets, including the Julie Bennell Cookbook Collection and the Margaret Scruggs Cookbook Collection); The Ribbon Archives; Genevieve Dixon Collection (1126 books); university archives and manuscript collection (2200 cubic feet). **Holdings:** 65,729 books and bound periodical volumes; 27,125 items in microforms; 575 AV programs. **Subscriptions:** 98 journals and other serials. **Services:** Interlibrary loan; copying; collections open to the public. **Automated Operations:** Computerized public access catalog, cataloging, and circulation. **Computerized Information Services:** DIALOG Information Services, Geac Library Information System, OCLC, BRS Information Technologies, MEDLINE. **Networks/Consortia:** Member of AMIGOS Bibliographic Council, Inc., Association for Higher Education of North Texas (AHE). **Special Catalogs:** Finder's Guide to Texas Women: A Celebration of History. **Remarks:** Alternate telephone number(s): 898-2665. FAX: (817)898-3726. **Staff:** Kim Grover-Haskins; Georgia Bonatis.

★ 16280 ★
Texas Woman's University - Center for the Study of Learning - Library (Educ)
Box 23029   Phone: (817)898-2045
Denton, TX 76204   Ruth M. Caswell, Dir.
Subjects: Reading - methodology, teaching, testing. **Holdings:** 1500 books; 150 other cataloged items. **Services:** Library open to the public by appointment for reference use. **Remarks:** An alternate telephone number is 898-2227.

★ 16281 ★
Texas Woman's University - F.W. and Bessie Dye Memorial Library (Med)
1810 Inwood Rd.   Phone: (214)689-6580
Dallas, TX 75235   Rod Koliha, Coord., Hea.Sci.Lib.
Founded: 1966. **Staff:** Prof 2; Other 5. **Subjects:** Nursing, occupational therapy, medical records, health care administration, psychology, physical therapy. **Holdings:** 23,877 books; 10,903 bound periodical volumes; 1791 bound theses, dissertations, and professional papers; 1271 volumes on microfilm; 1735 volumes on microfiche; 172 volumes on microcard. **Subscriptions:** 298 journals and other serials. **Services:** Interlibrary loan; copying; library open to the public for reference use only. **Automated Operations:** Computerized public access catalog and cataloging. **Computerized Information Services:** DIALOG Information Services, Geac Library Information System, MEDLINE, CINAHL, ERIC, Health Planning and Administrative Data Base. **Networks/Consortia:** Member of Health Libraries Information Network (HealthLINE), Association for Higher Education of North Texas (AHE), National Network of Libraries of Medicine - South Central Region, AMIGOS Bibliographic Council, Inc. **Remarks:** FAX: (214)689-6583. **Staff:** Susan Gilkeson, Libn.

★ 16282 ★
Texas Woman's University - Library Science Library (Info Sci)
School of Library and Information Studies   Phone: (817)898-2621
Denton, TX 76204-0905   Charles Wilt, Libn.
Founded: 1939. **Staff:** Prof 2; Other 8. **Subjects:** Library and information science, children's and young adult literature. **Holdings:** 20,100 books; 3000 bound periodical volumes; 291 reels of microfilm; 55 kits; 200 titles of library newsletters. **Subscriptions:** 125 journals. **Services:** Library open to the public. **Automated Operations:** Computerized public access catalog, cataloging, and circulation. **Computerized Information Services:** DIALOG Information Services, BRS Information Technologies, OCLC, Geac Library Information System. **Remarks:** FAX: (817)898-3198.

★ 16283 ★
Texas Woman's University - Library Science Library - Proyecto LEER (Educ)
School of Library and Information Studies   Phone: (817)898-2619
Denton, TX 76204   Gilda Baeza Ortega
Founded: 1967. **Subjects:** Spanish and bilingual (Spanish-English) materials. **Holdings:** 24,000 books, journals, and nonprint materials. **Services:** Interlibrary loan; research collection and advisory service available on a limited schedule to TWU students and to the public with restrictions; classes conducted for librarians, educators, and library school students. **Automated Operations:** Computerized public access catalog, cataloging, acquisitions, serials, and circulation. **Computerized Information Services:** OCLC. **Publications:** Proyecto LEER Bulletin, irregular. **Remarks:** FAX: (817)898-3198.

★ 16284 ★
Textile Museum - Arthur D. Jenkins Library (Art, Hist)
2320 S St., N.W.   Phone: (202)667-0441
Washington, DC 20008   Mary Samms, Libn.
Staff: Prof 1; Other 1. **Subjects:** Oriental rugs; ancient and ethnographic textiles - Islamic, Peruvian, Asian, Oriental, Central American, Southwest American, Native North American; textile conservation; traditional and contemporary needlework. **Holdings:** 13,000 books and periodicals; 5500 slides; 14 VF drawers; auction catalogs. **Subscriptions:** 144 journals and other serials. **Services:** Library open to the public for reference use only on a limited schedule. **Computerized Information Services:** FRANCIS; internal database. **Remarks:** FAX: (202)483-0994.

★ 16285 ★
Textile Research Institute - Library (Sci-Engr)
601 Prospect Ave.
PO Box 625   Phone: (609)924-3150
Princeton, NJ 08542   G. Eaton, Libn.
Founded: 1945. **Staff:** 1. **Subjects:** Fibers, chemistry, textiles, polymers, composites, physics, engineering, microscopy, cellulose. **Holdings:** 2000 books; 2500 bound periodical volumes; 50 VF drawers of reports, reprints, patents. **Subscriptions:** 100 journals and other serials. **Services:** Interlibrary loan (fee); copying; library open to the public by appointment. **Computerized Information Services:** DIALOG Information Services, NERAC; TRI Reprints and Publications. **Publications:** Books and journals received, semiannual; serials list, biannual. **Remarks:** FAX: (609)683-7836.

★ 16286 ★
Textron Defense Systems - Everett Library (Sci-Engr)
2385 Revere Beach Pkwy.   Phone: (617)381-4620
Everett, MA 02149-5900   Joanne M. Campbell, Libn.
Founded: 1955. **Staff:** Prof 1. **Subjects:** Gas dynamics, magnetohydrodynamics, laser technology, superconductivity, physics, plasma physics, chemistry, cardiovascular research. **Special Collections:** Magnetohydrodynamic power generation; Dr. Arthur Kantrowitz Collection (3000 items). **Holdings:** 20,000 books; 7500 bound periodical volumes; 33,000 technical reports; 315,500 reports on microfiche; 8 VF drawers of pamphlets; 13 VF drawers of reprints. **Subscriptions:** 636 journals and other serials. **Services:** Interlibrary loan; translation; SDI. **Computerized Information Services:** DIALOG Information Services, OCLC. **Remarks:** FAX: (617)381-4295.
        Formerly: Avco Research Laboratory Inc. - Textron Division.

★ 16287 ★
Textron Defense Systems - Research Library (Sci-Engr)
201 Lowell St.   Phone: (508)657-2632
Wilmington, MA 01887   Shirley Levinson, Libn.
Staff: Prof 2; Other 1. **Subjects:** Aerodynamics, chemistry, space technology, physics, instrumentation, electronics, missile technology. **Holdings:** 10,000 books; 8000 bound periodical volumes; 20,000 technical reports and documents in hardcopy and on microfiche. **Subscriptions:** 150 journals and other serials. **Services:** Interlibrary loan; library not open to the public. **Automated Operations:** Computerized public access catalog, cataloging, and acquisitions. **Computerized Information Services:** DIALOG Information Services, DTIC; internal database. **Remarks:** FAX: (508)657-3528.

★ 16288 ★
Textron, Inc. - Aerostructures Division - Technical Library (Sci-Engr)
Box 210   Phone: (615)360-4043
Nashville, TN 37202   Jan L. Haley, Tech.Libn.
Founded: 1982. **Staff:** Prof 1. **Subjects:** Engineering, aircraft, aeronautics, chemistry, metallurgy, materials science. **Holdings:** 1307 books; 3700 pamphlets; 1300 reels of microfilm; military standards and specifications; industry standards; publications of NASA, National Advisory Committee for Aeronautics (NACA), Air Force Materials Laboratory (AFML), Air Force Wright Aeronautical Laboratories (AFWAL), and Air Force Flight Dynamics Laboratory (AFFDL). **Subscriptions:** 165 journals and other serials. **Services:** Interlibrary loan (to local libraries); copying; library open to the public with restrictions. **Automated Operations:** Computerized public access catalog. **Computerized Information Services:** DIALOG Information Services, PFDS Online. **Publications:** Newsletter, monthly. **Remarks:** FAX: (615)361-2752.

★ 16289 ★
Textron Lycoming - Division Library (Sci-Engr, Bus-Fin)
550 Main St.   Phone: (203)385-2547
Stratford, CT 06497   Joyce Ceccarelli, Engr.Libn.
Founded: 1980. **Staff:** Prof 1. **Subjects:** Aerospace, engineering, business planning, manufacturing, training and development. **Holdings:** 7500 books; 50 bound periodical volumes; 5000 NASA and National Advisory Committee for Aeronautics (NACA) reports; 5500 ASME papers, 1956 to present; Society of Automotive Engineers (SAE) papers, 1955 to present; AIAA and AHS technical papers; 100,000 company reports, proposals, papers on microfilm; training and development audio- and videotapes. **Subscriptions:** 600 journals and other serials. **Services:** Interlibrary loan; SDI; library open to the public by appointment. **Automated Operations:** Computerized cataloging, acquisitions, serials, and circulation. **Computerized Information Services:** DIALOG Information Services, DTIC, NASA/RECON; internal databases. **Networks/Consortia:** Member of Southwestern Connecticut Library Council (SWLC). **Publications:** Periodicals List, annual; Monthly Newsletter, quarterly; user guide, annual. **Special Catalogs:** Microfilm holdings; research and development reports. **Remarks:** FAX: (203)385-2469.

★ 16290 ★
Thacher Proffitt & Wood - Library (Law)
2 World Trade Center, 39th Fl.   Phone: (212)912-7743
New York, NY 10048   Elisabeth Tavss Ohman, Libn.
Staff: Prof 1; Other 2. **Subjects:** Law - admiralty, English, banking, corporate, real estate, tax. **Holdings:** 15,000 books; 1000 bound periodical volumes; 8 VF drawers. **Subscriptions:** 200 journals and other serials; 10 newspapers. **Services:** Interlibrary loan; library not open to the public. **Computerized Information Services:** LEXIS, WESTLAW, DIALOG Information Services. **Remarks:** FAX: (212)912-7751.

★ 16291 ★
Thai Industrial Standards Institute - Standards Information Center (Sci-Engr)
Ministry of Industry
Rama VI St.
Bangkok 10400, Thailand   Phone: 2 2461991
Founded: 1968. **Staff:** 11. **Subjects:** Standardization. **Special Collections:** Standards; technical regulations and certification systems. **Holdings:** 438,070 volumes. **Subscriptions:** 210 journals and other serials. **Services:** Interlibrary loan; copying; current awareness; translation; enquiry services. **Computerized Information Services:** CD-ROM. **Publications:** TISI Bibliographies; Library Accession List, quarterly. **Special Catalogs:** TISI Standards Catalogue, annual. **Remarks:** Alternate telephone numbers(s): 2 2464086. FAX: 2 2478741. Telex: 84375 minidus th (Attn: tisi). Alternate telephone number(s): 2 2464086.

★ 16292 ★
Thailand - National Institute of Development Administration - Library and Information Center (Bus-Fin)
Klong Chan
Bangkapi
Bangkok 10240, Thailand   Phone: 2 3775070
                              Dr. Chirawan Bhakdibutr, Libn.
Founded: 1955. **Staff:** 79. **Subjects:** Development economics; social development; public administration; computer science; applied statistics; business administration; human resource development; library and information science. **Holdings:** 167,499 volumes; 1289 periodical titles; 22 newspaper titles; 1551 reels of microfilm; 1753 microfiche; 921 cassette tapes. **Services:** Interlibrary loan; SDI; library open to the public. **Computerized Information Services:** Thai Social Science Periodical Index, World Bank Monograph Serials, Who is Who in Thailand, Human Resource Management; NIDA Research Reports List (internal database). **Publications:** List of Acquisitions, monthly; NIDA Bulletin, bimonthly. **Special Indexes:** Index to Thai Periodical Literature, annual. **Remarks:** FAX: 2 3740748. Alternate telephone number(s): 2 3755497; 2 3775481.

★ 16293 ★
Thailand - National Library of Thailand (Area-Ethnic, Info Sci)
Samsen Rd.   Phone: 2 281-5212
Bangkok 10300, Thailand Mr. Prachark Wattananusit, Gift & Exch.Libn.
Subjects: History, literature, Buddhism, art, social and basic sciences. **Special Collections:** Praya Anumanrajadhon; Vichitravadakarn; music; Thai manuscripts and collections. **Holdings:** 1.2 million books; 1933 periodical titles; 24,771 AV programs; 5014 microforms; 132,490 manuscripts. **Services:** Interlibrary loan; copying; library open to the public. **Publications:** National bibliography; ISDS-SEA bulletin; bibliography of children's books. **Special Indexes:** Subject indexes. **Also Known As:** Ho Samut Haeng Chat. **Staff:** Mrs. Pranom Panya-ngam, Dir.

★ 16294 ★
Thayer County Museum - Historical & Genealogical Library (Hist)
P.O. Box 387   Phone: (402)768-2147
Belvidere, NE 68315   Jacqueline J. Williamson, Musm. Co-Cur.
Founded: 1970. **Subjects:** Thayer County history, past and present residents, Thayer family genealogies. **Holdings:** Family files; Thayer County Censuses, 1860-1910 on microfilm; Thayer County newspapers; tombstone transcriptions; genealogies; maps and atlases. **Services:** Copying; library open to the public at librarian's discretion on a seasonally variable schedule. **Remarks:** Alternate telephone number(s): (402)768-6845; 768-7313. Museum and library maintained by Thayer County Historical Society and Thayer County Genealogical Society. **Staff:** Virginia Priefert, Musm. Co-Cur.

THE DRUGSTORE Information Clearinghouse
See: **South Carolina (State) Commission on Alcohol and Drug Abuse** (15400)

★ 16295 ★
Theatre Historical Society Archives (Theater)
York Theatre Bldg., 2nd Fl., Ste. 200
152 N. York Rd.   Phone: (708)782-1800
Elmhurst, IL 60126   William T. Benedict, Adm.
Founded: 1969. **Staff:** Prof 1. **Subjects:** Theater architecture, theater. **Special Collections:** Chicago Architectural Photographing Co. (1000 negatives); Ben Hall Collection (photographs; clippings; memorabilia); Terry Helegen Photograph Collection; blueprints. **Holdings:** 500 books; 10,000 slides; 8000 negatives; index to 7900 U.S. theaters; antique postcards; artifacts. **Subscriptions:** 1000 journals and other serials. **Services:** Copying; library open to the public on Tuesdays or by appointment. **Publications:** Marquee, quarterly; annual publication on one theater or subject. **Remarks:** FAX: (708)782-1802. Answers research requests with three weeks prior notice. **Formerly:** Located in Chicago, IL.

Theatre Intime Archives
See: **Princeton University - William Seymour Theatre Collection** (13388)

★ 16296 ★
Thelen, Marrin, Johnson & Bridges - Law Library (Law)
2 Embarcadero Center   Phone: (415)392-6320
San Francisco, CA 94111   Ann Borkin, Hd.Libn.
Staff: Prof 3; Other 3. **Subjects:** Law. **Holdings:** 30,000 volumes. **Subscriptions:** 800 journals and other serials; 50 newspapers. **Services:** Interlibrary loan; library not open to the public. **Computerized Information Services:** DIALOG Information Services, LEXIS, NEXIS, WESTLAW, DataTimes, RLIN, Information America, LEGI-SLATE. **Networks/Consortia:** Member of CLASS. **Remarks:** FAX: (415)421-1068. Telex: 340906 THEMARSF. **Staff:** Todd Bennett, Assoc.Libn.; Dan Cunningham, Ref.Libn.

★ 16297 ★
Theosophical Book Association for the Blind, Inc. (Aud-Vis)
54 Krotora Hill   Phone: (805)646-2121
Ojai, CA 93023   Dennis Gottschalk, Dir.
Founded: 1910. **Staff:** 9. **Subjects:** Theosophy, science, healing, meditation, comparative religion, Yoga, philosophy, esoteric philosophy, spiritual awareness. **Holdings:** 1200 books; 600 tapes; magazines and pamphlets. **Services:** Library open to the public by mail. **Publications:** Braille Star Theosophist, quarterly. **Remarks:** Library holdings are in braille and on cassette tape.

★ 16298 ★
Theosophical Society - Hermes Library (Rel-Phil)
2807 W. 16th Ave., Suite 2
Vancouver, BC, Canada V6K 3C5   Phone: (604)733-5684
                              Diana Cooper, Libn.
Founded: 1927. **Staff:** Prof 1; Other 1. **Subjects:** Theosophy, philosophy, mythology, psychology, religious studies. **Holdings:** 3000 books; 325 bound periodical volumes; 300 audio and video cassettes; reprints and originals of rare theosophical journals; pamphlet file. **Subscriptions:** 30 journals and other serials. **Services:** Interlibrary loan; library open to the public with restrictions. **Publications:** Secret Doctrine Bibliography.

★ 16299 ★
Theosophical Society in America - Olcott Library & Research Center
(Rel-Phil)
1926 N. Main St.
Box 270   Phone: (708)668-1571
Wheaton, IL 60189-0270   Dorothy Abbenhouse, Natl.Pres.
Founded: 1926. **Staff:** 2. **Subjects:** Theosophy (wisdom traditions),
comparative religions, metaphysics, parapsychology, mysticism. **Special
Collections:** Boris DeZirkoff Collection (H.P. Blavatsky; 650 books); The
Theosophical Society in America's National Archives (400 books; 32 reels
of microfilm); rare works in subject areas; theosophical periodicals.
Holdings: 18,000 books; 547 bound periodical volumes; 1000 pamphlets;
1000 audio cassettes; 500 video cassettes. **Subscriptions:** 5 journals and other
serials. **Services:** Copying; library open to the public. **Automated
Operations:** Computerized circulation. **Networks/Consortia:** Member of
DuPage Library System. **Publications:** Selected annotated bibliographies -
for sale. **Special Catalogs:** Annotated reading lists of the library collection.
Staff: Lakshmi Narayanswami, Hd.Libn.

★ 16300 ★
Theosophical Society in Miami - Library (Rel-Phil)
119 N.E. 62nd St.   Phone: (305)754-4331
Miami, FL 33138   Carol L. Hurd, Contact
Staff: Prof 1. **Subjects:** Theosophy; religion, especially eastern; yoga;
philosophy; astrology; metaphysics. **Holdings:** 6000 books. **Services:**
Library open to the public.

Theosophical Society of Pasadena - Theosophical University
See: Theosophical University - Library (16301)

★ 16301 ★
Theosophical University - Library (Rel-Phil)
2416 N. Lake Ave.   Phone: (818)798-8020
Altadena, CA 91001   John P. Van Mater, Libn.
Founded: 1919. **Staff:** Prof 3; Other 3. **Subjects:** Theosophy, comparative
religion and mythology, ancient and modern philosophy and science,
occultism. **Special Collections:** Theosophical magazines, 1879 to present
(nearly complete); first editions of theosophical books. **Holdings:** 60,000
books; 8000 bound periodical volumes; 1000 theosophical pamphlets.
Subscriptions: 30 journals and other serials. **Services:** Interlibrary loan
(limited); library open to the public for reference use. **Remarks:** Maintained
by the Theosophical Society of Pasadena. **Staff:** I. Manuel Oderberg,
Res.Libn.; Ina Belderis, Asst.Libn.

Theosophy Hall - Library
See: United Lodge of Theosophists (16724)

Thermo Analytical/Los Angeles
See: TMA/ARLI (16377)

★ 16302 ★
Thermo King Corporation - Library (Sci-Engr)
314 W. 90th St.   Phone: (612)887-2336
Minneapolis, MN 55420   Julie Ann Ostrow, Corp.Libn.
Founded: 1973. **Staff:** Prof 1; Other .5. **Subjects:** Refrigerated transport, air
conditioning, refrigeration, heating, transportation, automotive engineering.
Special Collections: International Institute of Refrigeration (61 volumes).
Holdings: 3000 books; 2 VF drawers of patents; 10 VF drawers of
documents; 1600 reports; 2000 vendor catalogs; 10 drawers of microfilm; 7
VF drawers of domestic and international standards. **Subscriptions:** 135
journals and other serials. **Services:** Library not open to the public.
Automated Operations: Computerized cataloging. **Computerized
Information Services:** DIALOG Information Services. **Remarks:** FAX:
(612)887-2617. Telex: 29-0450.

★ 16303 ★
(Thessaloniki) American Center Library - USIS Library (Educ)
34, Metropoleos St.
Thessaloniki, Greece
Remarks: Maintained or supported by the U.S. Information Agency. Focus
is on materials that will assist peoples outside the United States to learn
about the United States, its people, history, culture, political processes, and
social milieux.

★ 16304 ★
Thetford Historical Society - Library (Hist)
Thetford, VT 05074   Phone: (802)785-4361
                                                    Charles Latham, Jr.
Founded: 1975. **Staff:** Prof 1. **Subjects:** Thetford history, local crafts and
manufacturing, Vermont history. **Special Collections:** Charles H.
Farnsworth Collection (6 linear feet of music history materials); Dean C.
Worcester Collection (15 linear feet of materials on the Philippines; 1890-
1921); Mary B. Slade Collection (30 linear feet of local history materials).
Holdings: 4000 books; 400 bound periodical volumes; 150 linear feet of
archival materials. **Subscriptions:** 2 journals and other serials. **Services:**
Copying; library open to the public.

Thibault & Associates, Inc. - Environmental Science Services
See: Environmental Science Services (5384)

★ 16305 ★
Thiele Kaolin Company - Research & Development Library (Sci-Engr)
Box 1056   Phone: (912)552-3951
Sandersville, GA 31082   Barbara W. Goodman, Tech.Sec.-Libn.
Founded: 1966. **Staff:** Prof 1; Other 1. **Subjects:** Clay beneficiation, kaolin,
geology, mineralogy, applied chemistry. **Holdings:** 801 books; 70 bound
periodical volumes; 13 VF drawers; 1372 patents. **Subscriptions:** 50 journals
and other serials. **Services:** Interlibrary loan; library open to the public with
restrictions. **Computerized Information Services:** Chemical Abstracts
Service (CAS), DIALOG Information Services; Paperchem, Claims Patents
(internal databases). Performs searches on fee basis. **Remarks:** FAX:
(912)552-4105.

★ 16306 ★
Thiokol Corporation - Technical Library (Sci-Engr)
P.O. Box 400006   Phone: (205)882-8255
Huntsville, AL 35815-1506   Craig Weckwarth, Supv.Doc.Cont.
Founded: 1949. **Staff:** Prof 3. **Subjects:** Rocket motors, solid fuels. **Holdings:**
1000 books; 3000 reports; 60,000 reels of microfilm. **Subscriptions:** 50
journals and other serials; 2 newspapers. **Services:** Interlibrary loan;
copying; library not open to the public. **Staff:** Mrs. Pat Fowler.

★ 16307 ★
Third Baptist Church - Library (Rel-Phil)
620 N. Grand   Phone: (314)533-7340
St. Louis, MO 63103   Jim Wilson, Media Dir.
Founded: 1943. **Staff:** 10. **Subjects:** Bible, church doctrine, church history,
church work, social sciences, literature, biography. **Holdings:** 6000 volumes;
AV programs. **Subscriptions:** 40 journals and other serials. **Services:** Library
open to the public with restrictions.

★ 16308 ★
Third World House - Library (Soc Sci)
August-Bebel-Strasse 62
W-4800 Bielefeld 1, Germany   Phone: 521 62864
Subjects: Third World countries and their development. **Holdings:** 3500
volumes. **Also Known As:** Dritte Welt Haus.

★ 16309 ★
Third World Resource Center (Soc Sci)
125 Tecumseh, W.   Phone: (519)252-1517
Windsor, ON, Canada N8X 1E8   Ellen Preuschat, Rsrc.Coord.
Staff: 3. **Subjects:** Aids to social action and development education,
disarmament and arms trade, foreign relations, human rights, natural
resources, Third World areas, native peoples, women's issues. **Holdings:**
2000 books; 194 reports and manuscripts; 40 vertical file boxes of articles;
32 simulation games; 200 videotapes, filmstrips, and slide shows; 70 kits.
Subscriptions: 62 journals and other serials. **Services:** Copying; center open
to the public. **Automated Operations:** Computerized cataloging.
Publications: Newsletter, 5/year; bibliographies. **Special Catalogs:** AV
Catalogue (booklet).

Thirteen/WNET Reference Services
See: Educational Broadcasting Corporation (5253)

★ 16310 ★
Thistletown Regional Centre - Library (Soc Sci)
Rexdale Campus
51 Panorama Court
Etobicoke, ON, Canada M9V 4L8   Phone: (416)326-0717
     Joy Shanfield, Supv., Libs.
Founded: 1962. **Staff:** Prof 1; Other 2. **Subjects:** Child psychiatry and psychology, family therapy, special education, adolescent psychiatry and psychology, juvenile corrections. **Holdings:** 3150 books; 2200 bound periodical volumes; 300 audiotapes; 7 VF drawers; 2 drawers of legislation materials. **Subscriptions:** 104 journals and other serials. **Services:** Interlibrary loan; library open to the public for reference use only. **Automated Operations:** Computerized cataloging. **Computerized Information Services:** DIALOG Information Services. **Publications:** Recent Acquisitions, quarterly - for internal distribution only. **Remarks:** Maintained by Ontario Ministry of Community and Social Services. FAX: (416)326-0644.

★ 16311 ★
Thjodskjalasafn Islands (Hist)
Laugavegur 162
Postholf R5 5390
Reykjavik, Iceland   Phone: 91 623393
     Olafur Asgeirsson, Dir.
Founded: 1900. **Subjects:** History. **Remarks:** FAX: 91 25720. **Also Known As:** National Archives of Iceland.

Thode Library of Science & Engineering
See: **McMaster University** (9953)

Carey S. Thomas Library
See: **Denver Conservative Baptist Seminary** (4776)

★ 16312 ★
Thomas College - Marriner Library (Bus-Fin)
W. River Rd.
Waterville, ME 04901   Phone: (207)873-0771
     Richard A. Boudreau, Libn.
Staff: Prof 1; Other 4. **Subjects:** Business. **Holdings:** 21,489 books and bound periodical volumes. **Subscriptions:** 244 journals and other serials; 12 newspapers. **Services:** Interlibrary loan; copying; library open to the public with restrictions. **Computerized Information Services:** DIALOG Information Services; CD-ROM (MaineCat).

★ 16313 ★
Thomas County Historical Society - Library (Hist)
1905 S. Franklin, Box 465
Colby, KS 67701   Phone: (913)462-6972
     Sue Ellen Taylor, Dir.
Founded: 1959. **Staff:** Prof 4; Other 4. **Subjects:** Local history. **Holdings:** 500 linear feet of microfilm, manuscripts, books, archives, photographs, slides, clippings, cassettes. **Subscriptions:** 42 journals and other serials. **Services:** Copying; library open to the public for reference use only. **Publications:** Newsletter, quarterly - to members; Golden Jubilee, 1935 reprint; Land of the Windmills, 1976; Golden Heritage of Thomas County, Kansas, 1979; A History of Thomas County, 1987 (all books).

Thomas Library
See: **Wittenberg University - Thomas Library** (20546)

★ 16314 ★
Thomas Memorial Hospital - Medical/Nursing Library (Med)
4605 MacCorkle Ave., S.W.
South Charleston, WV 25309   Drema A. Pierson, Dir., Ed. & Trng.
Founded: 1946. **Subjects:** Medicine, nursing. **Holdings:** 300 books; 80 bound periodical volumes. **Subscriptions:** 80 journals and other serials. **Services:** Interlibrary loan; copying; library open to the public with director's permission. **Computerized Information Services:** Access to MEDLINE (through West Virginia University Library). **Remarks:** Maintained by the Department of Education and Training. Alternate telephone number(s): 766-3790. FAX: (304)766-3600. **Staff:** Margret Poling.

★ 16315 ★
Thomas, Snell, Jamison, Russell, and Asperger et al - Library (Law)
2445 Capitol St.
Box 1461
Fresno, CA 93716   Phone: (209)442-0600
     Tina Louise Marquez, Law Libn.
Staff: Prof 1; Other 1. **Subjects:** Law - corporate, tax, real estate, probate; civil litigation. **Holdings:** 10,000 books; 500 bound periodical volumes; 350 cassette tapes. **Subscriptions:** 140 journals and other serials. **Services:** Library not open to the public. **Computerized Information Services:** LEXIS, Information America. **Remarks:** FAX: (209)442-5078.

★ 16316 ★
Boyce Thompson Institute for Plant Research - Library (Biol Sci)
Cornell University
Tower Rd.
Ithaca, NY 14853   Phone: (607)254-1250
     Sherry Hoard-Ashton, Libn.
Staff: 1. **Subjects:** Plant physiology and pathology, biochemistry, microbiology, molecular biology, environmental biology, entomology, ecology. **Holdings:** 4000 books; 1500 bound periodical volumes. **Subscriptions:** 250 journals and other serials. **Services:** Interlibrary loan; copying; library open to the public. **Computerized Information Services:** BITNET (electronic mail service). **Publications:** Specialized Table of Content (weekly). **Remarks:** Electronic mail address(es): ASHX@CORNELLC (BITNET).

C.Y. Thompson Library
See: **University of Nebraska, Lincoln** (18994)

★ 16317 ★
David Thompson Library - Special Collections (Hist)
1402 Fell St.
Nelson, BC, Canada V1L 6A6   Phone: (604)352-5188
     Roberta Griffiths, Mgr.
Founded: 1963. **Staff:** 2.5. **Subjects:** Kootenaiana. **Special Collections:** English as a second language collection. **Holdings:** 1414 volumes; 949 photographs; clipping file; microfilms. **Subscriptions:** 41 journals and other serials; 5 newspapers. **Services:** Interlibrary loan (limited); copying; microfilm copying; collections open to the public for reference use only. **Publications:** Kootenaiana: a listing of books, government publications, monographs, journals, pamphlets, and other materials relating to the Kootenay area, 1976. **Remarks:** Maintained by Canadian International College.

Floyd Thompson Library
See: **NASA - Langley Research Center** (10986)

Harold W. Thompson Folklife Archives
See: **New York (State) Historical Association - Library** (11663)

J. Thompson Psychiatry Library
See: **Yeshiva University - Albert Einstein College of Medicine - Department of Psychiatry** (20753)

★ 16318 ★
J. Walter Thompson Company - Information Center (Bus-Fin)
900 N. Michigan Ave.
Chicago, IL 60611   Phone: (312)951-4000
     Roberta Piccoli, V.P., Dir., Info.Serv.
Founded: 1921. **Staff:** Prof 2; Other 2. **Subjects:** Advertising, advertising research, market research, marketing, consumer products and services, consumer behavior. **Holdings:** 4000 books; 225 VF drawers; 1 million print advertisements; 1000 reels of microfilm. **Subscriptions:** 504 journals and other serials. **Services:** Interlibrary loan; center open to the public by appointment. **Computerized Information Services:** DIALOG Information Services, NEXIS, DataTimes, VU/TEXT Information Services, PRODUCTSCAN; internal databases. **Networks/Consortia:** Member of ILLINET. **Remarks:** FAX: (312)951-4571. Telex: 824275. **Staff:** Henry Anderson, Info.Spec.

★ 16319 ★
J. Walter Thompson Company - Information Center (Bus-Fin)
466 Lexington Ave.　　　　　　　Phone: (212)210-7267
New York, NY 10017　　　　　Carol Stankiewicz, Dir., Info.Serv.
Founded: 1918. **Staff:** Prof 2; Other 2. **Subjects:** Advertising, marketing, industry. **Special Collections:** Picture and art; consumer print advertisements. **Holdings:** 3000 books; 100 VF drawers; 1563 reels of microfilm; 2000 microfiche. **Subscriptions:** 200 journals and other serials. **Services:** Center open to SLA members and others by appointment. **Computerized Information Services:** DIALOG Information Services, NEXIS, NewsNet, Inc., Dow Jones News/Retrieval, MAID. **Remarks:** FAX: (212)210-7053. **Staff:** Christopher Brown, Info.Spec.

★ 16320 ★
J. Walter Thompson Company - Information Centre (Bus-Fin)
160 Bloor St., E.
Toronto, ON, Canada M4W 3P7　　　Phone: (416)920-9171
Founded: 1984. **Staff:** 1. **Subjects:** Advertising, marketing, business, creative media. **Special Collections:** Audiovisual collection; media collection. **Holdings:** 400 books; 200 other cataloged items; information file; annual reports. **Subscriptions:** 112 journals and other serials; 6 newspapers. **Services:** Copying; SDI; center open to the public with restrictions. **Special Indexes:** Information file, AV materials. **Remarks:** FAX: (416)926-7375.

J. Walter Thompson Company Archives
See: Duke University - Special Collections Department (5049)

John H. Thompson Memorial Library
See: Torrington Historical Society, Inc. (16428)

★ 16321 ★
Thompson & Knight - Library (Law)
3300 First City Center　　　　　Phone: (214)969-1428
Dallas, TX 75201　　　　　　　Anne E. Montgomery, Libn.
Founded: 1976. **Staff:** 6. **Subjects:** Law. **Holdings:** 20,000 volumes. **Subscriptions:** 75 journals and other serials. **Services:** Interlibrary loan; copying; library open to Dallas area law librarians only. **Computerized Information Services:** LEXIS, WESTLAW, Dow Jones News/Retrieval, DIALOG Information Services, Information America, DataTimes. **Remarks:** FAX: (214)969-1751. **Staff:** Bonnie Anthis, Info.Spec.; Kathleen O'Sullivan, Acq.; Mechele Manchen, Ser./Tech.Serv.; Donna Fowler, Ref.Spec.

★ 16322 ★
Thompson, Mann & Hutson - Law Library (Law)
1455 Pennsylvania Ave., Suite 1160
Washington, DC 20004　　　　　Phone: (202)783-1900
Subjects: Labor law. **Holdings:** 3000 books. **Subscriptions:** 20 journals and other serials. **Services:** Library not open to the public. **Computerized Information Services:** WESTLAW. **Remarks:** FAX: (202)625-4030.

★ 16323 ★
Thompson Memorial Medical Center - Health Sciences Library (Med)
466 E. Olive Ave.　　　　　　　Phone: (818)953-6574
Burbank, CA 91501　　　　　　Jeanne S. Dawes, Cons.Libn.
Founded: 1973. **Subjects:** Medicine, nursing, pharmacy, administration, allied health sciences. **Holdings:** 200 books; vertical files. **Subscriptions:** 4 journals and other serials. **Services:** Interlibrary loan; library not open to the public. **Computerized Information Services:** MEDLARS. **Networks/Consortia:** Member of San Fernando Valley Medical Library Group. **Formerly:** Burbank Community Hospital.

Nancy Thompson Library
See: Kean College of New Jersey (8595)

Thompson-Pell Research Center
See: Fort Ticonderoga Association, Inc. (6013)

R.C. Thompson Library
See: Maryland Rehabilitation Center (9755)

Robert L. Thompson Strategic Hospital
See: U.S. Air Force - Robert L. Thompson Strategic Hospital (16817)

W.F. Thompson Memorial Library
See: U.S. Natl. Marine Fisheries Service (17645)

Thomson Company - Altoona Mirror
See: Altoona Mirror - Library (428)

★ 16324 ★
Thomson Consumer Electronics, Inc. - Engineering Library (Sci-Engr)
600 N. Sherman Dr., Bldg. 6-123
Indianapolis, IN 46201　　　　Cassandra J. Lewis, Adm., Lib.Serv.
Founded: 1955. **Staff:** Prof 1. **Subjects:** Engineering, electronics, physics, chemistry, television, computers. **Holdings:** 2050 books; 800 bound periodical volumes. **Subscriptions:** 100 journals and other serials. **Services:** Interlibrary loan; library not open to the public. **Automated Operations:** Computerized cataloging. **Computerized Information Services:** DIALOG Information Services, WILSONLINE, OCLC. **Networks/Consortia:** Member of Central Indiana Area Library Services Authority (CIALSA), INCOLSA. **Publications:** The Elm, bimonthly - for internal distribution only. **Remarks:** FAX: (317)231-4158.

★ 16325 ★
Thomson Consumer Electronics, Inc. - Library (Sci-Engr)
1002 New Holland Ave.　　　　Phone: (717)295-6608
Lancaster, PA 17601　　　　　Mary Kathryn Noll, Libn.
Founded: 1989. **Staff:** Prof 1. **Subjects:** Electronics, television, electrical engineering, physics, chemistry, metallurgy, ceramics, mathematics. **Holdings:** 1000 books; 500 bound periodical volumes; 450 patents. **Subscriptions:** 12 journals and other serials. **Services:** Interlibrary loan; copying; library open to the public. **Computerized Information Services:** DIALOG Information Services.

★ 16326 ★
Thomson Consumer Electronics, Inc. - Picture Tube Division - Library
3301 S. Adams St.
P.O. Box 2001
Marion, IN 46952-8401
Founded: 1950. **Staff:** 1. **Subjects:** Vacuum tubes, television, electronics, physics, chemistry, glass, metals. **Holdings:** 2058 books; 1687 bound periodical volumes; 1200 pamphlets; 16 VF drawers of internal reports. **Remarks:** Currently inactive.

Thomson Newspaper Group - Financial Times of Canada
See: Financial Times of Canada (5699)

★ 16327 ★
Thomson, Rogers, Barristers & Solicitors - Library (Law)
390 Bay St., Suite 3100　　　　Phone: (416)868-3100
Toronto, ON, Canada M5H 1W2　　Dianne D. Sydij, Libn.
Staff: 1. **Subjects:** Law - commercial, motion picture, entertainment, copyright, insurance, aviation, taxation, real estate, municipal. **Holdings:** 10,000 volumes. **Services:** Library not open to the public.

W.J. Thomson Library
See: Scottish Agricultural College (14965)

★ 16328 ★
Thoreau Society, Inc. - Thoreau Lyceum - Library (Hum, Hist)
156 Belknap St.　　　　　　　Phone: (617)369-5912
Concord, MA 01742　　　　　　Anne McGrath, Cur.
Founded: 1967. **Staff:** Prof 1; Other 3. **Subjects:** Henry David Thoreau, American transcendentalism, natural history, Concord history, American literature. **Holdings:** 1500 volumes. **Services:** Library open to the public with restrictions. **Staff:** Brad Parker, Asst.; Richard O'Connor, Asst.Interp.

Dr. Max Thorek Library and Manuscript Room
See: **International Museum of Surgical Science** (8159)

Olaf H. Thormodsgard Law Library
See: **University of North Dakota** (19102)

Thorndike, Doran, Paine and Lewis Inc.
See: **Wellington Management Company** (20161)

★ 16329 ★
Thorndike Library (Law)
1300 Court House   Phone: (617)725-8077
Boston, MA 02108   Jean Roberts, Ed./Libn.
Founded: 1921. **Staff:** Prof 1. **Subjects:** Law. **Holdings:** 20,000 books; 525 bound periodical volumes. **Services:** Library is a private facility for court use only. **Remarks:** Chartered as Judges Library Corporation in 1921. Maintained by Massachusetts State Supreme Judicial Court. FAX: (617)248-8954.

Thorngate Library
See: **University of Wisconsin--Madison - Clinical Research Laboratories - Thorngate Library** (19589)

★ 16330 ★
C.W. Thornthwaite Associates Laboratory of Climatology - Library (Sci-Engr)
R.D. 1   Phone: (609)358-2350
Elmer, NJ 08318   William J. Superior, Pres.
Subjects: Climatology, meteorology. **Holdings:** Figures not available. **Publications:** Publications in Climatology, 2/year - for sale.

Harry Thornton Memorial Library
See: **Pensacola Museum of Art** (12920)

★ 16331 ★
Thorp, Reed & Armstrong - Library (Law)
One Riverfront Center   Phone: (412)394-2358
Pittsburgh, PA 15222   Donna M. Kielar, Lib.Dir.
Staff: 2. **Subjects:** Law - general corporate, labor, tax, medical; litigation. **Subscriptions:** 100 journals and other serials; 5 newspapers. **Services:** Interlibrary loan, copying, library not open to the public. **Computerized Information Services:** LEXIS, WESTLAW, Information America, Dun & Bradstreet Business Credit ServicesN. **Remarks:** FAX: (412)394-2555.

Thorpe Music Library
See: **Illinois Wesleyan University** (7709)

Thorvaldson Library
See: **University of Saskatchewan** (19298)

Thousand Islands Shipyard Museum, Inc.
See: **Antique Boat Museum, Inc.** (900)

Three Lions - Picture Library
See: **Superstock** (15882)

★ 16332 ★
3M - 53 Technical Library (Sci-Engr)
3M Center, 53-3E-02   Phone: (612)778-6270
St. Paul, MN 55144   Claire Z. Stokes, Supv.
Founded: 1989. **Staff:** Prof 1; Other 1. **Subjects:** Textiles, fluorine, chemistry, polymer chemistry, abrasives, plastics design. **Holdings:** 500 books; 2000 microfiche. **Subscriptions:** 118 journals and other serials. **Services:** Interlibrary loan; library open to the public with advance notice and a 3M visitor's pass. **Computerized Information Services:** DIALOG Information Services, STN International, ORBIT. **Publications:** Library Extract (newsletter), bimonthly - for internal distribution only. **Remarks:** FAX: (612)778-6271.

★ 16333 ★
3M - 201 Technical Library (Sci-Engr)
3M Center, 201-2S-00   Phone: (612)733-2445
St. Paul, MN 55144-1000   Mariann Cyr, Supv.
Founded: 1955. **Staff:** Prof 5; Other 3. **Subjects:** Chemistry, physics, polymer science, electronics, materials science. **Holdings:** 30,000 books; 50,000 bound periodical volumes; 750 volumes of chemical trade literature; 250 audiotapes; 500 videotapes; government documents on microfiche. **Subscriptions:** 825 journals and other serials. **Services:** Interlibrary loan; open to public with advance notice and a 3M visitor's pass. **Computerized Information Services:** DIALOG Information Services, NLM, BRS Information Technologies, STN International, ORBIT Search Service, Questel. **Networks/Consortia:** Member of Twin Cities Standards Cooperators, Metronet. **Publications:** Alert (acquisitions), biweekly; Bulletin Board - both for internal distribution only. **Special Catalogs:** Computerized List of Serials. **Remarks:** FAX: (612)736-0902. **Staff:** Mary E. Hansen; Elizabeth S. French; Eugene P. Danilenko; Debra R. Yndestad.

★ 16334 ★
3M - 209 Technical Library (Sci-Engr)
3M Center, 209-BC-06   Phone: (612)733-6973
St. Paul, MN 55144-1000   Alice E. Bresnahan, Sr.Tech.Libn.
Founded: 1959. **Staff:** Prof 1; Other 1. **Subjects:** Adhesives and adhesion, ceramics and glass, coatings, elastomers, imaging, organic chemistry, photographic chemistry, polymers, rubber technology, surface science. **Holdings:** 6000 books. **Subscriptions:** 240 journals and other serials. **Services:** Interlibrary loan; open to the public with advance notice and a 3M visitor's pass. **Computerized Information Services:** DIALOG Information Services, ORBIT Search Service, STN International, OCLC, EPIC, WILSONLINE. **Publications:** 209 Library Bulletin (acquisitions list), monthly - for internal distribution only. **Remarks:** FAX: (612)736-6352.

★ 16335 ★
3M - 230 Technical Library (Sci-Engr)
3M Center, 230-1S-12   Phone: (612)733-5017
St. Paul, MN 55144-1000   Elizabeth Sandness French, Tech.Libn.
Founded: 1935. **Staff:** Prof 1; Other 1. **Subjects:** Adhesives, elastomers, films, nonwovens, paper chemistry, rubber technology, packaging, plastics, polymers, coatings, converting technology, glass science, research and development management. **Special Collections:** Institute of Paper Chemistry papers; Institute of Paper Science and Technology papers. **Holdings:** 3500 books; chemical trade literature. **Subscriptions:** 140 journals and other serials. **Services:** Interlibrary loan; open to the public with advance notice and a 3M visitor's pass. **Computerized Information Services:** DIALOG Information Services, STN International, ORBIT Search Service, BRS Information Technologies, Mead Data Central, NEXIS, EPIC, NLM, WILSONLINE. **Publications:** Choice (acquisitions list) - for internal distribution only. **Remarks:** FAX: (612)736-3870.

★ 16336 ★
3M - 235 Technical Library (Sci-Engr)
3M Center, 235-1A-25   Phone: (612)733-2592
St. Paul, MN 55144   Amy Holzle, Libn.
Founded: 1966. **Staff:** Prof 1; Other 1. **Subjects:** Electronics, micrographics, optics, paper chemistry and technology, printing, reprographics, computer technology, imaging technology, hardgoods manufacturing technology. **Holdings:** 7200 books; 361 documents on microfilm. **Subscriptions:** 280 journals and other serials. **Services:** Interlibrary loan; open to the public with advance notice and a 3M visitor's pass. **Computerized Information Services:** DIALOG Information Services, STN International, ORBIT Search Service, OCLC EPIC, DTIC. **Publications:** Book Bin (acquisitions list), monthly - for internal distribution only.

★ 16337 ★
3M - 236 Technical Library (Sci-Engr, Comp Sci)
3M Center, 236-1E-09   Phone: (612)733-5751
St. Paul, MN 55144   Jan M. Curtis, Sr.Tech.Libn.
Founded: 1970. **Staff:** Prof 1; Other 1. **Subjects:** Chemistry, computers, electronics, electrical engineering, rubber, polymer science, magnetic recording. **Holdings:** 6000 books; 2 VF drawers of annual reports; 5 VF drawers of house organs; 15 VF drawers of trade literature. **Subscriptions:** 196 journals and other serials. **Services:** Interlibrary loan; open to the public with advance notice and a 3M visitor's pass. **Computerized Information Services:** DIALOG Information Services, STN International, ORBIT Search Service, Questel, DTIC, BRS Information Technologies. **Publications:** Recorder (acquisitions list), monthly - for internal distribution only. **Remarks:** FAX: (612)736-6890.

★ 16338 ★
3M - 251 Technical Library (Sci-Engr)
3M Center, 251-2A-06   Phone: (612)733-5236
St. Paul, MN 55144   Ramona R. Huppert, Libn.
Founded: 1955. **Staff:** Prof 1; Other 1. **Subjects:** Abrasives, automotive technologies, metallurgy, textiles, tribology, chemical specialties, ceramics. **Holdings:** 4360 books; 8690 microfiche; 218 reels of microfilm. **Subscriptions:** 222 journals and other serials. **Services:** Interlibrary loan; open to the public with advance notice and a 3M visitor's pass. **Computerized Information Services:** DIALOG Information Services, ORBIT Search Service, STN International. **Publications:** Focus (acquisitions list), bimonthly - for internal distribution only. **Remarks:** FAX: (612)736-2332.

★ 16339 ★
3M - 275 Library (Med)
3M Center, 275-1W-07   Phone: (612)733-1703
St. Paul, MN 55144   Eloise M. Jasken, Tech.Info.Spec.
Founded: 1969. **Staff:** Prof 2; Other 1. **Subjects:** Biochemistry, medicine, physiology, chemistry, pharmacology, biomaterials, business. **Holdings:** 6500 books; 7200 bound periodical volumes. **Subscriptions:** 450 journals and other serials. **Services:** Interlibrary loan; open to the public with advance notice and a 3M visitor's pass. **Computerized Information Services:** DIALOG Information Services, NLM, ORBIT Search Service, BRS Information Technologies. **Publications:** Connection (acquisitions list), monthly - for internal distribution only. **Formerly:** Its 270 Technical Library. **Staff:** Maryann Horn; Amy Lougren; Fred Morgan.

★ 16340 ★
3M - Austin Information Services (Sci-Engr)
6801 River Place Blvd.   Phone: (512)984-3236
Austin, TX 78726-9000   Erika C. Mittag, Supv.
Founded: 1984. **Staff:** Prof 1; Other 2. **Subjects:** Business and technical information for the electronic, telecommunications, and visual presentation industries. **Holdings:** 1500 books; manufacturer's catalogs on microfilm. **Subscriptions:** 280 journals and other serials. **Services:** Interlibrary loan; library open to the public with advance notice and a 3M visitor's pass. **Automated Operations:** Computerized public access catalog and serials. **Computerized Information Services:** DIALOG Information Services, BRS Information Technologies, Data-Star, NEXIS, Dow Jones News/Retrieval, STN International, ORBIT Search Service, NewsNet, Inc., WILSONLINE; DIALMAIL (electronic mail service). **Remarks:** FAX: (512)984-3237. Electronic mail address(es): 14982 (DIALMAIL).

★ 16341 ★
3M - Business Library (Bus-Fin)
3M Center, 220-1C-02   Phone: (612)733-9057
St. Paul, MN 55144   Rebekah E. Anderson, Supv.
Founded: 1952. **Staff:** Prof 5; Other 3. **Subjects:** Management, marketing, research and development, financial planning, personnel. **Holdings:** 3000 books; 10K reports for New York, American, and over the counter exchanges; 650 reels of microfilm; 50 VF. **Subscriptions:** 238 journals and other serials. **Services:** Interlibrary loan; open to the public with advance notice and a 3M visitor's pass. **Computerized Information Services:** DIALOG Information Services, NEXIS, TEXTLINE, ORBIT Search Service, Official Airline Guides, Inc. (OAG), WILSONLINE, BRS Information Technologies, Dow Jones News/Retrieval, VU/TEXT Information Services, DataTimes, INVESTEXT. **Publications:** Abbreviations - for internal distribution only. **Remarks:** FAX: (612)736-3940. **Staff:** Cheryl Boyd, Libn.; Helen Stassen, Libn.; Amy Lovgren, Libn.

★ 16342 ★
3M - Engineering and Vendor Library (Sci-Engr)
Bldg. 21-BW
Box 3331   Phone: (612)778-4264
St. Paul, MN 55133   Claire Z. Stokes, Supv.
Founded: 1956. **Staff:** Prof 3; Other 2. **Subjects:** Engineering. **Special Collections:** ANSI Standards Information. **Holdings:** 3000 books; 6000 vendor catalogs; 30,000 vendor catalogs on microfilm. **Subscriptions:** 220 journals and other serials. **Services:** Interlibrary loan; library open to the public with advance notice and a 3M visitor's pass. **Computerized Information Services:** DIALOG Information Services, NEXIS, OCLC, ORBIT Search Service, STN International, WILSONLINE. **Publications:** Spectrum, monthly - for internal distribution only. **Special Indexes:** Vendor Library Index (online). **Remarks:** FAX: (612)778-6364. **Staff:** L.K. Hoekstra; K. Jursik.

★ 16343 ★
3M - Information Services (Sci-Engr, Comp Sci, Med)
3M Center, 201-2S-09   Phone: (612)733-5402
St. Paul, MN 55144-1000   Barbara J. Peterson, Dir.
    Prof 43; Other 34. **Holdings:** Figures not available. **Services:** Services open to the public by appointment with restrictions. **Automated Operations:** Computerized public access catalog, cataloging, serials, and ILL. **Computerized Information Services:** DIALOG Information Services, Dow Jones News/Retrieval, VU/TEXT Information Services, Data-Star, Mead Data Central, OCLC, WILSONLINE, InvesText, CompuServe Information Service, Maxwell Macmillan Taxes Online, Official Airline Guide (OAG), PLASPEC, Questel, STN International; internal databases. **Remarks:** 3M Information Services is comprised of the 3M libraries listed. **Staff:** Martha Ellison, Current Awareness; Aletta Moore, Mgr., Lib. Network; Kristin K. Oberts, Tech.Mgr., Lib. Network; David Schrader, Mgr.Sys.Serv.; Thea Welsh, Supv.Tech.Serv.

★ 16344 ★
3M - Information Technology Library (Comp Sci)
3M Center, 224-2N-12   Phone: (612)733-1488
St. Paul, MN 55144   Rebekah E. Anderson, Libn.
Founded: 1990. **Staff:** 1. **Subjects:** Information technology, computing, data processing. **Holdings:** 250 books; reports. **Subscriptions:** 77 journals and other serials. **Services:** Interlibrary loan; library open to the public by appointment. **Computerized Information Services:** CD-ROM (Computer Select).

★ 16345 ★
3M - Law Library (Law)
P.O. Box 33355   Phone: (612)733-1460
St. Paul, MN 55133   C. Jean Johnson, Libn.
Staff: 2. **Subjects:** Law. **Holdings:** 20,000 volumes. **Services:** Library not open to the public. **Computerized Information Services:** DIALOG Information Services, LEXIS, WESTLAW. **Remarks:** FAX: (612)736-9469.

★ 16346 ★
3M - Patent and Technical Communications Services (Sci-Engr)
3M Center, 201-2C-12   Phone: (612)733-7670
St. Paul, MN 55144   Karen L. Flynn, Mgr.
Founded: 1962. **Staff:** Prof 8; Other 8. **Subjects:** U.S. and foreign patents. **Special Collections:** Complete U.S. Patent collection, 1963 to present (microfilm). **Holdings:** 2700 bound periodical volumes; foreign patents on aperture cards; 120,000 3M reports on microfiche. **Subscriptions:** 12 journals and other serials. **Services:** Executes patent searches and internal technical report searches for information on continuing basis for 3M's technical, engineering, and business staffs; open to the public with advance notice and 3M visitor's pass. **Computerized Information Services:** DIALOG Information Services, ORBIT Search Service, STN International, Questel, Mead Data Central. **Remarks:** FAX: (612)736-6495. **Staff:** Sharon M. Peterson; Victoria K. Veach; John M. Dudinyak; Margaret Hibberd; Kerin Gleason; Fred C. Morgan.

★ 16347 ★
3M Canada - Technical Information Centre (Sci-Engr)
Box 5757   Phone: (519)451-2500
London, ON, Canada N6A 4T1   Cheryl Stephenson, Tech.Libn.
Founded: 1973. **Staff:** Prof 1; Other 1. **Subjects:** Polymer chemistry, plastics and rubber, adhesives, chemical technology. **Holdings:** 1200 books; 900 items in vendor information file. **Subscriptions:** 300 journals and other serials. **Services:** Interlibrary loan; center not open to the public. **Automated Operations:** Computerized public access catalog, cataloging, acquisitions, serials, and circulation. **Computerized Information Services:** DIALOG Information Services, Info Globe, CAN/OLE, Dow Jones News/Retrieval, BRS Information Technologies, The Financial Post DataGroup, Infomart Online; Envoy 100 (electronic mail service). **Remarks:** FAX: (519)452-6142. Telex: 0645886. Electronic mail address(es): MMM.TECHINFO (Envoy 100).

★ 16348 ★
Thurber Consultants Ltd. - Library (Sci-Engr)
1445 W. Georgia St., Suite 200   Phone: (604)684-4384
Vancouver, BC, Canada V6G 2T3   Guy M. Robertson, Libn.
Founded: 1972. **Staff:** Prof 1; Other 3. **Subjects:** Geological engineering, geology, civil engineering. **Holdings:** 18,500 books; 6200 bound reports; 14,180 bound proposals; aerial photographs; maps. **Subscriptions:** 46 journals and other serials. **Services:** Copying; SDI; library open to the public upon approval of the librarian. **Computerized Information Services:** Pacific Rim Info-Search Corp. **Remarks:** FAX: (604)684-5124.

I.N. Thut World Education Center
See: **University of Connecticut - School of Education (18529)**

Thyssen-Bornemisza, Inc. - Information Handling Services - Global Engineering Documentation
See: **Global Engineering Documents (6511)**

★ 16349 ★
Tian Yi Ge Library (Area-Ethnic)
Ningbo, Zhejiang Province, People's Republic of China
Founded: 1561. **Subjects:** Chinese writings - Confucian classics, history, philosophy, belles-lettres. **Special Collections:** Rare editions of Song, Yuan, Ming, and Qing dynasties block-printed editions, handcopies of Ming and Qing manuscripts, rectified editions, copper and wooden type editions (total of 80,000 volumes); Ming dynasty district histories (271 titles); registers of candidates and papers of Imperial Examinations of Ming dynasty (389 titles). **Holdings:** 300,000 volumes.

Tibby Library
See: **University of Southern California - Catalina Marine Science Center (19323)**

Tice Memorial Library
See: **Cook County Hospital (4267)**

★ 16350 ★
Ticonderoga Historical Society - Library (Hist)
Hancock House
Moses Circle
Ticonderoga, NY 12883   Phone: (518)585-7868
Subjects: Local and area history, 1609 to present. **Holdings:** 10,000 volumes; correspondence; diaries; journals; logbooks; account books; business records; financial records; genealogical materials; public documents; maps; photographs. **Services:** Library open to the public.

Tierra Viva
See: **Friends of the Earth (6170)**

Tiffany Archives
See: **Corry Area Historical Society - Tiffany Archives (4342)**

★ 16351 ★
Tiffin University - Richard C. Pfeiffer Library (Bus-Fin)
139 Miami St.   Phone: (419)447-6442
Tiffin, OH 44883   Frances A. Fleet, Libn.
Staff: Prof 1; Other 1. **Subjects:** Business. **Holdings:** 14,300 books. **Subscriptions:** 105 journals and other serials; 10 newspapers. **Services:** Interlibrary loan; copying; library open to the public. **Computerized Information Services:** DIALOG Information Services. Performs searches on fee basis. **Networks/Consortia:** Member of Northwest Library District (NORWELD). **Remarks:** FAX: (416)447-9605.

Tilderquist Memorial Medical Library
See: **Miller-Dwan Medical Center (10399)**

★ 16352 ★
Tillamook County Pioneer Museum - Library (Hist)
2106 Second St.   Phone: (503)842-4553
Tillamook, OR 97141   M. Wayne Jensen, Jr., Dir.
Founded: 1935. **Subjects:** Northwest history and natural history, local history, genealogy. **Holdings:** Genealogy and county records; reference books; Tillamook Indian material; Tillamook County cemetery records; county newspapers. **Services:** Copying; library open to the public during museum hours.

★ 16353 ★
Timber Products Manufacturers - Library (Agri)
951 E. 3rd Ave.   Phone: (509)535-4646
Spokane, WA 99202   Greg R. Tichy, Mgr./Sec.
Founded: 1916. **Staff:** 9. **Subjects:** Regional timber products manufacturing, wholesale lumber and building materials distribution. **Holdings:** 1500 volumes; biographical archives. **Services:** Interlibrary loan; library not open to the public. **Remarks:** FAX: (509)534-6106.

★ 16354 ★
Time-Life Books Inc. - Editorial Reference Library (Hist, Rec, Publ)
777 Duke St., Suite 418   Phone: (703)838-7198
Alexandria, VA 22314   Louise D. Forstall, Hd.Libn.
Founded: 1976. **Staff:** Prof 2. **Subjects:** History - United States Civil War, American West; photography; gardening; fantasy; culinary arts; parenting; computer science; astronomy and space science; mysterious arts. **Special Collections:** Complete holdings of Time, Life, and Fortune magazines. **Holdings:** 20,000 books; 350 bound periodical volumes. **Subscriptions:** 175 journals and other serials. **Services:** Interlibrary loan; library not open to the public. **Computerized Information Services:** DIALOG Information Services. **Remarks:** FAX: (703)838-8017. **Staff:** Anne S. Heising, Libn.

★ 16355 ★
Time Warner, Inc. - Library (Publ)
Time & Life Bldg.
Rockefeller Center
New York, NY 10020   Phone: (212)522-3745
                                         Benjamin Lightman, Chf.Libn.
Founded: 1930. **Staff:** Prof 24; Other 91. **Subjects:** News reference topics. **Special Collections:** Reporting of Time, Inc. newsgathering services throughout the world. **Holdings:** 89,000 books; 500,000 folders of clippings and reports. **Subscriptions:** 1500 journals and other serials; 9 newspapers. **Services:** Library not open to the public. **Computerized Information Services:** DIALOG Information Services, Dow Jones News/Retrieval, Mead Data Central, DataTimes, NewsNet, Inc., INVESTEXT, VU/TEXT Information Services, Washington Alert Service, BASELINE, Warner Computer Systems, Inc, Reuters, Sovset. **Special Indexes:** Indexes to company magazines (card). **Remarks:** FAX: (212)522-0224. **Staff:** Dorothy Paulsen, Hd., Files; Patricia U. Rich, Hd., Ref.; Robert Kassinger, Hd., Index; Ellen Callahan, Hd.Bk.Serv.

★ 16356 ★
Time Warner, Inc. - Sports Library (Rec)
Radio City Sta., Box 614   Phone: (212)522-3397
New York, NY 10101   Peter Miller, Hd. Sports Libn.
Founded: 1960. **Staff:** Prof 4; Other 6. **Subjects:** Sports. **Special Collections:** Olympic Games Collection; Media Guides (college and professional sports). **Holdings:** 5000 books; 220 bound periodical volumes; 17,200 subject folders; 16,500 biographical folders. **Subscriptions:** 246 journals and other serials; 13 newspapers. **Services:** Library not open to the public. **Computerized Information Services:** DIALOG Information Services, VU/TEXT Information Services, DataTimes, NEXIS, Jockey Club Information Systems, BASELINE. **Publications:** Sports Source, quarterly - for internal distribution only. **Remarks:** FAX: (212)522-1719. **Staff:** Linda Ann Wachtel; Natasha Simon, Lib. Files Supv.; Judy Goldberg; Avi Kempinski.

★ 16357 ★
Timeplex, Inc. - Technical Library (Info Sci)
470 Chestnut Ridge Rd.   Phone: (201)391-6000
Woodcliff Lake, NJ 07675   Margit Linforth, Libn.
Staff: Prof 1. **Subjects:** Data communications, telecommunications, electronic engineering. **Holdings:** 500 books. **Subscriptions:** 200 journals and other serials. **Services:** Interlibrary loan; library not open to the public. **Computerized Information Services:** DIALOG Information Services. **Publications:** Monthly Acquisitions Bulletin. **Remarks:** FAX: (201)391-0779.

Times-Mirror Company - (Allentown) Morning Call
See: **(Allentown) Morning Call (385)**

★16358★
Times Publishing Company - News Library (Publ)
490 First Ave., S.
Box 1121   Phone: (813)893-8108
St. Petersburg, FL 33701   Cary Kenney, Lib.Dir.
Founded: 1923. **Staff:** Prof 15; Other 4. **Subjects:** Newspaper reference topics. **Holdings:** 5000 books; 60 VF drawers of reports and pamphlets; newspaper clippings; news and historical photographs; original maps and artwork; newspapers on microfilm and CD-ROM. **Services:** Library not open to the public. **Computerized Information Services:** NEXIS, DataTimes, VU/TEXT Information Services, Washington Alert Service, DIALOG Information Services, CompuServe Information Service, Florida State Legislature Systems, MEDLINE, Burrelle's Broadcast Database, Information America; CompuServe Information Service (electronic mail service). **Networks/Consortia:** Member of Tampa Bay Library Consortium, Inc. (TBLC). **Remarks:** Alternate telephone number(s): (813)893-8911 (information service). FAX: (813)893-8107. **Staff:** Barbara Hijek, Dp.Libn., Res.Coord.; Sammy Alzofon, Dp.Libn., Sys.

★16359★
Times Tribune - Library (Publ)
245 Lytton Ave.
Box 300   Phone: (415)853-5244
Palo Alto, CA 94302   Pam Allen, Hd.Libn.
Subjects: Newspaper reference topics. **Holdings:** 250 books; 200,000 file folders of clippings; 1404 reels of microfilm; 148,000 pictures; 200 state and county pamphlets and reports. **Subscriptions:** 5 newspapers. **Services:** Library not open to the public.

★16360★
Times-World Corporation - Newspaper Library (Publ)
Box 2491   Phone: (703)981-3279
Roanoke, VA 24010   Belinda Harris, Libn.
Founded: 1956. **Staff:** 3. **Subjects:** Newspaper reference topics. **Holdings:** 1500 books; newspaper clippings; pictures and biographical data; microfiche; by-line files; microfilm. **Subscriptions:** 18 journals and other serials. **Services:** Library not open to the public. **Computerized Information Services:** Produces Roanoke Times & World-News database (available online through VU/TEXT Information Services); VU/TEXT Information Services, NEXIS. **Remarks:** FAX: (703)981-3346. **Also Known As:** Roanoke Times & World-News.

★16361★
TIMET - Library (Sci-Engr)
c/o Titanium Metals
1999 Broadway, No.4300
Denver, CO 80202-5743   Phone: (303)296-5600
Subjects: Metallurgy, alloys, titanium. **Holdings:** Figures not available. **Remarks:** Telex: 823153.

★16362★
(Timisoara) Casa Corpului Didactic - Biblioteca (Educ)
Strada Gh. Doja 11   Phone: 61 19871
Timisoara, Romania   Iotcovici Persida
Founded: 1971. **Staff:** Prof 2. **Subjects:** Education sciences, literature, methodology of teaching, sciences. **Holdings:** 32,000 books. **Subscriptions:** 27 journals and other serials; 3 newspapers. **Services:** Interlibrary loan; library not open to the public.

★16363★
Timken Company - Research Library (Sci-Engr)
1835 Deuber Ave.   Phone: (216)471-2049
Canton, OH 44706   Patricia A. Cromi, Info.Anl.
Staff: Prof 1; Other 1. **Subjects:** Research management and planning, steel process research, bearing design, engineering research, materials handling. **Holdings:** 30,000 volumes; microfilm. **Subscriptions:** 290 journals and other serials. **Services:** Interlibrary loan; copying; SDI; library open to the public by appointment. **Automated Operations:** Computerized cataloging and acquisitions. **Computerized Information Services:** DIALOG Information Services, OCLC. **Networks/Consortia:** Member of OHIONET. **Remarks:** FAX: (216)471-2282.

★16364★
Timken Mercy Medical Center - Medical Library (Med)
1320 Timken Mercy Dr.   Phone: (216)489-1462
Canton, OH 44708   Nancy S. Erwin, Supv.
Staff: 1. **Subjects:** Medicine, nursing, and allied health sciences. **Holdings:** 4000 books; 4100 bound periodical volumes; 400 AV programs. **Subscriptions:** 200 journals and other serials. **Services:** Interlibrary loan. **Automated Operations:** Computerized cataloging. **Computerized Information Services:** Online systems. **Networks/Consortia:** Member of NEOUCOM Council Associated Hospital Librarians. **Remarks:** FAX: (216)489-1127.

Abigail Smith Timme Library
See: Ferris State University (5670)

Timpanogos Cave National Monument
See: U.S. Natl. Park Service (17785)

★16365★
Tin Information Center of North America (Sci-Engr)
1353 Perry St.   Phone: (614)424-6924
Columbus, OH 43201-3177   William B. Hampshire, Mgr.
Founded: 1949. **Staff:** Prof 3; Other 2. **Subjects:** Tin and its uses. **Special Collections:** Information File (28 subjects including tinplate, solders, bronze, bearings). **Holdings:** 350 volumes; 28 VF drawers of reports, manuscripts, patents; slides; films; photographs. **Subscriptions:** 45 journals and other serials. **Services:** Interlibrary loan; copying; library open to the public. **Publications:** Tin and Its Uses, quarterly; research reports; annual report of activities. **Remarks:** FAX: (614)424-6924.

★16366★
Carrie Tingley Hospital - Medical Library (Med)
1127 University Blvd., N.E.
Albuquerque, NM 87102   Phone: (505)272-5200
Staff: 1. **Subjects:** Orthopedics - pediatric, general; pediatric dysmorphology; pediatrics; rehabilitation. **Holdings:** 760 books; 250 bound periodical volumes; 200 resident research papers. **Subscriptions:** 12 journals and other serials. **Services:** Library not open to the public.

Helen C. Tingley Memorial Library
See: University of Maryland - School of Medicine - Department of Psychiatry (18799)

★16367★
Robert C. Tinker Library (Med)
3600 E. Harry   Phone: (316)689-5377
Wichita, KS 67218   Carol Matulka, Med.Libn.
Founded: 1942. **Staff:** Prof 2; Other 1. **Subjects:** Medicine, nursing, and allied health sciences, administration. **Holdings:** 4198 books; 1355 bound periodical volumes; 4247 books and journals in storage for recall; cassettes; records; AV programs and video cassettes. **Subscriptions:** 200 journals and other serials. **Services:** Interlibrary loan; copying; library open to hospital personnel and affiliated college/university students. **Computerized Information Services:** Online systems. Performs searches on fee basis. **Networks/Consortia:** Member of National Network of Libraries of Medicine - Midcontinental Region.

★16368★
Tioga County Historical Society Museum - Library (Hist)
110-112 Front St.   Phone: (607)687-2460
Owego, NY 13827   Jean Winnie Neff, Dir.
Founded: 1914. **Staff:** Prof 3. **Subjects:** Tioga County, Owego, and Southern Tier (New York) history and genealogy. **Services:** Copying; library open to the public.

★ 16369 ★
Tioga County Law Library (Law)
Court House
118 Main St.   Phone: (717)724-1906
Wellsboro, PA 16901   Shirley L. Kriner, Lib.Dir.
Subjects: Law. **Remarks:** No further information was supplied by respondent.

★ 16370 ★
Tippecanoe County Historical Association - Alameda McCollough Research & Genealogy Library (Hist)
909 South St.   Phone: (317)742-8411
Lafayette, IN 47901   Nancy Weirich, Libn.
Founded: 1925. **Staff:** Prof 3. **Subjects:** Genealogy; Indiana; Tippecanoe and local history. **Holdings:** 7000 books; 150 bound periodical volumes; 125 VF drawers of manuscripts and clippings; 40 scrapbooks; 575 reels of microfilm; 10,000 negatives; 2000 photographs. **Subscriptions:** 21 journals and other serials. **Services:** Copying; library open to the public with restrictions. **Publications:** Weatenotes (newsletter), monthly - to members; historical booklets and leaflets, annual - for sale. **Staff:** Sarah E. Cooke, Archv.

Tireman Learning Materials Library
See: **University of New Mexico - Tireman Learning Materials Library** (19049)

★ 16371 ★
(Tirgu Mures) Casa Corpului Didactic - Biblioteca (Educ, Soc Sci)
Strada Crinului 2   Phone: 54 30886
Tirgu Mures, Romania   Prof. Ioan Matepiuc
Founded: 1970. **Staff:** Prof 1. **Subjects:** Pedagogy, didactics, psychology, philosopy, arts, science. **Holdings:** 22,000 books; 501 didactic films. **Subscriptions:** 30 journals and other serials; 10 newspapers. **Services:** Interlibrary loan; library open to the public. **Staff:** Prof. Adriana Popa, Libn.

★ 16372 ★
Tiroler Landesmuseum Ferdinandeum - Bibliothek (Area-Ethnic, Geog-Map)
Museumstrasse 15   Phone: 0512 59489
A-6020 Innsbruck, Austria   Martin Bitschnau, Ph.D.
Founded: 1823. **Subjects:** Tirol and Trent provinces, bordering territories. **Holdings:** 150,000 books; 2100 bound periodical volumes; 1500 documents; 100 AV programs; 2000 manuscripts; 100 nonbook items. **Services:** Library open to the public for reference use only. **Remarks:** FAX: 5948988

Tishman Learning Center
See: **Montefiore Medical Center - Health Sciences Library/Tishman Learning Center** (10662)

★ 16373 ★
Titan Systems, Inc. - Library (Comp Sci)
1950 Old Gallows Rd., Suite 600
Vienna, VA 22182   Phone: (703)883-9200
Staff: Prof 1. **Subjects:** Artificial intelligence, advanced technology, defense systems, communications. **Holdings:** 200 monographs; 1000 reports. **Subscriptions:** 40 journals and other serials. **Services:** Interlibrary loan. **Computerized Information Services:** DIALOG Information Services, DTIC.

★ 16374 ★
Titanium Metals Corporation of America - Henderson Technical Library (Sci-Engr)
Box 2128   Phone: (702)564-2544
Henderson, NV 89009   Barbara Rosales, Tech.Libn.
Founded: 1952. **Staff:** 1. **Subjects:** Metallurgy, chemistry, physics, aerospace. **Holdings:** 16,000 books; technical reports and papers. **Subscriptions:** 30 journals and other serials. **Services:** Library not open to the public. **Automated Operations:** Computerized acquisitions. **Remarks:** FAX: (702)564-9038.

★ 16375 ★
(Titograd) Americki Centar - USIS Library (Educ)
Bulevar Octobarske Revolucije 100
YU-81000 Titograd, Yugoslavia
Remarks: Maintained or supported by the U.S. Information Agency. Focus is on materials that will assist peoples outside the United States to learn about the United States, its people, history, culture, political processes, and social milieux.

Paul Titus Memorial Library and School of Nursing Library
See: **St. Margaret Memorial Hospital** (14493)

★ 16376 ★
TLA Lighting Consultants, Inc. - Library (Plan)
72 Loring Ave.
Salem, MA 01970   Phone: (508)745-6870
Founded: 1970. **Staff:** 2. **Subjects:** Illumination, optics, lighting systems, architectural lighting design. **Holdings:** 150 books; 5000 bound periodical volumes; 250 reports; 75 manuscripts; 150 patents. **Subscriptions:** 35 journals and other serials. **Services:** Interlibrary loan; copying; library open to the public by appointment. **Remarks:** FAX: (508)741-4420. Telex: 6504370402 MCI UW.

★ 16377 ★
TMA/ARLI - Library (Sci-Engr)
160 Taylor St.   Phone: (818)357-3247
Monrovia, CA 91016   Dennis Wells, Lab.Mgr.
Subjects: Chemistry; environmental analysis; radioactive, organic, and inorganic materials; contamination and industrial hygiene. **Holdings:** 1000 volumes. **Computerized Information Services:** Internal database. **Remarks:** FAX: (818)359-5036. **Also Known As:** Thermo Analytical/Los Angeles.

★ 16378 ★
TMO/ANCI Management Affiliates - Library (Sci-Engr)
11 Todds Rd.   Phone: (203)438-3801
Ridgefield, CT 06877   Beverly Bondo
Founded: 1977. **Staff:** 1. **Subjects:** Technical standards, laboratory accreditation, product certification, quality system/registration, international equivalents. **Holdings:** 600 books; 100 bound periodical volumes; 1100 reports; 15,000 microfiche. **Subscriptions:** 90 journals and other serials; 6 newspapers. **Services:** Interlibrary loan; copying; library open to the public by appointment. **Computerized Information Services:** DIALOG Information Services. Contact Person: Chas W. Hyer, III. **Publications:** TMO Update Newsletter; TMO Survey Week Review of Federal Register; Commercial Laboratories - Profiles; Directory of State and Local Government Laboratory Accreditation/Designation Programs; Directory of Professional/Trade Organization Laboratory Accreditation/ Designation Programs; Directory of Quality Systems Assessment and Registration Organizations with National and International Accreditation. **Remarks:** FAX: (203)438-3801.

Tobacco and Health Research Institute
See: **University of Kentucky** (18759)

★ 16379 ★
Tobacco Institute - Information Center (Biol Sci, Med)
1875 Eye St., N.W., Suite 800
Washington, DC 20006   Phone: (202)457-9325
                        Maureen Booth, Res./Ref.Libn.
Founded: 1958. **Staff:** Prof 1; Other 1. **Subjects:** Tobacco history, smoking/ health controversy. **Holdings:** 2500 books; clippings; manuscripts; reports. **Subscriptions:** 200 journals and other serials; 10 newspapers. **Services:** Interlibrary loan; center not open to the public. **Automated Operations:** Computerized serials. **Computerized Information Services:** DIALOG Information Services, NEXIS, LEXIS, Dow Jones News/Retrieval, DataTimes, VU/TEXT Information Services. **Publications:** Tobacco state history series; Tobacco: Pioneer In American Industry; Tobacco Industry Profile; Tax Burden on Tobacco; related smoking and health pamphlets. **Staff:** Jennifer Dowden.

Tobacco Literature Service
See: **North Carolina State University** (11906)

★ 16380 ★

Tobacco Merchants Association of the U.S. - Howard S. Cullman Library (Agri)
Box 8019   Phone: (609)275-4900
Princeton, NJ 08543-8019   Thomas C. Slane, Ph.D., V.P.
Founded: 1915. **Staff:** Prof 2. **Subjects:** Tobacco industry and products. **Special Collections:** Complete collections of Tobacco Leaf and U.S. Tobacco Journal; trademark and brand files of tobacco products; smokers' articles. **Holdings:** 2000 books; 296 bound periodical volumes; 150 VF drawers of pamphlets, archives, and clippings; 18 shelves of government reports; 135 drawers of trademark file cards; 25 drawers of brand file cards. **Subscriptions:** 99 journals and other serials; 10 newspapers. **Services:** Copying; library open to the public for reference use by appointment only. **Publications:** List of publications - available upon request. **Special Indexes:** SYSTIM-INDEX (book); Cigarette Brand Directory (book). **Remarks:** FAX: (609)275-8379. **Staff:** Farrell Delman, Pres.

★ 16381 ★

Tobe Coburn School for Fashion Careers - Library
686 Broadway
New York, NY 10012
Defunct.

★ 16382 ★

Tobey Hospital - Stillman Library (Med)
High St.   Phone: (508)295-0880
Wareham, MA 02571   Athena Harvey, Libn.
Staff: Prof 1. **Subjects:** Medicine, surgery, nursing, hospital administration, basic sciences. **Holdings:** 1000 books; vertical files. **Subscriptions:** 50 journals and other serials; 5 newspapers. **Services:** Interlibrary loan; copying; library open to the public with restrictions. **Networks/Consortia:** Member of Southeastern Massachusetts Consortium of Health Science Libraries (SEMCO). **Publications:** Newsletter, quarterly - for internal distribution only.

Tobin Collection
See: **Marion Koogler McNay Art Museum** (9960)

Tocantins Memorial Library
See: **Thomas Jefferson University - Cardeza Foundation** (8359)

★ 16383 ★

Toccoa Falls College - Seby Jones Library (Rel-Phil)
Box 38   Phone: (404)886-6831
Toccoa Falls, GA 30598   Sarah Patterson, Hd.Libn.
Staff: Prof 2; Other 1. **Subjects:** Religion, Bible, theology, Christian education, missiology, teacher education, sacred music, communications. **Holdings:** 82,000 books; 3000 bound periodical volumes; 9500 AV programs; 1300 vertical files; 2000 microforms. **Subscriptions:** 500 journals and other serials; 5 newspapers. **Services:** Interlibrary loan; copying; library open to the public. **Staff:** Sara Patterson, Asst.Libn./Cat.

Ernst Toch Archive
See: **University of California, Los Angeles - Music Library** (18392)

A.M. Todd Rare Book Room
See: **Kalamazoo College - Upjohn Library** (8528)

Todd Library
See: **Rochester Museum and Science Center - Strasenburgh Planetarium** (13986)

★ 16384 ★

Todmorden Mills Heritage Museum and Art Centre (Hist)
850 Coxwell Ave.   Phone: (416)425-2250
Toronto, ON, Canada M4C 5R1   Susan Hughes, Cur.
Founded: 1967. **Staff:** Prof 2. **Subjects:** History of the Borough of East York, Don Valley, pioneer history, museology. **Special Collections:** Local History Archives for the Borough of East York; Photograph and Documentary Collection. **Holdings:** Photographs. **Services:** Library open to the public by appointment. **Remarks:** FAX: (416)466-4170. Maintained by the Borough of East York Department of Parks and Recreation.

Arnold B. Tofias Industrial Archives
See: **Stonehill College** (15814)

★ 16385 ★

Tokei Suri Kenkyujo - Toshoshitsu (Sci-Engr)
4 6 7 Minami azabu
Minato ku   Phone: 3 34461501
Tokyo 106, Japan   Giitiro Suzuki
Founded: 1944. **Staff:** Prof 1; Other 3. **Subjects:** Statistical mathematics. **Holdings:** 19,087 books; 14,681 bound periodical volumes; 30 reports. **Subscriptions:** 1972 journals and other serials. **Services:** Interlibrary loan; copying; library open to the public. **Remarks:** FAX: 3 34461695.

★ 16386 ★

Tokyo American Center - USIS Library (Educ)
ABC Bldg.
6-3, Shiba Koen 2-chome, Minato-ku
Tokyo 105, Japan
Remarks: Maintained or supported by the U.S. Information Agency. Focus is on materials that will assist peoples outside the United States to learn about the United States, its people, history, culture, political processes, and social milieux.

★ 16387 ★

Tokyo Ika Daigaku - Toshokan (Med)
6 7 1
Nishishinjuku, Shinjuku ku   Phone: 3 33426111
Tokyo 160, Tokyo, Japan   Tsuneo Tosaka
Founded: 1947. **Staff:** Prof 11; Other 6. **Subjects:** Medicine. **Holdings:** 54,165 books; 99,307 bound periodical volumes; 3118 microfiche; 8 reels of microfilm. **Subscriptions:** 2071 journals and other serials; 25 newspapers. **Services:** Interlibrary loan; copying; library open to the public. **Computerized Information Services:** JOIS (JICST On-Line Information System), DIALOG Information Services. Contact Person: Nobuko Takano. **Publications:** Holding List; TMCL News. **Remarks:** FAX: 3 33498277. Telex: 2322316.

★ 16388 ★

Toledo Blade - Library (Publ)
541 Superior St.   Phone: (419)245-6188
Toledo, OH 43660   Mary F. Mackzum, Hd.Libn.
Founded: 1926. **Staff:** Prof 2; Other 2. **Subjects:** Newspaper reference topics. **Holdings:** Bound volumes of newspapers; microforms. **Services:** Library not open to the public.

★ 16389 ★

Toledo Hospital - Medical Library (Med)
2142 N. Cove Blvd.   Phone: (419)471-5437
Toledo, OH 43606   Linda M. Tillman, Dir.
Staff: Prof 2; Other 5. **Subjects:** Medicine, nursing, allied health sciences. **Holdings:** 6687 books; 24,399 bound periodical volumes; video cassettes; audio cassettes; slides; filmstrips. **Subscriptions:** 610 journals and other serials. **Services:** Interlibrary loan; copying; SDI; library open to the public. **Automated Operations:** Computerized cataloging, circulation, and ILL. **Computerized Information Services:** BRS Information Technologies, MEDLARS. Performs searches on fee basis. **Networks/Consortia:** Member of National Network of Libraries of Medicine - Greater Midwest Region, Health Science Librarians of Northwest Ohio (HSLNO). **Special Catalogs:** Catalog for audiovisual materials (book). **Remarks:** FAX: (419)479-6953. **Staff:** Debbie Lyons, Asst.Dir.

★ 16390 ★
Toledo Law Association Library (Law)
Lucas County Court House   Phone: (419)245-4747
Toledo, OH 43624   Brenda Kelley, Dir./Law Libn.
Founded: 1870. **Staff:** Prof 1; Other 3. **Subjects:** Law. **Special Collections:** English and Canadian law. **Holdings:** 65,000 volumes. **Subscriptions:** 200 journals and other serials. **Services:** Interlibrary loan; library not open to the public. **Computerized Information Services:** WESTLAW, Hannah Legislative Service; Hannah Legislative Service (electronic mail service). Performs searches on fee basis. **Remarks:** FAX: (419)255-3577.

★ 16391 ★
Toledo-Lucas County Public Library - Business Department (Bus-Fin)
325 Michigan St.   Phone: (419)259-5208
Toledo, OH 43624   Joanne A. Kosanke, Dept.Mgr.
Staff: Prof 6; Other 1.5. **Subjects:** Business, economics, investment, trade. **Special Collections:** Phone directories (domestic and foreign); corporate annual reports representing 3500 companies; federal documents depository; import/export material; government procurement center (materials to help businesses win government contracts); career/vocational material center. **Holdings:** 41,000 books; 800 file envelopes of pamphlets. **Subscriptions:** 730 journals and other serials. **Services:** Interlibrary loan; copying; department open to the public. **Automated Operations:** Computerized public access catalog, cataloging, circulation, and acquisitions. **Computerized Information Services:** DIALOG Information Services, Dow Jones News/Retrieval, BRS Information Technologies; internal database. Performs searches on fee basis. **Networks/Consortia:** Member of OHIONET. **Remarks:** FAX: (419)255-1334.

★ 16392 ★
Toledo-Lucas County Public Library - Fine Arts and Audio Service Department (Art, Mus, Rec)
325 Michigan St.   Phone: (419)259-5226
Toledo, OH 43624   John C. Selzer, Dept.Mgr.
Staff: Prof 4; Other 1.5. **Subjects:** Art, music, sports, costume, architecture, photography, theater, dance, entertainment, antiques, collectibles, historic preservation. **Special Collections:** Framed prints for borrowing (600); sheet music (organ, 550; piano and voice, 4200; violin, 410); picture collection loan file (200,000). **Holdings:** 69,000 books; 750 phonograph records; 9200 cassettes; 3500 compact discs. **Subscriptions:** 204 journals. **Services:** Interlibrary loan; copying; department open to the public. **Automated Operations:** Computerized public access catalog, cataloging, and circulation. **Computerized Information Services:** Online systems. **Networks/Consortia:** Member of OHIONET. **Special Indexes:** Song Index. **Remarks:** FAX: (419)255-1334.

★ 16393 ★
Toledo-Lucas County Public Library - History-Travel-Biography Department (Hist, Geog-Map)
325 Michigan St.   Phone: (419)259-5200
Toledo, OH 43624   Donald C. Barnette, Jr., Dept.Mgr.
Staff: Prof 4; Other 1. **Subjects:** History, travel, geography, biography, archeology. **Holdings:** 106,488 books; 17,635 map sheets; duplicates of Toledo and northwest Ohio Collection for circulation; travel pamphlets. **Subscriptions:** 81 journals and other serials. **Services:** Interlibrary loan; copying; department open to the public. **Automated Operations:** Computerized public access catalog and cataloging. **Computerized Information Services:** InfoTrac. **Networks/Consortia:** Member of OHIONET. **Publications:** Booklists, irregular - to branch libraries. **Remarks:** FAX: (419)259-5313. **Staff:** Brian Nichols; Anthony Schafer; Delores Smith.

★ 16394 ★
Toledo-Lucas County Public Library - Literature/Fiction Department (Hum)
325 Michigan St.   Phone: (419)259-5224
Toledo, OH 43624   Susan I. Coburn, Dept.Mgr.
Staff: Prof 4; Other 1. **Subjects:** Literature, language. **Special Collections:** Large print materials; foreign language materials; Adult Literacy Center; criticism file. **Holdings:** 102,000 volumes. **Subscriptions:** 111 journals and other serials. **Services:** Interlibrary loan; copying; department open to the public. **Automated Operations:** Computerized public access catalog, cataloging, and circulation. **Networks/Consortia:** Member of OHIONET. **Publications:** Titles on Television, weekly - to local libraries. **Remarks:** FAX: (419)255-1334.

★ 16395 ★
Toledo-Lucas County Public Library - Local History & Genealogy Department (Hist)
325 Michigan St.   Phone: (419)259-5200
Toledo, OH 43624   James C. Marshall, Dept.Mgr.
Founded: 1941. **Staff:** Prof 5; Other 2. **Subjects:** Genealogy, local history, regional materials - Ohio, Indiana, Michigan, Illinois, Kentucky and original 13 colonies. **Special Collections:** Manuscripts dealing with local urban history (300 boxes); local picture collection (20,000 items); map collection of Ohio and Toledo area, 1800 to present (350 items); oral history interviews (200); Barbour Collection of Connecticut vital records (98 reels of microfilm); Family History Library catalog; International Genealogical Index. **Holdings:** 19,000 books; 1000 bound periodical volumes; 600 reels of microfilm; 2500 microfiche; 300 scrapbooks relating to the local area; 700 reels of microfilm of Ohio census, at ten-year intervals, 1820-1880, 1900, 1910; 800 reels of microfilm of Ohio Soundex census index, 1880, 1900, 1910; 284 reels of microfilm of Michigan census, at ten-year intervals, 1820-1880, 1900, 1910; 220 reels of microfilm of Michigan census index, 1880, 1900, 1910; 255 reels of microfilm of Kentucky census, at ten-year intervals, 1810-1880; 88 reels of microfilm of Kentucky census index, 1880; 465 reels of microfilm of Toledo Blade, 1835 to present; 381 reels of microfilm of Toledo Times, 1900-1975; Toledo City Council and Committee Minutes, 1837-1899; 41 reels of microfilm of probate court records, 1835-1966; 125 reels of microfilm of Common Pleas Civil Journals, 1835-1940; 10 reels of microfilm of birth and death records, 1858-1954; 36 reels of microfilm of city police department jail registrations, 1872-1921; 23 reels of microfilm of Lucas County naturalization records, 1853-1952. **Subscriptions:** 121 journals and other serials. **Services:** Copying; department open to the public. **Automated Operations:** Computerized public access catalog and cataloging. **Networks/Consortia:** Member of OHIONET. **Special Indexes:** Toledo Blade Obituary Index, 1837 to present; manuscript index; map index; picture index; oral history index; architectural index (all on cards); Blade computer index (1990 to present). **Remarks:** FAX: (419)243-4318.

★ 16396 ★
Toledo-Lucas County Public Library - Science and Technology Department (Sci-Engr)
325 Michigan St.   Phone: (419)259-5212
Toledo, OH 43624   Karen A. Wiggins, Dept.Mgr.
Staff: Prof 6; Other 1. **Subjects:** Physical and natural sciences, applied science and technology. **Special Collections:** Glass and glass technology (historical collection through 1975). **Holdings:** 96,417 books; depository for federal documents; 11,118 bound patent specifications, 1871-1965; patent specifications, 1966 to present, on microfilm; 15 drawers of microforms; pamphlets; clippings. **Subscriptions:** 611 journals and other serials. **Services:** Interlibrary loan; copying; department open to the public. **Automated Operations:** Computerized public access catalog, cataloging, and circulation. **Computerized Information Services:** DIALOG Information Services, BRS Information Technologies, STN International, U.S. Patent Classification System; InfoTrac; CD-ROM (Health Reference Center). **Networks/Consortia:** Member of OHIONET. **Remarks:** FAX: (419)255-1334.

★ 16397 ★
Toledo-Lucas County Public Library - Social Science Department (Soc Sci)
325 Michigan St.   Phone: (419)259-5200
Toledo, OH 43624   Jane Pinkston, Dept.Mgr.
Staff: Prof 7; Other 2. **Subjects:** Religion, law, sociology, psychology, education, philosophy. **Special Collections:** Government Documents depository; Foundation Center Depository; Library and Information Science Collection. **Holdings:** 90,000 books; 15,785 bound periodical volumes; pamphlets; maps; federal and state documents; Toledo newspapers on microfilm. **Subscriptions:** 339 journals and other serials; 59 newspapers. **Services:** Interlibrary loan; copying; department open to the public. **Automated Operations:** Computerized public access catalog and cataloging. **Computerized Information Services:** DIALOG Information Services, InfoTrac; CD-ROM. **Networks/Consortia:** Member of OHIONET. **Publications:** Beyond High School; Substance Abuse - A Pathfinder; Considering Home Schooling. **Remarks:** FAX: (419)243-4318.

★ 16398 ★
Toledo Museum of Art - Art Reference Library (Art)
Box 1013   Phone: (419)255-8000
Toledo, OH 43697   Anne O. Morris, Hd.Libn.
Founded: 1901. **Staff:** Prof 3. **Subjects:** History of art and decorative arts with special emphasis on glass, music. **Special Collections:** George W.

Stevens Collection (history of writing). **Holdings:** 41,868 books; 6111 bound periodical volumes; 9456 collection catalogs; 104 VF drawers; sales catalogs; 75 reels of microfilm; 335 microfiche. **Subscriptions:** 300 journals and other serials. **Services:** Interlibrary loan; copying; library open to the public. **Remarks:** FAX: (419)255-5638. **Staff:** Judith Friebert, Assoc.Libn.; Sharon Scott, Cat.

★ 16399 ★
Toledo Zoological Society - Library and Archives (Biol Sci)
2700 Broadway   Phone: (419)385-5721
Toledo, OH 43609   Linda Calcamuggio, Libn.
Founded: 1981. **Staff:** Prof 1. **Subjects:** Zoology, animal husbandry, endangered species, horticulture, natural history museums. **Holdings:** 1500 books; Toledo Zoo archives. **Subscriptions:** 120 journals and other serials. **Services:** Interlibrary loan; copying; library open to the public by appointment. **Remarks:** FAX: (419)385-6935.

J. Penrod Toles Learning Center
See: **New Mexico Military Institute - J. Penrod Toles Learning Center** (11522)

J.R.R. Tolkien Manuscript Collection
See: **Marquette University - Department of Special Collections and University Archives - Manuscript Collections Memorial Library** (9709)

★ 16400 ★
Tolland Genealogical Library (Hist)
Tolland Green
Box 47   Phone: (203)872-0138
Tolland, CT 06084   Prescott Libbey Brown, Chf.Libn.
Founded: 1986. **Staff:** 7. **Subjects:** Genealogy, local history. **Holdings:** 900 books; 300 pamphlets and magazines; 26 tapes. **Subscriptions:** 13 journals and other serials. **Services:** Library open to the public on a limited schedule.

Melvin B. Tolson Black Heritage Center
See: **Langston University** (8944)

Tomlinson Adult Learning Center
See: **Pinellas County School Board** (13069)

Tomlinson Library
See: **Arkansas Tech University** (1036)

★ 16401 ★
Tompkins Community Hospital - Robert Broad Medical Library (Med)
101 Dates Dr.   Phone: (607)274-4407
Ithaca, NY 14850   Sally Van Idistine, Libn.
Subjects: Surgery, medicine, nursing. **Holdings:** 500 books; 800 bound periodical volumes. **Subscriptions:** 70 journals and other serials. **Services:** Copying.

★ 16402 ★
D.A. Tompkins Memorial Library & Archives (Hist)
104 Courthouse Sq.   Phone: (803)637-4010
Edgefield, SC 29824   Diane W. Timmierman, Dir./Archv.
Founded: 1904. **Staff:** 1. **Subjects:** Antiquities of England, Ireland, Wales, and Normandy; history - American Colonial, South Carolina, Confederate. **Special Collections:** Antebellum home library of James Madison Abney. **Holdings:** 9000 volumes; Edgefield Advertiser, 1836-1902, on microfilm; 210 reels of microfilm of Edgefield County wills, probate records, equity, and guardianships. **Services:** Copying; library open to the public for reference use only. **Publications:** The Quill, monthly; Annals of Edgefield District, S.C., semiannual - both by subscription. **Staff:** Christine Hodgson.

Tompkins-McCaw Library
See: **Virginia Commonwealth University - Medical College of Virginia Campus** (19862)

★ 16403 ★
Tompkins, McGuire & Wachenfeld - Library
4 Gateway Ctr.
100 Mulberry St.   Phone: (201)622-3000
Newark, NJ 07102   Mary Beth Guenther, Libn.
Services: Library not open to the public. **Computerized Information Services:** LEXIS. **Remarks:** No further information was supplied by respondent.

★ 16404 ★
Tongass Historical Museum - Library (Area-Ethnic)
629 Dock St.   Phone: (907)225-5600
Ketchikan, AK 99901   Roxana Adams, Musm.Dir.
Founded: 1967. **Staff:** 4. **Subjects:** Alaska - forestry, mining, fishing, Indians. **Special Collections:** Ketchikan Spruce Mills manuscript collection (500 cubic feet); regional photographs of Alaskan industries and Indians (20,000). **Holdings:** 500 books; 500 cubic feet of regional archives. **Subscriptions:** 5 journals and other serials; 2 newspapers. **Services:** Copying; library open to the public for reference use only. **Computerized Information Services:** Internal database. **Remarks:** FAX: (907)225-5075. Library cooperates with Alaska State Historical Library, Pouch G, Juneau, AK 99801.

K. Ross Toole Archives
See: **University of Montana - Maureen & Mike Mansfield Library** (18987)

Toor Library
See: **Palm Springs Desert Museum - Toor Library & Hoover Natural Science Library** (12704)

★ 16405 ★
Topeka Genealogical Society Library (Hist)
Box 4048   Phone: (913)233-5762
Topeka, KS 66604-0048   Katy Matthews, Libn.
Founded: 1970. **Staff:** 21. **Subjects:** Genealogy, history. **Holdings:** 2500 books; 1800 bound periodical volumes; 520 holding boxes; Shawnee County Kansas burial records file; city directories; Kansas telephone directory; surname reference file. **Subscriptions:** 175 journals and other serials. **Services:** Copying; library open to the public with restrictions. **Publications:** Topeka Geneological Society Newsletter, quarterly; Topeka Geneological Society Quarterly Journal. **Remarks:** Library located at 2717 Indiana, Topeka, KS 66605. **Staff:** Carol Tyner, Per.Chm.

★ 16406 ★
Topeka State Hospital - Staff Library (Med)
2700 W. 6th St.   Phone: (913)296-4411
Topeka, KS 66606-1898   Laura E. Schafer, Libn.
Founded: 1950. **Staff:** Prof 1. **Subjects:** Psychiatry, psychology, psychiatric nursing, social work, chaplaincy training. **Special Collections:** Rare books and journals on the history of psychiatry (150 volumes). **Holdings:** 7000 books; 3000 bound periodical volumes. **Subscriptions:** 50 journals and other serials. **Services:** Interlibrary loan; copying (limited); library open to the public with approval of Director of Research and Education. **Networks/Consortia:** Member of National Network of Libraries of Medicine - Midcontinental Region. **Remarks:** FAX: (913)296-4289.

★ 16407 ★
Topeka Zoological Park - Zoo Library (Biol Sci)
635 Gage Blvd.   Phone: (913)272-5821
Topeka, KS 66606   Ron L. Kaufman, Zoo Educ.Coord.
Subjects: Natural history. **Holdings:** 1000 books; 60 bound periodical volumes; 70 AV programs. **Services:** Copying; library open to the public for reference use only. **Remarks:** FAX: (913)272-2539.

Helen Topping Architecture & Fine Arts Library
See: University of Southern California (19331)

★ 16408 ★
Toronto Board of Education - Education Centre Reference Library
(Educ)
155 College St.   Phone: (416)591-8183
Toronto, ON, Canada M5T 1P6   Joy Thomas, Mgr.
Founded: 1961. **Staff:** Prof 4.5; Other 10. **Subjects:** Education, psychology,
Canadian studies, literary criticism, women's studies, business, economics,
library science, science, technology. **Holdings:** 40,000 volumes; 5000 subject
vertical files; ERIC, Ontario Education Resources Information System
(ONTERIS), and MICROLOG microfiche. **Subscriptions:** 1200 journals
and other serials. **Services:** Interlibrary loan; copying; library open to the
public for reference use only. **Automated Operations:** Computerized public
access catalog. **Computerized Information Services:** DIALOG Information
Services, Info Globe, BRS Information Technologies, CAN/OLE, Infomart
Online, WILSONLINE, Refcatss, UTLAS. **Networks/Consortia:** Member
of Education Libraries Sharing of Resources Network (ELSOR).
Publications: Highlights, 3/year; Journal Contents, 3/year - for internal
distribution only. **Remarks:** FAX: (416)591-8186. **Staff:** M. Mohammed,
ILL.

★ 16409 ★
Toronto City Planning and Development Department - Library (Plan)
City Hall, 19th Fl., E.   Phone: (416)392-7185
Toronto, ON, Canada M5H 2N2   Deborah Fowler, Libn.
Founded: 1958. **Staff:** Prof 1; Other 2. **Subjects:** Urban planning, housing,
urban design, urban transportation, urban economy. **Special Collections:**
Staff reports (microfiche). **Holdings:** 7500 books. **Subscriptions:** 300 journals
and other serials. **Services:** Library open to the public for the use of staff
reports. **Publications:** Bibliography of Major Planning Publications.
Remarks: FAX: (416)392-0797.

★ 16410 ★
Toronto Dominion Bank - Department of Economic Research - Library
(Bus-Fin)
55 King St., W.   Phone: (416)982-8068
Toronto, ON, Canada M5K 1A2   Ann MacLeod, Libn.
Founded: 1960. **Staff:** Prof 1; Other 2. **Subjects:** Banking, finance,
economics, trade, industry. **Holdings:** 7000 books; 3000 pamphlets; 28 VF
drawers of weekly and monthly letters from financial institutions,
associations, and government; 16 VF drawers, 4 drawers of microfiche, and
900 pamphlet boxes of Statistics Canada publications; 250 pamphlet boxes
of annual reports from companies and banks. **Subscriptions:** 700 journals
and other serials; 23 newspapers. **Services:** Interlibrary loan; library open
to the public with librarian's permission. **Automated Operations:**
Computerized cataloging, acquisitions, and serials. **Computerized
Information Services:** Info Globe, DIALOG Information Services, Infomart
Online, Reuters; CD-ROMs (Disclosure Incorporated, Moody's Company
Data). **Publications:** Recent Additions to the Library, bimonthly - for
internal distribution only. **Remarks:** FAX: (416)982-6884. Telex: 06524267.

★ 16411 ★
**Toronto East General and Orthopaedic Hospital Inc. - Health Sciences
Library** (Med)
825 Coxwell Ave.   Phone: (416)469-6011
Toronto, ON, Canada M4C 3E7   Glenda West, Libn.
Founded: 1960. **Staff:** Prof 1; Other 1. **Subjects:** Medicine, nursing, allied
health sciences. **Special Collections:** History of medicine collection.
Holdings: 1750 books. **Subscriptions:** 175 journals and other serials.
Services: Interlibrary loan. **Computerized Information Services:**
MEDLARS, BRS Information Technologies. **Remarks:** FAX: (416)469-
6106.

★ 16412 ★
Toronto General Hospital - Fudger Medical Library (Med)
200 Elizabeth St.   Phone: (416)595-3429
Toronto, ON, Canada M5G 2C4   Jennifer Bayne, Chf.Libn.
Founded: 1964. **Staff:** Prof 1; Other 6. **Subjects:** Cardiovascular surgery,
obstetrics and gynecology, psychiatry, dermatology, neurosurgery, family
and community medicine. **Special Collections:** Drs. Brock, Delarue, and
Morley Collections (neurosurgery; 1000 volumes). **Holdings:** 8000 books;
15,000 bound periodical volumes; cassettes; tapes. **Subscriptions:** 472
journals and other serials. **Services:** Interlibrary loan; copying; SDI; library
open to the public by contacting chief librarian. **Publications:** Fudger
Medical Library (flyer) - available on request; bibliographies. **Remarks:**
FAX: (416)595-7005.

★ 16413 ★
Toronto Globe and Mail, Ltd. - Library (Publ)
444 Front St., W.   Phone: (416)585-5075
Toronto, ON, Canada M5V 2S9   Amanda Valpy, Chf.Libn.
Staff: Prof 6; Other 7. **Subjects:** Newspaper reference topics. **Holdings:** 8000
books; 7 million newspaper clippings; 1 million photographs; 40 VF drawers
of pamphlets; 5 million clippings on microfiche; 1500 reels of microfilm of
The Globe and Mail; 200,000 photographic negatives. **Subscriptions:** 200
journals and other serials; 20 newspapers. **Services:** Interlibrary loan; library
not open to the public. **Computerized Information Services:** DIALOG
Information Services, Dow Jones News/Retrieval, TEXTLINE, STM
Systems Corporation, PROFILE, Mead Data Central, Infomart Online,
Info Globe. **Special Indexes:** Index to negatives (online). **Staff:** Celia
Donnelly, Asst.Libn.

Toronto Harbour Commissioners - World Trade Centre Toronto
See: World Trade Centre Toronto (20631)

Toronto Jewish Congress - Albert J. Latner Jewish Public Library
See: Albert J. Latner Jewish Public Library (8970)

★ 16414 ★
Toronto Public Library - Canadiana Collection of Children's Books
(Hum)
Boys and Girls House
40 St. George St.   Phone: (416)393-7753
Toronto, ON, Canada M5S 2E4   Margaret Crawford Maloney, Hd.
Staff: Prof 3; Other 3. **Subjects:** Children's literature written or illustrated
by Canadians, about Canadians, or bearing a Canadian imprint. **Holdings:**
6000 books; 75 bound periodical volumes; manuscripts; original art.
Services: Copying (limited); collection open to the public for research use
only. **Special Indexes:** Chronological index; illustrators and engravers index;
publishers, booksellers, and printers index (all on cards). **Remarks:** FAX:
(416)393-7635. **Staff:** Jill Shefrin, Libn.; Dana Tenny, Libn.

★ 16415 ★
Toronto Public Library - Lillian H. Smith Collection of Children's
Books (Hum)
Boys and Girls House
40 St. George St.   Phone: (416)393-7753
Toronto, ON, Canada M5S 2E4   Margaret Crawford Maloney, Hd.
Founded: 1962. **Staff:** Prof 3; Other 3. **Subjects:** Children's literature in
English, 1910 to present. **Holdings:** 6500 books; manuscripts; original art.
Services: Copying (limited); collection open to the public for research use
only. **Special Indexes:** Chronological index; illustrators index; publishers
and printers index (all on cards). **Remarks:** Books in this collection represent
a qualitative selection of twentieth century publications. FAX: (416)393-
7635. **Staff:** Jill Shefrin, Libn.; Dana Tenny, Libn.

★ 16416 ★
Toronto Public Library - Marguerite G. Bagshaw Collection (Theater)
Boys and Girls House
40 St. George St.   Phone: (416)393-7746
Toronto, ON, Canada M5S 2E4   Mary Anne Cree, Br.Hd.
Founded: 1973. **Staff:** Prof 2; Other 1. **Subjects:** Puppetry, storytelling,
creative drama, mime. **Holdings:** 1089 books; 65 sets of puppets; 35 posters
on puppets; 12 toy theaters; 50 puppetry scripts; 40 display puppets; 64 VF
drawers; 145 AV items. **Subscriptions:** 2 journals and other serials. **Services:**
Interlibrary loan; copying; collection open to the public for reference use
only. **Remarks:** FAX: (416)393-7635. **Staff:** Joanne Schott, Subject Spec.

★ 16417 ★
Toronto Public Library - Merril Collection of Science Fiction,
Speculation and Fantasy (Hum, Rec)
40 St. George St.   Phone: (416)393-7748
Toronto, ON, Canada M5S 2E4   Lorna Toolis, Coll.Hd.
Founded: 1970. **Staff:** Prof 2; Other 1. **Subjects:** Speculative fiction - science
fiction, fantasy, and magic realism. **Special Collections:** Specialty publishers
collection, including Arkham House and Ace Double series, Cheap Street,
Morrigan, Axlotl, Carcosa House, Kerosina, NESFA, Gnome, Shasta and
Fantasy Press; Jules Verne Collection; UFO collection; multilingual
collection (primarily French, German, and Dutch, with Eastern European
and other languages). **Holdings:** 25,461 books; 17,627 periodicals; 1500
fanzine titles; 300 vertical file folders; 350 audio recordings; 40 fantasy
games; 150 videotapes. **Subscriptions:** 90 journals and other serials.
Services: Copying; main collection open to the public for reference use only.
Publications: Sol Rising, semiannual - to members. **Remarks:** Alternate
telephone number(s): 393-7749. FAX: (416)393-7635. **Staff:** Annette
Mocek, AV Libn.; Mary Cannings, Lib.Asst.

★ 16418 ★
Toronto Public Library - Osborne Collection of Early Children's Books
(Rare Book)
Boys and Girls House
40 St. George St.
Toronto, ON, Canada M5S 2E4   Margaret Crawford Maloney, Hd.
Founded: 1949. **Staff:** Prof 3; Other 3. **Subjects:** English children's literature, 14th century-1910; printing; book illustration; folklore; education; original art. **Special Collections:** Jean Thomson Collection of Original Art; Taylors of Ongar Collection; Queen Mary's Collection of Children's Books; Florence Nightingale Collection; G. A. Henty Collection. **Holdings:** 27,000 books; 800 bound periodical volumes; manuscripts; 1600 original pictures; engraved wood blocks. **Subscriptions:** 35 journals and other serials. **Services:** Copying (limited); collection open to the public for research use only. **Special Catalogs:** Osborne Collection of Early Children's Books: A Catalogue (2 volumes, 1975); selected exhibition catalogs. **Special Indexes:** Chronological index (book and card); illustrators and engravers index (book and card); publishers, booksellers, and printers index (book and card). **Remarks:** FAX: (416)393-7635. Facsimiles of Osborne Collection books and lecture series are available. **Staff:** Jill Shefrin, Libn.; Dana Tenny, Libn.

★ 16419 ★
Toronto Star Newspapers Ltd. - Library (Publ)
One Yonge St.   Phone: (416)869-4490
Toronto, ON, Canada M5E 1E6   Carol Lindsay, Chf.Libn.
Founded: 1923. **Staff:** Prof 4; Other 9. **Subjects:** Newspaper reference topics. **Special Collections:** Clipping files on subjects and personalities in the news; database of Toronto Star stories since 1986. **Holdings:** 3000 books; 400,000 photographs; reports; government documents. **Subscriptions:** 50 journals and other serials; 8 newspapers. **Services:** Library not open to the public. **Computerized Information Services:** Info Globe, VU/TEXT Information Services, Infomart Online, LEXIS, NEXIS, The Financial Post DataGroup; internal database. **Remarks:** FAX: (416)869-4416. Telex: 065 24387.

★ 16420 ★
Toronto Stock Exchange - Information Resource Centre (Bus-Fin)
The Exchange Tower
2 First Canadian Place, 3rd Fl.   Phone: (416)947-4653
Toronto, ON, Canada M5X 1J2   Mary Hum, Mgr.
Founded: 1939. **Staff:** 1. **Subjects:** Stock exchanges, securities industry, investment, economics, finance. **Special Collections:** Stock exchange publications (Toronto, Canadian, U.S., and others); Toronto Stock Exchange archives. **Holdings:** 2000 books; 2000 unbound reports, speeches, and leaflets; 7 drawers of clippings. **Subscriptions:** 300 journals and other serials; 11 newspapers. **Services:** Interlibrary loan. **Automated Operations:** Computerized cataloging, serials, and acquisitions. **Computerized Information Services:** DIALOG Information Services, Mead Data Central, Dow Jones News/Retrieval, QL Systems, Info Globe, Canada Systems Group (CSG), The Financial Post DataGroup, Infomart Online, CAN/LAW. **Publications:** Information Exchange, bimonthly - both for internal distribution only. **Remarks:** FAX: (416)947-4662. **Staff:** Shonna Fimrite, Sr.Info.Spec.;

★ 16421 ★
Toronto Sun Publishing Company - Library (Publ)
333 King St., E.   Phone: (416)947-2257
Toronto, ON, Canada M5A 3X5   Julie Kirsh, Chf.Libn.
Staff: Prof 1; Other 8. **Subjects:** Newspaper reference topics. **Holdings:** 200 books; newspaper clippings; Toronto Sun, 1971 to present, on microfilm; Toronto Telegram, 1887-1971, on microfilm. **Subscriptions:** 100 journals and other serials; 20 newspapers. **Services:** Library open to the public by appointment for a fee. **Automated Operations:** Computerized cataloging, acquisitions, and serials. **Computerized Information Services:** Info Globe, Infomart Online, DIALOG Information Services, VU/TEXT Information Services, NEXIS, LEXIS; internal database. **Remarks:** Staff will research questions submitted by mail, on a fee basis.

★ 16422 ★
Toronto Transit Commission - Engineering & Maintenance Library (Sci-Engr, Trans)
1910 Yonge St.   Phone: (416)393-4070
Toronto, ON, Canada M4S 3B2   Gerie N. Singh, Libn.
Staff: Prof 1. **Subjects:** Transportation, construction, design. **Holdings:** 3900 books; standards from the American Society for Testing and Materials, Canadian Standards Association, and Canadian Government Specifications Board. **Subscriptions:** 49 journals and other serials. **Services:** Library open to the public with restrictions. **Formerly:** Its Engineering & Construction Library.

★ 16423 ★
Toronto Transit Commission - Head Office Library (Trans)
1900 Yonge St.   Phone: (416)481-4252
Toronto, ON, Canada M4S 1Z2   Adrian Gehring, Lib.Techn.
Staff: Prof 1. **Subjects:** Transportation. **Special Collections:** Photograph collection; archival collection. **Holdings:** 3000 books. **Subscriptions:** 60 journals and other serials. **Services:** Library not open to the public. **Remarks:** FAX: (416)485-9394.

★ 16424 ★
Toronto Western Hospital - R.C. Laird Health Sciences Library (Med)
399 Bathurst St.   Phone: (416)369-5750
Toronto, ON, Canada M5T 2S8   Elizabeth A. Reid, Dir.
Founded: 1961. **Staff:** Prof 2; Other 6. **Subjects:** Medicine. **Holdings:** 2000 books; 10,000 bound periodical volumes. **Subscriptions:** 375 journals and other serials. **Services:** Interlibrary loan; library not open to the public. **Computerized Information Services:** MEDLARS, CAN/OLE, UTLAS, FELIX, DIALOG Information Services; Envoy 100 (electronic mail service). **Publications:** Acquisitions list - for internal distribution only. **Remarks:** FAX: (416)369-5326. Electronic mail address(es): OTTWH.LIB (Envoy 100).

★ 16425 ★
Torrance Memorial Medical Center - Medical Library (Med)
3330 W. Lomita Blvd.   Phone: (213)517-4720
Torrance, CA 90505   Anita N. Klecker, Med.Libn.
Founded: 1972. **Staff:** Prof 1; Other 1. **Subjects:** Medicine, surgery, cardiology, pediatrics, nursing, psychiatry, oncology. **Holdings:** 433 books; 27 videotapes. **Subscriptions:** 116 journals and other serials. **Services:** Interlibrary loan; copying; SDI; library open to health care professionals and students only. **Computerized Information Services:** MEDLARS, DIALOG Information Services. Performs searches on fee basis. **Networks/Consortia:** Member of National Network of Libraries of Medicine - Pacific Southwest Region. **Remarks:** FAX: (213)784-4816.

★ 16426 ★
(Torreon) Instituto Mexicano-Norteamericano de Relaciones Culturales - USIS Collection (Educ)
Rodriguez No. 351 Sur, 40 Piso
27000 Torreon, Coahuila, Mexico
Remarks: Maintained or supported by the U.S. Information Agency. Focus is on materials that will assist peoples outside the United States to learn about the United States, its people, history, culture, political processes, and social milieux.

Torreyson Library - Children's Literature Collection
See: University of Central Arkansas (18445)

★ 16427 ★
Torrington Community Hospital - Medical Library (Med)
2000 Campbell Dr.   Phone: (307)532-4181
Torrington, WY 82240   Kimberly Bingham, Info.Techn.
Founded: 1978. **Staff:** Prof 1. **Subjects:** Medicine, nursing, patient care. **Holdings:** 150 books. **Subscriptions:** 25 journals and other serials. **Services:** Interlibrary loan; copying; library open to medical professionals and students. **Remarks:** FAX: (307)532-4181, ext. 135. Maintained by Lutheran Hospitals and Homes.

★ 16428 ★
Torrington Historical Society, Inc. - John H. Thompson Memorial Library (Hist)
192 Main St.   Phone: (203)482-8260
Torrington, CT 06790   Mark McEachern, Exec.Dir.
Founded: 1944. **Staff:** Prof 2. **Subjects:** History - Torrington, Litchfield County, Connecticut. **Special Collections:** Connecticut Journal, 1782-1813; Litchfield Monitor, 1791-1795; Litchfield Enquirer, 1842-1941. **Holdings:** 5000 volumes; 200 boxes of microfilm; 8 file drawers containing 2500 newspapers; 800 sets of local architectural drawings. **Services:** Copying; library open to the public for reference use only. **Staff:** Gail Houck, Cur.

Tort Liability Research Library
See: Defense Research Institute, Inc. - Brief Bank (4703)

★ 16429 ★
Tory Tory Deslauriers & Binnington - Library (Law)
IBM Tower, 31st Fl.
Toronto Dominion Centre
P.O. Box 270   Phone: (416)865-7532
Toronto, ON, Canada M5K 1N2   Janet E. Macdonald, Mgr., Lib.Serv.
Staff: Prof 3; Other 3.5. **Subjects:** Canadian law. **Holdings:** 1500 books; 1500 bound periodical volumes; 5000 bound volumes of law reports. **Subscriptions:** 200 journals; 90 law reports; 10 newspapers. **Services:** Interlibrary loan; copying; SDI; library open to the public by appointment. **Computerized Information Services:** QL Systems, Info Globe, DIALOG Information Services, Canadian Tax Online, LEXIS, NEXIS, Infomart Online, CBANET, CAN/LAW, The Financial Post Information Service, INSIGHT, Dunsdata, Dow Jones News/Retrieval; internal database; Envoy 100, QUICKMAIL, DIALMAIL (electronic mail services). Performs searches on fee basis. **Remarks:** FAX: (416)865-7380. Electronic mail address(es): TORY.TORY (Envoy 100); Box 53 (QUICKMAIL). **Staff:** Mary Almey, Ref.Libn.; Margaret Bryan, Asst.Libn.

Toscanini Memorial Archives
See: New York Public Library for the Performing Arts - Music Division (11637)

★ 16430 ★
Total Petroleum Canada Ltd. - Library (Sci-Engr)
639 5th Ave., S.W., 6th Fl.   Phone: (403)267-3000
Calgary, AB, Canada T2P 0M9   Cheryl Fishleigh, Libn.
Staff: Prof 1. **Subjects:** Geology, geophysics, petroleum engineering, business management. **Special Collections:** Annual reports from different companies (200). **Holdings:** 4000 books; 100 bound periodical volumes; 1000 government documents; 50 research reports; 75 theses. **Subscriptions:** 200 journals and other serials. **Services:** Interlibrary loan; library open to the public by request. **Computerized Information Services:** ORBIT Search Service. **Publications:** News Letter, bimonthly - for internal distribution only. **Remarks:** FAX: (403)267-3006.

★ 16431 ★
Totem Heritage Center (Area-Ethnic)
c/o 629 Dock St.   Phone: (907)225-5900
Ketchikan, AK 99901   Roxana Adams, Musm.Dir.
Founded: 1976. **Staff:** Prof 3. **Subjects:** Northwest Coast Indian art, culture, and history. **Special Collections:** Northwest Coast totem poles (31). **Holdings:** 500 books; 150 bound periodical volumes; 2500 photographs; 50 manuscripts. **Subscriptions:** 3 journals and other serials. **Services:** Copying; center open to the public for reference use only. **Computerized Information Services:** Internal database. **Remarks:** FAX: (907)225-5075. Maintained by the City of Ketchikan Museum Department.

★ 16432 ★
Tottori University - Medical Library (Med)
86 Nishi cho
Yonago 683, Tottori, Japan   Phone: 859 331111
                 Prof. Tadao Itoh, D.M.Sc.
Founded: 1945. **Staff:** Prof 4; Other 7. **Subjects:** Medicine. **Holdings:** 47,000 books; 96,000 bound periodical volumes; 280 videotapes and compact discs. **Subscriptions:** 1449 journals and other serials; 13 newspapers. **Services:** Interlibrary loan; copying; library open to researchers and students in the field of medicine and related areas. **Computerized Information Services:** DIALOG Information Services, JOIS; internal databases; CD-ROM (MEDLINE). Contact Person: Tsutomu Shinji, Chf. of Lib.Serv. **Publications:** Contents sheets, weekly; bibliographic data on books with a list of special themes of Japanese journals, semimonthly. **Remarks:** FAX: 859 348079.

Sam Tour Library
See: American Standards Testing Bureau, Inc. (766)

Tourism Reference and Documentation Centre
See: Canada - Department of Industry, Science & Technology (2688)

★ 16433 ★
Touro College - Jacob D. Fuchsberg Law Center - Touro Law Center Library (Law)
300 Nassau Rd.   Phone: (516)421-2244
Huntington, NY 11743   Daniel P. Jordan, Jr., Hd.Law Libn.
Founded: 1980. **Staff:** 22.5. **Subjects:** Law, Jewish law. **Holdings:** 128,000 books; 1100 bound periodical titles; 110,000 nonbook items; 800 audiovisual programs. **Subscriptions:** 3300 journals and other serials; 20 newspapers. **Services:** Interlibrary loan; copying; library open to attorneys with a visitor pass or law students with proper identification. **Computerized Information Services:** LEXIS, WESTLAW, DIALOG Information Services. **Publications:** Judaica bibliography. **Remarks:** Alternate telephone number(s): (516)421-2320. FAX: (516)421-2675. **Staff:** Lois Markowitz; Beth Mobley; Susan Goss; Marsha Freeman; Marge Hudson.

★ 16434 ★
Touro Infirmary - Hospital Library Services (Med)
1401 Foucher St., 10th Fl., M Bldg.   Phone: (504)897-8102
New Orleans, LA 70115   Patricia J. Greenfield, Lib.Mgr.
Founded: 1947. **Staff:** Prof 1. **Subjects:** Clinical medicine, nursing. **Special Collections:** Elsie Waldhorn Cohn Memorial Collection (medical history); Jonas Rosenthal Memorial Ophthalmology Collection. **Holdings:** 2000 books; 5000 bound periodical volumes; 300 videotapes; 100 Audio-Digest tapes. **Subscriptions:** 200 journals and other serials. **Services:** Interlibrary loan; copying. **Automated Operations:** Computerized acquisitions. **Computerized Information Services:** NLM, BRS Information Technologies. **Networks/Consortia:** Member of National Network of Libraries of Medicine - South Central Region, New Orleans Area Health Science Libraries. **Remarks:** FAX: (504)897-8322.

★ 16435 ★
Tousimis Research Corporation, Inc. - Biodynamics Laboratory - Library (Biol Sci)
2211 Lewis Ave.
Box 2189
Rockville, MD 20847   Phone: (301)881-2450
                 Callie Thomas, Libn.
Subjects: Biomedical sciences, materials research, ultrastructure, microanalysis. **Holdings:** 10,000 volumes; 65,000 reprints. **Remarks:** Telex: 287296 (UR).

★ 16436 ★
Towers Perrin - Corporate Information Center (Bus-Fin)
100 Summit Lake Dr.   Phone: (914)745-4500
Valhalla, NY 10595   Jack Borbely, Dir., Info.Serv.
Founded: 1925. **Staff:** Prof 10; Other 9. **Subjects:** Compensation, retirement/pensions, employee benefits, U.S. companies and industries, international business, insurance. **Holdings:** 3000 books; 125 VF drawers of clippings, reports, pamphlets; company annual reports and proxy statements on microfiche. **Subscriptions:** 600 journals and other serials. **Services:** Interlibrary loan; copying; center open to SLA members by appointment. **Computerized Information Services:** DIALOG Information Services, LEXIS, NEXIS, INVESTEXT, VU/TEXT Information Services, BRS Information Technologies, Human Resource Information Network (HRIN), NewsNet, Inc., DataTimes, Dow Jones News/Retrieval, TEXTLINE. **Remarks:** FAX: (914)745-4555. **Staff:** Gail Leslie, Info.Spec.; Helen Garvey, Info.Spec.; Evy Frankel, Info.Spec.; Leslie Tobias, Info.Spec.; Julia Blanchard, Info.Spec.; Linda Panovich-Sachs, Info.Spec.; Nancy Audino, Supv., Sys.; Anne Ross, Supv., Corp.Info.Ctr.; Amy Scowen Walsh, Supv., Sys.Trng. and Sup.; Elizabeth Siracusa, Index Spec.

★ 16437 ★
Towers Perrin - Cresap - Library (Bus-Fin)
200 W. Madison   Phone: (312)609-9501
Chicago, IL 60606-3417   Janean Bowersmith, Res.Mgr.
Founded: 1975. **Staff:** Prof 1. **Subjects:** Business and industry. **Holdings:** 500 books; 1200 annual reports. **Subscriptions:** 50 journals and other serials. **Services:** Interlibrary loan; copying (limited). **Computerized Information Services:** DIALOG Information Services, DataTimes, VU/TEXT Information Services, Investext. **Networks/Consortia:** Member of Chicago Library System. **Remarks:** FAX: (312)609-9406. **Formerly:** Cresap - Library.

★ 16438 ★
Towers Perrin Co. - Cresap Library (Bus-Fin)
333 Bush St.   Phone: (415)773-3053
San Francisco, CA 94104   Victoria A. Barbero, Libn.
Staff: Prof 1; Other 1. **Subjects:** Business, management, human resources, strategy, utilities, communication. **Special Collections:** Actuarial library. **Holdings:** 200 books. **Subscriptions:** 54 journals and other serials. **Services:** Library open to SLA members. **Remarks:** FAX: (415)773-3071. **Formerly:** Cresap - Library.

Towers Perrin Co. - TPF & C
See: **TPF & C, Ltd.** (16442)

★ 16439 ★
Townley & Updike - Law Library (Law)
405 Lexington Ave.   Phone: (212)973-6050
New York, NY 10174   John S. Kostecky, Hd.Libn.
Staff: Prof 1; Other 2. **Subjects:** Law - labor, product liability, bankruptcy, securities, patent, trademark and copyright. **Holdings:** 15,000 volumes. **Subscriptions:** 60 journals and other serials; 10 newspapers. **Services:** Interlibrary loan; library not open to the public. **Computerized Information Services:** LEXIS, WESTLAW, DIALOG Information Services, Dow Jones News/Retrieval, DataTimes, LEGI-SLATE, NEXIS. **Remarks:** FAX: (212)370-1645; (212)370-1348.

John Wilson Townsend Room
See: **Eastern Kentucky University - John Grant Crabbe Library** (5147)

Townsend Memorial Library
See: **University of Mary Hardin-Baylor** (18797)

★ 16440 ★
Towson State University - Gerhardt Library of Musical Information (Mus)
Towson State University   Phone: (301)321-2839
Towson, MD 21204   Edwin L. Gerhardt, Cur.
Staff: Prof 2. **Subjects:** Music literature. **Special Collections:** Thomas A. Edison and the phonograph; John Philip Sousa and bands. **Holdings:** Figures not available for books; phonograph records; pictures; artifacts. **Services:** Copying, library open to the public by appointment. **Remarks:** Library does not have a collection of scores or manuscripts. Direct all library correspondence to Edwin L. Gerhardt, 4926 Leeds Ave., Baltimore, MD 21227. Phone: (301)242-0328. **Staff:** Dale E. Rauschenberg, Coord.

★ 16441 ★
Towson State University - Gerhardt Marimba & Xylophone Collection (Mus)
Towson State University   Phone: (410)830-2000
Towson, MD 21204   Dale Rauschenberg, Cur.
Founded: 1924. **Staff:** Prof 2. **Subjects:** Marimbas and xylophones. **Holdings:** Figures not available for books; VF drawers of materials on assorted marimbas, xylophones, and artifacts. **Services:** Copying; colllection open to the public by appointment. **Remarks:** The collection is a unique and comprehensive accumulation of marimba and xylophone lore. It includes literature, phonograph recordings, tape recordings, catalogs, music, methods, pictures, correspondence, miscellaneous information. It is not a collection of instruments. Direct all library correspondence to Edwin L. Gerhardt, 4926 Leeds Ave., Baltimore, MD 21227. Phone: (410)242-0328.

Harold S. Toy, M.D. Memorial Health Science Library
See: **Santa Rosa Health Care** (14818)

Tozzer Library
See: **Harvard University** (6999)

★ 16442 ★
TPF & C, Ltd. - Information Centre (Bus-Fin)
250 Bloor St., E., Suite 1100   Phone: (416)960-2600
Toronto, ON, Canada M4W 3N3 Rosemary Lindsay, Supv. of Info.Serv.
Founded: 1978. **Staff:** Prof 5; Other 2. **Subjects:** Employee benefits, compensation, communications, human resource management and information systems, insurance, management consulting, risk management. **Holdings:** 1700 books; 140 salary surveys; 540 Conference Board publications; 1000 annual reports; 750 vertical files; 10,000 internal reports on microfiche. **Subscriptions:** 350 journals and other serials. **Services:** Interlibrary loan; center not open to the public. **Automated Operations:** Computerized cataloging and serials. **Computerized Information Services:** DIALOG Information Services, Info Globe, Infomart Online, Reuters, Publinet Data Base, Mead Data Central; internal databases. **Publications:** Communique, weekly - for internal distribution only. **Special Indexes:** Index to internal reports (online). **Remarks:** FAX: (416)960-2819. TPF & C is an operating unit of Towers Perrin Co. **Staff:** Cathy Kiedrowski, Info.Serv.Spec.; Lorraine Flanigan, Info.Serv.Spec.; Maggie Fox, Info.Serv.Spec.; Karen Shirely, Info.Serv.Spec.

★ 16443 ★
TPF & C, Ltd. - Information Centre (Bus-Fin)
1800 McGill College Ave., 2nd Fl.   Phone: (514)982-2172
Montreal, PQ, Canada H3A 3J6   Dawn H. Chipps, Info.Spec.
Founded: 1976. **Staff:** Prof 2; Other 1. **Subjects:** Employee benefits, compensation, actuarial science, taxation, labor, social security, employee communications, insurance, human resource management. **Holdings:** 2000 books; 100 internal reports; 40 VF drawers of pamphlets and clippings; 1000 microfiche; AV materials. **Subscriptions:** 100 journals and other serials; 8 newspapers. **Services:** Center not open to the public. **Automated Operations:** Computerized cataloging and routing. **Publications:** Communique, weekly - for internal distribution only. **Special Indexes:** Internal reports index (computerized). **Remarks:** FAX: (514)982-9269. TPF & C is an operating unit of Towers Perrin Co. **Staff:** Monique Chaput, Info.Spec.

★ 16444 ★
TRA Architecture Engineering Planning Interiors - Library (Plan)
215 Columbia   Phone: (206)682-1133
Seattle, WA 98104   Dan Trefethen, Info.Mgr.
Founded: 1979. **Staff:** Prof 1; Other 1. **Subjects:** Architecture, engineering, airport planning and design, interior design, planning, graphic design. **Special Collections:** Airport/Aircraft Data File (4 VF drawers). **Holdings:** 1500 books; 2000 reports; 2000 manufacturer's product catalogs; 10,000 slides. **Subscriptions:** 154 journals and other serials. **Services:** Interlibrary loan; library not open to the public. **Computerized Information Services:** DIALOG Information Services. **Remarks:** FAX: (206)621-8782.

★ 16445 ★
Tracor Technology Resources, Inc. - Research Resources Information Center (Biol Sci)
1601 Research Blvd.   Phone: (301)251-4970
Rockville, MD 20850-3191   Ole Henriksen, Ph.D
Founded: 1976. **Staff:** Prof 5; Other 2. **Subjects:** Research - biomedical, animal, biotechnological, clinical. **Holdings:** Figures not available. **Services:** Center not open to the public. **Computerized Information Services:** Research Resources Reporter (internal database). **Publications:** Research Resources Reporter, monthly; research resources directories, annual; National Center for Research Resources Program Highlights, annual. **Special Indexes:** Research Resources Reporter Index, annual. **Remarks:** FAX: (301)251-4917. Maintained by U.S. National Institutes of Health - National Center for Research Resources. **Staff:** Jane Collins, Sci. Correspondent; J. Langsam, Sci.Correspondent.

★ 16446 ★
Tracy-Locke Advertising - Information Services Department (Bus-Fin)
200 Crescent Ct., Suite 900   Phone: (214)969-9000
Dallas, TX 75201   Susan Elam, Mgr., Info.Serv.
Founded: 1967. **Staff:** Prof 3; Other 1. **Subjects:** Advertising, marketing, consumer products. **Holdings:** 2000 books, research reports, directories; 2 VF drawers of clippings on Texas subjects; 40 VF drawers of data on various industries and products. **Subscriptions:** 250 journals and other serials. **Services:** Interlibrary loan; copying; department open to the public by appointment. **Automated Operations:** Computerized routing. **Computerized Information Services:** DIALOG Information Services, Dow Jones News/Retrieval, NEXIS, Dun & Bradstreet Business Credit Services, VU/TEXT Information Services, DataTimes, InvesText, MAID. **Remarks:** FAX: (214)855-2258. **Staff:** Libba Reid, Info.Spec.; Cheryl Martin, Tech.Serv.Asst.

★ 16447 ★
Trade Relations Council of the United States - Library (Bus-Fin)
1 Church St., Suite 601   Phone: (202)785-4194
Rockville, MD 20850   Eugene L. Stewart, Exec.Sec.
Subjects: Import/export trade, tariff, and allied subjects for the U.S., Japan, Taiwan, European Economic Community (EEC), Korea, and Canada. **Holdings:** Figures not available. **Services:** Library not open to the public. **Computerized Information Services:** Internal database. Performs searches on fee basis. Contact Person: Timothy Stewart, Pres., 785-4194. **Remarks:** FAX: (202)785-4188.

★ 16448 ★
Traffic Injury Research Foundation of Canada (TIRF) - Library (Med)
171 Nepean St., 6th Fl.
Ottawa, ON, Canada K2P 0B4   Phone: (613)238-5235
Staff: Prof 9; Other 2. **Subjects:** Road safety - behavioral, medical, pharmacological, statistical. **Holdings:** 800 books; 100 bound periodical volumes; 4500 technical reports, statistics reports, government publications, newsletters. **Subscriptions:** 53 journals and other serials. **Services:** Interlibrary loan; copying; center open to the public. **Computerized Information Services:** Traffic Fatality Database (internal database). **Publications:** Newsletter, quarterly. **Remarks:** FAX: (613)238-5292.

Trailside Nature Museum
See: **Westchester County Department of Parks, Recreation and Conservation** (20228)

★ 16449 ★
Train Collectors Association - Toy Train Reference Library (Rec)
Paradise Lane
Box 248   Phone: (717)687-8623
Strasburg, PA 17579   Patricia Baltadonis, Lib.Ck.
Founded: 1982. **Staff:** Prof 1; Other 3. **Subjects:** Toy and model trains. **Special Collections:** Manufacturer catalogs (2000); toy/model train serial publications (7200 issues of 200 titles). **Holdings:** 900 books; 95 bound periodical volumes; annual reports. **Subscriptions:** 27 journals and other serials. **Services:** Copying; library open to the public by appointment for reference use only. **Remarks:** FAX: (717)687-0742.

★ 16450 ★
Tranet - Library (Soc Sci)
Box 567   Phone: (207)864-2252
Rangeley, ME 04970   William N. Ellis, Exec.Dir.
Founded: 1976. **Staff:** 4. **Subjects:** Appropriate technology, alternative energy, alternative economics, social humanism, new ruralism. **Holdings:** 2000 books; 900 unbound magazines; 200 reports; 200 papers. **Subscriptions:** 50 journals and other serials. **Services:** Library open to the public. **Publications:** Tranet, bimonthly - to members.

★ 16451 ★
Trans Canada Pipelines Ltd. - Library (Energy)
27th Fl.
P.O. Box 1000, Sta. M   Phone: (403)267-6498
Calgary, AB, Canada T2P 4K5   Zaytoon Janjua, Supv., Lib.Serv.
Founded: 1957. **Staff:** Prof 2; Other 2. **Subjects:** Energy, pipelines, transmission, law. **Holdings:** 10,000 books. **Subscriptions:** 850 journals and other serials; 10 newspapers. **Services:** Interlibrary loan; copying; library open to the public with restrictions. **Automated Operations:** Computerized cataloging, acquisitions, serials, and circulation. **Computerized Information Services:** DIALOG Information Services, PFDS Online, QL Systems, Info Globe, Reuters Information Services (Canada) Limited, Infomart Online, Daily Oil Bulletin; A.G.A. GasNet, Envoy 100 (electronic mail services). **Publications:** New Books in the Library, monthly - for internal distribution only. **Remarks:** FAX: (403)267-6266. Electronic mail address(es): ILL.TCPLILL (Envoy 100). **Staff:** Rose Gruber, Libn.

★ 16452 ★
Trans Data Corporation - Library (Bus-Fin)
P.O. Box 39   Phone: (215)341-9650
Wayne, PA 19087-0039   Denise Moretti, III, Database Mgr.
Subjects: Financial services industry, retail finance, corporate banking. **Holdings:** Periodicals; reports. **Computerized Information Services:** Internal databases. **Remarks:** Toll-free telephone number(s): (800)456-3282. Parent organization is American Banker, Inc. (New York, NY). **Formerly:** Located in Salisbury, MD.

★ 16453 ★
Trans Mountain Pipe Line Company, Ltd. - Library (Energy)
1333 W. Broadway, Suite 900   Phone: (604)876-6711
Vancouver, BC, Canada V6H 4C2   S. O'Driscoll, Supv., Adm.Serv.
Subjects: Pipeline and oil industries, general collection. **Holdings:** 20,000 books; 200 bound periodical volumes; 20 AV programs. **Services:** Interlibrary loan; copying; library open to the public at librarian's discretion. **Computerized Information Services:** DIALOG Information Services, Info Globe, CAN/OLE. **Remarks:** FAX: (604)876-3911. Telex: 04-54301.

★ 16454 ★
Trans World Airlines, Inc. - Corporate Library (Trans)
110 S. Bedford Rd.   Phone: (914)242-3117
Mount Kisco, NY 10549   John Rossi, Dir.Adm.
Founded: 1965. **Staff:** Prof 1. **Subjects:** Air transportation. **Holdings:** 7000 books and bound periodical volumes; 1100 pamphlets; 7 VF drawers of annual reports; 350 volumes of company reports; travel surveys. **Subscriptions:** 210 journals and other serials. **Services:** Interlibrary loan; copying; library open to the public for reference use only on request. **Remarks:** FAX: (914)242-3109. **Also Known As:** TWA.

★ 16455 ★
Trans World Consulting Company, Inc. - Library (Sci-Engr)
383 S. Main St.   Phone: (203)668-5108
Windsor Locks, CT 06096   Margaret Straka, Libn.
Founded: 1972. **Staff:** 2. **Subjects:** Plastics and polymers - applications in aircraft and energy fields. **Holdings:** Books; reports; patents. **Services:** Library not open to the public. **Remarks:** FAX: (203)623-2560.

★ 16456 ★
Transalta Utilities Corporation - Library (Energy, Bus-Fin)
110 12th Ave., S.W.
P.O. Box 1900   Phone: (403)267-7388
Calgary, AB, Canada T2P 2M1   Shamim Kassam, Libn.
Staff: Prof 2; Other 2. **Subjects:** Electricity, management, reclamation. **Special Collections:** Electric Power Research Institute Research Reports. **Holdings:** 10,000 books; 800 annual reports; 1200 other cataloged items. **Subscriptions:** 600 journals and other serials; 50 newspapers. **Services:** Interlibrary loan; library open to the public at librarian's discretion. **Automated Operations:** Computerized cataloging, serials, and circulation. **Computerized Information Services:** PFDS Online, CAN/OLE, QL Systems, CANSIM, BRS Information Technologies, Info Globe. **Remarks:** FAX: (403)267-3727.

Transamerica Delaval Inc. - Biphase Energy Systems
See: **Biphase Energy Systems** (1849)

★ 16457 ★
Transamerica Occidental Life Insurance Company - Law Library (Law)
1150 S. Olive St., Suite T-2100   Phone: (213)742-3123
Los Angeles, CA 90015   Lynette Lawson, Mgr.
Staff: 1. **Subjects:** Insurance law, general law. **Holdings:** 9000 volumes. **Subscriptions:** 11 journals and other serials. **Services:** Library not open to the public. **Remarks:** FAX: (213)741-6623.

★ 16458 ★
Transco Energy Company - Corporate Library (Energy)
Box 1396   Phone: (713)439-2321
Houston, TX 77251   Cheryl L. Watson, Sr.Libn.
Founded: 1951. **Staff:** Prof 1. **Subjects:** Natural gas industry, petroleum industry. **Holdings:** 2000 books; 700 bound periodical volumes; 10 VF drawers of information files. **Subscriptions:** 300 journals and other serials. **Services:** Interlibrary loan; copying; library open to the public by appointment. **Computerized Information Services:** DIALOG Information Services, Dow Jones News/Retrieval, A.G.A. GasNet. **Publications:** Library Bulletin (acquisitions list), monthly. **Remarks:** Library located at 2800 S. Post Oak Rd., Houston, TX 77056. FAX: (713)439-2440; (713)439-2441.

★ 16459 ★
Transition Zone Horticultural Institute - The Arboretum at Flagstaff - Library (Agri)
S. Woody Mountain Rd.
P.O. Box 670   Phone: (602)774-1441
Flagstaff, AZ 86002   Judy Hite, Educ.Coord.
Founded: 1989. **Subjects:** Horticulture, forestry, landscape design. **Holdings:** 1200 books. **Services:** Interlibrary loan; copying; library open to the public by appointment. **Computerized Information Services:** Internal database. **Publications:** News from The Arboretum at Flagstaff, quarterly.

TRANSLab Library
See: **California (State) Department of Transportation - Materials & Research Library** (2539)

Transport Canada
See: **Canada - Transport Canada** (2867)

Transport and Road Research Laboratory
See: **Great Britain - Department of Transport** (6676)

★ 16460 ★
Transportation Association of Canada - Technical Information Service (Trans)
2323 St. Laurent Blvd.   Phone: (613)521-4052
Ottawa, ON, Canada K1G 4K6   Chris Hedges, Libn.
Founded: 1956. **Staff:** Prof 1. **Subjects:** Road construction, surface transportation, urban transit, transportation planning. **Holdings:** 16,000 books. **Subscriptions:** 200 journals and other serials. **Services:** Interlibrary loan; copying; service open to the public. **Automated Operations:** Computerized cataloging, circulation, and ILL. **Computerized Information Services:** DIALOG Information Services, ESA-QUEST, CAN/OLE. Performs searches on fee basis. **Publications:** Surface Transportation R & D in Canada, annual - by subscription; RTAC News, bimonthly - to members. **Remarks:** FAX: (613)521-6542.

★ 16461 ★
Transportation-Communications Union (TCU) - Library
3 Research Pl.
Rockville, MD 20850
Founded: 1980. **Subjects:** Rail industry; labor movement - law, history, statistics. **Special Collections:** Presidential Emergency Board documents (archival collection for disputes to which TCU was a party); historical collection of official union publications. **Holdings:** 2500 books; 30 VF drawers. **Remarks:** Currently inactive.

★ 16462 ★
Transportation Institute - Information Resource Center (Trans)
5201 Auth Way, 5th Fl.   Phone: (301)423-3335
Camp Springs, MD 20746   Stephan M. Barker, Mgr., Info.Rsrc.Ctr.
Founded: 1968. **Staff:** Prof 1. **Subjects:** Merchant marine, transportation, economics, statistics, labor management, manpower. **Holdings:** 1400 volumes; 4000 documents; 3000 newspaper clippings; 1000 Congressional documents; 1300 documents on microfiche. **Subscriptions:** 35 journals and other serials; 8 newspapers. **Services:** Interlibrary loan; library not open to the public. **Computerized Information Services:** DIALOG Information Services. **Publications:** Transportation Institute Library/New Acquisitions, monthly - for internal distribution only. **Staff:** Chung Tai Shen.

★ 16463 ★
Transportation Institute - Research Documentation Center (Trans)
303 Merrick Bldg.
North Carolina Agricultural & Tech. State Univ.
Greensboro, NC 27411   Phone: (919)334-7745
Subjects: Urban public transit, freight transportation, transportation for the elderly and handicapped, rural public transit, public transit finance, motor carrier deregulation. **Holdings:** 4000 reports and books; 250 microfiche; unbound periodicals. **Services:** Center open to the public by appointment. **Remarks:** FAX: (919)334-7093.

Transportation Research Board Library
See: **National Research Council** (11269)

Transportation Research Information Center (TRIC)
See: **U.S. Urban Mass Transportation Administration** (17955)

Transportation Research Information Service
See: **National Research Council** (11270)

Transportation Safety Board of Canada
See: **Canada - Transportation Safety Board of Canada** (2881)

Transportation Services Division
See: **Technical Services Laboratories, Inc.** (16031)

★ 16464 ★
Transylvanian World Federation - Library (Area-Ethnic)
Rua Pedro Zolcsak, 221
Sao Bernardo do Campo   Phone: 11 4488855
Sao Paulo, SP, Brazil   Ilona Abaligeti, Sec.
Founded: 1968. **Subjects:** Hungarians in Transylvania and Moldavia in Rumania. **Holdings:** 190 volumes; archival materials. **Services:** Library not open to the public. **Remarks:** FAX: 114587788. Telex: 1144536 CSAK BR. **Also Known As:** Erdelyi Vilagszovetseg.

★ 16465 ★
Traphagen School of Fashion - Ethel Traphagen Leigh Memorial Library (Art)
686 Broadway   Phone: (212)673-0300
New York, NY 10012   Janet Harris, Dir. of Oper.
Founded: 1923. **Staff:** Prof 2; Other 10. **Subjects:** Fashion design and illustration, history of costume, visual arts, art history, customs of mankind, American Indian arts and customs, interior decorating, architecture, fashion merchandising, fashion marketing, business management and marketing, textile arts and industry. **Special Collections:** Rare late 18th and 19th century fashion periodicals of France, England, Germany, and America; Harper's Bazaar and Vogue, from their inception to the present; Ethnic Costume publications of many nations and religions (lithographs, original drawings). **Holdings:** 5000 books; 600 bound periodical volumes; 4 VF drawers of clippings; 550 unbound periodicals; slides. **Subscriptions:** 35 journals and other serials. **Services:** Library open to the public by appointment for publication research. **Remarks:** Affiliated with Tobe Coburn School for Fashion Careers - Library.

Dr. Carl R. Trask Health Sciences Library
See: **Saint John Regional Hospital** (14330)

Trask Library
See: **Andover Newton Theological School** (861)

Travail Canada
See: **Canada - Labour Canada** (2760)

Travaux Publics Canada
See: **Canada - Public Works Canada** (2838)

Travel Industry Association of America - U.S. Travel Data Center
See: **U.S. Travel Data Center** (17952)

★ 16466 ★
Travel Professionals Association - Library (Rec)
216 S. Bungalow Park Ave.   Phone: (813)876-0286
Tampa, FL 33609   Claudine Dervoes
Staff: 2. **Subjects:** Travel industry. **Holdings:** 1600 volumes of reference books. **Services:** Library open to the public by appointment. **Remarks:** Toll-free telephone number(s): (800)226-0286.

Travel Weekly Library
See: **Reed Travel Group** (13773)

★ 16467 ★
Travelers Insurance Companies - The Information Exchange 2 GS (Bus-Fin)
One Tower Square
Hartford, CT 06183   Phone: (203)954-4636
Founded: 1922. **Staff:** 8. **Subjects:** Insurance, management, actuarial science. **Special Collections:** Company history; mortality tables. **Holdings:** 5800 volumes. **Subscriptions:** 400 journals and other serials; 8 newspapers. **Services:** Interlibrary loan; open to the public by appointment. **Automated Operations:** Computerized public access catalog, cataloging, serials, and circulation. **Computerized Information Services:** DIALOG Information Services, BRS Information Technologies, Human Resource Information Network (HRIN), NewsNet, Inc., LEXIS, NEXIS, Dow Jones News/Retrieval, InfoMaster. **Networks/Consortia:** Member of Capital Region Library Council (CRLC). **Publications:** Newsletter, quarterly. **Remarks:** FAX: (203)277-9167. **Staff:** Pat Alderson; Faye Titus; Kathy Corcoran; David Cyr; Bill Pape.

★ 16468 ★
Travelers Insurance Company - Engineering Division - Library (Sci-Engr)
One Tower Sq. 8SB   Phone: (203)277-5279
Hartford, CT 06183-4070   Jill Schuler
Staff: Prof 1; Other 1. **Subjects:** Safety engineering, industrial health. **Holdings:** 2000 books. **Subscriptions:** 200 journals and other serials. **Services:** Library not open to the public. **Remarks:** FAX: (203)954-6727.

★ 16469 ★
Traverse City Record-Eagle - Library (Publ)
120 W. Front St.   Phone: (616)946-2000
Traverse City, MI 49685   Dan Brown
Founded: 1980. **Staff:** 1. **Subjects:** Newspaper reference topics. **Holdings:** 750 books; archives, 1970 to present; microfilm, 1880 to present. **Services:** Library open to the public for reference use only. **Remarks:** FAX: (616)946-8273.

★ 16470 ★
(Traverse City) Regional Educational Media Center - REMC 2 - Central (Educ)
880 Parsons Rd.   Phone: (616)922-6217
Traverse City, MI 49684   Stephen M. Norvilitis, Dir.
Founded: 1968. **Staff:** Prof 1; Other 2. **Subjects:** Educational curriculum. **Holdings:** 15,000 videocassettes and 16mm films; computer software. **Services:** Center open to the public with restrictions. **Special Catalogs:** Catalogs of video holdings, 16mm film holdings, computer software. **Remarks:** FAX: (616)946-0417.

Travertine Nature Center Library
See: **U.S. Natl. Park Service - Chickasaw Natl. Recreation Area** (17690)

★ 16471 ★
Travis Avenue Baptist Church - Library (Rel-Phil)
3041 Travis Ave.   Phone: (817)924-4266
Fort Worth, TX 76110   Beth Andrews, Dir.
Founded: 1954. **Staff:** 4. **Subjects:** Religion, biography, history, literature. **Holdings:** 16,712 books; AV programs. **Subscriptions:** 30 journals and other serials; 2 newspapers. **Services:** Copying; library open to the public with restrictions. **Computerized Information Services:** Internal database.

Anthony P. Travisono Library
See: **American Correctional Association** (545)

★ 16472 ★
Tread of Pioneers Museum - Routt County Collection (Hist)
Box 774568
Steamboat Springs, CO 80477   Phone: (303)879-0240
Founded: 1981. **Subjects:** Local history and genealogy, skiing, ranching, mining. **Holdings:** 100 books; 8 file cabinets of manuscripts; photographs; scrapbooks; oral histories; clippings; 25 dissertations on microfilm; 1880 and 1890 census materials; maps. **Services:** Copying; library open to the public for reference use only.

★ 16473 ★
Treasure Hunting Research and Information Center (Rec)
P.O. Box 76
Patterson, LA 70392   John Reed, Dir.
Founded: 1986. **Staff:** Prof 5; Other 4. **Subjects:** Treasure hunting, ship wrecks, exploration, prospecting, adventure. **Special Collections:** Latin American lost cities (10 vertical files); legendary Amazons of Latin America (5 vertical files). **Holdings:** 1250 books; 350 bound periodical volumes; 250 vertical files. **Subscriptions:** 18 journals and other serials. **Services:** Center not open to the public. **Special Catalogs:** Catalog of treasure hunting clubs and organizations, periodicals, events, books, authors, and commercial enterprises (card). **Formerly:** Located in Gibson, LA.

★ 16474 ★
Treasure Island Museum - Library (Mil)
Bldg. One
Treasure Island   Phone: (415)395-5067
San Francisco, CA 94130-5000   Mary Gentry, Reg.
Founded: 1975. **Subjects:** Navy, Marine Corps, Coast Guard, China Clipper Flying Boats, Golden Gate International Exposition. **Holdings:** 1500 books; 60 bound periodical volumes. **Services:** Copying; library open to the public. **Remarks:** FAX: (415)395-5436.

★ 16475 ★
Trebas Institute - Resource Center (Mus)
451 St. Jean   Phone: (514)845-4141
Montreal, PQ, Canada H2Y 2R5   David P. Leonard, Pres.
Founded: 1979. **Staff:** Prof 1. **Subjects:** Music industry, recording arts and sciences, audio engineering, acoustics, electronic music synthesis. **Holdings:** 2000 books; 3000 periodicals. **Subscriptions:** 25 journals and other serials. **Services:** Center not open to the public. **Remarks:** FAX: (514)845-2581. Branch centers are maintained in Ottawa, ON; Toronto, ON; Vancouver, BC; and Hollywood, CA. **Formed by the merger of:** Trebas Institute of Recording Arts - MontreaL Campus Library and its Resource Center.

★ 16476 ★
Trebas Institute of Recording Arts - Montreal Campus Library/Resource Centre
451 Saint Jean
Montreal, PQ, Canada H2Y 2R5
Defunct. Holdings merged with Trebas Institute of Recording Arts.

Harleigh B. Trecker Library
See: **University of Connecticut** (18517)

★ 16477 ★
Tree of Life Press - Library and Archives (Publ)
420 N.E. Blvd.
Gainesville, FL 32601   Reva Pachefsky, Libn.
Founded: 1971. **Staff:** Prof 1; Other 1. **Subjects:** Infant language development, child development, graphic arts. **Special Collections:** Archives of the Tree of Life Press; Collection of the Art of Robert (Ishmael) Grabb, Jr. **Services:** Interlibrary loan; library open to the public by appointment. **Publications:** Newsletter; New Acquisitions; Listing of the Collection by Topic, all irregular.

★16478★

TreePeople - Environmental Resources Library
12601 Mulholland Dr.
Beverly Hills, CA 90210
Subjects: Forestry, air pollution, tropical rainforests, environmental issues.
Holdings: Articles. **Remarks:** Currently inactive.

Trends Publishing, Inc.
See: **Science Trends** (14943)

★16479★

Trenton Free Public Library - Art & Music Department (Art, Mus)
120 Academy St.
Box 2448   Phone: (609)392-7188
Trenton, NJ 08608   Shirley Michael, Dept.Hd.
Founded: 1967. **Staff:** Prof 1; Other 2. **Subjects:** Fine arts, music, applied arts, antiques, dance, photography. **Special Collections:** Collection of original oil and water color paintings (22 items); Archives of Trenton Area Music; Union List of Sacred Music. **Holdings:** 6500 books; 2700 bound periodical volumes; 4500 phonograph records; 30 VF drawers of pictures; 4 VF cabinets of orchestral scores and parts; 1 VF cabinet of choral parts; 300 pieces of sheet music; 205 16mm films. **Subscriptions:** 90 journals and other serials. **Services:** Interlibrary loan; copying; department open to the public. **Special Indexes:** Song index; paintings index; phonograph record index (all on cards); dance index; arias index. **Remarks:** FAX: (609)396-7655.

★16480★

Trenton Free Public Library - Business and Technology Department (Bus-Fin, Sci-Engr)
120 Academy St.   Phone: (609)392-7188
Trenton, NJ 08608   Richard Rebecca, Dept.Hd.
Founded: 1902. **Staff:** Prof 2; Other 2. **Subjects:** Business and finance, science and technology, labor, automotive industry, home repair, aviation. **Holdings:** 10,000 books; 2000 bound periodical volumes; 1000 annual reports (print and microfiche); 350 telephone directories; 300 trade directories; 25 VF drawers; loose-leaf financial services; daily stock price records (1962 to present); patent abstracts; Moodys manuals (1930s to present); ASTM Standards, 1988; National Fire Codes. **Subscriptions:** 250 journals and other serials. **Services:** Interlibrary loan; copying; department open to the public. **Computerized Information Services:** CD-ROMs (Moody's Company Data, EBSCO Electronic Information). **Special Indexes:** Indexes of various N.J. business publications. **Remarks:** FAX: (609)396-7655. **Staff:** Margaret Walsh, Sr.Libn.

★16481★

Trenton Free Public Library - Government Documents Collection (Info Sci)
120 Academy St.   Phone: (609)392-7188
Trenton, NJ 08608   Nan Wright, Hd., Ref.Dept.
Founded: 1910. **Staff:** Prof 1; Other 1. **Special Collections:** Federal, state, and local government documents; U.S. Government periodicals and serial sets. **Holdings:** 25,000 books; 1000 bound periodical volumes; 250,000 other cataloged items. **Subscriptions:** 150 journals and other serials. **Services:** Interlibrary loan; copying; collection open to the public. **Automated Operations:** Computerized cataloging. **Computerized Information Services:** OCLC, DIALOG Information Services, Auto - Graphics. **Networks/Consortia:** Member of PALINET. FAX: (609)396-7655. **Staff:** Joyce Bagnall, Libn.; Sharon Shrieves, Jr.Lib.Asst.

★16482★

Trenton Free Public Library - Trentoniana Collection (Hist)
120 Academy St.   Phone: (609)392-7188
Trenton, NJ 08608   Nan Wright, Hd., Ref.Dept.
Founded: 1910. **Staff:** Prof 1; Other 1. **Subjects:** Local history, genealogy. **Special Collections:** Early Trenton Fire Department minutes and records; New Jersey books and documents; archives of local organizations; local maps. **Holdings:** 4000 books; 403 bound periodical volumes; 26 VF drawers of photographs; 34 VF drawers; 175 maps and atlases; 5 VF drawers of manuscripts; 28 reels of film; 35 audiotapes; 47 oral histories; Trenton newspapers on microfilm; 5 pieces of Lenox china; 3 VF drawers of memorabilia; 30 boxes of unspecified materials. **Subscriptions:** 45 journals and other serials; 5 newspapers. **Services:** Copying; collection open to the public. **Remarks:** FAX: (609)396-7655. **Staff:** Richard Reeves, Sr.Lib.Asst.

★16483★

Trenton Psychiatric Hospital - Professional Library (Med)
Box 7500   Phone: (609)633-1572
West Trenton, NJ 08628   Elaine Scheuerer, Lib.Coord.
Founded: 1944. **Staff:** 1. **Subjects:** Psychiatry, psychotherapy, medicine, psychoanalysis, nursing. **Holdings:** 3550 books; 3000 bound periodical volumes; 5 VF drawers of pamphlets; 600 audio cassettes; 3 16mm films; 27 video cassettes; manuscripts; reports; clippings; 1 cabinet of phonograph records, tapes, filmstrips. **Subscriptions:** 92 journals and other serials. **Services:** Interlibrary loan; library open to the public for reference use only. **Computerized Information Services:** MEDLARS, BRS Information Technologies. **Networks/Consortia:** Member of Central Jersey Health Science Libraries Association (CJHSLA), Health Sciences Library Association of New Jersey (HSLANJ), BHSL. **Remarks:** FAX (609)396-5701.

★16484★

Trenton State College - Roscoe L. West Library - Special Collections (Hist)
Hillwood Lakes, CN-4700
Trenton, NJ 08650-4700   Phone: (609)771-2332
Founded: 1969. **Special Collections:** New Jersey (3537 volumes); Trenton State College Archives (815 items); 1432 historic textbooks; Trenton State faculty author collection (770 volumes); Trenton State College masters' theses (350 volumes); autograph collection (163 volumes); historic children's books (152 volumes); Feinstone Collection of the American Revolution (50 items); oral history collection (31 cassettes); Trenton State College alumni author collection (51 volumes); special illustrators collection (6 volumes); limited editions collection (13 volumes); early imprints collection (622 volumes). **Services:** Interlibrary loan (limited); copying; collections open to the public for reference use only. **Automated Operations:** Computerized public access catalog, cataloging, and circulation (NOTIS). **Computerized Information Services:** BRS Information Technologies, OCLC, WILSONLINE, DIALOG Information Services, Dow Jones News/Retrieval. **Networks/Consortia:** Member of PALINET. **Publications:** Guide to the Library, annual; - available on request; Periodical Holdings, biennial; Accessions List, monthly - both for internal distribution only. **Special Catalogs:** Catalog of the Feinstone Collection of the American Revolution (typed list). **Remarks:** FAX: (609)771-3299.

★16485★

(Trenton) Times - Library (Publ)
500 Perry St.
Box 847   Phone: (609)396-3232
Trenton, NJ 08605   Kathy Murphy, Hd.Libn.
Staff: Prof 1; Other 3. **Subjects:** Newspaper reference topics, state information on local political figures, highways. **Holdings:** Figures not available. **Subscriptions:** 16 journals and other serials; 6 newspapers. **Services:** Interlibrary loan; library not open to the public.

★16486★

Ralph Treves Workshop Features - Workshop Photos (Aud-Vis, Rec)
311 Lake Evelyn Dr.   Phone: (407)683-5167
West Palm Beach, FL 33411   Ralph Treves, Owner
Subjects: Manual crafts and skills, home improvements, hobby workshop projects, home security. **Special Collections:** Photographs illustrating techniques related to woodworking, home repair, and renovation. **Holdings:** 14,000 black/white photographs available for reproduction by magazines, public relations agencies, newspapers, book publishers.

★16487★

Harry C. Trexler Masonic Library (Rec)
1524 Linden St.   Phone: (215)434-2661
Allentown, PA 18102   Charles S. Canning, Libn., Cur.
Founded: 1930. **Staff:** 1. **Subjects:** Freemasonry, Masonic history. **Special Collections:** Writings of George Washington, Benjamin Franklin, Thomas Jefferson; Ars Quatuos Coronatorum; rare books; collection of Masonic and anti-Masonic documents and artifacts. **Holdings:** 7500 books and bound periodical volumes. **Subscriptions:** 15 journals and other serials. **Services:** Copying; library open to the public with restrictions. **Remarks:** Maintained by five Masonic lodges in Allentown.

Trexler Nurses' Library
See: **St. Luke's Hospital of Bethlehem, Pennsylvania - School of Nursing** (14482)

Scott Andrew Trexler II Memorial Library
See: **Lehigh County Historical Society** (9055)

★ 16488 ★
Tri Brook Group, Inc. - Library (Med)
999 Oakmont Plaza Dr., Suite 600   Phone: (708)990-8070
Westmont, IL 60559-5504   Sandra Rumbyrt, Libn.
Staff: Prof 1. **Subjects:** Health care management, health statistics. **Holdings:** 4000 volumes including government publications and reports. **Subscriptions:** 85 journals and other serials. **Services:** Interlibrary loan; library not open to the public. **Networks/Consortia:** Member of Fox Valley Health Science Library Consortium (FVHSL).

★ 16489 ★
Tri-City Jewish Center - Library (Rel-Phil)
2715 30th St.
Box 4087   Phone: (309)788-3426
Rock Island, IL 61204-4087   Faye Kershner, Chm.
Founded: 1951. **Subjects:** Judaica. **Holdings:** 5500 books. **Subscriptions:** 4 journals and other serials; 2 newspapers. **Services:** Library open to the public on a limited schedule.

★ 16490 ★
Tri-County Metropolitan District of Oregon (Tri-Met) - Library (Trans)
4012 S.E. 17th Ave.   Phone: (503)238-4814
Portland, OR 97202   Judy Weinsoft, Lib.Spec.
Founded: 1982. **Staff:** 1.5 **Subjects:** Public transit, urban transportation. **Holdings:** 3000 books. **Subscriptions:** 125 journals and other serials. **Services:** Interlibrary loan; copying; library open to the public by appointment. **Computerized Information Services:** DIALOG Information Services, LEXIS. **Remarks:** FAX: (503)239-6469.

★ 16491 ★
Tri-County Regional Planning Commission - Information Resource Center (Plan)
913 W. Holmes Rd., Suite 201   Phone: (517)393-0342
Lansing, MI 48910   Carrie Clinkscales, Exec.Asst.
Founded: 1956. **Staff:** 9. **Subjects:** Urban and regional planning. **Holdings:** Figures not available. **Services:** Center open to the public for reference use only. **Computerized Information Services:** Internal databases; AutoMail (electronic mail service). **Publications:** Planning reports on Clinton, Eaton, and Ingham counties, continuous updates. **Remarks:** FAX: (517)393-4424.

★ 16492 ★
Tri-County Regional Planning Commission - Library (Plan)
632 W. Jefferson St.
Morton, IL 61550-1540   Phone: (309)694-4391
Founded: 1958. **Subjects:** Land use, housing, open space and recreation, environment, transportation. **Special Collections:** Environmental Protection Agency (EPA) Special Environmental Technical Studies; depository for Federal Home Mortgage and Disclosure Act. **Holdings:** 450 books; 250 bound periodical volumes; 150 items of census information; transportation documents; local development codes; original of Standard Metropolitan Statistical Area maps; urban transportation planning package (special census tabulation). **Subscriptions:** 198 journals and other serials. **Services:** Interlibrary loan; copying; library open to the public for reference use only. **Computerized Information Services:** LINUS. **Networks/Consortia:** Member of Illinois State Data Center Cooperative (ISDCC). **Publications:** Annotated Bibliography of Agency Publications. **Remarks:** Alternate telephone number(s): 266-9941. **Staff:** John Boyle, Dir., Plan.; Cindy J. Bergstrand, Dir., Human Serv.

★ 16493 ★
Tri-County Technical College - Learning Resource Center (Sci-Engr, Educ)
Box 587   Phone: (803)646-8361
Pendleton, SC 29670   Nancy C. Griese, Hd.Libn.
Founded: 1963. **Staff:** Prof 2; Other 6. **Subjects:** Industrial electronics, business administration, secretarial science, machine shop, marketing, management, radio and television broadcasting, electronics engineering, veterinary technology, textile management, quality assurance, automated manufacturing, computer technology, criminal justice, dental assisting, surgical technology, practical nursing, nursing, medical lab, heating, ventilating, air conditioning, industrial mechanics. **Special Collections:** Black studies (300 items); Child Development (3000 items); Medical Lab Technicians (200 items). **Holdings:** 39,439 books; 4565 bound periodical volumes; 3868 AV programs. **Subscriptions:** 170 journals and other serials; 12 newspapers. **Services:** Interlibrary loan; copying; comprehensive audiovisual production services; center open to residents of Anderson, Oconee, and Pickens Counties, South Carolina. **Computerized Information Services:** OCLC. **Networks/Consortia:** Member of South Carolina Library Network. **Publications:** Quarterly and annual reports. **Special Catalogs:** Printed catalog of AV materials. **Staff:** Claudia Poore, Lib.Tech.Asst. III; Dianne Histt, Off.Mgr.; Willa Roland, Lib.Tech.Asst. III.

★ 16494 ★
Tri-State University - General Lewis B. Hershey Museum (Hist)
Hershey Hall   Phone: (219)665-4141
Angola, IN 46703   Robert Bricker, Dir.
Founded: 1970. **Subjects:** General Lewis B. Hershey. **Holdings:** Figures not available for books; memorabilia; articles. **Services:** Museum open to the public.

★ 16495 ★
Tri-State University - Perry T. Ford Memorial Library (Sci-Engr, Bus-Fin)
S. Darling St.   Phone: (219)665-4161
Angola, IN 46703   Mrs. Enriqueta G. Taboy, Lib.Dir.
Founded: 1962. **Staff:** Prof 3; Other 2. **Subjects:** Engineering, business, arts and sciences, elementary and secondary curricula. **Special Collections:** NACA and NASA publications; Smithsonian publications; NATO Advisory Group for Aerospace Research and Development (AGARD) publications. **Holdings:** 149,974 books; 13,601 bound periodical volumes; 3053 reels of microfilm; 712 phonograph records; 590 audio cassettes; 345 maps; 140 videotapes; 490 filmstrips; 31,665 other cataloged items; microfiche. **Subscriptions:** 601 journals and other serials; 19 newspapers. **Services:** Interlibrary loan; copying; library open to the public with restrictions on circulation. **Automated Operations:** Computerized cataloging and periodical maintenance. **Computerized Information Services:** Access to DIALOG Information Services, OCLC; CD-ROM. Performs searches on fee basis. **Networks/Consortia:** Member of Tri-ALSA, INCOLSA. **Publications:** Library Newsletter, monthly - for internal distribution only. **Remarks:** Alternate telephone number(s): 665-4162; 665-4163. FAX: (219)665-4292. **Staff:** Carolyn Cripe, Ref.Libn.; Linda Sebring, Cat.; Barbara Steel, Rd.Serv.

Triangle Club Archives
See: **Princeton University - William Seymour Theatre Collection** (13388)

Trianon Press Archive
See: **University of California, Santa Cruz - Dean E. McHenry Library** (18435)

★ 16496 ★
Tribble & Richardson, Inc. - Library (Env-Cons)
P.O. Box 13147   Phone: (912)474-6100
Macon, GA 31208-3147   Jan Turner, Libn.
Subjects: Environmental protection; engineering - civil, environmental, structural; water quality. **Holdings:** Figures not available. **Services:** Library not open to the public. **Remarks:** FAX: (912)474-8933.

★16497★
Trident Technical College - Main Campus Learning Resources Center
(Sci-Engr, Educ)
LD/M Box 10367   Phone: (803)572-6089
Charleston, SC 29411   Marion L. Vogel, Dean, Lrng.Rsrcs.
Founded: 1964. **Staff:** Prof 6; Other 5. **Subjects:** Engineering technology,
business and management, health sciences, automotive and industrial crafts,
horticulture, commercial graphics, paralegal studies, broadcasting, physical
sciences, radio and television electronics, humanities. **Special Collections:**
Archives; Sams Photofact Collection (Howard Sams Schematics for Radios
and Televisions; complete collection); engineering and technical books
(11,637). **Holdings:** 41,245 books; 39 bound periodical volumes; 325
government documents; 350 pamphlets in vertical file; 1602 reels of
microfilm; 50,699 microfiche; 51 realia; 668 phonograph records; 539
audiotapes; 1417 videotapes; 302 films; 37,696 slides; 1576 overhead
transparencies; 4 computer software programs. **Subscriptions:** 602 journals
and other serials; 13 newspapers. **Services:** Interlibrary loan; copying;
library open to the public for reference use only. **Automated Operations:**
Computerized public access catalog and circulation. **Computerized
Information Services:** DIALOG Information Services; CD-ROMs;
electronic mail. Performs searches on fee basis (free to students and college
faculty and staff). Contact Person: Beverly Powers-Schacht, Pub.Serv.Libn.
Networks/Consortia: Member of Charleston Academic Libraries
Consortium. **Publications:** Annual Report - to administrators and
administrative faculty, technical colleges in South Carolina, and their
academic libraries in 8 county area; Audiovisual Bibliography, irregular;
subject bibliographies. **Remarks:** FAX: (803)569-6484. **Staff:** Rose Marie
Huff, Acq.Libn.; Rosetta Martin, Ref.Libn.; Lisanne Hamilton,
Tech.Serv.Libn.

★16498★
Trieste Astronomical Observatory - Library (Sci-Engr)
Via Tiepolo 11
I-34131 Trieste, Italy   Phone: 40 3199111
Founded: 1753. **Staff:** 2. **Subjects:** Astronomy, astrophysics, astronomical
technology, radio astronomy, cosmology. **Holdings:** 8500 books; bound
periodical volumes; microfiche. **Subscriptions:** 90 journals and other serials.
Services: Library open to the public. **Computerized Information Services:**
ISIS; electronic mail. **Remarks:** FAX: 40 309418. Telex: 461137 OAT I.

Trimble Library
See: **Nazarene Bible College** (11355)

★16499★
**Trinidad and Tobago - Ministry of Education - Central Library Services
- West Indian Reference Library** (Area-Ethnic)
81 Belmont Circular Rd.   Phone: 6241130
Belmont, Trinidad and Tobago   Ann Clarke, Libn.
Staff: 13. **Subjects:** West Indies - history, culture, literature, social studies.
Special Collections: Legal deposit (4977 items). **Holdings:** 12,828 books;
17,621 bound periodical volumes; 50 cassette tapes. **Subscriptions:** 634
journals and other serials; 52 newspapers. **Services:** Interlibrary loan; library
open to the public. **Publications:** Trinidad & Tobago National Bibliography.
Staff: Vere Achong, Dir., Lib.Serv.

★16500★
Trinity Bible College - Fred J. Graham Library (Rel-Phil)
Ellendale, ND 58436   Phone: (701)349-5430
                                        Ruby Wesson, Libn.
Staff: Prof 1; Other 4. **Subjects:** Bible, theology, church work, evangelism,
Christian ministries, missions, business education, elementary education.
Special Collections: Pentecostal Works/Trinity Bible College archives.
Holdings: 60,971 books; 6968 bound periodical volumes; 685 book titles on
microfiche; 50 VF drawers. **Subscriptions:** 429 journals and other serials.
Services: Interlibrary loan; copying; library open to the community.
Automated Operations: Computerized cataloging. **Computerized
Information Services:** OCLC, EasyLink. **Networks/Consortia:** Member of
MINITEX Library Information Network.

★16501★
Trinity Church - Library (Rel-Phil)
107 N. State St.
Merrill, WI 54452   Phone: (715)536-5482
                                        Margaret Koch, Libn.
Remarks: No further information was supplied by respondent.

★16502★
Trinity Church - Parish Archives (Rel-Phil, Hist)
74 Trinity Place   Phone: (212)602-0848
New York, NY 10006   Phyllis Barr, Archv./Rec.Mgr./Cur.
Founded: 1980. **Staff:** Prof 3; Other 4. **Subjects:** Parish and diocesan history,
New York City history, U.S. history. **Holdings:** 1000 books; 3000 linear feet
of archival records; 10 cubic feet of microfilm. **Subscriptions:** 6 journals and
other serials. **Services:** Copying; education programs; archives open to the
public with restrictions. **Computerized Information Services:** Internal
database. **Remarks:** FAX: (212)602-0727. **Staff:** Irmgard Carras, Exhibit
Spec., Catherine Shisa, Musm.Educ.

★16503★
Trinity College - Archives (Hist)
1250 Michigan Ave, N.E.   Phone: (202)939-5000
Washington, DC 20017   Sr. Columba Mullaly, Ph.D., Archv.
Founded: 1965. **Staff:** Prof 1. **Subjects:** Trinity College archives. **Holdings:**
550 cubic feet of records, minutes, photographs, artifacts, college catalogs
(1899 to present), and student yearbooks (1911-1982). **Services:** Archives
open to the public with restrictions.

★16504★
Trinity College - Watkinson Library (Hum)
300 Summit St.   Phone: (203)297-2268
Hartford, CT 06106   Dr. Jeffrey H. Kaimowitz, Cur.
Founded: 1857. **Staff:** Prof 5; Other 2. **Subjects:** Americana (especially 19th
century), American Indians, black history, U.S. Civil War, British history
and topography, folklore, witchcraft, graphic arts, history of printing,
natural history, horology, philology (especially American Indian languages),
early voyages and travels, maritime history. **Special Collections:** Incunabula
and 16th century imprints (especially Trumbull-Prime Collection of
illustrated books); private press books (especially Ashendene Press); English
and American first editions (especially Frost, E.A. Robinson, Walter Scott);
18th and 19th century English and American periodicals; ornithology (6000
volumes); Barnard Collection of early American school books (7000
volumes); manuscripts of Charles Dudley Warner, Frost, E.A. Robinson,
Walter Scott, Henry Barnard, Ely Halperine-Kaminsky, Sibour, Nathan
Allen, Watkinson family, Hartford families, and other historical and literary
figures; American music (including jazz and blues and 18th and 19th century
religious and secular works in printed and manuscript form; 1100 song
sheets; 26,000 pieces of sheet music). **Holdings:** 165,000 books and bound
periodical volumes; atlases; 500 maps; printed ephemera including 100
indexed scrapbooks, advertisements, fashion plates, music and theater
programs, and valentines. **Subscriptions:** 40 journals and other serials.
Services: Copying; library open to the public for reference use only.
Automated Operations: Computerized cataloging. **Computerized
Information Services:** OCLC. **Networks/Consortia:** Member of NELINET,
Inc. **Publications:** Bibliographies, irregular. **Special Catalogs:** Exhibition
catalogs. **Remarks:** FAX: (203)297-2251. **Staff:** Karen B. Clarke, Asst.Cur.,
Ornithology.

Trinity College - Watkinson Library - Mark Twain Memorial
See: **Mark Twain Memorial** (16599)

★16505★
Trinity County Law Library (Law)
Courthouse
101 Court St.
Box 1258   Phone: (916)623-1201
Weaverville, CA 96093   Donna Regnani, Judicial Sec.
Subjects: Law. **Holdings:** 3326 volumes. **Services:** Library open to the
public.

★16506★
Trinity Episcopal Church - Ashton Library (Rel-Phil)
128 W. Hardin St.   Phone: (419)422-3214
Findlay, OH 45840   Kathryn J. Gambell, Libn.
Founded: 1960. **Staff:** 1. **Subjects:** Christianity, Episcopal Church.
Holdings: 650 books. **Subscriptions:** 2 journals and other serials. **Services:**
Library not open to the public.

★ 16507 ★
Trinity Episcopal Church - Library (Rel-Phil)
1500 State St.   Phone: (805)965-7419
Santa Barbara, CA 93101   Liese Fajardo, Libn.
Staff: Prof 2. **Subjects:** Religion. **Holdings:** 2475 books. **Services:** Library open to the public.

★ 16508 ★
Trinity Evangelical Divinity School - Rolfing Memorial Library (Rel-Phil)
2065 Half Day Rd.   Phone: (708)317-8150
Deerfield, IL 60015   Dr. Brewster Porcella, Libn.
Founded: 1897. **Staff:** Prof 4; Other 15. **Subjects:** Biblical studies, evangelicalism and fundamentalism, theology, Christian education, church history. **Special Collections:** Evangelical Free Church of America Archives (books; periodicals; 8 VF drawers); Trinity Evangelical Divinity School Archives. **Holdings:** 116,539 books; 29,371 bound periodical volumes; 45,153 microfiche; 6259 reels of microfilm. **Subscriptions:** 1020 journals and other serials; 9 newspapers. **Services:** Interlibrary loan; copying; library open to the public. **Automated Operations:** Computerized cataloging. **Computerized Information Services:** OCLC. **Networks/Consortia:** Member of ILLINET, North Suburban Library System (NSLS), Association of Chicago Theological Schools Library Council. **Staff:** Keith Wells, Ref.Libn.; Jacquelyn Allen, Cat.; Debe Gordon, Adm.Assoc.; Cheryl Felmlee, Acq.; Eleanor Warner, ILL.

★ 16509 ★
Trinity Evangelical Lutheran Church - Library & Media Center (Rel-Phil)
5th & Chestnut Sts.
Box 231   Phone: (215)257-6801
Perkasie, PA 18944   Charles Snyder, Libn.
Founded: 1962. **Staff:** Prof 3; Other 5. **Subjects:** Bible, church history, prayer, mission and ministry, Lutheran Christian education. **Special Collections:** Local and church history archives. **Holdings:** 7000 books; 1000 AV programs. **Subscriptions:** 50 journals and other serials. **Services:** Interlibrary loan; copying; library open to the public. **Automated Operations:** Computerized cataloging and acquisitions. **Publications:** Trinity Chimes (newsletter), monthly; Library News and Book Reviews.

★ 16510 ★
Trinity Lutheran Church - Library (Rel-Phil)
210 S. 7th St.
Box 188   Phone: (218)236-1333
Moorhead, MN 56560   Rodney Erickson, Libn.
Founded: 1959. **Staff:** Prof 3; Other 4. **Subjects:** Biblical studies, personal growth, doctrine, missions, church history. **Special Collections:** Interpreters Bible and Dictionary. **Holdings:** 4226 books. **Services:** Library open to the public.

★ 16511 ★
Trinity Lutheran Church - Library (Rel-Phil)
2802 Belvedere Dr.
Billings, MT 59102   Phone: (406)656-1021
Founded: 1960. **Staff:** 1. **Subjects:** Bible, secular history. **Holdings:** Figures not available.

★ 16512 ★
Trinity Lutheran Church - Library (Rel-Phil)
1904 Winnebago St.
Madison, WI 53704   Sharon Kenyon, Libn.
Founded: 1946. **Staff:** 5. **Subjects:** Religion, home and family, missions, juvenile and adult literature. **Special Collections:** Bible Study Aids (600). **Holdings:** 4800 books; 2 VF drawers of clippings; 80 pamphlets and tapes. **Subscriptions:** Interlibrary loan; copying; library open to area residents.

★ 16513 ★
Trinity Lutheran Hospital - Florence L. Nelson Memorial Library (Med)
3030 Baltimore Ave.   Phone: (816)751-2270
Kansas City, MO 64108   Cami L. Loucks, Dir.
Founded: 1970. **Staff:** Prof 2; Other 2. **Subjects:** Clinical medicine, preclinical medicine, nursing, hospital administration. **Special Collections:**

Nelson Local History Collection (30 volumes); archival collection; media contacts. **Holdings:** 4500 books; 2600 bound periodical volumes; 12 VF drawers of pamphlets; 800 reels of microfilm; 180 filmstrips; 4000 slides; 450 audio cassettes; 10 16mm films; 450 video cassettes. **Subscriptions:** 375 journals and other serials; 8 newspapers. **Services:** Interlibrary loan; copying; library open to qualified research specialists for reference use only. **Automated Operations:** Computerized cataloging and ILL. **Computerized Information Services:** MEDLINE, BRS Information Technologies, DIALOG Information Services; DOCLINE (electronic mail service). **Networks/Consortia:** Member of Kansas City Library Network, Inc. (KCLN), Kansas City Metropolitan Library Network (KCMLN). **Publications:** The Medical Library Infoline, quarterly - for internal distribution only. **Special Catalogs:** AV union list; serials union list. **Remarks:** FAX: (816)751-4594. **Staff:** Danae J. Duffin, Asst.Libn.; Brian R. Mattis, Media Techn.

Trinity Lutheran Hospital - North - Medical Information Retrieval Center
See: **Medical Information Retrieval Center - Consumer Health Information Research Institute** (10005)

★ 16514 ★
Trinity Lutheran Seminary - Hamma Library (Rel-Phil)
2199 E. Main St.   Phone: (614)235-4169
Columbus, OH 43209-2334   Richard H. Mintel, Dir., Lib.Serv.
Founded: 1830. **Staff:** Prof 3; Other 3. **Subjects:** Theology. **Special Collections:** Hymnals; catechisms. **Holdings:** 98,000 books; 10,000 bound periodical volumes. **Subscriptions:** 760 journals and other serials. **Services:** Interlibrary loan; copying; library open to the public for reference use only. **Automated Operations:** Computerized cataloging. **Computerized Information Services:** BRS Information Technologies, EPIC. **Networks/Consortia:** Member of OHIONET. **Remarks:** FAX: (614)238-0263. **Staff:** Linda Fry, Assoc.Libn.; Rodney Hutton, Bibliog.Libn.

★ 16515 ★
Trinity Medical Center - Angus L. Cameron Medical Library (Med)
Trinity Professional Bldg.
20 Burdick Expwy.   Phone: (701)857-5435
Minot, ND 58701   Barb Knight, NW Campus Libn.
Founded: 1928. **Staff:** Prof 1. **Subjects:** Medicine, nursing. **Holdings:** 3000 books; 13.000 bound periodical volumes; 2000 AV programs. **Subscriptions:** 150 journals and other serials. **Services:** Interlibrary loan; copying; SDI; library open to the public for reference use only. **Computerized Information Services:** MEDLINE; EasyLink (electronic mail service). Performs searches on fee basis. **Networks/Consortia:** Member of National Network of Libraries of Medicine - Greater Midwest Region, Northwest AHEC Library Information Network. **Remarks:** FAX: (701)857-5749. This is the Northwest Campus Library of the University of North Dakota School of Medicine.

★ 16516 ★
Trinity Memorial Hospital - Library (Med)
5900 S. Lake Dr.   Phone: (414)769-4028
Cudahy, WI 53110   Carl W. Baehr, Libn.
Founded: 1967. **Subjects:** Medicine, nursing, health care administration. **Holdings:** 1050 books; 2100 bound periodical volumes; 8 VF drawers of pamphlets; 4 VF drawers of news clippings. **Subscriptions:** 140 journals and other serials. **Services:** Interlibrary loan; library open to the public by appointment. **Computerized Information Services:** MEDLINE, DIALOG Information Services. **Networks/Consortia:** Member of Southeastern Wisconsin Health Science Library Consortium (SWHSL). **Remarks:** FAX: (414)769-4154.

★ 16517 ★
Trinity Presbyterian Church - Norman E. Hjorth Memorial Library (Rel-Phil)
Rte. 70 & W. Gate Dr.   Phone: (609)428-2050
Cherry Hill, NJ 08034   Bernice R. Ahlquist, Chm., Lib.Comm.
Founded: 1961. **Staff:** Prof 1; Other 5. **Subjects:** Christian life and education, Bible study. **Holdings:** 2500 books; 25 phonograph records. **Services:** Library open to congregation members.

★ 16518 ★
Trinity United Church of Christ - Edith L. Stock Memorial Library
    (Rel-Phil)
4700 S. Grand Blvd.
St. Louis, MO 63111   Phone: (314)352-6645
Founded: 1960. **Subjects:** Religion. **Holdings:** 2500 books; 60 phonograph records; 125 filmstrips. **Services:** Library open to the public.

Trinity United Methodist Church
See: **Central United Methodist Church - Library (3376)**

★ 16519 ★
Trinity United Methodist Church - Library (Rel-Phil)
2715 E. Jackson Blvd.
Elkhart, IN 46516   Jodie Trimmer, Libn.
    Phone: (219)294-7602
Staff: 1. **Subjects:** History of Methodism, United Methodist missions, religious study, social problems, devotions, United Methodist women. **Holdings:** 3900 books. **Services:** Library open to the public.

★ 16520 ★
Trinity United Presbyterian Church - Library (Rel-Phil)
13922 Prospect Ave.   Phone: (714)544-7850
Santa Ana, CA 92705   Patricia A. Veeh, Hd.Libn.
Founded: 1955. **Staff:** Prof 1; Other 6. **Subjects:** Bible, theology, psychology, church history, social concerns, missions, education, religions. **Special Collections:** Children's Library (2000 volumes). **Holdings:** 7500 books; 400 cassettes. **Subscriptions:** 25 journals and other serials. **Services:** Library open to the public with restrictions.

★ 16521 ★
Trinity University - Elizabeth Coates Maddux Library - Special
    Collections (Soc Sci, Hum)
715 Stadium Dr.
Box 56
San Antonio, TX 78212   Phone: (512)736-7355
Founded: 1869. **Special Collections:** Beretta Texana Collection (includes Encino Press Collection and Nicholson Collection); Mr. and Mrs. Walter F. Brown Rare Book Collection; J.F. Buenz Collection; Paul A. Campbell International Library of Man and Space; Sir Henry Hardman Pamphlet Collection; Ronald Hilton Latin American Collection; George P. Isbell Collection of Works by and about Logan Pearsall Smith; Helen Miller Jones Collection of American Literature; microfilm collection of the Municipal and Parochial Archives, States of Coahuila and Nuevo Leon, Mexico, 1599-1972; Malcolm Lowry Collection; Jim Maloney Aerospace Collection; C.W. Miller Collection of Manuscripts, Incunabula and Early Printed Books; Pat Ireland Nixon Texana Collection; Something Else Press/Avant-Garde Poetry Collection; Albert Steves, III, Collection of Works by and about Sir Winston Churchill; Decherd Turner Collection of William Morris' Kelmscott Press Editions; Harold F. Clark Economics Collection; Gilbert M. Denman, Jr., Collection of Ancient Greek, Roman, and Etruscan Art; Sir Henry Hardman Collection; Left Book Club Collection; Trinity University Archives; U.S. and selected Texas Government document depository (total 200,000 items). **Services:** Interlibrary loan; copying. **Computerized Information Services:** DIALOG Information Services, BRS Information Technologies, OCLC, STN International, MARCIVE, Inc., LIBS 100 System. **Networks/Consortia:** Member of AMIGOS Bibliographic Council, Inc., Council of Research & Academic Libraries (CORAL).

★ 16522 ★
Triodyne Consulting Engineers and Scientists - Safety Information
    Center (Sci-Engr)
5950 W. Touhy Ave.   Phone: (708)677-4730
Niles, IL 60648   Sharon I. Meyer, Dir. of Lib.Serv.
Founded: 1979. **Staff:** Prof 5; Other 3. **Subjects:** Engineering - forensic, mechanical, automotive, civil; industrial safety; chemistry; materials science. **Holdings:** 6650 books; 300 VF drawers of technical reports and patents; 143 VF drawers of manufacturers' literature; 45 VF drawers of engineering standards and specifications; 14 VF drawers of catalogs. **Subscriptions:** 212 journals and other serials. **Services:** Interlibrary loan; copying; SDI; center open to the public by appointment. **Automated Operations:** Computerized cataloging and acquisitions. **Computerized Information Services:** PFDS Online, OCLC, DIALOG Information Services, BRS Information Technologies. Performs searches on fee basis. **Networks/Consortia:** Member of ILLINET, North Suburban Library System (NSLS). **Special Indexes:** Permuted Index of Bibliographies on File (computer). **Remarks:** FAX: (708)647-2047. Jointly maintained by the Institute for Advanced Safety Studies. **Staff:** Cheryl Hansen, Engr.Ref.Libn.; Shirley W. Ruttenberg, Info.Anl.; Meredith L. Hamilton, Engr.Ref.Libn.; Kimberly Last, Tech.Serv.Libn.; Norene Kramer, Acq.; Jackie Schwartz, Circ.

Tripler Army Medical Center
See: **U.S. Army Hospitals (17052)**

Triton Biosciences Inc.
See: **Berlex Biosciences Inc. (1752)**

★ 16523 ★
Triton Environmental Consultants Ltd. - Library (Env-Cons)
120-13511 Commerce Pkwy.   Phone: (604)279-2093
Richmond, BC, Canada V6V 2L1   Louise Archibald, Libn.
Founded: 1980. **Subjects:** Environment, fisheries biology, engineering. **Holdings:** 6000 books. **Subscriptions:** 60 journals and other serials. **Services:** Interlibrary loan; library not open to the public. **Computerized Information Services:** DIALOG Information Services, CAN/OLE. **Remarks:** FAX: (604)279-2047.

★ 16524 ★
Triton Museum of Art - Drs. Ben and A. Jess Shenson Library (Art)
1505 Warburton Ave.   Phone: (408)247-3754
Santa Clara, CA 95050   Bill Atkins, Dir.
Founded: 1965. **Staff:** 10. **Subjects:** 19th and 20th century American art. **Special Collections:** Slide library of works of art in museum collection (400 slides). **Holdings:** 200 books; 300 exhibition catalogs and periodicals; 300 art newspapers; 300 art periodicals, 1919-1950; 12 volumes of news releases on Triton events. **Subscriptions:** 14 journals and other serials. **Services:** Library open to the public with restrictions.

Trolley Park
See: **Oregon Electric Railway Historical Society, Inc. (12520)**

Tropical Agricultural Research and Training Center
See: **Inter-American Institute for Cooperation on Agriculture - Tropical Agricultural Research and Training Center (8028)**

★ 16525 ★
Trotting Horse Museum - Peter D. Haughton Memorial Library (Rec)
240 Main St.   Phone: (914)294-6330
Goshen, NY 10924   Philip A. Pines, Dir.
Founded: 1951. **Staff:** Prof 4. **Subjects:** History of standard bred horses, history of harness racing, training horses, horses in literature, veterinary medicine. **Special Collections:** Currier & Ives trotting prints; sculpture. **Holdings:** 400 books; 200 bound periodical volumes; 4400 record books, sale catalogs, and racing records; videotapes; motion picture films. **Services:** Library open to the public with permission. **Automated Operations:** Computerized cataloging and acquisitions. **Computerized Information Services:** Internal database. **Publications:** Newsletter devoted to museum activities, quarterly. **Special Catalogs:** Catalog of Books Available (online). **Remarks:** FAX: (914)294-3467.

Harry M. Trowbridge Research Library
See: **Wyandotte County Historical Society and Museum (20653)**

★ 16526 ★
Troy Public Library - Special Collections (Hist)
510 W. Big Beaver Rd.   Phone: (313)524-3538
Troy, MI 48084   CoraEllen DeVinney, Dir.
Founded: 1963. **Staff:** 42.5. **Special Collections:** White House Memorabilia; Fran Teasdale Collection (Civil War history); depository for Oakland County Genealogical Society material. **Holdings:** 243,623 books; 133 bound periodical volumes; 105,569 microfiche; 3941 reels of microfilm. **Subscriptions:** 727 journals and other serials; 42 newspapers. **Services:** Interlibrary loan; copying; collections open to the public with restrictions. **Automated Operations:** Computerized public access catalog and circulation. **Computerized Information Services:** WILSEARCH, BRS/After Dark, DIALOG Information Services; internal database. **Networks/Consortia:** Member of Library Cooperative of Macomb (LCM), Michigan Library Consortium (MLC). **Publications:** FYI (staff newsletter); In Print (friends newsletter). **Remarks:** FAX: (313)524-2726. **Staff:** Marcia Rutledge, Hd., Adult Serv.

★ 16527 ★
Trudeau Institute Immunobiological Research Laboratories - Library
(Med)
Algonquin Ave.
Box 59   Phone: (518)891-3080
Saranac Lake, NY 12983   Helen Jarvis, Libn.
Founded: 1900. **Staff:** 1. **Subjects:** Immunobiological research. **Holdings:** 13,000 books and bound periodical volumes. **Subscriptions:** 120 journals and other serials. **Services:** Interlibrary loan; copying; library open to the public at librarian's discretion. **Publications:** Trudeau Institute Annual Report.

★ 16528 ★
True Vine Missionary Baptist Church - Library (Rel-Phil)
831 Broadway Ave.
Box 1051   Phone: (318)445-6730
Alexandria, LA 71302   Ruby Laroche, Libn.
Founded: 1947. **Staff:** Prof 3; Other 5. **Subjects:** Religion - philosophy, history, doctrine. **Holdings:** 2000 books; AV programs. **Subscriptions:** 4 journals and other serials. **Services:** Interlibrary loan; library open to other churches and the local community on a limited basis.

True West Archives
See: University of Texas at Austin - Barker Texas History Center (19379)

George W. Truett Memorial Library
See: First Baptist Church of Dallas - First Baptist Academy (5749)

Harry S Truman Institute for the Advancement of Peace
See: Hebrew University of Jerusalem (7102)

Harry S Truman Library
See: U.S. Presidential Libraries (17924)

★ 16529 ★
Trumbull Memorial Hospital - Wean Medical Library (Med)
1350 E. Market St.   Phone: (216)841-9379
Warren, OH 44482   Diane Richardson, Med.Libn.
Staff: Prof 1. **Subjects:** Medicine and allied health sciences. **Holdings:** 3500 books; 5500 bound periodical volumes. **Subscriptions:** 223 journals and other serials. **Services:** Interlibrary loan; copying; library open to the public at librarian's discretion. **Computerized Information Services:** MEDLINE. Performs searches on fee basis. **Networks/Consortia:** Member of NEOUCOM Council Associated Hospital Librarians. **Publications:** Wean Library News, bimonthly - to medical staff and dental service. **Remarks:** Contains the holdings of the former Trumbull Memorial Hospital - School of Nursing Library

Trunkline Gas - Library
See: Panhandle Eastern Corporation - Corporate Library (12725)

★ 16530 ★
Truth or Consequences Public Library - Southwest Collection (Hist)
325 Library Ln.
P.O. Box 311   Phone: (505)894-3027
Truth or Consequences, NM 87901-0311   Ellanie Sampson, Libn.
Subjects: Southwest history and culture. **Holdings:** 1500 books; 30 bound periodical volumes; 16 nonbook items. **Services:** Interlibrary loan; copying; library open to the public. **Remarks:** FAX: (505)894-7767.

Sojourner Truth Library
See: State University College at New Paltz (15708)

Sojourner Truth Room
See: Prince George's County Memorial Library System (13359)

Sojourner Truth Women's Resource Library
See: Women's Resource and Action Center (20562)

Truxtun-Decatur Naval Museum Library
See: U.S. Navy - Department Library (17800)

TRW, Inc. - Electromagnetic Systems Laboratories
See: ESL/Subsidiary of TRW, Inc. (5439)

★ 16531 ★
TRW, Inc. - Information Center/Government Relations
1000 Wilson Blvd., Suite 2700
Arlington, VA 22209
Defunct.

★ 16532 ★
TRW, Inc. - Operations & Support Group - Space & Defense Sector - Technical Information Center (Sci-Engr, Comp Sci)
One Space Park, Bldg. S., Rm. 1930   Phone: (213)812-4194
Redondo Beach, CA 90278   Ann W. Ellington, Mgr.
Founded: 1954. **Staff:** Prof 9; Other 14. **Subjects:** Defense, space systems, electronics, energy, computer technology. **Special Collections:** Records Retention Center; American Institute of Aeronautics and Astronautics (AIAA) papers; SAE papers; NASA reports and microfiche. **Holdings:** 36,000 books; 9000 bound periodical volumes; 155,000 technical documents; 377,500 microfiche of documents. **Subscriptions:** 700 journals and other serials; 10 newspapers. **Services:** Interlibrary loan; center not open to the public. **Computerized Information Services:** BRS Information Technologies, DTIC, NASA/RECON, DIALOG Information Services, STN International, PFDS Online, Mead Data Central. **Remarks:** Alternate telephone number(s): 812-4191. **Staff:** Gayle Berry, Ref.Supv.; Barbara Molinelli, Acq.Supv.; Jerry Cao, Sys.Adm.; William Gammon, Docs.Cont.

★ 16533 ★
TRW, Inc. - Systems Integration Group - Technical Information Center (Sci-Engr)
One Federal Systems Park Dr.   Phone: (703)734-6243
Fairfax, VA 22033-4416   Jill C. Mercury, Lib.Mgr.
Founded: 1965. **Staff:** Prof 1; Other 1. **Subjects:** Underwater acoustics, systems engineering, sonar and radar systems, computer science. **Holdings:** 5000 books and technical reports. **Subscriptions:** 85 journals and other serials. **Services:** Interlibrary loan; library not open to the public. **Computerized Information Services:** DIALOG Information Services, DTIC. **Networks/Consortia:** Member of Interlibrary Users Association (IUA). **Remarks:** Library located at 7600 Colshire Dr., McLean, VA 22102. FAX: (703)734-6601. **Formerly:** Its Technical Library.

Tryon Library
See: University of Pittsburgh - Pymatuning Laboratory of Ecology (19222)

Tryon Palace Restoration
See: North Carolina (State) Department of Cultural Resources (11887)

Tsentar za Nauchna Informacija po Meditsina i Zdraveopazvane
See: Bulgaria - Medical Academy - Center for Scientific Information in Medicine and Public Health (2346)

TSI - Mason Research Institute
See: TSI Mason Laboratories (16534)

★ 16534 ★
TSI Mason Laboratories - Information Services (Med)
57 Union St.   Phone: (508)791-0931
Worcester, MA 01608   Linda Wells, Info.Spec.
Founded: 1956. **Staff:** Prof 1. **Subjects:** Biomedical sciences, toxicology, pathology, immunobiology, endocrinology, reproductive physiology, biochemistry, tissue culture, veterinary medicine. **Special Collections:** Bioassay data on 3000 steroids. **Holdings:** 1700 books, technical reports, directories, abstracts, indexes, reprints, bibliographies. **Subscriptions:** 35 journals and other serials. **Services:** Interlibrary loan; library open to the public for reference use only. **Computerized Information Services:** DIALOG Information Services, MEDLINE, LEXIS, NEXIS. **Networks/ Consortia:** Member of Central Massachusetts Consortium of Health Related Libraries (CMCHRL), Massachusetts Health Sciences Libraries Network (MaHSLiN), Worcester Area Cooperating Libraries (WACL). **Remarks:** FAX: (508)753-1834. **Formerly:** TSI - Mason Research Institute.

★ 16535 ★
TU Electric - Library (Energy, Bus-Fin)
Box 660268   Phone: (214)954-5966
Dallas, TX 75266   Ann S. Midgett, Corp.Libn.
Founded: 1983. **Staff:** Prof 1; Other 2. **Subjects:** Electrical engineering, energy industry, business administration, power transmission and distribution, finance, economics. **Special Collections:** Electric Power Research Institute reports; utility company annual reports. **Holdings:** 7000 books; 10 drawers of microfiche. **Subscriptions:** 425 journals and other serials; 8 newspapers. **Services:** Interlibrary loan; library not open to the public. **Automated Operations:** Computerized cataloging and serials. **Computerized Information Services:** WILSONLINE, DataTimes, DIALOG Information Services, Dow Jones News/Retrieval, Dun & Bradstreet Business Credit Services, Knight-Ridder Unicom, EPRI, URAP; Utility Data Institute (UDI; electronic mail service). **Remarks:** FAX: (214)954-5453.

★ 16536 ★
Tuality Community Hospital - Health Sciences Library (Med)
335 S.E. 8th Ave.   Phone: (503)681-1121
Hillsboro, OR 97123   Natalie Norcross, Med.Libn.
Founded: 1980. **Staff:** Prof 1. **Subjects:** Clinical medicine, pharmacology, nursing, therapeutics, cardiovascular medicine. **Holdings:** 460 books; 109 bound periodical volumes. **Subscriptions:** 175 journals and other serials. **Services:** Interlibrary loan; copying; library open to the public by appointment. **Computerized Information Services:** MEDLINE, DIALOG Information Services; OnTyme Electronic Message Network Service (electronic mail service). **Networks/Consortia:** Member of Oregon Health Information Online (ORHION), Washington County Cooperative Library Services (WCCLS), Portland Area Health Sciences Librarians, Oregon Health Sciences Libraries Association (OHSLA). **Remarks:** FAX: (503)681-1729. Electronic mail address(es): TUALCH (OnTyme Electronic Message Network Service).

★ 16537 ★
Tuality Healthcare Foundation - Tuality Health Information Resource Center (Med)
Box 309
334 S.E. 8th Ave.   Phone: (503)681-1702
Hillsboro, OR 97123   Natalie Norcross, Med.Libn.
Founded: 1988. **Staff:** Prof 1. **Subjects:** Health, fitness, nutrition, diseases, support groups. **Holdings:** 635 books; 4500 pamphlets; 25 anatomical models and charts; 150 videotapes. **Subscriptions:** 70 journals and other serials. **Services:** Interlibrary loan; copying; library open to the public. **Automated Operations:** Computerized public access catalog and cataloging. **Computerized Information Services:** MEDLINE, DIALOG Information Services; OnTyme Electronic Message Network Service (electronic mail service). Performs searches free of charge. **Networks/Consortia:** Member of Washington County Cooperative Library Services (WCCLS). **Remarks:** FAX: (503)681-1761. Electronic mail address(es): TUALCH (OnTyme Electronic Message Network Service).

★ 16538 ★
(Tubingen) German-American Institute - USIS Collection (Educ)
Karlstrasse, 3   Phone: 7071 34071
W-7400 Tubingen, Germany   Karl Stroebel
Founded: 1952. **Staff:** 2. **Subjects:** United States. **Holdings:** 7500 books; 3000 microfiche; 2500 slides; 200 videotapes; 300 audiocassettes; 800 music cassettes. **Subscriptions:** 70 journals and other serials; 15 newspapers. **Services:** Interlibrary loan; library open to the public. **Remarks:** FAX: 7071 31873. Maintained or supported by the U.S. Information Agency. Focus is on materials that will assist peoples outside the United States to learn about the United States, its people, history, culture, political processes, and social milieux. **Staff:** Patricia Lech, Libn.

Tubists Universal Brotherhood Association (TUBA) Resource Library
See: Ball State University - Music Library (1442)

Tuck Memorial Museum
See: Meeting House Green Memorial and Historical Association, Inc. (10020)

Gerald Tucker Memorial Medical Library
See: National Jewish Center for Immunology and Respiratory Medicine (11221)

Tucker Library of the History of Medicine
See: University of Cincinnati - Medical Center Information and Communications - Cincinnati Medical Heritage Center (18475)

Mollie Sublett Tucker Memorial Medical Library
See: Memorial Hospital (10034)

★ 16539 ★
Tucson Citizen - Library (Publ)
Box 26767   Phone: (602)573-4570
Tucson, AZ 85726   Charlotte Kenan, Libn.
Founded: 1956. **Staff:** Prof 1.5. **Subjects:** Newspaper reference topics. **Holdings:** 600 books; Tucson Citizen on microfilm; 1 million clippings; 1200 microfilm jackets; 20 drawers of pamphlets, photographs, negatives; clipping files. **Subscriptions:** 70 journals and other serials; 10 newspapers. **Services:** Library not open to the public. **Remarks:** Library located at 4850 S. Park Ave., Tucson, AZ 85714. FAX: (602)573-4569.

★ 16540 ★
Tucson City Planning Department - Library (Plan)
Box 27210   Phone: (602)791-4234
Tucson, AZ 85726   Anna S. Sanchez, Plan.Libn.
Founded: 1974. **Staff:** Prof 1. **Subjects:** Land use and development, planning, zoning, energy, environmental protection, economic development. **Special Collections:** City of Tucson planning reports, 1930 to present; local census reports, 1940 to present; zoning codes. **Holdings:** 5000 books; 150 bound periodical volumes; 300 microfiche; 3 VF drawers; slides; tapes; maps. **Subscriptions:** 72 journals and other serials. **Services:** Interlibrary loan; copying; SDI; library open to the public for reference use only. **Automated Operations:** Computerized cataloging and circulation. **Publications:** Publications catalog, annual. **Remarks:** FAX: (602)791-4130.

★ 16541 ★
Tucson Electric Power Company - Library (Energy)
220 W. 6th
Box 711   Phone: (602)622-6661
Tucson, AZ 85702   Darlene K. Smith, Libn.
Founded: 1973. **Staff:** 2. **Holdings:** 1600 books. **Subscriptions:** 300 journals and other serials; 7 newspapers. **Services:** library not open to the public. **Computerized Information Services:** DIALOG Information Services, Dow Jones News/Retrieval. **Remarks:** FAX: (602)884-3844.

★ 16542 ★
Tucson General Hospital - Medical Library (Med)
3838 N. Campbell Ave.   Phone: (602)327-5431
Tucson, AZ 85717   Judy Snow
Founded: 1960. **Subjects:** Medicine, nursing, and allied health sciences. **Special Collections:** Osteopathic medicine; management. **Holdings:** 630 books; 122 bound periodical volumes; 283 videotapes; 140 audiotapes; 41 slide/tape sets. **Subscriptions:** 67 journals and other serials. **Services:** Interlibrary loan; copying. **Computerized Information Services:** MEDLINE; internal database. **Special Catalogs:** AV holdings (printout).

★ 16543 ★
Tucson Medical Center - Medical Library (Med)
Box 42195   Phone: (602)327-5461
Tucson, AZ 85733   Lynn Flance, Mgr., Lib.Serv.
Founded: 1961. **Staff:** Prof 1; Other 1. **Subjects:** Clinical medicine and related sciences. **Holdings:** 1200 books; 10,000 bound periodical volumes; 400 AV programs. **Subscriptions:** 300 journals and other serials. **Services:** Interlibrary loan; library not open to the public. **Automated Operations:** Computerized cataloging and ILL. **Computerized Information Services:** MEDLARS, Dataderm, BRS Information Technologies, WILSONLINE; CD-ROM (MEDLINE); OnTyme Electronic Message Network Service (electronic mail service). **Special Catalogs:** AV Catalog (book). **Staff:** Dolores Canez, Ser.

★ 16544 ★
Tucson Museum of Art - Library (Art)
140 N. Main   Phone: (602)623-4881
Tucson, AZ 85701   S.M. Sheila Mortonson, OSF, Libn.
Founded: 1974. **Staff:** Prof 1; Other 10. **Subjects:** Art - pre-Columbian, primitive, African, other ethnic groups, Spanish-Colonial, U.S., European, Western, local, contemporary. **Special Collections:** Pre-Columbian art (15,000 slides); Arizona artists (2500 slides; 16 VF drawers of biographies, periodical articles); Arizona Artists' Archives (papers of notable Arizona artists; hard copy, microfiche); Aztec and Mixtec Codices (6 facsimiles); biography (21 VF drawers of clippings, periodical articles, exhibition catalogs, illustrations) . **Holdings:** 7500 books; 700 unbound periodical volumes; 6500 slides. **Subscriptions:** 36 journals and other serials. **Services:** Copying; library open to the public for reference use only. **Publications:** Brochure, 4th edition, 1984; Spanish Colonial Art: Books in the Tucson Museum of Art Library, 1985. **Special Indexes:** Index to Arizona Artists (12 card file drawers).

★ 16545 ★
Tucson Pima Library - Government Collection (Soc Sci)
Box 27470   Phone: (602)791-4041
Tucson, AZ 85726-7470   Jo Riester, Mgr./Libn.
Founded: 1974. **Staff:** Prof 1; Other 1. **Subjects:** Local government, groundwater management, growth management, economic development, personnel. **Holdings:** 3287 books; 2200 periodical volumes; 800 local documents. **Subscriptions:** 175 journals and other serials; 8 newspapers. **Services:** Copying; SDI; library open to the public. **Automated Operations:** Computerized circulation and ILL. **Computerized Information Services:** DIALOG Information Services, LOGIN, TRAINET. Performs searches free of charge. **Publications:** GRL Update-New Arrivals, irregular - on request to other libraries. **Formerly:** Its Tucson Governmental Reference Library.

★ 16546 ★
Tucson Public Library - Steinheimer Collection of Southwestern Children's Literature (Hum)
200 S. 6th Ave.
Box 27470   Phone: (602)791-4393
Tucson, AZ 85701   Roberta Barg, Sr.Chf.Libn.
Founded: 1980. **Staff:** Prof 2; Other 2. **Subjects:** Southwestern children's literature, folklore, and nonfiction. **Holdings:** 2000 books, filmstrips, phonograph records, audio cassettes, videotapes. **Services:** Copying; collection open to the public. **Automated Operations:** Computerized cataloging, acquisitions, and circulation. **Remarks:** FAX: (602)791-5248. **Staff:** Kristi Bradford, Ch.Libn.

★ 16547 ★
Tufts University - Center for the Study of Drug Development - Library (Med)
136 Harrison Ave.   Phone: (617)956-0185
Boston, MA 02111   Drusilla Raiford, Res.Assoc.
Founded: 1976. **Staff:** Prof 1. **Subjects:** Drug development and regulation, pharmaceutical industry. **Special Collections:** Drug development and regulation file (15,000 items). **Holdings:** 2200 books; 160 bound periodical volumes; 13,000 reports, manuscripts, reprints. **Subscriptions:** 25 journals and other serials. **Services:** Library open to researchers by appointment. **Computerized Information Services:** BRS Information Technologies, DIALOG Information Services; Drug Development File (internal database). **Remarks:** FAX: (617)350-8425.

★ 16548 ★
Tufts University - Fletcher School of Law & Diplomacy - Edwin Ginn Library (Law, Soc Sci)
Medford, MA 02155   Phone: (617)627-3273
                                     Natalie Schatz, Libn.
Founded: 1933. **Staff:** Prof 3; Other 7. **Subjects:** International law and organization, world politics, economic development, international security studies. **Special Collections:** United Nations (80,000 microforms; 10,000 paper documents); Murrow Library (43,000 pieces of ephemera; 1600 books; 2 films; audiotapes); Cabot papers (10,000 pieces of ephemera). **Holdings:** 99,456 books and bound periodical volumes. **Subscriptions:** 1209 journals and other serials; 40 newspapers. **Services:** Interlibrary loan; copying; library open to the public. **Automated Operations:** Computerized public access catalog and circulation. **Computerized Information Services:** OCLC, DIALOG Information Services, NEXIS, ABI/INFORM, PAIS, Predicasts F & S Indexes. **Networks/Consortia:** Member of NELINET, Inc., Boston Library Consortium (BLC). **Remarks:** FAX: (617)628-5508. **Staff:** Barbara Boyce, Assoc.Libn.; Miriam Seltzer, Ref.Libn.

★ 16549 ★
Tufts University - Health Sciences Library (Med)
145 Harrison Ave.   Phone: (617)956-7481
Boston, MA 02111   Elizabeth K. Eaton, Ph.D., Dir.
Founded: 1900. **Staff:** Prof 11.2; Other 12. **Subjects:** Medicine, dentistry, veterinary medicine, nutrition. **Special Collections:** History of Medicine. **Holdings:** 36,589 books; 79,183 bound periodical volumes; 284 audiotapes; 222 slide titles; 3511 reels of microfilm; 7072 microcards; 742 videotapes; 11 phonograph records; 7 video discs. **Subscriptions:** 1439 journals and other serials; 6 newspapers. **Services:** Interlibrary loan; copying; SDI; faxing; library open to the public by subscription. **Automated Operations:** Computerized public access catalog, cataloging, acquisitions, circulation, serials, and ILL (DOCLINE). **Computerized Information Services:** DIALOG Information Services, BRS Information Technologies, PaperChase, NLM, OCLC, MEDLINE; internal database; BITNET (electronic mail service). Performs searches on fee basis. Contact Person: Elizabeth J. Richardson, Info.Serv.Libn., 956-6705. **Networks/Consortia:** Member of NELINET, Inc., Boston Library Consortium (BLC), National Network of Libraries of Medicine - New England Region. **Publications:** Library Guide; Brochures; New Acquisitions. **Remarks:** FAX: (617)350-8039. Electronic mail address(es): EEATON@6PAL.TUFTS.EDU (BITNET). **Staff:** Cora C. Ho, Dp.Dir.; Carolyn Waite, Hd., Tech.Serv.; Janet Holborow, Info.Serv.Libn.; Amy Lapidow, Info.Serv.Libn.; Anne Nou, Info.Serv.Libn.; Linda Van Horn, Network Libn.; Connie Wong, ILL Coord., Katie Daly, LRC Mgr.

★ 16550 ★
Tufts University - Knipp Physics Reading Room (Sci-Engr, Comp Sci)
Robinson Hall, Rm. 251   Phone: (617)629-3245
Medford, MA 02155   Wayne B. Powell, Engr./Sci.Libn.
Founded: 1955. **Staff:** Prof 1. **Subjects:** High energy physics, nuclear physics, solid state physics, quantum mechanics, electricity and magnetism, general relativity, astronomy, astrophysics. **Holdings:** 3500 bound periodical volumes; 1500 preprints. **Subscriptions:** 160 journals. **Services:** Interlibrary loan (through Wessell Library); library open to consortium members, others by permission. **Automated Operations:** Computerized public access catalog. **Networks/Consortia:** Member of Boston Library Consortium (BLC), NELINET, Inc. **Remarks:** FAX: (617)629-3002.

★ 16551 ★
Tufts University - Music Library (Mus)
Leir Hall   Phone: (617)381-3594
Medford, MA 02155   Brenda Chasen Goldman, Assoc.Libn., Mus.
Staff: Prof 1; Other 1. **Subjects:** Music theory and composition, history and literature of jazz, world music, western art music. **Holdings:** 26,000 books, scores, musical recordings. **Subscriptions:** 70 journals. **Services:** Interlibrary loan; copying; library open to the public at librarian's discretion. **Automated Operations:** Computerized public access catalog and circulation. **Computerized Information Services:** DIALOG Information Services; InterNet (electronic mail service). **Networks/Consortia:** Member of Boston Library Consortium (BLC), Boston Area Music Libraries (BAML). **Remarks:** Electronic mail address(es): BGOLDMAN@PEARL.TUFTS.EDU (InterNet).

★ 16552 ★
Tufts University - Nils Yngve Wessell Library - Special Collections (Hist)
Medford, MA 02155   Phone: (617)627-3737
                                     David R. McDonald, Dir.
Founded: 1960. **Staff:** 1. **Subjects:** History - University, United States, English; literature; religion (Universalism); music; environment; fine arts (stained glass). **Special Collections:** Hosea Ballou Collection; P.T. Barnum Collection; William Bentley Sermon Collection; Henri Goiran Collection; John Holmes Collection; Ryder Collection of Confederate Archives; Stearns Collection; Ritter Collection; Asa Alford Tufts Collection; Edwin Bolles Collection; Citizen's Clearinghouse for Hazardous Wastes. **Holdings:** 6000 books; 350 bound periodical volumes; 81 linear feet of manuscripts; 1912 linear feet of archival items; pamphlets. **Services:** Interlibrary loan; copying; SDI; library open to the public. **Networks/Consortia:** Member of Boston Library Consortium (BLC), NELINET, Inc. **Publications:** Brochures. **Remarks:** FAX: (617)627-3002; (617)627-3063. **Staff:** Barbara Tringali, Archv.Asst.

★ 16553 ★
Tufts University - Richard H. Lufkin Library (Sci-Engr)
Anderson Hall   Phone: (617)629-3245
Medford, MA 02155   Wayne B. Powell, Hd., Engr./Sci.Libn.
Founded: 1961. **Staff:** Prof 1; Other 1. **Subjects:** Engineering - civil, mechanical, electrical; engineering design; mathematics; physics; astronomy. **Holdings:** 23,000 books; 24,000 bound periodical volumes; 750 dissertations; 11,000 technical reports. **Subscriptions:** 400 journals and other serials. **Services:** Interlibrary loan (through Wessell Library); copying; library open to consortium members, others by permission. **Automated Operations:** Computerized public access catalog and circulation. **Computerized Information Services:** DIALOG Information Services, STN International; BITNET (electronic mail service). **Networks/Consortia:** Member of Boston Library Consortium (BLC), NELINET, Inc. **Remarks:** FAX: (617)629-3002.

★ 16554 ★
Tufts University - Rockwell Chemistry Library (Sci-Engr)
62 Talbot Ave.   Phone: (617)381-3439
Medford, MA 02155   Wayne B. Powell, Hd., Engr./Sci. Libn.
Staff: 1.5. **Subjects:** Chemistry, chemical engineering. **Holdings:** 6700 books; 7300 bound periodical volumes; 550 dissertations; 230 microforms. **Subscriptions:** 200 journals and other serials. **Services:** Interlibrary loan (through Wessell Library); copying; library open to consortium members, others by permission. **Automated Operations:** Computerized public access catalog and circulation. **Computerized Information Services:** DIALOG Information Services, STN International; BITNET (electronic mail service). **Networks/Consortia:** Member of Boston Library Consortium (BLC), NELINET, Inc. **Remarks:** FAX: (617)629-3002.

Tufts University - U.S.D.A. - Human Nutrition Center on Aging
See: U.S.D.A. - Human Nutrition Research Center on Aging (17202)

Tulane Regional Primate Research Center
See: Tulane University (16566)

★ 16555 ★
Tulane University - A.B. Freeman School of Business Administration - Turchin Library (Bus-Fin)
New Orleans, LA 70118   Phone: (504)865-5376
                                                 Dorothy Whittemore, Dir.
Founded: 1926. **Staff:** Prof 1; Other 3. **Subjects:** Accounting, finance, international business, marketing, behavioral analysis. **Special Collections:** Corporate financial history folders of annual reports and other documents (1000). **Holdings:** 30,007 volumes. **Subscriptions:** 500 journals and other serials. **Services:** Interlibrary loan; copying; library open to the University community.

★ 16556 ★
Tulane University - Architecture Library (Art, Plan)
Richardson Memorial Bldg., Rm. 202   Phone: (504)865-5391
New Orleans, LA 70118   Frances E. Hecker, Hd.
Founded: 1948. **Staff:** 2. **Subjects:** Architecture, city planning, preservation, technology. **Holdings:** 11,000 books; 1200 bound periodical volumes. **Subscriptions:** 325 journals and other serials. **Services:** Interlibrary loan; copying; library open to the public. **Automated Operations:** Computerized public access catalog. **Remarks:** FAX: (504)865-6773.

★ 16557 ★
Tulane University - Howard-Tilton Memorial Library - Louisiana Collection (Hist, Art)
New Orleans, LA 70118   Phone: (504)865-6773
                                                 Joan G. Caldwell, Hd.
Staff: 2. **Subjects:** Louisiana - history and politics, art and architecture, literature, genealogy. **Holdings:** 33,000 books and bound periodical volumes; 99 VF drawers of clippings, pamphlets, and other material; 29 VF drawers of pictures, portraits; 11 cases of maps; 54 boxes of Louisiana sheet music. **Subscriptions:** 75 journals and other serials; 6 newspapers. **Services:** Copying; collection open to the public with restrictions. **Automated Operations:** Computerized cataloging. **Computerized Information Services:** DIALOG Information Services, OCLC. **Special Indexes:** Indexes to books and periodicals, maps, sheet music (cards).

★ 16558 ★
Tulane University - Latin American Library (Area-Ethnic)
Howard-Tilton Memorial Library   Phone: (504)865-5681
New Orleans, LA 70118   Guillermo Nanez-Falcon, Ph.D., Dir.
Founded: 1924. **Staff:** Prof 1; Other 4.3. **Subjects:** Latin America - anthropology, archeology, art, history, economics, political science, sociology. **Special Collections:** Latin American Photographic Archive (19,000 photographs); Merle Greene Robertson Rubbings Collection (1400 rubbings of stone relief sculpture); William E. Gates Collections of Mexicana; Lewis Hanke Papers (18 VF drawers); France V. Scholes Collection (copies and notes of materials from the Archivo General de Indias of Seville and Archivo General de la Nacion of Mexico; 76 VF drawers); Nicolas Leon Collection; Ephraim George Squier Papers; Francisco Morazan Papers; George H. Pepper Papers on Indians of the American Southwest; Viceregal and Ecclesiastical Mexican Collection (3000 dossiers); William Walker Papers; Central American Printed Ephemera Collection; other collections relating to colonial and 19th century Mexico, Yucatan, and Chiapas. **Holdings:** 200,000 books; 615 linear feet of manuscripts; 4000 pamphlets; 3000 maps. **Subscriptions:** 1525 journals and other serials; 24 newspapers. **Services:** Interlibrary loan; copying; library open to the public. **Automated Operations:** Computerized cataloging and circulation. **Computerized Information Services:** DIALOG Information Services, OCLC. **Networks/Consortia:** Member of Center for Research Libraries (CRL), SOLINET. **Publications:** Catalog of Latin American Library, 1970 (9 volumes); supplements, 1970, 1974, 1978. **Remarks:** FAX: (504)865-6773. **Staff:** Ruth Olivera, Mss.Cat.; Martha Robertson, Rare Bks.; Maria Hernandez-Lehmann, Gifts, Exch., and Ser.

★ 16559 ★
Tulane University - Law Library (Law)
School of Law   Phone: (504)865-5952
New Orleans, LA 70118   David A. Combe, Libn.
Staff: Prof 10; Other 10. **Subjects:** Law - Roman, civil, maritime, comparative. **Holdings:** 480,000 volumes and microforms. **Subscriptions:** 6000 journals and other serials. **Services:** Interlibrary loan; library not open to the public. **Automated Operations:** Computerized public access catalog, acquisitions, serials, and circulation. **Computerized Information Services:** DIALOG Information Services, OCLC, PFDS Online, WESTLAW, DataTimes, ELSS (Electronic Legislative Search System), LEXIS, NEXIS. Performs searches on fee basis. **Networks/Consortia:** Member of SOLINET. **Staff:** Ray A. Lytle, Hd., Pub.Serv.; Mary McCorkle, Hd., Tech.Serv.; Katherine Nachod, Doc.Libn.; Mary Holt, Circ.Libn.; Barbara Matthews, Cat.; Margareta Horiba, Acq.Libn.; Kimberly Koko, Ref.Libn.; Kevin Houriban, Ref.Libn.; Ann Dewell, Cat.Libn.

★ 16560 ★
Tulane University - Manuscripts, Rare Books, and University Archive (Rare Book, Hist)
Howard-Tilton Memorial Library   Phone: (504)865-5685
New Orleans, LA 70118   Wilbur E. Meneray, Ph.D., Hd.
Founded: 1941. **Staff:** Prof 4; Other 7. **Subjects:** New Orleans and southern Louisiana history, politics, Civil War, economics, literature, religious and social history, 18th century to present; water transportation; natural history; English county history; Romanov Russian history and travel; American Revolution; science fiction; 19th-20th century English language first editions; Tulane University. **Special Collections:** George W. Cable Collection; Favrot Family papers (18th and early 19th century Louisiana); John Kennedy Toole papers; Ben Lucin Burman papers; Charles Colcock Jones papers (pre-Civil War minister and plantation owner in Georgia); Joseph Merrick Jones Steamboat Collection; Kuntz Collection (18th and early 19th century Louisiana); Albert Sidney and William Preston Johnston papers; Louisiana Historical Association Collection (Civil War papers); papers of U.S. Representatives F. Edward Hebert, Dave Treen, and T. Hale Boggs, Governor Sam Jones, and Mayor deLesseps S. Morrison; Political Ephemera Collection; William B. Wisdom Collections of William Faulkner and 19th and 20th century first editions; Lafcadio Hearn Collection; Robert Southey; Colonial Americana Collection; Tulane University (theses; dissertations; 1000 titles of archival materials; Board, Presidential, and deans' records); Jules C. Alciatore Collections of Stendhal; Midlo Bookplate Collection; Rosel Brown Science Fiction Collection; Southern Jewish Archive; Corinne Claiborne Boggs Papers (U.S. Representative papers); Frances Parkinson Keyes Collection. **Holdings:** 16,500 linear feet; 50,000 rare book titles. **Services:** Copying; archives open to the public with identification. **Automated Operations:** Computerized cataloging. **Computerized Information Services:** OCLC. **Networks/Consortia:** Member of SOLINET. **Publications:** The Favrot Family Papers (Volume I, 1690-1782; Volume II, 1783-1796; Volume III, 1797-1802); Pierre-Joseph Favrot's Education Manual for His Sons. **Special Catalogs:** Catalogs of the

Kuntz, Faulkner, and Hearn Collections; Favrot Library catalog; manuscript catalog; rare book catalog. **Staff:** Leon C. Miller, Mss.Libn.; Sylvia V. Metzinger, Rare Books Libn.; Robert G. Sherer, Ph.D., Univ.Archv.

★ 16561 ★
Tulane University - Mathematics Research Library (Sci-Engr)
Gibson Hall   Phone: (504)865-5727
New Orleans, LA 70118   Norbert Riedel, Prof., Math.
Founded: 1964. **Staff:** 1. **Subjects:** Graduate mathematics. **Holdings:** 12,800 books; 9000 bound periodical volumes; 133 Tulane math department dissertations. **Subscriptions:** 288 journals and other serials. **Services:** Interlibrary loan; copying; library open to the public with permission of librarian. **Automated Operations:** Computerized public access catalog and serials. **Staff:** Susan F. Bretz, Libn.

★ 16562 ★
Tulane University - Maxwell Music Library (Mus)
Howard-Tilton Memorial Library   Phone: (504)865-5642
New Orleans, LA 70118   Robert Curtis, Ph.D., Libn.
Staff: Prof 1; Other 3. **Subjects:** Music. **Holdings:** 33,606 volumes; 13,764 phonograph records, tapes, compact discs. **Subscriptions:** 202 journals and other serials. **Services:** Interlibrary loan; copying. **Computerized Information Services:** BITNET (electronic mail service). **Remarks:** Listening facilities are available. **Remarks:** FAX: (504)865-6773. Electronic mail address(es): LB08ILF@MUSIC.TCS.TULANE.EDU (BITNET).

★ 16563 ★
Tulane University - Newcomb College Center for Research on Women - Vorhoff Library (Soc Sci)
New Orleans, LA 70118   Phone: (504)865-5238
                                Susan Tucker
Founded: 1975. **Staff:** Prof 2; Other 3. **Subjects:** Women's education, women's labor, Southern women, motherhood. **Special Collections:** Archives of Newcomb College (300 cubic feet of archival materials); Scrapbooks of Southern Women Collection; Cookbook Collection. **Holdings:** 3055 books; 450 cubic feet of archival materials. **Subscriptions:** 76 journals and other serials. **Services:** Copying; library open to the public on fee basis. **Automated Operations:** Computerized cataloging (NOTIS). **Publications:** Contents Service; Bibliography and Reference Series; subject guide, biennial; Working Papers Series in Women's Studies.

★ 16564 ★
Tulane University - School of Medicine - Rudolph Matas Medical Library (Med, Biol Sci)
1430 Tulane Ave.   Phone: (504)588-5155
New Orleans, LA 70112-2699   William D. Postell, Jr., Med.Libn.
Founded: 1844. **Staff:** Prof 6; Other 8. **Subjects:** Medicine, public health. **Holdings:** 152,000 volumes. **Subscriptions:** 1200 journals. **Services:** Interlibrary loan; copying. **Computerized Information Services:** MEDLINE, DIALOG Information Services. **Networks/Consortia:** Member of National Network of Libraries of Medicine - South Central Region.

★ 16565 ★
Tulane University - Southeastern Architectural Archive (Art)
7001 Freret St.   Phone: (504)865-5697
New Orleans, LA 70118   William R. Cullison, Cur.
Staff: Prof 1; Other 1. **Subjects:** Architecture - general, Louisiana, Southeastern U.S. **Special Collections:** Garden Library of the New Orleans Town Gardeners. **Holdings:** 4 million items, including 3000 books; 500,000 architectural drawings; 15,000 photographs. **Services:** Copying; archive open to the public. **Publications:** Annual reports. **Special Catalogs:** Exhibit catalogs; catalog of the Garden Library of the New Orleans Town Gardeners.

★ 16566 ★
Tulane University - Tulane Regional Primate Research Center - Science Information Service (Biol Sci, Med)
18703 Rivers Rd.   Phone: (504)892-2040
Covington, LA 70433   Mercedes M. Fussell, Adm.Asst.
Founded: 1963. **Staff:** 1. **Subjects:** Infectious disease - acquired immunodeficiency syndrome (AIDS), leprosy, filariasis, malaria, pyelonephritis, prostatitis, treatment of viral infections with antiviral substances; neurobiology, reproductive physiology, urology, veterinary science, immunology, parasitology, primatology. **Holdings:** 4608 books; 4480 bound periodical volumes; 6 dissertations; 175 microfiche. **Subscriptions:** 64 journals and other serials. **Services:** Interlibrary loan; copying; SDI; service open to students, scientists, and researchers. **Automated Operations:** Computerized cataloging and ILL. **Computerized Information Services:** OCLC, MEDLINE, Louisiana Numerical Register (LNR). **Remarks:** FAX: (504)893-1352. **Formerly:** Its Delta Regional Primate Research Center.

★ 16567 ★
Tulane University - William Ransom Hogan Jazz Archive (Mus)
Howard-Tilton Memorial Library   Phone: (504)865-5688
New Orleans, LA 70118   Bruce B. Raeburn, Cur.
Founded: 1958. **Staff:** Prof 2; Other 2. **Subjects:** Classic New Orleans jazz, with related background material and a limited amount of material relating to later developments in jazz; blues; rhythm and blues; gospel music. **Special Collections:** Nick LaRocca Collection (2644 items); Al Rose Collection (6500 items); John Robichaux Collection (7219 items); Herbert A. Otto Collection (20 tapes); Robert W. Greenwood Collection (345 items); Robert Bradley Collection (1179 items); Roger Gulbrandsen Collection (4372 items); George Blanchin Collection (920 items); Orin Blackstone Collection (1432 items); Ted Demuth Collection (370 items); Gospel Music Collection (600 items); George Bing Collection (116 items); William Russell notes; Henry Kmen notes; Harry Souchon Collection; Edmond Souchon Collection; Ralston Crawford Collection; Ray Bauduc Collection; Joe Mares Collection; Knocky Parker Collection; Raymond Burke Collection. **Holdings:** 2200 books; 7000 photographs; 1750 oral history tapes; 10,000 pages of oral history summaries; 42,000 phonograph records; 1300 piano rolls; 142 cylinder recordings; 41,000 pieces of sheet music; 2500 magnetic tapes; 150 reels of motion picture film; 6 reels of microfilm; 100 videotapes; 25,655 miscellaneous notes, clippings, posters. **Subscriptions:** 461 journals and other serials. **Services:** Interlibrary loan; copying (copies of tape summaries and digests available); archive open to the public. **Automated Operations:** Computerized cataloging and circulation. **Computerized Information Services:** OCLC. **Publications:** List of publications - available upon request. **Special Catalogs:** Catalog of 78 rpm recordings, G.K. Hall (card); catalog of popular music in print (computerized). **Special Indexes:** Name index of New Orleans musicians, past and present (card); cross-reference index of oral history summaries (bands, persons, places). **Remarks:** FAX: (504)865-6773. **Staff:** Alma D. Williams, Asst. to Cur.; Kahne Parsons, Assoc.Cur., Print & Ms.Mat. ; Richard B. Allen, Cur., Oral Hist.

★ 16568 ★
Tulare County Free Library - California Historical Research Collection - Annie R. Mitchell Room (Hist)
200 W. Oak St.   Phone: (209)733-6954
Visalia, CA 93291-4993   Mary Anne Terstegge, Res.Rm.Libn.
Founded: 1920. **Staff:** 1. **Subjects:** Tulare county history, San Joaquin Valley history, Sequoia National Park, Kaweah Commonwealth Colony, Sierra Nevada Mountains. **Special Collections:** George W. Stewart Manuscript Collection on Sequoia/Kings Canyon National Parks and the California National Guard. **Holdings:** 3025 books; 29 bound periodical volumes; 39 VF drawers of pamphlets and pictures; 35 boxes. **Subscriptions:** 3 journals and other serials. **Services:** Copying; research collection open to the public on a limited schedule. **Computerized Information Services:** DIALOG Information Services, VU/TEXT Information Services. **Networks/Consortia:** Member of San Joaquin Valley Library System (SJVLS). **Special Indexes:** Los Tulares Index; index to Declarations of Intent and Petitions for Naturalization filed from 1855 to 1928 in Tulare County, California. **Remarks:** FAX: (209)730-2524.

★ 16569 ★
Tulare County Law Library (Law)
County Civic Center, Rm. 1
221 S. Mooney Blvd.   Phone: (209)733-6395
Visalia, CA 93291   Sharon Borbon, Law Lib.Coord.
Founded: 1892. **Staff:** 2. **Subjects:** Law and related subjects. **Holdings:** 19,300 volumes. **Computerized Information Services:** WESTLAW.

★ 16570 ★
Tulare Public Library - Inez L. Hyde Memorial Collection (Hist)
113 North F. St.
Tulare, CA 93274   Phone: (209)685-2342
Subjects: Genealogy, local history. **Holdings:** 3836 volumes; 2982 reels of microfilm; 3084 titles on 16,400 microfiche. **Services:** Genealogy Room open to the public with restrictions. **Staff:** Pat Ruiz, Libn.

Tullis Library/Resource Center
See: **Kansas State University, Salina** (8576)

Alice Tully Library
See: **Temple University - Esther Boyer College of Music - New School Institute** (16146)

★ 16571 ★
Tulsa City-County Library System - Business and Technology Department (Sci-Engr, Trans, Energy, Bus-Fin)
400 Civic Center   Phone: (918)596-7988
Tulsa, OK 74103   Karen S. Curtis, Dept.Hd.
Founded: 1920. **Staff:** Prof 8; Other 5. **Subjects:** Earth and petroleum sciences, energy technology, engineering, management, transportation, marketing, business, finance, computers. **Special Collections:** A.I. Levorsen Geology Collection (1600 books, serials, maps); General Land Office survey maps (18,000); C.R. Musgrave Transportation Library (700 items); local floodplain maps (90). **Holdings:** 60,000 books; 21,000 bound periodical volumes; 80,000 geologic and topographic maps; 2500 local government documents; 300,000 federal government documents; 800 telephone and city directories; 8000 periodicals and newspapers in microform; 11,000 state documents. **Subscriptions:** 1130 journals and other serials; 17 newspapers. **Services:** Interlibrary loan; copying; SDI; fee-based research; department open to the public. **Automated Operations:** Computerized cataloging, acquisitions, and circulation. **Computerized Information Services:** DIALOG Information Services, BRS Information Technologies, ORBIT Search Service, WILSONLINE, DataTimes, VU/TEXT Information Services, CompuServe Information Service; EDIC (internal database). **Networks/Consortia:** Member of Tulsa Area Library Cooperative (TALC), Oklahoma Telecommunications Interlibrary System (OTIS), AMIGOS Bibliographic Council, Inc. **Publications:** INFO, bimonthly. **Remarks:** FAX: (918)596- 7895. Department maintains Economic Development Information Center (EDIC). **Staff:** Robert Lieser, Libn.; Lisa Hansen, Libn.; Terri Combs, Libn.; Martha Gregory, EDIC/Info. II Libn.; Mary Moore, Libn.; Suanne Wymer, Libn.; Robert Sears, Libn.

★ 16572 ★
Tulsa County Law Library (Law)
Tulsa County Court House, Rm. 242
500 S. Denver   Phone: (918)596-5404
Tulsa, OK 74103   Susan Orchard, Dir.
Founded: 1949. **Staff:** Prof 1; Other 1. **Subjects:** Law. **Holdings:** 23,083 books and bound periodical volumes. **Services:** Copying; library open to the public. **Remarks:** FAX: (918)596-4509. **Staff:** Beatryce Henderson, Libn.

★ 16573 ★
Tulsa Historical Society - Library (Hist)
2501 W. Newton
Box 27303   Phone: (918)585-5520
Tulsa, OK 74149-0303   Robert Powers, Cur.
Founded: 1962. **Staff:** 1. **Subjects:** State and local history. **Holdings:** 600 cubic feet of reminiscences of pioneers, oral history tapes, diaries, business records, public documents, manuscript maps, and photographs. **Services:** Copying; library open to the public for reference use only. **Remarks:** FAX: (918)592-2248. **Formerly:** Tulsa County Historical Society.

Tulsa Medical College
See: **University of Oklahoma - Health Sciences Center - Tulsa Campus** (19133)

★ 16574 ★
Tulsa Regional Medical Center - L.C. Baxter Medical Library H230 (Med)
744 W. 9th   Phone: (918)599-5297
Tulsa, OK 74127   S. Jane Cooper, Lib.Dir.
Founded: 1960. **Staff:** Prof 1; Other 2. **Subjects:** General medicine, internal medicine, surgery, ophthalmology, otorhinolaryngology, allied health sciences. **Holdings:** 2500 books; 2200 bound periodical volumes; 1600 AV cassettes; 1900 slides. **Subscriptions:** 220 journals and other serials. **Services:** Interlibrary loan; copying; library open to the public for reference use only. **Networks/Consortia:** Member of National Network of Libraries of Medicine - South Central Region, Tulsa Area Library Cooperative (TALC). **Remarks:** FAX: (918)599-5829.

★ 16575 ★
Tulsa World-Tulsa Tribune - Library Department (Publ)
315 S. Boulder Ave.
Box 1770   Phone: (918)581-8583
Tulsa, OK 74102   Austin Farley, Libn.
Founded: 1941. **Staff:** Prof 1; Other 8. **Subjects:** Newspaper reference topics. **Holdings:** 700 books; 225,000 file envelopes of clippings; 50,000 file envelopes of photographs; 1200 reels of microfilm. **Services:** Copying (limited); library open to the public, appointments preferred. **Computerized Information Services:** DataTimes.

★ 16576 ★
Tulsa Zoological Park - Library (Biol Sci)
5701 E. 36th St., N.   Phone: (918)835-9453
Tulsa, OK 74115   Carol Eames, Educ.Cur.
Founded: 1976. **Staff:** Prof 1. **Subjects:** Zoology, zoo animal husbandry. **Holdings:** 1240 books; 1200 bound periodical volumes. **Subscriptions:** 14 journals and other serials. **Services:** Library open to the public for research purposes.

★ 16577 ★
(Tunis) Centre Culturel Americain - USIS Library (Educ)
2, Ave. de France
Tunis, Tunisia
Remarks: Maintained or supported by the U.S. Information Agency. Focus is on materials that will assist peoples outside the United States to learn about the United States, its people, history, culture, political processes, and social milieux.

★ 16578 ★
Tunisia - Archives Nationales de Tunisie (Hist)
Le Premier Ministere
Place du Gouvernement   Phone: 1 260556
1020 Tunis, Tunisia   Moncef Fakhfakh, Dir.
Founded: 1874. **Staff:** Prof 6; Other 2. **Subjects:** Administration, law, history, information sciences. **Holdings:** 4225 books; 910 bound periodical volumes; 6 kilometers of archives. **Services:** Copying; archives open to the public. **Special Catalogs:** Sommaire des registres fiscaux et administratifs aux Archives Nationales de Tunisie. **Remarks:** FAX: 1 569175.

Tunison Laboratory of Fish Nutrition
See: **U.S. Fish & Wildlife Service** (17506)

★ 16579 ★
Tuolumne County Genealogical Society - Library (Hist)
158 W. Bradford Ave.
Box 3956   Phone: (209)532-1317
Sonora, CA 95370   Metta Schafft, Lib.Coord.
Founded: 1979. **Staff:** 6. **Subjects:** Genealogy, county and state history. **Special Collections:** Tuolumne County and central California census records, 1850-1910 (microfilm); Tuolumne County vital statistics records, 1850-1950 (microfilm); C.H. Burden burial records, 1862-1950; California pioneer file (100 microfiche); Newspapers of Early California Collection; photograph collections. **Holdings:** 700 books; 250 bound periodical volumes; 250 reels of microfilm; 300 other cataloged items, including mining, cemetery, and school records; ancestor charts. **Services:** Copying; SDI; library open to the public. **Publications:** Golden Roots of the Mother Lode, quarterly. **Remarks:** Alternate telephone number(s): (209)532-1095. **Staff:** Viola McRae; Nell Holloway.

★ 16580 ★
Tuolumne County Law Library (Law)
Court House
2 S. Green St.   Phone: (209)533-5675
Sonora, CA 95370   Pamela Jarvis, Law Libn.
Subjects: Law. **Holdings:** 18,000 volumes. **Services:** Copying; library open by special request.

Turchin Library
See: Tulane University - A.B. Freeman School of Business
  Administration - Turchin Library (16555)

Rosalyn Tureck Archives
See: New York Public Library for the Performing Arts (11638)

★ 16581 ★
**Turkey - Scientific and Technical Research Council of Turkey - Turkish
  Scientific and Technical Documentation Center** (Sci-Engr)
Ataturk Bulvari No. 221
Kavaklidere   Phone: 4 1685300
TR-06100 Ankara, Turkey   Rezzan Kockar, Libn.
Founded: 1966. **Staff:** 9. **Subjects:** Basic and applied sciences, agriculture,
economics, industry, industrial management, medicine, information and
library science. **Holdings:** 13,500 volumes. **Subscriptions:** 304 journals and
other serials. **Services:** SDI; document delivery service. **Computerized
Information Services:** Online systems. **Remarks:** FAX: 4 1260489. Telex:
43186 BTAK TR. **Also Known As:** Turkiye Bilimsel ve Teknik Arastirma
Kurumu - Dokumantasyon Merkezi.

★ 16582 ★
Turkish Culture and Information Office (Area-Ethnic)
821 United Nations Plaza   Phone: (212)687-2194
New York, NY 10017   Oktay Ataman, Dir.
Founded: 1960. **Subjects:** Travel in Turkey. **Holdings:** Films; slides; posters,
brochures; maps. **Publications:** Sales Planning Guide, annual.

Turkish Scientific and Technical Documentation Center
See: Turkey - Scientific and Technical Research Council of Turkey
  (16581)

**Turkiye Bilimsel ve Teknik Arastirma Kurumu - Dokumantasyon
  Merkezi**
See: Turkey - Scientific and Technical Research Council of Turkey
  (16581)

Alexander Turnbull Library
See: New Zealand - National Library of New Zealand (11739)

★ 16583 ★
Turner, Collie & Braden, Inc. - Library and Information Services (Sci-
  Engr, Energy)
Box 130089   Phone: (713)267-2826
Houston, TX 77219   Suzette Broussard, Libn.
Founded: 1973. **Staff:** Prof 1, Other 1. **Subjects:** Hydraulic and sanitary
engineering, water resources in Texas, transportation. **Special Collections:**
Environmental Pollution and Control (2000 NTIS microfiche). **Holdings:**
10,000 books; 1500 bound periodical volumes; 2000 company reports.
Subscriptions: 145 journals and other serials. **Services:** Interlibrary loan;
copying; library open to the public by appointment. **Automated Operations:**
Computerized cataloging and serials. **Computerized Information Services:**
DIALOG Information Services, PFDS Online. **Remarks:** Library located at
5757 Woodway, Houston, TX 77057. FAX: (713)780-0838. **Staff:** Roberta
Franchville, Asst.Libn.

Don A. Turner County Law Library
See: San Bernardino County Law Library (14680)

Don A. Turner County Law Library, West End
See: San Bernardino County Law Library - West End Branch (14681)

J.A. Turner Professional Library
See: Peel Board of Education (12813)

Turner Memorial Library
See: Franklin Memorial Hospital (6096)

★ 16584 ★
Turner Museum - Archives (Art)
773 Downing St.   Phone: (303)834-0924
Denver, CO 80218   Douglas Graham, Founder
Founded: 1966. **Staff:** Prof 1; Other 1. **Subjects:** Artists Joseph Mallord
William Turner and Thomas Moran. **Special Collections:** Works by Turner
and Moran. **Holdings:** 1000 books; folios; photographs; documents.
Services: Interlibrary loan; copying; library open to the public. **Special
Catalogs:** J.M.W. Turner catalog; Thomas Moran catalog; Turner's Cosmic
Optimism.

Turpin Library
See: Dallas Theological Seminary (4570)

Willard Sherman Turrell Herbarium.
See: Miami University (10271)

★ 16585 ★
Turtle Bay Music School - Library (Mus)
244 E. 52nd St.   Phone: (212)753-8811
New York, NY 10022   Carmelo Ruta, Libn.
Founded: 1925. **Staff:** Prof 2; Other 2. **Subjects:** Music - piano, vocal,
instrumental, chamber, popular, classical. **Holdings:** 821 books; 8469 scores
and recordings. **Subscriptions:** 4 journals and other serials. **Services:** Library
open to enrolled students, faculty, and staff.

★ 16586 ★
Turun Yliopisto - Laaketieteellinen Tiedekuntakirjasto (Med)
Kiinamyllynkatu 10   Phone: 21 328621
SF-20520 Turku, Finland   Terttu Soini
Founded: 1943. **Staff:** Prof 5; Other 5. **Subjects:** Biomedical sciences.
Holdings: 54,000 books; 68,000 bound periodical volumes; 4600 microfiche;
6 CD-ROMs. **Subscriptions:** 1067 journals and other serials. **Services:**
Interlibrary loan; copying; library open to the public. **Computerized
Information Services:** Data-Star, DIALOG Information Services, KIBIC;
internal databases. **Remarks:** FAX: 21 331126. Telex: 62293.

★ 16587 ★
Turun Yliopisto - Matemaatiis Luonnontieteellinen Tiedekuntakirjasto
  (Biol Sci, Sci-Engr)
Yliopistonmaki   Phone: 21 6335463
SF-20500 Turku 50, Finland   Ilse Vahakyro, M.A.
Founded: 1954. **Staff:** Prof 4; Other 3. **Subjects:** Biology, geology, chemistry,
biochemistry, physical science. **Holdings:** 123,247 volumes. **Subscriptions:**
804 journals and other serials. **Services:** Interlibrary loan; copying; library
open to the public for reference use only. **Computerized Information
Services:** CD-ROMs. **Publications:** Catalogue on marine literature in the
Turku libraries, annual. **Remarks:** FAX: 921 6335050. Telex: 62123 TYK
SF.

★ 16588 ★
Tuscarawas County Genealogical Society - Library (Hist)
121 Fair Ave.   Phone: (216)364-4474
New Philadelphia, OH 44663   Susan Haloch, Libn.
Staff: Prof 2; Other 23. **Subjects:** Genealogy, local history. **Special
Collections:** Tuscarawas County records (55 volumes). **Holdings:** 357 books;
346 bound periodical volumes; 92 genealogical newsletters; 352 family
histories; 85 cemetery records; 24 local histories; 22 city directories; 10
passenger and ship records; 39 state histories; 18 court records; 60 war
records; 69 research guides; 88 church and sect histories; 259 city and county
histories; 27 colonial records; 4 alien country histories; 29 land records and
atlases; 25 printed census records; 27 phone books; 119 vital statistics
records; 149 reels of microfilm of probate, census, war, marriage, birth, and
death records. **Subscriptions:** 100 journals and other serials. **Services:**
Copying; library open to the public on a limited schedule. **Publications:**
Tuscarawas County Pioneer Footprints (newsletter), quarterly - to
members. **Special Indexes:** List of indexes - available upon request.

★ 16589 ★
Tuscarawas County Law Library Association (Law)
Court House   Phone: (216)364-3703
New Philadelphia, OH 44663   Diana L. O'Meara, Libn.
Staff: 1. **Subjects:** Law. **Holdings:** 17,000 volumes. **Services:** Interlibrary loan; copying; library open to the public. **Computerized Information Services:** WESTLAW. Performs searches on fee basis.

★ 16590 ★
Tusculum College - Instructional Materials Center (Educ)
Box 5036   Phone: (615)636-7324
Greeneville, TN 37743   Janie Douthat, Supv., IMC
Founded: 1973. **Staff:** Prof 5. **Subjects:** Education - general, special, elementary, early childhood, physical; children's literature. **Holdings:** 2450 books; 300 pamphlets; 75 filmstrips; 100 educational kits; 15 phonograph records; 15 film loops; 15 cassettes; 45 puzzles; 55 tests; 90 games; 30 charts; curriculum guides. **Subscriptions:** 19 journals and other serials; 2 newspapers. **Services:** Center open to the public. **Remarks:** FAX: (615)638-7166. **Staff:** Dr. Carol Hartman, Dir./Asst.Prof.; Dr. James T. Davis, Prof.; Dr. Dorothy Dennis, Asst.Prof.; Diane Skramstad, Assoc.Prof.; Dr. David Bow, Prof.

★ 16591 ★
Tuskegee University - Architecture Library (Art, Plan)
Willcox Bldg. A   Phone: (205)727-8351
Tuskegee, AL 36088   Linda K. Harvey, Hd.Libn.
Founded: 1964. **Staff:** Prof 1; Other 6. **Subjects:** Architecture, construction, science management, planning, historic preservation. **Special Collections:** Rare architectural book collection (520); African-American architects and architecture. **Holdings:** 8100 books; 525 bound periodical volumes; 89 theses; 22,678 slides; microfiche. **Subscriptions:** 125 journals and other serials. **Services:** Interlibrary loan; copying; SDI; library open to the public for reference use only. **Computerized Information Services:** Access to DIALOG Information Services. Performs searches on fee basis. Contact Person: Edna L. Williams, 727-8892. **Networks/Consortia:** Member of SOLINET. **Special Catalogs:** Library's Periodical Holdings (book). **Special Indexes:** Index to African-American architects and architecture collection.

★ 16592 ★
Tuskegee University - Hollis Burke Frissell Library-Archives (Area-Ethnic, Hist)
Main Library   Phone: (205)727-8888
Tuskegee, AL 36088   Daniel T. Williams, Archv.
Staff: Prof 1; Other 1. **Subjects:** African-American history, Tuskegee University history, civil rights, oral history. **Special Collections:** Washington Collection; Tuskegee University archives; Booker T. Washington papers (155 containers); George W. Carver papers (159 containers). **Holdings:** 25,000 books; 625 bound periodical volumes; 101 cabinets of Tuskegee University clipping files. **Subscriptions:** 39 journals and other serials; 19 newspapers. **Services:** Interlibrary loan; library open to the public on a limited schedule. **Computerized Information Services:** OCLC. **Networks/Consortia:** Member of Network of Alabama Academic Libraries (NAAL), CCLC. **Publications:** A Guide to the Special Collection and Archives of Tuskegee University (1974). **Remarks:** FAX: (205)727-9282. **Staff:** Edna L. Williams, Hd.Libn.

★ 16593 ★
Tuskegee University - School of Engineering Library (Sci-Engr, Energy)
Tuskegee, AL 36088   Phone: (205)727-8901
                                                   Frances F. Davis, Libn.
Founded: 1962. **Staff:** Prof 1; Other 1. **Subjects:** Engineering - electrical, mechanical, chemical, aerospace. **Holdings:** 14,500 books; 3700 bound periodical volumes; 19,000 Atomic Energy Commission materials; Energy Research Abstracts and Indexes. **Subscriptions:** 205 journals and other serials. **Services:** Library open to the public with restrictions. **Computerized Information Services:** DIALOG Information Services. **Networks/Consortia:** Member of Network of Alabama Academic Libraries (NAAL), SOLINET. **Remarks:** FAX: (205)727-8484.

★ 16594 ★
Tuskegee University - T.S. Williams Veterinary Medical Library (Med)
Patterson Hall   Phone: (205)727-8307
Tuskegee, AL 36088   Margaret K. Alexander, Libn.
Founded: 1949. **Staff:** Prof 1; Other 6. **Subjects:** Anatomy, physiology, pathology, pharmacology, microbiology, radiology. **Special Collections:** Small and large animal medicine and surgery. **Holdings:** 21,003 volumes; 194 reels of microfilm; 513 slide programs; 844 video programs; 49 filmstrips; 48 tape programs. **Subscriptions:** 442 journals and other serials. **Services:** Interlibrary loan (fee); copying; library open to the public for reference use only. **Computerized Information Services:** DIALOG Information Services, MEDLINE. Performs searches on fee basis. Contact Person: Margaret K. Alexander, Libn. **Networks/Consortia:** Member of CCLC, Network of Alabama Academic Libraries (NAAL). **Publications:** Library Newsletter, quarterly - for internal distribution only; AV/AT Programs of the Week - for internal distribution only. **Special Catalogs:** Tuskegee University School of Veterinary Medicine AV/AT Catalog of Programs. **Remarks:** FAX: (205)727-8442.

Charles Leaming Tutt Library
See: **Colorado College** (3940)

★ 16595 ★
Lyle Tuttle Tattooing - Tattoo Art Museum - Library (Art)
837 Columbus Ave.   Phone: (415)775-4991
San Francisco, CA 94133   Lyle Tuttle, Dir.
Founded: 1974. **Subjects:** Tattooing and related arts. **Special Collections:** George Burchett collection. **Holdings:** 200 books; drawings; tattoo equipment; memorabilia. **Services:** Copying; library open to the public. **Publications:** Tattoo Historian, 2/year; Tattoo '70; Tattoo Calendar Book, annual - all for sale.

Tuttleman Library
See: **Gratz College - Tuttleman Library** (6657)

Tutwiler Collection of Southern History and Literature
See: **Birmingham Public and Jefferson County Free Library - Linn-Henley Library for Southern Historical Research** (1859)

TV Guide Microfilm Library
See: **News America Publications, Inc. - TV Guide Microfilm Library** (11778)

★ 16596 ★
TV Ontario - Library (Educ, Info Sci)
P.O. Box 200, Station Q   Phone: (416)484-2651
Toronto, ON, Canada M4T 2T1   Ms. Rechilde Volpatti, Supv.
Founded: 1970. **Staff:** Prof 1; Other 2. **Subjects:** Educational television, television production, broadcasting, distance education, communications, adult education, children and television. **Holdings:** 20,000 books; TV Ontario documents, program guides, and newspaper clippings. **Subscriptions:** 200 journals and other serials. **Services:** Interlibrary loan; copying; library open to the public for reference use only. **Automated Operations:** Computerized public access catalog and circulation. **Computerized Information Services:** DIALOG Information Services, BRS Information Technologies, Questel, Info Globe, The Financial Post DataGroup, Infomart Online, CAN/OLE, UTLAS; Envoy 100 (electronic mail service). **Publications:** Journal articles, bimonthly - to staff and other libraries on request. **Remarks:** Distributes copies of its TV programs on videotape through its VIPS services to school boards, colleges, universities, and other educational institutions. Alternate telephone number(s): 484-2600. FAX: (416)484-7771. Telex: 0623547. Electronic mail address(es): LIBRARY.TVONTARIO (Envoy 100).

TWA
See: **Trans World Airlines, Inc.** (16454)

★ 16597 ★
Mark Twain Biblioteca - (San Jose) Centro Cultural Costarriense Norteamericano - USIS Collection (Educ)
Calle 37, Ave. Ctl-1
P.O. Box 1489-1000   Phone: 506 259433
San Jose, Costa Rica   Guisella Ruiz, Lib.Dir.
Founded: 1953. **Staff:** 4. **Subjects:** Social sciences, U.S. arts and humanities. **Holdings:** 9000 books. **Subscriptions:** 93 journals and other serials; 11 newspapers. **Services:** Interlibrary loan; copying; SDI; library open to the public. **Computerized Information Services:** LEGI-SLATE; CD-ROMs; LOGICAT (internal database). **Publications:** Article Alert; New Acquisitions. **Remarks:** FAX: 506 241480. Maintained or supported by the U.S. Information Agency. Focus is on materials that will assist peoples outside the United States to learn about the United States, its people, history, culture, political processes, and social milieux. **Staff:** Priscilla Hidalgo, Ref.Libn.; Mariela Aguilar, Outreach Libn.; Gisele Cartin, Tech.Serv.Libn.

★ 16598 ★
Mark Twain Birthplace Museum - Research Library (Hum)
Box 54   Phone: (314)565-3449
Stoutsville, MO 65283   John Cunning, Adm.
Founded: 1960. **Staff:** Prof 2. **Subjects:** Samuel L. Clemens (Mark Twain) - life and family. **Special Collections:** Manuscript used for the first British printing of The Adventures of Tom Sawyer and associated letters and documents. **Holdings:** 400 books. **Services:** Library open to the public for reference use only. **Remarks:** Maintained by Missouri State Department of Natural Resources.

★ 16599 ★
Mark Twain Memorial
351 Farmington Ave.   Phone: (203)297-2268
Hartford, CT 06106   Marianne J. Curling, Cur.
Founded: 1929. **Staff:** Prof 1. **Subjects:** Samuel L. Clemens and family. **Special Collections:** Samuel L. Clemens manuscript material, letters, clippings, pamphlets, documents; Clemens family papers; Candace Wheeler papers. **Holdings:** 3500 books; 100 bound periodical volumes; 7500 manuscript items. **Services:** Copying. **Automated Operations:** Computerized public access catalog. **Computerized Information Services:** OCLC. **Networks/Consortia:** Member of CTW Consortium. **Remarks:** FAX: (203)297-2251. Mark Twain Memorial collection is temporarily on deposit with the Trinity College - Watkinson Library. **Staff:** Margaret K. Powell, Cur., Ref./Mss. 001290 CTW

★ 16600 ★
Mark Twain Museum - Library (Hum)
208 Hill St.   Phone: (314)221-9010
Hannibal, MO 63401   Henry Sweets, Cur.
Founded: 1937. **Staff:** Prof 2; Other 3. **Subjects:** Mark Twain. **Special Collections:** Norman Rockwell paintings (15); first editions of Twain's works. **Holdings:** 600 books; 8 bound periodical volumes; periodicals, booklets, and pamphlets; scrapbooks of clippings; manuscript letters; 1 moving picture of Mark Twain. **Services:** Copying; library open only to special students with permission of curator. **Publications:** The Fence Painter, quarterly - by subscription; Hannibal: Mark Twain's Town. **Remarks:** Maintained by Mark Twain Home Foundation.

★ 16601 ★
Twentieth Century Fox Film Corporation - Research Library (Art, Hist)
10201 W. Pico Blvd.
Box 900   Phone: (213)203-2782
Beverly Hills, CA 90213   Kenneth Kenyon, Hd., Res.Dept.
Founded: 1924. **Staff:** Prof 2. **Subjects:** Architecture, house decoration, costume, travel, history, art. **Special Collections:** Wetzler and Tichy collections of World War II photographs (official U.S. and German Army photographs; 47 bound volumes). **Holdings:** 35,000 books; 5000 bound periodical volumes; 10,000 bound newspapers, pamphlets, plays; 345 VF drawers of photographs, clippings, maps; 600 research photographs bound in loose-leaf books. **Subscriptions:** 23 journals and other serials. **Services:** Interlibrary loan (fee); library not open to the public. **Special Catalogs:** Catalog of magazine articles and pictures (card). **Remarks:** FAX: (213)203-3645.

Twentieth Century-Fox Film Corporation Archives
See: **University of California, Los Angeles - Arts, Architecture and Urban Planning Library (18370)**

★ 16602 ★
Twentieth Century Fund - Library (Soc Sci)
41 E. 70th St.   Phone: (212)535-4441
New York, NY 10021   Nettie Gerduk, Libn.
Founded: 1935. **Staff:** Prof 1. **Subjects:** Economics, communications, international affairs, political science. **Holdings:** 1179 books. **Subscriptions:** 69 journals and other serials. **Services:** Interlibrary loan; library open to the public on request.

★ 16603 ★
Twentieth Century Trends Institute, Inc. - Source Library (Soc Sci)
c/o Darien High School
80 High School Ln.   Phone: (203)655-3981
Darien, CT 06820   Victoria Mark Anthony, Libn.
Subjects: Government, politics, economics, sociology, communications media, psychology. **Holdings:** 3194 books. **Subscriptions:** 175 journals and other serials. **Services:** Copying; library open to the public. **Special Indexes:** Articles index for subjects in library collection (card).

★ 16604 ★
Twenty First Century Electric Vehicles - Library (Sci-Engr)
8136 Byron Rd., Suite G   Phone: (213)945-6220
Whittier, CA 90606   Erwin Ulbrich
Founded: 1976. **Staff:** 1. **Subjects:** Electric vehicles; vehicles - engineering, displays, control; hybrid vehicles; electrical engineering. **Holdings:** 500 books; 1000 reports; slide sets; videotapes; 30 unbound periodicals. **Services:** Library open to the public by appointment. **Remarks:** Alternate telephone number(s): (213)696-4886.

★ 16605 ★
The Twins Foundation - Research Library (Soc Sci)
Box 6043   Phone: (401)274-8946
Providence, RI 02940-6043   Kay Cassill, Pres.
Founded: 1983. **Staff:** Prof 1; Other 2. **Subjects:** Twins and other multiple births - research, literature, arts, mythology, history. **Special Collections:** National Twin Registry (20,000 persons); The Twins Letter (5000 back issues). **Holdings:** 600 books; 2000 bound periodical volumes; 600 photographs and illustrations; 100 art works; 100 audiocassettes; 50 videotapes; 100 slides; 250 memorabilia; 10,000 clippings. **Services:** Library not open to the public. **Computerized Information Services:** National Twins Registry (internal database). Performs searches on fee basis. Contact Person: Anne Richards. **Publications:** The Twins Letter; various pamphlets. **Staff:** Germaine Dennaker.

★ 16606 ★
Tyler Courier-Times-Telegraph - Library (Publ)
Box 2030   Phone: (903)597-8111
Tyler, TX 75710   Margaret Dodd, Libn.
Staff: Prof 1. **Subjects:** Newspaper reference topics. **Holdings:** Newspapers, December, 1910 to present, on microfilm. **Subscriptions:** 35 newspapers. **Services:** Library open to the public. **Remarks:** FAX: (903)595-0335.

Tyler School of Fine Arts
See: **Temple University - Central Library System (16139)**

Tyrrell Historical Library
See: **Beaumont Public Library System (1624)**

Sallie M. Tyrrell, M.D. Memorial Library
See: **St. Margaret Hospital (14492)**

U

★ 16607 ★
U-Haul International, Inc. - Corporate Library (Bus-Fin, Trans)
2727 N. Central Ave. Phone: (602)263-6606
Phoenix, AZ 85004 Meg Maher, Libn.
Staff: Prof 3. **Subjects:** Management, marketing, transportation, engineering, personnel, insurance, law. **Holdings:** 6600 books; 43 bound periodical volumes; 55 VF drawers of corporate archives; 70 VF drawers of internal publications; 4 boxes of microfiche. **Subscriptions:** 560 journals and other serials. **Services:** Interlibrary loan; library not open to the public. **Publications:** Information System List of Publications, quarterly - for internal distribution only. **Special Indexes:** Publication Index, quarterly - for internal distribution only.

★ 16608 ★
U.P.E.C. Cultural Center - J.A. Freitas Library (Area-Ethnic, Hum)
1120-24 E. 14th St. Phone: (510)483-7676
San Leandro, CA 94577 Carlos Almeida, Dir.
Founded: 1964. **Staff:** Prof 1; Other 2. **Subjects:** Portuguese literature, history of Portuguese in California, Azores. **Holdings:** 8000 books; 30 bound periodical volumes; 50 reports; 140 archives; 20 microfilm; newspapers and historical documents. **Subscriptions:** 8 newspapers. **Services:** Interlibrary loan; copying; translations of works from Portuguese to English; library open to the public. **Remarks:** FAX: (510)483-5015.

U.S.
Filed as if spelled out United States

U.S.D.A.
Filed as if spelled out U.S. Dept. of Agriculture

UAW
See: United Automobile, Aerospace & Agricultural Implement Workers of America - Research Library (16687)

★ 16609 ★
UCAR Carbon Company, Inc. - Parma Technical Center - Technical Information Service (Sci-Engr)
Box 6116 Phone: (216)676-2223
Cleveland, OH 44101 Linda Riffle, Mgr.
Founded: 1945. **Staff:** Prof 2; Other 2. **Subjects:** Manufactured carbon and graphite, high temperature chemistry, metallurgy. **Holdings:** 12,000 books; 15,000 bound periodical volumes; 20,000 U.S. and foreign patents; 30,000 government documents and contract reports. **Subscriptions:** 450 journals and other serials. **Services:** Interlibrary loan; SDI; service open to the public with special permission and limited access. **Automated Operations:** Computerized cataloging. **Computerized Information Services:** DIALOG Information Services, STN International, WILSONLINE, PFDS Online; INDOC, ACCESS (internal databases). **Publications:** Biweekly bulletin (listing of references to carbon and graphite) - for internal distribution only; bibliography of carbon and graphite technology, 1945 to present. **Special Indexes:** Literature of carbon and graphite; U.S. and foreign patent indexes. **Formerly:** Union Carbide Corporation - Parma Technical Center. **Staff:** Mary D. Wood, Sr.Libn.

Uchu-ken Tosjo
See: Institute of Space and Astronautical Science - ISAS Library (7981)

UE (United Electrical Radio and Machine Workers of America) Archives
See: University of Pittsburgh - UE (United Electrical Radio and Machine Workers of America) Archives (19227)

★ 16610 ★
UFO Information Retrieval Center (Sci-Engr)
Points West No. 158
3131 W. Cochise Dr. Phone: (602)997-1523
Phoenix, AZ 85051-9501 Thomas M. Olsen, Pres.
Founded: 1966. **Staff:** Prof 1. **Subjects:** UFO sighting reports and related topics. **Special Collections:** Computer-machine-readable text and data. **Holdings:** 165 books; 160 bound periodical volumes; 50 volumes of unbound reports; 1100 Library of Congress cards on UFO topics; 50 purported photographs of UFO; 3 volumes of lecture and symposia AV programs. **Subscriptions:** 5 journals and other serials. **Services:** Center not open to the public; accepts written requests for information. **Computerized Information Services:** Internal databases. Performs searches on fee basis. **Publications:** The Reference for Outstanding UFO Sighting Reports, irregular - by mail order request; bibliography of currently available information on the UFO phenomenon - on request. **Special Indexes:** Verbatim text of anecdotal reports (online); inverted index for 160 categories of reported characteristics. **Remarks:** FAX: (602)870-3178. Phone calls received 24 hours/day.

★ 16611 ★
(Uganda) Public Libraries Board - Library (Info Sci)
P.O. Box 4262 Phone: 41 254661
Kampala, Uganda P. Birungi, Dir.
Founded: 1964. **Staff:** Prof 15; Other 82. **Subjects:** Ugandan public libraries - maintenance and management. **Holdings:** 72,866 books; Uganda government publications. **Subscriptions:** 4 newspapers. **Services:** Library open to the public. **Publications:** Accessions List; P.L.B. Newsletter. **Staff:** C.J. Endra; Ms. R.M. Mwayi; C.B. Nyamijunga; J. Ndawula; Ms. S. Nekusa; G. Tugaineyo; J. P. Erimu-Anyau; J. Nkubito; G. Luyimbazi; Ms. E. Barongo; B. N. Bagenda; J. Onyango; J. Oesetum.

Robert Uhlmann Medical Library
See: Menorah Medical Center (10092)

★ 16612 ★
Ukrainian Cultural and Educational Centre - Library (Area-Ethnic)
184 Alexander Ave., E. Phone: (204)942-0218
Winnipeg, MB, Canada R3B 0L6 Lydia Horocholyn, Libn.
Founded: 1944. **Staff:** Prof 1; Other 1. **Subjects:** Ukrainian history, literature, language, art, ethnography; Ukrainian settlement in Canada. **Special Collections:** Rare book collection (17th-19th century; 75 volumes); Koshetz Music Collection; Macenko Music Collection. **Holdings:** 40,000 books; 31,000 periodicals; 300 scores; 2000 slides. **Subscriptions:** 65 journals and other serials; 45 newspapers. **Services:** Copying; library open to the public for reference use only. **Remarks:** FAX: (204)943-2857.

★ 16613 ★
Ukrainian Engineers Society of America - Library (Sci-Engr)
2 E. 79th St. Phone: (201)224-9862
New York, NY 10021 George Honczarenko, Pres.
Founded: 1950. **Subjects:** Science and technology (in Ukrainian); development of the Ukraine. **Special Collections:** Engineering textbooks and handbooks in German and Russian; monographs, papers, reprints, theses, manuscripts authored by Ukrainian engineers and scientists in the U.S., Canada, and Germany, 1950 to present. **Holdings:** 400 volumes. **Subscriptions:** 15 journals and other serials; 5 newspapers. **Services:** Library not open to the public. **Publications:** Ukrainian Engineering News, quarterly; Bulletin, semiannual. **Remarks:** Branches of the society are located in Philadelphia, Chicago, Detroit, Cleveland, Boston, Buffalo, Minneapolis, New York, Washington, New Jersey, and Los Angeles.

★ 16614 ★
Ukrainian Medical Association of North America - Ukrainian Medical Archives and Library (Med)
2247 W. Chicago Ave. Phone: (312)278-6262
Chicago, IL 60632-4828 Dr. Paul Pundy, Dir.
Staff: Prof 2. **Subjects:** Medicine. **Special Collections:** Russian Medical Encyclopedia (30 volumes); Ukrainian medical journals and books (originals; copies; microfilm); medical books and journals in English, Russian, German, and Polish. **Holdings:** 1800 books; 200 bound periodical volumes; 8 VF drawers of clippings, pamphlets, unbound reports, photograph albums. **Services:** Interlibrary loan; library open to the public with written or telephone request. **Remarks:** FAX: (312)278-6962.

★ 16615 ★
Ukrainian Museum-Archives, Inc. (Area-Ethnic)
1202 Kenilworth Ave.   Phone: (216)781-4329
Cleveland, OH 44113-4424   Stepan Malanczuk, Hd.Libn.
Founded: 1952. **Staff:** 8. **Subjects:** Ukrainian Revolution, post World War II immigration of Ukrainians, religion, linguistics. **Special Collections:** Taras Shevchenko Collection (837 volumes); publications from the Ukrainian Revolution, 1917-1921. **Holdings:** 16,000 books; 250 bound periodical volumes; 1250 unbound periodicals; archival materials in Ukrainian. **Subscriptions:** 40 journals and other serials. **Services:** Copying; archives open to the public for reference use only.

★ 16616 ★
Ukrainian Museum of Canada - Library (Area-Ethnic)
910 Spadina Crescent, E.   Phone: (306)244-3800
Saskatoon, SK, Canada S7K 3H5   Rose Marie Fedorak, Cur.
Staff: Prof 1; Other 3. **Subjects:** Art, history, literature, ethnography in Ukrainian and English. **Special Collections:** Archives. **Holdings:** 6000 volumes; 7000 slides. **Subscriptions:** 40 journals and other serials. **Services:** Copying; library open to the public by appointment. **Automated Operations:** Computerized cataloging. **Computerized Information Services:** UTLAS; UTLAS (electronic mail service). **Publications:** Ukrainian Embroidery Design; Pobut Art-Heritage Patterns; Pysanka: Icon of the Universe. **Remarks:** FAX: (306)652-7620.

★ 16617 ★
Ukrainian National Federation - Library (Area-Ethnic)
297 College St.
Toronto, ON, Canada M5T 1S2   Phone: (416)921-0231
Founded: 1932. **Staff:** Prof 1; Other 2. **Subjects:** Ukraine, Ukrainians. **Special Collections:** Z. Knysh Collection (Organization of Ukrainian Nationalists; 1000 volumes). **Holdings:** 15,000 books; 400 bound periodical volumes; 3 VF drawers. **Subscriptions:** 20 journals and other serials; 10 newspapers. **Services:** Library open to the public. **Staff:** Nell Nakoneczny, Supv.; Yurij Serhijczuk, Techn.; John Pidkowich.

Ukrainian Public Library of Ivan Franko
See: **Ivan Franko Museum & Library Society, Inc.** (6100)

★ 16618 ★
Ukrainian Research Institute of Irrigated Farming - Library (Agri)
325908 Kherson, Ukraine   Phone: 59413
                                        N.P. Matsko
Founded: 1887. **Staff:** Prof 4. **Subjects:** Irrigated farming, plant growing, agrochemics, soil science, plant protecton, selection and seed breeding. **Holdings:** 36,051 books; 30,180 bound periodical volumes; 1320 reports. **Subscriptions:** 150 journals and other serials; 31 newspapers. **Services:** Interlibrary loan; library open to the public.

★ 16619 ★
Ukrainian Women's Association of Canada, St. John's Branch - Centennial Library (Area-Ethnic)
10611 110th Ave.   Phone: (403)457-1451
Edmonton, AB, Canada T5H 1H7   Mrs. Orasia Yereniuk, Libn.
Founded: 1967. **Staff:** 2. **Subjects:** Ukrainian embroidery, ceramics, woodcraft, and Easter egg writing, literature, geography, music, history, religion, biography; folk art; historical costumes; composers; art paintings; sculpture. **Holdings:** 2500 books. **Subscriptions:** 4 journals and other serials. **Services:** Library open to the public by appointment. **Computerized Information Services:** Internal database. **Remarks:** Alternate telephone number(s): (403)425-9692.

★ 16620 ★
Ukrainskij Institut Pocvovedenija i Agrochimii im. A.N. Sokolovskogo - Juznoe Otdelenie VASCHNIL - Naucnaja Biblioteka (Agri)
Cajkovskogo 4   Phone: 433392
Charkov 24, Ukraine   L.V. Kokhnjk
Founded: 1959. **Subjects:** Soil science, agrochemistry, agriculture, fertilization, soil physics, amelioration. **Holdings:** 30,800 books; 18,050 bound periodical volumes; 6900 reports; 44 microfiche; 101,000 reels of microfilm. **Subscriptions:** 15 journals and other serials; 13 newspapers. **Services:** Interlibrary loan; library open to the public.

★ 16621 ★
Edwin A. Ulrich Museum - Library/Archives (Art)
Wave Crest On-The-Hudson
Albany Post Rd.
P.O. Box 632   Phone: (914)229-7107
Hyde Park, NY 12538   Edwin A. Ulrich, Dir./Owner
Staff: 1. **Subjects:** Art - three generations of the Waugh family of American painters. **Special Collections:** Materials related to Samuel Bell Waugh (1814-1884), Frederick Judd Waugh (1861-1940), and Coulton Waugh (1896-1973); art reference books. **Holdings:** 200 books; other cataloged items. **Services:** Library open to the public.

★ 16622 ★
Herzog Anton Ulrich Museum - Library (Art)
Museumstr 1   Phone: 531 4842400
W-3300 Braunschweig, Germany   Eleonore Westermeier, Libn.
Founded: 1754. **Staff:** Prof 1. **Subjects:** Art history. **Holdings:** 45,000 volumes. **Subscriptions:** 120 journals and other serials. **Services:** Library open to the public. **Remarks:** FAX: 531 4842408.

★ 16623 ★
Ulster County Planning Board - Library (Plan)
244 Fair St.
Box 1800   Phone: (914)331-9300
Kingston, NY 12401   Dennis Doyle, Plan.Prin.
Subjects: Planning, transportation, recreation, environmental management, energy conservation. **Holdings:** 500 books; 1000 bound periodical volumes; pamphlets; newsletters; maps. **Subscriptions:** 20 journals and other serials.

Allen G. Umbreit Library
See: **Muskegon Community College** (10931)

★ 16624 ★
UMDNJ and Coriell Research Library (Med, Biol Sci)
401 Haddon Ave.   Phone: (609)757-7740
Camden, NJ 08103   Betty Jean Swartz, Libn.
Founded: 1989. **Staff:** Prof 2; Other 1. **Subjects:** Cancer, immunology, genetics, pediatrics, microbiology, cell biology, cytogenetics, molecular biology. **Holdings:** 9000 volumes. **Subscriptions:** 143 journals and other serials. **Services:** Interlibrary loan; copying; library open to the public. **Computerized Information Services:** MEDLARS, MEDLINE, DIALOG Information Services, BRS Information Technologies; InterNet (electronic mail service). Performs searches on fee basis. **Networks/Consortia:** Member of Health Sciences Library Association of New Jersey (HSLANJ), Southwest New Jersey Consortium for Health Information Services, BHSL, South Jersey Regional Library Cooperative, National Network of Libraries of Medicine - Middle Atlantic Region, Pinelands Consortium for Health Information. **Remarks:** FAX: (609)757-7713. Electronic mail address(es): LIBRARY@SOMA.UMDNJ.EDU (InterNet). **Staff:** Alisha Johnson, ILL.

William O. Umiker Medical Library
See: **St. Joseph Hospital - William O. Umiker Medical Library** (14380)

★ 16625 ★
John Umstead Hospital - Learning Resource Center (Med)
1003 12th St.   Phone: (919)575-7259
Butner, NC 27509   Brenda M. Ellis, Libn.
Founded: 1979. **Staff:** 1. **Subjects:** Psychiatry, neurology, nursing, medicine, sociology, psychology, geriatrics, child psychiatry. **Holdings:** 1500 books; 3175 bound periodical volumes. **Subscriptions:** 40 journals and other serials. **Services:** Interlibrary loan; copying; center open to the public. **Computerized Information Services:** NLM. **Networks/Consortia:** Member of Resources for Health Information (REHI). **Remarks:** FAX: (919)575-6322.

Umweltbundesamt - Informations- und Dokumentationssystem Umwelt - Zentrale Fachbibliothekumwelt
See: **Germany - Federal Environmental Agency - Environmental Information and Documentation System - Central Environmental Library (6443)**

★16626★
Uncap International, Inc. - Project Collectors Research Library (Rec)
2613 Huron St.   Phone: (213)222-2012
Los Angeles, CA 90065   James J. O'Connell, III, Cur.
Staff: 5. **Subjects:** Hobbies, history, culture. **Special Collections:** Numismatic and philatelic reference materials. **Holdings:** 6500 books; 500 bound periodical volumes; 32 books in microform; 10 slide sets; 200 periodicals and newsletters. **Services:** Library open to the public on fee basis. **Networks/Consortia:** Member of State of California Answering Network (SCAN). **Publications:** Booklist, annual.

Caroline M. Underhill Research Library
See: **Andover Historical Society (860)**

Daniel Underhill Music Library
See: **Swarthmore College (15901)**

Underwater Man Library Section
See: **Franklin Institute Science Museum - Library (6092)**

Underwood Law Library
See: **Southern Methodist University (15505)**

★16627★
Underwood-Memorial Hospital - Anthony J.D. Marino, M.D. Memorial Library (Med)
509 N. Broad St.   Phone: (609)845-0100
Woodbury, NJ 08096   Ellen K. Tiedrich, Libn.
Founded: 1951. **Staff:** Prof 1. **Subjects:** Medicine, nursing, and allied health sciences. **Holdings:** 3500 books; 100 bound periodical volumes; 1500 reels of microfilm. **Subscriptions:** 125 journals and other serials. **Services:** Interlibrary loan; copying; library open to the public by appointment. **Computerized Information Services:** BRS Information Technologies, MEDLINE; DOCLINE (electronic mail service). Performs searches on fee basis. **Networks/Consortia:** Member of National Network of Libraries of Medicine - Middle Atlantic Region, Health Sciences Library Association of New Jersey (HSLANJ), Pinelands Consortium for Health Information, BHSL. **Remarks:** Underwood-Memorial Hospital has a teaching affiliation with Thomas Jefferson University.

UNESCO - ICOM Museum Information Centre
See: **United Nations Educational, Scientific and Cultural Organization - International Council of Museums (16765)**

UNESCO - Institute for Education
See: **United Nations Educational, Scientific and Cultural Organization - Institute for Education (16763)**

UNESCO - Intergovernmental Oceanographic Commission - International Tsunami Information Center
See: **International Tsunami Information Center (8201)**

UNESCO - International Bureau of Education
See: **United Nations Educational, Scientific and Cultural Organization - International Bureau of Education (16764)**

UNESCO - International Centre for Theoretical Physics
See: **International Centre for Theoretical Physics (8077)**

UNESCO - International Council of Museums
See: **United Nations Educational, Scientific and Cultural Organization - International Council of Museums (16765)**

UNESCO - International Institute for Educational Planning
See: **International Institute for Educational Planning (8127)**

UNESCO - Principal Regional Office for Education in Asia and the Pacific
See: **United Nations Educational, Scientific and Cultural Organization - Principal Regional Office for Asia and the Pacific - Library (16766)**

UNESCO - Regional Office for Science and Technology for South and Central Asia
See: **United Nations Educational, Scientific and Cultural Organization - Regional Office for Science and Technology for South and Central Asia (16767)**

UNESCO - UNESCO Information Services Division
See: **United Nations Educational, Scientific and Cultural Organization - UNESCO Information Services Division (16768)**

★16628★
Unexpected Wildlife Refuge - Library (Env-Cons)
Unexpected Rd.
P. O. Box 765
Newfield, NJ 08344   Phone: (609)697-3541
                            Hope Sawyer Buyukmihci, Sec.
Founded: 1968. **Staff:** 2. **Subjects:** Humane education, beavers, wildlife. **Special Collections:** Works of Grey Owl, Canadian naturalist. **Holdings:** Figures not available. **Services:** Library open to the public for reference use only by appointment. **Publications:** The Beaver Defenders, quarterly - to members and by subscription. **Also Known As:** The Beaver Defenders.

★16629★
Uni-Bell PVC Pipe Association - Library (Sci-Engr)
2655 Villa Creek, Suite 155   Phone: (214)243-3902
Dallas, TX 75234   Robert P. Walker, Exec.Dir.
Founded: 1971. **Subjects:** Pipe and pipe products design. **Holdings:** 1000 volumes. **Services:** library not open to the public. **Remarks:** FAX: (214)243-3907.

★16630★
Uniao Cultural Brasil - Estados Unidos Library (Area-Ethnic, Educ)
Rua Cel. Oscar Porto 208
Paraiso   Phone: 11 8851233
04003 Sao Paulo, SP, Brazil   Roseli Ferreira De Azevedo, Lib.Hd.
Founded: 1942. **Staff:** 14. **Subjects:** Brazil and U.S. cultural exchange; English as a second language; Brazilian civilization; United States civilization; EFL study and teaching. **Special Collections:** United States Slide Collection; rare records. **Holdings:** 33,000 books; 4000 bound periodical volumes; 23,500 clippings; 4807 records; 30,644 color slides; 175 videotapes; 70 compact discs; 663 audiocassettes; 1731 slides (guides); 796 booklets (lyrics). **Subscriptions:** 65 journals and other serials; 5 newspapers. **Services:** Interlibrary loan; copying; SDI. **Publications:** INQUIRE (newsletter); annotated bibliographies. **Remarks:** 11 8850376. **Also Known As:** Brazil-U.S. Cultural Union - Library. **Staff:** Leila Maria Fernandes Duarte, Libn.; Rayssa Barbosa Figueiredo, Libn.

★16631★
Uniao Cultural Brasil - Estados Unidos Library - United States Resource Center (Hist, Hum)
Rua Cel. Oscar Porto 208
Paraiso   Phone: 11 8851233
04003 Sao Paulo, Brazil   Roseli Ferreira de Azevedo, Lib.Hd.
Subjects: American literature - criticism and interpretation; American art; United States - history. **Holdings:** 1200 books; 200 bound periodical volumes; 77 historical photographs.

★ 16632 ★
Unidynamics/Phoenix, Inc. - Library (Sci-Engr)
102 S. Litchfield Rd.
Goodyear, AZ 85338-1295   Phone: (602)932-8100
Founded: 1963. **Subjects:** Chemistry, biology, pyrotechnics, aeronautical engineering. **Holdings:** 2000 books; 1500 technical reports; 800 patents; 400 technical abstracts. **Remarks:** FAX: (602)932-8949.

★ 16633 ★
Unilever Research U.S., Inc. - Research Library (Sci-Engr)
45 River Rd.
Edgewater, NJ 07020   Terry Hauerstein, Mgr., Info. & Off.Serv.
Founded: 1950. **Staff:** Prof 4; Other 1. **Subjects:** Detergents, soaps, toiletries, fats and oils, chemistry. **Holdings:** 6000 books; 12,000 bound periodical volumes; reports; government documents. **Subscriptions:** 275 journals and other serials. **Services:** Library not open to the public. **Computerized Information Services:** DIALOG Information Services, PFDS Online, NLM, Chemical Abstracts Service (CAS). **Networks/Consortia:** Member of Bergen Passaic Regional Library Cooperative. **Staff:** Anne McDermott, Libn.; Nina Lesiga, Info.Chem.; Judith Cestero, Info.Chem.

★ 16634 ★
Union of American Hebrew Congregations - Synagogue Architectural and Art Library (Art)
838 Fifth Ave.
New York, NY 10021   Joseph C. Bernstein, Dir.
     Phone: (212)249-0100
Founded: 1950. **Staff:** Prof 1; Other 1. **Subjects:** History of synagogue architecture, contemporary synagogue art and architecture, art of Jewish interest, ceremonial objects. **Holdings:** 200 books; 50 bound periodical volumes; 3000 slides; 1000 photographs. **Services:** Interlibrary loan; copying; slide rental service; library open to the public by appointment. **Remarks:** FAX: (212)570-0895.

★ 16635 ★
Union of Banana-Exporting Countries - Library (Food-Bev)
Calle 50
Edificio del Bank of America, Piso 7
Apartado 4273   Phone: 636062
Panama 5, Panama   Nitzia Barrantes, Libn.
Founded: 1974. **Staff:** 3. **Subjects:** Banana - production, exportation, transport, commercialization, pricing, socioeconomic aspects. **Holdings:** 14,000 volumes. **Subscriptions:** 90 journals and other serials. **Services:** Interlibrary loan; copying; SDI; library open to the public. **Computerized Information Services:** SIBBANA, SIIBAN (internal databases). **Remarks:** Serves Latin America and the Caribbean. Now a coordinate center of the Regional Network for Information on Bananas and Plantains for Latin America and the Caribbean. FAX: 648355. Telex: 2568. **Also Known As:** Union de Paises Exportadores de Banano. **Staff:** Rogeldivers Salazar.

★ 16636 ★
Union Bank - Library (Bus-Fin)
445 S. Figueroa St.
Los Angeles, CA 90071   Phone: (213)236-4040
     John D. Shea, Adm.Off.
Staff: Prof 1. **Subjects:** Economics, banking. **Holdings:** 2500 books; 75 bound periodical volumes; 52 VF drawers of economic statistics, newsletters, government documents. **Subscriptions:** 75 journals and other serials; 5 newspapers. **Services:** Interlibrary loan; library open to the public. **Computerized Information Services:** NEXIS. **Remarks:** FAX: (213)236-4042.

★ 16637 ★
Union Bible College - Library (Rel-Phil)
434 S. Union St.
Westfield, IN 46074   Mabel S. Bigger, Lib.Dept.Supv.
     Phone: (317)896-9324
Founded: 1951. **Staff:** 2. **Subjects:** Bible, theology, Quaker history, general academic subjects. **Holdings:** 4000 volumes. **Subscriptions:** 32 journals and other serials. **Services:** Copying; library open to the public. **Formerly:** Union Bible Seminary.

★ 16638 ★
Union Camp Corp. - Technical Information Service (Sci-Engr)
3401 Princeton Pike   Phone: (609)844-7203
Lawrenceville, NJ 08648   Helen Lee, Libn.
Founded: 1963. **Staff:** Prof 1; Other 1. **Subjects:** Pulp and paper, chemistry, engineering. **Holdings:** 6000 books; 5000 bound periodical volumes. **Subscriptions:** 190 journals and other serials. **Services:** Interlibrary loan; copying; SDI; service open to the public by request. **Computerized Information Services:** Online systems. **Remarks:** FAX: (609)844-7455.

★ 16639 ★
Union Carbide Canada, Ltd. - Technical Centre Library (Sci-Engr)
104555 Metropolitan Blvd., E.
C.P. 700, Sta. P.A.T.   Phone: (514)640-6400
Montreal, PQ, Canada H1B 5K8   A.M. De Jesus, Libn.
Founded: 1963. **Staff:** Prof 1. **Subjects:** Chemistry, plastics technology. **Holdings:** 1400 volumes; R&D reports. **Subscriptions:** 86 journals and other serials. **Services:** Interlibrary loan; library not open to the public. **Computerized Information Services:** MEDLARS, PFDS Online, Canadian Centre for Occupational Health & Safety, STN International, iNET 2000. **Remarks:** FAX: (514)645-8149.

★ 16640 ★
Union Carbide Chemicals and Plastics Co., Inc. - Library (Sci-Engr)
Bldg. 770
Box 8361
South Charleston, WV 25303   Phone: (304)747-5119
     Alice S. Behr
Founded: 1948. **Staff:** Prof 1; Other 4. **Subjects:** Chemistry, chemical engineering, environmental sciences. **Holdings:** 100,000 books and bound periodical volumes. **Subscriptions:** 650 journals and other serials. **Services:** Interlibrary loan; copying; library open to the public with restrictions. **Formerly:** Union Carbide Corporation.

★ 16641 ★
Union Carbide Chemicals and Plastics Co., Inc. - Library & Technical Information Service (Sci-Engr)
777 Old Saw Mill River Rd.   Phone: (914)789-3703
Tarrytown, NY 10591-6799   Joan Schechtman, Mgr.
Founded: 1971. **Staff:** Prof 4; Other 3. **Subjects:** Chemistry, chemical engineering, metals and materials, surface science, catalysis, industrial gases, physics. **Holdings:** 60,000 volumes; 200 VF drawers of patents, internal reports, vendors bulletins, and catalogs; 3500 reels of microfilm; 4000 microfiche. **Subscriptions:** 900 journals and other serials. **Services:** Interlibrary loan; library not open to the public. **Automated Operations:** Computerized cataloging and circulation. **Computerized Information Services:** STN International, BRS Information Technologies, DIALOG Information Services, PFDS Online, OHS (Occupational Health Services, Inc.), Questel, Congressional Information Service, Inc. (CIS), Mead Data Central, Dow Jones News/Retrieval. **Publications:** Newsletter, monthly; Union List, annual - both for internal distribution only. **Remarks:** FAX: (914)789-2204. **Staff:** Cristina Puiu, Tech.Info.Sci.

★ 16642 ★
Union Carbide Coatings Service Corporation - Library (Sci-Engr)
1500 Polco St.
Box 24166
Indianapolis, IN 46224   Phone: (317)240-2520
     Mary Ann Brady, Tech.Libn.
Founded: 1956. **Staff:** Prof 1. **Subjects:** Metallurgy, mechanical engineering, advanced materials, high temperature coating technology. **Holdings:** 6700 books; 1800 bound periodical volumes. **Subscriptions:** 220 journals and other serials. **Services:** Interlibrary loan. **Computerized Information Services:** DIALOG Information Services. **Remarks:** FAX: (317)240-2426. Telex: 27413.

★ 16643 ★
Union Carbide Corporation - Business Research & Reference Service (Bus-Fin)
39 Old Ridgebury Rd., Rm. N2800   Phone: (203)794-5316
Danbury, CT 06817   Roger W. Miller, Mgr.
Staff: Prof 2; Other 2. **Subjects:** Management; marketing; finance; economics; chemicals. **Special Collections:** Marketing Research reports; financial reports; government statistics. **Holdings:** 9000 books; bound periodical volumes; 15 vertical files of pamphlets; 13 vertical files of statistics; 53 vertical files of financial reports. **Subscriptions:** 104 journals and other serials. **Services:** Interlibrary loan; library not open to the public. **Computerized Information Services:** DIALOG Information Services, BRS Information Technologies, PFDS Online, PIERS (Port Import/Export Reporting Service), NEXIS, Questel, VU/TEXT Information Services, Data-Star, WILSONLINE.

★16644★
Union Carbide Corporation - Law Department Library (Law)
Section E2
39 Old Ridgebury Rd.   Phone: (203)794-6396
Danbury, CT 06817   Roseanne M. Shea, Mgr., Info.Serv., Law Dept.
Founded: 1935. **Staff:** Prof 1; Other 1. **Subjects:** Law - antitrust, patent, labor, corporate. **Holdings:** 30,000 volumes; 3 VF drawers; 7 titles in microform; Federal Register, 1970 to present, in microform. **Subscriptions:** 200 journals and other serials. **Services:** Interlibrary loan; library not open to the public. **Automated Operations:** Computerized serials and cataloging. **Computerized Information Services:** LEXIS, WESTLAW, DIALOG Information Services, Dow Jones News/Retrieval, State Net, VU/TEXT Information Services; internal database. **Networks/Consortia:** Member of Southwestern Connecticut Library Council (SWLC). **Remarks:** FAX: (203)794-6238.

Union Carbide Corporation - Library
See: Union Carbide Chemicals and Plastics Co., Inc. - Library (16640)

Union Carbide Corporation - Parma Technical Center
See: UCAR Carbon Company, Inc. (16609)

★16645★
Union Carbide Corporation - Technical Information Center (Sci-Engr)
Bldg. 200
Box 670   Phone: (201)563-5730
Bound Brook, NJ 08805   Anna B. Coleman, Staff Coord.
Founded: 1957. **Staff:** Prof 2; Other 4. **Subjects:** Polymers, plastics, organic chemistry. **Holdings:** 10,000 books; 16,000 bound periodical volumes; U.S. patents on microfilm. **Subscriptions:** 500 journals and other serials. **Services:** Center not open to the public; services provided to employees only. **Automated Operations:** Computerized cataloging and serials. **Computerized Information Services:** DIALOG Information Services, NEXIS, NLM, PLASPEC, PFDS Online, STN International; internal database. Performs searches on fee basis. **Special Catalogs:** Serials and holdings locator (computer printout). **Special Indexes:** Literature Search Report Index (computer printout).

★16646★
Union Carbide Industrial Gases - Linde Center - Technical Library (Sci-Engr)
Box 44   Phone: (716)879-2031
Tonawanda, NY 14151   Sandra C. Anderson, Tech.Libn.
Founded: 1939. **Staff:** Prof 1; Other 1. **Subjects:** Engineering - cryogenic, chemical, mechanical; chemistry. **Holdings:** 8000 books; 4500 bound periodical volumes. **Subscriptions:** 252 journals and other serials. **Services:** Interlibrary loan. **Networks/Consortia:** Member of Western New York Library Resources Council (WNYLRC). **Remarks:** FAX: (716)879-2015.

★16647★
Union of Chambers of Commerce, Industry, and Maritime Commerce and Commodity Exchanges of Turkey - Library (Bus-Fin)
149 Ataturk Bulvari
Bakanliklar   Phone: 4 1177700
Ankara, Turkey   Lale Tugan
Founded: 1962. **Staff:** Prof 2; Other 1. **Subjects:** Economics, commerce, communications, managerial services, agriculture, law, political science. **Special Collections:** European Community publications (4100 items); Union of Chambers of Commerce, Industry, and Maritime Commerce and Commodity Exchanges of Turkey publications (1034 items; 1952 to present). **Holdings:** 14,750 books; 2465 bound periodical volumes; reports. **Subscriptions:** 76 journals and other serials; 10 newspapers. **Services:** Interlibrary loan; copying; library open to the public for reference use only. **Computerized Information Services:** ECHO, ESA/IRS, Data-Star, PFDS Online; internal databases. Performs searches. Contact Person: Aydogan Arkis, Sys.Anl. **Publications:** Bibliographies, annual and quarterly. **Remarks:** FAX: 4 1183268; 4 1178235. Telex: 44011; 46012; 42344. **Staff:** Aysel Calisir.

★16648★
Union Club - Library (Hist)
101 E. 69th St.   Phone: (212)606-3413
New York, NY 10021   Helen M. Allen, Libn.
Founded: 1836. **Subjects:** New York City history. **Holdings:** Figures not available. **Services:** library not open to the public.

★16649★
Union College - Ella Johnson Crandall Memorial Library - Special Collections (Rel-Phil)
3800 S. 48th St.   Phone: (402)488-2331
Lincoln, NE 68506   Deforest Nesmith, Lib.Dir. & Spec.Coll.
Staff: Prof 3; Other 2. **Special Collections:** Seventh-Day Adventism (early denominational books and periodicals); college archives. **Holdings:** 2600 books; 1000 bound periodical volumes; 60 VF drawers. **Services:** Interlibrary loan; copying; SDI; collections open to the public. **Automated Operations:** Computerized cataloging and circulation. **Computerized Information Services:** DIALOG Information Services; internal database. Performs searches on fee basis. Contact Person: DeForest Nesmith, Pub.Serv.Libn., ext. 403. **Networks/Consortia:** Member of NEBASE. **Remarks:** FAX: (402)486-2678.

★16650★
Union College - Schaffer Library - Special Collections (Hist, Sci-Engr, Rare Book)
Union College   Phone: (518)370-6277
Schenectady, NY 12308   Barbara Jones, Dir.
Special Collections: Bailey Collection of North American Wit and Humor (2800 volumes); Kellert Microscopy Collection (400 volumes); rare books (2000); manuscript collections; college archives; Schenectady Archives of Science and Technology. **Services:** Interlibrary loan; copying; collections open to the public for reference use only. **Automated Operations:** Computerized cataloging, acquisitions, serials, and ILL. **Computerized Information Services:** DIALOG Information Services, OCLC, BRS Information Technologies; SINS-Serials Information System (internal database). Contact Person: David Gerhan, Hd., Info.Serv. **Networks/Consortia:** Member of Capital District Library Council for Reference & Research Resources (CDLC). **Special Indexes:** Indexes to manuscripts in the Special Collections.

★16651★
Union County Historical Society - John B. Deans Memorial Library (Hist)
103 S. 2nd St.   Phone: (717)524-8666
Lewisburg, PA 17837   Gary W. Slear, Chm., Archv. & Musm.
Founded: 1963. **Staff:** 5. **Subjects:** Local history, genealogy. **Special Collections:** Oral traditions project (300 oral history tapes and transcripts; 10,000 slides and photographs). **Holdings:** 1500 books; 250 bound periodical volumes; 40 cubic feet of clippings; tax records on microfilm. **Services:** Copying; library open to the public. **Automated Operations:** Computerized cataloging and acquisitions. **Publications:** Biennial collection of manuscripts on local topics; regional studies of local crafts.

★16652★
Union County Law Library (Law)
Union County Court House
103 S. 2nd St.   Phone: (717)524-8641
Lewisburg, PA 17937   Ruth E. Shambach, Lib.Dir.
Subjects: Law. **Subscriptions:** 4 newspapers. **Services:** Library open to the public for reference use only. Attorneys may borrow reference materials. **Remarks:** FAX: (717)524-8644.

★16653★
Union Electric Company - Library (Sci-Engr, Bus-Fin)
1901 Chouteau Ave.
Box 149   Phone: (314)554-2913
St. Louis, MO 63166   Patricia F. Gatlin, Supv., Lib.Serv.
Founded: 1913. **Staff:** Prof 3; Other 1. **Subjects:** Business, environment, engineering, occupational safety and health, nuclear power, public utilities, public-private power. **Holdings:** 13,000 volumes; 30 linear feet of annual reports; 200 linear feet of pamphlets and scientific society papers; 144 linear feet of standards; 20 linear feet of technical reports. **Subscriptions:** 619 journals and other serials. **Services:** Interlibrary loan; copying; library open to the public by appointment. **Automated Operations:** Computerized serials and cataloging. **Computerized Information Services:** DIALOG Information Services, BRS Information Technologies, WILSONLINE; Knight-Ridder Unicom (electronic mail service). **Publications:** What's New (bulletin), monthly; Library Clipping Service, daily - both for internal distribution only. **Remarks:** FAX: (314)554-2401. **Staff:** Alison Verbeck, Tech.Libn.; Jean Jochum, Tech.Libn.

★ 16654 ★
Union Hospital - AtlantiCare Medical Center - Health Sciences Library
(Med)
500 Lynnfield St.   Phone: (617)581-9200
Lynn, MA 01904   Deborah T. Almquist, Dir., Lib.Serv.
Staff: Prof 1; Other 1. **Subjects:** Medicine, nursing, and allied health
sciences. **Holdings:** 1365 books; 3000 bound periodical volumes; 128 video
cassettes; 125 audio cassettes. **Subscriptions:** 140 journals and other serials.
Services: Interlibrary loan; copying; SDI; library open to the public.
Computerized Information Services: MEDLINE, MEDLARS; internal
databases; DOCLINE (electronic mail service). **Networks/Consortia:**
Member of North Atlantic Health Science Libraries (NAHSL),
Northeastern Consortium for Health Information (NECHI), Massachusetts
Health Sciences Libraries Network (MaHSLiN). **Remarks:** FAX: (617)581-
0720.

★ 16655 ★
Union Hospital - Medical Library (Med)
1000 Galloping Hill Rd.
Union, NJ 07083   Phone: (201)851-7234
Staff: Prof 1. **Subjects:** Medicine. **Holdings:** 800 monographs.
Subscriptions: 121 journals and other serials. **Services:** Interlibrary loan;
copying; library open to the public for reference use only. **Networks/
Consortia:** Member of Cosmopolitan Biomedical Library Consortium
(CBLC), Health Sciences Library Association of New Jersey (HSLANJ),
BHSL.

Union Internationale des Chemins de Fer
See: **International Railway Union - Documentation Center** (8177)

★ 16656 ★
Union League Club Library (Hist, Hum)
38 E. 37th St.
New York, NY 10016   Phone: (212)685-3800
Founded: 1863. **Staff:** Prof 1. **Subjects:** Civil War; American history. **Special
Collections:** Union League Club Archive. **Holdings:** 20,000 volumes.
Subscriptions: 40 journals and other serials; 8 newspapers. **Services:** Library
not open to the public. **Networks/Consortia:** Member of New York
Metropolitan Reference and Research Library Agency. **Publications:** ULC
Club Bulletin, monthly. **Special Indexes:** Index of paintings in Union
League Club.

★ 16657 ★
Union League of Philadelphia - Library (Hist)
140 S. Broad St.   Phone: (215)587-5594
Philadelphia, PA 19102   Lisa M. Bondura, Asst.Libn.
Founded: 1862. **Staff:** Prof 1. **Subjects:** American Civil War; Lincoln;
political history; Philadelphia and Pennsylvania history, biography. **Special
Collections:** League archives (document cases). **Holdings:** 25,000 books.
Subscriptions: 62 journals and other serials; 10 newspapers. **Services:**
Library and archives open to researchers with proper introduction.
Remarks: FAX: (215)563-7141.

Union Marocaine du Travail
See: **Moroccan Union of Work** (10743)

★ 16658 ★
Union Memorial Hospital - Library & Information Resources (Med)
201 E. University Pkwy.   Phone: (301)554-2294
Baltimore, MD 21218-2895   Beverly Gresehover, Mgr.
Staff: Prof 3; Other 1. **Subjects:** Hand surgery, medicine, orthopedics,
nursing. **Special Collections:** The hand (70 monographs; 17 journal
subscriptions); sports medicine (50 monographs; 14 journal subscriptions).
Holdings: 5000 books; 6600 bound periodical volumes; 1656 AV programs.
Subscriptions: 390 journals and other serials. **Services:** Interlibrary loan;
copying; SDI; literature searches; patient education; library open to health
care professionals and outside users with restrictions. **Computerized
Information Services:** MEDLARS, DIALOG Information Services, BRS
Information Technologies, NLM; Maryland MED-SIG - Union Library
(electronic mail service). **Networks/Consortia:** Member of National
Network of Libraries of Medicine - Southeastern/Atlantic Region,
Maryland Association of Health Science Librarians (MAHSL). **Staff:**
Connie Daugherty, Educ.Res.Libn.

★ 16659 ★
Union Memorial Hospital - Nursing Library (Med)
201 E. University Pkwy.   Phone: (301)554-2296
Baltimore, MD 21218   Beverly Gresehover, Lib.Mgr.
Founded: 1893. **Staff:** Prof 1; Other 7. **Subjects:** Nursing, medicine,
sociology, psychology, life sciences. **Holdings:** 3000 books; 807 bound
periodical volumes; 4 VF drawers of articles; 35 file boxes; 20 tapes; 50
cassettes. **Subscriptions:** 120 journals and other serials. **Services:**
Interlibrary loan; library not open to the public. **Publications:** Monthly Lists
of Acquisitions. **Remarks:** Alternate telephone number(s): 554-2647.

Union Mondial pour la Nature
See: **International Union for Conservation of Nature and Natural
Resources - Library** (8202)

Union Mondiale des Pioniers de Stockholm
See: **World Union of Stockholm Pioneers** (20632)

★ 16660 ★
Union National Bank and Trust Company - Library (Bus-Fin)
Univest Plaza
Broaden Main St.   Phone: (215)721-2400
Souderton, PA 18964   Delores Gasbarra, Libn.
Founded: 1966. **Staff:** 1. **Subjects:** Banking, audit controls, commercial and
installment lending, human resources, data processing. **Holdings:** 306 books;
295 other cataloged items; 200 tapes. **Subscriptions:** 50 journals and other
serials; 7 newspapers. **Services:** Library open to the public by appointment.

★ 16661 ★
Union Pacific Railroad Company - Marketing Information Office (Trans,
Bus-Fin)
1416 Dodge St., Rm. 620
Omaha, NE 68179   Phone: (402)271-5000
Founded: 1976. **Staff:** Prof 1. **Subjects:** Transportation, business. **Holdings:**
1200 books; 1000 annual reports. **Services:** Interlibrary loan. **Automated
Operations:** Computerized cataloging and serials. **Computerized
Information Services:** DIALOG Information Services, InvesText,
Disclosure Information Group, NEXIS, VU/TEXT Information Services,
Dow Jones News/Retrieval.

★ 16662 ★
**Union Pacific Resources Company - Technical Information Center-MS
3701** (Sci-Engr, Energy)
P.O. Box 7   Phone: (817)877-7793
Fort Worth, TX 76101-0007   Debra McCann, Mgr., Rec.Adm.
Staff: Prof 2. **Subjects:** Geology, geophysics, engineering, petroleum
industry, business, computer science. **Holdings:** 20,000 volumes.
Subscriptions: 200 journals and other serials. **Services:** Library not open to
the public. **Automated Operations:** Computerized cataloging, acquisitions,
serials, and circulation. **Computerized Information Services:** DIALOG
Información Services, PFDS Online. **Publications:** Acquisitions; Current
Awareness Bulletin; new books list; newsletter. **Remarks:** FAX: (817)877-
7794. **Remarks:** Alternate telephone number(s): (817)877-7729. **Staff:**
Connie Hildebrand, Libn.; Ann Gilmore, Libn.

★ 16663 ★
Union Pacific Resources Inc. - Production (Energy)
205 5th Ave., S.W., Suite 3600   Phone: (403)233-6500
Calgary, AB, Canada T2P 2V7   Joan Broadley, Lib.Techn.
Staff: 1. **Subjects:** Oil and gas production. **Holdings:** 400 books; 50 bound
periodical volumes; 100 reports. **Subscriptions:** 52 journals and other serials.
Services: Library not open to the public. **Automated Operations:**
INMAGIC. **Remarks:** FAX: (403)233-6789.

Union de Paises Exportadores de Banano
See: **Union of Banana-Exporting Countries** (16635)

★16664★
Union of Polish Composers - Library (Mus)
Rynek Starego Miasta 27
PL-00-272 Warsaw, Poland   Phone: 22 311741
Subjects: Polish music and composers. **Holdings:** 32,000 books; 13,000 recordings. **Remarks:** Telex: 816996 ZKPZG PL. **Also Known As:** Zwiazek Kompozytorow Polskich.

★16665★
Union Saint-Jean-Baptiste and Catholic Family Life Insurance - Mallet Library (Hist)
One Social St.   Phone: (401)769-0520
Woonsocket, RI 02895-9987   Sr. Charles Emile, Libn.
Founded: 1908. **Staff:** Prof 1. **Subjects:** Franco-American history, civilization, biography, social life, and customs; French-Canadian civilization, genealogy. **Special Collections:** Major Edmond Mallet's correspondence (600 letters). **Holdings:** 5117 books; 144 bound periodical volumes; 350 pamphlets; 30 sets of manuscript notes; 50 maps; 12 VF drawers; 39 dissertations; 17 drawers of photographs; 112 reels of microfilm; 850 French-Canadian and French phonograph records; 17 video cassettes. **Subscriptions:** 25 journals and other serials; 10 newspapers. **Services:** Copying; library open to the public for reference use only. **Also Known As:** Bibliotheque Mallet. **Formed by the merger of:** Union Saint-Jean-Baptiste and Catholic Family Life Insurance of Milwaukee, WI.

★16666★
Union Texas Petroleum Corporation - Library (Sci-Engr)
1330 Post Oak Rd.
Box 2120   Phone: (713)968-3282
Houston, TX 77252   Carolyn Marshall, Supv., Lib.
Staff: Prof 1. **Subjects:** Geology, geophysics, business, petroleum engineering. **Holdings:** 6000 books. **Subscriptions:** 330 journals and other serials. **Services:** Interlibrary loan; copying; library open to the public with restrictions. **Computerized Information Services:** DIALOG Information Services, PFDS Online; Datatrieve (internal database). **Remarks:** FAX: (713)968-2771.

★16667★
Union Theological Seminary - Burke Library (Rel-Phil)
3041 Broadway at 121st St.   Phone: (212)280-1504
New York, NY 10027   Milton C. Gatch, Dir.
Founded: 1838. **Staff:** Prof 6; Other 11. **Subjects:** Bible, theology, sacred music, church history, missions, ecumenics. **Special Collections:** McAlpin Collection of British History and Theology; Van Ess Collection; sacred music collection (including hymnology); Bonhoeffer Collection; Auburn Collection; archives; Missionary Research Library Collection. **Holdings:** 580,000 volumes; 148,000 microforms; 1800 media items. **Subscriptions:** 1815 journals. **Services:** Interlibrary loan; copying; library open to the public upon application. **Computerized Information Services:** RLIN, WILSONLINE, DIALOG Information Services. **Networks/Consortia:** Member of New York State Interlibrary Loan Network (NYSILL), SUNY/OCLC Library Network, Research Libraries Information Network (RLIN), New York Metropolitan Reference and Research Library Agency. **Special Catalogs:** Catalog of post-1975 holdings (microfiche). **Remarks:** FAX: (212)280-1456. **Staff:** Seth E. Kasten, Hd., Rd.Serv.; Andrew G. Kadel, Ref. & Rd.Serv.Libn.; Paul A. Byrnes, Hd., Coll.Mgt.Serv.; Michael A. Bereza, Hd., Tech.Serv.

Union Theological Seminary - Hymn Society in the United States and Canada, Inc.
See: Hymn Society in the United States and Canada, Inc. - National Headquarters - Library (7606)

★16668★
Union Theological Seminary in Virginia - Library (Rel-Phil)
3401 Brook Rd.   Phone: (804)355-0671
Richmond, VA 23227   Dr. John B. Trotti, Libn.
Founded: 1806. **Staff:** Prof 6; Other 22. **Subjects:** Bible, theology, church history. **Special Collections:** Presbyterian Church Archives (775 manuscript volumes); Human Relations Area Files (37,070 microfiche). **Holdings:** 270,149 volumes; 42,604 microfiche; 27,706 audio recordings; 2226 films; 2478 reels of microfilm; 706 microcards; 238 transparencies, maps, posters; 2113 phonograph records; 882 filmstrips; 629 videotapes; 27,164 slides; 599

kits and games. **Subscriptions:** 1555 journals and other serials. **Services:** Interlibrary loan; copying; library open to the public with restrictions on circulation. **Automated Operations:** Computerized cataloging and acquisitions. **Computerized Information Services:** OCLC, BRS Information Technologies. Performs searches on fee basis. Contact Person: Patsy Verreault, Ref.Libn. **Networks/Consortia:** Member of SOLINET, Richmond Area Libraries Cooperative. **Publications:** Scholar's Choice, semiannual - for sale. **Special Catalogs:** Reigner Recording Library Catalog. **Remarks:** (804)355-3919. **Staff:** Robert Benedetto, Assoc.Libn.; Hobbie Bryant, Acq.Libn.; Dorothy Thomason, Cat.; Linda Sue Quinn, Asst.Cat.; Ann Knox, Media Rsrcs.Dir.

★16669★
Union University - Albany Law School - Schaffer Law Library (Law)
80 New Scotland Ave.   Phone: (518)445-2340
Albany, NY 12208   Robert T. Begg, Dir.
Founded: 1851. **Staff:** Prof 8; Other 11. **Subjects:** Law. **Special Collections:** Anglo-American law. **Holdings:** 369,878 volumes. **Subscriptions:** 4000 journals and other serials. **Services:** Interlibrary loan; copying; library open to alumni, attorneys, state and federal agencies. **Automated Operations:** Computerized cataloging and serials. **Computerized Information Services:** LEXIS, DIALOG Information Services, NEXIS, VU/TEXT Information Services, WILSONLINE, WESTLAW, OCLC. **Networks/Consortia:** Member of Capital District Library Council for Reference & Research Resources (CDLC), New England Law Library Consortium (NELLCO). **Publications:** Directory; acquisitions list, monthly. **Remarks:** FAX: (518)445-2315. **Staff:** Robert Emery, Assoc.Dir.; Elizabeth Duncan, Tech.Serv.Libn.; Kenneth Botsford, Asst.Cat.; Mary Wood, Pub.Serv.Libn.; Robert Eaton, AV/Ref. Libn.; Nancy Lenahan, Govt.Docs.; Marcel Lajoy, Ref.

★16670★
Uniontown Hospital - Professional Library (Med)
500 W. Berkeley St.   Phone: (412)430-5191
Uniontown, PA 15401   Marilyn D. Miller, Dir.
Staff: Prof 1. **Subjects:** Medicine and allied health sciences. **Holdings:** 550 books; 2500 bound periodical volumes. **Subscriptions:** 75 journals and other serials. **Services:** Interlibrary loan; photocopying; library open to the public with restrictions. **Computerized Information Services:** MEDLARS, MEDLINE. Performs searches on fee basis. **Networks/Consortia:** Member of National Network of Libraries of Medicine - Middle Atlantic Region, Pittsburgh Regional Medical Library Group, Southeast Pittsburgh Library Consortium, BHSL. **Remarks:** FAX: (412)437-9950.

★16671★
Uniontown Hospital - School of Nursing - Library (Med)
Annette Home
500 W. Berkeley St.   Phone: (412)430-5348
Uniontown, PA 15401   Elizabeth A. Johnson, Libn.
Founded: 1904. **Staff:** Prof 1. **Subjects:** Nursing. **Holdings:** 4553 books; 240 bound periodical volumes; 555 audiocassettes; 24 charts; 170 computer disks; 13 filmloops; 224 filmstrips; 28 models; 15 motion pictures; 45 phonograph records; 2613 slides; 135 transparencies; 193 videocassettes. **Subscriptions:** 33 journals and other serials. **Services:** Interlibrary loan; copying; library open to the public with restrictions. **Networks/Consortia:** Member of Southeast Pittsburgh Library Consortium.

★16672★
Uniroyal Chemical Company, Inc. - Information Services/Library (Sci-Engr)
P.O. Box 117   Phone: (203)573-4509
Waterbury, CT 06720-0117   Patrica Ann Harmon, Libn.
Founded: 1988. **Staff:** Prof 1; Other 2. **Subjects:** Chemistry, rubber, agricultural chemicals, plastics. **Holdings:** 10,000 books; 10,000 bound periodical volumes; patents; pamphlets; dissertations; documents. **Subscriptions:** 350 journals and other serials. **Services:** Library open to the public by appointment. **Automated Operations:** Computerized serials and ILL. **Computerized Information Services:** DIALOG Information Services, ORBIT Search Service, NLM, STN International, Questel, Data-Star. **Remarks:** FAX: (203)573-3079.

★ 16673 ★
Uniroyal Chemical Ltd. - Research Laboratories Library (Sci-Engr)
120 Huron St.   Phone: (519)822-3790
Guelph, ON, Canada N1H 6N3   Lorna P. Cole, Mgr., Info.Serv./
                                         Leg.Lias.
Founded: 1943. **Staff:** Prof 2; Other 3. **Subjects:** Organic chemistry, plastics, rubber, composite materials. **Holdings:** 6000 books; 2555 bound periodical volumes; 44 drawers of reports, trade catalogs, patents, pamphlets; 900 reels of microfilm. **Subscriptions:** 350 journals and other serials. **Services:** Interlibrary loan; copying; SDI; library open to the public with restrictions. **Automated Operations:** Computerized public access catalog and serials. **Computerized Information Services:** DIALOG Information Services, QL Systems, Chemical Abstracts Service (CAS), CAN/OLE, PFDS Online, Info Globe, Questel; internal databases; Envoy 100 (electronic mail service). **Publications:** Library Bulletin, biweekly; Accessions List, monthly; Reports List, quarterly; Library Notes, irregular. **Special Catalogs:** Company research reports; periodical holdings (both computerized). **Remarks:** FAX: (519)821-1956. **Staff:** Alecia Lambert.

★ 16674 ★
Uniroyal Goodrich Tire Company - Akron Information Center (Sci-Engr)
600 S. Main St.   Phone: (216)374-3884
Akron, OH 44397-0001   Tom Oliver, Mgr.
Founded: 1971. **Staff:** Prof 1; Other 1. **Subjects:** Tires, rubber, polymers, elastomers, management. **Holdings:** 2500 books; 30 VF drawers of pamphlets. **Subscriptions:** 150 journals and other serials. **Services:** Interlibrary loan. **Computerized Information Services:** DIALOG Information Services, PFDS Online, Dow Jones News/Retrieval, STN International. **Networks/Consortia:** Member of OHIONET. **Special Catalogs:** Tire pamphlet file; Journal Holdings.

★ 16675 ★
UNISYS Corporation - Corporate Information Center (Sci-Engr, Comp Sci)
M.S. E3-112
P.O. Box 500   Phone: (215)986-2324
Blue Bell, PA 19424   Marlene V. Ross, Mgr.
Founded: 1952. **Staff:** Prof 1; Other 1. **Subjects:** Business, computer science, computer industry, programming, data communications, telecommunications. **Special Collections:** Computer industry market research reports. **Holdings:** 10,000 books; 1000 bound periodical volumes; 100 audio cassettes; 5000 unbound items. **Subscriptions:** 175 journals and other serials; 15 newspapers. **Automated Operations:** Computerized public access catalog (PALS), serials, and circulation. **Computerized Information Services:** OCLC, DIALOG Information Services, Dow Jones News/Retrieval, NEXIS; CD-ROMs. **Networks/Consortia:** Member of PALINET. **Remarks:** FAX: (215)986-5586.

UNISYS Corporation - Defense Systems Operations - Electronic & Information Systems Group
See: UNISYS Corporation - Paramax Systems Corporation (16678)

★ 16676 ★
UNISYS Corporation - Law Library (Law)
MS C-15W19
Box 500   Phone: (215)986-3050
Blue Bell, PA 19424   Marsha A. Frederick, Chf. Law Libn.
Staff: Prof 1; Other 1. **Subjects:** Law - labor, contract, patent, trademark, copyright. **Holdings:** 11,000 volumes. **Services:** Library not open to the public. **Computerized Information Services:** LEXIS, WESTLAW, DIALOG Information Services, ORBIT Search Service, DataTimes. **Remarks:** FAX: (215)986-3090.

★ 16677 ★
UNISYS Corporation - Library (Sci-Engr, Comp Sci)
D1Z04
322 North 2200 west   Phone: (801)594-5222
Salt Lake City, UT 84116   Brad Myers, Libn.
Founded: 1956. **Staff:** Other 1. **Subjects:** Computer science, engineering, management, business. **Holdings:** 3000 books; 500 symposia proceedings; 5000 technical reports and manuals. **Subscriptions:** 250 journals and other serials. **Services:** Interlibrary loan; library not open to the public. **Computerized Information Services:** OCLC, DIALOG Information Services. **Publications:** Acquisition list, monthly.

★ 16678 ★
UNISYS Corporation - Paramax Systems Corporation - Electronic Systems - Library (Sci-Engr, Comp Sci)
P.O. Box 64445, MSU1H24   Phone: (612)456-3016
St. Paul, MN 55164-0445   Linda M. Sellars, Mgr.
Staff: Prof 3; Other 3. **Subjects:** Computers, electronics, data processing, management, physics, chemistry, mathematics. **Holdings:** 25,000 books; 15,000 technical reports. **Subscriptions:** 600 journals and other serials. **Services:** Interlibrary loan; copying; services open to the public with restrictions. **Automated Operations:** Computerized cataloging and circulation. **Computerized Information Services:** DIALOG Information Services, DataTimes, DROLS; DIALMAIL (electronic mail service). **Publications:** Bulletin (selected magazine articles and new book list), monthly. **Remarks:** FAX: (612)456-3098. Paramax Systems Corporation is a UNISYS company. **Formerly:** UNISYS Corporation - Defense Systems Operations - Electronic & Information Systems Group. **Staff:** Virginia Van Horn, Libn.; Samira Saleh, Libn.

★ 16679 ★
UNISYS Corporation - Rancho Bernardo Technical Information Center (Sci-Engr)
10850 Via Frontera
Box 28810   Phone: (619)451-4448
San Diego, CA 92127   Rosemond M. Corey, Tech.Libn.
Founded: 1977. **Staff:** Prof 1. **Subjects:** Physics, semiconductors, electronics, statistics, quality control, management. **Special Collections:** Career education. **Holdings:** 800 books; 600 bound periodical volumes; 200 proceedings and specifications; 500 technical data tapes; AV programs. **Subscriptions:** 120 journals and other serials; 5 newspapers. **Services:** Interlibrary loan; not open to the public. **Computerized Information Services:** DIALOG Information Services, TRAINET; DIALMAIL, Mail Manager (electronic mail services). **Networks/Consortia:** Member of CLASS. **Remarks:** FAX: (619)451-4114.

★ 16680 ★
UNISYS Corporation - Roseville Information Center (Sci-Engr, Comp Sci)
Box 43942
St. Paul, MN 55164   Phone: (612)635-5833
Founded: 1965. **Staff:** Prof 1; Other 2. **Subjects:** Computers, engineering, electronics, programming, management, production methods. **Holdings:** 15,000 volumes; 6000 technical reports; 1000 audio cassettes; 700 video cassettes. **Subscriptions:** 400 journals and other serials; 25 newspapers. **Services:** Interlibrary loan (limited); center not open to the public. **Automated Operations:** Computerized cataloging, acquisitions, serials, and circulation (PALS). **Computerized Information Services:** DIALOG Information Services, DataTimes; MAPPER (internal database). **Special Indexes:** Online indexes to internal documents. **Remarks:** Center is located at 2470 Highcrest Rd., Roseville, MN 55113. **Remarks:** FAX: (612)635-7523. **Staff:** Kim Loskota, Tech.Libn.

★ 16681 ★
UNISYS Corporation - Technical Information Center (Comp Sci)
25725 Jeronimo Rd., MS-260   Phone: (714)380-5061
Mission Viejo, CA 92691   M. Patricia Feeney, Sr.Info.Res.Anl.
Founded: 1974. **Staff:** Prof 1. **Subjects:** Computer architecture, computer programming, software design, hardware engineering design, data communications, management. **Holdings:** 5000 books; 3500 technical reports; 3000 other cataloged items. **Subscriptions:** 160 journals and other serials. **Services:** Interlibrary loan; center open to the public at librarian's discretion. **Automated Operations:** Computerized public access catalog, cataloging, and circulation. **Computerized Information Services:** DIALOG Information Services, Reuter TEXTLINE; DIALMAIL (electronic mail service). **Publications:** Acquisitions Bulletin, monthly. **Remarks:** FAX: (714)380-5138.

★ 16682 ★
UNISYS Corporation - Technical Information Center (Sci-Engr, Comp Sci)
41100 Plymouth Rd.   Phone: (313)451-4512
Plymouth, MI 48170   Carol Smith Feder, Lib.Mgr.
Founded: 1973. **Staff:** Prof 1. **Subjects:** Computer technology, banking. **Holdings:** 1800 books. **Subscriptions:** 300 journals and other serials; 20 newspapers. **Services:** Interlibrary loan; center not open to the public. **Automated Operations:** Computerized public access catalog, cataloging, serials, and circulation. **Computerized Information Services:** DIALOG Information Services, OCLC; DIALMAIL (electronic mail service). **Networks/Consortia:** Member of Oakland Wayne Interlibrary Network (OWIN). **Publications:** Plymouth Info Center News, monthly - for internal distribution only. **Remarks:** FAX: (313)451-4414.

★ 16683 ★

UNISYS Corporation - Technical Information Resource Center (Comp Sci)
70 E. Swedesford Rd.
Box 517   Phone: (215)648-2214
Paoli, PA 19301   Gwen Smolnik, Libn.
Founded: 1949. **Staff:** 2. **Subjects:** Computer science, artificial intelligence, expert systems, natural language processing. **Special Collections:** UNISYS publications. **Holdings:** 3000 books; 1500 reports. **Subscriptions:** 160 journals and other serials; 25 newspapers. **Services:** Interlibrary loan; copying; SDI; center not open to the public. **Automated Operations:** PALS. **Computerized Information Services:** DIALOG Information Services; internal database. **Remarks:** Alternate telephone number(s): (215)648-2665. FAX: (215)648-2531. Electronic mail address(es): GWENS@GVLVI.UNISYS.COM. **Staff:** Judith Norton.

★ 16684 ★

UNISYS Defense Systems - Reston Research Library (Mil)
12010 Sunrise Valley Dr.   Phone: (703)620-7360
Reston, VA 22091-3407   Jennifer Hatfield, Libn.
Founded: 1984. **Staff:** 1. **Subjects:** Electronic Warfare, naval systems, signal processing. **Special Collections:** Military Specifications and Standards, GIDEP. **Holdings:** 5000 books. **Subscriptions:** 161 journals and other serials. **Services:** Interlibrary loan; copying; SDI; library open to the public by appointment. **Automated Operations:** Computerized cataloging, circulation, acquisitions, and serials. **Computerized Information Services:** DIALOG Information Services, USNI Military Database, OCLC, CompuServe Information Service; CORMAP, DISMAP, MAPPER (internal databases); InterNet, DIALOG Information Services, CompuServe Information Service (electronic mail services). **Remarks:** FAX: (703)620-7022; (703)620-7916. **Formerly:** UNISYS Corporation - Reston Research Library.

★ 16685 ★

UNISYS Defense Systems - Technical Information Center (Sci-Engr)
365 Lakeville Rd.   Phone: (516)574-2735
Great Neck, NY 11020   James Montalbano, Libn.
Staff: Prof 1. **Subjects:** Navigation, radar, electronics, telecommunications, optics, systems engineering. **Holdings:** 5600 books and bound periodical volumes. **Subscriptions:** 170 journals and other serials. **Services:** Interlibrary loan; center not open to the public. **Computerized Information Services:** DIALOG Information Services, DTIC, NEXIS, DataTimes. **Networks/ Consortia:** Member of Long Island Library Resources Council. **Publications:** Acquisitions Bulletin, monthly - for internal distribution only. **Remarks:** FAX: (516)574-1244. **Formerly:** UNISYS Corporation - Technical Information Center.

★ 16686 ★

Unitarian-Universalist Association - Archives (Rel-Phil)
Office of Public Information
25 Beacon St.   Phone: (617)742-2100
Boston, MA 02108   Deborah J. Weiner, Dir. of Pub.Info.
Subjects: History, religion, biography, churches, ministers. **Special Collections:** Records of Unitarian-Universalist Ministers and Churches. **Holdings:** Clippings; manuscripts; pictures; maps; correspondence. **Services:** Archives open to the public for research and reference. **Remarks:** FAX: (617)367-3237.

United Arts - Resources & Counseling Division
See: **Resources and Counseling for the Arts - Library** (13850)

★ 16687 ★

United Automobile, Aerospace & Agricultural Implement Workers of America - Research Library (Bus-Fin)
8000 E. Jefferson Ave.   Phone: (313)926-5386
Detroit, MI 48214   Jane C. Murphey, Hd.Libn.
Founded: 1947. **Staff:** Prof 2; Other 2. **Subjects:** Economics and collective bargaining in automobile, aerospace, and agricultural implement industries; labor economics; industrial relations; United Automobile Workers. **Special Collections:** Automation; plant closings; UAW collective agreements; testimonies and speeches of UAW officers and staff. **Holdings:** Figures not available for books and periodicals; U.S., state, and Canadian government documents; newspaper clippings; pamphlets; press releases; microforms.

Holdings: 33,000 books. **Subscriptions:** 370 journals and other serials; 8 newspapers. **Services:** Library not open to the public. **Automated Operations:** Computerized cataloging. **Computerized Information Services:** DIALOG Information Services, PFDS Online, LEXIS, Dow Jones News/ Retrieval, Info Globe, Data-Star, Bureau of Labor Statistics (BLS); internal databases. **Remarks:** FAX: (313)823-6016. **Also Known As:** UAW; International Union, United Automobile, Aerospace and Agricultural Implement Workers of America. **Staff:** Helen Hillman, Asst.Libn.

★ 16688 ★

United Bank Center Law Library (Law)
2 United Bank Center, Suite 1215
1700 Broadway
Denver, CO 80290-1201   Phone: (303)832-3335
Founded: 1954. **Staff:** Prof 2. **Subjects:** Law - tax, corporate, insurance, bankruptcy, real estate; estate planning. **Special Collections:** Code of Federal Regulations and Federal Register, 1975 to present; U.S. Statutes at Large. **Holdings:** 15,220 books; 330 bound periodical volumes. **Subscriptions:** 5 journals and other serials. **Services:** Interlibrary loan; library not open to the public. **Staff:** Yvette Ferree; Marilyn Walter

United Bible Societies - Archives
See: **American Bible Society - Library** (502)

★ 16689 ★

United Catalysts, Inc. - Technical Library (Sci-Engr)
Box 32370   Phone: (502)634-7200
Louisville, KY 40232   Betty B. Simms, Tech.Libn.
Founded: 1943. **Staff:** Prof 1. **Subjects:** Catalysis, chemistry, physics, engineering, mathematics, clays, management. **Special Collections:** Catalysis. **Holdings:** 4000 books; 1300 bound periodical volumes; 18,000 patents; 18 VF drawers of indexed technical reports; microfilm. **Subscriptions:** 50 journals and other serials. **Services:** Interlibrary loan; library open to the public by appointment. **Computerized Information Services:** DIALOG Information Services, ORBIT Search Service. **Publications:** Acquisition Bulletin; Patent Awareness Bulletin; Articles of Interest Bulletin. **Special Indexes:** Indexes to documents, pamphlets, and technical reports. **Remarks:** Library is located at 1227 S. 12th St., Louisville, KY 40210.

United Cerebral Palsy Association of Northwestern Connecticut, Inc.
See: **Community Associates of Connecticut, Inc.** (4073)

★ 16690 ★

United Cerebral Palsy of New York City, Inc. - Library (Med)
120 E. 23rd St.   Phone: (212)979-9700
New York, NY 10010   Richard Gordon, Lib.Adm.
Founded: 1959. **Staff:** Prof 2. **Subjects:** Cerebral palsy and allied subjects. **Holdings:** 524 books; 19 bound periodical volumes. **Subscriptions:** 13 journals and other serials; 5 newspapers. **Services:** Library open to the public. **Publications:** Update, quarterly. **Staff:** Peter Hollander, Adm.Asst.

★ 16691 ★

United Cerebral Palsy Research and Educational Foundation - Library (Med)
7 Penn Plaza, Suite 804
New York, NY 10001   Phone: (212)268-5962
Subjects: Cerebral palsy. **Remarks:** No further information was supplied by respondent.

★ 16692 ★

United Charities - Library (Soc Sci)
14 E. Jackson Blvd.   Phone: (312)986-4000
Chicago, IL 60604   Yolanda Fonseca, Libn./Rec.Mgr.
Staff: Prof 1; Other 1. **Subjects:** Social work, law. **Holdings:** 6700 books. **Subscriptions:** 167 journals and other serials. **Services:** Interlibrary loan; copying; library open to the public by appointment. **Automated Operations:** Computerized public access catalog. **Computerized Information Services:** DIALOG Information Services. **Networks/Consortia:** Member of Chicago Library System, ILLINET. **Publications:** New Acquisitions, monthly - for internal distribution only.

★ 16693 ★
United Church Board for World Ministries - Library (Rel-Phil)
475 Riverside Dr., 16th Fl.   Phone: (201)567-5292
New York, NY 10115   Virginia Stowe, Libn.
Founded: 1820. **Staff:** Prof 1. **Subjects:** Missions of United Church Board
for World Ministries and its predecessors (especially American Board of
Commissioners for Foreign Ministries), third world areas. **Holdings:** 3000
books; 200 bound periodical volumes. **Subscriptions:** 50 journals and other
serials. **Services:** Library open to the public at librarian's discretion.
Remarks: Archival records are located in Houghton Library, Harvard
University, Cambridge, MA 02138, and in the library of Lancaster
Theological Seminary, Lancaster, PA 17603.

★ 16694 ★
United Church of Canada - Essex Presbytery - Resource Centre (Rel-
Phil)
208 Sunset Ave.   Phone: (519)253-4232
Windsor, ON, Canada N9B 3A7   Betsy Hanson
Founded: 1972. **Staff:** Prof 1; Other 1. **Subjects:** Religion. **Holdings:** Books;
magazines; church and Sunday School material; filmstrip; records; cassettes;
posters; videotapes. **Subscriptions:** 14 journals and other serials. **Services:**
Center open to the public.

★ 16695 ★
United Church of Canada - Maritime Conference Archives (Hist, Rel-
Phil)
Falconer Room
640 Francklyn St.   Phone: (902)429-4819
Halifax, NS, Canada B3H 3B5   Carolyn Earle, Archv.
Staff: Prof 1. **Subjects:** History of the Congregational, Methodist,
Presbyterian churches , and The United Church of Canada in the Maritime
provinces of Canada, Gaspe, and Bermuda. **Special Collections:** McGregor
Papers; Black-McColl Papers; Geddie Letters. **Holdings:** Several thousand
books, pamphlets, manuscripts, photographs, microfilm, newspapers,
official church records. **Services:** Interlibrary loan; copying; assistance with
research; archives open to the public.

United Church of Canada - St. Stephen's College
See: **St. Stephen's College** (14592)

★ 16696 ★
United Church of Canada/Victoria University Archives (Hist)
Birge-Carnegie Bldg.
73 Queen's Park Crescent, E.   Phone: (416)585-4563
Toronto, ON, Canada M5S 1K7   Jean E. Dryden, Chf.Archv.
Founded: 1953. **Staff:** Prof 6; Other 4. **Subjects:** Religious and social history
of the United Church of Canada and its antecedent churches, biography,
Methodist and Presbyterian foreign missions activity, local church history,
international religious organizations operating in Canada. **Holdings:** 13,000
books; 5000 bound periodical volumes; 600 yearbooks; 500 theses and
documents; 9400 pamphlets; 8250 feet of manuscripts; 9351 pamphlets; 4700
reels of microfilm; 2900 tapes. **Subscriptions:** 43 journals and other serials.
Services: Interlibrary loan; copying; archives open to the public for reference
use only. **Special Indexes:** Indexes to the Christian Guardian, the Christian
Advocate, other Methodist and Presbyterian serials, and local church
records. **Remarks:** FAX: (416)585-4584. **Staff:** Ruth Dyck Wilson,
Asst.Chf.Arch.; Karen Banner, Libn.

United Church of Christ - Archives
See: **Evangelical and Reformed Historical Society - Lancaster Central
Archives and Library** (5503)

★ 16697 ★
United Church of Christ - South Dakota Conference - Archives (Rel-
Phil)
Center for Western Studies
Augustana College
Box 727
Sioux Falls, SD 57197   Phone: (605)336-4007
                                            Harry F. Thompson, Cur.
Founded: 1980. **Staff:** Prof 1. **Subjects:** History - Congregational Church,
Great Plains, American Indian; missionary work; American West. **Special
Collections:** Oahe Industrial School; Santee Normal Training School; Steven
R. Riggs; Alfred L. Riggs; Thomas L. Riggs; Louisa I. Riggs; Mary C.
Collins. **Holdings:** 150 books; 30 bound periodical volumes; 170 linear feet
of archival materials. **Services:** Copying; archives open to the public with
restrictions. **Automated Operations:** PALS. **Publications:** CWS Newsletter,
semiannual; Guide to the Archives of the South Dakota Conference of the
United Church of Christ, 1986 (book).

**United Church of Christ - Southeast Conference - Audio-Visual Resource
Library**
See: **Audio-Visual Resource Library** (1288)

★ 16698 ★
United Church of Christ (Evangelical and Reformed) - Church Library
(Rel-Phil)
Grand & Ohio Sts.
850 Douglas St.   Phone: (216)967-4539
Vermilion, OH 44089   Doris M. Feiszli, Chf.Libn.
Founded: 1954. **Staff:** Prof 1. **Subjects:** Religion, faith, devotions and prayer,
Bible, biography, missions. **Holdings:** 5000 books; AV programs. **Services:**
Library open to the public for reference use only.

★ 16699 ★
**United Church of Christ First Congregational Church of Woodstock -
John Eliot Library** (Rel-Phil)
Rte. 169   Phone: (203)928-2197
Woodstock, CT 06281   Mary E. de Treville, Libn.
Founded: 1980. **Subjects:** Religion, children's literature, philosophy,
psychology, parenting, self-help, literature, biography. **Holdings:** 1600
books; 3 bound periodical volumes; 10 reports; 2000 archival items; 60 AV
items. **Subscriptions:** 4 journals and other serials. **Services:** Library open to
the public.

United Church of Christ of New Hampshire - Church Media Center
See: **Church Media Center** (3684)

★ 16700 ★
United Church of Los Alamos - Library (Rel-Phil)
2525 Canyon Rd.
Box 1286   Phone: (505)662-2971
Los Alamos, NM 87544   Jan Sinclair, Libn.
Founded: 1967. **Staff:** Prof 1; Other 3. **Subjects:** Religion, psychology,
family, social problems, health, philosophy. **Holdings:** 3450 volumes.
Subscriptions: 10 journals and other serials. **Services:** Library open to the
public.

★ 16701 ★
United Church of Religious Science - Ernest Holmes College Library
(Rel-Phil)
3223 W. 6th St.
P.O. 75127   Phone: (213)388-2181
Los Angeles, CA 90075   Albert Wickham, M.S.L.S., Hd.Libn.
Founded: 1974. **Staff:** Prof 1. **Subjects:** "New Thought," Science of Mind,
philosophy, religion, science, mental and spiritual healing. **Special
Collections:** Science of Mind (200 items); New Thought (500 items); church
archives. **Holdings:** 9000 books; 300 audiotapes; 1000 metaphysical
pamphlets and booklets; 16 VF drawers of clippings and archival materials;
200 file boxes of past metaphysical, scientific, and news magazines.
Subscriptions: 70 journals and other serials. **Services:** Interlibrary loan;
library open to members. **Special Indexes:** Index to Science of Mind
Magazine.

★ 16702 ★
United Cooperatives of Ontario - Harman Library
Sta. A, P.O. Box 527
Mississauga, ON, Canada L5A 3A4
Remarks: Currently inactive.

★ 16703 ★
United Dairy Industry Association - Information Services Department
(Food-Bev)
6300 N. River Rd.   Phone: (708)696-1860
Rosemont, IL 60018   Charlotte Wilson, Dir.
Founded: 1956. **Staff:** Prof 2; Other 2. **Subjects:** Dairy products, food,
nutrition. **Holdings:** 3000 books; 50 VF drawers of reprints and pamphlets.
Subscriptions: 1000 journals and other serials. **Services:** Interlibrary loan;
copying; technical background information; library open to the public by
appointment. **Computerized Information Services:** DIALOG Information
Services, MEDLARS, NEXIS. **Networks/Consortia:** Member of Illinois
Health Libraries Consortium, North Suburban Library System (NSLS),
National Network of Libraries of Medicine - Greater Midwest Region.
Publications: Dairy Council Digest, bimonthly. **Remarks:** FAX: (708)696-
1033.

★ 16704 ★
United Daughters of the Confederacy - Caroline Meriwether Goodlett
   Library (Hist)
U.D.C. Headquarters Bldg.
328 North Blvd.   Phone: (804)355-1636
Richmond, VA 23220   Annette E. Wetzel, Chm., Lib.Comm.
Founded: 1957. **Staff:** 1. **Subjects:** Civil War causes and Reconstruction.
Holdings: 5000 books; diaries; letters; manuscripts; papers; clippings;
memorabilia; photographs. **Services:** Library open to members and qualified
historians and students by appointment.

★ 16705 ★
United Daughters of the Confederacy - Shropshire Upton Chapter -
   Confederate Memorial Museum - Library (Hist)
Box 365   Phone: (409)732-3277
Columbus, TX 78934   Myrah Jane Draper, Cur.
Founded: 1962. **Staff:** 5. **Subjects:** Civil War, local history. **Special
Collections:** Antique local art (handwork; paintings); gun collection; 1913
Colorado River flood photographs; bound early newspapers; Civil War
correspondence of George McCormick and John S. Shropshire; antique
photography collection; family collections. **Holdings:** Figures not available.
Services: Library open to the public by appointment and on a limited
schedule. **Remarks:** Museum located in old Tower Building, on Colorado
County Court House Square. **Staff:** Millycent Tait Cranek, Musm.Comm.
Member.

★ 16706 ★
United Daughters of the Confederacy - Texas Confederate Museum
   Library (Hist)
621 N. 7th St.   Phone: (817)752-4774
Waco, TX 76701   Edith F. Williams
Founded: 1903. **Staff:** 1. **Subjects:** Southern history, Confederate States of
America military records. **Holdings:** 600 books. **Services:** Library open to
the public on a limited schedule with permission. **Special Indexes:** Texas
Division UDC chapter histories; confederate grave records in Texas; ladies
of the Texas Confederate Women's Home; ancestor roster of Texas UDC
members; confederate markers and monuments in Texas. **Remarks:** FAX:
(817)752-4781. Affiliated with the Helen Marie Taylor Museum of Waco.
Formerly: Located in Austin, TX.

United Electrical Radio and Machine Workers of America Archives
See: **University of Pittsburgh - UE (United Electrical Radio and**
   Machine Workers of America) Archives (19227)

★ 16707 ★
United Empire Loyalists' Association of Canada - National Headquarters
   - National Loyalist Reference Library (Hist)
50 Baldwin St.   Phone: (416)591-1783
Toronto, ON, Canada M5T 1L4   Dorothy Chisholm, Off.Adm.
Founded: 1923. **Staff:** Prof 2; Other 1. **Subjects:** Loyalist history, history of
Loyalist families, genealogy, education. **Holdings:** Figures not available.
Services: Copying; library open to the public. **Special Catalogs:** Catalog of
holdings, 1963-1985 - for sale. **Remarks:** Library is said to contain one of
the best specialized collections in North America on United Empire
Loyalists.

★ 16708 ★
United Engineers & Constructors Inc. - Library (Sci-Engr, Energy)
100 Summer St.   Phone: (617)338-6239
Boston, MA 02110   Margaret Preston, Libn. and Rec.Mgr.
Founded: 1908. **Staff:** Prof 1; Other 1. **Subjects:** Engineering - power,
mechanical, structural, electrical, hvac, environmental-industrial;
architecture. **Holdings:** 10,000 books; 100 bound periodical volumes; 7000
other cataloged items, including 3000 standards and USGS maps of New
England and New York. **Subscriptions:** 230 journals and other serials.
Services: Interlibrary loan; library open to the public with permission.
Computerized Information Services: DIALOG Information Services,
NASA/RECON; internal databases. **Publications:** Library Bulletin,
monthly - for internal distribution only. **Special Indexes:** Union List of
Serials for UE & C Libraries. **Remarks:** FAX: (617)338-6239. Telex: 92-
8307.

★ 16709 ★
United Engineers & Constructors Inc. - Library (Sci-Engr, Energy)
30 S. 17th St.
Box 8223   Phone: (215)422-3374
Philadelphia, PA 19101   Marie S. Knup, Hd.Libn.
Founded: 1928. **Staff:** Prof 1. **Subjects:** Heavy construction; design
engineering and architecture; power plants; energy sources - nuclear, fossil
fuels, solar, geothermal; wastewater; sanitary engineering; environmental
protection; seismology; chemical process plants; iron and steel. **Special
Collections:** Standards from voluntary standards organizations (10,000);
Atomic Energy Commission, Nuclear Regulatory Commission, Energy
Research and Development Administration, and Department of Energy
licensing dockets on microfiche. **Holdings:** 4500 books; 5000 government
documents. **Subscriptions:** 300 journals and other serials; 10 newspapers.
Services: Interlibrary loan (by prior arrangement). **Automated Operations:**
Computerized cataloging. **Computerized Information Services:** DIALOG
Information Services, PFDS Online, BRS Information Technologies.
Special Indexes: KWOC Index. **Remarks:** FAX: (215)422-3060. United
Engineers & Constructors Inc. is a subsidiary of Raytheon Company.

★ 16710 ★
United Engineers & Constructors Inc. - Western Operations - Technical
   Information Center (Sci-Engr)
P.O. Box 5888   Phone: (303)843-2256
Denver, CO 80217   Judith A. Valdez, Info.Spec.
Founded: 1971. **Staff:** Prof 1; Other 1. **Subjects:** Petroleum technology;
engineering - chemical, mechanical, structural; mining; business. **Holdings:**
11,000 books; 250 bound periodical volumes; 1000 microfilm cartridges of
vendor catalogs. **Subscriptions:** 350 journals and other serials; 3 newspapers.
Services: Interlibrary loan; SDI; library open to the public by appointment.
Automated Operations: Computerized cataloging. **Computerized
Information Services:** Dun & Bradstreet Business Credit Services,
DIALOG Information Services, BRS Information Technologies, PASS;
internal database. **Remarks:** FAX: (303)843-2208. Library located at 5555
Greenwood Plaza Blvd., Englewood, CO 80111. **Formerly:** Its Stearns-
Roger Division - Technical Library.

★ 16711 ★
United Food and Commercial Workers International Union - Library
   (Bus-Fin)
Suffridge Bldg.
1775 K St., N.W.   Phone: (202)223-3111
Washington, DC 20006   Ellen Newton, Libn.
Founded: 1975. **Staff:** Prof 1; Other 1. **Subjects:** Labor and trade union
history, business, economics, agriculture, food industry, retail industry.
Holdings: 1300 books; 300 Bureau of Labor Statistics Reports; 25 U.S.D.A.
periodicals; 24 VF drawers of clippings and pamphlets. **Subscriptions:** 500
journals and other serials; 100 newspapers. **Services:** Interlibrary loan;
copying; SDI; library open to researchers by appointment. **Automated
Operations:** Computerized serials. **Computerized Information Services:**
LEXIS, NEXIS, VU/TEXT Information Services, DataTimes, DIALOG
Information Services. **Networks/Consortia:** Member of Washington Area
Labor Information Specialists (WALIS).

★ 16712 ★
United Fresh Fruit and Vegetable Association - Information Center
   (Food-Bev)
727 N. Washington   Phone: (703)836-3410
Alexandria, VA 22314   Laura Kinkle, Mgr., Info. & Res.
Staff: Prof 1. **Subjects:** Fresh fruits and vegetables - production, distribution,
marketing, nutrition, history. **Holdings:** 40,000 items; 500 VF drawers.
Subscriptions: 150 journals and other serials; 15 newspapers. **Services:**
Center open to the public by appointment only. **Automated Operations:**
Computerized cataloging and serials. **Computerized Information Services:**
DIALOG Information Services, Dialcom, Inc. Performs searches on fee
basis. **Publications:** The Produce Industry Fact Book, biannual - for sale:
The Encyclopedia of Produce, irregular - for sale. **Remarks:** FAX: (703)836-
7745.

★ 16713 ★
United Grain Growers Ltd. - Library (Agri)
433 Main St.
Box 6600   Phone: (204)944-5572
Winnipeg, MB, Canada R3C 3A7   Carole Rogers, Libn.
Staff: 1.5. **Subjects:** Grain handling and transportation, agricultural history,
company publications, agricultural economics, agricultural business,

marketing. **Holdings:** 3000 books; 150 vertical file boxes; 10 Statistics Canada publications. **Subscriptions:** 500 journals and other serials; 15 newspapers. **Services:** Interlibrary loan; copying; library open to the public with restrictions. **Automated Operations:** Computerized cataloging and acquisitions (INMAGIC). **Computerized Information Services:** DIALOG Information Services, CAN/OLE; Envoy 100 (electronic mail service). **Remarks:** FAX: (204)944-5454. Telex: 07 57809. Electronic mail address(es): UGG.LIB (Envoy 100).

United Grand Imperial Council
See: **Red Cross of Constantine - United Grand Imperial Council** (13759)

★ 16714 ★
United Health Services/Binghamton General Hospital - Stuart B. Blakely Memorial Library (Med)
Mitchell Ave.   Phone: (607)762-2110
Binghamton, NY 13903   Maryanne Donnelly, Mgr.
Founded: 1940. **Staff:** Prof 1; Other 2. **Subjects:** Medicine and nursing. **Holdings:** 9181 volumes; 568 audiotapes; 126 videotapes; 15 films; 132 slides; VF drawers of pamphlets. **Subscriptions:** 208 journals and other serials. **Services:** Interlibrary loan; library open to health professionals. **Automated Operations:** Computerized cataloging. **Computerized Information Services:** DIALOG Information Services, WILSONLINE, BRS Information Technologies, MEDLINE, OCLC; CD-ROM (MEDLINE). Performs searches on fee basis. **Networks/Consortia:** Member of National Network of Libraries of Medicine - Middle Atlantic Region, South Central Research Library Council (SCRLC). **Remarks:** An alternate telephone number is 762-2109. **Staff:** Mary-Carol Lindbloom, Asst.Mgr.

★ 16715 ★
United Health Services/Wilson Hospital - Learning Resources Department (Med)
33-57 Harrison St.   Phone: (607)763-6030
Johnson City, NY 13790   Maryanne Donnelly, Mgr., Lrng.Rsrcs.Dept.
Staff: Prof 4; Other 9. **Subjects:** Medicine, nursing, health sciences administration. **Holdings:** 6000 books; 5400 bound periodical volumes; 1800 video cassettes, slide/tape programs, models, films, charts. **Subscriptions:** 305 journals and other serials. **Services:** Interlibrary loan; self instructional learning lab; department open to the public for reference use only. **Automated Operations:** Computerized cataloging, circulation, reference searching, and ILL. **Computerized Information Services:** MEDLINE, OCLC, BRS Information Technologies, DIALOG Information Services, WILSONLINE; CD-ROM (MEDLINE). Performs searches on fee basis. **Networks/Consortia:** Member of South Central Research Library Council (SCRLC), Health Sciences Libraries Consortium (HSLC). **Staff:** Mary-Carol Lindbloom, Asst.Mgr.

★ 16716 ★
United Hospital - Library (Med)
1200 S. Columbia Rd.   Phone: (701)780-5187
Grand Forks, ND 58201   Patrice Conely, Med.Libn.
Founded: 1952. **Staff:** Prof 1; Other 1. **Subjects:** Medicine, nursing, allied health sciences. **Special Collections:** Patient Education Library. **Holdings:** 1000 books; 3 VF drawers of pamphlets. **Subscriptions:** 257 journals and other serials. **Services:** Interlibrary loan; copying; library open to the public. **Computerized Information Services:** MEDLARS, DIALOG Information Services; EasyLink (electronic mail service). Performs searches on fee basis. **Networks/Consortia:** Member of National Network of Libraries of Medicine - Greater Midwest Region, Valley Medical Network (VMN). **Remarks:** FAX: (701)780-5772. Electronic mail address(es): 62755140-GFH (EasyLink).

★ 16717 ★
United Hospital Center Inc. - Health Science Library (Med)
3 Hospital Plaza   Phone: (304)624-2230
Clarksburg, WV 26301   Deanna Black, Hea.Sci.Libn.
Staff: Prof 1. **Subjects:** Medicine, continuing education, health administration, health education. **Holdings:** 2600 books; 1400 bound periodical volumes; 260 microforms; 400 AV programs; 300 video cassettes; 500 audio cassettes. **Subscriptions:** 230 journals and other serials. **Services:** Interlibrary loan; copying; SDI; center open to the public. **Automated Operations:** Computerized serials. **Computerized Information Services:** MEDLARS, DIALOG Information Services. **Remarks:** FAX: (304)624-2909. **Formerly:** Its Information Center.

★ 16718 ★
United Hospital Fund of New York - Reference Library (Bus-Fin)
55 5th Ave., 16th Fl.   Phone: (212)645-2500
New York, NY 10003   Rochelle Yates, Libn.
Founded: 1941. **Staff:** Prof 1; Other 1. **Subjects:** Hospital management, health services research, fund raising, volunteer services. **Holdings:** 5000 books; 90 VF drawers of reports, documents, pamphlets, clippings. **Subscriptions:** 100 journals and other serials. **Services:** Interlibrary loan; copying; library open to the public by appointment. **Computerized Information Services:** DIALOG Information Services, MEDLARS. **Networks/Consortia:** Member of Manhattan-Bronx Health Sciences Library Consortia, New York Metropolitan Reference and Research Library Agency. **Remarks:** FAX: (212)727-2471.

★ 16719 ★
United Hospitals Medical Center - Library (Med)
15 S. 9th St.   Phone: (201)268-8774
Newark, NJ 07107   Charlene G. Taylor, Dir., Lib.Serv.
Founded: 1960. **Staff:** Prof 2; Other 2. **Subjects:** Medicine, nursing, ophthalmology, otorhinolaryngology, pediatrics, orthopedics, hospital administration. **Special Collections:** Learning Resource Center Collection. **Holdings:** 5000 books; 8000 bound periodical volumes; tapes; 6 VF drawers of pamphlets, clippings, reprints; 2 VF drawers and 3 shelves of archival materials; 1883 AV programs; 7 audio cassette subscriptions. **Subscriptions:** 250 journals and other serials. **Services:** Interlibrary loan; copying; current awareness services; library open to the public with restrictions. **Automated Operations:** Computerized serials and circulation. **Computerized Information Services:** MEDLINE, DIALOG Information Services. Performs searches on fee basis. **Networks/Consortia:** Member of Cosmopolitan Biomedical Library Consortium (CBLC), Health Sciences Library Association of New Jersey (HSLANJ), Essex Hudson Regional Library Cooperative. **Publications:** Library Informer (newsletter and acquisitions list), quarterly; bibliographies - to medical professionals. **Special Catalogs:** Children's Health Audiovisual Materials Project Catalog (pamphlet). **Remarks:** FAX: (201)482-6647. Alternate telephone number(s): 268-8776. **Staff:** Bill Paringer, Asst.Dir.

★ 16720 ★
United Illuminating - Library (Sci-Engr, Energy)
80 Temple St.   Phone: (203)777-7070
New Haven, CT 06506   Nick Dematties, Mgr., Admin.Serv.
Founded: 1979. **Staff:** Prof 1. **Subjects:** Electricity generation and distribution, energy resources, computer science, management, engineering. **Holdings:** 1600 books. **Subscriptions:** 448 journals and other serials. **Services:** Interlibrary loan; copying; library open to the public by appointment. **Computerized Information Services:** DIALOG Information Services, Utility Data Institute. **Publications:** Newsletter. **Remarks:** FAX: (203)777-7137.

★ 16721 ★
United Kingdom - Civil Aviation Authority (CAA) - Central Library (Trans)
CAA House
45-59 Kingsway   Phone: 71 8325912
London WC2B 6TE, England   Tony Doyle
Founded: 1972. **Staff:** Prof 8; Other 7. **Subjects:** Aviation, air traffic control, electronics, computing, radar, medicine. **Special Collections:** Aviation history collection. **Holdings:** 20,000 books; 30,000 bound periodical volumes; 17,000 reports. **Subscriptions:** 1700 journals and other serials; 100 newspapers. **Services:** Interlibrary loan; copying; library open to the public for reference use only. **Computerized Information Services:** DIALOG Information Services. **Remarks:** FAX: 71 8326262.

★ 16722 ★
United Kingdom - MOD Main Establishment - Libraries (Mil, Soc Sci)
Prince Consort Library
Knollys Road
Aldershot GU11 1PS, England   Phone: 252 349381
Founded: 1860. **Staff:** Prof 2; Other 5. **Subjects:** War studies, international relations, military history. **Special Collections:** HRH Prince Albert's Foundation Collection. **Holdings:** 60,000 books; 500 bound periodical volumes. **Subscriptions:** 50 journals and other serials; 10 newspapers. **Services:** Interlibrary loan; library open to the public at librarian's discretion.

★16723★
United Library of Garrett-Evangelical and Seabury-Western Theological Seminaries (Rel-Phil)
2121 N. Sheridan Rd.
Evanston, IL 60201   Phone: (708)866-3911
Founded: 1857. **Staff:** Prof 5; Other 4. **Subjects:** General theology, Wesleyana, British and American Methodism, Anglicana, Semitic languages and literature. **Special Collections:** Deering-Jackson Methodistica (500 titles); Keen Bible Collection; Hibbard Egyptian Collection. **Holdings:** 280,000 books. **Subscriptions:** 1400 journals and other serials. **Services:** Interlibrary loan; copying; library open to the public with restrictions with fee for borrowing. **Automated Operations:** Computerized cataloging, acquisitions, and serials (NOTIS). **Computerized Information Services:** OCLC. Contact Person: John Thompson. **Staff:** Alva R. Caldwell, Co-Dir.; Newland F. Smith, Co-Dir.

★16724★
United Lodge of Theosophists - Theosophy Hall - Library (Rel-Phil)
347 E. 72nd St.
New York, NY 10021   Phone: (212)535-2230
Founded: 1922. **Subjects:** Theosophy, comparative religion, Buddhism, Hinduism, philosophy, psychology, psychic research, mythology and symbolism, Christian church history, the heretics. **Special Collections:** Original editions of writings of H.P. Blavatsky and W.Q. Judge. **Holdings:** 6500 books; 325 bound periodical volumes. **Services:** Library open to the public.

★16725★
United McGill Corporation - Library (Env-Cons)
2400 Fairwood Ave.
P.O. Box 820
Columbus, OH 43207
Subjects: Acoustics, airflow technology, air pollution, commercial and industrial applications of noise control systems. **Holdings:** 5000 volumes. **Computerized Information Services:** Internal databases. **Remarks:** FAX: (614)444-0234.

★16726★
United Media Resource Center - Central Illinois Conference - Library (Rel-Phil)
1211 N. Park St.
P.O. Box 515
Bloomington, IL 61702-0515   Phone: (309)828-5092
                                Mary Lou Scott, Media Libn.
Founded: 1965. **Staff:** Prof 1; Other 1. **Subjects:** Religion - general, education; ethics. **Holdings:** 1000 books; maps; transparencies; 16mm films; videotapes; audiocassettes; records; periodicals. **Services:** Interlibrary loan (printed material only); library open to the public for reference use only. **Publications:** Catalog (every 5 years). **Remarks:** FAX: (309)829-8369. Library is affiliated with The United Methodist Church of Central Illinois Annual Conference, The Presbyterian Church USA of Great Rivers and Southeast Illinois Presbyteries.

★16727★
United Medical Center - Department of Library Services (Med)
501 10th Ave.   Phone: (309)757-2912
Moline, IL 61265   Connie M. Santarelli, Team Ldr.
Staff: Prof 3; Other 2. **Subjects:** Medicine, nursing. **Holdings:** 6000 books; AV programs. **Subscriptions:** 165 journals and other serials. **Services:** Interlibrary loan; copying; SDI; library open to the public for reference use only. **Computerized Information Services:** DIALOG Information Services, MEDLARS. **Networks/Consortia:** Member of ILLINET, Quad City Area Biomedical Consortium. **Remarks:** Alternate telephone number(s): (309)757-3107. FAX: (309)757-2081; (309)757-3106. **Formerly:** Lutheran Hospital and School for Nurses Library. **Staff:** Jeanne Gittings, Libn.; Ellen Proctor; Cathy Hassman, Libn.; Charlotte Fauble.

★16728★
United Methodist - Armstrong Chapel - Church Library (Rel-Phil)
5125 Drake Rd.   Phone: (513)561-4220
Cincinnati, OH 45243   Margaret L. Hallman
Founded: 1970. **Staff:** Prof 1; Other 6. **Subjects:** Theology; Bible - study, history; Christianity - education, life, practice; healing ministry; poetry; literature; biography. **Special Collections:** Children's literature collection. **Holdings:** 3000 books; 210 videotapes. **Services:** Copying; library open to the public. **Automated Operations:** Computerized cataloging. **Special Indexes:** Videotape index. **Remarks:** FAX: (513)561-3062.

★16729★
United Methodist Church - California-Nevada Annual Conference - Archives (Rel-Phil)
Graduate Theological Union
2400 Ridge Rd.   Phone: (415)952-5177
Berkeley, CA 94709   Dr. Stephen E. Yale, Dir.
Founded: 1873. **Staff:** 1. **Subjects:** Methodism, church history, Western Americana. **Special Collections:** Hymnbooks (1200). **Holdings:** 5000 books; 600 bound periodical volumes; 8000 archival items. **Subscriptions:** 2 journals and other serials. **Services:** Copying; library open to the public by appointment. **Computerized Information Services:** Internal database. **Remarks:** FAX: (510)649-1417.

United Methodist Church - California Pacific Conference - Archives
See: School of Theology at Claremont - Library (14924)

★16730★
United Methodist Church - Central Illinois Conference - Conference Historical Society Library (Rel-Phil)
1211 N. Park
P.O. Box 515   Phone: (309)828-5092
Bloomington, IL 61702-0515   Catharine W. Knight, Archv./Ck.
Staff: 2. **Subjects:** History of the Illinois Conference, 1824 to present; Methodism in Illinois; United Brethren and Evangelical Churches. **Holdings:** 1200 books and bound periodical volumes; local church histories; biographies; early conference journals on microfilm. **Services:** Library open to the public. **Publications:** Historical Messenger, quarterly. **Staff:** Bettie W. Story, Commun.Coord.

★16731★
United Methodist Church - Detroit Conference - Commission on Archives & History - Detroit Conference Archives (Hist)
Adrian College Library   Phone: (517)265-5161
Adrian, MI 49221   Rev. James G. Simmons, Archv.
Subjects: Methodist history - Michigan, regional, American; early Methodism in England; Michigan history. **Holdings:** 5600 books; 520 bound periodical volumes; 8200 letters; 600 photographs; 500 pamphlets; 782 church files; 888 minister files; 400 manuscripts. **Services:** Archives open to the public by appointment.

★16732★
United Methodist Church - Eastern Pennsylvania Annual Conference - Historical Society Library (Hist, Rel-Phil)
326 New St.   Phone: (215)925-7788
Philadelphia, PA 19106   Brian McCloskey, Adm.
Subjects: Methodist history and related subjects. **Special Collections:** Annual Conference Journals and Methodist Disciplines, 1784 to present; General Conference minutes of the United Methodist Church. **Holdings:** 7000 books and bound periodical volumes. **Services:** Library open to the public for reference use only.

★16733★
United Methodist Church - General Commission on Archives and History - Library and Archives (Rel-Phil)
36 Madison Ave.
Box 127   Phone: (201)408-3590
Madison, NJ 07940   Kenneth E. Rowe, Libn.
Founded: 1866. **Staff:** Prof 3; Other 3. **Subjects:** Church records of Methodist Episcopal Church, Methodist Episcopal Church (South), Methodist Protestant Church, Methodist Church, Evangelical United Brethren Church, United Brethren in Christ Church, Evangelical Church, Evangelical Association, United Evangelical Church; United Methodist Church. **Special Collections:** Board of Mission correspondence from missionaries and overseas conference journals; private papers of Methodist leaders and bishops. **Holdings:** 70,000 books; 1600 bound periodical volumes; 4 million archival items; 100,000 feet of microfilm; 100 tubes of blueprints. **Subscriptions:** 600 journals and other serials. **Services:** Interlibrary loan; copying; library open to the public with restrictions. **Computerized Information Services:** OCLC, RLIN, DIALOG Information Services. **Publications:** Historians' Digest (newsletter), quarterly; Methodist History, quarterly. **Remarks:** Includes the holdings of the Association of Methodist Historical Societies and the former E.U.B. His torical Society. Alternate telephone number(s): (201)822-2787 (archives). FAX: (201)408-3939 (library); (201)408-3909 (archives). **Staff:** William C. Beal, Jr., Archv.

★ 16734 ★
United Methodist Church - Historical Society of the Eastern
   Pennsylvania Conference - Archives Room (Rel-Phil)
Gossard Memorial Library
Lebanon Valley College   Phone: (717)867-2104
Annville, PA 17003   Rev. Jere R. Martin
Founded: 1957. **Subjects:** Eastern Conference materials, general former
Evangelical United Brethren Church materials. **Holdings:** 578 books; 42
bound periodical volumes; 463 conference proceedings; 53 VF drawers of
unbound archival materials. **Services:** Archives open to the public by
appointment. **Staff:** James O. Bemesderfer, Libn.; Rev. Robert M.
Daugherty, (215)666-9090.

United Methodist Church - Kansas East Conference - Commission on
   Archives and History
See: **Baker University - Archives and Historical Library** (1425)

★ 16735 ★
United Methodist Church - Kansas West Conference - Archives and
   History Depository (Rel-Phil)
Southwestern College Library
100 College St.   Phone: (316)221-4150
Winfield, KS 67156   Joanne Black, Archv.
Founded: 1928. **Staff:** 1. **Subjects:** Methodism, especially Kansas
Methodism. **Special Collections:** Journals of Kansas West Annual
Conference and predecessor conferences; disciplines of United Methodist
Church and predecessor denominations; unpublished histories of present
and former United Methodist, Methodist, Methodist Episcopal,
Evangelical, United Brethren in Christ, and Evangelical United Brethren
churches in geographic area of Kansas West Annual Conference. **Holdings:**
1000 volumes; church records; newspapers; manuscripts; memoirs;
obituaries. **Services:** Copying; archives open to the public by appointment.

★ 16736 ★
United Methodist Church - Nebraska Conference - Historical Center
   (Rel-Phil, Hist)
Old Main Building
Nebraska Wesleyan University
5000 St. Paul Ave.   Phone: (402)465-2175
Lincoln, NE 68504-2796   Bernice M. Boilesen, Cur.
Founded: 1942. **Staff:** Prof 1. **Subjects:** United Methodist history, Nebraska
Conference. **Special Collections:** Bible Collection (200); Conference
Journals - Methodist, 1856 to present, Evangelical United Brethren, 1880
to present; church histories; local church records. **Holdings:** 15,000 volumes.
Services: Copying; research; center open to the public.

★ 16737 ★
United Methodist Church - Peninsula Annual Conference - Commission
   on Archives and History - Barratt's Chapel Museum Library (Rel-
   Phil)
RD 2, Box 25   Phone: (302)335-5544
Frederica, DE 19946   Lynn Hobbs
Subjects: Methodism, religion, Delaware history. **Special Collections:**
Peninsula Conference; Wilmington Conference; Delaware Conference.
Holdings: Figures not available. **Services:** Copying.

★ 16738 ★
United Methodist Church - South Dakota Conference - Commission on
   Archives and History - Library (Rel-Phil, Hist)
1331 W. University Ave.
Box 460   Phone: (605)996-6552
Mitchell, SD 57301   Patricia A. Breidenbach, Archv.
Founded: 1969. **Staff:** Prof 1. **Subjects:** Religion, church history. **Special**
Collections: Bibles; hymnals; gospel song books; Methodist Quarterly
Review (1843-1930); United Methodist and E.U.B. Conference histories and
journals; United Methodist and predecessor denominations' disciplines and
histories; journals pertaining to conferences in South Dakota (1880 to
present); Methodist Quarterly Review (1843-1930). **Holdings:** 2800 books;
300 bound periodical volumes; 350 slides and cassettes; bibles; hymnals;
gospel song books. **Subscriptions:** 2 journals and other serials. **Services:**
Copying; library open to the public. **Remarks:** FAX: (605)996-1766.

★ 16739 ★
United Methodist Church - South Georgia Conference - Commission on
   Archives and History - Arthur J. Moore Methodist Museum - Library
   (Hist)
Epworth-by-the-Sea
P.O. Box 407   Phone: (912)638-4050
St. Simons Island, GA 31522   Mary McCook, Dir./Cur.
Founded: 1964. **Staff:** 2. Methodist history, Georgia history and Methodist
growth, coastal history, regional Methodist history (1736 to present), related
biographies. **Special Collections:** Archives of the South Georgia Conference
United Methodist Church; Wesley Collection (life works, early Methodism;
300 rare volumes); hymnal collection (100 volumes); 2 original John Wesley
letters; Bishop Arthur Moore papers. **Holdings:** 5000 volumes; 150 bound
periodical volumes; 20 documents; 6 AV programs. **Subscriptions:** 6
journals and other serials. **Services:** Copying; library open to the public for
reference use only. **Remarks:** Jointly maintained by South Georgia
Conference And Epworth By The Sea.

★ 16740 ★
United Methodist Church - Southern New England Conference -
   Historical Society Library (Rel-Phil, Hist)
745 Commonwealth Ave.   Phone: (617)353-3034
Boston, MA 02215   Myra V. Siegenthaler, Libn.
Subjects: New England Methodist history, Wesleyana. **Holdings:** 13,881
books; 300 bound periodical volumes; 200 other cataloged items; 1000
pamphlets; 8000 letters; 30 VF drawers on local churches. **Subscriptions:** 10
journals and other serials. **Services:** Copying; library open to the public.
Automated Operations: Computerized cataloging. **Remarks:** The library is
housed in the library of the Boston University - School of Theology and
serviced by that staff on a contract basis. FAX: (617)353-3061.

★ 16741 ★
United Methodist Church - Southern New Jersey Conference -
   Commission on Archives and History - Library (Hist)
Bishop's Wing
The Pennington School
112 W. Deleware Ave.
Pennington, NJ 08534   Rev. Robert B. Steelman, Hist.
Subjects: New Jersey Methodism, Wesleyism, genealogy. **Holdings:** Books;
bound periodical volumes; manuscripts; nonbook items. **Services:** Library
open to the public for reference use only. **Publications:** The Historical Trail.

★ 16742 ★
United Methodist Church - Wisconsin Conference - Archives (Hist, Rel-
   Phil)
P.O. Box 220   Phone: (608)837-7328
Sun Prairie, WI 53590-0220   Mary E. Schroeder, Archv./Hist.Libn.
Staff: Prof 1. **Subjects:** Church history. **Special Collections:** Diaries of
William Darwin Ames, 1857-1898; Journal of Michael Benson (1832-1919);
Journal of Joseph J. Austin (1838-1885; 120 pages). **Holdings:** 2000 books;
50 bound periodical volumes; 28 VF drawers of archival materials; 15 boxes
of newspapers. **Services:** Copying; archives open to the public on a limited
schedule. **Special Indexes:** Biographical indexes; church indexes. **Remarks:**
Library located at 750 Windsor St., Suite 302, Sun Prairie, WI 53590.

★ 16743 ★
United Methodist Church - Yellowstone Conference - Archives (Hist,
   Rel-Phil)
Rocky Mountain College
Adams Library
355 Broadwater Ave.   Phone: (406)256-1385
Billings, MT 59101   Rev. Ruth Wight, Chair
Staff: 1. **Subjects:** History of ministers and churches. **Special Collections:**
Personal papers of Brother Van Orsdel (Methodist circuit rider in Montana);
papers of other early-day Methodist ministers. **Holdings:** Books of historical
value; microfilm; church materials of historical importance; slides;
photographs; tapes; Conference Journals. **Services:** Archives open to the
public by appointment. **Special Catalogs:** List of United Methodist ministers
who served within conference boundaries.

★16744★
United Methodist Commission on Archives & History - Minnesota Annual Conference - Archives & Historical Library (Hist, Rel-Phil)
122 W. Franklin Ave., Rm. 400   Phone: (612)870-0058
Minneapolis, MN 55404   Thelma Boeder, Archv./Exec.Sec.
Founded: 1856. **Staff:** Prof 1. **Subjects:** United Methodist Church and Evangelical United Brethren history, particularly in the Minnesota Conference; Methodism. **Special Collections:** Records of many discontinued churches in Minnesota Conference; Church Disciplines; annual conference minutes; journals. **Holdings:** 2000 books; 100 bound periodical volumes; archival records. **Services:** Copying; library open to the public for reference use only.

★16745★
United Methodist Commission on Archives & History - Northwest Texas Annual Conference - Archives (Rel-Phil)
Jay-Rollins Library
McMurry College
Box 296   Phone: (915)691-2291
Abilene, TX 79697   Jewell Posey, Archv.
Staff: Prof 1; Other 1. **Subjects:** Church history. **Special Collections:** J.O. Haymes (6 boxes); O.P. Clark (1 box); Cal C. Wright (21 linear feet); Alsie H. Carleton (10 linear feet); J. Edmund Kirby (4 boxes); Mrs. C.C. Coffee (12 linear feet). **Holdings:** 459 books; 100 bound periodical volumes; 200 membership minutes; 2 VF drawers of local church histories; 25 boxes of unbound reports and publicity; 48 cases of sermon manuscripts; 2 boxes of videotapes and cassettes. **Services:** Copying; archives open to the public with restrictions.

★16746★
United Methodist Commission on Archives & History - South Carolina Conference - Historical Society Library (Rel-Phil)
Wofford College   Phone: (803)597-4309
Spartanburg, SC 29303-3663   Herbert Hucks, Jr., Cur.
Founded: 1856. **Staff:** 1. **Subjects:** Methodist history with particular reference to South Carolina Methodism. **Holdings:** 2000 books and bound periodical volumes; minutes of the South Carolina conference; letters; notes; manuscripts. **Services:** Library open to the public for reference use only.

★16747★
United Methodist Historical Society - Baltimore Annual Conference - Lovely Lane Museum Library (Rel-Phil, Hist)
2200 St. Paul St.   Phone: (410)889-4458
Baltimore, MD 21218   Rev. Edwin Schell, Exec.Sec./Libn.
Founded: 1855. **Staff:** Prof 2; Other 1. **Subjects:** Religion, Wesleyana, American church history, higher education, Methodism. **Special Collections:** Baltimore Conference Journal and papers; letters of Bishop Asbury; journals of early Methodist preachers; letters and notes of Bishop Coke; E. Stanley Jones and John F. Goucher papers; Maryland church records. **Holdings:** 5000 books; 280 bound periodical volumes; 18,000 reports, personal papers, church histories, clippings. **Subscriptions:** 30 journals and other serials; 3 newspapers. **Services:** Interlibrary loan; copying; library open to qualified researchers. **Publications:** Third Century Methodism, triennial; annual reports. **Special Catalogs:** United Methodist Clergy - Baltimore and Vicinity, 1773-1990 (card). **Staff:** Betty Ammons, Asst.Libn.

★16748★
United Methodist Publishing House - Library (Publ, Rel-Phil)
P.O. Box 801   Phone: (615)749-6335
Nashville, TN 37202   Rosalyn Lewis, Libn.
Founded: 1946. **Staff:** Prof 1; Other 2. **Subjects:** Methodist history, religion. **Special Collections:** Wesleyana (575 items). **Holdings:** 30,000 books; 4000 bound periodical volumes; 60 VF drawers; 1100 reels of microfilm. **Subscriptions:** 263 journals and other serials; 10 newspapers. **Services:** Interlibrary loan; copying; library open to the public for research use only. **Automated Operations:** Computerized cataloging. **Computerized Information Services:** OCLC, OCLC EPIC. **Networks/Consortia:** Member of SOLINET. **Remarks:** FAX: (615)749-6079. Library located at 201 Eighth Ave., S., Rm. 122.

★16749★
United Mortgage Bankers of America - Library (Bus-Fin)
800 Ivy Hill Rd.
Philadelphia, PA 19150   Gene Hatton, Exec.Dir.
Founded: 1962. **Subjects:** Minority mortgage brokering and banking. **Holdings:** 2000 volumes. **Publications:** Newsletter, monthly. **Remarks:** United Mortgage Bankers of America, Inc., a National Trade Association, seeks to provide members with the information and technical assistance necessary to enhance their businesses. The UMBA sponsors training sessions and educational programs in order to accomplish this goal. FAX: (215)247-1580.

★16750★
United Nations - Centre for Human Settlements (Habitat) - Information Office for North America and the Caribbean (Soc Sci)
130 Albert St., Suite 417
Ottawa, ON, Canada K1P 5G4   Phone: (613)235-6400
Staff: Prof 1; Other 2. **Subjects:** Human settlements issues. **Special Collections:** Government documentation relating to the 1976 United Nations Conference on Human Settlements; government-produced films on human settlements issues (over 200). **Holdings:** 50 published works on human settlements; documents; reports; information directories; videotapes; films. **Subscriptions:** 28 journals and other serials. **Services:** Interlibrary loan; office open to the public. **Publications:** Habitat News, 3/year; list of other publications - available on request. **Special Catalogs:** Film Catalog (English or French). **Remarks:** Center's headquarters is at Box 30030, Nairobi, Kenya. There are additional information offices in Amman, Bangkok, Budapest, Geneva, and Mexico City. FAX: (613)235-6226. Telex: 05 33137. **Also Known As:** Habitat.

★16751★
United Nations - Centre on Transnational Corporations - Library (Bus-Fin)
United Nations   Phone: (212)963-3352
New York, NY 10017   Samuel K.B. Asante, Dir., Adv./Info.Serv.Div.
Founded: 1976. **Staff:** 1. **Subjects:** Transnational corporations, foreign direct investment, foreign investment laws, contracts. **Special Collections:** Company directories; corporate reports; United Nations documents. **Holdings:** Figures not available. **Services:** Library open to public by written or telephone application. **Automated Operations:** Computerized cataloging. **Computerized Information Services:** DIALOG Information Services, Dow Jones News/Retrieval, Dun & Bradstreet Business Credit Services, PFDS Online; internal databases. **Publications:** List of publications - available on request. **Staff:** Luciana Marcell;-Koenig, TNC Affairs Off.; Paul Dysenchuk, Res.Asst./Libn.; Sharon Brandstein, Res.Asst./Bibliog.

★16752★
United Nations - Food and Agriculture Organization - David Lublin Memorial Library (Biol Sci, Agri)
Via delle Terme di Caracalla
I-00100 Rome, Italy   Phone: 6 57973703
Founded: 1909. **Staff:** 57. **Subjects:** Agriculture, food and nutrition, plant production, agricultural machinery, agro-industries, agro-forestry, sustainable development, statistics and economics in food and agriculture, fisheries, forestry, rural development, animal production. **Special Collections:** FAO publications, 1945 to present; International Institute of Agriculture Library, 1905-1945; incunabula (32). **Holdings:** 1 million volumes; 120,000 documents; 90,000 microfiche; 4 manuscripts. **Subscriptions:** 7000 journals and other serials. **Services:** Interlibrary loan; copying; SDI; library open to experts. **Automated Operations:** Computerized public access catalog, cataloging, and acquisitions. **Computerized Information Services:** DIALOG Information Services, ESA/IRS; produces FAO Documentation database, FAO Library Catalogue of Monographs database. **Publications:** FAO Documentation on Microfiche - by subscription; New Books in the DLML, monthly. **Special Catalogs:** AGLINET Union List; COM Catalogs of FAO Documentation, 1976 to present. **Remarks:** FAX: 57973152; 57826810. Telex: 610181 FAO I. Electronic mail address(es): 14938 (DIALMAIL). Acts as the coordinating center for the Worldwide Network of Agricultural Libraries (AGLINET), an international cooperative which ensures the availability of global information not held by participating libraries. **Staff:** T.M. Jaansoo-Boudreau, Chf., Ref./Doc.Info.Sect.; T. Ellis, Chf., Sel.Acq. & Ser; E. Corassacz, Doc., Proc.Sect.; M. O'Doherty, Doc., Proc.Sect.; C. Puccinelli, Nutrition Libn.; G. Gerusa, Stat.Libn.; J. Collins, Fisheries Libn.; S. Ayazi, Ref.Libn.; M. Zito, Ser.Libn.; G. Stergion, Sys.

★ 16753 ★
United Nations - International Court of Justice - Library (Law)
Peace Palace
Carnegieplein 2   Phone: 70 3924441
NL-2517 KJ The Hague, Netherlands   Arthur C. Eyffinger, Libn.
Founded: 1931. **Staff:** 4. **Subjects:** International public law, International Court of Justice. **Special Collections:** Permanent Court of International Justice publications; International Court of Justice publications. **Holdings:** 13,000 books; 17,000 bound periodical volumes; 50,000 United Nations documents; 500 microforms. **Subscriptions:** 200 journals and other serials. **Services:** Library not open to the public. **Computerized Information Services:** Internal database. **Publications:** Annual Bibliography of the International Court of Justice. **Remarks:** FAX: 70 3649928. Telex: 32323. **Staff:** Mrs. R.S.B. Van Megen, Dp.Libn.; M. Schiethart; G.J.F.J. Vooijs.

United Nations - International Telecommunication Union
See: International Telecommunication Union (8196)

★ 16754 ★
United Nations - Office of the United Nations Disaster Relief
   Coordinator - UNDRO Reference Library (Soc Sci)
Palais des Nations   Phone: 22 7346011
CH-1211 Geneva 10, Switzerland   Ingrid Nilsson, Ref.Libn.
Founded: 1976. **Staff:** 1. **Subjects:** Disaster relief and disaster management - mobilization, information on sites; prediction of natural disasters; disaster preparedness; forecasting and warning systems. **Holdings:** 4100 books, monographs, training materials, legislation, serial publications, and disaster classification lists. **Subscriptions:** 160 journals and other serials. **Services:** Interlibrary loan; copying; SDI; library open to disaster specialists, international organizations, IGOs and NGOs, students and governments. **Computerized Information Services:** Internal databases; Dialcom, Inc. (electronic mail service). **Publications:** List of new acquisitions; list of disaster related periodicals. **Remarks:** Electronic mail address(es): 141:UNX008 (Dialcom, Inc.). FAX: 22 7335623. Telex: 414242 dro ch.

United Nations - World Meteorological Organization
See: World Meteorological Organization (20625)

★ 16755 ★
United Nations Association of Turkey - Library
Arjantin Caddesi
Halia Sokak 8/1
Gaziosmanpasa
Ankara, Turkey
Subjects: Human rights. **Holdings:** 500 volumes. **Remarks:** Currently inactive. **Also Known As:** Birlesnris Milletler Turk Dernegi.

★ 16756 ★
United Nations Association of the United States of America - Greater
   St. Louis Chapter - Library (Soc Sci)
121 S. Meranec   Phone: (314)721-1961
St. Louis, MO 63105   Judith Domahidy, Libn.
Staff: 1. **Subjects:** International culture, United Nations, peace, conservation, nutrition, children's literature. **Holdings:** 1200 books; 143 files on U.N. member countries; U.N. publications; files on U.N. agencies; culture kits; slides; videotapes; flags. **Subscriptions:** 25 journals and other serials. **Services:** Interlibrary loan; copying; library open to the public. **Networks/Consortia:** Member of St. Louis Regional Library Network. **Publications:** UN Center Newsletter.

★ 16757 ★
United Nations Centre for Regional Development - UNCRD Library
   (Soc Sci)
Nagono 1-47-1
Nakamura-ku
Nagoya 450, Japan   Phone: 561-9377
                 Josefa S. Edralin, Info.Sys.Plan.
Founded: 1971. **Staff:** 2. **Subjects:** Regional development and planning in developing countries. **Special Collections:** Development and Planning Fields. **Holdings:** 18,500 books. **Subscriptions:** 660 journals and other serials. **Services:** Interlibrary loan; copying; SDI; library open to researchers. **Computerized Information Services:** Bibliographic Information System for Planning (BISPLAN) Project (internal database, 4,200 records). **Publications:** UNCRD Library's new acquisitions, bimonthly; Selected Articles on Local/Regional Development, quarterly. **Remarks:** Field project of United Nations Department of Technical Cooperation for Development. FAX: 561-9375. Telex: J59620 UNCENTRE.

★ 16758 ★
United Nations Centre for Science and Technology for Development -
   Reading Room (Sci-Engr)
1 United Nations Plaza, DC1-10th Fl.   Phone: (212)963-2478
New York, NY 10017   Kwaku Aning, Sr.Sci. Affairs Off.
Founded: 1987. **Staff:** Prof 2; Other 1. **Subjects:** Science and technology for development, international cooperation, international socio-economic development, environment, energy, international scientific communities. **Special Collections:** Environmentally Sound Technology Assessment collection; international energy collection; Advance Technology Alert System collection. **Holdings:** 400 books; 1000 reports. **Subscriptions:** 100 journals and other serials; 20 newspapers. **Services:** Interlibrary loan; library open to researchers, scholars, staff members, and delegations from permanent missions to the United Nations. **Computerized Information Services:** UNBIS, IDRC (internal databases). Performs searches. Contact Person: Kwaku Aning, Sr.Sci. Affairs Off. **Publications:** Weekly digests; seminar proceedings. **Remarks:** FAX: (212)963-1267. Telex: 422311 UN UI.

★ 16759 ★
United Nations Economic Commission for Latin America and the
   Caribbean - Library (Soc Sci)
Avenida Dag Hammarskjold
Casilla 179-D
Las Condes   Phone: 2 2085051
Santiago, Chile   Carmen Vera Arendt
Founded: 1948. **Staff:** 10. **Subjects:** Economic and social development of Latin America and Caribbean countries. **Special Collections:** Official documents of Latin American and Caribbean countries. **Holdings:** 50,000 volumes. **Subscriptions:** 3000 journals and other serials; 30 newspapers. **Services:** Interlibrary loan; copying; SDI; library open to the public. **Computerized Information Services:** BIBLOS, CEPAL, AUTOR, INT, IBRD, ADQ, SUS (internal databases). **Publications:** CEPALINDEX; Monthly Bulletin; Current Awareness Services; Special Bibliographies. **Remarks:** FAX: 2 2080252. Telex: 441054 UNSGO CZ; 340295 UNSTGO CK.

★ 16760 ★
United Nations Economic and Social Commission for Asia and the
   Pacific - Natural Resources Division - Energy Resources Section -
   Library (Energy)
United Nations Bldg.
Rajadamnern Ave.   Phone: 02 282-9161
Bangkok 10200, Thailand   Mr. N.P. Cummins, Libn.
Founded: 1947. **Staff:** 19. **Subjects:** Economic and social development, food and agriculture, industry, international trade, tourism, natural resources, energy, population, statistics, transport and communications, human settlements, environment. **Special Collections:** United Nations publications and documents. **Holdings:** 200,000 volumes. **Subscriptions:** 4000 journals and other serials; 31 newspapers. **Services:** Interlibrary loan; copying; SDI; library open to UN staff members, researchers, government officials, delegates of member countries, and post-graduate students. **Computerized Information Services:** EBIS. **Publications:** Asian Bibliography, semiannual; EBIS Register of Serials, biennial; ESCAP Documents and Publications, annual; Rural Development, annual; New Titles Received, monthly. **Remarks:** FAX: 02 282-9602. Telex: 82392 ESCAP TH. **Staff:** Mrs. Somwong Changkasiri, Libn.

★ 16761 ★
United Nations Economic and Social Commission for Asia and the
   Pacific - Statistics Division - UN/ESCAP Statistical Information
   Services - Library (Soc Sci)
United Nations Bldg.
Rajadamnern Ave.   Phone: 2 829161
Bangkok 10200, Thailand   Bishnu Dev Pant, Chf. of Sect.
Founded: 1948. **Staff:** 11. **Subjects:** Asia and the Pacific - socioeconomic data, demography, social statistics, national accounts, production, trade. **Holdings:** 14,000 bound volumes. **Services:** Library not open to the public. **Computerized Information Services:** Internal databases. Performs searches. **Remarks:** FAX: 2 28296022. Telex: 82392 ESCAP TH; 82315 ESCAP TH.

★16762★

United Nations Economic and Social Commission for Western Asia -
Library (Soc Sci)
P.O. Box 27
Amiriyah, Airport Rd.   Phone: 1 694351
Baghdad, Iraq   Ms. Ghazwa Malhas, Chf.Libn.
Founded: 1972. **Staff:** 4. **Subjects:** Western Asia - economic development, food security, integrated rural development, transfer of appropriate technology, women, environment, social development. **Special Collections:** ESCWA documents; United Nations documents. **Holdings:** 30,000 volumes; statistical materials, periodicals, conferences, reports, directories. **Services:** 400 journals and other serials; 15 newspapers. **Services:** Library open to UN staff and researchers. **Computerized Information Services:** Internal database. **Publications:** Library acquisitions list. **Remarks:** FAX: 1 694981. Telex: 21691,7,8 UNECWA JO. **Staff:** Mr. Malek Tannir; Mr. Zuheir Hussari; Mrs. Najwa Atieh; Mrs. Lina Traboulsi.

★16763★

United Nations Educational, Scientific and Cultural Organization -
Institute for Education - Library (Educ)
Feldbrunnenstrasse 58   Phone: 40 44 78 43
W-2000 Hamburg 13, Germany   Ursula Giere, Libn.
Subjects: Comparative education, educational research, lifelong education, curriculum development, learning strategies, evaluation, teacher training, literacy, continuing education in developing countries. **Holdings:** 45,000 volumes. **Remarks:** FAX: 4107723. Telex: 2164146. **Also Known As:** UNESCO.

★16764★

United Nations Educational, Scientific and Cultural Organization -
International Bureau of Education - Documentation Centre (Educ)
P.O. Box 199
CH-1211 Geneva 20, Switzerland   Phone: 22 7981455
Founded: 1926. **Staff:** Prof 3; Other 4. **Subjects:** UNESCO member states - educational organization, school systems, educational policies and reform. **Special Collections:** ERIC microfiche collection. **Holdings:** 100,000 books and documents; 1200 periodicals; 200 AV programs; 350,000 microfiche. **Subscriptions:** 182 journals and other serials. **Services:** Interlibrary loan; copying; center open to the public. **Automated Operations:** Computerized public access catalog, cataloging, acquisitions, serials, and circulation. **Computerized Information Services:** DIALOG Information Services, PFDS Online, Questel; CD-ROMs (ERIC, OCLC); IBEDOCS, IBECENT (internal databases); BITNET, UNESCO, ICC (electronic mail services). Performs searches on fee basis. **Publications:** Thematic bibliographies; directories; catalog. **Remarks:** Center located at 15, route des Morillons, 1218 Grand-Saconnex, Geneva, Switzerland. FAX: 22 7981486. Telex: 415 771 BIE. Electronic mail address(es): JTHOMAS@UNICC (BITNET). **Also Known As:** UNESCO:IBE. **Staff:** Wanda Rokicka; Felicity Nacereddine; Hoang Bao.

★16765★

United Nations Educational, Scientific and Cultural Organization -
International Council of Museums - UNESCO-ICOM Museum
Information Centre (Hum)
1, rue Miollis   Phone: 1 47340500
F-75732 Paris Cedex 15, France   Jane Sledge, Chf.
Founded: 1947. **Staff:** 3.5. **Subjects:** Museology, museography. **Special Collections:** Museum catalogs (32,000). **Holdings:** 3500 books; 600 unbound periodical titles; 7000 microfiche. **Subscriptions:** 600 journals and other serials; 2 newspapers. **Services:** Copying; center open to the public with restrictions. **Computerized Information Services:** ICOMMOS (internal database). Performs searches free of charge. **Publications:** Directory of African Museums (1990). **Remarks:** Alternate telephone number(s): 1 45682850. FAX: 1 43067862. **Formerly:** Its ICOM Documentation Centre. **Staff:** Elisabeth Jani; Patricia Poupeau; Lorenzo Parades.

★16766★

United Nations Educational, Scientific and Cultural Organization -
Principal Regional Office for Asia and the Pacific - Library (Educ)
P.O. Box 967
Prakanong Post Office   Phone: 2 3910879
Bangkok 10110, Thailand   Ms. C.L. Villanueva, Chf.
Founded: 1962. **Staff:** 5. **Subjects:** Education, culture, literacy, educational planning, educational facilities, communication, social and human sciences, natural science. **Special Collections:** UNESCO program documents.

Holdings: 65,000 monographs; 857 periodical titles; 8000 documents; 1500 microforms. **Subscriptions:** 36 journals and other serials; 3 newspapers. **Services:** Interlibrary loan; service open to the public. **Computerized Information Services:** Computerized Documentation Service/Integrated Set of Information Systems (CDS/ISIS). **Publications:** Accessions list; book reviews; bibliographies. **Special Indexes:** Periodicals of Asia and the Pacific. **Remarks:** FAX: 2 3910866. Telex: 20591 TH. **Also Known As:** UNESCO. **Staff:** Mrs. Pensri Tongyai; Mrs. Kanchana Soonsawad.

★16767★

United Nations Educational, Scientific and Cultural Organization -
Regional Office for Science and Technology for South and Central
Asia - ROSTSCA Library (Sci-Engr)
UNESCO House
8 Poorvi Marg, Vasant Vihar   Phone: 11 677310
New Delhi 110 057, Delhi, India   Mrs. Tripta Sondhi, Doc.
Founded: 1948. **Staff:** 1. **Subjects:** Science and technology, education, culture, communications. **Special Collections:** ROSTSCA reports; UNESCO publications; appropriate technology (120 volumes). **Holdings:** 26,700 books; 360 periodical titles; 60 films; 45 video cassettes, audiotapes; posters; photographs. **Subscriptions:** 10 journals and other serials; 3 newspapers. **Services:** Interlibrary loan; copying (limited); library open to the public. **Computerized Information Services:** Internal databases. **Publications:** ROSTSCA Bulletin - free upon request; reports, irregular. **Remarks:** Alternate telephone number(s): 676308; 676285. FAX: 11 6873351. Telex: ROSTIN 031-65896. **Also Known As:** UNESCO.

★16768★

United Nations Educational, Scientific and Cultural Organization -
UNESCO Information Services Division (Educ, Sci-Engr)
7, place de Fontenoy   Phone: 1 568-1000
F-75700 Paris, France   Mr. A.A. Bousso
Subjects: Education, science, culture. **Holdings:** 150,000 volumes. **Subscriptions:** 2000 journals and other serials. **Services:** Interlibrary loan; copying; SDI; services open to the public. **Computerized Information Services:** DIALOG Information Services; UNESBIB (internal database). **Remarks:** Telex: 270602. **Also Known As:** UNESCO.

★16769★

United Nations Environment Programme - International Register of
Potentially Toxic Chemicals - Library (Env-Cons)
Palais des Nations   Phone: 22 7985850
CH-1211 Geneva 10, Switzerland   Jan W. Huismans, Dir.
Founded: 1977. **Subjects:** Chemicals - physical and chemical properties, hazard identification and control, sampling methods, analytic methods, adverse effects, environmental impact, national and international control recommendations, toxicology, waste disposal. **Holdings:** 30,000 microfiche; 4500 monographs. **Subscriptions:** 120 journals and other serials. **Computerized Information Services:** DIALOG Information Services, NLM; produces International Register of Potentially Toxic Chemicals database. Performs searches. **Publications:** IRPTC Bulletin, semiannual. **Remarks:** Alternate telephone number(s): 22 7988400. FAX: 22 7332673. Telex: 415 465 UNE CH. Alternate telephone number(s): 22 7898400. Library is the international reference center for critical review on chemicals. **Staff:** Mrs. Phuong Minh Nguyen.

★16770★

United Nations Environment Programme - Library and Documentation
Centre (Env-Cons)
P.O. Box 30552   Phone: 2 230800
Nairobi, Kenya   Mary Dwyer Rigby, Chf.
Founded: 1973. **Staff:** 7. **Subjects:** Environment. **Holdings:** 20,000 books; 10,000 bound periodical volumes; 2 million documents; 150,000 nonbook items. **Subscriptions:** 450 journals and other serials; 15 newspapers. **Services:** Copying; SDI; library open to the public. **Automated Operations:** Computerized cataloging. **Computerized Information Services:** Internal databases. **Remarks:** FAX: 2 226890. Telex: 22068 UNEP KE. Alternate telephone number(s): 2 520600. **Staff:** Samuel Mwaniki, Cat.

★ 16771 ★
United Nations Environment Programme - Regional Office for Latin America - Library
Presidente Masaryk, 29, Piso 5
11570 Mexico City, DF, Mexico
Founded: 1975. **Subjects:** Environmental protection in Latin America and the Caribbean. **Holdings:** 6000 volumes. **Services:** Library not open to the public. **Remarks:** Currently inactive. **Also Known As:** Programa de las Naciones Unidas para el Medio Ambiente.

★ 16772 ★
United Nations Headquarters - Dag Hammarskjold Library (Soc Sci)
United Nations   Phone: (212)963-7412
New York, NY 10017   Jakob Van Heijst, Dir.
Founded: 1946. **Staff:** Prof 65; Other 86. **Subjects:** Political affairs, economics, national and international law, social affairs, international relations, science and technology, statistics, transnational corporations, history and activities of the United Nations. **Special Collections:** U.N. and specialized agencies documents; League of Nations documents; Woodrow Wilson Memorial Library (international affairs, 1918-1945); official gazettes of member states. **Holdings:** 400,000 volumes; 80,000 maps; 12,300 reels of microfilm; 50,000 microcards; 200,000 microfiche. **Subscriptions:** 8000 journals and other serials; 200 newspapers. **Services:** Interlibrary loan; library not open to the public. **Automated Operations:** Computerized cataloging and acquisitions. **Computerized Information Services:** NEXIS; UNBIS (internal database). **Publications:** List of publications - available on request. **Remarks:** FAX: (212)963-4879. Telex: 232422. **Staff:** Joseph L. Fuchs, Chf., Users' Serv.; Frank Nakada, Chf., Tech.Oper./Pubn.Serv.

★ 16773 ★
United Nations High Commissioner for Refugees - Center for Documentation on Refugees - Library (Soc Sci)
Case Postale 2500   Phone: 22 7398458
CH-1211 Geneva 2, Switzerland   Hans Thoolen, Chf.
Founded: 1986. **Staff:** 12. **Subjects:** Refugees - causes, flight, reception, durable solutions, protection and assistance. **Holdings:** 8500 documents in English, French, and Spanish; videotapes; microfiche; 250 periodicals. **Services:** Consultation; library open to the public. **Computerized Information Services:** REFLIT (Refugee Literature), REFINT (Refugee Instruments), REFLEG (Refugee Legislation), REFCAS (Refugee Case Law) (internal databases). Performs searches. **Publications:** Refugee Abstracts, quarterly - available by subscription; Ad hoc bibliographies on refugee women, children, health; EXCOM in Abstracts. **Remarks:** FAX: 22 7398682. Telex: 415740 HCR CH. Library located at 5-7 ave. de la Paix, Geneva.

★ 16774 ★
United Nations Institute for Namibia - Library (Area-Ethnic)
P.O. Box 33811   Phone: 228883
Lusaka, Namibia   Mr. P.C. Kulleen, Libn.
Subjects: Namibia - liberation struggle to post-independence reconstruction. **Holdings:** 16,000 monographs; 40,000 documents. **Subscriptions:** 150 journals and other serials. **Services:** Library open to bona fide researchers who are researching Namibia. **Automated Operations:** Computerized cataloging. **Computerized Information Services:** Socio-Economic Database on Namibia (internal database). **Remarks:** Alternate telephone number(s): 228884. FAX: 222661. Telex: ZA 41960.

★ 16775 ★
United Nations Institute for Training and Research - Library (Soc Sci)
801 United Nations Plaza   Phone: (212)963-8621
New York, NY 10017   Veta Randall, Libn.
Subjects: United Nations policy and efficacy; regional cooperation; policy choices and strategies for the future; energy and natural resources. **Special Collections:** Wilfred Jenks Memorial Collection (250 League of Nations documents). **Holdings:** 12,000 book titles; 105 periodical titles; 200,000 official and unofficial UN documents.

★ 16776 ★
United Nations Population Fund - Library (Soc Sci)
220 E. 42nd St., Rm. DN-1763   Phone: (212)297-5069
New York, NY 10017   Audun Gythfeldt, Chf.
Founded: 1975. **Staff:** Prof 2; Other 2. **Subjects:** Population, demography, family planning, economic development, population assistance,

contraception. **Holdings:** 5500 books; 2500 reprints. **Subscriptions:** 400 journals and other serials; 5 newspapers. **Services:** Interlibrary loan; copying; SDI; library open to graduate students and professional researchers. **Automated Operations:** Computerized cataloging. **Computerized Information Services:** DIALOG Information Services, NEXIS, MEDLINE, POPLINE; internal database. **Networks/Consortia:** Member of APLIC International Census Network, Consortium of Foundation Libraries (CFL). **Remarks:** FAX: (212)297-4914. **Staff:** David P. Rose, Tech.Serv. & Database Libn.

★ 16777 ★
United Negro College Fund, Inc. - Department of Archives and History (Educ)
500 E. 62nd St.   Phone: (212)326-1285
New York, NY 10021   Paula Williams, Asst.Archv.
Staff: Prof 3. **Subjects:** Higher education for blacks, history of philanthropy and fund raising. **Holdings:** 750 cubic feet. **Services:** Copying; department open to the public with restrictions.

United of Omaha Insurance Company
See: **Mutual of Omaha/United of Omaha Insurance Company** (10940)

★ 16778 ★
United Paperworkers International Union - Irene Glaus Memorial Library (Law, Soc Sci)
3340 Perimeter Hill Dr.
Box 1475   Phone: (615)834-8590
Nashville, TN 37202   Mary Alyce Dimoff, Libn.
Founded: 1981. **Staff:** Prof 1. **Subjects:** Labor relations, law, and history; occupational safety and health. **Special Collections:** UPIU Oral History Series (50 audio- and videotapes). **Holdings:** 6050 books; 758 bound periodical volumes; 4000 microfiche; 38 audiotapes; 61 videotapes; 76 16mm films; 1150 government documents; UPIU archival material (39 linear feet of folders, boxes, bound periodical volumes, microfilm). **Subscriptions:** 145 journals and other serials; 51 newspapers. **Services:** Interlibrary loan; library open to the public for reference use only. **Computerized Information Services:** LEXIS, NEXIS. **Remarks:** FAX: (615)834-7741.

United Press International and Reuters Photograph Libraries
See: **Bettmann - Bettmann Archive/Bettmann Newsphotos** (1798)

★ 16779 ★
United Samaritans Medical Center - Library (Med)
812 N. Logan Ave.   Phone: (217)443-5270
Danville, IL 61832   Janet Cronkhite, MLS.
Founded: 1921. **Staff:** Prof 1; Other 1. **Subjects:** Nursing, medicine, clinical pathology, pharmacy, physical therapy, radiology. **Holdings:** 3939 books. **Subscriptions:** 110 journals and other serials. **Services:** Interlibrary loan; copying; SDI; library not open to the public. **Computerized Information Services:** MEDLARS, MEDLINE; DOCLINE. **Networks/Consortia:** Member of East Central Illinois Consortium. **Remarks:** FAX: (217)443-1965.

★ 16780 ★
United Seaman's Service - American Merchant Marine Library Association - Public Library of the High Seas (Hum)
One World Trade Center, Suite 2161   Phone: (212)775-1038
New York, NY 10048   Ernest H. Pigott, Exec.Dir.
Founded: 1921. **Staff:** 4. **Special Collections:** William Bollman Collection (maritime history prior to World War I). **Holdings:** 3500 volumes. **Services:** Library not open to the public. **Publications:** Annual report. **Remarks:** FAX: (212)432-5492. The William Bollman Collection is on permanent loan to the U.S. Merchant Marine Academy, Kings Point, NY. Provides sea-going libraries for the educational, recreational, and self-help needs of officers and crews of the American Merchant Marine, Military Sealift Command, U.S. Coast Guard, and other ships. AMMLA books are available to seafarers in 6 AMMLA port offices in the United States, 11 United Seamen's Service Centers around the world, and are provided to U.S. flag ships through direct mail.

★16781★
United Services Automobile Association - Corporate Library C-1-E (Bus-Fin)
9800 Fredericksburg Rd.   Phone: (512)498-1524
San Antonio, TX 78288   Sylvia Phillips, Mgr., Lib.Serv.
Founded: 1967. **Staff:** Prof 2; Other 3. **Subjects:** Insurance, business, management, computer science. **Holdings:** 4000 books; 10 drawers of pamphlets and maps. **Subscriptions:** 300 journals and other serials; 10 newspapers. **Services:** Interlibrary loan; copying; current alerts; library open to the public by appointment. **Automated Operations:** Computerized cataloging. **Computerized Information Services:** DIALOG Information Services, PFDS Online, OCLC, Dun & Bradstreet Business Credit Services, Dow Jones News/Retrieval, NEXIS, DataTimes. Performs searches. **Networks/Consortia:** Member of AMIGOS Bibliographic Council, Inc., Council of Research & Academic Libraries (CORAL). **Staff:** Leslie Todd, Libn.

★16782★
United Society of Believers - The Shaker Library (Rel-Phil)
RR No. 1
Box 640   Phone: (207)926-4597
Poland Spring, ME 04274   Leonard Brooks, Dir.
Founded: 1882. **Staff:** Prof 3. **Subjects:** Shaker theology and history, biography, art, music, technology, herbology, historical agriculture, American communal societies. **Special Collections:** The Koreshan Unity; Christian Israelite Church; Religious Society of Friends. **Holdings:** 5000 volumes; 8000 manuscripts; 20 VF drawers of catalogs, labels, broadsides; 8 VF drawers of tracts and pamphlets; 13 VF drawers of photographs, slides, maps; 200 reels of microfilm. **Subscriptions:** 75 journals and other serials. **Services:** Library open to the public. **Automated Operations:** Computerized cataloging. **Publications:** The Shaker Quarterly; brochure/guide - available upon request. **Special Indexes:** Biographical index (card). **Staff:** Anne Gilbert, Archv./Libn.

U.S. Advisory Commission on Intergovernmental Relations
See: **Advisory Commission on Intergovernmental Relations** (97)

★16783★
U.S. Agency for International Development - A.I.D. Development Information Center (Soc Sci, Sci-Engr)
Rm. 105, SA-18   Phone: (703)875-4818
Washington, DC 20523-1801   Jeanne D. Tifft, Coord.
Founded: 1967. **Staff:** Prof 4; Other 4. **Subjects:** International economic development; foreign assistance administration; agricultural and rural development; education; health, nutrition, and population planning; technology transfer; energy; natural resources management; international trade; privatization. **Special Collections:** AID historical project and program documents (1958-1974; 20,000). **Holdings:** 8000 books; 75,000 AID foreign assistance project and program documents and research reports on microfiche. **Subscriptions:** 300 journals and newsletters. **Services:** Interlibrary loan; copying; library open to the public. **Automated Operations:** Computerized public access catalog. **Computerized Information Services:** Access to DIALOG Information Services, NEXIS, BRS Information Technologies, OCLC, Dun & Bradstreet Business Credit Services; AID Development Information System (internal database); MCI Mail (electronic mail service). Performs searches free of charge on internal database only; written request required. **Networks/Consortia:** Member of FEDLINK. **Publications:** New This Month (acquisitions bulletin) - to AID staff. **Remarks:** Library located at 1601 N. Kent St., Arlington, VA. FAX: (703)875-5269. Electronic mail address(es): INFO CDIE (MCI Mail). **Staff:** Mary Nelson, Ref.; Steven Shadle, Acq.; Tina Wilson-Romero, DIS Database Acq.; Joanne Tetrault, Ref.

U.S. Agency for International Development - Nitrogen Fixation by Tropical Agricultural Legumes
See: **Nitrogen Fixation by Tropical Agricultural Legumes** (11817)

U.S. Agency for International Development - Population Information Program
See: **Johns Hopkins University - Population Information Program** (8425)

★16784★
U.S. Agency for International Development - Research and Reference Services - Africa Bureau Information Center (Soc Sci)
Rm. 209 SA-18
Washington, DC 20523-1802   Phone: (703)875-4807
Founded: 1991. **Staff:** Prof 4. **Subjects:** Democratization, A.I.D. program in relation to Africa. **Holdings:** Figures not available. **Remarks:** FAX: (703)875-5269. Library provides information support to the U.S. Foreign Assistance Program to Africa under the Congressionally mandated Development Fund for Africa.

★16785★
U.S. Agency for International Development - Water & Sanitation for Health Project - Information Center (Env-Cons)
1611 N. Kent St., Rm. 1002   Phone: (703)243-8200
Arlington, VA 22209   Dan B. Campbell, Libn.
Staff: Prof 1. **Subjects:** Water supply, sanitation, environmental health, technology transfer. **Special Collections:** Rainwater catchments; guineaworm control; women in development. **Holdings:** 7000 reports and texts focusing on rural and peri-urban areas in developing countries; reports on 66 least-developed countries. **Subscriptions:** 35 journals and other serials; 50 newsletters. **Services:** Center open to the public. **Computerized Information Services:** DIALOG Information Services; internal databases. **Remarks:** FAX: (703)525-9137. Telex: WU1 64552. **Also Known As:** WASH Information Center.

U.S. Air Force - 3790 Medical Service Training Wing
See: **U.S. Air Force - Air Training Command - U.S. Air Force 3790 Medical Service Training Wing** (16810)

★16786★
U.S. Air Force - Aerospace Audiovisual Service - Records Center Branch (Aud-Vis, Mil)
1352 AVS/DOC, Bldg. 248   Phone: (714)382-6315
Norton AFB, CA 92409-5996   Clifton O. Bates, Chf., Rec.Ctr.
Staff: 3. **Subjects:** Army, Navy, and Marine Corps documentary film and U.S. Department of Defense film productions, 1950 to present; Air Force in World Wars I and II; Korean War; Vietnam War. **Holdings:** 120 million feet of motion picture film and video records. **Services:** Center open to the public with clearance through appropriate military service public affairs office. **Remarks:** Records center is the depository for all motion pictures or video materials created or acquired by the U.S. military prior to their retirement to the national archives.

★16787★
U.S. Air Force - Air Force Materiel Command - Rome Air Development Center - Technical Library (Sci-Engr)
R1 SUL Tech. Library
FL 2810   Phone: (315)330-7607
Griffiss AFB, NY 13441-5700   Rodney Heines, Chf.
Founded: 1942. **Staff:** Prof 2; Other 3. **Subjects:** Aeronautics, engineering, electronics, mathematics, photonics, computer science, artificial intelligence, radar, communications, electromagnetics, technology. **Holdings:** 19,000 books; 330,000 documents and technical reports. **Subscriptions:** 500 journals and other serials. **Services:** Interlibrary loan. **Computerized Information Services:** DIALOG Information Services, DTIC, OCLC. **Networks/Consortia:** Member of Central New York Library Resources Council (CENTRO). **Publications:** Accessions List. **Formerly:** U.S. Air Force - Air Force Systems Command.

★16788★
U.S. Air Force - Air Force Materiel Command - Rome Laboratory - Data & Analysis Center for Software (Comp Sci)
258 Genesee St., Suite 103   Phone: (315)734-3696
Utica, NY 13502   James J. Reed, DACS Dir.
Staff: Prof 5. **Subjects:** Software - engineering, technology, reliability, maintenance, productivity, research. **Holdings:** 107 books; 3442 conference proceedings papers; 2970 journal articles; 186 standards and regulations; 2066 theses, dissertations, and technical reports. **Subscriptions:** 36 journals and other serials. **Services:** Center open to the public for reference use only. **Automated Operations:** Computerized cataloging and retrieval. **Computerized Information Services:** Software Engineering Bibliographic Database (internal database). Performs searches on fee basis. **Publications:** Annual Annotated Bibliography; User's Guide to DACS Products & Services; DACS Newsletter; DACS Bulletin. **Remarks:** FAX: (315)734-3699. **Formerly:** U.S. Air Force - Air Force Systems Command - Rome Air Development Center. **Staff:** Barbara Radzisz, Info.Spec.

★ 16789 ★
U.S. Air Force - Air Force Civil Engineering Support Agency -
  Technical Information Center (Sci-Engr)
Bldg. 1120, Stop 21
FL 7050   Phone: (904)283-6285
Tyndall AFB, FL 32403-6001   Andrew D. Poulis, Chf.Tech.Info.Ctr.
Founded: 1975. **Staff:** Prof 2; Other 2. **Subjects:** Engineering - civil,
environmental, mechanical, electrical, chemical; readiness; fire research;
cost analysis. **Special Collections:** Rapid runway repair; geotechnical
centrifuges; bird air strike hazards; sonic boom research; hazardous wastes
minimization; privatization; environmental quality. **Holdings:** 7200 books;
30,000 hardcopy technical reports; 125,000 technical reports on microfiche;
150,000 military and commercial specifications and standards on microfilm;
3000 slides; 500 technical videotapes. **Subscriptions:** 525 journals; 10
newspapers. **Services:** Interlibrary loan; center open to Air Force
engineering and services personnel, Department of Defense and other
government agency personnel stationed at Tyndall AFB, and local residents
who can show need. **Automated Operations:** Computerized public access
catalog, cataloging, acquisitions, and serials. **Computerized Information
Services:** DIALOG Information Services, BRS Information Technologies,
OCLC, STN International, NASA/RECON, PFDS Online, Integrated
Technical Information System (ITIS), DTIC; BASIS/TECHLIB (internal
database). **Networks/Consortia:** Member of FEDLINK. **Publications:**
Databases Directory; Periodicals Directory, both annual - both for internal
distribution only; customized bibliographies; Current Awareness
bibliographies. **Remarks:** Alternate telephone number(s): 283-6270. FAX:
(904)283-6499. **Formerly:** Its Air Force Engineering and Services Center.
Staff: Virginia Davis, Cat.; Julie Herrlinger, Acq./ILL; Tamara Perez.

★ 16790 ★
U.S. Air Force - Air Force Communications Command - Technical
  Library (Info Sci)
TIC/RSIC (AFCC)   Phone: (618)256-4437
Scott AFB, IL 62225-6343   Sylvia J. Sefcik, Libn.
Founded: 1981. **Staff:** Prof 1; Other 2. **Subjects:** Telecommunications,
computers, electronics, engineering, mathematics, management. **Holdings:**
2500 books; 1400 technical reports; 3400 technical reports on microfiche.
Subscriptions: 139 journals and other serials; 6 newspapers. **Services:** Center
not open to the public. **Computerized Information Services:** DTIC, OCLC.
Networks/Consortia: Member of Kaskaskia Library System (KLS).
Publications: New Additions List, monthly. **Formerly:** Its Technical
Information Center.

★ 16791 ★
U.S. Air Force - Air Force Intelligence Command - AFIC Library (Sci-
  Engr, Comp Sci)
6960 ESG/MWL
FL7046, Bldg. 2017   Phone: (512)977-2617
San Antonio, TX 78243-5000   Carol-Anne Charbonneau, Libn.
Founded: 1965. **Staff:** Prof 3; Other 2. **Subjects:** Engineering,
telecommunications, computers, electronics, management, recreation.
Holdings: 20,000 books and bound periodical volumes; 1300 microforms;
2300 AV programs. **Subscriptions:** 517 journals and other serials; 31
newspapers. **Services:** Interlibrary loan; library open to the public with
restrictions. **Remarks:** FAX: (512)977-2390. **Formerly:** Its Electronic
Security Command - General Library. **Staff:** Bertha Nagelhout, Chf.Techn.;
Cynthia Madrigal, Techn.

★ 16792 ★
U.S. Air Force - Air Force Legal Services Agency (Law)
AFLSA/CCP Bldg. 5683
Bolling AFB   Phone: (202)767-1520
Washington, DC 20332-6128   Doneva M. Jones, Libn.
Founded: 1949. **Subjects:** Law. **Special Collections:** Criminal law. **Holdings:**
16,000 volumes. **Services:** Library open to the public. **Formerly:** Its Office
of the Judge Advocate General.

U.S. Air Force - Air Force Logistics Command
See: **U.S. Air Force - Air Force Materiel Command - U.S. Air Force**
  Museum (16804)

★ 16793 ★
U.S. Air Force - Air Force Manpower & Personnel Center - Morale,
  Welfare & Recreation Directorate - Air Force Library and
  Information Systems Branch (Info Sci)
AFMPC/DPMSPL   Phone: (512)652-4589
Randolph AFB, TX 78150-6001   Tony Dakan, Dir., USAF Lib. &
                                     Info.Sys.
Founded: 1943. **Staff:** 5. **Holdings:** Figures not available. **Services:** Library
not open to the public. **Publications:** AFLIS Update. **Remarks:** Section is
administrative headquarters for Air Force library services throughout the
world with a total of 340 library facilities and a book stock of more than 5
million volumes. Alternate telephone number(s): (512)652-3037. FAX:
(512)652-2383; (512)652-2380. **Staff:** Annette Gohlke, Asst.Dir.; Faye M.
Miller, Acq.Libn.

★ 16794 ★
U.S. Air Force - Air Force Materiel Command - Armament Division, Air
  Force Armament Laboratory - Technical Library (Sci-Engr)
WL/MNOI   Phone: (904)882-3212
Eglin AFB, FL 32542-5438   Bob Bailey, Chf.
Founded: 1955. **Staff:** Prof 3; Other 6. **Subjects:** Aeronautics, electronics,
physics, mathematics, biology, chemistry. **Holdings:** 13,000 books; 1500
bound periodical volumes; 150,000 technical reports; 250,000 reports on
microfiche; 15,000 reels of microfilm. **Subscriptions:** 431 journals and other
serials. **Services:** Interlibrary loan; library open to qualified users.
Computerized Information Services: DTIC, DIALOG Information
Services, OCLC, USNI Military Database. **Networks/Consortia:** Member
of FEDLINK. **Publications:** Accessions List, semimonthly - for internal
distribution only. **Formerly:** U.S. Air Force - Air Force Systems Command.
Staff: Frances Chambers, Open Lit.Libn.

★ 16795 ★
U.S. Air Force - Air Force Materiel Command - Armstrong Laboratory -
  Human Resources Directorate - Library (Soc Sci)
AL/HR-DOKL
FL 2870   Phone: (512)536-2651
Brooks AFB, TX 78235-5601   Orrine L. Woinowsk, Adm.Libn.
Founded: 1948. **Staff:** Prof 1; Other 1. **Subjects:** Psychology, mathematical
statistics, computer sciences. **Holdings:** 13,077 volumes; 5637 technical
reports; 3918 microforms. **Subscriptions:** 511 journals and other serials; 9
newspapers. **Services:** Interlibrary loan; copying; library open to the public
by appointment for reference use only. **Automated Operations:**
Computerized cataloging, serials, and ILL. **Computerized Information
Services:** OCLC, DIALOG Information Services; CD-ROMs; FAXON
LINX (electronic mail service). **Networks/Consortia:** Member of Health
Oriented Libraries of San Antonio (HOLSA), AMIGOS Bibliographic
Council, Inc., Council of Research & Academic Libraries (CORAL),
FEDLINK. **Remarks:** FAX: (512)536-2902. **Formerly:** U.S. Air Force - Air
Force Systems Command.

★ 16796 ★
U.S. Air Force - Air Force Materiel Command - Arnold Engineering
  Development Center - Technical Library (Sci-Engr)
FL 2804
Mail Stop 100   Phone: (615)454-4429
Arnold Air Force Base, TN 37389-9998   Gay D. Goethert, Lib.Supv.
Founded: 1952. **Staff:** Prof 4; Other 3. **Subjects:** Aerospace sciences,
aerodynamics, aircraft propulsion, optics, physics, computer science,
mathematics, chemistry, pollution, astronomy. **Special Collections:** NACA
and NASA reports (complete sets); American Institute of Aeronautics and
Astronautics papers on microfiche, 1963-1988. **Holdings:** 18,200 books;
8910 bound periodical volumes; 304,300 technical reports and documents;
241,070 microforms; 6 VF drawers of standards and specifications.
Subscriptions: 641 journals and other serials. **Services:** Interlibrary loan;
library not open to the public. **Automated Operations:** Computerized
cataloging. **Computerized Information Services:** DIALOG Information
Services, WILSONLINE, NASA/RECON, DTIC, OCLC. **Networks/
Consortia:** Member of SOLINET. **Publications:** Reports Accession List,
monthly; Book Accession Lists, irregular; Periodicals Holdings List,
irregular. **Remarks:** Alternate telephone number(s): 454-4430; 454-4432.
FAX: (615)454-5421. **Formerly:** U.S. Air Force - Air Force Systems
Command. **Staff:** Della C. Burch, Group Ldr., Lib.Div.; Brenda D. Warren,
Tech.Libn., Lib.Div.; Effie W. Boyd, Group Ldr., Doc.Div.

★ 16797 ★
U.S. Air Force - Air Force Materiel Command - Flight Test Center - Technical Library (Sci-Engr)
6510 TW/TSTL FL 2806   Phone: (805)277-3606
Edwards AFB, CA 93523-5000   Jolaine Lamb, Libn.
Founded: 1955. **Staff:** Prof 3; Other 3. **Subjects:** Aerodynamics, chemistry, physics, management, propulsion, mathematics. **Special Collections:** AFFTC technical reports; Astronautics Laboratory (AFSC) technical reports. **Holdings:** 27,000 books; 6000 bound periodical volumes; 10,000 society papers; 180,000 technical reports; 500 videotapes; audiotapes; periodicals on microfilm. **Subscriptions:** 500 journals and other serials. **Services:** Interlibrary loan; library not open to the public. **Computerized Information Services:** DIALOG Information Services, DTIC, OCLC. **Publications:** Current Contents of Periodicals; List of Books Received - both for internal distribution only. **Remarks:** FAX: (805)277-4892. DSN LINE: 527-2124/3606. **Formerly:** U.S. Air Force - Air Force Systems Command. **Staff:** Darrell Shiplett, Br.Libn.

★ 16798 ★
U.S. Air Force - Air Force Materiel Command - Human Systems Division - Armstrong Laboratory - Strughold Aeromedical Library (Med)
Brooks AFB, TX 78235-5301   Phone: (512)536-3321
                                          Fred W. Todd, Chf.Libn.
Founded: 1918. **Staff:** Prof 10; Other 9. **Subjects:** Aerospace medicine, bioastronautics, bionucleonics, clinical medicine, dentistry, life sciences. **Holdings:** 36,131 books; 110,421 bound periodical volumes; 55,244 microfiche; 156,237 technical reports. **Subscriptions:** 1008 journals and other serials; 6 newspapers. **Services:** Interlibrary loan; copying; SDI; library open by special permission. **Automated Operations:** Computerized cataloging. **Computerized Information Services:** DIALOG Information Services, DTIC, MEDLARS, NASA/RECON, OCLC, National Technical Information Service (NTIS), Federal Research in Progress (FEDRIP). **Networks/Consortia:** Member of National Network of Libraries of Medicine - South Central Region, Council of Research & Academic Libraries (CORAL), AMIGOS Bibliographic Council, Inc., Health Oriented Libraries of San Antonio (HOLSA). **Publications:** Library Accessions List; Strughold Researcher - both monthly. **Special Indexes:** KWIC index to current serials titles; Indexes to Aeromedical Reviews and Technical Reports for the School of Aerospace Medicine (book). **Remarks:** FAX: (512)536-2371. **Formerly:** U.S. Air Force - Air Force Systems command - Human Systems Division - Armstrong Laboratory - Strughold Aeromedical Lirary. **Staff:** Joseph J . Franzello, Chf., Pub.Serv.; Marilyn M. Goff, Chf., Tech.Proc.; Dewey A. Goff, Jr., Chf., Tech.Rpt.; Marion E. Green, Chf.Med.Ed.; Thomas Kerns, Med.Ed.; F. John Glowacz, Med.Ed.; Helen Post, ILL Libn.; Darlene Taylor, Cat.

★ 16799 ★
U.S. Air Force - Air Force Materiel Command - Library Division
HQ AFSC/DPSL
FL 2865, Andrews AFB   Phone: (301)981-2598
Washington, DC 20334-5000   Frances Quinn Deel, Dir., Command Libs.
Staff: Prof 1; Other 1. **Remarks:** Director of Command Libraries is responsible for establishing plans and policies for library service in 20 Air Force Systems Command technical and base libraries. FAX: (301)981-3091. **Formerly:** U.S. Air Force - Air Force Systems Command.

★ 16800 ★
U.S. Air Force - Air Force Materiel Command - Office of Scientific Research - Technical Information Services Division (Sci-Engr)
AFOSR/XOT
FL 2819, Bldg. 410
Bolling AFB   Phone: (202)767-4910
Washington, DC 20332-6448   Gloria Miller, Libn.
Founded: 1956. **Staff:** 3. **Subjects:** Physics, mathematics, aerospace sciences, chemistry, life sciences, computer sciences, materials science, electronics, environmental sciences. **Holdings:** 15,000 books. **Subscriptions:** 280 journals and other serials. **Services:** Interlibrary loan; library open to researchers on a limited schedule. **Computerized Information Services:** DTIC, OCLC. **Remarks:** FAX: (202)767-0466. **Formerly:** U.S. Air Force - Air Force Systems Command.

★ 16801 ★
U.S. Air Force - Air Force Materiel Command - Phillips Laboratory Geophysical Research Library (Sci-Engr)
Pl/TSML
FL 2807   Phone: (617)377-4895
Hanscom AFB, MA 01731-5000   Barbara Wrinkle, Lib.Dir.
Founded: 1945. **Staff:** Prof 8; Other 5. **Subjects:** Physical and environmental sciences, geophysics, meteorology, math and computer science, astronomy and astrophysics, electronics and electrical engineering, chemical and materials sciences. **Special Collections:** Asian Science Library (35,000 volumes); scientific manuscripts of 3rd and 4th Lords Rayleigh; early ballooning and aeronautics (200 volumes); rare books (2500 volumes). **Holdings:** 259,700 books and bound periodical volumes; 100,595 unbound technical reports; 1583 audio materials; 3177 reels of microfilm; 84,610 microfiche; 992 cassettes; 40 VF drawers of translations. **Subscriptions:** 1000 journals and other serials. **Services:** Interlibrary loan; copying; library open to the public with restrictions. **Automated Operations:** Computerized cataloging and serials. **Computerized Information Services:** DIALOG Information Services, OCLC, DTIC, Faxon Company; LINX Courier, DIALMAIL (electronic mail services). **Networks/Consortia:** Member of FEDLINK. **Publications:** Weekly Accessions List - for internal distribution only. **Remarks:** FAX: (617)377-5627. **Formerly:** U.S. Air Force - Air Force Systems Command - Phillips Laboratory - Research Library. **Staff:** John W. Armstrong, Sel.Libn.; Elfrieda L. Cavallari, Chf., Cat.; Elizabeth Duffek, Chf., Acq.

★ 16802 ★
U.S. Air Force - Air Force Materiel Command - Phillips Laboratory Technical Library (Mil)
PL/SUL
FL 2809   Phone: (505)846-4767
Kirtland AFB, NM 87117-6008   Barbara I. Newton, Chf.
Founded: 1947. **Staff:** Prof 6; Other 5. **Subjects:** Advanced weapons development, civil engineering, aeronautical systems, lasers, missile and space systems, electromagnetic pulse, optics, artificial intelligence. **Holdings:** 28,000 books; 10,000 cartridges of microfilm of periodicals; 350,000 technical reports; 150,000 microfiche of technical reports. **Subscriptions:** 1200 serials. **Services:** Interlibrary loan; copying; SDI; library open to the public for reference use only with permission of military authority. **Automated Operations:** STILAS. **Computerized Information Services:** DTIC, DIALOG Information Services, BRS Information Technologies, STN International, Integrated Technical Information System (ITIS), NASA/RECON, OCLC. **Networks/Consortia:** Member of FEDLINK. **Remarks:** FAX: (505)846-1194. **Formerly:** U.S. Air Force - Air Force Systems Command. **Staff:** Jo Janet Dean, Ref.Libn.; Harriet Foster, Ref.Libn.; Janet M. Jourdain, Supv.Libn., Tech.Proc.; Leslie G. Berwick, Cat.Libn.; Becky Smith, Cat.Libn.; Lee McLaughlin, Supv.Libn., Info.Serv.

★ 16803 ★
U.S. Air Force - Air Force Materiel Command - Technical Information Center
HQ AFSC/DPSLT
FL 2800, Andrews AFB
Washington, DC 20334-5000   Phone: (301)981-3551
Founded: 1952. **Staff:** Prof 1; Other 1. **Subjects:** Aerospace systems, management, energy, military affairs, operations research, government contracting, unconventional warfare, computer science. **Holdings:** 7700 books; 500 technical reports; 3000 reels of microfilm; 100 audio cassettes; 135 video cassettes. **Subscriptions:** 500 journals and other serials; 20 newspapers. **Services:** Interlibrary loan; center not open to the public. **Automated Operations:** Computerized cataloging. **Computerized Information Services:** DIALOG Information Services, DTIC. **Networks/Consortia:** Member of FEDLINK. **Formerly:** U.S. Air Force - Air Force Systems Command.

★ 16804 ★
U.S. Air Force - Air Force Materiel Command - U.S. Air Force Museum - Research Division Library (Mil)
Bldg. 489, Area B
Wright-Patterson AFB, OH 45433-   Phone: (513)255-4644
6518   Charles G. Worman, Chf., Res.Div.
Staff: Prof 3; Other 3. **Subjects:** History and technology of the United States Air Force and its predecessor organizations. **Holdings:** 200,000 documents, including aircraft technical orders, manuscripts, photographs, and drawings. **Services:** Copying (documents); library open to the public by appointment. **Remarks:** FAX: (513)255-3910. **Formerly:** U.S. Air Force - Air Force Logistics Command.

★ 16805 ★
U.S. Air Force - Air Force Materiel Command - Wright Aeronautical
Laboratories - Aerospace Structures Information & Analysis Center
(Sci-Engr)
P.O. Box 31041
Overlook Branch
Dayton, OH 45431   Phone: (513)255-6688
                                    Dr. Gordon Negaard, Dir.
Founded: 1973. **Staff:** Prof 2; Other 2. **Subjects:** Structures, computerized
analysis, aircraft, stress (mechanics), mathematics, fatigue. **Special
Collections:** Specialized and technical reports and publications dealing with
aircraft structural design and analysis. **Holdings:** 13,500 technical reports;
46,000 reports on microfiche. **Services:** Interlibrary loan; copying; center
open to Department of Defense agencies and their contractors.
Computerized Information Services: DIALOG Information Services,
DTIC, NASA/RECON. **Publications:** Newsletter, quarterly. **Remarks:**
FAX: (513)476-4682. **Formerly:** U.S. Air Force - Air Force Systems
Command. **Staff:** Richard D. Scibetta, Info.Spec.

★ 16806 ★
U.S. Air Force - Air Force Materiel Command Wright Laboratory
Technical Library - Technical Library (Sci-Engr)
WL/DOOT
Area B, Bldg. 22   Phone: (513)255-7454
Wright-Patterson AFB, OH 45433-6523   Carolyn Ray, Dir.
Founded: 1918. **Staff:** Prof 5; Other 7. **Subjects:** Aeronautics, avionics,
materials science, flight dynamics, physics, chemistry, mathematics,
electronics, engineering, logistics, propulsion, aerospace medicine, human-
factors engineering, management. **Special Collections:** Lahm & Chandler
Collection (aeronautics). **Holdings:** 63,000 books; 70,000 bound journals;
900,000 technical reports; microforms; military specifications; industry
standards. **Subscriptions:** 1100 journals and other serials. **Services:**
Interlibrary loan; library open to the public for reference use only.
Automated Operations: Computerized cataloging, acquisitions, and
circulation. **Computerized Information Services:** DIALOG Information
Services, ORBIT Search Service, STN International, NASA/RECON,
DTIC, MEDLARS, NEXIS, CIRC II. **Networks/Consortia:** Member of
Southwestern Ohio Council for Higher Education (SOCHE). **Remarks:**
FAX: (513)476-4826. Alternate telephone number(s): (513)255-3630.
Formerly: U.S. Air Force - Air Force Systems Command - Wright Research
and Development Center. **Staff:** Frankie Schverak, Cat./Sys.Coord.; Bill
Benson, Ser./Libn.; Ron Lundquist, Pub.Serv.Libn.; Dan Sell, Ref.Libn.;
Peri Switzer, Acq./Doc. Delivery Libn.

U.S. Air Force - Air Force Systems Command
See: **U.S. Air Force - Air Force Materiel Command - Armament**
Division, Air Force Armament Laboratory - Technical Library (16794)

U.S. Air Force - Air Force Systems Command - Phillips Laboratory -
Research Library
See: **U.S. Air Force - Air Force Materiel Command - Phillips Laboratory**
Geophysical Research Library (16801)

★ 16807 ★
U.S. Air Force - Air Training Command - Chanute Base Technical
Branch Library (Sci-Engr)
FL 3018, Bldg. 95
Chanute AFB, IL 61868-5000   Phone: (217)495-3191
                                    Esther E. Cornelius, Libn.
Founded: 1964. **Staff:** Prof 1. **Subjects:** Aerospace, electronics, metallurgy.
Holdings: 3000 books. **Subscriptions:** 63 journals and other serials. **Services:**
Interlibrary loan; library open to military personnel and their dependents.
Automated Operations: CLSI. **Networks/Consortia:** Member of Lincoln
Trail Libraries System (LTLS). Lincoln Trail Libraries System.

★ 16808 ★
U.S. Air Force - Air Training Command - Keesler Technical Training
Center - Academic Library (Sci-Engr, Mil)
3390 TCHTG/TTCOL
FL 3011
McClelland Hall, Bldg. 2818   Phone: (601)377-4295
Keesler AFB, MS 39534-5000   Verna Westerburg, Lib.Techn.
Founded: 1970. **Staff:** 2. **Subjects:** Communications, electronics,
management, military science, computer science, systems engineering.
Holdings: 4100 books; 125 periodicals. **Services:** Interlibrary loan; library
open to the public with restrictions. **Remarks:** FAX: (601)377-3745.

★ 16809 ★
U.S. Air Force - Air Training Command - Library Program (Sci-Engr,
Mil)
HQ ATC/DPSOL
FL 3000   Phone: (512)652-3410
Randolph AFB, TX 78150-5001   Margie S. Buchanan, Command Libn.
Staff: Prof 28; Other 99. **Subjects:** Aeronautics, astronautics, engineering,
leadership, military history, management, electronics. **Special Collections:**
World War II; weather and instrument flying; survival training; education;
vocational guidance; foreign affairs; foreign languages. **Holdings:** 450,910
books and bound periodical volumes; 4260 technical reports and documents;
256,000 microforms; 40,100 AV programs. **Subscriptions:** 6715 journals and
other serials; 580 newspapers. **Services:** Interlibrary loan; library not open
to the public. **Automated Operations:** Computerized cataloging,
acquisitions, serials, and ILL. **Computerized Information Services:** OCLC,
DTIC, Mead Data Central, DIALOG Information Services. **Networks/
Consortia:** Member of Council of Research & Academic Libraries
(CORAL), Lincoln Trail Libraries System (LTLS). **Remarks:** Command
Librarian is responsible for the administration, development, and operation
of 19 academic, technical, and base libraries in Air Training Command.
Information represents all 19 libraries. An alternate telephone number is
652-2573.

★ 16810 ★
U.S. Air Force - Air Training Command - U.S. Air Force 3790 Medical
Service Training Wing - Academic Library (Med)
3790 MSTW/CCAAL   Phone: (817)676-2736
Sheppard AFB, TX 76311-5465   Ms. Boyd, Supv.Libn.
Founded: 1956. **Staff:** Prof 1. **Subjects:** General medicine, biological science,
nursing, dentistry, pharmacy, hospital administration, management.
Holdings: 10,000 books; 1100 technical reports; 2000 pamphlets.
Subscriptions: 190 journals and other serials. **Services:** Interlibrary loan;
copying; library open to the public for reference use only. **Computerized
Information Services:** MEDLARS. **Remarks:** FAX: (817)676-2825.

★ 16811 ★
U.S. Air Force - Air University - Institute of Technology - Library (Sci-
Engr)
FL 3319
Bldg. 642, Area B   Phone: (513)255-3005
Wright-Patterson AFB, OH 45433-6583   James T. Helling, Dir.
Founded: 1946. **Staff:** Prof 9; Other 9. **Subjects:** Aeronautics, astronautics,
electrical engineering, computer engineering, management, logistics,
physics. **Holdings:** 48,037 books; 43,621 bound periodical volumes; technical
reports on microfiche; 62,084 other uncataloged items; Rand reports.
Subscriptions: 1234 journals and other serials; 24 newspapers. **Services:**
Interlibrary loan; library not open to the public. **Automated Operations:**
Integrated library system. **Computerized Information Services:** DIALOG
Information Services, DTIC, NASA/RECON, OCLC; InterNet (electronic
mail service). **Networks/Consortia:** Member of Southwestern Ohio Council
for Higher Education (SOCHE), FEDLINK. **Publications:** Computerized
Journal Holdings List. **Special Indexes:** Serials listing; index to AFIT-
owned AV materials. **Remarks:** FAX: (513)255-2791. Electronic mail
address(es): jhelling@eagle.afrt.af.mil. (InterNet). **Staff:** Helen L. Helton,
Chf., Tech.Serv.; Barry J. Boettcher, Chf., Rd.Serv.; Pam McCarthy, Lead
Libn.; Carol Sullivan, Sys.Libn.; Lenore Pursch, Cat.; Gwen Canada,
Ref.Libn.; Barbra Macke, Libn.; Dorothy Andserson, Ref.Libn.

★ 16812 ★
U.S. Air Force - Air University Library (Mil)
FL 3368   Phone: (205)953-2606
Maxwell AFB, AL 36112   Robert B. Lane, Dir.
Founded: 1946. **Staff:** Prof 30; Other 44. **Subjects:** Military science,
aeronautics, political science, military affairs. **Special Collections:** Air Force
Regulations. **Holdings:** 280,000 books; 120,000 bound periodical volumes;
510,000 cataloged military documents; 850,000 maps and charts; 8900 reels
of microfilm of serials and newspapers; 120,000 regulations and manuals;
9000 clippings and pamphlets. **Subscriptions:** 2000 journals and other
serials; 62 newspapers. **Services:** Interlibrary loan; copying; library open to
the public with restrictions. **Automated Operations:** Computerized
cataloging, acquisitions, and serials. **Computerized Information Services:**
BRS Information Technologies, DTIC, DIALOG Information Services,
NEXIS, OCLC; internal database. **Networks/Consortia:** Member of
SOLINET, FEDLINK, Network of Alabama Academic Libraries (NAAL).
Publications: Air University Library Index to Military Periodicals,
quarterly; Guide to Library Services, occasional; Roster of Subject

Specialists, annual; Special Bibliography Series, irregular; Selected Document Accessions, monthly - all for limited distribution. **Remarks:** FAX: (205)953-2329. Alternate telephone number(s): 953-2888. **Staff:** Marvin L. Borgman, Exec.Off and Chf.Cart. Helen N. Taliaferro, Chf., Rd.Serv.Div.; Regina A. Mayton, Chf., Sys.Div.; Tomma Pastorett, Chf.Bibliog.; Martha Stewart, Ed.; Gene Johnson, Chf., Adm.Serv.; Shirley B. Laseter Chf.Ref.Libn.; James L. Clark, Commun.Lib.Serv.

U.S. Air Force - Armament Laboratory
See: **U.S. Air Force - Air Force Materiel Command - Armament Division, Air Force Armament Laboratory - Technical Library (16794)**

U.S. Air Force - Armstrong Laboratory
See: **U.S. Air Force - Air Force Materiel Command - Human Systems Division - Armstrong Laboratory (16798)**

U.S. Air Force - Armstrong Laboratory - Human Resources Directorate
See: **U.S. Air Force - Air Force Materiel Command - Armstrong Laboratory - Human Resources Directorate - Library (16795)**

U.S. Air Force - Arnold Engineering Development Center
See: **U.S. Air Force - Air Force Materiel Command - Arnold Engineering Development Center (16796)**

★16813★
U.S. Air Force - Defense Finance & Accounting Service - Denver Center - Technical Information Center (Bus-Fin)
AFAFC/FL7040   Phone: (303)370-7566
Denver, CO 80279-5000   Alreeta Eidson, Chf.Adm.Libn.
Founded: 1951. **Staff:** Prof 2; Other 2. **Subjects:** Computer science, accounting, information management, business, management. **Holdings:** 9000 books; 110,000 Armed Forces and Department of Defense directives and other government documents. **Subscriptions:** 400 journals and other serials; 20 newspapers. **Services:** Interlibrary loan; copying; center open to federal employees. **Automated Operations:** Computerized public access catalog, cataloging, acquisitions, serials, and ILL. **Computerized Information Services:** OCLC, DIALOG Information Services, WILSONLINE; CD-ROMs. **Networks/Consortia:** Member of FEDLINK. **Publications:** Serials listing. **Remarks:** FAX: (303)370-7439. **Staff:** Judith D. Moisey, Ref.Libn.

U.S. Air Force - Electronic Security Command - General Library
See: **U.S. Air Force - Air Force Intelligence Command - AFIC Library (16791)**

★16814★
U.S. Air Force - Environmental Technical Applications Center - Air Weather Service Technical Library (Sci-Engr)
FL 4414   Phone: (618)256-2625
Scott AFB, IL 62225-5458   Walter S. Burgmann, Dir.
Founded: 1950. **Staff:** Prof 6; Other 9. **Subjects:** Meteorology, climatology. **Special Collections:** Meteorological and climatological data summarized for worldwide stations. **Holdings:** 15,505 books; 2352 bound periodical volumes; 60,477 hardcopy technical reports; 231,916 technical reports on microfiche. **Subscriptions:** 406 journals and other serials. **Services:** Interlibrary loan; center open to U.S. Government personnel and others through library referral. **Automated Operations:** Computerized circulation. **Computerized Information Services:** DTIC, DIALOG Information Services, OCLC. **Networks/Consortia:** Member of FEDLINK, ILLINET, St. Louis Regional Library Network, Kaskaskia Library System (KLS). **Remarks:** FAX: (618)256-3772. **Formerly:** Its Military Airlift Command. **Staff:** Kathryn E. Marshall, Hd.Libn.; Susan A. Tarbell, Cat.Libn.; Wayne E. McCollom, Chf., Ref.; George M. Horn, Tech.Ed.

U.S. Air Force - Flight Test Center
See: **U.S. Air Force - Air Force Materiel Command - Flight Test Center (16797)**

★16815★
U.S. Air Force - Headquarters Air Force Historical Research Agency (Mil)
HQ AFHRO/RF
Bldg. 1405 A   Phone: (205)953-5834
Maxwell AFB, AL 36112-6678 Col. Elliott V. Converse, III, Commander
Founded: 1942. **Staff:** Prof 20; Other 30. **Subjects:** Army Air Force, U.S. Air Force history. **Special Collections:** Unit histories, 1942 to present; oral history tapes and transcripts; Air Corps Tactical School course materials, 1920s-1930s; materials relating to USAF activities in the Southeast Asian war; aircraft record card collection; End of Tour reports; Karlsruhe Collection on the German Air Force; papers of select Air Force personnel. **Holdings:** 550,000 documents; 40,000 reels of microfilm; 2000 audiotapes. **Services:** Interlibrary loan (limited); copying; microfilm available for purchase; library open to the public for reference use on request, with restrictions on classified and some other selected documents. **Publications:** Bibliographies. **Special Catalogs:** Organizational catalogs reflecting the holdings by organization or special collection. **Remarks:** FAX: (205)953-7428. Alternate telephone number(s): 953-5342. **Formerly:** Its Headquarters USAF Historical Research Center. **Staff:** Lynn O. Gamma, Chf., Ref.Div.; Dr. Fred Shaw, Chf., Res.Div.; Carolyn Mandler, Chf., Accessions Div.; Capt. George Cully, Chf., Inquiries Div.

U.S. Air Force - Human Systems Division
See: **U.S. Air Force - Air Force Materiel Command - Human Systems Division - Armstrong Laboratory (16798)**

U.S. Air Force - Institute of Technology
See: **U.S. Air Force - Air University - Institute of Technology - Library (16811)**

U.S. Air Force - Military Airlift Command
See: **U.S. Air Force - Environmental Technical Applications Center (16814)**

U.S. Air Force - Office of the Judge Advocate General
See: **U.S. Air Force (16792)**

U.S. Air Force - Office of Scientific Research
See: **U.S. Air Force - Air Force Materiel Command - Office of Scientific Research - Technical Information Services Division (16800)**

U.S. Air Force - Office of the Surgeon General
See: **U.S. Army/U.S. Air Force - Offices of the Surgeons General (17079)**

★16816★
U.S. Air Force - Officer Training School - Library (Mil)
FL 3050, Bldg. 147   Phone: (512)671-4316
Lackland AFB, TX 78236-5000 Theresa B. Phillips, OTS Supv.Libn.
Staff: Prof 1; Other 2. **Subjects:** Military art and science, military history, leadership, management, communicative skills, physical fitness, defense studies. **Holdings:** 8000 books; 780 bound periodical volumes; 12,780 microfiche; 32 video recordings; 72 AV programs. **Subscriptions:** 96 journals and other serials; 9 newspapers. **Services:** Interlibrary loan; library not open to the public. **Automated Operations:** DataLinx. **Computerized Information Services:** NEXIS. **Remarks:** FAX: 473-2733 (Autovon Line).

U.S. Air Force - Phillips Laboratory
See: **U.S. Air Force - Air Force Materiel Command - Phillips Laboratory Geophysical Research Library (16801)**

★16817★
U.S. Air Force - Robert L. Thompson Strategic Hospital - Medical Library/SGEL (TX-Carswell AFB) (Med)
Carswell AFB, TX 76127   Phone: (817)782-4598
                             Jean Robbins, Med.Libn.
Founded: 1956. **Staff:** Prof 1. **Subjects:** Medicine, surgery, nursing, psychiatry, dentistry, orthopedics, veterinary medicine. **Holdings:** 3014 books; 2751 bound periodical volumes. **Subscriptions:** 240 journals and other serials; 9 newspapers. **Services:** Interlibrary loan; library not open to the public. **Remarks:** FAX: (817)782-4706.

U.S. Air Force - Rome Air Development Center
See: U.S. Air Force - Air Force Materiel Command - Rome Laboratory - Data & Analysis Center for Software (16788)

U.S. Air Force - Rome Laboratory
See: U.S. Air Force - Air Force Materiel Command - Rome Laboratory - Data & Analysis Center for Software (16788)

U.S. Air Force - School of Health Care Sciences
See: U.S. Air Force - Air Training Command - U.S. Air Force 3790 Medical Service Training Wing (16810)

★ 16818 ★
U.S. Air Force - Scott Air Force Base - Library (Mil)
Bldg. 1940,375 CSG/MWRL   Phone: (618)256-5100
Scott AFB, IL 62225   Kristen A. Campbell
Founded: 1926. **Staff:** Prof 2; Other 6. **Subjects:** Military science, military history, business administration, social sciences. **Special Collections:** Collections on aviation, intelligence, transportation, computer technology, construction, engineering, and related technology. **Holdings:** 37,000 books; 20,000 microfiche; 500 reels of microfilm; 900 videocassettes; 700 audiocassettes. **Subscriptions:** 435 journals and other serials; 19 newspapers. **Services:** Interlibrary loan; library not open to the public. **Automated Operations:** Computerized circulation. **Computerized Information Services:** LEXIS, NEXIS, DIALOG Information Services; DataLinx (electronic mail service). **Remarks:** FAX: (618)744-1948.

★ 16819 ★
U.S. Air Force - Strategic Air Command - Library Headquarters
HQS SAC/DPSOL
Offutt AFB, NE 68113-5001
Defunct.

★ 16820 ★
U.S. Air Force - Western Space and Missile Center - WSMC/PMET Technical Library (Sci-Engr)
FL 2827   Phone: (805)734-8232
Vandenberg AFB, CA 93437-6021   Carolyn Crowley-Hodina, Chf.Libn.
Founded: 1965. **Staff:** Prof 1; Other 4. **Subjects:** Aerospace vehicles, antennas, electronics, engineering, guided missiles, instrumentation, management, mathematics, propulsion. **Special Collections:** Radar; telemetry. **Holdings:** 11,000 books and bound periodical volumes; 2000 technical reports; 3400 maps; 41,000 microforms; environmental impact statements. **Subscriptions:** 410 journals and other serials; 24 newspapers. **Services:** Interlibrary loan; library open to military personnel, dependents, and civilian base employees. **Automated Operations:** Computerized cataloging. **Computerized Information Services:** DIALOG Information Services, STN International, NASA/RECON, OCLC, DTIC. **Networks/Consortia:** Member of CLASS, Total Interlibrary Exchange (TIE). **Publications:** Periodicals Holdings; New Acquisitions - both for internal distribution only. **Remarks:** FAX: (805)734-8232. DSN: 276-9745.

U.S. Air Force - Wright Laboratory
See: U.S. Air Force - Air Force Materiel Command Wright Laboratory Technical Library - Technical Library (16806)

U.S. Air Force - Wright Research and Development Center
See: U.S. Air Force - Air Force Materiel Command Wright Laboratory Technical Library - Technical Library (16806)

★ 16821 ★
U.S. Air Force Academy - Law Library (Law, Mil)
U.S. Air Force Academy, CO 80840   Phone: (719)472-3680
      Col. R. Lee, Prof. of Law
Subjects: Law - general, constitutional, governmental contract, international. **Holdings:** 5100 volumes. **Subscriptions:** 126 journals and other serials. **Services:** Library open to faculty and students only. **Staff:** Capt. H. Manson.

★ 16822 ★
U.S. Air Force Academy - Library (Mil, Sci-Engr)
U.S. Air Force Academy, CO   Phone: (719)472-2590
80840-5701   LTC Reiner H. Schaeffer, Dir. of Libs.
Founded: 1955. **Staff:** Prof 16; Other 33. **Subjects:** Science, technology, humanities, social sciences, military art and science, aeronautics. **Special Collections:** Archival materials relating to the Air Force Academy; Colonel Richard Gimbel Aeronautics History Library (20,000 items); falconry. **Holdings:** 336,293 books; 110,687 bound periodical volumes; 3845 phonograph records; 166,034 U.S. Government documents; 16,749 reels of microfilm; 514,178 reports on microfiche; 2000 maps. **Subscriptions:** 3587 journals and other serials; 39 newspapers. **Services:** Interlibrary loan; copying; library open to the public with permission of the director. **Automated Operations:** Computerized public access catalog, cataloging, acquisitions, and circulation. **Computerized Information Services:** DIALOG Information Services, PFDS Online, BRS Information Technologies, OCLC, NASA/RECON, MEDLARS, DTIC, LEGISLATE, LEXIS, NEXIS. **Networks/Consortia:** Member of FEDLINK, Plains and Peaks Regional Library Service System, Bibliographical Center for Research, Rocky Mountain Region, Inc. (BCR). **Publications:** Handbook; special bibliographies, irregular. **Remarks:** FAX: (719)472-4754. **Staff:** Donald J. Barrett, Asst.Dir., Pub.Serv.; Steven Maffeo, Asst.Dir., Tech.Serv.; Rita A. Jones, Chf., Cat.Br.; Marcia Mohn, Chf., Acq.Br.; Marie L. Nelson, Chf., Ref.Br.; Duane J. Reed, Spec.Coll.Libn.; M. Douglas Johnson, Chf., Sys.Mgt.Off.

★ 16823 ★
U.S. Air Force Academy - Medical Library (Med)
U.S. Air Force Academy, CO 80840-5300   Phone: (719)472-5107
      Jeanne Entze, Libn.
Staff: 1. **Subjects:** Medicine. **Holdings:** 4886 books. **Subscriptions:** 329 journals and other serials. **Services:** Interlibrary loan; copying; library open to the public for reference use only. **Automated Operations:** Computerized cataloging and circulation. **Computerized Information Services:** DIALOG Information Services, MEDLARS. **Networks/Consortia:** Member of Colorado Council of Medical Librarians.

★ 16824 ★
U.S. Air Force Base - Altus Base Library (Mil)
FL 4419   Phone: (405)482-8670
Altus AFB, OK 73523-5985   Bruce Gaver, Libn.
Staff: Prof 1; Other 5. **Subjects:** Military sciences. **Holdings:** 29,000 books; sound recordings; cassettes. **Subscriptions:** 175 journals and other serials; 30 newspapers. **Services:** Interlibrary loan; copying; library open to military and government employees only. **Automated Operations:** Computerized circulation (CLSI). **Computerized Information Services:** DIALOG Information Services, LEXIS, NEXIS.

★ 16825 ★
U.S. Air Force Base - Andrews Base Library (Mil)
FL 4425, Bldg. 1642   Phone: (301)981-6454
Washington, DC 20331-5984   Karen L. Connair, Lib.Dir.
Staff: Prof 1; Other 10. **Subjects:** Aerospace, military history, literature. **Holdings:** 30,000 books; 180 bound periodical volumes; 500 video cassettes; 500 audio cassettes; microforms; war games. **Subscriptions:** 300 journals and other serials; 15 newspapers. **Services:** Library not open to the public. **Computerized Information Services:** InfoTrac, NewsBank.

★ 16826 ★
U.S. Air Force Base - Barksdale Base Library (Mil)
FL 4608, 2SPTG/MWL   Phone: (318)456-4101
Barksdale AFB, LA 71110-5000   Sharon Austin, Base Libn.
Staff: Prof 2; Other 5. **Subjects:** Aviation, management, business, history. **Special Collections:** Louisiana history. **Holdings:** 39,071 books; 51,406 microforms; 1856 phonograph records. **Subscriptions:** 261 journals and other serials; 23 newspapers. **Services:** Interlibrary loan; copying; library open to base community, military retirees and families. **Computerized Information Services:** OCLC, Faxon Company. **Networks/Consortia:** Member of FEDLINK.

★ 16827 ★
U.S. Air Force Base - Base Library (Mil)
FL 4810
Unit 0665   Phone: (507)846249
APO Miami, FL 34001-5000   S.K. Murdoch, Base Libn.
Staff: Prof 2; Other 6. **Subjects:** Military arts and sciences, Latin America. **Holdings:** 39,272 books; 5992 AV materials. **Subscriptions:** 243 journals and other serials; 31 newspapers. **Services:** Interlibrary loan; copying; library open to persons with government identification. **Staff:** R.J. Ferland.

★ 16828 ★
U.S. Air Force Base - Beale Base Library (Mil)
FL 4686   Phone: (916)634-2706
Beale AFB, CA 95903-5000   David S. English, Base Libn.
Staff: Prof 1; Other 3. **Subjects:** Military art and science. **Holdings:** 30,000 books; 4000 phonograph records and tapes; 20,000 microfiche. **Subscriptions:** 450 journals and other serials. **Services:** Interlibrary loan; library not open to the public. **Computerized Information Services:** OCLC. **Special Indexes:** Periodical Holdings.

★ 16829 ★
U.S. Air Force Base - Bergstrom Base Library (Mil)
FL 4857   Phone: (512)369-3739
Bergstrom AFB, TX 78743-5000   Louise Saint-John, Base Libn.
Staff: Prof 1; Other 4. **Subjects:** Aeronautics, social sciences, mathematics, U.S. wars, U.S. and foreign history and travel, languages. **Holdings:** 30,255 books; 3 files of pamphlets on foreign countries; clippings file; 2104 phonograph records, tapes, filmstrips; 300 movie videotapes; 300 training and management videotapes. **Subscriptions:** 300 journals and other serials; 23 newspapers. **Services:** Interlibrary loan; library not open to the public. **Computerized Information Services:** OCLC, DIALOG Information Services. **Remarks:** Alternate telephone number(s): 369-3740.

★ 16830 ★
U.S. Air Force Base - Bolling Base Library (Mil)
FL 4400, Bolling AFB
Washington, DC 20332-5000   Phone: (202)767-4251
                                              D.L. Grinnell, Libn.
Staff: Prof 1; Other 4. **Special Collections:** Total Quality Management; Military Transition Business Management. **Holdings:** 25,000 books. **Subscriptions:** 124 journals and other serials. **Services:** Interlibrary loan; copying; faxing; computer work stations; library open to the public. **Remarks:** FAX: (202)404-8526.

★ 16831 ★
U.S. Air Force Base - Cannon Base Library (Mil)
FL 4855
Cannon AFB, NM 88103-5725   Phone: (505)784-2786
Staff: Other 7. **Subjects:** U.S. Air Force history, New Mexico history, Southwest, general topics. **Holdings:** 41,600 books; 54,800 microfiche; 4700 AV programs. **Subscriptions:** 382 journals and other serials; 59 newspapers. **Services:** Interlibrary loan; library not open to the public. **Computerized Information Services:** OCLC, DIALOG Information Services; FAXON LINX (electronic mail service).

★ 16832 ★
U.S. Air Force Base - Carswell Base Library (Mil)
FL 4689/Bldg. 1500
Carswell AFB, TX 76127-5225   Phone: (817)782-5230
Founded: 1943. **Staff:** 4. **Subjects:** General and technical collection, military science. **Special Collections:** Project Warrior; Air War College. **Holdings:** 31,720 books; 1574 other cataloged items; videotapes. **Subscriptions:** 191 journals and other serials; 20 newspapers. **Services:** Interlibrary loan; copying. **Computerized Information Services:** OCLC, DTIC, NTIS (U.S. National Technical Information Service). **Remarks:** Alternate telephone number(s): 782-7677. FAX: (817)782-7457.

★ 16833 ★
U.S. Air Force Base - Castle Base - Baker Library (Mil)
FL 4672, Bldg. 422   Phone: (209)726-2630
Castle AFB, CA 95342-5200   Caroline Frandsen-Cantillas, Base Libn.
Founded: 1956. **Staff:** Prof 1; Other 4. **Subjects:** Management, defense management, United States and military history, sociology, aeronautics. **Special Collections:** Total Quality Management. **Holdings:** 30,046 books; 30 bound theses; 3059 phonograph records and tapes; 1000 pamphlets; 196 reels of microfilm. **Subscriptions:** 255 journals and other serials; 20 newspapers. **Services:** Interlibrary loan; copying; library open to the public for reference use only. **Publications:** Minorities bibliographies - for internal distribution only.

★ 16834 ★
U.S. Air Force Base - Chanute Base Library (Mil)
FL 3018, Bldg. 95   Phone: (217)495-3191
Chanute AFB, IL 61868-5000   Esther E. Cornelius, Libn.
Founded: 1925. **Staff:** 9. **Subjects:** General and technical topics. **Holdings:** 30,000 volumes. **Subscriptions:** 308 journals and other serials. **Services:** Interlibrary loan; library open to active and retired military personnel and dependents and civilian base employees. **Networks/Consortia:** Member of Lincoln Trail Libraries System (LTLS). **Remarks:** FAX: (217)495-4314.

★ 16835 ★
U.S. Air Force Base - Charleston Base Library
FL 4418   Phone: (803)566-3320
Charleston AFB, SC 29404-5225   Janine Devereaux, Libn.
Staff: Prof 1; Other 5. **Holdings:** 25,500 books; 2600 phonograph records. **Subscriptions:** 125 journals and other serials; 20 newspapers. **Services:** Interlibrary loan; library not open to the public. **Computerized Information Services:** DIALOG Information Services, NEXIS. **Remarks:** FAX:(803)566-5354.

★ 16836 ★
U.S. Air Force Base - Davis-Monthan Base Library (Mil)
FL 4877   Phone: (602)750-4381
Davis-Monthan AFB, AZ 85707   Kathleen E. Baumwart, Base Libn.
Staff: 5. **Holdings:** 25,000 books; 3718 audiocassettes; 1077 videocassettes. **Subscriptions:** 160 journals and other serials; 20 newspapers. **Services:** Interlibrary loan; library open to military personnel, DOD civilians, retired personnel, and dependents. **Computerized Information Services:** OCLC, DIALOG Information Services. **Networks/Consortia:** Member of FEDLINK.

★ 16837 ★
U.S. Air Force Base - Dover Base Library (Mil)
436 CS6/MWL
FL 4497, Bldg. 443
Dover AFB, DE 19902-5225   Phone: (302)677-3992
Founded: 1953. **Staff:** Prof 1; Other 6. **Subjects:** Aviation, general topics. **Special Collections:** Military history; foreign policy. **Holdings:** 23,500 books; 35,000 microforms. **Subscriptions:** 230 journals and other serials; 14 newspapers. **Services:** Interlibrary loan; copying; library open to the public for reference use only. **Computerized Information Services:** NEXIS; FAXON LINX (electronic mail service). **Networks/Consortia:** Member of Kent Library Network (KLN). **Remarks:** FAX: (302)677-2900. Alternate telephone number(s): (302)677-3993; (302)677-3995. **Staff:** Robin E. Lank, Ch. Libn.

★ 16838 ★
U.S. Air Force Base - Dyess Base Library (Mil)
96 CSG/SSL   Phone: (915)696-2618
Dyess AFB, TX 79607-5000   Virginia King, Libn.
Founded: 1957. **Staff:** 3. **Subjects:** Social science, Air Force history. **Special Collections:** Texas history and literature. **Holdings:** 21,000 books; 1500 phonograph records. **Subscriptions:** 225 journals and other serials; 12 newspapers. **Services:** Interlibrary loan; library open to the public for reference use only. **Publications:** Book List, monthly.

★ 16839 ★
U.S. Air Force Base - Eaker Base Library (Mil)
FL 4634, Bldg. 555
Eaker AFB   Phone: (501)762-7286
Blytheville, AR 72317-5225   Laura Gilham, Lib.Mgr.
Staff: Prof 1; Other 3. **Subjects:** General collection. **Holdings:** 20,000 books. **Subscriptions:** 150 journals and other serials; 18 newspapers. **Services:** Interlibrary loan; library not open to the public.

★ 16840 ★
U.S. Air Force Base - Edwards Base Library (Mil)
6510th ABG/SSL, Stop 115
FL 2805, Bldg. 2665   Phone: (805)277-2375
Edwards AFB, CA 93523-5000   Orin M. Moyer, Libn.
Founded: 1942. **Staff:** Prof 1; Other 2. **Subjects:** Recreation, education. **Holdings:** 22,932 books; 319 bound periodical volumes; 608 phonograph records; 24 tapes; 694 reels of microfilm; 83 8mm films; 150 cassettes. **Subscriptions:** 350 journals and other serials. **Services:** Interlibrary loan; library not open to the public.

★16841★
U.S. Air Force Base - Eglin Base Library (Mil, Sci-Engr)
FL 2823   Phone: (904)882-5088
Eglin AFB, FL 32542   F.P. Morgan, Chf., Lib.Br.
Founded: 1942. **Staff:** Prof 2; Other 5. **Subjects:** Aeronautics, military art and science, counterinsurgency, aircraft and missile systems, mathematics, management. **Holdings:** 54,000 books; 2972 bound periodical volumes; 7346 reels of microfilm; 37,784 microfiche; 3715 recordings and tapes; 2064 video cassettes; 58 art prints; 2299 cassettes; 1083 compact discs. **Subscriptions:** 825 journals and other serials; 33 newspapers. **Services:** Interlibrary loan; library not open to the public. **Automated Operations:** Computerized circulation, cataloging, and ILL. **Computerized Information Services:** OCLC, DIALOG Information Services; CD-ROMs (ERIC, NEWSBANK, WILSON indexes). **Networks/Consortia:** Member of FEDLINK. **Publications:** Accessions list, bimonthly. **Staff:** Carole B. Steele, Asst.Libn.

★16842★
U.S. Air Force Base - Eielson Base Library (Mil)
343 RD CSPTS/CTRL
3340 Central Ave., Suite 1   Phone: (907)377-3174
Eielson AFB, AK 99702-2150   Cathy Rasmussen, Adm.Libn.
Staff: Prof 1; Other 4. **Subjects:** Air Force professional and technical material, fiction and nonfiction. **Special Collections:** Alaska; children's collection. **Holdings:** 32,000 volumes; 600 videotapes; 6000 phonograph records, compact discs, and audiotapes; 6 VF drawers. **Subscriptions:** 140 journals and other serials; 10 newspapers. **Services:** Interlibrary loan; copying; library open to military personnel and civilian base employees. **Remarks:** FAX: (907)377-1683.

★16843★
U.S. Air Force Base - Elmendorf Base Library (Mil)
FL5000   Phone: (907)552-3787
Elmendorf AFB, AK 99506   Mary M. Ezzell, Lib.Dir.
Staff: Prof 1; Other 9. **Subjects:** Military science. **Special Collections:** Alaska collection. **Holdings:** 67,000 books; 33,000 microforms. **Subscriptions:** 390 journals and other serials; 15 newspapers. **Services:** Interlibrary loan; library not open to the public.

★16844★
U.S. Air Force Base - England Base Library (Mil)
FL 4805, Bldg. 1213
England AFB, LA 71311-5725   Barbara Green, Libn.
Founded: 1952. **Staff:** Prof 1; Other 4. **Subjects:** Social and applied sciences, American history and literature. **Special Collections:** Louisiana. **Holdings:** 22,500 volumes; 2000 unbound periodicals; 1500 microfiche. **Subscriptions:** 115 journals and other serials; 12 newspapers. **Services:** Interlibrary loan; library not open to the public. **Publications:** Bibliographies, irregular.

★16845★
U.S. Air Force Base - Fairchild Base Library (Mil)
FL 4620   Phone: (509)247-5556
Fairchild AFB, WA 99011-5000   Sherry Ann Hokanson, Libn.
Staff: Prof 1; Other 5. **Subjects:** General and technical topics, military science, business, Northwest. **Special Collections:** Office collections (50). **Holdings:** 32,102 volumes; 2700 phonograph records and tapes; 15,724 microfiche; 539 compact discs. **Subscriptions:** 305 journals and other serials; 12 newspapers. **Services:** Interlibrary loan; copying; library open to military personnel, dependents, retirees, and civilian base employees. **Computerized Information Services:** OCLC, WLN; internal database. **Remarks:** FAX: (509)247-5938.

★16846★
U.S. Air Force Base - George Base Library
FL 4812
George AFB, CA 92394-5000
Defunct.

★16847★
U.S. Air Force Base - Goodfellow Base Library (Mil)
FL 3030, 3498 ABG/MWL   Phone: (915)654-3045
Goodfellow AFB, TX 76908-5000   Elaine C. Penner, Libn.
Staff: Prof 1; Other 6. **Subjects:** Military science, cryptology, foreign language, military intelligence, general topics. **Holdings:** 29,000 books; 33,000 microfiche. **Subscriptions:** 107 journals and other serials; 18 newspapers. **Services:** Interlibrary loan; copying; library open to the public with restrictions. **Computerized Information Services:** CD-ROM (NewsBank Electronic Index). **Remarks:** Alternate telephone number(s): 654-3232.

★16848★
U.S. Air Force Base - Grand Forks Base Library (Mil)
FL 4659
Grand Forks AFB, ND 58205-5000   Phone: (701)747-3046
Founded: 1970. **Staff:** Prof 1; Other 8. **Subjects:** Military science. **Holdings:** 30,000 books; 22 bound periodical volumes; 46,995 microfiche. **Subscriptions:** 250 journals and other serials; 46 newspapers. **Services:** Interlibrary loan; copying; library open to the public. **Automated Operations:** Computerized public access catalog, cataloging, and circulation. **Computerized Information Services:** OCLC. **Remarks:** FAX: (701)747-3491. **Staff:** Roberta Jurge, Supv.Techn.

★16849★
U.S. Air Force Base - Grissom Base Library (Mil)
FL 4654, Bldg. 303
Grissom AFB, IN 46971-5000   Phone: (317)689-2056
Founded: 1956. **Staff:** Prof 1; Other 3. **Subjects:** Military science, business management. **Special Collections:** MacNaughton Booklease Plan (800 volumes). **Holdings:** 24,346 books; 8772 AV programs. **Subscriptions:** 115 journals and other serials; 15 newspapers. **Services:** Interlibrary loan; copying; SDI; library open to military personnel, dependents, and civilians employed on base. **Automated Operations:** Computerized cataloging. **Computerized Information Services:** MARCIVE, Inc. **Publications:** Library Brochure, irregular. **Staff:** Sgt. Rodney Stain; Amn. Traci Whittaker; Nancy Briganti.

★16850★
U.S. Air Force Base - Gunter Base Library (Mil)
FL 3370   Phone: (205)279-3179
Gunter AFS, AL 36114   James Lee Clark, Base Libn.
Founded: 1950. **Staff:** Prof 1; Other 8. **Subjects:** Recreational materials, medicine, education, language, literature, history, military science, aviation, business. **Holdings:** 29,000 books; 2000 recordings, 400 cassette recordings. **Subscriptions:** 100 journals and other serials. **Services:** Library open to military personnel, dependents, and civilian base employees.

★16851★
U.S. Air Force Base - Hanscom Base Library (Mil)
FL 2835   Phone: (617)377-2177
Hanscom AFB, MA 01731-5000   T. Hathaway, Base Libn.
Staff: 5. **Subjects:** Military, technical, educational, and recreational topics. **Holdings:** 21,875 books; records; tapes. **Subscriptions:** 396 journals and other serials; 65 newspapers. **Services:** Interlibrary loan; copying; library open to the public for specific research. **Automated Operations:** Computerized cataloging. **Computerized Information Services:** OCLC. **Networks/Consortia:** Member of FEDLINK.

★16852★
U.S. Air Force Base - Hickam Base Library (Mil)
15 ABW/MWL, Bldg. 595
FL 5260   Phone: (808)449-7163
Hickam AFB, HI 96853-5000   Eleanor F. Ballou, Chf.Libn.
Staff: Prof 2; Other 12. **Subjects:** Military history, current foreign policy, U.S. Air Force, management, investments. **Holdings:** 62,892 volumes. **Subscriptions:** 300 journals and other serials; 30 newspapers. **Services:** Interlibrary loan; copying; library open to the public by appointment. **Computerized Information Services:** CD-ROM (ERIC). **Remarks:** FAX: (808)449-7166.

★16853★
U.S. Air Force Base - Holloman Base Library (Mil)
FL 4801   Phone: (505)479-3939
Holloman AFB, NM 88310   Cora E. Ahrens, Base Libn.
Staff: Prof 2; Other 7. **Subjects:** Military aerospace history, contemporary issues, the Southwest, business management, general topics. **Special Collections:** Southwest collection. **Holdings:** 30,000 books; 130 bound periodical volumes; 50 regional maps; 73,000 microfiche; 2000 phonograph records; 3000 cassettes; 2500 videotapes; 174 art prints; 3 VF drawers of pamphlets and clippings. **Subscriptions:** 550 journals and other serials; 50 newspapers. **Services:** Interlibrary loan; library not open to the public. **Automated Operations:** Computerized ILL. **Computerized Information Services:** OCLC, DIALOG Information Services. **Networks/Consortia:** Member of FEDLINK. **Remarks:** FAX: (505)479-3866. **Staff:** Carol Austin, Lib.Techn.

★ 16854 ★
U.S. Air Force Base - Homestead Base Library (Mil)
FL 4829   Phone: (305)257-8184
Homestead AFB, FL 33039-5000   Carolyn M. Covington, Lib.Dir.
Founded: 1955. **Staff:** Prof 2; Other 6. **Subjects:** Aeronautics, Florida.
Holdings: 31,000 books; 1004 audio and video cassettes; 20,000 microforms.
Subscriptions: 388 journals and other serials; 10 newspapers. **Services:**
Interlibrary loan; library not open to the public. **Automated Operations:**
Computerized cataloging. **Computerized Information Services:** DIALOG
Information Services, OCLC. **Networks/Consortia:** Member of FEDLINK.
Remarks: FAX: (305)258-6787. Autovon Line(s): 791-8184.

★ 16855 ★
U.S. Air Force Base - Hurlburt Base Library (Mil)
Hurlburt Field, FL 32544-5000   Phone: (904)884-6947
                                        Susan J. Whitson, Base Libn.
Founded::1945. **Staff:** Prof 2; Other 5. **Subjects:** General collection.
Holdings: 32,000 books. **Subscriptions:** 200 journals and other serials; 12
newspapers. **Services:** Interlibrary loan; library not open to the public.
Computerized Information Services: DIALOG Information Services
NEXIS. **Remarks:** FAX: (904)884-6050. **Staff:** Karen M. Blaker, Asst.Libn.

★ 16856 ★
U.S. Air Force Base - Keesler Base - McBride Library (Mil, Info Sci)
3380 ABG/MWL
FL 3010, Bldg. 2222   Phone: (601)377-2181
Keesler AFB, MS 39534-5225   William R. Province, Lib.Dir.
Founded: 1963. **Staff:** Prof 4; Other 15. **Subjects:** Telecommunications,
computer science, military history, warfare, literature, management science,
electronic and computer engineering. **Special Collections:** Professional
military education and leadership. **Holdings:** 55,500 books; 1709 bound
periodical volumes; 1700 AV programs; 2700 technical reports and
documents; 500 maps; 53,000 microforms. **Services:** Interlibrary loan; copying; SDI;
library open to military personnel, civil servants, and dependents.
Automated Operations: Computerized cataloging. **Computerized
Information Services:** DTIC, NTIS, OCLC, NEXIS. **Networks/Consortia:**
Member of FEDLINK. **Publications:** Classified List of Periodicals; Guide
to Use of Materials; special bibliographies. **Staff:** Joan Van Acker,
Tech.Libn.; Marty Madison, Cat.

★ 16857 ★
U.S. Air Force Base - Kelly Base Library (Mil)
FL 2050   Phone: (512)925-3214
Kelly AFB, TX 78241-5000   Mary L. McCarty, Act.Libn.
Founded: 1917. **Staff:** Prof 1; Other 7. **Subjects:** Aircraft, management,
business, auto and home repair, logistics, Civil Service Test, American
history, self-improvement, cooking. **Holdings:** 28,000 books; 620 reels of
microfilm; 1400 phonograph records; 850 video cassettes; 15,000 microfiche;
770 cassette tapes; 185 compact discs. **Subscriptions:** 215 journals and other
serials; 10 newspapers. **Services:** Interlibrary loan; copying; library open to
San Antonio area military personnel, civilian base employees, and
dependents. **Automated Operations:** MicroLinx. **Computerized Information
Services:** CD-ROMs. **Remarks:** FAX: (512)925-9853. **Staff:** Karen
Weiskittel.

★ 16858 ★
U.S. Air Force Base - Kirtland Base Library (Mil)
FL 4469   Phone: (505)844-1071
Kirtland AFB, NM 87117-5000   Martha K. Sumpter, Libn.
Founded::1945. **Staff:** Prof 2; Other 6. **Subjects:** Military history and science,
general education, Southwest. **Special Collections:** Project Warrior;
Southwest. **Holdings:** 40,820 books; 11,127 microfiche of periodicals; 348
tapes; 1957 phonograph records; 50 language records and tapes.
Subscriptions: 368 journals and other serials; 29 newspapers. **Services:**
Interlibrary loan; copying; library open to active and retired military
personnel, civilian base employees, and dependents for reference use only.
Automated Operations: Computerized circulation. **Computerized
Information Services:** DIALOG Information Services, NEXIS; FAXON
LINX (electronic mail service). **Publications:** New Acquisitions, monthly -
for internal distribution only. **Remarks:** FAX: (505)846-1372. **Staff:** Robert
C. Mathews, Ref.Libn.

★ 16859 ★
U.S. Air Force Base - Langley Base Library (Mil)
FL 4800   Phone: (804)764-2906
Langley AFB, VA 23665   Margaret E. Whitehill, Base Libn.
Founded: 1942. **Staff:** Prof 2; Other 14. **Subjects:** Military history, sociology,
foreign affairs, management. **Holdings:** 80,000 books; 16 mm films; video
cassettes; phonograph records; tapes. **Subscriptions:** 600 journals and other
serials. **Services:** Copying; document delivery service. **Automated
Operations:** Computerized circulation and ILL. **Computerized Information
Services:** OCLC, DIALOG Information Services, Dun & Bradstreet
Business Credit Services, FAXON. **Remarks:** FAX: (804)766-1468.

★ 16860 ★
U.S. Air Force Base - Laughlin Base Library (Mil)
FL 3099   Phone: (512)298-5119
Laughlin AFB, TX 78840   Vicky Crone, Supv.Lib.Techn.
Staff: Prof 1; Other 5. **Subjects:** Aviation; military history, art, and science;
management. **Holdings:** 19,000 books; 30,000 sheets of microfiche.
Subscriptions: 150 journals and other serials; 6 newspapers; 8 microfiche.
Services: Interlibrary loan; library open to DOD employees only.
Computerized Information Services: NEXIS.

★ 16861 ★
U.S. Air Force Base - Little Rock Base Library (Mil)
FL 4460, Bldg. 976
Little Rock AFB, AR 72099-5000   Phone: (501)988-6979
Founded: 1956. **Staff:** Prof 1; Other 6. **Subjects:** Military science,
aeronautics, management, social science. **Holdings:** 22,000 books.
Subscriptions: 150 journals and other serials; 10 newspapers. **Services:**
Interlibrary loan; library not open to the public. **Remarks:** FAX: (501)988-
3717.

★ 16862 ★
U.S. Air Force Base - Loring Base Library (Mil)
FL 4678   Phone: (207)999-2416
Loring AFB, ME 04751-5000   Jeanette M. Waters, Lib.Dir.
Founded: 1958. **Staff:** Prof 1; Other 5. **Subjects:** General topics. **Special
Collections:** Aeronautics. **Holdings:** 29,757 books; 508 phonograph records;
787 tapes; 123 compact discs; 273 videotapes; 43 software packages; 2000
maps and pamphlets; 39,991 microforms; 20 art prints; 13 war games.
Subscriptions: 290 journals and other serials; 42 newspapers. **Services:**
Interlibrary loan; library not open to the public. **Automated Operations:**
Computerized circulation (MicroLinx, DataLinx, Data Trek).

★ 16863 ★
U.S. Air Force Base - Lowry Base Library (Mil)
Lowry Technical Training Ctr.
FL 3059, ABG/SSL   Phone: (303)370-3093
Lowry AFB, CO 80230-5000   Helen C. McClaughry, Base Libn.
Founded: 1939. **Staff:** Prof 2; Other 4. **Subjects:** Electronics, missiles, space,
photography, nuclear weapons, avionics, intelligence, special instruments,
aeronautics, graphics, logistics, general collection with emphasis on military
subjects and education. **Holdings:** 40,000 books; 2000 recordings; 500
framed and unframed pictures; 800 video recordings. **Subscriptions:** 350
journals and other serials. **Services:** Interlibrary loan; library not open to the
public. **Automated Operations:** Computerized serials. **Networks/Consortia:**
Member of Central Colorado Library System (CCLS). **Publications:** New
Book List; Subject Bibliographies. **Remarks:** Alternate telephone number(s):
370-3836. FAX: (303)370-3796. **Staff:** Eileen Hogan, Asst.Libn.

★ 16864 ★
U.S. Air Force Base - Luke Base Library (Mil)
FL 4887   Phone: (602)856-7191
Luke AFB, AZ 85309-5725   M. Cecilia Rothschild, Libn.
Founded: 1951. **Staff:** Prof 1; Other 7. **Subjects:** General collection with
emphasis on aeronautics. **Special Collections:** Project Warrior; Arizona
history; quality management; careers. **Holdings:** 25,050 books; 378
phonograph records; 877 audio cassettes; 919 video cassettes; 38,784
microfiche; 138 compact disks. **Subscriptions:** 195 journals and other serials;
19 newspapers. **Services:** Interlibrary loan; copying; library open to active
duty and retired military personnel. **Automated Operations:** Computerized
ILL. **Computerized Information Services:** DIALOG Information Services.
Performs searches free of charge. **Networks/Consortia:** Member of
FEDLINK. **Remarks:** FAX: (602)935-2023.

★ 16865 ★
U.S. Air Force Base - Luke Base Medical Library (Med)
58th Medical Group/SGQL   Phone: (602)856-7585
Luke AFB, AZ 85309-5300   Sharon A. Primus, Med.Libn.
Founded: 1951. **Staff:** 1. **Subjects:** Medicine, dentistry. **Holdings:** 2200 books; 439 bound periodical volumes. **Subscriptions:** 75 journals and other serials. **Services:** Interlibrary loan; copying; library open to Department of Defense employees only. **Computerized Information Services:** MEDLINE. **Remarks:** FAX: (602)856-3615.

★ 16866 ★
U.S. Air Force Base - MacDill Base Library (Mil)
FL 4814   Phone: (813)830-3607
MacDill AFB, FL 33608-5050   Jean Jacob Phillips, Base Libn.
Staff: Prof 2; Other 7. **Subjects:** Military history, Middle East, Latin America, international affairs. **Holdings:** 28,214 books; 58,612 microforms; 104 framed art prints. **Subscriptions:** 414 journals and other serials; 67 newspapers. **Services:** Interlibrary loan; copying; SDI; library open to military personnel, Department of Defense civilians, and civilians attending on-base university classes. **Automated Operations:** Computerized cataloging. **Computerized Information Services:** DIALOG Information Services, OCLC, LEXIS, NEXIS. **Networks/Consortia:** Member of Tampa Bay Library Consortium, Inc. (TBLC). **Remarks:** FAX: (813)830-4416.

★ 16867 ★
U.S. Air Force Base - Malmstrom Base Library (Mil)
FL 4626   Phone: (406)731-2748
Malmstrom AFB, MT 59402-5000   Arden G. Hill, Libn.
Founded: 1957. **Staff:** 7. **Subjects:** General, aviation, alternative energy, and technical topics. **Holdings:** 27,528 books; 14 VF drawers; 1006 government publications; 3632 AV programs; 35,336 microforms. **Subscriptions:** 360 journals and other serials; 13 newspapers. **Services:** Interlibrary loan; library not open to the public. **Automated Operations:** Computerized public access catalog, cataloging, serials, and circulation. **Computerized Information Services:** OCLC.

★ 16868 ★
U.S. Air Force Base - March Base Library (Mil)
FL 4664   Phone: (714)655-2203
March AFB, CA 92518   Rose Moorhouse, Base Libn.
Staff: Prof 1; Other 5. **Subjects:** Aeronautics, education, political science, technology, general topics, children's literature. **Special Collections:** California Collection (250 items); International Relations (318 items); Caldecott/Newbery Collection; USC-SSMC Systems Management; Air War College. **Holdings:** 34,000 books; 203 maps; 1141 phonograph records; 1697 audiotapes; 978 video cassettes; 40 books on cassettes. **Subscriptions:** 204 journals and other serials; 14 newspapers. **Services:** Interlibrary loan; library open to military personnel and to civilians enrolled in on-base education courses. **Automated Operations:** Computerized public access catalog and circulation. **Computerized Information Services:** OCLC, DIALOG Information Services. **Networks/Consortia:** Member of San Bernardino, Inyo, Riverside Counties United Library Services (SIRCULS), FEDLINK.

★ 16869 ★
U.S. Air Force Base - Mather Base Library (Mil)
FL 3067   Phone: (916)364-4759
Mather AFB, CA 95655-5000   Jean-Marie Clemmons, Libn.
Founded: 1943. **Staff:** Prof 1; Other 3. **Subjects:** Aviation, military history, World War II history. **Holdings:** 30,000 books; 3300 microfiche; 2400 records and tapes; 400 video cassettes. **Subscriptions:** 184 journals and other serials. **Services:** Interlibrary loan; library not open to the public.

★ 16870 ★
U.S. Air Force Base - McChord Base Library (Mil)
62 ABG/SSL
FL 4479   Phone: (206)984-3454
McChord AFB, WA 98438-5000   Margaret Ono, Base Libn.
Founded: 1940. **Staff:** Prof 2; Other 5. **Subjects:** Aeronautics, military history, fiction. **Holdings:** 28,000 books. **Subscriptions:** 188 journals and other serials; 11 journals and other serials. **Services:** Interlibrary loan; library not open to the public. **Automated Operations:** Computerized serials and circulation. **Computerized Information Services:** DIALOG Information Services, NEXIS. Contact Person: Johna Sheller, Ref.Libn.

★ 16871 ★
U.S. Air Force Base - McClellan Base Library (Mil)
2852 ABG/MWL
FL 2040   Phone: (916)643-4640
McClellan AFB, CA 95652   Esther Sims, Libn.
Founded: 1941. **Staff:** Prof 1; Other 5. **Subjects:** Aeronautics, psychology, literature, government. **Special Collections:** Project Warrior (129 books); California description and travel (61 books). **Holdings:** 34,459 books; 5075 audio recordings; 157 reels of microfilm; 5111 microfiche; 697 videocassettes; 99 automotive repair manuals; 195 testing books; 51 games; 10 cameras; 47 sculptures and framed art works. **Subscriptions:** 220 journals and other serials; 14 newspapers. **Services:** Interlibrary loan; copying; library open to military personnel and dependents and civilian base employees. **Publications:** New book list, bimonthly; bibliographies, monthly.

★ 16872 ★
U.S. Air Force Base - McConnell Base Library (Mil)
FL 4621/Library   Phone: (316)652-4207
McConnell AFB, KS 67221-5000   Ann D. Moore, Base Libn.
Staff: Prof 2; Other 6. **Subjects:** Aeronautics, business, military history, children's collection, auto repair. **Holdings:** 35,516 books; 1453 audio cassettes; 564 records; 10 VF drawers; 851 videotapes; 103 compact discs; 58,508 microfiche; 1835 reels of microfilm. **Subscriptions:** 463 journals and other serials; 46 newspapers. **Services:** Interlibrary loan; library open to persons enrolled in outreach programs of Butler County Community College, Webster University, Kansas Newman, and Embry-Riddle Aviation University. **Automated Operations:** Computerized public access catalog, cataloging, serials, and circulation. **Computerized Information Services:** CD-ROM (Newsbank). **Publications:** Flyleaf, irregular; Calendar of Events, irregular. **Remarks:** FAX: (316)652-5418. **Staff:** Lois Gordon.

★ 16873 ★
U.S. Air Force Base - McGuire Base Library (Mil)
FL 4484   Phone: (609)724-2079
McGuire AFB, NJ 08641-5225   Audrey J. Marques, Base Libn.
Founded: 1948. **Staff:** Prof 1; Other 6. **Subjects:** General and technical topics. **Holdings:** 30,214 books; 54,274 micrifiche; 556 reels of microfilm. **Subscriptions:** 240 journals and other serials. **Services:** Interlibrary loan; copying; library open to the public for reference use only. **Computerized Information Services:** CD-ROMs (NewsBank, Periodical Abstracts). **Networks/Consortia:** Member of South Jersey Regional Library Cooperative. **Remarks:** FAX: (609)723-2952.

★ 16874 ★
U.S. Air Force Base - Minot Base Library (Mil)
5 SPTG/MWL
215 Missile Ave., Unit 1
                                           Phone: (701)723-3344
Minot AFB, ND 58705-5026   Wendy Davis, Libn.
Staff: 6. **Subjects:** Aeronautics, electronics, military history and science. **Special Collections:** Project Warrior (600 items); McNaughton Rental Collection; study guides; Air War College. **Holdings:** 27,013 books; 78 bound periodical volumes; 223 reels of microfilm; 1105 recordings; 4 VF drawers. **Subscriptions:** 597 journals and other serials; 41 newspapers. **Services:** Interlibrary loan; copying; library open to the public with restrictions. **Staff:** William E. Kendra, Lib.Dir.

★ 16875 ★
U.S. Air Force Base - Moody Base Library (Mil)
FL 4830
Moody AFB, GA 31699-5000   Phone: (912)333-3539
Founded: 1951. **Staff:** Prof 1; Other 4. **Subjects:** Aeronautics, science, history, general topics. **Holdings:** 23,968 books; 2251 phonograph records; 223 microfiche; 8000 videotapes; 300 filmstrips. **Subscriptions:** 337 journals and other serials; 21 newspapers. **Services:** Interlibrary loan; copying; library open to active and retired military personnel and dependents, Department of Defense personnel, and civilians enrolled in on-base educational programs. **Computerized Information Services:** OCLC, DIALOG Information Services.

★ 16876 ★

U.S. Air Force Base - Myrtle Beach Base Library (Mil)
FL 4806   Phone: (803)238-7195
Myrtle Beach AFB, SC 29579-5000   Nellie Moffitt, Base Libn.
Founded: 1956. **Staff:** Prof 1; Other 5. **Subjects:** Aeronautics, military science, electronics, business, general topics. **Special Collections:** Air War College Seminar books (military and political science). **Holdings:** 21,000 books; 1000 phonograph records and cassette tapes. **Subscriptions:** 200 journals and other serials. **Services:** Interlibrary loan; library not open to the public. **Remarks:** Maintains 43 office collections of 2500 books.

★ 16877 ★

U.S. Air Force Base - Nellis Base Library (Mil)
FL 4852, 554 CSG/SSL   Phone: (702)652-4484
Nellis AFB, NV 89191-5000   Sharron Cooper, Dir.
Founded: 1949. **Staff:** Prof 1; Other 9. **Subjects:** Aeronautics, business, management, military history, political science, general reference. **Holdings:** 46,125 books; 48,000 microforms; 8091 tapes and phonograph records; 58 16mm films; 2600 video cassettes; 1378 slides; 253 art prints; 202 strategy games; 504 computer software items; 295 video games. **Subscriptions:** 458 journals and other serials; 11 newspapers. **Services:** Interlibrary loan; Dial-A-Story Program; library open to the public for reference use only. **Automated Operations:** Computerized public access catalog and circulation. **Computerized Information Services:** DIALOG Information Services, OCLC, USNI Military Database, InfoTrac, NewsBank. **Remarks:** FAX: (702)643-0697.

★ 16878 ★

U.S. Air Force Base - Norton Base Library (Mil)
Bldg. 125   Phone: (714)382-7119
Norton AFB, CA 92409-5985   Joanna J. Hansen, Base Libn.
Founded: 1943. **Staff:** Prof 1; Other 8. **Subjects:** Aeronautics, business and management, military history, general topics. **Holdings:** 23,500 books. **Subscriptions:** 250 journals and other serials; 15 newspapers. **Services:** Interlibrary loan; copying; library open to the public for reference use only. **Networks/Consortia:** Member of San Bernardino, Inyo, Riverside Counties United Library Services (SIRCULS).

★ 16879 ★

U.S. Air Force Base - Offutt Base Library (Mil)
FL 4600   Phone: (402)294-2533
Offutt AFB, NE 68113-5000   Margaret A. Byrne, Libn.
Subjects: General collection. **Holdings:** 50,000 books and periodicals. **Services:** Library not open to the public.

★ 16880 ★

U.S. Air Force Base - Patrick Base Library (Mil)
FL 2520   Phone: (407)494-6881
Patrick AFB, FL 32925-6625   Katheryn Kessler, Adm.Libn.
Staff: Prof 1; Other 7. **Subjects:** Social science, engineering technology, history. **Special Collections:** Air War College; Total Quality Management. **Holdings:** 40,500 books; 4000 audio cassettes; 800 video cassettes. **Subscriptions:** 110 journals and other serials; 5 newspapers. **Services:** Interlibrary loan; library not open to the public. **Computerized Information Services:** OCLC. **Networks/Consortia:** Member of FEDLINK.

★ 16881 ★

U.S. Air Force Base - Peterson Base Library (Mil)
FL2500   Phone: (719)554-7462
Peterson AFB, CO 80914-5000   B.N. Coleman
Founded: 1950. **Staff:** Prof 1; Other 3. **Subjects:** Aeronautics, astronautics, business and management, military science, space sciences. **Holdings:** 31,874 books; 565 reports; 122,918 microfiche; 1016 reels of microfilm. **Subscriptions:** 697 journals and other serials; 13 newspapers. **Services:** Interlibrary loan; copying; library open to the public for reference use only. **Computerized Information Services:** DTIC; internal database. **Remarks:** FAX: (719)591-4553.

★ 16882 ★

U.S. Air Force Base - Pope Base Library (Mil)
317 CSG/MWRL
Bldg. 370   Phone: (919)394-2791
Pope AFB, NC 28308   Emily J. Borland, Base Libn.
Staff: Prof 1; Other 6. **Subjects:** Military science, business, general topics. **Holdings:** 21,000 books; 1500 phonograph records; 50 puzzles; 500 books in rental collection; 56,000 microfiche; 560 cassettes; 70 compact discs; 21 wargames; 42 computer software (wargames); 700 video cassettes; pamphlets; maps. **Subscriptions:** 302 journals and other serials; 24 newspapers. **Services:** Interlibrary loan; copying; preschool story service; library open to active and retired military personnel and dependents and to civilian base employees. **Automated Operations:** Computerized acquisitions, circulation, and serials. **Computerized Information Services:** DIALOG Information Services, OCLC; FAXON LINX (electronic mail service). **Networks/Consortia:** Member of FEDLINK, North Carolina Information Network (NCIN). **Remarks:** FAX: (919)394-2125.

★ 16883 ★

U.S. Air Force Base - Randolph Base Library (Mil)
FL 3089, Bldg. 584   Phone: (512)652-5578
Randolph AFB, TX 78150-5000   Lenore Shapiro, Base Libn.
Staff: Prof 1; Other 4. **Subjects:** U.S. Air Force history, World War II, aeronautics, management, applied science, literature. **Special Collections:** Air War College Seminar Book Collection; Texas history. **Holdings:** 30,000 books. **Subscriptions:** 280 journals and other serials; 15 newspapers. **Services:** Interlibrary loan; copying; library open to the public with restrictions. **Automated Operations:** Computerized cataloging and serials. **Computerized Information Services:** LEXIS, NEXIS. **Staff:** Ruth Francis; John Mullen.

★ 16884 ★

U.S. Air Force Base - Reese Base Library (Mil)
FL 3060   Phone: (806)885-3344
Reese AFB, TX 79489-5438   Mac Odom, Libn.
Founded: 1950. **Staff:** Prof 2; Other 2. **Subjects:** Aeronautics, management, travel, history, fiction. **Holdings:** 16,500 books. **Subscriptions:** 142 journals and other serials. **Services:** Interlibrary loan; library not open to the public.

★ 16885 ★

U.S. Air Force Base - Robins Base Library (Mil)
2853 ABG/MWL
FL 2060   Phone: (912)926-5411
Robins AFB, GA 31098-5000   Rosalind J. Jackson, Lib.Mgt.Spec.
Staff: Prof 1; Other 7. **Subjects:** General and technical topics. **Holdings:** 70,000 books. **Subscriptions:** 365 journals and other serials; 60 newspapers. **Services:** Interlibrary loan; library not open to the public. **Computerized Information Services:** DIALOG Information Services, PhoneDisc, NTIS, NewsBank. **Remarks:** FAX: (912)929-5954.

★ 16886 ★

U.S. Air Force Base - Sheppard Base Library (Mil)
FL 3020   Phone: (817)676-2687
Sheppard AFB, TX 76311-5000   Linda Fryar, Hd.Libn.
Staff: Prof 2; Other 8. **Subjects:** General and technical topics. **Holdings:** 40,000 books, 29,000 microforms; 3000 recordings. **Subscriptions:** 250 journals and other serials; 19 newspapers. **Services:** Interlibrary loan; copying; library open to the public with approval of base commander. **Remarks:** FAX: (817)855-8854.

★ 16887 ★

U.S. Air Force Base - Tinker Base Library (Mil)
2854 ABG/SSL
FL 2030, Bldg. 5702   Phone: (405)734-3083
Tinker AFB, OK 73145   Joy Leverett, Adm.Libn.
Founded: 1942. **Staff:** Prof 2; Other 10. **Subjects:** Aeronautics, engineering, management. **Special Collections:** Project Warrior; Technical Information Center; Technical Mission Support publications. **Holdings:** 33,411 books; 1467 phonograph records. **Subscriptions:** 547 journals and other serials; 20 newspapers. **Services:** Interlibrary loan; library open to the public with permission. **Computerized Information Services:** OCLC, DTIC. **Publications:** Subject Bibliographies. **Remarks:** FAX: (405)734-4174. **Staff:** Don Richardson, Asst.Libn.; Ann Irby, Acq./Coll.; Mary Burnside, Acq./Lib.; Debbie Robertis, TIC Libn.; David Moinette, Circ.; Linda Armor, Circ.

★ 16888 ★
U.S. Air Force Base - Travis Base Library (Mil)
Mitchell Memorial Library
60 SG/MWL
FL 4427   Phone: (707)424-3279
Travis AFB, CA 94535   Nina Jacobs, Libn.
Founded: 1956. **Staff:** Prof 1; Other 9. **Subjects:** Military science and
aviation, general topics. **Holdings:** 45,243 volumes. **Subscriptions:** 297
journals and other serials; 13 newspapers. **Services:** Interlibrary loan; library
not open to the public. **Computerized Information Services:** NEXIS,
DIALOG Information Services. **Networks/Consortia:** Member of North
Bay Cooperative Library System (NBCLS).

★ 16889 ★
U.S. Air Force Base - Tyndall Base Library (Mil)
325 SG/MWCL/45   Phone: (904)283-4287
Tyndall AFB, FL 32403-5725   Sheila Ray, Libn.
Staff: Prof 1; Other 5. **Subjects:** Aviation history, military science, business
management. **Holdings:** 23,000 books. **Subscriptions:** 300 journals and other
serials; 20 newspapers. **Services:** Interlibrary loan; library not open to the
public. **Computerized Information Services:** DIALOG Information
Services. **Remarks:** FAX: (904)283-3293.

★ 16890 ★
U.S. Air Force Base - Vance Base Library (Mil)
FL 3029   Phone: (405)249-7368
Vance AFB, OK 73705-5000   Tom L. Kirk, Chf.Libn.
Founded: 1941. **Staff:** Prof 1; Other 3. **Subjects:** General topics. **Holdings:**
16,750 books; 4500 phonograph records; 5000 microforms; 1100
videocassettes. **Subscriptions:** 118 journals and other serials; 9 newspapers.
Services: Interlibrary loan; library not open to the public. **Automated
Operations:** Computerized cataloging.

★ 16891 ★
U.S. Air Force Base - Vandenberg Base Library (Mil)
FL 4610, Bldg. 10343-A   Phone: (805)734-8232
Vandenberg AFB, CA 93437-5000   Joseph L. Buelna, Base Libn.
Founded: 1952. **Staff:** Prof 2; Other 10. **Subjects:** Military and general
topics. **Special Collections:** Military science; books for War College
students. **Holdings:** 42,000 books; 4000 nonbook items; 3600 reels of
microfilm of technical periodicals, 1970 to present. **Subscriptions:** 236
journals and other serials; 8 newspapers. **Services:** Interlibrary loan;
copying; library open to the public. **Automated Operations:** Computerized
public access catalog and circulation. **Computerized Information Services:**
DIALOG Information Services, InfoTrac, WILSONLINE. **Remarks:**
FAX: (805)734-1201.

★ 16892 ★
U.S. Air Force Base - Wheeler Base Library (Mil)
Bldg. 824   Phone: (808)656-1867
Wheeler AAF, HI 96854-5000   Karen J. Lewis, Libn.
Founded: 1960. **Staff:** Prof 1; Other 2. **Subjects:** Systems management,
Hawaiiana, military history. **Holdings:** 20,000 books; 14 VF drawers; 68
periodicals on microfilm; maps; phonograph records. **Subscriptions:** 208
journals and other serials; 20 newspapers. **Services:** Interlibrary loan;
copying; library open to military personnel and dependents. **Computerized
Information Services:** CD-ROM (WILSONDISC).

★ 16893 ★
U.S. Air Force Base - Whiteman Base Library (Mil)
FL 4625   Phone: (816)687-3089
Whiteman AFB, MO 65305-5000   Karen Hightill, Base Libn.
Founded: 1951. **Staff:** Prof 1; Other 3. **Subjects:** Military science. **Special
Collections:** Project Warrior; office collections (51). **Holdings:** 23,863
volumes; 900 audiotapes; 3552 microforms; 2000 phonograph records; 648
video cassettes; 4 VF drawers of clippings and pamphlets. **Subscriptions:** 114
journals and other serials; 18 newspapers. **Services:** Interlibrary loan; library
not open to the public. **Automated Operations:** Computerized public access
catalog and circulation.

★ 16894 ★
U.S. Air Force Base - Williams Base Library (Mil)
FL 3044
82 ABG/MML
Williams AFB, AZ 85240-5575   Phone: (602)988-5279
Founded: 1941. **Staff:** 2. **Subjects:** U.S. Air Force, airplanes, pilot training.
Special Collections: Project Warrior. **Holdings:** 18,684 books.
Subscriptions: 140 journals and other serials; 12 newspapers. **Services:**
Interlibrary loan; copying; library open to active and retired military
personnel and to Department of Defense civilians. **Remarks:** FAX:
(602)988-6630.

★ 16895 ★
U.S. Air Force Base - Wright-Patterson Base Library (Mil)
2750 ABW/SSL
Kittyhawk Ctr., Bldg. 1044   Phone: (513)257-4815
Wright-Patterson AFB, OH 45433-5000   Mary E. Rinas, Chf., Lib.Br.
Staff: Prof 1; Other 11. **Subjects:** Military art and science, business
management. **Special Collections:** Project Warrior (2176 items). **Holdings:**
55,000 books; AV programs. **Subscriptions:** 220 journals and other serials;
21 newspapers. **Services:** Interlibrary loan; copying; library open to the
public for reference use only.

★ 16896 ★
U.S. Air Force Hospital - 416 Medical Group - Library (NY-Griffiss
AFB) (Med)
Griffiss AFB, NY 13441-5300   Phone: (315)330-5917
                                           Patty Sbaraglia, Med.Libn.
Staff: 1. **Subjects:** Nursing, dental services, mental and social health,
surgery, internal medicine, food service. **Holdings:** 856 books. **Subscriptions:**
63 journals and other serials. **Services:** Interlibrary loan; library not open
to the public. **Publications:** Newsletter. **Special Catalogs:** Union list.
Remarks: FAX: (315)330-5849. **Formerly:** Its 416 Strategic Hospital.

★ 16897 ★
**U.S. Air Force Hospital - Air University Regional Hospital - Health
Sciences Library** (Med)
Maxwell AFB   Phone: (205)953-5852
Montgomery, AL 36112-5304   Patricia A. Kuther, Med.Lib.Techn.
Founded: 1956. **Staff:** Prof 1. **Subjects:** General medicine, surgery,
pathology, dentistry, nursing, veterinary medicine. **Holdings:** 4000 books
and bound periodical volumes. **Subscriptions:** 200 journals and other serials.
Services: Interlibrary loan; library not open to the public. **Computerized
Information Services:** MEDLARS. **Remarks:** FAX: (205)953-5621.

★ 16898 ★
U.S. Air Force Hospital - CTTC Hospital - Medical Library (IL -
Chanute AFB) (Med)
Chanute AFB, IL 61868-5300   Phone: (217)495-3068
                                           Gordon P. Laumer, Libn.
Staff: 1. **Subjects:** Medicine. **Holdings:** 1600 books. **Subscriptions:** 60
journals and other serials. **Services:** Interlibrary loan; library not open to the
public. **Networks/Consortia:** Member of East Central Illinois Consortium,
National Network of Libraries of Medicine - Greater Midwest Region.
Formerly: Its Chanute Technical Training Center - Medical Library.

★ 16899 ★
**U.S. Air Force Hospital - David Grant Medical Center - Medical
Library** (Med)
Travis AFB, CA 94535-5300   Phone: (707)423-7963
                                           V. Kay Hafner, Med.Libn./Dir.
Founded: 1958. **Staff:** Prof 1; Other 1. **Subjects:** Medicine, family practice,
dentistry, nursing. **Holdings:** 4938 books; 13,375 bound periodical volumes.
Subscriptions: 570 journals and other serials. **Services:** Interlibrary loan;
library not open to the public. **Computerized Information Services:**
MEDLARS, BRS Information Technologies, OCLC; OnTyme Electronic
Message Network Service (electronic mail service). Performs searches free
of charge. **Networks/Consortia:** Member of National Network of Libraries
of Medicine - Pacific Southwest Region, Northern California and Nevada
Medical Library Group (NCNMLG). **Remarks:** Alternate telephone
number(s): (707)423-5344.

★ 16900 ★
U.S. Air Force Hospital - Ehrling Bergquist Strategic Hospital - Medical Library (Med)
Attn: SGASAL
2501 Capehart Rd., Suite 1I13   Phone: (402)294-5499
Offutt AFB, NE 68113-2160   Jan Hatcher, Lib.Mgr.
Founded: 1966. Staff: 1. Subjects: Surgery and allied health sciences. Holdings: 2200 books. Subscriptions: 260 journals and other serials. Services: Interlibrary loan; copying; library open to the public for reference use only. Computerized Information Services: MEDLINE; DOCLINE (electronic mail service).

U.S. Air Force Hospital - Health Sciences Library (AL-Maxwell AFB)
See: U.S. Air Force Hospital - Air University Regional Hospital - Health Sciences Library (16897)

★ 16901 ★
U.S. Air Force Hospital - Malcolm Grow Medical Center - Medical Library/SGEL (Med)
Andrews AFB   Phone: (202)981-2354
Washington, DC 20331-5300   Carol J. Davidson
Staff: Prof 1. Subjects: Internal medicine, nursing, cardiology, surgery, dentistry, food service, psychology. Holdings: 8000 books; 4000 bound periodical volumes; clippings; maps; bibliographies; dissertations; reprints; pamphlets; tapes. Subscriptions: 300 journals and other serials. Services: Interlibrary loan; library not open to the public. Computerized Information Services: MEDLARS, OCLC. Performs searches free of charge. Networks/Consortia: Member of FEDLINK.

★ 16902 ★
U.S. Air Force Hospital - Medical Library (AK-Elmendorf AFB) (Med)
Elmendorf AFB, AK 99506-5300   Phone: (907)552-3383
                                  Donna M. Hudson, Libn.
Founded: 1952. Staff: Prof 1. Subjects: General and military medicine. Holdings: 4600 books; Subscriptions: 251 journals and other serials. Services: Interlibrary loan; copying; SDI; library open to the public for reference use only. Computerized Information Services: MEDLINE. Networks/Consortia: Member of National Network of Libraries of Medicine (NN/LM), Alaska Library Network (ALN). Publications: Holdings List, annual. Remarks: FAX: (907)552-8107.

★ 16903 ★
U.S. Air Force Hospital - Medical Library (CA-Mather AFB) (Med)
323 FTW Hospital/SGAL   Phone: (916)364-3179
Mather AFB, CA 95655-5300   Willis J. Collick, Med.Libn.
Staff: 1. Subjects: Medicine. Holdings: 960 books. Subscriptions: 102 journals and other serials. Services: Interlibrary loan; library not open to the public. Remarks: FAX: (916)364-3193.

★ 16904 ★
U.S. Air Force Hospital - Medical Library (FL-Patrick AFB) (Med)
Patrick AFB, FL 32925-5300   Phone: (407)494-8105
                                  Arlene S. Bilsky, Med.Lib.Techn.
Founded: 1968. Staff: Prof 1. Subjects: Medicine, surgery, nursing, pediatrics. Holdings: 800 books. Subscriptions: 60 journals and other serials. Services: Library not open to the public.

★ 16905 ★
U.S. Air Force Hospital - Medical Library (OK-Tinker AFB) (Med)
Tinker AFB, OK 73145   Phone: (405)734-8443
                                  Mary B. Mills, Lib.Techn.
Staff: 1. Subjects: Pediatrics, internal medicine, surgery, nursing. Holdings: 1263 books. Subscriptions: 93 journals and other serials. Services: Interlibrary loan; copying; library open to the public with restrictions. Computerized Information Services: MEDLARS. Networks/Consortia: Member of Greater Oklahoma City Area Health Sciences Library Consortium (GOAL). Remarks: FAX: (405)734-8248.

★ 16906 ★
U.S. Air Force Hospital - Medical Library (TX-Reese AFB) (Med)
64th Medical Squad   Phone: (806)885-3543
Reese AFB, TX 79459-5300   Gaylor Dickerson, Libn.
Staff: 2. Subjects: Medicine and medical specialties, dentistry. Holdings: 780 books. Subscriptions: 40 journals and other serials. Services: Library open to USAF personnel.

★ 16907 ★
U.S. Air Force Hospital - Medical Library (WA-Fairchild AFB) (Med)
92 Medical Group   Phone: (509)247-5353
Fairchild AFB, WA 99011-5300   Susan Coleman, Med.Libn.
Staff: 1. Subjects: General internal medicine, pediatrics, orthopedics, obstetrics and gynecology, family practice. Special Collections: Hyperbaric medicine; aerospace medicine; bioenvironmental engineering; environmental health. Holdings: 1260 books; 54 bound periodical volumes. Subscriptions: 48 journals and other serials; 6 newspapers. Services: Library not open to the public. Automated Operations: Computerized cataloging, acquisitions, and circulation. Computerized Information Services: MEDLINE, MARCIVE, Inc.; internal database. Remarks: FAX: (509)247-2245.

★ 16908 ★
U.S. Air Force Hospital - Sheppard Technical Training Center Hospital - Health Sciences Library (Med)
Sheppard AFB, TX 76311-5300   Phone: (817)676-6647
                                  Marilyn Lucas, Lib.Techn.
Staff: Prof 1. Subjects: Medicine, nursing, dentistry, pharmacy, hospital administration. Holdings: 6000 books; 2308 bound periodical volumes; 90 video cassettes. Subscriptions: 185 journals and other serials. Services: Interlibrary loan; library not open to the public. Automated Operations: Computerized cataloging. Computerized Information Services: Access to MEDLINE. Networks/Consortia: Member of National Network of Libraries of Medicine - South Central Region.

★ 16909 ★
U.S. Air Force Hospital - Wilford Hall U.S.A.F. Medical Center - Medical Library (SGEL) (Med)
Lackland AFB   Phone: (512)670-7204
San Antonio, TX 78236-5300   Rita F. Smith, Med.Libn.
Staff: Prof 2; Other 4. Subjects: Medicine, nursing, dentistry, hospital administration, veterinary medicine. Holdings: 9800 books; 13,800 bound periodical volumes; 4900 AV programs; 1825 reels of microfilm of journals. Subscriptions: 900 journals and other serials. Services: Interlibrary loan; library not open to the public. Computerized Information Services: DIALOG Information Services, MEDLINE. Remarks: FAX: (512)670-7030. Staff: Barbara Farwell, Asst.Libn.

★ 16910 ★
U.S. Air Force Hospital Medical Center - Medical Library (IL-Scott AFB) (Med)
Scott AFB, IL 62225   Phone: (618)256-7437
                                  Blanche A. Savage, Dir.
Staff: Prof 1; Other 1. Subjects: Medicine, nursing, dentistry, allied health sciences. Holdings: 8000 books; 4633 bound periodical volumes; 1500 pamphlets and tapes. Subscriptions: 325 journals and other serials; 5 newspapers. Services: Interlibrary loan; library not open to the public. Computerized Information Services: Online systems. Networks/Consortia: Member of Areawide Hospital Library Consortium of Southwestern Illinois (AHLC).

★ 16911 ★
U.S. Air Force Medical Center - Medical Library (MS-Keesler AFB) (Med)
SGEL   Phone: (601)377-6249
Keesler AFB, MS 39534-5300   Sherry N. Nave, Med.Libn.
Staff: Prof 1; Other 1. Subjects: Medicine, surgery, nursing, dentistry, allied health sciences. Holdings: 5000 books; 4000 bound periodical volumes; 1100 volumes on microfilm. Subscriptions: 500 journals and other serials. Services: Interlibrary loan; library not open to the public. Computerized Information Services: NLM, DIALOG Information Services. Networks/Consortia: Member of Mississippi Biomedical Library Consortium (MBLC), National Network of Libraries of Medicine - Southeastern/Atlantic Region. Remarks: FAX: (601)377-6127.

★16912★
U.S. Air Force Medical Center - Medical Library (OH-Wright-Patterson AFB) (Med)
SGEL/Bldg. 830A
Wright-Patterson AFB, OH 45433-5300   Phone: (513)257-4506
Staff: Prof 2; Other 2. **Subjects:** Clinical medicine, dentistry, veterinary medicine, hospital administration. **Special Collections:** Tropical medicine; plastic surgery; military and aerospace medicine. **Holdings:** 9000 books; 11,000 bound periodical volumes; 4000 AV programs; 45,000 microfiche. **Subscriptions:** 800 journals and other serials. **Services:** Interlibrary loan; SDI; library open to members of affiliated institutions only. **Automated Operations:** Computerized cataloging, acquisitions, and serials. **Computerized Information Services:** MEDLINE, DIALOG Information Services, BRS Information Technologies, OCLC. **Networks/Consortia:** Member of National Network of Libraries of Medicine - Greater Midwest Region. **Staff:** Cathy Constance, Ref.Libn.; Mary Auer, Adm.Libn.

U.S. Air Force Museum
See: U.S. Air Force - Air Force Materiel Command - U.S. Air Force Museum (16804)

U.S. Alcohol, Drug Abuse and Mental Health Administration - National Institute on Drug Abuse
See: National Institute on Drug Abuse - Addiction Research Center Library (11209)

★16913★
U.S. Armed Forces Institute of Pathology - Ash Library (Med)
Walter Reed Army Medical Center
Bldg. 54, Rm. 4077   Phone: (202)576-2983
Washington, DC 20306-6000   Ruth Li, Libn.
Founded: 1951. **Staff:** Prof 2; Other 5. **Subjects:** Pathology, medicine. **Special Collections:** Audiovisual Collection; microscopic slide set collection (pathology); Yakolev Collection (brain pathology). **Holdings:** 6500 books; 18,000 bound periodical volumes; 2270 2x2's; 2425 glass slides; 3000 Massachusetts General Hospital sets. **Subscriptions:** 450 journals and other serials. **Services:** Interlibrary loan; library copying; open to the public. **Automated Operations:** Computerized cataloging. **Computerized Information Services:** DIALOG Information Services, OCLC; ILS (internal database). **Special Catalogs:** Audiovisual Catalog. **Remarks:** FAX: (202)576-2113.

★16914★
U.S. Armed Forces Radiobiology Research Institute (AFRRI) - Library Services (Med)
National Naval Medical Ctr., Bldg. 42   Phone: (301)295-0443
Bethesda, MD 20889-5145   Ilse Vada, Adm.Libn.
Founded: 1962. **Staff:** Prof 2; Other 1. **Subjects:** Radiobiology, radiation physics, neurobiology, nuclear medicine, behavioral science, veterinary medicine. **Holdings:** 10,000 books; 20,000 bound periodical volumes; 6000 technical reports; Atomic Bomb Casualty Commission technical reports; 50,000 microfiche of U.S. Government-funded technical reports. **Subscriptions:** 200 journals and other serials; 6 newspapers. **Services:** Interlibrary loan; copying; library open to outside users who must register at reception desk of institute. **Automated Operations:** Computerized cataloging, acquisitions, and circulation. **Computerized Information Services:** BRS Information Technologies, MEDLINE, OCLC. **Networks/Consortia:** Member of FEDLINK, National Network of Libraries of Medicine - Southeastern/Atlantic Region, Interlibrary Users Association (IUA). **Publications:** Current Awareness, monthly; Acquisitions List, monthly. **Special Catalogs:** Union List of Serials-National Naval Medical Center (book). **Remarks:** Institute is part of the U.S. Defense Nuclear Agency. **Staff:** Martha R. Harris, Cat.; Myron K. Allman, Circ.

★16915★
U.S. Armed Forces School of Music - Reference Library (Mus)
NAVPHI Base, Little Creek   Phone: (804)464-7501
Norfolk, VA 23521   James Treier, SSG.
Founded: 1941. **Staff:** Prof 4. **Subjects:** Music - analysis, conducting, composition, counterpoint, harmony, theory, instruments; jazz; military music. **Special Collections:** Rare books (copyrights from 1753). **Holdings:** 3800 books; 4900 scores; 7000 phonograph records; 8500 instrumental methods; 175 compact discs; 7000 solos; 900 song books; 1900 reel-to-reel tapes. **Subscriptions:** 30 journals and other serials. **Services:** Library open to the public with restrictions. **Remarks:** Alternate telephone number(s): 464-7511. **Staff:** SSG M. Herold; SSG J. Park; MU1 R. Kawamura.

★16916★
U.S. Armed Forces Staff College - Library (Mil)
7800 Hampton Blvd.   Phone: (804)444-5155
Norfolk, VA 23511-6097   Gail Nicula, Dir.
Founded: 1947. **Staff:** Prof 7; Other 10. **Subjects:** Military science, national and international affairs, history. **Special Collections:** Military administrative publications (3500). **Holdings:** 7900 bound periodical volumes; 110,000 other cataloged items; 22,000 microforms; 65 drawers and 766 boxes of archival materials; 24 drawers of pamphlets. **Subscriptions:** 670 journals and other serials; 17 newspapers. **Services:** Interlibrary loan; bibliographic and reference services to other U.S. government libraries; library not open to the public. **Computerized Information Services:** DIALOG Information Services, OCLC, DTIC; internal database. **Networks/Consortia:** Member of FEDLINK. **Publications:** Library Accessions List, weekly; Current Periodical Review, weekly - both for internal distribution only. **Special Indexes:** Reference Information File; subject index to periodicals in defense area (card). **Remarks:** FAX: (804)444-5120. College operates under the direction of U.S. Department of Defense - National Defense University. **Staff:** Sandra R. Byrn, Chf., Tech.Serv.; Carolyn B. Orr, Chf., Rd.Serv.

★16917★
U.S. Arms Control and Disarmament Agency - Library (Soc Sci)
Dept. of State Bldg., Rm. 5840
320 21st St., N.W.   Phone: (202)647-5969
Washington, DC 20451   Diane A. Ferguson, Libn.
Staff: Prof 1. **Subjects:** Arms control and disarmament - political, military, and economical. **Holdings:** 3000 volumes; documents of the Committee on Disarmament, 1962 to present; Congressional documents; ACDA research reports and publications. **Subscriptions:** 190 journals and other serials; 12 newspapers. **Services:** Interlibrary loan; copying; library open to the public by advance arrangement. **Computerized Information Services:** NEXIS, LEXIS, DTIC. **Publications:** Annual Report; World Military Expenditures and Arms Transfers; Documents on Disarmament, all annual. **Remarks:** FAX: (202)647-6928. **Also Known As:** ACDA.

U.S. Army - Aeromedical Research Laboratory
See: U.S. Army - Medical Research & Development Command - Aeromedical Research Laboratory (16988)

U.S. Army - Air Defense Artillery School
See: U.S. Army - TRADOC - Air Defense Artillery School (17004)

★16918★
U.S. Army - Armament, Munitions & Chemical Command - Armament Research, Development & Engineering Center - Scientific & Tech.Info. Branch - Information Center (Sci-Engr, Mil)
ARDEC, Bldg. 59   Phone: (201)724-2914
Picatinny Arsenal, NJ 07806-5000   Normand L. Varieur, Chf., Sci. & Tech.Info.Br.
Founded: 1929. **Staff:** Prof 7; Other 11. **Subjects:** Explosives, propellants, pyrotechnics, armament, chemistry, physics. **Special Collections:** Government-Industry Data Exchange Program Reports; Archive of Frankford Arsenal (Philadelphia, PA); Archive of Picatinny Arsenal. **Holdings:** 70,000 books; 20,000 bound periodical volumes; 550,000 technical reports. **Subscriptions:** 890 journals and other serials. **Services:** Interlibrary loan; copying (limited); center open to the public for reference use only on request. **Automated Operations:** Computerized public access catalog, cataloging, acquisitions, serials, and circulation. **Computerized Information Services:** DIALOG Information Services, DTIC, OCLC; internal database; DDN Network Information Center (electronic mail service). **Networks/Consortia:** Member of FEDLINK, Northwest Regional Library Cooperative. **Remarks:** FAX: (201)724-3044. Electronic mail address(es): VARIEUR@PICA.ARMY.MIL (DDN Network Information Center). **Staff:** Ismail Haznedari, Supv.Libn.; Diane Gordon, Supv.Libn.; Kwang Hee Strieff, ILL Libn.; Patricia Ays, Sys.Libn.; Lester Baskin, Search Libn.

★16919★
U.S. Army - Armament, Munitions & Chemical Command - Benet Laboratories - Technical Library (Sci-Engr, Mil)
Watervliet Arsenal
Attn: SMCAR-CCB-TL Bldg. 40-3   Phone: (518)266-5613
Watervliet, NY 12189-4050   Susan A. Macksey, Chf., Sci./Tech.Info.Br.
Staff: Prof 1; Other 6. **Subjects:** Metallurgy, physics, ordnance, artillery, cannon, mortars, composite materials, mechanics. **Holdings:** 9000 books;

5500 bound periodical volumes; 20,000 technical documents. **Subscriptions:** 400 journals and other serials. **Services:** Copying; SDI; library open to the public on request subject to regulations. **Automated Operations:** Computerized cataloging, acquisitions, and serials. **Computerized Information Services:** DIALOG Information Services, OCLC, DTIC; DDN Network Information Center (electronic mail service). **Networks/Consortia:** Member of FEDLINK, Capital District Library Council for Reference & Research Resources (CDLC). **Publications:** Library Accession List. **Remarks:** FAX: (518)266-5603. Electronic mail address(es): SMACKSEY@PICA.ARMY.MIL (DDN Network Information Center).

★16920★

U.S. Army - Armament, Munitions & Chemical Command - Chemical Research, Development & Engineering Center - Technical Library (Sci-Engr)
Aberdeen Proving Ground, MD　　　　Phone: (301)671-2936
21010-5423　　　　C.R. Anaclerio, Chf., Info.Serv.Div.
Founded: 1919. **Staff:** Prof 3; Other 7. **Subjects:** Chemistry, chemical engineering. **Holdings:** 4500 books; 8630 bound periodical volumes; 260,000 government reports; 10,000 film cartridges. **Subscriptions:** 350 journals and other serials. **Services:** Interlibrary loan; library not open to the public. **Automated Operations:** Computerized cataloging and serials. **Computerized Information Services:** OCLC, DIALOG Information Services. **Networks/Consortia:** Member of FEDLINK. **Publications:** Periodical Holding List, irregular. **Staff:** E.F. Gier, Ref.Libn.; D.C. Smith, Ref.Libn.; P.A. D'Eramo, Tech.Info.Spec.

★16921★

U.S. Army - Armament, Munitions & Chemical Command - Technical Library (Sci-Engr)
HDQ AMCCOM
AMSMC-IMF-L
Rock Island, IL 61299-6000　　　　Phone: (309)782-5031
　　　　Cecelia J. Thorn-Olson, Libn.
Founded: 1958. **Staff:** Prof 1; Other 2. **Subjects:** Weapons and ammunition, production engineering, manufacturing technology. **Holdings:** 12,773 books; 5740 bound periodical volumes; 13,430 technical reports; 76,507 reports on microfiche. **Subscriptions:** 504 journals and other serials; 9 newspapers. **Services:** Interlibrary loan; SDI; library open to the public with restrictions. **Computerized Information Services:** DIALOG Information Services, DTIC, USNI Military Database, OCLC, NEXIS; CD-ROMs (Computer Library, NTIS Database, HMIS Database). **Networks/Consortia:** Member of Quad Cities Libraries in Cooperation (Quad-LINC), FEDLINK. **Publications:** Accession list, monthly - for internal distribution only; Military Reading List, annual. **Special Indexes:** Subject index of materiel status records (card).

U.S. Army - Armor School
See: **U.S. Army - TRADOC** (17006)

★16922★

U.S. Army - Aviation Applied Technology Directorate - Technical Library (Sci-Engr)
Aviation Applied Technology
Directorate
U.S. Army Aviation Research &
Development Activity　　　　Phone: (804)878-2963
Fort Eustis, VA 23604-5577　　　　Edwin P. Knihnicki, Adm.Libn.
Founded: 1945. **Staff:** Prof 2. **Subjects:** Aeronautical engineering, Army aircraft, composite structures, low speed aeronautics, aircraft flight control systems, flight safety and research, V/STOL aircraft, rotary wing aircraft. **Holdings:** 6000 books and bound periodical volumes; 91,000 hard copy and microfiche technical reports; 1 million engineering drawings and technical data on Army aircraft. **Subscriptions:** 200 journals and other serials. **Services:** Interlibrary loan; library not open to the public. **Automated Operations:** Computerized cataloging and serials. **Computerized Information Services:** DIALOG Information Services, DTIC, OCLC. **Networks/Consortia:** Member of FEDLINK, Shared Bibliographic Input Network. **Staff:** Gary Robertson, Libn.

★16923★

U.S. Army - Aviation Systems Command - Library and Information Center (Mil)
4300 Goodfellow Blvd.　　　　Phone: (314)263-2345
St. Louis, MO 63120-1798　　　　Grace C. Feng, Supv.Libn.
Founded: 1954. **Staff:** Prof 3; Other 5. **Subjects:** Aircraft - systems, components, procurements, performance; aircraft/helicopter services; aeronautical engineering. **Holdings:** 9077 books; 705 bound periodical volumes; 38,000 federal administrative publications; 36,000 technical reports. **Subscriptions:** 205 journals and other serials. **Services:** Interlibrary loan (fee); copying; library open to the public with government authorization. **Automated Operations:** Computerized cataloging. **Computerized Information Services:** DIALOG Information Services, DTIC, Aerospace Online; electronic mail service. **Networks/Consortia:** Member of FEDLINK. **Publications:** Selected New Books; Selected New Technical Reports, both quarterly - both for internal distribution only; Library Bulletin. **Remarks:** FAX: 693-2030 (Autovon Line); (314)263-2030. **Staff:** Paul Y. Fritts, Tech.Serv.Libn.; Mattie L. Jones, Pub.Serv.Libn.

★16924★

U.S. Army - Belvoir Research, Development & Engineering Center - Technical Library (Sci-Engr, Mil)
Bldg. 315　　　　Phone: (703)704-2143
Fort Belvoir, VA 22060-5606　　　　Linda Cheung, Chf., Tech.Lib.Div.
Staff: Prof 3; Other 2. **Subjects:** Vehicle drives, camouflage, amphibious vehicles, electric vehicles, detection and detectors, construction equipment, engineering, environmental control, gasahol, army equipment. **Holdings:** 15,000 books; 200 bound periodical volumes; 10,000 technical reports; 200 test reports. **Subscriptions:** 300 journals and other serials; 5 newspapers. **Services:** Interlibrary loan; library not open to the public. **Automated Operations:** Computerized cataloging. **Computerized Information Services:** DTIC, DIALOG Information Services, BRS Information Technologies, OCLC, DTIC. **Remarks:** Alternate telephone number(s): 664-5339. FAX: (703)355-3739. **Staff:** Janice Pepper, Ref.Libn., Doc.Sect.

★16925★

U.S. Army - Bruce C. Clarke Engineering School - Library (Mil, Sci-Engr)
3202 N. Nebraska Ave.　　　　Phone: (314)563-7986
Fort Leonard Wood, MO 65473　　　　Arlene Shaw, Engr.Sch.Libn.
Founded: 1935. **Staff:** 4. **Subjects:** Civil and military engineering, military and American history. **Special Collections:** Corps of Engineers history; rare books on military engineering and history from 16th to 19th centuries; Fort Belvoir history; Army unit history. **Holdings:** 20,000 books; 5000 bound periodical volumes; 17,000 photographs; 60,000 military publications; 1000 AV programs. **Subscriptions:** 160 journals and other serials. **Services:** Interlibrary loan; copying; SDI. **Automated Operations:** Computerized acquisitions. **Computerized Information Services:** DIALOG Information Services, DTIC, OCLC; Profs (electronic mail service). **Networks/Consortia:** Member of TRADOC Library and Information Network (TRALINET), FEDLINK. **Publications:** New Books List, quarterly; Periodicals List, annual. **Special Catalogs:** Author, title, and subject card catalogs to Engineer Magazine and staff studies/student papers; accession number cards for DTIC documents. **Remarks:** FAX: (314)563-7983. **Staff:** Donald Horvath, Ref.Libn.; Claretta Crawford, Lib.Techn.; Beverly Hall, Lib.Techn.

★16926★

U.S. Army - Center of Military History - 7th Infantry Division & Fort Ord Museum - Library (Mil)
Attn: AFZW-PTM-MUSEUM　　　　Phone: (408)242-4905
Fort Ord, CA 93941-5111　　　　Don DeVere, Cur.
Founded: 1982. **Staff:** Prof 3. **Subjects:** History - Fort Ord, 7th Infantry Division, Army. **Holdings:** 550 books; 300 volumes on microfiche. **Services:** Library open to the public for reference use only by appointment only. **Staff:** Barbara Hennig-Loomis, Cur.; June D. Villa, Reg.

★16927★

U.S. Army - Center of Military History - U.S. Army Museum, Presidio of Monterey - Library (Mil)
CDR, HQs, 7th Infantry Division
ATTN: AFZW-PTM-O
Fort Ord　　　　Phone: (408)242-4905
Presidio of Monterey, CA 93941-5111　　　　June Villa, Registrar
Staff: Prof 1; Other 1. **Subjects:** Monterey County - local and military history, archeology; Presidio of Monterey history; U.S. Army history and equipment. **Holdings:** 100 books; 220 microfiche; 8 VF drawers of clippings and reports. **Services:** Library open to the public by appointment for reference use. **Remarks:** Museum and library located at Bldg. 113, Cpl. Ewing Rd.

U.S. Army - Chemical Research, Development & Engineering Center
See: U.S. Army - Armament, Munitions & Chemical Command - Chemical Research, Development & Engineering Center (16920)

U.S. Army - Chemical School
See: U.S. Army - TRADOC - Chemical School (17009)

U.S. Army - Cold Regions Research & Engineering Laboratory
See: U.S. Army - Corps of Engineers - Cold Regions Research & Engineering Laboratory (16935)

★ 16928 ★
U.S. Army - Command and General Staff College - Combined Arms Research Library (Mil)
Bell Hall   Phone: (913)684-4035
Fort Leavenworth, KS 66027-6900   Martha Davis, Dir.
Founded: 1882. **Staff:** 32. **Subjects:** Military art and science, military history, military doctrine, political science, management, leadership, international relations. **Special Collections:** Combined Arms Command and U.S. Army Command and General Staff College Archives; rare books collection (military arts and sciences). **Holdings:** 181,077 books; 9528 bound periodical volumes; 268,230 documents; 1.2 million microforms. **Subscriptions:** 1500 journals and other serials; 51 newspapers. **Services:** Interlibrary loan; copying; library open to the public with restrictions. **Automated Operations:** Computerized public access catalog, cataloging, acquisitions, and circulation. **Computerized Information Services:** DIALOG Information Services, NEXIS, OCLC, U.S. Naval Institute (USNI), DTIC; DDN Network Information Center (electronic mail service). **Networks/Consortia:** Member of TRADOC Library and Information Network (TRALINET), FEDLINK. **Remarks:** FAX: (913)684-7308. Electronic mail address(es): DAVIS@LEAV-EMH.ARMY.MIL (DDN Network Information Center). **Staff:** Bertina Byers, Chf., Info.Serv.; Dan Dorris, Chf., Sup.Serv.; Alice Blaser, Acq.Libn.; Elizabeth Snowe, Archv.

★ 16929 ★
U.S. Army - Communications-Electronics Command - R & D Technical Library (Sci-Engr, Comp Sci)
Bldg. 2700, Attn: ASQNC-ELC-IS-L-R
Myer Ctr.   Phone: (908)544-2553
Fort Monmouth, NJ 07703-5703   Margaret Borden, Chf.
Founded: 1942. **Staff:** Prof 2. **Subjects:** Electronics, electrical engineering, chemistry, physics, computer science. **Holdings:** 49,000 books; 24,000 bound periodical volumes; 180,000 technical documents. **Subscriptions:** 390 journals and other serials. **Services:** Library not open to the public. **Automated Operations:** Computerized cataloging and acquisitions. **Computerized Information Services:** DIALOG Information Services, OCLC, Books in Print, SCI. **Networks/Consortia:** Member of FEDLINK.

★ 16930 ★
U.S. Army - Communications-Electronics Command - Technical Library (Sci-Engr)
CDR, USACeCOM
ASQNC-EIC-IS-L-M (Technical Library)   Phone: (908)532-1298
Fort Monmouth, NJ 07703-5007   Jerri Hooks, Libn.
Founded: 1940. **Staff:** Prof 2; Other 2. **Subjects:** Mathematics, electrical engineering, personnel management, physics, electronic engineering, chemistry, photography, test engineering. **Special Collections:** Historical file of official Signal Corps literature; complete collection of Department of the Army literature on electronic equipment (cataloged by type designation). **Holdings:** 4000 books; 100,000 technical manuals and related publications; 1000 manufacturers' catalogs; 2500 pamphlets. **Subscriptions:** 300 journals and other serials. **Services:** Interlibrary loan; library not open to the public. **Staff:** Marion Clinton, Libn.

★ 16931 ★
U.S. Army - Communications-Electronics Museum (Mil)
Bldg. 275, Kaplan Hall   Phone: (908)532-2440
Fort Monmouth, NJ 07703   Mindy Rosewitz, Musm.Dir.
Founded: 1955. **Staff:** Prof 2; Other 1. **Subjects:** History of communication and electronic research and development at Fort Monmouth, 1917 to present. **Holdings:** 1200 volumes of out-of-print books, technical manuals, pamphlets; 1000 photographs. **Services:** Library open to qualified researchers. **Publications:** History of Fort Monmouth, 1917-1989. **Remarks:** Alternate telephone number(s): 532-1682.

★ 16932 ★
U.S. Army - Community & Family Support Center - Library Program Office (Mil, Info Sci)
Hoffman Bldg. I, Rm. 1450   Phone: (703)325-9700
Alexandria, VA 22331-0510   Nellie B. Strickland, Div.Chf.
Staff: Prof 3; Other 2. **Subjects:** Library science. **Holdings:** 200 books. **Subscriptions:** 27 journals and other serials. **Services:** Interlibrary loan; library not open to the public. **Computerized Information Services:** OCLC; PROFS (electronic mail service). **Networks/Consortia:** Member of FEDLINK. **Publications:** Monthly newsletter; army regulations and directives pertaining to the Army Library Program. **Remarks:** FAX: (703)325-2519. Electronic mail address(es): STRICKNO%AEDDCLA@MELPAREMH1.ARMY.MIL (PROFS). Branch is administrative headquarters for the U.S. Army Morale, Welfare & Recreation Library Program, and establishes overall policy and procedures for the administration of over 203 general libraries, branches, bookmobiles, and technical processing centers. It also selects and purchases books for installation general libraries to supplement local acquisitions, and provides reading materials for isolated troop units and maneuver areas. **Staff:** Barbara Christine, Chf.Acq.Libn.; Lee Porter, Asst.Acq.Libn.

★ 16933 ★
U.S. Army - Concepts Analysis Agency - Technical Library (Comp Sci)
8120 Woodmont Ave.   Phone: (301)295-1530
Bethesda, MD 20814-2797   Bettie Littlejohn, Chf.Libn.
Founded: 1973. **Staff:** Prof 1; Other 1. **Subjects:** Artificial intelligence, computer science, operations research, military history. **Holdings:** 3500 books; 7800 federal, military, and civilian documents. **Subscriptions:** 218 journals and other serials. **Services:** Interlibrary loan; library not open to the public. **Computerized Information Services:** DIALOG Information Services, DTIC, OCLC, USNI (U.S. Naval Institute) Military Database, UMI (University Microfilms International). **Networks/Consortia:** Member of FEDLINK. **Remarks:** FAX: (202)295-1834.

★ 16934 ★
U.S. Army - Corps of Engineers - Alaska District Library (Mil, Sci-Engr)
CENPA-IM-S-L
Box 898   Phone: (907)753-2527
Anchorage, AK 99506-0898   Barbara J. Berg, Libn.
Remarks: No further information was supplied by respondent.

★ 16935 ★
U.S. Army - Corps of Engineers - Cold Regions Research & Engineering Laboratory - Library (Sci-Engr)
72 Lyme Rd.   Phone: (603)646-4221
Hanover, NH 03755-1290   Nancy C. Liston, Libn.
Founded: 1952. **Staff:** Prof 2; Other 2. **Subjects:** Civil engineering, physics, geology, hydrology, meteorology, geography, mathematics, engineering. **Special Collections:** Snow, ice, and frozen ground; cold regions environment and materials. **Holdings:** 18,000 books; 150,000 documents, reports, pamphlets, periodical articles; 30,000 articles on 460 reels of microfilm; 145,000 items on microfiche; 70 videotapes. **Subscriptions:** 750 journals and other serials. **Services:** Interlibrary loan; copying; SDI; library open to the public with restrictions. **Automated Operations:** Computerized cataloging. **Computerized Information Services:** DIALOG Information Services, PFDS Online; CD-ROMs; produces COLD database (available commercially); DIALMAIL (electronic mail service). **Networks/Consortia:** Member of Northern Libraries Colloquy, Corps of Engineers Network. **Publications:** Library accession bulletin; CRREL publications list; Bibliography on Cold Regions Science and Technology, irregular - by request. **Remarks:** Alternate telephone number(s): 646-4238. FAX: (603)646-4695. **Staff:** Elisabeth Hoffmeister.

★ 16936 ★
U.S. Army - Corps of Engineers - Construction Engineering Research Laboratory - Martha A. Blake Memorial Library (Sci-Engr)
Interstate Research Park
PO Box 9005
Champaign, IL 61826-9005   Phone: (217)373-7217
Founded: 1969. **Staff:** Prof 1; Other 1. **Subjects:** Environmental and structural engineering, construction materials and management, computer applications, civil engineering. **Holdings:** 9900 books; 1000 bound periodical volumes; 19,000 technical reports. **Subscriptions:** 550 journals and other serials. **Services:** Interlibrary loan; copying; library open to the public for

reference use only. **Computerized Information Services:** DIALOG Information Services, STN International, OCLC, DTIC. **Networks/Consortia:** Member of FEDLINK, ILLINET. **Publications:** New Acquisitions - for internal distribution only; library brochure. **Special Catalogs:** Catalog of laboratory reports. **Remarks:** FAX: (217)373-7222. **Formerly:** Its H.B. Zackrison Memorial Library.

★ 16937 ★

U.S. Army - Corps of Engineers - Detroit District - Canal Park Marine Museum - Library (Trans)
600 Lake Ave., S.   Phone: (218)727-2497
Duluth, MN 55802   C. Patrick Labadie, Dir.
Founded: 1973. **Staff:** 4.5. **Subjects:** Great Lakes shipping and ports; U.S. Army Corps of Engineers. **Special Collections:** Lake Superior Harbor navigation charts (200 items). **Holdings:** 2500 books; 900 bound periodical volumes; 30 AV programs; photographs. **Subscriptions:** 18 journals and other serials; 5 newspapers. **Services:** Copying; library open to the public by appointment. **Remarks:** FAX: (218)720-5270.

★ 16938 ★

U.S. Army - Corps of Engineers - Detroit District - Technical and Legal Library (Sci-Engr)
Box 1027   Phone: (313)226-6231
Detroit, MI 48231-1027   Michelle Dyer-Hurdon, Dist.libn.
Staff: Prof 1. **Subjects:** Engineering, environment, construction, water resources development, Great Lakes navigation, harbor structures, environmental and flood control. **Special Collections:** Detroit district technical reports and studies; district projects slide collection. **Holdings:** 3500 books; 5000 annual reports; government documents; climatological data. **Subscriptions:** 100 journals and other serials. **Services:** Interlibrary loan; copying; library open to the public by appointment; requests for service by non-government employees should be by written communication. **Automated Operations:** Computerized cataloging. **Computerized Information Services:** OCLC, DIALOG Information Services; internal database. **Networks/Consortia:** Member of FEDLINK. **Remarks:** FAX: (313)226-2056.

U.S. Army - Corps of Engineers - Engineer Topographic Laboratories
See: U.S. Army - Corps of Engineers - Topographic Engineering Center (16964)

U.S. Army - Corps of Engineers - Engineer Waterway Experiment Station
See: U.S. Army - Engineer Waterways Experiment Station (16966)

★ 16939 ★

U.S. Army - Corps of Engineers - Fort Worth District - Technical Library (Sci-Engr, Law)
819 Taylor St.
Box 17300
Fort Worth, TX 76102-0300   Phone: (817)334-2150
Founded: 1950. **Staff:** Prof 1; Other 1. **Subjects:** Law; engineering - civil, electrical, mechanical, safety; finance; nuclear science; ecology; environment. **Special Collections:** Air and water pollution; water resources development. **Holdings:** 15,000 books; 20,000 technical reports; army regulations; congressional documents; industry standards and specifications on microfiche; Federal Register, 1969 to present. **Subscriptions:** 500 journals and other serials; 50 newspapers. **Services:** Interlibrary loan; library open to the public for reference use only. **Automated Operations:** Computerized cataloging. **Computerized Information Services:** DIALOG Information Services, OCLC. **Networks/Consortia:** Member of FEDLINK.

★ 16940 ★

U.S. Army - Corps of Engineers - Galveston District - Library (Sci-Engr)
Box 1229   Phone: (409)766-3196
Galveston, TX 77553   Sheila Duckworth
Founded: 1945. **Staff:** 1. **Subjects:** Civil engineering, construction and operation of public works for navigation, flood control, environment, recreation, water resources, soil mechanics, law. **Special Collections:** Annual Reports of the Chief of Engineers, 1871 to present; Congressional documents, 1900-1978. **Holdings:** 8500 books; 2900 other cataloged items. **Subscriptions:** 170 journals and other serials; 10 newspapers. **Services:** Interlibrary loan; library open to the public for reference use except for classified material. **Automated Operations:** Computerized cataloging, acquisitions, and serials. **Computerized Information Services:** DIALOG Information Services, OCLC; internal database. **Networks/Consortia:** Member of FEDLINK. **Remarks:** FAX: (409)766-3905.

★ 16941 ★

U.S. Army - Corps of Engineers - Headquarters - Library (Sci-Engr)
20 Massachusetts Ave., N.W.   Phone: (202)272-1010
Washington, DC 20314-1000   James Dorsey, Chf., Lib.Br.
Founded: 1935. **Staff:** Prof 5; Other 3. **Subjects:** Civil engineering, Corps of Engineers. **Special Collections:** Panama Canal; Corps of Engineers papers and memoirs (500 volumes). **Holdings:** 100,000 books; 1500 bound periodical volumes; 45,000 technical reports; 200,000 microforms. **Subscriptions:** 400 journals and other serials; 5 newspapers. **Services:** Interlibrary loan; library not open to the public. **Automated Operations:** Computerized public access catalog, cataloging, acquisitions, serials, and circulation. **Computerized Information Services:** DIALOG Information Services, LEXIS, NEXIS, LEGI-SLATE; OnTyme Electronic Message Network Service (electronic mail service). **Networks/Consortia:** Member of FEDLINK. **Remarks:** FAX: (202)504-4436. Telex: 272-0839. **Staff:** Myra Craig, Sys.; Steve Balanda, Ref.; Robin Baird, Law.

★ 16942 ★

U.S. Army - Corps of Engineers - Humphreys Engineer Center - Technical Support Library (Sci-Engr)
Kingman Bldg., Rm. 3C02   Phone: (703)355-2387
Fort Belvoir, VA 22060-5580   Lois J. Carey, Chf., Lib.Br.
Founded: 1983. **Staff:** Prof 4; Other 2. **Subjects:** Water resources, hydraulics, civil engineering, beach erosion, rivers and harbours, navigation, computer science, management. **Special Collections:** Beach erosion board reports. **Holdings:** 20,000 books; technical reports; microforms; AV materials. **Subscriptions:** 475 journals and other serials. **Services:** Interlibrary loan. **Computerized Information Services:** OCLC, DIALOG Information Services, DTIC, OCLC EPIC; CD-ROM; OnTyme Electronic Message Network Service (electronic mail service). **Networks/Consortia:** Member of FEDLINK. **Publications:** Journals holdings list; new acquisitions. **Remarks:** FAX: (703)355-2896. **Staff:** Linda Cullen, Ref.Libn.; Patricia Kennedy, Acq.Libn.; Maryanne Randall, Cat.; Renate Craft, Libn.

★ 16943 ★

U.S. Army - Corps of Engineers - Huntington District - Library (Sci-Engr, Env-Cons)
502 8th St.   Phone: (304)529-5713
Huntington, WV 25701-2070   Sandra V. Morris, Libn.
Staff: Prof 1; Other 1. **Subjects:** Water resource development, environmental science, civil engineering, hydrology, water quality. **Special Collections:** Oral history collection (150 hours). **Holdings:** 11,800 books; 260 bound periodical volumes. **Subscriptions:** 80 journals and other serials; 10 newspapers. **Services:** Interlibrary loan; copying; SDI; library open to the public. **Automated Operations:** Computerized cataloging. **Computerized Information Services:** DIALOG Information Services, Washington Alert Service, OCLC, LEXIS, NEXIS; OnTyme Electronic Message Network Service, Email (electronic mail services). **Networks/Consortia:** Member of FEDLINK. **Remarks:** Alternate telephone number(s): 529-5435.

★ 16944 ★

U.S. Army - Corps of Engineers - Hydrologic Engineering Center - Library (Sci-Engr)
609 2nd St.   Phone: (916)756-1104
Davis, CA 95616   Gloria Briley, Ck.
Subjects: Hydrology, hydrologic modeling, hydrologic engineering, water resources planning and management, hydraulics. **Holdings:** 500 books; 500 unbound reports; 1000 documents. **Subscriptions:** 15 journals and other serials. **Services:** Interlibrary loan; copying; SDI; library open to the public with restrictions. **Remarks:** FAX: (916)756-8250.

★ 16945 ★

U.S. Army - Corps of Engineers - Jacksonville District - Technical Library - CESAJ-IM-CL (Biol Sci, Sci-Engr)
400 W. Bay St., Rm. G-13D
P.O. Box 4970   Phone: (904)791-3643
Jacksonville, FL 32232-0019   Oriana Brown West, District Libn.
Founded: 1978. **Staff:** Prof 2; Other 3. **Subjects:** Civil engineering, environmental resources, fish and wildlife, geology, coastal erosion, storms and hurricanes. **Special Collections:** Cross Florida Barge Canal; Central and Southern Florida Project for Flood Control and Other Purposes. **Holdings:** 8000 books; 13,000 reports; Congressional documents, 1940-1970. **Subscriptions:** 200 journals and other serials. **Services:** Interlibrary loan; copying; library open to the public for reference use only. **Automated Operations:** Computerized cataloging and circulation. **Computerized Information Services:** DIALOG Information Services, SDS, BRS Information Technologies, OCLC, Institute for Scientific Information (ISI). **Networks/Consortia:** Member of FEDLINK. **Publications:** Corps of Engineers Project Reports. **Remarks:** FAX: (904)791-2256. **Staff:** Linda Smith, Cons./Cat.

★ 16946 ★
U.S. Army - Corps of Engineers - Los Angeles District - Technical Library (Sci-Engr)
Box 2711   Phone: (213)894-5313
Los Angeles, CA 90053-2325   Connie Castillo, Libn. (Engr.)
Staff: Prof 1; Other 1. **Subjects:** Engineering, water resources, flood control, shoreline preservation, navigation, environmental studies, dams, earthquakes. **Special Collections:** U.S. Army Corps of Engineers histories. **Holdings:** 8000 books; 2000 technical reports; Congressional materials on Rivers and Harbors Act. **Subscriptions:** 120 journals and other serials. **Services:** Interlibrary loan; library open to the public by appointment. **Automated Operations:** Computerized cataloging. **Computerized Information Services:** DIALOG Information Services. **Remarks:** Library located at 300 N. Los Angeles St., Los Angeles, CA 90012.

★ 16947 ★
U.S. Army - Corps of Engineers - Lower Mississippi Valley Division - Mississippi River Commission - Technical Library (Sci-Engr)
1413 Walnut St.
Box 80   Phone: (601)634-5880
Vicksburg, MS 39180   Sherrie L. Moran, Libn.
Founded: 1943. **Staff:** Prof 2; Other 1. **Subjects:** Flood control, navigation, hydraulics. **Special Collections:** Mississippi River Commission historical documents (700). **Holdings:** 49,000 books; 200 bound periodical volumes; 700 reels of microfilm; 5000 microfiche. **Subscriptions:** 725 journals and other serials; 17 newspapers. **Services:** Interlibrary loan; library open to the public for reference use only. **Automated Operations:** Computerized cataloging, acquisitions, circulation, and serials. **Computerized Information Services:** DIALOG Information Services, OCLC, LEXIS, NEXIS, CQ Washington Alert Service, LEGI-SLATE; CD-ROM; OnTyme Electronic Message Network Service (electronic mail service). **Networks/Consortia:** Member of FEDLINK. **Publications:** List of publications received, monthly; Current Acquisitions, monthly; Technical Database Guide, annual; Library Handbook, biennial; Periodical Directory, annual. **Remarks:** FAX: (601)634-7707. **Staff:** Bettie R. Wiley, Libn.

★ 16948 ★
U.S. Army - Corps of Engineers - Memphis District - Library (Sci-Engr)
B-202 Clifford Davis Federal Bldg.   Phone: (901)544-3584
Memphis, TN 38103-1894   Carolyn Smith, Libn.
Founded: 1932. **Staff:** Prof 1. **Subjects:** Civil engineering, flood control, water resources, environment, computers and data processing. **Special Collections:** Lower Mississippi Valley. **Holdings:** 7500 books; 60 bound periodical volumes; 132 microforms. **Subscriptions:** 150 journals and other serials; 12 newspapers. **Services:** Interlibrary loan; library open to the public for reference use only. **Automated Operations:** Computerized cataloging. **Computerized Information Services:** DIALOG Information Services, OCLC; internal database. **Networks/Consortia:** Member of FEDLINK. **Special Indexes:** Current periodical list; monthly accessions list. **Remarks:** FAX: (901)544-3600.

★ 16949 ★
U.S. Army - Corps of Engineers - New England Division - Civil & Legal Library (Sci-Engr)
Bldg. 116N
424 Trapelo Rd.   Phone: (617)647-8118
Waltham, MA 02254-9149   Timothy P. Hays, Chf.
Founded: 1948. **Staff:** Prof 1; Other 1. **Subjects:** Water resources; hydrology; engineering - geotechnical, structural, civil; ecology. **Special Collections:** New England River Basin Collection; Boston Forts and Fortification (maps from World War II); Rhode Island Forts (World War II); Maine Forts (1910-1916, World War I); New England Navigation Condition Surveys of Harbors (1860-1960); New England photographic construction files (1950-1970); New England Division of Civil Works projects (1950-1960; 16mm film reels). **Holdings:** 10,000 books; 50 bound periodical volumes; 7000 reports; 5000 Corps of Engineers reports including reports on dredged materials; 1000 hydrology reports. **Subscriptions:** 400 journals and other serials; 20 newspapers. **Services:** Interlibrary loan; copying; library open to the public with identification. **Automated Operations:** Computerized cataloging and serials (LS/2000). **Computerized Information Services:** DIALOG Information Services, OCLC, LEXIS, NEXIS. **Networks/Consortia:** Member of FEDLINK. **Remarks:** FAX: (617)647-8455.

★ 16950 ★
U.S. Army - Corps of Engineers - North Atlantic Division - Technical Library
26 Federal Plaza
New York, NY 10278
Defunct.

★ 16951 ★
U.S. Army - Corps of Engineers - Omaha District - Library (Sci-Engr)
215 N. 17th St.   Phone: (402)221-3230
Omaha, NE 68102-4978   Wynne A. Tysdal, Libn.
Staff: Prof 1; Other 2. **Subjects:** Engineering, water resources, law, environmental resources. **Holdings:** Agency regulations and directives. **Subscriptions:** 553 journals and other serials. **Services:** Interlibrary loan; library open to the public for reference use only. **Automated Operations:** Computerized cataloging. **Computerized Information Services:** DIALOG Information Services, OCLC; CORPSMAIL (electronic mail service). **Networks/Consortia:** Member of FEDLINK. **Remarks:** Library serves both the District Office and the Missouri River Division Office. Alternate telephone number(s): 221-3229. FAX: (402)221-3029.

★ 16952 ★
U.S. Army - Corps of Engineers - Philadelphia District - Technical Library (Sci-Engr)
2nd & Chestnut Sts.
Philadelphia, PA 19106   Phone: (215)597-3610
Founded: 1974. **Staff:** Prof 1. **Subjects:** Engineering - civil, environmental, coastal. **Special Collections:** U.S. Army Corps of Engineers - Philadelphia District technical reports; U.S. Army Corps of Engineers Laboratory technical reports (3500). **Holdings:** 7000 books; 2 VF drawers of standards; 200 microfiche; 2 VF drawers of information files. **Subscriptions:** 115 journals and other serials. **Services:** Interlibrary loan; library open to the public with restrictions. **Automated Operations:** Computerized cataloging. **Computerized Information Services:** DIALOG Information Services, OCLC. **Networks/Consortia:** Member of FEDLINK. **Publications:** Accessions lists, monthly; bibliographies.

★ 16953 ★
U.S. Army - Corps of Engineers - Portland District - Library (Sci-Engr)
333 S.W. 1st.
Box 2946   Phone: (503)326-6016
Portland, OR 97208-2946   Jan Hayden, District Libn.
Founded: 1938. **Staff:** Prof 1; Other 1. **Subjects:** Engineering, law. **Special Collections:** Portland District and North Pacific Division Corps of Engineers reports. **Holdings:** 10,000 books. **Subscriptions:** 767 journals and other serials; 10 newspapers. **Services:** Interlibrary loan; library open to the public for reference use only. **Automated Operations:** Computerized cataloging and ILL. **Computerized Information Services:** DIALOG Information Services, OCLC. **Remarks:** FAX: (503)326-5548.

★ 16954 ★
U.S. Army - Corps of Engineers - Rock Island District - Technical Library (Sci-Engr)
Clock Tower Bldg.
PO Box 2004   Phone: (309)788-6361
Rock Island, IL 61204-2004   Nancy J. Larson-Bloomer, Libn. (Engr.)
Founded: 1975. **Staff:** Prof 1. **Subjects:** Civil engineering, hydraulics/locks and dams, flood plain management, construction, soil mechanics, environmental analysis. **Special Collections:** Hydraulics; Waterways Experiment Station technical reports; Water Resources Developments; construction. **Holdings:** 10,000 books; 15,000 technical reports; 5000 microfiche. **Subscriptions:** 150 journals and other serials. **Services:** Interlibrary loan; library open to the public by appointment. **Automated Operations:** Computerized cataloging and ILL (LS/2000). **Computerized Information Services:** DIALOG Information Services, OCLC, DTIC. **Networks/Consortia:** Member of FEDLINK, Quad Cities Libraries in Cooperation (Quad-LINC). **Publications:** Periodicals. **Remarks:** FAX: (309)788-9978.

★ 16955 ★
U.S. Army - Corps of Engineers - Sacramento District - Technical Information Center (Sci-Engr, Plan)
650 Capitol Mall, Rm. 7007 Phone: (916)557-6658
Sacramento, CA 95814-4794 Beatrice Alger, Dist.Libn.
Staff: Prof 1; Other 2. **Subjects:** Water, hydrology, hydraulics, environment, recreation planning, geology, architecture, construction. **Special Collections:** Annual Reports to the Chief of Engineers. **Holdings:** 25,000 volumes. **Subscriptions:** 220 journals and other serials; 5 newspapers. **Services:** Interlibrary loan; copying (limited); center open to the public with restrictions. **Automated Operations:** Computerized cataloging, acquisitions, circulation, and serials (LS/2000). **Computerized Information Services:** DIALOG Information Services, FAR On-line, OCLC EPIC; CD-ROM. **Networks/Consortia:** Member of FEDLINK. **Publications:** Library Bulletin, monthly - for internal distribution only. **Remarks:** FAX: (916)557-7843.

★ 16956 ★
U.S. Army - Corps of Engineers - St. Louis District - CASU Library and Information Services (Env-Cons, Sci-Engr)
1222 Spruce St. Phone: (314)539-6110
St. Louis, MO 63103-2822 Dr. Arthur R. Taylor, Chf.Libn.
Founded: 1968. **Staff:** Prof 1; Other 2. **Subjects:** Civil engineering, water resources, environment, wildlife management, recreation. **Holdings:** 9200 books; 6000 technical reports; microfilm. **Subscriptions:** 410 journals and other serials; 60 newspapers. **Services:** Interlibrary loan; copying; library open to the public. **Automated Operations:** Computerized cataloging, acquisitions, serials, and circulation. **Computerized Information Services:** OCLC, EPIC, DIALOG Information Services. **Networks/Consortia:** Member of FEDLINK. **Publications:** Periodical Holdings List, annual; Library Users Guide; New Books List, quarterly. **Special Catalogs:** Microfiche catalog of book and report collection. **Remarks:** FAX: (314)331-8677.

★ 16957 ★
U.S. Army - Corps of Engineers - St. Paul District - Map Files (Geog-Map)
1421 U.S. Post Office & Custom House Phone: (612)220-0560
St. Paul, MN 55101-1479 Al Santo, Lib.Techn.
Staff: Prof 1; Other 1. **Subjects:** Engineering, water resources, flood control, inland waterways, environmental planning. **Special Collections:** Mississippi River Continuous Survey, 1937 to present (83 sheets); Mississippi River Commission Charts, 1898 and 1915 (278 sheets); Brown Surveys of the Mississippi River, 1930 (129 sheets). **Holdings:** 70,000 engineering drawings; 10,000 maps and charts; 50,000 aerial photographs; 1000 field books. **Services:** Copying; files open to the public with restrictions. **Automated Operations:** Computerized circulation.

★ 16958 ★
U.S. Army - Corps of Engineers - St. Paul District - Technical Library (Sci-Engr)
1421 U.S. Post Office & Custom House Phone: (612)220-0680
St. Paul, MN 55101 Jean Marie Schmidt, Libn.
Founded: 1970. **Staff:** Prof 1. **Subjects:** Engineering, hydrology, water resources, dam construction, environmental studies, military history. **Special Collections:** Chief of Engineers Annual Reports, 1867 to present; Army Technical Manuals; Waterborne Commerce Statistics. **Holdings:** 6360 books; 9090 government reports, including Waterway Experiment Station reports and U.S. Geological Survey reports. **Subscriptions:** 391 journals and other serials. **Services:** Interlibrary loan; library open to the public for reference use only. **Computerized Information Services:** DIALOG Information Services, OCLC, DATANET. **Networks/Consortia:** Member of FEDLINK, Metronet. **Remarks:** FAX: (612)290-2256.

★ 16959 ★
U.S. Army - Corps of Engineers - Savannah District - Technical Library (Sci-Engr)
Box 889 Phone: (912)944-5462
Savannah, GA 31402-0889 Joseph T. Page, Chf.
Founded: 1968. **Staff:** Prof 1. **Subjects:** Engineering, geology, legislation, environmental and architectural science. **Holdings:** 6000 books; 7000 technical reports; 16,920 microforms, including 3000 reels of microfilm; technical standards and specifications. **Subscriptions:** 897 journals and other serials; 32 journals and other serials. **Services:** Interlibrary loan; copying; SDI; library open to the public at librarian's discretion. **Automated Operations:** Computerized cataloging. **Computerized Information Services:** DIALOG Information Services, LEXIS, NEXIS, OCLC. **Networks/Consortia:** Member of FEDLINK. **Remarks:** FAX: (912)944-5350.

★ 16960 ★
U.S. Army - Corps of Engineers - Seattle District - Library (Sci-Engr)
Box 3755 Phone: (206)764-3728
Seattle, WA 98124-2255 Pat J. Perry, District Libn.
Founded: 1940. **Staff:** Prof 2; Other 1. **Subjects:** Engineering; environment; hydraulics; construction - heating plant, military, marine; toxic cleanup; law. **Special Collections:** Army Field Law Library (9000 volumes); Eng/Tech Collection; Learning Center (self-guided classes; 1000 videotapes, audio cassettes, other AV programs; software tutors). **Holdings:** 12,000 books and reports; 30,000 technical reports on microfiche; 20,000 35mm slides; 5 drawers of pamphlets. **Subscriptions:** 400 journals and other serials; 25 newspapers. **Services:** Interlibrary loan; copying (limited); library open to the public for reference use only. **Automated Operations:** Computerized public access catalog, circulation, and serials (DataTrek). **Computerized Information Services:** DIALOG Information Services, DTIC, OCLC. **Networks/Consortia:** Member of FEDLINK. **Special Indexes:** District slide file index. **Remarks:** FAX: (206)764-6529; (206)764-3796. **Staff:** May Gin Carrell, Asst.Libn.

★ 16961 ★
U.S. Army - Corps of Engineers - South Atlantic Division - Technical Library (Sci-Engr)
77 Forsyth St., S.W., Rm. 313 Phone: (404)331-6620
Atlanta, GA 30335-6801 James D. Chestnut, Div.Libn.
Subjects: Civil engineering, water resources. **Holdings:** 3625 books. **Subscriptions:** 104 journals and other serials. **Services:** Interlibrary loan; copying; library open to the public for reference use only. **Automated Operations:** Computerized cataloging. **Computerized Information Services:** OCLC, DIALOG Information Services. **Networks/Consortia:** Member of FEDLINK, Georgia Online Database (GOLD).

★ 16962 ★
U.S. Army - Corps of Engineers - South Pacific Division - Library (Sci-Engr)
630 Sansome St., Rm. 720 Phone: (415)705-1520
San Francisco, CA 94111-2206 Mary G. Anderson, Div.Libn.
Staff: Prof 1. **Subjects:** Civil engineering, water resources. **Special Collections:** Corps of Engineers annual reports; Waterways Experiment Station Reports. **Holdings:** 4600 books; 10,000 bound reports. **Subscriptions:** 191 journals and other serials. **Services:** Interlibrary loan; library open to the public for reference use only. **Automated Operations:** Computerized cataloging. **Computerized Information Services:** DIALOG Information Services, OCLC. **Networks/Consortia:** Member of FEDLINK.

★ 16963 ★
U.S. Army - Corps of Engineers - Southwestern Division - Technical Library
1114 Commerce St.
Dallas, TX 75242-0216
Defunct.

★ 16964 ★
U.S. Army - Corps of Engineers - Topographic Engineering Center - Scientific & Technical Information Center (Sci-Engr)
Fort Belvoir, VA 22060-5546 Phone: (703)355-2656
Mildred L. Stiger, Chf.
Staff: Prof 1; Other 5. **Subjects:** Geodesy, photogrammetry, remote sensing, robotics, mapping. **Holdings:** 11,200 volumes; 390 bound periodical volumes; 2700 technical reports; 1923 microfiche. **Subscriptions:** 425 journals and other serials. **Services:** Interlibrary loan; copying; center open to government agencies and industry. **Automated Operations:** Computerized public access catalog, cataloging, and circulation. **Computerized Information Services:** DIALOG Information Services, DTIC, OCLC, SearchMaestro. **Networks/Consortia:** Member of FEDLINK. **Remarks:** FAX: (703)355-3176. **Formerly:** U.S. Army - Corps of Engineers - Engineer Topographic Laboratories. **Staff:** Dot K. Murphy.

★ 16965 ★
U.S. Army - Defense Logistics Agency - Defense Distribution Region West, Sharp Site - Community Recreation Library
Lathrop, CA 95331-5214
Defunct.

U.S. Army - Dugway Proving Ground
See: **Commander U.S. Army - Dugway Proving Ground** (4048)

U.S. Army - Engineer Topographic Laboratories
See: **U.S. Army - Corps of Engineers - Topographic Engineering Center**
(16964)

★ 16966 ★
U.S. Army - Engineer Waterways Experiment Station - Coastal
Engineering Information Analysis Center (Sci-Engr)
3909 Halls Ferry Rd.   Phone: (601)634-2012
Vicksburg, MS 39180-6199   Fred Camfield, Dir.
Subjects: Beach erosion, flood and storm protection, coastal and offshore
structures, navigation structures. **Holdings:** Center acts as a central
repository for the Corps of Engineers data collection under the field data
collection program for coastal engineering. The data includes wave statistics,
coastal currents, beach profiles, and aerial photographs. Center is supported
by holdings in the Research Library. **Services:** Interlibrary loan.
Publications: CERCular (information bulletin), quarterly; annotated
bibliography of publications of the Coastal Engineering Research Center.
Remarks: Engineer Waterways Experiment Station is part of U.S. Army -
Corps of Engineers.

★ 16967 ★
U.S. Army - Engineer Waterways Experiment Station - Concrete
Technology Information Analysis Center (Sci-Engr)
3909 Halls Ferry Rd.   Phone: (601)634-3264
Vicksburg, MS 39180-6199   Bryant Mather, Dir.
Subjects: Concrete materials and properties, concrete tests and analysis,
concrete construction, cements and pozzolans, reinforced concrete,
waterstops and jointing materials, grouts and grouting, adhesives and
coatings, corrosion in steel and concrete. **Holdings:** Center is supported by
holdings of the Research Library. **Services:** Interlibrary loan; copying.
Publications: List of publications - available on request.

★ 16968 ★
U.S. Army - Engineer Waterways Experiment Station - Hydraulic
Engineering Information Analysis Center (Sci-Engr)
3909 Halls Ferry Rd.   Phone: (601)634-2608
Vicksburg, MS 39180-6199   Bobby J. Brown, Dir.
Subjects: Hydraulics - river, harbor, tidal, closed conduit; flood control
structures; navigation structures; harbor protective structures; underwater
shock effects. **Holdings:** Center is supported by holdings in the Research
Library. **Services:** Interlibrary loan; copying.

★ 16969 ★
U.S. Army - Engineer Waterways Experiment Station - Pavements &
Soil Trafficability Information Analysis Center (Sci-Engr)
3909 Halls Ferry Rd.   Phone: (601)634-2734
Vicksburg, MS 39180-6199   Gerald W. Turnage, Dir.
Subjects: Soil trafficability, mobility, pavements, terrain evaluation.
Holdings: Center is supported by the collection of holdings in the Research
Library. **Services:** Interlibrary loan; copying. **Publications:** List of
publications - available on request.

★ 16970 ★
U.S. Army - Engineer Waterways Experiment Station - Research
Library (Sci-Engr)
3909 Halls Ferry Rd.   Phone: (601)634-2543
Vicksburg, MS 39180-6199   Carol McMillin, Chf., Res.Lib.
Founded: 1933. **Staff:** Prof 12; Other 15. **Subjects:** Hydraulics, soil
mechanics, concrete, weapons effects, mobility of vehicles, environmental
studies, explosive excavation, pavements, geology, computer science.
Holdings: 500,000 volumes, including microforms. **Subscriptions:** 1450
journals and other serials. **Services:** Interlibrary loan; copying; SDI; center
open to the public with restrictions. **Automated Operations:** Computerized
cataloging. **Computerized Information Services:** DTIC, DIALOG
Information Services, OCLC. **Publications:** List of Post Authorization
Reports, irregular; List of Translations of Waterways Experiment Station,
irregular - both to Corps of Engineers; List of Publications of the U.S. Army
Engineer Waterways Experiment Station, irregular; List of Translations of

Foreign Literature on Hydraulics, irregular; Bibliography on Tidal
Hydraulics, irregular; WES Engineering Computer Programs Library
Catalog, irregular - to Corps of Engineers; bibliographies. **Remarks:** FAX:
(601)634-2542. Supports the five Department of Defense Information
Analysis Centers established at the Waterways Experiment Station, which
do not have separate collections. **Staff:** Alfrieda Clark, Libn.; Hollis
Landrum, Info.Tech.Spec.; Don Kirby, Ref.Libn.; Helen Ingram, Ref.Libn.;
Debbie Carpenter, Chf., Tech.Ref. Unit; Paul Taccarino, Ref.Libn.;
Katherine Kennedy, Ref.Libn.; Richard Hancock, Cat.; Marita Sanders,
Chf., Tech.Proc.Acq. Unit; Jimmie Perry, Ref.Libn.

★ 16971 ★
U.S. Army - Engineer Waterways Experiment Station - Soil Mechanics
Information Analysis Center (Sci-Engr)
3909 Halls Ferry Rd.   Phone: (601)634-3376
Vicksburg, MS 39180-6199   Robert Larson
Subjects: Soil mechanics, soil dynamics, rock mechanics, foundation
engineering, earthquake engineering, engineering geology, earth dams,
subgrades. **Holdings:** Center is supported by holdings in the Research
Library. **Services:** Interlibrary loan; copying. **Publications:** Proceedings of
Symposium on Applications of the Finite Element Method in Geotechnical
Engineering; Microthesaurus of Soil Mechanics Terms; Evaluation
Statements and Abstracts of Recent Acquisitions on Soil Mechanics and
Related Subjects, bimonthly.

U.S. Army - Environmental Health Agency
See: **U.S. Army - Health Services Command - Environmental Hygiene**
Agency (16976)

★ 16972 ★
U.S. Army - Explosives Safety Technical Library (Mil)
USADACS
Attn: SMCAC-ESM   Phone: (815)273-8772
Savanna, IL 61074-9639   Jacqueline S. Bey
Founded: 1989. **Staff:** Prof 1; Other 1. **Subjects:** Ammunition, munitions,
explosives safety, accidents, incidents, chemicals, missiles, rockets. **Special**
Collections: Encyclopedia of Explosives and Related Items; Hazardous
Components Safety Data Sheets (HCSDS) aperture cards; DoD Explosives
Safety Board Minutes (archival holdings in microfilm reels). **Holdings:** 268
books; 2358 technical reports; 2800 regulatory publications. **Subscriptions:**
31 journals and other serials; 2 newspapers. **Services:** Interlibrary loan;
copying; library provides reference and bibliographic services to U.S.
government agencies. **Computerized Information Services:** DTIC,
DIALOG Information Services; explosives safety and accident/incident
data catalog (internal database); DDN Network Information Center
(electronic mail service). **Networks/Consortia:** Member of FEDLINK.
Publications: Accession list, monthly - for internal distribution only.
Remarks: FAX: (815)273-8769. Electronic mail address(es):
techlib@savanna-emhl.army.mil (DDN Network Information Center)

U.S. Army - Field Artillery School
See: **U.S. Army - TRADOC - Field Artillery School** (17010)

U.S. Army - Field Law Library
See: **U.S. Army - Corps of Engineers - Seattle District - Library** (16960)

★ 16973 ★
U.S. Army - Forces Command - Fort Meade Museum - Library (Mil)
Attn: AFKA-ZI-PTS-MU   Phone: (301)677-7054
Fort George G. Meade, MD 20755-5094   Robert S. Johnson, Cur.
Founded: 1963. **Staff:** 3. **Subjects:** U.S. and foreign army material culture
studies, general military history. **Special Collections:** Photographs of World
Wars I and II; weapons, uniforms and accoutrements, and other
memorabilia of the army. **Holdings:** 1000 books; 2000 Ft. Meade and 1st
U.S. Army archival materials. **Services:** Copying; library open to the public
by appointment. **Remarks:** Alternate telephone number(s): 677-6966.

★ 16974 ★
U.S. Army - Headquarters Services - Washington - Pentagon Library
(Mil)
The Pentagon, Rm. 1 A 518   Phone: (703)695-5346
Washington, DC 20310-6000   Louise Nyce, Dir.
Founded: 1850. **Staff:** Prof 18; Other 25. **Subjects:** Military science, law, political science, history, computer science, international affairs, technology, social science, management, administration. **Special Collections:** Army studies; regulatory publications; legislative histories; army unit histories. **Holdings:** 160,000 volumes; 435,000 documents. **Subscriptions:** 1500 journals and other serials. **Services:** Interlibrary loan; copying; SDI; library open to Department of Defense personnel only. **Automated Operations:** Computerized public access catalog, cataloging, acquisitions, serials, and circulation. **Computerized Information Services:** BRS Information Technologies, DIALOG Information Services, DMS/ONLINE, WESTLAW, LEXIS, NEXIS, DTIC, CQ Washington Alert Service, FBIS (Foreign Broadcast Information Service), LEGI-SLATE, ABI/INFORM, University Microfilms International (UMI), OCLC. **Networks/Consortia:** Member of FEDLINK. **Publications:** Selected Current Acquisitions List, monthly; subject bibliographies, irregular; briefing guides, irregular; Checklist of Periodical Holdings, annual. **Remarks:** FAX: (703)693-6543. **Staff:** Kathryn Earnest, Chf., Res. & Info.Div.; Irene Miner, Chf., Per.Br.; Mary Bob Vick, Chf., Tech./Automated Serv.Div.; Paula Vincent, Chf., Cat.Br.; Gail Henderson, Chf., Army Stud.Br.; Al Hardin, Chf., Law Br.; Menandra Whitmore, Chf., Acq.Br.

★ 16975 ★
U.S. Army - Health Services Command - Academy of Health Sciences -
Stimson Library (Med)
Bldg. 2840, Rm. 106   Phone: (512)221-8532
Fort Sam Houston, TX 78234-6100   Norma L. Sellers, Chf.Libn.
Founded: 1932. **Staff:** Prof 3; Other 6. **Subjects:** Military medicine, nursing, health care administration, management, psychiatry, veterinary medicine. **Holdings:** 34,000 books; 16,000 bound periodical volumes; 5800 technical reports; 2500 archival materials; 3500 items on microfilm; 1557 AV programs. **Subscriptions:** 560 journals and other serials. **Services:** Interlibrary loan; library open to the public for reference use only. **Computerized Information Services:** DIALOG Information Services, DTIC, MEDLINE. **Networks/Consortia:** Member of Council of Research & Academic Libraries (CORAL), Health Oriented Libraries of San Antonio (HOLSA). **Publications:** List of periodical holdings. **Staff:** Constance Baker, Ref.Libn.; Kay D. Livingston, Tech.Serv.

★ 16976 ★
U.S. Army - Health Services Command - Environmental Hygiene
Agency - Library (Med)
Bldg. E1570   Phone: (301)671-4236
Aberdeen Proving Ground, MD 21010   Krishan S. Goel, Libn.
Founded: 1955. **Staff:** Prof 1; Other 2. **Subjects:** Occupational medicine, safety and health; chemistry and toxicology; audiology; medical entomology; laser, microwave, and radiological safety and health; air and water pollution; sanitary engineering. **Special Collections:** National Institute for Occupational Safety and Health (NIOSH) and Environmental Protection Agency (EPA) reports. **Holdings:** 12,000 books; 8,000 bound periodical volumes; 8400 R&D reports; 3000 microfiche. **Subscriptions:** 400 journals and other serials. **Services:** Interlibrary loan; copying; SDI. **Automated Operations:** Computerized serials. **Computerized Information Services:** OCLC, DIALOG Information Services, MEDLINE.

U.S. Army - Health Services Command - Medical Research Institute of
Chemical Defense
See: U.S. Army - Medical Research & Development Command - Medical Research Institute of Chemical Defense (16990)

U.S. Army - Hydrologic Engineering Center
See: U.S. Army - Corps of Engineers - Hydrologic Engineering Center (16944)

U.S. Army - Infantry School
See: U.S. Army - TRADOC - Infantry School (17012)

★ 16977 ★
U.S. Army - Information Systems Command - Technical Library (Sci-
Engr, Info Sci)
Greely Hall, Rm. 2102
Attn: ASOP-DO-TL
Fort Huachuca, AZ 85613   Phone: (602)538-6202
Staff: 3. **Subjects:** Telecommunication, electronic engineering, computer science, electrical engineering, mathematics, optics. **Special Collections:** Department of Defense directives, instructions, and publications; Defense Communication Agency circulars; Fort Huachuca regulations and pamphlets; U.S. Army technical manuals; IEEE conferences. **Holdings:** 7800 books; 12,201 hard copy reports; 250,000 documents in microform; 1200 VSMF (Visual Search Microfilm File) microfilms; 3600 periodicals on microfilm; 25,000 military documents. **Subscriptions:** 512 journals and other serials; 16 newspapers. **Services:** Interlibrary loan; copying; library open to active and retired military and Department of Defense personnel. **Automated Operations:** Computerized circulation. **Computerized Information Services:** DIALOG Information Services, DTIC. **Networks/Consortia:** Member of FEDLINK. **Formerly:** U.S. Army Garrison - Technical Library.

★ 16978 ★
U.S. Army - Information Systems Software Center Command - Technical
Library (Comp Sci)
Stop H-9   Phone: (703)285-9872
Fort Belvoir, VA 22060-5456   Grace C. Corbin, Tech.Info.Spec.
Founded: 1968. **Staff:** Prof 1. **Subjects:** Data processing, computers, computer programming, operations research, functionally-oriented language, management information systems. **Holdings:** 2500 books; 3450 vendor manuals on computer hardware and programming; 1700 technical reports, hardcopy and microfiche; 1100 regulatory and standardization texts for federal and military ADP operations. **Subscriptions:** 70 journals and other serials. **Services:** Interlibrary loan; video self-study administration; library open to Department of Defense personnel for reference use only. **Computerized Information Services:** Internal database.

U.S. Army - The Institute of Heraldry
See: U.S. Army - Total Army Personnel Center - Personnel Service Support Directorate - The Institute of Heraldry (17003)

★ 16979 ★
U.S. Army - Institute of Surgical Research on Burns - Library (Med)
Bldg. 2653
Fort Sam Houston, TX 78234-5012   Phone: (512)221-4559
Subjects: Burns, scalds, surgical research. **Holdings:** 8800 volumes.

U.S. Army - Intelligence Center & School
See: U.S. Army - TRADOC - Intelligence Center & School (17013)

U.S. Army - Intelligence School, Devens
See: U.S. Army - TRADOC - Intelligence School, Devens (17014)

★ 16980 ★
U.S. Army - Intelligence & Threat Analysis Center - Library (Mil)
Attn: IAAII-PIL
Bldg. 213
Washington Navy Yard   Phone: (202)479-1964
Washington, DC 20374-2136   Dean A. Burns, Chf., Lib.
Staff: Prof 9; Other 5. **Subjects:** Military intelligence. **Special Collections:** Army threat documents. **Holdings:** Figures not available. **Subscriptions:** 580 journals and other serials; 20 newspapers. **Services:** Interlibrary loan (limited); facility not open to the public. **Automated Operations:** Computerized public access catalog, cataloging, and circulation. **Computerized Information Services:** DIALOG Information Services, NEXIS, INFOSOUTH. **Remarks:** Requests for classified documents should be submitted through channels. Contractors must submit requests through their contract monitors. All requests must include certification of need to know. FAX: (202)488-8846. **Staff:** Carol Norton, Chf., Ref.Sect.; Richard Cooper, Chf., Tech.Sect.; Holly Wilson, Libn.; Carol Wong, Libn.; Anita Parins, Libn.; Thomas Greene, Libn.; Betti Mack, Libn.

★ 16981 ★
U.S. Army - JFK Special Warfare Center & School - Marquat Memorial Library (Mil, Soc Sci)
Rm. 140, Kennedy Hall   Phone: (919)432-6503
Fort Bragg, NC 28307   Frank M. London, Supv.Libn.
Founded: 1952. **Staff:** Prof 2. **Subjects:** Military assistance, international studies, unconventional warfare, political science. **Holdings:** 45,000 volumes; pamphlets; documents; Human Relations Area Files on microfiche. **Subscriptions:** 274 journals and other serials; 20 newspapers. **Services:** Interlibrary loan; copying; library open to the public for reference use only. **Automated Operations:** Computerized cataloging and circulation. **Computerized Information Services:** OCLC, DTIC. **Networks/Consortia:** Member of FEDLINK. **Publications:** Accession List; Periodical Holdings List; library guide. **Remarks:** Alternate telephone number(s): 432-9222. **Staff:** Fred Fuller, Ref.Libn.; Mary Grooms, ILL.

★ 16982 ★
U.S. Army - Laboratory Command - Harry Diamond Laboratories - Technical Library (Sci-Engr)
2800 Powder Mill Rd. (SLCHD-SD-TL)   Phone: (301)394-2536
Adelphi, MD 20783-1197   Barbra L. McLaughlin, Chf.
Founded: 1959. **Staff:** Prof 4; Other 4. **Subjects:** Electronics, physics, engineering, chemistry, mathematics. **Holdings:** 34,900 books; 19,697 bound periodical volumes; 100,000 technical reports. **Subscriptions:** 752 journals and other serials. **Services:** Interlibrary loan; branch not open to the public. **Automated Operations:** Computerized cataloging. **Computerized Information Services:** DIALOG Information Services, OCLC, PFDS Online, DTIC. **Publications:** Accession List. **Remarks:** FAX: (301)394-1465.

★ 16983 ★
U.S. Army - Laboratory Command - Materials Technology Laboratory - Technical Library (Sci-Engr, Mil)
SLCMT-TML   Phone: (617)923-5460
Watertown, MA 02172-0001   M. Jims Murphy, Chf., Tech.Lib.
Founded: 1920. **Staff:** Prof 3; Other 3. **Subjects:** Materials science, mechanics, composite materials, metallurgy, nondestructive testing, chemistry, engineering, ceramics, polymer chemistry, military science, physics. **Holdings:** 25,000 books; 20,000 bound periodical volumes; 33,000 documents; 47,000 documents on microfiche; 913 volumes on microfiche/microfilm. **Subscriptions:** 650 journals and other serials; 15 newspapers. **Services:** Interlibrary loan; library not open to the public. **Computerized Information Services:** DIALOG Information Services, NASA/RECON, BRS Information Technologies, DTIC, OCLC. **Networks/Consortia:** Member of NELINET, Inc., FEDLINK. **Publications:** Monographs, annotated bibliographies, both irregular. **Staff:** Dolores R. Allen, Libn.; Judy H. Kesserich, Libn.

U.S. Army - Language Training Facility
See: U.S. Army - TRADOC - Language Training Facility (17015)

★ 16984 ★
U.S. Army - Letterman Army Institute of Research - Herman Memorial Library (Med)
Bldg. 1110
Presidio of San Francisco   Phone: (415)561-2600
San Francisco, CA 94129-6800   Richard Kempton
Founded: 1974. **Staff:** Prof 1; Other 2.5. **Subjects:** Biomedicine, nutrition. **Special Collections:** Military medical history collection. **Holdings:** 5400 books; 20,000 bound periodical volumes; 2000 reports. **Subscriptions:** 410 journals and other serials. **Services:** Interlibrary loan; library not open to the public. **Computerized Information Services:** DIALOG Information Services, DTIC, MEDLARS, OCLC; DOCLINE (electronic mail service). **Remarks:** FAX: (415)561-4138. Library is scheduled to close in 1993 due to closure of Army base.

U.S. Army - Logistics Library
See: U.S. Army - TRADOC - Logistics Library (17016)

★ 16985 ★
U.S. Army - Logistics Management Center - Technical Library (Sci-Engr, Mil)
Red River Army Depot   Phone: (903)334-3430
Texarkana, TX 75507-5000   Deborah Mack, Libn.
Founded: 1970. **Staff:** Prof 1. **Subjects:** Management; logistics; engineering - mechanical, electrical, safety, production, maintainability, industrial, software; computer management; quality and reliability. **Special Collections:** U.S. Military Regulations (3000); Intern Training Center Research Reports (600). **Holdings:** 18,900 books; 280 periodical volumes; 400 technical reports; 500 microfiche. **Subscriptions:** 197 journals and other serials. **Services:** Interlibrary loan; library not open to the public. **Automated Operations:** Computerized circulation. DTIC, OCLC, NTIS. **Publications:** Accessions list, quarterly. **Remarks:** Alternate telephone number(s): 334-3210. FAX: (903)334-3696.

U.S. Army - Materiel Command - Automated Logistic Management System Agency
See: Automated Logistic Management Systems Agency (1365)

U.S. Army - Materiel Command - Aviation Applied Technology Directorate
See: U.S. Army - Aviation Applied Technology Directorate (16922)

U.S. Army - Materiel Command - Communications-Electronics Command
See: U.S. Army - Communications-Electronics Command (16930)

★ 16986 ★
U.S. Army - Materiel Command - Headquarters - Technical Library (Mil)
Attn: AMCMM-L
5001 Eisenhower Ave.
Alexandria, VA 22333-0001   Phone: (703)274-8152
Founded: 1973. **Staff:** Prof 2; Other 3. **Subjects:** Management, mathematics and statistics, military affairs, data processing, social sciences and economics. **Holdings:** 20,000 volumes. **Subscriptions:** 302 journals and other serials; 24 newspapers. **Services:** Interlibrary loan; library not open to the public. **Automated Operations:** LS/2000, OCLC ACQ350, OCLC SC350. **Computerized Information Services:** DIALOG Information Services, DTIC, OCLC. **Networks/Consortia:** Member of FEDLINK. **Remarks:** FAX: (703)274-4991. **Staff:** Lynda Kennedy, Tech.Serv.Libn.

U.S. Army - Materiel Command - Laboratory Command
See: U.S. Army - Laboratory Command (16982)

U.S. Army - Materiel Command - Missile Command
See: U.S. Army - Missile Command & Marshall Space Flight Center (16996)

★ 16987 ★
U.S. Army - Materiel Command - Plastics Technical Evaluation Center (PLASTEC) - Library (Sci-Engr)
SMCAR-AET-O, Bldg. 355N
Armament Research, Development   Phone: (201)724-2778
& Engineering Ctr.   Suseela Chandrasekar,
Picatinny Arsenal, NJ 07806-5000   Tech.Info.Off.
Founded: 1960. **Staff:** Prof 1; Other 1. **Subjects:** Plastics, materials engineering, adhesives, organic matrix composites, compatibility of polymers with energetic materials, packaging materials. **Special Collections:** PLASTEC reports archives. **Holdings:** 2500 books; 200 bound periodical volumes; 58,000 technical reports; 20,000 reels of microfilm of military specifications and standards, commercial and foreign standards. **Subscriptions:** 50 journals and other serials. **Services:** Interlibrary loan; copying (limited); SDI; library open to the public by appointment. **Automated Operations:** Computerized cataloging. **Computerized Information Services:** DIALOG Information Services, DTIC, NASA/RECON; HAZARD, DETER, PLASTEC, COMPAT, MADPAC (internal databases). Performs searches on fee basis. Contact Person: Charles E. Yearwood, Chf., 724-4222. **Networks/Consortia:** Member of FEDLINK. **Publications:** State-of-the Art reports; PLASTEC reports; technical reports; technical notes; special bibliographies; evaluation reports - all released through the National Technical Information Service. **Special Catalogs:** Subject catalog for reports. **Remarks:** FAX: (201)361-7378. **Staff:** Len Silver, Onsite Contract Mgr.

U.S. Army - Materiel Command - Tank-Automotive Command
See: U.S. Army - Tank-Automotive Command (16999)

U.S. Army - Materiel Command - Test & Evaluation Command
See: Commander U.S. Army - Dugway Proving Ground (4048)

★ 16988 ★
U.S. Army - Medical Research & Development Command - Aeromedical Research Laboratory - Scientific Information Center (Med)
Box 577   Phone: (205)255-6907
Fort Rucker, AL 36362-5292   Diana L. Hemphill, Libn.
Founded: 1963. **Staff:** Prof 3. **Subjects:** Aviation medicine, medicine, vision, audiology, aviation psychology, acoustics, optics. **Special Collections:** All Aeromedical Research Laboratory Reports. **Holdings:** 15,000 books; 5000 bound periodical volumes; 15,000 documents; 2500 reels of microfilm; 1500 VF items; 50 magnetic tapes. **Subscriptions:** 425 journals and other serials. **Services:** Interlibrary loan; copying; center open to the public. **Automated Operations:** Computerized cataloging and circulation. **Computerized Information Services:** DIALOG Information Services, OCLC, NASA/RECON, DTIC. Performs searches for staff only. **Networks/Consortia:** Member of SEASHEL Consortium. **Publications:** Monthly Acquisitions; Periodical List, annual; special bibliographies; union list; bibliography of USAARL technical reports and letter reports. **Staff:** Linda Messer; Barbara Bethea; Udo Nowak.

★ 16989 ★
U.S. Army - Medical Research & Development Command - Biomedical Research & Development Laboratory - Technical Library (Biol Sci, Med)
Fort Detrick, Bldg. 568   Phone: (301)619-2502
Frederick, MD 21702-5010   Al Reynolds, Libn.
Founded: 1964. **Staff:** 2. **Subjects:** Biomedical engineering; pest management systems; entomology; environmental protection; air, land, and water pollution; solid waste and pesticide disposal; aquatic toxicology; occupational health. **Holdings:** 5500 books; 1500 bound periodical volumes; 6100 technical reprints, patents, reports; 1000 photographs; 2200 slides. **Subscriptions:** 220 journals and other serials. **Services:** Interlibrary loan (limited); copying; library open to the public on special request. **Computerized Information Services:** DIALOG Information Services, STN International, MEDLARS, OCLC, DTIC. **Networks/Consortia:** Member of FEDLINK. **Publications:** Reprints of journal publications - available on request; technical reports - available through DTIC.

★ 16990 ★
U.S. Army - Medical Research & Development Command - Medical Research Institute of Chemical Defense - Wood Technical Library (Med)
Bldg. E3100   Phone: (301)676-7045
Aberdeen Proving Ground, MD 21010-5425   Donna Hesson, Ref.Libn.
Founded: 1979. **Staff:** Prof 2; Other 2. **Subjects:** Pharmacology, biomedicine, psychology, biochemistry, medicine, toxicology. **Holdings:** 6192 books; 10,191 bound periodical volumes; 7776 reels of microfilm. **Subscriptions:** 1127 journals and other serials. **Services:** Interlibrary loan; copying; SDI; library open to the public for reference use only. **Automated Operations:** Computerized cataloging. **Computerized Information Services:** OCLC. **Networks/Consortia:** Member of FEDLINK. **Publications:** New Acquisitions List, monthly - to branches.

★ 16991 ★
U.S. Army - Medical Research & Development Command - Medical Research Institute of Infectious Diseases - Medical Library (Med)
Fort Detrick   Phone: (301)663-2717
Frederick, MD 21702-5011   Denise M. Lupp, Libn.
Staff: Prof 2; Other 1. **Subjects:** Medicine, microbiology, biochemistry. **Holdings:** 7600 books; 6500 bound periodical volumes; 6 shelves of contract reports; 22 shelves of miscellaneous reports. **Subscriptions:** 250 journals and other serials. **Services:** Interlibrary loan; library open to the public with restrictions.

★ 16992 ★
U.S. Army - Medical Research & Development Command - Walter Reed Army Institute of Research - Library (Med)
Walter Reed Army Medical Center   Phone: (202)576-3314
Washington, DC 20307-5100   V. Lynn Gera, Dir., Info.Rsrcs.Ctr./Lib.
Founded: 1946. **Staff:** Prof 4; Other 5. **Subjects:** Communicable diseases, immunology, dentistry, veterinary sciences, biochemistry, internal medicine, physiology, psychiatry, surgery, auto-immune deficiency syndrome. **Holdings:** 22,000 books; 11,000 bound periodical volumes. **Subscriptions:** 1000 journals and other serials. **Services:** Interlibrary loan; translations. **Automated Operations:** Computerized ILL (DOCLINE). **Computerized Information Services:** DIALOG Information Services, BRS Information Technologies, DTIC, OCLC; **Publications:** Union List of Biomedical Periodicals in the libraries of WRAIR, WRAMC and AFIP (Armed Forces Institute of Pathology), annual. **Remarks:** FAX: (202)576-0270.

★ 16993 ★
U.S. Army - Military Academy - Archives (Hist)
West Point, NY 10996-2099   Phone: (914)938-7073
                                       Suzanne M. Christoff, Archv.
Founded: 1954. **Staff:** Prof 2; Other 1. **Subjects:** History of the U.S. Military Academy and the Post of West Point; cadet personnel records, 1802 to present; alumni data on graduates, 1802-1905. **Holdings:** 30 cubic meters of archival materials, including 10 feet of sound recordings; 100,000 prints and negatives; official registers; yearbooks; catalogs. **Services:** Copying; archives open to the public by appointment.

★ 16994 ★
U.S. Army - Military Academy - Library (Mil, Hum, Sci-Engr)
West Point, NY 10966-1799   Phone: (914)938-2230
                                       Kenneth W. Hedman, Libn.
Founded: 1802. **Staff:** Prof 24; Other 35. **Subjects:** Military arts and sciences, military history, history of the U.S. Army, history of U.S. Military Academy, engineering and technology, social sciences, modern American literature. **Special Collections:** Early astronomy (170 items); military art and science (23,000 items); early atlases (200); Orientalia (3750 items); West Pointiana (3900 items); William Faulkner (600 first editions and criticisms). **Holdings:** 412,000 books; 50,000 bound periodical volumes; 27,000 other cataloged items; 135,000 documents; 375,000 microforms; 26,500 manuscripts; 8000 sound recordings. **Subscriptions:** 2200 journals; 56 newspapers. **Services:** Interlibrary loan; library open to the public by appointment. **Automated Operations:** Computerized cataloging and circulation. **Computerized Information Services:** DIALOG Information Services, OCLC; DDN Network Information Center (electronic mail service). **Networks/Consortia:** Member of SUNY/OCLC Library Network, Southeastern New York Library Resources Council (SENYLRC), FEDLINK. **Publications:** Friends of the West Point Library Newsletter, semiannual; subject bibliographies; archives and manuscript inventory lists. **Special Catalogs:** Subject Catalog of the Military Art and Science Collection in the Library of the United States Military Academy with Selected Author and Added Entries, including a Preliminary Guide to the Manuscript Collection (1969; 4 volumes); Official Records of the American Civil War: a researcher guide (1977); Catalog of the Orientalia Collection of the USMA Library (1977). **Special Indexes:** Subject index to selected military periodicals, 1916-1960. **Remarks:** FAX: (914)938-3752. **Staff:** Georgianna Watson, User Serv.Libn.; Joseph M. Barth, Coll.Dev.Libn.; Rona Steindler, Sys.Libn.; Angela H. Kao, Orientalia Libn.; Alan C. Aimone, Spec.Coll.Libn.; Nicholas S. Battipaglia, Jr., Math/Sci.Libn.; Gladys T. Calvetti, Cur. of Rare Bks.; Holbrook W. Yorke, AV Libn.; Judith Sibley, Maps & Mss.Libn.; Rose M. Robischon, Acq./Ser.Libn.; Paul T. Nergelovic, Govt.Docs.Libn.; Allen D. Hough, Ref.Libn.; Susan M. Lintelmann, Hum.Libn.; Linda E. Thompson, Circ.Libn.; Elizabeth J. Ince, Dir., Reading & Stud. Skill Ctr.; Wendy Swik, Mil.Aff.Libn.; Suzanne M. Christoff, Archv.; George Patail, Cat.; Larry Tietze, Cat.; Charlotte R. Snyder, ILL.

★ 16995 ★
U.S. Army - Military History Institute (Mil, Hist)
Carlisle Barracks, PA 17013-5008   Phone: (717)245-3611
                                       Nancy L. Gilbert, Asst.Dir., Lib.Serv.
Founded: 1967. **Staff:** Prof 19; Other 16. **Subjects:** Military history, U.S. and foreign history. **Special Collections:** Dyer Institute of Interdisciplinary Studies; Military Order of the Loyal Legion of the United States - Massachusetts Commandery Library. **Holdings:** 245,000 books; 8240 bound periodical volumes; 367,300 military publications; 5800 military unit histories; 59,600 reports and studies; 3000 hours of taped oral history

interviews; 5.5 million manuscripts; 730,000 photographs; 12,400 reels of microfilm. **Subscriptions:** 202 journals and other serials. **Services:** Interlibrary loan; copying; institute open to the public. **Automated Operations:** Computerized public access catalog, cataloging, and ILL. **Computerized Information Services:** OCLC. Performs searches free of charge. Contact Person: Judy Meck. **Networks/Consortia:** Member of FEDLINK. **Staff:** Col. Thomas W. Sweeney, Dir.; LTC Martin W. Andresen, Dp.Dir.; James Williams, Asst.Dir./Ed.Serv.; LTC Frederick Eiserman, Asst.Dir., Hist.Serv.Div.; Mary Lou Harris,Asst.Dir./Adm.Serv.; John Slonaker, Chf., Hist.Ref.Br.; Richard Sommers, Chf., Archv.Br.; Michael Winey, Chf., Spec.Coll.Br.; Ruth E. Hodge, Chf., Tech.Serv.Br.; Kathryn E. Davis, Asst.Dir., Sys.; Randall Rakers, Class.Archv.Techn.

U.S. Army - Military Police School
See: U.S. Army - TRADOC - Military Police School - Ramsey Library (17017)

★ 16996 ★
U.S. Army - Missile Command & Marshall Space Flight Center - Redstone Scientific Information Center - Scientific and Technical Library (Sci-Engr)
AMSMI-RD-CS-R   Phone: (205)876-3251
Redstone Arsenal, AL 35898-5241   Sybil H. Bullock, Dir.
Founded: 1949. **Staff:** Prof 19; Other 14. **Subjects:** Astronautics, astronomy, chemistry, engineering, management, mathematics, meteorology, physics. **Special Collections:** Rockets; missiles; space technology; lasers; Peenemuende Documents. **Holdings:** 250,996 books; 85,000 bound periodical volumes; 1.7 million documents and reports. **Subscriptions:** 4000 journals and other serials. **Services:** Interlibrary loan; copying; translations; center open to the public with restrictions on classified material. **Automated Operations:** Integrated library system (STILAS System). **Computerized Information Services:** DTIC, NASA/RECON, BRS Information Technologies, DIALOG Information Services, PFDS Online, Mead Data Central. **Networks/Consortia:** Member of Alabama Library Exchange, Inc. (ALEX), Network of Alabama Academic Libraries (NAAL). **Publications:** Literature surveys; library brochure; data compilations. **Special Catalogs:** Periodicals Catalog, semiannual - by request. **Remarks:** FAX: (205)880-0990.

U.S. Army - Office of the Surgeon General
See: U.S. Army/U.S. Air Force - Offices of the Surgeons General (17079)

★ 16997 ★
U.S. Army - Operational Test & Evaluation Command - TEXCOM - Headquarters - TEXCOM Experimentation Center - Technical Information Center (Mil, Sci-Engr)
Bldg. 177, Ft. Hunter Liggett   Phone: (408)385-2941
Jolon, CA 93928-5021   Carolyn I. Alexander, Chf.Libn.
Founded: 1966. **Staff:** Prof 2; Other 2. **Subjects:** Armor, behavioral sciences, experimental design, instrumentation, small arms, small unit organizations, helicopter warfare. **Holdings:** 8000 books and bound periodical volumes; 13,000 technical reports; 4000 publications; 50 pamphlets; 1200 microforms. **Subscriptions:** 300 journals and other serials; 10 newspapers. **Services:** Interlibrary loan; center not open to the public. **Computerized Information Services:** DIALOG Information Services, OCLC. **Networks/Consortia:** Member of Monterey Bay Area Cooperative Library System (MOBAC). **Publications:** Acquisitions List; Serials List, annual. **Remarks:** FAX: (408)385-0844. **Formerly:** U.S. Army - TEXCOM - Headquarters - TEXCOM Test & Experimentation Command - Experimentation Center - Technical Information Center, located at Fort Ord, CA. **Staff:** Dustin Miller, Ref.Libn.

★ 16998 ★
U.S. Army - Operational Test & Evaluation Command (OPTEC) - Technical Library (Sci-Engr, Mil)
4501 Ford Ave.   Phone: (703)756-2234
Alexandria, VA 22302-1458   Ava Dell Headley, Chf.
Founded: 1974. **Staff:** Prof 2; Other 1. **Subjects:** Test methodology, experimental/statistical design, instrumentation, reliability engineering, human engineering, combat arms/combat support weapon systems of U.S. Army. **Special Collections:** Army military publications (150 feet). **Holdings:** 5000 books; 2000 documents. **Subscriptions:** 225 journals and other serials; 9 newspapers. **Services:** Interlibrary loan; library not open to the public. **Computerized Information Services:** DIALOG Information Services, DTIC, OCLC EPIC. **Networks/Consortia:** Member of FEDLINK. **Publications:** Bibliography of USAOTEA/OPTEC Reports and Related Documents. **Remarks:** FAX: (202)756-4973. **Staff:** Marjorie Rust, ILL & Onl.Serv.

U.S. Army - Ordnance Center & School
See: U.S. Army - TRADOC - Ordnance Center & School (17018)

U.S. Army - Ordnance Missile, Munitions Center & School
See: U.S. Army - TRADOC - Ordnance Missile, Munitions Center & School (17019)

U.S. Army - Patton Museum of Calvary & Armor
See: U.S. Army - TRADOC - Patton Museum of Cavalry & Armor (17020)

U.S. Army - Pentagon Library
See: U.S. Army - Headquarters Services - Washington - Pentagon Library (16974)

U.S. Army - Plastics Technical Evaluation Center
See: U.S. Army - Materiel Command - Plastics Technical Evaluation Center (PLASTEC) (16987)

U.S. Army - Sergeants Major Academy
See: U.S. Army - TRADOC - Sergeants Major Academy (17022)

U.S. Army - Signal Center & Fort Gordon
See: U.S. Army - TRADOC - Signal Center & Fort Gordon (17023)

★ 16999 ★
U.S. Army - Tank-Automotive Command - TACOM Support Activity - General Library (Mil)
Bldg. 169
Selfridge Air Natl. Guard Base   Phone: (313)466-5088
Mt. Clemens, MI 48045   JoAnn Bonnett, Chf., Lib.Br.
Founded: 1971. **Staff:** Prof 2; Other 6. **Subjects:** History, military affairs, management. **Holdings:** 25,000 books; 5 VF drawers of pamphlets, maps, clippings; cassettes; phonograph records. **Subscriptions:** 280 journals and other serials; 15 newspapers. **Services:** Interlibrary loan; copying; library serves military personnel and their dependents, retirees, and civilians employed at TACOM and Selfridge ANG Base. **Automated Operations:** Computerized cataloging and ILL. **Computerized Information Services:** DIALOG Information Services; DIALMAIL (electronic mail service). **Networks/Consortia:** Member of FEDLINK.

★ 17000 ★
U.S. Army - Tank-Automotive Command - Technical Information Center (Sci-Engr, Mil)
Attn: ASQNC-TAC-DIT   Phone: (313)574-6543
Warren, MI 48397-5000   Louis X. Barbalas, Chf.
Staff: Prof 2; Other 1. **Subjects:** Automotive mechanics, materials science, physical science, military science, engineering. **Holdings:** 5900 books; administrative and military publications; 28,000 technical reports; 52 drawers of microfiche. **Subscriptions:** 20 journals and other serials. **Services:** Interlibrary loan; center open to government contractors on special request. **Computerized Information Services:** DTIC. Performs searches on fee basis. Contact Person: Leon Burg, 574-8803.

★ 17001 ★
U.S. Army - Test & Evaluation Command - White Sands Missile Range - Technical Library (Sci-Engr, Mil)
STEWS-IM-ST
White Sands Missile Range, NM   Phone: (505)678-1317
88002-5030   Laurel B. Saunders, Chf.Libn.
Founded: 1955. **Staff:** Prof 4; Other 8. **Subjects:** Optics, guided missiles, electronics, mathematics, physics, computers. **Special Collections:** Military specifications and industrial standards. **Holdings:** 30,000 books; 2000 bound periodical volumes; 180,000 microforms; 160,000 research and development reports; 4.1 million engineering drawings. **Subscriptions:** 440 journals and other serials. **Services:** Interlibrary loan; library not open to the public. **Automated Operations:** Computerized cataloging and acquisitions. **Computerized Information Services:** DIALOG Information Services, DTIC, OCLC, Government-Industry Data Exchange Program (GIDEP). **Publications:** Acquisitions of open literature and documents, annual; Bulletin, monthly; Periodical List, annual; GIDEP, monthly; Holdings Announcement List, irregular. **Staff:** Janice Haines, Chf., Doc.; Kathleen Hogan, Cat.

★ 17002 ★
U.S. Army - Test & Evaluation Command - Yuma Proving Ground - Technical Library (Sci-Engr, Mil)
Attn: ASQNC-TYU-IC-TL   Phone: (602)328-6549
Yuma, AZ 85365-9110   Katherine Ferguson, Libn.
Founded: 1965. **Staff:** 1. **Subjects:** Research and development, test and evaluation, engineering and technology, U.S. Army materiel. **Holdings:** 1200 books; 35,000 other cataloged items; 200,000 documents in microform, including 16mm visual search microfilm service. **Subscriptions:** 55 journals and other serials. **Services:** Interlibrary loan (for material with limited control); library not open to the public. **Computerized Information Services:** DTIC. **Remarks:** Alternate telephone number(s): 328-6218. **Staff:** Jean McCall, Lib.Techn.

U.S. Army - TEXCOM - Headquarters - TEXCOM Test & Experimentation Command
See: **U.S. Army - Operational Test & Evaluation Command - TEXCOM - Headquarters - TEXCOM Experimentation Center - Technical Information Center** (16997)

★ 17003 ★
U.S. Army - Total Army Personnel Center - Personnel Service Support Directorate - The Institute of Heraldry - Library (Mil)
Cameron Sta., Bldg. 15   Phone: (703)274-6544
Alexandria, VA 22304-5050   Ms. Nuala Barry, Libn.
Founded: 1962. **Staff:** Prof 1. **Subjects:** Heraldry, arts, colors, flags, lettering and decorations, history, medals, military history (chiefly U.S.), military insignia, military uniforms, seals, signs, symbolisms, weapons. **Special Collections:** Materials on uniforms, flags, and decorations of the U.S. Army, 1776 to present (2000 loose-leaf notebooks). **Holdings:** 22,600 volumes; 15 VF drawers. **Services:** Library open to the public by appointment. **Remarks:** Alternate telephone number(s): 274-6632.

★ 17004 ★
U.S. Army - TRADOC - Air Defense Artillery School - Library (Mil)
Bldg. 2, Wing E, Rm. 181   Phone: (915)568-5781
Fort Bliss, TX 79916-7027   Janet H. Barnhart, Supv.Libn.
Founded: 1944. **Staff:** Prof 2; Other 5. **Subjects:** Air defense - missiles, electronics; military arts and sciences, military and world history, technology. **Special Collections:** Archival collection of military subjects; Southwest Collection. **Holdings:** 19,610 books; 500 bound periodical volumes; 85,606 reports and documents on microfiche; 2840 reels of microfilm. **Subscriptions:** 124 journals and other serials; 11 newspapers. **Services:** Interlibrary loan; library not open to the public. **Automated Operations:** Computerized cataloging, acquisitions, and ILL. **Computerized Information Services:** OCLC, DTIC; PROFS (electronic mail services). **Staff:** Donna E. Ramsey, Libn.

★ 17005 ★
U.S. Army - TRADOC - Analysis Command - TRAC-WSMR Technical Research Center (Mil, Sci-Engr)
Attn: ATRC-WSS-R   Phone: (505)678-3135
White Sands Missile Range, NM 88002-5502 Julie A. Gibson, Adm.Libn.
Founded: 1977. **Staff:** Prof 1; Other 2. **Subjects:** Military science, ordnance, operations research, computer science, modelling. **Special Collections:** Defense Mapping Agency map collection. **Holdings:** 4400 books and bound periodical volumes; 57,000 technical reports. **Subscriptions:** 300 journals and other serials. **Services:** Interlibrary loan; center not open to the public. **Automated Operations:** Computerized cataloging, serials, and circulation. **Computerized Information Services:** DIALOG Information Services, BRS Information Technologies, DTIC, OCLC; Technical Library Information System database (internal database); LINX Courier (electronic mail service). **Networks/Consortia:** Member of TRADOC Library and Information Network (TRALINET), FEDLINK. **Publications:** New Acquisitions. **Remarks:** FAX: (505)678-5104.

★ 17006 ★
U.S. Army - TRADOC - Army Armor School - Library (Mil)
Gaffey Hall, 2369
Old Ironsides Ave.
ATSB-DOTD-L
Fort Knox, KY 40121-5200   Phone: (502)624-6231
          William H. Hansen, Chf.Libn.
Founded: 1941. **Staff:** Prof 2; Other 3. **Subjects:** Military science, history, political science, foreign affairs. **Holdings:** 20,000 books; 1000 bound periodical volumes; 14,092 Department of the Army publications; 138 reels of microfilm; 2432 student staff studies; 10,000 afteraction reports; 500,000 documents on microfiche. **Subscriptions:** 319 journals and other serials; 20 newspapers. **Services:** Interlibrary loan; library open to the public with restrictions on defense information. **Automated Operations:** Computerized cataloging and acquisitions. **Computerized Information Services:** DTIC, DIALOG Information Services. **Networks/Consortia:** Member of TRADOC Library and Information Network (TRALINET), Kentucky Library Network, Inc. (KLN). **Remarks:** FAX: (502)624-3365. **Staff:** Judy Stephenson, Ref.; Lorraine Mitchell, Cat. & Acq.; Gladys Burton, ILL; Janis Kendall, Circ.

★ 17007 ★
U.S. Army - TRADOC - Aviation Museum - Library/Archives (Mil)
Box 610   Phone: (205)255-4443
Fort Rucker, AL 36362   Regina C. Burns, Archv./Lib.Tech.
Staff: Prof 1; Other 1. **Subjects:** U.S. Army aviation, civilian aviation. **Special Collections:** Jackson Book Collection; Army Aviation Digest Photo Collection; Swenson papers; Silver Eagle papers; Hutton Collection; 1st Aviation Brigade files (Vietnam). **Holdings:** 2000 books; 924 bound periodical volumes; 5000 technical manuals on aircraft 375 linear ft. of papers and manuscripts dealing with Fort Rucker and Army Aviation history (figures include the holdings of special collections); 1100 microfiche; 600 films. **Services:** Interlibrary loan; library open by appointment to bona fide researchers only. **Computerized Information Services:** Internal database.

★ 17008 ★
U.S. Army - TRADOC - Aviation Technical Library (Mil, Sci-Engr)
Bldgs. 5906 & 5907   Phone: (205)255-4591
Fort Rucker, AL 36362-5163   Beverly M. Hall, Dir.
Founded: 1955. **Staff:** Prof 4; Other 6. **Subjects:** Aviation, international affairs, sciences, military history and science, education, management. **Special Collections:** Documents on history and development of army aviation. **Holdings:** 23,077 books; 107,714 documents. **Services:** Interlibrary loan; copying; SDI; library open to the public with restrictions. **Automated Operations:** Computerized cataloging and acquisitions. **Computerized Information Services:** DTIC, NASA/RECON, NEXIS, LEXIS, DIALOG Information Services, OCLC. **Networks/Consortia:** Member of FEDLINK. **Publications:** Acquisitions lists; subject bibliographies; handbooks. **Special Indexes:** Periodical holdings lists. **Staff:** James Lee, Tech.Serv.Libn.; Sherry Miller, Ref.Libn.; Beverly McMaster, Ref.Libn.

★ 17009 ★
U.S. Army - TRADOC - Chemical School - Fisher Library (Sci-Engr, Mil)
Bldg. 1081   Phone: (205)848-4414
Fort McClellan, AL 36205-5020   Richard Pastorett, Libn.
Founded: 1982. **Staff:** Prof 1; Other 4. **Subjects:** Chemical warfare, radiation protection, military history. **Special Collections:** Defense Department Technical Reports (2000); Defense Department documents (1500); rare books (150); Chemical School Archives (45 VF drawers). **Holdings:** 12,000 books; 10,000 documents; 200 periodical titles, 1977 to present, on microfilm. **Subscriptions:** 150 journals and other serials; 35 newspapers. **Services:** Interlibrary loan; library open to government agencies only. **Computerized Information Services:** DIALOG Information Services, OCLC, DTIC. **Networks/Consortia:** Member of TRADOC Library and Information Network (TRALINET).

★ 17010 ★
U.S. Army - TRADOC - Field Artillery School - Morris Swett Technical Library (Mil)
Snow Hall, Rm. 16, 19W   Phone: (405)351-4525
Fort Sill, OK 73503-0312   Martha H. Relph, Libn.
Founded: 1911. **Staff:** Prof 1; Other 3. **Subjects:** Military science and history, history of field artillery, political science, technology, management. **Special Collections:** U.S. Field Artillery Unit Histories; rare book collection. **Holdings:** 92,625 volumes; 45,000 other cataloged items; 138,713 microforms; 27,106 Department of the Army and Department of Defense publications. **Subscriptions:** 293 journals and other serials. **Services:** Interlibrary loan. **Computerized Information Services:** DTIC, OCLC. **Networks/Consortia:** Member of TRADOC Library and Information Network (TRALINET), Oklahoma Special Collections and Archives Network (OSCAN). **Publications:** Special bibliographies; checklists - irregular; century series bibliographies; subject headings and "U" Military Science Classification List. **Special Indexes:** Card index to military periodicals dating to mid-1800s; internal military science and subject indexes. **Remarks:** Autovon telephone numbers: 639-4525; 639-4477.

★17011★
U.S. Army - TRADOC - HQ/Fort Monroe Library & Intern Training Center (Mil)
ATLS-LT
Bldg. 133   Phone: (804)727-2821
Fort Monroe, VA 23651-5000   Frances M. Doyle, Adm.Libn.
Founded: 1824. **Staff:** Prof 2; Other 4. **Subjects:** Military science and history, management, training and education. **Special Collections:** Department of the Army publications (60,000). **Holdings:** 11,000 books; 375 bound periodical volumes; 3000 technical documents. **Subscriptions:** 350 journals and other serials; 10 newspapers. **Services:** Interlibrary loan; library open to Department of Defense personnel. **Computerized Information Services:** DIALOG Information Services, BRS Information Technologies, DTIC, OCLC; PROFS (electronic mail service). **Networks/Consortia:** Member of TRADOC Library and Information Network (TRALINET). **Publications:** Library Information Update, bimonthly - for internal distribution only. **Staff:** Dolores L. Hawn, Res.Libn.

★17012★
U.S. Army - TRADOC - Infantry School - Donovan Technical Library (Mil)
Infantry Hall, Bldg. 4, Rm. 101/102   Phone: (404)545-3390
Fort Benning, GA 31905-5452   Vivian S. Dodson, Chf., Lrng.Rsrcs.Div.
Founded: 1919. **Staff:** Prof 3; Other 4. **Subjects:** Military history, military art and science, political science, social science, national defense, foreign affairs, management, education. **Special Collections:** Map collection (12,000); rare military books (14,000). **Holdings:** 58,000 books and bound periodical volumes; 55,000 classified and unclassified documents. **Subscriptions:** 210 journals and other serials; 24 newspapers. **Services:** Interlibrary loan; library open to the public on a limited schedule. **Computerized Information Services:** DIALOG Information Services, DTIC. **Networks/Consortia:** Member of TRADOC Library and Information Network (TRALINET). **Remarks:** FAX: (404)545-7525.

★17013★
U.S. Army - TRADOC - Intelligence Center & School - Academic Library (Mil)
Alvarado Hall ATSI-TDS-L   Phone: (602)533-4100
Fort Huachuca, AZ 85613-6000   Chris Hurd, Chf.
Founded: 1970. **Staff:** Prof 3; Other 1. **Subjects:** Military intelligence, military history, foreign affairs, political science, terrorism. **Holdings:** 15,051 books; 864 VF documents; 2400 student research papers. **Subscriptions:** 300 journals and other serials; 20 newspapers. **Services:** Interlibrary loan; copying; SDI; library open to the public by appointment. **Automated Operations:** Computerized cataloging, acquisitions, serials, and ILL. **Computerized Information Services:** DIALOG Information Services, DTIC, OCLC; PROFS (electronic mail service). **Networks/Consortia:** Member of TRADOC Library and Information Network (TRALINET). **Staff:** Pauline Spanabel, Ref./Rd.Serv.Libn.

★17014★
U.S. Army - TRADOC - Intelligence School, Devens - Library and Information Services Division (Mil)
Commander, USAISD
Attn: ATSI-ETD-L   Phone: (508)796-3413
Fort Devens, MA 01433-6301   Dr. Lester E. Goodridge, Jr.
Founded: 1951. **Staff:** 3. **Subjects:** Military science, electronics, training/education. **Special Collections:** Cryptology; electronic warfare. **Holdings:** 6000 books; 844 bound periodical volumes; 19,000 noncommercial military publications. **Subscriptions:** 84 periodicals. **Services:** Interlibrary loan; library open to Department of Defense personnel only. **Automated Operations:** Computerized cataloging and acquisitions. **Computerized Information Services:** DIALOG Information Services, OCLC, DTIC; internal database; DDN (electronic mail service). **Networks/Consortia:** Member of TRADOC Library and Information Network (TRALINET), FEDLINK. **Remarks:** Autovon Line(s): 256-3413. FAX: 256-2033 (Autovon Line); (508)796-2033. Electronic mail address(es): CREWS@DEVENS-EMH.ARMY.MIL (DDN). **Staff:** Martha Rogers, Class.Lit.; Sandra Crews, Adm.

★17015★
U.S. Army - TRADOC - Language Training Facility - Library (Hum)
Bldg. 2844   Phone: (817)287-7394
Fort Hood, TX 76544-5056   Georgie C. Hodge
Founded: 1958. **Staff:** 1. **Subjects:** Books and texts in 40 foreign languages, area studies of foreign nations. **Special Collections:** Bible collection in 56 languages and dialects. **Holdings:** 8000 books; 2000 magnetic tapes; 4 VF drawers of pamphlets, articles. **Subscriptions:** 35 journals and other serials; 11 newspapers. **Services:** Interlibrary loan; library open to military members and their dependents, retired Army personnel.

★17016★
U.S. Army - TRADOC - Logistics Library (Mil, Bus-Fin)
Bldg. P-12500, Rm. B206   Phone: (804)734-1797
Fort Lee, VA 23801-6047   Katherine P. Sites, Chf.Libn.
Founded: 1971. **Staff:** Prof 3; Other 3. **Subjects:** Logistics, military history, management, computer science, social sciences, business and finance, food and nutrition. **Holdings:** 40,000 books; 425 bound periodical volumes; 60,000 U.S. Government publications; 100,000 unbound periodicals; 19,000 periodicals in microform. **Subscriptions:** 267 journals and other serials; 8 newspapers. **Services:** Interlibrary loan; copying; library open to the public for reference use only. **Automated Operations:** Computerized cataloging and acquisitions. **Computerized Information Services:** BRS Information Technologies, DIALOG Information Services, DTIC, OCLC; PROFS (electronic mail service). **Networks/Consortia:** Member of FEDLINK, TRADOC Library and Information Network (TRALINET). **Publications:** Quarterly Acquisition Newsletter; Library Handbook. **Remarks:** FAX: (804)734-2295. **Staff:** Dr. Laura Wilson, Asst.Libn.; Karen Perkins, Ref.Libn.; Virginia Gordon, ILL.

★17017★
U.S. Army - TRADOC - Military Police School - Ramsey Library (Mil, Law)
Bldg. 3181, Rm. 10   Phone: (205)238-3737
Fort McClellan, AL 36205   Martha M. Morgan, Supv.Libn.
Founded: 1941. **Staff:** Prof 2; Other 3. **Subjects:** Police science, education, military affairs, criminology, penology, military history, terrorism, psychology. **Special Collections:** Military Police Historical Collection. **Holdings:** 16,625 books; 2069 bound periodical volumes; 6500 paperbacks; 3675 reports; 1500 pamphlets; 30,000 military publications; 3537 microforms. **Subscriptions:** 248 journals and other serials; 23 newspapers. **Services:** Interlibrary loan; copying; library open to the public with restrictions. **Computerized Information Services:** DIALOG Information Services, DTIC; OPTIMIS (electronic mail service). Performs searches on fee basis. Contact Person: Margaret Pitts. **Networks/Consortia:** Member of TRADOC Library and Information Network (TRALINET). **Publications:** New book list. **Remarks:** FAX: (205)848-5885. Includes holdings of the Women's Army Corps School Library.

★17018★
U.S. Army - TRADOC - Ordnance Center & School - Library (Mil)
Attn: ATSL-SE-LI
Bldg. 3071, Simpson Hall   Phone: (301)278-5615
Aberdeen Proving Ground, MD 21005-5201 Janice C. Weston, Chf.Libn.
Founded: 1940. **Subjects:** Military science, ordnance, management, educational technology, military history. **Special Collections:** U.S. Department of the Army publications. **Holdings:** Books; bound periodical volumes; reports; classified documents; tape recordings; microfiche; microfilm. **Services:** Interlibrary loan; copying; library open to the public for reference use only with Security Office clearance. **Automated Operations:** Computerized cataloging and acquisitions. **Computerized Information Services:** DIALOG Information Services, OCLC, DTIC; PROFS (electronic mail service). **Networks/Consortia:** Member of TRADOC Library and Information Network (TRALINET), Maryland Interlibrary Organization (MILO). **Publications:** Monthly Acquisitions List; periodical listing, annual. **Remarks:** FAX: (301)278-8882. Electronic mail address(es): MON1 (WESTONJ; PROFS). **Staff:** Tracy A. Landfried, Ref.Libn.

★17019★
U.S. Army - TRADOC - Ordnance Missile, Munitions Center & School - OMMCS Technical Library (Sci-Engr)
Bldg. 3323, ATSK-AB   Phone: (205)876-7425
Redstone Arsenal, AL 35897-6280   Ronald W. Argentati, Chf.Libn.
Founded: 1959. **Staff:** Prof 2; Other 1. **Subjects:** Guided missiles, electrical engineering, mathematics, physics, management, education. **Holdings:** 17,100 books; 764 bound periodical volumes; 27,000 reports; 45 AV programs; 3000 microfiche; 3225 military publications. **Subscriptions:** 132 journals and other serials. **Services:** Interlibrary loan; library not open to the public. **Computerized Information Services:** DIALOG Information Services, BRS Information Technologies, OCLC, DTIC. **Networks/Consortia:** Member of TRADOC Library and Information Network (TRALINET). **Publications:** Acquisitions Listings, bimonthly; Library Guide. **Remarks:** FAX: (205)842-2193. **Staff:** Mark Iines, Ref.Libn.

★ 17020 ★
U.S. Army - TRADOC - Patton Museum of Cavalry & Armor - Emert L. Davis Memorial Library (Hist)
4554 Fayette Ave.
Box 208
Fort Knox, KY 40121-0208
Phone: (502)624-6350
David A. Holt, Libn.
Founded: 1975. **Staff:** Prof 1. **Subjects:** Armored fighting vehicles, General George S. Patton, Jr., armor warfare, Fort Knox history, unit histories. **Special Collections:** Colonel Robert J. Icks Collection of books, photographs, and unpublished material on armoured fighting vehicles. **Holdings:** 8400 books; 100 bound periodical volumes; 128 volumes of photographs; Fort Knox photographs and maps. **Subscriptions:** 15 journals and other serials. **Services:** Interlibrary loan; library open to researchers by appointment. **Publications:** Selected Bibliography: George S. Patton, Jr. (materials in library collection); United States Bullion Depository, Fort Knox, Kentucky: An Informal History (for sale).

★ 17021 ★
U.S. Army - TRADOC - School of the Americas - Library (Mil)
Bldg. 35
Attn: ATZL-SAS-LI
Fort Benning, GA 31905-6245
Phone: (404)545-4631
Richard M. Barone, Libn.
Founded: 1961. **Staff:** Prof 1; Other 3. **Subjects:** Military history, Latin American studies, control of narcotics. **Special Collections:** Spanish translations of Army publications. **Holdings:** 16,800 books; 515 bound periodical volumes; 20 VF drawers of pamphlets. **Subscriptions:** 190 journals and other serials. **Services:** Interlibrary loan; copying; library open to the public for reference use only. **Automated Operations:** TECHLIBplus. **Computerized Information Services:** OCLC, DTIC, INFO-SOUTH Latin American Information System, Latin America Forecast, Forum. **Networks/Consortia:** Member of TRADOC Library and Information Network (TRALINET), FEDLINK. **Remarks:** 90% of the collection is in Spanish. FAX: (404)545-1066.

★ 17022 ★
U.S. Army - TRADOC - Sergeants Major Academy - Othon O. Valent Learning Resources Center (Mil)
Bldg. 11294
Fort Bliss, TX 79918-1270
Phone: (915)568-8606
Marijean Murray, Supv.Libn.
Founded: 1972. **Staff:** 6. **Subjects:** Management, psychology, military history, leadership, military studies. **Special Collections:** Collection of rare books on military history and the history of the Non-Commissioned Officer Corps (500 items). **Holdings:** 42,000 books; 4835 bound periodical volumes; 20 archival materials; 900 AV programs; 41,000 microfiche; 5094 reels of microfilm. **Subscriptions:** 402 journals and other serials; 26 newspapers. **Services:** Interlibrary loan; copying; center open to the public for reference use only. **Computerized Information Services:** DIALOG Information Services. **Networks/Consortia:** Member of TRADOC Library and Information Network (TRALINET). **Staff:** Linda L. Gaunt; Melissa R. Cooper.

★ 17023 ★
U.S. Army - TRADOC - Signal Center & Fort Gordon - Conrad Technical Library (Mil, Sci-Engr)
Bldg. 29807
Fort Gordon, GA 30905-5081
Phone: (404)791-3922
Margaret H. Novinger, Chf.
Founded: 1950. **Staff:** Prof 3; Other 1. **Subjects:** Communications-electronics, computer science, military art and science. **Special Collections:** Signal Corps Collection. **Holdings:** 12,380 books; 1662 bound periodical volumes; 18,737 documents; 1169 periodical volumes on microfilm; 25 linear feet of pamphlets and monographs. **Subscriptions:** 343 journals and other serials. **Services:** Interlibrary loan; library open to the public with restrictions. **Computerized Information Services:** DIALOG Information Services, DTIC, OCLC. **Networks/Consortia:** Member of TRADOC Library and Information Network (TRALINET), Georgia Online Database (GOLD). **Remarks:** FAX: (404)791-5652. **Staff:** Janet M. Hansen; Linda L. Orne

★ 17024 ★
U.S. Army - TRADOC - Soldier Support Center - Main Library (Mil, Info Sci)
Bldg. 31
Fort Benjamin Harrison, IN 46216-5100
Phone: (317)542-4476
Mrs. Marina Griner, Supv.Libn.
Founded: 1957. **Staff:** Prof 4; Other 3. **Subjects:** Mass communications; journalism; management; military history, art, science; business; public

relations. **Special Collections:** Silver Anvils; Department of Defense publications; law collection. **Holdings:** 55,000 volumes; 425 AV programs; 2000 reports; 210,000 documents; 2000 microforms; 151 VF drawers. **Subscriptions:** 450 journals and other serials; 100 newspapers. **Services:** Interlibrary loan; copying; SDI; library open to the public for reference use only. **Automated Operations:** Computerized cataloging, acquisitions, and ILL. **Computerized Information Services:** DIALOG Information Services, OCLC. **Networks/Consortia:** Member of FEDLINK, TRADOC Library and Information Network (TRALINET). **Publications:** Library Guide; acquisition lists; newsletter, monthly; bibliographies; current awareness files. **Remarks:** Library serves U.S. Institute of Administration and Defense Information School. **Staff:** Thelma Shutt, Hd., Ref.Serv.; Eula Mallery, Hd., Tech.Serv.; Geneva Murphy, Hd., Pub.Serv.

★ 17025 ★
U.S. Army - TRADOC - Transportation & Aviation Logistics Schools - Information Center (Mil, Trans)
Bldg. 705, Rm. No. 36
Fort Eustis, VA 23604-5450
Phone: (804)878-5563
Marion J. Knihnicki, Chf.Libn.
Founded: 1944. **Staff:** Prof 3; Other 3. **Subjects:** Military transportation, military history, instructional technology. **Special Collections:** U.S. Army Transportation School Materials. **Holdings:** 45,397 books, bound periodical volumes, documents; 26,163 unbound periodicals and newspapers; 54,107 official publications; 22,251 miscellaneous items. **Subscriptions:** 450 journals and other serials; 8 newspapers. **Services:** Interlibrary loan; copying; center open to the public for reference use only. **Computerized Information Services:** DIALOG Information Services, BRS Information Technologies, DTIC, OCLC. **Networks/Consortia:** Member of TRADOC Library and Information Network (TRALINET). **Special Indexes:** Indexing Service for military transportation journals. **Staff:** Valerie Fashion-Dawson, Ref.Libn.; Richard Aubrey, Tech.Serv.Libn.

U.S. Army - Training & Doctrine Command
See: **U.S. Army - TRADOC** (17006)

★ 17026 ★
U.S. Army - Transportation Museum - Library (Trans)
Bldg. 300, Besson Hall
Fort Eustis, VA 23604-5260
Phone: (804)878-1115
Barbara A. Bower, Dir.
Founded: 1959. **Staff:** 6. **Subjects:** History of transportation in the U.S. Army and the Transportation Corps, 1914 to present. **Holdings:** 2000 books; 250 films; 3600 photographs; 58 periodical titles. **Services:** Copying; library open to the public. **Staff:** Carolyn Wright.

★ 17027 ★
U.S. Army - Troop Support Command - Natick Research, Development & Engineering Center - Technical Library (Sci-Engr)
Kansas St.
Natick, MA 01760-5040
Phone: (508)651-4249
Patricia Bremner, Chf.Libn.
Founded: 1946. **Staff:** Prof 4; Other 5. **Subjects:** Behavioral science, biochemistry, chemical and biological warfare, food science and technology, textiles and clothing, packaging technology, environmental medicine, chemistry, physics. **Special Collections:** U.S. Army Quartermaster research on food, clothing, footwear, and tentage. **Holdings:** 41,000 books; 20,000 bound periodical volumes; 54,000 technical reports. **Subscriptions:** 650 journals and other serials; 10 newspapers. **Services:** Interlibrary loan; library open to the public for reference use only. **Computerized Information Services:** DIALOG Information Services, OCLC, DTIC; electronic mail. **Networks/Consortia:** Member of FEDLINK, NELINET, Inc. **Publications:** Bibliography of Technical Publications, Papers, and Patents, annual; Technical Library Accessions List, bimonthly - for internal distribution only. **Staff:** Delia M. Cardinal, Acq.Libn.; Lisa A. Ethier, Cat.; Allyson N. Nolan, Ref.Libn.

U.S. Army - White Sands Missile Range
See: **U.S. Army - Test & Evaluation Command - White Sands Missile Range** (17001)

U.S. Army - Women's Army Corps School - Library
See: **U.S. Army - TRADOC - Military Police School - Ramsey Library** (17017)

U.S. Army - Yuma Proving Ground
See: U.S. Army - Test & Evaluation Command - Yuma Proving Ground (17002)

★ 17028 ★
U.S. Army and Air Force Exchange Service (AAFES) - Library/AD-A (Mil)
3911 S. Walton Walker Blvd.
Box 660202   Phone: (214)312-2110
Dallas, TX 75266-0202   Shirley C. Basa, Libn.
Staff: Prof 1; Other 1. **Subjects:** Military regulations, business and management. **Special Collections:** Exchange Service manuals; military history (40 volumes). **Holdings:** 1150 books; 820 binders of regulations; Department of Defense publications. **Subscriptions:** 34 journals and other serials. **Services:** Library not open to the public. **Computerized Information Services:** DIALOG Information Services, Startext; internal database. **Remarks:** FAX: (214)312-3000.

★ 17029 ★
U.S. Army Engineer Waterways Experiment Station - Environmental Information Analysis Center (Env-Cons)
3909 Halls Ferry Rd.   Phone: (601)634-3233
Vicksburg, MS 39180-6199   Roger T. Saucier, Dir.
Subjects: Environmental protection, conservation of natural resources, environmental engineering, water conservation. **Holdings:** Figures not available.

★ 17030 ★
U.S. Army in Europe (USAREUR) - Library and Resource Center (Mil)
HQ USAREUR and Seventh Army
Unit 29351
APO New York, NY 09014   Phone: 6221 577430
Founded: 1948. **Staff:** Prof 4; Other 4. **Subjects:** Military affairs, business, international relations, current events, political science, education. **Special Collections:** Evans Collection (early American imprints); Shaw-Shoemaker Collection; Western Americana; Gordon L. Cox Collection; Government Printing Office documents collection; U.N. Documents Collection; World War II; genealogy and local history; unit histories; campaigns. **Holdings:** 70,000 books; 3.25 million microforms; 12,760 reels of microfilm; 26,500 documents; 75 linear feet of pamphlets. **Subscriptions:** 600 journals and other serials; 21 newspapers. **Services:** Interlibrary loan; copying; SDI; center open to the public. **Automated Operations:** Computerized public access catalog, cataloging, and circulation. **Computerized Information Services:** DIALOG Information Services, OCLC; CD-ROMs; DDN Network Information Center, USAREUR (electronic mail services). **Networks/Consortia:** Member of FEDLINK. **Publications:** Subject bibliographies, irregular; periodical holdings, annual; InfoBrief, quarterly - for internal distribution only. **Special Indexes:** CD-ROM index (online). **Remarks:** Alternate telephone number(s): 6221 578129. **Staff:** Cheryl Hunter, Chf.; Eileen Diel, Supv., Ref.Serv.; Julia Foscue, Ref.Libn.; Linda Wooster, Ref.Libn.

U.S. Army Garrison - Technical Library
See: U.S. Army - Information Systems Command - Technical Library (16977)

★ 17031 ★
U.S. Army Hospitals - Bassett Army Community Hospital - Medical Library (Med)
Commander USA MEDDAC   Phone: (907)353-5194
Fort Wainwright, AK 99703-7300   George P. Kimmell, Lib.Techn.
Staff: Prof 1. **Subjects:** Surgery, obstetrics/gynecology, pediatrics, nursing, internal medicine, radiology. **Holdings:** 2450 books; 50 bound periodical volumes. **Subscriptions:** 110 journals and other serials. **Services:** Interlibrary loan; library open to the public for reference use only.

★ 17032 ★
U.S. Army Hospitals - Bayne-Jones Army Community Hospital - Medical Library (Med)
Fort Polk, LA 71459-6000   Phone: (318)531-3725
Cecelia B. Higginbotham, Med.Libn.
Staff: Prof 1; Other 1. **Subjects:** Medicine, pathology, hospital administration, dentistry. **Holdings:** 2300 monographs; 4000 bound periodical volumes. **Subscriptions:** 135 serials. **Services:** Interlibrary loan; copying; SDI; library open to the public by appointment. **Automated Operations:** Computerized cataloging and serials. **Computerized Information Services:** MEDLINE, OCLC, DIALOG Information Services. **Networks/Consortia:** Member of National Network of Libraries of Medicine - South Central Region, FEDLINK, Health Services Command Library Network (HSCLN). **Staff:** Patricia A. Derrigo, Lib.Techn.

★ 17033 ★
U.S. Army Hospitals - Blanchfield Army Community Hospital - Medical Library (Med)
Fort Campbell, KY 42223-1498   Phone: (502)798-8014
Lillian G. Graham, Med.Libn.
Founded: 1959. **Staff:** Prof 1; Other 1. **Subjects:** Medicine, allied health sciences. **Special Collections:** Ciba slide collection. **Holdings:** 5700 books; 2400 bound periodical volumes; video and audio cassettes. **Subscriptions:** 396 journals and other serials. **Services:** Interlibrary loan; copying; library open to medical personnel on limited basis. **Computerized Information Services:** MEDLARS, DIALOG Information Services. **Networks/Consortia:** Member of National Network of Libraries of Medicine - Greater Midwest Region, FEDLINK.

★ 17034 ★
U.S. Army Hospitals - Bliss Army Hospital - Medical Library (Med)
Fort Huachuca, AZ 85613-7040   Phone: (602)533-5668
Richard A. Sajac, Lib.Off.
Founded: 1969. **Staff:** Prof 1. **Subjects:** Clinical medicine, nursing, hospital administration. **Special Collections:** Medicine in World War II (especially surgery). **Holdings:** 1354 books; 951 bound and unbound periodical volumes; 112 audio cassettes. **Subscriptions:** 102 journals and other serials. **Services:** Interlibrary loan; copying; library open to the public with approval of Commander. **Computerized Information Services:** Dialcom, Inc. (electronic mail service). **Publications:** Quarterly Report - for internal distribution only. **Remarks:** FAX: (602)533-2930. Electronic mail address(es): MDU 0107 (Dialcom, Inc.). **Staff:** Ann E. Nichols, Libn.

★ 17035 ★
U.S. Army Hospitals - Brooke Army Medical Center - Medical Library (Med)
Bldg. 1001   Phone: (512)221-8182
Fort Sam Houston, TX 78234-6200   Kimmie Yu, Med.Libn.
Founded: 1914. **Staff:** Prof 1; Other 3. **Subjects:** Medicine, dentistry, nursing, allied health sciences, religion, social work. **Holdings:** 16,000 books; 23,500 bound periodical volumes. **Subscriptions:** 650 journals and other serials. **Services:** Interlibrary loan; library not open to the public. **Automated Operations:** Computerized cataloging. **Computerized Information Services:** MEDLINE, OCLC, DIALOG Information Services. **Networks/Consortia:** Member of Council of Research & Academic Libraries (CORAL), Health Oriented Libraries of San Antonio (HOLSA), National Network of Libraries of Medicine - South Central Region. **Remarks:** Alternate telephone number(s): 221-6119.

★ 17036 ★
U.S. Army Hospitals - Commander Silas B. Hays Army Community Hospital - Medical Library (Med)
Commander
USA MEDDAC
Attn: HSXT-CSD (Medical Library)   Phone: (408)242-2023
Fort Ord, CA 93941-5800   Bonnie Grewal, Med.Libn.
Staff: 2. **Subjects:** Medicine and allied health sciences. **Holdings:** 3000 books; 3500 bound periodical volumes. **Subscriptions:** 300 journals and other serials. **Services:** Interlibrary loan; copying. **Computerized Information Services:** MEDLINE, DIALOG Information Services, OCLC, MEDLARS, OPTIMIS (electronic mail service). Performs MEDLARS searches. **Networks/Consortia:** Member of National Network of Libraries of Medicine - Pacific Southwest Region. **Remarks:** Alternate telephone number(s): 242-6607 (Army); 899-0746 (Commercial). FAX: (408)394-7575.

★ 17037 ★
U.S. Army Hospitals - Cutler Army Community Hospital - Medical Library (Med)
Fort Devens, MA 01433-6401   Phone: (508)796-6728
Joan Stehn, Med.Libn.
Staff: Prof 1. **Subjects:** Medicine, surgery, nursing. **Holdings:** 1800 books; 1500 bound periodical volumes. **Subscriptions:** 130 journals and other serials. **Services:** Interlibrary loan; copying; library open to the public for reference use only. **Networks/Consortia:** Member of Northeastern Consortium for Health Information (NECHI).

★ 17038 ★
U.S. Army Hospitals - D.D. Eisenhower Army Medical Center - Medical Library (Med)
Fort Gordon, GA 30905-5650
Phone: (404)791-6765
Judy M. Krivanek, Med.Libn.
Staff: Prof 2; Other 2. **Subjects:** Surgery, psychiatry, internal medicine, dentistry, nursing. **Holdings:** 6114 books; 8969 bound periodical volumes. **Subscriptions:** 500 journals and other serials. **Services:** Interlibrary loan; library not open to the public.

★ 17039 ★
U.S. Army Hospitals - Darnall Army Hospital - Medical Library (Med)
Bldg. 36000
Phone: (817)288-8368
Fort Hood, TX 76544-5063
Frank M. Norton, Adm.Libn.
Staff: Prof 2; Other 1. **Subjects:** Medicine and allied health sciences. **Holdings:** 2600 books; 3500 bound periodical volumes; 400 videotapes. **Subscriptions:** 750 journals and other serials. **Services:** Interlibrary loan; copying; library open to medical professionals. **Automated Operations:** Computerized cataloging, acquisitions, serials, and circulation. **Computerized Information Services:** MEDLINE, DIALOG Information Services, OCLC. **Staff:** Jonella B. Lein, Tech.Info.Spec.

★ 17040 ★
U.S. Army Hospitals - Evans Army Community Hospital - Medical Library (Med)
Bldg. 7500
Phone: (719)579-7286
Fort Carson, CO 80913-5101
Roma A. Marcum, Med.Libn.
Staff: 3. **Subjects:** Medicine, nursing, allied health sciences, patient health education. **Holdings:** 4000 books; 13,000 bound periodical volumes; 360 AV programs; audiotapes. **Subscriptions:** 390 journals and other serials. **Services:** Interlibrary loan; copying; library open to the public with restrictions. **Computerized Information Services:** MEDLARS, OCLC, BRS Information Technologies, DIALOG Information Services; DOCLINE, Dialcom, Inc. (electronic mail services). **Networks/Consortia:** Member of FEDLINK, Colorado Council of Medical Librarians, Plains and Peaks Regional Library Service System, Bibliographical Center for Research, Rocky Mountain Region, Inc. (BCR). **Publications:** Hippocrates hieroglyphics (newsletter) - for internal distribution only. **Remarks:** Alternate telephone number(s): 579-7113. FAX: (719)579-7891. **Staff:** Phyllis Brown, Tech.Serv.; Helen V. Varsel, Circ.

★ 17041 ★
U.S. Army Hospitals - Fitzsimons Army Medical Center - Medical-Technical Library HSHG-ZBM (Med)
Aurora, CO 80045-5000
Phone: (303)361-3378
Alfreda H. Hanna, Adm.Libn.
Founded: 1947. **Staff:** Prof 3; Other 3. **Subjects:** Medicine and allied health sciences. **Holdings:** 12,000 books; 27,000 bound periodical volumes. **Subscriptions:** 830 journals and other serials. **Services:** Interlibrary loan; library not open to the public. **Automated Operations:** Computerized cataloging, serials, and ILL (DOCLINE). **Computerized Information Services:** DIALOG Information Services, BRS Information Technologies, DTIC, Current Contents; CD-ROMs (MEDLINE, CINAHL, HEALTH, PsycINFO, Compact Library: AIDS, PDQ-CD); TenTime (electronic mail service). **Networks/Consortia:** Member of Colorado Council of Medical Librarians, Health Services Command Library Network (HSCLN). **Remarks:** Alternate telephone number(s): (303)361-3407. FAX: (303)340-0528. **Staff:** Ellen Sue Coldren; Carol Deforest.

★ 17042 ★
U.S. Army Hospitals - General Leonard Wood Army Community Hospital - Medical Library (Med)
Fort Leonard Wood, MO 65473-5700
Phone: (314)596-9110
Ronald McNinch, Med.Libn.
Founded: 1950. **Staff:** Prof 1. **Subjects:** Medicine. **Holdings:** 3500 books; 200 bound periodical volumes. **Subscriptions:** 200 journals and other serials. **Services:** Interlibrary loan; library not open to the public. **Computerized Information Services:** MEDLARS. **Remarks:** FAX: (314) 596-9104.

★ 17043 ★
U.S. Army Hospitals - Irwin Army Hospital - Medical Library (Med)
Bldg. 600
Phone: (913)239-7874
Fort Riley, KS 66442-5036
Phyllis J. Whiteside, Med.Libn.
Staff: Prof 1. **Subjects:** Medicine, surgery, dentistry, nursing. **Holdings:** 1431 books; 782 bound periodical volumes; 455 reels of microfilm; 1063 microfiche. **Subscriptions:** 250 journals and other serials. **Services:** Interlibrary loan; copying; library open to the public with restrictions. **Computerized Information Services:** DIALOG Information Services, NLM; DDN Network Information Center (electronic mail service). **Networks/Consortia:** Member of National Network of Libraries of Medicine - Midcontinental Region, BHSL. **Publications:** Newsletter. **Remarks:** FAX: (913)239-7632. Electronic mail address(es): RILELIB@FTRILEY-AMEDD.ARMY.MIL (DDN Network Information Center).

★ 17044 ★
U.S. Army Hospitals - Keller Army Community Hospital - MEDDAC Library (Med)
Bldg. 900
Phone: (914)938-4883
West Point, NY 10996-1197
Halyna Barannik, Libn.
Staff: Prof 1. **Subjects:** Orthopedics, medicine, nursing. **Special Collections:** Sports medicine. **Holdings:** 2500 books; 2800 bound periodical volumes. **Subscriptions:** 212 journals and other serials. **Services:** Interlibrary loan. **Computerized Information Services:** DIALOG Information Services; CD-ROM (MEDLINE). **Networks/Consortia:** Member of Southeastern New York Library Resources Council (SENYLRC), Health Information Libraries of Westchester (HILOW), BHSL. **Remarks:** FAX: (914)938-5164.

★ 17045 ★
U.S. Army Hospitals - Kenner Army Community Hospital - Medical Library (Med)
Fort Lee, VA 23801-5260
Phone: (804)734-1339
Betty K. Lewis, Libn.
Subjects: Medicine. **Holdings:** 2200 volumes. **Services:** Library not open to the public.

★ 17046 ★
U.S. Army Hospitals - Letterman U.S. Army Hospital - Medical Library (Med)
Bldg. 1100, Rm. 338
Presidio of San Francisco
Phone: (415)561-2465
San Francisco, CA 94129-6700
Dixie Meagher, Adm.Libn.
Founded: 1918. **Staff:** Prof 2. **Subjects:** Medicine, nursing, psychology, hospital administration, military medical history. **Holdings:** 5000 books; 10,000 bound periodical volumes. **Subscriptions:** 325 journals and other serials. **Services:** Interlibrary loan; copying; SDI. **Automated Operations:** Computerized cataloging. **Computerized Information Services:** DIALOG Information Services, MEDLARS. **Networks/Consortia:** Member of San Francisco Biomedical Library Network, Northern California and Nevada Medical Library Group (NCNMLG). **Formerly:** Letterman Army Medical Center. **Staff:** Ken Tipton, Ref.Libn.

★ 17047 ★
U.S. Army Hospitals - Lyster Army Community Hospital - Medical Library (Med)
Bldg. 301
U.S. Army Aeromedical Center
Phone: (205)255-7350
Fort Rucker, AL 36362-5333
Mary Fran Prottsman, Med.Libn.
Staff: 1. **Subjects:** Medicine, nursing, veterinary medicine, aviation medicine, dentistry. **Holdings:** 2500 books; 2500 bound and microform periodical volumes. **Subscriptions:** 150 journals and other serials. **Services:** Interlibrary loan; copying; SDI; library open to the public for reference use only. **Computerized Information Services:** MEDLARS, BRS Information Technologies, OCLC, DIALOG Information Services; DOCLINE, Dialcom Inc. (electronic mail services). **Remarks:** Alternate telephone number(s): 255-7349.

★ 17048 ★
U.S. Army Hospitals - Madigan Army Medical Center - Medical Library (Med)
Attn: HSHJ-CLL
Phone: (206)967-6782
Tacoma, WA 98431-5000
Marcia I. Batchelor, Libn.
Founded: 1944. **Staff:** Prof 2; Other 2. **Subjects:** Medicine, dentistry, nursing, hospital administration, pharmacology. **Holdings:** 12,000 books; 13,000 bound periodical volumes; 1000 reels of microfilm; 100 video cassettes. **Subscriptions:** 750 journals and other serials. **Services:** Interlibrary loan; library not open to the public. **Computerized Information Services:** MEDLARS, BRS Information Technologies, OCLC; OnTyme Electronic Message Network Service (electronic mail service). **Networks/Consortia:** Member of FEDLINK. **Publications:** Information Sources and Resources, irregular - to personnel at the center and local medical libraries.

★ 17049 ★
U.S. Army Hospitals - Martin Army Community Hospital - Medical Library (Med)
Bldg. 9200 HSXB-CSD-L   Phone: (404)544-1341
Fort Benning, GA 31905-6100   Janice Missildimer, Med.Libn.
Founded: 1958. **Staff:** Prof 1; Other 1. **Subjects:** Medicine, allied health sciences. **Holdings:** 2300 books; 6008 bound periodical volumes; 500 audio cassette tapes. **Subscriptions:** 317 journals and other serials. **Services:** Interlibrary loan; library open to health care professionals for reference use only. **Computerized Information Services:** MEDLINE. **Networks/Consortia:** Member of National Network of Libraries of Medicine - Southeastern/Atlantic Region, Atlanta Health Science Libraries Consortium (AHSLC), Health Science Libraries Consortium of Central Georgia (HSLCG). **Publications:** Library Acquisitions; Internal News Bulletin, quarterly.

★ 17050 ★
U.S. Army Hospitals - McDonald Army Community Hospital - Medical Library (Med)
Fort Eustis, VA 23604-5549   Phone: (804)878-5800
                      Ruth E. Shepard, Libn.
Staff: 1. **Subjects:** Medicine, dentistry, nursing. **Holdings:** 1500 books; 1100 bound periodical volumes. **Subscriptions:** 100 journals and other serials. **Services:** Interlibrary loan; library open to the public for reference use only.

★ 17051 ★
U.S. Army Hospitals - Noble Army Hospital - Medical Library (Med)
HSXQ-DCS   Phone: (205)848-2411
Fort McClellan, AL 36205   Kathryn S. Aide, Lib.Techn.
Founded: 1951. **Staff:** 1. **Subjects:** Medicine and allied health sciences. **Holdings:** 2075 books; 614 bound periodical volumes. **Subscriptions:** 129 journals and other serials. **Services:** Interlibrary loan; copying; library open to the public for reference use only. **Networks/Consortia:** Member of Health Services Command Library Network (HSCLN), National Network of Libraries of Medicine - Southeastern/Atlantic Region.

★ 17052 ★
U.S. Army Hospitals - Tripler Army Medical Center - Medical Library (Med)
Honolulu, HI 96859-5000   Phone: (808)433-6391
                Linda Requena, Chf., Med.Lib.
Staff: Prof 2; Other 2. **Subjects:** Medicine, paramedical sciences, dentistry, nursing. **Holdings:** 15,000 books; 25,000 bound periodical volumes. **Subscriptions:** 800 journals and other serials. **Services:** Interlibrary loan; copying; SDI; library not open to the public. **Automated Operations:** Computerized cataloging. **Computerized Information Services:** MEDLINE, OCLC, DIALOG Information Services. **Networks/Consortia:** Member of FEDLINK, Medical Library Group of Hawaii. **Special Indexes:** Union Lists. **Remarks:** FAX: (808)433-4892.

★ 17053 ★
U.S. Army Hospitals - Walson Army Community Hospital - Medical Library (Med)
Fort Dix, NJ 08640-6734   Phone: (609)562-5741
Founded: 1959. **Staff:** 1. **Subjects:** Medicine, dentistry, nursing, psychiatry. **Holdings:** 4229 books; 20 microfiche; 1058 reels of microfilm; 39 AV titles. **Subscriptions:** 291 journals and other serials; 6 newspapers. **Services:** Interlibrary loan. **Networks/Consortia:** Member of National Network of Libraries of Medicine - Middle Atlantic Region. **Remarks:** FAX: (609)562-3333. **Formerly:** Walson Army Hospital. **Staff:** E. Pearl Crain, LIb.Techn.

★ 17054 ★
U.S. Army Hospitals - Walter Reed Army Medical Center - WRAMC Medical Library (Med)
Bldg. 2, Rm. 2G05   Phone: (202)576-1238
Washington, DC 20307-5001   Hoyt W. Galloway, Lib.Dir.
Staff: Prof 3; Other 7. **Subjects:** Clinical medicine, research, allied health sciences, history of medicine. **Special Collections:** Fred C. Ainsworth Endowment Library (history of military medicine); patient education. **Holdings:** 10,000 books; 18,000 bound periodical volumes. **Subscriptions:** 750 journals and other serials. **Services:** Interlibrary loan; library not open to the public. **Automated Operations:** Computerized public access catalog, cataloging, serials, circulation, and ILL. **Computerized Information Services:** DIALOG Information Services, DTIC, MEDLARS, NLM, MEDLINE; CD-ROM (MEDLINE); Dialcom, Inc. (electronic mail service). **Networks/Consortia:** Member of FEDLINK. **Publications:** WRAMC Medical Staff Bibliography. **Remarks:** FAX: (202)576-2478. **Staff:** Judy Hartman, Chf., Tech.Serv.; Ann Dougherty, Chf., Pub.Serv.; Virginia Velasco, ILL; Theresa Gabriel, Acq.

★ 17055 ★
U.S. Army Hospitals - William Beaumont Army Medical Center - Medical Library (Med)
Bldg. 7777, Rm. 2-246   Phone: (915)569-2580
El Paso, TX 79920-5001   Carolyn J. Rymer, Chf.Med.Libn.
Founded: 1931. **Staff:** Prof 2; Other 2. **Subjects:** Surgery, medicine, nursing, dentistry, trauma medicine. **Holdings:** 3000 books; 15,000 bound periodical volumes; 2000 periodical volumes on microfilm; 630 AV programs. **Subscriptions:** 600 journals and other serials. **Services:** Interlibrary loan; library not open to the public. **Computerized Information Services:** MEDLINE, DIALOG Information Services, OCLC, DTIC. **Networks/Consortia:** Member of National Network of Libraries of Medicine - South Central Region, Del Norte Biosciences Library Consortium. **Special Catalogs:** Catalog of Audiovisual Holdings (book). **Remarks:** FAX: (915)569-1534. **Staff:** Elaine W. Berg, Ref./Cat.Libn.

★ 17056 ★
U.S. Army Hospitals - Womack Army Medical Center - Medical Library (Med)
Fort Bragg, NC 28307-5000   Phone: (919)432-1819
                 Joan Hathaway, Med.Libn.
Founded: 1958. **Staff:** 3. **Subjects:** Medicine, dentistry, allied health sciences, orthopedics. **Holdings:** 3444 books; 3509 bound periodical volumes; 2 VF drawers of clippings, pamphlets, documents. **Subscriptions:** 197 journals and other serials. **Services:** Interlibrary loan; library not open to the public. **Automated Operations:** Computerized cataloging. **Computerized Information Services:** MEDLINE; Dialcom, Inc., DDN Network Information Center (electronic mail services). Performs searches free of charge. **Networks/Consortia:** Member of FEDLINK, Cape Fear Health Sciences Information Consortium (CFHSIC), National Network of Libraries of Medicine - Southeastern/Atlantic Region, South Central Health Information Network of North Carolina (SCHIN of NC). **Remarks:** FAX: (919)432-5851. Electronic mail address(es): BRAGGLIB@FTBRAGG-AMEDD.ARMY.MIL (DDN Network Information Center). **Formerly:** Womack Army Community Hospital.

U.S. Army Museum, Presidio of Monterey
See: **U.S. Army - Center of Military History - U.S. Army Museum, Presidio of Monterey** (16927)

★ 17057 ★
U.S. Army Post - Aberdeen Proving Ground Support Activity - Community Recreation Division - Post Library (Mil)
Bldg. 3320
Aberdeen Proving Ground, MD 21005-5001   Phone: (301)278-3417
Staff: Prof 2; Other 7. **Subjects:** Biography, world literature, auto repair, military history. **Holdings:** 40,382 books; 1700 cassettes. **Subscriptions:** 270 journals and other serials; 15 newspapers. **Services:** Interlibrary loan; library open to the military community. **Automated Operations:** Computerized cataloging. **Computerized Information Services:** DIALOG Information Services. Performs searches free of charge. **Networks/Consortia:** Member of FEDLINK. **Remarks:** FAX: (301)273-9337. Maintains branch library at Edgewood Area. **Staff:** Tina L. Pinnix.

★ 17058 ★
U.S. Army Post - Fort Belvoir - Library System (Mil)
Bldg. 1024   Phone: (703)664-6257
Fort Belvoir, VA 22060   Wendy S. Hill, Act.Dir.
Founded: 1939. **Staff:** Prof 6; Other 9. **Subjects:** Military science, social sciences, management. **Holdings:** 66,786 books; 20,000 documents; 1200 tapes; 8500 periodical volumes on microfilm. **Subscriptions:** 550 journals and other serials; 43 newspapers. **Services:** Interlibrary loan; library open to Department of Defense personnel and their families. **Automated Operations:** CLSI. **Computerized Information Services:** OCLC, DTIC. **Networks/Consortia:** Member of FEDLINK. **Formerly:** Its Van Noy Library. **Staff:** Phyllis Cassler, Ref.Libn.; Jane Drabkin, Pub.Serv.; Holly Hill, Tech.Serv.; Carolyn Graves, Tech.Serv.

★ 17059 ★
U.S. Army Post - Fort Benning - Sayers Memorial Library (Mil)
Bldg. 93   Phone: (404)545-4911
Fort Benning, GA 31905   John P. Cook, Supv.Libn.
Founded: 1920. **Staff:** Prof 3; Other 6. **Subjects:** Military science, art, management, business, general reference. **Holdings:** 65,000 books; 5000

bound and unbound periodicals; 1077 periodical volumes on microfilm; 2000 AV programs. **Subscriptions:** 365 journals and other serials; 30 newspapers. **Services:** Interlibrary loan; copying; library open to military personnel and civilian post employees. **Computerized Information Services:** DIALOG Information Services, BRS Information Technologies; PROFS (electronic mail service). **Networks/Consortia:** Member of Georgia Online Database (GOLD), TRADOC Library and Information Network (TRALINET). **Staff:** Barbara Jordan; Ann Pierce.

★ 17060 ★
U.S. Army Post - Fort Bragg - Library (Mil)
HQ, XVIII Airborne Corps & Fort Bragg
AFZA-PA-R   Phone: (919)396-6919
Fort Bragg, NC 28307-5000   Barbara A. Eller, Chf.Libn.
Founded: 1941. **Staff:** 14. **Subjects:** Military science, military history, education. **Holdings:** 78,156 books; 1 million microforms, including periodicals and special collections. **Subscriptions:** 651 journals and other serials; 32 newspapers. **Services:** Interlibrary loan; copying. **Computerized Information Services:** DIALOG Information Services.

★ 17061 ★
U.S. Army Post - Fort Carson - Grant Library (Mil)
Fort Carson, CO 80913   Phone: (719)579-2350
                                        Rebecca S. Harris
Staff: Prof 3; Other 11. **Subjects:** General collection. **Special Collections:** Colorado. **Holdings:** 32,386 books; 1802 sound recordings; 5400 pamphlets; 9000 microforms; 593 videotapes. **Subscriptions:** 252 journals and other serials; 20 newspapers. **Services:** Interlibrary loan; copying; library open to Fort Carson community members and active or retired military personnel. **Automated Operations:** Computerized cataloging and ILL. **Networks/Consortia:** Member of Plains and Peaks Regional Library Service System, FEDLINK, Bibliographical Center for Research, Rocky Mountain Region, Inc. (BCR). **Remarks:** Alternate telephone number(s): 579-2842. FAX: (719)576-0039.

★ 17062 ★
U.S. Army Post - Fort Clayton - Community Recreation Division - Library (Mil)
P.O. Drawer 933   Phone: 507-87-38-53
APO Miami, FL 34004-5000   John D. Paulding, Supv.Libn.
Staff: Prof 3; Other 6. **Subjects:** Military sciences, Latin America, Panama. **Holdings:** 60,000 books; 25,000 AV programs and reels of microfilm. **Subscriptions:** 300 journals and other serials; 30 newspapers. **Services:** Interlibrary loan; library not open to the public. **Publications:** Periodical holdings list. **Remarks:** Located in Panama. **Staff:** David Hunter, Ref.Libn.

U.S. Army Post - Fort Dix
See: U.S. Army Post - Training Center & Fort Dix (17076)

U.S. Army Post - Fort Gordon
See: U.S. Army - TRADOC - Signal Center & Fort Gordon (17023)

★ 17063 ★
U.S. Army Post - Fort Greely - Library (Mil)
P.O. Box 1107   Phone: (907)873-3217
Delta Junction, AK 99737   Alfred Preston, Adm.Libn.
Founded: 1949. **Staff:** Prof 1; Other 1. **Subjects:** Arctic region, war and history, general fiction. **Special Collections:** Arctic. **Holdings:** 23,900 volumes; 3610 AV programs. **Subscriptions:** 100 journals and other serials; 8 newspapers. **Services:** Interlibrary loan; library open to the public. **Computerized Information Services:** CD-ROM (LaserCat). **Networks/Consortia:** Member of Western Library Network (WLN). **Staff:** Betty Phillips, Lib.Techn.

★ 17064 ★
U.S. Army Post - Fort Hamilton - Library (Mil)
Bldg. 404   Phone: (718)630-4875
Brooklyn, NY 11252-5155   Amelia K. Sefton, Libn.
Founded: 1942. **Staff:** Prof 1; Other 1. **Subjects:** Military history, science, and tactics. **Special Collections:** Newyorkana Collection. **Holdings:** 27,000 volumes; phonograph records. **Services:** Interlibrary loan; library not open to the public. **Computerized Information Services:** DIALOG Information Services, OCLC. **Networks/Consortia:** Member of TRADOC Library and Information Network (TRALINET). **Remarks:** Alternate telephone number(s): 630-4101.

★ 17065 ★
U.S. Army Post - Fort Hood - Community Recreation Division - Casey Memorial Library (Mil)
Bldg. 18000   Phone: (817)287-5202
Fort Hood, TX 76544   Mary F. Rogerson, Adm.Libn.
Staff: Prof 4; Other 11. **Subjects:** General collection with emphasis on military science. **Holdings:** 69,000 books; 600 phonograph recordings; 800 videocassettes; 32,000 microforms. **Subscriptions:** 300 journals and other serials; 30 newspapers. **Services:** Interlibrary loan; copying; library open to military and Fort Hood employees. **Automated Operations:** Computerized cataloging and ILL. **Computerized Information Services:** DIALOG Information Services, OCLC; internal database. **Networks/Consortia:** Member of FEDLINK. **Publications:** Selected Subject Bibliographies, irregular. **Staff:** Pam Shelton, Cat.; Patsy Shields, Ref.; George Jung, Ref.

U.S. Army Post - Fort Jackson
See: U.S. Army Post - Training Command & Fort Jackson (17077)

★ 17066 ★
U.S. Army Post - Fort Lewis - Library System (Mil)
Bldg. 2109   Phone: (206)967-7736
Fort Lewis, WA 98433-5000   Patricia A. Louderback, Chf.Libn.
Founded: 1944. **Staff:** Prof 7; Other 18. **Subjects:** Military science, social sciences, psychology, mathematics, area studies, education, literature. **Special Collections:** Military affairs (8000 titles). **Holdings:** 110,000 books; 11,880 microforms; 3800 phonograph records, audiocassettes, videocassettes, art prints. **Subscriptions:** 610 journals and other serials. **Services:** Interlibrary loan; library not open to the public. **Computerized Information Services:** OCLC, DIALOG Information Services, WLN. **Networks/Consortia:** Member of Western Library Network (WLN). **Remarks:** Fort Lewis Library System consists of 1 main library, 3 branch libraries, and 1 field library. **Staff:** Bonnie Tucker, Main Post Libn.; Merry Magie, Br.Libn.; Elsa Largen, Proc.Ctr.; Ute Jarasitis, ILL; Mary Athey, Ch.Serv.; Deborah Mayers, Ref.Libn.; Jeremy Marshall, Ref.Libn.; Cathy Kargacin, Br.Libn.

★ 17067 ★
U.S. Army Post - Fort McPherson - Library System (Mil)
Bldg. 250   Phone: (404)752-2665
Fort McPherson, GA 30330-5000   Helen T. Kiss, Chf.Libn.
Staff: Prof 3; Other 5. **Subjects:** Military history. **Holdings:** 44,000 books; 11,000 Army and Department of Defense documents. **Subscriptions:** 450 journals and other serials; 15 newspapers. **Services:** Interlibrary loan; library not open to the public. **Computerized Information Services:** DIALOG Information Services, DTIC, OCLC. **Networks/Consortia:** Member of Georgia Online Database (GOLD), FEDLINK.

★ 17068 ★
U.S. Army Post - Fort Richardson - Library (Mil)
Bldg. 636   Phone: (907)862-9188
Fort Richardson, AK 99505   Doris A. Sheible, Lib.Dir.
Founded: 1950. **Staff:** Prof 1; Other 2. **Subjects:** Military science, Arctic regions, foreign languages. **Special Collections:** Military science; military history; Arctic region. **Holdings:** 44,500 books; 9300 microfiche; 7000 pamphlets; 3384 audiotapes and compact discs. **Subscriptions:** 172 journals and other serials; 23 newspapers. **Services:** Interlibrary loan; copying; reader's advisory; library open to the public for reference use only. **Networks/Consortia:** Member of Western Library Network (WLN).

★ 17069 ★
U.S. Army Post - Fort Riley - Libraries (Mil)
Bldg. 7264   Phone: (913)239-5305
Fort Riley, KS 66442-6416   Barbara Eussen, Chf.Libn.
Staff: Prof 2. **Subjects:** Military science. **Holdings:** 30,000 books; periodicals on microfilm; telephone books on microfiche; 1000 video cassettes. **Subscriptions:** 100 journals and other serials; 13 newspapers. **Services:** Interlibrary loan; copying. **Automated Operations:** Computerized cataloging and ILL. **Networks/Consortia:** Member of FEDLINK. **Staff:** Darrel Hoerle.

★ 17070 ★
U.S. Army Post - Fort Sam Houston - Library (Mil)
Bldg. 1222   Phone: (512)221-4702
Fort Sam Houston, TX 78234-5000   Alfonso J. Butcher, Post Libn.
Staff: Prof 4; Other 5. **Subjects:** Military history, management, health care administration, educational development. **Special Collections:** Local Military History; Military Archives (post returns for Fort Sam Houston). **Holdings:** 60,000 books; 2155 volumes on microfilm. **Subscriptions:** 200 journals and other serials; 18 newspapers. **Services:** Interlibrary loan; copying; library open to the public for reference use only. **Automated Operations:** Computerized cataloging. **Computerized Information Services:** DIALOG Information Services, OCLC. **Staff:** Mary Ann Deason, Lib.Coord.; Susan Artiglia, Ref.Libn.; Aurea Reyes, Cat.

★ 17071 ★
U.S. Army Post - Fort Stewart/Hunter AAF Library System (Mil)
Bldg. 411   Phone: (912)767-2828
Fort Stewart, GA 31314-6080   Richard D. Boyce, Chf.Libn.
Founded: 1942. **Staff:** Prof 4. **Subjects:** Military science, military history. **Special Collections:** Library of American Civilization (microfiche); Newsbank and Names in News; Korean language books and magazines; Library of English Literature (microfiche). **Holdings:** 76,833 books; 271 bound periodical volumes; 57,156 microfiche; phonograph records; cassettes; VF items; magnetic tapes. **Subscriptions:** 365 journals and other serials; 54 newspapers. **Services:** Interlibrary loan; copying; library open to military personnel and dependents. **Computerized Information Services:** OCLC, OCLC EPIC. **Networks/Consortia:** Member of Georgia Online Database (GOLD), FEDLINK. **Remarks:** FAX: (912)767-3794. The library system consists of the main post library, a branch library, and a bookmobile. **Staff:** M. Malinda Johnson, Post Libn.; Fred Berg, Ref.Libn.; Dawn Ryan, Tech.Serv.Libn.

★ 17072 ★
U.S. Army Post - Fort Story - Library (Mil)
Bldg. T-530   Phone: (804)422-7548
Fort Story, VA 23459-5067   Leslie A. Smail, Chf.
Staff: Prof 1; Other 2. **Subjects:** Military science and general collection. **Special Collections:** World War II. **Holdings:** 21,000 books; 600 videocassettes; 6 war games; 8 VF drawers of ephemera; 500 audiocassettes; 150 books on tape. **Subscriptions:** 110 journals and other serials; 6 newspapers. **Services:** Interlibrary loan; copying; library open to military personnel, retirees, civil service, and dependents only. **Computerized Information Services:** OCLC, DIALOG Information Services; PROFS (electronic mail service). **Networks/Consortia:** Member of FEDLINK, TRADOC Library and Information Network (TRALINET). **Remarks:** Alternate telephone number(s): 422-7525. Electronic mail address(es): SMAILL(MON1) (PROFS).

★ 17073 ★
U.S. Army Post - Fort Wainwright - Library (Mil)
Bldg. 3700   Phone: (907)353-7131
Fort Wainwright, AK 99703   Geraldine Smith, Adm.Libn.
Founded: 1951. **Staff:** Prof 2; Other 4. **Subjects:** General collection. **Special Collections:** Alaska and the Arctic; military. **Holdings:** 27,000 books; 6500 phonograph records, audio cassettes, compact discs; 2352 video cassettes. **Subscriptions:** 156 journals and other serials. **Services:** Interlibrary loan; library open to the general public for reference use only. **Networks/Consortia:** Member of Alaska Library Network (ALN), Western Library Network (WLN). **Remarks:** Alternate telephone number(s): 353-7131. **Staff:** Geraldine Smith; Nancy Kotarski.

★ 17074 ★
U.S. Army Post - Presidio of San Francisco - Post Library System
Bldg. 386
Presidio of San Francisco, CA 94129-5204
Defunct.

★ 17075 ★
U.S. Army Post - Training Center Engineer & Fort Leonard Wood - Bruce C. Clarke Community Library (Mil)
3202 N. Nebraska Ave.   Phone: (314)563-7169
Fort Leonard Wood, MO 65473-5125   Christine M. Reser, Chf.Libn.
Founded: 1941. **Staff:** Prof 5; Other 10. **Subjects:** Military affairs, history, government, social sciences, sports and recreation. **Special Collections:**

Children's collection; framed art reproductions. **Holdings:** 44,000 books; magazines on microfilm; college catalogs on microfiche; video cassettes; Newsbank, 1970-1990, on microfiche. **Subscriptions:** 180 journals and other serials; 20 newspapers. **Services:** Interlibrary loan; copying; library open to the public. **Automated Operations:** Computerized cataloging, acquisitions, and ILL. **Computerized Information Services:** BRS Information Technologies, DTIC, DIALOG Information Services; PROFS (electronic mail service). **Networks/Consortia:** Member of TRADOC Library and Information Network (TRALINET). **Remarks:** FAX: (314)563-5064. **Staff:** Tamara McAnally, Post Libn.; Freddie Siber, Ref.Libn.

★ 17076 ★
U.S. Army Post - Training Center & Fort Dix - General Library (Mil)
Hartford & Pointville Rds., Bldg. 5756   Phone: (609)562-4858
Fort Dix, NJ 08640-5111   Wanda C. James, Act.Chf.
Staff: 3. **Subjects:** General collection with emphasis on military science. **Holdings:** 77,000 books; 2000 reels of microfilm. **Subscriptions:** 250 journals and other serials; 10 newspapers. **Services:** Interlibrary loan; copying; library open to the public for reference use only. **Automated Operations:** Computerized cataloging and acquisitions. **Computerized Information Services:** BRS Information Technologies, DIALOG Information Services, OCLC; PROFS (electronic mail service). **Networks/Consortia:** Member of TRADOC Library and Information Network (TRALINET). **Remarks:** FAX: (609)562-3939.

★ 17077 ★
U.S. Army Post - Training Command & Fort Jackson - Thomas Lee Hall Post Library (Mil)
U.S. Army Main Lib., Community Recreation Div.
Bldg. 4679   Phone: (803)751-5589
Fort Jackson, SC 29207-5170   Fred A. Bush, Lib.Dir.
Founded: 1946. **Staff:** Prof 2. **Subjects:** Military history, business and management, auto repair, arts and crafts, children's literature. **Holdings:** 80,000 books; 130 framed art prints; 500 video cassettes; Newsbank, 1984-1991. **Subscriptions:** 300 journals and other serials; 15 newspapers. **Services:** Interlibrary loan; copying; library open to the public for reference use only. **Automated Operations:** Computerized acquisitions. **Computerized Information Services:** DIALOG Information Services, BRS Information Technologies; OPTIMIS, PROFS (electronic mail services). **Networks/Consortia:** Member of TRADOC Library and Information Network (TRALINET).

★ 17078 ★
U.S. Army Research Office - Technical Library (Sci-Engr)
Box 12211   Phone: (919)549-4227
Research Triangle Park, NC 27709-2211   Brenda Mann, Tech.Libn.
Staff: Prof 1; Other 2. **Subjects:** Physical sciences, engineering, materials, mathematics, geosciences, biology. **Holdings:** 2400 books. **Subscriptions:** 168 journals and other serials; 10 newspapers. **Services:** Library open to other government agencies. **Automated Operations:** Computerized cataloging. **Remarks:** FAX: (919)549-4310.

U.S. Army Topographic Engineering Center
See: **U.S. Army - Corps of Engineers - Topographic Engineering Center** (16964)

★ 17079 ★
U.S. Army/U.S. Air Force - Offices of the Surgeons General - Joint Medical Library (Med)
5109 Leesburg Pike, Rm. 670   Phone: (703)756-8028
Falls Church, VA 22041-3258   Diane Zehnpfennig, Lib.Dir.
Founded: 1969. **Staff:** Prof 1; Other 2. **Subjects:** Military and general medicine, hospital administration. **Special Collections:** Annual Report of the Surgeon General, U.S. Army, 1818 to present. **Holdings:** 13,000 books; 8000 bound periodical volumes; 500 microfiche; 200 pamphlets. **Subscriptions:** 430 journals and other serials. **Services:** Interlibrary loan; library open to the public for reference use only. **Computerized Information Services:** OCLC, DIALOG Information Services, DTIC, MEDLARS; OPTIMIS, Dialcom, Inc. (electronic mail services). **Remarks:** FAX: (703)756-0243. Electronic mail address(es): MDU0686 (Dialcom, Inc.).

★17080★
U.S. Army War College - Library (Mil)
Attn: AWCSL, Bldg. 122
Carlisle Barracks   Phone: (717)245-4319
Carlisle, PA 17013-5050   Bohdan I. Kohutiak, Dir.
Founded: 1951. **Staff:** 28. **Subjects:** Military science, strategy, international relations, leadership and management, international law, area studies. **Holdings:** 213,000 books and documents; 7209 bound periodical volumes; 54,501 uncataloged documents and theses; 4191 microforms; 2400 AV programs. **Subscriptions:** 964 journals and other serials; 38 newspapers. **Services:** Interlibrary loan; library not open to the public. **Automated Operations:** Computerized public access catalog, cataloging, acquisitions, serials, and circulation. **Computerized Information Services:** DIALOG Information Services; internal database; DDN Network Information Center (electronic mail service). **Networks/Consortia:** Member of FEDLINK. **Publications:** Periodicals Directory, annual; bibliographies, irregular; Library Acquisitions Bulletin. **Remarks:** FAX: (717)245-3323. Electronic mail address(es): KOHUTIAB@CARLISLE-EMH2.ARMY.MIL (DDN Network Information Center). **Staff:** Iqbal Junaid, Sys.Libn.; Lidwina J. Gole, Chf., Pub.Serv.; James J. Dorrian, Chf.Tech.Serv.

U.S. Attorney
See: **U.S. Dept. of Justice** (17263)

★17081★
U.S. Bancorp - Resource Library (Bus-Fin)
555 S.W. Oak St.
Portland, OR 97204   Phone: (503)275-5816
Founded: 1971. **Staff:** 1. **Subjects:** Banking and finance, management, personnel administration and supervision, education and training, psychology and sociology. **Special Collections:** History of U.S. National Bank of Oregon. **Holdings:** 1500 books; 455 AV cassettes. **Subscriptions:** 50 journals and other serials. **Services:** Library not open to the public. **Publications:** Resource Guide, annual update - for internal distribution only. **Remarks:** FAX: (503)275-4838. **Staff:** Judith A. Green, Rsrc.Libn.

United States Book Exchange
See: **Universal Serials & Book Exchange, Inc. - Library** (17976)

★17082★
United States Borax Research Corporation - Technical Information Department (Sci-Engr)
412 Crescent Way   Phone: (714)490-6064
Anaheim, CA 92801   Chitra Krishnaswamy, Mgr.
Founded: 1956. **Staff:** Prof 2; Other 3. **Subjects:** Chemistry, agriculture, mining, metallurgy, glass, ceramics, industrial minerals. **Holdings:** 4400 volumes; 2200 bound periodical volumes; 1500 government research reports; 6 VF drawers of patents; 14,000 company research reports; 12 drawers of microcards; 500 reels of microfilm. **Subscriptions:** 200 journals and other serials. **Services:** Interlibrary loan; copying; library open to the public for reference use only on request. **Computerized Information Services:** DIALOG Information Services, DTIC, NPIRS (National Pesticide Information Retrieval System); STAR (internal database). **Publications:** Library Bulletin, weekly - for internal distribution only. **Special Indexes:** Indexes to internal reports and patents (online). **Remarks:** FAX: (714)490-6062.

★17083★
U.S. Botanic Garden - Library (Biol Sci)
245 First St., S.W.   Phone: (202)226-4082
Washington, DC 20024   Holly Harmar Shimizu, Pub.Prog.Spec.
Subjects: Horticulture, botany. **Holdings:** 1000 books. **Services:** Library open to the public by appointment. **Publications:** Plant Culture Sheets. **Remarks:** Offers a Plant Information Service during weekday mornings at the above telephone number.

★17084★
U.S. Bureau of Alcohol, Tobacco and Firearms - National Laboratory Library (Sci-Engr)
1401 Research Blvd.   Phone: (301)294-0410
Rockville, MD 20850   Paula Deutsch, Lib.Techn.
Staff: 1. **Subjects:** Alcohol, analytical techniques, forensic sciences and photography, firearms, tobacco. **Holdings:** 6000 books; 4000 bound periodical volumes; 25 volumes of laboratory reports; government documents. **Subscriptions:** 100 journals and other serials. **Services:** Interlibrary loan; library not open to the public. **Automated Operations:** Computerized cataloging. **Computerized Information Services:** DIALOG Information Services, OCLC, Data-Star. **Networks/Consortia:** Member of FEDLINK. **Special Catalogs:** Technical publications of the ATF Laboratory System. **Remarks:** The Bureau of Alcohol, Tobacco and Firearms is part of the U.S. Department of the Treasury.

★17085★
U.S. Bureau of Alcohol, Tobacco and Firearms - Reference Library (Sci-Engr)
650 Massachusetts Ave. N.W.   Phone: (202)927-7890
Washington, DC 20226   Vicki R. Herrmann, Libn.
Founded: 1979. **Staff:** Prof 1. **Subjects:** Alcohol, tobacco, firearms, explosives. **Special Collections:** Tax and regulation history of the alcohol and tobacco industries in the United States (200 volumes). **Holdings:** 700 books; 100 bound periodical volumes; 1000 linear feet of indexed hearings, projects, tasks, and correspondence; 25 drawers of microfiche of historical documents. **Subscriptions:** 250 journals and other serials. **Services:** Interlibrary loan; copying; SDI; reading room open to the public; archives open to the public with written permission. **Automated Operations:** Computerized cataloging, serials, and circulation. **Computerized Information Services:** OCLC, NEXIS; internal database. Performs searches free of charge. **Special Indexes:** Index to correspondence; indexes to internal and bureau publications, rulings and procedures, relevant Treasury Decisions, archival projects, and legal memoranda.

U.S. Bureau of the Census - California State Census Data Center
See: **California State Census Data Center - Library** (2513)

★17086★
U.S. Bureau of the Census - Information Services Program - Atlanta Regional Office (Soc Sci)
1365 Peachtree St., N.E., 3rd Fl.
Capp Library
Atlanta, GA 30309-3112   Phone: (404)347-2274
Staff: 4. **Subjects:** U.S. census reports. **Holdings:** Figures not available. **Services:** Office open to the public. **Remarks:** FAX: (404)347-1707. **Staff:** Stephanie Staggers-Profit, Info.Serv.Spec.; Bea Piddock, Info.Serv.Spec.; Mary Beth Vetter, Info.Asst.

★17087★
U.S. Bureau of the Census - Information Services Program - Boston Regional Office - Library (Soc Sci)
10 Causeway St., Rm. 553   Phone: (617)565-7078
Boston, MA 02222-1084   Arthur G. Dukakis, Reg.Dir.
Staff: 4. **Subjects:** U.S. census reports. **Holdings:** 4000 books; 8 VF drawers; 1982 economic censuses, 1980 census reports (hard copy and microfiche); census maps. **Subscriptions:** 16 journals and other serials. **Services:** Copying; library open to the public. **Remarks:** FAX: (617)565-7108. **Staff:** Christine Payne, Info.Serv.Spec.

★17088★
U.S. Bureau of the Census - Information Services Program - Census Publication Center (Soc Sci)
6900 W. Jefferson
Lakewood, CO 80235   Phone: (303)969-7750
Subjects: U.S. census reports. **Holdings:** Figures not available. **Services:** Copying; statistical assistance; center open to the public. **Remarks:** FAX: (303)969-7020. **Staff:** Kendrick Ellwanger, Coord., Info.Serv.Prog.; Jerry O'Donnell, Info.Serv.Spec.; Pat Rodriguez, Census Info.Techn.; Homana Pawiki, Info.Serv.Spec.; Jackie Wells, Info.Serv.Spec.

★17089★
U.S. Bureau of the Census - Information Services Program - Charlotte Regional Office - Library (Soc Sci)
222 S. Church St., Suite 505
Charlotte, NC 28202   Phone: (704)371-6144
Founded: 1977. **Staff:** Prof 1; Other 1. **Subjects:** U.S. census reports. **Holdings:** 4000 books; 60 bound periodical volumes; 4 drawers of microfiche. **Services:** Copying; library open to the public for reference use only. **Computerized Information Services:** CD-ROMs. **Remarks:** FAX: (704)371-6515. **Staff:** Ken Wright, Info.Serv.Spec.; Nancy Olson, Info.Serv.Tech.; Dee Dee Hager, Info.Serv.Asst.

★17090★
U.S. Bureau of the Census - Information Services Program - Chicago Regional Office - Library (Soc Sci)
175 W Jackson Blvd., Rm. 557   Phone: (312)353-0980
Chicago, IL 60604   Stanley D. Moore, Reg.Dir.
Founded: 1975. **Staff:** Prof 3; Other 1. **Subjects:** U.S. census - population, housing, manufacturers, retail trade, agriculture, wholesale/service trades. **Holdings:** 3500 books; 350 bound periodical volumes; 200 series; Census Bureau computer tape technical documentation; 1980 census data on microfiche; census tract maps; block maps of Illinois and Indiana. **Services:** Copying (limited); assistance with census data through telephone access services; free census data access and use workshops; consultations; center open to the public. **Networks/Consortia:** Member of Illinois State Data Center Cooperative (ISDCC), Indiana State Data Center. **Publications:** Census Information Digest - to Illinois, Indiana, and Wisconsin regional users of census data. **Remarks:** FAX: (312)353-3824. **Staff:** Stephen Laue, Info.Serv.Spec.; Gregory Howard, Census Awareness Spec.; Dorothee McGrier, Info.Serv.Techn.; Angele Johnson, Info.Serv.Spec.; Al Castillo, Community Awareness Spec.

★17091★
U.S. Bureau of the Census - Information Services Program - Dallas Regional Office - Library (Soc Sci)
6303 Harry Hines Blvd., Suite 210   Phone: (214)767-7105
Dallas, TX 75235   Mickey Cole, Coord.
Founded: 1976. **Staff:** Prof 6; Other 2. **Subjects:** U.S. census reports. **Holdings:** 3500 volumes; 1980 census reports (hard copy and microfiche). **Subscriptions:** 12 journals and other serials. **Services:** Copying (limited); library open to the public. **Staff:** Willie DeBerry, Spec.; Marisela Lopez, Spec.; Paula Wright, Spec.; Tomas Zuniga, Spec.; Beverly Childs, Spec.

★17092★
U.S. Bureau of the Census - Information Services Program - Detroit Regional Office - Information Center (Soc Sci)
27300 W. 11 Mile Rd., Suite 200   Phone: (313)354-4654
Southfield, MI 48034   Vincent L. Kountz, Info.Serv.Spec.
Founded: 1977. **Staff:** Prof 2; Other 1. **Subjects:** U.S. census reports. **Special Collections:** 1980 Census for Michigan, Ohio, and West Virginia (microfiche). **Holdings:** 3550 volumes; federal and state publications. **Subscriptions:** 3 newspapers. **Services:** Copying; center open to the public. **Publications:** CAPPSULES, quarterly; Network Notes, quarterly. **Remarks:** FAX: (313)355-1259. **Formerly:** Located in Detroit, MI. **Staff:** Barbara Clayton, Census Data Spec.; Jane C. Garcia.

★17093★
U.S. Bureau of the Census - Information Services Program - Kansas City Office - Library (Soc Sci)
1 Gateway Center, Suite 500
4th & State St.
Kansas City, KS 66101   Phone: (913)236-3728
Staff: Prof 5; Other 1. **Subjects:** U.S. census reports - population, demographics. **Holdings:** Figures not available. **Services:** Copying; library open to the public. **Publications:** Midwest Messenger, quarterly - to selected mailing list. **Staff:** Cheryl Sorrell, Commun.Serv.Spec.; Bill Yates, Info.Spec.; Rachel Estrada, Commun.Serv.Spec.; Marietta Gumbel, Commun.Serv.Spec.

★17094★
U.S. Bureau of the Census - Information Services Program - Los Angeles Regional Office - Library (Soc Sci)
15350 Sherman Way, Suite 310   Phone: (818)904-6339
Van Nuys, CA 91406   Larry Hugg, Info.Serv.Spec.
Staff: Prof 4; Other 1. **Subjects:** U.S. census and survey reports - population, housing, economic, construction, agriculture, retail trade, manufactures, foreign trade. **Holdings:** Figures not available. **Services:** Library open to the public. **Computerized Information Services:** CD-ROM; CENDATA Information Service (internal database). **Publications:** Census and You, monthly. **Remarks:** Alternate telephone number(s): (213)479-5806. FAX: (818)892-6339. **Staff:** Jerry Wong, Info.Serv.Spec.; Reina Ornelas, Commun.Serv.Spec.; Una Kuan, Info.Serv.Spec.

★17095★
U.S. Bureau of the Census - Information Services Program - New York Regional Office - Library (Soc Sci)
26 Federal Plaza, Rm. 37-100
New York, NY 10278   Phone: (212)264-4730
Founded: 1976. **Staff:** 5. **Subjects:** U.S. census reports. **Holdings:** 15,000 volumes. **Services:** SDI (limited); library open to the public. **Staff:** Henry Palacios, Coord.; Margaret Padin-Bialo; Maria Morales-Harper, Info.Serv.Spec.; Beverly Wright, Info.Serv.Asst.; Rosemary Fogarty, Info.Serv.Asst.

★17096★
U.S. Bureau of the Census - Information Services Program - Philadelphia Regional Office - Library (Soc Sci)
105 S. Seventh St., 1st Fl.   Phone: (215)597-8313
Philadelphia, PA 19106   Fernando Armstrong, Prog.Coord.
Staff: 3. **Subjects:** U.S. census reports. **Holdings:** Census publications; 1980 census for Delaware, Maryland, New Jersey, and Pennsylvania on microfiche. **Services:** Data training activities; library open to the public. **Computerized Information Services:** CD-ROM (census data). **Remarks:** FAX: (215)597-7507.

★17097★
U.S. Bureau of the Census - Information Services Program - Seattle Regional Office (Soc Sci)
101 Stewart St., Suite 500
Seattle, WA 98101-1098   Phone: (206)728-5314
Staff: Prof 1. **Subjects:** U.S. decennial census reports, economic and agricultural census reports. **Special Collections:** Bureau of the Census Block Statistics and Census Tract Reports. **Holdings:** 5000 documents; maps; microfiche. **Services:** Copying; library open to the public. **Remarks:** FAX: (206)728-5336. **Staff:** Cam McIntosh, Info.Spec.; Alice Solomon, Info.Spec.

★17098★
U.S. Bureau of the Census - Library & Information Services Branch (Soc Sci)
Federal Bldg. No. 3, Rm. 2455   Phone: (301)763-5042
Washington, DC 20233   Jacqueline Fling, Pgm.Mgr./Hd.Libn.
Founded: 1952. **Staff:** Prof 8; Other 7. **Subjects:** Economics, population, public finance, survey and statistical methodology, urban studies, computers and technology, management. **Special Collections:** U.S. Census publications, 1790-1990 (60,000); census volumes, statistical yearbooks, bulletins of foreign governments (22,000); publications on electronic data processing. **Holdings:** 150,000 books; 850 bound periodical volumes; 200,000 microfiche; 28 drawers of congressional materials; census staff papers; 250 college catalogs; 25 CD-ROMs; 500 photographs. **Subscriptions:** 800 journals and other serials; 5 newspapers. **Services:** Interlibrary loan; copying; library open to the public. **Automated Operations:** Computerized cataloging, acquisitions, serials, and circulation. **Computerized Information Services:** DIALOG Information Services, LEXIS, NEXIS, OCLC, SMIS (Survey Methodology Information System), POPLINE, WILSONLINE, VU/TEXT Information Services, CQ (Congressional Quarterly Inc.), NewsNet, Inc., DataTimes, DunsPrint. **Networks/Consortia:** Member of FEDLINK. **Publications:** Information Exchange, bimonthly - available on request. **Remarks:** FAX: (301)763-7322. The Bureau of the Census is part of the U.S. Department of Commerce. **Staff:** Susan Austell, Hd.Sys.Libn.

★17099★
U.S. Bureau of Indian Affairs - Southwestern Indian Polytechnic Institute - Library (Educ)
9169 Coors Blvd., N.W.
Box 10146   Phone: (505)897-5340
Albuquerque, NM 87184   Paula M. Smith, Libn.
Founded: 1972. **Staff:** Prof 2; Other 1. **Subjects:** Vocational-technical curriculum, American Indians, recreational reading. **Special Collections:** American Indian Collection (2240 volumes; 25-35 newspapers and newsletters). **Holdings:** 26,000 books; 100 bound periodical volumes; 100 audio cassettes; 300 video cassettes; 16mm films. **Subscriptions:** 100 journals and other serials; 35 newspapers. **Services:** Interlibrary loan; center open to the public for reference use only. **Automated Operations:** Computerized circulation. **Publications:** Bibliographies. **Remarks:** The Bureau of Indian Affairs is part of the U.S. Department of the Interior. **Staff:** Helen F. Jojola, Hd.Techn.

★ 17100 ★
U.S. Bureau of Land Management - Alaska State Office - Alaska Resources Library (Biol Sci, Env-Cons)
222 W. 7th
No. 36   Phone: (907)271-5025
Anchorage, AK 99513   Martha L. Shepard, Dir.
Founded: 1972. **Staff:** Prof 4; Other 2. **Subjects:** Alaska - resources, wildlife, land management, forestry/vegetation; Arctic environment; pipelines; outer continental shelf; hydrology; pollution; engineering and geology; archeology. **Special Collections:** Alaskan map collection of original overlays; microfiche library of CRREL bibliography. **Holdings:** 45,000 volumes; 7000 maps. **Subscriptions:** 1200 journals and other serials. **Services:** Interlibrary loan; copying; library open to the public. **Computerized Information Services:** DIALOG Information Services, WLN, OCLC, WESTLAW, LEXIS; Dialcom Inc. Performs searches on fee basis. **Networks/Consortia:** Member of FEDLINK, Alaska Library Network (ALN). **Remarks:** FAX: (907)271-5965 **Staff:** Catherine Vitale, Acq.Libn.; Linda Tobiska, ILL Libn.

★ 17101 ★
U.S. Bureau of Land Management - California State Office - Library (Env-Cons)
2800 Cottage Way, Rm. E-2845   Phone: (916)978-4713
Sacramento, CA 95825   Louise Tichy, Mgt.Asst.
Staff: 2. **Subjects:** Land resources, recreation, environmental statements, U.S. statutes, interior land decisions, wildlife management, forestry, range management. **Holdings:** 3500 books; unbound periodicals. **Subscriptions:** 120 journals and other serials. **Services:** Interlibrary loan; copying; library open to the public for reference use only.

★ 17102 ★
U.S. Bureau of Land Management - Casper District Office - Library (Env-Cons)
1701 East E St.   Phone: (307)261-7613
Casper, WY 82601   Sandy Lindahl
Staff: 1. **Subjects:** Wildlife, fire, minerals, environmental impact statements, soil, hydrology. **Holdings:** Figures not available. **Subscriptions:** 12 journals and other serials. **Services:** Copying; library open to the public for reference use only. **Automated Operations:** Computerized cataloging.

★ 17103 ★
U.S. Bureau of Land Management - District Office Library (Plan)
HC 74-12533, Hwy. 20, W.   Phone: (503)573-5241
Hines, OR 97738   Kay Campbell, Libn.
Remarks: No further information was supplied by respondent.

★ 17104 ★
U.S. Bureau of Land Management - District Office Library (Plan)
1300 Airport Lane   Phone: (503)756-0100
North Bend, OR 97459-2023   Pat Richardson, Libn.
Founded: 1976. **Holdings:** 1500 books; 100 bound periodical volumes. **Subscriptions:** 4 journals and other serials; 4 newspapers. **Services:** Interlibrary loan; library open to the public.

★ 17105 ★
U.S. Bureau of Land Management - Eastern States Office - Library (Env-Cons)
350 S. Pickett St.   Phone: (703)461-1373
Alexandria, VA 22304   Vernadean White, Mgt.Asst.
Founded: 1975. **Staff:** Prof 1. **Subjects:** Land management and environmental assessment. **Holdings:** 10,000 books; BLM manuals; public lands law books; U.S. Department of the Interior manuals. **Subscriptions:** 50 journals and other serials. **Services:** Interlibrary loan; copying; library open to the public. **Remarks:** FAX: (703)461-1376.

★ 17106 ★
U.S. Bureau of Land Management - Library (Env-Cons)
Denver Federal Ctr., Bldg. 50
Box 25047   Phone: (303)236-6648
Denver, CO 80225-0047   Sandra Bowers, Hd.Libn.
Staff: Prof 2; Other 8. **Subjects:** Public lands, forestry, range and wildlife management, geology, minerals, oil shale. **Holdings:** 30,000 volumes.

Subscriptions: 500 journals and other serials. **Services:** Interlibrary loan; copying; library open to the public for reference use only. **Automated Operations:** Computerized cataloging. **Computerized Information Services:** DIALOG Information Services, PFDS Online, BRS Information Technologies, LEXIS, WESTLAW. **Networks/Consortia:** Member of FEDLINK, Central Colorado Library System (CCLS). **Remarks:** Library is headquarters library for the Bureau of Land Management, which is part of the U.S. Department of the Interior. Alternate telephone number(s): 236-6650. **Staff:** Barbara Campbell, Libn.

★ 17107 ★
U.S. Bureau of Land Management - Montana State Office Library (Env-Cons)
222 N. 32nd St.
Box 36800   Phone: (406)255-2759
Billings, MT 59107   Patricia J. Koch, Lib.Techn.
Founded: 1972. **Staff:** 1. **Subjects:** Water resources, land use, range management, wildlife, coal, minerals. **Special Collections:** Missouri River Basin Reports. **Holdings:** 13,000 books. **Subscriptions:** 201 journals and other serials; 15 newspapers. **Services:** Interlibrary loan; copying; library open to the public with restrictions. **Automated Operations:** Computerized cataloging and ILL. **Computerized Information Services:** OCLC. **Networks/Consortia:** Member of FEDLINK. **Remarks:** FAX: (406)255-2792.

★ 17108 ★
U.S. Bureau of Land Management - New Mexico State Office Information Center (Env-Cons)
P. O. Box 27115   Phone: (505)988-6047
Santa Fe, NM 87502-7115   Eileen G. Vigil, State Rec.Mgr.
Founded: 1967. **Staff:** Prof 2; Other 1. **Subjects:** Management - land resource, wildlife, recreation, minerals, range; environmental protection. **Special Collections:** U.S. Statutes at Large; Interior Board of Land Appeals decisions; Lindley on Mines, Volumes I and II; Environmental Statements. **Holdings:** 4500 books; 250 bound periodical volumes. **Services:** Interlibrary loan; copying; library open to the public for reference use only. **Computerized Information Services:** Dialcom Inc. (electronic mail service). **Remarks:** FAX: (505)988-6530.

★ 17109 ★
U.S. Bureau of Mines - Alaska Field Operations Center Library (Energy, Sci-Engr)
Box 020550   Phone: (907)364-2111
Juneau, AK 99802-0550   Bruce Bennett, Libn.
Founded: 1950. **Staff:** 1. **Subjects:** Mining, geology, engineering in Northern Regions, permafrost construction, mineral deposits of Alaska. **Special Collections:** U.S. Geological Survey publications on Alaska; U.S. Bureau of Mines publications; extensive publications on permafrost; state and territory of Alaska publications on mining and minerals. **Holdings:** 5500 volumes; 15,000 documents; 5500 titles on microfilm; 5000 maps. **Subscriptions:** 57 journals and other serials. **Services:** Interlibrary loan; copying; library open to the public. **Computerized Information Services:** OCLC; Mining Claims Information System (MCIS) (internal database). **Special Indexes:** Index of Bureau of Mines Publications on Alaska. **Remarks:** FAX: (907)364-3622. The Bureau of Mines is part of the U.S. Department of the Interior.

★ 17110 ★
U.S. Bureau of Mines - Albany Research Center Library (Sci-Engr)
1450 Queen Ave., S.W.   Phone: (503)967-5864
Albany, OR 97321-2198   Harry Brooks, Libn., Physical Sci.
Staff: Prof 1. **Subjects:** Metallurgy, chemistry, physics, chemical engineering, thermodynamics, materials, environmental science. **Special Collections:** Zirconium research; thermodynamics. **Holdings:** 20,000 books; 17,000 bound periodical volumes; 16,000 technical reports; 11,000 microfiche. **Subscriptions:** 152 journals and other serials. **Services:** Interlibrary loan; library open to the public for reference use only. **Computerized Information Services:** DIALOG Information Services, OCLC; internal databases. **Special Catalogs:** Journals list and online catalog. **Remarks:** FTS: 420-5864. FAX: (503)967-5986; (503)967-5936 (backup); 420-5936 (FTS).

★ 17111 ★
U.S. Bureau of Mines - Branch of Library Services - James Boyd
   Memorial Library (Sci-Engr)
Rm. 301, MS 2157
810 7th St., N.W.   Phone: (202)501-9755
Washington, DC 20241   Susan Whitmore, Hd.Libn.
Founded: 1965. **Staff:** Prof 2; Other 2. **Subjects:** Mining, minerals, metal
industry, statistics, economics, policy. **Special Collections:** Bureau of Mines
publications; mining company annual reports; international mining
statistics. **Holdings:** 10,000 monographs. **Subscriptions:** 90 journals and
other serials. **Services:** Library open to the public for reference use only with
permission of librarian. **Computerized Information Services:** OCLC.
Networks/Consortia: Member of FEDLINK. **Remarks:** FAX: (202)634-
4112. FTS: 241-9755. **Formerly:** U.S. Bureau of Mines - Branch of
Operations & Support - Library. **Staff:** Linda Evans, Asst.Libn.

U.S. Bureau of Mines - Branch of Operations & Support - Library
See: U.S. Bureau of Mines - Branch of Library Services - James Boyd
   Memorial Library (17111)

★ 17112 ★
U.S. Bureau of Mines - Charles W. Henderson Memorial Library (Sci-
   Engr)
Denver Federal Center, Bldg. 20   Phone: (303)236-0474
Lakewood, CO 80225   Betsy Chapel, Libn.
Founded: 1963. **Staff:** Prof 1. **Subjects:** Mining engineering, economics,
research, geology. **Holdings:** 21,000 books; 1380 bound periodical volumes;
2280 maps and charts; 11,100 bulletins; 2270 water supply papers.
Subscriptions: 60 journals and other serials; 6 newspapers. **Services:**
Interlibrary loan; copying; library open to the public with restrictions.
Computerized Information Services: DIALOG Information Services,
OCLC. **Networks/Consortia:** Member of FEDLINK.

★ 17113 ★
U.S. Bureau of Mines - Comminution Center - Reference Center (Sci-
   Engr)
115 EMRO
University of Utah   Phone: (801)581-8283
Salt Lake City, UT 84112   Sam Asihene, Info.Off.
Founded: 1982. **Staff:** Prof 3. **Subjects:** Minerals - control, comminution,
classification, models, wear. **Holdings:** 200 books and journals; 2000
scientific and technical papers; 2000 abstracts; 33 theses and dissertations on
comminution and related subjects; 2 videotapes. **Services:** Copying; center
open to the public. **Automated Operations:** Computerized cataloging.
Publications: Master List; Book of Abstracts, 2/year.

★ 17114 ★
U.S. Bureau of Mines - Reno Research Center - Library (Sci-Engr)
1605 Evans Ave.   Phone: (702)784-5348
Reno, NV 89512-2295   Sandy Crews, Lib.Techn.
Staff: Prof 1. **Subjects:** Chemistry, metallurgy, chemical engineering,
physics, geology. **Holdings:** 3349 books; 1775 bound periodical volumes;
16,000 reports, manuscripts, and documents. **Subscriptions:** 125 journals
and other serials. **Services:** Interlibrary loan; copying; library open to the
public for reference use only. **Computerized Information Services:** STN
International, DIALOG Information Services, CompuServe Information
Service.

★ 17115 ★
U.S. Bureau of Mines - Rolla Research Center - Library (Sci-Engr)
1300 Bishop Ave.
Box 280   Phone: (314)364-3169
Rolla, MO 65401   Betty Feeler, Libn.
Founded: 1921. **Staff:** 1. **Subjects:** Metallurgy and mining research.
Holdings: 2000 books; 200 bound periodical volumes; 2000 reports; U.S.
Bureau of Mines publications. **Subscriptions:** 33 journals and other serials.
Services: Interlibrary loan; library open to the public for reference use only.

★ 17116 ★
U.S. Bureau of Mines - Salt Lake City Research Center - Library (Env-
   Cons)
729 Arapeen Dr.   Phone: (801)524-6112
Salt Lake City, UT 84108   Kyo Okawa, Libn.
Staff: 1. **Subjects:** Metallurgy research, natural resources conservation,
environmental pollution, engineering, physical sciences. **Special Collections:**
Bureau of Mines publications (1500 bound volumes). **Holdings:** 10,700
books; 1250 bound periodical volumes; 39 notebooks of patents.
Subscriptions: 60 journals and other serials. **Services:** Interlibrary loan;
library open to the public for reference use only. **Computerized Information
Services:** ESA/IRS. **Remarks:** FAX: (801)524-6119.

★ 17117 ★
U.S. Bureau of Mines - SSI - Library (Sci-Engr, Energy)
Cochrans Mill Rd.
Box 18070   Phone: (412)892-4431
Pittsburgh, PA 15236   Kathleen M. Stabryla, Lead Libn.
Staff: Prof 3; Other 3. **Subjects:** Coal research, fossil fuels, mining, geology,
chemistry. **Special Collections:** U.S. Bureau of Mines publications (complete
set). **Holdings:** 165,000 books; 54,000 bound periodical volumes.
Subscriptions: 250 journals and other serials. **Services:** Interlibrary loan;
copying (limited); library open to the public for reference use only.
Computerized Information Services: DIALOG Information Services.
Networks/Consortia: Member of Pittsburgh Regional Library Center
(PRLC). **Remarks:** FAX: (412)892-4292. **Staff:** Bernard Kenney, Br.Libn.;
Chia-ling Wu, Libn.

★ 17118 ★
U.S. Bureau of Mines - TURC Technical Library (Sci-Engr, Energy)
University of Alabama
Capstone Dr.
Box L   Phone: (205)759-9427
Tuscaloosa, AL 35486-9777   Jean E. Daniel Moss, Lib.Techn.
Founded: 1938. **Staff:** 1. **Subjects:** Chemistry, metallurgy, thermodynamics,
physical chemistry, ceramics. **Special Collections:** Bureau of Mines
publications. **Holdings:** 2132 books; 200 bound periodical volumes; 3
drawers of photographs; 1 drawer of microfilm; 1 drawer of tapes.
Subscriptions: 100 journals and other serials; 7 newspapers. **Services:**
Interlibrary loan; library open to the public for reference use only.
Computerized Information Services: OCLC; Information Handling System
(internal database); CD-ROMs (PERSONNET, FPM). **Networks/
Consortia:** Member of FEDLINK. **Remarks:** FAX: (205)759-9440.
Formerly: Its Tuscaloosa Research Center - Reference Library.

★ 17119 ★
U.S. Bureau of Mines - Twin Cities Research Center - Library (Energy,
   Sci-Engr)
5629 Minnehaha Ave., S.   Phone: (612)725-4503
Minneapolis, MN 55417-3099   Marilynn R. Anderson, Libn.
Staff: Prof 1. **Subjects:** Mining engineering, metallurgy, mineral industries,
geology, industrial safety, conservation. **Holdings:** 7200 books; 2270 bound
periodical volumes; 95 VF drawers of reports, documents, patents.
Subscriptions: 220 journals and other serials. **Services:** Interlibrary loan;
library open to the public. **Computerized Information Services:** Infomaster,
OCLC EPIC.

★ 17120 ★
U.S. Bureau of Reclamation - Denver Office - Library (Sci-Engr)
Denver Federal Center
Box 25007   Phone: (303)236-6963
Denver, CO 80225   Carolyn McNee, Proj.Mgr.
Founded: 1930. **Staff:** Prof 3; Other 6. **Subjects:** Water resources
development; design, construction, and operation of dams, power plants,
pumping plants, canals, transmission lines; water quality. **Holdings:** 15,000
books; 14,000 bound periodical volumes; 20,000 archival items; 10,000
specifications; 20,000 internal reports; 10,000 reports on microfilm; 20,000
external reports; Government Publications Office publications.
Subscriptions: 1000 journals and other serials. **Services:** Interlibrary loan;
copying; SDI; library open to the public. **Automated Operations:**
Computerized cataloging, acquisitions, circulation, and periodical routing.
Computerized Information Services: DIALOG Information Services.
Networks/Consortia: Member of FEDLINK, Colorado Alliance of
Research Libraries (CARL). **Publications:** Recent Library Additions -
available on request; reclamation project histories. **Special Catalogs:**
Specialized internal reports (online). **Remarks:** The Bureau of Reclamation
is part of the U.S. Department of the Interior. **Staff:** Ruth Ann Zook,
Ref.Libn.; Nancy Urquhart, ILL.

★ 17121 ★
U.S. Bureau of Reclamation - Library (Sci-Engr)
2800 Cottage Way, Rm. W-1522   Phone: (916)978-5168
Sacramento, CA 95825-1898   Diane M. Johnson, Lib.Tech.
Founded: 1946. Staff: 1. Subjects: Water and land resources, power, agriculture. Holdings: 18,050 volumes. Subscriptions: 150 journals and other serials. Services: Interlibrary loan; copying; library open to the public for reference use only. Computerized Information Services: Internal database. Publications: Accession list, quarterly; magazine list, annual. Remarks: Alternate telephone number(s): 978-5169. FAX: (916)978-5284.

★ 17122 ★
U.S. Bureau of Reclamation - Technical Library (Env-Cons)
P. O. Box 61470   Phone: (702)293-8666
Boulder City, NV 89006-1470   Alma K. Spruill, File Ck.
Subjects: Water and power resources, hydrology, canals and other hydraulic structures, hydroelectric power, flood control, ecology, soil. Special Collections: Project histories for the lower Colorado region. Holdings: 25,000 volumes. Services: Interlibrary loan; library open to the public for reference use only. Remarks: FAX: (702)293-8615.

★ 17123 ★
United States Catholic Conference - Library (Rel-Phil)
3211 4th St., N.E.   Phone: (202)541-3193
Washington, DC 20017   Guy Wilson, Dir.
Founded: 1989. Staff: Prof 2; Other 1. Subjects: Theology; church - management, history; human rights; medical ethics; international relations. Special Collections: U.S. Catholic Conference and Vatican documents (1500 items); publications of Latin American Bishops' Conference (500 items). Holdings: 4500 books; 1250 bound periodical volumes; 250,000 archival items. Subscriptions: 125 journals and other serials; 5 newspapers. Services: Copying; library open to the public by appointment. Automated Operations: Computerized cataloging. Computerized Information Services: DIALOG Information Services. Performs searches. Publications: Internal newsletter, monthly. Special Indexes: Index of Papal statements (in progress).

★ 17124 ★
U.S. Cavalry Museum - Library (Mil)
Bldg. 205   Phone: (913)239-2737
Fort Riley, KS 66442   Terry Van Meter, Musm.Dir.
Founded: 1957. Staff: 6. Subjects: United States cavalry. Special Collections: Complete black/white 16mm sound set of 12 cavalry training films, 1940. Holdings: Books; annual reports of Secretary of War; Cavalry Journal; photographs; documents. Subscriptions: 12 journals and other serials. Services: Copying; library open to researchers with restrictions. Special Indexes: Index of archival holdings.

★ 17125 ★
U.S. Centers for Disease Control - CDC Information Center (Med)
1600 Clifton Rd., N.E.   Phone: (404)639-3396
Atlanta, GA 30333   Joan U. Kennedy, Chf.
Founded: 1947. Staff: Prof 10; Other 8. Subjects: Infectious diseases, epidemiology, laboratory medicine, medical entomology, microbiology, biochemistry, public health, preventive medicine, virology. Holdings: 12,000 books; 130 theses; 2600 U.S. Department of Health and Human Services publications. Subscriptions: 370 journals and other serials. Services: Interlibrary loan. Automated Operations: Computerized cataloging and serials. Computerized Information Services: BRS Information Technologies, DIALOG Information Services, MEDLARS, LEXIS, NEXIS, MEDIS, STN International, JURIS, LEGI-SLATE, National AIDS Information Clearinghouse, PaperChase; Current Contents on diskette; CD-ROMs (Compact Library: AIDS, MEDLINE, Electronic Encyclopedia, PC-SIG Library, Microsoft Bookshelf, CCINFOdisc, Computer Library); Public Health Network, BITNET (electronic mail services). Networks/Consortia: Member of FEDLINK, Atlanta Health Science Libraries Consortium (AHSLC), Georgia Health Sciences Library Association (GHSLA). Remarks: FAX: (404)639-1160. Telex: 549571. The Center for Disease Control is an agency of the U.S. Public Health Service. Staff: Mary Evelyn Gilbert, Chf., Info.Sup.Sect.; Susan Wilkin, Chf., Info.Mgt. Unit; Marilyn Mollenkamp, Chf., Info.Serv. Unit.

★ 17126 ★
U.S. Centers for Disease Control - CDC Information Center-Chamblee (Biol Sci, Med)
1600 Clifton Rd., N.E., 30/1321   Phone: (404)488-4167
Atlanta, GA 30333   Joan A. Redmond-Leonard, Tech.Info.Spec.
Staff: Prof 1. Subjects: Toxicology, clinical chemistry, vector biology and control, parasitic diseases. Holdings: 2000 books. Subscriptions: 180 journals and other serials. Services: Interlibrary loan. Automated Operations: Computerized cataloging and serials. Computerized Information Services: BRS Information Technologies, DIALOG Information Services, NLM, MEDLARS, LEXIS, NEXIS, MEDIS, STN International, JURIS, LEGI-SLATE, National AIDS Information Clearinghouse, PaperChase; Dialcom, Inc., BITNET, AMA/NET (electronic mail services). Remarks: FAX: (404)488-4766. Telex: 549571.

★ 17127 ★
U.S. Centers for Disease Control, - Division of Vector-Borne Infectious Diseases - Library (Biol Sci)
U.S. Public Health Service
P.O. Box 2087
Foothill Campus
Fort Collins, CO 80522-2087   Phone: (303)221-6400
Subjects: Microbiology, vector ecology, immunology. Holdings: Figures not available. Subscriptions: 104 journals and other serials. Services: Library not open to the public. Remarks: FAX: (303)221-6476.

★ 17128 ★
U.S. Centers for Disease Control - National Center for Chronic Disease Prevention and Health Promotion - Office on Smoking and Health - Technical Information Center (Med)
Mail Stop K-12
1600 Clifton Rd., N.E.   Phone: (404)488-5708
Atlanta, GA 30333   Christine Fralish, Chf.
Founded: 1965. Staff: Prof 5; Other 2. Subjects: Smoking, health, tobacco use. Holdings: 55,000 books, reprints, journal articles, and technical reports. Subscriptions: 40 journals and other serials. Services: Copying; answers written and telephone requests for information; center open to the public. Automated Operations: Computerized cataloging. Computerized Information Services: DIALOG Information Services; internal database. Publications: Report of the Surgeon General, irregular; Bibliography on Smoking and Health, annual - both available to libraries and professionals. Remarks: Center houses the world's leading resource materials on smoking and its effects on health. Center is located at 3005 Chamblee Tucker Rd., Rm. 1109, Tucker, GA. FAX: (404)488-5152. Formerly: Located in Rockville, MD.

U.S. Centers for Disease Control - National Institute for Occupational Safety & Health
See: U.S. Natl. Institute for Occupational Safety & Health (17611)

United States Chamber of Commerce-Spain
See: Spain-United States Chamber of Commerce - Library (15568)

★ 17129 ★
U.S.-China Business Council - Business Information Center (Bus-Fin)
1818 N St., N.W., Suite 500   Phone: (202)429-0340
Washington, DC 20036   Kathleen E. Syron, Mgr.
Staff: Prof 2; Other 4. Subjects: China - economy, trade, industry; U.S- foreign trade. Special Collections: Chinese export catalogs; trip reports. Holdings: 1250 books; periodicals; 20,000 microfiche; 35 VF drawers of clippings, reports, papers. Subscriptions: 75 journals and other serials. Services: Copying; center not open to the public. Computerized Information Services: Reuter TEXTLINE. Performs searches on fee basis. Remarks: FAX: (202)775-2476. Telex: 64517 NCUSCTUW.

★ 17130 ★
U.S. Coast Guard - Research and Development Center - Technical Information Center (Sci-Engr)
Avery Point   Phone: (203)441-2648
Groton, CT 06340   Martha F. Kendall, Tech.Libn.
Founded: 1979. Staff: 1. Subjects: Marine engineering, information systems, systems analysis, environmental safety, navigation systems, surveillance systems, marine fire research, ice technology. Special Collections: U.S. Coast Guard reports. Holdings: 1000 books; 1000 reports. Subscriptions: 250 journals and other serials; 12 newspapers. Services: Interlibrary loan; copying; SDI; center open to the public with permission. Automated Operations: Computerized cataloging. Computerized Information Services: OCLC, NERAC, Inc. Publications: Library Update, bimonthly. Remarks: FAX: (203)441-2792.

★17131★
U.S. Coast Guard - Support Center Library (Mil)
Governors Island, Bldg. S251   Phone: (212)668-7394
New York, NY 10004   Bessie Seymour, Libn.
Founded: 1966. **Staff:** Prof 2; Other 1. **Subjects:** Military history, seamanship, U.S. Coast Guard. **Holdings:** 30,000 volumes; phonograph records. **Subscriptions:** 105 journals and other serials. **Services:** Interlibrary loan; library open to the public for reference use only. **Staff:** Anson Huang, Asst.Libn.

★17132★
U.S. Coast Guard Academy - Library (Mil)
New London, CT 06320-4195   Phone: (203)444-8510
                                            Patricia A. Daragan, Hd.Libn.
Founded: 1876. **Staff:** Prof 5; Other 4. **Subjects:** Marine technology. **Special Collections:** U.S. documents depository. **Holdings:** 160,000 volumes; 20,221 government documents. **Subscriptions:** 1023 journals and other serials. **Services:** Interlibrary loan; government documents collection open to the public by appointment; library not open to the public. **Automated Operations:** Computerized cataloging, serials, acquisitions, and ILL. **Computerized Information Services:** DIALOG Information Services. **Networks/Consortia:** Member of FEDLINK. **Remarks:** The Coast Guard is part of the U.S. Department of Transportation. **Staff:** Pamela A. McNulty, Hd., Pub.Serv.; Robert E. Biega, Hd., Tech.Serv.; Sheila Lamb, Asst.Tech.Serv.; Nijole M. Crane, Ref.

★17133★
U.S. Coast Guard/Air Station - Base Library (Mil)
Bldg. 5205   Phone: (508)968-6456
Otis ANGB, MA 02542   Shirley Conant, Libn.
Founded: 1974. **Staff:** Prof 1; Other 1. **Subjects:** U.S. and European history, American literature, military engineering, social sciences, aeronautics, children's literature. **Special Collections:** Air Forces (600 volumes); aeronautics (900 volumes); World War II history (2000 volumes). **Holdings:** 40,000 books; 200 bound periodical volumes; 6 VF drawers of military base information; 3 VF drawers of pamphlets; maps. **Subscriptions:** 41 journals and other serials. **Services:** Interlibrary loan; copying; library open to the public.

U.S. Commission on Civil Rights
See: **Commission on Civil Rights (4054)**

★17134★
United States Committee for Refugees - Library (Soc Sci)
1025 Vermont Ave., N.W., Suite 920   Phone: (202)347-3507
Washington, DC 20005   Roger Winter, Dir.
Subjects: Refugee matters. **Holdings:** Figures not available. **Services:** Telephone referral and response to inquiries; library open to researchers on a limited basis. **Publications:** Refugee Reports (newsletter), monthly - by subscription; World Refugee Survey, annual; periodic issue papers. **Remarks:** FAX: (202)347-3418. United States Committee for Refugees is the publications and public information program of American Council for Nationalities Service, a private, nonprofit organization.

★17135★
U.S. Comptroller of the Currency - Library (Bus-Fin)
250 E St., N.W.   Phone: (202)874-4720
Washington, DC 20219   Robert A. Updegrove, Adm.Libn.
Founded: 1974. **Staff:** Prof 4; Other 4. **Subjects:** Law, banking, economics. **Holdings:** 43,500 volumes. **Subscriptions:** 500 journals and other serials; 12 newspapers. **Services:** Interlibrary loan; library open to the public with restrictions. **Automated Operations:** Computerized cataloging and serials. **Computerized Information Services:** DIALOG Information Services, WESTLAW, NEXIS, OCLC, Dun & Bradstreet Business Credit Services. **Networks/Consortia:** Member of FEDLINK. **Publications:** Recent Acquisitions and Journal Articles, monthly - to other banking libraries. **Remarks:** FAX: (202)874-5138. The Comptroller of the Currency is part of the U.S. Department of the Treasury. **Staff:** John Posniak, Asst.Libn.; Mary Pruitt, Cat.Libn.

U.S. Congress - Congressional Budget Office
See: **Congressional Budget Office (4170)**

U.S. Congress - House of Representatives
See: **U.S. House of Representatives (17555)**

U.S. Congress - Office of Technology Assessment
See: **U.S. Office of Technology Assessment (17914)**

U.S. Congress - Senate
See: **U.S. Senate (17938)**

★17136★
U.S. Council for Energy Awareness - Library (Energy)
1776 I St., N.W., Suite 400   Phone: (202)293-0770
Washington, DC 20006   Erin M. Nagorske, Mgr.
Founded: 1954. **Staff:** Prof 1. **Subjects:** Nuclear energy, radiation, nuclear waste management, nuclear regulation. **Holdings:** 6500 books and technical reports; conference papers. **Subscriptions:** 300 journals and other serials; 5 newspapers. **Services:** Interlibrary loan; library open to association members. **Computerized Information Services:** DIALOG Information Services. **Remarks:** FAX: (202)785-4019. Telex: 7108249602.

★17137★
U.S. Court of Appeals, 1st Circuit - Library (Law)
1208 U.S. Post Office & Courthouse   Phone: (617)223-9044
Boston, MA 02109   Karen M. Moss, Circuit Libn.
Founded: 1927. **Staff:** Prof 3; Other 4. **Subjects:** Federal law, administrative material. **Special Collections:** Selective U.S. Government depository; slip opinions of all U.S. Courts of Appeals. **Holdings:** 50,000 books; 3000 bound periodical volumes; 2000 unbound reports; 26 drawers of microfilm; 40 drawers of microfiche; Code of Federal Regulations; Federal Register and Congressional Record in microform. **Subscriptions:** 136 journals and other serials; 5 newspapers. **Services:** Interlibrary loan (to Boston area law libraries); library open to members of the bar. **Automated Operations:** Computerized cataloging. **Computerized Information Services:** WESTLAW, LEXIS, DIALOG Information Services, OCLC. **Networks/Consortia:** Member of NELINET, Inc., FEDLINK. **Remarks:** FAX: (617)223-9047. **Staff:** Susan Lee, Tech.Serv.Libn.; Kristie Randall, Ref.Libn.

★17138★
U.S. Court of Appeals, 2nd Circuit - Library (Law)
U.S. Court House, Rm. 2801, Foley Square
40 Centre St.   Phone: (212)791-1052
New York, NY 10007   Margaret J. Evans, Circuit Libn.
Founded: 1917. **Staff:** Prof 5; Other 6. **Subjects:** Law. **Special Collections:** Legislative and judiciary history. **Holdings:** 100,000 books; 4500 bound periodical volumes. **Subscriptions:** 138 journals and other serials; 5 newspapers. **Services:** Library open to the public at librarian's discretion. **Automated Operations:** Computerized cataloging. **Computerized Information Services:** LEXIS, DIALOG Information Services, OCLC, WESTLAW. **Networks/Consortia:** Member of FEDLINK. **Publications:** Acquisitions List and Comments; Library Report Letter. **Special Indexes:** Index to Second Circuit Slip Opinions (looseleaf). **Staff:** Champa S. Nittor, Dp.Dir.

★17139★
U.S. Court of Appeals, 3rd Circuit - Branch Library (Law)
U.S. Courthouse
844 King St.
Box 43   Phone: (302)573-6178
Wilmington, DE 19801   Judith F. Ambler, Libn.
Founded: 1974. **Staff:** Prof 2. **Subjects:** Law. **Holdings:** 20,000 books and bound periodical volumes. **Subscriptions:** 45 journals and other serials. **Services:** Copying; library open to the public for reference use only. **Computerized Information Services:** OCLC, LEXIS, NEXIS, WESTLAW. **Staff:** Lesley D. Lawrence, Asst.Libn.

★ 17140 ★
U.S. Court of Appeals, 3rd Circuit - Branch Library (Law)
U.S. Post Office & Court House
Box 1068   Phone: (201)645-3034
Newark, NJ 07101   Andrea Battel, Libn.
Founded: 1975. **Staff:** Prof 2; Other 1. **Subjects:** Law. **Holdings:** 19,000
books; 500 bound periodical volumes; 10,000 microfiche; 25 reels of
microfilm. **Subscriptions:** 50 journals and other serials; 3 newspapers.
Services: Copying; library open to members of the bar and pro se litigants.
Computerized Information Services: LEXIS, WESTLAW. **Special
Catalogs:** Case name files for slip opinions from the U.S. Court of Appeals,
3rd Circuit and the U.S. District Court for the District of New Jersey. **Staff:**
Dorothy Cordo, Asst.Libn.

★ 17141 ★
U.S. Court of Appeals, 3rd Circuit - Library (Law)
22409 U.S. Court House
601 Market St.   Phone: (215)597-2009
Philadelphia, PA 19106   Susan B. English, Circuit Libn.
Staff: Prof 6; Other 4. **Subjects:** Law. **Special Collections:** Selected
government documents. **Holdings:** 75,000 books; 4000 bound periodical
volumes. **Subscriptions:** 80 journals and other serials. **Services:** Interlibrary
loan (limited); copying; library open to the public with approval of librarian.
Computerized Information Services: LEXIS, DIALOG Information
Services, WESTLAW. **Networks/Consortia:** Member of FEDLINK.
Remarks: FAX: (215)597-6913. **Staff:** Shirley C. Harrison, Deputy Circuit
Libn.; Roberta Cross, Ref.Libn.; Elizabeth Snipes, Tech.Serv.Libn.; Karen
Richardson, Ref.Libn.

★ 17142 ★
U.S. Court of Appeals, 3rd Circuit - Pittsburgh Branch Library (Law)
512 U.S. Courthouse   Phone: (412)644-6485
Pittsburgh, PA 15219   Linda Schneider, Libn.
Staff: Prof 2; Other 1. **Subjects:** Law - U.S., Pennsylvania, New Jersey,
Virgin Islands, Delaware. **Holdings:** 22,000 books; 1100 bound periodical
volumes. **Subscriptions:** 85 journals and other serials; 6 newspapers.
Services: Interlibrary loan; copying; library open to the public.
Computerized Information Services: LEXIS, WESTLAW. **Special Indexes:**
Western District of Pennsylvania Opinions (by case name and subject; card);
Middle District of Pennsylvania Opinions (by case name and subject; card).
Remarks: FAX: (412)644-5975. **Staff:** Barbara Alexander Klein, Asst.Libn.

★ 17143 ★
U.S. Court of Appeals, 4th Circuit - Library (Law)
U.S. Courthouse, Rm. 424
10th & Main Sts.   Phone: (804)771-2219
Richmond, VA 23219   Peter A. Frey, Circuit Libn.
Founded: 1891. **Staff:** Prof 4; Other 4. **Subjects:** Law. **Holdings:** 60,000
volumes. **Services:** Interlibrary loan; copying; library open to judiciary and
members of the bar. **Computerized Information Services:** LEXIS,
WESTLAW. **Staff:** Elaine H. Woodward, Tech.Serv.Libn.; Alyene H.
McClure, Asst.Libn.; Elizabeth Bilyeu, Asst.Libn.

★ 17144 ★
U.S. Court of Appeals, 5th Circuit - Library (Law)
600 Camp St., Rm. 106   Phone: (504)589-6510
New Orleans, LA 70130   Kay E. Duley, Circuit Libn.
Staff: Prof 5; Other 5. **Subjects:** Law. **Holdings:** 50,000 books; 10,000 bound
periodical volumes; microfiche. **Subscriptions:** 200 journals and other
serials; 5 newspapers. **Services:** Interlibrary loan; copying; library open to
the public. **Automated Operations:** Computerized cataloging. **Computerized
Information Services:** OCLC, LEXIS, WESTLAW, DIALOG Information
Services. **Networks/Consortia:** Member of FEDLINK. **Remarks:** Maintains
branch libraries in Houston, San Antonio, and Brownsville, TX; Shreveport,
Baton Rouge, and Lafayette, LA; and Biloxi, and Jackson, MS. FAX:
(504)589-6517. **Staff:** Michael Smith, Dp. Circuit Libn.; Michelle Nader,
Asst.Libn.; Cassandra Dover, Asst.Libn.

★ 17145 ★
U.S. Court of Appeals, 6th Circuit - Library (Law)
317 U.S. Court House & Post Office Bldg.   Phone: (513)684-2678
Cincinnati, OH 45202   Kathy Joyce Welker, Circuit Libn.
Founded: 1894. **Staff:** Prof 4; Other 4. **Subjects:** Law. **Holdings:** 60,000
volumes. **Subscriptions:** 1444 journals and other serials. **Services:** Library

open to attorneys only. **Automated Operations:** Computerized cataloging
and acquisitions. **Computerized Information Services:** WESTLAW,
DIALOG Information Services, NEXIS, LEXIS. **Special Indexes:** Index of
Sixth Circuit Published Opinions. **Remarks:** Maintains branch libraries in
Cleveland, Columbus, Detroit, Grand Rapids, Memphis, Nashville, and
Toledo. **Staff:** Pamela Schaffner, Dp.Libn.; Barbara Overshiner, Ref.Libn.;
Elizabeth Bourner, Tech.Serv.Libn.

★ 17146 ★
U.S. Court of Appeals, 8th Circuit - Branch Library (Law)
Post Office and Courthouse
600 W. Capitol, Rm. 224   Phone: (501)324-5039
Little Rock, AR 72201   Kathryn C. Fitzhugh, Br.Libn.
Founded: 1981. **Staff:** Prof 1. **Subjects:** Law. **Holdings:** 16,000 books; 500
bound periodical volumes; 100 other cataloged items. **Subscriptions:** 64
journals and other serials. **Services:** Interlibrary loan; copying; library open
to members of the federal bar. **Automated Operations:** Computerized
cataloging. **Computerized Information Services:** OCLC, WESTLAW,
LEXIS. **Remarks:** FAX: (501)324-5158.

★ 17147 ★
U.S. Court of Appeals, 8th Circuit - Library (Law)
U.S. Court House
811 Grand Ave., Rm. 805   Phone: (816)426-2937
Kansas City, MO 64106   Margaret Tranne Pearce, Libn.
Founded: 1984. **Staff:** Prof 2. **Subjects:** Law. **Holdings:** 30,000 volumes.
Subscriptions: 100 journals and other serials; 5 newspapers. **Services:**
Library open to members of the bar. **Computerized Information Services:**
WESTLAW, LEXIS, DIALOG Information Services. **Networks/
Consortia:** Member of FEDLINK. **Remarks:** FAX: (816)426-2936. **Staff:**
Deborah Showalter-Johnson.

★ 17148 ★
U.S. Court of Appeals, 8th Circuit - Library (Law)
U.S. Court & Customs House, Rm. 503
1114 Market St.   Phone: (314)539-2930
St. Louis, MO 63101   Ann T. Fessenden, Circuit Libn.
Staff: Prof 4; Other 5. **Subjects:** Law. **Holdings:** 30,000 books; 1000 bound
periodical volumes. **Subscriptions:** 175 journals and other serials. **Services:**
Interlibrary loan; copying; library open to government attorneys, members
of the federal bar, and to the public with permission. **Automated Operations:**
Computerized cataloging. **Computerized Information Services:**
WESTLAW, LEXIS, NEXIS, OCLC, DIALOG Information Services.
Networks/Consortia: Member of FEDLINK. **Remarks:** FAX: (314)539-
3764. Branch libraries are located in Little Rock, AR; St. Paul, MN; Omaha,
NE; Des Moines, IA; Kansas City, MO; Minneapolis, MN; Fargo, ND;
Lincoln, NE. **Staff:** James Voelker, Dp. Circuit Libn.; Kirk Gregory, Ref./
Comp.Res.Libn.; Leann Genovese, Tech.Serv.Libn.

★ 17149 ★
U.S. Court of Appeals, 8th Circuit - Research Library (Law)
590 Federal Bldg.
316 N. Robert St.   Phone: (612)290-3177
St. Paul, MN 55101   Joyce Larson Schampel, Br.Libn.
Staff: 2. **Subjects:** Legal research topics. **Holdings:** 14,000 volumes.
Services: Interlibrary loan; copying; library open to the public.
Computerized Information Services: WESTLAW, LEXIS. **Staff:** Kathryn
Kratz, Res.Libn.

★ 17150 ★
U.S. Court of Appeals, 9th Circuit - Library (Law)
Box 020349   Phone: (907)586-7458
Juneau, AK 99802   Melody Prescott, Dp.Ck.
Subjects: Law. **Holdings:** 7000 volumes. **Services:** Library open to attorneys
and law students. **Remarks:** Library located at 709 W. 9th St., Juneau, AK
99801.

★ 17151 ★
U.S. Court of Appeals, 9th Circuit - Library (Law)
U.S. Courthouse, Rm. 6434
230 N. 1st Ave.   Phone: (602)379-3879
Phoenix, AZ 85025-0074   Timothy J. Blake, Asst.Libn.
Founded: 1980. **Staff:** Prof 2; Other 1. **Subjects:** Law. **Special Collections:** U.S. Government documents depository. **Holdings:** 25,000 books; 1400 bound periodical volumes. **Subscriptions:** 900 journals and other serials; 8 newspapers. **Services:** Interlibrary loan; U.S. Government documents depository open to the public; library not open to the public. **Computerized Information Services:** OCLC, LEXIS, NEXIS, WESTLAW, OCLC EPIC. **Networks/Consortia:** Member of FEDLINK. **Publications:** Library Update (newsletter); Library Guide, annual - for internal distribution only. **Remarks:** FAX: (602)379-3370. **Staff:** Evelyn Rayburn, Lib.Techn.; Gwen Gregory, Asst.Libn., Tech.Serv.

★ 17152 ★
U.S. Court of Appeals, 9th Circuit - Library (Law)
1702 U.S. Courthouse
312 N. Spring St.   Phone: (213)894-3636
Los Angeles, CA 90012   Joanne Mazza, Libn.
Founded: 1971. **Staff:** Prof 2; Other 2. **Subjects:** Law. **Holdings:** 34,000 books; 77,500 microfiche. **Services:** Interlibrary loan; library open to the public for reference use only. **Computerized Information Services:** WESTLAW, LEXIS, OCLC. **Remarks: Staff:** Nina Truex.

★ 17153 ★
U.S. Court of Appeals, 9th Circuit - Library (Law)
125 S. Grand Ave.   Phone: (818)405-7020
Pasadena, CA 91105   Kathryn A. Way, Law Libn.
Founded: 1985. **Staff:** Prof 1; Other 3. **Subjects:** Law. **Holdings:** 22,700 books; 1748 bound periodical volumes; 56,583 microfiche and ultrafiche. **Subscriptions:** 713 journals and other serials; 7 newspapers. **Services:** Library open to members of the bar. **Computerized Information Services:** WESTLAW, LEXIS. **Publications:** BiblioVista, quarterly - for internal distribution only. **Special Indexes:** Index to the Published Decisions & Orders of the Ninth Circuit (card). **Remarks:** FAX: (818)405-7077.

★ 17154 ★
U.S. Court of Appeals, 9th Circuit - Library (Law)
121 Spear St.
P.O. Box 193939
San Francisco, CA 94119-3939   Phone: (415)744-9590
      Elisabeth S. Knauff, Circuit Libn.
Founded: 1891. **Staff:** Prof 8; Other 5. **Subjects:** Law. **Holdings:** 71,793 volumes; 173,272 microforms. **Subscriptions:** 397 journals and other serials. **Services:** Interlibrary loan; library open to the public with restrictions. **Automated Operations:** Computerized cataloging. **Computerized Information Services:** LEXIS, WESTLAW, NEXIS, DIALOG Information Services, Washington Alert Service. **Special Indexes:** Index to current 9th Circuit opinions. **Staff:** Helen Hill, Dp. Circuit Libn.; Cheryl Blare, HQ Libn.; Deborah Celle, Ref.Libn.; Eric Wade, Ref.Libn.; Edward Hosey, Acq.Libn.; James Moldovan, Cat.Libn.

★ 17155 ★
U.S. Court of Appeals, 9th Circuit - Library (Law)
Pioneer Courthouse   Phone: (503)326-6042
Portland, OR 97204-1494   Scott M. McCurdy, Libn.
Staff: Prof 2.5. **Subjects:** Law. **Holdings:** 14,000 books; 400 bound periodical volumes. **Services:** Interlibrary loan; copying; library open to attorneys on day of court proceedings. **Computerized Information Services:** WESTLAW, LEXIS. **Remarks:** FAX: (503)326-7788. **Staff:** Dianne Schauer, Asst.Libn.

★ 17156 ★
U.S. Court of Appeals, 9th Circuit - Library (Law)
1018 U.S. Courthouse
1010 5th Ave.   Phone: (206)553-4475
Seattle, WA 98104   Timothy Sheehy, Br.Libn.
Founded: 1939. **Staff:** Prof 2; Other 2. **Subjects:** Law. **Holdings:** 24,199 books; 116,039 microfiche; 306 reels of microfilm. **Subscriptions:** 1319 journals and other serials. **Services:** Library open to the public for reference use only. **Computerized Information Services:** WESTLAW, LEXIS, NEXIS, ACES. **Remarks:** FAX: (206)553-4385. **Staff:** Karen Lasnick, Comp. Assisted Leg.Res. & Dist.Ct.Serv.Libn.; Jean Pasche, Govt.Doc.

★ 17157 ★
U.S. Court of Appeals, 10th Circuit - Library (Law)
U.S. Court House, Rm. C 411   Phone: (303)844-3591
Denver, CO 80294   J. Terry Hemming, Circuit Libn.
Staff: Prof 3; Other 3. **Subjects:** Law. **Holdings:** 35,000 volumes. **Services:** Interlibrary loan; copying; library open to the public. **Automated Operations:** Computerized cataloging. **Computerized Information Services:** LEXIS, WESTLAW. **Remarks:** FAX: (303) 844-5958. **Staff:** Catherine McGuire Eason, Dp. Circuit Libn. Ruthann Rehnborg, Asst.Lib., Tech.Serv.

★ 17158 ★
U.S. Court of Appeals, 10th Circuit - Oklahoma City Branch Library
(Law)
U.S. Courthouse, Rm. 5114
200 N.W. 4th St.   Phone: (405)231-4967
Oklahoma City, OK 73102   Jerry E. Stephens, U.S. Courts Libn.
Staff: Prof 1. **Subjects:** Law. **Special Collections:** Unpublished opinions of the Tenth Circuit. **Holdings:** U.S. code and statutes at large; law reviews and digests. **Subscriptions:** 175 journals and other serials; 3 newspapers. **Services:** Library open to the public for reference use only. **Computerized Information Services:** WESTLAW, LEXIS, NEXIS; internal database. **Remarks:** FAX: (405)231-5788.

★ 17159 ★
U.S. Court of Appeals, 11th Circuit - Library (Law)
56 Forsyth St., N.W.   Phone: (404)331-2510
Atlanta, GA 30303   Elaine P. Fenton, Circuit Libn.
Founded: 1980. **Staff:** Prof 5; Other 2. **Subjects:** Law. **Holdings:** 30,000 books; 5000 bound periodical volumes; 20 cabinets of microforms. **Subscriptions:** 200 journals and other serials; 6 newspapers. **Services:** Interlibrary loan; library open to attorneys only. **Automated Operations:** Computerized cataloging. **Computerized Information Services:** WESTLAW, LEXIS, NEXIS, DIALOG Information Services, VU/TEXT Information Services, OCLC; CD-ROM. **Networks/Consortia:** Member of FEDLINK. **Remarks:** FAX: (404)331-1255. **Staff:** Sara M. Straub, Dp. Circuit Libn.; Sue T. Lee, Ref.Libn.; Judith F. Newsom, Tech.Serv.Libn.; William M. Dunnahoo, Comp. Assisted Leg.Res.Asst.

★ 17160 ★
U.S. Court of Appeals, District of Columbia Circuit - Library (Law)
5518 U.S. Court House
3rd & Constitution Ave., N.W.   Phone: (202)535-3400
Washington, DC 20001   Nancy Lazar, Circuit Libn.
Founded: 1953. **Staff:** Prof 5. **Subjects:** Law. **Holdings:** 120,000 volumes. **Subscriptions:** 200 journals and other serials; 7 newspapers. **Services:** Interlibrary loan; copying; library open to the public at librarian's discretion. **Automated Operations:** Computerized cataloging and serials. **Computerized Information Services:** DIALOG Information Services, LEXIS, NEXIS, WESTLAW. **Networks/Consortia:** Member of FEDLINK. **Staff:** Theresa Santella, Dp. Circuit Libn.; Michelle Sea, Asst.Libn., Tech.Serv.; Linda Baltrusch, Asst.Libn., CALR; Mona Scott, Asst.Libn., Sys.

★ 17161 ★
U.S. Court of Appeals for the Federal Circuit - National Courts' Library
(Law)
717 Madison Pl., N.W., Rm. 218   Phone: (202)633-5871
Washington, DC 20439   Patricia M. McDermott, Libn.
Founded: 1967. **Staff:** Prof 3; Other 2. **Subjects:** Law, taxation, government contracts, patents and trademarks, international trade, veterans appeals, government employee appeals. **Holdings:** 38,454 books. **Subscriptions:** 90 journals and other serials; 6 newspapers. **Services:** Interlibrary loan; copying; library open to members of the Courts' Bar. **Automated Operations:** Computerized cataloging. **Computerized Information Services:** WESTLAW, LEXIS, NEXIS, LEGI-SLATE, OCLC, OCLC EPIC, DIALOG Information Services. **Networks/Consortia:** Member of FEDLINK. **Publications:** Notes from the Library; Library Guide. **Remarks:** FAX: (202)786-6586. **Staff:** David J. Lockwood, Asst.Libn.; Carol S. McClintock, Asst.Libn., Tech.Serv.

★17162★
U.S. Court of International Trade - Law Library (Law)
One Federal Plaza   Phone: (212)264-2816
New York, NY 10007   Simone-Marie Kleckner, Law Libn.
Founded: 1926. **Staff:** Prof 3; Other 3. **Subjects:** Law, customs, tariff, international trade, import, countervailing, antidumping, science and technology. **Special Collections:** Customs laws and procedures (3000 volumes); legislative histories of custom and trade laws; tariff schedules. **Holdings:** 50,000 volumes; 8700 bound periodical volumes; 8000 government documents; 12 VF drawers of pamphlets; microfiche. **Subscriptions:** 100 journals and other serials; 9 newspapers. **Services:** Interlibrary loan; copying; library open to the public by appointment. **Automated Operations:** Computerized cataloging. **Computerized Information Services:** LEXIS, NEXIS, WESTLAW, OCLC. **Networks/Consortia:** Member of FEDLINK. **Publications:** Library Newsletter, semiannual. **Remarks:** FAX: (212)264-1085. **Staff:** Ella Lidsky, Asst.Libn.; Anna Djirdjirian, Asst.Libn.

★17163★
U.S. Court of Military Appeals - Library (Law, Mil)
450 E St., N.W.   Phone: (202)272-1466
Washington, DC 20442   Mary S. Kuck, Libn.
Founded: 1952. **Staff:** Prof 2. **Subjects:** Law - military, criminal, evidence. **Special Collections:** Air Force, Army, Navy, and Marine Corps regulations pertaining to military justice. **Holdings:** 20,000 volumes. **Subscriptions:** 50 journals and other serials. **Services:** Interlibrary loan; library open to the public for reference use only on request. **Computerized Information Services:** WESTLAW. **Staff:** Agnes Kiang, Asst.Libn.

★17164★
U.S. Customs Service - Library and Information Center (Law)
1301 Constitution Ave., N.W., Rm. 3340   Phone: (202)566-5642
Washington, DC 20229   Patricia M. Dobrosky, Dir.
Founded: 1975. **Staff:** Prof 5; Other 4. **Subjects:** Law, law enforcement, economics, international trade, drugs. **Holdings:** 42,000 volumes. **Subscriptions:** 600 journals and other serials. **Services:** Interlibrary loan; copying; SDI; library open to the public for reference use only. **Automated Operations:** Computerized cataloging and acquisitions. **Computerized Information Services:** DIALOG Information Services, LEXIS, NEXIS, LEGI-SLATE, WESTLAW, OCLC. **Networks/Consortia:** Member of FEDLINK. **Publications:** Media Varia. **Remarks:** The Customs Service is part of the U.S. Department of the Treasury. **Staff:** Martha Glock, User Serv.Libn.; Cecilia Hlatshwayo, Bus. & Econ.Libn.

U.S. Defense Communications Agency
See: **U.S. Defense Information Systems Agency (17165)**

★17165★
U.S. Defense Information Systems Agency - Library and Information Center (Comp Sci, Info Sci)
Code BHL
701 S. Courthouse Rd.   Phone: (703)692-2468
Arlington, VA 22204-2199   Donald A. Guerriero, Lib.Dir.
Founded: 1974. **Staff:** Prof 5; Other 5. **Subjects:** Information systems, telecommunications, computer science, electronics, engineering, management, military science. **Holdings:** 20,000 books; 1500 technical reports. **Subscriptions:** 500 journals and other serials. **Services:** Interlibrary loan (limited); center not open to the public. **Automated Operations:** Integrated library system. **Computerized Information Services:** OCLC, DIALOG Information Services, DTIC, LEXIS, NEXIS, NewsNet, Inc.; CD-ROMs. **Networks/Consortia:** Member of FEDLINK. **Remarks:** FAX: (202)692-2045. Serves headquarters and field agencies of the Defense Information Systems Agency (DISA). The Defense Information Systems Agency is part of the U.S. Department of Defense. **Formerly:** U.S. Defense Communications Agency.

★17166★
U.S. Defense Intelligence Agency - Library DSP-2A (Mil)
Washington, DC 20340-3342   Phone: (202)373-3836
                Ruth Mullane, Chf., Ref.Lib.Br.
Founded: 1963. **Staff:** Prof 17; Other 17. **Subjects:** Intelligence - armed forces, transportation, political, scientific and technical, economic, sociological; communications and electronics. **Special Collections:**

Intelligence reports, documents, periodicals, video cassettes. **Holdings:** 85,000 books; 100,000 reports; 50,000 translations; 1.5 million microfiche; 2.5 million unbound reports; 1000 video cassettes. **Subscriptions:** 1500 journals and other serials. **Services:** Interlibrary loan; library not open to the public but public information act requests are satisfied. **Automated Operations:** Computerized public access catalog, cataloging, acquisitions, serials, and circulation. **Computerized Information Services:** DIALOG Information Services, NEXIS, OCLC; CD-ROMs. **Networks/Consortia:** Member of FEDLINK. **Remarks:** FAX: (202)373-3838. The Defense Intelligence Agency is part of the U.S. Department of Defense. **Formerly:** Its Library RTS-2A.

★17167★
U.S. Defense Logistics Agency - Defense Construction Supply Center (Sci-Engr)
Box 3990
ATTN: DCSC-SDRM   Phone: (614)238-3549
Columbus, OH 43216-5000   Charles Rutter, Chf.
Staff: 6. **Special Collections:** Total Quality Management (TQM) Library. **Holdings:** Specifications; manufacturers' catalogs; government specifications and standards. **Services:** Center not open to the public. **Staff:** Carole Gouda; Colleen Irvin; Linda Hackenbracht; Dorothy Jefferson.

★17168★
U.S. Defense Logistics Agency - Defense Contract Management Area Operations Milwaukee - Library (Mil)
310 W. Wisconsin Ave., Suite 340
Milwaukee, WI 53203   Nancy J. Slowinski, Oper.Sup.Asst.
Founded: 1965. **Staff:** 2. **Holdings:** Microfilm library of military standards; QPL qualified products lists; manufacturers' code books and miscellaneous publications. **Services:** Library open to the public for reference use only. **Automated Operations:** Computerized cataloging. **Computerized Information Services:** Online systems. Performs searches free of charge.

★17169★
U.S. Defense Logistics Agency - Defense General Supply Center - Center Library (Mil)
Richmond, VA 23297   Phone: (804)279-3215
Subjects: Management; military science; economics; political science; DoD, DLA, USAF, and Army regulations. **Holdings:** 6990 volumes; 280 boxes of unbound magazines; operating regulations and manuals. **Subscriptions:** 5 newspapers. **Services:** Library open to DGSC personnel only.

★17170★
U.S. Defense Logistics Agency - Defense Industrial Supply Center - Technical Data Management Division (Sci-Engr)
700 Robbins Ave.   Phone: (215)697-2757
Philadelphia, PA 19111-5096   Nancy J. Popson, Chf., Tech. Data Mgt.Div.
Founded: 1961. **Staff:** 86. **Subjects:** Industrial metals, plastics, and synthetic rubbers; engineering; management; industrial and general hardware. **Holdings:** 2000 books; 1.7 million aperture cards of manufacturers' drawings; 20,000 manufacturers' catalogs; 30,000 industry standards; 35,000 government specifications and standards; cartridge film file. **Services:** Division not open to the public.

★17171★
U.S. Defense Logistics Agency - Defense Logistics Services Center - Library (Mil, Comp Sci)
Federal Ctr.
74 N. Washington St.   Phone: (616)961-4957
Battle Creek, MI 49017-3084   Judith A. Hunsicker, Libn.
Founded: 1962. **Staff:** Prof 1. **Subjects:** Electronic data processing, adult education, management. **Holdings:** 3700 books; 414 government documents. **Subscriptions:** 174 journals and other serials. **Services:** Interlibrary loan; library open to the public for reference use only. **Automated Operations:** Computerized cataloging. **Computerized Information Services:** OCLC, BRS Information Technologies. **Networks/Consortia:** Member of FEDLINK.

★ 17172 ★
U.S. Defense Logistics Agency - Defense Personnel Support Center - Directorate of Medical Materiel - Medical Information Center (Med, Sci-Engr)
2800 S. 20th St., Bldg. 9-3-F   Phone: (215)737-2110
Philadelphia, PA 19101-8419   Ann Cline Tobin, Libn.
Founded: 1952. **Staff:** Prof 2. **Subjects:** Medicine, pharmacy, engineering. **Special Collections:** Military medicine. **Holdings:** 2500 books; 1500 unbound periodical volumes; military and federal specifications and industry standards on microfilm. **Subscriptions:** 62 journals and other serials. **Services:** Interlibrary loan; center not open to the public. **Automated Operations:** Computerized serials. **Computerized Information Services:** BRS Information Technologies, DIALOG Information Services, MEDLARS, DTIC, OCLC; DDN Network Information Center, InterNet (electronic mail services). **Networks/Consortia:** Member of FEDLINK. **Publications:** Directorate of Medical Materiel, monthly - for internal distribution only. **Remarks:** FAX: (215)737-8139. Electronic mail address(es): DPSC.DLA.MIL (DDN Network Information Center, InterNet). **Staff:** Clara McCollaum, Asst.Libn.

★ 17173 ★
U.S. Defense Logistics Agency - Headquarters Library (Mil, Comp Sci)
Cameron Sta., Rm. 4D120   Phone: (703)274-6055
Alexandria, VA 22304-6100   Barbara Federline, Chf.Libn.
Founded: 1962. **Subjects:** Management, automatic data processing. **Special Collections:** Military regulations (5000 items). **Holdings:** 8300 books; 300,000 microforms. **Subscriptions:** 290 journals and other serials. **Services:** Interlibrary loan; library open to the public by permission. **Automated Operations:** Computerized cataloging, serials, and circulation. **Computerized Information Services:** OCLC, SearchMaestro, EasyNet, WESTLAW, LEGI-SLATE, Dun & Bradstreet Business Credit Services, EBSCO Subscription Services, The Faxon Company, University Microfilms International (UMI), DTIC, Haystack. **Networks/Consortia:** Member of FEDLINK. **Remarks:** The Defense Logistics Agency is part of the U.S. Department of Defense. **Staff:** Barbara Sable, Asst.Libn.

★ 17174 ★
U.S. Defense Mapping Agency - Aerospace Center - Technical Library (Sci-Engr, Comp Sci)
3200 S. 2nd St.   Phone: (314)263-4267
St. Louis, MO 63118-3399   Barbara K. Bick, Chf.
Founded: 1943. **Staff:** Prof 1; Other 3. **Subjects:** Geodesy, computer science, earth sciences, astronomy, mathematics, management. **Holdings:** 20,000 books; 8000 scientific-technical reports. **Subscriptions:** 425 journals and other serials. **Services:** Interlibrary loan; library not open to the public. **Automated Operations:** Computerized cataloging, acquisitions, and circulation. **Computerized Information Services:** DTIC, OCLC, DIALOG Information Services. **Remarks:** Alternate telephone number(s): (314)263-4267. **Staff:** Bruce Brooks, Acq.

★ 17175 ★
U.S. Defense Mapping Agency - Hydrographic/Topographic Center - Library (Geog-Map)
Attn: MCD5
4600 Sangamore Rd.   Phone: (301)227-2103
Bethesda, MD 20816-5003   Janet G. Gee, Chf., Lib.Br.
Founded: 1871. **Staff:** Prof 26; Other 11. **Subjects:** Topography, cartography, hydrography, bathymetry, geodesy, toponomy. **Special Collections:** Department of Defense libraries of maps, geodetic data, foreign place names, nautical charts, bathymetric data. **Holdings:** 80,000 books, periodicals, documents; 550,000 maps; 44,000 charts; 4.5 million place names; 60,000 bathymetric surveys. **Subscriptions:** 550 journals and other serials. **Services:** Interlibrary loan (limited); library not open to the public. **Automated Operations:** Computerized cataloging. **Computerized Information Services:** DIALOG Information Services, PFDS Online; internal databases. **Publications:** Biweekly accessions listings. **Remarks:** FAX: (301)227-5059. The Defense Mapping Agency is part of the U.S. Department of Defense. **Formerly:** Located in Washington, DC.

U.S. Defense Nuclear Agency - Armed Forces Radiobiology Research Institute (AFRRI)
See: **U.S. Armed Forces Radiobiology Research Institute (AFRRI)** (16914)

★ 17176 ★
U.S. Defense Nuclear Agency - Technical Library (Sci-Engr)
Washington, DC 20305-1000   Phone: (202)325-1043
     Mrs. Bennie F. Maddox, Chf., Tech.Lib.Div.
Founded: 1947. **Staff:** Prof 2; Other 7. **Subjects:** Nuclear science and technology, nuclear weapons effects. **Holdings:** 4000 books; 150,000 technical reports. **Subscriptions:** 300 journals and other serials; 6 newspapers. **Services:** Interlibrary loan; library not open to the public. **Automated Operations:** Computerized cataloging and circulation. **Computerized Information Services:** NEXIS, DIALOG Information Services, DTIC; LAM (Local Automation Model; internal database). **Remarks:** The Defense Nuclear Agency is part of the U.S. Department of Defense.

U.S. Defense Technical Information Center - Chemical Warfare/ Chemical and Biological Defense Information Analysis Center
See: **Battelle Memorial Institute** (1565)

★ 17177 ★
U.S. Defense Technical Information Center - DTIC Los Angeles Regional Office (Mil)
222 N. Sepulveda Blvd., Rm. 906   Phone: (213)335-4170
El Segundo, CA 90245-4320   Barbara Busch, Mgr.
Founded: 1940. **Staff:** Prof 3. **Subjects:** Research and development funded by the U.S. Department of Defense. **Special Collections:** Information Analysis Center collections. **Holdings:** 2 million documents. **Services:** Microfiche-to-microfiche reproduction; office open to government agencies and U.S. Department of Defense registered and potential registered contractors. **Computerized Information Services:** DTIC. **Special Indexes:** Cumulative annual indexes (microfiche). **Remarks:** FAX: (213)335-3663. **Staff:** Dolores Pieper, Tech.Info.Spec.

★ 17178 ★
U.S. Defense Technical Information Center - Technical Library (Sci-Engr, Comp Sci)
Cameron Sta., Bldg. 5   Phone: (703)274-6833
Alexandria, VA 22304-6145   Rusty Delorie, Libn.
Founded: 1958. **Staff:** Prof 1; Other 1. **Subjects:** Computer and information sciences, physical sciences, engineering, life sciences. **Holdings:** 8000 books. **Subscriptions:** 175 journals and other serials. **Services:** Interlibrary loan; library not open to the public. **Automated Operations:** Computerized public access catalog, cataloging, and serials. **Computerized Information Services:** Produces the Defense Research, Development, Test, and Evaluation Online System (DROLS); DIALOG Information Services, PFDS Online, BRS Information Technologies, NEXIS, NASA/RECON, OCLC, WILSONLINE, STN International, SearchMaestro. **Networks/Consortia:** Member of FEDLINK. **Remarks:** This is an internal support library primarily for DTIC personnel.

U.S.D.A. - Agricultural Research Service - Bee Biology and Systematics Laboratory
See: **Bee Biology and Systematics Laboratory** (1650)

★ 17179 ★
U.S.D.A. - Agricultural Research Service - Central Great Plains Research Station - Library (Agri)
Box 400   Phone: (303)345-2259
Akron, CO 80720   Dr. A.D. Halvorson, Res.Ldr.
Founded: 1907. **Staff:** Prof 6; Other 12. **Subjects:** Agronomy, soils, water, plants, hydrology. **Holdings:** 250 books. **Subscriptions:** 26 journals and other serials. **Services:** Library not open to the public.

★ 17180 ★
U.S.D.A. - Agricultural Research Service - Cereal Crops Research Unit - Library (Agri)
501 N. Walnut St.   Phone: (608)262-3355
Madison, WI 53705   Debi Schaefer, Sec.
Founded: 1948. **Subjects:** Malting, brewing, cereal chemistry. **Holdings:** 500 volumes. **Remarks:** Center is jointly operated by University of Wisconsin, Madison.

★17181★
U.S.D.A. - Agricultural Research Service - Eastern Regional Research
  Center Library (Sci-Engr, Food-Bev)
600 E. Mermaid Lane   Phone: (215)233-6602
Philadelphia, PA 19118   Wendy H. Kramer, Adm.Libn.
Founded: 1940. Staff: Prof 1; Other 2.5. Subjects: Chemistry, biochemistry,
chemical engineering, food sciences, leather research, plant sciences,
microbiology, biotechnology, food safety, wool research. Holdings: 10,000
books; 40,000 bound periodical volumes. Subscriptions: 260 journals and
other serials. Services: Interlibrary loan; copying (limited); SDI; document
delivery service; library open to the public. Automated Operations:
Computerized cataloging, acquisitions, circulation, and ILL. Computerized
Information Services: DIALOG Information Services, OCLC; CD-ROM
(AGRICOLA); SprintMail (electronic mail service). Networks/Consortia:
Member of FEDLINK, National Network of Libraries of Medicine - Middle
Atlantic Region. Publications: Accession List, monthly; library newsletter,
quarterly. Remarks: Alternate telephone number(s): 233-6604; 233-6660.
FAX: (215)233-6606. Electronic mail address(es): LIB.ERRC (SprintMail).

★17182★
U.S.D.A. - Agricultural Research Service - Ft. Keogh Livestock and
  Range Research Laboratory - Library (Agri)
Montana State Univ.
Rte. 1, Box 2021
Miles City, MT 59301   Phone: (406)232-4970
Subjects: Animal science, range science. Holdings: 300 books; bound
periodical volumes. Remarks: FAX: (406)232-6375.

★17183★
U.S.D.A. - Agricultural Research Service - Honey Bee Research
  Laboratory - Library (Biol Sci)
2413 E. Hwy. 83   Phone: (512)968-3150
Weslaco, TX 78596   A.M. Collins, Res. Geneticist
Subjects: Apiculture, pesticides, beekeeping, honey bees, bee diseases,
Africanized bees, acarine parasites, insect pathology, entomology. Holdings:
480 books and bound periodical volumes; bulletins and reprints.
Subscriptions: 10 journals and other serials. Services: Library open to
graduate students in apiculture research. Remarks: FAX: (512)565-6133.

★17184★
U.S.D.A. - Agricultural Research Service - Horticultural Crops Research
  Laboratory - Library (Biol Sci)
2021 S. Peach Ave.   Phone: (209)453-3000
Fresno, CA 93727-5999   Marya Salmu, Libn.
Staff: Prof 1. Subjects: Horticulture, plant and insect pathology, stored-
product entomology, food science. Holdings: 2000 books; 600 bound
periodical volumes; government documents. Subscriptions: 74 journals and
other serials. Services: Library open to the public for reference use only.
Computerized Information Services: Internal database. Remarks: FAX:
(209)453-3011.

★17185★
U.S.D.A. - Agricultural Research Service - Horticultural Research
  Laboratory - Library (Biol Sci, Agri)
2120 Camden Rd.   Phone: (407)897-7301
Orlando, FL 32803   Ruby Glass, Libn.
Founded: 1970. Staff: 1. Subjects: Citrus - culture, breeding, processing,
insects; nematology; plant pathology and physiology; biochemistry;
transportation, storage, and marketing of fruits and vegetables. Special
Collections: Publications and reprints on citrus and related topics. Holdings:
1500 books; 1000 bound periodical volumes; reprints; slides and
photographs. Subscriptions: 100 journals and other serials. Services:
Interlibrary loan; copying (limited); library open to the staff and students of
nearby universities and experiment stations. Remarks: FAX: (407)897-7309.

★17186★
U.S.D.A. - Agricultural Research Service - Knipling-Bushland U.S.
  Livestock Insects Laboratory - Library (Biol Sci)
Box 232
Kerrville, TX 78029-0232   Phone: (512)257-3566
Founded: 1946. Subjects: Veterinary entomology. Holdings: 1000 books;
2000 bound periodical volumes. Subscriptions: 61 journals and other serials.
Services: Interlibrary loan; library open to the public. Computerized
Information Services: DIALOG Information Services; SprintMail
(electronic mail service). Remarks: FAX: (512)792-3637.

★17187★
U.S.D.A. - Agricultural Research Service - Meat Animal Research
  Center (Biol Sci, Food-Bev)
Box 166   Phone: (402)762-4106
Clay Center, NE 68933   Patricia L. Sheridan, Libn.
Founded: 1975. Staff: Prof 1. Subjects: Animals - science, breeding and
reproduction, nutrition; agricultural engineering; meats; production
systems. Holdings: 2500 books; 2700 bound periodical volumes.
Subscriptions: 153 journals and other serials. Services: Interlibrary loan;
copying; center open to the public with restrictions. Computerized
Information Services: OCLC, DIALOG Information Services, MEDLINE.
Networks/Consortia: Member of FEDLINK. Remarks: FAX: (402)762-
4148. Also Known As: Roman L. Hruska U.S. Meat Animal Research
Center.

★17188★
U.S.D.A. - Agricultural Research Service - National Animal Disease
  Center - Library (Biol Sci, Med)
2300 Dayton Ave.
P.O. Box 70   Phone: (515)239-8271
Ames, IA 50010   Janice K. Eifling, Libn.
Founded: 1961. Staff: Prof 1; Other 1. Subjects: Biomedicine, microbiology,
veterinary science. Holdings: 8000 books; 18,000 bound periodical volumes.
Subscriptions: 350 journals and other serials. Services: Interlibrary loan;
copying; ARS Current Awareness Literature Service; library open to
qualified researchers. Computerized Information Services: DIALOG
Information Services; DOCLINE (electronic mail service). Publications:
Library Notes, monthly - for internal distribution only; Periodical Holdings
List, annual; NADC Publications List, annual - available on request. Special
Catalogs: Catalog of literature references on animal diseases, 1800-1940
(microfilm). Remarks: FAX: (515)239-8458.

★17189★
U.S.D.A. - Agricultural Research Service - National Center for
  Agricultural Utilization Research - Library (Sci-Engr, Biol Sci)
1815 N. University St.   Phone: (309)685-4011
Peoria, IL 61604   Donald L. Blevins, Libn.
Founded: 1940. Staff: Prof 1; Other 1. Subjects: Organic chemistry,
biochemistry, microbiology, fermentation, plant physiology. Holdings:
40,000 volumes; 200 reels of microfilm. Subscriptions: 225 journals and
other serials. Services: Interlibrary loan; copying; SDI; library open to the
public. Automated Operations: Computerized cataloging. Computerized
Information Services: DIALOG Information Services, STN International,
OCLC; SprintMail (electronic mail service). Networks/Consortia: Member
of FEDLINK, Heart of Illinois Library Consortium (HILC), Illinois Valley
Library System. Remarks: FAX: (309)671-7065. Formerly: Its Northern
Regional Research Center Library.

★17190★
U.S.D.A. - Agricultural Research Service - National Soil Dynamics
  Laboratory - Library (Agri)
Box 792   Phone: (205)844-4741
Auburn, AL 36831-0792   Eddie C. Burt, Res.Ldr.
Founded: 1955. Staff: 1. Subjects: Tillage, traction, soil-machine relations,
soil reactions, earth-moving, conservation tillage, plant nutrient uptake,
cropping systems, rhizasphere. Special Collections: Translations of foreign
technical publications (60 bound volumes; 7000 other cataloged items).
Holdings: 400 books; 500 bound periodical volumes; 7000 other cataloged
items; 18,000 reports; 130 theses; 50 technical films; 5000 slides; 5000
photographs. Subscriptions: 30 journals and other serials. Services:
Interlibrary loan; library not open to the public. Remarks: FAX: (205)887-
8597.

U.S.D.A. - Agricultural Research Service - Northern Regional Research
  Center Library
See: U.S.D.A. - Agricultural Research Service - National Center for
  Agricultural Utilization Research - Library (17189)

★17191★
U.S.D.A. - Agricultural Research Service - Plum Island Animal Disease
  Center - Library (Agri, Med)
Box 848   Phone: (516)323-2500
Greenport, NY 11944-0848   Hugh Thomas, Libn.
Founded: 1954. Staff: Prof 1. Subjects: Virology, microbiology,
immunology, molecular biology, veterinary medicine, laboratory animal

sciences. **Special Collections:** Foreign animal diseases exotic to the U.S. **Holdings:** 14,000 books; 16,000 bound periodical volumes; 12,645 reprints; 85 VF drawers of pamphlets and reprints. **Subscriptions:** 166 journals and other serials. **Services:** Interlibrary loan; library not open to the public. **Computerized Information Services:** DIALOG Information Services, OCLC, EMERPRO; SCIENCEREF (internal database). **Networks/ Consortia:** Member of FEDLINK. **Special Catalogs:** Card catalog on foreign animal diseases; subject catalog (computerized).

★ 17192 ★
U.S.D.A. - Agricultural Research Service - Soil and Water Management
   Research Unit Library (Agri)
3793N 3600E   Phone: (208)423-5582
Kimberly, ID 83341   J. Sanborn, Libn.
Staff: Prof 2; Other 2. **Subjects:** Agriculture, agronomy, entomology, computers, plant and crop science, soil science, meteorology, ecology and environment, water and hydrology. **Holdings:** 1300 books; 1500 bound periodical volumes. **Subscriptions:** 50 journals and other serials. **Services:** Interlibrary loan; library open to the public for reference use only. **Computerized Information Services:** Internal database. **Publications:** New Book List - for internal distribution only. **Remarks:** FAX: (208)423-6555.

★ 17193 ★
U.S.D.A. - Agricultural Research Service - South Atlantic Area -
   Richard B. Russell Agricultural Research Center Library (Agri)
Box 5677   Phone: (404)546-3314
Athens, GA 30613   Jo Ann Schoonmaker, Libn.
Staff: Prof 2. **Subjects:** Agriculture, toxicology, food safety, plant physiology, animal science, poultry. **Holdings:** 6000 books; 340 bound periodical volumes. **Subscriptions:** 340 journals and other serials. **Services:** Interlibrary loan; copying; SDI; library open to the public. **Automated Operations:** Computerized cataloging and ILL. **Computerized Information Services:** DIALOG Information Services, OCLC, Chemical Abstracts Service (CAS), MEDLARS, PFDS Online; SprintMail (electronic mail service). **Networks/Consortia:** Member of FEDLINK, SOLINET. **Publications:** Newsletter. **Remarks:** FAX: (404)546-3412. **Staff:** Barbara Gazda, Lib.Tech.

★ 17194 ★
U.S.D.A. - Agricultural Research Service - Southern Regional Research
   Center (Sci-Engr, Food-Bev, Biol Sci)
1100 Robert E. Lee Blvd.
Box 19687   Phone: (504)286-4287
New Orleans, LA 70179   Suhad Wojkowski, Adm.
Founded: 1941. **Staff:** Prof 1; Other 2. **Subjects:** Chemistry, textiles, food processing, plant sciences, aquaculture, mechanical and chemical engineering, microscopy, electron microscopy, vegetable fats and oils, microbiology, statistics. **Special Collections:** Trade literature; U.S. and foreign patents in laboratory's fields of interest. **Holdings:** 35,000 volumes; 59 VF drawers of pamphlets, foreign patents, trade literature, reprints, translations and manuscripts; 68 shelves of U.S. patents. **Subscriptions:** 2000 journals and other serials. **Services:** Interlibrary loan; center open to the public for reference use only. **Automated Operations:** Computerized cataloging. **Computerized Information Services:** DIALOG Information Services, OCLC, BRS Information Technologies, MEDLARS. **Networks/ Consortia:** Member of FEDLINK. **Publications:** Accession List, monthly; bibliography on Aflatoxin and Byssinosis (card). **Remarks:** FAX: (504)286-4396.

★ 17195 ★
U.S.D.A. - Agricultural Research Service - Southwest Watershed
   Research Center (Env-Cons)
2000 E. Allen Rd.   Phone: (602)670-6381
Tucson, AZ 85719   E. Sue Anderson, Libn.
Founded: 1957. **Staff:** 1. **Subjects:** Water and soil conservation, sediment, runoff, erosion, rainfall, arid land ecosystems improvement, watershed protection, climate change. **Holdings:** 400 books; 150 bound periodical volumes. **Subscriptions:** 5 journals and other serials. **Services:** Center open to the public with restrictions. **Publications:** Bibliography of abstracts and papers. **Remarks:** FAX: (602)670-6493. **Formerly:** Its Aridland Watershed Management Research Unit.

★ 17196 ★
U.S.D.A. - Agricultural Research Service - Stored-Product Insects
   Research & Development Laboratory - Library (Biol Sci, Sci-Engr)
3401 Edwin St.
Box 22909   Phone: (912)233-7981
Savannah, GA 31403   M. Harriet Winiger, Lib.Techn.
Founded: 1965. **Staff:** Prof 1. **Subjects:** Stored-product insect control, entomology, chemistry, biology, insect-resistant packaging, mothproofing, insect rearing. **Holdings:** 4000 books; 9000 bound periodical volumes; 15 VF drawers of U.S.D.A. publications; 2000 slides; 3500 unbound journals; 17,000 reprints; 200 microfiche. **Subscriptions:** 100 journals and other serials. **Services:** Interlibrary loan; library open to the public with director's permission. **Computerized Information Services:** DIALOG Information Services; NAL (Natl. Agriculture Library, internal database). **Remarks:** FAX: (912)233-7981, ext. 294.

★ 17197 ★
U.S.D.A. - Agricultural Research Service - U.S. Water Conservation
   Laboratory - Library (Agri)
4331 E. Broadway Rd.
Phoenix, AZ 85040   Phone: (602)379-4356
Founded: 1961. **Staff:** Prof 1. **Subjects:** Agricultural and irrigation engineering, hydraulics, hydrology, soils, plant physiology, chemistry, meteorology, instrumentation, wastewater renovation, infrared remote sensing, plant stress. **Holdings:** 1300 books; 200 bound periodical volumes; laboratory annual reports; reports of Geological Survey and ARS Series. **Subscriptions:** 85 journals and other serials. **Services:** Library open to the public for reference use only. **Publications:** Listing of publications of laboratory staff members, annual. **Remarks:** FAX: (602)379-4355.

★ 17198 ★
U.S.D.A. - Agricultural Research Service - Western Regional Research
   Center Library (Agri, Food-Bev)
800 Buchanan St.   Phone: (510)559-5603
Albany, CA 94710   Rena Schonbrun, Libn.
Founded: 1940. **Staff:** Prof 1; Other 2. **Subjects:** Cereals, fruits and vegetables, field crops, food technology, pharmacology, chemistry, nutrition. **Holdings:** Figures not available. **Subscriptions:** 320 journals. **Services:** Interlibrary loan; copying; SDI; library open to the public by appointment. **Automated Operations:** Computerized cataloging. **Computerized Information Services:** DIALOG Information Services, OCLC. **Networks/ Consortia:** Member of FEDLINK. **Remarks:** FAX: (510)559-5777.

★ 17199 ★
U.S.D.A. - Animal and Plant Inspection Service - Animal Damage
   Control Program - Denver Wildlife Research Center - Library (Biol
   Sci, Env-Cons, Sci-Engr)
Federal Center, Bldg. 16
Box 25266   Phone: (303)236-7873
Denver, CO 80225-0266   Diana L. Dwyer, Libn.
Staff: Prof 2; Other 3. **Subjects:** Wildlife biology, zoology, ornithology, mammalogy, ecology, pesticides, animal damage control, analytical chemistry, statistics, agriculture. **Special Collections:** International collection of theses and dissertations on vertebrate pest management; wildlife reprints and technical reports. **Holdings:** 15,000 books; 650 bound periodical volumes; 1500 technical reports and reprints; 500 unbound periodical volumes. **Subscriptions:** 271 journals and other serials. **Services:** Interlibrary loan; copying; library open to the public with restrictions. **Automated Operations:** Computerized cataloging and ILL. **Computerized Information Services:** DIALOG Information Services, Chemical Information Systems, Inc. (CIS), LEXIS, NPIRS, STN International, OCLC; Predator Database, Bird Damage (internal databases). **Networks/ Consortia:** Member of FEDLINK. **Publications:** Acquisitions list, quarterly; Serials Holdings, irregular; publications list, annual. **Remarks:** FAX: (303)236-7863. Telex: 303 236 7863. **Formerly:** Its Science and Technology Program.

★ 17200 ★
U.S.D.A. - Argicultural Research Service - Grain Marketing Research
   Laboratory - Library (Agri)
1515 College Ave.   Phone: (913)776-2701
Manhattan, KS 66502   G. Glen Dalluge, Lib.Hd.
Founded: 1971. **Subjects:** Agriculture, grain science. **Holdings:** 1200 books; 200 bound periodical volumes. **Subscriptions:** 20 journals and other serials. **Services:** Library not open to the public. **Remarks:** FAX: (913)776-2792.

★ 17201 ★
U.S.D.A. - Economic Research Service - ERS Reference Center (Bus-Fin)
1301 New York Ave., Rm. B28   Phone: (202)219-0724
Washington, DC 20005-4788   D.J. Fusonie, Dir.
Staff: Prof 2; Other 2. **Subjects:** Agricultural economics. **Special Collections:** Comprehensive collection of the U.S.D.A. - Economic Research Service and U.S.D.A. - Economics and Statistics Service publications (unbound and/or on microfiche). **Holdings:** 16,000 monographs; 10,000 microforms. **Subscriptions:** 450 journals and other serials. **Services:** Copying (limited); center open to the public by appointment for reference use. **Automated Operations:** Computerized cataloging, circulation, and ILL. **Computerized Information Services:** DIALOG Information Services; CD-ROMS. **Networks/Consortia:** Member of FEDLINK. **Publications:** Newsletter, quarterly. **Special Catalogs:** Catalog to book collection; catalog to vertical file collection of articles (online and book); catalog to journal holdings. **Remarks:** FAX: (202)219-0760. **Staff:** Barbara Baker.

U.S.D.A. - Forest Service
See: **U.S. Forest Service** (17513)

★ 17202 ★
U.S.D.A. - Human Nutrition Research Center on Aging - Library (Med)
711 Washington St.   Phone: (617)556-3173
Boston, MA 02111   Kathleen L. Capellano, M.S., R.D.
Founded: 1988. **Staff:** Prof 1. **Subjects:** Nutrition, biomedical sciences, aging. **Holdings:** 500 books; 60 bound periodical volumes; 30 reports; 1200 publication archives. **Subscriptions:** 115 journals and other serials. **Services:** Library open to the public for reference use only by request. **Computerized Information Services:** CD-ROM (MEDLINE); diskettes (Current Contents: Life Sciences); BITNET (electronic mail service). **Publications:** HNRC Research Program Description, annual; HNRC publications listing, annual. **Remarks:** FAX: (617)556-3344. Electronic mail address(es): CAPELLAN-NI@HNRC.TUFTS.EDU (BITNET).

★ 17203 ★
U.S.D.A. - National Agricultural Library (Biol Sci, Agri, Sci-Engr)
10301 Baltimore Blvd.   Phone: (301)344-3755
Beltsville, MD 20705   Joseph H. Howard, Dir.
Founded: 1862. **Staff:** Prof 124; Other 88. **Subjects:** Plant science, forestry, horticulture, animal industry, veterinary medicine, aquaculture, entomology, soils and fertilizers, alternative farming, agricultural engineering, rural development, agricultural products, food and nutrition, home economics, biotechnology, agricultural trade and marketing. **Special Collections:** Layne R. Beaty papers (farm radio and television broadcasting); foreign and domestic nursery and seed trade catalogs; flock, herd, and stud books; rare book collection; AV collection on food and nutrition; apiculture; Forest Service Photo Collection; M. Truman Fossum Collection (floriculture); James M. Gwin Collection (poultry); Charles E. North Collection (milk sanitation); Pomology Collection (original pomological art); Charles Valentine Riley Collection (entomology); plant exploration photo collection; food and nutrition microcomputer software. **Holdings:** 2.1 million volumes; 948,647 microforms; 13,580 maps. **Subscriptions:** 27,000 journals and newspapers. **Services:** Interlibrary loan; copying; SDI; library open to the public. **Automated Operations:** Computerized public access catalog, cataloging, acquisitions, serials, circulation, and indexing. **Computerized Information Services:** DIALOG Information Services, BRS Information Technologies, OCLC; produces AGRICOLA; ISIS (internal databases); Dialcom Inc. (electronic mail service). **Networks/Consortia:** Member of FEDLINK. **Publications:** Agricultural Libraries Information Notes, monthly; Quick Bibliography, irregular; AGRICOLA (computerized tape service), monthly - for sale. **Remarks:** FAX: (301)344-5472. **Staff:** Maria Pisa, Asst.Dir.; Pamela Andre, Assoc.Dir.Automation; Sarah Thomas, Assoc.Dir.Tech.Serv.; Keith Russell, Assoc.Dir.Pub.Serv.

★ 17204 ★
U.S.D.A. - National Agricultural Library - Animal Welfare Information Center (Agri)
Beltsville, MD 20705   Phone: (301)344-3212
                 Jean Larson, Coord./Tech.Info.Spec.
Founded: 1986. **Staff:** Prof 4; Other 1. **Subjects:** Animals involved in research, testing, education, and exhibition - training in their care and use, pain and anesthesia, improved methodologies, reduction in usage, alternatives. **Holdings:** Figures not available. **Services:** Interlibrary loan; copying; center open to the public with restrictions. **Computerized Information Services:** DIALOG Information Services. Performs searches on fee basis. **Publications:** Quick bibliographies; special reference briefs; fact sheets; newsletter. **Remarks:** FAX: (301)344-5472. **Staff:** D'anna Berry, Tech.Info.Spec.; Janice Swanson, Tech.Info.Spec.

★ 17205 ★
U.S.D.A. - National Agricultural Library - Aquaculture Information Center (Agri)
10301 Baltimore Blvd., Rm. 304   Phone: (301)344-3704
Beltsville, MD 20705   Deborah T. Hanfman, Coord.Aquac.Info.Ctr.
Founded: 1984. **Staff:** Prof 3. **Subjects:** Aquaculture - aquatic plant culture, fish farming, mariculture, diseases of aquaculture species, harvesting/processing of aquaculture species. **Special Collections:** Virginia Institute of Marine Science Microfiche Collection on Aquaculture (10,500 microfiche); REGIS II: A Hypermedial/Expert System on African Aquaculture (diskette); AQUACULTURE I: A Pilot Full-Text CD-ROM (also available at various land-grant libraries); Agricultural collection. **Holdings:** 2.1 million volumes. **Subscriptions:** 26,000 current periodical titles. **Services:** Interlibrary loan; copying. **Automated Operations:** Computerized public access catalog, cataloging, indexing, circulation, acquisitions, and serials. **Computerized Information Services:** DIALOG Information Services, BRS Information Technologies; ALF (Agricultural Library Forum). Performs searches on fee basis (fee dependent upon user affiliation and professional time involved). **Publications:** Quick Bibliography Series, irregular; Aqua-Topics; AIC Series; directories and other resource materials. **Remarks:** The Aquaculture Information Center is one of 11 specialized centers within the National Agricultural Library. Alternate telephone number(s): 344-3558. FAX: (301)344-5472. **Staff:** Eileen McVey, Libn.; Ann Young, Tech.Info.Spec.; Nancy Thomson.

★ 17206 ★
U.S.D.A. - National Agricultural Library - Biotechnology Information Center (Agri)
10301 Baltimore Blvd., Rm. 1402   Phone: (301)344-3875
Beltsville, MD 20705   Robert D. Warmbrodt, Coord./Tech.Info.Spec.
Founded: 1985. **Staff:** Prof 2. **Subjects:** Biotechnology - plant, food, animal, regulation, and ethics. **Holdings:** 2 million volumes. **Subscriptions:** 22,000 journals and other serials. **Services:** Interlibrary loan; copying; center open to the public for reference use only. **Computerized Information Services:** DIALOG Information Services; InterNet (electronic mail service). Performs searches on fee basis. **Publications:** Bibliographies, 5-10/year. **Remarks:** FAX: (301)344-5472. Electronic mail address(es): RWARMBRODT@ASRR.ARSUSDA.GOV (InterNet).

★ 17207 ★
U.S.D.A. - National Agricultural Library - Food and Nutrition Information Center (Food-Bev)
10301 Baltimore Blvd., Rm. 304   Phone: (301)344-3719
Beltsville, MD 20705-2351   Sandra L. Facinoli, Coord.
Founded: 1971. **Staff:** Prof 3; Other 1. **Subjects:** Human nutrition research and education, food service management and food technology. **Special Collections:** Audiovisual materials (2500 AV programs); food and nutrition software demonstration center (150 programs). **Holdings:** 50,000 books; VF drawers. **Subscriptions:** 200 journals and other serials. **Services:** Interlibrary loan; copying; center open to the public with restricted lending. **Automated Operations:** Computerized cataloging. **Computerized Information Services:** DIALOG Information Services, AGRICOLA; Dialcom, Inc. (electronic mail service). Performs searches on fee basis. **Publications:** List of publications - available on request; assorted bibliographies on food and nutrition. **Remarks:** FAX: (301)344-3462. **Staff:** Shirley King Evans; Marcy Schveibinz; Natalie Updegrove.

U.S.D.A. - National Agricultural Library - National Arboretum
See: **U.S. Natl. Arboretum** (17608)

★ 17208 ★
U.S.D.A. - National Agricultural Library - Plant Genome Data and Information Center (Agri)
10301 Baltimore Blvd.   Phone: (301)344-3875
Beltsville, MD 20705   Susan McCarthy, Coord./Tech.Info.Spec.
Founded: 1990. **Staff:** Prof 10. **Subjects:** Molecular biology, mapping, large scale sequencing of nucleotides and polypeptides, computational genetics, database and software development for sequencing. **Holdings:** Figures not available. **Services:** Interlibrary loan; copying; center open to the public for reference use only. **Computerized Information Services:** DIALOG Information Services; InterNet (electronic mail service). Performs searches on fee basis. **Publications:** Newsletter, quarterly; bibliographies, 4-10/year. **Remarks:** FAX: (301)344-6098. Electronic mail address(es): SMCCARTHY@ASRR.ARSUSDA.GOV (InterNet).

★ 17209 ★
U.S.D.A. - National Agricultural Library - Rural Information Center
(Soc Sci)
10301 Baltimore Blvd., Rm. 304   Phone: (301)344-2547
Beltsville, MD 20705   Patricia La Caille John, Coord.
Founded: 1987. **Staff:** Prof 9; Other 4. **Subjects:** Economic development; small business development; city and county government services; government and private grants and funding sources; rural communities; community leadership; natural resources; rural health care - services, programs, issues. **Holdings:** Figures not available. **Services:** Interlibrary loan; copying; center open to the public. **Computerized Information Services:** DIALOG Information Services, Federal Assistance Programs Retrieval System (FAPRS), LOGIN, OLIADS (Online Intelligence and Decision Support), OCLC, NewsNet, Inc.; BITNET, InterNet (electronic mail services). Performs searches on fee basis. **Publications:** Rural Information Center Publication Series, irregular; Quick Bibliography Series, irregular. **Remarks:** Electronic mail address(es): NALRIC (BITNET, InterNet). Toll-free telephone number(s): (800)633-7701. **Staff:** M. Louise Reynnells, Tech.Info.Spec.; Terri Brown, Med.Libn.; Dorothy Heise, Libn.; Scott McKearney, Tech.Info.Spec.; Louise Murphy Simmons, Hea.Info.Spec.; Joy Zimmerman, Hea.Info.Spec.

★ 17210 ★
U.S.D.A. - National Agricultural Library - Technology Transfer Information Center (Agri)
10301 Baltimore Blvd., Rm. 1402   Phone: (301)344-3875
Beltsville, MD 20705-2351   Kathleen C. Hayes, Coord./Tech.Info.Spec.
Founded: 1989. **Staff:** Prof 2. **Subjects:** Technology transfer - legislation, methodology, evaluation, entrepreneurship; venture capital; partnerships; CRDAs; incubators; leadership; creativity; innovation; quality management. **Holdings:** Figures not available. **Services:** Interlibrary loan; copying; center open to the public for reference use only. **Computerized Information Services:** DIALOG Information Services. Performs searches on fee basis. **Remarks:** FAX: (301)344-6098. **Staff:** Bonnie Craighead

★ 17211 ★
U.S.D.A. - National Agricultural Library - Water Quality Information Center (Agri)
10301 Baltimore Blvd., Rm. 1402   Phone: (301)504-6077
Beltsville, MD 20705   Janice C. Kemp, Coord., WQIC
Founded: 1990. **Staff:** Prof 2. **Subjects:** Water - polution, quality, management, regulation; effect of agricultural practices on water quality and quantity. **Holdings:** Figures not available. **Services:** Interlibrary loan; copying; center open to the public for reference use only. **Computerized Information Services:** DIALOG Information Services, BRS Information Technologies, NLM; InterNet (electronic mail service). Performs searches. **Publications:** Bibliographies, 5-10/year. **Remarks:** FAX: (301)504-7098. Electronic mail address(es): JKEMP@ASRR.ARSUSDA.GOV (InterNet).

★ 17212 ★
U.S.D.A. - National Sedimentation Laboratory - Library (Env-Cons)
P.O. Box 1157   Phone: (601)232-2920
Oxford, MS 38655   Dr. C.K. Mutchler, Lab.Dir.
Staff: 1. **Subjects:** Erosion processes, sediment yield, water quality, water ecology. **Special Collections:** Reprints of articles published by the Scientific Staff of the National Sedimentation Laboratory. **Holdings:** 20,288 volumes. **Subscriptions:** 75 journals and other serials. **Services:** Library not open to the public; articles published by the Scientific Staff are available upon request. **Computerized Information Services:** CD-ROM (AGRICOLA, ProCite). **Publications:** List of staff publications available for distribution, upon request. **Remarks:** FAX: (601)232-2915.

★ 17213 ★
U.S.D.A. - Office of General Counsel - Law Library (Law)
Independence Ave. at 12th St., S.W.
Rm. M-1406, S Bldg.   Phone: (202)720-7751
Washington, DC 20250   Peter MacHare, Law Libn.
Founded: 1910. **Staff:** Prof 2; Other 2. **Subjects:** Law, legislative histories of federal acts of interest to the Department of Agriculture, federal administrative decisions (selective). **Holdings:** 116,277 books; 2404 bound periodical volumes; 49 reels of microfilm of Congressional Globe; 192,748 microfiche of the CIS microfiche library of the working papers of the U.S. Congress; 328 reels of microfilm of Federal Register, March 1936-December 1979; 615 reels of microfilm. **Subscriptions:** 115 journals and other serials. **Services:** Interlibrary loan (within metropolitan area); copying; library open to the public for reference use only. **Computerized Information Services:** LEXIS, WESTLAW, DIALOG Information Services. **Remarks:** FAX: (202)475-5682.

U.S.D.A. - Office of Governmental and Public Affairs
See: U.S.D.A. - Office of Public Affairs (17214)

★ 17214 ★
U.S.D.A. - Office of Public Affairs - Photography Division - Photograph Library (Aud-Vis, Agri)
14th & Independence Ave., S.W.
Washington, DC 20250   Phone: (202)720-6633
Staff: Prof 2; Other 4. **Subjects:** Agriculture, food production and marketing, land use. **Holdings:** 70,000 black/white photographs; 20,000 color slides. **Services:** Library open to the public by appointment. **Publications:** Filmstrips and Slide Sets of the USDA - free upon request. **Special Catalogs:** Catalog of USDA Photos. **Formerly:** U.S.D.A. - Office of Governmental and Public Affairs. **Staff:** Robert Hailstock, Vis.Info.Spec.

★ 17215 ★
U.S.D.A. - Sheep Experiment Station - Library (Agri)
Dubois, ID 83423   Phone: (208)374-5306
Founded: 1920. **Staff:** 1. **Subjects:** Animal breeding, animal genetics, reproduction. **Holdings:** Books; bound periodical volumes; reports. **Subscriptions:** 20 journals and other serials. **Services:** Library open to the public. **Computerized Information Services:** DIALOG Information Services. **Remarks:** FAX: (208)374-5582.

U.S.D.A. - Soil Conservation Service
See: U.S. Soil Conservation Service (17942)

U.S. Dept. of Commerce - Bureau of the Census
See: U.S. Bureau of the Census (17098)

★ 17216 ★
U.S. Dept. of Commerce - Economic Development Administration - Library (Soc Sci)
Main Commerce Bldg., Rm. H7315   Phone: (202)377-2127
Washington, DC 20230   Eli March, Tech.Asst.Spec.
Founded: 1981. **Subjects:** Economic development. **Holdings:** Figures not available.

★ 17217 ★
U.S. Dept. of Commerce - International Library (Bus-Fin)
121 S.W. Salmon, Suite 242
Portland, OR 97204   Phone: (503)326-3001
Staff: 1. **Holdings:** 50 books; 50 bound periodical volumes; 100 reports. **Subscriptions:** 25 journals and other serials; 10 newspapers. **Services:** Library not open to the public. **Computerized Information Services:** CD-ROMs (CIMS, National Trade Data Base). **Remarks:** FAX: (503)326-6351.

U.S. Dept. of Commerce - International Trade Administration
See: U.S. International Trade Administration (17562)

★ 17218 ★
U.S. Dept. of Commerce - Law Library (Bus-Fin)
14th & Penn St., N.W., Rm. 1894   Phone: (202)377-5517
Washington, DC 20230   Billie J. Grey, Dir.
Founded: 1904. **Staff:** Prof 3; Other 2. **Subjects:** International law, antitrust, government procurement. **Special Collections:** Congressional documents, circa 1930 to present. **Holdings:** 50,000 books; 1000 bound periodical volumes; 100,000 uncataloged items. **Subscriptions:** 200 journals and other serials. **Services:** Interlibrary loan (limited); library open to the public for reference use only. **Automated Operations:** Computerized public access catalog, cataloging, and serials. **Computerized Information Services:** LEXIS, WESTLAW, NEXIS. **Networks/Consortia:** Member of FEDLINK, CAPCON Library Network. **Remarks:** FAX: (202)377-0221. **Staff:** George L. Warde.

★ 17219 ★
U.S. Dept. of Commerce - Library (Bus-Fin)
14th & Constitution Ave., N.W., Rm. 8060   Phone: (202)377-3611
Washington, DC 20230   Anthony J. Steinhauser, Dir.
Founded: 1913. **Staff:** Prof 7; Other 5. **Subjects:** Economics, export-import, foreign trade, business, economic theory, economic conditions, statistics, marketing, industry, finance, legislation, management, telecommunications. **Special Collections:** U.S. Census; Department of Commerce publications; telecommunications. **Holdings:** 50,000 books and bound periodical volumes; 4300 reels of microfilm; 250,000 volumes of microfiche. **Subscriptions:** 1600 journals and other serials. **Services:** Interlibrary loan; copying; library open to the public for reference use only. **Automated Operations:** Computerized cataloging. **Computerized Information Services:** DIALOG Information Services, OCLC, PFDS Online, BRS Information Technologies, LEXIS, LEGI-SLATE, Mead Data Central. **Networks/Consortia:** Member of FEDLINK. **Publications:** Directory of Libraries in the U.S. Dept. of Commerce (COM 72-11147); Library Bulletin. **Special Catalogs:** Law catalog. **Remarks:** Contains the holdings of the U.S. Dept. of Commerce - National Telecommunications and Information Administration Library. **Staff:** Vera Whisenton, Chf., Rd.Serv.; Willene J. Gaines, Chf., Tech.Serv.; Marie Scroggs, Adm.Asst.; Lee Ruffin, ILL; Mary S. Hardison, Acq.Libn.; Uko Villemi, Cat.

U.S. Dept. of Commerce - National Institute of Standards and Technology
See: **U.S. Natl. Institute of Standards and Technology** (17624)

U.S. Dept. of Commerce - National Oceanic & Atmospheric Administration
See: **U.S. Natl. Oceanic & Atmospheric Administration** (17650)

U.S. Dept. of Commerce - National Oceanic & Atmospheric Administration - National Marine Fisheries Service
See: **U.S. Natl. Marine Fisheries Service** (17630)

U.S. Dept. of Commerce - National Oceanic & Atmospheric Administration - National Weather Service
See: **U.S. Natl. Weather Service** (17796)

★ 17220 ★
U.S. Dept. of Commerce - National Technical Information Service (Info Sci)
5285 Port Royal Rd.   Phone: (703)487-4650
Springfield, VA 22161   Don Johnson, Act.Dir.
Holdings: 1.8 million titles of non-classified U.S. government-sponsored and foreign research, development, and engineering reports, and other analyses prepared by federal agencies, their contractors, or grantees. **Services:** Current summaries (abstracts) of NTIS documents sold in paper or microform copy; microfiche service; bibliographic databases are available on magnetic tapes; source data files and software are available on magnetic tape and diskette. **Computerized Information Services:** DIALOG Information Services, BRS Information Technologies, PFDS Online, STN International, Data-Star. **Publications:** Abstract newsletters; journals, biweekly; published searches. **Special Catalogs:** Annual catalog of holdings. **Special Indexes:** Indexes to current abstracts published in weekly journals. **Remarks:** The service is a central source for the public sale of government-sponsored reports, software, and database services. NTIS has agreements with several hundred federal research-sponsoring organizations and foreign government sources to provide the most complete list of publications possible. **Remarks:** FAX: (703)321-8547. **Also Known As:** NTIS.

★ 17221 ★
U.S. Dept. of Commerce - Office of Technology Policy - Technology Administration - Library
14th St. & Constitution Ave., N.W., Rm. 7413
Washington, DC 20230
Founded: 1978. **Subjects:** Technology and innovation, productivity, quality of working life, economics, management, labor relations, public administration. **Holdings:** 5580 volumes; 2000 microfiche; 2000 clippings. **Remarks:** Currently inactive.

U.S. Dept. of Commerce - Patent & Trademark Office
See: **U.S. Patent & Trademark Office** (17918)

★ 17222 ★
U.S. Dept. of Defense - Armed Forces Pest Management Board - Defense Pest Management Information Analysis Center (Biol Sci, Sci-Engr)
Walter Reed Army Medical Center
Forest Glen Section   Phone: (301)427-5365
Washington, DC 20307-5001   CDR Timothy H. Dickens, Chf.
Founded: 1963. **Staff:** Prof 5; Other 5. **Subjects:** Vector biology and control, vector-borne disease, arthropods of medical importance, stored product insects, pesticides, pesticide application equipment, pest vertebrates, pest management, agronomy. **Holdings:** 196,000 articles and volumes. **Subscriptions:** 254 journals and other serials. **Services:** Copying; SDI; center open to employees of the Department of Defense and other federal agencies. **Automated Operations:** Computerized cataloging. **Computerized Information Services:** DIALOG Information Services; internal database; DDN Network Information Center (electronic mail service). **Publications:** Bibliographies; Technical Information Bulletin, bimonthly; Disease Vector Ecology Profiles (foreign countries). **Remarks:** FAX: (301)291-5466.

U.S. Dept. of Defense - Defense Advanced Research Projects Agency - Tactical Technology Center
See: **Battelle Memorial Institute - Tactical Technology Center** (1570)

U.S. Dept. of Defense - Defense Communications Agency
See: **U.S. Defense Information Systems Agency** (17165)

★ 17223 ★
U.S. Dept. of Defense - Defense Industrial Plant Equipment Center - Technical Data Repository & Library (Sci-Engr)
2163 Airways Blvd.   Phone: (901)775-6549
Memphis, TN 38114   Tom Dumser, Branch Chf.
Founded: 1963. **Staff:** Prof 1; Other 1. **Holdings:** 580 volumes; 20,000 administrative, manufacturers', and military technical publications; 2050 feet of manufacturers' commercial technical data. **Subscriptions:** 23 journals and other serials. **Services:** Interlibrary loan; library not open to the public. **Automated Operations:** Computerized serials.

U.S. Dept. of Defense - Defense Information Systems Agency
See: **U.S. Defense Information Systems Agency** (17165)

U.S. Dept. of Defense - Defense Intelligence Agency
See: **U.S. Defense Intelligence Agency** (17166)

U.S. Dept. of Defense - Defense Logistics Agency
See: **U.S. Defense Logistics Agency** (17173)

U.S. Dept. of Defense - Defense Mapping Agency
See: **U.S. Defense Mapping Agency** (17175)

U.S. Dept. of Defense - Defense Nuclear Agency
See: **U.S. Defense Nuclear Agency** (17176)

U.S. Dept. of Defense - Defense Systems Management College
See: **Defense Systems Management College - Library** (4705)

U.S. Dept. of Defense - Infrared Information and Analysis Center (IRIA)
See: **Environmental Research Institute of Michigan - Infrared Information Analysis Center (IRIA)** (5382)

U.S. Dept. of Defense - Joint Chiefs of Staff - National Defense University
See: U.S. Natl. Defense University (17609)

★ 17224 ★
U.S. Dept. of Defense - Language Institute - Aiso Library (Area-Ethnic, Hum)
Presidio   Phone: (408)647-5572
Monterey, CA 93944-5007   Gary D. Walter, Libn.
Founded: 1944. **Staff:** Prof 6; Other 7. **Subjects:** Foreign languages, linguistics, history and culture of foreign countries. **Holdings:** 100,000 books; 650 bound periodical volumes; 8 VF drawers of pamphlets and clippings; 65 reels of microfilm; 5000 video cassettes. **Subscriptions:** 800 journals and other serials; 250 newspapers. **Services:** Interlibrary loan; copying; library open to the public for reference use only on request. **Computerized Information Services:** DIALOG Information Services. **Remarks:** FAX: (408)647-5254. **Staff:** Carl Chan, Cat.; Pauline Kasper, Ref.; Adorjan de Galffy, Ref.; Ted Hamilton, Acq.; Margaret Graner, Electronic Media.

U.S. Dept. of Defense - National Defense University - Armed Forces Staff College
See: U.S. Armed Forces Staff College (16916)

★ 17225 ★
U.S. Dept. of Defense - National Defense University - Information Resources Management College - Library
Bldg. 175, Rm. 504
Washington Navy Yard
Washington, DC 20374
Defunct.

U.S. Dept. of Defense - Reliability Analysis Center
See: IIT Research Institute - Reliability Analysis Center (7664)

★ 17226 ★
U.S. Dept. of Defense - Still Media Records Center (Aud-Vis, Mil)
Code SSRC   Phone: (202)433-2166
Washington, DC 20374-1681   Jerry Le Tournal, Proj.Mgr.
Founded: 1980. **Staff:** Prof 20; Other 9. **Subjects:** Military activities, equipment, weapons, operations, personalities, history of military aviation, aircraft, ships, Vietnam. **Holdings:** Over 2 million color and black and white photographs. **Services:** Copying; reprints available on fee basis to unofficial requestors, free of charge to government agencies; center open to the public. **Remarks:** Collections for the Army date from 1955 to present; Air Force, 1954 to present; Navy, 1958 to present; and Marine Corps, 1959 to present. **Staff:** Michael Rusnak, Hd., Rec.Ctr.Mgt.Div.

U.S. Dept. of Defense - Under Secretary of Defense for Research and Engineering - Nondestructive Testing Information Analysis Center
See: Texas Research Institute, Inc. - Nondestructive Testing Information Analysis Center (16226)

U.S. Dept. of Defense - U.S. Uniformed Services University of the Health Sciences
See: U.S. Uniformed Services University of the Health Sciences (17954)

U.S. Dept. of Education - East Central Network for Curriculum Coordination
See: Sangamon State University - East Central Network for Curriculum Coordination (14793)

U.S. Dept. of Education - ERIC Processing and Reference Facility
See: ERIC Processing and Reference Facility (5411)

★ 17227 ★
U.S. Dept. of Education - Research Library (Educ)
555 New Jersey Ave., N.W.   Phone: (202)219-1884
Washington, DC 20208   Dr. Milbrey L. Jones, Chf.
Founded: 1973. **Staff:** Prof 5; Other 4. **Subjects:** Education, psychology, management, public and social policy, educational statistics, library and information science. **Special Collections:** Rare Book Collection (education); American Textbook Collection, 1786-1940; U.S. Office of Education Historical Collection, 1870-1980; Elaine Exton's papers; historical foreign language periodicals. **Holdings:** 250,000 books; 42,000 bound periodical volumes; 350,000 ERIC microfiche; 500 National Institute of Education archives reports collection; 3000 reels of microfilm; 40,000 microfiche. **Subscriptions:** 800 journals and other serials. **Services:** Interlibrary loan; copying; library open to the public with restrictions. **Automated Operations:** Computerized public access catalog and cataloging. **Computerized Information Services:** OCLC. **Networks/Consortia:** Member of FEDLINK. **Publications:** Acquisitions list, monthly; Periodical Holdings List. **Special Catalogs:** Catalog of Rare Books on Education; Early American Textbook Catalog; NIE Products Catalog. **Remarks:** FAX: (202)219-1696. **Staff:** Jo Anne S. Cassell, Asst.Libn.

U.S. Dept. of Education - Western Curriculum Coordination Center
See: Western Curriculum Coordination Center (WCCC) (20243)

★ 17228 ★
U.S. Dept. of Energy - Alaska Power Administration - Library (Energy)
2770 Sherwood Ln, No. 2B
Juneau, AK 99801   Phone: (907)586-7405
Subjects: Water and power resources, Alaska natural resources, engineering. **Special Collections:** Alaskan utilities. **Holdings:** 2275 books and journals; 325 gealogy record reports. **Subscriptions:** 30 journals and other serials. **Services:** Interlibrary loan; copying; library open to the public with restrictions. **Remarks:** FAX: (907)586-7270.

★ 17229 ★
U.S. Dept. of Energy - Albuquerque Operations Office - National Atomic Museum - Library and Public Document Room (Energy)
Box 5400   Phone: (505)845-4378
Albuquerque, NM 87185-5400   Diana Leute Zepeda, Libn.
Founded: 1975. **Staff:** Prof 1. **Subjects:** Nuclear waste management, nuclear weapons history. **Special Collections:** Waste Isolation Pilot Project (1000 items); Uranium Mill Tailings Remedial Action (UMTRA; 300 items). **Holdings:** 2200 books; 4000 reports; 7000 microfiche. **Subscriptions:** 10 journals and other serials. **Services:** Copying; library open to the public with restrictions on borrowing. **Computerized Information Services:** Integrated Technical Information System (ITIS). Performs searches on fee basis.

U.S. Dept. of Energy - Argonne National Laboratory
See: Argonne National Laboratory (975)

U.S. Dept. of Energy - Atmospheric Turbulence & Diffusion Division
See: U.S. Natl. Oceanic & Atmospheric Administration - Atmospheric Turbulence & Diffusion Division (17646)

U.S. Dept. of Energy - Battelle-Northwest - Pacific Northwest Laboratory
See: Battelle-Northwest - Pacific Northwest Laboratory (1572)

U.S. Dept. of Energy - Bettis Atomic Power Laboratory
See: Westinghouse Electric Corporation - Bettis Atomic Power Laboratory (20311)

★ 17230 ★
U.S. Dept. of Energy - Bonneville Power Administration - Library (Energy, Sci-Engr)
905 N.E. 11th Ave.
Box 3621   Phone: (503)230-4171
Portland, OR 97232   Karen L. Hadman, Chf., Lib.Br.
Founded: 1939. **Staff:** Prof 6; Other 5. **Subjects:** Electrical engineeering, law, energy conservation, electric utility industry, management, computer science. **Special Collections:** Bonneville Power Administration publications and reports. **Holdings:** 50,000 volumes; 75,000 microfiche. **Subscriptions:** 1200 journals and other serials. **Services:** Interlibrary loan; library open to the public. **Automated Operations:** Computerized cataloging, acquisitions, circulation, and serials. **Computerized Information Services:** DIALOG Information Services, BRS Information Technologies, LEXIS, NEXIS. **Publications:** Research guides, irregular - all distributed internally and by request. **Remarks:** FAX: (503)230-4550. **Staff:** Monte J. Gittings, Engr.Libn.; Jean Connors, Law Libn.; Linda L. Kuriger, Power Mgt.Libn.

★17231★
U.S. Dept. of Energy - Bonneville Power Administration - Ross Library-
   EL (Energy)
Box 491   Phone: (206)690-2617
Vancouver, WA 98666   John A. Fenker, Libn.
Founded: 1982. Subjects: Energy. Special Collections: Internal technical
and laboratory reports; federal, military, and industry standards; EPRI
reports depository. Holdings: Figures not available. Services: Interlibrary
loan; library open to the public for reference use only. Computerized
Information Services: DIALOG Information Services, BRS Information
Technologies, TOXNET, Chemical Information Systems, Inc. (CIS);
OnTyme Electronic Message Network Service (electronic mail service).
Special Catalogs: Catalog of internal technical and laboratory reports.
Special Indexes: Index to internal technical and laboratory reports.
Remarks: FTS: 425-2617.

U.S. Dept. of Energy - Brookhaven National Laboratory
See: Brookhaven National Laboratory (2220)

U.S. Dept. of Energy - Conservation and Renewable Energy Inquiry and
   Referral Service
See: Conservation and Renewable Energy Inquiry and Referral Service
   (4218)

U.S. Dept. of Energy - EG&G Idaho, Inc. - Idaho National Engineering
   Laboratory
See: EG&G Idaho, Inc. - Idaho National Engineering Laboratory (5268)

★17232★
U.S. Dept. of Energy - Energy Information Administration - National
   Energy Information Center (Energy)
Forrestal Bldg., Rm. 1F-048   Phone: (202)586-8800
Washington, DC 20585   Nancy Nicoletti, Chf.
Staff: Prof 13; Other 2. Subjects: Energy - petroleum, electric power, nuclear
power, coal and synthetic fuels, renewable energy resources, natural gas;
energy statistics. Services: Center open to the public; responds to telephone
and letter inquiries. Remarks: FAX: (202)586-0727.

★17233★
U.S. Dept. of Energy - Energy Library (Energy)
Washington, DC 20585   Phone: (202)586-9534
                                 Denise B. Diggin, Chf., Lib.Br.
Founded: 1947. Staff: Prof 10; Other 10. Subjects: Energy resources and
technologies; economic, environmental, and social aspects of energy; energy
regulation; energy statistics; management. Special Collections: International
Atomic Energy Agency (IAEA) Publications; legislative histories relating
to Atomic Energy Commission (AEC) and Energy Research and
Development Administration (ERDA); ERDA, Federal Energy
Administration (FEA), and DOE technical reports. Holdings: 1 million
volumes of books, journals, technical reports, government documents.
Subscriptions: 1600 journals and other serials. Services: Interlibrary loan;
copying; SDI; library open to DOE headquarters staff and authorized
contractors. Automated Operations: Computerized public access catalog,
cataloging, acquisitions, serials, and circulation. Computerized Information
Services: DIALOG Information Services, ORBIT Search Service, NEXIS,
Integrated Technical Information System (ITIS), MEDLARS, Wharton
Econometric Forecasting Associates, BRS Information Technologies,
Questel, Reuters, Value Line Data Services, NASA/RECON, STN
International, Reuters Information Services (Canada) Limited, OCLC,
LEXIS, NewsNet, Inc. Networks/Consortia: Member of FEDLINK.
Publications: Data Bases Available at the Energy Library, irregular; Energy
Library Guide to Services; New at the Energy Library (accessions list).

★17234★
U.S. Dept. of Energy - Environmental Measurements Laboratory
   Library (Energy, Sci-Engr)
376 Hudson St.   Phone: (212)620-3606
New York, NY 10014   Rita D. Rosen, Tech.Libn.
Founded: 1947. Staff: Prof 1. Subjects: Physics, chemistry, environmental
science, radiation physics. Holdings: 2000 books; 1800 bound periodical
volumes; 30,000 technical reports; 35,000 reports in microform.
Subscriptions: 125 journals and other serials. Services: Interlibrary loan;
library not open to the public. Computerized Information Services:
DIALOG Information Services. Remarks: FAX: (212)620-3600.

U.S. Dept. of Energy - Federal Energy Regulatory Commission
See: Federal Energy Regulatory Commission (5627)

★17235★
U.S. Dept. of Energy - Field Office, Nevada - Technical Library (Sci-
   Engr, Energy)
Mail Stop 505
P.O. Box 98518   Phone: (702)295-1274
Las Vegas, NV 89193-8518   Cynthia Ortiz, Tech.Libn. II
Founded: 1969. Staff: Prof 2; Other 2. Subjects: Nuclear explosives,
radiation bioenvironmental effects, geology, hydrology, alternate energy
sources, radioactive waste storage, environmental restoration. Special
Collections: Peaceful uses of nuclear explosions. Holdings: 3050 books;
54,700 technical reports; 88,250 microfiche of technical reports; 7 file
drawers of clippings; 400 maps. Subscriptions: 220 journals and other
serials. Services: Interlibrary loan; copying; library open to the public by
prior arrangement. Computerized Information Services: Integrated
Technical Information System (ITIS), DIALOG Information Services,
LEXIS, NEXIS. Remarks: FAX: (702)295-1371; (702)295-1372. Formerly:
Its Nevada Operations Office.

★17236★
U.S. Dept. of Energy - Field Office, San Francisco - Energy Information
   Center (Energy)
1333 Broadway   Phone: (510)273-4428
Oakland, CA 94612   Estella M. Angel, Info.Coord., Energy Info.Ctr.
Subjects: Energy. Holdings: Energy Research Abstracts; selected Energy
Information Administration (EIA) publications, analyses, energy data
reports, statistics, and forecasts. Services: Center open to the public for
reference use only. Remarks: Alternate telephone number(s): (510)273-4135.
FAX: (510)273-6207. Center serves as the DOE's Public Reading Room in
northern California. Formerly: Its San Francisco Operations Office.

U.S. Dept. of Energy - Inhalation Toxicology Research Institute
See: Lovelace Biomedical & Environmental Research Institute, Inc. -
   Inhalation Toxicology Research Institute (9404)

U.S. Dept. of Energy - Knolls Atomic Power Laboratory
See: Knolls Atomic Power Laboratory (8768)

U.S. Dept. of Energy - Laboratory of Biomedical and Environmental
   Sciences
See: University of California, Los Angeles - Laboratory of Biomedical
   and Environmental Sciences (18388)

U.S. Dept. of Energy - Lawrence Berkeley Laboratory
See: Lawrence Berkeley Laboratory (9001)

U.S. Dept. of Energy - Lawrence Livermore National Laboratory
See: Lawrence Livermore National Laboratory - Technical Information
   Department Library (9009)

U.S. Dept. of Energy - Los Alamos National Laboratory
See: University of California - Los Alamos National Laboratory (18298)

U.S. Dept. of Energy - Martin Marietta Energy Systems Inc.
See: Martin Marietta Energy Systems Inc. - Libraries (9736)

U.S. Dept. of Energy - Mason & Hanger-Silas Mason Company, Inc.
See: Mason & Hanger-Silas Mason Company, Inc. (9775)

★ 17237 ★
U.S. Dept. of Energy - Morgantown Energy Technology Center - Library
(Energy)
Box 880   Phone: (304)291-4184
Morgantown, WV 26507-0880   Matthew Marsteller, Libn.
Founded: 1953. **Staff:** Prof 2; Other 2. **Subjects:** Coal and fossil fuel, petroleum, chemistry, chemical engineering, geology, coal gasification. **Special Collections:** U.S. Office of Coal Research reports (100); U.S. Dept. of Energy publications; U.S. Bureau of Mines publications (complete). **Holdings:** 10,000 books; 7000 bound periodical volumes; 1500 reports; 20 VF drawers of patents. **Subscriptions:** 110 journals and other serials. **Services:** Interlibrary loan; copying; library open to the public. **Computerized Information Services:** OCLC, PFDS Online, DIALOG Information Services; EasyLink (electronic mail service). **Publications:** Annual publications list. **Remarks:** FAX: (304)291-4403. Telex: 62958572 (EasyLink). **Staff:** Beth DiGiustino; Sheila Propst; Maria Hall.

U.S. Dept. of Energy - National Renewable Energy Laboratory
See: National Renewable Energy Laboratory - Library (11267)

U.S. Dept. of Energy - Nevada Operations Office
See: U.S. Dept. of Energy - Field Office, Nevada - Technical Library (17235)

U.S. Dept. of Energy - Oak Ridge National Laboratory
See: Oak Ridge National Laboratory (12186)

★ 17238 ★
U.S. Dept. of Energy - Office of General Counsel Law Library (Law)
1000 Independence Ave., S.W., Rm. 6A 156   Phone: (202)586-4848
Washington, DC 20585   Clara Smith, Chf. Law Libn.
Founded: 1975. **Staff:** Prof 2. **Subjects:** Law - energy, environmental, contract, administrative, patents; statutes. **Holdings:** 40,000 volumes; microfiche. **Subscriptions:** 270 journals and other serials. **Services:** Interlibrary loan; copying (limited); library open to the public for reference use only. **Computerized Information Services:** LEXIS, JURIS, WESTLAW. **Staff:** Paula Lipman, Asst.Libn.

U.S. Dept. of Energy - Plant Research Laboratory
See: Michigan State University - Plant Research Laboratory (10334)

U.S. Dept. of Energy - Reynolds Electrical and Engineering Company, Inc.
See: Reynolds Electrical and Engineering Company, Inc. - Coordination and Information Center (13862)

U.S. Dept. of Energy - San Francisco Operations Office
See: U.S. Dept. of Energy - Field Office, San Francisco - Energy Information Center (17236)

U.S. Dept. of Energy - Sandia National Laboratories
See: Sandia National Laboratories (14778)

U.S. Dept. of Energy - Stanford Linear Accelerator Center
See: Stanford Linear Accelerator Center (15642)

U.S. Dept. of Energy - Westinghouse Environmental Management Co. of Ohio
See: Westinghouse Environmental Management Co. of Ohio (20321)

U.S. Dept. of Energy - Westinghouse Savannah River Co.
See: Westinghouse Savannah River Co. (20323)

U.S. Dept. of Energy Historian Archives Office
See: Reynolds Electrical and Engineering Company, Inc. - Coordination and Information Center (13862)

U.S. Dept. of Health and Human Services - AMS Information Clearinghouse
See: National Arthritis and Musculoskeletal and Skin Diseases Information Clearinghouse (11047)

★ 17239 ★
U.S. Dept. of Health and Human Services - Library and Information Center - Cohen Bldg.
330 Independence Ave., S.W., Rm. G-619
Washington, DC 20201
Defunct.

U.S. Dept. of Health and Human Services - National Arthritis and Musculoskeletal and Skin Diseases Information Clearinghouse
See: National Arthritis and Musculoskeletal and Skin Diseases Information Clearinghouse (11047)

U.S. Dept. of Health and Human Services - National Center on Child Abuse and Neglect (NCCAN) - Clearinghouse on Child Abuse & Neglect Information
See: Clearinghouse on Child Abuse and Neglect Information (3788)

U.S. Dept. of Health and Human Services - National Center on Child Abuse and Neglect (NCCAN) - Clearinghouse on Family Violence Information
See: Clearinghouse on Family Violence Information (3790)

U.S. Dept. of Health and Human Services - National Digestive Diseases Information Clearinghouse
See: National Digestive Diseases Information Clearinghouse (11148)

U.S. Dept. of Health and Human Services - National Institute on Alcohol Abuse and Alcoholism
See: National Institute on Alcohol Abuse and Alcoholism (11205)

★ 17240 ★
U.S. Dept. of Health and Human Services - Policy Information Center - HHH Bldg. (Soc Sci, Med)
200 Independence Ave., S.W., Rm. 438 F   Phone: (202)245-6445
Washington, DC 20201   Carolyn Solomon, Tech.Info.Spec.
Founded: 1974. **Staff:** Prof 2; Other 1. **Subjects:** Health, income maintenance and support, social services. **Special Collections:** Department of Health and Human Services evaluation, short term evaluative research, policy-oriented projects; Health and Human Services Inspector General's program inspections and audits; reports from the CBO, GAO, OTA, the Institute of Medicine, and the National Research Council's Committee on National Statistics (both part of the National Academy of Sciences). **Holdings:** 4000 reports and executive summaries. **Services:** Copying; center open to the public for reference use only. **Automated Operations:** Computerized cataloging and circulation. **Computerized Information Services:** PIC On-line (internal database). Performs searches free of charge. **Publications:** Compendium of Health and Human Services Evaluations and Other Relevant Studies, annual; Users Guide to the PIC; Poilcy Information Center MEMORANDUM, quarterly. **Special Indexes:** Indexes of program names, sponsoring agencies, and subject names. **Remarks:** Evaluation/research reports are made available to the public through the National Technical Information Service (NTIS), U.S. Dept. of Commerce, Springfield, VA. **Staff:** Joan Turek-Brezina, Dir., Div. of Tech.Sup. & Computer.

U.S. Dept. of Health and Human Services - Social Security Administration
See: U.S. Social Security Administration (17939)

★17241★
U.S. Dept. of Housing and Urban Development - Library (Soc Sci, Plan)
451 7th St., S.W., Rm. 8141   Phone: (202)708-2370
Washington, DC 20410   Marianna Graham, Proj.Mgr.
Founded: 1934. **Subjects:** Housing, community development, urban planning, sociology, law, mortgage and construction finance, architecture, land use, intergovernmental relations. **Special Collections:** HUD publications; HUD management evaluation reports, including audit reports. **Holdings:** 720,000 items. **Subscriptions:** 2200 journals and other serials. **Services:** Interlibrary loan; copying (limited); library open to the public. **Automated Operations:** Integrated library system. **Computerized Information Services:** OCLC. **Networks/Consortia:** Member of FEDLINK. **Publications:** Recent Library Acquisitions; Library Periodicals List. **Special Indexes:** Special reports indexes. **Remarks:** FAX: (202)708-1485. The HUD Library is operated by Aspen Systems Corporation under contract to the U.S. Department of Housing and Urban Development.

★17242★
U.S. Dept. of Housing and Urban Development - Photography Library
  (Aud-Vis)
451 7th St., S.W., Rm. B-146   Phone: (202)245-6935
Washington, DC 20410   John B. Jones, Photo.Libn.
Staff: Prof 1. **Subjects:** Housing, urban development, housing for the elderly, housing renewal. **Special Collections:** Instant Rehab (Core) in New York City (500 color slides; 150 black/white negatives); Operation Breakthrough; Johnstown Flood Disaster. **Holdings:** 200,000 black/white negatives; 40,000 color slides; 10,000 black/white prints. **Services:** Interlibrary loan; library open to the public by appointment only. **Remarks:** FAX: (202)708-3720.

★17243★
·U.S. Dept. of Housing and Urban Development - Region IV - Library
Richard B. Russell Fed. Bldg., Rm. 676
75 Spring St., S.W.
Atlanta, GA 30303-3388
Founded: 1968. **Subjects:** Housing, planning, urban development, economic analysis, law, statistics. **Special Collections:** Housing and Urban Affairs (2700 microfiche; 1000 titles). **Holdings:** 17,000 books; 87 bound periodical volumes; Federal Register, 1967 to present, on microfilm; 12 VF drawers. **Remarks:** Currently inactive.

★17244★
U.S. Dept. of Housing and Urban Development - Region VI - Library
  (Law)
1600 Throckmorton
Box 2905   Phone: (817)885-5874
Fort Worth, TX 76113-2905   Susan Hayes, Libn./Paralegal Spec.
Founded: 1966. **Subjects:** Law - Arkansas, Texas, Oklahoma, Louisiana, New Mexico. **Holdings:** Figures not available. **Services:** Library open to the public for reference use only. **Remarks:** FAX: (817)885-5629.

★17245★
U.S. Dept. of the Interior - Adams National Historic Site - Stone Library (Rare Book)
135 Adams St.
P.O. Box 531   Phone: (617)773-1177
Quincy, MA 02169   Judith McAlister Curtis, Cur.
Founded: 1870. **Special Collections:** Books belonging to four generations of the Adams family, including Presidents John and John Quincy Adams. **Holdings:** 14,000 books; 600 reels of microfilm. **Services:** Library open to the public for reference use only by permission; a staff member is present at all times during library visits. **Automated Operations:** Computerized cataloging. **Computerized Information Services:** ANCS (internal database). **Remarks:** FAX: (617)471-9683. Many volumes are presentation copies from the authors to the presidents. The oldest book is a New Testament and concordance printed in Germany in 1521.

U.S. Dept. of the Interior - Bureau of Indian Affairs
See: U.S. Bureau of Indian Affairs (17099)

U.S. Dept. of the Interior - Bureau of Land Management
See: U.S. Bureau of Land Management (17106)

U.S. Dept. of the Interior - Bureau of Mines
See: U.S. Bureau of Mines (17109)

U.S. Dept. of the Interior - Bureau of Reclamation
See: U.S. Bureau of Reclamation (17120)

U.S. Dept. of the Interior - Fish & Wildlife Service
See: U.S. Fish & Wildlife Service (17496)

U.S. Dept. of the Interior - Geological Survey
See: U.S. Geological Survey (17539)

★17246★
U.S. Dept. of the Interior - Indian Arts and Crafts Board (Art)
18th & C Sts., N.W., Rm. 4004-MIB   Phone: (202)208-3773
Washington, DC 20240   Robert G. Hart, Gen.Mgr.
Founded: 1935. **Subjects:** Contemporary Native American arts and crafts. **Services:** Prepares answers or makes referrals for inquiries concerning contemporary Native American arts and crafts of the U.S.; no facilities maintained for researchers. **Publications:** Source Directory of Indian, Eskimo and Aleut Owned and Operated Arts and Crafts Businesses. **Remarks:** The Indian Arts and Crafts Board serves Indians, Eskimos, Aleuts, and the general public as an information, promotional, and advisory clearinghouse for all matters pertaining to the development of authentic Native American arts and crafts.

★17247★
U.S. Dept. of the Interior - Law Branch Library (Law)
1849 C St., N.W., Rm. 7100W   Phone: (202)208-4571
Washington, DC 20240   Vickki Nozer, Act.Lib.
Founded: 1975. **Staff:** Prof 2; Other 2. **Subjects:** Law - public land, Indian, natural resources, administrative, environmental. **Special Collections:** Pre-Federal Register regulations of the Department of the Interior (1000 pieces); Native American Legal Materials (500 microfiche). **Holdings:** 30,000 books; 2000 bound periodical volumes; 10,000 microfiche; 1000 reels of microfilm; 3000 microfiche of Indian Claims Commission materials; 10 reels of microfilm of executive orders; 1000 microfiche of Council of State Governments publications; 700 legislative histories. **Subscriptions:** 801 journals and other serials. **Services:** Library open to the public for reference use only. **Automated Operations:** Computerized cataloging and acquisitions. **Computerized Information Services:** Online systems; Public Land Order Status System (internal database). **Networks/Consortia:** Member of FEDLINK. **Publications:** Law Library Update, monthly - for internal distribution only; Selected List of Federal Register Items of Interest to the Department of the Interior, weekly. **Special Indexes:** Statutory Index to the Legislative History Collection; Index to Microfilmed Public Lands Withdrawal Orders; Index to the Files on the Passage of PL96-487, Alaska National Interest Lands Conservation Act. **Remarks:** FAX: (202)268-4714.

★17248★
U.S. Dept. of the Interior - Minerals Management Service - Alaska Outer Continental Shelf Regional Library (Env-Cons)
949 E. 36th Ave., Rm. 110   Phone: (907)271-6000
Anchorage, AK 99508-4302   Christine R. Huffaker, Libn.
Founded: 1976. **Staff:** 5. **Subjects:** Environmental science, geophysics, geology, socioeconomic assessment, petroleum engineering, paleotology, marine sciences, biological sciences. **Holdings:** 8000 books; 1500 bound periodical volumes. **Subscriptions:** 100 journals and other serials; 10 newspapers. **Services:** Library not open to the public. **Automated Operations:** Computerized cataloging. **Computerized Information Services:** LEXIS, NEXIS, OCLC, DIALOG Information Services, ORBIT Search Service. **Networks/Consortia:** Member of FEDLINK, Alaska Library Network (ALN). **Remarks:** Alternate telephone number(s): (907)271-6435. FAX: (907)561-4860.

U.S. Dept. of the Interior - National Park Service
See: U.S. Natl. Park Service (17661)

★ 17249 ★
U.S. Dept. of the Interior - Natural Resources Library (Env-Cons, Energy)
18th & C Sts., N.W.
Washington, DC 20240   Phone: (202)208-5815
Founded: 1949. **Subjects:** Conservation, energy and power, land use, parks, American Indians, fish and wildlife, mining, law, management. **Special Collections:** Archival collection of materials published by Department of Interior (150,000 items). **Holdings:** 600,000 books; 90,000 bound periodical volumes; 7000 reels of microfilm; 40,000 unbound periodical volumes; 300,000 microfiche. **Subscriptions:** 6000 journals and other serials. **Services:** Interlibrary loan; copying; library open to the public with restrictions. **Automated Operations:** Computerized cataloging, acquisitions, serials, circulation, and ILL. **Computerized Information Services:** DIALOG Information Services, NEXIS, OCLC, Washington Alert Service, WESTLAW, JURIS, LEXIS. **Networks/Consortia:** Member of FEDLINK. **Publications:** Departmental Manual Subject Index: FPM, FAR, and IPMR Additions; Law Library Update; Selected List of Federal Register Items of Interest to the Department of Interior. **Remarks:** FAX: (202)208-5048. Library operated by Aspen System Corporation under contract to the Department of the Interior. Government manager, tel. (202)208-5435.

★ 17250 ★
U.S. Dept. of Justice - Antitrust Branch Library (Law)
10th & Pennsylvania Ave., N.W.
Rm. 3310   Phone: (202)514-2431
Washington, DC 20530   Mary E. Clarity, Libn.
Staff: Prof 2; Other 2. **Subjects:** Antitrust law, administrative law, business, economics. **Special Collections:** Legislative histories. **Holdings:** 33,000 volumes. **Subscriptions:** 300 journals and other serials. **Services:** Interlibrary loan; library not open to the public. **Automated Operations:** Computerized cataloging and acquisitions. **Computerized Information Services:** DIALOG Information Services, NEXIS, LEXIS, JURIS, LEGI-SLATE, Dow Jones News/Retrieval, Dun & Bradstreet Business Credit Services, VU/TEXT Information Services, DataTimes, Washington Alert Service, OCLC, DATALIB. **Networks/Consortia:** Member of FEDLINK. **Remarks:** FAX: (202)514-0589. A branch library is maintained at 555 4th St., N.W., Rm. B1-615, Washington, DC 20001. **Staff:** Charles Swindle.

★ 17251 ★
U.S. Dept. of Justice - Bureau of Justice Statistics - Drugs and Crime Data Center and Clearinghouse (Law)
1600 Research Blvd.   Phone: (800)666-3332
Rockville, MD 20850   Candice Byrne, Libn.
Founded: 1987. **Staff:** 5. **Subjects:** Illegal drugs, drug law violations, drug-related crime, drug-using offenders in the criminal justice system, the impact of drugs on criminal justice administration. **Special Collections:** State drug control strategies (complete sets for 1989, 1990, 1991, and 1992). **Holdings:** 7500 documents; 5 VF drawers of clippings. **Subscriptions:** 10 journals and other serials. **Services:** Copying; SDI; center open to the public. **Computerized Information Services:** Internal database. Performs searches free of charge. **Publications:** Publications list; State Drug Resources: A National Directory; Federal Drug Data for National Policy; Drugs and Crime Facts, annual; fact sheets; selected bibliographies. **Remarks:** FAX: (301)251-5747.

★ 17252 ★
U.S. Dept. of Justice - Bureau of Prisons - Library (Law)
320 First St., N.W.
Washington, DC 20534   Phone: (202)307-3029
Founded: 1960. **Staff:** Prof 1; Other 2. **Subjects:** Criminology, corrections, criminal psychology. **Holdings:** 2591 books and bound periodical volumes; 65 periodicals; 500 items in information file; 50 annual reports. **Subscriptions:** 40 journals and other serials. **Services:** Interlibrary loan; library open to those in correctional work and related fields, including graduate students doing research in corrections. **Computerized Information Services:** OCLC, DIALOG Information Services.

★ 17253 ★
U.S. Dept. of Justice - Bureau of Prisons - National Institute of Corrections - NIC Information Center (Law)
1790 30th St., Suite 130   Phone: (303)939-8877
Boulder, CO 80301   Coralie Whitmore
Founded: 1980. **Subjects:** Prisons, jails, probation, parole, community corrections. **Holdings:** 12,000 documents. **Subscriptions:** 200 journals and other serials. **Services:** Interlibrary loan; copying; center open to the public. **Automated Operations:** Computerized public access catalog, cataloging, acquisitions, serials, and circulation. **Computerized Information Services:** DIALOG Information Services, RLIN, OCLC EPIC. **Networks/Consortia:** Member of Central Colorado Library System (CCLS), Criminal Justice Information Exchange Group. **Publications:** Corrections Information Series. **Remarks:** FAX: (303)442-3412. **Staff:** Eileen Conway, Rsrc.Coord.; Barbara Sudol, Libn.; Pat Scholes, Corrections Spec.; Annmarie Jensen, Corrections Spec.; Rod Botloms, Corrections Spec.; Jo Gustafson, Corrections Spec.

★ 17254 ★
U.S. Dept. of Justice - Civil Branch Library (Law)
10th & Pennsylvania Ave., N.W., Rm. 3344   Phone: (202)514-3523
Washington, DC 20530   Roger N. Karr, Libn.
Staff: Prof 3; Other 2. **Subjects:** Law, customs, bankruptcy, government contracts, commercial law, admiralty, aviation, patents, trademarks, copyright. **Special Collections:** Legislative histories. **Holdings:** 35,000 volumes. **Subscriptions:** 100 journals and other serials. **Services:** Interlibrary loan; library not open to the public. **Automated Operations:** Computerized cataloging and acquisitions. **Computerized Information Services:** DIALOG Information Services, LEXIS, NEXIS, JURIS, LEGI-SLATE, Dow Jones News/Retrieval, WESTLAW, DataTimes, Washington Alert Service, DATALIB, OCLC, VU/TEXT Information Services. **Networks/Consortia:** Member of FEDLINK. **Remarks:** Maintains branch libraries at 601 D. St., N.W., Rm. 8443, Washington, DC 20530 and 550 11th St., N.W., Rm. 8100, Washington, DC 20530. **Staff:** Bertus Lee; Carol Watkin.

★ 17255 ★
U.S. Dept. of Justice - Civil Rights Branch Library (Soc Sci, Law)
10th & Pennsylvania Ave., N.W., Rm. 7618   Phone: (202)514-4098
Washington, DC 20530   Catherine D. Harman, Libn.
Staff: Prof 1; Other 1. **Subjects:** Civil rights, constitutional law, demographics. **Holdings:** 8000 volumes. **Subscriptions:** 50 journals and other serials. **Services:** Interlibrary loan; library not open to the public. **Automated Operations:** Computerized cataloging and acquisitions. **Computerized Information Services:** JURIS, WESTLAW, LEXIS, NEXIS, DIALOG Information Services, LEGI-SLATE, VU/TEXT Information Services, DataTimes, Washington Alert Service, DATALIB, OCLC. **Networks/Consortia:** Member of FEDLINK. **Remarks:** A branch library is maintained at 320 1st St., N.W., Rm. 1066, Washington, DC 20530.

★ 17256 ★
U.S. Dept. of Justice - Criminal Branch Library (Law)
1400 New York Ave., N.W.
Bond Bldg., Rm. 7100   Phone: (202)514-1141
Washington, DC 20530   Diane L. Smith, Libn.
Staff: Prof 3; Other 1. **Subjects:** Federal criminal law, procedure and evidence. **Special Collections:** White collar, computer, and organized crime; espionage and terrorism. **Holdings:** 16,000 volumes. **Subscriptions:** 64 journals and other serials. **Services:** Interlibrary loan; library not open to the public. **Automated Operations:** Computerized acquisitions and cataloging. **Computerized Information Services:** JURIS, LEXIS, NEXIS, WESTLAW, DIALOG Information Services, LEGI-SLATE, VU/TEXT Information Services, DataTimes, Washington Alert Service. **Networks/Consortia:** Member of FEDLINK. **Staff:** Susan Glaize; Martin Schwartz.

U.S. Dept. of Justice - Drug Enforcement Administration
See: U.S. Drug Enforcement Administration (17454)

★ 17257 ★
U.S. Dept. of Justice - Environment and Natural Resources Branch Library (Law)
10th & Pennsylvania Ave., N.W., Rm. 2333   Phone: (202)514-2768
Washington, DC 20530   Leola Decker, Libn.
Staff: Prof 3; Other 1. **Subjects:** Civil cases regarding lands, titles, water rights, Indian claims, hazardous waste, public works, pollution control,

marine resources, fish and wildlife, environment. **Special Collections:** Legislative histories. **Holdings:** 18,000 volumes. **Subscriptions:** 84 journals and other serials. **Services:** Interlibrary loan; library not open to the public. **Automated Operations:** Computerized cataloging and acquisitions. **Computerized Information Services:** JURIS, DIALOG Information Services, LEXIS, NEXIS, LEGI-SLATE, WESTLAW, VU/TEXT Information Services, DataTimes, Washington Alert Service, OCLC, DATALIB. **Networks/Consortia:** Member of FEDLINK. **Remarks:** A branch library is maintained 601 Pennsylvania Ave., N.W., Rm. 6308, Washington, DC 20530. **Formerly:** Its Land and Natural Resources - Branch Library. **Staff:** Edward Wolff; Kendra Swe

U.S. Dept. of Justice - Federal Bureau of Investigation
See: **U.S. Federal Bureau of Investigation** (17488)

U.S. Dept. of Justice - Foreign Claims Settlement Commission of the United States
See: **Foreign Claims Settlement Commission of the United States** (5973)

★17258★
U.S. Dept. of Justice - Main Library (Law, Bus-Fin)
10th & Pennsylvania Ave., N.W., Rm. 5400   Phone: (202)514-2133
Washington, DC 20530   Daphne B. Sampson, Dir.
Founded: 1831. **Staff:** Prof 15; Other 4. **Subjects:** Law, business, and allied subjects. **Special Collections:** Legislative histories; Department of Justice publications. **Holdings:** 200,000 volumes; 300,000 microform equivalent volumes. **Subscriptions:** 800 journals. **Services:** Interlibrary loan; library open to the public by appointment. **Automated Operations:** Computerized cataloging and acquisitions. **Computerized Information Services:** DIALOG Information Services, OCLC, LEXIS, JURIS, NEXIS, LEGI-SLATE, Dow Jones News/Retrieval, WESTLAW, VU/TEXT Information Services, CQ (Congressional Quarterly, Inc.), Washington Alert Service, DataTimes, DATALIB. **Networks/Consortia:** Member of FEDLINK. **Publications:** Consolidated Periodicals Guide; Database Guide; Consolidated Legislative History List; Library Handbook. **Remarks:** FAX: (202)371-0570. **Staff:** Christine Rudy, Asst.Dir., Lib.Serv.; Kristina Kelley, Chf., Res.; Winifred Hart, Chf., Coll.; Richard Shrout, Asst.Dir., Tech.Serv.; Daire McCabe, Chf., Acq.; Camille Simmons, Chf., Cat.

U.S. Dept. of Justice - National Institute of Corrections
See: **U.S. Dept. of Justice - Bureau of Prisons - National Institute of Corrections** (17253)

★17259★
U.S. Dept. of Justice - National Institute of Justice - Library (Soc Sci, Law)
633 Indiana Ave., N.W., Rm. 900   Phone: (202)307-5883
Washington, DC 20531   Barbara L. Owen, Libn.
Founded: 1970. **Staff:** 1. **Subjects:** Law enforcement, police science, criminology, juvenile delinquency, courts, corrections, white collar crime, spouse and child abuse, victims. **Holdings:** 5500 books; 1000 U.S. Government documents. **Subscriptions:** 100 journals and other serials. **Services:** Interlibrary loan; copying; library open to the public for reference use only. **Computerized Information Services:** DIALOG Information Services, OCLC. **Networks/Consortia:** Member of FEDLINK. **Remarks:** FAX: (202)307-6394. Affiliated with National Criminal Justice Reference Service in Rockville, MD.

★17260★
U.S. Dept. of Justice - National Institute of Justice - National Criminal Justice Reference Service (Soc Sci, Law)
1600 Research Blvd.
Box 6000   Phone: (301)251-5500
Rockville, MD 20850   Richard S. Rosenthal, Prog.Dir.
Founded: 1972. **Subjects:** Law enforcement, criminal and juvenile justice, white collar crime, public corruption, courts, corrections, crime prevention/ security, evaluations and research, criminology, victim/witness assistance, dispute resolution. **Holdings:** 110,000 books, research reports, articles; 40,000 documents on microfiche. **Subscriptions:** 200 journals and other serials. **Services:** Interlibrary loan; referrals; public reading room. **Computerized Information Services:** DIALOG Information Services. Performs searches on fee basis. **Networks/Consortia:** Member of Criminal Justice Information Exchange Group. **Publications:** Monthly Accessions List; Microfiche Packages; Directory of Criminal Justice Information Sources; DIALOG User's Manual. **Special Catalogs:** National Institute of Justice Catalog. **Special Indexes:** Document Retrieval Index (microfiche); index to microfiche collection. **Remarks:** Toll-free telephone number(s): (800)851-3420. FAX: (301)251-5212.

★17261★
U.S. Dept. of Justice - Tax Branch Library (Bus-Fin, Law)
10th & Pennsylvania Ave., N.W., Rm. 4335   Phone: (202)514-2819
Washington, DC 20530   Jacqueline Lee, Libn.
Staff: Prof 2; Other 1. **Subjects:** Federal tax law, bankruptcy. **Special Collections:** Legislative histories. **Holdings:** 21,000 volumes. **Subscriptions:** 50 journals and other serials. **Services:** Interlibrary loan; library not open to the public. **Automated Operations:** Computerized cataloging and acquisitions. **Computerized Information Services:** JURIS, LEXIS, NEXIS, WESTLAW, DIALOG Information Services, Maxwell Macmillan Taxes Online, DATALIB, OCLC, DataTimes, VU/TEXT Information Services, Washington Alert Service. **Networks/Consortia:** Member of FEDLINK. **Remarks:** A branch library is maintained 555 4th St., N.W., Rm. 7607, Washington, DC 20530. **Staff:** John Davis.

★17262★
U.S. Dept. of Justice - United States Attorney, Central District of California - Library (Law)
1214 U.S. Court House
312 N. Spring St.   Phone: (213)894-2419
Los Angeles, CA 90012   Dennis Yanaihara, Dir.
Staff: Prof 1; Other 1. **Subjects:** Law. **Holdings:** 13,000 volumes. **Services:** Library not open to the public.

★17263★
U.S. Dept. of Justice - United States Attorney, District of New Jersey - Law Library (Law)
970 Broad St.
Newark, NJ 07102   Phone: (201)645-2851
Staff: Prof 1. **Subjects:** Law. **Holdings:** 6000 volumes. **Services:** Library not open to the public. **Computerized Information Services:** JURIS.

★17264★
U.S. Dept. of Justice - United States Attorney, Eastern District of Pennsylvania - Library (Law)
3310 U.S. Courthouse
601 Market St.   Phone: (215)597-2161
Philadelphia, PA 19106   Susan J. Falken, Lib.Dir
Staff: Prof 1; Other 2. **Subjects:** Criminal law. **Special Collections:** Briefs of the 3rd circuit; indictments of the 3rd circuit. **Holdings:** 25,000 books. **Subscriptions:** 12 journals and other serials; 10 newspapers. **Services:** Interlibrary loan; copying. **Computerized Information Services:** NEXIS, VU/TEXT Information Services, WESTLAW, JURIS. **Special Indexes:** Briefs of the Third Circuit. **Remarks:** FAX: (215)597-8773.

★17265★
U.S. Dept. of Justice - United States Attorney, Northern District of Illinois - Library (Law)
1500 Dirksen Federal Bldg.
219 S. Dearborn St.   Phone: (312)353-5338
Chicago, IL 60604   Mary Alice Stack, Libn.
Staff: Prof 1. **Subjects:** Federal law. **Holdings:** 12,000 volumes. **Services:** Interlibrary loan; library not open to the public. **Computerized Information Services:** JURIS, WESTLAW, LEXIS.

★17266★
U.S. Dept. of Justice - United States Attorney, Southern District of New York - Library (Law)
1 St. Andrew's Plaza, 6th Fl.   Phone: (212)791-0029
New York, NY 10007   Barbara J. Zelenko, Hd.Libn.
Staff: Prof 1; Other 3. **Subjects:** Law. **Holdings:** 20,000 books; law memoranda; manuscripts; 12 VF drawers of clippings; sample indictment file; 6 VF drawers of sample charge files. **Subscriptions:** 91 journals and other serials. **Services:** Interlibrary loan; library not open to the public. **Computerized Information Services:** JURIS, LEXIS.

★17267★
U.S. Dept. of Labor - Bureau of Labor Statistics - Information and Advisory Branch - Self Service Data Users' Center (Bus-Fin)
201 Varick St., Rm. 808
New York, NY 10014   Phone: (212)337-2400
Founded: 1949. **Staff:** 3. **Subjects:** Labor force, employment, productivity, industrial relations, occupational outlook, occupational health and safety statistics, consumer and producer price indexes. **Holdings:** 500 books; 1500 bound periodical volumes; 5000 pamphlets. **Subscriptions:** 100 journals and other serials. **Services:** Copying; center open to the public. **Remarks:** Maintains 24-hour recordings providing information on national and regional Consumer Price Indexes, Producer Price Indexes, unemployment rates, and weekly research findings. **Formerly:** Its Information and Advisory Section.

★ 17268 ★
U.S. Dept. of Labor - Bureau of Labor Statistics - North Central Regional Office Reference Library (Bus-Fin)
230 S. Dearborn St., 9th Fl.   Phone: (312)353-1880
Chicago, IL 60604   Ronald M. Guzicki, Supv. Economist
Staff: Prof 4; Other 4. **Subjects:** Labor force, price indexes, productivity, occupational safety and health, compensation, industrial relations. **Holdings:** Bureau of Labor Statistics bulletins, reports, and news releases. **Services:** Library open to the public for reference use only. **Computerized Information Services:** LABSTAT (internal database). **Remarks:** FAX: (312)353-1886. **Staff:** Leslie Matthews, Economist; Rita Erickson, Economist; Paul LaPorte, Economist.

★ 17269 ★
U.S. Dept. of Labor - Library (Bus-Fin)
200 Constitution Ave., N.W., Rm. N-2445   Phone: (202)523-6992
Washington, DC 20210   Theresa Turner, Mgr.
Founded: 1917. **Staff:** 14. **Subjects:** Economics, labor. **Special Collections:** Trade union constitutions, proceedings, and journals. **Holdings:** 535,000 volumes; labor papers on microfilm. **Subscriptions:** 2200 journals. **Services:** Interlibrary loan (limited); copying; library open to the public for reference use only. **Automated Operations:** Computerized cataloging, acquisitions, and circulation. **Computerized Information Services:** OCLC, DIALOG Information Services, BRS Information Technologies, LEXIS, NEXIS, JURIS. **Networks/Consortia:** Member of FEDLINK.

★ 17270 ★
U.S. Dept. of Labor - Library - Law Library Division (Law)
200 Constitution Ave., N.W., Rm. N-2445   Phone: (202)523-6992
Washington, DC 20210   Judy Kestell, Law Libn.
Founded: 1940. **Staff:** Prof 1; Other 2. **Subjects:** Labor law. **Holdings:** 30,000 volumes. **Subscriptions:** 2000 journals and other serials; 1005 newspapers. **Services:** Interlibrary loan; copying; library open to the public. **Automated Operations:** Computerized acquisitions. **Computerized Information Services:** WESTLAW, LEXIS, NEXIS, Washington Alert Service, OCLC. **Networks/Consortia:** Member of FEDLINK.

★ 17271 ★
U.S. Dept. of Labor - Mine Safety & Health Administration - Informational Services Library (Sci-Engr)
P.O. Box 25367   Phone: (303)231-5449
Denver, CO 80225   James A. Greenhalgh, Libn.
Founded: 1979. **Staff:** Prof 1; Other 3. **Subjects:** Mine safety and health, mining industry. **Special Collections:** Federal standards. **Holdings:** 2000 books and bound periodical volumes; 7000 government documents on microfiche; 5000 Bureau of Mines reports; 9000 Mines Safety & Health Administration reports; 4 CD-ROMs of chemical information. **Subscriptions:** 105 journals and other serials. **Services:** Interlibrary loan; copying; library open to the public. **Automated Operations:** Computerized cataloging and serials. **Computerized Information Services:** DIALOG Information Services, NLM, Integrated Technical Information System (ITIS), Occupational Health Services, Inc. (OHS), OCLC; CD-ROMs. **Publications:** New Publications List, quarterly.

★ 17272 ★
U.S. Dept. of Labor - Mine Safety & Health Administration - National Mine Health and Safety Academy - Informational Services Branch (Bus-Fin, Sci-Engr)
Airport Rd.
Box 1166   Phone: (304)256-3100
Beckley, WV 25802-1166   Becky Farley, Chf., ISB
Founded: 1976. **Staff:** Prof 1; Other 4. **Subjects:** Mine and industrial safety, industrial health, management, education. **Special Collections:** Audiovisual materials on mine safety; government publications on mine safety. **Holdings:** 8800 books; 723 films; 600 video cassettes; 115,000 microfiche; 740 reels of microfilm; 300 audio cassettes; 400 slide/tape sets; 200 slide sets. **Subscriptions:** 125 journals and other serials; 5 newspapers. **Services:** Copying; SDI; center open to the public for reference use only. **Automated Operations:** Computerized cataloging. **Computerized Information Services:** DIALOG Information Services; Accident Data Analysis (internal database). Performs searches free of charge. **Publications:** News clips; acquisitions list, both irregular. **Remarks:** FAX: (304)256-3100.

U.S. Dept. of Labor - Occupational Safety and Health Administration
See: U.S. Dept. of Labor - OSHA (17277)

★ 17273 ★
U.S. Dept. of Labor - OSHA - Billings Area Office Library (Med)
19 N. 25th St.   Phone: (406)657-6649
Billings, MT 59101   Bonnie Albright, Ck.
Founded: 1974. **Staff:** 1. **Subjects:** Safety and health in the workplace. **Holdings:** 500 books; microfilm. **Services:** Library open to the public. **Automated Operations:** Computerized cataloging. **Remarks:** FAX: (406)657-6389.

★ 17274 ★
U.S. Dept. of Labor - OSHA - Office of Training & Education - Library (Med)
1555 Times Dr.   Phone: (708)297-4810
Des Plaines, IL 60018   Linda Vosburgh, Libn.
Founded: 1972. **Staff:** Prof 1. **Subjects:** Industrial hygiene, occupational safety, industrial toxicology. **Special Collections:** Occupational Safety and Health Audiovisual Collection (1194 videocassettes, slide/tape sets, and films). **Holdings:** 2200 books; 1200 government documents; 1082 standards. **Subscriptions:** 46 journals and other serials. **Services:** Library open to the public for reference use only. **Computerized Information Services:** OSHA Computerized Information System (internal database). **Special Catalogs:** Resource Center Construction Audiovisual Catalog. **Remarks:** FAX: (708)297-4874.

★ 17275 ★
U.S. Dept. of Labor - OSHA - Region III Library (Med)
3535 Market St., Suite 2100   Phone: (215)596-1201
Philadelphia, PA 19104   Barbara Goodman, Libn.
Staff: Prof 2. **Subjects:** Occupational health and safety, industrial hygiene, toxic substances. **Special Collections:** National Institute of Occupational Safety and Health (NIOSH) documents; OSHA standards; industry standards. **Holdings:** 1500 books. **Services:** Library open to the public. **Computerized Information Services:** DIALOG Information Services, OCLC, MEDLARS; OCIS (internal database). **Networks/Consortia:** Member of FEDLINK. **Remarks:** FAX: (215)596-4872. **Staff:** Connie Dale.

★ 17276 ★
U.S. Dept. of Labor - OSHA - Region X Library (Med)
1111 3rd Ave., Suite 715   Phone: (206)553-5930
Seattle, WA 98101-3212   Donna M. Hoffman, Libn.
Founded: 1971. **Staff:** Prof 1. **Subjects:** Industrial hygiene, toxic substances, industrial safety, toxicology, safety, engineering. **Special Collections:** ANSI Standards; NIOSH documents. **Holdings:** 1000 titles. **Subscriptions:** 10 journals and other serials. **Services:** Interlibrary loan; copying; library open to the public for reference use only. **Computerized Information Services:** NLM, DIALOG Information Services; OCIS (OSHA Computerized Information System, internal database). **Networks/Consortia:** Member of FEDLINK. **Publications:** Acquisitions list, quarterly - for internal distribution only. **Special Indexes:** Standards Interpretations Index (unbound).

★ 17277 ★
U.S. Dept. of Labor - OSHA - Technical Data Center (Sci-Engr, Med)
200 Constitution Ave., N.W.
Rm. N-2625   Phone: (202)523-9700
Washington, DC 20210   Thomas A. Towers, Dir.
Founded: 1972. **Staff:** Prof 8; Other 6. **Subjects:** Occupational safety, industrial hygiene, toxicology, control technology, hazardous materials, fire safety, electrical safety, noise, carcinogens, material safety, farm safety, process safety, ergonomics, occupational health nursing, blood-borne pathogens, indoor air quality. **Holdings:** 12,000 books and bound periodical volumes; 250,000 microfiche; 2000 technical documents; 3000 standards and codes. **Subscriptions:** 250 journals and other serials. **Services:** Interlibrary loan; copying; center open to the public for reference use only. **Computerized Information Services:** DIALOG Information Services, PFDS Online, BRS Information Technologies, Chemical Information Systems, Inc. (CIS), NLM; NIOSHTIC, OCIS, TIRS (internal databases). **Networks/Consortia:** Member of FEDLINK. **Publications:** TDC User Reference Guide. **Remarks:** FAX: (202)523-5046. **Staff:** Shirley Marshall, Tech.Info.Spec.; Denise E. Hayes, Tech.Info.Spec.; Marija Hughes, Tech.Info.Spec.; Elaine C. Johnson, Tech.Info.Spec.; James Towles, Tech.Info.Spec.; Robert Turnage, Tech.Info.Spec.; Elaine G. Bynum, Docket Off.

★ 17278 ★
U.S. Dept. of State - Library (Soc Sci, Hist, Law)
Washington, DC 20520   Phone: (202)647-1062
Founded: 1789. **Staff:** Prof 12; Other 7. **Subjects:** International relations, diplomatic history, international law, treaties and agreements, political history, economic conditions, social and cultural developments, ideologies and trends, law. **Holdings:** 650,000 books. **Subscriptions:** 1100 journals and other serials. **Services:** Interlibrary loan; library may be consulted by special arrangement. **Automated Operations:** Computerized cataloging and circulation. **Computerized Information Services:** DIALOG Information Services, BRS Information Technologies, Mead Data Central, LEGI-SLATE, Dow Jones News/Retrieval, RLIN, WILSONLINE, VU/TEXT Information Services, DataTimes, G.CAM. **Networks/Consortia:** Member of FEDLINK. **Staff:** Dan O. Clemmer, Chf., Rd.Serv.

★ 17279 ★
U.S. Dept. of State - Office of the Legal Adviser - Law Library, L/EX/LL (Law)
Dept. of State, Rm. 6422
2201 C St., N.W.   Phone: (202)647-4130
Washington, DC 20520-6310   Randall J. Snyder, Law Libn.
Founded: 1920. **Staff:** Prof 2. **Subjects:** Law - international, foreign, comparative, U.S. **Holdings:** 90,000 volumes. **Subscriptions:** 500 journals and other serials. **Services:** Library not open to the public. **Automated Operations:** Computerized cataloging and serials. **Computerized Information Services:** LEXIS, WESTLAW, DIALOG Information Services, JURIS. **Networks/Consortia:** Member of FEDLINK. **Special Catalogs:** International Court of Justice, Arbitration, and International Law Treatises catalogs. **Staff:** Odell Dehart.

U.S. Dept. of Transportation - Coast Guard
See: **U.S. Coast Guard** (17132)

U.S. Dept. of Transportation - Federal Aviation Administration
See: **U.S. Federal Aviation Administration** (17485)

U.S. Dept. of Transportation - Federal Highway Administration
See: **U.S. Federal Highway Administration** (17492)

★ 17280 ★
U.S. Dept. of Transportation - Library (Trans)
400 7th St., S.W.
M-493.3, Rm. 2200   Phone: (202)366-0746
Washington, DC 20590   Lawrence E. Leonard, Lib.Dir.
Founded: 1969. **Staff:** Prof 15; Other 12. **Subjects:** Highways, aviation, marine transportation, law, urban mass transit, railroads. **Special Collections:** Aviation reports (28,120 volumes); aviation technical publications (2300 titles). **Holdings:** 310,474 books; 49,282 bound periodical volumes; 80 pamphlet boxes of state highway department maps; 40,000 pamphlets in VF drawers; 548,067 microforms. **Subscriptions:** 2100 journals and other serials; 5 newspapers. **Services:** Interlibrary loan; copying; division open to the public for limited reference use. **Automated Operations:** Computerized cataloging, acquisitions, serials, and ILL. **Computerized Information Services:** DIALOG Information Services, JURIS, NEXIS, LEXIS, OCLC, WESTLAW, DunsPrint. **Networks/Consortia:** Member of FEDLINK. **Publications:** Selected Library Acquisitions, quarterly - for official distribution. **Special Indexes:** Periodicals Index File on transportation, 1921-1982 (card). **Remarks:** The 10-A Services Section, M-493.2, library is located at 800 Independence Ave., S.W., Washington, DC 20591 and the telephone number is 267-3113. The library director can be reached at 366-2565. The telephone number for law is 366-0749. Subject scope of the 10-A library stresses air transportation, aeronautics, and related subjects. There is also a Coast Guard law collection located at 2100 2nd St., S.W., Washington, DC 20593, telephone 267-2536. **Staff:** Dorothy Poehlman, Chf., Info.Serv.Br.; Cecily V. Wood, Chf., Tech.Serv.Br.; William Mills, Chf., Acq.Sect.; Mon-hua Mona Kuo, Chf., Cat.Sect.; Loretta A. Norris, Chf., Law Serv.Sect.; Thomas M. Haggerty, Chf., 10A Serv.Sect.; Mary Jo Burke, Chf., HQ Serv.Sect.

U.S. Dept. of Transportation - Maritime Administration - U.S. Merchant Marine Academy
See: **U.S. Merchant Marine Academy** (17607)

U.S. Dept. of Transportation - National Highway Traffic Safety Administration
See: **U.S. Natl. Highway Traffic Safety Administration** (17610)

★ 17281 ★
U.S. Dept. of Transportation - Research and Special Programs Administration - John A. Volpe National Transportation Systems Center - Technical Reference Center (Trans)
Kendall Square   Phone: (617)494-2306
Cambridge, MA 02142   Susan C. Dresley, Lib.Dir.
Founded: 1970. **Staff:** Prof 7; Other 2. **Subjects:** Transportation. **Holdings:** 20,000 books; 650 bound periodical volumes; 350,000 microfiche. **Subscriptions:** 150 journals and other serials; 5 newspapers. **Services:** Interlibrary loan; center open to the public for reference use only. **Automated Operations:** Computerized public access catalog, cataloging, and circulation. **Computerized Information Services:** OCLC, DIALOG Information Services, LEGI-SLATE. **Networks/Consortia:** Member of FEDLINK. **Publications:** Bibliography of technical reports, irregular; TRC Bulletin (acquisitions list), monthly. **Remarks:** FAX: (617)494-2497. **Staff:** Robert Perreault, ILL; Marilyn Gross, Tech.Serv.

U.S. Dept. of Transportation - Urban Mass Transportation Administration
See: **U.S. Urban Mass Transportation Administration** (17955)

U.S. Dept. of the Treasury - Bureau of Alcohol, Tobacco and Firearms
See: **U.S. Bureau of Alcohol, Tobacco and Firearms** (17084)

U.S. Dept. of the Treasury - Comptroller of the Currency
See: **U.S. Comptroller of the Currency** (17135)

U.S. Dept. of the Treasury - Customs Service
See: **U.S. Customs Service** (17164)

★ 17282 ★
U.S. Dept. of the Treasury - Information & Library Services - Treasury Department Library (Bus-Fin, Law)
Main Treasury Bldg., Rm. 5030   Phone: (202)566-2777
Washington, DC 20220   Susanne B. Perella, Asst.Dir., Info. & Lib.Serv.
Founded: 1789. **Staff:** Prof 7; Other 10. **Subjects:** Taxation, public finance, law, domestic and international economics and economic conditions. **Holdings:** 80,100 books and bound periodical volumes; 323,400 microfiche; 7200 reels of microfilm. **Subscriptions:** 800 journals and other serials; 6 newspapers. **Services:** Interlibrary loan; copying; library open to the public by appointment for reference use only. **Automated Operations:** Computerized acquisitions and serials. **Computerized Information Services:** DIALOG Information Services, LEXIS, NEXIS, OCLC, TEXTLINE, Dow Jones News/Retrieval, Washington Alert Service, JURIS-DATA. **Networks/Consortia:** Member of FEDLINK. **Remarks:** FAX: (202)566-8066. **Staff:** Mary Pope, Chf., Tech.Serv.Br.; Michael Conklin, Chf., Rd.Serv.Br.

U.S. Dept. of the Treasury - Internal Revenue Service
See: **U.S. Internal Revenue Service** (17561)

★ 17283 ★
U.S. Dept. of Veterans Affairs (AL-Birmingham) - Medical Center Library (Med)
700 S. 19th St.   Phone: (205)933-8101
Birmingham, AL 35233   Mary Ann Knotts, Chf., Lib.Serv.
Founded: 1953. **Staff:** Prof 4; Other 1. **Subjects:** Medicine, dentistry, nursing, hospital administration. **Holdings:** 1000 books; 2487 bound periodical volumes; 1000 AV programs. **Subscriptions:** 300 journals and other serials. **Services:** Interlibrary loan; copying; SDI; library open to the public with restrictions. **Computerized Information Services:** NLM, BRS Information Technologies, DIALOG Information Services; VALNET (internal database). **Networks/Consortia:** Member of VALNET, Jefferson County Hospital Librarians' Association. **Remarks:** FAX: (205)933-8101. **Formerly:** U.S. Veterans Administration. **Staff:** Henrietta Mims, Patient Educ.Libn.; Jane Groves, Med.Libn.; Gail Frey, Proj.Libn.; J. Burt, AV.

★ 17284 ★
U.S. Dept. of Veterans Affairs (AL-Montgomery) - Medical Center Library (142D) (Med)
215 Perry Hill Rd.   Phone: (205)272-4670
Montgomery, AL 36193   George Marangoly
Founded: 1940. **Staff:** Prof 2. **Subjects:** Medicine, allied health sciences. **Holdings:** 600 books; 175 videocassettes (restricted use); unbound periodicals. **Subscriptions:** 200 journals. **Services:** Interlibrary loan; copying; library open to the public for reference use only. **Computerized Information Services:** MEDLINE; electronic mail. **Networks/Consortia:** Member of VALNET. **Remarks:** FAX: (205)272-4670, ext. 4231. **Staff:** Susan J. Helms, Asst.Libn.

★ 17285 ★
U.S. Dept. of Veterans Affairs (AL-Tuscaloosa) - Medical Center Library (Med)
701 Loop Rd. E.   Phone: (205)554-2000
Tuscaloosa, AL 35404   Olivia S. Maniece, Chf.Libn.
Founded: 1932. **Staff:** Prof 2; Other 1. **Subjects:** Psychiatry, nursing, geriatrics and gerontology, community mental health. **Special Collections:** Psychiatry; geriatrics and gerontology; community mental health. **Holdings:** 1751 books; 981 bound periodical volumes; 150 other cataloged items; 200 manuscripts, reports, clippings. **Subscriptions:** 24 newspapers. **Services:** Interlibrary loan; copying; SDI; library open to the public. Performs searches free of charge. **Computerized Information Services:** MEDLINE; MAILMAN, FORUM (electronic mail services). Performs searches free of charge. **Networks/Consortia:** Member of VALNET, Tuscaloosa Health Science Library Association (THeSLA). **Publications:** News-O-Gram. **Remarks:** FAX: (205)553-3760, ext. 2358. **Staff:** Betsy S. Pertzog, Med.Libn.

★ 17286 ★
U.S. Dept. of Veterans Affairs (AL-Tuskegee) - Medical Center Library (Med)
Tuskegee, AL 36083   Phone: (205)727-0550
     Artemisia J. Junier, Chf., Lib.Serv.
Founded: 1948. **Staff:** Prof 4; Other 2. **Subjects:** Medicine, patient education. **Holdings:** 28,000 books; 9500 bound periodical volumes; 2800 AV programs. **Subscriptions:** 586 journals and other serials. **Services:** Interlibrary loan; copying; library open to the public with restrictions. **Automated Operations:** Computerized cataloging, acquisitions, serials, and circulation. **Computerized Information Services:** NLM; MAILMAN (electronic mail service). **Networks/Consortia:** Member of VALNET. **Remarks:** FTS: 534-3647. **Staff:** Inez C. Pinkard, Med.Libn.; Elaine P. McGee, Libn.; Charlie P. Tarver, Libn.

★ 17287 ★
U.S. Dept. of Veterans Affairs (AR-Fayetteville) - Medical Center Library Service (142D) (Med)
1100 N. College Ave.   Phone: (501)444-5096
Fayetteville, AR 72701   Kimberly Megginson, Chf., Lib.Serv.
Founded: 1946. **Staff:** Prof 1; Other 1.5. **Subjects:** Medicine, nursing, allied health sciences. **Special Collections:** Patient Health Education (102 AV materials; 108 monographs). **Holdings:** 3125 books; 1900 microfilm and unbound periodical volumes; 604 AV items. **Subscriptions:** 211 journals and other serials. **Services:** Interlibrary loan; copying; SDI; library open to the public for reference use only. **Automated Operations:** Computerized cataloging and ILL. **Computerized Information Services:** MEDLARS, BRS Information Technologies; DOCLINE, FORUM/ARFAY (electronic mail services). Performs searches free of charge. **Networks/Consortia:** Member of VALNET, National Network of Libraries of Medicine - South Central Region. **Publications:** Patient Health Education AV Catalog. **Remarks:** FAX: (501)444-5054.

★ 17288 ★
U.S. Dept. of Veterans Affairs (AR-Little Rock) - Hospital Libraries (Med)
4300 W. 7th St.   Phone: (501)660-2044
Little Rock, AR 72205   George M. Zumwalt, Chf., Lib.Serv.
Founded: 1950. **Staff:** Prof 3; Other 1. **Subjects:** Medicine, surgery, nursing, psychiatry, psychology, social work, dietetics. **Holdings:** 3580 books; 6500 bound periodical volumes; 1 16mm motion picture; 527 videocassettes; 77 audiocassettes; 69 slide programs. **Subscriptions:** 340 journals and other serials. **Services:** Interlibrary loan; copying; SDI; library open to professionals and health science students. **Computerized Information**

Services: BRS Information Technologies, MEDLINE. **Remarks:** Above data includes the holdings of the U.S. Veterans Administration Hospital Library in North Little Rock, which has consolidated its library service with the Little Rock Hospital Library. Patients' libraries contain an additional 7000 volumes. **Remarks:** FAX: (501)660-2044, ext. 3048. **Staff:** Michael M. Blanton, Hea.Sci.Libn., LR Div.

★ 17289 ★
U.S. Dept. of Veterans Affairs (AZ-Phoenix) - Medical Center Library (142D) (Med)
650 E. Indian School Rd.   Phone: (602)222-6411
Phoenix, AZ 85012   Susan Harker, Chf., Lib.Serv.
Founded: 1946. **Staff:** Prof 2; Other 1. **Subjects:** Medicine, nursing, allied health sciences. **Special Collections:** Staff development; patient education. **Holdings:** 2081 books; 3560 bound periodical volumes; AV programs. **Subscriptions:** 396 journals. **Services:** Interlibrary loan; copying; SDI; library open to the public for reference use only. **Computerized Information Services:** DIALOG Information Services, MEDLARS; OnTyme Electronic Message Network Service (electronic mail service). **Networks/Consortia:** Member of VALNET, Central Arizona Biomedical Libraries (CABL). **Publications:** Acquisitions List, quarterly; Journal Holdings, annual - to staff and other libraries. **Remarks:** Patients' library contains additional volumes. FAX: (602)222-7377. Electronic mail address(es): VAL/AZPHO (OnTyme Electronic Message Network Service). **Staff:** Mark Simmons, Med.Libn.

★ 17290 ★
U.S. Dept. of Veterans Affairs (AZ-Prescott) - Health Sciences Library (Med)
Prescott, AZ 86313   Phone: (602)445-4860
     Carol Clark, Chf., Lib.Serv.
Staff: Prof 1; Other 1. **Subjects:** Medicine, nursing, surgery, dentistry, allied health sciences, administration. **Holdings:** 600 books; 300 AV programs; 30 titles on microfilm. **Subscriptions:** 140 journals and other serials; 10 newspapers. **Services:** Interlibrary loan; library not open to the public. **Computerized Information Services:** MEDLARS, BRS Information Technologies. **Networks/Consortia:** Member of VALNET.

★ 17291 ★
U.S. Dept. of Veterans Affairs (AZ-Tucson) - Medical Center Library (142D) (Med)
3601 S. 6th Ave.   Phone: (602)792-1450
Tucson, AZ 85723   William E. Azevedo, Chf., Lib.Serv.
Staff: 2. **Subjects:** Medicine, nursing, surgery, neurology, psychiatry, radiology, management, patient health education. **Holdings:** 3204 books; 7802 bound periodical volumes; 968 volumes on microfilm. **Subscriptions:** 320 journals and other serials. **Services:** Interlibrary loan; copying; library open to qualified reseachers. **Computerized Information Services:** MEDLINE, MEDLARS, BRS Information Technologies. **Networks/Consortia:** Member of VALNET. **Remarks:** FAX: (602)792-1450, ext. 5160.

★ 17292 ★
U.S. Dept. of Veterans Affairs (CA-Fresno) - Hospital Medical Library (Med)
2615 E. Clinton Ave.   Phone: (209)228-5341
Fresno, CA 93703   Cynthia K. Meyer, Chf., Lib.Serv.
Founded: 1950. **Staff:** Prof 2; Other 2. **Subjects:** Medicine, nursing, allied health sciences. **Holdings:** 4250 books; 7527 bound periodical volumes. **Subscriptions:** 362 journals and other serials. **Services:** Interlibrary loan; copying; SDI; library open to the public for reference use only. **Computerized Information Services:** MEDLARS, DIALOG Information Services, MEDLINE. **Networks/Consortia:** Member of VALNET, Area Wide Library Network (AWLNET), Northern California and Nevada Medical Library Group (NCNMLG), National Network of Libraries of Medicine - Pacific Southwest Region. **Remarks:** FAX: (209)228-6924. **Staff:** Nancy Crossfield, Med.Libn.; Tom Warren, ILL Techn.

★ 17293 ★
U.S. Dept. of Veterans Affairs (CA-Livermore) - Medical Library (Med)
4951 Arroyo Rd.   Phone: (510)447-2560
Livermore, CA 94550   Sandra Lynch, Libn.
Founded: 1925. **Staff:** Prof 1; Other 1. **Subjects:** Medicine, nursing, allied health sciences. **Holdings:** 1300 books; 2365 bound periodical volumes; 128 AV programs; 204 boxes of microfilm. **Subscriptions:** 188 journals and other serials. **Services:** Interlibrary loan; copying; library open to the public for reference use only. **Networks/Consortia:** Member of VALNET.

★ **17294** ★
U.S. Dept. of Veterans Affairs (CA-Loma Linda) - Hospital Library Service (142D) (Med)
11201 Benton St.   Phone: (714)422-3063
Loma Linda, CA 92357   Kathleen M. Puffer, Chf.
Founded: 1977. **Staff:** Prof 2; Other 2. **Subjects:** Medicine. **Holdings:** 2500 books. **Subscriptions:** 500 journals and other serials. **Services:** Interlibrary loan; copying; SDI; library open to the public. **Automated Operations:** Computerized public access catalog and circulation. **Computerized Information Services:** DIALOG Information Services, MEDLINE; MAILMAN, FORUM (electronic mail services). **Networks/Consortia:** Member of VALNET, San Bernardino, Inyo, Riverside Counties United Library Services (SIRCULS), Inland Empire Medical Library Cooperative (IEMLC). **Remarks:** FAX: (714)422-3164. Electronic mail address(es): CALOL (MAILMAN). **Staff:** Elizabeth Smith.

★ **17295** ★
U.S. Dept. of Veterans Affairs (CA-Long Beach) - Medical Center Library (Med)
5901 E. 7th St., 142B   Phone: (213)494-5529
Long Beach, CA 90822   Karen Vogel, Chf., Lib.Serv.
Founded: 1946. **Staff:** Prof 4; Other 3. **Subjects:** Medicine and allied health sciences, patient education. **Holdings:** 6100 books; 9000 bound periodical volumes; 1141 other volumes; AV programs. **Subscriptions:** 650 journals and other serials. **Services:** Interlibrary loan; copying; library open to the public for reference use only. **Automated Operations:** Computerized acquisitions, circulation, serials, and AV holdings. **Computerized Information Services:** DIALOG Information Services, BRS Information Technologies, MEDLARS; OnTyme Electronic Message Network Service (electronic mail service). **Networks/Consortia:** Member of VALNET. **Remarks:** Patients' library contains an additional 3050 volumes. FAX: (213)494-5447. **Staff:** Patti Flynn, Patient Libn.; Meredith Mitchell, Med.Libn.; Kathy Verdugo, AV Libn.

★ **17296** ★
U.S. Dept. of Veterans Affairs (CA-Los Angeles) - Medical Research Library (Med)
W142-D
Wilshire & Sawtelle Sts.   Phone: (310)824-3102
Los Angeles, CA 90073   Christa Buswell, Chf., Lib.Serv.
Staff: Prof 1. **Subjects:** Biochemistry, immunology, microbiology, molecular biology, physiology, ultrastructural research, metabolism. **Holdings:** 3400 books; 6200 bound periodical volumes. **Subscriptions:** 125 journals and other serials. **Services:** Interlibrary loan; library not open to the public. **Automated Operations:** Computerized acquisitions and serials. **Computerized Information Services:** MEDLARS. **Networks/Consortia:** Member of VALNET, National Network of Libraries of Medicine - Pacific Southwest Region. **Publications:** Quarterly Newsletter - for internal distribution only.

★ **17297** ★
U.S. Dept. of Veterans Affairs (CA-Los Angeles) - Wadsworth Medical Library (Med)
W142-D
Wilshire & Sawtelle Blvds.   Phone: (301)824-3102
Los Angeles, CA 90073   Christa Buswell, Chf., Lib.Serv.
Staff: Prof 5; Other 4. **Subjects:** Clinical medicine, surgery, dentistry, nursing, epilepsy, geriatrics, nutrition, social work. **Special Collections:** Patient Education Resource Library (500 volumes); AV collection (400 programs). **Holdings:** 6044 books; 12,557 bound periodical volumes; pamphlet file of monographs. **Subscriptions:** 480 journals and other serials; 12 newspapers. **Services:** Interlibrary loan; SDI; library open to the public for reference use only. **Automated Operations:** Computerized cataloging. **Computerized Information Services:** MEDLINE; Checkmate (internal database). **Networks/Consortia:** Member of VALNET, CLASS, National Network of Libraries of Medicine - Pacific Southwest Region, Metropolitan Cooperative Library System (MCLS). **Publications:** Library Newsletter, quarterly - for internal distribution and to VALNET members.

★ **17298** ★
U.S. Dept. of Veterans Affairs (CA-Martinez) - Medical Center Staff Library
150 Muir Rd.
Martinez, CA 94553
Defunct.

★ **17299** ★
U.S. Dept. of Veterans Affairs (CA-Palo Alto) - Medical Center - Medical Libraries (Med)
3801 Miranda Ave.   Phone: (415)493-5000
Palo Alto, CA 94304   C.R. Gallimore, Chf., Lib.Serv.
Founded: 1922. **Staff:** Prof 4; Other 2. **Subjects:** Medicine, behavioral sciences. **Holdings:** 13,000 books; 13,000 bound periodical volumes; 5000 recreational books. **Subscriptions:** 690 journals and other serials; 6 newspapers. **Services:** Interlibrary loan; copying; libraries open to the public by appointment. **Networks/Consortia:** Member of VALNET.

★ **17300** ★
U.S. Dept. of Veterans Affairs (CA-San Diego) - Medical Center Library (142D) (Med)
3350 La Jolla Village Dr.   Phone: (619)552-8585
San Diego, CA 92161   Chris Drew, Chf., Lib.Serv.
Founded: 1972. **Staff:** Prof 2; Other 5. **Subjects:** Medicine, patient education, management, self development. **Holdings:** 11,000 bound periodical volumes; 500 reels of microfilm; 700 AV programs. **Subscriptions:** 520 journals and other serials. **Services:** Interlibrary loan; copying; SDI; library open to the public at librarian's discretion. **Computerized Information Services:** BRS Information Technologies, MEDLARS. **Networks/Consortia:** Member of VALNET, National Network of Libraries of Medicine - Pacific Southwest Region. **Publications:** Medical Library Update, monthly - for internal distribution only; Journal Holdings List, annual - internal and Southern California VA hospitals. **Remarks:** Patients' Health Information Collection contains an additional 2000 items. **Staff:** Joanne Metcalf, Med.Libn.

★ **17301** ★
U.S. Dept. of Veterans Affairs (CA-San Francisco) - Medical Center Library Service (142D) (Med)
4150 Clement St.   Phone: (415)221-4810
San Francisco, CA 94121   William Koch, Chf., Lib.Serv.
Founded: 1947. **Staff:** Prof 4; Other 1. **Subjects:** Health sciences. **Special Collections:** AIDS; patient education. **Holdings:** 5500 books; 20,000 bound periodical volumes. **Subscriptions:** 400 journals and other serials. **Services:** Interlibrary loan; library not open to the public. **Computerized Information Services:** BRS Information Technologies, DIALOG Information Services, MEDLARS; FORUM (electronic mail service). **Networks/Consortia:** Member of VALNET, San Francisco Biomedical Library Network. **Remarks:** Includes a Patient Education Resource Center and AIDS Information Center. FAX: (415)750-6919. **Staff:** Sen Yee, Patient Educ.Libn.; Anne Ludvik, Med.Libn.; Michael Howe, AIDS Info.Ctr.Libn.

★ **17302** ★
U.S. Dept. of Veterans Affairs (CO-Denver) - Library Service (142D) (Med)
1055 Clermont St.
Denver, CO 80220   Phone: (303)393-2821
Founded: 1947. **Staff:** Prof 2; Other 2. **Subjects:** Medicine and allied clinical sciences. **Holdings:** 3000 books; 5000 bound periodical volumes; 200 pamphlets. **Subscriptions:** 250 journals and other serials. **Services:** Interlibrary loan; SDI; library open to the public for reference use only. **Computerized Information Services:** MEDLARS, BRS Information Technologies; DOCLINE (electronic mail service). **Networks/Consortia:** Member of VALNET. **Remarks:** FAX: (303)333-4935. Patients' library contains an additional 4000 volumes.

★ **17303** ★
U.S. Dept. of Veterans Affairs (CO-Fort Lyon) - Medical Library (Med)
VA Medical Center (567/142D)   Phone: (303)456-1260
Fort Lyon, CO 81038   Helen S. Bradley, Chf., Lib.Serv.
Founded: 1922. **Staff:** Prof 1; Other 3. **Subjects:** Psychiatry, nursing, geriatrics, psychology. **Holdings:** Figures not available. **Services:** Interlibrary loan; copying; library open to the public. **Automated Operations:** Computerized ILL (DOCLINE). **Computerized Information Services:** CD-ROMs (MEDLINE, PsycLIT, Nursing & Allied Health Database, Healthline); internal database; MAILMAN (electronic mail service). Performs searches free of charge. **Networks/Consortia:** Member of Arkansas Valley Regional Library Service System, Plains and Peaks Regional Library Service System, VALNET. **Remarks:** FAX: (719)384-3189.

★ 17304 ★
U.S. Dept. of Veterans Affairs (CO-Grand Junction) - Medical Center
  Medical Library (Med)
2121 North Ave.   Phone: (303)242-0731
Grand Junction, CO 81501   Lynn L. Bragdon, Chf., Lib.Serv.
Founded: 1948. **Staff:** Prof 1; Other 1. **Subjects:** Medicine, surgery.
Holdings: 1200 books; 900 bound periodical volumes. **Subscriptions:** 130
journals and other serials. **Services:** Interlibrary loan; library open to health
care professionals. **Automated Operations:** Computerized ILL
(DOCLINE). **Computerized Information Services:** MEDLARS, BRS
Information Technologies, DIALOG Information Services; VALOR
(internal database); MAILMAN (electronic mail service). **Networks/**
Consortia: Member of VALNET, National Network of Libraries of
Medicine - Midcontinental Region, Pathfinder Regional Library Service
System, Colorado Council of Medical Librarians. **Remarks:** Patients' library
contains an additional 1600 volumes. FAX: (303)244-1309. FTS: 322-0386.

★ 17305 ★
U.S. Dept. of Veterans Affairs (CT-Newington) - Health Sciences
  Library (Med)
555 Willard Ave.   Phone: (203)667-6702
Newington, CT 06111   Lynn A. Lloyd
Founded: 1938. **Staff:** Prof 1; Other 1. **Subjects:** Medicine, geriatrics.
Holdings: 2279 books; 1700 bound periodical volumes. **Subscriptions:** 180
journals and other serials. **Services:** Interlibrary loan; copying; library open
to the public for reference use only. **Computerized Information Services:**
MEDLINE, BRS Information Technologies; CD-ROMs (CINAHL,
MEDLINE).**Networks/Consortia:** Member of VALNET, Connecticut
Association of Health Science Libraries (CAHSL). **Remarks:** FAX:
(203)667-6767.

★ 17306 ★
U.S. Dept. of Veterans Affairs (CT-West Haven) - Medical Center
  Library (Med)
950 Campbell Ave.   Phone: (203)932-5711
West Haven, CT 06516   Joan McGinnis, Chf., Lib.Serv.
Founded: 1953. **Staff:** Prof 1; Other 1. **Subjects:** Medicine, psychiatry,
psychology. **Holdings:** 6500 books; 9000 bound periodical volumes; AV
programs. **Subscriptions:** 360 journals and other serials. **Services:**
Interlibrary loan; copying; library open to area health professionals for
reference use only. **Automated Operations:** Computerized cataloging and
serials. **Computerized Information Services:** DIALOG Information
Services, MEDLARS, BRS Information Technologies, OCLC; CD-ROM.
Networks/Consortia: Member of VALNET, Connecticut Association of
Health Science Libraries (CAHSL). **Remarks:** Patients' library contains an
additional 2000 volumes. **Staff:** Gail LoScola, Techn.

★ 17307 ★
U.S. Dept. of Veterans Affairs (DC-Washington) - General Counsel's
  Law Library (026H) (Law)
810 Vermont Ave., N.W., Rm. 1039   Phone: (202)233-2159
Washington, DC 20420   Jay D. Farris, Law Libn.
Staff: Prof 1; Other 2. **Subjects:** Law, with emphasis on veterans' laws.
Special Collections: Current state codes. **Holdings:** 25,000 volumes.
Services: Interlibrary loan; copying; library is for official use of the Veterans
Administration and other government agencies. **Computerized Information**
Services: WESTLAW. **Remarks:** Alternate telephone number(s): (202)233-
6442; 233-6443. FAX: (202)233-6444. **Staff:** Mary Reiman, Asst. Law Libn.

★ 17308 ★
U.S. Dept. of Veterans Affairs (DC-Washington) - Headquarters Central
  Office Library (142D) (Med)
810 Vermont Ave., N.W.   Phone: (202)566-1715
Washington, DC 20420   Diane Wiesenthal, Act.Chf.
Founded: 1930. **Staff:** Prof 3; Other 4. **Subjects:** Medicine, health care
administration, veterans affairs, management. **Special Collections:**
Historical material relating to Veterans Administration. **Holdings:** 11,000
books; 9000 bound periodical volumes; 500 AV programs; slides.
Subscriptions: 555 journals and other serials. **Services:** Interlibrary loan;
copying; SDI; library open to the public for reference use only.
Computerized Information Services: DIALOG Information Services, BRS
Information Technologies, MEDLARS, NEXIS. **Networks/Consortia:**
Member of VALNET, District of Columbia Health Sciences Information
Network (DOCHSIN), FEDLINK. **Publications:** Acquisitions List,
quarterly; Journal Holdings List, annual; fact sheets, annual; brochure,
biennial. **Remarks:** Alternate telephone number(s): (202)233-5907 (ILL).
FAX: (202)233-4764; (202)535-7539.

★ 17309 ★
U.S. Dept. of Veterans Affairs (DC-Washington) - Medical Center
  Library (Med)
50 Irving St., N.W.   Phone: (202)745-8262
Washington, DC 20422   Anne Crozier, Chf.Libn.
Staff: Prof 2; Other 1. **Subjects:** General medicine, surgery. **Holdings:** 2000
books; 4300 bound periodical volumes. **Subscriptions:** 230 journals and
other serials. **Services:** Interlibrary loan. **Computerized Information**
Services: MEDLARS, BRS Information Technologies. **Remarks:** FAX:
(202)745-8632. **Staff:** Robert Mohrman, Med.Libn.

★ 17310 ★
U.S. Dept. of Veterans Affairs (DC-Washington) - Office of Technology
  Transfer - Resource Center (Med)
VA Prosthetics Research & Development Center
103 S. Gay St.
Baltimore, MD 21202   Phone: (301)962-1800
Founded: 1949. **Subjects:** Prosthetics, sensory aids, orthotics, spinal cord
injury, rehabilitation, bioengineering. **Holdings:** 3600 books; 2500 technical
and contractor reports. **Subscriptions:** 150 journals and other serials.
Services: Interlibrary loan; copying; center open to the public for reference
use only and with permission. **Networks/Consortia:** Member of Maryland
Interlibrary Organization (MILO). **Remarks:** FAX: (301)962-9670.

★ 17311 ★
U.S. Dept. of Veterans Affairs (DC-Washington) - VA Library Network
  (VALNET) (Med)
810 Vermont Ave., N.W.   Phone: (202)535-7337
Washington, DC 20420   Wendy Carter, Asst., Lib.Prog.
Founded: 1930. **Staff:** 2. **Subjects:** Medicine, allied health sciences, health
care administration, veterans affairs, management, medical education.
Special Collections: Dept. of Veterans Affairs archival materials. **Holdings:**
695,000 books; 155,000 AV programs; pamphlets; microforms; government
documents. **Subscriptions:** 3400 journals and other serials. **Services:**
Interlibrary loan; copying; SDI; library open to the public. **Automated**
Operations: Computerized cataloging, serials, and ILL. **Computerized**
Information Services: BRS Information Technologies, DIALOG
Information Services, MEDLARS, NEXIS, OCLC; VALOR (internal
database); MAILMAN, ALIX (electronic mail services). **Publications:** List
of publications - available on request. **Remarks:** The division administers the
libraries in 176 VA facilities throughout the U.S. with a combined staff of
350 library professionals and 350 nonprofessionals. Figures given represent
combined holdings. Learning Resources Center is headquarters of
VALNET. FTS: 535-7337. FAX: (202)535-7539.

★ 17312 ★
U.S. Dept. of Veterans Affairs (DE-Wilmington) - Center Medical
  Library (Med)
1601 Kirkwood Hwy.   Phone: (302)633-5354
Wilmington, DE 19805   Donald A. Passidomo, Chf.Libn.
Founded: 1940. **Staff:** Prof 1; Other 1. **Subjects:** General medicine, surgery,
dentistry, nursing, allied health sciences. **Holdings:** 5000 books; 6000 bound
periodical volumes; 1600 AV programs; medical journals on microfilm.
Subscriptions: 325 journals and other serials. **Services:** Interlibrary loan;
copying (for ILL); SDI; library open to medical staff and affiliated students
only. **Automated Operations:** Computerized cataloging. **Computerized**
Information Services: MEDLINE. **Networks/Consortia:** Member of
VALNET, Wilmington Area Biomedical Library Consortium (WABLC).
Publications: Acquisitions List, quarterly - to hospital staff. **Remarks:** FAX:
(302)633-5540.

★ 17313 ★
U.S. Dept. of Veterans Affairs (FL-Bay Pines) - Medical Library (142D)
  (Med)
Bay Pines, FL 33504   Phone: (813)398-9366
                    Ann A. Conlan, Chf., Lib.Serv.
Staff: Prof 3; Other 1. **Subjects:** Medicine, surgery, psychiatry, nursing,
radiology, dentistry. **Special Collections:** Gerontology. **Holdings:** 6000
books; 2000 bound periodical volumes. **Subscriptions:** 475 journals and
other serials. **Services:** Interlibrary loan; library not open to the public.
Computerized Information Services: DIALOG Information Services,
MEDLINE; CD-ROM; DOCLINE (electronic mail service). **Networks/**
Consortia: Member of VALNET, Tampa Bay Medical Library Network.
Remarks: FAX: (813)398-6661, ext. 4366. Electronic mail address(es):
33504A (DOCLINE). **Staff:** Arnold Jasen, AV Libn.

★17314★
U.S. Dept. of Veterans Affairs (FL-Gainesville) - Hospital Library (Med)
Archer Rd. Phone: (904)376-1611
Gainesville, FL 32608-1197 Marylyn E. Gresser, Chf., Lib.Serv.
Founded: 1967. **Staff:** Prof 2; Other 1. **Subjects:** Health education, neurology, surgery, internal medicine, nursing, pathology, pharmacology, ophthalmology, psychiatry, radiology. **Holdings:** 6657 books; 2500 periodical volumes; journal volumes on microfilm. **Subscriptions:** 358 journals and other serials; 9 newspapers. **Services:** Interlibrary loan; copying; library open to those in the medical or paramedical fields. **Computerized Information Services:** BRS Information Technologies, MEDLINE. **Networks/Consortia:** Member of VALNET. **Publications:** New Books List, quarterly; Medical Library Policies & Journal Holdings, annual.

★17315★
U.S. Dept. of Veterans Affairs (FL-Lake City) - Medical Center -
Learning Resource Center (Med)
801 S. Marion St. Phone: (904)755-3016
Lake City, FL 32055-5898 Jacqueline B. Rahman, Chf., Lib.Serv.
Staff: Prof 1; Other 2. **Subjects:** Medicine, surgery, nursing, and allied health sciences; hospital administration; patient education. **Holdings:** 4229 books; 2800 bound periodical volumes; 846 AV programs; 300 talking books; 10 VF drawers; 2500 volumes on microfilm; 30 software programs. **Subscriptions:** 309 journals and other serials; 15 newspapers. **Services:** Interlibrary loan; copying; microcomputer; center open for reference use to professionals and lay persons requiring health information. **Automated Operations:** Computerized ILL. **Computerized Information Services:** NLM; MAILMAN (electronic mail service). **Networks/Consortia:** Member of VALNET. **Publications:** Acquisitions Bulletin, bimonthly; Annual Journal List; Health Education List, annual. **Remarks:** FAX: (904)755-3016. Patients' library contains an additional 5300 volumes and 3000 paperbacks.

★17316★
U.S. Dept. of Veterans Affairs (FL-Miami) - Medical Library (Med)
1201 N.W. 16th St. Phone: (305)324-3187
Miami, FL 33125 Mark A. Petersen, Chf.Libn.
Founded: 1947. **Staff:** Prof 2; Other 3. **Subjects:** Medicine, nursing, psychology, allied health sciences. **Holdings:** 3347 books; 5518 bound periodical volumes; 447 AV programs. **Subscriptions:** 681 journals and other serials. **Services:** Interlibrary loan; library not open to the public. **Computerized Information Services:** MEDLINE, BRS Information Technologies; DOCLINE, MAILMAN (electronic mail services). **Networks/Consortia:** Member of VALNET. **Publications:** Serials Holding List; Acquisitions List bimonthly. **Remarks:** FAX: (305)324-3118. **Staff:** Cecy Rowen, ILL Techn.

★17317★
U.S. Dept. of Veterans Affairs (FL-Tampa) - Medical Library (Med)
James A. Haley Veterans Hospital
13000 N. Bruce B. Downs Blvd. Phone: (813)972-7531
Tampa, FL 33612 Nancy Bernal, Chf.Libn.
Founded: 1972. **Staff:** Prof 2; Other 1. **Subjects:** Internal medicine, psychiatry, nursing, geriatrics. **Holdings:** 3667 books; 2281 bound periodical volumes. **Subscriptions:** 383 journals and other serials. **Services:** Interlibrary loan; library not open to the public. **Computerized Information Services:** MEDLARS, BRS Information Technologies, WILSONLINE; CD-ROMs (CD Plus/Medline, CD Plus Health, CINAHL, Health Index). **Networks/Consortia:** Member of VALNET, Tampa Bay Medical Library Network. **Staff:** Charlotte Truitt, Med.Libn.

★17318★
U.S. Dept. of Veterans Affairs (GA-Atlanta) - Medical Center - Medical
Library (Med)
1670 Clairmont Rd. Phone: (404)321-6111
Decatur, GA 30033 Eugenia H. Abbey, Chf.Libn.
Founded: 1945. **Staff:** Prof 2; Other 3. **Subjects:** Medicine, health and social sciences. **Special Collections:** Patient health education collection (343 books, 12 journals, and 17 AV programs). **Holdings:** 3733 books; 7000 bound periodical volumes; 278 AV programs. **Subscriptions:** 454 journals and other serials. **Services:** Interlibrary loan; copying; SDI; library open to the public for reference use only. **Computerized Information Services:** MEDLINE; MAILMAN (electronic mail service). **Networks/Consortia:** Member of VALNET, Atlanta Health Science Libraries Consortium (AHSLC), Georgia Online Database (GOLD). **Remarks:** Patients' library contains an additional 3872 books, 51 journals, 63 AV programs, and 354 large prints. FAX: (404)248-6858. **Staff:** Rita Clifton, Patients' Libn.

★17319★
U.S. Dept. of Veterans Affairs (GA-Augusta) - Medical Center Library
(Med)
1 Freedom Way Phone: (404)733-0188
Augusta, GA 30910 Elizabeth Northington, Chf., Lib.Serv.
Founded: 1937. **Staff:** Prof 4; Other 3. **Subjects:** Medicine, nursing, psychiatry, allied health sciences. **Holdings:** 4801 books; 2497 bound periodical volumes; 3 VF drawers. **Subscriptions:** 299 journals and other serials; 15 newspapers. **Services:** Interlibrary loan; copying; SDI; library open to the public for reference use only. **Computerized Information Services:** OCLC, BRS Information Technologies, MEDLARS. **Networks/Consortia:** Member of VALNET. **Remarks:** Patients' library contains an additional 7706 volumes. **Remarks:** FAX: (404)823-3920. **Staff:** Anita Bell, Asst.Chf., Lib.Serv.; Billy Houke, Med.Libn.; Sandra Morse, Patient Educ.Libn.

★17320★
U.S. Dept. of Veterans Affairs (GA-Dublin) - Center Library (Med)
Carl Vinson VA Medical Center Phone: (912)272-1210
Dublin, GA 31021 Steve Toepper, Chf., Lib.Serv.
Founded: 1948. **Staff:** Prof 1; Other 2. **Subjects:** Medicine, nursing and allied health sciences. **Holdings:** 3708 books; AV programs; microfilm. **Subscriptions:** 280 journals and other serials. **Services:** Interlibrary loan; copying; library open to medical professionals only. **Computerized Information Services:** MEDLINE. **Networks/Consortia:** Member of VALNET, Health Science Libraries Consortium of Central Georgia (HSLCG). **Remarks:** Patients' library contains an additional 9447 volumes.

★17321★
U.S. Dept. of Veterans Affairs (IA-Des Moines) - Medical Center
Library (Med)
38800 30th Phone: (515)271-5824
Des Moines, IA 50310 Clare M. Jergens, Chf., Lib.Serv.
Founded: 1934. **Staff:** Prof 1; Other 2. **Subjects:** Medicine, nursing, psychiatry, radiology, psychology, audiology, surgery, patient education, dentistry. **Special Collections:** Dept. of Veterans Affairs networked audiovisual programs; patient health education. **Holdings:** 3824 books; 4227 bound periodical volumes; Network for Continuing Medical Education videocassettes. **Subscriptions:** 405 journals and other serials. **Services:** Interlibrary loan; copying; library open to the public for reference use only. **Computerized Information Services:** DIALOG Information Services, MEDLINE; FORUM, DOCLINE (electronic mail services). **Networks/Consortia:** Member of VALNET, National Network of Libraries of Medicine - Greater Midwest Region, Polk County Biomedical Consortium (PCBC). **Publications:** Source (newsletter), quarterly - for internal distribution only; periodicals holdings list, annual - for internal distribution and to consortia and VALNET members. **Remarks:** FAX: (515)271-5877. Electronic mail address(es): JERGENS,CLARE@DES (FORUM).

★17322★
U.S. Dept. of Veterans Affairs (IA-Iowa City) - Medical Center Library
(Med)
Iowa City, IA 52246 Phone: (319)339-7163
Helene Petty, Chf., Lib.Serv.
Founded: 1952. **Staff:** Prof 2. **Subjects:** Medicine, allied health sciences. **Holdings:** 2415 books; 455 AV programs. **Subscriptions:** 209 journals and other serials. **Services:** Interlibrary loan; copying; SDI; library open to health professionals. **Automated Operations:** Computerized ILL. **Computerized Information Services:** NLM, BRS Information Technologies; DOCLINE (electronic mail service). **Networks/Consortia:** Member of VALNET. **Remarks:** FAX: (319)339-7077.

★17323★
U.S. Dept. of Veterans Affairs (IA-Knoxville) - Medical Center Library
(Med)
Knoxville, IA 50138 Phone: (515)842-3101
R.B. Sayers, Chf.Libn.
Founded: 1921. **Staff:** Prof 2; Other 3. **Subjects:** Psychiatry, psychology, medicine, nursing. **Holdings:** 10,500 books; 3000 bound periodical volumes; 400 other cataloged items. **Subscriptions:** 400 journals and other serials; 20 newspapers. **Services:** Interlibrary loan; SDI. **Computerized Information Services:** MEDLINE, BRS Information Technologies. **Networks/Consortia:** Member of VALNET. **Remarks:** FAX: (515)828-5084. **Staff:** Judith L. Gottshall, Med.Libn.

★ 17324 ★
U.S. Dept. of Veterans Affairs (ID-Boise) - Medical Center Library
(142D) (Med)
500 W. Fort St.   Phone: (208)338-7206
Boise, ID 83702-4598   Gordon Carlson, Chf.Libn.
Founded: 1929. **Staff:** Prof 1; Other 1. **Subjects:** Clinical medicine. **Holdings:** 1800 books; 2894 bound periodical volumes; 450 AV programs. **Subscriptions:** 210 journals and other serials. **Services:** Interlibrary loan; library open to health science professionals and students. **Computerized Information Services:** MEDLARS; MESSAGES (electronic mail service). **Networks/Consortia:** Member of VALNET, Boise Valley Health Sciences Library Consortium. **Remarks:** FAX: (208)389-7990.

★ 17325 ★
U.S. Dept. of Veterans Affairs (IL-Chicago) - Lakeside Hospital Medical Library (Med)
333 E. Huron St.   Phone: (312)943-6600
Chicago, IL 60611   Lydia Tkaczuk, Chf., Lib.Serv.
Founded: 1954. **Staff:** Prof 2; Other 1. **Subjects:** Medicine and allied health sciences. **Special Collections:** Patient education. **Holdings:** 5000 books; 3500 bound periodical volumes; 200 other cataloged items; 2 VF drawers of pamphlets. **Subscriptions:** 250 journals and other serials. **Services:** Interlibrary loan; copying. **Computerized Information Services:** MEDLINE. **Networks/Consortia:** Member of National Network of Libraries of Medicine - Greater Midwest Region, VALNET, Metropolitan Consortium of Chicago, ILLINET. **Staff:** Cheryl Kinnaird, Med.Libn.

★ 17326 ★
U.S. Dept. of Veterans Affairs (IL-Chicago) - West Side Medical Center Library Service (142D) (Med)
820 S. Damen Ave.   Phone: (312)633-2116
Chicago, IL 60612   Susan L. Thompson, Chf., Lib.Serv.
Founded: 1953. **Staff:** Prof 3; Other 3. **Subjects:** Medicine and allied health sciences. **Holdings:** 5300 books; 4275 unbound periodical volumes; 12 linear feet of VF materials; 2400 AV programs. **Subscriptions:** 473 journals and other serials. **Services:** Interlibrary loan; SDI; library open to the public. **Computerized Information Services:** MEDLARS, BRS Information Technologies. **Networks/Consortia:** Member of VALNET, Metropolitan Consortium of Chicago, Chicago Library System. **Remarks:** FAX: (312)633-2110. **Staff:** Ina Ostertag, Med.Libn.

★ 17327 ★
U.S. Dept. of Veterans Affairs (IL-Danville) - Medical Center Library (Med)
Danville, IL 61832   Phone: (217)431-6520
                                         Edward J. Poletti, Chf., Lib.Serv.
Staff: Prof 1; Other 3. **Subjects:** Psychiatry, psychology, medicine, allied health sciences. **Holdings:** 2900 books; 2275 bound periodical volumes; 342 reels of microfilm. **Subscriptions:** 250 journals and other serials. **Services:** Interlibrary loan; library open to health care community for reference use. **Computerized Information Services:** MEDLINE, BRS Information Technologies. **Networks/Consortia:** Member of VALNET. **Publications:** New Titles List, quarterly - for internal distribution only. **Remarks:** Patients' library contains an additional 3000 volumes.

★ 17328 ★
U.S. Dept. of Veterans Affairs (IL-Hines) - Library Services (142D) (Med)
Edward Hines, Jr. Medical Center   Phone: (708)216-2000
Hines, IL 60141   Lendell Beverly, Chf., Lib.Serv.
Staff: Prof 4; Other 4. **Subjects:** Hospital administration, medicine, nursing, allied health sciences. **Holdings:** 8000 books; 23,000 bound periodical volumes. **Subscriptions:** 950 journals and other serials. **Services:** Interlibrary loan; copying; library open to the public. **Automated Operations:** Computerized acquisitions. **Computerized Information Services:** MEDLINE, BRS Information Technologies, DIALOG Information Services. **Networks/Consortia:** Member of VALNET, National Network of Libraries of Medicine - Greater Midwest Region, Suburban Library System (SLS), Metropolitan Consortium of Chicago. **Remarks:** Patients' libraries contain an additional 9000 volumes. FAX: (708)343-1126. **Staff:** John Cline, Med.Libn.; Ann Novacich, Libn.; Marian Daley, Libn.

★ 17329 ★
U.S. Dept. of Veterans Affairs (IL-Marion) - Hospital Library (Med)
W. Main St., 142-D   Phone: (618)993-4114
Marion, IL 62959   Arlene M. Dueker, Chf., Lib.Serv.
Staff: Prof 1; Other 1. **Subjects:** Medicine, surgery. **Holdings:** 956 books. **Subscriptions:** 156 journals and other serials. **Services:** Interlibrary loan; library open to the public with restrictions. **Automated Operations:** Computerized cataloging. **Computerized Information Services:** MEDLARS; MAILMAN (electronic mail service). **Networks/Consortia:** Member of VALNET. **Remarks:** FAX: (618)993-4176. Affiliated with Southern Illinois University Medical School.

★ 17330 ★
U.S. Dept. of Veterans Affairs (IL-North Chicago) - Medical Library
(142D) (Med)
3001 Green Bay Rd.   Phone: (708)688-1900
North Chicago, IL 60064   William E. Nielsen, Chf., Lib.Serv.
Staff: Prof 5; Other 1. **Subjects:** Psychiatry, psychology, medicine, allied health sciences. **Holdings:** 4600 books; 2 VF drawers; 700 AV programs. **Subscriptions:** 450 journals and other serials. **Services:** Interlibrary loan; copying; library open to health science professionals. **Computerized Information Services:** BRS Information Technologies, MEDLINE. **Networks/Consortia:** Member of VALNET, Northeastern Illinois Library Consortium. **Publications:** Newsletter; New Book List; bibliographies. **Remarks:** Alternate telephone number(s): (708)688-4525. **Staff:** Sylvia Ryan, Media Libn.; Lou Ann Moore, Med.Libn.

★ 17331 ★
U.S. Dept. of Veterans Affairs (IN-Fort Wayne) - Medical Center Library Service (Env-Cons)
2121 Lake Ave.   Phone: (219)460-1490
Fort Wayne, IN 46805   Margaret O. Fulsom, Chf., Lib.Serv.
Founded: 1950. **Staff:** Prof 1; Other 1. **Subjects:** Medicine, nursing, patient education. **Holdings:** 1226 books; 169 volumes of unbound periodicals; 431 AV programs; 138 microforms. **Subscriptions:** 165 journals and other serials; 10 newspapers. **Services:** Interlibrary loan; copying; SDI; library open to the public for reference use only. **Automated Operations:** Computerized cataloging, serials, acquisitions, and ILL. **Computerized Information Services:** MEDLARS, BRS Information Technologies. **Networks/Consortia:** Member of VALNET, Tri-ALSA, Northeast Indiana Health Sciences Libraries. **Remarks:** FAX: (219)460-1364. Patients' library contains an additional 2442 volumes.

★ 17332 ★
U.S. Dept. of Veterans Affairs (IN-Indianapolis) - Medical Center Library (Med)
1481 W. 10th St.   Phone: (317)635-7401
Indianapolis, IN 46202   Lori L. Klein, Chf., Lib.Serv.
Founded: 1952. **Staff:** Prof 2; Other 2. **Subjects:** General medicine, surgery, nursing, psychiatry, allied health sciences. **Holdings:** 4000 books; 4400 bound periodical volumes; 3000 reels of microfilm; 800 AV programs. **Subscriptions:** 400 journals and other serials. **Services:** Interlibrary loan; copying; SDI; library open to the public. **Automated Operations:** Computerized cataloging. **Computerized Information Services:** MEDLINE, BRS Information Technologies; MESSAGES (electronic mail service). **Networks/Consortia:** Member of VALNET, Central Indiana Health Science Library Consortium. **Publications:** Acquisitions List, quarterly; AV list; serials list. **Remarks:** FAX: (317)269-6376. **Staff:** Linda J. Bennett, Med.Libn.

★ 17333 ★
U.S. Dept. of Veterans Affairs (IN-Marion) - Hospital Medical Library
(Med)
1700 E. 38th St.   Phone: (317)677-3110
Marion, IN 46952   Karen A. Davis, Chf., Lib.Serv.
Founded: 1930. **Staff:** Prof 2; Other 1. **Subjects:** Medicine, with special emphasis on psychiatry and psychology. **Special Collections:** NCME video cassette library; Patient Health Education Collection (674 books). **Holdings:** 4074 books; 7352 bound periodical volumes (also in microform); government documents; slides; audio and video cassettes; microforms. **Subscriptions:** 190 journals and other serials; 40 newspapers. **Services:** Interlibrary loan; copying; library open to local health care community. **Automated Operations:** Computerized cataloging, serials, and ILL. **Computerized Information Services:** MEDLARS, BRS Information Technologies; MAILMAN (electronic mail service). **Networks/Consortia:** Member of VALNET, Eastern Indiana Area Library Services Authority (EIALSA), National Network of Libraries of Medicine - Greater Midwest Region, INCOLSA. **Remarks:** Patients' library contains an additional 4782 volumes, with emphasis on patient health education. FAX: (317)677-3111. **Staff:** Alice Clouser, Patient Libn.

★ 17334 ★
U.S. Dept. of Veterans Affairs (KS-Leavenworth) - Center Medical
   Library (142D) (Med)
4101 S. Fort St.
Traffic Way   Phone: (913)682-2000
Leavenworth, KS 66048   Bennett F. Lawson, Chf., Lib.Serv.
Staff: Prof 2; Other 1. **Subjects:** Medicine, allied health sciences. **Holdings:** 3535 books; 4743 bound periodical volumes; 1400 periodical volumes on microfilm. **Subscriptions:** 230 journals and other serials. **Services:** Interlibrary loan; copying; library open to the public for reference use only. **Computerized Information Services:** MEDLINE, BRS Information Technologies, DIALOG Information Services; OnTyme Electronic Message Network Service (electronic mail service). **Networks/Consortia:** Member of VALNET. **Remarks:** Patients' library contains an additional 15,006 volumes. **Staff:** Jan Gosselin, Med.Libn.

★ 17335 ★
U.S. Dept. of Veterans Affairs (KS-Topeka) - Dr. Karl A. Menninger
   Medical Library (142D) (Med)
2200 S.W. Gage Blvd.   Phone: (913)272-3111
Topeka, KS 66622   Eris R. Kirby, Chf., Lrng.Rsrcs.Serv.
Founded: 1946. **Staff:** Prof 3; Other 2. **Subjects:** Psychiatry, internal medicine, pathology, neurology, surgery, rehabilitation medicine, psychology, social service, fine arts. **Holdings:** 19,000 books; 5800 bound periodical volumes; 13 VF drawers of clippings, reprints, original papers. **Subscriptions:** 340 journals and other serials. **Services:** Interlibrary loan; library open to the public for reference use only. **Computerized Information Services:** MEDLINE, BRS Information Technologies. **Networks/Consortia:** Member of VALNET. **Remarks:** Holdings include patients' library of approximately 9200 volumes. **Staff:** Nancy Vaughn, Med.Libn.; Rosemarie Adkins, Tech.Serv.Libn.

★ 17336 ★
U.S. Dept. of Veterans Affairs (KS-Wichita) - Medical & Regional
   Office Center - Library Service (142D) (Med)
5500 E. Kellogg   Phone: (316)651-3612
Wichita, KS 67218   Alice H. Schad, Chf., Lib.Serv.
Founded: 1933. **Staff:** Prof 1; Other 1. **Subjects:** Medicine, nursing, allied health sciences, social sciences, patient health education, veterans affairs. **Holdings:** 2000 books; 1155 bound periodical volumes; 1306 reels of microfilm; 4 VF drawers of pamphlets; 414 AV programs. **Subscriptions:** 427 journals and other serials. **Services:** Interlibrary loan; copying; SDI; library open to the public for reference use only. **Automated Operations:** Computerized serials. **Computerized Information Services:** BRS Information Technologies, DOCLINE, MEDLARS, MEDLINE; Checkmate (internal database); OnTyme Electronic Message Network Service, FORUM (electronic mail services). **Networks/Consortia:** Member of VALNET. **Publications:** Journal holdings list, annual; acquisitions list, quarterly. **Remarks:** Library located at 5500 E. Kellogg, Wichita, KS 67218. Patients' library contains an additional 3500 volumes. FAX: (316)651-3669. Electronic mail address(es): KSWIC (FORUM).

★ 17337 ★
U.S. Dept. of Veterans Affairs (KY-Lexington) - Medical Center
   Libraries (Med)
142D
Leestown Rd. and Cooper Dr. Divisions   Phone: (606)281-4916
Lexington, KY 40511   Deborah Kessler
Founded: 1931. **Staff:** Prof 3; Other 2. **Subjects:** Psychology, psychiatry, nursing, medicine, surgery, social sciences, patient health education. **Holdings:** 7000 books; 5000 bound periodical volumes. **Subscriptions:** 260 journals and other serials; 60 newspapers. **Services:** Interlibrary loan; copying; SDI; library open to the public with restrictions. **Computerized Information Services:** MEDLINE, BRS Information Technologies; FORUM (electronic mail service). **Networks/Consortia:** Member of VALNET, Kentucky Health Sciences Library Consortium. **Remarks:** Electronic mail address(es): LEXINGTON.VA.GOV (FORUM). **Staff:** Lillian Hutcheson, Libn.; Gail Rutledge, Techn.; Katrina Scott, Techn.

★ 17338 ★
U.S. Dept. of Veterans Affairs (KY-Louisville) - Hospital Library (Med)
800 Zorn Ave.   Phone: (502)895-3401
Louisville, KY 40206-1499   James F. Kastner, Chf.Libn.
Founded: 1946. **Staff:** Prof 3; Other 2. **Subjects:** Clinical medicine, surgery, nursing, psychiatry, social work. **Holdings:** 3600 books; 8000 bound

periodical volumes; 24,000 volumes of journals in microform; 1325 AV programs. **Subscriptions:** 510 journals and other serials. **Services:** Interlibrary loan; library not open to the public. **Automated Operations:** Computerized cataloging. **Computerized Information Services:** MEDLINE, DIALOG Information Services; MAILMAN (electronic mail service). **Networks/Consortia:** Member of VALNET, Kentucky Health Sciences Library Consortium, State Assisted Academic Library Council of Kentucky (SAALCK), Kentucky Library Network, Inc. (KLN). **Remarks:** FAX: (502)895-3401, ext. 333. **Staff:** Lynn Thomason, Med.Libn.; Kathy Train, Med.Libn.

★ 17339 ★
U.S. Dept. of Veterans Affairs (LA-Alexandria) - Medical Center
   Medical Library (Med)
Shreveport Hwy.   Phone: (318)473-0010
Alexandria, LA 71301   Nancy M. Guillet, Chf., Lib.Serv.
Founded: 1930. **Staff:** Prof 2; Other 3. **Subjects:** Medicine, employee development, patient education and recreation. **Holdings:** 1568 books; 2475 bound periodical volumes; 61 maps and atlases; 481 AV programs. **Subscriptions:** 226 journals and other serials; 7 newspapers. **Services:** Interlibrary loan; copying (limited); SDI; library open to medical and health professionals. **Computerized Information Services:** MEDLARS, BRS Information Technologies; MAILMAN (electronic mail service). Performs searches free of charge. **Networks/Consortia:** Member of VALNET, National Network of Libraries of Medicine - South Central Region, Health Sciences Library Association of Louisiana. **Remarks:** FAX: (318)473-0010, ext. 2244. Patients' library contains an additional 4638 volumes and 57 periodical subscriptions.

★ 17340 ★
U.S. Dept. of Veterans Affairs (LA-New Orleans) - Medical Center
   Library (Med)
1601 Perdido St.   Phone: (504)589-5272
New Orleans, LA 70146   Donna L. Patsfield, Chf., Lib.Serv.
Founded: 1945. **Staff:** Prof 2; Other 1. **Subjects:** Medicine, nursing, dentistry, surgery, allied health sciences. **Holdings:** 2100 books; 2482 bound periodical volumes. **Subscriptions:** 220 journals and other serials. **Services:** Interlibrary loan; library not open to the public. **Computerized Information Services:** BRS Information Technologies, MEDLINE. **Networks/Consortia:** Member of VALNET. **Remarks:** Patients' library contains an additional 2000 volumes. FAX: (504)589-5916. **Staff:** Mary Hess, Med.Libn.

★ 17341 ★
U.S. Dept. of Veterans Affairs (LA-Shreveport) - Overton Brooks
   Medical Center Library (Med)
510 E. Stoner
Shreveport, LA 71101-4295   Phone: (318)424-6036
Founded: 1950. **Staff:** Prof 2. **Subjects:** General medicine. **Holdings:** 1920 books; 1497 bound periodical volumes. **Subscriptions:** 213 journals and other serials; 3 newspapers. **Services:** Interlibrary loan; library not open to the public. **Computerized Information Services:** MEDLINE; DOCLINE (electronic mail service). **Networks/Consortia:** Member of VALNET.

★ 17342 ★
U.S. Dept. of Veterans Affairs (MA-Bedford) - Edith Nourse Rogers
   Memorial Veterans Hospital - Medical Library (Med)
200 Springs Rd.   Phone: (617)275-7500
Bedford, MA 01730   Sanford S. Yagendorf, Chf., Lib.Serv.
Founded: 1928. **Staff:** Prof 3; Other 3. **Subjects:** Psychiatry, geriatrics. **Holdings:** 6855 books; 3488 bound periodical volumes; 1702 boxes of microfilm; 776 tapes. **Subscriptions:** 270 journals and other serials. **Services:** Interlibrary loan; SDI; library open to the public for reference use only. **Computerized Information Services:** DIALOG Information Services, BRS Information Technologies, MEDLINE; OnTyme Electronic Message Network Service (electronic mail service). **Networks/Consortia:** Member of Boston Biomedical Library Consortium, WELEXACOL, Northeastern Consortium for Health Information (NECHI). **Publications:** Medical Library Newsletter, quarterly; acquisition list, monthly - to hospital staff. **Remarks:** Patients' library contains an additional 10,000 volumes. **Staff:** Irmeli Kilburn, Med.Libn.

★17343★
U.S. Dept. of Veterans Affairs (MA-Boston) - Hospital Medical Library
(142D) (Med)
150 S. Huntington Ave.   Phone: (617)739-3434
Boston, MA 02130   John F. Connors, Chf., Lib.Serv.
Founded: 1952. **Staff:** Prof 4; Other 2. **Subjects:** General medicine, surgery, allied health sciences, patient education. **Holdings:** 3000 books; 12,000 bound periodical volumes. **Subscriptions:** 391 journals and other serials. **Services:** Interlibrary loan; copying; SDI; library open to the public with restrictions. **Computerized Information Services:** MEDLINE, BRS Information Technologies. **Networks/Consortia:** Member of VALNET, Boston Biomedical Library Consortium. **Remarks:** Patients' library contains an additional 5344 volumes. **Staff:** Irmeli Kilburn, Med.Libn.

★17344★
U.S. Dept. of Veterans Affairs (MA-Boston) - Outpatient Clinic Library
Service (142D) (Med)
251 Causeway St.   Phone: (617)248-1170
Boston, MA 02114   John F. Connors, Chf., Lib.Serv.
Founded: 1975. **Staff:** Prof 1. **Subjects:** Health sciences, patient health education. **Holdings:** 3000 books; 1836 periodical volumes on microfilm; 1000 patient education pamphlets. **Subscriptions:** 145 journals and other serials. **Services:** Interlibrary loan; copying; SDI; library open to the public. **Automated Operations:** Computerized ILL. **Computerized Information Services:** DIALOG Information Services, BRS Information Technologies. **Networks/Consortia:** Member of VALNET, Massachusetts Health Sciences Libraries Network (MaHSLiN), National Network of Libraries of Medicine - New England Region. **Publications:** Newsletter, 4/year; bibliographies; new acquisitions list, monthly. **Remarks:** FAX: (617)248-1451. FTS: 8-835-9542. **Staff:** Ann Samson, Libn.

★17345★
U.S. Dept. of Veterans Affairs (MA-Brockton) - Medical Center Library
(Med)
940 Belmont St.   Phone: (508)583-4500
Brockton, MA 02401   Suzanne N. Noyes, Chf., Lib.Serv.
Founded: 1953. **Staff:** Prof 2; Other 3. **Subjects:** Psychiatry, psychology, hospital administration, nursing, medicine, alcoholism, drug abuse. **Holdings:** 4200 books; 5000 bound periodical volumes; 400 other cataloged items. **Subscriptions:** 450 journals and other serials. **Services:** Interlibrary loan; copying; library open to the public. **Computerized Information Services:** MEDLINE, DIALOG Information Services, BRS Information Technologies; MAILMAN (electronic mail service). **Networks/Consortia:** Member of VALNET, National Network of Libraries of Medicine - New England Region, Southeastern Massachusetts Cooperating Libraries (SMCL), Southeastern Massachusetts Consortium of Health Science Libraries (SEMCO). **Remarks:** Patients' library contains an additional 5,000 volumes. FAX: (508)583-4500, ext. 797.

★17346★
U.S. Dept. of Veterans Affairs (MA-Northampton) - Medical Center
Library (Med)
N. Main St.   Phone: (413)584-4040
Northampton, MA 01060   Dorothy E. Young, Act.Chf., Lib.Serv.
Founded: 1935. **Staff:** Prof 2; Other 3. **Subjects:** Neurology, psychiatry, psychology, nursing, medicine. **Holdings:** 3500 books; 283 bound periodical volumes; 4039 volumes on microfilm; 1041 unbound periodical volumes. **Subscriptions:** 234 journals and other serials. **Services:** Interlibrary loan; library open to the public for reference use only. **Computerized Information Services:** BRS Information Technologies. **Networks/Consortia:** Member of VALNET, Western Massachusetts Health Information Consortium, Massachusetts Health Sciences Libraries Network (MaHSLiN), BHSL. **Remarks:** FAX: (413)582-3039. Patients' library contains an additional 11,000 volumes.

★17347★
U.S. Dept. of Veterans Affairs (MD-Baltimore) - Medical Center Library
Service (142D) (Med)
3900 Loch Raven Blvd.   Phone: (301)467-9932
Baltimore, MD 21218   Deborah A. Stout, Chf., Lib.Serv.
Staff: Prof 1; Other 1. **Subjects:** Medicine, surgery, nursing. **Holdings:** 2000 books; 4000 bound periodical volumes; 200 AV programs; staff and VA publications; pamphlets. **Subscriptions:** 300 journals and other serials. **Services:** Interlibrary loan; copying; SDI; library open to the public for reference use only. **Computerized Information Services:** BRS Information Technologies, NLM; DOCLINE (electronic mail service). **Networks/Consortia:** Member of VALNET. **Publications:** Acquisitions List, monthly - for internal distribution only. **Remarks:** Patients' library contains an additional 2000 volumes including AV programs, vocational and patient health education collections.

★17348★
U.S. Dept. of Veterans Affairs (MD-Fort Howard) - Hospital Library
(Med)
9600 N. Point Rd.   Phone: (301)687-8729
Fort Howard, MD 21052-3035   Joanne M. Bennett, Chf.Libn.
Founded: 1941. **Staff:** Prof 1; Other 1. **Subjects:** Medicine. **Holdings:** 1800 books; 2262 bound periodical volumes. **Subscriptions:** 160 journals and other serials. **Services:** Interlibrary loan; copying; library open to the public by permission. **Computerized Information Services:** MEDLINE, BRS Information Technologies. **Networks/Consortia:** Member of VALNET. **Remarks:** FAX: (301)687-8849.

★17349★
U.S. Dept. of Veterans Affairs (MD-Perry Point) - Medical Center
Medical Library (Med)
Perry Point, MD 21902   Phone: (301)642-2411
                                   Barbara A. Schultz, Chf., Lib.Serv.
Founded: 1947. **Staff:** Prof 3; Other 1. **Subjects:** Psychiatry, nursing, geriatrics. **Holdings:** 3800 books; 4000 bound periodical volumes; 660 cassettes; 12 VF drawers of clippings, pamphlets, reprints. **Subscriptions:** 200 journals and other serials. **Services:** Interlibrary loan; copying; library open to the public for reference use only. **Computerized Information Services:** BRS Information Technologies, NLM. **Networks/Consortia:** Member of VALNET, Maryland Association of Health Science Librarians (MAHSL). **Remarks:** Patients' library contains an additional 11,000 volumes. **Remarks:** FAX: (410)642-1103. **Staff:** Jane Robillard, Med.Libn.

★17350★
U.S. Dept. of Veterans Affairs (ME-Togus) - Medical & Regional Office
Center - Learning Resources Services (Med)
Togus, ME 04330   Phone: (207)623-5773
                                     Melda W. Page, Chf.Libn.
Founded: 1933. **Staff:** Prof 4; Other 4. **Subjects:** Social sciences/psychiatry, medicine, alcoholism, nursing, dentistry, hospital administration. **Special Collections:** Patient health education (1000 items). **Holdings:** 4000 books; 3800 bound periodical volumes; 2000 AV programs; 400 serial titles in microform; 3100 other cataloged items. **Subscriptions:** 570 journals and other serials; 50 newspapers. **Services:** Interlibrary loan; copying; SDI; library open to the public. **Automated Operations:** Computerized acquisitions and serials. **Computerized Information Services:** DIALOG Information Services, NLM, BRS Information Technologies, WILSONLINE; MAILMAN, FORUM, DOCLINE (electronic mail services). Performs searches on fee basis. Contact Person: Christopher Bovie, Med.Libn. **Networks/Consortia:** Member of VALNET, Health Science Library and Information Cooperative of Maine (HSLIC). **Publications:** Medical Library Newsletter, quarterly; Patients' Library Newssheet, weekly. **Remarks:** FAX: (207)623-5766. Electronic mail address(es): METOG (FORUM). **Staff:** June C. Roullard, Med.Libn.; Judy Littlefield, Supv.Lib.Techn.; Gary Pelletier, ILL; Don Kluck, AV Spec.; Jane Gillis, Illus.

★17351★
U.S. Dept. of Veterans Affairs (MI-Allen Park) - Medical Center
Library Service (142D) (Med)
Southfield and Outer Dr.   Phone: (313)562-3380
Allen Park, MI 48101   Arlene Devlin, Chf., Lib.Serv.
Founded: 1939. **Staff:** Prof 2; Other 3. **Subjects:** Surgery, oncology, internal medicine, psychiatry, psychology, health management. **Special Collections:** Health information for patients; patient record slide collection; complete works of Sigmund Freud; Armed Forces Institute of Pathology (AFIP) Pathology Series. **Holdings:** 8000 books; 10,000 bound periodical volumes; 1500 reels of microfilm. **Subscriptions:** 450 journals and other serials; 10 newspapers. **Services:** Interlibrary loan; copying; SDI; library open to the public with restrictions. **Automated Operations:** Computerized acquisitions. **Computerized Information Services:** DIALOG Information Services, BRS Information Technologies, MEDLARS; internal database; OnTyme Electronic Message Network Service (electronic mail service). **Networks/Consortia:** Member of VALNET. **Publications:** Acquisitions list, quarterly; journal list, annual. **Staff:** Mary Jo Durivage, Med.Libn.

★17352★
U.S. Dept. of Veterans Affairs (MI-Ann Arbor) - Hospital Library (Med)
2215 Fuller Rd.   Phone: (313)761-5385
Ann Arbor, MI 48105   Vickie Smith, Chf.Libn.
Founded: 1953. **Staff:** Prof 1; Other 1. **Subjects:** Medicine, patient education. **Holdings:** 4610 books; 3610 bound periodical volumes. **Subscriptions:** 345

journals and other serials. **Services:** Interlibrary loan; copying; SDI; library open to the public with restrictions. **Computerized Information Services:** MEDLINE, BRS Information Technologies. **Networks/Consortia:** Member of VALNET, Washtenaw-Livingston Library Network (WLLN). **Remarks:** FAX: (313)761-7197.

★ 17353 ★
U.S. Dept. of Veterans Affairs (MI-Battle Creek) - Medical Center - Library Service (142D) (Med)
Battle Creek, MI 49016   Phone: (616)966-5600
                        Charles T. Coker, Chf., Lib.Serv.
Founded: 1925. **Staff:** Prof 1; Other 3. **Subjects:** Psychiatry, neurology, psychology. **Holdings:** 2554 books; 913 bound periodical volumes; 1856 volumes of journals on microfilm. **Subscriptions:** 423 journals and other serials; 21 newspapers. **Services:** Interlibrary loan; copying; library open to the public. **Automated Operations:** Computerized cataloging. **Computerized Information Services:** MEDLINE; MAILMAN (electronic mail service). Performs searches free of charge. **Networks/Consortia:** Member of VALNET.

★ 17354 ★
U.S. Dept. of Veterans Affairs (MI-Iron Mountain) - Medical Center Library (Med)
E. H St.   Phone: (906)774-3300
Iron Mountain, MI 49801   Jeanne M. Durocher, Chf., Lib.Serv.
Founded: 1950. **Staff:** Prof 1; Other 1. **Subjects:** Medicine, surgery, nursing, patient education, allied health. **Holdings:** 900 books; 1553 bound periodical volumes; 15 files of patient education materials; 550 videocassettes; 77 filmstrips and slide/tape kits. **Subscriptions:** 253 journals and other serials; 20 newspapers. **Services:** Interlibrary loan; SDI; library open to the public for reference use only. **Automated Operations:** Computerized cataloging. **Computerized Information Services:** MEDLINE; Mailman (electronic mail service). **Networks/Consortia:** Member of VALNET, UP Health Sciences Libraries Consortium, Michigan Health Sciences Libraries Association (MHSLA), Mid-Peninsula Library Cooperative. **Remarks:** FAX: (906)779-3107. Patients' library contains an additional 1500 volumes.

★ 17355 ★
U.S. Dept. of Veterans Affairs (MI-Saginaw) - Aleda E. Lutz VA Medical Center Library (Med)
1500 Weiss St.   Phone: (517)793-2340
Saginaw, MI 48602   Nancy R. Dingman, Chf., Lib.Serv.
Founded: 1950. **Staff:** Prof 1. **Subjects:** Medicine, surgery, nursing, health education. **Special Collections:** Respiratory, coronary, and intensive care; computer information and management. **Holdings:** 2000 books; periodicals in microform; 300 AV programs; health education pamphlets. **Subscriptions:** 150 journals and other serials. **Services:** Interlibrary loan; patient education; SDI; library open to hospital personnel only. **Automated Operations:** Access to computerized cataloging, acquisitions, serials, and ILL. **Computerized Information Services:** MEDLINE, DIALOG Information Services. **Networks/Consortia:** Member of VALNET, National Network of Libraries of Medicine - Greater Midwest Region, Michigan Health Sciences Libraries Association (MHSLA). **Remarks:** FAX: (517)791-2224. Patients' library contains an additional 1000 volumes and a large collection of health educational AV, print, and pamphlet materials.

★ 17356 ★
U.S. Dept. of Veterans Affairs (MN-Minneapolis) - Medical Center Library Service (142D) (Med)
1 Veterans Dr.   Phone: (612)725-2000
Minneapolis, MN 55417   Dorothy P. Sinha, Chf.
Founded: 1946. **Staff:** Prof 4; Other 4. **Subjects:** General medicine, psychology, pre-clinical sciences, biomedical research. **Holdings:** 5500 books; 11,000 bound periodical volumes; 1500 volumes on microfilm; 1000 AV programs. **Subscriptions:** 450 journals and other serials; 5 newspapers. **Services:** Interlibrary loan; SDI; patient education; library not open to the public. **Computerized Information Services:** MEDLINE, DIALOG Information Services, BRS Information Technologies; MAILMAN (electronic mail service). Performs searches on fee basis. **Networks/Consortia:** Member of VALNET, National Network of Libraries of Medicine - Greater Midwest Region, Twin Cities Biomedical Consortium (TCBC). **Publications:** Acquisitions list, quarterly; special bibliographies; list of journal holdings, annual; patient education publications. **Remarks:** Patient Education Center/Library has print and nonprint collections in health care field for patients, families, and staff. FAX: (612)725-2046. **Staff:** Kathy Mackay, Libn., Patient Educ.Ctr.; Barbara Winge, Med.Libn.; Diane Hoisington, Med.Libn.

★ 17357 ★
U.S. Dept. of Veterans Affairs (MN-St. Cloud) - Medical Center Library (Med)
4801 8th St., N.   Phone: (612)255-6342
St. Cloud, MN 56303   Marjorie Hammer, Chf., Lib.Serv.
Founded: 1924. **Staff:** Prof 2; Other 1. **Subjects:** General medicine, psychiatry, nursing, geriatrics. **Holdings:** 2200 books; 1000 bound periodical volumes; microfilm. **Subscriptions:** 250 journals and other serials. **Services:** Interlibrary loan; library open to health care professionals, students, and local residents for reference use only. **Computerized Information Services:** MEDLARS; MAILMAN (electronic mail service). Performs searches. **Networks/Consortia:** Member of VALNET. **Remarks:** FAX: (612)255-6494. Patients' library contains an additional 4000 volumes. **Staff:** Richard Barnes.

★ 17358 ★
U.S. Dept. of Veterans Affairs (MO-Columbia) - Hospital Library (Med)
800 Stadium Rd.   Phone: (314)443-2511
Columbia, MO 65201   Mark Fleetwood, Act.Chf., Lib.Serv.
Founded: 1972. **Staff:** Prof 2; Other 1. **Subjects:** Medicine, surgery. **Special Collections:** Patient education (267 books; 67 AV programs). **Holdings:** 4400 books; 2000 bound periodical volumes. **Subscriptions:** 300 journals and other serials; 14 newspapers. **Services:** Interlibrary loan; copying; SDI; library open to the public for reference use only. **Automated Operations:** Computerized cataloging and serials. **Computerized Information Services:** MEDLARS, BRS Information Technologies, DIALOG Information Services; CD-ROM (MEDLINE); MAILMAN (electronic mail service). **Networks/Consortia:** Member of VALNET.

★ 17359 ★
U.S. Dept. of Veterans Affairs (MO-Kansas City) - Medical Center Library (Med)
4801 Linwood Blvd.   Phone: (816)861-4700
Kansas City, MO 64128   Shirley C. Ting, Chf., Lib.Serv.
Founded: 1952. **Staff:** Prof 2; Other 1. **Subjects:** Medicine, surgery, neurology, nursing, psychology, psychiatry. **Special Collections:** Patient education. **Holdings:** 3528 books; 5278 bound periodical volumes; 907 AV programs. **Subscriptions:** 178 journals and other serials. **Services:** Interlibrary loan; copying; SDI; library open to the public for reference use only. **Automated Operations:** Computerized cataloging, acquisitions, serials, and ILL (DOCLINE). **Computerized Information Services:** MEDLINE; internal database; MESSAGES (electronic mail service). **Networks/Consortia:** Member of VALNET, National Network of Libraries of Medicine - Midcontinental Region, Kansas City Library Network, Inc. (KCLN). **Remarks:** Patients' library contains an additional 1721 volumes. FAX: (816)861-4700, ext. 3680. **Staff:** Geanne Garrette, Med.Libn.; Monty Williams.

★ 17360 ★
U.S. Dept. of Veterans Affairs (MO-Poplar Bluff) - Library Service (142D) (Med)
John J. Pershing Veterans Administration Medical Center
1500 N. Westwood Blvd.   Phone: (314)686-4151
Poplar Bluff, MO 63901   Genise E. Denton, Chf., Lib.Serv.
Founded: 1951. **Staff:** Prof 1. **Subjects:** Medicine. **Holdings:** 1305 books; AV equipment and programs. **Subscriptions:** 170 journals and other serials; 19 newspapers. **Services:** Interlibrary loan; copying; SDI; library open to the public. **Computerized Information Services:** MEDLARS, BRS Information Technologies. **Networks/Consortia:** Member of VALNET. **Remarks:** Patients' library contains an additional 7972 books and 44 periodicals.

★ 17361 ★
U.S. Dept. of Veterans Affairs (MO-St. Louis) - Library Service (142D) - Jefferson Barracks Division Library (Med)
St. Louis, MO 63125   Phone: (314)894-6630
                        John Chesmelewski, Libn.
Staff: Prof 4; Other 3. **Subjects:** Medicine and allied health sciences. **Special Collections:** Geriatrics. **Holdings:** 5500 books; 9000 bound periodical volumes; 9800 reels of microfilm; 978 AV programs. **Subscriptions:** 650 journals and other serials. **Services:** Interlibrary loan; copying; SDI; library open to the public. **Computerized Information Services:** Philnet, DIALOG Information Services, MEDLARS; MAILMAN (electronic mail service). **Networks/Consortia:** Member of VALNET, Saint Louis Medical Librarians Consortia. **Remarks:** FAX: (314)894-6613. Patients' library contains an additional 750 volumes. Library Service also operates the John Cochran Division Library. **Staff:** Ann Repetto, Libn.; Barbara Paulick, Libn.

★ 17362 ★
U.S. Dept. of Veterans Affairs (MO-St. Louis) - Library Service (142D)
- John Cochran Division Library (Med)
915 Grand Blvd.   Phone: (314)289-6421
St. Louis, MO 63106   Alfreida Keeling, Libn.
Staff: Prof 4; Other 3. **Subjects:** Medicine and allied health sciences. **Special Collections:** Geriatrics. **Holdings:** 5500 books; 9000 bound periodical volumes; 9800 reels of microfilm; 978 AV programs. **Subscriptions:** 650 journals and other serials. **Services:** Interlibrary loan; copying; SDI; library open to the public. **Computerized Information Services:** Philnet, DIALOG Information Services, MEDLARS; MAILMAN (electronic mail service). **Networks/Consortia:** Member of VALNET, Saint Louis Medical Librarians Consortia. **Remarks:** FAX: (314)289-6321. Patients' library contains an additional 750 volumes. Library Service also operates the Jefferson Barracks Division Library. **Staff:** Ann Repetto, Libn.; Barbara Paulick, Libn.

★ 17363 ★
U.S. Dept. of Veterans Affairs (MS-Jackson) - Medical Center Library
(Med)
1500 E. Woodrow Wilson Dr.   Phone: (601)364-1273
Jackson, MS 39216   Carol Sistrunk, Chf.Libn.
Founded: 1946. **Staff:** Prof 2; Other 1. **Subjects:** Medicine and allied health sciences. **Holdings:** 1800 books; 2750 bound periodical volumes; 2000 volumes of journals on microfilm; 275 AV software programs. **Subscriptions:** 200 journals and other serials; 5 newspapers. **Services:** Interlibrary loan; copying; SDI; library open to the public by permission. **Automated Operations:** Computerized circulation. **Computerized Information Services:** MEDLINE, BRS Information Technologies; MAILMAN (electronic mail service). **Networks/Consortia:** Member of VALNET, Central Mississippi Consortium of Medical Libraries, Mississippi Biomedical Library Consortium (MBLC). **Remarks:** Patients' library contains an additional 500 volumes.

★ 17364 ★
U.S. Dept. of Veterans Affairs (MT-Fort Harrison) - Medical Center
Library (Med)
Veterans Administration   Phone: (406)442-6410
Fort Harrison, MT 59636   Charles Grasmick, Chf., Lib.Serv.
Staff: Prof 1. **Subjects:** Medicine, internal medicine, surgery. **Holdings:** 1484 books. **Subscriptions:** 268 journals and other serials; 10 newspapers. **Services:** Interlibrary loan; library open to the public with restrictions. **Computerized Information Services:** MEDLARS, BRS Information Technologies; DOCLINE, VAINET (electronic mail services). **Networks/Consortia:** Member of VALNET, Helena Area Health Sciences Library Consortium (HAHSLC). **Remarks:** Patients' library contains an additional 4013 volumes. FAX: (406)442-6410, ext. 7344.

★ 17365 ★
U.S. Dept. of Veterans Affairs (MT-Miles City) - Medical Center
Library (Med)
Miles City, MT 59301   Phone: (406)232-3060
                                         Gail Shaw Wilkerson, Chf., Lib.Serv.
Founded: 1951. **Staff:** 1. **Subjects:** Medicine. **Holdings:** 1500 volumes. **Subscriptions:** 100 journals and other serials. **Services:** Interlibrary loan; library not open to the public. **Automated Operations:** Computerized ILL. **Computerized Information Services:** MEDLARS. **Networks/Consortia:** Member of VALNET. **Remarks:** FAX: (406)232-3060. Patients' library contains an additional 1500 volumes.

★ 17366 ★
U.S. Dept. of Veterans Affairs (NC-Asheville) - Medical Center Library
(Med)
Asheville, NC 28805   Phone: (704)298-7911
                                         Jane Lambremont, Chf., Lib.Serv.
Staff: Prof 1; Other 1. **Subjects:** General and cardiopulmonary medicine, thoracic surgery, nursing. **Holdings:** 2000 books; 3000 bound periodical volumes. **Subscriptions:** 334 journals and other serials. **Services:** Interlibrary loan; copying; library open to medical professionals. **Automated Operations:** Computerized serials. **Computerized Information Services:** NLM; MAILMAN (electronic mail service). **Networks/Consortia:** Member of VALNET.

★ 17367 ★
U.S. Dept. of Veterans Affairs (NC-Durham) - Medical Center Library
(Med)
508 Fulton St.   Phone: (919)286-6929
Durham, NC 27705   Jeffrey F. Kager, Chf., Lib.Serv.
Founded: 1953. **Staff:** Prof 3; Other 2. **Subjects:** Clinical medicine, pre-clinical sciences, allied health sciences, management, research, patient health education. **Holdings:** 1600 books; 9000 bound periodical volumes; 2600 reels of microfilm; 70 microfiche; 927 AV programs. **Subscriptions:** 360 journals and other serials; 13 newspapers. **Services:** Interlibrary loan; SDI; library open to the public with restrictions. **Computerized Information Services:** MEDLINE, BRS Information Technologies, Net-Search; CD-ROM (SilverPlatter); MAILMAN, OnTyme Electronic Message Network Service (electronic mail services). **Networks/Consortia:** Member of VALNET. **Publications:** Medical Library Journal Holdings, annual; Library Guide, irregular. **Remarks:** FAX: (919)286-6859. **Staff:** Stephen Perlman, Med.Libn.; Douglas Young, Med.Libn.

★ 17368 ★
U.S. Dept. of Veterans Affairs (NC-Fayetteville) - Medical Center
Library Service (142D) (Med)
2300 Ramsey St.   Phone: (919)822-7072
Fayetteville, NC 28301   Diana Akins, Chf., Lib.Serv.
Founded: 1940. **Staff:** Prof 1; Other 1. **Subjects:** Medicine, nursing, dentistry, patient education, allied health sciences. **Holdings:** 2500 books; 3978 periodicals; 467 AV programs. **Subscriptions:** 400 journals and other serials. **Services:** Interlibrary loan; copying; SDI; library open to students and physicians. **Computerized Information Services:** MEDLINE, BRS Information Technologies, DIALOG Information Services; DOCLINE (electronic mail service). **Networks/Consortia:** Member of VALNET, Cape Fear Health Sciences Information Consortium (CFHSIC). **Remarks:** Patients' library contains an additional 1500 volumes and patient health education resource center. **Remarks:** FAX: (919)822-7072.

★ 17369 ★
U.S. Dept. of Veterans Affairs (NC-Salisbury) - Medical Center Library
(Med)
1601 Brenner Ave.   Phone: (704)638-9000
Salisbury, NC 28144   Nancy Smith, Lrng.Rsrcs.Serv.
Founded: 1953. **Staff:** Prof 3; Other 3. **Subjects:** Psychology, psychiatry, nursing, internal medicine, alcoholism, surgery, gerontology, dentistry. **Special Collections:** Business and management. **Holdings:** 2700 books; 1500 AV programs. **Subscriptions:** 475 journals and other serials. **Services:** Interlibrary loan; library open to health science professionals. **Automated Operations:** Computerized ILL (DOCLINE). **Computerized Information Services:** BRS Information Technologies, MEDLINE. Performs searches on fee basis. **Networks/Consortia:** Member of VALNET. **Publications:** Newsletter, monthly - for internal distribution only. **Remarks:** FAX: (704)638-3341. Patients' library contains an additional 2300 books. **Staff:** Nancy J. Stine, Med.Libn.; Mary C. Cullop, Hea.Educ.Libn.

★ 17370 ★
U.S. Dept. of Veterans Affairs (ND-Fargo) - Center Library (Med)
2101 Elm St.   Phone: (701)232-3241
Fargo, ND 58102   James Robbins, Chf., Lib.Serv.
Founded: 1945. **Staff:** Prof 2. **Subjects:** Medicine, dentistry, nursing, social work, hospital administration. **Holdings:** 3100 books; pamphlets; bibliographies. **Subscriptions:** 296 journals and other serials. **Services:** Interlibrary loan; copying; library open to the public with restrictions. **Computerized Information Services:** MEDLINE, HEALTH, CINAHL. Performs searches on fee basis. **Networks/Consortia:** Member of VALNET, Valley Medical Network (VMN). **Remarks:** Patients' library services and patient education material available. FAX: (701)239-3775. **Staff:** Jane Borland, SE Campus Libn.

★ 17371 ★
U.S. Dept. of Veterans Affairs (NE-Grand Island) - Hospital Library
(Med)
2201 N. Broadwell St.   Phone: (308)382-3660
Grand Island, NE 68803   Shirley J. Barthelman, Chf., Lib.Serv.
Founded: 1950. **Staff:** Prof 1. **Subjects:** Medicine, surgery, nursing. **Holdings:** 1074 books. **Subscriptions:** 110 journals and other serials. **Services:** Interlibrary loan; copying; loan services from Library of Congress and regional libraries for blind and physically handicapped; library open to the public by permission. **Computerized Information Services:** MEDLINE, MEDLARS. **Remarks:** Patients' library contains an additional 1000 volumes and large print books.

★17372★
U.S. Dept. of Veterans Affairs (NE-Lincoln) - Medical Center Library (142D) (Med)
600 S. 70th St.   Phone: (402)489-3802
Lincoln, NE 68510   Mrs. Swoboda, Libn.
Staff: 1. **Subjects:** Medicine and allied health sciences. **Holdings:** 1650 titles; 1028 bound periodical volumes; 1436 boxes of microfilm (periodicals); 700 AV programs. **Subscriptions:** 218 journals and other serials; 5 newspapers. **Services:** Interlibrary loan; copying; library open to qualified medical personnel. **Automated Operations:** Computerized acquisitions and circulation. **Computerized Information Services:** NLM. **Networks/Consortia:** Member of VALNET, Lincoln Health Science Library Group (LHSLG). **Remarks:** Patients' library contains an additional 2200 volumes. FAX: (402)486-7840.

★17373★
U.S. Dept. of Veterans Affairs (NE-Omaha) - Hospital Library (Med)
4101 Woolworth Ave.   Phone: (402)449-0652
Omaha, NE 68105   Ronald L. Fingerson, Chf., Lib.Serv.
Founded: 1950. **Staff:** Prof 1; Other 1. **Subjects:** Medicine and allied health sciences. **Holdings:** 872 books; 1014 AV programs. **Subscriptions:** 259 journals and other serials; 25 newspapers. **Services:** Interlibrary loan; copying; library open to the public by request. **Computerized Information Services:** MEDLARS; DOCLINE (electronic mail service). **Networks/Consortia:** Member of VALNET, ICON. **Remarks:** FAX: (402)449-0692.

★17374★
U.S. Dept. of Veterans Affairs (NH-Manchester) - Medical Center Library (Med)
718 Smyth Rd.   Phone: (603)624-4366
Manchester, NH 03104   Martha Roberts, Chf., Lib.Serv.
Founded: 1950. **Staff:** Prof 1; Other 1. **Subjects:** Medicine, surgery, nursing. **Holdings:** 1650 books. **Subscriptions:** 168 journals and other serials; 7 newspapers. **Services:** Interlibrary loan; copying; SDI; library open to the public with restrictions. **Computerized Information Services:** BRS Information Technologies, NLM; MAILMAN, DOCLINE (electronic mail services). **Networks/Consortia:** Member of VALNET. **Remarks:** FAX: (603)626-6503.

★17375★
U.S. Dept. of Veterans Affairs (NJ-East Orange) - Medical Center Library (142D) (Med)
385 Tremont Ave.   Phone: (201)676-1000
East Orange, NJ 07018-1095   David Madden, Chf., Lib.Serv.
Founded: 1952. **Staff:** Prof 3; Other 3. **Subjects:** General medicine. **Holdings:** 11,000 books; 16,000 bound periodical volumes; 900 AV programs. **Subscriptions:** 400 journals and other serials. **Services:** Interlibrary loan; library not open to the public. **Automated Operations:** Computerized acquisitions and serials. **Computerized Information Services:** BRS Information Technologies, DIALOG Information Services, MEDLINE. **Networks/Consortia:** Member of VALNET. **Staff:** Judith Grace, AV Libn./ILL.

★17376★
U.S. Dept. of Veterans Affairs (NJ-Lyons) - Hospital Library (Med)
Knollcroft Rd.   Phone: (908)604-5822
Lyons, NJ 07939   James G. Delo, Chf., Lib.Serv.
Founded: 1930. **Staff:** Prof 2; Other 1. **Subjects:** Psychiatry, neurology, psychology, medicine, nursing, patient health education. **Special Collections:** Psychiatry. **Holdings:** 7500 books; 5200 bound periodical volumes; 500 AV programs; 14 newspapers. **Subscriptions:** 300 journals and other serials; 5 newspapers. **Services:** Interlibrary loan; copying; library open to the public for reference use only. **Computerized Information Services:** BRS Information Technologies, MEDLINE; MUMPS (internal database). **Networks/Consortia:** Member of VALNET, MEDCORE. **Remarks:** FAX: (908)604-5837. Patients' library contains an additional 8500 volumes. **Staff:** Marian Krugman, Patients' Libn.

★17377★
U.S. Dept. of Veterans Affairs (NM-Albuquerque) - Medical Center Library (Med)
2100 Ridgecrest Dr., S.E.   Phone: (505)256-2786
Albuquerque, NM 87108   Nancy Myer, Chf., Lib.Serv.
Founded: 1932. **Staff:** Prof 2; Other 2. **Subjects:** Medicine, surgery, nursing, psychiatry. **Holdings:** 1530 books; 8537 bound periodical volumes; 500 reels

of microfilm of journals. **Subscriptions:** 393 journals and other serials; 10 newspapers. **Services:** Interlibrary loan; copying; library open to the public by special permission. **Computerized Information Services:** MEDLINE, DIALOG Information Services. **Networks/Consortia:** Member of VALNET, New Mexico Consortium of Biomedical and Hospital Libraries. **Remarks:** Patients' library contains an additional 1225 volumes. FAX: (505)256-2870. Also serves the Kirtland Air Force Base Hospital. **Staff:** Phyllis L. Kregstein, Biomed.Libn.

★17378★
U.S. Dept. of Veterans Affairs (NV-Reno) - Medical Center - Library Services (142D) (Med)
1000 Locust St.   Phone: (702)328-1471
Reno, NV 89520   Christine J. Camp, Chf., Lib.Serv.
Staff: Prof 3; Other 1. **Subjects:** Clinical medicine, gerontology. **Holdings:** 2850 books; 500 AV items. **Subscriptions:** 300 journals and other serials. **Services:** Interlibrary loan; SDI; library open to the public. **Computerized Information Services:** DIALOG Information Services, MEDLARS; MAILMAN, (electronic mail service). **Networks/Consortia:** Member of VALNET, Northern California and Nevada Medical Library Group (NCNMLG). **Remarks:** FAX: (702)328-1732. **Staff:** Kelly Boyer, Libn.; Stephen Stanley, Med. Media.

★17379★
U.S. Dept. of Veterans Affairs (NY-Albany) - Medical Center Library (142D) (Med)
113 Holland Ave.   Phone: (518)462-3311
Albany, NY 12208   Halyna L. Korhun
Founded: 1951. **Staff:** Prof 2; Other 2. **Subjects:** Medicine, social services, nursing, mental health. **Holdings:** 2000 books; 2300 bound periodical volumes; 210 AV programs. **Subscriptions:** 302 journals and other serials. **Services:** Interlibrary loan; copying; SDI; library open to the public for reference use only. **Automated Operations:** Computerized acquisitions and ILL. **Computerized Information Services:** BRS Information Technologies, OCLC; MAILMAN, DOCLINE (electronic mail services). **Networks/Consortia:** Member of VALNET, Capital District Library Council for Reference & Research Resources (CDLC). **Publications:** Medical library handbook; patient pamphlet list; patient library handbook; journal holdings list; new book list; AV list. **Remarks:** FAX: (518)462-5457. **Staff:** Mary Jo Maloney, Med.Libn.; Steve Long, Ill.

★17380★
U.S. Dept. of Veterans Affairs (NY-Batavia) - Medical Center Library (Med)
Redfield Pkwy.   Phone: (716)343-7500
Batavia, NY 14020   Madeline A. Coco, Chf.Libn.
Founded: 1934. **Staff:** Prof 1; Other 1. **Subjects:** General medicine, surgery, nursing, pathology, radiology. **Holdings:** 1700 books; 1700 bound periodical volumes. **Subscriptions:** 99 journals and other serials. **Services:** Interlibrary loan; copying; library open to medical professionals and students. **Computerized Information Services:** MEDLINE. **Networks/Consortia:** Member of VALNET, Western New York Library Resources Council (WNYLRC). **Remarks:** Patients' library contains an additional 4500 volumes.

★17381★
U.S. Dept. of Veterans Affairs (NY-Bath) - Medical Center Library Service (142D) (Med)
Bath, NY 14810   Phone: (607)776-2111
    Sally Ann Hillegas, Chf., Lib.Serv.
Founded: 1930. **Staff:** Prof 1; Other 1. **Subjects:** Geriatrics, chronic diseases, general internal medicine, long term care. **Holdings:** 1282 books; 125 video cassettes; 600 periodical volumes on microfilm. **Subscriptions:** 116 journals and other serials; 8 newspapers. **Services:** Interlibrary loan. **Computerized Information Services:** MEDLINE; MAILMAN (electronic mail service). **Networks/Consortia:** Member of South Central Research Library Council (SCRLC). **Publications:** Newsletter. **Remarks:** Patients' library contains an additional 10,231 volumes.

★ 17382 ★
U.S. Dept. of Veterans Affairs (NY-Bronx) - Medical Center Library
(Med)
130 W. Kingsbridge Rd.   Phone: (212)579-1631
Bronx, NY 10468   Margaret M. Kinney, Chf.Libn.
Founded: 1946. **Staff:** Prof 3; Other 2. **Subjects:** Medicine and allied health sciences. **Holdings:** 20,244 volumes. **Subscriptions:** 395 journals and other serials. **Services:** Interlibrary loan; library open to the public with restrictions. **Computerized Information Services:** Online systems. **Networks/Consortia:** Member of VALNET, Medical Library Center of New York (MLCNY), New York Metropolitan Reference and Research Library Agency. **Publications:** Bibliographica Media (current awareness), monthly. **Remarks:** Patients' library contains an additional 5000 volumes. **Staff:** Mr. Sumitte De Soyza; Kathleen O'Hogan.

★ 17383 ★
U.S. Dept. of Veterans Affairs (NY-Brooklyn) - Medical Center Library
(Med)
800 Poly Place   Phone: (718)836-6600
Brooklyn, NY 11209   Francine Tidona
Founded: 1947. **Staff:** Prof 3; Other 3. **Subjects:** Medicine, surgery, psychiatry, psychology, nursing, social work. **Holdings:** 6685 books; 7226 bound periodical volumes; 106 video cassettes; 138 slide sets; 6 films. **Subscriptions:** 477 journals and other serials. **Services:** Interlibrary loan; library not open to the public. **Automated Operations:** Computerized cataloging. **Computerized Information Services:** MEDLINE, DIALOG Information Services, BRS Information Technologies; DOCLINE, (electronic mail services). **Remarks:** FAX: (718)630-3573. **Staff:** Halyna Liszczynskyj, Med.Libn.

★ 17384 ★
U.S. Dept. of Veterans Affairs (NY-Buffalo) - Medical Center Library
Service (Med)
3495 Bailey Ave.   Phone: (716)834-9200
Buffalo, NY 14215   Betty A. Withrow, Chf.Libn.
Founded: 1950. **Staff:** Prof 3; Other 1. **Subjects:** Medicine, surgery, nursing, management, patient education. **Holdings:** 2000 books; 9000 periodical volumes; 700 AV programs. **Subscriptions:** 400 journals and other serials. **Services:** Interlibrary loan; copying; SDI; library open to the public for reference use only. **Computerized Information Services:** BRS Information Technologies, NLM. **Networks/Consortia:** Member of VALNET, Western New York Library Resources Council (WNYLRC), National Network of Libraries of Medicine - Middle Atlantic Region, Library Consortium of Health Institutions in Buffalo (LCHIB). **Publications:** Newsletter, bimonthly; Serial Holdings List; AV Holdings List; Patient Education Bibliography. **Remarks:** Patients' library contains an additional 5000 volumes. FAX: (716)862-3758. **Staff:** Russell Hall, Med.Libn.; James Mendola, Med.Libn.

★ 17385 ★
U.S. Dept. of Veterans Affairs (NY-Canandaigua) - Medical Center
Library (142D) (Med)
Canandaigua, NY 14424   Phone: (716)396-3649
        Peter Fleming, Chf., Lib.Serv.
Founded: 1933. **Staff:** Prof 1; Other 2. **Subjects:** Psychiatry, psychology, medicine, nursing, alcoholism, geriatrics. **Holdings:** 4000 books; 612 bound periodical volumes; 2488 other volumes. **Subscriptions:** 240 journals and other serials. **Services:** Interlibrary loan; SDI; library open to the public for reference use only. **Automated Operations:** Computerized cataloging. **Computerized Information Services:** NLM, BRS Information Technologies. **Networks/Consortia:** Member of Rochester Regional Library Council (RRLC). **Remarks:** FAX: (716)396-3650. Patients' library contains an additional 7270 volumes.

★ 17386 ★
U.S. Dept. of Veterans Affairs (NY-Castle Point) - Department of
Medicine and Surgery - Library Service (Med)
Castle Point, NY 12511   Phone: (914)831-2000
        Jeffrey Nicholas, Chf., Lib.Serv.
Staff: Prof 1; Other 1. **Subjects:** Spinal cord injuries, surgery, nursing education, geriatric medicine, dentistry. **Holdings:** 1966 books; 649 periodicals on microfilm; 286 audio cassettes; 129 video cassettes. **Subscriptions:** 130 journals and other serials; 5 newspapers. **Services:** Interlibrary loan; copying; SDI; library open to the public for reference use only. **Computerized Information Services:** MEDLINE, BRS Information Technologies; VALOR (internal database). **Networks/Consortia:** Member of VALNET, Southeastern New York Library Resources Council (SENYLRC). **Remarks:** FAX: (914)831-2000, ext. 5246.

★ 17387 ★
U.S. Dept. of Veterans Affairs (NY-Montrose) - Medical Library (Med)
Franklin Delano Roosevelt Veterans Medical Ctr.   Phone: (914)737-4400
Montrose, NY 10548   Bruce S. Delman, Ph.D., Chf., Lib.Serv.
Founded: 1950. **Staff:** Prof 4; Other 2. **Subjects:** Psychiatry, psychology, medicine, social work, nursing, geriatrics. **Special Collections:** Patient Education Collection. **Holdings:** 7422 books; 1600 bound periodical volumes; 2800 boxes of microfilm; 1250 AV programs. **Subscriptions:** 615 journals and other serials; 8 newspapers. **Services:** Interlibrary loan; copying; SDI; library open to the public by permission. **Computerized Information Services:** MEDLARS; MAILMAN (electronic mail service). **Networks/Consortia:** Member of VALNET, Health Information Libraries of Westchester (HILOW), New York Metropolitan Reference and Research Library Agency. **Publications:** Medical Library News, bimonthly - to staff members and VA hospitals. **Remarks:** Patients' library contains an additional 5067 volumes. **Staff:** Won Kim, Asst.Libn.; Jeffrey Garverick, Med.Libn.; Ann Aaron, Patients Libn.

★ 17388 ★
U.S. Dept. of Veterans Affairs (NY-New York) - Medical Center Library
(142D) (Med)
423 E. 23rd St.   Phone: (212)686-7500
New York, NY 10010   Karin Wiseman, Chf.Libn.
Founded: 1955. **Staff:** Prof 4; Other 5. **Subjects:** Medicine, surgery, neurology, psychiatry, nursing. **Holdings:** 5000 books; 5684 bound periodical volumes. **Subscriptions:** 500 journals and other serials; 10 newspapers. **Services:** Interlibrary loan; library open to affiliated medical professionals and public with METRO Referral. **Computerized Information Services:** MEDLINE, BRS/COLLEAGUE. **Networks/Consortia:** Member of VALNET, Medical Library Center of New York (MLCNY). **Remarks:** Patients' library contains an additional 5344 volumes. FAX: (212)951-3367. **Staff:** Niki Buettner, Med.Libn.; Lily Hom, Gen.Libn.

★ 17389 ★
U.S. Dept. of Veterans Affairs (NY-Northport) - Health Science Library
(Med)
Middleville Rd.   Phone: (516)261-4400
Northport, NY 11768   Caryl Kazen, Chf., Lib.Sect.
Staff: Prof 4; Other 2. **Subjects:** Medicine, allied health sciences, psychiatry, dentistry. **Special Collections:** Geriatrics; hospital administration. **Holdings:** 5000 books; 2000 AV programs. **Subscriptions:** 530 journals and other serials. **Services:** Interlibrary loan; library open to the public for reference use only. **Computerized Information Services:** MEDLINE, BRS Information Technologies, DIALOG Information Services. **Networks/Consortia:** Member of VALNET, Medical & Scientific Libraries of Long Island (MEDLI), Long Island Library Resources Council, BHSL. **Remarks:** FAX: (516)754-7992. **Staff:** Marc Horowitz, AV Libn.; Robert Toronto, Libn.; Kathleen Kesser, Libn.

★ 17390 ★
U.S. Dept. of Veterans Affairs (NY-Syracuse) - Medical Center Library
(Med)
Irving Ave. & University Pl.   Phone: (315)476-7461
Syracuse, NY 13210   June M. Mitchell, Chf., Lib./LRC Serv.
Founded: 1953. **Staff:** Prof 3. **Subjects:** Clinical medicine, surgery, nursing, psychology, social work. **Holdings:** 3000 books; 2625 bound and microform periodical volumes; 350 pamphlets. **Subscriptions:** 190 journals and other serials. **Services:** Library open to the public for reference use only. **Automated Operations:** Computerized ILL (DOCLINE). **Computerized Information Services:** MEDLINE, OCLC, BRS Information Technologies; MAILMAN (electronic mail service). **Networks/Consortia:** Member of VALNET, Central New York Library Resources Council (CENTRO). **Remarks:** FAX: (315)476-7461, ext. 2647. Patients' library contains an additional 10,000 volumes, including management and patient education collections. Learning Resources Center, established in 1975, contains many AV programs in patient education, staff instruction and training. **Staff:** Kay A.W. Root, Med.Libn.; E. Nancy Hellwig, AV Libn.

★ 17391 ★
U.S. Dept. of Veterans Affairs (OH-Brecksville) - Medical Library
(142D) (Med)
10000 Brecksville Rd.   Phone: (216)526-3030
Brecksville, OH 44141   Janet Monk Gillette, Chf., Reg.Lib.Serv.
Founded: 1961. **Staff:** Prof 3; Other 3. **Subjects:** Psychology, nursing, psychiatry, social work, clinical medicine. **Holdings:** 4807 volumes; 20

dissertations; 1900 AV programs. **Subscriptions:** 300 journals and other serials. **Services:** Interlibrary loan; SDI; library open to the public. **Computerized Information Services:** MEDLARS, DIALOG Information Services, BRS Information Technologies. **Networks/Consortia:** Member of VALNET. **Remarks:** Patients' library contains an additional 2000 volumes. FAX: (216)838-6045. **Staff:** Mary Conway, Med.Libn.; John C. White, AV Libn.

★ 17392 ★
U.S. Dept. of Veterans Affairs (OH-Chillicothe) - Medical Library (142D) (Med)
Chillicothe, OH 45601   Phone: (614)773-1141
                                         John A. Package, Chf., Lib.Serv.
Founded: 1947. **Staff:** Prof 3; Other 3. **Subjects:** Psychiatry, medicine, allied health sciences. **Holdings:** 2793 volumes. **Subscriptions:** 373 journals and other serials. **Services:** Interlibrary loan; copying; SDI. **Computerized Information Services:** MEDLARS, BRS Information Technologies. **Networks/Consortia:** Member of VALNET. **Remarks:** Patients' library contains an additional 3713 volumes. FAX: (614)772-7041. **Staff:** Merle Alexander; Jennifer Gray, AV Libn.; Sue Starr; G.J. Cordle; Daisy Justice.

★ 17393 ★
U.S. Dept. of Veterans Affairs (OH-Cincinnati) - Medical Center Library (Med)
3200 Vine St.   Phone: (513)559-6691
Cincinnati, OH 45220   Judith Alfred, Chf., Lrng.Rsrcs.Serv.
Founded: 1954. **Staff:** Prof 2. **Subjects:** Medicine, mental health, nursing, surgery. **Special Collections:** PERC (Patient Education Resource Center). **Holdings:** 10,036 volumes. **Subscriptions:** 318 journals and other serials. **Services:** Interlibrary loan; SDI; library open to the public. **Automated Operations:** Computerized cataloging, serials, acquisitions, and ILL. **Computerized Information Services:** NLM, BRS Information Technologies; MAILMAN (electronic mail service). **Networks/Consortia:** Member of VALNET. **Remarks:** FAX: (513)559-6694. **Staff:** Robert Mohrman, Med.Libn.

★ 17394 ★
U.S. Dept. of Veterans Affairs (OH-Dayton) - Medical Center Library Service (142D) (Med)
4100 W. Third St.   Phone: (513)268-6511
Dayton, OH 45428   Lendell L. Beverly, Chf., Lib.Serv.
Founded: 1867. **Staff:** Prof 5; Other 4. **Subjects:** Medicine, nursing, hospital administration, patient education, local VA history. **Special Collections:** Dayton VA history; patient education. **Holdings:** 7000 books; 4840 bound periodical volumes. **Subscriptions:** 500 journals and other serials. **Services:** Interlibrary loan; copying; SDI; library open to the public for reference use only. **Automated Operations:** Computerized public access catalog, serials, circulation, ILL (DOCLINE). **Computerized Information Services:** BRS Information Technologies, NLM, DIALOG Information Services. **Networks/Consortia:** Member of VALNET, National Network of Libraries of Medicine - Greater Midwest Region. **Publications:** Fact Sheet; new book list, quarterly; Library Link Up (newsletter), monthly; Resources for Managers and Supervisors; Total Quality Management Bibliography. **Special Catalogs:** AV Catalog. **Remarks:** Patients' library contains an additional 5000 volumes. FAX: (513)262-2181. **Staff:** Jim Koegel, AV Libn.; Miriam Carrigg-Wise, Ref.Libn.; Melissa Rumbarger, Hist.; Peter Sullivan, Patient Educ.Libn.

★ 17395 ★
U.S. Dept. of Veterans Affairs (OK-Muskogee) - Medical Center Library (Med)
1101 Honor Height Dr.   Phone: (918)683-3261
Muskogee, OK 74401   Jeanine Brown, Chf., Lib.Serv.
Staff: Prof 1; Other 2. **Subjects:** Medicine, nursing, allied health sciences. **Holdings:** 3269 books; 4584 bound periodical volumes; 737 AV programs. **Subscriptions:** 275 medical journals; 12 newspapers. **Services:** Interlibrary loan; copying; SDI; library open to the public for reference use only. **Automated Operations:** Computerized cataloging and acquisitions. **Computerized Information Services:** MEDLARS, BRS Information Technologies; MAILMAN (electronic mail service). **Networks/Consortia:** Member of VALNET, Oklahoma Health Sciences Library Association (OHSLA). **Remarks:** Patients' library contains an additional 3076 volumes and 172 patient education programs. FAX: (918)683-0488.

★ 17396 ★
U.S. Dept. of Veterans Affairs (OK-Oklahoma City) - Medical Center Library (Med)
921 N.E. 13th St.   Phone: (405)270-0501
Oklahoma City, OK 73104   Verlean Delaney, Chf.Libn.
Founded: 1946. **Staff:** 3. **Subjects:** Medicine, patient health education. **Holdings:** 2243 books; 459 AV programs; talking books. **Subscriptions:** 310 journals and other serials. **Services:** Interlibrary loan; copying; SDI; library open to the public for reference use only. **Computerized Information Services:** MEDLINE, BRS Information Technologies; DOCLINE, MAILMAN (electronic mail services). **Networks/Consortia:** Member of VALNET, Greater Oklahoma City Area Health Sciences Library Consortium (GOAL), Metronet. **Publications:** Library Notes, biweekly - for internal distribution. **Remarks:** FAX: (405)270-5145. **Staff:** Delores Loudermilk, Libn.

★ 17397 ★
U.S. Dept. of Veterans Affairs (OR-Portland) - Medical Library (Med)
Box 1034   Phone: (503)220-8262
Portland, OR 97207   Mara R. Wilhelm, Chf., Lib.Serv.
Staff: Prof 3; Other 2. **Subjects:** Medicine, nursing, allied health sciences, psychology, basic sciences. **Special Collections:** Patient Health Information. **Holdings:** 7681 books; 6010 bound periodical volumes; journals on microfilm. **Subscriptions:** 613 journals; 111 administrative serials. **Services:** Interlibrary loan; copying; SDI; library open to the public for reference use only. **Computerized Information Services:** MEDLARS, BRS Information Technologies; CD-ROMs (MEDLINE, CINAHL); OnTyme Electronic Message Network Service (electronic mail service). **Networks/Consortia:** Member of VALNET, Oregon Health Sciences Libraries Association (OHSLA). **Publications:** Acquisitions List - for internal distribution only. **Remarks:** FAX: (503)721-7816. Electronic mail address(es): VAPO (OnTyme Electronic Message Network Service). **Staff:** Cathy M. Jordan; Sandra Brayson.

★ 17398 ★
U.S. Dept. of Veterans Affairs (OR-Portland) - Vancouver Division - Medical Library (Med)
Box 1035   Phone: (206)696-4061
Portland, OR 97207   Mara R. Wilhelm, Chf., Lib.Serv.
Founded: 1946. **Staff:** 1. **Subjects:** Medicine. **Special Collections:** Patient Health Information. **Holdings:** Figures not available. **Services:** Interlibrary loan; SDI; library open to the public for reference use only. **Computerized Information Services:** MEDLARS, BRS Information Technologies; OnTyme Electronic Message Network Service (electronic mail service). **Networks/Consortia:** Member of VALNET. **Remarks:** FAX: (206)690-0340. Electronic mail address(es): CLASS.VAPOV (OnTyme Electronic Message Network Service). **Staff:** Cathy Jordan, Libn.

★ 17399 ★
U.S. Dept. of Veterans Affairs (OR-Roseburg) - Medical Center Library Service (Med)
913 N.W. Garden Valley Blvd.   Phone: (503)440-1000
Roseburg, OR 97470   Hope Reenstjerna
Staff: Prof 1; Other 1. **Subjects:** Medicine, patient education, management, nursing. **Holdings:** 4400 books; 500 AV programs; 40 journals on microfilm. large-print materials. **Subscriptions:** 300 journals and other serials; 6 newspapers. **Services:** Interlibrary loan; copying; SDI; library open to the public when referred by another librarian. **Automated Operations:** Computerized public access catalog and circulation. **Computerized Information Services:** NLM, BRS Information Technologies; MAILMAN (electronic mail service). **Networks/Consortia:** Member of VALNET, Oregon Health Information Online (ORHION), Oregon Health Sciences Libraries Association (OHSLA). **Publications:** Newsletter, quarterly - for internal distribution and to other librarians.

★ 17400 ★
U.S. Dept. of Veterans Affairs (OR-White City) - Library (Med)
8495 Crater Lake Hwy.   Phone: (503)826-2111
White City, OR 97503   Sarah Fitzpatrick, Chf., Lib.Serv.
Staff: Prof 2; Other 1. **Subjects:** Medicine. **Holdings:** 11,000 books; 762 bound periodical volumes. **Subscriptions:** 362 journals and other serials; 4 newspapers. **Services:** Interlibrary loan; library not open to the public. **Computerized Information Services:** MAILMAN (electronic mail service). **Networks/Consortia:** Member of VALNET. **Staff:** Margaret C. Rose, Libn.

★ 17401 ★
U.S. Dept. of Veterans Affairs (PA-Altoona) - James E. Van Zandt
  Medical Center - Library Service (142D) (Med)
2907 Pleasant Valley Blvd.   Phone: (814)943-8164
Altoona, PA 16602-4377   Dorothy McCorvey, Chf.,Lib.Serv.
Founded: 1950. **Staff:** Prof 1; Other 1. **Subjects:** Medicine, patient education,
management. **Holdings:** 5089 books; 500 periodical volumes; 1355 reels of
microfilm and AV programs. **Subscriptions:** 220 journals and other serials;
43 newspapers. **Services:** Interlibrary loan; copying; SDI; library open to the
public with restrictions. **Automated Operations:** Computerized cataloging.
Computerized Information Services: BRS Information Technologies, NLM;
FILEMAN (internal database); MAILMAN (electronic mail service).
Networks/Consortia: Member of Central Pennsylvania Health Sciences
Library Association (CPHSLA), VALNET. **Publications:** Orientation
booklets for patients and medical staff.

★ 17402 ★
U.S. Dept. of Veterans Affairs (PA-Butler) - Medical Center Library
  (Med)
325 New Castle Rd.   Phone: (412)287-4781
Butler, PA 16001   Dianne Hohn, Chf., Lib.Serv.
Founded: 1946. **Staff:** Prof 2; Other 1. **Subjects:** Nursing, general medicine.
Holdings: 1200 books; 3000 periodical volumes, bound and in microform.
Subscriptions: 100 journals and other serials; 10 newspapers. **Services:**
Interlibrary loan; copying; library open to the public for reference use only.
Computerized Information Services: BRS Information Technologies.
Networks/Consortia: Member of VALNET. **Remarks:** Patients' library
contains an additional 4000 volumes. **Staff:** Donna D. Blose, Libn.

★ 17403 ★
U.S. Dept. of Veterans Affairs (PA-Coatesville) - Medical Center
  Library (142D) (Med)
1400 Black Horse Hill Rd.   Phone: (215)383-0288
Coatesville, PA 19320-2097   Mary Lou Burton, Chf., Lib.Serv.
Founded: 1930. **Staff:** Prof 3; Other 3. **Subjects:** Psychiatry, neurology,
medicine, nursing, psychology. **Holdings:** 7200 books; 8000 bound
periodical volumes; 10 VF drawers of information files; 1500 AV programs.
Subscriptions: 150 journals and other serials; 5 newspapers. **Services:**
Interlibrary loan; copying; library open to health service personnel only.
Automated Operations: Computerized serials. **Computerized Information
Services:** BRS Information Technologies, MEDLARS; CD-ROM
(MEDLINE, CINAHL, PsycLIT). **Networks/Consortia:** Member of
VALNET, Consortium for Health Information & Library Services (CHI).
Remarks: Patients' library contains an additional 5000 volumes. FAX:
(215)383-0245. FTS: 489-7245. **Staff:** Andrew Henry, Libn.; Mary L.
Walters, Libn.

★ 17404 ★
U.S. Dept. of Veterans Affairs (PA-Erie) - Medical Center Library
  (Med)
135 E. 38th St.   Phone: (814)868-6207
Erie, PA 16504   Robert M. Schnick, Chf., Lib.Serv.
Founded: 1951. **Staff:** Prof 1; Other 2. **Subjects:** Medicine, nursing,
geriatrics, quality assurance. **Special Collections:** The classics of medicine
library (70 volumes). **Holdings:** 3000 books; 4000 reels of periodical
microfilm. **Subscriptions:** 120 journals and other serials; 15 newspapers.
Services: Interlibrary loan; copying; SDI. **Automated Operations:**
Computerized cataloging. **Computerized Information Services:**
MEDLARS; FILEMAN (internal database); MAILMAN (electronic mail
service). **Networks/Consortia:** Member of VALNET, Erie Area Health
Information Library Cooperative (EAHILC), Northwest Interlibrary
Cooperative of Pennsylvania (NICOP). **Publications:** Periodicals holdings
list, annual - for internal distribution only. **Remarks:** FAX: (814)868-6240.

★ 17405 ★
U.S. Dept. of Veterans Affairs (PA-Lebanon) - Medical Center Library
  (Med)
State Drive   Phone: (717)272-6621
Lebanon, PA 17042   David E. Falger, Chf., Lib.Serv.
Founded: 1947. **Staff:** Prof 3; Other 3. **Subjects:** Medicine, aging and
geriatrics, psychiatry. **Holdings:** 2433 books; 1250 periodical volumes on
microfilm. **Subscriptions:** 305 journals and other serials; 31 newspapers.
Services: Interlibrary loan; copying (limited); library open to the public with
restrictions. **Computerized Information Services:** DIALOG Information
Services, MEDLINE, BRS Information Technologies; MAILMAN,

DOCLINE (electronic mail services). **Networks/Consortia:** Member of
VALNET, National Network of Libraries of Medicine - Middle Atlantic
Region, Central Pennsylvania Health Sciences Library Association
(CPHSLA). **Publications:** Quarterly newsletter. **Remarks:** Patients' library
contains an additional 7100 books. FAX: (717)272-2867. **Staff:** Barbara E.
Deaven, Med.Libn.; Michelle Clark, Patients' Libn.

★ 17406 ★
U.S. Dept. of Veterans Affairs (PA-Philadelphia) - Medical Center
  Library (142D) (Med)
University & Woodland Aves.   Phone: (215)823-5860
Philadelphia, PA 19104   Carol R. Glatt, Chf., Lib.Serv.
Founded: 1953. **Staff:** Prof 2; Other 2. **Subjects:** Medicine and allied health
sciences. **Holdings:** 4275 books; 7350 bound periodical volumes.
Subscriptions: 451 journals and other serials. **Services:** Interlibrary loan;
copying; SDI; library open to the public by permission. **Computerized
Information Services:** BRS Information Technologies, MEDLINE;
DOCLINE, MAILMAN (electronic mail services). **Networks/Consortia:**
Member of VALNET, Delaware Valley Information Consortium (DEVIC),
National Network of Libraries of Medicine - Middle Atlantic Region.
Publications: Holdings list, quarterly. **Remarks:** FAX: (215)823-5108.
Electronic mail address(es): LIBIB=19104D (DOCLINE). **Staff:** Angela
Chow, Libn.

★ 17407 ★
U.S. Dept. of Veterans Affairs (PA-Pittsburgh) - Medical Center Library
  Service (142D) (Med)
Highland Dr.   Phone: (412)365-5515
Pittsburgh, PA 15206   Sandra Mason, Chf.
Founded: 1953. **Staff:** Prof 2; Other 1. **Subjects:** Psychiatry, general
medicine, neurology, nursing, social work. **Holdings:** 3319 books; 8 VF
drawers of pamphlets; 458 video cassettes. **Subscriptions:** 298 journals and
other serials; 6 newspapers. **Services:** Interlibrary loan; library not open to
the public. **Computerized Information Services:** MEDLARS, BRS
Information Technologies. **Networks/Consortia:** Member of VALNET.
Publications: Bibliographies. **Remarks:** Patients' library contains an
additional 6310 volumes. FAX: (413)365-4809.

★ 17408 ★
U.S. Dept. of Veterans Affairs (PA-Pittsburgh) - Medical Center Library
  Service (142D) (Med)
University Dr. C   Phone: (412)692-3259
Pittsburgh, PA 15240   Terrie R. Wheeler, Libn.,MLS
Founded: 1946. **Staff:** Prof 3; Other 2. **Subjects:** Medicine, surgery,
gerontology, and allied health sciences. **Holdings:** 2200 books; 12,400 bound
periodical volumes. **Subscriptions:** 400 journals and other serials. **Services:**
Interlibrary loan; copying; SDI. **Computerized Information Services:**
MEDLARS; MAILMAN (electronic mail service). **Networks/Consortia:**
Member of VALNET, BHSL. **Publications:** New acquisitions lists.
Remarks: Alternate telephone number(s): (412)692-3260. FAX: (412)692-
3265. **Staff:** Tuula Beazell, Libn.; Norma Lodico, Libn.

★ 17409 ★
U.S. Dept. of Veterans Affairs (PA-Wilkes-Barre) - Medical Center
  Library (Med)
1111 E. End Blvd.   Phone: (717)824-3521
Wilkes-Barre, PA 18711   Bruce D. Reid, Chf., Lib.Serv.
Founded: 1950. **Staff:** Prof 2; Other 2. **Subjects:** Medicine, allied health
sciences. **Special Collections:** Internal Medicine. **Holdings:** 3900 books;
2600 bound periodical volumes; journals on microfilm. **Subscriptions:** 234
journals and other serials. **Services:** Interlibrary loan; library open to the
public with restrictions. **Computerized Information Services:** MEDLINE,
BRS Information Technologies; MAILMAN (electronic mail service).
Networks/Consortia: Member of VALNET, Northeastern Pennsylvania
Bibliographic Center (NEPBC), Health Information Library Network of
Northeastern Pennsylvania (HILNNEP). **Remarks:** Patients' library
contains an additional 3500 volumes. **Remarks:** FAX: (717)821-7264. **Staff:**
Jay Sufferen, Libn.

★ 17410 ★
U.S. Dept. of Veterans Affairs (PR-San Juan) - Hospital Library (Med)
VA Medical & Regional Office Ctr.
1 Veteran Plaza   Phone: (809)758-7575
San Juan, PR 00927-5800   Raquel A. Walters, Chf., Lib.Serv.
Founded: 1947. **Staff:** Prof 2; Other 2. **Subjects:** Medicine and specialties, nursing, surgery and specialties, dietetics and nutrition. **Holdings:** 8598 books and bound periodical volumes; AV programs. **Subscriptions:** 610 journals and other serials. **Services:** Interlibrary loan; library open to the public through sharing agreements with community institutions. **Computerized Information Services:** NLM. **Publications:** Annual Periodical Holding List; Quarterly New Medical Books List; Annual Library Orientation Guide. **Remarks:** Patients' library contains an additional 8745 volumes with special collections on the Caribbean, management, talking books. **Staff:** Virginia E. Budet, Patients' Libn.

★ 17411 ★
U.S. Dept. of Veterans Affairs (RI-Providence) - Health Sciences Library (Med)
Davis Park   Phone: (401)457-3001
Providence, RI 02908   Nicola F. Pallotti, Lib.Techn.
Founded: 1949. **Staff:** Prof 2. **Subjects:** Medicine, nursing, and allied health sciences. **Holdings:** 2249 books; AV programs. **Subscriptions:** 261 journals and other serials. **Services:** Interlibrary loan; copying; SDI; library open to the public for reference use only. **Computerized Information Services:** MEDLINE, BRS Information Technologies; DOCLINE, VALNET (electronic mail services). **Networks/Consortia:** Member of North Atlantic Health Science Libraries (NAHSL), Association of Rhode Island Health Sciences Librarians (ARIHSL). **Remarks:** Patients' library contains patient health education collection. FAX: (401)457-3097.

★ 17412 ★
U.S. Dept. of Veterans Affairs (SC-Columbia) - William Jennings Bryan-Dorn Veterans Hospital - Library (Med)
VA Medical Center   Phone: (803)776-4000
Columbia, SC 29201   Charletta P. Felder, Chf., Lib.Serv.
Founded: 1933. **Staff:** Prof 2. **Subjects:** Medicine, surgery, nursing, dentistry, psychiatry. **Holdings:** 3817 books; 3200 bound periodical volumes; 15 drawers of microfilm; 800 AV programs. **Subscriptions:** 250 journals and other serials; 12 newspapers. **Services:** Interlibrary loan; copying; SDI; library open to the public. **Computerized Information Services:** MEDLINE; OnTyme Electronic Message Network Service (electronic mail service). **Networks/Consortia:** Member of VALNET, Columbia Area Medical Librarians' Association (CAMLA). **Remarks:** Patients' library contains an additional 6500 volumes. **Staff:** Emily E. Clyburn, Staff Libn.

★ 17413 ★
U.S. Dept. of Veterans Affairs (SD-Fort Meade) - Medical Center Library Service (142D) (Med)
113 Comanche Rd.   Phone: (605)347-2511
Fort Meade, SD 57741-1099   Gene Stevens, Chf., Lib.Serv.
Founded: 1942. **Staff:** Prof 1, Other 1. **Subjects:** Medicine and allied health sciences. **Holdings:** 1000 books; 700 volumes of journals on microfilm; 220 AV programs. **Subscriptions:** 140 journals and other serials. **Services:** Interlibrary loan; copying; library open to the public. **Computerized Information Services:** MEDLINE; MAILMAN (electronic mail service). Performs searches free of charge. **Networks/Consortia:** Member of VALNET, South Dakota Library Network (SDLN). **Remarks:** Patients' library contains an additional 3700 titles. FAX: (605)347-5460.

★ 17414 ★
U.S. Dept. of Veterans Affairs (SD-Hot Springs) - Center Library (Med)
Hot Springs, SD 57747   Phone: (605)745-2013
                                                   Carole W. Miles, Chf., Lib.Serv.
Staff: Prof 1; Other 1. **Subjects:** Geriatrics, surgery. **Holdings:** 845 books; 781 bound periodical volumes. **Subscriptions:** 108 journals and other serials. **Services:** Interlibrary loan; library open to the medical community. **Remarks:** Patients' library contains an additional 10,135 volumes. FAX: (605)745-2082.

★ 17415 ★
U.S. Dept. of Veterans Affairs (SD-Sioux Falls) - Medical & Regional Office Center - Medical Library (Med)
2501 W. 22nd St.
Box 5046   Phone: (605)336-3230
Sioux Falls, SD 57117   Raisa Cherniv, Chf., Lib.Serv.
Staff: Prof 2; Other 2. **Subjects:** General medicine and allied health. **Special Collections:** AV medical collection (1200 programs). **Holdings:** 3800 books; 4631 bound periodical volumes; 4968 reels of microfilm; 800 AV programs. **Subscriptions:** 300 journals and other serials; 50 newspapers. **Services:** Interlibrary loan; copying; SDI; library open to medical and allied health professionals. **Computerized Information Services:** NLM, BRS Information Technologies. **Networks/Consortia:** Member of VALNET. **Remarks:** Patients' library contains an additional 2984 volumes. FAX: (605)333-6893.

★ 17416 ★
U.S. Dept. of Veterans Affairs (TN-Johnson City) - Medical Center Library (Med)
Mountain Home, TN 37684   Phone: (615)926-1171
                                                   Nancy Dougherty, Chf., Lib.Serv.
Staff: Prof 2; Other 1. **Subjects:** Medicine and allied health sciences. **Holdings:** 2925 books; 3681 bound periodical volumes. **Subscriptions:** 315 journals and other serials. **Services:** Interlibrary loan; library open to the public with restrictions. **Automated Operations:** Computerized ILL. **Computerized Information Services:** MEDLARS, BRS Information Technologies; MAILMAN (electronic mail service). **Networks/Consortia:** Member of VALNET, Tri-Cities Area Health Sciences Libraries Consortium. **Remarks:** Patients' library contains an additional 18,000 volumes. FAX: (615)926-1171, ext. 7289. **Staff:** Joan Warden, Libn.; Lisa Kornblau, Libn.

★ 17417 ★
U.S. Dept. of Veterans Affairs (TN-Memphis) - Medical Center Library (Med)
1030 Jefferson Ave.   Phone: (901)523-8990
Memphis, TN 38104   Mary Virginia Taylor, Chf., Lib.Serv.
Founded: 1941. **Staff:** Prof 2; Other 2. **Subjects:** Medicine, dentistry, nursing. **Holdings:** 4650 books; 3377 bound periodical volumes; microfilm. **Subscriptions:** 250 journals and other serials. **Services:** Interlibrary loan; SDI; library open to the public for reference use only. **Computerized Information Services:** BRS Information Technologies, MEDLINE; MAILMAN (electronic mail service). **Networks/Consortia:** Member of VALNET, Association of Memphis Area Health Science Libraries (AMAHSL). **Remarks:** FAX: (901)523-8990, ext. 5657. Patients' library contains an additional 2000 volumes.

★ 17418 ★
U.S. Dept. of Veterans Affairs (TN-Murfreesboro) - Medical Center Library Service (Med)
Murfreesboro, TN 37130   Phone: (615)893-1360
                                                   Joy W. Hunter, Chf., Lib.Serv.
Staff: Prof 3; Other 1. **Subjects:** Psychiatry, medicine, nursing, geriatrics. **Holdings:** 2800 books; 1200 bound periodical volumes; 1200 AV programs. **Subscriptions:** 280 journals and other serials. **Services:** Interlibrary loan; library not open to the public. **Automated Operations:** Computerized cataloging and serials. **Computerized Information Services:** BRS Information Technologies, MEDLINE. **Networks/Consortia:** Member of VALNET. **Publications:** Libragram, quarterly - for internal distribution only. **Remarks:** Patients' library contains patient education and wellness materials. FAX: (615)893-2490. **Staff:** Marie Eubanks, Med.Libn.; Ruby H. Nichols, Patients' Libn.

★ 17419 ★
U.S. Dept. of Veterans Affairs (TN-Nashville) - Medical Center Library Service (Med)
1310 24th Ave., S.   Phone: (615)327-4751
Nashville, TN 37212   Barbara A. Meadows, Chf., Lib.Serv.
Founded: 1946. **Staff:** Prof 2; Other 1. **Subjects:** Medicine, nursing, dentistry, surgery. **Holdings:** 2843 books; 2600 bound periodical volumes; 775 AV programs; 2757 periodical volumes on microfilm. **Subscriptions:** 356 journals and other serials. **Services:** Interlibrary loan; copying; library open to the public for reference use only. **Automated Operations:** Computerized cataloging, acquisitions, ILL, and serials. **Computerized Information Services:** MEDLINE; CD-ROM; VALNET (electronic mail service). **Networks/Consortia:** Member of VALNET, Mid-Tennessee Health Sciences Librarians Consortium (MTHSLC). **Remarks:** FAX: (615)327-4751, ext. 5803. **Staff:** A. Faye Kulp, Med.Libn.

★ 17420 ★
U.S. Dept. of Veterans Affairs (TX-Amarillo) - Hospital Library (Med)
Amarillo, TX 79106   Phone: (806)354-7877
Founded: 1941. **Staff:** Other 1. **Subjects:** General medicine, surgery, nursing, dentistry. **Special Collections:** Staff and patient education collection (550 AV programs; 150 pamphlet titles). **Holdings:** 3894 books; periodicals on microfilm. **Subscriptions:** 235 journals and other serials. **Services:** Interlibrary loan; copying; library open to area medical personnel only. **Computerized Information Services:** MAILMAN (electronic mail service). **Networks/Consortia:** Member of VALNET. **Publications:** Medical Newsletter, quarterly; serials listing. **Special Catalogs:** Patient Education Materials Catalog.

★ 17421 ★
U.S. Dept. of Veterans Affairs (TX-Big Spring) - Hospital Library (Med)
2400 S. Gregg St.   Phone: (915)263-7361
Big Spring, TX 79720   Don Fortner
Founded: 1950. **Staff:** Prof 1. **Subjects:** General medicine, surgery. **Holdings:** 700 books; **Subscriptions:** 40 journals and other serials. **Services:** Interlibrary loan; library open to qualified health personnel only. **Computerized Information Services:** MEDLARS.

★ 17422 ★
U.S. Dept. of Veterans Affairs (TX-Bonham) - Sam Rayburn Memorial Veterans Center - Medical Library (Med)
E. 9th & Lipscomb Sts.   Phone: (903)583-2111
Bonham, TX 75418   Elizabeth J. Alme, Chf., Lib.Serv.
Founded: 1951. **Staff:** Prof 1; Other 3. **Subjects:** Medicine and allied health sciences. **Holdings:** 1011 books; 110 Audio-Digest tapes. **Subscriptions:** 152 journals and other serials. **Services:** Interlibrary loan; copying; SDI; library open to the public with restrictions. **Computerized Information Services:** MEDLARS, BRS Information Technologies; MAILMAN (electronic mail service). Performs searches free of charge. **Networks/Consortia:** Member of VALNET. **Remarks:** Patients' library contains an additional 4423 books. FAX: (214)583-2111, ext. 6304.

★ 17423 ★
U.S. Dept. of Veterans Affairs (TX-Dallas) - Library Service (142D) (Med)
4500 S. Lancaster Rd.   Phone: (214)372-7025
Dallas, TX 75216   Nancy A. Clark, Chf., Lib.Serv.
Founded: 1940. **Staff:** Prof 2; Other 2. **Subjects:** Medicine, surgery, allied health sciences, management. **Special Collections:** Patient health information. **Holdings:** 4500 books; 10,000 bound periodical volumes; 4500 volumes on microfilm; 1000 AV programs. **Subscriptions:** 480 journals and other serials. **Services:** Interlibrary loan; SDI; library open to health care personnel. **Automated Operations:** Computerized cataloging. **Computerized Information Services:** MEDLARS, BRS Information Technologies; MAILMAN (electronic mail service). **Networks/Consortia:** Member of VALNET, Health Libraries Information Network (HealthLINE). **Remarks:** FAX: (214)372-7939. **Staff:** Shirley A. Campbell, Med.Libn.

★ 17424 ★
U.S. Dept. of Veterans Affairs (TX-Houston) - Medical Center Library (Med)
2002 Holcombe Blvd.   Phone: (713)791-1414
Houston, TX 77030   Jerry E. Barrett
Staff: Prof 3; Other 2. **Subjects:** Medicine. **Holdings:** 2864 books; 7500 periodical volumes. **Subscriptions:** 235 journals and other serials. **Services:** Interlibrary loan; library open to qualified users. **Computerized Information Services:** MEDLINE. **Networks/Consortia:** Member of VALNET.

★ 17425 ★
U.S. Dept. of Veterans Affairs (TX-Kerrville) - Health Sciences Library (Med)
Memorial Blvd.   Phone: (512)896-2020
Kerrville, TX 78028   Lois A. Johnson, Chf., Lib.Serv.
Founded: 1922. **Staff:** Prof 1. **Subjects:** Medicine and allied health sciences. **Holdings:** 2300 books; journals, 1967 to present, on microfilm; 400 video cassettes and 16mm films. **Subscriptions:** 125 journals and other serials. **Services:** Interlibrary loan; copying; SDI; AV loans; library open to the public for reference use only. **Automated Operations:** Computerized circulation. **Computerized Information Services:** MEDLINE; OnTyme Electronic Message Network Service (electronic mail service). **Networks/Consortia:** Member of National Network of Libraries of Medicine - South Central Region, Health Oriented Libraries of San Antonio (HOLSA), VALNET. **Publications:** Library Newsletters; Guide to New Media Titles; New Book List, all quarterly; Guide to the Use of the Health Sciences Library.

★ 17426 ★
U.S. Dept. of Veterans Affairs (TX-Marlin) - Medical Center Library Service (142D) (Med)
1016 Ward St.   Phone: (817)883-3511
Marlin, TX 76661   Mavis Williams, Act.Chf.
Founded: 1950. **Staff:** Prof 1; Other 1. **Subjects:** Medicine, nursing, allied health sciences, health care administration. **Holdings:** 780 books; 1031 periodical volumes on microfilm; unbound reports; pamphlets. **Subscriptions:** 112 journals and other serials. **Services:** Interlibrary loan; copying; library open to the public. **Networks/Consortia:** Member of VALNET. **Remarks:** FAX: (817)883-3511. Telex: 246 728 1246.

★ 17427 ★
U.S. Dept. of Veterans Affairs (TX-San Antonio) - Medical Center Library Service (142D) (Med)
7400 Merton Minter Blvd.   Phone: (512)617-5300
San Antonio, TX 78284   Elosia Mitchell, Chf.
Founded: 1973. **Staff:** Prof 2; Other 2. **Subjects:** Medicine, allied health sciences. **Holdings:** 4367 books; 5000 microfilm volumes; 503 AV programs. **Subscriptions:** 565 journals and other serials; 21 newspapers. **Services:** Interlibrary loan; library not open to the public. **Computerized Information Services:** NLM, BRS Information Technologies; DOCLINE, MAILMAN (electronic mail services). **Networks/Consortia:** Member of VALNET, Health Oriented Libraries of San Antonio (HOLSA), Council of Research & Academic Libraries (CORAL). **Publications:** Library Newsletter, quarterly; Library Handbook, annual; subject bibliographies - for internal distribution only. **Remarks:** FAX: (512)694-5246.

★ 17428 ★
U.S. Dept. of Veterans Affairs (TX-Temple) - Medical Center Medical Library (Med)
Olin E. Teague Veterans Adm. Ctr.
1901 S. First St.   Phone: (817)778-4811
Temple, TX 76504   Barbara A. Ward, Chf., Lib.Serv.
Founded: 1942. **Staff:** Prof 3; Other 3. **Subjects:** Medicine, surgery, nursing, dentistry. **Special Collections:** Patient education. **Holdings:** 3500 books; 9038 bound periodical volumes; 8 VF drawers of clippings and pamphlets; 17 VF drawers of audio cassettes; 260 video cassette tapes. **Subscriptions:** 500 journals and other serials; 12 newspapers. **Services:** Interlibrary loan; copying. **Computerized Information Services:** NLM, BRS Information Technologies. **Networks/Consortia:** Member of VALNET, TAMU Consortium of Medical Libraries. **Remarks:** FAX: (817)771-4532. **Staff:** Elizabeth McCullough, Med.Libn.; Ruth Hempel, Med.Libn.

★ 17429 ★
U.S. Dept. of Veterans Affairs (TX-Waco) - Medical Center Library (Med)
4800 Memorial Dr.   Phone: (817)752-6581
Waco, TX 76711   Barbara H. Hobbs, Chf., Lib.Serv.
Founded: 1932. **Staff:** Prof 4; Other 4. **Subjects:** Psychiatry, neurology, psychology, nursing, gerontology, posttraumatic stress. **Holdings:** 3153 volumes; 1219 volumes on microfilm; 1046 AV programs; 8 VF drawers. **Subscriptions:** 320 journals and other serials. **Services:** Interlibrary loan; copying; library open to the public with restrictions. **Computerized Information Services:** MEDLINE, BRS Information Technologies; DOCLINE (electronic mail service). **Networks/Consortia:** Member of VALNET, National Network of Libraries of Medicine - South Central Region. **Publications:** Medical Library Newsletter, monthly - for internal distribution only. **Remarks:** FAX: (817)752-6581, ext. 6614. Electronic mail address(es): 76703A (DOCLINE). **Staff:** JoAnn Greenwood, Med.Libn.

★ 17430 ★
U.S. Dept. of Veterans Affairs (UT-Salt Lake City) - Hospital Medical Library (Med)
500 Foothill Dr.   Phone: (801)584-1209
Salt Lake City, UT 84148   Carl Worstell, Chf.Libn.
Staff: Prof 3; Other 4. **Subjects:** Medicine, surgery, psychiatry, emergency medicine, research, allied health sciences. **Special Collections:** Hospital Satellite Network Collection (170 videotapes). **Holdings:** 3000 books; 11,262 bound periodical volumes; 1696 reels of microfilm; 85 video cassettes; 240 pamphlets; 1830 other cataloged items. **Subscriptions:** 325 journals and other serials. **Services:** Interlibrary loan; copying; SDI; library open to the public for reference use only. **Computerized Information Services:** DIALOG Information Services, BRS Information Technologies, MEDLARS; MAILMAN, OnTyme Electronic Message Network Service,

DOCLINE (electronic mail services). **Networks/Consortia:** Member of VALNET, National Network of Libraries of Medicine - Midcontinental Region, Utah Health Sciences Library Consortium (UHSLC). **Publications:** Journal and audiovisual holdings lists, annual. **Remarks:** Patients' library contains an additional 2000 volumes. FAX: (801)584-1251. **Staff:** Kirk L. Davis, Libn.; Barbara B. Windley, Libn.

★ 17431 ★
U.S. Dept. of Veterans Affairs (VA-Hampton) - Medical Center Library (Med)
Hampton, VA 23667 Phone: (804)722-9961
Jacqueline Bird, Chf., Lib.Serv.
Staff: Prof 3; Other 1. **Subjects:** Surgery, medicine, nursing, psychology, patient education. **Holdings:** 4000 books; 800 bound periodical volumes; 7500 unbound periodicals volumes. **Subscriptions:** 425 journals and other serials. **Services:** Interlibrary loan (limited); library not open to the public. **Computerized Information Services:** BRS Information Technologies, MEDLINE. **Networks/Consortia:** Member of VALNET. **Publications:** Book lists, quarterly; special bibliographies. **Remarks:** Patients' library contains an additional 6000 volumes. FAX: (804)722-2988. **Staff:** Lori Beudoin, Med.Libn.; Sharon Durio, Med.Libn.

★ 17432 ★
U.S. Dept. of Veterans Affairs (VA-Richmond) - Hospital Library (Med)
1201 Broad Rock Blvd. Phone: (804)230-0001
Richmond, VA 23249 Eleanor Rollins, Chf., Lib.Serv.
Founded: 1945. **Staff:** Prof 2; Other 2. **Subjects:** Medicine, psychology, sociology. **Holdings:** 4000 books; 6000 bound periodical volumes; 1000 AV programs; 1000 volumes on microfilm. **Subscriptions:** 830 journals and other serials. **Services:** Interlibrary loan; copying; library open to the public with restrictions. **Remarks:** FAX: (804)230-0001, ext. 1961.

★ 17433 ★
U.S. Dept. of Veterans Affairs (VA-Salem) - Medical Center Library (Med)
1970 Roanoke Blvd. Phone: (703)982-2463
Salem, VA 24153 Jean A. Kennedy, Chf.Libn.
Founded: 1946. **Staff:** Prof 2; Other 2. **Subjects:** Medicine, psychiatry, nursing, allied health sciences. **Holdings:** 5100 books; 1220 AV programs. **Subscriptions:** 251 journals and other serials. **Services:** Interlibrary loan; SDI; library open to community health professionals. **Computerized Information Services:** MEDLARS, BRS Information Technologies. **Networks/Consortia:** Member of VALNET, Southwestern Virginia Health Information Librarians (SWVAHILI). **Publications:** Medical Library Books and AVs Bulletin, quarterly. **Remarks:** FAX: (703)983-1079. Patients' library contains an additional 8423 volumes. **Staff:** Susan B. DuGrenier, Patients' Libn.

★ 17434 ★
U.S. Dept. of Veterans Affairs (VT-White River Junction) - Medical & Regional Office Center - Library Service (Med)
White River Junction, VT 05001 Phone: (802)295-9363
Richard Haver, Chf., Lib.Serv.
Staff: Prof 1; Other 1. **Subjects:** Medicine, surgery, psychiatry, nursing. **Holdings:** 1000 books. **Subscriptions:** 240 journals and other serials. **Services:** Interlibrary loan; library not open to the public. **Automated Operations:** Computerized cataloging. **Computerized Information Services:** NLM, BRS Information Technologies, DIALOG Information Services, ; CD-ROM (MEDLINE Knowledge Finder); MAILMAN (electronic mail service). **Networks/Consortia:** Member of VALNET, Health Science Libraries of New Hampshire & Vermont (HSL-NH/VT). **Remarks:** FAX: (802)296-5150.

★ 17435 ★
U.S. Dept. of Veterans Affairs (WA-Seattle) - Hospital Medical Library (Med)
1660 S. Columbian Way, 142-D Phone: (206)764-2065
Seattle, WA 98108 Maryanne Blake, Chf., Lib.Serv.
Staff: Prof 2; Other 1. **Subjects:** Medicine. **Special Collections:** Health education program. **Holdings:** 1620 books; 4000 bound periodical volumes; 570 AV programs. **Subscriptions:** 365 journals and other serials. **Services:** Interlibrary loan; SDI; library open to the public for reference use only. **Computerized Information Services:** MEDLINE, BRS Information Technologies. **Networks/Consortia:** Member of VALNET, Seattle Area Hospital Library Consortium (SAHLC). **Publications:** Medical Library Newsletter, irregular - for internal distribution only. **Staff:** Mia Hannula, Med.Libn.

★ 17436 ★
U.S. Dept. of Veterans Affairs (WA-Spokane) - Medical Center Library (Med)
N. 4815 Assembly St. Phone: (509)328-4521
Spokane, WA 99205 Mary Curtis-Kellett, Chf., Lib.Serv.
Founded: 1950. **Staff:** Prof 1; Other 1. **Subjects:** Medicine and allied health sciences. **Special Collections:** Health Information Center. **Holdings:** 1441 books; 978 bound periodical volumes; 502 video cassettes; 15 models; pamphlets; patient teaching charts. **Subscriptions:** 168 journals and other serials. **Services:** Interlibrary loan; library not open to the public. **Computerized Information Services:** BRS Information Technologies, MEDLARS; OnTyme Electronic Message Network Service (electronic mail service). **Networks/Consortia:** Member of VALNET, Inland Northwest Health Sciences Libraries (INWHSL). **Remarks:** Patients' library contains an additional 100 volumes. FAX: (509)325-7922. Electronic mail address(es): CLASS.VAS (OnTyme Electronic Message Network Service).

★ 17437 ★
U.S. Dept. of Veterans Affairs (WA-Tacoma) - Medical Center Library Service (Med)
American Lake Phone: (206)582-8440
Tacoma, WA 98493 Dennis L. Levi, Chf., Lib.Serv.
Founded: 1924. **Staff:** Prof 2; Other 1. **Subjects:** Psychiatry, psychology, general medicine, nursing. **Holdings:** 1761 books; 2 VF drawers of pamphlets. **Subscriptions:** 262 journals and other serials; 33 newspapers. **Services:** Interlibrary loan; SDI; library open to the public for reference use only. **Computerized Information Services:** MEDLARS, BRS Information Technologies, MIALMAN, DOCLINE, OnTyme Electronic Message Network Service (electronic mail services). **Networks/Consortia:** Member of VALNET. **Remarks:** FAX: (206)582-8440. VAT (OnTyme Electronic Message Network Service); WAAME (Mailman). Patients' library contains an additional 3807 volumes. **Staff:** Enid Laulicht.

★ 17438 ★
U.S. Dept. of Veterans Affairs (WA-Walla Walla) - Hospital Library (Med)
77 Wainwright Dr. Phone: (509)525-5200
Walla Walla, WA 99362 Max J. Merrell, Chf.Libn.
Staff: Prof 1. **Subjects:** Medicine, surgery, nursing, allied health sciences. **Holdings:** 1500 books; 700 volumes of journals. **Subscriptions:** 100 journals and other serials. **Services:** Interlibrary loan; copying; SDI; library open to the public for reference use only; borrowing by special permission of librarian. **Computerized Information Services:** MEDLINE. **Networks/Consortia:** Member of VALNET, Western Library Network (WLN). **Special Catalogs:** VA Medical District Union List of Audiovisuals in Walla Walla. **Remarks:** Patients' library contains an additional 1000 volumes. FAX: (509)525-5200, ext. 2663.

★ 17439 ★
U.S. Dept. of Veterans Affairs (WI-Madison) - William S. Middleton Memorial Veterans Hospital - Library (Med)
2500 Overlook Terr. Phone: (608)256-1901
Madison, WI 53705 Phyllis E. Goetz, Chf., Lib.Serv.
Founded: 1951. **Staff:** Prof 1; Other 2. **Subjects:** General medicine. **Holdings:** 6303 books; 15,700 bound periodical volumes; 2566 journal volumes on microfilm. **Subscriptions:** 268 journals and other serials. **Services:** Interlibrary loan; library not open to the public. **Computerized Information Services:** MEDLINE; VALNET (internal database); MAILMAN, DOCLINE (electronic mail services). **Networks/Consortia:** Member of South Central Wisconsin Health Science Libraries Consortium, VALNET. **Remarks:** FAX: (608)262-7685

★ 17440 ★
U.S. Dept. of Veterans Affairs (WI-Milwaukee) - Medical Center Library (Med)
5000 W. National Ave. Phone: (414)384-2000
Milwaukee, WI 53295 Maureen L. Farmer, Chf., Lib.Serv.
Founded: 1946. **Staff:** Prof 3; Other 3. **Subjects:** Medicine, nursing, dentistry, allied health sciences. **Holdings:** 5500 books; 5000 bound periodical volumes; 2000 AV programs. **Subscriptions:** 525 journals and other serials. **Services:** Interlibrary loan; SDI; library open to the public with restrictions. **Automated Operations:** Computerized serials. **Computerized Information Services:** MEDLARS, BRS Information Technologies, DIALOG Information Services; internal database; DOCLINE, MAILMAN (electronic mail services). **Networks/Consortia:** Member of VALNET, Southeastern Wisconsin Health Science Library Consortium (SWHSL). **Remarks:** FAX: (414)382-5334. Patients' library contains an additional 20,000 volumes. **Staff:** Janice Curnes, Med.Libn.; Cathy Peterson, Patient Libn.

★ 17441 ★
U.S. Dept. of Veterans Affairs (WI-Tomah) - Medical Center Library
(142D) (Med)
Tomah, WI 54660   Phone: (608)372-1716
                                          Xena C. Kenyon, Chf., Lib.Serv.
Founded: 1947. **Staff:** Prof 2; Other 4. **Subjects:** Psychiatry, neurology,
general medicine, psychology, nursing, aging. **Holdings:** 2612 books; 171
bound periodical volumes; 1344 volumes of unbound journals; 596
periodical volumes on microfilm; 278 AV programs. **Subscriptions:** 235
journals and other serials. **Services:** Interlibrary loan; copying; library open
to the public. **Automated Operations:** Computerized ILL (DOCLINE).
Computerized Information Services: MEDLINE, BRS Information
Technologies; MAILMAN (electronic mail service). Performs searches free
of charge. **Networks/Consortia:** Member of VALNET. **Publications:**
Acquisitions List; special bibliographies. **Remarks:** Patients' library contains
an additional 5381 volumes, 106 periodical titles, and 299 AV programs.
FAX: (608)372-6670. **Staff:** Glen Salter, Med.Libn.

★ 17442 ★
U.S. Dept. of Veterans Affairs (WV-Beckley) - Library Service (Med)
200 Veterans Ave.   Phone: (304)255-2121
Beckley, WV 25801   Lois M. Watson, Chf., Lib.Serv.
Founded: 1951. **Staff:** Prof 1. **Subjects:** Medicine, nursing, surgery.
Holdings: 1004 volumes; 973 journal volumes; 2 VF drawers of patient
education pamphlets; Audio-Digest tapes; microfilm. **Subscriptions:** 117
journals and other serials. **Services:** Interlibrary loan; copying; library open
to college students by appointment. **Computerized Information Services:**
MEDLARS. **Networks/Consortia:** Member of VALNET. **Remarks:**
Patients' library contains an additional 1911 volumes.

★ 17443 ★
U.S. Dept. of Veterans Affairs (WV-Clarksburg) - Medical Center
Library Service (Med)
Rte. 98   Phone: (304)623-3461
Clarksburg, WV 26301   Wanda F. Kincaid, Chf.,Lib.Serv.
Founded: 1950. **Staff:** Prof 1; Other 1. **Subjects:** Medicine. **Holdings:** 1415
books; 2330 bound periodical volumes. **Subscriptions:** 194 journals and
other serials; 10 newspapers. **Services:** Interlibrary loan; copying; library
open to the public for reference use only. **Computerized Information
Services:** NLM; DOCLINE, MAILMAN (electronic mail services).
Networks/Consortia: Member of VALNET. **Remarks:** Patients' library
contains an additional 3448 volumes.

★ 17444 ★
U.S. Dept. of Veterans Affairs (WV-Huntington) - Medical Center
Library (Med)
1540 Spring Valley Dr.   Phone: (304)429-6741
Huntington, WV 25704   Bruce Thornlow, Chf., Lib.Serv.
Founded: 1931. **Staff:** Prof 1; Other 1. **Subjects:** Clinical medicine. **Holdings:**
1000 books; Audio-Digest tapes; microfilm. **Subscriptions:** 189 journals and
other serials. **Services:** Interlibrary loan; SDI; library open to the public with
restrictions. **Automated Operations:** Computerized ILL (DOCLINE).
Computerized Information Services: MEDLINE. **Networks/Consortia:**
Member of VALNET, West Virginia Biomedical Information Network,
Huntington Health Science Library Consortium. **Remarks:** FAX: (304)429-
6741, ext. 2267.

★ 17445 ★
U.S. Dept. of Veterans Affairs (WV-Martinsburg) - Center Medical
Library (Med)
Martinsburg, WV 25401   Phone: (304)263-0811
                                           Barbara S. Adams, Chf.Libn.
Founded: 1945. **Staff:** Prof 2; Other 2. **Subjects:** Medicine, surgery, allied
health sciences. **Holdings:** 3000 books; 5435 bound periodical volumes; 996
AV programs; 53 titles on microfilm. **Subscriptions:** 300 journals and other
serials. **Services:** Interlibrary loan; copying. **Computerized Information
Services:** MEDLINE; MAILMAN (electronic mail service). **Networks/
Consortia:** Member of VALNET. **Remarks:** Patients' library contains an
additional 6400 volumes. **Staff:** Geraldine Meyer, Med.Lib.Techn.

★ 17446 ★
U.S. Dept. of Veterans Affairs (WY-Cheyenne) - Medical and Regional
Office Center - Library Service (1420) (Med)
2360 E. Pershing Blvd.   Phone: (307)778-7321
Cheyenne, WY 82001   Kerry Skidmore, Chf., Lib.Serv.
Founded: 1932. **Staff:** Prof 1. **Subjects:** Medicine, nursing. **Holdings:** 1265
books; 2063 volumes of journals, bound and on microfilm; 300
videocassettes. **Subscriptions:** 142 journals and other serials; 15 newspapers.
Services: Interlibrary loan; copying; SDI; library open to the public.
Computerized Information Services: MEDLINE; CD-ROMs (MEDLINE,
CINAHL); internal database. **Networks/Consortia:** Member of VALNET.
Remarks: FAX: (307)778-7356. Patients' library contains an additional 150
volumes.

★ 17447 ★
U.S. Dept. of Veterans Affairs (WY-Sheridan) - Medical Center Library
(Med)
Sheridan, WY 82801   Phone: (307)672-1661
                                           Pat Carlson, Library Head
Staff: Prof 1; Other 2. **Subjects:** Psychiatry, psychology, medicine, nursing,
administration. **Holdings:** 2250 books; 250 bound periodical volumes; 1620
periodical volumes on microfilm; 2000 AV programs. **Subscriptions:** 300
journals and other serials. **Services:** Interlibrary loan; copying; library open
to the public. **Computerized Information Services:** MEDLARS, BRS
Information Technologies; MAILMAN (electronic mail service).
Networks/Consortia: Member of VALNET, Health Sciences Information
Network (HSIN), Northeastern Wyoming Medical Library Consortium.
Remarks: Patients' library contains an additional 5000 volumes. FAX:
(307)672-1652.

★ 17448 ★
U.S. District Court - Eastern District of New York - Library (Law)
225 Cadman Plaza, E.   Phone: (718)330-7483
Brooklyn, NY 11201   John T. Saiz, Law Libn.
Founded: 1965. **Staff:** Prof 3. **Subjects:** Federal, state, and municipal law.
Holdings: 35,000 volumes.**Subscriptions:** 100 journals and other serials.
Services: Library not open to the public. **Computerized Information
Services:** WESTLAW, LEXIS, OCLC. **Staff:** Kenneth Edmonds, Nirmala
Singh.

★ 17449 ★
U.S. District Court - Law Library (Law)
222 W. 7th Ave., No. 31   Phone: (907)271-5655
Anchorage, AK 99513-7586   Catherine Davidson, Libn.
Staff: Prof 1; Other 1. **Subjects:** Law. **Holdings:** 15,708 books; 833 bound
periodical volumes; 530 pamphlets. **Subscriptions:** 94 journals and other
serials. **Services:** Library open to the public with restrictions. **Computerized
Information Services:** WESTLAW, LEXIS. **Remarks:** FAX: (907)271-
5564.

★ 17450 ★
U.S. District Court - Library (Law)
U.S. Court House
300 Ala Moana Blvd., Rm. C-309
Box 50128   Phone: (808)541-1797
Honolulu, HI 96850   Patricia L. Butson, Libn.
Staff: 1. **Subjects:** Law. **Holdings:** 25,000 volumes. **Services:** Library
primarily serves U.S. Court personnel. **Computerized Information Services:**
LEXIS, WESTLAW, OCLC.

★ 17451 ★
U.S. District Court - Library (Law)
213 U.S. Courthouse
620 S.W. Main   Phone: (503)326-6042
Portland, OR 97205-3080   Scott McCurdy, Libn.
Staff: Prof 2. **Subjects:** Law. **Holdings:** 15,000 volumes. **Services:**
Interlibrary loan; library open to attorneys on day of hearing. **Computerized
Information Services:** WESTLAW, LEXIS. **Remarks:** FAX: (503)326-
7788. **Staff:** Diane Schauer, Asst.Libn.

★ 17452 ★
U.S. District Court - Library (Law)
150 Chardon Ave.
Federal Bldg., Rm. 121   Phone: (809)766-5740
Hato Rey, PR 00918   Ana Milagros Rodriguez, Libn.
Staff: 1. **Subjects:** Law. **Holdings:** 15,000 volumes. **Subscriptions:** 250
journals and other serials. **Services:** Copying; library not open to the public.

★ 17453 ★
**U.S. District Court - Northern California District - Louis E. Goodman
  Memorial Library** (Law)
450 Golden Gate Ave.
Box 36060   Phone: (415)556-7979
San Francisco, CA 94102   Lynn E. Lundstrom, Libn.
Founded: 1964. **Staff:** Prof 2; Other 1. **Subjects:** Federal and state law.
Holdings: 33,198 books; **Subscriptions:** 6 newspapers. **Services:** Interlibrary
loan; copying; library open to attorneys practicing before the court and
judges. **Computerized Information Services:** LEXIS, WESTLAW. **Staff:**
Therese M. Cason, Asst.Libn.

★ 17454 ★
U.S. Drug Enforcement Administration - Library (Law)
Washington, DC 20537   Phone: (202)307-8932
                                          Morton S. Goren, Libn.
Founded: 1959. **Staff:** Prof 3; Other 1. **Subjects:** Narcotic addiction,
dangerous drug abuse, law and legislation, law enforcement, drug abuse
education, international control. **Holdings:** 10,000 books; 24 VF drawers.
Subscriptions: 300 journals and other serials. **Services:** Interlibrary loan;
library not open to the public. **Computerized Information Services:**
DIALOG Information Services. **Publications:** Accession list, monthly.
Remarks: The Drug Enforcement Administration is part of the U.S.
Department of Justice. **Remarks:** FAX: (202)307-8939.

U.S. Electromagnetic Compatibility Analysis Center
See: IIT Research Institute - Electromagnetic Compatibility Analysis
  Center (7660)

★ 17455 ★
U.S. English - Mary Cavitt Memorial Library (Hum)
818 Connecticut Ave., N.W., Suite 200   Phone: (202)833-0100
Washington, DC 20006   Scipio Garling
Founded: 1983. **Staff:** Prof 1. **Subjects:** English language, bilingual
education, linguistics. **Holdings:** 1500 books; reports; manuscripts;
monographs; testimonies; editorials; news clippings; videotapes; audiotapes.
Services: Copying; library open to the public by appointment. **Computerized
Information Services:** AskSam (internal database). **Publications:** UPDATE,
6/year. **Remarks:** FAX: (202)833-0108. **Staff:** Kathleen Carroll

★ 17456 ★
**U.S. Environmental Protection Agency - Andrew W. Breidenbach
  Environmental Research Library** (Env-Cons, Sci-Engr)
26 W. Martin Luther King Dr.   Phone: (513)569-7705
Cincinnati, OH 45268   Stephena E. Harmony, Hd.Libn./Coord.
Founded: 1971. **Staff:** Prof 5; Other 7. **Subjects:** Water - pollution, quality,
research; hazardous waste; chemistry; environmental studies;
biotechnology. **Special Collections:** Hazardous Waste Collection; risk
assessment collection; solid waste; Management Collection; EPA approved
test methods. **Holdings:** 20,000 books; 7000 bound periodical volumes;
200,000 reports on microfiche; 1000 documents. **Subscriptions:** 803 journals
and other serials. **Services:** Interlibrary loan; SDI; library open to the public
for reference use only. **Automated Operations:** Computerized cataloging,
serials, and circulation. **Computerized Information Services:** DIALOG
Information Services, BRS Information Technologies, NLM, Occupational
Health Services, Inc. (OHS), Chemical Information Systems, Inc. (CIS),
STN International; CD-ROMs; internal database; EPA/IRC Bulletin Board
(electronic mail service). **Networks/Consortia:** Member of National
Network of Libraries of Medicine - Greater Midwest Region, FEDLINK.
Publications: EPA Library Journal Holdings Report, annual - to EPA
libraries; Computerized Literature Searching and Data Bases; library
accessions list, monthly. **Special Catalogs:** COM catalog; Hazardous Waste;
Solid Waste; EPA/NOAA Library Information Network Catalog.
Remarks: FAX: (513)569-7709.

★ 17457 ★
**U.S. Environmental Protection Agency - Atmospheric Sciences Model
  Division - Library** (Env-Cons)
Research Triangle Park, NC 27711   Phone: (919)541-4536
                                          Evelyn M. Poole-Kober,
                                          Tech.Pubns.Ed.
Founded: 1971. **Subjects:** Air pollution, meteorology. **Holdings:** 1200 books;
13,000 hardcopy documents and technical reports; microfiche.
Subscriptions: 125 journals and other serials. **Services:** Interlibrary loan;
center open to Environmental Protection Agency (EPA) personnel and
others under contract to the agency.

★ 17458 ★
**U.S. Environmental Protection Agency - Central Regional Laboratory -
  Library** (Env-Cons)
839 Bestgate Rd.   Phone: (301)266-9180
Annapolis, MD 21401   Ann Menninger Johnson, Libn.
Founded: 1964. **Staff:** Prof 1. **Subjects:** Water quality management, marine
environment, biological indicators, mathematical modeling, toxic
substances. **Special Collections:** Scientific studies of Chesapeake Bay.
Holdings: 1500 books; 5000 reprints; 150 Annapolis Field Office/CRL
publications; 10,000 EPA reports on microfiche; EPA R&D reports.
Subscriptions: 60 journals and other serials. **Services:** Interlibrary loan;
library open to the public for reference use only. **Remarks:** FAX: (301)266-
9180.

★ 17459 ★
**U.S. Environmental Protection Agency - Eastern Environmental
  Radiation Lab - Library** (Sci-Engr)
1504 A Ave.   Phone: (205)270-3400
Montgomery, AL 36114-5000   Charles M. Petko, Supv., Spec.Serv.
Founded: 1960. **Subjects:** Analytical chemistry of radionuclides, radon, and
radon measurement, electronic products, microwave energy, nuclear power
reactors and their environmental effects. **Holdings:** 1050 books; 4000
technical reports; 7000 technical reports on microfiche. **Subscriptions:** 120
journals and other serials. **Services:** Interlibrary loan; library not open to the
public. **Remarks:** FAX: (205)270-3454.

★ 17460 ★
**U.S. Environmental Protection Agency - Environmental Monitoring and
  Systems Laboratory - Library** (Env-Cons)
944 E. Harmon Ave.   Phone: (702)798-2648
Las Vegas, NV 89119   Camille Clark Wallin, Libn.
Founded: 1970. **Staff:** 2. **Subjects:** Environmental and nuclear science.
Holdings: 1533 books; 1200 reports; 65,000 microfiche. **Subscriptions:** 184
journals and other serials; 11 newspapers. **Services:** Interlibrary loan; library
open to the public for reference use only. **Computerized Information
Services:** OCLC. **Networks/Consortia:** Member of FEDLINK. **Remarks:**
FAX: (702)798-2637. **Staff:** Mary Forrester, ILL/Ser.Techn.

★ 17461 ★
**U.S. Environmental Protection Agency - Environmental Research
  Laboratory, Athens - Library** (Sci-Engr)
College Station Rd.   Phone: (404)546-3154
Athens, GA 30613-7799   Janice Sims, Info.Spec.
Founded: 1967. **Staff:** Prof 1. **Subjects:** Sanitary engineering, chemistry,
biology, environmental systems, aquatic biology. **Holdings:** 5000 books;
3500 government documents; 100 journals on microfilm. **Subscriptions:** 75
journals and other serials. **Services:** Interlibrary loan; copying; SDI; library
open to the public. **Automated Operations:** Computerized cataloging and
circulation. **Computerized Information Services:** DIALOG Information
Services, Chemical Information Systems, Inc. (CIS), STN International.

★ 17462 ★
**U.S. Environmental Protection Agency - Environmental Research
  Laboratory, Corvallis - Library** (Env-Cons)
200 S.W. 35th St.   Phone: (503)754-4600
Corvallis, OR 97333   Renie Cain McVeety, Libn.
Founded: 1966. **Staff:** Prof 1; Other 2. **Subjects:** Effects of air, water, and
soil pollutants on the ecosystem; freshwater ecosystems; toxic substances;
wildlife toxicology; hazardous waste; biotechnology; global climate. **Special
Collections:** Acid rain and air pollution effects (28,000 documents).
Holdings: 4000 books; 9000 reports; 22,000 microforms. **Subscriptions:** 120
journals and other serials. **Services:** Interlibrary loan; copying; library open
to the public for reference use only. **Automated Operations:** Computerized
cataloging and circulation. **Computerized Information Services:** OCLC,
DIALOG Information Services, NLM. **Networks/Consortia:** Member of
FEDLINK. **Remarks:** FAX: (503)457-4799; (503)457-4600 (confirmation
number).

★ 17463 ★
U.S. Environmental Protection Agency - Environmental Research Laboratory, Gulf Breeze - Library (Biol Sci)
Sabine Island   Phone: (904)934-9218
Gulf Breeze, FL 32561   Elizabeth Pinnell, Libn.
Founded: 1967. **Staff:** Prof 1; Other 2. **Subjects:** Pathobiology, ecology, aquatic toxicology, microbiology, biotechnology. **Special Collections:** Environmental publications for northwest Florida. **Holdings:** 5000 volumes; 6000 reprints; 38,000 publications on microfiche. **Subscriptions:** 240 journals and other serials. **Services:** Interlibrary loan; SDI; library open to the public for reference use only. **Automated Operations:** Computerized cataloging and circulation. **Computerized Information Services:** DIALOG Information Services, OCLC, NLM, STN International; EPALIT (internal database). **Networks/Consortia:** Member of FEDLINK. **Publications:** Publications List and Special Bibliographies; Computerized Library Systems Directory - available on request. **Remarks:** FAX: (904)934-9201.

★ 17464 ★
U.S. Environmental Protection Agency - Environmental Research Laboratory, Narragansett - Library (Biol Sci)
27 Tarzwell Dr.   Phone: (401)782-3000
Narragansett, RI 02882   Rose Ann Gamache, Libn.
Founded: 1966. **Staff:** 1. **Subjects:** Biological oceanography, marine ecology, biomedical science, fisheries biology, chemistry. **Holdings:** 15,000 technical reports and collected reprints; microforms. **Subscriptions:** 45 journals and other serials. **Services:** Interlibrary loan; copying; library open to the public with restrictions. **Automated Operations:** Computerized cataloging and serials. **Computerized Information Services:** Online systems.

★ 17465 ★
U.S. Environmental Protection Agency - Headquarters Library (Env-Cons)
Rm. 2904 PM-211-A
401 M St., S.W.   Phone: (202)260-5921
Washington, DC 20460-0001   Lois Ramponi, Hd.Libn./Coord.
Founded: 1971. **Staff:** Prof 12; Other 12. **Subjects:** Water - pollution, quality, supply; air pollution; noise abatement; radiation; hazardous wastes; solid waste management; resource recovery; pesticides; chemistry and toxicology; social, economic, legislative, legal, administrative, and management aspects of environmental policy. **Special Collections:** Hazardous waste; management; international, information resources management. **Holdings:** 15,500 books; 23,000 hardcopy documents and technical reports; 330,000 documents and reports from the EPA and its predecessor agencies on microfiche; newspapers, abstracts and indexes, periodicals on microfilm. **Subscriptions:** 625 journals, abstracts, indexes, newsletters, and newspapers. **Services:** Interlibrary loan; SDI; library open to the public with restrictions. **Automated Operations:** Computerized cataloging, circulation, serials, and ILL. **Computerized Information Services:** DIALOG Information Services, LEXIS, NEXIS, Chemical Information Systems, Inc. (CIS), NLM, Washington Alert Service; internal databases. **Networks/Consortia:** Member of FEDLINK. **Publications:** Journal Holdings Report, annual - to other libraries; ACCESS EPA series - Bibliographic Series, irregular - free upon request; Newsletterr, monthly - to EPA Headquarters staff only. **Remarks:** Headquarters of U.S. Environmental Protection Agency. FAX: (202)382-7883; (202)382-7884. **Staff:** Gretl Cox, Hd., Tech.Serv.; Michelle Tsai, Coll.Dev.; John Butsch, INFOTERRA Libn.; Mary Stevanus, Ref.Libn.; Felice Sacks, Hd., Hazardous Waste Lib.; Craig Lelansky, Ref.Libn.; Mary Beth Weaver, Water Libn.; Carol Stiles, Gen.Ref.Libn.; Robin Cook, Gen.Ref.Libn.

★ 17466 ★
U.S. Environmental Protection Agency - Library (Env-Cons)
2890 Woodbridge Ave.
Bldg. 209, MS-245   Phone: (908)321-6762
Edison, NJ 08837-3679   Dorothy Szefczyk, Lib.Techn.
Founded: 1967. **Staff:** 1. **Subjects:** Water pollution, water quality, environmental quality, air pollution, toxic substances, hazardous wastes. **Holdings:** 3000 books; 10,000 federal and state reports; 100,000 microfiche. **Subscriptions:** 60 journals and other serials. **Services:** Interlibrary loan; copying; library open to the public. **Computerized Information Services:** DIALOG Information Services, OCLC. **Publications:** Selected Acquisitions - distributed within the region and to other EPA libraries. **Remarks:** FAX: (908)321-6613.

★ 17467 ★
U.S. Environmental Protection Agency - Library Services (Env-Cons)
MD 35   Phone: (919)541-2777
Research Triangle Park, NC 27711   John Knight, Chf., Info.Serv.
Founded: 1970. **Staff:** Prof 4; Other 2. **Subjects:** Air pollution, its effects on health, control technologies. **Special Collections:** APTIC (Air Pollution Technical Information Center) Collection; Environmental Protection Agency document distribution center. **Holdings:** 4000 volumes; 4470 technical reports; 200,000 microfiche. **Subscriptions:** 500 journals and other serials. **Services:** Interlibrary loan; copying; SDI; library open to the public for reference use only. **Automated Operations:** Computerized public access catalog, cataloging, serials, and circulation. **Computerized Information Services:** DIALOG Information Services, MEDLINE, Chemical Information Systems, Inc. (CIS); CD-ROM; APTIC (internal database); Dialcom, Inc. (electronic mail service). **Networks/Consortia:** Member of FEDLINK. **Publications:** Combined serials list for the Environmental Protection Agency - Library Services, the National Institute of Environmental Health Sciences Library, and RTP. **Remarks:** FAX: (919)541-1405. **Staff:** Rosemary Thorn, Dir., Lib.Serv.; Bess Villeponteaux, Asst.Dir., Lib.Serv.; Sharon Arnette, Hd., ILL

★ 17468 ★
U.S. Environmental Protection Agency - Motor Vehicle Emission Laboratory - Library (Sci-Engr)
2565 Plymouth Rd.   Phone: (313)668-4311
Ann Arbor, MI 48105   Debra Talsma, Libn.
Founded: 1968. **Staff:** Prof 1. **Subjects:** Automotive engineering, air pollution from mobile sources, alternative fuels for motor vehicles. **Special Collections:** Society of Automotive Engineers (SAE) papers (4000); EPA final and technical reports (1000). **Holdings:** 360 books; 15,000 reports on microfiche; 300 legislative documents; patents. **Subscriptions:** 64 journals and other serials. **Services:** Interlibrary loan; copying; library open to the public. **Computerized Information Services:** Electronic mail service. **Special Catalogs:** EPA Motor Vehicle Emission Laboratory final and technical report listing. **Remarks:** FAX: (313)668-8368 (Attn.: Libn.). Electronic mail address(es): EPA 6476.

★ 17469 ★
U.S. Environmental Protection Agency - National Enforcement Investigations - EPA-NEIC Library (Env-Cons)
Denver Federal Center, Bldg. 53
Box 25227   Phone: (303)236-5122
Denver, CO 80225   Dorothy Biggs, Libn.
Founded: 1972. **Staff:** Prof 1. **Subjects:** Environmental law, water quality, industrial and agricultural pollution abatement practices, air pollution, pesticides, hazardous wastes, chemistry. **Holdings:** 2000 volumes; 750,000 microfiche; technical reports; R&D reports; conference documents; state of the art abatement practices for municipal, industrial, and agricultural pollution. **Subscriptions:** 95 journals and other serials. **Services:** Interlibrary loan; copying; SDI; library open to the public with restrictions. **Automated Operations:** Computerized cataloging and circulation. **Computerized Information Services:** DIALOG Information Services, NLM, WESTLAW, Chemical Information Systems, Inc. (CIS), BRS Information Technologies, VU/TEXT Information Services, DataTimes, JURIS, Chemical Abstracts Service (CAS), LEXIS, NEXIS, STN International; Hazardous Waste Database (internal database); All-In-One (electronic mail service). **Networks/Consortia:** Member of FEDLINK. **Publications:** News Extras from the Information Center, bimonthly - to staff. **Remarks:** (303)236-5116. Electronic mail address(es): EPA2339 (All-In-One). **Staff:** Barbara Greenman.

★ 17470 ★
U.S. Environmental Protection Agency - National Small Flows Clearinghouse - Library (Env-Cons)
West Virginia Univ.
617 Spruce St.
P.O. Box 6064   Phone: (800)624-8301
Morgantown, WV 26506-6064   John L. Mow
Subjects: Small communities, wastewater management, alternative sewers, onsite systems, finance, public education. **Special Collections:** Bibliographic database collection (3000 articles). **Holdings:** 3000 reports. **Services:** Library not open to the public. **Computerized Information Services:** Internal databases. **Publications:** Design Modules; public education videos; Small Flows & Pipeline (newsletter). **Remarks:** FAX: (304)293-3161. May use electronic bulletin board system to request a search of any in-house database at (800)544-1936.

★ 17471 ★
U.S. Environmental Protection Agency - ORD - Risk Reduction Engineering Laboratory - Releases Control Branch - Technical Information Exchange
MS-104
Woodbridge Ave.
Edison, NJ 08837
Defunct.

★ 17472 ★
U.S. Environmental Protection Agency - Region 1 Library (Env-Cons)
JFK Federal Bldg.   Phone: (617)565-3300
Boston, MA 02203   Peg Nelson, Reg.Libn.
Founded: 1970. Staff: Prof 2; Other 1. Subjects: Solid and hazardous waste, air and water pollution, pesticides and toxicology, environment. Special Collections: Hazardous Waste Collection; test methods; wetlands. Holdings: 10,000 books, government documents, technical reports; 100,000 microfiche. Subscriptions: 150 journals and other serials. Services: Interlibrary loan; copying; library open to the public with borrowing through ILL only. Automated Operations: Computerized cataloging. Computerized Information Services: BRS Information Technologies, DIALOG Information Services, Chemical Information Systems, Inc. (CIS), NLM. Networks/Consortia: Member of FEDLINK. Special Indexes: Index to EPA Test Methods. Staff: Judy Saravis.

★ 17473 ★
U.S. Environmental Protection Agency - Region 1 Research Library for Solid Waste, HER-CAN6 (Env-Cons)
JFK Federal Bldg.   Phone: (617)573-9687
Boston, MA 02203   Fred Friedman, Libn.
Founded: 1989. Staff: 1.7. Subjects: Solid waste education, recycling, materials transformation, waste. Holdings: 100 books; 2000 reports; 2000 documents. Subscriptions: 50 journals and other serials. Services: Interlibrary loan; copying. Computerized Information Services: LEXIS, NEXIS; internal databases.

★ 17474 ★
U.S. Environmental Protection Agency - Region 2 Library (Env-Cons)
26 Federal Plaza, Rm. 402   Phone: (212)264-2881
New York, NY 10278   Eveline M. Goodman, Hd.Libn.
Founded: 1965. Staff: Prof 1. Subjects: Hazardous waste; acid rain; energy; pollution - ocean, water, air. Special Collections: Hazardous Waste in the region: New York, New Jersey, Puerto Rico, Virgin Islands. Holdings: 2200 books; 2700 reports; 250,000 microfiche. Subscriptions: 62 journals and other serials. Services: Interlibrary loan; library open to the public for reference use only. Automated Operations: Computerized cataloging. Computerized Information Services: DIALOG Information Services, OCLC; Hazardous Waste Database (internal database). Networks/Consortia: Member of FEDLINK. Publications: Acquisitions list, monthly. Remarks: FAX (212)264-5433.

★ 17475 ★
U.S. Environmental Protection Agency - Region 3 Information Resource Center (Env-Cons)
841 Chestnut St.   Phone: (215)597-0580
Philadelphia, PA 19107   Diane M. McCreary, Libn.
Founded: 1972. Staff: Prof 2; Other 2. Subjects: Environmental sciences and law, management, economics, toxicology. Special Collections: Wetland ecology; hazardous waste. Holdings: 14,000 books; 8000 technical reports; 121,000 microfiche. Subscriptions: 200 journals and other serials. Services: Interlibrary loan; copying; center open to the public for reference use only. Automated Operations: Computerized cataloging and circulation. Computerized Information Services: DIALOG Information Services, MEDLARS, TOXNET, LEXIS, Chemical Information Systems, Inc. (CIS); Hazardous Waste Database (internal database). Networks/Consortia: Member of FEDLINK. Publications: User's guide; bimonthly acquisitions list; periodical holdings list; subject bibliographies. Staff: Dawn Scellenberger.

★ 17476 ★
U.S. Environmental Protection Agency - Region 4 Library (Env-Cons)
345 Courtland St.   Phone: (404)347-4216
Atlanta, GA 30365   Pricilla Pride, Hd.Libn.
Founded: 1973. Staff: Prof 3; Other 2. Subjects: Pollution - water, air, noise; solid waste management; toxic substances; Southeastern U.S. ecology.

Special Collections: Environmental impact statements. Holdings: 4000 books; 110,000 EPA documents on microfiche; 20,000 EPA documents. Subscriptions: 200 journals and other serials. Services: Interlibrary loan; copying; SDI; library open to the public. Automated Operations: Computerized cataloging, acquisitions, serials, and circulation. Computerized Information Services: OCLC, DIALOG Information Services, NLM, National Pesticide Information Retrieval System (NPIRS); Hazardous Waste Database, Integrated Risk Information System (IRIS); CD-ROMs; Dialcom, Inc. (electronic mail service). Networks/Consortia: Member of FEDLINK. Publications: Monthly Acquisitions; newsletter - both for internal distribution only. Special Catalogs: Hazardous Waste Collection (online); EPA Library (online). Remarks: FAX: (404)347-4486. Electronic mail address(es): EPA 9415 (Dialcom, Inc.). Staff: Beverly Fulwood, Superfund Libn.; John Nemeth, Ref.Libn.

★ 17477 ★
U.S. Environmental Protection Agency - Region 5 Library (PL-12 J) (Env-Cons)
77 W. Jackson Blvd., 12th Fl.   Phone: (312)353-2022
Chicago, IL 60604   Ms. Lou W. Tilley, Reg.Libn.
Founded: 1972. Staff: Prof 3; Other 4. Subjects: Water quality and supply; air quality and air pollution; solid waste management; pesticides; radiation; noise; energy; hazardous wastes; toxic substances; environmental science; environmental law with emphasis on the Great Lakes and six states in the region: Illinois, Indiana, Michigan, Minnesota, Ohio, Wisconsin. Special Collections: Environmental Protection Agency and predecessor agency reports (complete set); Air Pollution Technical Information Center (APTIC) microfiche file. Holdings: 17,000 books; 21,000 state and federal documents; 12 VF drawers; 56 VF drawers of microforms. Subscriptions: 395 journals and other serials. Services: Interlibrary loan; copying; library open to the public for reference use. Computerized Information Services: PFDS Online, BRS Information Technologies, DIALOG Information Services, MEDLARS, Chemical Information Systems, Inc. (CIS), OCLC, NEXIS, LEXIS; DCS, Hazardous Waste Database (internal databases); All-in-One (electronic mail service). Publications: Region V Library Selected Acquisitions, bimonthly - internal distribution and to libraries on request; Fact Sheet/Brochure, irregular; bibliographies. Remarks: FAX: (312)353-1155. Electronic mail address(es): EPA 9559 (All-in-One). Staff: Penny Boyle, Libn.; Lisha Li, GLNPO Lib.Tech.

★ 17478 ★
U.S. Environmental Protection Agency - Region 7 Library (Env-Cons)
726 Minnesota Ave.   Phone: (913)551-7241
Kansas City, KS 66101   Barbara MacKinnon, Reg.Libn.
Founded: 1970. Staff: 2. Subjects: Air and water pollution, solid waste, pesticides. Holdings: 2300 books; 4600 technical reports; 125,000 technical reports on microfiche. Subscriptions: 100 serials. Services: Interlibrary loan. Computerized Information Services: DIALOG Information Services, Hazardous Waste Database (internal database). Remarks: FAX: (913)551-7467.

★ 17479 ★
U.S. Environmental Protection Agency - Region 8 Library (Env-Cons)
999 18th St., Suite 500   Phone: (303)293-1444
Denver, CO 80202-2405   Barbara L. Wagner, Reg.Libn.
Founded: 1973. Staff: Prof 1; Other 3. Subjects: Water, air, solid waste management, pesticides, radiation, noise, toxic substances, energy. Special Collections: Microfiche collections of EPA technical reports. Holdings: 4500 books; 22,000 EPA and technical reports; 26,000 titles on microfiche. Subscriptions: 350 journals and other serials. Services: Interlibrary loan; library open to the public on a limited schedule. Automated Operations: Computerized cataloging and circulation. Computerized Information Services: DIALOG Information Services, OCLC; EPA Online Library System (internal database); All-In-One (electronic mail service). Publications: Library New Titles, monthly - available in the library. Remarks: FAX: (303)293-1647. Electronic mail address(es): EPA9869 (All-In-One).

★ 17480 ★
U.S. Environmental Protection Agency - Region 9 Library (Env-Cons)
75 Hawthorne St., 13th Fl.   Phone: (415)774-1510
San Francisco, CA 94105   Linda Vida-Sunnen, Hd.Libn.
Founded: 1969. Staff: Prof 3; Other 3. Subjects: Environment; water and air pollution; pesticides; hazardous waste; environmental health and law for California, Arizona, Nevada, Hawaii, and the Pacific Islands. Special

Collections: Oswer Directives; Record(s) of Decisions; hazardous waste collection; EPA Reports; Toxic Release Inventory (on microfiche). **Holdings:** 4000 books; 250,000 reports; 300,000 reports on microfiche. **Subscriptions:** 250 journals and other serials. **Services:** Interlibrary loan; library open to the public for reference use only. **Automated Operations:** Computerized public access catalog, cataloging, and circulation. **Computerized Information Services:** DIALOG Information Services, OCLC, TOXNET; Hazardous Waste Database, Integrated Risk Information System (IRIS), Clean Lakes Database, Toxic Release Inventory (internal databases). **Publications:** Acquisitions list, quarterly - to EPA staff and mailing list; Fact Sheets Services Brochure. **Special Indexes:** Annual journal holding list. **Remarks:** FAX: (415)744-1474. **Staff:** Deborra Samuels, Ref .Libn.; Bernadette Adams, Ref.Libn.

★ 17481 ★
U.S. Environmental Protection Agency - Region 10 Library (Env-Cons)
1200 6th Ave.   Phone: (206)442-1289
Seattle, WA 98101   Julienne Sears, Reg.Libn.
Founded: 1971. **Staff:** Prof 2; Other 1. **Subjects:** Environmental pollution. **Holdings:** EPA technical reports. **Subscriptions:** 100 journals and other serials. **Services:** Interlibrary loan; library open to the public for reference use only. **Automated Operations:** Computerized cataloging and circulation. **Computerized Information Services:** OCLC.

★ 17482 ★
U.S. Environmental Protection Agency - Robert S. Kerr Environmental Research Laboratory - Research Library (Env-Cons)
Kerr Lab Rd.
P.O. Box 1198   Phone: (405)332-8800
Ada, OK 74820   Joyce Williams Bergin, Lib.Dir.
Founded: 1966. **Staff:** Prof 1; Other 3. **Subjects:** Environment, ground water, chemistry, microbiology, soil science, hydrology, modeling. **Holdings:** 3000 monographs; 72,000 microfiche; 10,000 other cataloged items. **Subscriptions:** 85 journals and other serials. **Services:** Interlibrary loan; telephone reference for the public. **Automated Operations:** EPA's Online Library System. **Computerized Information Services:** DIALOG Information Services, IRIS; CD-ROMs. All-In-One (electronic mail service). **Remarks:** FAX: (8)743-2256 (FTS); (405)332-8800 (commercial). Electronic mail address(es): EPA8603, RSKERL.LIBRARY.EMB (All-In-One).

★ 17483 ★
U.S. Equal Employment Opportunity Commission - Library (Soc Sci, Law)
1801 L St., N.W., Rm. 6502   Phone: (202)663-4630
Washington, DC 20507   Susan D. Taylor, Lib.Dir.
Founded: 1964. **Staff:** Prof 2; Other 3. **Subjects:** Employment discrimination, minorities, women, aged, handicapped, testing, labor law, civil rights. **Special Collections:** Equal Employment Opportunity Commission Publications. **Holdings:** 25,000 books. **Subscriptions:** 300 journals and other serials; 8 newspapers. **Services:** Interlibrary loan; copying; SDI; library open to the public by appointment. **Computerized Information Services:** LEXIS, DIALOG Information Services, WESTLAW, LEGI-SLATE, OCLC. **Networks/Consortia:** Member of FEDLINK. **Publications:** Library service and selected bibliographies, brochure. **Remarks:** FAX: (202)663-4629. **Also Known As:** EEOC. **Staff:** Mary Grady, Res.Libn.

★ 17484 ★
U.S. Executive Office of the President - Libraries (Soc Sci)
725 17th St., N.W., Rm. G-102   Phone: (202)395-3654
Washington, DC 20503   Mary H. Anton, Dir.
Founded: 1978. **Staff:** Prof 15; Other 15. **Subjects:** U.S. budget, international trade, past and current administrations, politics, government policy, political science, Presidency, economics, federal legislation. **Holdings:** 53,000 volumes; 660,000 pieces of microfiche; 7500 reels of microfilm. **Subscriptions:** 1000 journals and other serials; 20 newspapers. **Services:** Interlibrary loan; copying; SDI; library open to the public by appointment for items unique to this library. **Automated Operations:** Computerized cataloging, acquisitions, serials, and circulation. **Computerized Information Services:** DIALOG Information Services, VU/TEXT Information Services, WESTLAW, LEXIS, NEXIS, LEGI-SLATE, Dialcom Inc., OCLC, Dun & Bradstreet Business Credit Services, DataTimes, JURIS. **Networks/Consortia:** Member of FEDLINK.

★ 17485 ★
U.S. Federal Aviation Administration - Aeronautical Center Library, AAC-66D (Sci-Engr)
6500 S. MacArthur
Box 25082   Phone: (405)680-4709
Oklahoma City, OK 73125   Virginia C. Hughes, Libn.
Founded: 1962. **Staff:** Prof 1. **Subjects:** Aeronautics, airplanes, mathematics, avionics, electronics, management. **Holdings:** Books; periodicals; technical reports. **Subscriptions:** 52 journals and other serials. **Services:** Interlibrary loan; library open to the public. **Computerized Information Services:** OCLC, DIALOG Information Services. **Networks/Consortia:** Member of FEDLINK. **Remarks:** The Federal Aviation Administration is part of the U.S. Department of Transportation. **Also Known As:** FAA.

★ 17486 ★
U.S. Federal Aviation Administration - Civil Aeromedical Institute Library, AAM 400a (Med, Biol Sci)
6500 S. MacArthur Blvd.
Box 25082   Phone: (405)680-4398
Oklahoma City, OK 73125   Janice Varner Nakagawara, Med.Libn.
Founded: 1963. **Staff:** Prof 1. **Subjects:** Aviation medicine, biochemistry, psychology, human factors, toxicology, occupational hygiene. **Special Collections:** Aviation medicine. **Holdings:** 8000 books; 12,000 bound periodical volumes; 20,000 unbound reports. **Subscriptions:** 200 journals and other serials. **Services:** Interlibrary loan; copying; SDI; library open to the public with restrictions. **Automated Operations:** Computerized public access catalog and cataloging. **Computerized Information Services:** MEDLARS, DIALOG Information Services, ORBIT Search Service, OCLC. **Remarks:** Alternate telephone number(s): 680-6804; 680-4398. FAX: (405)680-4813; 747-4813.

★ 17487 ★
U.S. Federal Aviation Administration - Technical Center Library (ACM-651) (Trans)
Atlantic City International Airport   Phone: (609)484-5772
Atlantic City, NJ 08405   Robert Mast, Br. Mgr.
Founded: 1958. **Staff:** Prof 4; Other 2. **Subjects:** Air traffic control, collision avoidance, aviation safety, radar, navigation, configuration management. **Special Collections:** Addison B. Johnson Air Traffic Control Resource Center; Air Traffic Safety Information Center. **Holdings:** 7000 books; 3500 bound periodical volumes; 2000 technical reports; 80,000 unbound, uncataloged technical reports. **Subscriptions:** 400 journals and other serials. **Services:** Interlibrary loan; copying; SDI; facility open to the public. **Automated Operations:** Computerized cataloging, acquisitions, serials, and circulation. **Computerized Information Services:** DIALOG Information Services, DTIC, NASA/RECON, OCLC; internal databases. Performs searches on fee basis. **Networks/Consortia:** Member of FEDLINK. **Publications:** Acquisitions List; custom bibliographies. **Remarks:** FAX (609)484-5126. **Staff:** Dr. Nancy Boylan, Tech.Info.Spec.; Harry Kemp, Tech.Info.Spec.; Ruth Farrell, Libn.

★ 17488 ★
U.S. Federal Bureau of Investigation - F.B.I. Academy - Library (Law)
Quantico, VA 22135   Phone: (703)640-1135
          I. John Vasquez, Unit Chf.
Founded: 1972. **Staff:** Prof 3; Other 10. **Subjects:** Law enforcement, police, criminal justice. **Holdings:** 35,000 books; 1300 bound periodical volumes; 11,000 government documents; 6800 vertical file materials; 6000 items in law library; 22,000 microfiche. **Subscriptions:** 525 journals and other serials; 6 newspapers. **Services:** Interlibrary loan; SDI; library open to the public by special permission only. **Computerized Information Services:** DIALOG Information Services, NEXIS, OCLC, LEXIS. **Publications:** Subject bibliographies - available upon request. **Special Catalogs:** Periodicals holdings list, annual; audiovisual catalog, annual. **Remarks:** FAX: (703)640-1452. The Federal Bureau of Investigation is part of the U.S. Department of Justice. **Staff:** Sandra Coupe, Libn.; Bertha Scott, Libn.

★ 17489 ★
U.S. Federal Communications Commission - Library (Info Sci, Law)
1919 M St., N.W.   Phone: (202)632-7100
Washington, DC 20554   Gloria Thomas, Supv.Libn.
Founded: 1934. **Staff:** Prof 2; Other 2. **Subjects:** Telecommunications, electrical engineering, law, economics, public utility regulation, public administration, management, statistics. **Special Collections:** Legislative histories of Communications Act of 1934 and allied statutes; congressional

hearings in the area of telecommunications. **Holdings:** 45,000 books; 123 bound periodical volumes; 6200 VF materials; 3000 reels of microfilm. **Subscriptions:** 305 journals and other serials. **Services:** SDI; library open to the public for reference use only. **Automated Operations:** Computerized cataloging, serials, and circulation. **Computerized Information Services:** WESTLAW, LEXIS, NEXIS, DIALOG Information Services, OCLC; Citator (internal database). **Publications:** Acquisitions list, bimonthly. **Also Known As:** FCC.

★ 17490 ★
U.S. Federal Deposit Insurance Corporation - Library (Bus-Fin)
550 17th St., N.W.   Phone: (202)898-3631
Washington, DC 20429   Carole Cleland, Chf.Libn.
Founded: 1935. **Staff:** Prof 2. **Subjects:** Banking, finance, economics, law. **Special Collections:** State banking commissioners annual reports. **Holdings:** 65,000 volumes. **Subscriptions:** 750 journals and other serials. **Services:** Interlibrary loan; copying; library open to the public with restrictions. **Computerized Information Services:** DIALOG Information Services, WESTLAW, LEXIS, NEXIS, Dun & Bradstreet Business Credit Services, OCLC, Information America, Prentice Hall Online, TRW, Trans Unim, CBI/Equitax. **Networks/Consortia:** Member of FEDLINK. **Publications:** Recent Acquisitions, quarterly. **Special Indexes:** KWIC banking index (online). **Remarks:** FAX: (202)898-3984. **Also Known As:** FDIC. **Staff:** Diana Smith, Asst.Chf.Libn.; Len Samowitz, Mgr.Ref.Serv.; Mary Kathryn Wilson, Coord., Reg & Tech.Serv.

★ 17491 ★
U.S. Federal Election Commission - National Clearinghouse on Election Administration - Document Center (Soc Sci)
999 E St., N.W.   Phone: (202)219-3670
Washington, DC 20463   Penelope Bonsall, Dir.
Founded: 1976. **Staff:** Prof 5. **Subjects:** Elections administration, federal election results, federal and state election laws and procedures, census data, contract research projects. **Holdings:** 1000 volumes; state legislative research reports. **Services:** Center open to the public. **Remarks:** Toll-free telephone number(s): (202)219-3880.

★ 17492 ★
U.S. Federal Highway Administration - Office of the Chief Counsel - Law Library (Trans, Law)
400 Seventh St., S.W., Rm. 4232   Phone: (202)366-1388
Washington, DC 20590   Sherie A. Abbasi, Law Libn.
Staff: Prof 1. **Subjects:** Highways and roads. **Special Collections:** Legislative histories of highways, 1909 to present. **Holdings:** Figures not available. **Services:** Library open to the public by appointment. **Computerized Information Services:** WESTLAW, LEXIS, NEXIS, LEGI-SLATE; internal databases; OnTyme Electronic Message Network Service (electronic mail service). **Publications:** Federal laws and material relating to the Federal Highway Administration, biennial. **Remarks:** FAX: (202)366-7499 (Rm. 4213). The Federal Highway Administration is part of the U.S. Department of Transportation.

★ 17493 ★
U.S. Federal Judicial Center - Information Services (Law)
1520 H St., N.W., Rm. B-102   Phone: (202)633-6365
Washington, DC 20005   Roger Karr, Sr.Res.Libn.
Founded: 1968. **Staff:** Prof 2; Other 3. **Subjects:** Judicial administration, court management, civil and criminal procedure. **Special Collections:** Local Federal court rules. **Holdings:** 11,000 books. **Subscriptions:** 380 journals and other serials. **Services:** Interlibrary loan; copying; services open to the public by appointment. **Computerized Information Services:** OCLC, DIALOG Information Services, LEXIS, WESTLAW. **Networks/Consortia:** Member of FEDLINK. **Special Catalogs:** Catalog of Center publications, annual. **Remarks:** FAX: (202)786-6389. **Staff:** Matt P. Sarago.

★ 17494 ★
U.S. Federal Maritime Commission - Library (Law, Trans)
1100 L St., N.W.   Phone: (202)523-5762
Washington, DC 20573   Mary Ellen Daffron, Libn.
Founded: 1961. **Staff:** Prof 1; Other 1. **Subjects:** Law, shipping law, marine transportation, economics. **Special Collections:** Containerization (intermodal transportation); shipping; legislation. **Holdings:** 12,800 books; 238 bound periodical volumes; 20 legislative histories; 1500 congressional hearings and reports. **Subscriptions:** 150 journals and other serials; 8 newspapers. **Services:** Interlibrary loan; copying; library open to the public. **Computerized Information Services:** WESTLAW, VU/TEXT Information Services, DIALOG Information Services. **Publications:** Library Acquisitions, bimonthly - for internal distribution only. **Remarks:** FAX: (202)523-3782.

★ 17495 ★
U.S. Federal Trade Commission - Library (Bus-Fin, Law)
6th St. & Pennsylvania Ave., N.W., Rm. 630
Washington, DC 20580   Phone: (202)326-2395
Founded: 1915. **Staff:** Prof 9; Other 12. **Subjects:** Antitrust, consumerism, advertising, economics, law, business, accounting. **Holdings:** 120,000 volumes; 275,000 microforms. **Subscriptions:** 1000 journals and other serials. **Services:** Interlibrary loan; copying; library open to the public. **Automated Operations:** Computerized cataloging, acquisitions, and serials (GEAC Advance). **Computerized Information Services:** DIALOG Information Services, LEXIS, NEXIS, OCLC, VU/TEXT Information Services, WESTLAW, Dow Jones News/Retrieval, ELSS (Electronic Legislative Search System), Prentice Hall Online, TRW Business Profiles, CBI, Information America. **Networks/Consortia:** Member of FEDLINK. **Publications:** Monthly Library Bulletin; Bibliography Series; Periodicals Holdings List; Legislative Histories Holdings List. **Remarks:** FAX: (202)326-2050. **Also Known As:** FTC. **Staff:** Elaine Sullivan, Mgr., Lib.Serv.; Denise Ottie, Mgr., Info.Ctr.

★ 17496 ★
U.S. Fish & Wildlife Service - Abernathy Salmon Culture Technology Center - Research and Information Center (Biol Sci)
1440 Abernathy Rd.   Phone: (206)425-6072
Longview, WA 98632   David A. Leith, Dir.
Founded: 1942. **Staff:** 10. **Subjects:** Fish culture, feeding salmonids, water reuse, diseases of fish, temperature, hatchery techniques. **Holdings:** 125 books; 175 bound periodical volumes; 2125 other cataloged items; 5 drawers of reprints. **Subscriptions:** 25 journals and other serials. **Services:** Interlibrary loan; center not open to the public. **Remarks:** FAX: (206)636-1855. The Fish & Wildlife Service is part of the U.S. Department of the Interior.

★ 17497 ★
U.S. Fish & Wildlife Service - Fish Farming Experimental Laboratory - Fisheries Research Library (Biol Sci)
Box 860   Phone: (501)673-4484
Stuttgart, AR 72160   Joyce Cooper, Dir.
Founded: 1962. **Staff:** Prof 1. **Subjects:** Aquaculture technologies; warmwater fish culture; crawfish culture; fish health, physiology, and nutrition; fish parasitology. **Holdings:** 1135 volumes; 9500 reprints. **Subscriptions:** 150 journals and other serials. **Services:** Interlibrary loan; copying (limited); library open to the public. **Remarks:** FAX: (501)673-7710.

★ 17498 ★
U.S. Fish & Wildlife Service - Library (Biol Sci)
1011 E. Tudor Rd.   Phone: (907)786-3358
Anchorage, AK 99503   Nancy Tileston, Libn.
Staff: Prof 1; Other 1. **Subjects:** Alaska fisheries and wildlife. **Special Collections:** U.S. Fish and Wildlife Service publications; Alaska Department of Fish and Game publications; gray literature on Alaskan fish and wildlife issues. **Holdings:** 10,000 monographs and monographic serials. **Subscriptions:** 80 journals and other serials. **Services:** Library open to the public. **Computerized Information Services:** DIALOG Information Services, LEXIS, OCLC; internal databases. **Networks/Consortia:** Member of Alaska Library Network (ALN), FEDLINK. **Remarks:** FAX: (907)786-3625.

★ 17499 ★
U.S. Fish & Wildlife Service - National Fisheries Contaminant Research Center - Library (Env-Cons, Agri)
4200 New Haven Rd.   Phone: (314)875-5399
Columbia, MO 65201   Ell-Piret Multer, Dir.
Founded: 1959. **Staff:** Prof 2. **Subjects:** Pesticides, agricultural chemicals, pollution, environmental contaminants, environmental chemistry. **Holdings:** 4500 books; 1500 bound periodical volumes; 20,000 reprints; 34,500 microfiche. **Subscriptions:** 100 journals and other serials. **Services:** Interlibrary loan; copying; library open to the public. **Computerized Information Services:** OCLC, OCLC EPIC; CD-ROM; CompuServe Information Service (electronic mail service). **Remarks:** FAX: (314)876-1896. Electronic mail address(es): R8NFCRC (CompuServe Information Service).

★ 17500 ★
U.S. Fish & Wildlife Service - National Fisheries Research Center -
  Great Lakes - John Van Oosten Library (Biol Sci, Env-Cons)
1451 Green Rd.   Phone: (313)994-3331
Ann Arbor, MI 48105   Ann Zimmerman, Libn.
Founded: 1965. **Staff:** Prof 1. **Subjects:** Fishery biology, aquatic ecology,
pesticide, contaminants and water pollution, Great Lakes. **Holdings:** 3000
books; 2100 bound periodical volumes; 40,000 reprints. **Subscriptions:** 163
journals and other serials. **Services:** Interlibrary loan; copying; library open
to the public. **Automated Operations:** Computerized cataloging.
Computerized Information Services: DIALOG Information Services, BRS
Information Technologies, OCLC. **Networks/Consortia:** Member of
FEDLINK, Michigan Library Consortium (MLC). **Remarks:** FTS: 378-
1210. FAX: (313)994-3331, ext. 273. Fax via FTS: 378-1273.

★ 17501 ★
U.S. Fish & Wildlife Service - National Fisheries Research Center -
  Library (Biol Sci, Agri)
Box 818   Phone: (608)783-6451
La Crosse, WI 54602-0818   Rosalie A. Schnick, Tech.Info.Spec.
Founded: 1959. **Staff:** Prof 1; Other 2. **Subjects:** Fish management,
toxicology, pharmacology, fish culture and physiology, limnology. **Special
Collections:** Complete sets of volumes of early studies on fish culture, fish
diseases, and fishery biology. **Holdings:** 6000 books; 300 bound periodical
volumes; 15,000 reprints; 10,000 leaflets and pamphlets. **Subscriptions:** 200
journals and other serials. **Services:** Interlibrary loan; library open to the
public for reference use only on request. **Computerized Information
Services:** DIALOG Information Services, OCLC. **Publications:** List of
Serials - available on request. **Remarks:** FAX: (608)783-6606.

★ 17502 ★
U.S. Fish & Wildlife Service - National Fisheries Research Center
  (Leetown) - Technical Information Services (Biol Sci, Sci-Engr, Agri)
Box 700   Phone: (304)725-8461
Kearneysville, WV 25430   Joyce A. Mann, Tech.Info.Off.
Founded: 1959. **Staff:** Prof 3. **Subjects:** Aquaculture; fish - diseases,
nutrition, pathology, physiology, bacteriology, virology, parasitology,
culture, immunology, chemotherapy, freshwater biology. **Special
Collections:** Fish diseases (15,000 reprints); fish culture (8000 reports and
reprints). **Holdings:** 22,000 books; 23,000 reprints; 13 VF drawers of staff
publications. **Subscriptions:** 400 journals and other serials. **Services:**
Interlibrary loan; copying; services open to the public with restrictions.
Automated Operations: Computerized cataloging. **Computerized
Information Services:** DIALOG Information Services, OCLC. **Networks/
Consortia:** Member of FEDLINK. **Remarks:** Statistics include the holdings
of the National Fishery Research and Development Laboratory in
Wellsboro, Pennsylvania and the Tunison Laboratory of Fish Nutrition in
Cortland, New York, and its Field Station in Hagerman, Idaho. **Staff:** Vi
Catrow, Libn.

★ 17503 ★
U.S. Fish & Wildlife Service - Northern Prairie Wildlife Research
  Center - Library (Biol Sci, Env-Cons)
Rte. 1, Box 96C   Phone: (701)252-5363
Jamestown, ND 58401-9736   Kirsten M. Lahlum, Libn.
Founded: 1965. **Staff:** Prof 1. **Subjects:** Wildlife management and research,
avian biology, plant and animal ecology, predation, waterfowl, global
climate change. **Holdings:** 3000 books; 2300 bound periodical volumes.
Subscriptions: 150 journals and other serials. **Services:** Interlibrary loan;
copying; library open to qualified persons by permission. **Computerized
Information Services:** DIALOG Information Services, OCLC. **Networks/
Consortia:** Member of FEDLINK, MINITEX Library Information
Network. **Remarks:** FAX: (701)252-4217.

★ 17504 ★
U.S. Fish & Wildlife Service - Office of Audio-Visual - Library (Aud-
Vis)
1849 C St., N.W., Rm. 3444   Phone: (202)208-5634
Washington, DC 20240   Steve Hillebrand, Chf.
Staff: 1. **Subjects:** Wildlife, especially birds and endangered species.
Holdings: 15,000 still photographs and color transparencies. **Services:**
Photographs may be consulted by authors, editors, publishers, and
conservationists. library open to the public by appointment. **Remarks:**
Library prefers all requests to be submitted in writing, specifying the species
(endangered or nonendangered) to be researched. Requests are filled within
two weeks, although larger requests may take longer.

★ 17505 ★
U.S. Fish & Wildlife Service - Patuxent Wildlife Research Center -
  Library (Biol Sci, Env-Cons)
Laurel, MD 20708   Phone: (301)498-0235
                                       Lynda Garrett, Libn.
Founded: 1942. **Staff:** Prof 1; Other 1. **Subjects:** Wildlife, especially birds;
environmental pollution; endangered species; biostatistics. **Holdings:** 9000
books; 35,000 reprints and pamphlets. **Subscriptions:** 250 journals and other
serials. **Services:** Interlibrary loan; copying; library open to the public for
reference use only. **Automated Operations:** Computerized cataloging and
ILL. **Computerized Information Services:** DIALOG Information Services,
OCLC; CD-ROM (Fish and Wildlife Worldwide). **Networks/Consortia:**
Member of Maryland Interlibrary Organization (MILO), FEDLINK.
Remarks: FAX: (301)498-0363.

★ 17506 ★
U.S. Fish & Wildlife Service - Tunison Laboratory of Fish Nutrition -
  Library (Biol Sci, Agri)
3075 Gracie Rd.   Phone: (607)753-9391
Cortland, NY 13045   James Meade, Dir.
Founded: 1932. **Staff:** 9. **Subjects:** Fish nutrition and physiology, fishery
biology, general nutrition and physiology. **Holdings:** 750 books; 500 bound
periodical volumes; 5500 reprints. **Services:** Interlibrary loan; copying;
library open to the public for reference use only. **Remarks:** FAX: (607)753-
0259. Library is part of the National Fisheries Research Center,
Kearneysville, WV.

★ 17507 ★
U.S. Food & Drug Administration - Center for Devices & Radiological
  Health - Library HFZ-46 (Med)
1390 Piccard Dr.   Phone: (301)427-1235
Rockville, MD 20850   Harriet Albersheim, Chf.Libn.
Founded: 1976. **Staff:** Prof 4; Other 3. **Subjects:** Ultrasonics, lasers, medical
devices, artificial organs, biomedical engineering, biomaterials, radiology,
radiobiology, radiation, nuclear medicine, radiological health, radiation
hazards, emission, microwaves. **Special Collections:** National Council on
Radiation Protection and Measurements reports; Radiation Effects
Research Foundation technical reports. **Holdings:** 7000 books; periodical
titles (bound and microfilm). **Subscriptions:** 800 journals and other serials.
Services: Interlibrary loan; library open to qualified users for research in
subject field. **Computerized Information Services:** DIALOG Information
Services, MEDLARS, BRS Information Technologies, OCLC. **Networks/
Consortia:** Member of FEDLINK. **Publications:** Newsletter, irregular.
Remarks: FAX: (301)427-1997.

★ 17508 ★
U.S. Food & Drug Administration - Center for Food Safety & Applied
  Nutrition - Library (Food-Bev, Sci-Engr)
200 C St., S.W., Rm. 3321, HFF-37   Phone: (202)245-1235
Washington, DC 20204   Michele R. Chatfield, Dir.
Staff: Prof 6; Other 5. **Subjects:** Chemistry, analytical chemistry, toxicology,
food technology, nutrition, medicine, biology, cosmetics. **Holdings:** 12,000
books; 1500 reports, documents, pamphlets; 18,000 cartridges of microfilm.
Subscriptions: 900 journals and other serials. **Services:** Interlibrary loan;
SDI; library open to the public. **Automated Operations:** Computerized
cataloging and serials. **Computerized Information Services:** DIALOG
Information Services, MEDLARS, BRS Information Technologies, OCLC.
Networks/Consortia: Member of FEDLINK. **Special Catalogs:** Union List
of Periodicals in conjunction with other federal libraries. **Remarks:** FAX:
(202)245-6694. The Food & Drug Administration is part of the U.S. Public
Health Service. **Also Known As:** FDA. **Staff:** Lee Bernstein, Ref.Libn.; Joan
Gilbert, Tech.Serv.Libn.; Anna McGowan, Tech.Info.Spec.; Karen Smith,
Ref.Libn.; Bruce Marquette, Beltsville Res. Complex, Libn.

★ 17509 ★
U.S. Food & Drug Administration - Fishery Research Branch - Library
  (Biol Sci)
Box 158   Phone: (205)694-4480
Dauphin Island, AL 36528   Patsy C. Purvis, Libn.
Staff: Prof 12; Other 11. **Subjects:** Aquaculture, microbiology, marine
biology, chemistry. **Holdings:** 400 books. **Subscriptions:** 30 journals and
other serials. **Services:** Library open to the public by special arrangement.
Remarks: FAX: (205)694-4477.

★17510★

U.S. Food & Drug Administration - National Center for Toxicological Research - Library (Biol Sci)
Jefferson, AR 87102   Phone: (501)543-7389
                                                              Billie Gough, Supv.Libn.
Founded: 1972. **Staff:** Prof 2; Other 2. **Subjects:** Toxicology, chemistry, teratogenesis, carcinogenesis, mutagenesis, biochemistry. **Special Collections:** Bacteriology. **Holdings:** 15,000 books; 500 bound periodical volumes. **Subscriptions:** 250 journals and other serials. **Services:** Interlibrary loan; SDI; library open to the public for reference use only. **Automated Operations:** Computerized cataloging. **Computerized Information Services:** DIALOG Information Services, MEDLARS, OCLC. **Networks/Consortia:** Member of FEDLINK, AMIGOS Bibliographical Council, Inc. **Remarks:** FAX: (501)543-7610. **Staff:** Mary Moss.

★17511★

U.S. Food & Drug Administration - Winchester Engineering & Analytical Center - Library (Med)
109 Holton St.   Phone: (617)729-5700
Winchester, MA 01890   James Fritzgerald, Dir.
Founded: 1961. **Staff:** 1. **Subjects:** Radiology, medical roentgenology, chemistry, physics, nuclear science, oceanography, statistics, medicine, electronics. **Holdings:** 1000 books; 710 bound periodical volumes; technical documents; miscellaneous reports; 20 VF drawers of unbound materials. **Subscriptions:** 109 journals and other serials. **Services:** Interlibrary loan; copying; library open to the public for reference use only upon request.

U.S. and Foreign Commercial Service
See: **U.S. International Trade Administration** (17562)

★17512★

U.S. Forest Service - Forest Engineering Research Project - Library (Biol Sci)
George W. Andrews Forestry Sciences Laboratory
Devall St.   Phone: (205)826-8700
Auburn University, AL 36849   Dr. Bryce J. Stokes, Project Ldr.
Staff: 1. **Subjects:** Forest engineering, timber harvesting, forest machinery, harvesting systems, forest soils, forest roads. **Holdings:** 300 books; 100 bound periodical volumes; 10,000 reports. **Subscriptions:** 10 journals and other serials. **Services:** Copying; library open to the public for reference use only. **Computerized Information Services:** Internal database. **Remarks:** FAX: (205)821-0037.

★17513★

U.S. Forest Service - Forest Products Laboratory - Library (Sci-Engr, Agri, Biol Sci)
One Gifford Pinchot Dr.   Phone: (608)231-9313
Madison, WI 53705-2398   Roger Scharmer, Libn.
Founded: 1910. **Staff:** Prof 2; Other 5. **Subjects:** Forest products utilization, energy from wood, paper and pulp, wood engineering, wood process and protection, timber, wood products economics. **Special Collections:** Forest products utilization. **Holdings:** 56,300 books and bound periodical volumes; 30,300 technical reports; 20,000 bulletins, reports, reprints; 6100 patents; 5900 microforms. **Subscriptions:** 550 journals. **Services:** Interlibrary loan; copying (limited); library open to the public. **Computerized Information Services:** DIALOG Information Services; internal database. **Remarks:** The Forest Service is part of the U.S. Department of Agriculture. **Staff:** Julie Blankenburg, Asst.Libn.

★17514★

U.S. Forest Service - Forestry Sciences Laboratory - Library (Biol Sci)
5985 Hwy. K
Box 898   Phone: (715)362-7474
Rhinelander, WI 54501   Deanna J. Okimosh
Founded: 1957. **Subjects:** Biotechnology, biology, botany, genetics, silviculture, horticulture. **Holdings:** 3000 books; 2300 bound periodical volumes. **Subscriptions:** 33 journals and other serials. **Services:** Interlibrary loan; library open to the public for reference use only. **Remarks:** FAX: (715)362-7816.

★17515★

U.S. Forest Service - FS Info NW (Biol Sci)
University of Washington, Mail Stop AQ-15   Phone: (206)543-7484
Seattle, WA 98195   Kay F. Denfeld, Libn.
Founded: 1976. **Staff:** Prof 2; Other 3. **Subjects:** Forestry, natural resources. **Holdings:** Figures not available. **Services:** Interlibrary loan; service not open to the public. **Computerized Information Services:** DIALOG Information Services; FS Info (internal database); InterNet (electronic mail service). **Networks/Consortia:** Member of Forest Service Information Network. **Publications:** Monthly Alert (library bibliography). **Remarks:** FAX: (206)553-1190. Electronic mail address(es): DENFELD@U.WASHINGTON.EDU (InterNet). Jointly maintained with University of Washington. **Also Known As:** FS INFO NW. **Staff:** Susan Cudnohfsky, Asst.Libn.

U.S. Forest Service - Gila Natl. Forest
See: **U.S. Natl. Park Service - Gila Cliff Dwellings Natl. Monument** (17721)

★17516★

U.S. Forest Service - History Unit Reference Collection (Hist)
14th and Independence, S.W.
Auditors Bldg. 2-C
P.O. Box 69090   Phone: (202)205-1059
Washington, DC 20090-6090   Terry West, Hist.
Founded: 1971. **Staff:** 1. **Subjects:** Forest Service administrative history, conservation history, natural resource management, land use history, agency timber management policy and practices. **Special Collections:** Forest Service manuals and handbooks, 1880s to 1930s. **Holdings:** 100 books; 10 bound periodical volumes; 500 documents; 20 manuscripts. **Services:** Copying (limited); collection open to the public by appointment for reference use. **Publications:** History Line, 2/year (newsletter); reports, occasional. **Remarks:** FAX: (202)205-0885.

★17517★

U.S. Forest Service - Intermountain Research Station - Library (Env-Cons, Agri)
324 25th St.   Phone: (801)625-5444
Ogden, UT 84401   Carol A. Ayer, Tech.Info.Off.
Founded: 1962. **Staff:** Prof 3; Other 8. **Subjects:** Management - forest, range, watershed; forest fires; wildlife; forest disease, economics, utilization, and insects. **Holdings:** 7000 books; 2500 bound periodical volumes; 29,000 reprints, pamphlets, translations; 6 files of microfiche; 4 drawers of microfilm. **Subscriptions:** 450 journals and other serials. **Services:** Interlibrary loan; library open to the public. **Automated Operations:** Computerized public access catalog and cataloging. **Computerized Information Services:** DIALOG Information Services, OCLC; FS INFO (internal database). Performs searches free of charge on internal database only. **Networks/Consortia:** Member of FEDLINK. **Publications:** FS INFO Monthly Alert. **Remarks:** FAX: (801)625-5129. **Also Known As:** U.S. Forest Service - FS INFO-Intermountain. **Staff:** Irene E. Voit; Richard Cacciato.

★17518★

U.S. Forest Service - Northeastern Forest Experiment Station - Library (Biol Sci)
359 Main Rd.   Phone: (614)363-0023
Delaware, OH 43015   Sheryl A. Dew, Lib.Techn.
Founded: 1961. **Staff:** 1. **Subjects:** Economics; silviculture; forest botany, mensuration, utilization, management, entomology and pathology, resources and conservation; watershed management. **Holdings:** 1000 books; 1200 bound periodical volumes. **Subscriptions:** 160 journals and other serials. **Services:** Library open to the public. **Computerized Information Services:** OCLC, DIALOG Information Services; FS INFO (internal database). **Remarks:** FAX: (614)363-1437.

★17519★

U.S. Forest Service - Pacific Northwest Research Station - Forestry Sciences Laboratory - FS INFO Alaska (Agri, Biol Sci)
2770 Sherwood Ln., Suite 2A   Phone: (907)586-7810
Juneau, AK 99801-8545   Lori Erbs, Biol.Libn.
Founded: 1961. **Staff:** 2. **Subjects:** Boreal forestry, fisheries, wildlife, entomology, recreation, rainforest ecology. **Holdings:** 2500 books; 3000 bound periodical volumes; 24,000 pamphlets, reprints, and reports; 15,000

government serial documents; 250 maps and charts; 1500 photographs; 150 reels of microfilm and microfiche. **Subscriptions:** 224 journals and other serials. **Services:** Interlibrary loan; journal routing; library open to the public with restrictions on circulation. **Computerized Information Services:** DIALOG Information Services, FS-INFO; CD-ROM (WLN on LaserCat). **Networks/Consortia:** Member of Forest Service Information Network. **Publications:** Accession Lists, quarterly; Periodicals and Serials Holdings Lists; Station Publication Lists; special subject bibliographies, all irregular. **Remarks:** FAX: (907)586-7848. **Formerly:** Its Library.

★17520★
U.S. Forest Service - Pacific Southwest Forest and Range Experiment Station - Library (Biol Sci, Agri, Env-Cons)
800 Buchanan St.   Phone: (510)559-6300
Albany, CA 94710   Brian Lym, Sta.Libn.
Founded: 1960. **Staff:** Prof 1; Other 4. **Subjects:** Forest management, silviculture, watershed management, computers and statistics, wildlife management, environmental protection. **Holdings:** 40,000 volumes, documents, offprints, reprints, preprints, bulletins, research notes. **Subscriptions:** 602 journals and other serials. **Services:** Interlibrary loan; copying; center open to the public for reference use only. **Automated Operations:** Computerized public access catalog and cataloging. **Computerized Information Services:** DIALOG Information Services, RLIN, OCLC; internal databases. **Networks/Consortia:** Member of Forest Service Information Network. **Publications:** WESTFORNET Monthly Alert. **Special Indexes:** FAMULUS-based indexes and abstract collections. **Also Known As:** U.S. Forest Service - FS-INFO-PSW. **Staff:** Ellen Dreibelbis, Doc. Delivery/ILL; Sandra Stasenka, Ser./Acq.

★17521★
U.S. Forest Service - Recreation, Wilderness, & Cultural Resources (Hist)
·630 Sansome St.   Phone: (415)705-2819
San Francisco, CA 94111   Linda Marie Lux, Hist.
Subjects: History of the National Forests in California - logging, mining, grazing, forestry, recreation, subsistence uses; history of California Indians, Euro-Americans, Chinese, other cultural and ethnic groups in the National Forests, prehistory to present. **Holdings:** 2500 manuscripts, records, oral history materials; historic photographs. **Services:** Copying; center open to the public by appointment during business hours.

★17522★
U.S. Forest Service - Rocky Mountain Forest & Range Experiment Station - Library (Biol Sci, Agri)
240 W. Prospect St.   Phone: (303)498-1268
Fort Collins, CO 80526   Frances J. Barney, Libn.
Founded: 1966. **Staff:** Prof 2; Other 2. **Subjects:** Forest management, shelterbelts, wildland valuation, resource economics, snow and watershed management, forest entomology and pathology, wildlife habitats, disturbed site reclamation, atmospheric deposition, nematology, ecology of arid lands, history of forestry in Rocky Mountains. **Special Collections:** World Mistletoe Literature (on Famulus retrieval system; 7000 references); Boyce Index to Forest Pathology Literature (30 card file drawers). **Holdings:** 15,000 books; 5000 bound periodical volumes; 20,000 unbound serials; 10 VF drawers of reprints; 150 reels of microfilm of Oxford Catalog and periodicals; 1200 dissertations; 4 VF drawers of Rocky Mountain Station historical material. **Subscriptions:** 650 journals and other serials. **Services:** Interlibrary loan; copying; library open to the public for reference use only. **Computerized Information Services:** DIALOG Information Services, BRS Information Technologies, OCLC, LS/2000. **Networks/Consortia:** Member of Forest Service Information Network. **Remarks:** FAX: (303)498-1010. **Staff:** Robert W. Dana, Tech.Info.Spec.

★17523★
U.S. Forest Service - Southern Forest Experiment Station - Institute of Tropical Forestry - Library (Biol Sci, Env-Cons)
Call Box 25000   Phone: (809)766-5335
Rio Piedras, PR 00928-2500   Gisel Reyes
Staff: 3. **Subjects:** Tropical forestry and ecology, wildlife management. **Holdings:** 50,000 items. **Subscriptions:** 100 journals and other serials. **Services:** Interlibrary loan; copying; library open to the public for reference use only. **Automated Operations:** Computerized mailing list for dissemination of institute's publications. **Computerized Information Services:** DIALOG Information Services; FS INFO-ON LINE (internal database). **Publications:** ITF Annual Letter. **Remarks:** FAX: (809)250-6924. Telex: 23 7401032.

★17524★
U.S. Forest Service - Southern Forest Experiment Station Library (Agri, Biol Sci)
Postal Service Bldg., Rm. T-10210
701 Loyola Ave.   Phone: (504)589-3935
New Orleans, LA 70113   Cheryl Rademacher, Ck.
Founded: 1921. **Staff:** 1. **Subjects:** Forest management, economics, and utilization; range and watershed management; forest disease, fire, and insects; wildlife habitat. **Holdings:** Figures not available. **Services:** Interlibrary loan; copying; library open to the public. **Remarks:** FAX: (504)589-3961.

★17525★
U.S. General Accounting Office - Boston Regional Office - Technical Information Services (Bus-Fin)
10 Causeway St., Rm. 575   Phone: (617)565-7474
Boston, MA 02222-1030   Jennifer Arns, Computer Prog./Anl.
Staff: Prof 1. **Subjects:** Auditing, public administration, health care financing, environmental protection, national security, government contracting, financial services. **Special Collections:** All GAO publications (20 VF drawers); Comptroller General Decisions (published and unpublished); legislative histories. **Holdings:** Public laws; appropriation hearings; technical reports; Congressional documents; U.S. Code; Code of Federal Regulations. **Subscriptions:** 71 journals and other serials. **Services:** Interlibrary loan; open to the public by appointment only. **Computerized Information Services:** Library of Congress Information System (LOCIS), DataTimes, VU/TEXT Information Services, LEXIS, NEXIS, DIALOG Information Services; internal database. **Networks/Consortia:** Member of FEDLINK. **Remarks:** Alternate telephone number(s): (617)565-7563.

★17526★
U.S. General Accounting Office - Information Services Center (Law, Bus-Fin)
441 G St., N.W., Rm. 6430   Phone: (202)275-3691
Washington, DC 20548   Phyllis Christenson, Dir.
Founded: 1949. **Staff:** Prof 23; Other 32. **Subjects:** Law, accounting and auditing, management, public policy, program evaluation, information technology. **Special Collections:** Federal departmental regulatory material; legislative history collection; GAO Historical Collection; GAO reports (in microform). **Holdings:** 125,000 volumes; 1 million microfiche. **Subscriptions:** 1600 journals; 3000 serials; 18 newspapers. **Services:** Interlibrary loan; center open to the public for reference use only. **Automated Operations:** Computerized cataloging and acquisitions. **Computerized Information Services:** BRS Information Technologies, DataTimes, DIALOG Information Services, LEXIS, NEXIS, OCLC, USNI Military Database, VU/TEXT Information Services, WESTLAW, WILSONLINE, JURIS, SCORPIO (Subject-Content-Oriented Retriever for Processing Information Online); internal databases. **Networks/Consortia:** Member of FEDLINK. **Publications:** Library Focus, monthly; Library & Information Services Handbook; subject bibliographies, irregular; GAO Library Periodicals. **Remarks:** FAX: (202)275-0373; (202)275-0373. Alternate telephone number(s): 275-5180. **Also Known As:** GAO. **Staff:** Ellen Swain, Mgr., Tech.Lib.; Carol Hillier, Mgr., Law Lib.; Marcia Talley, Mgr., Tech.Serv.

★17527★
U.S. General Accounting Office - Philadelphia Regional Resource Center (Bus-Fin)
841 Chestnut St., Suite 760   Phone: (215)574-4052
Philadelphia, PA 19107   Linda Carnevale Skale, Tech.Info.Spec.
Founded: 1979. **Staff:** Prof 1. **Subjects:** Accounting, U.S. legislation. **Special Collections:** Decisions of the U.S. Comptroller General, 1921 to present; GAO Legislative History Microfiche Collection (through 96th Congress); Congressional agencies' material. **Holdings:** 500 books; General Accounting Office annual reports, 1961 to present; complete set of Public Laws from 90th Congress to present; U.S. House Committee on Appropriations hearings. **Subscriptions:** 64 journals and other serials. **Services:** Interlibrary loan; copying; SDI; center open to the public by appointment. **Computerized Information Services:** DIALOG Information Services, Library of Congress Information System (SCORPIO), Mead Data Central, OCLC, VU/TEXT Information Services, DataTimes, U.S. House of Representatives Legislative Information and Status System (LEGIS); internal database. **Remarks:** FAX: (215)574-4082.

★ 17528 ★
U.S. General Accounting Office - San Francisco Regional Office - Library (Bus-Fin)
301 Howard St., Suite 1200   Phone: (415)904-2000
San Francisco, CA 94105   Linda F. Sharp, Tech.Info.Spec.
Founded: 1976. **Staff:** Prof 1; Other 1. **Subjects:** Auditing, program evaluation, legislation. **Special Collections:** U.S. General Accounting Office Audit Reports; annual reports. **Holdings:** 10 VF drawers of reports on microfiche. **Subscriptions:** 30 journals and other serials. **Services:** Library open to the public by appointment. **Computerized Information Services:** Online systems.

U.S. General Services Administration
See: **General Services Administration** (6348)

★ 17529 ★
U.S. Geological Survey - Earth Resources Observation Systems (EROS) Data Center - Technical Reference Unit (Sci-Engr)
EROS Data Center   Phone: (605)594-6102
Sioux Falls, SD 57198   K.C. Wehde, Tech.Ref. Unit Coord.
Founded: 1974. **Staff:** Prof 1. **Subjects:** Remote sensing, natural resources. **Special Collections:** ERTS reports (microfiche). **Holdings:** 3000 books; 200 bound periodical volumes; 6000 microfiche; 2000 reports; 2000 periodicals. **Subscriptions:** 55 journals and other serials. **Services:** Interlibrary loan; unit open to the public. **Automated Operations:** Computerized cataloging. **Remarks:** FAX: (605)594-6589.

★ 17530 ★
U.S. Geological Survey - Earth Science Information Center (ESIC) (Geog-Map)
Federal Center, Stop 504
Box 25046
Denver, CO 80225   Phone: (303)236-5829
   W. Graser, Info.Ctr.Chf.
Founded: 1947. **Staff:** 15. **Subjects:** Topographic maps, aerial photography, space imagery, orthophotoquads, digital data, land use. **Special Collections:** Out of print topographic quadrangles (266 reels of microfilm). **Holdings:** 480 VF drawers of maps; 1 million aerial photographs. **Services:** Copying; center open to the public for reference use only. **Computerized Information Services:** Internal database. **Special Indexes:** Topographic and orthophotoquad advance material index (map indexes available for each state). **Remarks:** FAX: (303)236-8654.

★ 17531 ★
U.S. Geological Survey - Earth Science Information Center (ESIC) (Geog-Map)
507 National Center   Phone: (703)860-6045
Reston, VA 22092   John T. Wood, Chf.
Founded: 1974. **Staff:** 26. **Subjects:** Earth science: geologic, hydrologic and topographic; maps and charts; aerial and space photos; satellite and radar imagery; geodetic control; digital cartographic/geographic data (tapes); related earth science and cartographic data. **Holdings:** Cartographic Catalog (29,000 entries); Aerial Photo Summary Record System (234,000 air photo project records); Map and Chart Information System (254,000 map records). **Computerized Information Services:** Internal databases. **Publications:** Publications of the USGS, monthly; ESIC Newsletter, semiannual; technical user guides, as needed. **Special Indexes:** Indexes to numerous U.S.G.S. map products, semiannual. **Remarks:** ESIC provides information on earth science, cartographic, and geographic data produced by federal agencies, states, and commercial organizations. FAX: (703)648-5939.

★ 17532 ★
U.S. Geological Survey - Earth Science Information Center (ESIC) - Library (Energy, Sci-Engr)
4230 University Dr., Rm. 101   Phone: (907)786-7011
Anchorage, AK 99508-4664   Elizabeth C. Behrendt, Geog.
Founded: 1951. **Subjects:** Geology, water resources, oil and gas, minerals. **Special Collections:** U.S. Geological Survey (USGS) open-file reports on Alaska (1000); all USGS topographic and thematic maps for Alaska; USGS world and U.S. maps. **Holdings:** 16,000 books; departmental publications; State of Alaska publications. **Subscriptions:** 40 journals and other serials. **Services:** Copying; library open to the public for reference use only. **Computerized Information Services:** Earth Science Data Directory; CD-ROMs (Earth Science Library); internal databases. **Special Catalogs:** Lists of all U.S.G.S. publications on Alaska (card); Catalog of Holdings of USGS Main Library, Reston VA (book, CD-ROM). **Remarks:** FTS: 868-7011. FAX: (907)786-7050.

★ 17533 ★
U.S. Geological Survey - Earth Science Information Center (ESIC) MS 532 (Geog-Map)
345 Middlefield Rd., MS 532   Phone: (415)329-4309
Menlo Park, CA 94025-3591   Glenn Ireland, Chf.
Founded: 1977. **Staff:** 20. **Subjects:** Maps and charts, aerial photography, geodetic control, digital data. **Special Collections:** Original map reproduction material on separate data plates. **Holdings:** 25 million photographs and images. **Services:** Copying; photograph reproduction; cartographic research, reference, and technical advice; center open to the public. **Automated Operations:** Computerized cataloging, acquisitions, and circulation. **Computerized Information Services:** Internal database. Performs most searches free of charge. Contact Person: Dennis Cole, Chf., User Serv., 329-4357. **Publications:** Topographic, geologic, water resources, and conservation brochures; directories. **Special Catalogs:** Microform catalogs. **Special Indexes:** Published map and advanced materials indexes. **Remarks:** FAX: (415)329-5130. Alternate telephone number(s): (415)329-4362 (Data Acq.). **Staff:** Gerald Greenberg, Chf., Data Acq.

★ 17534 ★
U.S. Geological Survey - Flagstaff Field Center - Branch Library (Sci-Engr, Geog-Map)
2255 N. Gemini Dr.   Phone: (602)527-7008
Flagstaff, AZ 86001   Jenny Bronk, Lib.Tech.
Founded: 1964. **Staff:** 2. **Subjects:** Earth sciences, space sciences. **Holdings:** 31,000 volumes; 30,000 maps. **Subscriptions:** 150 journals and other serials. **Services:** Interlibrary loan; library open to the public for reference use only. **Computerized Information Services:** OCLC; internal database.

★ 17535 ★
U.S. Geological Survey - Ice and Climate Project - Glacier Inventory Photo Library (Sci-Engr, Aud-Vis)
University of Puget Sound   Phone: (206)593-6516
Tacoma, WA 98416   David R. Hirst, Photo.
Founded: 1960. **Staff:** 1. **Subjects:** Glaciers, glacier features, mountainous regions, conterminous U.S. **Special Collections:** Aerial photographs of glaciated areas in western U.S., Canada, and Alaska (100,000 black/white images, 1960 to present). **Holdings:** Figures not available. **Services:** Copying; library open to the public with restrictions. **Remarks:** FAX: (206)383-7967.

★ 17536 ★
U.S. Geological Survey - Library (Sci-Engr)
345 Middlefield Rd., MS955   Phone: (415)329-5090
Menlo Park, CA 94025-3591   Nancy Blair, Adm.Libn.
Founded: 1953. **Staff:** Prof 3; Other 10. **Subjects:** Geology, geophysics, oceanography. **Special Collections:** California Information Center; photograph library; Earth Sciences Education Center. **Holdings:** 300,000 volumes; 50 drawers of microforms; 35,000 maps; 30 drawers of photographs. **Subscriptions:** 1500 journals and other serials. **Services:** Interlibrary loan; SDI; library open to the public for reference use only. **Automated Operations:** Computerized public access catalog, cataloging, serials, and circulation. **Computerized Information Services:** DIALOG Information Services, RLIN, OCLC. **Remarks:** FAX: (415)329-5132. **Staff:** Ellen White, Ref.Libn.; Diane Rafferty, Ref.Libn.

★ 17537 ★
U.S. Geological Survey - Library (Sci-Engr)
Box 25046
Mail Stop 914
Denver, CO 80225   Phone: (303)236-1000
   Marilyn Stark, Reg.Libn.
Founded: 1948. **Staff:** Prof 7; Other 13. **Subjects:** Geology, mineral and water resources, mineralogy, physics, paleontology, petrology, chemistry, soil and environmental sciences. **Special Collections:** Photographic Library (300,000 items); Field Records Library (80,000 items). **Holdings:** 175,000 books; 60,000 bound periodical volumes; 75,000 other cataloged items; 15,000 microforms; 65,000 topographic maps of U.S.; 1500 geologic world maps; 7000 USGS maps in series (complete); 20,000 reports and pamphlets. **Subscriptions:** 1600 journals and other serials. **Services:** Interlibrary loan; library open to the public for reference use only. **Automated Operations:** Computerized cataloging and circulation. **Computerized Information Services:** DIALOG Information Services, PFDS Online, STN International; DIALMAIL (electronic mail service). **Networks/Consortia:** Member of Central Colorado Library System (CCLS). **Remarks:** FAX: (303)236-0015. **Staff:** M. Elaine Watson, ILL Libn.; Isabella Hopkins, Spec.Coll.Libn.; Tommie Ann Gard, Ref.Circ.Libn.

★ 17538 ★
U.S. Geological Survey - Library (Sci-Engr)
8011A Cameron Rd.   Phone: (512)873-3020
Austin, TX 78753   Julie Menard, Libn.
Staff: Prof 1; Other 1. **Subjects:** Hydrology, hydrogeology, hydrologic and environmental engineering, water quality. **Special Collections:** U.S.G.S Professional Papers (complete collection); U.S.G.S. Water Supply Papers (complete collection). **Holdings:** 3000 books; 5000 technical reports. **Subscriptions:** 20 journals and other serials. **Services:** Interlibrary loan; library open to the public for reference use only. **Automated Operations:** Computerized cataloging and ILL. **Computerized Information Services:** DIALOG Information Services, OCLC. **Networks/Consortia:** Member of FEDLINK. **Remarks:** FAX: (512)873-3090.

★ 17539 ★
U.S. Geological Survey - Library System (Sci-Engr)
12201 Sunrise Valley Dr.
National Center, Mail Stop 950   Phone: (703)648-4302
Reston, VA 22092   Barbara A. Chappell, Chf.Libn.
Founded: 1882. **Staff:** Prof 27; Other 31. **Subjects:** Geology, mineralogy, mineral resources, water resources, petrology, paleontology. **Special Collections:** George F. Kunz Collection of Gems and Precious Stones; Douglas C. Alverson Collection of Russian Geological Books. **Holdings:** 799,000 volumes; 326,000 maps; 270,000 pamphlets; 370,000 microforms; doctoral dissertations on microfilm and microfiche; NTIS report literature on microfiche. **Subscriptions:** 9250 journals and other serials. **Services:** Interlibrary loan; copying; SDI; library open to the public with borrowing restricted to interlibrary loan. **Automated Operations:** Computerized cataloging, serials, and circulation. **Computerized Information Services:** DIALOG Information Services, WILSONLINE, ORBIT Search Service, STN International, LS/2000, UMI, OCLC; CD-ROMs; Geoindex (internal database). **Networks/Consortia:** Member of FEDLINK. **Remarks:** FAX: (703)648-6373. The Geological Survey is part of the U.S. Department of the Interior. **Staff:** Edward H. Liszewski, Assoc.Chf.Libn.; Virginia L. Major, Hd., Geologic Inquiries; Bruce Keck, Asst.Libn., Coll.Mgt. & Access; Margaret Merryman, Hd.Acq. & Exchange; Carol Borsik, Sys.Libn.; Elizabeth Whiting, Hd.Cat.; Carol Messick, Hd.Ref. & Circ.; Robert Bier, Hd., Cart.Info.Ctr.

★ 17540 ★
U.S. Geological Survey - National Mapping Division Assistance Facility - Library
Stennis Space Center
SSC, MS 39529
Founded: 1973. **Subjects:** Remote sensing, mapping, platforms and sensors, electromagnetic energy, cultural features and other man-related aspects of remote sensing, animal and plant life, geology and meteorology, hydrology and astronomy, data processing and management, digital cartography. **Special Collections:** Photo interpretation keys (87). **Holdings:** 1200 books; 183 bound periodical volumes; 15,000 documents on microfiche; 50 state map indices. **Remarks:** Currently inactive.

★ 17541 ★
U.S. Geological Survey - Water Resources Division - Colorado Water Resources Library (Env-Cons)
Denver Federal Center, Bldg. 53
Box 25046, Stop 415   Phone: (303)236-4882
Lakewood, CO 80225-0046   April Kobayashi, Libn.
Founded: 1973. **Staff:** Prof 1; Other 1. **Subjects:** Water resources, limnology, coal, oil shale. **Special Collections:** Annual reports of the Colorado River Basin, Arkansas River Basin, Missouri River, and Rio Grande River; U.S. Geological Survey Water Supply Papers (complete set); oil shale material. **Holdings:** 3800 books; 5000 pamphlets and serials; 2000 microfiche; 10 videotapes. **Subscriptions:** 35 journals and other serials. **Services:** Interlibrary loan; copying (limited); library open to the public for reference use only. **Automated Operations:** Computerized cataloging. **Computerized Information Services:** OCLC, DIALOG Information Services. **Remarks:** FAX: (303)236-4912. Branch libraries located at Pueblo, Grand Junction, and Meeker, Colorado.

★ 17542 ★
U.S. Geological Survey - Water Resources Division - Information Resource Center (Env-Cons)
5957 Lakeside Blvd.
Indianapolis, IN 46278   Phone: (317)290-3333
Founded: 1977. **Staff:** 1. **Subjects:** Hydrology, water resources in Indiana, geology, water pollution. **Holdings:** 7000 books; 225 reports on microfiche; 600 maps; 1000 reprints. **Subscriptions:** 15 journals and other serials. **Services:** Center open to the public for reference use only.

★ 17543 ★
U.S. Geological Survey - Water Resources Division - Library (Env-Cons)
Federal Bldg., Rm. 428
301 S. Park
Drawer 10076   Phone: (406)449-5263
Helena, MT 59626-0076   Cynthia J. Harksen, Libn.
Staff: Prof 1. **Subjects:** Water resources and development, water quality, floods. **Special Collections:** U.S. Geological Survey water supply papers, bulletins, professional papers. **Holdings:** 10,000 items. **Subscriptions:** 10 journals and other serials. **Services:** Interlibrary loan; copying; library open to the public for reference use only. **Automated Operations:** Computerized cataloging. **Computerized Information Services:** OCLC. **Networks/Consortia:** Member of FEDLINK.

★ 17544 ★
U.S. Geological Survey - Water Resources Division - Library (Env-Cons)
6417 Normandy Ln.   Phone: (608)276-3802
Madison, WI 53719-1133   Susan L. Ziegler, Ed.Asst.
Staff: 1. **Subjects:** Surface and ground water, water quality. **Special Collections:** Complete set of WRD Wisconsin publications. **Holdings:** 2500 books; 550 water supply papers; 475 professional papers; 140 bulletins; 180 circulars. **Subscriptions:** 10 journals and other serials. **Services:** Library open to the public for reference use only. **Remarks:** FAX: (608)276-3817.

★ 17545 ★
U.S. Geological Survey - Water Resources Division - National Water Data Exchange and Water Data Storage and Retrieval System (Sci-Engr)
National Center, Mail Stop 421   Phone: (703)648-6848
Reston, VA 22092   Dr. James S. Burton, Prog.Mgr.
Founded: 1976. **Staff:** Prof 9; Other 2. **Subjects:** Surface water stage and discharge, chemical quality parameters, radiochemistry, sedimentology, pesticide and biological concentrations in water, ground and surface water levels, flood frequency and flood inundation mapping. **Holdings:** 486,075 descriptions of sites that collect water data; 2000 descriptions of organizations that have water data and water related information. **Services:** Data and water information dissemination, water data exchange, and water data indexing; system open to the public on fee basis. **Computerized Information Services:** DIALOG Information Services; CD-ROMs; Master Water Data Index, Water Data Sources Directory (internal databases). **Publications:** List of publications - available on request. **Remarks:** FAX: (703)648-5704. The National Water Data Exchange provides access to the Water Data Storage and Retrieval System (WATSTORE) of the U.S. Geological Survey and the Storage and Retrieval System (STORET) of the U.S. Environmental Protection Agency. **Formerly:** Its National Water Data Storage & Retrieval System and Water Resources Scientific Information Center. **Also Known As:** NAWDEX, WATSTORE.

★ 17546 ★
U.S. Geological Survey - Water Resources Division - National Water Information Clearinghouse (Env-Cons)
National Center, Mail Stop 423   Phone: (703)648-6832
Reston, VA 22092   Donald L. Bingham, Info.Ctr.Hd.
Founded: 1990. **Staff:** Prof 3; Other 1. **Subjects:** Water related information and data. **Special Collections:** Water-related educational materials. **Holdings:** Figures not available. **Services:** Water-data indexing; literature abstracting; data-systems modernization. **Computerized Information Services:** Provides access to U.S. Geological Survey National Water Information System. **Remarks:** FAX: (703)648-5704. Toll-free telephone number(s): (800)H2O-9000. The National Water Information Clearinghouse is a new and emerging program designed to manage and coordinate the exchange of water resources information with Federal, State, and local governmental agencies, academia, industry, and the general public. **Also Known As:** NWIC.

★ 17547 ★
U.S. Geological Survey - Water Resources Division - New York District - Library (Sci-Engr)
343 Court House
Box 1669   Phone: (518)472-3107
Albany, NY 12201   Margaret Phillips, Hydro.Techn.
Subjects: Geochemistry, hydrology, geology, climatology. **Special Collections:** Acid Precipitation Collection (reprints and documents). **Holdings:** 6500 books; 250 pamphlet boxes of periodicals; 1000 maps; climatological data; 950 hydrologic investigations; atlases. **Subscriptions:** 50 journals and other serials. **Services:** Library open to the public for reference use only. **Computerized Information Services:** DIALOG Information Services, ORBIT Search Service, OCLC; Ground Water Site Inventory, Automated Data Processing System, Water Quality System, Water-Use (internal databases). **Remarks:** FAX: (518)472-2805.

★17548★

U.S. Geological Survey - Water Resources Division - New York
Subdistrict - Library
5 Aerial Way
Syosset, NY 11791   Phone: (516)938-8830
Subjects: Water resources, geology of Long Island. **Special Collections:** U.S. Geological Survey's professional papers; water supply papers; water resources investigations. **Holdings:** 300 books; 27 bound periodical volumes. **Services:** Library open to the public with restrictions.

★17549★

U.S. Geological Survey - Water Resources Division - Reading Room
(Sci-Engr, Geog-Map)
4501 Indian School Rd., N.E., Suite 200   Phone: (505)262-5362
Albuquerque, NM 87110   Cindy Shattuck
Founded: 1958. **Staff:** Prof 1. **Subjects:** Hydrology, geology of New Mexico. **Special Collections:** Topographic and geologic maps. **Holdings:** 1427 books; 10,012 bound periodical volumes; 19,965 unbound periodicals and reports; 855 microfiche. **Subscriptions:** 374 journals and other serials. **Services:** Interlibrary loan; copying; room open to the public for reference use only on Wednesdays. **Remarks:** FAX: (505)262-5398.

★17550★

U.S. Geological Survey - Water Resources Division - Water Resources
Scientific Information Center (Env-Cons)
425 National Center   Phone: (703)648-6820
Reston, VA 22092   Raymond A. Jensen, Chf.
Founded: 1966. **Staff:** Prof 3. **Subjects:** Nature and properties of water; water cycle and hydrology; water supply augmentation and conservation; water quantity management and control; water quality management and protection; water resources planning and water law; resources data; networks, techniques, and computer applications; engineering works and hydraulics; reviews, bibliographies, and other water literature products and services. **Computerized Information Services:** Produces Water Resources Abstracts available through DIALOG Information Services and on CD-ROM. **Publications:** Selected Water Resources Abstracts, available by subscription; Water Resources Thesaurus, 1980 - for sale; Abstracting and Indexing Guide - free upon request. **Remarks:** FAX: (703)648-5704. All acquisitions are eventually deposited with the U.S. Geological Survey Library, Reston, VA. **Also Known As:** WRSIC.

★17551★

U.S. Geological Survey - Water Resources Library (Env-Cons)
W. Aspinall Federal Bldg., Rm. 201
4th & Rood Ave.
Box 2027   Phone: (303)245-5257
Grand Junction, CO 81502   Dannie L. Collins, Subdistrict Chf.
Staff: Prof 2. **Subjects:** Water resources, water quality, geological and atmospheric conditions as they pertain to water. **Holdings:** 1534 books; 1014 bound periodical volumes; 669 volumes of basic data reports; 3880 maps; 110 decisions on names in the U.S.; 55 reels of microfilm of well log data for Colorado; 179 volumes of professional papers. **Services:** Interlibrary loan; copying; library open to the public with restrictions. **Publications:** Water Resources Data, Colorado; Water Year 1987; Missouri River Basin; Rio Grande River Basin.

★17552★

U.S. Geological Survey - Western Mineral Resources Library (Sci-Engr)
656 U.S. Court House
920 W. Riverside Ave.   Phone: (509)353-2641
Spokane, WA 99201   Kathy Linale, Lib.Techn.
Founded: 1948. **Staff:** 2. **Subjects:** Geology and allied sciences. **Special Collections:** U.S. Geological Survey publications (almost complete run). **Holdings:** Figures not available for books and bound periodical volumes; 1200 shelf feet of topographic maps of Pacific Northwest states and Alaska; state publications related to geology of Idaho, Washington, Montana, and Oregon. **Subscriptions:** 15 journals and other serials. **Services:** Library open to the public with restrictions. **Remarks:** FAX: (509)747-8980.

★17553★

United States Golf Association - Golf House Museum & Library (Rec)
P.O. Box 708   Phone: (201)234-2300
Far Hills, NJ 07931   Karen Bednarski, Libn./Musm.Cur.
Founded: 1938. **Staff:** Prof 2. **Subjects:** Golf. **Holdings:** 9000 books; 440 bound periodical volumes; 52 scrapbooks of newspaper clippings. **Subscriptions:** 25 journals and other serials. **Services:** Library open to the public for reference use only. **Remarks:** FAX: (201)234-0319. **Staff:** Andrew Mutch, Asst.Cur.

★17554★

U.S. Hockey Hall of Fame - Library (Rec)
Hat Trick Ave.
Box 657   Phone: (218)744-5167
Eveleth, MN 55734   Robert T. Scott, Exec.Dir.
Founded: 1973. **Subjects:** Ice hockey. **Special Collections:** College hockey rulebooks. **Holdings:** Unbound periodicals; newspapers; guide books; programs; scrapbooks. **Subscriptions:** 6 newspapers. **Services:** Library open to serious researchers only.

★17555★

U.S. House of Representatives - Library (Law)
B-18 Cannon Bldg.   Phone: (202)225-0462
Washington, DC 20515   E. Raymond Lewis, Libn.
Founded: 1792. **Staff:** 4. **Subjects:** Legislation, law. **Special Collections:** Congressional documents, Continental Congress to present. **Holdings:** 225,000 volumes. **Services:** Use of library restricted to members and committees of Congress and their staffs, except by special permission. **Publications:** Index to Congressional Committee Hearings in the House.

★17556★

U.S. Information Agency - Library Programs Division (Info Sci)
301 4th St., S.W., Rm. 314   Phone: (202)619-4915
Washington, DC 20547   Donald C. Hausrath, Dir.
Founded: 1943. **Staff:** 48. **Subjects:** American culture, American studies. **Holdings:** 50,000 books; periodicals; documents; microforms; AV programs. **Subscriptions:** 700 journals and other serials; 20 newspapers. **Services:** Interlibrary loan; library not open to the public. **Computerized Information Services:** Family of five databases, Public Diplomacy Query (internal databases). **Remarks:** Agency functions as service headquarters for 143 USIS libraries in 85 countries abroad, and also provides support to library programs in 27 Binational Centers. FAX: (202)619-6670.

★17557★

U.S. Information Agency - USIA Library (Soc Sci)
301 4th St., S.W., E/CLR Rm. 135   Phone: (202)619-4700
Washington, DC 20547   Donald Hausrath, Chf., Lib.Prog.Div.
Founded: 1955. **Staff:** Prof 29; Other 16. **Subjects:** International affairs, Americana, area studies, communication. **Special Collections:** Agency historical collection (5500 volumes). **Holdings:** 70,000 books; 27,000 bound periodical volumes; 85 VF drawers of clippings and documents; 90,500 microforms. **Subscriptions:** 840 journals and other serials; 12 newspapers. **Services:** Interlibrary loan; copying; SDI; library open to the public by appointment. **Automated Operations:** Computerized cataloging. **Computerized Information Services:** DIALOG Information Services, OCLC, NEXIS, VU/TEXT Information Services, DataTimes, LEGISLATE, WILSONLINE; internal database; DIALMAIL (electronic mail service). **Networks/Consortia:** Member of FEDLINK. **Publications:** USIA Library Bulletin, monthly; Calendar of Coming Events and Anniversaries, quarterly; Periodical Holdings, annual - all for internal distribution only. **Special Indexes:** Program Materials Index (PMI; online); index to government documents (online). **Remarks:** FAX: (202)485-1879. **Staff:** Helen Amabile, Dp.Chf., Lib.Prog.; Connie Moraff, Chf., Tech.Serv.; Nelia Dunbar, Chf., Ref.Br.; William Mitchell, Chf., Bibliog.Br.

U.S. Information Center for the Universal Decimal Classification
See: **University of Maryland, College Park - College of Library & Information Services (18804)**

★17558★

United States Information Service - Library (Soc Sci)
150 Wellington St., 3rd Fl.   Phone: (613)238-4470
Ottawa, ON, Canada K1P 5A4   Kyle Ward, Lib.Dir.
Founded: 1961. **Staff:** Prof 3. **Subjects:** United States - politics and government, legislation and policy; Canadian/American relations. **Special Collections:** United States Code Annotated; Code of Federal Regulations; selected U.S. Government publications; current speeches. **Holdings:** 3000 books and government documents; 14 VF drawers of clippings; telephone directories of major U.S. cities. **Subscriptions:** 80 journals and other serials. **Services:** Interlibrary loan; locates addresses and backgrounds of U.S. departments and institutions; provides information on U.S. laws, legislation, and documents; library open to the public with restrictions. **Computerized Information Services:** DIALOG Information Services, Info Globe, Infomart

Online, Public Diplomacy Query (PDQ), LEGI-SLATE; DIALMAIL (electronic mail service). **Networks/Consortia:** Member of FEDLINK. **Publications:** Library News; Article Alert. **Special Catalogs:** U.S. Official Publications in Selected Canadian Libraries. **Remarks:** FAX: (613)563-7701. Electronic mail address(es): 14517 (DIALMAIL). Provides educational advising service to students wishing to study in the U.S. as well as information on institutions of higher education and sources of financial aid. **Staff:** Allison Abraszko, Ref.Libn.; Gail McKeating, Libn./Educ.Adv.

U.S. Institute of Administration and Defense Information School
See: **U.S. Army - TRADOC - Soldier Support Center - Main Library** (17024)

★ 17559 ★
U.S. Institute of Peace - Jeannette Rankin Library Program (Soc Sci)
1550 M St., N.W., Suite 700   Phone: (202)457-1700
Washington, DC 20005-1708   Jeanne L. Bohlen, Dir.
Founded: 1988. **Staff:** 3. **Subjects:** International peace, conflict resolution. **Holdings:** 3700 books. **Subscriptions:** 135 journals and other serials; 6 newspapers. **Services:** Interlibrary loan; copying; library open to the public by appointment. **Computerized Information Services:** DIALOG Information Services, NEXIS, RLIN, OCLC, WILSONLINE, Institute for Global Communication. **Networks/Consortia:** Member of FEDLINK. **Publications:** List of publications - available on request. **Remarks:** FAX: (202)429-6063. **Staff:** Denise Dowdell, Ref.Libn.

★ 17560 ★
U.S. Interagency Advanced Power Group - Power Information Center (Sci-Engr, Energy)
Horizon Data Corporation
10700 Parkridge Blvd., Suite 250   Phone: (703)758-0531
Reston, VA 22091   Judy Hanst, Proj.Mgr.
Founded: 1960. **Staff:** Prof 4. **Subjects:** Electrical power conditioning; pulse power; superconductivity; mechanical heat engines and auxiliary components; chemical, nuclear, solar-thermal, and photovoltaic magnetohydrodynamics; systems. **Holdings:** 4000 project briefs and project reports. **Services:** Center open to government employees. **Publications:** Project Briefs, monthly; meeting proceedings; roster, annual. **Special Indexes:** Indexes to briefs, monthly and semiannual indexes. **Remarks:** FAX: (703)758-9713. **Formerly:** Located in Washington, DC. **Staff:** Daniel DeVoe, Prog.Coord.

★ 17561 ★
U.S. Internal Revenue Service - Law Library (Law)
Internal Revenue Service Bldg., Rm. 4324
1111 Constitution Ave., N.W.   Phone: (202)566-6342
Washington, DC 20224   Geraldine F. Katz, Chf.
Founded: 1917. **Staff:** Prof 8; Other 10. **Subjects:** Federal tax law, international taxation, accounting, management, business, finance. **Special Collections:** Historical collection of Internal Revenue publications and tax forms; legislative histories of all Internal Revenue acts and related statutes. **Holdings:** 100,000 volumes. **Subscriptions:** 1200 journals and other serials; 8 newspapers. **Services:** Interlibrary loan (to government agencies only); library open to government employees on official business. **Automated Operations:** Computerized cataloging, acquisitions, and serials. **Computerized Information Services:** LEXIS, DIALOG Information Services, Maxwell Macmillan Taxes Online, WESTLAW, Dow Jones News/Retrieval, WILSONLINE, OCLC. **Networks/Consortia:** Member of FEDLINK. **Publications:** Library Bulletin, biweekly. **Remarks:** FAX: (202)377-6975. The Internal Revenue Service is part of the U.S. Department of the Treasury. **Also Known As:** IRS. **Staff:** Susan N. Cushing, Cat.; Jill H. Klein, Acq.; Minnie Sue Ripy, Ref.; Luanne Karr, Digest Group; Jule McCartney, Ref.; Rosemary Coskey, Ref.;Catherine Duffy, Leg.Res.; Brenda Cope, Leg.Res.

★ 17562 ★
U.S. International Trade Administration - U.S. and Foreign Commercial Service - Albuquerque Branch Office Library (Bus-Fin)
625 Silver, SW, Suite 320   Phone: (505)766-2070
Albuquerque, NM 87102   Elizabeth S. Stillie, Trade Ref.Asst.
Staff: 1. **Subjects:** International trade, export. **Holdings:** Foreign country directories. **Services:** Provides international export marketing services for U.S. Dept. of Commerce. **Computerized Information Services:** Dept. of Commerce - Commercial Information Management Services (CIMS; internal database). **Remarks:** FAX: (505)766-1057.

★ 17563 ★
U.S. International Trade Administration - U.S. and Foreign Commercial Service - Anchorage District Office Library (Bus-Fin)
4201 Tudor Center Dr., No. 319   Phone: (907)271-6237
Anchorage, AK 99508-5916   Charles F. Becker, Dir.
Holdings: 1000 volumes, including Census Bureau publications, Alaska and international commerce reference files. **Services:** Copying; library open to the public. **Publications:** Alaska World Trade U.S.A., monthly. **Special Indexes:** Alaska International Trade Directory. **Remarks:** FAX: (907)271-6242.

★ 17564 ★
U.S. International Trade Administration - U.S. and Foreign Commercial Service - Atlanta District Office Library (Bus-Fin)
4360 Chamblee Dunwoody Rd., Suite 310   Phone: (404)452-9102
Atlanta, GA 30341   Rachel Bailey, Trade Spec.
Staff: Prof 1. **Subjects:** Demographic and economic statistics, foreign trade, patents, copyrights. **Holdings:** 600 books; 32 bound periodical volumes. **Subscriptions:** 31 journals and other serials. **Services:** Copying; library open to the public. **Computerized Information Services:** DIALOG Information Services, PFDS Online, BRS Information Technologies. **Publications:** Census and foreign trade publications.

★ 17565 ★
U.S. International Trade Administration - U.S. and Foreign Commercial Service - Baltimore District Office - Library
413 U.S. Customhouse
40 S. Gay St.
Baltimore, MD 21202
Subjects: International trade, export expansion. **Holdings:** 3 bookcases; trade directories; tariff schedules; FT series publications. **Remarks:** Currently inactive.

★ 17566 ★
U.S. International Trade Administration - U.S. and Foreign Commercial Service - Birmingham District Office Library (Bus-Fin)
Berry Bldg., 3rd Fl.
2015 2nd Ave., N., Rm. 302   Phone: (205)731-1331
Birmingham, AL 35203   Charles T. Lidikay
Founded: 1954. **Staff:** 4. **Holdings:** 170 books; reports; departmental and Census Bureau publications. **Subscriptions:** 28 journals and other serials. **Services:** Library open to the public. **Remarks:** FAX: (205)731-0076.

★ 17567 ★
U.S. International Trade Administration - U.S. and Foreign Commercial Service - Boston District Reference Room (Bus-Fin)
World Trade Center, Boston
Commonwealth Pier, Suite 307   Phone: (617)565-8576
Boston, MA 02210   Frank J. O'Connor, Dir.
Founded: 1930. **Staff:** 14. **Subjects:** Business, commerce, international trade. **Holdings:** 960 linear feet of reference files. **Services:** Library open to the public. **Publications:** Trade World New England Newsletter, irregular. **Remarks:** FAX: (617)565-8530.

★ 17568 ★
U.S. International Trade Administration - U.S. and Foreign Commercial Service - Buffalo District Office Library (Bus-Fin)
1312 Federal Bldg.
111 W. Huron St.
Buffalo, NY 14202   Phone: (716)846-4191
Holdings: 100 volumes, including Census Bureau reports and international and domestic trade publications. **Services:** Library open to the public. **Remarks:** FAX: (716)846-5290.

★ 17569 ★
U.S. International Trade Administration - U.S. and Foreign Commercial Service - Charleston District Office Library (Bus-Fin)
405 Capitol St., Suite 809   Phone: (304)347-5123
Charleston, WV 25301   Roger L. Fortner, Dir.
Subjects: Exporting, patents, copyright. **Holdings:** 4400 volumes, including departmental publications, International Trade Administration directories, West Virginia state pamphlets and studies. **Services:** Library open to the public. **Remarks:** FAX: (304)347-5408.

★ 17570 ★
U.S. International Trade Administration - U.S. and Foreign Commercial Service - Chicago District Office Library (Bus-Fin)
Mid-Continental Plaza Bldg., Rm. 1406
55 E. Monroe
Chicago, IL 60603
Phone: (312)353-4450
Constance V. Green, Libn.
Founded: 1940. **Staff:** 1. **Subjects:** Business economics, population (census), foreign trade statistics. **Special Collections:** Census materials; foreign trade directories. **Holdings:** 5000 books; 5000 pamphlets; 500 bibliographies. **Subscriptions:** 30 journals and other serials. **Services:** Library open to the public.

★ 17571 ★
U.S. International Trade Administration - U.S. and Foreign Commercial Service - Cincinnati District Office Library (Bus-Fin)
9504 Federal Office Bldg.
550 Main St.
Cincinnati, OH 45202
Phone: (513)684-2944
Gordon B. Thomas, Dir.
Subjects: Domestic and international trade. **Holdings:** 16 bookcase sections of statistical data, catalogs, trade journals, industry reports, department publications, directories, and Census Bureau materials; 10 VF drawers. **Services:** Library open to the public. **Computerized Information Services:** National Trade Data Base; CIMS/FTI (internal database). **Remarks:** FAX: (513)684-3200.

★ 17572 ★
U.S. International Trade Administration - U.S. and Foreign Commercial Service - Dallas District Office Library (Bus-Fin)
World Trade Center, Suite 170
2550 Stemmos Fwy.
P.O. Box 581409
Dallas, TX 75258
Phone: (214)767-0542
Donald Schilke, Dir.
Subjects: Domestic and foreign commerce. **Holdings:** 3725 volumes. **Services:** Library open to the public. **Remarks:** FAX: (214)767-8240.

★ 17573 ★
U.S. International Trade Administration - U.S. and Foreign Commercial Service - Des Moines District Office Library (Soc Sci)
817 Federal Bldg.
210 Walnut St.
Des Moines, IA 50309
Phone: (515)284-4222
John H. Steuber, Dir.
Subjects: Foreign trade and census statistics. **Holdings:** Figures not available. **Services:** Library open to the public.

★ 17574 ★
U.S. International Trade Administration - U.S. and Foreign Commercial Service - Detroit District Office Library (Bus-Fin)
477 Michigan Ave., Suite 1140
Detroit, MI 48226
Phone: (313)226-3650
Edward Chirstie, Dir.
Subjects: Economics, marketing, trade, census. **Holdings:** 100 volumes; 4 drawers of international trade statistics on microfiche. **Subscriptions:** 10 journals and other serials. **Services:** Library open to the public. **Computerized Information Services:** DIALOG Information Services; internal database. **Publications:** Business America - Michigan Newsletter, monthly; Bugs, Bytes & Glitches (newsletter), quarterly. **Remarks:** FAX: (313)226-3657.

★ 17575 ★
U.S. International Trade Administration - U.S. and Foreign Commercial Service - Greensboro District Office Library (Bus-Fin)
Box 1950
Greensboro, NC 27402
Phone: (919)333-5345
Samuel P. Troy, RMD
Subjects: Domestic and foreign commerce. **Holdings:** 1400 volumes. **Subscriptions:** 15 journals and other serials. **Services:** Library open to the public. **Computerized Information Services:** DIALOG Information Services; Automatic Information Transfer System (internal database). **Remarks:** FAX: (919)333-5158.

★ 17576 ★
U.S. International Trade Administration - U.S. Foreign and Commercial Service - Hartford District Office Library (Bus-Fin)
450 Main St., Rm. 610B
Hartford, CT 06103
Phone: (203)240-3530
Subjects: Census statistics, country files. **Holdings:** Figures not available. **Services:** Library open to the public. **Remarks:** FAX: (203)240-3473.

★ 17577 ★
U.S. International Trade Administration - U.S. and Foreign Commercial Service - Houston District Office Library (Bus-Fin)
515 Rusk Ave., Rm. 2625
Houston, TX 77002
Phone: (713)229-2578
James D. Cook, Dir.
Subjects: Commerce, business. **Holdings:** 600 volumes, including departmental publications. **Services:** Library open to the public.

★ 17578 ★
U.S. International Trade Administration - U.S. and Foreign Commercial Service - Little Rock District Office Library (Bus-Fin)
320 W. Capitol, Suite 811
Little Rock, AR 72201
Phone: (501)324-5794
Mary Hayward, Sec.
Founded: 1979. **Staff:** Prof 3. **Subjects:** International trade. **Holdings:** 1000 books; 35 bound periodical volumes; departmental and Census Bureau publications. **Subscriptions:** 25 journals and other serials; 5 newspapers. **Services:** Library open to the public for reference use only. **Computerized Information Services:** National Trade Data Base (NTDB).

★ 17579 ★
U.S. International Trade Administration - U.S. and Foreign Commercial Service - Miami District Office Library
Federal Bldg., Rm. 224
51 S.W. First Ave.
Miami, FL 33130
Defunct.

★ 17580 ★
U.S. International Trade Administration - U.S. and Foreign Commercial Service - Milwaukee District Office Library (Bus-Fin)
Federal Bldg., Rm. 596
517 E. Wisconsin Ave.
Milwaukee, WI 53202
Phone: (414)297-3473
J.E. Brown, Dir.
Subjects: Economic and market research, technology, foreign trade statistics. **Holdings:** 6000 volumes. **Services:** Library open to the public. **Computerized Information Services:** National Trade Data Board (internal database). **Remarks:** FAX: (414)297-3470.

★ 17581 ★
U.S. International Trade Administration - U.S. and Foreign Commercial Service - Minneapolis District Office Library (Bus-Fin)
108 Federal Bldg.
110 S. 4th St.
Minneapolis, MN 55401-2227
Phone: (612)348-1638
Mary Hobbs, Trade Spec.
Staff: Prof 1. **Subjects:** Census, marketing, government statistics, foreign trade, area development. **Special Collections:** Directories. **Holdings:** Figures not available. **Services:** Interlibrary loan; library open to the public. **Computerized Information Services:** National Trade Data Base (NTDB). **Remarks:** FAX: (612)348-1650.

★ 17582 ★
U.S. International Trade Administration - U.S. and Foreign Commercial Service - Nashville District Office Library (Bus-Fin)
404 James Robertson Pkwy., Rm. 114
Nashville, TN 37219-1505
Phone: (615)736-5161
Jim Charlet, Dir.
Founded: 1930. **Staff:** Prof 4; Other 2. **Subjects:** International trade, economic studies, foreign trade regulations, customs procedures. **Holdings:** 1000 books; 77 bound periodical volumes; 3000 other cataloged items. **Subscriptions:** 27 journals and other serials; 6 newspapers. **Services:** Interlibrary loan; copying; library open to the public for reference use only. **Computerized Information Services:** Foreign Traders Index (FTI); CD-ROM (National Trade Data Base); internal database. Performs searches on fee basis. **Remarks:** FAX: (615)736-2454. **Staff:** Beverly Reed, Trade Ref.Asst.

★ 17583 ★
U.S. International Trade Administration - U.S. and Foreign Commercial Service - New Orleans District Office Library (Bus-Fin)
World Trade Center, Rm. 432
2 Canal St.   Phone: (504)589-6546
New Orleans, LA 70130   Paul L. Guidry, Dir.
Staff: 4. **Subjects:** Foreign trade statistics. **Holdings:** Foreign phone books and foreign directories. **Services:** Library open to the public for export information only. **Computerized Information Services:** National Trade Data Base (NTDB). **Remarks:** FAX: (504)589-2337.

★ 17584 ★
U.S. International Trade Administration - U.S. and Foreign Commercial Service - New York District Office Market Information Center (Bus-Fin)
26 Federal Plaza   Phone: (212)264-0630
New York, NY 10278   Stuart Werner, Tech.Info.Spec.
Founded: 1925. **Staff:** Prof 1; Other 2. **Subjects:** Censuses, business censuses, business, foreign trade, marketing. **Special Collections:** Foreign and domestic trade directories. **Holdings:** 1000 books; 26 VF drawers of international marketing and business information. **Subscriptions:** 35 journals and other serials; 5 newspapers. **Services:** Copying; center open to the public. **Computerized Information Services:** Internal database. **Remarks:** FAX: (212)264-1356.

★ 17585 ★
U.S. International Trade Administration - U.S. and Foreign Commercial Service - Philadelphia District Office Library (Bus-Fin)
475 Allendale Rd., Suite 202   Phone: (215)962-4980
King of Prussia, PA 19406   Robert Kistler, Dir.
Subjects: Industry, foreign business, international marketing. **Holdings:** 800 volumes; Department of Commerce publications. **Services:** Library not open to the public.

★ 17586 ★
U.S. International Trade Administration - U.S. and Foreign Commercial Service - Phoenix District Office Library (Bus-Fin)
230 N. 1st Ave., Rm. 3412   Phone: (602)379-4324
Phoenix, AZ 85025   Donald W. Fry, Dir.
Founded: 1946. **Staff:** Prof 5. **Subjects:** Technology, census, agriculture, business, education, transportation, Indians, importing and exporting, Arizona statistics. **Holdings:** 6000 books; 1500 other volumes. **Services:** Library open to the public. **Remarks:** FAX: (602)379-4324.

★ 17587 ★
U.S. International Trade Administration - U.S. and Foreign Commercial Service - Pittsburgh District Office Library (Bus-Fin)
2002 Federal Bldg.
1000 Liberty Ave.   Phone: (412)644-2850
Pittsburgh, PA 15222   John A. McCartney, Dir.
Subjects: Foreign commerce, census, international trade. **Holdings:** 1000 volumes; 140 VF drawers of government pamphlets, reports, and statistics. **Subscriptions:** 30 journals and other serials. **Services:** Library open to the public. **Remarks:** FAX: (412)644-4875.

★ 17588 ★
U.S. International Trade Administration - U.S. and Foreign Commercial Service - Richmond District Office Library (Bus-Fin)
8010 Federal Bldg.
400 N. 8th St.   Phone: (804)771-2246
Richmond, VA 23240   Philip A. Ouzts, Dir.
Subjects: Census, business economics, foreign trade. **Holdings:** 1300 volumes. **Subscriptions:** 7 journals and other serials. **Services:** Library open to the public. **Computerized Information Services:** National Trade Data Bank (internal database). **Remarks:** FAX: (804)771-2390.

★ 17589 ★
U.S. International Trade Administration - U.S. and Foreign Commercial Service - St. Louis District Office Library (Bus-Fin)
7911 Forsyth Blvd., Suite 610   Phone: (314)425-3302
St. Louis, MO 63105   Sandra Gerley, Dp.Dir.
Subjects: Exports, foreign trade. **Holdings:** 1500 volumes. **Services:** Interlibrary loan; library open to the public.

★ 17590 ★
U.S. International Trade Administration - U.S. and Foreign Commercial Service - Salt Lake City District Office Library (Bus-Fin)
324 S. State St., Suite 105   Phone: (801)524-5116
Salt Lake City, UT 84111   Stephen P. Smoot, Dir.
Founded: 1945. **Subjects:** Business economics. **Holdings:** 200 books. **Services:** Library open to the public. **Remarks:** FAX: (801)524-5886.

★ 17591 ★
U.S. International Trade Administration - U.S. and Foreign Commercial Service - San Juan District Office - Business Library (Bus-Fin)
Chardon Ave.
Federal Office Bldg., Rm. G-55   Phone: (809)766-5555
Hato Rey, PR 00918   Enrique Vilella, Dir.
Staff: 4. **Subjects:** Market statistics, international economics, and marketing, export/import, commerce between Puerto Rico and United States. **Holdings:** 1000 volumes; international manufacturers' directories. **Services:** Copying; library open to the public.

★ 17592 ★
U.S. International Trade Administration - U.S. and Foreign Commercial Service - Savannah District Office Library (Bus-Fin)
120 Barnard St., A-107   Phone: (912)652-4204
Savannah, GA 31401   Barbara H. Prieto, Trade Spec.
Subjects: Census and other department publications, foreign and domestic trade directories, market research, foreign trade and tariff regulations. **Holdings:** 1800 volumes. **Services:** Library open to the public.

★ 17593 ★
U.S. International Trade Commission - Law Library (Law)
500 E St., S.W., Rm. 614   Phone: (202)205-3287
Washington, DC 20436   Steven J. Kover, Hd.
Founded: 1972. **Staff:** Prof 2; Other 1. **Subjects:** U.S. trade and patent law. **Special Collections:** Legislative histories of U.S. trade and tariff acts; U.S. International Trade Commission reports. **Holdings:** 10,000 books; 700 bound periodical volumes. **Subscriptions:** 70 journals and other serials. **Services:** Interlibrary loan; copying; library open to the public. **Automated Operations:** Computerized cataloging. **Computerized Information Services:** WESTLAW, LEGI-SLATE, OCLC. **Publications:** Bibliography of Law Journal Articles on Statutes Administered by the U.S.I.T.C. and Related Subjects. **Remarks:** FAX: (202)205-3111. **Staff:** Maureen Bryant, Law Libn.

★ 17594 ★
U.S. International Trade Commission - National Library of International Trade (Soc Sci)
500 E St., S.W.   Phone: (202)205-2630
Washington, DC 20436   Barbara J. Pruett, Chf.,Lib.Serv.
Founded: 1917. **Staff:** Prof 6; Other 6. **Subjects:** U.S. trade policy, international trade, foreign trade statistics, tariffs. **Holdings:** 90,000 volumes. **Subscriptions:** 2500 journals and other serials. **Services:** Interlibrary loan except for legislative histories; copying; library open to the public by appointment. **Automated Operations:** Computerized cataloging, acquisitions, serials, and circulation. **Computerized Information Services:** OCLC, DIALOG Information Services, LEGI-SLATE, Mead Data Central (for staff use only). **Networks/Consortia:** Member of FEDLINK. **Staff:** Katharine Loughney, Hd., Ref./Res.Serv.; Elizabeth A. Root, Hd., Tech.Serv.

U.S. Interstate Commerce Commission
See: Interstate Commerce Commission (8211)

★ 17595 ★
U.S. League of Savings Institutions - Library (Bus-Fin)
1709 New York Ave., N.W.   Phone: (202)637-8920
Washington, DC 20006   Katherine Harahan, Libn.
Staff: Prof 1; Other 2. **Subjects:** Savings and loans, economics. **Special Collections:** Savings and loan congressional materials; general historical data. **Holdings:** 8000 books. **Subscriptions:** 200 journals and other serials; 15 newspapers. **Services:** Interlibrary loan; library open to the public at librarian's discretion. **Computerized Information Services:** Washington Alert Service, Congressional Quarterly Inc. (CQ), NEXIS.

★ **17596** ★
U.S. League of Savings Institutions - Library (Bus-Fin)
1709 New York Ave., N.W., Suite 801   Phone: (202)637-8900
Washington, DC 20006   Kent Harahand, Chf.Libn.
Staff: Prof 2. **Subjects:** Savings and loans, housing finance and mortgages, savings banks, banking services, electronic funds transfer. **Holdings:** 3000 books; 300 bound periodical volumes; 70 VF drawers. **Subscriptions:** 200 journals and other serials; 7 newspapers. **Services:** Interlibrary loan; copying; library open to the public with restrictions. **Automated Operations:** Computerized cataloging. **Computerized Information Services:** DIALOG Information Services, Mead Data Central, Dow Jones News/Retrieval, OCLC. **Remarks:** FAX: (312)938-2541. **Formerly:** Located in Chicago, IL. **Staff:** Ronald Stoner, Lib.Rsrcs.Coord.

U.S. Library of Congress
See: **Library of Congress** (9107)

★ **17597** ★
United States Lifesaving Association - Library & Information Center (Med)
425 E. McFridge Dr.   Phone: (312)294-2332
Chicago, IL 60605   Joe Pecoraro, Pres.
Founded: 1964. **Staff:** Prof 1. **Subjects:** Open-water lifeguarding, rescue procedures, first aid and resuscitation, ocean environment, marine safety, flood rescue procedures. **Special Collections:** Films and photographs of open-water lifeguard subjects; lifeguard manuals from United States and World Lifesaving. **Holdings:** 1000 U.S. Lifesaving Magazines; 1000 lifesaving photographs. **Services:** Library not open to the public. **Automated Operations:** Computerized acquisitions. **Publications:** Annual Reports; Emergency Services, annual; Lifeguarding and Marine Safety; Beach Information; Guidelines for Open-Water Lifeguard Training. **Remarks:** Sponsors the American Lifesaving Emergency Response Team (A.L.E.R.T.) to respond to floods and water disasters throughout the United States.

U.S. Livestock Insects Laboratory
See: **U.S.D.A. - Agricultural Research Service** (17186)

★ **17598** ★
U.S. Marine Corps - Camp Pendleton Library System (Mil)
Marine Corps Base
Bldg. 1122   Phone: (619)725-5104
Camp Pendleton, CA 92055-5000   Patrick J. Carney, Lib.Dir.
Founded: 1950. **Staff:** Prof 3; Other 17. **Subjects:** Military art and science. **Holdings:** 110,070 books and bound periodical volumes; 22 VF drawers of pamphlets; 49,058 microforms; 115 films; 1897 phonograph records. **Subscriptions:** 636 journals and other serials; 27 newspapers. **Services:** Interlibrary loan; copying; library open to the public for reference use only on request. **Automated Operations:** Computerized cataloging, circulation, and serials. **Publications:** Library Bulletin, irregular - for internal distribution only. **Remarks:** Maintains three base branch libraries and a bookmobile. **Staff:** Mrs. Vernese B. Thompson, Cons.

★ **17599** ★
U.S. Marine Corps - Commanding General (856) - Logistics Base - Technical Support Library (Sci-Engr, Mil)
Rm. 321-Code 851-4   Phone: (912)439-6470
Albany, GA 31704-5000   Patricia Williams, Tech.Libn.
Founded: 1966. **Staff:** 1. **Subjects:** Physical science, engineering, ordnance, electronics, military science. **Special Collections:** Marine Corps publications. **Holdings:** 25,000 books; 40,000 military specifications and standards on microfilm; 200 Army handbooks and bulletins. **Subscriptions:** 40 journals and other serials. **Services:** Interlibrary loan; library not open to the public. **Automated Operations:** Computerized acquisitions.

★ **17600** ★
U.S. Marine Corps - Historical Center Library (Mil)
Washington Navy Yard, Bldg. 58   Phone: (202)433-4253
Washington, DC 20374-0580   Evelyn A. Englander, Libn.
Staff: Prof 1; Other 1. **Subjects:** U.S. Marine Corps history, history of amphibious warfare, general naval and military history. **Special Collections:** Marine Corps-published periodicals and newspapers; Marine Corps

doctrinal publications; personal papers of famous figures in Marine Corps history. **Holdings:** 30,000 books; 500 bound periodical volumes; 6500 pamphlets; 5000 maps; 4000 reels of microfilm; 1987 linear feet of research papers. **Subscriptions:** 50 journals and other serials; 18 newspapers. **Services:** Interlibrary loan; copying; library open to the public. **Automated Operations:** Computerized cataloging and ILL. **Computerized Information Services:** OCLC. **Networks/Consortia:** Member of FEDLINK. **Publications:** Fortitudine (newsletter of Marine Corps history), quarterly. **Special Catalogs:** Marine Corps Historical Publications Catalog; Oral History Catalog; Personal Papers Catalog. **Remarks:** FAX: (202)433-7265. Alternate telephone number(s): 433-3447.

★ **17601** ★
U.S. Marine Corps - Kaneohe Air Station Library (Mil)
Bldg. 219   Phone: (808)254-6301
Kaneohe Bay, HI 96863-5010   Murray R. Visser, Supv.Libn.
Founded: 1951. **Staff:** Prof 1; Other 5. **Subjects:** Military history, U.S. Marine Corps. **Special Collections:** Hawaiiana; children's literature; commandant's professional reading collection. **Holdings:** 33,076 books; 31,949 microforms; 8610 paperback books; 917 VF items; 1579 phonograph records. **Subscriptions:** 159 journals and other serials; 14 newspapers. **Services:** Interlibrary loan; copying; faxing; library open to military dependents and to civilians who work on base. **Automated Operations:** Computerized public access catalog. **Computerized Information Services:** Internal databases. **Special Indexes:** Leatherneck index, 1950-1990; Marine Corps Gazette Index, 1952-1990. **Remarks:** FAX: (808)254-3503.

★ **17602** ★
U.S. Marine Corps - Marine Band Library (Mil, Mus)
Marine Barracks
8th & I Sts., S.E.   Phone: (202)433-4298
Washington, DC 20390-5000   D. Michael Ressler, Chf.Libn.
Founded: 1880. **Staff:** Prof 5. **Subjects:** Band music, orchestra music, instrumental ensembles, national anthems, piano music, dance band. **Special Collections:** History of the Marine Band archives (photographs, 1864 to present; program files, 1898 to present; daily activities logs, 1916 to present; published material; tour and biographical information and memorabilia of former Marine Bandsmen); Military Music Collection (John Philip Sousa Collection); Victor Grabel/John Philip Sousa Music Library); The Sousa Band Encore Books; personal items of Sousa Band members John J. Heney, Sr., Walter F. Smith, Earle Polling, and Rudolph Becker). **Holdings:** 600 books; 40,000 pieces of sheet music. **Subscriptions:** 20 journals and other serials. **Services:** Library open to the public by appointment. **Computerized Information Services:** Internal database. **Remarks:** FAX: (202)433-4752.

★ **17603** ★
U.S. Marine Corps - Recruit Depot - Library (Mil, Hist)
Bldg. 7W, MCRD   Phone: (619)524-1850
San Diego, CA 92140   Usha Arya, Hd.Libn.
Founded: 1932. **Staff:** Prof 1; Other 5. **Subjects:** History, humanities, social and behavioral sciences, physical education. **Special Collections:** Professional military education. **Holdings:** 50,000 books; bound periodical volumes; videotapes; audiotapes. **Subscriptions:** 100 journals and other serials; 10 newspapers. **Services:** Interlibrary loan; copying; library open to the public at librarian's discretion.

★ **17604** ★
U.S. Marine Corps - Special Services - Camp H.M. Smith Library (Mil)
Bldg. 27   Phone: (808)477-6348
Honolulu, HI 96861   Evelyn Mau, Libn.
Founded: 1966. **Staff:** Prof 1; Other 2. **Subjects:** Marine Corps. **Holdings:** 10,000 books. **Subscriptions:** 60 journals and other serials; 8 newspapers. **Services:** Interlibrary loan; library not open to the public.

★ **17605** ★
U.S. Marine Corps University - James Carson Breckinridge Library (Mil, Soc Sci)
Marine Corps Research Center TU-05RCL   Phone: (703)640-2248
Quantico, VA 22134-5010   Pearce S. Grove, Lib.Dir.
Founded: 1928. **Staff:** Prof 5; Other 5. **Subjects:** Military art and science, history, naval art and science, political and social science. **Special Collections:** Amphibious operations; Marine Corps; federal documents depository, 1967 to present. **Holdings:** 75,000 books and bound periodical

volumes; 4500 unbound periodicals; 3600 reels of microfilm; 4000 documents. **Subscriptions:** 254 journals and other serials; 11 newspapers. **Services:** Interlibrary loan; copying; library open to the public by permission. **Automated Operations:** Computerized cataloging. **Computerized Information Services:** OCLC. **Networks/Consortia:** Member of FEDLINK. **Publications:** New Acquisitions List, quarterly; Current Contents of Selected Military Periodicals, bimonthly - both for limited distribution. **Remarks:** FAX: (703)262-8088. **Staff:** Mary J. Porter, Ref.Libn.; David C. Brown, Cat.Libn.; Patricia A. Salchert, Ref.Libn.; JoAnn H. Payne, Acq.; A. Kerry Strong, Archv.

★ 17606 ★
U.S. Maritime Administration - National Maritime Research Center - Maritime Technical Information Facility
Kings Point, NY 11024-1699
Defunct.

★ 17607 ★
U.S. Merchant Marine Academy - Schuyler Otis Bland Memorial Library (Trans)
Steamboat Rd.   Phone: (516)773-5501
Kings Point, NY 11024   Dr. George J. Billy, Chf.Libn.
Founded: 1944. **Staff:** Prof 4; Other 3. **Subjects:** Marine engineering, nautical science, maritime history and economics. **Special Collections:** William Bollman Collection (maritime history). **Holdings:** 220,000 volumes; 7500 bound periodical volumes, 97,000 microfiche; 3700 reels of microfilm; 50 films; 12 VF drawers of maritime research reports; 400 maps; 17,000 other cataloged items. **Subscriptions:** 1246 journals and other serials; 8 newspapers. **Services:** Interlibrary loan; copying; library open to the public for reference use only. **Automated Operations:** Computerized cataloging. **Computerized Information Services:** DIALOG Information Services, OCLC; internal databases. **Networks/Consortia:** Member of Long Island Library Resources Council. **Publications:** Acquisitions List, monthly; Library Handbook, annual; Periodicals Holdings List, annual; Oil Spills and Tanker Regulations bibliographies. **Remarks:** The Academy is operated by the Maritime Administration of the U.S. Department of Transportation. **Staff:** Marilyn Stern, Tech.Serv.Libn.; Esther W. Bovarnick, Rd.Serv.Libn.

U.S. NASA
See: **NASA** (10980)

U.S. National Aeronautics and Space Administration
See: **NASA** (10980)

★ 17608 ★
U.S. Natl. Arboretum - Library (Biol Sci)
3501 New York Ave., N.E.
Washington, DC 20002   Phone: (202)475-4828
Staff: 2. **Subjects:** Botany, taxonomy, floristics, horticulture, gardening, plant genetics and breeding. **Special Collections:** Nursery and seed trade catalogs (3 VF drawers); Mary Cokely Wood Ikebana Collection (75 volumes); floral prints; early photographs of U.S. Department of Agriculture Plant Exploration trips; U.S. Department of Agriculture photographs of agricultural practices of early 20th century; Bonsai; U.S. Plant Patent File (5400); Carlton R. Ball Collection on Salix (25 volumes); Arie F. den Boer manuscripts on crabapples (967 folders). **Holdings:** 7000 books; 500 periodical titles; 4 VF drawers of pamphlets and clippings. **Subscriptions:** 175 journals and other serials. **Services:** Interlibrary loan (through National Agricultural Library only); SDI; library open to the public by appointment for on-site research only. **Computerized Information Services:** DIALOG Information Services, ISIS. **Remarks:** FAX: (202)475-5252. A branch of the National Agricultural Library of the U.S. Department of Agriculture. **Staff:** Susan Chapman, Libn.; Wayne Olsen, Libn.

★ 17609 ★
U.S. Natl. Defense University - Library (Mil)
Fort Lesley J. McNair
4th & P Sts., S.W.   Phone: (202)287-9460
Washington, DC 20319-6000   Sarah A. Mikel, Dir.
Founded: 1976. **Staff:** Prof 15; Other 18. **Subjects:** Military history and science, manpower and industrial mobilization, political science, national

security affairs, international relations, management of resources, joint and combined operations, strategic studies, wargaming. **Special Collections:** Personal papers of Maxwell D. Taylor, Lyman L. Lemnitzer, George S. Brown, Andrew J. Goodpaster, Paul D. Adams, and Frank S. Besson, Jr.; speeches on industrial mobilization by J. Carlton Ward, Jr.; Hudson Institute Papers; early editions of Marshal de Saxe; Libraries of Arthur W. Radford, Hoffman Nickerson (both on military history), Roland H. del Mar (Latin America), and Ralph L. Powell (China). **Holdings:** 230,000 books and bound periodical volumes; 2900 nonprint items; 1200 linear feet of local history materials. **Subscriptions:** 1400 journals and newspapers. **Services:** Interlibrary loan; library open to the public by appointment (some special collections restricted). **Automated Operations:** Computerized public access catalog, cataloging, acquisitions, serials, and circulation. **Computerized Information Services:** DIALOG Information Services, LS/2000, DLSIE, Info-South, LEXIS, NEXIS, EPIC, OCLC, Washington Alert Service, DTIC; CD-ROMs. **Networks/Consortia:** Member of FEDLINK. **Publications:** Handbook, biennial; subject pathfinders and bibliographies, irregular. **Remarks:** FAX: (202)287-9102. The National Defense University operates under the direction of the Chairman of the Joint Chiefs of Staff of the U.S. Department of Defense. **Staff:** Ann Parham, Chf., Res. & Info.Serv.; Ann Sullivan, Ref.Libn.; Teresa Chapman, Info.Spec.; Jeannemarie Faison, Ref.Libn.; Dolores Knight, Ref.Libn.; Rosemary Marlowe-Dziuk, Ref.Libn.; Mary T. Quintero, Ref.Libn.; Howard Hume, Dp.Dir./Chf., Automation & Tech.Serv.; Benard Strong, Chf., Tech.Serv.; Lydia Y. Luh, Ser.Cat.; Alta Linthicum, Sys.Libn.; Susan Lemke, Chf., Spec.Coll., Archv. & Hist.; Mary Stuart-Taylor, Coll. Control Libn.; Mary Ruth Duncan, Monographic Cat.

★ 17610 ★
U.S. Natl. Highway Traffic Safety Administration - Technical Reference Division (Sci-Engr, Trans)
400 7th St., S.W., Rm. 5110   Phone: (202)366-2768
Washington, DC 20590   Jerome A. Holiber, Chf.
Founded: 1967. **Staff:** Prof 9; Other 3. **Subjects:** Motor vehicle safety, highway safety, alcohol countermeasures for driving safety, automobile occupant protection, emergency medical services. **Special Collections:** NHTSA Research Reports; Federal Motor Vehicle Safety Standards Docket; Compliance Test Reports; Defects Investigation Reports; Recall Campaigns; Crash Test Reports. **Holdings:** 2500 books; 48,000 reports; 600,000 microfiche. **Subscriptions:** 80 journals and other serials. **Services:** Interlibrary loan (limited); copying; division open to the public for reference use only. **Computerized Information Services:** Manufacturer's Service Bulletins, Consumer Complaints, Recall Campaigns, Defects Investigation (internal databases). Performs searches on fee basis. **Remarks:** The National Highway Traffic Safety Administration is part of the U.S. Department of Transportation. **Staff:** Dawn Gordy, Tech.Info.Spec.; Clara Wampler, Tech.Info.Spec.; Paulette Twine, Tech.Info.Spec.; Frances Bean, Tech.Info.Spec.; Grace Ogden, Tech.Info.Spec.; Robert Hornickle, Tech.Info.Spec.; David Doernberg, Tech.Info.Spec.; Jeanette Chow, Tech.Info.Spec.

★ 17611 ★
U.S. Natl. Institute for Occupational Safety & Health - Taft Center C-21 - Library (Med)
4676 Columbia Pkwy.   Phone: (513)533-8321
Cincinnati, OH 45226   Colleen M. Herrington, Supv.Libn.
Founded: 1970. **Staff:** Prof 3; Other 3. **Subjects:** Occupational safety and health, industrial hygiene and toxicology. **Special Collections:** NIOSHTIC and CIS microfiche. **Holdings:** 10,000 books; 10,000 bound periodical volumes. **Subscriptions:** 400 journals and other serials. **Services:** Interlibrary loan; library open to the public. **Automated Operations:** Computerized ILL. **Computerized Information Services:** OCLC. **Networks/Consortia:** Member of FEDLINK. **Remarks:** Institute is a branch of U.S. Centers for Disease Control. **Staff:** Lawrence Q. Foster, Hd.Libn.; Lucy Schoolfield, Libn.

★ 17612 ★
U.S. Natl. Institute of Standards and Technology - Alloy Phase Diagram Data Center (Sci-Engr)
NIST
Bldg. 223, Rm. B-152   Phone: (301)975-6043
Gaithersburg, MD 20899   Dr. Benjamin Burton, Dir.
Staff: Prof 1. **Subjects:** Alloy phase stability and phase diagrams. **Holdings:** Collection of alloy phase diagram evaluations and related compilations. **Subscriptions:** 10 journals and other serials. **Services:** Center open to the public with restrictions. **Computerized Information Services:** Alloy Phase Diagram Database (internal database); BITNET (electronic mail service).

Publications: List of publications - available on request. **Special Indexes:** Compilations of Binary Ti- Al- and Fe-based alloy phase diagrams. **Remarks:** Alternate telephone number(s): 975-6044. FAX: (301)972-2128. Electronic mail address(es): BURTON@NBSENH (BITNET). The National Institute of Standards and Technology is part of the U.S. Department of Commerce.

★ 17613 ★
U.S. Natl. Institute of Standards and Technology - Atomic Energy Levels Data Center (Energy)
Physics Bldg., Rm. A155   Phone: (301)975-3221
Gaithersburg, MD 20899   Dr. William C. Martin, Physicist
Founded: 1945. **Staff:** Prof 3. **Subjects:** Atomic energy levels and spectra. **Holdings:** 7000 reprints of pertinent papers on atomic energy levels and spectra. **Services:** Copying; center open to the public. **Automated Operations:** Computerized cataloging. **Computerized Information Services:** Internal databases (references, 1984 to present; levels and wavelenghts data, 1978 to present); BITNET (electronic mail service). **Publications:** Bibliography on Atomic Energy Levels and Spectra, quadrennial - to users of the Data Center; Compilations of Atomic Energy Levels, 1-2/year. **Special Catalogs:** Current information on atomic spectra which covers information not yet published in bibliographies (online). **Remarks:** FAX: (301)975-3038. Telex: TRT 197674 NIST UT. Electronic mail address(es): AEL@NISTCS2 (BITNET). **Staff:** Dr. J. Sugar, Physicist; Arlene F. Musgrove, Tech.Info.Spec.

★ 17614 ★
U.S. Natl. Institute of Standards and Technology - Chemical Thermodynamics Data Center (Sci-Engr)
Chemistry Bldg., Rm. A151   Phone: (301)975-2529
Gaithersburg, MD 20899   Eugene S. Domalski, Group Ldr.
Subjects: Chemical thermodynamics, molecular parameters, correlation of physical properties. **Holdings:** 250 books; 117 bound periodical volumes; 33 reels of microfilm; 26.5 meters of unbound journals; microfilm file of 50,000 papers on experiments. **Services:** Center open to the public. **Automated Operations:** Computerized acquisitions (limited). **Computerized Information Services:** Chemical Abstracts Service (CAS), STN International, Chemical Information Systems, Inc. (CIS); BITNET (electronic mail service). **Publications:** NBS Tables of Chemical Thermodynamic Properties; bibliography of papers on thermochemical and related measurements (60,000 entries); JANAF Thermochemical Tables (3rd edition). **Special Indexes:** Index to thermochemical measurements coded by substance and property measured (card, 250,000 entries, with computer tape backup). **Remarks:** FAX: (301)926-4513. Telex: 197674 NIST OT. Electronic mail address(es): GENE@NBS (BITNET). **Staff:** David Neumann, Data Anl.; Donald Archer, Data Anl.; T.L. Jobe, Info.Spec.; David Garvin, Sci.

★ 17615 ★
U.S. Natl. Institute of Standards and Technology - Data Center on Atomic Transition Probabilities (Sci-Engr)
Physics Bldg., Rm. A267   Phone: (301)975-3204
Gaithersburg, MD 20899   Dr. W.L. Wiese, Dir.
Founded: 1960. **Staff:** Prof 1. **Subjects:** Atomic transition probabilities. **Holdings:** Complete and up-to-date files of publications on atomic transition probabilities (5800 articles). **Subscriptions:** 5 journals and other serials. **Services:** Numerical data provided on atomic transition probabilities; center open to the public. **Automated Operations:** Computerized cataloging. **Computerized Information Services:** Internal database (bibliographic and numerical data); BITNET (electronic mail service). **Publications:** Bibliographies and critically-evaluated data tables. **Remarks:** FAX: (301)975-3038. Telex: TRT197674 NIST UT. Electronic mail address(es): FUHR@NISTCS2 (BITNET). **Staff:** J.R. Fuhr, Physicist.

★ 17616 ★
U.S. Natl. Institute of Standards and Technology - Fire Research Information Services (Sci-Engr)
Bldg. 224, Rm. A252   Phone: (301)975-6862
Gaithersburg, MD 20899   Nora H. Jason, Proj.Ldr.
Founded: 1971. **Staff:** 2. **Subjects:** Fire research and safety, combustion, combustion toxicology, arson, fabric flammability, fire modeling, suppression, building fires, extinguishment. **Holdings:** 400 books and bound periodical volumes; 34,000 technical reports and conference proceedings. **Subscriptions:** 90 journals and other serials. **Services:** Interlibrary loan; services open to the public. **Computerized Information Services:** FIREDOC. **Publications:** Fire Research Publications, annual. **Remarks:** FAX: (301)975-4052.

★ 17617 ★
U.S. Natl. Institute of Standards and Technology - Fluid Mixtures Data Center (Sci-Engr)
Division 838.02
325 Broadway   Phone: (303)497-5964
Boulder, CO 80303-3328   Daniel G. Friend, Dir.
Founded: 1980. **Subjects:** Thermophysical properties of fluids and mixtures - natural gas, synthetic gas, coal conversion products, chemicals, refrigerants, cryogens. **Holdings:** 1000 volumes. **Subscriptions:** 60 journals and other serials. **Services:** Library open to the public. **Computerized Information Services:** Internal database; BITNET (electronic mail service). **Remarks:** FAX: (303)497-5224. FTS: 8-320-5964. Telex: 592811. Electronic mail address(es): DFRIEND@NISTCS2 (BITNET).

★ 17618 ★
U.S. Natl. Institute of Standards and Technology - Fundamental Constants Data Center (Sci-Engr)
Bldg. 221, Rm. B160   Phone: (301)975-4220
Gaithersburg, MD 20899   Dr. Barry N. Taylor, Mgr., Data Ctr.
Founded: 1970. **Staff:** Prof 1. **Subjects:** Fundamental constants, precision measurement. **Holdings:** 10,000 journal article reprints, mid 1960s to present. **Subscriptions:** 12 journals and other serials. **Services:** Center not open to the public. **Publications:** Periodic compilation of sets of recommended values of the fundamental physical constants. **Remarks:** FAX: (301)975-3038. Telex: 197674 NIST UT.

★ 17619 ★
U.S. Natl. Institute of Standards and Technology - Ion Kinetics and Energetics Data Center (Sci-Engr)
Chemistry Bldg., Rm. A267   Phone: (301)975-2000
Gaithersburg, MD 20899   Dr. Sharon G. Lias, Dir.
Founded: 1963. **Staff:** 2. **Subjects:** Ionization potentials, appearance potentials, heats of formation of positive ions, proton affinity, electron affinity, ion-molecule reaction rate constants. **Holdings:** 6000 reprints. **Services:** Center open to the public. **Publications:** A Bibliography on Ion-Molecule Reactions, NBS Technical Note 291; Ionization Potentials, Appearance Potentials, and Heats of Formation of Gaseous Positive Ions, NSRDS-NBS 26; Energetics of Gaseous Ions, J. Phys. Chem. Ref. 6, Suppl. 1 (1977); The Measurement of Ionization and Appearance Potentials, International J. Mass Spectro. Ion Phys 20, 139 (1976); Ionization Potential and Appearance Potential Measurements, NSRDS-NBS 71 (1971-1981); Evaluated Gas Basicities and Proton Affinities (1984); Gas-phase Ion and Neutral Thermochemistry (1988).

U.S. Natl. Institute of Standards and Technology - Joint Institute for Laboratory Astrophysics (JILA)
See: **University of Colorado--Boulder - Joint Institute for Laboratory Astrophysics (JILA) - Reading Room (18501)**

★ 17620 ★
U.S. Natl. Institute of Standards and Technology - Metallurgy Division - Diffusion in Metals Data Center (Sci-Engr)
Bldg. 223, Rm. A153   Phone: (301)975-6157
Gaithersburg, MD 20899   John R. Manning, Dir.
Staff: Prof 1. **Subjects:** Solid-state and liquid diffusion, diffusion coatings, oxidation, permeation, electromigration, thermomigration. **Special Collections:** Atomic motion in solids (25,000 documents). **Holdings:** 500 books; 10,000 reports on microfilm. **Services:** Center open to the public for reference use only. **Publications:** Diffusion in Copper and Copper Alloys.

★ 17621 ★
U.S. Natl. Institute of Standards and Technology - National Center for Standards and Certification Information (Sci-Engr)
TRF Bldg., Rm. 163   Phone: (301)975-4040
Gaithersburg, MD 20899   JoAnne R. Overman, Supv.Tech.Info.Spec.
Founded: 1965. **Staff:** 4. **Subjects:** Engineering and product standards, specifications, test methods, analytical methods, codes, and recommended practices; certification rules and programs; standardization; international, foreign, U.S., and state government standards and regulations. **Holdings:** Figures not available for books; U.S. national and industry standards; U.S. Government standards; foreign national standards; international standards; unbound articles; pamphlets; reports; monographs; microform files. **Services:** Information and referral services; center open to the public for reference use only. **Computerized Information Services:** Internal databases. **Publications:** List of publications - available on request. **Remarks:** This collection of standards and related information is the largest and most comprehensive of its kind in the United States. It is located at Quince Orchard Rd. & Rte. 270, Gaithersburg, MD. FAX: (301)926-1559. Telex: TRT 197674 NIST UT. **Staff:** Mike Squires, Tech.Info.Spec.; Brenda Umberger, Tech.Info.Asst.; A. Diane Lay, Tech.Info.Spec.

★ 17622 ★
U.S. Natl. Institute of Standards and Technology - Phase Diagrams for Ceramists - Data Center (Sci-Engr)
Matls. Bldg., Rm. A-215   Phone: (301)975-5761
Gaithersburg, MD 20899   Stephen W. Freiman, Supv.
Staff: Prof 3. **Subjects:** Chemical phase equilibria data - phase diagrams of nonmetallic, inorganic substances. **Services:** Inquiries about phase diagrams are answered. **Publications:** Phase Diagrams for Ceramists, irregular - for sale by American Ceramic Society. **Remarks:** Jointly sponsored by the U.S. National Institute of Standards and Technology and the American Ceramic Society. **Staff:** Helen Ondik, Oper.Mgr.

★ 17623 ★
U.S. Natl. Institute of Standards and Technology - Photon and Charged Particle Data Center (Sci-Engr)
Radiation Physics Bldg., Rm. C311   Phone: (301)975-5552
Gaithersburg, MD 20899   Stephen M. Seltzer, Mgr.
Founded: 1952. **Staff:** Prof 5. **Subjects:** Electrons, positrons, protons, and other charged particles; photons; bremsstrahlung; stopping power and range tables; photon cross sections: Compton scattering atomic and nuclear photoeffect, pair production, and atomic form factors; x-ray attenuation coefficients; critical evaluations; radiation dosimetry. **Holdings:** 5 VF drawers of x-ray and Gamma ray total cross section reprints and reports; 20 VF drawers of partial cross sections, applications to shielding, radiometric gauging, x-ray crystallography, and other related reprints; 5 VF drawers of photonuclear data reprints. **Services:** Will answer inquiries; library open to the public with professional interest in the field. **Publications:** Evaluation of Collision Stopping Power of Elements and Compounds for Electrons and Positrons, 1982; Bremsstrahlung Energy Spectra from Electrons with Kinetic Energy 1 keV - 10 GeV Incident on Screened Nuclei and Orbital Electrons of Neutral Atoms with Z=1-100, 1986; Pair, Triplet and Total Atomic Cross Sections (and Mass Attenuation Coefficients) for 1 MeV - 100 GeV Photons in Elements Z=1-100, 1980; Bibliography of Photon Total Cross Section (Attenuation Coefficient) Measurements 10 eV - 13.5 GeV and Comparison with Theoretical Values 0.1 - 100 keV, 1986; Photonuclear Data-Abstract Sheets, 1955-1982 (Z=1-95). **Special Indexes:** Photonuclear Data Index, 1955-1972, 1973-1981. **Remarks:** Alternate telephone number(s): 975-5550. FAX: (301)869-7682. **Staff:** M.J. Berger; J.H. Hubbell; E.B. Saloman.

★ 17624 ★
U.S. Natl. Institute of Standards and Technology - Research Information Center (Sci-Engr)
E106 Administration Bldg.   Phone: (301)975-3052
Gaithersburg, MD 20899   Patricia W. Berger, Off., Info.Serv.
Founded: 1901. **Staff:** 49. **Subjects:** Physical sciences, chemistry, metrology, engineering, materials science, computer science, technology, statistics, mathematics, robotics. **Special Collections:** Reference Collection of the Office of Standard Reference Data; museum collection of scientific apparatus and other memorabilia of the past work of the National Bureau of Standards and the National Institute of Standards and Technology; oral history collection; history of metrology and standardization; intergovernmental affairs. **Holdings:** 250,000 books and bound periodical volumes; scientific artifacts and historical files, AV collection. **Subscriptions:** 2500 journals and other serials. **Services:** Interlibrary loan; copying (limited); center open to the public for reference use only. **Automated Operations:** Computerized public access catalog, cataloging, acquisitions, serials, circulation, and ILL. **Computerized Information Services:** DIALOG Information Services, PFDS Online, BRS Information Technologies, NLM, LEXIS, NEXIS, Chemical Information Systems, Inc. (CIS), NASA/RECON, Integrated Technical Information System (ITIS), Institute for Scientific Information (ISI), Mead Data Central, OCLC, Government-Industry Data Exchange Program (GIDEP); CD-ROMs; BITNET (electronic mail service). **Networks/Consortia:** Member of FEDLINK, Interlibrary Users Association (IUA). **Publications:** Monthly bulletin; special catalogs; finding aids. **Remarks:** FAX: (301)869-8071; (301)869-6787 (ILL). Electronic mail address(es): pberger@enh.nist.gov (BITNET). The National Institute of Standards and Technology is part of the U.S. Department of Commerce. **Staff:** Karma A. Beal, Hist.Info.Spec.; Marvin A. Bond, Chf., Info.Sys. & Equipment; Sami Klein, Chf., Res.Info.Serv.

★ 17625 ★
U.S. Natl. Institutes of Health - Division of Computer Research & Technology - Library (Comp Sci, Sci-Engr)
9000 Rockville Pike
Bldg. 12A, Rm. 3018   Phone: (301)496-1658
Bethesda, MD 20892   Ellen Moy Chu, Libn.
Founded: 1966. **Staff:** Prof 2; Other 2. **Subjects:** Computer applications in biomedical sciences, computer science, mathematics, statistics, information science. **Holdings:** 6600 books and reports; 530 bound periodical volumes; 9 drawers of microfilm. **Subscriptions:** 200 journals. **Services:** Interlibrary loan; SDI; library open to the public by special permission. **Automated Operations:** Computerized public access catalog, cataloging, acquisitions, serials, and circulation. **Computerized Information Services:** DIALOG Information Services, NLM, NEXIS, LEXIS, OCLC, STN International; BITNET, InterNet, OCLC (electronic mail services). **Networks/Consortia:** Member of FEDLINK. **Remarks:** FAX: (301)402-0007. Electronic mail address(es): ELC@NIHDCRTL (BITNET). **Staff:** Anita McGregor; Anita Florentino.

★ 17626 ★
U.S. Natl. Institutes of Health - Library (Med, Biol Sci)
9000 Rockville Pike
Bldg. 10, Rm. 1L-25   Phone: (301)496-2447
Bethesda, MD 20892   Carolyn P. Brown, Chf.Libn.
Founded: 1903. **Staff:** Prof 26; Other 29. **Subjects:** Medicine, health sciences, chemistry, pathology, physiology, biology. **Holdings:** 85,000 books; 152,000 bound periodical volumes; 17,000 microforms. **Subscriptions:** 5300 journals and other serials. **Services:** Interlibrary loan; copying; SDI; library open to the public for reference use only. **Automated Operations:** Computerized cataloging, acquisitions, serials and circulation. **Computerized Information Services:** DIALOG Information Services, BRS Information Technologies, STN International, NLM, OCLC, NEXIS. **Networks/Consortia:** Member of FEDLINK. **Publications:** Current and Noncurrent Journals in the NIH Library, biennial; Recent Additions to the NIH Library, monthly. **Remarks:** Institutes are a part of the U.S. Public Health Service. **Remarks:** FAX: (301)402-0254. **Staff:** Maxine Hanke, Dp.Chf.; Jennylind C. Boggess, Sys.Libn.; Rosalie H. Stroman, Chf., Rd.Serv.Sect.; Lisa C. Wu, Chf., Tech.Serv.; Elsie Cerutti, Chf., Ref. & Bibliog.Serv.; Patricia A. Barnes, ILL Libn.; Joan Daghita, Hd., Circ.; Margarett Kunz, Hd., Acq.

U.S. Natl. Institutes of Health - National Arthritis and Musculoskeletal and Skin Disease Information Clearinghouse
See: **National Arthritis and Musculoskeletal and Skin Diseases Information Clearinghouse** (11047)

★ 17627 ★
U.S. Natl. Institutes of Health - National Cancer Institute - Frederick Cancer Research & Development Center - Scientific Library (Med)
Box B - Bldg. 549   Phone: (301)846-1093
Frederick, MD 21702-1013   Susan W. Wilson, Dir.
Founded: 1972. **Subjects:** Cancer biology, biological and chemical carcinogenesis, acquired immunodeficiency syndrome, biomedical research. **Holdings:** 16,000 books; 24,000 bound periodical volumes; 2600 reels of microfilm of periodicals. **Subscriptions:** 718 journals and other serials. **Services:** Interlibrary loan; SDI; library open to the public with restrictions. **Automated Operations:** Computerized serials. **Computerized Information Services:** Online systems. **Networks/Consortia:** Member of FEDLINK. **Publications:** Accessions list, monthly; Serial holdings list, annual.

U.S. Natl. Institutes of Health - National Digestive Diseases Information Clearinghouse
See: **National Digestive Diseases Information Clearinghouse** (11148)

U.S. Natl. Institutes of Health - National Heart, Lung, and Blood Institute - Education Programs' Information Center
See: **National Heart, Lung, and Blood Institute - Education Programs' Information Center** (11193)

U.S. Natl. Institutes of Health - National Institute on Aging
See: **National Institute on Aging** (11204)

★17628★
U.S. Natl. Institutes of Health - National Institute of Allergy &
Infectious Diseases - Rocky Mountain Laboratory Library (Med, Biol
Sci)
Hamilton, MT 59840   Phone: (406)363-3211
                                        Leza Serha Hamby, Med.Libn.
Founded: 1932. Staff: Prof 1. Subjects: Medicine, virology, bacteriology,
immunology, entomology, chemistry, parasitology, pathology,
microbiology, biochemistry, biology, sexually transmitted disease. Holdings:
6000 books; 22,000 bound periodical volumes. Subscriptions: 287 journals
and other serials. Services: Interlibrary loan (limited); library not open to
the public. Computerized Information Services: WLN, MEDLARS;
OnTyme Electronic Message Network Service (electronic mail service).
Remarks: FAX: (406)363-3211 ext. 204. (voice); (406)363-6406 (direct).

U.S. Natl. Institutes of Health - National Institute of Arthritis and
Muskuloskeletal and Skin Diseases
See: National Institute of Arthritis and Muskuloskeletal and Skin
Diseases (11207)

U.S. Natl. Institutes of Health - National Institute of Dental Research
See: National Institute of Dental Research (11208)

U.S. Natl. Institutes of Health - National Institute of Environmental
Health Sciences
See: National Institute of Environmental Health Sciences (11210)

U.S. Natl. Institutes of Health - National Library of Medicine
See: U.S. National Library of Medicine (17629)

U.S. Natl. Institutes of Health - Research Resources Division - Tracor
Technology Resources, Inc.
See: Tracor Technology Resources, Inc. (16445)

U.S. Natl. Labor Relations Board
See: National Labor Relations Board (11225)

★17629★
U.S. National Library of Medicine (Med)
8600 Rockville Pike   Phone: (301)496-6308
Bethesda, MD 20894   Donald A.B. Lindberg, M.D., Dir.
Founded: 1836. Staff: Prof 310; Other 204. Subjects: Medicine, health
sciences, dentistry, public health, nursing, biomedical research. Special
Collections: History of medicine (pre-1914); Prints and Photographs
Collection; modern manuscripts. Holdings: 700,000 books; 920,000 bound
periodical volumes; 2.3 million manuscripts; 57,000 pictures; 293,000
microforms; 282,000 theses; 172,000 pamphlets; 50,000 AV programs;
microfilm. Subscriptions: 21,600 journals and other serials. Services:
Interlibrary loan; copying; SDI; library open to the public. Automated
Operations: Computerized cataloging, acquisitions, serials, and indexing.
Computerized Information Services: MEDLARS, MEDLINE; SprintMail
(electronic mail service). Publications: NLM News (newsletter) - to the
public. Special Catalogs: NLM Current Catalog; NLM Audiovisuals
Catalog, both quarterly with annual cumulation. Special Indexes: Index
Medicus; Abridged Index Medicus, both monthly with annual cumulation.
Remarks: FAX: (301)496-4450. Headquarters of National Network of
Libraries of Medicine (formerly Regional Medical Library Network).
Library is a branch of U.S. Public Health Service - National Institutes of
Health. Also Known As: NLM.

U.S. National Library of Medicine - Toxicology Information Response
Center
See: Oak Ridge National Laboratory - Toxicology Information Response
Center (12192)

★17630★
U.S. Natl. Marine Fisheries Service - Auke Bay Fisheries Laboratory -
Fisheries Research Library (Biol Sci, Env-Cons)
11305 Glacier Hwy.   Phone: (907)789-6010
Juneau, AK 99801-8626   Paula Johnson, Libn.
Founded: 1960. Staff: Prof 1; Other 1. Subjects: Biological sciences,
fisheries, oceanography, water pollution. Special Collections: Scandinavian
fisheries periodicals; International North Pacific Fisheries Commission
documents; Pribiloff Island Log Books. Holdings: 11,500 books; 2700 bound
periodical volumes; 500 manuscripts; 1500 reprints; 2000 translations; 105
reels of microfilm; 40 microfiche and microcard titles; 1500 slides.
Subscriptions: 202 journals and other serials. Services: Interlibrary loan;
copying; library open to the public. Computerized Information Services:
DIALOG Information Services. Publications: Accession List. Remarks:
Alternate telephone number(s): 789-6009. FAX: (907)789-6094. The
National Marine Fisheries Service is part of the National Oceanic &
Atmospheric Administration of the U.S. Department of Commerce.
Formerly: Located in Auke Bay, AK.

★17631★
U.S. Natl. Marine Fisheries Service - Charleston Laboratory - Library
(Biol Sci, Food-Bev)
217 Fort Johnson Rd.
P.O. Box 12607   Phone: (803)762-1200
Charleston, SC 29422-2607   Lois F. Winemiller, Chf., Tech.Info.Serv.
Subjects: Chemistry, food science and technology, nutrition, microbiology,
biology. Holdings: 8000 volumes. Subscriptions: 150 journals and other
serials. Services: Interlibrary loan; library open to the public by special
request. Computerized Information Services: DIALOG Information
Services. Networks/Consortia: Member of FEDLINK, FEDLINK.
Remarks: FAX: (803)762-1200.

★17632★
U.S. Natl. Marine Fisheries Service - Honolulu Laboratory - Library
(Biol Sci)
2570 Dole St.   Phone: (808)943-1221
Honolulu, HI 96822-2396   Sandra L. Abbott-Stout, Libn.Hd.
Founded: 1950. Staff: Prof 1. Subjects: Marine biology, ichthyology, tuna,
oceanography. Holdings: 3800 books. Subscriptions: 200 journals and other
serials. Services: Interlibrary loan; copying; library open to qualified
researchers for reference only. Remarks: FAX: (808)943-1290.

★17633★
U.S. Natl. Marine Fisheries Service - Milford Laboratory Library (Biol
Sci, Env-Cons)
212 Rogers Ave.
Milford, CT 06460   Phone: (203)783-4200
Subjects: Fisheries, marine biology, aquaculture, cytology, genetics,
ecology, microbiology, physiology, biochemistry, microscopy, statistics,
marine pollution. Special Collections: Reprints (primarily fisheries and
related subjects); U.S. Bureau of Fisheries and NOAA/NMFS documents,
1874 to present. Holdings: 3300 books; 1500 bound periodical volumes; 1800
slides. Subscriptions: 100 journals and other serials. Services: Interlibrary
loan; library open to the public for reference use only with permission.
Automated Operations: Computerized cataloging. Computerized
Information Services: OCLC, DIALOG Information Services. Remarks:
FAX: (203)783-4217.

★17634★
U.S. Natl. Marine Fisheries Service - Mississippi Laboratories - Library
(Biol Sci)
3209 Frederic St.
Drawer 1207   Phone: (601)762-4591
Pascagoula, MS 39568-1207   Sally Glynn, Libn.
Staff: Prof 1. Subjects: Marine biology, fishery and fishing gear research,
marine resources, microbiology, chemistry. Holdings: 2000 books; 1800
bound periodical volumes; 3000 reprints. Subscriptions: 150 journals and
other serials. Services: Interlibrary loan; copying; library open to the public.
Computerized Information Services: DIALOG Information Services,
OCLC. Networks/Consortia: Member of FEDLINK, U.S. Natl. Oceanic &
Atmospheric Administration Southeastern Area Resources Cooperative
(NOAASARC). Remarks: FAX: (601)769-9200.

★ 17635 ★
U.S. Natl. Marine Fisheries Service - National Marine Mammal
  Laboratory - Library (Biol Sci)
7600 Sand Point Way, N.E., Bldg. 4   Phone: (206)526-4013
Seattle, WA 98115-0070   Sherry Pearson, Tech.Info.Spec.
Staff: 1. **Subjects:** Marine mammals. **Holdings:** 1700 books and bound
periodical volumes; 145 VF drawers of reprints. **Subscriptions:** 137 journals
and other serials. **Services:** Interlibrary loan; library open to the public.
Remarks: FAX: (206)526-6615.

★ 17636 ★
U.S. Natl. Marine Fisheries Service - Northeast Fisheries Center -
  Library (Biol Sci, Env-Cons)
Woods Hole, MA 02543   Phone: (508)548-5123
                         Lynn Forbes, Libn.
Founded: 1893. **Staff:** Prof 1. **Subjects:** Fishery biology, marine biology,
oceanography, management and law of fisheries. **Special Collections:**
Research documents of the former International Commission for the
Northwest Atlantic Fisheries (ICNAF) and the current Northwest Atlantic
Fisheries Organization (NAFO); annual meeting documents of the
International Council for the Exploration of the Sea (I.C.E.S.). **Holdings:**
7000 bound periodicals and other cataloged items; 50 films; 2000 slides;
scrapbooks of newspaper clippings and photographs, 1940-1967; archives.
Subscriptions: 50 journals and other serials. **Services:** Interlibrary loan;
copying; library open to the public. **Automated Operations:** Computerized
cataloging. **Computerized Information Services:** DIALOG Information
Services, OCLC. Performs searches on fee basis. **Networks/Consortia:**
Member of FEDLINK. **Special Catalogs:** Collected Reprints of the
Northeast Fisheries Center, 1977 to 1983; Serials List. **Remarks:** FAX:
(508)548-5124.

★ 17637 ★
U.S. Natl. Marine Fisheries Service - Northeast Fisheries Center -
  Oxford Laboratory Library (Biol Sci, Env-Cons)
Oxford, MD 21654   Phone: (301)226-5193
                         Susie K. Hines, Libn.
Founded: 1961. **Staff:** Prof 1. **Subjects:** Marine shellfish and fish pathology,
marine resource investigations. **Special Collections:** U.S. government
publications on fisheries. **Holdings:** 4350 books; 4700 bound periodical
volumes; 40,000 reprints and pamphlets. **Subscriptions:** 125 journals and
other serials. **Services:** Interlibrary loan; copying; library open to the public
for reference use only. **Computerized Information Services:** DIALOG
Information Services, OCLC. **Networks/Consortia:** Member of FEDLINK.
Publications: Annual Publications List; Serials Holding List, annual;
Dissertations and Theses Collection of the Oxford Laboratory Library.

★ 17638 ★
U.S. Natl. Marine Fisheries Service - Northwest & Alaska Fisheries
  Center - Library (Biol Sci, Env-Cons)
2725 Montlake Blvd., E.   Phone: (206)553-7795
Seattle, WA 98112   Patricia Cook, Libn.
Staff: Prof 2. **Subjects:** Fisheries, oceanography, chemistry, biochemistry,
food technology, statistics, marine biology. **Holdings:** 32,000 volumes; 4000
files of reprints; 3000 files of translations. **Subscriptions:** 220 journals and
other serials. **Services:** Interlibrary loan; library open to the public for
reference use only. **Computerized Information Services:** OCLC; CD-ROM
(Aquatic Sciences and Fisheries Abstracts); internal database; SCIENCEnet
(electronic mail service). **Networks/Consortia:** Member of FEDLINK.
Remarks: FAX: (206)553-4304. Electronic mail address(es):
P.COOK.NMFS (SCIENCEnet).

★ 17639 ★
U.S. Natl. Marine Fisheries Service - Panama City Laboratory - Library
  (Biol Sci, Env-Cons)
3500 Delwood Beach Rd.   Phone: (904)234-6541
Panama City, FL 32408   Rosalie Shaffer, Tech.Info.Spec.
Founded: 1972. **Staff:** Prof 1. **Subjects:** Fishery science, marine biology,
oceanography, zoology, ecology. **Holdings:** 3000 books; 8500 technical
reports; 300 periodical titles; 200 dissertations; 8000 reprints. **Subscriptions:**
150 journals and other serials. **Services:** Interlibrary loan; copying; library
open to the public. **Computerized Information Services:** DIALOG
Information Services. **Networks/Consortia:** Member of U.S. Natl. Oceanic
& Atmospheric Administration Library & Information Network.
Publications: List of contributions, annual; serials holdings list, annual.
Remarks: FAX: (904)234-6543.

★ 17640 ★
U.S. Natl. Marine Fisheries Service - Sandy Hook Laboratory - Lionel
  A. Walford Library (Biol Sci, Env-Cons)
U.S. Dept. of Commerce NOAA -Bg
74 Magruder Rd.   Phone: (908)872-3035
Highlands, NJ 07732   Claire L. Steimle, Libn.
Founded: 1961. **Staff:** Prof 1; Other 1. **Subjects:** Fisheries, environmental
problems, marine invertebrates, biological and chemical oceanography,
plankton behavior, microbiology, New York Bight. **Special Collections:**
Fishery Bulletins and Reports to Commissioner of Fisheries; Special
Pollution Collection (150 volumes). **Holdings:** 6000 books; 4500 bound
periodical volumes; 14,000 documents. **Subscriptions:** 300 journals and
other serials. **Services:** Interlibrary loan; copying (limited); library open to
the public by appointment. **Computerized Information Services:** DIALOG
Information Services, OCLC; CD-ROM (ASFA); SCIENCEnet (electronic
mail service). **Publications:** Bibliographies. **Remarks:** Alternate telephone
number(s): (908)872-3034. FAX: (908)872-3088. Electronic mail
address(es): NMFS.SANDYHOOK.LIB (SCIENCEnet).

★ 17641 ★
U.S. Natl. Marine Fisheries Service - Southeast Fisheries Center -
  Miami Laboratory Library (Biol Sci)
75 Virginia Beach Dr.   Phone: (305)361-4229
Miami, FL 33149   Harriet Corvino, Lib.Techn.
Founded: 1965. **Staff:** Prof 1. **Subjects:** Marine biology, fish, fisheries.
Special Collections: Reprint collection (7000 concerning fish, fish eggs, and
larvae). **Holdings:** 20,500 books and bound periodical volumes.
Subscriptions: 350 journals and other serials. **Services:** Interlibrary loan;
copying; library open to the public with restrictions. **Automated Operations:**
Computerized cataloging, acquisitions, and serials. **Computerized
Information Services:** DIALOG Information Services, OCLC. Performs
searches on fee basis. **Networks/Consortia:** Member of FEDLINK.

★ 17642 ★
U.S. Natl. Marine Fisheries Service - Southeast Fisheries Center - Rice
  Library (Biol Sci, Env-Cons)
Pivers Island   Phone: (919)728-3595
Beaufort, NC 28516-9722   Ann Bowman Manooch, Libn.
Founded: 1949. **Staff:** Prof 1. **Subjects:** Fish, fisheries, marine biology,
radioecology, oceanography. **Holdings:** 15,000 books and bound periodical
volumes; 200 linear feet of unbound materials. **Subscriptions:** 380 journals
and other serials. **Services:** Interlibrary loan; library open to the public with
restrictions. **Automated Operations:** Computerized public access catalog,
cataloging, and ILL. **Computerized Information Services:** DIALOG
Information Services; CD-ROM (Aquatic Sciences and Fisheries Abstracts).
Publications: List of Serials. **Remarks:** Alternate telephone number(s): 728-
8713.

★ 17643 ★
U.S. Natl. Marine Fisheries Service - Southwest Fisheries Science
  Center - Library (Biol Sci, Env-Cons)
8604 La Jolla Shores Dr.
Box 271   Phone: (619)546-7038
La Jolla, CA 92038-0271   Debra A. Losey, Tech.Info.Spec.
Founded: 1965. **Staff:** Prof 1; Other 1. **Subjects:** Fisheries, oceanography,
marine biology and ecology, marine mammals, Antarctic biology. **Holdings:**
2700 books; 12,000 periodical volumes; 9000 pamphlets. **Subscriptions:** 200
journals and other serials. **Services:** Interlibrary loan; copying; SDI; library
open to the public for reference use only. **Automated Operations:**
Computerized cataloging. **Computerized Information Services:** DIALOG
Information Services, OCLC; internal database (reprints and internal
reports); DIALMAIL, SCIENCEnet (electronic mail services). **Networks/
Consortia:** Member of FEDLINK. **Remarks:** Figures include Inter-
American Tropical Tuna Commission Collection. FAX: (619)546-7003.
Telex: 91-033712-71. Electronic mail address(es): NMFS.SW.LIBRARY
(SCIENCEnet). U.S. National Marine Fisheries Service is part of the U.S.
Department of Commerce - National Oceanic & Atmospheric
Administration.

★ 17644 ★
U.S. Natl. Marine Fisheries Service - Tiburon Laboratory Library (Biol
  Sci, Env-Cons)
3150 Paradise Dr.   Phone: (415)435-3149
Tiburon, CA 94920   Gareth Penn, Libn.
Founded: 1962. **Staff:** Prof 1. **Subjects:** Marine biology, fishery science,
commercial fishing, sport fisheries, oceanography. **Special Collections:**

Collection of W.H. Rich on Salmon; Dr. Victor L. Loosanoff Reprint Collection (commercial mollusks); Susumu Kato Shark Reprint Collection (shark taxonomy). **Holdings:** 2800 books; 2700 bound periodical volumes; 12,000 reprints. **Subscriptions:** 250 journals and other serials. **Services:** Interlibrary loan; library open to the public for reference use only. **Automated Operations:** Computerized cataloging and ILL. **Computerized Information Services:** DIALOG Information Services, OCLC. **Networks/Consortia:** Member of FEDLINK. **Publications:** Occasional reprints. **Remarks:** FAX: (415)435-3675.

★17645★
U.S. Natl. Marine Fisheries Service - W.F. Thompson Memorial Library (Biol Sci, Env-Cons)
Box 1638   Phone: (907)487-4961
Kodiak, AK 99615   Nancy L. Matt, Libn.
Founded: 1971. **Staff:** 1. **Subjects:** Fisheries, biology, chemistry, fishery food science, Alaska fishing research. **Special Collections:** Collection of W.F. Thompson, leader in Alaska fishery research. **Holdings:** 2500 books; 3300 bound periodical volumes; leaflets; circulars; reports; biological reports. **Subscriptions:** 90 journals and other serials; 5 newspapers. **Services:** Interlibrary loan; copying; library open to the public by permission. **Computerized Information Services:** DIALOG Information Services; access to NOAA internal database. **Remarks:** FAX: (907)487-4960.

★17646★
U.S. Natl. Oceanic & Atmospheric Administration - Atmospheric Turbulence & Diffusion Division - Library (Sci-Engr, Energy)
Box 2456   Phone: (615)576-0061
Oak Ridge, TN 37831   Barbara S. Johnson, Adm.Off.
Founded: 1964. **Staff:** 1. **Subjects:** Air pollution, forest meteorology, climatic studies. **Holdings:** 2500 volumes; 6000 technical reports and reprints. **Subscriptions:** 60 journals and other serials. **Services:** Library open to the public for reference use only. **Remarks:** FAX: (615)576-1327. Laboratory is operated for the Department of Energy as a division of the National Oceanic & Atmospheric Administration's Air Resources Laboratory. **Staff:** Lala Chambers.

★17647★
U.S. Natl. Oceanic & Atmospheric Administration - Geophysical Fluid Dynamics Laboratory - Library (Sci-Engr)
Box 308   Phone: (609)452-6550
Princeton, NJ 08542   Gail T. Haller, Libn.
Founded: 1968. **Staff:** Prof 1. **Subjects:** Meteorology, climatology, oceanography, fluid dynamics. **Special Collections:** Russian monographs on meteorology and climatology (200 volumes); atmospheric sciences collection. **Holdings:** 8000 books; 1600 bound periodical volumes; 3000 technical reports; 50 atlases; 30 films. **Subscriptions:** 120 journals and other serials. **Services:** Interlibrary loan; copying; library open to the public. **Automated Operations:** Computerized cataloging and serials. **Computerized Information Services:** DIALOG Information Services, OCLC; internal database; SCIENCEnet, InterNet (electronic mail services). **Networks/Consortia:** Member of FEDLINK. **Publications:** GFDL Activities and Plans, annual; bibliography of the works of L.S. Gandin, Russian meteorologist. **Remarks:** FAX: (609)987-5063. Electronic mail address(es): NOAA.GFDL.LIBRARY (SCIENCEnet); gth@gfdl.gov (InterNet).

★17648★
U.S. Natl. Oceanic & Atmospheric Administration - Great Lakes Environmental Research Laboratory Library (Sci-Engr)
2205 Commonwealth Blvd.   Phone: (313)668-2242
Ann Arbor, MI 48105   Barbara J. Carrick, Libn.
Staff: Prof 1; Other 2. **Subjects:** Great Lakes - hydraulics, hydrology, limnology, limnologic systems, meteorological weather data, physical oceanography, water characteristics, modeling, water quality control; information analysis. **Holdings:** 9000 books; 200 bound periodical volumes; 217 reels of microfilm of Great Lakes Archives, 1841-1952; 12 VF drawers of pamphlets; 124 agency publications. **Subscriptions:** 210 journals and other serials. **Services:** Interlibrary loan; copying; library open to the public for reference use only. **Computerized Information Services:** Online systems. **Publications:** List of publications - available on request.

★17649★
U.S. Natl. Oceanic & Atmospheric Administration - Library and Information Services Division (Sci-Engr)
7600 Sand Point Way, N.E., E/OC43, Bldg. 3   Phone: (206)526-6241
Seattle, WA 98115-0070   Maureen Woods, Libn.
Founded: 1980. **Staff:** Prof 1; Other 1. **Subjects:** Physical and chemical oceanography, marine pollution, geochemistry, meteorology, atmospheric physics, ocean engineering, mathematics, statistics, climatology. **Holdings:** 5500 books and technical reports. **Subscriptions:** 220 journals and other serials. **Services:** Interlibrary loan; copying; SDI; center open to the public for reference use only. **Automated Operations:** Computerized cataloging, acquisitions, and serials. **Computerized Information Services:** DIALOG Information Services, OCLC; NOAA LINC (Library and Information Network Catalog; internal database). **Networks/Consortia:** Member of FEDLINK.

★17650★
U.S. Natl. Oceanic & Atmospheric Administration - Library and Information Services Division - Main Library (Geog-Map, Sci-Engr)
6009 Executive Blvd.   Phone: (301)443-0237
Rockville, MD 20852   Carol Watts, Div.Dir.
Founded: 1846. **Staff:** Prof 15; Other 16. **Subjects:** Geodesy, surveying, oceanography, geophysics, geodetic and hydrographic surveying, photogrammetry, nautical and aeronautical cartography, fisheries, geodetic astronomy, meteorology, climatology, hydrology, atmospheric physics, ocean engineering, mathematics, computer science. **Special Collections:** Rare book collection (includes scientific treatises from the 16th and 17th centuries). **Holdings:** 654,000 volumes; 100,100 bound periodical volumes; 100,400 bound documents; 19,500 microfiche; 34,000 reports, maps, charts, data publications. **Subscriptions:** 9040 journals and other serials. **Services:** Interlibrary loan; copying; SDI; library open to the public for reference use only. **Automated Operations:** Computerized cataloging, serials, and acquisitions. **Computerized Information Services:** DIALOG Information Services, PFDS Online, BRS Information Technologies, NEXIS, NLM, LEGI-SLATE, OCLC. **Networks/Consortia:** Member of FEDLINK. **Publications:** Acquisitions list; list of other publications - available on request. **Remarks:** The National Oceanic & Atmospheric Administration is part of the U.S. Department of Commerce. Provides consultative and technical guidance to 33 NOAA libraries and information centers with highly specialized collections in meteorology, climatology, hydrology, marine biology, fisheries science located throughout the U.S. Maintains branches in Miami, FL and Seattle, WA. FAX: (301)443-0237. **Also Known As:** NOAA. **Staff:** Janice Beattie, Reg.Libs.Coord.; Lynda Kuntz, Sys.

★17651★
U.S. Natl. Oceanic & Atmospheric Administration - Miami Regional Library/AOML (Sci-Engr)
4301 Rickenbacker Causeway   Phone: (305)361-4428
Miami, FL 33149   Linda Pikula, Lib.Dir.
Founded: 1970. **Staff:** Prof 1; Other 1. **Subjects:** Oceanography, tropical meteorology, marine geology, ocean chemistry, applied mathematics, physics. **Special Collections:** U.S. Coast and Geodetic Survey Report, 1866-1982. **Holdings:** 12,000 volumes; 19,000 technical reports; 750 atlases and symposia; 12,000 microforms; 750 charts and maps. **Subscriptions:** 151 journals and other serials. **Services:** Interlibrary loan; library open to the public. **Automated Operations:** Computerized cataloging and serials. **Computerized Information Services:** DIALOG Information Services, BRS Information Technologies; NOAALINK (internal database); OMNET (electronic mail service). **Networks/Consortia:** Member of U.S. Natl. Oceanic & Atmospheric Administration Southeastern Area Resources Cooperative (NOAASARC). **Publications:** New acquisitions list, monthly. **Remarks:** FAX: (305)361-4449. Electronic mail address(es): AOML.LIBRARY (OMNET).

★17652★
U.S. Natl. Oceanic & Atmospheric Administration - Mountain Administrative Support Center - Information Resources Division - Library (Sci-Engr, Comp Sci)
325 Broadway MC5   Phone: (303)497-3271
Boulder, CO 80303   John J. Welsh, Chf., Info.Rsrcs.Div.
Founded: 1954. **Staff:** Prof 5; Other 9. **Subjects:** Mathematics, electronics engineering, atmospheric science, aeronomy, computer science, telecommunications, radio physics, oceanography, marine sciences, astrophysics, cryogenics, radio engineering, physics, astronomy. **Holdings:** 45,540 books; 29,661 bound periodical volumes; 12,931 technical reports; 131,330 titles on microfiche; 175 audio cassettes; 21 compact discs.

Subscriptions: 907 journals and other serials. **Services:** Interlibrary loan; copying; library open to the public for reference use only. **Automated Operations:** Computerized public access catalog, cataloging, acquisitions, serials, and circulation. **Computerized Information Services:** DIALOG Information Services, PFDS Online, BRS Information Technologies, Integrated Technical Information System (ITIS), NASA/RECON, DTIC, OCLC, STN International. **Networks/Consortia:** Member of Bibliographical Center for Research, Rocky Mountain Region, Inc. (BCR), FEDLINK. **Publications:** Library Notes, weekly - for internal distribution only; Library Brochure - available upon request. **Remarks:** FAX: (303)497-3890. **Staff:** Jean Bankhead, Hd., Ref.Serv./ILL; Sara Martin, Hd., Tech.Serv.; Jane Watterson, Ref.Libn.; Katherine Day, Ref.Libn.

★ 17653 ★
U.S. Natl. Oceanic & Atmospheric Administration - National Environmental Satellite, Data, & Information Service - National Oceanographic Data Center (Biol Sci, Sci-Engr)
Universal Bldg., Rm. 401
1825 Connecticut Ave., N.W.   Phone: (202)606-4594
Washington, DC 20235   Bruce C. Douglas, Dir.
Founded: 1961. **Staff:** 86. **Subjects:** Oceanography - physical, chemical, biological. **Holdings:** Digital oceanographic data: oceanographic station and bathythermograph data covering the world's oceans; marine pollution and marine biological data from selected offshore areas of the U.S.; surface and subsurface current data; wind/wave data from environmental buoys offshore of the U.S.; global wind/wave data derived from altimeter measurements of the U.S. Navy GEOSAT; data from special projects such as the Climatological Atlas of the World Ocean. **Services:** Data inventory searches; selective retrieval and output of data; referral services; center open to the public. **Automated Operations:** Computerized data retrieval and presentation. **Computerized Information Services:** SprintMail, SCIENCEnet, Space Physics Analysis Network (SPAN) (electronic mail services). **Publications:** List of publications - available on request; NODC User's Guide (which describes data holdings, products, and services) - free upon request. **Remarks:** Center located at Universal South Bldg., 1825 Connecticut Ave., N.W., Washington, DC 20235. Alternate telephone number(s): 673-5561. FAX: (202)673-5586. Electronic mail address(es): NODC:WDCA (SprintMail, SCIENCEnet); NODC:SERVICES (Space Physics Analysis Network). **Staff:** Robert Lockerman, User Serv.

★ 17654 ★
U.S. Natl. Oceanic & Atmospheric Administration - National Environmental Satellite, Data, & Information Services - National Climatic Data Center - Library (Sci-Engr)
Federal Bldg.   Phone: (704)259-0677
Asheville, NC 28801-2696   Linda D. Preston, Libn.
Founded: 1962. **Staff:** 1. **Subjects:** Climatology, meteorology, oceanography, weather records. **Special Collections:** Past weather records. **Holdings:** 10,455 books; 700 bound periodical volumes; 29 reels of microfilm; 2000 microfiche; 94,000 pamphlets; 8 atmospheric models. **Subscriptions:** 1000 journals and other serials. **Services:** Interlibrary loan; copying; library open to the public with restrictions. **Computerized Information Services:** DIALOG Information Services, DTIC, BRS Information Technologies, OCLC. **Remarks:** FAX: (704)672-0246. Telex: 6502643731.

★ 17655 ★
U.S. Natl. Oceanic & Atmospheric Administration - National Geodetic Information Center - Geodetic Reference Services (Sci-Engr)
11400 Rockville Pike   Phone: (301)443-8316
Rockville, MD 20852   Grace C. Sollers, Tech.Info.Spec.
Founded: 1975. **Staff:** Prof 2. **Subjects:** Geodesy. **Holdings:** 50,000 books; 10,000 bound periodical volumes; reports; manuscripts; agency records, publications, surveys. **Subscriptions:** 50 journals and other serials. **Services:** Copying; services open to the public for reference use only. **Computerized Information Services:** Social Science Data Libraries. **Publications:** Geodetic & Charting Publications, June 1991 - free upon request; National Geodetic Survey, August 1991 - free upon request. **Remarks:** FAX: (301)881-0154.

★ 17656 ★
U.S. Natl. Oceanic & Atmospheric Administration - National Hurricane Center - Library (Sci-Engr)
Gables 1 Tower, 6th Fl.
1320 S. Dixie Hwy.   Phone: (305)666-0413
Coral Gables, FL 33146   Linda Pikula, Lib.Dir.
Staff: Prof 1. **Subjects:** Meteorology - tropical, hurricane, satellite. **Special Collections:** Films of clouds and rainband as planes penetrate hurricanes.

Holdings: 5000 volumes; contractor reports; college, government, and private meteorological reports; maps and hemispheric information on microfilm; films of reconnaissance and research flights into hurricanes; photopanel films of instrument panel of planes in hurricane flight; film of radar in planes; printouts of processed data on information from hurricane flights. **Subscriptions:** 30 journals and other serials. **Services:** Interlibrary loan; copying; library open to the public for reference use only. **Automated Operations:** Computerized public access catalog. **Computerized Information Services:** DIALOG Information Services, BRS Information Technologies, NOAA (internal database); OMNET (electronic mail service) (through AOML/NOAA Library). **Remarks:** FAX: (305)665-8526. **Also Known As:** Technical Library for Tropical and Hurricane Meteorology.

★ 17657 ★
U.S. Natl. Oceanic & Atmospheric Administration - National Ocean Service - Cartographic Support Unit (Geog-Map)
6501 Lafayette Ave.   Phone: (301)436-6990
Riverdale, MD 20737   Elaine Downs, Chf.
Founded: 1938. **Subjects:** Cartographic information, U.S. nautical and aeronautical charts, U.S. and Canadian topographical maps, special maps. **Special Collections:** Civil War maps (800); early city plans; 19th century nautical charts; 16th, 17th, and 18th century historical expedition maps; Great Lakes nautical charts (6500). **Holdings:** 138,000 cartographic publications of the 19th century; 8000 aeronautical charts, 1927 to present; 22 atlases; 214 American Revolution maps; 500,000 other cataloged items. **Services:** Copying; library open to the public for reference use only.

★ 17658 ★
U.S. Natl. Oceanic & Atmospheric Administration - National Sea Grant College Program - National Sea Grant Depository (Biol Sci)
Pell Library Bldg.
URI-Bay Campus   Phone: (401)792-6114
Narragansett, RI 02882   Cynthia Murray, Mgr.
Founded: 1970. **Staff:** Prof 1; Other 2. **Subjects:** Oceanography, aquaculture, marine recreation, fisheries, marine education, marine law and policy. **Holdings:** 28,000 documents; reprints; technical reports; books; annual reports; newsletters. **Services:** Interlibrary loan; depository open to the public. **Computerized Information Services:** SGNET (internal database); SGNET Email (electronic mail service). Performs searches. **Publications:** Sea Grant Abstracts, quarterly. **Remarks:** FAX: (401)792-6160. **Staff:** Joyce Winn, Loan Libn.

★ 17659 ★
U.S. Natl. Oceanic & Atmospheric Administration - National Severe Storms Laboratory - Library (Sci-Engr)
1313 Halley Circle   Phone: (405)366-0421
Norman, OK 73069   Mary Meacham, Libn.
Founded: 1972. **Staff:** Prof 1. **Subjects:** Meteorology, climatology, storm morphology . **Holdings:** 1500 volumes; films; slides; video recordings; climatological data. **Subscriptions:** 40 journals and other serials. **Services:** Interlibrary loan; library open to the public. **Remarks:** FAX: (405)366-0472.

★ 17660 ★
U.S. Natl. Oceanic & Atmospheric Administration - ORA/SAL Climate Applications Branch (Env-Cons)
Federal Bldg., Rm. 200
608 E. Cherry St.   Phone: (314)875-5263
Columbia, MO 65201   Rita B. Terry, Libn.
Staff: 1. **Subjects:** Climatology, ecology, crop production, world food supply, energy consumption. **Holdings:** 100 volumes; raw climatological data; reprint/report file. **Subscriptions:** 75 journals and other serials. **Services:** Branch open to the public for reference use only. **Automated Operations:** Computerized cataloging. **Remarks:** FAX: (314)875-5268.

★ 17661 ★
U.S. Natl. Park Service - Abraham Lincoln Birthplace Natl. Historic Site - Library (Hist)
2995 Lincoln Farm Rd.   Phone: (502)358-3874
Hodgenville, KY 42748   Gary V. Talley, Chf., Interp.
Founded: 1916. **Staff:** 4. **Subjects:** Abraham Lincoln. **Special Collections:** Thomas Lincoln Land Records (microfilm; photostats); Lincoln Farm Association Collection (photographs; documents). **Holdings:** 200 books and bound periodical volumes. **Services:** Library open to the public with restrictions. **Remarks:** The National Park Service is part of the U.S. Department of the Interior. **Remarks:** FAX: (502)358-9474.

★ 17662 ★
U.S. Natl. Park Service - Acadia Natl. Park - Islesford Historical Museum - Library (Geog-Map, Hist)
P.O. Box 177
Bar Harbor, ME 04609   Phone: (207)244-9224
Founded: 1926. **Staff:** 1 **Subjects:** History of old Acadia, eastern Maine, and the Canadian Maritime Provinces, 1640-1933. **Special Collections:** Schooner trade from Cranberry Isles, 1796-1890 (ships' logs; freight slips; pilot slips; papers; documents); Cranberry Isles and Mount Desert real estate and town papers; early history of Acadia National Park. **Holdings:** 1300 books and pamphlets; 7500 archival items including papers, manuscripts, genealogical data, maps, photographs. **Services:** Museum open to the public in July and August and for reference use by appointment.

★ 17663 ★
U.S. Natl. Park Service - Allegheny Portage Railroad Natl. Historic Site - Johnstown Flood National Memorial Library (Trans, Hist)
P.O. Box 355   Phone: (814)886-8176
St. Michael, PA 15951   Gregory J. Zaborowski, Hist.
Founded: 1964. **Staff:** Prof 2. **Subjects:** Railroad, 1800-1945; transportation and canals of Pennsylvania, 1830-1850; Johnstown Flood of 1889; steel industry. **Holdings:** 200 volumes; 12 rare documents; old newspaper files; slides; photographs. **Services:** Library open to the public for reference use only. **Remarks:** Alternate telephone number(s): 495-4643. FAX: (814)886-5857; 495-7181. **Staff:** Barbara A. Zaborowski, libn., MLS.

★ 17664 ★
U.S. Natl. Park Service - Allegheny Portage Railroad Natl. Historic Site - Library (Trans, Hist)
Box 247   Phone: (814)886-6153
Cresson, PA 16630   Gregory J. Zaborowkski, Hist.
Founded: 1964. **Staff:** Prof 2; Other 1. **Subjects:** Canals, 1800-1860; railroads, 1800-1945; transportation; natural history. **Holdings:** 120 volumes; 12 rare documents; old newspaper files. **Services:** Library open to the public for reference use only. **Remarks:** FAX: (814)886-6117. **Staff:** Barbara A. Zaborowkski, Libn.

★ 17665 ★
U.S. Natl. Park Service - Andrew Johnson Natl. Historic Site - Library (Hist)
College & Depot Sts.
Box 1088   Phone: (615)638-3551
Greeneville, TN 37744-1088   Jim Small, Chf.Pk. Ranger
Special Collections: Andrew Johnson (65 volumes); The Presidency (21 volumes); Tennessee history (50 volumes); Civil War and Reconstruction history (22 volumes). **Holdings:** 200 books, periodicals, pamphlets, Park Service documents and publications. **Services:** Library open to the public for reference use only.

★ 17666 ★
U.S. Natl. Park Service - Antietam Natl. Battlefield - Visitor Center Library (Hist)
Box 158
Sharpsburg, MD 21782   Phone: (301)432-5125
Staff: 2. **Subjects:** Civil War, especially the Battles of South Mountain and Antietam; regimental histories; park history. **Special Collections:** Henry Kyd Douglas Collection; Park Service and Washington County publications. **Holdings:** 980 books; 3 VF drawers of periodicals; 6 VF drawers of reports, manuscripts, transcripts, and copies of diaries, slides, photographs, news articles, and park history; 16mm films; microfilms; tapes; maps. **Services:** Copying; library open to the public by appointment for reference use only. **Staff:** Ted Alexander.

★ 17667 ★
U.S. Natl. Park Service - Apostle Islands Natl. Lakeshore - Library (Hist)
Old Courthouse Bldg.
Rte. 1, Box 4   Phone: (715)779-3397
Bayfield, WI 54814   Kayci Cook, Chf., Interp.
Founded: 1970. **Staff:** 1. **Subjects:** Apostle Islands natural and cultural history, Great Lakes region, National Park Service history. **Special Collections:** Research reports on the natural and cultural history of Apostle Islands National Lakeshore (200). **Holdings:** 800 books; 150 bound periodical volumes; 4000 VF items; 60 oral history tapes; 40 reels of microfilm; 150 microfiche; 300 planning documents. **Subscriptions:** 42 journals and other serials. **Services:** Library open to the public by appointment for reference use only. **Computerized Information Services:** PROCOMM PLUS (electronic mail service). **Networks/Consortia:** Member of Northwest Wisconsin Library System (NWLS). **Special Indexes:** Index to research reports. **Remarks:** FAX: (715)779-3049.

★ 17668 ★
U.S. Natl. Park Service - Appomattox Court House Natl. Historical Park - Library (Hist)
Box 218   Phone: (804)352-8987
Appomattox, VA 24522   Ronald G. Wilson, Pk.Hist.
Staff: Prof 2; Other 2. **Subjects:** Civil War, history of Park and Village of Appomattox. **Holdings:** 1000 books; 3700 artifacts and maps. **Services:** Library open to the public for reference use only. **Special Indexes:** Confederate enlisted men who surrendered at Appomattox (card). **Remarks:** FAX: (804)352-0135. **Staff:** Jon Montgomery, Supt.

★ 17669 ★
U.S. Natl. Park Service - Arlington House, the Robert E. Lee Memorial - Library (Hist)
Turkey Run Park   Phone: (703)557-0613
McLean, VA 22101   Agnes Downey Mullins, Cur.
Staff: 1. **Subjects:** Robert E. Lee, George W.P. Custis, Arlington House. **Special Collections:** 19th century sheet music. **Holdings:** 500 books; 100 pamphlets; 70 Custis and Lee family and associated family manuscripts. **Subscriptions:** 2 journals and other serials. **Services:** Library open to the public by appointment. **Remarks:** Library located in the Arlington National Cemetery, Arlington, VA.

★ 17670 ★
U.S. Natl. Park Service - Assateague Island Natl. Seashore - Library (Biol Sci)
Rte. 611 7206 Natl. Seashore Ln.   Phone: (301)641-1443
Berlin, MD 21811   Chris Seymour, Interp.Spec.
Founded: 1965. **Staff:** 2. **Subjects:** Marine biology, botanical sciences, zoological sciences, geography. **Special Collections:** Research documents and reprint abstracts of seashore environments (250). **Holdings:** 500 books; 6500 color slides of Assateague Island and environs. **Subscriptions:** 3 journals and other serials. **Services:** Library open to the public with restrictions. **Remarks:** FAX: (301)641-1099.

★ 17671 ★
U.S. Natl. Park Service - Aztec Ruins Natl. Monument - Library (Hist)
Box 640   Phone: (505)334-6174
Aztec, NM 87410   Terry Nichols, Pk. Ranger
Founded: 1923. **Staff:** Prof 1. **Subjects:** Archeology, natural history, National Park Service history. **Holdings:** 500 books; 5 VF drawers of maps; pamphlets; 16 volumes of ruins stabilization reports. **Services:** Library open to the public with restrictions.

★ 17672 ★
U.S. Natl. Park Service - Badlands Natl. Park - Library (Hist)
Box 6   Phone: (605)433-5361
Interior, SD 57750   Midge Johnston, Bus.Mgr.
Founded: 1961. **Staff:** 1. **Subjects:** Natural history, paleontology, geology, National Park Service. **Holdings:** 3500 books; 500 bound periodical volumes. **Subscriptions:** 10 journals and other serials. **Services:** Library open to the public for reference use only. **Remarks:** Maintained by Badlands Natural History Association and Badlands National Park.

★ 17673 ★
U.S. Natl. Park Service - Bandelier Natl. Monument - Library (Hist)
HCR 1, Box 1, Suite 15   Phone: (505)672-3861
Los Alamos, NM 87544   Al Seidenkranz, Chf. of Interp.
Staff: 2. **Subjects:** Bandelier National Monument excavations and stabilization; archeology, ethnology, and natural history of the Southwest. **Holdings:** 1400 books; vertical file; 1 box of cassette tapes of guest speakers and oral history; annual and monthly reports of Southwest monuments, 1933-1940; monthly report of superintendent, 1941-1978; unpublished excavation and stabilization reports; excavation maps. **Services:** Library open to researchers by request. **Publications:** Trail Guides for Frijoles Canyon and Tsankawi - for sale.

★17674★
U.S. Natl. Park Service - Bent's Old Fort National Historic Site -
    Library (Hist)
35110 Hwy. 194 E.   Phone: (719)384-2596
La Junta, CO 81050   Donald C. Hill, Supt.
Founded: 1960. **Staff:** 1. **Subjects:** Fur trade, Santa Fe Trail, Bent's Fort, Cheyenne and Arapaho Indians, Mexican War, Southwest. **Special Collections:** Missouri Historical Society Republican News (1828-1850; microfilm); Fur Trade Ledgers (William Abee and Michel Zillard); American Fur Company Papers (37 reels of microfilm). **Holdings:** 1000 books; 82 nonbook items; 1 AV program. **Subscriptions:** 3 journals and other serials. **Services:** Copying; library open to the public by appointment.

★17675★
U.S. Natl. Park Service - Big Hole Natl. Battlefield - Library (Hist)
Box 237   Phone: (406)689-3155
Wisdom, MT 59761   Jock F. Whitworth, Unit Mgr.
Staff: 2. **Subjects:** Nez Perce War of 1877. **Holdings:** 280 books. **Services:** Library open to researchers. **Computerized Information Services:** SEA DOG (electronic mail service). **Remarks:** FAX: (406)689-3151.

★17676★
U.S. Natl. Park Service - Bighorn Canyon Natl. Recreation Area -
    Library (Hist)
Box 458   Phone: (406)666-2412
Fort Smith, MT 59035   Paul Gordon, Pk. Ranger
Founded: 1967. **Staff:** Prof 1. **Subjects:** Local history, Crow Indian history, ethnology, wildlife, geology, botany, archeology. **Special Collections:** National Park Service reports and management plans for Bighorn Canyon National Recreation Area; government reports on Crow Indians of Montana. **Holdings:** 1370 books. **Subscriptions:** 14 journals and other serials. **Services:** Interlibrary loan; library open to the public.

★17677★
U.S. Natl. Park Service - Booker T. Washington Natl. Monument -
    Library (Hist)
Rte. 3, Box 310   Phone: (703)721-2094
Hardy, VA 24101   Richard Saunders, Chf.Interp. & Rsrcs.Mgt.
Subjects: Booker T. Washington, black history, local agriculture in the mid-19th century, Appalachian culture. **Special Collections:** Correspondence and documents relating to Burroughs plantation, birthplace of Booker T. Washington. **Holdings:** 600 books; photographs. **Services:** Interlibrary loan; copying (limited); library open to the public.

★17678★
U.S. Natl. Park Service - Cabrillo Natl. Monument - Library &
    Information Center (Hist, Env-Cons)
1800 Cabrillo Memorial Dr.
P.O. Box 6670   Phone: (619)557-5450
San Diego, CA 92166   Terry DiMattio, Supt.
Founded: 1966. **Staff:** Prof 3. **Subjects:** Spanish exploration, history, lighthouses, plants, natural history, marine animals. **Special Collections:** Spanish exploration and settlement (300 volumes); national parks (100 volumes). **Holdings:** 1500 books; 20 bound periodical volumes; photographs; slides. **Subscriptions:** 15 journals and other serials. **Services:** Library open to the public for reference use only. **Remarks:** FAX: (619)557-5469. **Staff:** Edmond E. Roberts, Chf., Interp.; Howard Overton, Chf. Ranger.

★17679★
U.S. Natl. Park Service - Cape Cod Natl. Seashore - Library (Env-Cons,
    Hist)
Marconi Station Site   Phone: (508)349-3785
South Wellfleet, MA 02663   G. Franklin Ackerman, Chf., Interp.
Founded: 1961. **Staff:** 1. **Subjects:** Ecology, local history, botany, earth sciences. **Special Collections:** U.S. Life Saving Service annual reports, 1879-1914; Rhodora Journal of the New England Botanical Club (26 volumes); sea stories by W. Clark Russell (54 titles). **Holdings:** 2300 books. **Subscriptions:** 45 journals and other serials. **Services:** Interlibrary loan; library open to the public for reference use only.

★17680★
U.S. Natl. Park Service - Cape Hatteras National Seashore - Library
    (Hist, Biol Sci)
Rte. 1, Box 675   Phone: (919)473-2111
Manteo, NC 27954   Penny Ambrose, Sec./Libn.
Founded: 1955. **Staff:** Prof 1. **Subjects:** History and natural history of North Carolina Outer Banks. **Holdings:** 4000 items in technical reference file; 200 microforms. **Subscriptions:** 30 journals and other serials. **Services:** Interlibrary loan; library open to the public by appointment. **Remarks:** FAX:(919)473-2595.

★17681★
U.S. Natl. Park Service - Cape Lookout Natl. Seashore - Library (Env-
    Cons)
3601 Bridges St., Suite F   Phone: (919)240-1409
Morehead City, NC 28557-2913   William A. Harris, Supt.
Founded: 1976. **Staff:** 2. **Subjects:** Seashore ecology, geology, Outer Banks history, marine natural history, barrier island ecology, lighthouses and life-saving, local history. **Holdings:** 2000 volumes. **Subscriptions:** 15 journals and other serials. **Services:** Library open to the public for reference use only with permission of park superintendent. **Remarks:** FAX: (919)240-1644. Library located at the District Office, Harkers Island, NC., tel. (919)728-2250.

★17682★
U.S. Natl. Park Service - Capulin Volcano Natl. Monument - Library
    (Sci-Engr, Biol Sci)
Capulin Volcano National Monument   Phone: (505)278-2201
Capulin, NM 88414   Mary J. Karraker, Supt.
Founded: 1981. **Staff:** Prof 2. **Subjects:** Volcanos, area history, pre-history, Indian culture/history, flora/fauna/mammals, National Park service history, military history. **Holdings:** 751 books. **Subscriptions:** 6 journals and other serials; 2 newspapers. **Services:** Interlibrary loan; library open to the public. **Remarks:** FAX: (505)278-2211. **Staff:** J.J. Wallis, Pk. Ranger.

★17683★
U.S. Natl. Park Service - Carl Sandburg Home Natl. Historic Site -
    Museum/Library (Hum, Hist)
1928 Little River Rd.   Phone: (704)693-4178
Flat Rock, NC 28731   Kenneth Hulick, Supt.
Founded: 1969. **Staff:** Prof 2. **Subjects:** Carl Sandburg, local history. **Holdings:** 9000 books. **Services:** Library open to the public by appointment as a museum only; available to researchers by appointment. **Automated Operations:** Computerized cataloging. **Remarks:** This historic house contains part of Carl Sandburg's personal working library.

★17684★
U.S. Natl. Park Service - Carlsbad Caverns Natl. Park - Library (Biol
    Sci, Sci-Engr)
3225 National Parks Hwy.
Carlsbad, NM 88220   Phone: (505)885-8884
Staff: 1. **Subjects:** Geology, botany, zoology, paleontology, parks and conservation, regional history. **Special Collections:** Photograph collection. **Holdings:** 4000 books; 150 bound periodical volumes; 2500 reprints. **Subscriptions:** 25 journals and other serials. **Services:** Library open to the public for reference use only on request. **Remarks:** FAX: (505)885-4557.

★17685★
U.S. Natl. Park Service - Castillo de San Marcos Natl. Monument &
    Fort Matanzas Natl. Monument - Library (Hist)
One Castillo Dr.   Phone: (904)829-6506
St. Augustine, FL 32084-3699   Luis R. Arana, Hist.
Subjects: Florida's colonial history, 1518-1833, especially the construction and repair of Castillo de San Marcos and Fort Matanzas. **Special Collections:** Spanish and British records concerning Florida's colonial history; East Florida Papers (Spanish military, administrative, ecclesiastical, financial, and personal records of the territory; 175 reels of microfilm). **Services:** Library open to the public by appointment.

★ 17686 ★
U.S. Natl. Park Service - Chaco Culture Natl. Historical Park - Study Library (Sci-Engr, Hist)
Star Rte. 4, Box 6500
Bloomfield, NM 87413
Phone: (505)786-7014
Lawrence A. Belli, Supt.
Staff: 1. **Subjects:** Chaco and Southwest archeology, Southwest cultural and natural history, park planning. **Special Collections:** Unpublished records of park administrative history, early explorations; historic photographs. **Holdings:** 2000 books; 500 bound periodical volumes. **Subscriptions:** 12 journals and other serials. **Services:** Library open to the public with approval of superintendent. **Remarks:** FAX: (505)786-7061.

★ 17687 ★
U.S. Natl. Park Service - Chamizal Natl. Memorial - Library (Hist)
Federal Bldg., Suite D-301
800 S. San Marcial
El Paso, TX 79905
Phone: (915)532-7273
Founded: 1967. **Staff:** 1. **Subjects:** Border disputes between U.S. and Mexico, Mexican and Spanish drama, political evolution in Mexico, U.S. and Mexican history, biology. **Holdings:** 1200 books; historic documents and manuscripts on border disputes. **Subscriptions:** 10 journals and other serials. **Services:** Library open to the public for reference use only. **Remarks:** FAX: (915)532-7240.

★ 17688 ★
U.S. Natl. Park Service - Chesapeake & Ohio Canal National Historical Park - C & O Canal NHP Resource Library (Hist)
Box 4
Sharpsburg, MD 21782
Phone: (301)739-4200
Gordon Gay, Cf. of Interp.
Founded: 1971. **Staff:** 1. **Subjects:** History - canals, American canals, C & O Canal, area, natural. **Special Collections:** Canal workers collection (audiotapes, transcripts); historical photograph file (canal life, historical structures, canal families); chronological history of the C & O Canal Company, 1828-1924; archives (manuscripts). **Holdings:** 1500 books; 10 VF drawers; bound periodical volumes. **Subscriptions:** 5 journals and other serials. **Services:** Copying; library open to the public by appointment. **Remarks:** FAX: (301)739-5275.

★ 17689 ★
U.S. Natl. Park Service - Chickamauga-Chattanooga National Military Park - Library (Hist)
P.O. Box 2128
Fort Oglethorpe, GA 30742
Phone: (404)866-9241
Daniel W. Brown, Supt.
Subjects: Battle of Chickamauga, Battle of Chattanooga, American Civil War, Southeast Tennessee, Northwest Georgia. **Special Collections:** Manuscript collection. **Holdings:** 3000 books; 30 linear feet of documents; 25 AV programs. **Services:** Copying; library open to the public by appointment. **Staff:** James Ogden, III, Hist.

★ 17690 ★
U.S. Natl. Park Service - Chickasaw Natl. Recreation Area - Travertine Nature Center Library (Biol Sci)
Box 201
Sulphur, OK 73086
Phone: (405)622-3165
Beth Hagler-Martin, Chf.Pk.Interp.
Founded: 1969. **Staff:** 4. **Subjects:** Biological sciences, botany, zoology, American Indians, U.S. history, astronomy, geology, natural resources. **Holdings:** 800 books; 5 boxes of pamphlets; 80 boxes of periodicals. **Subscriptions:** 31 journals and other serials. **Services:** Library open to the public.

★ 17691 ★
U.S. Natl. Park Service - Clara Barton National Historic Site - Library (Hist)
5801 Oxford Rd.
Glen Echo, MD 20812
Phone: (301)492-6245
William R. Morris, Site Mgr.
Founded: 1975. **Staff:** 3.5. **Subjects:** Clara Barton, American Red Cross, 19th century architecture, 19th century women's history, Civil War. **Holdings:** 500 books; 200 bound periodical volumes; 30 AV programs; 500 photos; 2000 slides; 1 manuscript. **Subscriptions:** 4 journals and other serials. **Services:** Library open by appointment to researchers for reference use only. **Remarks:** FAX: (301)492-5384. Library is housed in Clara Barton's last home, which was the first permanent headquarters of the American Red Cross.

★ 17692 ★
U.S. Natl. Park Service - Coronado Natl. Memorial - Archives (Hist, Area-Ethnic)
401 E. Montezuma Canyon Rd.
Hereford, AZ 85615
Phone: (602)366-5515
Ed Lopez, Supt.
Staff: 7. **Subjects:** Coronado expedition, history and cultural contributions of the Spanish Empire, history of Spanish-Mexican movement into the United States and northwest Mexico, 1500 to present. **Special Collections:** Formation and development of the Coronado National Memorial (8 linear feet). **Holdings:** 464 books; 9 videotapes. **Services:** Archives open to researchers for reference use only. **Remarks:** FAX: (602)366-5705.

★ 17693 ★
U.S. Natl. Park Service - Coulee Dam Natl. Recreation Area (Hist)
P.O. Box 37
Coulee Dam, WA 99116
Phone: (509)633-9441
Lynne Dubiel, South Dist.Interp.
Founded: 1966. **Staff:** 2. **Subjects:** Military history, 1880-1900; Colville Indian Agency, 1900-1930; history and natural sciences of the Upper Columbia River Valley. **Special Collections:** Artifactual study collection of Fort Spokane. **Holdings:** 5 volumes of copies of historical news articles and diaries; 9 volumes of professional research reports. **Services:** Center open to the public for reference use only. **Automated Operations:** Computerized cataloging.

★ 17694 ★
U.S. Natl. Park Service - Crater Lake Natl. Park - Library (Hist, Biol Sci)
Box 7
Crater Lake, OR 97604
Phone: (503)594-2211
Gregg Fauth, Asst.Chf., Interp.
Founded: 1930. **Staff:** Prof 1. **Subjects:** Geology, botany, zoology, cultural and natural history. **Special Collections:** Crater Lake Nature Notes. **Holdings:** 1500 books; 100 bound periodical volumes; 6 VF drawers of journal articles and similar material. **Subscriptions:** 8 journals and other serials. **Services:** Library open to the public for reference use only.

★ 17695 ★
U.S. Natl. Park Service - Craters of the Moon National Monument - Library (Sci-Engr)
P.O. Box 29
Arco, ID 83213
Phone: (208)527-3257
Lee Taylor-Edmonston, Pk. Ranger/Interp.
Staff: 1. **Subjects:** Volcanic geology, wildlife biology, botany, environmental education, history. **Holdings:** 2972 books; 293 journals, technical reports, and research documents; field guides and manuals; 12 AV programs. **Services:** Library open by appointment to qualified researchers. **Remarks:** FAX: (208)527-3073.

★ 17696 ★
U.S. Natl. Park Service - Cumberland Gap Natl. Historical Park - Library (Hist)
Box 1848
Middlesboro, KY 40965-1848
Phone: (606)861-2006
Daniel A. Brown, Hist.
Founded: 1959. **Staff:** 1. **Subjects:** History, folklife, natural history, transportation. **Special Collections:** Hensly Settlement Oral History Collection (on local Appalachian culture; 87 tapes). **Holdings:** 1250 books; 200 bound periodical volumes; 50 documents. **Services:** Library open to the public by appointment for research. **Automated Operations:** Computerized public access catalog. **Computerized Information Services:** NPS Library Program (internal database).

★ 17697 ★
U.S. Natl. Park Service - Custer Battlefield Natl. Monument - Library (Hist)
Box 39
Crow Agency, MT 59022-0039
Phone: (406)638-2622
Douglas C. McChristian, Chf.Hist.
Founded: 1952. **Staff:** 2. **Subjects:** Battle of Little Big Horn, George Custer, Western history, Indian wars. **Special Collections:** Elizabeth B. Custer Correspondence Collection; Walter M. Camp papers. **Holdings:** 3000 books; 500 bound periodical volumes; 15,000 artifacts, relics, and correspondences; 19 reels of microfilm; rare book and manuscript collection. **Subscriptions:** 10 journals and other serials. **Services:** Copying; library open to the public for reference use only by appointment. **Special Indexes:** Photographic Index of Sioux, Cheyenne, Crow, and 7th Cavalry. **Remarks:** FAX: (406)638-2623. **Staff:** John A. Doerner, Libn.

★ 17698 ★
U.S. Natl. Park Service - De Soto Natl. Memorial - Library (Hist)
75th St., N.W.   Phone: (813)792-0458
Bradenton, FL 34209-9656   Elias Ramirez-Diaz, Pk. Ranger
Staff: Prof 4; Other 1. **Subjects:** Spanish exploration; general exploration; American, Florida, and natural history. **Holdings:** 1128 volumes. **Subscriptions:** 5 journals and other serials; 2 newspapers. **Services:** Library open to the public for reference use only. **Remarks:** FAX: (813)792-5094.

★ 17699 ★
U.S. Natl. Park Service - Death Valley Natl. Monument - Reference and Research Library (Biol Sci, Sci-Engr)
Death Valley, CA 92328   Phone: (714)786-2331
                                           Shirley A. Harding, Cur.
Founded: 1933. **Staff:** Prof 1; Other 2. **Subjects:** Death Valley geology, history, and research; biological sciences. **Special Collections:** Graduate theses in the natural and cultural sciences prepared from Death Valley data (50 volumes). **Holdings:** 5500 books; 50 bound periodical volumes; 60 boxes of pamphlets and reprints; 55 boxes of unbound periodicals; 3 VF drawers of folders on National Park System areas. **Subscriptions:** 14 journals and other serials; 7 newspapers. **Services:** Interlibrary loan; copying; library open to the public on written request. **Remarks:** FAX: (619)786-2344.

★ 17700 ★
U.S. Natl. Park Service - Denali Natl. Park and Preserve - Library (Biol Sci, Hist)
Box 9   Phone: (907)683-2294
Denali Park, AK 99755   Melanie Heacox, East Dist. Naturalist
Staff: Prof 1.5. **Subjects:** Natural history, history, Denali Naional Park research data. **Holdings:** 2000 books. **Subscriptions:** 22 journals and other serials. **Services:** Library open to the public for reference use only.

★ 17701 ★
U.S. Natl. Park Service - Dinosaur Natl. Monument - Dinosaur Quarry - Library (Sci-Engr, Biol Sci)
Box 128
Jensen, UT 84035   Phone: (801)789-2115
Founded: 1962. **Subjects:** Paleontology, geology, area history, wildlife management, natural history. **Holdings:** 3500 volumes. **Subscriptions:** 15 journals and other serials. **Services:** Library open to the public by appointment.

★ 17702 ★
U.S. Natl. Park Service - Edison Natl. Historic Site - Archives (Sci-Engr, Hist)
Main St. and Lakeside Ave.   Phone: (201)736-0550
West Orange, NJ 07052   George D. Tselos, Archv.
Founded: 1887. **Staff:** Prof 2; Other 5. **Subjects:** Invention, science, electricity, botanic research, chemistry, geology, business, early motion pictures, phonographs and recorded music. **Holdings:** 10,000 volumes; 4.5 million pages of Edison's personal and laboratory correspondence and documents; business records of Edison Industries and Thomas Alva Edison, Inc.; 3000 notebooks kept by Edison and his workers; 60,000 photographic images. **Subscriptions:** 12 journals and other serials. **Services:** Copying (limited); archives open to the public by appointment. **Computerized Information Services:** Photographic Collection Database, Motion Picture Collection Database (internal databases). **Publications:** The Papers of Thomas A. Edison (microfilm and letterpress edition). **Remarks:** FAX: (201)736-8496.

★ 17703 ★
U.S. Natl. Park Service - Effigy Mounds Natl. Monument - Library (Sci-Engr, Biol Sci)
R.R. 1, Box 25A
Harpers Ferry, IA 52146   Phone: (319)873-3491
                                           Thomas A. Munson, Supt.
Founded: 1949. **Staff:** Prof 1. **Subjects:** Archeology, anthropology, ethnology, local history, natural sciences. **Special Collections:** Ellison Orr manuscripts and library (1000 items). **Holdings:** 2600 books. **Subscriptions:** 17 journals and other serials. **Services:** Library open to the public for reference use only.

★ 17704 ★
U.S. Natl. Park Service - Everglades Natl. Park - Reference Library (Biol Sci)
Box 279   Phone: (305)242-7800
Homestead, FL 33030   Dan Foxen, Musm.Cur.
Founded: 1964. **Staff:** Prof 1. **Subjects:** Birds, botany, marine biology and ecology, wildlife biology, aquatic ecology, hydrology, national parks, South Florida natural history and water resources. **Holdings:** 6525 books and bound periodical volumes; 10,500 pamphlets and reprints; 635 maps; 945 microforms. **Subscriptions:** 110 journals and other serials. **Services:** Interlibrary loan; copying (limited); library open to the public. **Remarks:** FAX: (305)248-3913. **Staff:** Vivie Thue, Asst.Libn.

★ 17705 ★
U.S. Natl. Park Service - Fire Island Natl. Seashore - Headquarters Library (Hist, Sci-Engr)
120 Laurel St.   Phone: (516)289-4810
Patchogue, NY 11772   Mardi Butt, Interp.Spec.
Staff: 1. **Subjects:** Barrier Island geology, marine biology, oceanography, history. **Holdings:** 5000 books; 1000 other cataloged items. **Services:** Copying; library open to the public for reference use only. **Remarks:** FAX: (516)289-4898.

★ 17706 ★
U.S. Natl. Park Service - Florissant Fossil Beds Natl. Monument - Library (Sci-Engr)
Box 185   Phone: (719)748-3253
Florissant, CO 80816   Margaret Johnston, Chf., I & RM
Founded: 1970. **Subjects:** Geology, paleontology, natural history. **Holdings:** 600 books and scientific papers; historical documents; photographs. **Services:** Library open to the public upon request. **Remarks:** FAX: (719)748-3164. **Staff:** Doris Kneuer.

★ 17707 ★
U.S. Natl. Park Service - Fort Davis Natl. Historic Site - Library (Hist)
Box 1456   Phone: (915)426-3224
Fort Davis, TX 79734   Kevin G. Cheri, Supt.
Founded: 1963. **Subjects:** Frontier military history. **Special Collections:** Colonel Benjamin H. Grierson Manuscript Collection (10,000 letters and documents, 1840-1920, on microfilm). **Holdings:** 1700 books; 100 pamphlets and magazines; 60 copies of frontier military maps; 10 manuscripts and theses; 185 reels of microfilm of records of Fort Davis. **Subscriptions:** 5 journals and other serials; 3 newspapers. **Services:** Library open to the public for reference use only. **Remarks:** FAX: (915)426-3122. **Staff:** Mary Williams, Pk. Ranger.

★ 17708 ★
U.S. Natl. Park Service - Fort Laramie Natl. Historic Site - Library (Hist)
Box 86   Phone: (307)837-2221
Fort Laramie, WY 82212   Steven R. Fullmer, Pk. Ranger
Founded: 1955. **Staff:** 1. **Subjects:** Frontier military history, Western history, Oregon-California-Mormon trails, Plains Indians. **Holdings:** 3500 books; 200 reels of microfilm. **Services:** Copying; library open to scholars for reference use only.

★ 17709 ★
U.S. Natl. Park Service - Fort Larned Natl. Historic Site - Library (Hist)
Rte. 3   Phone: (316)285-6911
Larned, KS 67550-9733   Steven R. Linderer, Supt.
Founded: 1966. **Staff:** 1. **Subjects:** Fort Larned, 1859-1878; Plains Indians; Santa Fe Trail; military history; Indian Wars, 1848-1890; museum conservation and preservation. **Holdings:** 775 books; 110 reels of microfilm; 10 binders of national archives. **Subscriptions:** 10 journals and other serials. **Services:** Library open to the public by appointment. **Remarks:** FAX: (316)285-3571.

★ 17710 ★
U.S. Natl. Park Service - Fort McHenry Natl. Monument & Historic Shrine - Library (Mil, Hist)
E. Fort Ave.   Phone: (301)962-4290
Baltimore, MD 21230-5393   Scott S. Sheads, Pk. Ranger/Hist.
Founded: 1958. **Staff:** 1. **Subjects:** War of 1812, The Star-Spangled Banner, 1814 Battle of Baltimore, The Chesapeake Campaign 1813-1815, Civil War, Rodman Cannon 1861-1889, U.S. Corps of Engineers 1807-1933, World War I (U.S. Army General Hospital Number 2), World War II, U.S. Coast Guard Training Station, 1942-1945. **Special Collections:** Historical & Archeological Research Project (HARP); register of more than 10,000 political prisoners and Confederate prisoners of war held at Fort McHenry during the Civil War; War of 1812 Baltimore newspapers (microfilm). **Holdings:** 50,000 copies of documents from the National Archives; 150 reels of microfilm; maps, 1775-1991; photographs; archeological data; vertical files; reels of microfilm; reports; videocassettes. **Subscriptions:** 10 journals and other serials. **Services:** Library open to the public by appointment. **Remarks:** FAX: (301)962-2500.

★ 17711 ★
U.S. Natl. Park Service - Fort Necessity Natl. Battlefield - Library (Hist)
The National Pike
RD 2, Box 528   Phone: (412)329-5512
Farmington, PA 15437   Marilyn H. Parris, Supt.
Founded: 1962. **Staff:** 2. **Subjects:** Battle of Great Meadows (July 3, 1754), French and Indian War, 19th century transportation in western Pennsylvania, fauna and flora of the region. **Holdings:** 1250 books. **Services:** Library open to the public by appointment. **Remarks:** FAX: (412)329-8682.

★ 17712 ★
U.S. Natl. Park Service - Fort Pulaski Natl. Monument - Library (Hist)
Box 30757   Phone: (912)786-5787
Savannah, GA 31410-0757   Kimberly A. Walsh, Pk. Ranger
Founded: 1924. **Staff:** Prof 3. **Subjects:** Siege of Fort Pulaski, 1862; Civil War; Fort Pulaski restoration, 1933-1940; American historic preservation; Colonial history of Georgia; Siege of Savannah, 1779. **Special Collections:** Complete set of War of the Rebellion, Official Records of the Union and Confederate Armies and Navies. **Holdings:** 920 books; 300 other cataloged items; 20 linear feet of VF on Civilian Conservation Corps research on historic sites in Florida, Georgia, and South Carolina, 1934-1940; 2600 photographs, 1862-1866 and 1930-1960. **Services:** Interlibrary loan; copying (limited); library open to the public with restrictions. **Remarks:** FAX: (912)786-6023. **Staff:** Talley Kirkland; John Breen.

★ 17713 ★
U.S. Natl. Park Service - Fort Sumter Natl. Monument - Library (Hist)
1214 Middle St.   Phone: (803)883-3123
Sullivan's Island, SC 29482   John Tucker, Supt.
Founded: 1948. **Staff:** 1. **Subjects:** Civil War, Revolutionary War, Fort Sumter, Fort Moultrie, U.S. Seacoast fortifications, artillery, South Carolina, firearms, conservation. **Special Collections:** War of the Rebellion, Official Records of the Union and Confederate Armies (128 volumes); Naval Records (30 volumes); American Revolution naval documents. **Holdings:** 700 books; 200 bound periodical volumes; 250 maps; 650 pamphlets. **Subscriptions:** 10 journals and other serials. **Services:** Library open to the public for reference use only by reservation. **Staff:** Joseph McGill, Jr., Libn.

★ 17714 ★
U.S. Natl. Park Service - Fort Union Natl. Monument - Library (Hist)
Watrous, NM 87753   Phone: (505)425-8025
                                                            Harry C. Myers, Supt.
Founded: 1956. **Staff:** 2. **Subjects:** Santa Fe Trail and Fort Union history, military history, Western Americana. **Special Collections:** Rare books on the Santa Fe Trail and Fort Union; Fort Union documents (on microcards and microfilm). **Holdings:** 3000 books. **Subscriptions:** 10 journals and other serials. **Services:** Library open to the public by appointment for reference use only. **Remarks:** FAX: (505)454-1155.

★ 17715 ★
U.S. Natl. Park Service - Fort Vancouver Natl. Historic Site - Library (Hist)
612 E. Reserve St.   Phone: (206)696-7655
Vancouver, WA 98661   Robert D. Appling, Supv./Pk. Ranger
Founded: 1948. **Staff:** Prof 2. **Subjects:** Hudson's Bay Company, fur trade, Western expansion. **Special Collections:** Archeological and historical reports on old Fort Vancouver. **Holdings:** 1300 books; 200 bound periodical volumes; historical pamphlets; 60 historic documents. **Subscriptions:** 4 journals and other serials. **Services:** Library open to the public for reference use only. **Automated Operations:** Computerized cataloging. **Remarks:** Jointly maintained by Pacific Northwest National Parks Association. **Staff:** Don Dinsmore, Pk. Ranger.

★ 17716 ★
U.S. Natl. Park Service - Frederick Douglass National Historic Site - Library (Hist)
1411 W St., S.E.   Phone: (202)426-5962
Washington, DC 20020   Douglas E. Stover, Musm.Cur.
Founded: 1877. **Staff:** 3. **Subjects:** History, biography, science, geography, philosophy. **Special Collections:** History of Women's Suffrage (4 volumes); Executive Documents, 1820-1895. **Holdings:** 2000 books. **Subscriptions:** 14 journals and other serials. **Services:** Library open to researchers by appointment for reference use only. **Computerized Information Services:** Internal database. **Remarks:** FAX: (202)426-0880. **Also Known As:** National Capital Park-East - Douglass Private Collection.

★ 17717 ★
U.S. Natl. Park Service - Frederick Law Olmsted Natl. Historic Site - Archives (Plan)
99 Warren St.   Phone: (617)566-1689
Brookline, MA 02146   Elizabeth S. Banks, Cur.
Staff: Prof 3; Other 4. **Subjects:** Landscape architecture, urban design, city planning. **Special Collections:** 19th and early 20th century photographic prints of parks, landscapes, estates, and urban design in European cities and towns (8 linear feet). **Holdings:** 1000 books; 650 bound periodical volumes; 150,000 landscape architectural drawings, 1860-1979; 60,000 photographic prints of Olmsted landscape jobs in the U.S. and Canada; 30 linear feet of landscape job planting lists. **Services:** Copying; archives open to scholars by appointment. **Staff:** Lee C. Farrow, Archv.; Joyce Connolly, Ref.Archv.

★ 17718 ★
U.S. Natl. Park Service - Fredericksburg & Spotsylvania Natl. Military Park - Library (Hist)
120 Chatham Ln.   Phone: (703)373-4461
Fredericksburg, VA 22405   Robert K. Krick, Chf.Hist.
Founded: 1927. **Staff:** 3. **Subjects:** Civil War in Virginia. **Special Collections:** Southern Historical Society Papers; Confederate Military History; Confederate veterans; War of Rebellion: the Official Records of the Union and Confederate Armies. **Holdings:** 5500 books; 250 bound periodical volumes; 3000 manuscript items; 1300 reels of microfilm; 10 drawers of maps. **Subscriptions:** 13 journals and other serials; 3 newspapers. **Services:** Copying; library open to the public by appointment. **Remarks:** FAX: (703)371-1907.

★ 17719 ★
U.S. Natl. Park Service - George Washington Carver Natl. Monument - Library (Hist)
Box 38   Phone: (417)325-4151
Diamond, MO 64840   Shirley Baxter, Pk.Ranger
Staff: Prof 1. **Subjects:** George Washington Carver, black history, national parks. **Special Collections:** Carver Collection (3019 archives and artifacts); original Carver letters (97 items). **Holdings:** 246 books; 130 documents and technical reports; 50 maps and charts; 1505 pictures and study prints; 16 VF drawers of park administrative records. **Subscriptions:** 14 journals and other serials. **Services:** Interlibrary loan; copying; library open to the public for historic research. **Publications:** Monumental News (newsletter), quarterly - free upon request. **Special Catalogs:** Carver Collection. **Remarks:** FAX: (417)325-4231.

★ 17720 ★
U.S. Natl. Park Service - Gettysburg Natl. Military Park - Cyclorama Center Library (Hist)
Gettysburg, PA 17325   Phone: (717)334-1124
              Kathleen G. Harrison, Hist.
Founded: 1893. **Staff:** 2. **Subjects:** Battle of Gettysburg, Civil War, Lincoln, Eisenhower at Gettysburg, 19th century life, environment. **Special Collections:** Eisenhower oral history (100 tapes); William H. Tipton photographs (2500). **Holdings:** 4600 books; 25 VF drawers; 1700 maps and plans; 180 reels of microfilm. **Subscriptions:** 20 journals and other serials. **Services:** Copying (limited); library open to the public by appointment. **Remarks:** FAX: (717)334-1891.

★ 17721 ★
U.S. Natl. Park Service - Gila Cliff Dwellings Natl. Monument - Visitor Center Library (Hist)
Rte. 11, Box 100   Phone: (505)536-9461
Silver City, NM 88061   Eric Finkelstein
Founded: 1967. **Staff:** 1. **Subjects:** Archeology, natural history, Mogollon Indians. **Special Collections:** Mogollon Indian artifacts. **Holdings:** 300 books. **Subscriptions:** 3 journals and other serials. **Services:** Library open to the public for reference use only. **Remarks:** Consolidated with U.S. Forest Service to serve Gila National Forest.

★ 17722 ★
U.S. Natl. Park Service - Glacier Natl. Park - George C. Ruhle Library (Env-Cons, Biol Sci)
West Glacier, MT 59936   Phone: (406)888-5441
             Beth Dunagan, Pk.Libn.
Founded: 1975. **Staff:** 1. **Subjects:** Glacier Park history, environment, geology, glaciology, mammals, Plains Indians. **Special Collections:** Schultz books on the Plains Indians. **Holdings:** 13,000 books; 3000 reprints; 10,000 museum specimens. **Subscriptions:** 27 journals and other serials; 6 newspapers. **Services:** Library open to the public for reference use only. **Remarks:** FAX: (406)888-5581.

★ 17723 ★
U.S. Natl. Park Service - Grand Canyon Natl. Park - Research Library (Biol Sci, Sci-Engr)
P.O. Box 129   Phone: (602)638-7768
Grand Canyon, AZ 86023   Valerie Meyer, Libn.
Founded: 1931. **Staff:** 1. **Subjects:** Grand Canyon region - geology, zoology, botany, ethnology, archeology, anthropology, history; Colorado Plateau; archeology. **Special Collections:** Grand Canyon Collection (2750 items). **Holdings:** 10,600 books; 300 bound periodical volumes; 85 video recordings; 80 manuscripts; river journals; clippings; reprints; oral histories. **Subscriptions:** 72 journals and other serials. **Services:** Interlibrary loan; copying; research; library open to the public by appointment for reference use only. **Automated Operations:** Computerized public access catalog. **Computerized Information Services:** National Production Service, DIALOG Information Services. **Networks/Consortia:** Member of Colorado Alliance of Research Libraries (CARL). **Remarks:** FAX: (602)638-7797.

★ 17724 ★
U.S. Natl. Park Service - Grand Portage Natl. Monument - Library (Hist)
Box 666
Grand Marais, MN 55604   Phone: (218)387-2788
Subjects: American-Canadian fur trade, Chippewa Indian culture, Canadian-Minnesota exploration and history. **Special Collections:** Wisconsin Historical Collection (21 volumes); journals of the Hudson's Bay Company (24 volumes); works of Samuel De Champlain (6 volumes). **Holdings:** 900 books; 100 bound periodical volumes. **Services:** Library open to the public with restrictions.

★ 17725 ★
U.S. Natl. Park Service - Grand Teton Natl. Park - Library (Biol Sci)
Drawer 170
Moose, WY 83012   Phone: (307)733-2880
Founded: 1929. **Subjects:** Grand Teton National Park - fauna, flora, history, geology; Western history. **Holdings:** 1500 books; pamphlets; 1000 historic photographs. **Subscriptions:** 15 journals and other serials. **Services:** Library not open to the public.

★ 17726 ★
U.S. Natl. Park Service - Grant-Kohrs Ranch Natl. Historic Site (Hist)
Box 790   Phone: (406)846-2070
Deer Lodge, MT 59722   Neysa Dickey, Chf. of Interp.
Subjects: History - ranching, local, Western U.S., natural; interpretation. **Special Collections:** Frontier cattle era collection; oral histories. **Holdings:** 1500 volumes. **Services:** Library open to the public for reference use only. **Remarks:** FAX: (406)846-3962.

★ 17727 ★
U.S. Natl. Park Service - Great Smoky Mountains Natl. Park - Library (Biol Sci, Hist)
Gatlinburg, TN 37738   Phone: (615)436-1296
             Annette Evans, Libn.
Founded: 1935. **Staff:** Prof 1. **Subjects:** Natural sciences, area history, pioneer and oral history, environment, geology, park history. **Special Collections:** Naturalists' journals; historic maps; memorabilia of early settlers; archival collection (18,000 black and white photographs; 250 linear feet of files); Research/Resource Management Report Series (66). **Holdings:** 6000 books; bound periodical volumes; theses and dissertations; VF drawers of technical papers and clippings; 123 tapes and transcriptions; records; films. **Subscriptions:** 30 journals and other serials. **Services:** Interlibrary loan (limited); center open to the public for reference use only.

★ 17728 ★
U.S. Natl. Park Service - Haleakala Natl. Park - Library (Biol Sci)
Box 369
Makawao, HI 96768   Phone: (808)572-9306
Founded: 1916. **Staff:** 2. **Subjects:** Botany, zoology, Hawaiiana, geology, ecology, parks, archeology. **Special Collections:** IBP-Island Ecosystems (of Hawaii; 75). **Holdings:** 560 books; 18 file boxes of pertinent subject material. **Subscriptions:** 2 journals and other serials. **Services:** Library open to the public for reference use only on request. **Computerized Information Services:** Internal database. **Remarks:** FAX: (808)572-1304. **Staff:** Vikki Greive.

★ 17729 ★
U.S. Natl. Park Service - Harpers Ferry Center Library (Hist, Mil)
Harpers Ferry, WV 25425   Phone: (304)535-6261
             David Nathanson, Chf.Libn.
Founded: 1971. **Staff:** Prof 5; Other 5. **Subjects:** American history, natural history, museology, decorative arts, photography, American military history. **Special Collections:** U.S. National Park Service Research Reports (20,000 items); Historic Furnishings Library (4000 volumes); Harold L. Peterson Collection (military art and science, firearms; 4000 volumes); Vera Craig Pictorial Archive of American Interiors (250 items); U.S. PatenT Label Collection, 1872-1945 (500 boxes); Museology Library (2000 volumes); National Park Service History Collection (2000 books; 200 bound periodical volumes; 600 boxes of archival/manuscript materials; 120 films; 1100 museum artifacts; 1000 hours of oral history tapes); National Park Service Historic Photograph Collection (900.000 items). **Holdings:** 29,000 books; 500 bound periodical volumes; 120 shelf feet of unbound periodicals; 25 VF drawers of pamphlets; 220 reels of microfilm; 15,000 microfiche; 1150 19th and 20th century trade catalogs; 2000 rare books. **Subscriptions:** 350 journals and other serials. **Services:** Interlibrary loan; copying; library open to the public for reference use only. **Automated Operations:** Computerized public access catalog, cataloging, and ILL. **Computerized Information Services:** DIALOG Information Services, Conservaton Information Network, OCLC, OCLC EPIC. **Networks/Consortia:** Member of FEDLINK. **Publications:** New Accessions at HFC Library, monthly; NPS Library Management Notes Series. **Special Catalogs:** Guide to the Trade Catalog Collection, 1984; Guide to the NPS Reports Collection; Collecting, Using and Preserving Oral History in the National Park Service, 1984; Reprint File; NPS Oral History Survey, 1981; Sunshine and Shadows: A Catalog of Civil War Regimental Histories and Personal Narratives in NPS Libraries, 1986. **Special Indexes:** Inventories of archival/manuscript collections; index to The Courier: Newsmagazine of the National Park Service, 1982-1990 (ondisc); trade catalog collection index (ondisc); illustration index (in progress). **Remarks:** FAX: (304)535-6492. **Staff:** Thomas DuRant, Picture Libn.; Nancy L. Potts, ILL Off.; Bryce Workman, Graphic Res.; Marilyn Wandrus, Graphic Res.; Susan Myers, Graphics Mgr.; Diann McCoy, Kpr., Oral Hist.Coll.

★ 17730 ★

U.S. Natl. Park Service - Harpers Ferry Natl. Historical Park - Library
(Hist)
Box 65
Harpers Ferry, WV 25425   Phone: (304)535-6163
Founded: 1962. **Staff:** 1. **Subjects:** John Brown, Armory, Civil War, Black history of education, local and general U.S. history, natural science, military science. **Holdings:** 2168 books; 230 historical newspapers; 224 research reports on historic structures, sites, archeology, and related histories; 53 college catalogs; 58 binders of unpublished correspondence and papers; booklet and document file; historic and modern photographs; 166 reels of microfilm. **Services:** Library open to the public by appointment and for reference use only. **Remarks:** FAX: (304)535-6244.

★ 17731 ★

U.S. Natl. Park Service - Hawaii Volcanoes Natl. Park - Library (Biol Sci, Sci-Engr)
Hawaii National Park, HI 96718   Phone: (808)967-7311
                                          Dick Rasp, Chf.Pk.Interp.
Founded: 1916. **Staff:** 1. **Subjects:** Volcanology, zoology, botany, ancient culture of Hawaiians. **Holdings:** 2450 books; 470 bound periodical volumes; 1620 pamphlets; 2000 black/white photographs; 3000 slides. **Subscriptions:** 17 journals and other serials. **Services:** Library open to the public by appointment for reference use only.

★ 17732 ★

U.S. Natl. Park Service - Homestead Natl. Monument - Research Library (Hist)
R.R. 3, Box 47   Phone: (402)223-3514
Beatrice, NE 68310-9416   Randall K. Baynes, Supt.
Founded: 1936. **Staff:** Prof 2; Other 6. **Subjects:** U.S. public lands policy and Western expansion, U.S. agricultural history, Nebraska history, ecology and natural history. **Special Collections:** Museum Study Collection on the homesteading experience and the local area of Nebraska (189 books). **Holdings:** 1000 books; 60 bound periodical volumes; 40 park archives. **Services:** Library open to the public for reference use only.

★ 17733 ★

U.S. Natl. Park Service - Hopewell Furnace Natl. Historic Site - Library (Hist)
2 Mark Bird Ln.   Phone: (215)582-8773
Elverson, PA 19520   Derrick M. Cook, Supt.
Founded: 1938. **Staff:** 1. **Subjects:** 18th and 19th century ironmaking. **Special Collections:** Hopewell Furnace Records (80 items); name file for persons associated with the Hopewell Furnace during its 113 years of operation. **Holdings:** 1000 books; 100 unpublished reports; 10,000 furnace documents; microfilm. **Subscriptions:** 3 journals and other serials. **Services:** Library open to the public by appointment for reference use only. **Special Indexes:** Hopewell Source Material Index. **Remarks:** FAX: (215)582-2768.

★ 17734 ★

U.S. Natl. Park Service - Horseshoe Bend Natl. Military Park - Library (Hist)
Rte. 1, Box 103   Phone: (205)234-7111
Daviston, AL 36256   Dwight Dixon, Chf. Ranger
Staff: Prof 3; Other 5. **Subjects:** Battle of Horseshoe Bend, Creek Indians, War of 1812. **Holdings:** 400 books; 35 bound periodical volumes; letters; maps; documents. **Services:** Copying; library open to the public by appointment.

★ 17735 ★

U.S. Natl. Park Service - Independence Natl. Historical Park - Library (Hist)
313 Walnut St.   Phone: (215)597-8047
Philadelphia, PA 19106   Shirley A. Mays, Lib.Techn.
Founded: 1951. **Staff:** Prof 1. **Subjects:** American history, Philadelphia and Pennsylvania history, arts and crafts. **Special Collections:** Independence Hall Association Papers; Judge Edwin O. Lewis Papers. **Holdings:** 10,000 books; 800 bound periodical volumes; 200 manuscripts; 604 reels of microfilm; 150 resource studies reports; 150,000 research note cards; 17,000 photographs; 60,000 slides. **Subscriptions:** 34 journals and other serials. **Services:** Interlibrary loan; library open to the public for reference use only. **Remarks:** FAX: (215)597-1548. Library is located at 120 S. Third St., Philadelphia, PA. **Staff:** David C.G. Dutcher, Chf., Div. of Hist. & Hist.Archv.

★ 17736 ★

U.S. Natl. Park Service - Jefferson Natl. Expansion Memorial - Library
(Hist)
11 N. 4th St.   Phone: (314)425-4468
St. Louis, MO 63102   Thomas Dewey
Founded: 1961. **Staff:** 1. **Subjects:** Westward expansion, St. Louis and Missouri history, fur trade, Thomas Jefferson, Lewis & Clark. **Special Collections:** Grace Lewis Miller Collection on Meriwether Lewis. **Holdings:** 4200 books; 175 linear feet of archival material on park history; photographs; research reports. **Subscriptions:** 50 journals and other serials. **Services:** Copying; library open to the public for reference use only by appointment. **Remarks:** FAX: (314)425-4570.

★ 17737 ★

U.S. Natl. Park Service - John Muir National Historic Site - Research Library (Hist)
4202 Alhambra Ave.   Phone: (510)228-8860
Martinez, CA 94553   Mary Kline, Chf., Interp.
Subjects: John Muir. **Holdings:** Figures not available. **Services:** Library open to the public with restrictions. **Remarks:** FAX: (510)228-1729.

★ 17738 ★

U.S. Natl. Park Service - Joshua Tree National Monument - Library
(Hist)
74485 Natl. Monument Dr.   Phone: (619)367-7511
Twentynine Palms, CA 92277   Bill Truesdell, Chf.Interp.
Subjects: Desert - natural science, history, mining; regional archeology. **Special Collections:** Elizabeth Crozer Campbell Collection. **Holdings:** 800 books. **Services:** Library open to the public for reference use only. **Staff:** Betty Hammett, VIP Prog.

★ 17739 ★

U.S. Natl. Park Service - Kennesaw Mountain Natl. Battlefield Park - Library (Hist)
P.O. Box 1610   Phone: (404)427-4686
Marietta, GA 30061   Richard J. Hanks, Chf.Interp. & Rsrcs.Mgr.
Founded: 1939. **Staff:** 2. **Subjects:** Civil War, 19th century American history, Georgia history. **Holdings:** 1000 books; 20 diaries; 25 reels of microfilm; 20 manuscripts and letters; 6 films. **Services:** Library open to serious researchers by appointment for reference use only. **Remarks:** FAX: (404)427-1760.

★ 17740 ★

U.S. Natl. Park Service - Kings Mountain Natl. Military Park - Library
(Hist)
Box 40   Phone: (803)936-7921
Kings Mountain, NC 28086   James J. Anderson, Chf. Ranger
Founded: 1941. **Subjects:** Revolutionary War history. **Holdings:** 601 volumes; 12 reports; 1 reel of microfilm. **Subscriptions:** 10 journals and other serials, 2 newspapers. **Services:** Library open to the public with restrictions.

★ 17741 ★

U.S. Natl. Park Service - Klondike Gold Rush National Historical Park - Library (Hist)
P.O. Box 517   Phone: (907)983-2921
Skagway, AK 99840   Clay R. Alderson, Supt.
Founded: 1976. **Staff:** 2. **Subjects:** Klondike Gold Rush, Alaska cultural and natural history, 19th century material culture. **Holdings:** 1000 books; 12 AV programs; 68 reels of microfilm; 14 feet of manuscripts; 3000 photographs; newspapers; documents. **Subscriptions:** 2 journals and other serials. **Services:** Library open to the public. **Remarks:** FAX: (907)983-2046. **Staff:** Betsy Duncan-Clark, Interp.Spec.

★ 17742 ★

U.S. Natl. Park Service - Lake Mead Natl. Recreation Area - Library
601 Nevada Hwy.
Boulder City, NV 89005-2426
Founded: 1962. **Subjects:** Lake Mead - history, geology, plants, animals, archeology; National Park Service. **Holdings:** 850 books; 1000 other cataloged items. **Remarks:** Currently inactive.

★ 17743 ★
U.S. Natl. Park Service - Lava Beds Natl. Monument - Library (Sci-Engr, Hist)
Box 867   Phone: (916)667-2282
Tulelake, CA 96134   Gary Hathaway, Chf., Div. of Interp.
Founded: 1933. **Staff:** Prof 1; Other 1. **Subjects:** History of Modoc War, 1872-1873; geology and volcanology; natural history; Indian ethnography; archeology. **Holdings:** 2100 books. **Services:** Copying; library open to the public by appointment for reference use only. **Automated Operations:** Computerized cataloging. **Remarks:** FAX: (916)667-2284.

★ 17744 ★
U.S. Natl. Park Service - Lincoln Boyhood Natl. Memorial - Library (Hist)
Lincoln City, IN 47552   Phone: (812)937-4541
    Paul D. Guraedy, Supt.
Founded: 1962. **Staff:** 1. **Subjects:** Abraham Lincoln, pioneer life, state and local history. **Special Collections:** Interpretive Museum for the 1816-1830 period of Lincoln's life. **Holdings:** 1000 books; 25 bound periodical volumes; pamphlets; maps; documents. **Subscriptions:** 16 journals and other serials. **Services:** Copying; library open to the public for reference use only. **Publications:** Handout copies of information about Lincoln. **Remarks:** FAX: (812)937-9929.

★ 17745 ★
U.S. Natl. Park Service - Longfellow Natl. Historic Site - Library (Hum)
105 Brattle St.   Phone: (617)876-4491
Cambridge, MA 02138   Elizabeth S. Banks, Cur.
Staff: Prof 1; Other 2. **Subjects:** European literature and languages, American literature, H.W. Longfellow's works, Dante, Scandinavian literature. **Holdings:** 10,000 books, bound periodical volumes, pamphlets; 175 linear feet of Longfellow-Wadsworth-Appleton-Dana family papers. **Services:** Library open to the public during the week for bona fide scholarly use only.

★ 17746 ★
U.S. Natl. Park Service - Lyndon B. Johnson Natl. Historical Park - Library (Hist)
Box 329   Phone: (512)868-7128
Johnson City, TX 78636   John T. Tiff, Pk. Ranger/Hist.
Founded: 1970. **Staff:** Prof 1; Other 1. **Subjects:** Lyndon B. Johnson and his family, Texas hill country history, local natural history. **Special Collections:** Oral history collection on life and times of LBJ (500 tapes). **Holdings:** 2000 books; 750 slides; 20 VF drawers of pamphlets; artifacts; 125 reels of 35mm microfilm of historic newspapers. **Services:** Copying (limited); library open to the public for reference use only for approved research.

★ 17747 ★
U.S. Natl. Park Service - Manassas Natl. Battlefield Park - Library (Hist)
6511 Sudley Rd.   Phone: (703)361-1865
Manassas, VA 22110   Kenneth Apschnikat, Supt.
Founded: 1940. **Staff:** Prof 3. **Subjects:** Civil War - history, biographies, medicine, surgery, uniforms, equipment; campaigns and battles of First and Second Manassas (Bull Run); general military works. **Special Collections:** Fitz-John Porter Collection; James Brewerton Ricketts Collection; T.C.H. Smith Papers (photostat); journal of Abner Doubleday, 1862 (photocopy); Franklin B. Hough Papers (photostat). **Holdings:** 1500 books; 92 bound periodical volumes; 200 contemporary photographs; 100 photostats of Civil War-related newspapers; 1000 photostats of documents, diaries, and memoirs; 100 maps; bibliography files on First and Second Manassas. **Services:** Copying; library open to the public by appointment. **Computerized Information Services:** Internal database. **Remarks:** FAX: (703)361-4067. **Staff:** James Burgess, Pk. Ranger; Edmund Raus, Chf.Hist.; Keith Snyder, Pk. Ranger.

★ 17748 ★
U.S. Natl. Park Service - Martin Luther King, Jr. National Historic Site - Library (Soc Sci)
522 Auburn Ave., N.E.   Phone: (404)331-3920
Atlanta, GA 30312   John Huth, Pk. Ranger
Subjects: Dr. Martin Luther King, Jr., Civil Rights Movement, black history, black Atlanta history, historic preservation. **Holdings:** 200 books. **Services:** Library not open to the public. **Remarks:** FAX: (404)331-1064.

★ 17749 ★
U.S. Natl. Park Service - Mesa Verde Natl. Park - Research Library (Hist)
Box 38   Phone: (303)529-4475
Mesa Verde Natl. Park, CO 81330   Ramona Hutchinson, Dir.
Founded: 1906. **Staff:** Prof 1. **Subjects:** Archeology, ethnology, anthropology, history. **Special Collections:** Early historical and archeological documents of Mesa Verde Natl. Park. **Holdings:** 6790 books; 150 bound periodical volumes; 47 filing boxes of unbound documents. **Subscriptions:** 42 journals and other serials. **Services:** Interlibrary loan; library materials available to researchers by appointment. **Computerized Information Services:** SEADOG (electronic mail service). **Networks/Consortia:** Member of Southwest Regional Library Service System (SWRLSS), Colorado Alliance of Research Libraries (CARL). **Remarks:** FAX: (303)529-4454. Electronic mail address(es): 12/1490 (SEADOG). **Formerly:** Its Museum Library.

★ 17750 ★
U.S. Natl. Park Service - Midwest Archeological Center - Research Library (Soc Sci)
Federal Bldg., Rm. 474
100 Centennial Mall N.   Phone: (402)437-5392
Lincoln, NE 68508-3873   Rene A. Botts, Archv.Techn.
Founded: 1969. **Staff:** Prof 1. **Subjects:** Archeology of the mid-continental United States, National Park Service, American Indians. **Holdings:** 400 books; 5600 bound periodical volumes; 2000 volumes of manuscripts; 150 volumes of government publications. **Subscriptions:** 45 journals and other serials. **Services:** Library not open to the public.

★ 17751 ★
U.S. Natl. Park Service - Midwest Regional Office Library (Hist)
1709 Jackson St.
Omaha, NE 68102-2571   Phone: (402)221-3471
Founded: 1935. **Staff:** 1. **Subjects:** Midwestern Americana, ethnology, anthropology. **Special Collections:** Pacific railroad surveys; early Western travel; Westerners brand book. **Holdings:** 6250 books; special historical research, interpretive planning, historic structures, and salvage archeology reports. **Subscriptions:** 15 journals and other serials. **Services:** Library open to the public for reference use only. **Remarks:** FAX: (402)221-3461.

★ 17752 ★
U.S. Natl. Park Service - Moores Creek Natl. Battlefield - Library (Hist)
Box 69   Phone: (919)283-5591
Currie, NC 28435   Dusty Shultz, Supt.
Founded: 1960. **Staff:** Prof 1. **Subjects:** North Carolina history, American Revolution, national parks, environment, Highland Scots. **Holdings:** 325 books; 100 bound volumes of periodicals and historical papers. **Services:** Library open to the public for reference use only. **Remarks:** FAX: (919)283-5351.

★ 17753 ★
U.S. Natl. Park Service - Morristown Natl. Historical Park - Library (Hist)
Washington Place   Phone: (201)539-2016
Morristown, NJ 07960   James L. Kochan, Cur.
Founded: 1955. **Staff:** Prof 2. **Subjects:** History of the American Revolution; Continental Army; Morristown encampments - 1777, 1779-1780; Colonial Americana; George Washington; New Jersey local history. **Special Collections:** Lloyd W. Smith Manuscript Collection; Morristown National Historical Park manuscript collection; Ford family papers; Lidgerwood Collection of Hessian transcripts; diary of Sylvanus Seeley. **Holdings:** 40,000 books; 300 bound periodical volumes; 1000 pamphlets; 75 linear feet of manuscripts; 800 reels of microfilm. **Subscriptions:** 40 journals and other serials. **Services:** Copying; library open to the public. **Automated Operations:** Computerized cataloging (Automated National Catalog System). **Special Catalogs:** Guide to the Manuscript Collection; Guide to Hessian Documents of the American Revolution, 1776-1783. **Remarks:** FAX: (201)645-4531.

★ 17754 ★
U.S. Natl. Park Service - Mound City Group Natl. Monument - Library
(Hist)
16062 State Rte. 104   Phone: (614)774-1125
Chillicothe, OH 45601   William Gibson, Supt.
Staff: Prof 1. **Subjects:** Archeology, Hopewell and other prehistoric Indian cultures of Ohio, environment and environmental education, Ohio history. **Special Collections:** Reports of archeological research on Hopewell and Adena cultures conducted at monument; Hopewell Archeological Conference papers, 1978. **Holdings:** 1800 books; 650 magazines, reports, unbound articles. **Subscriptions:** 8 journals and other serials. **Services:** Copying; library open to the public for reference use only by request. **Staff:** Robert Petersen, Pk. Ranger.

★ 17755 ★
U.S. Natl. Park Service - Mount Rainier Natl. Park - Library (Rec)
Tahoma Woods, Star Rte.
Ashford, WA 98304-9751   Phone: (206)569-2211
Remarks: No further information was supplied by respondent.

★ 17756 ★
U.S. Natl. Park Service - Mount Rushmore Natl. Memorial - Library
(Hist)
Box 268   Phone: (605)574-2523
Keystone, SD 57751   Fred Banks, Jr., Supv.Pk. Ranger
Founded: 1964. **Staff:** 3. **Subjects:** American history, Mount Rushmore history, natural history of the Black Hills, history of South Dakota, national parks. **Special Collections:** Development of Mount Rushmore (documents on administrative history); color slide file (5000). **Holdings:** 960 books; 5 VF drawers of subject files; 6 VF drawers of black and white photo files. **Subscriptions:** 30 journals and other serials. **Services:** Library open to the public by appointment. **Remarks:** FAX: (605)574-2307.

★ 17757 ★
U.S. Natl. Park Service - Natchez Trace Parkway - Library & Visitor Center (Hist)
R.R. 1, NT-143
Tupelo, MS 38801   Phone: (601)842-1572
Founded: 1963. **Staff:** 1. **Subjects:** History, natural history, national parks. **Special Collections:** Papers and letters related to Choctaw and Chickasaw Indians (200 items). **Holdings:** 2300 books; 200 bound periodical volumes; 1000 color slides; 10,000 negatives. **Subscriptions:** 10 journals and other serials. **Services:** Interlibrary loan; copying; library open to the public.

★ 17758 ★
U.S. Natl. Park Service - National Capital Region - Rock Creek Nature Center Library (Biol Sci)
5200 Glover Rd., N.W.   Phone: (202)426-6829
Washington, DC 20015   David R. Smith, Supv.Pk. Ranger
Subjects: Birds, mammals, reptiles, astronomy, park and milling history, environment and environmental education. **Holdings:** 1000 books; 32 boxes of clippings and photographs; unbound journals. **Services:** Library open to the public for reference use only. **Publications:** Mimeographed nature leaflets.

★ 17759 ★
U.S. Natl. Park Service - Nez Perce Natl. Historical Park - Library
(Hist)
Box 93   Phone: (208)843-2261
Spalding, ID 83551   Frank Walker, Supt.
Founded: 1965. **Staff:** 1. **Subjects:** Nez Perce Indians, Nez Perce War, Indian ethnology, history of the Northwest and Idaho, Western history. **Holdings:** 1200 books; 4000 historical photographs. **Services:** Library open to the public with restrictions by appointment. **Computerized Information Services:** Internal database. **Remarks:** FAX: (208)843-2001.

★ 17760 ★
U.S. Natl. Park Service - Olympic Natl. Park - Pioneer Memorial Museum - Library (Biol Sci)
3002 Mount Angeles Rd.   Phone: (206)452-4501
Port Angeles, WA 98362   Henry C. Warren, Chf.Pk. Naturalist
Founded: 1938. **Staff:** 1. **Subjects:** Natural history, Northwest Coast Indians, Olympic National Park. **Special Collections:** Manuscript material and reports relating to exploration and settlement of the Olympic Peninsula; correspondence, memoranda, reports, and photographs relating to the establishment and administration of Olympic National Park. **Holdings:** 2000 books; 6 VF drawers of clippings and articles relating to natural and human history of Olympic National Park. **Services:** Copying; library open to the public by appointment.

★ 17761 ★
U.S. Natl. Park Service - Organ Pipe Cactus Natl. Monument - Library
(Hist)
Rte. 1, Box 100   Phone: (602)387-6849
Ajo, AZ 85321   Caroline Wilson, Interp.Spec.
Founded: 1937. **Staff:** 1. **Subjects:** Natural and cultural history, ecology of the Sonoran Desert and the Southwest, U.S. Natl. Park Service history and policies. **Holdings:** 1500 books and bound periodical volumes; research reports and manuscripts. **Services:** Library open to park employees and approved researchers.

★ 17762 ★
U.S. Natl. Park Service - Pea Ridge Natl. Military Park - Library (Hist)
Pea Ridge, AR 72751   Phone: (501)451-8122
                               Douglas Keller, Act.Chf.Interp.
Founded: 1960. **Subjects:** Battle of Pea Ridge, Civil War west of the Mississippi, regimental histories, Indians of the Civil War, arms and equipment, medicine. **Special Collections:** Battle of Pea Ridge (30 reels of microfilm; 15 reports). **Holdings:** 450 books; letters; clippings. **Services:** Library open to the public for reference use only.

★ 17763 ★
U.S. Natl. Park Service - Perry's Victory & International Peace Memorial - Library (Hist)
Box 549   Phone: (419)285-2184
Put-In-Bay, OH 43456   Richard Lusardi, Supt.
Staff: 10.5. **Subjects:** Naval victory of Oliver H. Perry over British at the Battle of Lake Erie, War of 1812; Lake Erie Islands. **Special Collections:** Construction of memorial designed by Freedlander and Seymour. **Holdings:** 700 books; 2 VF drawers of reports and correspondence from Centennial Commission and subsequent organizations; 2 VF drawers of pamphlets; 1200 photographs. **Services:** Library open to the public by appointment. **Remarks:** FAX: (419)285-2516.

★ 17764 ★
U.S. Natl. Park Service - Petersburg Natl. Battlefield - Library (Hist)
Box 549   Phone: (804)732-3531
Petersburg, VA 23804   Christopher M. Calkins, Hist./Pk. Ranger
Founded: 1926. **Staff:** Prof 2. **Subjects:** Civil War, Petersburg. **Holdings:** 1900 books; 200 bound periodical volumes; 500 maps; 200 letters and documents. **Subscriptions:** 10 journals and other serials. **Services:** Copying (limited); library open to the public by appointment. **Remarks:** FAX: (804)732-0835. **Staff:** John R. Davis, Chf., Interp.

★ 17765 ★
U.S. Natl. Park Service - Petrified Forest Natl. Park - Library (Sci-Engr, Hist)
Petrified Forest Natl. Park, AZ 86028   Phone: (602)524-6228
                                        Mary Knight
Founded: 1906. **Subjects:** Petrified wood, geology, paleontology, natural and cultural history. **Special Collections:** Paleontology library (papers and reports on continental Triassic deposits of the world). **Holdings:** 4200 books and bound periodical volumes. **Subscriptions:** 19 journals and other serials. **Services:** Library open to the public by appointment; paleontology library open to bona fide researchers by appointment only. **Remarks:** FAX: (602)524-3567.

★ 17766 ★
U.S. Natl. Park Service - Pipestone Natl. Monument - Library & Archives (Hist)
Box 727   Phone: (507)825-5464
Pipestone, MN 56164   Vincent J. Halvorson, Supt.
Subjects: Archeology, history, ethnology of the early Indian occupation of the Northern Plains; white exploration and settlement of the region. **Special Collections:** Publications relating to ceremonial pipes and Indian smoking customs. **Holdings:** 430 volumes; manuscripts; reports; clippings; microfilm; photographs; slides. **Subscriptions:** 12 journals and other serials; 2 newspapers. **Services:** Library open to the public for reference use only.

★ 17767 ★
U.S. Natl. Park Service - Point Reyes Natl. Seashore - Library (Biol Sci)
Point Reyes, CA 94956   Phone: (415)663-1092
                         Carlin Finke, Pk. Ranger
Subjects: Natural history, Indians, environmental education, geology, California history, sea life, mammals, botany, National Park Service. **Holdings:** 2500 books; 2075 bound periodical volumes; 425 other cataloged items; reports. **Services:** Library open to the public for reference use only by special arrangement. **Remarks:** FAX: (415)663-8132. **Staff:** Carlin Finke, Libn.Cat.

★ 17768 ★
U.S. Natl. Park Service - Pu'uhonua o Honaunau Natl. Historical Park - Library (Hist)
Box 129   Phone: (808)328-2288
Honaunau, HI 96726   Blossom Sapp, Pk. Ranger
Founded: 1961. **Staff:** 9. **Subjects:** Hawaiian culture and history; National Park Service. **Holdings:** 400 books; 180 manuscripts. **Services:** Library open to the public for reference use only. **Automated Operations:** Computerized cataloging. **Remarks:** FAX: (808)328-9485. **Staff:** Katherine K. Domingo, Supv.Pk. Ranger; Jerry Y. Shimoda, Supt.

★ 17769 ★
U.S. Natl. Park Service - Richmond Natl. Battlefield Park - Library (Hist)
3215 E. Broad St.
Richmond, VA 23223   Phone: (804)226-1981
Founded: 1936. **Staff:** 4. **Subjects:** Civil War, national parks, museums. **Holdings:** 1000 books; local newspapers on microfilm; Chimborazo Hospital records. **Services:** Library open to the public for reference use only by appointment. **Remarks:** FAX: (804)226-7077.

★ 17770 ★
U.S. Natl. Park Service - Rocky Mountain National Park - Library (Biol Sci, Hist)
Estes Park, CO 80517   Phone: (303)586-2371
                    Helen M. Burgener, Lib.Techn.
Staff: Prof 1. **Subjects:** Rocky Mountain National Park - history, geology, plant and animal ecology; Western history. **Special Collections:** Enos Mills Collection (28 books; personal letters); William Allen White Collection (16 books by and about White); unpublished MAps of park area before and during its early days. **Holdings:** 3090 books; 220 bound periodical volumes; 151 theses; 75 boxes of clippings and reports; 4 volumes of maps; 63 oral history tapes and cassettes. **Subscriptions:** 26 journals and other serials. **Services:** Interlibrary loan; copying; library open to the public on a limited schedule for reference use only, under the supervision of park personnel. **Remarks:** FAX: (303)586-3565.

★ 17771 ★
U.S. Natl. Park Service - Rocky Mountain Regional Office - Library (Rec, Hist)
12795 W. Alameda Pkwy.
Box 25287   Phone: (303)969-2715
Denver, CO 80225-0287   Janette Wesley, Libn.
Founded: 1971. **Staff:** Prof 1; Other 2. **Subjects:** National parks and monuments, outdoor recreation, ecology, landscape and historic architecture, American history. **Special Collections:** Brochures and pamphlets on individual national parks and monuments (3000 items). **Holdings:** 25,000 books, reports, documents, and dissertations. **Subscriptions:** 300 journals and other serials; 10 newspapers. **Services:** Interlibrary loan; copying; library open to the public for reference use only. **Automated Operations:** Computerized ILL. **Computerized Information Services:** OCLC. **Networks/Consortia:** Member of FEDLINK. **Remarks:** FAX: (303)969-2717.

★ 17772 ★
U.S. Natl. Park Service - Russell Cave Natl. Monument - Library (Sci-Engr)
Rte. 1, Box 175   Phone: (205)495-2672
Bridgeport, AL 35740   Russell Cave, Supt.
Staff: 6. **Subjects:** General and state archeology, biology, National Park Service, history, nature. **Special Collections:** Miscellaneous points and shards (1500). **Holdings:** 420 books; 4 unbound manuscripts. **Services:** Library open to the public for reference use only. **Staff:** Larry Beane, Pk. Ranger.

★ 17773 ★
U.S. Natl. Park Service - Salem Maritime Natl. Historic Site - Library (Hist)
Custom House, Derby St.   Phone: (508)744-4323
Salem, MA 01970   John M. Frayler, Hist.
Founded: 1937. **Staff:** 1. **Subjects:** Maritime history, Essex County and local history, recreation and conservation. **Holdings:** 900 books; 250 periodicals; 3 VF drawers of Custom House records; pamphlets; clippings; historic prints. **Services:** Copying (limited); library open to the public by appointment.

U.S. Natl. Park Service - San Francisco Maritime Natl. Historical Park
See: National Maritime Museum (11234)

★ 17774 ★
U.S. Natl. Park Service - Saratoga Natl. Historical Park - Library (Hist)
684 Rte. 32   Phone: (518)664-9821
Stillwater, NY 12170   S. Paul Okey, Pk.Hist.
Founded: 1948. **Staff:** 1. **Subjects:** Battles of Saratoga, military campaign of 1777, American Revolution, National Park System. **Special Collections:** Primary source materials (microfilm). **Holdings:** 500 books; 500 maps; 500 photographs; 1000 slides; 100 unbound reports and primary source transcript groupings. **Services:** Library open to the public by appointment.

★ 17775 ★
U.S. Natl. Park Service - Saugus Iron Works Natl. Historic Site - Library (Hist)
244 Central St.   Phone: (617)233-0050
Saugus, MA 01906   Frank Studinski, Supv.Pk. Ranger
Founded: 1969. **Staff:** Prof 2; Other 1. **Subjects:** Early iron technology, 17th century life, natural history, Americana. **Holdings:** 500 books. **Services:** Library open to the public for reference use only.

★ 17776 ★
U.S. Natl. Park Service - Scotts Bluff Natl. Monument - Library (Hist)
Box 27
Gering, NE 69341   Phone: (308)436-4340
Founded: 1935. **Staff:** 1. **Subjects:** Westward movement, Oregon Trail. **Holdings:** 890 books and diaries. **Services:** Library open to the public for reference use only.

★ 17777 ★
U.S. Natl. Park Service - Shenandoah Natl. Park - Library (Rec)
Rte. 4
Box 348   Phone: (703)999-3283
Luray, VA 22835-9051   Patressa G. Kearns, Pk.Libn.
Founded: 1967. **Staff:** 1. **Subjects:** Natural history. **Holdings:** 1650 books; 10 bound periodical collections; 500 reports. **Subscriptions:** 57 journals and other serials. **Services:** Interlibrary loan; library not open to the public.

★ 17778 ★
U.S. Natl. Park Service - Shiloh Natl. Military Park - Library (Hist)
Box 67   Phone: (901)689-5275
Shiloh, TN 38376   George A. Reaves, Chf.Interp. & Rsrcs.Mgt.
Founded: 1894. **Subjects:** Battle of Shiloh, American Civil War, military arms and equipment. **Holdings:** 1000 books; 200 unbound periodicals; 150 monographs; 200 letters from Civil War personnel. **Services:** Library open to the public for reference use only.

★ 17779 ★
U.S. Natl. Park Service - Sitka Natl. Historical Park - Library (Hist)
Box 738   Phone: (907)747-6281
Sitka, AK 99835   Tim Stone, Chf.Pk. Ranger
Founded: 1965. **Staff:** Prof 1. **Subjects:** Pacific Northwest Coast Indians, arts and crafts, ethnology, archeology, Southeast Alaska history, natural history, Russian American history. **Special Collections:** Park archives; Old Kasaan National Monument. **Holdings:** 1500 books; 200 clippings and special papers; 55 tapes; 14 films. **Services:** Library open to the public with permission and by advance request. **Computerized Information Services:** CompuServe Information Service (electronic mail service). **Remarks:** FAX: (907)747-5938.

★ 17780 ★

U.S. Natl. Park Service - Southwest Regional Office - Library (Sci-Engr)
P.O. Box 728   Phone: (505)988-6840
Santa Fe, NM 87504-0728   Amalin Ferguson, Libn.
Staff: Prof 2; Other 1. **Subjects:** Southwestern archeology, Indians of the Southwest, Western U.S. history, natural history, history of the National Park Service. **Special Collections:** National Park Service publications and reports (3000). **Holdings:** 30,000 books; 500 unbound periodical volumes; 300 videotapes; 3000 manuscripts; 800 prints and negatives; 6000 slides; 150 maps. **Subscriptions:** 25 journals and other serials. **Services:** Copying; library open to the public for reference use only. **Automated Operations:** Computerized public access catalog. **Computerized Information Services:** DIALOG Information Services, OCLC; CD-ROM (WLN). **Remarks:** FAX: (505)988-6876 ATTN: LIBRARY. Library holds many unpublished manuscripts and institutional reports not available elsewhere. These are primarily concerned with park units comprising the Southwest Region of the National Park Service.

★ 17781 ★

**U.S. Natl. Park Service - Springfield Armory Natl. Historic Site -
  Library and Archives** (Mil)
1 Armory Square   Phone: (413)734-8551
Springfield, MA 01105   Barbara Higgins Aubrey, Libn.
Staff: Prof 3. **Subjects:** Small armaments, military science, industrial history. **Special Collections:** Manuscript papers of 20th century inventors John C. Garand and John D. Pedersen. **Holdings:** 2000 books; 36 bound periodical volumes; 1300 periodicals; 4 VF drawers of papers, reports, histories, memorabilia; 22 theses; 3500 maps and drawings; 214 reels of microfilm; 181 films; 18,000 photographic images; oral history tapes; 138 linear feet of archives (1880-1968). **Services:** Copying (limited); library open to the public for reference use only. **Staff:** Stanislaus Skarzynski, Photo.Archv.; Dru Bronson-Geoffroy, Archv.

★ 17782 ★

U.S. Natl. Park Service - Statue of Liberty-Ellis Island Library (Hist)
Statue of Liberty National Monument
Liberty Island   Phone: (212)363-5803
New York, NY 10004   Diana Pardue, Chf., Musm.Serv.
Founded: 1972. **Staff:** 2. **Subjects:** Statue of Liberty and Ellis Island history, immigration/emigration, ethnic groups, National Park Service. **Special Collections:** Augustus F. Sherman Collection of Ellis Island photographs (141 prints); Statue of Liberty and Ellis Island Collection (8 VF drawers; 1302 prints); immigrant oral history (600 tapes; 500 transcripts); American Museum of Immigration, Inc. archives (20 boxes). **Holdings:** 2000 books; 6102 photographs; 2141 negatives; 16,400 slides; 3300 aperture cards; 165 microfiche; 65 reports; 80 manuscripts; 78 films; 3 VF drawers of research papers; 280 videotapes. **Subscriptions:** 5 journals and other serials. **Services:** Interlibrary loan; copying; tape and photograph duplication; library open to the public by appointment. **Remarks:** FAX: (212)363-8347. Alternate telephone number(s): (212)363-5804. **Staff:** Barry Morino; Jeff Dosik.

★ 17783 ★

U.S. Natl. Park Service - Stones River Natl. Battlefield - Library (Hist)
3501 Old Nashville Hwy.   Phone: (615)893-9501
Murfreesboro, TN 37129   Mary Ann Peckham, Pk.Supt.
Founded: 1932. **Staff:** 2. **Subjects:** American history, Civil War history, environmental education, National Park Service. **Special Collections:** Regimental files on units participating in battle of Stones River (250). **Holdings:** 500 books; 10 Civil War manuscripts. **Subscriptions:** 5 journals and other serials. **Services:** Interlibrary loan; copying; library open to bona fide researchers. **Special Indexes:** Regimental index; map index. **Remarks:** FAX: (615)893-9508. **Staff:** Elizabeth C. Cook, Pk. Ranger.

★ 17784 ★

U.S. Natl. Park Service - Theodore Roosevelt Natl. Park - Library
  (Hist)
Medora, ND 58645   Phone: (701)623-4466
                                        Bruce M. Kaye, Chf. Naturalist
Founded: 1947. **Staff:** 2. **Subjects:** Theodore Roosevelt; open range cattle industry; environment and ecology; area, natural, and cultural history; National Park Service. **Holdings:** 2500 books; 60 boxes of unbound pamphlets and manuscripts; 50 boxes of unbound periodicals; 50 reports, manuscripts, and dissertations. **Subscriptions:** 30 journals and other serials. **Services:** Library open to the public for reference use only. **Staff:** William Gleason, Dist. Naturalist.

★ 17785 ★

U.S. Natl. Park Service - Timpanogos Cave Natl. Monument - Library
  (Sci-Engr)
Timpanogos Cave
R.R. 3, Box 200   Phone: (801)756-5238
American Fork, UT 84003   Ray Pugsley, Ld.Pk. Ranger
Founded: 1922. **Staff:** 1. **Subjects:** Speleology, Utah geology, history, natural sciences, biology, environmental education. **Holdings:** 600 books; 300 unbound periodicals. **Subscriptions:** 10 journals and other serials. **Services:** Library open to the public for reference use only. **Remarks:** FAX: (801)756-5661.

★ 17786 ★

U.S. Natl. Park Service - USS Arizona Memorial - Library (Mil)
1 Arizona Memorial Place   Phone: (808)422-2771
Honolulu, HI 96818   Daniel Martinez, Hist.
Founded: 1980. **Staff:** 30. **Subjects:** Pearl Harbor attack; early Pacific War (1941-1942); USS Arizona Battleship; underwater archaeology; causes of the Pacific War. **Special Collections:** Oral history (200 audio- and videotapes, transcriptions); Pearl Harbor, 1909-1941 (10,000 items); Museum Collection (3000 artifacts). **Holdings:** 700 books; 100 AV programs; 1000 photographs; 2000 manuscripts; newspapers. **Subscriptions:** 26 journals and other serials. **Services:** Copying; library open to the public by appointment. **Computerized Information Services:** Internal database (under development). **Special Indexes:** Index to Photo, Library, and Museum Collections. **Remarks:** FAX: (808)541-3168. **Staff:** Donald Magee, Supt.

★ 17787 ★

U.S. Natl. Park Service - Vicksburg Natl. Military Park - Library (Hist)
3201 Clay St.   Phone: (601)636-0583
Vicksburg, MS 39180   Terry Winschel, Pk.Hist.
Founded: 1899. **Staff:** 1. **Subjects:** Vicksburg campaign, U.S.S. Cairo. **Special Collections:** Vicksburg campaign manuscript collections (12,000). **Holdings:** 600 books; 300 folders of other cataloged items. **Subscriptions:** 3 journals and other serials. **Services:** Library open to the public for reference use only by appointment. **Remarks:** FAX: (601)636-9497.

★ 17788 ★

**U.S. Natl. Park Service - Walnut Canyon Natl. Monument - Reference
  Library** (Biol Sci)
Walnut Canyon Rd.   Phone: (602)526-3367
Flagstaff, AZ 86004   Rueben Honahnie
Founded: 1940. **Staff:** 1. **Subjects:** Walnut Canyon and Southwest archeology, natural history, park policies, park histories. **Special Collections:** Bureau of American Ethnology (14 annual reports dating from 1881 through 1908). **Holdings:** 700 books. **Subscriptions:** 2 journals and other serials. **Services:** Interlibrary loan; library open to the public for reference use only. **Remarks:** FAX: (602)556-9419.

★ 17789 ★

**U.S. Natl. Park Service - Western Archeological and Conservation
  Center - Museum Collections Repository - Archives and Research
  Library** (Biol Sci, Soc Sci)
1415 N. 6th Ave.   Phone: (602)670-6501
Tucson, AZ 85705   W. Richard Horn, Chf.Libn.
Founded: 1953. **Staff:** Prof 2; Other 4. **Subjects:** Archeology, ethnology, and history of the Southwest; natural history - geology, botany, biology. **Special Collections:** Archives of archeological projects of the Southwestern U.S.; unpublished archeological reports. **Holdings:** 18,000 books; 5000 bound periodical volumes; 160,000 photographic images. **Subscriptions:** 100 journals and other serials. **Services:** Interlibrary loan. **Automated Operations:** Computerized cataloging. **Computerized Information Services:** OCLC; National Park Service Library Database (internal database); CD-ROM (WLN). **Networks/Consortia:** Member of FEDLINK. **Remarks:** FAX: (602)762-6503. **Staff:** Lynn M. Mitchell, Archv.; Johanna M. Alexander, Pub.Serv.Libn.

★ 17790 ★

**U.S. Natl. Park Service - Western Regional Office - Regional Resources
  Library** (Hist)
600 Harrison St., Suite 600   Phone: (415)744-3963
San Francisco, CA 94107-7372   Gordon Chappell, Reg.Hist.
Subjects: History, archeology, historic architecture of National Park Service areas in California, Nevada, Arizona, Hawaii, Guam, Saipan, and American Samoa. **Holdings:** 3800 books; 50 VF drawers of manuscripts, photographs, research files, clippings, and archival materials. **Services:** Copying; library open to the public for reference use only.

★ 17791 ★
U.S. Natl. Park Service - William Howard Taft Natl. Historic Site -
Library (Hist)
2038 Auburn Ave.
Cincinnati, OH 45219   Phone: (513)684-3262
Founded: 1969. **Subjects:** William Howard Taft, National Park Service.
Special Collections: Taft family papers; Charles Taft, II papers (7000 items).
Holdings: 300 books; William Howard Taft Memorial Association papers.
Services: Library open to the public with restrictions.

★ 17792 ★
U.S. Natl. Park Service - Wupatki Natl. Monument - Library (Hist)
HC 33, Box 444A
Flagstaff, AZ 86001   Phone: (602)556-7040
Staff: 1. **Subjects:** Archeology, ethnology, natural history. **Special**
Collections: Wupatki Archeology collection. **Holdings:** 1000 books; 200
bound periodical volumes; 800 pamphlets. **Subscriptions:** 3 journals and
other serials. **Services:** Library open to the public for reference use only.
Remarks: FAX: (602)556-7071.

★ 17793 ★
U.S. Natl. Park Service - Yellowstone Association - Research Library
(Hist, Sci-Engr)
Box 117   Phone: (307)344-7381
Yellowstone Park, WY 82190   Patricia Cole, Bus.Mgr.
Founded: 1931. **Staff:** 2. **Subjects:** History of Yellowstone area, science.
Special Collections: Haynes Guides to Yellowstone, 1894-1966;
superintendents' reports, 1872 to present. **Holdings:** 11,000 books; 15,000
reprints; 4 drawers of manuscripts; 36 drawers of reprint material and
clippings; maps. **Subscriptions:** 65 journals and other serials. **Services:**
Interlibrary loan; copying; library open to the public with restrictions. **Staff:**
Beverly Whitman, Lib.Techn.; Barbara Zafft, Lib.Techn.

★ 17794 ★
U.S. Natl. Park Service - Yosemite Natl. Park - Research Library (Hist,
Biol Sci)
Box 577   Phone: (209)372-0280
Yosemite National Park, CA 95389   Linda Eade, Res.Libn.
Founded: 1923. **Staff:** 2. **Subjects:** History and natural history of Yosemite
National Park. **Holdings:** 9000 books; 900 bound periodical volumes; 36 VF
drawers; 150 boxes of historical documents; maps; black and white
photographs. **Subscriptions:** 100 journals and other serials. **Services:**
Interlibrary loan; library open to the public.

★ 17795 ★
U.S. Natl. Park Service - Zion Natl. Park - Library (Biol Sci)
Springdale, UT 84767   Phone: (801)772-3256
                                          Jill Blumenthal, Pk.Libn.
Founded: 1930. **Staff:** Prof 1. **Subjects:** Natural sciences, Utah history,
natural resources management. **Holdings:** 3000 books. **Subscriptions:** 25
journals and other serials; 3 newspapers. **Services:** Library open to the public
for reference use only. **Remarks:** The interpretive, scientific, and historical
programs of the park are assisted by the Zion Natural History Association.

★ 17796 ★
U.S. Natl. Weather Service - Central Region Headquarters - Library
(Sci-Engr)
601 E. 12th St., Rm. 1836   Phone: (816)426-5672
Kansas City, MO 64106   Beverly D. Lambert, Meteorological Techn.
Staff: 1. **Subjects:** Meteorology, climatology, hydrology. **Holdings:** 1708
volumes. **Subscriptions:** 12 journals and other serials. **Services:** Interlibrary
loan; copying (limited); library open to the public for reference use only.
Remarks: The National Weather Service is part of the National Oceanic &
Atmospheric Administration of the U.S. Department of Commerce.

U.S. Natl. Weather Service - International Tsunami Information Center
See: International Tsunami Information Center (8201)

★ 17797 ★
U.S. Natl. Weather Service - Weather Service Nuclear Support Office -
Library (Sci-Engr)
2753 S. Highland
Box 94227   Phone: (702)295-1235
Las Vegas, NV 89193-4227   Daisy G. Ross, Off.Serv.Asst.
Founded: 1956. **Staff:** 1. **Subjects:** Meteorology, nuclear science. **Holdings:**
300 volumes. **Subscriptions:** 17 journals and other serials. **Services:** Library
not open to the public.

U.S. Naval.
See: U.S. Navy - Naval (17809)

★ 17798 ★
U.S. Navy - CEC/Seabee Museum - Library
Code 22M NCBC
Port Hueneme, CA 93010
Defunct. Holdings absorbed by its Naval Facilities Engineering Command
Historical Program Division.

★ 17799 ★
U.S. Navy - Coastal Systems Station - Technical Information Services
Branch (Sci-Engr, Mil)
Code N1222 Technical Library   Phone: (904)234-4381
Panama City, FL 32407-5000   Myrtle J. Rhodes, Supv.Libn.
Founded: 1945. **Staff:** Prof 4; Other 4. **Subjects:** Mine and ordnance
countermeasures, acoustic countermeasures, amphibious operations
support, naval diving and salvage support, inshore warfare, coastal
technology. **Holdings:** 16,000 books; 5000 bound periodical volumes; 80,000
technical reports; 15,000 microforms. **Subscriptions:** 414 journals and other
serials; 5 newspapers. **Services:** Interlibrary loan; copying; SDI; library open
to outside users cleared by Security Office. **Automated Operations:**
Computerized cataloging, acquisitions, serials, and circulation.
Computerized Information Services: DIALOG Information Services,
DTIC, Integrated Technical Information System (ITIS); internal databases.
Publications: OFFLINE, monthly. **Special Catalogs:** Computer-generated
subject catalogs. **Formerly:** Its Naval Coastal Systems Center. **Staff:** B.
Householder, Ref./NWPL; Nadine Iferd, Acq./Ser.; D. Hines, Doc.Cat./
DTIC; Angelia Whatley, Bk.Cat./INTEL; Schurron Finklea, Circ.

★ 17800 ★
U.S. Navy - Department Library (Mil)
Bldg. 44
Washington Navy Yard   Phone: (202)433-4131
Washington, DC 20374-0571   John E. Vajda, Dir.
Founded: 1800. **Staff:** Prof 7; Other 2. **Subjects:** Naval history, naval art and
science, polar studies, naval and military biography, maritime law, naval
ordnance, voyages. **Special Collections:** Congressional documents; Reports
of the Secretary of the Navy; manuscripts; American Revolution maps and
charts; rare books (7000); Truxtun-Decatur Naval Museum Library.
Holdings: 170,000 books; 32,000 bound periodical volumes; 10,000
pamphlets; 10,000 reels of microfilm. **Subscriptions:** 400 journals and other
serials. **Services:** Interlibrary loan; copying; library open to the public.
Automated Operations: Computerized cataloging. **Computerized**
Information Services: DIALOG Information Services, DTIC, OCLC.
Networks/Consortia: Member of FEDLINK. **Publications:** Accession List,
quarterly; Subject Bibliographies, irregular. **Remarks:** FAX: (202)433-9553.
Alternate telephone number(s): (202)433-4132. **Staff:** Susana C. Wang, Hd.,
Tech.Serv.Sect.; Jean Hort, Hd., Ref./Rd.Serv.Sect.; Glenn Helm, ILL;
Tonya Montgomery, Circ.

U.S. Navy - Fleet Analysis Center (FLTAC) - Library
See: U.S. Navy - Naval Warfare Assessment Center - Technical Library/
C-012L (17895)

★ 17801 ★
U.S. Navy - Fleet Anti-Submarine Warfare Training Center, Atlantic -
Technical Library (Sci-Engr, Mil)
Norfolk, VA 23511-6495   Phone: (804)444-1660
                                          D.S. Kolick, Libn.
Founded: 1956. **Staff:** Prof 1; Other 3. **Subjects:** Antisubmarine warfare,
equipment, vehicles, oceanography, tactics, antisubmarine warfare foreign
capabilities. **Holdings:** 10,000 books; 200 bound periodical volumes.
Subscriptions: 22 journals and other serials. **Services:** Maintains operation
orders and post exercise results on major ASW exercises; maintains retrieval
system compatible with similar library in San Diego; U.S. government
clearance for secret and cognizant, bureau "Need to Know" certification for
individual user within the Department of Defense only. **Publications:**
Quarterly Accession List - to military commands.

★ 17802 ★
U.S. Navy - Fleet Anti-Submarine Warfare Training Center, Pacific - Tactical Library (Mil)
Pacific Nimitz Blvd. at Harbor Dr.
San Diego, CA 92147   Phone: (619)524-1908
Subjects: Tactical documents. **Holdings:** 3000 bound periodical volumes. **Subscriptions:** 100 journals and other serials. **Services:** Library open to contractors with proper clearance on a need-to-know basis. **Staff:** Vicky McCuan, Tactical Libn.

★ 17803 ★
U.S. Navy - Fleet Combat Direction Systems Support Activity - TISO Library
200 Catalina Blvd.
San Diego, CA 92147
Defunct.

U.S. Navy - Marine Corps
See: U.S. Marine Corps (17604)

★ 17804 ★
U.S. Navy - Military Sealift Command - Technical Information Center
Bldg. 210, Rm. 212a
Washington Navy Yard
Washington, DC 20398-5100
Defunct. Holdings absorbed by the Navy Yard Library in Washington, DC.

★ 17805 ★
U.S. Navy - National Naval Medical Center - Edward Rhodes Stitt Library (Med)
Bethesda, MD 20889-5000   Phone: (301)295-1184
Jerry Meyer, Lib.Dir.
Founded: 1902. **Staff:** Prof 2; Other 2. **Subjects:** Medicine and allied health sciences. **Special Collections:** Pastoral Counseling Collection (500 volumes); Video Cassette Collection (950 tapes); Hospital Management Collection (4000 volumes); History of Medicine Collection (3000 volumes). **Holdings:** 70,000 volumes; 2000 audiotapes. **Subscriptions:** 890 journals. **Services:** Interlibrary loan; library not open to the public. **Automated Operations:** Computerized cataloging. **Computerized Information Services:** MEDLINE, BRS Information Technologies. **Publications:** Stitt Notes. **Remarks:** Contains the holdings of the former U.S. Navy - Naval School of Health Sciences - Library. **Staff:** Jean Jacobsen.

★ 17806 ★
U.S. Navy - National Naval Medical Command - Naval Dental School - National Naval Dental Clinic - William L. Darnall Library (Med)
Bethesda, MD 20889-5077   Phone: (301)295-0080
Patricia A. Evans, Chf., Lrng.Rsrc.Div.
Staff: Prof 1. **Subjects:** Dentistry, medicine. **Holdings:** 8500 books. **Subscriptions:** 85 journals and other serials. **Services:** Interlibrary loan; copying (limited); library open to command personnel and others with authorization from the director of the Naval Dental School.

★ 17807 ★
U.S. Navy - Nautilus Memorial - Submarine Force Library and Museum (Mil)
Box 571   Phone: (203)449-3558
Groton, CT 06349-5000   William P. Galvani, Dir.
Founded: 1964. **Staff:** Prof 4. **Subjects:** Submarine history. **Special Collections:** Submarines and their inventors ; U.S. Navy and foreign submarines; biographical file of submariners; U.S. submarine patrol reports of World War II and the Korean War; German submarine patrol reports and war diaries of World War II; Naval Submarine Base, Groton, 1868 to present; J.P. Holland and Simon Lake papers; blue print collection; glassplate negative collection; correspondance; U.S. submarine cachets; submarine paintings and photographs. **Holdings:** 5000 books; 20,000 photographs; technical manuals. **Subscriptions:** 15 journals and other serials. **Services:** Memorial and museum open to the public; library open to the public by appointment. **Publications:** Museum brochure; KLAXON Submarine Data Book; Teacher's Guide. **Remarks:** Toll-free telephone number(s): (800)343-0079. Serves as the repository for the records and history of the U.S. Submarine Force, from its beginnings at the turn of the century to the modern Navy. **Staff:** Martha Barber, Archv.Asst.; Wendy Gulley, Archv.Asst.

★ 17808 ★
U.S. Navy - Naval Academy - Nimitz Library (Mil)
589 McNair Rd.   Phone: (301)267-2194
Annapolis, MD 21402-5029   Prof. Richard A. Werking, Lib.Dir.
Founded: 1845. **Staff:** Prof 20; Other 31. **Subjects:** Naval science, naval history, history, international relations, biography, technology, science. **Special Collections:** Benjamin Collection (1150 volumes of early works on electricity); Weidorn Collection (900 volumes containing colorplates); Guggenheim Collection (2950 volumes, including literary first editions); Steichen Collection (10,000 photographs); Somers Submarine Collection (1000 volumes, vertical files, photographs). **Holdings:** 342,000 books; 96,500 bound periodical volumes; 18,500 reels of microfilm; 115,800 government documents. **Subscriptions:** 2200 journals and other serials; 34 newspapers. **Services:** Interlibrary loan; copying; library open to the public with restrictions. **Automated Operations:** Computerized public access catalog, cataloging, acquisitions, and circulation. **Computerized Information Services:** DIALOG Information Services, OCLC; DDN Network Information Center, BITNET, InterNet (electronic mail services). **Networks/Consortia:** Member of FEDLINK. **Publications:** Nimitz Library Newsletter and Guide to the Nimitz Library, both irregular; Serials Holdings List, biennial. **Remarks:** FAX: (301)267-3669. Electronic mail address(es): Q21031@N1.USNA.NAVY.MIL (DDN Network Information Center). **Staff:** John P. Cummings, Assoc.Dir.; Robert A. Lambert, Assoc.Libn., Tech.Serv.; Alice S. Creighton, Asst.Libn., Spec.Coll.; Barbara Parker, Asst.Libn., Coll.Dev.; Genevieve Clemens, Asst.Libn., Automated Serv.

★ 17809 ★
U.S. Navy - Naval Aerospace Medical Institute - Library (Med)
Bldg. 1953, Code 03L   Phone: (904)452-2256
Pensacola, FL 32508-5600   Ruth T. Rogers, Adm.Libn.
Founded: 1940. **Staff:** Prof 1; Other 2. **Subjects:** Aviation and aerospace medicine, medical specialties, basic sciences. **Holdings:** 10,000 books; 10,000 bound periodical volumes. **Subscriptions:** 300 journals and other serials. **Services:** Interlibrary loan; library not open to the public. **Computerized Information Services:** BRS Information Technologies. **Remarks:** FAX: (904)452-4479.

U.S. Navy - Naval Air Development Center - Technical Information Branch
See: U.S. Navy (17826)

★ 17810 ★
U.S. Navy - Naval Air Engineering Center - Naval Air Warfare Center, Aircraft Division - Technical Library, Code 7312 (Sci-Engr)
Lakehurst, NJ 08733-5000   Phone: (908)323-2368
Connie Priestly, Supv.
Founded: 1917. **Staff:** 2. **Subjects:** Aerodynamics, aeronautics, astronautics, aviation medicine, electronics, mechanical engineering, guided missiles, ground support equipment, mathematics. **Special Collections:** NASA reports. **Holdings:** 6000 books; 4000 unbound periodical volumes; 56,000 technical reports. **Subscriptions:** 150 journals and other serials. **Services:** Interlibrary loan; library not open to the public. **Publications:** List of Accessions Received by NAEC Library, bimonthly - for internal distribution only.

★ 17811 ★
U.S. Navy - Naval Air Propulsion Center - Technical Data Center (Sci-Engr)
Box 7176   Phone: (609)896-5609
Trenton, NJ 08628   Robert Malone, Libn.
Founded: 1955. **Staff:** 1. **Subjects:** Aircraft engines and fuels. **Holdings:** 1000 books; 1000 unbound periodical volumes; 7500 technical reports; 1000 government specifications. **Subscriptions:** 104 journals and other serials. **Services:** Interlibrary loan; center open to outside users by appointment. **Publications:** Accessions list, 5/year - limited distribution.

★ 17812 ★
U.S. Navy - Naval Air Station (CA-Alameda) - Library (Mil)
Bldg. 2, Wing 3   Phone: (510)263-3030
Alameda, CA 94501-5051   Mrs. Ranjan Bhashyam-Tambe, Sta.Libn.
Founded: 1940. **Staff:** Prof 1; Other 4. **Subjects:** Navy and other military branches, careers and education, women and minorities. **Special Collections:** Materials on and about California; Janes's books. **Holdings:** 29,848 volumes; 200 bound periodical volumes; 10 VF drawers of pamphlets and clippings; 10 shelves of periodicals; 1495 phonograph records/tapes (mainly popular music). **Subscriptions:** 60 journals and other serials; 7 newspapers. **Services:** Interlibrary loan; copying; library open to the public with visitor permit. **Publications:** Library News - basewide distribution.

★ 17813 ★
U.S. Navy - Naval Air Station (CA-Lemoore) - Library (Mil)
Bldg. 821   Phone: (209)998-4634
Lemoore, CA 93246-5001   Lois C. Gruntorad, Libn.
Founded: 1961. **Staff:** Prof 1; Other 2. **Subjects:** U.S. Navy, biography, history, science. **Holdings:** 20,000 books. **Subscriptions:** 55 journals and other serials; 8 newspapers. **Services:** Interlibrary loan; copying; library open to students, civil employees, and active duty military personnel. **Networks/Consortia:** Member of San Joaquin Valley Library System (SJVLS).

★ 17814 ★
U.S. Navy - Naval Air Station (CA-North Island) - Library (Mil, Sci-Engr)
Bldg. 650
Box 29
San Diego, CA 92135-5016   Phone: (619)545-8230
                                  Sharon Nelson, Adm.Libn.
Staff: Prof 1; Other 2. **Subjects:** Naval aviation and history. **Holdings:** 22,000 books; 20 drawers of pamphlets. **Subscriptions:** 50 journals and other serials; 6 newspapers. **Services:** Interlibrary loan; copying; library open to the public by appointment. **Networks/Consortia:** Member of Serra Cooperative Network.

★ 17815 ★
U.S. Navy - Naval Air Station (FL-Jacksonville) - Library (Mil, Sci-Engr)
Bldg. 620, Box 52   Phone: (904)772-3415
Jacksonville, FL 32212-0052   Martha Lynne Baldwin, Libn.
Founded: 1941. **Staff:** Prof 1; Other 1. **Subjects:** World War II, naval history and aviation. **Special Collections:** CND Professional Reading Program; Recycling Collection. **Holdings:** 28,000 books; 200 bound periodical volumes; 5 drawers of microfiche. **Subscriptions:** 117 journals and other serials; 10 newspapers. **Services:** Interlibrary loan; library not open to the public. **Remarks:** Alternate telephone number(s): 772-3433.

★ 17816 ★
U.S. Navy - Naval Air Station (FL-Key West) - Library (Mil)
Bldg. A508   Phone: (305)292-2116
Key West, FL 33040-5000   Betty Lindstrand, Lib.Techn.-in-Charge
Staff: 1. **Subjects:** Naval air history, naval history. **Holdings:** 7500 books. **Subscriptions:** 50 journals and other serials. **Services:** Library not open to the public.

★ 17817 ★
U.S. Navy - Naval Air Station (FL-Pensacola) - Station Library (Mil, Sci-Engr)
Bldg. 633   Phone: (904)452-4362
Pensacola, FL 32508-5000   Judith A. Walker, Hd.Libn.
Staff: Prof 1; Other 2.5. **Subjects:** Naval aviation, Navy; naval history. **Special Collections:** Historical archives for naval installations in the area. **Holdings:** 24,000 books; 500 bound periodical volumes; 1136 volumes of microforms of periodical backfiles; 8 VF drawers of clippings and pamphlets on local history. **Subscriptions:** 181 journals and other serials; 22 newspapers. **Services:** Interlibrary loan (limited); library open to the public. **Computerized Information Services:** MOLLI (internal database). **Networks/Consortia:** Member of Panhandle Library Access Network (PLAN).

★ 17818 ★
U.S. Navy - Naval Air Station (FL-Whiting Field) - Library (Mil)
Bldg. 1417   Phone: (904)623-7274
Milton, FL 32570   Eva K. Locke, Libn.
Staff: Prof 1. **Subjects:** Naval aviation, U.S. Navy, United States history. **Holdings:** 13,000 books. **Subscriptions:** 58 journals and other serials; 6 newspapers. **Services:** Interlibrary loan; library not open to the public. **Publications:** Naval Education and Training Program Development Center General Library News Memorandum, monthly - for internal distribution only.

★ 17819 ★
U.S. Navy - Naval Air Station (HI-Barbers Point) - Library (Mil)
Barbers Point, HI 96862-5050   Phone: (808)684-5217
                                             Kenneth Ornstein
Founded: 1943. **Staff:** Prof 1; Other 3. **Subjects:** Military affairs, naval aviation. **Special Collections:** Hawaiiana; "Welcome Aboard" packets describing naval bases and their locales for transferring personnel; Learning Center (SAT and other test preparation guides). **Holdings:** 18,469 books; 9238 microfiche. **Subscriptions:** 75 journals and other serials; 4 newspapers. **Services:** Interlibrary loan; copying; library open to active duty military personnel and their dependents, military retirees, and civilian employees of the station. **Remarks:** FAX: (808)682-4437.

★ 17820 ★
U.S. Navy - Naval Air Station (NV-Fallon) - Library (Mil)
Commanding Officer for Station Library   Phone: (702)426-2599
Fallon, NV 89406   Denise H. Koster
Staff: Prof 1. **Subjects:** Naval history, naval aviation. **Holdings:** 15,000 books. **Subscriptions:** 75 journals and other serials; 10 newspapers. **Services:** Interlibrary loan; copying; library open to persons with authorised entry to the Naval Air Station. **Remarks:** FAX: (702)423-0735.

★ 17821 ★
U.S. Navy - Naval Air Station (TN-Memphis) - Library (Mil, Sci-Engr)
Bldg. S-78   Phone: (901)873-5683
Millington, TN 38054   Suzanne Miles, Libn.
Staff: Prof 1; Other 5. **Subjects:** Electronics, avionics, aeronautics, navigation, military history and biography, geography. **Special Collections:** "Welcome Aboard" (packets from worldwide military installations). **Holdings:** 38,000 books; 450 bound periodical volumes; 600 phonograph records. **Subscriptions:** 115 journals and other serials; 9 newspapers. **Services:** Interlibrary loan; library open to active and retired military personnel and dependents and civilian employees. **Remarks:** Autovon Line(s): (8) 966-5683.

★ 17822 ★
U.S. Navy - Naval Air Station (TX-Corpus Christi) - Library (Mil)
Station Library, Bldg. 5   Phone: (512)939-3574
Corpus Christi, TX 78419   Sharon F. Scott, Libn.
Founded: 1941. **Staff:** 1. **Subjects:** U.S. Navy, World War II, aeronautics. **Holdings:** 18,000 books; 8 VF drawers of clippings, pamphlets, pictures, maps. **Subscriptions:** 67 journals and other serials. **Services:** Interlibrary loan; copying; library open to the public by permission.

★ 17823 ★
U.S. Navy - Naval Air Systems Command - Technical Information & Reference Center AIR-5004 (Sci-Engr)
Washington, DC 20361   Phone: (703)692-9006
                          Patricia Ames, Hd., Tech.Info. & Ref.Ctr.
Founded: 1922. **Staff:** Prof 3; Other 3. **Subjects:** Aeronautics, weapon systems, management, mathematics, materials, electronics. **Special Collections:** Technical manuals; naval aviation. **Holdings:** 10,000 books; 1600 bound periodical volumes; 50,000 technical reports. **Subscriptions:** 125 journals and other serials. **Services:** Interlibrary loan; copying; library serves government agencies and contractors only. **Automated Operations:** Computerized cataloging. **Computerized Information Services:** DIALOG Information Services, DTIC, OCLC. **Networks/Consortia:** Member of FEDLINK. **Publications:** Accessions list, bimonthly. **Remarks:** FAX: (703)746-0848. **Staff:** Candace Parker, Ref.Libn.; Amy Tursky, Ref.Libn.

★ 17824 ★
U.S. Navy - Naval Air Test Center - Central Library (Mil, Sci-Engr)
Bldg. 407   Phone: (301)863-1927
Patuxent River, MD 20670   Suzanne M. Ryder, Dir.
Founded: 1943. **Staff:** Prof 2.5; Other 6. **Subjects:** Engineering, aviation, military science and history, management, computer science, science. **Holdings:** 60,000 books; 15,000 government documents. **Subscriptions:** 400 journals and other serials; 25 newspapers. **Services:** Interlibrary loan; copying; department open only to base personnel and retired military with the exception of a government documents depository that serves all residents of Southern Maryland. **Automated Operations:** Computerized cataloging. **Computerized Information Services:** DIALOG Information Services, DTIC, NASA/RECON, Government-Industry Data Exchange Program (GIDEP). **Networks/Consortia:** Member of FEDLINK. **Staff:** Patricia Aud, Info.Spec.

★ 17825 ★
U.S. Navy - Naval Air Warfare Center - Aircraft Division - Technical Library (Sci-Engr)
Dept. 765
6000 E. 21st St.   Phone: (317)353-7765
Indianapolis, IN 46219-2189   Louise Boyd, Supv.
Founded: 1945. **Staff:** 5. **Subjects:** Mathematics, electronics, electrical engineering, physics, metallurgy, avionics equipment. **Holdings:** 11,000 books; 2000 microfiche; 20,000 technical reports. **Subscriptions:** 450 journals and other serials. **Services:** Interlibrary loan; library not open to the public. **Computerized Information Services:** ORBIT Search Service. **Remarks:** FAX: (317)353-3122. **Formerly:** Its Naval Avionics Center.

★ 17826 ★
U.S. Navy - Naval Air Warfare Center - Aircraft Division Warminster (Sci-Engr)
Code 8131
Warminster, PA 18974-5000   Phone: (215)441-1698
    Mary Hellings, Adm.
Founded: 1944. **Subjects:** Naval aviation, air and ship navigation, aerospace medicine, systems engineering, computer science, crew systems. **Special Collections:** Defense reports; NASA reports. **Holdings:** 30,000 books; 20,000 bound periodical volumes; 400,000 technical reports including microfiche. **Subscriptions:** 650 journals. **Services:** Interlibrary loan; library open to Department of Defense personnel and approved government contractors. **Automated Operations:** Computerized cataloging. **Computerized Information Services:** DIALOG Information Services, DTIC, NASA/RECON, OCLC, BRS Information Technologies. **Networks/Consortia:** Member of FEDLINK. **Remarks:** FAX: (215)441-3818. **Formerly:** Its Naval Air Development Center - Technical Information Branch.

★ 17827 ★
U.S. Navy - Naval Amphibious Base (CA-Coronado) - Library (Mil)
San Diego, CA 92155   Phone: (619)437-3026
    Nadine Bangsberg, Adm.Libn.
Founded: 1950. **Staff:** Prof 1; Other 2. **Subjects:** Naval history, amphibious operations, guerrilla warfare, Vietnam, World War II. **Holdings:** 25,000 books; 159 bound periodical volumes; 3000 tapes and phonograph records; 2000 paperbacks. **Subscriptions:** 125 journals and other serials; 8 newspapers. **Services:** Interlibrary loan; library not open to the public. **Publications:** Subject bibliographies; Book List, monthly - for internal distribution only.

★ 17828 ★
U.S. Navy - Naval Amphibious School - John Sidney McCain Amphibious Warfare Library (Mil)
Bldg. 3504 NAB LCREEK
Norfolk, VA 23521-5290   Phone: (804)464-7467
    Carolyn G. Jones, Dir., Lib.Serv.
Founded: 1965. **Staff:** 2. **Subjects:** Amphibious warfare, military arts and sciences, leadership, management. **Holdings:** 2700 books; 3000 documents. **Subscriptions:** 50 journals and other serials. **Services:** Interlibrary loan; library open to qualified researchers.

U.S. Navy - Naval Avionics Center
See: **U.S. Navy - Naval Air Warfare Center - Aircraft Division - Technical Library** (17825)

★ 17829 ★
U.S. Navy - Naval Civil Engineering Laboratory - Information Management and Services (Sci-Engr)
Code L06C
Port Hueneme, CA 93043-5003   Phone: (805)982-1124
    Bryan Thompson, Lib.Dir.
Founded: 1948. **Staff:** Prof 4; Other 2. **Subjects:** Engineering, ocean engineering, construction materials, environmental protection, energy, soil mechanics. **Holdings:** 16,000 books; 7000 bound periodical volumes; 20,000 technical reports. **Subscriptions:** 600 journals and other serials; 5 newspapers. **Services:** Interlibrary loan; copying; library open to the public by appointment. **Automated Operations:** Computerized public access catalog, cataloging, acquisitions, serials, and circulation. **Computerized Information Services:** DIALOG Information Services, DTIC, NASA/RECON, OCLC, MELVYL (University of California On-Line Union Catalog), STN International. **Networks/Consortia:** Member of FEDLINK, Total Interlibrary Exchange (TIE). **Publications:** New on the Shelf, monthly. **Remarks:** FAX: (805)982-1409. **Staff:** Josephine Walsh, Libn.; Jo Ann Van Reenan, Libn.; Reinaldo Acosta, ILL.

U.S. Navy - Naval Coastal Systems Center
See: **U.S. Navy** (17799)

★ 17830 ★
U.S. Navy - Naval Command, Control and Ocean Surveillance Center - Technical Libraries (Sci-Engr)
Code 964
San Diego, CA 92152-5000   Phone: (619)553-4879
    Joan Buntzen, Hd., Tech.Libs.Br.
Founded: 1977. **Staff:** Prof 7; Other 15. **Subjects:** Electronics, physics, ocean engineering, underwater ordnance, marine biology, the Arctic, communications, oceanography, artificial intelligence, robotics. **Holdings:** 60,000 books; 60,000 bound periodical volumes; 100,000 technical reports. **Subscriptions:** 1500 journals and other serials. **Services:** Interlibrary loan; copying; SDI; libraries open to the public on a need-to-know basis. **Automated Operations:** Computerized cataloging, acquisitions, circulation, and serials. **Computerized Information Services:** DIALOG Information Services, BRS Information Technologies, PFDS Online, DATALIB, OCLC, NASA/RECON, WILSONLINE, DTIC. **Networks/Consortia:** Member of FEDLINK, OCLC Pacific Network. **Publications:** List of periodical holdings, annual; New Publications, biweekly; Current Awareness, monthly. **Remarks:** FAX: (619)553-4882. Technical libraries include holdings of the Topside Technical Library Branch, the Bayside Technical Library, and the Hawaii library. **Formerly:** Its Naval Ocean Systems Center. **Staff:** Kathy Wright, Hd., Bayside Lib.

★ 17831 ★
U.S. Navy - Naval Computer & Telecomm Station - Technical Information Office (Sci-Engr, Comp Sci)
Bldg. 143, Washington Navy Yard   Phone: (202)433-5700
Washington, DC 20374   Octavia J. Ross, Libn.
Founded: 1964. **Staff:** 1. **Subjects:** Electronic data processing, management, data communications, mathematics, naval science. **Holdings:** 5400 books; 218 bound periodical volumes; 3006 technical documents; 113 microfiche. **Subscriptions:** 186 journals and other serials. **Services:** Interlibrary loan; copying; library open to Department of Defense employees. **Automated Operations:** Computerized circulation. **Special Catalogs:** Catalog of project documentation (computer printout). **Remarks:** FAX: (202)433-0491. **Formerly:** Its Regional Data Automation Center - Technical Library.

★ 17832 ★
U.S. Navy - Naval Construction Battalion Center - Library (Sci-Engr, Mil)
Code 1922G, Bldg. No. 65
Port Hueneme, CA 93043-5000   Phone: (805)982-4411
    Diana Hoslett, Libn.
Staff: Prof 1; Other 3. **Subjects:** Naval history, construction, building trades, guerilla warfare, engineering, survival. **Holdings:** 30,000 books. **Subscriptions:** 100 journals and other serials. **Services:** Interlibrary loan; copying; library open to the public with restrictions.

★ 17833 ★
U.S. Navy - Naval Dental Research Institute - Thomas S. Meyer Memorial Library (Med)
Bldg. 1-H
Great Lakes, IL 60088-5259   Phone: (708)688-5647
    Myra J. Portis, Lib.Tech.
Founded: 1967. **Staff:** 1. **Subjects:** Clinical dentistry, basic sciences, oral biology, dental research. **Holdings:** 1800 books; 3800 bound periodical volumes. **Subscriptions:** 85 journals and other serials. **Services:** Interlibrary loan; library not open to the public. **Computerized Information Services:** MEDLARS. **Networks/Consortia:** Member of Northeastern Illinois Library Consortium, North Suburban Library System (NSLS).

★ 17834 ★
U.S. Navy - Naval Education and Training Center - Library System (Mil)
Main Library Bldg. 114
Newport, RI 02841-5002   Phone: (401)841-3044
    James F. Aylward, Adm.
Founded: 1917. **Staff:** Prof 3; Other 4. **Subjects:** Military and naval science, naval history, technology, curriculum background. **Holdings:** 85,560 books; 250 bound periodical volumes; 10 VF drawers; 2300 microforms; 2500 NAV manuals; 1700 audio programs; military documents. **Subscriptions:** 274 journals and other serials; 28 newspapers. **Services:** Interlibrary loan; copying; library open to the public with Naval Command permission. **Computerized Information Services:** DTIC. **Remarks:** The NETC Library System includes the main library, Officer Candidate School Library, Chaplains School Library, Brig Library, and the Naval Hospital Patients' Library. FAX: (401)841-2265. An alternate telephone number is 841-4352. **Staff:** Robert S. Wessells, Asst.Libn.; Paul Cotsoridis, Hd., Circ. Control.

★ 17835 ★

U.S. Navy - Naval Electronic Systems Engineering Center - Technical Library (Mil)
Box 55   Phone: (804)396-7688
Portsmouth, VA 23705   Beatrice L. Neal
Subjects: Naval Science. **Holdings:** Naval technical manuals; military specifications; Department of Defense directives. **Services:** Library not open to the public.

★ 17836 ★

U.S. Navy - Naval Electronics Systems Engineering Center - San Diego Technical Library (Sci-Engr)
Code 103
P.O. Box 85137   Phone: (619)524-2900
San Diego, CA 92186-5137   N.K. Leiser, Hd.Libn.
Founded: 1967. **Staff:** 2. **Subjects:** Electronics, engineering, antennas, finance, computers, business administration. **Special Collections:** U.S. Navy Electronic Equipment; DOD Electronic Equipment; naval engineering drawings. **Holdings:** 6000 books; 5000 reports; 11,000 other cataloged items. **Subscriptions:** 123 journals and other serials. **Services:** Interlibrary loan; library open to Department of Defense contractors. **Computerized Information Services:** IHS Haystack; Paradox, Navy Engineering Drawing Asset Locator System (internal databases). **Special Catalogs:** Subject; Equipment nomenclature.

★ 17837 ★

U.S. Navy - Naval Explosive Ordnance Disposal Technology Center - Technical Library (Sci-Engr)
Naveod Technical Center   Phone: (301)743-6817
Indian Head, MD 20640-5070   Anne Gifford, Hd.Libn.
Staff: Prof 1; Other 6. **Subjects:** U.S. and foreign ordnance, explosives. **Special Collections:** Explosive ordnance disposal procedures, tools, and equipment. **Holdings:** 15,000 books; 140,000 documents; 48,000 engineering drawings; 700 photographs; 25,000 microfiche; 60 reels of microfilm. **Subscriptions:** 250 journals and other serials. **Services:** Interlibrary loan; copying; library not open to the public. **Automated Operations:** Computerized public access catalog, cataloging, acquisitions, serials, and circulation. **Computerized Information Services:** DIALOG Information Services, BRS Information Technologies, OCLC. **Publications:** Accession List, monthly. **Remarks:** FAX: (301)743-6927.

★ 17838 ★

U.S. Navy - Naval Facilities Engineering Command - Historical Program Division (Hist, Mil)
Naval Construction Battalion Ctr.,   Phone: (805)982-5563
Code 223   Dr. Vincent A. Transano,
Port Hueneme, CA 93043   MAUFAC Command Hist.
Founded: 1943. **Staff:** 7. **Subjects:** History of the Naval Facilities Engineering Command, the Naval Construction Force (Seabees), and the Navy's Civil Engineering Corps, 1940 to present. **Special Collections:** Records of the Naval Facilities Engineering Command (acquisition, construction, and maintenance of the naval shore establishment in the U.S. and abroad); Naval Construction Force records (operational accomplishments of the combat construction branch of the U.S. Navy); Civil Engineers Corps records (the evolving role of the civil engineer in the U.S. Navy). **Holdings:** 12,000 cubic feet of records. **Services:** Copying; open to the public during business hours. **Formed by the merger of:** Its Naval Facilities Engineering Command Historian and its CEC/Seabee Museum - Library.

★ 17839 ★

U.S. Navy - Naval Facilities Engineering Command - Northern Division - Design Division Library (Sci-Engr)
Bldg. 77-L
Philadelphia Naval Base   Phone: (215)897-6482
Philadelphia, PA 19112-5094   John Fidler, Br.Hd.
Staff: Prof 1; Other 2. **Subjects:** Civil engineering, architectural design, mechanical and electrical engineering, management. **Special Collections:** Navy manuals (200). **Holdings:** 2000 books; 500 unbound reports and documents. **Subscriptions:** 64 journals and other serials. **Services:** Library not open to the public. **Automated Operations:** Computerized cataloging. **Computerized Information Services:** Internal database. **Publications:** Design Library Newsletter, quarterly - for internal distribution only.

★ 17840 ★

U.S. Navy - Naval Facility Centerville Beach Station - Library (Mil)
Ferndale, CA 95536   Phone: (707)786-9531
                                         Sean Aragon
Staff: 1. **Subjects:** U.S. Navy. **Special Collections:** Navy periodicals (1000). **Holdings:** 2759 books. **Subscriptions:** 20 journals and other serials; 2 newspapers. **Services:** Library not open to the public. **Publications:** Library information articles, monthly. **Remarks:** FAX: (707)786-9235.

★ 17841 ★

U.S. Navy - Naval Health Research Center - Walter L. Wilkins Bio-Medical Library (Med)
Box 85122   Phone: (619)553-8425
San Diego, CA 92186-5122   Mary Aldous, Libn.
Founded: 1959. **Staff:** Prof 1; Other 2. **Subjects:** Environmental and stress medicine, psychiatry, medical information systems, work physiology, biological sciences, social medicine, enhanced performance, sleep research, military medicine, sustained operations, sports medicine. **Special Collections:** Prisoners of War studies. **Holdings:** 10,000 books; 6944 bound periodical volumes; 10,000 technical reports; 410 audiotapes. **Subscriptions:** 350 journals and other serials. **Services:** Interlibrary loan; library open to the public with restrictions. **Automated Operations:** Computerized cataloging and serials. **Computerized Information Services:** DIALOG Information Services, BRS Information Technologies, MEDLARS, OCLC, DTIC; OnTyme Electronic Message Network Service (electronic mail service). **Publications:** Periodicals holding list. **Remarks:** FAX: (619)553-9389.

★ 17842 ★

U.S. Navy - Naval Historical Center - Operational Archives Branch (Mil, Hist)
Bldg. 57, Washington Navy Yard   Phone: (202)433-3170
Washington, DC 20374-0571   Bernard F. Cavalcante, Br.Hd.
Founded: 1942. **Staff:** Prof 9; Other 2. **Subjects:** U.S. Naval history, naval operations, naval archives, naval biography. **Special Collections:** CNO records; oral history interview transcripts; China repository; aviation histories; materials relating to World War II and post-war operations. **Holdings:** 10,000 feet of records and documents, including 1200 feet of action and operational reports, 1941-1953; 900 feet of naval command war diaries, 1941-1953; 570 feet of miscellaneous records and publications, 1931-1950. **Services:** Copying (limited); reading room open to the public. **Publications:** List of open collections and publications - available on request. **Remarks:** FAX: (202)433-3593. **Staff:** Regina T. Akers, Archv.; Ariana A. Jacob, Archv.; Kathleen M. Lloyd, Archv.; John L. Hodges, Archv.; Paul A. Breck, Archv.; Kathleen L. Rohr, Archv.; Judith W. Short, Archv.; Richard M. Walker, Archv.

★ 17843 ★

U.S. Navy - Naval Historical Center - Photographic Section (Aud-Vis)
Washington Navy Yard
Washington, DC 20374-0571   Phone: (202)433-2765
Staff: Prof 2. **Subjects:** Visual aspects of naval history, including weapons, wars, U.S. and foreign naval ships. **Holdings:** 200,000 photographs, prints, drawings, posters. **Services:** Copying; section open to the public.

★ 17844 ★

U.S. Navy - Naval Hospital (CA-Camp Pendleton) - Medical Library (Med)
Camp Pendleton, CA 92055-5008   Phone: (619)725-1322
                                         Christina D. Inouye, Med.Libn.
Founded: 1949. **Staff:** Prof 1; Other 1. **Subjects:** General medicine, nursing, family practice. **Holdings:** 1000 books; 4800 bound periodical volumes; 1100 AV programs. **Subscriptions:** 200 journals and other serials. **Services:** Interlibrary loan; library open to the public for reference use only. **Computerized Information Services:** NLM. **Networks/Consortia:** Member of National Network of Libraries of Medicine - Pacific Southwest Region. **Publications:** Newsletter. **Remarks:** Autovon Line(s): 365-1322.

★ 17845 ★

U.S. Navy - Naval Hospital (CA-Oakland) - Medical Library (Med)
8750 Mountain Blvd.   Phone: (510)639-2031
Oakland, CA 94627-5000   Harriet V. Cohen, Adm.Libn.
Staff: Prof 2; Other 1. **Subjects:** Medicine, nursing, paramedical sciences, psychiatry. **Holdings:** 8000 books; 10,000 bound periodical volumes.

Subscriptions: 400 journals and other serials. **Services:** Interlibrary loan; library not open to the public. **Computerized Information Services:** MEDLINE, BRS Information Technologies, OCLC; DOCLINE (electronic mail service). **Networks/Consortia:** Member of National Network of Libraries of Medicine - Pacific Southwest Region. **Publications:** Serials List, annual; New Book List, monthly - to department heads. **Staff:** Robin L. Holloway, Med.Libn.

★ 17846 ★
U.S. Navy - Naval Hospital (CA-San Diego) - Medical and General Libraries (Med)
San Diego, CA 92134   Phone: (619)532-7950
                             Marilyn Schwartz, Chf.Libn.
Founded: 1923. **Staff:** Prof 3; Other 2. **Subjects:** Medicine, nursing, dentistry, hospital administration. **Holdings:** 14,340 books; 15,204 bound periodical volumes. **Subscriptions:** 724 journals. **Services:** Interlibrary loan; copying; SDI; library open to military personnel. **Computerized Information Services:** DIALOG Information Services, MEDLINE, BRS Information Technologies; OnTyme Electronic Message Network Service (electronic mail service). **Publications:** List of journal subscriptions, annual; recent acquisitions, quarterly; Library Newsletter, quarterly. **Remarks:** FAX: (619)532-9293. **Staff:** Jan B. Dempsey, Ref.Libn.

★ 17847 ★
U.S. Navy - Naval Hospital (FL-Jacksonville) - Medical Library (Med)
Jacksonville, FL 32214   Phone: (904)777-7583
                                Bettye W. Stilley, Med.Libn.
Founded: 1942. **Staff:** Prof 1. **Subjects:** Medicine. **Holdings:** 1500 books; 2400 bound periodical volumes; 500 other cataloged items. **Subscriptions:** 162 journals and other serials. **Services:** Interlibrary loan; library not open to the public. **Computerized Information Services:** MEDLARS, BRS/COLLEAGUE.

★ 17848 ★
U.S. Navy - Naval Hospital (FL-Orlando) - Medical Library (Med)
Orlando, FL 32813   Phone: (407)646-4959
                           Nancy B. Toole, Med.Libn.
Staff: Prof 1. **Subjects:** Clinical medicine. **Holdings:** 1032 books; 500 bound periodical volumes; 625 videocassettes. **Subscriptions:** 86 journals and other serials. **Services:** Interlibrary loan; library not open to the public. **Automated Operations:** Computerized public access catalog (LUIS). **Computerized Information Services:** MEDLINE, DAVIS.

★ 17849 ★
U.S. Navy - Naval Hospital (FL-Pensacola) - Medical Library (Med)
Pensacola, FL 32512-5000   Phone: (904)452-6635
                                  Mrs. Connie C. Walker, Med.Libn.
Staff: Prof 1; Other 1. **Subjects:** Medicine, allied health sciences. **Holdings:** 1200 books; 15,000 bound periodical volumes. **Subscriptions:** 150 journals and other serials. **Services:** Interlibrary loan; library not open to the public. **Computerized Information Services:** BRS/COLLEAGUE.

★ 17850 ★
U.S. Navy - Naval Hospital (Guam) - Medical Library (Med)
PSC490
Box 7747
FPO AP
San Francisco, CA 96540-1649   Phone: (671)344-9250
                                      Alice E. Hadley, Med.Libn.
Founded: 1954. **Staff:** Prof 1. **Subjects:** Medicine, nursing, dentistry, surgery, obstetrics. **Holdings:** 1800 books; 1300 bound periodical volumes. **Subscriptions:** 115 journals and other serials. **Services:** Interlibrary loan; copying; library open to medical professionals. **Computerized Information Services:** MCI, CompuServe Information Service (electronic mail services). **Remarks:** FAX: (671)477-4960. Electronic mail address(es): MCI:383-8217 (MCI); 72627,1575 (CompuServe Information Service).

★ 17851 ★
U.S. Navy - Naval Hospital (IL-Great Lakes) - Medical Library (Med)
Bldg. 200-H   Phone: (708)688-4601
Great Lakes, IL 60088-5230   Bryan Parhad, Med.Libn.
Founded: 1945. **Staff:** Prof 1; Other 1. **Subjects:** Medicine, surgery, dentistry, nursing. **Holdings:** 1500 books; 5260 bound periodical volumes. **Subscriptions:** 237 journals and other serials. **Services:** Interlibrary loan; library not open to the public. **Computerized Information Services:** BRS Information Technologies. **Networks/Consortia:** Member of National Network of Libraries of Medicine - Greater Midwest Region, Northeastern Illinois Library Consortium, North Suburban Library System (NSLS). **Publications:** Annual Journals Holdings List. **Remarks:** FAX: (708)688-3346.

★ 17852 ★
U.S. Navy - Naval Hospital (NC-Camp Lejeune) - Medical Library (Med)
Camp Lejeune, NC 28542   Phone: (919)451-4076
                                Gladys Dixon, Lib.Techn.
Founded: 1941. **Staff:** 1. **Subjects:** Medicine and allied health sciences. **Holdings:** 2124 books; 4936 bound periodical volumes. **Subscriptions:** 151 journals and other serials. **Services:** Interlibrary loan; library not open to the public. **Remarks:** FAX: (919)451-4012.

★ 17853 ★
U.S. Navy - Naval Hospital (PA-Philadelphia) - Medical Library (Med)
17th & Pattison Aves.   Phone: (215)897-8038
Philadelphia, PA 19145-5199   Giovina Cavacini, Libn.
Founded: 1917. **Staff:** Prof 1. **Subjects:** Medicine, allied health sciences. **Holdings:** 6000 books; 8000 bound periodical volumes; Audio-Digest tapes. **Subscriptions:** 275 journals and other serials. **Services:** Interlibrary loan; copying; library open to the public with restrictions. **Computerized Information Services:** NLM. **Networks/Consortia:** Member of National Network of Libraries of Medicine - Middle Atlantic Region. **Remarks:** Alternate telephone number(s): (215)897-8000.

★ 17854 ★
U.S. Navy - Naval Hospital (RI-Newport) - Medical Library (Med)
Cypress & 3rd Sts.   Phone: (401)841-4512
Newport, RI 02841-5003   Winifred M. Jacome, Med.Lib.Techn.
SStaff: 1. **Subjects:** Medicine and allied health sciences, dentistry, orthopedics, ophthalmology. **Holdings:** 2100 books; Audio-Digest tapes, 1990 to present; 2938 journal volumes. **Subscriptions:** 176 journals and other serials. **Services:** Interlibrary loan; copying; library open to the public for reference use only. **Automated Operations:** Computerized ILL (DOCLINE). **Computerized Information Services:** MEDLARS. **Networks/Consortia:** Member of Association of Rhode Island Health Sciences Librarians (ARIHSL), North Atlantic Health Science Libraries (NAHSL), BHSL. **Remarks:** FAX: (401)841-1321; (401)841-4766.

★ 17855 ★
U.S. Navy - Naval Hospital (TN-Memphis) - General/Medical/Audiovisual Library (Med)
Millington, TN 38054   Phone: (901)873-5846
                              G.R. Counts, Lib.Techn.
Founded: 1942. **Staff:** 1. **Subjects:** Dentistry, medicine, nursing. **Holdings:** 5800 volumes. **Subscriptions:** 50 journals and other serials. **Services:** Library open to patients, staff, and their dependents. **Computerized Information Services:** Access to online systems. **Networks/Consortia:** Member of Association of Memphis Area Health Science Libraries (AMAHSL), National Network of Libraries of Medicine (NN/LM). **Remarks:** FAX: (901)873-5928. **Formerly:** Its General and Medical Library.

★ 17856 ★
U.S. Navy - Naval Hospital (TX-Corpus Christi) - Patricia M. Sessions Memorial Library (Med)
Corpus Christi, TX 78419   Phone: (512)939-3863
                                  Charles C. Rosecrans, Hd., Educ. & Trng.Dept.
Founded: 1941. **Staff:** 2. **Subjects:** Medicine, surgery, nursing, allied health sciences. **Holdings:** Bound periodical volumes; reports; archives; other cataloged items. **Subscriptions:** 110 journals and other serials. **Services:** Interlibrary loan; library not open to the public. **Networks/Consortia:** Member of Coastal Bend Health Sciences Library Consortium (CBHSLC).

★ 17857 ★
U.S. Navy - Naval Hospital (VA-Portsmouth) - Medical Library (Med)
Bldg. 215   Phone: (804)398-5383
Portsmouth, VA 23708-5100   Suad Jones, Med.Libn.
Staff: Prof 2; Other 2. **Subjects:** Medicine, dentistry, nursing, allied health sciences. **Holdings:** 7155 books; 15,997 bound periodical volumes; 1371 cartridges of microfilm. **Subscriptions:** 590 journals and other serials. **Services:** Interlibrary loan; copying; SDI; library open to the public for reference use only on request. **Computerized Information Services:** MEDLINE, OCLC, BRS Information Technologies, DIALOG Information Services; OnTyme Electronic Message Network Service (electronic mail service). **Publications:** Medical Library/News/Acquisitions/Publications, irregular - for internal distribution only. **Staff:** Jane Pellegrino.

★ 17858 ★
U.S. Navy - Naval Hospital (WA-Bremerton) - Medical Library (Med)
Bremerton, WA 98314   Phone: (206)478-9316
                                                         Jane Easley, Libn.
Founded: 1947. **Staff:** 1. **Subjects:** Medicine, nursing, administration.
Holdings: 1300 books; 2700 bound periodical volumes. **Subscriptions:** 185
journals and other serials. **Services:** Interlibrary loan; copying; library open
to qualified medical personnel. **Computerized Information Services:** NLM.
Publications: Bibliographies.

★ 17859 ★
U.S. Navy - Naval Institute - Oral History Office (Mil, Hist)
118 Maryland Ave.   Phone: (410)268-6110
Annapolis, MD 21402-5035   Paul Stillwell, Dir., Oral Hist.
Founded: 1969. **Staff:** Prof 3. **Subjects:** Naval biography, Coast Guard
biography, naval aviation. **Special Collections:** Admiral Nimitz Collection;
POLARIS interviews; WAVE interviews; early black naval officers.
Holdings: 175 bound volumes containing 90,000 pages of transcripts; tapes
of 215 individual memoirs. **Services:** Library open to researchers. **Remarks:**
Copies of some volumes available for loan by mail; copies of all bound
volumes are also available in the special collections at the Nimitz Library
of the U.S. Naval Academy, Annapolis, MD and the Naval Historical
Center, Washington Navy Yard, Washington, DC. FAX: (410)269-7940.

★ 17860 ★
U.S. Navy - Naval Institute - Reference & Photographic Library (Mil)
Annapolis, MD 21402   Phone: (301)268-6110
                                                         Patty M. Maddocks, Dir.
Staff: 4. **Subjects:** U.S. and foreign Navy - ships, aircraft, personalities,
weapons; American Revolution; Civil War; World War I; World War II;
Korean War; Vietnam War; Desert Storm. **Special Collections:** James C.
Fahey Ship and Aircraft Collection of U.S. Navy; "Our Navy" collection;
Miller Collection. **Holdings:** 4000 books; 100 bound periodical volumes; 100
oral history materials; 100 bound volumes of proceedings. **Subscriptions:**
103 journals and other serials. **Services:** Copying; library open to the public.
Computerized Information Services: Internal databases. **Publications:** U.S.
Naval Institute Proceedings; Naval History Magazine; Naval Review.
Special Indexes: Proceedings Index; Navy Oral History Index; Naval
History Index. **Remarks:** FAX: (301)269-7940. Telex: 187-114 Airs Corps
PHX. **Staff:** Mary E. Straight, Photo.Archv.; Dottie Sappington, Photo.
Sales; Linda Cullen, Magazine/Bk.Ed.; Virginia Schultz, Photo. Sales Ck.

★ 17861 ★
U.S. Navy - Naval Maritime Intelligence Center (Mil)
4301 Suitland Rd.
Code DS-31   Phone: (301)763-1606
Washington, DC 20390   Peggy Mechanic, Hd., Tech.Lib.Serv.
Founded: 1944. **Staff:** Prof 5; Other 20. **Subjects:** Military intelligence,
science and technology. **Special Collections:** Russian Language technical
book and manual collection (4500). **Holdings:** 5000 books; 50,000 reports;
50,000 documents. **Subscriptions:** 1000 journals and other serials; 30
newspapers. **Services:** Interlibrary loan; division not open to the public.
Automated Operations: Computerized cataloging, acquisitions, serials, and
circulation. **Computerized Information Services:** DIALOG Information
Services, BRS Information Technologies, OCLC. **Publications:** Weekly
Accession Bulletin; Periodicals Collection, updated annually. **Remarks:**
FAX: (301)763-3528. **Formerly:** Its Naval Technical Intelligence Center.
Staff: Donnie McCants, Hd., Ref.Serv.; Betty Vicino, Hd., Tech.Serv.

★ 17862 ★
**U.S. Navy - Naval Medical Research Institute - Medical Research
   Library** (Med)
Bldg. 17 Stop 2 NNMC   Phone: (202)295-2186
Bethesda, MD 20889-5055   Phyllis R. Blum, Adm.Libn.
Founded: 1942. **Staff:** Prof 1; Other 2. **Subjects:** Infectious diseases, casualty
care, hyperbaric medicine, experimental surgery, transplantation, military
medicine. **Special Collections:** Naval Medical Research Institute Reports,
1943 to present. **Holdings:** 5000 books. **Subscriptions:** 250 journals and
other serials. **Services:** Interlibrary loan; copying; SDI; division open to the
public for reference use only. **Automated Operations:** Computerized
cataloging. **Computerized Information Services:** DIALOG Information
Services, OCLC, BRS Information Technologies; internal database.
Networks/Consortia: Member of FEDLINK, Interlibrary Users
Association (IUA). **Publications:** Summaries of Research; Union List of
Serials, both annual. **Remarks:** Alternate telephone number(s): 295-2188.
Formerly: Its Information Services Division.

★ 17863 ★
U.S. Navy - Naval Military Personnel Command - Technical Library
   (Bus-Fin, Mil)
NMPC-013DD
Arlington Annex, Rm. 1429   Phone: (703)614-2073
Washington, DC 20370   Rufus E. Lassiter, Libn.
Founded: 1946. **Staff:** Prof 2. **Subjects:** Military personnel administration,
education, psychology, management, statistics. **Holdings:** 4000 books; 146
VF drawers of technical reports. **Subscriptions:** 350 journals and other
serials. **Services:** Interlibrary loan; copying; library open to naval personnel
and other government agencies. **Remarks:** Alternate telephone number(s):
(703)614-1271. **Staff:** Steven E. Norris, Asst.Libn.

★ 17864 ★
**U.S. Navy - Naval Observatory - Matthew Fontaine Maury Memorial
   Library** (Sci-Engr)
34th and Massachusetts Ave., N.W.   Phone: (202)653-1499
Washington, DC 20392-5100   Brenda G. Corbin, Libn.
Founded: 1843. **Staff:** Prof 2. **Subjects:** Astronomy, astrophysics, celestial
mechanics, geophysics, mathematics, physics. **Special Collections:** Rare
books, 1482-1800 (astronomy, navigation, mathematics; 800 volumes).
Holdings: 75,000 volumes; slides; microfiche; maps; manuscripts; archives.
Subscriptions: 200 journals and other serials. **Services:** Interlibrary loan;
copying (both limited); library open to graduate students. **Automated
Operations:** Computerized cataloging. **Computerized Information Services:**
OCLC, DIALOG Information Services; InterNet (electronic mail service).
Networks/Consortia: Member of FEDLINK. **Publications:** Naval
Observatory Publications - restricted distribution; Acquisitions List,
quarterly. **Remarks:** FAX: (202)653-1497. Telex: 710 822 1970. Electronic
mail address(es): LIB@PHOBOS.USNO.NAVY.MIL (InterNet). **Staff:**
Gregory A. Shelton.

U.S. Navy - Naval Ocean Systems Center
See: **U.S. Navy - Naval Command, Control and Ocean Surveillance
   Center** (17830)

U.S. Navy - Naval Oceanographic Atmospheric Research
See: **U.S. Navy - Naval Research Laboratory/Monterey - Library**
   (17871)

★ 17865 ★
**U.S. Navy - Naval Oceanographic Office - Matthew Fontaine Maury
   Oceanographic Library** (Sci-Engr)
NSTL   Phone: (601)688-4017
Bay St. Louis, MS 39522   Kay Miller, Supv.Libn.
Founded: 1871. **Staff:** Prof 4; Other 3. **Subjects:** Oceanography - biological,
chemical, geological, physical; ocean engineering; cartography;
photogrammetry; meteorology; marine technology. **Special Collections:**
Domestic and foreign sailing directions; International Hydrographic Bureau
publications and oceanographic expeditions; Naval Oceanographic Office
publications. **Holdings:** 120,000 books, bound periodical volumes,
documents, translations, pamphlets; 10,000 microforms. **Subscriptions:** 500
journals and other serials. **Services:** Interlibrary loan; copying; library open
to the public. **Automated Operations:** Computerized public access catalog,
cataloging, and circulation. **Computerized Information Services:** DTIC,
NASA/RECON, DIALOG Information Services. **Networks/Consortia:**
Member of FEDLINK. **Publications:** Accessions List, monthly - for
internal distribution only. **Remarks:** FAX: (601)688-4191. **Staff:** Ann
Loomis, Libn.; Martha Elbers, Libn.; Dianne Sellier, Tech.Info.Spec.

★ 17866 ★
U.S. Navy - Naval Ordnance Station - Library Branch (Sci-Engr)
Indian Head, MD 20640-5000   Phone: (301)743-4742
                                                         Charles F. Gallagher, Libn.
Founded: 1960. **Staff:** Prof 1; Other 5. **Subjects:** Explosives and propellants,
missiles and rockets, aerospace technology, chemistry, chemical
engineering, management. **Holdings:** 9000 books; 5500 bound periodical
volumes; 40,000 domestic and foreign research reports; 7400 microcards;
microfiche. **Subscriptions:** 400 journals and other serials. **Services:**
Interlibrary loan; branch not open to the public. **Automated Operations:**
Computerized cataloging and serials. **Computerized Information Services:**
DTIC, DIALOG Information Services, LS/2000; LINX Courier (electronic
mail service). **Networks/Consortia:** Member of FEDLINK. **Publications:**
Accessions Bulletin - for internal distribution only. **Remarks:** Alternate
telephone number(s): 743-4743. FAX: (301)743-4192.

★ 17867 ★

U.S. Navy - Naval Ordnance Station - Technical Library (Sci-Engr, Mil)
Code 7053-W-2-5   Phone: (502)364-5662
Louisville, KY 40214-5001   Elizabeth T. Miles, Libn.
Founded: 1961. **Staff:** 2. **Subjects:** Naval ordnance, engineering. **Holdings:** 2400 books; 75 bound periodical volumes; 3500 technical reports; 100,000 government specifications. **Subscriptions:** 100 journals and other serials. **Services:** Interlibrary loan; library open to the public with restrictions. **Computerized Information Services:** HAYSTACK. **Remarks:** Alternate telephone number(s): 364-5667.

★ 17868 ★

U.S. Navy - Naval Postgraduate School - Dudley Knox Library (Sci-Engr, Mil)
Monterey, CA 93943-5002   Phone: (408)646-2341
    Paul Spinks, Dir. of Libs.
Founded: 1906. **Staff:** Prof 15; Other 21. **Subjects:** Engineering, physical sciences, naval science, operations research, administrative sciences, international affairs. **Special Collections:** Christopher Buckley, Jr. Library (naval and maritime history; 8000 volumes). **Holdings:** 289,968 books; 86,212 bound periodical volumes; 555 videotapes; 110,000 research reports; 19,800 pamphlets; 537,914 microforms. **Subscriptions:** 1500 journals and other serials; 20 newspapers. **Services:** Interlibrary loan; copying; SDI; library open to the public with some facilities limited to authorized personnel. **Automated Operations:** Computerized public access catalog, cataloging, acquisitions, and serials. **Computerized Information Services:** DIALOG Information Services, RLIN, DTIC; SABIRS III (internal database); OnTyme Electronic Message Network Service, BITNET (electronic mail service). **Networks/Consortia:** Member of CLASS, Monterey Bay Area Cooperative Library System (MOBAC), SOUTHNET. **Publications:** Library Periodicals: Current Subscriptions and Earlier Holdings, annual; This is Your Library, annual - both for internal distribution only. **Remarks:** FAX: (408)646-2842. Electronic mail address(es): 2982p@NAVPGS (BITNET). **Staff:** Bobbie Carr, Assoc.Libn.; Anna Lee Bernstein, Hd., Acq.Div.; Roger Martin, Hd., Rd.Serv.Div.; Norma Dobay, Hd., Res.Rpt.Div.; Leslie Navari, Hd., Bibliog. Control Div.

★ 17869 ★

U.S. Navy - Naval Research Laboratory - Ruth H. Hooker Research Library and Technical Information Center (Sci-Engr)
Code 4820   Phone: (202)767-2357
Washington, DC 20375-5000   Laurie E. Stackpole, Chf.Libn.
Founded: 1927. **Staff:** Prof 9; Other 16. **Subjects:** Physics, chemistry, electronics, materials, systems. **Special Collections:** Microcomputer Software Support Center (software; related reference materials). **Holdings:** 150,000 books and bound periodical volumes; 1 million reports on microfiche; 350,000 paper reports. **Subscriptions:** 2000 journals and other serials. **Services:** Interlibrary loan; library open to other government personnel with prior arrangement (excludes report collection). **Automated Operations:** Computerized cataloging, circulation, acquisitions, and serials. **Computerized Information Services:** DIALOG Information Services, STN International, OCLC EPIC, CompuServe Information Service, DTIC, DROLS, LEXIS, NEXIS; DDN Network Information Center (electronic mail service). **Networks/Consortia:** Member of FEDLINK. **Publications:** A Users' Guide to the Ruth H. Hooker Technical Library; Holdings List of Periodicals in the Ruth H. Hooker Library of the Naval Research Laboratory (book). **Remarks:** Alternate telephone number(s): 767-2269. FAX: (202)767-3352. Electronic mail address(es): NRL4820@CCF.NRL.NAVY.MIL (DDN Network Information Center). **Staff:** Eileen Pickenpaugh, Dp.Libn. & Hd., Lib.Serv.Sect.; Carolyn Thomas, Hd., Lib.Rsrcs.Sect.; Murray Bradley, Hd., Doc.Sect.

★ 17870 ★

U.S. Navy - Naval Research Laboratory - Underwater Sound Reference Detachment - Technical Library (Sci-Engr)
3909 S. Summerlin Ave.
Box 568337
Orlando, FL 32856-8337   Phone: (407)857-5238
    Marge Tarnowski, Libn.
Founded: 1947. **Staff:** 2. **Subjects:** Underwater sound, electroacoustics, electronics, mathematics, physics, standards. **Holdings:** 6000 books; 5053 technicl reports; 5144 documents on microfiche. **Subscriptions:** 130 journals and other serials. **Services:** Library not open to the public. **Computerized Information Services:** DIALOG Information Services, OCLC. **Networks/Consortia:** Member of Central Florida Library Consortium (CFLC). **Publications:** USRD Library Bulletin - for internal distribution only.

★ 17871 ★

U.S. Navy - Naval Research Laboratory/Monterey - Library (Sci-Engr)
Monterey, CA 93943-5006   Phone: (408)647-4791
    Joanne M. May, Libn.
Founded: 1971. **Staff:** Prof 1. **Subjects:** Meteorology. **Holdings:** 2900 books; 3000 bound periodical volumes; 7560 technical reports; 30,000 microfiche. **Subscriptions:** 125 journals and other serials. **Services:** Interlibrary loan; copying; SDI; library open to Department of Defense only. **Computerized Information Services:** DIALOG Information Services. **Publications:** Library Bulletin, biweekly - for internal distribution only. **Remarks:** FAX: (408)647-4769. **Formerly:** Its Naval Oceanographic Atmospheric Research.

★ 17872 ★

U.S. Navy - Naval School - Civil Engineer Corps Officers - Moreell Library (Sci-Engr)
CECOS, Moreell Library, Code C-35   Phone: (805)982-2826
Port Hueneme, CA 93043-5002   Deborah Gunia, Lib.Dir.
Founded: 1946. **Staff:** Prof 1; Other 1. **Subjects:** Engineering and construction management, economic analysis, civil engineering. **Special Collections:** Admiral Ben Moreell Collection (1100 volumes and correspondence). **Holdings:** 7982 books; 370 bound periodical volumes; 7468 reports and 7500 texts; 4500 course materials; 300 microfiche. **Subscriptions:** 75 journals and other serials; 3 newspapers. **Services:** Interlibrary loan; copying; library open to the public upon written request. **Computerized Information Services:** OCLC. **Networks/Consortia:** Member of FEDLINK. **Remarks:** FAX: (805)982-2918.

★ 17873 ★

U.S. Navy - Naval Sea Support Center, Pacific - Library (Mil)
Code 400T
PO Box 85548
San Diego, CA 92186-5548   Phone: (619)524-2330
    Linda West
Founded: 1979. **Staff:** 1.75. **Subjects:** Naval ships - hull, mechanical, and electrical systems; naval ordnance. **Holdings:** 70,000 naval technical documents. **Subscriptions:** 30 journals and other serials. **Services:** Library open to those who can officially establish a need to know. **Computerized Information Services:** Internal database. **Remarks:** FAX: (619)524-2230.

★ 17874 ★

U.S. Navy - Naval Sea Systems Command - Technical Library 04TD2L (Sci-Engr)
Rm. 1S15, National Center, Bldg. 3   Phone: (703)602-3349
Washington, DC 20362-5101   Elmer E. Long, III, Hd.Libn.
Founded: 1976. **Staff:** Prof 2; Other 2. **Subjects:** Engineering - marine, electrical, mechanical, nuclear; naval architecture and ordnance; marine propulsion; acoustics; shipbuilding. **Special Collections:** Complete sets of RINA Transactions and U.S. Naval Institute Proceedings. **Holdings:** 25,000 books; 2700 bound periodical volumes; 2500 technical manuals; 7000 microforms. **Subscriptions:** 150 journals and other serials. **Services:** Interlibrary loan; copying; SDI; library open to authorized navy contractors and Department of Defense components. **Automated Operations:** Computerized cataloging and circulation. **Computerized Information Services:** OCLC, DIALOG Information Services. **Networks/Consortia:** Member of FEDLINK. **Publications:** FOCUS (list of acquisitions), quarterly - to authorized Department of Defense components. **Staff:** W. Marie Crawley, Tech.Info.Spec.; Don Erickson, Libn.

★ 17875 ★

U.S. Navy - Naval Ship Systems Engineering Station Headquarters - Technical Library (Sci-Engr)
Bldg. 619, Naval Base   Phone: (215)897-7078
Philadelphia, PA 19112   Kathleen Schollenberger, Libn.
Founded: 1979. **Staff:** Prof 2; Other 3. **Subjects:** Engineering - marine, mechanical, electrical; chemistry; metallurgy. **Holdings:** 40,000 books and Navy manuals; microforms. **Subscriptions:** 150 journals and other serials. **Services:** Interlibrary loan; library not open to the public. **Computerized Information Services:** DIALOG Information Services, DTIC.

★ 17876 ★

U.S. Navy - Naval Shipyard (CA-Long Beach) - Technical Library (Sci-Engr)
Code 244.13, Bldg. 300, Rm. 358   Phone: (213)547-6515
Long Beach, CA 90822-5099   Flora Yapp, Libn.
Founded: 1943. **Staff:** Prof 1; Other 2. **Subjects:** Naval architecture, ship repair and maintenance, electronic equipment, mechanical equipment,

industrial management, occupational safety. **Special Collections:** Naval Sea Systems Command Technical Publications. **Holdings:** 3350 books; 225,000 technical manuals and reports; 177,000 microfilm copies of military specifications and standards; 1000 microfiche; 4000 American Society for Testing and Materials (ASTM) specifications; government reports relating to U.S. Fleet. **Subscriptions:** 25 journals and other serials. **Services:** Interlibrary loan; library open to Department of Defense contractors. **Publications:** Acquisitions list, irregular.

★ 17877 ★
U.S. Navy - Naval Shipyard (CA-Mare Island) - Science and Technology Library (Sci-Engr)
Code 202.13, Stop T-4
Vallejo, CA 94592-5100
Phone: (707)646-2532
Jane E. Oswitt, Adm.Libn.
Founded: 1950. **Staff:** Prof 2; Other 1. **Subjects:** Naval shipbuilding and repair; engineering - nuclear, civil, mechanical, electrical; materials science; occupational safety and health; physics. **Holdings:** 12,000 books; 1200 bound periodical volumes; 6800 technical reports; specifications and standards. **Subscriptions:** 150 journals and other serials. **Services:** Interlibrary loan; library not open to the public. **Automated Operations:** Computerized cataloging and ILL. **Computerized Information Services:** DIALOG Information Services, DTIC, OCLC. **Networks/Consortia:** Member of FEDLINK, National Network of Libraries of Medicine - Pacific Southwest Region. **Publications:** Bulletin, monthly; periodical list, irregular.

★ 17878 ★
U.S. Navy - Naval Shipyard (HI-Pearl Harbor) - Technical Library (Sci-Engr)
Code 244.5, Box 400
Pearl Harbor, HI 96860-5350
Phone: (808)474-0023
Lincoln H.S. Yu, Libn.
Founded: 1951. **Staff:** Prof 1; Other 9. **Subjects:** Engineering, naval shipbuilding. **Holdings:** 40,000 volumes. **Services:** Library not open to the public.

★ 17879 ★
U.S. Navy - Naval Shipyard (NH-Portsmouth) - Technical Library (Sci-Engr)
Code 542.2
Portsmouth, NH 03801-2590
Phone: (207)438-5506
Jeanne Aspimwall, Tech.Libn.
Founded: 1947. **Staff:** Prof 1; Other 1. **Subjects:** Submarines, naval architecture, marine and nuclear engineering, mathematics, noise and vibration, electrical engineering, materials, management. **Special Collections:** Society of Naval Architects and Marine Engineers Transactions, 1893 to present (complete set). **Holdings:** 20,000 books and bound periodical volumes; 13,000 technical reports; 4 VF drawers of reprints and pamphlets; 350 reels of microfilm; videotapes. **Subscriptions:** 180 journals and other serials. **Services:** Interlibrary loan; copying; library open to the public with restrictions.

★ 17880 ★
U.S. Navy - Naval Shipyard (PA-Philadelphia) - Technical Data Library (Sci-Engr)
Philadelphia Naval Base
Philadelphia, PA 19112
Phone: (215)897-3220
Marie Cunningham, Tech.Libn.
Founded: 1946. **Staff:** Prof 4. **Subjects:** Naval science and architecture; engineering - marine, electrical, mechanical; electronics; mathematics. **Special Collections:** Shipbuilding; naval engineering. **Holdings:** 10,000 books; 100 bound periodical volumes; 51,000 technical manuals; 5000 microfiche; 2000 cartridges of microfilm. **Subscriptions:** 203 journals and other serials. **Services:** Interlibrary loan (limited to Department of Defense); library not open to the public. **Remarks:** FAX: (215)897-3496. **Staff:** Dewey Green; Paulette Minard; Valerie Johnson.

★ 17881 ★
U.S. Navy - Naval Shipyard (SC-Charleston) - Technical Library (Sci-Engr)
Naval Base
Code 202.3, Bldg. 234, Rm. 204
Charleston, SC 29408-6100
Phone: (803)743-4071
Leola Gadsden, Lib.Techn.
Founded: 1946. **Staff:** 4. **Subjects:** Naval engineering and architecture, electronics, management, ordnance, mathematics. **Holdings:** 1000 books; 100,000 technical manuals; 1000 reports and pamphlets. **Subscriptions:** 60 periodicals. **Services:** Interlibrary loan; library not open to the public.

★ 17882 ★
U.S. Navy - Naval Shipyard (VA-Norfolk) - Technical Library (Sci-Engr)
Code 202.3, Bldg. 29, 2nd Fl.
Portsmouth, VA 23709-5000
Phone: (804)396-5674
Patsy J. Scott, Supv.Lib.Techn.
Subjects: Engineering, management, mathematics, physics, chemistry, mechanical trades. **Holdings:** 6000 books; 2500 reports; 50,000 technical manuals; 40 reels of magnetic tape. **Subscriptions:** 200 journals and other serials. **Services:** Interlibrary loan; library not open to the public.

★ 17883 ★
U.S. Navy - Naval Station Library (CA-San Diego) (Mil)
Box 224
San Diego, CA 92136
Phone: (619)556-1249
Karen High, Adm.Libn.
Staff: Prof 1; Other 3. **Subjects:** Naval history, World War II. **Special Collections:** Auxiliary Library Service Collection for Naval Officers (professional reading). **Holdings:** 26,782 books; 400 bound periodical volumes. **Subscriptions:** 161 journals and other serials; 17 newspapers. **Services:** Interlibrary loan; copying; library open to the public for reference use only. **Publications:** Current Subscriptions & Periodicals Holdings List, annual; Classified List of Periodicals, annual; Selected Acquistions List/ Naval Station General Library Bulletin, bimonthly; bibliographies; reading lists. **Remarks:** Alternate telephone number(s): 556-5450.

★ 17884 ★
U.S. Navy - Naval Station Library (FL-Mayport) (Mil)
Box 235
Mayport, FL 32228
Phone: (904)246-5393
Harvey C. Palmer, Lib.Mgr.
Staff: Prof 1; Other 1. **Subjects:** Naval history, military art and science, navigation. **Special Collections:** Chiltons Motor Repair Books. **Holdings:** 12,800 books. **Subscriptions:** 69 journals and other serials; 9 newspapers. **Services:** Interlibrary loan; library not open to the public.

★ 17885 ★
U.S. Navy - Naval Submarine Medical Research Laboratory - Medical Library (Med)
Naval Submarine Base New London
Box 900
Groton, CT 06340
Phone: (203)449-3629
Elaine M. Gaucher, Libn.
Founded: 1945. **Staff:** Prof 1; Other 1. **Subjects:** Submarine medicine, diving, physiology, psychology. **Holdings:** 4343 books; 8468 bound periodical volumes; 7000 documents; 1400 microforms; 1200 internal reports. **Subscriptions:** 175 journals and other serials. **Services:** Interlibrary loan; copying; library open to doctors, hospital staff, corpsmen, and researchers. **Automated Operations:** Computerized circulation. **Computerized Information Services:** BRS Information Technologies, MEDLARS, DTIC, DIALOG Information Services. **Networks/Consortia:** Member of Connecticut Association of Health Science Libraries (CAHSL). **Publications:** Submarine Medical Research Laboratory Reports. **Remarks:** FAX: (203)449-4809. **Staff:** Thomas Tremblay.

★ 17886 ★
U.S. Navy - Naval Supply Center - Technical Library (Sci-Engr, Mil)
937 North Harbor Dr.
Mail Code 103
San Diego, CA 92132-5044
Phone: (619)556-8484
Founded: 1950. **Staff:** 1. **Subjects:** Electronics; ordnance; weapons; fire control systems; aviation; engineering - automotive, electrical, mechanical. **Holdings:** 25,355 books and bound periodical volumes; 3136 reels of microfilm; 35,700 microfiche of military specifications and standards. **Subscriptions:** 10 journals and other serials. **Services:** Library open to qualified individuals.

★ 17887 ★
U.S. Navy - Naval Support Activity - Library (Hum)
Bldg. 47
7500 Sand Point Way, N.E.
Seattle, WA 98115
Phone: (206)526-3577
Bob Kinsedahl, Libn.
Founded: 1932. **Staff:** Prof 1. **Subjects:** Nonfiction, fiction, science, art, mystery, science fiction, history, military history. **Holdings:** 12,000 volumes; pamphlets. **Subscriptions:** 30 journals and other serials. **Services:** Library serves station personnel, retired military personnel, and dependents.

★ 17888 ★
U.S. Navy - Naval Surface Warfare Center - Technical Library (Sci-Engr, Mil)
Dahlgren Division
Mail Code E231   Phone: (703)663-8994
Dahlgren, VA 22448   Dr. J. Marshal Hughes, II, Hd.
Founded: 1953. **Staff:** Prof 14; Other 12. **Subjects:** Mathematics, electronics, physics, weapons systems, management, chemistry, materials. **Special Collections:** Independent Research and Development Navy/Industry Collection (AEGIS, electronic warfare, Tomahawk). **Holdings:** 220,000 books; 8000 bound periodical volumes; 11,200 periodical volumes on microfilm; 375,000 documents. **Subscriptions:** 553 journals and other serials. **Services:** Interlibrary loan; copying; SDI; library open with restrictions to government agencies and contractors. **Automated Operations:** Computerized cataloging. **Computerized Information Services:** DIALOG Information Services, NASA/RECON, Integrated Technical Information System (ITIS), DTIC; internal database. **Publications:** Accession Lists, biweekly; SDI, daily. **Remarks:** The Technical Library is composed of the Dahlgren, VA and Silver Spring, MD libraries. Figures represent the combined holdings of the libraries. FAX: (703)663-7165.

★ 17889 ★
U.S. Navy - Naval Surface Warfare Center - White Oak Library (Sci-Engr, Mil)
10901 New Hampshire Ave.   Phone: (202)394-1922
Silver Spring, MD 20903-5000   Katharine R. Wallace, Supv.Libn.
Founded: 1944. **Staff:** Prof 9; Other 7. **Subjects:** Naval ordnance, explosives, aerodynamics, physics, chemistry, engineering. **Holdings:** 40,000 books; 750 periodical titles; 160 periodical titles on microfilm; 200,000 technical reports. **Subscriptions:** 550 journals and other serials. **Services:** Interlibrary loan; copying (limited); library open to other government agencies and contractors. **Automated Operations:** Computerized cataloging. **Computerized Information Services:** DIALOG Information Services, National Technical Information System (NTIS), DTIC, OCLC; internal database. **Networks/Consortia:** Member of Interlibrary Users Association (IUA). **Remarks:** FAX: (202)394-3096. **Staff:** Charlotte Mullinix, Libn.; Catheryn Lee, Libn.; Jon Sellin, Info.Spec.; Sara Happel, Libn.; Judith Blatt, Libn.; Heda Van Deveuter, Libn.; David Glenn, Info.Spec.; Dale Sharrick, Libn.

★ 17890 ★
U.S. Navy - Naval Test Pilot School - Research Library (Sci-Engr, Mil)
Naval Air Test Center   Phone: (301)863-4411
Patuxent River, MD 20670   Robert B. Richards, Hd. of Academics
Founded: 1950. **Staff:** Prof 1; Other 1. **Subjects:** Aeronautical engineering, aircraft flight testing, propulsion, aircraft systems, space engineering. **Special Collections:** Aero engineering; flight testing; atmospheric propulsion. **Holdings:** 750 books; 5500 reports. **Subscriptions:** 10 journals and other serials. **Services:** Library open to U.S. government agencies.

★ 17891 ★
U.S. Navy - Naval Training Center - Library (Mil)
Bldg. 177   Phone: (619)524-5562
San Diego, CA 92133-3000   Jim Koizumi, Lib.Supv.
Founded: 1924. **Staff:** Prof 1; Other 3. **Subjects:** Naval art and science. **Special Collections:** Naval history; U.S. Naval Institute Proceedings, 1800 to present. **Holdings:** 40,000 books; 18,180 microforms. **Subscriptions:** 125 journals and other serials; 11 newspapers. **Services:** Interlibrary loan; copying; library open to the public with restrictions.

★ 17892 ★
U.S. Navy - Naval Undersea Warfare Center Division, Newport - Technical Library (Sci-Engr, Mil)
Bldg. 103   Phone: (401)841-4338
Newport, RI 02841-4421   Mary N. Barravecchia, Hd.Libn.
Staff: Prof 4. **Subjects:** Antisubmarine warfare, undersea warfare and surveillance, underwater ordnance, target detection. **Holdings:** 14,000 books; 425,000 technical documents. **Subscriptions:** 425 journals and other serials. **Services:** Interlibrary loan; library not open to the public. **Automated Operations:** Computerized cataloging (LIMASYS). **Computerized Information Services:** DIALOG Information Services, PFDS Online, DTIC, BRS Information Technologies. **Networks/Consortia:** Member of FEDLINK. **Publications:** Technical reports. **Remarks:** FAX: (401)841-3699. **Formerly:** Its Naval Underwater Systems Center. **Staff:** Philip Tomposki, Ref.Libn.; Carolyn Prescott, Libn.; George Scheck.

U.S. Navy - Naval Underwater Systems Center
See: **U.S. Navy - Naval Undersea Warfare Center Division, Newport - Technical Library** (17892)

★ 17893 ★
U.S. Navy - Naval Underwater Systems Center - New London Technical Library (Sci-Engr, Mil)
Bldg. 80   Phone: (203)440-4365
New London, CT 06320   David R. Hanna, Hd.Libn.
Founded: 1970. **Staff:** Prof 3; Other 4. **Subjects:** Underwater acoustics, ordnance, surveillance; antisubmarine warfare. **Holdings:** 35,000 volumes; 425,000 technical documents; 425,000 government reports on microfiche. **Subscriptions:** 505 journals and other serials. **Services:** Interlibrary loan; library not open to the public. **Automated Operations:** Computerized cataloging. **Computerized Information Services:** DIALOG Information Services, PFDS Online, DTIC, BRS Information Technologies, OCLC, Library Management & Retrieval System (LMARS). **Networks/Consortia:** Member of FEDLINK. **Publications:** Periodical holding list. **Remarks:** FAX: (203)440-6543. **Staff:** Charles Logan, Cat.; Jerome Barner, Ref.; Lorraine McKinney, Bks. & Per.

★ 17894 ★
U.S. Navy - Naval War College - Library (Mil, Hist)
Newport, RI 02841-5010   Phone: (401)841-2641
                                            Robert E. Schnare, Dir.
Founded: 1884. **Staff:** Prof 13; Other 20. **Subjects:** History - naval, military, diplomatic; management; leadership; organizational and behavioral theory; political science; military and naval art and science; international relations; international law; economics; history. **Special Collections:** Pre-1900 books (naval and military history, art and science, and geography); the Navy and Narrangansett Bay (manuscripts, personal papers, and oral histories); College Archives. **Holdings:** 166,000 books and bound periodical volumes; 82,000 classified documents; 23,000 periodical volumes in microform. **Subscriptions:** 735 journals and other serials. **Services:** Interlibrary loan; library open to the public with permission. **Automated Operations:** Computerized cataloging and ILL. **Computerized Information Services:** OCLC, WILSONLINE, DTIC, DIALOG Information Services; LOGDUS (internal database). **Networks/Consortia:** Member of FEDLINK, NELINET, Inc., Consortium of Rhode Island Academic and Research Libraries, Inc. (CRIARL). **Publications:** Faculty Guide, annual. **Remarks:** Alternate telephone number(s): 841-3052 (Ref.); 841-4386 (ILL). FAX: (401)841-1140. **Staff:** Michael Riggle, Hd., Rd.Serv.; Doris B. Ottaviano, Hd., Ref.Br.; Robin Lima, ILL; Evelyn Cherpak, Hd., Naval Hist.Coll.; Lucille Rosa, Hd., Tech.Serv.; Loretta Silvia, Coll.Dev.Libn.

★ 17895 ★
U.S. Navy - Naval Warfare Assessment Center - Technical Library/C-012L (Sci-Engr)
Corona, CA 91718-5000   Phone: (714)273-4467
                                         Marilyn Anderson, Tech.Libn.
Founded: 1953. **Staff:** Prof 1; Other 1. **Subjects:** Electronics, computers, mathematics, management. **Holdings:** 6000 books; 1400 bound periodical volumes; 450 reels of microfilm. **Subscriptions:** 120 journals and other serials; 5 newspapers. **Services:** Interlibrary loan; library not open to the public. **Computerized Information Services:** Online systems. **Publications:** Accessions List, biweekly - for internal distribution only. **Formerly:** Its Fleet Analysis Center (FLTAC) - Library.

★ 17896 ★
U.S. Navy - Naval Weapons Center - Library Division (Sci-Engr, Mil)
Mail Code 343   Phone: (619)939-3389
China Lake, CA 93555   Mary-Deirdre Croaggio, Hd., Lib.
Founded: 1946. **Staff:** Prof 8; Other 18. **Subjects:** Rockets, missiles, propellants, explosives, chemistry, physics, electronics, aerodynamics, parachutes. **Holdings:** 17,000 books; 50,000 bound periodical volumes; 150,000 reports; 750,000 microfiche of technical reports. **Subscriptions:** 900 journals and other serials. **Services:** Interlibrary loan; restricted access to library. **Automated Operations:** Computerized serials, document retrieval, and catalog production. **Computerized Information Services:** DIALOG Information Services, DTIC, RLIN, NASA/RECON. **Networks/Consortia:** Member of FEDLINK, CLASS. **Publications:** Accession List of Technical Reports, bimonthly; Periodicals Table of Contents List, weekly; Periodicals List, annual; Guide to the Use of NWC Technical Library; Accession List of Books, monthly. **Staff:** Sandra M. Friedman, Hd., Customer Serv.Br.; Alice A. Pastorius, Act.Hd., Info. Access Br.

★ 17897 ★
U.S. Navy - Naval Weapons Station - Command Library (Mil)
Code 012L   Phone: (213)594-7142
Seal Beach, CA 90740-5000   Barbara J. Galbraith
Founded: 1943. **Staff:** Prof 6. **Subjects:** Ordnance and explosives, statistics and mathematics, naval and military science, chemistry and technology, materials and standards, electronics and optics. **Holdings:** 11,000 books; 13,000 technical manuals; 400,000 aperture cards; 7000 magnetic tapes; microforms. **Subscriptions:** 440 journals and other serials; 10 newspapers. **Services:** Interlibrary loan; copying; SDI. **Automated Operations:** Computerized cataloging, acquisitions, serials, and circulation. **Computerized Information Services:** NASA Research and Development Contracts Search File, NTIS Bibliographic Data Base, USNI Military Database. **Publications:** Weaponeer (newsletter), weekly - for internal distribution only. **Remarks:** The Naval Weapons Station is one of three facilities that comprise the Command Library. Additional facilities are located at the Naval Warfare Assessment Center, Corona, CA 91720-5000; and Naval Weapons Station, Fallbrook, CA 92028. **Staff:** Jerry Hawk, Supv.; Marilyn Anderson, Corona Libn.; Geraldine Stone, Seal Beach Libn.

★ 17898 ★
U.S. Navy - Naval Weapons Station - Library (Sci-Engr, Mil)
Bldg. 705   Phone: (804)887-4726
Yorktown, VA 23691-5000   Eleanor Lacy Sorokatch, Libn.
Founded: 1961. **Staff:** Prof 1. **Subjects:** Naval mines, missiles, torpedoes, corrosion, depth charges, explosives, underwater weapons, engineering. **Holdings:** 10,000 books; 5000 technical reports. **Subscriptions:** 135 journals and other serials. **Services:** Interlibrary loan; copying; library open to qualified persons by permission. **Publications:** Accession Lists, monthly.

★ 17899 ★
U.S. Navy - Naval Weapons Support Center - Library (Sci-Engr, Mil)
Code 016   Phone: (812)854-3143
Crane, IN 47522-5000   Anne Johnson, Supv.Tech.Info.Spec.
Founded: 1958. **Staff:** 7. **Subjects:** Explosives, ammunition, pyrotechnics, engineering, military science, electronics. **Holdings:** 4300 books. **Subscriptions:** 100 journals and other serials. **Services:** Interlibrary loan; library not open to the public. **Computerized Information Services:** DTIC, DIALOG Information Services, OCLC. **Networks/Consortia:** Member of Four Rivers Area Library Services Authority (ALSA), INCOLSA.

★ 17900 ★
U.S. Navy - Navy Personnel Research & Development Center - Library (Soc Sci)
Code 041   Phone: (619)553-7841
San Diego, CA 92152-6800   Char-Lou Dinger, Libn.
Founded: 1953. **Staff:** Prof 1; Other 3. **Subjects:** Industrial and social psychology, education, computer technology, human factors, management science. **Holdings:** 15,000 books; 4700 bound periodical volumes; 100,000 technical reports. **Subscriptions:** 450 journals and other serials. **Services:** Interlibrary loan; copying; library open to the public with a need to know. **Automated Operations:** Computerized cataloging and circulation. **Computerized Information Services:** DIALOG Information Services, OCLC; internal database. **Networks/Consortia:** Member of FEDLINK. **Publications:** Accessions list, weekly; periodical list, annual. **Remarks:** Alternate telephone number(s): 553-7842; 553-7846.

★ 17901 ★
U.S. Navy - Office of the Chief of Naval Research - Library (Biol Sci, Sci-Engr, Mil)
Code 01231L
800 N. Quincy St.   Phone: (202)696-4415
Arlington, VA 22217-5000   W.F. Rettenmaier, Jr., Libn.
Founded: 1948. **Staff:** 2. **Subjects:** Biological and medical sciences, physical and chemical sciences, naval and marine sciences, social sciences. **Holdings:** 150 reference books. **Subscriptions:** 260 journals and other serials; 5 newspapers. **Services:** Interlibrary loan; library not open to the public. **Computerized Information Services:** DIALOG Information Services, OCLC. **Networks/Consortia:** Member of FEDLINK. **Remarks:** FAX: (202)696-5383.

★ 17902 ★
U.S. Navy - Office of the General Counsel - Law Library (Law, Mil)
Crystal Plaza 5, Rm. 450   Phone: (703)602-2750
Washington, DC 20360-5110   Erika Teal, Hd.Libn.
Founded: 1949. **Staff:** Prof 2. **Subjects:** Government contracts, civilian personnel law. **Holdings:** 30,000 books; 1400 bound periodical volumes. **Services:** Interlibrary loan; copying (both limited); library open to authorized federal government employees. **Automated Operations:** Computerized cataloging. **Computerized Information Services:** DIALOG Information Services, WESTLAW. **Networks/Consortia:** Member of FEDLINK. **Remarks:** FAX: (703)602-4532. **Staff:** Mary Williams, Ref.Libn.

★ 17903 ★
U.S. Navy - Office of the Judge Advocate General - Law Library (Law, Mil)
Code 64.3
Hoffman Bldg. 2
200 Stovall St.   Phone: (703)325-9565
Alexandria, VA 22332-2400   Susan S. Roach, Hd.
Staff: Prof 3; Other 4. **Subjects:** Law - military, international, criminal. **Special Collections:** Opinions of the Judge Advocate General (unpublished); Decisions of the U.S. Navy Court of Military Review (unpublished). **Holdings:** 50,000 volumes; 29 VF drawers. **Subscriptions:** 95 journals and other serials. **Services:** Interlibrary loan; library open to the public by appointment. **Computerized Information Services:** OCLC, WESTLAW; SHIPS (electronic mail service). **Networks/Consortia:** Member of FEDLINK. **Remarks:** Supports 300 field libraries. FAX: (202)325-2158. **Staff:** Mary Carver, Acq.

★ 17904 ★
U.S. Navy - Pacific Missile Test Center - Technical Library (Sci-Engr)
Code 1018, Bldg. 511A   Phone: (805)989-8156
Point Mugu, CA 93042   Veronica L. Briggs, Libn.
Founded: 1948. **Staff:** Prof 1; Other 1. **Subjects:** Aeronautics, mathematics, electronics, astronautics, meteorology, oceanography, naval history, physics, radar technology. **Holdings:** 17,000 books; 9000 bound periodical volumes; 1000 reels of microfilm. **Subscriptions:** 100 journals and other serials. **Services:** Interlibrary loan; library open to Department of Defense personnel and others with librarian's permission. **Networks/Consortia:** Member of Total Interlibrary Exchange (TIE). **Publications:** Bibliographies.

★ 17905 ★
U.S. Navy - Puget Sound Naval Shipyard - Engineering Library (Mil)
Code 203.5   Phone: (206)476-2767
Bremerton, WA 98314-5000   Marilyn Drengson, Libn.
Founded: 1936. **Staff:** Prof 1. **Subjects:** Engineering, naval architecture, management, computer science, Navy ships and history. **Holdings:** 12,000 books; 10,000 industry standards. **Subscriptions:** 281 journals and other serials. **Services:** Interlibrary loan; library not open to the public. **Computerized Information Services:** DIALOG Information Services. **Remarks:** FAX: (206)476-6186.

U.S. Navy - Regional Data Automation Center - Technical Library
See: U.S. Navy - Naval Computer & Telecomm Station (17831)

★ 17906 ★
U.S. Navy - Strategic Systems Programs - Technical Library (Sci-Engr, Mil)
Blbc CM3   Phone: (703)607-1240
Arlington, VA 22002   Leonard Broomfield, Tech.Lib.Br.Hd.
Staff: Prof 1; Other 2. **Subjects:** Missile technology, mathematics, electronics, solid propellants, management. **Holdings:** 2500 books; 40,000 technical reports; 4 VF drawers of pamphlets. **Subscriptions:** 175 journals and other serials. **Services:** Interlibrary loan; library open to persons with appropriate security clearance and need-to-know. **Automated Operations:** Computerized cataloging. **Computerized Information Services:** DIALOG Information Services, OCLC. **Networks/Consortia:** Member of FEDLINK. **Formerly:** Located in Washington, DC.

★ 17907 ★
U.S. Navy - Submarine Force Library & Museum - Library (Mil)
Naval Submarine Base New London
Box 571　　　　　　　　　Phone: (203)449-3558
Groton, CT 06349-5000　　　William Galuani, Cur.
Founded: 1955. **Subjects:** Submarine history - U.S. and general. **Special Collections:** U.S. submarine history collection (individual volumes for each submarine in U.S. history); U.S. submarines in World War II (300 war patrol reports). **Holdings:** 8000 books; 200 bound periodical volumes; 2000 documents; 100 films. **Services:** Library open to the public for reference use only and by appointment. **Remarks:** Toll-free telephone number(s): (800)343-0079. **Staff:** Theresa Cass, Archv.

★ 17908 ★
U.S. Navy - Supervisor of Shipbuilding, Conversion and Repair -
Technical Library (Sci-Engr, Mil)
U.S. Naval Station, Code 244 TL
32nd St. & Harbor Dr.
Box 119　　　　　　　　　Phone: (619)556-1021
San Diego, CA 92136-5119　　Patricia Parker, Lib.Techn.
Founded: 1960. **Staff:** Prof 2; Other 2. **Subjects:** Ship systems, ordnance, electronics, engineering. **Holdings:** 100,000 books and bound periodical volumes; 500 reels of microfilm of military and federal specifications; 300 reels of microfilm of design information files; manuals and textbooks. **Subscriptions:** 10 journals and other serials. **Services:** Interlibrary loan; library open to federal personnel and government contractors. **Remarks:** Alternate telephone number(s): (619)556-1011.

★ 17909 ★
U.S. Navy - U.S. Marine Corps Air Station (MCAS El Toro) - Station
Library (Mil)
Bldg. 280　　　　　　　　　Phone: (714)726-2569
Santa Ana, CA 92709-5007　　Karen L. Hayward, Adm.Libn.
Founded: 1942. **Staff:** Prof 5; Other 2. **Subjects:** Genreal, military history and science, biography, social science. **Special Collections:** Early California history; U.S. Marine Corps and military aviation history; Library of American Civilization (LAC; microfiche). **Holdings:** 55,000 books and bound periodical volumes; 19,000 volumes in microform; microfiche. **Subscriptions:** 200 journals and other serials; 13 newspapers. **Services:** Interlibrary loan; library not open to the public. **Automated Operations:** Computerized cataloging, acquisitions, and circulation. **Remarks:** FAX: (714)726-2575.

★ 17910 ★
U.S. Navy - U.S. Marine Corps Air Station (MCAS Tustin) - Station
Library (Mil)
Bldg. 2　　　　　　　　　Phone: (714)726-7265
Tustin, CA 92710　　　　　Karen L. Hayward, Sta.Libn.
Founded: 1945. **Staff:** Prof 1; Other 4. **Subjects:** Military history, biography, social science. **Holdings:** 18,109 books. **Subscriptions:** 64 journals and other serials; 6 newspapers. **Services:** Interlibrary loan; library not open to the public.

★ 17911 ★
U.S. News & World Report - Library (Publ)
2400 N St., N.W.　　　　　Phone: (202)955-2350
Washington, DC 20037-1196　Kathleen Trimble, Lib.Dir.
Founded: 1933. **Staff:** Prof 13; Other 8. **Subjects:** Current events, government, politics, history, economics, law. **Holdings:** 10,000 books; 2000 volumes of congressional hearings and reports; 2500 vertical files; 6600 newspaper clipping files; 9000 biographical files; 100 newspaper and periodical titles in microform. **Subscriptions:** 600 journals and other serials; 30 newspapers. **Services:** Interlibrary loan; library not open to the public. **Automated Operations:** Computerized public access catalog, cataloging, acquisitions, serials, and circulation. **Computerized Information Services:** DIALOG Information Services, VU/TEXT Information Services, DataTimes, Dow Jones News/Retrieval, BRS Information Technologies, WILSONLINE, Washington Alert Service, Reuter TEXTLINE, FT PROFILE, NEXIS, Periscope, Public Opinion Location Library (POLL), LEXIS, BASELINE, NewsNet, Inc., Info Globe, Burrelle's Broadcast, Reuters Country Reports, OCLC. **Networks/Consortia:** Member of CAPCON Library Network. **Publications:** Library guide with periodicals list (online) - for internal distribution only. **Special Indexes:** Index to U.S. News & World Report (printed, through 1979; card, 1980-1986; online, 1987 to present). **Remarks:** FAX: (202)955-2506. **Staff:** Kate Forsyth, Asst.Dir.; Judith Katzung, Newspaper File Mgr.; Nancy Langford, Index Ed.; Anne Bradley, Online Database Coord.; Jamie Russell, Mgr., New York Bur.

★ 17912 ★
U.S. Nuclear Regulatory Commission - Law Library (Law)
1 White Flint, N., 15-B-11　　Phone: (301)492-1526
Washington, DC 20555　　Charlotte Carnahan, Chf., Legal Info.Serv.
Staff: Prof 3. **Subjects:** Law - nuclear energy, environmental, administrative. **Special Collections:** Publications of the Joint Committee on Atomic Energy, 1945-1975 (complete set); AEC and NRC Reports, 1956 to present. **Holdings:** 10,000 books; 1500 bound periodical volumes; 500 technical documents; 20 drawers of Federal Register, Congressional Record, law journals in microform. **Subscriptions:** 113 journals and other serials. **Services:** Interlibrary loan; library open to the public when librarian is present. **Computerized Information Services:** LEXIS, WESTLAW. **Publications:** Law Library News, monthly - for internal distribution only. **Special Catalogs:** Administrative Law Article File (card, loose-leaf); Law Review Articles & Speeches (loose-leaf). **Special Indexes:** Significant Federal Court Case File - AEC and NRC issues (loose-leaf). **Remarks:** FAX: (301)443-7725. **Also Known As:** NRC. **Staff:** Sauci S. Churchill, Law Libn.; Christine Pierpoint, Leg.Spec.

★ 17913 ★
U.S. Nuclear Regulatory Commission - Public Document Room (Energy)
Washington, DC 20555　　　Phone: (202)634-3273
　　　　　　　　　　　Elizabeth Yeates, Br.Chf.
Subjects: Nuclear power - licensing and regulation of nuclear facilities and materials, Advisory Committee on Reactor Safeguards activities, commission meetings, export and import licenses, Freedom of Information Act requests, nuclear waste management, rulemakings, research work sponsored by the NRC, and allied nuclear safety topics. **Holdings:** 1.75 million documents in print and microfiche. **Services:** Copying; room open to the public. **Computerized Information Services:** Internal database. **Publications:** Public Document Room User's Guide; accession lists; How to Use the PDR Accession Lists. **Remarks:** FAX: (202)634-3343. Library located at 2120 L St., N.W., Lower Level, Washington, D.C. 20037. Room does not maintain collections of formally published books or periodicals. Requests may be made in person or by telephone, mail, or fax.

U.S. Office of Education - Region VI - Educational Resources
Information Center
See: **Dallas Public Library - J. Erik Jonsson Central Library - History**
and Social Sciences Division (4567)

U.S. Office of Personnel Management
See: **Office of Personnel Management** (12251)

★ 17914 ★
U.S. Office of Technology Assessment - Information Center (Plan, Sci-
Engr)
Congress of the United States　　Phone: (202)228-6150
Washington, DC 20510　　　Gail M. Kouril, Mgr., Info.Serv.
Founded: 1974. **Staff:** Prof 3; Other 2. **Subjects:** Technology assessment, future, science policy. **Holdings:** 6000 books; 300,000 microfiche; 1000 documents in VF drawers. **Subscriptions:** 500 journals and other serials; 6 newspapers. **Services:** Interlibrary loan; copying; SDI; center open to the public with restrictions. **Automated Operations:** Computerized cataloging, acquisitions, serials, and circulation. **Computerized Information Services:** DIALOG Information Services, MEDLINE, Library of Congress Information System (LOCIS), House Information Systems (HIS), NEXIS, LEXIS, Dow Jones News/Retrieval. **Networks/Consortia:** Member of FEDLINK. **Publications:** FOCUS (newsletter), biweekly. **Special Indexes:** Quotation, a computerized index of Office of Technology Assessment publications. **Remarks:** FAX: (202)228-6150. The Office of Technology Assistance is under the direction of the U.S. Congress. **Staff:** Debra McCurry, Ref./ILL; Linda Jo Trout, Ref.

★ 17915 ★
U.S. Office of Thrift Supervision - Law Library (Law, Bus-Fin)
1700 G St., N.W.　　　　　Phone: (202)906-6470
Washington, DC 20552　　　Joyce A. Potter, Chf.Lib.Serv.
Founded: 1933. **Staff:** 4. **Subjects:** Law, savings and loan associations. **Holdings:** 24,000 volumes. **Services:** Interlibrary loan; library not open to the public. **Automated Operations:** Computerized cataloging. **Computerized Information Services:** LEXIS, NEXIS, OCLC, WESTLAW, Washington Alert Service. **Remarks:** FAX: (202)906-7495; 789-2670. **Staff:** Shirley Bornstein, Libn./Cat.; Eileen Forest, Acq.Techn.

★17916★
U.S. Office of Thrift Supervision - Research Library (Bus-Fin)
1700 G St., N.W.   Phone: (202)906-6296
Washington, DC 20552   Cheryl Wright, Libn.
Founded: 1935. **Staff:** Prof 2; Other 2. **Subjects:** Real estate, finance, banking, savings and loan, business, economics. **Special Collections:** Files of annual reports of savings and loan supervisory authorities. **Holdings:** 25,000 volumes; 12 VF drawers of pamphlets and statistical reports. **Subscriptions:** 575 journals and other serials; 14 newspapers. **Services:** Interlibrary loan; copying; library open to the public on request. **Automated Operations:** Computerized cataloging and serials. **Computerized Information Services:** DIALOG Information Services, Dow Jones News/Retrieval, DunsPrint, NEXIS, OCLC. **Publications:** Library Handbook; Library Bulletin, monthly; Acquisition List, monthly - limited distribution. **Special Catalogs:** Union List of Serials.

★17917★
U.S. Olympic Committee - Olympic Resource & Information Center (Med)
Dept. Information Resources
1750 E. Boulder St.   Phone: (719)578-4622
Colorado Springs, CO 80909   Cindy Slater, Mgr., Dept.Info.Rsrcs.
Founded: 1981. **Staff:** Prof 2; Other 2. **Subjects:** Sports medicine - exercise physiology, biomechanics, sports psychology, vision and dental screening, athletic training, injury prevention and treatment, health maintenance and conditioning, coaching science. **Holdings:** 3500 books; unbound periodicals; 2000 reprints; sports rulebooks; U.S. Olympic Committee central files of photographs, slides, and 16mm films; N.G.B. constitutions and by-laws. **Subscriptions:** 400 journals and other serials; 5 newspapers. **Services:** Interlibrary loan; copying; SDI; center open to the public for reference use only. **Automated Operations:** Computerized cataloging, serials, ILL, and indexes. **Computerized Information Services:** PFDS Online, DIALOG Information Services, BRS Information Technologies. **Networks/Consortia:** Member of Bibliographical Center for Research, Rocky Mountain Region, Inc. (BCR), Colorado Council of Medical Librarians. **Remarks:** FAX: (719)632-5352. **Staff:** Carrie Clifton, Libn.

★17918★
U.S. Patent & Trademark Office - Scientific and Technical Information Center (Sci-Engr)
Crystal Plaza Bldg. 3
2021 Jefferson Davis Hwy.   Phone: (703)308-0810
Arlington, VA 22202   Henry Rosicky, Prog.Mgr.
Founded: 1836. **Staff:** Prof 33; Other 38. **Subjects:** Technology, applied science. **Special Collections:** Foreign patents (20 million in numerical arrangement); Project XL. **Holdings:** 195,000 books and bound periodical volumes; 435 titles on microfilm; U.S. Government documents depository (selective). **Subscriptions:** 1500 journals and other serials. **Services:** Interlibrary loan; copying; library open to the public for reference use only. **Automated Operations:** Computerized cataloging, serials, and circulation. **Computerized Information Services:** DIALOG Information Services, OCLC, PFDS Online, STN International, Chemical Abstracts Service (CAS), DTIC, Questel, Automated Patent Searching (APS); IG-Suite Sequence Database (internal database). **Networks/Consortia:** Member of FEDLINK. **Publications:** Biotech Newsletter. **Remarks:** FAX: (703)308-0989. The Patent & Trademark Office is part of the U.S. Department of Commerce. **Staff:** Kay H. Melvin, Chf., Sci.Lit.Div.; Kathleen Dell'Orto, Chf. Foreign Docs.Div.; Michael Moore, Chf., Chem./Biotech Div.

★17919★
U.S. Peace Corps - Library (Soc Sci, Sci-Engr)
1990 K St., N.W., Rm. E-5333   Phone: (202)606-3307
Washington, DC 20526   Marian P. Francois, Dir.
Founded: 1966. **Staff:** Prof 1; Other 2. **Subjects:** Peace Corps, developing countries in Asia, Africa, Latin America, the South Pacific Islands, Caribbean, Central Europe; economic development; cross-cultural studies; community development; appropriate technology; women in development, voluntarism. **Special Collections:** Foreign language learning materials. **Holdings:** 27,000 books; 54 shelves of folder materials. **Subscriptions:** 265 journals and other serials. **Services:** Interlibrary loan; copying; SDI; division open to the public. **Automated Operations:** Computerized cataloging. **Computerized Information Services:** DIALOG Information Services, OCLC, NEXIS. **Networks/Consortia:** Member of FEDLINK. **Publications:** List of Acquisitions, monthly; country and specialized bibliographies and resource lists. **Special Indexes:** Country and vertical file indexes (online). **Remarks:** FAX: (202)606-3110.

★17920★
U.S. Postal Service - Library (Bus-Fin)
475 L'Enfant Plaza, S.W.   Phone: (202)268-2904
Washington, DC 20260   Jane F. Kennedy, Gen.Mgr.
Founded: 1955. **Staff:** Prof 5; Other 7. **Subjects:** Management, law, engineering, economics, marketing, electronic data processing. **Special Collections:** History and operation of U.S. Postal Service. **Holdings:** 55,000 volumes; 40,000 microforms; 59,000 government documents. **Subscriptions:** 1600 journals and other serials. **Services:** Interlibrary loan; copying; library open to the public for reference use only. **Computerized Information Services:** OCLC, DIALOG Information Services, LEXIS, WESTLAW, NEXIS, Dun & Bradstreet Business Credit Services, Dow Jones News/Retrieval. **Remarks:** FAX: (202)554-1388. **Staff:** Jerry Mansfield, Hd.Ref.; Robert F. Gardner, Hd., Tech.Serv.

★17921★
U.S. Presidential Libraries - Dwight D. Eisenhower Library (Hist)
S.E. 4th St.   Phone: (913)263-4751
Abilene, KS 67410   Daniel D. Holt, Dir.
Founded: 1961. **Staff:** Prof 25; Other 10. **Subjects:** Dwight D. Eisenhower - life, presidency, military career; World War II. **Special Collections:** Papers of Dwight D. Eisenhower and his associates. **Holdings:** 24,000 books; 21 million pages of manuscripts; 12,000 government documents; 23,000 items in VF drawers; 250,000 photographs; 2205 hours of sound recordings; 4055 reels of microfilm; 675,000 feet of motion picture film. **Subscriptions:** 75 journals and other serials. **Services:** Interlibrary loan (limited); copying; library open to the public on written application to the director. **Publications:** Overview (newsletter), quarterly - available on request; Dwight D. Eisenhower: A Selected Bibliography of Periodical and Dissertation Literature. **Special Catalogs:** List of Holdings, biennial - available on request; registers to manuscript collections. **Remarks:** Maintained by the National Archives & Records Administration.

★17922★
U.S. Presidential Libraries - Franklin D. Roosevelt Library (Hist)
511 Albany Post Rd.   Phone: (914)229-8114
Hyde Park, NY 12538   William R. Emerson, Dir.
Founded: 1941. **Staff:** Prof 11; Other 7. **Subjects:** The New Deal, 1933-1940; World War II; Franklin D. Roosevelt; American naval history, 1775-1945; American political and social history, 1900-1950. **Special Collections:** Papers of Franklin and Eleanor Roosevelt and various associates; American children's books, 18th-19th centuries; Franklin D. Roosevelt's naval history library, manuscripts, and ship models; Americana and Hudson Valley local history books and manuscripts; Archives of the Livingston Family, 1680-1880; papers of Henry Morgenthau Jr. **Holdings:** 45,000 books; 79,000 pamphlets and serials; 16 million manuscripts; 130,000 photographs; 21,000 museum objects; 2500 reels of microfilm; 500 microfiche; 300,000 feet of motion picture film; 1100 phonograph records; 1000 audiotapes. **Subscriptions:** 40 journals and other serials. **Services:** Interlibrary loan; copying; library open to the public upon application. **Networks/Consortia:** Member of Southeastern New York Library Resources Council (SENYLRC). **Publications:** Franklin D. Roosevelt and Conservation, 1911-1945, 2 volumes, 1957; Calendar of Speeches and Other Published Statements of Franklin D. Roosevelt, 1910-1920; Franklin D. Roosevelt and Foreign Affairs, 10 volumes, 1979; Era of Franklin D. Roosevelt: A Selected Bibliography of Periodical, Essay, and Dissertation Literature, 1945-1971; The Roosevelt-Churchill Messages (microfilm); The Press Conferences of Franklin D. Roosevelt, 1933-1945 (microfilm). **Remarks:** Maintained by National Archives & Records Administration. **Staff:** Verne Newton, Dir.; Sheryl Griffith, Libn.; Frances M. Seeber, Asst.Dir.; Raymond Teichman, Supv.Archv.; Mark Renovitch, AV Archv.; Alycia Vivona, Musm.Reg.

★17923★
U.S. Presidential Libraries - Gerald R. Ford Library (Hist)
1000 Beal Ave.   Phone: (313)668-2218
Ann Arbor, MI 48109   Frank Mackaman, Dir.
Founded: 1981. **Staff:** Prof 12; Other 2. **Subjects:** Gerald R. Ford's Presidency, 1974-1977; U.S. domestic, social, and foreign policies; U.S. party politics; Gerald Ford biography. **Special Collections:** Papers of Gerald R. Ford, 1948 to present; papers of Federal Reserve Board Chairman Arthur Burns, 1969-1978 (199 feet); Market Opinion Research President Robert Teeter papers, 1967-1977 (25 feet); National Council for U.S.-China Trade records, 1973-1982 (307 feet); Gerald R. Ford scrapbooks, 1929 to present (31 feet; 71 volumes); White House staff files, 1974-1977. **Holdings:** 8500 books; 50 bound periodical volumes; 9000 linear feet of archival/manuscripts collections; 312,000 still photographs; 2600 audiotapes; 780,000

feet of film; 765 videotapes; 460 reels of microfilm. **Subscriptions:** 34 journals and other serials. **Services:** Interlibrary loan (limited); copying; library open to the public; research grants program. **Computerized Information Services:** PRESNET (internal database). Performs searches free of charge. **Publications:** Historical Materials in Gerald Ford Library (guide) - free upon request. **Special Catalogs:** Inventory of each archival collection (print). **Special Indexes:** Keyword index to Ford Presidential statements (card); index to Ford daily appointments and trips (database); PRESNET index to White House and other files. **Remarks:** FAX: (313)668-2341. Maintained by the National Archives and Records Administration. **Staff:** David A. Horrocks, Supv.Archv.; Richard Holzhausen, AV Archv.

★ 17924 ★

U.S. Presidential Libraries - Harry S Truman Library (Hist)
U.S. Hwy. 24 & Delaware St.   Phone: (816)833-1400
Independence, MO 64050   Dr. Benedict K. Zobrist, Dir.
Founded: 1957. **Staff:** Prof 9; Other 20. **Subjects:** Career and administration of President Harry S Truman. **Holdings:** 38,178 books; 2264 bound periodical volumes; 13.9 million manuscripts on paper; 92,888 other printed items; 460 oral history interviews; 25 VF drawers. **Subscriptions:** 75 journals and other serials. **Services:** Interlibrary loan; copying; library open to the public by written application. **Publications:** Harry S Truman Library/Institute Newsletter: Whistlestop, quarterly. **Special Catalogs:** Historical Materials in the Harry S Truman Library (book). **Remarks:** Maintained by National Archives & Records Administration. **Staff:** Dr. George H. Curtis, Asst.Dir.

★ 17925 ★

U.S. Presidential Libraries - Herbert Hoover Library (Hist)
West Branch, IA 52358   Phone: (319)643-5301
                Richard Norton Smith, Dir.
Founded: 1962. **Staff:** Prof 8; Other 14. **Subjects:** Herbert Hoover, 20th century history with special emphasis on the period 1920-1960. **Special Collections:** Manuscripts of George Akerson, American Child Health Association, Arthur A. Ballantine, Harriet C. Brown, Herbert D. Brown, Delph E. Carpenter, William R. Castle, Kenneth W. Colegrove, Colorado River Commission, George C. Drescher, Ralph Evans, Frederick M. Feiker, James P. Goodrich, Harold R. Gross, George Hastings, Bourke B. Hickenlooper, Herbert Hoover, Lou Henry Hoover, Hoover Commissions of 1947 and 1953, Theodore G. Joslin, Rose Wilder Lane, Irwin B. Laughlin, Robert H. Lucas, Nathan W. MacChesney, William P. MacCracken, Hanford MacNider, Verne Marshall, Ferdinand L. Mayer, John F. Meck, Felix Morley, William C. Mullendore, Bradley Nash, Gerald Nye, Maurice Pate, Westbrook Pegler, John F. Shafroth, Truman Smith, Oscar C. Stine, Lewis H. Strauss, French Strother, Charles C. Tansill, Henry J. Taylor, Walter Trohan, Ray Lyman Wilbur, Hugh R. Wilson, Richard L. Wilson, Robert E. Wood. **Holdings:** 23,700 volumes; 40,750 photographs; 154,941 feet of motion picture film; 2799 reels of microfilm; 81 microfiche; 11,695 pages of oral history transcripts; 452 hours of sound recordings; 78 audiodiscs; 51 hours of video. **Subscriptions:** 23 journals and other serials. **Services:** Interlibrary loan (limited); copying; library open to researchers who apply in writing. **Special Catalogs:** Book catalog; photographs; finding aids and selected indexes for manuscript collections; Historical Materials in the Herbert Hoover Presidential Library - free upon request. **Remarks:** FAX: (319)643-5825. Maintained by National Archives & Records Administration. **Staff:** Mildred Mather, Archv.-Libn.

★ 17926 ★

U.S. Presidential Libraries - Jimmy Carter Library (Hist)
One Copenhill Ave.   Phone: (404)331-3942
Atlanta, GA 30307   Dr. Donald B. Schewe, Dir.
Founded: 1986. **Staff:** Prof 8; Other 20. **Subjects:** Presidency of Jimmy Carter. **Holdings:** Papers of Jimmy Carter during his presidency (27 million pages). **Subscriptions:** 25 journals and other serials. **Services:** Copying; library open to the public. **Automated Operations:** Computerized cataloging and acquisitions. **Computerized Information Services:** DIALOG Information Services, WILSONLINE. **Networks/Consortia:** Member of FEDLINK. **Remarks:** FAX: (404)730-2215. Maintained by National Archives & Records Administration. **Staff:** John Patillo, Libn.; Sylvia Naguib, Musm.Cur.

★ 17927 ★

U.S. Presidential Libraries - John F. Kennedy Library (Hist, Hum)
Columbia Point   Phone: (617)929-4500
Boston, MA 02125   Charles U. Daly, Dir.
Founded: 1963. **Staff:** Prof 16; Other 40. **Subjects:** John F. Kennedy and his administration, mid-20th century American politics and government.

Special Collections: Oral history; Robert Kennedy papers; Ernest Hemingway papers. **Holdings:** 35,000 volumes; 30 million manuscript pages; 2.2 million pages of records of the Democratic National Committee; 500,000 pages of collections of personal papers; 40,000 pages of oral history interviews; 12,500 museum objects; 2500 reels of records and papers; 150,000 photographs; 5400 sound recordings; 6.5 million feet of motion picture film. **Subscriptions:** 8 journals and other serials. **Services:** Interlibrary loan; copying; library open to the public. **Special Catalogs:** Historical Materials in the John F. Kennedy Library. **Remarks:** FAX: (617)929-4538. Maintained by National Archives & Records Administration. **Staff:** E. William Johnson, Chf.Archv.; Ronald E. Whealan, Libn.; David F. Powers, Musm.Cur.; Allan B. Goodrich, AV Archv.

★ 17928 ★

U.S. Presidential Libraries - Lyndon B. Johnson Library and Museum (Hist)
2313 Red River St.   Phone: (512)482-5137
Austin, TX 78705   Harry J. Middleton, Dir.
Founded: 1971. **Staff:** Prof 22; Other 6. **Subjects:** Lyndon B. Johnson - career, administration, family, papers; U.S. Presidency; American political, social, and economic history, 1937 to present. **Special Collections:** Oral history interviews; individual personal papers. **Holdings:** 16,369 books; 4406 unbound periodicals; 4926 transcripts of Congressional hearings; 31.5 million archives-manuscript pages; 614,453 photographs; 7401 video recordings; 13,096 sound recordings; 37,101 museum items; 824,773 feet of motion picture film; 14 VF drawers of periodical articles; 5 VF drawers of papers and dissertations; 13 VF drawers of newspaper clippings. **Subscriptions:** 13 journals and other serials. **Services:** Interlibrary loan (limited); copying; library open to the public. **Publications:** The Lyndon B. Johnson Library - to visitors; Historical Materials in the Lyndon Baines Johnson Library (list of holdings) - free upon request. **Special Catalogs:** Finding aids to papers of Lyndon B. Johnson as President, Congressman, Senator, and Vice President (notebook form); finding aids to oral histories. **Special Indexes:** Variety of searches on researcher topics - free upon request. **Remarks:** Maintained by National Archives & Records Administration. FAX: (512)478-9104 (LBJ Foundation). **Staff:** Charles W. Corkran, Asst.Dir.; Christina Houston, Supv.Archv.; David C. Humphrey, Sr.Archv.; Gary Yarrington, Musm.Cur.; Frank Wolfe, Chf., Tech.Serv.; Katherine Frankum, Adm.Off.

★ 17929 ★

U.S. Presidential Libraries - Ronald Reagan Library (Hist)
40 Presidential Dr.   Phone: (805)522-8444
Simi Valley, CA 93065   Dr. Ralph Bledsoe, Dir.
Founded: 1991. **Staff:** Prof 22; Other 8. **Subjects:** Ronald Reagan, presidency, the 1980s - U.S. history, U.S. politics, U.S. government, world history. **Special Collections:** Presidential Records (1981-89; 43 million pages); personal papers and financial records relating to Ronald Reagan (1981-89; 4 million pages); audiovisual collection (1.5 million still photographs; 20,000 videotapes; 22,000 audiocassettes); museum objects (75,000). **Holdings:** 15,000 books; 47 million pages of archives; 6000 microfiche; 25 reels of microfilm; 38,000 serials. **Services:** Interlibrary loan (limited); library open to the public. **Computerized Information Services:** Document index to select portion of presidential records (internal database). Performs searches. **Publications:** Preliminary List of Holdings. **Remarks:** FAX: (805)522-9621.

★ 17930 ★

U.S. Presidential Museum - Library of the Presidents (Hist)
622 N. Lee St.   Phone: (915)332-7123
Odessa, TX 79761   B.R. Reese, Musm.Dir.
Founded: 1964. **Staff:** Prof 2; Other 10. **Subjects:** U.S. Presidents, presidential candidates, Vice Presidents, First Ladies, political parties, campaigns. **Holdings:** 4000 volumes; 500 volumes of rare and first edition books; unbound periodicals. **Subscriptions:** 53 journals and other serials. **Services:** Library open to the public for reference use only by appointment on a limited schedule.

U.S. Public Health Service - Centers for Disease Control
See: U.S. Centers for Disease Control (17125)

U.S. Public Health Service - Food & Drug Administration
See: U.S. Food & Drug Administration (17508)

U.S. Public Health Service - Health Resources and Services Administration - National Center for Education in Maternal and Child Health
See: National Center for Education in Maternal and Child Health - Library (11102)

U.S. Public Health Service - Mescalero Public Health Service Hospital
See: Mescalero Public Health Service Hospital (10172)

U.S. Public Health Service - National Center for Health Statistics
See: National Center for Health Statistics (11103)

U.S. Public Health Service - National Institutes of Health
See: U.S. Natl. Institutes of Health (17626)

U.S. Public Health Service - Navajo Area Indian Health Service - Gallup Indian Medical Center
See: Gallup Indian Medical Center (6236)

★ 17931 ★
U.S. Public Health Service - Office of Disease Prevention and Health Promotion - ODPHP National Health Information Center (OHIC) (Med)
Box 1133   Phone: (301)565-4167
Washington, DC 20013-1133   Linda Malcolm, Proj.Dir.
Staff: Prof 10; Other 3. **Subjects:** Health, nutrition, health promotion. **Holdings:** 900 books; 50 bound periodical volumes; 44 VF drawers of pamphlets and clippings. **Subscriptions:** 75 journals and other serials. **Services:** Copying; center open to the public by appointment. **Automated Operations:** Computerized inventory control. **Computerized Information Services:** DIALOG Information Services, BRS Information Technologies, MEDLARS; internal database. **Publications:** Healthfinder series, irregular; resource guides to health topics of current interest. **Special Catalogs:** Address and contact information for over 1200 health-related organizations (machine-readable format). **Remarks:** Center located at 1010 Wayne Ave., Suite 300, Silver Spring, MD 20910. Toll-free telephone number(s): (800)336-4797. FAX: (301)565-5112. **Staff:** Sheila Richard, Info.Serv.Mgr.

U.S. Public Health Service - Office for Substance Abuse Prevention - National Clearinghouse for Alcohol and Drug Information
See: National Clearinghouse for Alcohol and Drug Information (11115)

★ 17932 ★
U.S. Public Health Service - Parklawn Health Library (Med, Soc Sci)
5600 Fishers Ln., Rm. 13-12   Phone: (301)443-2665
Rockville, MD 20857   Bruce N. Yamasaki, Lib.Dir.
Founded: 1969. **Staff:** Prof 6; Other 8. **Subjects:** Delivery of health services, drug abuse, health planning, health care statistics, health services research, mental health, social aspects of health care, emergency medical services. **Special Collections:** Public Health Service Numbered Report Series; Vital Statistics of the U.S.; Public Health Service Contract Reports. **Holdings:** 30,000 books; 2000 bound periodical volumes; 10,000 NTIS reports on microfiche. **Subscriptions:** 1200 journals and other serials. **Services:** Interlibrary loan; copying; SDI; library open to the public for reference use only. **Automated Operations:** Computerized public access catalog, acquisitions, and circulation. **Computerized Information Services:** DIALOG Information Services, MEDLARS, BRS Information Technologies, OCLC; Emergency Medical Services Database (internal database). **Publications:** Current Awareness; Parklawn Health Library Bulletin, monthly - both to mailing list; Periodical List - free upon request. **Special Indexes:** KWOC index. **Remarks:** FAX: (301)443-2269.

★ 17933 ★
U.S. Public Health Service - Parklawn Health Library - PGC Branch Library (Med)
6525 Bellcrest Rd.   Phone: (301)436-6147
Hyattsville, MD 20782   Karen Stakes, Lib.Dir.
Founded: 1977. **Staff:** Prof 1; Other 2. **Subjects:** Health services, drug abuse, health planning, health care statistics, health services research, mental health, social aspects of health care, emergency medical services. **Holdings:** 3000 books. **Subscriptions:** 400 journals and other serials. **Services:** Interlibrary loan. **Automated Operations:** Computerized public access catalog and circulation. **Computerized Information Services:** MEDLARS, DIALOG Information Services, BRS Information Technologies. **Publications:** Current Awareness Service; Recent Acquisitions List; Guide to Library Resources. **Remarks:** FAX: (301)436-8008.

U.S. Public Health Service Archive
See: Reynolds Electrical and Engineering Company, Inc. - Coordination and Information Center (13862)

★ 17934 ★
U.S. Public Health Service Hospital - Gillis W. Long Hansen's Disease Center - Medical Library (Med)
Carville, LA 70721   Phone: (504)642-4748
          Anna Belle Steinbach, Med.Libn.
Staff: Prof 2. **Subjects:** Hansen's disease, dermatology, general medicine, bone and joint surgery, rehabilitation, physical therapy, immunology, microbiology, nursing. **Special Collections:** Leprosy Archives (all material published in English about leprosy, 1958 to present). **Holdings:** 5000 books; 10,000 unbound items. **Subscriptions:** 130 journals and other serials. **Services:** Interlibrary loan; copying; SDI; library open to the public for reference use only. **Computerized Information Services:** MEDLARS. **Networks/Consortia:** Member of National Network of Libraries of Medicine - South Central Region, Health Sciences Library Association of Louisiana. **Special Indexes:** Hansen's Disease Index (card). **Remarks:** FAX: (504)642-4729.

★ 17935 ★
U.S. Railroad Retirement Board - Library (Soc Sci, Law)
844 Rush St.   Phone: (312)751-4926
Chicago, IL 60611   Kay G. Collins, Hd.Libn.
Founded: 1940. **Staff:** Prof 2. **Subjects:** Law, legislation, social sciences. **Holdings:** 50,000 volumes; 83 VF drawers of legislative materials; 28 VF drawers of miscellaneous unbound materials. **Subscriptions:** 179 journals and other serials. **Services:** Interlibrary loan; library open to the public by appointment. **Computerized Information Services:** LEGI-SLATE, LEXIS, OCLC. **Networks/Consortia:** Member of FEDLINK, Chicago Library System. **Publications:** Quarterly Accessions List, quarterly. **Staff:** Katherine M. Tsang, Asst.Libn.

U.S. Refractories
See: General Refractories Company (6345)

★ 17936 ★
U.S. Securities and Exchange Commission - Library (Bus-Fin)
450 5th St., N.W.   Phone: (202)272-2618
Washington, DC 20549   Jeane Sessa, Chf.Libn.
Founded: 1934. **Staff:** Prof 5; Other 2. **Subjects:** Accounting, corporations, economics, finance, government, investments, law, public utilities, securities, statistics, stock exchanges. **Special Collections:** Legislative histories of statutes administered by agency. **Holdings:** 80,000 books; 5000 bound periodical volumes. **Subscriptions:** 500 journals and other serials. **Services:** Interlibrary loan; library open to the public by appointment. **Computerized Information Services:** LEXIS, OCLC. **Publications:** Library Bulletin, monthly. **Also Known As:** SEC. **Staff:** Raymond J. Kramer, Asst.Libn.

★ 17937 ★
U.S. Securities and Exchange Commission - Public Reference Library (Bus-Fin)
500 W. Madison, Ste. 1400   Phone: (312)353-7433
Chicago, IL 60606   Wilberta Moulthrop, Chf.Ref.Libn.
Founded: 1940. **Staff:** Prof 1; Other 3. **Subjects:** Securities laws, SEC releases and special studies. **Holdings:** Financial statements; corporate

annual reports; 20,000 files of reports by publicly owned companies on microfiche; registration statements, applications, and financial data for regional broker/dealers and investment advisors; annual reports for registered investment companies. **Services:** Copying; library open to the public. **Remarks:** Other repositories of this same information are located in SEC headquarters in Washington, DC and a regional office in New York City. Requests for copies of documents should be sent to Disclosure Incorporated, 5161 River Road, Bethesda, MD 20816. **Also Known As:** SEC.

★17938★
U.S. Senate - Library (Soc Sci)
Capitol Bldg., Suite S-332   Phone: (202)224-7106
Washington, DC 20510   Roger K. Haley, Senate Libn.
Founded: 1871. **Staff:** Prof 8; Other 13. **Subjects:** Legislation, government, political science, history, biography, economics. **Special Collections:** House and Senate bills and resolutions; committee hearings; legislative proceedings and debates. **Holdings:** 150,000 volumes; 1 million microforms. **Subscriptions:** 200 journals and other serials; 10 newspapers. **Services:** Library not open to the public. **Automated Operations:** Computerized cataloging and circulation. **Computerized Information Services:** NEXIS, LEXIS, DIALOG Information Services, VU/TEXT Information Services, DataTimes, WESTLAW, OCLC; House Information System (HIS), Library of Congress Information System (LOCIS), Senate LEGIS, SLCC (internal databases). Performs searches free of charge. **Networks/Consortia:** Member of FEDLINK. **Publications:** Presidential Vetoes. **Remarks:** FAX: (202)224-0879. **Staff:** Ann C. Womeldorf, Asst.Libn.; Gregory C. Harness, Hd.Ref.Libn.; Thea Koehler, Ref.Libn.; Anne Sporn, Ref.Libn.; Leona Pfund, Hd.Cat.; Thomas McCray, Lib. Automation Coord.; Patricia Schmid, Cat.

U.S. Small Business Administration
See: **Small Business Administration** (15226)

★17939★
U.S. Social Security Administration - Branch Library (Bus-Fin, Med)
Van Ness Centre, Rm. 206
4301 Connecticut Ave., N.W.   Phone: (202)282-7000
Washington, DC 20008   Linda Del Bene, Libn.
Founded: 1972. **Staff:** Prof 1; Other 1. **Subjects:** Social Security programs, retirement, economics, disability insurance, income maintenance, pension benefits, health insurance, medical care. **Special Collections:** Research Grant Reports and Contract Reports of SSA and Office of Research and Statistics. **Holdings:** 9000 books; 100 bound periodical volumes; 200 pamphlets; 500 microforms. **Subscriptions:** 260 journals and other serials. **Services:** Interlibrary loan; copying; library open to the public with permission. **Publications:** Periodicals list. **Remarks:** FAX: (202)282-7219.

★17940★
U.S. Social Security Administration - Information Resources Branch - Library Services Section (Soc Sci, Bus-Fin, Med)
Altmeyer Bldg., Rm. 570
P.O. Box 17330   Phone: (301)965-6107
Baltimore, MD 21235   M. Joyce Donohue
Founded: 1942. **Staff:** Prof 4; Other 3. **Subjects:** Social insurance, medical and hospital economics, operations research, management, personnel administration, supervision and training, electronic data processing, law, health insurance, business and management. **Holdings:** 83,280 books; 1250 bound periodical volumes; 600,000 microfiche; 4700 ultrafiche. **Subscriptions:** 1447 journals and other serials. **Services:** Interlibrary loan; copying (limited); library open to the public for reference use only on request. **Automated Operations:** Computerized public access catalog, cataloging, acquisitions, and circulation. **Computerized Information Services:** DIALOG Information Services, BRS Information Technologies, LEXIS, NEXIS, LEGI-SLATE, JURIS, OCLC. **Publications:** SSA Library Notes, monthly; Bibliographic Quick Lists; Legislative Notes (guide to particular Social Security laws) - all free upon request. **Special Indexes:** Index to legislative information (card). **Remarks:** The Social Security Administration is part of the U.S. Department of Health and Human Services. **Staff:** Leo Hollenbeck, Chf.Ref.Libn.; Celeste Huecker, Chf.Tech.Serv.Libn.; Eugene Malkowski, Tech.Serv.Libn.

★17941★
U.S. Social Security Administration - International Studies and Organizations Staff - Reference Room (Law)
4301 Connecticut Ave., N.W.
Van Ness Centre, Suite 200 A   Phone: (202)282-7270
Washington, DC 20008   Ms. Concepcion McNeace, Tech.Info.Spec.
Founded: 1978. **Staff:** Prof 1. **Subjects:** Social security, disability, work injuries, and health care laws, unemployment, and family allowances in foreign countries. **Special Collections:** Foreign annual yearbooks, 1965 to present; International Labor Organization, Organization for Economic Cooperation and Development (OECD), and International Social Security Association publications. **Holdings:** 5500 volumes; 36 VF drawers of clippings on international subjects. **Subscriptions:** 153 journals and other serials. **Services:** Room open to the public by appointment. **Computerized Information Services:** Readmore. **Publications:** Social Security Programs throughout the World, biennial. **Remarks:** FAX: (202)282-7219.

★17942★
U.S. Soil Conservation Service - National Photographic Library (Aud-Vis, Env-Cons)
Box 2890   Phone: (202)447-2889
Washington, DC 20013   Tim McCabe, Natl.Photo.Spec.
Founded: 1935. **Staff:** Prof 2. **Subjects:** Soil erosion, conservation practices. **Holdings:** 10,000 photographs. **Services:** Library open to the public with restrictions. **Remarks:** The Soil Conservation Service is part of the U.S. Department of Agriculture. **Staff:** Tim McCabe, Vis.Info.Spec.

★17943★
United States Space Education Association - G.L. Borrowman Astronautics Library (Sci-Engr)
P.O. Box 1032   Phone: (306)584-9526
Weyburn, SK, Canada S4H 2L3   Gerald L. Borrowman, Chf.Libn.
Founded: 1978. **Staff:** Prof 2. **Subjects:** Astronautics, American and Soviet space programs, Apollo and Gemini projects, space shuttle. **Holdings:** 2000 books; 2000 bound periodical volumes; press kits and photographs. **Subscriptions:** 32 journals and other serials. **Services:** Library not open to the public.

★17944★
United States Space Education Association - USSEA Media Center (Sci-Engr)
746 Turnpike Rd.   Phone: (717)367-3265
Elizabethtown, PA 17022-1161   Stephen M. Cobaugh, Intl.Pres.
Founded: 1973. **Staff:** 5. **Subjects:** NASA space program, space sciences, solar power, science fiction. **Special Collections:** NASA Technical Publications (3500 documents); Solar Power Abstracts (250 documents). **Holdings:** 3000 books; 500 bound periodical volumes; 5000 slides, photographs, and cassettes; 2500 brochures and reports; 5000 clippings. **Subscriptions:** 30 journals and other serials. **Services:** Copying; center open to the public with restrictions. **Publications:** Space Age Times, bimonthly; USSEA Update, monthly. **Remarks:** USSEA is a worldwide, non-profit, non-partisan organization dedicated to promoting peaceful space exploration, seeking to archieve goals through both professionals and the layman.

★17945★
United States Sports Academy - Library (Rec)
One Academy Dr.   Phone: (205)626-3303
Daphne, AL 36526   Jeff Calametti, Hd.Libn.
Staff: Prof 2. **Subjects:** Sports, including medicine, research and management; fitness; coaching. **Holdings:** 3064 books; 8 VF drawers of clippings; 271 cassette tapes; films; slides; 100 videotapes; periodicals on microfiche. **Subscriptions:** 220 journals and other serials. **Services:** Interlibrary loan; copying; library open to the public for reference use only. **Automated Operations:** Computerized cataloging and circulation. **Computerized Information Services:** OCLC, BRS Information Technologies, MEDLARS. Performs searches on fee basis. **Networks/Consortia:** Member of Network of Alabama Academic Libraries (NAAL). **Publications:** Handbook; Shelflist (acquisitions list), monthly. **Special Catalogs:** Books by discipline (computer printout). **Remarks:** FAX: (205)626-1149. **Staff:** Nena Shelley, Asst.Libn.; Jacque Frey, Comp.Spec.

U.S. Steel Group
See: USX Corporation - U.S. Steel Group (19705)

★17946★
U.S. Supreme Court - Library (Law)
One First St., N.E.　　　　　　Phone: (202)479-3000
Washington, DC 20543　　　　Shelley L. Dowling, Libn.
Founded: 1832. **Staff:** Prof 11; Other 14. **Subjects:** Law, legislative histories. **Special Collections:** Records and briefs of the Supreme Court, 1832 to present; Gerry Collection (23,000 volumes). **Holdings:** 295,000 books; 110,000 microforms; 20,000 bound periodical volumes. **Subscriptions:** 4050 journals and other serials. **Services:** Copying; library open to members of Supreme Court Bar and congressional attorneys. **Automated Operations:** Computerized cataloging, acquisitions, serials, and circulation. **Computerized Information Services:** DIALOG Information Services, NEXIS, OCLC, LEXIS, WESTLAW, Library of Congress Information System (LOCIS), JURIS, RLIN, VU/TEXT Information Services, House Information Systems (HIS), USC Current. **Networks/Consortia:** Member of FEDLINK. **Remarks:** FAX: (202)479-3477. **Staff:** Linda Maslow, Asst.Libn., Res.; Rosalie Sherwin, Asst.Libn., Tech.Serv.; Diane Smith, Asst.Libn., Circ.

★17947★
U.S. Tax Court - Library (Law)
400 Second St., N.W.　　　　　Phone: (202)376-2707
Washington, DC 20217　　　　Jeanne R. Bonynge, Libn.
FO 1924. **Staff:** Prof 3; Other 3. **Subjects:** Federal tax law - income, estate, gift. **Holdings:** 40,000 books; 7900 bound periodical volumes; 380,000 Index-Digest card file of federal tax cases; Congressional Record, Federal Register, and federal tax legislation on microfiche. **Subscriptions:** 90 journals and other serials. **Services:** Interlibrary loan (limited); library not open to the public. **Automated Operations:** Computerized serials. **Computerized Information Services:** Washington Alert Service, LEXIS, OCLC, WESTLAW, CCH Access, DIALOG Information Services, Dow Jones News/Retrieval. **Networks/Consortia:** Member of FEDLINK. **Publications:** Library Bulletin, monthly - to Tax Court personnel. **Special Indexes:** File of tax cases arranged by case name, Internal Revenue code section, and subject (card). **Staff:** Elsa B. Silverman, Asst.Libn.; Tania Andreeff, Paralegal Spec.

★17948★
U.S. Team Handball Federation - Administrative Office Library (Rec)
1750 E. Boulder St.　　　　　　Phone: (719)578-4582
Colorado Springs, CO 80909　　Dr. Peter Buehning, Pres.
Staff: 1. **Subjects:** Team handball - rules, equipment, technique, coaching, refereeing, history. **Holdings:** Books; films; videotapes; pamphlets. **Services:** Library open to the public with restrictions. **Publications:** Team Handball USA. **Remarks:** Alternate telephone number(s): 632-5551, ext. 3290. FAX: (719)475-1240. Telex: 45 2424.

★17949★
United States Testing Company, Inc. - Library (Sci-Engr)
1415 Park Ave.　　　　　　　　Phone: (201)792-2400
Hoboken, NJ 07030　　　　　　Phyllis Keegan
Founded: 1930. **Staff:** Prof 1; Other 1. **Subjects:** Biology; chemistry; consumer products; engineering - materials, physical, electronics, product, nuclear; environmental testing; paper; plastics; textiles. **Holdings:** 5000 military and government specifications. **Subscriptions:** 150 journals and other serials. **Services:** Library not open to the public. **Remarks:** FAX: (201)656-0636. Telex: 7607729.

★17950★
U.S. Tobacco - R & D Library (Sci-Engr)
800 Harrison St.　　　　　　　Phone: (615)271-2347
Nashville, TN 37203　　　　　Barbara Borrelli, Libn.
Founded: 1983. **Staff:** Prof 1. **Subjects:** Tobacco. **Holdings:** 1800 books; 600 bound periodical volumes. **Subscriptions:** 101 journals and other serials. **Services:** Library not open to the public. **Computerized Information Services:** DIALOG Information Services, STN International. **Remarks:** FAX: (615)271-2192.

★17951★
United States Trademark Association - Law Library (Law)
6 E. 45th St.　　　　　　　　　Phone: (212)986-5880
New York, NY 10017　　　　Charlotte Jones, Mng.Ed./Libn.
Founded: 1878. **Staff:** 20. **Subjects:** Trademarks. **Holdings:** 1800 books; 73 bound periodical volumes. **Subscriptions:** 40 journals and other serials. **Services:** Library open to the public. **Remarks:** FAX: (212)687-8267.

★17952★
U.S. Travel Data Center - Library (Bus-Fin)
2 Lafayette Centre
1133 21st St., N.W.　　　　　　Phone: (202)293-1040
Washington, DC 20036　　　　Suzanne D. Cook, Exec.Dir.
Founded: 1973. **Staff:** 14. **Subjects:** Travel and tourism. **Holdings:** 3000 research documents; 3800 government documents; 250 unpublished travel research reports; 15,000 clippings; 20 tapes. **Subscriptions:** 27 journals and other serials. **Services:** Library not open to the public. **Special Catalogs:** Publications Catalog, annual - free upon request. **Remarks:** FAX: (202)293-3155. Affiliated with Travel Industry Association of America. **Staff:** Susan Weil, Mgr., Mktg.

★17953★
United States Trust Company - Investment Library (Bus-Fin)
114 W. 47th. St.　　　　　　　Phone: (212)852-1000
New York, NY 10036　　　　　Rafael Tamargo
Founded: 1958. **Staff:** Prof 1; Other 2. **Subjects:** Finance, investments, banking, securities. **Holdings:** 300 volumes; 1000 unbound periodicals; 2750 corporate files. **Subscriptions:** 80 journals and other serials; 7 newspapers. **Services:** Interlibrary loan; copying; library open to clients and employees. **Automated Operations:** Computerized cataloging, acquisitions, and serials. **Computerized Information Services:** DIALOG Information Services, NEXIS, FINSTAT, LEXIS, Dow Jones News/Retrieval.

★17954★
U.S. Uniformed Services University of the Health Sciences - Learning Resource Center (Med)
4301 Jones Bridge Rd.　　　　Phone: (301)295-3350
Bethesda, MD 20814-4799　　Chester J. Pletzke, Assoc.Prof. & Dir.
Founded: 1976. **Staff:** Prof 8; Other 23. **Subjects:** Medicine, military medicine. **Holdings:** 118,109 books and journals. **Subscriptions:** 1327 journals and other serials. **Services:** Interlibrary loan; copying; center open to the public. **Automated Operations:** Computerized public access catalog, cataloging, acquisitions, serials, and circulation. **Computerized Information Services:** DIALOG Information Services, NLM, OCLC; USUHS Information System (internal database); CD-ROMs; InterNet, BITNET (electronic mail service). **Networks/Consortia:** Member of FEDLINK, National Network of Libraries of Medicine - Southeastern/Atlantic Region. **Publications:** Research Series Guide; Exhibit Bibliographies, both irregular - both for internal distribution only. **Remarks:** FAX: (301)295-3431. Electronic mail address(es): PLETZKE@USUHS (BITNET). The University is under the direction of the U.S. Department of Defense. **Staff:** Janice Powell Muller, Hd., Tech.Serv.; Judith Torrence, Hd., Ref. & Info.Serv.; Stephen Brown, Microcomputers.

★17955★
U.S. Urban Mass Transportation Administration - Transportation Research Information Center (TRIC) (Trans)
400 7th St., S.W., Rm. 6100　　Phone: (202)366-9157
Washington, DC 20590　　Pauline D'Antignac, Trans.Res.Spec.
Staff: Prof 3. **Subjects:** Urban transportation - bus and paratransit systems, rail and construction technology, new systems and technology, service and methods, planning and analysis, management resources. **Holdings:** 4000 reports. **Services:** Copying; SDI; center open to the public by appointment; responds to inquiries. **Computerized Information Services:** DIALOG Information Services. **Publications:** UMTA Abstracts, annual - for sale. **Remarks:** FAX: (202)366-3765. The Urban Mass Transportation Administration is part of the U.S. Department of Transportation and sponsors the Urban Mass Transportation Research Information Service (UMTRIS), a computer-based information system operated by the Transportation Research Board (TRB) of the National Academy of Sciences. UMTRIS contains transportation information from domestic and international sources and is available on DIALOG Information Services File 63. **Staff:** Marina Drancsak, Liaison.

U.S. Veterans Administration
See: U.S. Dept. of Veterans Affairs (17283)

United States Volleyball Association Archives
See: Ball State University - Bracken Library - Archives & Special
Collections (1438)

U.S. Water Conservation Laboratory
See: U.S.D.A. - Agricultural Research Service (17197)

★ 17956 ★
U.S.S. Massachusetts Memorial Committee, Inc. - Archives & Technical
Library (Sci-Engr, Hist)
Battleship Cove   Phone: (508)678-1100
Fall River, MA 02721   Mark Newton, Educ.Coord./Cur.
Founded: 1982. **Staff:** Prof 1. **Subjects:** Naval engineering and ordnance,
naval radio and radar, shipboard ephemera, World War II naval history,
battleship systems. **Holdings:** 300 books; 200 bound periodical volumes;
films; videotapes; 75 shelf feet of blueprints; 35 reels of microfilm; voice
recordings of first U.S. fleet raids on Japan; 250 pages of correspondence.
Services: Copying; library open to the public by appointment with one-time
research fee. **Publications:** Bibliographies. **Remarks:** FAX: (508)674-5597.

★ 17957 ★
U.S.S.R. Academy of Sciences - Astronomical Council - Center for
Astronomical Data - Library (Sci-Engr)
Pjatnitskaya, 48   Phone: 095 2331702
109017 Moscow, Russia   M.S. Nikitina, Chf. of Lib.
Founded: 1947. **Staff:** Prof 2. **Subjects:** Astronomy, physics, mathematics,
mechanics, electronics, philosophy. **Holdings:** 23,000 bound volumes; 44
microfiche; 61 catalogs. **Subscriptions:** 118 journals and other serials.
Services: Interlibrary loan; library open to the public. **Computerized**
Information Services: Internal database. **Remarks:** Alternate telephone
number(s): 231-54-61. FAX: 231-20-81. Telex: 411576 ASCON SU.

★ 17958 ★
U.S.S.R. Academy of Sciences - Library (Sci-Engr)
Birzhevaya liniya 1   Phone: 2183692
198034 St. Petersburg, Russia   Valeri P. Leonov
Founded: 1714. **Staff:** Prof 755; Other 129. **Subjects:** Science. **Special**
Collections: Manuscripts; rare and ancient books; map materials; reference
sources; Oriental pieces; Academy-decorated, medal-winning, and
prizewinning research papers. **Holdings:** 7.1 million books; 8 million bound
periodical volumes; 115,939 microfiche; 59,318 reels of microfilm; 17,116
manuscripts. **Subscriptions:** 10,000 journals and other serials; 25,590
newspapers. **Services:** Interlibrary loan; SDI; library open to the public for
reference use only. **Computerized Information Services:** SCI (internal
database). Contact Person: Elena I. Zagorskaya. **Publications:** Academy-
Issued Publications, annual; 275th Anniversary brochure, 1989; pamphlets.
Special Indexes: Union index of bibliographies issued in the USSR.
Remarks: Founded by Peter I, the library is Russia's oldest science library.

★ 17959 ★
United Steelworkers of America - Library (Law, Bus-Fin)
234 Eglinton Ave., E., 7th Fl.   Phone: (416)487-1571
Toronto, ON, Canada M4P 1K7   Lesley Stodart, Libn.
Founded: 1963. **Staff:** Prof 1. **Subjects:** Canadian law, labor law, economics,
health and safety, labor, business, mining industry, steel industry. **Special**
Collections: Current USWA collective agreements (20,000); Steelabour
magazine, January 1946 to present; Royal Commission reports, 1930s to
present. **Holdings:** 5000 books; 200 bound periodical volumes; local union
publications; government documents. **Subscriptions:** 200 journals and other
serials; 6 newspapers. **Services:** Interlibrary loan; copying; library open to
the public by appointment. **Computerized Information Services:** Info Globe,
Infomart Online, InvesText. **Remarks:** FAX: (416)487-8826.

United Technologies Corporation - Carrier Corporation
See: Carrier Corporation (3096)

★ 17960 ★
United Technologies Corporation - Chemical Systems Division - Library
(Sci-Engr)
Box 49028   Phone: (408)776-5995
San Jose, CA 95161-9028   Karen Ream Schaffer, Libn.
Founded: 1959. **Staff:** Prof 1. **Subjects:** Chemical propulsion and
technology, mechanical and aeronautical engineering. **Special Collections:**
National Advisory Committee for Aeronautics (NACA) Annual Reports,
1915-1959. **Holdings:** 5500 books; 2000 bound periodical volumes; 1850
microfilm cartridges; 6700 microfiche; 25,000 other cataloged items.
Subscriptions: 153 journals and other serials. **Services:** Interlibrary loan;
library not open to the public. **Computerized Information Services:** NASA/
RECON, DIALOG Information Services, DTIC, Chemical Abstracts
Service (CAS). **Networks/Consortia:** Member of CLASS. **Publications:**
Library Bulletins, irregular - for internal distribution only. **Remarks:** FAX:
(408)776-4444.

★ 17961 ★
United Technologies Corporation - Library & Information Services (Sci-
Engr)
United Technologies Research Center   Phone: (203)727-7478
East Hartford, CT 06108   Jean G. Mayhew, Mgr.
Founded: 1939. **Staff:** Prof 24; Other 22. **Subjects:** Aerospace sciences and
engineering, business, power plants and energy conversion, metals and
materials, electronics, lasers, optics, physics, chemistry. **Holdings:** 55,000
book titles; 15,000 bound periodical volumes; 120,000 technical reports and
preprint titles; 250,000 microfiche. **Subscriptions:** 1200 journals and other
serials. **Services:** Interlibrary loan (limited); library not open to the public.
Automated Operations: Computerized cataloging and circulation.
Computerized Information Services: DIALOG Information Services, PFDS
Online, Dow Jones News/Retrieval, BRS Information Technologies, DTIC,
LEXIS, NEXIS, NewsNet, Inc., NLM, TEXTLINE, VU/TEXT
Information Services, STN International, WILSONLINE, NASA/
RECON, Integrated Technical Information System (ITIS), Electronic
Materials Information Service (EMIS); UTOC (internal database).
Publications: UTLIS Bulletin, monthly; Technical Topics, monthly;
Business Contents, semimonthly - all for internal distribution only.
Remarks: FAX: (203)727-7316. **Staff:** Rita Yeh, Supv., Lib.Sys.; John
Goncar, Supv., Tech.Serv.; Noreen Steele, Supv., Br.Libs.

United Technologies Corporation - Norden Systems, Inc.
See: Norden Systems, Inc. (11839)

United Technologies Corporation - Pratt and Whitney Canada Inc.
See: Pratt and Whitney Canada Inc. (13307)

★ 17962 ★
United Technologies Corporation - Pratt & Whitney Information
Services (Sci-Engr)
400 Main St., MS 169-31   Phone: (203)565-0385
East Hartford, CT 06108   Mary "Dottie" Moon, Sr.Libn.
Founded: 1961. **Staff:** Prof 2; Other 3.5. **Subjects:** Materials, aerospace
technology, chemistry, engineering, human resources, computers, business,
gas turbine engines, manufacturing. **Holdings:** 6000 books; 1500 bound
periodical volumes; 5200 technical reports. **Subscriptions:** 225 journals and
other serials. **Services:** Interlibrary loan; services not open to the public.
Automated Operations: Computerized public access catalog and circulation.
Computerized Information Services: DIALOG Information Services,
NEXIS, PFDS Online, BRS Information Technologies, LEXIS, Chemical
Abstracts Service (CAS), Aerospace Online, VU/TEXT Information
Services, EdVent (Educational Events) Data Base, Global Report,
WILSONLINE, NewsNet, Inc., DRI/McGraw-Hill, Dow Jones News/
Retrieval, Reuter TEXTLINE. **Remarks:** Alternate telephone number(s):
565-0386. FAX: (203)565-9060. **Staff:** Barbara E. Rankin.

★ 17963 ★
United Technologies Corporation - Sikorsky Aircraft Division - Library
and Information Services S339A (Sci-Engr)
6900 Main St.   Phone: (203)386-4713
Stratford, CT 06601-1381   Gail C. Smith, Lib.Mgr.
Founded: 1945. **Staff:** Prof 2; Other 1. **Subjects:** Aeronautics, engineering,
helicopters, management. **Special Collections:** Helicopter and vertical
takeoff and landing (VTOL) aircraft data. **Holdings:** 3300 books; 90,000

technical government reports. **Subscriptions:** 170 journals and other serials. **Services:** Interlibrary loan; copying; library open to the public with restrictions. **Automated Operations:** Computerized public access catalog, cataloging, acquisitions, and circulation. **Computerized Information Services:** PFDS Online, DIALOG Information Services, NEXIS, NewsNet, Inc., DTIC, WILSONLINE, Aerospace Online; PROFS (electronic mail service). **Publications:** Library Bulletin of new materials - for internal distribution only. **Remarks:** FAX: (203)386-6020. **Staff:** Candy L. Quinn, Libn.; Steve Zelinger, Assoc.Libn.

★ 17964 ★
United Telecommunications, Inc. - US Sprint - Corporate Library (Info Sci)
2330 Shawnee Mission Pkwy. Phone: (913)624-8500
Shawnee Mission, KS 66205 Desi Bravo, Mgr.
Founded: 1980. **Staff:** Prof 5; Other 4. **Subjects:** Telecommunications, data communications, telephone engineering, information management, office automation. **Holdings:** 20,000 books, reports, annual reports, subject files, company files. **Subscriptions:** 323 journals and other serials. **Services:** Center open to the public by appointment. **Automated Operations:** Computerized cataloging. **Computerized Information Services:** DIALOG Information Services, VU/TEXT Information Services, Telescope, Dow Jones News/Retrieval, NewsNet, Inc., InvesText, CompuServe Information Service; internal database; SprintMail (electronic mail service). **Networks/Consortia:** Member of Kansas City Metropolitan Library Network (KCMLN). **Publications:** Information Newsletter, monthly; Trade Talk, daily (electronic newspaper) - for internal distribution only. **Remarks:** FAX: (913)624-3225. Electronic mail address(es): CORP.LIBRARY (SprintMail). **Staff:** Brenda Ward; Sara Hill; Schelley Scamman; Barbara Jolley.

★ 17965 ★
United Theological Seminary - Library (Rel-Phil)
1810 Harvard Blvd. Phone: (513)278-5817
Dayton, OH 45406 Elmer J. O'Brien, Libn./Prof.
Founded: 1872. **Staff:** Prof 3; Other 2. **Subjects:** Theology. **Special Collections:** Evangelical United Brethren Church Collection (8000 items). **Holdings:** 118,527 volumes. **Subscriptions:** 513 journals and other serials; 5 newspapers. **Services:** Interlibrary loan; copying; library open to the public by application with references. **Automated Operations:** Computerized cataloging, acquisitions, and serials. **Computerized Information Services:** DIALOG Information Services, OCLC. **Networks/Consortia:** Member of Southwestern Ohio Council for Higher Education (SOCHE). **Remarks:** FAX: (513)278-1218. **Staff:** Paul Schrodt, Asst.Libn.; Betty A. O'Brien, Ref.Libn.

★ 17966 ★
United Theological Seminary of the Twin Cities - Library (Rel-Phil)
3000 5th St., N.W. Phone: (612)633-4311
New Brighton, MN 55112 Arthur L. Merrill, Dir.
Founded: 1962. **Staff:** Prof 3; Other 4. **Subjects:** Theology, church history, education, sociology, psychology, philosophy. **Holdings:** 69,000 volumes; 318 films and filmstrips; 580 microforms; 101 videotapes; 982 cassettes and tapes. **Subscriptions:** 282 journals and other serials. **Services:** Interlibrary loan; copying; library open to the public. **Computerized Information Services:** Joint consortium catalog/intelligent catalog (internal database). **Networks/Consortia:** Member of Minnesota Theological Libraries Association (MTLA), MINITEX Library Information Network. **Remarks:** FAX: (612)633-4315. **Staff:** Susan Ebbers, Libn.; Dale Dobias, Tech.Serv.

★ 17967 ★
United Way of America - Information Center (Soc Sci)
701 N. Fairfax St. Phone: (703)836-7100
Alexandria, VA 22314-2088 Nell Benton
Founded: 1934. **Staff:** 1. **Subjects:** History and management of social and human services, fund raising, philanthropy, voluntarism. **Special Collections:** Archives of United Way of America. **Holdings:** 600 books; 5000 monographs and research reports. **Subscriptions:** 300 journals and other serials. **Services:** Interlibrary loan; center open to area researchers and human service professionals by appointment. **Automated Operations:** Computerized cataloging, acquisitions, and serials. **Computerized Information Services:** DIALOG Information Services. **Publications:** Digest of Selected Reports - to members and others by subscription. **Remarks:** FAX: (703)683-7840.

★ 17968 ★
United Way/Crusade of Mercy - Library (Soc Sci)
560 E. Lake St. Phone: (312)906-2345
Chicago, IL 60661-1499 Sally J. Barnum, Mgr.
Founded: 1977. **Staff:** Prof 1; Other 1. **Subjects:** Social services, fund raising, social statistics, nonprofit management, voluntarism. **Special Collections:** United Way/Crusade of Mercy and predecessor agency archives (United Way of Chicago, Welfare Council of Metropolitan Chicago, Community Fund of Chicago, Council for Community Services, Crusade of Mercy; 250 titles); United Way/Crusade of Mercy and United Way of Chicago central files. **Holdings:** 10,000 books; 300 reports on microfiche. **Subscriptions:** 200 journals and other serials; 5 newspapers. **Services:** Interlibrary loan; SDI; library open to the public by appointment. **Automated Operations:** Computerized cataloging. **Computerized Information Services:** OCLC. **Networks/Consortia:** Member of ILLINET, National Network of Libraries of Medicine - Greater Midwest Region, Chicago Library System. **Publications:** Recent Acquisitions, bimonthly - to staff and local libraries by request. **Remarks:** FAX: (312)876-0721.

United Way Information Service for the Aging
See: First Call For Help - Milwaukee (5754)

★ 17969 ★
United Way of the Lower Mainland - Social Planning and Research Department Library (Soc Sci)
1625 W. 8th Ave. Phone: (604)731-7781
Vancouver, BC, Canada V6J 1T9 Jennifer Cleathero, Libn.
Founded: 1965. **Staff:** 1. **Subjects:** Family violence, income security, housing, social problems, child abuse and child sexual abuse, social services planning. **Special Collections:** United Way of the Lower Mainland publications (200 titles). **Holdings:** 3000 books and bound reports; 2500 unbound reports, pamphlets, and ephemera. **Subscriptions:** 75 journals and other serials. **Services:** Interlibrary loan; copying; library open to the public for reference use only. **Remarks:** FAX: (604)731-0631.

★ 17970 ★
United Way Volunteer and Information Center - Library (Soc Sci)
3600 8th Ave., S., Suite 504 Phone: (205)323-0000
Birmingham, AL 35222 Ken Smith, Info. & Referral Coord.
Subjects: Voluntarism. **Holdings:** Figures not available. **Services:** Library open to the public. **Computerized Information Services:** Internal database. **Remarks:** Alternate telephone number(s): (205)251-5131.

United World Colleges - Lester B. Pearson College of the Pacific
See: Lester B. Pearson College of the Pacific (12810)

★ 17971 ★
Unity of Fairfax - Library (Rel-Phil)
2854 Hunter Mill Rd. Phone: (703)281-1767
Oakton, VA 22124 Alice Segura, Libn.
Staff: Prof 1; Other 2. **Subjects:** Religion, metaphysics. **Holdings:** 1000 books. **Services:** Library open to the public.

★ 17972 ★
Unity Medical Center - Library (Med)
550 Osborne Rd. Phone: (612)780-6774
Fridley, MN 55432 Aggie Koutroupas, Libn.
Founded: 1973. **Staff:** Prof 1; Other 1. **Subjects:** Medicine, nursing, and allied health sciences. **Holdings:** 800 books; 3000 bound periodical volumes. **Subscriptions:** 108 journals and other serials. **Services:** Interlibrary loan; copying; library open to the public. **Automated Operations:** Computerized cataloging. **Computerized Information Services:** MEDLARS, MEDLINE. **Networks/Consortia:** Member of Twin Cities Biomedical Consortium (TCBC). **Remarks:** FAX: (612)780-6783.

★ 17973 ★
Universal City Studios - Research Department Library (Art, Hist)
100 Universal City Plaza Phone: (818)777-2493
Universal City, CA 91608 Sherri Seeling, Hd., Res.Dept.
Founded: 1916. **Staff:** Prof 1; Other 6. **Subjects:** American West, Americana, costume, literature, art and architecture, wars, film history, history, biography. **Holdings:** 30,000 books; 700 bound periodical volumes; 6000 files of clippings, stills, brochures, pictures, illustrations, slides and transparencies for background research on film and television projects. **Subscriptions:** 90 journals and other serials. **Services:** Library not open to the public. **Computerized Information Services:** NEXIS, LEXIS, OCLC. **Special Indexes:** Clipping file index; pictorial magazine index. **Remarks:** FAX: (818)777-8854. **Staff:** Margaret Ross, Res.Spec.

Universal Flavor Corporation - Hurty-Peck Library of Beverage Literature
See: **Hurty-Peck Library of Beverage Literature** (7589)

★ 17974 ★
Universal Foods Corporation - Technical Information Center (Biol Sci, Food-Bev)
6143 N. 60th St.   Phone: (414)535-4307
Milwaukee, WI 53218   Aileen Mundstock, Tech.Info.Spec.
Founded: 1951. **Staff:** Prof 1. **Subjects:** Fermentation industry, biotechnology, biochemistry, microbiology, chemistry, quality control, product development, engineering. **Holdings:** 4000 books and bound periodical volumes; patents; internal reports. **Subscriptions:** 60 journals and other serials. **Services:** Copying (limited); center open to the public with restrictions. **Automated Operations:** Computerized cataloging, acquisitions, circulation, and serials. **Computerized Information Services:** DIALOG Information Services, STN International, NLM. **Networks/Consortia:** Member of Library Council of Metropolitan Milwaukee, Inc. (LCOMM).

★ 17975 ★
Universal Postal Union - International Bureau - Library (Bus-Fin)
Weltpostr. 4   Phone: 31 43 22 11
CH-3000 Berne 15, Switzerland   Arne J. Johnsen, Assit. Counsellor
Subjects: Postal service. **Holdings:** 10,000 volumes. **Remarks:** FAX: 31 432210. Telex: 912761 UPU CH. **Also Known As:** Bureau International de l'Union Postale Universelle.

★ 17976 ★
Universal Serials & Book Exchange, Inc. - Library (Info Sci)
2969 W. 25th St.   Phone: (216)241-6960
Cleveland, OH 44113   John T. Zubal, Pres.
Founded: 1948. **Staff:** Prof 7. **Subjects:** U.S. and foreign publications, library science. **Special Collections:** Bibliographies. **Holdings:** 5 million items, including bound and unbound journals, books, microforms, and government documents. **Subscriptions:** 25 journals and other serials; 2 newspapers. **Services:** Document delivery; copying; library open to librarians on fee basis. **Computerized Information Services:** OCLC. Performs searches on fee basis. **Publications:** For Members Only (catalog and newsletter), irregular-to members. **Remarks:** FAX: (216)241-6966. Telex: 298256. USBE is a nonprofit library cooperative, organized to facilitate the redistribution of library resources and to extend the availability of publications. **Also Known As:** USBE, Inc; United States Book Exchange. **Staff:** Michael T. Zubal, V.P.; Marilyn C. Zubal, Treas.; Paul L. Csank, Sec.; Jean Marie Zubal, Oper.Mgr.

★ 17977 ★
Universala Esperanto-Asocio - Biblioteko Hector Hodler (Hum)
Nieuwe Binnenweg 176   Phone: 10 4361044
NL-3015 BJ Rotterdam, Netherlands   Rob Moerbeek
Founded: 1908. **Subjects:** Esperanto literature, history of Esperanto movement and organizations, interlinguistics. **Holdings:** 13,500 books; 150 bound periodical volumes. **Services:** Library open to the public for reference use only. **Remarks:** FAX: 10 4361751. Telex: 23721 uea nl.

★ 17978 ★
Universidad de los Andes - Biblioteca General (Sci-Engr, Hum)
Apdo. Aereo 4976
Carrera 1-Este, 18-A-10   Phone: 1 2866309
Bogota, Colombia   Angela Maria Mejia de Restrepo, Dir.
Founded: 1948. **Subjects:** Science; engineering - electrical, mechanical, civil, industrial; computer sciences; humanities. **Special Collections:** Antique and rare books. **Holdings:** 85,000 titles; 6000 documents; 4500 nonbook materials; United Nations university publications depository. **Subscriptions:** 640 journals and other serials. **Services:** Interlibrary loan; copying; library open to the public with restrictions. **Automated Operations:** NOTIS. **Computerized Information Services:** DIALOG Information Services. Performs searches on fee basis. Contact Person: Nohelia Rios Ocampo. **Publications:** Incunables de la Universidad de los Andes; Libros publicados entre 1501 y 1600; La Expedicion Botanica. **Remarks:** FAX: 1 2841890. Telex: 42343 Unand Co. **Staff:** Maria Victoria Franco.

★ 17979 ★
Universidad Autonoma Agraria Antonio Narro - Biblioteca (Agri, Sci-Engr)
Doctor Egidio G. Rebonato
Apdo Postal No. 342   Phone: 84 173100
Saltillo, Coahuila, Mexico   Luz Elena Perez Mata
Founded: 1923. **Subjects:** Science - agricultural, applied, social. **Holdings:** 19,727 books; 10,596 bound periodical volumes; 16,194 microfiche. **Subscriptions:** 142 journals and other serials; 4 newspapers. **Services:** Interlibrary loan; copying; library open to the public for reference use only. **Computerized Information Services:** Banco de Tesis Regional (internal database). **Remarks:** FAX: 84 173022.

★ 17980 ★
Universidad Autonoma de Barcelona - Facultad de Ciencias de la Informacion - Biblioteca (Info Sci)
Campus Universitario   Phone: 3 5811492
E-08193 Bellaterra, Spain   Antonia Galceran
Founded: 1972. **Staff:** Prof 4; Other 5. **Subjects:** Mass media, broadcasting, advertising, journalism, television, public relations. **Special Collections:** Instituto Oficial de Radio y TV. **Holdings:** 28,000 books; 20,000 bound periodical volumes; 49 microfiche; 143 reels of microfilm; 6 videotapes. **Subscriptions:** 381 journals and other serials. **Services:** Interlibrary loan; copying; library open to the public. **Automated Operations:** VTLS. **Special Catalogs:** Cataleg de Publicacions Periodiques 1989. **Remarks:** FAX: 93 5812339.

★ 17981 ★
Universidad Autonoma Chapingo - Biblioteca Central (Agri)
56230 Chapingo, Mexico   Phone: 91595 42200
                              Rosa Maria Ojeda
Staff: Prof 9; Other 41. **Subjects:** Agronomy, forestry, soils, animal science, plant breeding, rural sociology. **Special Collections:** Mexican agricultural congresses (500 publications). **Holdings:** 75,000 books; 150,000 bound periodical volumes. **Subscriptions:** 350 journals and other serials. **Services:** Interlibrary loan; copying; library open to the public. **Publications:** Lista de Tesis de las Escuelas de Agricultura, Ganaderia y Medicina Veterinaria de la Rep. Mexicana, 1856-1985.

★ 17982 ★
Universidad Boliviana Mayor de San Andres - Facultad de Ciencias de la Salud - Biblioteca (Med)
Av Saavedra 2246
Casilla 12148   Phone: 2 42442
La Paz, Bolivia   Hugo Morales Bellido, Bib.
Founded: 1973. **Staff:** Prof 5; Other 5. **Subjects:** Medicine, health sciences, odontology, pharmacy, nursing, nutrition. **Holdings:** 7000 books; 2000 bound periodical volumes; slides. **Subscriptions:** 11 journals and other serials. **Services:** Library not open to the public. **Computerized Information Services:** CD-ROMs (POPLINE, MEDLINE, LILACS); En Disco Duro LIBOCS (internal database). **Publications:** Boletin de Informaciones. **Remarks:** FAX: 2 359593.

★ 17983 ★
Universidad de Caldas - Centro de Biblioteca e Informacion Cientifica Enrique Mejia Ruiz (Med, Agri)
Apdo. Aereo 275   Phone: 968-855-240
Manizales, Colombia   Elsie Duque de Ramirez, Dir.
Subjects: Medicine, agriculture, veterinary medicine, law, education, social sciences, humanities. **Holdings:** 30,000 books; 25,000 bound periodical volumes; 300 AV programs; 100 microforms; 50 rare books. **Services:** Interlibrary loan; copying; SDI; library open to the public. **Computerized Information Services:** MEDLARS, MEDLINE. Performs searches on fee basis.

★ 17984 ★
Universidad Catolica Argentina - Facultad de Filosofia y Letras - Biblioteca (Soc Sci, Hum)
1869 Batolome Mitre
1039 Buenos Aires, Bs As, Argentina   Phone: 1 402238
Founded: 1960. **Staff:** Prof 1; Other 1. **Subjects:** Philosophy, history, psychology, literature, education sciences, theology. **Special Collections:** Index Thomisticus; Pauly Wissowwa; Commentaria in Aristotelis Graeca. **Holdings:** 42,000 books; 450 bound periodical volumes. **Subscriptions:** 3 journals and other serials. **Services:** Library open to other universities and investigators only. **Computerized Information Services:** MICROSIS. **Publications:** SAPIENTIA; LETRAS; RES GESTA; Actas de Jornadas; Estudios Micrograficos EDUCA.

Universidad Catolica del Norte - Unidad de Biblioteca y Documentacion
See: Catholic University of North (3167)

★ 17985 ★
Universidad Central de Venezuela - Facultad de Agronomia - Biblioteca
(Agri)
Apdo 4579   Phone: 43 22212
Maracay, Venezuela   Alex Moreno Sotomayor
Staff: Prof 4; Other 10. **Subjects:** Agriculture. **Holdings:** 15,000 books; 300 bound periodical volumes; 3000 reports. **Subscriptions:** 280 journals and other serials. **Services:** Interlibrary loan (local only); copying; SDI; library open to the public with restrictions - loans restricted to local users only. **Automated Operations:** Computerized cataloging. **Computerized Information Services:** CAB International, SESAME, BIOSIS; CDS ISIS. **Remarks:** FAX: 43 463242; 43 454175.

★ 17986 ★
Universidad Central de Venezuela - Instituto de Medicina Experimental -
Biblioteca (Biol Sci, Med)
Humberto Garcia Arocha
Ciudad Universitaria Sabana Grande
Apdo 50587   Phone: 2 6626540
Caracas 1051, Venezuela   Alecia Freites De Acosta
Founded: 1941. **Staff:** Prof 3. **Subjects:** Biochemistry, pharmacology, physiology, physiopathology. **Holdings:** 40,337 books; 50 microfiche; 100 reels of microfilm. **Subscriptions:** 389 journals and other serials. **Services:** Interlibrary loan; copying; SDI; library open to the public. **Computerized Information Services:** MEDLINE; CD-ROM (LILACS); internal database. **Publications:** Boletin Informativo-Sinabid; Directorio de Bibliotecas Biomedicas y Afines; Informes Anuales. **Remarks:** FAX: 2 6622480. Telex: 27495.

★ 17987 ★
Universidad de Concepcion - Facultad de Ciencias Agropecuarias y
Forestales - Biblioteca (Agri)
Avda Vicente Mendez 595
Casilla 537   Phone: 42 226333
Chillan, Chile   Lya Hernandez Palominos, Jefe de Biblioteca
Founded: 1955. **Staff:** Prof 3; Other 3. **Subjects:** Agronomy, veterinary science, agricultural science, forest science, land and cattle sciences. **Holdings:** 18,000 books; 120 bound periodical volumes; 5000 reports; 4000 theses. **Services:** Interlibrary loan; library not open to the public. **Computerized Information Services:** DIALOG Information Services, Chemical Abstracts. **Remarks:** FAX: 42 221507.

★ 17988 ★
Universidad de Cordoba - Escuela Tecnica Superior de Ingenieros
Agronomos - Biblioteca (Agri)
Avda Menendez Pidal s7n
E-14004 Cordoba, Spain   Phone: 57 218438
Founded: 1972. **Staff:** Prof 2; Other 2. **Subjects:** Agriculture, economy, physics, chemistry, statistics, mathematics, engineering. **Holdings:** 31,000 books; 50 bound periodical volumes; theses. **Subscriptions:** 350 journals and other serials. **Services:** Interlibrary loan; copying; SDI; library open to the public. **Computerized Information Services:** Internal database. **Special Catalogs:** Serial catalog (until 1986). **Remarks:** FAX: 957 218563. **Staff:** Guzman Garcia; Juan Alfredo.

★ 17989 ★
Universidad de Costa Rica - Sistema de Bibliotecas, Documentacion e
Informacion (Sci-Engr, Hum, Med, Law)
Ciudad Universitaria "Rodrigo Facio"   Phone: 536163
San Jose, Costa Rica   Maria Julia Vargas Bolanos, Prof., Dir.
Founded: 1946. **Staff:** 114. **Subjects:** Religion, humanities, literature, history, geography, medicine, philosophy, education, philology, chemistry, computer science, geology, mathematics, architecture, economics, physics, engineering, law, pharmacy and pharmacology, microbiology, dentistry, agriculture, fine arts, sociology, administration, anthropology. **Special Collections:** Rare books; atomic energy collection. **Holdings:** 322,036 books; 20,838 AV items; theses. **Subscriptions:** 9942 journals and other serials. **Services:** Interlibrary loan; copying; SDI; library open to the public with restrictions. **Computerized Information Services:** DIALOG Information Services. Performs searches on fee basis. Contact Person: Sra. Maria Eugenia

Solano Mendez. **Publications:** Boletin Bibliografico; Boletines Diseminacion de la Informacion; Publicacion Trabajos Finales de Graduacion; Publicacion "Serie Bibliografica." **Remarks:** Includes the holdings of the following libraries: Biblioteca Carlos Monge Alfaro, Biblioteca Luis Demetrio Tinoco, Biblioteca de Derecho, and Biblioteca de Farmacia. FAX: 506 249367. Telex: UNICORI 2544. **Staff:** Maritza Bonilla; Sonia Gutierrez; Hernan Rodriguez; Maria Rosa Rojas; Maria Eugenia Solano; Julia Urena; Aurora Zamora.

★ 17990 ★
Universidad Nacional Autonoma de Mexico - Direccion General de
Bibliotecas - Biblioteca Central (Hum, Soc Sci)
Ciudad Universitaria
Circuito Interior   Phone: 915 550-52-15
04510 Mexico City, DF, Mexico   Adolfo Rodriguez Gallardo, Dir.Gen.
Subjects: Humanities, social sciences, physical sciences, medicine, health sciences, arts. **Special Collections:** Rare books (16th-19th centuries). **Holdings:** 350,000 books; 40,000 bound periodical volumes; 5000 microforms. **Services:** Interlibrary loan; copying; library open to the public. **Computerized Information Services:** LIBRUNAM. Contact Person: Angela Pacheco. **Publications:** List of publications - available on request. **Special Catalogs:** Catalogo Colectivo de Publicaciones Periodicas de la UNAM; Informe de Labores de la Direccion General de Bibliotecas. **Also Known As:** National Autonomous University of Mexico. **Staff:** Eugenio Romero Hernandez, Subdir., Serv.

★ 17991 ★
Universidad Nacional Autonoma de Mexico - Facultad de Medicina -
Biblioteca (Med)
Brasil Num. 33, 1er Piso
Antigua Escuela de Santo Domingo
Plaza Santo Domingo   Phone: 5 261275
06020 Mexico City, DF, Mexico   Dr. Nicolas Leon
Founded: 1956. **Staff:** Prof 2; Other 2. **Subjects:** Medicine - history, philosophy, Mexican, 18th and 19th centuries. **Special Collections:** Mexican Codex. **Holdings:** 20,000 books; 500 bound periodical volumes. **Subscriptions:** 10 journals and other serials. **Services:** Interlibrary loan; copying; library open to the public. **Computerized Information Services:** MEDLINE; CD-ROM. Contact Person: Carmen Castaneda; Bernardo Martinez. **Special Catalogs:** Catalog of Thesis in Medicine of the 19th Century; Catalog of Books in Medicine in the 19th Century.

★ 17992 ★
Universidad Nacional Autonoma de Mexico - Instituto de Investigaciones
Esteticas - Biblioteca (Art)
Ciudad Universitaria
Alvaro Obragon   Phone: 6652465
04510 Mexico City, DF, Mexico   Carmen Block Iturriaga
Staff: 9. **Subjects:** Mexican arts - pre-Columbian, colonial, 19th century, modern, contemporary; literature; music; dance; theater; cinema. **Holdings:** 20,000 volumes. **Services:** Interlibrary loan; copying; library open to the public. **Computerized Information Services:** Internal database. **Remarks:** FAX: 6654740. **Also Known As:** National Autonomous University of Mexico - Institute of Aesthetics Research - Library. **Staff:** Jose de Jesus Hernandez Flores.

★ 17993 ★
Universidad Nacional Autonoma de Mexico - Instituto de Investigaciones
Historicas - Biblioteca Rafael Garcia Granados (Hist)
3er Circuito Cultural Universitario
Ciudad de la Investigacion en Humanidades
Ciudad Universitaria   Phone: 5 548-82-05
04510 Mexico City, DF, Mexico   Marianela Heredia Abarca, Libn./Adm.
Founded: 1954. **Staff:** Prof 2; Other 5. **Subjects:** History of Mexico, Latin America, Spain; world history; writing of history; history of science and technology. **Special Collections:** Rafael Garcia Granados; Pedro Bosch-Gimpera; Juan Comas; Manuel Maldonado; Koerdell y Fernado Anaya Monroy. **Holdings:** 30,000 books; 5000 bound periodical volumes; 850 theses; 2000 pamphlets; 300 reels of microfilm; 1000 microfiche. **Subscriptions:** 380 journals and other serials. **Services:** Interlibrary loan; copying; SDI; library open to the public for reference use only. **Automated Operations:** Computerized cataloging. **Special Catalogs:** De articulos de publicaciones periodicas (incomplete). **Special Indexes:** De tesis sobre Historia de Mexico presentadas en Estados Unidos y Canada, reproducidas por University Microfilms International (book). **Also Known As:** National Autonomous University of Mexico - Institute of Historical Research - Rafael Garcia Granados Library. **Staff:** Carmen Manzano, Chf., Lib.Serv.

★ 17994 ★

Universidad Nacional Autonoma de Mexico - Instituto de Investigaciones en Matematicas Aplicadas en Sistemas - Biblioteca (Sci-Engr)
Edificio llMAS 20 piso
Circuito Exterior C.U.
04510 Mexico City, DF, Mexico　　　Phone: 5 505215
Staff: Prof 4; Other 4. **Subjects:** Applied mathematics, electronics, numerical analysis, computation, statistics. **Holdings:** 17,000 books; 15,000 bound periodical volumes. **Subscriptions:** 392 journals and other serials. **Services:** Interlibrary loan; copying; library open to the public. **Automated Operations:** Computerized acquisitions, cataloging, and serials. **Remarks:** FAX: 5 500047.

★ 17995 ★

Universidad Nacional de Cuyo - Facultad de Ciencias Agrarias - Biblioteca (Agri)
Almte Brown 500　　　Phone: 61 960469
5505 Chacras de Coria, Mza., Argentina　　　Fanny Beatriz Arago
Founded: 1942. **Staff:** Prof 1; Other 6. **Subjects:** Agronomy, food sciences, forestry. **Holdings:** 16,300 books; 2770 bound periodical volumes. **Subscriptions:** 678 journals and other serials. **Services:** Interlibrary loan; copying; library open to the public. **Remarks:** FAX: 61 960469.

★ 17996 ★

Universidad Nacional del Sur - Departamento de Ciencias Agrarias - Biblioteca (Agri)
Complejo Palihue　　　Phone: 91 21942
8000 Bahia Blanca, Argentina　　　Prof. Antonio M. Squillace
Founded: 1980. **Staff:** Prof 2; Other 3. **Subjects:** Agronomy, soils, plant physiology, biology, hydrology, genetics. **Services:** Interlibrary loan, copying, library open to the public for reference use only. **Remarks:** FAX: 91 27876. Telex: 81758 PPINQ-AR.

★ 17997 ★

Universidad Santa Maria la Antigua - Biblioteca (Bus-Fin, Law)
Apartado 6-1696
El Dorado　　　Phone: 361311
Panama, Panama　　　Prof. Jorge Kam Rios, Lib.Dir.
Founded: 1969. **Staff:** 8. **Subjects:** Mathematics, finance, economics, management, Catholicism, accounting, law. **Special Collections:** Panamanian collection (7000 volumes). **Holdings:** 48,363 books; 12,000 bound periodical volumes; 3000 theses. **Subscriptions:** 1600 journals and other serials; 14 newspapers. **Services:** Library open to the public with restrictions. **Publications:** New Books List, monthly. **Remarks:** Alternate telephone number(s): 36-1311; 36-1226; 36-1003. **Staff:** Emeterio Quintero Romos, Title Classifier Libn.

★ 17998 ★

Universidad de Valparaiso - Facultad de Medicina - Biblioteca Central (Med)
Hontaneda 2653 Casilla 92-V　　　Phone: 32 212011
Valparaiso, Chile　　　Lina Rosales
Founded: 1965. **Staff:** Prof 5; Other 4. **Subjects:** Medicine, nursing, psychology, chemiistry, pharmacy, obstetrics. **Holdings:** Figures not available. **Services:** Interlibrary loan; copying; library open to health professionals. **Computerized Information Services:** CD-ROMs (MEDLINE, LILACS, POPLINE). **Publications:** New titles. **Remarks:** FAX: 56 32217612.

★ 17999 ★

Universidade Federal do Parana - Setor de Ciencias da Saude - Biblioteca (Med)
Rua Padre Camargo 280
CP 441　　　Phone: 41 22642011
80001 Curitiba, Parana, Brazil　　　Suzana G.G. Castilho, Hd.Libn.
Founded: 1912. **Staff:** Prof 5; Other 15. **Subjects:** Medicine, nutrition, OPS/OMS publications, nursing, research methodology. **Special Collections:** Theses (3500). **Holdings:** 21,000 books; 80 microfiche; 34 videocassettes. **Services:** Interlibrary loan; copying; library open to the public for reference use only. **Computerized Information Services:** MEDLINE; UFPR Book Catalog Subject Headings On-line (internal database); CD-ROMs (MEDLINE, LILACS, POPLINE). Contact Person: Selma R.R. Conte. **Publications:** Current awareness bulletin, monthly. **Remarks:** Alternate telephone number(s): 412 2624147. FAX: 412 2642243. Telex: 412-5100.

★ 18000 ★

Universidade Federal do Rio Grande do Sul - Biblioteca Central (Soc Sci, Hist)
Avenida Paulo Gama
C.P. 2303　　　Phone: 512 281633
90001 Porto Alegre, RS, Brazil　　　June Magda Rosa Scharnberg, Dir.
Founded: 1971. **Subjects:** Philosophy, social sciences, literature, history. **Special Collections:** Rare books (7000 volumes). **Holdings:** 52,000 books; 674 bound periodical volumes; 719 nonbook materials. **Subscriptions:** 163 journals and other serials; 6 newspapers. **Services:** Interlibrary loan; copying; library open to the public. **Computerized Information Services:** DIALOG Information Services, CNPq, ARUANDA/SERPRO, SEMEAR/IBICT, FGV. Performs searches on fee basis. Contact Person: Sonia Falcetta, Libn. **Publications:** Noticia Bibliografica; annual report. **Remarks:** Maintains 27 branch libraries. FAX: 512 273777. Telex: 051 1055.

★ 18001 ★

Universidade Federal de Rio Grande do Sul - Faculdade de Medicina - Biblioteca (Med)
Rua Ramiro Barcelos, 2350 2
Andar
Cala 2217
90210 Porto Alegre, Rio Grande do　　　Phone: 512 316699
Sul, Brazil　　　Rosaria Maria Lucia Geremia, Libn.
Founded: 1898. **Staff:** Prof 6; Other 10. **Subjects:** Internal medicine, surgery, public health. **Special Collections:** Theses (3291; 1900 to present). **Holdings:** 13,645 books; 60 microfiche. **Subscriptions:** 335 journals and other serials. **Services:** Interlibrary loan; copying; library open to the public. **Computerized Information Services:** DIALOG Information Services; SABI (internal database); CD-ROMs (MEDLINE, POPLINE, LILACS). **Remarks:** FAX: 512 302185.

★ 18002 ★

Universidade Federal Rural do Rio de Janeiro - Biblioteca Central (Agri)
Antiga Rodovia
Rio Sao Paulo km 47　　　Phone: 21 6821864
23851 Seropedica, RJ, Brazil　　　Maria Helena Sleutjes, Dir.
Founded: 1948. **Staff:** Prof 13; Other 42. **Subjects:** Agronomy, social sciences, geology, veterinary science, animal husbandry, technology. **Special Collections:** Costa Lima collection (insects of Brazil). **Holdings:** 47,000 books; 3000 titles of bound periodical volumes; 300 microfiche; 60 videotapes. **Subscriptions:** 5 journals and other serials. **Services:** Interlibrary loan; copying; library open to the public. **Computerized Information Services:** BIBLIODATA-CALCO (internal database). **Publications:** Bibliografia de Olericultura. **Special Catalogs:** Catalogo de Periodicos. **Remarks:** FAX: 21 6821120. Telex: 021-34411.

★ 18003 ★

Universidade de Lisboa - Faculdade de Medicina - Biblioteca Central (Med)
Av Prof Egas Moniz　　　Phone: 1 7972966
P-1600 Lisbon, Portugal　　　Emilia Calado Clamote
Founded: 1911. **Staff:** Prof 5; Other 5. **Subjects:** Medicine. **Holdings:** 87,000 books; 600 bound periodical volumes. **Subscriptions:** 160 journals and other serials. **Services:** Interlibrary loan; copying; library open to the public. **Computerized Information Services:** DIALOG Information Services; PORBASE (internal database). **Remarks:** FAX: 764059.

★ 18004 ★

Universidade de Sao Paulo - Campus de Piracicaba - Divisao de Biblioteca Documentacao (Agri, Biol Sci, Env-Cons, Soc Sci)
Av. Padua Dias, No. 11
CP 09　　　Phone: 194 330011
13400 Piracicaba, SP, Brazil　　　Janeti L. Bombini de Moura, Lib.Hd.
Founded: 1901. **Staff:** Prof 24; Other 39. **Subjects:** Agriculture, ecology, biotechnology, genetics, food technology, economics. **Special Collections:** Interamerican Institute for Cooperation on Agriculture collection; International Agricultural Exchange Association collection; Food and Agriculture Organization collection. **Holdings:** 90,000 books; 50,000 bound periodical volumes; CD-ROMs; diskettes. **Subscriptions:** 700 journals and other serials; 6 newspapers. **Services:** Interlibrary loan; copying; SDI; library open to the public for reference use only. **Computerized Information Services:** DIALOG Information Services; internal databases. **Publications:** Journal Contents; News in the Library. **Remarks:** FAX: 194 341611. Telex: 019 11 41 EALQ.

★ 18005 ★
Universidade de Sao Paulo - Escola de Communicacoes e Artes -
  Biblioteca (Info Sci, Art, Theater)
Av. Prof. Lucio M Rodrigues 443
Cidade Universitaria   Phone: 11 8133222
05508 Sao Paulo, SP, Brazil   Vera Alice Ferreira de Moraes
Founded: 1970. **Staff:** Prof 43. **Subjects:** Communication, fine arts, music, theatre, mass media, library science, cinema, radio, television, public relations, marketing, tourism. **Holdings:** 20,600 books; 11,800 bound periodical volumes; 1211 films; 355 videocassettes; 19,000 slides; 3000 photographs; 9400 scores; 6000 records; 3500 audiocassettes; 1940 theses; 1200 pamphlets and folders; 2000 art exhibition catalogues; 1200 theatre programs; 1000 theatre items. **Subscriptions:** 372 journals and other serials; 43 newspapers. **Services:** Interlibrary loan; copying; SDI; library open to the public. **Computerized Information Services:** Internal database. **Publications:** Periodicals Summary on Library Science, Music, Fine Arts, and Mass Communication; Bibliographical Bulletin. **Remarks:** FAX: 11 8154272. Telex: 11 80629.

★ 18006 ★
Universidade de Sao Paulo - Instituto de Ciencias Matematicas -
  Biblioteca (Sci-Engr)
Av Dr Carlos Batelho 1465   Phone: 162 712214
13560 Sao Carlos, Brazil   Zelma M. Varella Guerrini
Founded: 1972. **Staff:** Prof 3; Other 6. **Subjects:** Mathematics - computation, statistics, applied. **Special Collections:** Lecture Notes in Mathematics (1450 vols.); Lecture Notes in Computer Science (472 vols.); Die Grundlehren der Mathematischen Wissenschaften (290 vols.); Graduate Texts in Mathematics (121 vols.). **Holdings:** 19,000 books; 25,000 bound periodical volumes; 100 microfiche; 1500 theses. **Subscriptions:** 300 journals and other serials. **Services:** Interlibrary loan; copying; SDI; library not open to the public. **Computerized Information Services:** DEDALUS (internal database). **Publications:** Catalogo de Publicacoes Periodicas; Producao Cientifica; Guia da Biblioteca; Sumarios Correntes; Notas do ICMSC/USP. **Remarks:** FAX: 162 711038; Telex: 162.408 UVSI.

★ 18007 ★
Universita di Firenze - Biblioteca di Storia e Letteratura Nordamericana
  (Area-Ethnic, Hum)
Facotta di Magistero
Via San Gallo 10   Phone: 55 2757943
I-50129 Florence, Italy   Prof. Mario Materazi, Dir.
Founded: 1945. **Staff:** Prof 2. **Subjects:** United States - history, literature, literary criticism, social sciences, politics; ethnic studies. **Special Collections:** Italian Immigration to the United States (more than 1000 books, periodicals, and other items); Lost Cause Press (Americanistica on microcards; 4000 titles). **Holdings:** 32,000 books; 1100 bound periodical volumes; 5200 microfiche; 920 reels of microfilm. **Subscriptions:** 65 journals and other serials. **Services:** Interlibrary loan; copying; library open to scholars not part of the Italian university system upon presentation of letter of introduction. **Remarks:** Alternate telephone number(s): 55 2757940 (reading room).

★ 18008 ★
Universita di Milano - Facolta di Medicina Veterinaria - Biblioteca
  (Med, Biol Sci)
Via Celoria 10   Phone: 2 58352281
I-20133 Milan, Italy   Maria Alessandra Dall'era
Founded: 1808. **Staff:** Prof 5; Other 3. **Subjects:** Veterinary medicine, zoology. **Holdings:** 33,000 books; 1340 bound periodical volumes. **Subscriptions:** 530 journals and other serials. **Services:** Copying; library open to the public. **Computerized Information Services:** DIALOG Information Services; SBM (internal database). **Remarks:** FAX: 2 2367788.

★ 18009 ★
Universita di Napoli - Facolta di Agraria - Biblioteca Centrale (Agri)
Via dell'Universita 95   Phone: 273739
I-80055 Porticii, Italy   Olimpia Petriccione
Founded: 1872. **Subjects:** Agriculture, biology. **Holdings:** Figures not available. **Services:** Library open to the public. **Publications:** Bollettino delle nuove accessioni. **Special Catalogs:** Catalogo periodici.

★ 18010 ★
Universita di Padova - Istituto di Storia della Medicina e Biblioteca
  Pinali - Sezione Antica (Med)
Via G. Falloppio 50   Phone: 49 8751220
I-35121 Padova, Italy   Prof. Loris Premuda
Founded: 1954. **Staff:** Prof 2. **Subjects:** Medical history. **Special Collections:** Cere oculistiche. **Holdings:** 28,300 books; 624 bound periodical volumes; 1070 diagrams; 680 photographs. **Subscriptions:** 76 journals and other serials. **Publications:** Acta Medicae Historiae Patavina (review); Attivita dell'Istituto di Storia della Medicina. **Remarks:** FAX: 49 8754286.

★ 18011 ★
Universita di Padova - Seminario Matematico - Biblioteca (Sci-Engr)
Via G.B. Belzoni 7
I-35131 Padova, Italy   Phone: 49 831959
Founded: 1914. **Staff:** Prof 1; Other 2. **Subjects:** Mathematics, computer sciences. **Holdings:** 20,000 books; 30,000 bound periodical volumes. **Subscriptions:** 512 journals and other serials. **Services:** Interlibrary loan; copying; library open to the public for reference use only. **Computerized Information Services:** CD-ROMs (MathSci, CompactMATH); SBN (internal database). **Remarks:** FAX: 49 8758596.

★ 18012 ★
Universita di Palermo - Facolta di Agraria - Biblioteca (Agri)
Viale delle Scienze   Phone: 91 6521086
I-90128 Palermo, Italy   Dr. Oliveri Domenico
Founded: 1948. **Staff:** Prof 3; Other 4. **Subjects:** Agricure. **Holdings:** 25,000 books. **Subscriptions:** 350 journals and other serials. **Services:** Interlibrary loan; copying; library open to the public for reference use only. **Computerized Information Services:** DOBIS Canadian Online Library System; M.A.G.I.C. On Line (internal database). **Contact Person:** Antonina Foto. **Remarks:** FAX: 91 481546.

★ 18013 ★
Universita di Perugia - Facolta di Agraria - Biblioteca Centrale (Agri)
Borgo XX Giugno 74   Phone: 75 5856004
I-06100 Perugia, Italy   Dr. Giovanna Ascani Panella, Lib.Mgr.
Founded: 1912. **Staff:** Prof 3; Other 4. **Subjects:** Agriculture, livestock, entomology, food science, census. **Special Collections:** ATTI dei Comizi agrari (agricultural education, 235 volumes). **Holdings:** 33,600 books; 54,815 bound periodical volumes; 9600 reports; 1 archive. **Subscriptions:** 278 journals and other serials; 3 newspapers. **Services:** Copying; SDI; library open to the public. **Computerized Information Services:** ESA/IRS; DOBIS/LIBIS (internal databases). **Contact Person:** M. Aiuti, Asst.Libn. **Publications:** ANNALI. **Remarks:** Alternate telephone number(s): 75 5856005. FAX: 75 36298.

★ 18014 ★
Universita di Siena - Facolta di Medicina e Chirurgia - Biblioteca
  Centrale (Med)
Le Scotte   Phone: 577 45156
I-53100 Siena, Italy   Deonilla Pizzi
Founded: 1976. **Staff:** Prof 15. **Subjects:** Medicine, biochemistry, biology. **Special Collections:** Medical books (17th-19th centuries). **Holdings:** 10,000 books; 100,000 bound periodical volumes; videotapes. **Subscriptions:** 1000 journals and other serials. **Services:** Interlibrary loan; copying; SDI; library open to the public. **Automated Operations:** Computerized public access catalog. **Computerized Information Services:** NLM, ECHO, EUROBASES, BRS Information Technologies, DIALOG Information Services, ESA/IRS; EARN/BITNET (electronic mail service). **Contact Person:** Lucia Maffei, Hd. of Doc.Serv. **Publications:** Linee di Ricerca e Pubblicazioni; Universita degli Studi; Faculta di Medicina e Chirurgia, Vol. 1. **Remarks:** FAX: 577 286202. Electronic mail address(es): PIZZI@SIVAX.CINECA.IT (EARN/BITNET).

★ 18015 ★
Universita di Trieste - Dipartimento di Science Matematiche - Biblioteca
  (Sci-Engr)
Piazzale Europa 1
I-34127 Trieste, Italy   Phone: 40 5603254
Founded: 1949. **Staff:** Prof 1. **Subjects:** Mathematics. **Holdings:** 23,000 books. **Subscriptions:** 200 journals and other serials. **Services:** Interlibrary loan; copying; library open to the public. **Automated Operations:** Computerized acquisitions and circulation (IBM Filing Assistant). **Special Catalogs:** Catalog of Journals - for internal distribution only. **Remarks:** FAX: 40 5603256.

★ 18016 ★
Universitas Tarumanagara - Fakultas Kedokteran - Perpustakaan (Med)
Jl Let Jend S Parman 1
Jakarta, Indonesia   Ms. Siti Sumarningsih, Libn.
Founded: 1979. **Staff:** Prof 1; Other 4. **Subjects:** Medicine, nursing, and allied health sciences. **Special Collections:** WHO publications (500). **Holdings:** 7000 books; 90 bound periodical volumes. **Subscriptions:** 48 journals and other serials. **Services:** Copying; library open to the public. **Publications:** Accession list.

★ 18017 ★
Universitat Bern - Medizinhistorisches Institut - Bibliothek (Med)
Buhlstr 26
CH-3012 Berne, Switzerland   Phone: 31 658486
Founded: 1963. **Staff:** Prof 2; Other 1. **Subjects:** History of medicine. **Special Collections:** Collections of manuscripts, museum objects, and illustrations. **Holdings:** 35,000 books; 10,000 bound periodical volumes. **Subscriptions:** 35 journals and other serials. **Services:** Interlibrary loan; copying; library open to the public. **Remarks:** FAX: 31 245449. **Staff:** Prof. U. Boschung; P. Burkhalter.

Universitat Bochum - Archaeologie - Bibliothek
See: University of Bochum - Institute for Archeology - Library (18250)

★ 18018 ★
Universitat Bochum - Englisches Seminar - Bibliothek (Hum)
Gebaude GB 6/41 5/41
Postfach 102148
W-4630 Bochum, Germany   Phone: 234 7002595
                                     Ingrid Perk
Founded: 1963. **Staff:** Prof 1. **Subjects:** Shakespeare, comtemporary literature, history and culture of England and America, linguistics. **Special Collections:** Microbook Library of American Civilization (12,500 microfiches); technical dictionaries collection. **Holdings:** 75,000 books; 7 microfiche; 220 reels of microfilm; 190 audiocassettes; 238 records; 430 videotapes. **Subscriptions:** 96 journals and other serials; 3 newspapers. **Services:** Interlibrary loan; library open to the public for reference use only. **Remarks:** FAX: 234 7002001. Telex: 17 234 356.

★ 18019 ★
Universitat Bonn - Englisches Seminar - Bibliothek (Hum)
Regina-Pacis-Weg 5
W-5300 Bonn 1, Germany   Phone: 228 737368
Founded: 1887. **Staff:** Prof 1; Other 3. **Subjects:** English and American literature; Canadian studies; English language and linguistics. **Holdings:** 63,000 books; 14,000 bound periodical volumes; 8 microfiche titles; 215 reels of microfilm; 680 AV materials. **Subscriptions:** 162 journals and other serials; 3 newspapers. **Services:** Interlibrary loan; copying; library open to the public for reference use only. **Staff:** Monika Nokel-Belau, Libn.; Claire Waldecker, Libn.

Universitat Bonn - Kunsthistorisches Institut - Bibliothek
See: University of Bonn - Institute of the History of Arts - Library (18251)

★ 18020 ★
Universitat Bonn - Medizinhistorisches Institut - Bibliothek (Med)
Sigmund Freud Str 25
Venusberg   Phone: 228 2802003
W-5300 Bonn 1, Germany   Frau G. Nettekoven, Dipl.-Bibl.
Founded: 1943. **Staff:** Prof 1. **Subjects:** History of medicine. **Special Collections:** Dia collection (3370 items). **Holdings:** 27,009 books; 3392 bound periodical volumes; 7 reels of microfilm; 1034 dissertations; 5466 offprints; 19 videotapes. **Subscriptions:** 83 journals and other serials. **Services:** Copying; library open to the public. **Publications:** Chronik.

★ 18021 ★
Universitat Erlangen-Nurnberg - Lehrstuhle fur Englische Philologie - Institut fur Anglistik und Amerikanistik - Bibliothek (Hum)
Bismarckstr 1
W-8520 Erlangen, Germany   Phone: 9131 852935
Founded: 1890. **Staff:** Prof 1; Other .5. **Subjects:** English literature, English linguistics, American literature. **Special Collections:** English personal names; emblematics; Shaftesbury; American narrative fiction of the 19th and 20th centuries. **Holdings:** 63,000 books; 200 microfiche; 50 reels of microfilm. **Subscriptions:** 70 journals and other serials; 6 newspapers. **Services:** Library not open to the public.

★ 18022 ★
Universitat Frankfurt - Didaktisches Zentrum - Bibliothek (Educ)
Senckenberganiage 15   Phone: 69 7983595
W-6000 Frankfurt, Germany   Reinhard Koch
Founded: 1972. **Staff:** Prof 1. **Subjects:** Teacher education, German as a foreign language, media didactics, adult education, university science didactics and research, methods of foreign language acquisitions. **Holdings:** 19,000 books; 970 bound periodical volumes. **Subscriptions:** 77 journals and other serials. **Services:** Library open to the public for reference use only. **Publications:** New Acquisitions, quarterly.

★ 18023 ★
Universitat Frankfurt - Mathematishes Seminar - Bibliothek (Sci-Engr)
Robert Mayer Str 8   Phone: 69 7983420
W-6000 Frankfurt, Germany   Dr. K. Hainer
Founded: 1914. **Staff:** Prof 1.5. **Subjects:** Mathematics. **Holdings:** 20,622 books; 15,333 bound periodical volumes. **Subscriptions:** 243 journals and other serials. **Services:** Library open to the public.

★ 18024 ★
Universitat Freiburg - Englisches Seminar I und II - Bibliothek (Hum)
KG IV   Phone: 761 2034580
W-7800 Freiburg, Germany   Mrs. F. Vrba, Libn.
Founded: 1935. **Staff:** Prof 1; Other 1. **Subjects:** English literature, linguistics, Celtic literature, American literature, literary sciences. **Holdings:** 4800 books; 2000 bound periodical volumes; 450 reels of microfilm. **Subscriptions:** 100 journals and other serials; 2 newspapers. **Services:** Interlibrary loan; library open to the public for reference use only, books loaned over the weekend only.

★ 18025 ★
Universitat Giessen - Fachbereichsbibliothek Anglistik und Amerikanistik (Hum)
Otto Behaghel Str 10   Phone: 641 7025558
W-6300 Giessen, Germany   Birgit Jesberg
Founded: 1919. **Staff:** Prof 1. **Subjects:** Literature - English, Commonwealth, American; literary criticism. **Holdings:** 65,000 books; 4500 reels of microfilm; 600 videotapes; 500 sound recordings. **Subscriptions:** 110 journals and other serials; 6 newspapers. **Services:** Library not open to the public. **Computerized Information Services:** HEBIS-KAT (internal database).

★ 18026 ★
Universitat Giessen - Institut fur Agrarpolitik und Marktforschung - Bibliothek (Agri)
Senckenbergstr 3   Phone: 641 7028344
W-6300 Giessen, Germany   Prof. Dr. E. Wohlken
Founded: 1946. **Subjects:** Agricultural politics, agricultural market research, statistics, econometrics. **Holdings:** 16,100 books; 370 bound periodical volumes. **Subscriptions:** 119 journals and other serials; 3 newspapers. **Services:** Copying; library open to university members only.

★ 18027 ★
Universitat Giessen - Institut fur Geschichte der Medizin - Bibliothek (Hist)
Jheringstr 6   Phone: 641 7024200
W-6300 Giessen, Germany   Prof. Dr. Jost Benedum
Subjects: History of medicine. **Holdings:** 1400 books; 300 bound periodical volumes. **Services:** Library open to the public. **Publications:** 375 Jahre Medizin in Giessen, 1607-1982 (1983); Funfundzwanzig Jahre Institut fur Geschichte der Medizin an der Justus-Liebig-Universitat Giessen, 1965-1990 (1990); Arbeiten zur Geschichte der Medizin in Giessen.

★ 18028 ★
Universitat Giessen - Mathematisches Institut - Bibliothek (Sci-Engr)
Arndstr 2
W-6300 Giessen, Germany   Phone: 641 7022564
Founded: 1864. **Staff:** Prof 1. **Subjects:** Mathematics. **Holdings:** 13,800 books; 10,000 bound periodical volumes. **Subscriptions:** 300 journals and other serials. **Services:** Library open to the public.

★ 18029 ★
Universitat Goettingen - Abteilung Geschichte der Medizin - Bibliothek
(Hist)
Nikolausberger Weg 7b
W-3400 Goettingen, Germany   Phone: 551 399007
Founded: 1967. Staff: Prof 1. Subjects: History of Medicine. Holdings:
18,000. Subscriptions: 35 journals and other serials. Services: Library open
to the public. Remarks: FAX: 551 399554.

★ 18030 ★
Universitat Goettingen - Mathematisches Institut - Bibliothek (Sci-Engr)
Bunsenstr 3-5
W-3400 Goettingen, Germany   Phone: 551 397776
Founded: 1880. Subjects: Mathematics. Holdings: 18,000 books; 16,000
bound periodical volumes. Subscriptions: 220 journals and other serials.
Services: Library open to the public.

★ 18031 ★
Universitat Goettingen - Seminar fur Englische Philologie - Bibliothek
(Hum)
Humboldtallee 13
W-3400 Goettingen, Germany   Phone: 551 397554
Founded: 1888. Staff: Prof 1; Other 1. Subjects: Literature - Old English,
Elizabethan, eighteenth-century English, nineteenth-century English;
history of the English language; English syntax. Holdings: 51,000 books and
bound periodical volumes; 800 microfiche and reels of microfilm.
Subscriptions: 115 journals and other serials. Services: Library open to the
public.

★ 18032 ★
Universitat Graz - Institut fur Mathematik - Bibliothek (Sci-Engr)
Heinrichstr. 36
A-8010 Graz, Austria   Phone: 316 3805159
Founded: 1895. Staff: 1. Subjects: Mathematics. Holdings: 20,000 books;
10,500 bound periodical volumes; 2000 reports. Subscriptions: 320 journals
and other serials. Services: Interlibrary loan; library open to the public.
Remarks: FAX: 316 381454.

★ 18033 ★
Universitat Hamburg - Institut fur Angewandte Botanik - Bibliothek
(Biol Sci)
Marseiller Str 7
W-2000 Hamburg 36, Germany   Phone: 40 41232371
                                        Dr. H. Wurm
Founded: 1883. Staff: Prof 2. Subjects: Applied botany, plant protection,
agricultural chemistry, seed testing. Holdings: 90,000 books and periodical
volumes. Subscriptions: 314 journals and other serials. Services: Library
open to the public. Remarks: FAX: 40 41236593.

★ 18034 ★
Universitat Hamburg - Institut fur Geschichte der Medizin - Bibliothek
(Med)
Martinistrasse 52
W-2000 Hamburg 20, Germany   Phone: 40 4683141
                                        Prof. Ursula Weisser
Founded: 1962. Staff: Prof 1. Subjects: Medical history. Subscriptions: 18
journals and other serials. Services: Library open to the public.

★ 18035 ★
**Universitat Hamburg - Institut fur Hydrobiologie und
Fischereiwessenschaft - Bibliothek** (Biol Sci)
Zeiseweg 9
W-2000 Hamburg 50, Germany   Phone: 40 41236699
                                        Deta Axnick, Libn.
Founded: 1964. Staff: Prof 1. Subjects: Hydrobiology, fisheries sciences,
limnology, biological oceanography. Holdings: 16,000 books; 44,000
reprints. Subscriptions: 150 journals and other serials. Services: Interlibrary
loan; copying; library open to the public for reference use only.
Computerized Information Services: Internal databases. Publications:
Reports of the Centre of Marine and Climate Research; reprints list.

★ 18036 ★
**Universitat Hamburg - Institut fur Seerecht und Seehandelsrecht -
Bibliothek** (Law)
Heimhuder Str 71
W-2000 Hamburg, Germany   Phone: 40 41235921
Founded: 1984. Staff: Prof 1. Subjects: Law of the sea, maritime law,
transportation law. Holdings: 8000 books; 3200 bound periodical volumes.
Subscriptions: 99 journals and other serials; 3 newspapers. Services: Library
open to the public. Staff: Roland Petersen; Stella Schmidt.

★ 18037 ★
**Universitat Hamburg - Seminar fur Afrikanische Sprachen und Kulturen
- Bibliothek** (Area-Ethnic)
Mittelweg 177   Phone: 40 41234874
W-2000 Hamburg 13, Germany   Heidi Werbetz, Libn.
Founded: 1909. Subjects: Africa - languages, history, culture, literature,
music. Holdings: 20,000 books; 350 microfiche and microfilm; computer
cassettes and tapes. Subscriptions: 95 journals and other serials. Services:
Interlibrary loan; library open to the public.

★ 18038 ★
**Universitat Hamburg - Seminar fur Handels Schiffahrts und
Wirtschaftsrecht - Bibliothek** (Law)
Schluterstr. 28   Phone: 40 41234579
W-2000 Hamburg 13, Germany   Prof. Dr. Karsten Schmidt
Founded: 1919. Staff: Prof 10; Other 5. Subjects: Law - commercial,
corporate, anti-trust, intellectual property, economic, transportation; unfair
trade practices. Holdings: 32,000 books; 54 bound periodical volumes; 10
reports; microfiche. Subscriptions: 54 journals and other serials. Services:
Library open to the public. Publications: Hamburger Beitrage zum
Handels-, Schiffahrts- und Wirtschaftsrecht. Remarks: FAX: 40 41236638.
Telex: 214732.

★ 18039 ★
Universitat Hannover - Institut fur Mathematik - Bibliothek (Sci-Engr)
Welfengarten 1   Phone: 511 7622894
W-3000 Hannover, Germany   Dr. W. Heinermann, Academic Dir.
Founded: 1880. Staff: 3. Subjects: Mathematics, pure mathematics, logic,
algebraic geometry. Holdings: 23,000 books; 6800 bound periodical
volumes; 2100 bound periodical volumes; 2100 reports. Subscriptions: 221
journals and other serials. Services: Library open to students only.
Automated Operations: FORTRAN. Remarks: Telex: 923868 inih-d.

★ 18040 ★
Universitat Heidelberg - Institut fur Soziologie - Bibliothek (Soc Sci,
Area-Ethnic)
Sandgasse 9   Phone: 6221 542983
W-6900 Heidelberg, Germany   Silvia Henninger, Dipl.-Bibl.
Staff: Prof 1; Other 8. Subjects: Sociology, ethnology. Special Collections:
Africa; Sicily; philosophy. Holdings: 60,000 books. Subscriptions: 100
journals and other serials. Services: Interlibrary loan; library open to the
public.

★ 18041 ★
**Universitat Hohenheim - Landesanstalt fur Landwirtschaftliche Chemie -
Bibliothek** (Agri)
Emil Wolff Str 14
Postfach 700562   Phone: 711 4592735
W-7000 Stuttgart 70, Germany   G. Drescher
Subjects: Agriculture; chemistry - analytical, environmental. Holdings:
3500 books; 2300 bound periodical volumes. Subscriptions: 10 journals and
other serials. Remarks: FAX: 711 4593495.

★ 18042 ★
Universitat Innsbruck - Institut fur Alte Geschichte - Bibliothek (Hist)
Innrain 52   Phone: 5222 7243531
A-6020 Innsbruck, Austria   Dr. G. Kipp, Univ.-Doz.
Founded: 1885. Subjects: Ancient history, ancient Near East, ancient Egypt,
ancient church history, Old Testament times, social anthropology.
Holdings: 11,500 books; 11,000 slide sets. Subscriptions: 23 journals and
other serials. Services: Library open to the public.

★ 18043 ★
Universitat Innsbruck - Medizinisch-Biologische Fachbibliothek (Biol Sci)
Fritz Pregl Str 3/2   Phone: 512 5072112
A-6020 Innsbruck, Austria   Dr. Walter Neuhauser, Mag.Dr.
Founded: 1979. **Staff:** Prof 2. **Subjects:** Life sciences. **Holdings:** 70,000 bound periodical volumes; 100 microfiche. **Subscriptions:** 480 journals and other serials. **Services:** Interlibrary loan; copying; library open to the public. **Computerized Information Services:** MEDLINE. Contact Person: A.T. Deutsch, Libn.

Universitat Innsbruck - Universitatsbiliothek - Fakultatsbibliothek fur Bauingenieurwessen und Architektur
See: **University of Innsbruck - University Library - Library of the Faculty of Civil Engineering and Architecture (18702)**

★ 18044 ★
Universitat Koln - Historische Seminar - Anglo Amerkanische Abteilung - Bibliothek (Hist)
Albertus Magnus Pl
W-5000 Cologne 41, Germany   Phone: 221 4703020
Founded: 1952. **Staff:** Prof 1. **Subjects:** American history, British history. **Holdings:** 32,000 books; 6000 microfiche; 2200 reels of microfilm; 2150 microcards. **Subscriptions:** 30 journals and other serials. **Services:** Library open to the public for reference use only.

Universitat Koln - Kunsthistorisches Institut - Bibliothek
See: **University of Cologne - Institute of Art History (18488)**

★ 18045 ★
Universitat Koln - Seminar fur Mathematik und ihre Didaktik - Bibliothek (Sci-Engr)
Gronewaldstr 2
W-5000 Cologne 41, Germany   Phone: 221 4704749
Founded: 1965. **Staff:** Prof 1; Other 1. **Subjects:** Mathematics, cognitive psychology, mathematical education. **Holdings:** 11,500 books; 1430 bound periodical volumes; 90 reports. **Subscriptions:** 52 journals and other serials. **Services:** Library not open to the public. **Remarks:** FAX: 221 4705174.

★ 18046 ★
Universitat Mainz - Fachbereichsbibliothek Mathematik (Sci-Engr)
Staudingerweg 9
Postfach 3980   Phone: 6131 392693
W-6500 Mainz, Germany   Gislinde Thiessen, Libn.
Founded: 1946. **Staff:** Prof 1; Other 2. **Subjects:** Mathematics. **Holdings:** 18,800 books; 17,000 bound periodical volumes; theses. **Subscriptions:** 210 journals and other serials. **Services:** Copying; library open to the public with restrictions. **Publications:** Berichte zur Stochastik; Mainzer Seminarberichte. **Remarks:** FAX: 6131 394389.

★ 18047 ★
Universitat Mainz - Institut fur Ethnologie und Afrika Studien - Bibliothek (Area-Ethnic, Soc Sci)
Forum Universitatis
Eingang 6
Postfach 3980   Phone: 6131 392798
W-6500 Mainz, Germany   Dr. Ulla Schild
Founded: 1946. **Staff:** Prof 1. **Subjects:** Social anthropology, African literature, American Indians, African studies, Indonesia. **Special Collections:** Janheinz Jahn Library (African literature - 14,000 volumes, 40 journals). **Holdings:** 34,300 books; 80 bound periodical volumes; 3 archival items. **Services:** Copying; library open to the public on a limited schedule. **Remarks:** FAX: 6131 393730.

★ 18048 ★
Universitat Mainz - Seminar fur Englische Philogie - Bibliothek l (Hum, Hist)
Welderweg 18
Postfach 3980   Phone: 6131 393367
W-6500 Mainz, Germany   Alfred Hornung, Ph.D.
Founded: 1950. **Staff:** Prof 1; Other 3. **Subjects:** Great Britain, Canada, and U.S. - literature, language, linguistics, history and culture. **Special Collections:** Early Colonial Literature and Culture Collection. **Holdings:** 85,000 books; 15,000 bound periodical volumes; 1000 microfiche; 400 reels of microfilm. **Subscriptions:** 160 journals and other serials; 3 newspapers. **Services:** Copying; library open to the public. **Computerized Information Services:** HEBIS (internal database). Contact Person: Karla Lemm. **Remarks:** FAX: 6131 395100.

★ 18049 ★
Universitat Mannheim - Bibliothek der Fakultat fur Mathematik und Informatik (Sci-Engr)
Seminargebaude A5
Postf. 103462   Phone: 621 2925326
W-6800 Mannheim 1, Germany   Dr. Manfield Kleiss
Founded: 1968. **Staff:** Prof 2; Other 10. **Subjects:** Mathematics, informatics. **Holdings:** 45,000 books. **Subscriptions:** 310 journals and other serials. **Services:** Library open to the public (materials are loaned during weekends only). **Publications:** Library List of Journals.

★ 18050 ★
Universitat Munchen - Amerika-Institut - Bibliothek (Area-Ethnic)
Schellingstr 3   Phone: 89 21802841
W-Munich 40, Germany   Dorothea Scheid, Libn.
Founded: 1948. **Staff:** Prof 1. **Subjects:** North America - culture, literature, history. **Holdings:** 43,000 books; 5000 bound periodical volumes. **Subscriptions:** 100 journals and other serials; 3 newspapers. **Services:** Interlibrary loan; copying; library open to the public for reference use only. **Remarks:** Alternate telephone number(s): 89 21802730.

★ 18051 ★
Universitat Munchen - Institut fur Politik und Offentliches Recht - Bibliothek (Law)
Prof. Huber Pl. 2   Phone: 89 21802791
W-8000 Munich 22, Germany   Dr. Peter Badura
Founded: 1932. **Staff:** Prof 1; Other 8. **Subjects:** Constitutional law, administrative law, German public law, political science. **Holdings:** 45,900 books and bound periodical volumes; 650 uncataloged items. **Subscriptions:** 74 journals and other serials. **Services:** Copying; library open to the public with restrictions.

★ 18052 ★
Universitat Munchen - Institut fur Volkerkunde und Afrikanistik - Bibliothek (Area-Ethnic)
Ludwigstr 27
W-8000 Munich 22, Germany   Phone: 89 2180
Founded: 1956. **Subjects:** Systematic ethnology, Atlanten, South Africa, Ethiopia, archeology of Africa, Dias, cultural anthropology, Indonesia, Madagascar. **Holdings:** 16,300 books; 64 bound periodical volumes. **Subscriptions:** 64 journals and other serials. **Services:** Interlibrary loan; copying; library open to the public weekends only. **Computerized Information Services:** Internal database. **Remarks:** Alternate telephone number(s): 89 2853.

★ 18053 ★
Universitat Munchen - Mathematisches Institut - Bibliothek (Sci-Engr, Comp Sci)
Theresienstr. 39   Phone: 89 23944500
W-8000 Munich 2, Germany   Prof. O. Forster
Founded: 1893. **Staff:** Prof 2. **Subjects:** Mathematics, physics, computer science. **Holdings:** 25,398 books; 17,334 bound periodical volumes. **Subscriptions:** 272 journals and other serials. **Services:** Library open to the public with restrictions. **Computerized Information Services:** LARS (internal database). Contact Person: Dr. E. Schafer. **Remarks:** FAX: 89 2805248.

★ 18054 ★
Universitat Munster - Westf. Wilhelms - Institut fur Altertumskunde - Bibliothek (Hist)
Domplatz 20-22   Phone: 251 834558
W-4400 Munster, Germany   Regine Binder, Dipl.Bibl.
Founded: 1883. **Staff:** Prof 2. **Subjects:** Classical philology (Greek and Latin language and literature), ancient history, classical antiquity, philosophy, papyrology, epigraphy. **Special Collections:** Ancient Orientalistic collection. **Holdings:** 50,000 books; 300 reels of microfilm. **Subscriptions:** 720 journals and other serials. **Services:** Interlibrary loan; copying; library open to the public for reference use only.

★ 18055 ★
Universitat Salzburg - Institut fur Anglistik und Amerikanistik -
   Bibliothek (Hum)
Akademiestr 24   Phone: 662 80444400
A-5020 Salzburg, Austria   Dr. Leo Truchlar, Hd. of Dept.
Founded: 1964. **Subjects:** English and American literature, linguistics, and civilization; methodology of teaching English as a second language. **Holdings:** 44,000 books; 5000 bound periodical volumes; 2 reels of microfilm. **Subscriptions:** 119 journals and other serials; 6 newspapers. **Services:** Interlibrary loan; library not open to the public.

★ 18056 ★
Universitat Salzburg - Institut fur Erziehungswissenschaften - Bibliothek
   (Educ)
Akademiestr. 26
A-5020 Salzburg, Austria   Phone: 662 8044
Founded: 1964. **Staff:** Prof 2. **Subjects:** Education, psychology, didactics, teaching, sociology, education systems, history of education. **Holdings:** 16,000 books; 1700 bound periodical volumes. **Subscriptions:** 65 journals and other serials. **Services:** Copying; library open to the public for reference use only. **Remarks:** Alternate telephone number(s): 662 4030. **Staff:** Dr. Monika Rothbucher; Mag. Maria Strasser.

★ 18057 ★
Universitat Wien - Fachbibliothek fuer Anglistik und Amerikanistik
   (Hum)
Universitatsstr 7   Phone: 222 401032511
A-1010 Vienna, Austria   Dr. Harald Mittermann
Founded: 1885. **Staff:** Prof 3. **Subjects:** English language, English linguistics, British literature, American and other anglophone literature, cultural studies. **Holdings:** 58,000 books; bound periodical volumes; 75 microfiche and microfilm titles; computer disks and tapes; CD-ROMs. **Subscriptions:** 60 journals and other serials. **Services:** Interlibrary loan; copying; library open by special permission. **Automated Operations:** Computerized public access catalog. **Computerized Information Services:** BITNET (electronic mail service). **Remarks:** FAX: 222 4020533 (Attn. Mittermann). Electronic mail address(es): a7541dae@awiunill (BITNET).

Universitat Wien - Fachbibliothek fur Botanik
See: **University of Vienna - Botany Library** (19490)

★ 18058 ★
Universitat Wien - Fachbibliothek fur Kunstgeschichte (Art)
Universitatsstr 7   Phone: 222 43002503
A-1010 Vienna, Austria   Dr. Schikola Gertraut
Staff: Prof 1; Other 1. **Subjects:** Art history, architecture, Byzantine art. **Holdings:** 70,000 books; microfiche; microfilm. **Services:** Copying; library open to the public for reference use only. **Publications:** Wiener Jahrbuch f.Kunstgeschichte. **Remarks:** FAX: 222 4028510.

★ 18059 ★
Universitat Wurzburg - Institut fur Geschichte der Medizin - Bibliothek
   (Hist)
Koellikerstr 6 (Ruckgeb)   Phone: 931 31716
W-8700 Wurzburg, Germany   Dr. Gundolf Keil, Ph.D., M.D.
Founded: 1953. **Staff:** Prof 4. **Subjects:** History - medicine, science, technology, pharmacy, culture, arts. **Special Collections:** Medieval medicine collection. **Holdings:** 59,935 books; 14,875 bound periodical volumes; 74.75 million archival items; 454 reels of microfilm; 600 medical instruments. **Subscriptions:** 648 journals and other serials; 45 newspapers. **Services:** Interlibrary loan; library not open to the public.

Universitat Zurich - Kunstgeschichtliches Seminar - Bibliothek
See: **University of Zurich - Institute for Art History - Library** (19663)

★ 18060 ★
Universitat Zurich - Medizinhistorisches Institut and Museum -
   Bibliothek (Med)
Ramistr 71   Phone: 1 2572199
CH-8006 Zurich, Switzerland   Heidi Seger
Founded: 1951. **Staff:** Prof 1; Other 1. **Subjects:** History of medicine, medical biographies, history of science, history of surgical instruments. **Holdings:** 100,000 books, bound periodical volumes, theses, manuscripts, microfiche, and microfilm. **Subscriptions:** 80 journals and other serials. **Services:** Interlibrary loan; copying; library open to the public. **Remarks:** FAX: 1 2572349.

★ 18061 ★
Universitatea Din Timisoara Institutul Agronomic - Biblioteca (Agri)
Calea Aradului 119
Catsuta Postala 136   Phone: 61 41424
1900 Timisoara, Romania   Laura Demetrovici
Founded: 1946. **Staff:** Prof 10. **Subjects:** Agriculture, veterinary medicine, food industry, animal husbandry, horticulture. **Holdings:** 49,000 books; 106,000 bound periodical volumes. **Services:** Interlibrary loan; library open to the public. **Remarks:** Telex: 71386 UA tim R.

Universitats- und Landesbibliothek Sachsen-Anhalt
See: **Martin Luther Universitat Halle-Wittenberg** (9731)

Universitatsbibliothek Hannover und Technische Informationsbibliothek
See: **University Library of Hannover and Technical Information Library**
   (18764)

★ 18062 ★
Universite d' Aix Marseille II - Bibliotheque - Section Medecine-
   Odontologie (Med)
27 bd Jean Moulin
F-13385 Marseille Cedex 5, France   Phone: 91 834356
Staff: Prof 22; Other 4. **Subjects:** Medicine, paramedicine, odontology. **Holdings:** 70,000 books; 200,000 bound periodical volumes; 200 microfiche; theses. **Subscriptions:** 800 journals and other serials. **Services:** Interlibrary loan; copying; library open to the public with restrictions. **Computerized Information Services:** Questel, Data-Star, SUNIST; Intervatel (internal database). **Contact Person:** A.M. Descat, Bibliothecaire. **Special Catalogs:** Catalogue des Periodiques. **Remarks:** FAX: 91 796115.

★ 18063 ★
Universite de Caen - Bibliotheque de l'Universite - Section Medecine
   Pharmacie (Med)
Av de la Cote de Nacre
F-14032 Caen Cedex, France   Phone: 31068206
Founded: 1972. **Staff:** Prof 5; Other 4. **Subjects:** Medicine, pharmacy. **Holdings:** 15,000 books; 3000 dissertations. **Subscriptions:** 470 journals and other serials. **Services:** Interlibrary loan; copying; SDI; library open to the public by appointment. **Computerized Information Services:** Questel, G.CAM, NLM, Data-Star, DIALOG Information Services, SUNIST. **Special Catalogs:** Local union catalogue of biomedical serials. **Remarks:** FAX: 31068207.

★ 18064 ★
Universite de Geneve - Section de Mathematiques - Bibliotheque (Sci-
   Engr)
2/4 rue du Lievre   Phone: 22 435068
CH-1211 Geneva 24, Switzerland   Mrs. Bernard Jujez, Hd.
Founded: 1899. **Staff:** Prof 3. **Subjects:** Pure mathematics, statistics, numerical analysis, probability. **Holdings:** 17,000 books; 3629 bound periodical volumes. **Subscriptions:** 300 journals and other serials. **Services:** Interlibrary loan; copying; library open to the public with restrictions. **Automated Operations:** Computerized public access catalog (SIBIL-REBUS).

★ 18065 ★
Universite Laval - Bibliotheque Generale (Area-Ethnic, Hum)
Cite Universitaire   Phone: (418)656-3344
Ste. Foy, PQ, Canada G1K 7P4   Claude Busque, Lib.Hd.
Subjects: French Canadian and Quebec studies; French Canadian folklore; Quebec geography; ethnic groups from Quebec and Canada; French and French Canadian literature; 19th century French musical press; law; philosophy of science; philosophy - Aristotelian, Thomist, and French modern. **Holdings:** Figures not available. **Services:** Interlibrary loan; copying; SDI; library open to the public for reference use only. **Computerized Information Services:** DIALOG Information Services, QL Systems, CAN/OLE, RESORS (Remote Sensing On-Line Retrieval System), BADADUQ, WILSONLINE, International Development Research Centre (IDRC), SOQUIJ, LaborLine, MEDLINE, BRS Information Technologies, Questel, CANSIM, Info Globe, PFDS Online; InterNet (electronic mail service). **Remarks:** FAX: (418)656-7897.

Electronic mail address(es): bonnelly@vm.ulaval.ca (InterNet). **Staff:** Denis Kronstrom, Asst.Lib.Hd.; Agathe Garon, Media Chf.; Adele Bertrand-Gosselin, Gen.Ref.; Remi Boucher, Gen.Ref.; Philippe Morneau, Gen. Ref.; Jacques Robidas, Gen.Ref.; Louise Ranger, Gen.Ref.; Melanie Sainte-Marie, Gen.Ref.; Madeleine Robin, Art & Architecture; Louise Dion, Geography & Ecology; Monique Mailloux, History; Robert Crispo, Journalism Info.; Denis LeMay, Law; Christine Lachance, Law; Francine Rousseau, Literature & Language; Claude Beaudry, Music; Gilles Paradis, Philosophy & Psychology; Pierre Guilemette, Pol., Econ.; Nicole Deschenes, Sci.Admin.; Yolande Taillon, Educ.Sci.; Gaetan Drolet, Soc.Sci.; Maurice Mathieu, Theology; Colette Sanfacon, Transparencies; Gary Ross, Films & Video; Flora Veress, Films & Video; Yves Tessier, Maps & Atlas; Helene Genest, Online/SDI Serv.

★ 18066 ★
Universite Laval - Bibliotheque Scientifique (Sci-Engr, Med, Agri)
Quebec, PQ, Canada G1K 7P4   Phone: (418)656-3967
Alain Bourque, Hd.
Founded: 1973. **Staff:** Prof 10; Other 24. **Subjects:** Science, technology, medical and paramedical sciences, agriculture, forestry, food and nutrition, wood science technology and forest ecology (mycories), animal science, soils, phytopathology, electrochemistry and corrosion, noise pollution, wind energy. **Holdings:** 100,000 books; 200,000 bound periodical volumes; 16,153 reels of microfilm; 18,526 microfiches. **Subscriptions:** 2738 journals and other serials; 30 newspapers. **Services:** Interlibrary loan; copying; library open to the public for reference use only. **Automated Operations:** Computerized cataloging, acquisitions, serials, and circulation. **Computerized Information Services:** DIALOG Information Services, BRS Information Technologies, QL Systems, Questel, MEDLARS, RESORS (Remote Sensing On-line Retrieval System), Info Globe, WILSONLINE, International Development Research Centre (IDRC), CAN/OLE, PFDS Online; CD-ROMs (MEDLINE, CINAHL, CCINFOdisc, Pollution/Toxicology, AGRICOLA, FSTA (Food Science and Technology Abstracts), ASFA (Aquatic Sciences and Fisheries Abstracts), COMPENDEX, MATHFILE). **Staff:** Michel Dagenais, Sci.; Louise DeLisle, Forestry; Doris Dufour, Med.Sci.; Jean Morel, Med.Sci.; Lorraine Vallieres, Med.Sci.; Robert Giroux, Agri.; Louise Marcil, Sci.; Richard Laverdiere, Tech.; Yolande Taillon, Agri.

★ 18067 ★
Universite Laval - International Centre for Research on Language Planning (Hum)
Pavillon De Koninck, 2nd Fl.   Phone: (418)656-3232
Ste. Foy, PQ, Canada G1K 7P4   Claude Rocheleau, Lib.Techn.
Founded: 1967. **Staff:** 3. **Subjects:** Bilingualism; bilingual education; language - teaching, learning, planning, rights, contact; computer linguistics. **Special Collections:** Commission on Bilingualism and Biculturalism; Commission Gendron; Commission Bibeau; Report of the Bilingual Districts Advisory Board. **Holdings:** 6000 books; 30,000 documents; 250 reels of microfilm. **Subscriptions:** 50 journals and other serials. **Services:** Copying; center open to the public. **Automated Operations:** Computerized cataloging and acquisitions. **Computerized Information Services:** BIBELO (internal database). **Publications:** List of publications - available upon request. **Remarks:** FAX: (418)656-2019 (CIRAL-FAC.LETTRES). **Also Known As:** Centre International de Recherche en Amenagement Linguistique.

★ 18068 ★
Universite de Liege - Bibliotheque de la Faculte de Medecine (Med)
CHU Sart Tilman   Phone: 41 307500
B-4000 Liege 1, Belgium   Francoise Noel-Lambot, Dr.Sc.
Founded: 1988. **Staff:** Prof 4; Other 8. **Subjects:** Medicine, preclinical sciences, microbiology. **Holdings:** 50,000 books; 1000 theses. **Subscriptions:** 1000 journals and other serials; 10 newspapers. **Services:** Interlibrary loan; copying; SDI; library open to the public upon registration and payment of access fee. **Computerized Information Services:** DIMDI; LIBER (internal database); CD-ROMs. **Publications:** Nouvelles Scientifiques, weekly. **Special Catalogs:** Catalog of serials; catalog of theses. **Remarks:** FAX: 41 307506.

★ 18069 ★
Universite de Liege - Unite de Documentation - Mathematique (Sci-Engr)
Av des Tilleuls 15   Phone: 41 669377
B-4000 Liege, Belgium   Paul Chauveheid
Staff: Prof 2. **Subjects:** Mathematics, statistics. **Holdings:** 25,000 books; reports; archives. **Subscriptions:** 200 journals and other serials. **Services:** Interlibrary loan; copying; library open to the public. **Computerized Information Services:** STN International; LIBER (internal database).

★ 18070 ★
Universite de Lille - UFR d'Anglais - Bibliotheque (Hum)
BP 149   Phone: 20336274
F-59653 Villeneuve d'Ascq Cedex, France   Nicole Gabet
Founded: 1953. **Staff:** Prof 1; Other 5. **Subjects:** British literature, American literature, British civilization, American civilization, English language. **Holdings:** 28,000 books; 1200 documents; videocassettes. **Subscriptions:** 61 journals and other serials. **Services:** Interlibrary loan; copying; library open to the public.

★ 18071 ★
Universite de Moncton - Bibliotheque de Droit (Law)
Moncton, NB, Canada E1A 3E9   Phone: (506)858-4547
Simonne Clermont, Law Libn.
Founded: 1978. **Staff:** Prof 2; Other 7. **Subjects:** Law. **Holdings:** 39,100 books; 47,162 bound serial volumes; 26,299 AV programs. **Subscriptions:** 915 journals and other serials. **Services:** Interlibrary loan; copying; library open to the public for reference use only. **Computerized Information Services:** QL Systems, CAN/LAW. Performs searches on fee basis. **Publications:** Liste selective des nouvelles acquisitions. **Remarks:** FAX: (506)858-4534. **Staff:** Carmel Allain, Cat.

★ 18072 ★
Universite de Moncton - Centre d'Etudes Acadiennes (Area-Ethnic)
Moncton, NB, Canada E1A 3E9   Phone: (506)858-4085
Ronald Labelle, Dir.
Founded: 1968. **Staff:** Prof 5; Other 3. **Subjects:** Acadian history, genealogy, and folklore. **Holdings:** 12,300 books and pamphlets; 3240 reels of microfilm; 1458 feet of manuscripts; 3435 reels of magnetic tape of Acadian folk tales and songs. **Subscriptions:** 52 journals and other serials; 10 newspapers. **Services:** Interlibrary loan (limited); copying; center open to the public. **Computerized Information Services:** Envoy 100 (electronic mail service). **Publications:** Contact-Acadie, irregular. **Remarks:** FAX: (506)858-4086. Electronic mail address(es): PEB NBMOU (Envoy 100). **Staff:** Gilles Chiasson, Libn.; Ronnie-Gilles Leblanc, Archv.; Kenneth Breau, Univ.Archv.; Stephen White, Geneal.

★ 18073 ★
Universite de Moncton - Faculte des Sciences de l'Education - Centre de Ressources Pedagogiques (Educ)
Moncton, NB, Canada E1A 3E9   Phone: (506)858-4356
Berthe Boudreau, Dir.
Founded: 1973. **Staff:** Prof 2; Other 2. **Subjects:** Education: instructional material on the subject studies in public schools. **Holdings:** 32,000 books, kits, and tests; 28,172 slides; 1052 filmstrips; 1577 pictures; 1992 transparencies. **Services:** Copying; center open to New Brunswick teachers. **Automated Operations:** Computerized cataloging and circulation. **Publications:** Newsletter, monthly - for internal distribution only. **Staff:** Leonard Gallant, Ref.Libn.

★ 18074 ★
Universite de Montreal - Audiovideotheque (Aud-Vis)
Pavillon Marie-Victorin
90, Vincent-d'Indy
Salle C-415   Phone: (514)343-7344
Montreal, PQ, Canada H3C 3J7   Ginette Gagnier, Libn.
Staff: Prof 1; Other 4. **Holdings:** 10,368 AV programs. **Services:** Interlibrary loan; library open to the public with restrictions. **Automated Operations:** Computerized cataloging and acquisitions. **Special Catalogs:** Catalogue des documents audiovisual. **Remarks:** FAX: (514)343-2349.

★ 18075 ★
Universite de Montreal - Bibliotheque d'Amenagement (Art, Plan)
Pavillon 5620
av. Darlington
Salle 1004   Phone: (514)343-7177
Montreal, PQ, Canada H3C 3J7   Vesna Blazina, Libn.
Founded: 1964. **Staff:** Prof 3; Other 9. **Subjects:** Architecture, landscape architecture, design, city planning, urbanism. **Holdings:** 39,442 books; 11,422 bound periodical volumes; 39,645 slides; 1202 microforms; 2970 AV programs. **Subscriptions:** 641 journals and other serials. **Services:** Interlibrary loan; copying; library open to the public with restrictions. **Automated Operations:** Computerized cataloging and acquisitions. **Computerized Information Services:** DIALOG Information Services, CAN/OLE, Questel; DIAME (internal database). **Publications:** Acquisitions list, monthly - limited distribution; Bibliographie guides (slides); Periodicals list - limited distribution. **Staff:** Ginette Melancon-Bolduc; Nevart Nairy Gunjian.

★ 18076 ★
Universite de Montreal - Bibliotheque de Bibliotheconomie (Info Sci)
Pavillon Lionel-Groulx
3150, avenue Jean-Brillant
2e etage, salle C-2059   Phone: (514)343-6047
Montreal, PQ, Canada H3C 3J7   Clement Tremblay, Libn.
Founded: 1961. **Staff:** Prof 1; Other 3. **Subjects:** Library science, information science, records management. **Holdings:** 30,032 books; 8055 bound periodical volumes; 5615 microforms; 570 reports. **Subscriptions:** 739 journals and other serials. **Services:** Interlibrary loan; copying; library open to the public with restrictions. **Automated Operations:** Computerized cataloging, acquisitions, and circulation. **Publications:** Acquisitions list, monthly - limited distribution; guide de l'usager. **Special Catalogs:** Periodicals list. **Remarks:** FAX: (514)343-2348. **Staff:** Myloan Duong, Libn.

★ 18077 ★
Universite de Montreal - Bibliotheque de Biologie (Biol Sci)
Pavillon Marie-Victorin
90, avenue Vincent-d'Indy
Salle G-210   Phone: (514)343-7073
Montreal, PQ, Canada H3C 3J7   Robert Gauthier, Libn.
Founded: 1962. **Staff:** Prof 2; Other 7. **Subjects:** Biology, zoology, ecology, herpetology, cell biology, pysiology, molecular biology, entomology, ornithology, mammalogy, ethology, ichthyology, protozoology. **Holdings:** 19,674 books; 20,147 bound periodical volumes; 2304 microforms; 158 reports; 98 AV programs; 166 slides. **Subscriptions:** 461 journals and other serials. **Services:** Interlibrary loan; copying; library open to the public with restrictions. **Automated Operations:** Computerized cataloging and acquisitions. **Computerized Information Services:** DIALOG Information Services, CAN/OLE, MEDLINE, Questel; CD-ROMs (FM Waves CD-ROM, Current Contents Search); InterNet (electronic mail service). **Publications:** Acquisitions list, irregular - limited distribution; Periodical list - limited distribution; User Guide (general); User Guides (specialized). **Remarks:** FAX: (514)343-2349. Electronic mail address(es): WALLER@EME.UMONTREAL.CA (InterNet). **Staff:** Marc Waller.

★ 18078 ★
Universite de Montreal - Bibliotheque de Botanique (Biol Sci)
Jardin Botanique
4101 est, rue Sherbrooke
Salle 334   Phone: (514)872-8495
Montreal, PQ, Canada H1X 2B2   Robert Gauthier, Libn.
Founded: 1925. **Staff:** 1. **Subjects:** General botany, taxonomy, genetics, evolution, paleobotany, ecology, plant physiology, mycology, algology, bryology, plant biotechnology. **Holdings:** 10,094 books; 12,106 bound periodical volumes; 27,676 microforms; 15,127 slides; 6301 photographs; 18,917 reports. **Subscriptions:** 241 journals and other serials. **Services:** Interlibrary loan; copying; library open to the public with restrictions. **Automated Operations:** Computerized acquisitions. **Publications:** Acquisitions list, monthly - limited distribution; User Guide.

★ 18079 ★
Universite de Montreal - Bibliotheque de Chimie (Sci-Engr)
Pavillon principal
Salle H-715   Phone: (514)343-6459
Montreal, PQ, Canada H3C 3J7   Josee Schepper, Libn.
Founded: 1963. **Staff:** Prof 1; Other 4. **Subjects:** Chemistry, organic chemistry, analytic chemistry. **Holdings:** 8776 books; 16,223 bound periodical volumes; 11,597 microforms; 540 slides. **Subscriptions:** 309 journals and other serials. **Services:** Interlibrary loan; copying; library open to the public with restrictions. **Automated Operations:** Computerized cataloging and acquisitions. **Computerized Information Services:** DIALOG Information Services, CAN/OLE, Questel, STN International, Sadtler Research Laboratories; CD-ROM (Current Contents Search); InterNet (electronic mail service). **Publications:** Acquisitions list, monthly - limited distribution; User Guide; Periodical list - limited distribution. **Remarks:** FAX: (514)343-5878. Electronic mail address(es): SANANIKO@UMONTREAL.CA (InterNet). **Staff:** Malivana Sananikone, Libn.

★ 18080 ★
Universite de Montreal - Bibliotheque de Droit (Law)
Pavillon Maximilien-Caron
3101, chemin de la Tour
4e etage, salle 4433   Phone: (514)343-7095
Montreal, PQ, Canada H3C 3J7   Clement Tremblay, Libn.
Founded: 1942. **Staff:** Prof 5; Other 16. **Subjects:** Law. **Special Collections:** Public law; civil law; history of law. **Holdings:** 82,373 books; 77,434 bound periodical volumes; 38,338 microforms; 1004 reports. **Subscriptions:** 1427 journals and other serials. **Services:** Interlibrary loan; copying; library open to the public. **Automated Operations:** Computerized cataloging and acquisitions. **Computerized Information Services:** CAN/LAW, QL Systems, Societe Quebecoise d'Information Juridique (SOQUIJ); CD-ROMs (Index to Legal Periodicals, Legaltrac). **Publications:** Guide du lecteur; la Classification Roy; liste des abreviations frequemment utilisees; le fichier systematique; guides bibliographiques. **Remarks:** FAX: (514)343-2348. **Staff:** Georges Clonda; Yvon Desbiens; Brigitte Butticaz; Huguette Renaud; Suzane Roumain.

★ 18081 ★
Universite de Montreal - Bibliotheque d'Education Physique (Educ, Rec)
Cepsum
2100, boul. Edouard-Montpetit
8e etage, salle 8259   Phone: (514)343-6765
Montreal, PQ, Canada H3C 3J7   Johanne Hopper, Libn.
Founded: 1966. **Staff:** Prof 1; Other 6. **Subjects:** Physical education, sports, physiology, psychology, education. **Holdings:** 20,662 books; 7432 bound periodical volumes; 18,348 microforms; 1982 reports; 153 AV programs. **Subscriptions:** 350 journals and other serials. **Services:** Interlibrary loan; copying; library open to the public with restrictions. **Automated Operations:** Computerized cataloging and acquisitions. **Computerized Information Services:** CAN/OLE; CD-ROM (SPORT Discus). **Publications:** Acquisitions list; periodicals list - both limited distribution. **Staff:** Lise Mayband.

★ 18082 ★
Universite de Montreal - Bibliotheque Education/Psychologie/ Communication (Educ)
Pavillon Marie-Victorin
90, avenue Vincent-d'Indy
3e etage, salle G-305   Phone: (514)343-7242
Montreal, PQ, Canada H3C 3J7   Tamara Rosenthal, Libn.
Founded: 1965. **Staff:** Prof 4; Other 18. **Subjects:** Education, pedagogy, psychology, communication, school administration, educational applications of computers. **Special Collections:** Rey-Herme Collection (3500 volumes); Villeneuve Collection (8150 volumes). **Holdings:** 86,376 books; 35,595 bound periodical volumes; 412,052 microforms. **Subscriptions:** 1470 journals and other serials. **Services:** Interlibrary loan; copying; library open to the public with restrictions. **Automated Operations:** Computerized cataloging and acquisitions. **Computerized Information Services:** DIALOG Information Services, CAN/OLE, Questel, MEDIOADOQ, APO; CD-ROMs (ERIC, PsycLIT); InterNet (electronic mail service). **Publications:** Acquisitions list; list of serials; list of reference works; list of dissertations - all limited distribution; Guide to CD-ROM. **Special Catalogs:** Rey-Herme Collection Catalog. **Remarks:** FAX: (514)343-2349. Electronic mail address(es): RIOUXMT@ERE.UMONTREAL.CA; SARRASIN@ERE.UMONTREAL.CA; PERRAULT@ERE.UMONTREAL.CA (InterNet). **Staff:** Marie-Therese Rioux; Vincent Perrault; Pierre Casno; Louis-Raymond Sarrasin.

★ 18083 ★
Universite de Montreal - Bibliotheque de Geographie (Geog-Map)
520, chemin Cote Ste-Catherine
Salle 339   Phone: (514)343-8063
Montreal, PQ, Canada H3C 3J7   Paquerette Ranger, Libn.
Staff: 1. **Subjects:** Geography. **Holdings:** 8488 books; 4570 bound periodical volumes; 116 microforms; 120 reports. **Subscriptions:** 211 journals and other serials. **Services:** Interlibrary loan; copying; library open to the public with restrictions. **Automated Operations:** Computerized cataloging, acquisitions, and circulation.

★18084★

Universite de Montreal - Bibliotheque de Geologie (Sci-Engr)
Ecole Polytechnique
2500, chemin de Polytechnique
4e etage, salle C-408-5
Montreal, PQ, Canada H3C 3J7
Phone: (514)343-6831
Robert Gauthier, Libn.
Founded: 1965. **Staff:** Prof 1; Other 1. **Subjects:** Geology, mineralogy, paleontology, geomorphology, mining, volcanology, geophysics. **Holdings:** 7649 books; 17,058 bound periodical volumes; 1019 microforms; 3525 reports. **Subscriptions:** 305 journals and other serials. **Services:** Interlibrary loan; copying; library open to the public with restrictions. **Automated Operations:** Computerized cataloging and acquisitions. **Publications:** Acquisitions list; periodicals list - both have limited distribution; Users Guide. **Staff:** Clement Arwas, Libn.

★18085★

Universite de Montreal - Bibliotheque d'Informatique (Info Sci, Comp Sci)
Pavillon principal
Salle M-615
Montreal, PQ, Canada H3C 3J7
Phone: (514)343-6819
Jules Giroux, Libn.
Founded: 1966. **Staff:** Prof 1; Other 4. **Subjects:** Computer science, applied linguistics, operations research, systems theory, programming. **Holdings:** 13,089 books; 6229 bound periodical volumes; 4926 microforms; 11,485 reports; 452 slides; 27 AV programs. **Subscriptions:** 338 journals and other serials. **Services:** Interlibrary loan; copying; library open to the public with restrictions. **Automated Operations:** Computerized acquisitions. **Computerized Information Services:** DIALOG Information Services, CAN/OLE, Questel; CD-ROM (INSPEC Ondisc); InterNet (electronic mail service). **Publications:** Acquisitions list, monthly; periodical list - both for limited distribution; User Guide. **Remarks:** FAX: (514)343-5878. Electronic mail address(es): PARADISC@ERE.UMONTREAL.CA (InterNet). **Staff:** Carole Paradis.

★18086★

Universite de Montreal - Bibliotheque des Lettres et Sciences Humaines (Soc Sci, Hum)
Pavillon Samuel-Bronfman
Salle 1030
Montreal, PQ, Canada H3C 3J7
Phone: (514)343-7430
Paquerette Ranger, Libn.
Founded: 1968. **Staff:** Prof 18; Other 49. **Subjects:** Anthropology, criminology, demography, history, French studies, linguistics, philosophy, industrial relations, political science, economics, social service, sociology, science history, science policy, comparative literature, art history, African studies, theology. **Holdings:** 970,311 books; 212,783 bound periodical volumes; 539,410 microforms; 19,875 AV programs; 4500 reports. **Subscriptions:** 4716 journals and other serials. **Services:** Interlibrary loan; copying; library open to the public with restrictions. **Automated Operations:** Computerized cataloging, acquisitions, and circulation. **Computerized Information Services:** DIALOG Information Services, CAN/OLE, Questel; CD-ROMs. Performs searches on fee basis. **Publications:** Bibliographic guides; guide de l'usager; guides to CD-ROM. **Special Catalogs:** Journals and periodicals list (on microfilm); Preliminary Inventory of Landmarks of Science Collection. **Remarks:** FAX: (514)343-2348. **Staff:** Monique LeCavalier; Michel Theriault; Andre Audy; Marie Brisebois-Mathieu ; Ghylaine Brodeur; Jerry Bull; Nicole Chamberland; Yolande Menard; Jihad Farhat; Andre Fleury; Luc Girard; Lise Lambert; Elias Maalouf; Luce Payette.

★18087★

Universite de Montreal - Bibliotheque de Mathematiques (Sci-Engr)
Pavillon 5620
av. Darlington
Salle 1004
Montreal, PQ, Canada H3C 3J7
Phone: (514)343-6703
Jules Giroux, Libn.
Founded: 1966. **Staff:** Prof 1; Other 3. **Subjects:** Mathematics, statistics. **Holdings:** 20,500 books; 15,227 bound periodical volumes; 2554 microforms; 4470 reports; 123 AV programs. **Subscriptions:** 347 journals and other serials. **Services:** Interlibrary loan; copying; library open to the public with restrictions. **Automated Operations:** Computerized acquisitions. **Computerized Information Services:** DIALOG Information Services, CAN/OLE, Questel; CD-ROM (MathSci). **Publications:** Reports of Higher Mathematics Seminars, 3/year; acquisitions list, monthly; periodical list - both for limited distribution; User Guide.

★18088★

Universite de Montreal - Bibliotheque de Medecine Veterinaire (Med)
3200, rue Sicotte
Salle 2121
St. Hyacinthe, PQ, Canada J2S 7C6
Phone: (514)773-8521
Bernard Bedard, Libn.
Founded: 1948. **Staff:** Prof 1; Other 4. **Subjects:** Veterinary medicine, animal science. **Special Collections:** French veterinary theses (14,164). **Holdings:** 31,259 books; 14,568 bound periodical volumes; 166 reports; 4408 microforms; 1581 government publications; 302 slides; 273 AV programs. **Subscriptions:** 472 journals and other serials. **Services:** Interlibrary loan; copying; library open to the public. **Automated Operations:** Computerized cataloging and acquisitions. **Computerized Information Services:** DIALOG Information Services, MEDLINE, CABCD, Merck & Co., VET, SESAME; TELUM (internal database). **Publications:** Liste de Nouvelles Acquisitions, irregular - limited distribution; publications lists on veterinary information; periodical list - limited distribution. **Staff:** Jean-Paul Jette.

★18089★

Universite de Montreal - Bibliotheque de Musique (Mus)
Pavillon de la faculte de musique
200, avenue Vincent-d'Indy
Salle B-287
Montreal, PQ, Canada H3C 3J7
Phone: (514)343-6432
Marc Joanis, Libn.
Founded: 1952. **Staff:** Prof 2; Other 7. **Subjects:** Music, ethnomusicology. **Holdings:** 11,545 books; 3006 bound periodical volumes; 15,527 phonograph records; 2122 slides; 25,558 scores; 10,985 microforms; 618 AV materials. **Subscriptions:** 263 journals and other serials. **Services:** Interlibrary loan; copying; library open to the public with restrictions. **Automated Operations:** Computerized cataloging and acquisitions. **Publications:** Acquisitions list - for internal distribution only. **Special Catalogs:** Periodicals list - for internal distribution only. **Staff:** Claude Soulard.

★18090★

Universite de Montreal - Bibliotheque d'Optometrie (Med)
3750, avenue Jean-Brillant
Salle 220
Montreal, PQ, Canada H3C 3J7
Phone: (514)343-7674
Danielle Tardif, Libn.
Founded: 1964. **Staff:** 2. **Subjects:** Optometry. **Holdings:** 4627 books; 5638 bound periodical volumes; 2592 slides; 139 reports; 2132 microforms; 307 AV programs. **Subscriptions:** 129 journals and other serials. **Services:** Interlibrary loan; copying; library open to the public with restrictions. **Automated Operations:** Computerized cataloging, acquisitions, and serials. **Publications:** Periodical list; acquisitions list, monthly - limited distribution.

★18091★

Universite de Montreal - Bibliotheque Para-Medicale (Med)
Pavillon Marguerite d'Youville
2375, chemin Cote Ste-Catherine
2e etage, salle 2120
Montreal, PQ, Canada H3C 3J7
Phone: (514)343-6180
Johanne Hopper, Libn.
Founded: 1963. **Staff:** Prof 3; Other 11. **Subjects:** Nursing, health administration, nutrition, epidemiology, environmental health, audiology, ergotherapy, orthophonics, physiotherapy, social and preventive medicine, gerontology and geriatrics. **Holdings:** 52,942 books; 19,797 bound periodical volumes; 27,305 microforms; 1673 slides; 1386 AV programs; 3357 reports. **Subscriptions:** 1600 journals and other serials. **Services:** Interlibrary loan; copying; library open to the public with restrictions. **Automated Operations:** Computerized cataloging acquisitions, and serials. **Computerized Information Services:** DIALOG Information Services, MEDLINE; CD-ROMs (CINAHL-CD, MEDLINE). **Publications:** Periodical list; acquisitions list, monthly - limited distribution; guide de l'usager. **Staff:** Lucille Larose-Ouimet; Louise Paradis.

★18092★

Universite de Montreal - Bibliotheque de Physique (Sci-Engr)
Pavillon principal
Salle H-825
Montreal, PQ, Canada H3C 3J7
Phone: (514)343-6613
Jules Giroux, Libn.
Founded: 1966. **Staff:** Prof 1; Other 3. **Subjects:** Physics, astrophysics, astronomy, biophysics, plasma physics, quantic mechanics, optics. **Holdings:** 13,770 books; 18,461 bound periodical volumes; 1531 reports; 83 microforms. **Subscriptions:** 235 journals and other serials. **Services:** Interlibrary loan; copying; library open to the public with restrictions. **Automated Operations:** Computerized cataloging and acquisitions. **Computerized Information Services:** DIALOG Information Services, CAN/OLE, Questel; CD-ROM (INSPEC Ondisc); InterNet (electronic mail service). **Publications:** Acquisitions list, monthly; periodical list - both for limited distribution; user guide. **Remarks:** FAX: (514)343-5878. Electronic mail address(es): CADETJ@ERE.UMONTREAL.CA (InterNet). **Staff:** Janine Cadet.

★18093★
Universite de Montreal - Bibliotheque de Psycho-Education (Educ)
750 est, boul. Gouin
2e etage, salle 201   Phone: (514)385-2556
Montreal, PQ, Canada H3C 3J7   Tamara Rosenthal, Libn.
Founded: 1970. **Staff:** Prof 1; Other 2. **Subjects:** Child psychology, rehabilitation of maladjusted children, social adaptation, social psychology, developmental psychology, psychopothology. **Holdings:** 10,905 books; 2014 bound periodical volumes; 88 microforms; 135 reports; 110 slides. **Subscriptions:** 145 journals and other serials. **Services:** Interlibrary loan; library open to the public with restrictions. **Automated Operations:** Computerized cataloging and acquisitions. **Computerized Information Services:** DIALOG Information Services, Questel; CD-ROM (PsycLIT). **Publications:** Acquisitions list; periodical list - both for internal distribution only.

★18094★
Universite de Montreal - Bibliotheque de la Sante (Med)
Pavillon principal
Salle L-623   Phone: (514)343-6826
Montreal, PQ, Canada H3C 3J7   Diane Raymond-Clerk, Libn.
Founded: 1962. **Staff:** Prof 7; Other 24. **Subjects:** Medicine, dentistry, pharmacy. **Holdings:** 85,740 books; 110,930 bound periodical volumes; 3193 microforms; 12,720 slides; 1089 reports; 886 AV programs. **Subscriptions:** 2469 journals and other serials. **Services:** Interlibrary loan; copying; library open to the public with restrictions. **Automated Operations:** Computerized cataloging and acquisitions. **Computerized Information Services:** DIALOG Information Services, CAN/OLE, MEDLINE, Questel; CD-ROMs (Current Contents Search, Life Sciences Collection CD-ROM, Drugdex System, MEDLINE, Science Citation Index). **Publications:** Acquisitions list - limited distribution; guide de l'usager. **Special Catalogs:** Periodicals list. **Remarks:** FAX: (514)343-2530. **Staff:** Bernard Bedard; Danielle Tardif; Helene Lalime; Therese Leclerc; Helene Julien.

★18095★
Universite de Montreal - Centre de Documentation de Criminologie (Soc Sci)
3150, rue Jean-Brillant   Phone: (514)343-6534
Montreal, PQ, Canada H3C 3J7   Aniela Belina, Resp.
Founded: 1964. **Staff:** Prof 2; Other 1. **Subjects:** Criminology, corrections, law enforcement, juvenile delinquency. **Holdings:** 2000 books; 7000 documents, theses, research reports, government reports, and statistics. **Subscriptions:** 80 journals and other serials. **Services:** Copying; center open to the public with restrictions. **Computerized Information Services:** Internal database. **Publications:** List of publications; acquisitions list - by subscription. **Remarks:** FAX: (514)343-2269.

★18096★
Universite de Montreal - Centre de Recherche sur les Transports - Information Centre (Trans)
C.P. 6128, Succursale A   Phone: (514)343-7575
Montreal, PQ, Canada H3C 3J7   Sylvie Hetu, Libn.
Founded: 1971. **Staff:** Prof 1. **Subjects:** Transportation, road safety. **Holdings:** 250 books; 40 bound periodical volumes; 11,000 technical reports; 400 microfiche. **Subscriptions:** 80 journals and other serials. **Services:** Interlibrary loan; copying; SDI; center open to the public for reference use only. **Automated Operations:** Computerized cataloging. **Computerized Information Services:** DIALOG Information Services, Questel, CAN/OLE. Performs searches on fee basis. **Remarks:** FAX: (514)343-7121. Telex: 05 24 146 BIBPOLYTEC.

Universite de Montreal - Clinical Research Institute of Montreal
See: **Clinical Research Institute of Montreal/ - Medical Library** (3836)

★18097★
Universite de Montreal - Departement de Demographie - Centre de Documentation (Soc Sci)
C.P. 6128, Succursale A   Phone: (514)343-6111
Montreal, PQ, Canada H3C 3J7   Micheline Frechette, Doc.
Founded: 1966. **Staff:** Prof 1. **Subjects:** Census, vital statistics, mortality, marriages, fertility, population theory and policy, migration, geographical distribution and ethnic groups, historical demography, aging, health, linguistic groups, demography of the Third World. **Special Collections:** Census of Canada, 1850 to present; vital statistics of Canada, 1921 to present; Canadian Yearbook, 1900 to present; Quebec Yearbook, 1914 to present. **Holdings:** 5000 books; 3000 bound periodical volumes; 4200 reprints, dissertations, and unbound reports. **Subscriptions:** 200 journals and other serials. **Services:** Interlibrary loan; copying; center open to the public. **Remarks:** FAX: (514)343-2309.

Universite de Montreal - Ecole des Hautes Etudes Commerciales de Montreal
See: **Ecole des Hautes Etudes Commerciales de Montreal** (5205)

Universite de Montreal - Ecole Polytechnique de Montreal
See: **Ecole Polytechnique de Montreal** (5209)

★18098★
Universite de Montreal - Service des Collections Speciales (Hist, Rare Book)
Pavillon Samuel-Bronfman
Salle 4030   Phone: (514)343-7753
Montreal, PQ, Canada H3C 3J7   Genevieve Bazin, Libn.
Founded: 1984. **Staff:** Prof 2; Other 2. **Subjects:** Canadian history, rare books. **Special Collections:** The Louis Melzack Collection of Canadian Books (4000 volumes); The L.F. Georges Baby Collection of Canadian Books (3500 volumes); Collection Pariseau (history of sciences, 4000 volumes); Collection Rey-Herme (education, 3500 volumes). **Holdings:** 68,421 books. **Services:** Copying; collection open to the public. **Automated Operations:** Computerized cataloging and acquisitions. **Special Catalogs:** Catalogue de la Collection de Canadiana Louis Melzack; Catalogue des Imprimes de la Collection Baby (1989). **Remarks:** FAX: (514)343-2348. **Staff:** Marie-Marthe Boucher.

★18099★
Universite de Paris I - Institut de Sciences Mathematiqueset Economiques Appliquees (ISMEA) - Bibliotheque (Bus-Fin)
11 rue Pierre et Marie Curie   Phone: 1 46337342
F-75005 Paris, France   Macrino Suarez
Founded: 1944. **Staff:** Prof 3. **Subjects:** Development, history of economic thought, international economy, economic theory, statistics and economics, agricultural economy. **Holdings:** 17,101 books; 602 bound periodical volumes. **Subscriptions:** 401 journals and other serials. **Services:** Interlibrary loan; copying; library open to doctoral students, researchers, and professors. **Remarks:** FAX: 1 40510661.

★18100★
Universite de Paris V (Rene Descartes) - Bibliotheque de l'Universite - U.E.R. Medicale Paris Quest (Med)
Hopital Ambroise Pare
9, av Charles-de-Gaulle
F-92104 Boulogne-Billancourt   Phone: 1 49095457
Cedex, France   Marie-Dominique Allen-Papillon
Founded: 1971. **Staff:** Prof 2; Other 1. **Subjects:** Medicine. **Holdings:** 3800 books; 3000 microfiche; 8000 slide sets. **Subscriptions:** 100 journals and other serials. **Services:** Interlibrary loan; library open to the public. **Computerized Information Services:** MEDLINE; CD-ROM (MEDLINE).

★18101★
Universite de Paris XI - Bibliotheque Universitaire - Centre Scientifique d'Orsay (Biol Sci, Sci-Engr)
Campus Universitaire
Bat 307   Phone: 1 69416979
F-91405 Orsay Cedex, France   Marie-France Such
Founded: 1962. **Staff:** Prof. 47. **Subjects:** Physics. biology, mathematic, chemistry, geology, history of science. **Special Collections:** Maison de la Chimie (12,000 books, 4000 serials). **Holdings:** 88,000 books; 400,000 bound periodical volumes; 20,000 microfiche. **Subscriptions:** 282 journals and other serials; 10 newspapers. **Services:** Interlibrary loan; copying; SDI; library open to the public. **Remarks:** FAX: 1 69416181. Telex: 601 460 F.

★18102★
Universite de Paris XI - Bibliotheque Universitaire - Section Medecine (Kremlin Bicetre) (Med)
63 rue Gabriel Peri   Phone: 49596780
F-94276 Le Kremlin Bicetre, France   F. Bayle, Cons.
Founded: 1969. **Staff:** Prof 8; Other 1. **Subjects:** Medicine. **Holdings:** 15,000 books; theses. **Subscriptions:** 414 journals and other serials. **Services:** Interlibrary loan; copying; SDI; library open to the public with restrictions. **Computerized Information Services:** Questel. **Remarks:** FAX: 49596778.

★ 18103 ★
Universite du Quebec - Bibliotheque (Educ)
2875, blvd. Laurier   Phone: (418)657-3551
Ste. Foy, PQ, Canada G1V 2M3   Paule Royer, Dir.
Founded: 1972. **Staff:** Prof 1; Other 1. **Subjects:** Higher education, administration, information processing. **Holdings:** 2000 books; 1000 Quebec and federal publications; 200 Quebec statutes. **Subscriptions:** 153 journals and other serials. **Services:** Interlibrary loan; copying; mediatheque open to the public for reference use only. **Automated Operations:** Computerized cataloging and serials. **Computerized Information Services:** Online systems. **Remarks:** FAX: (418)657-2132. **Formerly:** Its centre de Documentation.

★ 18104 ★
Universite du Quebec - Ecole Nationale d'Administration Publique - Centre de Documentation (Soc Sci, Bus-Fin)
945, ave. Wolfe   Phone: (418)657-2485
Ste. Foy, PQ, Canada G1V 3J9   Michel Gelinas, Libn.
Founded: 1969. **Staff:** Prof 2; Other 7. **Subjects:** Public administration, management, economics, political science, international administration. **Holdings:** 55,000 books; 8300 pamphlets; 1010 dissertations; 347 theses. **Subscriptions:** 1100 journals and other serials; 7 newspapers. **Services:** Interlibrary loan; copying; center open to the public. **Automated Operations:** Computerized cataloging, acquisitions, and circulation. **Computerized Information Services:** DIALOG Information Services, Questel, BADADUQ, MINISIS. **Publications:** Vient de paraitre; Bulletin signaletique des acquisitions; Guide bibliographique en administration publique; Administration publique canadienne, bibliographie; Thesaurus multilingue en administration publique; Liste cumulative des publications et rapports de recherche de personnel de l'Enap. **Remarks:** FAX: (418)657-2620. Maintains a branch library at 1001 Sherbrooke E., Suite 300, Montreal, PQ, Canada H2L 4Z1. **Staff:** Carole Urbain, Libn.

★ 18105 ★
Universite du Quebec - Ecole Nationale d'Administration Publique - Centre de Documentation ENAP-Montreal (Bus-Fin)
1001 Sherbrooke   Phone: (514)522-3641
Montreal, PQ, Canada H2L 421   Carole Urbain, Libn.
Founded: 1977. **Staff:** Prof 1; Other 3. **Subjects:** Public and urban administration, management, international studies. **Holdings:** 10,000 volumes; 300 annual reports of federal and provincial government and international organizations; 2500 microfiche. **Subscriptions:** 330 journals and other serials; 5 newspapers. **Services:** Interlibrary loan; copying; SDI; center open to the public. **Automated Operations:** Computerized cataloging and circulation. **Computerized Information Services:** DIALOG Information Services, Questel, DOBIS, BADADUQ; POSTE, Envoy 100 (electronic mail services). **Publications:** Vient de Paraitre - for internal distribution only. **Remarks:** FAX: (514)522-8222.

Universite du Quebec - Institut Armand-Frappier
See: Institut Armand-Frappier (7864)

Universite du Quebec - Mediatheque
See: Universite du Quebec - Bibliotheque (18103)

★ 18106 ★
Universite du Quebec en Abitibi-Temiscamingue - Bibliotheque (Educ)
425, Boul. du College
Box 8000   Phone: (819)762-0971
Rouyn-Noranda, PQ, Canada J9X 5M5   Serge Allard, Dir.
Founded: 1971. **Staff:** Prof 3; Other 14. **Subjects:** Education, administration. **Special Collections:** Northwest Quebec (Abitibi-Temiscamingue; 6608 documents; 4 newspaper titles; 10,622 slides and AV programs); Societe du Developpement de la Baie James documents (20,000). **Holdings:** 75,129 books; 318,390 microforms; 9026 AV programs. **Subscriptions:** 279 journals and other serials. **Services:** Interlibrary loan; copying; library open to the public with restrictions. **Computerized Information Services:** DIALOG Information Services, BADADUQ. **Remarks:** FAX: (819)797-4727. Electronic mail address(es): PEB.QRUQR (Envoy 100). **Staff:** Levis Tremblay, Tech.Serv.; Andre Beland, Ref.Libn.; Gisele Neas, ILL.

★ 18107 ★
Universite du Quebec a Chicoutimi - Paul-Emile Boulet Bibliotheque - Cartotheque (Geog-Map)
555, blvd. de l'Universite   Phone: (418)545-5031
Chicoutimi, PQ, Canada G7H 2B1   Gilles Caron, Dir.
Founded: 1969. **Subjects:** Regional studies - northern Quebec. **Holdings:** 16,130 topographical maps; 10,129 thematic maps; 35,368 aerial photographs; 88 satellite photographs; 758 atlases; 6388 geological reports; 855 theses (geology and geography); 4263 monographs. **Subscriptions:** 43 journals and other serials; 10 newspapers. **Services:** Interlibrary loan; SDI; library open to the public. **Automated Operations:** Computerized cataloging, acquisitions, and circulation. **Computerized Information Services:** DIALOG Information Services, PFDS Online, BRS Information Technologies, CAN/OLE, CAN/SDI, MEDLINE, Questel, FRI Information Services Ltd., DOBIS Canadian Online Library System, BADADUQ; DOMYNO (internal database); Envoy 100 (electronic mail service). Performs searches on fee basis. **Remarks:** Alternate telephone number(s): 545-5011. FAX: (418)545-5012. Telex: 051 36108. **Staff:** Jacques Tremblay, Supv.; Francoise Lange, Libn./Map Libn.

★ 18108 ★
Universite du Quebec a Hull - Bibliotheque (Soc Sci, Hum)
C.P. 1250, Succursale B   Phone: (819)595-2370
Hull, PQ, Canada J8X 3X7   Monique Legere, Dir.
Founded: 1972. **Staff:** Prof 6; Other 13. **Subjects:** Business, international relations, education, social sciences, nursing, computer science, art and linguistics. **Holdings:** 90,000 books; 19,000 bound periodical volumes; 5820 microforms. **Subscriptions:** 2359 journals and other serials; 6 newspapers. **Services:** Interlibrary loan; SDI; library open to the public. **Automated Operations:** Computerized public access catalog, cataloging, acquisitions, serials, and circulation. **Computerized Information Services:** DIALOG Information Services, BRS Information Technologies, BADADUQ, Questel; CD-ROMs; Envoy 100 (electronic mail service). Performs searches on fee basis. Contact Person: Gilles Bergeron, Pub.Serv.Libn., 595-2373. **Publications:** Annual reports; list of periodicals. **Remarks:** FAX: (819)595-3924; 595-4459 (Pub.Serv.). Electronic mail address(es): PEB.QHU (Envoy 100). **Staff:** Danielle Boisvert, Ref.Libn.; Daniel Pouliot, Ref.Libn.; Louise Grondines, Cat.Libn.; Monique Picard, Cat.Libn.; Jacques Cloutier, Acq.

★ 18109 ★
Universite du Quebec a Montreal - Audiovideotheque (Aud-Vis)
C.P. 8889, Succursale A   Phone: (514)987-4332
Montreal, PQ, Canada H3C 3P8   Huguette Tanguay, AV Libn.
Staff: Prof 1; Other 2. **Subjects:** Sexology, administration, earth sciences, psychology, education. **Holdings:** 3137 films and videotapes; 43,540 slides. **Services:** Library open to the public with restrictions. **Computerized Information Services:** BADADUQ. **Remarks:** FAX: (514)987-4070.

★ 18110 ★
Universite du Quebec a Montreal - Bibliotheque des Arts (Art)
C.P. 8889, Succursale A   Phone: (514)987-6134
Montreal, PQ, Canada H3C 3P3   Daphne Dufresne, Dir.
Founded: 1944. **Staff:** Prof 1; Other 10. **Subjects:** Painting, sculpture, art history, Canadian art, design, engraving, dance. **Holdings:** 66,200 books; 7000 bound periodical volumes; 138,000 slides; 1600 microforms; 20 VF drawers of clippings on Canadian art. **Subscriptions:** 364 journals and other serials. **Services:** Interlibrary loan; copying; library open to university students. **Automated Operations:** Computerized cataloging, circulation, and acquisitions. **Computerized Information Services:** BADADUQ, DIALOG Information Services, DOBIS Canadian Online Library System, Questel, RLIN. **Remarks:** FAX: (514)987-4070. **Staff:** Patricia Black.

★ 18111 ★
Universite du Quebec a Montreal - Bibliotheque de Musique (Mus)
C.P. 8889, Succursale A   Phone: (514)987-3934
Montreal, PQ, Canada H3C 3P3   Daphne Dufresne, Dir.
Founded: 1977. **Staff:** Prof 1; Other 3. **Subjects:** Music education and therapy, musicology. **Special Collections:** Canadian Broadcasting Corporation (CBC) Music Program archives, 1940-1983. **Holdings:** 7812 books; 657 bound periodical volumes; 17,487 scores; 14,499 phonograph records; 13,079 tape records. **Subscriptions:** 137 journals and other serials. **Services:** Interlibrary loan; copying; library open to the public. **Automated Operations:** Computerized cataloging, circulation, and acquisitions. **Computerized Information Services:** BADADUQ. **Remarks:** FAX: (514)987-4070. **Staff:** Gerald Parker.

★18112★
Universite du Quebec a Montreal - Bibliotheque des Sciences (Sci-Engr)
C.P. 8889, Succursale A
Montreal, PQ, Canada H3C 3P3
Phone: (514)987-3570
Conrad Corriveau, Dir.
Staff: Prof 3; Other 9. **Subjects:** Chemistry, biology, mathematics, physics, geology, technology, computer science. **Holdings:** 55,000 books; 33,000 bound periodical volumes; 2600 microforms; 600 dissertations. **Subscriptions:** 900 journals and other serials. **Services:** Interlibrary loan; copying; library open to the public with restrictions. **Automated Operations:** Computerized cataloging, acquisitions, and circulation. **Computerized Information Services:** DIALOG Information Services, BADADUQ, CAN/OLE, BRS Information Technologies; Envoy 100 (electronic mail service). **Special Catalogs:** Lists of periodical and monograph holdings (computer printout). **Remarks:** FAX: (514)987-3115. **Staff:** Jean Juneau, Ref.Libn.; Mychelle Boulet, Ref.Libn.; Bibiane Dostie, Libn.

★18113★
Universite du Quebec a Montreal - Bibliotheque des Sciences de l'Education (Educ)
C.P. 8889, Succursale A
Montreal, PQ, Canada H3C 3P3
Phone: (514)987-6174
Andre Champagne, Dir.
Staff: Prof 3; Other 8. **Subjects:** Continuing teacher education, elementary and secondary education, physical education, disadvantaged and exceptional child education, hearing and learning disabilities, professional and vocational information, vocational education, pre-school education, neurokinetics. **Special Collections:** ERIC documents, EDUQ, Microform publications college and human development and performance, microlog. **Holdings:** 53,000 books; 8000 bound periodical volumes; 320,000 ERIC microfiche; 3900 microcards; 820 reels of microfilm; 125 film loops. **Subscriptions:** 562 journals and other serials. **Services:** Interlibrary loan; copying; SDI; library open to the public. **Automated Operations:** Computerized public access catalog, cataloging, acquisitions, and circulation. **Computerized Information Services:** BRS Information Technologies, DIALOG Information Services, BRS/After Dark, Questel, PFDS Online, MEDLINE, CAN/OLE, BADADUQ, WILSONLINE, International Development Research Centre (IDRC); CD-ROMs (ERIC, CD:EDUCATION, Education Library, SPORT Discus); SIGIRD (Systeme integre de gestion des ressources documentaires) (internal database). Performs searches on fee basis. **Special Catalogs:** Lists of periodical holdings (printout). **Remarks:** FAX: (514)987-7994. **Staff:** Lucie Verreault, Ref.Libn.; Danielle Malette, Ref.Libn.; Monique Gaucher, Libn.

★18114★
Universite du Quebec a Montreal - Bibliotheque des Sciences Juridiques (Law, Soc Sci)
C.P. 8889, Succursale A
Local A-2183
Montreal, PQ, Canada H3C 3P3
Phone: (514)987-6184
Micheline Drapeau, Dir.
Founded: 1974. **Staff:** Prof 3; Other 7. **Subjects:** Jurisprudence; social security; law - consumer and environmental protection, constitutional, family, fiscal, health, housing, labor, poverty, public education, social; immigration and civil rights. **Holdings:** 35,284 volumes; 6 VF drawers of microfiche; 101 magnetic tapes; 413 reels of microfilm. **Subscriptions:** 498 journals and other serials. **Services:** Interlibrary loan; copying; library open to the public with restrictions. **Automated Operations:** Computerized cataloging, acquisitions, and circulation. **Computerized Information Services:** BADADUQ. **Staff:** Claudio Antonelli, Ref.Libn.; Jean-Paul Reid, Ref.Libn.

★18115★
Universite du Quebec a Montreal - Cartotheque (Geog-Map)
C.P. 8889, Succursale A
Montreal, PQ, Canada H3C 3P3
Phone: (514)987-3133
Pierre Roy, Cart.
Staff: Prof 1; Other 2. **Subjects:** Cartography, aerial photography. **Holdings:** 12,850 books; 800 bound periodical volumes; 504,988 aerial photographs; 56,617 maps. **Services:** Library open to the public. **Computerized Information Services:** BADADUQ. **Remarks:** FAX: (514)987-7787.

★18116★
Universite du Quebec a Montreal - Centre de Documentation Economie-Administration (Soc Sci)
C.P. 8889, Succursale A
Montreal, PQ, Canada H3C 3P8
Phone: (514)987-6136
Monique Cote, Libn.
Founded: 1971. **Staff:** Prof 1; Other 1. **Subjects:** Economics, administration, urban studies. **Holdings:** 40,920 corporation reports, public documents, university studies; 7923 microforms. **Subscriptions:** 731 journals and other serials. **Services:** Center open to the public. **Automated Operations:** Computerized acquisitions. **Computerized Information Services:** BADADUQ, MINISIS. **Publications:** Nouveautes and periodical highlights, monthly.

★18117★
Universite du Quebec a Montreal - Centre de Documentation en Sciences Humaines (Soc Sci)
C.P. 8889, Succursale A
Montreal, PQ, Canada H3C 3P3
Phone: (514)987-6138
Catherine Passerieux, Libn.
Staff: Prof 1; Other 1. **Subjects:** Political parties, labor unions, feminism, urban movements, Latin America, Eastern Europe, ethnic studies. **Special Collections:** Quebec labor union archives; Quebec and Canadian political party archives; Quebec feminist movement archives. **Holdings:** 1021 books; 72 boxes of archives; 365 linear feet of bound periodical volumes; 25 VF drawers; 320 reels of microfilm; 12 linear feet of microfilm; 900 maps. **Subscriptions:** 58 journals and other serials. **Services:** Interlibrary loan; copying; center open to the public. **Automated Operations:** Computerized cataloging and acquisitions. **Computerized Information Services:** BADADUQ.

★18118★
Universite du Quebec a Montreal - Institut National de la Recherche Scientifique-Urbanisation - Bibliotheque (Plan)
3465 Durocher
Montreal, PQ, Canada H2X 2C6
Phone: (514)499-4018
Helene Houde, Libn.
Founded: 1970. **Staff:** Prof 20; Other 18. **Subjects:** Urban and regional planning, demography, sociology, economics. **Holdings:** 5000 books. **Subscriptions:** 300 journals and other serials. **Services:** Interlibrary loan; copying; library open to the public. **Automated Operations:** Computerized cataloging and circulation. **Publications:** Etudes et documents; rapports de recherche, both irregular. **Remarks:** FAX: (514)499-4000. **Also Known As:** INRS-Urbanisation.

★18119★
Universite du Quebec a Montreal - Institut National de la Recherche Scientifique-Urbanisation - Cartotheque (Geog-Map)
3465 Durocher, Local 225
Montreal, PQ, Canada H2X 2C6
Phone: (514)499-4033
Christiane Desmarais, Cart.
Founded: 1973. **Staff:** Prof 1. **Subjects:** Cartography - urban and topographic. **Special Collections:** Land-use plans for Montreal, 1958-1990; fire insurance plans of Quebec, 1885-1973. **Holdings:** 118 atlases; 78 bound periodical volumes; 8577 topographic maps; 14,560 urban maps; 17 reels of microfilm. **Services:** Interlibrary loan; copying; library open to the public. **Special Catalogs:** Catalogs by area and subject. **Remarks:** FAX: (514)499-4065.

★18120★
Universite du Quebec a Pointe-Claire - Institut National de la Recherche Scientifique-Sante - Bibliotheque (Med, Biol Sci)
245 Hymus Blvd.
Pointe-Claire, PQ, Canada H9R 1G6
Phone: (514)630-8800
Gilbert LeBlanc
Founded: 1972. **Staff:** Prof 1. **Subjects:** Pharmacology, biochemistry, environment. **Holdings:** 7000 books. **Subscriptions:** 125 journals and other serials. **Services:** Interlibrary loan; copying; library open to the public. **Computerized Information Services:** DIALOG Information Services, MEDLARS; internal database. **Remarks:** FAX: (514)630-8850.

★18121★
Universite du Quebec a Rimouski - Cartotheque (Geog-Map)
300, ave. des Ursulines
Rimouski, PQ, Canada G5L 3A1
Phone: (418)723-1986
Yves Michaud, Map Libn.
Founded: 1971. **Staff:** Prof 1. **Subjects:** Cartography, aerial photography. **Special Collections:** Canadian, Quebec, East Quebec, lower St. Lawrence, and Gaspesia region maps. **Holdings:** 850 books; 900 atlases; 25,000 maps; 22,000 aerial photographs; 100 other cataloged items. **Services:** Library open to the public. **Publications:** Information cartologique, irregular; repertoire cartobibliographique sur la region de l'est du Quebec. **Remarks:** FAX: (418)724-1525.

★18122★
Universite du Quebec a Rimouski - Department of Oceanography - Bibliotheque (Biol Sci)
300 Allee des Ursulines
Rimouski, PQ, Canada G5L 3A1
Phone: (418)724-1476
Gaston Dumont
Founded: 1969. **Staff:** Prof 8; Other 18. **Subjects:** Oceanography, marine biology, marine resources, regional development. **Special Collections:** Documentation Regionale (5000 documents on lower St. Lawrence and

Gaspe Peninsula, eastern Quebec). **Holdings:** 200,000 books; 50,000 bound periodical volumes; 320 meters of archives; 3900 microfiche; 8800 reels of microfilm. **Subscriptions:** 3600 journals and other serials. **Services:** Interlibrary loan; copying; SDI; library open to the public. **Computerized Information Services:** DIALOG Information Services, CAN/OLE, Questel, BADADUQ; ESQUEDOC (internal database); Envoy 100 (electronic mail service). Contact Person: Christian Bielle, Ref.Hd. **Remarks:** FAX: (418)724-1525. Telex: 051-31623. Electronic mail address(es): PEB.QRU (Envoy 100).

★18123★
Universite du Quebec a Trois-Rivieres - Cartotheque (Geog-Map)
Pavillon Leon-Provancher
C.P. 500   Phone: (819)376-5099
Trois-Rivieres, PQ, Canada G9A 5H7   Marie Lefebvre, Cart.
Staff: Prof 1. **Subjects:** Cartography, aerial photography. **Special Collections:** Maps of the Trois-Rivieres region. **Holdings:** 2087 books and bound periodical volumes; 42,900 maps; 229 atlases; 3 globes; 5 relief models; 51,400 aerial photographs. **Services:** Library open to the public. **Publications:** Guide de l'usager, 1987 - both for sale. **Remarks:** The map collection is administered by the Department of Humanities.

★18124★
Universite de Saint Etienne - Bibliotheque de l'Universite - Section Sciences (Sci-Engr)
21 rue Dr Paul Michelon   Phone: 77 421500
F-42023 Saint Etienne Cedex 02, France   Marinette Junique
Founded: 1969. **Staff:** Prof 5; Other 2. **Subjects:** Mathematics, physics, chemistry, biology, computing, geology. **Holdings:** 15,000 books; 200 bound periodical volumes; 25,000 microfiche. **Subscriptions:** 100 journals and other serials. **Services:** Interlibrary loan; library open to the public. **Computerized Information Services:** Questel, ESA/IRS. Contact Person: D. Shatrafil, Libn. **Remarks:** FAX: 77 421575.

★18125★
Universite de Sherbrooke - Bibliotheque des Sciences (Sci-Engr)
2500, blvd. Universite   Phone: (819)821-7099
Sherbrooke, PQ, Canada J1K 2R1   Roger B. Bernier, Resp.
Founded: 1960. **Staff:** Prof 2; Other 6. **Subjects:** Biology; mathematics; computer science; chemistry; physics; engineering - chemical, civil, mechanical, electrical. **Holdings:** 57,350 books; 73,100 bound periodical volumes. **Subscriptions:** 1006 journals and other serials. **Services:** Interlibrary loan; copying; SDI; library open to the public. **Automated Operations:** Computerized cataloging and circulation. **Computerized Information Services:** DIALOG Information Services, QL Systems, Questel, PFDS Online, CAN/OLE, ESA/IRS; CD-ROMs (COMPENDEX PLUS, PolTox, General Science Index, CCINFOdisc); Envoy 100 (electronic mail service). **Publications:** Liste des Periodiques, annual; Guide Bibliographique en Sciences Pures et Appliquees; Guide Bibliographique en Biologie; Guide Bibliographique en Chimie; Guide Bibliographique en Mathematiques; Guide Bibliographique en Physique; Guide Bibliographique en Genie Chimique; Guide Bibliographique en Genie Civil; Guide Bibliographique en Genie Mecanique; Guide Bibliographique en Genie Electrique; Guide Bibliographique en Environnement. **Remarks:** FAX: (819)821-7935. Telex: 05-836149. Electronic mail address(es): PEB.QSHERUS (Envoy 100). **Staff:** Benoit Legault.

★18126★
Universite de Sherbrooke - Faculte de Medecine - Bibliotheque des Sciences de la Sante (Med)
Centre Hospitalier Universitaire   Phone: (819)564-5297
Sherbrooke, PQ, Canada J1H 5N4   Germain Chouinard, Dir.
Founded: 1965. **Staff:** Prof 2; Other 6. **Subjects:** Health sciences. **Holdings:** 58,571 volumes. **Subscriptions:** 974 journals and other serials. **Services:** Interlibrary loan; copying; SDI; library open to the public with restrictions. **Automated Operations:** Computerized public access catalog, cataloging, and circulation. **Computerized Information Services:** NLM, DIALOG Information Services, BRS Information Technologies, PFDS Online, MEDLINE, CAN/OLE; CD-ROM (MEDLINE); Envoy 100, NETNORTH (electronic mail services). Performs searches on fee basis. **Remarks:** Electronic mail address(es): PEB.QSHERC (Envoy 100); QIAA@UDESVM (NETNORTH). **Staff:** Mireille Lapierre.

★18127★
Universite de Sherbrooke - Programme de Recherche sur l'amiante (Sci-Engr)
Information Center   Phone: (819)821-7566
Sherbrooke, PQ, Canada J1K 2R1   Mrs. Asta Sokov, Dir.
Founded: 1977. **Staff:** Prof 1. **Subjects:** Asbestos - chemistry, geology, biology, physics, industry, sanitary engineering, commercial aspects, economics, law, medicine, social sciences. **Holdings:** 500 bound volumes; 35,000 journal articles. **Subscriptions:** 12 journals and other serials. **Services:** Current awareness. **Computerized Information Services:** Produces ASBEST database (available online through QL Systems); internal databases; Envoy 100 (electronic mail service). **Publications:** New acquisitions list. **Remarks:** FAX: (819)821-7939. Electronic mail address(es): PFB.QSHERURA.21 (Envoy 100). **Also Known As:** University of Sherbrooke - Asbestos Research Program.

★18128★
Universite St-Paul - Bibliotheque (Rel-Phil)
223 Main   Phone: (613)236-1393
Ottawa, ON, Canada K1S 1C4   Barbara Hicks, Chf.Libn.
Founded: 1937. **Staff:** Prof 4; Other 14. **Subjects:** Religious sciences, philosophy, canon law, medieval studies, theology, Bible, church history. **Holdings:** 375,000 books; 100,000 bound periodical volumes; 5000 reels of microfilm; 85,000 microfiche; 3000 manuscripts on microfilm. **Subscriptions:** 1100 journals and other serials. **Services:** Interlibrary loan; copying; library open to the public with restrictions. **Computerized Information Services:** Envoy 100 (electronic mail service). **Remarks:** FAX: (613)782-3005. Electronic mail address(es): ILL.OOSU (Envoy 100). Maintained by Oblate Fathers.

Universite de Sudbury
See: **University of Sudbury** (19359)

★18129★
Universite de Yaounde - Centre Universitaire des Sciences de la Sante - Bibliotheque (Med)
Yaounde, Cameroon   Phone: 220651
                            Vincent Boumsong
Founded: 1969. **Staff:** Prof 1; Other 9. **Subjects:** Medicine, nursing, and allied health sciences. **Holdings:** 26,000 books. **Subscriptions:** 239 journals and other serials. **Services:** Interlibrary loan; library open to students and medical and paramedical staff with permission. **Remarks:** FAX: 311224.

★18130★
Universiteit van Amsterdam - Faculteit Wiskunde en Informatica - Bibliotheek (Sci-Engr)
Plantage Muidergracht 24   Phone: 20 5255470
NL-1018 TV Amsterdam, Netherlands   Dr. F.J. Kroon, Libn.
Subjects: Mathematics, logic, computer science. **Special Collections:** Heyting Archive. **Holdings:** 18,000 books; 445 meters of bound periodical volumes; 50 meters of reports. **Subscriptions:** 352 journals and other serials. **Services:** Interlibrary loan; copying; library open to the public. **Automated Operations:** Computerized public access catalog. **Remarks:** FAX: 20 5255101.

Universiteit van Amsterdam - Kunsthistorisch Instituut - Bibliotheek
See: **University of Amsterdam - Art History Department - Library** (18206)

Universiteit van Amsterdam - Vakgroep Arabische en Islamitische Studien - Bibliotheek
See: **University of Amsterdam - Institute for Modern Near Eastern Studies - Department of Arabic & Islamic Studies - Library** (18207)

★18131★
Universiteit Antwerpen - Universitaire Faculteiten Sint-Ignatius Antwerpen - Bibliotheek van het Ruusbroecgenootschap (Rel-Phil)
Prinsstraat 13   Phone: 3 2204367
B-2000 Antwerp, Belgium   Frans Hendrickx, Libn.
Staff: 2. **Subjects:** History of ascetic and mystic devotion, history of spirituality, church history, cloisters, religious art and folklore. **Special Collections:** Rare books, 1470-1800 (35,000); saints and devotional prints (35,000); manuscripts, 12th-20th centuries (500). **Holdings:** 108,000 volumes; 600 reels of microfilm. **Subscriptions:** 400 journals and other serials. **Services:** Interlibrary loan; copying; library open to the public. **Computerized Information Services:** VUBIS. Performs searches on fee basis. **Remarks:** FAX: 3 2204420. **Also Known As:** Ruusbroecgenootschap Centrum voor Spiritualiteit. **Staff:** Inge Wouters, Asst.Libn.

★ 18132 ★
Universites de Montpellier - Bibliotheque Interuniversitaire - Section Medecine (Med)
2 rue Ecole de Medecine   Phone: 67 662777
F-34000 Montpellier Cedex, France   Christiane Nicq
Staff: 15. **Subjects:** Biomedicine. **Special Collections:** Archives, 12th century to 19th century; History of Medicine collection; drawing collection, 16th century to 18th century; French, Italian, and Flemish medical schools manuscripts (800). **Holdings:** 400,000 books; 1000 microfiche; 1000 reels of microfilm. **Subscriptions:** 700 journals and other serials. **Services:** Interlibrary loan; copying; SDI; library open to the public for reference use only. **Computerized Information Services:** Data-Star, Questel; SIBIL (internal database). Contact Person: A. Dujol, Libn. **Remarks:** FAX: 67661924.

Universites de Montpellier - Institut d'Archeologie et d'Histoire de l'Art - Bibliotheque
See: **University of Montpellier - Institute of Archaeology and History of Art - Library (18991)**

★ 18133 ★
Universites de Paris - Bibliotheque Litteraire Jacques Doucet (Hum)
10 place du Pantheon   Phone: 1 43296100
F-75005 Paris, France   Francais Chapon, Cons. en Chef
Founded: 1929. **Staff:** Prof 3; Other 3. **Subjects:** French literature; illustrated books; modern bindings. **Special Collections:** Collections of Bergson, Mallarme, Valeryanum, Gide, Char, Tzara, Andre Breton, Mauriac, Jouhan Deau, Suares, Milosz, Charles Du Bos, Reverdy, Desnos, Leiris, Barney. **Holdings:** 30,000 books; 700,000 letters and manuscripts. **Services:** Interlibrary loan; library open to qualified researchers. **Special Catalogs:** Collection de Catalogues Partiels (Valery, Rene Char, Eluard, Florence Gould, Natalie Barney, Francois Mauriac).

★ 18134 ★
Universites de Paris I, III, IV, V, VII - Bibliotheque de la Sorbonne (Hist, Sci-Engr, Hum)
47, rue des Ecoles   Phone: 1 40463027
F-75230 Paris Cedex 05, France   Claude Jolly, Dir.
Founded: 1765. **Staff:** 121. **Subjects:** History; linguistics; literature - French, Slavic, foreign; history of science and technology; psychology; sociology; philosophy; religious studies; university history. **Special Collections:** Archives de l'ancienne universite; early theology and history. **Holdings:** 3.2 million books; 13,000 bound periodical volumes; 2141 manuscripts. **Subscriptions:** 5500. journals and other serials **Services:** Interlibrary loan; copying; library open to the public with restrictions. **Computerized Information Services:** FRANCIS (French Retrieval Automated Network for Current Information in Social and Human Sciences), Frantext. Performs searches on fee basis. Contacts: F. Borione, 40463062; M.T. Prinot, 40463041. **Publications:** Melanges de la Bibliotheque de la Sorbonne (11 volumes); Collection de la Bibliotheques de la Sorbonne (20 volumes). **Special Catalogs:** Catalogue des manuscrits; Inventorie des Livres de XVIe Siecle. **Remarks:** FAX: 1 40463044.

★ 18135 ★
Universites de Rennes I - Section Sante - Bibliotheque (Med)
13 Av. du Professeur Leon Bernard   Phone: 99 591544
F-35043 Rennes Cedex, France   A. Roussel
Founded: 1958. **Staff:** Prof 6.5; Other 8.5. **Subjects:** Medicine, pharmacy. **Holdings:** Figures not available. **Subscriptions:** 540 journals and other serials. **Services:** Interlibrary loan; copying; library open to the public. **Computerized Information Services:** CD-ROM (MEDLINE). **Remarks:** FAX: 99337831.

★ 18136 ★
Universites de Strasbourg - Departement de Mathematiques - Bibliotheque (Sci-Engr)
7 rue Rene Descartes Esplanade   Phone: 88416306
F-67084 Strasbourg, France   Christine Disdier, Libn.
Staff: Prof 4. **Subjects:** Mathematics, probability, computer science, physics. **Holdings:** 27,000 books; 20,000 bound periodical volumes. **Subscriptions:** 459 journals and other serials. **Services:** Interlibrary loan; copying; library open to researchers only. **Computerized Information Services:** CCN; internal database; CD-ROM (MathSci).

★ 18137 ★
Universitetet i Bergen - Universitetsbiblioteket - Avd. Det Matematisk-Naturvitenskapelige Fakultet (Sci-Engr)
Allegaten 41   Phone: 5 213264
N-5007 Bergen, Norway   Dag Vaula, Dept.Libn.
Founded: 1977. **Staff:** Prof 8; Other 2. **Subjects:** Science, technology. **Holdings:** 40,000 books; 50,000 bound periodical volumes; 3000 archival items. **Subscriptions:** 800 journals and other serials. **Services:** Interlibrary loan; copying; library open to staff and students. **Computerized Information Services:** DIALOG Information Services, STN International, ESA/IRS. **Remarks:** FAX: 5 325527. Telex: 42877 ubbrb n.

★ 18138 ★
Universitetet i Oslo - Det Matematisk-Naturvitenskapelige Fakultetsbibliotek (Sci-Engr)
Fysikkbygningen
Postboks 1063 Blindern   Phone: 2 856151
N-0316 Oslo 3, Norway   Tor Blekastad
Founded: 1948. **Staff:** Prof 21.25; Other 15. **Subjects:** Natural sciences, mathematics, informatics. **Holdings:** 750,000 volumes. **Subscriptions:** 6200 journals and other serials; 21 newspapers. **Services:** Interlibrary loan; copying; SDI; library open to the public. **Computerized Information Services:** DIALOG Information Services, ESA/IRS, STN International. Contact Person: Inger Wiborg, Univ.Bibl. **Remarks:** FAX: 2 692499. Telex: 76639 UBMNF.

★ 18139 ★
Universitetet i Oslo - Nordisk Institutt for Sjorett - Library (Trans, Law)
Karl Johansgt 47
Dormus media   Phone: 2 429010
N-0162 Oslo 1, Norway   Kirsten Al-Araki
Founded: 1963. **Staff:** Prof 1.5. **Subjects:** Maritime law, transportation law, oil and gas law. **Holdings:** 14,500 books; 5500 bound periodical volumes. **Subscriptions:** 280 journals and other serials; 5 newspapers. **Services:** Interlibrary loan; copying; library open to the public. **Automated Operations:** Computerized public access catalog (BIBSYS). **Remarks:** FAX: 2 336308.

★ 18140 ★
Universitetet i Tromso - Avdelingsbibliotek for Museumsvirksomhet (Soc Sci, Biol Sci, Sci-Engr)
Tromso Museum Folkeparken   Phone: 83 45006
N-9000 Tromso, Norway   Tor Sveum
Founded: 1872. **Staff:** Prof 1.5; Other 1. **Subjects:** Northern Norway - archeology, anthropology, local history, zoology, botany, geology. **Holdings:** 80,000 books. **Services:** Interlibrary loan; copying; library open to the public. **Computerized Information Services:** DIALOG Information Services, BRS Information Technologies, Questel, BLAISE, DBI; BIBSYS (internal database). **Remarks:** FAX: 83 89158.

★ 18141 ★
Universiti Pertanian Malaysia - Perpustakaan (Agri)
Serdang, Selangor, Malaysia   Phone: 3 9486101
                                      Mr. Syed Salim Agha
Founded: 1971. **Staff:** Prof 37; Other 120. **Subjects:** Agriculture, forestry, veterinary science, agricultural engineering, agricultural economics, fishery. **Special Collections:** Malaysiana (6000 volumes). **Holdings:** 230,000 books; 54,000 bound periodical volumes; 28,728 microfiche; 2265 reels of microfilm; 23,888 AV materials. **Subscriptions:** 6106 journals and other serials; 12 newspapers. **Services:** Library open to registered users only. **Computerized Information Services:** DIALOG Information Services, AGRIS; Management & Utilization of Wastes, UPM Staff Publications, Malaysian Environment, Fish Diseases, Food Technology in Malaysia (internal databases). Contact Person: Ms. Badilah Saad. **Publications:** UPM Staff Publications, annual; Malaysian Agricultural Bibliography; Malaysian Agricultural Information Bulletin, quarterly. **Remarks:** FAX: 3 9483745. Alternate telephone number(s): 3 9486110. Telex: UNIPER MA37454. **Staff:** Kamsiah Mohd. Ali, Libn., Trng. Unit.

★18142★

Universities Federation for Animal Welfare - Library (Biol Sci)
8 Hamilton Close
South Mimms
Potters Bar, Herts. EN6 3QD, England   Phone: 707 58202
Subjects: Animals - welfare, management, care, use in science. **Holdings:** 2000 volumes. **Remarks:** FAX: 707 49279.

★18143★

Universities Field Staff International
4600 Sunset Ave.
Box 243
Indianapolis, IN 46208
Defunct.

★18144★

Universities Research Association - Fermi National Accelerator Laboratory - Library (Sci-Engr)
Box 500, MS 109   Phone: (708)840-3401
Batavia, IL 60510   Paula Garrett, Lib.Adm.
Founded: 1967. **Staff:** Prof 2; Other 2. **Subjects:** High energy physics, particle accelerators, particle physics. **Special Collections:** High-energy physics preprints. **Holdings:** 12,000 books; 8000 bound periodical volumes; 4000 preprints and reports; 3000 microfiche. **Subscriptions:** 200 journals and other serials. **Services:** Interlibrary loan; library open to the public for reference use only. **Automated Operations:** Computerized public access catalog, cataloging. **Computerized Information Services:** SPIRES, DIALOG Information Services, STN International, OCLC; BITNET (electronic mail service). **Networks/Consortia:** Member of DuPage Library System, ILLINET. **Remarks:** The Universities Research Association operates under contract to the U.S. Department of Energy. FAX: (708)840-4343. Telex: 910-230-3233. Electronic mail address(es): FNAL (BITNET). **Staff:** May West, Asst.Libn.

★18145★

The University of Adelaide - Waite Agricultural Research Institute - Library (Agri, Biol Sci)
Glen Osmond, SA 5064, Australia   Phone: 8 3722310
Founded: 1925. **Staff:** Prof 2; Other 5. **Subjects:** Crop, pasture, and animal production; agricultural biochemistry; agronomy; crop ecology; genetics; plant breeding; animal sciences; systematic botany; entomology; plant physiology and pathology; soil science; horticulture; plant and agricultural biotechnology. **Holdings:** 50,000 volumes. **Subscriptions:** 502 journals and other serials; 742 exchange journals; 6 newspapers. **Services:** Interlibrary loan; copying. **Automated Operations:** Computerized public access catalog and cataloging. **Computerized Information Services:** DIALOG Information Services, AUSTRALIS, STN International, Australian Bibliographic Network (ABN), Australian MEDLINE; BRS Information Technologies. Performs searches on fee basis. **Remarks:** FAX: 8 3791636. Telex: UNIVAD AA 89141. Maintained by University of Adelaide. **Staff:** Ellen A. Randva, Libn.; Angela C. Mills.

★18146★

University of Adelaide - Waite Agricultural Research Institute - Library (Agri)
Glen Osmond, SA 5064, Australia   Phone: 8 3722312
                                             Ellen Randva
Founded: 1924. **Staff:** Prof 2; Other 3.5. **Subjects:** Agriculture, biochemistry, chemistry, plant physiology, pathology, animal sciences, entomology. **Holdings:** 20,000 books; 30,000 bound periodical volumes; 340 archival items. **Subscriptions:** 633 journals and other serials. **Services:** Interlibrary loan; copying; SDI; library open to the public for reference use only. **Computerized Information Services:** DIALOG Information Services, STN International, AUSTRALIS, Australian Medline Service; BITNET (electronic mail service). Contact Person: Angela Mills, Asst.Libn. **Publications:** Institute's biennial report - available for exchange purposes. **Remarks:** FAX: 8 3791636; Telex: UNIVAD AA89141. Electronic mail address(es):erandva@library.adelaide.edu.au (BITNET).

★18147★

University Affiliated Cincinnati Center for Developmental Disorders - Research Library (Med, Educ)
Pavilion Bldg.
3300 Elland Ave.   Phone: (513)559-4626
Cincinnati, OH 45229   Arlene Johnson, Dir.
Founded: 1960. **Staff:** Prof 2; Other 3. **Subjects:** Developmental disabilities, mental retardation, learning disabilities, special education, pediatrics, neurology, nutrition, rehabilitation, psychology, social work, vocational counseling. **Special Collections:** Library for parents of exceptional children (1000 books and 500 pamphlet titles for distribution); Toy Library for Special Children; bibliotherapy collection. **Holdings:** 17,000 books; 2000 bound periodical volumes; 100 AV programs; 175,000 reprint articles relating to developmental disorders and pediatrics; 4 VF drawers of staff publications; 10,000 slides. **Subscriptions:** 250 journals and other serials. **Services:** Interlibrary loan; copying; SDI; library open to the public with restrictions and for reference only. **Computerized Information Services:** BRS Information Technologies, NLM, MEDLINE. **Networks/Consortia:** Member of National Network of Libraries of Medicine - Greater Midwest Region. **Publications:** Library Bulletin, quarterly - for internal and limited outside distribution. **Special Indexes:** Card index to reprint file. **Remarks:** Affiliated with University of Cincinnati and Cincinnati Children's Hospital. **Staff:** Jenny Swerdlow, Cat.; Cathy Etter, Asst.Lib.Res.; Alison Kissling, Asst.Lib.Res.

★18148★

University of Agricultural Sciences - Library (Agri)
GKVK Campus   Phone: 812 330153
Bangalore 560 065, Karnataka, India   K.T. Somashekar
Founded: 1965. **Staff:** Prof 10; Other 29. **Subjects:** Agriculture, horticulture, veterinary science, dairy science, home economics. **Special Collections:** Food and Agriculture Organization collection (1500 items). **Holdings:** 128,108 books; 39,132 bound periodical volumes; 10,267 reports; 2784 theses; 167 microfiche; 78 maps; 68 reels of microfilm. **Subscriptions:** 1051 journals and other serials; 6 newspapers. **Services:** Interlibrary loan; copying; SDI. **Publications:** Select Bibliographies. **Special Catalogs:** Catalogue of theses; Union Catalogue of Serials. **Remarks:** Telex: 8458393 UASK IN.

★18149★

University of Agriculture Malaysia - Bintulu Campus - Library (Agri)
PO Box 396   Phone: 86 35911
97008 Bintulu, Malaysia   Margaret Simeng
Founded: 1974. **Staff:** Prof 3; Other 22. **Subjects:** Agriculture, forestry, science, social sciences. **Special Collections:** Borneo Collections (1000 titles). **Holdings:** 55,801 books; 2107 bound periodical volumes; 1179 microfiche; 75 reels of microfilm; 217 videotapes; 243 maps. **Subscriptions:** 400 journals and other serials; 12 newspapers. **Services:** Interlibrary loan; copying; SDI; library open to registered members. **Publications:** Library Acquisition List; Library Handbook; Serials Holdings; Audio-Visual Holdings. **Remarks:** FAX: 86 35835.

★18150★

University of Akron - American History Research Center (Hist)
Bierce Library   Phone: (216)972-7670
Akron, OH 44325-1702   John V. Miller, Jr., Dir.
Founded: 1970. **Staff:** Prof 2; Other 2. **Subjects:** State and local history, business, labor, politics, religion, social services. **Special Collections:** Records and papers of Akron Area Chamber of Commerce, Akron Mayors John Ballard and Roy Ray, Canal Society of Ohio, General Tire and Rubber Company, B.F. Goodrich Company, John S. Knight, Lighter-than-Air Society, Ohio Edison Company, Congressman John F. Seiberling. **Holdings:** 4100 cubic feet of historical documents. **Services:** Center open to the public. **Networks/Consortia:** Member of Ohio Network of American History Research Centers (ONARCH). **Remarks:** FAX: (216)972-6383. **Staff:** George V. Hodowznec.

★18151★

University of Akron - Archives of the History of American Psychology (Soc Sci)
Simmons Hall   Phone: (216)972-7285
Akron, OH 44325-4302   John A. Popplestone, Dir.
Founded: 1965. **Staff:** Prof 1; Other 4. **Subjects:** American psychology. **Special Collections:** Papers of E.A. Doll, H.H. Goddard, H.S. Hollingworth, Leta Hollingworth, K. Koffka, A. Maslow, M. Scheerer, W. Shipley, E.C. Tolman; historical laboratory equipment (600 items). **Holdings:** 18,000 books; 2000 linear feet of documents; 70 linear feet of ephemeral and fugitive material; 5000 tests; 3000 photographs; 5500 films; 350 audiotapes. **Services:** Copying; archives open to the public by appointment. **Remarks:** FAX: (216)972-6990.

★ 18152 ★
University of Akron - Art Slide Library (Art)
150 E. Exchange St.   Phone: (216)972-5962
Akron, OH 44325   James R. Crowe, Slide Libn.
Founded: 1978. **Staff:** Prof 1; Other 5. **Subjects:** Art history, textile, fiber art, photography, museums, advertising, architecture, computer graphic. **Special Collections:** Egyptian slide collection. **Holdings:** 868 books; 55,000 slides. **Subscriptions:** 25 journals and other serials. **Services:** Library not open to the public.

★ 18153 ★
University of Akron - Audio-Visual Services (Aud-Vis)
63 Bierce Library   Phone: (216)972-7811
Akron, OH 44325-1704   Stanley W. Akers, Dir., AV Serv.
Founded: 1952. **Staff:** Prof 2; Other 3. **Holdings:** Media equipment, university-produced and general media software. **Services:** Center open to campus and nonprofit groups. **Computerized Information Services:** MEDIANET (internal database); InterNet (electronic mail service). **Remarks:** FAX: (216)972-6383. Electronic mail address(es): TELNET MEDIA.AVS.UAKRON.EDU (InterNet). **Staff:** Thomas B. Bennett.

★ 18154 ★
University of Akron - Center for Peace Studies - Library (Soc Sci)
Akron, OH 44325-6201   Phone: (216)972-6513
                     John F. Seiberling, Dir.
Staff: 1. **Subjects:** Peace movements and their history; internationalism; human rights; peace education. **Special Collections:** Library of World Peace Studies (5000 microfiche). **Holdings:** 400 books; 2 VF drawers of peace societies and organizations; 2 VF drawers of academic peace programs. **Subscriptions:** 15 journals and other serials. **Services:** Copying; library open to the public. **Publications:** Human Rights bibliography (card).

★ 18155 ★
University of Akron - Herman Muehlstein Rare Book Collection (Rare Book)
Bierce Library
Akron, OH 44325   Phone: (216)972-7670
Staff: Prof 1. **Subjects:** American and English literature, American history. **Holdings:** 1500 volumes. **Services:** Collection open to the public. **Computerized Information Services:** OCLC; VTLS (internal database). Performs searches on fee basis. **Remarks:** FAX: (216)972-6383.

★ 18156 ★
University of Akron - Music Resource Center (Mus)
School of Music   Phone: (216)972-7111
Akron, OH 44325   Nancy L. Stokes, Dir.
Subjects: Music. **Holdings:** 1500 books; 12,000 scores; 6000 sound recordings. **Services:** Interlibrary loan; copying; library open to the public; circulation limited to students and faculty. **Computerized Information Services:** DIALOG Information Services. Performs searches on fee basis.

★ 18157 ★
University of Akron - School of Law - C. Blake McDowell Law Center (Law)
Akron, OH 44325-2902   Phone: (216)972-7330
                      Paul Richert, Law Libn.
Founded: 1965. **Staff:** Prof 5; Other 6. **Subjects:** Anglo-American law. **Holdings:** 210,000 volumes. **Subscriptions:** 832 periodicals. **Services:** Interlibrary loan; copying; library open to the public. **Computerized Information Services:** LEXIS, OCLC, WESTLAW; BITNET, InterNet (electronic mail services). **Publications:** Acquisition List, monthly - for internal distribution only. **Remarks:** FAX: (216)258-2343. Electronic mail address(es): RIPR@AKRONVM (BITNET); RIPR@UAKRON.EDU (InterNet). **Staff:** Robbie Robertson, Acq.Coord.; Anne McFarland, Assoc. Law Libn.; Kyle Passmore, Asst. Law Libn.; Jill Williams, Asst. Law Libn.; Deborah Bobinets, Asst. Law Libn.

★ 18158 ★
University of Akron - Science and Technology Library (Sci-Engr, Biol Sci, Comp Sci)
104 Auburn Science Center   Phone: (216)972-7195
Akron, OH 44325-3907   Norma Pearson, Hd.
Founded: 1967. **Staff:** Prof 3; Other 3. **Subjects:** Biology; chemistry; physics; mathematics; computer science; geology; polymer science; nursing and allied health sciences; engineering - biomedical, chemical, civil, computer, electrical, mechanical, polymer. **Holdings:** 80,000 volumes. **Subscriptions:** 2300 journals and other serials. **Services:** Copying; library open to the public. **Automated Operations:** Computerized public access catalog, cataloging, serials, and circulation. **Computerized Information Services:** DIALOG Information Services, BRS Information Technologies, Chemical Abstracts Service (CAS), OCLC; CD-ROMs; VTLS (internal database). Performs searches on fee basis. **Networks/Consortia:** Member of Center for Research Libraries (CRL), OHIONET, NEOMARL. **Staff:** Ann Bolek, Physical Sci.Libn.; Robert Rittenhouse, Physical Sci. & Engr.Libn.; J.B. Hill, Ref.Libn.

University of Akron - Science and Technology Library - John H. Gifford Memorial Library & Information Center
See: **American Chemical Society - Rubber Division** (524)

★ 18159 ★
University of Akron - University Archives (Hist)
Bierce Library   Phone: (216)972-7670
Akron, OH 44325-1702   John V. Miller, Jr., Dir. of Archv.Serv.
Founded: 1965. **Staff:** Prof 2; Other 2. **Subjects:** University of Akron. **Holdings:** 4000 cubic feet of archival materials, 1870 to present. **Services:** Archives open to the public. **Computerized Information Services:** BITNET (electronic mail service). **Remarks:** FAX: (216)972-6383. Electronic mail address(es): D2JVM@AKRONVM (BITNET). **Staff:** George V. Hodowznec.

★ 18160 ★
University of Alabama - Business Library (Bus-Fin)
P.O. Box 870266   Phone: (205)348-6096
Tuscaloosa, AL 35487-0266   Lee E. Pike, Hd.
Founded: 1925. **Staff:** Prof 3; Other 4. **Subjects:** Accounting, banking, economics, finance, human resource management, marketing, international business, management, real estate, transportation, business law, insurance, management science, statistics. **Special Collections:** Corporate reports (90,793). **Holdings:** 90,054 books; 45,575 bound periodical volumes; 246,753 microforms; 3000 bound annual report volumes. **Subscriptions:** 1600 journals and other serials. **Services:** Interlibrary loan; copying; library open to the public. **Automated Operations:** Computerized public access catalog, cataloging, and circulation. **Computerized Information Services:** DIALOG Information Services, PFDS Online, BRS Information Technologies, OCLC, Dow Jones News/Retrieval, Dun & Bradstreet Business Credit Services; CD-ROM (ABI/INFORM). Performs searches on fee basis. **Networks/Consortia:** Member of Network of Alabama Academic Libraries (NAAL), SOLINET, Center for Research Libraries (CRL). **Special Catalogs:** Corporate report catalog (card). **Remarks:** FAX: (205)348-8833. **Staff:** Karen J. Chapman, Bus.Ref.Libn.

★ 18161 ★
University of Alabama - Center for Business and Economic Research - Library (Bus-Fin)
P.O. Box 870221   Phone: (205)348-6191
Tuscaloosa, AL 35487   Annette Watters
Founded: 1930. **Staff:** Prof 10; Other 5. **Subjects:** Demography, economics. **Holdings:** 1000 books; 50 bound periodical volumes. **Subscriptions:** 20 journals and other serials; 2 newspapers. **Services:** Copying; library open to the public for reference use only. **Computerized Information Services:** CD-ROMs. Performs searches. Contact Person: Deborah Hamilton, Asst.Dir. **Remarks:** FAX: (205)348-2951.

★ 18162 ★
University of Alabama - College of Community Health Sciences - Health Sciences Library (Med)
P.O. Box 870378   Phone: (205)348-1360
Tuscaloosa, AL 35487-0378   Lisa Rains Russell, Chf.Med.Libn.
Founded: 1973. **Staff:** Prof 3; Other 6. **Subjects:** Primary care, clinical medicine, nursing. **Special Collections:** AV programs on clinical medicine

(2000). **Holdings:** 8000 books; 16,000 bound periodical volumes; 16 VF drawers of pamphlets and clippings. **Subscriptions:** 475 journals and other serials. **Services:** Interlibrary loan; copying; library open to health care professionals. **Computerized Information Services:** MEDLARS, DIALOG Information Services, OCLC. Performs searches on fee basis. Contact Person: Barbara Doughty, Med.Ref.Libn., 348-1364. **Networks/Consortia:** Member of SOLINET. **Staff:** Martha Tillotson, Tech.Serv./Sys.Libn.

★18163★
University of Alabama - Eric and Sarah Rodgers Library for Science and Engineering (Sci-Engr)
P.O. Box 870266
Tuscaloosa, AL 35487-0266   Phone: (205)348-2100
Founded: 1990. **Staff:** Prof 2; Other 4. **Subjects:** Natural sciences, physical sciences, engineering, mathematics, computer science. **Holdings:** 70,000 books; 130,000 bound periodical volumes; 62,092 microfiche, 783 reels of microfilm; NASA documents. **Subscriptions:** 1700 journals and other serials. **Services:** Interlibrary loan; copying; library open to the public. **Automated Operations:** Computerized public access catalog, cataloging, and circulation (NOTIS). **Computerized Information Services:** DIALOG Information Services, ORBIT Search Service, Chemical Abstracts Service (CAS), STN International; CD-ROMs (NTIS Bibliographic Data Base, General Science Index). Performs searches. Contact Person: Kebede Gessesse, Ref.Libn. **Networks/Consortia:** Member of Network of Alabama Academic Libraries (NAAL), SOLINET, Center for Research Libraries (CRL). **Remarks:** FAX: (205)348-2113. **Staff:** Linda G. Ackerson, Ref.Libn.

★18164★
University of Alabama - McLure Education Library (Educ)
P.O. Box 870266   Phone: (205)348-6055
Tuscaloosa, AL 35487-0266   Sharon Lee Stewart, Sr.Libn.
Founded: 1928. **Staff:** Prof 2; Other 4. **Subjects:** Administration and educational leadership; special education; curriculum and instruction; health and human performance; behavioral studies; fine arts education. **Special Collections:** Curriculum Laboratory; Children's Collection; history of education in America. **Holdings:** 137,647 books; 14,719 bound periodical volumes; 507,843 microforms; 3 VF drawers of newsletters; 6 VF drawers of additional material. **Subscriptions:** 901 journals and other serials. **Services:** Interlibrary loan; copying; microfiche-to-microfiche copying; microfiche-to-paper copying; microfilm-to-paper copying; library open to the public. **Automated Operations:** Computerized public access catalog, cataloging, and circulation (NOTIS). **Computerized Information Services:** DIALOG Information Services, OCLC, BRS Information Technologies, PFDS Online; CD-ROM (ERIC). **Networks/Consortia:** Member of SOLINET, Network of Alabama Academic Libraries (NAAL), Center for Research Libraries (CRL). **Publications:** Education Library Resources. **Remarks:** FAX: (205)348-8833. **Staff:** Helga Visscher, Ref.Libn.

★18165★
.**University of Alabama - Natural Gas Supply Information Center** (Energy)
205 Tom Bevill Bldg.
Box 870211   Phone: (205)348-2839
Tuscaloosa, AL 35487   Ron W. Henderson, Info.Spec.
Founded: 1985. **Staff:** Prof 1; Other 1. **Subjects:** Coalbed methane; alternative energy sources; oil and gas petroleum industry; coal. **Holdings:** 654 books; 12 basin reports; 618 petrophysical logs; 783 technical reports; 200 vertical files and ephemera; 60 maps; unbound periodicals. **Subscriptions:** 18 journals and other serials. **Services:** Copying; SDI; center open to the public for reference use only. **Automated Operations:** Computerized cataloging and acquisitions. **Computerized Information Services:** COMETBIB (internal database). Performs searches free of charge. **Publications:** Bibliographies, irregular. **Special Indexes:** Index to well logs; index to vertical files. **Remarks:** FAX: (205)348-9268. **Formerly:** Its Coalbed Methane Information Center.

★18166★
University of Alabama - School of Law - Alabama Law Review - Library (Law)
P.O. Box 870382   Phone: (205)348-5300
Tuscaloosa, AL 35487-0382   Randall Quarles, Ed.-in-Chf.
Staff: 1. **Subjects:** Federal and state law. **Holdings:** 3366 books; 361 bound periodical volumes. **Subscriptions:** 25 journals and other serials. **Services:** Library not open to the public. **Computerized Information Services:** WESTLAW, LEXIS. **Publications:** Alabama Law Review, 3/year - by subscription. **Remarks:** FAX: (205)348-1112.

★18167★
University of Alabama - School of Law Library (Law)
Box 870383   Phone: (205)348-1113
Tuscaloosa, AL 35487-0383   Robert Marshall
Founded: 1872. **Staff:** Prof 5; Other 6. **Subjects:** Law. **Special Collections:** U.S. Supreme Court Justice Hugo L. Black Book Collection. **Holdings:** 211,423 books; 30,476 bound periodical volumes; 43,000 microforms. **Subscriptions:** 2726 journals and other serials; 10 newspapers. **Services:** Interlibrary loan; copying; library open to the public. **Computerized Information Services:** LEXIS, DIALOG Information Services, WESTLAW. **Networks/Consortia:** Member of Consortium of South Eastern Law Libraries, Network of Alabama Academic Libraries (NAAL). **Remarks:** FAX: (205)348-1112. **Staff:** David Lowe, Comp.Serv.Ref.; Ruth Weeks, Cat.; Paul Pruitt, Ref./Coll.Dev.; Penny C. Gibson, Pub.Serv.Libn.

★18168★
University of Alabama - University Map Library (Geog-Map)
Box 870322   Phone: (205)348-6028
Tuscaloosa, AL 35487   Thomas J. Kallsen, Map Lib.Supv.
Founded: 1971. **Staff:** Prof 1; Other 1. **Subjects:** Place name research; maps - U.S., Alabama, geology, natural resources, world, Europe. **Special Collections:** Winn-Dixie Atlas Collection (140 thematic atlases); Place Names Research Center of the United States. **Holdings:** 475 books; 270,000 maps; 70,000 aerial photographs; 130 relief models. **Services:** Interlibrary loan; SDI; library open to the public with restrictions on circulation. **Publications:** Map Library: University of Alabama (brochure).

★18169★
University of Alabama - William Stanley Hoole Special Collections Library (Hum, Rare Book)
Box 870266   Phone: (205)348-5512
Tuscaloosa, AL 35487-0266   Joyce H. Lamont, Asst. Dean, Spec.Coll.
Founded: 1947. **Staff:** Prof 5; Other 3. **Subjects:** Alabamiana, travels in the South East, southern Americana, early imprints, state documents. **Special Collections:** Rare books (22,500); manuscripts (30 million); university archives (18 million items); Alabamiana (60,000 volumes); black folk music (250 magnetic tapes); oral history (875 magnetic tapes); maps (25,000). **Holdings:** 46,000 books; 12,500 theses, dissertations, and pamphlets. **Subscriptions:** 135 journals and other serials. **Services:** Interlibrary loan; copying; library open to the public. **Automated Operations:** NOTIS. **Computerized Information Services:** OCLC. **Networks/Consortia:** Member of SOLINET, Network of Alabama Academic Libraries (NAAL), Center for Research Libraries (CRL). **Special Indexes:** Finding aids for manuscripts and archival collections. **Remarks:** FAX: (205)348-8833.

★18170★
University of Alabama at Birmingham - Computer and Information Sciences Research Library (Comp Sci)
Campbell Hall, Rm. 115A   Phone: (205)934-2213
Birmingham, AL 35294   Barrett Bryant, Fac.Lib.Rep.
Founded: 1982. **Staff:** 2. **Subjects:** Computer science, parallel processing, artificial intelligence, software engineering, programming languages, computer graphics. **Holdings:** 1000 unbound periodicals; 1000 technical reports; 1000 manuscripts. **Subscriptions:** 20 journals and other serials; 10 newspapers. **Services:** Library not open to the public. **Automated Operations:** Computerized cataloging, acquisitions, and serials. **Computerized Information Services:** InterNet (electronic mail service). **Publications:** Department of Computer and Information Sciences Technical Report Series, 25-30/year - free upon request. **Remarks:** FAX: (205)934-5473. Electronic mail address(es): bryant@cis.uab.edu (InterNet).

★18171★
University of Alabama at Birmingham - Lister Hill Library of the Health Sciences (Med)
UAB Station   Phone: (205)934-5460
Birmingham, AL 35294   Virginia Algermissen, Dir.
Founded: 1945. **Staff:** Prof 15; Other 38. **Subjects:** Medicine, dentistry, nursing, public health, optometry, allied health fields. **Special Collections:** Reynolds Historical Library (rare medical books and manuscripts; 10,000 items); Alabama Museum of the Health Sciences (medical history; 10,700 items); Multi-Media Services (2910 AV programs). **Holdings:** 99,516 books; 136,084 bound periodical volumes; 366.5 linear feet of archival material; 35,303 microforms. **Subscriptions:** 2872 journals and other serials; 5 newspapers. **Services:** Interlibrary loan; copying; faxing; microcomputer lab; SDI; library open to the public for reference use only. **Automated**

Operations: Computerized public access catalog, cataloging, acquisitions, serials, and circulation. **Computerized Information Services:** MEDLARS, BRS Information Technologies, NLM, DIALOG Information Services, WILSONLINE, MEDLINE, CCML; CD-ROMs; OnTyme Electronic Message Network Service (electronic mail service). Performs searches on fee basis. Contact Person: Nancy Clemmons, Hd., Ref.Serv., 934-2230. **Networks/Consortia:** Member of SOLINET, Network of Alabama Academic Libraries (NAAL). **Publications:** Rare Books and Collections of the Reynolds Historical Library: A Bibliography, 1968; Update (newsletter), bimonthly; Reynolds Library Associates Newsletter, 3/year. **Remarks:** FAX: (205)934-3545. **Staff:** Nancy Farnum, Coord., Multi-Media Serv.; Jay Harris, Hd., Coll.Dept.; B.J. Gramka, Hd., Cat.; Jack Smith, Micro Lab.

★ 18172 ★

University of Alabama at Birmingham - School of Medicine - Anesthesiology Library (Med)
Department of Anesthesiology
619 19th St., S.   Phone: (205)934-6500
Birmingham, AL 35233-1924   A.J. Wright, Clin.Libn.
Founded: 1980. **Staff:** Prof 1; Other 1. **Subjects:** Anesthesia, pain management. **Special Collections:** Anesthesia History Collection (400 articles and monographs). **Holdings:** 1236 books; 1117 bound periodical volumes; 100 cassettes; 110 videotapes. **Subscriptions:** 105 journals and other serials. **Services:** Interlibrary loan; copying; SDI; library open to the public for reference use only. **Automated Operations:** Computerized cataloging. **Computerized Information Services:** NLM, DIALOG Information Services; BITNET, InterNet (electronic mail services). Performs searches on fee basis. **Networks/Consortia:** Member of Jefferson County Hospital Librarians' Association. **Publications:** A Core List of Anesthesia Monographs and Serials, annual. **Special Indexes:** Historical Files List; Journal Holdings List. **Remarks:** FAX: (205)975-5033. Electronic mail address(es): MEDS002@UABDPO (BITNET); MEDS002@UABDPO.DPO.UAB.EDU (InterNet).

★ 18173 ★

University of Alabama in Huntsville - Special Collections (Hist, Sci-Engr)
Library   Phone: (205)895-6523
Huntsville, AL 35899   J.M. Perreault, Hd., Spec.Coll.
Staff: Prof 1; Other 2. **Subjects:** Alabama politics and government, space sciences, astronomy, ballistics, science fiction. **Special Collections:** Congressman Robert E. Jones papers (correspondence, office files, and personal papers); university archives; Space Collection (Willy Ley Collection of space sciences; ballistics and rocketry; science fiction; Saturn history documentation; Peenemunde Archive 66; Rudolf Herrmann Collection; Gerhard Reisig Collection). **Holdings:** 1224 linear feet of files, books, and journals. **Services:** Copying; collections open to qualified scholars. **Computerized Information Services:** Internal databases. **Remarks:** FAX: (205)895-6862. **Staff:** Helen Tygielski, Space.

★ 18174 ★

University of Alaska - Institute of Marine Science - Seward Marine Station Library (Biol Sci, Sci-Engr)
Box 730   Phone: (907)224-5261
Seward, AK 99664   Dwight Ittner, Libn.
Staff: 1. **Subjects:** Physical and chemical oceanography, aquaculture, marine biology, marine botany. **Special Collections:** Aquaculture reprint collection. **Holdings:** 3000 books; 400 bound periodical volumes; 10,200 reprints; 2300 technical reports; 2000 hydrographic charts. **Subscriptions:** 100 journals and other serials. **Services:** Interlibrary loan; library open to the public with restrictions. **Remarks:** FAX: (907)224-3392.

★ 18175 ★

University of Alaska, Anchorage - Arctic Environmental Information and Data Center (Soc Sci, Energy)
707 A St.   Phone: (907)279-4523
Anchorage, AK 99501   Dr. Douglas Segar, Dir.
Founded: 1972. **Staff:** Prof 17; Other 6. **Subjects:** Alaska - environment, fisheries, glaciology, land use planning, oil pollution, energy resources, coastal zone management; arctic research; Alaska climate records; natural resources management and planning. **Special Collections:** Depository for Arctic Petroleum Operators Association and Alaska Oil and Gas Association (AOGA) reports; Annual Reports of the 13 Alaska Native Regional Corporations; ARCO Arctic Environmental Reports Collection. **Holdings:** 8800 books; 2000 photographs of Alaska; 11,500 microfiche;

reports; pamphlets; maps. **Subscriptions:** 65 journals and other serials. **Services:** Center open to the public. **Computerized Information Services:** DIALOG Information Services; internal databases; BITNET, OMNET (electronic mail services). Performs searches. **Publications:** List of publications - available on request. **Remarks:** FAX: (907)276-6847. Since 1972 the Center has been involved at one level or another in all major resource management issues in Alaska, from assisting in Native land selection under the Alaska Native Claims Settlement Act to evaluating the environmental effects of development projects. The Center has written sociocultural impact studies, and provided background analyses on policy and development questions debated by the International Whaling Commission, the U.S. Congress, and the Alaska legislature. It is also one of twelve designated CMAS (Computer Mapping and Analysis System) stations in the U.S. for the National Oceanographic and Atmospheric Administration (NOAA). It operates the Alaska Climate Center, which conducts climate-related research and houses historic data files on the state's climatology and meteorology including wind, snowpack, and solar radiation records. The Center also houses liaison offices of the U.S. Arctic Research Commission and the National Oceanographic and Atmospheric Administration, Alaska region.

★ 18176 ★

University of Alaska, Anchorage - Consortium Library (Hist, Mus)
3211 Providence Dr.   Phone: (907)786-1825
Anchorage, AK 99508   Barbara J. Sokolov, Dir.
Founded: 1973. **Staff:** 46. **Subjects:** Health science, education, psychology, history, literature. **Special Collections:** Alaskana and Polar Regions Collection; sheet music collection; rare books; maps; archives and manuscripts. **Holdings:** 393,210 books and bound periodical volumes; 2254.2 cubic feet of archival items; 38,171 microforms. **Subscriptions:** 3441 journals and other serials. **Services:** Interlibrary loan; copying; collections open to the public. **Computerized Information Services:** DIALOG Information Services, PFDS Online, OCLC, VU/TEXT Information Services; University of Alaska Computer Network (internal database). **Networks/Consortia:** Member of Alaska Library Network (ALN), Western Library Network (WLN). **Publications:** Guide to UAA Archives. **Special Catalogs:** Catalog of Sheet Music at the UAA Library. **Remarks:** FAX: (907)786-6050. **Formerly:** Its Library - Special Collections. **Staff:** Tohook P. Chang; Ronald L. Lantaret; Nancy L. Lesh; Catherine Innes-Taylor; Alden M. Rollins; William P. Siemens; Clara Sitter; Dennis F. Walle.

University of Alaska, Anchorage - Energy Extension Service - Energy Resource and Information Center
See: Alaska (State) Energy Extension Service (218)

★ 18177 ★

University of Alaska, Anchorage - Library - Archives & Manuscripts Department (Hist)
3211 Providence Dr.   Phone: (907)786-1849
Anchorage, AK 99508   Dennis F. Walle, Archv./Mss.Cur.
Founded: 1979. **Staff:** Prof 1; Other 3. **Special Collections:** University archives (350 record series) and historical manuscripts (375 collections); social, political, and cultural organizations, business records, papers of individuals and families (2350 cubic feet). **Services:** Department open to the public with restrictions. **Publications:** Annual Report; Guide to R.T. Harris Family Collection, 1981; Guide to the Fred Wildon Fickett Collection, 1985; Guide to the Victor C. Rivers Family Collection, 1986; Guide to the Manuscript Collections at the University of Alaska Anchorage, 1990; occasional guides to specific collections. **Special Catalogs:** Unpublished internal guide containing collection and university record inventories.

★ 18178 ★

University of Alaska, Anchorage - Library - Government Documents (Info Sci)
3211 Providence Dr.   Phone: (907)786-1874
Anchorage, AK 99508   Alden Rollins, Gov.Docs.Libn.
Founded: 1973. **Special Collections:** Government documents. **Holdings:** 220,000 volumes. **Services:** Interlibrary loan; copying; library open to the public. **Computerized Information Services:** DIALOG Information Services, WILSONLINE, VU/TEXT Information Services; OnTyme Electronic Message Network Service, OCLC, WLN (electronic mail services). Performs searches on fee basis. **Networks/Consortia:** Member of Alaska Library Network (ALN), Western Library Network (WLN). **Publications:** Census Alaska: Number of Inhabitants, 1792-1970. **Special Indexes:** Anchorage Documents File, 1970-1979. **Remarks:** FAX: (907)786-6050.

★ 18179 ★

University of Alaska, Fairbanks - Agricultural & Forestry Experiment
  Station - Palmer Research Center (Agri)
533 E. Fireweed   Phone: (907)745-3257
Palmer, AK 99645   G. Allen Mitchell, Assoc.Dir.
Founded: 1950. **Staff:** 1. **Subjects:** Agriculture, soil science, crop science,
animal science, statistics, plant pathology. **Holdings:** 1800 books; 4000
bound periodical volumes; 40,500 abstracts on cards. **Subscriptions:** 20
journals and other serials. **Services:** Interlibrary loan; copying (limited);
library open to the public. **Remarks:** FAX: (907)746-2677.

★ 18180 ★

University of Alaska, Fairbanks - Alaska Native Language Center -
  Research Library (Area-Ethnic)
Fairbanks, AK 99775-0120   Phone: (907)474-7874
                                             Michael Krauss, Dir.
Founded: 1972. **Staff:** Prof 6; Other 3. **Subjects:** Alaskan native,
Athabaskan, Eyak, Tlingit, Haida, Tsimshian, and Eskimo-Aleut languages;
Amerindian linguistics. **Holdings:** 8000 books, journals, unpublished papers,
field notes, and archival materials. **Services:** Copying (limited); library open
to the public for reference use only with permission. **Computerized
Information Services:** BITNET (electronic mail service). **Publications:** List
of publications - available on request. **Remarks:** Said to contain practically
everything written in or on any Alaska native language, including languages
shared in Canada and the Soviet Union. FAX: (907)474-6586. Electronic
mail address(es): FYANLP@ALASKA (BITNET).

★ 18181 ★

University of Alaska, Fairbanks - Alaska and Polar Regions Department
  (Hist)
Elmer E. Rasmuson Library   Phone: (907)479-7261
Fairbanks, AK 99775-1005   David A. Hales, Hd.
Founded: 1965. **Staff:** Prof 7; Other 18. **Subjects:** Alaska - history, business,
anthropology, sciences, university, politics; Arctic; Antarctic. **Special
Collections:** Alaska and Polar Regions Books (Alaska 55,000; Canada 6500;
Greenland 2500; Siberia 4500; Antarctica 4000); Alaska historical
photographs (500,000); rare books (4000); rare maps (500); oral history; U.S.
Documents (Alaska, 160,000); Alaska manuscripts and congressional
papers (3000 cubic feet); University archives (2000 cubic feet). **Holdings:**
11,000 microforms; 6000 historical and university audiotapes; 300
videotapes; 730 reels of archival movie film; 2000 cubic feet of university
archives; 5000 cubic feet of manuscripts. **Subscriptions:** 930 journals and
other serials; 50 newspapers. **Services:** Interlibrary loan; copying; archives
open to the public. **Computerized Information Services:** CD-ROM (Polar
Pac); Ancestors, Bibliography of Alaska and Polar Regions, of Alaska,
Alaska Manuscript Maps, Wenger Anthropological Eskimo database,
Project Jukebox Oral History database (internal databases); electronic mail.
Networks/Consortia: Member of Western Library Network (WLN).
Publications: Guide to Holdings of the University Archives and Manuscript
Collections (microfiche); Bibliography of Alaskana (microfiche); Russian
Sources on American History (Shur Collection); Into the 80's with Alaskan
environmental impact statements (bibliography); Alaska Natives: a guide to
current reference sources in the Rasmuson Library; historic Alaska
documents translation series (8 titles); Elmer E. Rasmuson Library
Occasional Papers (11 titles); Guide to Historical Photographs in the Elmer
E. Rasmusen Library. **Special Indexes:** Oral History Index; Index to the
Anthropological Papers of the University of Alaska; Index to Historical
Photographs; Alaska Newspaper Microfilm and Paper Holdings; Pioneers
of Alaska Index; University of Alaska Theses (1926 to present); Rare Maps
Title Listing; Bibliography of Alaska and Polar Regions - guides to
congressional papers of Anthony J. Dimond , Mike Gravel, Ralph J. Rivers,
Howard W. Pollock; unpublished indexes for all processed manuscript
collections. **Remarks:** FAX: (907)474-6841. **Staff:** Eugene West, Arctic
Bibliog.; Albert Fowler, Archv.; Gretchen Lake, Asst.Archv.; Marvin Falk,
Rare Bk.Cur.; William Schneider, Oral Hist.Cur.; Ronald Inouye, Ed.

★ 18182 ★

University of Alaska, Fairbanks - Biosciences Library (Med, Biol Sci)
Fairbanks, AK 99775-0300   Phone: (907)474-7442
                                             Dwight Ittner, Libn.
Founded: 1973. **Staff:** Prof 1; Other 3. **Subjects:** Health sciences, veterinary
medicine, fish biology and fisheries, animal physiology, microbiology, plant
pathology, ocean sciences, molecular biology. **Holdings:** 50,792 books;
22,071 bound periodical volumes; 2543 volumes in microform.
Subscriptions: 550 journals and other serials. **Services:** Interlibrary loan;
copying; library open to the public. **Automated Operations:** Computerized

public access catalog, cataloging, and circulation. **Computerized
Information Services:** DIALOG Information Services, BRS Information
Technologies, QL Systems, PFDS Online; OnTyme Electronic Message
Network Service, DIALMAIL, SCIENCEnet, EBSCONET (electronic
mail services). **Networks/Consortia:** Member of National Network of
Libraries of Medicine - Pacific Northwest Region, Western Library Network
(WLN), Alaska Library Network (ALN). **Remarks:** FAX: (907)474-7820.
Electronic mail address(es): UAFAWR (OnTyme Electronic Message
Network Service); UAF.Bio.Library (SCIENCEnet). Includes the holdings
of the Institute of Marine Science - Library. **Formerly:** Its Bio-Medical
Library.

★ 18183 ★

University of Alaska, Fairbanks - College of Rural Alaska - Resource
  Center (Educ)
Gruening Bldg., Rm. 717
Fairbanks, AK 99775-0420   Phone: (907)474-6474
Founded: 1974. **Staff:** 1. **Subjects:** Cross-cultural education, psychology, and
sociology; Alaska Native studies; rural development. **Special Collections:**
Small High School Project curriculum materials (1000 items). **Holdings:**
5000 books; 150 unpublished theses and research reports; 4000 VF items;
3500 government publications. **Services:** Center open to the public on a
limited schedule. **Computerized Information Services:** BITNET (electronic
mail service). **Special Catalogs:** Catalog of the Small High Schools Project
(book). **Remarks:** FAX: (907)474-5451. Electronic mail address(es):
FYPUBL@ALASKA (BITNET).

★ 18184 ★

University of Alaska, Fairbanks - Geophysical Institute - Keith B.
  Matheu Library (Sci-Engr)
Fairbanks, AK 99775-0800   Phone: (907)479-7503
                                             Julia H. Triplehorn, Libn.
Founded: 1949. **Staff:** Prof 1; Other 2. **Subjects:** Physics, astronomy,
geophysics, geology, mathematics, electronic engineering, meteorology,
solar terrestrial science, geothermal energy, glaciology, solid earth sciences,
oceanography, remote sensing, polar phenomena, atmospheric chemistry,
atmospheric sciences, space sciences, aeronomy, volcanology,
geochronology, permafrost. **Special Collections:** Alaska Earthquake
Photographs; International Geophysical Year materials; Alaska and Arctic
Climate Data; arctic air chemistry. **Holdings:** 10,178 titles; 38,387 books and
bound periodical volumes; technical reports and data. **Subscriptions:** 270
journals and other serials. **Services:** Interlibrary loan; library open to the
public. **Computerized Information Services:** DIALOG Information
Services, ORBIT Search Service, NASA/RECON, RESORS (Remote
Sensing On-line Retrieval System), QL Systems, STN International;
BITNET (electronic mail service). **Networks/Consortia:** Member of
Western Library Network (WLN). **Remarks:** FAX: (907)474-7290.
Electronic mail address(es): FYGILIB@ALASKA (BITNET).

★ 18185 ★

University of Alaska, Fairbanks - Wildlife Library (Biol Sci)
Department of Biology and Wildlife   Phone: (907)474-7174
Fairbanks, AK 99775   Carol Button, Lib. Aide
Staff: 1. **Subjects:** Wildlife management, animal ecology, mammalogy, plant
ecology, wildlife economics, outdoor recreation, Arctic ecology. **Special
Collections:** Government reports. **Holdings:** 300 volumes; 10,000 reprints.
Subscriptions: 31 journals and other serials. **Services:** Interlibrary loan;
copying; library open to the public. **Computerized Information Services:**
Reprint collection emphasizing Alaskan, arctic-sub-arctic birds and
mammals (internal database). **Special Catalogs:** Termatrex cataloging of
reprints (taxonomy, geographic area, date). **Remarks:** FAX: (907)474-6967.

University of Alberta - Alberta Law Foundation - Health Law Institute
See: Health Law Institute (7078)

★ 18186 ★

University of Alberta - Centre for Subatomic Research (Sci-Engr)
Edmonton, AB, Canada T6G 2N5   Phone: (403)492-3637
                                             Llanca Letelier, Sec.
Staff: Prof 1. **Subjects:** Subatomic physics, intermediate energy. **Holdings:**
803 books; 1849 bound periodical volumes; 112 theses; 597 preprints and
reprints of internal research reports; 2564 external reports. **Subscriptions:**
3 journals and other serials. **Services:** Library open to the public for
reference use only. **Computerized Information Services:** BITNET
(electronic mail service). **Publications:** Progress Report; preprints of
research papers, talks, and theses. **Remarks:** FAX: (403)492-3408.
Electronic mail address(es): SAPH@UALTAMTS (BITNET). **Formerly:**
Its Nuclear Research Centre.

★18187★
University of Alberta - Computing Science Reading Room (Sci-Engr,
  Comp Sci)
604 General Services Bldg.   Phone: (403)492-7538
Edmonton, AB, Canada T6G 2H1   Linda Needham, Lib.Techn.
Founded: 1968. **Staff:** 1. **Subjects:** Computing science, mathematics,
statistics, engineering. **Holdings:** 4500 books; 500 bound periodical volumes;
3500 technical reports; 200 theses. **Subscriptions:** 200 journals and other
serials. **Services:** Interlibrary loan; room open to the public. **Automated
Operations:** Computerized public access catalog. **Remarks:** FAX: (403)492-
4327.

★18188★
**University of Alberta - Department of Geography - William C. Wonders
  Map Collection** (Geog-Map)
B-7 H.M. Tory Bldg.   Phone: (403)492-4760
Edmonton, AB, Canada T6G 2H4   Ronald Whistance-Smith,
     Coord.Rsc.Servs.
Founded: 1966. **Staff:** Prof 1; Other 2. **Subjects:** Topography, geology,
geography, cartography, history, soils, aerial photography, Canada, Eastern
Europe. **Holdings:** 2872 atlases; 484 gazetteers; 2100 reference books; 45
titles of bound periodicals; 3000 unbound reports; 12 reels of microfilm of
maps; 281 reels of microfilm of air photographs; 32 cartobibliographies on
microfilm; 14,000 map and air photo index titles on microfiche; 377,548 map
titles; 1 million air photographs; 101 relief models. **Subscriptions:** 175
journals and other serials. **Services:** Interlibrary loan; copying; collection
open to the public with restrictions. **Computerized Information Services:**
BITNET (electronic mail service). **Remarks:** FAX: (403)492-7508.
Electronic mail address(es): GEOG@MTS.UCS.UALBERTA.CA
(BITNET).

★18189★
**University of Alberta - Department of Rural Economy - Eric Richard
  Berg Memorial Library** (Agri)
504 General Services Bldg.   Phone: (403)492-0815
Edmonton, AB, Canada T6G 2H1   Barbara Johnson, Libn.
Founded: 1963. **Staff:** Prof 2; Other 1. **Subjects:** Agricultural economics,
rural sociology, forest economics. **Special Collections:** Department theses
(260); Statistics Canada catalogs (230); U.S. Department of Agriculture
titles (45). **Holdings:** 14,000 books; 520 bound periodical volumes; 2 VF
drawers of archives; government documents, textbooks, and university
documents. **Subscriptions:** 280 journals and other serials; 8 newspapers.
Services: Interlibrary loan; copying; SDI; library open to the public with
restrictions. **Automated Operations:** Computerized cataloging.
Computerized Information Services: Monographic holdings (internal
database). **Special Catalogs:** Department theses list; department
publications list; various subject area search strategies (printouts). **Remarks:**
FAX: (403)492-0268.

★18190★
University of Alberta - Developmental Disabilities Centre - Library
  (Med)
6-123A Education North   Phone: (403)492-4439
Edmonton, AB, Canada T6G 2G5   Henny de Groot, Adm.Asst.
Founded: 1967. **Staff:** 3. **Subjects:** Biology, medicine, neurology,
psychology, education. **Holdings:** 250 books and bound periodical volumes;
50 other cataloged items. **Services:** Interlibrary loan; library not open to the
public. **Computerized Information Services:** BITNET (electronic mail
service). **Remarks:** FAX: (403)492-1318. Electronic mail address(es):
USEROOPS@UALTAMTS (BITNET).

★18191★
University of Alberta - Devonian Botanic Garden - Library (Biol Sci)
Edmonton, AB, Canada T6G 2E9   Phone: (403)987-3054
Founded: 1971. **Subjects:** Horticulture, botany, gardening, landscape design.
Holdings: 2000 books. **Subscriptions:** 2 journals and other serials. **Services:**
Library open to the public with restrictions. **Remarks:** FAX: (403)987-4141.

★18192★
**University of Alberta - Division of Educational Research Services -
  Technical Library** (Educ, Comp Sci)
3-104 Education Bldg. N.   Phone: (403)492-3762
Edmonton, AB, Canada T6G 2G5   Rina Perez, Libn.
Staff: Prof 1; Other 1. **Subjects:** Computers, computer-based instruction,
statistics and research design. **Holdings:** 4000 books and bound periodical

volumes. Educational Testing Service Research Bulletins, 1963 to present.
Subscriptions: 46 journals and other serials. **Services:** Interlibrary loan;
copying; library open to the public with restrictions. **Automated Operations:**
Computerized cataloging. **Remarks:** FAX: (403)432-7219. Affiliated with
Department of Educational Psychology - Test Library. **Staff:** Gwen Parker,
Libn.; Angela Chalkley, Libn.

★18193★
University of Alberta - Faculte St-Jean - Bibliotheque (Area-Ethnic,
  Hum)
8406 Rue Marie-Anne Gaboury (91e)   Phone: (403)465-8711
Edmonton, AB, Canada T6C 4G9   Juliette J. Henley, Hd.Libn.
Founded: 1910. **Staff:** Prof 2; Other 4. **Subjects:** French-Canadian and
Western Canadian history, ethnology, French and French-Canadian
literature, French language resources in education, arts, humanities, social
sciences, and science. **Special Collections:** French government documents
(10,000 items). **Holdings:** 110,000 items (mainly in French); 3500 bound
periodical volumes; 1600 reels of microfilm; 16,000 microfiche.
Subscriptions: 300 journals and other serials; 9 newspapers. **Services:**
Interlibrary loan; SDI; library open to the public for reference use only.
Automated Operations: Computerized cataloging and acquisitions.
Computerized Information Services: Services Documentaires Multimedias
(SDM), BRS Information Technologies, Termium, INFOPUQ, Banque de
Terminologie du Quebec (BTQ), UTLAS; CD-ROMs. Performs searches on
fee basis. Contact Person: Jacqueline Girouard, Ref.Libn. **Remarks:** FAX:
(403)465-8760.

★18194★
University of Alberta - H.T. Coutts Library (Educ)
Faculty of Education Bldg.   Phone: (403)492-1460
Edmonton, AB, Canada T6G 2G5   Kathleen DeLong, Area Coord.
Founded: 1945. **Staff:** Prof 9; Other 46. **Subjects:** Education, teaching
materials, children's literature. **Special Collections:** Historical Textbook
Collection; William S. Gray Reading Collection (on microfiche). **Holdings:**
242,331 volumes; 356,334 titles on microfiche; 7768 reels of microfilm;
28,606 nonbook titles; 9920 newspaper clippings; 13,677 theses; ERIC,
ONTERIS, and MICROLOG education collection microfiche.
Subscriptions: 879 journals. **Services:** Interlibrary loan; copying; library
open to the public for reference use only. **Automated Operations:**
Computerized acquisitions and circulation. **Computerized Information
Services:** DIALOG Information Services, BRS Information Technologies,
SPIRES; CD-ROM (PsycLIT, SPORT Discus, International Encyclopedia
of Education). **Special Indexes:** Alberta Education Index; Index to Faculty
of Education theses held by library (computer printout); picture and art slide
indexes; index to record collection; index to curriculum guides. **Staff:** Josie
Tong, Hd., Ref.; Leslie Aitken, Coll.Coord.; Grant Kayler, Hd., Access
Serv.

★18195★
University of Alberta - Humanities and Social Sciences Library (Hum,
  Soc Sci)
Rutherford Library   Phone: (403)492-3794
Edmonton, AB, Canada T6G 2J4   Deborah Dancik, Area Coord.
Founded: 1972. **Staff:** Prof 14; Other 47. **Subjects:** Humanities, social
sciences, business and commerce, physical education, library science.
Holdings: 1.4 million volumes; 150,000 bound periodical volumes; 2.3
million microforms. **Subscriptions:** 7600 journals and other serials; 125
newspapers. **Services:** Interlibrary loan; copying; SDI; library open to the
public for reference use only. **Automated Operations:** Computerized
cataloging, acquisitions, and circulation. **Computerized Information
Services:** DIALOG Information Services, BRS Information Technologies,
International Development Research Centre (IDRC), Info Globe, CAN/
OLE, Infomart Online; internal database; Envoy 100 (electronic mail
service). Performs searches on fee basis. Telephone 492-5791. **Publications:**
Library Guide. **Special Indexes:** Business Annual Reports Index. **Remarks:**
FAX: (403)492-4327. **Staff:** B. Champion, Ref.Libn.; G. Olson, Ref.Libn.;
W. Quoika-Stanka, Ref.Libn.; K. West, Bus.Libn.; K. Wikeley, Ref.Libn.;
M. McClary, Per./Microforms Libn.; F. Ziegler, Tech.Serv. and Coll.Libn.;
C.D. Sharplin, Ref.Libn.; S. Manwaring, Hd.Govt.Pubns.Libn.; Ione
Hooper, Asst.Bus.Libn.; Deborah Scott-Douglas, Asst.Bus.Libn.; Janet
Williamson, Ref.Libn.; Alan Rutkowski, Ref.Libn.; Fern Russell,
Bibliog.Instr.Libn.

★18196★
University of Alberta - Humanities and Social Sciences Library - Bruce Peel Special Collections Library (Rare Book, Hum, Hist)
Rutherford South   Phone: (403)492-5998
Edmonton, AB, Canada T6G 2J4   John Charles, Spec.Coll.Libn./Hd.
Founded: 1964. **Staff:** Prof 2; Other 4. **Subjects:** Western Canadiana; prairie provinces; English literature, 1600-1940; Canadian drama; European drama, 17th-18th centuries; California history; European history, 1500-1900; book arts. **Special Collections:** John Bunyan (early editions; 245 volumes); Milton (early editions; 165 volumes); Salzburg (16th-18th century editions of canon law and ecclesiastical works; 700 volumes); Cuala Press (250 items including broadsides); D.H. Lawrence (early editions; 290 volumes); Grabhorn Press (600 volumes); 19th century English theater playbills (900); Curwen Press (Curwen's own in-house collection of their publications, 1920-1956; 1000 volumes, 3000 ephemera, scrapbooks, posters); Gregory Javitch Collection on North and South American Indians (emphasis on treaties, warfare, language, and ceremonial dances; 900 volumes); 19th and 20th century book arts (emphasis on Victorian chromo-lithography, Canadian fine printing, contemporary book works, and artists' books; 1500 volumes); Georg Kaiser Archiv (39 boxes and photocopies of manuscripts); Ariel Bension Collection (Sephardic manuscripts and texts; 10 volumes; 350 manuscripts); Wordsworth (153 volumes of facsimiles of Dove Cottage manuscripts); Black Sparrow Press archives, 1966-1970 (archives for first 94 publications). **Holdings:** 85,000 volumes; 14,250 volumes of University of Alberta dissertations and theses; 48 volumes of diaries and typescripts on Alberta early settlers and local history. **Subscriptions:** 10 journals and other serials. **Services:** Interlibrary loan; copying (both limited); library open to the public. **Automated Operations:** Computerized cataloging. **Publications:** Library Editions, semiannual. **Remarks:** FAX: (403)492-4327. **Staff:** Jeannine Green, Spec.Coll.Libn.; Carolynne Poon, Conservator.

★18197★
University of Alberta - Humanities and Social Sciences Library - Government Publications (Soc Sci)
Edmonton, AB, Canada T6G 2J8   Phone: (403)492-3776
                    Sally Manwaring, Hd.Govt.Pubns.Libn.
Founded: 1964. **Staff:** Prof 2.5; Other 5. **Subjects:** Economics, political science, business, history, sociology. **Holdings:** 290,000 books and bound periodical volumes; 1.2 million microforms. **Subscriptions:** 4050 journals and other serials. **Services:** Interlibrary loan; copying; open to the public. **Automated Operations:** Computerized public access catalog, cataloging, and serials. **Computerized Information Services:** DIALOG Information Services; SPIRES (internal database). **Publications:** Statistical sources in the library, a selected bibliography, 1974; Descriptive guide to government publications of Canada, Great Britain, the United States and international bodies, 1977; Selected Accessions List, bimonthly - for internal distribution and by request. **Special Indexes:** KWOC index to uncataloged acquisitions. **Staff:** David Sharplin, Asst.Govt.Pubns.Libn.

★18198★
University of Alberta - Humanities and Social Sciences Library - Winspear Business Reference Room (Bus-Fin)
1-18 Business Bldg.   Phone: (403)492-5652
Edmonton, AB, Canada T6G 2R6   Kathy West, Bus. & Econ.Libn.
Staff: Prof 2; Other 3. **Subjects:** Business. **Special Collections:** Canadian annual reports, 1975 to present; Canadian prospectuses, 1981-1988; U.S. annual reports; 10K reports, 1975 to present; U.S. proxy statements, 1987 to present; Statistical Reference Index; Corporate and Industry Research Reports; Disclosure Canada; Disclosure USA. **Holdings:** 5249 books; 88 drawers of microfiche; 50 lateral file drawers of annual reports. **Services:** Interlibrary loan; copying; room open to the public. **Computerized Information Services:** DIALOG Information Services, BRS Information Technologies, Info Globe, The Financial Post DataGroup, Canadian Financial Database (C.F.D.); internal database; CD-ROMs (ABI/INFORM, Canadian Business and Current Affairs). Performs searches on fee basis. Contact Persons: Ione Hooper, Asst.Bus.Libn.; Deborah Scott-Douglas, Asst.Bus.Libn.

★18199★
University of Alberta - John A. Weir Memorial Law Library (Law)
Law Centre   Phone: (403)492-3371
Edmonton, AB, Canada T6G 2H5   Lillian MacPherson, Law Libn.
Founded: 1921. **Staff:** Prof 6; Other 12. **Subjects:** Anglo-American law. **Holdings:** 78,905 books; 113,850 bound periodical volumes; 92,474 microforms; 832 AV programs. **Subscriptions:** 3230 journals and other serials. **Services:** Interlibrary loan; copying; library open to the public with

restrictions. **Automated Operations:** Computerized cataloging and acquisitions. **Computerized Information Services:** LEXIS, WESTLAW, CAN/LAW, WILSONLINE, Info Globe, DIALOG Information Services, QL Systems, LAWCENTRE, SOQUIJ, CBA/NET; CD-ROMs; internal databases; Envoy 100, QUICKMAIL, NETNORTH (electronic mail services). Performs reference searches free of charge; performs searches through LAWSEARCH for a fee. Contact Person: M. Lefebvre, (403)421-8660. **Publications:** Acquisitions list. **Special Indexes:** Alberta Case Locator; index of all Alberta Queen's Bench, Court of Appeal and written Provincial Court decisions (online). **Remarks:** FAX: (403)492-7546. Electronic mail address(es): ILL.AEUL (Envoy 100); BOX 113 (QUICKMAIL). **Staff:** C. Ewaskiw, Coll.Dev.Libn.; M. Storozuk, Ref. & Tech.Libn.; S. Wilkins, Ref.Libn.; C. Rollins, Ref.Libn.; B. Burrows, Coll.Mgt.Libn.

★18200★
University of Alberta - John W. Scott Health Sciences Library (Med)
2K328 Walter McKinsey Center   Phone: (403)492-3899
Edmonton, AB, Canada T6G 2R7   Sylvia R. Chetner, Area Coord.
Staff: Prof 8; Other 17. **Subjects:** Medicine, nursing, dentistry, pharmacy, rehabilitation medicine, health services administration. **Special Collections:** Rawlinson Historical Collection (1000 volumes). **Holdings:** 177,425 books and bound periodical volumes; 7657 microfiche. **Subscriptions:** 2150 journals and other serials. **Services:** Interlibrary loan; copying; SDI; library open to the public with restrictions. **Automated Operations:** Computerized cataloging, acquisitions, and circulation. **Computerized Information Services:** DIALOG Information Services, PFDS Online, BRS Information Technologies, CAN/OLE, MEDLINE, CD-ROMs (MEDLINE, PSYCHINFO, CINAHL, Health Planning and Administrative Data Base). **Special Indexes:** Index to Alberta Medical Bulletin (card). **Remarks:** FAX: (403)432-6960. **Staff:** L. Starr, Coord., Ref.Serv.; J. Buckingham, Coord., Coll.Mgt.; J. Irving, Supv., Circ.Serv. & Doc. Delivery; S. Shores, Libn.; M. Dorgan, Libn.; L. Sutherland, Libn.; Linda Slater, Libn.

★18201★
University of Alberta - Legal Resource Centre - Library (Law)
Faculty of Extension
10049 81st Ave.   Phone: (403)492-5732
Edmonton, AB, Canada T6E 1W7   Elaine Hutchinson, Libn.
Founded: 1975. **Staff:** Prof 2; Other 4. **Subjects:** Law for the layperson, criminal law, public legal education, family and juvenile law, business law, native rights. **Special Collections:** Pamphlets (3000 titles). **Holdings:** 30,000 books and AV programs. **Subscriptions:** 454 journals and other serials. **Services:** Copying; library open to the public. **Automated Operations:** Computerized cataloging. **Computerized Information Services:** QL Systems, SPIRES; LRCDATA (internal database). **Publications:** Law Now, monthly magazine; Bibliography of Law-Related AV Materials (book); Legal Resource Centre Pamphlet List (book); Legal Materials for Alberta Public Libraries (book). **Special Indexes:** Index of Holdings on Microfiche - limited distribution. **Remarks:** FAX: (403)492-1857. Toll-free telephone number(s): (800)232-1961.

★18202★
University of Alberta - Mathematics Library (Sci-Engr)
Central Academic Bldg.   Phone: (403)432-3529
Edmonton, AB, Canada T6G 2J8   M. Ahmad, Supv.
Founded: 1964. **Staff:** 1. **Subjects:** Pure mathematics, applied mathematics, applied probability, statistics. **Holdings:** 18,908 books; 28,161 bound periodical volumes. **Subscriptions:** 579 journals and other serials. **Services:** Interlibrary loan; copying; SDI; library open to the public. **Computerized Information Services:** DOBIS Canadian Online Library System. **Publications:** Library manual.

University of Alberta - Nuclear Research Centre
See: **University of Alberta (18186)**

★18203★
University of Alberta - Science and Technology Library (Sci-Engr)
Edmonton, AB, Canada T6G 2J8   Phone: (403)492-2728
                    Margo Young, Area Coord.
Founded: 1963. **Staff:** Prof 7; Other 15. **Subjects:** Physical and life sciences, engineering, agriculture, forestry, household economics. **Special Collections:** Solar and wind energy. **Holdings:** 400,000 books and bound periodical volumes. **Subscriptions:** 4800 journals and other serials. **Services:**

Interlibrary loan; copying; SDI; library open to the public. **Automated Operations:** Computerized cataloging, acquisitions, and circulation. **Computerized Information Services:** DIALOG Information Services, PFDS Online, CAN/OLE, QL Systems, BRS Information Technologies, Info Globe, STN International, Knowledge Index; Envoy 100, DIALMAIL, BITNET (electronic mail services). Performs searches on fee basis. **Remarks:** Alternate telephone number(s): 492-7912 (reference). FAX: (403)492-4327. **Staff:** David Jones, Coll.Coord.; Vera Kunda, Ref.Coord.; Susan Moysa, Ref.Libn.; John Miletich, Ref.Libn.; Sandra Campbell, Ref.Libn.; Marianne Jamieson, Ref.Libn.; Randy Reichardt, Ref.Libn.

★ 18204 ★
University of Alberta - Stanley Taylor Sociology Reading Room (Soc Sci)
Dept. of Sociology   Phone: (403)492-3916
Edmonton, AB, Canada T6G 2H4   Kerri Calvert, Lib.Asst.
Founded: 1965. **Staff:** Prof 1; Other 1. **Subjects:** Sociology, demography, criminology, statistics and methodology. **Special Collections:** Canadian Census; World Fertility Survey Materials. **Holdings:** 10,200 books; 600 bound periodical volumes; 304 dissertations; 3500 reprints and conference papers. **Subscriptions:** 182 journals and other serials. **Services:** Room open to the public for reference use only. **Computerized Information Services:** SPIRES; BITNET (electronic mail service). **Publications:** New Materials List. **Remarks:** FAX: (403)492-2589. Electronic mail address(es): USERSRRR@UALTAMTS (BITNET).

★ 18205 ★
University of Alberta - University Computing Systems - Data Library (Info Sci)
352 General Services Bldg.   Phone: (403)492-5212
Edmonton, AB, Canada T6G 2H1   Charles Humphrey, Data Lib.Coord.
Founded: 1977. **Staff:** Prof 2. **Subjects:** Social sciences, literature. **Holdings:** 3500 files of machine-readable statistical and textual data on magnetic tapes and disks. **Services:** Interlibrary loan; SDI; library open to the public. **Automated Operations:** Computerized cataloging and acquisitions. **Computerized Information Services:** ICPSR Guide, SMIS Database (internal databases); BITNET (electronic mail service). **Special Catalogs:** Data Library Catalogue (online and book), biennial. **Remarks:** Library located at Central Academic Bldg., Rm. 2-19, Edmonton, AB T6G 2H1. Alternate telephone number(s): 492-2741. Electronic mail address(es): UADL@MTS.UCS.UALBERTA.CA (BITNET).

★ 18206 ★
University of Amsterdam - Art History Department - Library (Art)
Johannes Vermeerstraat 17   Phone: 20 5253002
NL-1071 DK Amsterdam, Netherlands   M. Versteeg
Founded: 1929. **Staff:** Prof 3.5. **Subjects:** Art, 16th-18th century painting, 18th-20th century architecture, art history, manuscript illumination. **Holdings:** 68,320 books; 6757 bound periodical volumes; 18 microfiche. **Subscriptions:** 146 journals and other serials. **Services:** Interlibrary loan; copying; library open to the public for reference use only. **Automated Operations:** Computerized public access catalog. **Also Known As:** Universiteit van Amsterdam - Kunsthistorisch Instituut - Bibliotheek.

★ 18207 ★
University of Amsterdam - Institute for Modern Near Eastern Studies - Department of Arabic & Islamic Studies - Library (Area-Ethnic, Hum)
Oute Turfmarkt 141 (achter)   Phone: 20 5254424
NL-1012 GC Amsterdam, Netherlands   Dr. Arie Schippers
Founded: 1956. **Staff:** Prof 1.5. **Subjects:** Arabic language, literature and history; Islamology; documentation of the Arabic world; Turkish, Kurdish, and Semitic linguistics. **Holdings:** 20,000 books; 5000 bound periodical volumes. **Subscriptions:** 35 journals and other serials; 2 newspapers. **Services:** Interlibrary loan; library open to the public at librarian's discretion. **Remarks:** FAX: 20 5254681. **Also Known As:** Universiteit van Amsterdam - Vakgroep Arabische en Islamitische Studien - Bibliotheek.

University of Amsterdam - International Information Center and Archives for the Women's Movement
See: International Information Center and Archives for the Women's Movement (8121)

★ 18208 ★
University of Arizona - Arid Lands Information Center (Sci-Engr)
845 N. Park Ave.   Phone: (602)621-1955
Tucson, AZ 85719   Barbara Hutchinson, Dir.
Founded: 1968. **Staff:** Prof 3; Other 2. **Subjects:** Deserts of the world - international research, economic crops, remote sensing. **Special Collections:** MUSAT:sra (Summer Rainfall Agriculture; 14,000 items); West Africa Collection (1500 items); Dryland Forestry (1500 items); Jojoba, Guayule (1300 items). **Holdings:** 30,000 volumes; 100 environmental impact statements. **Subscriptions:** 30 journals and other serials. **Services:** Copying; SDI; center open to the public with restrictions. **Automated Operations:** Computerized cataloging. **Computerized Information Services:** DIALOG Information Services, BRS Information Technologies; Dialcom, Inc. (electronic mail service). Performs searches on fee basis. **Publications:** List of publications - available on request. **Remarks:** Alternate telephone number(s): 621-7897. FAX: (602)621-3816. Telex: 1561507 ARIDUX. **Staff:** Carla Casler, Libn.

★ 18209 ★
University of Arizona - Arizona Health Sciences Center Library (Med)
1501 N. Campbell Ave.   Phone: (602)626-6121
Tucson, AZ 85724   Rachael K. Anderson, Dir.
Founded: 1967. **Staff:** Prof 15; Other 23. **Subjects:** Medicine and allied health sciences; preclinical sciences. **Special Collections:** Hugh H. Smith Collection/Public Health (300 volumes). **Holdings:** 76,396 books; 99,426 bound periodical volumes; 3253 AV program titles; 20 drawers of microforms. **Subscriptions:** 3623 journals and other serials. **Services:** Interlibrary loan; copying; SDI; library open to the public. **Automated Operations:** Computerized public access catalog, cataloging, acquisitions, serials, and circulation. **Computerized Information Services:** DIALOG Information Services, BRS Information Technologies; CD-ROM (MEDLINE); OnTyme Electronic Message Network Service (electronic mail service). Performs searches on fee basis. Contact Person: Fred Heidenreich, Hd., Ref.Serv., 626-7724. **Networks/Consortia:** Member of AMIGOS Bibliographic Council, Inc., National Network of Libraries of Medicine - Pacific Southwest Region. **Publications:** Media Software Titles (subject list); Bulletin, bimonthly. **Remarks:** FAX: (602)626-2831. **Staff:** Jeanette C. McCray, Assoc.Dir.; Marilyn McCarthy, Hd., Loan Serv.; Mary Rhoads, Outreach Serv.; Frances Chen, Ser.Libn.; Nancy Condit, Cat.Libn.; Catherine Wolfson, Acq.Libn.; David Piper, Hd., Mic rocomputer Serv.

★ 18210 ★
University of Arizona - Arizona State Museum Library (Hist)
Tucson, AZ 85721   Phone: (602)621-4695
    Mary Graham
Founded: 1958. **Staff:** Prof 1; Other 2. **Subjects:** Southwestern and Mesoamerican anthropology, museum studies. **Special Collections:** Kelemen Collection of Latin American art and architecture (1000 items). **Holdings:** 40,000 volumes; 500 bound periodical volumes. **Subscriptions:** 150 journals and other serials. **Services:** Interlibrary loan; copying; library open to the public. **Remarks:** FAX: (602)621-2976.

★ 18211 ★
University of Arizona - Center for Creative Photography (Art)
Olive St. at Speedway Blvd.   Phone: (602)621-7968
Tucson, AZ 85721   Tim Troy, Libn.
Founded: 1975. **Staff:** Prof 11; Other 5. **Subjects:** Photography. **Special Collections:** Photographic archives (including those of Ansel Adams, Edward Weston, W. Eugene Smith, Richard Avedon). **Holdings:** 12,000 books; 2000 bound periodical volumes; 600 reels of microfilm; 36 feet of biographical files; 500 oral history videotapes. **Subscriptions:** 100 journals and other serials. **Services:** Interlibrary loan; copying; center open to the public. **Automated Operations:** Computerized cataloging. **Computerized Information Services:** OCLC EPIC. **Publications:** The Archive, irregular. **Remarks:** FAX: (602)621-9444. **Staff:** Terence Pitts, Dir.; Nancy Solomon, Pubns.Coord.; Anne Sullivan, Registrar; Marcia Tiede, Cat.; Amy Rule, Archv.; Nancy Lutz, Asst.Dir.; Victor LaViola, Cur. of Educ.

★ 18212 ★
University of Arizona - College of Architecture Library (Art, Plan)
Tucson, AZ 85721   Phone: (602)621-2498
    Shannon Paul, Libn.
Founded: 1961. **Staff:** Prof 3; Other 5. **Subjects:** Architectural design, desert architecture, urban planning, building technology, historic preservation, design communication. **Holdings:** 13,000 books; 2100 bound periodical

volumes; 29,000 slides. **Subscriptions:** 110 journals and other serials. **Services:** Copying; library open to the public for reference use only. **Computerized Information Services:** DIALOG Information Services. Performs searches on fee basis. **Publications:** Library acquisitions list, monthly. **Remarks:** FAX: (602)621-8700. **Staff:** R. Brooks Jeffery; Madelyn Cook.

★ 18213 ★
University of Arizona - College of Law Library (Law)
Tucson, AZ 85721 Phone: (602)621-1413
Ronald L. Cherry, Dir.
Founded: 1915. **Staff:** Prof 8; Other 6. **Subjects:** Law. **Special Collections:** Natural resources; law relating to American Indians; Latin American law. **Holdings:** 199,441 volumes; 110,122 volumes in microform. **Subscriptions:** 3318 journals and other serials; 12 newspapers. **Services:** Interlibrary loan; copying; library open to the public for reference use only. **Automated Operations:** Computerized cataloging. **Computerized Information Services:** LEXIS, WESTLAW. **Remarks:** FAX: (602)621-3138. **Staff:** Robert Genovese, Asst.Libn., Tech.Serv.; Edward White, Asst.Libn., Pub.Serv.; Francisco Avalos, Foreign Libn., Spec.Coll.; Carol G. Elliott, Ref.Libn.; Karen Norvelle, Cat.Libn.; Jacquelyn Casper, Ref.Libn.

★ 18214 ★
University of Arizona - Department of Atmospheric Sciences - Institute of Atmospheric Physics - Library (Sci-Engr)
Bldg. No. 81 Physics-Atmospheric
Science, Rm. 546 Phone: (602)621-6831
Tucson, AZ 85721 Carol Knapp, Libn.
Founded: 1953. **Staff:** 1. **Subjects:** Physical and dynamical meteorology, cloud physics, atmospheric dynamics, thunderstorm electricity, micrometeorology. **Special Collections:** Manuscripts, publications, and library of Dr. James E. McDonald. **Holdings:** 2800 monographs and conference proceedings; 2500 bound periodical volumes; 200 volumes of bound sets of meteorological maps; 83 theses and dissertations by IAP students; 4000 reprints of journal articles; 19,000 technical reports, technical memoranda, publications of U.S. governmental agencies, and others. **Subscriptions:** 96 journals and other serials. **Services:** Copying; library open to the public for reference use only. **Publications:** Science and Conscience: an annotated bibliography of the writings of Dr. James E. McDonald.

University of Arizona - Division of Media & Instructional Services - Film Library
See: **University of Arizona - Film Collection** (18218)

★ 18215 ★
University of Arizona - Economic and Business Research - Library (Bus-Fin, Soc Sci)
College of Business & Public Administration Phone: (602)621-2155
Tucson, AZ 85721 Pia Montoya
Staff: 2. **Subjects:** Economic, demographic, and industrial data for Arizona; employment; labor and productivity; travel and tourism. **Special Collections:** Regional econometric models for Pima and Maricopa counties and state of Arizona. **Holdings:** 7000 items. **Subscriptions:** 250 journals and other serials; 6 newspapers. **Services:** Library open to the public for reference use only. **Computerized Information Services:** Arizona Economic Indicators Database (internal database). **Remarks:** FAX: (602)621-2150. An alternate telephone number is 621-2109. **Formerly:** Its Division of Economic and Business Research.

★ 18216 ★
University of Arizona - Environmental Psychology Program - Library
Department of Psychology
Tucson, AZ 85721
Founded: 1980. **Subjects:** Environmental psychology, behavior and environment, post occupancy evaluations. **Special Collections:** Edward T. Hall Library (2529 items). **Holdings:** 1200 books; 100 bound periodical volumes; 3500 other cataloged items. **Remarks:** Currently inactive. Holdings sent to University of Kansas - Spencer Research Library in Lawrence, KS.

★ 18217 ★
University of Arizona - Environmental Research Laboratory - Library (Biol Sci)
Tucson International Airport
2601 E. Airport Dr. Phone: (602)741-1990
Tucson, AZ 85706 Nancy Sprague, Info.Spec.
Subjects: Aquaculture, seawater irrigation, controlled environment agriculture, solar energy, controlled ecological systems, environmental engineering. **Holdings:** 1800 books. **Subscriptions:** 45 journals and other serials. **Services:** Library open to the public for reference use only. **Automated Operations:** Computerized cataloging. **Computerized Information Services:** Current Contents Search. **Remarks:** FAX: (602)573-0852. Telex: 165580.

★ 18218 ★
University of Arizona - Film Collection (Aud-Vis)
1325 E. Speedway Blvd. Phone: (602)621-3282
Tucson, AZ 85719 Carrie Russell, Media Libn.
Founded: 1919. **Staff:** Prof 1; Other 3. **Special Collections:** Archive collection of television commercials; Gallagher Memorial Film Collection. **Holdings:** 6500 16mm motion pictures in active collection. **Services:** Library open to the public for reference use only. **Networks/Consortia:** Member of Consortium of College and University Media Centers (CCUMC). **Publications:** The Leader, 2/year.

★ 18219 ★
University of Arizona - Government Documents Department (Info Sci)
University Library Phone: (602)621-4871
Tucson, AZ 85721 Cynthia E. Bower, Hd.Docs.Libn.
Founded: 1907. **Staff:** Prof 3; Other 6. **Subjects:** Business and economics, environmental studies, American history, politics and government, foreign relations, health care, education, law enforcement and criminal justice. **Special Collections:** Selected holdings of National Archives microfilm (5000 reels); U.S. Congressional hearings and committee prints, 1869-1981 (100,000 microfiche); current Arizona documents. **Holdings:** 950,000 printed documents; 300,000 ERIC microfiche; 750,000 other microfiche; 6200 reels of microfilm. **Subscriptions:** 3200 journals and other serials. **Services:** Interlibrary loan; copying; department open to the public. **Automated Operations:** Computerized circulation. **Computerized Information Services:** DIALOG Information Services, OCLC, LEGI-SLATE, OCLC EPIC; CD-ROMs; Federal electronic bulletin boards. **Publications:** Documents Despatch, bimonthly - free upon request. **Special Indexes:** Geographic index to environmental impact statements (card file). **Remarks:** FAX: (602)621-9733. **Staff:** Robert P. Mitchell, Govt.Docs.Libn.; Atifa Rawan, Govt.Docs.Libn.

★ 18220 ★
University of Arizona - Herbarium (Biol Sci)
113 Shantz Bldg. Phone: (602)621-7243
Tucson, AZ 85721 Charles T. Mason, Jr.
Founded: 1891. **Staff:** Prof 2. **Subjects:** Plants - Southwestern United States, Mexico. **Holdings:** 292,000 plant specimens. **Services:** Herbarium open to the public.

★ 18221 ★
University of Arizona - Map Collection (Geog-Map)
University Library Phone: (602)621-2596
Tucson, AZ 85721 Charlene M. Baldwin, Hd. Map Libn.
Founded: 1955. **Staff:** Prof 2.5; Other 5. **Subjects:** Geology, mines and mineral resources, history, topography, climate, water resources, Arizona and Southwestern U.S., Mexico, Latin America, arid lands. **Special Collections:** Frank A. Schilling Military Collection (military post of the Southwest; 60 maps); Maurice Garland Fulton Collection (history of the Southwest; 59 maps). **Holdings:** 5000 books; 300 bound periodical volumes; 273,000 sheet maps; 17,000 aerial photographs; 15 globes; 26,000 microfiche; 176 relief models; 2126 reels of microfilm. **Subscriptions:** 50 journals and other serials. **Services:** Interlibrary loan; copying; collection open to the public. **Automated Operations:** Computerized cataloging, acquisitions, and circulation. **Computerized Information Services:** OCLC, DIALOG Information Services, OCLC EPIC; CD-ROM (databases and atlases); BITNET, InterNet (electronic mail services). **Publications:** Pimeria, Bulletin of the Map Collection, University of Arizona Library - free upon request. **Remarks:** FAX: (602)621-9733 (University Library). Electronic mail address(es): BALDWIN@ARIZRVAX (BITNET); BALDWIN@CCIT.ARIZONA.EDU (InterNet). **Staff:** Christine E. Kollen, Map Cat.Libn.; Jack Mount, Map & Sci.Eng.Ref.Libn.; Christine Ziegler, Lib.Spec.

★ 18222 ★
University of Arizona - Media Center (Aud-Vis, Educ)
Library - B104   Phone: (602)621-6409
Tucson, AZ 85721   Bonnie L. Travers, Hd. Media Ctr.Libn.
FO 1977. **Staff:** Prof 3; Other 7. **Subjects:** Nonprint materials for elementary through college levels, K-12 textbooks, juvenile trade books. **Special Collections:** University 16mm Film Collection (5900 titles). **Holdings:** 24,500 juvenile trade books; 11,000 textbooks; 17,000 nonprint titles; 1100 reference books and serials. **Services:** Center open to the public. **Automated Operations:** Computerized cataloging, acquisitions, and circulation. **Computerized Information Services:** DIALOG Information Services, EPIC; CD-ROM (A-V Online); InterNet, BITNET (electronic mail services). Performs searches on fee basis (limited). **Publications:** Classic Film Series Program, annual. **Special Catalogs:** Media Center film and videotape catalog (book); Media Center Archival Radio Program List (book). **Remarks:** FAX: (602)621-9733. Electronic mail address(es): btravers@ccit.arizona.edu (InterNet); btravers@arirvax (BITNET). **Staff:** Carrie S. Russell, Media Libn.

★ 18223 ★
University of Arizona - Museum of Art Library (Art)
Tucson, AZ 85721   Phone: (602)621-7567
                                                Barbara Kittle, Libn.
Remarks: No further information was supplied by respondent.

★ 18224 ★
University of Arizona - Music Collection (Mus)
Tucson, AZ 85721   Phone: (602)621-7009
                                Charles W. King, Act.Hd.Mus.Libn.
Founded: 1959. **Staff:** Prof 2; Other 4. **Subjects:** Music - classical, ethnic, folk, popular. **Special Collections:** National Flute Association Music Library; International Trombone Association Resource Library; Arizona and Southwest; historical popular sheet music. **Holdings:** 49,000 scores; 15,250 pieces of classical sheet music; 37,400 pieces of popular sheet music; 21,875 phonograph records and tapes; microforms. **Subscriptions:** 280 journals and other serials. **Services:** Interlibrary loan; copying; collection open to the public. **Automated Operations:** Computerized circulation. **Computerized Information Services:** Internal databases; BITNET (electronic mail service). **Special Catalogs:** National Flute Association Music Library Catalog, 1989 - for sale to members and libraries; International Trombone Association Catalog, 1990 - for sale to members and libraries. **Special Indexes:** Song, piano and jazz indexes (card); band music and children's songs indexes (online). **Remarks:** Music books and journals housed separately. FAX: (602)621-9733. Electronic mail address(es): DHSMITH@ARIZRVAX (BITNET).

★ 18225 ★
University of Arizona - Office of Arid Lands Studies - Bioresources Research Library (Energy)
250 E. Valencia   Phone: (602)741-1691
Tucson, AZ 85706   Jan Taylor, Lib.Asst.
Staff: Prof 1; Other 2. **Subjects:** Energy - resource development, research, biomass production and conversion, solar. **Holdings:** 100 books; 700 other cataloged items. **Subscriptions:** 12 journals and other serials. **Services:** Copying; library open to the public for reference use only. **Computerized Information Services:** DIALOG Information Services. Performs searches on fee basis. Contact Person: Barbara Hutchinson, Libn., 621-7897. **Remarks:** FAX: (602)741-1468.

★ 18226 ★
University of Arizona - Optical Sciences Center - Fred A. Hopf Library (Sci-Engr)
Tucson, AZ 85721   Phone: (602)621-4022
                                                Cathy Alexander
Founded: 1968. **Staff:** 1. **Subjects:** Optics, optical physics, optical engineering. **Special Collections:** SPIE Proceedings. **Holdings:** 4500 books; 400 bound periodical volumes; 400 theses and dissertations. **Subscriptions:** 25 journals and other serials. **Services:** Copying; library open to the public with prior approval. **Computerized Information Services:** DIALOG Information Services. **Remarks:** FAX: (602)623-9034. Alternate telephone number(s): 621-8154.

★ 18227 ★
University of Arizona - Oriental Studies Collection (Area-Ethnic)
University Library   Phone: (602)621-6380
Tucson, AZ 85721   Ju-yen Teng, Hd. Oriental Stud.Libn.
Founded: 1964. **Staff:** Prof 3; Other 1. **Subjects:** Humanities and social sciences of China and Japan; vernacular language materials - Chinese, Japanese. **Holdings:** 146,831 books; 625 bound periodical volumes; 900 reels of microfilm. **Subscriptions:** 500 journals and other serials; 15 newspapers. **Services:** Interlibrary loan; copying; collection open to the public. **Automated Operations:** Computerized cataloging and circulation. **Computerized Information Services:** InterNet (electronic mail service). **Remarks:** FAX: (602)621-9733. Electronic mail address(es): jyteng@ccit.arizona.edu (InterNet). **Staff:** Gene Hsiao, Oriental Stud.Libn./Cat.; Shizuko Radbill, Lib.Spec.

★ 18228 ★
University of Arizona - Poetry Center (Hum)
1216 N. Cherry Ave.   Phone: (602)321-7760
Tucson, AZ 85719   Alison Deming, Dir.
Founded: 1960. **Staff:** Prof 1; Other 1. **Subjects:** Poetry. **Holdings:** 24,000 books and periodicals; 770 phonograph records and audiotapes; 60 videotapes. **Subscriptions:** 200 journals and other serials. **Services:** Center open to the public; sponsors a series of poetry readings annually. **Publications:** Poetry Center Newsletter, 4/year; 25th Anniversary Anthology, 1985; Reading Series Announcements.

★ 18229 ★
University of Arizona - Science-Engineering Library (Sci-Engr, Agri)
Tucson, AZ 85721   Phone: (602)621-6394
                                Donald G. Frank, Hd.Sci.Engr.Libn.
Founded: 1963. **Staff:** Prof 8; Other 6.5. **Subjects:** Agriculture, astronomy, biology, chemistry, computer science, engineering, forestry, geology, hydrology, mathematics, mining and metallurgy, optical science, physics. **Special Collections:** Arid lands. **Holdings:** 520,000 volumes; 1.4 million microforms; 27,000 government documents; 3000 pamphlets. **Subscriptions:** 10,000 journals and other serials. **Services:** Interlibrary loan; copying; SDI; library open to the public. **Automated Operations:** Computerized public access catalog and circulation. **Computerized Information Services:** DIALOG Information Services, BRS Information Technologies, OCLC, STN International, Chemical Abstracts Service (CAS); CD-ROMS; BITNET (electronic mail service). Performs searches on fee basis. **Networks/Consortia:** Member of AMIGOS Bibliographic Council, Inc. **Publications:** SEL News. **Remarks:** Alternate telephone number(s): 621-6384. FAX: (602)621-9733. Electronic mail address(es): DGFRANK@ARIZRUAX (BITNET). **Staff:** Janet Fore, Sci.Engr.Ref.Libn.; Douglas Jones, Sci.Engr.Ref.Libn.; Robert Mautner, Sci.Engr.Ref.Libn.; Jack Mount, Map & Sci.Engr.Ref.Libn.; Beth Brin, Sci.Engr.Ref.Libn.; Nancy Simons, Cat. & Sci.Engr.Ref.Libn.; Jeanne Pfander, Sci.Engr.Ref.Libn.; Chestalene Pintozzi, Sci.Engr.Ref.Libn.; Kathy Whitley, Sci.Engr.Ref.Libn.

★ 18230 ★
University of Arizona - Space Imagery Center (Sci-Engr)
Lunar & Planetary Laboratory
Tucson, AZ 85721   Phone: (602)621-4861
Founded: 1977. **Staff:** Prof 1; Other 2. **Subjects:** Space photography, planetary sciences. **Holdings:** 750,000 images of planets and satellites taken from spacecraft and earth-based telescopes; 1000 maps; 23 atlases; 5000 35mm slides. **Services:** Center open to the public with restrictions. **Automated Operations:** Computerized cataloging. **Computerized Information Services:** Internal database. **Remarks:** FAX: (602)621-4933.

★ 18231 ★
University of Arizona - Special Collections Department (Hist, Hum)
University Library   Phone: (602)621-2101
Tucson, AZ 85721   Louis A. Hieb, Hd.Spec.Coll.Libn.
Founded: 1958. **Staff:** Prof 4; Other 3. **Subjects:** Arizona, University of Arizona archives, Southwest, science fiction, history of science. **Special Collections:** Frank Holme Collection; Thomas Wood Stevens Collection; Lewis W. Douglas Papers; War Relocation Authority Papers; Hubbell Trading Post Papers; Bukowski and Wakoski Poetry Collections; Black Sparrow Press Archives. **Holdings:** 150,000 volumes; 800 manuscript collections. **Subscriptions:** 900 journals and other serials and newspapers. **Services:** Copying; department open to the public. **Automated Operations:** Computerized acquisitions, serials, and circulation. **Computerized Information Services:** DIALOG Information Services, BRS Information Technologies, STN International. **Special Indexes:** Arizona Index; Arizona Daily Star Index. **Remarks:** FAX: (602)621-4619. **Staff:** Roger Myers, Mss.Libn.

★ **18232** ★
University of Arkansas, Fayetteville - Chemistry/Biochemistry Library
(Sci-Engr, Comp Sci)
Chemistry Bldg.   Phone: (501)575-2028
Fayetteville, AR 72701   Carolyn DeLille, Hd. of Lib.
Founded: 1932. **Staff:** Prof 1; Other 4. **Subjects:** Chemistry, mathematics, physics, chemical technology, computer science, biochemistry, biology, medicine. **Special Collections:** Eva Dickson Greene collection; Harrison Hale collection. **Holdings:** 11,137 books; 15,871 bound journals. **Subscriptions:** 259 journals and other serials. **Services:** Interlibrary loan; copying; library open to the public. **Formerly:** Its Chemistry Library.

★ **18233** ★
University of Arkansas, Fayetteville - Fine Arts Library (Art, Plan)
Fayetteville, AR 72701   Phone: (501)575-4708
    Norma Mosby, Fine Arts Libn.
Staff: Prof 1; Other 18. **Subjects:** Art, architecture, music, city planning, interior design, landscape architecture. **Holdings:** 42,000 books; 7400 bound periodical volumes; 225 reels of microfilm; 1500 microfiche; 15 slide sets. **Subscriptions:** 200 journals and other serials. **Services:** Interlibrary loan; copying; SDI; library open to the public. **Computerized Information Services:** OCLC. **Networks/Consortia:** Member of AMIGOS Bibliographic Council, Inc. **Remarks:** The special collections, recordings, microforms, and some rare books are housed in Mullins Library.

★ **18234** ★
University of Arkansas, Fayetteville - Map Collection (Geog-Map)
University Library   Phone: (501)575-3177
Fayetteville, AR 72701   Janet B. Dixon, Map Libn.
Staff: 3. **Subjects:** Maps - U.S. topography and geology, world topography, transportation, geology. **Special Collections:** Historical maps of Arkansas and region; Sanborn Fire Insurance maps of Arkansas towns. **Holdings:** 120,000 map sheets. **Services:** Copying; collection open to the public. **Computerized Information Services:** DIALOG Information Services, BRS Information Technologies, STN International, PFDS Online; CD-ROMs (including atlases of Arkansas and world). Performs searches on fee basis. Contact reference department, 575-6645. **Networks/Consortia:** Member of AMIGOS Bibliographic Council, Inc. **Remarks:** FAX: (501)575-6656.

★ **18235** ★
University of Arkansas, Fayetteville - School of Law - Robert A. Leflar Law Center (Law)
Fayetteville, AR 72701   Phone: (501)575-5604
    Louise Lindsey, Int.Dir.
Founded: 1924. **Staff:** Prof 5; Other 5. **Subjects:** Law. **Special Collections:** Selective government depository; agricultural law. **Holdings:** 210,000 books; 30,000 bound periodical volumes. **Subscriptions:** 1634 journals and other serials; 6 newspapers. **Services:** Copying; library open to the public for reference use only. **Computerized Information Services:** LEXIS, WESTLAW, LEGI-SLATE. **Networks/Consortia:** Member of Mid-America Law School Library Consortium. **Remarks:** FAX: (501)575-5604. **Staff:** Cathy Chick, Assoc.Libn.; Claudia Driver, Asst.Libn.; Sally J. Kelley, Asst.Libn., Agri. Law. Ruth Parlin, Assoc.Libn.

★ **18236** ★
University of Arkansas, Fayetteville - Special Collections Division (Hist, Hum)
Fayetteville, AR 72701-1201   Phone: (501)575-4101
    Michael J. Dabrishus, Cur.
Founded: 1967. **Staff:** Prof 3; Other 8. **Subjects:** Arkansas - history, literature, politics, culture, and folklore; Ozark folklore; international education. **Special Collections:** John Gould Fletcher Collection (1983 volumes); Otto Ernest Rayburn Library of Folklore (838 volumes); Dime Novel Collection (1630 items); Haldeman-Julius Little Blue Books (2404 items); Robert Owen Collection (273 items). **Holdings:** 42,000 books; 12,000 bound periodical volumes; 8500 linear feet of manuscripts; 300 linear feet of university archives; 100,500 photographs; 365 rare maps. **Subscriptions:** 950 journals and other serials. **Services:** Interlibrary loan; copying; division open to the public with restrictions. **Computerized Information Services:** OCLC. **Networks/Consortia:** Member of AMIGOS Bibliographic Council, Inc. **Publications:** A Guide to Selected Manuscripts Collections in the University of Arkansas Library, 1976; Manuscript Resources for Women's Studies, 1989; Manuscript Resources for the Civil War, 1990. **Special Catalogs:** Card catalog of published titles; unpublished finding aids to manuscript collections. **Special Indexes:** Index to selected Arkansas periodicals (card); Arkansas Sheet Music Index (online). **Staff:** Andrea E. Cantrell, Assoc.Libn.; Ethel C. Simpson, Assoc.Libn.; Janet B. Dixon, Asst.Libn.

★ **18237** ★
University of Arkansas, Little Rock - Arkansas Institute for Economic Advancement - Research Library (Soc Sci, Bus-Fin)
2801 S. University   Phone: (501)569-8521
Little Rock, AR 72204   Crata Castleberry, Res.Libn.
Founded: 1960. **Staff:** Prof 1; Other 2. **Subjects:** Business and economics, industrial development, labor statistics, resources for Arkansas, demographics, government and taxes. **Holdings:** 9500 books; 285 bound periodical volumes; census data for U.S. and Arkansas, 1900 to present. **Subscriptions:** 200 journals and other serials; 5 newspapers. **Services:** Copying; library open to the public for reference use only. **Automated Operations:** Computerized public access catalog. **Computerized Information Services:** DIALOG Information Services. Performs searches on fee basis. **Remarks:** Contains the holdings of the Arkansas State Data Center.

★ **18238** ★
University of Arkansas, Little Rock - Pulaski County Law Library (Law)
400 W. Markham   Phone: (501)324-9444
Little Rock, AR 72201   Lynn Foster, Dir.
Founded: 1965. **Staff:** Prof 5; Other 8.5. **Subjects:** Law. **Holdings:** 213,000 books; 1200 audiocassettes. **Subscriptions:** 3663 journals and other serials. **Services:** Interlibrary loan; copying; library open to the public. **Computerized Information Services:** LEXIS, NEXIS, WESTLAW, DIALOG Information Services. **Networks/Consortia:** Member of AMIGOS Bibliographic Council, Inc. **Remarks:** FAX: (501)371-0167. **Staff:** James Martin, Pub.Serv.; Greta Boeringer, Ref./Docs.; Jada Aitchison, Acq.; Susan Goldner, Cat.

★ **18239** ★
University of Arkansas, Monticello - Library - Special Collections (Hist)
Box 3599   Phone: (501)367-6811
Monticello, AR 71655   William F. Droessler, Libn.
Special Collections: Arkansas Collection (1000 items and miscellaneous pamphlets); government documents (75,000). **Services:** Interlibrary loan; copying; collections open to the public. **Automated Operations:** Computerized cataloging and ILL.

★ **18240** ★
University of Arkansas, Pine Bluff - John Brown Watson Memorial Library (Soc Sci)
N. University Blvd.
U.S. Hwy. 79   Phone: (501)541-6825
Pine Bluff, AR 71601   E.J. Fontenette, Libn.
Founded: 1938. **Staff:** 1. **Subjects:** History and biography, emigration, sociology, literature, slavery and emancipation, education, music, religion, economics. **Special Collections:** Afro-American Literature; Paul Laurence Dunbar papers (9 reels of microfilm). **Holdings:** 4615 books; 65 bound periodical volumes; 73 reels of microfilm of the Pittsburgh Courier; 4 recordings; 4 films; 18 overhead transparencies; periodicals on microfilm. **Subscriptions:** 41 journals and other serials; 10 newspapers. **Services:** Interlibrary loan; copying; library open to the public. **Computerized Information Services:** OCLC. **Networks/Consortia:** Member of AMIGOS Bibliographic Council, Inc.

★ **18241** ★
University of Arkansas for Medical Sciences - Library (Med)
Slot 586
4301 W. Markham   Phone: (501)686-5980
Little Rock, AR 72205-7186   Audrey Newcomer, Dir.
Founded: 1879. **Staff:** Prof 12; Other 25. **Subjects:** Medical sciences. **Holdings:** 151,448 books and bound periodical volumes; 2200 AV programs. **Subscriptions:** 1545 journals and other serials. **Services:** Interlibrary loan; copying; library open to the public for reference use only. **Automated Operations:** Computerized public access catalog, cataloging, circulation, and serials. **Computerized Information Services:** OCLC, BRS Information Technologies, DIALOG Information Services, MEDLINE; BITNET (electronic mail service). **Networks/Consortia:** Member of AMIGOS Bibliographic Council, Inc., National Network of Libraries of Medicine - South Central Region, South Central Academic Medical Libraries Consortium (SCAMEL). **Remarks:** FAX: (501)686-6745. **Staff:** Neil Kelley, Assoc.Dir./Hd., Pub.Serv.; Sally Kasalko, Hd., Ref.Div.; Jean Ann Moles, Hd., Ser.Div.; Edwina Walls,Hd., Spec.Coll.; Margaret Ann Johnson, Hd., ILL Div.; Amanda Saar, Hd., Circ.Div.; Mary Hawks, Hd., Cat. & Book Acq.Div.; Jan Hart, Hd., LRC; Rena Sheffer, Ref./BI Libn.

★ 18242 ★
University of Arkansas for Medical Sciences - Northwest Area Health
  Education Center - Library (Med)
1125 N. College   Phone: (501)521-7615
Fayetteville, AR 72703   Connie M. Wilson, Libn.
Founded: 1975. Staff: Prof 1; Other 1. Subjects: Medicine, nursing, and allied health sciences. Holdings: 1500 books; 3260 bound periodical volumes. Subscriptions: 168 journals and other serials. Services: Interlibrary loan; copying; SDI; library open to the public for reference use only. Automated Operations: Computerized cataloging. Computerized Information Services: MEDLINE, BRS Information Technologies, OCLC; DOCLINE (electronic mail service). Publications: From the Shelf, irregular - to mailing list. Special Catalogs: Library Guide. Remarks: Library has been designated as the regional information center for the Northwest Arkansas area and serves health professionals in an eleven county area. It is located at Washington Regional Medical Center.

★ 18243 ★
University of the Arts - Audiovisual Department - Film Library
  (Theater)
320 S. Broad St.
3rd Fl. Furness   Phone: (215)875-5463
Philadelphia, PA 19102   Brian Feeney, Dir., AV Serv.
Founded: 1968. Staff: Prof 1; Other 4. Subjects: Silent films - early experimental and comedy, black and white feature films. Holdings: 300 films. Services: Library open to the public for reference use only. Networks/Consortia: Member of Tri-County Library Consortium. Remarks: FAX: (215)875-5467.

★ 18244 ★
University of the Arts - University Libraries (Art, Theater, Mus)
320 S. Broad St.   Phone: (215)875-1111
Philadelphia, PA 19102   Stephen Bloom, Dir.
Staff: Prof 5; Other 8. Subjects: Visual arts, theater, dance, music, humanities. Special Collections: Book Arts; Textiles. Holdings: 77,393 books; 8649 bound periodical volumes; 1500 reproductions; 9800 phonograph records; 267 compact discs; 103,980 pictures; 149,671 slides; 400 volumes of archival materials; 233 cassettes; 391 boxes of microfilm; 400 microfiche; 185 videotapes. Subscriptions: 300 journals and other serials. Services: Interlibrary loan; copying; library open to the public for reference use only. Automated Operations: Computerized cataloging. Computerized Information Services: CD-ROMs (Art Index, Readers' Guide). Performs searches on fee basis. Networks/Consortia: Member of PALINET. Remarks: FAX: (215)875-5467. Includes the holdings of the music and slide libraries. Staff: Carol Homan Graney, Assoc.Dir.; Martha Hall, Vis.Rsrcs.Coord.; Sara MacDonald, Ref.Libn.; Mark Germer, Mus.Libn.

★ 18245 ★
University of Auckland - Centre for Continuing Education - Library
  (Educ, Soc Sci)
Old Arts Bldg.
22 Princess St.   Phone: 9 737999
Auckland 1, New Zealand   Mary Ann Crick
Founded: 1949. Staff: Prof 1. Subjects: Adult education, women's studies. Holdings: 20,251 books; 340 bound periodical volumes. Subscriptions: 52 journals and other serials. Services: Library not open to the public. Automated Operations: Computerized public access catalog, cataloging, acquisitions, and serials (INMAGIC). Publications: Bibliography of adult education holdings; bibliography of women's studies holdings. Remarks: FAX: 9 3033429.

University Avenue Church of Christ Library and Institute for Christian
  Studies Library
See: Institute for Christian Studies - Library (7915)

★ 18246 ★
University of Baltimore - Langsdale Library - Archives & Special
  Materials Section - Reference Department (Plan, Soc Sci)
1420 Maryland Ave.   Phone: (301)625-3135
Baltimore, MD 21201   Steve P. Labash, Ref.Dept.Hd.
Staff: Prof 2. Subjects: Baltimore - history, planning, urban renewal, housing, community development, social welfare, family planning, business, church activities; accounting. Special Collections: Oral histories; records of

organizations and associations important to the economic, political, and social development of the Baltimore region (80 collections); WMAR-TV Newsfilm Collection (7 million feet); Herwood Accounting Collection (2000 volumes); Steamship Historical Society of America Library; U.S. and Maryland Document Depository; corporate annual and 10K reports (5000 editions for 1000 companies). Holdings: 10,000 books; 11,000 cubic feet of manuscripts and archives. Services: Copying; department open to the public. Automated Operations: Computerized cataloging. Computerized Information Services: Internal database. Performs searches on fee basis. Publications: Baltimore's Past: A Directory of Historical Sources; Urban Information Thesaurus; The Records of Baltimore's Private Organizations. Special Indexes: Subject index; file folder heading index. Formerly: Its Special Collections Department. Staff: Ann House, Libn.; Thomas Hollowak, Archv.

★ 18247 ★
University of Baltimore - Law Library (Law)
1415 Maryland Ave.   Phone: (301)625-3400
Baltimore, MD 21201   Emily R. Greenberg, Libn.
Founded: 1925. Staff: Prof 8; Other 9. Subjects: Anglo-American law. Holdings: 130,000 books; 95,000 microforms. Subscriptions: 2000 journals and other serials. Services: Interlibrary loan; copying; SDI; library open to members of Maryland Bar. Computerized Information Services: OCLC, WESTLAW, LEXIS; BITNET, InterNet (electronic mail services). Networks/Consortia: Member of CAPCON Library Network, Colorado Alliance of Research Libraries (CARL). Remarks: FAX: (301)625-3402. Electronic mail address(es): eajqerg@ube.ub.umd.edu (InterNet). Staff: Will Tress, Assoc.Libn.; Patricia Behles, Govt.Doc.Libn.; Jane Cupit, Ref.Libn.; Mary Paige Smith, Tech.Serv.Libn.; Robin Klein, Ref.Libn.; Robert Pool, Ref.Libn.; Harvey Morrell, Circ./Ref.Libn.

★ 18248 ★
University of Barcelona - Centre for International Historical Studies -
  CEHI Library (Area-Ethnic, Hist)
Carrer de Brusi, 61   Phone: 3 2004567
E-08006 Barcelona, Spain   Jordi Planes, Hd., Res.
Founded: 1949. Staff: 7. Subjects: Spain - contemporary history, Spanish Civil War, Francoist period, modern social movements, national liberation movements. Holdings: 35,000 books; 6000 bound periodical volumes; documents; microforms. Services: Copying; library open to the public for reference use only. Publications: Estudis d'Historia Agraria; ACACIA (Moviments socials). Special Indexes: Indice Historico Espanol. Remarks: FAX: 3 4144454. Staff: Olga Giralt; Lourdes Prades; Francesc Amoros.

★ 18249 ★
University of Birmingham - School of Manufacturing and Mechanical
  Engineering - Ergonomics Information Analysis Centre - Library (Sci-Engr)
Edgbaston
Birmingham B15 2TT, England   Phone: 21 4144239
Founded: 1968. Staff: Prof 1. Subjects: Ergonomics, human factors, human engineering, human-computer interaction. Holdings: 850 volumes; 128,000 abstracts; 13,000 reports. Subscriptions: 120 journals and other serials. Services: Library open to the public. Computerized Information Services: Internal database. Publications: Ergonomics Abstracts, 6/year available by subscription; specialized bibliographies; list of bibliographies - available on request. Remarks: FAX: 21 4143476. Formerly: Its Centre for Ergonomics and Operational Research. Staff: Ms. C. Stapleton.

★ 18250 ★
University of Bochum - Institute for Archeology - Library (Hist)
Gebaude GA 2/51
Postfach 102148
W-4630 Bochum, Germany   Phone: 0234 7002528
Founded: 1965. Staff: 1. Subjects: Classical archeology. Special Collections: Topographical literature and reports of 17th-19th century travelers in Greece and Asia Minor. Holdings: 12,000 books; 6000 bound periodical volumes; 200 reels of microfilm. Subscriptions: 78 journals and other serials. Services: Library open to the public. Computerized Information Services: DYABOLA (internal database). Contact Person: Dr. Hayo Heinrich. Remarks: FAX: 0234 7002001. Telex: 17234356. Also Known As: Universitat Bochum - Archaeologie - Bibliothek.

★ 18251 ★
University of Bonn - Institute of the History of Arts - Library (Art)
Regina-Pacis-Weg 1
W-5300 Bonn 1, Germany   Phone: 228 737598
Founded: 1872. **Staff:** Prof 2; Other 2. **Subjects:** Art history, art, architecture, applied arts, early Christian and Byzantine art. **Holdings:** 120,000 books; 13,000 bound periodical volumes; 15,000 microfiche; 200,000 dispositives. **Subscriptions:** 600 journals and other serials. **Services:** Library open to scholars and students. **Remarks:** FAX: 228 735579. Telex: 886657 unibod. **Also Known As:** Universitat Bonn - Kunsthistorisches Institut - Bibliothek.

★ 18252 ★
University of Bridgeport - Magnus Wahlstrom Library - Special Collections (Hum)
126 Park Ave.   Phone: (203)576-4740
Bridgeport, CT 06601   William Calhoon, Act.Univ.Libn.
Staff: Prof 7; Other 10. **Subjects:** Exploration, literature, graphic arts, Socialist-Labor movement, political science, history, health sciences. **Special Collections:** McKew Parr Memorial Collection (exploration); Starr Collection (English literature); Lincolniana (manuscripts; clippings; photographs). **Holdings:** 300,000 books. **Subscriptions:** 1400 journals and other serials; 10 newspapers. **Services:** Interlibrary loan; collections open to the public. **Automated Operations:** Computerized cataloging and ILL. **Computerized Information Services:** DIALOG Information Services, OCLC. Performs searches on fee basis. **Networks/Consortia:** Member of Southwestern Connecticut Library Council (SWLC), NELINET, Inc. **Remarks:** FAX: (203)576-4791. **Staff:** Teri Oparanozie; Michael Brent; Karen Smiga; Harold Hammond; Terry McCarthy.

★ 18253 ★
University of Bridgeport - School of Law - Law Library (Law)
126 Park Ave.   Phone: (203)576-4056
Bridgeport, CT 06601   Ann M. DeVeaux, Lib.Dir.
Founded: 1978. **Staff:** Prof 9; Other 5. **Subjects:** Law - federal, state, international. **Holdings:** 250,000 volumes; legal treatises; journals; government documents. **Subscriptions:** 2700 journals and other serials. **Services:** Interlibrary loan; library open to the public. **Automated Operations:** Computerized cataloging. **Computerized Information Services:** WESTLAW, LEXIS, NEXIS, DIALOG Information Services; internal databases. **Networks/Consortia:** Member of NELINET, Inc., New England Law Library Consortium (NELLCO). **Remarks:** FAX: (203)576-4236. **Staff:** Tina Delucia, Ref.Libn.; Larry Raftery, Ref.Libn.; Judith Parisi, Cat.Libn.; Michael Hughes, Assoc.Dir.; Mary Ellen Lomax, Ser.Mgr.; Maritza Ramirez, Comp.Mgr.; Valerie Jones, Acq.Lib.; Barbara Agonito, Adm.Serv.Coord.

★ 18254 ★
University of Bristol - University Library (Hum)
Tyndall Ave.   Phone: 272 303030
Bristol BS8 1TJ, England   Geoffrey Ford, Libn.
Founded: 1909. **Staff:** 90. **Subjects:** Arts, engineering, law, medicine, social sciences. **Special Collections:** English Novel to 1850; Penguin Books Collection and publishing archives; business histories; early science and philosophy; British General Election addresses; I.K. Brunel workbooks and papers (railroad builder/engineer); Pinney papers (17th-19th century); landscape gardening; Wiglesworth Ornithological Library; early medical works; Eyles Collection of early geology. **Holdings:** 1 million books, periodicals, and pamphlets; 130,000 microforms; manuscripts. **Subscriptions:** 6300 journals and other serials. **Services:** Interlibrary loan. **Computerized Information Services:** DIALOG Information Services, Data-Star, ESA/IRS, DIMDI; Telecom Gold, Janet (electronic mail service). **Remarks:** FAX: 272 255334. Telex: 9312110824. Electronic mail address(es): 79:LLA1028 (TELECOM GOLD); LIBRARY@UK.AC.BRISTOL (JANET).

★ 18255 ★
University of British Columbia - Asian Library (Area-Ethnic)
1871 West Mall   Phone: (604)822-2427
Vancouver, BC, Canada V6T 1Z2   Linda Joe, Hd.
Founded: 1960. **Staff:** Prof 3.5; Other 4. **Subjects:** East Asia (mainly China and Japan) - history, classics, language, literature, philosophy, Buddhism, fine arts, archeology, economics, political science, sociology, anthropology, education; South Asia - history, language, literature, religion; Indonesia - humanities, social sciences. **Special Collections:** P'u-pan Collection (45,000 volumes in Chinese, including 320 editions of the 10th-17th centuries and 270 gazetteers). **Holdings:** 311,661 volumes in East Asian languages; 39,260 volumes in Indic languages; 2810 periodical titles of Japanese government publications; 5099 reels of microfilm; 20,284 microfiche. **Subscriptions:** 1328 journals and other serials; 26 newspapers. **Services:** Interlibrary loan; copying; library open to the public for reference use only; annual fee required for circulation. **Automated Operations:** Computerized public access catalog. **Computerized Information Services:** OCLC, DOBIS Canadian Online Library System, UTLAS, RLIN; BITNET, InterNet (electronic mail services). **Publications:** Reference lists, irregular; Bibliography on the History of the Chinese Book & Calligraphy, 1970; a descriptive catalog of valuable manuscripts and rare books from China (P'u-pan Collection) by Dr. Yi-t'ung Wang, 1959 (book form, mimeographed). **Special Indexes:** Title index to P'u-pan Collection (in Chinese, on cards); Periodicals in Asian Studies (book form; revised edition 1971; 3rd edition, 1979). **Remarks:** FAX: (604)882-5207. Electronic mail address(es): USERLINJ@UBCMTSL (BITNET); LINDA-JOE@LIBRARY.UBC.CA (InterNet). **Staff:** Tsuneharu Gonnami, Ref.Libn. (Japanese); Shui-Yim Tse, Ref.Libn. (Chinese); Miseli Jeon, Ref.Libn. (Korean); Mandakranta Bose, Bibliog.Assoc. (Indic); Anthony Hardy, Bibliog.Assoc. (Indonesia).

★ 18256 ★
University of British Columbia - Biomedical Branch Library (Med)
Vancouver General Hospital
700 W. 10th Ave.   Phone: (604)875-4505
Vancouver, BC, Canada V5Z 1L5   Nancy P. Forbes, Act.Lib.Hd.
Founded: 1952. **Staff:** Prof 2; Other 4. **Subjects:** Clinical medicine. **Holdings:** 13,193 books; 17,552 bound periodical volumes. **Subscriptions:** 562 journals and other serials. **Services:** Interlibrary loan (through Woodward Biomedical Library); copying; library open to the public for reference use only. **Automated Operations:** Computerized circulation. **Computerized Information Services:** NLM, BRS Information Technologies, DIALOG Information Services; CD-ROM (Compact MedBase). **Remarks:** FAX: (604)875-4689.

University of British Columbia - British Columbia Rehabilitation Society
See: British Columbia Rehabilitation Society - G.F. Strong Centre (2172)

★ 18257 ★
University of British Columbia - Charles Crane Memorial Library (Aud-Vis)
1874 East Mall   Phone: (604)822-6111
Vancouver, BC, Canada V6T 1Z1   Paul E. Thiele, Hd.Libn.
Founded: 1968. **Staff:** 6. **Subjects:** University and college texts, reference materials, literature, research, and reports for the blind, visually impaired, and handicapped nonprint readers. **Special Collections:** Electronic, optical, and mechanical reading aids for the blind; Crane ABC - Alternate Book Centre. **Holdings:** 40,000 talking books on cassette and reel tapes; 25,000 braille volumes; 300 large print volumes; 500 printed books on blindness and disability. **Subscriptions:** 12 journals and other serials (recorded, braille, large print, and ordinary print). **Services:** Interlibrary loan; search and location service of books and materials for the blind and handicapped; sales of duplicate copies of talking books; recordings of books on demand (Crane Library Recording Centre has eight sound studios, high speed duplicating and mixing facilities). **Computerized Information Services:** BRS Information Technologies, ABLEDATA, CANUC:H, DOBIS; Envoy 100 (electronic mail service). Performs searches on fee basis. **Publications:** Crane Works in Progress, monthly (computer-produced); FUNSTUFF: Recreational and Leisure Materials in the Crane Collection, 1982; FUNSTUFF TOO!, 1989. **Remarks:** FAX: (604)822-6113. Telex: 04-51233 UBC PURCH VCR. Electronic mail address(es): CRANE (Envoy 100). **Staff:** Judith C. Thiele, Ref. & Coll.Libn.

★ 18258 ★
University of British Columbia - Curriculum Laboratory (Educ)
Scarfe Bldg.
2125 Main Mall   Phone: (604)228-3767
Vancouver, BC, Canada V6T 1Z5   Howard Hurt, Hd.Libn.
Founded: 1965. **Staff:** Prof 3; Other 11. **Subjects:** Educational theory and methods, children's literature. **Special Collections:** Historical textbooks (4000); French Collection (12,000 volumes). **Holdings:** 120,000 books; 6000 bound periodical volumes; 500 slide sets; 36 drawers of pamphlets; 1000 kits; 5000 pictures; 200 jackdaws; 1000 posters; 1400 transparencies; 100 maps; 2000 filmstrips; 2000 audiotapes; 1500 videotapes. **Subscriptions:** 600 journals and other serials. **Services:** Interlibrary loan; copying; SDI; open

to the public for reference use only. **Automated Operations:** Computerized cataloging, acquisitions, serials, and circulation. **Computerized Information Services:** DIALOG Information Services, PFDS Online, BRS Information Technologies, ERIC; Envoy 100 (electronic mail service). **Publications:** Orientation brochure; bibliographies. **Remarks:** FAX: (604)228-2309. Electronic mail address(es): curr.lab (Envoy 100). **Staff:** Lee-Ann Bryant, Ref.Libn.; Jo-Anne Naslund, Ref.Libn.

★ 18259 ★
University of British Columbia - Data Library (Info Sci, Comp Sci)
6356 Agricultural Rd., Rm. 206   Phone: (604)822-5587
Vancouver, BC, Canada V6T 1Z2   Ms. Hilde Colenbrander, Hd., Data Lib.
Founded: 1972. **Staff:** Prof 2; Other 1. **Subjects:** Social sciences, humanities, sciences. **Special Collections:** Canada census, 1961, 1966, 1971, 1976, 1981, 1986; Canadian Institute of Public Opinion surveys, 1945-1991 (400 subfiles of data). **Holdings:** 1000 books; 6000 files and subfiles of machine-readable data; 2000 codebooks. **Subscriptions:** 86 journals and other serials. **Services:** Copying of data files where contracts allow; library open to the public with restrictions on some files. **Automated Operations:** Computerized public access catalog. **Computerized Information Services:** Internal databases; BITNET, InterNet (electronic mail services). **Special Catalogs:** Data Library Catalogue (COM), irregular. **Remarks:** The Data Library, jointly operated by the UBC Library and University Computing Services, acquires, organizes, and maintains a collection of nonbibliographic, quantatative, and text data files in computer-readable form. **Remarks:** FAX: (604)822-5116. Electronic mail address(es): USERDLDB@UBCMTSG (BITNET); HILDE–COLENBRADER@MTSG.UBL.CA (InterNet).

★ 18260 ★
University of British Columbia - Department of Chemical Engineering - Chemical Engineering Reading Room (Sci-Engr, Energy)
Chemical Engineering Bldg.
2216 Main Mall
Vancouver, BC, Canada V6T 1W5   Phone: (604)228-3238
Staff: 1. **Subjects:** Biochemical and biomedical engineering, oil and gas, pulp and paper, heat transfer, fluidized and spouted beds. **Holdings:** 1907 books; departmental bachelors', masters', and Ph.D. theses; fourth year summer essays. **Subscriptions:** 26 journals and other serials. **Services:** Room open to the public. **Automated Operations:** Computerized cataloging. **Special Catalogs:** Union catalog of books and serials held by the six engineering reading rooms. **Special Indexes:** Indexes to fourth year summer essays and bachelors' theses (card). **Remarks:** FAX: (604)228-6003.

★ 18261 ★
University of British Columbia - Department of Civil Engineering - Civil Engineering Reading Room (Sci-Engr)
CEME Bldg., Rm. 1203
2324 Main Mall
Vancouver, BC, Canada V6T 1W5   Phone: (604)228-2120
Staff: 1. **Subjects:** Engineering - geotechnical, coastal, ocean; structures; construction; management; water resources; hydrology; environmental pollution. **Holdings:** 1785 books; departmental masters' and Ph.D. theses and other publications. **Subscriptions:** 66 journals and other serials. **Services:** Room open to the public. **Automated Operations:** Computerized cataloging. **Special Catalogs:** Union catalog of books and serials held by the six engineering reading rooms. **Special Indexes:** Index to theses (card). **Remarks:** FAX: (604)228-6901.

★ 18262 ★
University of British Columbia - Department of Electrical Engineering - Electrical Engineering Reading Room (Sci-Engr)
2356 Main Mall
Vancouver, BC, Canada V6T 1W5   Phone: (604)228-2872
Staff: 1. **Subjects:** Applied electromagnetics, biomedical engineering, solid state microelectronics, communications and signal processing, systems and control, digital system design, software engineering. **Holdings:** 670 books; departmental masters' and Ph.D. theses. **Subscriptions:** 102 journals and other serials. **Services:** Room open to the public. **Automated Operations:** Computerized cataloging. **Special Catalogs:** Union catalog of books and serials held by the six engineering reading rooms. **Special Indexes:** Index to departmental theses (card). **Remarks:** FAX: (604)228-6059.

★ 18263 ★
University of British Columbia - Department of Geography - Geographic Information Centre (Geog-Map)
1984 West Mall   Phone: (604)228-3048
Vancouver, BC, Canada V6T 1Z2   Rosemary J. Cann, Libn.
Staff: Prof 1. **Subjects:** Maps, air photography. **Special Collections:** Tri-Met air photo coverage of British Columbia; provincial/federal air photo indexes for British Columbia and the Yukon. **Holdings:** 202,763 air photos; 8748 air photo index maps; 48,417 maps; 16,993 publications. **Subscriptions:** 56 journals and other serials. **Services:** Interlibrary loan (limited); center open to the public. **Computerized Information Services:** Internal database. **Remarks:** FAX: (604)228-6150.

★ 18264 ★
University of British Columbia - Department of Mechanical Engineering - Mechanical Engineering Reading Room (Sci-Engr)
CEME Bldg., Rm. 1203
2324 Main Mall
Vancouver, BC, Canada V6T 1W5   Phone: (604)228-2120
Staff: 1. **Subjects:** Engineering - wind, design, industrial; solid mechanics; vibration; fluid mechanics; aerodynamics; bioengineering; applied statistics; space dynamics; energy conversion; nuclear safety. **Holdings:** 1291 books; departmental masters' and Ph.D theses and other departmental publications. **Subscriptions:** 24 journals and other serials. **Services:** Room open to the public. **Automated Operations:** Computerized cataloging. **Special Catalogs:** Union catalog of books and serials held by the six engineering reading rooms. **Special Indexes:** Index to departmental theses (card). **Remarks:** FAX: (604)228-2403.

★ 18265 ★
University of British Columbia - Department of Metals and Materials Engineering - Metals and Materials Engineering Reading Room (Sci-Engr)
Metallurgy Bldg., Rm. 319
6350 Stores Rd.
Vancouver, BC, Canada V6T 1W5   Phone: (604)228-2676
Staff: 1. **Subjects:** Mathematical modeling, ceramics, hydrometallurgy, composites, welding, metallurgical kinetics. **Holdings:** 1499 books; departmental masters' and Ph.D. theses. **Subscriptions:** 44 journals and other serials. **Services:** Room open to the public. **Automated Operations:** Computerized cataloging. **Special Catalogs:** Union catalog of books and serials held by the six engineering reading rooms. **Special Indexes:** Index to theses (card). **Remarks:** FAX: (604)228-3619.

★ 18266 ★
University of British Columbia - Department of Mining and Mineral Process Engineering - Mining and Mineral Process Engineering Reading Room (Sci-Engr)
Forward Bldg., Rm. 319
6350 Stores Rd.
Vancouver, BC, Canada V6T 1W5   Phone: (604)228-2540
Staff: 1. **Subjects:** Mining, mineral processing, geology. **Special Collections:** Mine proposals (200). **Holdings:** 1137 books; departmental masters' and Ph.D. theses. **Subscriptions:** 14 journals and other serials. **Services:** Room open to the public. **Automated Operations:** Computerized cataloging. **Special Catalogs:** Union catalog of books and serials held by the six engineering reading rooms. **Special Indexes:** Index to theses (card); Index to mining companies' mine proposals. **Remarks:** FAX: (604)228-5599.

★ 18267 ★
University of British Columbia - Eric W. Hamber Memorial Library (Med)
Children's Hospital
4480 Oak St.   Phone: (604)875-2154
Vancouver, BC, Canada V6H 3V4   Pat Lysyk, Libn.
Founded: 1982. **Staff:** Prof 1; Other 3. **Subjects:** Clinical medicine, pediatrics, obstetrics and gynecology. **Holdings:** 7127 books; 5157 bound periodical volumes. **Subscriptions:** 399 journals and other serials. **Services:** Interlibrary loan; copying; SDI; library open to the public. **Automated Operations:** Computerized cataloging, acquisitions, serials, and circulation. **Computerized Information Services:** DIALOG Information Services, BRS Information Technologies, NLM; CD-ROMs (MEDLINE, CINAHL, Current Contents: Life Sciences); internal databases; InterNet (electronic mail service). **Networks/Consortia:** Member of Health Sciences Library Network. **Remarks:** FAX: (604)875-2195. Electronic mail address(es): PAT–LYSYK@Library.ubc.ca (InterNet).

★ 18268 ★

University of British Columbia - Faculty of Commerce & Business Administration - David and Dorothy Lam Management Research Library (Bus-Fin)
HA No. 307
2053 Main Mall   Phone: (604)822-8470
Vancouver, BC, Canada V6T 1Y8   Diana Chan, Adm.Libn.
Founded: 1985. **Staff:** Prof 2; Other 4. **Subjects:** Finance, accounting, marketing, sales management, industrial relations, Asia-Pacific business, urban land economics, transportation, management information systems, management science, policy, real estate. **Holdings:** 5000 books; 6000 bound periodical volumes; 12,500 corporate annual reports; 3000 microfiche; 6 file cabinets of working papers; 2 file cabinets of collective agreements; 120 Canadian Government serials. **Subscriptions:** 1000 journals and other serials; 12 newspapers. **Services:** Copying; SDI; library open to card holders. **Automated Operations:** Computerized cataloging, acquisitions, and serials. **Computerized Information Services:** DIALOG Information Services, Reuters Information Services (Canada), Info Globe, The Financial Post DataGroup, Infomart Online; CD-ROMs (ABI/INFORM, COMPUSTAT PC PLUS: Corporate Text). Performs searches on fee basis. **Publications:** Directory of Business Computerized Databases, annual - for sale; Library Source Guides 1-20, irregular - for internal distribution only; management bibliographies on various topics, irregular - for sale. **Special Catalogs:** Author/title/series book catalog; subject catalog; journal list; working paper catalog. **Special Indexes:** Working Paper Quarterly Checklist (printout); Index to corporate annual reports (printout); Investment Index. **Remarks:** FAX: (604)822-8467.

★ 18269 ★

University of British Columbia - Fine Arts Library (Art)
University Library
1956 Main Mall   Phone: (604)822-3943
Vancouver, BC, Canada V6T 1Z1   Hans Burndorfer, Hd.
Founded: 1948. **Staff:** Prof 3; Other 6. **Subjects:** Fine arts, architecture, community and regional planning, history of costume and dance, artistic photography, fashion design. **Holdings:** 80,000 books; 30,000 bound periodical volumes; 45,000 pamphlets; 4000 photographs; 50,000 pictures; 70,000 exhibition catalogs; 60,000 clippings; 8000 microforms. **Subscriptions:** 400 journals and other serials. **Services:** Interlibrary loan; copying; library open to the public with restrictions. **Automated Operations:** Computerized cataloging, serials, and circulation. **Computerized Information Services:** DIALOG Information Services, RLIN; Envoy 100 (electronic mail service). **Publications:** Reference guides; bibliographies. **Special Catalogs:** Catalogs of exhibitions, pictures, planning pamphlets and clippings, Canadian art and artists, fashion design, and designers. **Remarks:** FAX: (604)822-6465. **Staff:** Diana Cooper, Fine Arts Ref.Libn.; Peggy McBride, Plan.Ref.Libn.

★ 18270 ★

University of British Columbia - Government Publications & Microforms Divisions (Info Sci)
University Library
P.O. Box 2194   Phone: (604)822-2584
Vancouver, BC, Canada V6B 3V7   Jocelyn Godolphin, Hd.
Founded: 1964. **Staff:** Prof 5; Other 8. **Subjects:** Publications from all levels of government and from all parts of the world; varied subjects on microforms. **Holdings:** 3.9 million microforms; 590,000 uncataloged government publications. **Subscriptions:** 8500 government publications. **Services:** Interlibrary loan; copying; divisions open to the public. **Automated Operations:** Computerized acquisitions, serials and processing. **Computerized Information Services:** Envoy 100, BITNET, InterNet (electronic mail services). **Remarks:** FAX: (604)822-9122. Electronic mail address(es): UBC.GP (Envoy 100); USERJOHD@UBCMTSL (BITNET); JOCELYN–GODOLPHIN@LIBRARY.UBC.CA (InterNet). **Staff:** Theresa Iverson, Proc.Libn.; Patrick Willoughby, Ref.Libn.; Mary Luebbe, Ref.Libn.; Susan Mathew, Ref.Libn.

★ 18271 ★

University of British Columbia - Humanities and Social Sciences Division (Soc Sci, Hum)
University Library
1956 Main Mall   Phone: (604)822-2725
Vancouver, BC, Canada V6T 1Z1   Jocelyn Godolphin, Hd.
Founded: 1984. **Staff:** Prof 8; Other 6. **Subjects:** Religion, language and literature, philosophy, history, linguistics, classical studies, theater, film, sociology, business administration, anthropology, commerce, economics,

psychology, geography, political science, education, physical education, library science. **Holdings:** 65,000 books and bound periodical volumes; annual reports of 850 companies. **Subscriptions:** 11,390 journals and other serials. **Services:** Interlibrary loan; copying; division open to the public. **Automated Operations:** Computerized cataloging, acquisitions, and serials. **Computerized Information Services:** DIALOG Information Services, CAN/OLE, QL Systems, Infomart Online, The Financial Post DataGroup, STM Systems Corporation, Questel, Info Globe, Reuters Information Services (Canada), BRS Information Technologies, WILSONLINE; Services Documentaines Multimedia, SIRLS, SDIProfiles, Canadian Politics Bibliography (internal databases); Envoy 100, BITNET, InterNet (electronic mail services). Performs searches on fee basis. **Publications:** Reference bibliographies and "Start Here" guides, irregular - on request. **Remarks:** FAX: (604)822-9122 Electronic mail address(es): USERLHUM@LIBRARY.UBC.CA (InterNet); USERLHUM@UBCMTSL.BITNET. **Staff:** Helene Redding, Libn.; Elizabeth Caskey, Libn.; Seonaid Lamb, Libn.; Iza Laponce, Libn.; Dorothy Martin, Libn.; Pia Christensen, Libn.; Joseph Jones, Libn.; Ture Erickson, Libn.; Les Karpinski, libn.

★ 18272 ★

University of British Columbia - Law Library (Law)
1822 East Mall   Phone: (604)822-2275
Vancouver, BC, Canada V6T 1Z1   Thomas J. Shorthouse, Law Libn.
Founded: 1945. **Staff:** Prof 3; Other 12. **Subjects:** Law. **Holdings:** 220,000 books and bound periodical volumes; law reports; statutes; legal journals; monographs. **Subscriptions:** 3100 journals and other serials. **Services:** Interlibrary loan; copying; library open to the public with restrictions. **Automated Operations:** Computerized cataloging, acquisitions, and circulation. **Computerized Information Services:** QL Systems, DIALOG Information Services, WESTLAW, LEXIS; Envoy 100 (electronic mail service). **Special Indexes:** Periodicals in Canadian law libraries: a Union List (online and published). **Remarks:** FAX: (604)822-6864. Electronic mail address(es): UBC.LAW (Envoy 100). **Staff:** Allen H. Soroka, Asst.Libn., Ref.; Mary E. Mitchell, Ref.Libn.

★ 18273 ★

University of British Columbia - MacMillan Forestry/Agriculture Library (Agri, Biol Sci)
MacMillan Bldg.
2357 Main Mall   Phone: (604)822-3609
Vancouver, BC, Canada V6T 1Z4   Lore Brongers, Hd.
Founded: 1967. **Staff:** Prof 1.5; Other 4. **Subjects:** Agricultural sciences, aquaculture, food science, forestry, forest products. **Holdings:** 62,143 books and bound periodical volumes; 90,843 unbound government publications; 200 annual reports; 57,065 microfiche; 317 reels of microfilm. **Subscriptions:** 1300 journals. **Services:** Interlibrary loan; copying; SDI; library open to the public. **Automated Operations:** Computerized serials and circulation. **Computerized Information Services:** CAN/SDI, CAN/OLE, DIALOG Information Services; Document Retrieval System (internal database). Performs searches on fee basis. **Staff:** Deborah Wilson, Ref.Libn.

★ 18274 ★

University of British Columbia - Map Library (Geog-Map)
University Library
1956 Main Mall   Phone: (604)822-2231
Vancouver, BC, Canada V6T 1Y3   Tim Ross, Map Libn.
Founded: 1964. **Staff:** Prof 1; Other 3. **Subjects:** Maps, cartography, map librarianship, travel. **Holdings:** 3346 books; 3343 atlases; 530 gazetteers; 163,000 maps; 140 pamphlet boxes of tourist literature and city guides; 13,459 microfiche. **Subscriptions:** 30 journals and other serials. **Services:** Copying; library open to the public. **Computerized Information Services:** CD-ROMs. **Publications:** Acquisitions list, 2/year; bibliographies, occasional; guide to collections. **Remarks:** Alternate telephone number(s): 822-6191. FAX: (604)822-3893.

★ 18275 ★

University of British Columbia - Marjorie Smith Library
School of Social Work
6201 Cecil Green Park Rd.
Vancouver, BC, Canada V6T 1W5
Defunct. Holdings absorbed by other University of British Columbia libraries.

★ 18276 ★
University of British Columbia - Mathematics Library (Comp Sci, Sci-Engr)
1984 Main Mall　　　　　　　　　　Phone: (604)822-3826
Vancouver, BC, Canada V6T 1W5　Bonita Stableford, Hd., Sci.Div. &
　　　　　　　　　　　　　　　　　　　　　　Math.Lib.
Founded: 1966. **Staff:** 2. **Subjects:** Mathematics, computer science, statistics. **Holdings:** 31,737 books and bound periodical volumes. **Subscriptions:** 459 journals and other serials. **Services:** Interlibrary loan; library open to the public. **Computerized Information Services:** OnTyme Electronic Message Network Service, Envoy 100 (electronic mail services). **Remarks:** FAX: (604)228-3893. Electronic mail address(es): UBC (OnTyme Electronic Message Network Service); UBC.SCI.MATH (Envoy 100).

★ 18277 ★
University of British Columbia - Music Library (Mus)
6361 Memorial Rd.　　　　　　　　Phone: (604)822-3589
Vancouver, BC, Canada V6T 1Z2　　Hans Burndorfer, Hd.
Founded: 1948. **Staff:** Prof 1.5; Other 2. **Subjects:** Music. **Holdings:** 65,000 books and scores; 4000 reels of microfilm; 15,000 recordings. **Subscriptions:** 150 journals and other serials. **Services:** Interlibrary loan; copying; library open to the public. **Remarks:** FAX: (604)822-3893. **Staff:** Kirsten Walsh, Mus.Ref.Libn.

★ 18278 ★
University of British Columbia - Patent Search Service (PATSCAN)
　(Info Sci)
Science Division, Main Library
1956 Main Mall　　　　　　　　　　Phone: (604)822-5404
Vancouver, BC, Canada V6T 1Y3　　Ronald Simmer, Patent Libn.
Founded: 1986. **Staff:** 1.5. **Subjects:** Patents, patent searching. **Special Collections:** U.S. and European Patent Abstracts (CD-ROM). **Holdings:** Reference works and manuals; Canadian patent index database; Canadian patent office records; U.S. Official Gazette (1916 to present). **Subscriptions:** 6 journals and other serials. **Services:** Interlibrary loan; copying; SDI; library open to the public on a restricted schedule. **Computerized Information Services:** DIALOG Information Services, PFDS Online, STN International; Envoy 100 (electronic mail service). Performs searches on fee basis. **Publications:** PATSCAN Newsletter. **Remarks:** FAX: (604)822-3893. Electronic mail address(es): PATSCAN (Envoy 100).

★ 18279 ★
University of British Columbia - St. Paul's Hospital Health Sciences
　Library (Med)
1081 Burrard St.　　　　　　　　　Phone: (604)631-5425
Vancouver, BC, Canada V6Z 1Y6　　Barbara J. Saint, Hd.
Founded: 1950. **Staff:** Prof 1; Other 4. **Subjects:** Health sciences. **Holdings:** 5000 books; 2 VF drawers of pamphlets. **Subscriptions:** 225 journals and other serials. **Services:** Interlibrary loan; copying; SDI; library open to the public. **Automated Operations:** Computerized cataloging, acquisitions, serials, and circulation. **Computerized Information Services:** DIALOG Information Services, BRS Information Technologies, NLM, CAN/OLE, QL Systems; Envoy 100 (electronic mail services). Performs searches on fee basis. **Publications:** Newsletter, irregular - for internal distribution only. **Special Catalogs:** Periodical holdings (book), annual. **Remarks:** FAX: (604)631-5013. Electronic mail address(es): UBC.WOOD.REF (Envoy 100)

★ 18280 ★
University of British Columbia - School of Library, Archival and
　Information Studies Reading Room (Info Sci)
1956 Main Mall, Rm. 831　　　　　Phone: (604)228-2704
Vancouver, BC, Canada V6T 1Y3　Wendy Halferdahl, Adm.Asst.
Founded: 1961. **Staff:** Prof 1; Other 1. **Subjects:** Librarianship, archival studies, information science, publishing and book trade. **Holdings:** 3000 cataloged books and bound periodical volumes; uncataloged annual reports, newsletters, publishers' catalogs, course materials. **Subscriptions:** 130 journals and other serials. **Services:** Room open to the public with restrictions. **Computerized Information Services:** Envoy 100 (electronic mail service). **Remarks:** FAX: (604)228-3893. Electronic mail address(es): UBC.SLAIS (Envoy 100).

★ 18281 ★
University of British Columbia - Science Division (Sci-Engr)
University Library
1956 Main Mall　　　　　　　　　　Phone: (604)822-3295
Vancouver, BC, Canada V6T 1Y3　Bonita Stableford, Hd., Sci.Div. &
　　　　　　　　　　　　　　　　　　　　　　Math.Lib.
Founded: 1960. **Staff:** Prof 3.25; Other 2. **Subjects:** Chemistry, physics, engineering, mathematics, geology, astronomy. **Special Collections:** Rand Corporation Depository, 1970 to present. **Holdings:** 235,000 volumes; ANSI standards; CSA standards. **Subscriptions:** 3200 journals and other serials. **Services:** Interlibrary loan; copying; patent searching; division open to the public. **Computerized Information Services:** CAN/OLE, DIALOG Information Services, QL Systems, Chemical Abstracts Service (CAS); OnTyme Electronic Message Network Service, Envoy 100 (electronic mail services). **Special Indexes:** Index to IEEE Publications held at UBC; Index to conference proceedings in journal issues. **Remarks:** FAX: (604)822-3893. Electronic mail address(es): UBC (OnTyme Electronic Message Network Service); UBC.SCI.MATH (Envoy 100). **Staff:** Helen Mayoh, Ref.Libn.; Sundaram Venkataraman, Ref.Libn.; Jack McIntosh, Ref.Libn.; Janice Kreider, Ref.Libn.

★ 18282 ★
University of British Columbia - Special Collections and University
　Archives Division
University Library
1956 Main Mall　　　　　　　　　　Phone: (604)822-2521
Vancouver, BC, Canada V6T 1Z1　Anne Yandle, Hd., Spec.Coll.
Founded: 1960. **Staff:** Prof 4; Other 5. **Subjects:** Canadian history, travel, and literature; Pacific Northwest; early children's literature; historical cartography; 19th century English and Anglo-Irish literature; University of British Columbia; labor and business history; Arctic explorations. **Special Collections:** Colbeck Collection (English and Anglo-Irish belles lettres; 20,000 books); Robert Burns Collection (700 books); Thomas J. Wise Collection (200 books); University Archives and Historical Manuscripts Collections (7000 linear feet); Howay-Reid Collection of Pacific Northwest Americana; Robertson Collection of English dictionaries . **Holdings:** 77,000 books and bound periodical volumes; 21,000 pamphlets; 25,000 maps; 70,000 photographs; 2000 audiotapes; 86 films. **Subscriptions:** 140 journals and other serials. **Services:** Copying; division open to the public. **Automated Operations:** Computerized cataloging, acquisitions, and serials. **Publications:** Published guides to manuscript, Colbeck and dictionary collections. **Remarks:** FAX: (604)822-3893. **Staff:** Chris Hives, Univ.Archv.; George Brandak, Mss.Cur.; Frances Woodward, Ref.Libn.

★ 18283 ★
University of British Columbia - Spencer Entomological Museum -
　Library (Biol Sci)
Dept. of Zoology　　　　　　　　　Phone: (604)822-3379
Vancouver, BC, Canada V6T 1Z4　G.G.E. Scudder, Dir.
Founded: 1953. **Staff:** Prof 2. **Subjects:** Entomology. **Holdings:** 350 books; 8000 reprints; 50 series of unbound journals. **Services:** Copying; library open to the public at the discretion of the director. **Special Catalogs:** Subject catalog for reprints. **Remarks:** FAX: (604)822-2416. **Staff:** S. Cannings, Cur.

★ 18284 ★
University of British Columbia - Wilson Recordings Collection (Aud-Vis)
1958 Main Mall　　　　　　　　　　Phone: (604)228-2534
Vancouver, BC, Canada V6T 1W5　Joan Sandilands, Hd.
Founded: 1941. **Staff:** 2. **Subjects:** Literature, music, show business. **Holdings:** 30,000 phonograph records; 7000 compact discs. **Services:** Collection open to the public. **Automated Operations:** Computerized public access catalog, cataloging, and circulation. **Special Indexes:** Author/composer, number, performer/conductor, distinctive title.

★ 18285 ★
University of British Columbia - Woodward Biomedical Library (Med, Biol Sci)
2198 Health Sciences Mall　　　　Phone: (604)822-2762
Vancouver, BC, Canada V6T 1W5　Johann van Reenen, Hd.
Founded: 1950. **Staff:** Prof 12; Other 26. **Subjects:** Medicine, zoology, botany, dentistry, pharmacy, nursing, rehabilitation medicine, nutrition. **Special Collections:** Historical Collection in Science and Medicine (5000 volumes; pictures; manuscripts; letters; reprints; artifacts). **Holdings:** 180,208 books; 149,452 bound periodical volumes; 35,878 microforms. **Subscriptions:** 4044 journals and other serials. **Services:** Interlibrary loan; copying; SDI; library open to the public (library card must be purchased to

borrow materials). **Automated Operations:** Computerized public access catalog, acquisitions, serials, and circulation. **Computerized Information Services:** NLM, DIALOG Information Services, CAN/OLE, BRS Information Technologies, QL Systems, STN International; CD-ROM (MEDLINE, BIOSIS); Envoy 100, OnTyme Electronic Message Network Service, BITNET, InterNet (electronic mail services). Performs searches on fee basis. **Networks/Consortia:** Member of Health Sciences Library Network. **Remarks:** Alternate telephone numbers are 822-4440 and 822-5461. FAX: (604)822-5596. Electronic mail address(es): BCW (Envoy 100); JOHANN–VAN–REENEN@LIBRARY,UBC,CA (InterNet); USERLJVR@UBCMTSL (BITNET). **Staff:** Elsie De Bruijn, Assoc.Libn.; Lynne Hallonquist, Life Sci.Bibliog.; Lee Perry, Hist.Coll.; Diana Kent, Ref.Libn.; Dan Heino, Ref.Libn.; Pat Lysyk, Ref.Libn.; William Parker, Ref.Libn.; Florence Doidge, Circ.Libn.; Stephanie Dykstra, Ref.Libn.; Margaret Price, Ref.Libn.; Helen Chan, Ref.Libn.

★ 18286 ★
University of Calgary - Canadian Institute of Resources Law - Library (Law, Energy)
BioSciences Bldg., Rm. 430M   Phone: (403)220-3200
Calgary, AB, Canada T2N 1N4   Evangeline S. Case, Pubn.Off.
Subjects: Canadian energy regulation, oil and gas law. **Holdings:** 600 books; 30 book shelves of Canadian regulatory tribunal publications. **Subscriptions:** 25 journals and other serials. **Services:** Copying; library open to the public with permission. **Remarks:** FAX: (403)282-6182.

★ 18287 ★
University of Calgary - Com/Media Film/Video Library (Aud-Vis)
2500 University Dr., N.W.   Phone: (403)220-3721
Calgary, AB, Canada T2N 1N4   Wendy Stephens, Supv.
Founded: 1969. **Staff:** Prof 4. **Subjects:** Social sciences. **Special Collections:** Film study collection (392 titles). **Holdings:** 3400 16mm film titles; 3200 videotape titles; 41 slide sets; 8 videodisc titles; 9 VF drawers of distributors' catalogs. **Subscriptions:** 65 journals and other serials. **Services:** Interlibrary loan; library open to the public with restrictions. **Automated Operations:** Computerized cataloging. **Computerized Information Services:** DOBIS Canadian Online Library System. **Special Catalogs:** Catalog of film and videotape holdings (book) - for sale. **Remarks:** FAX: (403)282-4497.

★ 18288 ★
University of Calgary - Education Materials Centre (Educ)
Education Tower, Rm. 402
2500 University Dr., N.W.   Phone: (403)220-5637
Calgary, AB, Canada T2N 1N4   David Brown, Dir.
Founded: 1963. **Staff:** Prof 2; Other 6. **Subjects:** Teaching methods, elementary and secondary curriculum, children's literature. **Special Collections:** Archive collection of Alberta curriculum guides and texts. **Holdings:** 55,000 books; 5000 pictures; 1500 sound recordings; 300 video cassettes; 4000 filmstrips; 2500 kits; 3000 slides. **Subscriptions:** 170 journals and other serials. **Services:** Copying; center open to the public for reference use only. **Automated Operations:** Computerized public access catalog, cataloging, acquisitions, and circulation. **Computerized Information Services:** CD-ROM (ERIC, CD:Education). **Remarks:** Maintained by Faculty of Education. **Staff:** Pearl Herscovitch, Curric.Libn.

★ 18289 ★
University of Calgary - Gallagher Library of Geology & Geophysics (Sci-Engr)
2500 University Dr., N.W.,   Phone: (403)220-6042
Calgary, AB, Canada T2N 1N4   Midge King, Libn.
Founded: 1974. **Staff:** Prof 1; Other 2. **Subjects:** Sedimentary and petroleum geology, geophysics. **Holdings:** 20,000 books; 15,000 bound periodical volumes; 10,000 government publications; 2300 maps; 550 microforms; 52 slide sets. **Subscriptions:** 100 journals and other serials. **Services:** Interlibrary loan; copying; library open to the public. **Automated Operations:** Computerized cataloging, acquisitions, and circulation. **Computerized Information Services:** CAN/OLE, SPIRES Data Base Management, DIALOG Information Services; NETNORTH, BITNET, Envoy 100 (electronic mail services). Performs searches on fee basis. **Special Catalogs:** University of Calgary Theses in Geology and Geophysics (printout). **Remarks:** FAX: (403)282-6837. Electronic mail address(es): MHKING@UNCAMULT (BITNET).

★ 18290 ★
University of Calgary - Kananaskis Centre for Environmental Research - Library (Env-Cons, Biol Sci)
Calgary, AB, Canada T2N 1N4   Phone: (403)220-5355
                                     Grace LeBel, Libn.
Staff: 1. **Subjects:** Chemistry, biology, environmental research. **Special Collections:** Field guides and environmental collection. **Holdings:** 4000 books; 3000 unpublished reports and theses. **Subscriptions:** 5 journals and other serials; 2 newspapers. **Services:** Library open to the public with restrictions. **Remarks:** FAX: (403)673-3671.

★ 18291 ★
University of Calgary - Law Library (Law)
2500 University Dr., N.W.   Phone: (403)220-5090
Calgary, AB, Canada T2N 1N4   Olga Margaret Kizlyk, Law Libn.
Founded: 1975. **Staff:** Prof 4; Other 10. **Subjects:** Law. **Holdings:** 102,000 volumes; 52,000 microforms. **Subscriptions:** 2200 journals and other serials. **Services:** Interlibrary loan; copying; library open to the public. **Automated Operations:** Computerized public access catalog, cataloging, acquisitions, and circulation. **Computerized Information Services:** QL Systems, DIALOG Information Services, WESTLAW, LEXIS, UTLAS; NETNORTH, Envoy 100, QUICKMAIL (electronic mail services). **Remarks:** FAX: (403)282-3000. Electronic mail address(es): 47107@UCDASVM1 (NETNORTH); Box 55 (QUICKMAIL); UNCAMULT (BITNET). **Staff:** Dani Pahulje; Umesh Vyas; Mary Hemmings, Tech.Serv.

★ 18292 ★
University of Calgary - Mackimmie Library - Humanities/Arts/Social Sciences Area (Art, Hum)
2500 University Dr., N.W.   Phone: (403)220-3601
Calgary, AB, Canada T2N 1N4   Yvonne R. Hinks, Hd. &
                                     Philosophy Libn.
Founded: 1966. **Staff:** Prof 9; Other 15. **Subjects:** Literature; art; drama; classics; music; philosophy; religious studies; Germanic, Slavic, and Romance languages; linguistics; economics; sociology; archaeology; anthropology; history; political science. **Special Collections:** Canadian Authors Manuscripts; Canadian Architectural Archives. **Holdings:** Figures not available. **Services:** Interlibrary loan; copying; SDI; library open to the public. **Automated Operations:** Computerized cataloging, acquisitions, and circulation. **Computerized Information Services:** DIALOG Information Services, PFDS Online, CAN/OLE, QL Systems, Info Globe, Dow Jones News/Retrieval, SPIRES; internal databases; Envoy 100, AOSS, NETNORTH (electronic mail services). Performs searches on fee basis. Contact Person: Saundra Lipton, Rd.Stud./Classics Libn., 220-3793. **Remarks:** Library maintains the Government Publications Division and newspapers for the main University Library. FAX: (403)282-6837. **Staff:** Nora Robins, Asst.Hd., Coll. & Hist./Political Sci.Libn.; Apollonia Lang Steele, Asst.Hd., Pers. & Spec.Coll.Libn.; William Sgrazzutti, Mus.Libn.; Kathy Zimon, Arts Libn.; Jan Roseneder, English Libn.; Rhys Williams, Govt.Pubns.Libn.; Rosvita Vaska, Germanic/Slavic; Cindy Murrell, Drama/Theater; Joanne Henning, Canadian Lit.Libn.; Deb deBruijn, Econ.Libn.; Ada-Marie Atkins Nechka, Linguistics Libn.; Sharon Neary, Archeo., Anthropology, Sociology Libn.

★ 18293 ★
University of Calgary - Mackimmie Library - Humanities/Arts/Social Sciences Area - Special Collections Division (Hum)
2500 University Dr., N.W.   Phone: (403)220-5972
Calgary, AB, Canada T2N 1N4   Apollonia Lang Steele, Spec.Coll.Libn.
Founded: 1966. **Staff:** Prof 1; Other 3. **Subjects:** Canadian literature, Canadian music. **Special Collections:** Papers of Hugh MacLennan, Alice Munro, Mordecai Richler, Brian Moore, W.O. Mitchell, Christie Harris, Robert Kroetsch, Rudy Weibe, George Ryga, Gwen Ringwood, Len Peterson, Michael Cook, Joanna Glass, Aritha van Herk, Sharon Pollock, John Murrell, Grant MacEwan, James Gray, Bruce Hutchison, Alden Nowlan, Clark Blaise, John Metcalf, Lois Kerr; Morris Surdin (papers; musical scores; Canadian Broadcasting Corporation scripts); E.C.W. Press. **Holdings:** 30,000 books and periodical volumes; 875 meters of manuscripts and archives. **Subscriptions:** 10 journals and other serials. **Services:** Copying; collections open to the public. **Automated Operations:** Computerized cataloging and acquisitions. **Computerized Information Services:** BITNET (electronic mail service). **Publications:** Published inventories of The Hugh MacLennan Papers; The Rudy Wiebe Papers: First Accession; The Robert Kroetsch Papers: First Accession; The Alice Munro Papers: First Accession; The Joanna M. Glass Papers; The W.O. Mitchell

Papers; The Alice Munro Papers: Second Accession; The Brian Moore Papers: First Accession and Second Accession; The Mordecai Richler Papers; The Gwen Pharis Ringwood Papers; The Aritha van Herk Papers: First Accession; The Sharon Pollock Papers: First Accession; The Miriam Mandel Papers; The Clark Blaise Papers: First Accession and Second Accession. **Remarks:** FAX: (403)282-6837. Electronic mail address(es): ASTEELE@UNCAMULT (BITNET).

★ 18294 ★

University of Calgary - Medical Library (Med)
Health Sciences Centre
3330 Hospital Dr., N.W.   Phone: (403)220-6858
Calgary, AB, Canada T2N 4N1   Andras Kirchner, Med.Libn.
Founded: 1968. **Staff:** Prof 3; Other 14.5. **Subjects:** Health sciences with special emphasis on family practice. **Holdings:** 99,924 volumes; 15,140 microforms; 50 films; 446 videotapes; 332 slide/tape programs; 1250 cassettes. **Subscriptions:** 1613 journals and other serials. **Services:** Interlibrary loan; copying; SDI; library open to the public. **Automated Operations:** Computerized cataloging and acquisitions. **Computerized Information Services:** DIALOG Information Services, CAN/OLE, MEDLARS; CD-ROMs (MEDLINE, PsycLIT, BIOSIS); Envoy 100, NETNORTH, InterNet (electronic mail services). Performs searches on fee basis. Contact Person: D.I.H. Cole, Asst.Med.Libn., 220-3750. **Special Catalogs:** Union list of serials of Calgary area hospital libraries. **Remarks:** FAX: (403)282-7992. Electronic mail address(es): ILL.ACUM (Envoy 100); 47106@UCDASVM1 (NETNORTH); 47106@UCDASVM1.ADMIN.UCALGARY.CA (InterNet). **Staff:** Judith Osborne, Coll.Dev.Libn.

★ 18295 ★

University of Calgary - University Libraries - Sciences/Professions Area (Sci-Engr, Env-Cons)
2500 University Dr., N.W.   Phone: (403)220-5598
Calgary, AB, Canada T2N 1N4   Gretchen Ghent, Hd.
Staff: Prof 7; Other 11. **Subjects:** Physical and biological sciences, engineering, geology and geophysics, northern studies, environment and architecture, urban and regional planning, mathematics and computing science, nursing, communication studies, education, social welfare, physical education/sport sciences, management, psychology, rehabilitation studies. **Special Collections:** Arctic Institute of North America Collection; maps and aerial photographs; Management Resource Center. **Holdings:** Figures not available for books, bound periodical volumes, and microforms; 150,000 maps; 600,000 aerial photographs. **Services:** Library open to the public. **Automated Operations:** Computerized public access catalog. **Computerized Information Services:** DIALOG Information Services, BRS Information Technologies, CAN/SDI, DOBIS Canadian Online Library System, CAN/OLE, QL Systems, SPIRES, STN International, PFDS Online; NOMADS (internal database); CD-ROMs (MEDLINE, PsychLit, ERIC, CINAHL, SOCIOFILE, DISS.ABS., SPORT, BIOSIS, COMPENDEX); Envoy 100 (electronic mail service). Performs searches on fee basis. Contact Person: Alane Wilson, Online Coord. & Educ.Libn., 220-3462. **Remarks:** FAX: (403)282-6837. Electronic mail address(es): 47109@UCDASVM1 (BITNET, NETNORTH). **Staff:** Laurie Moffat, Asst. Area Hd. & Nurs.Libn.; Eric Tull, EVDS Libn. & Northern Studies; Darlene Warren, Bio./Chem./Physics Libn.; Elizabeth Watson, Engr.Libn.; Helen Clarke, Map/Airphoto Libn.; Shelagh Mikulak, Mgt.Libn.; Elaine Bouey, Soc. Welfare Libn.; E. Chris Hayward, Commun.Stud.Libn.; Ruth Borst-Boyd, Tourism Libn.

★ 18296 ★

University of California - Bodega Marine Laboratory - Library (Biol Sci)
P.O. Box 247   Phone: (707)875-2015
Bodega, CA 94923   Eleanor S. Uhlinger
Founded: 1964. **Staff:** Prof 1. **Subjects:** Marine invertebrates. **Special Collections:** Bodega Marine Laboratory Student Reports (1931 to present). **Holdings:** 5000 books; 12,000 bound periodical volumes; 2400 site reports. **Subscriptions:** 93 journals and other serials. **Services:** Interlibrary loan; copying; library open to the public for reference use only. **Automated Operations:** Computerized public access catalog. **Computerized Information Services:** DIALOG; internal databases; InterNet, BITNET, Usenet (electronic mail services). **Remarks:** Electronic mail address(es): ucdbml@avis.edu (InterNet); ucdbml@avis (BITNET); uunet!ucdavis!ucdbml (Usenet). FAX: (707)875-2089.

★ 18297 ★

University of California - Kearney Agricultural Center - Electronic Library (Agri)
9240 S. Riverbend Ave.   Phone: (209)891-2500
Parlier, CA 93648   Louise Ferguson, Contact
Founded: 1961. **Staff:** Prof 20; Other 60. **Subjects:** Agronomy, agricultural economics, entomology, nematology, plant pathology, pomology, viticulture, vegetable crops, water science, biological control. **Holdings:** CD-ROMs. **Services:** Center open to the public by permission. **Computerized Information Services:** CD-ROMs (AGRICOLA, Current Contents); MELVYL (internal database).

★ 18298 ★

University of California - Los Alamos National Laboratory - Library (Sci-Engr)
MS-P362   Phone: (505)667-4448
Los Alamos, NM 87545   Richard Luce, Hd.Libn.
Founded: 1943. **Staff:** Prof 14; Other 24. **Subjects:** Military and peaceful uses of nuclear energy, physics, chemistry, materials science, engineering, earth sciences, mathematics and computers. **Special Collections:** Biomedicine (40,000 volumes). **Holdings:** 150,000 books; 200,000 bound periodical volumes; 1 million technical reports; 500 reels of motion picture film; videos. **Subscriptions:** 2300 journals and other serials. **Services:** Interlibrary loan; copying; internal translation; library open to the public for reference use only on a limited schedule. **Automated Operations:** Computerized public access catalog, cataloging, acquisitions, serials, and circulation. **Computerized Information Services:** DIALOG Information Services, ORBIT Search Service, BRS Information Technologies, Integrated Technical Information System (ITIS), RLIN, NLM, NASA/RECON, DTIC, NEXIS, STN International, CompuServe Information Service, WILSONLINE, NewsNet, Inc., Washington Alert Service, DataTimes, Dow Jones News/Retrieval, VU/TEXT Information Services, USNI Military Database, Videolog, WESTLAW, IRIS, CAN/SND, New Mexico Legalnet; Los Alamos Authors (internal database); CD-ROMs; InterNet, BITNET, ITIS, STNMAIL, RLIN (electronic mail services). **Publications:** What's New. **Special Catalogs:** Card catalog for technical reports; computer listing of laboratory sponsored unclassified publications. **Remarks:** FAX: (505)665-2948. The laboratory is operated by the University of California for the U.S. Department of Energy. **Staff:** Theresa Connaughton, Act.Dp.Hd.Libn.; Jackie Stack, Act.Info. Access Libn.; Carol Nielson, Ref.Libn.; Donna Berg, Ref.Libn.; Ann Beyer, Ref.Libn.; Betty Burnett, Ref.Libn.; Marie Harper Ref.Libn.; Jeane Strub, Ref.Libn.; Joan Stover, Rpt.Libn.; Jackson Carter, Tech.Libn.; Sharon Smith, Tech.Libn.; Irma Holtkamp, Tech.Libn.; Kathryn Varjabedian, Act.Cat.Libn.

University of California, Berkeley - Alcohol Research Group
See: **Alcohol Research Group** (328)

★ 18299 ★

University of California, Berkeley - Anthropology Library (Soc Sci)
230 Kroeber Hall   Phone: (510)642-2400
Berkeley, CA 94720   Dorothy A. Koenig, Libn.
Founded: 1956. **Staff:** Prof 1; Other 2. **Subjects:** Anthropology. **Holdings:** 64,784 volumes; 2318 microforms; 1999 pamphlets. **Subscriptions:** 965 journals and other serials. **Services:** Interlibrary loan (through 307 General Library); copying; library open for reference use with restrictions on circulation. **Computerized Information Services:** InterNet (electronic mail service). **Remarks:** Alternate telephone number(s): 642-2419. Electronic mail address(es): DKOENIG@LIBRARY.BERKELEY.EDU (InterNet).

★ 18300 ★

University of California, Berkeley - Architecture Slide Library (Art)
315 Wurster Hall   Phone: (510)642-3439
Berkeley, CA 94720   Maryly Snow, Libn.
Founded: 1936. **Staff:** 3. **Subjects:** Architecture, architectural history, city and regional planning, urbanism, design, building sciences, landscape architecture, and allied subjects. **Special Collections:** Denise Scott Brown Collection; William Wheaton Collection; M.R. Jay Collection. **Holdings:** 200,000 slides and photographs. **Services:** Library open to the public with limited circulation. **Automated Operations:** Computerized public access catalog. **Computerized Information Services:** INGRES, Image Query (internal databases); InterNet (electronic mail service). **Remarks:** FAX: (510)643-9576. Electronic mail address(es): SLIDES@CED.BERKELEY.EDU. (InterNet).

★ 18301 ★
University of California, Berkeley - Asian American Studies Library
    (Area-Ethnic)
3407 Dwinelle Hall   Phone: (510)642-2218
Berkeley, CA 94720   Mrs. Wei Chi Poon, Hd.Libn.
Founded: 1970. **Staff:** Prof 1; Other 2.5. **Subjects:** Asians in the U.S., past
and present. **Special Collections:** Chinese American Research Collection
(archival materials in English and Chinese; 38,113 items). **Holdings:** 63,579
volumes; 5000 slides; 106 videotapes; 26 16mm films. **Subscriptions:** 167
journals and other serials; 134 newspapers. **Services:** Library open to the
public with restrictions on circulation. **Publications:** A Guide for
Establishing Asian American Core Collection; Directory of Asian American
Collections in the United States. **Remarks:** FAX: (510)642-6456.

★ 18302 ★
University of California, Berkeley - Astronomy-Mathematics-Statistics
    Library (Sci-Engr)
100 Evans Hall   Phone: (510)642-3381
Berkeley, CA 94720   Ralph H. Moon, Libn.
Founded: 1959. **Staff:** Prof 1; Other 3. **Subjects:** Astronomy, pure and
applied mathematics, statistics, mathematics of computer science. **Holdings:**
72,000 volumes. **Subscriptions:** 1288 journals and other serials. **Services:**
Interlibrary loan (through 307 General Library); copying; library open to
the public for reference use with restricted circulation. **Computerized
Information Services:** CD-ROMs (MathSci); InterNet (electronic mail
service). **Remarks:** Electronic mail address(es):
MATH@LIBRARY.BERKELEY.EDU (InterNet).

★ 18303 ★
University of California, Berkeley - Bancroft Library (Hist, Rare Book)
Berkeley, CA 94720   Phone: (510)642-3781
                                       Peter E. Hanff, Interim Dir.
Founded: 1859. **Staff:** Prof 19; Other 27. **Special Collections:** Bancroft
Collection (history of western North America, especially Rocky Mountain
states to the Pacific Coast and from Panama to Alaska with greatest
emphasis on California and Mexico); Rare Books (incunabula; 403); rare
European, English, U.S., and South American imprints; fine printing of all
periods and places (emphasis on modern English and American typography,
medieval manuscript books and documents, papyri); University Archives;
Regional Oral History Office (recollections of persons who have contributed
to the development of the West and the nation); Mark Twain Papers
(collection of the author's manuscripts, correspondence, related
documentary material, and the editorial program to publish it); history of
science and technology, especially in California. **Holdings:** 427,913 volumes;
32,061 linear feet of manuscripts; 21,600 maps and atlases; 2.38 million
pictures and portraits; 71,178 microforms; 10,816 recordings; 2850 motion
pictures. **Subscriptions:** 1519 journals and other serials. **Services:**
Interlibrary loan (limited to microfilm; through General Library); copying
(limited); library open to the public. **Automated Operations:** Computerized
cataloging. **Publications:** A Guide to the Manuscripts of the Bancroft
Library, Volumes 1 and 2, Berkeley, 1963 and 1972; Bancroftiana
(newsletter), 2/year - to Friends of The Bancroft Library. **Special Catalogs:**
A Catalog of the Bancroft Collection, 1964, and supplements (book).
Remarks: FAX: (510)643-7891.

★ 18304 ★
University of California, Berkeley - Biochemistry Library
430 Barker Hall
Berkeley, CA 94720
Defunct.

★ 18305 ★
University of California, Berkeley - BioSciences Library (Biol Sci)
40 Giannini Hall   Phone: (510)642-2531
Berkeley, CA 94720   Beth Weil, Libn.
Founded: 1930. **Staff:** Prof 4; Other 8.5. **Subjects:** Agriculture, anatomy,
botany, cell biology, environmental sciences, molecular biology, biology,
nutrition, pest management, physiology. **Special Collections:** Holl
Collection of Cookbooks; Rare Book Collection (17th-19th century natural
history; 4000 volumes). **Holdings:** 356,465 volumes; 50,615 pamphlets and
reprints; 1543 reels of microfilm; 23,470 microfiche. **Subscriptions:** 6794
journals and other serials. **Services:** Interlibrary loan (through 307 General
Library); copying; library open to the public for reference use with restricted
circulation. **Computerized Information Services:** DIALOG Information
Services, BRS Information Technologies, NLM, RLIN, STN International;

InterNet (electronic mail service). **Special Indexes:** California Index -
Publications of the California Agricultural Experimentation Station (card).
Remarks: FAX: (510)642-4612. Electronic mail address(es):
BIOS@LIBRARY.BERKELEY.EDU (InterNet). **Staff:** Norma kobzina,
Hd.Info.Serv.; Ingrid Radkey, Ref.Libn.; Barbara Glendenning, Ref.Libn.,
Hd.Circ./ Doc . Delivery Serv.

★ 18306 ★
University of California, Berkeley - Botanical Garden - Library (Biol
    Sci)
Centennial Dr.   Phone: (510)643-8040
Berkeley, CA 94720   Robert Ornduff, Cur.
Founded: 1890. **Staff:** Prof 1. **Subjects:** Horticulture, plant taxonomy,
botanical gardens. **Holdings:** 1000 books; 30 feet of other cataloged items.
Subscriptions: 20 journals and other serials. **Services:** Library open to the
public for reference use only. **Computerized Information Services:** Internal
database; BITNET (electronic mail service). **Remarks:** FAX: (510)642-
4612. Electronic mail address(es): BOTGARD@NATURE (BITNET).
Staff: Holly Forbes, Asst.Cur.

★ 18307 ★
University of California, Berkeley - Business & Economics Library (Soc
    Sci, Bus-Fin)
30 Stephens Hall   Phone: (510)643-6471
Berkeley, CA 94720   Milt Ternberg, Hd.
Founded: 1964. **Staff:** Prof 2; Other 7. **Subjects:** Economics, business
administration, labor, public policy. **Special Collections:** Labor union
publications. **Holdings:** 117,165 volumes; 1.09 million microforms.
Subscriptions: 2747 journals and other serials. **Services:** Interlibrary loan
(through 307 General Library); copying; library open to the public, special
borrowers' card required. **Computerized Information Services:** DIALOG
Information Services, WILSONLINE, Dow Jones News/Retrieval, BRS
Information Technologies, RLIN, LEXIS, NEXIS; InterNet (electronic
mail service). Performs searches on fee basis. Contact Person: Wendy
Diamond, Assoc.Libn., 643-6471. **Publications:** Berkeley Business Guides,
annual - free upon request. **Remarks:** FAX: (510)643-7871. Electronic mail
address(es): MTERNBER@LIBRARY.BERKELEY.EDU (InterNet).
Formerly: Its Business/Social Science Library.

★ 18308 ★
University of California, Berkeley - California Public Employee
    Relations Library (Bus-Fin)
2521 Channing Way, Rm. 302
Berkeley, CA 94720   Phone: (510)643-6811
Subjects: Public employee relations in California, including public schools,
local government, special districts, safety services, state and higher
education employers and employees. **Holdings:** Research materials - Figures
not available. **Services:** library open to the public for reference use only.

★ 18309 ★
University of California, Berkeley - Center for Chinese Studies - Library
    (Area-Ethnic)
2223 Fulton St.   Phone: (510)642-6510
Berkeley, CA 94720   Chi-Ping Chen, Libn.
Founded: 1959. **Staff:** 3.5. **Subjects:** Social sciences of Peoples' Republic of
China, Chinese Communist Movement (1921 to present). **Special
Collections:** KEIO Collection (29 reels of microfilm); Hatano Collection (41
reels of microfilm); Union Research Institute Classified File on
Contemporary China, 1949-1975 (650 microfiche); Chen Cheng Collection
(20 reels of microfilm); Wen Shih Tzu Liao Collection (1000 volumes);
videotape collection of television programs from the People's Republic of
China (480 videotapes); People's University Reprint Series of selected
articles published in the People's Republic of China (social science; 50 serial
titles; 1150 microfiche). **Holdings:** 47,000 volumes; 40 drawers of microfilm;
4250 items in VF drawers; newspaper clippings. **Subscriptions:** 325 journals
and other serials; 48 newspapers. **Services:** Interlibrary loan (through 307
General Library); copying; library open to the public. **Computerized
Information Services:** RLIN; MELVYL, GLADIS (internal databases);
InterNet (electronic mail service). **Publications:** Bilingual lists of Chinese
yearbooks in major U.S. libraries; Wen Shih Tzu Liao collection; Chinese-
language newspapers at University of California and Stanford libraries; list
of materials on the June 4, 1989 Tiananmen Square Incident. **Remarks:**
FAX: (510)643-7062. Electronic mail address(es):
ccsl@library.Berkeley.edu (InterNet). **Staff:** Annie Chang, LA IV; John
Sweeney, LA III; Jeffery Kapellas, LA II.

★ 18310 ★
University of California, Berkeley - Center for Media & Independent Learning (Aud-Vis)
2176 Shattuck Ave.   Phone: (510)642-0460
Berkeley, CA 94704   Mary Beth Almeda, Dir.
Founded: 1915. **Staff:** Prof 2; Other 14. **Subjects:** Anthropology, sciences, social studies and social issues, education, arts. **Special Collections:** Documentaries; anthropology; education; ecology; ethnic studies; health and medical sciences; film studies; women. **Holdings:** 3800 films and videotapes in rental collection; 450 films and videotapes for sale. **Services:** Film rental and preview before purchase; center open to the public; rental film distribution limited to continental U.S. **Automated Operations:** Computerized cataloging and film reservation system. **Networks/Consortia:** Member of Consortium of College and University Media Centers (CCUMC). **Publications:** Brochures; newsletters; books; study guides. **Special Catalogs:** Rental catalogs; sales catalogs. **Remarks:** FAX: (510)643-8683. **Formerly:** Its Extension Media Center.

★ 18311 ★
University of California, Berkeley - Chemistry Library (Sci-Engr)
100 Hildebrand Hall   Phone: (510)642-3753
Berkeley, CA 94720   Laura Osegueda, Hd., Chem.Lib.
Founded: 1948. **Staff:** Prof 1.5; Other 5. **Subjects:** Chemistry - inorganic, organic, physical; chemical kinetics, thermodynamics, and engineering; electrochemistry; transport and mass transfer; polymer chemistry. **Special Collections:** Russian monographs and serials obtained on exchange; U.S. chemical patents (20,000). **Holdings:** 62,000 volumes; 31,300 microforms; 322 pamphlets. **Subscriptions:** 768 journals and other serials. **Services:** Interlibrary loan (through 307 General Library); copying; library open for reference use with restricted circulation. **Automated Operations:** Computerized public access catalog and circulation. **Computerized Information Services:** DIALOG Information Services, Chemical Abstracts Service (CAS); BITNET (electronic mail service). **Remarks:** FAX: (510)642-8369. Electronic mail address(es): CHEM@LIBRARY.BERKELEY.EDU (BITNET). **Staff:** Diana J. Bunting, Ref.Libn.; Patrick Duke, Circ.Supv.; David Rapp, Circ.Asst.

★ 18312 ★
University of California, Berkeley - Chicano Studies Library (Area-Ethnic)
3404 Dwinelle Hall   Phone: (510)642-3859
Berkeley, CA 94720   Lillian Castillo-Speed, Coord.
Founded: 1970. **Staff:** Prof 3; Other 6. **Subjects:** Chicano, Mexican American, Spanish speaking/surname people in U.S.; Raza; farmworkers; bilingual and biculturalgroups. **Special Collections:** Retrospective Newspaper Collection, 1844-1943; Chicano Art Color Transparencies (4000); Chicano Posters (800). **Holdings:** 5000 volumes; 150 bound periodical volumes; 4300 other cataloged items; 1500 microforms; 350 audiotapes; 10 videotapes; 5 films; 5000 slides; 20 maps; 1000 noncurrent journal titles; 150 linear feet of archives. **Subscriptions:** 400 journals and other serials; 75 newspapers. **Services:** Interlibrary loan; library open to the public. **Computerized Information Services:** Internal database; CD-ROM (Chicano Database); UNIX (electronic mail service). **Networks/Consortia:** Member of Chicano Information Management Consortium of California. **Publications:** List of publications - available on request. **Special Indexes:** Chicano Periodical Index; the Chicano Index. **Remarks:** Electronic mail address(es): chicslib@garnet.berkeley.edu (UNIX). Library located at 104 Wheeler Hall. **Staff:** Carlos Delgado, Ser.Coord.

★ 18313 ★
University of California, Berkeley - Data Archive & Technical Assistance (Soc Sci)
Survey Research Center
2538 Channing Way
Berkeley, CA 94720   Phone: (510)642-6571
Founded: 1958. **Staff:** Prof 2; Other 2. **Subjects:** Sociology, political science, psychology, survey research methods, statistics, opinion polls, U.S. Census, economics, health, vital statistics. **Special Collections:** Unpublished reports on social science, topics employing survey research methods. **Holdings:** 1000 volumes; 2000 studies on computer tapes; questionnaires, interview forms, codebooks, and data sets of past U.S. and foreign surveys; news releases of Gallup, Harris, L.A. Times, and California polls. **Subscriptions:** 40 journals and other serials. **Services:** Copying; magnetic tape reproduction and downloading to diskette of data sets from past surveys; library open to the public for reference use only. **Computerized Information Services:** BITNET (electronic mail service). **Publications:** UC DATA Research Reports. **Special Catalogs:** Catalog of available material, annual - by subscription. **Remarks:** FAX: (510)643-8292. Electronic mail address(es): CENSUS85@UCBCMSA (BITNET). **Staff:** Ilona Einowski, Data Archv.; Fred Gey, Data Archv.

★ 18314 ★
University of California, Berkeley - Earth Sciences Library (Sci-Engr)
230 Earth Sciences Bldg.   Phone: (510)642-2997
Berkeley, CA 94720   Phil Hoehn, Hd.Libn.
Founded: 1961. **Staff:** Prof 1; Other 2. **Subjects:** Geology, geophysics, seismology, physical geography, climatology, paleontology. **Holdings:** 99,000 volumes; 18,600 microforms; 2500 pamphlets; 55,000 maps. **Subscriptions:** 2600 journals and other serials. **Services:** Interlibrary loan (through 307 General Library); copying; library open for reference use with limited circulation. **Automated Operations:** Computerized public access catalog. **Computerized Information Services:** InterNet (electronic mail service). **Remarks:** Electronic mail address(es): EART@LIBRARY.BERKELEY.EDU (ITN).

★ 18315 ★
University of California, Berkeley - Earthquake Engineering Research Center Library (Sci-Engr)
1301 S. 46th St.   Phone: (510)231-9403
Richmond, CA 94804   Katherine A. Frohmberg, Info.Sys.Mgr.
Founded: 1972. **Staff:** Prof 2; Other 1. **Subjects:** Engineering - earthquake, civil, geotechnical, structural; geology; seismology; natural hazards mitigation. **Holdings:** 40,000 items including 3200 nonbook materials. **Subscriptions:** 297 journals and other serials. **Services:** Interlibrary loan; copying; faxing; SDI; library open to the public. **Automated Operations:** Computerized cataloging. **Computerized Information Services:** DIALOG Information Services, OCLC, NISEE Data Base; MELVYL (University of California On-Line Union Catalog); BITNET, InterNet (electronic mail services). Performs searches on fee basis. **Publications:** Abstract Journal in Earthquake Engineering, semiannual - by subscription; UCB/EERC reports, irregular - by subscription or single issues; Library Acquisitions Alert - free upon request; EERC News - free upon request. **Remarks:** Library materials are in English, Asian, and other Indo-European languages. Alternate telephone number(s): 231-7401. FAX: (510)231-9471. Electronic mail address(es): EERCLIB@SHAKE.EERC.BERKELEY.EDU (InterNet). **Staff:** Shirley Joy Svihra, Libn.

★ 18316 ★
University of California, Berkeley - East Asian Library (Area-Ethnic)
208 Durant Hall   Phone: (510)642-2556
Berkeley, CA 94720   Donald H. Shively, Hd.
Founded: 1947. **Staff:** Prof 7; Other 13. **Subjects:** Publications in Chinese, Japanese, Korean, Manchu, Mongolian, and Tibetan languages, primarily in the humanities and social sciences. **Special Collections:** Asami Library of Yi dynasty Korean books and manuscripts; Murakami Library of Meiji literature, 1868-1911 (7200); Chohyo-kaku and other collections of Chinese stone and bronze rubbings (2700); Japanese woodblock and lithograph maps, 17th to early 20th centuries (2403 sheets); Doi Gakken collection of Chinese poetry and prose by Japanese writers; Soshin and Motoori collections of xylographic editions of Tokugawa and early Meiji periods and the Kihon section containing publications of the 100 years prior to World War II; Rare Books Room collection devoted to pre-1795 Chinese and pre-1868 Japanese imprints. **Holdings:** 645,159 volumes; 6892 manuscripts; 14,015 microforms; 5058 prints and photographs; 520 video materials. **Subscriptions:** 4297 journals and other serials; 74 newspapers. **Services:** Interlibrary loan (through Rm. 307 Main Library); copying; library open to the public with restrictions. **Computerized Information Services:** RLIN, BITNET, InterNet (electronic mail services). **Networks/Consortia:** Member of Research Libraries Information Network (RLIN). **Special Catalogs:** Book Catalog, 1968, first supplement, 1973; Asami Library, 1969; Edo Printed Books at Berkeley, 1990. **Remarks:** FAX: (510)643-7891. Electronic mail address(es): EAL@UBLIBRA.BITNET (BITNET); EAL@LIBRARY.BERKELEY.EDU (InterNet). **Staff:** Rose Chang; Yong Kyu Choo; Christa Chow; Jean Han; Hisayuki Ishimatsu; C.P. Chen.

★ 18317 ★
University of California, Berkeley - Education/Psychology Library (Educ)
2600 Tolman Hall   Phone: (510)642-4208
Berkeley, CA 94720   Barbara Kornstein, Libn.
Founded: 1924. **Staff:** Prof 2; Other 5. **Subjects:** Education, psychology, and allied subjects. **Special Collections:** Children's and young adult collection. **Holdings:** 118,000 volumes; 297,000 microforms; ERIC microfiche. **Subscriptions:** 1842 journals and other serials. **Services:** Interlibrary loan (through 307 General Library); copying; library open to the public. **Computerized Information Services:** DIALOG Information Services, BRS Information Technologies, NLM. **Remarks:** An alternate telephone number is 642-2475. **Staff:** Sonya Kaufman, Hd., Ref.Serv.

★18318★
University of California, Berkeley - Entomology Library (Biol Sci)
Wellman Hall, Rm. 210
Berkeley, CA 94720
Phone: (510)642-2030
Nancy Axelrod, Hd.
Founded: 1943. **Staff:** 1. **Subjects:** Entomology, parasitology, helminthology, biological control, insect pathology, and allied subjects. **Holdings:** 15,000 volumes; 17,050 pamphlets and reprints; 4 sound recordings. **Subscriptions:** 350 journals and other serials. **Services:** Interlibrary loan (through 307 General Library); copying; library open to the public for reference use with restricted circulation.

★18319★
University of California, Berkeley - Environmental Design Library (Art, Plan)
210 Wurster Hall
Berkeley, CA 94720
Phone: (510)642-4818
Elizabeth Byrne, Libn.
Founded: 1905. **Staff:** Prof 2; Other 3. **Subjects:** Architecture, city and regional planning, landscape architecture. **Special Collections:** Beatrix Jones Farrand Collection (early and rare landscape architectural history). **Holdings:** 170,000 volumes; 10,000 microforms. **Subscriptions:** 1450 journals and other serials. **Services:** Interlibrary loan (through 307 Main Library); copying; library open to the public for reference use with restricted circulation. **Computerized Information Services:** DIALOG Information Services, RLIN; InterNet (electronic mail service). Performs searches on fee basis. **Remarks:** FAX: (510)643-7891. Electronic mail address(es): ENVI@LIBRARY.BERKELEY.EDU (InterNet). **Staff:** Kathryn Wayne, Arch.Libn.

★18320★
University of California, Berkeley - Executive Library (Office of the President) (Educ)
300 Lakeside Dr., 17th Fl.
Oakland, CA 94612
Phone: (510)987-9462
Rebecca G. Lhermitte
Founded: 1966. **Staff:** 1. **Subjects:** Higher education and its administration. **Holdings:** University documents. **Subscriptions:** 44 journals and other serials. **Services:** Library not open to the public. **Computerized Information Services:** DIALOG Information Services. **Remarks:** Library provides reference and advisory service to the Office of the President of the University. FAX: (510)987-0328. Electronic mail address(es): LPPLIB@UCCVMA (BITNET).

★18321★
University of California, Berkeley - Forest Products Library (Sci-Engr)
1301 S. 46th St.
Richmond, CA 94804
Phone: (510)231-9549
Founded: 1963. **Staff:** Prof 1; Other 1. **Subjects:** Wood chemistry; pulp and paper technology; adhesives; wood preservation; timber physics; identification and anatomy of wood; tree growth and development; wood seasoning; biomass energy - pyrolysis, gosification; wood machining. **Holdings:** 10,655 volumes; 4616 pamphlets; 668 microforms. **Subscriptions:** 300 journals and other serials. **Services:** Interlibrary loan (through 307 General Library); copying; library open to the public. **Computerized Information Services:** DIALOG Information Services, Conservation Information Network (CIN); GLADIS, MELVYL (internal databases); InterNet (electronic mail service). **Special Catalogs:** List of FPL staff publications, biennial. **Remarks:** FAX: (510)231-9535. Electronic mail address(es): PEVANS@LIBRARY.BERKELEY.EDU (InterNet). **Staff:** Norma Kobzina, Act.Libn., Coll. & Pub.Serv.

★18322★
University of California, Berkeley - Forestry Library (Env-Cons, Biol Sci)
260 Mulford Hall
Berkeley, CA 94720
Phone: (510)642-2936
Founded: 1948. **Staff:** 2. **Subjects:** Forestry, agroforestry, conservation, wildlife management, and related subjects. **Special Collections:** Rudy Grah Agroforestry Collection; Metcalf-Fritz Photograph Collection (6400 photographs of western forestry, 1910-1960). **Holdings:** 32,000 volumes; 85 manuscripts; 1500 maps; microforms; 8000 unbound pamphlets. **Subscriptions:** 1400 journals and other serials. **Services:** Interlibrary loan (through 307 General Library); copying; library open to the public for reference use with restricted circulation. **Automated Operations:** Computerized public access catalog. **Computerized Information Services:** DIALOG Information Services, FS INFO (Forest Service Information Network - Forestry Online); MELVYL, GLADIS (internal databases); InterNet (electronic mail service). **Remarks:** FAX: (510)643-5438. Electronic mail address(es): fore@LIBRARY.BERKELEY.EDU (InterNet). **Staff:** Beth Weil, Libn.; Norma Kobzina, Libn.

★18323★
University of California, Berkeley - Giannini Foundation of Agricultural Economics - Research Library (Agri)
248 Giannini Hall
Berkeley, CA 94720
Phone: (510)642-7121
Grace Dote, Libn.
Founded: 1930. **Staff:** Prof 1; Other 2. **Subjects:** Agriculture - economics, labor, land utilization, valuation and tenure, marketing and transportation problems, cost of production and marketing studies; agricultural economic developments in Lesser Developed Countries; water resources economics; conservation of natural resources. **Special Collections:** Federal state market news reports from most major U.S. cities, 1920-1982. **Holdings:** 19,000 volumes; 140,000 pamphlets; 3800 microforms; 140 maps. **Subscriptions:** 3000 journals and other serials. **Services:** Copying; library open to qualified researchers for reference use only. **Automated Operations:** Computerized public access catalog. **Computerized Information Services:** InterNet (electronic mail service). **Publications:** Economic research of interest to agriculture, triennial - to mailing list; Material Added to the Giannini Foundation Library, 10/year - by subscription. **Remarks:** FAX: (510)643-8911. Electronic mail address(es): DOTE@ARE.BERKELEY.EDU (InterNet).

★18324★
University of California, Berkeley - Government Documents Library (Info Sci)
General Library
Berkeley, CA 94720
Phone: (510)642-2568
Gary R. Peete, Hd.
Founded: 1938. **Staff:** Prof 6; Other 12. **Subjects:** U.S., state, and international foreign governmental affairs and politics; economics; demography; history; industry and commerce; international organizations. **Holdings:** 357,885 books; 579,444 microforms. **Subscriptions:** 20,000 journals and other serials. **Services:** Interlibrary loan (through Interlibrary Lending Division); copying; department open to the public. **Computerized Information Services:** DIALOG Information Services, BRS Information Technologies; MELVYL, GLADIS (internal databases). **Staff:** Charles Eckman, Assoc.Libn.; Andrea Sevetson, Asst.Libn.; Elizabeth Sibley, Libn.; M. Miller, Assoc.Libn.; Ken Logan, Libn.

★18325★
University of California, Berkeley - Graduate School of Journalism - Library (Info Sci)
140 North Gate Hall
Berkeley, CA 94720
Phone: (510)642-0415
David Martinez, Hd.Libn.
Founded: 1977. **Staff:** Prof 1; Other 1. **Subjects:** Print journalism, photojournalism, broadcasting. **Special Collections:** Major authors collection (225 volumes). **Holdings:** 2525 books; 500 bound periodical volumes; 480 theses; 4 VF drawers of pamphlets; unbound periodicals; newspapers. **Subscriptions:** 75 journals and other serials; 25 newspapers. **Services:** Copying; library open to the public with restrictions.

★18326★
University of California, Berkeley - Institute of Governmental Studies - Library (Soc Sci)
Moses Hall, Rm. 109
Berkeley, CA 94720
Phone: (510)642-1472
Terry Dean, Hd.Libn.
Founded: 1920. **Staff:** Prof 3; Other 7. **Subjects:** Administration, metropolitan problems, planning, finance, taxation, welfare, criminology, personnel, local government, political science. **Holdings:** 421,416 pamphlets and documents; 39,963 microforms. **Subscriptions:** 2129 journals and other serials. **Services:** Interlibrary loan; copying; library open to the public. **Automated Operations:** Computerized cataloging. **Computerized Information Services:** OCLC. **Networks/Consortia:** Member of CLASS. **Remarks:** FAX: (510)642-3020. **Staff:** Ronald Heckart, Libn.; Marc Levin, Libn.

★18327★
University of California, Berkeley - Institute of Industrial Relations - Library (Soc Sci, Bus-Fin)
2521 Channing Way, Rm. 110
Berkeley, CA 94720
Phone: (510)642-1705
Terence K. Huwe, Libn.
Founded: 1948. **Staff:** Prof 2; Other 2. **Subjects:** Industrial relations, labor, and allied social science topics. **Special Collections:** Tenth Regional War Labor Board Collection (World War II). **Holdings:** 57,000 cataloged items; 3000 uncataloged items. **Subscriptions:** 1000 journals and other serials. **Services:** Interlibrary loan; library open for reference use with restricted circulation. **Computerized Information Services:** DIALOG Information Services.

★ 18328 ★
University of California, Berkeley - Institute of International Studies Library - Carl G. Rosberg International Studies Library (Soc Sci)
340 Stephens Hall   Phone: (510)642-3633
Berkeley, CA 94720   Colette Myles, Hd.Libn.
Founded: 1921. **Staff:** Prof 1; Other 2. **Subjects:** International politics, international organizations, economic development, political and social change, area studies. **Special Collections:** Current political and economic newsletters from Latin America, Africa, and the Middle East; **Holdings:** 9900 volumes; 3200 pamphlets. **Subscriptions:** 200 journals and other serials; 5 newspapers. **Services:** Interlibrary loan; library open to the public. **Computerized Information Services:** MELVYL, GLADIS (internal databases). **Remarks:** FAX: (510)643-5045.

★ 18329 ★
University of California, Berkeley - Institute of Transportation Studies Library (Trans)
412 McLaughlin Hall   Phone: (510)642-3604
Berkeley, CA 94720   Michael Kleiber, Hd.Libn.
Founded: 1948. **Staff:** Prof 3; Other 4. **Subjects:** Transportation. **Holdings:** 137,000 volumes; 15 VF drawers of newspaper clippings; visual aids; 1500 maps; 104,000 microfiche. **Subscriptions:** 3000 journals and other serials. **Services:** Interlibrary loan; copying; library open to the public for reference use only. **Automated Operations:** Computerized cataloging. **Computerized Information Services:** DIALOG Information Services, OCLC; MELVYL, PATH (internal databases). **Publications:** Library References, irregular. **Special Indexes:** Index to 65,000 articles (card and online). **Remarks:** FAX: (510)642-1246. **Staff:** Daniel Krummes, Tech.Serv.Libn.; Catherine Cortelyou, Pub.Serv.Libn.

★ 18330 ★
University of California, Berkeley - Kresge Engineering Library (Sci-Engr, Comp Sci)
110 Bechtel Engineering Center   Phone: (510)642-3339
Berkeley, CA 94720   Camille Wanat, Hd.
Staff: Prof 2.5; Other 4. **Subjects:** Engineering - civil, mineral, mechanical, nuclear, electrical, industrial; computer science; operations research; naval architecture; materials science; mining and metallurgy. **Special Collections:** Industry standards. **Holdings:** 154,361 books; 600,000 technical reports on paper and in microform. **Subscriptions:** 2181 journals and other serials. **Services:** Interlibrary loan (through 307 Main Library); copying; library open to the public for reference use only. **Automated Operations:** Computerized cataloging, acquisitions, and circulation. **Computerized Information Services:** DIALOG Information Services, RLIN, OCLC, STN International; GLADIS, MELVYL (internal databases); InterNet (electronic mail service). Performs searches on fee basis for campus community only. Contact Person: Ann Jensen, Ref.Libn., 643-5575. **Remarks:** Electronic mail address(es): engi@library.berkeley.edu (InterNet).

★ 18331 ★
University of California, Berkeley - Law Library (Law)
230 Boalt Hall   Phone: (510)642-4044
Berkeley, CA 94720   Robert Berring, Libn.
Founded: 1907. **Staff:** Prof 16; Other 17. **Subjects:** Law - Anglo-American, foreign, international. **Special Collections:** Robbins Collection (canon and ecclesiastical law); Colby Collection (mining law); Robbins Collection (civil and medieval law). **Holdings:** 560,000 volumes; 662,000 microforms; 963 sound recordings; 175 manuscripts; 400,000 court briefs and theses. **Subscriptions:** 8253 journals and other serials. **Services:** Interlibrary loan; library open to the public for reference use only. **Computerized Information Services:** LEXIS, NEXIS, DIALOG Information Services, INNOPAC, RLIN, OCLC, WESTLAW. **Networks/Consortia:** Member of Research Libraries Information Network (RLIN). **Remarks:** The Graduate Theological Union Library works cooperatively with the Canon Law Collection. **Remarks:** FAX: (510)643-5039. **Also Known As:** Garret W. McEnerney Law Library.

University of California, Berkeley - Lawrence Berkeley Laboratory
See: **Lawrence Berkeley Laboratory** (9001)

★ 18332 ★
University of California, Berkeley - Lawrence Hall of Science - Science Education Library (Educ, Sci-Engr)
Lawrence Hall of Science
Centennial Dr.   Phone: (510)642-1334
Berkeley, CA 94720   Marian Drabkin, Libn.
Subjects: Science and mathematics teaching and education materials. **Special Collections:** Science collection for children through junior high school. **Holdings:** Tradebooks and textbooks (pre-school through 12th grade); periodicals; curriculum materials. **Subscriptions:** 70 journals and other serials. **Services:** Library open to the public for reference use only on a limited schedule; lending limited to members of Lawrence Hall of Science. **Computerized Information Services:** MELVYL, GLADIS (internal databases).

★ 18333 ★
University of California, Berkeley - Library School Library (Info Sci)
2 South Hall   Phone: (510)642-2253
Berkeley, CA 94720   Dorothy A. Koenig, Libn.
Founded: 1946. **Staff:** Prof 1; Other 2. **Subjects:** Library science and history of libraries; printing, publishing, and book trade; information storage, retrieval, policy, and services; archives and records management; bibliographical organization, theory, and methods; bibliography, history, and criticism of children's literature. **Holdings:** 49,659 volumes; 1288 microforms; 4701 pamphlets; 501 sound recordings. **Subscriptions:** 1349 journals and other serials. **Services:** Interlibrary loan (through 307 General Library); copying; library open to the public. **Computerized Information Services:** InterNet (electronic mail service). **Publications:** Selected Additions to the Library School Library, bimonthly - free. **Remarks:** Electronic mail address(es): DKOENIG@LIBRARY.BERKELEY.EDU (InterNet).

★ 18334 ★
University of California, Berkeley - Map Room (Geog-Map)
137 Library   Phone: (510)642-4940
Berkeley, CA 94720   Philip Hoehn, Libn.
Founded: 1917. **Staff:** Prof 1; Other 2. **Subjects:** Worldwide maps, national and regional atlases. **Holdings:** 4110 volumes; 300,673 maps; 51,605 aerial photographs; 536 pamphlets; 38,559 microforms. **Subscriptions:** 100 journals and other serials. **Services:** Interlibrary loan (through Interlibrary Lending Service); copying; room open to the public. **Automated Operations:** Computerized public access catalog and cataloging. **Computerized Information Services:** OCLC, RLIN; BITNET (electronic mail service). **Networks/Consortia:** Member of Research Libraries Information Network (RLIN). **Remarks:** Electronic mail address(es): MAPS@UCBLIBRA.BITNET; MAPS@LIBRARY.BERKELEY.EDU (BITNET).

★ 18335 ★
University of California, Berkeley - Music Library (Mus)
240 Morrison Hall   Phone: (510)642-2623
Berkeley, CA 94720   John H. Roberts, Hd.
Founded: 1947. **Staff:** Prof 3; Other 5. **Subjects:** History of Western music; history of opera; 18th century instrumental music; contemporary American and European music; ethnomusicology; Afro-American, Indic, Indonesian, and Japanese music; historiography of music. **Special Collections:** Connick and Romberg Opera Collections (10,000 scores); music manuscripts of the 11th-15th centuries (1200 titles); music manuscripts of the 20th century (200 titles); Chambers Campanology Collection; Cortot Opera Collection (60 collections); Cortot Opera Collection (400 scores); Italian instrumental music (1000 manuscripts); opera libretti (5000). **Holdings:** 143,000 volumes; 36,000 sound recordings; 6000 early music manuscripts; 11,500 microforms. **Subscriptions:** 1200 journals and other serials. **Services:** Interlibrary loan (through 307 Main Library); copying; library open to the public for reference use; circulation available to users with valid borrower's cards. **Automated Operations:** Computerized cataloging. **Computerized Information Services:** RLIN, DIALOG Information Services, OCLC; internal database; InterNet (electronic mail service). **Networks/Consortia:** Member of Research Libraries Information Network (RLIN). **Special Catalogs:** Duckles and Elmer Thematic Catalog of a Manuscript Collection of 18th Century Italian Instrumental Music, 1963; Catalog of the Opera Collections (UCB & UCLA), 1983; Catalog of Pre-1900 Vocal Manuscripts in the Music Library, 1988. **Remarks:** FAX: (510)643-7891. Electronic mail address(es): MUSI@LIBRARY.BERKELEY.EDU (InterNet). **Staff:** Leah Emdy; Elisabeth Aurelle; Julie Jeffrey; Elisabeth Rebman; Judy Tsou; Sophia Sinkevich; Stephen Mendoza.

★ 18336 ★

University of California, Berkeley - Native American Studies Library
(Area-Ethnic)
3415 Dwinelle Hall   Phone: (510)642-2793
Berkeley, CA 94720   Rosalie McKay, Libn.
Staff: 6. **Subjects:** Native Americans. **Special Collections:** Annual Reports of the Commissioner of Indian Affairs, 1849-1949; Survey of the Conditions of the Indians of the U.S., 1929-1944; Records of the Bureau of Indian Affairs, Record Group 75: Indian Census, 1885-1941; Harvard University Peabody Museum papers and memoirs, 1896-1957; Indian Rights Association papers, 1864-1973; Bureau of American Ethnology annual reports and bulletins; Indian Claims Commission reports; water rights; special collection on California Indians. **Holdings:** 30,000 cataloged items; 7800 monographs; dissertations on microfilm; 150 phonograph records; 200 cassettes; 67 reel-to-reel tapes; 90 videotapes; newsclipping files. **Subscriptions:** 300 Indian newsletters and journals. **Services:** Library open to the public for reference use only, circulation available for University of California students, faculty, and staff. **Remarks:** Library located at 103 Wheeler, Berkeley, CA.

★ 18337 ★

University of California, Berkeley - Newspaper/Microform Room (Rare Book)
444 Main Library   Phone: (510)642-3536
Berkeley, CA 94720   Asya Usvitsky, Hd.
Staff: 2. **Special Collections:** Rare newspapers, 1600 to present; foreign newspaper collection (Latin American, Indian, Russian); California newspaper collection (including ethnic and alternative papers). **Holdings:** 20,869 bound volumes and bundles of newsprint; 132,858 reels of microfilm; 209,021 microfiche; 210,778 microcards and microprints. **Subscriptions:** 350 newspapers. **Services:** Interlibrary loan; copying; room open to the public. **Automated Operations:** Computerized public access catalog, cataloging, and acquisitions. **Computerized Information Services:** Electronic mail. **Special Catalogs:** Geographic and chronological catalog of newspapers held by the Newspaper/Microform Room.

★ 18338 ★

University of California, Berkeley - Optometry Library (Med)
490 Minor Hall   Phone: (510)642-1020
Berkeley, CA 94720   Alison Howard, Hd.
Founded: 1949. **Staff:** Prof 1; Other 1. **Subjects:** Optometry, physiological optics, ophthalmology. **Holdings:** 8041 volumes; 668 pamphlets; 414 microforms; 251 sound recordings; 3300 slides; 120 video recordings; 30 motion pictures. **Subscriptions:** 188 journals and other serials. **Services:** Interlibrary loan (through 307 General Library); copying; library open to the public for reference use only. **Computerized Information Services:** DIALOG Information Services, BRS Information Technologies; InterNet (electronic mail service). **Publications:** Acquisition lists, monthly - to local and related libraries. **Remarks:** Electronic mail address(es): OPTO@LIBRARY.BERKELEY.EDU (InterNet).

★ 18339 ★

University of California, Berkeley - Physics Library (Sci-Engr)
Berkeley, CA 94720   Phone: (510)642-3122
                                            Diane M. Brown, Hd.
Founded: 1948. **Staff:** Prof 1; Other 2. **Subjects:** Physics and allied sciences. **Holdings:** 42,752 volumes; 1615 microforms; 358 pamphlets; 20 sound recordings; 6 computer files; 75 videocasettes. **Subscriptions:** 444 journals and other serials. **Services:** Interlibrary loan (through 307 Main Library); copying; library open to the public. **Automated Operations:** Computerized public access catalog, cataloging, and acquisitions. **Computerized Information Services:** DIALOG Information Services, STN International, BRS Information Technologies; MELVYL (internal database); InterNet (electronic mail service). Performs searches on fee basis. **Networks/Consortia:** Member of Research Libraries Information Network (RLIN). **Publications:** Acquisitions List, monthly. **Remarks:** FAX: (510)643-8497. Electronic mail address(es): PHYS@LIBRARY.BERKELEY.EDU (InterNet).

★ 18340 ★

University of California, Berkeley - Program in Population Research - Library (Soc Sci)
2234 Piedmont Ave.   Phone: (510)642-9800
Berkeley, CA 94720   Andrew Ruppenstein, Lib.Asst.
Founded: 1978. **Subjects:** Demography - historical, statistical, mathematical, ethnographic, economic. **Holdings:** 2300 volumes.

Subscriptions: 20 journals and other serials. **Services:** Library open to the public for reference use only. **Computerized Information Services:** Internal database; InterNet (electronic mail service). **Remarks:** Electronic mail address(es): DEMLIB@QAL.BERKELEY.EDU (InterNet); RUPPEN@QAL.BERKELEY.EDU (InterNet).

★ 18341 ★

University of California, Berkeley - Public Health Library (Med)
42 Earl Warren Hall   Phone: (510)642-2511
Berkeley, CA 94720   Thomas J. Alexander, Libn.
Founded: 1947. **Staff:** Prof 6; Other 6. **Subjects:** Public health, epidemiology, biostatistics, hospital administration, environmental health, maternal and child health, biomedical science (laboratory), occupational health, toxicology. **Holdings:** 80,121 volumes; 10,000 pamphlets; 1100 microforms. **Subscriptions:** 2151 journals and other serials. **Services:** Interlibrary loan (through 307 General Library); copying; library open to the public for reference use only. **Computerized Information Services:** DIALOG Information Services, BRS Information Technologies, NLM, Chemical Abstracts Service (CAS); InterNet (electronic mail service). Performs searches on fee basis for campus community only. **Remarks:** FAX: (510)642-7623. Electronic mail address(es): TALEXAND@LIBRARY.BERKELEY.EDU (InterNet). **Staff:** Patricia Stewart, Ref.Libn.; Charleen Kubota, Ref.Libn.; Mary Ann Mahoney, Ref.Libn.; Juta Savage, Ref.Libn.; Cristina Campbell, Asst.Hd.

★ 18342 ★

University of California, Berkeley - School of Public Health - Labor Occupational Health Program Library (Bus-Fin, Med)
2515 Channing Way   Phone: (510)642-5507
Berkeley, CA 94720   Donna Jarvis
Founded: 1974. **Staff:** 1. **Subjects:** Chemical and physical occupational hazards, medical and industrial hygiene, standards and regulations, workers' compensation and education. **Special Collections:** Papers and pamphlets on occupational health topics; resource center for information on the hazards of video display terminals; special files on indoor air quality; hazardous waste; workers' compensation; AIDS in the Workplace. **Holdings:** 2200 books; 180 unbound periodicals; newspaper clipping file. **Subscriptions:** 50 journals and other serials; 110 newspapers. **Services:** Copying; library open to the public for reference use only. **Publications:** Labor Occupational Health Program Monitor (newsletter), bimonthly - by subscription; list of publications - available upon written request. **Remarks:** FAX: (510)643-5698.

★ 18343 ★

University of California, Berkeley - Social Welfare Library (Soc Sci)
227 Haviland Hall   Phone: (510)642-4432
Berkeley, CA 94720   Lora L. Graham, Supv.
Founded: 1963. **Staff:** 2. **Subjects:** Social welfare. **Holdings:** 21,446 volumes. **Subscriptions:** 245 journals and other serials. **Services:** Interlibrary loan (through 307 General Library); copying; library open to the public for reference use only. **Computerized Information Services:** Social Work Abstracts Database. **Staff:** Barbara Kornstein, Libn.

★ 18344 ★

University of California, Berkeley - South/Southeast Asia Library
(Area-Ethnic)
438 Library   Phone: (510)642-3095
Berkeley, CA 94720   Kenneth R. Logan, Libn.
Founded: 1970. **Staff:** Prof 1; Other 2. **Subjects:** South and Southeast Asian countries (Afghanistan, Bangladesh, Bhutan, India, Nepal, Pakistan, Sri Lanka, Brunei, Myanmar, Indonesia, Cambodia, Laos, Malaysia, Philippines, Singapore, Thailand, and Vietnam) - social sciences, humanities. **Special Collections:** Ghadar Party Collection; Nepal Collection; Thai Collection; modern Hindi, Indonesian, and Malay literature; government publications on India and Indonesia. **Holdings:** 400,000 monographs; dissertations; microfilm; pamphlets; manuscripts; videotapes; sound recordings; maps. **Subscriptions:** 5000 journals and other serials; 50 newspapers. **Services:** Interlibrary loan; copying; library open to the public. **Automated Operations:** Computerized public access catalog, cataloging, acquisitions, and serials. **Computerized Information Services:** MELVYL, GLADIS (internal databases); InterNet (electronic mail service). **Publications:** South Asians in North America: An Annotated and Selected Bibliography; Analysis of Southeast Asian Materials at the University of California, Berkeley. **Special Catalogs:** Catalog of South Asia by language; catalog of Southeast Asian countries (card). **Remarks:** FAX: (510)643-7891. Telex: 910 3667114 UC BERK BERK. Electronic mail address(es): SSEA@LIBRARY.BERKELEY.EDU (InterNet).

★ 18345 ★
University of California, Berkeley - University Extension - Continuing Education of the Bar - Library (Law)
2300 Shattuck Ave.   Phone: (510)642-5343
Berkeley, CA 94704   Virginia Polak, Libn.
Founded: 1960. **Staff:** Prof 1; Other 2. **Subjects:** Law. **Holdings:** 8000 volumes. **Subscriptions:** 221 journals and other serials; 7 newspapers. **Services:** Interlibrary loan; library; not open to the public. **Computerized Information Services:** WESTLAW, LEXIS. **Publications:** Recent Acquisitions, bimonthly - for internal distribution only. **Remarks:** FAX: (415)642-3788.

★ 18346 ★
University of California, Berkeley - University Herbarium - Library (Biol Sci)
6701 San Pablo Ave.
Oakland, CA 94608   Phone: (510)642-2465
Subjects: Botany. **Special Collections:** History of the University Herbarium, 1870s to present (field books kept by collectors; correspondence; transactions information; photographs of persons and events related to the Herbarium). **Holdings:** 100 linear feet of archival materials. **Services:** Copying; library open to the public during business hours. **Remarks:** FAX: (510)643-5390.

★ 18347 ★
University of California, Berkeley - Virus Laboratory - Library (Biol Sci)
229 Stanley Hall
Berkeley, CA 94720   Phone: (510)642-1722
Subjects: Virology - molecular, cell; virus laboratory science. **Holdings:** Figures not available. **Subscriptions:** 60 journals and other serials. **Services:** Library not open to the public. **Remarks:** FAX: (510)643-9290.

★ 18348 ★
University of California, Berkeley - Water Resources Center Archives (Env-Cons)
410 O'Brien Hall   Phone: (510)642-2666
Berkeley, CA 94720   Gerald J. Giefer, Libn.
Founded: 1956. **Staff:** Prof 1; Other 3. **Subjects:** Water as a natural resource, water resources development and management, municipal and industrial water uses and problems, reclamation and irrigation, flood control, waste disposal, coastal engineering, water quality, water law. **Special Collections:** Ocean engineering (20,000 pieces); manuscript collection of papers of men prominent in western water development (4290). **Holdings:** 112,602 volumes; 5201 maps; 1085 microforms; 8322 manuscripts. **Subscriptions:** 1830 journals and other serials. **Services:** Interlibrary loan; copying; archives open to the public. **Automated Operations:** Computerized cataloging. **Computerized Information Services:** OCLC; CD-ROMs (selected water resources abstracts). Performs searches on fee basis. **Publications:** Selected Recent Accessions, bimonthly; Archives series (monographs), irregular; list of other publications - available upon request. **Remarks:** FAX: (510)642-9143.

★ 18349 ★
University of California, Davis - Agricultural Economics Branch Library (Agri)
Voorhies Hall   Phone: (916)752-1540
Davis, CA 95616   Susan Casement, Libn.
Founded: 1951. **Staff:** Prof 1; Other 1.5. **Subjects:** Agricultural economics; agricultural business; land, resource, and consumer economics; international agriculture. **Holdings:** 7664 volumes; 259,538 pamphlets. **Subscriptions:** 888 journals and other serials. **Services:** Copying; library open to the public for reference use only. **Automated Operations:** Computerized public access catalog. **Computerized Information Services:** InterNet, BITNET (electronic mail services). **Remarks:** FAX: (916)752-8572. Electronic mail address(es): SDCASEMENT@UCDAVIS.UCDAVIS.EDU (InterNet).

★ 18350 ★
University of California, Davis - Arboretum - Library (Biol Sci)
Davis, CA 95616   Phone: (916)752-2498
                                          Judy Schneider
Founded: 1975. **Staff:** Prof 1; Other 2. **Subjects:** Botany, horticulture, gardening. **Special Collections:** California native plants; Indian uses of native plants. **Holdings:** 1000 books; 20 bound periodical volumes; unbound periodicals; vertical files. **Subscriptions:** 14 journals and other serials. **Services:** Library open to the public for reference use only.

★ 18351 ★
University of California, Davis - Environmental Toxicology Department - Toxicology Documentation Center (Env-Cons)
Davis, CA 95616-8588   Phone: (916)752-2587
                                          Dr. Ming-Yu Li, Doc.Spec.
Founded: 1966. **Staff:** Prof 1; Other 2. **Subjects:** Pesticides, environmental pollutants, toxic metals, PCBs, air and water pollutants, food additives and toxicants, hazardous wastes management. **Special Collections:** Pesticide chemical and subject files. **Holdings:** 5000 books; 3500 bound periodical volumes; 65,000 classified abstract cards; 36,000 items on pesticides in VF drawers; 41,000 items in subject files on environmental pollutants, toxic metals and elements, hazardous substances, and waste management. **Subscriptions:** 100 journals and other serials. **Services:** Center open to the public for reference use only with special permission. **Computerized Information Services:** NLM, DIALOG Information Services, STN International; MELVYL, Pesticide Data Bank (internal databases).

★ 18352 ★
University of California, Davis - Institute of Governmental Affairs - Library (Soc Sci, Plan)
Davis, CA 95616-8617   Phone: (916)752-2045
                                          Jean Stratford, Hd.Libn.
Founded: 1962. **Staff:** Prof 2. **Subjects:** Macroeconomics; public policy; East Asian business and economics; demographics; state and local government; taxation; farm labor; agricultural policy; the Johnson presidency and the Vietnam War; politics; election statistics. **Special Collections:** East Asian Business and Development Research Archive; Presidential Studies Archive. **Holdings:** 16,927 volumes; 4862 pamphlets; 17 manuscript units. **Subscriptions:** 661 journals and other serials. **Services:** Interlibrary loan; library open to researchers, students, and public. **Automated Operations:** Computerized cataloging and circulation. **Computerized Information Services:** DIALOG Information Services, ASIA Online, LEXIS, NEXIS, BITNET (electronic mail service). **Publications:** Ex Libris (newsletter). **Remarks:** FAX: (916)752-2835. Electronic mail address(es): JSSTRATFORD@UCDAVIS; SMMACKAY@UCDAVIS (BITNET). **Staff:** Shelagh M. MacKay.

★ 18353 ★
University of California, Davis - Loren D. Carlson Health Sciences Library (Med)
Davis, CA 95616   Phone: (916)752-1214
                                          Jo Anne Boorkman, Hd.Libn.
Founded: 1966. **Staff:** Prof 7; Other 24. **Subjects:** Medicine, veterinary medicine, primatology. **Special Collections:** Veterinary historical collection. **Holdings:** 55,917 books; 167,750 bound periodical volumes; 13,642 microforms; 430 AV programs. **Subscriptions:** 3854 journals and other serials. **Services:** Interlibrary loan; copying; SDI; library open to the public - fee card required for borrowing. **Automated Operations:** Computerized cataloging, acquisitions, serials, and circulation. **Computerized Information Services:** NLM, BRS Information Technologies, DIALOG Information Services, OCLC; InterNet (electronic mail service). Performs searches on fee basis. **Networks/Consortia:** Member of National Network of Libraries of Medicine - Pacific Southwest Region. **Publications:** HSL News, irregular - to library clientele. **Remarks:** FAX: (916)752-4718. Electronic mail address(es): JABOURKMAN@CDAVIS.EDU (InterNet). **Staff:** Carolyn Kopper, Hd.Ref.Serv.; Rebecca Davis, Coord. Online Serv.; Judy Welsh, Ref.Libn.; Karleen Darr, Hd., Tech.Serv.; Judith Levitt, Hd., Coll.Dev.; Kenneth Firestein, Data Serv.Libn.

★ 18354 ★
University of California, Davis - Medical Center Library (Med)
4301 X St., Rm. 1005   Phone: (916)734-3529
Sacramento, CA 95817   Terri L. Malmgren, Hd.Libn.
Founded: 1970. **Staff:** Prof 2; Other 5. **Subjects:** Medicine, nursing, and allied health sciences. **Holdings:** 8772 books; 14,423 bound periodical volumes; 2565 AV programs 3883 microforms. **Subscriptions:** 767 journals and other serials. **Services:** Copying; library open to the public for reference use only. **Computerized Information Services:** MEDLINE, DIALOG Information Services; InterNet, BITNET (electronic mail services). **Networks/Consortia:** Member of Mountain Valley Library System, National Network of Libraries of Medicine - Pacific Southwest Region, Sacramento Area Health Sciences Librarians (SAHSL). **Publications:** Monthly Newsletter/Acquisitions List - for internal distribution only. **Remarks:** FAX: (916)734-7418. Electronic mail address(es): MCLILL@UCDAVIS.EDU (InterNet); MCLILL@UCDAVIS (BITNET). **Staff:** Kathleen O. Rainey, Ref./Educ.Serv.Libn.

★ 18355 ★
University of California, Davis - Michael and Margaret B. Harrison Western Research Center (Hist)
Department of Special Collections
Shields Library   Phone: (916)752-1621
Davis, CA 95616   Michael Harrison, Dir.
Founded: 1981. **Staff:** Prof 1. **Subjects:** History and development of the trans-Mississippi West, mid-19th century to present; American Indians; ethnic studies; military, local, and economic history; sociology; folklore; exploration and travel; geography; religious studies, especially the Catholic and Mormon churches; literature; art and architecture; history of printing. **Special Collections:** Books from Western fine presses; correspondence with 20th century artists, writers, and enthusiasts of the American West; original works of art. **Holdings:** 18,995 volumes. **Subscriptions:** 107 journals and other serials. **Services:** Center open to the public by appointment only.

★ 18356 ★
University of California, Davis - Physical Sciences Library (Sci-Engr)
University Library   Phone: (916)752-0459
Davis, CA 95616   Marlene Tebo, Hd.Libn.
Founded: 1971. **Staff:** Prof 4; Other 13. **Subjects:** Chemistry, engineering, geology, mathematics, physics, statistics. **Special Collections:** Depository for DOE documents and selected NASA documents. **Holdings:** 129,378 books; 135,472 bound periodical volumes; 1 million DOE and NASA microforms and Nuclear Regulatory Commission dockets; 10,948 maps; 116,437 additional microforms; 33,146 research reports; 1937 vertical files. **Subscriptions:** 5173 journals and other serials. **Services:** Interlibrary loan; copying; library open to the public. **Automated Operations:** Computerized public access catalog, cataloging, and circulation. **Computerized Information Services:** DIALOG Information Services, STN International. **Networks/Consortia:** Member of Center for Research Libraries (CRL). **Remarks:** FAX: (916)752-4719. **Staff:** Johanna Ross, Libn.; John Ward, Libn.; Carol LaRussa, Libn.; Ann Preston, Staff Supv.

★ 18357 ★
University of California, Davis - School of Law - Law Library (Law)
Davis, CA 95616   Phone: (916)752-3327
                                                  Judy Janes, Act. Law Libn.
Founded: 1963. **Staff:** Prof 5; Other 13. **Subjects:** Law - U.S., California, international, comparative, and foreign; common law countries. **Special Collections:** Depository for federal and California documents. **Holdings:** 247,407 volumes; 77,873 volumes in microform. **Subscriptions:** 6345 journals and other serials. **Services:** Interlibrary loan; copying; library open to the public. **Automated Operations:** Computerized public access catalog. **Computerized Information Services:** LEXIS, RLIN, WESTLAW; MELVYL (internal database); electronic mail. **Remarks:** FAX: (916)752-8766.

★ 18358 ★
University of California, Davis - University Libraries - Special Collections (Agri, Biol Sci, Hum)
Davis, CA 95616   Phone: (916)752-1621
                                                  John Skarstad, Act.Hd., Spec.Coll.
Founded: 1966. **Staff:** 5.65. **Special Collections:** Rare books - agriculture, American literature (18th, 19th, and 20th centuries), avant garde poetry, botany, English history, literature and religion (16th- 20th centuries), fine printing (1000 volumes), minor British poets (1789-1979, 15,000 volumes), performing arts, pomology, viticulture and enology; manuscripts - agricultural technology (18 collections, 1000.8 linear feet), agriculture (23 collections, 61.4 linear feet), animal science (12 collections, 62.8 linear feet), apiculture (11 collections, 42.2 linear feet), art and architecture (19 collections, 82.6 linear feet), California history (21 collections, 295.7 linear feet), entomology (12 collections, 52 linear feet), food processing and technology (12 collections, 2823 linear feet), language and literature (50 collections, 335.2 linear feet), natural resources (6 collections, 104 linear feet), performing arts (74 collections, 549.55 linear feet), plant science (17 collection, 294.6 linear feet), political science (18 collections, 273.4 linear feet), United States history (10 collections, 190.6 linear feet), viticulture and enology (25 collections, 397.8 linear feet); University Archives (2605.3 linear feet). **Services:** Copying; collections open to the public for reference use only. **Automated Operations:** Computerized cataloging. **Computerized Information Services:** MELVYL (internal database). **Publications:** Guide to Manuscript Collections; Toby Cole Archives Finding Aid. **Special Indexes:** F. Hal Higgins Collection Index (2 volumes); Agricultural Technology Manuals Index (2 volumes). **Remarks:** FAX: (916)752-3148. **Staff:** Axel Borg, Viticulture & Enology Bibliog.

★ 18359 ★
University of California, Davis - Women's Resources & Research Center - Library (Soc Sci)
10 Lower Freeborn Hall   Phone: (916)752-3373
Davis, CA 95616   Joy Fergoda, Libn.
Founded: 1975. **Staff:** 1. **Subjects:** Women's issues, concerns, and research. **Special Collections:** Native and Pioneer Women in Yolo and Solano Counties, California (oral history collection; 28 tapes; 2 photograph albums). **Holdings:** 4500 books; 7500 vertical file materials; 650 audiotapes. **Subscriptions:** 130 journals and other serials; 14 newspapers. **Services:** Copying; library open to the public for reference use only.

★ 18360 ★
University of California, Irvine - Biological Sciences Library (Biol Sci)
Irvine, CA 92717   Phone: (714)856-6730
                                                  Margaret Aguirre, Lib.Asst. IV
Founded: 1967. **Staff:** 7. **Subjects:** Biological sciences. **Holdings:** 20,000 volumes. **Subscriptions:** 800 journals and other serials. **Services:** Interlibrary loan; copying; library open to the public with restrictions. **Automated Operations:** Computerized serials. **Remarks:** A branch of the Biomedical Library. An alternate telephone number is 856-7515.

★ 18361 ★
University of California, Irvine - Biomedical Library (Med)
Box 19556   Phone: (714)856-6652
Irvine, CA 92713   J. Michael Homan, Asst.Univ.Libn. for the Sci.
Founded: 1969. **Staff:** Prof 5; Other 11. **Subjects:** Medicine. **Holdings:** 156,000 volumes; 5635 audio cassettes; 1245 microfiche; pamphlet file. **Subscriptions:** 2555 journals and other serials. **Services:** Interlibrary loan; copying; SDI; library open to the public. **Automated Operations:** Computerized cataloging, acquisitions, serials, and circulation. **Computerized Information Services:** BRS Information Technologies, BRS Information Technologies, DIALOG Information Services; Performs searches on fee basis. **Networks/Consortia:** Member of National Network of Libraries of Medicine - Pacific Southwest Region. **Remarks:** FAX: (714)856-7909. **Staff:** Rochelle Minchow, Hd.Pub.Serv.; Judith Bube, Hd., Acq./Ser.; Stephen Clancy, Ref.Libn.; Barbara Lucas, Ref.Libn.; Kathryn Pudlock, Ref.Libn.

★ 18362 ★
University of California, Irvine - Institute of Transportation Studies - Information Center
330 Berkeley Pl.
Irvine, CA 92717
Subjects: Urban transportation. **Holdings:** 10,000 books and reports; 800 bound periodical volumes; 6700 NTIS technical reports on microfiche; 600 dissertations. **Subscriptions:** 55 journals and other serials. **Services:** Interlibrary loan; SDI; center open to the public. **Remarks:** Currently inactive.

★ 18363 ★
University of California, Irvine - Medical Center Library (Med)
Rt. 82
101 City Dr., S., Bldg. 22A   Phone: (714)634-5585
Orange, CA 92668   Susan Russell, Hd.Libn.
Staff: Prof 2; Other 5. **Subjects:** Clinical medicine. **Holdings:** 28,000 volumes; 4 VF drawers; 10 filmstrips; 100 slide and cassette programs; 130 videotapes; 200 software diskettes. **Subscriptions:** 825 journals and other serials. **Services:** Interlibrary loan; copying; SDI; library open to the public. **Automated Operations:** Computerized serials and circulation. **Computerized Information Services:** DIALOG Information Services, PFDS Online, BRS Information Technologies, MEDLINE. **Remarks:** The Medical Center Library is a branch of the Biomedical Library.

★ 18364 ★
University of California, Irvine - University Library - Department of Special Collections (Hum, Hist)
Box 19557   Phone: (714)856-7227
Irvine, CA 92713   Sylvester E. Klinicke, Act.Hd., Spec.Coll.
Founded: 1965. **Staff:** Prof 4; Other 1. **Subjects:** Californiana, dance, literary criticism and theory, 16th-18th century French literature, British naval history, orchids, book illustration. **Special Collections:** Meadows Collection of California history (5000 volumes); Menninger Collection in Horticulture

(1800 volumes); Rene Wellek Collection of the History of Criticism (4500 volumes); Hans Waldmuller Thomas Mann Collection (2000 volumes); contemporary small press poetry collection (6000 titles); 20th century political pamphlets (2500 titles); books and manuscripts of Ross Macdonald, Kathleen Raine, and Alfonso Sastre. **Holdings:** 53,000 books; 1500 bound periodical volumes; 200,000 manuscripts; 300 maps; 12,000 photographs. **Subscriptions:** 25 journals and other serials. **Services:** Department open to qualified researchers. **Automated Operations:** Computerized public access catalog and cataloging (MELVYL). **Computerized Information Services:** ANTPAC (internal database); electronic mail. **Publications:** Centennial Bibliography of Orange County California (1989). FAX: (714)725-2472. **Staff:** Eddie Yeghiayan, Cur., Lit. Theory/Criticism Colls.; Sharon G. Pugsley, Reg.Hist.Mss.Libn.; Irene Wechselberg, Mss.Libn.

★ 18365 ★
University of California, Los Angeles - American Indian Studies Center -
  Library (Area-Ethnic)
3220 Campbell Hall   Phone: (213)825-7315
Los Angeles, CA 90024-1548   Velma S. Salabiye, Libn.
Founded: 1971. **Staff:** Prof 1; Other 1. **Subjects:** American Indians - government relations, history, literature, art, language; Indians in California; works of Indian authorship. **Special Collections:** Dissertations and theses by and about American Indians; Indian newspapers and journals. **Holdings:** 6500 volumes; 4805 pamphlets. **Subscriptions:** 90 serials. **Services:** Copying; library open to the public with restrictions. **Computerized Information Services:** ORION (internal database). **Remarks:** FAX: (213)206-7060.

★ 18366 ★
University of California, Los Angeles - Architecture & Urban Planning
  Library
1302 Perloff Hall
Los Angeles, CA 90024-1467
Defunct. Merged with University of California, Los Angeles - Theater Arts Library, Art Library, and Elmer Belt Library of Vinciana to form University of California, Los Angeles - Arts, Architecture and Urban Planning Library.

★ 18367 ★
University of California, Los Angeles - Archive of Popular American
  Music (Mus)
1102 Schoenberg Hall
405 Hilgard Ave.   Phone: (213)825-1665
Los Angeles, CA 90024-1490   Victor Cardell, Hd.Libn.
Founded: 1965. **Staff:** Prof 1; Other 1. **Subjects:** American popular music, 1820 to present, including theater, motion picture, and radio and television music. **Holdings:** 12,000 volumes; 900 serial titles; 566 manuscripts; 550 method books; 27,000 orchestrations; 335,374 sheet music imprints; 8000 scores; 334 cylinders; 50,000 phonograph records; 47,146 audio discs; 1247 audiocassettes; 600 audio reels; 882 compact discs; 78 reels of microfilm; 18 microfiche. **Subscriptions:** 5 journals and other serials. **Services:** Copying (limited); archive open to the public by appointment for reference use only. **Computerized Information Services:** BITNET (electronic mail service). **Special Indexes:** Sheet music index; sound recordings index (both incomplete). **Remarks:** Access presently limited to cataloged materials. Electronic mail address(es): ECZ5POP@UCLAMVS (BITNET).

★ 18368 ★
University of California, Los Angeles - Art Library
2250 Dickson Art Center
Los Angeles, CA 90024-1392
Defunct. Merged with University of California, Los Angeles - Architecture & Urban Planning Library, Theater Arts Library, and Elmer Belt Library of Vinciana to form University of California - Arts, Architecture and Urban Planning Library.

★ 18369 ★
University of California, Los Angeles - Art Library - Elmer Belt Library
  of Vinciana
Dickson Art Center
Los Angeles, CA 90024-1392
Defunct. Merged with University of California, Los Angeles - Architecture & Urban Planning Library, Art Library, and Theater Arts Library to form University of California, Los Angeles - Arts, Architecture and Urban Planning Library.

★ 18370 ★
University of California, Los Angeles - Arts, Architecture and Urban
  Planning Library (Theater, Art, Plan)
2250 Dickson Art Center   Phone: (310)825-3817
Los Angeles, CA 90024   Anne Hartmere, Hd.Libn.
Subjects: Theater, film, television, radio, art, art and architectural history, design, photography, Italian Renaissance, Leonardo da Vinci, Renaissance technology, art theory, architecture, urban planning. **Special Collections:** Twentieth Century-Fox Film Corporation Archive (motion picture scripts, legal files, stills, 1915 to present; production files, 1952-1982; television scripts and stills, 1960s-1980s); Columbia Pictures Corporation (motion picture stills, 1950s-1980s); Paramount Pictures Corporation (black-and-white keysets for 645 motion picure productions, 1920s-1940s); RKO Archive (1929-1956; scripts, music files, story submission files, production information files); Metro-Goldwyn-Meyer, Inc. (architectural set plans for motion picture productions, 1917-1950; collection of screenplays, 1924-1960); professional papers and archives of writers, producers, directors, actors, and production companies, including Waldo Salt, Jean Renoir, Michael Wilson, Emmet Lavery, Mark Robson, Herbert Leonard (Naked City), Stirling Silliphant, Jack Webb, Larry Gelbart, Bruce Geller, Arthur Rowe (Fantasy Island), Gene Roddenberry (Star Trek), Smothers Brothers, Charlton Heston, William Wyler, Don Fedderson, Allan Joslyn, Tony Barrett, Gene Reynolds, Dan Curtis (Dark Shadows), Irwin Allen, Arnold Rosen (Carol Burnett Show), and Burt Metcalf (MASH); Alcoa Presents Collection; Hallmark Hall of Fame (radio and television scripts, 1951-1984); Home Box Office; Hollywood Television Theater; Terrence O'Flaherty Collection (history of television, 1952-1986; program and network presskits and publicity photographs); Walter Lantz Animation Archive; Film Poster Collection (1915 to present, 2500 titles, including Swedish and Polish items); Lobby Card Collection (1920s to present, 5000 titles); Judith A. Hoffberg Collection of Bookworks and Artists' Publications (3000 volumes); Archives of Dr. Elmer Belt and Kate Trauman Steinitz; graphics collection. **Holdings:** 177,000 volumes; 60,065 manuscripts; 3.5 million production stills and portrait shots (1905 to present); 15,000 screenplays and scripts for teleplays; scripts of 55 radio programs and 600 television series; 45,000 slides; 102,000 clippings; 2500 motion picture programs and presskits; 251,931 pamphlets; 533,276 pictorial items; 16,541 microfiche; 779 reels of microfilm; 166 VF drawers of uncataloged serials, clippings, museum catalogs, one-person exhibition catalogs, and announcements; 500 unbound and bound periodical volumes; 8 VF drawers of pamphlets and clippings; 22 file boxes of clippings; 19 file boxes of articles arranged by author; 30 file boxes of magazines; 4 sound recordings; documents. **Subscriptions:** 2235 journals and other serials. **Services:** Interlibrary loan; copying; library open to the public. **Automated Operations:** Computerized cataloging, acquisitions, and serials (MELVYL). **Computerized Information Services:** DIALOG Information Services, BRS Information Technologies. **Publications:** Leonardo Bibliography. **Special Catalogs:** Motion Pictures: A Catalog of Books, Periodicals, Screen Plays, and Productions, 1 volume, 1976. **Special Indexes:** Princeton Index of Christian Art; Decimal Index to the Art of the Low Countries (DIAL); Index of Jewish Art; Marburger Index. **Formed by the merger of:** University of California, Los Angeles Art Library, Architecture and Urban Planning Library, Elmer Belt Library of Vinciana, and Theater Arts Library. **Staff:** Raymond Soto, Theatre Arts Libn.; Brigitte Kueppers, Spec.Coll.Libn.; Raymond Reece, Art Libn. .

★ 18371 ★
University of California, Los Angeles - Asian American Studies Center
  Reading Room (Area-Ethnic)
3230 Campbell Hall   Phone: (213)825-5043
Los Angeles, CA 90024-1546   Marjorie Lee, Coord.
Staff: 3. **Subjects:** Asian American studies. **Holdings:** 4000 volumes; 450 slides; 8 multimedia kits; 150 sound recordings; 2 filmstrips; 10 maps; 160 manuscripts; 3000 pamphlets; 60 government documents; 5 video recordings. **Subscriptions:** 30 journals and other serials; 25 newspapers. **Services:** Room open to the public. **Publications:** Asian American Library Resources at University of California, Los Angeles - available upon request.

★ 18372 ★
University of California, Los Angeles - Brain Information Service (Med)
Center for Health Sciences, No. 43-367   Phone: (213)825-3417
Los Angeles, CA 90024   Michael H. Chase, Dir.
Founded: 1964. **Staff:** Prof 1. **Subjects:** Neurosciences, alcohol and driving, sleep. **Holdings:** Figures not available. **Services:** Service open to researchers. **Publications:** Sleep Research, annual; Alcohol, Drugs and Driving, quarterly. **Remarks:** FAX: (213)206-3499.

University of California, Los Angeles - Center for 17th and 18th Century Studies
See: University of California, Los Angeles - William Andrews Clark Memorial Library (18402)

★ 18373 ★
University of California, Los Angeles - Center for Afro-American Studies - Library (Area-Ethnic)
1232 Campbell Hall
405 Hilgard Ave.   Phone: (213)825-6060
Los Angeles, CA 90024-1545   Gladys Lindsay, Lib.Hd.
Founded: 1969. **Staff:** Prof 1; Other 4. **Subjects:** Afro-American studies. **Special Collections:** Black history photograph collection (250 items). **Holdings:** 5265 volumes; 540 35mm slides; 283 photographs; 78 videotapes; 410 audiotapes; 2350 pamphlets; 34 audio reels; 35 monographs. **Subscriptions:** 62 journals and other serials; 19 newspapers. **Services:** Copying; library open to the public. **Publications:** Afro-American Library Resources at UCLA, 1980; Graduate Research in Afro-American Studies, 1942-1980. **Remarks:** FAX: (213)206-3421.

★ 18374 ★
University of California, Los Angeles - Center for Finance and Real Estate - Real Estate Research Library (Bus-Fin)
AGSM, Rm. 2292   Phone: (213)825-3977
Los Angeles, CA 90024-1481   Kathleen Connell, Dir.
Founded: 1987. **Staff:** Prof 2; Other 2. **Subjects:** Transportation, housing and real estate, land use, environment, planning, urban sociology. **Special Collections:** Reprints; journals; articles; Council of Planning Libraries bibliographies, 1-176; Housing and Urban Development (Miscellaneous reports). **Holdings:** 3450 books; 30,500 pamphlets; 41 maps; 6000 government pamphlets and census materials; clippings; 1 volume of bound newspapers. **Subscriptions:** 178 journals and other serials. **Services:** Interlibrary loan; copying; center open to the public on a limited schedule. **Computerized Information Services:** Framework (internal database). **Remarks:** Contains the holdings of the former University of California, Los Angeles - Housing Real Estate & Urban Land Studies Program Collection. **Remarks:** FAX: (213)825-0822.

★ 18375 ★
University of California, Los Angeles - Chemistry Library (Sci-Engr)
4238 Young Hall   Phone: (213)825-3342
Los Angeles, CA 90024-1569   Marion C. Peters, Hd.Libn.
Founded: 1947. **Staff:** Prof 1; Other 2. **Subjects:** Chemistry - organic, inorganic, analytical, physical; biochemistry. **Special Collections:** Morgan Memorial Collection (history of chemistry). **Holdings:** 64,493 volumes; 1196 reels of microfilm; 13,363 microfiche; 1144 microcards; U.S. chemical patents, 1952 to present, in microform. **Subscriptions:** 736 journals and other serials. **Services:** Interlibrary loan; copying; SDI; library open to the public. **Automated Operations:** Computerized circulation, cataloging, acquisitions, and serials. **Computerized Information Services:** DIALOG Information Services, BRS Information Technologies, Chemical Abstracts Service (CAS), Institute for Scientific Information (ISI); ORION, MELVYL (internal databases); BITNET (electronic mail service). Performs searches on fee basis. **Remarks:** Electronic mail address(es): ECZ5CHM@UCLAMVS (BITNET).

★ 18376 ★
University of California, Los Angeles - Chicano Studies Research Library (Area-Ethnic)
1112 Campbell Hall
405 Hilgard Ave.   Phone: (213)206-6052
Los Angeles, CA 90024-1380   Richard Chabran, Chicano Stud.Libn.
Founded: 1969. **Staff:** Prof 1; Other 2. **Subjects:** Immigration, labor, higher education, school desegregation, Raza women, Chicano literature, U.S.-Mexico relations. **Special Collections:** Ron Lopez papers; Latino Community Development Archive; Casa Collection; Mexico-U.S. Relations Archive; Magdalena Mora Archive; Jose Ortiz papers; Grace Montanes Davis Papers. **Holdings:** 9900 books; 200 bound periodical volumes; 1100 manuscripts; 1680 theses and dissertations; 90 16mm films and videotapes; 5100 clippings and pamphlets; 100 student papers; 658 reels of microfilm; 136 posters; 3 multimedia kits; 319 pictorial items; 333 sound recordings; 140 cassettes; 120 audiotapes; 8 filmstrips; 800 volumes of newspapers; 22 realia; 30 maps; 335 slides. **Subscriptions:** 82 journals and other serials; 30 newspapers. **Services:** Interlibrary loan; copying; library open to the public for reference use only. **Automated Operations:** Computerized public access catalog and cataloging. **Computerized Information Services:** ORION (internal database). **Publications:** Aztlan; monographs; working papers; policy papers. **Remarks:** FAX: (213)206-1784.

★ 18377 ★
University of California, Los Angeles - Computer Science Department - Archives (Comp Sci)
3440 Boelter Hall   Phone: (213)825-4317
Los Angeles, CA 90024-1596   Sharon Marcus, Libn.
Founded: 1973. **Staff:** Prof 1. **Subjects:** Computer science. **Special Collections:** Institute of Electrical and Electronics Engineers Repository Collection. **Holdings:** 3000 books; 181 bound periodical volumes; 10,000 technical reports; 3000 dissertations, theses, and microfiche. **Subscriptions:** 150 journals. **Services:** Interlibrary loan; archives not open to the public. **Automated Operations:** Computerized circulation. **Remarks:** FAX: (213)825-2273.

★ 18378 ★
University of California, Los Angeles - Department of Art History - Visual Resource Collection & Services (Art)
3239 Dickson Art Center
405 Hilgard Ave.   Phone: (213)825-3725
Los Angeles, CA 90024   David K. Ziegler, Sr.Musm.Sci.
Founded: 1958. **Staff:** Prof 3; Other 7. **Subjects:** Painting, sculpture, applied art, and architecture - European, Islamic, Japanese, Indian, American, Chinese, African; Pre-Columbian, Oceanic, and American Indian art; contemporary art forms. **Special Collections:** The Burton Holmes Collection (hand-tinted lantern slides, 1886-1937; 19,000) **Holdings:** 260,000 slides. **Services:** Collection not open to the public. **Automated Operations:** Computerized cataloging and acquisitions. **Computerized Information Services:** Internal database. **Special Indexes:** Artists and architects index to slide collection and manuscript index by title and location (both punched cards). **Staff:** Susan Rosenfeld, Asst. Slide Cur.; Marth Godfrey, Asst. Slide Cur.

★ 18379 ★
University of California, Los Angeles - Department of Special Collections (Hist, Hum)
University Research Library, Fl. A   Phone: (213)825-4988
Los Angeles, CA 90024-1575   David Zeidberg, Hd.Libn.
Founded: 1946. **Staff:** Prof 6; Other 16. **Subjects:** Californiana; motion pictures; radio; television; dance; blacks in entertainment and literature; Japanese in America; history of photography; folklore, including broadside ballads, songsters, hymnals, American almanacs; university archives; popular culture, including pulp magazines and comic books. **Special Collections:** Michael Sadleir Collection of 19th century English fiction; Ahmanson-Murphy Collections of Aldines and Early Italian Printing; Sir Maurice Holmes Collection of Captain Cook; English and American auction catalogs; early children's books; Bodoni imprints; Spinoza Collection; 1500 manuscript collections, including papers of William Starke Rosecrans, Franz Werfel, Henry Stevens, John Houseman, Ralph Bunche; oral history interviews; Near Eastern manuscripts (Arabic, Turkish, Persian, Armenian); books and manuscripts of Henry Miller, Norman Douglas, Aldous Huxley, Edward Gordon Craig, Gertrude Stein, Maria Edgeworth, Raymond Chandler. **Holdings:** 182,555 volumes; 19.7 million manuscripts; 632 volumes of newspapers; 238,409 pieces of ephemera and clippings; 46,730 pamphlets; 673,225 pictorial items; 2188 historical maps; 12,684 reels of microfilm; 205 sound recordings; 4719 slides; 3028 videotapes. **Subscriptions:** 339 journals and other serials. **Services:** Copying (limited); department open to the public for reference use only. **Automated Operations:** Computerized cataloging, acquisitions, serials, and circulation. **Computerized Information Services:** OCLC; ORION (internal database); BITNET (electronic mail service). Performs searches free of charge. **Publications:** Bibliographies of Henry Miller, Kenneth Rexroth, and Lawrence Durrell. **Remarks:** Alternate telephone number(s): 825-4879. FAX: (213)206-1864. Electronic mail address(es): ECZ5DAV@UCLAMVS (BITNET). **Staff:** James Davis, Rare Bks.Libn.; Anne Caiger, Mss.Libn.; Charlotte Brown, Univ.Archv./Asst.Hd.; Dale Treleven, Dir., Oral Hist.Prog.; Paul Naiditch, Pubn.Ed.

★ 18380 ★
University of California, Los Angeles - Education & Psychology Library
390 Powell Library Bldg.
Los Angeles, CA 90024-1516
Defunct. Holdings absorbed by the University of California, Los Angeles - University Research Library and Laboratory of Biomedical and Environmental Sciences - Library.

★ 18381 ★
University of California, Los Angeles - Engineering & Mathematical Sciences Library (Sci-Engr)
8270 Boelter Hall   Phone: (213)825-6515
Los Angeles, CA 90024-1600   Audrey Jackson
Founded: 1945. **Staff:** Prof 4; Other 7. **Subjects:** Astronomy, atmospheric science, mathematics, computer science, engineering. **Special Collections:** Technical Reports Collection (including depository items from NASA). **Holdings:** 227,758 volumes; 3842 reels of microfilm; 1.8 million technical reports on microfiche; 68,201 hard copy technical reports. **Subscriptions:** 3632 journals and other serials. **Services:** Interlibrary loan; copying; document delivery; library open to the public. **Automated Operations:** Computerized cataloging, acquisitions, and serials. **Computerized Information Services:** DIALOG Information Services, STN International; ORION (internal database); BITNET, DDN Network Information Center (electronic mail services). Performs searches on fee basis. **Remarks:** Electronic mail address(es): ECZSPTL@UCLAMVS (BITNET). **Staff:** Bruce E. Pelz, Ref.Libn.; Karen L. Andrews, Ref.Libn.; Charlene Silverstein, Hd., Circ.; Michael Hernandez, Hd., Acq.; Aggi Raeder, Ref.Libn.

★ 18382 ★
University of California, Los Angeles - English Reading Room (Hum)
1120 Rolfe Hall   Phone: (213)825-4511
Los Angeles, CA 90024-1528   Tim Strawn, Hd.
Founded: 1950. **Staff:** 1. **Subjects:** English and American literature, literary criticism. **Special Collections:** Josephine Miles Poetry Collection (contemporary poetry; 1200 volumes). **Holdings:** 25,000 volumes. **Subscriptions:** 151 journals and other serials. **Services:** Copying; library open to the public. **Computerized Information Services:** ORION (internal database); InterNet (electronic mail service). **Remarks:** Electronic mail address(es): ECZ5TIM@MVS.OAC.UCLA.EDU (InterNet).

★ 18383 ★
University of California, Los Angeles - Ethnomusicology Archive (Mus)
1630 Schoenberg Hall
405 Hilgard Ave.   Phone: (213)825-1695
Los Angeles, CA 90024-1657   Louise S. Spear, Dir.
Founded: 1961. **Staff:** Prof 2. **Subjects:** Ethnomusicology. **Holdings:** 10,000 sound recordings. **Services:** Archive open to the public with restrictions. **Computerized Information Services:** OCLC; UCLA'S ORION (internal database); BITNET, InterNet (electronic mail services). **Remarks:** FAX: (213)206-0422. Electronic mail address(es): ECZ5LOU@UCLAMVS (BITNET); ECZ5LOU@MVS.OAC.UCLA.EDU (InterNet). **Staff:** Maureen A. Russell.

★ 18384 ★
University of California, Los Angeles - Geology-Geophysics Library (Sci-Engr)
Geology Bldg., Rm. 4697   Phone: (213)825-1055
Los Angeles, CA 90024-1567   Michael M. Noga, Hd.
Founded: 1940. **Staff:** Prof 1; Other 2. **Subjects:** Geology, geophysics, planetary sciences, paleontology, geochemistry, space physics. **Special Collections:** California geology; UCLA geology, geophysics, and geochemistry theses and dissertations. **Holdings:** 101,456 volumes; 190 reels of microfilm; 18,495 microfiche; 5466 maps; 3 globes. **Subscriptions:** 2256 journals and other serials. **Services:** Interlibrary loan; copying; library open to the public. **Automated Operations:** Computerized acquisitions and serials. **Computerized Information Services:** DIALOG Information Services, STN International; MELVYL, ORION (internal databases); BITNET (electronic mail service). Performs searches on fee basis. **Remarks:** Electronic mail address(es): ECZ5GEO@UCLAMVS (BITNET).

★ 18385 ★
University of California, Los Angeles - Henry J. Bruman Map Library (Geog-Map)
Bunche Hall, Rm. A-253   Phone: (213)825-3526
Los Angeles, CA 90024-1468   Carlos B. Hagen-Lautrup, Dir.
Founded: 1957. **Staff:** Prof 1; Other 3. **Subjects:** Nautical and aeronautical charts, map intelligence materials, topographic maps, city plans. **Special Collections:** Latin America and Pacific Ocean materials. **Holdings:** 7798 books; 504,222 flat maps; 2436 technical reports; 48,583 VF of city plans and road maps; 3168 atlases; 2535 aerial photographs; 12,033 microcards; 38 slides; 943 pictorial items. **Subscriptions:** 349 journals and other serials. **Services:** Interlibrary loan; copying; library open to the public on a limited schedule for reference use only. **Publications:** Latitude - a newsletter of selected acquisitions, annual; technical reports.

★ 18386 ★
University of California, Los Angeles - Institute for Social Science Research - Social Science Data Archive (Soc Sci)
405 Hilgard Ave.   Phone: (213)825-0711
Los Angeles, CA 90024-1484   Elizabeth Stephenson, Data Archv.
Founded: 1977. **Staff:** Prof 2; Other 1. **Subjects:** Social science. **Special Collections:** California Polls; Los Angeles Metropolitan Area Surveys; National Center for Health Statistics data repository; Southern California Social Surveys. **Holdings:** 1783 volumes. **Subscriptions:** 12 serials. **Services:** Archive open to the public with restrictions. **Automated Operations:** Computerized cataloging. **Computerized Information Services:** ORION (internal database). **Publications:** ISSR, quarterly. **Special Indexes:** Index of women's studies machine-readable data files; Index of the Southern California Social Surveys; index of machine-readable data files for multi-ethnic research. **Remarks:** FAX: (213)206-4453.

★ 18387 ★
University of California, Los Angeles - John E. Anderson Graduate School of Management - Library (Bus-Fin)
405 Hilgard Ave.   Phone: (213)825-3138
Los Angeles, CA 90024-1460   Robert Bellanti, Hd.
Founded: 1961. **Staff:** Prof 4; Other 7. **Subjects:** All fields of management and business administration, accounting-information systems, business economics, computers and information systems, finance and investments, personnel and industrial relations, international and comparative management studies, arts management, marketing, operations research, sociotechnical systems/behavioral science, urban land economics. **Special Collections:** Robert E. Gross Collection of Rare Books in Business and Economics; Dean Emeritus Neil H. Jacoby Collection; Goldsmiths'-Kress Collection of Rare Books in Business and Economics (microfilm). **Holdings:** 140,924 volumes; 86,920 hardcopy annual and 10K reports of corporations; 326,499 microcards and microfiche; 2675 pamphlets; 8076 reels of microfilm of journals and newspapers. **Subscriptions:** 2865 journals and other serials. **Services:** Interlibrary loan; copying; library open to the public for reference use only. **Automated Operations:** Computerized public access catalog, cataloging, acquisitions, serials, and circulation. **Computerized Information Services:** DIALOG Information Services, OCLC, BRS Information Technologies, Dow Jones News/Retrieval, NewsNet, Inc.; ORION (internal database). Performs searches on fee basis. Contact Person: Karen Sternheim, Ref.Libn., 825-3047. **Networks/Consortia:** Member of CLASS. **Staff:** Caroline Sisneros, Tech.Serv.Sect.; Rita Costello, Coll.Dev./Ref.; Arturo Esparza, Circ.Sect.; Eloisa Yeargain, Ref.Libn.

★ 18388 ★
University of California, Los Angeles - Laboratory of Biomedical and Environmental Sciences - Library (Env-Cons, Med)
900 Veteran Ave.   Phone: (213)825-8741
Los Angeles, CA 90024-1786   Janet D. Carter, Libn.
Founded: 1955. **Staff:** Prof 1; Other 1. **Subjects:** Biochemistry, nuclear medicine, environmental science, cell biology. **Special Collections:** Depository for U.S. Atomic Energy Commission reports. **Holdings:** 37,650 bound volumes (books and journals); 100,000 reports on microfiche; 1550 technical reports. **Subscriptions:** 166 journals and other serials. **Services:** Library open to the public with restrictions. **Computerized Information Services:** MEDLINE, DIALOG Information Services, BRS Information Technologies; ORION, MELVYL (internal databases); BITNET (electronic mail service). **Publications:** Annual reports. **Remarks:** Electronic mail address(es): EFU0JDC@UCLAMVS (BITNET). The Laboratory of Biomedical and Environmental Sciences operates under contract to the U.S. Department of Energy.

★ 18389 ★
University of California, Los Angeles - Law Library (Law)
School of Law Bldg.
405 Hilgard Ave.   Phone: (213)825-7826
Los Angeles, CA 90024-1458   Myra Saunders, Law Libn.
Founded: 1949. **Staff:** Prof 9; Other 16. **Subjects:** Law. **Special Collections:** Anglo-American legal materials; David Bernard Memorial Aviation Law Library. **Holdings:** 411,917 volumes; 204,306 microcards and microfiche; 1169 sound recordings; 44,326 government documents; 182 manuscripts; 2 maps; 1755 reels of microfilm. **Subscriptions:** 7239 journals and other serials. **Services:** Interlibrary loan; library open to the public with restrictions. **Computerized Information Services:** LEXIS, NEXIS, WESTLAW, Legaltrac; ORION, MELVYL (internal databases). **Remarks:** FAX: (213)206-3680. **Staff:** Adrienne Adan, Assoc. Law Libn. for Tech.Serv.; Val Russell, Assoc. Law Libn. for Pub.Serv.

★ 18390 ★
University of California, Los Angeles - Louise Darling Biomedical
  Library (Med, Biol Sci)
Center for Health Sciences
10833 Le Conte Blvd.   Phone: (213)825-5781
Los Angeles, CA 90024-1798   Alison Bunting, Biomed.Libn.
Founded: 1947. **Staff:** Prof 21; Other 31. **Subjects:** Medicine, dentistry,
nursing, public health, psychology, biology, microbiology, botany, zoology.
Special Collections: Near Eastern Medical Manuscripts (12th-19th
centuries); Japanese medical books and prints; classics in ornithology and
mammalogy from the Donald R. Dickey Library of Vertebrate Zoology; S.
Weir Mitchell Collection (history of medical science); Dr. M.N. Beigelman
Collection (classics in ophthalmology); Florence Nightingale Collection;
John A. Benjamin Collection of Medical History. **Holdings:** 494,550
volumes; 48 manuscripts; 472 maps; 3796 reels of microfilm; 670,018
microfiche; 3480 sound recordings; 6588 pamphlets; 31,590 slides; 9496
pictorial items; 5 filmstrips; 5 motion pictures; 1983 video recordings; 13
videodiscs; 15 machine-readable data files. **Subscriptions:** 8545 journals and
other serials. **Services:** Interlibrary loan; copying; SDI; library open to the
public. **Automated Operations:** Computerized cataloging, acquisitions,
serials, and circulation. **Computerized Information Services:** NLM, BRS
Information Technologies, DIALOG Information Services; ORION
(internal database); OnTyme Electronic Message Network Service
(electronic mail service). Performs searches on fee basis. **Publications:**
UCLA Biomedical Library: Brief Guide to Its Facilities, Policies and
Services, annual - free upon request. **Remarks:** Library is headquarters of
the Pacific Southwest Regional Medical Library Service (PSRMLS).
Alternate telephone number(s): 825-6098. FAX: (213)206-8675. **Staff:** Gail
Yokote, Assoc.Biomed.Libn.-Pub.Serv. ; Pat L. Walter,
Assoc.Biomed.Libn.-Tech.Serv.; Beryl Glitz, Assoc.Dir., PSRMLS.

★ 18391 ★
University of California, Los Angeles - Mathematics Reading Room (Sci-
  Engr)
Mathematics Science Bldg., Rm. 5379   Phone: (310)825-4930
Los Angeles, CA 90024-1554   Christine Morton, Lib.Hd.
Founded: 1948. **Staff:** 2. **Subjects:** Mathematics. **Holdings:** 9200 books;
11,100 bound periodical volumes; reports and reprints; preprints of faculty
and students; 259 departmental dissertations. **Subscriptions:** 146 journals
and other serials. **Services:** Copying; reading room open to the public with
restrictions. **Remarks:** FAX: (310)206-6673.

★ 18392 ★
University of California, Los Angeles - Music Library (Mus)
1102 Schoenberg Hall
405 Hilgard Ave.   Phone: (213)825-4882
Los Angeles, CA 90024-1490   Gordon Theil, Hd.
Founded: 1942. **Staff:** Prof 3; Other 4. **Subjects:** Music, musicology, music
education. **Special Collections:** 17th and 18th century Venetian libretti
(1300); ballads and songs of the British Isles; film and television recordings
and manuscript score collection; Ernst Toch Archive; Erich Zeisl Archive;
John Vincent Archive; Clarence V. Mader Archive. **Holdings:** 52,418
volumes; 66,514 scores; 150,000 manuscripts; 5424 reels of microfilm; 40,311
sound recordings; 1919 slides; 366 pictorial items; 11,278 pamphlets.
Subscriptions: 1237 journals and other serials. **Services:** Interlibrary loan;
copying; library open to the public. **Automated Operations:** Computerized
acquisitions and text editing. **Computerized Information Services:** BRS
Information Technologies, DIALOG Information Services; BITNET,
InterNet (electronic mail services). Performs searches. **Publications:** The
Full Score (newsletter), 3/year; Guide to UCLA Music Library, annual - all
free upon request. **Special Catalogs:** Exhibit catalogs - free upon request.
Special Indexes: Tune-dex/song-dex (10,000 song cards). **Remarks:** FAX:
(213)206-3374. Electronic mail address(es): ECZ5MUS@UCLAMVS
(BITNET); ECZ5MUS@OAC.UCLA.EDU (InterNet). **Staff:** Marsha
Berman, Mus.Libn., Ref.Serv.; Stephen M. Fry, Mus.Libn., Coll.Dev.

★ 18393 ★
University of California, Los Angeles - Oral History Program Library
  (Hist)
136 Powell Library   Phone: (213)825-4932
Los Angeles, CA 90024-1575   Dale E. Treleven, Dir.
Founded: 1959. **Staff:** Prof 5; Other 12. **Subjects:** Arts in southern
California, architecture, civil liberties, printing and bookselling, politics and
government, university history, Los Angeles black leadership; water
resources. **Holdings:** 350 volumes of tape transcriptions. **Services:** Copying;
library open to the public. **Computerized Information Services:** OCLC;
MELVYL, ORION (internal databases). **Special Catalogs:** Catalog of
holdings (bound). **Remarks:** FAX: (213)206-1864. **Staff:** Richard Candida
Smith, Prin.Ed.; Alva Moore Stevenson, Adm.Asst.

★ 18394 ★
University of California, Los Angeles - Physical Sciences & Technology
  Libraries (Sci-Engr)
213 Kinsey Hall   Phone: (213)825-6515
Los Angeles, CA 90024-1500   Michael Sullivan, Hd.Libn.
Founded: 1975. **Staff:** Prof 11; Other 20. **Subjects:** Physical sciences,
engineering, mathematics. **Holdings:** 500,000 books; 1.7 million microfiche;
840 pamphlets; 8 sound recordings; 68,273 government documents; 3541
maps; 28 videotapes. **Subscriptions:** 7212 journals and other serials.
Services: Interlibrary loan; copying; SDI; document delivery; library open
to the public. **Automated Operations:** Computerized public access catalog,
cataloging, acquisitions, and serials. **Computerized Information Services:**
DIALOG Information Services, BRS Information Technologies, STN
International, Questel; ORCON (internal database); BITNET (electronic
mail service). Performs searches on fee basis. Contact Person: Aggi Raeder,
825-2649. **Remarks:** Administrative unit for Chemistry, Engineering and
Mathematical Sciences, Geology/Geophysics, and Physics Libraries
including centralized cataloging and interlibrary loan service. Electronic
mail address(es): ECZ5PTL@UCLAMVS (BITNET). **Staff:** Dorothy
McGarry, Hd.Cat.; Sara Shatford Layne, Hd., ILL.

★ 18395 ★
University of California, Los Angeles - Physics Library (Sci-Engr)
213 Kinsey Hall   Phone: (213)825-4792
Los Angeles, CA 90024-1500   Michael V. Sullivan, Libn.
Founded: 1947. **Staff:** Prof 1; Other 2. **Subjects:** Physics - solid state, high
energy and particle, plasma, condensed matter, low temperature,
mathematical; elementary particles; acoustics; astrophysics and applied
fields. **Special Collections:** SLAC High Energy Preprint Library (10,558).
Holdings: 45,558 volumes. **Subscriptions:** 627 journals and other serials.
Services: Interlibrary loan; copying; library open to the public for reference
use only. **Automated Operations:** Computerized public access catalog,
acquisitions, and serials. **Computerized Information Services:** DIALOG
Information Services, STN International, SPIRES; BITNET, PI-NET
(electronic mail services). Performs searches on fee basis. **Remarks:**
Electronic mail address(es): ECZ5PYY@UCLAMVS (BITNET). **Staff:**
Elaine Adams, Operational Hd.

★ 18396 ★
University of California, Los Angeles - Public Affairs Service (Soc Sci,
  Plan)
405 Hilgard   Phone: (213)825-3135
Los Angeles, CA 90024-1575   Lauri Kram, Hd.
Founded: 1971. **Staff:** Prof 6; Other 11. **Subjects:** Government, social and
economic problems and development, local and regional planning, industrial
relations, ethnic studies, social welfare, politics and political parties.
Holdings: 317,095 volumes; 707,357 microfiche and microcards; 18,082
pamphlets. **Subscriptions:** 17,117 serials. **Services:** Interlibrary loan;
copying; service open to the public with restrictions. **Automated Operations:**
Computerized public access catalog, acquisitions, and serials. **Computerized
Information Services:** DIALOG Information Services, BRS Information
Technologies; BITNET (electronic mail service). Performs searches on fee
basis. Contact Person: Chere Negaard, Pub.Serv.Libn. **Remarks:** FAX:
(213)206-3374. Electronic mail address(es): ECZ5PAS@UCLAMVS
(BITNET). **Staff:** Eudora Loh, Docs.Libn.; Roberta Medford, Docs.Libn.;
Barbara Silvernail, Docs.Libn.; Betty Takahashi, Docs.Libn.

★ 18397 ★
University of California, Los Angeles - Richard C. Rudolph East Asian
  Library (Area-Ethnic)
405 Hilgard Ave.   Phone: (213)825-4836
Los Angeles, CA 90024-1575   James K.M. Cheng, Hd.
Founded: 1948. **Staff:** Prof 4; Other 14.5. **Subjects:** East Asia - art,
archeology, history, literature, Buddhism, linguistics, political science,
religion, sociology, humanities, social science (in the Chinese, Japanese, and
Korean languages). **Holdings:** 314,606 volumes; 3409 reels of microfilm;
1790 microcards; 2600 newspaper volumes; 719 pamphlets. **Subscriptions:**
2774 journals and other serials; 45 newspapers. **Services:** Interlibrary loan;
copying; library open to the public. **Computerized Information Services:**
OCLC; BITNET (electronic mail service). **Remarks:** FAX: (213)206-4960.
Electronic mail address(es): ECZ5ORI@UCLAMVS (BITNET).

★ 18398 ★
University of California, Los Angeles - Theater Arts Library
22478 University Research Library
Los Angeles, CA 90024-1575
Defunct. Merged with University of California, Los Angeles - Architecture & Urban Planning Library, Art Library, and Elmer Belt Library of Vinciana to form University of California, Los Angeles - Arts, Architecture and Urban Planning Library.

★ 18399 ★
University of California, Los Angeles - UCLA Film and Television Archive - Research and Study Center (Aud-Vis)
46 Powell Library
405 Hilgard Ave.   Phone: (213)206-5388
Los Angeles, CA 90024-1517   Robert Rosen, Dir.
Founded: 1965. **Staff:** Prof 20; Other 24. **Subjects:** U.S. theatrical films and broadcast television programs, theatrical newsreels, films of recognized importance in world film history, television news programs, animated films. **Special Collections:** Paramount Collection (740 prints); Twentieth Century-Fox Collection (750 prints); Warner Brothers Collection (1200 prints and negatives); Republic Pictures Collection (3000 prints and negatives); Universal Pictures Collection (100 prints); Columbia Pictures Collection (300 prints); RKO Pictures Collection (700 prints); Animated Film Study Collection (1000 prints); China Film Study Collection (100 prints); Exploitation Film Study Collection (1000 prints); Hearst Newsreel Library (27 million feet); Collection of Television Technology and Design (300 pieces); Television News and Public Affairs Collection (60,000 programs); Hallmark Hall of Fame Collection (150 programs); Alcoa Collection (150 programs); Paramount Telefilm Collection (500 prints); Jack Benny Radio and Television Collection (1200 programs); Los Angeles Area Emmy Awards Nominees and Winners, 1965 to present (2000 programs); National Emmy Awards Nominees and Winners (1000 programs). **Holdings:** 40,000 motion picture prints and negatives; 25,000 television films and tapes. **Services:** Interlibrary loan (limited); archive open to the public for scholarly and project-oriented research only. **Automated Operations:** Computerized public access catalog and cataloging. **Publications:** Film calendar, monthly; special program brochures. **Remarks:** FAX: (213)206-5392. **Staff:** Eric Aijala, Asst. Film Presrv.; Blaine Bartell, Newsreel Presrv.; Daniel Einstein, Television Archv.; Geoffrey Gilmore, Hd., Prog.; Robert Gitt, Presrv.Supv.; Jere Guldin, Vault Mgr.; Howard Hays, Commercial Serv.Mgr.; Charles Hopkins, Motion Pict.Archv.; Eric Jerstad, Asst. Commercial Serv.Mgr.; Jane Magree, Cat.; Deborah Miller, Admin.Coord.; Edward Richmond, Cur.; Geoffrey Stier, Asst. to Dir.; Martha Yee, Cat.Supv.; Steven Ricci, Mgr., Res. and Stud.Ctr.; Andrea Kalas, Asst.Mgr., Res. and Stud.Ctr.

★ 18400 ★
University of California, Los Angeles - University Elementary School Library (Hum)
1017 Seeds U.E.S. Bldg.   Phone: (213)825-4928
Los Angeles, CA 90024-1619   Judith Kantor, Hd.Libn.
Founded: 1920. **Staff:** Prof 1; Other 1. **Subjects:** Children's literature. **Special Collections:** Folk literature; poetry collection. **Holdings:** 17,366 volumes; 50 bound periodical volumes; 750 pamphlets; 347 bibliographies. **Subscriptions:** 40 journals and other serials. **Services:** Interlibrary loan; library open to the public with restrictions. **Automated Operations:** Computerized cataloging and acquisitions. **Staff:** Jenifer S. Abramson, Libn.

★ 18401 ★
University of California, Los Angeles - Wayland D. Hand Library of Folklore and Mythology (Hist)
Los Angeles, CA 90024   Phone: (213)825-4242
                                            Joseph F. Nagy, Dir.
Staff: Prof 1; Other 2. **Subjects:** Folklore and folk literature, mythology, folk music and folk song, folklife, material culture, folk arts, ethnology. **Special Collections:** Western European folklore atlases; Ralph Steele Boggs Collection of Latin American folklore. **Holdings:** 3060 books; 867 bound periodical volumes; 173 boxes and 3 VF drawers of reprints, pamphlets, and clippings; 946 reels of microfilm; 222 cassettes; 2046 tapes; 11,000 phonograph records. **Subscriptions:** 108 journals and other serials. **Services:** Library open to the public by appointment to visiting scholars. **Publications:** American Ethnic Bibliography; Bibliography of Games and Other Play Activities. **Special Catalogs:** Ralph Steele Boggs Collection of Latin American Folklore (card). **Remarks:** Maintained by the Center for the Study of Comparative Folklore and Mythology.

★ 18402 ★
University of California, Los Angeles - William Andrews Clark Memorial Library (Hum)
2520 Cimarron St.   Phone: (213)731-8529
Los Angeles, CA 90018-2098   Thomas Wright, Libn.
Founded: 1934. **Staff:** Prof 4; Other 7. **Subjects:** English civilization, 1640-1750; Eric Gill; John Dryden; Oscar Wilde; Montana history; fine printing. **Holdings:** 80,000 volumes; 14,500 manuscripts. **Subscriptions:** 200 journals and other serials. **Services:** Copying; microfilm reader-printer; library open to the public for research purposes. **Automated Operations:** Computerized public access catalog and cataloging. **Computerized Information Services:** OCLC, RLIN, Eighteenth Century Short Title Catalogue (ESTC); ORION, MELVYL (internal databases); BITNET (electronic mail service). Performs searches on fee basis. **Remarks:** FAX: (213)731-8617. Library awards fellowships for research conducted in residence. Affiliated with University of California, Los Angeles - Center for 17th and 18th Century Studies. **Staff:** Michael Halls, Ref.Libn.

★ 18403 ★
University of California, Riverside - Bio-Agricultural Library (Biol Sci, Agri)
Riverside, CA 92521   Phone: (714)787-3238
                                            John E. Cooper, Hd.
Founded: 1967. **Staff:** Prof 5; Other 10. **Subjects:** Biochemistry, biology, biomedical sciences, citrus and desert horticulture, entomology, environmental sciences, nematology, pest management, plant pathology, plant sciences, soil sciences-agricultural engineering. **Special Collections:** Citrus Collection (citrus fruits and citrus industry in California); desert ecology; arid land research; collections on jojoba, guayule, and dates. **Holdings:** 170,036 volumes. **Subscriptions:** 1921 journals and other serials. **Services:** Interlibrary loan; copying; SDI; library open to the public. **Automated Operations:** Computerized public access catalog, acquisitions, serials, and circulation. **Computerized Information Services:** DIALOG Information Services, BRS Information Technologies, NLM, STN International, MEDLINE; MELVYL (internal database); CD-ROMs (AGRICOLA, CAB Abstracts, Cambridge Life Sciences). **Networks/Consortia:** Member of San Bernardino, Inyo, Riverside Counties United Library Services (SIRCULS). **Remarks:** FAX: (714)787-3285.

★ 18404 ★
University of California, Riverside - California Museum of Photography - Research and Study Center (Art)
Riverside, CA 92521   Phone: (714)787-4787
                                            Roy McJunkin, Coll.Mgr.
Founded: 1973. **Staff:** Prof 8; Other 6. **Subjects:** Photography, art. **Special Collections:** Keystone-Mast Collection (major world events and sites, 1880-1930; 350,000 stereo photographs); University Print Collection (20,000 photographs of extraordinary artistic and historical value); Bingham Collection, 1851 to present (8000 cameras). **Holdings:** 10,000 books; exhibition catalogs, photography periodicals. **Services:** Copying; museum open to the public by appointment. **Computerized Information Services:** Internal database. **Publications:** CMP Bulletin, quarterly - to members; calendar, bimonthly - to members and others on request. **Remarks:** FAX: (714)787-4797. **Staff:** Edward W. Earle, Cur.; Deborah Klochko, Cur.; Kevin Boyle, Ex. Designer.

★ 18405 ★
University of California, Riverside - Deep Canyon Desert Research Center - Library (Biol Sci)
Box 1738   Phone: (619)341-3655
Palm Desert, CA 92261   Allan Muth, Ph.D., Resident Dir.
Founded: 1958. **Subjects:** Desert - biology, climatology, archeology, geology; ecology; hydrology. **Special Collections:** Rare books about the desert. **Holdings:** 350 books; 392 bound periodical volumes; 240 dissertations, theses, and professional reports; maps; aerial photographs; slides. **Services:** Library open to scientists by appointment with prior approval of Resident Director. **Also Known As:** Its Philip L. Boyd Deep Canyon Desert Research Center.

★ 18406 ★
University of California, Riverside - Education Services Library (Educ)
Box 5900   Phone: (714)787-3715
Riverside, CA 92517   Peter Bliss, Hd., Educ.Serv.
Founded: 1970. **Staff:** 2. **Subjects:** Education. **Holdings:** 27,000 volumes, including textbooks, children's literature, kits with cassettes and tapes, curriculum guides, study prints, software, educational tests, videotapes. **Services:** Library open to the public. **Special Catalogs:** Children's literature collection, textbook collection, curriculum guides, nonbook materials, and test collection. **Remarks:** FAX: (714)787-3285.

★ 18407 ★
University of California, Riverside - English Department Library (Hum)
Humanities Bldg.   Phone: (714)787-3792
Riverside, CA 92521   Elizabeth Lang, Hd.
Founded: 1965. **Staff:** 1. **Subjects:** English and American literature and bibliography; literary reference and criticism. **Special Collections:** Olga W. Vickery Collection of Southern Literature (73 volumes); Mortimer Proctor Memorial Collection (1000 volumes); Marion W. Singleton Memorial Collection (220 volumes). **Holdings:** 4420 volumes; 300 pamphlets; 268 recordings; 41 cassettes. **Subscriptions:** 34 journals and other serials; 23 audiotapes. **Services:** Library open to the university community. **Computerized Information Services:** MELVYL (internal database); CD-ROM (Oxford English Dictionary).

★ 18408 ★
University of California, Riverside - Government Publications
   Department - Library (Info Sci, Law)
P.O. Box 5900   Phone: (714)787-3226
Riverside, CA 92517-5900   Margaret Mooney, Dept.Hd.
Staff: Prof 2; Other 6. **Subjects:** U.S. and California governments, international organizations. **Special Collections:** Law Collection (National Reporter System; federal and California statutory and administrative law). **Holdings:** 30,000 volumes; 400,000 government documents; 60,000 microforms. **Services:** Interlibrary loan; library open to the public. **Computerized Information Services:** DIALOG Information Services, BRS Information Technologies; CD-ROMs; U.S. Depository Item Numbers Database (internal database); BITNET (electronic mail service). Performs searches on fee basis. **Remarks:** FAX: (714)787-3285. Electronic mail address(es): GOVPUB@UCRVMS (BITNET).

★ 18409 ★
University of California, Riverside - Map Section - Library (Geog-Map)
P.O. Box 5900   Phone: (714)787-3226
Riverside, CA 92517   Margaret Mooney, Map Libn.
Founded: 1963. **Staff:** Prof 1; Other 1. **Subjects:** All areas of the world with emphasis on the western hemisphere. **Special Collections:** U.S. Geological Survey topographic maps (depository); Defense Mapping Agency Topographic Center maps (depository). **Holdings:** 65,000 sheet maps; 2000 folded maps; 1500 atlases. **Subscriptions:** 10 journals and other serials. **Services:** Library open to the public. **Automated Operations:** Computerized cataloging. **Computerized Information Services:** BITNET (electronic mail service). **Remarks:** FAX: (714)787-3285. Electronic mail address(es): GOVPUB@UCRVMS (BITNET).

★ 18410 ★
University of California, Riverside - Media Library (Aud-Vis)
A-127 Olmsted Hall   Phone: (714)787-5606
Riverside, CA 92521-0140   Jim Glenn, Hd.
Staff: 1. **Subjects:** Foreign languages, film study, biomedical sciences, music, biology, history, psychology, sociology, ethnic studies, art/photography, art history, science fiction. **Holdings:** 193 16mm films; 1400 video cassettes; 390 audio cassettes; 8051 slides; 23 videodiscs. **Services:** Library open to the public for reference use only. **Computerized Information Services:** Internal database. Performs searches.

★ 18411 ★
University of California, Riverside - Music Library (Mus)
Riverside, CA 92521   Phone: (714)787-3137
                                          John W. Tanno, Assoc.Univ.Libn.
Founded: 1963. **Staff:** Prof 1; Other 2. **Subjects:** Musicology, composition and theory, organology, performance practice. **Special Collections:** Books on bells and carillons (200 titles); Niels Wilhelm Gade Collection (all editions and arrangements of his works); Oswald Jonas Memorial Archive, incorporating the Heinrich Schenker Archive. **Holdings:** 35,000 volumes; 20,000 scores; 12,000 phonograph records; 1000 compact discs; 130 reels of microfilm. **Subscriptions:** 250 journals and other serials. **Services:** Interlibrary loan; copying; library open to the public. **Computerized Information Services:** MELVYL (internal database); BITNET (electronic mail service). **Remarks:** FAX: (714)787-3285. Electronic mail address(es): TANNO@UCRVMS (BITNET).

★ 18412 ★
University of California, Riverside - Physical Sciences Library (Sci-Engr)
Riverside, CA 92517   Phone: (714)787-3511
                                          Carol S. Resco, Hd.Libn.
Founded: 1961. **Staff:** Prof 3; Other 8. **Subjects:** Astronomy, chemistry, physics, geology, geophysics, physical geography, computer science, soil and environmental science and engineering. **Special Collections:** Geologic maps (10,000); Sadtler, Coblentz, and API/MCA spectra; U.S. Geological Survey open file reports. **Holdings:** 115,420 volumes; 18,128 microforms; 1129 reels of microfilm. **Subscriptions:** 1454 journals and other serials. **Services:** Interlibrary loan; copying; library open to the public. **Automated Operations:** Computerized acquisitions, serials, and circulation. **Computerized Information Services:** DIALOG Information Services, BRS Information Technologies, PFDS Online, STN International, WILSONLINE; BITNET, InterNet (electronic mail services). **Networks/Consortia:** Member of San Bernardino, Inyo, Riverside Counties United Library Services (SIRCULS). **Special Catalogs:** Map catalog (online). **Remarks:** FAX: (714)787-2223. Electronic mail address(es): PHYSCI@URVMS (BITNET). **Staff:** Barbara Haner, Ref.Libn.; Lizbeth Langston, Ref.Libn.

★ 18413 ★
University of California, Riverside - Special Collections (Hum)
Box 5900   Phone: (714)787-3233
Riverside, CA 92517-5900   Sidney E. Berger, Hd., Spec.Coll.
Founded: 1968. **Staff:** Prof 3; Other 1. **Special Collections:** 20th century English literature; Ezra Pound (700 volumes); Juan Silvano Godoi Collection (45 volumes; 57 boxes); Eaton Collection of Fantasy and Science Fiction (65,000 volumes; 6500 periodicals; 25,000 items of fanzines); historical collection of children's literature (2000 volumes); Thomas Hardy Theater Collection; Skinner-Ropes Collection (7000 manuscripts, 1843-1917, including 5 Civil War diaries and extensive Californiana); Sadakichi Hartmann Collection (47 boxes); Oswald Jonas/Heinrich Schenker Collection (71 boxes); Jack Hirschman poetry (2700 sheets of manuscripts); William Blake Collection (900 volumes); Niels Gade Collection (600 scores); German National Socialism (5000 volumes); photography (3000 volumes); Osuna Photographic Archive on the Mexican Revolution (427 glass plates); Tomas Rivera Archive, (192 boxes); utopias (500 volumes); women (5000 volumes); history of citriculture; date growing; Paraguay (1000 volumes); B. Traven (240 volumes; 1 box of manuscripts); William Walker (75 volumes); manuscripts and papers of Robert L. Forward, Gregory Benford, and others; university archives (1300 items; 52 tapes); Riverside City Archives (on deposit). **Holdings:** 110,000 volumes; 150,000 manuscripts; 13,000 photographs. **Services:** Interlibrary loan; copying; collections open to the public. **Automated Operations:** INNOVACQ. **Computerized Information Services:** MELVYL (internal database); BITNET (electronic mail service). **Publications:** Dictionary Catalog of J. Lloyd Eaton Collection of Science Fiction and Fantasy Literature; Oswald Jonas Memorial Collection; The Sadakichi Hartmann Papers: A Descriptive Inventory. **Remarks:** FAX: (714)787-3285. Electronic mail address(es): SPCOLSEB@UCRVMS (BITNET). **Staff:** Araxie P. Churukian; George E. Slusser.

★ 18414 ★
University of California, San Diego - Biomedical Library (Biol Sci, Med)
9500 Gilman Dr., 0175B   Phone: (619)534-3253
La Jolla, CA 92093-0175   Mary Horres, Libn.
Founded: 1963. **Staff:** Prof 7; Other 15. **Subjects:** Clinical and pre-clinical medicine, biology. **Holdings:** 182,845 volumes. **Subscriptions:** 3314 journals and other serials. **Services:** Interlibrary loan; copying; library open to the public. **Automated Operations:** Computerized public access catalog, acquisitions, circulation, and serials. **Computerized Information Services:** MEDLINE, NLM, BRS Information Technologies, OCLC, DIALOG Information Services. Performs searches on fee basis. **Networks/Consortia:** Member of National Network of Libraries of Medicine - Pacific Southwest Region. **Remarks:** FAX: (619)534-1202. **Staff:** Beverly Renford, Hd., Pub.Serv.; Anne Prussing, Hd., Tech.Serv.

★ 18415 ★
University of California, San Diego - Center for Magnetic Recording
   Research - Information Center (Sci-Engr)
9500 Gilman Dr.   Phone: (619)534-6213
La Jolla, CA 92093-0401   Dawn E. Talbot, Info.Mgr.
Founded: 1984. **Staff:** Prof 1; Other 1. **Subjects:** Magnetic recording technology, magnetic media, optical recording technology. **Holdings:** 1677 books. **Subscriptions:** 71 journals and other serials. **Services:** Center open

to the public. **Automated Operations:** Computerized cataloging and acquisitions. **Computerized Information Services:** DIALOG Information Services, STN International, NewsNet, Inc., PFDS Online; internal databases; InterNet, BITNET, DIALMAIL (electronic mail services). **Publications:** CMRR Information Bulletin - to sponsoring companies; CMRR Report - free upon request. **Remarks:** Alternate telephone number(s): (619)534-6199. FAX: (619)534-2720. Electronic mail address(es): dTALBOT@UCSD.EDU (InterNet); DTALBOT@UCSD (BITNET).

★ 18416 ★
University of California, San Diego - International Relations & Pacific Studies Library (Bus-Fin)
La Jolla, CA 92093-0175   Phone: (619)534-1413
                                  Karl Lo, Libn.
Founded: 1986. **Staff:** Prof 5; Other 5. **Subjects:** Economics, business, and international relations in East Asia and Latin America. **Special Collections:** Pacific Economic Cooperation Conference collection. **Holdings:** 29,005 volumes. **Subscriptions:** 2033 journals and other serials. **Services:** Interlibrary loan, copying, library open to the public. **Automated Operations:** Computerized public access catalog and circulation. **Computerized Information Services:** DIALOG Information Services, DataTimes, Dow Jones News/Retrieval, INFO-SOUTH Latin American Information System, LEXIS, NEXIS, Nikkei Telecom, OCLC, Reuter TEXTLINE, Delphi En Espanol. **Publications:** PacificScope (newsletter), quarterly. **Remarks:** FAX: (619)534-8526. **Staff:** Harold Colson, Hd., Pub.Serv.; Maryanne Reilly, Hd., Tech.Serv./Korean Stud.Libn.; Richard Wang, Chinese Stud.Libn.; Eiji Yutani, Japanese Stud.Libn.

★ 18417 ★
University of California, San Diego - Medical Center Library (Med)
225 Dickinson St.   Phone: (619)543-6520
San Diego, CA 92103-8828   Christine Chapman, Hd.Libn.
Founded: 1966. **Staff:** Prof 2; Other 5. **Subjects:** Medicine, nursing. **Holdings:** 26,523 volumes. **Subscriptions:** 780 journals and other serials. **Services:** Interlibrary loan; copying; SDI; library open to the public. **Automated Operations:** Computerized public access catalog, circulation, acquisitions, and serials. **Computerized Information Services:** NLM, BRS Information Technologies, DIALOG Information Services; BITNET (electronic mail service). Performs searches on fee basis. **Networks/Consortia:** Member of National Network of Libraries of Medicine - Pacific Southwest Region. **Remarks:** FAX: (619)534-3289. Electronic mail address(es): CCHAPMAN@UCSD.EDU (BITNET). Library is a branch of the Biomedical Library. **Staff:** Barbara Slater, Ref.Libn.

★ 18418 ★
University of California, San Diego - Science & Engineering Library (Sci-Engr, Comp Sci)
O175E   Phone: (619)534-4579
La Jolla, CA 92093-0175   William Goff, Act.Hd.
Founded: 1965. **Staff:** Prof 4; Other 14. **Subjects:** Mathematics, chemistry, physics, computer science, engineering, astronomy. **Holdings:** 176,000 volumes; 263,000 reports on microfiche. **Subscriptions:** 2345 journals and other serials. **Services:** Interlibrary loan; copying; library open to the public. **Computerized Information Services:** DIALOG Information Services, STN International, BRS Information Technologies, Data-Star, ORBIT Search Service, EPIC; BITNET (electronic mail service). **Remarks:** FAX: (619)534-5583. Electronic mail address(es): DKEGEL@UCSD; SWILLHITE@UCSD; CHIGHTOW@UCSD (BITNET). **Staff:** Deborah Kegel, Hd., Pub.Serv.; Christy Hightower, Ref.Libn.; Sherry Willhite, Chem.Spec.

★ 18419 ★
University of California, San Diego - Scripps Institution of Oceanography Library (Sci-Engr, Biol Sci)
9500 Gilman Dr., 0175C   Phone: (619)534-3274
La Jolla, CA 92093-0175   William J. Goff, Libn.
Founded: 1913. **Staff:** Prof 4; Other 17. **Subjects:** Oceanography, marine biology, geophysics, geological sciences, meteorology, climatology. **Special Collections:** Expedition literature; rare books; SIO Archives. **Holdings:** 223,000 volumes; 65,000 maps and charts; 50,000 microforms. **Subscriptions:** 3500 journals and other serials. **Services:** Interlibrary loan; document delivery; copying; library open to the public. **Automated Operations:** Computerized cataloging, circulation, acquisitions, and serials. **Computerized Information Services:** DIALOG Information Services, STN

International; MELVYL (internal database); CD-ROMs (Aquatic Sciences and Fisheries Abstracts (ASFA), Arctic and Antarctic Regions, Biological Abstracts, GeoRef, Aerospace Database); SprintMail, InterNet, BITNET (electronic mail services). Performs searches on fee basis. Contact Person: Peter Brueggeman, Hd., Pub.Serv. **Networks/Consortia:** Member of CLASS, OCLC Pacific Network. **Publications:** Newsletter/Acquisitions List, bimonthly; SIO Contributions, annual. **Special Indexes:** Finding aids for archival collections (online). **Remarks:** FAX: (619)534-5269. Electronic mail address(es): [SCRIPPS.LIBRARY/OMNET]MAIL/USA (SprintMail); scrippsill@ ucsd.edu (InterNet); scrippsill@ucsd (BITNET). **Staff:** Deborah Day, Archv.; Susan Jurist, Hd., Tech.Serv.; Phyllis Lett, Ref.Asst.

★ 18420 ★
University of California, San Diego - University Libraries (Hum, Sci-Engr, Biol Sci)
9500 Gilman Dr., 0175G   Phone: (619)534-3336
La Jolla, CA 92093-0175   Phyllis S. Mirsky, Act.Univ.Libn.
Founded: 1961. **Staff:** Prof 101; Other 272. **Subjects:** Marine sciences, Latin American studies, Melanesian studies, magnetic recording, medicine, Pacific studies. **Special Collections:** Baja California Collection; Pacific voyages; Spanish Civil War; Archive for New Poetry. **Holdings:** 2.05 million volumes. **Subscriptions:** 23,784 journals and other serials. **Services:** Interlibrary loan; copying; libraries open to the public. **Automated Operations:** Computerized cataloging, circulation, and serials. **Computerized Information Services:** DIALOG Information Services, OCLC, PFDS Online, BRS Information Technologies, Association of Research Libraries (ARL). **Networks/Consortia:** Member of Center for Research Libraries (CRL), CLASS. **Publications:** Bibliography of the Hill Collection of Pacific Voyages. **Remarks:** Figures given include holdings of the Central University Library and six branch libraries. FAX: (619)534-4970. **Staff:** George J. Soete, Assoc.Univ.Libn.; R. Bruce Miller, Asst.Univ.Libn.; Jacqueline Hanson, Asst.Univ.Libn.; Garrett Bowles, Mus.Libn.; Kari Lucas, Undergraduate Libn.; Karen Feeney, Acq.Libn.; Karl Lo, Intl.Rel. & Pacific Studies Lib.; Susan Starr, Govt.Docs. & Maps. Barbara Tillett, Cat.Libn.; Chris D. Ferguson, Ref.Libn.; Virginia Steel, Circ.Libn.; Lynda Claassen, Spec.Coll.Libn.; Louise Schaper, Sys.Libn.; Bill Goff, Act.Sci. and Engr.; Mary Horres, Biomedical Lib.

★ 18421 ★
University of California, San Francisco - Center on Deafness - Library (Soc Sci)
3333 California St., Suite 10   Phone: (415)476-4980
San Francisco, CA 94143-1208   Karen Guma, Libn.
Founded: 1988. **Subjects:** Mental health, psychosocial, and linguistic aspects of deafness. **Holdings:** 200 volumes. **Subscriptions:** 11 journals and other serials; 4 newspapers. **Services:** Library not open to the public. **Computerized Information Services:** BITNET (electronic mail service). **Remarks:** TDD number is 476-7600. FAX: (415)476-8102. Electronic mail address(es): UCCD.MENTAL.HEALTH (BITNET).

★ 18422 ★
University of California, San Francisco - Hastings College of the Law - Legal Information Center (Law)
200 McAllister St.   Phone: (415)565-4750
San Francisco, CA 94102   Gail Winson, Act.Dir.
Founded: 1878. **Staff:** Prof 10; Other 11. **Subjects:** Law. **Special Collections:** U.S. and California Documents Depository. **Holdings:** 345,542 volumes; 156,475 volumes in microform; 3010 audiocassettes. **Subscriptions:** 6590 journals and other serials. **Services:** Interlibrary loan; copying; center open to the public. **Automated Operations:** Computerized public access catalog, circulation, cataloging, acquisitions, and serials (INNOPAC). **Computerized Information Services:** WESTLAW, OCLC, LEXIS, NEXIS, DIALOG Information Services, RLIN, ELSS (Electronic Legislative Search System), BRS Information Technologies, Legitech, DataTimes, Dow Jones News/Retrieval, Reuters, StateNet, VU/TEXT Information Services, WILSONLINE; STAR (internal databases); CD-ROM (WILSONDISC); ALANET (electronic mail service). **Networks/Consortia:** Member of Bay Area Library and Information System (BALIS), CLASS. **Publications:** Legal Notice, 2/year; New Books, bimonthly - both available on request; Hastings Legal Information Center Handbook, annual. **Remarks:** Alternate telephone number(s): 565-4761. FAX: (415)621-4859. **Staff:** Linda Weir, Pub.Serv.Libn.; Daniel Taysom, Comp.Serv.Libn.; Susan Campbell, Circ.Libn.; Mary Glennon, Tech.Serv.Libn.; Laura Peritore, Ref./C A Docs.Libn.; Veronica Maclay, U.S. Docs.Libn.; Rebecca Holland, Ser.Libn./Hd.Cat.; Grace Takatani, Cat.; Dorothy Mackay-Collins, Cur./ Archv.

★ 18423 ★
University of California, San Francisco - Library and Center for Knowledge Management (Med)
530 Parnassus Ave.   Phone: (415)476-8293
San Francisco, CA 94143-0840   Richard E. Lucier, Univ.Libn.
Founded: 1864. **Staff:** Prof 19; Other 54. **Subjects:** Health sciences, medicine, dentistry, pharmacy, nursing. **Special Collections:** History of Health Sciences; Oriental Medicine; homeopathy; Osleriana; California medicine; university archives. **Holdings:** 691,041 volumes. **Subscriptions:** 5459 journals and other serials. **Services:** Interlibrary loan; copying; library open to public with restricted circulation. **Automated Operations:** Computerized public access catalog, cataloging, acquisitions, and serials (MELVYL). **Computerized Information Services:** MEDLINE, OCLC, BRS Information Technologies, DIALOG Information Services; InterNet, BITNET (electronic mail services). Performs searches on fee basis. Contact Person: Elisabeth Bell, Ref.Div., 476-8031. **Networks/Consortia:** Member of National Network of Libraries of Medicine - Pacific Southwest Region, San Francisco Consortium. **Remarks:** FAX: (415)476-4653. Electronic mail address(es): rel@ucsfvm.uscf.edu (InterNet). **Staff:** Karen A. Butter, Dir., Info.Rsrcs & Serv.; Richard S. Cooper, Dir., Fin., Plan. & Adm.

★ 18424 ★
University of California, San Francisco - Medical Library - Oriental Collection (Med)
San Francisco, CA 94143-0840   Phone: (415)476-8101
Founded: 1954. **Staff:** 2. **Subjects:** History of medicine in Japan and China; Chinese medicine; development of Western medicine in China and Japan. **Special Collections:** Japanese woodblock prints on popular medicine in Japan (400 sheets); medical history in Japan during the Edo Period (1600-1868); Chinese and Japanese rare medical books (in vernacular). **Holdings:** 13,984 volumes; 1260 bound periodical volumes; 309 nonbook items. **Subscriptions:** 51 journals and other serials. **Services:** Interlibrary loan; copying; collection open to the public with restrictions. **Automated Operations:** Computerized public access catalog and ILL. **Computerized Information Services:** OCLC; MELVYL (internal database). **Remarks:** FAX: (415)476-7940.

★ 18425 ★
University of California, San Francisco - Mount Zion Medical Center - Harris M. Fishbon Memorial Library (Med)
Box 7921   Phone: (415)885-7378
San Francisco, CA 94120   Gail Sorrough, Dir.
Staff: Prof 2; Other 2. **Subjects:** Medicine, geriatrics, cardiology, pediatrics, psychiatry. **Special Collections:** History of medicine. **Holdings:** 15,000 books; 30,000 bound periodical volumes; 1300 AV programs. **Subscriptions:** 350 journals and other serials. **Services:** Interlibrary loan; library not open to the public. **Automated Operations:** Computerized acquisitions, serials, circulation, and ILL (DOCLINE). **Computerized Information Services:** MEDLARS, DIALOG Information Services. Performs searches on fee basis. **Networks/Consortia:** Member of San Francisco Biomedical Library Network, Bay Area Library and Information Network, National Network of Libraries of Medicine - Pacific Southwest Region, Northern California and Nevada Medical Library Group (NCNMLG).

★ 18426 ★
University of California, Santa Barbara - Arts Library (Art, Mus)
Santa Barbara, CA 93106   Phone: (805)893-3613
    Lynette Korenic, Hd./Art Libn.
Founded: 1966. **Staff:** Prof 4; Other 10. **Subjects:** Art history, studio art, musicology, music performance, music composition, music theory, ethnomusicology, history of photography. **Special Collections:** Art Exhibition Catalog Collection (74,000); Archive of Art Auction Catalogs (43,000); Archive of Recorded Vocal Music (25,000 78rpm phonograph records); Bernard Herrmann Collection (75,000 phonograph records, 41,000 scores, 2400 compact discs, 9000 audiotapes). **Holdings:** 185,000 volumes; 70,000 phonograph records; 137,428 microforms; 277 videotapes; 5000 audiotapes; 1700 compact discs; 38,000 scores. **Subscriptions:** 907 journals and other serials. **Services:** Interlibrary loan; copying; library open to the public. **Automated Operations:** Computerized cataloging, acquisitions, and circulation. **Computerized Information Services:** DIALOG Information Services, OCLC, RLIN; CD-ROMs; internal database; BITNET (electronic mail service). **Networks/Consortia:** Member of Research Libraries Information Network (RLIN). **Special Indexes:** Art Exhibition Catalog Subject Index (1978); catalog of Archive of Recorded Vocal Music (online). **Remarks:** FAX: (805)893-4676. Electronic mail address(es): BM.A3Z@RLG (BITNET). **Staff:** Susan Bower, Asst.Hd./Mus.Libn.; Martin Silver, Mus.Libn.; Susan Lentz, Art Libn.

★ 18427 ★
University of California, Santa Barbara - Black Studies Library Unit (Area-Ethnic)
Santa Barbara, CA 93106   Phone: (805)893-2922
    Sylvia Y. Curtis, Black Studies Libn.
Founded: 1971. **Staff:** Prof 1; Other 1. **Subjects:** African-American studies, African area studies, Caribbean studies, Black literature and history. **Holdings:** 7000 books; 5 VF drawers of newspaper clippings; 5 VF drawers of pamphlets; 100 posters; catalogs from black colleges and universities. **Subscriptions:** 101 journals and other serials. **Services:** Interlibrary loan; SDI; library open to the public. **Automated Operations:** Computerized cataloging, acquisitions, serials, and circulation. **Computerized Information Services:** DIALOG Information Services, BRS Information Technologies, WILSONLINE; BITNET (electronic mail service). Performs searches on fee basis to members of the University of California community. **Publications:** New Acquisitions List & Announcements - to researchers, patrons, and on request. **Remarks:** FAX: (805)893-4676. Electronic mail address(es): SYCSB@UCCMUSA (BITNET).

★ 18428 ★
University of California, Santa Barbara - Department of Special Collections (Rare Book, Hum)
University Library   Phone: (805)893-3420
Santa Barbara, CA 93106   David Tambo, Dept.Hd.
Staff: Prof 3.5 Other 4. **Subjects:** Printing; Abraham Lincoln; Civil War; antislavery; U.S. westward expansion; Aldous Huxley; Samuel Beckett; Henry James; Robinson Jeffers; Charles Bukowski; W. Somerset Maugham; avant-garde literature; Stopes Birth Control Collection; Californiana; Colombian novels; Mauritius; Spanish Inquisition; French revolutionary pamphlets; book arts; Christmas books; press books; Romaine Trade Catalog Collection; evolution; Pear Tree Press; Rudge Press; Mme. Lotte Lehman Archive; Pearl Chase Collection; Stuart L. Bernath Collection; Morris Ernst Banned Book Collection; Humanistic Psychology Archive; self-help graphics and art collection; California Ethnic and Multicultural Archives. **Holdings:** 200,000 books and pamphlets; 750,000 manuscripts; 4000 theses; 2000 reels of microfilm; 15,000 microcards. **Subscriptions:** 120 journals and other serials. **Services:** Interlibrary loan; copying; collections open to qualified individuals. **Automated Operations:** NOTIS. **Computerized Information Services:** DIALOG Information Services, RLIN, MELVYL. **Networks/Consortia:** Member of Research Libraries Information Network (RLIN). **Remarks:** Alternate telephone number(s): (805)893-3062. FAX: (805)893-4676. **Staff:** Elizabeth Witherell, Ms.Cur.; David Russell, Oral Hist.; Salvador Guerena, CEMA Dir.

University of California, Santa Barbara - Department of Special Collections - The American Institute of Wine and Food
See: **The American Institute of Wine & Food** (642)

★ 18429 ★
University of California, Santa Barbara - East Asian Studies Collection (Area-Ethnic)
University Library   Phone: (805)893-2365
Santa Barbara, CA 93106   Cathy Chiu, East Asian Libn.
Founded: 1967. **Staff:** Prof 2; Other 1. **Subjects:** East Asia - materials in Chinese and Japanese languages, primarily in the humanities and social sciences. **Holdings:** 76,700 books; 15,279 bound periodical volumes; 1653 microforms. **Subscriptions:** 364 journals and other serials; 16 newspapers. **Services:** Interlibrary loan; collection open to the public. **Computerized Information Services:** RLIN; BITNET (electronic mail service). **Networks/Consortia:** Member of Research Libraries Information Network (RLIN). **Remarks:** FAX: (805)893-4676. Electronic mail address(es): LB10Chiu@UCSBUXA (BITNET). **Staff:** Sung-in Ch'oe, Assoc.Libn.

★ 18430 ★
University of California, Santa Barbara - Government Publications Department (Info Sci)
University Library   Phone: (805)893-2863
Santa Barbara, CA 93106   Lucia Snowhill, Dept.Hd.
Founded: 1960. **Staff:** Prof 5; Other 6. **Subjects:** Federal, state, local, foreign and international government publications. **Holdings:** 628,700 hard copy government publications; 828,000 microforms. **Subscriptions:** 5900 journals and other serials. **Services:** Interlibrary loan; department open to the public. **Computerized Information Services:** DIALOG Information Services; BITNET (electronic mail service). **Remarks:** FAX: (805)893-4676. Electronic mail address(es): LB10GOVE@UCSBUXA (BITNET). **Staff:** Carol Doyle, Foreign & Intl.Docs.Libn.; Janet Martorana, Local Docs.Libn.; Barbara Silver, State Docs.Libn.; Rosemary Meszaros, U.S. Docs.Libn.; Scott Jackson, California Docs.Libn.

★ 18431 ★
University of California, Santa Barbara - Library - Chicano Studies Collection (Area-Ethnic)
University Library
Santa Barbara, CA 93106   Phone: (805)893-2756
Founded: 1971. **Staff:** Prof 1; Other 1. **Subjects:** Chicano literature, history, and cultural arts; Mexico/U.S. border; social sciences; bibliography; bilingual education. **Special Collections:** Chicano Studies Serial Collection (300 titles on microfilm); Chicano Studies Literary Videotape Series. **Holdings:** 12,000 volumes; 11,000 articles, pamphlets and news clippings; 381 microfilms (books and serials); 20 titles on microfiche; 360 videocassettes. **Subscriptions:** 175 journals and other serials. **Services:** Interlibrary loan; copying; collection open to the public for reference use only. **Automated Operations:** Computerized public access catalog and cataloging. **Computerized Information Services:** DIALOG Information Services, BRS Information Technologies, RLIN, OCLC. **Networks/Consortia:** Member of Center for Research Libraries (CRL), Chicano Information Management Consortium of California. **Publications:** Chicanos: A Checklist of Current Materials, biennial - free upon request; Dia de los Muertos (illustrated essay and bibliography); Guide to Library Research in Chicano Studies; list of additional publications - free upon request. **Remarks:** FAX: (805)893-4676. **Also Known As:** Coleccion Tloque Nahuaque.

★ 18432 ★
University of California, Santa Barbara - Library - Humanistic Psychology Archive (Soc Sci)
University Library   Phone: (805)893-8147
Santa Barbara, CA 93106   David Russell, Humanistic Psych.Archv.
Subjects: Humanistic psychology, humanistic psychiatry, the Human Potential Movement. **Holdings:** Books; reports; early draft manuscripts of books and articles; diaries and personal journals; current and back organizational catalogs; program announcements; files; papers; correspondence; posters; audio and video records and tapes; photographs; films; slides. **Remarks:** Co-sponsored by the Association for Humanistic Psychology.

★ 18433 ★
University of California, Santa Barbara - Map and Imagery Laboratory - Library (Geog-Map)
Santa Barbara, CA 93106   Phone: (805)893-2779
    Larry Carver, Hd.
Founded: 1967. **Staff:** Prof 2; Other 6. **Subjects:** Remotely sensed imagery - digital and analog; physical and biological science mapping; land use mapping; topographic mapping. **Special Collections:** Landsat 1 and 2 original imagery; Teledyne-Geotronics aerial photography (1927-1984; includes Fairchild photographic library); Johnson Space Center's AgriSTARS and LACIE original research materials; Mark Hurd Aerial Survey's Santa Barbara Sales Library; U.S. Geological Survey and U.S. Corps of Engineers backfiles of historic topographic mapping; Earth Resources Observation Systems (EROS) and Earth Observation Satellite Co. (EOSAT) browse holdings (complete set). **Holdings:** 3.5 million images; 4000 atlases and gazetteers; 380,000 maps; 54,000 microfiche; EROS microforms; nautical charts; cartographic data in digital form. **Subscriptions:** 50 journals and other serials. **Services:** Interlibrary loan (limited); training on cartographic/remote sensing interpretation/ information transfer lab equipment by prior arrangement; computer manipulation of spatial data in digital form. **Automated Operations:** Computerized public access catalog. **Computerized Information Services:** Earth Resources Observation System (EROS), NASA/AMES, Earth Observation Satellite Co. (EOSAT), RLIN; internal databases; BITNET (electronic mail service). Performs searches free of charge. Telephone 893-4049. **Networks/Consortia:** Member of Total Interlibrary Exchange (TIE). **Remarks:** FAX: (805)893-4676. Telex: 910 334 4902 UCSBLIBSNC. Electronic mail address(es): lb08lgc@UCSBVM (BITNET). **Staff:** Mary Larsgaard, Asst.Hd.

★ 18434 ★
University of California, Santa Barbara - Sciences-Engineering Library (Biol Sci, Sci-Engr)
Santa Barbara, CA 93106   Phone: (805)893-2765
    Robert Sivers, Dept.Hd.
Founded: 1966. **Staff:** Prof 7; Other 9. **Subjects:** Biological sciences; engineering - chemical, electrical, mechanical, nuclear; chemistry; computer science; environmental science; geography; geology; mathematics; materials science; physics; oceanography, speech and hearing. **Holdings:** 475,000

volumes; 800,000 technical and contract reports. **Subscriptions:** 5700 journals and other serials. **Services:** SDI; library open to the public. **Computerized Information Services:** DIALOG Information Services, RLIN, STN International; MELVYL, PEGASUS (internal databases); CD-ROMs; BITNET (electronic mail service). **Publications:** Literature guides in earth sciences, environmental sciences, water resources, energy, marine science, speech and hearing, remote sensing, artificial intelligence, and robotics. **Remarks:** Offers library tours and classes. Alternate telephone number(s): 893-2647 (Dept.Hd.). FAX: (805)893-8620. Electronic mail address(es): rmsivers@ucsbuxa (BITNET). **Staff:** Chuck Huber, Materials Sci./Chem./Nuclear Engr. Al Krichmar, Comp.Sci./Elec.Engr./ Speech & Hearing; Jim Markham, Ocean./Botany/Aquatic Biol.

★ 18435 ★
University of California, Santa Cruz - Dean E. McHenry Library (Hist, Hum)
Santa Cruz, CA 95064   Phone: (408)459-2711
    Allan J. Dyson, Univ.Libn.
Founded: 1962. **Staff:** Prof 32; Other 100. **Subjects:** Astronomy, women's studies, literature, local history. **Special Collections:** Thomas Carlyle; Kenneth Patchen; Gregory Bateson; Robert Heinlein; South Pacific; Santa Cruz local history including pre-statehood and Mexican local government archives; Trianon Press Archive; fine printing; Californiana. **Holdings:** 1 million volumes; 2149 manuscript units; 161,677 maps; 19,685 reels of microfilm; 453,199 microfiche; 75,331 microprints; 72,112 government documents; 24,833 audio items; 2041 videotapes; 33 multi-media kits; 610 motion pictures; 24 filmstrips; 14,447 pictures; 229,647 slides. **Subscriptions:** 10,004 journals and other serials. **Services:** Interlibrary loan; copying; library open to the public. **Automated Operations:** Computerized public access catalog, cataloging, acquisitions, serials, and circulation. **Computerized Information Services:** OCLC, RLIN; BITNET (electronic mail service). Performs searches. **Networks/Consortia:** Member of Monterey Bay Area Cooperative Library System (MOBAC). **Remarks:** FAX: (408)459-8206. Electronic mail address(es): LIBOFF@UCSCM (BITNET). **Staff:** Rita Bottoms, Hd., Spec.Coll.; Wayne Mullin, Hd., Access Serv.; Marion Taylor, Hd., Coll.Plan.; Janis Dickens, Hd., Media Serv.; Arturo Flores, Hd., Ref.Serv.

★ 18436 ★
University of California, Santa Cruz - Map Collection (Geog-Map)
Dean E. McHenry Library   Phone: (408)459-2364
Santa Cruz, CA 95064   Stanley D. Stevens, Map Libn.
Founded: 1966. **Staff:** Prof 1; Other 1. **Subjects:** Cartography, aerial photography. **Special Collections:** The Hihn Archive (land ownership maps and records of Frederick Augustus Hihn, F.A. Hihn Company, Capitola-Hihn Company, Santa Cruz Water Company, and Valencia-Hihn Company); Sanborn maps on color film of 5-county Monterey Bay area cities; historical maps of Santa Cruz County and the four adjacent counties; depository library for complete topographical coverage of the United States. **Holdings:** 160,000 maps; 34,000 aerial photographs; 30,000 microfiche; 4000 Sanborn maps on film mounted into slides. **Subscriptions:** 20 journals and other serials. **Services:** Interlibrary loan (limited); copying; collection open to the public. **Computerized Information Services:** OCLC; BITNET (electronic mail service). **Special Catalogs:** Catalog of Aerial Photos in the Map Collection of the University Library, 1928 to present (loose-leaf binder). **Remarks:** FAX: (408)459-8206. Electronic mail address(es): SDSMAPS@UCSCM (BITNET).

★ 18437 ★
University of California, Santa Cruz - Regional History Project (Hist)
Dean E. McHenry Library   Phone: (408)459-2847
Santa Cruz, CA 95064   Randall Jarrell, Dir.
Founded: 1965. **Staff:** Prof 1; Other 1. **Subjects:** California and central California Coast area: social, economic, agricultural and governmental history, transportation, principal industries, UCSC institutional history. **Holdings:** Transcripts of interviews; photographs of interviewees. **Services:** Project open to researchers on request, for reference use only. **Publications:** Bibliography - available on request. **Special Indexes:** Master regional history index. **Remarks:** FAX: (408)459-8206. Transcripts are on deposit at Special Collections, McHenry Library of University California, Santa Cruz, in the Bancroft Library of University of California, Berkeley, and some are available on microfilm through the New York Times Oral History Program.

★ 18438 ★
University of California, Santa Cruz - Science Library (Biol Sci, Sci-Engr)
Santa Cruz, CA 95064   Phone: (408)459-2886
                                        Victoria Welborn, Sci.Libn.
Founded: 1969. **Staff:** Prof 6; Other 7. **Subjects:** Astronomy, biology, chemistry, computer sciences, earth sciences, mathematics, physics. **Special Collections:** Lick Observatory Library (40,000 volumes; 750 serials). **Holdings:** 216,022 volumes. **Subscriptions:** 4217 journals and other serials. **Services:** Interlibrary loan; copying; library open to the public. **Automated Operations:** Computerized public access catalog, cataloging, acquisitions, and circulation. **Computerized Information Services:** DIALOG Information Services, BRS Information Technologies, STN International, NLM. **Remarks:** FAX: (408)459-2797. **Staff:** Steven Watkins, Asst.Hd.; George Keller, Sci.Ref.Libn.; Wei Wei, Sci.Ref.Libn.; Fred Yuengling, Sci.Ref.Libn.; Julie Kowalewski, Hd., Circ./Oper.

★ 18439 ★
University of Cambridge - Faculty of Archaeology and Anthropology - Haddon Library (Hist)
Downing St.   Phone: 223 333505
Cambridge CB2 3DZ, England   Mr. Aidan Baker
Founded: 1936. **Staff:** Prof 1; Other 2. **Subjects:** Archeology, social anthropology, biological anthropology. **Special Collections:** Burkitt Bequest; De Navarro Bequest; McBurney Bequest; Frazer Bequest (partial); Haddon Bequest (partial); rare books collection (600 volumes). **Holdings:** 26,000 books; 21,000 bound periodical volumes; 16,000 reports. **Subscriptions:** 548 journals and other serials. **Services:** Interlibrary loan; copying; library open to the public with restrictions. **Publications:** Library guide, annual. **Remarks:** FAX: 223 333503.

★ 18440 ★
University of Cambridge - Fitzwilliam Museum - Department of Manuscripts & Printed Books (Rare Book)
Trumpington St.   Phone: 223 332900
Cambridge CB2 1RB, England   Paul Woudhuysen, Keeper
Founded: 1816. **Staff:** Prof 2; Other 2. **Subjects:** Rare books, manuscripts and printed music, autograph letters, illuminated manuscripts, literary and historical manuscripts, music. **Special Collections:** Founder's library; McClean Manuscripts/Books; Marley Manuscripts/Books; incunabula; private press books. **Holdings:** 250,000 bound periodical volumes. **Subscriptions:** 250 journals and other serials. **Services:** Copying; library open to the public with letter of application and recommendation. **Automated Operations:** Computerized cataloging. **Publications:** Catalogs of collections. **Remarks:** FAX: 223 332923.

★ 18441 ★
University of Cambridge - Library (Rare Book, Hum, Sci-Engr)
West Rd.   Phone: 223 333000
Cambridge CB3 9DR, England   Dr. F.W. Ratcliffe, Univ.Libn.
Staff: Prof 44; Other 188. **Subjects:** Theology, religion, philosophy, psychology, social sciences, law, sciences, fine arts, entertainment and sports, technology, engineering, agriculture, anthropology, archeology, genealogy, history, geography, Western literature, linguistics, Oriental languages and literature, bibliography. **Special Collections:** Acton Library; adversaria (printed books with annotations); almanacs; armorial bindings; Madden Collection of Ballads, 1750-1850 (16,354 broadsides); bookplates and book stamps; book sales catalogs; Cambridge Collection, 1750-1850 (3500); Darwin Library; early English printed books, 1501-1701; Ely diocesan and chapter records; incunabula (4300); Bradshaw Collection of Irish Books; Peterborough Cathedral Library; portraits; Taylor-Schechter Genizah Collection (100,000 fragments of vellum and paper from the depository of an ancient synagogue in Cairo); university archives, 13th century to the present (charters of privilege; letters and mandates; records of the University Press, 16th-early 20th century; plans for university buildings; university papers); War Collection (World War I; pamphlets and ephemeral publications); British and Foreign Bible Society Library; Hunter-Macalpurie history of psychiatry; Library & Archives of Royal Greenwich Observatory. **Holdings:** 4.8 million volumes; 84,000 reels of microfilm; 1 million maps; 889,000 microfiche; 130,000 manuscripts. **Subscriptions:** 58,800 journals and other serials. **Services:** Interlibrary loan; copying; library open to the public with restrictions. **Automated Operations:** Computerized public access catalog, cataloging, and circulation. **Computerized Information Services:** Online systems. Performs searches on fee basis. **Publications:** Bibliographies; guides to the library; exhibition handlists. **Special Catalogs:** Catalogs to: AV material, ballads, Cambridge

Collection, chapbooks, dissertations, Far Eastern books, incunabula, manuscripts, maps and atlases, microforms, music, official publications, pamphlets, university archives; additional published catalogs of special collections - for sale. **Remarks:** FAX: 223 333160. Telex: 81395. **Staff:** R.W. Welbourn, Dp.Libn.; D.J. Hall, Adm.; V.H. King, Accessions; Mrs. P. Harris, Admissions; C.J. Sendall, Automation; A.F. Jesson, Bible Soc.; A.G. Farrant, Binding & Cons.; J.R.H. Taylor, Cat.; C.A. Simmonds, Comp. Search Serv./Ser.; A.J. Illes, Copyright; P.M. Meadows, Ely Ecclesiastical Archv.; W.A. Noblett, European Doc.Ctr./Official Pubns.; S.M. Lees, ILL; P.N.R. Zutshi, Mss./Univ.Archv.; R.H. Fairclough, Maps; R.M. Andrewes, Mus.; S.C. Reif, Oriental & Other Lang./Taylor-Schechter Genizah Res.; B.E. Eaden, Per.; G.D. Bye, Photo.; B. Jenkins, Rare Bks.; N.J. Hancock, Rd.Serv.; Miss A.R. Darvall, Ref.Serv.; A.J. Perkins, Royal Greenwich Observatory Archv.; P. Ayris, Union Cat.

★ 18442 ★
University of Cambridge - Pure Mathematical and Mathematical Statistics Library (Sci-Engr)
16 Mill Ln.
Cambridge CB2 1SB, England   Phone: 223 337998
Founded: 1965. **Staff:** 1.5. **Subjects:** Pure mathematics, mathematical statistics, probability theory, operations research, geometry, theory of numbers. **Holdings:** 19,257 books; 2677 bound periodical volumes; 3670 offprints. **Subscriptions:** 63 journals and other serials. **Services:** Library not open to the public. **Publications:** Library Guide, for internal distribution only. **Staff:** T.J. Ransford, M.A./Ph.D.; J.R. Norris, M.A./Ph.D.; Kay Roper, Asst.Libn.

★ 18443 ★
University of Cape Town - African Studies Library (Area-Ethnic)
Leslie Social Science Bldg.   Phone: 21 6503107
Rondebosch 7700, Republic of South Africa   Ms. M.P. Richards
Staff: 10. **Subjects:** Southern Africa, Africa. **Holdings:** 10,000 volumes. **Subscriptions:** 300 journals and other serials. **Services:** Interlibrary loan; copying; SDI; library open to the public for reference use only. **Remarks:** FAX: 21 6503714. Telex: 5-20327. **Formerly:** Its Centre for African Studies Library.

★ 18444 ★
University of Central Arkansas - Torreyson Library - Archives & Special Collections (Hist)
Conway, AR 72032   Phone: (501)450-3418
                                        Tom W. Dillard, Dir., Archv.
Founded: 1986. **Staff:** 2. **Subjects:** Arkansas - history, culture, literature, geography. **Special Collections:** Ted R. Worley Papers; F. Hampton Roy Papers; Arkansas Symphony Orchestra Records; Arkansas Repertory Theater Records. **Holdings:** 21,200 books; 100 manuscripts; 15,000 photographic images; 300 pamphlets; 400 maps. **Subscriptions:** 137 journals and other serials. **Services:** Copying; collections open to the public with restrictions. **Publications:** Finding aids to all manuscript collections. **Special Catalogs:** Catalog of published titles and selected manuscript collections (online).

★ 18445 ★
University of Central Arkansas - Torreyson Library - Children's Literature Collection (Educ)
Conway, AR 72032   Phone: (501)450-5203
                                        Dr. Willie Hardin
Founded: 1948. **Subjects:** Children's literature. **Holdings:** 20,787 volumes. **Subscriptions:** 25 journals and other serials. **Services:** Interlibrary loan; copying; SDI; collection open to the public with restrictions. **Remarks:** FAX: (501)327-9938. **Staff:** Carol Powers.

University of Central Florida - Florida Solar Energy Center
See: **Florida Solar Energy Center** (5883)

★ 18446 ★
University of Central Oklahoma - Library - Microforms Research Center
(Aud-Vis)
Serials-1
Central State University Library   Phone: (405)341-2980
Edmond, OK 73060-0192   Dr. John L. Lolley, Dir., Lib.Serv.
Subjects: Education, business, liberal arts, mathematics, science and
technology. **Holdings:** Over 400,000 microforms of periodicals, newspapers,
and special collections. **Services:** Interlibrary loan; copying; center open to
the public. **Automated Operations:** Computerized cataloging, acquisitions,
and serials. **Computerized Information Services:** BRS Information
Technologies, DIALOG Information Services, OCLC, DataTimes,
WILSONLINE. **Networks/Consortia:** Member of AMIGOS Bibliographic
Council, Inc. **Remarks:** Alternate telephone number(s): (405)341-2883.
Formerly: Central State University.

★ 18447 ★
University of Chicago - D'Angelo Law Library (Law)
1121 E. 60th St.   Phone: (312)702-9631
Chicago, IL 60637   Judith M. Wright, Law Libn.
Founded: 1902. **Staff:** Prof 9; Other 13. **Subjects:** Law - Anglo-American,
foreign, international. **Special Collections:** U.S. Supreme Court Briefs and
Records. **Holdings:** 524,639 volumes. **Subscriptions:** 7429 journals and other
serials. **Services:** Interlibrary loan; library not open to the public. **Automated
Operations:** Computerized public access catalog, cataloging, circulation,
and acquisitions. **Computerized Information Services:** LEXIS, OCLC,
WESTLAW, DIALOG Information Services; CD-ROMs. **Networks/
Consortia:** Member of Center for Research Libraries (CRL), ILLINET.
Publications: Selected List of Recent Publications Added to the Library,
bimonthly; Law Library Handbook, annual. **Remarks:** FAX: (312)702-
0730. **Staff:** Charles Ten Brink, Hd., Pub.Serv.; Lorna Tang, Hd.,
Tech.Serv.; Adolf Sprudz, Foreign Law Libn.

University of Chicago - Argonne National Laboratory
See: Argonne National Laboratory (975)

★ 18448 ★
University of Chicago - Art and Architecture Collection (Art)
Joseph Regenstein Library, Rm. 420
1100 E. 57th St.   Phone: (312)702-8438
Chicago, IL 60637   Katherine Haskins, Bibliog/Art & Class.Archeo.
Founded: 1938. **Staff:** Prof 1; Other 5. **Subjects:** Art and architecture -
ancient through modern; history of photography. **Holdings:** 60,000 volumes.
Subscriptions: 500 journals and other serials. **Services:** Collection not open
to the public. **Computerized Information Services:** OCLC. **Networks/
Consortia:** Member of Center for Research Libraries (CRL), ILLINET.
Special Catalogs: Union Art Catalog (includes the holdings of major
Chicago art libraries, through 1980). **Remarks:** FAX: (312)702-0853.

★ 18449 ★
University of Chicago - Business and Economics Collection (Bus-Fin)
Joseph Regenstein Library
1100 E. 57th St.   Phone: (312)702-8716
Chicago, IL 60637   Jennette S. Rader, Bus./Econ.Libn.
Staff: Prof 2; Other 1. **Subjects:** Economics, economic and business history,
finance, management, accounting. **Holdings:** 375,000 books. **Subscriptions:**
4000 journals and other serials. **Services:** Interlibrary loan; copying;
collection open to the public with restrictions. **Automated Operations:**
Computerized public access catalog, cataloging, acquisitions, and
circulation. **Computerized Information Services:** DIALOG Information
Services, VU/TEXT Information Services, WILSONLINE, OCLC, BRS
Information Technologies; CD-ROMs (Lotus One Source, ABI/INFORM,
EconLit); InterNet (electronic mail service). **Networks/Consortia:** Member
of Center for Research Libraries (CRL), ILLINET. **Remarks:** FAX:
(312)702-0853. Electronic mail address(es):
JENN@MIDWAY.UCHICAGO.EDU;
LLN2@MIDWAY.UCHICAGO.EDU (InterNet). **Staff:** Paul Belloni,
Ref.Libn.

★ 18450 ★
University of Chicago - Department of Art - Max Epstein Archive (Art)
Joseph Regenstein Library, Rm. 420
1100 E. 57th St.   Phone: (312)702-7080
Chicago, IL 60637   Benjamin Withers, Cur.
Founded: 1938. **Staff:** 2. **Subjects:** General art. **Special Collections:**
Photographs of medals in the Courtauld Institute and the British Museum;
Armenian Architectural Collection; Harold R. Willoughby Collection of
Byzantine Manuscripts and New Testament Iconography. **Holdings:**
550,000 mounted photographs. **Services:** Archive open to the public by
appointment. **Special Indexes:** Decimal Index of Arts in the Lowlands
(DIAL). **Remarks:** FAX: (312)702-0853.

★ 18451 ★
University of Chicago - East Asian Collection (Area-Ethnic, Hum)
Joseph Regenstein Library
1100 E. 57th St.   Phone: (312)702-8432
Chicago, IL 60637   Tai-loi Ma, Cur.
Founded: 1936. **Staff:** Prof 7; Other 14. **Subjects:** Chinese classics,
philosophy, history, archeology, biography, social sciences, literature, and
art; Japanese history, social sciences, and literature; Korean history, social
sciences, and literature. **Special Collections:** Chinese classics; Chinese local
gazetteers; rare books. **Holdings:** 301,000 volumes in Chinese; 144,000
volumes in Japanese; 9000 volumes in Korean; 6400 volumes in Tibetan,
Mongol, and Manchu; 7700 volumes of Western language reference works;
21,000 microforms. **Subscriptions:** 3700 journals and other serials. **Services:**
Interlibrary loan; copying; collection open to qualified visitors.
Computerized Information Services: BITNET (electronic mail service).
Networks/Consortia: Member of Center for Research Libraries (CRL),
Research Libraries Information Network (RLIN), ILLINET. **Publications:**
Reference List: Chinese Local Histories, 1969; Far Eastern Serials, 1977;
Daisaku Ikeda Collection of Japanese Religion and Culture, 1977. **Special
Catalogs:** Author-title catalog of Chinese Collection (8 volumes); author-
title catalog of Japanese Collection (4 volumes); classified catalog and subject
index of the Chinese and Japanese Collections (6 volumes), 1974; 12 volume
First Supplement to above catalogs, 1981. **Remarks:** FAX: (312)702-0853.
Electronic mail address(es): bm.cio@rlg.(BITNET). **Staff:** Wen-Pai Tai,
Chinese Libn.; Eizaburo Okuizumi, Japanese Libn.; Jai Hsyatsao, Hd.Cat.

★ 18452 ★
University of Chicago - John Crerar Library (Biol Sci, Sci-Engr, Med)
5730 S. Ellis   Phone: (312)702-7715
Chicago, IL 60637   Patricia K. Swanson, Asst.Dir. for Sci.Libs.
Founded: 1892. **Staff:** Prof 8; Other 30. **Subjects:** Astronomy; astrophysics;
biological sciences, including biochemistry, botany, physiology, and
zoology; chemistry; clinical medicine; computer science; engineering;
geophysical sciences, including geology, meteorology, and oceanography;
history of medicine; history of science; mathematics; physics; statistics;
technology. **Holdings:** 443,100 books; 683,785 bound periodical volumes.
Subscriptions: 7000 journals and other serials. **Services:** Interlibrary loan;
copying; library open to the public. **Automated Operations:** Computerized
public access catalog, cataloging, acquisitions, and circulation.
Computerized Information Services: BRS Information Technologies,
DIALOG Information Services, Chemical Abstracts Service (CAS),
MEDLARS, OCLC; CD-ROMs; InterNet (electronic mail service).
Performs searches on fee basis. Contact Person: Ammiel Prochovnick, 702-
8337. **Networks/Consortia:** Member of Center for Research Libraries
(CRL), ILLINET, National Network of Libraries of Medicine - Greater
Midwest Region. **Remarks:** FAX: (312)702-3022. Alternate telephone
numbers are: Science Libraries administration (312)702-7720; Access
Services (312)702-7409. Electronic mail address(es):
JCLS@MIDWAY.UCHICAGO.EDU (InterNet). The John Crerar
Collection of Rare Books and Archives is housed in the Joseph Regenstein
Library. **Staff:** Kathleen Zar, Hd., Ref. & Subj.Serv.; James Vaughan, Hd.,
Access Serv.

★ 18453 ★
University of Chicago - Map Collection (Geog-Map)
Joseph Regenstein Library
1100 E. 57th St.   Phone: (312)702-8761
Chicago, IL 60637   Christopher Winters, Geog./Anthrop./Maps/Bibliog.
Founded: 1929. **Staff:** Prof 1; Other 4. **Subjects:** Maps, atlases, charts, aerial
photographs. **Special Collections:** 19th and 20th century topographic maps
of Europe and America; 19th and 20th century urban plans (American and
foreign); depository for maps of the U.S. Geological Survey, the U.S.
Defense Mapping Agency, the Superintendent of Documents, U.S. National

Oceanic and Atmospheric Administration, Central Intelligence Agency, and Canadian Surveys and Mapping Branch. **Holdings:** 2000 books; 360,000 maps; 9000 aerial photographs. **Subscriptions:** 20 journals and other serials. **Services:** Interlibrary loan (contingent on condition of materials); copying; collection open to the public with restrictions. **Computerized Information Services:** InterNet, BITNET (electronic mail services). **Networks/Consortia:** Member of Center for Research Libraries (CRL), ILLINET. **Publications:** Maps of the Soviet Union at the University of Chicago Map Collection; Maps of Chicago at the University of Chicago Map Collection; The University of Chicago Map Collection: A Brief Guide; Cartographic Materials at the University of Chicago Library. **Remarks:** FAX: (312)702-0853. Electronic mail address(es): WINT@MIDWAY.UCHICAGO.EDU (InterNet); UCLWINT@UCHIMVS1 (BITNET).

★ 18454 ★
University of Chicago - Middle Eastern Collection (Area-Ethnic)
Joseph Regenstein Library, Rm. 560
1100 E. 57th St.   Phone: (312)702-8425
Chicago, IL 60637-1502   Bruce D. Craig, Bibliog., Middle East Stud.
Founded: 1924. **Staff:** Prof 3, Other 6. **Subjects:** Middle Eastern and Islamic studies. **Special Collections:** Middle East Documentation Center (government documents; medieval archives and manuscripts). **Holdings:** 250,000 books; 100,000 bound periodical volumes. **Subscriptions:** 2000 journals and other serials; 50 newspapers. **Services:** Interlibrary loan; library not open to the public. **Computerized Information Services:** BITNET, InterNet (electronic mail services). **Networks/Consortia:** Member of ILLINET, Center for Research Libraries (CRL). **Publications:** Middle Eastern Serials in the Middle East Department; A Handlist of Islamic Manuscripts and Documents in Microformat in the Middle East Department; A List of Uncatalogued Manuscripts in Microformat in the Middle East Department; Official Gazettes in the Middle East Department; A Handlist of Books and Lithographs in Microformat in the Middle East Department. **Special Catalogs:** Catalogue of the Ottoman and Persian Microform Projects of the University of Chicago. **Remarks:** FAX: (312)702-0853. Telex: 282131. Electronic mail address(es): UCLABBO@UCHIMVS1 (BITNET); ABBO@MIDWAY.UCHICAGO.EDU (InterNet).

★ 18455 ★
University of Chicago - Music Collection (Mus)
Joseph Regenstein Library
1100 E. 57th St.   Phone: (312)702-8451
Chicago, IL 60637   Hans Lenneberg, Mus.Libn.
Founded: 1940. **Staff:** Prof 1; Other 5. **Subjects:** Music, musicology, ethnomusicology, theory. **Special Collections:** Chicago Jazz Archive (2000 hours of recordings). **Holdings:** 110,000 books; 6500 reels of microfilm; 14,000 recordings. **Subscriptions:** 400 journals and other serials. **Services:** Interlibrary loan; collection not open to the public. **Automated Operations:** Computerized public access catalog, cataloging, acquisitions, and circulation. **Computerized Information Services:** OCLC; InterNet (electronic mail service). **Networks/Consortia:** Member of Center for Research Libraries (CRL), ILLINET. **Remarks:** FAX: (312)702-0853. Electronic mail address(es): Len3@midway.uchicago; how@midway.uchicago (InterNet). **Staff:** Edna Christopher, Cat.; Standley Howell, Pub.Serv.; Richard Wang, Sr.Res. Fellow, Chicago Jazz Archive.

★ 18456 ★
University of Chicago - National Opinion Research Center (NORC) - Paul B. Sheatsley Library (Soc Sci)
1155 E. 60th St.   Phone: (312)753-7679
Chicago, IL 60637   Patrick Bova, Libn.
Founded: 1941. **Staff:** Prof 1; Other 1. **Subjects:** Sociology, public opinion research, statistics, economics, demography, political science, education, public health. **Special Collections:** Current domestic and foreign public opinion polls. **Holdings:** 7000 books; 24 VF drawers; NORC numbered research reports; data and materials from NORC studies; NORC field materials. **Subscriptions:** 150 journals and other serials. **Services:** Interlibrary loan; copying; library open to qualified users. **Computerized Information Services:** DIALOG Information Services, WILSONLINE, VU/TEXT Information Services, DataTimes. **Networks/Consortia:** Member of Chicago Library System. **Publications:** Bibliography of publications, annual - free to mailing list. **Remarks:** FAX: (312)753-7886.

★ 18457 ★
University of Chicago - Oriental Institute - Archives (Area-Ethnic, Hist)
1155 E. 58th St.   Phone: (312)702-9520
Chicago, IL 60637-1569   John A. Larson, Musm.Archv.
Staff: Prof 1; Other 4. **Subjects:** Ancient Near East, Near Eastern archeology, Egyptology, Assyriology, Syro-Palestinian archeology, Achaemenid Persian art. **Special Collections:** The Director's Files, 1919 to present; the personal papers of James Henry Breasted, Harold H. Nelson, William F. Edgerton, Keith C. Seele, Nabia Abbott, Wilhelm Spiegelberg, W. Max Muller, Raymond O. Bowman, Klaus Baer, Charles F. Nims, and Georg Steindorff; field records and publication materials of the institute's archeological field expeditions in the Near East: The Epigraphic and Architectural Survey in Egypt, The Anatolian Expedition (Alishar Huyuk), The Megiddo Expedition, The Persepolis Expedition, The Nippur Expedition, The Iraq Expedition (Khorsabad, Tell Asmar, Tell Agrab, Khafajah), and The Prehistoric Expedition (Jarmo). **Holdings:** 200 VF drawers; 100,000 black and white photographic images, 1905 to present. **Services:** Copying; archives open to qualified scholars by appointment. **Special Catalogs:** The 1905-1907 Breasted Expeditions to Egypt and the Sudan: A Photographic Study (2 volumes); Persepolis and Ancient Iran; The 1919/1920 Expedition to the Near East; Ptolemais Cyrenaica (all on microfiche). **Remarks:** FAX: (312)702-9853.

★ 18458 ★
University of Chicago - Oriental Institute - Research Archives (Area-Ethnic)
1155 E. 58th St.   Phone: (312)702-9537
Chicago, IL 60637-1569   Charles E. Jones, Res.Archv.
Founded: 1973. **Staff:** Prof 1; Other 2. **Subjects:** Egyptology, Cuneiform studies, Near Eastern archeology, Northwest Semitic languages. **Holdings:** 16,966 books; 8037 bound periodical volumes; 9000 pamphlets; 2700 maps. **Subscriptions:** 650 journals and other serials. **Services:** Archives open to members of The Oriental Institute. **Automated Operations:** Mac Library System. **Computerized Information Services:** BITNET (electronic mail service). **Publications:** Oriental Institute Research Archives Acquisitions List. **Remarks:** FAX: (312)702-9853. Electronic mail address(es): CHARLES–JONES.ORINST@MEMPHIS-ORINST.UCHICAGO (BITNET).

★ 18459 ★
University of Chicago - Social Services Administration Library (Soc Sci, Med)
969 E. 60th St.   Phone: (312)702-1199
Chicago, IL 60637   Eileen Libby, Libn.
Founded: 1965. **Staff:** Prof 1; Other 3. **Subjects:** Social services, American and foreign social work, public welfare, mental health, urban policy, social problems, child welfare, health care, aged, psychotherapy. **Holdings:** 26,000 books; 1800 bound periodical volumes; 6500 pamphlets; 6510 microforms. **Subscriptions:** 400 journals and other serials. **Services:** Interlibrary loan (through main university library); copying; library open to the public with restrictions. **Automated Operations:** Computerized public access catalog, cataloging, and acquisitions. **Computerized Information Services:** DIALOG Information Services, PFDS Online, OCLC. **Networks/Consortia:** Member of Center for Research Libraries (CRL), ILLINET. **Publications:** Selected List of New Acquisitions, monthly. **Remarks:** FAX: (312)702-0874.

★ 18460 ★
University of Chicago - Southern Asia Collection (Area-Ethnic)
Joseph Regenstein Library
1100 E. 57th St.   Phone: (312)702-8430
Chicago, IL 60637   James H. Nye, Bibliog., Southern Asia
Founded: 1959. **Staff:** Prof 1; Other 3. **Subjects:** Humanities and social sciences in thirty South Asian and many Western languages; Indology; regional history and culture; economics; geography; art history. **Special Collections:** Albert Mayer papers; Gitel Steed papers; Bhubaneshwar Archive on Modern Orissa; monographic series in Sanskrit, Prakrit, and Pali. **Holdings:** 234,600 books; 43,930 bound periodical volumes; 50 VF drawers of pamphlets and ephemera. **Subscriptions:** 4666 journals and other serials; 15 newspapers. **Services:** Interlibrary loan (through main university library); copying; collection open to the public with restrictions. **Automated Operations:** Computerized public access catalog, cataloging, acquisitions, and circulation. **Computerized Information Services:** DIALOG Information Services, PFDS Online, OCLC, RLIN. **Networks/Consortia:** Member of Center for Research Libraries (CRL), ILLINET. **Publications:** Guide to the Albert Mayer Papers. **Special Catalogs:** Pamphlet Collection Card Catalog. **Remarks:** FAX: (312)702-0853. Telex: 282 131.

★ 18461 ★
University of Chicago - Special Collections (Rare Book, Hum)
Joseph Regenstein Library
1100 E. 57th St.   Phone: (312)702-8705
Chicago, IL 60637   Alice Schreyer, Cur.
Founded: 1891. **Staff:** 13. **Special Collections:** Ludwig Rosenberger
Collection of Judaica; Donnelley Collection (fine printing and the history of
printing); John Crerar Collection of the history of science and medicine;
Grant Collection of English Bibles; William E. Barton Collection of
Lincolniana; Frank Collection (anatomical illustration); Durrett Collection
(history of Kentucky and the Ohio River Valley); Encyclopaedia Britannica
Collection (books for children, particularly of the nineteenth century);
Croue Collection of Balzac's Works; American Bible Union and
Hengstenberg Collections (early theology and Biblical criticism); Littlefield
Collection (early American schoolbooks); Samuel Harper Collection
(Russian political pamphlets, 1902-1946); Lincke Collection (German
popular fiction, 1790-1850); Hirsch-Bernays Collection (Continental
literature); Celia and Delia Austrian Collection (English drama to 1800);
Eckels Collection of Cromwelliana; Heinemann Goethe Collection; Helen
and Ruth Regenstein Collection (rare books in English and American
literature); personal papers of William Beaumont, Saul Bellow, Stephen A.
Douglas, William H. English, Elijah Grant, John Gunther, Salmon O.
Levinson, Fielding Lewis, Frank O. Lowden, Wyndham Robertson, Julius
Rosenwald, Joel T. Hart, Joshua Lacy Wilson, George Nicholas, Michael
Polanyi, and others; Sir Nicholas Bacon Collection (papers and manorial
records relating to estates in Norfolk and Suffolk); office files of Poetry: A
Magazine of Verse, including the personal papers of Harriet Monroe; life
records of Geoffrey Chaucer; The Canterbury Tales transcripts and
photostats of manuscripts; Samuel R. and Marie-Louise Rosenthal
Collection (northern Italian documents); Wieboldt-Rosenwald Collection
(photostats of German folksongs); Edgar J. Goodspeed Collection (New
Testament manuscripts); University of Chicago Archives, including papers
of George Herbert Mead, Robert M. Hutchins, S. Chandrasekhar, Enrico
Fermi, Robert Herrick, William Vaughn Moody, Howard Taylor Ricketts,
Thomas C. Chamberlin, Hermann E. von Holst, William F. Ogburn, Ernest
W. Burgess, Charles E. Merriam, James Franck, and other members of the
faculty. **Holdings:** 250,000 volumes; 6 million manuscripts and archival
materials. **Services:** Copying; library open to the public. **Automated
Operations:** Computerized public access catalog, cataloging, and
acquisitions. **Publications:** Guide to the Records of the Carnegie Council on
Children (1982); Historical Documents from Northern Italy: A Guide to the
Samuel R. and Marie-Louise Rosenthal Collection (1984); A Guide to the
Historical Records of the John Crerar Library 1828-1984 (1991); Guide to
the John A. Simpson Papers (1991). **Remarks:** FAX: (312)702-0853. **Staff:**
Daniel Meyer, Asst.Cur., Mss. and Archv.

★ 18462 ★
University of Chicago - Yerkes Observatory Library (Sci-Engr)
Williams Bay, WI 53191   Phone: (414)245-5555
                                            J.A. Bausch, Asst. in Chg.
Founded: 1897. **Staff:** 1. **Subjects:** Astronomy, astrophysics. **Holdings:**
15,000 books; 10,000 bound periodical volumes. **Subscriptions:** 150 journals
and other serials. **Services:** Interlibrary loan; copying; library open to the
public by appointment. **Computerized Information Services:** InterNet
(electronic mail service). **Networks/Consortia:** Member of Center for
Research Libraries (CRL). **Remarks:** FAX: (414)245-9805. Electronic mail
address(es): JAB@TYCHO.UCHICAGO.EDU (InterNet).

★ 18463 ★
**University of Chicago Hospitals - Pharmaceutical Services - Drug
   Information Service** (Med)
5841 S. Maryland Ave.   Phone: (312)702-1388
Chicago, IL 60637   Lora L. Armstrong, R.Ph., Dir.
Founded: 1975. **Staff:** Prof 1. **Subjects:** Pharmacy, biopharmaceutics,
clinical pharmacology. **Holdings:** 300 books; 50 bound periodical volumes;
100 boxes of journals; MICROMEDEX; Drug Information System.
Subscriptions: 28 journals and other serials. **Services:** Service open to the
public. **Automated Operations:** Computerized formulary maintenance.
Computerized Information Services: NLM. **Publications:** Topics in Drug
Therapy, monthly - by subscription. **Special Indexes:** Formulary. **Remarks:**
FAX: (312)702-9082.

★ 18464 ★
University of Cincinnati - Archives and Rare Books Department (Hum,
   Rare Book)
Carl Blegen Library, 8th Fl.   Phone: (513)556-1959
Cincinnati, OH 45221-0113   Alice M. Cornell, Hd. & Univ.Archv.
Founded: 1973. **Staff:** Prof 1; Other 2. **Subjects:** University of Cincinnati,
Southwestern Ohio, 18th century English literature, travel and exploration,
North American Indians, baseball history, history of the book. **Holdings:**
Rare Book Collection (16,000); University Archives (6000 linear feet);
Urban Studies Collection (2700 linear feet); Ohio Network Collection (3000
linear feet); Baseball Research Collection (15 linear feet); History of Design
Collection; University Biographical File (42 linear feet); university theses
and dissertations; Southwest Ohio Public Records (177 reels of microfilm).
Subscriptions: 4 journals and other serials. **Services:** Copying; department
open to the public with restrictions. **Automated Operations:** Computerized
public access catalog and cataloging. **Computerized Information Services:**
Hamilton County Records Database (internal database). **Networks/
Consortia:** Member of Greater Cincinnati Library Consortium (GCLC),
Ohio Network of American History Research Centers (ONARCH),
OHIONET. **Remarks:** FAX: (513)556-2113. Electronic mail address(es):
ARCHIVES@UCBEH (BITNET). **Staff:** Kevin Grace, Asst.Hd.; Lois
Hughes, Tech.Asst.

★ 18465 ★
**University of Cincinnati - College Conservatory of Music - Gorno
   Memorial Music Library** (Mus)
Carl Blegen Library, Rm. 417   Phone: (513)556-1970
Cincinnati, OH 45221-0152   Robert O. Johnson, Hd.
Founded: 1949. **Staff:** Prof 3; Other 3. **Subjects:** Music performance, history,
and theory; musicology; dance; broadcasting; theater arts; music education.
Special Collections: Everett Helm Collection (1500 items); Leigh Harline
Collection (500 items); Anatole Chujoy Memorial Dance Collection (700
items). **Holdings:** 30,000 bound volumes; 38,000 scores; 29,000 sound
recordings; 6000 microforms. **Subscriptions:** 600 journals and other serials.
Services: Interlibrary loan; copying; library open to the public for reference
use only. **Automated Operations:** Computerized public access catalog and
cataloging. **Networks/Consortia:** Member of Greater Cincinnati Library
Consortium (GCLC), OHIONET. **Remarks:** FAX: (513)556-2113. **Staff:**
Mark Palkovic, Rec.Libn.; Paul Cauthen, Mus.Cat.

★ 18466 ★
University of Cincinnati - Curriculum Resources Center (Educ, Aud-Vis)
Carl Blegen Library, Rm. 600   Phone: (513)556-1430
Cincinnati, OH 45221-0219   Dr. Gary Lare, Libn.
Founded: 1971. **Staff:** Prof 1; Other 4. **Subjects:** Curriculum resources,
primary and secondary education and teaching. **Holdings:** 32,000 books; 655
tests; 2000 microfiche; 10,500 AV programs; elementary and secondary
school textbooks; children's books; curriculum guides; teaching activities
books. **Subscriptions:** 120 journals and other serials. **Services:** Center open
to the public for reference use only. **Automated Operations:** Computerized
public access catalog and cataloging. **Computerized Information Services:**
ERIC, Microsoft Bookshelf, Academic American Encyclopedia, AV Online.
Networks/Consortia: Member of Greater Cincinnati Library Consortium
(GCLC), OHIONET. **Remarks:** Center offers media equipment services and
maintains media production and computer labs. FAX: (513)556-2113.

★ 18467 ★
University of Cincinnati - Department of Environmental Health Library
   (Med)
Kettering Laboratory Library
3223 Eden Ave.   Phone: (513)558-1721
Cincinnati, OH 45267-0056   Sherrie Kline, Sr.Res.Assoc./Libn.
Founded: 1930. **Staff:** Prof 1; Other 3. **Subjects:** Environmental health,
toxicology, physiology, analytical chemistry, statistics. **Special Collections:**
Industrial health. **Holdings:** 6000 books; 4500 bound periodical volumes; 78
VF drawers of reprints, reports, translations; 400 microfiche; 565
unpublished reports. **Subscriptions:** 175 journals and other serials. **Services:**
Interlibrary loan; copying; SDI; library open to professional personnel.
Automated Operations: Computerized cataloging and ILL. **Computerized
Information Services:** Data-Star, DIALOG Information Services,
MEDLARS, STN International; CD-ROM (MEDLINE, PolTox,
CANCER-CD, CCINFO). **Networks/Consortia:** Member of National
Network of Libraries of Medicine - Greater Midwest Region. **Remarks:**
FAX: (513)558-4397.

★ 18468 ★
University of Cincinnati - Design, Architecture, Art & Planning Library
  (Art)
800 Alms Bldg.   Phone: (513)556-1320
Cincinnati, OH 45221-0016   Jane Carlin, Hd.
Founded: 1929. **Staff:** Prof 1; Other 3. **Subjects:** Architecture,
art history, art education, planning, interior design, industrial design,
fine arts, fashion design, urban studies, health planning, graphic
design. **Special Collections:** Ladislas Segoe Collection (city planning;
200 volumes); artists' publications. **Holdings:** 40,000 books; 9965
serial volumes; 2448 microforms; 100 planning reports. **Subscriptions:**
500 journals and other serials. **Services:** Interlibrary loan; copying;
library open to the public. **Automated Operations:** Computerized
public access catalog and cataloging. **Computerized Information
Services:** DIALOG Information Services, RLIN; MIQ (internal database).
Performs searches on fee basis. **Networks/Consortia:** Member of
Greater Cincinnati Library Consortium (GCLC), OHIONET. **Special
Catalogs:** Artists' publications catalog. **Remarks:** FAX:
(513)556-3288.

★ 18469 ★
University of Cincinnati - Engineering Library (Sci-Engr)
880 Baldwin Hall   Phone: (513)556-1550
Cincinnati, OH 45221-0018   Dorothy F. Byers, Hd.
Founded: 1911. **Staff:** Prof 2; Other 3. **Subjects:** Engineering -
environmental, nuclear, civil, mechanical, aerospace, chemical,
metallurgical, electrical, industrial, computer; material science and
engineering; engineering mechanics. **Holdings:** 30,000 books; 30,000
bound periodical volumes; 2 cabinets of journals on microfilm; 1 cabinet
of NASA on microfiche; 26 cabinets of AEC/DOE on microfiche; technical
reports. **Subscriptions:** 900 journals and other serials. **Services:**
Interlibrary loan; copying; library open to the public. **Automated
Operations:** Computerized public access catalog and cataloging.
Computerized Information Services: DIALOG Information Services;
CD-ROMs (ASTI, Compendex, Water Resources Abstracts, METADEX,
Aerospace Database). Performs searches on fee basis. **Networks/
Consortia:** Member of Greater Cincinnati Library Consortium (GCLC),
OHIONET. **Remarks:** FAX: (513)556-2654. **Staff:** James W. Clasper,
Engr.Ref.Libn.

★ 18470 ★
University of Cincinnati - Geology/Physics Library (Sci-Engr, Geog-
  Map)
225 Braunstein Hall   Phone: (513)556-1324
Cincinnati, OH 45221-0153   Marianna Wells, Hd.
Founded: 1907. **Staff:** Prof 2; Other 3. **Subjects:** Geology -
general, paleontology, sedimentology, physical geography; physics -
classical and modern, condensed matter, high-energy, nuclear, particle,
atmospheric, terrestrial, biophysics. **Special Collections:** S.V.
Hvabar-Exxon Guidebook Collection (1500 guidebooks of U.S. and
Canada); Isay Balinkin Color Collection. **Holdings:** 49,496 books;
37,442 bound periodical volumes; 586 dissertations; 106,125 maps.
Subscriptions: 553 journals and other serials. **Services:** Interlibrary
loan; library open to the public. **Automated Operations:** Computerized
public access catalog and cataloging. **Networks/Consortia:** Member of
Greater Cincinnati Library Consortium (GCLC), OHIONET. **Remarks:**
FAX: (513)556-2161. **Staff:** Richard Spohn, Hd. of Pub.Serv.

★ 18471 ★
University of Cincinnati - George Elliston Poetry Collection (Hum)
646 Langsam Library   Phone: (513)556-1570
Cincinnati, OH 45221-0033   James Cummins, Cur.
Founded: 1951. **Staff:** Prof 1. **Subjects:** 20th century poetry.
Special Collections: Rare book collection (300 titles). **Holdings:**
9617 books; 702 bound periodical volumes; 413 phonograph records.
Subscriptions: 88 journals and other serials. **Services:** Collection
open to the public for reference use only. **Automated Operations:**
Computerized public access catalog and cataloging. **Publications:**
Calendar of events, 3/year. **Remarks:** FAX: (513)556-2161.

★ 18472 ★
University of Cincinnati - German-Americana Collection (Area-Ethnic)
Blegen Library   Phone: (513)556-1958
Cincinnati, OH 45221-0133   Don Heinrich Tolzmann, Sr.Libn.
Founded: 1974. **Staff:** Prof 1. **Subjects:** German-American
literature, history, and culture. **Special Collections:** Fick Collection;
Goebel Collection; Niers Collection; Wolff Collection; Helmecke
Collection.

Holdings: 2000 books; 250 bound periodical volumes; 1000 other
cataloged items. **Services:** Copying; collection open to the public for
reference use only. **Computerized Information Services:** BITNET
(electronic mail service). **Special Catalogs:** Catalog of the German-
Americana Collection, University of Cincinnati, 1990. **Remarks:** FAX:
(513)556-2113. Alternate telephone number(s): 556-1859.

★ 18473 ★
University of Cincinnati - John Miller Burnam Classical Library (Hum)
Carl Blegen Library, Rm. 320   Phone: (513)556-1315
Cincinnati, OH 45221-0191   Jean Susorney Wellington, Hd.
Founded: 1900. **Staff:** Prof 1; Other 1.5. **Subjects:** Bronze Age
Aegean and classical archeology, Greek and Latin languages and
literature, Greek and Latin paleography and epigraphy, Byzantine and
modern Greece, modern Greek language and literature, ancient history.
Special Collections: Paleography Collection (1500 volumes); Modern
Greek Collection (29,000 volumes). **Holdings:** 104,500 books; 21,000
bound periodical volumes; 13,500 Programmschriften and dissertations;
3300 offprints; 6000 microforms; 180 sound recordings; 732 maps.
Subscriptions: 2000 journals and other serials. **Services:** Interlibrary
loan; copying; library open to the public for reference use only.
Automated Operations: Computerized public access catalog and
cataloging. **Computerized Information Services:** DIALOG Information
Services; DYABOLA (internal database). **Networks/Consortia:** Member
of Greater Cincinnati Library Consortium (GCLC), OHIONET. **Special
Catalogs:** Catalog of the Modern Greek Collection, University of
Cincinnati, 5 volumes (1978); The Modern Greek Collection in the Library
of the University of Cincinnati, by Niove Kyparissiotis (1960). **Remarks:**
FAX: (513)556-2113.

★ 18474 ★
University of Cincinnati - Mathematics Library (Sci-Engr, Comp Sci)
840 Old Chemistry Bldg.   Phone: (513)556-1330
Cincinnati, OH 45221-0025   John H. Tebo, Hd.
Founded: 1973. **Staff:** 2. **Subjects:** Pure and applied mathematics,
including complex analysis, functional analysis, mathematical logic,
topology, differential geometry, probability, and statistics; computer
science. **Holdings:** 19,687 books; 13,838 bound periodical volumes.
Subscriptions: 510 journals and other serials. **Services:** Interlibrary
loan; copying; library open to the public. **Automated Operations:**
Computerized public access catalog and cataloging. **Computerized
Information Services:** DIALOG Information Services; CD-ROM (MathSci
Disc, SciTech Reference Plus); BITNET (electronic mail service).
Networks/Consortia: Member of Greater Cincinnati Library Consortium
(GCLC), OHIONET. **Remarks:** FAX: (513)556-3417. Electronic mail
address(es): TEBO@UCBEH.SAN.UC.EDU (BITNET).

★ 18475 ★
University of Cincinnati - Medical Center Information and
  Communications - Cincinnati Medical Heritage Center (Hist, Med)
121 Wherry Hall
Eden & Bethesda Aves.   Phone: (513)558-5120
Cincinnati, OH 45267-0574   Billie Broaddus, Dir.
Founded: 1977. **Staff:** Prof 2. **Subjects:** History of medicine and
pharmacy. **Special Collections:** Tucker Library of the History of
Medicine (1500 items); Albert B. Sabin, M.D. Archives (polio research);
Robert A. Kehoe Archives (environmental health); Leon Goldman, M.D.
Archives (laser medicine, history); Mussey Collection (19th century
medicine; 4000 items); Daniel Drake Historical Collection (60 items; 30
manuscripts); hospital records, 1837-1940. **Holdings:** 32,000 books;
3782 bound periodical volumes; 10,000 pamphlets; 3100 linear feet of
archives; 5000 photographs; 51 oral history videotapes; 150 diplomas
and certificates; 2000 medical instruments; 109 pharmacy jars (Cantagalli
15th century replicas produced in 1890s). **Subscriptions:** 15 journals
and other serials. **Services:** Interlibrary loan; copying; services open
to the public with restrictions. **Automated Operations:** Computerized
public access catalog. **Computerized Information Services:** NLM, BRS
Information Technologies. **Special Catalogs:** Tucker Library of the
History of Medicine (book); Guide to the Mussey Medical and Scientific
Library. **Remarks:** FAX: (513)558-0175. **Staff:** Doris A. Haag.

★ 18476 ★
University of Cincinnati - Medical Center Information and
  Communications - Libraries (Med)
231 Bethesda Ave.   Phone: (513)558-5627
Cincinnati, OH 45267-0574   Nancy M. Lorenzi, Ph.D.
Founded: 1974. **Staff:** Prof 13; Other 20. **Subjects:** Medicine,
biomedical sciences, pharmacy. **Special Collections:** History of
medicine, especially

local. **Holdings:** 53,701 books; 89,214 bound periodical volumes; 47,461 monographs. **Subscriptions:** 3057 journals and other serials. **Services:** Interlibrary loan; copying; SDI; library open to the public. **Automated Operations:** Computerized public access catalog, cataloging, acquisitions, serials, and ILL. **Computerized Information Services:** DIALOG Information Services, BRS Information Technologies, MEDLINE, NLM; MIQ (Medical Information Quick; internal database); OnTyme Electronic Message Network Service (electronic mail service). Performs searches on fee basis. **Networks/Consortia:** Member of National Network of Libraries of Medicine - Greater Midwest Region. **Publications:** New from the MCIC Libraries, monthly - to library patrons. **Special Catalogs:** Media Resources Center Catalog. **Remarks:** Alternate telephone number(s): 558-4941. FAX: (513)558-0175. **Formerly:** Its Health Sciences Library.

★ 18477 ★
University of Cincinnati - Medical Center Information and Communications - Nursing Educational Resources (Med)
3110 Vine St.   Phone: (513)558-8378
Cincinnati, OH 45221-0038   Leslie Schick, Dir., Lib.Serv.
Staff: Prof 2; Other 3. **Subjects:** Nursing, clinical medicine, gerontology, education, sociology. **Special Collections:** Phoebe Kandel Historical Collection (history of nursing). **Holdings:** 20,000 volumes; 500 AV programs. **Subscriptions:** 475 journals and other serials. **Services:** Interlibrary loan; copying; SDI; open to the public by permission. **Automated Operations:** Computerized public access catalog and cataloging. **Computerized Information Services:** BRS Information Technologies, DIALOG Information Services, NLM; CD-ROMs; Medical Information Quick (internal database). Performs searches on fee basis. **Remarks:** FAX: (513)558-9102. Includes holdings of the Levi Memorial Library. **Staff:** Priscilla Mitchell.

★ 18478 ★
University of Cincinnati - Observatory Library (Sci-Engr)
c/o Geology/Physics Library   Phone: (513)556-1324
Cincinnati, OH 45221-0153   Marianna Wells, Hd.
Founded: 1845. **Subjects:** Astronomy. **Special Collections:** Rare books. **Holdings:** 13,000 volumes. **Subscriptions:** 115 journals and other serials. **Services:** Library open to the public by appointment only. **Remarks:** Maintained by University of Cincinnati - Geology/Physics Library. FAX: (513)556-2161.

★ 18479 ★
University of Cincinnati - Oesper Chemistry-Biology Library (Sci-Engr, Biol Sci)
503 Rieveschl Hall   Phone: (513)556-1498
Cincinnati, OH 45221-0151   Margret Lippert, Hd.
Staff: Prof 1; Other 2. **Subjects:** Chemistry, biology, history of chemistry. **Holdings:** 39,900 books; 42,000 bound periodical volumes; 271 reels of microfilm; 3190 microfiche. **Subscriptions:** 985 journals and other serials. **Services:** Interlibrary loan; copying; library open to the public, ID card required for check out of materials. **Automated Operations:** Computerized public access catalog and cataloging. **Computerized Information Services:** STN International, DIALOG Information Services, NLM, PFDS Online, BRS Information Technologies; CD-ROMs (Biological Abstracts, Science Citation Index); BITNET (electronic mail service). **Networks/Consortia:** Member of Greater Cincinnati Library Consortium (GCLC), OHIONET. **Remarks:** FAX: (513)556-2161. Electronic mail address(es): LIPPERT@UCBEH (BITNET).

★ 18480 ★
University of Cincinnati - OMI College of Applied Science - Timothy C. Day Technical Library (Sci-Engr)
2220 Victory Pkwy.   Phone: (513)556-6594
Cincinnati, OH 45206-2822   Rosemary Young, Libn.
Founded: 1828. **Staff:** Prof 1; Other 2. **Subjects:** Computer science, electrical and mechanical engineering technology, chemical technology, construction science, fire science technology. **Holdings:** 34,000 books; 500 senior design theses; 1500 reels of microfilm; 2000 microfiche; 75 videotapes; 120 diskettes. **Subscriptions:** 200 journals and other serials; 8 newspapers. **Services:** Interlibrary loan; copying; SDI; library open to the public for reference use only. **Automated Operations:** Computerized public access catalog and cataloging. **Computerized Information Services:** DIALOG Information Services. Performs searches on fee basis. **Networks/Consortia:** Member of Greater Cincinnati Library Consortium (GCLC), OHIONET. **Remarks:** FAX: (513)556-4217.

University of Cincinnati - Physics Library
See: **University of Cincinnati - Geology/Physics Library** (18470)

★ 18481 ★
University of Cincinnati - Raymond Walters College - Library (Med)
9555 Plainfield Rd.   Phone: (513)745-5710
Cincinnati, OH 45236   Lucy Wilson, Coll.Libn.
Staff: Prof 5; Other 6. **Special Collections:** Dental hygiene. **Holdings:** 50,000 books; 12,000 microforms. **Subscriptions:** 671 journals and other serials; 16 newspapers. **Services:** Interlibrary loan; copying; SDI; library open to the public. **Automated Operations:** Computerized public access catalog, cataloging, and serials. **Computerized Information Services:** DIALOG Information Services; CD-ROMs (ERIC, ACADEMIC INDEX). Performs searches on fee basis for community members. Contact Person: Gerald Nidich, Ref.Libn. **Networks/Consortia:** Member of OHIONET, Greater Cincinnati Library Consortium (GCLC). **Publications:** New & Novel, quarterly - to college faculty. **Remarks:** FAX: (513)745-5767. **Staff:** Paul Vash, Ref.Libn.; Mike Sanders, Media Libn.; Rose Neyhouse, Microcomputer Lab.Supv.

★ 18482 ★
University of Cincinnati - Robert S. Marx Law Library (Law)
Law School   Phone: (513)556-3016
Cincinnati, OH 45221-0142   Taylor Fitchett, Hd.Libn.
Founded: 1832. **Staff:** Prof 8; Other 7. **Subjects:** Law - general, comparative, international; government documents. **Special Collections:** Morgan Collection on Human Rights (800 volumes). **Holdings:** 323,149 volumes. **Subscriptions:** 3000 journals and other serials; 20 newspapers. **Services:** Interlibrary loan; copying; library open to the public for reference use only. **Automated Operations:** Computerized public access catalog, cataloging, and circulation. **Computerized Information Services:** LEXIS, WESTLAW, NEXIS. **Networks/Consortia:** Member of Ohio Regional Consortium of Law Libraries (ORCLL). **Remarks:** FAX: (513)556-6265. **Staff:** Janet W. Smith, Cat.; Patricia Denham, Hd., Presrv.Archv.; Mark Dinkelacker, Ref.; Charles Parsons, ILL/Govt.Doc.; Swarn Varma, Asst.Cat.; James Hart, Hd., Pub.Serv.; Mariann Morales-Lebron, Ref.; Cynthia Aninao, Circ.; John W. Hopkins, Hd., Tech.Serv.; Ruth Levor, Hd., Govt.Docs.; Ruth Long, Ref.; Jack Montgomery, Acq.; Mike Church, Asst.Acq.

University of Cincinnati - University Affiliated Cincinnati Center for Developmental Disorders
See: **University Affiliated Cincinnati Center for Developmental Disorders** (18147)

★ 18483 ★
University Club Library (Hum)
1 W. 54th St.   Phone: (212)572-3418
New York, NY 10019   Andrew J. Berner, Dir.
Founded: 1865. **Staff:** Prof 4; Other 1. **Subjects:** Literature; history - Civil War, World Wars I and II; collegiana; biography. **Special Collections:** Rare books, Tinker, Darrow, Rudge Collections (fine printing and printing history); Bicklehaupt Collection of Sporting Books; Southern Society Collection of Books about the South; George Cruikshank. **Holdings:** 100,000 books; 1500 bound periodical volumes; 15 VF drawers of New York newspapers in microform; 25 VF drawers of University Club Archives. **Subscriptions:** 150 journals and other serials; 20 newspapers. **Services:** Copying; library open to serious scholars by appointment. **Automated Operations:** Computerized cataloging and circulation. **Publications:** The Illuminator - limited distribution. **Remarks:** FAX: (212)586-9095. **Staff:** Jane Reed, Assoc.Libn.; Kan Kin, Tech.Serv.Libn.; Laurie Bolger, Cons.Tech; Jennifer Whitman, Libn.Asst.

University of Coimbra - Institute of Anthropology
See: **Portugal - Ministry of Education - Institute of Anthropology** (13261)

★ 18484 ★
University College of Cape Breton - Beaton Institute - Eachdraidh Archives (Hist, Area-Ethnic)
Box 5300   Phone: (902)539-5300
Sydney, NS, Canada B1P 6L2   Dr. R.J. Morgan, Dir.
Founded: 1957. **Staff:** Prof 3; Other 2. **Subjects:** Cape Breton Island - history, labor history, Gaelic literature, folklore, political history, industrial

history; traditional Scottish music of Cape Breton Island; genealogy. **Special Collections:** John Parker Nautical Collection (8.7 meters); Gaelic and Scottish collection (3000 volumes); political papers; Micmac Indian, Acadian, and other ethnic collections (manuscripts; audio- and videotapes). **Holdings:** 5000 books; 200 bound periodical volumes; 300 unbound reports; 50,000 photographs; 1000 maps; 200 meters of manuscripts; 5 VF drawers of clippings; 600 reels of microfilm; 200 large scrapbooks; 3500 tapes; 600 slides; 50 videotapes. **Subscriptions:** 10 journals and other serials. **Services:** Copying; archives open to the public. **Computerized Information Services:** QL Systems; K-MAN (internal database). **Remarks:** FAX: (902)562-0119. **Staff:** Dr. Mary K. Macleod, Asst.Dir.; Elizabeth Planetta, Res.Assoc.

★ 18485 ★
University College Dublin - School Architecture Richview - Architecture Library (Plan)
Richview
Clonskeagh Rd
Dublin 14, Ireland

Phone: 1 7062741
Julia Barrett, Libn.

Founded: 1981. **Staff:** Prof 2.5; Other 3. **Subjects:** Architecture, urban planning, construction, regional planning, interior design. **Special Collections:** Ordinance survey maps for Ireland; history of architecture slide collection; trade literature collection. **Holdings:** 15,300 books; 3675 bound periodical volumes; 300 reports; 600 microfiche; 100 reels of microfilm; 12,000 slides; 80 videotapes; maps. **Subscriptions:** 231 journals and other serials. **Services:** Interlibrary loan; copying; library open to the public. **Automated Operations:** Computerized public access catalog. **Computerized Information Services:** Electronic mail service. **Remarks:** FAX: 1 2830329.

★ 18486 ★
University College of Medical Sciences - Library (Med)
Dilshad Garden, Shahdara
Delhi 110 095, India

Phone: 2282971
R. Kumar, Libn.

Founded: 1971. **Staff:** Prof 4; Other 8. **Subjects:** Medical sciences. **Holdings:** 10,000 books; 10,000 bound periodical volumes; 300 reports. **Subscriptions:** 221 journals and other serials; 5 newspapers. **Services:** Interlibrary loan; copying; SDI; library open to persons with an introduction letter from a concerned organization, and upon permission of the college librarian. **Computerized Information Services:** MEDLINE; internal database. **Publications:** List of New Additions in the College Library. **Remarks:** Alternate telephone number(s): 2282974.

★ 18487 ★
University of Cologne - Central Archives for Empirical Social Research (Soc Sci)
Bachemer Strasse 40
W-5000 Cologne 41, Germany

Phone: 221 476940
Dr. Erwin K. Scheuch, Dir.

Founded: 1960. **Staff:** 50. **Subjects:** Surveys - social, population, panel studies, cross-national studies; survey methodology. **Special Collections:** Election studies. **Holdings:** 13,000 monographs, reports, unpublished papers; complete primary materials for 1900 surveys. **Subscriptions:** 100 journals and other serials; 5 newspapers. **Services:** Archives open to the public with restrictions. **Computerized Information Services:** Internal database; EARN (electronic mail service). Performs searches on fee basis. **Publications:** List of Archive Holdings; additional publications available. **Remarks:** FAX: 221 4769444. **Staff:** Ekkehard Mochmann, Mgr.

★ 18488 ★
University of Cologne - Institute of Art History - Library (Art)
St. Laurentius 8
W-5000 Cologne 41, Germany

Phone: 221 4702508
Karin Dolle, Dipl.-Bibl.

Founded: 1930. **Staff:** Prof 1; Other 4. **Subjects:** History of art. **Holdings:** 79,000 books. **Subscriptions:** 100 journals and other serials. **Services:** Library not open to the public. **Also Known As:** Universitat Koln - Kunsthistorisches Institut - Bibliothek.

★ 18489 ★
University of Colorado--Boulder - Academic Media Services (Aud-Vis)
Stadium Bldg., Gate 11, Rm. 360
Campus Box 379
Boulder, CO 80309

Phone: (303)492-7341
Dr. Daniel Niemeyer, Dir.

Founded: 1923. **Staff:** Prof 1; Other 3. **Subjects:** Social studies, science, arts and humanities, language, general areas. **Special Collections:** 16mm educational films and videotapes covering most subject areas for primary,

elementary, junior, senior, college, and adult groups. **Holdings:** 4000 16mm films; 500 videotapes. **Services:** Interlibrary loan; audio- and videotape duplication; services open to the public. **Automated Operations:** Computerized public access catalog. **Networks/Consortia:** Member of Consortium of College and University Media Centers (CCUMC), Colorado Alliance of Research Libraries (CARL). **Special Catalogs:** University of Colorado Instructional Film Video Catalog. **Staff:** Jan Sichel, Mgr., Media Lib.

★ 18490 ★
University of Colorado--Boulder - Art and Architecture Library (Art)
Campus Box 184
Boulder, CO 80309-0184

Phone: (303)492-7955
Liesel Nolan

Founded: 1966. **Staff:** Prof 1; Other 1.5. **Subjects:** Fine arts, art history, photography, architecture, landscape and urban design and planning. **Special Collections:** Artist's books; art exhibition catalogs, 1962 to present. **Holdings:** 76,000 volumes. **Subscriptions:** 400 journals and other serials. **Services:** Interlibrary loan; copying; library open to the public. **Automated Operations:** Computerized public access catalog and circulation. **Computerized Information Services:** DIALOG Information Services; InterNet (electronic mail service). **Networks/Consortia:** Member of Colorado Alliance of Research Libraries (CARL). **Remarks:** FAX: (303)492-2185. Electronic mail address(es): reflib–aa@CUBLDR.COLORADO.EDU (InterNet).

★ 18491 ★
University of Colorado--Boulder - Business Research Division - Business & Economic Collection (Bus-Fin)
Campus Box 420
Boulder, CO 80309

Phone: (303)492-8227
Richard Nobbekind, Dir.

Founded: 1915. **Staff:** 6. **Subjects:** National and Colorado economic data, finance, marketing, real estate, insurance, management. **Holdings:** 4500 volumes. **Subscriptions:** 65 journals and other serials. **Services:** Copying; collection open to the public. **Remarks:** FAX: (303)492-3620. **Staff:** Gin Hayden.

★ 18492 ★
University of Colorado--Boulder - Business Research Division - Travel Reference Center (Bus-Fin)
Campus Box 420
Boulder, CO 80309

Phone: (303)492-5056
C.R. Goeldner, Dir.

Founded: 1969. **Staff:** 2. **Subjects:** Travel, tourism, recreation, leisure. **Holdings:** 40 books; 2 VF drawers of travel papers, speeches, and miscellaneous publications; 8000 other cataloged items. **Subscriptions:** 20 journals and other serials. **Services:** Copying; center open to the public (with fee). **Computerized Information Services:** Internal database. **Remarks:** FAX: (303)492-3620. **Staff:** Gin Hayden; Cindy Di Persio.

★ 18493 ★
University of Colorado--Boulder - Center for Economic Analysis - Library (Bus-Fin)
Economics Bldg. 208
Campus Box 257
Boulder, CO 80309

Phone: (303)492-7413
Michael Greenwood

Founded: 1964. **Staff:** Prof 2; Other 1. **Subjects:** Economics. **Holdings:** 500 volumes. **Subscriptions:** 15 journals and other serials. **Services:** Interlibrary loan (limited); library not open to the public.

★ 18494 ★
University of Colorado--Boulder - Earth Sciences Library (Sci-Engr)
Campus Box 184
Boulder, CO 80309-0184

Phone: (303)492-6133
Suzanne T. Larsen

Staff: Prof 1; Other 1.5. **Subjects:** Physical geology, historical geology, mineralogy, paleontology, geophysics, geochemistry, oceanography, Quaternary period, physical geography. **Holdings:** 38,000 volumes (including government publications); 47,705 microforms. **Subscriptions:** 325 journals and other serials. **Services:** Interlibrary loan; copying; library open to the public. **Automated Operations:** Computerized public access catalog and circulation. **Computerized Information Services:** DIALOG Information Services, BRS Information Technologies, STN International; CD-ROMs; InterNet (electronic mail service). **Networks/Consortia:** Member of Colorado Alliance of Research Libraries (CARL). **Remarks:** FAX: (303)492-2185. Electronic mail address(es): REFLIB–ES@CUBLDR.COLORADO.EDU (InterNet).

★ 18495 ★

University of Colorado--Boulder - East Asiatic Library (Area-Ethnic, Hum)
Campus Box 184   Phone: (303)492-8822
Boulder, CO 80309-0184   Shi-Lai Chu, Act.Hd.
Founded: 1989. **Staff:** 1. **Subjects:** Humanities - Chinese, Japanese. **Holdings:** 25,000 volumes. **Services:** Interlibrary loan; copying; library open to the public. **Computerized Information Services:** InterNet (electronic mail service). **Remarks:** FAX: (303)492-2185. Electronic mail address(es): REFLIB-EA@CUBLDR.COLORADO.EDU (InterNet).

★ 18496 ★

University of Colorado--Boulder - Engineering Library (Sci-Engr)
Campus Box 184   Phone: (303)492-5396
Boulder, CO 80309-0184   Sharon Gause
Founded: 1965. **Staff:** Prof 1.5; Other 2. **Subjects:** Engineering. **Holdings:** 108,063 volumes; 57,633 titles on microfilm and microfiche. **Subscriptions:** 888 journals. **Services:** Interlibrary loan; copying; library open to the public. **Automated Operations:** Computerized public access catalog and circulation. **Computerized Information Services:** DIALOG Information Services, BRS Information Technologies; CD-ROMs; InterNet (electronic mail service). **Networks/Consortia:** Member of Colorado Alliance of Research Libraries (CARL). **Remarks:** FAX: (303)492-4012. Electronic mail address(es): REFLIB–ENG@CUBLDR.COLORADO.EDU (InterNet). **Staff:** Linda Rogers.

★ 18497 ★

University of Colorado--Boulder - Government Publications Library (Info Sci)
Campus Box 184   Phone: (303)492-8834
Boulder, CO 80309-0184   Timothy Byrne
Founded: 1940. **Staff:** Prof 3; Other 4. **Subjects:** Government publications - federal, state, foreign, international; technical reports - NTIS, DOD, DOE, NASA. **Holdings:** 1.4 million documents; 10,500 reels of microfilm; 2.7 million microcards and microfiche; 169,900 microprints; documents depository for United Nations, European Communities, GATT. **Subscriptions:** 10,200 journals and other serials. **Services:** Interlibrary loan; copying; library open to the public. **Computerized Information Services:** Congressional Information Service, Inc. (CIS), DIALOG Information Services, NTIS, LEGI-SLATE; CD-ROMs; InterNet (electronic mail service). **Networks/Consortia:** Member of Colorado Alliance of Research Libraries (CARL). **Remarks:** FAX: (303)492-2185. Electronic mail address(es): REFLIB–GP@CUBLDR.COLORADO.EDU (InterNet). **Staff:** Laura Carter; Dan O'Mahony.

★ 18498 ★

University of Colorado--Boulder - Institute of Arctic & Alpine Research - Reading Room (Sci-Engr)
Rose M. Litman Research Lab.
Campus Box 450   Phone: (303)492-1867
Boulder, CO 80309   Martha Andrews, Prof.Res.Asst.
Staff: 1. **Subjects:** Arctic and Alpine environments, meteorology, climatology, geomorphology, hydrology, palynology, Quaternary geology, glaciology, plant and animal ecology. **Holdings:** 2400 books; 4200 reports; 300 maps; 200 microfiche; 290 theses. **Subscriptions:** 225 journals and other serials. **Services:** Room open to serious researchers for reference use only. **Computerized Information Services:** DIALOG Information Services; CD-ROMs; internal databases; SCIENCEnet (electronic mail service). **Publications:** Niwot Ridge Bibliography (online). **Special Catalogs:** Monograph & serial catalog (ondisc). **Special Indexes:** List of INSTAAR Publications, 1968-1990 (print and online). **Remarks:** FAX: (303)492-6388. Electronic mail address(es): INSTAAR.LIBRARY (SCIENCEnet).

★ 18499 ★

University of Colorado--Boulder - Institute of Behavioral Science - Natural Hazards Research and Applications Information Center (Soc Sci)
IBS Bldg. 6
Campus Box 482   Phone: (303)492-6818
Boulder, CO 80309   Dave Morton, Lib.Asst.
Founded: 1972. **Staff:** 1. **Subjects:** Natural hazards and disasters; socioeconomic, psychological, and political effects of disasters. **Holdings:** 5000 volumes; 200 departmental publications; 45 VF drawers. **Subscriptions:** 20 journals and other serials. **Services:** Interlibrary loan; copying (both limited); center open to the public. **Computerized Information**

Services: HAZBIB (internal database); InterNet (electronic mail service). Performs searches free of charge. **Publications:** Monograph series (52 publications); working papers (72); special publications (24); bibliographies (29); newsletter - free upon request in the U.S; Quick Response Reports (45). **Remarks:** FAX: (303)492-6924. Electronic mail address(es): HAZARDS@VAXF.COLORADO.EDU (InterNet).

★ 18500 ★

University of Colorado--Boulder - Joint Institute for Laboratory Astrophysics (JILA) - Atomic Collision Cross Section Data Center (Sci-Engr)
Campus Box 440
Boulder, CO 80309   Phone: (303)492-7801
Founded: 1963. **Staff:** Prof 2. **Subjects:** Low-energy atomic collision; collisions of low-energy electrons and photons with atoms and simple molecules; low-energy heavy-particle collisions; lasers. **Holdings:** 23,000 documents on microfiche. **Services:** Center open to the public for reference use only. **Computerized Information Services:** Internal database; BITNET (electronic mail service). **Publications:** Annotated bibliographies on time-share disk files and hard copies. **Remarks:** FAX: (303)492-5235. Electronic mail address(es): SKROG@JILA (BITNET). **Staff:** Dr. John T. Broad; Stephen Krog.

★ 18501 ★

University of Colorado--Boulder - Joint Institute for Laboratory Astrophysics (JILA) - Reading Room (Sci-Engr)
Campus Box 440
Boulder, CO 80309   Phone: (303)492-5097
Founded: 1962. **Subjects:** Nuclear physics, astronomy. **Holdings:** 600 volumes. **Subscriptions:** 60 journals and other serials. **Services:** Room not open to the public. **Remarks:** Institute jointly maintained with the U.S. National Institute for Standards and Technology.

★ 18502 ★

University of Colorado--Boulder - Law Library (Law)
Campus Box 402   Phone: (303)492-7534
Boulder, CO 80309-0402   Barbara A. Bintliff, Dir.
Founded: 1892. **Staff:** Prof 7; Other 6. **Subjects:** Law, international law. **Holdings:** 263,838 volumes. **Subscriptions:** 2550 journals and other serials. **Services:** Interlibrary loan; copying; library open to the public with restrictions. **Automated Operations:** Computerized public access catalog, cataloging, acquisitions, circulation, and ILL. **Computerized Information Services:** WESTLAW, LEXIS, NEXIS, OCLC; C.A.R.L. (internal database). **Networks/Consortia:** Member of Central Colorado Library System (CCLS). **Publications:** User's guide, annual - internal use only. **Remarks:** FAX: (303)492-2707. **Staff:** Richard Jost, Hd., Tech.Serv.; Jane Thompson, Hd., Pub.Serv.; Barbara J. Allen, Coll.Dev.; Stacy Dorian, Ref./ Govt.Docs.; Leanne Walther, Ref.Libn.; Roberta Studwell, Assoc.Dir.

★ 18503 ★

University of Colorado--Boulder - Map Library (Geog-Map)
Campus Box 184   Phone: (303)492-7578
Boulder, CO 80309-0184   Susan Lowenberg, Cur.
Staff: 1.5. **Holdings:** General map collection (166,000 sheets). **Services:** Interlibrary loan; copying; library open to the public. **Computerized Information Services:** InterNet (electronic mail service). **Remarks:** FAX: (303)492-2185. Electronic mail address(es): reflib–sci@CUBLDR.Colorado.edu (InterNet).

★ 18504 ★

University of Colorado--Boulder - Music Library (Mus)
Campus Box 184   Phone: (303)492-8093
Boulder, CO 80309-0184   Karl Kroeger
Founded: 1959. **Staff:** Prof 2; Other 4. **Subjects:** Music. **Special Collections:** American Music Research Center (8000 items including tune books, comic operas, psalters); Lumpkin Folk Song Collection (research collection); manuscripts of composers Cecil Effinger and Normand Lockwood; papers of musicologist Erich Katz; popular sheet music collection (10,000 items); 18th century comic opera, California Mission music, early New England singing schools, Moravian music. **Holdings:** 58,000 volumes; 34,000 phonograph records, phonotapes, and compact discs; 34,000 scores. **Subscriptions:** 250 journals and other serials. **Services:** Interlibrary loan; copying; library open to the public. **Automated Operations:** Computerized public access catalog and circulation. **Computerized Information Services:** DIALOG Information Services; InterNet (electronic mail service). **Networks/Consortia:** Member of Colorado Alliance of Research Libraries (CARL). **Publications:** Gloria Dei: Story of California Mission Music (1975). **Remarks:** FAX: (303)492-2185. Electronic mail address(es): REFLIB–MUS@CUBLDR.COLORADO.EDU (InterNet). **Staff:** Nancy F. Carter.

★ 18505 ★

University of Colorado--Boulder - Oliver C. Lester Library of Mathematics and Physics (Sci-Engr)

Campus Box 184   Phone: (303)492-8231
Boulder, CO 80309-0184   Allen Wynne
Founded: 1963. **Staff:** Prof 1; Other 2. **Subjects:** Mathematics, astrogeophysics, physics, computer theory and programming languages, astrophysics. **Special Collections:** High Energy Physics (4500 preprints and reports). **Holdings:** 39,126 books; 39,840 bound periodical volumes; 2700 microforms; 169 linear feet of government documents. **Subscriptions:** 950 journals and other serials. **Services:** Interlibrary loan; copying; library open to the public. **Automated Operations:** Computerized public access catalog and circulation. **Computerized Information Services:** DIALOG Information Services, BRS Information Technologies; CD-ROMs; InterNet (electronic mail service). **Networks/Consortia:** Member of Colorado Alliance of Research Libraries (CARL). **Remarks:** FAX: (303)492-2185. Electronic mail address(es): REFLIB–MP@CUBLDR.COLORADO.EDU (InterNet).

★ 18506 ★

University of Colorado--Boulder - Science Library (Sci-Engr, Biol Sci)

Campus Box 184   Phone: (303)492-5136
Boulder, CO 80309-0184   David M. Fagerstrom
Founded: 1940. **Staff:** Prof 2.5; Other 2. **Subjects:** Chemistry; biology - molecular, cellular, developmental, environmental, organismic, population; psychology; pharmacy; speech pathology; audiology; artificial intelligence; exercise physiology. **Holdings:** 194,000 volumes; 22,150 microforms. **Subscriptions:** 2230 journals and other serials. **Services:** Interlibrary loan; copying; SDI; library open to the public. **Automated Operations:** Computerized public access catalog and circulation. **Computerized Information Services:** DIALOG Information Services, BRS Information Technologies, STN International, NASA/RECON, RLIN, MEDLINE; CD-ROMs; InterNet (electronic mail service). **Networks/Consortia:** Member of Colorado Alliance of Research Libraries (CARL). **Remarks:** FAX: (303)492-2185. Electronic mail address(es): REFLIB–SCI@CUBLDR.COLORADO.EDU (InterNet). **Staff:** Daria Carle; Susan Lowenberg.

★ 18507 ★

University of Colorado--Boulder - Special Collections Department (Rare Book)

Campus Box 184
Boulder, CO 80309-0184   Phone: (303)492-6144
Founded: 1939. **Staff:** Prof 2; Other 2. **Special Collections:** Photography; Bibles in many languages; Epsteen Collection (children's literature); Willard Collection (17th-19th century pamphlets); Aileen Fisher Manuscripts; Gene Fowler Manuscripts; Bowen Collection (French Revolution); Aldous Huxley; David Lavender Manuscripts; Hugh MacDiarmid; John Masefield; Florence Crannell Means Manuscripts; Tour Collection (history of metallurgy); mountaineering; Samuel French Plays; Dickson Leavens Collection (silver money); Pettit Collection (Edward Young); 18th century English literature; 20th century English and American literature; Ashendene Press; Doves Press; Kelmscott Press; Limited Editions Club; Nonesuch Press; Vale Press; Jean Stafford Manuscripts; Marjorie Seiffert Manuscripts; history of meteorology; John D. MacDonald Collection; M. Creighton Collection (Renaissance Papacy); Florence Becker Lennon Collection (20th century poetry); Franklin Folsom and Mary Elting Manuscripts; Creamer Collection (19th century English literature); Kempner Collection (history of mathematics); Veazie Collection (philosophy); Camille Cummings Collection (Elliot Paul); 20th century photography collection. **Holdings:** 45,000 volumes. **Subscriptions:** 30 journals and other serials. **Services:** Interlibrary loan; department open to the public. **Special Catalogs:** The Henry Pettit/Edward Young Collection (1989); exhibit catalogs. **Remarks:** FAX: (303)492-2185. **Staff:** A. Carol Klemme.

★ 18508 ★

University of Colorado--Boulder - Western Historical Collections/ University Archives (Hist)

Campus Box 184   Phone: (303)492-7242
Boulder, CO 80309-0184   Bruce Montgomery
Founded: 1918. **Staff:** Prof 3. **Subjects:** Colorado history, 19th and 20th century American West, political leadership, organized labor, professional organizations, citizen activism, radiation and health, women's history, environmental history, business and industry. **Special Collections:** Women's International League for Peace and Freedom Papers; National Farmers

Union Archives; Edward P. Costigan Papers; Western Federation of Miners and International Union of Mine, Mill and Smelter Workers Archives; James G. Patton Papers; International Typographical Union Archive; Carl Johnson Papers; Elwood Brooks Papers; Western History Association Papers; Colorado Library Association Archives; Oil, Chemical and Atomic Workers Union; Wayne Aspinall Papers; Ray Kogovsek Papers; Frank Delaney Papers; Gary Hart Papers; Friends of the Earth Papers. **Holdings:** 16,000 linear feet of historical manuscripts; 5200 linear feet of university archives; 2000 linear feet of newspapers; 14,000 volumes; 180,000 photographs; pamphlets; maps; microfilm. **Services:** Copying; collection open to the public for reference use only. **Computerized Information Services:** InterNet (electronic mail service). **Publications:** A Guide to Manuscript Collections (1982); guides to individual manuscript collections - for sale. **Remarks:** FAX: (303)492-2185. Electronic mail address(es): MONTGOMERY–B@CUBLDR.COLORADO.EDU (InterNet).

★ 18509 ★

University of Colorado--Boulder - William M. White Business Library (Bus-Fin, Info Sci)

Campus Box 184   Phone: (303)492-8367
Boulder, CO 80309-0184   Carol Krismann
Founded: 1970. **Staff:** Prof 3; Other 3. **Subjects:** Information systems, management and organization, finance, accounting, marketing, transportation, management science, banking, real estate, insurance, taxation. **Special Collections:** Douglas H. Buck Financial Records Collection (101,000 annual and 10K reports on microfiche). **Holdings:** 68,500 volumes; 2000 serials on microfilm. **Subscriptions:** 620 journals; 15 newspapers. **Services:** Interlibrary loan; copying; library open to the public. **Automated Operations:** Computerized public access catalog and circulation. **Computerized Information Services:** DIALOG Information Services, BRS Information Technologies, LEXIS, NEXIS; CD-ROMs (ABI/INFORM, LEXIS, NEXIS, InfoTrac, Compact DISCLOSURE, National Trade Data Base, COMPUSTAT PC); InterNet (electronic mail service). **Networks/ Consortia:** Member of Colorado Alliance of Research Libraries (CARL). **Remarks:** FAX: (303)492-3620. Electronic mail address(es): reflib–bus@CUBLDR.COLORADO.EDU (InterNet). **Staff:** Martha Jo Sani, Asst.Libn.; Yolanda Maloney, Asst.Libn.

★ 18510 ★

University of Colorado--Denver - Auraria Library - Archives and Special Collections (Soc Sci)

Lawrence at 11th St.   Phone: (303)556-8373
Denver, CO 80204   Rutherford W. Witthus, Hd., Archv. & Spec.Coll.
Staff: Prof 1; Other 2. **Subjects:** State and local government, civil liberties, higher education. **Special Collections:** Murray Seasongood Library; National Municipal League, Records, 1894-1986 (200 linear feet); National Repository of State and Local Policy; Auraria Higher Education Center Archives (220 linear feet). **Holdings:** 2000 books; archives (442 linear feet); manuscripts (477 linear feet). **Services:** Interlibrary loan; copying; collections open to the public. **Automated Operations:** Computerized public access catalog, cataloging, acquisitions, serials, and circulation. **Computerized Information Services:** DIALOG Information Services, OCLC; BITNET (electronic mail service). Performs searches on fee basis. Contact Person: Mara Sprain, Computer Res.; 556-8371. **Networks/ Consortia:** Member of Colorado Alliance of Research Libraries (CARL). **Remarks:** Contains the holdings of the former National Civic League, Inc. - Murray Seasongood Library. FAX: (303)556-3528. Electronic mail address(es): RWITTHUS@CUDENVER (BITNET).

★ 18511 ★

University of Colorado Health Sciences Center - Denison Memorial Library (Med)

4200 E. 9th Ave.   Phone: (303)270-5158
Denver, CO 80262   Rick Forsman, Act.Dir.
Founded: 1924. **Staff:** Prof 11; Other 27. **Subjects:** Medicine, nursing, dentistry, allied health sciences. **Special Collections:** James J. Waring History of Medicine Collection. **Holdings:** 87,501 books; 135,242 bound periodical volumes; 3716 AV programs; 194 computer software titles. **Subscriptions:** 2112 journals and other serials. **Services:** Interlibrary loan (fee); copying; library open to the public. **Automated Operations:** Computerized public access catalog, cataloging, acquisitions, serials, and circulation. **Computerized Information Services:** OCLC, DIALOG Information Services, BRS Information Technologies, NLM; CD-ROM (SilverPlatter Information, Inc.); EasyLink, BITNET (electronic mail services). Performs searches on fee basis. Contact Person: Martha Burroughs, Online Serv.Coord., 270-5158. **Networks/Consortia:** Member of

National Network of Libraries of Medicine - Midcontinental Region. **Publications:** Currents, bimonthly. **Remarks:** FAX: (303)270-7227; (303)270-6255. **Staff:** Pat Nelson, Asst.Dir.; Marla Graber, Hd., Cat.; Vicki Milam, Hd., Ser. & Acq.; Sandra Arnesen, Hd., Lrng.Rsrc.Ctr.; Carole Hirschfield, Hd., Circ.; C. Martise Cooper, Hd., Info.Mgt.Ed.Dept.

★ 18512 ★
University of Colorado Health Sciences Center - Rene A. Spitz Psychiatric Library (Med)
4200 E. 9th Ave., C-249   Phone: (303)394-7039
Denver, CO 80262   Irwin Berry, Libn.
Founded: 1967. **Staff:** Prof 1. **Subjects:** Psychiatry, psychoanalysis. **Holdings:** 2900 books; 350 bound periodical volumes; 2550 unbound journals; 100 cassettes. **Subscriptions:** 15 journals and other serials. **Services:** Interlibrary loan; copying; library open to the public with restrictions. **Networks/Consortia:** Member of Colorado Council of Medical Librarians.

★ 18513 ★
University Community Hospital - Medical Library (Med)
3100 E. Fletcher Ave.   Phone: (813)972-7236
Tampa, FL 33613   Gwen E. Walters, Lib.Dir.
Founded: 1974. **Staff:** 2.75. **Subjects:** Medicine, nursing, allied health sciences, health care delivery and administration. **Holdings:** 1740 books; 715 bound periodical volumes; 168 periodicals in microform; 28 file drawers of microfilm; 16 file drawers of microfiche; slides; audiotapes. **Subscriptions:** 464 journals and other serials. **Services:** Interlibrary loan; copying; SDI; library open to the public by appointment. **Automated Operations:** Computerized cataloging, acquisitions, and serials. **Computerized Information Services:** DIALOG Information Services, MEDLARS, OCLC, BRS Information Technologies; DOCLINE, OnTyme Electronic Message Network Service (electronic mail services). Performs searches. **Networks/Consortia:** Member of Tampa Bay Medical Library Network, Tampa Bay Library Consortium, Inc. (TBLC), Florida Library Network (FLN). **Remarks:** FAX: (813)972-7854. **Staff:** Sharon Henrich, Med.Libn.

★ 18514 ★
University of Connecticut - Bartlett Arboretum - Library (Biol Sci, Agri)
151 Brookdale Rd.   Phone: (203)322-6971
Stamford, CT 06903   Sharon Morrisey, Dir.
Founded: 1965. **Staff:** Prof 1. **Subjects:** Horticulture, plant science, botany, arboriculture. **Special Collections:** Materials on conifers, rhododendrons, and floras. **Holdings:** 2500 books; 1000 bound periodical volumes; 30 VF drawers. **Subscriptions:** 25 journals and other serials. **Services:** Library open to the public.

★ 18515 ★
University of Connecticut - Center for Real Estate & Urban Economic Studies - Real Estate Reference & Documents Room (Bus-Fin, Plan)
U-41-RE, Rm. 426
368 Fairfield Rd.   Phone: (203)486-3227
Storrs, CT 06268   Katherine A. Stadtmueller, Asst.Dir.
Founded: 1966. **Staff:** Prof 6; Other 4. **Subjects:** Real estate, urban studies, housing, finance, land use. **Holdings:** 4000 volumes. **Subscriptions:** 65 journals and other serials. **Services:** Interlibrary loan; room open to the public with restrictions. **Publications:** List of publications - available on request. **Remarks:** FAX: (203)486-0349.

★ 18516 ★
University of Connecticut - Frank B. Cookson Music Library (Mus)
876 Coventry Rd.
Box U-153   Phone: (203)486-2502
Storrs, CT 06269-1153   Dorothy McAdoo Bognar, Hd.Mus.Libn.
Staff: Prof 2; Other 2. **Subjects:** Music. **Holdings:** 11,300 books; 2200 bound periodical volumes; 13,000 scores; 25,000 phonograph records; 670 compact discs; 800 reels of microfilm; 570 microfiche sheets; 100 videotapes. **Subscriptions:** 200 journals and other serials. **Services:** Interlibrary loan; listening system; video viewing; library open to the public for reference use only. **Automated Operations:** Computerized cataloging. **Computerized Information Services:** OCLC. **Networks/Consortia:** Member of NELINET, Inc. **Publications:** Guide to the Music Library, irregular - for internal distribution only. **Special Catalogs:** Catalog of piano music and vocal music in collections (card). **Special Indexes:** Music periodicals list (printout). **Staff:** Joseph Scott.

★ 18517 ★
University of Connecticut - Harleigh B. Trecker Library (Soc Sci, Bus-Fin)
1800 Asylum Ave.   Phone: (203)241-4704
West Hartford, CT 06117   James Estrada
Founded: 1985. **Staff:** Prof 6; Other 5. **Subjects:** Business, insurance, data processing, economics, child study, psychoanalysis, psychology, social work, sociology, social security, social welfare, psychiatry, social research, criminology and corrections, recreation. **Holdings:** 93,000 volumes; 35 drawers of pamphlets; 70 drawers of annual reports and company histories; 3700 reels of microfilm of business and insurance periodicals and newspapers and social science materials. **Subscriptions:** 897 journals and other serials; 17 newspapers. **Services:** Interlibrary loan; copying; library open to the public for reference use only. **Automated Operations:** Computerized cataloging and circulation. **Computerized Information Services:** DIALOG Information Services, BRS Information Technologies, Disclosure Information Group, OCLC; CD-ROMs; PROFS, BITNET (electronic mail services). Performs searches on fee basis. **Networks/Consortia:** Member of NELINET, Inc., Capital Region Library Council (CRLC). **Remarks:** Alternate telephone number(s): 241-4869. FAX: (203)241-4790. Electronic mail address(es): HBTLIB1@UCONNVM (BITNET). **Staff:** Marilyn Noronha, Ref.Libn.; Francine DeFranco, Soc.Work Ref.Libn.; Beverley Manning, Cat.Libn.; Norma Holmquist, Bus.Ref.Libn.; Janice Lambert, Access Serv.Libn.

★ 18518 ★
University of Connecticut - Health Center - Lyman Maynard Stowe Library (Med)
P.O. Box 4003   Phone: (203)679-2839
Farmington, CT 06034-4003   Ralph Arcari, Dir.
Founded: 1966. **Staff:** Prof 17; Other 20. **Subjects:** Medicine, dentistry, nursing, allied health sciences. **Special Collections:** Learning Resources Center collection of audiovisuals (6693 items in health sciences). **Holdings:** 55,024 books; 108,247 bound periodical volumes; 329 computer software programs; 5 drawers of pamphlets. **Subscriptions:** 2309 journals and other serials. **Services:** Interlibrary loan; copying; SDI; library open to the public. **Automated Operations:** Computerized public access catalog, cataloging, acquisitions, serials, circulation, and ILL. **Computerized Information Services:** MEDLINE, DIALOG Information Services, OCLC, LS/2000, BRS Information Technologies; CD-ROM (MEDLINE, Science Citation Index, POPLINE); EasyLink (electronic mail service). Performs searches on fee basis. **Networks/Consortia:** Member of Capital Region Library Council (CRLC), Connecticut Association of Health Science Libraries (CAHSL), NELINET, Inc., National Network of Libraries of Medicine - New England Region. **Publications:** Library Newsletter, quarterly; Regional Medical Library Newsletter, quarterly. **Remarks:** FAX: (203)679-4046. Telex: 710-423-5521. **Staff:** Marion Levine, Assoc.Dir.; Jacqueline Lewis, Circ./ILL Libn.; Barbara J. Frey, Hd.Ref.Libn.; Lorna Wright, Automation/Tech.Serv.; Alberta Richetelle, Hd., HEALTHNET; Lynn White, Comp.Educ.Ctr.; Linda Walton, Reg.Med.Lib.Prog.

★ 18519 ★
University of Connecticut - Homer Babbidge Library - Special Collections (Soc Sci, Hum)
Storrs, CT 06269-1005   Phone: (203)486-2524
                                           Richard H. Schimmelpfeng, Dir., Spec.Coll.
Founded: 1881. **Staff:** Prof 4. **Special Collections:** Charles Olson Archives; Turkish language collection; Puerto Rican Collection; Madrid Collection; Spanish periodicals and newspapers; Gaines Americana Collection; Kays Horse Collection; Alternative Press Collection; little magazines; Edwin Way Teale Archives; Chilean history and literature; Jose Toribio Medina Collection; modern German drama; French language and dialects; Luis Camoens; Powys Brothers; American socialist and communist pamphlets and periodicals; children's illustrated books; sundials; ice skating; history of nursing. **Holdings:** 46,000 books; 147,302 bound periodical volumes. **Services:** Interlibrary loan; copying; collections open to the public. **Automated Operations:** Computerized circulation. **Computerized Information Services:** OCLC. **Publications:** Bibliography series, irregular; HARVEST, irregular. **Remarks:** FAX: (203)486-3593. **Staff:** Ellen E. Embardo, Cur., Alternative Press Coll.; Richard Fyffe, Cur., Lit. & Cultural Archv.; Darlene Waller, Cur., Hispanic Coll.

★ 18520 ★
University of Connecticut - Institute of Materials Science - Reading Room (Sci-Engr)
Storrs, CT 06269-3136
Phone: (203)486-4623
Tom Saxton, Asst. to Dir.
Staff: 1. **Subjects:** Metallurgy, polymer science, materials science. **Holdings:** 50 books; 200 bound periodical volumes. **Subscriptions:** 95 journals and other serials. **Services:** Copying; room open to the public.

★ 18521 ★
University of Connecticut - Institute of Public and Urban Affairs - Library
421 Whitney Rd.
Box U-106
Phone: (203)486-4518
Storrs, CT 06268-0106
Richard C. Kearney, Dir.
Founded: 1963. **Staff:** Prof 2; Other 2. **Subjects:** State and local urban affairs. **Special Collections:** Connecticut town and city materials; special reports from Connecticut agencies; New Cities. **Holdings:** 350 books; 200 pamphlets. **Subscriptions:** 11 journals and other serials. **Services:** Copying; library open to the public with restrictions. **Remarks:** FAX: (203)486-3347.

★ 18522 ★
University of Connecticut - Institute for Social Inquiry (Soc Sci)
341 Mansfield Rd., Rm. 421
Box U-164
Phone: (203)486-4440
Storrs, CT 06269-1164
Everett C. Ladd, Jr., Exec.Dir.
Founded: 1968. **Staff:** Prof 13; Other 19. **Subjects:** Public opinion surveys conducted nationally, internationally, and at state levels. **Holdings:** Over 10,000 surveys. **Subscriptions:** Poll releases, journals, serials, and electronic data files. **Services:** Provides instruction in the use of social data; engages in original data collection, including the Connecticut Poll; conducts workshops and seminars; assists in the administration of special research projects involving social survey data. **Computerized Information Services:** DIALOG Information Services, Public Opinion Location Library (POLL). **Publications:** The Public Perspective, bimonthly; Data Acquisitions, biennial; Profiles of the American Collection, annual. **Remarks:** FAX: (203)486-6308. Electronic mail address(es): SSDCK@UCONNVM. The institute is a local archive of survey and aggregate data in machine readable form and serves as a multipurpose research and teaching facility for the social sciences. It also hosts the archival development component, user services, and Office of the Executive Director of the Roper Center (see the description of the Roper Center for further information). **Staff:** Lois Timms-Ferrara, User Serv.Coord.; G. Donald Ferree, Assoc.Dir.

★ 18523 ★
University of Connecticut - Labor Education Center - Information Center (Bus-Fin)
One Bishop Circle, Rm. 210
Box U-13
Phone: (203)486-3417
Storrs, CT 06269-4013
Mark E. Sullivan, Act.Dir.
Founded: 1946. **Subjects:** Labor studies, industrial relations. **Holdings:** 300 volumes. **Subscriptions:** 20 journals and other serials. **Services:** Center open to the public with restrictions. **Computerized Information Services:** Human Resource Information Network (HRIN).

★ 18524 ★
University of Connecticut - Law School Library (Law)
120 Sherman St.
Phone: (203)241-4636
Hartford, CT 06105-2289
Dennis J. Stone, Law Libn.
Founded: 1942. **Staff:** Prof 11; Other 3. **Subjects:** Law. **Holdings:** 240,000 books; 900 AV programs; 4450 reels of microfilm; 550,000 microfiche; government documents depository. **Subscriptions:** 4200 journals and other serials. **Services:** Interlibrary loan; copying; library open to the public for reference use only. **Automated Operations:** Computerized cataloging, acquisitions, and circulation. **Computerized Information Services:** LEXIS, WESTLAW, OCLC, RLIN; BITNET (electronic mail service). **Networks/Consortia:** Member of New England Law Library Consortium (NELLCO), NELINET, Inc. **Remarks:** FAX: (203)241-4612. Electronic mail address(es): LAWLIB9@UCONNUM (BITNET). **Staff:** Marsha Baum, Dp.Dir.; Kathleen McLeod, Ref.Libn.; Jui-Chung Cheng, Computer/Media Spec.; Andrea Joseph, Rd.Serv.Libn.; Marcella Montagano, Govt.Docs.Libn.

★ 18525 ★
University of Connecticut - Map Library (Geog-Map)
Homer Babbidge Library
Phone: (203)486-4589
Storrs, CT 06269-1005
Thornton P. McGlamery, Map Libn.
Founded: 1976. **Staff:** Prof 1; Other 1. **Subjects:** Maps, cartography, history of cartography, computer cartography, remote sensing, travel. **Special Collections:** Petersen Collection, photostat collection of 19th century New England towns; enlarged photostats of manuscript working charts of the U.S. Coast Survey. **Holdings:** 156,000 maps; 15 VF drawers of aerial photographs; 28 VF drawers of U.S. Geological Survey reports; 6 VF drawers of map publisher and dealer catalogs; Sanborn Fire Insurance Maps for Connecticut on microfilm; Digital cartographic data; 91 horizontal map cases; 16 vertical map cases. **Subscriptions:** 5 journals and other serials. **Services:** Interlibrary loan; large format copying; library open to the public. **Automated Operations:** Computerized cataloging, acquisitions, serials, and circulation. **Computerized Information Services:** Earth Science Information Center (ESIC); internal databases.

★ 18526 ★
University of Connecticut - Marine Sciences Institute - Library (Biol Sci)
Avery Point
Phone: (203)445-3426
Groton, CT 06340
Constance B. Cooke
Founded: 1967. **Staff:** Prof 2. **Subjects:** Marine biology, physical oceanography, chemical oceanography. **Special Collections:** Army Corps of Engineers collection of dredging materials (600 items); hydrographic charts, 1832-1876 (300). **Holdings:** 5000 books; 2000 bound periodical volumes; 500 reports. **Services:** Interlibrary loan; copying; library open to the public for reference use only. **Computerized Information Services:** OCLC, Aquatic Sciences and Fisheries Abstracts (ASFA), Institute for Scientific Information (ISI) Science Citation Index, InfoTrac; ReQuest (internal database). **Remarks:** FAX: (203)445-3498. Alternate telephone number(s): (203)445-3427.

★ 18527 ★
University of Connecticut - Pharmacy Library and Learning Center (Med)
Box U-92
Phone: (203)486-2218
Storrs, CT 06269-1092
Sharon Giovenale, Dir.
Staff: Prof 2. **Subjects:** Pharmaceutics, pharmacology, pharmacognosy, pharmaceutical chemistry, health care services. **Holdings:** 5000 books; 16,000 bound periodical volumes; 5 VF drawers of pamphlets and clippings; 300 AV programs; 400 reels of microfilm of periodicals. **Subscriptions:** 244 journals and other serials. **Services:** Interlibrary loan; copying; library open to the public for reference use only. **Computerized Information Services:** BRS Information Technologies, NLM, DIALOG Information Services; CD-ROMs (MEDLINE, current 5 years; International Pharmaceutical Abstracts). **Remarks:** FAX: (203)486-4998. **Staff:** David Keighley, Media Spec.

★ 18528 ★
University of Connecticut - Roper Center for Public Opinion Research (Soc Sci)
Box 440
Phone: (203)486-4440
Storrs, CT 06268-0440
Everett C. Ladd, Exec.Dir.
Founded: 1946. **Staff:** Prof 13; Other 19. **Subjects:** Survey data contributed by the world's major survey organizations. **Special Collections:** Gallup Opinion Surveys, 1936 to present; Yankelovich, Clancy Shulman surveys for Time magazine; CBS/New York Times; ABC/Washington Post; NBC/Associated Press; Los Angeles Times; National Opinion Research Center (NORC); Roper Organization; international surveys conducted by United States Information Agency, International Research Associates, Gallup Affiliates, Brule Ville Associes, and Commission of European Communities (Eurobarometer). **Holdings:** 11,000 public opinion surveys. **Services:** Data set reproduction; data analysis; search and retrieval; duplication of questionnaires and codebooks; copying; center open to the public. **Computerized Information Services:** POLL (Public Opinion Location Library; internal database). Performs searches on fee basis. Contacts: Lois Timms-Ferrara, John Benson, Marc Maynard, Marilyn Potter. **Publications:** Study listings organized by country; The Public Perspective, bimonthly; Data Aquisitions, biennial; Profiles of the American Collection, annual. **Remarks:** FAX: (203)486-6308. Since 1977, the Roper Center has operated through a formal partnership of the University of Connecticut and Williams College. The University of Connecticut branch of the Roper Center, which has primary operating responsibilities, is housed administratively within the Institute for Social Inquiry. **Staff:** Anne-Marie Mercure, Mgr., Archv.

★ 18529 ★
University of Connecticut - School of Education - I.N. Thut World Education Center (Educ)
P.O. Box U-93   Phone: (203)486-0244
Storrs, CT 06269-2093   Ms.Byunghwa Yoo, Graduate Asst.
Founded: 1971. **Staff:** Prof 2; Other 2. **Subjects:** Education - multicultural, international, global, bilingual-bicultural, urban; education for development. **Special Collections:** The Peoples of Connecticut oral histories (150); artifacts collection for teaching about other cultures and nations. **Holdings:** 800 books; 1000 documents; 110 sets of slides; 20 videotapes. **Subscriptions:** 40 journals and other serials. **Services:** Interlibrary loan; copying; center open to the public. **Automated Operations:** Computerized cataloging, acquisitions, serials, and circulation. **Computerized Information Services:** Online systems. **Publications:** Annual report; publications list; annotated bibliography on Peace Studies; Tootline: Newsletter of The Isaac N. Thut World Education Center, semiannual. **Special Catalogs:** Catalog of Asian and Middle Eastern Studies resources in Connecticut; curriculum guides for the Peoples of Connecticut, World Education Monograph Series, Multicultural Educational Research Methodologies Series. **Remarks:** Alternate telephone number(s): 486-0243. **Staff:** Dr. Patricia Snyder Weibust, Co-Dir.; Dr. Frank A. Stone, Co-Dir.

★ 18530 ★
University of Connecticut - Storrs Agricultural Experiment Station - Library (Agri)
U-10, Rm. 211
1376 Storrs Rd.   Phone: (203)486-3535
Storrs, CT 06269-4010   Louis J. Pierro, Assoc.Dir.
Founded: 1887. **Subscriptions:** 23 journals and other serials. **Computerized Information Services:** BITNET (electronic mail service). **Remarks:** Library functions as an information center for faculty and administrative use. Holdings partially housed in conference room, the remainder distributed to small departmental libraries in six other locations. FAX: (203)486-4128. Electronic mail address(es): CAGADM02@UCONNVM (BITNET).

★ 18531 ★
University of Connecticut - Waterbury Regional Campus - Library (Agri)
32 Hillside Ave.   Phone: (203)757-6795
Waterbury, CT 06710-2288   Janet M. Swift
Founded: 1946. **Staff:** Prof 3; Other 2. **Special Collections:** Philemon J. Hewitt Apicultural Collection (200 books; 8 current subscriptions; 35 back runs of periodicals). **Services:** Interlibrary loan; copying; library open to the public. **Computerized Information Services:** BITNET (electronic mail service). **Remarks:** FAX: (203)754-8540. Electronic mail address(es): WBLADMO1@UCONNVM (BITNET).

★ 18532 ★
University of Dayton - Law School Library (Soc Sci, Law)
300 College Park   Phone: (513)229-2314
Dayton, OH 45469   Prof. Thomas L. Hanley, Dir.
Founded: 1974. **Staff:** Prof 4; Other 8. **Subjects:** Law, political science, social sciences. **Holdings:** 200,000 volumes; government documents. **Subscriptions:** 702 journals and other serials; 15 newspapers. **Services:** Interlibrary loan; copying; library open to the public for reference use only. **Automated Operations:** Computerized public access catalog, cataloging, circulation, and ILL. **Computerized Information Services:** LEXIS, WESTLAW, OCLC. **Networks/Consortia:** Member of Southwestern Ohio Council for Higher Education (SOCHE), Ohio Regional Consortium of Law Libraries (ORCLL). **Publications:** Recent Acquisitions List, monthly; Annual Report. **Staff:** Theodora Artz, Hd., Acq.Dept.; Geraldine Wernersbach, Hd., Ref./Circ.Dept.; Karen Wilhoit, Hd., Cat.Dept.

★ 18533 ★
University of Dayton - Marian Library (Rel-Phil)
300 College Park   Phone: (513)229-4214
Dayton, OH 45469-1390   Rev. Thomas A. Thompson, Dir.
Founded: 1943. **Staff:** Prof 4; Other 4. **Subjects:** Virgin Mary in theology, devotions, belles lettres, art, music. **Special Collections:** Clugnet Collection (Marian shrines; 8000 items); religious art (300 volumes). **Holdings:** 78,000 volumes; 53,300 clippings; 200 reels of microfilm; 2 boxes of American bishops' pastoral letters; 2200 slides; 4 manuscripts; 5000 pictures; 10,000 holy cards; postcards of Marian shrines and art; 15 albums of postage stamps; 1000 photographs; 300 medals; 80 phonograph records; 330 audio cassettes; 30 videocassettes. **Subscriptions:** 110 journals and other serials; 10

newspapers. **Services:** Interlibrary loan; copying; library open to the public. **Publications:** Marian Library Studies, annual - available by subscription; Marian Library Newsletter, 2/year - free upon request. **Special Catalogs:** Union catalog of Marian holdings in selected North American libraries. **Special Indexes:** Author/title indexes to proceedings of International Mariological Congresses: 1950, 1954, 1958, 1965, 1971, 1975; indexes to selected journals. **Staff:** William Fackovec, S.M., Cat./Bibliog.; Anne E. Moss, Cat.

★ 18534 ★
University of Dayton - Roesch Library - Rare Books (Rare Book)
300 College Park Ave., 7th Fl.   Phone: (513)229-3669
Dayton, OH 45469   Raymond H. Nartker, Rare Bks.Libn.
Founded: 1965. **Staff:** Prof 1. **Subjects:** First editions of 19th and early 20th century English and American literature; works of Paul Laurence Dunbar, Booth Tarkington, Charles Craddock, George Bar McCutcheon; Lincoln and the Civil War; theology; church history; canon law. **Holdings:** 7400 volumes; limited editions club books. **Services:** Copying; library open to the public by appointment.

★ 18535 ★
University of Dayton - Roesch Library - University Archives/Special Collections (Hum)
300 College Park Ave., 3rd Fl.   Phone: (513)229-4267
Dayton, OH 45469-1360   Kerrie A. Moore, Archv./Spec.Coll.Libn.
Founded: 1970. **Staff:** Prof 1. **Subjects:** University of Dayton, science fiction, Dayton Performing Arts. **Special Collections:** University archives (889 linear feet); Science Fiction Writers of America (SFWA) Collection (1339 books); Urban Schnurr Collection; Victory Theatre Papers; Charles W. Whalen Congressional Papers, 1966-1978 (464 boxes); Michael Polanyi Papers; Catholic Council on Civil Liberties (CCCL) Papers; Association for Creative Change Papers. **Holdings:** 1339 linear feet. **Services:** Copying; collections open to the public for reference use only. **Automated Operations:** Computerized public access catalog and cataloging. **Computerized Information Services:** DIALOG Information Services, BRS Information Technologies, OCLC EPIC. **Networks/Consortia:** Member of Southwestern Ohio Council for Higher Education (SOCHE). **Special Catalogs:** Catalogs of archives and SFWA Collection (card and online). **Special Indexes:** Inventories of Schnurr, Whalen, Polanyi, and CCCL Collections.

★ 18536 ★
University of Dayton - School of Education - Curriculum Materials Center - 0514 (Educ)
Chaminade Hall 114
300 College Park   Phone: (513)229-3140
Dayton, OH 49469   Ann Raney, Dir.
Founded: 1955. **Staff:** 1. **Subjects:** Elementary and secondary textbooks, children's literature, teacher education. **Holdings:** 15,224 books; 215 bound periodical volumes; 81 sets of transparencies; 2200 filmstrips; 600 records; 60 models; 400 material kits; 223 cartridges; 480 sets of charts and posters; 1500 other teaching aids; 56 VF drawers; 724 tests/assessments; master's projects for School of Education. **Subscriptions:** 65 journals and other serials. **Services:** Center open to the public. **Computerized Information Services:** Internal database. **Publications:** Monthly News Bulletin, bimonthly during academic year - to faculty and students. **Special Catalogs:** Book and nonprint material collection catalog.

★ 18537 ★
University of Delaware - Archives (Hist)
78 E. Delaware Ave.   Phone: (302)451-2750
Newark, DE 19716   Jean K. Brown, Dir. of Rec.Mgt. & Archv.Serv.
Founded: 1969. **Staff:** Prof 2; Other 3. **Subjects:** University of Delaware history. **Holdings:** 10,750 theses and dissertations; 320 bound periodical volumes; 5600 cubic feet of records; 950 reels of AV programs; 9000 photographs and negatives. **Services:** Copying; archives open to the public for approved research projects. **Automated Operations:** Computerized cataloging.

★ 18538 ★
University of Delaware - Center for Research and Evaluation of Applied Technology in Education - Library
College of Education
Willard Hall Education Bldg., Rm. 303C
Newark, DE 19716
Defunct.

★ 18539 ★
University of Delaware - College of Urban Affairs and Public Policy - Library
Graham Hall
Newark, DE 19716
Subjects: Government, economics, and sociology (primarily Delaware); census information on all school districts in New Castle County. **Holdings:** 2000 books. **Remarks:** Currently inactive.

★ 18540 ★
University of Delaware - Department of Music - Music Resource Center (Mus)
Newark, DE 19716
Phone: (302)451-8130
J. Michael Foster, Supv.
Founded: 1979. **Staff:** Prof 1. **Subjects:** Music. **Holdings:** 2600 books; 4500 scores; 5700 phonograph records; 800 tape recordings. **Services:** Center open to the public with restrictions.

★ 18541 ★
University of Delaware - Disaster Research Center (Soc Sci)
Newark, DE 19716
Phone: (302)451-6618
Dr. E.L. Quarantelli
Founded: 1963. **Staff:** Prof 4. **Subjects:** Disaster research, sociology of disaster and mass emergencies. **Holdings:** 6000 books; 15,000 reports and articles; 250 dissertations and theses; documents. **Subscriptions:** 175 journals and other serials. **Services:** Copying; library open to the public. **Computerized Information Services:** BITNET (electronic mail service). **Publications:** Publications List, semiannual - free upon request. **Remarks:** FAX: (302)451-2828. Electronic mail address(es): ACJ00984@UDACSVM (BITNET).

★ 18542 ★
University of Delaware - Education Resource Center (Educ)
013 Willard Hall Education Bldg.
Phone: (302)831-2335
Newark, DE 19716
Beth G. Anderson, Dir.
Founded: 1972. **Staff:** Prof 2.5. **Subjects:** Curriculum materials in elementary science and mathematics, elementary language arts, occupational education, special education, elementary social studies, reading, marine studies. **Special Collections:** Multicultural children's collection (6000 items). **Holdings:** 21,000 books; AV programs and kits; microcomputer laboratory; videodiscs. **Subscriptions:** 25 education journals. **Services:** Center open to the public. **Computerized Information Services:** Special Education Mini Center (internal database); BITNET (electronic mail service). **Networks/Consortia:** Member of Delaware Learning Resource System (DLRS). **Remarks:** FAX: (302)831-3569. Electronic mail address(es): HPS09074@UDELVM (BITNET). The multicultural children's collection is on permanent loan from UNICEF - Information Center on Children's Cultures. **Staff:** Allison Kaplan; James Cayz; Jennifer Taylor.

★ 18543 ★
University of Delaware - Library - Agriculture Library (Agri)
002 Townsend Hall
Phone: (302)831-2530
Newark, DE 19717-1303
Frederick B. Getze, Libn.
Founded: 1888. **Staff:** Prof 1; Other 1. **Subjects:** Agriculture and related areas in biology and chemistry, veterinary medicine. **Special Collections:** State agricultural experiment station documents; Unidel History of Horticultural Landscape Architecture (housed at Morris Library). **Holdings:** Figures not available. **Services:** Interlibrary loan; copying; library open to the public. **Automated Operations:** Computerized public access catalog, cataloging, acquisitions, serials, circulation, and ILL. **Computerized Information Services:** DIALOG Information Services, RLIN, BRS Information Technologies, OCLC; CD-ROM (AGRICOLA). Performs searches on fee basis. **Networks/Consortia:** Member of Center for Research Libraries (CRL), PALINET. **Staff:** Margaret Welshmer, Hd., Br.Libs.Dept.

★ 18544 ★
University of Delaware - Library - Chemistry & Biochemistry/Chemical Engineering Library (Sci-Engr)
202 Brown Laboratory
Phone: (302)831-2993
Newark, DE 19716
Margaret Welshmer, Hd., Br.Libs.Dept.
Founded: 1938. **Staff:** 1. **Subjects:** Chemistry and chemical engineering. **Special Collections:** Unidel History of Chemistry Collection (housed at Morris Library). **Holdings:** 10,072 books; 11,363 bound periodical volumes; 2969 microfilm. **Subscriptions:** 1227 journals and other serials. **Services:** Interlibrary loan; copying; library open to the public. **Automated Operations:** Computerized cataloging, acquisitions, serials, circulation, and ILL. **Computerized Information Services:** DIALOG Information Services, BRS Information Technologies, Association of Research Libraries (ARL), STN International, Chemical Abstracts Service (CAS), RLIN, OCLC. **Networks/Consortia:** Member of Center for Research Libraries (CRL), PALINET.

★ 18545 ★
University of Delaware - Library - Marine Studies Library (Biol Sci, Sci-Engr)
Harry L. Cannon Marine Studies Laboratory
Phone: (302)645-4290
Lewes, DE 19958
Dorothy Allen, Lib.Coord.
Founded: 1973. **Staff:** Prof 1; Other .5. **Subjects:** Marine biology and geology, physical and chemical oceanography. **Special Collections:** All publications of Delaware College of Marine Studies; Sea Grant publications. **Holdings:** 7200 books; 4100 bound periodical volumes; 5300 reprints. **Subscriptions:** 196 journals and other serials. **Services:** Interlibrary loan; copying; library open to the public. **Automated Operations:** Computerized public access catalog, cataloging, acquisitions, serials, and circulation. **Computerized Information Services:** DIALOG Information Services, OCLC, RLIN, BRS Information Technologies, STN International, Chemical Abstracts Service (CAS); CD-ROM (Aquatic Sciences and Fisheries Abstracts (ASFA)); BITNET (electronic mail service). Performs searches on fee basis. Telephone (302)645-4293. **Networks/Consortia:** Member of Center for Research Libraries (CRL), PALINET. **Remarks:** FAX: (302)645-4007. **Staff:** Margaret Welshmer, Hd., Br.Libs.Dept.

★ 18546 ★
University of Delaware - Library - Physics Library (Sci-Engr)
221 Sharp Laboratory
Phone: (302)831-2323
Newark, DE 19716
Mayra Focht, Lib.Coord.
Staff: 1. **Subjects:** Physics, astronomy, astrophysics, mathematics, engineering. **Holdings:** Figures not available. **Services:** Interlibrary loan; library open to the public. **Automated Operations:** Computerized cataloging, acquisitions, serials, circulation, and ILL. **Computerized Information Services:** DIALOG Information Services, RLIN, BRS Information Technologies, OCLC. **Networks/Consortia:** Member of Center for Research Libraries (CRL), PALINET. **Staff:** Margaret Welshmer, Hd., Br.Libs.Dept.

★ 18547 ★
University of Denver - College of Law - Westminster Law Library (Law)
1900 Olive St. - LTLB
Phone: (303)871-6188
Denver, CO 80220
Barbara Greenspahn, Dir.
Founded: 1898. **Staff:** Prof 9; Other 8. **Subjects:** Law. **Holdings:** 244,072 books, bound periodical volumes, microforms, government documents. **Subscriptions:** 3000 journals and other serials. **Services:** Interlibrary loan; copying; library open to current members and alumni, and to all others on a fee basis. **Automated Operations:** Computerized cataloging, acquisitions, serials, and circulation. **Computerized Information Services:** DIALOG Information Services, WESTLAW, LEXIS, InfoTrac. **Networks/Consortia:** Member of Colorado Alliance of Research Libraries (CARL). **Remarks:** FAX: (303)871-6411. **Staff:** Gary Alexander, Coll.Dev.Libn.; David Burrows, User Serv.Libn.; Susan Madison, Bibliog. Access Libn.; Mary Wilder, Curric./Instr.Libn.; Sheila Green, User Serv.Libn.; Esther Crawford, User Serv.Libn.; Catherine Pabich, User Serv.Libn.; Elaine Jurries, Info. Sources Mgt.Libn.

★ 18548 ★
University of Denver - Penrose Library - Special Collections (Hist)
2150 E. Evans Ave.
Phone: (303)871-3428
Denver, CO 80208-0287
Steven Fisher, Cur.
Founded: 1864. **Special Collections:** Judaica (17,000 volumes); Husted Culinary Collection (8000 items); Miller Civil War Collection (1000 items); Davidson Folklore Collection (1000 items). **Services:** Interlibrary loan; copying; collections open to the public. **Automated Operations:** Computerized cataloging, acquisitions, serials, and circulation. **Computerized Information Services:** Online systems. **Networks/Consortia:** Member of Colorado Alliance of Research Libraries (CARL).

★ 18549 ★
University of Detroit Mercy - Dental Library (Med)
2931 E. Jefferson Ave.   Phone: (313)446-1817
Detroit, MI 48207   M. Agnes Shoup, Dir.
Founded: 1932. **Staff:** Prof 2; Other 3. **Subjects:** Dentistry. **Holdings:** 13,000 books; 15,000 bound periodical volumes. **Subscriptions:** 450 journals and other serials. **Services:** Interlibrary loan; copying; SDI; library open to the public for reference use only. **Automated Operations:** Computerized cataloging. **Computerized Information Services:** MEDLINE, DIALOG Information Services. Performs searches on fee basis. **Networks/Consortia:** Member of Michigan Library Consortium (MLC). **Publications:** Acquisitions, quarterly. **Formerly:** Its School of Dentistry Library. **Staff:** Beverly Dorrah, Libn.

★ 18550 ★
University of Detroit Mercy - Evening Business and Administration Library
651 E. Jefferson
Detroit, MI 48226
Defunct.

★ 18551 ★
University of Detroit Mercy - McNichols Campus Library Media Center (Aud-Vis)
4001 W. McNichols Rd.   Phone: (313)993-1075
Detroit, MI 48221   William Gould-McElhone, Hd., Lib. Media Serv.
Founded: 1961. **Staff:** Prof 4. **Subjects:** History, literature, language arts, fine arts, education, business and management, sociology, psychology, science, mathematics, religious studies, philosophy, economics, political science, music. **Holdings:** 2002 phonograph records and sets; 1533 filmstrips and filmstrip sets with sound; 181 slides and slide sets with sound; 659 models and games; 252 videocassettes and 16mm films; 389 audiocassettes and sets; 1740 transparencies and sets; 275 testing materials titles; 146 compact discs; reference materials. **Services:** Interlibrary loan; AV equipment pool; projection rooms; group study room; photography; AV software production; audiocassettes duplication; graphic design, production, and duplication; punch binding; desktop publishing; picture framing; laminating; dry mounting; center open to the public with restrictions. **Automated Operations:** Computerized public access catalog and circulation. **Computerized Information Services:** PROFS (electronic mail service). **Networks/Consortia:** Member of Michigan Library Consortium (MLC). **Publications:** Bibliography of Recent Acquisitions, annual. **Remarks:** FAX: (313)993-1780. Electronic mail address(es): WAYNEST1 WMCELHO (PROFS). **Staff:** Sue Homant, Hd., Ref.

★ 18552 ★
University of Detroit Mercy - School of Law Library (Law)
651 E. Jefferson Ave.   Phone: (313)596-0241
Detroit, MI 48226   Byron D. Cooper, Dir.
Founded: 1912. **Staff:** Prof 5; Other 7. **Subjects:** Law - United States, Canada, England. **Holdings:** 220,000 volumes; 50,000 volumes in microform. **Subscriptions:** 1800 journals and other serials; 12 newspapers. **Services:** Interlibrary loan; copying; library open to the public. **Automated Operations:** Computerized cataloging. **Computerized Information Services:** LEXIS, NEXIS, DIALOG Information Services, WESTLAW, VU/TEXT Information Services, BRS Information Technologies, ELSS (Electronic Legislative Search System). **Networks/Consortia:** Member of Michigan Library Consortium (MLC). **Publications:** Law Library Guide, annual - to students; Current Acquisitions List, monthly. **Remarks:** FAX: (313)596-0245. **Staff:** Colleen M. Hickey, S.S.J., Assoc.Dir.; Mary E. Hayes, Ref.Libn.; Gene P. Moy, Docs./Circ.Libn.; Katherine A. Cooper, Res.Spec.; Lida Keem, Tech.Serv.

★ 18553 ★
University of the District of Columbia - Georgia/Harvard Campus - Harvard Street Library (Educ)
1100 Harvard St., N.W.   Phone: (202)673-7018
Washington, DC 20009   Melba Broome, Supv.
Staff: Prof 3; Other 1. **Subjects:** Education, human ecology. **Special Collections:** Trevor Arnett Library of Black Culture (8000 reels of microfilm); Miner-Wilson Collection (2000 rare books); legislative history of Federal City College. **Holdings:** 111,000 books; 10,000 bound periodical volumes; 150,000 microforms; archives. **Subscriptions:** 500 journals and other serials; 6 newspapers. **Services:** Interlibrary loan; copying; library open to the public with restrictions. **Networks/Consortia:** Member of Consortium of Universities of the Washington Metropolitan Area. **Special Catalogs:** Catalog of Miner-Wilson Collection; District of Columbia Teachers College Library (book catalog). **Staff:** Taro G. Gehani, Acq.Libn.; Elizabeth M. Thompson, Media Serv.Libn.; Anne Robinson, Media Serv.Libn.

★ 18554 ★
University of the District of Columbia - Learning Resources Division (Soc Sci, Hist)
4200 Connecticut Ave., N.W.
MB 4102   Phone: (202)282-7536
Washington, DC 20008   Albert J. Casciero, Dir.
Staff: 68. **Special Collections:** Human Relations Area Files (microfiche); Atlanta University Black Culture Collection; Water Resources (625 items); University of D.C. archives (513 linear feet); slavery source materials (962 microfiche); Schombury Clipping File (9500 microfiche). **Holdings:** 498,792 books; 584,020 microfiche. **Subscriptions:** 2610 journals and other serials; 25 newspapers. **Services:** Interlibrary loan; copying; SDI; division open to the public with restrictions. **Automated Operations:** Computerized cataloging and circulation. **Computerized Information Services:** DIALOG Information Services, OCLC. Performs searches on fee basis. Contact Person: Veronica Nance, 282-3091. **Networks/Consortia:** Member of CAPCON Library Network, Washington Research Library Consortium. **Publications:** Access brochures. **Remarks:** FAX: (202)282-3102. **Staff:** Melba Broome; Ulysses Cameron; Robert Artisst; Bruce Cheeks; Taro Gehani; Anthony Gittens; R. Leroy Hooper; Katie Inmon; Albertine Johnson; Edward S. Jones; Raoul Kulberg; Parvin Kujoory; Darrell Lemke; Jack Martinelli; Eugene Miller; John S. Page; Gemma Park; Chet Sarangapani; I'Yao Shen; Willard Taylor; Kay Varnado; Maria Willis; Clement Goddard.

★ 18555 ★
University of Dubuque Theological Seminary - Library (Rel-Phil)
2000 University   Phone: (319)589-3215
Dubuque, IA 52001   Joel L. Samuels, Dir., Libs.
Staff: Prof 6; Other 4. **Subjects:** Theology, missions, ecumenical studies. **Special Collections:** Hymnals; Lutheran irenics and polemics. **Holdings:** 222,256 volumes. **Subscriptions:** 800 journals and other serials; 10 newspapers. **Services:** Interlibrary loan; copying; library open to the public. **Automated Operations:** Computerized cataloging, serials, and circulation. **Computerized Information Services:** OCLC, DIALOG Information Services, BRS Information Technologies. Performs searches free of charge. **Publications:** STD Library Bulletin, monthly - for internal distribution only. **Remarks:** Includes the holdings of the Couchman Memorial Library located at 2050 University Ave. and the Ficke-Laird Library. Alternate telephone number(s): 589-0265. **Staff:** Vera L. Robinson, Cat.; Mary Anne Knefel, Ref.Libn.; Debbie Fliegel, Ref.Libn.; Carolynne Lathrop, Ref.Libn.

★ 18556 ★
University of Dusseldorf - Research Division for Philosophy Information and Documentation - Philosophy Information Service (Rel-Phil)
Universitatstrasse 1   Phone: 211 3112913
W-4000 Dusseldorf 1, Germany   Dr. Norbert Henrichs, Hd.
Founded: 1967. **Staff:** Prof 3; Other 7. **Subjects:** Philosophy, philosophy of science, logic, anthropology, metaphysics, ethics. **Special Collections:** Letters of Philosophers, 1750-1850 (300,000 pages). **Holdings:** 70,000 volumes. **Subscriptions:** 150 journals and other serials. **Services:** Interlibrary loan; SDI; service open to the public. **Automated Operations:** Computerized public access catalog, cataloging, and serials. **Computerized Information Services:** Produces Epistolographie Data Base; PHILIS (international philosophical periodicals; internal database); electronic mail service. Performs searches free of charge. **Remarks:** FAX: 211 342229. Telex: 8587348 uni d.

★ 18557 ★
University of Florida - Agricultural Research & Education Center - Library (Agri)
Box 728   Phone: (904)692-1792
Hastings, FL 32145-0728   M.J. Campbell, Off.Mgr.
Founded: 1940. **Staff:** 1. **Subjects:** Agriculture, vegetable production. **Holdings:** 350 books; 240 bound periodical volumes; 100 unbound periodicals; 1400 unbound agricultural bulletins and pamphlets. **Subscriptions:** 28 journals and other serials. **Services:** Library open to the public for reference use only. **Remarks:** FAX: (904)692-2195.

★ 18558 ★
University of Florida - Aquatic Plant Information Retrieval System (APIRS) (Biol Sci)
7922 N.W. 71st St.   Phone: (904)392-1799
Gainesville, FL 32606   Victor Ramey, Coord.Ed./Media Comm.
Founded: 1980. **Staff:** Prof 3; Other 2. **Subjects:** Aquatic plants - biology, control, utilization, ecology. **Holdings:** 1000 books; 32,000 other cataloged

items. **Services:** Interlibrary loan; copying; center open to the public for reference use only. **Automated Operations:** Computerized cataloging, acquisitions, and document indexing. **Computerized Information Services:** Aquatic Plant Information Retrieval System (internal database). Performs searches free of charge. **Publications:** Aquaphyte, biennial - free upon request; bibliographic database searches (computer printout). **Remarks:** FAX: (904)392-3462. **Staff:** Karen Brown, Sr.Info.Spec.; Jeri Friedman, Info.Spec.

★18559★
University of Florida - Architecture & Fine Arts Library (Art)
201 FAA   Phone: (904)392-0222
Gainesville, FL 32611   Edward H. Teague, AFA Libn.
Founded: 1965. **Staff:** Prof 2; Other 2.5. **Subjects:** Architecture, visual arts, interior design, building construction, landscape architecture, urban design. **Holdings:** 75,000 volumes; 12 VF drawers; 7400 architectural drawings, photographs, postcards; 20 drawers of Historic American Buildings Survey drawings and pictures; 32,000 microforms. **Subscriptions:** 640 journals and other serials. **Services:** Interlibrary loan; copying; library open to the public. **Computerized Information Services:** RLIN, DIALOG Information Services; CD-ROM (Art Index); BITNET (electronic mail service). **Publications:** New Books Received, monthly. **Special Indexes:** Index to the Reference Collection. **Remarks:** FAX: (904)392-7251. Electronic mail address(es): EDTEAG@NERVM (BITNET). **Staff:** James M. Glenn.

★18560★
University of Florida - Borland Health Sciences Library (Med)
P.O. Box 4426   Phone: (904)359-6516
Jacksonville, FL 32231   Carolyn G. Hall, Dir.
Founded: 1964. **Staff:** Prof 3; Other 4. **Subjects:** Medicine, public health, nursing, allied health sciences, dentistry. **Holdings:** 3500 books; 25,000 bound periodical volumes. **Subscriptions:** 575 journals and other serials. **Services:** Interlibrary loan; copying. **Computerized Information Services:** MEDLINE, DIALOG Information Services, BRS/COLLEAGUE; OnTyme Electronic Message Network Service (electronic mail service). **Remarks:** FAX: (904)355-3310. **Staff:** Deborah Lawless, Instr.Libn.; Pamela Neumann, Asst.Libn.

★18561★
University of Florida - Center for Health Policy Research - Library (Med)
Box J-177, Health Science Center   Phone: (904)392-2571
Gainesville, FL 32610   Michael Miller, Dir.
Founded: 1981. **Subjects:** Medical care regulation and administration, health economics. **Holdings:** 1500 volumes.

★18562★
University of Florida - Center for Latin American and Tropical Art - Library (Art)
University Art Gallery
102 FAB   Phone: (904)392-0201
Gainesville, FL 32611   Karen Valdes, Dir.
Founded: 1965. **Staff:** 2. **Subjects:** Art - Latin American, African, Asian, Indian. **Holdings:** 100 catalogs. **Subscriptions:** 4 journals and other serials. **Services:** Interlibrary loan (limited); library not open to the public. **Remarks:** FAX: (904)392-3802. **Staff:** Dana Moore, Reg.

University of Florida - Center for Wetlands Reference Library
See: **University of Florida** (18590)

★18563★
University of Florida - Central Florida Research and Education Center - Leesburg Library (Biol Sci, Agri)
Inst. of Food & Agricultural Sciences
5336 University Ave.   Phone: (904)787-3423
Leesburg, FL 34748   Dr. Donald L. Hopkins, Asst.Ctr.Dir.
Founded: 1930. **Staff:** 2. **Subjects:** Plant pathology, vegetable crops, fruit crops, entomology. **Holdings:** 1267 volumes; 5335 indexed reprints; 109 unbound journals; 4250 abstract cards; 21,345 index cards. **Subscriptions:** 51 journals and other serials. **Services:** Library not open to the public. **Remarks:** FAX: (904)392-8940.

★18564★
University of Florida - Citrus Research & Education Center - Lake Alfred Library (Agri, Biol Sci)
Inst. of Food & Agricultural Sciences
700 Experiment Station Rd.   Phone: (813)956-1151
Lake Alfred, FL 33850   Pamela K. Russ, Assoc.Univ.Libn.
Founded: 1935. **Staff:** Prof 1. **Subjects:** Chemistry, botany, entomology, nematology, agronomy. **Special Collections:** Yothers Rare Book Collection (citrus). **Holdings:** 5250 books; 8300 bound periodical volumes; 850 documents; 24 VF drawers of citrus reprints; 1620 Florida Geological Survey maps. **Subscriptions:** 85 journals and other serials. **Services:** Copying; library open to the public for reference use only. **Automated Operations:** Computerized ILL. **Computerized Information Services:** DIALOG Information Services, STN International. **Special Indexes:** Citrus card file (author and subject). **Remarks:** FAX: (813)956-4631.

★18565★
University of Florida - Coastal & Oceanographic Engineering Department - Coastal Engineering Archives (Sci-Engr)
433 Weil Hall   Phone: (904)392-2710
Gainesville, FL 32611   Helen Twedell, Sr.Lib.Techn.
Founded: 1973. **Staff:** 2. **Subjects:** Florida beaches, beach erosion, sediment transport, coastal vegetation, nearshore oceanography, estuarine circulation. **Holdings:** 654 books; 400 microforms; 710 cataloged coastal and oceanographic reports and technical reports; 985 reports about Florida; 9000 other cataloged items. **Subscriptions:** 41 journals and other serials. **Services:** Interlibrary loan; copying; archives open to the public for reference use only. **Publications:** Acquisitions list; Monthly wave data. **Remarks:** FAX: (904)392-3466.

★18566★
University of Florida - College of Education Library (Educ)
1500 Norman Hall   Phone: (904)392-0707
Gainesville, FL 32611   David Shontz, Hd./Asst.Libn.
Staff: Prof 2; Other 3. **Subjects:** Education, child development, higher education, psychology, counseling, children's literature. **Holdings:** 108,804 books; 10,655 bound periodical volumes; 349,287 ERIC microfiche; 792 reels of microfilm. **Subscriptions:** 570 journals and other serials. **Services:** Interlibrary loan; copying; public-access microcomputers; library open to the public. **Automated Operations:** Computerized cataloging. **Computerized Information Services:** RLIN, DIALOG Information Services, BRS Information Technologies, WILSONLINE. Performs searches on fee basis. **Remarks:** FAX: (904)392-7159. **Staff:** Linda Sparks, Assoc.Libn.

★18567★
University of Florida - Data Tape Library (Info Sci)
513 Library West   Phone: (904)392-0796
Gainesville, FL 32611   Bill Covey, Sys.Off.Hd.
Founded: 1970. **Staff:** Prof 3; Other 4. **Subjects:** Census data, business data. **Holdings:** 6145 machine readable data tapes; 5168 computer disks; 1816 data diskettes. **Services:** Library open to the public with restrictions. **Automated Operations:** Computerized public access catalog (NOTIS), cataloging, acquisitions, circulation, and serials. **Computerized Information Services:** OCLC; internal database. **Staff:** Tom Kinney, Sys.Libn.; Suzy Shaw, Sys.Libn.

★18568★
University of Florida - Documents Library (Info Sci)
254 Library West   Phone: (904)392-0367
Gainesville, FL 32611   Jan Swanbeck, Ch./Univ.Libn.
Founded: 1907. **Staff:** Prof 5; Other 9. **Subjects:** Government publications - United States, foreign, international, Florida, and other states. **Holdings:** 2900 volumes; 663,310 documents; 1.03 million microfiche and microprint. **Services:** Interlibrary loan; copying; library open to the public. **Computerized Information Services:** LEGI-SLATE; CD-ROMs; BITNET (electronic mail service). **Remarks:** FAX: (904)392-7251. Electronic mail address(es): JANSWAN@NERVM (BITNET). **Staff:** Gary Cornwell, Assoc.Libn./Asst.Ch.; Sally Cravens, Univ.Libn., State & Local; Mary Gay Anderson, Asst.Libn./Intl.Docs.; Kate Zumbro, Inst. Foreign Docs.

★ 18569 ★
University of Florida - Everglades Research & Education Center - Belle Glade Library (Biol Sci, Agri)
Inst. of Food & Agricultural Sciences
Box 8003
Belle Glade, FL 33430
Phone: (407)996-3062
Joan Blemman, Libn.
Staff: 1. **Subjects:** Agriculture, soils science, rice, vegetables, sugarcane, tropical botany, animal science, crops science, horticulture science. **Holdings:** 5000 books; 3700 bound periodical volumes. **Subscriptions:** 171 journals and other serials. **Services:** Interlibrary loan; copying; library open to the public for reference use only. **Publications:** AREC Research Reports EES.

★ 18570 ★
University of Florida - Florida Museum of Natural History - Simpson Library of Paleontology (Sci-Engr, Biol Sci)
Museum Rd.
Gainesville, FL 32611
Phone: (904)392-1721
Dr. S. David Webb, Cur.
Founded: 1971. **Subjects:** Invertebrate and vertebrate paleontology, geology, natural history, ecology. **Special Collections:** Personal collections of books and reprints of G.G. Simpson, D. Nicol, and F.S. MacNeil. **Holdings:** 4000 books; 2000 bound periodical volumes; 70,000 reprints and separates; 30 dissertations. **Subscriptions:** 20 journals and other serials. **Services:** Library open to visiting scientists for reference use only. **Remarks:** FAX: (904)392-8783. **Formerly:** Its Florida State Museum. **Staff:** Roger Portell, Coll.Mgr.; Kevin Schindler, Bio.

★ 18571 ★
University of Florida - Gulf Coast Research & Education Center - Bradenton Library (Biol Sci)
Inst. of Food & Agricultural Sciences
5007 60th St., E.
Bradenton, FL 34203
Phone: (813)751-7636
Tracey Revels, Libn.
Staff: 1. **Subjects:** Plant pathology, entomology, vegetable crops, horticulture. **Holdings:** 550 books; 900 bound periodical volumes. **Subscriptions:** 40 journals and other serials. **Services:** Library not open to the public.

★ 18572 ★
University of Florida - Health Science Library (Med)
Box J-206
Gainesville, FL 32611
Phone: (904)392-4016
Ted F. Srygley, Dir.
Founded: 1956. **Staff:** Prof 11; Other 30. **Subjects:** Medicine, basic medical sciences, nursing, pharmacy, veterinary medicine, allied health sciences, dentistry. **Holdings:** 243,215 volumes; 2760 films and tapes; 4610 microfiche; Ciba collection of slides. **Subscriptions:** 2592 journals and other serials. **Services:** Interlibrary loan (fee); copying; library open to the public by permission. **Computerized Information Services:** MEDLARS, DIALOG Information Services, STN International, WILSONLINE, Maxwell Online, Inc., OCLC. **Networks/Consortia:** Member of SOLINET. **Publications:** Library Bulletin; Library Handbook; Acquisitions list; annual periodical list. **Remarks:** FAX: (904)392-6803. **Staff:** Esther Jones, Pub.Serv.Libn.; Leonard Rhine, Tech.Serv.Libn.

★ 18573 ★
University of Florida - Isser and Rae Price Library of Judaica (Hist, Rel-Phil)
406 Smathers Library
Gainesville, FL 32611
Phone: (904)392-0308
Robert Singerman, Libn.
Founded: 1977. **Staff:** Prof 1. **Subjects:** Judaism, Jewish history, Holocaust, Hebrew and Yiddish language and literature, Israel and Zionism, Rabbinic literature, Hebrew scriptures. **Special Collections:** Festschriften; community histories. **Holdings:** 43,700 books and bound periodical volumes; 748 reels of microfilm; 2905 microfiche. **Subscriptions:** 400 journals and other serials. **Services:** Interlibrary loan; copying. **Automated Operations:** Computerized cataloging. **Computerized Information Services:** OCLC; RLIN. **Networks/Consortia:** Member of SOLINET. **Publications:** AMUDIM, annual - free upon request. **Special Catalogs:** Catalog to pre-1881 Hebrew and Yiddish imprints (card). **Remarks:** FAX: (904)392-7251.

★ 18574 ★
University of Florida - Latin American Collection (Area-Ethnic)
4th Fl., Library East
Gainesville, FL 32611
Phone: (904)392-0360
Dr. Peter Stern
Founded: 1967. **Staff:** Prof 2; Other 2. **Subjects:** Latin America, Caribbean and Circum-Caribbean, Brazil. **Special Collections:** Caribbean Collection (45,880 books; 203 current periodicals; 13,494 reels of microfilm); Latin American Collection (186,065 books; 1103 periodicals; 19,370 reels of microfilm; 6806 microcards; 12,255 microfiche). **Holdings:** 6200 dissertations on microfilm; 123 atlases; Latin American vertical file. **Subscriptions:** 1334 journals and other serials; 38 newspapers. **Services:** Interlibrary loan; collection open to the public.

★ 18575 ★
University of Florida - Legal Information Center (Law)
Gainesville, FL 32611
Phone: (904)392-0417
Dr. Betty W. Taylor, Dir./Prof.
Founded: 1909. **Staff:** Prof 12; Other 14. **Subjects:** Law - tax, labor, statutory, water resources, property and public, international, admiralty, Latin American. **Holdings:** 310,009 volumes; 945,236 microforms; 332 computer disks. **Subscriptions:** 8186 journals and other serials. **Services:** Interlibrary loan; copying; library open to the public by permission. **Automated Operations:** Computerized cataloging, serials, circulation, and acquisitions. **Computerized Information Services:** LEXIS, WESTLAW, OCLC, DIALOG Information Services, Legaltrak, RLIN. **Networks/Consortia:** Member of SOLINET. **Remarks:** FAX: (904)392-8727. **Staff:** A.R. Donnelly, Assoc.Libn. & Assoc.Dir.; Robert Munro, Law Libn.; Pamela D. Williams, Assoc.Libn. & Asst.Dir.; Carole Grooms, Assoc.Libn., Cat.; Susy B. Potter, Assoc.Libn., Circ.; James Flavin, Asst.Libn., AV; Rosalie Sanderson, Assoc.Libn., Ref.; James Gates, Assoc.Libn. & Asst.Dir.; Mark Bergeron, Comp.Serv.; Brian Burns, AV.

★ 18576 ★
University of Florida - Map and Imagery Library (Geog-Map)
Marston Science Library, Rm. 110
Gainesville, FL 32611
Phone: (904)392-2825
Dr. HelenJane Armstrong, Map Libn.
Staff: Prof 1; Other 2. **Subjects:** Maps, aerial photographs and remote sensing images including the specialized areas of Latin America, Africa, and Southeastern United States. **Special Collections:** Erwin Raisz Collection of Maps and Cartographic Papers; Sanborn Historical Maps of Florida Cities (6000). **Holdings:** 387,000 maps; 158,735 aerial photographs; 2000 remote sensing and satellite images in print, on digital tapes, and on cartridges; 110 relief models; 151 transparencies; 1977 microforms; 957 photograph negatives. **Services:** Library open to the public. **Automated Operations:** Computerized cataloging (NOTIS). **Computerized Information Services:** OCLC, RLIN. **Publications:** Acquisitions List, irregular.

★ 18577 ★
University of Florida - Marston Science Library (Sci-Engr)
Gainesville, FL 32611-2020
Phone: (904)392-2759
Carol Drum, Libn. & Dept.Ch.
Founded: 1987. **Staff:** Prof 10; Other 18. **Subjects:** Science, engineering, chemistry, physics, astronomy, food and agricultural sciences, geology, biological science, mathematics. **Holdings:** 505,515 books; 1.16 million microforms; 289,324 documents. **Subscriptions:** 9719 journals and other serials. **Services:** Interlibrary loan; copying; library open to the public. **Automated Operations:** Computerized cataloging, acquisitions, serials, and circulation (NOTIS). **Computerized Information Services:** DIALOG Information Services, OCLC, PFDS Online, STN International, RLIN, WILSONLINE; BITNET (electronic mail service). Performs searches on fee basis. **Remarks:** FAX: (904)392-7251. Electronic mail address(es): CDRUM@NERVM (BITNET). **Staff:** Barry Hartigan, Sci.Bibliog.; Denise Beaubien, Electronics Formats Unit Hd.; Pam Cenzer, Ser./Binding Unit Hd.; Stephanie Haas, Docs. Unit Hd.; Alice Primack, Info. Literacy Unit Hd.; Marijka Willis, Circ. Unit Hd.; Anita Battiste, Ref. Unit Hd.

★ 18578 ★
University of Florida - Music Library (Mus)
231 Music Bldg.
Gainesville, FL 32611-2051
Phone: (904)392-6678
Robena Eng Cornwell, Assoc.Univ.Libn.
Founded: 1972. **Staff:** Prof 1; Other 1.5. **Subjects:** Music. **Special Collections:** Didiere Graeffe Collection; Eugene E. Grissom Trombone Library. **Holdings:** 19,647 books; 8536 scores; 2478 bound periodical volumes; 2502 microfiche; 6206 phonograph records; 3005 tapes; 516 compact discs; 1113 VF titles; 916 reels of microfilm; 126 videocassettes. **Subscriptions:** 145 journals and other serials. **Services:** Interlibrary loan; copying; library open to the public with restrictions. **Automated Operations:** Computerized cataloging. **Computerized Information Services:** BITNET (electronic mail service). **Remarks:** Electronic mail address(es): ROBCORN@NERVM (BITNET).

★18579★

University of Florida - North Florida Research & Education Center - Quincy Library
Rte. 3, Box 4370
Quincy, FL 32351
Subjects: Agriculture. **Holdings:** Figures not available. **Remarks:** Currently inactive.

★18580★

University of Florida - P.K. Yonge Laboratory School - Mead Library (Educ)
1080 S.W. 11th St.
Gainesville, FL 32601
Phone: (904)392-1554
Iona Malanchuk, Hd.Libn.
Founded: 1934. **Staff:** Prof 2.5; Other 2.5. **Subjects:** Materials for grades K-12. **Holdings:** 20,251 volumes; 146 maps; 519 recordings; 897 filmstrips; 4 slide-tape sets; 13 audio cassettes; 152 videotapes; 1344 microfiche; 4 games; 26 kits; 35 posters; 506 slides; 16 computer software programs. **Subscriptions:** 122 journals and other serials. **Services:** Interlibrary loan; computer workstations; library open to qualified persons. **Automated Operations:** Computerized public access catalog (LUIS). **Computerized Information Services:** CD-ROMs (WILSONDISC, Information Finder, Mammals: A Multimedia Encyclopedia, Social Issues Resources Series, PC Globe); BITNET (electronic mail service). **Remarks:** FAX: (904)392-7159. Electronic mail address(es): IONMALA@NERVM (BITNET). **Staff:** Penny Chou, AV Libn.

★18581★

University of Florida - Research & Education Center - Fort Lauderdale Library (Agri, Biol Sci)
Inst. of Food & Agricultural Sciences
3205 College Ave.
Fort Lauderdale, FL 33314
Phone: (305)475-8990
Staff: Prof 1. **Subjects:** Ornamental horticulture, entomology, turf science, plant pathology, soils, aquatic weeds science, environmental quality, urban entomology. **Holdings:** 1200 books; 360 bound periodical volumes. **Subscriptions:** 65 serials. **Services:** Library open to the public with restrictions for reference use only. **Computerized Information Services:** Access to online systems. **Publications:** Conference proceedings; Library Bulletin. **Remarks:** FAX: (305)475-4125. **Staff:** Janet Yaeger.

★18582★

University of Florida - Space Astronomy Laboratory - Library (Sci-Engr)
1810 N.W. 6th St.
Gainesville, FL 32609
Phone: (904)371-4778
Jerry L. Weinberg, Dir.
Founded: 1973. **Subjects:** Atmospheric physics, astronomy, space astronomy, spacecraft environments, space instrumentation, nuclear physics/astrophysics. **Special Collections:** Magnetic tapes of observations from Skylab, Space Shuttle Mission 3, Pioneer 10 and 11; ESA GIOTTO Halley Mission; ground observations of zodiacal light and background starlight. **Holdings:** 200 volumes. **Subscriptions:** 25 journals and other serials. **Services:** Interlibrary loan; library open to the public for reference use only.

★18583★

University of Florida - Special Collections - Baldwin Library (Hum)
208 Smathers Library
Gainesville, FL 32611
Phone: (904)392-0369
Bernard F. McTigue, Ch., Dept. of Spec.Coll.
Founded: 1979. **Staff:** Prof 1. **Subjects:** Historical children's literature. **Holdings:** 84,000 books, periodicals, and manuscripts. **Services:** Copying. **Computerized Information Services:** BITNET (electronic mail service). **Remarks:** FAX: (904)392-7251. Electronic mail address(es): BERMCTI@NERVM (BITNET). **Staff:** Rita Smith.

★18584★

University of Florida - Special Collections - Belknap Collection for the Performing Arts (Mus, Theater)
1 Smathers Library
Gainesville, FL 32611
Phone: (904)392-0322
Bernard F. McTigue, Ch., Dept. of Spec.Coll.
Founded: 1953. **Staff:** Prof 2; Other 2. **Subjects:** Dance, opera, music, theater, film. **Special Collections:** Ringling Collection (early playbills; engravings; prints; photographs); 19th and 20th century American and British playbills; Florida performing arts files; popular sheet music collection; Sarah Belknap Correspondence and Guides to the Performing Arts. **Holdings:** 4200 books; 912 bound periodicals; 912 scores; 200,000 souvenir programs, prints and photographs, clippings, correspondence, posters. **Subscriptions:** 60 journals and other serials. **Services:** Copying; collection open to the public. **Automated Operations:** LUIS. **Computerized Information Services:** BITNET (electronic mail service). **Publications:** Ballet close ups (1941); Florida Index (1966); Guide to Dance Periodicals (1950); Guide to Performing Arts (1960); Guide to Musical Arts (1957). **Remarks:** FAX: (904)392-7251. Electronic mail address(es): BERMCTI@NERVM (BITNET). **Staff:** Mary Jane Daicoff.

★18585★

University of Florida - Special Collections - P.K. Yonge Library of Florida History (Hist)
1 Smathers Library
Gainesville, FL 32611
Phone: (904)392-0319
Elizabeth Alexander, Libn.
Founded: 1944. **Staff:** Prof 1; Other 2. **Subjects:** Florida history and prehistory. **Special Collections:** Stetson Collection (photostats of documents from the Archivo General de Indias, Sevilla, relating to Spanish activity in the Southeastern borderlands, 1518-1819; 150,000); East Florida Papers (archives of the Second Spanish Administration of East Florida, 1784-1821; 178 reels of microfilm); Papeles de Cuba (Spanish West and East Florida, 1784-1819; 761 reels of microfilm). **Holdings:** 28,000 books and bound periodical volumes; 2500 maps; 19th and 20th century Florida, Georgia, South Carolina, Tennessee newspapers on microfilm; miscellaneous manuscripts; microfilm and photocopies of Colonial British and Spanish Florida materials. **Subscriptions:** 98 journals and other serials; 60 newspapers. **Services:** Library open to adults for reference use only. **Computerized Information Services:** BITNET (electronic mail service). **Publications:** The Florida Situado; Los Sobrevivientes De La Florida. **Remarks:** FAX: (904)392-7251. Electronic mail address(es): BERMCTI@NERVM (BITNET).

★18586★

University of Florida - Special Collections - Rare Books & Manuscripts (Rare Book, Hum)
1 Smathers Library
Gainesville, FL 32611
Phone: (904)392-0321
Carmen Russell Hurff, Cur.
Founded: 1950. **Staff:** Prof 2. **Subjects:** 17th, 18th, and 19th century English and American literature; English theology (especially 17th century); modern English and American poetry; history of ideas; Irish literary revival. **Special Collections:** Printing and graphic arts; Rochambeau papers; John Wilson Croker papers; Margaret Dreier Robins papers; Bromsen-Medina and Harrisse collections of Latin American bibliography; Jeremie papers (Haiti); Sir Walter Scott; Florida authors: papers of Alden Hatch, Zora Neale Hurston, John D. MacDonald, Edith Pope, Marjorie Kinnan Rawlings, Frank O'Connor, and Lillian Smith; manuscripts of Lady Gregory; P.D. Howe Collection (New England authors' first printings and manuscripts; 6000 volumes); Kohler Collection of Victorian Theology; French Drama (1760-1960). **Holdings:** 64,000 books; 350 bound periodicals; 575 linear feet of manuscripts; 99 linear feet of pamphlets. **Subscriptions:** 74 journals and other serials. **Services:** Copying (limited); library open to the public. **Computerized Information Services:** OCLC, RLIN; BITNET (electronic mail service). **Networks/Consortia:** Member of SOLINET. **Special Catalogs:** Descriptive author catalogs (Howe Library I-V in print). **Special Indexes:** Manuscript collection index (loose-leaf). **Remarks:** FAX: (904)392-7251. Electronic mail address(es): BERMCTI@NERVM. **Staff:** David Lashmet, Asst.Cur.

★18587★

University of Florida - Special Collections - University Archives and University Collection (Hist)
208 Smathers Library
Gainesville, FL 32611
Phone: (904)392-6547
Carla Kemp, Univ.Archv./Libn.
Founded: 1951. **Staff:** Prof 2; Other 1. **Subjects:** University history. **Holdings:** 25,000 volumes; 1100 cubic feet of manuscripts from faculty, staff, alumni; 1566 linear feet of university publications, theses, dissertations, newspapers, yearbooks, ephemera, and photographs. **Services:** Copying; archives open to the public. **Computerized Information Services:** BITNET (electronic mail service). **Remarks:** FAX: (904)392-7251. Electronic mail address(es): BERMCTI@NERVM (BITNET). **Staff:** Carl Van Ness, Asst.Univ.Archv./Asst.Univ.Libn.

★ 18588 ★
University of Florida - Transportation Research Center (Trans)
512 Weil Hall   Phone: (904)392-0378
Gainesville, FL 32611-2083   Charles E. Wallace, Dir.
Founded: 1972. **Subjects:** Transportation engineering and planning, traffic engineering. **Holdings:** 100 books; 3000 government and private reports; 236 videotapes. **Subscriptions:** 10 journals and other serials. **Services:** Copying; center open to the public by appointment. **Computerized Information Services:** BITNET, InterNet (electronic mail services). **Publications:** Research publications, 12/year. **Remarks:** FAX: (904)392-3224. Electronic mail address(es): UFTRC@NERVM.UFL.EDU (BITNET, InterNet). **Staff:** Betty Sampson.

★ 18589 ★
University of Florida - Tropical Research & Education Center -
     Homestead Library (Biol Sci, Agri)
Inst. of Food & Agricultural Sciences
18905 S.W. 280th St.   Phone: (305)246-6340
Homestead, FL 33031   R.M. Baranowski, Dir.
Staff: 14. **Subjects:** Plant pathology, entomology, plant nutrition, horticulture, tropical foliage plants, soil science, tropical exotics, tissue culture. **Special Collections:** Collection on all aspects of mango culture and tropical and subtropical fruits. **Holdings:** 3200 books; 750 bound periodical volumes. **Subscriptions:** 75 journals and other serials. **Services:** Library not open to the public. **Remarks:** FAX: (305)246-7003. **Staff:** N. Cruz, Libn.

★ 18590 ★
University of Florida - Wetland and Water Resources Research Center -
     Reference Library (Env-Cons)
Phelps Laboratory   Phone: (904)392-2424
Gainesville, FL 32611-2061   G. Ronnie Best, Dir.
Founded: 1973. **Staff:** 3 **Subjects:** Wetlands research, ecosystems modeling, energy analysis, reclamation, water resources, water resource management. **Holdings:** 900 books; 16 VF drawers of unbound reports; 160 theses and dissertations; 90 technical reports. **Subscriptions:** 9 journals and other serials. **Services:** Library open to the public. **Computerized Information Services:** Internal databases. **Remarks:** FAX: (904)392-3624. **Formerly:** Its Center for Wetlands Reference Library.

★ 18591 ★
University of Florida - Whitney Laboratory - Library (Biol Sci)
9505 Ocean Shore Blvd.
St. Augustine, FL 32086-8623   Phone: (904)461-4000
Founded: 1975. **Subjects:** Neurobiology, marine biology, physiology, molecular biology, cell biology. **Holdings:** 1000 books. **Subscriptions:** 43 journals and other serials. **Services:** Library open to the public for reference use only. **Computerized Information Services:** DIALOG Information Services, NLM. Contact Person: John Young, Comp.Sys.Anl. **Remarks:** FAX: (904)461-4008.

★ 18592 ★
University of Frankfurt - Department of Biology - Library for Biological
     Sciences (Biol Sci)
Siesmayerstr 58
Postfach 11 19 32
W-6000 Frankfurt am Main, Germany   Phone: 69 7983748
Founded: 1958. **Staff:** Prof 1; Other 1. **Subjects:** Zoology, botany, anthropology. **Holdings:** 20,521 books; 14,456 bound periodical volumes; 598 microfiche. **Subscriptions:** 92 journals and other serials. **Services:** Library open to scholars and students. **Computerized Information Services:** Internal database. Contact Person: Mrs. C. Ecterbruch, Dipl.Bibl. **Also Known As:** J. W. Goethe-Universitat - Fachbereich Biologie - Arbeitsbibliothek.

★ 18593 ★
University of Georgia - Coastal Plain Experiment Station Library (Agri)
Moore Hwy.
Box 748   Phone: (912)386-3447
Tifton, GA 31793   Patricia M. Griffin, Sta.Libn.
Founded: 1924. **Staff:** 2. **Subjects:** Agricultural research. **Holdings:** 14,500 volumes; 450 theses and dissertations. **Subscriptions:** 400 journals and other serials. **Services:** Interlibrary loan; copying; library primarily for use of research personnel at the station. **Computerized Information Services:** DIALOG Information Services; BITNET (electronic mail service). **Remarks:** FAX: (912)386-7005. Electronic mail address(es): LIBR-TIF@TIFTON (BITNET).

★ 18594 ★
University of Georgia - College of Education - Curriculum Materials
     Center (Educ)
Aderhold Hall   Phone: (706)542-2996
Athens, GA 30602   Janet Lawrence, Libn.
Founded: 1987. **Staff:** Prof 1; Other 8. **Subjects:** Juvenile and young adult literature, K-12 curriculum materials. **Special Collections:** The Osborne Collection: Toronto Public Library Early English Children's Books (30 volumes). **Holdings:** 21,000 books; 5 VF drawers; 6 cabinet drawers of microfiche; Kraus Curriculum Guides on microfiche, 1970 to present; audio recordings; videotapes; posters; maps; charts; slides; computer software; tests. **Subscriptions:** 84 journals and other serials. **Services:** Interlibrary loan; center open to the public with restrictions. **Automated Operations:** Computerized public access catalog and circulation. **Computerized Information Services:** Internal database; PROFS, BITNET (electronic mail services). **Publications:** Information brochure and resource lists. **Remarks:** Electronic mail address(es): CMC@UGA (BITNET).

★ 18595 ★
University of Georgia - Data Services (Soc Sci)
University of Georgia Libraries   Phone: (706)542-0727
Athens, GA 30602   Hortense L. Bates, Hd.
Founded: 1986. **Staff:** Prof 1; Other 2. **Subjects:** Census, social and political sciences, public opinion polls. **Holdings:** 1300 books; 1400 reels of magnetic tape. **Services:** Services open to the public with restrictions. **Automated Operations:** Computerized cataloging, acquisitions, and circulation. **Computerized Information Services:** Internal numeric databases. Performs searches on fee basis.

★ 18596 ★
University of Georgia - Department of Records Management &
     University Archives (Hist)
4th Fl., Old Section
Ilah Dunlap Little Memorial Library   Phone: (706)542-8151
Athens, GA 30602   Dr. John Carver Edwards, C.A.Rec.Off./Archv.
Founded: 1972. **Staff:** 4. **Subjects:** Presidential papers, administrative records, student records, fiscal records. **Special Collections:** Ecological Society of America Collection; Institute of Ecology Archives. **Holdings:** 10,500 cubic feet of university archival material. **Services:** Archives open to the public.

★ 18597 ★
University of Georgia - Georgia Center for Continuing Education -
     Library (Educ)
Athens, GA 30602   Phone: (706)542-2071
     Deanna Britton, Libn.
Founded: 1957. **Staff:** Prof 1; Other 3. **Subjects:** Adult and continuing education, conference programming, management, educational technology. **Holdings:** 2708 books. **Subscriptions:** 150 journals and other serials; 8 newspapers. **Services:** Interlibrary loan; copying; library open to the public. **Automated Operations:** Computerized public access catalog. **Computerized Information Services:** CD-ROM (ERIC); BITNET, PROFS (electronic mail services). **Publications:** Brochure; newsletter; new book list. **Remarks:** FAX: (706)542-5990. Electronic mail address(es): GCLIB@UGA (BITNET).

★ 18598 ★
University of Georgia - Georgia Experiment Station Library (Agri)
1109 Experiment St.   Phone: (706)228-7238
Griffin, GA 30223-1797   M. Kay Mowery, Libn.
Founded: 1924. **Staff:** Prof 1; Other 1. **Subjects:** Agriculture and related sciences. **Special Collections:** Georgia Agicultural Experiment Stations publications. **Holdings:** 30,000 volumes. **Subscriptions:** 500 journals and other serials. **Services:** Interlibrary loan; library open to the public with restrictions. **Computerized Information Services:** DIALOG Information Services; Current Contents on Diskette: Agriculture, Biology, & Environmental Sciences; Current Contents on Diskette: Life Sciences; CD-ROMs (AGRICOLA, CRIS, GPO Monthly Catalog, CAB Abstracts); BITNET InterNet (electronic mail services). **Remarks:** FAX: (706)228-7270. Electronic mail address(es): LIBR-GRF@GRIFFIN (BITNET); LIBR-GRF@GRIFFIN.UGA.EDU (InterNet).

★ 18599 ★
University of Georgia - Government Documents Department (Info Sci)
University of Georgia Libraries
Athens, GA 30602
Phone: (706)542-8949
Susan C. Field, Hd., Govt.Docs.Dept.
Founded: 1907. **Staff:** Prof 5; Other 5. **Special Collections:** U.S. Government publications; Georgia state and United Nations documents; British and West German Parliamentary debates and papers; official gazettes of France; regional U.S. Government document depository, 1977 to present; selective depository for Canadian documents. **Holdings:** Figures not available. **Services:** Interlibrary loan; department open to the public. **Computerized Information Services:** BITNET (electronic mail service). **Publications:** Documents in Georgia. **Special Indexes:** U.S. agency and shelflist; Georgia shelflist, keyword, and title; U.N. shelflist and title; Canada shelflist and series title. **Staff:** Carol Wheeler, Doc.Ref.Libn.; Susan Tuggle, Doc.Ref.Spec.; John Wilcox, Doc.Ref.Libn.

★ 18600 ★
University of Georgia - Hargrett Rare Book and Manuscript Library
(Rare Book, Hist)
University of Georgia Libraries
Athens, GA 30602
Phone: (706)542-7123
Thomas E. Camden, Hd.
Founded: 1933. **Staff:** Prof 5; Other 7. **Subjects:** Georgiana, Civil War, small press and fine printing, theater arts, southern culture, English and American literature, British local history, music, photography. **Special Collections:** Georgiana (125,000 volumes); DeRenne Collection (Georgiana); Egmont papers; Charles Coburn Collection; Charles C. Jones Collection; Telamon Cuyler Collection; Olin Downes Collection; Ward Morehouse Collection; Paris Music Hall Collection; Freddy Wittop Collection; Keith Read Collection; Margaret Mitchell papers; Lillian Smith papers. **Holdings:** 125,000 rare books; 100,000 Georgiana volumes; 4.2 million manuscripts. **Subscriptions:** 200 journals and other serials; 12 newspapers. **Services:** Department open to the public. **Computerized Information Services:** Galin (internal database). **Special Catalogs:** Unpublished guides to manuscripts. **Remarks:** FAX: (706)542-6522. **Staff:** Joseph Cote, Georgiana; Mary Ellen Brooks, Rare Bks.; Nancy Stamper, Rare Bks.; Larry Gulley, Mss.

★ 18601 ★
University of Georgia - Law Library (Law)
Athens, GA 30602
Phone: (706)542-8480
Erwin C. Surrency, Dir.
Staff: Prof 8; Other 10. **Subjects:** Law. **Holdings:** 322,173 volumes; 4379 reels of microfilm; 231,310 microfiche. **Subscriptions:** 1190 journals and other serials; 11 newspapers. **Services:** Interlibrary loan; copying; library open to the public. **Computerized Information Services:** LEXIS, WESTLAW, OCLC. **Publications:** List of Acquisitions. **Special Indexes:** Index to legal publications in the state of Georgia (cards). **Remarks:** FAX: (706)542-5556. **Staff:** Jose R. Pages, Acq.Libn.; Carol Ramsey, Cat.Libn.; Martha N. Hampton, Law Ser.Libn.; Diana Duderwicz, Asst.Cat.Libn.; Sally Curtis Askew, Asst.Pub.Serv.Libn.; James M. Whitehead, Asst.Pub.Serv.Libn.; Carol A. Watson, Asst.Pub.Serv.Libn.

★ 18602 ★
University of Georgia - Richard B. Russell Memorial Library (Soc Sci)
University of Georgia Libraries
Athens, GA 30602
Phone: (706)542-5788
Sheryl B. Vogt, Dept.Hd.
Founded: 1974. **Staff:** 6.5. **Subjects:** 20th century Georgia politics; U.S. Congress; civil rights; agriculture, defense, and armed services legislation. **Holdings:** 6505 linear feet; 80 collections; AV materials; photographs; memorabilia. **Services:** Interlibrary loan; copying; library open to the public; visiting scholars should write for application to do research. **Computerized Information Services:** BITNET, ALANET (electronic mail services). **Remarks:** FAX: (706)542-6522. Electronic mail address(es): SBVOGT@UGA (BITNET); ALA1593 (ALANET). **Staff:** Lenore Richey, Archv.Assoc.; Pam Hackbart-Dean, Archv.Assoc.

★ 18603 ★
University of Georgia - Science Library (Sci-Engr)
Athens, GA 30602
Phone: (706)542-0691
Arlene E. Luchsinger, Hd.
Staff: Prof 13; Other 22. **Subjects:** Science, technology, agriculture, home economics, medicine, veterinary medicine. **Holdings:** 740,000 books. **Subscriptions:** 4035 journals and other serials. **Services:** Interlibrary loan; copying; library open to the public. **Automated Operations:** Computerized public access catalog, acquisitions, and circulation. **Computerized Information Services:** DIALOG Information Services, BRS Information Technologies, OCLC, PFDS Online; BITNET, ALANET (electronic mail services). **Networks/Consortia:** Member of SOLINET. **Remarks:** FAX: (706)542-6523. Electronic mail address(es): SCIADMIN@UGA (BITNET).

★ 18604 ★
University of Georgia - Science Library - Map Collection (Geog-Map)
University of Georgia Libraries
Athens, GA 30602
Phone: (706)542-0690
John Sutherland, Map Cur.
Staff: Prof 2; Other 1. **Subjects:** Topography, geology, natural resources, climate, population. **Special Collections:** Sanborn Atlas Sheets of Georgia (7100). **Holdings:** 220,000 aerial photographs; 338,732 maps; 1800 atlases. **Services:** Interlibrary loan; copying; collection open to the public. **Computerized Information Services:** OCLC, BITNET (electronic mail service). **Publications:** Selected Acquisitions; Sanborn Fire Insurance Maps of Georgia Held by the Map Collection; Atlases in the Map Collection; Aerial Photograph coverage of Georgia Held by the Map Collection. **Remarks:** FAX: (706)542-6253. Electronic mail address(es): JSUTHERL@UGA (BITNET). **Staff:** Paige G. Andrew, Map Cat.

★ 18605 ★
University of Georgia - Science Library - Sapelo Marine Institute -
Library (Biol Sci)
Sapelo Island, GA 31327
Phone: (912)485-2133
Lorene Townsend, Lib. Subject Spec.
Founded: 1953. **Staff:** 1. **Subjects:** Ecology, marine biology. **Holdings:** 6000 periodical volumes. **Subscriptions:** 85 journals and other serials. **Services:** Interlibrary loan; copying. **Computerized Information Services:** BITNET (electronic mail service). **Publications:** Collected Reprints. **Remarks:** FAX: (912)485-2133. Electronic mail address(es): LORENE@UGA (BITNET).

★ 18606 ★
University of Georgia - Skidaway Institute of Oceanography - Library
(Sci-Engr, Biol Sci)
Box 13687
Savannah, GA 31406-0687
Phone: (912)598-2474
Tom A. Turner, Libn.
Founded: 1970. **Staff:** Prof 1. **Subjects:** Oceanography, marine resources, fisheries, marine pollution, geochemistry, marine research. **Special Collections:** Climatological data for Georgia and adjacent states; sea surface isotherm records, 1960 to 1979; Gulf Stream data, 1966 to present. **Holdings:** 3700 books; 6500 bound periodical volumes; 8000 reports, documents, and unbound serials. **Subscriptions:** 170 journals and other serials; 35 newsletters. **Services:** Interlibrary loan; copying; library open to the public with restrictions. **Automated Operations:** Computerized cataloging, acquisitions, and serials (through University of Georgia Libraries). **Computerized Information Services:** DIALOG Information Services; CD-ROMs (Aquatic Sciences & Fisheries Abstracts, Life Sciences Collection); BITNET (electronic mail service). **Publications:** Serials holdings list; Technical Reports of the Georgia Marine Science Center. **Remarks:** FAX: (912)598-2310. Electronic mail address(es): TTURNER@UGA (BITNET). The library is a branch of the University of Georgia Libraries, but the Skidaway Institute of Oceanography is a separate research unit of the University System of Georgia. The library is a NOAA Associate Library.

★ 18607 ★
University of Georgia - State Botanical Garden of Georgia - Library
(Biol Sci)
2450 S. Milledge Ave.
Athens, GA 30605
Phone: (404)542-1244
Lee Meinersmann
Founded: 1975. **Staff:** 1. **Subjects:** Plants, gardening, horticulture, botany, landscape design, floral crafts. **Holdings:** 1000 books. **Subscriptions:** 5 journals and other serials. **Services:** Library open to the public for reference use only. **Remarks:** FAX: (404)542-3091.

★ 18608 ★
University of Ghana - Institute of African Studies - Library (Hum)
P.O. Box 73
Legon
Accra, Ghana
Phone: 21 775512
Olive Akpebu
Founded: 1961. **Staff:** 7. **Subjects:** Africa - art, music, dance, drama, literature, history, languages, economics, political systems. **Holdings:** 18,173 volumes; manuscripts; AV programs. **Subscriptions:** 113 journals and other serials; 5 newspapers. **Services:** Interlibrary loan; copying; SDI; library open to the public. **Publications:** Accessions list; contents list to periodicals.

★ 18609 ★
University of Groningen - Polemological Institute - Library (Soc Sci)
Oude Kijk in 't Jatstraat 5/9   Phone: 3150 635656
NL-9712 EA Groningen, Netherlands   Ms. Digna van Boven, Lib.Hd.
Founded: 1962. **Staff:** 1. **Subjects:** Conflicts in the international system; theories of international relations; relations between United States and its allies, 1945 to present; conflict, political violence, and war; armament; arms race; defense expenditures; effects of war; conflict resolution and peace; peace research. **Special Collections:** American Congressional publications. **Holdings:** 13,000 books. **Subscriptions:** 200 journals and other serials. **Services:** Interlibrary loan; copying; SDI; library open to the public on a limited schedule. **Remarks:** FAX: 3150 635603. **Also Known As:** Polemologisch Instituut.

★ 18610 ★
University of Guam - Micronesian Area Research Center - Pacific Collections (Area-Ethnic)
U.O.G. Sta.
Mangilao, GU 96923   Phone: (671)344-4473
Founded: 1967. **Staff:** Prof 3. **Subjects:** Micronesia, Oceania, Philippines, World War II. **Special Collections:** Spanish manuscripts; South Pacific Commission depository; Guam Constitutional Convention Papers; A.B. Won Pat Papers (300 boxes). **Holdings:** 25,000 books; 5000 bound periodical volumes; 80 VF drawers of clippings and pamphlets; 1000 slides; 30 VF drawers containing 15,000 photographs; 58 boxes of microfiche; 1300 reels of microfilm; 500 boxes of archives; 2000 sheets of maps and charts; 220 tapes; 500 cartons of manuscripts. **Subscriptions:** 300 journals and other serials. **Services:** Copying (limited); collection open to the public for reference use only. **Publications:** Bibliographies. **Special Indexes:** Photographs and manuscripts indexes. **Remarks:** FAX: (617)734-7403. **Staff:** Marjorie Driver, Cur., Spanish Docs.; William Wuerch, Archv.; Cecilia L. Salvatore, Ref.Libn.

★ 18611 ★
University of Guelph - Humanities and Social Sciences Division - Map Collection (Geog-Map)
McLaughlin Library   Phone: (519)824-4120
Guelph, ON, Canada N1G 2W1   J. Black, Chf.Libn.
Founded: 1968. **Subjects:** Cartography, agriculture, climatology, economics, geology, historiology, hydrology, land use, population, soils, topography, transportation. **Special Collections:** Canada Company maps; Scotland. **Holdings:** 70,180 maps; 2035 atlases; 105 gazetteers; indexes; cartobibliographies; cartographic equipment. **Services:** Interlibrary loan (limited); copying; collection open to the public. **Automated Operations:** Computerized public access catalog (CD-ROM; accessible via InterNet), cataloging, acquisitions, serials, and circulation. **Computerized Information Services:** BRS Information Technologies, CAN/OLE, DIALOG Information Services, Info Globe, QL Systems, International Development Research Center (IDRC); CD-ROMs (Sociofile, CAB, AGRICOLA, PAIS, SSCI, Dissertation Abstracts, Microlog: Canadian Research Index, ABI/INFORM, Tourism and Travel Index, BBC Domesday System); ALANET, Envoy 100, BITNET (electronic mail services). Performs searches on fee basis. **Remarks:** FAX: (519)824-6931. Electronic mail address(es): GUELPH.MAIL (Envoy 100). **Staff:** Flora Francis, Hd., Map Coll., Soc.Sci.Div.; Bernard Katz, Hd., Hum. & Soc.Sci.Div.

★ 18612 ★
University of Guelph - University Library (Soc Sci, Agri, Hum)
Guelph, ON, Canada N1G 2W1   Phone: (519)824-4120
       Dr. John B. Black, Chf.Libn.
Founded: 1964. **Staff:** Prof 31; Other 115. **Subjects:** Agriculture; veterinary medicine; arts; humanities; social sciences; pure, natural, and applied sciences. **Special Collections:** Theatre Archives; Bernard Shaw Collection; Scottish Collection; L.M. Montgomery; Apiculture. **Holdings:** 2.4 million volumes. **Subscriptions:** 13,600 journals and other serials. **Services:** Interlibrary loan; copying; SDI; library open to the public. **Automated Operations:** Computerized public access catalog, cataloging, acquisitions, serials, circulation, documents, and maps. **Computerized Information Services:** QL Systems, CAN/OLE, BRS Information Technologies, WILSONLINE, MEDLARS, Info Globe, International Development Research Centre (IDRC), RESORS (Remote Sensing On-Line Retrieval System), DIALOG Information Services; internal databases; ALANET, BITNET, NETNORTH, CoSy, Envoy 100 (electronic mail services). Performs searches on fee basis. Contact Person: Ellen M. Pearson, Assoc.Libn. **Networks/Consortia:** Member of Ontario Council of University Libraries (OCUL). **Publications:** Reports, irregular; Library Newsletter;

bibliography series, irregular; Collection Update, annual. **Remarks:** Library catalog is available on CD-ROM. FAX: (519)824-6931. Electronic mail address(es): GUELPH.MAIL (Envoy 100). **Staff:** L.T. Porter, Assoc.Libn., Sys./Tech.Proc.; V.A. Gillham, Assoc.Libn., Pub.Serv.; F.J. Stewart, Hd., Bus.Off.; P.L. Hock, Hd., Circ. & Interlib.Serv.; J.M. Kaufman, Hd., Doc. & Media Rsrc.Ctr.; B.M.L. Katz, Hd., Hum. & Soc.Sci.Div.; D.C. Hull, Hd., Sci. & Vet.Sci.Div.; E.L. Tom, Hd., Tech.Proc.Div.; N.C. Sadek, Archv. & Spec.Coll.; T.D. Sauer, Hd., Acq. & Coll.Div.; C.P. Pawley, Lib. Personnel

★ 18613 ★
University of Haifa - Library - Special Collections (Hist)
Mount Carmel   Phone: 4 240289
31905 Haifa, Israel   Prof. Shmuel Sever, Dir. & Hd. of Lib. Studies
Founded: 1963. **Staff:** 55. **Subjects:** Humanities; social sciences; mathematics; computers; law; Israel - history, geography, archeology. **Special Collections:** Judaica; Kibbutz studies; the Holocaust; Yiddish studies. **Holdings:** 585,880 books; 156,140 bound periodical volumes; 23,709 reports; 153,849 slides; 3559 AV items; 398,622 microfiche. **Subscriptions:** 14,669 journals and other serials. **Services:** Interlibrary loan; copying; SDI; library open to the public with restrictions. **Automated Operations:** Computerized public access catalog (ALEPH). **Computerized Information Services:** Haifa On-Line Bibliographic Text System (HOBITS; internal database); BITNET (electronic mail service). **Special Indexes:** Index to Hebrew Periodicals. **Remarks:** Alternate telephone number(s): 4 240497; 4 246650. FAX: 4 257753. Telex: 46660 UNIHA IL. Electronic mail address(es): MAILBOX@LIB.HAIFA.AC.IL (BITNET, InterNet). **Staff:** Lia Koffler, Hd., Media Dept.; Mrs. Pnina Erez, Hd., Per.Dept.; Esther Merman, Hd., Rd.Serv. & Adm.; Mr. Elhanan Adler, Asst.Dir.

★ 18614 ★
University of Hartford - Hartt School of Music - Allen Memorial Library (Mus)
West Hartford, CT 06117   Phone: (203)243-4491
       Linda Solow Blotner, Mus.Libn.
Founded: 1920. **Staff:** Prof 2; Other 3. **Subjects:** Music. **Special Collections:** Robert E. Smith Record Collection (30,000 phonograph records); Kalmen Opperman Collection (clarinet); Stuart Smith Collection (manuscripts and publications). **Holdings:** 14,000 books; 1500 bound periodical volumes; 30,000 pieces of music; 20,000 phonograph records; 1700 audiotapes; 160 reels of microfilm; 600 compact discs; 200 videocassettes. **Subscriptions:** 330 journals and other serials. **Services:** Interlibrary loan; copying; library open to the public for reference use only. **Automated Operations:** Computerized cataloging. **Computerized Information Services:** OCLC; BITNET (electronic mail service). **Networks/Consortia:** Member of NELINET, Inc., Hartford Consortium for Higher Education, Capital Region Library Council (CRLC). **Remarks:** Electronic mail address(es): BLOTNER@HARTFORD; HICKNER@HARTFORD (BITNET). **Staff:** Paula L. Hickner, Asst.Mus.Libn.; Philip Ponella, Hd., Circ. & Reserves; Kristine Day, Cat.Asst.; Anne Lee, Proc.Asst.

★ 18615 ★
University of Hartford - William H. Mortensen Library - Anne Bunce Cheney Library (Art)
200 Bloomfield Ave.   Phone: (203)243-4397
West Hartford, CT 06117   Jean J. Miller, Art Libn.
Founded: 1963. **Staff:** Prof 1; Other 1. **Subjects:** Art history, art education, applied art, decorative arts, crafts, photography, typography. **Holdings:** 11,581 books; 1686 bound periodical volumes; 15,303 mounted reproductions; 3473 pamphlets. **Subscriptions:** 85 journals and other serials. **Services:** Interlibrary loan; copying; library open to the public. **Computerized Information Services:** OCLC. **Networks/Consortia:** Member of NELINET, Inc., Capital Region Library Council (CRLC), Hartford Consortium for Higher Education.

★ 18616 ★
University of Hartford - William H. Mortensen Library - Science and Engineering Library (Sci-Engr)
200 Bloomfield Ave.   Phone: (203)243-4404
West Hartford, CT 06117   Larry Noroanha
Founded: 1967. **Staff:** Prof 2; Other 10. **Subjects:** Chemistry, biology, physiological psychology, mathematics, physics, earth sciences, engineering. **Special Collections:** History of Science (300 volumes). **Holdings:** 23,597 books; 29,698 bound periodical volumes; microforms; 90 masters' theses. **Subscriptions:** 750 journals and other serials. **Services:** Interlibrary loan;

copying; library open to the public for reference use only. **Automated Operations:** Computerized cataloging. **Computerized Information Services:** DIALOG Information Services, OCLC. **Networks/Consortia:** Member of Hartford Consortium for Higher Education, Capital Region Library Council (CRLC), NELINET, Inc. **Publications:** Listing of Periodical Holdings - to consortium members. **Staff:** Jenny Wong, Asst.Libn.

★ 18617 ★
University of Hawaii - Asia Collection (Area-Ethnic)
Hamilton Library
2550 The Mall   Phone: (808)956-8116
Honolulu, HI 96822   Lan Hiang Char, Act.Hd.
Founded: 1962. **Staff:** Prof 11; Other 1. **Subjects:** East, Southeast, and South Asia. **Special Collections:** Sakamaki Collection (Ryukyus); Kajiyama Collection (Japanese language); Tun Huang Manuscripts (Chinese language); Imanishi Hakushi Shushu Chosenbon (Korean historical resources); Kyujunggak Collection (archival material from the Yi Dynasty Royal Library); United Presbyterian Mission Correspondence of the 19th and early 20th centuries from and to missions in East Asia, South Asia, and Southeast Asia; despatches from U.S. Consuls and Ministers to East Asia, South Asia, and Southeast Asia (19th and early 20th centuries). **Holdings:** 595,870 volumes; 37,080 reels of microfilm; 148,225 microfiche. **Subscriptions:** 9102 journals and other serials; 112 newspapers. **Services:** Interlibrary loan; copying; collection open to the public. **Automated Operations:** Computerized public access catalog, cataloging, serials, and circulation. **Computerized Information Services:** RLIN, OCLC. **Networks/Consortia:** Member of Research Libraries Information Network (RLIN), Colorado Alliance of Research Libraries (CARL). **Remarks:** FAX: (808)956-5968. **Staff:** Masato Matsui, Japanese Lang.; Chau Mun Lau, Chinese Bibliog.; Lynette Wageman, S. Asia Spec.; Katherine Yoshimura, Asia Libn.; Alice Mak, Philippines; Shiro Saito, Philippines; Patricia Polansky, Russian Bibliog.; Alan Kamida, Spec.Proj.

★ 18618 ★
University of Hawaii - Center for Korean Studies - Library (Area-Ethnic)
1881 East-West Rd.   Phone: (808)948-7041
Honolulu, HI 96822   Sam Suk Hahn, Libn.
Founded: 1972. **Staff:** Prof 2. **Subjects:** Korea. **Special Collections:** Archival collection of Tongjihoe organization (Honolulu); George and Evelyn McCune Collection; Doo Soo Suh Collection; Eugene I. Knez Collection. **Holdings:** 22,500 items (6500 titles), including 700 serial titles; 825 reels of microfilm of doctoral dissertations; 71 16mm films; 226 reels of microfilm of newspapers; 97 lectures and 12 conference/workshops on audio cassette; 12 cassette-slide sets; sound recordings. **Subscriptions:** 105 journals and other serials; 11 newspapers. **Services:** Copying; film showings; library open to the public with restrictions. **Publications:** The Tongjihoe Collection: A List of Archival Materials; informal acquisitions lists; bibliographies. **Remarks:** An alternate telephone number is 948-6391. FAX: (808)948-6388. **Staff:** Deanna Lee, Adm.Off.

★ 18619 ★
University of Hawaii - John A. Burns School of Medicine - Pacific Basin Rehabilitation Research & Training Center Library (Med)
Rehabilitation Hospital of the Pacific
226 N. Kuakini St., Rm. 233   Phone: (808)537-5986
Honolulu, HI 96817   Joanne Yamada, Commun.Spec.
Subjects: Rehabilitation, disabled/disability, Pacific Basin, low-technology (orthotics, prosthetics), research, manpower development training, communications. **Holdings:** 240 books; 188 bound periodical volumes. **Subscriptions:** 198 journals and other serials; 268 serial newsletters. **Services:** Interlibrary loan; copying; center open to the public with restrictions. **Remarks:** FAX: (808)531-8691.

University of Hawaii - Nitrogen Fixation by Tropical Agricultural Legumes
See: **Nitrogen Fixation by Tropical Agricultural Legumes** (11817)

★ 18620 ★
University of Hawaii - Pacific Bio-Medical Research Center - Library (Biol Sci)
41 Ahui St.   Phone: (808)539-7300
Honolulu, HI 96813   Dr. Barbara H. Gibbons, Res.
Founded: 1967. **Staff:** 1. **Subjects:** Biochemistry, cell biology, developmental morphology, molecular biology. **Special Collections:** Reprints of papers by C.F.W. McClure. **Holdings:** 700 bound periodical volumes. **Subscriptions:** 15 journals and other serials. **Services:** Copying; library open to the public with restrictions. **Remarks:** FAX: (808)599-4817.

★ 18621 ★
University of Hawaii - Public Services - Government Documents & Maps (Info Sci, Geog-Map)
Hamilton Library
2550 The Mall   Phone: (808)956-8230
Honolulu, HI 96822   Virginia Richardson, Hd.
Founded: 1945. **Staff:** Prof 3; Other 5. **Holdings:** 63,872 bound volumes; public documents of official U.S. agencies, including U.S. Geological Survey, Defense Mapping Agency, and National Ocean Service (regional depository), state agricultural departments and experiment stations, United Nations and its affiliated agencies (including UNESCO, Food and Agriculture Organization, World Bank, World Health Organization), European Economic Community (EEC), and selected British, Australian, and New Zealand parliamentary documents; 631,937 unbound parts; 1.3 million microforms; 136,000 maps; 86,000 aerial photographs. **Subscriptions:** 60 journals and other serials. **Services:** Interlibrary loan; copying; collection open to the public. **Staff:** Mabel Suzuki, Docs.Libn.; Verna Young, Docs.Libn.

★ 18622 ★
University of Hawaii - School of Public Health - Library (Med)
1960 East-West Rd., Rm. D 206   Phone: (808)956-8666
Honolulu, HI 96822   Virginia (Ginny) Tanji, Hd.Libn.
Founded: 1968. **Staff:** Prof 1; Other 2. **Subjects:** Public health, health services planning and administration, environmental health, population studies, quantitative health sciences, health education, maternal and child health, public health nutrition, international health, population and family planning studies, gerontology. **Holdings:** 12,000 books; 1200 bound periodical volumes; 1500 theses and dissertations. **Subscriptions:** 200 journals and other serials. **Services:** Interlibrary loan; copying; library open to the public. **Automated Operations:** Computerized ILL (DOCLINE). **Computerized Information Services:** MEDLARS, DIALOG Information Services, OCLC; CD-ROM (MEDLINE, HealthPlan, CCINFOdisc); BITNET, EDUNET (electronic mail services). Performs searches on fee basis. **Networks/Consortia:** Member of National Network of Libraries of Medicine - Pacific Southwest Region. **Special Indexes:** Index to the School of Public Health Collection of Student Papers (book). **Remarks:** FAX: (808)944-3986. Electronic mail address(es): TANJI@UHUNIX.UHCC.HAWAII.EDU (EDUNET); TANJI@UHUNIX (BITNET).

★ 18623 ★
University of Hawaii - Social Science Research Institute (Soc Sci)
Porteus Hall 704
2424 Maile Way   Phone: (808)956-8930
Honolulu, HI 96822   Donald M. Topping, Dir.
Founded: 1974. **Subjects:** Research in the social sciences with emphasis on Hawaii and the Pacific; anthropology; language acquisition; oral history; linguistics; telecommunications; health and social sciences; development studies; cognitive studies. **Holdings:** Figures not available. **Services:** Institute not open to the public. **Computerized Information Services:** Internal databases; electronic mail service. **Publications:** Oceanic Linguistics, semiannual; Asian and Pacific Archeology Series; Hawaii Series (annotated bibliographies); Oceanic Linguistics: Special Publications (monographs); PALI Language Texts; newsletter. **Remarks:** FAX: (808)956-2884.

★ 18624 ★
University of Hawaii - Special Collections - Archives and Manuscripts (Hist)
Sinclair Library
2425 Campus Rd.   Phone: (808)956-6673
Honolulu, HI 96822   Dr. Nancy Morris, Assoc.Lib.Spec.
Founded: 1968. **Staff:** 2. **Subjects:** University of Hawaii. **Holdings:** Noncurrent official records of the university, faculty, and staff; miscellaneous historical material about the university; manuscript material related to Hawaii and the Pacific. **Services:** Copying; archives open to the public. **Computerized Information Services:** BITNET (electronic mail service). **Publications:** Guides to holdings; specialized finding aids. **Remarks:** Electronic mail address(es): JIMC@UHCCUX (BITNET). **Staff:** James F. Cartwright, Univ.Archv.

★ 18625 ★
University of Hawaii - Special Collections - Hawaii War Records
   Depository (Hist)
Hamilton Library
2550 The Mall   Phone: (808)956-8245
Honolulu, HI 96822   James Cartwright, Univ.Archv.
Founded: 1943. **Subjects:** Hawaii in World War II. **Holdings:** 200 linear feet of books, transcripts, photographs, microfilm, letters, memoranda, diaries, narratives, pamphlets, articles, government documents. **Services:** Depository open to the public. **Computerized Information Services:** BITNET (electronic mail service). **Remarks:** Alternate telephone number(s): 956-8264. Electronic mail address(es): JIMC@UHCCUX (BITNET). **Staff:** Nancy Morris, Staff Cons.; Eleanor Au, Staff Cons.

★ 18626 ★
University of Hawaii - Special Collections - Hawaiian Collection (Area-Ethnic)
Hamilton Library
2550 The Mall   Phone: (808)956-8264
Honolulu, HI 96822   Dr. Chieko Tachihata, Hawaiian Cur.
Founded: 1927. **Staff:** Prof 2. **Subjects:** Hawaiian Islands, languages, Captain Cook, state and county government documents, children's literature, Hawaiian language materials, ethnic materials. **Special Collections:** Rare Hawaiiana; 19th century Hawaiian business and literary manuscripts (20 linear feet); oral history collections (30.5 linear feet of reel-to-reel tapes, audio cassettes, bound transcripts). **Holdings:** 105,479 volumes; 8590 reels of microfilm; audiovisual materials; 39 linear feet of pamphlets; audiotapes of oral history; oral history transcripts; University of Hawaii theses and dissertations. **Subscriptions:** 2077 journals and other serials. **Services:** Interlibrary loan; copying; collection open to the public. **Computerized Information Services:** Hawaiian sheet music (internal database); InterNet, BITNET (electronic mail services). **Publications:** Acquisitions list, quarterly; Dissertations and Theses, University of Hawaii at Manoa, annual. **Special Catalogs:** Union catalog of Hawaiian holdings of several Honolulu libraries (card); file of University of Hawaii theses by fields of study (card). **Remarks:** FAX: (808)956-5968. Electronic mail address(es): chieko@uhccux.uhcc.hawaii.edu (InterNet); chieko@uhunix (BITNET). **Staff:** Dr. Michaelyn Chou, Hd. of Pub.Serv./Oral Hist.

★ 18627 ★
University of Hawaii - Special Collections - Jean Charlot Collection
   (Art, Hum)
Hamilton Library, Rm. 501
2550 The Mall   Phone: (808)956-2849
Honolulu, HI 96822   Dr. Nancy Morris, Charlot Libn.
Staff: 1. **Subjects:** French artist and writer Jean Charlot, 1898-1979. **Holdings:** Art works, documents, and working papers of and relating to Charlot: oil paintings, mural drawings, sketchbooks, and prints by Charlot; published and unpublished writings by Charlot; private documents, including Charlot's daily journal; tape-recorded interviews; correspondence; reminiscences; Charlot's personal library of over 1500 items; works by other artists, including Orozco, Siquieros, Rivera, Edward Weston, Ben Shahn, Louis Elshemius, and Hawaiian artists; prints by Posada and Daumier; Mexican folk art; documents by or relating to other artists and scholars. **Services:** Collection open to the public by appointment.

★ 18628 ★
University of Hawaii - Special Collections - Pacific Collection (Area-Ethnic)
Hamilton Library
2550 The Mall   Phone: (808)956-2851
Honolulu, HI 96822   Karen Peacock, Ph.D, Cur.
Founded: 1959. **Staff:** Prof 3. **Subjects:** Pacific Islands - government, economics, law, linguistics, vernacular texts, art, literature, anthropology, history, politics, geography, business; Melanesia; Micronesia; Polynesia. **Special Collections:** Depository for microfilm issued by PAMBU (Pacific Manuscripts Bureau), Canberra; out-of-state theses; depository for South Pacific Commission documents; Trust Territory Archives (microfilm); rare Pacific materials. **Holdings:** 68,000 volumes. **Subscriptions:** 1650 journals and other serials. **Services:** Photocopying via ILL; collection open to the public. **Computerized Information Services:** Hawaiian and Pacific Journal Contents (pre 1989) (internal database); electronic mail. **Publications:** Acquisitions List. **Special Indexes:** Trust Territory Archives Index (online). **Remarks:** FAX: (808)956-5968. **Staff:** Renee Heyum, Emeritus Pacific Cur.; Lynette Furuhashi, Pacific Spec.

★ 18629 ★
University of Hawaii - Special Collections - Rare Books (Rare Book)
Hamilton Library
2550 The Mall   Phone: (808)956-2844
Honolulu, HI 96822   Eleanor C. Au, Hd., Spec.Coll.
Staff: Prof 1. **Holdings:** Authors - Jack London, Mark Twain, Herman Melville, C.W. Stoddard; Book Arts Collection; juvenile books; historical text books; Social Movement Collection. **Services:** Collection open to the public for reference use only.

★ 18630 ★
University of Hawaii - Waikiki Aquarium - Library (Biol Sci)
2777 Kalakaua Ave.   Phone: (808)923-9741
Honolulu, HI 96815   Carol Hopper, Ph.D., Act.Libn.
Founded: 1980. **Staff:** Prof 1. **Subjects:** Hawaii-South Pacific region - marine aquarium technology, zoology, oceanography, vertebrata, invertebrata, mollusca, sharks, ichthyology, environment and ecosystems. **Special Collections:** Waikiki Aquarium Archives; Dr. Spencer Tinker Collection; aquarium guides; collection of out-of-print Aquarium Management magazines. **Holdings:** 2020 books; 150 journals and newsletters; 11 VF drawers of reprints; reports. **Subscriptions:** 153 journals and other serials. **Services:** Copying; SDI; library open to the public for reference use only by request. **Publications:** Directory of Public Aquaria of the World; Directory of Aquarium Specialists; Directory of Aquarium Libraries of the U.S., irregular; nature pamphlets; Kilo i'a, Looking at the Sea (newsletter), bimonthly; acquisitions list - for internal distribution only. **Special Catalogs:** Subject catalog (selected subjects only) for reprints (card). **Remarks:** FAX: (808)923-1771.

★ 18631 ★
University of Hawaii - William S. Richardson School of Law Library
   (Law)
2525 Dole St.   Phone: (808)956-7583
Honolulu, HI 96822   John E. Pickron, Law Libn.
Founded: 1973. **Staff:** Prof 5; Other 4. **Subjects:** Anglo-American and Hawaiian law. **Holdings:** 215,000 volumes. **Subscriptions:** 2400 journals and other serials. **Services:** Interlibrary loan (through graduate library); copying; library open to the public. **Automated Operations:** Computerized public access catalog and cataloging. **Computerized Information Services:** LEXIS, NEXIS; internal database. **Remarks:** FAX: (808)956-6402. **Staff:** Ted Kwok, Ref.Libn.; Dennis Ladd, Ref.Libn.; Nancy Westcott, Tech.Serv.Libn.

★ 18632 ★
University of Health Sciences - Mazzacano Hall Library (Med)
2105 Independence Blvd.   Phone: (816)283-2290
Kansas City, MO 64124   Marilyn J. DeGeus, Dir. of Lib.
Founded: 1916. **Staff:** Prof 3; Other 3. **Subjects:** Clinical medicine, basic science. **Special Collections:** Osteopathic medicine. **Holdings:** 47,993 books; 18,018 bound periodical volumes; 194 cassette tape titles; 2554 slide titles; 2293 videotapes; 1 microfiche; 2 transparencies; 24 teaching models; 24 three-dimensional disc titles; 168 computer programs; 891 x-ray radiographs; 64 16mm films. **Subscriptions:** 300 journals and other serials. **Services:** Interlibrary loan; copying; library open to the public for reference use only. **Automated Operations:** Computerized cataloging. **Computerized Information Services:** MEDLINE, TOXLINE, OCLC, OCLC EPIC, BRS Information Technologies, DIALOG Information Services; DOCLINE (electronic mail service). Performs searches on fee basis. Contact Person: Bonnie Anderson, Ref.Libn., (816)283-2294. **Networks/Consortia:** Member of Kansas City Library Network, Inc. (KCLN), National Network of Libraries of Medicine - Midcontinental Region. **Publications:** Mazzacano Hall Library Handbook. **Remarks:** FAX: (816)283-2303. **Staff:** Lynn Mousseau, Cat.

★ 18633 ★
University of Health Sciences-Chicago Medical School - Learning
   Resources Center (Med)
3333 Green Bay Rd.   Phone: (708)578-3242
North Chicago, IL 60064   Nancy W. Garn, Dir. & Asst. Dean
Founded: 1912. **Staff:** Prof 6; Other 17. **Subjects:** Medicine, psychology, and allied health sciences. **Special Collections:** Grants Resource Center. **Holdings:** 19,775 books; 72,076 bound periodical volumes; 20,000 volumes on 2800 reels of microfilm; 3 drawers of residency catalogs; 150 dissertations; 3 drawers of elective catalogs; 8 drawers of pamphlets. **Subscriptions:** 1301 journals and other serials; 7 newspapers. **Services:** Interlibrary loan;

copying; center open to the public with letter of introduction. **Automated Operations:** Computerized cataloging, serials, and ILL. **Computerized Information Services:** BRS Information Technologies, DIALOG Information Services, OCLC. **Publications:** Calendar of Events, weekly; Grants Resource Center Report, bimonthly; Current Monographs and Serials Newsletter, monthly; LRC Guide, annual; Journal Holdings List, annual; bibliographies, irregular; subject guides, irregular. **Special Catalogs:** AV Catalog, annual. **Remarks:** Center is a Resource Library of the Greater Midwest Regional Medical Library Network (Region 3). FAX: (708)578-3401. **Staff:** Pat McQueen, Hd., Tech.Serv.; Kevin Robertson, ILL Libn.; Sharyn Fradin, Assoc.Dir.; Peter Nierenberger, Hd.Ref. Online Serv.

★ 18634 ★
University of Helsinki - Department of Mathematics - Library (Sci-Engr)
Hallituskatu 15   Phone: 0 1912853
SF-00100 Helsinki 10, Finland   Prof. Lauri Myrberg
Founded: 1937. **Staff:** Prof 3. **Subjects:** Mathematics and its applications. **Holdings:** 35,000 bound volumes. **Subscriptions:** 452 journals and other serials. **Services:** Interlibrary loan; copying; library open to advanced students and staff of the university. **Computerized Information Services:** STN International; HELKA (internal database). **Remarks:** FAX: 0 1913213. **Also Known As:** Helsingin Yliopisto - Matematiikan Laitoksen Kirjasto.

★ 18635 ★
University of Helsinki - Library (Hum, Info Sci)
Unioninkatu 36
P.O. Box 312   Phone: 0 191 2740
SF-00171 Helsinki, Finland   Inger Osterman, Libn./Hd., Pub.Serv.
Subjects: Humanities. **Special Collections:** National Library of Finland; Slavonic Collection, 1828-1917 (300,000 volumes); 200 other special collections. **Holdings:** 2.7 million volumes; 300,000 microforms. **Subscriptions:** 6941 journals and other serials; 426 newspapers. **Services:** Interlibrary loan; copying; SDI; library open to the public. **Computerized Information Services:** KDOK/Minttu, DIALOG Information Services, Questel, Libris; CD-ROMs. Performs searches on fee basis. **Publications:** Finnish national bibliography; bibliographies - both for sale. **Remarks:** National Library of Finland is an archival collection; no interlibrary loans or circulation are allowed. FAX: 0 1912719. Telex: HYK SF 121538.

★ 18636 ★
University Hospital - Health Sciences Library (Med)
1350 Walton Way   Phone: (404)823-5078
Augusta, GA 30910-3599   Jane B. Wells, Libn.
Founded: 1959. **Staff:** Prof 1; Other 1. **Subjects:** Medicine, nursing, allied health sciences. **Holdings:** 5000 books; 450 bound periodical volumes. **Subscriptions:** 300 journals and other serials. **Services:** Interlibrary loan; library not open to the public. **Computerized Information Services:** Internal database.

★ 18637 ★
University Hospital and Clinic - Herbert L. Bryans Memorial Library (Med)
1200 W. Leonard St.   Phone: (904)436-9187
Pensacola, FL 32501   Ms. Sammie Campbell, Med.Rec.
Founded: 1985. **Staff:** Prof 1. **Subjects:** Medicine, dentistry, nursing, dietetics, hospital administration. **Holdings:** 300 books. **Subscriptions:** 8 journals and other serials. **Services:** Interlibrary loan; copying; library open to the public with restrictions. **Remarks:** AV programs are available through the Pensacola Education Program. **Staff:** Marilyn E. Lee.

★ 18638 ★
University Hospitals of Cleveland & Case Western Reserve University - Department of Pathology - Library (Med)
2085 Adelbert Rd.   Phone: (216)368-2482
Cleveland, OH 44106   Jeanette W. Nagy, Dir.
Founded: 1930. **Staff:** Prof 1. **Subjects:** Pathology, biochemistry, obstetrics, gynecology, surgery, neuropathology, immunology, histology, cytology. **Holdings:** 2000 books; 7000 bound periodical volumes; reprints; theses; dissertations. **Subscriptions:** 75 journals and other serials. **Services:** Library open to the public with restrictions.

★ 18639 ★
University of Houston - Allied Geophysical Laboratories - Milton B. Dobrin Library (Sci-Engr)
Allied Geophysical Laboratories Bldg.
4800 Calhoun   Phone: (713)749-7336
Houston, TX 77204-4231   Gloria Bellis, Libn.
Founded: 1984. **Staff:** Prof 1. **Subjects:** Geophysics, geology. **Holdings:** 4500 books; 132 bound periodical volumes. **Subscriptions:** 6 journals and other serials. **Services:** Copying; library open to members of the Allied Geophysical Laboratories Consortium. **Automated Operations:** Computerized public access catalog and cataloging. **Remarks:** FAX: (713)749-4169.

University of Houston - Audiovisual Services
See: University of Houston - University Media Services (18645)

★ 18640 ★
University of Houston - College of Optometry Library (Med)
Houston, TX 77204-6052   Phone: (713)749-2411
                                            Suzanne Ferimer, Dir., Lrng.Rsrcs.
Founded: 1952. **Staff:** Prof 1; Other 2. **Subjects:** Optometry, ocular diagnosis and management, community and public health, contact lenses, pediatric optometry, optics, physiological optics, ocular drugs. **Holdings:** 13,300 books and bound periodical volumes; 500 audiocassettes; 3 drawers of vertical files, bibliographies, reports; 170 videocassettes; 70 slide-tape presentations; 310 pamphlets. **Subscriptions:** 125 journals and other serials. **Services:** Interlibrary loan; copying; library open to the public with restrictions. **Automated Operations:** Computerized cataloging, acquisitions, and circulation. **Computerized Information Services:** DIALOG Information Services, PFDS Online, NLM, BRS Information Technologies. **Networks/Consortia:** Member of AMIGOS Bibliographic Council, Inc., Houston Area Research Library Consortium (HARLIC). **Remarks:** FAX: (713)749-3867.

★ 18641 ★
University of Houston - College of Pharmacy Library (Med)
Houston, TX 77204-5511   Phone: (713)749-1566
                                            Derral Parkin, Libn.
Founded: 1947. **Staff:** Prof 1; Other 4. **Subjects:** Chemistry, pharmacy, pharmaceuticals, toxicology, pharmacognosy, pharmacology. **Special Collections:** History and biography of pharmacy and medicine. **Holdings:** 15,487 books and bound periodical volumes; pharmaceutical catalogs. **Subscriptions:** 154 journals and other serials. **Services:** Interlibrary loan; copying; library open to the public. **Automated Operations:** Computerized cataloging, acquisitions, and circulation. **Computerized Information Services:** BRS Information Technologies, DIALOG Information Services, NLM, STN International. **Networks/Consortia:** Member of AMIGOS Bibliographic Council, Inc., Houston Area Research Library Consortium (HARLIC). **Publications:** Quarterly acquisitions list - for internal distribution only. **Remarks:** FAX: (713)749-3867.

★ 18642 ★
University of Houston - Law Library (Law)
Houston, TX 77204-6390   Phone: (713)749-3191
                                            Jon S. Schultz, Dir.
Staff: Prof 11; Other 6. **Subjects:** Law. **Holdings:** 218,696 volumes; 5000 Texas Supreme Court briefs; 580,665 microfiche. **Subscriptions:** 1733 journals and other serials. **Services:** Interlibrary loan; copying; library open to the public with permission. **Automated Operations:** Computerized cataloging, acquisitions, and serials. **Computerized Information Services:** LEXIS, WESTLAW. **Networks/Consortia:** Member of AMIGOS Bibliographic Council, Inc. **Remarks:** FAX: (713)749-2567.

★ 18643 ★
University of Houston - Libraries - Special Collections (Hist, Hum)
Houston, TX 77204-2091   Phone: (713)749-2726
                                            Pat Bozeman, Hd. of Spec.Coll.
Staff: Prof 1; Other 3. **Subjects:** Texana; Western history; Houston, British, and American authors; Latin drama. **Special Collections:** George Fuermann City of Houston Collection; W.B. Bates Collection of Texana; James E. & Miriam A. Ferguson Papers (3 boxes); Jones Drama Collection (1500 volumes); Israel Shreve papers (25); James V. Allred papers (100 linear feet); Larry McMurtry manuscripts (60 boxes); Beverly Lowry manuscripts (5

boxes); Jan de Hartog manuscripts (19 boxes); Aldous Huxley manuscripts (3 boxes); historical railroad and Western hemisphere maps; Kenneth Patchen Collection (188 items); Fritz Leiber Collection (23 boxes); Cheryl Crawford Collection (9 boxes); Houston Sangerbund Collection (8 boxes); George Kirksey papers (16 boxes); William Wilberforce Edgerton Civil War letters (2 boxes); Sylvan Karchmer papers (19 boxes); Vassar Miller papers (15 boxes); university archives. **Holdings:** 50,000 books; 2000 bound periodical volumes. **Subscriptions:** 11 journals and other serials. **Services:** Collections open to the public with supervision. **Special Catalogs:** W.B. Bates Collection Catalog; Robinson Jeffers Collection Catalog; John Updike Catalog; Luyet Memorial Collection in Cryobiology Catalog; African-American authors catalog; children's literature catalog; Celebrating Literary Diversity: Selected Authors. **Special Indexes:** Examples of Early, Rare and Fine Printing in Special Collections; Manuscript Collection: Compendium of Finding Aids. **Remarks:** FAX: (713)749-3867.

★ 18644 ★
University of Houston - Music Library (Mus)
Houston, TX 77204-4893   Phone: (713)749-2534
                       Samuel R. Hyde, Libn.
Founded: 1975. **Staff:** Prof 1; Other 1.5. **Subjects:** Music. **Holdings:** 40,242 books, bound periodical volumes, scores. **Subscriptions:** 187 journals and other serials. **Services:** Interlibrary loan; copying; library open to the public for reference use only. **Automated Operations:** Computerized cataloging, acquisitions, and circulation. **Computerized Information Services:** DIALOG Information Services. **Networks/Consortia:** Member of AMIGOS Bibliographic Council, Inc., Houston Area Research Library Consortium (HARLIC). **Remarks:** (713)749-3867.

★ 18645 ★
University of Houston - University Media Services (Aud-Vis)
Houston, TX 77204-2090   Phone: (713)749-2361
                       Joe Schroeder, Dir.
Founded: 1927. **Staff:** Prof 6; Other 11. **Holdings:** 2570 films, videotapes, and AV modules. **Services:** Full media services to administration, research, and instructional programs: television, photographic, audio, and graphic production; media distribution; media supplies; electronic maintenance; instruction development; Instructional Television Fixed Service (ITFS) broadcast studio/classroom; satellite uplink and downlink teleconference service. **Publications:** Annual report; newsletter. **Remarks:** FAX: (713)749-2364. **Formerly:** Its Audiovisual Services. **Staff:** James Joplin, Asst.Dir., Prod.Serv.; Umesh Kapur, Asst.Dir., Tech.Serv.; Betty Bishop, Coord., Educ. LRC.

★ 18646 ★
University of Houston - William R. Jenkins Architecture and Art Library (Art, Plan)
Houston, TX 77204-4431   Phone: (713)743-2340
                   Margaret Culbertson, Libn.
Founded: 1961. **Staff:** Prof 1; Other 2. **Subjects:** Architecture, art, urban design, photography. **Holdings:** 55,000 books and bound periodical volumes. **Subscriptions:** 225 journals and other serials. **Services:** Interlibrary loan; library open to the public for reference use only. **Automated Operations:** Computerized cataloging, acquisitions, and circulation. **Computerized Information Services:** DIALOG Information Services, PFDS Online, BRS Information Technologies, RLIN. **Networks/Consortia:** Member of AMIGOS Bibliographic Council, Inc., Houston Area Research Library Consortium (HARLIC). **Remarks:** FAX: (713)749-3867.

University of Houston, Victoria
See: Victoria College/University of Houston, Victoria (19826)

★ 18647 ★
University of Idaho - Bureau of Public Affairs Research - Library (Soc Sci)
Moscow, ID 83843   Phone: (208)885-6563
                       Florence Heffron
Founded: 1959. **Staff:** 1. **Subjects:** State and local politics and administration. **Holdings:** Reference books, pamphlets, reports, periodicals, newsletters, and other publications of governmental research bureaus and state and local agencies throughout the nation. **Services:** Research and training services for state and local government agencies in Idaho.

★ 18648 ★
University of Idaho - Herbarium - Library (Biol Sci)
Dept. of Biological Sciences   Phone: (208)885-6798
Moscow, ID 83843   Douglass Henderson, Dir.
Founded: 1889. **Staff:** Prof 1. **Subjects:** Botany, phytogeography, plant classification. **Holdings:** 1200 books; 3000 bound periodical volumes; 2000 reports; 150 microfiche; botanical monographs; scientific reprints; floral manuals; botanical indices. **Subscriptions:** 7 journals and other serials. **Services:** Library open to the public only upon special request. **Computerized Information Services:** Poaceae of Idaho, Flora of East Central Idaho (internal databases).

★ 18649 ★
University of Idaho - Humanities Library (Hum)
Moscow, ID 83843   Phone: (208)885-6584
                   Gail Z. Eckwright, Libn.
Founded: 1906. **Staff:** Prof 3; Other 2. **Subjects:** Literature, music, language, art, philosophy, architecture. **Holdings:** 145,752 books; 36,441 bound periodical volumes; 129,349 volumes in microform. **Subscriptions:** 2575 journals and other serials; 99 newspapers. **Services:** Interlibrary loan; copying; library open to the public. **Automated Operations:** Computerized public access catalog, cataloging, acquisitions, and serials. **Computerized Information Services:** DIALOG Information Services; OnTyme Electronic Message Network Service (electronic mail service). Performs searches on fee basis. **Networks/Consortia:** Member of Western Library Network (WLN). **Publications:** The Bookmark, 4/year. **Remarks:** FAX: (208)885-6817. **Staff:** Dora Mih, Ref.Libn.; Ruth Cochran, Ref.Libn.

★ 18650 ★
University of Idaho - Idaho Geological Survey - Library (Sci-Engr)
Morrill Hall, Rm. 332   Phone: (208)885-7991
Moscow, ID 83843   Earl H. Bennett, Dir.
Founded: 1920. **Staff:** Other 1. **Subjects:** Geology, mineral resources. **Special Collections:** Geology and mineral resources of Idaho. **Holdings:** 3000 volumes. **Services:** Copying. **Publications:** List of publications - available on request.

★ 18651 ★
University of Idaho - Idaho Water Resources Research Institute - Technical Information Center & Reading Room
Moscow, ID 83843
Staff: 2. **Subjects:** Water resources, resource economics, outdoor recreation, groundwater, irrigation, wild and scenic rivers, water seepage, agriculture, water law, precipitation distribution, small hydroelectric developments. **Holdings:** 4000 books and bound periodical volumes. **Remarks:** Currently inactive.

★ 18652 ★
University of Idaho - Law Library (Law)
College of Law   Phone: (208)885-6521
Moscow, ID 83843   Leinaala R. Seeger, Dir.
Founded: 1911. **Staff:** Prof 4; Other 5. **Subjects:** Law. **Special Collections:** Idaho records and briefs. **Holdings:** 137,458 volumes. **Subscriptions:** 3224 journals and other serials. **Services:** Interlibrary loan; copying. **Automated Operations:** Computerized public access catalog and cataloging. **Computerized Information Services:** LEXIS, NEXIS, WESTLAW, DIALOG Information Services; CARL, BITNET, WLN, InterNet (electronic mail services). **Networks/Consortia:** Member of Western Library Network (WLN). **Publications:** American Indian Law Holdings List, annual. **Remarks:** FAX: (208)885-7609. Electronic mail address(es): LAWLIB@IDUI1 (BITNET); LAWLIB@IDUI1.UIDAHO.EDU (InterNet). **Staff:** James R. Carlson, Jr., Assoc. Law Libn.Pub.Serv.; Ruth P. Funabiki, Assoc.Law Libn.Tech.Serv.; John M. Madden, Asst. Law Libn.

★ 18653 ★
University of Idaho - Pacific Northwest Anthropological Archives (Hist)
Laboratory of Anthropology   Phone: (208)885-6123
Moscow, ID 83843   Roderick Sprague, Dir.
Founded: 1975. **Staff:** Prof 1; Other 1. **Subjects:** Pacific Northwest - archeology, ethnography, ethnohistory, historical archeology, physical anthropology. **Holdings:** 10,000 photocopies and other materials relating to the archeology and physical anthropology of the Pacific Northwest. **Subscriptions:** 14 journals and other serials. **Services:** Copying; archives open to the public. **Remarks:** FAX: (208)885-5878.

★ 18654 ★
University of Idaho - Science and Technology Library (Biol Sci, Sci-Engr)
Moscow, ID 83843   Phone: (208)885-6235
    Donna Hanson, Libn.
Founded: 1906. **Staff:** Prof 3; Other 1. **Subjects:** Forestry, agriculture, mining and geology, entomology, engineering, physical sciences, biological sciences, U.S. patent depository. **Holdings:** 160,489 books; 132,028 bound periodical volumes; 4727 microforms. **Subscriptions:** 6439 journals and other serials. **Services:** Interlibrary loan; copying; library open to the public. **Automated Operations:** Computerized public access catalog, cataloging, acquisitions, and serials. **Computerized Information Services:** DIALOG Information Services; OnTyme Electronic Message Network Service (electronic mail service). Performs searches on fee basis. **Networks/Consortia:** Member of Western Library Network (WLN). **Remarks:** FAX: (208)885-6817. **Staff:** John Kawula, Ref.Libn.(Sci.); Diane Prorak, Ref.Libn.(Sci.)

★ 18655 ★
University of Idaho - Social Science Library (Soc Sci)
Moscow, ID 83843   Phone: (208)885-6344
    Dennis Baird, Libn.
Founded: 1906. **Staff:** Prof 3; Other 2. **Subjects:** History, education, political science, sociology, business and economics. **Holdings:** 199,380 books; 49,494 bound periodical volumes; 969,983 government publications; 184,714 volumes in microform and ERIC microfiche; 184,144 sheet maps. **Subscriptions:** 3222 journals and other serials. **Services:** Interlibrary loan; copying; library open to the public. **Automated Operations:** Computerized public access catalog, cataloging, acquisitions, and serials. **Computerized Information Services:** DIALOG Information Services; OnTyme Electronic Message Network Service (electronic mail service). Performs searches on fee basis. **Networks/Consortia:** Member of Western Library Network (WLN). **Remarks:** FAX: (208)885-6817. **Staff:** Lily Wai, Doc.Libn.; Robert Bolin, Ref.Libn.

★ 18656 ★
University of Idaho - Special Collections Library (Hum)
Moscow, ID 83843-4198   Phone: (208)885-7951
    Terry Abraham, Hd., Spec.Coll.
Staff: Prof 3; Other 2. **Subjects:** Idaho and Pacific Northwest, State of Idaho publications, University of Idaho archives, Sir Walter Scott, Ezra Pound, Western Americana. **Holdings:** 42,823 volumes; 1267 bound periodical volumes; 98,858 prints and photographs; 3715 cubic feet of manuscripts; 811 cubic feet of archives; 100 cubic feet of maps, vertical files, oral history materials, and other items. **Subscriptions:** 643 journals and other serials. **Services:** Copying; library open to the public for reference use only. **Automated Operations:** Computerized public access catalog, cataloging, acquisitions, and serials. **Computerized Information Services:** BITNET, InterNet (electronic mail services). **Networks/Consortia:** Member of Western Library Network (WLN). **Remarks:** FAX: (208)885-6817. Electronic mail address(es): LIBRSPEC@IDUI1 (BITNET); LIBRSPEC@IDUI1.CSRV.UIDAHO.EDU (InterNet). **Staff:** Ralph Nielsen, Spec.Proj.Libn.; Richard C. Davis, Mss.-Archv.Libn.

★ 18657 ★
University of Illinois - Agriculture Library (Agri)
226 Mumford Hall
1301 W. Gregory Dr.   Phone: (217)333-2416
Urbana, IL 61801   Carol Boast, Libn.
Founded: 1915. **Staff:** Prof 4; Other 5. **Subjects:** Agricultural economics, animal science, agricultural engineering, crops, horticulture, food science and technology, agricultural history, forestry, soils. **Holdings:** 70,000 volumes; 600 microforms. **Subscriptions:** 2850 journals and other serials. **Services:** Interlibrary loan; copying; library open to the public. **Automated Operations:** Computerized cataloging, acquisitions, serials, and circulation. **Computerized Information Services:** BRS Information Technologies, DIALOG Information Services; internal database. **Publications:** Selected New Acquisitions List, bimonthly. **Remarks:** FAX: (217)244-0398. **Staff:** Maria Porta, Asst.Libn.; Ken Carlborg, Sr.Proj.Cat.

★ 18658 ★
University of Illinois - Applied Life Studies Library (Educ, Rec)
Main Library, Rm. 146
1408 W. Gregory Dr.   Phone: (217)333-3615
Urbana, IL 61801   Mary Beth Allen, Hd.Libn.
Founded: 1949. **Staff:** Prof 1; Other 2. **Subjects:** Leisure studies; education - physical, health, safety, driver; sport science - biomechanics, medicine,

psychology, sociology, history; dance. **Special Collections:** Avery Brundage Collection (1600 volumes). **Holdings:** 21,074 volumes; 1200 theses; 6 VF drawers of pamphlets; 10,536 microcards; 15,219 microfiche. **Subscriptions:** 488 journals and other serials. **Services:** Interlibrary loan; copying. **Automated Operations:** Computerized circulation. **Computerized Information Services:** Online systems; BITNET (electronic mail service). Performs searches on fee basis. **Publications:** Acquisition list, quarterly - to faculty, students, and others on request. **Remarks:** FAX: (217)244-0398. Electronic mail address(es): MCCANDLE@UIUCVMD (BITNET).

★ 18659 ★
University of Illinois - Asian Library (Area-Ethnic)
325 Main Library
1408 W. Gregory Dr.
Urbana, IL 61801   Phone: (217)333-1501
Founded: 1965. **Staff:** Prof 5; Other 6. **Subjects:** East Asia, South Asia, Southeast Asia, and Middle East - history, literature, languages, economics, sociology, anthropology, art, political science. **Holdings:** 250,000 books. **Subscriptions:** 1000 journals and other serials. **Services:** Interlibrary loan; copying; library open to the public. **Computerized Information Services:** RLIN; internal databases. **Remarks:** FAX: (217)244-0398. The University of Illinois Rare Book Room contains a collection of Japanese rare books. **Staff:** Narindar K. Aggarwal, Assoc. Asian Libn.; Karen Wei, Chinese Libn.

★ 18660 ★
University of Illinois - Asian Library - South and West Asian Division (Area-Ethnic)
325 Main Library
1408 W. Gregory Dr.   Phone: (217)333-2492
Urbana, IL 61801   Narindar K. Aggarwal, Assoc. Asian Libn.
Founded: 1964. **Staff:** Prof 1; Other 2. **Subjects:** South and West Asia - languages, literature, history, culture. **Holdings:** 98,000 books; 150 bound periodical volumes. **Services:** Interlibrary loan; division open to the public.

★ 18661 ★
University of Illinois - Biology Library (Biol Sci)
101 Burrill Hall
407 S. Goodwin   Phone: (217)333-3654
Urbana, IL 61801   Elisabeth B. Davis, Libn.
Founded: 1884. **Staff:** Prof 2; Other 12. **Subjects:** Biology, botany, entomology, biophysics, genetics, ecology, microbiology, physiology, zoology. **Special Collections:** Oberholser reprint collection on ornithology; microfiche collection of vascular plant types from botanical gardens and herbaria. **Holdings:** 117,000 volumes. **Subscriptions:** 2058 journals and other serials. **Services:** Interlibrary loan; copying; SDI; library open to the public by permit. **Automated Operations:** Computerized cataloging, acquisitions, and circulation. **Computerized Information Services:** DIALOG Information Services, NLM, BRS Information Technologies; BITNET (electronic mail service). Performs searches on fee basis. **Publications:** List of New Acquisitions, monthly; Guides to the Literature Held in the Biology Library. **Staff:** Diane Schmidt.

★ 18662 ★
University of Illinois - Chemistry Library (Sci-Engr)
255 Noyes Laboratory
505 S. Mathews   Phone: (217)333-3737
Urbana, IL 61801   Tina E. Chrzastowski, Chem.Libn.
Founded: 1892. **Staff:** Prof 1; Other 3. **Subjects:** Chemistry - analytical, inorganic, organic, physical; biochemistry; chemical engineering. **Holdings:** 70,000 volumes; 925 films and microfiche. **Subscriptions:** 840 journals and other serials. **Services:** Interlibrary loan; copying; library open to the public. **Automated Operations:** Computerized public access catalog and circulation. **Computerized Information Services:** DIALOG Information Services, Chemical Abstracts Service (CAS), OCLC. **Publications:** List of Acquisitions, monthly.

★ 18663 ★
University of Illinois - City Planning and Landscape Architecture Library (Plan)
203 Mumford Hall
1301 W. Gregory Dr.   Phone: (217)333-0424
Urbana, IL 61801   Mary D. Ravenhall, Libn.
Founded: 1912. **Staff:** Prof 1; Other 1. **Subjects:** City and regional planning, landscape architecture, urban studies. **Holdings:** 21,706 volumes; 14,000 pamphlets. **Subscriptions:** 544 journals and other serials. **Services:** Interlibrary loan; copying; library open to the public by permit from Main Library. **Automated Operations:** Computerized public access catalog and circulation. **Publications:** Acquisitions List, irregular - to mailing list. **Remarks:** FAX: (217)244-0398; 244-6649.

★ 18664 ★
University of Illinois - Classics Library (Hum)
419A Main Library
1408 W. Gregory Dr.   Phone: (217)333-1124
Urbana, IL 61801   Danuta Gorecki
Subjects: Classical languages and literatures, Roman and Greek history and civilizations, classical archeology. **Special Collections:** Dittenberger-Vahlen Collection. **Holdings:** 48,110 volumes. **Subscriptions:** 380 journals and other serials. **Services:** Interlibrary loan; library open to the public.

★ 18665 ★
University of Illinois - College of Engineering - Engineering Documents
  Center (Sci-Engr)
112 Engineering Hall
1308 W. Green St.   Phone: (217)244-6271
Urbana, IL 61801   Mu-chin Cheng, Doc.Libn.
Founded: 1966. **Staff:** Prof 1. **Subjects:** Engineering. **Holdings:** 10,000 technical reports. **Services:** Interlibrary loan; copying; center open to the public. **Automated Operations:** Computerized cataloging. **Special Indexes:** Engineering Documents Center Index, annual.

★ 18666 ★
University of Illinois - Commerce Library (Bus-Fin)
Rm. 101, Main Library
1408 W. Gregory Dr.   Phone: (217)333-3619
Urbana, IL 61801   M. Balachandran, Libn.
Staff: Prof 3; Other 8. **Subjects:** Economics, business administration, accounting, finance. **Holdings:** 57,376 volumes; 157,073 company annual and 10K reports on microfiche; 1330 working papers. **Subscriptions:** 1923 journals and other serials. **Services:** Interlibrary loan; library open to the public by permit. **Automated Operations:** Computerized circulation. **Computerized Information Services:** BRS Information Technologies, DIALOG Information Services; CD-ROMs (ABI/INFORM, Standard & Poor's COMPUSTAT Services, Inc., CD/Corporate, PAIS on CD-ROM, Business Periodicals Index). Performs searches on fee basis. **Publications:** Acquisitions List, 10/year - for internal distribution only. **Staff:** J. Phillips, Asst.Libn.; J. Thompson, Asst.Libn.

★ 18667 ★
University of Illinois - Communications Library (Info Sci)
122 Gregory Hall   Phone: (217)333-2216
Urbana, IL 61801   Diane Carothers, Commun.Libn.
Founded: 1933. **Staff:** Prof 1; Other 2. **Subjects:** Advertising, broadcasting, journalism, magazines, newspapers, public relations, communication theory, mass communications, photography, publishing, typography, motion pictures. **Special Collections:** D'Arcy Collection (advertising clippings from magazines and newspapers, 1890-1970; 2 million clippings). **Holdings:** 14,000 volumes. **Subscriptions:** 525 journals and other serials; 36 newspapers. **Services:** Interlibrary loan; copying; library open to the public with permit from Main Library. **Automated Operations:** Computerized public access catalog and circulation. **Publications:** Acquisition List (annotated), quarterly.

★ 18668 ★
University of Illinois - Coordinated Science Laboratory Library (Sci-Engr)
1101 W. Springfield, Rm. 269 A   Phone: (217)333-4368
Urbana, IL 61801   Mary Allison, Info.Spec.
Founded: 1951. **Staff:** Prof 1. **Subjects:** Electrical engineering, computers and control, physics, systems theory, artificial intelligence. **Holdings:** 3000 books; 2200 bound periodical volumes; 250 technical reports and dissertations. **Subscriptions:** 137 journals and other serials. **Services:** Copying; SDI; library open to the public for reference use only. **Computerized Information Services:** BITNET (electronic mail service). **Remarks:** FAX: (217)244-1764. Electronic mail address(es): NORTH@VICSL.CSL.VIVC.EDU (BITNET).

★ 18669 ★
University of Illinois - Documents Library (Info Sci)
200D Main Library
1408 W. Gregory Dr.   Phone: (217)333-1056
Urbana, IL 61801   Susan E. Bekiares, Hd.
Founded: 1980. **Staff:** Prof 4; Other 3. **Subjects:** Statistics, legislation, regulation, historical bibliography. **Special Collections:** U.S. Government and Illinois state; research and development reports. **Holdings:** 110,000 volumes; 1.3 million microfiche. **Subscriptions:** 6000 journals and other serials. **Services:** Interlibrary loan; copying; library open to the public for reference use only. **Automated Operations:** Computerized public access catalog, cataloging, acquisitions, serials, and circulation. **Computerized Information Services:** BRS Information Technologies, OCLC, DIALOG Information Services; internal databases. Performs searches on fee basis. Contact Person: Mary Gassmann, Docs.Libn. **Networks/Consortia:** Member of ILLINET. **Staff:** John Littlewood, Docs.Libn.; Mary Mallory, Docs.Libn.; Raeann Dossett, Docs.Libn.

★ 18670 ★
University of Illinois - Education and Social Science Library (Soc Sci)
100 Main Library
1408 W. Gregory Dr.   Phone: (217)333-2305
Urbana, IL 61801   Susan Klingberg, Sociology Spec.Libn.
Staff: Prof 5; Other 9. **Subjects:** Education, anthropology, psychology, political science, social work, sociology, speech and hearing science. **Special Collections:** Arms Control Collection; C.W. Odell Test Collection (7900 educational and psychological tests); ERIC microfiche; children's literature collection; Human Relations Area Files; U.N. official records; parapsychology and the occult; curriculum collection. **Holdings:** 209,348 volumes. **Subscriptions:** 2155 journals and other serials. **Services:** Interlibrary loan; copying; library open to the public on a limited basis. **Automated Operations:** Computerized circulation. **Computerized Information Services:** CD-ROMs. **Publications:** Bibliographies, occasional. **Staff:** J. Williams, Applied Social Sci.Spec.Libn.; N. O'Brien, Educ.Spec.Libn.; E. Sutton, Anthropology/Psych.Spec.Libn.

★ 18671 ★
University of Illinois - Engineering Library (Sci-Engr)
221 Engineering Hall
1308 W. Green St.   Phone: (217)333-3576
Urbana, IL 61801   William Mischo, Engr.Libn.
Staff: Prof 5; Other 5. **Subjects:** Engineering - aeronautical, agricultural, astronautical, ceramic, civil, computer, electrical, materials, mechanical, metallurgical, nuclear; bioengineering; computer science; theoretical and applied mechanics. **Special Collections:** U.S. National Advisory Committee for Aeronautics (NACA) Depository Sets, 1915-1958; U.S. NASA Depository Sets, 1978 to present. **Holdings:** 175,000 volumes. **Subscriptions:** 3200 journals and other serials. **Services:** Interlibrary loan; copying; library open to the public with permit. **Automated Operations:** Computerized public access catalog, serials, and circulation. **Computerized Information Services:** DIALOG Information Services, BRS Information Technologies, STN International. Performs searches on fee basis. **Remarks:** Alternate telephone number(s): 333-7497. **Staff:** Melvin G. DeSart, Asst.Engr.Libn.; Jounghyoun Kim Lee, Asst.Engr.Libn.; Barbara Loomis, Asst.Engr.Libn.; Timothy Cole, Asst.Emgr.Libn.

★ 18672 ★
University of Illinois - English Library (Hum)
321 Library
1408 W. Gregory Dr.   Phone: (217)333-2220
Urbana, IL 61801   William S. Brockman, Libn.
Founded: 1908. **Staff:** Prof 2. **Subjects:** English literature - early, medieval, Renaissance, 17th-20th centuries; American literature; philology; folk tales; worldwide cinema and theater. **Holdings:** 34,588 volumes. **Subscriptions:** 595 journals and other serials. **Services:** Interlibrary loan; copying; library open to the public. **Computerized Information Services:** DIALOG Information Services. **Staff:** Robert Jones.

★ 18673 ★
University of Illinois - Geology Library (Sci-Engr)
223 Natural History Bldg.
1301 W. Green St.   Phone: (217)333-1266
Urbana, IL 61801   Lois Pausch, Libn.
Founded: 1959. **Staff:** Prof 1; Other 3. **Subjects:** Geology, mineralogy, paleontology, geomorphology, geophysics, geochemistry, oceanography, stratigraphy, petrology. **Special Collections:** History of Geology (early and rare items in geology); biographies of geologists. **Holdings:** 80,000 volumes; 54,000 geological maps. **Subscriptions:** 2000 journals and other serials. **Services:** Interlibrary loan; copying. **Automated Operations:** Computerized public access catalog. **Computerized Information Services:** Online systems; electronic mail service. Performs searches on fee basis.

★ 18674 ★

University of Illinois - Herbarium (Biol Sci)
Dept. of Plant Biology
505 S. Goodwin Ave.   Phone: (217)333-2522
Urbana, IL 61801   Almut G. Jones, Herbarium Cur.
Founded: 1868. **Staff:** Prof 1; Other 1. **Subjects:** Plants - Illinois, North
America, international. **Holdings:** 530,000 botanical specimens. **Remarks:**
FAX: (217)244-7246.

★ 18675 ★

University of Illinois - History and Philosophy Library (Rel-Phil, Hist)
424 Main Library
1408 W. Gregory Dr.   Phone: (217)333-1091
Urbana, IL 61801   Martha Friedman, Libn.
Founded: 1918. **Staff:** Prof 2; Other 3. **Subjects:** Medieval and modern
philosophy; religious studies; history - American, European, Far Eastern,
Latin American. **Special Collections:** Horner Lincoln Collection (10,000
books, pamphlets, broadsides; manuscripts; microfilm). **Holdings:** 21,311
volumes. **Subscriptions:** 1500 journals and other serials. **Services:**
Interlibrary loan (through Main Library). **Automated Operations:**
Computerized circulation. **Staff:** Priscilla Yu, Asst.Libn.

★ 18676 ★

University of Illinois - Home Economics Library (Agri, Food-Bev)
905 S. Goodwin Ave.   Phone: (217)333-0748
Urbana, IL 61801   Barbara C. Swain, Libn.
Founded: 1957. **Staff:** Prof 1; Other 1. **Subjects:** Family and consumer
economics, foods and nutrition, home economics education, human
development and family ecology, textiles, apparel, interior design, food
science. **Holdings:** 18,000 volumes; 2608 slides. **Subscriptions:** 302 journals
and other serials. **Services:** Interlibrary loan; library open to the public by
permit from Main Library. **Computerized Information Services:** DIALOG
Information Services, WILSONLINE. Performs searches on fee basis.
Publications: Selected List of New Books, quarterly.

★ 18677 ★

**University of Illinois - Housing Research & Development Program -
Library** (Plan)
1204 W. Nevada
Urbana, IL 61801   Phone: (217)333-7330
Founded: 1969. **Staff:** 1. **Subjects:** Housing for the elderly, housing design,
community development, low-income housing, environmental psychology,
government programs. **Holdings:** 2000 books; 8 VF drawers of clippings,
reports, pamphlets, brochures, maps. **Subscriptions:** 37 journals and other
serials. **Services:** Library open to the public for reference use only. **Remarks:**
FAX: (217)244-5527.

★ 18678 ★

University of Illinois - Illinois Historical Survey (Hist)
346 Main Library
1408 W. Gregory Dr.   Phone: (217)333-1777
Urbana, IL 61801   John Hoffmann, Libn.
Founded: 1910. **Staff:** Prof 1; Other 1. **Subjects:** Illinois history. **Special
Collections:** Religious Society of Friends; communitarianism; Illinois labor;
German immigration. **Holdings:** 14,000 volumes; 1750 maps; 800 linear feet
of archives and manuscripts; 700 reels of microfilm of manuscripts; 3500 VF
items. **Subscriptions:** 30 journals and other serials. **Services:** Interlibrary
loan; copying; library open to the public for reference and research only.
Publications: Manuscripts guide to collections at the University of Illinois
at Urbana-Champaign; Guide to the Heinrich A. Rattermann Collection of
German-American Manuscripts; Guide to the Papers in the John Hunter
Walker Collection, 1911-1953.

★ 18679 ★

University of Illinois - Illinois State Natural History Survey - Library
(Biol Sci)
196 Natural Resources Bldg.
607 E. Peabody   Phone: (217)333-6892
Champaign, IL 61820   Carla G. Heister, Libn.
Founded: 1858. **Staff:** Prof 1; Other 1. **Subjects:** Economic entomology,
conservation biology, aquatic ecology, botany, wildlife ecology,
environmental quality, biodiversity studies, biogeography. **Holdings:** 36,500
volumes. **Subscriptions:** 1037 journals and other serials. **Services:**

Interlibrary loan; copying; SDI; library open to the public for reference use
only. **Automated Operations:** Computerized cataloging, acquisitions, and
circulation. **Computerized Information Services:** BRS Information
Technologies, DIALOG Information Services, OCLC; BITNET (electronic
mail service). Performs searches on fee basis. **Networks/Consortia:** Member
of ILLINET. **Publications:** Selected acquisitions list, bimonthly. **Remarks:**
FAX: (217)333-4949. Electronic mail address(es): HEISTER@UIUCVMD
(BITNET).

★ 18680 ★

**University of Illinois - Institute of Labor and Industrial Relations
Library** (Bus-Fin)
504 E. Armory   Phone: (217)333-2380
Champaign, IL 61820   Margaret A. Chaplan, Libn.
Founded: 1947. **Staff:** Prof 1; Other 2. **Subjects:** Labor and industrial
relations. **Holdings:** 11,000 volumes; 30,000 VF items; 796 reels of
microfilm; 3600 microfiche; 53 audio cassettes. **Subscriptions:** 450 journals
and other serials. **Services:** Interlibrary loan; copying; library open to the
public. **Automated Operations:** Computerized public access catalog,
cataloging, and circulation. **Computerized Information Services:** DIALOG
Information Services, BRS Information Technologies, PFDS Online;
DIALMAIL, BITNET (electronic mail services). Performs searches on fee
basis. **Publications:** ILIR Library Selected Recent Acquisitions, weekly - for
internal distribution only. **Remarks:** FAX: (217)244-4091.

★ 18681 ★

University of Illinois - Law Library (Law)
104 Law Bldg.
504 E. Pennsylvania Ave.   Phone: (217)333-2914
Champaign, IL 61820   Richard Surles, Dir.
Founded: 1897. **Staff:** Prof 7; Other 10. **Subjects:** Law and related social
sciences. **Special Collections:** Depository for U.S., Illinois State, and
European Economic Community documents; Archives of the American
Association of Law Libraries. **Holdings:** 473,000 volumes; 33,856
microcards; 1330 reels of microfilm; 433,132 microfiche; 2957 pamphlets.
Subscriptions: 6376 journals and other serials. **Services:** Interlibrary loan;
copying; library open to the public. **Computerized Information Services:**
LEXIS, WESTLAW, OCLC; LCS (internal database). **Publications:**
Research Aids. **Staff:** Fred Mansfield, Bibliog.; Cheryl Nyberg, Docs./
Ref.Libn.; Jane Williams, Ref.; Sandra Klein, Records/Ref.Libn.

★ 18682 ★

University of Illinois - Library and Information Science Library (Info
Sci)
306 Main Library
1408 W. Gregory Dr.   Phone: (217)333-3804
Urbana, IL 61801   Patricia F. Stenstrom, Libn.
Founded: 1906. **Staff:** Prof 1; Other 2. **Subjects:** Library and information
science. **Holdings:** 21,701 volumes; 1762 microfiche. **Subscriptions:** 1556
journals and other serials. **Services:** Interlibrary loan; copying; library open
to the public with permit from Main Library. **Automated Operations:**
Computerized public access catalog and circulation. **Computerized
Information Services:** WILSONLINE, DIALOG Information Services;
CD-ROM. Performs searches on fee basis. **Remarks:** Alternate telephone
number(s): 333-4456.

★ 18683 ★

University of Illinois - Map and Geography Library (Geog-Map)
418 Main Library
1408 W. Gregory Dr.   Phone: (217)333-0827
Urbana, IL 61801   David A. Cobb, Map & Geog.Libn.
Founded: 1944. **Staff:** Prof 2; Other 1. **Subjects:** Maps, geography, Illinois
aerial photography, atlases, gazetteers. **Special Collections:** Sanborn fire
insurance maps for Illinois cities; Cavagna Library (16th-19th century maps
of Italy); 19th century U.S. coastal charts. **Holdings:** 15,000 volumes;
150,000 aerial photographs; 370,000 maps; 475 reels of microfilm.
Subscriptions: 700 journals and other serials. **Services:** Interlibrary loan;
copying; library open to the public. **Automated Operations:** Computerized
cataloging. **Computerized Information Services:** OCLC. **Networks/
Consortia:** Member of ILLINET. **Publications:** Biblio, quarterly;
Acquisition Policy Statement. **Special Catalogs:** Catalog of Aerial
Photographs in the Map and Geography Library; Sanborn Maps; State
Atlases in the University of Illinois Library; List of Illinois County Atlases;
List of Illinois Topographic Maps; List of Gazetteers in the Map and
Geography Library.

★ 18684 ★
University of Illinois - Mathematics Library (Sci-Engr, Comp Sci)
216 Altgeld Hall
1409 W. Green St.   Phone: (217)333-0258
Urbana, IL 61801   Nancy D. Anderson, Libn.
Staff: Prof 2; Other 2. **Subjects:** Pure and applied mathematics, mathematical physics, statistics, computer sciences. **Holdings:** 75,000 volumes; 750 microforms; AV programs. **Subscriptions:** 1000 journals and other serials. **Services:** Interlibrary loan; copying; library open to the public. **Automated Operations:** Computerized public access catalog and circulation. **Computerized Information Services:** Current Journals of Interest to Mathematicians (internal database); electronic mail service. **Publications:** List of Acquisitions, bimonthly - to mailing list. **Remarks:** FAX: (217)244-0398.

★ 18685 ★
University of Illinois - Modern Languages and Linguistics Library
(Hum)
425 Main Library
1408 W. Gregory Dr.   Phone: (217)333-0076
Urbana, IL 61801   Sara de Mundo Lo, Libn.
Founded: 1911. **Staff:** Prof 4; Other 3. **Subjects:** Romance and Germanic language and literature, comparative literature, linguistics. **Special Collections:** Linguistic atlases; International Cinema Collection; Proust Collection; Chicano-Borico Collection. **Holdings:** 17,000 books; 800 bound periodical volumes. **Subscriptions:** 400 journals and other serials; 40 newspapers. **Services:** Interlibrary loan; copying; library open to the public. **Automated Operations:** Computerized circulation. **Computerized Information Services:** DIALOG Information Services, BRS Information Technologies; BITNET (electronic mail service). **Publications:** The Stentor, irregular - to faculty; user's guide - free upon request. **Remarks:** Electronic mail address(es): GHUETING@UIUC.VMD (BITNET). **Staff:** Tom Kilton; Gail Hueting; Pat Cardenas.

★ 18686 ★
University of Illinois - Music Library (Mus)
Music Bldg.   Phone: (217)333-1173
Urbana, IL 61801   William M. McClellan, Mus.Libn.
Founded: 1943. **Staff:** Prof 4; Other 8. **Subjects:** Music performance and research. **Special Collections:** Pre-1800 music manuscripts and editions (emphasis on medieval and Renaissance vocal music, lute and keyboard music sources; 2000 titles on microfilm); American popular sheet music, 1830-1970 (vocal; 100,000 titles); Rafael Joseffy Collection (19th century piano music; 2000 titles); Joseph Szigeti Collection (19th-20th century violin music manuscripts and editions; 700 titles); choral reference collection (single copies of octavos; 40,000 titles); recorded concerts and programs of the School of Music, 1950 to present (3000 reels of tape). **Holdings:** 40,000 volumes; 150,000 scores and parts; 10,000 reels of microfilm; 2422 microcards; 2000 microfiche; 80,000 phonograph records; 4 VF drawers of pamphlets; audio cassettes; compact discs; video cassettes. **Subscriptions:** 1300 journals and other serials. **Services:** Interlibrary loan; copying; library open to the public. **Automated Operations:** Computerized public access catalog and circulation. **Computerized Information Services:** Internal database. **Networks/Consortia:** Member of ILLINET. **Staff:** Jean Geil, Mus.Spec.Coll.Coord.; Richard Burbank, Mus.Cat.Coord.; Leslie Troutman, Mus. User Serv.Coord.

University of Illinois - National Clearinghouse on Marital and Date Rape
See: **National Clearinghouse on Marital and Date Rape** (11118)

★ 18687 ★
University of Illinois - Newspaper Library (Info Sci)
Main Library, Rm. 1
1408 W. Gregory Dr.
Urbana, IL 61801   Phone: (217)333-1509
Staff: 2. **Subjects:** Newspapers. **Holdings:** 11,018 volumes; 77,078 reels of microfilm; 8810 microcards. **Subscriptions:** 55 journals and other serials; 670 newspapers. **Services:** Interlibrary loan; copying; library open to the public. **Publications:** Holdings of Subject Classified Newspapers; general newspapers in microform - backfiles; Foreign Newspapers Currently Received; U.S. Newspapers Currently Received; Labor Newspapers Currently Received; Labor Newspapers on Microfilm and Other Special Listings, revised and reissued biennial; English Language Foreign Newspapers; Third World Newspapers.

★ 18688 ★
University of Illinois - Physics/Astronomy Library (Sci-Engr)
204 Loomis Laboratory
1110 W. Green St.   Phone: (217)333-2101
Urbana, IL 61801   David Stern, Physics/Astronomy Libn.
Founded: 1948. **Staff:** Prof 1; Other 2. **Subjects:** Physics - solid state, nuclear, theoretical, medical; fluorescence dynamics; complex systems; astronomy and astrophysics; magnetism; optics. **Holdings:** 34,300 volumes. **Subscriptions:** 400 journals and other serials. **Services:** Interlibrary loan; copying; library open to the public with permit. **Automated Operations:** Computerized public access catalog and circulation. **Computerized Information Services:** BRS Information Technologies, DIALOG Information Services, STN International, OCLC; BITNET (electronic mail service). **Publications:** Acquisitions list; dedicated issues of journals list, both monthly. **Special Catalogs:** Conference file keyword index (card).

★ 18689 ★
University of Illinois - Rare Book and Special Collections Library (Rare Book)
346 Main Library
1408 W. Gregory Dr.   Phone: (217)333-3777
Urbana, IL 61801   Nancy Romero, Hd. Libn.
Staff: Prof 4; Other 1. **Subjects:** Sixteenth and seventeenth century editions of classical authors, Bibles, catechisms and sermons, grammars, and dictionaries; English and American literature and history; Italian drama, history, and biography; history of science. **Special Collections:** Milton Collection (3000 volumes); Ingold Shakespeare Collection; Clayton Papers, 1579-1744 (3020 original letters and documents); Cobbett Collection; 17th century newsletters; Proust correspondence; Meine Collection of American Humor; Harwell Collection of Confederate Imprints; Hollander Collection on Economics; Baskette Collection on Freedom of Expression; Nickell Collection of 18th Century English Literature; Winston S. Churchill Collection; Carl Sandburg Collection; H.G. Wells Collection; emblem books of Germany and low countries, 16th and 17th centuries; Japanese rare books; W.S. Merwin Archives; Motley Theater Design Collection. **Holdings:** 141,535 books, manuscripts, pamphlets, and early periodicals; 26,870 reels of microfilm. **Subscriptions:** 55 journals and other serials. **Services:** Interlibrary loan; copying (limited); room open to the public. **Special Catalogs:** Book catalog (1972, 11 volumes; Supplement, 1978, 2 volumes). **Staff:** N. Fredrick Nash; Gene Rinkel.

University of Illinois - Rehabilitation Education Center - National Publications Library
See: **National Publications Library** (11257)

★ 18690 ★
University of Illinois - Ricker Library of Architecture and Art (Art)
208 Architecture Bldg.   Phone: (217)333-0224
Urbana, IL 61801   Jane Block, Hd.
Founded: 1873. **Staff:** Prof 2; Other 3. **Subjects:** Architecture, historic preservation, fine arts, applied arts, art education, art history, history of photography, industrial design, graphic design. **Holdings:** 51,094 volumes. **Subscriptions:** 617 journals and other serials. **Services:** Interlibrary loan; library open to the public. **Automated Operations:** Computerized circulation. **Computerized Information Services:** RLIN, AVERY, SCIPIO, DIALOG Information Services; electronic mail service.

★ 18691 ★
University of Illinois - Slavic and East European Library (Area-Ethnic)
225 Main Library   Phone: (217)333-1349
Urbana, IL 61801   Robert Burger, Libn.
Staff: Prof 6; Other 12. **Subjects:** Slavic languages, social sciences, humanities. **Holdings:** 600,000 books and bound periodical volumes; 80,000 volumes in microform. **Subscriptions:** 3000 journals and other serials. **Services:** Interlibrary loan; copying; library open to the public with permit from Main Library. **Automated Operations:** Computerized circulation. **Computerized Information Services:** DIALOG Information Services, BRS Information Technologies, RLIN, OCLC, InfoTrac; internal databases; EasyLink (electronic mail service). Performs searches on fee basis. **Remarks:** Maintains Slavic Reference Service which handles bibliographic and reference questions in the humanities and social sciences. **Staff:** Larry Miller, Slavic Acq.Libn.; Dmytro Shtohryn, Slavic Cat.Libn.; Darinka Craft; Margaret Olson.

★ 18692 ★

University of Illinois - Survey Research Laboratory - SRL Library (Soc Sci)
909 W. Oregon St., Suite 300   Phone: (217)333-7109
Urbana, IL 61801-3856   Mary A. Spaeth, Survey Res.Info.Coord.
Founded: 1967. **Staff:** Prof 1. **Subjects:** Survey research, consumer behavior. **Holdings:** 1450 books; 1800 unbound periodicals; 67 VF drawers of government publications, reprints, newsletters, reports, pamphlets, catalogs. **Subscriptions:** 20 journals and other serials. **Services:** Library open to researchers for reference use only. **Publications:** Survey Research (newsletter), quarterly - to supporting organizations and qualified researchers. **Remarks:** FAX: (217)244-4408.

★ 18693 ★

University of Illinois - University Archives (Educ)
University Library, Rm. 19
1408 W. Gregory Dr.   Phone: (217)333-0798
Urbana, IL 61801   Maynard Brichford, Univ.Archv.
Founded: 1963. **Staff:** Prof 2; Other 1. **Subjects:** Higher education, graduate education, teaching, research, public service, science and technology, humanities, student life, business archives, agriculture, fraternities, library science, librarianship, athletics, physical education. **Holdings:** 7906 cubic feet of office records; 3533 cubic feet of faculty papers; 1239 cubic feet of publications; 1473 cubic feet of American Library Association (ALA) archives; 11.5 million historical manuscripts; scrapbooks; clippings; pamphlets; microfilm; videotapes; photographs; sound recordings. **Services:** Copying; archives open to the public. **Computerized Information Services:** PARADIGM (internal database). **Publications:** Annual Report; Guide to University Archives; Manuscripts Guide to Collections at the University of Illinois at Urbana-Champaign; Guide to ALA Archives. **Special Catalogs:** Recorded series control (5106 cards); supplementary finding aids (lists, publications, narrative descriptions, file guides); PARADIGM online series and subject control and data processing listings. Series are arranged by source and record groups and subgroups are described in the University Archives Classification Guide. **Staff:** William Maher, Asst.Archv.

★ 18694 ★

University of Illinois - Veterinary Medicine Library (Med)
1257 Vet. Med. Basic Sciences Bldg.
2001 S. Lincoln Ave.   Phone: (217)333-2193
Urbana, IL 61801   Mitsuko Williams, Hd.
Founded: 1952. **Staff:** Prof 2; Other 2. **Subjects:** Pathology, physiology, pharmacology, bacteriology, veterinary science, parasitology, toxicology. **Special Collections:** German dissertations in veterinary science. **Holdings:** 33,746 volumes; 4 VF drawers of pamphlets. **Subscriptions:** 838 journals and other serials. **Services:** Interlibrary loan; copying; library open to the public. **Automated Operations:** Computerized circulation. **Computerized Information Services:** DIALOG Information Services, BRS Information Technologies, NLM; CD-ROM (MEDLINE); diskette (Current Contents). **Publications:** Newsletter; new acquisitions list, quarterly. **Remarks:** FAX: (217)333-4628. **Staff:** Priscilla Smiley, Asst.Libn.

★ 18695 ★

University of Illinois at Chicago - College of Medicine at Peoria - Library of the Health Sciences (Med)
P.O. Box 1649   Phone: (309)671-8490
Peoria, IL 61656   Trudy Landwirth, Hea.Sci.Libn., Peoria
Founded: 1971. **Staff:** Prof 2; Other 6. **Subjects:** Medicine, basic sciences, nursing. **Holdings:** 25,862 books; 24,397 bound periodical volumes; 1884 AV programs; 5500 government documents; 1269 microfiche. **Subscriptions:** 502 journals and other serials. **Services:** Interlibrary loan; copying; SDI; library open to the public for reference use only. **Automated Operations:** Computerized circulation (NOTIS). **Computerized Information Services:** NLM, BRS Information Technologies, DIALOG Information Services, Statewide Library Computer System (LCS), OCLC; CD-ROMs (MEDLINE, CINAHL). Contact Person: Jo Dorsch, Asst.Hea.Sci.Libn., Peoria. **Networks/Consortia:** Member of National Network of Libraries of Medicine - Greater Midwest Region, Heart of Illinois Library Consortium (HILC), Illinois Valley Library System. **Publications:** Library Guide; Current List of Serials; Subject List of Current Serials. **Special Catalogs:** Subject Guide to Audiovisual Holdings. **Remarks:** Library located at One Illini Dr., Peoria, IL 61605. FAX: (309)671-8495.

★ 18696 ★

University of Illinois at Chicago - College of Medicine at Rockford - Woodruff L. Crawford Branch Library of the Health Sciences (Med)
1601 Parkview Ave.   Phone: (815)395-5650
Rockford, IL 61107   Don Lanier, Hea.Sci.Libn., Rockford
Founded: 1971. **Staff:** Prof 2; Other 6.5. **Subjects:** Medicine, biomedical sciences. **Holdings:** 22,419 books; 26,437 bound periodical volumes; 358 pamphlets; 11,768 slides. **Subscriptions:** 414 journals and other serials; 7 newspapers. **Services:** Interlibrary loan; copying; SDI; library open to the public. **Automated Operations:** Computerized cataloging, acquisitions, serials, circulation, and ILL. **Computerized Information Services:** NLM, BRS Information Technologies, OCLC, WILSONLINE, DIALOG Information Services, Statewide Library Computer System (LCS); DOCLINE, BITNET (electronic mail services). Performs searches on fee basis. Contact Person: Karen Wark, Ref.Libn., 395-5650. **Networks/Consortia:** Member of National Network of Libraries of Medicine - Greater Midwest Region, Northern Illinois Library System (NILS). **Remarks:** FAX: (815)395-5655. Electronic mail address(es): U35673@ U1CVM (BITNET). **Staff:** Debbie Adrian, Circ.; Carrol Nelson, ILL; Jeanette Gawronski, Info.Serv.; Carol Frate, Tech.Serv.; Tom Waugh, Ser.

★ 18697 ★

University of Illinois at Chicago - Energy Resources Center - Documents Center (Energy)
412 S. Peoria St.
Box 4348   Phone: (312)996-4490
Chicago, IL 60680   James Hartnett, Dir.
Staff: Prof 1; Other 1. **Subjects:** Energy - resources, policy, conservation, technology; alternative energy technologies; electric utility statistics. **Special Collections:** Heat and mass transfer (225 monographs; 15 journal subscriptions). **Holdings:** 4000 books; 100 bound periodical volumes; 2 VF drawers of clippings; 3 VF drawers of pamphlets; 100 maps; 100 reports on microfiche. **Subscriptions:** 120 journals and other serials. **Services:** Interlibrary loan; copying; SDI; center open to the public. **Computerized Information Services:** DIALOG Information Services, BRS Information Technologies. **Networks/Consortia:** Member of Chicago Library System. **Publications:** Illinois Energy Newsletter - free upon request. **Staff:** James Wiet, Dir.Asst.

★ 18698 ★

University of Illinois at Chicago - Library of the Health Sciences (Med)
1750 W. Polk St.
Chicago, IL 60612   Phone: (312)996-8974
Founded: 1881. **Staff:** Prof 27; Other 72. **Subjects:** Medicine, dentistry, nursing, pharmacy, public health, behavioral sciences, allied health professions. **Special Collections:** Kiefer Collection (urology; 2000 volumes); herbals and pharmacopoeias (500 volumes); Bailey Collection (neurology and psychiatry; 1000 volumes); medical center archives. **Holdings:** 643,697 volumes; 35,030 document titles; 881 linear feet of archives. **Subscriptions:** 7634 journals and other serials. **Services:** Interlibrary loan; SDI; library open to the public. **Automated Operations:** Computerized cataloging, serials, and circulation. **Computerized Information Services:** NLM, BRS Information Technologies, STN International, DIALOG Information Services, OCLC, NOTIS, Statewide Library Computer System (LCS); CD-ROM (MEDLINE); BITNET (electronic mail service). **Networks/Consortia:** Member of ILLINET, National Network of Libraries of Medicine - Greater Midwest Region. **Publications:** Information Services Department guides to various special segments of the literature of the health sciences. **Special Catalogs:** Percival Bailey Catalog of Neurology and Psychiatry; Joseph Kiefer Catalog of Urology; Dental Literature Collection; Pharmacopoeias, Formularies, and Dispensatories; Warren Henry Cole - a bibliography; Catalog of pre-fire Chicago imprints (1844-1873) - all for sale. **Remarks:** Library is the Region 3 Regional Medical Library of the National Library of Medicine. FAX: (312)996-1899. Electronic mail address(es): U50534@UICVM (BITNET). **Staff:** Ann C. Weller, Deputy Libn.; Robert Adelsperger, Hd., Spec.Coll.; Stephen Van Houten, Hd.Cat.; Darel Robb, Hd., Ser./Acq.; Karen Dahlen, Hd., Info.Serv.; Ruby S. May, Assoc.Dir., Greater Midwest Reg.Med.Lib. Network; Kim Goldman, Prog.Coord.; Ruth Fenske, Libn., Hea.Sci., Urbana; Trudy Landwirth, Hea.Sci.Libn., Peoria; Donald Lanier, Hea.Sci.Libn., Rockford.

★ 18699 ★
University of Illinois at Chicago - Library of the Health Sciences,
  Urbana (Med)
102 Medical Sciences Bldg.
506 S. Matthews   Phone: (217)333-4893
Urbana, IL 61801   Ruth E. Fenske, Hea.Sci.Libn.
Founded: 1971. **Staff:** Prof 2; Other 6. **Subjects:** Medicine, nursing, medical applications of magnetic resonance imaging. **Holdings:** 24,909 books; 9312 bound periodical volumes; 2358 pamphlets; 1724 AV programs. **Subscriptions:** 650 journals and other serials. **Services:** Library open to the public. **Automated Operations:** Computerized cataloging, acquisitions, serials (NOTIS), and circulation (LCS). **Computerized Information Services:** BRS Information Technologies, NLM, DIALOG Information Services; CD-ROMs (MEDLINE, CINAHL); BITNET (electronic mail service). **Networks/Consortia:** Member of National Network of Libraries of Medicine - Greater Midwest Region, ILLINET, East Central Illinois Consortium. **Remarks:** FAX: (217)359-3619. Electronic mail address(es): FENSKE@UIUCVMD (BITNET). **Staff:** Victoria G. Pifalo.

★ 18700 ★
University of Illinois at Chicago - Science Library (Sci-Engr)
Science & Engineering South Bldg.
Box 8198   Phone: (312)996-5396
Chicago, IL 60680   Julie M. Hurd, Sci.Libn.
Founded: 1970. **Staff:** Prof 2; Other 4. **Subjects:** Chemistry, biology, geology, physics. **Special Collections:** Sadtler Research Laboratories Standard Collections of Spectra; industry standards and codes. **Holdings:** 59,728 books; 69,710 bound periodical volumes; 89,822 technical reports (hard copy and microform). **Subscriptions:** 1656 journals and other serials. **Services:** Interlibrary loan; copying; library open to the public for reference use only. **Automated Operations:** Computerized public access catalog and circulation. **Computerized Information Services:** OCLC, DIALOG Information Services, STN International, WILSONLINE, Northwestern Online Total Integrated Systems (NOTIS), BRS Information Technologies, Statewide Library Computer System (LCS). **Publications:** Bibliography of Materials Relating to Spectra. **Remarks:** FAX: (312)996-7822. **Staff:** Gladys Odegaard, Asst.Sci.Libn.; Helen Badawi, Circ.Supv.

★ 18701 ★
University of Illinois at Chicago - University Library - Map Section
  (M/C 234) (Geog-Map)
Box 8198   Phone: (312)996-5277
Chicago, IL 60680   Marsha L. Selmer, Map Libn.
Founded: 1957. **Staff:** Prof 1; Other 1. **Subjects:** Maps, atlases, aerial photographs. **Special Collections:** Historic Urban Plans (complete set); 16th-19th century maps of the Russian Empire and Eastern Europe; 19th century maps of Illinois; 17th-18th century maps of the Great Lakes; aerial photographs and photomaps of Chicago and northeastern Illinois; fire insurance maps of Chicago. **Holdings:** 157,834 maps; 915 atlases; 3850 aerial photographs. **Subscriptions:** 3 journals and other serials. **Services:** Interlibrary loan; section open to the public. **Computerized Information Services:** BITNET (electronic mail service). **Publications:** Information brochure, irregular - free upon request. **Remarks:** FAX: (312)413-0424. Electronic mail address(es): LIB-MAPS@UICVM (BITNET).

★ 18702 ★
University of Innsbruck - University Library - Library of the Faculty of
  Civil Engineering and Architecture (Sci-Engr, Plan)
Technikerstr 13   Phone: 5222 2184080
A-6020 Innsbruck, Austria   Peter Unteregger, Ph.D.
Founded: 1975. **Staff:** Prof 8. **Subjects:** Civil engineering, architecture, mathematics, geodesy, environment, regional planning. **Holdings:** 130,000 books; 50,000 bound periodical volumes; 3000 reports; 200 microfiche; 10 reels of microfilm. **Subscriptions:** 1200 journals and other serials; 5 newspapers. **Services:** Interlibrary loan; copying; SDI; library open to the public. **Also Known As:** Universitat Innsbruck - Universitatsbiliothek - Fakultatsbibliothek fur Bauingenieurwesen und Architektur.

★ 18703 ★
University of International Business and Economics - Library (Bus-Fin)
Beijing 100029, People's Republic of China   Phone: 1 4225522
       Shi Shiyu, Dean of the Lib.
Founded: 1954. **Staff:** 48. **Subjects:** World economics, international trade, languages, international law, English language. **Special Collections:** Remarkable editions of Chinese and foreign books (Chinese block-printed editions and hand copies of Ming and Qing dynasties; foreign editions of customhouse publications; 5000 volumes); Chinese customhouse publications, 1850s-1949. **Holdings:** 310,000 volumes; 604 periodicals. **Subscriptions:** 1400 journals and other serials. **Services:** Copying. **Formerly:** Beijing Institute of Foreign Trade. **Also Known As:** UIBE. **Staff:** Xinhou Liu; Chang Lian Xue; Xiashong Qiu.

★ 18704 ★
University of Iowa - Art Library (Art)
Art Bldg.   Phone: (319)335-3089
Iowa City, IA 52242   Harlan Sifford, Libn.
Staff: Prof 1; Other 1. **Subjects:** Art. **Holdings:** 74,550 volumes. **Services:** Interlibrary loan; copying.

★ 18705 ★
University of Iowa - Biology Library (Biol Sci)
301 Zoology Bldg.   Phone: (319)335-3083
Iowa City, IA 52242   Leo Clougherty, Libn.
Staff: Prof 1; Other 1. **Subjects:** Zoology. **Holdings:** 39,036 volumes. **Services:** Interlibrary loan; copying.

★ 18706 ★
University of Iowa - Business Library (Bus-Fin)
College of Business Administration
Phillips Hall   Phone: (319)335-3077
Iowa City, IA 52242   David Martin, Bus.Libn.
Founded: 1965. **Staff:** Prof 2; Other 1. **Subjects:** Management, labor relations, labor unions, accounting, finance. **Special Collections:** Major labor union periodicals. **Holdings:** 25,098 volumes. **Services:** Interlibrary loan; copying.

★ 18707 ★
University of Iowa - Chemistry-Botany Library (Biol Sci, Sci-Engr)
Iowa City, IA 52242   Phone: (319)335-3085
       Leo Clougherty, Libn.
Staff: Prof 1; Other 1. **Subjects:** Botany, chemistry, and related fields. **Holdings:** 81,145 volumes. **Services:** Interlibrary loan; copying.

★ 18708 ★
University of Iowa - College of Education - Curriculum Resources
  Laboratory (Educ)
N140 Lindquist Center   Phone: (319)335-5616
Iowa City, IA 52242   Paula O. Brandt, Coord.
Staff: Prof 2; Other 3. **Subjects:** Children's books; adolescent novels; special, elementary, and secondary education curriculum materials. **Special Collections:** K-12 textbooks (11,000); curriculum guides (6000). **Holdings:** 29,000 books; 4000 AV programs, games, computer diskettes, picture sets, and other nonprint materials. **Subscriptions:** 12 journals and other serials. **Services:** Copying; laboratory open to the public. **Publications:** Newsletter, irregular; topical bibliographies. **Remarks:** FAX: (319)335-5386. **Staff:** Carol Vogt, Ref.Libn.

★ 18709 ★
University of Iowa - Engineering Library (Sci-Engr)
106 Engineering Bldg.   Phone: (319)335-6047
Iowa City, IA 52242   John W. Forys, Libn.
Staff: Prof 1; Other 1. **Subjects:** Engineering, science, technology. **Holdings:** 91,335 volumes. **Services:** Interlibrary loan.

★ 18710 ★
University of Iowa - Geology Library (Sci-Engr)
136 Trowbridge Hall   Phone: (319)335-3084
Iowa City, IA 52242   Louise Zipp, Libn.
Founded: Prof 1; Other 1. **Subjects:** Sedimentology, crystallography, mineralogy, structural geology, petrology, geochemistry, geophysics, engineering geology. **Holdings:** 48,747 volumes. **Services:** Interlibrary loan.

★ 18711 ★
University of Iowa - Health Sciences Library (Med)
Health Sciences Library Bldg.   Phone: (319)335-9871
Iowa City, IA 52242   David S. Curry, Libn.
Founded: 1870. **Staff:** Prof 8; Other 7. **Subjects:** Medicine, speech pathology, dentistry, nursing, pharmacy. **Special Collections:** John Martin History of Medicine Collection. **Holdings:** 236,554 volumes. **Services:** Interlibrary loan; copying. **Automated Operations:** Computerized cataloging and serials. **Computerized Information Services:** MEDLINE. **Networks/Consortia:** Member of National Network of Libraries of Medicine - Greater Midwest Region. **Remarks:** FAX: (319)335-9897.

★ 18712 ★
University of Iowa - Iowa Social Science Institute - Data Archive (Soc Sci)
345 Schaeffer Hall   Phone: (319)335-2367
Iowa City, IA 52242   Prof. Arthur Miller, Dir.
Founded: 1987. **Staff:** Prof 4; Other 1. **Subjects:** Political science, sociology, history, geography, economics, law, psychology, health care. **Special Collections:** Des Moines Register and Tribune public opinion polls; Heartland Poll (annual survey of Iowa and six surrounding states); machine-readable bibliographies on legislative behavior and communist political systems; Soviet public opinion poll on social, economic, political, and international relations issues (administered in Russia, Lithuania, and Ukraine; May 1990, May 1991, and May 1992). **Holdings:** 3000 data sets. **Services:** Archive open to the public. **Computerized Information Services:** Internal database; BITNET (electronic mail service). **Publications:** Annual Heartland Poll code books. **Special Indexes:** Listing of archive holdings; index of survey items on legislative behavior. **Remarks:** FAX: (319)335-2070. Electronic mail address(es): BDALZIWY@UIAMVS (BITNET). **Staff:** Mary E. Losch, Prog.Dir.; C.H. Lu, Tech.Dir.; Brian T. Dalziel, Data Archv.Mgr.

★ 18713 ★
University of Iowa - Iowa Urban Community Research Center - Reference Library (Soc Sci)
W170 Seashore Hall   Phone: (319)335-2525
Iowa City, IA 52242   Prof. Lyle W. Shannon, Dir.
Founded: 1958. **Staff:** 3. **Subjects:** U.S. Census, vital statistics and public health, population and demography, minority groups, juvenile delinquency and crime. **Special Collections:** Selected series of U.S. Census, 1910 to present. **Holdings:** 1000 books; 25 drawers of reprints, publications; punched cards and tapes on all studies conducted, 1958 to present. **Subscriptions:** 30 journals and other serials. **Services:** Library open to the public. **Publications:** Monograph series - for sale. **Remarks:** FAX: (319)335-2509.

University of Iowa - Laboratory for Political Research
See: University of Iowa - Iowa Social Science Institute (18712)

★ 18714 ★
University of Iowa - Law Library (Law)
Law Center   Phone: (319)335-9104
Iowa City, IA 52242   Arthur Bonfield, Dir.
Founded: 1866. **Staff:** Prof 12; Other 13. **Subjects:** Anglo-American law. **Holdings:** 154,390 books; 360,245 bound serial volumes; U.S. Supreme Court records and briefs in microform. **Subscriptions:** 1809 journals and other serials; 10 newspapers. **Services:** Interlibrary loan; copying; library open to the public with restrictions on circulation. **Computerized Information Services:** LEXIS, WESTLAW, RLIN; CD-ROMs (WILSONDISC, GPO Index on CD-ROM). Performs searches on fee basis. Contact Person: Tom Eicher, Ref., 335-9038. **Networks/Consortia:** Member of Research Libraries Information Network (RLIN). **Remarks:** FAX: (319)335-9019. **Staff:** Katherine Belgum, Exec. Law Libn.; Caitlin Robinson, Tech.Serv.; Virginia Melroy, Cat.; Mary Ertl, Acq.; Sue Emde, Docs.; Karen Nobbs, Hd.Cat.; John Bengstrom, Circ.; Sandra Keller, Ref.; Suzanne Fleury, Hd.Ref.; Sherri Wolleat, Bibliog.Proc.

★ 18715 ★
University of Iowa - Map Collection (Geog-Map)
Main Library   Phone: (319)335-5920
Iowa City, IA 52242-1460   L.S. Zipp, Act. Map Libn.
Founded: 1965. **Staff:** 1. **Special Collections:** Aerial photographs of Iowa; Sanborn Fire Insurance maps of Iowa. **Holdings:** 300,000 maps and aerial photographs; 4200 atlases. **Subscriptions:** 10 journals and other serials. **Services:** Collection open to the public. **Automated Operations:** NOTIS. **Computerized Information Services:** BITNET, InterNet (electronic mail services). **Networks/Consortia:** Member of Research Libraries Information Network (RLIN). **Remarks:** FAX: (319)335-5830. Electronic mail address(es): CADLSZTS@UIAMVS (BITNET).

★ 18716 ★
University of Iowa - Mathematics Library (Sci-Engr)
MacLean Hall   Phone: (319)335-3076
Iowa City, IA 52242   Christine Kerckhove, Libn.
Staff: Prof 1; Other 1. **Subjects:** Mathematics. **Holdings:** 47,267 volumes. **Services:** Interlibrary loan; copying.

★ 18717 ★
University of Iowa - Music Library (Mus)
Music Bldg.   Phone: (319)335-3086
Iowa City, IA 52242   Joan O. Falconer, Libn.
Founded: 1957. **Staff:** Prof 1; Other 2. **Subjects:** Music. **Holdings:** 78,379 volumes. **Services:** Interlibrary loan; copying; library open to the public. **Special Catalogs:** Annotated catalog of rare music items in the libraries of the University of Iowa.

★ 18718 ★
University of Iowa - Office of the State Archaeologist - Document Collection (Sci-Engr, Hist)
317 Eastlawn   Phone: (319)335-2395
Iowa City, IA 52242   Julianne Loy Hoyer, Docs.Cur.
Founded: 1978. **Staff:** Prof 1. **Subjects:** Archeology, anthropology, geomorphology, soil surveys, ethnology, physical anthropology. **Special Collections:** All published and unpublished archeological surveys and excavations performed in Iowa; office archives. **Holdings:** 2000 books; 18,000 other items. **Subscriptions:** 45 journals and other serials. **Services:** Copying; SDI; collection open to the public for reference use only. **Automated Operations:** Computerized cataloging. **Computerized Information Services:** Internal database of site records and catalog sheets. **Publications:** Bibliography on Mesquakie Indians. **Special Indexes:** Index to the Journal of the Iowa Archeological Society and Newsletter. **Remarks:** FAX: (319)335-2776.

★ 18719 ★
University of Iowa - Physics Library (Sci-Engr)
Physics Research Center   Phone: (319)335-3082
Iowa City, IA 52242   Dorothy M. Persson, Libn.
Staff: Prof 1; Other 1. **Subjects:** Physics. **Holdings:** 46,134 volumes. **Services:** Interlibrary loan; copying.

★ 18720 ★
University of Iowa - Psychology Library (Soc Sci)
Iowa City, IA 52242   Phone: (319)335-2405
                                             Dorothy M. Persson, Libn.
Staff: Prof 1; Other 2. **Subjects:** Psychology. **Holdings:** 54,886 volumes. **Services:** Interlibrary loan; copying.

★ 18721 ★
University of Iowa - Special Collections Department (Rare Book)
Main Library   Phone: (319)335-5921
Iowa City, IA 52242   Robert A. McCown, Hd.
Staff: Prof 4; Other 3. **Special Collections:** Brewer-Leigh Hunt Collection (2200 volumes; 3520 leaves of manuscript; 1635 manuscript letters); Iowa Authors Collection (10,000 volumes; 3000 manuscripts); Bollinger-Lincoln Collection (4600 volumes; 480 pamphlets); History of Hydraulics Collection (550 volumes); university archives (4000 linear feet of papers; 4000 volumes); French medals, 1848 (842); original Ding Darling cartoons (6000); right-wing ephemeral publications (1100 titles). **Holdings:** 75,000 rare books; 450 manuscript collections of personal and corporate records. **Services:** Department open to the public. **Publications:** Books at Iowa, semiannual - to members of the Friends of the University of Iowa Libraries. **Special Indexes:** The Wallace Papers: An Index to the Microfilm Editions of the Henry A. Wallace Papers (1975), 2 volumes; A Guide To Resources for the Study of the Recent History of the U.S. (1977). **Staff:** Earl M. Rogers, Cur. of Archv.; David E. Schoonover, Cur. of Rare Bks.; Richard M. Kolbet, Spec.Coll.Libn.

★ 18722 ★
University of Iowa - Translation Laboratory (Hum)
W 615 Seashore Hall   Phone: (319)335-2002
Iowa City, IA 52242   Gertrud G. Champe, Dir.
Founded: 1982. **Staff:** Prof 1; Other 3. **Subjects:** Translation, interpreting, international research, subtitling. **Special Collections:** Completed translations (1000). **Holdings:** 200 books; 1200 bilingual documents. **Services:** Laboratory open to the public. **Remarks:** FAX: (319)335-2951.

★ 18723 ★
University of Kansas - Department for Spain, Portugal, & Latin America
  (Area-Ethnic)
Watson Library   Phone: (913)864-3351
Lawrence, KS 66045-2800   Shelley Miller
Staff: Prof 1; Other 1. **Subjects:** Latin America - literature, history, social sciences. **Special Collections:** Central America; 19th century Guatemala; Costa Rica; Paraguay. **Holdings:** 200,000 volumes in Spanish and Portuguese. **Services:** Interlibrary loan; copying; collection open to the public. **Automated Operations:** Computerized cataloging, serials, and circulation. **Computerized Information Services:** BITNET (electronic mail service). **Remarks:** FAX: (913)864-3855. Electronic mail address(es): SMILLER@UKANVM (BITNET).

★ 18724 ★
University of Kansas - Department of Special Collections (Hist, Hum)
Spencer Research Library   Phone: (913)864-4334
Lawrence, KS 66045-2800   Alexandra Mason, Spencer Libn.
Founded: 1953. **Staff:** Prof 7; Other 2. **Subjects:** 17th and 18th century English history, economics, literature; history of ornithology; European Renaissance and early modern history, economics, politics; discovery and exploration; Latin America; history of botany; Anglo-Irish literature. **Special Collections:** Summerfield Collection of Renaissance and Early Modern Books (7400 volumes including 130 incunabula); Roger Clubb Memorial Collection of Books in Anglo-Saxon Types (300 books); Brodie of Brodie Collection of 17th to 19th century pamphlets (1200 items); Edmund Curll Collection (750 books); English Poetical Miscellanies, 18th century (500 books); Melvin French Revolutionary Collection (9000 items); Realey Collection of Walpoliana (500 items); Robert Horn Collection of Panegyrics on the Duke of Marlborough (200 items); 18th century English Pamphlet Collection (15,000 items); James Joyce Collection (900 books); Rainer Maria Rilke Collection (1700 items); W.B. Yeats Collection (650 items); New American Poetry Collection (6000 items); Ellis Ornithology Collection (15,000 volumes, pamphlets, letters, drawings, and manuscripts); Linnaeus Collection (1750 volumes); Children's Literature, 18th to 20th century (6500 volumes); H.L. Mencken (780 volumes, scrapbooks, manuscripts); Science Fiction (7000 items); O'Hegarty Anglo-Irish Literature and History (12,000 volumes); manuscripts and documents in medieval, early modern, and modern literature, history, and science (480,000 items); Bond Collection of 18th century English newspapers and periodicals; paleography and manuscript studies; Frank Lloyd Wright Collection (books; blueprints; clippings; photographs; manuscripts); Griffith Collection on Guatemala; W.D. Paden Collection of Tennyson; World Science Fiction Depository; Howey Collection of Economics and Economic History to 1850 (3500 volumes). **Holdings:** 193,733 books and periodicals; 888 rare maps; 2092 photographs; 1700 linear feet of manuscripts. **Services:** Copying; department open to the public for reference use only. **Automated Operations:** Computerized cataloging and serials. **Computerized Information Services:** OCLC, RLIN; BITNET (electronic mail service). **Networks/Consortia:** Member of Bibliographical Center for Research, Rocky Mountain Region, Inc. (BCR). **Publications:** A Guide to the Collections, 1987. **Special Catalogs:** Catalog of manuscripts (loose-leaf); exhibit catalogs, irregular - available upon request. **Special Indexes:** Indexes of provenance, printers, methods of illustration (card); Boys-Mizener first-line index to English poetical miscellanies (card); chronological indexes to books and manuscripts. **Remarks:** Electronic mail address(es): AMASON@UKANVM (BITNET). **Staff:** William L. Mitchell, Consrv.Libn.; Ann Hyde, Mss.Libn.; Sarah E. Haines, Botany Libn.; L.E.J. Helyar, Cur. in Graphics; Robert Melton, Asst.Libn.; Richard Clement, Asst.Libn.

★ 18725 ★
University of Kansas - Documents Collection (Info Sci)
6001 Malott Hall   Phone: (913)864-4662
Lawrence, KS 66045-2800   Donna Koepp, Doc./Maps Libn.
Founded: 1869. **Staff:** Prof 2; Other 4. **Subjects:** Census, U.S. legislative history, British parliamentary history. **Special Collections:** Regional depository for U.S. documents; United Nations depository; official publications of the United Kingdom; Organization for Economic Cooperation and Development and European Community publications; Kansas State census on microfilm; Joint Publications Research Service (JPRS) publications in microform. **Holdings:** 894,610 documents; 726,651 microforms. **Subscriptions:** 2817 journals and other serials. **Services:** Interlibrary loan; copying; collection open to the public. **Computerized Information Services:** OCLC; CD-ROMs (Impact, CIS/Index, FBIS); BITNET (electronic mail service). **Networks/Consortia:** Member of Bibliographical Center for Research, Rocky Mountain Region, Inc. (BCR), Kansas Library Network. **Publications:** Duplicate List of Regional

Depository, monthly - to other depository libraries. **Remarks:** FAX: (913)864-5380. Electronic mail address(es): DOCSMAP@UKANVM (BITNET). **Staff:** Julie Hoff, Asst.Doc./Maps Libn.

★ 18726 ★
University of Kansas - East Asian Library (Area-Ethnic)
Watson Library   Phone: (913)864-4669
Lawrence, KS 66045-2800   Eugene Carvalho, Libn.
Founded: 1964. **Staff:** Prof 2. **Subjects:** Chinese and Japanese history, literature, language, culture; contemporary China; contemporary Japan. **Holdings:** 134,076 books and bound periodical volumes. **Subscriptions:** 722 journals and other serials; 15 newspapers. **Services:** Interlibrary loan; copying; library open to the public. **Automated Operations:** Computerized cataloging, serials, and circulation. **Computerized Information Services:** OCLC; BITNET (electronic mail service). **Networks/Consortia:** Member of Bibliographical Center for Research, Rocky Mountain Region, Inc. (BCR), Kansas Library Network. **Remarks:** Materials primarily in Chinese, Japanese, and Korean languages. Electronic mail address(es): ECARVALH@UKANVM (BITNET). **Staff:** Vickie Doll, Chinese Bibliog.

★ 18727 ★
University of Kansas - Institute for Public Policy and Business Research
  (Soc Sci)
607 Blake Hall   Phone: (913)864-3701
Lawrence, KS 66045-2800   Thelma Helyar, Libn.
Founded: 1985. **Staff:** Prof 1. **Subjects:** Survey research; economic indicators; economic, community, and rural development; census data; data processing; econometric models; demographics; policy studies; statistics. **Holdings:** 9000 volumes. **Subscriptions:** 200 journals and other serials. **Services:** Interlibrary loan; copying; institute open to the public. **Publications:** Kansas Statistical Abstract and the Kansas Business Review, quarterly. **Remarks:** Institute is affiliated with the Kansas State Data Center.

★ 18728 ★
University of Kansas - Journalism Reading Room (Info Sci)
William Allen White School of Journalism
210 Flint Hall   Phone: (913)864-4755
Lawrence, KS 66045-2800   Yvonne Martinez, Libn.
Founded: 1955. **Staff:** Prof 1. **Subjects:** Newspaper journalism, mass communications, broadcasting, graphic arts, advertising. **Holdings:** Figures not available. **Services:** Copying; room open to the public.

★ 18729 ★
University of Kansas - Kansas Collection (Hist)
220 Spencer Research Library   Phone: (913)864-4274
Lawrence, KS 66045-2800   Sheryl K. Williams, Cur.
Founded: 1892. **Staff:** Prof 4; Other 3. **Subjects:** Kansas and Great Plains - social movements, business and economic history, social and cultural history, politics, travel; regional African-American history. **Special Collections:** Overland diaries; Kansas State documents depository; J.J. Pennell Collection of photographs and negatives, 1891-1923 (40,000 items); Wilcox Collection of Contemporary Political Movements, 1960 to present (6500 books; 6000 serials; 84,000 pieces of ephemera); Jules Bourquin Collection of photographs, 1898-1959 (30,000); J.B. Watkins Land Mortgage Company Records, 1864-1946 (627 linear feet); regional African-American history. **Holdings:** 97,536 volumes; 8524 linear feet of manuscripts; 1.4 million photographs; 81,815 glass negatives; 9397 sheets and volumes of maps; 4260 cartoons. **Subscriptions:** 1575 journals and other serials; 50 newspapers. **Services:** Interlibrary loan; copying; collection open to the public. **Automated Operations:** Computerized cataloging and serials. **Computerized Information Services:** OCLC; BITNET (electronic mail service). **Networks/Consortia:** Member of Bibliographical Center for Research, Rocky Mountain Region, Inc. (BCR), Kansas Library Network. **Remarks:** Electronic mail address(es): SWILLIAM@UKANVM (BITNET). **Staff:** Nicolette Bromberg, Photoarchv.; Rebecca Schulte, Asst.Cur.; Deborah Dandridge, Field Archv.

★ 18730 ★
University of Kansas - Map Library (Geog-Map)
6001 Malott Hall   Phone: (913)864-4420
Lawrence, KS 66045-2800   Donna Koepp, Doc./Maps Libn.
Founded: 1950. **Staff:** Prof 2. **Subjects:** Cartography, Kansas aerial photography, U.S. Congressional serial set maps, 1789-1969. **Holdings:** 3498

volumes; 282,317 maps; 98,000 aerial photographs. **Subscriptions:** 93 journals and other serials. **Services:** Interlibrary loan; copying; library open to the public. **Automated Operations:** Computerized cataloging and serials. **Computerized Information Services:** OCLC; CD-ROMs (SUPERMAP, TIGER, PC USA, PC GLOBE); BITNET (electronic mail service). **Networks/Consortia:** Member of Bibliographical Center for Research, Rocky Mountain Region, Inc. (BCR), Kansas Library Network. **Remarks:** FAX: (913)864-5380. Electronic mail address(es): DOCSMAP@UKANVM (BITNET). **Staff:** Jennie Dienes, Asst.Libn.

★ 18731 ★
University of Kansas - Marian and Fred Anschutz Science Library (Sci-Engr, Biol Sci)
Lawrence, KS 66045-2800   Phone: (913)864-4928
                                          Kathleen Neeley, Sci.Libn.
Founded: 1989. **Staff:** Prof 5; Other 7. **Subjects:** Chemistry, physics, pharmacy, biology, geology, medicine, astronomy, history of science, general science, computer science, mathematics. **Holdings:** 352,194 volumes; 19,001 government documents; 108,546 microforms. **Subscriptions:** 5500 journals and other serials. **Services:** Interlibrary loan; library open to the public. **Automated Operations:** Computerized public access catalog, cataloging, serials, and circulation. **Computerized Information Services:** STN International, DIALOG Information Services, PFDS Online, BRS Information Technologies, NLM, OCLC; CD-ROM (MEDLINE). **Networks/Consortia:** Member of Bibliographical Center for Research, Rocky Mountain Region, Inc. (BCR), Kansas Library Network. **Remarks:** FAX: (913)864-5380. Electronic mail address(es): KNEELEY@UKANVM (BITNET). **Staff:** Judith Emde, Asst.Sci.Libn.; Lorraine Knox, Asst.Sci.Libn.; Connie Powell, Asst.Sci.Libn.; Julie Waters, Asst.Sci.Libn.

★ 18732 ★
University of Kansas - Medical Center - Clendening History of Medicine Library (Med)
History of Medicine Dept.
39th & Rainbow Blvd.   Phone: (913)588-7040
Kansas City, KS 66103   Susan B. Case, Rare Bks.Libn.
Founded: 1945. **Staff:** 3. **Subjects:** Medicine - history, philosophy, ethics; history of science. **Special Collections:** Jager Collection (pathology); Clendening History of Anesthesia Collection; Shaw Collection (History of Plastic Surgery); Skinner Collection (History of Roentgenology); Hayden Collection (History of Hematology/microscopy). **Holdings:** 26,000 books; 2000 bound periodical volumes; 50 AV programs; 2000 artifacts; 2000 photograph/etched portraits; 500 manuscripts. **Subscriptions:** 58 journals and other serials. **Services:** Interlibrary loan; copying; library open to the public by appointment. **Automated Operations:** Computerized public access catalog and cataloging. **Computerized Information Services:** OCLC. **Staff:** Barbara Stephens.

★ 18733 ★
University of Kansas - Medical Library - Archie R. Dykes Library of the Health Sciences (Med)
2100 W. 39th St.   Phone: (913)588-7166
Kansas City, KS 66103   James L. Bingham, Dir.
Founded: 1906. **Staff:** Prof 15; Other 29. **Subjects:** Basic sciences, clinical medicine, allied health sciences, nursing, social work. **Special Collections:** Educational Resource Center. **Holdings:** 55,947 books; 84,902 bound periodical volumes. **Subscriptions:** 1750 journals and other serials. **Services:** Interlibrary loan; copying; SDI; library open to the public with restrictions (reference use only for outside users). **Automated Operations:** Computerized public access catalog, cataloging, serials, circulation, acquisitions, and ILL. **Computerized Information Services:** BRS Information Technologies, NLM, OCLC, DIALOG Information Services; CD-ROMs (MEDLINE, CINAHL, PsycLIT, ERIC, HealthPlan, Science Citation Index). Performs searches on fee basis. **Networks/Consortia:** Member of Kansas City Library Network, Inc. (KCLN), National Network of Libraries of Medicine - Midcontinental Region. **Remarks:** FAX: (913)588-7304. **Staff:** Linda Davies, Asst.Dir.Educ.Tech.; Robert Pisciotta, Asst.Dir.Tech.Serv.; Cheryl Pace, Hd., Ref.; Cecile Doty, Hd., Cat.; Kathleen West, Hd., Acq.; D.A. Thomas, Dir. of Educ.; Shelli Crocker, Ref.; Christina Ernst, Ref.; Jane Carver, Hd., ILL; Gene Pace, Educ.Tech.; Carol Massoth, Educ.Tech; Grant James, Educ.Tech.; Lee Hancock, Educ.Tech.

★ 18734 ★
University of Kansas - Murphy Library of Art and Architecture (Art)
Helen Foresman Spencer Museum of Art   Phone: (913)864-3020
Lawrence, KS 66045-2800   Susan V. Craig, Art & Arch.Libn.
Founded: 1970. **Staff:** Prof 1; Other 3. **Subjects:** Art, design, photography, architecture, art history. **Special Collections:** Ephemeral collection of museum and gallery publications. **Holdings:** 93,997 volumes; pamphlet files on artists. **Subscriptions:** 770 journals and other serials. **Services:** Interlibrary loan; copying; library open to the public. **Automated Operations:** Computerized cataloging, serials, and circulation. **Computerized Information Services:** OCLC, RLIN, DIALOG Information Services (through Watson Library); BITNET (electronic mail service). **Networks/Consortia:** Member of Bibliographical Center for Research, Rocky Mountain Region, Inc. (BCR), Kansas Library Network. **Remarks:** Electronic mail address(es): SCRAIG@UKANVM (BITNET).

★ 18735 ★
University of Kansas - Regents Center - Library (Educ, Bus-Fin)
9900 Mission Rd.   Phone: (913)341-4554
Shawnee Mission, KS 66206   Nancy J. Burich, Libn.
Founded: 1976. **Staff:** Prof 1; Other 3. **Subjects:** Education, business, engineering management, journalism management, architectural management, public administration, social welfare, health services administration. **Special Collections:** Reavis Reading Room. **Holdings:** 14,200 books; 11,072 microforms. **Subscriptions:** 300 journals and other serials; 8 newspapers. **Services:** Interlibrary loan; copying; library open to the public with restrictions. **Automated Operations:** Computerized public access catalog and serials. **Computerized Information Services:** DIALOG Information Services, BRS Information Technologies; CD-ROMs (ABI/INFORM, ERIC, PsycLIT, Newspaper Abstracts Ondisc, Periodical Abstracts Ondisc, Business Dateline, SWAB). **Remarks:** FAX: (913)341-3301.

★ 18736 ★
University of Kansas - School of Law Library (Law)
Green Hall   Phone: (913)864-3025
Lawrence, KS 66045-2800   Peter C. Schanck, Dir.
Founded: 1904. **Staff:** Prof 5; Other 7. **Subjects:** Law. **Special Collections:** Basic collection in the law of Great Britain, Canada, and other common law countries; Russian law (includes complete code of the Russian Empire, 1801-1894). **Holdings:** 231,932 bound volumes; 84,000 volumes in microform. **Subscriptions:** 3700 journals and other serials. **Services:** Interlibrary loan; copying; library open to the public. **Automated Operations:** Computerized cataloging. **Computerized Information Services:** LEXIS, WESTLAW, NEXIS, DIALOG Information Services, WILSONLINE. **Networks/Consortia:** Member of Kansas Library Network, Mid-America Law School Library Consortium. **Publications:** Weekly List of Acquisitions - for internal distribution only; Readers' Handbook; Guide for Readers No. 14: University of Kansas Law Library; subject bibliographies. **Staff:** Fritz Snyder, Assoc.Dir. for Res. & Acq.; Mary D. Burchill, Assoc.Dir. for Adm. & Automation; Mon Yin Lung, Hd., Tech.Serv.; Louise Hanson, Pub.Serv.Libn.

★ 18737 ★
University of Kansas - Slavic Collection (Area-Ethnic)
Watson Library   Phone: (913)864-3957
Lawrence, KS 66045-2800   Gordon Anderson, Dir.
Founded: 1954. **Staff:** Prof 4; Other 1. **Subjects:** Slavic literature, languages, linguistics, history, social sciences, Slavic-language science titles. **Special Collections:** 16th-18th century Slavic imprints, especially Polish; World War II materials, especially Ukrainian and Polish memoirs; Yugoslav literature and languages; Russian and Polish emigre literature. **Holdings:** 187,600 volumes in Slavic languages; 69,600 volumes in translation or in West European languages; 90,000 bound periodical volumes. **Subscriptions:** 1000 journals and other serials; 34 newspapers. **Services:** Interlibrary loan; collection open to authorized users. **Automated Operations:** Computerized public access catalog, cataloging, acquisitions, serials, and circulation. **Computerized Information Services:** OCLC; BITNET (electronic mail service). **Networks/Consortia:** Member of Bibliographical Center for Research, Rocky Mountain Region, Inc. (BCR), Kansas Library Network. **Remarks:** GANDERSD@UKANVM (BITNET). **Staff:** Michael Biggins Cat.Libn., S. Slavic Bibliog.; Brad Schaffner, Russian/Soviet Bibliog.; Margaret Winchell, Cat.Libn.; Maria Alexander, Slavic Acq.

★ 18738 ★
University of Kansas - Spahr Engineering Library (Sci-Engr)
Lawrence, KS 66045-2800   Phone: (913)864-3866
                                       LeAnn Weller, Libn.
Staff: Prof 1; Other 3. **Subjects:** Engineering. **Holdings:** 55,985 books and bound periodical volumes. **Subscriptions:** 1239 journals and other serials. **Services:** Interlibrary loan; copying; library open to the public. **Automated Operations:** Computerized cataloging and serials. **Computerized Information Services:** DIALOG Information Services, PFDS Online, OCLC, BRS Information Technologies; BITNET (electronic mail service). **Networks/Consortia:** Member of Bibliographical Center for Research, Rocky Mountain Region, Inc. (BCR), Kansas Library Network. **Remarks:** Electronic mail address(es): LWELLER@UKANVM (BITNET).

★ 18739 ★
University of Kansas - Thomas Gorton Music Library (Mus)
448 Murphy Hall   Phone: (913)864-3496
Lawrence, KS 66045-2800   Susan Hitchens, Libn.
Founded: 1953. **Staff:** Prof 1; Other 1. **Subjects:** Music. **Holdings:** 49,083 books and scores; 97,407 sound recordings; 7668 microforms. **Services:** Interlibrary loan; copying; library open to the public. **Automated Operations:** Computerized cataloging and serials. **Computerized Information Services:** OCLC; BITNET (electronic mail service). **Networks/Consortia:** Member of Bibliographical Center for Research, Rocky Mountain Region, Inc. (BCR), Kansas Library Network. **Remarks:** Electronic mail address(es): HITCHENS@UKANVM (BITNET).

★ 18740 ★
University of Kansas - University Archives (Hist)
422 Spencer Research Library   Phone: (913)864-4188
Lawrence, KS 66045-2800   John M. Nugent, Univ.Archv.
Founded: 1969. **Staff:** Prof 3. **Subjects:** University of Kansas. **Special Collections:** University records, 1866 to present; faculty papers; D'Ambra photographs, 1925-1970. **Holdings:** 25,818 volumes; 633,723 negatives; 246,985 photographs; 2724 tapes; 17,183 linear feet of university records; 4362 reels of 16mm film; 528 reels of microfilm; 1416 videotapes. **Services:** Interlibrary loan; copying; archives open to the public with restrictions. **Computerized Information Services:** OCLC. **Networks/Consortia:** Member of Bibliographical Center for Research, Rocky Mountain Region, Inc. (BCR), Kansas Library Network. **Staff:** Edward Kehde, Archv.; Barry Bunch, Archv.I.

★ 18741 ★
University of Kansas - University Information Center (Hist)
Burge Union   Phone: (913)864-3506
Lawrence, KS 66045   Susan Elkins, Coord.
Founded: 1970. **Staff:** Prof 1; Other 19. **Subjects:** University of Kansas; Lawrence/Kansas City area. **Holdings:** 100 volumes; university papers; topical files. **Services:** Copying; center open to the public. **Publications:** Lecture List; Travel and Transportation Information; Bank Guide; Abbreviation and Acronym Directory for University of Kansas - all for internal distribution only.

★ 18742 ★
University of Kentucky - Adelle Dailey Music Library (Mus)
116 Fine Arts Bldg.   Phone: (606)257-2800
Lexington, KY 40506-0022   Lewis P. Bowling, Mus.Libn.
Staff: Prof 1; Other 2. **Subjects:** Music - history, theory, education; applied music. **Special Collections:** Alfred Cortot Collection (265 early theory books). **Holdings:** 44,560 books and scores; 3500 bound periodical volumes; 10,440 phonograph records; 678 compact discs; 1595 cassettes; 107 video recordings; 7000 microforms. **Subscriptions:** 262 journals and other serials. **Services:** Interlibrary loan; copying; library open to the public with check-out privileges for residents of Kentucky. **Automated Operations:** Computerized public access catalog, cataloging, and acquisitions. **Computerized Information Services:** OCLC, DIALOG Information Services, RLIN; CDBUYS (internal database); BITNET (electronic mail service). **Networks/Consortia:** Member of SOLINET. **Remarks:** FAX: (606)257-4104. Electronic mail address(es): LBOWLING@UKCC.UKY.EDU (BITNET).

★ 18743 ★
University of Kentucky - Agriculture Library (Biol Sci, Agri)
N 24 Agricultural Science Ctr., N.   Phone: (606)257-2758
Lexington, KY 40546-0091   Antoinette P. Powell, Dir.
Founded: 1905. **Staff:** Prof 3; Other 6. **Subjects:** Agriculture, forestry, veterinary medicine, food, nutrition, entomology, horticulture, botany, landscape architecture. **Holdings:** 34,267 books; 56,386 bound periodical volumes; 3169 reels of microfilm; 82,099 microfiche; 10,070 U.S. Department of Agriculture publications; 3907 unbound materials. **Subscriptions:** 2118 journals and other serials; 10 newspapers. **Services:** Interlibrary loan; copying; library open to the public. **Automated Operations:** Computerized public access catalog, cataloging, and circulation. **Computerized Information Services:** OCLC, DIALOG Information Services, BRS Information Technologies; AGMAILER (internal database); CD-ROM (AGRICOLA, STN International, CAB Abstracts, AGRIS); BITNET (electronic mail service). Performs searches on fee basis. **Networks/Consortia:** Member of SOLINET. **Publications:** Monthly Acquisitions List - available upon request. **Remarks:** FAX: (606)258-4719. Electronic mail address(es): TONILIB@UKCC.UKY.EDU (BITNET). **Staff:** Lillian Mesner, Tech.Serv.; Patricia Wilson, Pub.Serv.

★ 18744 ★
University of Kentucky - Biological Sciences Library (Biol Sci)
313 Thomas Hunt Morgan Bldg.   Phone: (606)257-5889
Lexington, KY 40506-0225   Brad Grissom, Biol.Sci.Libn.
Founded: 1963. **Staff:** Prof 1; Other 1. **Subjects:** Microbiology, biology, molecular and cell biology, botany, zoology, virology, endocrinology, ecology and evolutionary biology, developmental biology. **Holdings:** 19,992 books; 23,772 bound periodical volumes; 1425 microforms. **Subscriptions:** 650 journals and other serials. **Services:** Interlibrary loan; copying; library open to the public. **Automated Operations:** Computerized public access catalog and circulation. **Computerized Information Services:** OCLC, DIALOG Information Services, BRS Information Technologies; CD-ROM (Biological Abstracts); BITNET (electronic mail service). **Networks/Consortia:** Member of SOLINET. **Publications:** Acquisitions List, 4/year. **Remarks:** FAX: (606)257-5889. Electronic mail address(es): BGRISSOM@UKCC (BITNET).

★ 18745 ★
University of Kentucky - Center for Applied Energy Research (Energy)
3572 Iron Works Pike   Phone: (606)257-0309
Lexington, KY 40511-8433   Theresa K. Wiley, Lib.Mgr.
Founded: 1974. **Staff:** Prof 1; Other 1. **Subjects:** Coal, oil shale, energy. **Holdings:** 8200 books; 846 bound periodical volumes; 44,000 technical reports in microform. **Subscriptions:** 40 journals and other serials. **Services:** Interlibrary loan; library open to the public for reference use only. **Automated Operations:** Computerized cataloging. **Computerized Information Services:** DIALOG Information Services, OCLC, STN International; InterNet (electronic mail service). Performs searches on fee basis. **Networks/Consortia:** Member of Kentucky Library Network, Inc. (KLN). **Publications:** Research Reports - for sale. **Remarks:** FAX: (606)257-0220. Electronic mail address(es): LIBRARY@CAER.UKY.EDU (InterNet). Official sales agent for IEA Coal Research, London.

★ 18746 ★
University of Kentucky - Chemistry-Physics Library (Sci-Engr)
150 Chemistry-Physics Bldg.   Phone: (606)257-5954
Lexington, KY 40506-0055   Maggie Johnson, Libn.
Founded: 1963. **Staff:** Prof 1; Other 1. **Subjects:** Chemistry, physics, astronomy. **Holdings:** 9960 books; 39,522 bound periodical volumes; 236 reels of microfilm. **Subscriptions:** 492 journals and other serials. **Services:** Interlibrary loan; copying; library open to the public. **Automated Operations:** Computerized public access catalog and circulation. **Computerized Information Services:** STN International, DIALOG Information Services, TOXNET, Knowledge Index; BITNET (electronic mail service). Performs searches on fee basis. **Remarks:** FAX: (606)257-5954. Electronic mail address(es): MJOHNSON@UKCC (BITNET).

★ 18747 ★
University of Kentucky - Education Library (Educ)
205 Dickey Hall   Phone: (606)257-7977
Lexington, KY 40506   Mary Vass, Libn.
Staff: Prof 1; Other 2. **Subjects:** Education, juvenile literature, counseling. **Special Collections:** Juvenile and young adult collection (16,337 volumes).

Holdings: 65,175 volumes; 11,240 bound periodical volumes; 410,515 microfiche; 230 reels of microfilm. **Subscriptions:** 308 journals and other serials. **Services:** Interlibrary loan; copying; SDI; library open to the public with restrictions. **Automated Operations:** Computerized public access catalog and circulation. **Computerized Information Services:** DIALOG Information Services, BRS Information Technologies. Performs searches on fee basis. **Networks/Consortia:** Member of SOLINET. **Publications:** Newsletter/Acquisitions List, irregular - for internal distribution only. **Remarks:** Alternate telephone number(s): 257-1351. FAX: (606)257-7977.

★ 18748 ★
University of Kentucky - Edward Warder Rannells Art Library (Art, Theater)
4 King Library N.   Phone: (606)257-3938
Lexington, KY 40506-0039   Meg Shaw, Libn.
Staff: Prof 1; Other 1. **Subjects:** Art, theater, photography. **Holdings:** 27,806 books; 7121 bound periodical volumes; 70 reels of microfilm; 812 microfiche; 36 VF drawers of pamphlets and catalogs. **Subscriptions:** 206 journals and other serials. **Services:** Interlibrary loan; copying; library open to the public. **Automated Operations:** Computerized cataloging and circulation. **Computerized Information Services:** DIALOG Information Services, BRS Information Technologies. Performs searches on fee basis. **Remarks:** FAX: (606)257-4908.

★ 18749 ★
University of Kentucky - George W. Pirtle Geological Sciences Library (Sci-Engr)
100 Bowman Hall   Phone: (606)257-5730
Lexington, KY 40506-0059   Mary Spencer, Act.Libn.
Founded: 1923. **Staff:** Prof 1; Other 1. **Subjects:** Petroleum geology and paleontology, mining geology, hydrogeology, tectonics, geophysics, volcanology, remote sensing, mineralogy, petrology, geochemistry, all aspects of geology including regional and economic. **Special Collections:** Depository for all U.S. Geological Survey maps; Repository of Black Shale Documents by U.S. Department of Energy researchers. **Holdings:** 14,515 books; 32,134 bound periodical volumes; 122,082 maps; 412 reels of microfilm; 15,794 microfiche. **Subscriptions:** 1150 journals and other serials. **Services:** Interlibrary loan; copying; library open to the public. **Automated Operations:** Computerized public access catalog and circulation. **Computerized Information Services:** OCLC EPIC; Kentucky Earth Sciences Bibliographic Information Database (internal database); CD-ROM (Index to publications of U.S. Geological Survey); BITNET (electronic mail service). **Networks/Consortia:** Member of SOLINET. **Publications:** Acquisition list, bimonthly; theses listing; periodicals list, both annual. **Remarks:** FAX: (606)257-5730. Electronic mail address(es): KLIMRS@UKCC.UKY.EDU (BITNET).

★ 18750 ★
University of Kentucky - Hunter M. Adams Architecture Library (Plan, Art)
College of Architecture
200 Pence Hall   Phone: (606)257-1533
Lexington, KY 40506-0041   Daniel H. Hodge, Libn.
Founded: 1962. **Staff:** Prof 1; Other 1. **Subjects:** Architecture, landscape architecture, city and urban planning, historic preservation, alternative energy sources, construction, interior design. **Special Collections:** Rare books; Le Corbusier (300 volumes); Kentucky architecture. **Holdings:** 20,365 books; 8290 bound periodical volumes; 608 sets of architectural plans and drawings; 606 reels of microfilm; 1904 microfiche; 3550 VF items; 50 cassettes. **Subscriptions:** 230 journals and other serials. **Services:** Interlibrary loan; copying; library open to the public. **Automated Operations:** Computerized public access catalog and circulation. **Computerized Information Services:** DIALOG Information Services, OCLC, RLIN; BITNET (electronic mail service). Performs searches on fee basis. **Networks/Consortia:** Member of SOLINET. **Publications:** Quarterly Newsletter; Acquisitions List; Library Guide. **Remarks:** FAX: (606)257-4305. Electronic mail address(es): DHHODGE@UKCC.UKY.EDU (BITNET).

★ 18751 ★
University of Kentucky - Law Library (Law)
College of Law
Lexington, KY 40506-0048   Phone: (606)257-8346
                                                    Mark Linneman, Dir.
Founded: 1908. **Staff:** Prof 4; Other 7. **Subjects:** Law. **Special Collections:** Kocourek Collection on Jurisprudence; Records and Briefs on U.S. Supreme

Court (1897 to present); Natural Resource law (Coal law). **Holdings:** 198,708 books; 167,746 U.S. Government publications (partial depository); 568,518 microfiche; 1549 microfilms; 1264 audiotapes; 147 videotapes. **Subscriptions:** 3263 journals and other serials; 10 newspapers. **Services:** Interlibrary loan; copying; library open to the public. **Automated Operations:** Computerized public access catalog, cataloging, acquisitions, circulation, and ILL. **Computerized Information Services:** OCLC, LEXIS, WESTLAW. **Networks/Consortia:** Member of SOLINET, Center for Research Libraries (CRL). **Publications:** Acquisitions List, monthly; table of contents for periodicals received, weekly; Users Manual, annual. **Remarks:** FAX: (606)258-1061. **Staff:** Cheryl Jones, Dp.Dir./Pub.Serv.Libn.; Ebba Jo Sexton, Tech.Serv.Libn.; Sue Burch, Circ./Ref.Libn.

★ 18752 ★
University of Kentucky - Margaret I. King Library - Government Publications/Maps Department (Info Sci)
Lexington, KY 40506-0039   Phone: (606)257-3139
                                                    Sandra McAninch, Hd.,
                                                    Govt.Pubns./Maps Dept.
Founded: 1967. **Staff:** Prof 2; Other 6. **Subjects:** Government publications - U.S., Canada, Great Britain, Kentucky, and other states of the U.S.; United Nations documents; European Communities documents; technical reports. **Special Collections:** Sanborn Fire Insurance Maps for Kentucky. **Holdings:** 1 million hard copy documents; 2.1 million microform documents. **Subscriptions:** 9964 journals and other serials. **Services:** Interlibrary loan; copying; department open to the public. **Computerized Information Services:** LEGI-SLATE, OCLC EPIC, Economic Bulletin Board (EBB); CD-ROMs. **Publications:** Let's Talk Documents. **Remarks:** FAX: (606)257-1563. **Staff:** Roxanna Jones, Asst.Docs.Libn.

★ 18753 ★
University of Kentucky - Margaret I. King Library - Government Publications/Maps Department - Map Collection (Geog-Map)
Lexington, KY 40506-0039   Phone: (606)257-1853
                                                    Gwen Curtis, Hd. of Map Coll.
Founded: 1973. **Staff:** 2. **Subjects:** Cartography. **Special Collections:** Kentucky maps, 1875 to present; Southeastern U.S. maps, 1800 to present; Sanborn Insurance Maps of Kentucky cities (7895 sheets; 3000 maps on microfilm); Defense Mapping Agency Depository (20,000 sheets). **Holdings:** 1770 books and atlases; 11,440 cataloged maps; 67,125 uncataloged maps and aerial photographs. **Subscriptions:** 5 journals and other serials. **Services:** Interlibrary loan; copying; collection open to the public with limited circulation. **Automated Operations:** Computerized public access catalog, cataloging, and circulation. **Computerized Information Services:** OCLC. **Networks/Consortia:** Member of SOLINET. **Publications:** Selected Acquisitions Bulletin, quarterly - to faculty and other libraries. **Remarks:** Kentucky maps published before 1875 are housed in the Special Collections Department of the King Library; geology and hydrology maps are housed in the George W. Pirtle Geological Sciences Library. FAX: (606)257-1563.

★ 18754 ★
University of Kentucky - Margaret I. King Library - Special Collections and Archives (Hist)
11 King Library N.   Phone: (606)257-8611
Lexington, KY 40506-0039   William Marshall, Asst.Dir.,
                                                    Spec.Coll. & Archv.
Founded: 1946. **Staff:** Prof 6; Other 7. **Subjects:** Kentuckiana, 20th century politics, Appalachia, English Romantic and Victorian literature, Miltoniana, history of printing, typography and the fine press. **Holdings:** 125,726 volumes; 9951 linear feet of manuscripts; 9418 linear feet of archives; 377,613 photographs; 19,696 reels of microfilm; 3197 oral history interviews; 9566 audiotapes; 3264 videotapes. **Subscriptions:** 850 journals and other serials. **Services:** Interlibrary loan; copying; collections open to the public. **Automated Operations:** Computerized public access catalog and cataloging. **Computerized Information Services:** OCLC; internal database. Performs searches on fee basis. **Networks/Consortia:** Member of SOLINET. **Special Catalogs:** Applied Anthropology Documentation Project; catalogs to Dime Novel collection, Science Fiction Collection, Milton Collection, Cortot Collection, Kentucky Imprint Collection; theses catalog; rare book collection; Guide to Selected Manuscripts (Kentuckiana); Guide to Appalachian Regional Commission Collection; catalogs to photographic archives, microfilm, and manuscripts. **Remarks:** (606)257-8379. **Staff:** Terry Birdwhistoll, Archv., Oral Hist.; Kate Black, Appalachian Libn.; Bill Cooper, Modern Political Papers; Claire McCann, Pub.Serv.; Terry Warth, Cat.

★ 18755 ★
University of Kentucky - Mathematical Sciences Library (Sci-Engr, Comp Sci)
OB-9 Patterson Office Tower   Phone: (606)257-8365
Lexington, KY 40506-0027   Julie Moseley, Libn.
Staff: Prof 1; Other 1. **Subjects:** Mathematics, computer science, statistics. **Holdings:** 19,116 books; 14,455 bound periodical volumes. **Subscriptions:** 470 journals and other serials. **Services:** Interlibrary loan; copying; library open to the public. **Automated Operations:** Computerized public access catalog, cataloging, and circulation. **Computerized Information Services:** DIALOG Information Services, BRS Information Technologies, OCLC; CD-ROM (MathSci Disc); BITNET (electronic mail service). Performs searches on fee basis. **Publications:** Monthly acquisitions list; newsletter, irregular; annual report. **Remarks:** FAX: (606)257-8365. Electronic mail address(es): CSENN@UKCC.UKY.EDU (BITNET).

★ 18756 ★
University of Kentucky - Medical Center Library (Med)
Lexington, KY 40536-0084   Phone: (606)233-5726
                                              Omer Hamlin, Jr., Dir.
Founded: 1957. **Staff:** Prof 10; Other 18. **Subjects:** Medicine, dentistry, nursing, pharmacy, allied health sciences. **Special Collections:** Harvey Collection; Servetus Collection. **Holdings:** 76,811 books; 97,010 bound periodical volumes; 1084 reels of microfilm; 2372 AV programs. **Subscriptions:** 1884 journals and other serials. **Services:** Interlibrary loan (fee); copying; SDI; Grateful Med and BRS training; library open to health science personnel. **Automated Operations:** Computerized public access catalog, cataloging, circulation, and ILL. **Computerized Information Services:** MEDLINE, DIALOG Information Services, BRS Information Technologies, OCLC; CD-ROM (MEDLINE). **Networks/Consortia:** Member of National Network of Libraries of Medicine - Greater Midwest Region, SOLINET, Kentucky Library Network, Inc. (KLN). **Remarks:** FAX: (606)258-1040; 233-6805 (ILL). **Staff:** Janet Stith, Asst.Dir. for Pub.Serv.; Karl Heinz-Boewe, Circ.Libn.; Bev Hilton, AV Libn.; Lynne Bowman, Cat.Libn.; Bernadette Baldini, Asst.Dir., Tech.Serv.; Stephanie Allen, Ref.Libn.; Edwina Theirl, ILL Libn.; Mark Ingram, Ref.Libn.; Cindy Cline, Ser.Libn.

★ 18757 ★
University of Kentucky - Morris Library and Information Center (Biol Sci)
108 Gluck Equine Research Center   Phone: (606)257-1192
Lexington, KY 40546-0099   Susan Byars, Libn.
Founded: 1989. **Staff:** 1. **Subjects:** Horses. **Holdings:** 250 books. **Subscriptions:** 60 journals and other serials. **Services:** SDI; document delivery; library open to the public. **Computerized Information Services:** BRS Information Technologies, EquineLine, Bloodstock Research Information Services, Inc.; CD-ROM (MEDLINE, SPORT Discus, AGRICOLA). **Remarks:** FAX: (606)257-8542.

★ 18758 ★
University of Kentucky - Robert E. Shaver Library of Engineering (Energy, Sci-Engr)
355 Anderson Hall   Phone: (606)257-2965
Lexington, KY 40506-0046   Russell H. Powell, Libn.
Founded: 1965. **Staff:** Prof 2; Other 1. **Subjects:** Environment; coal mining and processing; robotics and manufacturing; transportation; engineering mechanics; energy; engineering - civil, mechanical, electrical, chemical, metallurgical. **Holdings:** 32,574 monographs; 28,348 bound periodical volumes; 2263 reels of microfilm; 80,819 microfiche. **Subscriptions:** 650 journals; 319 irregular serials. **Services:** Interlibrary loan; copying; library open to the public with restrictions on borrowing. **Automated Operations:** Computerized cataloging and circulation. **Computerized Information Services:** DIALOG Information Services, OCLC. **Networks/Consortia:** Member of SOLINET. **Remarks:** FAX:(606)258-1911. **Staff:** Adil Razeeq.

University of Kentucky - Technology Applications Center
See: **NASA/University of Kentucky - Technology Applications Center** (10992)

★ 18759 ★
University of Kentucky - Tobacco and Health Research Institute - Library (Med)
Cooper and University Drs.   Phone: (606)257-2877
Lexington, KY 40546-0236   Laura McIlwain, Data Libn.
Founded: 1966. **Staff:** Prof 2.5. **Subjects:** Tobacco products, diseases, passive smoking, cessation of smoking, maternal smoking, legislation. **Computerized Information Services:** BRS Information Technologies; computerized data base on all aspects of tobacco and health (65,000 scientific articles with keywords and abstracts where available; internal database). **Remarks:** FAX: (606)258-1077.

★ 18760 ★
University of King's College - King's College Library (Rel-Phil, Hum)
6350 Coburg Rd.   Phone: (902)422-1271
Halifax, NS, Canada B3H 2A1   Drake Petersen, Act.Hd.Libn.
Founded: 1789. **Staff:** Prof 2; Other 3. **Subjects:** Theology, Canadiana, philosophy, history, literature, classics, journalism. **Special Collections:** Incunabula and rare books (25,000 volumes); William Inglis Morse Canadiana Collection; Journalism Resource Collection; Weldon Loyalist China Collection (porcelain); Kingdon Library (Tractarian theology); Dr. Bray Associates Libraries. **Holdings:** 90,000 books and bound periodical volumes; college archives. **Subscriptions:** 192 journals and other serials; 25 newspapers. **Services:** Interlibrary loan; library open to the public with restrictions. **Special Catalogs:** Incunabula. **Remarks:** FAX: (902)423-3357. **Staff:** Patricia Chalmers, Asst.Libn., Coll.; Elaine Galey, Asst.Libn., Sys.

★ 18761 ★
University of La Verne - American Armenian International College - Library (Area-Ethnic)
1950 3rd St.   Phone: (714)593-3511
La Verne, CA 91750   Mr. Nishan Basmadjian, Libn.
Founded: 1976. **Staff:** Prof 1; Other 4. **Subjects:** Armenia - literature, history, church history, architecture, music, art, theatre. **Special Collections:** Armenian genealogy (229 reels of microfilm). **Holdings:** 13,300 books; 14 videocassettes. **Subscriptions:** 33 journals and other serials; 27 newspapers. **Services:** Interlibrary loan; copying; library open to the public by appointment.

★ 18762 ★
University of La Verne - College of Law at La Verne - Law Library (Law)
1950 3rd St.   Phone: (714)593-7184
La Verne, CA 91750   Alla Buckrinskaya, Dir.
Founded: 1978. **Staff:** Prof 1; Other 3. **Subjects:** Law. **Special Collections:** Juvenile Law (3080 volumes); California State and U.S. Government depositories. **Holdings:** 43,275 volumes; 6573 bound periodical volumes; 4288 government documents; 320 audio cassettes; 38,381 volumes on microfiche. **Subscriptions:** 456 journals and other serials. **Services:** Interlibrary loan; copying; library open to the public. **Automated Operations:** Computerized cataloging. **Computerized Information Services:** WESTLAW, OCLC, DIALOG Information Services; MCI Mail (electronic mail service). **Remarks:** FAX: (714)593-5139.

★ 18763 ★
University of La Verne - College of Law at San Fernando Valley - Law Library (Law)
5445 Balboa Blvd.   Phone: (818)981-4529
Encino, CA 91316   Alla Buckrinskaya, Libn.
Founded: 1962. **Staff:** 5. **Subjects:** Law. **Holdings:** 44,436 volumes; 30,509 volumes on microform. **Subscriptions:** 180 journals and other serials. **Services:** Interlibrary loan; copying; library open to the public with restrictions. **Automated Operations:** Computerized cataloging. **Computerized Information Services:** DIALOG Information Services, WESTLAW. **Remarks:** A depository for California state government documents. FAX: (818)789-1557.

★ 18764 ★
University Library of Hannover and Technical Information Library (Sci-Engr)
Universitatsbibliothek und TIB
Welfengarten 1B   Phone: 511 7622268
W-3000 Hannover 1, Germany   Dr. Gerhard Schlitt, Dir.
Founded: 1959. **Staff:** Prof 77; Other 154. **Subjects:** Engineering, physics, mathematics, chemistry. **Holdings:** 3 million volumes; 1 million reels of

microfilm. **Subscriptions:** 20,000 journals and other serials. **Services:** Interlibrary loan; copying; library open to the public. **Automated Operations:** Computerized public access catalog (TIBKAT) and cataloging. **Computerized Information Services:** DIALOG Information Services, ESA/IRS, STN International, DIMDI, Zeitschriftendatenbank (ZDB); DIALMAIL, STN International (electronic mail services). Performs searches on fee basis. **Special Catalogs:** Periodicals list: ZV 89. **Remarks:** Serves as central national library for science and engineering. FAX: 511 715936. Telex: 922 168 tibhn d. Electronic mail address(es): 331 K (STN International); 11 343 /TIBORDER (DIALMAIL). **Also Known As:** Universitatsbibliothek Hannover und Technische Informationsbibliothek. **Staff:** Jobst Tehnzen, Dp.Libn.; Dr. Wolfgang Zick, Dp.Libn.

★18765★
University of London - Charing Cross and Westminster Medical School - Library (Med)
St. Dunstan Rd.
London W6 8RP, England   Phone: 81 8467152
Founded: 1834. **Staff:** Prof 6; Other 2. **Subjects:** Medicine. **Special Collections:** Charing Cross Collection (200 volumes.). **Holdings:** 20,000 books. **Subscriptions:** 300 journals and other serials; 4 newspapers. **Services:** Interlibrary loan; copying; SDI; library open to the public for a fee. **Computerized Information Services:** Data-Star; CD-ROM (MEDLINE). Contact Person: H. Hague, Asst.Libn. **Remarks:** FAX: 81 8467222.

★18766★
University of London - Wye College - Library (Agri)
Wye   Phone: 233 812401
Ashford TN25 5AH, England   Mrs. E.M. Lucas, Libn.
Founded: 1900. **Staff:** Prof 3; Other 2.5. **Subjects:** Agriculture; horticulture; rural environmental studies; agricultural economics; agrarian development; farm business. **Special Collections:** Early books on agriculture and horticulture; Crundale Rectorial Library. **Holdings:** 35,000 books; 20,000 bound periodical volumes. **Subscriptions:** 600 journals and other serials; 3 newspapers. **Services:** Interlibrary loan; copying; library open for genuine research in relevant subject areas only. **Computerized Information Services:** DIALOG Information Services. Contact Person: Mrs. W.D. Sage, Asst.Libn. **Remarks:** FAX: 233 813320.

★18767★
University of Louisville - Allen R. Hite Art Institute - Margaret M. Bridwell Art Library (Art)
Belknap Campus   Phone: (502)588-6741
Louisville, KY 40292   Gail R. Gilbert, Hd./Art Libn.
Founded: 1956. **Staff:** Prof 1; Other 1. **Subjects:** Art - Renaissance, medieval, ancient, American; modern architecture; landscape architecture; German sculpture; art history; photography; textiles; graphic design; interior design. **Special Collections:** Robert J. Doherty Typography Collection; Ainslie Hewett Bookplate Collection. **Holdings:** 54,000 volumes; 840 posters; 13,000 folders of artists' files and information files. **Subscriptions:** 265 journals and other serials. **Services:** Interlibrary loan; library open to the public for reference use only. **Automated Operations:** Computerized public access catalog and circulation. **Computerized Information Services:** BITNET (electronic mail service). **Remarks:** Electronic mail address(es): GRGILB@ULKYVM (BITNET).

★18768★
University of Louisville - Department of Rare Books and Special Collections (Rare Book, Hum)
Belknap Campus   Phone: (502)588-6762
Louisville, KY 40292   Delinda S. Buie, Cur.
Founded: 1837. **Staff:** Prof 2; Other 1. **Subjects:** Astronomy-mathematics, World War I, literary first editions, popular culture, Irish Literary Renaissance literature, American humor, Louisvilliana. **Special Collections:** Bullitt Collection (rare astronomy and mathematics; 400 items); Arthur Rackham Collection (500 books, manuscripts, original art); Edgar Rice Burroughs Collection (25,000 items); H.L. Mencken Collection (500 items); Graham Greene Collection (300 items); Lawrence Durrell Collection (200 items); J.D. Salinger Collection (200 items); American Humor (3000 items); Lafcadio Hearn Collection (200 items); World War I Collection (2000 items); Mosher Press (1000 volumes); Roger Manvell Collection of Theater & Film History (20,000 items); Irish Literary Renaissance Collection (3500 volumes, manuscripts, and ephemera. **Holdings:** 70,000 books and periodicals; 165 linear feet of manuscripts. **Subscriptions:** 7 journals and other serials. **Services:** Interlibrary loan; copying; photography of items that cannot be copied; department open to the public for reference use only. **Also Known As:** University of Louisville - John L. Patterson Room. **Staff:** George McWhorter, Cur., Burroughs Coll.

★18769★
University of Louisville - Dwight Anderson Memorial Music Library (Mus)
2301 S. 3rd St.   Phone: (502)588-5659
Louisville, KY 40292   Richard Griscom, Libn.
Founded: 1947. **Staff:** Prof 2; Other 5. **Subjects:** Music. **Special Collections:** Early American Sheet Music; Kentucky imprints; Kentucky composers; Louisville Orchestra Commissioning Project materials; Jean Thomas "Traipsin' Woman" Collection; Isidore Philipp Archive; Ricasoli Collection. **Holdings:** 20,852 books and bound periodical volumes; 24,316 scores; 907 microtext and microfilm titles; 13,801 sound recordings; 20,000 uncataloged items. **Subscriptions:** 161 Periodicals. **Services:** Interlibrary loan; copying; library open to the public. **Automated Operations:** Computerized cataloging and circulation. **Computerized Information Services:** OCLC; BITNET, InterNet (electronic mail services). **Networks/Consortia:** Member of SOLINET. **Publications:** Gamut (newsletter). **Remarks:** Electronic mail address(es): RWGRIS01@ULKYVM (BITNET); rwgris01@ulkyvm.et.louisville.edu (InterNet). **Staff:** Karen Little, Asst.Hd.Libn.

University of Louisville - John L. Patterson Room
See: University of Louisville - Department of Rare Books and Special Collections (18768)

★18770★
University of Louisville - Kersey Library (Sci-Engr)
Belknap Campus   Phone: (502)588-6297
Louisville, KY 40292   Carol S. Brinkman, Hd.Libn.
Staff: Prof 2; Other 5.5. **Subjects:** Applied mathematics; computer science; engineering - chemical, electrical, mechanical, civil, industrial, nuclear, environmental; physics; chemistry; mathematics; statistics; astronomy; history of science and technology; general science. **Holdings:** 93,565 volumes; 29,139 microforms. **Subscriptions:** 1304 journals and other serials. **Services:** Copying; library open to the public. **Computerized Information Services:** Online systems.

★18771★
University of Louisville - Kornhauser Health Sciences Library (Med)
Louisville, KY 40292   Phone: (502)588-5771
                                 Leonard M. Eddy, Dir.
Founded: 1836. **Staff:** Prof 9; Other 13. **Subjects:** Medicine, dentistry, nursing, allied health sciences, medical history. **Special Collections:** Horine Anesthesia Collection; Gardner Collection in the History of Psychiatry; Charles Caldwell Collection. **Holdings:** 58,820 books; 104,080 bound periodical volumes; 3886 AV programs. **Subscriptions:** 1715 journals. **Services:** Interlibrary loan; library open to the public. **Automated Operations:** Computerized public access catalog, cataloging, acquisitions, serials, and circulation. **Computerized Information Services:** BRS Information Technologies, NLM, DIALOG Information Services, OCLC; CD-ROM; BITNET, InterNet (electronic mail services). Performs searches. **Networks/Consortia:** Member of National Network of Libraries of Medicine - Greater Midwest Region. **Publications:** Bio-Echo, monthly. **Remarks:** FAX: (502)588-5300. Electronic mail address(es): LMEDD01@ULKYVM (BITNET). **Staff:** Neal Nixon, Hd., Tech.Serv.; Parthenia Durrett, Circ.; Diane Nichols, Pub.Serv.Libn.; Nancy Utterback, Hd., Pub.Serv.; Sherrill Redmon, Archv.; Kathleen Curlovic, Cat.; Maura Ellison, Ser.; Gwendolyn Snodgrass, Coll.Dev.Libn.; Michel Atlas, Ref.Libn.; Elizabeth McKinney, ILL Supv.

★18772★
University of Louisville - Photographic Archives (Hist)
Belknap Campus   Phone: (502)588-6752
Louisville, KY 40292   James C. Anderson, Cur. & Hd.
Founded: 1962. **Staff:** Prof 1; Other 3. **Subjects:** History of Louisville; 20th century social history; American industry; oil industry; photography - historic, artistic, documentary, commercial. **Special Collections:** Antique media and equipment; Lou Block Collection; Will Bowers Collection; Bradley Studio/Georgetown Collection; Theodore M. Brown/Robert J. Doherty Collection; Caldwell Tank Company Collection; Cooper Collection; erotic photography; Fine Print Collection; Arthur Y. Ford albums; Forensic Photography Collection; U.S. Corps of Engineers (Louisville District) Collection; Vida Hunt Francis Collection; Mary D. Hill Collection; Joseph Krementz Collection; Macauley Collection; Manvell Collection (film stills); Boyd Martin Collection; Kate Matthews Collection; Metropolitan Sewer District Collection; R.G. Potter Collection; J.C. Rieger

Collection; Royal Photo Studio Collection; Jean Thomas Collection; World Wars I and II photographs; Caufield and Shook of Louisville Collection; Roy E. Stryker Collections, including Standard Oil Company of New Jersey Collection. **Holdings:** 1000 books; 10,000 pages of manuscripts; 1 million photographs and photograph-related items. **Subscriptions:** 20 journals and other serials. **Services:** Interlibrary loan; copying; photographic print service; library open to the public. **Automated Operations:** Computerized cataloging. **Computerized Information Services:** Internal databases; BITNET (electronic mail service). **Publications:** Exhibition catalogs, irregular; Guide to Collections - for sale. **Remarks:** FAX: (502)588-8753. Electronic mail address(es): JCANDE01@ULKYVM (BITNET).

★ 18773 ★
University of Louisville - School of Law Library (Law)
Belknap Campus   Phone: (502)588-6392
Louisville, KY 40292   David Ensign, Law Libn.
Founded: 1926. **Staff:** Prof 6; Other 7. **Subjects:** Law. **Special Collections:** Correspondence of Mr. Justice Brandeis (250,000 items) and Mr. Justice Harlan, 1833-1911 (1500 items). **Holdings:** 219,638 volumes and microform volume equivalents. **Subscriptions:** 4240 journals and other serials. **Services:** Interlibrary loan; library open to the public with restrictions. **Computerized Information Services:** LEXIS, WESTLAW. **Remarks:** FAX: (502)588-0862. **Staff:** Shelley Burgett, Tech.Serv./Govt.Docs.; Doris Geoghegan, Hd., Tech.Serv.; Robin Harris, Pub.Serv.; Joyce Pearson, Intl. Law/Ref.

★ 18774 ★
University of Louisville - University Archives and Records Center (Hist)
Ekstrom Library   Phone: (502)588-6674
Louisville, KY 40292   William J. Morison, Dir./Univ.Archv.
Founded: 1973. **Staff:** Prof 7; Other 2. **Subjects:** History of the university and its predecessor schools; political, social, economic, and cultural history of Louisville and the geographic region; regional business. **Special Collections:** Louis D. Brandeis papers (184 reels of microfilm); Louisville and Nashville Railroad Company records (155 linear feet; 39 reels of microfilm; 46 oral history interviews); Louisville Orchestra records (150 linear feet; 19 oral history interviews); Louisville Defender records and Frank L. Stanley papers (13.75 linear feet; 13 reels of microfilm; 2 oral history interviews); Presbyterian Community Center records (8 linear feet); Louisville YWCA records (51.5 linear feet); Simmons University records (5 linear feet); Isaac W. Bernheim papers; D.W. Griffith papers (1897-1954; 36 reels of microfilm); Kentucky medical history (1801-1940; 32 reels of microfilm). **Holdings:** 6055 linear feet of archives and personal papers; 1550 linear feet of local government archives; 2335 linear feet of Kentuckiana Historical Collections, records of local organizations, and personal papers of area individuals and families; 1027 reels of microfilm; 77 microfiche; oral history materials. **Subscriptions:** 14 journals and other serials. **Services:** Copying; microfilming; archives and manuscripts open to the public with restrictions. **Automated Operations:** Computerized cataloging. **Computerized Information Services:** BITNET (electronic mail service). **Publications:** A Place Where Historical Research May Be Pursued: Selected Primary Sources in the University of Louisville Archives; Papers of Louis D. Brandeis at the University of Louisville, Microfilm Edition, 1981; D.W. Griffith Papers 1897-1954: Guide to the Microfilm Edition, 1982. **Remarks:** FAX: (502)588-8753. Electronic mail address(es): WJMORI01@ULKYVM (BITNET). **Staff:** Thomas Owen, Assoc.Archv.; Janet Hodgson, Assoc.Archv.; Sherrill Redmon, Assoc.Archv.; Margaret Merrick, Assoc.Archv.; L. Dale Patterson, Assoc.Archv.; Larry Raymond, Hd., Microform Lab.; Colleen Schiavone, Proj.Archv.; Sherri Pawson, Off.Mgr.

★ 18775 ★
University of Louisville - University Archives and Records Center - Oral History Center (Hist)
Ekstrom Library   Phone: (502)588-6674
Louisville, KY 40292   William J. Morison, Dir./Univ.Archv.
Founded: 1968. **Staff:** Prof 2. **Subjects:** History of Louisville, Kentucky, including the Louisville Orchestra; prominent citizens; university history; the Louisville and Nashville Railroad; photography; Jewish history; local government; African American history; Kentucky distilling industry; Bernheim Forest. **Holdings:** 1179 interviews. **Services:** Copying; copies of tapes, finding aids, and selected transcripts available; center open to the public. **Computerized Information Services:** BITNET (electronic mail service). **Remarks:** FAX: (502)588-8753. Electronic mail address(es): LDPATT01@ULKYVM (BITNET). **Staff:** L. Dale Patterson, Co-Dir.; Carl G. Ryant, Co-Dir.

★ 18776 ★
University of Louisville - Urban Research Institute - Library (Soc Sci)
College of Urban and Public Affairs   Phone: (502)588-7990
Louisville, KY 40292   Ron Crouch, Dir., KY State Data Ctr.
Founded: 1980. **Staff:** Prof 3; Other 1. **Subjects:** Population, social, and economic demography of Kentucky, housing assessment, public opinion surveys, public administration, municipal planning, criminal justice surveys and statistics. **Special Collections:** Census Publications; Bureau of Economic Analysis Publications; Kentucky State Government Publications; Census maps for Kentucky, 1970, 1980, and 1990 (1000). **Holdings:** 5000 books; 200 computer tapes; computer printouts; maps; microfiche. **Subscriptions:** 37 journals and other serials. **Services:** Copying; library open to the public. **Computerized Information Services:** Internal database; CD-ROMs (Census tapes). **Publications:** Quarterly newsletter; Periodic Kentucky Data Publications. **Remarks:** The Urban Research Institute operates the Kentucky State Data Center i n cooperation with the U.S. Bureau of the Census, disseminating population, housing, and economic census data. It also works with other agencies as coordinator of the Kentucky Business Industry Data Network, which provides economic data. It has 60 affiliate agencies including Area Development districts, Small Business Development Centers, Regional and University Libraries.

University of Lowell
See: **University of Massachusetts at Lowell** (18834)

★ 18777 ★
University of Maine - Ira C. Darling Center Library (Biol Sci, Sci-Engr)
Walpole, ME 04573   Phone: (207)563-3146
       Louise M. Dean, Libn.
Founded: 1967. **Staff:** Prof 1. **Subjects:** Marine biology; oceanography - biological, physical, chemical, geological; fisheries; aquaculture. **Holdings:** 10,550 books and bound periodical volumes; 8000 reprints; 1500 microforms. **Subscriptions:** 190 journals and other serials. **Services:** Interlibrary loan; copying; library open to the public. **Automated Operations:** Computerized public access catalog. **Remarks:** FAX: (207)563-3119.

★ 18778 ★
University of Maine - Northeast Archives of Folklore and Oral History (Hist)
Dept. of Anthropology
S. Stevens Hall   Phone: (207)581-1891
Orono, ME 04469   Edward D. Ives, Dir.
Founded: 1964. **Staff:** Prof 2; Other 2. **Subjects:** Folklore, oral history. **Special Collections:** Folksong; lumbering and river driving; folklife of Maine and the Maritime Provinces. **Holdings:** 2200 cataloged accessions; 6000 photographs of lumbering and other aspects of folklife. **Subscriptions:** 600 journals and other serials. **Services:** Copying; archives open to the public. **Publications:** Northeast Folklore, annual. **Special Indexes:** Place names, personal names, song titles, subjects. **Staff:** Mary O'Meara, Assoc.Dir.

★ 18779 ★
University of Maine - Raymond H. Fogler Library - Special Collections Department (Hist)
Orono, ME 04469   Phone: (207)581-1686
       Muriel Sanford, Spec.Coll.Libn.
Founded: 1970. **Staff:** Prof 1.5; Other 2. **Subjects:** State of Maine, maritime history. **Special Collections:** State of Maine Collection (16,000 volumes); Maine State Documents Collection (8500 titles); University Collection (13,725 items); Clinton L. Cole Marine Library (4550 volumes); O'Brien Collection of American Negro History and Culture (1600 items); Philip H. Taylor Collection of Modern History, War, and Diplomacy (1200 volumes); Thoreau Fellowship Papers. **Holdings:** 35,000 books; 475 bound periodical volumes; 1700 archive boxes of manuscripts on Maine; 2500 maps of Maine; 5600 reels of microfilm; 36 Maine newspapers. **Services:** Interlibrary loan; copying; library open to the public. **Automated Operations:** Computerized public access catalog, acquisitions, serials, and indexing. **Special Catalogs:** A Catalog of the Clinton L. Cole Collection (1972). **Special Indexes:** Maine Times Index; Down East Magazine Index; Maine Campus Index; Elderberry Times Index; Maine Fish and Wildlife Index (each in card or book form); Shaker Quarterly Index. **Remarks:** FAX: (207)581-1653. **Staff:** Melvin Johnson, Spec.Coll.Libn.

★18780★
University of Maine - Raymond H. Fogler Library - Tri-State Regional Document Depository (Info Sci)
Orono, ME 04469   Phone: (207)581-1680
        Francis R. Wihbey, Hd., Govt.Docs./Microforms Dep
Founded: 1907. **Staff:** Prof 1; Other 5. **Subjects:** Government, Canada, New Brunswick, Agricultural Experiment Stations, maps and atlases, forestry. **Special Collections:** Regional depository of U.S. documents; selective depository of U.S. National Oceanic and Atmospheric Administration and Canadian documents; Army Map Service; Defense Mapping Agency; U.S. Department of Agriculture Soil Survey and U.S. Geological Survey maps. **Holdings:** 1.6 million documents, including 475,000 microforms and maps (82,000 sheet, 120,000 bound, 27,000 in microform). **Subscriptions:** 7000 journals and other serials. **Services:** Interlibrary loan; copying; SDI; depository open to the public. **Computerized Information Services:** BRS Information Technologies, OCLC, DIALOG Information Services, Integrated Technical Information System (ITIS); internal databases. Performs searches on fee basis. Contact Person: Dick Swain, 581-1673. **Publications:** Newsletter to U.S. Government Document Depositories in Tri-State Region, irregular. **Special Catalogs:** Maine Agricultural Experiment Station publications (card); Canadian Forest Service and Forest Research Centres publications (card). **Special Indexes:** Index guide to 1980 census microfiche set (Maine tables). **Remarks:** FAX: (207)581-1653.

★18781★
University of Maine at Presque Isle - Library - Special Collections (Hist)
181 Main St.   Phone: (207)764-0311
Presque Isle, ME 04769-2888   Anna McGrath, Spec.Coll.Libn.
Founded: 1980. **Staff:** Prof 2; Other 1. **Subjects:** Maine - authors, town and city histories, Aroostook County. **Special Collections:** Aroostook County, Maine Collection (1750 volumes); Maine Collection (1250 volumes). **Holdings:** 10 bound periodical volumes; 336 Maine maps; 20 reels of microfilm; 30 tapes; 1500 Maine documents; 16 VF drawers; 3 boxes of photographs; scrapbooks; Civil War memorabilia. **Subscriptions:** 5 newspapers. **Services:** Interlibrary loan; copying; collections open to the public by appointment. **Automated Operations:** Computerized public access catalog, cataloging, acquisitions, serials, and circulation. **Computerized Information Services:** OCLC; URSUS (internal database). **Networks/Consortia:** Member of NELINET, Inc. **Special Indexes:** Index to Star Herald (1986 to present). **Staff:** Nancy Roe, Cat.

★18782★
University of Maine School of Law - Donald L. Garbrecht Law Library (Law)
246 Deering Ave.   Phone: (207)780-4829
Portland, ME 04102   William Wells, Lib.Dir. & Assoc.Prof. of Law
Founded: 1961. **Staff:** Prof 9; Other 6. **Subjects:** Law. **Holdings:** 250,000 books and books in microform. **Subscriptions:** 2600 journals and other serials. **Services:** Interlibrary loan; copying; SDI; library open to the public with restrictions. **Automated Operations:** Computerized cataloging, acquisitions, and ILL. **Computerized Information Services:** LEXIS, NEXIS, WESTLAW, DIALOG Information Services, RLIN. **Networks/Consortia:** Member of CLASS, New England Law Library Consortium (NELLCO). **Remarks:** FAX: (207)780-4913. **Staff:** Anne K. Myers, Asst. Law Libn.; Ramona L. Moore, Ser.Libn.; Tom French, Asst. Law Libn.; Patricia M. Milligan, Cat.; Suzanne I. Parent, Acq.Libn.; Hugh Hill, Ref.Libn.; Lynn Wilcox, Sr. Law Cat.

★18783★
University of Manitoba - Agriculture Library (Biol Sci, Agri)
W212 Agriculture Bldg.   Phone: (204)474-6334
Winnipeg, MB, Canada R3T 2N2   Judith Harper, Hd.
Founded: 1906. **Staff:** Prof 1; Other 2. **Subjects:** Agriculture, animal science, plant science, entomology, agricultural economics, soil science, food science. **Holdings:** 20,000 volumes. **Subscriptions:** 330 journals and other serials. **Services:** Interlibrary loan; SDI; library open to the public. **Automated Operations:** Computerized cataloging, acquisitions, serials, circulation, and ILL. **Computerized Information Services:** DIALOG Information Services, CAN/OLE, UTLAS; Envoy 100 (electronic mail service). Performs searches on fee basis. **Remarks:** FAX: (204)261-7467. Telex: 07 587721. Electronic mail address(es): UM.LIB.ADMIN; ILL.MWU (both Envoy 100).

★18784★
University of Manitoba - Albert D. Cohen Management Library (Bus-Fin)
207 Drake Centre Bldg.   Phone: (204)474-8440
Winnipeg, MB, Canada R3T 2N2   Dennis Felbel, Hd.Libn.
Founded: 1971. **Staff:** Prof 1; Other 5. **Subjects:** Accounting, finance, marketing, business administration, actuarial and management sciences. **Holdings:** 22,000 volumes; annual reports for 1000 companies (past 5 years). **Subscriptions:** 375 journals and other serials. **Services:** Interlibrary loan; library open to the public. **Automated Operations:** Computerized cataloging, acquisitions, serials, circulation, and ILL. **Computerized Information Services:** DIALOG Information Services, MEDLARS, CAN/OLE, BRS Information Technologies, UTLAS; CD-ROMs (ABI/INFORM, Canadian Business and Current Affairs); Envoy 100 (electronic mail service). Performs searches on fee basis. **Remarks:** FAX: (204)261-9281. Telex: 07 587721. Electronic mail address(es): UM.LIB.ADMIN; ILL.MWU (both Envoy 100).

★18785★
University of Manitoba - Architecture & Fine Arts Library (Art, Plan)
206 Architecture Bldg.   Phone: (204)474-9216
Winnipeg, MB, Canada R3T 2N2   Mary Lochhead, Hd.Libn.
Founded: 1916. **Staff:** Prof 2; Other 9. **Subjects:** Architecture, interior design, fine arts, city planning, landscape architecture, environmental studies. **Holdings:** 61,500 volumes; 1200 maps; 700 art reproductions; 500 student projects; 5000 product catalogs; 50 VF drawers of miscellaneous material. **Subscriptions:** 450 journals and other serials. **Services:** Interlibrary loan. **Automated Operations:** Computerized cataloging, acquisitions, serials, circulation, and ILL. **Computerized Information Services:** CD-ROM (Art Index). **Special Indexes:** Indexes to maps, vertical file, reproductions, and product catalogs. **Remarks:** FAX: (204)269-8357. Electronic mail address(es): UM.LIB.ADMIN; ILL.MWU (both Envoy 100). **Staff:** Love Negrych, Ref.Libn.

★18786★
University of Manitoba - D.S. Woods Education Library (Educ)
100 Education Bldg.   Phone: (204)474-9976
Winnipeg, MB, Canada R3T 2N2   David Thirlwall, Hd.
Founded: 1935. **Staff:** Prof 3; Other 10. **Subjects:** Education, physical education. **Special Collections:** Manitoba school textbooks (18,000 volumes). **Holdings:** 64,000 volumes; 431,000 ERIC microfiche. **Subscriptions:** 625 journals and other serials. **Services:** Interlibrary loan; library open to the public. **Automated Operations:** Computerized cataloging, acquisitions, serials, circulation, and ILL. **Computerized Information Services:** UTLAS, DIALOG Information Services, CAN/OLE, BRS Information Technologies; Envoy 100 (electronic mail service). Performs searches on fee basis. **Special Indexes:** KWIC Indexes to Records, Adolescent Literature, Standardized Tests. **Remarks:** FAX: (204)261-9282. Telex: 07 587721. Electronic mail address(es): UM.LIB.ADMIN; ILL.MWU (both Envoy 100). **Staff:** Richard Ellis, Ref.Libn.; Sheila Andrich, Ref.Libn.

★18787★
University of Manitoba - Donald W. Craik Engineering Library (Sci-Engr)
351 Engineering Bldg.   Phone: (204)474-6360
Winnipeg, MB, Canada R3T 2N2   Norma Godavari, Hd.
Founded: 1907. **Staff:** Prof 2; Other 5. **Subjects:** Engineering - civil, electrical, computer, agricultural, geological, mechanical, industrial. **Holdings:** 68,000 volumes; 30,800 government publications; 20,000 microfiche. **Subscriptions:** 720 journals and other serials. **Services:** Interlibrary loan; SDI; library open to the public. **Automated Operations:** Computerized cataloging, acquisitions, serials, circulation, and ILL. **Computerized Information Services:** CAN/OLE, Infomart Online, DIALOG Information Services, QL Systems, MEDLINE, UTLAS, BRS Information Technologies; BITNET, Envoy 100 (electronic mail services). Performs searches on fee basis. **Special Indexes:** KWIC Index to Standards. **Remarks:** FAX: (204)261-9234. Telex: 07 587721. Electronic mail address(es): NGODAVA@CCM.UMANITOBA.CA (BITNET); N.GODAVARI (Envoy 100). **Staff:** Bharpur Khangura, Ref.

★18788★
University of Manitoba - E.K. Williams Law Library (Law)
401 Robson Hall   Phone: (204)474-9995
Winnipeg, MB, Canada R3T 2N2   Neil Campbell, Hd.Libn.
Founded: 1922. **Staff:** Prof 3; Other 11. **Subjects:** Law. **Holdings:** 138,000 volumes; 56,000 microfiche. **Subscriptions:** 1800 journals and other serials.

Services: Interlibrary loan; reference service for members of legal profession residing in Manitoba. **Automated Operations:** Computerized cataloging, serials, circulation, and ILL. **Computerized Information Services:** QL Systems, UTLAS, WESTLAW, DIALOG Information Services, LEXIS, Info Globe, CAN/LAW; Envoy 100, BITNET (electronic mail services). Performs searches on fee basis for members of the legal profession. **Publications:** Bibliographies - to legal professionals. **Remarks:** FAX: (204)275-5266. Telex: 07 587721. Electronic mail address(es): UM.LIB.ADMIN; ILL.MWU (both Envoy 100); CAMPBELL@CCM.UMANITOBA.CA (BITNET). **Staff:** Debra Bedford Benson, Cat.; John Eaton, Ref.

★ 18789 ★
University of Manitoba - Elizabeth Dafoe Library (Hum, Soc Sci, Area-Ethnic)
Winnipeg, MB, Canada R3T 2N2   Phone: (204)474-9844
                                      Nicole Michaud-Oystryk
Founded: 1885. **Staff:** Prof 12; Other 39. **Subjects:** Humanities, social sciences, nursing, social work, human ecology. **Special Collections:** Slavic collection (55,000 volumes); Icelandic collection (25,000 volumes); rare books, including incunabula and medieval manuscripts (35,000 volumes); university archives (1278 linear feet); manuscript collection specializing in prairie literature and Western Canadian agricultural history (561 linear feet); Winnipeg Tribune collection of newspaper clippings (11,000 subject files) and photographs (250,000). **Holdings:** 792,000 volumes; 411,000 government publications; 523,000 microfiche; 48,000 reels of microfilm; 97,000 maps; theses. **Subscriptions:** 4600 journals and other serials. **Services:** Interlibrary loan; SDI; library open to the public with restrictions. **Automated Operations:** Computerized cataloging, acquisitions, serials, circulation, and ILL. **Computerized Information Services:** DIALOG Information Services, CAN/OLE, BRS Information Technologies, WILSONLINE, UTLAS, MEDLARS; internal databases; Envoy 100 (electronic mail service). Performs searches on fee basis. Contact Person: Sharon Tully, 474-6590. **Special Indexes:** KWIC Indexes to Microform Collections, Uncataloged Collections, Photographs, Theses, University Publications, Patents. **Remarks:** FAX: (204)275-2597. Telex: 07 587721. Electronic mail address(es): ILL.MWU (Envoy 100). **Staff:** Jim Blanchard, Hd., Ref.; June Dutka, Hd., Govt.Pubns.; Richard E. Bennett, Hd., Archv./Spec.Coll.; Nevenka West, Hd., Slavic Coll.; Sigrid Johnson, Icelandic Coll.

★ 18790 ★
University of Manitoba - Medical Library (Med)
Medical College Bldg.
770 Bannatyne Ave.   Phone: (204)788-6342
Winnipeg, MB, Canada R3T 0W3   Michael Tennenhouse, Act.Hd.
Founded: 1895. **Staff:** Prof 5; Other 17. **Subjects:** Medicine and basic medical sciences. **Special Collections:** History of Medicine. **Holdings:** 106,000 volumes. **Subscriptions:** 1500 journals and other serials. **Services:** Interlibrary loan; reference services for members of the medical profession residing in Manitoba; library open to qualified users. **Automated Operations:** Computerized cataloging, acquisitions, serials, circulation, and ILL. **Computerized Information Services:** UTLAS, MEDLINE, DIALOG Information Services, BRS Information Technologies, MEDLARS, CAN/OLE, DOBIS Canadian Online Library System; Envoy 100, BITNET (electronic mail services). Performs searches on fee basis. Contact Person: Keir Reavie, Pub.Serv.Libn. **Publications:** Bibliographies - to medical professionals. **Remarks:** FAX: (204)772-0094. Telex: 07 587721. Electronic mail address(es): ILL.MWM (Envoy 100); MTENNEN@CCM.UMANITOBA.CA (BITNET). **Staff:** Beverly Brown, Cat.; Natalia Pohorecky, Ref.Libn.; H. Davoodifar, Ext.Libn.

★ 18791 ★
University of Manitoba - Music Library (Mus)
223 Music Bldg.   Phone: (204)474-9567
Winnipeg, MB, Canada R3T 2N2   Vladimir Simosko, Hd.
Founded: 1965. **Staff:** Prof 1; Other 2. **Subjects:** Music reference and research, historical musicology, instruments and voice, theory and analysis of music. **Holdings:** 17,700 volumes; 6000 phonograph records; 32,500 items of performance music; composers' works and scores. **Subscriptions:** 150 journals and other serials. **Services:** Interlibrary loan; library open to the public with restrictions on borrowing. **Automated Operations:** Computerized cataloging, acquisitions, serials, circulation, and ILL. **Computerized Information Services:** UTLAS, DIALOG Information Services, CAN/OLE; Envoy 100 (electronic mail service). Performs searches on fee basis. Contact Person: Sharon Tully, 474-6590. **Special Indexes:** KWIC Indexes to Performance Tapes, Sound Recordings, Performance Music. **Remarks:** FAX: (204)275-0800. Telex: 07 587721. Electronic mail address(es): UM.LIB.ADMIN; ILL.MWU (both Envoy 100).

★ 18792 ★
University of Manitoba - Neilson Dental Library (Med)
780 Bannatyne Ave.   Phone: (204)788-6635
Winnipeg, MB, Canada R3E 0W3   Anne Thornton-Trump, Hd.Libn.
Founded: 1958. **Staff:** Prof 1; Other 3. **Subjects:** Dentistry, dental hygiene. **Holdings:** 23,400 volumes; 1500 pamphlets. **Subscriptions:** 380 journals and other serials. **Services:** Interlibrary loan; library open to medical and dental professionals. **Automated Operations:** Computerized circulation. **Computerized Information Services:** UTLAS, MEDLINE, CAN/OLE; Envoy 100 (electronic mail service). Performs searches on fee basis. **Remarks:** FAX: (204)774-2539. Electronic mail address(es): ILL.MWUD (Envoy 100).

★ 18793 ★
University of Manitoba - St. John's College - Library (Hum, Rel-Phil)
400 Dysart Rd.   Phone: (204)474-8542
Winnipeg, MB, Canada R3T 2M5   Patrick D. Wright, Libn.
Founded: 1849. **Staff:** Prof 1; Other 2. **Subjects:** Religion, Canadian studies, humanities. **Holdings:** 60,000 volumes. **Subscriptions:** 150 journals and other serials. **Services:** Interlibrary loan; library open to the public. **Remarks:** FAX: (204)275-1498.

★ 18794 ★
University of Manitoba - St. Paul's College - Library (Rel-Phil)
119 St. Paul's College   Phone: (204)474-8585
Winnipeg, MB, Canada R3T 2M6   Earle C. Ferguson, Act.Hd.
Founded: 1931. **Staff:** Prof 1; Other 3. **Subjects:** Theology, philosophy, history, English literature. **Special Collections:** Index Thomisticus; Vatican archives on microfilm (transactions and correspondence pertaining to Canada, 1668 to present; in progress). **Holdings:** 75,000 volumes. **Subscriptions:** 120 journals and other serials. **Services:** Interlibrary loan; library open to the public. **Automated Operations:** Computerized circulation. **Publications:** List of new acquisitions. **Remarks:** FAX: (204)275-5421.

★ 18795 ★
University of Manitoba - Science Library (Biol Sci, Sci-Engr)
211 Machray Hall   Phone: (204)474-8171
Winnipeg, MB, Canada R3T 2N2   Ada M. Ducas, Hd., Sci.Lib.
Founded: 1906. **Staff:** Prof 4; Other 9. **Subjects:** Physical, mathematical, earth, and biological sciences; computer science; pharmacy; statistics; botany; chemistry; astronomy; zoology. **Holdings:** 131,000 volumes. **Subscriptions:** 1170 journals and other serials. **Services:** Interlibrary loan; library open to the public with restrictions. **Automated Operations:** Computerized cataloging, acquisitions, serials, circulation, and ILL. **Computerized Information Services:** CAN/OLE, MEDLARS, DIALOG Information Services, UTLAS, BRS Information Technologies; Envoy 100 (electronic mail service). Performs searches on fee basis. **Remarks:** FAX: (204)275-3492. Telex: 07 587721. Electronic mail address(es): UM.LIB.ADMIN; ILL.MWU (both Envoy 100). **Staff:** M. Gregg, Ref.Libn.; L. Newell, Ref.Libn.; M. Speare, Ref.Libn.

★ 18796 ★
University of Mary - Library (Rel-Phil)
7500 University Dr.   Phone: (701)255-7500
Bismarck, ND 58504   Cheryl M. Bailey, Dir.
Founded: 1959. **Staff:** Prof 2; Other 3. **Subjects:** Theology, philosophy, education, music, history, nursing, business. **Holdings:** 50,000 books; 2000 bound periodical volumes; 5000 records, audiocassettes, videocassettes; 2000 reels of microfilm of back files of magazines. **Subscriptions:** 495 journals and other serials. **Services:** Interlibrary loan; copying; library open to the public with restrictions. **Computerized Information Services:** OCLC. **Networks/Consortia:** Member of North Dakota Network for Knowledge, Northwest AHEC Library Information Network, MINITEX Library Information Network. **Remarks:** FAX: (701)255-7690.

★ 18797 ★
University of Mary Hardin-Baylor - Townsend Memorial Library (Educ)
9th & Wells
UMHB Sta., Box 8016   Phone: (817)939-4637
Belton, TX 76513   Robert Strong, Libn.
Founded: 1845. **Staff:** Prof 4; Other 2.5. **Subjects:** Education, religion, business, nursing. **Special Collections:** McFadden-Texas Collection; Bell

County History; University Archives and History. **Holdings:** 83,000 books; 11,500 bound periodical volumes; 70,000 microforms. **Subscriptions:** 822 journals and other serials; 8 newspapers. **Services:** Interlibrary loan; copying; library open to the public for reference use only. **Automated Operations:** Computerized cataloging and ILL. **Computerized Information Services:** OCLC, DIALOG Information Services, OCLC EPIC, PRODIGY. **Networks/Consortia:** Member of AMIGOS Bibliographic Council, Inc. **Remarks:** FAX: (817)939-4642. Contains the holdings of the former Central Counties Center for Mental Health & Mental Retardation Services - Information Resource Center. **Staff:** Denise Karimkhani, Asst.Libn.; Teresa Buck, Asst.Libn.; Audrey Giles, Asst.Libn.

★18798★
University of Maryland - Center for Environmental & Estuarine Studies - Chesapeake Biological Laboratory - Library (Biol Sci)
Box 38   Phone: (410)326-4281
Solomons, MD 20688   Kathleen A. Heil, Libn.
Founded: 1925. **Staff:** Prof 1. **Subjects:** Fisheries research; marine research, biology, zoology; oceanography; aquatic microbiology; ecosystems studies; environmental chemistry and toxicology. **Special Collections:** Freshwater sponge reprints; shellfish reprints (1200); larvel fishes reprints (7000). **Holdings:** 5000 books; 25,000 bound periodical volumes; 3500 reports and documents; 2000 manuscripts; 1000 archival items; 10,000 reprints; 55 VF drawers of laboratory publications; 600 retrospective titles. **Subscriptions:** 202 journals and other serials. **Services:** Interlibrary loan; copying; SDI; library open to the public for reference use only. **Computerized Information Services:** DIALOG Information Services. **Networks/Consortia:** Member of Maryland Interlibrary Organization (MILO). **Publications:** Newsletter, monthly; annual bibliography of serials - both for internal distribution only. **Remarks:** FAX: (410)326-6342.

★18799★
University of Maryland - School of Medicine - Department of Psychiatry - Helen C. Tingley Memorial Library (Med)
Maryland Psychiatric Research Ctr.
Box 21247   Phone: (301)455-7667
Catonsville, MD 21228   Nancy Flowers, Libn.
Staff: Prof 1. **Subjects:** Psychiatry, allied health sciences. **Holdings:** 400 volumes; 50 bound periodical volumes; 50 audio cassettes; 50 reference works. **Subscriptions:** 15 journals and other serials. **Services:** Interlibrary loan; library not open to the public.

★18800★
University of Maryland, Baltimore - Health Sciences Library (Med)
111 S. Greene St.   Phone: (301)328-7545
Baltimore, MD 21201   Frieda O. Weise, Dir.
Founded: 1813. **Staff:** Prof 24; Other 36. **Subjects:** Medicine, dentistry, pharmacy, nursing, social work. **Special Collections:** Crawford Medical Historical Collection; Cordell Medical Historical Collection; Grieves Dental Historical Collection; historical book collections in pharmacy, social work, and nursing. **Holdings:** 148,119 books; 153,921 bound periodical volumes; University of Maryland archives. **Subscriptions:** 2968 journals and other serials. **Services:** Interlibrary loan; copying; library open to qualified public for reference use only. **Automated Operations:** Computerized cataloging, serials, and circulation. **Computerized Information Services:** OCLC, DIALOG Information Services, BRS Information Technologies, Current Contents, MEDLINE, MICROMEDEX; internal databases; BITNET (electronic mail service). Performs searches on fee basis. Contact Person: M.J. Tooey, Asst.Dir., Info.Serv., 328-7373. **Networks/Consortia:** Member of National Network of Libraries of Medicine - Southeastern/Atlantic Region, PALINET, Maryland Interlibrary Organization (MILO). **Remarks:** FAX: (301)328-8403. Electronic mail address(es): FWEISE@UMAB (BITNET). **Staff:** Diana Cunningham, Assoc.Dir., Rsrc.Mgt.; Gary Freiburger, Asst.Dir., Sys./Automation.

★18801★
University of Maryland, Baltimore - School of Law - Marshall Law Library (Law)
20 N. Paca St.   Phone: (410)328-7185
Baltimore, MD 21201   Barbara S. Gontrum, Dir.
Founded: 1843. **Staff:** Prof 12; Other 19. **Subjects:** Law. **Special Collections:** U.S. Government document depository. **Holdings:** 305,000 volumes; microforms. **Subscriptions:** 4246 journals and other serials. **Services:** Interlibrary loan; copying; library open to the public. **Automated Operations:** Computerized public access catalog, cataloging, and circulation. **Computerized Information Services:** LEXIS, OCLC, DIALOG Information Services, WESTLAW. **Networks/Consortia:** Member of PALINET. **Remarks:** FAX: (410)328-8354. **Staff:** David Grahek, Assoc.Dir.; Pamela Bluh, Asst.Dir., Tech.Serv.; Maxine Grosshans, Res.Libn.; Dennis Guion, Asst.Dir., Info.Serv.; Deborah McCalpin, Info.Serv.Libn.; Peter Burslem, Sys.Libn.

★18802★
University of Maryland, Cambridge - Horn Point Environmental Lab - Library (Biol Sci)
Box 775   Phone: (301)228-8200
Cambridge, MD 21613   Darlene Windsor, Lib.Techn.
Founded: 1973. **Staff:** Prof 1. **Subjects:** Marine sciences, oceanography, seafood science, fisheries, aquaculture, water quality, water resources. **Special Collections:** Reprints (5000); Environmental Protection Agency reports (975); Contribution numbers (450); National Resource Inventory (NRI) reference numbers (596); U.S. Fish & Wildlife Service reports (80). **Holdings:** 1439 books; 1312 bound periodical volumes; 300 unbound reports; 61 theses; 2450 microfiche; 84 reels of microfilm; 10 file cabinets of reprints. **Subscriptions:** 80 journals and other serials. **Services:** Interlibrary loan; copying; library open to the public. **Computerized Information Services:** DIALOG Information Services; Enable (internal database); SCIENCEnet, Telmail (electronic mail services). **Networks/Consortia:** Member of Maryland Interlibrary Organization (MILO). **Publications:** Contributions (1973-1983). **Remarks:** FAX: (301)476-5490.

★18803★
University of Maryland, College Park - College of Library & Information Services - Library (Info Sci)
Hornbake Library Bldg., Rm. 4105   Phone: (301)405-2066
College Park, MD 20742   William G. Wilson, Libn.
Founded: 1965. **Staff:** Prof 1; Other 5. **Subjects:** Organization of knowledge, bibliography, administration, information science, computer applications for libraries, juvenile books, communication. **Holdings:** 51,500 books; 8000 bound periodical volumes; 2000 pamphlets; 150 VF drawers of pamphlets and reports; 21,000 microforms; 1500 nonprint items (540 titles); 100 software programs. **Subscriptions:** 325 journals and other serials. **Services:** Interlibrary loan; copying; library open to the public with limited circulation. **Automated Operations:** Computerized cataloging, acquisitions, and serials. **Computerized Information Services:** Internal database. **Publications:** Orientation handouts. **Remarks:** FAX: (301)314-9145.

★18804★
University of Maryland, College Park - College of Library & Information Services - U.S. Information Center for the Universal Decimal Classification (Info Sci)
College Park, MD 20742   Phone: (301)405-2057
                                Hans H. Wellisch, Dir.
Staff: Prof 1. **Subjects:** Universal Decimal Classification (UDC). **Special Collections:** UDC schedules in English and in the major languages of Europe and Asia. **Holdings:** 500 books. **Services:** Interlibrary loan; copying; center open to the public. **Remarks:** FAX: (301)314-9145.

★18805★
University of Maryland, College Park - Computer Science Center - Program Library (Info Sci, Comp Sci)
College Park, MD 20742   Phone: (301)405-4261
                                Barbara Rush, Mgr., Lib.Serv.
Founded: 1963. **Staff:** Prof 2; Other 2. **Subjects:** Computer science, information science, mathematics, statistics. **Special Collections:** System Reference Libraries for UNIVAC 1100 series; reference manuals for IBM CMS; Digital Equipment Corporation Reference Collection. **Holdings:** 3500 books; 750 bound periodical volumes; 5000 technical reports; 30 computer newsletters from universities; 300 software packages for IBM and Macintosh personal computers. **Subscriptions:** 200 journals and other serials. **Services:** Copying; library open to the public for reference use only. **Automated Operations:** Computerized public access catalog. **Computerized Information Services:** CD-ROM (Computer Select); BITNET (electronic mail service). **Remarks:** FAX: (301)314-9220. Electronic mail address(es): PLBARB@UMDD.UMD.EDU (BITNET). Center provides microcomputers for faculty and staff for short loan periods. **Staff:** Kathy Campoli, Asst.Libn.

★ 18806 ★
University of Maryland, College Park - M. Lucia James Curriculum Laboratory (Educ)
Division of Educational Technology Center
College of Education   Phone: (301)405-3173
College Park, MD 20742   Frances Weinstein, Libn.
Staff: Prof 1; Other 4. **Subjects:** Education - elementary, secondary, teacher, special, art, early childhood, curriculum development; guidance and counseling. **Special Collections:** Curriculum guides from many states and major U.S. (5900); Microcomputer Courseware (95); special subject collections by subject/name. **Holdings:** 18,500 volumes; reports of curriculum projects; 1860 multimedia kits and manipulative teaching aids; 48 VF drawers; 28 VF drawers of resource materials; 894 standardized test specimen sets. **Services:** Copying; transparency making; laboratory open to the public for reference use only. **Publications:** Bibliographies; recent acquisitions and special reports on curriculum materials - to students, staff, and faculty of the College of Education.

★ 18807 ★
University of Maryland, College Park - Maryland Center for Quality and Productivity - Library (Bus-Fin)
College of Business and Management   Phone: (301)405-2189
College Park, MD 20742   Tom Tuttle, Dir.
Founded: 1977. **Staff:** Prof 4; Other 3. **Subjects:** Productivity, productivity measurement, management development, participative management, labor-management cooperation, gainsharing. **Holdings:** 1100 books. **Subscriptions:** 30 journals and other serials. **Publications:** Maryland Workplace (newsletter), bimonthly - free upon request. **Remarks:** FAX: (301)454-0179.

★ 18808 ★
University of Maryland, College Park - National Clearinghouse for Commuter Programs (Soc Sci, Trans)
1195 Stamp Student Union   Phone: (301)314-5274
College Park, MD 20742   Dr. Barbara Jacoby, Dir.
Staff: Prof 1; Other 2. **Subjects:** Student commuters, housing, transportation, tenant/landlord relations, orientation. **Holdings:** 8 VF drawers of manuscripts, reports, and handbooks. **Services:** Copying; clearinghouse open to the public by appointment. **Publications:** The Commuter, quarterly - to members; Serving Commuter Students: Examples of Good Practice; Commuter Students: References & Resources. **Remarks:** FAX: (301)314-9634.

★ 18809 ★
University of Maryland, College Park Libraries - Architecture Library (Art, Plan)
College Park, MD 20742   Phone: (301)405-6317
                                              Leslie E. Abrams, Hd.
Founded: 1967. **Staff:** Prof 1; Other 2. **Subjects:** Architecture, urban design. **Special Collections:** Collection on world expositions, 1851-1937 (500 volumes, pamphlets, clippings, engravings, and memorabilia). **Holdings:** 33,800 books; 6000 bound periodical volumes. **Subscriptions:** 137 journals and other serials. **Services:** Interlibrary loan; copying; library open to the public for reference use only. **Automated Operations:** Computerized public access catalog, cataloging, acquisitions, and circulation. **Publications:** Access to Architectural Literature (series of research and informational guides). **Remarks:** FAX: (301)314-9583.

★ 18810 ★
University of Maryland, College Park Libraries - Architecture Library - National Trust for Historic Preservation Library Collection (Plan)
College Park, MD 20742   Phone: (301)405-6320
                                              Sally R. Sims Stokes, Cur.
Founded: 1949. **Staff:** Prof 1; Other 3. **Subjects:** All aspects of historic preservation including architecture, tax incentives, building restoration, zoning. **Special Collections:** Postcards, 1903-1914 (18,500); National Park Service historic structures reports repository. **Holdings:** 12,000 books; bound periodical volumes; 13,000 vertical files; 1000 microfiche of newspaper clippings; research reports. **Subscriptions:** 300 journals and other serials. **Services:** Library open to the public by appointment for research. **Automated Operations:** Computerized cataloging, acquisitions, and circulation. **Computerized Information Services:** OCLC. **Special Indexes:** G.K. Hall Index to Historic Preservation Periodicals (index to articles in periodicals received in the National Trust Library, 1988); Supplement, 1992. **Remarks:** FAX: (301)314-9583.

★ 18811 ★
University of Maryland, College Park Libraries - Art Library (Art)
College Park, MD 20742   Phone: (301)405-9061
                                              Courtney A. Shaw, Hd.Libn.
Founded: 1979. **Staff:** Prof 2; Other 2. **Subjects:** Art history, studio art, art education, decorative and applied arts, historic textiles and photography. **Special Collections:** Decimal Index to the Art of the Low Countries; microfiche collections; Index photographique d'art de France; emblem books; Marburg Index; Alinari; art reproduction collection; picture collection; Index of American Design. **Holdings:** 76,776 books; VF drawers; 27,000 art reproduction files. **Subscriptions:** 351 journals; 284 serials. **Services:** Interlibrary loan; copying; library open to the public for reference use only. **Automated Operations:** Computerized public access catalog, cataloging, acquisitions, and circulation. **Computerized Information Services:** DIALOG Information Services, RLIN, OCLC, OCLC EPIC; CD-ROM (Art Index); InterNet (electronic mail service). Performs searches on fee basis. **Publications:** Directory of Maryland Artists; Art Related Bookstores in the Washington Metropolitan Area; Directory of Local Art Museums. **Remarks:** FAX: (301)314-9146. Electronic mail address(es): CS20@UMAIL.UMD.EDU (InterNet).

★ 18812 ★
University of Maryland, College Park Libraries - Charles E. White Memorial Library (Sci-Engr)
College Park, MD 20742   Phone: (301)405-9078
                                              Elizabeth W. McElroy, Hd.
Staff: Prof 2; Other 2. **Subjects:** Chemistry, biochemistry, microbiology, nuclear chemistry. **Holdings:** 55,000 books; 28,500 bound periodical volumes; 2000 cartridges of microfilm; 1300 dissertations. **Subscriptions:** 550 journals and other serials. **Services:** Interlibrary loan; copying; library open to the public for reference use only. **Automated Operations:** Computerized cataloging and circulation. **Computerized Information Services:** OCLC, DIALOG Information Services, MEDLINE, STN International, Chemical Abstracts Service (CAS); CD-ROMs (MEDLINE, Science Citation Index). Performs searches on fee basis. **Staff:** Sylvia D. Evans.

★ 18813 ★
University of Maryland, College Park Libraries - Engineering & Physical Sciences Library (Sci-Engr)
College Park, MD 20742   Phone: (301)405-9157
                                              Herbert N. Foerstel, Hd., Br.Libs.
Founded: 1953. **Staff:** Prof 6; Other 11. **Subjects:** Aeronautics and astronautics; astronomy; computer science; electronics; engineering - aerospace, chemical, civil, electrical, industrial, mechanical; geology; materials science; mathematics; oceanography; physics; textile technology; transportation; space sciences. **Special Collections:** ANSI Standards; Patent Depository Library (complete patent backfile, 1789 to present); R. von Mises Collection (1100 titles; 217 boxes of reprints); Max Born Collection (theoretical mathematics and physics; 650 titles; 6 boxes of reprints); NASA Reference Report collection (complete set; 1 million documents on microfiche). **Holdings:** 150,000 books; 150,000 bound periodical volumes; 259,600 hardcopy reports; 1.84 million reports on microfiche; 220,000 reports on microcard; 11,187 reels of microfilm. **Subscriptions:** 2930 journals and other serials. **Services:** Interlibrary loan; copying; library open to the public for reference use only. **Automated Operations:** Computerized public access catalog, cataloging, acquisitions, and circulation. **Computerized Information Services:** DIALOG Information Services, DTIC, OCLC, Current Contents; CD-ROMs (Applied Science & Technology Index, CITIS, Dissertation Abstracts, MathSci, NTIS, SCI, Selected Water Resources Abstracts, Supertech Abstracts Plus, CASSIS/CD-ROM). **Publications:** New Books List, monthly - to departments and library representatives. **Staff:** Gloria Chawla; Judy Erickson; Jim Miller; Mary Pawlowski; Dave Wilt.

★ 18814 ★
University of Maryland, College Park Libraries - Hornbake Library - East Asia Collection (Area-Ethnic)
College Park, MD 20742-7011   Phone: (301)405-9133
                                              Frank Joseph Shulman, Cur.
Founded: 1963. **Staff:** Prof 3; Other 1. **Subjects:** Social sciences (Japanese, Chinese, and Korean languages); modern Japanese, Chinese, and Korean history, literature, and culture. **Holdings:** 60,000 books; 17,000 bound periodical volumes; 500 reels of microfilm. **Subscriptions:** 800 journals and other serials; 29 newspapers. **Services:** Interlibrary loan; collection open to the public for reference use only. **Staff:** Kuang-Yao Fan; Kenneth Tanaka; Connie Tomita Galmeijer.

★ 18815 ★
University of Maryland, College Park Libraries - Hornbake Library -
  Government Documents/Map Room (Info Sci, Geog-Map)
College Park, MD 20742   Phone: (301)405-9165
                                    Hugh A. O'Connor, Hd., Govt.Docs/Maps
Staff: Prof 2; Other 4. **Subjects:** U.S. Federal Government documents,
maps, documents of international agencies. **Special Collections:** U.S.
Government documents regional depository (1 million); United Nations
documents (30,000); topographic maps (100,000). **Holdings:** 1 million
documents; 130,000 maps; 2000 reels of microfilm; 30 cabinets of microfiche.
Services: Interlibrary loan; copying; room open to the public. **Computerized**
Information Services: DIALOG Information Services, OCLC, LEGI-
SLATE, LEXIS; CD-ROMs. Performs searches free of charge in most cases.
Networks/Consortia: Member of Maryland Interlibrary Organization
(MILO). **Remarks:** FAX: (301)314-9416.

★ 18816 ★
University of Maryland, College Park Libraries - Hornbake Library -
  Marylandia Department (Rare Book)
College Park, MD 20742-7011   Phone: (301)405-9212
                                                Peter H. Curtis, Cur.
Staff: Prof 2; Other 2. **Subjects:** Maryland history - political, social,
economic, industrial, agricultural. **Special Collections:** Maryland state,
county, and municipal documents (400 linear feet); maps of Maryland and
Chesapeake Bay region; University of Maryland, College Park theses and
dissertations. **Holdings:** 60,000 volumes; 50 drawers of maps. **Subscriptions:**
300 journals and other serials. **Services:** Department open to the public for
reference use only. **Computerized Information Services:** Internal database.
Remarks: FAX: (301)314-9419.

★ 18817 ★
University of Maryland, College Park Libraries - McKeldin Library -
  Gordon W. Prange Collection & Archive (Area-Ethnic)
College Park, MD 20742-7011   Phone: (301)405-9348
                                          Paul S. Koda, Prange Coll.Proj.Dir.
Founded: 1963. **Staff:** Prof 3; Other 3. **Subjects:** World War II (Pacific area).
Special Collections: Allied Occupation of Japan, 1945-1952 (50,000
Japanese-language monographs; 13,000 titles of Japanese magazines; 17,000
titles of Japanese newspapers; 24 file cabinets of unique censored materials
from Supreme Commander, Allied Powers' Censorship Detachment);
papers of Justin Williams, Sr. (69 filing boxes of material relating to political
aspects of the Allied Occupation of Japan). **Services:** Collection and
Archives open for scholarly use only. **Publications:** Microfilm Edition of
Censored Periodicals, 1945-1949 (User's Guide to the Gordon W. Prange
Collection, I). **Special Catalogs:** Newspapers and periodicals from period of
Allied Occupation of Japan (card files); guide to Justin Williams Papers.
Remarks: FAX: (301)314-9408.

★ 18818 ★
University of Maryland, College Park Libraries - McKeldin Library -
  Historical Manuscripts and Archives Department (Hist)
College Park, MD 20742-7011   Phone: (301)405-9058
                                                Lauren R. Brown, Cur.
Founded: 1972. **Staff:** Prof 2; Other 1. **Special Collections:** Personal and
organizational papers related to the Maryland region (Thomas Bray papers;
Maryland Division/American Association of University Women Archives);
papers of leading Maryland political leaders and organizations (Millard
Tydings papers; Maryland League of Women Voters Archives); archives of
trade unions (Cigar Makers; Marine & Shipbuilding Workers; Tobacco
Workers; Bakery & Confectionery Workers); Cuba Company Archives;
Association for Childhood Education International Archives; Association
for Intercollegiate Athletics for Women Archives; Maryland Sheet Music
Collection; University of Maryland, College Park archives (archival record
groups; university publications; faculty papers; photographs; memorabilia);
National Public Broadcasting Archives. **Holdings:** 10,500 cubic feet.
Services: Department open to the public for reference use only.
Publications: Personal and Organizational Papers Relating to Maryland,
1978; Greenbelt: A Guide to Further Sources, 1981; University Fact Book,
1981. **Remarks:** FAX: (301)314-9416. **Staff:** Anne Turkos, Asst.Cur.

★ 18819 ★
University of Maryland, College Park Libraries - McKeldin Library -
  Katherine Anne Porter Library (Hum)
College Park, MD 20742-7011   Phone: (301)405-9255
                                            Blanche Ebeling-Koning, Cur.
Founded: 1968. **Staff:** Prof 1; Other 1. **Subjects:** The personal library and
memorabilia of author Katherine Anne Porter. **Holdings:** 5000 books.
Services: library open to the public for reference use only. **Networks/**
Consortia: Member of Colorado Alliance of Research Libraries (CARL).
Remarks: FAX: (301)454-9485.

★ 18820 ★
University of Maryland, College Park Libraries - McKeldin Library -
  Rare Books and Literary Manuscripts Department (Rare Book)
College Park, MD 20742-7011   Phone: (301)405-9255
                                            Blanche T. Ebeling-Koning, Cur.
Staff: Prof 1. **Subjects:** Rare books and manuscripts in a wide range of
scholarly fields. **Special Collections:** Djuna Barnes Collection; Katherine
Anne Porter Collection; Freytag von Loringhoven Collection; manuscripts
of contemporary American and British authors, including T.S. Eliot, Robert
Frost, William Faulkner, John Dos Passos, Thom Gunn, Carl Bode,
Ferdinand Reyher, Reed Whittemore, and Ernest Hemingway; history of
books, typography, and printing; William Morris and the Kelmscott Press;
German Expressionism; Mazarinades; 19th and 20th century American and
British literature; Savoy regional history; 16th-19th century French politics
and economics; French and Spanish drama; pamphlets on slavery. **Holdings:**
60,000 books. **Services:** Department open to the public for reference use
only. **Networks/Consortia:** Member of Colorado Alliance of Research
Libraries (CARL). **Special Indexes:** Guide to the William Morris Collection
(typescript); inventory of the Bode, Reyher, Whittemore, Barnes, and Porter
manuscript collections (typescript). **Remarks:** FAX: (301)454-4985.

★ 18821 ★
University of Maryland, College Park Libraries - Music Library (Mus)
College Park, MD 20742   Phone: (301)405-9215
                                                Neil Ratliff, Hd.
Founded: 1958. **Staff:** Prof 4. **Subjects:** Music, dance. **Special Collections:**
American Bandmasters Association Research Center; Music Educators
National Conference Historical Center; College Band Directors National
Association Archives; National Association of College Wind and Percussion
Instructors Research Center; International Clarinet Society Research
Center; Archives of the Music Library Association; Archives of the United
States Branch of the International Association of Music Libraries, Archives,
and Documentation Centers; The Irving and Margery Lowens Collection of
Musical Americana and Music Criticism; Jacob Coopersmith Collection of
Handeliana; Wallenstein Collection of Orchestra Music (29,628 items);
Contemporary Music Project (CMP) Lending Service; Archives of the
American Society of University Composers; Archives of the International
Society for Music Education; Archives of the Society for Ethnomusicology;
Archives of the Mid-West International Band and Orchestra Clinic.
Holdings: 40,000 volumes; 80,000 scores; 45,000 phonograph records; 671
VF drawers. **Subscriptions:** 324 journals and other serials. **Services:**
Interlibrary loan; copying; library open to the public for reference use only.
Automated Operations: Computerized cataloging, acquisitions, serials, and
circulation. **Computerized Information Services:** DIALOG Information
Services, PFDS Online. **Publications:** Guide to the Coopersmith Collection
of Handeliana at the University of Maryland; Catalog of the International
Clarinet Society Score Collection. **Staff:** Philip Vandermeer, Ref./
Circ.Libn.; Bruce D. Wilson, Cur., Spec.Coll.; Morgan Cundiff, Piano
Archv.Libn.

★ 18822 ★
University of Maryland, College Park Libraries - Music Library -
  International Piano Archives at Maryland (Mus)
Hornbake Library, 3210   Phone: (301)405-9215
College Park, MD 20742   Neil Ratliff, Hd.
Founded: 1965. **Staff:** Prof 2. **Subjects:** Music, performance practice, piano,
harpsichord. **Special Collections:** Archival papers and recordings of Abram
Chasins, Gary Graffman, Josef Hofmann, Jan Holcman, William Kapell,
Arthur Loesser, Jerome Lowenthal, Nadia Reisenberg, David Barnett, Erno
Balogh, Inga Hoegsbro Christensen, Artur Balsam, Joseph Bloch, Jorge
Bolet, Bruce Hungerford, Raymond Lewenthal, Margaret Leng Tan, and
Beveridge Webster. **Holdings:** 1800 books and pamphlets; 75 manuscripts;
8000 reproducing piano rolls; 15,000 33rpm phonograph records; 8500
78rpm phonograph records; 6000 piano scores; 1600 audiotapes; 1500
compact discs. **Services:** Copying; archives open to the public with
restrictions. **Publications:** IPAM Newsletter, irregular - free upon request.
Special Catalogs: Catalog of the Reproducing Piano Roll Collection.
Remarks: Alternate telephone number(s): 454-6903. **Staff:** Morgan Cundiff,
Piano Archv.Libn.

★ 18823 ★
University of Maryland, College Park Libraries - Nonprint Media
  Services (Aud-Vis)
Hornbake Library, Rm. 4210   Phone: (301)405-9236
College Park, MD 20742-7011   Allan C. Rough, Hd.
Founded: 1972. **Staff:** Prof 2; Other 10. **Special Collections:** Video cassettes
of Watergate hearings (162); NOVA (series) videocassettes (275); BBC

Shakespeare Series (complete plays on video cassette); U.S. Air Force Film Collection (600); U.S.D.A. Food and Nutrition Information Center's Deposit AV Collection (3500 items); Pioneers in Science and Technology (30 videocassettes); Maryland Public Television Archives (953 videocassettes); The Complete Iran Contra Hearings (100 videocassettes); The National Public Broadcasting Archives at Maryland, including The Corporation for Public Broadcasting (1000 videocassettes), National Association of Education Broadcasters, National Education Radio Archives (5600 reels of audiotapes). **Holdings:** 150 laser videodiscs; 48 slide sets; 1200 16mm films; 4500 videocassettes; 3200 audio cassettes. **Services:** Services open to public by arrangement with department head. **Automated Operations:** Computerized public access catalog and circulation. **Computerized Information Services:** InterNet (electronic mail service). **Publications:** Subject "Mediagraphies" (media bibliographies, 110). **Remarks:** FAX: (301)314-9419. Electronic mail address(es): AR21@UMAIL.UMD.EDU (InterNet). **Staff:** Angela Domanico, Oper.Supv.; Linda Sarigol, Film Unit Supv.; Jeffrey Wagner, Electronic Media Sys.Engr.; Carleton Jackson, Ref.Libn.

★ 18824 ★
University of Massachusetts - Cranberry Experiment Station (Agri)
Glen Charlie Rd.
Box 569
East Wareham, MA 02538
Phone: (508)295-2213
Irving E. Demoranville, Dept.Hd.
Subjects: Cranberry culture and history. **Holdings:** Figures not available. **Services:** Station open to the public.

★ 18825 ★
University of Massachusetts - Five College Astronomy Department - Astronomy Reading Room (Sci-Engr)
Graduate Research Tower B, Rm. 517G
Amherst, MA 01003
Phone: (413)545-4301
Subjects: Astronomy. **Holdings:** Preprints; journals. **Remarks:** FAX: (413)545-0648. Telex: 95-5491. Department serves Amherst College, Hampshire College, Mount Holyoke College, Smith College, and the University of Massachusetts.

★ 18826 ★
University of Massachusetts - Labor Relations & Research Center Library (Bus-Fin)
Draper Hall
Amherst, MA 01003
Phone: (413)545-3870
Janice Tausky, Libn.
Founded: 1965. **Staff:** 2. **Subjects:** Industrial relations. **Holdings:** 5000 books; 10,000 pamphlets. **Subscriptions:** 400 journals and other serials. **Services:** Interlibrary loan; copying; library open to the public with restrictions. **Computerized Information Services:** DIALOG Information Services. **Publications:** LRRC Library users' guide. **Staff:** Shameem Syed, Asst.Libn.

★ 18827 ★
University of Massachusetts - Library - Special Collections and Archives (Rare Book)
Amherst, MA 01003
Phone: (413)545-2780
Linda Seidman, Act.Lib.Hd.
Founded: 1867. **Staff:** Prof 1; Other 2. **Subjects:** History of botany and entomology to 1900; historical geography and cartography of Northeastern United States to 1900; history of Massachusetts and New England; antislavery movement in New England; travel and tourism in New England, New York, and eastern Canada; Massachusetts; African-American studies; labor and business history. **Special Collections:** Alspach Yeats Collection (600 items); Federal Land Bank Collection (cartography, county maps and atlases; 270 items); Robert Francis Collection (100 items); Binet French Revolution Collection (1524 items); Massachusetts Pamphlet Collection (985 items); Benjamin Smith Lyman Collection (Japan; 2000 items); Papers of W.E.B. Du Bois, Horace Mann Bond, Erasmus Darwin Hudson, John Haigis, Maurice Donahue, Sol Barkin, J. William Belanger, Kenyon Butterfield, Harvey Swados, Robert Francis, Joseph Obrebski, William Smith Clark, Thomas Copeland; Records of American Writing Paper Co., Northampton Cutlery Co., George H. Gilbert Co., Rodney HuntCo., Granite Cutters International Association, Carpenters unions of Western Massachusetts, New England Joint Board of Textile Workers Union of America, American Dialect Society, University of Massachusetts. **Holdings:** 19,000 books; 7000 linear feet of records, manuscripts, clippings, photographs, maps, building plans, microfilm, audiotapes. **Services:** Copying; collections open to the public. **Computerized Information Services:** OCLC. **Networks/Consortia:** Member of NELINET, Inc., HILC, Inc.

★ 18828 ★
University of Massachusetts - Massachusetts Water Resources Research Center - Library (Env-Cons)
Blaisdell House
Amherst, MA 01003
Phone: (413)545-2842
John R. Cole, Ph.D.
Founded: 1974. **Subjects:** Water resources, environment, acid precipitation. **Special Collections:** Acid Rain Monitoring Project (ARM) publications (data from 1982 to present); Massachusetts state-wide surface water monitoring. **Holdings:** 3000 books; 1000 bound periodical volumes. **Services:** Interlibrary loan; copying; library open to the public. **Automated Operations:** Computerized cataloging.

★ 18829 ★
University of Massachusetts - Morrill Biological & Geological Sciences Library (Biol Sci, Sci-Engr)
214 Morrill Science Center
Amherst, MA 01003
Phone: (413)545-2674
Laurence M. Feldman, Libn.
Founded: 1963. **Staff:** Prof 3; Other 6. **Subjects:** Biochemistry; biology; botany; entomology; environmental sciences; forestry, wildlife, and fisheries biology; geography; geology; microbiology; nursing; plant and soil sciences; plant pathology; public health; veterinary and animal sciences; zoology. **Special Collections:** Arthur Cleveland Bent (ornithology); Guy Chester Crampton (entomology and evolutionary biology). **Holdings:** 100,000 volumes; 125,000 maps. **Subscriptions:** 1000 journals and other serials. **Services:** Interlibrary loan; copying; library open to the public for reference use only; borrowing privileges upon application. **Computerized Information Services:** BRS Information Technologies, DIALOG Information Services. **Networks/Consortia:** Member of Boston Library Consortium (BLC), NELINET, Inc. **Publications:** New Acquisitions List, weekly - for internal and limited external distribution; Literature Guides, irregular - for internal distribution only. **Staff:** Alena Chadwick, Br.Libn.; James L. Craig, Biol.Sci.Libn.

★ 18830 ★
University of Massachusetts - Music Library (Mus)
Fine Arts Center, Rm. 149
Amherst, MA 01003
Phone: (413)545-2870
Pamela Juengling, Mus.Libn.
Staff: Prof 1; Other 3. **Subjects:** Music. **Special Collections:** Alma Werfel Collection; Howard LeBow Collection; Philip Bezanson papers. **Holdings:** 15,000 books; 4000 bound periodical volumes; 12,000 scores; 13,000 sound recordings; 600 other cataloged items. **Subscriptions:** 250 journals and other serials. **Services:** Interlibrary loan; copying; listening facilities; library open to the public. **Automated Operations:** Computerized cataloging and acquisitions. **Computerized Information Services:** DIALOG Information Services, BRS Information Technologies, NLM, OCLC. Performs searches on fee basis. Contact Person: Virginia Craig, 545-0150. **Networks/Consortia:** Member of NELINET, Inc. **Special Catalogs:** Catalog of recording analytics (card).

★ 18831 ★
University of Massachusetts - Physical Sciences Library (Sci-Engr)
Graduate Research Center
Amherst, MA 01003
Phone: (413)545-1370
Eric Esau, Libn.
Founded: 1971. **Staff:** Prof 3; Other 6. **Subjects:** Engineering - chemical, civil, electrical, industrial, mechanical; chemistry; physics and astronomy; mathematics and statistics; aeronautics and astronautics; computer science; food technology; polymer science; wood technology. **Holdings:** 115,000 books; 74,000 bound periodical volumes; 800,000 technical reports on microfiche; U.S. patents, 1950 to present. **Subscriptions:** 900 journals and other serials. **Services:** Interlibrary loan; copying; library open to the public for reference use only; borrowing privileges on application. **Automated Operations:** Computerized public access catalog, cataloging, acquisitions, and circulation. **Computerized Information Services:** DIALOG Information Services, U.S. Patent Classification System, STN International. **Networks/Consortia:** Member of Boston Library Consortium (BLC). **Staff:** Linda Arny, Ref./Asst.Br.Libn.; Selma Etter, Ref.Libn.

★ 18832 ★
University of Massachusetts at Boston, Harbor Campus - Joseph P. Healey Library - Dept. of Archives and Special Collections (Hist)
Boston, MA 02125
Phone: (617)287-5944
William P. Quinn, Act.Dir.
Founded: 1965. **Staff:** Prof 1; Other 2. **Subjects:** Local urban history, peace and social protest, social welfare institutions, Dorchester local history, community action. **Special Collections:** Massachusetts Society for the

Prevention of Cruelty to Children collection; Boston Children's Aid Society collection; Dorchester House collection; Gold Star Parents for Amnesty collection; Urban Planning Aid collection; New England Free Press collection; WGBH's Vietnam: A Television History Archives; Thompson's Island Collection. **Holdings:** 6000 books; 200 bound periodical volumes; 2000 feet of archival material. **Subscriptions:** 4 journals and other serials; 5 newspapers. **Services:** Copying; library open to the public. **Automated Operations:** Computerized public access catalog. **Publications:** A Guide to the Archives and Special Collections, 1991. **Staff:** Elizabeth R. Mock, Univ.Archv. & Cur. of Spec.Coll.

★ 18833 ★
University of Massachusetts at Dartmouth - Library Communications Center - Robert F. Kennedy Assassination Archive (Hist)
North Dartmouth, MA 02747   Phone: (508)999-8686
                                                  Helen Koss, Univ.Archv.
Founded: 1985. **Staff:** Prof 1; Other 1. **Subjects:** Robert F. Kennedy assassination, U.S. assassinations, political violence. **Special Collections:** Nelson-Castellano Collection; Robert Blair Kaiser Collection; Lowenstein-Stone Collection. **Holdings:** 100 books; 100 boxes of manuscripts; 300 audiotapes; 200 photographs. **Services:** Copying; archive open to the public with restrictions. **Automated Operations:** Computerized cataloging. **Computerized Information Services:** DIALOG Information Services, BRS Information Technologies. Performs searches on fee basis. Contact Person: Charles McNeil. **Networks/Consortia:** Member of NELINET, Inc., Southeastern Massachusetts Cooperating Libraries (SMCL). **Remarks:** FAX: (508)996-9759. **Formerly:** Southeastern Massachusetts University.

★ 18834 ★
University of Massachusetts at Lowell - Center for Lowell History (Hist)
40 French St.   Phone: (508)934-4998
Lowell, MA 01852   Martha Mayo, Dir.
Founded: 1971. **Staff:** Prof 2; Other 4. **Subjects:** Middlesex Canal; Lowell, Massachusetts; hydraulics; women in industry; textile manufacturing; immigrants; Warren H. Manning. **Special Collections:** Lowell Historical Society Collection; Middlesex Canal Collection; Proprietors of Locks & Canals Collection; Manning Collection; University Archives; Olney Collection (textile books); Boston & Maine Railroad Historical Society Collection; Lowell Museum Collection; Greater Lowell Chapter of the American Association of University Women Records; John I. Coggeshall Collection; Katherine Davis Collection; Paul E. Tsongas Collection; Jack Kerouac Collection; Flather Collection; Lambert Collection; Oral History Collection; Commodore Collection; Nursing Collection; Riddick Collection. **Holdings:** 28,000 volumes; records and manscripts; 6000 maps and plans; 1000 hours of oral histories; 30,000 photographs; 25 paintings; 2000 reels of microfilm. **Services:** Copying; photographic reproduction; collections open to the public. **Special Indexes:** Multiple cross index of photographs; inventories of most records and manuscript collections. **Remarks:** Alternate telephone number(s): 934-4998. **Formerly:** University of Lowell.

★ 18835 ★
University of Massachusetts Medical School & Worcester District Medical Society - Library (Med)
55 N. Lake Ave.   Phone: (508)856-2511
Worcester, MA 01655   Donald J. Morton, Lib.Dir.
Founded: 1966. **Staff:** Prof 9; Other 13. **Subjects:** Medicine, health sciences, human biology. **Special Collections:** Scientific government publications depository; history of medicine. **Holdings:** 43,340 books; 104,191 bound periodical volumes. **Subscriptions:** 2481 journals and other serials. **Services:** Interlibrary loan; copying; SDI; library open to the public. **Automated Operations:** Computerized cataloging and serials. **Computerized Information Services:** MEDLINE, BRS Information Technologies, DIALOG Information Services, PFDS Online, MEDLARS, OCLC; electronic mail service. **Networks/Consortia:** Member of Worcester Area Cooperating Libraries (WACL), Central Massachusetts Consortium of Health Related Libraries (CMCHRL), C/W MARS, Inc. **Remarks:** FAX: (508)856-5899. **Staff:** Annanaomi Sams, Asst.Dir., Pub. & Tech.Serv.; Michael Guercio, Asst.Dir., Ancillary Serv.

University of Mauritius - Mauritius Sugar Industry Research Institute
See: **Mauritius Sugar Industry Research Institute** (9852)

University Mayor of San Andres - National Scientific and Technological Documentation Center
See: **Bolivia - National Scientific and Technological Documentation Center** (1949)

★ 18836 ★
University Medical Center of Southern Nevada - Medical Library (Med)
2040 W. Charleston Blvd., Suite 500   Phone: (702)383-2368
Las Vegas, NV 89102   Aldona Jonynas, Dir., Lib.Serv.
Founded: 1964. **Staff:** Prof 1; Other 1. **Subjects:** Medicine, nursing. **Holdings:** 6500 books; 8329 bound periodical volumes; 336 bound indexes; 95 vertical files; 5 boxes of staff publications; 600 symposia; 700 audiocassettes and videotapes. **Subscriptions:** 250 journals and other serials. **Services:** Interlibrary loan; copying; bibliographic searches (limited); library open to the public for reference use only. **Automated Operations:** Computerized ILL and request routing (DOCLINE). **Computerized Information Services:** MEDLINE, NLM; OnTyme Electronic Message Network Service (electronic mail service). **Remarks:** FAX: (702)383-2369. Electronic mail address(es): CLASS.SONVMH (OnTyme Electronic Message Network Service).

★ 18837 ★
University of Medicine and Dentistry of New Jersey - George F. Smith Library (Med)
30 12th Ave.   Phone: (201)456-4580
Newark, NJ 07103-2706   Madeline Taylor, Dir.
Staff: Prof 11.5; Other 19.5. **Subjects:** Health sciences. **Special Collections:** Rare book collection; archival collection. **Holdings:** 68,000 books; 80,000 bound periodical volumes; AV programs. **Subscriptions:** 2500 journals and other serials. **Services:** Interlibrary loan; copying; SDI; library open to the public for reference use only. **Automated Operations:** Computerized public access catalog, cataloging, acquisitions, serials, and circulation. **Computerized Information Services:** BRS Information Technologies, NLM, OCLC, miniMEDLINE. Performs searches on fee basis. Contact Person: Sushila Kapadia, Info.Sys.Supv., 456-5318. **Networks/Consortia:** Member of National Network of Libraries of Medicine - Middle Atlantic Region, Essex Hudson Regional Library Cooperative. **Publications:** Periodicals holdings, biennial; Library Newsletter, 4/year. **Special Catalogs:** Media Catalog (book); Rare Book Catalog (book). **Remarks:** FAX: (201)456-6949. **Staff:** Victor A. Basile, Univ.Libn.; George Sprung, Ref.Libn.; Melvin White, Chf., Circ.; Jackie K. Bush, Asst.Chf., Circ.; Valentine Allen, ILL; Laura Barrett, AV Libn.; Janice Rettino, Dir., Univ.Lib.Sys.; Robert Cupryk, Ref.Libn.; Daria Gorman, Chf.Cat.; Beth Lapow, Acq.Libn.; Barbara Irwin, Oral Hist. Archv.; Barbara Packard, Tech.Serv.Libn.; Lynn Baltimore, Clin.Libn.; Laura Mayer, Proj.Mgr.; Martha Loesch, Cat.; Lois Densky, Archv.

★ 18838 ★
University of Medicine and Dentistry of New Jersey - Robert Wood Johnson Library of the Health Sciences (Med)
CN 19   Phone: (201)937-7606
New Brunswick, NJ 08903   Mary R. Scanlon, Lib.Dir.
Founded: 1982. **Staff:** Prof 3; Other 5. **Subjects:** Clinical medicine, hospital administration, nursing. **Holdings:** 6613 books; 20,891 bound periodical volumes; 310 AV programs. **Subscriptions:** 631 journals and other serials. **Services:** Interlibrary loan; copying; library open to the public for reference use only. **Automated Operations:** Computerized serials and circulation. **Computerized Information Services:** miniMEDLINE, MEDLINE, BRS Information Technologies, DIALOG Information Services; CD-ROMs (MEDLINE, CINAHL); DOCLINE (electronic mail service). Performs searches on fee basis. Contact Person: Kerry O'Rourke, Info.Mgmt.Libn., 937-7604. **Networks/Consortia:** Member of MEDCORE, Health Sciences Library Association of New Jersey (HSLANJ), BHSL. **Publications:** Library Rounds, bimonthly - available upon request. **Remarks:** FAX: (201)937-7826. **Staff:** Robert Gessner, Info.Mgt.Libn.

★ 18839 ★
University of Medicine and Dentistry of New Jersey - Robert Wood Johnson Medical School - Media Library (Med)
675 Hoes Ln.   Phone: (908)463-4671
Piscataway, NJ 08854-5635   Zana Etter, Dir.
Founded: 1970. **Staff:** Prof 1; Other 2. **Subjects:** Medicine, allied health sciences. **Special Collections:** Lecture notes and sample exams (18 VF drawers); Pathology videodisks (CAI programs). **Holdings:** 750 books; 1300 AV programs; 400 tapes of lectures; 18 VF drawers; 2 VF drawers of

software programs. **Services:** Interlibrary loan; copying; library open to the public for reference use only. **Automated Operations:** Computerized public access catalog and circulation. **Computerized Information Services:** CD-ROM (MEDLINE, Material Safety Data Sheets (MSDS), CCINFOdisc); InterNet (electronic mail service). **Networks/Consortia:** Member of MEDCORE. **Special Catalogs:** Network for Continuing Medical Education (NCME) videotape collection (print); Audiovisual Catalog (print). **Remarks:** Alternate telephone number(s): 463-4460. FAX: (908)463-4117.

★ 18840 ★
University of Medicine and Dentistry of New Jersey - School of Osteopathic Medicine - Health Sciences Library (Med)
Ambulatory Health Care Ctr.
301 S. Central Plaza, Suite 1100
Laurel Rd.   Phone: (609)346-6800
Stratford, NJ 08084   Judith Schuback Cohn, Lib.Dir.
Founded: 1974. **Staff:** Prof 3; Other 4. **Subjects:** Medicine, nursing, hospital administration, allied health sciences. **Special Collections:** Osteopathy. **Holdings:** 6500 books; 12,000 bound periodical volumes; 300 AV programs; 2 vertical files; 200 reels of microfilm. **Subscriptions:** 610 journals and other serials. **Services:** Interlibrary loan; copying; SDI; library open to the public by appointment. **Automated Operations:** Computerized cataloging. **Computerized Information Services:** MEDLARS, BRS Information Technologies, DIALOG Information Services. Performs searches on fee basis. Contact Person: Janice K. Skica, Pub.Serv.Libn., 346-6810. **Networks/Consortia:** Member of BHSL, Health Sciences Library Association of New Jersey (HSLANJ), Pinelands Consortium for Health Information. **Publications:** Selected Aquisitions and Monthly Micro Lab Schedules. **Remarks:** FAX: (609)435-8246. **Staff:** Micki McIntyre, Info.Mgt.Libn.; Zuleika Rodriguez, ILL; Elaine Mayweather, Circ./ILL; Kevin Block, Circ./Ser.

★ 18841 ★
University of Melbourne - School of Mathematical Sciences - Library (Sci-Engr)
Parkville, VIC 3052, Australia   Phone: 3 3446607
         Alan Burns
Founded: 1977. **Staff:** Prof 1. **Subjects:** Mathematics, computer science, mathematical statistics, mathematical physics. **Holdings:** 8300 books; 3500 bound periodical volumes; 500 reports; 1500 microfiche; 500 reels of microfilm. **Subscriptions:** 200 journals and other serials. **Services:** Interlibrary loan; copying; library open to staff and research students of other institutions. **Automated Operations:** Computerized public access catalog. **Computerized Information Services:** ACSNET (electronic mail service). **Remarks:** FAX: 3 3481148. Telex: AA35185. Electronic mail address(es): aburns@mulga.cs.mu.oz.au (ACSNET).

★ 18842 ★
University of Miami - Dorothy & Lewis Rosenstiel School of Marine & Atmospheric Sciences - Library (Biol Sci, Sci-Engr)
4600 Rickenbacker Causeway   Phone: (305)361-4007
Miami, FL 33149   Kay K. Hale, Libn.
Founded: 1941. **Staff:** Prof 2; Other 3. **Subjects:** Marine sciences (especially tropical), biology, fisheries, marine geology and geophysics, ocean engineering, physical and chemical oceanography, atmospheric sciences, marine affairs. **Holdings:** 18,000 books; 32,000 bound periodical volumes; 25,000 reprints; 560 reels of microfilm; 5182 microfiche; 1242 microcards; 45 sets of oceanographic expedition reports; 850 atlases; 3000 nautical charts; 45 videotapes. **Subscriptions:** 1100 journals and other serials. **Services:** Interlibrary loan; copying; SDI; library open to the public for reference use only. **Automated Operations:** Computerized public access catalog. **Computerized Information Services:** DIALOG Information Services, OCLC; CD-ROMs; DIALMAIL, SCIENCEnet (electronic mail services). **Networks/Consortia:** Member of SOLINET, Florida Library Network (FLN), South East Florida Library Information Network (SEFLIN). **Publications:** Serials list; accessions list. **Remarks:** Alternate telephone number(s): (305)361-4021. FAX: (305)361-9306. Telex: 317454. Electronic mail address(es): 15057 (DIALMAIL); RSMAS.LIBRARY (SCIENCEnet). **Staff:** Helen Albertson, Asst.Libn.

★ 18843 ★
University of Miami - Intelligent Computer Systems Research Institute - Library (Comp Sci)
P.O. Box 248235   Phone: (305)284-5195
Coral Gables, FL 33124   David B. Hertz, Ph.D.
Founded: 1983. **Subjects:** Computer systems, artificial intelligence, expert systems, neural networks. **Holdings:** 2000 volumes. **Subscriptions:** 30

journals and other serials. **Services:** Library open to students. **Computerized Information Services:** Internal database; BITNET (electronic mail service). **Remarks:** FAX: (305)284-6526. Telex: 519308. Electronic mail address(es): DUMICS@SER (BITNET).

★ 18844 ★
University of Miami - Lowe Art Museum Library (Art)
1301 Stanford Dr.   Phone: (305)284-3536
Coral Gables, FL 33124-6310   Martha Kent, Archv.
Founded: 1971. **Staff:** 1. **Subjects:** Art and art history. **Holdings:** 3500 books; 1000 unbound periodical volumes; 4000 museum exhibition catalogs; 1000 slides. **Subscriptions:** 6 journals and other serials. **Services:** Library open to the university community by appointment. **Remarks:** FAX: (305)284-2024.

★ 18845 ★
University of Miami - Morton Collectanea (Biol Sci)
Box 8204   Phone: (305)284-3741
Coral Gables, FL 33124   Dr. Julia F. Morton, Dir.
Founded: 1932. **Staff:** Prof 1; Other 2. **Subjects:** Economic botany. **Special Collections:** Tropical fruits and vegetables; poisonous plants; medicinal plants; edible wild plants; aquatic plants; honeybee plants; horticulture. **Holdings:** 5900 books; 4000 unbound journals; 186 VF drawers of plant species subject files; agricultural abstracts. **Subscriptions:** 25 journals and other serials. **Services:** Copying; consultations; library open to scientists and students from other institutions. **Publications:** Communications; papers presented at scientific meetings; reprints. **Remarks:** Conducts field investigations and lectures. FAX: (305)284-2035.

★ 18846 ★
University of Miami - Otto G. Richter Library - Archives & Special Collections Division (Hist)
Coral Gables, FL 33124-0320   Phone: (305)284-3247
    William E. Brown, Jr., Hd., Archv. & Spec.Coll.
Founded: 1978. **Staff:** Prof 3; Other 4. **Subjects:** University history, Floridiana, Cuba and Cuban exiles, Jamaica, Colombia, Latin America, American literature. **Special Collections:** University Archives (1680 linear feet); Mark F. Boyd Collection; Minnie Moore Willson Collection; American Literary Agency Collection, 1948-1986; Bernhardt E. Muller Collection; A. Curtis Wilgus Collection; The Truth About Cuba Committee, Inc. Collection; Jackie Gleason Collection (occultism, psychical research, spiritualism, movie pictures, actors and actresses; 1700 books; 141 volumes of periodicals); Cuban Exile Periodical Collection; David Masnata Collection; August S. Houghton Collection; David Ewen Collection; Walter T. Swingle Collection. **Holdings:** 35,000 books; 22,890 volumes of periodicals; 300 manuscript collections; dissertations; masters' theses; audiotapes; audio and videocassettes; 5000 maps; 25,000 photographs. **Services:** Copying; department open to the public for scholarly research. **Computerized Information Services:** Electronic mail. **Remarks:** FAX: (305)655-7352. **Staff:** Esperanza B. Varona, Asst.Libn.; John McMinn, Cat.

★ 18847 ★
University of Miami - School of Law Library (Law)
Box 248087   Phone: (305)284-2250
Coral Gables, FL 33124-0247   Westwell R. Daniels, Law Libn.
Founded: 1928. **Staff:** Prof 18; Other 23. **Subjects:** Law - Anglo-American, Latin American, Caribbean area, European, international. **Holdings:** 280,556 volumes; 378,131 microforms. **Subscriptions:** 5992 journals and other serials. **Services:** Interlibrary loan; library open to those doing legal research. **Automated Operations:** Computerized public access catalog, cataloging, acquisitions, circulation, and serials. **Computerized Information Services:** LEXIS, NEXIS, WESTLAW, DIALOG Information Services, OCLC, RLIN. **Networks/Consortia:** Member of SOLINET. **Remarks:** FAX: (305)284-3554. **Staff:** Felice K. Lowell, Asst.Libn.; Warren Rosmarin, Assoc.Libn.; Edgardo Rotman, Foreign and Intl. Law Libn.; Beth Gwynn, Ref.Libn.; Leila Mestrits, Cat.; Michael Petit, Acq.Libn.; Althea Gerrard, Act.Circ.Libn.; Sonia Luna-Lamas, Ser.Libn.; Gordon Russell, Hd. of Ref.; Scott Schaffer, Ref.; Lennye Wellins, Adm.Asst.; Ellen Greenfield, Sys.Mgr.; Nora de la Garza, Hd., Retrieval Serv.

★ 18848 ★
University of Miami - School of Medicine - Bascom Palmer Eye
Institute - Mary and Edward Norton Library of Ophthalmology (Med)
Anne Bates Leach Eye Hospital
900 N.W. 17th St.
Box 016880   Phone: (305)326-6078
Miami, FL 33101   Reva Hurtes, Libn.
Founded: 1962. **Staff:** Prof 1; Other 2. **Subjects:** Ophthalmology, visual
optics, visual physiology and anatomy. **Special Collections:** Historical and
rare books (3000 volumes). **Holdings:** 15,000 volumes; AV programs.
Subscriptions: 200 journals and other serials. **Services:** Interlibrary loan;
copying; SDI; library open to the public on a limited basis. **Automated**
Operations: Computerized cataloging. **Computerized Information Services:**
BRS Information Technologies. **Remarks:** FAX: (305)326-6374.

★ 18849 ★
University of Miami - School of Medicine - Louis Calder Memorial
Library (Med)
Box 016950   Phone: (305)547-6441
Miami, FL 33101   Henry L. Lemkau, Jr., Dir.
Founded: 1952. **Staff:** Prof 10; Other 28. **Subjects:** Medicine, nursing.
Special Collections: Weinstein Collection (paramedical sciences; 461
volumes); Ophthalmology Collection (10,641 volumes); History of Medicine
Collection (3832 volumes); Florida Collection (429 volumes); rare books
(1036 volumes). **Holdings:** 62,791 books; 106,914 bound periodical volumes;
620 Florida pamphlets; 263 linear feet of archives; 20 linear feet of clipping
files; 1821 illustrations; 212 medallions; 1226 portraits; 347 dissertations;
353 volumes of faculty publications. **Subscriptions:** 2434 journals and other
serials. **Services:** Interlibrary loan; copying; SDI; library open to health
science personnel and institutions of Southern Florida. **Automated**
Operations: Computerized public access catalog, cataloging, serials,
acquisitions, circulation, fund accounting, and ILL. **Computerized**
Information Services: MEDLINE, DIALOG Information Services, BRS
Information Technologies, PFDS Online, OCLC, MEDLINE; Plusnet 2
(internal database); DOCLINE, OnTyme Electronic Message Network
Service (electronic mail services). Performs searches on fee basis. Contact
Person: Vislava Tylman, Assoc.Dir./Educ. & Ref.Serv., 54 7-6648.
Networks/Consortia: Member of National Network of Libraries of
Medicine - Southeastern/Atlantic Region, Miami Health Sciences Library
Consortium (MHSLC), SOLINET, Consortium of Southern Biomedical
Libraries (CONBLS). **Publications:** Bulletin; guide; Fee Structure;
Periodicals Currently Received; Annual Report. **Remarks:** FAX: (305)325-
8853 (Administration); (305)324-4089 (ILL). Electronic mail address(es):
CLASS.CALDER/FL (OnTyme Electronic Message Network Service).
Staff: August La Rocco, Hea.Info. Network; Erica Powell, Hd., LRC;
Teresita D. Sayus, Circ.Libn.; Yanira Garcia, Ref.Libn.; Isabel Caballero,
Ref.Libn.; Van Afes, Hd., Tech.Serv.; James Clark, Hd., ILL; Frank Yanes,
Mgr., Auto.Sys.; Amalia De La Vega, Hd., Acq. & Ser.; Suzetta C. Burrows,
Vice Chair; Mary P. Dillon, Assoc.Dir./Database & Coll.Dev.; Thomas
Williams, Assoc.Dir./Sys. Integration & Access Serv.

★ 18850 ★
University of Miami - School of Music - Albert Pick Music Library
(Mus)
Coral Gables, FL 33124   Phone: (305)284-2429
                                    Nancy Zavac, Mus.Libn.
Founded: 1957. **Staff:** Prof 2; Other 5. **Subjects:** Music. **Special Collections:**
Autographed recordings (composers and performers); ethnic recordings,
especially Latin American, Yiddish, jazz; Inter-American Music Archive;
Larry Taylor/Billy Matthews Musical Theatre Archive (15,000 recordings;
20,000 pieces of sheet music and scores; 800 books; 550 compact discs; 100
piano rolls); Handleman Institute of Recorded Sound Archives (25,000
uncataloged recordings); Yiddish music scores and recordings. **Holdings:**
36,000 scores; 25,500 recordings. **Subscriptions:** 180 journals and other
serials. **Services:** Interlibrary loan; library open to the public for reference
use only. **Automated Operations:** Computerized cataloging. **Computerized**
Information Services: OCLC. **Networks/Consortia:** Member of SOLINET.
Special Catalogs: Inter-American Music Archive (card); Catalog to Larry
Taylor/Billy Matthews Musical Theater Archive (online). **Staff:** Cheryl
Gowing, Mus.Cat.

★ 18851 ★
University of Michigan - Aerospace Engineering Library (Sci-Engr)
221 Aerospace Engineering Bldg.   Phone: (313)764-7200
Ann Arbor, MI 48109-2140   Kathy Stolaruk, Res.Sec. II
Staff: Prof 1. **Subjects:** Aerospace science, plasma physics, fluid mechanics,
aerodynamics, mathematics, structures and elasticity. **Holdings:** 3000 books;

8000 bound periodical volumes; NASA reports and departmental
dissertations. **Subscriptions:** 25 journals and other serials. **Services:** Library
open to the public with permission of the department chairman. **Remarks:**
FAX: (313)763-0578.

★ 18852 ★
University of Michigan - Alfred Taubman Medical Library (Med)
1135 E. Catherine   Phone: (313)764-1210
Ann Arbor, MI 48109-0726   Suzanne Grefsheim, Hd.Libn.
Founded: 1920. **Staff:** Prof 10.25; Other 26. **Subjects:** Basic medical sciences,
clinical medicine, nursing, pharmacy, history of medicine. **Special**
Collections: Crummer Collection (History of Medicine); Warthin Collection
(Dance of Death). **Holdings:** 424,490 volumes. **Subscriptions:** 3200 journals
and other serials. **Services:** Interlibrary loan. **Automated Operations:**
Computerized cataloging, acquisitions, serials, and circulation.
Computerized Information Services: DIALOG Information Services, BRS
Information Technologies, PFDS Online, NLM, RLIN; CD-ROMs;
BITNET, InterNet (electronic mail services). **Networks/Consortia:**
Member of National Network of Libraries of Medicine - Greater Midwest
Region. **Remarks:** FAX: (313)763-1473. **Staff:** Diane Schwartz, Asst.Hd.;
Helen F. Meranda, Coll.Dev.; Whitney K. Field, Circ.Hd.; Nadia Lalla,
Info.Serv.Libn.; Doris M. Mahony, Ref.Libn.; Barbara L. Shipman,
Tech.Sys.; Carole Weber, Hd., Tech.Proc.

★ 18853 ★
University of Michigan - Art & Architecture Library and Computer Lab
(Art, Plan)
2106 Art & Architecture Bldg.   Phone: (313)764-1303
Ann Arbor, MI 48109   Peggy Ann Kusnerz, Libn.
Staff: Prof 2.5; Other 3.5. **Subjects:** Architecture, urban and regional
planning, landscape architecture, art, graphic design, photography. **Special**
Collections: Jens Jensen landscape drawings. **Holdings:** 55,000 books; 82 VF
drawers of pamphlets; 1500 photographs; 72,000 slides; 1000 maps; 477
prints; 2000 drawings; computer software programs. **Subscriptions:** 550
journals and other serials. **Services:** Interlibrary loan; copying; library open
to the public with restrictions. **Automated Operations:** Computerized
cataloging, acquisitions, and circulation. **Computerized Information**
Services: RLIN, DIALOG Information Services. Performs searches on fee
basis. **Networks/Consortia:** Member of Research Libraries Information
Network (RLIN). **Publications:** Guide Series - available upon request.
Remarks: Library includes computer facilities for U of M faculty, staff, and
students. **Staff:** Dorothy Shields, Assoc.Libn.; Yolanda Jones, Asst.Libn.

★ 18854 ★
University of Michigan - Asia Library (Area-Ethnic)
Hatcher Graduate Library, 4th Fl. Phone: (313)764-0406
Ann Arbor, MI 48109-1205   Weiying Wan, Hd.
Founded: 1947. **Staff:** Prof 7; Other 6. **Subjects:** East Asian humanities and
social sciences, including anthropology, archeology, calligraphy,
communism, drama, theater, economics, education, ethics, fine arts,
geography, history, journalism, linguistics, phonology, library science,
military history, military science, music, political science, religion,
sociology. **Special Collections:** Union Research Institute Classified Files on
China; Red Guards materials and classified files on the Cultural Revolution;
rare editions of Chinese fiction in Japanese collections; Ming local gazetteers
and literary collections; National Peking Library Rare Book Collection on
microfilm; British Public Record Office Archives on China; Tun-huang
materials from Beijng, Taipei, the British Museum, and the Bibliotheque
Nationale; Japanese local history, materials on the Occupation of Japan;
Japanese literature; Japanese Diet Proceedings; Bartlett Collection of
Botanical Works and Materia Medica; Kamada Collection of Pre-war
Japanese Works. **Holdings:** 268,575 volumes in Chinese; 216,568 volumes
in Japanese; 4118 volumes in Korean; 21,443 reels of microfilm and 21,205
sheets of microfiche in Chinese; 7451 reels of microfilm and 5041 sheets of
microfiche in Japanese. **Subscriptions:** 1795 journals and other serials; 79
newspapers. **Services:** Interlibrary loan; copying. **Remarks:** FAX: (313)763-
5080. **Staff:** Yasuko Matsudo, Asst.Hd.; Choo Won Suh, Sr. Japanese Libn.;
Sharon Ying, Chinese Cat.Supv.; Wei-Yi Ma, Chinese Bibliog.; Mei-Ying
Lin, Chinese Cat.; Takaharu Yamakawa, Japanese Cat.

★ 18855 ★
University of Michigan - Biological Station Library (Biol Sci)
Pellston, MI 49769   Phone: (616)936-2337
                                   Dorothy Riemenschneider, Hd.
Subjects: Zoology, botany, ichthyology, parasitology, entomology,
limnology, ornithology. **Holdings:** 14,000 volumes; 2200 station papers.

Subscriptions: 69 journals and other serials. **Services:** Library open to the public for reference use only (library open only during summer). **Computerized Information Services:** Internal databases. **Remarks:** Library is managed by the University of Michigan Natural Science Library in Ann Arbor, MI, telephone (313)764-1494.

★ 18856 ★
University of Michigan - Center for the Education of Women - Library (Soc Sci)
330 E. Liberty   Phone: (313)998-7080
Ann Arbor, MI 48104-2289   Mary Lee Jensen, Libn.
Founded: 1965. **Staff:** Prof 1; Other 1. **Subjects:** Women - employment, education, status, counseling, career development. **Special Collections:** Women's organizations collection (3 cubic feet); women in science series (20 audio- and videotapes). **Holdings:** 700 books; 2000 organizational reports, government publications, dissertations, manuscripts, unpublished papers; 1 cubic foot of clippings; Michigan Occupational Information System computer software and microfiche. **Subscriptions:** 50 journals and other serials. **Services:** Copying; library open to the public. **Computerized Information Services:** BRS Information Technologies, MERIT/UMNET; electronic mail service. **Publications:** Acquisition List, quarterly; selected topical bibliographies - all free upon request; Directory of Special Collections/Libraries Independent of the University of Michigan Library System, irregular. **Remarks:** FAX: (313)936-7787.

★ 18857 ★
University of Michigan - Chemistry Library (Sci-Engr)
2000 Chemistry Bldg.   Phone: (313)764-7337
Ann Arbor, MI 48109-1055   Tracy Primich, Chem.Libn.
Staff: Prof 1; Other 2. **Subjects:** Chemistry. **Special Collections:** Beilstein; Sadtler Proton NMR Spectra. **Holdings:** 70,000 volumes; Chemical Abstracts. **Subscriptions:** 400 journals and other serials. **Services:** Interlibrary loan; copying; library open to the public for reference use only. **Automated Operations:** Computerized public access catalog and circulation. **Computerized Information Services:** DIALOG Information Services, RLIN, STN International; InterNet (electronic mail service). **Remarks:** Electronic mail address(es): TRACY–PRIMICH@UM.CC.UMICH.EDU (InterNet).

★ 18858 ★
University of Michigan - Dentistry Library (Med)
1100 Dental Bldg.   Phone: (313)764-1526
Ann Arbor, MI 48109-1078   Susan I. Seger, Hd.Libn.
Founded: 1908. **Staff:** Prof 1; Other 3. **Subjects:** Dentistry. **Special Collections:** Rare Book Collection (875). **Holdings:** 49,560 volumes; 25 VF drawers of pamphlets. **Subscriptions:** 698 journals and other serials. **Services:** Interlibrary loan; copying; library open to the public for reference use only. **Automated Operations:** Computerized public access catalog, cataloging, acquisitions, and circulation. **Computerized Information Services:** BRS Information Technologies, MEDLINE, WILSONLINE, PsycINFO. **Networks/Consortia:** Member of National Network of Libraries of Medicine - Greater Midwest Region, Research Libraries Information Network (RLIN). **Publications:** Library Information Guide; Special Subject Bibliographies. **Special Indexes:** Index of M.S. theses (card). **Remarks:** FAX: (313)764-4477. **Staff:** Kari Tant, Circ.Supv.

★ 18859 ★
University of Michigan - Department of Geological Sciences - Subsurface Laboratory Library (Sci-Engr)
1006 C.C. Little Bldg.   Phone: (313)764-9405
Ann Arbor, MI 48109-1063   Joyce M. Budai, Dir.
Staff: Prof 1; Other 5. **Subjects:** Geology, stratigraphy, sedimentary rocks, sedimentation, sedimentary geochemistry. **Special Collections:** Michigan well history central system file; subsurface geology materials and information. **Holdings:** 500 well cores; cuttings for 4000 wells; petrophysical logs for 2300 wells. **Services:** Interlibrary loan; copying; library open to the public. **Automated Operations:** Computerized cataloging and acquisitions. **Computerized Information Services:** MICRO Data Management System (internal database); BITNET (electronic mail service). Performs searches on fee basis. **Special Catalogs:** Core, mounted strip log, unmounted cuttings, electric log, and descriptive log catalogs. **Remarks:** FAX: (313)763-4690.

★ 18860 ★
University of Michigan - Department of Rare Books and Special Collections - Library (Rare Book)
711 Hatcher Graduate Library   Phone: (313)764-9377
Ann Arbor, MI 48109-1205   Peggy E. Daub, Hd.
Founded: 1913. **Staff:** Prof 5; Other 4. **Subjects:** Rare books on all branches of knowledge. **Special Collections:** Worcester Philippine Collection; imaginary voyages; history of science; English and American drama; incunabula; manuscripts - biblical, medieval, renaissance, modern, Islamic; papyri (7000 items); theater collections; Shakespeare; information science and micrographics; military art and science; documents of the Weimar Republic and Nazi periods; Labadie Collection (social protest movements). **Holdings:** 195,000 books, bound periodical volumes, pamphlets, nonbook materials; 105 linear feet of vertical files; 650 linear feet of modern manuscripts. **Subscriptions:** 650 journals, newspapers, and other serials. **Services:** Interlibrary loan; copying (both limited); collection open to qualified researchers. **Automated Operations:** Computerized public access catalog, cataloging, acquisitions, and circulation. **Computerized Information Services:** OCLC; Labadie Database (internal database); MTS (electronic mail service). Performs searches free of charge. Contact Person: R. Anne Okey, Labadie Coll.Libn. **Networks/Consortia:** Member of Research Libraries Information Network (RLIN). **Special Catalogs:** Exhibition checklists and occasional catalogs. **Staff:** Kathryn L. Beam, Ms.Libn.; Edward C. Weber, Hd., Labadie Coll.

★ 18861 ★
University of Michigan - Engineering-Transportation Library (Trans, Sci-Engr)
312 Undergraduate Library Bldg.   Phone: (313)764-7494
Ann Arbor, MI 48109-1185   Daisy T. Wu
Founded: 1903. **Staff:** Prof 3; Other 5.5. **Subjects:** All divisions and aspects of engineering except nuclear engineering; all divisions and aspects of transportation. **Holdings:** 450,000 volumes. **Subscriptions:** 2600 journals and other serials. **Services:** Interlibrary loan; copying. **Computerized Information Services:** DIALOG Information Services, PFDS Online, NASA/RECON, Chemical Abstracts Service (CAS), BRS Information Technologies, DTIC, VU/TEXT Information Services, U.S. Patent Classification System; BITNET, EDUNET (electronic mail services). **Publications:** Library News, monthly - free upon request. **Remarks:** FAX: (313)763-9813. Electronic mail address(es): USERLELN@UB.CC.UMICH.EDU. **Staff:** Robert Schwarzwalder, Coord. for Info.Serv.; Theresa Lee, Coll.Dev. & Info.Serv.

★ 18862 ★
University of Michigan - English Language Institute and Linguistics Library (Educ)
3003 North University Bldg.   Phone: (313)747-0478
Ann Arbor, MI 48109   Patricia M. Aldridge, Libn.
Founded: 1960. **Staff:** 2. **Subjects:** Teaching English as a foreign language, teaching modern foreign language, English grammar, linguistics, psycholinguistics, sociolinguistics, bilingual education, language laboratories, foreign students in the U.S. **Holdings:** 6750 books and pamphlets; 400 boxed volumes of periodicals; 32 VF drawers; 15 series of Working Papers; 60 videotapes; audiotapes; microfiche; microfilm. **Subscriptions:** 105 journals and other serials. **Services:** Interlibrary loan; copying; library open to the public for reference use only on request. **Computerized Information Services:** Internal database. **Remarks:** Includes the holdings of the Linguistics Department Library. FAX: (313)763-0369.

★ 18863 ★
University of Michigan - Fine Arts Library (Art)
260 Tappan Hall   Phone: (313)764-5405
Ann Arbor, MI 48109   Deirdre D. Spencer, Hd.
Founded: 1949. **Staff:** Prof 1; Other 2. **Subjects:** History of art and architecture. **Holdings:** 65,000 volumes; 32 VF drawers. **Subscriptions:** 265 journals and other serials. **Services:** Interlibrary loan; library open to the public for reference use only. **Automated Operations:** public access catalog. **Computerized Information Services:** DIALOG Information Services, RLIN, WILSONLINE; BITNET (electronic mail service). **Remarks:** FAX: (313)763-5080. Electronic mail address(es): USERGD62@UMICHUM (BITNET).

★ 18864 ★
University of Michigan - History of Art Department - Archives of Asian Art (Art)
Tappan Hall, Rm. 50
519 S. State   Phone: (313)764-5555
Ann Arbor, MI 48109-1357   Wendy Holden, Sr.Assoc.Cur.
Staff: Prof 2; Other 3. **Subjects:** Art - Chinese, Japanese, South and Southeast Asian. **Special Collections:** Photographs of paintings from the National Palace Museum, Taiwan; Indian Buddhist cave sites; Thai art; Islamic manuscripts. **Holdings:** 80,000 photographs and mounted reproductions. **Services:** Archives open to the public for reference use only; slides and photographs of Chinese and Japanese paintings available for sale to institutions. **Staff:** Naseem Banerji, Asst.Cur.

★ 18865 ★
University of Michigan - History of Art Department - Collection of Slides and Photographs (Art)
110 Tappan Hall   Phone: (313)763-6114
Ann Arbor, MI 48109-1357   Joy Blouin, Cur.
Founded: 1946. **Staff:** Prof 6; Other 35. **Subjects:** History of art. **Holdings:** 270,000 35mm transparencies; 30,000 lantern slides; 190,000 photographs and mounted reproductions. **Services:** Illustrative material provided to history of art faculty for lectures and research. **Remarks:** FAX: (313)747-4121.

★ 18866 ★
University of Michigan - Hopwood Room (Hum)
1006 Angell Hall   Phone: (313)764-6296
Ann Arbor, MI 48109   Andrea Beauchamp, Prog.Assoc.
Staff: 1. **Subjects:** Contemporary literature. **Special Collections:** Hopwood Awards manuscripts. **Holdings:** Figures not available.

★ 18867 ★
University of Michigan - Information and Library Studies Library (Info Sci)
300 Hatcher Graduate Library   Phone: (313)764-9375
Ann Arbor, MI 48109-1205   Mary Townsend, Libn.
Staff: Prof 1; Other 1. **Subjects:** Library science, history of libraries, history of publishing, history of bookselling, history of the book, bibliography, children's literature, online information services, information storage and retrieval, micrographics. **Special Collections:** Award winning children's and young adult books. **Holdings:** 58,767 books; 491 dissertations; 453 reels of microfilm; 2608 sheets of microfiche; 100 AV programs. **Subscriptions:** 575 journals and other serials. **Services:** Interlibrary loan; library open to the public. **Automated Operations:** Computerized cataloging, acquisitions, circulation, and serials. **Computerized Information Services:** DIALOG Information Services, RLIN, BRS Information Technologies, WILSONLINE, PsycINFO, PAIS. **Networks/Consortia:** Member of Research Libraries Information Network (RLIN).

★ 18868 ★
University of Michigan - Institute for Social Research - Inter-University Consortium for Political and Social Research (Info Sci)
Box 1248   Phone: (313)764-2570
Ann Arbor, MI 48106   Richard C. Rockwell, Exec.Dir.
Founded: 1962. **Staff:** Prof 13; Other 27. **Subjects:** International and national social, economic, and political data: elections, census; international relations; aging and the aging process; crime, deviance, and criminal justice; recreation and leisure. **Holdings:** 2300 collections of machine-readable data representing 29,000 discrete data files. **Services:** Services open to the public on a fee basis. **Automated Operations:** Computerized public access catalog, cataloging, and acquisitions. **Computerized Information Services:** CDNet; ICPSR Guide, ICPSR Variables, ICPSR Rollcalls, SMIS (Survey Methodology Information System) (internal databases); BITNET, InterNet, NSFNet (electronic mail services). Performs searches on fee basis. **Publications:** Guide to Resources and Services, annual; annual report; ICPSR's Bulletin, quarterly; codebooks. **Remarks:** FAX: (313)764-8041, Alternate telephone number(s): 763-5010. **Also Known As:** ICPSR. **Staff:** Erik W. Austin, Dir., Arch.Dev.; Janet K. Vavra, Tech.Dir.

★ 18869 ★
University of Michigan - Institute for Social Research - Library (Soc Sci)
426 Thompson St.
P.O. Box 1248   Phone: (313)764-8513
Ann Arbor, MI 48106   Mrs. Adye Bel Evans, Libn.
Staff: Prof 1; Other 1. **Subjects:** Social psychology, industrial psychology, mental health, economic behavior. **Holdings:** 3000 books, monographs, unpublished papers, and research reports comprising publications of institute staff; 1000 research reports produced by other survey institutions. **Subscriptions:** 150 journals and other serials. **Services:** Interlibrary loan; copying; library open to the public for reference use only. **Publications:** Bibliography of institute-authored publications, annual with five-year cumulations.

★ 18870 ★
University of Michigan - Kresge Business Administration Library (Bus-Fin)
School of Business Administration, K3330   Phone: (313)764-7356
Ann Arbor, MI 48109-1234   Dr. Elaine K. Didier, Dir.
Founded: 1925. **Staff:** Prof 7.5; Other 10. **Subjects:** General business, accounting, finance, marketing, statistics, international business, human resource management, organizational behavior. **Special Collections:** Career Resources Center (files of 500 companies). **Holdings:** 210,000 volumes; corporate annual reports; 10Ks and proxies; working papers. **Subscriptions:** 3200 journals and other serials. **Services:** Library open to the public. **Automated Operations:** Computerized cataloging (RLIN). **Computerized Information Services:** DIALOG Information Services, Dow Jones News/Retrieval, ABI/INFORM, InfoTrac; CD-ROMs (Business Periodicals Ondisc, Compact Disclosure, CD/Private Plus, CIRR On Disc, F & S Indexes, Moody's International, National Newspaper Index); BITNET (electronic mail service). **Networks/Consortia:** Member of Research Libraries Information Network (RLIN), Michigan Library Consortium (MLC). **Publications:** Bibliographies highlighting resources and services. **Remarks:** FAX: (313)763-5688. Electronic mail address(es): @UMICHUM (BITNET). **Staff:** JoAnn Sokkar; Aline Soules; Jane Lucas; Nancy Karp; Katherine Pittsley; Elizabeth Foss; Susan Pritts.

★ 18871 ★
University of Michigan - Law Library (Law)
Legal Research Bldg.   Phone: (313)764-9322
Ann Arbor, MI 48109-1210   Margaret A. Leary, Dir.
Founded: 1859. **Staff:** Prof 11; Other 32. **Subjects:** Anglo-American law, foreign law, international law, international organizations, Roman law, legal bibliography. **Holdings:** 718,240 volumes. **Subscriptions:** 11,139 journals and other serials. **Services:** Interlibrary loan; copying; library open to the public. **Automated Operations:** Computerized public access catalog, cataloging, acquisitions, serials, and circulation. **Computerized Information Services:** LEXIS, WESTLAW, DIALOG Information Services. **Networks/Consortia:** Member of Research Libraries Information Network (RLIN). **Remarks:** FAX: (313)936-3884. **Staff:** Bobbie Snow, Chf.Circ.Libn.; Evelyn L. Smith, Chf., Tech.Serv.Libn.; Barbara Vaccaro, Chf.Ref.Libn.

★ 18872 ★
University of Michigan - Map Library (Geog-Map)
825 Hatcher Graduate Library   Phone: (313)764-0407
Ann Arbor, MI 48109-1205   Karl E. Longstreth, Libn. Head
Staff: Prof 1; Other 2. **Subjects:** Maps - topographic, geologic, political, thematic; nautical charts; history of cartography. **Holdings:** 250,000 sheet maps; 7000 monographs, serials, atlases, gazetteers; cartobibliographies; 2400 aerial photographs; satellite images. **Subscriptions:** 50 journals and other serials. **Services:** Copying; library open to the public. **Automated Operations:** Computerized public access catalog (NOTIS), cataloging, acquisitions, serials, and circulation. **Computerized Information Services:** BITNET, InterNet (electronic mail services). **Remarks:** FAX: (313)763-5080. Electronic mail address(es): MAP–LIBRARY@UB.CC.UMICH.EDU (InterNet); USERLGG3@UMICHUB (BITNET). **Staff:** Jerry Thornton, Cat.; David M. Moore, Supv.

★ 18873 ★
University of Michigan - Mathematics Library (Sci-Engr)
3027 Angell Hall   Phone: (313)764-7266
Ann Arbor, MI 48109-1003   Jack W. Weigel, Libn.
Founded: 1930. **Staff:** 1 **Subjects:** Mathematics, statistics, history of mathematics, actuarial mathematics. **Holdings:** 60,500 volumes; 758 reels of microfilm; 586 dissertations. **Subscriptions:** 786 journals and other serials. **Services:** Interlibrary loan; library open to the public for reference use only. **Computerized Information Services:** DIALOG Information Services, STN International. Performs searches on fee basis.

★ 18874 ★
University of Michigan - Matthaei Botanical Gardens - Library (Biol Sci)
1800 N. Dixboro Rd.   Phone: (313)998-7061
Ann Arbor, MI 48105-9741   Katherine R. French, Interp. Botanist
Subjects: Botany, horticulture, ethnobotany. **Holdings:** 3776 volumes; 8 VF drawers of brochures and clippings. **Subscriptions:** 8 journals and other serials. **Services:** Library open to the public for reference use only by appointment. **Remarks:** FAX: (313)998-6205.

★ 18875 ★
University of Michigan - Michigan Historical Collections - Bentley
   Historical Library (Hist)
1150 Beal   Phone: (313)764-3482
Ann Arbor, MI 48109-2113   Francis X. Blouin, Jr., Dir.
Founded: 1935. **Staff:** Prof 13; Other 6. **Subjects:** Michigan - history, religion, urban affairs, education, business; University of Michigan; politics and government of Michigan and United States; ethnic groups. **Special Collections:** Philippine Islands; Sino-American relations; printed and manuscript holdings on temperance and prohibition in the U.S. **Holdings:** 50,000 volumes; 29,000 linear feet of manuscripts and archives; 4500 collections; 2000 maps; 350 reels of microfilm of newspapers; 32 VF drawers; 500,000 photographs. **Subscriptions:** 176 journals and other serials. **Services:** Interlibrary loan (limited); copying; library open to the public. **Automated Operations:** Computerized cataloging and serials. **Computerized Information Services:** RLIN. **Networks/Consortia:** Member of Research Libraries Information Network (RLIN). **Publications:** Annual Report; Bulletins, annual; Bentley Historical Library (newsletter), annual; Bibliographical series, irregular; Guide to the Michigan Historical Collections. **Staff:** William K. Wallach, Asst.Dir.; Thomas Powers, Archv.; Nancy Bartlett, Ref.Archv.; James Craven, Consrv.; Kenneth Scheffel, Assoc.Archv.; Leonard Coombs, Assoc.Archv.; Marjorie Barritt, Assoc.Archv.; Christine Weideman, Assoc.Archv.; Gregory Kinney, Asst.Archv.; Ann Flowers, Asst.Archv.; Karen Mason, Asst.Archv.

★ 18876 ★
University of Michigan - Michigan Information Transfer Source (MITS)
   (Info Sci)
106 Hatcher Graduate Library   Phone: (313)763-5060
Ann Arbor, MI 48109-1205   Pamela J. MacKintosh, Dir.
Founded: 1980. **Staff:** Prof 2.5; Other 12. **Services:** Interlibrary loan; SDI; bibliographies, patents, translations. **Computerized Information Services:** DIALOG Information Services, BRS Information Technologies, PFDS Online, VU/TEXT Information Services, WILSONLINE, OCLC, Dow Jones News/Retrieval. **Networks/Consortia:** Member of Research Libraries Information Network (RLIN). **Publications:** Fee-Based Services: Issues & Answers (1988) - for sale; brochure; bibliographies. **Remarks:** MITS provides research and information services to business, industry, and individuals on a cost recovery basis. Fee schedule available upon request. FAX: (313)936-3630.

★ 18877 ★
University of Michigan - Museums Library (Biol Sci)
2500 Ruthven Museums Bldg.   Phone: (313)764-0467
Ann Arbor, MI 48109   Dorothy Riemenschneider, Hd.
Founded: 1928. **Staff:** Prof 1.5. **Subjects:** Natural history with emphasis on systematic and taxonomic works. **Special Collections:** Anthropology; paleontology; botany; birds; herpetology; fish; insects; mammals; mollusks. **Holdings:** 110,000 volumes. **Subscriptions:** 1400 journals and other serials. **Services:** Interlibrary loan; copying; library open to the public. **Automated Operations:** Computerized public access catalog. **Computerized Information Services:** DIALOG Information Services, RLIN, BRS Information Technologies. **Networks/Consortia:** Member of Research Libraries Information Network (RLIN).

★ 18878 ★
University of Michigan - Music Library (Mus)
3250 Earl V. Moore Bldg., N. Campus   Phone: (313)764-2512
Ann Arbor, MI 48109-2085   Calvin Elliker, Hd. of Mus.Lib.
Founded: 1942. **Staff:** Prof 2; Other 4. **Subjects:** Music. **Special Collections:** Rare book collection; women's music collection (2000 scores); American popular music collection. **Holdings:** 85,000 books and scores; 3000 reels of microfilm; 24,000 recordings. **Subscriptions:** 550 journals and other serials. **Services:** Interlibrary loan; copying; library open to the public for reference use only. **Automated Operations:** Computerized public access catalog, cataloging, acquisitions, and circulation. **Computerized Information Services:** RLIN. **Networks/Consortia:** Member of Research Libraries Information Network (RLIN). **Special Catalogs:** Women's music collection catalog.

★ 18879 ★
University of Michigan - Natural Science Library (Sci-Engr, Biol Sci)
3140 Natural Science Bldg.   Phone: (313)764-1494
Ann Arbor, MI 48109-1048   Patricia Morris
Founded: 1917. **Staff:** Prof 1.5; Other 2. **Subjects:** Biology, geology, natural resources. **Special Collections:** U of M masters' theses. **Holdings:** 184,000 volumes; 2600 masters' theses. **Subscriptions:** 1800 journals and other serials. **Services:** Copying; library open to the public for reference use. **Automated Operations:** Computerized public access catalog and circulation. **Computerized Information Services:** DIALOG Information Services, BRS Information Technologies, RLIN; CD-ROMs (Biological Abstracts, Science Citations). **Networks/Consortia:** Member of Research Libraries Information Network (RLIN). **Remarks:** FAX: (313)764-3829.

★ 18880 ★
University of Michigan - North Engineering Library (Energy, Biol Sci)
1100 Dow   Phone: (313)764-5298
Ann Arbor, MI 48109   Daisy T. Wu
Founded: 1974. **Staff:** 2.5. **Subjects:** Nuclear power, nuclear engineering, reactor design and construction, radiation utilization and effects, natural science aspect of the Great Lakes, limnology, biophysics, biochemistry. **Holdings:** 70,000 volumes; 40,000 hardcopy Atomic Energy Commission and DOE reports; 80,000 AEC microcards; 1 million AEC and DOE microfiche. **Subscriptions:** 200 journals and other serials. **Services:** Interlibrary loan; copying; library open to the public. **Computerized Information Services:** DIALOG Information Services, BRS Information Technologies, PFDS Online, NASA/RECON; BITNET, EDUNET (electronic mail services). **Remarks:** FAX: (313)764-4487. Electronic mail address(es): LELN@UB.CC.UMICH.EDU.

★ 18881 ★
University of Michigan - Physics-Astronomy Library (Sci-Engr)
290 Dennison Bldg.   Phone: (313)764-3442
Ann Arbor, MI 48109-1090   Jack W. Weigel, Libn.
Founded: 1924. **Staff:** Prof 1.25; Other 2. **Subjects:** Astronomy, history of astronomy, physics, history of physics, applied mathematics. **Holdings:** 67,000 volumes; 82 reels of microfilm; 578 technical reports; 810 dissertations. **Subscriptions:** 507 journals and other serials. **Services:** Interlibrary loan; library open to the public for reference use only. **Computerized Information Services:** DIALOG Information Services, STN International. Performs searches on fee basis. **Remarks:** FAX: (313)763-8646. **Staff:** Dottie Riemenschneider.

★ 18882 ★
University of Michigan - School of Education - Instructional Research
   and Information Services (Educ, Info Sci, Comp Sci)
3014 School of Education
Corner East and South University Avenues   Phone: (313)764-0519
Ann Arbor, MI 48109-1259   Claire Sandler, Dir.
Founded: 1979. **Staff:** Prof 4; Other 4. **Subjects:** Elementary and secondary education, higher education, microcomputers, media services. **Special Collections:** Resource Center (microcomputers; textbooks; curriculum guides; teaching aids; AV programs); Media Services. **Holdings:** 2500 books; 8600 textbooks; 1400 dissertations; 600 microcomputer programs; 260 curriculum guides. **Subscriptions:** 40 journals and other serials. **Services:** Copying; demonstration and evaluation of curriculum materials, microcomputers, and software; consultation; workshops; services open to the public. **Computerized Information Services:** CD-ROM (ERIC). **Special Catalogs:** Software catalog (computerized). **Remarks:** FAX: (313)763-1229. **Staff:** Donna Estabrook, Rsrc.Ctr.; Ron Miller, Media Serv.

★ 18883 ★
University of Michigan - School of Public Health - Department of
   Population Planning and International Health - Reference Collection
   (Soc Sci, Med)
Ann Arbor, MI 48109-2029   Phone: (313)764-5464
Staff: Prof 2. **Subjects:** National and international population policy and family planning; educational and medical aspects of family planning; family planning systems; demography. **Holdings:** 500 books; 6000 unbound reports and documents; 1000 country files representing 70 countries; family planning program data; reprints; documents; conference proceedings. **Subscriptions:** 100 journals and other serials. **Services:** Collection open to the public for reference use only. **Computerized Information Services:** POPLINE, DIALOG Information Services. **Special Catalogs:** Holdings lists of country files, journals, and serials.

★ 18884 ★
University of Michigan - School of Public Health - Public Health Library (Med)
M2030 School of Public Health
Ann Arbor, MI 48109
Phone: (313)936-1391
Sandra C. Dow, Hd.Libn.
Founded: 1943. **Staff:** Prof 2; Other 3. **Subjects:** Public health, environmental and industrial health, epidemiology, population planning, health services management and policy, biostatistics, health behavior, health education. **Holdings:** 68,000 volumes. **Subscriptions:** 420 journals and other serials. **Services:** Interlibrary loan; library open to other state university faculty and students in Michigan. **Automated Operations:** Computerized cataloging, acquisitions, serials and circulation. **Computerized Information Services:** DIALOG Information Services, BRS Information Technologies, NLM. **Networks/Consortia:** Member of Research Libraries Information Network (RLIN). **Remarks:** FAX: (313)763-9851. **Staff:** Cassandra Hartnett, Asst.Libn.; Helen Coltman, Circ.Supv.

★ 18885 ★
University of Michigan - Social Work Library (Soc Sci)
1548 Frieze Bldg.
Ann Arbor, MI 48109
Phone: (313)764-5169
Darlene P. Nichols, Assoc.Libn.
Founded: 1958. **Staff:** Prof 1; Other 2. **Subjects:** Social work. **Holdings:** 40,000 books; 100 boxes of pamphlets. **Subscriptions:** 250 journals and other serials. **Services:** Interlibrary loan; consultation; library open to the public with restrictions. **Computerized Information Services:** BRS Information Technologies, DIALOG Information Services; InterNet, BITNET (electronic mail services). **Publications:** Accessions list, semiannual - for internal distribution only; library newsletter and information leaflets - available on request. **Remarks:** FAX: (313)764-0259. Electronic mail address(es): SOCIAL–WORK–LIBRARY@UM.CC.UMICH.EDU (InterNet); userleld@umichum (BITNET).

★ 18886 ★
University of Michigan - Sumner & Laura Foster Library (Soc Sci)
Lorch Hall, Rm. 265
Ann Arbor, MI 48109-1220
Phone: (313)763-6609
Catherine C. Weber, Libn.
Founded: 1985. **Staff:** Prof 1; Other 7. **Subjects:** Economics, international development, public policy. **Special Collections:** African government documents (10,500 items); Sharfman Collection (economics); Livestock in Africa documentation (500 items). **Holdings:** 2000 books; 300 series of working papers and research reports; Dissertations from U of M economics students (1980 to present). **Subscriptions:** 354 journals and other serials. **Services:** Copying; SDI; library open to the public with restrictions. **Computerized Information Services:** Internal databases. **Publications:** Working Papers Acquisition Bulletin, monthly - for internal distribution only. **Staff:** Margo Williams, Asst. to Libn.

★ 18887 ★
University of Michigan - Transportation Research Institute - Research Information & Publications Center (Trans)
2901 Baxter Rd.
Ann Arbor, MI 48109-2150
Phone: (313)764-2171
Ann C. Grimm, Hd.Libn.
Founded: 1966. **Staff:** Prof 2; Other 3. **Subjects:** Highway safety, accident investigation, biomechanics, injury mechanics, driver behavior and characteristics, vehicle dynamics, shipbuilding, automotive industry. **Holdings:** 74,000 documents. **Subscriptions:** 200 journals and other serials. **Services:** Copying; center open to the public for reference use only. **Computerized Information Services:** DIALOG Information Services; internal database. **Publications:** UMTRI Research Review, bimonthly - by subscription; Transportation Research Information (acquisitions list), weekly - available on exchange or by subscription. **Remarks:** FAX: (313)936-1081. **Staff:** Robert Sweet, Asst.Libn.

★ 18888 ★
University of Michigan - William L. Clements Library (Hist)
909 S. University Ave.
Ann Arbor, MI 48109-1190
Phone: (313)764-2347
John C. Dann, Dir.
Founded: 1923. **Staff:** Prof 6; Other 3. **Subjects:** Rare Americana to 1877 - discovery and exploration, early settlement, Indian relations, colonial wars, American Revolution, beginnings of federal government, Northwest Territory, War of 1812, early reforms, Westward movement, Civil War, arts and crafts. **Holdings:** 60,000 volumes; 350 manuscript collections, 1740-1900; 36,000 printed and manuscript maps; 40,000 pieces of sheet music, 1790-1920; American newspapers, 1750-1876; prints. **Services:** Library open to the public with interview. **Computerized Information Services:** RLIN.

Networks/Consortia: Member of Research Libraries Information Network (RLIN). **Publications:** American Magazines and Historical Chronicle, 2/year - to members of Clement Library Associates. **Special Catalogs:** Guide to Manuscript Collections; Division of Maps; Guide to Manuscript Maps; Author/Title Catalog of Americana 1493-1860 in The William L. Clements Library (book, 7 volumes). **Staff:** Richard W. Ryan, Cur. of Bks.; Arlene P. Shy, Hd., Rd.Serv.; David Bosse, Cur. of Maps; Robert S. Cox, Cur. of Mss.; John C. Harriman, Mng.Ed.

★ 18889 ★
University of Michigan, Dearborn - Center for Armenian Research and Publication - Information Center (Area-Ethnic)
4901 Evergreen Rd.
Dearborn, MI 48128-1591
Phone: (313)593-5181
Dennis R. Papazian, Dir.
Founded: 1985. **Staff:** Prof 2; Other 3. **Subjects:** Armenia, Middle East, Holocaust, USSR, genocide. **Special Collections:** U.S. State Department Archives on Armenia (microfilm); Armenian Review (microfilm; complete set); Armenian Architecture collection (microfiche). **Holdings:** 3000 books; 500 reports; archival items; microfiche; microfilm; vertical file of clippings. **Subscriptions:** 3 journals and other serials; 6 newspapers. **Services:** Copying; center open to the public for reference use only. **Computerized Information Services:** Internal databases. Performs searches. Contact Person: Gerald Ottenbreit. **Remarks:** FAX: (313)593-5452.

★ 18890 ★
University Microfilms International - Library (Publ)
300 N. Zeeb Rd.
Ann Arbor, MI 48106
Phone: (313)761-4700
Joseph J. Fitzsimmons, Pres. & CEO, UMI
Founded: 1938. **Staff:** Prof 5. **Subjects:** Early English printed books, incunabula, early American printed books, early English and American periodicals, out-of-print books. **Holdings:** 1 million dissertations; 175 major research collections; 17,000 periodicals on microfilm; 7000 newspapers. **Services:** Library not open to the public. **Computerized Information Services:** ABI/INFORM, Newspaper Abstracts, Business Dateline, Pharmaceutical News Index (PNI); CD-ROM (Periodical Abstracts Ondisc); DATRIX (doctoral research information; internal database). **Publications:** UMI Newsletter; Collections Guides and Indexes; Special Bibliographies; Dissertation Abstracts International; Masters Abstracts; Monograph Abstracts; American Doctoral Dissertations. **Special Catalogs:** Serials in Microform Catalog; Books on Demand Catalog. **Special Indexes:** Comprehensive Dissertation Index; Japanese Technical Abstracts and Japanese Current Research. **Remarks:** FAX: (313)761-1204. Telex: 211607-UMI-UR.

★ 18891 ★
University of Minnesota - Ames Library of South Asia (Area-Ethnic)
Wilson Library, S-10
309 19th Ave., S.
Minneapolis, MN 55455
Phone: (612)624-4857
Donald Clay Johnson, Hd.
Founded: 1908. **Staff:** Prof 1. **Subjects:** South Asia - history, economics, political science, art, literature, philology, philosophy, religion, music. **Special Collections:** French India (400 volumes); Portuguese India (includes the Trois Johnson Collection; 1500 volumes); Sanskrit series (4000 volumes). **Holdings:** 150,000 volumes; 8924 microforms; 20 feet of manuscripts; 1162 AV programs. **Subscriptions:** 755 journals and other serials; 7 newspapers. **Services:** Interlibrary loan; copying; library open to the public for reference use only. **Computerized Information Services:** Electronic mail. **Networks/Consortia:** Member of MINITEX Library Information Network, Research Libraries Information Network (RLIN). **Special Catalogs:** G.K. Hall catalog, 16 vols., 1980. **Special Indexes:** Author-subject index of the Journal of Indian History; author-subject index of 19th century pamphlet collection. **Remarks:** FAX: (612)626-9353. **Staff:** Emiko Weeks.

★ 18892 ★
University of Minnesota - Architecture Library (Art, Plan)
160 Architecture Bldg.
89 Church St., S.E.
Minneapolis, MN 55455
Phone: (612)624-6383
Joon Mornes, Act.Hd.
Founded: 1913. **Staff:** Prof 1; Other 1. **Subjects:** Architecture, planning, landscape architecture, design methodology, energy conservation, interior design, environmental psychology. **Holdings:** 36,038 volumes; 661 AV programs; 278 microforms; pamphlets; theses. **Subscriptions:** 195 journals and other serials. **Services:** Interlibrary loan; copying; library open to the public for reference use only. **Computerized Information Services:** Internal database. **Networks/Consortia:** Member of MINITEX Library Information Network, Research Libraries Information Network (RLIN). **Special Catalogs:** Thesis, video cassette, and pamphlet catalogs (card).

★ 18893 ★
University of Minnesota - Bell Museum of Natural History - Library
  (Biol Sci)
10 Church St., S.E.   Phone: (612)624-1639
Minneapolis, MN 55455   Tom English, Hd.
Staff: Prof 1. **Subjects:** Ornithology, ethology, mammalogy, herpetology, animal behavior, taxonomy, amphibians. **Holdings:** 12,660 volumes; 66 AV programs. **Subscriptions:** 362 journals and other serials. **Services:** Interlibrary loan; library open to the public for reference only. **Networks/Consortia:** Member of MINITEX Library Information Network, Research Libraries Information Network (RLIN).

★ 18894 ★
University of Minnesota - Bio-Medical Library (Med, Biol Sci)
450 Diehl Hall
505 Essex St., S.E.   Phone: (612)626-3260
Minneapolis, MN 55455   Ellen Nagle, Dir.
Founded: 1892. **Staff:** Prof 11; Other 39. **Subjects:** Medicine and allied health sciences, nursing, dentistry, pharmacy, public health, biology. **Holdings:** 369,656 volumes; 2089 AV programs; 139,000 monographs; 51 manuscripts; 53,230 microforms. **Subscriptions:** 4718 journals and other serials. **Services:** Interlibrary loan; copying; SDI; library open to the public for reference use only. **Automated Operations:** Computerized cataloging, acquisitions, and serials. **Computerized Information Services:** BRS Information Technologies, NLM, PFDS Online, DIALOG Information Services; Minnesota MEDLine (internal database); CD-ROMs; BITNET (electronic mail service). Performs searches on fee basis. Contact Person: Janet Arth, Assoc.Libn. **Networks/Consortia:** Member of National Network of Libraries of Medicine - Greater Midwest Region, MINITEX Library Information Network, Research Libraries Information Network (RLIN). **Publications:** Bio-Medical Library Bulletin. **Remarks:** FAX: (612)626-3824. Electronic mail address(es): E-NAGL@UMINN1 (BITNET). Library offers Biomedical Information Service (BIS), a fee-based service for corporate clients. **Staff:** Vicki Glasgow, Hd., Biomed.Info.Serv.; Gertrude Foreman, Hd., Pub.Serv.; Margaret Lindorfer, Circ.; Dorothy Bohn, Hd. of Coll.Dev.; Mary Mueller, Hd., Lib.Instr.; M. Kathryn Robbins, Coord. of Ref. Desk. Serv.; Ruth Makinen, Hd., Tech.Serv.

★ 18895 ★
University of Minnesota - Bio-Medical Library - Owen H. Wangensteen Historical Library of Biology and Medicine (Biol Sci, Med)
568 Diehl Hall
505 Essex St., S.E.   Phone: (612)626-6881
Minneapolis, MN 55455   Elaine Challacombe, Cur.
Founded: 1967. **Staff:** Prof 1; Other 1. **Subjects:** Health sciences, surgery, nursing, tuberculosis, pharmacy, medicine. **Special Collections:** Burch Ophthalmology Collection; Mackall Mushroom Collection; Cole Collection of Orthopedic Surgery; Minnesota Association of Public Health Archives; Spink Brucellosis Collection; Minnesota Health Science Libraries Association Archives; medical and pharmaceutical artifacts. **Holdings:** 46,261 books; 409 feet of manuscripts and archival material; 790 microforms. **Subscriptions:** 14 journals and other serials. **Services:** Copying; library open to the public. **Automated Operations:** Computerized cataloging, acquisitions, and serials. **Computerized Information Services:** BITNET (electronic mail service). **Networks/Consortia:** Member of MINITEX Library Information Network, Research Libraries Information Network (RLIN). **Special Indexes:** Index to author presentation copies. **Remarks:** FAX: (612)626-2454. Electronic mail address(es): E-CHAL@UMINN1 (BITNET).

★ 18896 ★
University of Minnesota - Business Reference Service (Bus-Fin)
Wilson Library, 2nd Fl.
309 19th Ave., S.   Phone: (612)624-9066
Minneapolis, MN 55455   Judy Wells, Hd.
Staff: Prof 3; Other 2. **Subjects:** Business, finance and investments, marketing, accounting, management information systems, computer hardware and software, insurance, management science, transportation. **Holdings:** 6511 volumes; 1352 documents, 108,420 microforms. **Subscriptions:** 8530 journals and other serials. **Services:** Interlibrary loan; copying; service open to the public for reference use only. **Computerized Information Services:** DIALOG Information Services, BRS Information Technologies, DataTimes. **Networks/Consortia:** Member of MINITEX Library Information Network, Research Libraries Information Network (RLIN).

★ 18897 ★
University of Minnesota - Business Reference Service - Deloitte Haskins & Sells Tax Research Room (Bus-Fin)
Wilson Library, 2nd Fl.
309 19th Ave., S.   Phone: (612)624-9066
Minneapolis, MN 55455   Judy Wells, Hd.
Founded: 1978. **Subjects:** Taxation. **Holdings:** 1207 volumes; 1907 tax pamphlets. **Services:** Copying; room open to the public for reference use only. **Networks/Consortia:** Member of Research Libraries Information Network (RLIN).

★ 18898 ★
University of Minnesota - Center for Youth Development and Research
386 McNeal Hall
1985 Buford Ave.   Phone: (612)624-3700
St. Paul, MN 55108   Jerry Beker, Dir.
Founded: 1970. **Subjects:** Youth. **Holdings:** 500 books; 1000 clippings; 100 county reports. **Remarks:** Currently inactive.

★ 18899 ★
University of Minnesota - Charles Babbage Institute Collection (Comp Sci)
103 Walter Library
117 Pleasant St., S.E.   Phone: (612)624-5050
Minneapolis, MN 55455   Bruce Bruemmer, Archv.
Founded: 1980. **Staff:** Prof 2. **Subjects:** History - information processing, information storage and retrieval systems, computers, programming languages, computing; computer industry. **Holdings:** 400 volumes; 2500 linear feet of documents, oral interview transcripts, records; 24,000 photographs and other AV material; 1062 microforms. **Services:** Copying; collection open to researchers. **Automated Operations:** Computerized public access catalog. **Computerized Information Services:** Internal database; BITNET (electronic mail service). **Networks/Consortia:** Member of Research Libraries Information Network (RLIN), MINITEX Library Information Network. **Publications:** Newsletter, quarterly - free upon request. **Remarks:** FAX: (612)624-2841. Electronic mail address(es): B-BRUE@UMINN1 (BITNET). **Staff:** Kevin D. Corbitt, Asst.Archv.

★ 18900 ★
University of Minnesota - Children's Literature Research Collections (Hum)
109 Walter Library
117 Pleasant St., S.E.   Phone: (612)624-4576
Minneapolis, MN 55455   Karen Nelson Hoyle, Cur.
Founded: 1949. **Staff:** Prof 1; Other 1. **Subjects:** Children's books - first editions, manuscripts, illustrations; children's literary history and criticism; children's periodicals; American and British dime novels, periodicals, story papers, pulps; Big Little Books; comic books. **Special Collections:** Kerlan Collection (52,000 books; manuscript materials for 2600 titles; illustration materials for 3300 titles; correspondence); Hess Collection (48,000 dime novels, periodicals, story papers, pulps; 561 Big Little Books; 1200 comic books); Wanda Gag Collection (33 books; manuscript and illustration materials for 8 titles); Gustaf Tenggren Collection (150 books; illustration materials for 78 titles); Children's Periodicals Collection (64 19th century American titles; 26 19th century British titles); Series Books Collection (8000 books); Edward S. Ellis Collection (57 periodicals; 217 dime novels; 1090 books; 325 non-English titles; 15 linear feet of related materials); Beulah Counts Rudolph Collection of Figurines, Wall Hangings and Book Marks (400 figurines; 68 wall hangings; 700 book marks); Paul Bunyan Collection (140 books; 8 linear feet of related materials); Newberry and Caldecott Award Books; Minnesota Authors and Illustrators; Mildred L. Batcholder Award books; Tomie de Paola, Jean Craighead George, Marguerite Henry, Katherine Paterson, Charles Mikolaycak, Madeleine L'Engle, and others; Translation of Classics to English; Non-English Language books (including Scandanavian, 3600 titles). **Holdings:** 60,000 monographs; 833 feet of manuscripts; 2511 illustrations; 127 microforms. **Subscriptions:** 30 journals and other serials. **Services:** Copying (limited); collections open for research upon application. **Automated Operations:** Computerized public access catalog. **Computerized Information Services:** Internal database. **Networks/Consortia:** Member of Research Libraries Information Network (RLIN), MINITEX Library Information Network. **Publications:** List of brochures and bibliographies - available on request. **Special Catalogs:** The Kerlan Collection: Manuscripts and Illustrations, 1985 (book); Girls Series Books, 1991 (book). **Remarks:** FAX: (612)624-8518.

★ 18901 ★
University of Minnesota - Classical Studies Department - Seminar Library (Hum)
309 Folwell Hall
9 Pleasant St., S.E. Phone: (612)625-5353
Minneapolis, MN 55455 Asst.Prof. Oliver Nicholson, Libn.
Staff: Prof 1. **Subjects:** Latin, Greek, classical civilization. **Special Collections:** Classics Curriculum Library of elementary and intermediate texts. **Holdings:** 2000 volumes. **Services:** Copying; library open to the public with restrictions.

★ 18902 ★
University of Minnesota - Department of Linguistics - Linguistics and ESL Library (Hum)
152 Klaeber Ct.
320 16th Ave., S.E. Phone: (612)624-3528
Minneapolis, MN 55455 Karen Frederickson, Prin.Sec.
Subjects: Linguistics, English as a second language. **Holdings:** 1400 books. **Subscriptions:** 80 journals and other serials. **Services:** Library open to the public on a limited schedule.

★ 18903 ★
University of Minnesota - Department of Obstetrics and Gynecology - Litzenberg-Lund Library (Med)
PO Box 395 UMHC
420 Delaware St., S.E. Phone: (612)626-2645
Minneapolis, MN 55455 Sarah Sturey, Lib.Mgr.
Founded: 1978. **Staff:** 1. **Subjects:** Obstetrics, gynecology, reproductive endocrinology, gynecologic oncology, gynecologic surgery, maternal-fetal medicine. **Special Collections:** Historical medical and obstetrics-gynecology books. **Holdings:** 330 books; 300 bound periodical volumes. **Subscriptions:** 14 journals and other serials. **Services:** Interlibrary loan; copying; library not open to the public. **Automated Operations:** Computerized public access catalog (LUMINA). **Computerized Information Services:** BRS/COLLEAGUE, MEDLARS, MEDLINE. Performs searches. **Remarks:** The Litzenberg-Lund Library is sponsored by the University of Minnesota Medical School's Department Of Obstetrics & Gynecology, University Women's Health Physicians, and donations.

★ 18904 ★
University of Minnesota - Drug Information Services (Med)
3-106 Health Science Unit F
308 Harvard St., S.E. Phone: (612)624-6492
Minneapolis, MN 55455 Gail Weinberg
Founded: 1970. **Staff:** Prof 2; Other 1. **Subjects:** Psychosocial aspects and research findings of drugs of abuse, alternatives to drug abuse, school curricula, drug abuse in business, treatment and prevention of drug abuse, alcoholism. **Holdings:** 29,000 books, bound periodical volumes, reprints; pamphlets. **Subscriptions:** 90 journals and other serials. **Services:** Interlibrary loan; copying; services open to the public. **Automated Operations:** Computerized ILL (DOCLINE). **Computerized Information Services:** BRS Information Technologies, NLM; DRUGINFO (internal database). Performs searches on fee basis. **Networks/Consortia:** Member of Twin Cities Biomedical Consortium (TCBC), Substance Abuse Librarians and Information Specialists (SALIS). **Publications:** DIS Update, 4/year. **Special Catalogs:** Thesaurus for DRUGINFO database. **Remarks:** The center is part of the College of Pharmacy and the University of Minnesota Hospital's Department of Pharmacy. **Also Known As:** DIS.

★ 18905 ★
University of Minnesota - East Asian Library (Area-Ethnic)
Wilson Library, S-75
309 19th Ave., S. Phone: (612)624-9833
Minneapolis, MN 55455 Yuan Zhou, Hd.
Staff: 1.75. **Subjects:** China and Japan - language and literature, history and politics, philosophy and religion; Asian art history. **Holdings:** 98,330 volumes; 2130 microforms; 6 maps. **Subscriptions:** 490 journals and other serials. **Services:** Interlibrary loan; copying; library open to the public for reference use only. **Automated Operations:** Computerized public access catalog. **Computerized Information Services:** Internal database. **Networks/Consortia:** Member of MINITEX Library Information Network, Research Libraries Information Network (RLIN). **Remarks:** FAX: (612)626-9353. **Staff:** Yuh Shiow Wang.

★ 18906 ★
University of Minnesota - Economics Research Library (Bus-Fin)
525 Science Classroom Bldg.
222 Pleasant St., S.E. Phone: (612)625-2307
Minneapolis, MN 55455 Wendy Williamson, Libn.
Founded: 1969. **Staff:** 1. **Subjects:** Economics, econometrics, mathematics. **Holdings:** 4000 books; 35,000 working papers; 4000 reprints. **Subscriptions:** 50 journals and other serials. **Services:** Library open to university faculty and students on a limited schedule. **Computerized Information Services:** Dataflex (internal database); InterNet (electronic mail service). **Publications:** Recent Acquisitions, monthly. **Remarks:** FAX: (612)624-0209. Electronic mail address(es): williams@mec.econ.umn.edu (InterNet).

★ 18907 ★
University of Minnesota - Education/Psychology Reference Service (Educ, Info Sci)
110 Walter Library
117 Pleasant St., S.E. Phone: (612)624-4185
Minneapolis, MN 55455 James Hodson, Hd.
Founded: 1962. **Staff:** Prof 4; Other 1. **Subjects:** Education, psychology, library science. **Special Collections:** Educational Testing Service; tests (microfiche); history of education (microfiche); psychological tests. **Holdings:** 225,000 volumes; 550,000 microforms; college catalogs on microfiche; ERIC microfiche; annual reports from college and university libraries. **Subscriptions:** 6000 journals and other serials. **Services:** Interlibrary loan; copying; SDI; library open to the public for reference use only. **Computerized Information Services:** DIALOG Information Services, BRS Information Technologies, WILSONLINE, DataTimes; BITNET (electronic mail service). **Networks/Consortia:** Member of MINITEX Library Information Network, Research Libraries Information Network (RLIN). **Remarks:** Electronic mail address(es): X-EDUREF@UMINN1 (BITNET). **Staff:** Don Osier; Pat Stark; Lowell Olson.

★ 18908 ★
University of Minnesota - Eric Sevareid Journalism Library (Info Sci)
121 Murphy Hall
206 Church St., S.E. Phone: (612)625-7892
Minneapolis, MN 55455 Kathleen Hansen, Assoc.Prof./Libn.
Founded: 1941. **Staff:** Prof 1; Other 1. **Subjects:** Mass communications, newspaper journalism, broadcasting, magazine journalism, graphic arts, advertising, international communication, public relations, behavioral research, media management, visual communication. **Special Collections:** Thomas Heggen Memorial Library (creative writing; 1000 items); Eric Sevareid Papers (29 reels of microfilm). **Holdings:** 7100 books; 1300 bound periodical volumes; 1000 pamphlets; 218 theses. **Subscriptions:** 160 journals and other serials; 40 newspapers. **Services:** Interlibrary loan; copying; library open to the public. **Automated Operations:** Computerized cataloging. **Computerized Information Services:** DIALOG Information Services, VU/TEXT Information Services, DataTimes; BITNET (electronic mail service). Performs searches on fee basis. **Networks/Consortia:** Member of Research Libraries Information Network (RLIN). **Remarks:** FAX: (612)626-7755. Electronic mail address(es): K-HANS@UMINN1 (BITNET).

★ 18909 ★
University of Minnesota - ESTIS/INFORM (Info Sci)
108 Walter Library
117 Pleasant St. S.E. Phone: (612)624-2356
Minneapolis, MN 55455 Kathy Fouty, Hd.
Computerized Information Services: OCLC; BITNET (electronic mail service). **Networks/Consortia:** Member of Center for Research Libraries (CRL), Research Libraries Information Network (RLIN), MINITEX Library Information Network. **Remarks:** ESTIS/INFORM is a service unit that provides fee-based document delivery for business, industry, and individuals. Scope includes literature in business, law, government, education, psychology, humanities, sciences, and social sciences. Services include photocopying of articles and book loans. Interlibrary loan service provided for material within scope as well as science and technology literature. Referrals of requests are made to other campus fee-based services as appropriate. Fee schedule available on request. FAX: (612)624-8518. Electronic mail address(es): P-MCKI@UMINN1 (BITNET). **Formerly:** University of Minnesota - INFORM.

★ 18910 ★
University of Minnesota - Government Publications Library (Info Sci)
409 Wilson Library
309 19th Ave., S.   Phone: (612)624-5073
Minneapolis, MN 55455   Julia F. Wallace, Dir.
Staff: Prof 3; Other 5. **Subjects:** Government publications. **Special Collections:** Regional depository for U.S. documents; Minnesota state documents depository; Canadian depository; United Nations depository; European Community depository; Organization for Economic Cooperation and Development (OECD) documents; Organization of American States (OAS) documents. **Holdings:** 2000 books; 2.4 million documents; 593,500 microforms; 10 AV programs. **Subscriptions:** 1202 journals and other serials. **Services:** Interlibrary loan; copying; library open to the public for reference use only; loans made with acceptable borrowing cards. **Computerized Information Services:** DIALOG Information Services, LEGI-SLATE, Datanet; BITNET, InterNet (electronic mail services). **Networks/Consortia:** Member of MINITEX Library Information Network, Research Libraries Information Network (RLIN), Center for Research Libraries (CRL). **Remarks:** FAX: (612)626-9353. Electronic mail address(es): X-GOVREF@UMINN1 (BITNET); X-GOVREF@vm1.spcs.umn.edu (InterNet).

★ 18911 ★
University of Minnesota - Hormel Institute - Library (Sci-Engr)
801 16th Ave., N.E.   Phone: (507)433-8804
Austin, MN 55912   Judith A. Mullen, Libn.
Founded: 1948. **Staff:** 1. **Subjects:** Lipid and membrane chemistry and biochemistry. **Holdings:** 1800 books; 8000 bound periodical volumes. **Subscriptions:** 100 journals and other serials. **Services:** Interlibrary loan; copying; library open to the public with permission. **Automated Operations:** Computerized cataloging. **Computerized Information Services:** STN International, MEDLARS, OCLC. **Networks/Consortia:** Member of MINITEX Library Information Network, Southeast Library System (SELS). **Remarks:** Alternate telephone number(s): 437-9607. FAX: (507)437-9606.

★ 18912 ★
University of Minnesota - Humanities/Social Sciences Library - Learning Resources Center - Non-Print Library (Aud-Vis)
15 Walter Library
117 Pleasant St., S.E.   Phone: (612)624-1584
Minneapolis, MN 55455   Daniel Donnelly, Hd.
Founded: 1965. **Staff:** 3. **Subjects:** Foreign languages, liberal arts, science, agriculture, ethnic materials, graphic materials. **Holdings:** 755 books; 11,500 sound recordings; 2500 video programs; 10,000 slides. **Subscriptions:** 3 journals and other serials. **Services:** Center open to the public for reference use only. **Automated Operations:** Computerized public access catalog (LUMINA). **Computerized Information Services:** BITNET (electronic mail service). **Remarks:** FAX: (612)624-8518. Electronic mail address(es): D-DONN@UMINN1 (BITNET).

★ 18913 ★
University of Minnesota - Immigration History Research Center (Area-Ethnic)
826 Berry St.   Phone: (612)627-4208
St. Paul, MN 55114   Joel Wurl, Cur.
Founded: 1965. **Staff:** Prof 2; Other 1. **Subjects:** East, Central, and South European and Near Eastern immigration and ethnic groups in the United States, 1880 to present, with emphasis on Finns, Italians, and Slavic peoples; ethnic labor and political movement; ethnic churches, presses, and fraternal organizations; resettlement of refugees after World War II; immigrant welfare agencies; Ukraine and Ukrainians. **Special Collections:** Records of the American Council for Nationalities Service, Jugoslav Socialist Federation, American Latvian Association, Tyomies Society, National Slovak Society, United Ukrainian American Relief Committee, and other ethnic organizations; papers of Anthony Capraro, Alexander A. Granovsky, Philip K. Hitti, Karol T. Jaskolski, Joseph C. Roucek, Theodore Saloutos, and other ethnic scholars and leaders; public ations of ethnic presses and organizations. **Holdings:** 46,800 volumes, including 3000 serial titles and files of 900 newspapers; 1685 AV programs; 65 maps; 4500 feet of manuscripts; 5403 microforms. **Subscriptions:** 488 journals and other serials. **Services:** Interlibrary loan (microfilm only); copying (limited); collection open for research upon application. **Networks/Consortia:** Member of Research Libraries Information Network (RLIN). **Publications:** The IHRC: A Guide to Collections, 1991 - for sale; Spectrum (IHRC journal), irregular - by subscription; IHRC News, 3/year - available upon request; conference proceedings; reprints; preservation manuals; survey guides; microfilm guides - all for sale; publications brochure - available upon request. **Staff:** Rudolph J. Vecoli, Dir.; Halyna Myroniuk, Asst.Cur.

★ 18914 ★
University of Minnesota - Industrial Relations Center - Reference Room (Bus-Fin)
Management & Economics, West Campus
271 19th Ave., S.   Phone: (612)624-7011
Minneapolis, MN 55455   Georgianna Herman, Libn. & Supv.
Founded: 1945. **Staff:** Prof 2; Other 3. **Subjects:** Personnel administration, labor relations, human resource management, collective bargaining, industrial sociology, labor economics, industrial psychology. **Special Collections:** Publications from industrial relations centers in the U.S. (6000). **Holdings:** 14,000 books; 5000 bound periodical volumes; 120 VF drawers of subject files; 5500 government documents; 570 volumes of court cases, labor arbitration awards, and other loose-leaf reporting services. **Subscriptions:** 140 journals and other serials; 60 labor union newspapers. **Services:** Copying; reference room open to the public. **Computerized Information Services:** DIALOG Information Services; internal database. **Remarks:** FAX: (612)624-8360. **Staff:** Mariann Nelson, Lib.Asst.

University of Minnesota - INFORM
See: **University of Minnesota - ESTIS/INFORM** (18909)

★ 18915 ★
University of Minnesota - James Ford Bell Library (Hist)
462 Wilson Library
309 19th Ave., S.   Phone: (612)624-1528
Minneapolis, MN 55455   Carol Urness, Cur.
Founded: 1953. **Staff:** Prof 2. **Subjects:** History of European overseas expansion to 1800. **Holdings:** 15,016 volumes; 200 reels of microfilm. **Services:** Copying; collection open to the public for reference use only. **Automated Operations:** Computerized public access catalog. **Computerized Information Services:** Internal database. **Networks/Consortia:** Member of Research Libraries Information Network (RLIN), MINITEX Library Information Network. **Publications:** The Merchant Explorer, annual - on request and to selected libraries. **Special Catalogs:** The James Ford Bell Library: an annotated catalog of original source materials relating to the history of European expansion, 1400-1800 (1981). **Remarks:** FAX: (612)626-9353. **Staff:** Bradley Oftelie, Asst.Cur.

★ 18916 ★
University of Minnesota - John R. Borchert Map Library (Geog-Map)
Wilson Library, S-76
309 19th Ave., S.   Phone: (612)624-4549
Minneapolis, MN 55455   Brent Allison, Hd.
Founded: 1940. **Staff:** Prof 2; Other 2. **Subjects:** Cartography, history of cartography, geographic information systems. **Special Collections:** Ames Library of South Asia Map Collection of India; early maps of Minnesota. **Holdings:** 6544 books, atlases, bound periodical volumes; 372,428 documents; 244,894 maps; 55 microforms; 172,614 aerial photographs; AV programs; pamphlets. **Subscriptions:** 40 journals and other serials. **Services:** Interlibrary loan (limited); copying; library open to the public with restrictions. **Automated Operations:** Computerized public access catalog. **Computerized Information Services:** BITNET (electronic mail service). **Networks/Consortia:** Member of MINITEX Library Information Network, Research Libraries Information Network (RLIN). **Special Indexes:** Aerial photography summary record system. **Remarks:** FAX: (612)626-9353. Electronic mail address(es): B-ALLI@UMINN1 (BITNET). **Staff:** John A. Olson.

★ 18917 ★
University of Minnesota - Landscape Arboretum - Elmer L. & Eleanor J. Andersen Horticultural Library (Biol Sci)
3675 Arboretum Dr.   Phone: (612)443-2440
Chanhassen, MN 55317   Richard T. Isaacson, Hd.
Founded: 1973. **Staff:** Prof 1; Other 2. **Subjects:** Horticulture, botany, natural science, landscape architecture. **Special Collections:** Wildflowers (botanical illustrations); Frances R. Williams Collection (publications on the genus Hosta); seed and nursery catalogs. **Holdings:** 9524 volumes; 555 AV programs; 9 feet of manuscripts; 1388 microforms. **Subscriptions:** 487 journals and other serials. **Services:** Library open to the public for reference use only; arboretum plant locater. **Networks/Consortia:** Member of Research Libraries Information Network (RLIN).

★18918★
University of Minnesota - Law Library (Law)
120 The Law Center
Minneapolis, MN 55455
Phone: (612)625-4300
Joan S. Howland, Dir.
Founded: 1888. **Staff:** Prof 10; Other 16. **Subjects:** Law - Anglo-American, foreign. **Special Collections:** Scandinavian law; American Indians; British Commonwealth legal materials, including Indian and Pakistani legal materials. **Holdings:** 519,236 volumes; 1.13 million microforms. **Subscriptions:** 9629 journals and other serials. **Services:** Interlibrary loan; copying; faxing; 24-hour study hall available; library open to the public for reference use only. **Automated Operations:** Computerized cataloging, serials, acquisitions, and circulation. **Computerized Information Services:** LEXIS, WESTLAW, LEGI-SLATE, DIALOG Information Services, NEXIS, RLIN, OCLC; BITNET, InterNet (electronic mail services). **Networks/Consortia:** Member of MINITEX Library Information Network. **Publications:** Newsletter, bimonthly; Law Library Guide; Pathfinders. **Remarks:** FAX: (612)625-3487. Electronic mail address(es): UMINN1 (BITNET); VM1.SPCS.UMN.EDU (InterNet). **Staff:** Suzanne Thorpe, Asst.Dir./Pub.Serv.; Margaret Axtmann, Asst.Dir./Tech.Serv.; Milagros R. Rush, Acq./Ser.; Katherine Hedin, Cat.; Nancy McCormick, Circ.; George Jackson, Ref.; Tami Gierloff, Ref.; Julia Wentz, Ref.; Claire Stuckey, Cat.

★18919★
University of Minnesota - Machine Readable Data Center (Soc Sci)
50 Humphrey Ctr.
301 19th Ave., S.
Minneapolis, MN 55454
Phone: (612)624-4389
Wendy Treadwell, Coord.
Founded: 1967. **Staff:** Prof 1; Other 2. **Subjects:** Demographics, economics, agriculture. **Special Collections:** U.S. Decennial Census, 1970 to present; Bureau of Economic Analysis tables, 1969 to present; Current Population Survey Annual Demographic File, 1967 to present. **Holdings:** 600 books; 300 computer tapes, CD-ROMs, diskettes. **Subscriptions:** 4 journals and other serials. **Services:** Copying; center open to the public with restrictions. **Computerized Information Services:** InterNet, BITNET (electronic mail services). **Publications:** CONNECTION (newsletter), bimonthly. **Remarks:** FAX: (612)626-9353. Electronic mail address(es): W-TREA@UMINN1 (BITNET); W-TREA@VM1.SPCS.UMN.EDU (InterNet). Center is a tape depository of the Minnesota State Data Center.

★18920★
University of Minnesota - Manuscripts Division (Hist)
826 Berry St.
St. Paul, MN 55114
Phone: (612)627-4199
Alan K. Lathrop, Cur.
Founded: 1970. **Staff:** Prof 1. **Special Collections:** Literary Manuscripts Collections - papers of Gordon R. Dickson (63 linear feet), Clifford D. Simak (10 linear feet), John Berryman (55 linear feet), Frederick Manfred (90 linear feet), H.P. Lovecraft (87 items), Arthur Motley (195 linear feet); Performing Arts Archives - records of Guthrie Theater (400 linear feet), Minnesota Orchestra (450 linear feet); Twin Cities scenic design studios scenic backdrop renderings (2000 items); Northwest Architectural Archives - records of American Terra Cotta Company, Purcell and Elmslie, architects (100,000 items), Morrel and Nichols Landscape Architects (48 linear feet), Ellerbe Architects (20 linear feet), Liebenberg and Kaplan Architects (840 linear feet), L.S. Buffington Drawings Collection (2200 items), Close Associates architects (40 linear feet); trade catalog collection (6100 items). **Holdings:** 200 volumes of stock plan books; 10,235 feet of manuscripts; 4099 microforms; 30,175 photographs and recordings; 7 maps. **Subscriptions:** 4 journals and other serials. **Services:** Copying; division open for research upon application. **Automated Operations:** Computerized public access catalog. **Computerized Information Services:** RLIN; BITNET, InterNet (electronic mail services). **Networks/Consortia:** Member of Research Libraries Information Network (RLIN), MINITEX Library Information Network. **Special Indexes:** Index to architectural archives by building name, identifying media, and type of documentation (card). **Remarks:** Electronic mail address(es): A-LATH@UMINNI (BITNET); A-LATH@VMI.SPCS.UMN.EDU (InterNet).

★18921★
University of Minnesota - Mathematics Library (Sci-Engr)
Vincent Hall, Rm. 310
206 Church St., S.E.
Minneapolis, MN 55455
Phone: (612)624-9395
Janice Griggs
Staff: Prof 1; Other 1. **Subjects:** Pure mathematics, theoretical statistics. **Holdings:** 31,397 volumes, 12 microforms. **Subscriptions:** 358 journals and other serials. **Services:** Interlibrary loan; copying; library open to the public

for reference use only. **Computerized Information Services:** DIALOG Information Services, BRS Information Technologies; BITNET (electronic mail service). **Networks/Consortia:** Member of MINITEX Library Information Network, Research Libraries Information Network (RLIN). **Remarks:** Electronic mail address(es): J-GRIG@UMINN1 (BITNET).

★18922★
University of Minnesota - Middle East Library (Area-Ethnic)
Wilson Library, S-30
309 19th Ave., S.
Minneapolis, MN 55455
Phone: (612)624-1012
Nassif Youssif, Hd.
Founded: 1967. **Staff:** Prof 1; Other 1. **Subjects:** Arabic, Hebrew, Persian, and Turkish languages, literature, and history. **Special Collections:** Middle Eastern vernaculars (50,000 volumes). **Holdings:** 57,500 volumes; 111 AV programs; 18 microforms; 28 government documents; 3 maps. **Subscriptions:** 250 journals and other serials; 32 newspapers. **Services:** Interlibrary loan; library open to the public for reference use only. **Automated Operations:** Computerized public access catalog. **Computerized Information Services:** Internal database. **Networks/Consortia:** Member of MINITEX Library Information Network, Research Libraries Information Network (RLIN). **Remarks:** FAX: (612)626-9353.

★18923★
University of Minnesota - Minnesota Center for Philosophy of Science - Departmental Library (Rel-Phil, Sci-Engr)
309 Ford Hall
224 Church St., S.E.
Minneapolis, MN 55455
Phone: (612)625-6635
Steve Lelchuk, Sec.
Subjects: Philosophy of science, physics, psychology; theoretical physics; psychology; logic (mathematical). **Holdings:** 1000 books; reprints; manuscripts. **Services:** Library open to center members only. **Computerized Information Services:** BITNET (electronic mail service). **Remarks:** FAX: (612)626-8380. Electronic mail address(es): PHILOSCI@UMNACVX (BITNET). **Staff:** Ronald Giere, Dir.

★18924★
University of Minnesota - Minnesota Extension Service - Dial-U Insect and Plant Information Clinic (Biol Sci)
145 Alderman Hall
1970 Folwell Ave.
St. Paul, MN 55108
Dr. Mark Ascerno, Dial-U Coord.
Founded: 1983. **Staff:** Prof 4; Other 8. **Subjects:** Horticulture, plant pathology, entomology. **Holdings:** 200 books; 400 extension fact sheets and bulletins. **Subscriptions:** 15 journals and other serials. **Remarks:** This is a telephone information service that can be reached by metropolitan area residents calling 1-976-0200. Caller is automatically charged a special fee when information number is used. **Staff:** Deborah Brown, Horticulture Ext.Spec.; Jeff Hahn, Entomology Ext.Educ.; Cynthia Ash, Plant Pathology Ext.Educ.

★18925★
University of Minnesota - Music Library (Mus)
70 Ferguson Hall
2106 4th St., S.
Minneapolis, MN 55455
Phone: (612)624-5890
Laura K. Probst, Hd.
Founded: 1947. **Staff:** Prof 2; Other 2. **Subjects:** Musicology; music history; opera; theory and composition; vocal, instrumental, and orchestra music; ethnomusicology; folk music; music therapy; music education; keyboard music. **Special Collections:** Donald N. Ferguson Collection of Rare Books and Scores (336 volumes); Operas of 18th & early 19th centuries (175 volumes); Ritzen Collection of Sound Recordings (2200 phonograph records); Latin American music scores (450 volumes); Berger Band Library (335 volumes); Stanley E. Hubbard Music Collection (KSTP radio library; 23,000 items). **Holdings:** 60,823 books, bound periodical volumes, scores; 42,303 AV programs; 1885 microforms. **Subscriptions:** 300 journals and other serials. **Services:** Interlibrary loan; copying; library open to the public for reference use only. **Computerized Information Services:** DIALOG Information Services, BRS Information Technologies, PFDS Online. **Networks/Consortia:** Member of MINITEX Library Information Network, Research Libraries Information Network (RLIN). **Remarks:** FAX: (612)626-9353.

★ 18926 ★
University of Minnesota - Newman Center - Lenore Scallen Library
(Rel-Phil)
1701 University Ave., S.E.   Phone: (612)331-3437
Minneapolis, MN 55414   Larry Conley, Campus Minister
Founded: 1958. **Staff:** Prof 1; Other 1. **Subjects:** Theology, philosophy, humanities, ethics, medical ethics, social issues. **Special Collections:** Newman Center history. **Holdings:** 10,000 books and bound periodical volumes; 195 tapes; 1 box of Newman publications; pamphlets; clippings. **Subscriptions:** 37 journals and other serials. **Services:** Library open to the public on a limited schedule.

★ 18927 ★
University of Minnesota - St. Anthony Falls Hydraulic Laboratory -
Lorenz G. Straub Memorial Library (Sci-Engr)
Mississippi River at 3rd Ave., S.E.   Phone: (612)627-4587
Minneapolis, MN 55414   Patricia Swanson, Ed.
Founded: 1964. **Staff:** 2. **Subjects:** Hydraulics, hydrology, fluid mechanics, water resources, hydropower. **Holdings:** 2000 books; 10,000 other cataloged items. **Subscriptions:** 15 journals and other serials. **Services:** Copying; library open to the public. **Remarks:** Alternate telephone number(s): 627-4011. FAX: (612)627-4609.

★ 18928 ★
University of Minnesota - Science and Engineering Library (Sci-Engr)
108 Walter Library
117 Pleasant St., S.E.
Minneapolis, MN 55455   Phone: (612)624-0224
Founded: 1985. **Staff:** Prof 7; Other 45. **Subjects:** Engineering, chemistry, general science and technology, physics, geology, astronomy, history of science and technology. **Special Collections:** Archive for the History of Quantum Physics; Helmut Heinrich Parachute Technology Collection. **Holdings:** 437,939 books and bound periodical volumes; 92,681 maps; 31,403 microfiche; 2478 reels of microfilm; 250,000 government documents; 3 feet of manuscripts; 896 AV programs. **Subscriptions:** 3976 journals and other serials. **Services:** Interlibrary loan; copying; SDI (fee); library open to the public. **Automated Operations:** Computerized public access catalog. **Computerized Information Services:** DIALOG Information Services, BRS Information Technologies, PFDS Online; internal database; BITNET (electronic mail service). Contact: ESTIS, 624-2356. **Networks/Consortia:** Member of MINITEX Library Information Network, Research Libraries Information Network (RLIN). **Remarks:** FAX: (612)624-8518. **Staff:** Sandra Moline; Raymond Bohling; John Butler; Jody Kempf; Gary Fouty; Donald Marion; Kathy Fouty.

★ 18929 ★
University of Minnesota - Social and Administrative Pharmacy Reading
Room (Med)
7-159 Health Sciences Unit F
308 Harvard St., S.E.   Phone: (612)624-2487
Minneapolis, MN 55455   Ronald S. Hadsall, Ph.D, Dir.
Staff: 2. **Subjects:** Pharmacy, drugs, health service. **Holdings:** 340 books; 425 bound periodical volumes; 4000 NTIS reports on microfiche; government publications; Ph.D. dissertations. **Subscriptions:** 75 journals and other serials. **Services:** Room open to the public with permission. **Remarks:** FAX: (612)625-9931.

★ 18930 ★
University of Minnesota - Social Welfare History Archives (Soc Sci)
101 Walter Library
117 Pleasant St., S.E.   Phone: (612)624-6394
Minneapolis, MN 55455   David Klaassen, Archv.
Founded: 1964. **Staff:** Prof 1; Other 2. **Subjects:** Social welfare, settlement movement, professional social work, voluntary associations, recreation, health. **Special Collections:** records and files of Survey Associates, National Federation of Settlements, Young Men's Christian Association (YMCA) of the U.S.A., National Association of Social Workers, United Neighborhood Houses of New York, and others; social service organization materials (600 linear feet); contemporary feminist periodicals and pamphlets (100 linear feet). **Holdings:** 10,134 books; 7213 feet of manuscripts; 1563 microforms; 20,044 AV programs. **Subscriptions:** 65 journals and other serials. **Services:** Interlibrary loan (limited); copying; archives open for research upon application. **Automated Operations:** Computerized public access catalog. **Computerized Information Services:** Internal database. **Networks/Consortia:** Member of Research Libraries Information Network (RLIN), MINITEX Library Information Network. **Publications:** Guide to Holdings, 1979; Descriptive Inventories of Collections in the Social Welfare History Archives. **Remarks:** FAX: (612)624-8518.

University of Minnesota - Social Welfare History Archives - Young
Men's Christian Association of the USA - YMCA of the USA
Archives
See: YMCA of the USA - Archives (20760)

★ 18931 ★
University of Minnesota - Special Collections and Rare Books Library
(Rare Book)
466 Wilson Library
309 19th Ave. S.   Phone: (612)624-3855
Minneapolis, MN 55455   Austin J. McLean, Cur.
Staff: Prof 2; Other 1. **Subjects:** History, literature, philosophy, astronomy, 17th century England and Holland, private press books, fortification, Scandinavian travel, art, Austrian history. **Special Collections:** Walter de la Mare; Henry Miller; John Galsworthy; Franklin Delano Roosevelt; Sinclair Lewis; John Steinbeck; Sherlock Holmes; Charles Dickens - Edwin Drood; modern Greek literature; Thomas Wolfe; World War I pamphlets (6000); black literature (3500 volumes); Swedish Americana; Vincent Starrett; August Strindberg photomechanics collection; ballooning; silent film scores. **Holdings:** 125,000 books and bound periodical volumes. **Subscriptions:** 20 journals and other serials. **Services:** Copying; library open to the public for reference use only. **Automated Operations:** Computerized public access catalog. **Computerized Information Services:** Interal database. **Networks/Consortia:** Member of Research Libraries Information Network (RLIN), MINITEX Library Information Network. **Special Indexes:** Card indexes to places, dates, printers of books before 1700; card index to private press books by press, printer, designers; card indexes of provenance, manuscripts, signed bindings. **Remarks:** FAX: (612)626-9353. **Staff:** John Jenson, Asst.Cur.

★ 18932 ★
University of Minnesota - Statistics Reading Room (Sci-Engr)
270a Vincent Hall
206 Church St., S.E.   Phone: (612)625-8046
Minneapolis, MN 55455   Seymour Geisser, Dir.
Founded: 1963. **Staff:** 4. **Subjects:** Statistics. **Holdings:** 238 books; 274 bound periodical volumes; 30 bound theses; 567 School of Statistics technical reports. **Subscriptions:** 10 journals and other serials. **Services:** Room open to graduate students for reference use only. **Remarks:** FAX: (612)624-8868.

★ 18933 ★
University of Minnesota - Underground Space Center - Library (Energy)
790 Civil and Mineral Engr. Bldg.
500 Pillsbury Dr., S.E.   Phone: (612)624-0066
Minneapolis, MN 55455   Sara B. Hanft
Founded: 1977. **Staff:** Prof 8. **Subjects:** Earth sheltered housing, energy, underground space use, rock and soil mechanics, alternative energy financing and legislation, building codes. **Holdings:** 150 books; 200 technical papers; 600 documents; 900 clippings. **Subscriptions:** 20 journals and other serials. **Services:** Library open to the public for reference use only. **Computerized Information Services:** Internal database. **Publications:** Building Foundation Design Handbook; Earth Sheltered Housing Design; Earth Sheltered Homes - all for sale; Insulation Materials; Frost Heaving; Basement Insulation; Slab-on-Grade Insulation; Drainage Systems (fact sheets) - all free upon request. **Special Indexes:** Professionals involved in underground construction (computer listings). **Remarks:** FAX: (612)624-0293. Telex: 9102504002. **Staff:** Dr. Ray Sterling, Dir.

★ 18934 ★
University of Minnesota - University Archives (Hist)
10 Walter Library
117 Pleasant St., S.E.   Phone: (612)624-0562
Minneapolis, MN 55455   Penelope Krosch, Hd.
Founded: 1928. **Staff:** Prof 1; Other 2. **Subjects:** University of Minnesota. **Special Collections:** Papers of people and organizations connected with the university. **Holdings:** 75,604 books, bound periodical volumes, dissertations; 13,800 linear feet of manuscripts; 40 VF drawers of ready reference material; 1440 microforms; 44,000 AV programs; 383 maps. **Subscriptions:** 658 journals and other serials. **Services:** Copying; archives open to bona fide researchers. **Automated Operations:** Computerized public access catalog. **Computerized Information Services:** Internal database; BITNET (electronic mail service). **Networks/Consortia:** Member of Research Libraries Information Network (RLIN), MINITEX Library Information Network. **Special Indexes:** Indexes for 7 major university publications (card); index of photograph collection. **Remarks:** Electronic mail address(es): P-KROS@UMINN1 (BITNET).

★ 18935 ★
University of Minnesota - University Counseling Services - Career Resource Center (Educ)
302 Eddy Hall
192 Pillsbury Dr., S.E. Phone: (612)624-8344
Minneapolis, MN 55455 Kevin J. Nutter, Ph.D., Ctr.Dir.
Staff: 2. **Subjects:** Educational and career planning. **Holdings:** 200 books; national and international college catalog collections (complete); 1200 college catalogs on microfiche; 300 occupational files; 36 cassette tapes on careers and personal development; 2 computerized career development programs. **Services:** Center open to the public with restrictions.

★ 18936 ★
University of Minnesota - University Film and Video (Aud-Vis)
Minneapolis, MN 55414 Phone: (612)627-4270
  Judith A. Gaston, Dir.
Founded: 1913. **Staff:** Prof 2; Other 8. **Subjects:** General collection. **Holdings:** 9750 16mm films; 13,500 prints. **Subscriptions:** 20 journals and other serials. **Services:** Library open to the public. **Automated Operations:** Computerized circulation. **Remarks:** FAX: (612)627-4280. **Staff:** R. Kay Cooper, Media Spec.

★ 18937 ★
University of Minnesota - Wilson Library - Scandanavian Collection (Area-Ethnic)
309 19th Ave., S. Phone: (612)624-5860
Minneapolis, MN 55455 Mariann Tiblin, Bibliog.
Subjects: Scandinavian humanities and social sciences. **Special Collections:** Jeppe Aakjaer Collection (110 volumes); Scandinavian Children's Literature Collection (700 volumes); Par Lagerkvist Collection (158 volumes); Scandinavian maps; Scandinavian Travels Collection; August Strindberg Collection (800 volumes); Swedish Royal Decrees, 1649-1824 (2655); Tell G. Dahllof Collection of Swedish-Americana (10,000 volumes). **Holdings:** 200,000 volumes (in general and periodical Wilson Library collections). **Subscriptions:** 200 journals and other serials; 5 newspapers. **Services:** Interlibrary loan; copying; collection open to the public. **Computerized Information Services:** DIALOG Information Services, BRS Information Technologies, PFDS Online. **Networks/Consortia:** Member of MINITEX Library Information Network, Research Libraries Information Network (RLIN). **Remarks:** FAX: (612)626-9353. Materials in the Scandinavian Collection are located in various departments of the University Libraries.

★ 18938 ★
University of Minnesota, Crookston - Kiehle Library - Media Resources (Agri, Bus-Fin)
Crookston, MN 56716-0801 Phone: (218)281-6510
  Harold J. Opgrand, Dir., Media Rsrcs.
Founded: 1966. **Staff:** Prof 3. **Subjects:** Agriculture, horsemanship, business, foods, hospitality, hotel management. **Special Collections:** Minnesota State Depository materials; Equine Resource Center. **Holdings:** 27,858 books; 130 periodicals on microfilm; 1783 AV programs. **Subscriptions:** 920 journals and other serials; 55 newspapers. **Services:** Interlibrary loan; copying; resources open to the public, AV materials available for on-site use only. **Automated Operations:** Computerized public access catalog, cataloging, and ILL. **Computerized Information Services:** OCLC, DIALOG Information Services; CD-ROMs. Performs searches on fee basis. Contact Person: Owen Williams, Ref.Libn. **Networks/Consortia:** Member of MINITEX Library Information Network, Northern Lights Library Network (NLLN). **Special Indexes:** Index to Crookston Daily Times. **Remarks:** FAX: (218)281-3392. **Staff:** Krista Proulx, Per./ILL Libn.

★ 18939 ★
University of Minnesota, Duluth - Geography Department - Map Library (Geog-Map)
324 Cina Hall Phone: (218)726-6226
Duluth, MN 55812 Kurt A. Schroeder, Asst.Prof., Geog.
Subjects: Topography - Minnesota, North Dakota, South Dakota, Iowa, Wisconsin, Michigan, Illinois. **Special Collections:** Great Lakes nautical maps; world map series; Canadian topographic maps. **Holdings:** 1000 books; 30,000 maps. **Services:** Library open to the public. **Remarks:** Alternate telephone number(s): 726-6300.

★ 18940 ★
University of Minnesota, Duluth - Health Science Library (Med)
10 University Dr. Phone: (218)726-8587
Duluth, MN 55812 Diane C.P. Ebro, Dir.
Founded: 1971. **Staff:** Prof 2; Other 2. **Subjects:** Medicine, allied clinical health, veterinary medicine, forensic medicine, nursing, biochemistry, behavioral science. **Holdings:** 21,782 books; 46,835 bound periodical volumes; 3000 pamphlets; 3784 reels of microfilm. **Subscriptions:** 691 journals and other serials. **Services:** Interlibrary loan; copying; SDI; library open to the public. **Automated Operations:** Computerized cataloging and serials. **Computerized Information Services:** DIALOG Information Services, PFDS Online, NLM, BRS Information Technologies, OCLC; BITNET, InterNet (electronic mail services). **Networks/Consortia:** Member of National Network of Libraries of Medicine - Greater Midwest Region, MINITEX Library Information Network, Arrowhead Professional Libraries Association (APLA). **Special Catalogs:** Serials Holding List. **Remarks:** Alternate telephone number(s): 726-8100. FAX: (218)726-6205. Electronic mail address(es): LIB@UMNDUL (BITNET); DEBRO@UB.D.UMN.EDU (InterNet). Maintained by the University of Minnesota , Duluth Library. **Staff:** Martha Eberhart, Life Sci.Ref./Online Serv.; Mary Palzer, ILL.

★ 18941 ★
University of Minnesota, Duluth - Natural Resources Research Institute (NRRI) - Natural Resources Library (Biol Sci)
5013 Miller Trunk Hwy. Phone: (218)720-4235
Duluth, MN 55811 Susan R. Hendrickson, Lib.Mgr.
Founded: 1985. **Staff:** Prof 1; Other 2. **Subjects:** Forest products, minerals, peat, ecosystems, environmental chemistry. **Holdings:** 5200 books; 2075 microfiche. **Subscriptions:** 250 journals and other serials. **Services:** Interlibrary loan; copying; library open to the public. **Automated Operations:** Computerized public access catalog, acquisitions, serials, and ILL. **Computerized Information Services:** DIALOG Information Services, PFDS Online, OCLC. **Networks/Consortia:** Member of MINITEX Library Information Network. **Publications:** Nature Today, monthly - available upon request. **Remarks:** FAX: (218)720-4219.

University of Minnesota, Duluth - Northeast Minnesota Historical Center
See: **Northeast Minnesota Historical Center** (11971)

University of Minnesota, Morris - West Central Minnesota Historical Center
See: **West Central Minnesota Historical Center** (20185)

★ 18942 ★
University of Minnesota, St. Paul - Biochemistry Library (Biol Sci, Sci-Engr)
406 Biological Sciences Ctr.
1445 Gortner Ave. Phone: (612)624-1292
St. Paul, MN 55108 Jeffrey Dains, Lib.Asst.
Staff: 1. **Subjects:** Biochemistry, plant biochemistry, animal biochemistry, chemistry of cereals and cereal products, genetics, cell biology. **Holdings:** 22,815 volumes; 8188 microforms. **Subscriptions:** 278 journals and other serials. **Services:** Interlibrary loan (through Central Library, St. Paul Campus); copying; library open to the public for reference use. **Networks/Consortia:** Member of MINITEX Library Information Network, Research Libraries Information Network (RLIN).

★ 18943 ★
University of Minnesota, St. Paul - Central Library (Biol Sci, Agri)
1984 Buford Ave. Phone: (612)624-1212
St. Paul, MN 55108 Richard L. Rohrer, Dir.
Founded: 1890. **Staff:** Prof 7; Other 19. **Subjects:** Agricultural economics and engineering, agricultural and home economics education, home economics, agronomy and plant genetics, animal science, horticultural sciences, biological sciences, applied statistics, food science and nutrition, plant pathology, soil science. **Special Collections:** U.S.D.A. Depository materials; agricultural experiment station, extension, and international agricultural exchange publications. **Holdings:** 168,685 volumes; 454,127 documents; 231 AV programs; 39,038 microforms. **Subscriptions:** 3525 journals and other serials. **Services:** Interlibrary loan; copying; BASIS (fee-based services); library open to the public for reference use. **Computerized Information Services:** BRS Information Technologies, DIALOG Information Services, PFDS Online; BITNET (electronic mail service). **Networks/Consortia:** Member of MINITEX Library Information Network, Research Libraries Information Network (RLIN). **Remarks:** FAX: (612)624-9245.

★ 18944 ★
University of Minnesota, St. Paul - Entomology, Fisheries and Wildlife Library (Biol Sci)
1980 Folwell Ave.
375 Hodson Hall
St. Paul, MN 55108   Phone: (612)624-9288
       Loralee Kerr, Hd.
Founded: 1905. **Staff:** Prof 1; Other 1. **Subjects:** Entomology, fisheries, wildlife, pesticides, limnology, aquatic biology. **Special Collections:** Bee collection (800 monographs; 87 journal titles). **Holdings:** 37,454 books and bound periodical volumes; 37,459 documents; 90 maps; 1824 AV programs; 6695 microforms. **Subscriptions:** 757 journals and other serials. **Services:** Interlibrary loan; copying; library open to the public for reference use only. **Computerized Information Services:** DIALOG Information Services, BRS Information Technologies. **Networks/Consortia:** Member of MINITEX Library Information Network, Research Libraries Information Network (RLIN).

★ 18945 ★
University of Minnesota, St. Paul - Forestry Library (Biol Sci, Env-Cons)
B50 NRAB
2003 Upper Buford Circle
St. Paul, MN 55108   Phone: (612)624-3222
       Jean Albrecht, Hd.
Founded: 1899. **Staff:** Prof 1; Other 1. **Subjects:** Forestry, forest products, outdoor recreation, conservation of natural resources, hydrology, range management, aerial photogrammetry, remote sensing, pulp and paper. **Holdings:** 28,935 books and bound periodical volumes; 72,219 documents; 4206 maps; 675 AV programs; 2327 microforms. **Subscriptions:** 1167 journals and other serials. **Services:** Interlibrary loan (through Central Library, St. Paul Campus); copying; library open to the public for reference use only. **Computerized Information Services:** DIALOG Information Services. **Networks/Consortia:** Member of MINITEX Library Information Network, Research Libraries Information Network (RLIN). **Publications:** Social Sciences in Forestry: A Current Selected Bibliography and Index, quarterly - available on a fee basis. **Remarks:** Operates in conjunction with U.S. Forest Service - North Central Forest Experiment Station (NCFES). The Forestry Library contains partial holdings of the former NCFES Library.

★ 18946 ★
University of Minnesota, St. Paul - Plant Pathology Library (Biol Sci)
395 Borlaug Hall
1991 Upper Buford Circle
St. Paul, MN 55108   Phone: (612)625-9777
       Erik Biever, Lib.Asst.
Founded: 1909. **Staff:** 1. **Subjects:** Phytopathology, mycology, air pollution effects on vegetation. **Holdings:** 8442 books and bound periodical volumes; 66 AV programs; 216 microforms; maps. **Subscriptions:** 127 journals and other serials. **Services:** Interlibrary loan (through Central Library, St. Paul Campus); copying; library open to the public for reference use. **Networks/Consortia:** Member of MINITEX Library Information Network, Research Libraries Information Network (RLIN).

★ 18947 ★
University of Minnesota, St. Paul - Veterinary Medical Library (Med)
450 Veterinary Science Bldg.
1971 Commonwealth Ave.
St. Paul, MN 55108   Phone: (612)624-4281
       Livija Carlson, Hd.
Staff: Prof 1; Other 2. **Subjects:** Veterinary medicine. **Special Collections:** German veterinary theses. **Holdings:** 44,366 books and bound periodical volumes; 18,564 documents; 66 AV programs; 723 microforms; dissertations. **Subscriptions:** 1057 journals and other serials. **Services:** Interlibrary loan; copying; library open to the public for reference use only. **Computerized Information Services:** BITNET, InterNet (electronic mail services). **Networks/Consortia:** Member of MINITEX Library Information Network, Research Libraries Information Network (RLIN). **Special Catalogs:** Pamphlet and documents catalogs. **Remarks:** Electronic mail address(es): M-BERG@UMINN1 (BITNET); M-BERG@VM1.SPCS.UMN.EDUC (InterNet).

★ 18948 ★
University of Minnesota, Waseca - UMW Library
1000 University Dr., S.W.
Waseca, MN 56093
Defunct.

★ 18949 ★
University of Mississippi - Archives & Special Collections/ Mississippiana (Hum, Hist)
J.D. Williams Library   Phone: (601)232-7408
University, MS 38677   Dr. Thomas M. Verich, Univ.Archv.
Founded: 1975. **Staff:** Prof 1; Other 3. **Subjects:** Mississippi and Southern subjects and authors, Afro-American fiction. **Special Collections:** Lumber archives of lumber industry of southern Mississippi (268 linear feet); William Faulkner Collection (2000 volumes); Wynn Collection of Faulkner editions; Senator Pat Harrison Collection (51 linear feet including photographs); Arthur Palmer Hudson Folklore Collection (5 linear feet); David L. Cohn Collection (12 linear feet); Stark Young Collection (3.5 linear feet); Revolutionary War Letters (1 linear foot); Rayburn Collection of Paper Americana (36 linear feet); Herschel Brickell Collection (4000 manuscript items; 3400 volumes; 150 linear feet); William Faulkner Rowan Oak Literary Manuscript Collection; literary papers of Ellen Douglas, Barry Hannah, and Beth Henley (33 linear feet); James Silver papers (20 linear feet); Aldrich Collection (10 linear feet); William R. Ferris Collection (350 linear feet). **Holdings:** 32,000 books; 3000 bound periodical volumes; 2000 manuscripts; 525 linear feet of University of Mississippi archival materials; 221 linear feet of Thomas G. Abernathy papers; 67 linear feet of Carroll Gartin papers, 1913-1966; 485 linear feet of John E. Rankin papers, 1882-1960; 164 linear feet of William M. Whittington papers, 1878-1962; 180 linear feet of William M. (Fishbait) Miller papers (all papers are unprocessed); 9.5 linear feet of Henry H. Bellamann papers, 1882-1945; 80 linear feet of James W. Garner papers. **Subscriptions:** 150 journals and other serials. **Services:** Copying; archives open to the public. **Staff:** Althea Church, Sr.Lib.Asst.; Sharron Eve Sarthou, Sr.Lib.Asst.

★ 18950 ★
University of Mississippi - Bureau of Business & Economic Research Library
School of Business Administration
University, MS 38677
Subjects: Economics, business, public finance, government. **Holdings:** 5000 documents; Mississippi documents. **Remarks:** Currently inactive.

★ 18951 ★
University of Mississippi - John Davis Williams Library - Austin A. Dodge Pharmacy Library (Med)
215A Faser Hall   Phone: (601)232-7381
University, MS 38677   Nancy F. Fuller, Libn.
Founded: 1965. **Staff:** Prof 1; Other 2. **Subjects:** Pharmacy, medicine, organic chemistry, pharmacy administration, botany (pharmacognosy). **Holdings:** 32,400 books, bound periodical volumes, reels of microfilm, AV programs; 128 dissertations and graduate theses from School of Pharmacy. **Subscriptions:** 425 journals and other serials. **Services:** Interlibrary loan; copying; library open to the public for reference use. **Automated Operations:** Computerized public access catalog and circulation (CLSI). **Computerized Information Services:** BRS Information Technologies, DIALOG Information Services, NLM, MEDLINE, Chemical Abstracts Service (CAS), OCLC; CD-ROM (Index Medicus, International Pharmaceutical Abstracts). **Networks/Consortia:** Member of Association of Memphis Area Health Science Libraries (AMAHSL), Mississippi Biomedical Library Consortium (MBLC).

★ 18952 ★
University of Mississippi - John Davis Williams Library - Blues Archive (Mus)
Farley Hall   Phone: (601)232-7753
University, MS 38677   Tinsley E. Silcox, Mus.Libn./Blues Archv.
Founded: 1984. **Staff:** Prof 3. **Subjects:** Music - blues, gospel, American traditional; folklore. **Special Collections:** Goldstein Folklore Collection (10,000 volumes; 5600 recordings); B.B. King Collection (9100 recordings); Living Blues Archival Collection (22 feet of archives; 20,000 recordings); Trumpet Record Company (10 feet of archives). **Holdings:** 12,000 books; 200 bound periodical volumes; 38,000 phonograph records; 39 feet of manuscripts and archives; 525 posters; 6.5 feet of photographs; 400 audiocassettes; 150 videocassettes; 2000 pamphlets; 175 feet of unbound periodicals. **Subscriptions:** 40 journals and other serials. **Services:** Copying; archive open to the public. **Automated Operations:** Computerized cataloging. **Computerized Information Services:** OCLC. **Networks/Consortia:** Member of SOLINET. **Special Catalogs:** Finding aids to manuscript and archival collections. **Remarks:** FAX: (601)232-7753. **Staff:** Glenn Lemieux, Cat.; Walter Liniger, Res.Assoc.

★ 18953 ★
University of Mississippi - Medical Center - Rowland Medical Library
(Med)
2500 N. State St.   Phone: (601)984-1290
Jackson, MS 39216   Ada M. Seltzer
Founded: 1955. **Staff:** Prof 11; Other 12. **Subjects:** Medicine, nursing, allied health, dentistry. **Holdings:** 33,084 books; 103,852 bound periodical volumes; 12,516 microfiche; 535 reels of microfilm. **Subscriptions:** 2205 journals and other serials; 4 newspapers. **Services:** Interlibrary loan; copying; SDI; library open to the public for reference use only. CD-ROM databases not available to the public. **Automated Operations:** Ameritech LS/2000 (Integrated library system). **Computerized Information Services:** MEDLARS, DIALOG Information Services, BRS Information Technologies; EasyLink (electronic mail service). Contact Person: Virginia Seagrest, Assoc.Dir., Pub.Serv. **Publications:** Handbook; quarterly newsletter. **Remarks:** FAX: (601)984-1262. Electronic mail address(es): 62027657; 62033291 (EasyLink).

★ 18954 ★
University of Mississippi - Public Policy Research Center (Soc Sci)
University, MS 38677   Phone: (601)232-5407
                                                     Carol M. Hopkins, Libn.
Founded: 1945. **Staff:** Prof 1. **Subjects:** State, local, and national government; public administration and regional governance. **Special Collections:** Mississippi Collection (500 volumes). **Holdings:** 5500 volumes; 10 VF drawers of publications and clippings; 85 dissertations and masters' theses. **Subscriptions:** 200 journals and other serials. **Services:** Library open to qualified researchers. **Publications:** Public Administration Survey, quarterly; monographs, irregular. **Staff:** Mr. Dana B. Brammer, Dir.

★ 18955 ★
University of Mississippi - School of Law Library (Law)
University, MS 38677   Phone: (601)232-7361
                                                 Herbert E. Cihak, Dir. of Law Lib.
Founded: 1854. **Staff:** Prof 6; Other 7. **Subjects:** American and international law. **Special Collections:** Papers of Senator Eastland (1600 linear feet), Senator Cochran (75 linear feet), Congressman Lott (40 linear feet), and Judge Smith (20 linear feet); space law (500 volumes). **Holdings:** 132,000 volumes; 114,000 microforms. **Subscriptions:** 2200 journals and other serials. **Services:** Interlibrary loan; copying; library open to the public with restrictions. **Automated Operations:** Computerized public access catalog, serials, circulation, and acquisitions. **Computerized Information Services:** LEXIS, WESTLAW, OCLC. **Networks/Consortia:** Member of SOLINET, Consortium of South Eastern Law Libraries. **Remarks:** FAX: (601)232-7731. **Staff:** Sherry Young, Ref./Computer Serv.Libn.; Bernard Scherr, Pub.Serv.Libn.; Catherine Swanson, Tech.Serv.Libn.; Eugenia Minor, Cat./Docs.Libn.; Linda Scott, Ref.Libn.

★ 18956 ★
University of Mississippi - University Museums - Library (Art)
University, MS 38677   Phone: (601)232-7073
                                                 Bonnie J. Krause, Dir. of Musms.
Founded: 1939. **Subjects:** Art, folk art, antiquities, antiques, exhibit catalogs. **Holdings:** 300 books. **Services:** Library open to the public with supervision. **Special Indexes:** Subscription Index.

★ 18957 ★
University of Missouri--Columbia - A.G. Unklesbay Geological Sciences Library (Sci-Engr)
201 Geology Bldg.   Phone: (314)882-4860
Columbia, MO 65211   Robert Heidlage, Lib.Asst.
Founded: 1875. **Staff:** 1. **Subjects:** Paleontology, stratigraphy, sedimentology, geochemistry, geomorphology, hydrology. **Holdings:** 66,012 volumes; 145,002 maps; 7959 microforms. **Subscriptions:** 686 journals and other serials. **Services:** Interlibrary loan; copying; library open to the public for reference use; materials circulate to library card holders only. **Automated Operations:** Computerized cataloging and acquisitions. **Computerized Information Services:** CD-ROM (Geological Reference File); BITNET (electronic mail service). **Networks/Consortia:** Member of Center for Research Libraries (CRL). **Remarks:** Electronic mail address(es): GEOLBOB@UMCVMB. **Formerly:** Its Geology Library.

★ 18958 ★
University of Missouri--Columbia - Anthropology Museum - Archives
Dept. of Anthropology
104 Swallow Hall
Columbia, MO 65211
Defunct.

★ 18959 ★
University of Missouri--Columbia - Business and Public Administration Research Center - Library
10 Professional Bldg.   Phone: (314)882-4805
Columbia, MO 65211   Dr. Edward H. Robb, Dir.
Staff: 5. **Subjects:** Missouri and national business and economics-agriculture, banking, construction, economic forecast, education, employment, government, demographics, prices and welfare. **Holdings:** 8000 volumes; 1300 computer tapes. **Computerized Information Services:** Internal databases. Performs searches on fee basis. **Remarks:** FAX: (314)882-5563.

★ 18960 ★
University of Missouri--Columbia - Center for Economic Education - Library (Bus-Fin)
Dept. of Economics
Professional Bldg.   Phone: (314)882-3803
Columbia, MO 65211   Karen Hallows, Dir.
Founded: 1970. **Staff:** 2. **Subjects:** Economic education. **Holdings:** 2000 volumes. **Subscriptions:** 5 journals and other serials. **Services:** Library open to the public. **Publications:** Newsletters, quarterly; Econ Echo. **Remarks:** FAX: (314)882-2697. **Staff:** Marilyn Keffer.

University of Missouri--Columbia - College of Veterinary Medicine - OFA Hip Displasia Registry
See: Orthopedic Foundation for Animals - OFA Hip Dysplasia Registry (12583)

★ 18961 ★
University of Missouri--Columbia - Columbia Missourian - Newspaper Reference Library (Publ)
Box 917   Phone: (314)882-4876
Columbia, MO 65205   Rhonda Glazier, Newspaper Ref.Libn.
Staff: Prof 1; Other 1. **Subjects:** Newspaper reference topics, Columbia, Boone County, Missouri, University of Missouri. **Holdings:** 100 books; 64,000 biographical clippings files; 17,400 subject clippings files; 16,500 photograph and illustration files; 560 pamphlet files; historical clippings, from 1920s to present. **Services:** Interlibrary loan; copying; SDI; library open to the public for reference use only. **Computerized Information Services:** DIALOG Information Services, Dow Jones News/Retrieval, CompuServe Information Service, VU/TEXT Information Services, The Source Information Network; internal database. Performs searches on fee basis. **Special Indexes:** Subject index to file cards and clippings; references to Columbia Missourian, Columbia Missourian Weekly, and Columbia Daily Tribune, 1977-1990. **Remarks:** FAX: (314)882-9002. Library located at 9th and Elm, Columbia, MO 65201.

★ 18962 ★
University of Missouri--Columbia - Department of Geography - Map Collection (Geog-Map)
3 Stewart Hall   Phone: (314)882-8370
Columbia, MO 65211   Christopher L. Salter, Chm.
Founded: 1950. **Subjects:** Missouri, Anglo-America. **Special Collections:** Maps and state agency documents on Missouri. **Holdings:** 4200 maps; 166 atlases; 480 wall maps. **Services:** Collection open to the public. **Remarks:** FAX: (314)884-4239.

★ 18963 ★
University of Missouri--Columbia - Engineering Library (Sci-Engr)
2017 Engineering Bldg.   Phone: (314)882-2379
Columbia, MO 65211   Judy S. Pallardy, Hd., Sci.Br./Engr.Libn.
Founded: 1906. **Staff:** Prof 1; Other 2. **Subjects:** Engineering - chemical, civil, electrical, industrial, mechanical, aerospace, agricultural, nuclear. **Holdings:** 70,544 volumes. **Subscriptions:** 613 journals and other serials.

Services: Interlibrary loan; copying; library open to the public with restrictions on borrowing. **Automated Operations:** Computerized public access catalog and circulation. **Computerized Information Services:** DIALOG Information Services, PFDS Online, BRS Information Technologies, STN International, OCLC; CD-ROMs (DIALOG OnDisc, COMPENDEX); BITNET (electronic mail service). Performs searches on fee basis. **Networks/Consortia:** Member of Center for Research Libraries (CRL), Missouri Library Network Corp. (MLNC). **Publications:** New Book List, monthly - to engineering faculty. **Remarks:** Electronic mail address(es): ENGJUDY@UMCVMB (BITNET).

★ 18964 ★
University of Missouri--Columbia - Freedom of Information Center (Info Sci)
20 Walter Williams Hall   Phone: (314)882-4856
Columbia, MO 65211   M. Kathleen Edwards, Mgr.
Founded: 1958. **Staff:** 2. **Subjects:** Governmental, societal, and economic controls on information. **Holdings:** 171 volumes; pamphlets; clippings; reprints; government documents; professional newsletters. **Subscriptions:** 150 journals and other serials. **Services:** Collecting and indexing information on the public's right to know; copying; reference and referral on over 1000 subjects on demand; center open to the public. **Remarks:** FAX: (314)882-8044.

★ 18965 ★
University of Missouri--Columbia - J. Otto Lottes Health Sciences Library (Med)
Columbia, MO 65212   Phone: (314)882-7033
Dean Schmidt, Dir.
Founded: 1903. **Staff:** Prof 9; Other 13. **Subjects:** Medicine, nursing, hospital administration. **Holdings:** 189,884 volumes; 230 microforms; 500 tapes; 150 motion pictures; 400 AV programs; 25 phonograph records; 2000 slides. **Subscriptions:** 1991 journals and other serials. **Services:** Interlibrary loan; copying; SDI; library open to the public. **Automated Operations:** Computerized cataloging, acquisitions, serials, circulation, and ILL. **Computerized Information Services:** WILSONLINE, MEDLINE, BRS Information Technologies, DIALOG Information Services, PFDS Online; POAC (internal database); BITNET (electronic mail service). Performs searches on fee basis. Contact Person: Diane Johnson, Hd., Info.Serv., 882-6141. **Networks/Consortia:** Member of National Network of Libraries of Medicine - Midcontinental Region. **Remarks:** FAX: (314)882-5574. Electronic mail address(es): HSLDEAN@UMCVMB (BITNET). **Staff:** Richard Rexroat, Hd., Tech.Serv.; Shelley Worden, Hd., Coll.Mgt.; Alice Edwards, Ill.

★ 18966 ★
University of Missouri--Columbia - Journalism Library (Info Sci)
117 Walter Williams Hall   Phone: (314)882-7502
Columbia, MO 65202   Patricia P. Timberlake, Libn.
Founded: 1908. **Staff:** Prof 1; Other 6. **Subjects:** Advertising, broadcasting, journalism, magazines, news writing and management, newspaper publishing, photography, public relations, semantics, typography, linotype. **Holdings:** 23,341 books; 6214 bound periodical volumes. **Subscriptions:** 350 journals and newspapers. **Services:** Interlibrary loan; copying; library open to the public with restrictions. **Computerized Information Services:** DIALOG Information Services, BRS Information Technologies, LEXIS, NEXIS, Dow Jones News/Retrieval, VU/TEXT Information Services; BITNET, InterNet (electronic mail services). **Special Indexes:** Journalism Index. **Remarks:** FAX: (314)882-4823; (314)882-8044. Electronic mail address(es): EIIISPT@UMCVMB (BITNET, InterNet).

★ 18967 ★
University of Missouri--Columbia - Math Sciences Library (Sci-Engr, Comp Sci)
206 Math Sciences Bldg.   Phone: (314)882-7286
Columbia, MO 65211   Dixie L. Fingerson, Lib.Asst.
Founded: 1968. **Staff:** 2. **Subjects:** Mathematics, computer science, statistics. **Holdings:** 44,586 volumes. **Subscriptions:** 443 journals and other serials. **Services:** Interlibrary loan; library open to the public for reference use only. **Automated Operations:** Computerized public access catalog and circulation. **Computerized Information Services:** BITNET (electronic mail service). **Networks/Consortia:** Member of Center for Research Libraries (CRL), Missouri Library Network Corp. (MLNC). **Publications:** New Book List, monthly - to faculty. **Remarks:** Electronic mail address(es): MTHDIXIE@UMCVMB (BITNET).

★ 18968 ★
University of Missouri--Columbia - Medical Informatics Group - Library
605 Lewis Hall
Columbia, MO 65211   Phone: (314)882-7296
Founded: 1977. **Subjects:** Health care technology, health services research, computer applications in medicine. **Special Collections:** Medical Information Systems (2600 entries), including Drug Information Systems (290 entries) and Hospital Information Systems (600 entries); Microprocessors (200 entries); Medical Imaging (2000 entries), including Computerized Tomography (1200 entries) and Ultrasound (600 entries); End-Stage Renal Disease (460 entries); Medical Competency Examination (290 entries); Hospital Technology Costs (500 entries); Mental Health Information Systems (1200 entries). **Holdings:** 1200 books; 2000 unbound periodicals; 6000 reprints; 800 pamphlets, clippings, manuscripts, and reports. **Remarks:** Currently inactive.

★ 18969 ★
University of Missouri--Columbia - Missouri Institute of Mental Health - Library (Med)
5400 Arsenal St.   Phone: (314)644-8838
St. Louis, MO 63139-1494   Mary E. Johnson, Lib.Dir.
Founded: 1962. **Staff:** Prof 1; Other 4. **Subjects:** Psychiatry, neurology, psychology, biochemistry, nursing. **Holdings:** 10,000 books; 14,000 bound periodical volumes; 7 VF drawers; 250 films and videocassettes; 650 audio cassettes; 50 microforms. **Subscriptions:** 400 journals and other serials. **Services:** Interlibrary loan; copying; SDI; library open to the public. **Automated Operations:** Computerized cataloging, serials, circulation, and ILL. **Computerized Information Services:** DIALOG Information Services, BRS Information Technologies, OCLC, Philnet, PHILSOM, ALANET. Performs searches on fee basis. **Networks/Consortia:** Member of St. Louis Regional Library Network, National Network of Libraries of Medicine - Midcontinental Region. **Publications:** Missouri Institute of Mental Health Faculty Publications. **Remarks:** Alternate telephone number(s): 644-8860. FAX: (314)644-8839. **Formerly:** University of Missouri, Columbia - Missouri Institute of Psychiatry Library.

★ 18970 ★
University of Missouri--Columbia - Museum of Art and Archaeology - Library (Art)
1 Pickard Hall   Phone: (314)882-3591
Columbia, MO 65211   Morteza Sajadian, Dir. of Musm.
Founded: 1957. **Subjects:** Art history, archeology. **Holdings:** 560 books; 5160 exhibition and sales catalogs. **Services:** Library open to the public with restrictions. **Remarks:** FAX: (314)884-4039.

★ 18971 ★
University of Missouri--Columbia - School of Law Library (Law)
Hulston Hall   Phone: (314)882-4597
Columbia, MO 65211   Susan D. Csaky, Prof., Dir./Law Libn.
Founded: 1872. **Staff:** Prof 6; Other 7. **Subjects:** Law. **Special Collections:** Lawson Collection (criminal law and criminology); U.S. and state government document depository. **Holdings:** 201,200 volumes; 329,322 microforms. **Subscriptions:** 3747 journals and other serials. **Services:** Interlibrary loan; copying; library open to the public with restrictions. **Automated Operations:** Computerized public access catalog and cataloging. **Computerized Information Services:** LEXIS, NEXIS, OCLC, WESTLAW, DIALOG Information Services; BITNET, InterNet (electronic mail services). Performs searches on fee basis. Contact Person: Jo Ann Humphreys, Comp.Serv./Assoc. Law Libn., 882-2935. **Networks/Consortia:** Member of Mid-America Law School Library Consortium, Libraries of the University of Missouri Information Network (LUMIN), Missouri Library Network Corp. (MLNC). **Publications:** Law Library Guide; Selected Acquisitions List. **Remarks:** FAX: (314)882-9676. Electronic mail address(es): LAWLIB@UMCVMB (BITNET); LAWLIBJH@UMCVMB.MISSOURI.EDU (InterNet). **Staff:** Needra Jackson, Hd., Pub.Serv./Law Libn.; Erlene Rickerson, Hd., Tech.Serv./Law Libn.; Wai-On Vianne Tang, Asst.Hd., Tech.Serv./Law Libn.; Steve Lambson, Asst.Hd., Pub.Serv./Law Libn.

★ 18972 ★
University of Missouri--Columbia - Special Collections (Hist)
Ellis Library, Rm. 401   Phone: (314)882-0076
Columbia, MO 65201   Margaret A. Howell, Hd., Spec.Coll.
Staff: Prof 1; Other 2. **Subjects:** American and church history, history of printing. **Special Collections:** Rare book collection; Thomas Moore Johnson

Collection of Philosophy; Frank Luther Mott Collection of American Best Sellers; University of Missouri Collection; Anthony C. DeBellis Collection of Italian Literature; William Peden Short Story Collection; 19th century British pamphlets; Comic Art Collection; Weinberg Journalists in Fiction Collection. **Holdings:** 44,200 books; 1700 bound periodical volumes; 4.8 million microforms. **Subscriptions:** 270 journals and other serials; 23 newspapers. **Services:** Interlibrary loan; copying (both limited); collections open to the public. **Automated Operations:** Computerized cataloging, acquisitions, and serials. **Computerized Information Services:** Internal database; ALANET, BITNET (electronic mail services). Performs searches free of charge. **Special Catalogs:** Primary Resources in History; Guide to the Microform Collections of the University of Missouri-Columbia Libraries, 1987. **Remarks:** FAX: (314)882-8044. Electronic mail address(es): UMO.ALMONY (ALANET); ELSMHOW@UMCVMB (BITNET).

★ 18973 ★
University of Missouri--Columbia - Veterinary Medical Library (Med)
W218 Veterinary Medicine   Phone: (314)882-2461
Columbia, MO 65211   Trenton Boyd, Libn.
Founded: 1951. **Staff:** Prof 1; Other 2. **Subjects:** Veterinary medicine. **Holdings:** 20,819 books; 21,958 bound periodical volumes; 740 microforms. **Subscriptions:** 406 journals and other serials; 5 newspapers. **Services:** Interlibrary loan; copying; library open to the public. **Automated Operations:** Computerized cataloging, acquisitions, and serials. **Computerized Information Services:** MEDLINE, DIALOG Information Services, PFDS Online, BRS Information Technologies. **Remarks:** FAX: (314)882-2950.

University of Missouri--Columbia - Western Historical Manuscript Collection
See: Western Historical Manuscript Collection (20250)

University of Missouri--Kansas City - Conservatory Library
See: University of Missouri--Kansas City - Music Library (18977)

★ 18974 ★
University of Missouri--Kansas City - Health Sciences Library (Med)
2411 Holmes   Phone: (816)235-1880
Kansas City, MO 64108   Marilyn Sullivan, Chf.Libn.
Founded: 1967. **Staff:** Prof 6; Other 6. **Subjects:** Medicine, nursing. **Holdings:** 16,072 books; 55,594 serial volumes; 3158 AV titles; 43,000 items in microform. **Subscriptions:** 722 journals and other serials. **Services:** Interlibrary loan; copying; SDI; library open to members of the health sciences community. **Automated Operations:** Computerized public access catalog.**Computerized Information Services:** DIALOG Information Services, BRS Information Technologies, MEDLARS, Data-Star; internal database. **Networks/Consortia:** Member of Kansas City Library Network, Inc. (KCLN). **Remarks:** Contains the archives of the American Nurses' Association. **Staff:** Jeanne Sarkis, Sr.Clin.Med.Libn./Ref.Coord.; Kelly Parish, Online Serv.Coord.; Marlene Smith, AV Med.Libn.; Mark Yates, ILL.

★ 18975 ★
University of Missouri--Kansas City - Law Library (Law)
School of Law
5100 Rockhill Rd.   Phone: (816)235-1650
Kansas City, MO 64110   Prof. Patricia Harris, Law Lib.Dir.
Staff: Prof 5; Other 6. **Subjects:** Law. **Holdings:** 154,045 volumes; 202,413 microfiche; 395 reels of microfilm. **Subscriptions:** 4714 journals and other serials. **Services:** Interlibrary loan; copying; library open to the public. **Automated Operations:** Computerized cataloging, acquisitions, and serials. **Computerized Information Services:** LEXIS, WESTLAW, INNOVACQ Automated Library System, OCLC; LUMIN (internal database). **Remarks:** FAX: (816)444-6560. **Staff:** J. William Draper, Pub.Serv.; Inas El-Sayed, Tech.Serv.; Larry MacLachlan, Pub.Serv.; Nancy Stancel Tech.Serv.

★ 18976 ★
University of Missouri--Kansas City - Miller Nichols Library - Marr Sound Archives (Mus)
5100 Rockhill Rd.   Phone: (816)235-2798
Kansas City, MO 64110-2499   Prof. Gaylord Marr, Cur.
Founded: 1986. **Staff:** 2.5. **Subjects:** Music - popular American, jazz, folk, country, classical opera; historic voices and events. **Special Collections:** Dave E. Dexter, Jr. Collection; Leith Stevens Collection. **Holdings:** 100,000 sound recordings; recordings by Kansas City artists. **Services:** Copying (limited); archives open to the scholarly community. **Computerized Information Services:** CD-ROM (Search CD450). **Publications:** ARSC Journal. **Remarks:** FAX: (816)333-5584. **Staff:** Chuck Haddix, Sound Recording Spec.

★ 18977 ★
University of Missouri--Kansas City - Music Library (Mus)
Miller Nichols Library
5100 Rockhill Rd.   Phone: (816)235-1675
Kansas City, MO 64110   Peter Munstedt, Mus.Libn.
Founded: 1906. **Staff:** Prof 1; Other 1. **Subjects:** Music. **Special Collections:** Archives of the Midwest Center for American Music (manuscripts of regional and national composers, including Amy Beach and Paul Creston; 12 collections); popular American sheet music (50,000 items); popular American dance band music (8000 items); American hymnals (1500 items); Warner Brothers Film Music Collection (12,000 scores). **Holdings:** 50,911 volumes; 18,047 recordings. **Subscriptions:** 285 journals and other serials. **Services:** Interlibrary loan; copying (limited). **Automated Operations:** Computerized public access catalog. **Computerized Information Services:** Popular American Sheet Music Collection, Popular American Dance Band Music Collection (internal databases); BITNET (electronic mail service). **Publications:** Inventories for all music manuscript collections. **Remarks:** FAX: (816)333-5584. Electronic mail address(es): PMUNSTEDT@UMKCVAX1 (BITNET). **Formerly:** Its Conservatory Library.

★ 18978 ★
University of Missouri--Kansas City - School of Dentistry Library (Med)
650 E. 25th St.   Phone: (816)235-2030
Kansas City, MO 64108   Ann Marie Corry, Dental Libn.
Founded: 1920. **Staff:** Prof 1; Other 3. **Subjects:** Dentistry. **Holdings:** 12,893 books; 10,388 bibliographic volumes of periodicals. **Subscriptions:** 336 journals and other serials. **Services:** Interlibrary loan; copying; library open to the public for reference use only. **Automated Operations:** Computerized public access catalog and ILL (DOCLINE). **Computerized Information Services:** BRS Information Technologies, MEDLINE, DIALOG Information Services, OCLC EPIC, Quest. **Networks/Consortia:** Member of Kansas City Library Network, Inc. (KCLN). **Remarks:** FAX: (816)235-2157.

★ 18979 ★
University of Missouri--Kansas City - Snyder Collection of Americana (Hist)
Miller Nichols Library
5100 Rockhill Rd.   Phone: (816)235-1534
Kansas City, MO 64110   Marilyn Carbonell, Asst.Dir., Coll.Dev.
Founded: 1937. **Subjects:** Political campaign literature; Civil War; Indians of North America; Kansas and Missouri - history, travel, biography, fiction, poetry; 19th century Americana; early Missouri and Kansas imprints. **Holdings:** 24,837 volumes. **Subscriptions:** 10 journals and other serials. **Services:** Interlibrary loan; copying (both limited). **Automated Operations:** Computerized public access catalog. **Computerized Information Services:** BITNET (electronic mail service). **Remarks:** Alternate telephone number(s): 235-1580. FAX: (816)333-5584. Electronic mail address(es): MCARBONELL@UMKCVAX1 (BITNET).

University of Missouri--Kansas City - Western Historical Manuscript Collection
See: Western Historical Manuscript Collection (20251)

★ 18980 ★
University of Missouri--Rolla - Curtis Laws Wilson Library (Sci-Engr)
Rolla, MO 65401   Phone: (314)341-4227
                                             Ronald Bohley, Libn.
Founded: 1871. **Staff:** Prof 9; Other 19. **Subjects:** Mining, metallurgy, engineering, geology, earth sciences. **Special Collections:** U.S. Geological Survey publications; U.S. Bureau of Mines publications. **Holdings:** 433,000 volumes; 330,000 titles on microform. **Subscriptions:** 1500 journals and other serials; 20 newspapers. **Services:** Interlibrary loan; copying; library open to the public. **Automated Operations:** Computerized cataloging, serials, and circulation. **Computerized Information Services:** DIALOG Information Services, OCLC, STN International; BITNET (electronic mail service). **Networks/Consortia:** Member of Missouri Library Network Corp. (MLNC). **Remarks:** FAX: (314)341-4233. Electronic mail address(es): C0655@UMRVMB (BITNET). **Staff:** Jean Eisenman, Asst.Dir., Pub.Serv.; Bruce Gilbert, Asst.Dir., Tech.Serv.; Gloria Ho, Cat.; Andy Stewart, Ref.; Janet McKean, Ref.; Amy Prendergast, Ref.; Laura Hunter, Cat.; George Barnett, Ref.

University of Missouri--Rolla - Western Historical Manuscript Collection
See: Western Historical Manuscript Collection (20252)

★ 18981 ★
University of Missouri--St. Louis - Health Sciences Library (Med)
8001 Natural Bridge Rd.   Phone: (314)553-5909
St. Louis, MO 63121   Cheryle J. Cann, Hd.Libn.
Founded: 1981. **Staff:** Prof 1; Other 1.5. **Subjects:** Nursing science, vision science. **Holdings:** 6670 books; 3877 bound periodical volumes; 758 AV programs; 223 reels of microfilm; 4188 microfiche. **Subscriptions:** 200 journals and other serials. **Services:** Interlibrary loan; copying; SDI (upon written request); library open to the public. **Automated Operations:** Computerized cataloging. **Computerized Information Services:** OCLC, BRS Information Technologies; BITNET, InterNet (electronic mail services). Performs searches on fee basis. **Networks/Consortia:** Member of St. Louis Regional Library Network, Libraries of the University of Missouri Information Network (LUMIN), Association of Visual Science Librarians (AVSL), Saint Louis Medical Librarians Consortia. **Publications:** Self-Guided Tour of the Health Sciences Library - to students, faculty, and staff; recent acquisitions list, monthly - to faculty, staff, and Association of Visual Science Librarians members; Library Skills Exercises. **Remarks:** FAX: (314)553-5281. Electronic mail address(es): C1749f@UMSLVMA (BITNET).

★ 18982 ★
University of Missouri--St. Louis - Thomas Jefferson Library - Special Collections (Soc Sci, Hum)
8001 Natural Bridge Rd.   Phone: (314)553-5050
St. Louis, MO 63121   Joan G. Rapp, Dir.
Founded: 1963. **Subjects:** Utopian literature and social theory; U.S. Government Documents Depository; Colonial Latin American history. **Holdings:** 7000 books. **Subscriptions:** 12 journals and other serials; 5 newspapers. **Services:** Interlibrary loan; copying; collections open to the public. **Automated Operations:** Computerized public access catalog and circulation. **Computerized Information Services:** DIALOG Information Services, BRS Information Technologies, OCLC, RLIN; BITNET (electronic mail service). Performs searches on fee basis. **Contact Person:** Theresa Norton, 553-5059. **Networks/Consortia:** Member of St. Louis Regional Library Network, Missouri Library Network Corp. (MLNC). **Remarks:** FAX: (314)553-5853. Electronic mail address(es): C1749A@UMSLVMA (BITNET). **Staff:** Genevieve Owens, Hd., Coll.Dev.

★ 18983 ★
University of Missouri--St. Louis - Ward E. Barnes Education Library (Educ)
8001 Natural Bridge Rd.   Phone: (314)553-5572
St. Louis, MO 63121   Virginia Workman, Hd.Libn.
Founded: 1976. **Staff:** Prof 2; Other 5. **Subjects:** Education, children's literature, curriculum materials. **Holdings:** 32,321 books; 5079 bound periodical volumes; 14,724 K-12 textbooks; 15,542 curriculum guides (4868 hardcopy; 10,674 on microfiche); 434,838 ERIC microfiche; 1793 tests (786 standardized; 1007 unpublished); 6795 children's literature books. **Subscriptions:** 295 journals and other serials. **Services:** Interlibrary loan; library open to the public with restrictions. **Automated Operations:** Computerized public access catalog and circulation. **Computerized Information Services:** BRS Information Technologies; CD-ROM (ERIC). Performs searches on fee basis. **Networks/Consortia:** Member of St. Louis Regional Library Network, Missouri Library Network Corp. (MLNC). **Remarks:** FAX: (314)553-5281. Alternate telephone number(s): 553-5188. **Staff:** Peter Monat, Ref.Libn.

University of Missouri--St. Louis - Western Historical Manuscript Collection
See: Western Historical Manuscript Collection (20253)

★ 18984 ★
University of Missouri--St. Louis - Women's Center (Soc Sci)
211 Clark Hall
8001 Natural Bridge Rd.   Phone: (314)553-5380
St. Louis, MO 63121   Joanne Grubb, Dir.
Staff: 3. **Subjects:** Women - politics, psychology, medicine; male sex roles. **Holdings:** 450 books; 500 unbound periodicals; 8 VF drawers of clippings and reports. **Subscriptions:** 6 newspapers. **Services:** Center open to the public with permission.

★ 18985 ★
University of Montana - Bureau of Business and Economic Research - Library (Bus-Fin)
School of Business Administration   Phone: (406)243-5113
Missoula, MT 59812   James Sylvester, Statistician
Staff: 1. **Subjects:** Economic indicators in the United States and Montana; regional economics with emphasis on Montana and northern Rocky Mountain area; wood products industry. **Special Collections:** Montana, Idaho, and Wyoming Forest Industry Data Systems; County Data Packages, Montana. **Holdings:** Figures not available. **Subscriptions:** 52 journals and other serials. **Services:** Copying; library open to the public with restrictions. **Publications:** List of publications - available on request. **Remarks:** FAX: (406)248-2086.

★ 18986 ★
University of Montana - Maureen & Mike Mansfield Library - Instructional Media Services (Aud-Vis)
Social Sciences Bldg.   Phone: (406)243-4070
Missoula, MT 59812   Devon Chandler, Ed.D., Dir.
Founded: 1962. **Staff:** Prof 4; Other 10. **Subjects:** Audiovisual materials. **Special Collections:** Montana Committee for the Humanities-Media Collection; U.S.D.A. Forest Service, Northern Region, Film Library. **Holdings:** 75,819 AV programs; 1638 films; 2444 videotapes; 13,959 sound recordings; 57,683 slides, filmstrips, art prints, study prints, transparencies, kits, computer files, models, realia, maps, and globes. **Services:** Interlibrary loan; film rentals; copying; audio and video reproduction; services open to the public with restrictions. **Automated Operations:** Computerized cataloging and acquisitions. **Computerized Information Services:** AVLINE, WLN, OCLC; internal databases; BITNET, InterNet (electronic mail services). Performs searches on fee basis. **Contact Person:** Karen C. Driessen, Media Libn. **Networks/Consortia:** Member of Western Library Network (WLN), Consortium of College and University Media Centers (CCUMC). **Special Catalogs:** Film catalog, biannual - to Consortium of University Film Centers members; IMS Review - for internal distribution only; video catalogs. **Special Indexes:** Internal bibliographies in humanities, poetry, ethnic music, Japanese materials, and Montana. **Remarks:** FAX: (406)243-4067. Electronic mail address(es): IMS-FILMVID@LEWIS.UMT.EDU (BITNET, InterNet). **Staff:** Robert Wachtel, Media Serv.Coord.; Linda Harris, Media Circ.Coord.; Gerald Kling, Photo.; Harriet Ranney, Act.Mus.Libn.

★ 18987 ★
University of Montana - Maureen & Mike Mansfield Library - K. Ross Toole Archives (Hist)
Missoula, MT 59812   Phone: (406)243-2053
       Dale L. Johnson, Archv.
Staff: Prof 1. **Subjects:** Montana - business history, forest industries; politics and government. **Special Collections:** James W. Gerard Collection; Mike Mansfield Collection; James E. Murray Collection; Joseph M. Dixon Collection; Dorothy M. Johnson Collection; Chet Huntley Collection. **Holdings:** 1000 oral histories; 30,000 photographs; 8500 feet of manuscripts. **Services:** Copying; archives open to the public. **Networks/Consortia:** Member of Western Library Network (WLN). **Publications:** People Will Talk: Oral History Collection of the Mansfield Library.

★ 18988 ★
University of Montana - Office of Career Services - Career Resource Center
Lodge Rm. 148
Missoula, MT 59812
Defunct.

★ 18989 ★
University of Montana - School of Law - Law Library (Law)
Missoula, MT 59812   Phone: (406)243-6171
       Maurice M. Michel, Dir.
Founded: 1911. **Staff:** Prof 3; Other 2. **Subjects:** Law. **Special Collections:** Indian law. **Holdings:** 122,103 books. **Subscriptions:** 822 journals and other serials. **Services:** Interlibrary loan; copying; library open to the public for reference use only. **Computerized Information Services:** WESTLAW, LEXIS. **Remarks:** FAX: (406)243-2576. **Staff:** Carole A. Granger.

★ 18990 ★

University of Montana - Wilderness Institute - LIbrary (Env-Cons)
Forestry Bldg., Rm. 207
Missoula, MT 59812   Phone: (406)243-5361
Founded: 1974. **Staff:** 2. **Subjects:** Wildlands management, scenic and wild rivers, wildlife. **Holdings:** 3000 file documents (including Forest Plans, environmental impact statements, and wilderness-related studies). **Services:** Library open to the public for reference use only. **Computerized Information Services:** Internal database. **Publications:** Words on Wilderness (newsletter). **Staff:** Mimi Lockman; Susan VanRooy.

★ 18991 ★

University of Montpellier - Institute of Archaeology and History of Art - Library (Hist)
Route de Mende
BP 5043
F-34032 Montpellier Cedex, France   Phone: 67142376
Founded: 1957. **Staff:** 1. **Subjects:** Antiquity. **Special Collections:** Charles Dugas Bequest (pottery and architecture in antiquity). **Holdings:** 12,000 books. **Subscriptions:** 200 journals and other serials. **Services:** Library open to the public. **Publications:** Revue Archiologigue de Narbonnaise. **Remarks:** FAX: 67142377. **Also Known As:** Universites de Montpellier - Institut d'Archeologie et d'Histoire de l'Art - Bibliotheque.

★ 18992 ★

University of Nebraska, Lincoln - Architecture Library (Art, Plan)
308 Architectural Hall   Phone: (402)472-1208
Lincoln, NE 68588-0108   Kay Logan-Peters, Arch.Libn.
Staff: Prof 1; Other 2. **Subjects:** Architecture, community and regional planning. **Holdings:** 21,714 books; 10,261 bound periodical volumes; 1858 volumes on microfilm; 6936 volumes on microfiche; 48 VF drawers; 35,000 slides. **Subscriptions:** 796 journals and other serials. **Services:** Interlibrary loan; library open to the public. **Automated Operations:** Integrated library system. **Computerized Information Services:** DIALOG Information Services, BRS Information Technologies (through Love Library); internal database; InterNet (electronic mail service). **Networks/Consortia:** Member of NEBASE. **Remarks:** FAX: (402)472-5131. Electronic mail address(es): ARCHMAIL@UNLLIB.UNL.EDU (InterNet).

★ 18993 ★

University of Nebraska, Lincoln - Biological Sciences Library (Biol Sci)
Manter Hall 402   Phone: (402)472-2756
Lincoln, NE 68588-0118   Richard E. Voeltz, Assoc.Prof.
Founded: 1895. **Staff:** Prof 1; Other 2. **Subjects:** Botany, zoology, microbiology, immunology. **Holdings:** 31,546 books; 41,863 bound periodical volumes; 563 microforms. **Subscriptions:** 860 journals and other serials. **Services:** Interlibrary loan; copying; library open to the public. **Automated Operations:** Computerized circulation. **Computerized Information Services:** DIALOG Information Services; Current Contents on Diskette: Life Sciences; InterNet (electronic mail service). **Publications:** Acquisitions list, monthly - for internal distribution only. **Remarks:** FAX: (402)472-5131. Electronic mail address(es): BIOLMAIL@UNLLIB.UNL.EDU (InterNet).

★ 18994 ★

University of Nebraska, Lincoln - C.Y. Thompson Library (Biol Sci, Sci-Engr, Agri)
East Campus   Phone: (402)472-2802
Lincoln, NE 68583-0717   Rebecca Bernthal, Interim Dir.
Staff: Prof 4; Other 5. **Subjects:** Agriculture, home economics, textiles, wildlife conservation, human development, nutrition, applied sciences, speech pathology, special education, dentistry, dental hygiene, oral surgery. **Special Collections:** Entomology collection containing many rare volumes. **Holdings:** 138,500 books; 138,200 bound periodical volumes; 26,608 microforms. **Subscriptions:** 4700 journals and other serials; 10 newspapers. **Services:** Interlibrary loan; copying; library open to the public. **Automated Operations:** Integrated library system. **Computerized Information Services:** DIALOG Information Services; CD-ROMs; internal database; InterNet (electronic mail service). Performs searches on fee basis. **Publications:** Acquisitions list, monthly - for internal distribution only. **Remarks:** FAX: (402)472-7005. Electronic mail address(es): CYTMAIL@UNLLIB.UNL.EDU (InterNet). Contains the holdings of the former Dentistry Library. **Staff:** Dana Boden, Asst.Prof.; Vicki Eastman, Lib.Spec.; Barbara Ganger, Asst.Prof.; Lyle Schreiner, Prof.

★ 18995 ★

University of Nebraska, Lincoln - Center for Great Plains Studies (Hist, Art)
205 Love Library   Phone: (402)472-6220
Lincoln, NE 68588-0475   Martha Kennedy, Cur.
Founded: 1980. **Staff:** Prof 1; Other 5. **Subjects:** Western Americana. **Special Collections:** William Henry Jackson Photographs; Patricia J. and Stanley H. Broder Collection of Indian Painting; Richard Lane Collection of Western Fiction. **Holdings:** 6500 books; 500 photographs; 300 paintings; 200 sculptures; 100 drawings and graphics. **Services:** Copying; center open to the public. **Automated Operations:** Computerized public access catalog and cataloging. **Publications:** Great Plains Quarterly; exhibition catalogs; Great Plains Research.

★ 18996 ★

University of Nebraska, Lincoln - Chemistry Library (Sci-Engr)
Hamilton Hall 427   Phone: (402)472-2739
Lincoln, NE 68588-0305   Richard E. Voeltz, Assoc.Prof.
Founded: 1930. **Staff:** Prof 1; Other 1. **Subjects:** Chemistry, chemical engineering. **Holdings:** 15,707 books; 26,036 bound periodical volumes; 1508 microforms. **Subscriptions:** 825 journals and other serials. **Services:** Interlibrary loan; copying; library open to the public. **Automated Operations:** Computerized circulation. **Computerized Information Services:** DIALOG Information Services; InterNet (electronic mail service). **Publications:** Acquisitions list, monthly - for internal distribution only. **Remarks:** FAX: (402)472-5131. Electronic mail address(es): CHEMMAIL@UNLLIB.UNL.EDU (InterNet).

★ 18997 ★

University of Nebraska, Lincoln - College of Law Library (Law)
East Campus   Phone: (402)472-3547
Lincoln, NE 68583-0902   Sally H. Wise, Dir. of Law Lib./Assoc.Prof.
Founded: 1891. **Staff:** Prof 5; Other 6. **Subjects:** Anglo-American law. **Special Collections:** U.S. taxation. **Holdings:** 170,583 volumes; 108,613 volumes in microform. **Subscriptions:** 2730 journals and other serials. **Services:** Interlibrary loan; copying; library open to the public for reference use only. **Automated Operations:** Computerized public access catalog, cataloging, acquisitions, and serials. **Computerized Information Services:** LEXIS, WESTLAW; InterNet (electronic mail service). **Networks/Consortia:** Member of Mid-America Law School Library Consortium. **Remarks:** FAX: (402)472-5185. Electronic mail address(es): LAWLINE@UNLLIB.UNL.EDU (InterNet). **Staff:** Brian D. Striman, Hd.,Tech.Serv.; Mitchell J. Fontenot, Ref.Libn.; Timothy P. Kelly, Ref.Libn.; Rebecca Trammell, Assoc.Dir./Hd., Pub.Serv.

★ 18998 ★

University of Nebraska, Lincoln - Engineering Library (Sci-Engr)
Nebraska Hall, 2nd Fl. W.   Phone: (402)472-3411
Lincoln, NE 68588-0516   Alan V. Gould, Assoc.Prof.
Founded: 1973. **Staff:** Prof 2; Other 3. **Subjects:** Engineering. **Special Collections:** Government Printing Office depository; patent depository. **Holdings:** 40,916 books; 53,793 bound periodical volumes (3186 titles); 535,000 microfiche; 6738 reels of microfilm. **Subscriptions:** 1106 journals and other serials. **Services:** Interlibrary loan; copying; library open to the public. **Automated Operations:** Integrated Library System. **Computerized Information Services:** DIALOG Information Services; CD-ROM (CASSIS); InterNet (electronic mail service). Performs searches on fee basis. **Publications:** Acquisitions list, monthly - for internal distribution only. **Remarks:** FAX: (402)472-5131. Electronic mail address(es): ENGLIBM@UNLLIB.UNL.EDU (InterNet). **Staff:** Larry Thompson, Asst.Prof.

★ 18999 ★

University of Nebraska, Lincoln - Geology Library (Sci-Engr)
Bessey Hall, Rm. 10   Phone: (402)472-2653
Lincoln, NE 68588-0332   Agnes Adams, Assoc.Prof.
Founded: 1895. **Staff:** Prof 1; Other 1. **Subjects:** Geology. **Special Collections:** Geological and topographic maps (92,000). **Holdings:** 13,244 books; 28,329 bound periodical volumes. **Subscriptions:** 1854 journals and other serials. **Services:** Interlibrary loan; copying; library open to the public. **Automated Operations:** Integrated Library System (IRIS). **Computerized Information Services:** DIALOG Information Services, OCLC, BRS Information Technologies; internal databases; CD-ROMs; InterNet (electronic mail service). **Networks/Consortia:** Member of NEBASE. **Publications:** Acquisitions list, monthly - for internal distribution only. **Remarks:** FAX: (402)472-5131. Electronic mail address(es): Geolmail@unllib.unl.edu (InterNet).

★ 19000 ★
University of Nebraska, Lincoln - Mathematics Library (Sci-Engr)
Oldfather Hall, Rm. 907　　　　　　Phone: (402)472-6900
Lincoln, NE 68588-0361　　　　Larry Thompson, Asst.Prof.
Founded: 1966. **Staff:** Prof 1; Other 1. **Subjects:** Mathematics, statistics. **Holdings:** 9117 books; 9832 bound periodical volumes. **Subscriptions:** 300 journals and other serials. **Services:** Interlibrary loan; copying; library open to the public. **Automated Operations:** Integrated Library System. **Computerized Information Services:** DIALOG Information Services; InterNet (electronic mail service). **Publications:** Acquisitions list, monthly - for internal distribution only. **Remarks:** FAX: (402)472-5131. Electronic mail address(es): MATHMAIL@UNLLIB.UNL.EDU (InterNet).

★ 19001 ★
University of Nebraska, Lincoln - Music Library (Mus)
30 Westbrook Music Bldg.　　　　Phone: (402)472-6300
Lincoln, NE 68588-0101　　　　Susan Messerli, Mus.Libn.
Founded: 1980. **Staff:** Prof 1; Other 3. **Subjects:** Music - history, literature, theory, performance. **Special Collections:** Guenther Collection of Passion Music (313 items); Ruth Etting Collection (707 scores, recordings, photographs, and scrapbooks); Zinnecker Jazz Collection (434 LP sound recordings); Labaree Jazz Collection (529 45rpm sound recordings). **Holdings:** 29,261 books and scores; 3708 bound periodical volumes; 12,184 sound recordings; 1494 microform units. **Subscriptions:** 164 journals and other serials. **Services:** Interlibrary loan; copying; library open to the public. **Automated Operations:** Integrated Library System. **Computerized Information Services:** PFDS Online, OCLC; InterNet (electronic mail service). **Networks/Consortia:** Member of NEBASE. **Remarks:** FAX: (402)472-5131. Electronic mail address(es): SUSANM@UNLLIB.UNL.EDU (InterNet).

★ 19002 ★
University of Nebraska, Lincoln - Nebraska Career Information System (Educ)
421 Nebraska Hall　　　　　　Phone: (402)472-2570
Lincoln, NE 68588-0552　　　　Fay G. Larson, Dir.
Founded: 1978. **Staff:** Prof 3; Other 1. **Special Collections:** Occupational briefs (557); Nebraska School and Program Information; military occupations; programs of study; state information on employment and education. **Services:** System open to persons involved in career counseling. **Computerized Information Services:** Internal database. Performs searches on fee basis. **Remarks:** This is a career information system available by lease agreement to schools and social agencies for career guidance support. FAX: (402)472-5907.

★ 19003 ★
University of Nebraska, Lincoln - Physics Library (Sci-Engr)
Brace Laboratory, Rm. 104　　　　Phone: (402)472-1209
Lincoln, NE 68588-0112　　　　Larry Thompson, Asst.Prof.
Founded: 1965. **Staff:** Prof 1; Other 1. **Subjects:** Physics, astronomy. **Holdings:** 9279 books; 16,257 bound periodical volumes; 65 microforms. **Subscriptions:** 279 journals and other serials. **Services:** Interlibrary loan; copying; library open to the public. **Automated Operations:** Integrated library system. **Computerized Information Services:** DIALOG Information Services; InterNet (electronic mail service). **Publications:** Acquisitions list, weekly - for internal distribution only. **Remarks:** FAX: (402)472-5131. Electronic mail address(es): PHYSMAIL@UNLLIB.UNL.EDU (InterNet).

★ 19004 ★
University of Nebraska, Lincoln - State Museum - Harold W. Manter Laboratory - Library (Biol Sci)
W-529 Nebraska Hall
16th and W Sts.　　　　　　　Phone: (402)472-3334
Lincoln, NE 68588-0514　　Mary Hanson Pritchard, Prof. & Cur.
Founded: 1971. **Staff:** 5. **Subjects:** Parasitology. **Special Collections:** Collection of articles on parasitology (58,000 reprints). **Holdings:** 5050 books; 525 bound periodical volumes; 3500 scientific photographs. **Subscriptions:** 15 journals and other serials. **Services:** Library open to the public by appointment for reference use. **Computerized Information Services:** Internal databases; BITNET, InterNet, UUCP Mail (electronic mail services). **Publications:** Contributions from the Harold W. Manter Laboratory, irregular; University Library exchange list and request; Technical Bulletins, irregular. **Remarks:** The laboratory is a research unit encompassing specimen collections, a specialized library for parasitological research, and a National Resource Center for Parasitology. FAX: (402)472-2410. Telex: LCN 484340 UNL. Electronic mail address(es): MHP@UNLINFO.UNL.EDU (BITNET, InterNet, UUCP Mail).

★ 19005 ★
University of Nebraska, Lincoln - University Archives and Special Collections (Hist, Hum)
308 Love Library　　　　　　Phone: (402)472-2531
Lincoln, NE 68588-0410　　　Joseph G. Svoboda, Prof./Hd.
Founded: 1968. **Staff:** Prof 1; Other 1.5. **Subjects:** Nebraskana, World Wars I and II, ethnicity, French Revolution, railroads, American folklore, university archives. **Special Collections:** Mari Sandoz Collection (210 feet); Benjamin A. Botkin Collection (500 feet; 10,000 volumes); Charles E. Bessey papers (45 feet); Charles M. Russell Collection (50 feet; 500 volumes); Czech Heritage Collection (300 feet of manuscripts, newspapers, periodicals; 6000 volumes; 200 reels of microfilm of newspapers); Christlieb Collection of Western Americana (3000 volumes); Mazour Collection of Russian History and Culture (5200 volumes); Latvian Collection (5 feet; 2000 volumes); Frank H. Shoemaker Collection. **Holdings:** 44,000 books; 1000 bound periodical volumes; 5000 cubic feet of university archives; 20,000 volumes of university theses and dissertations; 20 linear feet of manuscripts; 20 linear feet of glass negative plates and prints. **Services:** Copying; collections open to the public. **Computerized Information Services:** InterNet (electronic mail service). **Remarks:** FAX: (402)472-5131. Electronic mail address(es): JOES@UNLLIB.UNL.EDU (InterNet).

★ 19006 ★
University of Nebraska, Omaha - Center for Public Affairs Research - Library (Soc Sci)
Peter Kiewit-Conference Center
1313 Farnam-on-the-Mall　　　　Phone: (402)595-2311
Omaha, NE 68182　　　　Melanie Hayes, Staff Sec.
Founded: 1972. **Staff:** 2. **Subjects:** Census, community development and planning, economics, employment, government, public administration. **Holdings:** 1000 books; 250 manuscripts. **Subscriptions:** 24 journals and other serials. **Services:** Copying; library open to the public for reference use only. **Computerized Information Services:** Neb-Index (internal database); BITNET (electronic mail service). **Publications:** Newsletters, semiannual; research monographs; Nebraska Policy Choices series. **Remarks:** Electronic mail address(es): HIMBERGR@UNOMA1(BITNET). Houses the Nebraska State Data Center; FAX: (402)595-2366.

★ 19007 ★
University of Nebraska, Omaha - University Library - Special Collections (Hist, Publ)
Omaha, NE 68182-0237　　　　Phone: (402)554-2640
　　　　　　　　Robert S. Runyon, Lib.Dir.
Founded: 1908. **Special Collections:** Arthur Paul Afghanistan Collection; Abattoir Editions; Mary L. Richmond Cummington Press Collection; Edna Cole Postcard Collection; Icarian Collection; Wright Morris; Weldon Kees; Wayne C. Lee; Seven Anderton; WPA Historical Manuscripts on Omaha; Nebraska writers; Omaha history; fine presses. **Services:** Copying; collections open to the public by appointment. **Automated Operations:** Computerized cataloging and circulation. **Computerized Information Services:** DIALOG Information Services, BRS Information Technologies, WILSONLINE. Performs searches on fee basis. Contact Person: Robert Nash, 554-2884. **Publications:** Bibliography on Afghanistan (in progress). **Remarks:** FAX: (402)554-3215.

★ 19008 ★
University of Nebraska at Kearney - Calvin T. Ryan Library - Special Collections (Hist)
905 W. 25th　　　　　　　Phone: (308)236-4218
Kearney, NE 68847　　　　John Mayeski, Lib.Dir.
Founded: 1906. **Special Collections:** Nebraska history (2046 volumes); local history (707 cataloged items; 16,883 uncataloged items); Curriculum Collection (8973 cataloged titles; 8348 uncataloged titles; 71,378 nonbook items; 20 VF drawers). **Services:** Interlibrary loan; copying; collections open to the public. **Computerized Information Services:** DIALOG Information Services, OCLC, ERIC, BRS Information Technologies. Performs searches on fee basis. **Networks/Consortia:** Member of NEBASE. **Formerly:** Kearney State College.

★ 19009 ★
University of Nebraska at Kearney - Nebraska Vocational Curriculum Resource Center (Educ)
W. Campus-209　　　　　　Phone: (308)234-8462
Kearney, NE 68849　　　　Lyle Colsden, Dir.
Founded: 1973. **Staff:** Prof 1; Other 1. **Subjects:** Vocational education, home economics, industrial arts, industrial technology, career education, business

education, agriculture. **Holdings:** 9500 books; 500 AV items; curriculum guides. **Services:** Interlibrary loan; library open to the public. **Automated Operations:** Computerized circulation. **Computerized Information Services:** BRS Information Technologies; Vocational Data (internal database). **Publications:** Newsletter, annual. **Remarks:** FAX: (308)234-8669. **Formerly:** Kearney State College - Nebraska Vocational Education Curriculum Center.

★ 19010 ★

University of Nebraska at Omaha - Medical Center - McGoogan Library of Medicine (Med)
600 S. 42nd St.   Phone: (402)559-4006
Omaha, NE 68198-6705   Nancy N. Woelfl, Ph.D., Dir.
Founded: 1902. **Staff:** Prof 17; Other 33. **Subjects:** Medicine, nursing, pharmacy, psychiatry, allied health sciences. **Special Collections:** History of medicine; Nebraska Archives of Medicine; H. Winnett Orr Historical Collection (American College of Surgeons). **Holdings:** 79,721 books; 146,097 bound periodical volumes; 681 microforms; 25 VF drawers of archives. **Subscriptions:** 2365 journals and other serials. **Services:** Interlibrary loan (fee); copying; SDI; library open to the public. **Automated Operations:** Computerized cataloging, circulation, serials, and ILL. **Computerized Information Services:** DIALOG Information Services, NLM, BRS Information Technologies, WILSONLINE, PaperChase, CINAHL; BITNET (electronic mail service). **Remarks:** FAX: (402)559-5498. Contains the holdings of Eppley Institute for Research in Cancer & Allied Diseases - Library. Library serves as headquarters for the National Network of Libraries of Medicine - Midcontinental Region. **Staff:** Mary E. Helms, Assoc.Dir., Tech.Serv.; A. James Bothmer, Assoc.Dir., Pub.Serv.; Godfrey S. Belleh, Hd., Cat.; Joann Crocker, Hd., Coll.Dev.; Tom Gensichen, Sys.Libn.; Charlene R. Maxey-Harris, Educ.Coord.; Kathleen L. Cardwell, User Educ.Libn.; Roxanne R. Cox, Hd., Ref.; Mary J. Van Antwerp, Ref.; Rosita Nouravarsani, Ref.; Helen Yam, Hd., Presrv./Hist., Med.; Deborah H. Ward, Assoc.Dir., NNLM-MR; Claire E. Gadzikowski, Network Coord., NNLM-MR; Margaret P. Mullaly-Quijas, Outreach Coord., NNLM-MR; Nancy A. Morrow, Online Serv.Coord., NNLM-MR; Melissa J. Kaus, Online Serv.Inst., NNLM-MR; Molly A. Youngkin, Educ.Coord., NNLM-MR.

★ 19011 ★

University of Nevada--Las Vegas - Gaming Resource Center (Rec)
4505 Maryland Pkwy.   Phone: (702)739-3252
Las Vegas, NV 89154-7001   Susan Jarvis, Dir.
Founded: 1966. **Staff:** Prof 2; Other 2. **Subjects:** Gambling, horse racing, lotteries, cards. **Holdings:** 5000 books; 250 bound periodical volumes; 1500 clippings. **Subscriptions:** 205 journals and other serials; 10 newspapers. **Services:** Copying; center open to the public. **Automated Operations:** Computerized cataloging, acquisitions, serials, and circulation. **Computerized Information Services:** BITNET, InterNet (electronic mail services). **Publications:** A Gambling Bibliography, 1972 (based on the collection, listing over 1700 items). **Special Catalogs:** Gambling Catalog, a list of monographs from the research collection at the University of Nevada, Las Vegas, 1978. **Remarks:** FAX: (702)739-3050. Electronic mail address(es): susanj@nevada.edu (InterNet); susanj@nevada2 (BITNET).

★ 19012 ★

University of Nevada--Reno - Basque Studies Program (Area-Ethnic)
Library/322   Phone: (702)784-4854
Reno, NV 89557   Ellen Brow, Basque Studies Libn.
Founded: 1967. **Staff:** Prof 1. **Subjects:** Basque culture, history, language, literature. **Holdings:** 24,000 books; 2000 bound periodical volumes; 64 boxes of archives; 140 reels of microfilm; 17,000 slides; 550 cassettes and phonograph records. **Subscriptions:** 70 journals and other serials; 7 newspapers. **Services:** Interlibrary loan; copying; collection open to the public. **Computerized Information Services:** WOLFPAC (internal database); InterNet (electronic mail service). **Networks/Consortia:** Member of Information Nevada. **Publications:** Basque Studies Program Newsletter, semiannual - free upon request; Basque Studies Program Occasional Papers Series - for sale. **Remarks:** FAX: (702)784-6010. Electronic mail address(es): BASQUE@EQUINOX.UNR.EDU (InterNet).

★ 19013 ★

University of Nevada--Reno - Desert Research Institute - Library (Sci-Engr)
Box 60220   Phone: (702)677-3155
Reno, NV 89506   Shirley M. Smith, Dir.
Founded: 1966. **Staff:** Prof 1; Other 2. **Subjects:** Atmospheric physics, meteorology, weather modification, Antarctic studies, air pollution, water

resources, biological sciences, quaternary sciences. **Holdings:** 10,500 books; 4505 bound periodical volumes; 2392 bound government publications; 21,371 unbound government publications; 973 technical reports; 4620 microforms. **Subscriptions:** 274 journals and other serials. **Services:** Interlibrary loan; copying; library open to the public. **Computerized Information Services:** DIALOG Information Services; InterNet (electronic mail service). **Networks/Consortia:** Member of CLASS. **Remarks:** Alternate telephone number(s): 673-7402 (Tuesdays and Thursdays). FAX: (702)677-3157; 673-7397. Electronic mail address(es): SHIRLEY@WHEELER (InterNet). Maintains a branch library in Las Vegas, NV. **Staff:** Eva Sowers, Tech.Libn.; Linda Reichlin, Tech.Libn., ILL; Gary Hanneman, Lib.Comp.Spec.

★ 19014 ★

University of Nevada--Reno - Engineering Library (262) (Sci-Engr)
Scrugham Engineering/Mines Bldg., Rm. 228   Phone: (702)784-6945
Reno, NV 89557-0044   Glee Willis, Engr.Libn.
Founded: 1962. **Staff:** Prof 1; Other 2. **Subjects:** Engineering - civil, electrical, mechanical; computer science. **Holdings:** 21,189 books; 14,608 bound periodical volumes; 1905 government documents; 521 pamphlets; 1642 microfiche; 28 reels of microfilm; 1432 uncataloged standards. **Subscriptions:** 718 journals; 5 newspapers. **Services:** Interlibrary loan; copying; SDI; library open to the public. **Automated Operations:** Computerized public access catalog, acquisitions, serials, and circulation. **Computerized Information Services:** DIALOG Information Services, BRS Information Technologies, STN International; BITNET, InterNet (electronic mail services). Performs searches on fee basis. **Networks/Consortia:** Member of Information Nevada, CLASS. **Publications:** New Book List, monthly - free upon request. **Remarks:** FAX: (702)784-1751. Electronic mail address(es): WILLIS@EQUINOX (BITNET); WILLIS@UNR.EDU (InterNet).

★ 19015 ★

University of Nevada--Reno - Film & Video Library (Aud-Vis)
Getchell Library/322   Phone: (702)784-6037
Reno, NV 89557   Michael Simons, Educ. Media Libn.
Founded: 1955. **Staff:** Prof 1; Other 2. **Subjects:** Education, child development, anthropology, psychology, political science. **Special Collections:** Nevada films and videos; BBC productions of Shakespeare plays (37); Eyes on the Prize; A Walk Through the 20th Century; Vietnam: A Television History; America by Design; The Human Mind; The Constitution: That Delicate Balance; The Spice of Life; The Planet Earth; The Day the Universe Changed; The Shaping of the Western World. **Holdings:** 2000 16mm films; 2500 video cassettes. **Services:** Library open to the public on fee basis. **Automated Operations:** Computerized public access catalog (WolfPAC). **Networks/Consortia:** Member of Consortium of College and University Media Centers (CCUMC). **Publications:** Film and video catalogs and addenda. **Staff:** Ruth Hart; Joyce Oberman.

★ 19016 ★

University of Nevada--Reno - Government Publications Department (Info Sci)
Library/322
Reno, NV 89557   Phone: (702)784-6579
Founded: 1907. **Staff:** Prof 2; Other 3. **Subjects:** Government - Nevada, federal; United Nations. **Special Collections:** Patents, 1961 to present - NACA, AEC, Rand, Yucca Mountain Propposed Nuclear Waste Repository. **Holdings:** 1.05 million documents; 1.5 million microforms. **Services:** Interlibrary loan; department open to the public. **Computerized Information Services:** DIALOG Information Services, BRS Information Technologies, RLIN, U.S. Patent Classification System, Nevada Legislative Information System; InterNet (electronic mail service). Performs searches on fee basis. **Publications:** Selected List of Publications Received, monthly. **Remarks:** FAX: (702)784-1751. Electronic mail address(es): GPD@UNSSU.UNR.EDU (InterNet). **Staff:** Duncan Aldrich, Hd., Govt.Pubns.Dept.; Janita Jobe, U.S. Govt.Pubns.Libn.

★ 19017 ★

University of Nevada--Reno - Life and Health Sciences Library (Sci-Engr, Med)
Fleischmann College of Agriculture Bldg./206   Phone: (702)784-6616
Reno, NV 89557   Susan Stewart, Libn.
Founded: 1958. **Staff:** Prof 1; Other 2. **Subjects:** Biology, agriculture, nursing, health resources, speech pathology and audiology, medical technology. **Special Collections:** USDA, FAO, WHO. **Holdings:** 28,983

books; 23,826 bound periodical volumes; 8032 bound government reports; 67,913 unbound government reports; 417 reels of microfilm; 12,762 microfiche. **Subscriptions:** 664 journals. **Services:** Interlibrary loan; copying; library open to the public. **Automated Operations:** Computerized cataloging, acquisitions, serials, and circulation. **Computerized Information Services:** DIALOG Information Services, STN International; InterNet (electronic mail service). Performs searches on fee basis. **Networks/Consortia:** Member of Nevada Medical Library Group (NMLG). **Publications:** New Book List, monthly - free upon request. **Remarks:** FAX: (702)784-1751. Electronic mail address(es): LHSL@EQUINOX.UNR.EDU (InterNet). **Staff:** Dorothy Good, Sr.Supv.

★ 19018 ★
University of Nevada--Reno - Mines Library (Sci-Engr)
Getchell Library, Rm. 2/322   Phone: (702)784-6596
Reno, NV 89557-0044   Linda P. Newman, Libn.
Founded: 1952. **Staff:** Prof 2; Other 3. **Subjects:** Earth science; engineering - mining, chemical, metallurgical; physical geography. **Special Collections:** Theses on the geology of Nevada. **Holdings:** 16,700 books; 16,500 bound periodical volumes; 740 reels of microfilm; 123,300 maps; 28,500 microfiche; 8500 bound government reports; 18,900 unbound government reports. **Subscriptions:** 440 journals; 6 newspapers. **Services:** Interlibrary loan; copying; library open to the public with restrictions on borrowing. **Automated Operations:** Computerized public access catalog, acquisitions, and serials. **Computerized Information Services:** DIALOG Information Services, BRS Information Technologies; InterNet, BITNET (electronic mail services). Performs searches on fee basis. **Networks/Consortia:** Member of Information Nevada. **Publications:** New Books and Maps List, quarterly - free upon request; Mackay School of Mines Thesis List, 1908-1983 - for sale; Mineral Waste and Recovery Bibliography. **Special Indexes:** Nevada Mining and Geology File (44,600 cards). **Remarks:** FAX: (702)784-1751. Electronic mail address(es): 1NEWMAN@EQUINOX.UNR.EDU (InterNet); MINLIB@EQUINOX.UNR.EDU (InterNet); 1NEWMAN@EQUINOX (BITNET). **Staff:** Glee Willis.

★ 19019 ★
University of Nevada--Reno - Physical Sciences Library (Sci-Engr)
Chemistry Bldg., Rm. 316/218   Phone: (702)784-6716
Reno, NV 89557   Ann Eagan, Libn.
Founded: 1965. **Staff:** Prof 1; Other 2. **Subjects:** Chemistry, physics. **Holdings:** 10,602 books; 19,715 bound periodical volumes; 88 reels of microfilm; 3659 microfiche. **Subscriptions:** 294 journals and other serials. **Services:** Interlibrary loan; copying; SDI; library open to the public. **Automated Operations:** Computerized public access catalog, acquisitions, serials, and circulation. **Computerized Information Services:** DIALOG Information Services, STN International, Chemical Abstracts Service (CAS); InterNet (electronic mail service). Performs searches on fee basis. **Networks/Consortia:** Member of CLASS, Information Nevada. **Publications:** New Book List, monthly. **Remarks:** Electronic mail address(es): PHYL@EQUINOX.UNR.EDU (InterNet).

★ 19020 ★
University of Nevada--Reno - Research and Educational Planning Center
College of Education, Rm. 200
Reno, NV 89557
Defunct.

★ 19021 ★
University of Nevada--Reno - Savitt Medical Library (Med)
Savitt Medical Sciences Bldg./306   Phone: (702)784-4625
Reno, NV 89557   Joan S. Zenan, Dir.
Founded: 1978. **Staff:** Prof 2; Other 6. **Subjects:** Medicine and allied health sciences. **Special Collections:** Medical archives of Nevada. **Holdings:** 43,000 volumes. **Subscriptions:** 471 journals and other serials. **Services:** Interlibrary loan; copying; library open to the public. **Automated Operations:** Computerized public access catalog and cataloging. **Computerized Information Services:** Online systems; CD-ROM (MEDLINE); OnTyme Electronic Message Network Service, InterNet (electronic mail services). **Networks/Consortia:** Member of National Network of Libraries of Medicine - Pacific Southwest Region. **Publications:** University of Nevada School of Medicine Faculty Bibliography. **Remarks:** FAX: (702)784-4569. Electronic mail address(es): UNRMDZ (OnTyme Electronic Message Network Service); JOANZ@UQUINOX.UNR.EDU (InterNet). **Staff:** Laurie Potter, Ref.Libn.; Rosalyn Casey, Ser. & Acq.; Elizabeth McDonald, ILL; Jeannine Funk, Cat. & Acq.; Donna Packard, Circ.; Shawntay Beck, Adm.Serv.; Judy Dimitriadis, Ser. and Cat.

★ 19022 ★
University of Nevada--Reno - Special Collections Department/University Archives (Hist)
University Library   Phone: (702)784-6538
Reno, NV 89557-0044   Robert E. Blesse, Hd.
Founded: 1963. **Staff:** Prof 1; Other 4. **Subjects:** Nevada history, 20th century poetry and fiction, anthropology, ethnography, architecture, women in the trans-Mississippi West, magic, witchcraft, history of printing, university archives, mining, water and land use. **Special Collections:** Nevada Collection; Great Basin Anthropological Collection; Nevada fiction; Women in the West; Modern Authors Collection (170 English and American writers prominent after 1910); University of Nevada, Reno archives; History of Printing and the Book Arts Collection; Nevada Architectural Archives; Senator Alan Bible papers; Virginia & Truckee Railroad Collection; Samuel Johnson; Robert Burns; George Stewart. **Holdings:** 52,000 books; 600 bound periodical volumes; 4100 linear feet of manuscripts; 110,000 photographs; 4800 maps; 17,000 architectural drawings. **Subscriptions:** 31 journals and other serials. **Services:** Copying; department open to the public for reference use only. **Computerized Information Services:** InterNet (electronic mail service). **Special Catalogs:** Specialized subject and form catalogs (card); guides to manuscript collections. **Remarks:** FAX: (702)784-4529. Electronic mail address(es): SPECARCH@EQUINOX.UNR.EDU (InterNet).

★ 19023 ★
University of New Brunswick - Education Resource Centre (Educ)
D'Avray Hall
P.O. Box 7500   Phone: (506)453-3516
Fredericton, NB, Canada E3B 5H5   Andrew Pope, Hd.
Founded: 1973. **Staff:** Prof 2; Other 6. **Subjects:** Education, home economics. **Special Collections:** Micmac-Maliseet Institute (1070 volumes); Children's Literature Collection (6832 volumes). **Holdings:** 42,849 books; 4149 bound periodical volumes; 445,536 microfiche; 28 VF drawers of pamphlets; 17,763 AV and instructional programs. **Subscriptions:** 305 journals and other serials. **Services:** Interlibrary loan; copying; center open to the public. **Automated Operations:** Computerized cataloging. **Computerized Information Services:** CD-ROM (Eric); PHOENIX (internal database). Performs searches free of charge. **Remarks:** FAX: (506)453-4596. **Staff:** Patricia Johnston, Asst.Libn.

★ 19024 ★
University of New Brunswick - Engineering Library (Sci-Engr)
P.O. Box 440   Phone: (506)453-4747
Fredericton, NB, Canada E3B 3J7   Everett Dunfield, Hd.
Founded: 1967. **Staff:** Prof 2; Other 6. **Subjects:** Engineering - civil, mechanical, geological, electrical, forestry, surveying, chemical; computer science; transportation; bioengineering. **Holdings:** 25,500 books; 14,700 bound periodical volumes; 86,000 reports on microfiche and microfilm; 1375 theses; 142 films and slide sets; 15,200 reports, pamphlets, and clippings. **Subscriptions:** 735 journals and other serials; 5 newspapers. **Services:** Interlibrary loan; copying; SDI; library open to the public. **Automated Operations:** Computerized cataloging. **Computerized Information Services:** CAN/OLE, DIALOG Information Services, BRS Information Technologies, STN International; ENLIST, PHOENIX (internal databases); BITNET (electronic mail service). Performs searches on fee basis. **Publications:** Bibliographies and manuals - for internal and patron use only. **Remarks:** FAX: (506)453-4596. Electronic mail address(es): SLOAN@UNB.CA (BITNET). **Staff:** Steven Sloan.

★ 19025 ★
University of New Brunswick - Harriet Irving Library - Archives and Special Collections (Hum, Hist)
P.O. Box 7500   Phone: (506)453-4748
Fredericton, NB, Canada E3B 5H5   Mary Flagg, Mgr./Res.Off.
Founded: 1931. **Staff:** 9. **Subjects:** University and New Brunswick history, maritime history, Canadian literature. **Special Collections:** Hathaway Collection of Canadian Literature (3600 volumes); maritime history (4600 volumes); Beaverbrook Special Collections (1981 volumes). **Holdings:** 30,000 books; 4500 linear feet of bound periodical volumes; 1700 linear feet of university archives; 1600 linear feet of historical and literary manuscripts; 3500 photographs; personal papers. **Services:** Interlibrary loan; copying; collections open to the public. **Automated Operations:** Computerized cataloging and acquisitions. **Computerized Information Services:** Envoy 100, Datapac (electronic mail services). **Special Catalogs:** Maritime Pamphlet Collection: An Annotated Catalogue (online). **Remarks:** FAX: (506)453-4596. **Staff:** Francesca Holyoke; Marlene Power.

★ 19026 ★
University of New Brunswick - Law Library (Law)
Ludlow Hall
Bag Service No. 44999   Phone: (506)453-4734
Fredericton, NB, Canada E3B 6C9   C. Anne Crocker, Law Libn.
Founded: 1892. **Staff:** 10. **Subjects:** Law and common law. **Special Collections:** Lord Beaverbrook Legal Collection. **Holdings:** 93,204 books and bound periodical volumes; 16,374 volumes in microform; 67 AV titles. **Subscriptions:** 1765 journals and other serials. **Services:** Interlibrary loan; copying; library open to the public. **Automated Operations:** Computerized cataloging. **Computerized Information Services:** WESTLAW, QL Systems, LEXIS, UTLAS; PHOENIX (internal database); InterNet (electronic mail service). Performs searches on fee basis. Contact Person: John Sadler, Ref.Libn. **Publications:** Acquisitions List, monthly - on exchange. **Remarks:** FAX: (506)453-5186. Electronic mail address(es): ACROCKER@UNB.CA (InterNet). **Staff:** Janet Moss, Cat./Docs. Libn.

★ 19027 ★
University of New Brunswick - Science Library (Biol Sci, Sci-Engr)
P.O. Box 7500   Phone: (506)453-4601
Fredericton, NB, Canada E3B 5H5   Eszter L.K. Schwenke, Hd.
Staff: Prof 2; Other 5. **Subjects:** Forestry, biology, chemistry, geology, mathematics, physics. **Special Collections:** Forestry Collection (11,000 pamphlets). **Holdings:** 41,532 books; 41,600 bound periodical volumes; 800 theses; 435 reels of microfilm; 11,620 microcards; 51,065 microfiche. **Subscriptions:** 880 journals and other serials. **Services:** Interlibrary loan; copying; SDI; library open to the public. **Computerized Information Services:** DIALOG Information Services, CAN/OLE, QL Systems, Chemical Abstracts Service (CAS), STN International, Information Retrieval System for the Sociology of Leisure and Sport (SIRLS), MEDLINE; PHOENIX (internal database); Envoy 100 (electronic mail service). Performs searches on fee basis. **Special Indexes:** ENLIST, forestry pamphlet file (online and printout); GEOSCAN, New Brunswick mineral assessment file (microfiche). **Remarks:** Alternate telephone number(s): 453-4602. FAX: (506)453-3518.

★ 19028 ★
University of New England - Orange Agricultural College - Library (Agri)
Leeds Parade
PO Box 883   Phone: 63 635594
Orange, NSW 2800, Australia   Robyn Schwartz
Founded: 1973. **Subjects:** Agriculture, business, management, environmental science, horticulture, animal husbandry. **Holdings:** 25,000 books; 8000 bound periodical volumes; 850 reports; 85 microfiche; 2000 videotapes, maps, audiocassettes, and kits. **Subscriptions:** 500 journals and other serials; 15 newspapers. **Services:** Interlibrary loan; copying; SDI; library open to the public for reference use only. **Computerized Information Services:** DIALOG Information Services, AUSTRALIS; CD-ROMs (CAB Abstracts, CLANN-CD Cat, AUSTROM); ILANET, KEYLINK (electronic mail services). Contact Person: Stephen Doyle, Rd.Serv.Libn. **Publications:** Library Guide; Periodicals List; Reports List; Video List. **Remarks:** FAX: 63 635590. Electronic mail address(es): MLN 200300 (ILANET); ORN 001 (KEYLINK).

★ 19029 ★
University of New Hampshire - Biological Sciences Library (Biol Sci, Agri)
Kendall Hall   Phone: (603)862-1018
Durham, NH 03824   Barbara Farah, Coord., Engr. & Sci.Libs.
Staff: Prof 1; Other 2. **Subjects:** General biology, agriculture, natural resources, forestry, botany, microbiology, zoology, entomology, animal science, plant science, nutrition, biochemistry, genetics. **Holdings:** 75,000 volumes. **Subscriptions:** 800 journals and other serials. **Services:** Interlibrary loan; copying; library open to limited public use. **Automated Operations:** Computerized cataloging and acquisitions. **Computerized Information Services:** DIALOG Information Services, OCLC; CD-ROMs (AGRICOLA, MEDLINE, Biological Abstracts). Performs searches at cost. **Networks/Consortia:** Member of NELINET, Inc., New Hampshire College & University Council Library Policy Committee (NHCUC). **Remarks:** FAX: (603)862-2637. **Staff:** David Lane, Biol.Sci.Br.Libn.

★ 19030 ★
University of New Hampshire - Chemistry Library (Sci-Engr)
Parsons Hall   Phone: (603)862-4168
Durham, NH 03824   Barbara D. Farah, Libn.
Staff: Prof 1; Other 1. **Subjects:** Chemistry. **Holdings:** 21,027 volumes. **Subscriptions:** 147 journals. **Services:** Interlibrary loan; copying; library open to the public. **Automated Operations:** Computerized cataloging, acquisitions, and circulation. **Computerized Information Services:** OCLC, DIALOG Information Services, STN International. **Networks/Consortia:** Member of NELINET, Inc., New Hampshire College & University Council Library Policy Committee (NHCUC). **Remarks:** FAX: (603)862-4112.

★ 19031 ★
University of New Hampshire - Department of Instructional Services - Film Library (Aud-Vis)
Dimond Library   Phone: (603)862-2240
Durham, NH 03824   Colleen Kendoll-Piel, Mgr., Instr.Serv.
Founded: 1946. **Staff:** Prof 13; Other 8. **Special Collections:** Lotte Jacobi Photo Archive. **Holdings:** 2300 educational films for all ages. **Services:** Films available for rent; library open to the public. **Computerized Information Services:** InterNet (electronic mail service). **Special Catalogs:** Instructional Film Catalog (book). **Remarks:** FAX: (603)862-2241. Electronic mail address(es): C–PIEZ@UNHH.UNH.EDU (InterNet). **Staff:** Gary Samson, Filmmaker-Photog.; Dorothy Ahlgren, TV Producer-Supv.; Celine Chaisson, Film Dist.

★ 19032 ★
University of New Hampshire - Engineering-Math Library (Sci-Engr, Comp Sci)
Kingsbury Hall   Phone: (603)862-4168
Durham, NH 03824   Barbara D. Farah, Libn.
Founded: 1949. **Staff:** Prof 1; Other 2. **Subjects:** Engineering - mechanical, civil, electrical, chemical; mathematics; materials science; computer science. **Holdings:** 45,890 volumes. **Subscriptions:** 742 journals and other serials. **Services:** Interlibrary loan; copying; library open to the public. **Automated Operations:** Computerized cataloging, acquisitions, and circulation. **Computerized Information Services:** DIALOG Information Services, STN International; CD-ROM. **Networks/Consortia:** Member of NELINET, Inc., New Hampshire College & University Council Library Policy Committee (NHCUC). **Remarks:** FAX: (603)862-4112.

★ 19033 ★
University of New Hampshire - New Hampshire Water Resource Research Center - Library (Env-Cons)
218 Science/Engineering Research Bldg.   Phone: (603)862-2144
Durham, NH 03824   Thomas P. Ballestero, Dir.
Founded: 1965. **Staff:** Prof 1; Other 2. **Subjects:** Theoretical, analytical, and practical evaluation of hydrologic phenomena including evaporation and transpiration, watershed management, groundwater, water law and economics, interbasin transfers, water conservation, radon, aquifer remediation, and stream hydraulics. **Holdings:** 520 books and bound periodical volumes; 6361 pamphlets; 7500 reports and documents. **Subscriptions:** 16 journals and newsletters. **Services:** Library open to the public. **Publications:** Research reports and associated publications. **Special Catalogs:** Keyterm and title catalogs; shelf list; publication catalog. **Remarks:** FAX: (603)862-2030.

★ 19034 ★
University of New Hampshire - Physics Library (Sci-Engr)
DeMeritt Hall   Phone: (603)862-1740
Durham, NH 03824   Barbara D. Farah, Libn.
Founded: 1965. **Staff:** Prof 1; Other 1. **Subjects:** Physics. **Holdings:** 18,000 books; 12,000 bound periodical volumes; 120 theses; 70 film loops. **Subscriptions:** 140 journals and other serials. **Services:** Interlibrary loan; copying; library open to the public. **Automated Operations:** Computerized cataloging and acquisitions. **Computerized Information Services:** DIALOG Information Services, STN International, OCLC. **Networks/Consortia:** Member of NELINET, Inc., New Hampshire College & University Council Library Policy Committee (NHCUC). **Remarks:** FAX: (603)862-4112.

★19035★
University of New Hampshire - Sea Grant - Marine Resources Center
(Biol Sci)
Kingman Farm   Phone: (603)749-1565
Durham, NH 03824-3512   Marie Polk, Ed./Info.Spec.
Founded: 1978. **Staff:** 1. **Subjects:** Sea Grant/Marine and related research. **Special Collections:** University of New Hampshire faculty, staff, and student books, reports, journal article reprints, and theses (750 items). **Holdings:** 100 books; 2000 reports. **Services:** Copying; library open to the public. **Computerized Information Services:** Internal database. **Remarks:** FAX: (603)743-3997.

★19036★
University of New Hampshire - Special Collections (Hist, Hum)
University of New Hampshire Library   Phone: (603)862-2714
Durham, NH 03824   Michael C. York
Founded: 1974. **Staff:** Prof 1; Other 2. **Subjects:** New Hampshire. **Special Collections:** University of New Hampshire dissertations (10,000 volumes); Robert Frost (250 volumes); Milne Angling Collection (3000 volumes); Proper Shaker Collection (500 volumes); New Hampshire (21,000 volumes); Early New Hampshire Imprints (900 volumes); historical juvenile books (1200); Society for the Protection of New Hampshire Forests Archive; Edward MacDowell papers; Lotte Jacobi papers; Amy Cheney Beach papers; Donald Hall papers; Galway Kinnell papers; Charles Simic papers; Senator Norris Cotton papers; Senator Thomas McIntyre papers; university archives. **Holdings:** 45,000 books; 3200 linear feet of manuscripts; 1900 linear feet of university records. **Services:** Copying; collections open to the public. **Remarks:** FAX: (603)862-2637. **Staff:** William E. Ross, Hd.

★19037★
University of New Hampshire - State and Regional Indicators Archive
(Soc Sci)
128 Horton Social Science Ctr.   Phone: (603)862-1888
Durham, NH 03824   Murray A. Straus, Dir.
Founded: 1979. **Staff:** Prof 1. **Subjects:** U.S. state and regional social science statistics - politics, economics, culture, society, social stress, pornography, violence, sexual assault, medical resources, health, and allied topics. **Holdings:** 1000 books; 20 bound periodical volumes; reprints; clippings; machine-readable files. **Services:** Archive open to the public. **Computerized Information Services:** Internal database. Performs searches on fee basis. **Remarks:** FAX: (603)862-2030. The Archive collects data on the 50 states and the District of Columbia in order to facilitate research that uses the states of the U.S. as units of analysis.

University of New Mexico - Anderson Room
See: University of New Mexico - Special Collections Department (19047)

★19038★
University of New Mexico - Art Museum - Raymond Jonson Archives
(Art)
1909 Las Lomas Rd., N.E.   Phone: (505)277-4967
Albuquerque, NM 87131   Tiska Blankenship, Assoc.Cur.
Founded: 1950. **Staff:** 5. **Subjects:** Modernism, Transcendental Painting Group, Dane Rudhyar, Hilaire Hiler, music, poetry. **Special Collections:** Jonson's personal books, correspondence, manuscripts, photographs, news clippings, diaries. **Holdings:** 800 books. **Services:** Copying; archives open to the public by appointment. **Computerized Information Services:** Internal databases. **Remarks:** FAX: (505)277-0708.

★19039★
University of New Mexico - Bainbridge Bunting Memorial Slide Library
(Aud-Vis)
College of Fine Arts   Phone: (505)277-6415
Albuquerque, NM 87131   Sheila Hannah, Dir.
Founded: 1972. **Staff:** Prof 3. **Subjects:** History of art, architecture, photography, Native American arts, Spanish Colonial arts, Pre-Columbian arts. **Holdings:** 300,000 slides. **Services:** Library not open to the public. **Staff:** Margaret Hedges Favour, Coll.Mgr.; Carroll Botts, Circ.Supv.

University of New Mexico - Bell Room
See: University of New Mexico - Special Collections Department (19047)

★19040★
University of New Mexico - Bureau of Business & Economic Research Data Bank (Soc Sci, Bus-Fin)
1920 Lomas Blvd., N.E.   Phone: (505)277-6626
Albuquerque, NM 87131-6021   Kevin Kargacin, Hd., Info.Serv.
Founded: 1945. **Staff:** Prof 3; Other 3. **Subjects:** New Mexico - economics, income, employment, demographics, census. **Special Collections:** Census of Population and Housing for New Mexico, 1940-1990; 1970 census printouts for small areas; 1980 and 1990 census products (comprehensive set). **Holdings:** 14,000 cataloged publications. **Subscriptions:** 400 journals and other serials. **Services:** Copying; bureau open to the public. **Automated Operations:** Computerized cataloging. **Computerized Information Services:** New Mexico County Profiles, New Mexico Economic Indicators (internal databases). **Publications:** New Mexico Business, monthly - by subscription. **Remarks:** FAX: (505)277-7066. **Staff:** James A. McCormick, Prog. Specialist.

★19041★
University of New Mexico - Centennial Science and Engineering Library
(Sci-Engr)
Albuquerque, NM 87131   Phone: (505)277-4412
                         Harry Llull, Dir.
Founded: 1988. **Staff:** 16. **Subjects:** Science, engineering, geography, transportation. **Special Collections:** Patent depository (1833 to present). **Holdings:** 300,000 volumes; 1.4 million microfiche; 170,111 maps; 7029 air photos; government documents; technical reports. **Subscriptions:** 2100 journals and other serials. **Services:** Interlibrary loan; copying; library open to the public. **Computerized Information Services:** DIALOG Information Services, STN International, BRS Information Technologies, OCLC, RLIN; CD-ROMs; BITNET, InterNet (electronic mail services). Performs searches on fee basis. Contact Person: Diana Northrup, Online Serv., Biol. & Chem. Bibliog. **Networks/Consortia:** Member of Colorado Alliance of Research Libraries (CARL). **Publications:** Centennial Science and Engineering Library Newsletter and New Books List, monthly - in paper and electronic editions. **Remarks:** FAX: (505)277-0702. Electronic mail address(es): HLLULL@UNMB (BITNET, InterNet). **Staff:** Donna Cromer, Ref., Physics & Electrical Engr.Bibliog.; Andrea Testi, Coll., Math.Bibliog.; Dena Adams, Patents & Govt.Docs., Civil Engr.Bibliog.; Emily Terrell, Mechanical Engr.Bibliog.; Dan Mahoney, Chem. & Nuclear Engr.Bibliog.; Heather Rex, Map Libn., Geol. & Geog. Bibliog.

University of New Mexico - Coronado Room
See: University of New Mexico - Special Collections Department (19047)

★19042★
University of New Mexico - Fine Arts Library (Art, Mus)
Albuquerque, NM 87131-1501   Phone: (505)277-2357
                       James B. Wright, Dir.
Founded: 1963. **Staff:** Prof 8; Other 3. **Subjects:** Art, music, architecture, photography. **Special Collections:** Manuel Areu Zarzuela Collection; Bernice Frost Piano Music Archive; John David Robb Archive of Southwestern Music; art exhibition catalogs; Gigante Collection (orchestra bowing markings). **Holdings:** 103,500 books; 32,000 sound recordings. **Subscriptions:** 350 journals and other serials. **Services:** Listening center; copying; library open to the public. **Automated Operations:** Computerized public access catalog, cataloging, acquisitions, serials, and circulation. **Computerized Information Services:** DIALOG Information Services; BITNET (electronic mail service). **Remarks:** FAX: (505)277-6019. Electronic mail address(es): JWRIGHT@UNMB (BITNET). **Staff:** Nancy Pistorius, Assoc.Libn.

★19043★
University of New Mexico - Learning Resource Center/Library (Sci-Engr)
4000 University Dr.   Phone: (505)662-5919
Los Alamos, NM 87544   Linda G. Schappert, Dir.
Founded: 1984. **Staff:** Prof 1; Other 2. **Subjects:** Science, mathematics, computer science, fine arts, business, southwestern United States. **Holdings:** 9000 books. **Subscriptions:** 106 journals and other serials; 6 newspapers. **Services:** Interlibrary loan; copying; center open to New Mexico residents. **Automated Operations:** Computerized cataloging and ILL. **Computerized Information Services:** OCLC. **Networks/Consortia:** Member of New Mexico Consortium of Academic Libraries (NMCAL).

★ 19044 ★

University of New Mexico - Medical Center Library (Med)
North Campus   Phone: (505)277-2548
Albuquerque, NM 87131   Erika Love, Dir.
Founded: 1963. **Staff:** Prof 12; Other 29. **Subjects:** Medicine, basic sciences, nursing, pharmacy, Indian health, dental hygiene, allied health sciences. **Special Collections:** New Mexico medical history and public health; Medical Center archives; Indian health papers; oral histories of New Mexico physicians. **Holdings:** 51,895 books; 8260 bound periodical volumes; 1881 AV programs. **Subscriptions:** 1904 titles. **Services:** Interlibrary loan; SDI; outreach programs for New Mexico health personnel; library open to the public. **Automated Operations:** Computerized cataloging, acquisitions, serials, and circulation. **Computerized Information Services:** OCLC, NLM, BRS Information Technologies, DIALOG Information Services, PFDS Online; BITNET, InterNet (electronic mail services). Performs searches on fee basis. **Networks/Consortia:** Member of National Network of Libraries of Medicine - South Central Region, AMIGOS Bibliographic Council, Inc., South Central Academic Medical Libraries Consortium (SCAMEL), New Mexico Consortium of Academic Libraries (NMCAL). **Publications:** Adobe Medicus - to user community and selected U.S. medical libraries. **Remarks:** FAX: (505)277-5350. Electronic mail address(es): MEDLIB@UNMB (BITNET); ELOVE@BIBLIO.UNM.EDU (InterNet). **Staff:** Cecile C. Quintal, Assoc.Dir.; Jon Eldredge, Chf., Coll.Dev.; Deborah Graham, Hd., Biomedical Info.Serv.; Lisa Kindrick, Sys. & Automation Libn.; Caroline Mann, Network Coord.; Richard Evans, Electronic Commun.Chf.; Tom Peterson, Sys.

★ 19045 ★

University of New Mexico - Museum of Southwestern Biology - Library (Biol Sci)
Biology Bldg.   Phone: (505)277-5340
Albuquerque, NM 87131-1091   William L. Gannon, Coll.Mgr.
Founded: 1950. **Staff:** Prof 1. **Subjects:** Mammals, evolution, systematics, biology, ecology, behavior. **Holdings:** 1500 books; 1500 bound periodical volumes; 500 reports; 20 archival items; 6 microfiche; 50 theses/dissertations; 4600 reprints. **Subscriptions:** 16 journals and other serials. **Services:** Library open to the public by appointment. **Computerized Information Services:** Internal databases; BITNET (electronic mail service). **Remarks:** FAX: (505)2773411. Electronic mail address(es): WGANNON@UNMB (BITNET).

★ 19046 ★

University of New Mexico - School of Law Library (Law)
1117 Stanford, N.E.   Phone: (505)277-6236
Albuquerque, NM 87131-1441   Anita Morse, Dir.
Founded: 1950. **Staff:** Prof 4; Other 16. **Subjects:** Law. **Special Collections:** American Indian law; Community Land Grant Law; Mexican and Latin American legal materials. **Holdings:** 197,614 volumes; 657,155 microforms (109,526 volume equivalents); 12,000 New Mexico Supreme Court records and briefs. **Subscriptions:** 2700 journals and other serials; 21 newspapers. **Services:** Interlibrary loan; copying; library open to the public. **Automated Operations:** Computerized cataloging, acquisitions, serials, and circulation. **Computerized Information Services:** LEXIS, DIALOG Information Services, OCLC, WESTLAW. **Networks/Consortia:** Member of AMIGOS Bibliographic Council, Inc. **Publications:** A Guide to the School of Law Library; Annual New Acquisitions List - both to members of the New Mexico State Bar, judicial offices, and patrons; New Titles Received. **Special Catalogs:** Catalog of American Indian Law. **Remarks:** FAX: (505)277-0068. **Staff:** Lorraine Lester, Dp.Dir.; Eileen Cohen, Assoc.Libn.; David Epstein, Circ. Revenue Coll.Hd.; William Jacoby, Circ.Coll.Hd.; Dana Dorman, Cat.; Tom Huesemann, Acq.

★ 19047 ★

University of New Mexico - Special Collections Department - Center for Southwest Research (Hist)
General Library   Phone: (505)277-6898
Albuquerque, NM 87131   Michael Miller, Hd.
Founded: 1950. **Staff:** Prof 3; Other 12. **Subjects:** History of the American West, New Mexico history, history of Mexico and Latin America, Indians of the Southwest, southwestern architectural history. **Special Collections:** Doris Duke Collection (982 oral history tapes); Pioneer Foundation (527 tapes). **Holdings:** 36,700 volumes; 2100 tape recordings; 3150 linear feet of manuscript material; 17,000 photographs; 250 videocassettes. **Subscriptions:** 121 journals and other serials. **Services:** Copying (limited); center open to the public. **Publications:** Annual report. **Remarks:** The Special Collections Department consists of six divisions: the Anderson Room, containing

Western Americana; the Coronado Room collection on the history and culture of New Mexico; the Bell Room, housing the rare book collection; the manuscript collections and architectural records, which are also housed separately; the University Archives; and the Oral History Program. Alternate telephone number(s): 277-7171. FAX: (505)277-6019. **Staff:** Kathlene Ferris, Archv.; Stella De Sa Rego, Cur., Photo.; Jan Barnhart, Cur., John Gaw Meem Archv. of SW Arch.; Russ Davidson, Cur., Latin Amer.Coll.; Terry Gugliotta, Univ.Archv.; Barbara Johnson, Archv. & Mss.; Rose Diaz, Oral Hist./Commun.Rel.; John Grassham, Spec.Coll., Ref.Res.; Kathy Gienger, Acq.; Judith Murphy, Cons.; Carlos Vasquez, Oral Hist.

★ 19048 ★

University of New Mexico - Technology Application Center (Sci-Engr)
2808 Central Ave., S.E.   Phone: (505)277-3622
Albuquerque, NM 87131-6031   Stanley A. Morain, Dir.
Founded: 1965. **Staff:** Prof 14; Other 7. **Subjects:** Remote sensing, earth photography, geographic information systems. **Special Collections:** Remote sensing bibliography (citations). **Holdings:** 10K slides of earth-oriented photography. **Subscriptions:** 20 journals and other serials; 3 newspapers. **Services:** Image processing; short courses; visiting scientist program; photograph search service; center open to the public. **Computerized Information Services:** NASA/RECON, EROS Data Center; Dialcom Inc., NASAMAIL (electronic mail services). Performs searches on fee basis. **Publications:** Remote Sensing of Natural Resources Quarterly Literature Review. **Remarks:** Center is a NASA facility for transferring Earth observing technology. FAX: (505)277-3614. Telex: 660461 ASBKS UNM ABQ. **Also Known As:** TAC. **Staff:** Mike Inglis, Assoc.Dir.; Amy Budge, Photo. Search Serv.

★ 19049 ★

University of New Mexico - Tireman Learning Materials Library (Educ, Hist)
Albuquerque, NM 87131   Phone: (505)277-3856
                                Susan Deese, Dir.
Founded: 1965. **Staff:** Prof 3. **Subjects:** Children's and young adult's fiction; curriculum materials for kindergarten through high school. **Holdings:** 11,393 books and bound periodical volumes; 1782 nonbook titles (filmstrips, kits, games, software, videocassettes, audiocassettes, records, prints); 384 reference titles; 13,600 Evaluation Center items; 3 VF drawers of publishers' catalogs. **Subscriptions:** 13 journals and other serials. **Services:** Interlibrary loan; library open to the public with borrower's card. **Automated Operations:** Computerized cataloging, acquisitions, serials, and circulation. **Computerized Information Services:** InterNet (electronic mail service). **Remarks:** Library houses a regional evaluation center for state instructional materials. FAX: (505)277-6019. **Staff:** Deborah Cole, Coll.Maint.Mgr.; Karen Olson, Asst.Dir.; Shirley Pareo, Circ.Supv.

University of New Mexico - University Archives
See: **University of New Mexico - Special Collections Department** (19047)

★ 19050 ★

University of New Mexico - William J. Parish Memorial Library (Bus-Fin)
Albuquerque, NM 87131-1496   Phone: (505)277-5912
                                Judith Bernstein, Dir.
Founded: 1969. **Staff:** Prof 3; Other 7. **Subjects:** Economics, management, accounting, finance, personnel, marketing, international management, travel and tourism, real estate, management information systems. **Holdings:** 83,100 books; 52,139 serial volumes; 68,236 10K and annual reports; 118,427 microforms. **Subscriptions:** 1400 journals and other serials. **Services:** Interlibrary loan; copying; library open to the public with limited circulation. **Automated Operations:** Computerized public access catalog, cataloging, acquisitions, serials, and circulation. **Computerized Information Services:** DIALOG Information Services, PFDS Online, BRS Information Technologies, OCLC; CD-ROMs; InterNet, BITNET (electronic mail services). Performs searches on fee basis. Contact Person: Mary Beth Johnson, Asst.Dir., 277-9242. **Networks/Consortia:** Member of AMIGOS Bibliographic Council, Inc. **Publications:** Annual report; newsletter, monthly; monthly new acquisitions list - for internal distribution only; guides to the collection. **Remarks:** Electronic mail address(es): ROSEN@HYDRA.UNM.EDU (InterNet). **Staff:** Peter Ives, Ref.Libn.; Carolyn Mountain, Ibero-Amer.Spec.; Vanessa Moats, Oper.Mgr.

★ 19051 ★
University of New Orleans - Center for Economic Development - Library
(Soc Sci)
BA 368, Lakefront Campus   Phone: (504)286-6663
New Orleans, LA 70148   Kay Chapoton, Libn.
Founded: 1978. **Subjects:** Housing, trade, real estate, development, small business, international trade. **Holdings:** 500 volumes. **Services:** Library not open to the public.

★ 19052 ★
University of New Orleans - Earl K. Long Library - Archives &
    Manuscripts/Special Collections Department (Hist)
Lake Front   Phone: (504)286-7273
New Orleans, LA 70148   D. Clive Hardy, Archv., Hd. of Dept.
Founded: 1968. **Staff:** Prof 3; Other 16. **Subjects:** New Orleans - ethnic groups, labor unions, legal records, businesses, history, culture. **Special Collections:** Crabites Collection of Egyptology (printed materials, primarily books); Frank Von der Haar Collection of William Faulkner (printed materials, primarily books); Orleans Parish School Board Collection; Chamber of Commerce of New Orleans Collection; Louisiana Supreme Court Collection; Marcus Christian Collection; Audubon Park Commission Collection; National Association for the Advancement of Colored People - New Orleans Branch Collection; Jean Lafitte National Historical Park Collection. **Holdings:** 4800 volumes; 11,000 linear feet of manuscripts and archival records. **Subscriptions:** 12 journals and other serials. **Services:** Interlibrary loan (limited); copying; department open to the public. **Special Catalogs:** Special Collections at the University of New Orleans; The Frank A. Von der Haar Collection. **Remarks:** Alternate telephone number(s): 286-6543. FAX: (504)286-7277. **Staff:** Marie E. Windell, Lib.Assoc. III; Beatrice R. Owsley, Lib.Assoc. III.

★ 19053 ★
University of New South Wales - Biomedical Library (Med, Biol Sci, Soc Sci)
POB 1   Phone: 2 6972663
Kensington, NSW 2033, Australia   Monica Davis
Subjects: Medicine, biological sciences, psychology, food science and technology, pastoral sciences, biotechnology. **Holdings:** 80,000 books; 250,000 bound periodical volumes; 500 reports; 30,000 microfiche; 500 reels of microfilm; 1500 audio-visual materials. **Subscriptions:** 2150 journals and other serials. **Services:** Interlibrary loan; copying; library open to the public. **Automated Operations:** Computerized public access catalog. **Computerized Information Services:** OZLINE, DIALOG Information Services, ESA/IRS, BRS Information Technologies. **Remarks:** FAX: 2 6627312.

★ 19054 ★
University of Niamey - Research Institute for the Social Sciences -
    Library (Hum)
B.P. 318   Phone: 735141
Niamey, Niger   M. Saidou Harouna, Libn.
Subjects: Sociology, linguistics, archeology, history, geography. **Holdings:** 20,000 volumes. **Services:** Interlibrary loan; copying; library open to the public for reference use only. **Remarks:** Telex: 5258 UNINIM. **Formerly:** Its Research Institute for the Human Sciences.

University of North
See: **Catholic University of North** (3167)

University of North Carolina - Mossbauer Effect Data Center
See: **Mossbauer Effect Data Center** (10770)

★ 19055 ★
University of North Carolina at Asheville - Southern Highlands
    Research Center (Hist)
Asheville, NC 28804   Phone: (704)251-6645
    William Buchanan, Dir.
Subjects: Western North Carolina, 1833 to present; Appalachia. **Special Collections:** Asheville and Buncombe County photograph collection; papers of U.S. Representative Roy A. Taylor concerning the proposed Mount Mitchell National Park; oral history recordings of mountaineers (200); collections of black, Jewish, Greek, and other ethnic groups in Appalachia; Tom Wolfe Collection. **Holdings:** 50 linear feet of records and photographs. **Services:** Copying; center open to the public. **Remarks:** Alternate telephone number(s): 251-6111. FAX: (704)251-6012. Center is housed in the University's Ramsey Library.

★ 19056 ★
University of North Carolina at Chapel Hill - Alfred T. Brauer Library
(Sci-Engr, Comp Sci)
CB 3250 Phillips Hall   Phone: (919)962-2323
Chapel Hill, NC 27599   Dana M. Sally, Math/Physics Libn.
Founded: 1920. **Staff:** Prof 1; Other 4. **Subjects:** Mathematics, physics, statistics, computer science, operations research, astronomy. **Holdings:** 93,112 volumes; 995 technical reports; 1247 microfiche; 172 audiotapes. **Subscriptions:** 933 journals. **Services:** Interlibrary loan; copying; library open to the public. **Automated Operations:** Computerized cataloging. **Computerized Information Services:** OCLC, DIALOG Information Services; BITNET (electronic mail service). **Networks/Consortia:** Member of SOLINET. **Publications:** List of new books received, monthly; special subject bibliographies, irregular - both available on request. **Remarks:** Electronic mail address(es): UNCDSA@UNC (BITNET).

★ 19057 ★
University of North Carolina at Chapel Hill - Center for Alcohol Studies
    - Library (Med)
CB 7175 UNC School of Medicine, Bldg. A   Phone: (919)966-5678
Chapel Hill, NC 27514   Dr. Amir Rezvani, Asst.Dir.
Staff: Prof 1. **Subjects:** Alcohol research, alcoholism. **Holdings:** 250 books; 3000 reprints; clippings. **Subscriptions:** 5 journals and other serials. **Services:** Interlibrary loan; copying; library open to the public. **Publications:** Activities Report, annual - free upon request. **Remarks:** FAX: (919)966-5679.

★ 19058 ★
University of North Carolina at Chapel Hill - Center for Early
    Adolescence - Information Services Division (Educ)
D2 Carr Mill Town Ctr.   Phone: (919)966-1148
Carrboro, NC 27510   James Rosinia, Dir. of Info.Serv.
Founded: 1979. **Staff:** Prof 2; Other 1. **Subjects:** Young adolescents - biological, cognitive, psychological, and social development; middle schools and junior high schools; youth advocacy/services; sexuality and sex education; after-school care; literacy; at-risk youth. **Holdings:** 9000 books and articles; statistics. **Subscriptions:** 135 journals and other serials. **Services:** Phone and mail reference; copying; center open to the public. **Publications:** Common Focus (newsletter), irregular - free upon request; assorted bibliographies, resource lists, monographs, and curricula on early adolescence - for sale. **Remarks:** FAX: (919)966-7657. Center is part of the School of Medicine. **Staff:** Roberta Lloyd, Info.Spec.

★ 19059 ★
University of North Carolina at Chapel Hill - F. Stuart Chapin, Jr.
    Planning Library (Plan)
CB 3140 New East   Phone: (919)962-3985
Chapel Hill, NC 27599   Linda S. Drake, City & Reg.Plan.Libn.
Founded: 1949. **Staff:** 2. **Subjects:** Urban planning, land use, housing and community development, transportation, environmental planning, regional economics. **Special Collections:** Planning document collection; John Nolan Collection of misc. papers. **Holdings:** 16,423 books; 1679 bound periodical volumes; 8675 documents; 6066 microforms; 577 audiocassettes; 3797 slides; 11 videocassettes. **Subscriptions:** 275 journals and other serials. **Services:** Interlibrary loan; copying; library open to the public. **Automated Operations:** Computerized cataloging. **Publications:** Acquisitions list, irregular; Library Notes - for internal distribution only.

★ 19060 ★
University of North Carolina at Chapel Hill - Geology Library (Sci-Engr)
CB 3315 Mitchell Hall   Phone: (919)962-2386
Chapel Hill, NC 27599-3315   Miriam L. Sheaves, Libn.
Staff: Prof 1; Other 1. **Subjects:** Geology, geophysics, paleontology, oceanography. **Holdings:** 44,000 volumes; 42,000 map sheets; 15,000 microforms; partial depository of U.S. Geological Survey topographic and geologic maps. **Subscriptions:** 850 journals and other serials. **Services:** Interlibrary loan; copying; library open to the public. **Computerized Information Services:** DIALOG Information Services; CD-ROMs (GeoRef, Earth Science Library, Publications of the U.S. Geological Survey); BITNET (electronic mail service). **Remarks:** Electronic mail address(es): UNCMLS@UNC (BITNET).

★ 19061 ★

University of North Carolina at Chapel Hill - Health Sciences Library
(Med)
Chapel Hill, NC 27599-7585　　　　　Phone: (919)966-2111
　　　　　　　　　　　　　　　　　　Carol G. Jenkins, Dir.
Founded: 1952. **Staff:** Prof 25; Other 32. **Subjects:** Medicine, nursing, dentistry, public health, pharmacy, allied health sciences. **Special Collections:** History of Health Sciences. **Holdings:** 84,000 books; 170,000 bound periodical volumes; 4600 AV programs. **Subscriptions:** 3462 journals and other serials. **Services:** Interlibrary loan; copying; SDI; microcomputer learning center; library open to the public. **Automated Operations:** Computerized public access catalog, cataloging, acquisitions, serials, and ILL (DOCLINE). **Computerized Information Services:** BRS Information Technologies, DIALOG Information Services, NLM, OCLC, MEDLINE, LOANSOME DOC; CD-ROMs. Performs searches on fee basis. **Networks/Consortia:** Member of National Network of Libraries of Medicine - Southeastern/Atlantic Region, SOLINET, North Carolina Area Health Education Centers Program Library and Information Services Network, Triangle Research Libraries Network (TRLN). **Publications:** Annual Report; News & Views, semimonthly - to mailing list. **Special Catalogs:** Audiovisual union catalogs (online). **Remarks:** FAX: (919)966-1537. **Staff:** Gary Byrd, Asst.Dir.; Mona Couts, Asst.Dir.; Jim Curtis, Asst.Dir.; Marjory Waite, Hd., Acq.Serv.; Susan Lyon, Hd., Circ.Serv.; Steven Squires, Hd., Cat.Serv.; Diane Futrelle, Hd., Lrng.Rsrcs.Serv.; Diane McKenzie, Act.Hd., Info.Serv. ; Margaret Moore, Hd., Info.Mgt.Educ.; Carolyn Lipscomb, Asst. to Dir.; Diana McDuffee, AHEC LIS Network Coord.

★ 19062 ★

University of North Carolina at Chapel Hill - Highway Safety Research Center - Library (Trans)
CB 3430 134 1/2 E. Franklin St.　　　　Phone: (919)962-8701
Chapel Hill, NC 27599　　　　　　　　Anita H. Speed, Libn.
Founded: 1970. **Staff:** Prof 1; Other 1. **Subjects:** Highway safety, accident and investigation analysis, driver education and licensing, restraint systems usage and effectiveness, traffic records, evaluation of highway safety programs. **Special Collections:** North Carolina traffic data (traffic accidents, arrest/disposition reports, driver licensing, and driver improvement programs). **Holdings:** 21,000 books, documents, technical reports; 575 bound periodical volumes; 38,000 research reports on microfiche. **Subscriptions:** 125 journals and other serials. **Services:** Interlibrary loan; copying; library open to the public for reference use only. **Automated Operations:** Computerized public access catalog. **Computerized Information Services:** DIALOG Information Services. **Remarks:** FAX: (919)962-8710.

★ 19063 ★

University of North Carolina at Chapel Hill - Institute of Government - Library (Soc Sci)
CB 3330 Knapp Bldg.　　　　　　　　Phone: (919)966-4130
Chapel Hill, NC 27599-3330　　　　　Patricia A. Langelier, Libn.
Founded: 1930. **Staff:** Prof 1; Other 2. **Subjects:** Public administration, state and local government, public law. **Holdings:** 12,000 books; 2400 bound periodical volumes; 24,543 pamphlets. **Subscriptions:** 815 journals and other serials; 12 newspapers. **Services:** Interlibrary loan; copying; library open to the public. **Automated Operations:** Computerized public access catalog and acquisitions. **Computerized Information Services:** LEXIS, DIALOG Information Services, Online North Carolina Legislative Bill Status and History; internal database; BITNET (electronic mail service). Performs searches free of charge (limited). **Networks/Consortia:** Member of Triangle Research Libraries Network (TRLN). **Publications:** Acquisitions List, bimonthly. **Remarks:** FAX: (919)966-4762.

★ 19064 ★

University of North Carolina at Chapel Hill - Institute of Marine Sciences - Library (Biol Sci)
3407 Arendell St.　　　　　　　　　　Phone: (919)726-6841
Morehead City, NC 28557　　　　　　Brenda B. Bright, Libn.
Founded: 1948. **Staff:** Prof 1; Other 1. **Subjects:** Biological oceanography, marine ecology, malacology, ichthyology, mycology, carcinology, sedimentology, microbiology, marine biology, coastal geomorphology, ocean dynamics. **Special Collections:** Various species of mollusks, crustaceans, fish, marine algae, and fungi. **Holdings:** 1440 books; 3252 bound periodical volumes; 103 dissertations. **Subscriptions:** 300 journals and other serials. **Services:** Interlibrary loan; copying; library open to the public for reference use only. **Publications:** Separates of research staff publications, annual - on exchange basis. **Remarks:** FAX: (919)726-2426.

★ 19065 ★

University of North Carolina at Chapel Hill - Institute of Outdoor Drama - Archives (Theater)
CB 3240 NCNB Plaza　　　　　　　　Phone: (919)962-1328
Chapel Hill, NC 27599-3240　　　　　Scott J. Parker, Dir.
Founded: 1963. **Staff:** Prof 1; Other 2. **Subjects:** Architecture, lighting, scripts, organization, finance, personnel, promotion and publicity, production, planning. **Holdings:** 21 VF drawers of documents, souvenir programs, articles, manuscripts, dissertations, photographs, theses, clippings. **Services:** Archives not open to the public. **Publications:** U.S. Outdoor Drama (newsletter), quarterly; Outdoor Historical Drama in America (directory), annual; assorted bulletins on phases of outdoor drama.

★ 19066 ★

University of North Carolina at Chapel Hill - Institute for Research in Social Science - Data Library (Soc Sci)
CB 3355 Manning Hall, Rm. 10　　　　Phone: (919)966-3346
Chapel Hill, NC 27599　　　　　　　　John Reed, Dir.
Founded: 1969. **Staff:** Prof 5; Other 2. **Subjects:** Census data, election data, student attitude data, mass political behavior, political systems, socioeconomic data, social systems/socialization, international and cross-national public opinion polls. **Special Collections:** Public Opinion Poll conducted by Louis Harris & Associates, Inc., 1963 to present; Carolina Polls, 1976 to present; USA Today Polls; Atlanta Journal Constitution Polls; other North Carolina and Southern polls. **Holdings:** 2500 machine-readable data files. **Services:** Data sets disseminated for a fee; library open to the public. **Automated Operations:** Computerized cataloging. **Computerized Information Services:** Harris Question Retrieval System, North Carolina Information System (internal databases). **Publications:** List of publications - available upon request. **Remarks:** FAX: (919)962-IRSS. **Also Known As:** Louis Harris Data Center. **Staff:** Sue A. Dodd, Libn.; Josephine Marsh, Data.Proc.; David Sheaves, Libn.; Ed Bachmann, Census Cons.

★ 19067 ★

University of North Carolina at Chapel Hill - John N. Couch Biology Library - Botany Section (Biol Sci)
301 Coker Hall, CB 3280　　　　　　　Phone: (919)962-3783
Chapel Hill, NC 27599-3280　　　　　William R. Burk, Biol.Libn.
Founded: 1926. **Staff:** Prof 1; Other 1. **Subjects:** Mycology, plant physiology, genetics, economic botany, algae, world floras, horticulture, cytology, ecology, plant taxonomy, paleobotany, molecular biology. **Special Collections:** Rare books in mycology (1000 volumes); collected papers of university botanists (reprints and photocopies; 21 volumes containing 916 published works). **Holdings:** 35,392 volumes; 1757 maps; 15,231 microforms; 9000 mycological reprints. **Subscriptions:** 676 journals and other serials. **Services:** Interlibrary loan; copying; library open to the public. **Computerized Information Services:** DIALOG Information Services; BITNET (electronic mail service). **Publications:** Library Literature Guides on botanical topics, irregular - for internal distribution only. **Special Indexes:** Index to mycological pamphlet collection (card). **Remarks:** FAX: (919)962-1625. Electronic mail address(es): WMRBURK@UNC (BITNET).

★ 19068 ★

University of North Carolina at Chapel Hill - John N. Couch Biology Library - Zoology Section (Biol Sci)
213 Wilson Hall, CB 3280　　　　　　　Phone: (919)962-2264
Chapel Hill, NC 27599-3280　　　　　Joan E. Jones, Asst.Biol.Libn.
Founded: 1940. **Staff:** Prof 1; Other 1. **Subjects:** Invertebrate and vertebrate zoology, cell biology, genetics, physiology, evolution, molecular biology, embryology, behavior, ecology. **Holdings:** 33,000 volumes. **Subscriptions:** 550 journals and other serials. **Services:** Interlibrary loan; copying; library open to the public. **Computerized Information Services:** DIALOG Information Services; BITNET (electronic mail service). **Remarks:** FAX: (919)962-1625. Electronic mail address(es): JEPAR@UNC (BITNET).

★ 19069 ★

University of North Carolina at Chapel Hill - Kenan Chemistry Library (Sci-Engr)
269 Venable Hall, CB 3290　　　　　　Phone: (919)962-1188
Chapel Hill, NC 27599　　　　　　　　Jimmy Dickerson, Chem.Libn.
Staff: Prof 1; Other 2. **Subjects:** All branches of chemistry. **Special Collections:** Venable History of Science Collection (850 volumes). **Holdings:** 47,203 volumes; 2752 microforms. **Subscriptions:** 735 journals and other serials. **Services:** Interlibrary loan; copying; library open to the public with restrictions. **Computerized Information Services:** Chemical Abstracts Service (CAS). **Publications:** Monthly new book list - free upon request.

★19070★
University of North Carolina at Chapel Hill - Law Library (Law)
CB 3385 Van Hecke-Wettach Bldg.   Phone: (919)962-1321
Chapel Hill, NC 27599   Laura N. Gasaway, Dir.
Founded: 1923. **Staff:** Prof 9; Other 12. **Subjects:** Law. **Special Collections:** Native American law. **Holdings:** 265,911 volumes; 477,200 microforms. **Subscriptions:** 5341 journals and other serials. **Services:** Copying; library open to the public. **Computerized Information Services:** WESTLAW, LEXIS, DIALOG Information Services, OCLC; BITNET (electronic mail service). **Networks/Consortia:** Member of Triangle Research Libraries Network (TRLN), COSELL. **Publications:** Library User's Guide; LLUNCCH Times (newsletter), monthly. **Remarks:** FAX: (919)962-1193. Electronic mail address(es): UNCLNG@UNC (BITNET). **Staff:** Timothy L. Coggins, Assoc.Dir.; Carol Nicholson, Tech.Serv.Libn.; Terri Saye, Cat.Libn.; Julia Best, Ser.Libn.; Martha Barefoot, Ref./User Serv.Libn.; Janice Hammett, Ref./User Serv.Libn.; Deborah Webster, Ref./Comp.Serv.Libn.; Marguerite Most, Ref./Instr.Serv.Libn.

★19071★
University of North Carolina at Chapel Hill - Maps Collection (Geog-Map)
CB 3928 Wilson Library   Phone: (919)962-3028
Chapel Hill, NC 27599   Celia D. Pratt, Map Libn.
Staff: Prof 1; Other 1. **Subjects:** Cartography. **Holdings:** 219,200 maps, including maps from the Defense Mapping Agency, National Ocean Service, U.S. Geological Survey, CIA, and U.S. Forest Service; 1350 atlases; 690 reference works and cartobibliographies; 410 gazetteers. **Subscriptions:** 26 journals and other serials. **Services:** Interlibrary loan (limited); copying; collection open to the public. **Computerized Information Services:** BITNET (electronic mail service). **Remarks:** FAX: (919)962-0484. Electronic mail address(es): CDPMAPS@UNC (BITNET).

★19072★
University of North Carolina at Chapel Hill - Music Library (Mus)
CB 3320 Hill Hall   Phone: (919)966-1113
Chapel Hill, NC 27599   Ida Reed, Mus.Libn.
Founded: 1935. **Staff:** Prof 3; Other 3. **Subjects:** Music, music literature, musicology. **Special Collections:** Opera; history of music theory; the sonata; early American music collection; American shape-note tunebook collection. **Holdings:** 38,500 volumes; 64,500 volumes of music; 30,000 sound recordings; 4700 reels of microfilm; 2300 microcards; 500 microfiche. **Subscriptions:** 724 journals and other serials. **Services:** Interlibrary loan; copying. **Computerized Information Services:** OCLC; internal databases; BITNET (electronic mail service). **Networks/Consortia:** Member of SOLINET. **Publications:** Newsletter, quarterly. **Special Indexes:** Rare materials (online); recorded vocal music (online); recorded pre-1700 music (online); song anthology index; record anthology vocal index; music biography index; early American music index; American shape-note tunebook collection index; place/date/publisher index for rare materials. **Remarks:** Electronic mail address(es): IDAREED@UNC (BITNET). **Staff:** Charles Croissant, Mus.Cat.; Ruth McTyre, Pub.Serv.Libn.

★19073★
University of North Carolina at Chapel Hill - North Carolina Collection (Hist, Rare Book)
CB 3930 Wilson Library   Phone: (919)962-1172
Chapel Hill, NC 27599-3930   H.G. Jones, Cur.
Founded: 1844. **Staff:** Prof 7; Other 7. **Subjects:** North Caroliniana; books about North Carolina or by North Carolinians. **Special Collections:** Sir Walter Raleigh Collection (by and about Raleigh); Thomas Wolfe Collection (by and about Wolfe); Bruce Cotten Collection (fine and rare North Caroliniana). **Holdings:** 189,883 volumes; 4349 maps; 4045 broadsides; 13,000 manuscripts; 14,025 reels of microfilm; 406,000 pictures; 180,000 mounted newspaper clippings. **Subscriptions:** 3000 journals and other serials. **Services:** Interlibrary loan; copying; collection open to the public with identification. **Computerized Information Services:** Internal databases; BITNET (electronic mail service). **Publications:** Annual Report; North Caroliniana Society Imprints, irregular. **Remarks:** FAX: (919)962-0484. Electronic mail address(es): HGJONES@UNC (BITNET). **Staff:** Alice R. Cotten, Ref.Hist.; Robert G. Anthony, Jr., Coll.Dev.Libn.; Eileen McGrath, Cat.; Lula Avent, Cat.; R. Neil Fulghum, Kpr., NNC Gallery; Jerry W. Cotten, Photo.Archv.

★19074★
University of North Carolina at Chapel Hill - Occupational Safety & Health Educational Resource Center - OSHERC Library (Med)
311 Pittsboro St., C.B. No. 7410   Phone: (919)966-5001
Chapel Hill, NC 27599-7410   Mary Ellen Tucker, Libn.
Founded: 1979. **Staff:** Prof 1; Other 1. **Subjects:** Industrial hygiene; occupational medicine, occupational health nursing, and safety. **Special Collections:** Audiovisual training materials (150); research reports, theses, and dissertations of UNC Environmental Sciences graduate students; UNC Rubber Industry Study research reports (50). **Holdings:** 2500 books. **Subscriptions:** 18 journals and other serials. **Services:** Copying; library open to the public with restrictions. **Automated Operations:** Computerized cataloging. **Computerized Information Services:** DIALOG Information Services, NIOSH Data Base; CD-ROM. Performs searches on fee basis. **Remarks:** FAX: (919)966-4711.

★19075★
University of North Carolina at Chapel Hill - Rare Book Collection (Rare Book)
Wilson Library 024A, CB No. 3936   Phone: (919)962-1143
Chapel Hill, NC 27599   Charles B. McNamara, Cur.
Staff: Prof 5.5; Other 3. **Subjects:** History of the book, incunabula, English and American literature, French history, Americana. **Special Collections:** Bernard J. Flatow Collection of Early Latin American Cronistas; George Baer Collection of Fine Bindings; Jacques Barzun and Wendell Hertig Taylor Collection of Crime and Detection; Mary Shore Cameron Collection of Sherlock Holmes; Confederate Imprint Collection; Bowman Gray Collection relating to World Wars I and II; Hanes Collection of Estienne Imprints; Hanes Incunabula Collection; Archibald Henderson Collection of George Bernard Shaw; Roland Holt Collection of American Theater; Walter Hooper Collection of C.S. Lewis; William Henry Hoyt Collection of French History; Kellam Collection of "The Night Before Christmas"; Clifford and Glady Lyons Collection of Robert Frost; Mazarinades Collection; John Murray and Smith-Elder Imprints Collection; J.M. Dent & Sons Inprints Collection; Southern Pamphlets Collection; Ticknor and Fields Collection; William A. Whitaker Collections of Charles Dickens, George Cruikshank, Samuel Johnson and His Circle, and William Makepeace Thackeray; Victorian Bindings; Richard H. Wilmer, Jr. Collection of Civil War Novels. **Holdings:** 100,000 books; 16,000 graphics; 1170 manuscripts. **Subscriptions:** 20 journals and other serials. **Services:** Interlibrary loan; copying; collection open to the public with restrictions. **Automated Operations:** Computerized cataloging. **Computerized Information Services:** BITNET (electronic mail service). **Publications:** Hanes Lectures. **Remarks:** FAX: (919)962-0484. Electronic mail address(es): UNAMAR@UNC (BITNET). **Staff:** Roberta Engleman, Rare Bks.Cat.; Elizabeth Chenault, Pub.Serv.Libn.; Jan Paris, Cons.

★19076★
University of North Carolina at Chapel Hill - School of Information and Library Science Library (Info Sci)
114 Manning Hall, CB 3360   Phone: (919)962-8361
Chapel Hill, NC 27599   Elizabeth J. Laney, Libn.
Founded: 1931. **Staff:** 2. **Subjects:** Librarianship, documentation, communication, publishing, automation, information, management, education. **Special Collections:** Historical collection of children's literature in the United States; annual reports and newsletters of libraries and related institutions. **Holdings:** 75,000 books and bound periodical volumes; 1559 reels of microfilm; 2618 microcards and microfiche; 1600 documents in report literature collection; 3480 AV programs; 27,879 pamphlet and VF materials. **Subscriptions:** 1854 journals and other serials. **Services:** Interlibrary loan; copying; library open to the public. **Computerized Information Services:** WILSONLINE; CD-ROM (Library Literature); BITNET (electronic mail service). **Publications:** Acquisitions list, monthly; annual report. **Remarks:** FAX: (919)962-8071. Electronic mail address(es): Whey@ils.unc.adu (BITNET).

★19077★
University of North Carolina at Chapel Hill - Sloane Art Library (Art)
Hanes Art Center, CB 3405   Phone: (919)962-2397
Chapel Hill, NC 27599-3405   Philip A. Rees, Art Libn.
Founded: 1958. **Staff:** Prof 1; Other 1. **Subjects:** Art. **Holdings:** 75,000 volumes; 14,480 microfiche; 320 reels of microfilm. **Subscriptions:** 400 journals and other serials. **Services:** Interlibrary loan; copying; library open to the public with limited circulation. **Remarks:** FAX: (919)962-0484.

★ 19078 ★

University of North Carolina at Chapel Hill - Southern Historical Collection & Manuscripts Department (Hist)
CB 3926 Wilson Library   Phone: (919)962-1345
Chapel Hill, NC 27599   David O. Moltke-Hansen, Dir./Cur.
Founded: 1930. **Staff:** Prof 5; Other 4. **Subjects:** Southern history and culture, southern folk music, University history, American and English literature. **Holdings:** Over 12 million manuscript items organized into over 4400 collections; 2.8 million items in University of North Carolina archives; 14,000 microforms; 2300 AV programs; 42,000 audio recordings; 1200 maps; 48,000 photographs. **Services:** Copying; department open to the public for reference use only. **Computerized Information Services:** OCLC; internal database; BITNET (electronic mail service). **Publications:** The Southern Historical Collection: A Guide to Manuscripts, 1970 (supplement, 1976). **Remarks:** FAX: (919)962-0484. Electronic mail address(es): DAVIDMH@UNC (BITNET). **Staff:** Michael G. Martin, Jr., Univ.Archv.; Tim West, Tech.Serv.Archv.; Richard A. Shraeder, Pub.Serv.Archv.; Michael Casey, Sound & Image Libn.

★ 19079 ★

University of North Carolina at Charlotte - Southeast Waste Exchange - Library (Env-Cons)
Charlotte, NC 28223   Phone: (704)547-4289
                                                          Maxie L. May
Founded: 1980. **Staff:** Prof 3; Other 1. **Subjects:** Waste exchange. **Holdings:** Figures not available. **Computerized Information Services:** Electronic bulletin board. **Special Catalogs:** Waste Watcher, bimonthly. **Remarks:** FAX: (704)547-3178.

★ 19080 ★

University of North Carolina at Greensboro - Dance Collection (Hum)
Jackson Library, Special Collections   Phone: (919)334-5246
Greensboro, NC 27412   Emilie Mills, Spec.Coll.Libn.
Staff: Prof 1; Other 2. **Subjects:** History of the dance, modern dance, dance notation. **Special Collections:** Early dance books, 16th-18th centuries (100 volumes). **Holdings:** 3000 volumes. **Subscriptions:** 40 journals and other serials. **Services:** Collection open to the public for research.

★ 19081 ★

University of North Carolina at Greensboro - Eugenie Silverman Baizerman Archive (Art)
Jackson Library, Special Collections
Greensboro, NC 27412   Phone: (919)334-5246
Staff: Prof 1; Other 2. **Subjects:** Art. **Holdings:** 2000 items. **Services:** Archive open to the public but manuscript materials are not available. **Special Catalogs:** Catalog of Special Collections' Manuscripts and Archives.

★ 19082 ★

University of North Carolina at Greensboro - George Herbert Collection (Hum)
Jackson Library, Special Collections
Greensboro, NC 27412   Phone: (919)334-5246
Staff: Prof 2; Other 1. **Special Collections:** George Herbert Collection of books, 17th-20th centuries; Cross-Bias Newsletter, 1975 to present; Friends of Bemerton miscellanea (50 items). **Holdings:** 270 books; 4 dissertations on Herbert on microfilm. **Services:** Copying; collection open to the public for research.

★ 19083 ★

University of North Carolina at Greensboro - Girls Books in Series (Hum)
Jackson Library, Special Collections
Greensboro, NC 27412   Phone: (919)334-5246
Staff: Prof 1; Other 2. **Subjects:** Children's literature. **Holdings:** 1800 books. **Services:** Collection open to the public for research.

★ 19084 ★

University of North Carolina at Greensboro - Lois Lenski Collection (Hum, Rare Book)
Jackson Library, Special Collections
Greensboro, NC 27412   Phone: (919)334-5246
Subjects: Children's literature. **Holdings:** Lois Lenski Collection (5000 books, manuscripts, original drawings, correspondence, photographs, clippings, and ephemera); early children's books, 18th-19th centuries (1500). **Services:** Copying (limited); collection open to public for research.

★ 19085 ★

University of North Carolina at Greensboro - Luigi Silva Collection (Mus)
Jackson Library, Special Collections
Greensboro, NC 27412   Phone: (919)334-5246
Staff: Prof 1; Other 2. **Subjects:** History and teaching of the cello. **Special Collections:** Luigi Silva Library of the History and Teaching of the Cello. **Holdings:** 200 books; 20 bound periodical volumes; 73 boxes of manuscripts and printed scores; 80 bound volumes of chamber music. **Services:** Copying; collection open to the public for research. **Special Catalogs:** Catalog of the cello collections at University of North Carolina at Greensboro: Part I: The Luigi Silva Collection (1978).

★ 19086 ★

University of North Carolina at Greensboro - Physical Education History Collection (Educ)
Jackson Library, Special Collections
Greensboro, NC 27412   Phone: (919)334-5246
Subjects: Physical activity, training, theory; gymnastics; dance history. **Special Collections:** Gymnastics books dating from the 16th century; early dance books and landmark works on all types of physical activity, training, and theory, 16th century-early 1900s in English and several foreign languages. **Holdings:** 1500 books and pamphlets. **Services:** Collection open to the public for research.

★ 19087 ★

University of North Carolina at Greensboro - Printing Collection (Rare Book)
Jackson Library, Special Collections
Greensboro, NC 27412   Phone: (919)334-5246
Staff: Prof 1; Other 2. **Subjects:** Private presses, history of printing, 20th century illustrated books. **Special Collections:** Modern fine printing and the art of the book; 19th century American publishers' trade bindings; American publishers' cloth, early period. **Holdings:** 1500 volumes. **Services:** Collection open to the public for research.

★ 19088 ★

University of North Carolina at Greensboro - Randall Jarrell Collection (Hum)
Jackson Library, Special Collections
Greensboro, NC 27412   Phone: (919)334-5246
Staff: Prof 1; Other 2. **Subjects:** Randall Jarrell. **Holdings:** 300 books; over 3000 manuscript items; 10 films and tapes; 6 recordings. **Services:** Copying; collection open to the public for research. **Remarks:** Includes microfilm of Randall Jarrell manuscripts held at the New York Public Library, Berg Collection.

★ 19089 ★

University of North Carolina at Greensboro - Saul Baizerman Archive (Art)
Jackson Library, Special Collections
Greensboro, NC 27412   Phone: (919)334-5246
Staff: Prof 2; Other 1. **Subjects:** Saul Baizerman, sculptor (1889-1957). **Holdings:** Drawings, sketches, photographs of sculptures completed and in progress; exhibition catalogs, reviews, journals, personal memorabilia (2100 items). **Services:** Archive open to the public with restrictions on unpublished material. **Special Indexes:** Special Collections' Manuscripts and Archives (description with box listings).

★ 19090 ★

University of North Carolina at Greensboro - Way & Williams Collection (Publ)
Jackson Library, Special Collections
Greensboro, NC 27412   Phone: (919)334-5246
Holdings: Way & Williams Collection (100 books, manuscripts, correspondence, and original drawings and artwork of a Chicago literary publishing firm, 1895-1898). Important associations include Will Bradley, Maxfield Parrish, William Allen White. **Services:** Collection open to public for research.

★ 19091 ★
University of North Carolina at Greensboro - Woman's Collection (Soc Sci)
Jackson Library, Special Collections
Greensboro, NC 27412   Phone: (919)334-5246
Staff: Prof 1; Other 2. **Subjects:** Women - education, history, suffrage; history of costume; women authors; manners and morals; child raising and family life. **Special Collections:** Women in the 17th-19th centuries. **Holdings:** 5000 books; 254 bound periodical volumes. **Services:** Copying; collection open to the public for research. **Publications:** The Woman's Collection, A Check-list of Holdings, 1975.

★ 19092 ★
University of North Carolina at Greensboro - Woman's Detective Fiction Collection (Hum)
Jackson Library, Special Collections
Greensboro, NC 27412   Phone: (919)334-5246
Staff: Prof 2; Other 1. **Subjects:** Women detectives in American fiction, 1867-1967. **Holdings:** 2200 books. **Services:** Copying (limited); collection open to the public for research.

★ 19093 ★
University of North Carolina at Wilmington - William Madison Randall Library - Helen Hagan Rare Book Room (Rare Book)
601 S. College Rd.   Phone: (919)395-3276
Wilmington, NC 28403-3297   Eugene W. Huguelet, Dir., Lib.Serv.
Staff: 1.25. **Subjects:** History of the lower Cape Fear area of North Carolina (including Brunswick, Columbus, New Hanover, and Pender counties), 1700 to present; Civil War; early science and technology; music, 1850-1960. **Special Collections:** Papers of Congressman Alton Lennon Thomas J. Armstrong; local history collection (including land grants from George II and property documents); collections relating to desegregation and civil rights in New Hanover County; collection of ephemera about North Carolina artists and art institutions. **Holdings:** 1300 books; 515 linear feet of archival material; 2000 78rpm records. **Services:** Interlibrary loan; copying; room open to the public by appointment. **Automated Operations:** Computerized public access catalog, cataloging, serials, and circulation. **Computerized Information Services:** DIALOG Information Services, BRS Information Technologies, Chemical Abstracts Service (CAS), WILSONLINE, OCLC; EasyLink, LINX Courier (electronic mail services). Performs searches on fee basis. **Networks/Consortia:** Member of SOLINET. **Publications:** Descriptive inventory of the Armstrong papers; descriptive inventory of the Johnston and Virginia Hall Avery papers; descriptive inventory of the McGuire Collection of Letters from Black Soldiers (World War II); Laura Harriss Howell Music Collection; bibliography. **Special Indexes:** Manuscript register; North Carolina Visual Arts and Artists Index (card). **Remarks:** FAX: (919)395-3863. **Staff:** Lana D. Taylor, Ref./Spec.Coll.Libn.

★ 19094 ★
University of North Dakota - Chemistry Library (Sci-Engr)
224 Abbott Hall   Phone: (701)777-2741
Grand Forks, ND 58202   Evelyn Cole, Sec.
Staff: 1. **Subjects:** Chemistry - electrochemistry, environmental, inorganic, organometallic, medicinal. **Holdings:** 4600 books; 7700 bound periodical volumes; 611 microfiche; 21,510 microcards; 24 reels of microfilm. **Subscriptions:** 170 journals and other serials. **Services:** Interlibrary loan; library open to the public. **Automated Operations:** Computerized public access catalog, circulation, acquisitions, and serials. **Networks/Consortia:** Member of MINITEX Library Information Network, North Dakota Network for Knowledge. **Remarks:** FAX: (701)777-3319.

★ 19095 ★
University of North Dakota - Elwyn B. Robinson Department of Special Collections (Hist)
Chester Fritz Library   Phone: (701)777-4625
Grand Forks, ND 58202   Sandra Beidler, Hd., Archv. & Spec.Coll.
Founded: 1963. **Staff:** Prof 2; Other 2. **Subjects:** History - North and South Dakota, Northern Great Plains, Plains Indian, women, environmental; agrarian radicalism; Nonpartisan League (North Dakota); genealogy; oral history. **Special Collections:** North Dakota Book Collection (13,250 volumes); Fred G. Aandahl Book Collection (1350 volumes); Family History/Genealogy Collection (2300 volumes); North Dakota State Documents (40,000); university archives (1200 linear feet); Orin G. Libby Manuscript Collection (6000 linear feet). **Holdings:** 16,900 books; 7200

linear feet of manuscript material; 3725 reels of microfilm; 44,000 photographs; 2000 AV items. **Services:** Copying; department open to the public. **Automated Operations:** Computerized public access catalog and acquisitions. **Publications:** University of North Dakota Theses and Dissertations on North Dakota, 1895-1971, 1972; Reference Guide to North Dakota History and Literature, 1979; Reference Guide to the Orin G. Libby Manuscript Collection (Volume 1, 1975; Volume 2, 1983; Volume 3, 1985). **Special Catalogs:** Subject Guide to the Orin G. Libby Manuscript Collection, 1979; Guide to Genealogical/Family History Sources, 1984; Guide to Norwegian Bygdeboker, 1989. **Special Indexes:** Index to the Dakota Student (newspaper); index to the Alumni Review (newspaper); Guide to University Archives, University of North Dakota; Guide to Audio-Visual Productions: Video Tapes; Guide to Adio-Visual Productions: Films; Guide to Audio/Visual Productions: Audio Tapes. **Special Indexes:** Subject Index Guide to Orin G. Libby Photographic Collections; Subject Index Guide to University Archives Photographic Collection; Index to the Grand Forks City Council Minutes, 1882-1958; Index to the W.P. Davies Newspaper Column Collection. **Remarks:** FAX: (701)777-3319. **Staff:** Amy Christianson, Spec.Coll.Asst.

★ 19096 ★
University of North Dakota - Energy and Mineral Research Center - Energy Library (Energy)
University Sta., Box 8213   Phone: (701)777-5132
Grand Forks, ND 58202   DeLoris Smith, Lib.Assoc.
Founded: 1951. **Staff:** Prof 1. **Subjects:** Fossil energy conversion, coal, lignite. **Holdings:** 3500 books; 760 bound periodical volumes; U.S. Department of Energy reports; 229 periodical titles. **Subscriptions:** 108 journals and other serials. **Services:** Interlibrary loan (through Chester Fritz Library); copying; SDI; library open to the public. **Automated Operations:** Computerized public access catalog, circulation, acquisitions, and serials. **Computerized Information Services:** DIALOG Information Services, PFDS Online, BRS Information Technologies, Performs searches on fee basis. **Networks/Consortia:** Member of MINITEX Library Information Network. **Remarks:** FAX: (701)777-3319.

★ 19097 ★
University of North Dakota - Engineering Library (Sci-Engr)
Harrington Hall, University Sta.   Phone: (701)777-3040
Grand Forks, ND 58202   Kay Olesen, Lib.Assoc.
Staff: 1. **Subjects:** Engineering - chemical, civil, electrical, industrial, mechanical. **Holdings:** 13,120 books; 9380 bound periodical volumes; 6024 microfiche; 715 reels of microfilm. **Subscriptions:** 353 journals and other serials. **Services:** Interlibrary loan; copying; library open to the public. **Automated Operations:** Computerized public access catalog, circulation, acquisitions, and serials. **Computerized Information Services:** DIALOG Information Services, PFDS Online. **Networks/Consortia:** Member of MINITEX Library Information Network, North Dakota Network for Knowledge. **Remarks:** FAX: (701)777-3319.

★ 19098 ★
University of North Dakota - Geology Library (Sci-Engr)
Leonard Hall, University Sta.   Phone: (701)777-3221
Grand Forks, ND 58202   Kathleen Spencer, Lib.Assoc.
Staff: 1. **Subjects:** Geology, paleontology, petroleum engineering, North Dakota geology. **Special Collections:** Depository for state geological surveys publications; U.S. Geological Survey and U.S. Bureau of Mines publications; U.S.G.S. open-file reports for North Dakota. **Holdings:** 12,421 books; 18,622 bound periodical volumes; 86 microfiche; 210 reels of microfilm; 130,000 U.S. Geological Survey topographic maps; 7700 other maps. **Subscriptions:** 756 journals and other serials. **Services:** Interlibrary loan; copying; library open to the public. **Automated Operations:** Computerized public access catalog, circulation, acquisitions, and serials. **Computerized Information Services:** DIALOG Information Services. **Networks/Consortia:** Member of MINITEX Library Information Network, North Dakota Network for Knowledge. **Remarks:** Alternate telephone number(s): 777-2408. FAX: (701)777-3319.

★ 19099 ★
University of North Dakota - Institute for Ecological Studies - Environmental Resource Center - Library (Env-Cons)
Box 8278   Phone: (701)777-2851
Grand Forks, ND 58202   Rod Sayler, Dir.
Founded: 1972. **Staff:** 2. **Subjects:** Ecology, land use, water and air pollution, chemical and biological contaminants, wildlife, environmental education, energy, nonrenewable resources. **Holdings:** 1000 books; 600 research reports; 1000 environmental impact statements; 12 drawers of pamphlets; 600 maps. **Services:** Interlibrary loan; copying; SDI; center open to the public. **Automated Operations:** Computerized public access catalog, circulation, acquisitions, and serials.

★ 19100 ★
University of North Dakota - Math-Physics Library (Sci-Engr)
211 Witmer Hall   Phone: (701)777-3319
Grand Forks, ND 58202   Connie Karel, Sec.
Staff: 1. **Subjects:** Field theory, solid state physics, mathematical physics, thin films, mathematical analysis, mathematical models. **Holdings:** 9275 books; 8250 bound periodical volumes. **Subscriptions:** 230 journals and other serials. **Services:** Interlibrary loan; library open to the public. **Automated Operations:** Computerized public access catalog, circulation, acquisitions, and serials. **Networks/Consortia:** Member of MINITEX Library Information Network, North Dakota Network for Knowledge.

★ 19101 ★
University of North Dakota - Music Library (Mus)
Hughes Fine Arts Center
Grand Forks, ND 58202   Phone: (701)777-2817
Founded: 1974. **Staff:** 2. **Subjects:** Music. **Holdings:** 4000 phonograph records; 4000 scores. **Subscriptions:** 28 journals and other serials. **Services:** Interlibrary loan; copying; library open to the public, phonograph records do not circulate. **Automated Operations:** Computerized public access catalog, circulation, acquisitions, and serials. **Remarks:** FAX: (701)777-3319.

★ 19102 ★
University of North Dakota - Olaf H. Thormodsgard Law Library (Law)
Grand Forks, ND 58202-9003   Phone: (701)777-2204
                                         Gary D. Gott, Dir.
Founded: 1899. **Staff:** Prof 6; Other 3. **Subjects:** Law. **Holdings:** 113,780 bound volumes; 99,758 volumes in microform; 598,547 microfiche; 766 reels of microfilm; 508 AV programs. **Subscriptions:** 2514 journals and other serials. **Services:** Interlibrary loan; copying; library open to the public with restrictions. **Automated Operations:** Computerized public access catalog, cataloging, and circulation. **Computerized Information Services:** LEXIS, WESTLAW, OCLC; EasyLink (electronic mail service). Performs searches on fee basis. Contact Person: Ted Smith, Dir., Att.Serv., 777-3354. **Networks/Consortia:** Member of MINITEX Library Information Network, CLASS. **Remarks:** FAX: (701)777-2217. Electronic mail address(es): 62013724 (EasyLink). **Staff:** Donald D. Olson, Bibliog.Anl.; Patricia Folkestad, Circ.Asst.; Dennis Fossum, Acq.Libn.; Rhonda Schwartz, Ser.Libn.; Kaaren Pupino, Circ.Libn.; Kim Balow, Ser.Libn.; Sarah Scheuring, Bus.Mgr.; Christopher Noe, Hd. of Pub.Serv.; Ted Smith, ILL.

★ 19103 ★
University of North Dakota - School of Medicine - Harley E. French Library of the Health Sciences (Med)
Grand Forks, ND 58202-9002   Phone: (701)777-3993
                                         Lila Pederson, Interim Dir.
Founded: 1949. **Staff:** Prof 5; Other 5.5. **Subjects:** Medicine, nursing, physical therapy. **Special Collections:** Dr. French Collection (books by and about doctors; history of medicine); human nutrition research and trace elements; anesthesia. **Holdings:** 32,500 books; 42,000 bound periodical volumes; 1600 AV programs; 1500 volumes on microfiche. **Subscriptions:** 1124 journals and other serials. **Services:** Interlibrary loan; copying; library open to the public. **Automated Operations:** Computerized public access catalog, cataloging, ILL, and circulation. **Computerized Information Services:** OCLC, MEDLARS, BRS Information Technologies, WILSONLINE; CD-ROM (MEDLINE, CINAHL); EasyLink, DOCLINE (electronic mail services). Performs searches on fee basis. **Networks/Consortia:** Member of National Network of Libraries of Medicine - Greater Midwest Region, MINITEX Library Information Network. **Publications:** Biomedia Report, 3/year. **Special Catalogs:** Serials list, annual. **Remarks:** FAX: (701)772-0405. Electronic mail address(es): 62755136 (EasyLink). **Staff:** Michael Safratowich, Bibliog.Cont.; Lorraine Ettl, Pub.Serv.; Connie Kroll, ILL.

University of North Dakota - School of Medicine - Northwest Campus Library
See: Trinity Medical Center - Angus L. Cameron Medical Library (16515)

★ 19104 ★
University of North Texas Libraries - Media Library (Aud-Vis)
Box 12898   Phone: (817)565-2691
Denton, TX 76203-2898   Sharon G. Almquist, Act.Hd.
Founded: 1976. **Staff:** Prof 1; Other 15. **Subjects:** Gerontology, education, psychology, business, sciences, film studies. **Special Collections:** Gerontological Film Collection (490 titles). **Holdings:** 1989 reels of motion picture film; 1425 video cassettes; 79 laser discs; 2142 filmstrips; 2475 phonograph records; 3251 phonotapes; 36,096 slides; 231 transparencies; 65 kits; 428 microcomputer discs. **Subscriptions:** 12 journals and other serials. **Services:** Interlibrary loan; library open to the public for reference use only. **Automated Operations:** Computerized public access catalog, cataloging, and circulation. **Computerized Information Services:** AV-Online (internal database). **Networks/Consortia:** Member of Consortium of College and University Media Centers (CCUMC), Association for Higher Education of North Texas (AHE). **Special Catalogs:** Gerontological Film Collection catalog, bimonthly. **Remarks:** FAX: (817)565-2599. **Staff:** Matthew L. Fox, Tech.Spec.; Vernon A. Stephens, Reservations.

★ 19105 ★
University of North Texas Libraries - Oral History Collection (Hist)
University Sta., Box 13734   Phone: (817)565-2549
Denton, TX 76203   Dr. Ronald E. Marcello, Dir.
Founded: 1963. **Staff:** Prof 1; Other 1. **Subjects:** Texas governors and legislators, World War II, New Deal, integration, business history, institutional history, politics, Holocaust. **Holdings:** 945 books; 1056 oral history tapes. **Services:** Copying; collection open to the public with restrictions. **Publications:** Bulletin, Oral History Collection.

★ 19106 ★
University of North Texas Libraries - Rare Book Room (Rare Book)
North Texas Sta., Box 5188   Phone: (817)565-2769
Denton, TX 76203-5188   Dr. Kenneth Lavender, Cur., Rare Bk., Texana Coll.
Founded: 1981. **Staff:** Prof 1; Other 3. **Subjects:** Travel, children's literature, Texana, 18th century English literature. **Special Collections:** Larry McMurtry (63 typescripts; proof copies; signed editions); Mary Webb (50 books, manuscripts, and realia); Willa Cather (49 first editions and related materials). **Holdings:** 7000 books; 110 manuscripts. **Subscriptions:** 8 journals and other serials. **Services:** Room open to the public with restrictions. **Automated Operations:** Computerized public access catalog. **Networks/Consortia:** Member of AMIGOS Bibliographic Council, Inc., Association for Higher Education of North Texas (AHE). **Special Catalogs:** Catalogue of Webb Collection (card); Printers' File (card); catalog of children's literature (card); catalog of 18th century holdings. **Remarks:** FAX: (817)565-2599.

★ 19107 ★
University of Northern Colorado - University Archives (Hist)
James A. Michener Library   Phone: (303)351-1525
Greeley, CO 80639-9986   Mary Linscome, Archv.
Staff: Prof 1; Other 1. **Subjects:** University archives, including faculty publications. **Special Collections:** Papers and manuscripts of James A. Michener and other authors; International Gladiolus Hall of Fame Collection; Hazel E. Johnson local history/college collection. **Holdings:** 2000 books; 2000 linear feet of papers and manuscripts; other cataloged items. **Services:** Interlibrary loan; copying; archives open to the public. **Networks/Consortia:** Member of Colorado Alliance of Research Libraries (CARL).

★ 19108 ★
University of Northern Iowa - Rod Library - Special Collections (Hist)
Cedar Falls, IA 50613   Phone: (319)273-6307
                                         Gerald L. Peterson, Spec.Coll.Libn.
Staff: Prof 1; Other 1. **Subjects:** Education, Iowa history. **Special Collections:** American fiction first editions, proofs, and manuscripts (5000 volumes); university archives. **Holdings:** 9000 books; 1620 cubic feet of manuscripts. **Services:** Interlibrary loan; copying; collections open to the public. **Remarks:** FAX: (319)273-2913.

★ 19109 ★
University of Notre Dame - Architecture Library (Art, Plan)
218 Architectural Bldg.   Phone: (219)239-6654
Notre Dame, IN 46556   Robert Havlik, Libn.
Founded: 1963. **Staff:** Prof 1; Other 2. **Subjects:** Architecture, architectural engineering, city planning, landscape architecture, architectural history. **Holdings:** 16,000 volumes; 8 VF drawers. **Subscriptions:** 90 journals and other serials. **Services:** Interlibrary loan; copying; library open to the public for reference use only. **Computerized Information Services:** DIALOG Information Services, WILSONLINE, RLIN, Avery Index to Architectural Periodicals. **Remarks:** FAX: (219)239-6772. **Staff:** Linda Messersmith, Supv.

★ 19110 ★
University of Notre Dame - Archives (Hist)
607 Hesburgh Library   Phone: (219)239-6448
Notre Dame, IN 46556   Dr. Wendy Clauson Schlereth, Univ.Archv.
Founded: 1875. **Staff:** Prof 5; Other 6. **Subjects:** American Catholicism, University of Notre Dame. **Holdings:** 12,000 linear feet of manuscripts and archival material. **Services:** Copying; archives open to the public for reference use only. **Computerized Information Services:** Internal databases. **Publications:** Guides to microfilmed collections - for sale.

★ 19111 ★
University of Notre Dame - Chemistry/Physics Library (Sci-Engr)
231 Nieuwland Science Hall
Notre Dame, IN 46556   Phone: (219)239-7203
Founded: 1963. **Staff:** Prof 1; Other 2. **Subjects:** Chemistry - analytical, biochemistry, environmental, inorganic, organic, photochemistry, polymer, solid-state, stereo, theoretical; physics - acoustical, astrophysics, biophysics, computer, cryogenics, elementary particle, high energy, mathematical, nuclear, radio, solid-state, technical. **Holdings:** 41,095 volumes. **Subscriptions:** 429 journals. **Services:** Interlibrary loan; copying; library open to the public for reference use only. **Computerized Information Services:** DIALOG Information Services, BRS Information Technologies, Chemical Abstracts Service (CAS). Performs searches on fee basis. **Remarks:** FAX: (219)239-6772. **Staff:** Judy Kendall, Supv.

★ 19112 ★
University of Notre Dame - Department of Special Collections (Hum, Rare Book)
102 Hesburgh Library   Phone: (219)239-5610
Notre Dame, IN 46556   Sophia K. Jordan, Hd.
Staff: Prof 1; Other 3. **Subjects:** Theology, English literature, sports and games, botany. **Special Collections:** John Zahm Collection on Dante (5000 items); John Bennett Shaw Collection on Chesterton (2000 items); Rare Books Collection (25,000 items); Father Edmund P. Joyce, C.S.C., International Sports Research Collection (600,000 items); Edward L. Greene Collection on Botany (4000 items); Notre Dame Collection (9000 items); Catholic Americana Collection (5000 pamphlets; 6000 parish histories); Conway Collection on Edward Gorey (500 items); Eric Gill Collection (1300 items); Hackenbruch Collection of Early American Newspapers (3000 issues); Medieval and Renaissance Manuscripts (65 items); Robert H. Gore Numismatic Collection (4400 coins and bills); Theodore S. Weber Collection of Penguin Publications (12,000 items); Modern Manuscript Collection (2000 items); Captain Francis O'Neill Collection on Irish Music (1000 items); David J. Butler Collection of Maps of Ireland (84). **Holdings:** 52,000 books; 2000 manuscripts. **Subscriptions:** 100 journals and other serials. **Services:** Copying; department open to the public. **Automated Operations:** NOTIS. **Computerized Information Services:** DIALOG Information Services, WILSONLINE, BRS Information Technologies, OCLC; internal databases; BITNET (electronic mail service). **Networks/Consortia:** Member of Four Rivers Area Library Services Authority (ALSA). **Publications:** Access (newsletter). **Special Catalogs:** Exhibit catalogues; Incunabula Typographica, 1979; Catalogue of Medieval and Renaissance Manuscripts, 1978. **Remarks:** FAX: (219)239-6772. Electronic mail address(es): LLTB46@IRISHMVS (BITNET). **Staff:** Laura Fuderer, Libn., Rare Bks.; Jethrow Kyles, Cur., Joyce Sports Res.Coll.

★ 19113 ★
University of Notre Dame - Engineering Library (Sci-Engr)
149 Fitzpatrick Hall of Engineering   Phone: (219)239-6665
Notre Dame, IN 46556   Robert J. Havlik, Engr.Libn.
Founded: 1932. **Staff:** Prof 1; Other 3. **Subjects:** Engineering - civil, aerospace, mechanical, electrical, chemical; biotechnology; computer

science and engineering; earth sciences. **Holdings:** 30,000 books; 20,000 bound periodical volumes; 15,000 microfiche. **Subscriptions:** 800 journals and other serials. **Services:** Interlibrary loan; copying; library open to the public for reference use only. **Computerized Information Services:** DIALOG Information Services, BRS Information Technologies. **Networks/Consortia:** Member of INCOLSA. **Publications:** New Book List. **Remarks:** FAX: (219)239-6672. **Staff:** Regina Olson, Supv.

★ 19114 ★
University of Notre Dame - International Studies Resource Center (Soc Sci)
213 Hesburgh Library   Phone: (219)239-6166
Notre Dame, IN 46556   Stephen M. Hayes, Supv.
Founded: 1986. **Staff:** Prof 1; Other 2. **Subjects:** International relations; foreign policy; diplomacy; Latin America; political, social, and economic development; armament and disarmament. **Holdings:** 1859 boxes of newspaper clippings; 85 files of pamphlets; 21 films on Central America; 1100 working papers and technical reports. **Subscriptions:** 5 journals and other serials; 10 newspapers; 28 newsletter. **Services:** Center open to the public. **Automated Operations:** NOTIS. **Computerized Information Services:** DIALOG Information Services, BRS Information Technologies, Dow Jones News/Retrieval, RLIN, OCLC, WILSONLINE; BITNET, InterNet (electronic mail services). **Remarks:** FAX: (219)239-6772. Electronic mail address(es): LINSBK@IRISHMUS (BITNET); @IRISHMUS.CC.ND.EDU (InterNet). **Staff:** Susan Saavedra.

★ 19115 ★
University of Notre Dame - Law School - Kresge Law Library (Law)
Box 535   Phone: (219)239-7024
Notre Dame, IN 46556   Roger F. Jacobs, Dir.
Founded: 1869. **Staff:** Prof 8; Other 11. **Subjects:** Law. **Holdings:** 310,000 volumes. **Subscriptions:** 838 journals; 4103 serials. **Services:** Interlibrary loan; copying; library open to the public. **Automated Operations:** Computerized cataloging, acquisitions, and serials. **Computerized Information Services:** LEXIS, WESTLAW, DIALOG Information Services, NEXIS. **Networks/Consortia:** Member of INCOLSA. **Remarks:** FAX: (219)239-6371. **Staff:** Granville Cleveland, Asst.Dir., Stud.Empl.; Joseph Thomas, Cat.Libn.; Lucy Payne, Res.Libn.; Dwight King, Hd.Res.Dept.; Janis Johnston, Assoc.Dir., Tech.Serv. Patti Ogden, Res.Libn.; Carmela Kinslow, Circ./ILL Libn.

★ 19116 ★
University of Notre Dame - Life Sciences Research Library (Biol Sci)
B149 Galvin Life Sciences Bldg.   Phone: (219)239-7209
Notre Dame, IN 46556   Dorothy Coil, Libn.
Founded: 1938. **Staff:** Prof 1; Other 2. **Subjects:** Biology, genetics, microbiology, entomology, molecular biology, ecology, aquatic biology, parasitology, gnotobiology. **Holdings:** 25,000 volumes. **Subscriptions:** 600 journals and other serials. **Services:** Interlibrary loan; copying; library open to the public for reference use only. **Automated Operations:** NOTIS. **Computerized Information Services:** DIALOG Information Services, MEDLARS, WILSONLINE. **Remarks:** FAX (219)239-6772. **Staff:** Judy Mahoney, Supv.

★ 19117 ★
University of Notre Dame - Mathematics Library (Sci-Engr)
200 Computing Center
Notre Dame, IN 46556   Phone: (219)239-7278
Founded: 1962. **Staff:** Prof 1; Other 2. **Subjects:** Pure mathematics, applied mathematics. **Holdings:** 21,859 volumes. **Subscriptions:** 274 journals and other serials. **Services:** Interlibrary loan; copying; library open to the public for reference use only. **Computerized Information Services:** STN International; internal database. **Remarks:** FAX: (219)239-6772. **Staff:** Karen Lanser, Supv.

★ 19118 ★
University of Notre Dame - Medieval Institute Library (Hist)
715 Hesburgh Library   Phone: (219)239-7420
Notre Dame, IN 46556   Sophia K. Jordan, Hd.
Founded: 1946. **Staff:** Prof 1; Other 2. **Subjects:** Medieval studies. **Special Collections:** Frank M. Folsom Ambrosiana Microfilm & Photograph Collection; medieval education; medieval manuscripts; medieval seals. **Holdings:** 60,000 volumes; 15,000 microforms; 12 VF drawers. **Subscriptions:** 300 journals and other serials. **Services:** Interlibrary loan; copying; library open to the public for reference use only. **Computerized Information Services:** Ambrosiana Cataloging Project Database (internal database); CD-ROM (Thesaurus Linguae Graecae Canon of Greek Authors and Works). **Remarks:** FAX: (219)239-6772. **Staff:** Dr. Marina Smyth, Supv.; Dr. Louis Jordan, Bibliog.

★19119★
University of Notre Dame - Radiation Laboratory - Radiation Chemistry
   Data Center (Sci-Engr)
Notre Dame, IN 46556   Phone: (219)239-6527
                                  Dr. Alberta B. Ross, Supv.
Founded: 1965. **Staff:** Prof 4; Other 3. **Subjects:** Radiation chemistry,
photochemistry. **Holdings:** 120,000 data files. **Services:** Center open to
scientists on request. **Computerized Information Services:** RCDC
Bibliographic Database (internal database); BITNET (electronic mail
service). **Publications:** Biweekly List of Papers on Radiation Chemistry and
Photochemistry with indexed annual cumulation; Thesaurus for Radiation
Chemistry. **Remarks:** FAX: (219)239-8068. Electronic mail address(es):
RCDC@NDRADLAB. **Staff:** Dr. W.P. Helman; Dr. Gordon Hug; Dr. Ian
Carmichael.

★19120★
University of Notre Dame - Snite Museum of Art - Library (Art)
Notre Dame, IN 46556   Phone: (219)239-5466
Staff: Prof 1. **Subjects:** Art. **Holdings:** 2700 books; 3000 unbound
periodicals. **Services:** Copying; library open to the public with restrictions.

★19121★
University of Oklahoma - Architecture Library (Plan)
830 Van Vleet Oval   Phone: (405)325-5521
Norman, OK 73019   Ilse Davis, Lib.Techn.
Founded: 1929. **Subjects:** Architecture; landscape architecture; design -
urban, environmental, interior; construction science. **Special Collections:**
Lt. Orville S. Witt Memorial Collection. **Holdings:** 14,000 books.
Subscriptions: 48 journals and other serials. **Services:** Interlibrary loan.

★19122★
University of Oklahoma - Biological Station Library (Biol Sci)
HC-71 Box 205
Kingston, OK 73439   Phone: (405)564-2463
Founded: 1947. **Staff:** Prof 4. **Subjects:** Aquatic ecology, fisheries, reservoir
limnology. **Special Collections:** Lake Texoma Collection (1200 items); Riggs
Collection (fishes and fisheries; 5550 items); Greenbank Collection (fishes
and fisheries; 2081 items). **Holdings:** 3238 volumes; 4927 reprints.
Subscriptions: 30 journals and other serials. **Services:** Library open to
qualified persons. **Special Indexes:** Indexes to Lake Texoma Collection and
reprints. **Remarks:** FAX: (405)564-2479.

★19123★
University of Oklahoma - Carl Albert Center Congressional Archives
   (Hist, Soc Sci)
630 Parrington Oval, Rm. 202   Phone: (405)325-5401
Norman, OK 73019   John M. Caldwell, Archv.
Founded: 1986. **Staff:** Prof 1.5; Other 1. **Subjects:** U.S. Congress, Oklahoma,
American Southwest. **Special Collections:** Archival collection of 51
members of U.S. Congress. **Holdings:** 4500 cubic feet of manuscripts,
photographs, audio- and videotapes, political ephemera. **Services:** Copying;
archives open to the public with restrictions. **Automated Operations:**
Computerized cataloging. **Computerized Information Services:** Internal
database. **Special Indexes:** University of Oklahoma Congressional Record
Series. **Remarks:** FAX: (405)325-6419. **Staff:** Judy D. Day, Asst.Archv.

★19124★
University of Oklahoma - Center for Economic and Management
   Research - Library (Bus-Fin)
307 W. Brooks St., Rm. 4   Phone: (405)325-2931
Norman, OK 73019-0450   Fariba Williams, Lib.Techn. II
Staff: 1. **Subjects:** Statistics on Oklahoma business and economic conditions;
economic aspects of energy. **Holdings:** 600 books; 50 bound periodical
volumes; 1600 government documents; 24 VF drawers of reports.
Subscriptions: 150 journals and other serials; 8 newspapers. **Services:**
Copying; library open to the public with restrictions. **Publications:**
Oklahoma Business Bulletin, monthly; Statistical Abstract of Oklahoma,
annual. **Remarks:** FAX: (405)325-7688. **Staff:** Fariba Williams.

★19125★
University of Oklahoma - Chemistry-Mathematics Library (Sci-Engr)
Physical Sciences Center, 207   Phone: (405)325-5628
Norman, OK 73019   Dan Chandler, Chem.-Math.Libn.
Founded: 1921. **Staff:** Prof 1; Other 1. **Subjects:** Chemistry, mathematics.
Holdings: 50,000 volumes; 12,787 microforms. **Subscriptions:** 586 journals
and other serials. **Services:** Interlibrary loan; copying; library open to the
public for reference use only. **Automated Operations:** Computerized public
access catalog and circulation (NOTIS). **Computerized Information**
Services: DIALOG Information Services, STN International, BRS
Information Technologies, OCLC. Performs searches on fee basis.
Networks/Consortia: Member of AMIGOS Bibliographic Council, Inc.,
Research Libraries Information Network (RLIN).

★19126★
University of Oklahoma - Engineering Library (Sci-Engr)
Norman, OK 73019   Phone: (405)325-2941
                                      Jimmie L. Lee
Staff: Prof; Other 1. **Subjects:** Engineering - electrical, mechanical,
chemical, geological, industrial, petroleum, civil, aerospace; computer
science; environmental science; materials science. **Holdings:** 60,000 books;
50,000 microforms. **Subscriptions:** 625 journals and other serials. **Services:**
Interlibrary loan; copying; library open to the public. **Automated**
Operations: Computerized circulation and cataloging. **Computerized**
Information Services: DIALOG Information Services, PFDS Online, BRS
Information Technologies, STN International, NASA/RECON.
Networks/Consortia: Member of AMIGOS Bibliographic Council, Inc.

★19127★
University of Oklahoma - Fine Arts Library (Mus, Art)
007 Catlett Music Center
Jacobson Hall, Rm. 203   Phone: (405)325-2841
Norman, OK 73019   Jan Seifert, Fine Arts Libn.
Founded: 1986. **Staff:** Prof 1; Other 3. **Subjects:** Music, art, dance. **Special**
Collections: Spencer Norton Collection; Joseph Benton Collection; Bixler
Files; Harrison Kerr Collection. **Holdings:** 42,845 books, bound periodical
volumes, and scores; 424 reels of microfilm; 108 microcards; 1937
microfiche. **Subscriptions:** 114 journals. **Services:** Interlibrary loan; copying;
SDI; library open to the public. **Automated Operations:** Computerized
public access catalog, cataloging, and circulation. **Computerized**
Information Services: DIALOG Information Services, PFDS Online, BRS
Information Technologies, OCLC, WILSONLINE, DataTimes, PHINet
FedTax Database; RLG, BITNET, NOTIS-L (electronic mail services).
Performs searches on fee basis. **Networks/Consortia:** Member of AMIGOS
Bibliographic Council, Inc., Research Libraries Information Network
(RLIN). **Remarks:** Alternate telephone number(s): 325-4243 FAX:
(405)325-7618. Electronic mail address(es): QA6305@UOKMVSA
(BITNET). **Staff:** Dennis Mosser, Supv.

★19128★
University of Oklahoma - Geology Library (Sci-Engr)
100 E. Boyd
Energy Center R220   Phone: (405)325-6451
Norman, OK 73019-0628   Claren M. Kidd, Libn.
Founded: 1904. **Staff:** Prof 1; Other 1. **Subjects:** Geology, paleontology,
mineralogy, palynology, petroleum geology, geochemistry, geophysics,
oceanography, hydrology. **Special Collections:** Theses on Oklahoma
geology. **Holdings:** 83,200 volumes; 138,021 maps; 248,913 PI completion
cards for Oklahoma. **Subscriptions:** 1000 journals and other serials.
Services: Interlibrary loan; copying; library open to the public. **Automated**
Operations: Computerized circulation. **Computerized Information Services:**
BITNET (electronic mail service). **Networks/Consortia:** Member of
Research Libraries Information Network (RLIN), AMIGOS Bibliographic
Council, Inc. **Remarks:** FAX: (405)325-3180. Electronic mail address(es):
UA2431@UOKMVSA (BITNET).

★19129★
University of Oklahoma - Harry W. Bass Collection in Business History
   (Bus-Fin, Hist)
401 W. Brooks   Phone: (405)325-3941
Norman, OK 73019   Dr. Daniel A. Wren, Cur.
Founded: 1955. **Staff:** Prof 1; Other 2. **Subjects:** History - business,
economic, management. **Special Collections:** Sears Roebuck catalogs on
microfilm; rare books in economic history; archives of the J. & W. Seligman
& Co., Inc. (76 bound letter books, 19th and early 20th centuries; 23,000

pages and 6 linear feet of modern archival material; 325 engraved stock certificates). **Holdings:** 20,832 books; 1460 bound periodical volumes; 1750 pamphlets; 382 reels of microfilm; 10,000 microfiche; 30 magnetic tapes. **Subscriptions:** 23 journals and other serials. **Services:** Collection open to the public. **Special Catalogs:** Catalogs of the Collection, irregular. **Staff:** Sydona Baroff, Libn.

★ 19130 ★
University of Oklahoma - Health Sciences Center - Dean A. McGee Eye
   Institute - Library (Med)
Department of Ophthalmology
608 Stanton L. Young Blvd.   Phone: (405)271-6085
Oklahoma City, OK 73104   Sheri Greenwood, Med.Libn.
Staff: Prof 1. **Subjects:** Ophthalmology. **Holdings:** 1200 books; 1000 bound periodical volumes; 30 slide sets; 84 video cassettes. **Subscriptions:** 34 journals and other serials. **Services:** Interlibrary loan; SDI; library open to medical personnel only. **Computerized Information Services:** MEDLARS, BRS Information Technologies. **Networks/Consortia:** Member of Greater Oklahoma City Area Health Sciences Library Consortium (GOAL).

★ 19131 ★
University of Oklahoma - Health Sciences Center - Department of
   Surgery Library (Med)
P.O. Box 26901, RM 4SP305   Phone: (405)271-5506
Oklahoma City, OK 73190   Linda R. O'Rourke, Med.Libn.
Founded: 1976. **Staff:** Prof 1. **Subjects:** Surgery - general, plastic, neurosurgery, thoracic and cardiovascular, oral; emergency medicine and trauma. **Holdings:** 3349 volumes. **Subscriptions:** 90 journals and other serials. **Services:** Interlibrary loan; copying; SDI; library open to affiliated surgical personnel. **Computerized Information Services:** DIALOG Information Services, MEDLARS. **Remarks:** FAX: (405)271-3919.

★ 19132 ★
University of Oklahoma - Health Sciences Center - Robert M. Bird
   Health Sciences Library (Med)
1000 Stanton L. Young Blvd.
Box 26901   Phone: (405)271-2285
Oklahoma City, OK 73190-3046   C.M. Thompson, Jr., Dir.
Founded: 1928. **Staff:** Prof 10; Other 28. **Subjects:** Medicine, dentistry, nursing, public health, pharmacy, allied health subjects. **Holdings:** 71,334 books; 204,196 bound periodical volumes. **Subscriptions:** 2563 journals and other serials. **Services:** Interlibrary loan; copying; SDI; library open to the public for reference use only. **Automated Operations:** NOTIS. **Computerized Information Services:** DIALOG Information Services, MEDLARS, OCLC. Performs searches on fee basis. **Networks/Consortia:** Member of AMIGOS Bibliographic Council, Inc., Oklahoma Telecommunications Interlibrary System (OTIS), National Network of Libraries of Medicine - South Central Region, Metronet. **Publications:** Guide, annual; Footnote, bimonthly. **Remarks:** Alternate telephone numbers are 271-2670 and 271-2672. FAX: (405)271-3297. **Staff:** Barbara B. Peshel, Monograph Serv.; Virgil L. Jones, Ref.Libn.; Joe Ward, Ref.Libn.; Judy Wilkerson, Ser.Serv.; Jack Wagner, Cat.; Joy Summers-Ables, Access Serv.; Sandra Martin, Ref.Serv.; Jennifer Goodson, Ref.Libn.; Susan Staples, Ref.Libn.

★ 19133 ★
University of Oklahoma - Health Sciences Center - Tulsa Campus -
   Library (Med)
2808 S. Sheridan   Phone: (918)838-4616
Tulsa, OK 74129   Janet Minnerath, Lib.Dir.
Staff: Prof 1; Other 5. **Subjects:** Medicine. **Holdings:** 4000 books; 21,076 bound periodical volumes. **Subscriptions:** 674 journals and other serials. **Services:** Interlibrary loan; copying; SDI; library open to the public. **Automated Operations:** Computerized cataloging. **Computerized Information Services:** NLM, BRS Information Technologies. Performs searches on fee basis. **Networks/Consortia:** Member of AMIGOS Bibliographic Council, Inc., South Central Academic Medical Libraries Consortium (SCAMEL), Tulsa Area Library Cooperative (TALC). **Remarks:** FAX: (918)838-4624.

★ 19134 ★
University of Oklahoma - History of Science Collections (Sci-Engr, Hist)
401 W. Brooks, Rm. 524   Phone: (405)325-2741
Norman, OK 73019   Dr. Marilyn Ogilvie, Cur.
Founded: 1951. **Staff:** Prof 2; Other 4. **Subjects:** History of science and technology. **Special Collections:** DeGolyer, Klopsteg, Crew, Sally Hall,

Nielsen, Lacy, ADF, and Harlow Collections. **Holdings:** 75,000 volumes; 881 photographs, prints, pictures; 4378 volumes on microfilm; 671 volumes on microcards; 19,617 volumes in microprint; 232 volumes on microfiche; 18.15 cubic feet of manuscripts; 2848 pamphlets. **Subscriptions:** 83 journals and other serials. **Services:** Copying (limited); microfilming; collections open to the public by permission. **Automated Operations:** Computerized cataloging and circulation. **Computerized Information Services:** Association of Research Libraries (ARL), DIALOG Information Services, PFDS Online, OCLC, BRS Information Technologies. **Networks/Consortia:** Member of AMIGOS Bibliographic Council, Inc., Research Libraries Information Network (RLIN). **Special Catalogs:** Short-title Catalog (online and microfiche). **Special Indexes:** Alphabetical and chronological index to journal articles (card). **Staff:** Marcia M. Goodman, Hist. of Sci.Libn.

★ 19135 ★
University of Oklahoma - Law Library (Law)
300 Timberdell Rd.   Phone: (405)325-4311
Norman, OK 73019   Scott B. Pagel, Dir.
Founded: 1909. **Staff:** Prof 7.5; Other 7. **Subjects:** Law. **Special Collections:** Law - Indian, water, agriculture, natural resources; Indian land titles. **Holdings:** 173,859 volumes; 75,760 volumes in microform. **Subscriptions:** 3377 journals and other serials; 25 newspapers. **Services:** Interlibrary loan; copying; library open to legal researchers, law students, faculty. **Automated Operations:** Computerized cataloging and acquisitions. **Computerized Information Services:** LEXIS, WESTLAW, DIALOG Information Services, VU/TEXT Information Services, DataTimes; InterNet (electronic mail service). **Networks/Consortia:** Member of AMIGOS Bibliographic Council, Inc., Mid-America Law School Library Consortium. **Publications:** Law Library Newsletter, monthly; User's Guide; Research Guide. **Remarks:** FAX: (405)325-6282. Electronic mail address(es): SAO490@UOKMVSA.BACKBONE.UOKNOR.EDU (InterNet). **Staff:** Marilyn K. Nicely, Tech.Serv.Libn.; Maria E. Protti, Assoc.Dir.

★ 19136 ★
University of Oklahoma - Limited Access Collection (Hum)
401 W. Brooks, Rm. 509   Phone: (405)325-2048
Norman, OK 73019   Dr. Marilyn Ogilvie, Cur.
Staff: Prof 2; Other 1. **Subjects:** Literature, history. **Special Collections:** Lois Lenski Children's Literature Collection; Bizzell Bible Collection. **Holdings:** 12,199 volumes. **Services:** Copying (limited); collection open to the public by permission. **Automated Operations:** Computerized cataloging and circulation. **Computerized Information Services:** DIALOG Information Services, Association of Research Libraries (ARL), PFDS Online, OCLC. **Networks/Consortia:** Member of AMIGOS Bibliographic Council, Inc., Research Libraries Information Network (RLIN), Center for Research Libraries (CRL). **Staff:** Marcia M. Goodman, Libn.

★ 19137 ★
University of Oklahoma - Physics-Astronomy Library (Sci-Engr)
219 Nielsen Hall   Phone: (405)325-2887
Norman, OK 73019-0225   Zora Sampson, Lib.Techn. II
Founded: 1948. **Staff:** Prof 1; Other 1. **Subjects:** Quantum mechanics, high energy physics, astronomy, astrophysics, classical physics. **Special Collections:** Atlases of the northern and southern skies. **Holdings:** 9000 books; 11,000 bound periodical volumes. **Subscriptions:** 205 journals and other serials. **Services:** Interlibrary loan; library open to the public for reference use only. **Computerized Information Services:** DIALOG Information Services, STN International, BRS Information Technologies; BITNET (electronic mail service). Performs searches on fee basis. **Networks/Consortia:** Member of AMIGOS Bibliographic Council, Inc., Research Libraries Information Network (RLIN). **Remarks:** FAX: (405)325-7557. Electronic mail address(es): OA5305@UOKMVSA (BITNET). Alternate telephone number(s): 325-5628.

★ 19138 ★
University of Oklahoma - Science and Public Policy Program - Library
   (Env-Cons, Sci-Engr)
100 E. Boyd Room R208   Phone: (405)325-2554
Norman, OK 73019   Mary Morrison, Libn.
Staff: Prof 1. **Subjects:** Energy policy, impact assessment, environmental policy, regional studies, technology assessment, information transfer, science policy, hazardous and solid waste management alternatives, alternative transportation fuels. **Holdings:** 7000 books and documents; unbound periodicals; 3 cabinets of information files. **Subscriptions:** 24 journals and other serials. **Services:** Copying; library open to the public for reference use only. **Computerized Information Services:** Catalog of acquisitions, 1984 to present (internal database). **Remarks:** FAX: (405)325-7695.

University of Oklahoma - Tulsa Medical College
See: University of Oklahoma - Health Sciences Center - Tulsa Campus (19133)

★ 19139 ★

University of Oklahoma - Western History Collections (Hist)
630 Parrington Oval, Rm. 452   Phone: (405)325-3641
Norman, OK 73019   Donald L. DeWitt, Cur.
Founded: 1927. **Staff:** Prof 5; Other 4. **Subjects:** American Indian, Oklahoma, American Southwest, American Trans-Mississippi West, recent U.S. history. **Special Collections:** Cherokee Nation Papers; Patrick J. Hurley papers; E.E. Dale papers; Frank E. Phillips Collection; Alan Farley Collection; Henry B. Bass Collection; Norman Brillhart Collection. **Holdings:** 55,000 books; 9000 linear feet of manuscripts; 250,000 items in photographic archives; 20,000 microforms; 3600 maps; 1400 transcripts, tapes, and discs of oral history; 5000 pamphlets and documents; 1500 linear feet of University of Oklahoma archives; newspapers, posters, broadsides. **Subscriptions:** 52 journals and other serials; 17 newspapers. **Services:** Copying (limited); collections open to the public. **Automated Operations:** Computerized cataloging. **Computerized Information Services:** RLIN, OCLC. **Networks/Consortia:** Member of Research Libraries Information Network (RLIN). **Publications:** Guide to Regional Manuscripts in Division of Manuscripts of University of Oklahoma Library, 1960, American Indian Resource Materials in the Western History Collection, 1990. **Special Catalogs:** Catalogs of individual collections; catalog of microform holdings. **Staff:** Bradford Koplowitz, Asst.Cur.; John R. Lovett, Jr., Libn.; Charles E. Rand, Photo. & Univ.Archv.; Shirley Clark, Adm.Asst.

★ 19140 ★

University of the Orange Free State - Rabie Sanders Library (Agri, Env-Cons, Food-Bev)
Faculty of Agriculture
P.O. Box 339   Phone: 51 4012533
Bloemfontein 9300, Republic of South Africa   Mrs. J.E. Engelbrecht
Founded: 1958. **Staff:** Prof 1; Other 2. **Subjects:** Agricultue - economics, agronomy, meteorology, soil science; animal husbandry; food science and technology. **Holdings:** 140,000 books; 80,000 bound periodical volumes; 72 microfiche; 12 reels of microfilm. **Subscriptions:** 400 journals and other serials. **Services:** Interlibrary loan; copying; library open to the public with restrictions. **Computerized Information Services:** Kousidex (index of local publications).

★ 19141 ★

University of Oregon - Architecture and Allied Arts Library (Art, Plan)
200 Lawrence Hall   Phone: (503)346-3637
Eugene, OR 97403-1206   Sheila M. Klos, Hd.Libn.
Founded: 1915. **Staff:** Prof 3.5; Other 3. **Subjects:** Architecture, fine and applied arts, interior architecture, landscape architecture, urban design, art history, historic preservation, computer graphics, arts administration. **Holdings:** 54,000 volumes; 30,000 prints and photographs; 260,000 slides; 500 original architectural drawings; 200 sets of blueprints. **Subscriptions:** 420 journals and other serials. **Services:** Interlibrary loan (through Knight Library); copying; library open to the public. **Automated Operations:** Computerized public access catalog, cataloging, acquisitions, serials, and circulation. **Computerized Information Services:** RLIN, DIALOG Information Services, OCLC, BRS Information Technologies; internal databases; CD-ROM (Art Index). Performs searches on fee basis. **Staff:** James H. Carmin, Ref.Libn.; Marian Fincher, Ref.Libn.; Christine Sundt, Slide & Photo.Cur.

★ 19142 ★

University of Oregon - Career Information Center (Educ)
221 Hendricks Hall
Box 3257   Phone: (503)686-3235
Eugene, OR 97403   Lawrence H. Smith, Dir.
Founded: 1972. **Staff:** 1. **Subjects:** Career awareness and planning, job search, interview techniques, resume and cover-letter writing. **Holdings:** 350 books; 150 feet and shelves of pamphlets from professional organizations; 3 VF drawers of employer files. **Subscriptions:** 4 journals and other serials; 2 newspapers. **Services:** Center open to the public; will answer mail or phone questions from those interested in career planning. **Publications:** Career Information Center Bibliography of Resources, 1990.

★ 19143 ★

University of Oregon - Career Information System (Educ)
1787 Agate St.   Phone: (503)346-3872
Eugene, OR 97403   Michael Neill, Dir.
Founded: 1971. **Staff:** Prof 12; Other 15. **Subjects:** Occupations, study and training programs, education, financial aid, career development, computer systems for guidance. **Holdings:** 3000 volumes; occupational information in 300 areas; 130 programs of study and training. **Subscriptions:** 35 journals and other serials. **Services:** Copying; open to the public. **Computerized Information Services:** BITNET (electronic mail service). **Publications:** Updated issues of printouts, annual - by subscription. **Remarks:** FAX: (503)346-5890. Electronic mail address(es): MNEILL@OREGON(BITNET). Provides technical assistance, research, and development for operators of the Career Information System nationwide. Operates the Career Information System for schools, colleges, and agencies in Oregon. Operates a clearinghouse for the National Association of Computer-Based Systems for Career Information.

★ 19144 ★

University of Oregon - Center for Advanced Technology in Education - CATE Resource Center (Educ, Comp Sci)
1787 Agate St., Rm. 104   Phone: (619)564-3311
Eugene, OR 97403   Patricia Jones, Mgr.
Founded: 1965. **Staff:** Prof 1; Other 1. **Subjects:** Computers in education, instructional technology, educational software, media production. **Special Collections:** International Council for Computers in Education (1270 volumes); Instructional Technology (682 volumes). **Holdings:** 1952 books; 1150 titles of educational computer software. **Services:** Copying; center open to the public. **Automated Operations:** Computerized cataloging and serials. **Computerized Information Services:** Internal database. **Remarks:** FAX: (503)346-5890.

★ 19145 ★

University of Oregon - Computing Center - Library (Comp Sci)
Eugene, OR 97403   Phone: (503)346-4402
Founded: 1965. **Staff:** Prof 2; Other 2. **Subjects:** Computer science, microcomputers, educational computing. **Special Collections:** Newsletters from academic computing centers and computing organizations (200). **Holdings:** 1500 books; 500 computer manuals; 125 computer-related journals; hardware/software directories; vertical files of pamphlets and brochures. **Subscriptions:** 125 journals; 200 newsletters. **Services:** Interlibrary loan; SDI; library open to the public. **Automated Operations:** Computerized cataloging and routing of periodicals and newsletters. **Computerized Information Services:** BITNET (electronic mail service). **Publications:** Quarterly reports - for internal distribution only; accessions lists, irregular; series of specialized bibliographies - both available on request. **Special Indexes:** Index to current periodicals. **Remarks:** FAX: (503)346-4397. Electronic mail address(es): DKAUF@OREGON; VKM@OREGON (BITNET). **Staff:** Deborah Kaufman; Vickie Nelson.

★ 19146 ★

University of Oregon - Department of English - Randall V. Mills Archives of Northwest Folklore (Hist)
Eugene, OR 97403   Phone: (503)346-3925
                                      Bill Goldsmith, Archv.
Founded: 1965. **Staff:** Prof 1. **Subjects:** Folksongs, Bigfoot lore, logger lore, oral history, folklore and folklife. **Special Collections:** Robert Winslow Gordon Collection (folksongs and ballads); Randall V. Mills Collection (dialect studies, proverbs, place names, railroad and steamship lore); Otillie Seybolt Dialect Studies; Webfoots and Bunchgrassers Oregon Folk Art Slide Collection. **Holdings:** 300 books; 300 bound periodical volumes; 3500 unbound fieldwork projects; 18 dissertations/theses; 40 folkloric videocassettes; 1500 slides on general folklife; 700 audiotapes. **Services:** Copying; archives open to researchers. **Remarks:** Alternate telephone number(s): (503)346-3539.

★ 19147 ★

University of Oregon - Documents & Public Affairs Service (Info Sci)
University Library   Phone: (503)346-3070
Eugene, OR 97403   Thomas A. Stave, Hd.
Staff: Prof 2; Other 1. **Subjects:** U.S., Oregon, Canadian, and British Government documents; international intergovernmental organizations, including the U.N. and European Communities; Oregon local government land use planning documents. **Holdings:** 379,000 documents; 460,000 microforms. **Subscriptions:** 3000 journals and other serials. **Services:**

Interlibrary loan; copying; collection open to the public. **Computerized Information Services:** DIALOG Information Services, BRS Information Technologies; CD-ROMs (CASSIS, GPO). **Special Indexes:** Index to thesis projects of the University of Oregon Department of Planning, Public Policy and Management (PPPM); index to local land use planning documents of Oregon cities and counties. **Remarks:** FAX: (503)346-3094. **Staff:** David M. Barber, Oregon, Foreign & Intl.Docs.

★ 19148 ★
University of Oregon - Environmental Studies Center (Env-Cons, Energy)
Eugene, OR 97403-5223   Phone: (503)346-5006
Founded: 1971. **Staff:** Prof 1; Other 3. **Subjects:** Ecology, environmental issues, energy, conservation. **Holdings:** 3000 books; periodicals; back issues of scientific reports. **Subscriptions:** 100 environmental journals and other serials. **Services:** Center open to the public with restrictions. **Special Catalogs:** Catalog of Environmental Studies programs.

★ 19149 ★
University of Oregon - Herbarium - Library (Biol Sci)
Dept. of Biology   Phone: (503)346-3033
Eugene, OR 97403   David H. Wagner
Staff: Prof 1. **Subjects:** Botany. **Holdings:** 300 books; 100 reports; archives. **Subscriptions:** 5 journals and other serials. **Services:** Library open to the public for reference use only. **Remarks:** FAX: (503)346-6056.

★ 19150 ★
University of Oregon - Institute of Recreation Research & Service (Rec)
Esslinger Hall, Rm. 180   Phone: (503)346-3396
Eugene, OR 97403-1273   Larry Lin, Ph.D., Dir.
Founded: 1970. **Subjects:** Leisure services management, therapeutic recreation, basic and applied leisure research. **Special Collections:** L.S. Rodney Collection. **Holdings:** 200 books; 2000 bound periodical volumes; 700 studies; 1000 park and recreation materials; clippings. **Services:** Library not open to the public. **Publications:** Technical report series; monographs. **Remarks:** FAX: (503)346-2841. **Staff:** Larry L. Neal, Dir.; Gaylene Carpenter, Asst.Dir.

★ 19151 ★
University of Oregon - Instructional Media Center (Aud-Vis)
University Library   Phone: (503)346-3091
Eugene, OR 97403   James V. Mahoney, Jr., Dir.
Staff: Prof 3; Other 11. **Subjects:** Instructional media. **Holdings:** 1450 films and film loops; 826 filmstrips; 264 media kits; 1500 videotapes. **Services:** Center open to the public for reference use only. **Networks/Consortia:** Member of Consortium of College and University Media Centers (CCUMC). **Publications:** IMC Newsletter, quarterly - to faculty and staff. **Special Catalogs:** IMC Film Videotape and Catalog. **Remarks:** FAX: (503)346-3094. **Staff:** William C. Leonard, Hd., Graphic Arts Serv. Howard A. Lindstrom, Asst.Dir., IMC.

★ 19152 ★
University of Oregon - Law Library (Law)
Eugene, OR 97403-1221   Phone: (503)346-3088
                    Dennis R. Hyatt, Libn.
Founded: 1884. **Staff:** Prof 5; Other 5. **Subjects:** Law. **Holdings:** 145,378 volumes; 612,733 microforms. **Subscriptions:** 2865 journals and other serials. **Services:** Interlibrary loan; copying. **Automated Operations:** Computerized public access catalog, cataloging, and acquisitions. **Computerized Information Services:** OCLC, LEXIS, DIALOG Information Services, WESTLAW, Oregon Legislative Information Service. **Remarks:** FAX: (503)686-3094. **Staff:** Mary Clayton, Assoc. Law Libn.; Ann C. Fletcher, Asst. Law Libn., Pub.Serv.; Lelah Conrad, Asst. Law Libn., Tech.Serv.

★ 19153 ★
University of Oregon - Map and Aerial Photography Library (Geog-Map)
165 Condon Hall   Phone: (503)346-3051
Eugene, OR 97403-1218   Peter L. Stark, Hd.
Founded: 1968. **Staff:** Prof 1; Other 1. **Subjects:** Cartographic materials, aerial photography. **Special Collections:** Oregon maps; Oregon aerial photographs. **Holdings:** 2315 volumes, including atlases; 231,840 maps; 410,000 aerial photographs. **Subscriptions:** 7 journals and other serials. **Services:** Interlibrary loan; copying; library open to the public for reference use only. **Computerized Information Services:** Electronic mail. **Publications:** Acquisitions list, semiannual - by exchange. **Special Indexes:** Shelf list of map collection; index to aerial photography of Oregon. **Remarks:** FAX: (503)346-3094. **Formerly:** Its Map Library.

★ 19154 ★
University of Oregon - Mathematics Library (Comp Sci, Sci-Engr)
University Library   Phone: (503)346-3023
Eugene, OR 97403-1229   Isabel A. Stirling, Hd.Libn.
Staff: Prof 1. **Subjects:** Mathematics, computer science. **Holdings:** 30,000 volumes. **Subscriptions:** 400 journals and other serials. **Services:** Copying. **Computerized Information Services:** BITNET, InterNet (electronic mail services). **Remarks:** FAX: (503)346-3012. Electronic mail address(es): STIRLING@OREGON.UOREGON.EDU (BITNET, InterNet). **Staff:** Luise Walker, Ref.Libn.

★ 19155 ★
University of Oregon - Microforms and Recordings Department (Aud-Vis)
University Library   Phone: (503)346-3080
Eugene, OR 97403-1299   Rory A. Funke, Hd.
Founded: 1980. **Staff:** 4. **Holdings:** 1.3 million microforms; 25,000 phonograph records; 2500 tapes; 1200 compact discs. **Services:** Interlibrary loan; copying; department open to the public. **Publications:** Oregon Newspapers on Microfilm, 1989. **Remarks:** FAX: (503)346-3094.

University of Oregon - Nepal/USAID Project Archives
See: **American Nepal Education Foundation - Wood Nepal Library (696)**

★ 19156 ★
University of Oregon - Oregon Institute of Marine Biology - Library (Biol Sci)
Charleston, OR 97420   Phone: (503)888-2581
Staff: 1. **Subjects:** Marine biology, ecology, environmental research, comparative physiology of blood pigments of vertebrates and invertebrates. **Special Collections:** Student reports. **Holdings:** 3000 books; 300 maps; 150 topographic maps; 2500 reprints; 2000 slides; herbarium collection of local flora. **Subscriptions:** 30 journals and other serials. **Services:** Interlibrary loan; copying; library open to the public for reference use only. **Automated Operations:** Computerized cataloging and acquisitions. **Computerized Information Services:** DIALOG Information Services, BRS Information Technologies, Chemical Abstracts Service (CAS). Performs searches on fee basis. Contact Person: Isabel Stirling, Hd., Sci.Lib., 686-3075. **Remarks:** FAX: (503)888-3250.

★ 19157 ★
University of Oregon - Orientalia Collection (Hist, Area-Ethnic)
Knight Library   Phone: (503)346-3096
Eugene, OR 97403-1299   Robert Felsing, Orient.Bibliog.
Staff: Prof 2; Other 2. **Subjects:** East Asia - history, language, literature, Buddhism, humanities, social sciences. **Holdings:** 76,740 volumes; 286 reels of film. **Subscriptions:** 406 journals and other serials. **Services:** Interlibrary loan; copying; collection open to the public. **Remarks:** FAX: (503)346-3094. **Staff:** Daphne Wang, Cat.; Sharon Domier, Cat.

★ 19158 ★
University of Oregon - Science Library (Biol Sci, Sci-Engr)
University Library   Phone: (503)346-3075
Eugene, OR 97403-5201   Isabel A. Stirling, Hd.Libn.
Staff: Prof 3; Other 5. **Subjects:** Basic sciences, physics, chemistry, biological sciences, neuroscience, geology, computer science, astronomy. **Holdings:** 185,000 volumes. **Subscriptions:** 3800 journals and other serials. **Services:** Interlibrary loan (through Knight Library); copying. **Computerized Information Services:** DIALOG Information Services, BRS Information Technologies, Chemical Abstracts Service (CAS), STN International; BITNET, InterNet (electronic mail services). **Remarks:** FAX: (503)346-3012. Electronic mail address(es): STIRLING@OREGON.UOREGON.EDU (BITNET, InterNet). **Staff:** Bradley Wycoff, Ref.Libn.; Pamela White, Ref.Libn.; Luise Walker, Ref.Libn.

★ 19159 ★
University of Oregon - Special Collections Department (Hist)
University Library   Phone: (503)346-3068
Eugene, OR 97403   Fraser Cocks, Cur.
Founded: 1948. **Staff:** Prof 3; Other 2. **Subjects:** Political, social, economic, and literary history of the United States in the 19th and 20th centuries, with

emphasis on Oregon and the Pacific Northwest. **Special Collections:** Manuscript Collection (materials of political conservatives, authors and illustrators of children's literature, writers of western fiction, women writers of speculative fiction, missionaries to the Far East, and women in Oregon politics, 1960 to present; Pacific Northwest authors, architects, politicians, and business figures); Photograph Collection (primarily negatives of the Pacific Northwest, Alaska, Appalachia, and Far East); Rare Book Collection (western Americana, Bodoni Imprints, early European imprints, travels and voyages, Oriental art, manuscripts, pulp magazines, and Esperanto language books and journals); Oregon Collection (circulating collection of books and journals on all phases and periods of Oregon history, life, and letters). **Holdings:** 70,000 volumes; 20 million manuscripts; 130,000 photographic images; 75,000 architectural drawings; 20,000 pieces of sheet music. **Subscriptions:** 880 journals and other serials. **Services:** Interlibrary loan (from the Oregon Collection); copying (limited). **Special Catalogs:** Catalog of Manuscripts in the University of Oregon Library, 1971 (book); Catalog of the George Alan Connor Esperanto Collection, 1978 (pamphlet); Inventory of the Papers of Senator Wayne L. Morse, 1974 (book); Inventory of the Papers of T. Coleman Andrews, 1967 (pamphlet); Catalog of the Louis Conrad Rosenberg Collection, 1978 (pamphlet); Jane C. Grant Papers: A Collection of the University of Oregon Library, 1985 (pamphlet); Guide to Manuscript Collections Documenting Women in Society, 1989 (pamphlet); checklist of missionary collections, 1988 (pamphlet). **Remarks:** FAX: (503)346-3094. **Staff:** James Fox, Rare Bks. & Photo.Libn.; Victoria A. Jones, Cur. of Mss.

University of Oslo - Institute and Museum for Social Anthropology
See: **University of Oslo Library - Faculty of Social Sciences Library** (19161)

★19160★
University of Oslo - Library (Biol Sci, Med, Law, Info Sci)
N-0242 Oslo 2, Norway   Phone: 2 553630
                                      Jan Erik Roed, Libn.
Founded: 1811. **Staff:** 304. **Subjects:** Natural sciences, medicine, dentistry, law, humanities, theology, social sciences. **Holdings:** 4 million books; 550,000 microforms; 40,000 manuscripts. **Services:** Interlibrary loan; copying; SDI; library open to the public. **Computerized Information Services:** UBO:BOK. Performs searches on fee basis. **Publications:** National Bibliography. **Remarks:** Library is the legal depository for Norway and serves as the national library. FAX: 2 434497. Telex: 76078 ub n.

★19161★
University of Oslo Library - Faculty of Social Sciences Library (Soc Sci)
Moltke Moes vei 31
Eilert Sundts hus
Postboks 1098 - Blindern   Phone: 2 855050
N-0317 Oslo 3, Norway   Ms. Per Pharo, Faculty Libn.
Founded: 1966. **Staff:** 31. **Subjects:** Social anthropology, sociology, education, psychology, economics, political science, media and communication, women's research. **Holdings:** 235,000 volumes. **Subscriptions:** 2400 journals and other serials; 80 newspapers. **Services:** Interlibrary loan; copying; branch open to the public. **Computerized Information Services:** DIALOG Information Services, DIMDI; CD-ROMs; UBO:BOK, BIBSYS (internal databases). **Publications:** Dewey Kontrollregister; Dewey subject register. **Remarks:** FAX: 2 564135. Contains the holdings of the University of Oslo - Institute for Social Sciences and Museum for Social Anthropology, the Women's Research Center, and Institute of Nursing Research. **Staff:** Brita Lysne Kvam, Lib.Info.Asst. Faculty Libn.; Bredo Berntsen, Political Sci.; Hilde K. Bjerkholt, Educ.; Jan Fredenborg, Psych.; Sabine Basedow Ameln, Econ.; Berit Lund, Media/Commun.; Stein Erik Johansen, Sociology; Hana Konupek, Info./Tech.; Nancy Frank, Soc. Anthropology.

★19162★
University of Osteopathic Medicine and Health Sciences - Media Library (Med)
3200 Grand Ave.   Phone: (515)271-1430
Des Moines, IA 50312   Larry D. Marquardt, Lib.Dir.
Founded: 1898. **Staff:** Prof 3; Other 2. **Subjects:** Osteopathic and podiatric medicine, physician assisting, physical therapy, health care administration. **Special Collections:** Historical and archival collection (1600 volumes). **Holdings:** 30,382 volumes. **Subscriptions:** 489 journals and other serials. **Services:** Interlibrary loan; copying; SDI; library open to the public for reference use only. **Automated Operations:** Computerized cataloging and

ILL. **Computerized Information Services:** MEDLARS, BRS Information Technologies, OCLC; DOCLINE (electronic mail service). Performs searches on fee basis. **Networks/Consortia:** Member of Polk County Biomedical Consortium (PCBC), National Network of Libraries of Medicine - Greater Midwest Region, Bibliographical Center for Research, Rocky Mountain Region, Inc. (BCR).

★19163★
University of Ottawa - Health Sciences Library (Med)
451 Smyth Rd., No. 1020   Phone: (613)787-6431
Ottawa, ON, Canada K1H 8M5   Myra Owen, Dir.
Founded: 1982. **Staff:** Prof 3; Other 7. **Subjects:** Medicine, nursing, kinanthropology, physiotherapy, human kinetics. **Special Collections:** Graduate theses in medicine. **Holdings:** 47,677 books; 48,736 bound periodical volumes; 540 filmstrips; 263 videocassettes; 820 audiocassettes. **Subscriptions:** 1311 journals and other serials. **Services:** Interlibrary loan; copying; library open to the public with limited borrowing privileges. **Automated Operations:** Computerized public access catalog, cataloging, acquisitions, and circulation. **Computerized Information Services:** Infomart Online, DIALOG Information Services, MEDLARS, CAN/OLE; CD-ROMs (MEDLINE, HEALTH, CINA, CCINFO); Envoy 100 (electronic mail service). **Remarks:** FAX: (613)787-6430. Telex: 0533338. Electronic mail address(es): ILL.OOUH (Envoy 100). **Staff:** Michelle LeBlanc, Ref.; Cathering Mackellar, Ref.

★19164★
University of Ottawa - Law Library (Law)
Fauteux Hall, 4th Fl.
57 Louis Pasteur   Phone: (613)564-4943
Ottawa, ON, Canada K1N 9A5   Jules Lariviere, Dir.
Founded: 1973. **Staff:** Prof 4; Other 17. **Subjects:** Civil law (Quebec), common law. **Holdings:** 73,144 books; 84,887 bound periodical volumes; 28,064 microforms. **Subscriptions:** 2450 journals and other serials; 12 newspapers. **Services:** Interlibrary loan (through Morisset Library); copying; library open to the public for reference use only. **Automated Operations:** Computerized public access catalog, circulation, acquisitions, and cataloging. **Computerized Information Services:** QL Systems, LEGALTRAC; Envoy 100 (electronic mail service). **Remarks:** FAX: (613)564-9886. Telex: 0533338. Electronic mail address(es): OOU.ILL.OOU (Envoy 100). **Staff:** Ophelia Meza, Ref.; Mr. Chin-Shih Tang, Ref.; Susan Mowers, Ref.

★19165★
University of Ottawa - Map Library (Geog-Map)
Morisset Library
65 University St., Rm. 353   Phone: (613)564-6830
Ottawa, ON, Canada K1N 9A5   Grace Welch
Founded: 1968. **Staff:** Prof 2; Other 3. **Subjects:** Geography - general, physical, urban; urban planning; map coverage of Ottawa and the national capital region, Ontario, Quebec, Northern Canada, Bolivia, Chile, Colombia, Ecuador, Peru, French-speaking Africa. **Holdings:** 135,630 sheet maps; 569 wall maps; 2235 atlases; 15 globes; 254,097 aerial photographs; 8207 reference books; 427 bound periodical volumes. **Subscriptions:** 60 journals and other serials. **Services:** Interlibrary loan; copying; library open to the public. **Automated Operations:** Computerized public access catalog, cataloging, and acquisitions. **Computerized Information Services:** Envoy 100 (electronic mail service). **Publications:** Acquisitions List, annual. **Remarks:** FAX: (613)564-9886. Telex: 0533338. Electronic mail address(es): OOU.ILL.OOU (Envoy 100). **Staff:** Frank Williams, Cat.

★19166★
University of Ottawa - Media Library (Aud-Vis)
No. 022 - 65 University   Phone: (613)564-2374
Ottawa, ON, Canada K1N 9A5   Guillaume Blais
Founded: 1971. **Staff:** Prof 1; Other 10. **Subjects:** Audiovisual materials - literature, fine arts, social science, classical studies, geography, cinema. **Holdings:** 174 phonograph records; 978 audiocassettes; 1588 films; 1463 videocassettes; 176,665 slide sets. **Services:** Interlibrary loan; library open to the public with restrictions. **Automated Operations:** Computerized public access catalog, cataloging, and acquisitions. **Computerized Information Services:** CD-ROM (A-V Online); Envoy 100 (electronic mail service). Performs searches. **Special Catalogs:** AV Catalog. **Remarks:** FAX: (613)564-9886. Telex: 0533338. Electronic mail address(es): OOU.ILL.OOU (Envoy 100).

★ 19167 ★
University of Ottawa - Morisset Library (Hum, Soc Sci)
65 University   Phone: (613)564-6880
Ottawa, ON, Canada K1N 9A5   Suzanne St-Jacques, Dir.
Founded: 1904. **Staff:** Prof 17; Other 51. **Subjects:** Humanities and social sciences. **Special Collections:** Rare book collection (19,920 books). **Holdings:** 176,107 bound periodical volumes; 707,402 monographs; 1.1 million microfiche; 761,119 government documents. **Subscriptions:** 6054 journals and other serials. **Services:** Interlibrary loan; copying; library open to the public. **Automated Operations:** Computerized public access catalog, cataloging, acquisitions, and circulation. **Computerized Information Services:** DIALOG Information Services, Infomart Online, CAN/OLE, BRS Information Technologies, Questel, SDM, Info Globe; MINISIS (internal database); CD-ROMs (ERIC, PsychLit, SPORT, CBCA, TERMIUM); Envoy 100 (electronic mail service). **Publications:** Subject bibliographies. **Remarks:** FAX: (613)564-9886. Telex: 0533338. Electronic mail address(es): OOU.ILL.OOU (Envoy 100). Library is a depository for publications of the Canadian federal government, the province of Ontario, and the United Nations and its affiliates. **Staff:** Richard Greene, Univ.Chf.Libn.; Jean LeBlanc, Asst.Libn., Coll. & Pub.Serv.; David Holmes, Asst.Libn., Tech.Serv. & Sys.; Dale Ward, Hd., Ref.; Hera Arevian, Hd., Coll.; Ginette Mageau, Hd., Loan Serv.; Marilyn Rennick, Hd., Spec.Serv.

★ 19168 ★
University of Ottawa - Music Library (Mus)
50 University, No. 302   Phone: (613)564-5717
Ottawa, ON, Canada K1N 9A5   Debra Begg, Libn.
Founded: 1970. **Staff:** Prof 1; Other 2. **Subjects:** Music. **Holdings:** 3208 books; 25,195 scores; 7868 phonograph records; 851 tapes. **Services:** Interlibrary loan (through Morisset Library). **Automated Operations:** Computerized public access catalog, acquisitions, and cataloging. **Computerized Information Services:** Envoy 100 (electronic mail service). **Remarks:** FAX: (613)564-9886. Telex: 0533338. Electronic mail address(es): OOU.ILL.OOU (Envoy 100). Book collection and journals housed at Morisset Library.

★ 19169 ★
University of Ottawa - Teacher Education Library (Educ)
145 Jean-Jacques Lussier, No. 245   Phone: (613)564-5986
Ottawa, ON, Canada K1N 9A5   Jan Kolaczek, Libn.
Founded: 1974. **Staff:** Prof 2; Other 5. **Subjects:** Teacher education, elementary and secondary teaching in both French and English languages, education theory. **Special Collections:** Curriculum documents; educational software; test collection (2268 tests). **Holdings:** 36,996 volumes; 2442 bound periodical volumes; 575 filmstrips and film loops; 32 multimedia kits; 3362 mounted photographs; 43 sound recordings; 8020 microforms. **Subscriptions:** 203 journals and other serials. **Services:** Interlibrary loan (through Morisset Library); copying; library open to the public with restrictions on borrowing. **Computerized Information Services:** CD-ROMs (Eric, ONTERIS, GROLIER, Canadian Education Index); Envoy 100 (electronic mail service). **Remarks:** FAX: (613)564-9886. Telex: 0533338. Electronic mail address(es): OOU.ILL.OOU (Envoy 100). **Also Known As:** Bibliotheque de la Formation a l'Enseignement. **Staff:** Therese Nguyen, Ref.

★ 19170 ★
University of Ottawa - Vanier Science & Engineering Library (Sci-Engr)
11 Marie Curie   Phone: (613)564-2324
Ottawa, ON, Canada K1N 9A5   S. Elizabeth Reicker, Dir.
Founded: 1962. **Staff:** Prof 4; Other 9. **Subjects:** Science, engineering. **Special Collections:** Academic dissertations in science and technology accepted by the university. **Holdings:** 85,133 books; 56,730 bound periodical volumes; 34,296 microfiche. **Subscriptions:** 1393 journals and other serials. **Services:** Interlibrary loan; copying; library open to the public with restrictions on borrowing. **Automated Operations:** Computerized public access catalog, cataloging, acquisitions, and circulation. **Computerized Information Services:** Online systems; CD-ROMs (COMPENDEX, BIOSIS); EVY (electronic mail service). **Remarks:** FAX: (613)564-9886. Telex: 0533338. Electronic mail address(es): ILL.OOUM (Envoy 100). **Staff:** Edith Arbach, Ref.; Lynette Ng, Ref.; Ann Sung, Ref.

★ 19171 ★
University of Oxford - Queen Elizabeth House - International Development Centre - Library (Bus-Fin)
21 St. Giles
Queen Elizabeth House   Phone: 865 273590
Oxford OX1 3LA, England   Mrs. S.L. Allcock, Libn. & Info.Serv.Mgr.
Founded: 1989. **Staff:** Prof 1; Other 3. **Subjects:** Development economics, agricultural economics, international relations, Commonwealth history. **Special Collections:** News cuttings (1949 to present). **Holdings:** 30,000 books; 30,000 bound periodical volumes. **Subscriptions:** 600 journals and other serials; 6 newspapers. **Services:** Interlibrary loan; copying; SDI; library open to the public for reference use only. **Computerized Information Services:** Oxford Library System (OLIS, internal database); VANET (electronic mail service). **Publications:** Acquisitions lists; list of periodical articles, quarterly; library guide. **Remarks:** FAX: 865 273607. Telex: 83147 Attn QEH. Electronic mail address(es): ALLCOCK@OXFORD (VANET). **Formed by the merger of:** Institute of Commonwealth Studies and Institute of Agricultural Economics.

★ 19172 ★
University of the Pacific - Holt-Atherton Department of Special Collections (Hist)
Stockton, CA 95211   Phone: (209)946-2404
                                          Thomas W. Leonhardt, Dean
Founded: 1947. **Staff:** Prof 2; Other 1. **Subjects:** Californiana, Western Americana, Pacific Northwest, Northern San Joaquin Valley, gold mining, Western authors, Native Americans, economic development of the West, ethnic history in California. **Special Collections:** Early California exploration; fur trade; John Muir papers (900 volumes, 16,500 items); Jack London family collection; Shutes Collection on Lincoln and the Civil War; Perrin Collection on William Morris and Victoriana. **Holdings:** 30,000 books; 2928 bound periodical volumes; 75 linear feet of VF pamphlets; 30,000 photographs; 700 maps; 2000 linear feet of manuscripts. **Subscriptions:** 116 journals and other serials. **Services:** Interlibrary loan (limited); copying; library open to the public. **Automated Operations:** Computerized cataloging. **Computerized Information Services:** RLIN, BRS Information Technologies, DIALOG Information Services, ALANET (electronic mail service). Performs searches on fee basis. Contact Person: Karen Snure. **Networks/Consortia:** Member of 49-99 Cooperative Library System. **Publications:** Monographs; Bibliographic Guides to Archives. **Remarks:** FAX: (209)946-2810. Electronic mail address(es): ALA1641 (ALANET). **Also Known As:** Stuart Library of Western Americana. **Staff:** Ms. Daryl Morrison, Spec.Coll.

University of the Pacific - School of Dentistry
See: **California Pacific Medical Center/University of the Pacific School of Dentistry (2498)**

★ 19173 ★
University of the Pacific - Science Library (Sci-Engr, Med)
Stockton, CA 95211   Phone: (209)946-2940
                                          Marlene M. Hurley, Sci.Libn.
Founded: 1955. **Staff:** Prof 1; Other 2. **Subjects:** Pharmacy and pharmacology, medicine, chemistry, drug information. **Special Collections:** Iowa Drug Literature Information Service. **Holdings:** 17,770 books; 23,000 bound periodical volumes; 82,745 index cards; 1600 reels of microfilm; 9478 microcards; 12,000 microfiche. **Subscriptions:** 371 journals and other serials. **Services:** Interlibrary loan; copying; library open to the public. **Automated Operations:** Computerized cataloging, acquisitions, serials, and ILL (DOCLINE). **Computerized Information Services:** DIALOG Information Services, BRS Information Technologies, STN International. Performs searches on fee basis. **Networks/Consortia:** Member of 49-99 Cooperative Library System, Central Association of Libraries (CAL), Northern California and Nevada Medical Library Group (NCNMLG), North San Joaquin Health Sciences Library Consortium. **Remarks:** FAX: (209)946-2810. **Staff:** Dorothy Masters, Day Supv.; Rosemary Mann, Night Supv.

★ 19174 ★
University of Pennsylvania - Annenberg School for Communication - Library (Info Sci)
3620 Walnut St.   Phone: (215)898-7027
Philadelphia, PA 19104-6220   Susan G. Williamson, Libn.
Founded: 1962. **Staff:** Prof 1; Other 2. **Subjects:** Theory and research of communication; telecommunications; mass media communication; interpersonal communication; social psychology of communication;

communications economics; history and technology of broadcasting. **Special Collections:** Annenberg Faculty Publications; 16mm film and video catalogs; annual reports of leading U.S. communications companies and U.S. public television stations. **Holdings:** 25,899 volumes; 40 VF drawers of pamphlets and clippings; 451 theses and dissertations; 698 reels of microfilm; 10,085 microfiche. **Subscriptions:** 311 journals and other serials; 10 newspapers. **Services:** Interlibrary loan; library open to the public for reference use only. **Computerized Information Services:** DIALOG Information Services, BRS Information Technologies; RLIN, OCLC; CD-ROMs. **Networks/Consortia:** Member of PALINET, Research Libraries Information Network (RLIN). **Publications:** Thesaurus of Subject Headings for Television: A Vocabulary for Indexing Script Collections, 1989; Index to the Annenberg Television Script Archive: Volume 1, 1976-1977; Selected New Acquisitions, biennial; Selected Reference Sources in Communications - free upon request. **Remarks:** FAX: (215)898-2024.

★19175★
University of Pennsylvania - Archive of Folklore & Folklife (Area-Ethnic)
3440 Market St., Suite 370   Phone: (215)898-7352
Philadelphia, PA 19104   Dr. Kenneth Goldstein, Dir.
Subjects: Folklore, folklife, music, New Foundland folksong, West Indies, Virginia and Pennsylvania, American Folklore Society. **Special Collections:** Mac Edward Leach Collections from New Foundland, Nova Scotia, and Jamaica; Kenneth Goldstein Collection (New Foundland, Labrador, North Carolina, Great Britain, and Ireland); Horace and Jane Beck Collection (West Indies); Samuel Bayard recordings (western Pennsylvania); Jacob Elder Collection (Trinidad); Ray Birdwhistell Collection of Americana and American Humor; Niles C. Geerhold Popular Music Collection; John Diamond Folk Music Recordings. **Holdings:** 500 volumes; 4000 phonograph records; dissertations; files of student papers and other items. **Subscriptions:** 10 journals and other serials; 3 newspapers. **Services:** Copying; archive open to the public. **Computerized Information Services:** RLIN. Performs searches on fee basis. **Remarks:** Archives are open on a limited schedule during the summer months. **Staff:** Stephanie Wardwell.

★19176★
University of Pennsylvania - Archives and Records Center (Hist)
North Arcade, Franklin Field   Phone: (215)898-7024
Philadelphia, PA 19104-6320   Mark Frazier Lloyd, Dir.
Founded: 1945. **Staff:** Prof 9; Other 4. **Subjects:** University history, history of institutions of higher learning in the United States, American intellectual life, the Philadelphia community in which the university lives. **Special Collections:** University of Pennsylvania academic and administrative records; University community life (student activities, alumni organizations, organizations of faculty and administrators, and other University-related groups); personal and professional papers (University officers, faculty, students, alumni, and benefactors); University history-related papers (individuals and organizations). **Holdings:** 2500 volumes; 12,500 cubic feet of archives and manuscripts; 22,000 photographs, drawings, prints, paintings, and other visual materials; 150 cubic feet of University decorative arts and memorabilia; 450 current and retrospective serial titles. **Subscriptions:** 160 serials. **Services:** Photocopying; microfilming; archives open to the scholarly public. **Computerized Information Services:** RLIN; Minaret MARC-AMC (internal databases). **Networks/Consortia:** Member of Philadelphia Area Consortium of Special Collections Libraries (PACSCL). **Publications:** Protocols for the University Archives and Records Center (1990); The University Archives and Records Center: A Guide to Records Management (1986); Guide to the Archives of the University of Pennsylvania from 1740 to 1820 (1978). **Remarks:** FAX: (215)573-2036. Electronic mail address(es): LLOYD@AI.QUAKER.UPENN.EDU. **Staff:** Hamilton Y. Elliott, Assoc.Dir.; Theresa R. Snyder, Asst.Dir.; Sandra Markham, Hd., Pub.Serv.; Gail Pietrzyk, Pub.Serv.Archv.; L. Blake Cheney, Univ.Recs.Mgr.

University of Pennsylvania - The Arnold and Mabel Beckman Center for the History of Chemistry
See: **University of Pennsylvania - National Foundation for History of Chemistry - Library** (19190)

★19177★
University of Pennsylvania - Biddle Law Library (Law)
3400 Chestnut St.   Phone: (215)898-7478
Philadelphia, PA 19104-6279   Prof. Elizabeth S. Kelly, Libn./Prof.
Founded: 1886. **Staff:** Prof 17; Other 16. **Subjects:** American and foreign legislation; reports of Anglo-American and other judicial decisions;

administrative regulations and decisions; law - Anglo-American, foreign, canon, Roman, international. **Special Collections:** Trent Collection on the Black Lawyer in America. **Holdings:** 409,532 volumes; 412,194 microfiche; 3987 reels of microfilm. **Subscriptions:** 5771 journals and other serials. **Services:** Interlibrary loan; copying; library open to the public for reference use only. **Computerized Information Services:** DIALOG Information Services, ELSS (Electronic Legislative Search System), VU/TEXT Information Services, RLIN, LEXIS, WESTLAW, OCLC, LegalTrac, CIS Masterfile, BRS Information Technologies, Dow Jones News/Retrieval. **Networks/Consortia:** Member of Research Libraries Information Network (RLIN), PALINET, Mid-Atlantic Law Library Cooperative (MALLCO). **Remarks:** FAX: (215)898-6619. **Staff:** Patricia Callahan, Assoc.Dir., Tech.Serv.; Marie S. Newman, Assoc.Dir., Pub.Serv.; Marta Tarnawsky, Assoc.Dir., Foreign & Intl. Law; Cynthia Arkin, Assoc.Dir., Coll.Dev.

★19178★
University of Pennsylvania - Biomedical Library (Med)
Johnson Pavilion
36th & Hamilton Walk   Phone: (215)898-5817
Philadelphia, PA 19104-6060   Valerie A. Pena, Libn.
Founded: 1931. **Staff:** Prof 13; Other 17. **Subjects:** Medicine, biology, nursing, health care, basic sciences. **Holdings:** 155,170 volumes; 919 AV programs. **Subscriptions:** 2726 journals and other serials. **Services:** Interlibrary loan; copying; orientations; workshops; library open to the public for reference use only. **Computerized Information Services:** DIALOG Information Services, BRS Information Technologies, NLM, PaperChase, RLIN, OCLC; CD-ROMs; DOCLINE (electronic mail service). **Networks/Consortia:** Member of Research Libraries Information Network (RLIN), National Network of Libraries of Medicine - Middle Atlantic Region, PALINET, Health Sciences Libraries Consortium (HSLC). **Publications:** Newsletter, quarterly - for internal distribution only. **Remarks:** FAX: (215)573-2075. **Staff:** Wallace McLendon, Assoc.Dir., Pub.Serv.; Linda Rosenstein, Assoc.Dir., Tech.Serv.

★19179★
University of Pennsylvania - Chemistry Library (Sci-Engr)
231 S. 34th St.   Phone: (215)898-2177
Philadelphia, PA 19104-6323   Carol Carr, Libn.
Founded: 1967. **Staff:** Prof 1; Other 1. **Subjects:** Biochemistry; chemistry - inorganic, organic, physical. **Holdings:** 25,678 books. **Subscriptions:** 270 journals and other serials. **Services:** Interlibrary loan; copying; library open to the public. **Computerized Information Services:** STN International, DIALOG Information Services, BRS Information Technologies, RLIN, OCLC; BITNET (electronic mail service). Performs searches on fee basis. **Networks/Consortia:** Member of Research Libraries Information Network (RLIN), PALINET. **Remarks:** FAX: (215)898-0741. Electronic mail address(es): CARR@AI.RELAY.UPENN.EDU(BITNET).

★19180★
University of Pennsylvania - East Asia Collection (Hum)
Van Pelt Library
3420 Walnut St.   Phone: (215)898-3205
Philadelphia, PA 19104-6206   Karl Kahler, East Asian Bibliog.
Founded: 1938. **Staff:** Prof 1; Other 2. **Subjects:** Buddhism, pre-modern Japanese literature, pre-modern Chinese literature, Chinese history (Ming and Ch'ing dynasties). **Holdings:** 102,270 books; 2000 reels of microfilm. **Subscriptions:** 200 journals and other serials; 10 newspapers. **Services:** Interlibrary loan; copying; library open to the public with restrictions. **Automated Operations:** Computerized public access catalog. **Computerized Information Services:** DIALOG Information Services, BRS Information Technologies, OCLC, RLIN; BITNET (electronic mail service). Performs searches. **Networks/Consortia:** Member of Research Libraries Information Network (RLIN). **Remarks:** FAX: (215)898-0559. Electronic mail address(es): BM.PEO@RLG (BITNET).

★19181★
University of Pennsylvania - Edgar Fahs Smith Memorial Collection in the History of Chemistry (Sci-Engr, Med)
Van Pelt Library   Phone: (215)898-7089
Philadelphia, PA 19104-6206   Christine A. Ruggere, Cur.
Founded: 1931. **Subjects:** History of chemistry, alchemy, chemical biography, chemical engineering, chemical industry, early medicine, metallurgy, mineralogy, pharmacy, pyrotechnics. **Holdings:** 3000 portraits, prints, and engravings; Robert Boyle and Joseph Priestley collections of manuscripts and printed material; imprints; 300 late 19th century German

chemical dissertations; 8 boxes of Archives of the Division of Chemical Education, American Chemical Society; assorted manuscript collections (inventories available upon request). **Subscriptions:** 18 journals and other serials. **Services:** Interlibrary loan; copying; collection open to the public. **Computerized Information Services:** RLIN. **Networks/Consortia:** Member of Research Libraries Information Network (RLIN). **Special Catalogs:** Catalog of the Edgar Fahs Smith Memorial Collection in the History of Chemistry, 1960; Catalog of Manuscripts in the Libraries of the University of Pennsylvania to 1800, 1965; Franklin catalogs (online). **Remarks:** FAX: (215)898-0559.

★19182★
University of Pennsylvania - Fine Arts Library (Art, Plan)
Furness Bldg.
220 S. 34th St.   Phone: (215)898-8325
Philadelphia, PA 19104-6308   Alan E. Morrison, Libn.
Founded: 1890. **Staff:** Prof 2; Other 10. **Subjects:** Architecture, city planning, history of art, landscape architecture, regional planning, historic preservation, appropriate technology. **Special Collections:** Rare architectural books, 16th to 20th century. **Holdings:** 105,000 volumes; 59,000 mounted photographs; 335,000 35mm slides. **Subscriptions:** 770 journals and other serials. **Services:** Interlibrary loan; copying; library open to the public for reference use only. **Computerized Information Services:** DIALOG Information Services, RLIN, Conservation Information Network. **Networks/Consortia:** Member of Research Libraries Information Network (RLIN), PALINET. **Remarks:** FAX: (215)573-2066. **Staff:** Micheline Nilsen, Slide Libn.

★19183★
University of Pennsylvania - Henry Charles Lea Library (Hist)
Van Pelt Library
3420 Walnut St.   Phone: (215)898-7088
Philadelphia, PA 19104-6206   Daniel Traister, Hon.Cur.
Founded: 1924. **Subjects:** Medieval and Renaissance history, church history, canon law, the Inquisition, magic, witchcraft. **Special Collections:** Manuscripts, 12th-18th centuries (600 volumes). **Holdings:** 18,000 volumes. **Services:** Interlibrary loan; copying; library open to the public. **Networks/Consortia:** Member of Research Libraries Information Network (RLIN), PALINET. **Special Catalogs:** Catalog of Manuscripts in the Libraries of the University of Pennsylvania to 1800 (book). **Remarks:** Holdings available through Christine A. Ruggere, Curator of Special Collections, Van Pelt Library.

★19184★
University of Pennsylvania - Horace Howard Furness Memorial Library (Hum)
Van Pelt Library
3420 Walnut St.   Phone: (215)898-7552
Philadelphia, PA 19104-6206   Georgianna Ziegler, Cur.
Founded: 1932. **Staff:** Prof 1. **Subjects:** Shakespeare, medieval to 17th century English drama, theater history. **Special Collections:** Playbills, promptbooks, and pictures; dissertations on Shakespeare and his contemporaries (2000 reels of microfilm); STC Collection. **Holdings:** 20,000 volumes. **Subscriptions:** 37 journals and other serials. **Services:** Library open to qualified scholars and students. **Automated Operations:** Computerized public access catalog. **Computerized Information Services:** RLIN, ESTC. **Networks/Consortia:** Member of Research Libraries Information Network (RLIN), PALINET. **Remarks:** FAX: (215)898-0559.

★19185★
University of Pennsylvania - John Penman Wood Library of National Defense (Mil)
504 Hollenback Center
3000 South St.   Phone: (215)898-7757
Philadelphia, PA 19104-6325   Loretta Miller, Coord./Asst.Libn.
Founded: 1928. **Staff:** 1. **Subjects:** Officer education and production; leadership, organization, and management; operations, tactics, and strategy; logistics, supply, and transportation; military biography and history; principles of war, weaponry, and war gaming; medical services. **Holdings:** 15,500 books; 66 bound periodical volumes. **Services:** Interlibrary loan; library open to the public for reference use only. **Computerized Information Services:** BITNET (electronic mail service). **Remarks:** FAX: (609)386-9874. Alternate telephone number(s): 898-7756. Electronic mail address(es): MILLER@AL.QUAKER (BITNET).

★19186★
University of Pennsylvania - Lippincott Library (Bus-Fin)
Van Pelt-Dietrich Library Center
3420 Walnut St.   Phone: (215)898-5924
Philadelphia, PA 19104-6207   Michael Halperin, Hd.Libn.
Founded: 1927. **Staff:** Prof 9; Other 13. **Subjects:** Applied economics, econometrics, business, management, finance, multinational enterprises, marketing, accounting, insurance, labor, industrial relations, transportation, statistics, regional science, operations research, real estate. **Holdings:** 210,000 volumes; 4200 reels of microfilm; 224,000 microfiche and microcards. **Subscriptions:** 5610 journals and other serials. **Services:** Interlibrary loan; copying; library open to the public. **Computerized Information Services:** DIALOG Information Services, BRS Information Technologies, NEXIS, VU/TEXT Information Services, RLIN, OCLC, Dow Jones News/Retrieval, Data-Star, Datastream International Ltd; CD-ROMs. **Networks/Consortia:** Member of Research Libraries Information Network (RLIN), PALINET. **Remarks:** FAX: (215)898-2261. **Staff:** Ruth Pagell, Assoc.Libn.

★19187★
University of Pennsylvania - Map Library (Geog-Map)
Hayden Hall
240 S. 33rd St.
Philadelphia, PA 19104-6316   Phone: (215)898-5725
Subjects: Regional, U.S., and international maps. **Special Collections:** Depository for U.S. Geological Survey, National Ocean Survey Charts, Defense Mapping Agency, and Canadian Geological Survey. **Holdings:** 120,000 maps. **Services:** Copying; map enlarger; library open to the public by appointment.

★19188★
University of Pennsylvania - Mathematics-Physics-Astronomy Library (Sci-Engr)
Rittenhouse Laboratory   Phone: (215)898-8173
Philadelphia, PA 19104-6317   Margaret Dominy, Libn.
Founded: 1948. **Staff:** Prof 1; Other 1. **Subjects:** Astronomy, mathematics, physics. **Holdings:** 59,000 volumes. **Subscriptions:** Journals and other serials. **Services:** Interlibrary loan; copying; library open to the public for reference use only. **Computerized Information Services:** DIALOG Information Services, SPIRES, STN International, RLIN, OCLC; CD-ROMs. **Networks/Consortia:** Member of Research Libraries Information Network (RLIN), PALINET. **Remarks:** FAX: (215)573-2009. Electronic mail address(es): DOMINY@AI.RELAY.UPENN.EDU.

★19189★
University of Pennsylvania - Morris Arboretum Library (Biol Sci)
9414 Meadowbrook Ave.
Philadelphia, PA 19118   Phone: (215)247-5777
Founded: 1932. **Subjects:** Ornamental horticulture, garden history (especially Victorian period), floristic botany, urban forestry and silviculture, plant exploration. **Holdings:** 5000 books; 2500 bound periodical volumes. **Subscriptions:** 100 journals and other serials. **Services:** Interlibrary loan; library open to the public for reference use only. **Remarks:** FAX: (215)248-4439. **Staff:** Timothy R. Tomlinson, Assoc.Dir.; Ann F. Rhoads, Dir. of Botany.

★19190★
University of Pennsylvania - National Foundation for History of Chemistry - Library (Sci-Engr)
3401 Walnut St., Suite 460B   Phone: (215)898-4896
Philadelphia, PA 19104-6228   Dr. Arnold W. Thackray, Dir.
Founded: 1982. **Staff:** Prof 7; Other 5. **Subjects:** History of chemistry, chemical engineering, chemical process industries. **Holdings:** 50,000 books; 6000 bound periodical volumes; 500 manuscripts, 10 patents, 100 reels of microfilm; 100 artifacts; 200 oral history transcripts; 60 medals. **Subscriptions:** 20 journals and other serials. **Services:** Copying; center open to the public. **Publications:** Beckman Center News. **Remarks:** Jointly sponsored by the American Chemical Society, the American Institute of Chemical Engineers, and the University of Pennsylvania, the Foundation operates through the Arnold and Mabel Beckman Center for the History of Chemistry and the Donald F. and Mildred Topp Othmer Library of Chemical History. Foundation activities include oral history interviews, preparation of traveling exhibits, travel grants, and the location of manuscripts and archival records in the history of chemistry, chemical engineering, and the chemical process industries. Also administers a

program of fellowships and grants. Affiliated with the American Society for Biochemistry and Molecular Biology, the American Society for Mass Spectrometry, The Chemists' Club, and the Electrochemical Society. **FAX:** (215)898-3327. **Staff:** J.J. Bohning, Asst.Dir., Oral Hist.; Irene Lukoff, Asst.Dir., Dev.; Larry Friedman, Assoc.Dir.; O. Thedor Benfey, Asst.Dir., Pubns./Ed., Beckman Center News.

University of Pennsylvania - New Bolton Center - Jean Austin Du Pont Library
See: University of Pennsylvania - School of Veterinary Medicine (19196)

★ 19191 ★
University of Pennsylvania - Population Studies Center - Demography Library (Soc Sci)
3718 Locust Walk   Phone: (215)898-5375
Philadelphia, PA 19104-6298   Lisa A. Newman, Libn.
Founded: 1970. **Staff:** Prof 1; Other 1. **Subjects:** Foreign and United States census, population organizations, demographic surveys, statistics. **Special Collections:** Foreign censuses for 50 countries (varying years); statistical materials for 113 countries; United Nations repository; World Fertility Survey repository; John D. Durand Collection (historical demography). **Holdings:** 12,000 books; 600 bound periodical volumes; reprints; dissertations. **Subscriptions:** 75 journals and other serials. **Services:** Interlibrary loan; library not open to the public but special requests will be taken from related interest institutions. **Automated Operations:** Computerized cataloging and acquisitions. **Computerized Information Services:** NLM, DIALOG Information Services. **Networks/Consortia:** Member of APLIC International Census Network. **Publications:** Acquisitions List, monthly - to related interest institutions. **Remarks:** FAX: (215)898-2124.

★ 19192 ★
University of Pennsylvania - School of Dental Medicine - Leon Levy Library (Med)
4001 Spruce St.   Phone: (215)898-8969
Philadelphia, PA 19104-6041   Patricia Heller, Libn.
Founded: 1914. **Staff:** Prof 2; Other 4. **Subjects:** Dentistry, oral biology, history of dentistry. **Special Collections:** Rare dental books (1400). **Holdings:** 52,438 volumes. **Subscriptions:** 434 journals and other serials. **Services:** Interlibrary loan; copying; library open to the public for reference use only. **Computerized Information Services:** DIALOG Information Services, MEDLINE, RLIN. Performs searches on fee basis. **Networks/ Consortia:** Member of Research Libraries Information Network (RLIN), PALINET, Health Sciences Libraries Consortium (HSLC), National Network of Libraries of Medicine - Middle Atlantic Region. **Remarks:** Alternate telephone number(s): 898-8978. **Remarks:** FAX: (215)898-7985. **Staff:** Helen Sziget, Asst.Libn.

★ 19193 ★
University of Pennsylvania - School of Engineering and Applied Science - Library (Sci-Engr)
203 Moore Bldg.
200 S. 33rd St.   Phone: (215)898-8135
Philadelphia, PA 19104-6314   Gretchen Sneff, Libn.
Founded: 1926. **Staff:** 2.5. **Subjects:** Electrical engineering, electronics, computers, information science, optics, systems engineering. **Special Collections:** Robotics. **Holdings:** 30,000 volumes. **Subscriptions:** 325 journals and other serials. **Services:** Interlibrary loan; copying; library open to the public for reference use only. **Computerized Information Services:** DIALOG Information Services, BRS Information Technologies, STN International, RLIN, OCLC. **Networks/Consortia:** Member of Research Libraries Information Network (RLIN), PALINET. **Remarks:** FAX: (215)573-2010.

★ 19194 ★
University of Pennsylvania - School of Engineering and Applied Science - Library (Sci-Engr)
217 Towne Bldg.
220 S. 33rd St.   Phone: (215)898-7266
Philadelphia, PA 19104-6315   Gretchen Sneff, Libn.
Founded: 1947. **Staff:** 2.5. **Subjects:** Engineering - chemical, civil, metallurgical, mechanical, aeronautical, transportation, environmental; materials science; bioengineering. **Special Collections:** Depository for

NASA reports; robotics; heat transfer; fluid mechanics. **Holdings:** 75,000 volumes; 165,500 microfiche; 100 videotapes. **Subscriptions:** 584 journals and other serials. **Services:** Interlibrary loan; copying; library open to the public for reference use only. **Computerized Information Services:** DIALOG Information Services, BRS Information Technologies, STN International, RLIN, OCLC; CD-ROMs. **Networks/Consortia:** Member of Research Libraries Information Network (RLIN), PALINET. **Remarks:** FAX: (215)573-2011.

★ 19195 ★
University of Pennsylvania - School of Medicine - Clinical Epidemiology Unit - Library (Med)
2L NEB/S2
Philadelphia, PA 19104   Phone: (215)898-4623
Founded: 1978. **Subjects:** Medicine, clinical epidemiology, public health, statistics. **Holdings:** 30 books. **Services:** Library not open to the public. **Remarks:** FAX: (215)573-5315; (215)573-5325. **Staff:** Brian L. Strom, M.D., Dir.

★ 19196 ★
University of Pennsylvania - School of Veterinary Medicine - C.J. Marshall Memorial Library (Med)
3800 Spruce St.   Phone: (215)898-8874
Philadelphia, PA 19104-6008   Lillian D. Bryant, Libn.
Founded: 1908. **Staff:** Prof 1; Other 2. **Subjects:** Veterinary and comparative medicine, animal husbandry. **Holdings:** 31,255 volumes; 18 VF drawers of pamphlets, bulletins, and annual reports. **Subscriptions:** 332 journals and other serials. **Services:** Interlibrary loan; copying; library open to the public for reference use only. **Automated Operations:** Computerized ILL (DOCLINE). **Computerized Information Services:** DIALOG Information Services, MEDLINE, RLIN, OCLC; electronic mail. **Networks/Consortia:** Member of Research Libraries Information Network (RLIN), PALINET, National Network of Libraries of Medicine - Middle Atlantic Region, Health Sciences Libraries Consortium (HSLC). **Remarks:** FAX: (215)573-2007. Statistics include holdings of the New Bolton Center Library in Kennett Square.

★ 19197 ★
University of Pennsylvania - Special Collections (Hum, Rare Book)
Van Pelt Library
3420 Walnut St.   Phone: (215)898-7088
Philadelphia, PA 19104-6206   Daniel H. Traister, Cur., Spec.Coll.
Founded: 1941. **Staff:** Prof 5. **Subjects:** Literature - English, American, Spanish, Italian, German, classical, neo-Latin; French drama; history of agriculture; cryptography; ancient and early modern philosophy. **Special Collections:** Jonathan Swift (1400 volumes); English novel to 1820 (3000 volumes); Torquato Tasso, 16th and 17th centuries (350 volumes); Aristotle editions and commentaries before 1750 (1200 manuscript and printed volumes); Elzevir imprints (2500 volumes); Latin American history and religion, 17th-19th centuries (1500 volumes); Benjamin Franklin imprints (200 volumes); Philadelphia Society for the Promotion of Agriculture (1500 manuscript and printed volumes); French Revolution (25,000 items in 1460 volumes); Roman Catholic and Anglo-Catholic theology and liturgy (1000 volumes); University of Pennsylvania medical dissertations, 18th and 19th centuries (800 volumes); Indic manuscripts (50 volumes); collections of manuscripts by and about authors, artists, and public figures; Marian Anderson; Berchtesgaden interrogations, 1945; Robert Montgomery Bird; Van Wyck Brooks; Carey & Lea, Publishers; Theodore Dreiser; James T. Farrell; Howard Fast; Waldo Frank; John Haviland; Francis Hopkinson; William C. Lengel; Horace Liveright; H.L. Mencken; S. Weir Mitchell; Lewis Mumford; John Rowe Parker; Francis Daniel Pastorius; William Pepper; Ezra Pound; Arthur Hobson Quinn; Samuel J. Randall; Burton Rascoe; Ada Rehan; Agnes Repplier; Jurgis Saulys; George Seldes; Gilbert Seldes; May Sinclair; Robert E. Spiller and the Archive of the Literary History of the United States; Alma Mahler Werfel; Franz Werfel; Samuel Wetherill and Wetherill business records; Walt Whitman; Carl Zigrosser. **Holdings:** 250,000 books; 3500 linear feet of manuscripts. **Services:** Interlibrary loan; copying; collections open to the public by appointment. **Computerized Information Services:** RLIN. **Networks/Consortia:** Member of Research Libraries Information Network (RLIN), PALINET. **Special Catalogs:** Catalogs to European manuscripts to 1800 (1965), 16th century imprints (1976), English 17th century imprints (1978), Spanish drama of the Golden Age (1971), Aristotle Collection (1961), Maclure Collection of the French Revolution (1966), and Marian Anderson Collection (1981 - all in book form). **Remarks:** FAX: (215)898-0559. **Staff:** Christine A. Ruggere, Cur., E.F. Smith Coll.; Nancy M. Shawcross, Cur., Mss.; Dr. Georgianna Ziegler, Cur., Furners Lib.; Elizabeth Mosimann.

★ 19198 ★
University of Pennsylvania - The University Museum of Archaeology/
  Anthropology - Museum Library (Soc Sci)
33rd & Spruce Sts.   Phone: (215)898-7840
Philadelphia, PA 19104-6324   Jean S. Adelman, Libn.
Founded: 1887. **Staff:** Prof 1; Other 2. **Subjects:** Archeology, anthropology, ethnology. **Special Collections:** Brinton Collection of 19th century American Indian linguistics and ethnology (2000 titles). **Holdings:** 100,000 volumes; 5000 pamphlets; 80 reels of microfilm. **Subscriptions:** 900 journals and other serials. **Services:** Interlibrary loan; copying; library open to the public for reference use only. **Computerized Information Services:** RLIN, OCLC; CD-ROMs; electronic mail. **Networks/Consortia:** Member of Research Libraries Information Network (RLIN), PALINET. **Remarks:** FAX: (215)573-2008.

University of Petroleum and Minerals
See: **King Fahd University of Petroleum and Minerals (5551)**

University of Philadelphia - Marriage Council of Philadelphia
See: **Marriage Council of Philadelphia (9715)**

★ 19199 ★
University of the Philippines - Asian Center - Library (Area-Ethnic)
Diliman
Quezon City, Metro Manila, Philippines   Violeta V. Encarnacion, Libn.
Subjects: Philippines - history, culture, politics; Asia - history, society, culture, politics, language, literature. **Special Collections:** Association of Southeast Asian Nations (ASEAN) documents; news clippings of the Philippines, 1965 to present (1965-1982 on microfiche). **Holdings:** 35,181 books, bound periodical volumes, and monographs; pamphlets. **Subscriptions:** 17 journals and other serials; 5 newspapers. **Services:** Interlibrary loan; library open to bona fide University students, faculty, staff, and officers; room use is available for visiting scholars, researchers, and alumni.

★ 19200 ★
University of Pittsburgh - Afro-American Library (Area-Ethnic)
Hillman Library, First Floor   Phone: (412)648-7714
Pittsburgh, PA 15260   Pearl E. Woolridge
Founded: 1969. **Staff:** Prof 1; Other 1. **Subjects:** History, political science, literature, literary criticism, social sciences, culture and the arts, blacks in Western Pennsylvania. **Special Collections:** Atlanta University Black Culture Collection (microfilm); W.E.B. Dubois papers (microfilm); papers of the Congress of Racial Equality (microfilm); black history and landmarks in Western Pennsylvania (80 slides). **Holdings:** 16,936 volumes; 6 VF drawers of clippings and pamphlets. **Subscriptions:** 82 journals and other serials; 27 newspapers. **Services:** Interlibrary loan; library open to the public. **Automated Operations:** Computerized public access catalog, cataloging, acquisitions, serials, and circulation. **Networks/Consortia:** Member of Pittsburgh Regional Library Center (PRLC), Oakland Library Consortium. **Remarks:** FAX: (412)648-1245.

★ 19201 ★
University of Pittsburgh - Allegheny Observatory - Library (Sci-Engr)
159 Riverview Airway   Phone: (412)321-2400
Pittsburgh, PA 15260   Sandra S. Kerbel, Interim Hd.
Founded: 1868. **Staff:** 1. **Subjects:** Astronomy, astrometry. **Special Collections:** British and French Astronomical Association publications, 1800 to present; exchange publications from over 500 observatories throughout the world. **Holdings:** 3927 volumes. **Subscriptions:** 28 journals and other serials. **Services:** Interlibrary loan; library open to the public for reference use only. **Automated Operations:** Computerized public access catalog, cataloging, acquisitions, serials, and circulation. **Computerized Information Services:** BITNET (electronic mail service). **Publications:** Allegheny Observatory reports, irregular - to other observatories on exchange, free to libraries upon request. **Remarks:** All inquiries concerning this library should be directed to Sandra Kerbel, Engineering Library, 126 Benedum Hall; telephone: 624-9620. FAX: (412)321-0606. Electronic mail address(es): KERBEL@PITVMS (BITNET).

★ 19202 ★
University of Pittsburgh - Archives (Hist)
363 Hillman Library   Phone: (412)648-7998
Pittsburgh, PA 15260   Rebecca A. Abromitis, Assoc.Archv.
Founded: 1966. **Staff:** Prof 1. **Subjects:** University of Pittsburgh history and records; higher education records. **Special Collections:** Thomas Parran papers (Surgeon General of the U.S., 1936-1948, and a founder of the World Health Organization). **Holdings:** 3641 books; 305 bound periodical volumes; 2445 linear feet of manuscripts; 28,164 microforms; 1085 films; 9809 photographs; 696 sound recordings; 254 slides; 439 drawings and prints. **Subscriptions:** 74 journals and other serials. **Services:** Copying; archives open to the public. **Special Indexes:** Indexes to University publications (card); unpublished inventories to specific record groups and collections. **Remarks:** FAX: (412)648-1245.

★ 19203 ★
University of Pittsburgh - Archives of Industrial Society (Hist)
363-H Hillman Library   Phone: (412)648-7977
Pittsburgh, PA 15260   Frank A. Zabrosky, Cur.
Founded: 1963. **Staff:** Prof 2.5; Other 1. **Subjects:** History - urban, labor, ethnic. **Special Collections:** 497 collections (primarily manuscripts) of individuals, businesses, churches, institutions, organizations, labor unions, and ethnic groups; municipal records of Pittsburgh, Allegheny, and Allegheny County; Pittsburgh City Photographer Collection; oral history tapes. **Holdings:** 933 volumes; 10,854 linear feet of manuscripts; 1889 items in microform; 4925 reels of 16mm film; 82 phonograph records; 905 tape cassettes; 615 maps; 788 architectural drawings, plans, and sketches; 83,493 photographic images: glass plates, negatives, and prints. **Subscriptions:** 22 journals and other serials. **Services:** Copying; use of collections may be subject to conditions of owner/donor; access to archives is conditional. **Networks/Consortia:** Member of Oakland Library Consortium. **Publications:** Inventories of specific collections - for sale. **Special Catalogs:** Resources on the Ethnic and the Immigrant in the Pittsburgh Area, 1979 (book). **Special Indexes:** Indexes to the microfilmed correspondence of directors, acting directors, and selected astronomers among the records of the Allegheny Observatory. **Remarks:** FAX: (412)648-1245. **Staff:** John Thompson, Assoc.Archv.

★ 19204 ★
University of Pittsburgh - Barco Law Library (Law)
3900 Forbes Ave.   Phone: (412)648-1330
Pittsburgh, PA 15260   Jenni Parrish, Dir.
Founded: 1895. **Staff:** Prof 6; Other 12. **Subjects:** Law, taxation, labor law, international trade. **Holdings:** 153,000 volumes; 446,000 microfiche; 1700 reels of microfilm. **Subscriptions:** 3800 journals and other serials. **Services:** Interlibrary loan; library open to the public. **Automated Operations:** Computerized public access catalog, cataloging, acquisitions, serials, and circulation (NOTIS). **Computerized Information Services:** LEXIS, WESTLAW, DIALOG Information Services. **Networks/Consortia:** Member of Pittsburgh Regional Library Center (PRLC), Mid-Atlantic Law Library Cooperative (MALLCO). **Remarks:** FAX: (412)648-1352. **Staff:** Nickie Singleton, Assoc. Law Libn.; Cynthia Larter, Asst. Law Libn.; Marc Silverman, Asst. Law Libn.; Elizabeth Bedford Krebs, Cat.Libn.; Spencer Clough, Pub.Serv.Libn.

★ 19205 ★
University of Pittsburgh - Bevier Engineering Library (Sci-Engr)
126 Benedum Hall   Phone: (412)624-9620
Pittsburgh, PA 15261   Sandra S. Kerbel, Hd.
Founded: 1956. **Staff:** Prof 2; Other 3. **Subjects:** Engineering - chemical, civil, electrical, industrial, mechanical, metallurgical, petroleum, environmental, mining, materials; bioengineering; energy resources. **Special Collections:** Selected depository for U.S. Department of Energy, Environmental Protection Agency, and selected National Bureau of Standards documents; Advisory Group for Aerospace Research and Development depository set. **Holdings:** 60,084 volumes; 59,726 microfiche; 3247 reels of microfilm; 3926 U.S. documents; 100 nonprint items. **Subscriptions:** 965 journals. **Services:** Interlibrary loan; copying; library open to the public. **Automated Operations:** Computerized public access catalog, cataloging, acquisitions, serials, and circulation. **Computerized Information Services:** DIALOG Information Services, OCLC, STN International, PFDS Online. Performs searches on fee basis. **Networks/Consortia:** Member of Pittsburgh Regional Library Center (PRLC), Center for Research Libraries (CRL), Oakland Library Consortium. **Remarks:** FAX: (412)624-8103.

★19206★
University of Pittsburgh - Biological Sciences and Psychology Library
(Biol Sci)
A-217 Langley Hall   Phone: (412)624-4490
Pittsburgh, PA 15260   Drynda L. Johnston, Hd.
Founded: 1961. **Staff:** Prof 1; Other 3. **Subjects:** Biological sciences,
biophysics, biochemistry, psychology, behavioral neurosciences. **Holdings:**
62,781 volumes; 4300 microfiche. **Subscriptions:** 846 journals and other
serials. **Services:** Interlibrary loan; copying; library open to the public for
reference use only. **Automated Operations:** Computerized public access
catalog, cataloging, acquisitions, serials, and circulation. **Computerized
Information Services:** DIALOG Information Services. **Networks/
Consortia:** Member of Pittsburgh Regional Library Center (PRLC),
National Network of Libraries of Medicine - Middle Atlantic Region,
Oakland Library Consortium. **Remarks:** FAX: (412)624-1809.

★19207★
University of Pittsburgh - Chemistry Library (Sci-Engr)
200 Alumni Hall   Phone: (412)624-8294
Pittsburgh, PA 15260   Margarete Bower, Libn.
Staff: Prof 1; Other 2. **Subjects:** Chemistry - organic, physical, analytical;
inorganic, chemistry of natural products; spectroscopy. **Holdings:** 28,123
books; 17,000 bound periodical volumes; 145 government documents; 1091
microforms; spectral files and indices. **Subscriptions:** 238 journals and other
serials. **Services:** Interlibrary loan; copying; library open to the public.
Automated Operations: Computerized public access catalog, cataloging,
acquisitions, serials, and circulation. **Computerized Information Services:**
OCLC, DIALOG Information Services, STN International. Performs
searches on fee basis. **Networks/Consortia:** Member of Pittsburgh Regional
Library Center (PRLC), Oakland Library Consortium. **Publications:**
Monthly Acquisitions List. **Remarks:** FAX: (412)624-8296.

★19208★
University of Pittsburgh - Computer Science Library (Comp Sci)
200 Alumni Hall   Phone: (412)624-8294
Pittsburgh, PA 15260   Margarete Bower, Libn.
Founded: 1956. **Staff:** Prof 1; Other 2. **Subjects:** Computer science - theory,
programming languages, operating systems, database theory, graphics,
networking, software engineering, artificial intelligence, computer
management. **Holdings:** 11,582 books; 4500 bound periodical volumes; 6000
technical reports; 98 microforms. **Subscriptions:** 140 journals and other
serials. **Services:** Interlibrary loan; copying; library open to the public.
Automated Operations: Computerized public access catalog, cataloging,
acquisitions, serials, and circulation. **Computerized Information Services:**
OCLC, DIALOG Information Services, STN International. **Networks/
Consortia:** Member of Pittsburgh Regional Library Center (PRLC),
Oakland Library Consortium. **Remarks:** FAX: (412)624-8296.

★19209★
University of Pittsburgh - Darlington Memorial Library (Hist)
Cathedral of Learning   Phone: (412)624-4491
Pittsburgh, PA 15260   Charles E. Aston, Jr., Hd., Spec.Coll.
Founded: 1918. **Staff:** Prof 1; Other 1. **Subjects:** Colonial Americana, pre-
1870 Pennsylvania and Ohio Valley history. **Special Collections:** O'Hara
Darlington Collection (first editions of 19th century English novels).
Holdings: 17,905 books; 1507 bound periodical volumes; 273 bound volumes
of newspapers; 4570 pamphlets; 290 prints; 901 maps; 45 linear feet of
manuscripts. **Services:** Copying; library open to the public for reference use
only. **Computerized Information Services:** OCLC; internal database.
Publications: Guide to Manuscripts Collection; Women in Historical
Perspective: Guide to the Resources in the Darlington Memorial Library.
Remarks: FAX: (412)648-1245.

★19210★
University of Pittsburgh - East Asian Library (Area-Ethnic)
201 Hillman Library   Phone: (412)648-8185
Pittsburgh, PA 15260   Dr. Thomas C. Kuo, Cur.
Founded: 1960. **Staff:** Prof 4; Other 4. **Subjects:** Chinese, Japanese, and
Korean humanities and social sciences. **Special Collections:** Complete Sets
of Ku-chin t'u-shu chi-ch'eng Synthesis of Books and Illustrations of
Ancient and Modern Times (800 volumes of the 1934 photolithographic
edition of the 1728 original collection); Ssu-k'u ch'uan-shu Complete
Library in Four Branches of Literature (10,230 titles of a facsimile
reproduction of the Imperial Palace block print edition of 1782); Shgaku
zasshi, 1889 to present; Rekishi-Gaku Kenkyu, 1928 to present. **Holdings:**

160,286 volumes; 16,837 bound periodical volumes; 1947 microfiche; 4435
reels of microfilm. **Subscriptions:** 1234 journals and other serials. **Services:**
Interlibrary loan; library open to the public with restrictions. **Automated
Operations:** Computerized public access catalog, cataloging, acquisitions,
serials, and circulation. **Networks/Consortia:** Member of Pittsburgh
Regional Library Center (PRLC), Oakland Library Consortium.
Publications: A Selected List of Outstanding New Acquisitions, quarterly.
Special Catalogs: East Asian Periodicals and Serials (1970); Catalog of
Microfilms of the East Asian Library of the University of Pittsburgh (1971);
The Chinese Local History - Descriptive Holding List (1969). **Remarks:**
FAX: (412)648-1245. **Staff:** Agnes Wen, Tech.Serv.Libn.; Lisa Woo,
Chinese Bibliog./Cat.; Sachie Noguchi, Japanese Bibliog./Cat.

★19211★
University of Pittsburgh - Falk Library of the Health Sciences (Med)
Scaife Hall, 2nd Fl.   Phone: (412)648-8824
Pittsburgh, PA 15261   P. Mickelson, Dir.
Founded: 1957. **Staff:** Prof 18; Other 24. **Subjects:** Medicine, biology,
dentistry, nursing, pharmacy, public health, allied health professions.
Special Collections: History of medicine and dental medicine (12,000 items);
history of anesthesia (400 items). **Holdings:** 292,865 volumes. **Subscriptions:**
1761 journals and other serials. **Services:** Interlibrary loan; copying; library
open to the public with restrictions. **Automated Operations:** Computerized
public access catalog, cataloging, acquisitions, serials, and circulation.
Computerized Information Services: MEDLINE, BRS Information
Technologies, DIALOG Information Services. **Networks/Consortia:**
Member of National Network of Libraries of Medicine - Middle Atlantic
Region, Health Sciences Libraries Consortium (HSLC). **Remarks:** FAX:
(412)648-9020. Contains the holdings of the former University of Pittsburgh
- Ciocco Library. **Staff:** Jeremy Shellhase, Assoc.Dir., Res.Mgt.; June
Bandemer, Ref.Libn.; Charles Wessel, Coord., Hosp.Lib.Serv.; Alice Kuller,
Ref.Libn.; Sally Wilson, Ser.Libn.; Jonathon Erlen, Hist.Med.Libn.; Carol
Struble, Hd., Cat.Dept.; David Ginn, Assoc.Dir., Info.Serv.; Jill Foust,
Ref.Libn.; Susan Biery, Ref.Libn.; Katherine Schilling, Ref.Libn.; Caroline
Arms, Hd., Microcomputer & Media Ctr.

★19212★
University of Pittsburgh - Foster Hall Collection (Mus)
Stephen Foster Memorial
Forbes Ave.   Phone: (412)624-4100
Pittsburgh, PA 15260   Dr. Deane L. Root, Cur.
Founded: 1931. **Staff:** Prof 2.5; Other 3. **Subjects:** Life and works of Stephen
Collins Foster; American music history. **Holdings:** 1000 books; 565
periodical titles; 7000 pieces of 19th century sheet music; 2000 20th century
scores and collections for vocal and instrumental ensembles; 2500 magazine
and newspaper articles; 225 music manuscripts; 2000 photographs; 300
broadsides; 1000 78rpm phonograph records; 100 LP phonograph records;
75 cylinders; 60 music-box discs; 19 organ cylinders; 80 cassette tapes; 1080
songbooks; 250 songsters; 110 plays and poems; 10 oil portraits; 35 art
works; 11 statutes; 3000 uncataloged pieces of music; Foster instruments and
artifacts; collection archives. **Subscriptions:** 2 journals and other serials.
Services: Interlibrary loan; copying; collection open to the public by
appointment. **Automated Operations:** Computerized public access catalog
and cataloging. **Computerized Information Services:** OCLC. **Publications:**
The Music of Stephen C. Foster (complete works, 1990); research
monographs; cassette recordings of 19th century American music; out-of-
print publications on Foster; postcards; notecards - all for sale. **Special
Indexes:** Partial index with files for arrangers, broadsides, derivata,
magazines, recordings, pictures, scores, and songbooks (card). **Staff:** Laurie
Sampsel, Cat.Libn.

★19213★
**University of Pittsburgh - Graduate School of Public & International
Affairs/Economics Library** (Soc Sci)
1G12 Forbes Quadrangle   Phone: (412)648-7575
Pittsburgh, PA 15260   F.M. McKenna, Hd.
Founded: 1958. **Staff:** Prof 3; Other 4. **Subjects:** Public administration,
urban affairs, international security, diplomacy and negotiation, economic
and social development, international affairs, regional economics,
econometrics, economic theory, international trade and finance, money and
banking, demography, statistics, comparative systems. **Holdings:** 132,747
books; 4785 bound periodical volumes; 3000 pamphlets; 3500 microforms.
Subscriptions: 1109 journals and other serials. **Services:** Interlibrary loan;
library open to the public for reference use only. **Automated Operations:**
Computerized public access catalog, cataloging, acquisitions, serials, and
circulation. **Computerized Information Services:** DIALOG Information

Services, OCLC, Reuters Information Services (Canada). Performs searches on fee basis. **Networks/Consortia:** Member of Pittsburgh Regional Library Center (PRLC), Oakland Library Consortium. **Publications:** Economic Books: Current Selections, quarterly - available by subscription. **Remarks:** FAX: (412)648-7569. Contains the holdings of the former University of Pittsburgh - Economics/Collection in Regional Economics. **Staff:** Mary Lois Kepes, Libn.; Debora Rougeux, Libn.

★ 19214 ★
University of Pittsburgh - Henry Clay Frick Fine Arts Library (Art)
Pittsburgh, PA 15260   Phone: (412)648-2410
       Ray Anne Lockard, Hd.
Founded: 1927. **Staff:** Prof 1; Other 2.5. **Subjects:** Art of the Western World, with emphasis on Byzantine, early Christian, Medieval, Renaissance, and modern periods; Oriental art; studio arts. **Special Collections:** Medieval illuminated manuscript facsimiles. **Holdings:** 70,963 volumes; 14,070 microforms; 1518 pamphlets; 89 facsimiles and Oriental scrolls. **Subscriptions:** 418 journals and other serials. **Services:** Interlibrary loan; library open to the public for reference use only. **Automated Operations:** Computerized public access catalog, cataloging, and acquisitions. **Computerized Information Services:** DIALOG Information Services. **Networks/Consortia:** Member of Pittsburgh Regional Library Center (PRLC), Oakland Library Consortium. **Special Catalogs:** Exhibitions Catalog File; Art Sales Catalog File. **Remarks:** FAX: (412)648-7568.

★ 19215 ★
University of Pittsburgh - Human Relations Area Files (Soc Sci)
233 Hillman Library   Phone: (412)648-7722
Pittsburgh, PA 15260   Karen Meharra, Hd., Microforms/Current Per.
Staff: 3. **Subjects:** Anthropology and related behavioral sciences. **Holdings:** 23,036 microfiche. **Services:** Files open to the public for reference use only. **Computerized Information Services:** DIALOG Information Services, BRS Information Technologies; internal database. **Remarks:** FAX: (412)648-1245.

★ 19216 ★
University of Pittsburgh - Joseph M. Katz Graduate School of Business - Library (Bus-Fin)
130 Mervis Hall   Phone: (412)648-1669
Pittsburgh, PA 15260   Dr. Susan Neuman, Hd.
Founded: 1961. **Staff:** Prof 2; Other 4. **Subjects:** Econometrics, economics, business, management, accounting, industrial labor relations, behavioral science in business, business and society, marketing, finance. **Holdings:** 44,633 books; 4000 bound periodical volumes; 1823 reels of microfilm; 120,684 microfiche; annual reports of companies listed on New York and American Stock Exchanges on microfiche; 12 VF drawers of pamphlets. **Subscriptions:** 899 journals and other serials. **Services:** Interlibrary loan; copying; library open to the public for reference use only. **Automated Operations:** Computerized public access catalog, cataloging, acquisitions, serials, and circulation. **Computerized Information Services:** DIALOG Information Services, BRS Information Technologies, Reuters, VU/TEXT Information Services, Dow Jones News/Retrieval, ABI/INFORM, COMPACT DISCLOSURE. **Networks/Consortia:** Member of Pittsburgh Regional Library Center (PRLC), Oakland Library Consortium. **Publications:** Bimonthly Acquisitions List. **Remarks:** FAX: (412)648-1586. **Staff:** Dennis Smith, Ref.Libn.

★ 19217 ★
University of Pittsburgh - Latin American Collection (Area-Ethnic)
171 Hillman Library   Phone: (412)648-7734
Pittsburgh, PA 15260   Eduardo Lozano, Libn., Latin Amer.Stud.
Founded: 1967. **Staff:** Prof 4; Other 1.5. **Subjects:** Latin America - humanities, social sciences. **Special Collections:** Cuban Collection (16,000 volumes); Bolivian Collection (13,150 volumes; 1150 Bolivian political pamphlets); Human Relations Area File (1325 sources). **Holdings:** 287,500 books; 54,000 bound periodical volumes; 62,320 microforms; 1790 maps; 725 dissertations; 90 videocassettes and films; 200 audiotapes and records. **Subscriptions:** 7330 journals and other serials; 24 newspapers. **Services:** Interlibrary loan; copying; collection open to the public. **Automated Operations:** Computerized public access catalog, cataloging, acquisitions, serials, and circulation. **Computerized Information Services:** DIALOG Information Services, BRS Information Technologies, NEXIS, VU/TEXT Information Services, OCLC, INFO SOUTH, HAPI. Performs searches on fee basis. Contact Person: Fern Brody, 624-4438. **Networks/Consortia:** Member of Pittsburgh Regional Library Center (PRLC), Oakland Library Consortium. **Publications:** Cuban Periodicals in the University of Pittsburgh Libraries, 5th edition, 1991. **Special Catalogs:** Catalog of Latin American Periodicals (indexed by country and subject); Catalog of the Bolivian Collection (author and subject indexes). **Remarks:** FAX: (412)648-1245. Alternate telephone number(s): 648-7735.

★ 19218 ★
University of Pittsburgh - Mathematics Library (Sci-Engr)
430 Thackeray Hall   Phone: (412)624-8205
Pittsburgh, PA 15260   Sandra S. Kerbel, Hd.
Founded: 1963. **Staff:** Prof 1. **Subjects:** Mathematics - pure, applied, numerical; statistics. **Holdings:** 20,500 volumes; 83 reels of microfilm; 868 microfiche. **Subscriptions:** 247 journals. **Services:** Interlibrary loan; copying; library open to the public. **Automated Operations:** Computerized public access catalog, cataloging, and acquisitions. **Computerized Information Services:** DIALOG Information Services. **Networks/Consortia:** Member of Pittsburgh Regional Library Center (PRLC), Center for Research Libraries (CRL), Oakland Library Consortium. **Remarks:** FAX: (412)624-8103.

★ 19219 ★
University of Pittsburgh - NASA Industrial Applications Center (NIAC) (Sci-Engr, Info Sci, Comp Sci)
823 William Pitt Union   Phone: (412)648-7000
Pittsburgh, PA 15260   Lani F. Hummel, Dir.
Founded: 1963. **Staff:** Prof 15; Other 2. **Subjects:** Science and technology, business and marketing, computer and information sciences. **Holdings:** 1 million microfiche. **Services:** Center provides a wide range of technology management services including information retrieval; technical analyses and assessments; market intelligence; product enhancement; applications development; database system development; database creation; special multidisciplinary studies and international projects; document procurement. **Computerized Information Services:** DIALOG Information Services, PFDS Online, NASA/RECON; internal databases. **Publications:** United States Political Science Documents (USPSD) annual reference guide (hardcopy and online). **Remarks:** FAX: (412)648-7003. **Staff:** Jan P. Miller, Dir., Sys. & Oper.; John G. Hennon, Mgr., Info.Anl.

★ 19220 ★
University of Pittsburgh - Physics Library (Sci-Engr)
208 Engineering Hall   Phone: (412)624-8770
Pittsburgh, PA 15260   Sandra S. Kerbel, Interim Hd.
Founded: 1953. **Staff:** Prof 1; Other 1. **Subjects:** Physics - nuclear, high energy, atomic, molecular, solid state, quantum optics, atmospheric, low temperature; relativity; astrophysics; earth and planetary sciences. **Holdings:** 35,323 books; 17,000 bound periodical volumes; 1498 microforms. **Subscriptions:** 280 journals and other serials. **Services:** Interlibrary loan; copying; library open to the public. **Automated Operations:** Computerized public access catalog, cataloging, acquisitions, serials, and circulation. **Computerized Information Services:** OCLC, DIALOG Information Services, STN International; BITNET (electronic mail service). Performs searches on fee basis. **Networks/Consortia:** Member of Pittsburgh Regional Library Center (PRLC), Oakland Library Consortium. **Publications:** Monthly Acquisitions List. **Remarks:** FAX: (412)624-3239. Electronic mail address(es): KERBEL@PITUMS (BITNET).

★ 19221 ★
University of Pittsburgh - Presbyterian-University Hospital - Medical Staff Library (Med)
DeSoto at O'Hara Sts.   Phone: (412)647-3287
Pittsburgh, PA 15213   Charles B. Wessel, Coord., Hosp.Lib.Serv.
Founded: 1943. **Staff:** Prof 2; Other 2. **Subjects:** Clinical medicine, surgery. **Holdings:** 1500 books; 2875 bound periodical volumes; 639 Audio-Digest tapes. **Subscriptions:** 120 journals and other serials. **Services:** Interlibrary loan; copying; SDI; library open to the public with restrictions. **Computerized Information Services:** DIALOG Information Services, BRS Information Technologies, MEDLARS. Performs searches on fee basis. **Remarks:** FAX: (412)648-9020. **Staff:** Alice B. Kuller, Clin.Libn.

★ 19222 ★
University of Pittsburgh - Pymatuning Laboratory of Ecology - Tryon Library (Env-Cons)
R.R. 1, Box 7   Phone: (814)683-5813
Linesville, PA 16424   Dolores E. Smith, Sec./Libn.
Founded: 1949. **Staff:** 1. **Subjects:** Ecology, field biology, limnology, animal behavior. **Holdings:** 2100 books; 200 bound periodical volumes. **Subscriptions:** 11 journals and other serials. **Services:** Copying; library open to the public with restrictions. **Publications:** Special publications of Pymatuning Laboratory, irregular. **Remarks:** FAX: (814)683-2302.

★ 19223 ★
University of Pittsburgh - School of Library & Information Science - Library (Info Sci)
135 N. Bellefield Ave.   Phone: (412)624-4710
Pittsburgh, PA 15260   Elizabeth T. Mahoney, Hd.
Founded: 1966. **Staff:** Prof 2; Other 3. **Subjects:** Library science, information science, telecommunications, children's literature. **Special Collections:** Historical children's literature; Clifton Fadiman Collection of 20th Century Children's Literature; children's television archives, including archives of Mr. Roger's Neighborhood. **Holdings:** 80,608 books; 4618 microforms; 8.5 linear feet of manuscripts; 838 videotaped programs. **Subscriptions:** 1375 journals and other serials. **Services:** Interlibrary loan; copying; library open to the public with restrictions. **Automated Operations:** Computerized public access catalog, cataloging, and acquisitions. **Computerized Information Services:** DIALOG Information Services, BRS Information Technologies, OCLC EPIC; CD-ROMs; ALANET (electronic mail service). **Networks/Consortia:** Member of Pittsburgh Regional Library Center (PRLC), Oakland Library Consortium. **Remarks:** FAX: (412)624-4062. **Staff:** Thomas B. Wall, Pub.Serv.

★ 19224 ★
University of Pittsburgh - School of Social Work - Buhl Library (Soc Sci)
Hillman Library, First Fl.   Phone: (412)648-7716
Pittsburgh, PA 15260   Cathy Whittaker, Libn.
Founded: 1938. **Staff:** Prof 1. **Subjects:** Social work, social policy research, community studies, family interaction, child welfare, gerontology, juvenile justice. **Special Collections:** Classified Abstract Archive of Alcohol Literature (19,000 cards). **Holdings:** 17,514 volumes; 22 VF drawers. **Subscriptions:** 117 journals and other serials. **Services:** Interlibrary loan; library open to the public. **Automated Operations:** Computerized public access catalog, cataloging, acquisitions, serials, and circulation. **Computerized Information Services:** DIALOG Information Services, BRS Information Technologies, OCLC. **Networks/Consortia:** Member of Pittsburgh Regional Library Center (PRLC), Oakland Library Consortium. **Remarks:** FAX: (412)648-1245.

★ 19225 ★
University of Pittsburgh - Special Collections Department (Rare Book, Hum)
363 Hillman Library   Phone: (412)648-8190
Pittsburgh, PA 15260   Charles E. Aston, Jr., Hd.
Founded: 1966. **Staff:** Prof 2; Other 3. **Subjects:** Incunabula, early printed books, little presses, English and American first editions, fine presses and woodcut illustrations, 20th century poetry, early American textbooks, 20th century Spanish literature, theater programs and playbills, detective and mystery stories, modern dance, popular culture, science fiction, history and philosophy of science. **Special Collections:** Hervey Allen Collection; Mary Roberts Rinehart Collection; Ramon Gomez de la Serna Collection; Curtis Theater Collection; Nietz Old Textbook Collection; Bernard S. Horne Memorial-Izaak Walton Compleat Angler Collection; Anna Pavlowa-Karl G. Heinrich Collection; Archive of Popular Culture; Archives of Scientific Philosophy (including: Rudolf Carnap Collection, Hans Reichenbach papers, Frank P. Ramsey papers); Walter and Martha Leuba Collection; Bollingen Collection; Cooperative Movement Collection; Tomas G. Masaryk papers; Lawrence Lee Collection. **Holdings:** 55,119 volumes; 662 feet of manuscripts and archives; 1561 broadsides and dealer catalogs; 860 photographs; 351 posters; 506,189 theater programs; 52,750 theater history clippings; 442 sheet music scores; 2670 pamphlets; 1943 microforms; 12,110 prints; 355 slides; 34 recordings; 4937 acting editions and scripts. **Subscriptions:** 225 journals and other serials; 15 newspapers. **Services:** Copying; department open to the public for reference use only. **Computerized Information Services:** OCLC; internal database. **Special Catalogs:** Card files on printers, book designers, typography, paper, book illustration, and collection inventories. **Remarks:** FAX: (412)648-1245. **Staff:** W. Gerald Heverly, Libn. for Archv. of Sci. Philosophy & Gen.Ms.Coll.

★ 19226 ★
University of Pittsburgh - Theodore M. Finney Music Library (Mus)
Music Bldg.   Phone: (412)624-4130
Pittsburgh, PA 15260   Dr. Norris L. Stephens, Libn.
Founded: 1966. **Staff:** Prof 1; Other 2. **Subjects:** Music. **Special Collections:** Pre-1800 music and music literature (1000 items); Fidelis Zitterbart (1000 manuscripts); Adolph Foerster (290 manuscripts and printed music); Ethelbert Nevin (100 manuscripts and printed music); William Steinberg

(800 items). **Holdings:** 42,538 books and scores; 1900 bound periodical volumes; 1404 microforms; 19,000 pieces of sheet music; 100 photographs and prints; 18,000 sound recordings; 754 slides; 6 linear feet of manuscripts and archives. **Subscriptions:** 144 journals and other serials. **Services:** Interlibrary loan; copying; library open to the public. **Automated Operations:** Computerized cataloging, acquisitions, and serials. **Computerized Information Services:** DIALOG Information Services, BRS Information Technologies, OCLC. Performs searches on fee basis. **Networks/Consortia:** Member of Pittsburgh Regional Library Center (PRLC), Oakland Library Consortium. **Remarks:** FAX: (412)624-4180.

★ 19227 ★
University of Pittsburgh - UE (United Electrical Radio and Machine Workers of America) Archives (Bus-Fin)
363 Hillman Library   Phone: (412)648-7099
Pittsburgh, PA 15260   Dr. David L. Rosenberg, UE
                                               Archv., Cur., Labor Coll.
Founded: 1976. **Staff:** Prof 1. **Subjects:** Industrial unionism, labor and laboring classes, labor disputes, regional deindustrialization. **Special Collections:** Records of the National Office of the UE (1936 to present), UE districts, UE locals; records of assorted other Western Pennsylvania labor organizations including Service Employees, Teachers, Brewers, Shipbuilders, Tile Layers, and Communications Workers; company personnel records (USX Duquesne Works, LTV, A.M. Byers). **Holdings:** 2000 linear feet of records, including correspondence, organizers' reports, memoranda, and conference board files; 2500 photographs; 55 audiocassettes; 100 videotapes. **Services:** Most recent 25 years of records closed to public; limited access to older material. **Remarks:** Alternate telephone number(s): 648-7977. FAX: (412)648-1245.

★ 19228 ★
University of Pittsburgh - University Center for Instructional Resources (Aud-Vis)
A114 LIS Bldg.   Phone: (412)648-7240
Pittsburgh, PA 15260   Dr. J. Fred Gage, Dir.
Founded: 1968. **Staff:** Prof 16; Other 18. **Subjects:** Education, psychology, anthropology, history, life sciences, sociology, women's studies, black studies, film studies, administration of justice, labor history. **Special Collections:** Faces of Change (25 film series produced by American Universities' field staff; anthropological films on five countries); Maurice Falk Medical Fund (20 films); Ascent of Man series; Civilisation series; Europe the Mighty Continent series; World at War series; collections of films on aging, labor history, and film studies. **Holdings:** 1343 16mm films; reference books on nonprint media; 79 games; 39 kits; 20 transparency sets; 58 slide sets; 147 filmstrips; 1387 video recordings; 883 audio recordings; 27 manipulatives; 159 videodiscs. **Subscriptions:** 30 journals and other serials. **Services:** Free loan for university classroom use; video duplication; center open to the public with restrictions. **Automated Operations:** Computerized cataloging. **Computerized Information Services:** OCLC. **Networks/Consortia:** Member of Consortium of College and University Media Centers (CCUMC), American Film & Video Association. **Special Catalogs:** University of Pittsburgh Film Catalog, 1978, supplement, 1979, 1981, 1982, 1984; various mediagraphies; video recording catalog, January 1985. **Remarks:** FAX: (412)648-8812.

★ 19229 ★
University of Pittsburgh - Western Psychiatric Institute and Clinic - Library (Med)
3811 O'Hara St.   Phone: (412)624-2378
Pittsburgh, PA 15213   Barbara A. Epstein, Dir.
Founded: 1942. **Staff:** Prof 5; Other 6. **Subjects:** Psychiatry, behavioral science, mental health. **Holdings:** 61,170 volumes; 2400 audio- and videotapes. **Subscriptions:** 548 journals and other serials. **Services:** Interlibrary loan; copying; SDI; library open to the public for reference use only; borrowers must be affiliated with a university hospital or mental health center. **Automated Operations:** Computerized public access catalog, cataloging, serials, circulation and video booking. **Computerized Information Services:** MEDLINE, DIALOG Information Services, BRS Information Technologies, OCLC; CD-ROMs. Performs searches on fee basis. Contact Person: Donna Strawbridge, Ref.Libn. **Networks/Consortia:** Member of Health Sciences Libraries Consortium (HSLC), Pittsburgh Regional Library Center (PRLC), National Network of Libraries of Medicine - Middle Atlantic Region. **Publications:** Booklist of New Books Cataloged - general distribution; Current Awareness Series - by subscription. **Special Catalogs:** Video Catalog. **Remarks:** FAX: (412)624-6042. **Staff:** Patricia Reavis, AV & Ref.Libn.; Meliza Jackson, Patients' Libn.; Ester Saghafi, Ref./Cat.Libn.; Daniel Kudelka, Circ./ILL.

University of Poona - Gokhale Institute of Politics and Economics
See: Gokhale Institute of Politics and Economics (6531)

★ 19230 ★
University of Portland - Wilson W. Clark Memorial Library - Special Collections (Hist, Agri)
5000 N. Willamette Blvd.
Box 83017   Phone: (503)283-7111
Portland, OR 97283-0017   Rev. Joseph P. Browne, C.S.C., Dir.
Founded: 1901. **Staff:** Prof 6; Other 9. **Special Collections:** Salvador J. Macias Collection of Spanish Literature (750 volumes); David W. Hazen Collection in American History (4000 volumes); Daniel Buckley Forestry Collection (500 volumes); Anthony Juliano Drama Collection (800 volumes). **Holdings:** 310,000 volumes; 7000 government documents. **Subscriptions:** 1500 journals and other serials; 25 newspapers. **Services:** Interlibrary loan; copying; collections open to the public for reference use only. **Automated Operations:** Computerized cataloging, acquisitions, and serials. **Computerized Information Services:** DIALOG Information Services, BRS Information Technologies, OCLC; CD-ROMs (ERIC, CINAHL, PsycLIT, Compact Disclosure, ABI/INFORM); BITNET (electronic mail service). **Networks/Consortia:** Member of Northwest Association of Private Colleges & Universities (NAPCU). **Publications:** Philobiblon, monthly - for internal distribution only. **Special Indexes:** KWOC title index to government documents collection, quarterly. **Remarks:** FAX: (503)283-7491. Electronic mail address(es): BROWNE@UDFPORT (BITNET). **Staff:** Pam Horan, Govt.Docs.Libn.; L. Nadene Miller, Ref.Libn.; Susan Hinken, Tech.Serv.Libn.; Margaret Kleszynski, Spec.Serv.Libn.; Roxanne Dimyan, Asst.Ref.Libn.

★ 19231 ★
University Presbyterian Church - Ann Inglett Library (Rel-Phil)
1127 8th St.   Phone: (205)758-5422
Tuscaloosa, AL 35401   Margaret Memory, Libn.
Remarks: No further information was supplied by respondent.

★ 19232 ★
University of Prince Edward Island - Robertson Library, Archives and Special Collections (Area-Ethnic)
Charlottetown, PE, Canada C1A 4P3   Phone: (902)566-0536
                                              C.M. Crockett, Chf.Libn.
Founded: 1975. **Staff:** Prof 9; Other 19. **Special Collections:** Prince Edward Island collection. **Holdings:** 8400 books; 140 bound periodical volumes; clippings; pamphlets; government documents; microforms. **Subscriptions:** 20 journals and other serials; 6 newspapers. **Services:** Library open to the public with restrictions. **Computerized Information Services:** CAN/OLE, MEDLARS, DIALOG Information Services; Envoy 100 (electronic mail service). **Special Catalogs:** U.P.E.I. Archives Card Catalogue; P.E.I. Collection Card Catalogue. **Remarks:** Alternate telephone number(s): (902)566-0696. FAX: (902)566-0420. **Staff:** F.L. Pigot, Ref.Libn.

★ 19233 ★
University Publications of America - Library (Publ)
4520 East-West Hwy., Suite 800   Phone: (301)657-3200
Bethesda, MD 20814-3389   Robert E. Lester, Media Spec./Res.Coord.
Staff: 1. **Subjects:** History - U.S. diplomatic, social, economic, political, Anglo-American, science, legal, military intelligence, World War II, labor. **Holdings:** 450 books; 150,000 reels of microfilm. **Services:** Library not open to the public. **Remarks:** Subsidiary of Congressional Information Service, Inc.

★ 19234 ★
University of Puerto Rico - Agricultural Experiment Station - Library (Agri, Biol Sci)
P.O. Box 21630   Phone: (809)767-9705
Rio Piedras, PR 00928   Joan P. Hayes, Libn.
Founded: 1915. **Staff:** Prof 1; Other 2. **Subjects:** Agriculture, biology, botany, animal production, chemistry, food technology, rum research. **Holdings:** 33,124 volumes; 273,413 pamphlets, technical reports, annual reports. **Subscriptions:** 895 journals and other serials. **Services:** Interlibrary loan; copying; library open to the public for reference use only. **Publications:** Book List, irregular; Monthly Library List - to staff members and government libraries. **Special Indexes:** Index to the Journal of Agriculture of the University of Puerto Rico (book and card); indexes to Revista de Agricultura de Puerto Rico and Caribbean Journal of Science (both on cards).

★ 19235 ★
University of Puerto Rico - Humacao University College - Library (Sci-Engr, Hum)
CUH-Sta.   Phone: (809)850-9305
Humacao, PR 00792   Ramon A. Budet, Dir.
Founded: 1962. **Staff:** Prof 12; Other 16. **Subjects:** Natural sciences, applied sciences, electronics, social sciences, social welfare, special education. **Special Collections:** Puerto Rican collection (4227 books; 121 periodicals). **Holdings:** 88,906 volumes; 3257 bound periodical volumes; 6108 unbound periodicals; 752 phonograph records; 1495 reels of microfilm; 68 cassettes; 4375 documents; 128 maps. **Subscriptions:** 700 journals and other serials; 21 newspapers. **Services:** Interlibrary loan; copying; library open to the public. **Automated Operations:** NOTIS. **Computerized Information Services:** DIALOG Information Services, WILSONLINE, ERIC, HAPI; InterNet (electronic mail service). **Publications:** List of New Acquisitions; Desde la Biblioteca, irregular; Mundo Bibliografico, quarterly. **Remarks:** FAX: (809)852-4638. Electronic mail address(es): R–Budet@CUHAD.UPR.CLU.EDU (InterNet). **Staff:** Angela M. Ruiz, Pub.Serv.Libn.; Lilia E. Mendez, Automation Libn.; Ana L. Mendez, Cat.Libn.; Maria I. Hernandez, Acq.Libn.

★ 19236 ★
University of Puerto Rico - Law Library (Law)
Box L   Phone: (809)763-7199
San Juan, PR 00931   P. Michael Whipple, Law Libn.
Founded: 1903. **Staff:** Prof 10; Other 32. **Subjects:** Law - common, civil, international. **Special Collections:** Rare Puerto Rican Law Books Collection. **Holdings:** 195,807 books; bound periodical volumes. **Subscriptions:** 4313 journals and other serials; 5 newspapers. **Services:** Interlibrary loan; copying; library open to the public. **Computerized Information Services:** LEXIS, WESTLAW, InfoTrac, Compuclerk; CD-ROM (Compuley). **Remarks:** FAX: (809)764-2660. **Staff:** Marta E. Perez, Hd., Circ. & Reserve; Ivonne Quintero, Cat.; Josefina Bulerin, Docs. & Ser.Dept.; Carmen M. Melendez, Ref.; Miguel A. Rivera, Ref.; Orietta Ayala, Hd., Acq.Dept.; Esther Villarino, Cat.; Maria M. Otero, Hd., Ref.Dept.; Pedro Padilla, Ref.

★ 19237 ★
University of Puerto Rico - Library System - Arts Collection (Art)
Box 23302, UPR Sta.   Phone: (809)764-0000
Rio Piedras, PR 00931-3302   Oscar Mestey, Hd.
Founded: 1985. **Staff:** 4. **Subjects:** Fine arts, dance. **Special Collections:** Graphic materials collection (1374 items); art exhibition catalogs collection (4419 items); dance archive. **Holdings:** 15,749 books; 195 slides; 490 vertical file items. **Services:** Copying; library open to the public with restrictions. **Automated Operations:** Computerized cataloging and acquisitions (NOTIS). **Computerized Information Services:** DIALOG Information Services. **Publications:** Listado anotado de recursos de la Coleccion de las Artes; indice de las artes, both irregular - both free upon request. **Special Catalogs:** Graphic materials (card); art exhibitions catalogs (card). **Remarks:** FAX: (809)763-5685. Telex: 385 9172.

★ 19238 ★
University of Puerto Rico - Library System - Business Administration Library (Bus-Fin)
Box 23302, UPR Sta.   Phone: (809)764-0000
Rio Piedras, PR 00931-3302   Regina Favale de Marin, Hd.Libn.
Founded: 1983. **Staff:** Prof 2; Other 7. **Subjects:** Management, marketing, accounting, finance, computer sciences, statistics. **Holdings:** 18,643 books; 15,303 bound periodical volumes; 6404 readings; 228 dissertations; 150 slides; 639 microfiches; 5813 microfilms; 49 cassette tapes; 4 filmstrips; 35 films; 28 videocassettes. **Subscriptions:** 559 journals and other serials. **Services:** Interlibrary loan; copying; library open to the public with restrictions. **Automated Operations:** Computerized cataloging and acquisitions (NOTIS). **Computerized Information Services:** DIALOG Information Services. **Remarks:** FAX: (809)763-5685. Telex: 385 9172. **Staff:** Carmen Adria Emeric, Libn.

★ 19239 ★
University of Puerto Rico - Library System - Caribbean and Latin American Studies Collection (Area-Ethnic)
Box 21927 UPR Sta.   Phone: (809)764-0000
Rio Piedras, PR 00931-3302   Almaluces Figueroa, Hd.Libn.
Founded: 1946. **Staff:** Prof 2; Other 3. **Subjects:** The Caribbean - economics, statistics, trade, tourism, education, political science, demography. **Special**

Collections: Rare books on the Caribbean. Holdings: 111,506 books; 22,960 bound periodical volumes; 1443 maps; 38,160 microfiche; 7808 reels of microfilm; 12 VF drawers of studies; 20 VF drawers of minutes of the Caribbean Organization and Caribbean Commission Meetings; 5093 dissertations on microfiche; pamphlets; official documents; UNESCO publications. Subscriptions: 67 journals and other serials. Services: Interlibrary loan; copying; library open to the public with restrictions. Automated Operations: Computerized acquisitions and cataloging. Computerized Information Services: DIALOG Information Services. Publications: ACURIL Newsletter, irregular - for members. Remarks: Telex: 385 9172. Staff: Carmen Romero, Libn.

★19240★
University of Puerto Rico - Library System - Gerardo Selles Sola
　Library (Educ)
Box 23302, UPR Sta.　　　　　　　Phone: (809)764-0000
Rio Piedras, PR 00931-3302　　Alba Sanchez de Estebanez, Hd.Libn.
Founded: 1946. Staff: Prof 2; Other 4. Subjects: Education, psychology, educational philosophy, educational sociology, curriculum, counseling and guidance. Special Collections: Public school textbook collection, 1900 to present (2488 textbooks). Holdings: 24,654 books; 3679 bound periodical volumes; 425 pictures; 2498 readings; 378 pamphlets; 616 slides; 27 microfiche; 90 microfilms; 30 cassettes; 23 filmstrips; 28 films; 47 video cassettes; 28 VF drawers of clippings; 200 unbound reports. Subscriptions: 127 journals and other serials. Services: Interlibrary loan; copying; collection open to the public for reference use only. Automated Operations: Computerized cataloging and acquisitions (NOTIS). Computerized Information Services: DIALOG Information Services. Remarks: FAX: (809)763-5685. Telex: 385 9172.

★19241★
University of Puerto Rico - Library System - Historical Research Center
　(Hist)
Box 22802, UPR Sta.　　　　　　　Phone: (809)764-0000
Rio Piedras, PR 00931　　Maria Dolores Luque de Sanchez, Dir.
Staff: Prof 3; Other 5. Subjects: Puerto Rico, the Caribbean, Latin America. Special Collections: Personal documents. Holdings: 3837 books; 4862 bound periodical volumes; 76 theses; 7122 reprints; 6472 translations; 14,210 reels of microfilm; 11,563 microfiche. Services: Center open to the public. Publications: Boletin del Centro de Investigaciones Historicas, annual - by subscription; Los primeros pasos: Una bibliografia para empezara investigar la historia de Puerto Rico (book). Special Indexes: Guia descriptiva de los fondos existentes en el Centro de Investigaciones Historicas (pamphlet). Remarks: FAX: (809)763-5899. Also Known As: Centro de Investigaciones Historicas (CIH). Staff: Inette Perez Vega, Assoc.Res.; Jose Cruz Arrigoilia, Asst.Res.; Nelly Voyquez, Asst.Res.; Margarita Flores, Asst.Res.

★19242★
University of Puerto Rico - Library System - Josefina de Toro Fulladosa
　Collection (Hum)
Box 23302, UPR Sta.　　　　　　　Phone: (809)764-0000
Rio Piedras, PR 00931-3302　　Natividad Torres, Hd.Libn.
Founded: 1985. Staff: Prof 1; Other 1. Subjects: History (Americana), literature, religion. Special Collections: Rare books collection (9360 items); Genaro Cautino Collection; Nemours Collection (Haiti). Holdings: 7595 books; 987 manuscripts; 16 photographs; 72 engravings; 648 documents; 39 maps. Services: Library open to the public with restrictions. Automated Operations: Computerized cataloging and acquisitions (NOTIS). Computerized Information Services: DIALOG Information Services. Remarks: FAX: (809)763-5685. Telex: 385 9172.

★19243★
University of Puerto Rico - Library System - Library and Information
　Science Library (Info Sci)
Box 23302, UPR Sta.　　　　　　　Phone: (809)764-0000
Rio Piedras, PR 00931-3302　　Vilma Rivera de Bayron, Hd.Libn.
Founded: 1969. Staff: Prof 1; Other 3. Subjects: Library science, information science. Special Collections: Juvenile collection (3768 items). Holdings: 22,449 books; 5377 bound periodical volumes; 227 catalogs; 1144 pamphlets; 26 microfiche; 177 microfilms; 42 microcards; 261 posters; 78 transparencies; 195 slides; 66 cassette tapes; 19 tapes and records; 8 filmstrips; 6 films; 60 videocassettes. Subscriptions: 1340 journals and other serials. Services: Interlibrary loan; copying; library open to the public with restrictions. Automated Operations: Computerized cataloging and acquisitions (NOTIS). Computerized Information Services: DIALOG

Information Services, WILSONLINE, ERIC, Compuclerk. Publications: Egebiana, irregular; Servicio de Alerta, irregular - both by subscrpition; BCBI Inform; bibliographies by subject. Special Indexes: Index to Boletin de la Sociedad de Bibliotecarios de Puerto Rico (card); subject index to newspapers and journal articles on Puerto Rican librarianship. Remarks: FAX: (809)764-2890. Telex: 385 9172.

★19244★
University of Puerto Rico - Library System - Library Services for the
　Physically Handicapped (Educ)
Box 23302, UPR Sta.　　　　　　　Phone: (809)764-0000
Rio Piedras, PR 00931-3302　　Ludim Diaz, Hd.Libn.
Founded: 1971. Staff: 2. Subjects: Blind - education, printing, writing systems, rehabilitation; literature; history; languages. Special Collections: Braille collection (670 volumes); large type collection (139 volumes); audiovisual kits (788 items); large type and relief maps (69 titles). Holdings: 471 books; 1294 unbound periodicals; 582 maps; 572 cassette tapes; 41 open reel tapes; 2739 records. Subscriptions: 17 journals and other serials. Services: Interlibrary loan; copying; library open to the public for reference use only. Automated Operations: Computerized cataloging and acquisitions (NOTIS). Computerized Information Services: DIALOG Information Services. Networks/Consortia: Member of National Library Service for the Blind & Physically Handicapped (NLS). Special Catalogs: Holdings transcribed in Braille (card). Special Indexes: Vertical file subject index of blind and physically handicapped materials. Remarks: FAX: (809)763-5685. Telex: 385 9172.

★19245★
University of Puerto Rico - Library System - Monserrate Santana de
　Pales Library (Soc Sci, Educ)
Box 23302, UPR Sta.　　　　　　　Phone: (809)764-0000
Rio Piedras, PR 00931-3302　　Lillian Oliveras, Hd.Libn.
Founded: 1972. Staff: Prof 2; Other 3. Subjects: Social work, counseling, rehabilitation, child abuse, family relations, social services, psychopathology, medical social work. Holdings: 10,602 books; 6235 bound periodical volumes; 4053 readings; 477 documents; 1924 pamphlets; 417 dissertations; 44 microfilms; 5 filmstrips; 14 films; 2 video cassettes. Subscriptions: 93 journals and other serials. Services: Interlibrary loan; copying; library open to the public with restrictions. Automated Operations: Computerized cataloging and acquisitions (NOTIS). Computerized Information Services: DIALOG Information Services. Publications: Bibliographies; manuals; new acquisitions; journal titles list. Special Indexes: Journals' articles index; newspapers articles index (social work, counseling, and rehabilitation; both on card). Remarks: FAX: (809)763-5685. Telex: 385 9172. Staff: Magdalena Arce, Libn.

★19246★
University of Puerto Rico - Library System - Music Library (Mus)
Box 23302, UPR Sta.　　　　　　　Phone: (809)764-0000
Rio Piedras, PR 00931-3302　　Aurelio Huertas, Hd.Libn.
Founded: 1953. Staff: Prof 1; Other 4. Subjects: Music. Holdings: 9740 books; 10,223 bound periodical volumes; 10,080 scores; 458 microfiche; 940 microfilms; 129 microcards; 824 cassette tapes; 321 open reel tapes; 24,741 records; 45 videocassettes; 423 compact discs. Subscriptions: 100 journals and other serials. Services: Interlibrary loan; copying; library open to the public with restrictions. Automated Operations: Computerized cataloging and acquisitions (NOTIS). Computerized Information Services: DIALOG Information Services. Remarks: FAX: (809)763-5685. Telex: 385 9172.

★19247★
University of Puerto Rico - Library System - Natural Sciences Library
　(Sci-Engr)
Box 22446, UPR Sta.　　　　　　　Phone: (809)764-0000
Rio Piedras, PR 00931-2446　　Evangelina Perez, Hd.Libn.
Founded: 1954. Staff: Prof 2; Other 6. Subjects: Pure sciences, applied sciences, mathematics, chemistry, physics, geology, astronomy, botany, zoology, biology, environmental sciences. Holdings: 42,319 books; 62,000 bound periodical volumes; 800 readings; 254 pamphlets; 41 dissertations; 503 microfiche; 1583 micrfilms; 28,320 microcards; 155 filmstrips; 3992 pictures and photographs; 207 films; 4 videocassettes. Subscriptions: 1081 journals and other serials. Services: Interlibrary loan; copying; library open to the public with restrictions. Automated Operations: Computerized public access catalog, cataloging, and acquisitions. Computerized Information Services: DIALOG Information Services, MEDLINE; BITNET, InterNet (electronic mail services). Publications: Biblionotas, irregular - free upon request. Remarks: FAX: (809)764-2890. Telex: 385 9172. Staff: Josefina Mir.

★ 19248 ★

University of Puerto Rico - Library System - Planning Library (Plan)
Box 23302, UPR Sta.   Phone: (809)764-0000
Rio Piedras, PR 00931-3302   Carmen Orlandi, Hd.Libn.
Founded: 1965. **Staff:** Prof 1; Other 3. **Subjects:** Planning - urban, regional, economic, social, environmental; agriculture. **Special Collections:** Maps and plans. **Holdings:** 16,208 books; 4264 bound periodical volumes; 10,122 readings; 3149 government documents; 579 pamphlets; 508 maps; 140 slides; 113 microfiche; 45 microfilms. **Subscriptions:** 327 journals and other serials. **Services:** Interlibrary loan; copying; library open to the public with restrictions. **Automated Operations:** Computerized cataloging and acquisitions (NOTIS). **Computerized Information Services:** DIALOG Information Services. **Special Indexes:** Revista Interamericana de Planificacion Index (card); Plerus Index (card). **Remarks:** FAX: (809)763-5685. Telex: 385 9172.

★ 19249 ★

University of Puerto Rico - Library System - Public Administration Library (Bus-Fin, Soc Sci)
Box 21839, UPR Sta.   Phone: (809)764-0000
Rio Piedras, PR 00931-3302   Aracelis Sosa, Hd.Libn.
Founded: 1948. **Staff:** 5. **Subjects:** Public administration, public policy, administrative law, personnel administration, labor legislation, organization theory. **Holdings:** 15,331 books; 2761 bound periodical volumes; 4450 readings; 317 documents; 15,930 pamphlets; 1360 student reports; 574 microfiche; 462 microfilms. **Subscriptions:** 72 journals and other serials. **Services:** Interlibrary loan; copying; library open to the public with restrictions. **Automated Operations:** Computerized cataloging and acquisitions (NOTIS). **Computerized Information Services:** DIALOG Information Services. **Special Indexes:** Index to Revista de Administracion Publica UPR, 1964 to present (card); Index to Dissertations (Theses and Seminars). **Remarks:** FAX: (809)763-5685. Telex: 385 9172.

★ 19250 ★

University of Puerto Rico - Library System - Public Communications Library (Info Sci)
Box 23302, UPR Sta.   Phone: (809)764-0000
Rio Piedras, PR 00931-3302   Aura Lopez, Hd.Libn.
Founded: 1977. **Staff:** Prof 1; Other 3. **Subjects:** Radio, television, movies, journalism, communications, public relations, publicity. **Holdings:** 8498 books; 2596 bound periodical volumes; 147 catalogs; 4130 readings; 37 documents; 1379 pamphlets; 180 dissertations; 68 photographs; 312 transparencies; 1289 slides; 456 microfilms; 7 microcards; 70 cassette tapes; 35 tapes and records; 12 filmstrips; 182 films; 153 videocassettes. **Subscriptions:** 231 journals and other serials. **Services:** Interlibrary loan; copying; library open to the public with restrictions. **Automated Operations:** Computerized cataloging and acquisitions (NOTIS). **Computerized Information Services:** DIALOG Information Services. **Publications:** Bibliographies. **Special Indexes:** Index to El Mundo, El Nuevo Dia, El Reportero, El Vocero, The San Juan Star, Claridad; news articles and information in local and international communications (card). **Remarks:** FAX: (809)764-5685. Telex: 385 9172.

★ 19251 ★

University of Puerto Rico - Library System - Puerto Rican Collection (Area-Ethnic)
Box 23302, UPR Sta.   Phone: (809)764-0000
Rio Piedras, PR 00931-3302   Maria E. Ordonez, Hd.Libn.
Founded: 1940. **Staff:** Prof 4; Other 8. **Subjects:** Puerto Rican humanities and social sciences; Puerto Ricans. **Special Collections:** Rare 19th century books, printed in or dealing with Puerto Rico; 19th century newspapers; Puerto Rican graphics, manuscripts, photographs, and other AV items. **Holdings:** 91,694 books; 130,609 bound periodical volumes; 78,523 government documents; 2670 manuscripts; 1852 photographs; 3879 posters; 146 engravings; 94 seriegraphs; 322 maps; 5931 microfilms; 308 microcards. **Subscriptions:** 35 journals and other serials. **Services:** Interlibrary loan; copying; collection open to the public with restrictions. **Automated Operations:** Computerized cataloging and acquisitions (NOTIS). **Computerized Information Services:** DIALOG Information Services. Performs searches on fee basis. Contact Person: Olga Hernandez. **Special Catalogs:** Photograph catalog (card). **Special Indexes:** Indexes to Puerto Rican journals; El Mundo Newspaper (card). **Remarks:** FAX: (809)763-5685. Telex: 385 9172. **Staff:** Sonia Ibarra, Libn.; Maria P. Soto, Libn.; Elisa Vazquez, Libn.

★ 19252 ★

University of Puerto Rico - Library System - Zenobia y Juan Ramon Jimenez Room (Hum)
Box 23302, UPR Sta.   Phone: (809)764-0000
Rio Piedras, PR 00931-3302   Raquel Sarraga, Hd.Libn.
Founded: 1955. **Staff:** Prof 2; Other 2. **Subjects:** Spanish literature, modernism. **Special Collections:** Zenobia and Juan Ramon Jimenez Collection (64,886 items). **Holdings:** 9292 books; 5146 unbound periodical volumes; 50,475 manuscripts; 3110 pictures and photographs; 79 slides; 54 tapes and records; 2 films; 9 videocassettes. **Services:** Copying; library open to the public with restrictions. **Automated Operations:** Computerized cataloging and acquisitions (NOTIS). **Computerized Information Services:** DIALOG Information Services. **Special Indexes:** Index of Spanish poetry (card). **Remarks:** FAX: (809)763-5685. Telex: 385 9172. **Staff:** Carmen L. Busquets.

★ 19253 ★

University of Puerto Rico - Mayaguez Campus Library - Marine Sciences Collection (Biol Sci)
Mayaguez, PR 00709   Phone: (809)832-4040
      Sheila Dunstan, Hd.
Founded: 1954. **Staff:** Prof 2; Other 1. **Subjects:** Marine biology; marine invertebrates; fish biology; marine botany; aquaculture; oceanography - chemical, physical, geological, biological. **Special Collections:** Reprints on Marine Sciences (11,373). **Holdings:** 1341 books; 3932 bound and unbound periodicals; 7042 documents; 170 theses; 17 reels of microfilm; 361 microfiche; 2 tapes. **Subscriptions:** 208 journals and other serials. **Services:** Interlibrary loan; copying; collection open to the public for reference use only on request. **Computerized Information Services:** OCLC, DIALOG Information Services. Performs searches on fee basis. Contact Person: Ada C. Ramgolam or Jeanette Valentin. **Publications:** Department of Marine Sciences Contributions, annual - on exchange. **Staff:** Tomasita Martinez de Hernandez, Asst.Libn.

★ 19254 ★

University of Puerto Rico - Mayaguez Campus Library - Research and Development Center of the Caribbean - Energy and Environment Collection (Energy)
PO Box 5000, College Sta.   Phone: (809)832-1408
Mayaguez, PR 00708   Mrs. Lirio Ivette Lorenzo-Rivera, Act.Hd.
Founded: 1960. **Staff:** Prof 1; Other 2. **Subjects:** Energy - solar, biomass, wind; ocean thermal energy conversion; energy conversion and conservation; marine sciences; terrestrial ecology; aquatic ecology; electrochemistry; health and safety; environmental health; nuclear energy; engineering; resources conservation. **Holdings:** 5175 books; 2262 bound periodical volumes; 38,414 documents; 73,499 microcards; 105,159 microfiche; 410 films; 96 dissertations; 22 videocassettes; 88 open reel magnetic cassettes. **Subscriptions:** 11 journals and other serials. **Services:** Interlibrary loan; copying; SDI; collection open to the public. **Publications:** CEER Collection Bulletin of Information, monthly; List of Internal Publications Under PRNC and CEER. **Remarks:** Alternate telephone number(s): (809)832-4040, ext. 2080. FAX: (809)834-8025. Collection is part of University of Puerto Rico - Mayaguez Campus Library - Special Collections. **Formerly:** Its Special Collections - Center for Energy and Environment Research Reading Room - Energy Collection.

★ 19255 ★

University of Puerto Rico - Mayaguez Campus Library - Special Collections (Sci-Engr, Hum)
Main Library
Post St.   Phone: (809)833-8600
Mayaguez, PR 00708   Prof. Grace Quinones-Seda, Lib.Dir.
Founded: 1911. **Subjects:** Engineering, agriculture, marine sciences, chemistry, physics, biology, business, literature. **Special Collections:** Puerto Rican Collection (11,774 volumes); theses (1669); government documents (496,659 items); Alfred Stern Collection (209 manuscrpits); Music and Oral History Collection (6973 records); Center for Energy and Environmental Research (5138 items); Marine Sciences (1584). **Holdings:** 191,018 books; 68,591 bound periodical volumes; 27 linear feet of manuscripts; 235,266 microfiche; 12,470 microfilm; 1092 films; 1094 magnetic tapes; 5794 maps; 22,329 slides; 1416 videocassettes; 675 filmstrips; 908 transparencies; 270 posters; 64 computer programs; 86,218 microcards. **Services:** Interlibrary loan; copying; SDI; collections open to the public with special permission. **Automated Operations:** Computerized public access catalog, cataloging, acquisitions, and circulation. **Computerized Information Services:** DIALOG Information Services, OCLC; internal databases; UPRENET,

MARNET (internal databases). Performs searches on fee basis. Contact Person: Ada C. Ramgolam or Jeanette Valentin. **Networks/Consortia:** Member of SOLINET. **Publications:** Lista de Nuevas Adquisiciones, monthly; bibliographies, occasional; list of theses, annual. **Special Indexes:** Index of the Carribean Journal of Science. **Remarks:** FAX: (809)834-3031. Telex: 385 44 71. **Staff:** Isaura Gonzalez, Hd., Puerto Rican Coll.; Eneida M. Vicente, Hd., Mus.Coll.; Lirio Ivette Lorenzo, Hd., Ctr., Energy & Env.Res.; Marta S. Tomassini, Hd., Govt.Docs.

★ 19256 ★
University of Puerto Rico - Medical Sciences Campus - Library (Med)
P.O. Box 365067   Phone: (809)751-8199
San Juan, PR 00936-5067   Ana Isabel Moscoso, Dir.
Founded: 1950. **Staff:** Prof 8; Other 23. **Subjects:** Medicine, dentistry, public health, pharmacy, allied health sciences, nursing. **Special Collections:** Puerto Rican Health Sciences Collection; Dr. Bailey K. Ashford Collection; AIDS Information Center. **Holdings:** 33,465 book titles; 80,778 bound periodical volumes; 5000 clippings; 700 reprints; 1000 pamphlets. **Subscriptions:** 1437 journals and other serials. **Services:** Interlibrary loan; copying; library open to the public with restrictions. **Computerized Information Services:** MEDLINE, BRS Information Technologies. Performs searches on fee basis. Contact Person: Francisca Corrada, Ref.Libn. **Networks/Consortia:** Member of National Network of Libraries of Medicine - Middle Atlantic Region. **Special Indexes:** Author index to Boletin de la Asociacion Medica de Puerto Rico (card); Saludhos; Revista de Educadores en Salud; Homines; Boletin del Colegio de Profesionales de la Enfermeria; Revista de Adminstracion Publica; Revista de Psiquiatria y Salud Mental; Superacion; Informe Epidemiologico. **Remarks:** FAX: (809)759-6713. **Staff:** Leticia Perez, Ser.Libn.; Nilca I. Parrilla, Cat.Libn.; Aura Panepinto, Spec.Coll.; Margarita Gonzalez, Ref.Libn.

★ 19257 ★
University of Puget Sound - School of Law - Law Library (Law)
Norton Clapp Law Ctr.
950 Broadway Plaza   Phone: (206)591-2970
Tacoma, WA 98402-4470   Anita M. Steele, Dir.
Founded: 1972. **Staff:** Prof 8; Other 10. **Subjects:** Law. **Holdings:** 136,783 books and bound periodical volumes; 118,346 volumes in microform; 5171 reels of microfilm; 710,075 microfiche. **Subscriptions:** 3480 journals and other serials; 5 newspapers. **Services:** Interlibrary loan; copying; library open to the public with limited circulation. **Automated Operations:** Computerized cataloging, acquisitions, and serials. **Computerized Information Services:** InfoTrac, RLIN, LEXIS, WESTLAW, DIALOG Information Services, WILSONLINE, DataTimes, VU/TEXT Information Services; DIALMAIL, OnTyme Electronic Message Network Service (electronic mail services). **Networks/Consortia:** Member of Western Library Network (WLN). **Publications:** Student Library Handbook. **Remarks:** FAX: (206)591-6313. **Staff:** Faye Jones, Asst.Law Libn.; Betty Warner, Acq. & Fin.Rec.; Suzanne Harvey, Bibliog.Sys.Libn. (Cat.); Roger Becker, Sys. Strategist Law Libn.; Bob Menanteaux, Info.Serv.Libn. (Ref.); Kelly Kunsch, Ref.Libn.; Marilyn Harhai, Ref.Libn.

★ 19258 ★
University of Queensland Gatton College - J.K. Murray Library (Agri, Rec, Food-Bev)
Lawes, QLD 4343, Australia   Phone: 74 601111
                                          Mr. E.R. McLay
Staff: Prof 3; Other 6. **Subjects:** Agriculture, hospitality, tourism, food technology. **Holdings:** 46,000 books; 19,000 bound periodical volumes. **Subscriptions:** 1000 journals and other serials. **Services:** Interlibrary loan; copying; library open to the public for reference use only. **Computerized Information Services:** DIALOG Information Services; COJAK (internal database). **Remarks:** FAX: 74 601499. Telex: QUCOL AA 40866.

★ 19259 ★
University of Redlands - Armacost Library (Hum)
1249 E. Colton Ave.   Phone: (714)335-4022
Redlands, CA 92374   Fred E. Hearth, Lib.Dir.
Founded: 1909. **Staff:** Prof 7; Other 10.75. **Special Collections:** Music and musical scores; British and American literature; religion; Farquhar Collection of California and the Great Southwest; Harley F. and Florence Ayscough Macnair Far East Collection; James Irvine Foundation Map Collection. **Computerized Information Services:** DIALOG Information Services, BRS Information Technologies; CD-ROMs (ERIC, PsycLIT, Academic Index, National Newspaper Index, WILSONDISC, InfoTrac); internal databases. Contact Person: William Kennedy, Ref.Libn. **Publications:** The Helen and Vernon Farquhar Collection of California and the Great Southwest. **Remarks:** FAX: (714)335-3403.

University of Regina - Bilingual Centre
See: University of Regina (19261)

★ 19260 ★
University of Regina - Education Branch Library (Educ)
Regina, SK, Canada S4S 0A2   Phone: (306)585-4642
                                          Mr. Del Affleck, Hd.
Staff: Prof 3; Other 6. **Subjects:** Education, children's literature. **Special Collections:** School Demonstration Library (38,011 items); curriculum laboratory (34,382 items); Historic Textbook Collection (595 items); French Collection. **Holdings:** 154,592 books; 15,515 bound periodical volumes; 448,471 microfiche; 25,174 microfilms; 107,751 AV materials. **Subscriptions:** 766 journals and other serials. **Services:** Interlibrary loan; copying; library open to the public with restrictions. **Automated Operations:** Computerized cataloging and acquisitions (through Main Library). **Computerized Information Services:** DIALOG Information Services, BRS Information Technologies, QL Systems, Prima Telematic Inc., Info Globe, CAN/OLE, WILSONLINE, The Financial Post DataGroup, ERIC; NetNorth (electronic mail service). Performs searches on fee basis. Contact Person: Marianne Thauberger, Ref.Libn. **Remarks:** FAX: (306)586-9862. **Staff:** Liv Thorseth, French Serv.Libn.

★ 19261 ★
University of Regina - Language Institute - Library (Hum)
Regina, SK, Canada S4S 0A2   Phone: (306)585-4177
                                          Richard Lapointe
Founded: 1972. **Staff:** 1. **Subjects:** Bilingualism; translation; Francophones in Western Canada - history, sociology, literature. **Holdings:** 4000 books. **Subscriptions:** 10 journals and other serials; 10 newspapers. **Services:** Library open to the public. **Remarks:** FAX: (306)585-5183. **Formerly:** Its Bilingual Centre. **Also Known As:** Institut de Formation Linguistique.

★ 19262 ★
University of Regina - Map Library (Geog-Map)
Regina, SK, Canada S4S 0A2   Phone: (306)585-4401
Founded: 1968. **Staff:** 2. **Subjects:** Cartography. **Special Collections:** Historical urban plans and aerial photographs (15,000). **Holdings:** 5000 volumes; 65,000 maps; 15,000 aerial photographs; 800 microforms; 15 globes. **Subscriptions:** 28 journals and other serials. **Services:** Copying; library open to the public with restrictions. **Publications:** List of special acquisitions; list of atlases; list of wall maps; list of class-sets; Map Library Resources; Map Library Brochure.

★ 19263 ★
University Research Corporation - Library (Soc Sci)
7200 Wisconsin Ave., Suite 600   Phone: (301)654-8338
Bethesda, MD 20814   Dawn Lee, Dir.
Subjects: International health, health education, criminal justice, housing rehabilitation, management and evaluation. **Special Collections:** Alcohol and drug abuse (300 volumes and VF materials). **Holdings:** 1000 books; 3500 other cataloged items; 30 VF drawers. **Subscriptions:** 25 journals and other serials; 20 newspapers. **Services:** Interlibrary loan; library not open to the public. **Computerized Information Services:** DIALOG Information Services, MEDLARS, BRS Information Technologies.

★ 19264 ★
University of Rhode Island - Art Department - Slide Library (Art)
Fine Arts Center   Phone: (401)792-2771
Kingston, RI 02881   Linda Mugica, Cur.
Founded: 1960. **Subjects:** Arts - fine, graphic, applied; architecture; photography. **Holdings:** 70,000 slides. **Subscriptions:** 10 journals and other serials. **Services:** Library open to faculty and students.

★ 19265 ★
University of Rhode Island - International Center for Marine Resource Development - Library (Sci-Engr, Biol Sci)
Main Library   Phone: (401)792-2938
Kingston, RI 02881   Mrs. J. Alexander, Libn.
Founded: 1973. **Staff:** Prof 1; Other 2. **Subjects:** Fisheries, aquaculture, coastal zone management in developing countries. **Holdings:** 13,000 books and documents. **Subscriptions:** 200 journals and other serials. **Services:** Interlibrary loan; copying (limited); library open to the public. **Computerized Information Services:** Online systems (through Main Library). **Publications:** Titles on artisanal fisheries; list of other publications - available on request. **Remarks:** FAX: (401)789-3342.

★ 19266 ★
University of Rhode Island - Pell Marine Science Library (Biol Sci, Sci-Engr)
Narragansett, RI 02882-1197   Phone: (401)792-6161
      Janice F. Sieburth, Hd.
Founded: 1959. **Staff:** Prof 1; Other 3. **Subjects:** Oceanography, marine biology and geology, fisheries, atmospheric sciences. **Special Collections:** Marine and polar expeditionary reports (123 shelf feet). **Holdings:** 13,800 books; 18,750 bound periodical volumes; 1342 sheets of U.S. nautical charts; 16,000 reprints of scientific papers. **Subscriptions:** 970 journals and other serials. **Services:** Interlibrary loan; copying; library open to the public. **Automated Operations:** Computerized circulation and serials. **Computerized Information Services:** DIALOG Information Services, OCLC; internal database; CD-ROMs. Performs searches on fee basis. **Publications:** Graduate School of Oceanography, University of Rhode Island, GSO Abstracts, annual - by exchange. **Remarks:** FAX: (401)792-6160. **Staff:** Roberta Dorant, Pub. Serv.Libn.; Deborah Sanford, Serv.Libn.

★ 19267 ★
University of Rhode Island - Rhode Island Oral History Project (Hist)
Library - Special Collections   Phone: (401)792-2594
Kingston, RI 02881   David C. Maslyn, Hd., Spec.Coll.
Founded: 1972. **Staff:** 2. **Subjects:** Millworkers of Rhode Island and their social milieu, 1900 to present; Narragansett Indians; university history; local Franco-American community; state jewelry industry; Rhode Island's Islands (Block, Prudence, Conanicut); Galilee fisherman; immigrants; women's suffrage; town government (Yankee ingenuity). **Holdings:** 311 tapes of interviews; 70 tapes and transcripts of interviews on 1938 hurricane; typescripts of taped interviews of mill workers. **Services:** Project open to the public. **Remarks:** FAX: (401)792-4608.

★ 19268 ★
University of Rhode Island - Special Collections (Rare Book)
Library   Phone: (401)792-2594
Kingston, RI 02881   David C. Maslyn, Hd., Spec.Coll.
Founded: 1966. **Staff:** Prof 1; Other 1. **Special Collections:** Rare books (7171 volumes); Rhode Island Collection (3448 volumes); Whitman (296 volumes); Pound (582 volumes); Millay (163 volumes); Robinson (150 volumes); herbals; fine press books; printing presses, 1830-1840; working presses - Albion, Adams, Washington. **Holdings:** 10,800 volumes; theses; 2345 linear feet of university archives; 3411 linear feet of personal papers; 13,000 maps; 16 VF drawers of ephemera. **Services:** Copying; collections open to the public with restrictions. **Computerized Information Services:** OCLC. **Networks/Consortia:** Member of Rhode Island Library Network (RHILINET), NELINET, Inc., Consortium of Rhode Island Academic and Research Libraries, Inc. (CRIARL). **Publications:** Internal finding aids; New Leaves Press - Library Keepsakes. **Remarks:** FAX: (410)792-4608.

★ 19269 ★
University of Richmond - E. Claiborne Robins School of Business - Business Information Center (Bus-Fin)
Boatwright Library   Phone: (804)289-8666
Richmond, VA 23173   Littleton M. Maxwell, Dir.
Founded: 1962. **Staff:** Prof 1; Other 2. **Subjects:** Business administration, accounting, economics, finance, management, marketing. **Holdings:** 30,000 books; 6000 bound periodical volumes; 300 cassettes; 20 file cabinets of annual reports; 6 file cabinets of vertical files. **Subscriptions:** 1020 journals and other serials; 18 newspapers. **Services:** Interlibrary loan; copying; SDI; library open to the public. **Automated Operations:** Computerized cataloging. **Computerized Information Services:** DIALOG Information Services, PFDS Online, BRS Information Technologies, OCLC, InfoTrac, Standard & Poor's Corporation, Disclosure Information Group, Dun & Bradstreet Business Credit Services, Dow Jones News/Retrieval; BITNET (electronic mail service). Performs searches on fee basis. **Networks/Consortia:** Member of SOLINET, Richmond Area Libraries Cooperative. **Publications:** E. Claiborne Robins School of Business Information Center Briefs. **Special Indexes:** Business and Economic update (online); Marketing Proceedings (online). **Remarks:** FAX: (804)289-8757.

★ 19270 ★
University of Richmond - Music Library (Mus)
Richmond, VA 23173   Phone: (804)289-8286
      Bonlyn G. Hall, Mus.Libn.
Founded: 1955. **Staff:** Prof 1; Other 10. **Subjects:** Music. **Holdings:** 450 books; 8090 33rpm phonograph records; 1400 compact discs; 300 audiocassettes; 8400 scores. **Subscriptions:** 50 journals and other serials. **Services:** Interlibrary loan; copying; library open to the public. **Automated Operations:** Computerized public access catalog, cataloging, circulation, and acquisitions (DYNIX Automated Library System).

★ 19271 ★
University of Richmond - Science Library (Biol Sci, Sci-Engr)
Richmond, VA 23173   Phone: (804)289-8261
      Melanie M. Hillner, Dir.
Staff: Prof 1; Other 3. **Subjects:** Chemistry, biology, physics, mathematics, computer science; health and sport science. **Holdings:** 25,000 books; 28,590 bound periodical volumes. **Subscriptions:** 553 journals and other serials. **Services:** Interlibrary loan; copying; SDI; library open to the public. **Computerized Information Services:** BRS Information Technologies, DIALOG Information Services, STN International. Performs searches on fee basis. **Networks/Consortia:** Member of Richmond Area Libraries Cooperative, Richmond Health Information Group. **Remarks:** FAX: (804)289-8482.

★ 19272 ★
University of Richmond - William T. Muse Memorial Law Library (Law)
Richmond, VA 23173   Phone: (804)289-8225
      Steven D. Hinckley, Law Libn.
Staff: Prof 5; Other 7. **Subjects:** Law. **Special Collections:** Environmental law. **Holdings:** 120,283 books; 67,892 volumes in microform. **Subscriptions:** 2957 journals and other serials; 10 newspapers. **Services:** Interlibrary loan; library open to the public for reference use only. **Automated Operations:** Computerized public access catalog, cataloging, circulation, acquisitions, and serials (DYNIX Automated Library System). **Computerized Information Services:** LEXIS, OCLC, WESTLAW, DIALOG Information Services, NEXIS, VU/TEXT Information Services. **Networks/Consortia:** Member of SOLINET, COSELL. **Publications:** The Museletter (newsletter), quarterly; Selected List of Recent Acquisitions, monthly - both for internal distribution only; Research Guide to Environmental Law, 1988 - available on request. **Remarks:** FAX: (804)289-8683. **Staff:** Joyce Manna Janto, Dp.Dir.; Sally H. Wambold, Tech.Serv.Libn.; Lucinda D. Harrison-Cox, Sys./Ref.Libn.; Paul M. Birch, Comp.Serv./Ref.Libn.

★ 19273 ★
University of Rochester - Art Library (Art)
Rush Rhees Library
River Campus   Phone: (716)275-4476
Rochester, NY 14627   Stephanie Frontz, Libn.
Founded: 1955. **Staff:** Prof 1; Other 1. **Subjects:** Architecture, sculpture, painting, photography, graphic arts, decorative arts. **Holdings:** 40,000 books; 9000 bound periodical volumes; 28 VF drawers of clippings, phamphlets, and ephemera; 50 videotapes. **Subscriptions:** 300 journals and other serials. **Services:** Interlibrary loan; copying; library open to the public for reference use only. **Computerized Information Services:** OCLC, RLIN. **Networks/Consortia:** Member of Rochester Regional Library Council (RRLC), Research Libraries Information Network (RLIN).

★ 19274 ★
University of Rochester - Asia Library (Area-Ethnic)
Rush Rhees Library
River Campus   Phone: (716)275-4489
Rochester, NY 14627   Datta S. Kharbas, Libn.
Founded: 1965. **Staff:** Prof 1; Other 1. **Subjects:** Chinese, Japanese, and Indian history and philosophy; Japanese, Chinese, Sanskrit, Hindi, and Marathi language and literature. **Special Collections:** Asahi Shinbum on microfilm; Times of India, 1861-1889 (Indian gazetteers on microfilm); India census, 1881-1971. **Holdings:** 101,000 books; 14,000 bound periodical volumes. **Subscriptions:** 380 journals and other serials; 10 newspapers. **Services:** Interlibrary loan; copying; library open to the public on written request. **Computerized Information Services:** DIALOG Information Services, BRS Information Technologies. **Special Catalogs:** Catalog of the East Asia Collection.

★ 19275 ★
University of Rochester - Carlson Library (Biol Sci, Sci-Engr)
Computer Studies Bldg.
River Campus   Phone: (716)275-4465
Rochester, NY 14627   Arleen Somerville, Libn.
Founded: 1987. **Staff:** Prof 4; Other 6. **Subjects:** Chemistry, biology, mathematics, statistics, computer science, engineering, geology. **Holdings:** 84,000 books; 67,000 bound periodical volumes; 12,700 computer science technical reports; computer software. **Subscriptions:** 2100 journals and other serials. **Services:** Interlibrary loan; copying; library open to the public for reference use only. **Computerized Information Services:** DIALOG Information Services, BRS Information Technologies, STN International, OCLC, RLIN; internal database. **Remarks:** Includes the geology holdings of its former Geology/Map Library. **Staff:** Isabel Kaplan; Diane Reiman; Christine Sheetz.

★19276★
University of Rochester - Charlotte Whitney Allen Library (Art)
Memorial Art Gallery
500 University Ave.   Phone: (716)473-6226
Rochester, NY 14607   Lucy Harper, Libn.
Founded: 1913. **Staff:** Prof 1. **Subjects:** Art history, architecture, museology. **Holdings:** 21,000 books; 2200 bound periodical volumes; 2600 unbound museum bulletins and annual reports; 12,000 slides; 24 VF drawers of clippings, exhibition catalogs, and pamphlets; gallery archives; Sotheby Parke-Bernet and Christie's auction sales catalogs, 1952 to present; historical scrapbooks of Memorial Art Gallery. **Subscriptions:** 85 journals and other serials. **Services:** Interlibrary loan; copying; library open to the public. **Computerized Information Services:** CD-ROM (Art Index); File list of Gallery Archives and Artist Index to Exhibitions at the Memorial Art Gallery (internal databases). **Networks/Consortia:** Member of Rochester Regional Library Council (RRLC), Research Libraries Information Network (RLIN).

★19277★
University of Rochester - Computing Resources Center (Comp Sci)
Rush Rhees Library   Phone: (716)275-4475
Rochester, NY 14627   Barbara Moore, Asst.Dir. of Libs./Comp.Sys.
Founded: 1985. **Staff:** Prof 4. **Subjects:** Computer application, microcomputers, networking, computer product information, academic computing. **Holdings:** 800 books; 700 software titles. **Subscriptions:** 150 journals and other serials. **Services:** Interlibrary loan; copying; SDI; microcomputer equipment and consulting; center open to the public on fee basis. **Automated Operations:** Computerized public access catalog, cataloging, and circulation. **Computerized Information Services:** DIALOG Information Services, OCLC, RLIN, BRS Information Technologies; CD-ROMs (Computer Library, PC-SIG, Microsoft Bookshelf, Grolier Encyclopedia, Blue Sail Disk, EduCorp); BITNET (electronic mail service). Performs searches on fee basis. Contact Person: Sandy Lundquist, Comp.Serv.Libn., 275-6350. **Networks/Consortia:** Member of Rochester Regional Library Council (RRLC), Research Libraries Information Network (RLIN). **Publications:** CompUteR, monthly - by subscription. **Special Indexes:** Index to software titles (computer printout). **Remarks:** Electronic mail address(es): LUNDQ@UORDBV (BITNET). **Formerly:** Its Computing and Reserve Library (C.A.R.L.). **Staff:** Fran Versace, Co-Mgr., UCC; Shirley Ricker, Ref.Libn./Comp.Serv.Libn.; Sandy Lunquist, Comp.Serv.Libn.

★19278★
University of Rochester - Department of Rare Books and Special Collections (Hist, Rare Book)
River Campus   Phone: (716)275-4477
Rochester, NY 14627   Peter Dzwonkoski, Hd.
Founded: 1930. **Staff:** Prof 4; Other 2. **Subjects:** Rare books; literary and historical manuscripts; university archives; local history; Restoration and 19th century British theater and drama; history of law and political theory; 19th century American political history. **Special Collections:** Thomas E. Dewey papers; William Henry Seward papers; Thurlow Weed papers; Guzzetta Collection of Leonardo da Vinci; Ellwanger & Barry Horticultural Library; Upstate New York Historical Collection; Susan B. Anthony; George Eastman; Lewis Henry Morgan; Robert Southey; Arthur Wing Pinero; Henry James; Benjamin Disraeli; Sean O'Casey; Collins Collection of Alfred Tennyson; John Masefield; Claude Bragdon; Berlove Collection of Christopher Morley; Ross Collection of John Ruskin (400 volumes); Victoriana; Markiewicz Collection of Children's Books; Frederick Exley Archive; John Gardner Archive; Thomas McGuane manuscripts; Jerre Mangione Archive; John A. Williams Archive; Hubbell Collection (books illustrated with mounted photographs); 19th and early 20th century trade-bindings; Tauchnitz Editions; Roycroft Press; local imprints through 1860. **Holdings:** 90,000 volumes; 2.5 million manuscripts; 500,000 archival items; 8 VF drawers of ephemera. **Subscriptions:** 20 journals and other serials. **Services:** Copying; department open to qualified scholars. **Automated Operations:** Computerized cataloging. **Computerized Information Services:** OCLC, RLIN. **Publications:** Library Bulletin, irregular - to friends and institutions. **Special Catalogs:** Exhibition catalogs, irregular. **Special Indexes:** Registers and letter writer/recipient index to manuscript collections. **Staff:** Karl S. Kabelac, Mss.Libn.; Mary Huth, Asst.Hd.; Evelyn Walker, Rare Bk.Libn.

★19279★
University of Rochester - Eastman School of Music - Sibley Music Library (Mus)
27 Gibbs St.   Phone: (716)274-1350
Rochester, NY 14604   Mary Wallace Davidson, Libn.
Founded: 1904. **Staff:** Prof 7; Other 11.5. **Subjects:** Music. **Special Collections:** Pougin Collection (books on French music and theater); Krehbiel Collection (folk music); Gordon Collection (chamber music); Oskar Fleischer Collection (10th-16th century manuscripts); Olshki Collection (16th-17th century Italian printers). **Holdings:** 297,226 volumes; 56,874 phonograph records; 1400 manuscripts, autograph letters; 100,000 pieces of early American sheet music; 22,000 items in the choral octavo collection; 750 volumes of clippings. **Subscriptions:** 670 journals and other serials. **Services:** Interlibrary loan; copying; library open to the public for reference use only. **Automated Operations:** Computerized public access catalog, cataloging, and ILL. **Computerized Information Services:** BITNET (electronic mail service). **Networks/Consortia:** Member of SUNY/OCLC Library Network, Research Libraries Information Network (RLIN). **Special Catalogs:** Catalog of Sound Recordings, 1977 (14 volumes). **Special Indexes:** Pre-1949 Periodical Index (card). **Remarks:** Electronic mail address(es): SMMD@UORVM (BITNET). **Staff:** Dr. Louise Goldberg, Rare Bks.Libn./Coord., Ref.Serv.; Jennifer Bowen, Cat.; Laura Snyder, Cat.; Ann Snyder, Cat.; Sion T. Honea, Cons.; Monica Mashner, Circ.Supv.

★19280★
University of Rochester - Government Documents and Microtext Center (Info Sci)
Rush Rhees Library   Phone: (716)275-4484
Rochester, NY 14627   Kathleen E. Wilkinson, Govt.Docs.Libn.
Founded: 1880. **Staff:** Prof 1; Other 4. **Subjects:** Documents - U.S. Congress, U.S. Bureau of the Census, New York State, women's studies, black studies, North American Indians, American and British literature. **Special Collections:** Goldsmiths'-Kress Collection (economic literature); slavery; papers of William Henry Seward and of the National Association for the Advancement of Colored People (NAACP); Early English Books; American Fiction; History of Women; Early British Periodicals. **Holdings:** 380 books; 428,000 uncataloged government documents in paper; 914,200 uncataloged government documents in microform; 2.4 million other microforms. **Subscriptions:** 10 journals and other serials. **Services:** Interlibrary loan; copying; center open to the public. **Computerized Information Services:** DIALOG Information Services, BRS Information Technologies. **Remarks:** FAX: (716)473-1906.

★19281★
University of Rochester - Laboratory for Laser Energetics - Library (Sci-Engr)
250 E. River Rd.
Rochester, NY 14623   Phone: (716)275-4479
Founded: 1976. **Staff:** Prof 1; Other 1. **Subjects:** Plasma physics, inertial fusion, high energy lasers, x-ray diffraction, optical materials and coatings. **Holdings:** 2000 books; 1000 bound periodical volumes; 25,000 DOE Contractor Reports. **Subscriptions:** 80 journals and other serials. **Services:** Interlibrary loan; copying; SDI; library open to the public by appointment. **Automated Operations:** Computerized cataloging. **Computerized Information Services:** DIALOG Information Services, BRS Information Technologies, NEXIS, WILSONLINE, STN International, OCLC, RLIN. **Networks/Consortia:** Member of Research Libraries Information Network (RLIN), Rochester Regional Library Council (RRLC), New York State Interlibrary Loan Network (NYSILL). **Publications:** New Books List; New Reports, both irregular. **Staff:** Kenneth Harper.

★19282★
University of Rochester - Management Library (Bus-Fin)
Rush Rhees Library
River Campus   Phone: (716)275-4482
Rochester, NY 14627   Violanda Burns, Libn.
Founded: 1962. **Staff:** Prof 2.5; Other 1.5. **Subjects:** Management, accounting, economics, finance, marketing, manufacturing management, operations research and management, quantitative business methods, computer and information science, behavioral science in industry. **Holdings:** 130,547 volumes; 250,850 microfiche. **Subscriptions:** 2597 journals and other serials. **Services:** Interlibrary loan; library open to the public. **Automated Operations:** Computerized public access catalog, cataloging, and circulation. **Computerized Information Services:** DIALOG Information Services, NEXIS, Dow Jones News/Retrieval, BRS Information Technologies, OCLC, RLIN; CD-ROMs (CD/Corporate, ABI/INFORM,

Laser Disclosure, General Business File, EconLit, PTS F&S Indexes). **Networks/Consortia:** Member of Research Libraries Information Network (RLIN). **Publications:** Rochester Management Bibliographies, irregular. **Remarks:** FAX: (716)473-1906. **Staff:** Gregg Ames, Libn.; Datta S. Kharbas, Libn.

★ 19283 ★
University of Rochester - Map Center (Geog-Map, Sci-Engr)
Rush Rhees Library   Phone: (716)275-4489
Rochester, NY 14627   Datta S. Kharbas
Founded: 1960. **Staff:** Prof 1; Other 1. **Subjects:** Maps and atlases. **Holdings:** 100,000 maps. **Networks/Consortia:** Member of Research Libraries Information Network (RLIN), Rochester Regional Library Council (RRLC), New York State Interlibrary Loan Network (NYSILL).

★ 19284 ★
University of Rochester - Physics-Optics-Astronomy Library (Sci-Engr)
374 Bausch & Lomb Bldg.   Phone: (716)275-8605
Rochester, NY 14627   Kenneth Harper, Libn.
Founded: 1960. **Staff:** Prof 1; Other 1. **Subjects:** Astronomy and astrophysics; physics - condensed matter, biological, high energy/particle, nuclear; optics. **Special Collections:** Preprints in High Energy Physics. **Holdings:** 12,500 books; 11,500 bound periodical volumes; 500 patents; 950 theses; preprints and reports. **Subscriptions:** 375 journals and other serials. **Services:** Interlibrary loan; copying; SDI; library open to the public. **Automated Operations:** Computerized public access catalog, cataloging, and circulation. **Computerized Information Services:** DIALOG Information Services, BRS Information Technologies, STN International, Stanford Public Information Retrieval System (SPIRES); High Energy Physics Preprints (internal database). **Networks/Consortia:** Member of New York State Interlibrary Loan Network (NYSILL), Research Libraries Information Network (RLIN), Rochester Regional Library Council (RRLC). **Publications:** New Books List, quarterly. **Remarks:** FAX: (716)473-4524.

★ 19285 ★
University of Rochester - Rossell Hope Robbins Library (Hum)
River Campus   Phone: (716)275-0110
Rochester, NY 14627   Alan Lupack, Cur.
Founded: 1987. **Staff:** Prof 1. **Subjects:** Literature - Middle English, Old English, Old French, Anglo-Norman; manuscript studies; medieval studies. **Holdings:** 15,000 books; 400 bound periodical volumes; 5000 offprints. **Subscriptions:** 40 journals and other serials. **Services:** Library open to the public for reference use only. **Publications:** Robbins Library Bibliographies.

★ 19286 ★
University of Rochester - School of Medicine & Dentistry - Edward G. Miner Library (Med)
601 Elmwood Ave.   Phone: (716)275-3364
Rochester, NY 14642   Lucretia McClure, Med.Libn.
Founded: 1923. **Staff:** Prof 11; Other 15. **Subjects:** Medicine, nursing, psychiatry, dental research. **Special Collections:** Edward W. Mulligan History of Medicine Collection; Edward G. Miner Yellow Fever Collection. **Holdings:** 220,000 volumes. **Subscriptions:** 3074 journals and other serials. **Services:** Interlibrary loan; copying. **Automated Operations:** Computerized cataloging. **Computerized Information Services:** DIALOG Information Services, BRS Information Technologies, OCLC, MEDLINE. **Networks/ Consortia:** Member of Rochester Regional Library Council (RRLC), National Network of Libraries of Medicine - Middle Atlantic Region. **Publications:** Bulletin, monthly - to medical personnel and institutions. **Remarks:** FAX: (716)275-4799. Also serves the School of Nursing and Strong Memorial Hospital.

★ 19287 ★
University of St. Mary of the Lake - Mundelein Seminary - Feehan Memorial Library (Rel-Phil)
Mundelein, IL 60060   Phone: (708)566-6401
                                       Bro. Henry Baldwin, F.S.C.
Founded: 1929. **Staff:** Prof 1; Other 3. **Subjects:** Ancient Christian literature, medieval theology, Catholic theology. **Special Collections:** Irish history, language, literature. **Holdings:** 150,000 books; 25,000 bound periodical volumes; 610 reels of microfilm; 401 microcards. **Subscriptions:** 450 journals and other serials; 5 newspapers. **Services:** Interlibrary loan; copying. **Computerized Information Services:** OCLC. **Networks/Consortia:** Member of Association of Chicago Theological Schools Library Council. **Remarks:** FAX: (708)566-7330.

★ 19288 ★
University of San Diego - Legal Research Center (Law)
Alcala Park   Phone: (619)260-4542
San Diego, CA 92110-2492   Nancy Carol Carter, Dir.
Founded: 1954. **Staff:** Prof 9; Other 12. **Subjects:** Law. **Special Collections:** Selective government documents depository. **Holdings:** 289,676 volumes. **Subscriptions:** 4241 journals and other serials; 20 newspapers. **Services:** Interlibrary loan; center open to the public. **Automated Operations:** Computerized cataloging. **Computerized Information Services:** LEXIS, WESTLAW, DIALOG Information Services, OCLC, RLIN; InterNet, BITNET (electronic mail services). **Remarks:** FAX: (619)260-4616. **Staff:** Georgia Briscoe, Hd., Tech.Serv.; Kathy Whistler, Cat.; Franklin Weston, Hd., Ref.; Michael White, Ref.; Margaret McDonald, Ref.; Loren Stamper, Cat.; Brent Bernau, Assoc.Dir.; Sushila Selness, Hd., Docs./Microforms.

★ 19289 ★
University of San Francisco - School of Law Library (Law)
Kendrick Hall 2130 Fulton St.   Phone: (415)666-6679
San Francisco, CA 94117-1080   Virginia Kelsh, Law Libn./Prof.
Founded: 1912. **Staff:** Prof 5; Other 7. **Subjects:** Anglo-American law. **Holdings:** 114,673 volumes; 804 reels of microfilm; 696,585 microfiche; 314 audio cassettes. **Subscriptions:** 2463 journals and other serials; 10 newspapers. **Services:** Interlibrary loan; library open to the public with restrictions. **Automated Operations:** Computerized cataloging. **Computerized Information Services:** LEXIS, WESTLAW; CD-ROM. **Remarks:** FAX: (415)666-2345. **Staff:** Donna Hughes-Oldenburg, Cat.Libn.; Jean Stefancic, Tech.Serv.Libn.; Marian Shostrom, Pub.Serv.Libn.; Lee Ryan, Ref.Libn.

★ 19290 ★
University of San Francisco - Special Collections Department/Donohue Rare Book Room (Rare Book)
Richard A. Gleeson Library
2130 Fulton St.   Phone: (415)666-2036
San Francisco, CA 94117   Benjamin Watson, Rare Bks.Libn.
Staff: Prof 1. **Subjects:** 16th and 17th century English religious history; Jesuitica; graphic arts; San Francisco area private press books; English and American literature of the 19th and 20th centuries. **Special Collections:** St. Thomas More and English Contemporaries; recusant literature; Robert Graves (first editions; translations; manuscripts; letters); Charles Carroll of Carrollton (books; letters; account books; ephemera); Robinson Jeffers (first editions; manuscripts; letters); Madeline Gleason Poetry Archive and Collection of San Francisco Poets; A.E. Housman (first editions); Laurence Housman (first editions and letters); 1890s collection, including Arthur Symons, Oscar Wilde, Norman Gale, George Moore, and William Watson (1 box of manuscripts); Max Beerbohm Collection; Norman and Charlotte Strouse Collection of Richard Le Gallienne (first editions; manuscripts; letters); collections of other authors, including Mary Webb, James Hanley, and Vincent Starrett; Mr. and Mrs. S. Gale Herrick Collection of the Gregynog Press; William P. Barlow, Jr. Collection of the Daniel Press; M. Wallace Friedman Collection of L. Frank Baum and Oziana; Norman and Charlotte Strouse Collections of: The Book Club of California, Allen Press, Victor Hammer, Hammer Creek Press, John Henry Nash, Officina Bodoni, and the Peregrine Press; Theodore M. and Frances B. Lilienthal Grabhorn Press Collection; Lawton Kennedy-Printer Archive and the R.S. Speck Collection of the Kennedy Press; Overbrook Press; Albert Sperisen Collection of Eric Gill (books; prints; woodblocks; drawings; letters; ephemera); The Colt Press, Toyon Press, Black Vine Press, and James McNeill Whistler; Chauncey D. Leake, Jr. Collection of Abattoir Press, Ives St. Press, Prairie Press, Red Ozier Press, and Yellow Barn Press; Graham Greene collection (first editions, manuscripts, letters); William Everson (books; letters; ephemera); Tamalpais Press of Roger Levenson (complete archive); Scholartis Press; Poltroon Press; Plantin Press; Rather Press (complete collection); Cranium Press (complete archive); Five Trees Press (archive); Black Stone Press (complete collection); Twowindows Press (complete collection); John De Pol (wood engraver); Bird in Hand Press; Turkey Press; Mallette Dean Archive; James E. Beard of St. Helena Archive; Grace Hoper Press Archive; Clark Pamphlet File (political, social, and military literature, 1914-1939); Van Houten Collection (Spanish manuscripts, correspondence of Jose de Piedade, 1784-1818, and Marie Guadalupe de Lencastre, 1679-1691, relating to missions in Mexico and South America); Adolph Sutro Archive-Sutro Baths and Sutro Tunnel (6 boxes); George Poultney Theatre typscripts, 19th and 20th century drama (273 items); Ernest Born Collection; Rev. Peter C. Yorke Collection; George Tyrell-Modernist controversy, 1890-1910; Winterburn Bookplate Collection; W. Phillip Barrett (bookplate designer); Eidenmuller Collection of American Women's Suffrage; Kenneth Ball Collection of Christmas Literature; Dorothy Payne (bookplate designer); The Reed O. Hunt Archive

of President Nixon's Commission on Financial Structure & Regulation, 1970-1972 (6 boxes); Dr. David Hyatt and the National Conference of Christians and Jews, 1973 to present (8 boxes); San Francisco and California Fiction Collection (1300 volumes); Monsignor George Lacombe Archive of Medieval Philosophy (6 boxes); The V.C.C. Collum Carnac and Mother-Goddess Research Archive (7 boxes); incunabula (55); Albrecht Durer prints (87); Mihail Chemiakin art works. **Holdings:** 20,000 volumes; photographs; prints; letters; manuscripts. **Subscriptions:** 6 journals and other serials. **Services:** Copying; collections open to the public. **Computerized Information Services:** OCLC. **Publications:** Occasional keepsakes; announcements of exhibitions; brochure briefly describing collections is available upon request. **Special Catalogs:** Files of presses, prints, manuscripts, letters, provenance, bindings, bookplates, chronology (card). **Remarks:** The special collections were started in 1951. The Donohue Room was dedicated in 1972. FAX: (415)666-2233. **Also Known As:** University of San Francisco - Countess Bernardine Murphy Donohue Rare Book Room.

★ 19291 ★
University of Saskatchewan - Education Branch Library (Educ)
Saskatoon, SK, Canada S7N 0W0   Phone: (306)966-5973
                                       Debbie McGugan, Hd.
Founded: 1970. **Staff:** Prof 2; Other 8. **Subjects:** Education, school librarianship, music education, curriculum materials for grades K-12, children's literature. **Holdings:** 129,987 volumes; 519,046 microforms; 11,307 AV programs; 8120 pamphlets; 269 maps; 40,060 pictures; music scores and recordings. **Subscriptions:** 475 journals and other serials. **Services:** Interlibrary loan; copying; library open to the public with restrictions. **Computerized Information Services:** DIALOG Information Services, BRS Information Technologies; Envoy 100 (electronic mail service). **Remarks:** FAX: (306)966-6040; (306)966-8719. **Staff:** MaryLynn Gagne, Ref.Libn.

★ 19292 ★
University of Saskatchewan - Engineering Branch Library (Sci-Engr)
Saskatoon, SK, Canada S7N 0W0   Phone: (306)966-5976
                                       D. Salt, Hd., Sci. and Engr. Libs.
Staff: Prof 2; Other 4. **Subjects:** Engineering - mechanical, electrical, civil, agricultural; computational science. **Holdings:** 60,000 volumes; 2800 pamphlets; 3800 documents; 6000 microforms. **Subscriptions:** 950 journals and other serials. **Services:** Library open to the public with restrictions. **Automated Operations:** Computerized public access catalog and circulation. **Computerized Information Services:** DIALOG Information Services, PFDS Online, BRS Information Technologies, CAN/OLE; Envoy 100, BITNET, InterNet (electronic mail services). Performs searches on fee basis. **Remarks:** Alternate telephone number(s): 966-5978. FAX: (306)966-8710. Telex: 074-2659. Electronic mail address(es): SALT@SKLIB.USASK.CA (InterNet). **Staff:** E. Wilson, Br.Supv.

★ 19293 ★
University of Saskatchewan - Geology/Physics Library (Sci-Engr)
Saskatoon, SK, Canada S7N 0W0   Phone: (306)966-6047
                                       G.D. Armstrong, Sci.Libn.
Staff: Prof 1; Other 3. **Subjects:** Geological sciences, physics. **Holdings:** 67,000 volumes; 11,000 bound periodical volumes; 700 microforms; 10,000 maps. **Subscriptions:** 679 journals and other serials. **Services:** Interlibrary loan; SDI; library open to the public with restrictions. **Automated Operations:** Computerized public access catalog, cataloging, acquisitions, serials, and circulation. **Computerized Information Services:** DIALOG Information Services, CAN/OLE, STN International, QL/SEARCH; Envoy 100, InterNet (electronic mail services). **Remarks:** Alternate telephone numbers are 966-6048 and 966-6049. FAX: (306)966-6040. Electronic mail address(es): G.ARMSTRONG (Envoy 100); ARMSTRONGG@SKLIB.USASK.CA (InterNet).

★ 19294 ★
University of Saskatchewan - Health Sciences Library (Med)
Saskatoon, SK, Canada S7N 0W0   Phone: (306)966-5991
                                       Dr. Wilma P. Sweaney, Libn.
Founded: 1951. **Staff:** Prof 2; Other 6. **Subjects:** Medicine, clinical and basic sciences, nursing, dentistry, biochemistry, microbiology, pharmacology, physiology, physical therapy, cancer research. **Holdings:** 95,630 volumes; 11,045 slides; 171 cassettes; 45 kits; 20 realia. **Subscriptions:** 1454 journals and other serials. **Services:** Interlibrary loan; copying; library open to medical professionals. **Automated Operations:** Computerized public access catalog and circulation. **Computerized Information Services:** MEDLARS, BRS Information Technologies, DIALOG Information Services, QL Systems, PFDS Online; Envoy 100 (electronic mail service). Performs searches on fee basis. **Remarks:** FAX: (306)966-8718. Electronic mail address(es): ILL.SSUM (Envoy 100). **Staff:** Joan MacLaine, Ref.Libn.

★ 19295 ★
University of Saskatchewan - Law Library (Law)
College of Law Bldg.   Phone: (306)966-5999
Saskatoon, SK, Canada S7N 0W0   Edward Stanek, Law Libn.
Founded: 1915. **Staff:** Prof 2; Other 6. **Subjects:** Law. **Holdings:** 115,325 volumes; 12,048 microforms; 16,199 documents; 34,364 pamphlets; 118 AV programs. **Subscriptions:** 1392 journals and other serials. **Services:** Interlibrary loan; copying; library open to the public with courtesy card. **Computerized Information Services:** QL Systems. **Staff:** Ken Whiteway, Rd.Serv.Libn.

University of Saskatchewan - Lutheran Theological Seminary
See: **Lutheran Theological Seminary (9466)**

★ 19296 ★
University of Saskatchewan - Native Law Centre - Library (Law)
159 Diefenbaker Centre   Phone: (306)966-6195
Saskatoon, SK, Canada S7N 0W0   Mary Tastad, Libn.
Founded: 1979. **Staff:** Prof 1; Other 1. **Subjects:** Law, native studies. **Special Collections:** Mackenzie Valley Pipeline Inquiry (archival materials); Canadian native rights cases (reported and unreported, relating to aboriginal, treaty, and Indian Act issues). **Holdings:** 3000 books; cases. **Subscriptions:** 40 journals and other serials; 12 newspapers. **Services:** Interlibrary loan; copying; library open to the public. **Remarks:** FAX: (306)966-8517.

University of Saskatchewan - St. Andrew's College
See: **St. Andrew's College (14228)**

University of Saskatchewan - St. Thomas More College
See: **St. Thomas More College (14598)**

★ 19297 ★
University of Saskatchewan - Special Collections (Hist)
University Library   Phone: (306)966-6030
Saskatoon, SK, Canada S7N 0W0   Shirley Martin, Hd.
Founded: 1919. **Staff:** Prof 1; Other 1. **Subjects:** Prairie provinces, pre-Confederation history, Canadian church history. **Special Collections:** Shortt Library of Canadiana; P.A. Sorokin Papers and Library; Morton Manuscripts on Rupert's Land and North-West Territories to 1940 (45 linear feet). **Holdings:** 42,250 volumes; 6800 pamphlets; 100 linear feet of manuscripts; 4677 photographs. **Subscriptions:** 20 journals and other serials. **Services:** Copying; collections open to the public. **Automated Operations:** Computerized public access catalog, cataloging, acquisitions, and circulation. **Computerized Information Services:** GEAC Library Information System; InterNet (electronic mail service). **Special Catalogs:** Louis Riel and the Rebellions in the Northwest: an Annotated Bibliography of Material in Special Collections, 1985 (book). **Remarks:** Alternate telephone number(s): 966-6029. FAX: (306)966-6040. Electronic mail address(es): MARTINS@SKLIB.USASK.CA (InterNet).

★ 19298 ★
University of Saskatchewan - Thorvaldson Library (Sci-Engr)
Thorvaldson Bldg.   Phone: (306)966-6038
Saskatoon, SK, Canada S7N 0W0   G.D. Armstrong, Sci.Libn.
Staff: Prof 1; Other 3. **Subjects:** Chemistry, pharmacy, chemical engineering, nutrition and dietetics. **Holdings:** 16,000 books; 5000 bound periodical volumes; 100 microforms. **Subscriptions:** 493 journals and other serials. **Services:** Interlibrary loan; SDI; library open to the public with restrictions. **Automated Operations:** Computerized public access catalog, cataloging, acquisitions, serials, and circulation. **Computerized Information Services:** DIALOG Information Services, CAN/OLE, Chemical Abstracts Service (CAS), STN International; Envoy 100, InterNet (electronic mail services). Performs searches on fee basis. **Remarks:** Alternate telephone number(s): 966-4681. FAX: (306)966-6040. Electronic mail address(es): G.ARMSTRONG (Envoy 100); ARMSTRONGG@SKLIB.USASK.CA (InterNet).

★ 19299 ★
University of Saskatchewan - Veterinary Medicine Library (Med)
Western College of Veterinary Medicine   Phone: (306)966-7206
Saskatoon, SK, Canada S7N 0W0   John V. James, Vet.Med.Libn.
Founded: 1965. **Staff:** Prof 1; Other 2. **Subjects:** Veterinary medicine, animal science. **Holdings:** 32,000 books; 30,000 bound periodical volumes. **Subscriptions:** 556 journals and other serials. **Services:** Interlibrary loan; library open to the public. **Computerized Information Services:** DIALOG Information Services, MEDLINE, CAN/OLE, GEAC Library Information System; CD-ROM (MEDLINE, CAB Abstracts). Performs searches on fee basis. **Publications:** New Acquisitions, monthly; Bulletin, quarterly. **Remarks:** FAX: (306)966-8747. Alternate telephone number(s): 966-7205.

★ 19300 ★
University of Scranton - Center For Eastern Christian Studies - Library (Rel-Phil)
Scranton, PA 18510   Phone: (717)941-6116
     Rev. Thomas F. Sable, S.J., Libn.
Founded: 1952. **Staff:** Prof 1; Other 2. **Subjects:** Eastern Christian theology and liturgy, patristics, church history, Russian history, ecumenism. **Special Collections:** Tyszkiewicz Collection (557 volumes); rare book collections (623 volumes). **Holdings:** 12,337 books; 2008 bound periodical volumes; typescript reports of Vatican II; 11 boxes of typescript manuscript. **Subscriptions:** 39 journals and other serials; 8 newspapers. **Services:** Library open to scholars, staff, faculty, and students; fee for outside users. **Automated Operations:** Computerized cataloging. **Computerized Information Services:** BITNET (electronic mail service). **Remarks:** FAX: (717)941-6369. Electronic mail address(es): SABLE@SCRANTON (BITNET).

University of Sherbrooke - Abestos Research Program
See: **Universite de Sherbrooke - Programme de Recherche sur l'amiante** (18127)

★ 19301 ★
University of Sind - Institute of Sindhology - Research Library (Area-Ethnic)
Jamshoro, Pakistan   Phone: 221 71125
     Abdul Qadir Junejo, Dir. of Sindhology
Founded: 1962. **Staff:** Prof 2; Other 24. **Subjects:** Sind - history, literature, religion, fine arts, linguistics, social science. **Special Collections:** Sind archives (4851 archival materials). **Holdings:** 90,343 books; 14,581 bound periodical volumes; 1411 manuscripts; 21 newspaper titles; 5000 bound volumes of newspapers. **Subscriptions:** 45 journals and other serials; 18 newspapers. **Services:** Copying; library open to the public for reference use only. **Automated Operations:** Computerized public access catalog. **Special Catalogs:** Catalogue of Manuscripts, Sindhi periodicals, and list of archival material; list of government publications of pre-partition period. **Staff:** Sayed Ghulam Mohammed Shah, Jr.Asst.Libn.; Gul Mohammed N. Mughol, Libn.; Ghulam Asghir Soomro, Jr.Asst.Libn.

★ 19302 ★
University of the South - Archives and Special Collections (Hist)
duPont Library   Phone: (615)598-1387
Sewanee, TN 37375   Anne Armour, Dir., Univ.Archv./Spec.Coll.
Founded: 1868. **Staff:** Prof 1; Other 2. **Subjects:** University history, Protestant Episcopal Church in the South, local and regional history. **Special Collections:** Papers of Leonidas Polk (850 items); correspondence and diaries of Charles T. Quintard (1200 items); sermons of Walter Dakin (100 items); Papers of George Scarbrough; Fairbanks Historical Collection; J. Morgan Soaper Library Collection. **Holdings:** 12,500 books; 500,000 manuscripts and photographs. **Services:** Interlibrary loan; copying; archives open to the public. **Computerized Information Services:** OCLC. **Networks/Consortia:** Member of SOLINET.

★ 19303 ★
University of the South - School of Theology Library (Rel-Phil)
SPO   Phone: (615)598-1267
Sewanee, TN 37375-4006   Thomas Edward Camp, Libn.
Founded: 1879. **Staff:** Prof 3; Other 1. **Subjects:** Theology, Biblical studies, church music and art, church history, religious biography, liturgy and ritual, Episcopal Church in the U.S.A. **Special Collections:** Bayard H. Jones Liturgical Library; journals of Diocesan Conventions of the Episcopal Church; journals of General Convention of Episcopal Church, 1790 to present. **Holdings:** 110,000 books; 15,250 bound periodical volumes; 2000 pamphlets. **Subscriptions:** 1055 journals and other serials. **Services:** Interlibrary loan; copying; library open to the public. **Automated Operations:** Computerized public access catalog, cataloging and acquisitions. **Computerized Information Services:** DIALOG Information Services; CD-ROM (Religion Index); internal database. Performs searches on fee basis. **Networks/Consortia:** Member of SOLINET. **Remarks:** FAX: (615)598-1145. **Staff:** Anne Flint, Tech.Serv.Libn.; Charles Van Heck, Asst.Libn. for Pub.Serv.

★ 19304 ★
University of South Alabama - College of Medicine - Biomedical Library (Med)
Library 312   Phone: (205)460-7043
Mobile, AL 36688   Spencer Marsh, Dir.
Founded: 1972. **Staff:** Prof 7; Other 13. **Subjects:** Medicine, nursing, and allied health sciences. **Holdings:** 30,960 books; 51,495 bound periodical volumes; 613 reels of microfilm of periodicals; 7958 microfiche; AV programs. **Subscriptions:** 1963 journals and other serials. **Services:** Interlibrary loan (fee); copying; SDI; library open to the public with restrictions. **Automated Operations:** Computerized cataloging, acquisitions, circulation, serials, and ILL (DOCLINE). **Computerized Information Services:** BRS Information Technologies, NLM, OCLC. Performs searches on fee basis. **Networks/Consortia:** Member of SOLINET, Consortium of Southern Biomedical Libraries (CONBLS). **Publications:** Acquisitions & Information Letter, quarterly - free upon request. **Remarks:** FAX: (205)460-7638. **Staff:** Patricia M. Rodgers, Tech.Serv.Coord.; Sr. Mary Giles Peresich, Cat.; Geneva Bush, Pub.Serv.Coord.; Judith Burnham, Info.Serv.Libn.

★ 19305 ★
University of South Alabama - Library - Special Collections (Hist)
University Blvd.   Phone: (205)460-7028
Mobile, AL 36688   Jim Damico, Dir.
Founded: 1964. **Subjects:** Local history, Alabama authors. **Holdings:** 942 books; university archival materials; masters' theses. **Services:** Library open to the public with restrictions for reference use only. **Automated Operations:** Computerized cataloging. **Computerized Information Services:** OCLC, DIALOG Information Services, BRS Information Technologies.

★ 19306 ★
University of South Carolina - Coleman Karesh Law Library (Law)
Law Center   Phone: (803)777-5942
Columbia, SC 29208   Bruce S. Johnson, Law Libn.
Founded: 1867. **Staff:** Prof 7; Other 7. **Subjects:** Law. **Special Collections:** South Carolina Legal History Collection; selected federal depository. **Holdings:** 218,148 volumes; 579,969 microfiche; 2718 reels of microfilm; 1705 audiocassettes; 134 video cassettes. **Subscriptions:** 4664 journals and other serials; 11 newspapers. **Services:** Interlibrary loan; copying; library open to the public. **Automated Operations:** Computerized cataloging. **Computerized Information Services:** LEXIS, WESTLAW, OCLC. **Networks/Consortia:** Member of SOLINET. **Remarks:** FAX: (803)777-9405. **Staff:** Steve Huang, Assoc. Law Libn.; Joseph R. Cross, Jr., Hd., Rd.Serv.; Mary M. McCormick, Ref.Libn.; Melissa M. Surber, Acq./Ser.Libn.; Diana Osbaldiston, Cat.Libn.; Cassandra S. Gissendanner, Cat.Libn.

★ 19307 ★
University of South Carolina - Computer Services Division Reference Room (Comp Sci)
1244 Blossom St.   Phone: (803)777-6015
Columbia, SC 29208   Alma Kinzley, Mgr.
Founded: 1982. **Staff:** Prof 1; Other 4. **Subjects:** Computer hardware and software. **Holdings:** 200 books. **Subscriptions:** 80 journals and other serials. **Services:** Copying; SDI; room open to members of the university community. **Automated Operations:** Computerized cataloging. **Publications:** Network, monthly - for internal distribution only. **Remarks:** FAX: (803)777-4760.

★ 19308 ★
University of South Carolina - Institute of Public Affairs - Library (Soc Sci)
Columbia, SC 29208 Phone: (803)777-8156
Pinkie Whitfield, Pubns.Dir.
Founded: 1947. **Staff:** Prof 1. **Subjects:** State and local government, public finance, public personnel administration. **Special Collections:** State of South Carolina reference materials and U.S. census information. **Holdings:** 300 books; 1500 South Carolina documents; 5000 federal and state documents. **Subscriptions:** 203 journals and other serials. **Services:** Library open to the public for reference use only. **Automated Operations:** Computerized cataloging. **Computerized Information Services:** North Carolina State's Polinet (electronic mail service). **Publications:** Bibliography of bureau publications.

★ 19309 ★
University of South Carolina - School of Medicine Library (Med)
Columbia, SC 29208 Phone: (803)733-3344
R. Thomas Lange, Dir.
Founded: 1975. **Staff:** Prof 6; Other 16. **Subjects:** Medicine. **Holdings:** 20,000 books; 51,400 bound periodical volumes; 900 AV programs; 4280 reels of microfilm. **Subscriptions:** 1120 journals and other serials. **Services:** Interlibrary loan; copying; SDI; library open to the public, with services to medical professionals only. **Automated Operations:** Computerized public access catalog, cataloging, acquisitions, serials, circulation, and ILL. **Computerized Information Services:** OCLC, DIALOG Information Services, PFDS Online, Library and Information Services (LIS), BRS Information Technologies, MEDLARS; OnTyme Electronic Message Network Service, DOCLINE (electronic mail services). **Networks/Consortia:** Member of SOLINET, Columbia Area Medical Librarians' Association (CAMLA), South Carolina Health Information Network (SCHIN). **Special Catalogs:** Southeastern Medical Periodicals Union List; South Carolina Union List of Medical Periodicals, annual - free to participating libraries, for sale to individuals. **Remarks:** FAX: (803)733-1509. **Staff:** Julie Johnson McGowan, Assoc.Dir.; Felicia Yeh-Lin, Cat.Libn.; Loretta Westcott, Cir.Libn.; Karen Warren, Ser.Libn.; Sarah Gable, Ref.Libn.

★ 19310 ★
University of South Carolina - South Caroliniana Library (Hist)
Columbia, SC 29208 Phone: (803)777-3131
Allen H. Stokes, Libn.
Founded: 1840. **Staff:** Prof 5; Other 7. **Subjects:** South Caroliniana. **Holdings:** 90,327 books and pamphlets; 2.1 million manuscripts; 500,000 issues of South Carolina newspapers; 2095 maps; 14,371 reels of microfilm; 14,000 pictures; 400 pieces of sheet music. **Subscriptions:** 225 journals and other serials; 81 newspapers. **Services:** Interlibrary loan; copying; library open to the public for reference use only. **Publications:** A Guide to the Manuscript Collection of the South Caroliniana Library. **Staff:** Eleanor Richardson, Ref.Libn.; Herbert Hartsook, Cur., Modern S.C. Polit. Coll.; Thomas L. Johnson, Asst.Libn.

★ 19311 ★
University of South Carolina - Thomas Cooper Library - Map Library (Geog-Map)
Columbia, SC 29208 Phone: (803)777-2802
David C. McQuillan, Map Libn.
Founded: 1897. **Staff:** Prof 1. **Subjects:** Maps. **Holdings:** 200,000 maps; 2000 atlases; 90,000 aerial photographs; U.S. Geological Survey depository; Defense Mapping Agency depository. **Services:** Copying; library open to the public for reference use only. **Computerized Information Services:** PC-Globe, PC-USA, US ATLAS, Electromap World Atlas, World Weather Disc, GEODEX (internal databases); BITNET (electronic mail service). **Remarks:** FAX: (803)777-4661. Electronic mail address(es): LI00003@UNIVSCVM (BITNET).

★ 19312 ★
University of South Carolina - Thomas Cooper Library - Rare Books & Special Collections Department (Rare Book)
Columbia, SC 29208 Phone: (803)777-8154
Roger Mortimer, Hd., Spec.Coll.
Staff: Prof 1; Other 2. **Subjects:** Theology and church history, American and British history, voyages, Scottish literature, British and American literature, early geology, 18th century botany and natural history, ornithology, history of books and printing. **Special Collections:** 19th Century American and

English Literary Annuals; Muggletonianism; Left Book Club; Alfred Chapin Rogers Collection of 18th Century American History; Francis Lord Collection of the American Civil War; papers of Lord Allen of Hurtwood; John Osman Collection on Braun & Hogenberg City Views; G. Ross Roy Collection of Burnsiana and Scottish Literature; Sir Walter Scott Collection; Ewelme Collection of Robert Bridges; Rodger Tarr Collection of Thomas Carlyle; Robert Louis Stevenson Collection; Victorian Literature Collection; Historical Children's Literature; Walt Whitman Collection; Robert Frost Collection; Special Collection of Modern American Literature; Thomas Cooper Collection of Early Geology and Natural History; John James Audubon Collection; Claudia Lea Phelps Camellia Collection; Richard Wingate Lloyd Collection of Early Botany. **Holdings:** 40,000 books; 3000 manuscripts. **Services:** Interlibrary loan; copying; department open to the public for reference use only. **Computerized Information Services:** Internal databases. **Publications:** A Load of Gratitude: Audubon and South Carolina; Aspects of the Western Religious Heritage; Aspects of French Culture. **Remarks:** FAX: (803)777-9503.

★ 19313 ★
University of South Carolina - University Archives (Hist)
McKissick Museum Phone: (803)777-7251
Columbia, SC 29208 John R. Heiting, Archv.
Founded: 1976. **Staff:** Prof 3; Other 2. **Subjects:** University history. **Special Collections:** 19th century library records; photographs (30 cubic feet). **Holdings:** 3500 cubic feet of archives; student yearbooks, 1899 to present; minutes of faculty senate and board of trustees meetings, 1803-1962. **Services:** Copying; archives open to the public. **Publications:** University Archives Preliminary Guide; Guide to University Archives Photographic Collection. **Staff:** Gary Keith, Asst.Univ.Archv.

University of South Dakota - Center for the Study of the History of Musical Instruments - Shrine to Music Museum
See: **Shrine to Music Museum** (15146)

★ 19314 ★
University of South Dakota - Chemistry Library (Sci-Engr)
Pardee Laboratory Phone: (605)677-5487
Vermillion, SD 57069 Jan Small, Sec.
Subjects: Chemistry, chemical physics, history and philosophy of science. **Special Collections:** A.M. Pardee Historical Book Collection (420 volumes). **Holdings:** 1029 books; 3771 bound periodical volumes. **Subscriptions:** 109 journals and other serials. **Services:** Interlibrary loan; copying; library open to the public with restrictions on circulation. **Remarks:** FAX: (605)677-5073.

★ 19315 ★
University of South Dakota - Christian P. Lommen Health Sciences Library (Med)
School of Medicine
414 E. Clark Phone: (605)677-5347
Vermillion, SD 57069-2390 David A. Hulkonen, Dir.
Founded: 1907. **Staff:** Prof 3; Other 7. **Subjects:** Anatomy, physiology, pharmacology, microbiology, pathology, biochemistry, nursing, dental hygiene, medical technology, clinical medicine. **Special Collections:** History of Medicine; medical school archives. **Holdings:** 38,000 books; 47,000 bound periodical volumes; 900 AV programs. **Subscriptions:** 1012 journals and other serials. **Services:** Interlibrary loan; copying; SDI; reference; consultation services for hospitals; library open to the public. **Automated Operations:** Computerized public access catalog, cataloging, circulation, and serials. **Computerized Information Services:** OCLC, BRS Information Technologies, MEDLARS, PHILSOM; MEDLINE, PHILSOM, DOCLINE (electronic mail service). Performs searches on fee basis. Contact Person: Barbara Papik, Hd. User Serv. **Networks/Consortia:** Member of National Network of Libraries of Medicine - Greater Midwest Region, MINITEX Library Information Network, South Dakota Library Network (SDLN). **Publications:** Accessions list, monthly. **Special Catalogs:** South Dakota Union List of Health Science Serials. **Special Indexes:** Index to faculty publications (computer printout). **Remarks:** FAX: (605)677-5124. **Staff:** Gene Sederstrom, Hd., Tech.Serv.; Muriel Schamber, ILL. Grace Linden, Circ.

★ 19316 ★
University of South Dakota - Governmental Research Library (Soc Sci)
Vermillion, SD 57069   Phone: (605)677-5702
                                             Steven H. Feimer, Dir.
Founded: 1939. **Staff:** Prof 1. **Subjects:** State and local government, public administration, South Dakota government, political behavior, public finance, American Indians, public law, legislative apportionment. **Holdings:** 600 books; 40 bound periodical volumes. **Subscriptions:** 20 journals and other serials. **Services:** Copying; library open to the public for reference use only. **Publications:** Public Affairs; Reports, irregular; Special Projects, irregular.

★ 19317 ★
University of South Dakota - I.D. Weeks Library - Richardson Archives
   (Hist)
Vermillion, SD 57069   Phone: (605)677-5450
                                             Karen Zimmerman, Archv.
Founded: 1967. **Staff:** Prof 1. **Subjects:** History - Western U.S., frontier, South Dakota; American Indians. **Special Collections:** University Archives. **Holdings:** 10,500 books; 3528 linear feet of manuscripts. **Services:** Copying; archives open to the public with permission. **Automated Operations:** Computerized cataloging and acquisitions. **Computerized Information Services:** BITNET (electronic mail service). Performs searches on fee basis. **Networks/Consortia:** Member of MINITEX Library Information Network, South Dakota Library Network (SDLN). **Publications:** Guide to Collection - available upon request. **Remarks:** FAX: (605)677-5488. Electronic mail address(es): uzktl0@sdnet (BITNET).

★ 19318 ★
University of South Dakota - McKusick Law Library (Law)
414 E. Clark   Phone: (605)677-5259
Vermillion, SD 57069   John F. Hagemann, Law Libn.
Founded: 1901. **Staff:** Prof 7; Other 2. **Subjects:** Law - U.S., English, Canadian. **Special Collections:** Law - agricultural, Indian, family, water, tax, professional responsibility; arts and the law; South Dakota Supreme Court briefs (65 VF drawers); U.S. Circuit Court, 8th Circuit slip opinions. **Holdings:** 122,625 bound volumes; 6 VF drawers of pamphlets; 97,116 microfiche; 4 VF drawers of archives. **Subscriptions:** 1762 journals and other serials; 11 newspapers. **Services:** Interlibrary loan (fee); copying; SDI; library open to the public. **Automated Operations:** Computerized public access catalog, serials, acquisitions, and ILL. **Computerized Information Services:** LEXIS, WESTLAW, NEXIS; InterNet (electronic mail service). Performs searches on fee basis. Contact Person: Debbie Despain, Ref./Comp.Libn. **Networks/Consortia:** Member of MINITEX Library Information Network, South Dakota Library Network (SDLN), Mid-America Law School Library Consortium. **Publications:** Bibliography of periodical articles related to Indian law; Guide to the Law Library; Locator Guide. **Special Indexes:** List of Periodicals; Survey of Bibliographies and Indexes. **Remarks:** FAX: (605)677-5413. Electronic mail address(es): DDESPAIN@CHARLIE.USD.EDU (InterNet). **Staff:** Mary Jensen, Dir.; Candice Spurlin, Circ./ILL Libn.; Delores Jorgenson, Cat.Libn.; Karyl Knodel, Ser.Libn.; Barbara Heisinger, Coll.Libn.

★ 19319 ★
University of South Florida - Division of Learning Technologies - Film
   & Video Distribution Library (Aud-Vis)
4202 Fowler Ave.   Phone: (813)974-2874
Tampa, FL 33620   Jacqueline D. Fechter, Film/Video Distribution
Staff: Prof 3; Other 1. **Subjects:** Education, special education, social studies, literature, fine arts, management. **Special Collections:** Physical Education for the Handicapped (19 titles); Protocol Materials for Teacher Training (62 titles). **Holdings:** 1700 16mm films; 200 video cassettes. **Services:** Library open to the public with rental fee for film usage. **Networks/Consortia:** Member of Consortium of College and University Media Centers (CCUMC). **Special Catalogs:** Triennial book catalog of currently available film titles, updated with annual supplements - on request. **Formerly:** Its Film & Video Library.

★ 19320 ★
University of South Florida - Florida Mental Health Institute - Library
   (Med, Soc Sci)
13301 Bruce B. Downs Blvd.   Phone: (813)974-4471
Tampa, FL 33612   Ardis Hanson, Asst.Univ.Libn./Act.Dir.
Founded: 1974. **Staff:** Prof 2; Other 1. **Subjects:** Psychology and psychiatry; AIDS; epidemiology; aging, child, and family programs; forensics;

community mental health; social work. **Special Collections:** Florida Mental Health Institute Archives; AIDS/HIV collection. **Holdings:** 9650 books; 62 bound periodical volumes; 2500 unbound periodicals; 450 state and government documents; 60 microforms; 280 audio- and videocassettes; 74 kits; 82 computer diskettes. **Subscriptions:** 190 journals and other serials. **Services:** Interlibrary loan; copying; SDI; library open to the public with restrictions. **Automated Operations:** Integrated library system (NOTIS). **Computerized Information Services:** ERIC; CD-ROM (PsycLIT); internal databases. **Networks/Consortia:** Member of SOLINET. **Remarks:** FAX: (813)974-4406. **Staff:** Brian A. Greene, Tech.Serv.

★ 19321 ★
University of South Florida - Health Sciences Center Library (Med)
12901 Bruce B. Downs Blvd.
Box 31   Phone: (813)974-2399
Tampa, FL 33612   Beverly Shattuck, Dir.
Founded: 1971. **Staff:** Prof 7; Other 17. **Subjects:** Medicine, nursing, public health, allied health sciences. **Holdings:** 106,021 volumes. **Subscriptions:** 1504 journals and other serials. **Services:** Interlibrary loan; copying; SDI; library open to the public for health related research. **Automated Operations:** Computerized cataloging, serials, and acquisitions. **Computerized Information Services:** MEDLINE, DIALOG Information Services, OCLC; CD-ROMs (PsycLIT, CINAHL, MEDLINE); OnTyme Electronic Message Network Service (electronic mail service). Performs searches on fee basis. **Networks/Consortia:** Member of Tampa Bay Medical Library Network, Consortium of Southern Biomedical Libraries (CONBLS), SOLINET. **Publications:** Occasional papers. **Remarks:** FAX: (813)974-4930. **Staff:** Judy Johnston, Assoc.Dir.; Sarah Harmon, Tech.Serv.; Donna Doelling, Ref.Dept.; Gwen Wolff, Educ.Coord.; Larry Cramer, AV Dept.

★ 19322 ★
University of South Florida - Library - Special Collections Department
   (Hum, Hist)
4202 E. Fowler Ave.   Phone: (813)974-2731
Tampa, FL 33620   Thomas Jay Kemp
Staff: Prof 2; Other 4. **Subjects:** Floridiana, 19th and early 20th century American literature with emphasis on juvenile fiction. **Special Collections:** Florida Collection (20,000 volumes; maps; photographs; other items); Hudson Collection of Hard Cover Boys and Girls Series Books (9000 volumes); Dime Novel Collection (9000 items); Early American Textbook Collection (2000 volumes); Dobkin Collection of 19th Century American Literature (25,000 volumes); American Toybook Collection (600 items); Cigar Box Art (cigar labels, progressive proof books, and cigar industry memorabilia; 1000 proof books; 25,000 labels, bands, and other items); 19th century American Almanacs (900); 19th century American Printed Ephemera (10,000 advertising and greeting cards); Florida Postcards (7000); G.A. Henty Collection (500 volumes); Mosher Press Publications (700 volumes); 19th century American songsters and songbooks (200 volumes); NCNB Black American Music Collection (5000 pieces of sheet music); Florida Sheet Music Collection (500 items); Miniature Book Collection (600 items); Acting Editions of 19th century American Plays (1000 items). **Services:** Interlibrary loan (limited); copying; collections open to public. **Automated Operations:** Computerized cataloging. **Computerized Information Services:** OCLC. **Networks/Consortia:** Member of SOLINET. **Publications:** Ex Libris, irregular; 19th Century Tampa-Family Reconstitution Project; University of South Florida Library Bibliographic Series (American Boys' Series Books, 1900-1980; American Anthropomorphic Animal Series, 1900-1987). **Special Indexes:** USF Index. **Staff:** Paul Eugen Camp, Univ.Libn.

University of Southern California - Arnold Schoenberg Institute
See: **Arnold Schoenberg Institute** (14916)

★ 19323 ★
University of Southern California - Catalina Marine Science Center -
   Tibby Library (Biol Sci)
Big Fisherman Cove
Box 398
Avalon, CA 90704   Phone: (213)743-6792
Founded: 1969. **Staff:** Prof 1. **Subjects:** Marine biology, oceanography, marine ecology, invertebrate zoology. **Holdings:** 700 books; 100 bound periodical volumes. **Subscriptions:** 10 journals and other serials. **Services:** Interlibrary loan; copying; library open to the public at librarian's discretion. **Remarks:** Alternate telephone number(s): 743-6793; 743-7882. FAX: (213)510-1364.

★19324★
University of Southern California - Crocker Business and Accounting Libraries (Bus-Fin)
University Park   Phone: (213)740-8520
Los Angeles, CA 90089-1421   Judith A. Truelson, Hd.
Founded: 1967. **Staff:** Prof 3; Other 4. **Subjects:** Accounting and taxation, finance, marketing, decision systems, organizational behavior, business economics, management, investments, multinational business. **Holdings:** 71,000 books; 12,500 bound periodical volumes; 15,000 reels of microfilm; 500,000 microfiche, including annual reports. **Subscriptions:** 1650 journals and other serials; 50 newspapers. **Services:** Library open to the public. **Computerized Information Services:** DIALOG Information Services, BRS Information Technologies, PFDS Online. **Publications:** Selected subject bibliographies - for internal distribution only; Top Fifty Acquisitions, monthly - for internal distribution only. **Remarks:** FAX: (213)747-7263. **Staff:** Lillian Yang, Hd., Accounting Lib.; Deborah Bryson, Tech.Serv./ Ref.Libn.

★19325★
University of Southern California - Dentistry Library (Med)
DEN 201
University Park - MC 0641   Phone: (213)740-6476
Los Angeles, CA 90089-0641   Frank O. Mason, Dental Libn.
Founded: 1897. **Staff:** Prof 2; Other 3. **Subjects:** Dentistry, medicine, allied sciences. **Special Collections:** History of Dentistry (400 volumes). **Holdings:** 17,325 books; 11,500 bound periodical volumes; 2300 test files; 2519 AV programs and filmstrips; 1142 reading files. **Subscriptions:** 645 journals and other serials. **Services:** Interlibrary loan (fee); copying; SDI; library open to the public with Library card. **Automated Operations:** Computerized public access catalog, cataloging, acquisitions, serials, circulation, and ILL (DOCLINE). **Computerized Information Services:** DIALOG Information Services, OCLC, MEDLARS, MEDLINE; InterNet, OnTyme Electronic Message Network Service, (electronic mail service). Performs searches on fee basis. Contact Person: John Glueckert, Ref.Libn., 743-2884. **Networks/Consortia:** Member of National Network of Libraries of Medicine - Pacific Southwest Region, CLASS. **Publications:** List of Recently Acquired Titles, bimonthly - for internal distribution only. **Remarks:** FAX: (213)748-8565. Electronic mail address(es): fmason@phad.hsc.usc.edu (InterNet).

★19326★
University of Southern California - East Asian Library (Area-Ethnic)
University Park   Phone: (213)740-1772
Los Angeles, CA 90089-0182   Ken Klein, Hd., East Asian Lib.
Founded: 1956. **Staff:** Prof 2; Other 1. **Subjects:** East Asian social sciences and humanities with emphasis on Korean language. **Holdings:** 56,000 volumes. **Subscriptions:** 300 journals and other serials. **Services:** Interlibrary loan; copying; library open to the public for reference use only. **Computerized Information Services:** BITNET (electronic mail service). **Networks/Consortia:** Member of Research Libraries Information Network (RLIN). **Remarks:** Alternate telephone number(s): 740-3378. FAX: (213)749-1221. Electronic mail address(es): BM.EAZ@RLG (BITNET). **Staff:** Joy Kim, Hd., Korean Heritage Lib.

★19327★
University of Southern California - Emery Stoops and Joyce King-Stoops Education Library (Educ)
University Park   Phone: (213)740-1781
Los Angeles, CA 90089-0182   Linda Weber, Hd., Educ.Libn.
Founded: 1924. **Staff:** Prof 2; Other 3. **Subjects:** Education and related subjects, instructional technology, educational psychology, international education, sociology of education, higher education, early childhood education. **Special Collections:** Curriculum Collection (7839 texts and 6532 courses); juvenile books (6500 volumes); tests (1815); Donald E. Wilson Collection of Old Textbooks (200 volumes); Jean Burton Clark Higher Education Browsing Area (400 volumes). **Holdings:** 150,000 books; 7000 bound periodical volumes; 140 AV programs; 31 films; 390,000 microfiche; 12 VF drawers of pamphlets; 5000 reels of microfilm. **Subscriptions:** 501 journals and other serials. **Services:** Interlibrary loan; copying; library open to the public for reference use only. **Automated Operations:** Computerized cataloging, acquisitions, and circulation. **Computerized Information Services:** DIALOG Information Services. **Remarks:** FAX: (213)743-0864. **Staff:** Mark Merbaum, Assoc.Prof.

★19328★
University of Southern California - Gerontology Library (Soc Sci)
120 Gerontology - MC 0191   Phone: (213)740-5990
Los Angeles, CA 90089-0191   Stella Fu, Hd., Gerontology Lib.
Founded: 1966. **Staff:** Prof 1; Other 1. **Subjects:** Gerontology. **Special Collections:** Doctoral dissertations on aging and gerontology, 1934-1985 (microfilm); reprints collection (2000 items); Leonard Davis School of Gerontology Masters' Theses Collection; SCAN microfiche collection. **Holdings:** 10,000 books; 750 bound periodical volumes; 1500 reels of microfilm of dissertations. **Subscriptions:** 105 journals; 200 newsletters and other serials. **Services:** Interlibrary loan; copying; center open to the public for reference use only. **Automated Operations:** Computerized public access catalog, cataloging, acquisitions, and circulation. **Computerized Information Services:** RLIN, DIALOG Information Services, BRS Information Technologies. **Networks/Consortia:** Member of Research Libraries Information Network (RLIN). **Publications:** A Bibliography of Doctoral Dissertations on Aging from American Institutions of Higher Learning, 1934-1969 through 1976-1978; Journal of Gerontology, 1971-1988, annual. **Remarks:** FAX: (213)749-1221.

★19329★
University of Southern California - Hancock Library of Biology & Oceanography (Biol Sci)
University Park   Phone: (213)740-7542
Los Angeles, CA 90089-0372   Jean E. Crampon, Hd., Hancock Lib.
Founded: 1944. **Staff:** Prof 2; Other 3. **Subjects:** Marine biology, oceanography, zoology, botany, paleontology. **Special Collections:** Early scientific expeditions; natural history. **Holdings:** 25,963 books; 81,578 bound periodical volumes; scientific reprints and pamphlets. **Subscriptions:** 2299 journals and other serials. **Services:** Interlibrary loan; copying; library open to researchers. **Automated Operations:** Computerized cataloging. **Computerized Information Services:** OCLC, DIALOG Information Services, BRS Information Technologies. **Remarks:** FAX: (213)740-5142. **Staff:** Melinda Hayes, Coll.Dev./Cons.Libn.

★19330★
University of Southern California - Health Sciences Campus - Norris Medical Library (Med)
2003 Zonal Ave.   Phone: (213)342-1116
Los Angeles, CA 90033-4582   Nelson J. Gilman, Libn./Dir.
Founded: 1928. **Staff:** Prof 14; Other 27. **Subjects:** Medicine, pharmacy, occupational therapy, physical therapy. **Special Collections:** History of Medicine; Ethnopharmacology of American Indians; Far West Medicine. **Holdings:** 45,895 books; 94,602 bound periodical volumes; 40,229 slides; 8865 microfiche; 105 reels of microfilm; 2855 audiocassettes; 1080 videocassettes; 74 films; 46 filmstrips; 26 phonograph discs; 975 floppy discs; 6 compact discs; 40 video discs. **Subscriptions:** 2604 journals and other serials. **Services:** Interlibrary loan; copying; SDI; library open to the public for reference use only. **Automated Operations:** Computerized cataloging, acquisitions, serials, and circulation. **Computerized Information Services:** DIALOG Information Services, MEDLARS, PFDS Online, BRS Information Technologies, OCLC; USCInfo (internal database); OnTyme Electronic Message Network Service, InterNet (electronic mail services). Performs searches on fee basis. **Networks/Consortia:** Member of CLASS, National Network of Libraries of Medicine - Pacific Southwest Region, Health Information to Community Hospitals (HITCH). **Publications:** A Guide to Drug Information and Literature: An Annotated Bibliography; Learning Resources Newsletter; Library Newsletter; all bimonthly; Information, irregular; Computerized Acquisitions Tracking System (CATS); occasional papers. **Remarks:** Alternate telephone number(s): 342-1111. FAX: (213)221-1235. Telex: 494 9018. Electronic mail address(es): MEDLIB@PHAD.HSC.USC.EDU (InterNet); USCNML (OnTyme Electronic Message Network Service). **Staff:** Diane Johnson, Ref.Libn.; Teresa Manthey, Ref.Libn.; Dudee Chiang, Ref.Libn.; Bill Clintworth, Assoc.Dir., Info.Serv.; Elizabeth Wood, Hd. of Ref.; Eileen Eandi, Ref.Libn.; Jan Nelson, Ref.Libn.; Janis Brown, Assoc.Dir., Educ.Rsrcs.; Alice Karasick, Acq./Ser.Libn.; Margaret Wineburgh-Freed, Cat.Libn.; David Morse, Assoc.Dir., Coll.Rsrcs.; Louise Adams, Circuit-Rider Libn.; Pamela Corley, Ref.Libn.; Joan Mircheff, AV Acq.Libn.

★19331★
University of Southern California - Helen Topping Architecture & Fine Arts Library (Art, Plan)
University Park   Phone: (213)740-1956
Los Angeles, CA 90089-0292   Amy Navratil Ciccone, Hd.
Founded: 1925. **Staff:** Prof 2; Other 3. **Subjects:** Art history, history of architecture, architectural design, studio arts, photography, museum

studies, city planning. **Special Collections:** Primary source material in architectural history of Southern California; contemporary art; artists books. **Holdings:** 60,000 books; 5500 bound periodical volumes; 28 VF drawers of architecture and fine arts materials; 8 VF drawers of city planning materials; 200,000 slides; 10 VF drawers of exhibition catalogs. **Subscriptions:** 250 journals and other serials. **Services:** Interlibrary loan; copying; library open to the public. **Automated Operations:** Computerized public access catalog, cataloging, acquisitions, and circulation. **Computerized Information Services:** RLIN, DIALOG Information Services, BRS Information Technologies; USCInfo (internal database). **Networks/Consortia:** Member of Research Libraries Information Network (RLIN). **Special Catalogs:** East Asian Art catalog (card). **Special Indexes:** Guide to Indexes in the Architecture & Fine Arts Library; Guide to Vertical File. **Remarks:** FAX: (213)749-1221. **Staff:** Deborah Barlow, Ref.Libn.

★ 19332 ★

University of Southern California - Information Sciences Institute - Technical Library (Comp Sci)
4676 Admiralty Way   Phone: (213)822-1511
Marina Del Rey, CA 90292   Linda Louie, Hd.Libn.
Founded: 1972. **Staff:** Prof 1; Other 2. **Subjects:** Computer science, mathematics, electronics, cognitive psychology, linguistics. **Holdings:** 2800 books; 1700 bound periodical volumes; 7000 technical reports. **Subscriptions:** 120 journals and other serials. **Services:** Interlibrary loan; library not open to the public. **Automated Operations:** Computerized cataloging, acquisitions, serials, and circulation. **Computerized Information Services:** DIALOG Information Services; BITNET (electronic mail service). **Publications:** Newsletter, monthly. **Remarks:** FAX: (213)823-6714. Electronic mail address(es): techlib@isi.edu (BITNET).

★ 19333 ★

University of Southern California - Institute of Safety and Systems Management - Library (Sci-Engr)
SSM Library
University Park - MC 0021   Phone: (213)740-7053
Los Angeles, CA 90089-0021   Marco A. Ruiz, Act.Libn.
Founded: 1966. **Subjects:** Safety, systems, and decision science; systems management; human factors; biomechanics. **Special Collections:** Safety and Systems Management. **Holdings:** 10,000 books; 1270 bound periodical volumes; annual reports; proceedings; indexes; abstracts; safety newsletters and related serials. **Subscriptions:** 50 journals and other serials; 10 newspapers. **Services:** Interlibrary loan; copying; library open to the public with restrictions. **Automated Operations:** Computerized cataloging. **Computerized Information Services:** OCLC. Performs searches on fee basis. **Publications:** List of acquisitions, bimonthly - for internal distribution only. **Remarks:** The library serves 10 Study Centers in California. Alternate telephone number(s): 743-6999.

★ 19334 ★

University of Southern California - Law Library (Law)
University Park - MC 0072   Phone: (213)740-6482
Los Angeles, CA 90089-0072   Albert Brecht, Dir.
Founded: 1896. **Staff:** Prof 10; Other 11. **Subjects:** Anglo-American law, legal history, legal literature, taxation, law and social sciences. **Special Collections:** Legislative history of Internal Revenue Acts. **Holdings:** 237,633 books; 364,382 microforms; 230 shelves of documents; 1021 audiotapes and video cassettes. **Subscriptions:** 3866 journals and other serials. **Services:** Interlibrary loan; copying; SDI; library open to the public. **Automated Operations:** Computerized cataloging, acquisitions, and serials. **Computerized Information Services:** LEXIS, WESTLAW, DIALOG Information Services, NEXIS, WILSONLINE, BRS Information Technologies, DataQuick, ORION, Legaltrac, RLIN. **Networks/Consortia:** Member of Research Libraries Information Network (RLIN). **Publications:** Acquisition list, monthly; library guide, irregular; newsletter, semiannual; subject guide to secondary sources, irregular. **Remarks:** FAX: (213)740-7179. **Staff:** Pauline Aranas, Assoc.Dir.; Leonette Williams, Asst.Dir., Tech.Serv.; Paul George, Asst.Dir.Pub.Serv.; Susan McGlamery, Ref.; Robert Jones, Ref.; Hazel Lord, Access Serv.; Elizabeth Scherer, Cat.; Gregg Silvis, Comp.Serv.; Lisa Moske, Acq.

★ 19335 ★

University of Southern California - Library - Boeckmann Center for Iberian and Latin American Studies (Area-Ethnic)
Doheny Memorial Library
University Park   Phone: (213)740-3566
Los Angeles, CA 90089-0182   Barbara J. Robinson, Cur.
Founded: 1985. **Staff:** Prof 1; Other 3. **Subjects:** Latin American studies, history, and literature; Iberian studies; Spanish literature; Portuguese literature. **Special Collections:** Cervantes Collection (1000 volumes); Maximilian Collection (250 volumes); Central American Collection (12,000 titles); Cuban Collection (20,000 volumes); Tauromaquia Collection (100 volumes); early 19th century Mexican hacienda manuscripts (15 volumes); pamphlet collection (4000 volumes). **Holdings:** 100,000 books; bound periodical volumes. **Subscriptions:** 31 journals and other serials. **Services:** Interlibrary loan; copying; center open to the public for reference use only. **Automated Operations:** Computerized public access catalog, acquisitions, circulation. **Computerized Information Services:** RLIN, OCLC; USCInfo (internal database); BITNET (electronic mail service). **Networks/Consortia:** Member of Center for Research Libraries (CRL). **Publications:** Las Noticias (newsletter), monthly - available on request. **Remarks:** FAX: (213)749-1221. Electronic mail address(es): BROBINSO@USCVM (BITNET).

★ 19336 ★

University of Southern California - Library - Cinema-Television Library and Archives of Performing Arts (Theater)
Doheny Memorial Library   Phone: (213)740-8906
Los Angeles, CA 90089-0182   Stephen Hanson, Act.Hd.
Founded: 1964. **Staff:** Prof 1; Other 2. **Subjects:** Motion pictures, television, radio. **Special Collections:** MGM Collection, 1918-1958 (1900 titles, including screenplay drafts, synopses, and treatments); Warner Bros. Archives (all files from Burbank studio through 1967); Twentieth Century-Fox Script Collection, 1919-1967 (900 titles); Universal Pictures Collection (800 boxes); motion picture and television clippings and ephemera (175 feet); U.S. theater programs (50 feet); motion picture and portrait stills (140 feet); 206 collections of memorabilia from directors, writers, producers, composers, art directors, and actors. **Holdings:** 18,000 volumes; 250 reels of microfilm; 427 cartridges of videotape of David Wolper productions, 1962-1972; teleplay collection; screenplay collection; 1700 reels and cartridges of audiotape; 1200 soundtracks and original cast recordings. **Subscriptions:** 220 journals and other serials. **Services:** Interlibrary loan (limited); copying; library open to the public for reference use only. **Networks/Consortia:** Member of Performing Arts Libraries Network of Greater Los Angeles (PALNET). **Special Catalogs:** Catalog of Screenplays; Catalog of Audiotapes; pressbook catalog. **Special Indexes:** Index of Collections (looseleaf); An Index to Screenplays, Interviews and Special Collections (1975); An Index to Warner Bros. Archives; An Index to Universal Pictures Collection; index to motion picture stills and portraits. **Remarks:** FAX: (213)747-3301.

★ 19337 ★

University of Southern California - Library - Department of Special Collections (Hist)
University Park   Phone: (213)740-5946
Los Angeles, CA 90089-0182   Victoria Steele, Hd., Spec.Coll.
Founded: 1963. **Staff:** Prof 4; Other 3. **Subjects:** History - general, western, aeronautical; bibliography; fine printing; evolution; philosophy, Los Angeles, British East India, theater. **Special Collections:** Printing Arts collection (includes the Richard Hoffman Collection). **Holdings:** 130,000 volumes; 1.4 million manuscripts; 1.3 million clippings. **Subscriptions:** 54 journals and other serials. **Services:** Interlibrary loan; department open to researchers for reference use only. **Publications:** Special Collections (brochure). **Remarks:** Alternate telephone number(s): 743-2923. **Remarks:** FAX: (213)749-1221. **Staff:** John Ahouse, Asst.Hd., Spec.Coll.; Marje Schuetze-Coburn, Feuchtwanger Libn.; Marion Schulman, Gen.Bibliog.

★ 19338 ★

University of Southern California - Library - Department of Special Collections - American Literature Collection (Hum)
University Park   Phone: (213)740-5946
Los Angeles, CA 90089-0182   John Ahouse, Asst.Hd.,Spec.Coll.
Founded: 1940. **Staff:** Prof 1. **Subjects:** American literature, especially 1850 to present. **Special Collections:** Hamlin Garland papers (12,000 items); Jack London Collection (300 items); Willard S. Morse Collections of Ambrose Bierce, William Dean Howells, Sinclair Lewis, and Frank Norris; Paul Bowles Collection; Kenneth Rexroth Collection; archives of Charles

Bukowski, Lawrence Ferlinghetti, Lawrence Lipton, Jack Hirschman, and Tom Clark; Poets Garden Collection (Ruth LePrade). **Holdings:** 38,000 books; 19,000 manuscripts. **Subscriptions:** 20 journals and other serials. **Services:** Interlibrary loan; copying; collection open to researchers for reference use only. **Special Indexes:** Index to Hamlin Garland Collection (book); List of Manuscript Collections (loose-leaf). **Remarks:** FAX: (213)749-1221.

★ 19339 ★
University of Southern California - Library - Department of Special Collections - Feuchtwanger Memorial Library (Hist, Area-Ethnic)
Dept. of Special Collections
University Park   Phone: (213)740-5946
Los Angeles, CA 90089-0182   Marje Schuetze-Coburn, Hd.
Founded: 1959. **Staff:** Prof 2. **Subjects:** German literature and culture, exile studies, the French Revolution, Judaica, history of art. **Holdings:** 30,000 books; 30 bound periodical volumes; 75 cubic feet of manuscripts; correspondence; photographs; films. **Services:** Copying; library open to qualified researchers. **Computerized Information Services:** BITNET (electronic mail service). **Remarks:** FAX: (213)749-1221. Electronic mail address(es): SCHUETZE@USCVM (BITNET). **Staff:** Harold Von Hofe, Cur.

★ 19340 ★
University of Southern California - Library - Regional History Collection (Hist)
University Park   Phone: (213)743-3147
Los Angeles, CA 90089-0182   Victoria Steele, Hd., Spec.Coll.
Founded: 1940. **Staff:** Prof 2; Other 1. **Subjects:** Southern California politics. **Special Collections:** Hearst Collection (1.2 million photographs; 220,000 negatives, metal plates, clippings); Edmund G. Brown, Jr. Collection (2000 boxes); Craig Hosmer Collection (248 boxes); Thomas Rees Collection (117 boxes); Alphonzo Bell Collection (200 boxes); Yvonne Burke Collection (410 boxes); Eugene Biscailuz Collection; Houston Flournoy Collection; Frank D. Lanterman Collection; Gordon McDonough Collection; John Rousselot Collection; Home Front Collection; Century Freeway Collection; California Historical Society Collection. **Services:** Interlibrary loan; copying; collection open to the public by appointment. **Automated Operations:** Computerized cataloging, acquisitions, serials, and circulation. **Computerized Information Services:** RLIN, OCLC. **Special Indexes:** Governor Edmund G. Brown, Jr. Collection: An Inventory. **Remarks:** FAX: (213)749-1221. **Staff:** John Ahouse, Asst.Hd., Spec.Coll.

★ 19341 ★
University of Southern California - Music Library (Mus)
University Park   Phone: (213)740-0183
Los Angeles, CA 90089-0182   Rodney D. Rolfs, Hd., Mus.Lib.
Founded: 1952. **Staff:** Prof 1; Other 2; **Subjects:** Music. **Holdings:** 15,000 volumes; 18,000 phonograph records; 4000 cassettes; 40,000 scores. **Subscriptions:** 145 journals and other serials. **Services:** Interlibrary loan; copying; library. **Remarks:** FAX: (213)749-1221.

★ 19342 ★
University of Southern California - NASA Industrial Application Center (NIAC) (Sci-Engr)
3716 S. Hope St., Rm. 200   Phone: (213)743-6132
Los Angeles, CA 90007-4344   Robert Stark, Dir.
Founded: 1967. **Staff:** 10. **Subjects:** Aerodynamics; aircraft; auxiliary systems; biosciences; biotechnology; chemistry; communications; computers; electronic equipment; electronics; facilities research and support; fluid mechanics; geophysics; instrumentation and photography; machine elements and processes; masers; metallic and nonmetallic materials; mathematics; meteorology; navigation; nuclear engineering; physics - general, atomic, molecular, nuclear, plasma, solid state; propellants; propulsion systems; space - radiation, sciences, vehicles; structural mechanics; thermodynamics and combustion; patents; trademarks; business and market information. **Holdings:** 750,000 NASA technical reports on microfiche. **Services:** Technology services include Current Awareness Information Services (current awareness search; standard interest profile; monthly manual search of any source) and Retrospective Information Services (retrospective search; one time search of any source for period desired); center open to the public. **Computerized Information Services:** NIAC/USC has at its disposal the data banks of NASA, DIALOG Information Services, ORBIT Search Service, NLM, Data-Star, VU/TEXT Information Services, DataTimes, BRS Information Technologies, and STN

International; DIALMAIL, Dialcom, Inc., NASAMAIL (electronic mail services). **Publications:** NIACCESS - the Tecnology Transfer Newsletter of the NASA Industrial Application Center. **Remarks:** NIAC/USC is a nonprofit organization whose purpose is to disseminate technological information to U.S. industry and to implement NASA's Technology Utilization Program in the Western U.S. FAX: (213)746-9043. **Staff:** Martin Zeller, Mgr., Info.Serv.; Walter Goldenrath, Ph.D., Tech.Couns.

★ 19343 ★
University of Southern California - Philosophy Library (Hum)
University Park   Phone: (213)740-7434
Los Angeles, CA 90089-0182   LaVonne Wuertz, Act.Hd.
Founded: 1930. **Staff:** Prof 1; Other 1. **Subjects:** Philosophy. **Special Collections:** W.T. Harris Collection; Gomperz Collection (3500 volumes; 2000 pamphlets). **Holdings:** 49,000 books; 5800 bound periodical volumes. **Subscriptions:** 180 journals and other serials. **Services:** Interlibrary loan; copying; library open to the public for reference use only. **Remarks:** FAX: (213)749-1221.

★ 19344 ★
University of Southern California - Population Research Laboratory - Library (Soc Sci)
University Park, Research Annex 385   Phone: (213)743-2950
Los Angeles, CA 90007   Prof. Maurice D. Van Arsdol, Jr., Dir.
Founded: 1960. **Subjects:** Population, demography, census, human ecology, urban sociology. **Special Collections:** U.S. Census of Population and Housing, 1940, 1950, 1960, 1970, 1980; Latin American census. **Holdings:** 6000 U.S. Bureau of Census reports, vital statistics reports, United Nations reports, maps, computer tapes, journals, books, reprints, dissertations, newsletters, pamphlets, bibliographies. **Subscriptions:** 30 journals and other serials. **Services:** Library open to the public upon request. **Remarks:** FAX: (213)743-7408.

★ 19345 ★
University of Southern California - School of Architecture - Gamble House - Greene and Greene Library (Art)
Huntington Library
Virginia Steele Scott Gallery
1151 Oxford Rd.   Phone: (818)405-2232
San Marino, CA 91108   Doris N. Gertmenian, Lib.Comm.Chm.
Founded: 1968. **Subjects:** Architecture, Charles and Henry Greene, Craftsman Period, Tiffany glass, arts and crafts. **Special Collections:** Drawings, blueprints, books, magazines, photographs of the Greene brothers, their contemporaries, and the Arts and Crafts movement; Greene brothers' personal memorabilia, client clippings and files. **Holdings:** 800 books; 125 bound periodical volumes; pamphlets and photographs; 4 pamphlet file cabinets; 20 map drawers of plans and drawings; 190 file boxes. **Subscriptions:** 5 journals and other serials. **Services:** Copying; library open to the public by appointment. **Staff:** Randell L. Makison; Edward R. Bosley.

★ 19346 ★
University of Southern California - Science & Engineering Library (Sci-Engr)
University Park   Phone: (213)740-4416
Los Angeles, CA 90089-0481   Julie Kwan, Hd., Sci. & Engr.Lib.
Founded: 1970. **Staff:** Prof 4; Other 6. **Subjects:** Chemistry, physics, biological sciences, engineering, mathematics, geology, astronomy, computer science. **Holdings:** 110,000 books; 120,000 bound periodical volumes; 27,000 technical reports; 252,000 microforms. **Subscriptions:** 2230 journals. **Services:** Interlibrary loan; copying; library open to the public for reference use only. **Computerized Information Services:** DIALOG Information Services, STN International; InterNet (electronic mail service). **Remarks:** Alternate telephone number(s): 740-4424. FAX: (213)749-1221. Electronic mail address(es): jkwan@vm.usc.edu (InterNet). **Staff:** Bruce Bennion, Assoc.Prof.; Najwa Hanel, Ref./Info.Serv.Libn.

★ 19347 ★
University of Southern California - Social Work Library (Soc Sci)
University Park   Phone: (213)740-1777
Los Angeles, CA 90089-0411   Ruth Britton, Hd.Social Work Lib.
Founded: 1971. **Staff:** Prof 1; Other 1. **Subjects:** Social work, social welfare, child welfare, mental health, community organizations, social problems. **Special Collections:** California Social Welfare History Archives; Hispanic

Mental Health Collection (200 volumes); unpublished masters' research papers (500). **Holdings:** 35,000 books; 2300 bound periodical volumes; 300 linear feet of other uncataloged items. **Subscriptions:** 125 journals and other serials. **Services:** Interlibrary loan; copying; library open to the public for reference use only. **Automated Operations:** Computerized cataloging, acquisitions, and circulation. **Computerized Information Services:** DIALOG Information Services, BRS Information Technologies; Email (electronic mail service). **Publications:** New Acquisitions; Current Contents of Selected Journals, both monthly - both for internal distribution only. **Remarks:** FAX: (213)740-1776.

★ 19348 ★
University of Southern California - Von Kleinsmid Library (Soc Sci)
University Park   Phone: (213)740-1768
Los Angeles, CA 90089-0182   Janice Hanks, Hd., Von Kleinsmid Lib.
Founded: 1928. **Staff:** Prof 3; Other 4. **Subjects:** International relations, political science, public administration, urban and regional planning, economic development, international economic relations. **Special Collections:** International documents collection; planning documents collection. **Holdings:** 182,000 books; 7550 reels of microfilm; 81,000 microfiche. **Subscriptions:** 1850 journals and other serials; 72 newspapers. **Services:** Interlibrary loan; copying; library open to the public for reference use only. **Automated Operations:** Computerized public access catalog and circulation. **Computerized Information Services:** BRS Information Technologies, DIALOG Information Services; USCInfo (14 internal databases). **Publications:** Newsletter; Selected Recent Acquisitions, monthly - local distribution. **Remarks:** FAX: (213)749-1221. **Staff:** Sharon Geltner, Ref./Access Serv.Libn.; Ken Klein, Hd., East Asian Lib.

University of Southern California Medical Center
See: Los Angeles County and University of Southern California Medical Center (9338)

★ 19349 ★
University of Southern Colorado - Library - Special Collections (Soc Sci, Area-Ethnic)
2200 Bonforte Blvd.   Phone: (719)549-2714
Pueblo, CO 81001   Beverly A. Moore, Libn.
Founded: 1933. **Staff:** 19. **Special Collections:** Slavic Heritage Collection (2000 volumes and uncataloged items); U.S. Government publications depository (250,000 documents). **Services:** Library open to the public on a restricted basis. **Remarks:** FAX: (719)549-2738. Slavic Heritage Collection is currently inactive.

★ 19350 ★
University of Southern Indiana - Special Collections and University Archives (Hist)
8600 University Blvd.   Phone: (812)464-1896
Evansville, IN 47712-3595   Gina R. Walker, Certified Archv.
Founded: 1972. **Staff:** Prof 1; Other 1. **Subjects:** Regional and university history, communal societies, petroleum, geology, theater and film, children's literature. **Special Collections:** University Archives (70 cubic feet); Center for Communal Studies (560 volumes; 70 tapes; 25 linear feet); Sun Oil Geology Collection (130 VF drawers); Mead Johnson Archives (75 linear feet); Indiana labor history (18 linear feet). **Holdings:** 3500 books; 1100 linear feet of manuscripts; 300 oral history tapes; archives; maps; photographs; slides. **Subscriptions:** 10 journals and other serials. **Services:** Interlibrary loan; copying; collections open to the public. **Automated Operations:** Computerized cataloging and circulation (NOTIS). **Computerized Information Services:** OCLC. **Networks/Consortia:** Member of Area 2 Library Services Authority (ALSA 2), INCOLSA. **Publications:** A Preliminary Guide to the Special Collections of Indiana State University Evansville, 1975. **Special Catalogs:** Guides to collections (typescript, looseleaf), with updates; selected holdings of USI and other area repositories. **Remarks:** FAX: (812)465-1693.

★ 19351 ★
University of Southern Maine - Office of Sponsored Research - Library (Soc Sci)
96 Falmouth St.   Phone: (207)780-4411
Portland, ME 04103   Janet F. Brysh, Libn.
Founded: 1973. **Staff:** Prof 1. **Subjects:** Maine - state, county, economic, and social data; economic and environmental resources; health/social welfare;

population/housing; manpower; taxes; education. **Special Collections:** Regional collection for Foundation Center of New York (open collection). **Holdings:** 1500 books; 300 other cataloged items; 44 VF drawers of state and federal agency reports and documents, data compilations; 95 newsletters and bulletins; microfiche aperture cards of IRS tax exempt foundations for Maine. **Subscriptions:** 65 journals and other serials; 5 newspapers. **Services:** Interlibrary loan; copying; library open to the public. **Publications:** A Directory of Maine Foundations; list of other publications - available on request. **Remarks:** FAX: (207)780-4417. Library houses all research reports produced by the Human Services Development Institute, Health Policy Unit, and Child Welfare Research Center.

★ 19352 ★
University of Southern Maine - Small Business Development Center - Business Information Service (Bus-Fin)
96 Falmouth St.   Phone: (207)780-4420
Portland, ME 04103   Janice E. Tisdale, Mgr.
Founded: 1977. **Staff:** 2.5. **Subjects:** Business. **Special Collections:** Starting a Business collection (books; pamphlets). **Holdings:** 600 volumes; 12 VF drawers of clippings; telephone directories for Maine, Massachusetts, and major U.S. cities. **Subscriptions:** 30 journals and other serials. **Services:** Copying; service open to the public. **Remarks:** FAX: (207)780-4810.

★ 19353 ★
University of Southern Mississippi - Geology Department - Library (Sci-Engr)
Southern Sta., Box 5044   Phone: (601)266-4526
Hattiesburg, MS 39406-5044   Dr. Maurice A. Meylan, Prof.
Founded: 1972. **Staff:** 2. **Subjects:** Geology. **Special Collections:** State geological publications; United States Geological Survey geological publications; foreign geological publications; publications related to petroleum industry and nuclear waste storage; oil well logs (50,000). **Holdings:** 20,000 volumes. **Subscriptions:** 10 journals and other serials. **Services:** Library open to the public with permission of Geology Department. **Computerized Information Services:** BITNET (electronic mail service). **Remarks:** FAX: (601)266-5800. Electronic mail address(es): MAMEYLAN@USMCP6 (BITNET).

★ 19354 ★
University of Southern Mississippi - McCain Library and Archives (Hist)
Southern Sta., Box 5148   Phone: (601)266-4345
Hattiesburg, MS 39406-5148   Terry S. Latour, Dir.
Founded: 1976. **Staff:** Prof 6; Other 3. **Subjects:** Mississippiana, genealogy, Civil War, Confederate States of America, children's literature, British and American literary criticism, political cartoons. **Special Collections:** Papers of Theodore G. Bilbo, William M. Colmer, Governor Paul B. Johnson; Cleanth Brooks Literature Collection; de Grummond Children's Literature Research Collection; papers and illustrations of Ezra Jack Keats; Ernest A. Walen Collection of Confederate Literature; Collection of Rare Books; Association of American Editorial Cartoonists Collection; genealogy collection; University Archives; Association of American Railroads Collection; Gulf, Mobile & Ohio Railroad Collection. **Holdings:** 73,000 volumes; 7500 linear feet of manuscripts and illustrations. **Subscriptions:** 220 journals and other serials; 64 newspapers. **Services:** Interlibrary loan; copying (both limited); library open to the public for reference use only. **Automated Operations:** Computerized cataloging and serials. **Computerized Information Services:** OCLC. **Networks/Consortia:** Member of SOLINET. **Publications:** Juvenile Miscellany, 2/year - by subscription. **Staff:** Angela R. Jones, Ref.Libn./Cat.; Dolores A. Jones, Cur.; Anne H. Lundin, Asst.Cur.; Henry L. Simmons, Libn.

★ 19355 ★
University of Southwestern Louisiana - Center for Louisiana Studies (Hist)
Box 4-0831   Phone: (318)231-6027
Lafayette, LA 70504   Glenn R. Conrad, Dir.
Staff: Prof 5; Other 2. **Subjects:** Louisiana history. **Special Collections:** Louisiana Colonial Records; Women in Louisiana Collection; folklore and folklife. **Holdings:** Photographs; magnetic tapes; documents; microfilm. **Services:** Copying; center open to the public with restrictions. **Publications:** USL History Series; USL Architecture Series; Louisiana Language and Life Series. **Staff:** Carl A. Brasseaux, Asst.Dir.; Rebecca Batiste, Ed.Asst.

★ 19356 ★

**University of Southwestern Louisiana - Jefferson Caffery Louisiana
Room - Southwestern Archives and Manuscripts Collection** (Hist,
Area-Ethnic)
Dupre Library
302 E. St. Mary Blvd.   Phone: (318)231-6031
Lafayette, LA 70503   Dr. I. Bruce Turner, Hd., Archv. & Spec.Coll.
Founded: 1962. **Staff:** Prof 2; Other 2. **Subjects:** Cajun and Creole culture;
history - state, local, university; horticulture; Louisiana politics; agriculture;
literature; petroleum; genealogy. **Special Collections:** USL Oral History
Program (50 tapes); Robert and Edwin Broussard papers (160 feet);
Louisiana state documents; Zimmer papers (State Conservation
Commission hearing reports); Jefferson Caffery Collection; David R.
Williams Papers; Ollie Tucker Osborne Papers; Ernest J. Gaines Papers;
Edwin W. Willis Papers; John M. Parker Papers; Mary Alice Fontenot
Papers; Godchaux Family Papers/Louisiana State Rice Milling Company
records (200 feet); Freeland Collection (photographic images); Acadian
Folklore Collection (1000 taped interviews and field recordings); Rice
Millers Association Archives; university archives (1000 linear feet); rare
books (emphasis on Renaissance architecture, horticulture, and French
literature). **Holdings:** 20,000 volumes; 36 VF drawers of clippings and
pamphlets; 1700 theses; 250 manuscript collections (2000 linear feet); 1000
audiotapes; microforms. **Subscriptions:** 50 journals and other serials.
Services: Copying; microfilming; collection open to the public. **Automated
Operations:** Computerized cataloging and circulation. **Computerized
Information Services:** DOBIS Canadian Online Library System, OCLC;
InterNet (electronic mail service). **Special Indexes:** Unpublished guides to
manuscript collections; Bayou State Periodical Index, annual. **Remarks:**
Alternate telephone number(s): 231-5702. FAX: (318)231-5841. Electronic
mail address(es): TURNER@USL.EDU, JSK8711@usl.edu (InterNet).
Staff: Jean S. Kiesel, LA Rm.Libn.

University of Steubenville - Human Life Center
See: **Human Life Center - Library (7527)**

★ 19357 ★

**University of Strathclyde - National Centre for Training and Education
in Prosthetics and Orthotics - Library** (Med)
Curran Bldg.
131 St. James Rd.   Phone: 41 5524400
Glasgow G4 0LS, Scotland   Heather Smart, Info.Off.
Staff: Prof 1. **Subjects:** Prosthetics, orthotics, rehabilitation engineering.
Holdings: 8500 bound volumes. **Subscriptions:** 200 journals and other
serials. **Services:** SDI. **Computerized Information Services:** Produces
RECAL Offline. **Remarks:** FAX: 41 5521283. Telex: 77472 UNSLIB G.

★ 19358 ★

University of Sudbury - Jesuit Archives (Hist, Rel-Phil)
Sudbury, ON, Canada P3E 2C6   Phone: (705)673-5661
                                                         Lucien Michand, S.J.
Founded: 1913. **Staff:** Prof 1. **Subjects:** French-Canadian and Catholic
institutions in the Sudbury area, Manitoulin Island, Indians, Jesuit
missionaries in Northern Ontario, Ste. Anne parish, St. Ignace/Sault Ste.
Marie parish, French education in Ontario, Manitoulin Ojibway missions,
Detroit and Windsor 18th century missions among the French and Hurons,
Thunder Bay missions. **Special Collections:** Societe historique du Nouvel-
Ontario (85 volumes); College du Sacre-Coeur Archives; papers of Romanet,
Racette, and Hurtubise (10 boxes each). **Holdings:** 350 books; 200 bound
periodical volumes; 150 pamphlets; 18 cassettes; 60 maps; 300 photographic
portraits; 60 photograph albums; 450 boxes of archival material. **Services:**
Copying; archives open to the public on request. **Remarks:** Alternate
telephone number(s): 673-1061. Most of the holdings are in French.

★ 19359 ★

University of Sudbury - Library (Rel-Phil, Area-Ethnic)
Sudbury, ON, Canada P3E 2C6   Phone: (705)673-5661
                                                         Olga Beaulieu, Dir. of Lib.
Founded: 1960. **Staff:** 3. **Subjects:** Religion, philosophy, Native studies,
folklore. **Holdings:** 42,000 books; 4600 bound periodical volumes.
Subscriptions: 153 journals and other serials; 12 newspapers. **Services:**
Interlibrary loan; copying; library open to the public. **Automated
Operations:** Computerized public access catalog, cataloging, and
circulation. **Remarks:** FAX: (705)673-4912. **Also Known As:** Universite de
Sudbury.

★ 19360 ★

University of Sussex - University Library (Soc Sci, Hum)
Falmer   Phone: 273 606755
Brighton, East Sussex BN1 9QL, England   A.N. Peasgood, Libn.
Founded: 1961. **Staff:** 68. **Subjects:** General collection. **Special Collections:**
European Communities documents; Paris Commune of 1871 (2500 items);
Rudyard Kipling papers; papers of Leonard and Virginia Woolf; Tom
Harrisson Mass-observation Archive; sheet music (the former J & W
Chester Subscription Library; 50,000 pieces); Travers Collection of early
printed books. **Holdings:** 500,000 books; 150,000 bound periodical volumes;
5000 AV items; 720,000 microforms; 1500 boxes of manuscripts.
Subscriptions: 4000 journals and other serials; 10 newspapers. **Services:**
Interlibrary loan; copying; SDI; library open to the public with restrictions.
Computerized Information Services: DIALOG Information Services, ESA/
IRS, STN International, Data-Star, PFDS Online, BLAISE Online Services;
BITNET, Dialcom, Inc. (electronic mail services). Performs searches on fee
basis. **Publications:** Handlists of Special Collections. **Special Catalogs:**
Catalogue of the Travers Collection in the University of Sussex Library,
1990. **Remarks:** FAX: 273 678441. Electronic mail address(es):
LIBRARY@CLUSTER.SUSSEX.AC.UK   (BITNET);   79:LLA1001
(Dialcom, Inc.). **Staff:** T. Framroze; C.P. Ravilious; P.T. Stone; R.C.
Young.

★ 19361 ★

University of Swaziland - Faculty of Agriculture - Library (Agri)
PO   Phone: 10483021
Luyengo, Swaziland   Ms. M. Mavuso
Founded: 1966. **Staff:** Prof 3; Other 7. **Subjects:** Agricultural education,
agricultural economics, animal production, crop production; home
economics, land use. **Holdings:** 16,000 books; 6000 bound periodical
volumes; 5500 reports. **Subscriptions:** 97 journals and other serials; 4
newspapers. **Services:** Interlibrary loan; copying; library open to the public
at librarian's discretion. **Computerized Information Services:** CD-ROM
(CAB/CTA). Contact Person: Julian J. Massawe. **Publications:** Staff
publications. **Remarks:** Telex: 2080 WD.

★ 19362 ★

University of Sydney - Badham Library (Biol Sci, Agri)
Badham Bldg
Science Rd   Phone: 2 6922728
Sydney, NSW 2006, Australia   Pamela Leuzinger
Staff: Prof 2; Other 3.5. **Subjects:** Science - Biological, veterinary;
agriculture. **Holdings:** 47,000 books; 50,000 bound periodical volumes; 6
CD-ROMs. **Subscriptions:** 2500 journals and other serials. **Services:**
Interlibrary loan; copying; library open to the public for reference use only.
Computerized Information Services: DIALOG Information Services.
Contact Person: Karin Smith, Ref.Libn. **Publications:** Library guides.
Remarks: FAX: 2 6923852.

★ 19363 ★

University of Tennessee - Arboretum Society - Library (Biol Sci)
Univ. of Tenn. Experiment Station & Arboretum
901 Kerr Hollow Rd.   Phone: (615)483-3571
Oak Ridge, TN 37830   Richard M. Evans, Supv., Forestry Sta.
Founded: 1965. **Staff:** 2. **Subjects:** Forestry, ecology, botany, horticulture,
trees and shrubs, landscaping, floriculture. **Holdings:** 200 books; bulletins,
journals, and plant lists from major arboreta in the United States and
abroad. **Subscriptions:** 5 journals and other serials. **Services:** Copying
(limited); library open to the public for reference use only.

**University of Tennessee - Institute for Public Service - Municipal
Technical Advisory Service**
See: **Municipal Technical Advisory Service (10864)**

★ 19364 ★

University of Tennessee - Map Library (Geog-Map)
Hoskins Library, Rm.15   Phone: (615)974-4315
Knoxville, TN 37996-4006   James Minton, Asst.Prof./Hd., Map Lib.
Founded: 1989. **Staff:** Prof 1; Other 2. **Subjects:** Geological maps,
hydrographic maps, World War II, topographic maps, U.S. Government
agencies (U.S. Geological Survey, DMA, NOS). **Holdings:** 300,000 sheet
maps; 200 atlases; 300 reference titles. **Services:** Interlibrary loan; copying;
library open to the public. **Automated Operations:** Computerized public
access catalog. **Computerized Information Services:** Internal databases.
Networks/Consortia: Member of SOLINET. **Remarks:** FAX: (615)974-
2708.

★19365★
University of Tennessee at Knoxville - Agriculture-Veterinary Medicine Library (Agri, Med)
Veterinary Medicine Teaching Hospital   Phone: (615)974-7338
Knoxville, TN 37996-4500   Don Jett, Libn.
Founded: 1880. **Staff:** Prof 2; Other 4. **Subjects:** Agriculture, veterinary medicine. **Holdings:** 111,000 volumes. **Subscriptions:** 2500 journals and other serials. **Services:** Interlibrary loan; library open to the public for reference use only. **Computerized Information Services:** DIALOG Information Services, MEDLINE, Integrated Technical Information System (ITIS). **Remarks:** FAX: (615)974-4732. **Staff:** Ann Vlera.

★19366★
University of Tennessee at Knoxville - College of Law - Public Law Institute Library
1505 W. Cumberland Ave.
Knoxville, TN 37996
Defunct.

★19367★
University of Tennessee at Knoxville - College of Law Library (Law)
1505 W. Cumberland Ave.   Phone: (615)974-4381
Knoxville, TN 37996-1800   William J. Beintema, Dir.
Founded: 1890. **Staff:** Prof 4.75. Other 9. **Subjects:** Law. **Special Collections:** Depository of U.S. documents (10,000); constitutional law books and materials in braille (948 volumes). **Holdings:** 325,801 volumes. **Subscriptions:** 3895 journals and other serials; 16 newspapers. **Services:** Interlibrary loan; copying; library open to the public. **Automated Operations:** Computerized cataloging. **Computerized Information Services:** LEXIS, WESTLAW. Performs searches on fee basis. **Staff:** Reba A. Best, Asst.Libn., Tech.Serv.; D. Cheryn Picquet, Assoc. Law Libn., Adm.; Steve R. Thorpe, Asst.Libn., Pub.Serv.

★19368★
University of Tennessee at Knoxville - George F. DeVine Music Library (Mus)
Music Bldg., Rm. 301   Phone: (615)974-3474
Knoxville, TN 37996-2600   Pauline S. Bayne, Libn.
Founded: 1971. **Staff:** Prof 1; Other 4.5. **Subjects:** Music. **Special Collections:** Galston-Busoni Music Collection (manuscripts; photographs; memorabilia; 2000 scores for piano); Grace Moore memorabilia, photographs, autographed and annotated scores; David Van Vactor Collection (manuscripts; sketchbooks; first editions; original recordings). **Holdings:** 32,500 volumes; 16,000 recordings. **Subscriptions:** 300 journals and other serials. **Services:** Interlibrary loan; copying; library open to the public. **Computerized Information Services:** DIALOG Information Services, BRS Information Technologies, OCLC, RLIN, EPIC, WILSONLINE; InterNet, BITNET (electronic mail services). **Remarks:** FAX: (615)974-2708. Electronic mail address(es): BAYNE@UTKVX (BITNET); BAYNE@UTKVK.UTK.EDU (InterNet).

★19369★
University of Tennessee at Knoxville - Medical Center - Preston Medical Library (Med)
1924 Alcoa Hwy.   Phone: (615)544-9525
Knoxville, TN 37920   Doris Prichard, Dir.
Founded: 1966. **Staff:** Prof 2; Other 3. **Subjects:** Surgery and trauma, pediatrics, hematology, immunology, obstetrics, gynecology. **Holdings:** 3000 books; 26,000 bound periodical volumes. **Subscriptions:** 512 journals and other serials. **Services:** Interlibrary loan; copying; SDI; library open to the public with limited circulation. **Computerized Information Services:** MEDLINE, MEDLARS. Performs searches on fee basis. Contact Person: Connie Talbott, Database Search. **Networks/Consortia:** Member of Knoxville Area Health Sciences Library Consortium (KAHSLC), Tennessee Health Science Library Association (THeSLA). **Remarks:** FAX: (615)544-9527. **Staff:** Shelley Paden, Libn.

★19370★
University of Tennessee at Knoxville - Special Collections (Hist)
Knoxville, TN 37996-4006   Phone: (615)974-4480
     Dr. James Lloyd, Spec.Coll.Libn.
Founded: 1959. **Staff:** Prof 1; Other 3. **Subjects:** Tennesseana, 19th century American fiction, Southern Indians, early imprints. **Special Collections:** Estes Kefauver Collection (political papers and memorabilia; 1204 feet); Radiation Research Archives (435 feet); William Congreve Collection. **Holdings:** 40,000 books; 4550 feet of processed manuscripts. **Services:** Copying; collection open to the public with restrictions. **Publications:** Libray Development Review, annual. **Special Catalogs:** Rare books catalog (card); unpublished registers and calendars to manuscript collections. **Remarks:** FAX: (615)974-2708.

★19371★
University of Tennessee at Memphis - Health Sciences Library (Med)
877 Madison Ave.   Phone: (901)528-5638
Memphis, TN 38163   John Patruno, Dir.
Founded: 1913. **Staff:** Prof 8; Other 20. **Subjects:** Medicine, dentistry, nursing, pharmacy, allied health sciences, social work. **Special Collections:** Wallace Collection (books authored by University of Tennessee personnel). **Holdings:** 35,505 books; 165,142 bound periodical volumes; 130 microforms; 306 slide programs; 403 filmstrips; 220 films; 2312 video and audio cassettes. **Subscriptions:** 1975 journals and other serials. **Services:** Interlibrary loan; copying; library open to the public for reference use only. **Automated Operations:** Computerized public access catalog, cataloging, acquisitions, circulation, serials, and ILL (DOCLINE). **Computerized Information Services:** OCLC, DIALOG Information Services, MEDLINE, BRS Information Technologies; CD-ROMs (MEDLINE Knowledge Finder, CINAHL); internal database; BITNET (electronic mail service). Performs searches on fee basis. **Networks/Consortia:** Member of SOLINET. **Remarks:** FAX: (901)528-7235. Electronic mail address(es): UTLIBRARY@UTMEM1 (BITNET). **Staff:** Anne Carroll Bunting, Hd., Tech.Serv.Dept.; Frances Verble, Bibliog.Cont.Libn.; Ronald R. Sommer, Spec.Proj.Libn.; Richard Nollan, Br.Libn.; Lois Bellamy, Automated Serv.Libn.; Glenda Mendina, Hd., Access Serv.; Susan Selig, Assoc.Libn.

★19372★
University of Tennessee at Tullahoma - Space Institute - Library (Sci-Engr)
MS 20   Phone: (615)455-0631
Tullahoma, TN 37388-8897   Mary M. Lo, Hd.Libn.
Founded: 1965. **Staff:** Prof 2; Other 2. **Subjects:** Engineering - aeronautical, mechanical, electrical, metallurgical; fluid mechanics; MHD power generation; lasers; propulsion; physics; artificial intelligence; mathematics; aerodynamics; propulsion; space science and technology; computer science. **Holdings:** 16,720 books; 945 bound periodical volumes; 44,300 reports; 175,000 microforms; 312 dissertations; 100 patents. **Subscriptions:** 176 journals and other serials. **Services:** Interlibrary loan; copying; library open to the public by appointment. **Automated Operations:** Computerized cataloging and ILL. **Computerized Information Services:** DIALOG Information Services, NASA/RECON. Performs searches on fee basis. **Networks/Consortia:** Member of SOLINET. **Remarks:** FAX: (615)454-2354. **Staff:** Marjorie Joseph, Libn.

★19373★
University of Texas - Institute of Texan Cultures at San Antonio - Library (Area-Ethnic)
801 S. Bowie St.
P.O. Box 1226   Phone: (512)226-7651
San Antonio, TX 78294   James C. McNutt, Dir., Res. & Coll.
Founded: 1968. **Staff:** Prof 1; Other 3. **Subjects:** Texas ethnic history and regional folklore. **Special Collections:** Photographic collection (46,000 indexed copy negatives on Texas subjects); San Antonio Light negative collection (600,000 negatives made from 1924 to 1988 and retired from the newspaper morgue); Zintgraff collection of commercial photographs (450,000 negatives from 1928-1987); San Antonio Express News negative collection (750,000 negatives; partial coverage 1950-1980; complete coverage 1980-1987). **Holdings:** 6000 books; 87 bound periodical volumes; 100 VF drawers; 600 transcribed oral histories; slides; videotapes; filmstrips. **Subscriptions:** 110 journals and other serials. **Services:** Interlibrary loan; copying; reproduction and sale of photographs; library open to the public by appointment for reference use. **Computerized Information Services:** Internal database. **Networks/Consortia:** Member of Council of Research & Academic Libraries (CORAL). **Publications:** The Texians and the Texans (series of 17 ethnic pamphlets); The Ethnic Series (10 books); Young Readers (series of 5 books); Texans: A Story of Texan Cultures for Young People (textbook); books on various Texas topics; The Melting Pot (cookbook). **Special Indexes:** Subject index to photography, VF drawers, and oral histories. **Remarks:** FAX: (512)222-8564. **Staff:** Diane Bruce, Lib.Hd.

★19374★
University of Texas - M.D. Anderson Cancer Center - Research Medical Library (Med)
Texas Medical Center   Phone: (713)792-2282
Houston, TX 77030   Sara Jean Jackson, Dir.
Founded: 1945. **Staff:** Prof 5; Other 9. **Subjects:** Cancer, radiological physics, cell biology. **Special Collections:** Rare books and early treatises on cancer (600 volumes). **Holdings:** 45,000 volumes. **Subscriptions:** 1200

journals and other serials. **Services:** Interlibrary loan; copying; library open to the public for reference use only. **Automated Operations:** Computerized cataloging and circulation. **Computerized Information Services:** Online systems. **Networks/Consortia:** Member of AMIGOS Bibliographic Council, Inc., National Network of Libraries of Medicine - South Central Region. **Remarks:** FAX: (713)797-6513. **Also Known As:** University of Texas System Cancer Center.

★ 19375 ★
University of Texas at Arlington - Libraries - Division of Special Collections (Hist)
Box 19497   Phone: (817)273-3393
Arlington, TX 76019   Dr. Gerald D. Saxon, Asst.Dir., Spec.Coll.
Founded: 1974. **Staff:** Prof 12; Other 8. **Subjects:** Texana; Mexican war; history - cartographic, Meso-American, Texas labor and politics. **Special Collections:** Jenkins Garrett Library (Texana and Mexican war; 16,743 items); Cartographic History Library (5000 items); Fort Worth Star-Telegram Archive (790,000 items); Basil Clemons Photographic Collection (20,000 items); Robertson Colony Collection. **Holdings:** 20,000 books; 561 bound periodical volumes; 5350 maps, pieces of sheet music, graphics; 3100 linear feet of manuscripts; 1000 folders of newspapers; 4 VF drawers of clippings. **Subscriptions:** 35 journals and other serials. **Services:** Copying; division open to the public. **Automated Operations:** Computerized public access catalog, cataloging, serials, and circulation. **Networks/Consortia:** Member of AMIGOS Bibliographic Council, Inc. **Publications:** Papers Concerning Robertson's Colony in Texas UTA Press, annual; Compass Rose (newsletter), semiannual. **Special Indexes:** Guide to the Historical Manuscripts, Archival, and Oral History Collections in Special Collections (book). **Remarks:** FAX: (817)273-3392. **Staff:** Dr. Malcolm D. McLean, Hd., Robertson Colony Coll.; Jane Boley, Univ.Archv., Tex. Labor & Pol.; Marcelle Hull, Adm.Asst.; Maritza Arrigunaga, Meso-American Coll.; Shirley Rodnitzky, Spec. in Hist.Photo. & Nonbook Mtls.; Ann Kelley, Cat.; Betsey Hudon, Fort Worth Star-Telegram Archv.; Sally Gross, Libn.; Kit Goodwin, M.W. Bibliog./Exhibits; G. Tom Kellam, Archv.

★ 19376 ★
University of Texas at Austin - Architecture & Planning Library (Art, Plan)
General Libraries, BTL 200   Phone: (512)495-4620
Austin, TX 78713-7330   Eloise E. McDonald, Arch. & Plan.Libn.
Founded: 1926. **Staff:** Prof 1; Other 2.5. **Subjects:** Architecture, architectural history, historic preservation, city and regional planning, interior design. **Special Collections:** Architectural Drawings Collection (131,825 drawings). **Holdings:** 32,200 books; 8494 bound periodical volumes; 17,810 HUD 701 depository items; 388 reels of microfilm; 7750 microfiche. **Subscriptions:** 316 journals and other serials. **Services:** Interlibrary loan; copying; library open to the public. **Computerized Information Services:** DIALOG Information Services, BRS Information Technologies, DataTimes, Questel, Avery Index to Architectural Periodicals; UTCAT (internal database). **Publications:** Library Guide. **Remarks:** FAX: (512)495-4347. **Staff:** Lila Stillson, Cur., Arch. Drawings Coll.

★ 19377 ★
University of Texas at Austin - Artificial Intelligence Laboratory - Information Center (Comp Sci)
Computer Sciences Dept.
Taylor Hall, Rm. 2.124   Phone: (512)471-9556
Austin, TX 78712   Bess Sullivan, Sr.Tech.Sec.
Founded: 1985. **Staff:** 1. **Subjects:** Artificial intelligence, system documentation, computer science. **Special Collections:** Reports from 9 University of Texas research centers, 1959 to present. **Holdings:** 250 volumes; 5000 technical reports on microfiche; 275 technical reports. **Services:** Center open to the public with special permission. **Computerized Information Services:** ARPAnet (electronic mail service). **Publications:** Artificial Intelligence Laboratory Technical Report Series, quarterly. **Remarks:** Alternate telephone number(s): 471-9562. FAX: (512)471-8885. Electronic mail address(es): bess@cs.utexas.edu (ARPAnet).

★ 19378 ★
University of Texas at Austin - Audio Visual Library (Aud-Vis)
Peter T. Flawn Academic Center 101
General Libraries   Phone: (512)495-4467
Austin, TX 78713-7330   Gary Lay, Supv.
Founded: 1963. **Staff:** 5. **Subjects:** Audiovisual materials for instructional use and research, all subjects. **Holdings:** 1120 cassettes; 270 filmstrips; 10,118 phonograph records; 181 phonotapes; 6680 slides; 1892 videocassettes; 543 compact discs; 2743 films. **Services:** Library open to the public. **Computerized Information Services:** UTCAT (internal database). **Publications:** Library Guide. **Remarks:** FAX: (512)495-4347.

★ 19379 ★
University of Texas at Austin - Barker Texas History Center (Hist)
General Libraries, SRH 2.109   Phone: (512)495-4515
Austin, TX 78713-7330   Dr. Don E. Carleton, Dir.
Staff: Prof 8; Other 15. **Subjects:** Texas history, literature, and folklore; Texas state documents; University of Texas publications and history; Southern and Western history. **Special Collections:** Sound archives (1586 audiocassettes; 27,247 phonograph records; 4468 audiotapes; 1028 videocassettes; 85 videotapes); dime novel collection; Kell Frontier Collection; Austin papers; Bexar Archives; Bryan papers; T.S. Henderson papers; James S. Hogg papers; Ashbel Smith papers; John Henry Faulk papers; Pompeo Coppini-Waldine Tauch papers; Jesse Jones papers; James Wells papers; Martin M. Crane papers; Luther M. Evans Collection; James Harper Starr papers; James Farmer papers; True West Archives; Field Foundation Archives; Natchez Trace Collection; Russell Lee Photograph Collection; R.C. Hickman Photograph Collection; Robert Runyon Photograph Collection. **Holdings:** 144,996 volumes; 3000 linear feet of university records; 32,462 linear feet of nonuniversity records; 31,650 maps; 3800 titles of historic Texas and Southern newspapers; 760,327 documents; 11,887 slides; 100 VF drawers of clippings; 1500 scrapbooks; 17,996 reels of microfilm; 1363 microfiche; 4293 tapes of oral recordings. **Subscriptions:** 548 periodicals; 673 other serials. **Services:** Interlibrary loan; copying; center open to the public. **Publications:** Newsletter; Archives Guide; Library Guide. **Remarks:** FAX: (512)495-4542. **Staff:** Katherine Adams, Asst.Dir.; Ralph Elder, Pub.Serv.; Alison Beck, Archv. & Mss.; John Wheat, Sound Archv.; Barbara Griffith, Oral Hist.Coll.

★ 19380 ★
University of Texas at Austin - Benson Latin American Collection (Area-Ethnic)
General Libraries, SRH 1.108   Phone: (512)495-4520
Austin, TX 78713-7330   Laura Gutierrez-Witt, Hd.Libn.
Founded: 1921. **Staff:** Prof 5; Other 19. **Subjects:** Latin American anthropology, art, culture, economics, education, geography, government, history, law, literature, music, philology, philosophy, religion, science; Mexican American history, social sciences, and literature; studies on Hispanics in the U.S. **Special Collections:** Genaro Garcia; Joaquin Garcia Icazbalceta; Luis Garcia Pimentel; Alejandro Prieto; W.B. Stephens; Diego Munoz; Manuel Gondra; Hernandez y Davalos; Sanchez Navarro family; Simon Lucuix Rio de La Plata Library (21,000 volumes); Arturo Taracena Flores Library (Guatemala; 10,000 titles); Pedro Martinez Reales Gaucho Collection; Pablo Salce Arredondo Collection of Mexican Manuscripts and Imprints; Julio Cortazar Literary Papers; St. John del Rey Mining Company Archives from Brazil; Chicano Writers Manuscript Collection; Archive of the League of United Latin American Citizens; Raza Unida Party Archive (5 linear feet); Economy Furniture Company Strike Collection (3 linear feet); Carlos Castaneda Collection (35 linear feet); Eleuterio Escobar Collection (15 linear feet); Carlos Villalongin Dramatic Company Archives (247 playscripts; 32 photographs; 15 playbills and notices). **Holdings:** 597,321 volumes; 4 million pages of manuscripts; 20,186 reels of microfilm; 19,264 maps; 16,616 microfiche; 20,086 pages of broadsides; 22,100 prints and photographs; 10,000 volumes of newspapers; 1586 phonograph records; 3661 slides. **Subscriptions:** 24,494 journals and other serials. **Services:** Interlibrary loan; copying; collection open to the public for reference use only. **Computerized Information Services:** UTCAT (internal database); BITNET (electronic mail service). **Publications:** Bibliographic Guide to Latin American Studies; Benson Latin American Serials List (microfiche); Mexican American Archives in the Benson Collection: A Supplement for Educators; Archives and Manuscripts on Microfilm in the Nettie Lee Benson Latin American Collection: A Checklist; Mexican American Archives in the Benson Collection: A Guide for Users; Inventory of the Records of the Cuban Consulate, Key West, Florida, 1886-1961, on microfilm; Revolution and Counterrevolution in Guatemala, 1944-1963: An Annotated Bibliography of Materials in the Benson Latin American Collection. **Special Catalogs:** Catalog of the Benson Latin American Collection. **Remarks:** FAX: (512)495-4568. Electronic mail address(es): LLLGW@UTXDP (BITNET). Includes the holdings of University of Texas, Austin - Mexican American Library Program. **Staff:** Ann Hartness, Asst.Hd.Libn.; Jane Garner, Archv.; Donald Gibbs, Bibliog.; Anne Jordan, Rare Bks.Libn.; Margo Gutierrez, Mexican Amer.Stud.Libn.

★ 19381 ★
University of Texas at Austin - Bureau of Business Research - Information Services (Bus-Fin)
Box 7459, University Sta.   Phone: (512)471-5180
Austin, TX 78713   Rita J. Wright, Libn.
Founded: 1926. **Staff:** Prof 1; Other 1. **Subjects:** Texas - demographics, economics, industries. **Holdings:** 1200 books; Texas and U.S. Government

documents; 1990 Census tapes; other states' manufacturing directories. **Subscriptions:** 500 journals and other serials. **Services:** Copying; services open to the public. **Computerized Information Services:** Directory of Texas Wholesalers, Directory of Texas Manufacturers, TexLib database of Texas economic and demographic data (internal databases). Performs searches on fee basis. **Publications:** Texas Trade and Professional Associations, biennial; Texas Fact Book, 1992. **Remarks:** FAX: (512)471-1063.

★19382★
University of Texas at Austin - Bureau of Economic Geology - Reading Room/Data Center (Sci-Engr)
Box X, University Sta.
Austin, TX 78713-7508   L.E. Garner, Data Ctr.Supv.
Staff: Prof 1; Other 5. **Subjects:** Texas geology, mineral resources, nuclear waste repositories, Texas water resources, petroleum industry, general geology. **Special Collections:** Maps (100 VF drawers); aerial photographs (200,000 frames); well logs (100,000); well data (2000 notebooks). **Holdings:** 7000 books. **Subscriptions:** 50 journals and other serials. **Services:** Copying; room open to the public for reference use only. **Remarks:** FAX: (512)471-0140. **Staff:** David Koran, Read.Rm. Staff; Daniel Ortuno, G.L.F. Staff.

★19383★
University of Texas at Austin - Center for Intercultural Studies in Folklore and Ethnomusicology - Library (Hist)
Student Services Bldg., Rm. 3.106   Phone: (512)471-1288
Austin, TX 78712   Dr. Steven Feld, Dir.
Founded: 1970. **Staff:** 1. **Subjects:** Folklore, anthropology, sociology, ethnomusicology. **Holdings:** 900 books; 540 bound periodical volumes; 600 articles. **Subscriptions:** 18 journals and other serials. **Services:** Library open to the public.

★19384★
University of Texas at Austin - Center for Transportation Research (Trans)
3208 Red River St., Suite 200   Phone: (512)472-8875
Austin, TX 78705   Bennett Claire Ponsford, Lib.Asst. III
Founded: 1980. **Staff:** Prof 1. **Subjects:** Transportation planning, transportation and highway engineering. **Holdings:** 50 books; 2000 reports. **Subscriptions:** 25 journals and other serials. **Services:** Interlibrary loan; center not open to the public. **Computerized Information Services:** DIALOG Information Services, OCLC EPIC. **Remarks:** FAX: (512)480-0235.

★19385★
University of Texas at Austin - Chemistry Library (Sci-Engr)
General Libraries, WEL 2.132
Austin, TX 78713-7330   Phone: (512)495-4602
Staff: Prof 1; Other 2. **Subjects:** Chemistry, biochemistry, nutrition, chemical engineering. **Holdings:** 64,787 volumes; 165 reels of microfilm; 4509 microfiche. **Subscriptions:** 613 journals and other serials. **Services:** Interlibrary loan; copying; library open to the public. **Computerized Information Services:** DIALOG Information Services, STN International; UTCAT (internal database). **Publications:** Library Guide. **Remarks:** FAX: (512)471-8696. **Also Known As:** John W. Mallet Chemistry Library.

★19386★
University of Texas at Austin - Classics Library (Hum)
General Libraries, WAG 1   Phone: (512)495-4690
Austin, TX 78713-7330   Bonny Keyes, Supv.
Founded: 1967. **Staff:** 2. **Subjects:** Greek and Latin literature, classical civilization, Greek and Latin languages, classical archeology, Greek and Roman history, epigraphy, numismatics. **Holdings:** 21,547 books; 2207 bound periodical volumes. **Subscriptions:** 150 journals and other serials. **Services:** Interlibrary loan; library open to the public. **Computerized Information Services:** UTCAT (internal database). **Publications:** Library Guide. **Remarks:** FAX: (512)475-4347.

★19387★
University of Texas at Austin - Documents Collection (Info Sci)
General Libraries, PCL 2.400   Phone: (512)495-4262
Austin, TX 78713-7330   Paul Rascoe, Libn.
Staff: Prof 1; Other 5. **Subjects:** U.S. Government documents, U.N. documents. **Holdings:** 231,450 U.S. documents; 105,256 U.N. documents; 24,832 microfiche. **Services:** Interlibrary loan; copying; collection open to the public. **Computerized Information Services:** CD-ROM; UTCAT (internal database); InterNet (electronic mail service). **Remarks:** FAX: (512)495-4296. Electronic mail address(es): prascoe@emx.utexas.edu (InterNet).

★19388★
University of Texas at Austin - East Asian Library Program (Area-Ethnic)
General Libraries, PCL 4.114   Phone: (512)495-4323
Austin, TX 78713-7330   Kevin Lin, East Asian Studies Libn.
Staff: Prof 1; Other 2. **Subjects:** China and Japan; art; history, especially of Meiji Period in Japan; politics; economics and statistics; anthropology; philosophy; literature; Chinese and Japanese linguistics. **Holdings:** 70,225 volumes; 12,405 microfiche; 786 reels of microfilm. **Subscriptions:** 369 journals and other serials. **Services:** Interlibrary loan; copying; collection open to the public. **Remarks:** FAX: (512)495-4347.

★19389★
University of Texas at Austin - Engineering Library (Sci-Engr)
General Libraries, ECJ 1.300   Phone: (512)495-4500
Austin, TX 78713-7330   Susan B. Ardis, Libn.
Staff: Prof 3; Other 6. **Subjects:** Engineering - aerospace, civil, electrical, computer, mechanical, petroleum; engineering mechanics. **Holdings:** 151,484 volumes; industry standards; product catalogs; military specifications; U.S. Patent Depository Library (full patents, 1950 to present). **Subscriptions:** 1874 journals and other serials. **Services:** Interlibrary loan; copying; library open to the public. **Computerized Information Services:** DIALOG Information Services, BRS Information Technologies, STN International, CASSIS (Classification and Search Support Information System), Questel; UTCAT (internal database); BITNET (electronic mail service). **Publications:** Library Guide. **Remarks:** FAX: (512)495-4507. Electronic mail address(es): LYAA132@UTXVM (BITNET). Maintains the Balcones Library Service Center, a satellite location. **Also Known As:** Richard W. McKinney Engineering Library. **Staff:** Larayne Dallas, Asst.Libn.

★19390★
University of Texas at Austin - Fine Arts Library (Art, Mus, Theater)
General Libraries, FAB 3.200   Phone: (512)495-4480
Austin, TX 78713-7330   Marcia Parsons, Hd.Libn.
Staff: Prof 4; Other 12. **Subjects:** Art history, aesthetics, studio art, philosophy of art, art education, play production, drama education, theatrical designing, playwriting, dance, dance history, music, performance, composition, ethnomusicology, music education, music theory, musicology. **Special Collections:** Historical Music Recordings Collection. **Holdings:** 169,548 books; 15,049 bound periodical volumes; 33,616 phonograph records; 5035 compact discs; 2646 tapes; 2190 audiocassettes; 1041 videocassettes; 305 videodiscs; 1704 slides; 5648 reels of microfilm; 23,158 microfiche; 992 microcards. **Subscriptions:** 1206 journals and other serials. **Services:** Interlibrary loan; copying; library open to the public. **Computerized Information Services:** DIALOG Information Services; UTCAT (internal database). **Publications:** Library Guide. **Remarks:** FAX: (512)495-4347. **Staff:** Karl F. Miller, AV Libn. and Cur., Hist.Mus. Recordings Coll.; David Hunter, Mus.Libn.; Janine Henri, Art Libn.

★19391★
University of Texas at Austin - Geology Library (Sci-Engr)
General Libraries, GEO 302   Phone: (512)495-4680
Austin, TX 78713-7330   Dennis Trombatore, Libn.
Staff: Prof 1; Other 2. **Subjects:** Geology, paleontology, mineralogy, geophysics, petroleum and marine geology, volcanology. **Holdings:** 89,680 volumes; 336 reels of microfilm; 17,290 microfiche; 43,826 geological maps. **Subscriptions:** 1122 journals and other serials. **Services:** Interlibrary loan; copying; library open to the public. **Computerized Information Services:** UTCAT (internal database). **Publications:** Library Guide. **Remarks:** FAX: (512)471-6983. **Also Known As:** Joseph C. Walter, Jr. and Elizabeth C. Walter Geology Library.

★19392★
University of Texas at Austin - Harry Ransom Humanities Research Center (Hum)
Box 7219   Phone: (512)471-8944
Austin, TX 78713-7219   Dr. Thomas F. Staley, Dir.
Founded: 1956. **Staff:** Prof 14; Other 24. **Subjects:** 20th century American, English, and French literature; photography; theater arts; book arts; English and American authors including James Agee, Maxwell Anderson, W.H. Auden, Samuel Barclay Beckett, the Brownings, Baron George Gordon Byron, Joseph Conrad, Hart Crane, e.e. cummings, Charles Dickens, T.S. Eliot, William Faulkner, E.M. Forster, John Fowles, Graham Greene, Thomas Hardy, Lillian Hellman, James Joyce, D.H. Lawrence, William

Somerset Maugham, Henry Miller, Arthur Miller, Edgar Allan Poe, Ezra Pound, G.B. Shaw, the Sitwells, Dylan Thomas, H.G. Wells, Tennessee Williams, William Carlos Williams, and William Yeats; modern French authors including Celine, Cocteau, Genet, Gide, Giraudoux, and Sartre; modern French musical scores including Ravel, Roussel, Faure, Debussy, and Satie. **Special Collections:** Norman Bel Geddes (250,000 items); Gloria Swanson Archives (500,000 items); Alfred A. and Blanche Knopf Library and Publishing Archives (100,000 items); David O. Selznick Film Archives (1 million items); Robert Lee Wolff Collection (19th century fiction; 18,000 volumes); Miriam Lutcher Stark Library (10,000 items); John Henry Wrenn Library (6000 items); Pforzheimer Library of English Literature to 1700 (1010 items); Giorgio Uzielli Aldine Collection (287 items). **Holdings:** 1 million books; 30,000 linear feet of manuscripts; 5 million photographic images; 3000 linear feet of clippings, playbills, and miscellaneous files; 80,000 pieces of literary iconography. **Subscriptions:** 200 journals and other serials. **Services:** Photoduplication and photoreproduction performed by staff only. **Computerized Information Services:** OCLC, RLIN. **Networks/Consortia:** Member of AMIGOS Bibliographic Council, Inc., Research Libraries Information Network (RLIN). **Publications:** The Library Chronicle, 4/year; bibliographies; bibliographical monographs. **Special Catalogs:** Exhibition catalogs; catalogs of collections. **Remarks:** Alternate telephone number(s): 471-9119. FAX: (512)471-9646. **Staff:** Sally Leach, Assoc.Dir.; Mary Beth Bigger, Asst.Dir.; Richard Oram, Pub.Serv.Libn.; Catherine Henderson, Res.Libn.; W.H. Crain, Sr.Cur., Theater Arts Coll.; Roy Flukinger, Cur., Theater Arts, Photo. and Film; Maria X. Wells, Cur., Italian Coll.; Carlton Lake, Exec.Cur., French Coll.; Sue Murphy, Cur., Art Coll.; James G. Stroud, Chf.Cons.Off.

★19393★
University of Texas at Austin - Harry Ransom Humanities Research Center - Theatre Arts and Film Collections (Theater)
P.O. Box 7219   Phone: (512)471-9122
Austin, TX 78713   Dr. Thomas Staley, Dir.
Staff: Prof 3; Other 5. **Special Collections:** Gloria Swanson Collection; Norman Bel Geddes Collection (2500 technical drawings, 5000 sketches, 800 renderings, 5000 photographs, 5 models, 3000 leaves of MS documentation); David O. Selznick Collection (scenarios; music; artwork; photographs; correspondence; contracts and other legal papers); Ernest Lehman Collection (screenplays; production notes; correspondence); MGM Matte Drawings (1400); Albert Davis Collection (theatrical artifacts, including posters, programs, and photographs collected between 1874-1942); Messmore Kendall Collection (theatrical materials, including letters, engravings, programs, opera liberetti, and extra-illustrated books); Robert Downing Collection on the History and Theory of the Theatre (books; photographs; typescripts of plays; Lacy acting editions; American plays inscribed by their authors; sketches, floor plans, lightplots, and prompt scripts from productions for which Mr. Downing was stage manager); Hoblitzelle Interstate Circuit Collection (450,000 cinema artifacts, 1900-1973, including photographs, publicity materials, lobbby cards, and records of the circuits movie houses); John Gassner Collection (3000 books; typescripts and holograph manuscripts; pamphlets; reviews; clippings; play manuscripts; letters; photographs; magazines; personal memorabilia); Stanley Marcus Collection of Sicilian Marionettes (60); papers of Edith Evans, Marie Tempest, Pat Rooney, Frances Starr, Lucy Barton, B. Iden Payne, E.P. Conkle; Jule Styne Musical Collection (original manuscript scores of individual songs and entire productions; libretti; typed manuscripts and published versions of musicals; publicity materials; correspondence; stage directions); W.H. Crain Collection (original designs of costumes and scenery; posters; scrapbooks; sheet music, including that from the Ziegfeld Follies; Marquis de Cuevas Archive; film stills and posters; music hall sheet music; prompt scripts); Joe E. Ward Collection (19th and 20th century circus memorabilia, including photographs, letters, programs, playbills, route books, costumes); Donald Albery Collection (correspondence; legal papers; minutes; financial records; designs; notes of telephone conversations and other materials); B.J. Simmons Collection (29,000 costume designs and documentation, 1880-1960); Fred Fehl Collection of Theatre and Dance Photographs (200,000 photographs; 250,000 negatives; programs); Norman Dawn Collection (164 Special Effects layout cards); Jay Presson Allen Collection (90 film, theater, television scripts); Alfred Junge Collection (400 original movie set designs; 200 design photographs). **Holdings:** 42,000 books; 40,000 bound periodical volumes; 100 films and videotapes. **Subscriptions:** 50 journals and other serials. **Services:** Copying; library open to the public by appointment for reference use. **Remarks:** FAX: (512)471-9646. **Staff:** Dr. William H. Crain, Cur.; Charles Bell, Cur. of Film; Roy Flukinger, Cur. of Photo.

★19394★
University of Texas at Austin - Hogg Foundation for Mental Health - Library (Soc Sci)
W.C. Hogg Bldg., Rm. 301   Phone: (512)471-5041
Austin, TX 78713   Allison Chandler Supancic, Libn.
Founded: 1962. **Staff:** 2. **Subjects:** Psychology, psychiatry, gerontology, learning disabilities, parenting, social work, sociology, education, family life. **Special Collections:** Regional Foundation Library (depository of the Foundation Center in N.Y.; Internal Revenue Service tax returns from private foundations in Texas); collection on foundations and philanthropy, grant seeking, proposal writing, and fund-raising information. **Holdings:** 1700 books; 300 foundation annual reports. **Subscriptions:** 16 journals and newsletters. **Services:** Library open to the public. **Remarks:** FAX: (512)471-9608.

★19395★
University of Texas at Austin - Institute for Geophysics - Library (Sci-Engr)
8701 Mopac Blvd.   Phone: (512)471-0499
Austin, TX 78759-8345   Larry Cook, Libn.
Founded: 1973. **Staff:** Prof 1; Other 3. **Subjects:** Geophysics, marine geology, seismology. **Special Collections:** Caribbean; Central America; Gulf of Mexico; Antarctic; Data Archive/Library: Multichannel Seismic Film Master Library; Multichannel Seismic Digital Tape Library (20,000); Underway Geophysical (Analog Data) Data Base; Underway Geophysical Digital Data Base; Worldwide Underway Geophysical Data Base (digital); Global Digital Seismograph Network Database; abstracts of conference proceedings. **Holdings:** 4402 books; 2503 bound periodical volumes; 65 VF drawers of reprints; 185 theses; 2348 maps; technical reports. **Subscriptions:** 194 journals and other serials. **Services:** Interlibrary loan; copying; library open to the public for reference use only. **Computerized Information Services:** DIALOG Information Services, OCLC; TexMail (electronic mail service). **Publications:** Publications, Theses, Holdings, and Technical Reports, annual; Serial Holdings, annual. **Special Indexes:** Caribbean region (online; in preparation).

★19396★
University of Texas at Austin - Library and Information Science Collection (Info Sci)
General Libraries, PCL 6.102   Phone: (512)495-4210
Austin, TX 78713-7330   Mary Lynn Rice-Lively, Libn.
Staff: Prof 1; Other 1.5. **Subjects:** Library functions, organization, and administration; information science; children's and young adult literature; archives and records management. **Holdings:** 40,817 LIS volumes; 1005 reels of microfilm; 560 microfiche; 63 videocassettes; 113 filmstrips; 536 microcards; 316 cassettes; 15 slides; 15,076 volumes of youth collection. **Subscriptions:** 486 journals and other serials. **Services:** Interlibrary loan; copying; collection open to the public. **Computerized Information Services:** UTCAT (internal database); BITNET (electronic mail service). **Publications:** Brochure. **Remarks:** FAX: (512)495-4296. Electronic mail address(es): LYAA@UTXVM (BITNET).

★19397★
University of Texas at Austin - Life Science Library (Biol Sci)
General Libraries, MAI 220   Phone: (512)495-4630
Austin, TX 78713-7330   Nancy Elder, Libn.
Staff: Prof 2; Other 4. **Subjects:** Botany, microbiology, zoology, genetics, molecular biology, ecology, marine biology, pharmacy, pharmacology, pharmacognosy, pharmaceutical administration. **Special Collections:** Gray Herbarium Index. **Holdings:** 157,946 volumes; 1658 reels of microfilm; 28,100 microfiche; 1032 microcards; 107 cassettes. **Subscriptions:** 2248 journals and other serials. **Services:** Interlibrary loan; copying; library open to the public. **Computerized Information Services:** DIALOG Information Services, BRS Information Technologies, NLM; UTCAT (internal database); CD-ROMs (MEDLINE, Life Sciences Collection, Compact Cambridge International Pharmaceutical Abstracts); BITNET (electronic mail service). **Publications:** Library Guide. **Remarks:** FAX: (512)495-4638. Electronic mail address(es): LLNIE@UTXDP (BITNET).

★19398★
University of Texas at Austin - Map Collection (Geog-Map)
General Libraries, PCL 1.306   Phone: (512)495-4275
Austin, TX 78713-7330   Stephen Littrell, Map Libn.
Staff: Prof 1; Other 1. **Subjects:** Maps. **Special Collections:** Depository for U.S. Geological Survey topographic quadrangles; Canadian topographic

maps; maps from U.S. Defense Mapping Agency, Special Foreign Currency Program, U.S. Air Force, and U.S. National Ocean Survey. **Holdings:** 845 volumes; 246,000 maps; 12 globes; 506 microfiche. **Subscriptions:** 16 journals and other serials. **Services:** Interlibrary loan; copying; collection open to the public. **Computerized Information Services:** BITNET (electronic mail service). **Remarks:** FAX: (512)495-1790. Electronic mail address(es): LITTRELL@EMX.UTEXAS.EDU (BITNET).

★ 19399 ★
University of Texas at Austin - Marine Science Institute - Library (Biol Sci)
P.O. Box 1267   Phone: (512)749-6723
Port Aransas, TX 78373-1267   Ruth Grundy, Libn.
Founded: 1941. **Staff:** Prof 1; Other 1. **Subjects:** Marine science in the areas of botany, chemistry, ecology, geology, physiology, zoology. **Holdings:** 12,000 books; 45,000 bound periodical volumes; documents; maps; 1000 exchange journals. **Subscriptions:** 160 journals and other serials. **Services:** Interlibrary loan; copying; library open to the public. **Computerized Information Services:** DIALOG Information Services; SCIENCEnet (electronic mail service). **Publications:** Contributions in Marine Science, irregular. **Remarks:** Alternate telephone number(s): 749-6778. FAX: (512)749-6725. Electronic mail address(es): R.Grundy (SCIENCEnet). **Staff:** Rebecca Ford, Ref./ILL.

University of Texas at Austin - Mexican American Library Program
See: University of Texas at Austin - Benson Latin American Collection (19380)

★ 19400 ★
University of Texas at Austin - Middle Eastern Library Program (Area-Ethnic)
General Libraries, PCL 5.104   Phone: (512)495-4322
Austin, TX 78713-7330   Abazar Sepehri, Middle Eastern Studies Libn.
Founded: 1963. **Staff:** Prof 1; Other 4. **Subjects:** Arabic, Persian, and Turkish language and literature; general Middle East studies in the vernacular and western languages. **Special Collections:** Yemni manuscripts; Kasravi Collection. **Holdings:** 71,819 books; 5034 bound periodical volumes; 967 reels of microfilm; 4865 microfiche. **Subscriptions:** 502 journals and other serials. **Services:** Interlibrary loan; copying; collection open to the public. **Computerized Information Services:** UTCAT (internal database); BITNET (electronic mail service). **Publications:** Library Guide (introductory brochure); Arabic and Persian Periodicals in the Middle East Collection; The Z Note. **Remarks:** FAX: (512)495-1790. Electronic mail address(es): LLAS@UTXDP (BITNET).

★ 19401 ★
University of Texas at Austin - Natural Fibers Research and Information Center (Agri)
P.O. Box 7459   Phone: (512)495-1616
Austin, TX 78713-7459   Julia Kveton Apodaca, Res.Assoc.
Founded: 1947. **Staff:** 2. **Subjects:** Agricultural and economic statistics; export and import statistics; natural fibers - cotton, wool, mohair; oilseeds; production; climatological data. **Special Collections:** A.B. Cox Memorial Collection. **Holdings:** 500 books; 100 bound periodical volumes; 10,000 pamphlets, circulars; climatological summaries; fiber and fabric educational resources. **Subscriptions:** 100 journals and other serials. **Services:** Information and referrals to phone, letter, and visitor inquiries about natural fibers and the textile industry; center open to the public for reference use only. **Publications:** The Climates of the Texas Counties; The History of Cotton in Texas; Natural Fibers and Food Protein Production in Texas: An Economic Profile; Naturally Colored Cotton: A New Niche in Texas Natural Fibers Market (working paper); Marketing on Cotton Spinning Qualities. **Remarks:** FAX: (512)495-1063.

★ 19402 ★
University of Texas at Austin - Physics-Mathematics-Astronomy Library (Sci-Engr)
General Libraries, RLM 4.200   Phone: (512)495-4610
Austin, TX 78713-7330   Molly White, Libn.
Staff: Prof 1; Other 2. **Subjects:** Astronomy, physics, mathematics. **Holdings:** 77,482 volumes; 266 reels of microfilm; 1500 strips of 35mm microfilm. **Subscriptions:** 772 journals and other serials. **Services:** Interlibrary loan; copying; library open to the public. **Computerized Information Services:** UTCAT (internal database). **Publications:** Library Guide. **Remarks:** FAX: (512)495-4507. **Also Known As:** John M. Kuehne Physics-Math-Astronomy Library.

★ 19403 ★
University of Texas at Austin - Population Research Center Library (Soc Sci)
1800 Main Bldg.   Phone: (512)471-5514
Austin, TX 78712   Gera E. Draayer, Dir., Lib. Core
Founded: 1960. **Staff:** Prof 3. **Subjects:** Population and census data, human ecology and fertility. **Special Collections:** International census publications (covers 85% of all bona fide national population censuses taken; 27,000 items). **Holdings:** 6500 books; 30 file drawers of reprints, unbound reports, and other ephemera; 440 linear feet of periodicals; 200 microfiche; 1117 reels of microfilm. **Subscriptions:** 80 journals and other serials. **Services:** Interlibrary loan; copying; library open to qualified researchers. **Computerized Information Services:** CD-ROMs (NLM, POPLINE). **Networks/Consortia:** Member of APLIC International Census Network. **Publications:** International Population Census Bibliography; Handbook of National Population Censuses (30). **Remarks:** FAX: (512)471-4886.

★ 19404 ★
University of Texas at Austin - Sam Rayburn Foundation - Library (Hist)
Bonham, TX 75418   Phone: (214)583-2455
                                   H.G. Dulaney, Lib.Dir.
Founded: 1957. **Staff:** Prof 4; Other 2. **Subjects:** History of Congress and its leaders; history of political parties; Texas history, especially in 4th Congressional District. **Special Collections:** Congressional documents from the First Continental Congress to present. **Holdings:** 15,000 books; 100 bound periodical volumes; 30 VF drawers of personal papers and correspondence (microfilm) of Honorable Sam Rayburn, Speaker; Presidential letters to the Speaker; original letters from his mother to the Speaker; tape recordings of his speeches. **Subscriptions:** 10 journals and other serials. **Services:** Library open to the public with restrictions. **Publications:** Newsletter, semiannual. **Special Indexes:** Guide to contents of Speaker's papers. **Remarks:** Library is also a museum concerning the career of Speaker Rayburn. Library is a branch library of the University of Texas, Austin. **Staff:** Doretha Gay; Kimberly Burpo; MacPhelan Reese; Jesse Higgs; Henry Harris; Thomas Rice.

★ 19405 ★
University of Texas at Austin - School of Law - Tarlton Law Library (Law)
727 E. 26th St.   Phone: (512)471-7726
Austin, TX 78705   Roy M. Mersky, Prof./Dir. of Res.
Founded: 1883. **Staff:** Prof 23; Other 18. **Subjects:** Law - Anglo-American, foreign, international. **Special Collections:** U.S. Government depository; rare books; Texas Legal Resource Center on Child Abuse and Neglect; European communities depository; U.N. documents; papers of Tom C. Clark, U.S. Supreme Court Assoc. Justice; briefs of U.S. Supreme Court, 5th Circuit Court of Appeals (Texas cases) and Texas courts. **Holdings:** 639,984 books and bound periodical volumes; 19,610 microcards; 8052 reels of microfilm; 709,942 microfiche. **Subscriptions:** 7398 journals and other serials. **Services:** Interlibrary loan; SDI; library open to the public. **Automated Operations:** Computerized cataloging, acquisitions, and ILL. **Computerized Information Services:** LEXIS, WESTLAW, DIALOG Information Services, BRS Information Technologies, RLIN, DataTimes, NEXIS; InfoTrac. **Networks/Consortia:** Member of Research Libraries Information Network (RLIN). **Publications:** Tarlton Law Library Legal Bibliography Series; Guide to Tarlton Law Library; Symposium on the Tom C. Clark Papers; Tarlton Law Library Triennial Report; Tarlton Law Library Annual Report, Notes from the Tarlton Law Library, all irregular; Contents Pages of Legal Periodicals, weekly. **Special Indexes:** Index to Periodical Articles Related to Law. **Remarks:** FAX: (512)471-0243. **Staff:** Gwyn Anderson, Admin.Assoc.; Brian Quigley, Asst.Dir. for Bibliog.Serv.; Barbara Bridges, Docs.Libn.; Mike Widener, Archv.; David Burch, Comp.Serv.Coord.; Betty Cogswell, Cat.; Adrienne deVergie, Cat.; Susan Evangelist, Admin.Asst.; David Gunn, Hd. of Ref.; Mary Ann Nelson, Assoc. Law Libn.; Monika Szakasits, Ser./Cont. Unit Supv.; John Petesch, Cat.; Jon Pratter, Foreign & Intl. Law Libn.; Pierrette Moreno, Ser./Acq.Libn.; Marlyn Robinson, Ref.Libn.; Barbara Wascheca, Hd. of Cat.; Michael Wilson, Reserve Libn.; Kathie George, Bibliog.Rec.Libn.; Juan Zabala, Lib.Bus.Mgr.; Mary Elizabeth, Act.Dir., Leg.Rsrc.Ctr.

★ 19406 ★
University of Texas at Austin - South Asian Library Program (Area-Ethnic)
General Libraries, PCL 5.108   Phone: (512)495-4330
Austin, TX 78713-7330   Merry Burlingham, South Asia Libn.
Staff: Prof 1; Other 2. **Subjects:** South Asia - languages, literature, history, anthropology, religions, arts, and music. **Special Collections:** Censuses and

gazetteers of British India (microfiche); University of Pennsylvania Sanskrit Manuscript Collection (microfiche). **Holdings:** 200,000 books and bound periodical volumes. **Subscriptions:** 1800 journals and other serials; 8 newspapers. **Services:** Interlibrary loan; library open to the public. **Computerized Information Services:** BITNET (electronic mail service). **Remarks:** FAX: (512)495-4296. Electronic mail address(es): LYAA101@UTXVM (BITNET). Holdings include materials primarily in English, Hindi, Malayalam, Sanskrit, Pali, Prakrit, and Urdu. Some volumes are available in all South Asian regional languages.

★ 19407 ★

University of Texas at Austin - Textbook and Curriculum Collection (Educ)
General Libraries, PCL 2.430   Phone: (512)495-4260
Austin, TX 78713-7330   Philip Schwartz, Educ.Bibliog.
Staff: Prof 1. **Special Collections:** Textbooks submitted for adoption by the state, grades K-12; curriculum guides of Texas Education Agency and other school districts; textbooks published prior to 1900; bilingual education materials; selected comercially published curriculum guides. **Holdings:** 14,440 textbooks and curriculum guides. **Services:** Interlibrary loan; copying; collection open to the public. **Remarks:** FAX: (512)495-4296.

★ 19408 ★

University of Texas at Austin - Wasserman Public Affairs Library (Soc Sci)
General Libraries
Sid Richardson Hall, 3.243   Phone: (512)495-4400
Austin, TX 78712-1282   Olive Forbes, Hd.Libn.
Staff: Prof 2; Other 10. **Subjects:** Politics and government, public administration and finance, social problems and policy, U.S. and Texas statutory and administrative law, civil rights, discrimination, public welfare, pollution and environmental policy, education, regional and municipal planning, public health, evaluation research. **Special Collections:** Budgets and financial reports for selected cities, counties, and states; Texas state documents; selective U.S. documents depository, 1968 to present and Canadian documents depository, 1984 to present; urban documents, 1980 to present (microfiche). **Holdings:** 68,057 volumes; 187,530 documents; 233 phonotapes; 140 cassettes; 251 videocassettes; 83 videotapes; 2146 reels of microfilm; 133,828 microfiche. **Subscriptions:** 259 journals and other serials. **Services:** Copying; multi-media room; library open to the public. **Computerized Information Services:** LEXIS, NEXIS, DIALOG Information Services, OCLC; CD-ROMs; UTCAT (internal database). **Remarks:** FAX: (512)495-4347. **Staff:** Tshering Doma, Asst.Hd.Libn.

University of Texas at Austin - Winedale Historical Center
See: Winedale Historical Center (20482)

★ 19409 ★

University of Texas at Dallas - Center for Translation Studies - Translation Library (Hum)
McDermott Library
P.O. Box 830688
Richardson, TX 75083-0688   Phone: (214)690-2092
Founded: 1984. **Subjects:** Literary translations. **Holdings:** Literary works in translation; original source-language texts. **Services:** Library open to the public. **Computerized Information Services:** Internal database. **Remarks:** Emphasis of library is on translations published since 1980.

★ 19410 ★

University of Texas at Dallas - Geological Information Library (Energy, Sci-Engr)
4925 Greenville Ave., Suite 100   Phone: (214)363-1078
Dallas, TX 75206   Edward J. Earle, Dir.
Founded: 1969. **Staff:** Prof 1; Other 3. **Subjects:** Geosciences, oil and gas, energy resources. **Special Collections:** Well logs; maps; scout tickets; production data; completion cards; well histories. **Holdings:** 8500 books; 2500 bound periodical volumes. **Subscriptions:** 18 journals and other serials. **Services:** Copying; fax service; library open to the public with restrictions. **Computerized Information Services:** Petroleum Information Corporation, Dwight's Energydata, Inc. **Special Indexes:** Well log index (online). **Remarks:** FAX: (214)373-4608.

★ 19411 ★

University of Texas at El Paso - Documents/Maps Department (Info Sci, Geog-Map)
Library   Phone: (915)747-5685
El Paso, TX 79968-0582   David Larkin
Founded: 1974. **Staff:** Prof 1; Other 4. **Subjects:** Economics and business, political science, geology, history, sociology, sciences. **Special Collections:** U.S. documents depository (161,955 items); Texas documents depository (17,382 items); U.S. Geological Survey maps depository; National Oceanic and Atmospheric Administration maps; Defense Mapping Agency (total map collection 100,146 items). **Holdings:** 183,834 volumes; 290,466 microfiche; 160,100 microprints.**Subscriptions:** 3764 journals and other serials; 58 newspapers. **Services:** Interlibrary loan; copying; department open to the public with restrictions. **Computerized Information Services:** DIALOG Information Services, BRS Information Technologies, OCLC. **Networks/Consortia:** Member of AMIGOS Bibliographic Council, Inc. **Special Indexes:** Subject index to microforms (card); subject and area index to maps (card). **Remarks:** FAX: (915)747-5327.

★ 19412 ★

University of Texas at El Paso - Institute of Oral History (Hist)
Liberal Arts 334
El Paso, TX 79968   Phone: (915)747-5508
Staff: Prof 1; Other 2. **Subjects:** History - El Paso and Ciudad Juarez, Chihuahua, University of Texas, El Paso; Mexican Americans; the Border; Mexican Revolution; Border Labor History. **Holdings:** 550 manuscripts; 900 magnetic tapes. **Services:** Institute open to the public. **Special Catalogs:** Catalog of Oral History Program; interviewee and subject files (card).

★ 19413 ★

University of Texas at El Paso - Library - S.L.A. Marshall Military History Collection (Mil, Hist)
El Paso, TX 79968-0582   Phone: (915)747-5697
Thomas F. Burdett, Cur.
Founded: 1974. **Staff:** 1. **Subjects:** Military history from antiquity to the present with emphasis on World Wars I and II, British colonial wars, Vietnamese conflict, Israeli wars, Korean War. **Special Collections:** Brigadier General S.L.A. Marshall papers (74 linear feet of papers; 42 linear feet of memorabilia); Rear Admiral Edwin C. Parsons papers (10 linear feet); Major General Frank S. Ross papers (2 linear feet); Colonel Kimbrough S. Brown papers (20 linear feet); Major Edward F. Hinkle papers (1 linear foot). **Holdings:** 10,925 books; miscellaneous collections of military papers. **Services:** Copying; collection open to the public for reference use only. **Computerized Information Services:** DIALOG Information Services, BRS Information Technologies, OCLC. **Networks/Consortia:** Member of AMIGOS Bibliographic Council, Inc. **Publications:** Newsletter, irregular. **Remarks:** FAX: (915)747-5327.

★ 19414 ★

University of Texas at El Paso - Library - Special Collections (Hum)
El Paso, TX 79968-0582   Phone: (915)747-5697
Ann Massmann, Act.Hd.
Founded: 1919. **Staff:** 3.5. **Special Collections:** Southwest and Border Studies (11,075 volumes); rare books (7950); western fiction (2550 books); art (4625 books); Judaica (2425 books); Hertzog (1450 books); Mexican Archives on microfilm (2400 reels); oral history (1285 reels; 386 transcripts); manuscripts and photographs (3000 linear feet); military history (10,925 books); Chicano studies (2850 books). **Holdings:** 47,775 books. **Subscriptions:** 3 journals and other serials. **Services:** Interlibrary loan (limited); copying; collections open to the public. **Computerized Information Services:** DIALOG Information Services, BRS Information Technologies, OCLC. **Networks/Consortia:** Member of AMIGOS Bibliographic Council, Inc. **Publications:** Guide to the Oral History Collection. **Special Catalogs:** Mexico and the Southwest: Microfilm Holdings of Historical Documents and Rare books at the University of Texas at El Paso Library; The Border Finder: The Border Studies Bibliography. **Remarks:** FAX: (915)747-5327.

★ 19415 ★

University of Texas Health Science Center at Houston - Dental Branch Library (Med)
6516 John Freeman Ave.   Phone: (713)792-4094
Houston, TX 77225   Leah Krevit, Dir.
Founded: 1943. **Staff:** Prof 2; Other 2. **Subjects:** Dentistry. **Special Collections:** History of dentistry. **Holdings:** 13,675 books; 12,856 bound periodical volumes; 525 videotapes; theses. **Subscriptions:** 340 journals and other serials. **Services:** Interlibrary loan; copying; library open to the public for reference use only. **Automated Operations:** Computerized public access catalog, cataloging, circulation, serials, and ILL. **Computerized Information Services:** BRS Information Technologies, OCLC, LS/2000. **Remarks:** FAX: (713)792-4188. **Staff:** Robert C. Park, Cat.Libn.

★19416★
University of Texas Health Science Center at San Antonio - Briscoe Library (Med)
7703 Floyd Curl Dr.   Phone: (512)567-2400
San Antonio, TX 78284-7940   Virginia M. Bowden, Lib.Dir.
Founded: 1968. **Staff:** Prof 18; Other 44. **Subjects:** Health related sciences, nursing, dentistry. **Special Collections:** History of medicine (5000 volumes). **Holdings:** 99,338 books; 95,321 bound periodical volumes; 3304 AV programs. **Subscriptions:** 2904 journals and other serials. **Services:** Interlibrary loan; copying; SDI; library open to the public for reference use only. **Automated Operations:** Computerized public access catalog, cataloging, acquisitions, serials, circulation, and ILL (DOCLINE). **Computerized Information Services:** DIALOG Information Services, OCLC, BRS Information Technologies, NLM, miniMEDLINE; BITNET (electronic mail service). **Networks/Consortia:** Member of AMIGOS Bibliographic Council, Inc., Council of Research & Academic Libraries (CORAL), South Central Academic Medical Libraries Consortium (SCAMEL), Health Oriented Libraries of San Antonio (HOLSA). **Publications:** Library News. **Remarks:** FAX: (512)567-2490; (512)567-2463. **Staff:** Sallieann Swanner, Assoc.Dir., Sys.; Daniel Jones, Asst.Dir., Coll.Dev.; Evelyn Olivier, Asst.Dir., Adm.Serv.; Rajia Tobia, Assoc.Dir., Pub.Serv.; Ingrid Hendrix, Clin.Info.Serv.; Susan Beck, Cat.; Janna Lawrence, Online Serv./Inst.Serv.Coord.; Anne Comeaux, Sys.; Ellen Hanks, Coll.Dev. Monographs/Ref.; Bonnie O'Connor, Brady/Green Libn.; Claudia Kaufman, ILL/Microcomp.Serv.Libn.; Linda Siegal, Info.Serv.; Pat Hawthorne, Admin.Serv.; Gina Sink, Info.Serv.; Mary Jo Dwyer, AHEC/CLHIN Libn.

★19417★
University of Texas Health Science Center at San Antonio - Briscoe Library - Brady/Green Library (Med)
4502 Medical Dr.   Phone: (512)270-3938
San Antonio, TX 78284-4402   Bonnie O'Connor, Brady/Green Libn.
Founded: 1958. **Staff:** Prof 1; Other 2. **Subjects:** Obstetrics, pediatrics, family practice, ambulatory care, general medicine. **Holdings:** 1350 books; 4225 bound periodical volumes. **Subscriptions:** 121 journals. **Services:** Interlibrary loan; copying; SDI; library open to the public. **Automated Operations:** Computerized public access catalog, cataloging, acquisitions, and serials. **Computerized Information Services:** DIALOG Information Services, WILSONLINE, BRS Information Technologies, MEDLARS; LIS (internal database). Performs searches on fee basis. **Networks/Consortia:** Member of Health Oriented Libraries of San Antonio (HOLSA). **Publications:** Brady/Green Library Newsletter, quarterly - for internal distribution only. **Remarks:** Alternate telephone numbers are 270-3939 and 270-3940.

★19418★
University of Texas Health Science Center at Tyler - Watson W. Wise Medical Research Library (Med)
Box 2003   Phone: (903)877-7354
Tyler, TX 75710   Elaine Wells, Dir., Lib.Serv.
Founded: 1978. **Staff:** Prof 2; Other 3. **Subjects:** Lung and heart diseases, biochemistry, oncology, nursing, surgery, molecular biology, internal medicine. **Holdings:** 3000 books; 7000 bound periodical volumes; 900 AV programs; 600 reels of microfilm. **Subscriptions:** 408 journals and other serials. **Services:** Interlibrary loan; copying; SDI; library open to the public. **Automated Operations:** Computerized public access catalog, cataloging, serials, acquisitions, AND ILL (DOCLINE). **Computerized Information Services:** OCLC, DIALOG Information Services, NLM; InterNet, BITNET (electronic mail services). Performs searches on fee basis. **Networks/Consortia:** Member of National Network of Libraries of Medicine - South Central Region, East Texas Health Sciences Consortium, AMIGOS Bibliographic Council, Inc. **Remarks:** FAX: (903)877-2221. Electronic mail address(es): CRAIG@UTHSCSA1 (BITNET); CRAIG@ELZIP.UTHSCSA.EDU (InterNet). **Staff:** Thomas B. Craig, Asst. to Dir.

★19419★
University of Texas Medical Branch at Galveston - Moody Medical Library (Med)
9th & Market St.   Phone: (409)772-1971
Galveston, TX 77550-2782   Brett A. Kirkpatrick, Dir.
Founded: 1891. **Staff:** Prof 14; Other 44. **Subjects:** Medicine, nursing, history of medicine, allied health sciences. **Special Collections:** History of medicine; medical prints and portraits. **Holdings:** 91,212 books; 140,461 bound periodical volumes; 1814 AV programs. **Subscriptions:** 2883 journals

and other serials. **Services:** Interlibrary loan; copying; SDI; library open to the public. **Automated Operations:** Computerized public access catalog, cataloging, serials, and circulation. **Computerized Information Services:** MEDLINE, BRS Information Technologies, DIALOG Information Services, OCLC; MEDICAT (internal database). Performs searches on fee basis. Contact Person: Larry J. Wygant, Assoc.Dir., Pub.Serv., 772-2387. **Networks/Consortia:** Member of AMIGOS Bibliographic Council, Inc., National Network of Libraries of Medicine - South Central Region, Houston Area Research Library Consortium (HARLIC). **Publications:** The Truman G. Blocker, Jr., History of Medicine Collections (book). **Remarks:** FAX: (409)765-9852. **Staff:** Mary M. Asbell, Clin.Libn.; Alexander C. Bienkowski, Ref./AV Libn.; Dr. Inci A. Bowman, Cur., Hist./Med.; Gary C. Rasmussen, Assoc.Dir., Auto. & Tech.Serv.; Patricia A. Ciejka, Chf.Clin.Libn.; Lynn Burke, Clin.Libn.; Deirdre R. Becker, Ref./ILL Libn.; Ellen C. Wong, Med.Cat.; Mary Vaughn, Ref./Educ.Spec.; Elaine F. Jones, Ref.

★19420★
University of Texas Mental Sciences Institute - UT Psychiatry Library (Med)
1300 Moursund Ave.   Phone: (713)792-7711
Houston, TX 77030   Felicia S. Chuang, Libn.
Founded: 1959. **Staff:** Prof 2; Other 1. **Subjects:** Psychiatry, psychopharmacology, clinical psychology, gerontology, drug abuse. **Holdings:** 10,600 books; 5000 bound periodical volumes; 64 dissertations on microfilm; 735 journal volumes on microfilm. **Subscriptions:** 235 journals and other serials. **Services:** Interlibrary loan; copying; SDI; library open to the public. **Automated Operations:** Computerized public access catalog, cataloging, and circulation. **Computerized Information Services:** DIALOG Information Services, MEDLARS; TEXSEARCH (internal database). **Networks/Consortia:** Member of National Network of Libraries of Medicine - South Central Region. **Remarks:** FAX: (713)794-1425.

★19421★
University of Texas Southwestern Medical Center at Dallas - Library (Med)
5323 Harry Hines Blvd.   Phone: (214)688-3368
Dallas, TX 75235   Kathryn Hoffman, Dir.
Founded: 1943. **Staff:** Prof 21; Other 37. **Subjects:** Medicine, biochemistry, biological science, medical specialities. **Special Collections:** Medical history. **Holdings:** 214,580 volumes; 3078 AV programs; 10,011 microforms. **Subscriptions:** 2518 journals and other serials; 5 newspapers. **Services:** Interlibrary loan; copying; SDI; library open to the public. **Automated Operations:** Computerized public access catalog, cataloging, serials, and circulation. **Computerized Information Services:** DIALOG Information Services, OCLC, BRS Information Technologies. **Networks/Consortia:** Member of National Network of Libraries of Medicine - South Central Region, Association for Higher Education of North Texas (AHE), AMIGOS Bibliographic Council, Inc., South Central Academic Medical Libraries Consortium (SCAMEL). **Publications:** Library Newsletter - to faculty and by request; Annual Report - by request. **Remarks:** Alternate telephone number(s): 688-2626. FAX: (214)688-3277. **Staff:** Patricia McKeown, Sys.Libn.; Tim Judkins, Asst.Dir., Tech.Serv.; Marilyn McKay, Media Libn.; Laura Wilder, Hd., Info.Serv.; Kathryn Connell, Hd., Access Serv.; Bill Maina, Hd., Coll.Dev./Acq.; Glenn Bunton, Sys.Libn.; Penny Billings, Info.Serv.Libn.; Cynthia Peterson, Hd., Cat.; Marty Adamson, Asst.Dir., Sys./Tech.; Melissa Scott, P.R. Libn.; Mohammad Mury, Cat.; Diane Hudson, Microcomp.Libn.; Sandy Otto, Info.Serv.Libn.; Cathy Schack, Ser.Libn.; Helen Mayo, Asst.Dir.Pub.Serv.; Nancy Trask, Info.Serv.Libn.; Mitch Walters, Hd., Ser.

University of Texas System Cancer Center
See: **University of Texas - M.D. Anderson Cancer Center** (19374)

★19422★
University of Tokyo - Earthquake Research Institute - Library (Sci-Engr)
1-1 Yayoi, 1-Chome
Bunkyo-ku
Tokyo 113, Japan   Phone: 33 812-2111
                                          Mamoru Ito, Libn.
Subjects: Seismology. **Holdings:** 42,000 volumes.

★ 19423 ★
University of Tokyo - Institute of Industrial Science - Library (Sci-Engr)
22-1 Roppongi, 7-Chome
Minato-ku
Tokyo 106, Japan   Phone: 33 402-6231
Subjects: Applied physics and mechanics, mechanical engineering, naval architecture, industrial chemistry, metallurgy, building, civil engineering, instrumentation, composite materials, functional electronics. **Holdings:** 144,198 volumes. **Remarks:** FAX: 33 402-5078. Telex: 0242 3216 IISTYO.

★ 19424 ★
University of Toledo - College of Law Library (Law)
2801 W. Bancroft St.   Phone: (419)537-2733
Toledo, OH 43606   Janet L. Wallin, Law Libn.
Staff: Prof 5; Other 6. **Subjects:** Law. **Special Collections:** Josef L. Kunz Collection (international and comparative law; 1000 volumes). **Holdings:** 140,936 books and bound periodical volumes; 30,842 volumes in microform. **Subscriptions:** 2808 journals and other serials. **Services:** Interlibrary loan; library open to the public. **Automated Operations:** Computerized cataloging and ILL. **Computerized Information Services:** LEXIS, OCLC. **Publications:** Recent Acquisitions List, monthly - available upon request. **Staff:** P. Michael Whipple, Assoc. Law Libn.; Diane S. Bitter, Cat.; Theodore A. Potter, Acq.; Clara Smith, Circ.; Joseph Fugere, Evening Supv.

★ 19425 ★
University of Toledo - Ward M. Canaday Center (Hum)
William S. Carlson Library   Phone: (419)537-4480
Toledo, OH 43606   Barbara L. Floyd, Act.Dir.
Staff: Prof 3; Other 2. **Subjects:** 20th century American poetry, Southern authors, and black American literature; university history; history of books and printing; Toledo glass industry. **Special Collections:** Ezra Pound Collection (400 volumes); William Faulkner Collection (500 volumes); Black American Poetry, 1920 to present (1000 volumes); William Dean Howells Collection (150 volumes); Herbert W. Martin Collection (15 feet); Etheridge Knight Collection (10 feet); Libbey-Owens-Ford Corporation archives (150 feet); Richard T. Gosser Collection (20 feet); Jean Gould Collection (11 feet); university archives (2000 feet); J.H. Leigh Hunt (100 volumes); Scott Nearing (50 volumes); T.S. Eliot (200 volumes); William Carlos Williams (75 volumes); Marianne Moore (75 volumes); Broadside Press (200 items); Women's Social History, 1840-1920 (1200 volumes). **Holdings:** 25,000 books; 3000 linear feet of archives and manuscripts. **Services:** Copying; center open to the public. **Automated Operations:** Computerized public access catalog and cataloging. **Computerized Information Services:** BITNET (electronic mail service). **Publications:** Friends of the University of Toledo Libraries; exhibition catalogs. **Special Catalogs:** Catalog to special collections (card). **Remarks:** FAX: (419)537-2726. Electronic mail address(es): FAC1734@UOFT1 (BITNET). **Staff:** April Dougal, Mss.Proc.

★ 19426 ★
University of Toronto - A.E. Macdonald Ophthalmic Library (Med)
1 Spadina Crescent, Rm.116   Phone: (416)978-2635
Toronto, ON, Canada M5S 2J5   Elizabeth A. Le Ber
Founded: 1965. **Staff:** 1. **Subjects:** Ophthalmology. **Special Collections:** Historical collection. **Holdings:** 1250 volumes; 750 bound periodical volumes; reprints of publications by Ophthalmology Department members, 1950 to present. **Subscriptions:** 40 journals and other serials. **Services:** Interlibrary loan; library not open to the public.

★ 19427 ★
University of Toronto - Anthropology Reading Room (Soc Sci)
Sidney Smith Hall, Rm. 560A   Phone: (416)978-3028
100 St. George St.   Prof. P. Stuart Macadam, Chm.,
Toronto, ON, Canada M5S 1A1   Dept.Lib.Comm.
Founded: 1967. **Staff:** 1. **Subjects:** Archeology; anthropology - physical, social, cultural; linguistics. **Special Collections:** Human Relations Area Files. **Holdings:** 5000 volumes; 61,900 microforms. **Services:** Reading room open to the public with restrictions. **Publications:** Accession list, monthly - for internal distribution only. **Special Catalogs:** Department of Anthropology publications; International Biological Program reports. **Remarks:** FAX: (416)978-3217.

★ 19428 ★
University of Toronto - Astronomy Library (Sci-Engr)
60 St. George St., Rm. 1306   Phone: (416)978-4268
Toronto, ON, Canada M5S 1A7   Marlene Cummins, Libn.
Founded: 1935. **Staff:** Prof 1. Other 1. **Subjects:** Astronomy, astrophysics. **Holdings:** 20,000 books, bound periodical volumes, observatory publications. **Subscriptions:** 480 journals and other serials. **Services:** Interlibrary loan; copying; library open to the public for reference use only. **Computerized Information Services:** InterNet (electronic mail service). **Publications:** Acquisitions list, weekly. **Special Indexes:** Preprint index; Selected Astronomy Book Reviews. **Remarks:** FAX: (416)978-3921. Electronic mail address(es): astlibr@vela.astro.utoronto.ca (InterNet).

★ 19429 ★
University of Toronto - Audio-Visual Library (Aud-Vis)
9 King's College Circle   Phone: (416)978-6520
Toronto, ON, Canada M5S 2E8   Liz Avison, Hd.Libn.
Staff: Prof 3; Other 7. **Subjects:** Media, broadcasting. **Holdings:** 358 books; 1229 films; 2125 videocassettes; 525 sound recordings. **Subscriptions:** 43 journals and other serials. **Services:** Interlibrary loan; copying; videotape dubbing; library open to the public. **Remarks:** FAX: (416)978-8707.

★ 19430 ★
University of Toronto - Banting & Best Department of Medical Research - Library (Med)
Best Institute, Rm. 304
112 College St.   Phone: (416)978-2588
Toronto, ON, Canada M5G 1L6   Colin Savage
Founded: 1953. **Staff:** 1. **Subjects:** Medicine, physiology, diabetes, insulin, anticoagulants, lipid metabolism. **Holdings:** 7814 volumes. **Subscriptions:** 32 journals and other serials. **Remarks:** FAX: (416)978-7666.

★ 19431 ★
University of Toronto - Centre of Criminology - Library (Law, Soc Sci)
130 St. George St., Suite 8055   Phone: (416)978-7068
Toronto, ON, Canada M5S 1A5   Catherine J. Matthews, Libn.
Founded: 1963. **Staff:** Prof 2; Other 2. **Subjects:** Criminology. **Holdings:** 20,035 volumes; 250 files of newspaper clippings (by subject); 2100 reprints. **Subscriptions:** 197 journals and other serials. **Services:** Interlibrary loan; copying; library open to the public with deposit required for borrowing. **Publications:** Criminology Library Acquisitions List, 3/year. **Remarks:** FAX: (416)978-7666.

★ 19432 ★
University of Toronto - Centre for Industrial Relations - Jean & Dorothy Newman Library (Bus-Fin)
123 St. George St.   Phone: (416)978-2928
Toronto, ON, Canada M5S 2E8   Elizabeth Perry, Libn.
Founded: 1968. **Staff:** Prof 2; Other 2. **Subjects:** Labor relations, labor economics, personnel administration, industrial psychology, industrial sociology, labor law, manpower training. **Special Collections:** Labor union archives (constitutions; newspapers; proceedings; clippings). **Holdings:** 10,924 volumes; 950 linear feet of clippings, reprints, photocopies, reports, pamphlets, statistics, documents. **Subscriptions:** 329 journals and other serials. **Services:** Copying; library open to the public for reference use only. **Remarks:** FAX: (416)978-5696.

★ 19433 ★
University of Toronto - Centre for Urban and Community Studies - Resource Room (Plan)
455 Spadina Ave.   Phone: (416)978-4478
Toronto, ON, Canada M5S 2G8   Judith Kjellberg, Info.Off.
Founded: 1980. **Staff:** 2. **Subjects:** Urban studies. **Special Collections:** Canadian housing collection; local urban issues in Toronto; urban issues in developing countries. **Holdings:** 2000 documents, manuscripts, research papers. **Subscriptions:** 25 journals and other serials. **Services:** Interlibrary loan; library open to the public with restrictions. **Computerized Information Services:** Internal databases. **Publications:** Newsletter, 4/year. **Remarks:** FAX: (416)978-7162. **Staff:** Asako Yoshida, Info.Asst.

★ 19434 ★
University of Toronto - Department of Chemistry Library (Sci-Engr)
Lash-Miller Bldg., Rms. 429-433
80 St. George St.   Phone: (416)978-3587
Toronto, ON, Canada M5S 2T4   Mary Power, Sec.
Founded: 1938. **Staff:** 2. **Subjects:** Chemistry-analytical, inorganic, organic, physical. **Holdings:** 19,350 volumes. **Subscriptions:** 194 journals and other serials. **Remarks:** FAX: (416)978-8775.

★ 19435 ★
University of Toronto - Department of Computer Science - Computer Library (Comp Sci)
Engineering Annex, Rm. 206
11 King's College Rd.   Phone: (416)978-2987
Toronto, ON, Canada M5S 2E7   Stephanie Johnston, Libn.
Founded: 1950. **Staff:** Prof 1; Other 1. **Subjects:** Computers, information retrieval, numerical analysis, automatic translation. **Special Collections:** Abstracts on cards. **Holdings:** 13,286 volumes; 304 microforms. **Subscriptions:** 186 journals and other serials. **Services:** Interlibrary loan. **Special Catalogs:** Punched card title listings. **Remarks:** FAX: (416)978-7666.

★ 19436 ★
University of Toronto - Department of Physics Library (Sci-Engr)
McLennan Physical Labs., Rm. 211
60 St. George St.   Phone: (416)978-5188
Toronto, ON, Canada M5S 1A7   B. Chu, Libn.
Founded: 1910. **Staff:** Prof 1; Other 1. **Subjects:** Physics, geophysics. **Holdings:** 28,109 volumes. **Subscriptions:** 233 journals and other serials. **Services:** Interlibrary loan. **Remarks:** FAX: (416)978-5848.

★ 19437 ★
University of Toronto - Department of Zoology Library (Biol Sci)
Ramsey-Wright Bldg., Rm. 225
25 Harbord St.   Phone: (416)978-3515
Toronto, ON, Canada M5S 1A1   Kim Gallant
Staff: 1. **Subjects:** Zoology, aquatic biology. **Holdings:** 86,533 volumes; 71,101 indexed reprints and articles. **Subscriptions:** 225 journals and other serials. **Remarks:** FAX: (416)978-8532.

★ 19438 ★
University of Toronto - Earth Sciences Library (Biol Sci)
5 Bancroft Ave.   Phone: (416)978-3538
Toronto, ON, Canada M5S 1A5   Jennifer Mendelsohn, Libn.
Founded: 1989. **Staff:** Prof 6. **Subjects:** Botany, bacteriology, biology, agriculture, paleobotany, horticulture, biochemistry, forestry, geology. **Holdings:** 75,757 volumes. **Remarks:** FAX: (416)978-7666. **Staff:** Elizabeth Vitek khoo.

★ 19439 ★
University of Toronto - East Asian Library (Area-Ethnic)
Robarts Library, Rm. 8049
130 St. George St.   Phone: (416)928-3300
Toronto, ON, Canada M5S 1A5   Anna U, Libn.
Staff: Prof 3. **Subjects:** East Asia. **Special Collections:** Mu Collection (Chinese rare books); Chinese local histories; modern Japanese literature (13,000 volumes). **Holdings:** 231,435 volumes; 9175 microforms. **Subscriptions:** 568 journals and other serials. **Services:** Interlibrary loan; copying; library open to the public for reference use only. **Remarks:** FAX: (416)978-1608. **Staff:** Teresa Hsieh

★ 19440 ★
University of Toronto - Faculty of Architecture and Landscape Architecture - Library (Plan)
230 College St.   Phone: (416)978-2649
Toronto, ON, Canada M5S 1A1   Pamela Manson-Smith, Libn.
Founded: 1922. **Staff:** Prof 1; Other 1. **Subjects:** Architecture, urban and regional planning. **Holdings:** 18,872 volumes; 10 meters of VF materials. **Subscriptions:** 100 journals and other serials. **Services:** Interlibrary loan; copying; library open to the public for reference use only. **Remarks:** FAX: (416)978-7666.

★ 19441 ★
University of Toronto - Faculty of Dentistry Library (Med)
124 Edward St., Rm. 267   Phone: (416)979-4560
Toronto, ON, Canada M5G 1G6   Susan Goddard, Fac.Libn.
Founded: 1925. **Staff:** Prof 2; Other 2.5. **Subjects:** Dentistry, medicine, health sciences. **Special Collections:** Phyllis M. Smith Collection (rare books and catalogs). **Holdings:** 24,522 books and bound periodical volumes; 493 microforms; 82 videotapes; 128 slide/tape sets; 10.5 linear feet of clippings, pamphlets, and other vertical file materials. **Subscriptions:** 194 journals and other serials. **Services:** Interlibrary loan; copying; SDI; library open to the public with restrictions. **Computerized Information Services:** MEDLINE, CAN/OLE; CD-ROM (MEDLINE); CAN/OLE (electronic mail service). Performs searches on fee basis. Contact Person: Teresa Helik, Libn. **Publications:** Filling the Gap, quarterly - to faculty and dental libraries. **Special Catalogs:** The Rare Books Collection of the Dental Library, University of Toronto and the Harry R. Abbott Memorial Library, 1978; staff articles file (cards). **Remarks:** FAX: (416)979-4566. Electronic mail address(es): FGH25001 (CAN/OLE).

★ 19442 ★
University of Toronto - Faculty of Education Library (Educ)
371 Bloor St., W.   Phone: (416)978-3224
Toronto, ON, Canada M5S 2R7   Diana George, Chf.Libn.
Founded: 1906. **Staff:** Prof 3; Other 6. **Subjects:** Education - history, philosophy, psychology, administration, general methodology. **Special Collections:** Authorized school textbooks from the 19th century. **Holdings:** 40,578 volumes; 10,777 microforms; government documents; picture collection. **Subscriptions:** 236 journals and other serials. **Services:** Interlibrary loan; copying; library open to the public. **Publications:** Bibliographic aids for teachers. **Remarks:** FAX: (416)978-6775.

★ 19443 ★
University of Toronto - Faculty of Engineering Library (Sci-Engr)
Sandford Fleming Bldg., Rm 2402
10 King's College Rd.   Phone: (416)978-6494
Toronto, ON, Canada M5S 1A4   Elaine Granatstein, Libn.
Staff: Prof 2; Other 6. **Subjects:** Engineering - civil, mechanical, industrial, chemical, electrical; engineering science and technology; metallurgy; aerospace science. **Holdings:** 112,895 volumes; 18,710 microforms. **Subscriptions:** 1606 journals and other serials. **Services:** Interlibrary loan; copying. **Remarks:** FAX: (416)978-7666.

★ 19444 ★
University of Toronto - Faculty of Law Library (Law)
78 Queen's Park Crescent   Phone: (416)978-8580
Toronto, ON, Canada M5S 1A1   Ann Rae, Libn.
Staff: Prof 4; Other 14. **Subjects:** Law. **Special Collections:** Raoul Collection in International Law (4500 volumes). **Holdings:** 175,373 volumes. **Subscriptions:** 2680 journals and other serials. **Services:** Interlibrary loan; library open to the public with restrictions on borrowing. **Remarks:** FAX: (416)978-7666.

★ 19445 ★
University of Toronto - Faculty of Library and Information Science Library (Info Sci)
140 St. George St.   Phone: (416)978-7060
Toronto, ON, Canada M5S 1A1   Diane Henderson, Chf.Libn.
Founded: 1928. **Staff:** Prof 4; Other 6. **Subjects:** Library and information science, Canadian bibliography, printing, history of libraries and publishing. **Special Collections:** Library-related annual reports and calendars; subject analysis; systems. **Holdings:** 110,804 volumes; 29 meters of pamphlets and newspaper clippings; 30,901 microforms; 25 drawers of reprint files. **Subscriptions:** 1530 journals and other serials. **Services:** Interlibrary loan; copying; library open to the public. **Automated Operations:** Computerized cataloging, serials, and indexes. **Computerized Information Services:** UTLAS, DIALOG Information Services, CAN/SDI; Envoy 100 (electronic mail service). Performs searches on fee basis. Contact Person: Ellen Jones, Pub.Serv.Libn. **Publications:** Library and Information Science Update, monthly - by subscription. **Special Indexes:** Automated index to ERIC and NTIS reports; KWOC index to reprint files. **Remarks:** FAX: (416)978-5762.

★19446★
University of Toronto - Faculty of Management Studies Library (Bus-Fin)
246 Bloor St., W.   Phone: (416)978-3421
Toronto, ON, Canada M5S 1V4   Vicki Whitemell, Libn.
Founded: 1950. **Staff:** Prof 1; Other 4. **Subjects:** Accounting, marketing, finance, organizational behavior, statistics, management science, administration, industrial relations, business mathematics. **Special Collections:** Working papers of North American and European business schools. **Holdings:** 18,500 volumes; 6223 microforms; 51 meters of VF materials. **Subscriptions:** 1200 journals and other serials. **Services:** Interlibrary loan; copying; library open to the public for reference use only. **Publications:** Business Research: Basic Reference Sources; Selected List of Recent Acquisitions, every six weeks. **Special Indexes:** Index to working paper collection (list file). **Remarks:** FAX: (416)978-5433. The Faculty of Management Studies Library is affiliated with the university's Centre for Industrial Relations Information Service.

★19447★
University of Toronto - Faculty of Music Library (Mus)
Edward Johnson Bldg.   Phone: (416)978-3734
Toronto, ON, Canada M5S 1A1   Kathleen McMorrow, Libn.
Founded: 1945. **Staff:** Prof 4; Other 12. **Subjects:** Music - theory, history, biography. **Special Collections:** Creighton Collection of Violin Recordings; rare book room; Cobbett Chamber Music Collection; Fisher Collection (historical books, music, and instruments). **Holdings:** 155,001 volumes; 45,455 pieces of sheet music; 124,536 sound recordings. **Subscriptions:** 637 journals and other serials. **Services:** Interlibrary loan; copying; library open to the public for music-related research. **Remarks:** FAX: (416)978-7666. **Staff:** S.M. Sawa, Asst.Libn.; Steven Pallay, Cat.Libn.; James Creighton, Recordings Archv.

★19448★
University of Toronto - Faculty of Pharmacy - R.O. Hurst Library (Med)
25 Russell St.   Phone: (416)978-2872
Toronto, ON, Canada M5S 1A1   Sylvia Newman, Libn.
Staff: Prof 1; Other 1. **Subjects:** Pharmacy, chemistry, history of pharmacy and medicine. **Special Collections:** R.O. Hurst Collection of Pharmacopoeias; history of pharmacy. **Holdings:** 9775 volumes. **Subscriptions:** 122 journals and other serials. **Services:** Interlibrary loan. **Remarks:** FAX: (416)978-7666.

★19449★
University of Toronto - Fine Arts Library (Art)
100 St. George St.   Phone: (416)978-5006
Toronto, ON, Canada M5S 1A1   Andrea Retfalvi, Libn.
Founded: 1934. **Staff:** Prof 1; Other 1. **Subjects:** History and techniques of fine arts. **Special Collections:** Photographs of illustrated Bibles of the 12th and 13th centuries (8500); exhibition and sales catalogs. **Holdings:** 25,520 books; 92,118 photographs. **Services:** Library not open to the public. **Special Indexes:** Subject index to Bible illustrations. **Remarks:** FAX: (416)978-7666.

★19450★
University of Toronto - General Library - Science and Medicine Department (Sci-Engr, Med, Food-Bev)
Toronto, ON, Canada M5S 1A5   Phone: (416)978-2284
    Ms. G. Heaton, Hd.
Staff: Prof 12; Other 29. **Subjects:** Technology (excluding engineering), science, medicine, nursing, anatomy, food sciences, bacteriology, industrial hygiene. **Holdings:** 695,710 volumes; 85,929 microforms. **Subscriptions:** 3106 journals and other serials. **Services:** Interlibrary loan; copying; department open to the public with restrictions. **Remarks:** Alternate telephone number(s): 978-2280. FAX: (416)978-7666.

★19451★
University of Toronto - Institute for Aerospace Studies - Library (Sci-Engr)
4925 Dufferin St.   Phone: (416)667-7712
Downsview, ON, Canada M3H 5T6   Judy Mills, Libn.
Founded: 1950. **Staff:** Prof 1; Other 1. **Subjects:** Aeronautical and aerospace engineering, gas dynamics, materials science. **Special Collections:** UTIAS reviews, technical notes, reports, and theses. **Holdings:** 80,000 monographs and reports. **Subscriptions:** 113 journals and other serials. **Services:** Interlibrary loan (fee); copying; library open to the public. **Automated Operations:** Computerized public access catalog and cataloging. **Computerized Information Services:** CAN/OLE, DIALOG Information Services; UTIAS Catalog (internal database). **Remarks:** FAX: (416)667-7799.

★19452★
University of Toronto - Institute of Child Study - Library (Educ)
45 Walmer Rd.   Phone: (416)978-4897
Toronto, ON, Canada M5R 2X2   Miriam Herman, Admin.Asst.
Staff: 1. **Subjects:** Child psychology and development, assessment and counselling, early childhood education. **Holdings:** 7800 volumes; 600 pamphlets. **Subscriptions:** 42 journals and other serials. **Services:** Library open to the public for reference use only.

★19453★
University of Toronto - Institute for Policy Analysis - Library (Soc Sci)
150 St. George St.   Phone: (416)978-8623
Toronto, ON, Canada M5S 2E9   U. Gutenburg, Lib.Techn.
Staff: 1. **Subjects:** Economics. **Holdings:** 6276 volumes. **Subscriptions:** 5 journals and other serials. **Services:** Copying; library open to the public. **Remarks:** FAX: (416)978-5519.

★19454★
University of Toronto - Knox College - Caven Library (Rel-Phil)
59 St. George St.   Phone: (416)978-4504
Toronto, ON, Canada M5S 2E6   A. Burgess, Libn.
Founded: 1845. **Staff:** Prof 2; Other 1. **Subjects:** Theology (Presbyterian), philosophy, social ethics, Reformation era church history. **Special Collections:** Reproductions of Biblical codices; early editions of Bibles and commentaries; reproductions of medieval illuminated manuscripts; John Calvin Collection. **Holdings:** 69,629 volumes; 1650 microforms. **Subscriptions:** 313 journals and other serials. **Services:** Interlibrary loan; copying; library open to the public. **Remarks:** FAX: (416)978-7666.

★19455★
University of Toronto - Map Library (Geog-Map)
130 St. George St., Rm. 1001   Phone: (416)978-3372
Toronto, ON, Canada M5S 1A5   Joan Winearls, Map Libn.
Staff: Prof 2; Other 3. **Subjects:** Geography, cartography. **Holdings:** 13,088 books and atlases; 220,962 maps; 285,735 aerial photographs. **Subscriptions:** 42 journals and other serials. **Services:** Interlibrary loan; copying; library open to the public. **Publications:** Accessions list, bimonthly. **Remarks:** FAX: (416)978-1603.

★19456★
University of Toronto - Mathematics Library (Sci-Engr)
Sidney Smith Hall, Rm. 2124
100 St. George St.   Phone: (416)978-8624
Toronto, ON, Canada M5S 1A1   Richard D. Pullin, Libn.
Founded: 1970. **Staff:** Prof 1; Other 1. **Subjects:** Mathematics. **Holdings:** 25,972 volumes. **Subscriptions:** 555 journals and other serials. **Services:** Interlibrary loan; library not open to the public. **Remarks:** FAX: (416)978-4107.

★19457★
University of Toronto - Pathology Library (Med)
Banting Institute, Rms. 108-109
100 College St.   Phone: (416)978-2558
Toronto, ON, Canada M5G 1L5   Sophia Duda, Libn.
Founded: 1923. **Staff:** 1. **Subjects:** Pathology, immunology, bacteriology. **Holdings:** 4163 volumes. **Subscriptions:** 71 journals and other serials. **Services:** Interlibrary loan; copying. **Remarks:** FAX:(416)978-7666.

★19458★
University of Toronto - Pontifical Institute of Mediaeval Studies - Library (Hist)
113 St. Joseph St., 4th Fl.   Phone: (416)926-7146
Toronto, ON, Canada M5S 1J4   Rev. Donald Finlay, Libn.
Founded: 1929. **Staff:** Prof 3; Other 2. **Subjects:** Medieval life and thought. **Special Collections:** Gordon Taylor Microfilm Collection; Etienne Gilson Collection; Gerald B. Phelan Archives. **Holdings:** 85,000 books; 11,600 bound periodical volumes; 2.5 million pages on microfilm. **Subscriptions:** 150 journals and other serials. **Services:** Interlibrary loan; copying; library open to bona fide scholars with letters of introduction.

★19459★
University of Toronto - St. Michael's College - John M. Kelly Library (Rel-Phil)
113 St. Joseph St.   Phone: (416)926-7111
Toronto, ON, Canada M5S 1J4   Rev. Donald Finlay, Libn.
Founded: 1929. Staff: Prof 9; Other 14. Subjects: Humanities, medieval studies, theology. Special Collections: Counter Reformation; G.K. Chesterton; J.H. Newman; Roy Campbell; Stathas Collection (Spain); Etienne Gilson Archive. Holdings: 236,000 volumes; 6 linear feet of VF material; 7250 microforms; 16,417 slides. Subscriptions: 1600 journals and other serials; 25 newspapers. Services: Interlibrary loan; copying; library open to the public. Automated Operations: Computerized cataloging. Computerized Information Services: UTLAS. Publications: Pamphlets on the Counter Reformation and Newman collections. Special Catalogs: Catalog of the Pontifical Institute Library (book). Remarks: St. Michael's College Library is affiliated with the University of Toronto's Pontifical Institute of Mediaeval Studies Library. Staff: Louise H. Girard, Assoc.Libn.; Evelyn Collins, Hd., Ref.; Bea Lawford, Circ.; Margaret Ivor, Circ.; Andrew West, Hd., Tech.Serv.

★19460★
University of Toronto - Thomas Fisher Rare Book Library (Rare Book, Hist, Hum)
120 St. George St.   Phone: (416)978-5285
Toronto, ON, Canada M5S 1A5   Richard G. Landon, Dir.
Founded: 1955. Staff: Prof 10; Other 11. Subjects: English literature, Canadian literature, European literature, theater history, history, Canadian history, philosophy and theology, science, history of medicine, art, book arts and bibliography, rare books. Special Collections: Fisher Collection (Shakespeare editions and Shakespeareana; 3000 volumes); Endicott Collection (works by British authors whose careers fall between 1880 and 1930; 4500 volumes); DeLury Collection of Anglo-Irish Literature (5000 volumes); Duncan Collection (editions of D.H. Lawrence, Richard Aldington, Max Beerbohm, Norman Douglas, and Aldous Huxley; 800 volumes); Yellowback Collection (popular Victorian reading, fiction and nonfiction; 400 volumes); manuscript collections of Canadian authors, including Earle Birney, Margaret Atwood, Mazo De La Roche, Duncan Campbell Scott, Ernest Buckler, Leonard Cohen, Mavis Gallant, Dennis Lee, Gwendolyn McEwan, John Newlove, Raymond Souster, Josef Skvorecky, W.A. Deacon; Canadian literary periodicals; Rousseau Collection (700 volumes); Voltaire Collection (900 volumes); Italian play collection (especially Renaissance period; 6500 volumes); Rime Collection (Italian lyric verse; 700 volumes); Buchanan Collection (Spanish and Italian literature and historical works; 1700 volumes); Petlice Collection (Czechoslovakian works not allowed to be published in Czechoslovakia; 200 volumes); Bagnani Collection (editions of Petronius Arbiter; 200 volumes); Juvenile Drama Collection (6000 sheets; 150 volumes); papers of Dora Mavor Moore, Canadian director and founder of the New Play Society; French Revolution pamphlets (900); Spanish Civil War Collection (650 volumes); Shelden Collection of Australiana (1500 volumes); Czechoslovakia '68 Collection and Czechoslovakian History and Politics Collection (2500 volumes); Radio Free Europe Collection (3000 items); NSZZ Solidarnosc Collection (materials relating to the Solidarity movement in Poland; 1500 items); 17th and 18th century British history; Canadian history, discovery, and exploration (30,000 manuscripts; 1200 maps, plans, and insurance plans of Canadian towns); Kenny Collection (socialist and radical Canadian material; 2500 volumes); Woodsworth Collection of Co-operative Commonwealth Federation Material (700 items); Maclean Hunter and Southam Press Collections (periodicals and trade journals; 310 titles); papers of Mark Gayn, Canadian foreign correspondent, 1909-1981; historical manuscript collections and papers of eminent Canadians, including J.B. Tyrrell, James Mavor, Sir Alan MacNab, Sir Edmund Walker; James Forbes Collection (17th century theological works; 1600 volumes); Aristotle Collection (300 volumes); Bacon Collection (250 volumes); Hobbes Collection (500 volumes); Locke Collection (170 volumes); Bertrand Russell Collection (published works by and about Russell; 10,000 volumes); Science Collection (emphasis on Renaissance astronomy, physics, mechanics, and on English experimental science of the 17th and 18th centuries; 4500 volumes); Galileo Collection (300 volumes); James L. Baillie Collection of (ornithology; 3000 items); Darwin Collection (2000 volumes); Einstein Collection (300 volumes); Bronowski Collection (books and papers); Simcoe Collection (military science; 360 volumes); Victorian Natural History Collection (1700 volumes); Jason A. Hannah Collection (first and significant editions of medical works from classical times to the 20th century; 6000 volumes); Sir Frederick Banting Collection (books and manuscripts, including records of experiments leading to insulin; Fisher Hollar Collection (etchings by Wenceslaus Hollar, 1607-1677; 100 volumes; 3500 etchings); John E. Langdon Collection (silver and silversmiths; 1000 volumes); G.M. Miller Collection (architectural plans for

buildings in Toronto region, 1888-1952; 1300 plans); L.B. Duff Collection and reference collections (arts of the books, collectors, bibliography; 1500 volumes); Stanbrook Abbey Press Collection (125 volumes); Middle Hill Press Collection (325 volumes); Thoreau MacDonald Collection (illustrator; 300 volumes); Birdsall Collection (binders' finishing tools, 18th and 19th centuries; 3000); booksellers' catalogs. Holdings: 263,189 books; 3423 linear feet of manuscripts. Services: Interlibrary loan; copying (both limited); library open to the public. Automated Operations: Computerized cataloging. Computerized Information Services: UTLAS. Publications: A Brief Guide to the Collections - free upon request. Special Catalogs: Manuscript collection finding aids; chronological file for Canadiana holdings (card); autograph, bookplate, association, binding, and printers' files (all card); exhibition catalogs, 5-6/year - free upon request. Remarks: FAX: (416)978-1667. Staff: Katharine Martyn, Hd./Mss.Libn.; E. Anne Jocz, Hd.Cat.; Emrys Evans, Cons. & Binder.

★19461★
University of Toronto - University Archives (Hist)
Fisher Library
120 St. George St.   Phone: (416)978-2277
Toronto, ON, Canada M5S 1A5   Garron Wells, Univ.Archv.
Founded: 1965. Staff: Prof 2; Other 3. Subjects: University of Toronto, higher education. Holdings: 13,858 linear feet of publications of and about the university, theses, manuscripts, clippings, photographs, plans, tape recordings, motion picture films. Services: Interlibrary loan; copying; archives open to the public. Special Catalogs: Finding aids in typescript. Remarks: FAX: (416)978-1667. Staff: Harold Averill, Asst.Archv.; Lorraine O'Donnell, Spec. Media Archv.

★19462★
University of Toronto - University of Trinity College - Library (Rel-Phil, Hum)
6 Hoskin Ave.   Phone: (416)978-2653
Toronto, ON, Canada M5S 1H8   Linda Wilson Corman, Hd.Libn.
Staff: Prof 3; Other 7. Subjects: Anglican theology, English Literature, classics, philosophy, French and German literature. Special Collections: Bishop Strachan Collection (500 volumes); S.P.C.K. Collection (400 volumes). Holdings: 128,322 books and bound periodical volumes. Subscriptions: 315 journals and other serials. Services: Interlibrary loan; copying; library open to the public for reference use only. Automated Operations: Computerized cataloging. Computerized Information Services: BRS Information Technologies. Remarks: FAX: (416)978-7666. Staff: Lesie Del Bianco, Asst.Libn.

★19463★
University of Toronto - Victoria University - Library (Hum, Soc Sci)
71 Queen's Park Crescent, E.   Phone: (416)978-3821
Toronto, ON, Canada M5S 1K7   Dr. Robert C. Brandeis, Chf.Libn.
Staff: Prof 5; Other 22. Subjects: Humanities, social sciences, theology. Special Collections: E.J. Pratt Manuscript Collection; Coleridge Collection (350 books and manuscripts); Tennyson Collection (500 books and periodical articles); Wesleyana Collection (800 books); Woolf/Bloomsbury/ Hogarth Press Collection (500 books); Church of Christ Disciples Archives; Hymnology (500 hymn books). Holdings: 232,160 volumes; 150 Emmanuel College theses. Subscriptions: 508 journals and other serials. Services: Interlibrary loan; copying; library open to the public registration. Automated Operations: Computerized cataloging. Remarks: FAX: (416)585-4584. Victoria University Library houses its Arts College Collection in the E.J. Pratt Library, which also houses the Centre for Reformation and Renaissance Studies Collection (14,000 volumes). Victoria's Theological Collection is housed in the Emmanuel College Library.

★19464★
University of Toronto - Wycliffe College - Leonard Library (Rel-Phil)
Hoskin Ave.   Phone: (416)979-2870
Toronto, ON, Canada M5S 1H7   Adrienne Taylor, Coll.Libn.
Founded: 1880. Staff: Prof 1; Other 2. Subjects: Theology. Special Collections: Cody Memorial Library (mainly homiletics). Holdings: 46,124 volumes; 2200 pamphlets; maps. Subscriptions: 109 journals and other serials. Services: Interlibrary loan; copying; library open to the public by permission. Automated Operations: Computerized cataloging. Remarks: FAX: (416)978-7666.

University of Trinity College
See: **University of Toronto (19462)**

University of Trondheim - Norwegian Institute of Technology
See: **The Technical University Library of Norway (16033)**

★ 19465 ★
University of Tulsa - College of Law Library (Law)
3120 E. Fourth Place   Phone: (918)631-2459
Tulsa, OK 74104   Richard E. Ducey, Dir./Assoc.Prof.
Founded: 1923. **Staff:** Prof 5; Other 7. **Subjects:** Law. **Special Collections:** American Indian law; Energy Law and Policy Collection. **Holdings:** 245,911 volumes, including microfiche. **Subscriptions:** 3804 journals and other serials; 8 newspapers. **Services:** Interlibrary loan; copying; library open to members, excluding government documents. **Automated Operations:** Computerized public access catalog, cataloging, acquisitions, circulation, periodicals, and ILL. **Computerized Information Services:** LEXIS, NEXIS, OCLC, WESTLAW, LegalTrac; CD-ROM (WILSONDISC, Intelligent Catalog, CIS/Index). Performs limited searches on fee basis. Contact Person: Melanie Nelson, Pub.Serv./ILL/Circ. **Networks/Consortia:** Member of AMIGOS Bibliographic Council, Inc., Mid-America Law School Library Consortium. **Remarks:** FAX: (918)631-3556. Includes holdings of the University of Tulsa Law Research Center. **Staff:** Sue Sark, Asst.Dir./Coll.Dev.; Katherine J. Tooley, Tech.Serv.; Kathy Kane, Pub.Serv./Gov.Docs.

★ 19466 ★
University of Tulsa - McFarlin Library - Special Collections (Hum, Hist)
600 S. College Ave.   Phone: (918)631-2496
Tulsa, OK 74104   Sidney F. Huttner, Cur.
Founded: 1894. **Staff:** Prof 2; Other 4. **Subjects:** 20th century British and American literature; Indian history, law, and policy; World War I; Proletarian literature; American fiction regarding Vietnam; performing arts. **Special Collections:** Cyril Connolly Library and papers; Andre Deutsch Archive (London publisher, 1950-1988); Edmund Wilson Library; Richard Ellmann papers; Richard Murphy papers; Jean Rhys papers; Paul Scott papers; Muriel Spork papers; Rebecca West papers; Stevie Smith papers; Shleppey Indian Collection; J.B. Milam Library (Cherokee materials); Indian Claims Commission Archives; University Archives. **Holdings:** 100,000 books; 1000 bound periodical volumes; 55 boxes of Alice Robertson papers; 200,000 British and American 20th century literary manuscripts; 300 pieces of 20th century American Indian art; 150 territorial maps. **Subscriptions:** 20 journals and other serials. **Services:** Interlibrary loan; copying; collections open to the public on written application. **Automated Operations:** Computerized public access catalog, cataloging, acquisitions, and serials. **Computerized Information Services:** DIALOG Information Services, OCLC; RLG, BITNET, InterNet (electronic mail services). **Networks/Consortia:** Member of Tulsa Area Library Cooperative (TALC), Oklahoma Special Collections and Archives Network (OSCAN), AMIGOS Bibliographic Council, Inc., Research Libraries Information Network (RLIN). **Publications:** Women Writers in McFarlin Special Collections; The Paul and Lucie Leon/James Joyce Collection; The Anna Kavan papers; keepsake series; guides to manuscript collections - available on request; finding aids. **Remarks:** FAX: (918)631-3791. Electronic mail address(es): BM.TUL (RLG); SHUTTNER@TULSA (BITNET); SFH@VAX2.UTULSA.EDU (InterNet). **Staff:** Lori N. Curtis, Asst.Cur.

★ 19467 ★
University United Methodist Church - Library (Rel-Phil)
2000 S. Locust St.   Phone: (505)522-8220
Las Cruces, NM 88001   Marjorie Neher, Libn.
Founded: 1970. **Staff:** 1. **Subjects:** The Bible, Christian living, marriage, divorce, parenthood, prayer, Methodist church, John Wesley. **Holdings:** 3310 books; 11 maps; 22 audio cassettes. **Subscriptions:** 2 journals and other serials. **Services:** Library open to the public.

★ 19468 ★
University of Utah - Audio-Visual Division (Aud-Vis)
Marriott Library, 4th Fl.   Phone: (801)581-6283
Salt Lake City, UT 84112   Ralph E. Kranz, AV Libn.
Founded: 1967. **Staff:** Prof 1; Other 25. **Subjects:** Music, drama, poetry, art, dance, social sciences, sciences, architecture, film studies, microcomputer software. **Holdings:** 5000 audio cassettes; 20,000 phonograph records; 21,118 slides; 250 filmstrips; 100 films; 7361 audiotapes; 10,000 videocassettes; 2000 compact discs. **Services:** Division open to the public with restrictions. **Computerized Information Services:** OCLC; BITNET, InterNet (electronic mail services). **Networks/Consortia:** Member of Bibliographical Center for Research, Rocky Mountain Region, Inc. (BCR). **Publications:** Music and video bibliographies. **Remarks:** Division maintains a microcomputer center with 150 computers. FAX: (801)581-4882. Electronic mail address(es): RKRANZ@UTAH.LIB.EDU (BITNET); KTUDDENH@MLMC.LIB.UTAH.EDU (microcomputer center; InterNet). **Staff:** Reid Sondrup, AV Assoc.; Joni Clayton, AV Asst.; Ken Tuddenham, Comp.Ctr.Coord.; Ken Tuddenham, Coord., Micro Comp.Ctr; Bryan Morris, PC/Network Mgr.; Richard Glaser, Macintosh Mgr.

★ 19469 ★
University of Utah - Documents Division (Info Sci)
Marriott Library
Salt Lake City, UT 84112   Phone: (801)581-8394
Staff: Prof 4; Other 8. **Subjects:** Energy research and development, business and economics, statistics, geological and earth sciences, legislative documents, presidential materials, patents. **Special Collections:** Energy research and development reports, 1950 to present; Congressional committee prints on microfiche (15,100 prints); Congressional committee hearings on microfiche (29,400 hearings); American Statistics Index Nondepository Collection on microfiche (complete set); United Nations Depository Collection; Federal Documents Depository Collection; U.S. Patents, 1971 to present. **Holdings:** 550,000 volumes. **Subscriptions:** 1700 journals and other serials. **Services:** Interlibrary loan; copying; division open to the public. **Computerized Information Services:** DIALOG Information Services, PFDS Online, BRS Information Technologies, CASSIS; CD-ROM (Automated Patent Searching); BITNET (electronic mail service). **Remarks:** FAX: (801)585-3464. **Staff:** Maxine R. Haggerty, Doc.Acq.Libn.; David L. Morrison, Patents Docs.Libn.; Michele A. Widera, Intl.Doc.Libn.

★ 19470 ★
University of Utah - Human Relations Area Files (Soc Sci)
Marriott Library
Salt Lake City, UT 84112   Phone: (801)581-7024
Founded: 1950. **Staff:** Prof 1. **Subjects:** Anthropology, behavioral sciences, geography, history, psychology, sociology, political science. **Holdings:** 5000 books; 3.5 million records on microfiche. **Services:** Files open to the public for reference use only.

★ 19471 ★
University of Utah - Instructional Media Services (Educ)
207 Milton Bennion Hall   Phone: (801)581-6112
Salt Lake City, UT 84112   James R. Baird, Dir.
Founded: 1952. **Staff:** 32. **Subjects:** Social and behavioral sciences, literature, history, science, mathematics. **Holdings:** 5303 film and video titles. **Services:** T.V. distribution/production; photography and graphics; AV equipment service; instructional design; services open to the public on a fee basis. **Special Catalogs:** University of Utah Film Video Library Catalog and Supplement. **Remarks:** FAX: (801)581-7987. **Staff:** Jan Bruckman, Coll.Dev.Coord.

★ 19472 ★
University of Utah - Law Library (Law)
College of Law   Phone: (801)581-6438
Salt Lake City, UT 84112   Rita Reusch, Dir.
Founded: 1910. **Staff:** Prof 6; Other 11. **Subjects:** Law. **Holdings:** 185,000 volumes; 410,000 microfiche; 1000 reels of microfilm; 425 cassettes. **Subscriptions:** 2150 journals and other serials; 10 newspapers. **Services:** Interlibrary loan; copying; library open to the public. **Automated Operations:** Computerized public access catalog, cataloging, serials, acquisitions, and circulation. **Computerized Information Services:** RLIN, WESTLAW, LEXIS, NEXIS, LegalTrac; CD-ROM (WILSONDISC); InterNet (electronic mail service). **Networks/Consortia:** Member of Research Libraries Information Network (RLIN). **Publications:** Acquisitions, monthly; User Guide, miscellaneous bibliographies. **Remarks:** FAX: (801)581-6897. Electronic mail address(es): REUSCH@EDU-UTAH-LAW-ADMIN1 (InterNet). **Staff:** Lee Warthen, Asst.Dir./Hd. of Pub.Serv.; Ellen Ouyang, Tech.Serv.Libn.; Linda Stephenson, Ref.Libn.; Suzanne Miner, Ref.Libn.; Tom Oertel, Circ.Libn.

★ 19473 ★
University of Utah - Map Library (Geog-Map)
158 Marriott Library   Phone: (801)581-7533
Salt Lake City, UT 84112   Barbara Cox, Map Libn.
Staff: Prof 1. **Subjects:** Maps. **Holdings:** 400 books; 140,000 maps; 100 photographs. **Services:** Interlibrary loan; copying; library open to the public. **Automated Operations:** Computerized cataloging and circulation. **Computerized Information Services:** BITNET (electronic mail service). **Remarks:** FAX: (801)581-4882. Electronic mail address(es): BCOX@UTAHLIB (BITNET).

★ 19474 ★
University of Utah - Mathematics Library (Sci-Engr)
121 JWB   Phone: (801)581-6208
Salt Lake City, UT 84112   Carol Szoke, Math.Lib.Supv.
Founded: 1965. **Staff:** 2. **Subjects:** Mathematics. **Holdings:** 7000 books; 8500 bound periodical volumes; 1400 technical reports. **Subscriptions:** 255 journals and other serials. **Services:** Interlibrary loan; copying; library open to the public. **Automated Operations:** Computerized cataloging and circulation (NOTIS). **Computerized Information Services:** BITNET (electronic mail service). **Remarks:** FAX: (801)581-4882. Electronic mail address(es): CSZOKE@UTAHLIB (BITNET).

★ 19475 ★
University of Utah - Middle East Library (Area-Ethnic)
Marriott Library   Phone: (801)581-6311
Salt Lake City, UT 84112   Mr. Ragai N. Makar, Hd.
Staff: Prof 1; Other 3. **Subjects:** Humanities; language and literature; political science; social sciences; Islamic studies and history; Arabic, Hebrew, Persian, and Turkish culture and civilization. **Special Collections:** Arabic papyrus and paper documents (9th-11th centuries; 1560 items; 3400 rare books); Arabic, Persian, and Turkish manuscripts (250 items); Fayez Sayegh Collection; Zaki Abushadi Collection; Martin Levey Collection on the history of Arabic science (10,000 items); Arabic and Greek manuscripts (2255 reels of microfilm); illustrated history of Rashid al-Din; Arab League manuscripts collection (470 reels of microfilm); manuscript Qurans; Iranian newspapers on microfilm, 1978-1984; Kabbalah manuscripts collection (65 reels of microfilm); U.S. Department of State, Affairs of Turkey documents, 1910-1929 (125 reels of microfilm); U.S. Department of State Internal and Foreign Affairs of Egypt (79 reels of microfilm); Hebrew journals on microfiche (19th and early 20th centuries). **Holdings:** 138,000 books; 14,200 periodical volumes; 3800 reels of microfilm; 4000 microfiche. **Subscriptions:** 504 journals and other serials; 40 newspapers and newsletters. **Services:** Interlibrary loan; copying (limited); library open to the public for reference use only. **Automated Operations:** Computerized cataloging, acquisitions, and circulation. **Computerized Information Services:** Association of Research Libraries (ARL), DIALOG Information Services, PFDS Online, Performs searches on fee basis. Contact Person: Ruth Frear, 581-7533. **Networks/Consortia:** Member of Utah College Library Council (UCLC), Bibliographical Center for Research, Rocky Mountain Region, Inc. (BCR). **Publications:** Aziz S. Atiya Library for Middle East Studies Arabic Collection, 3 volumes; Middle East Bibliographic Bulletin, triennial. **Remarks:** FAX: (801)581-4882. **Staff:** Judy Jarrow, Asst.Libn.

★ 19476 ★
University of Utah - Special Collections Department (Hist)
Marriott Library   Phone: (801)581-8863
Salt Lake City, UT 84112   Gregory C. Thompson, Asst.Dir., Spec.Coll.
Founded: 1935. **Staff:** Prof 5; Other 35. **Subjects:** Utah, Mountain West, Mormons, Indians. **Special Collections:** Annie Clark Tanner Memorial Trust Fund; Utah, the Mormons and the West; university contracts. **Holdings:** 93,750 books; 5525 periodical titles; 30,000 theses and dissertations; 1771 federal documents; 15,161 folders of clippings; 10,100 folders of pamphlets; 12,000 linear feet of manuscripts; 600,000 photographs; 15,000 AV items; 2257 linear feet of archives. **Subscriptions:** 1680 journals and other serials; 170 newspapers. **Services:** Interlibrary loan; copying (both limited); department open to the public for reference use only. **Automated Operations:** Computerized public access catalog, cataloging, acquisitions, serials, and circulation. **Computerized Information Services:** Internal database. **Publications:** Registers to manuscript collections; guides for subject areas; manuscript inventories; manuscript name and subject index. **Special Indexes:** Analytic index for serials and pamphlets; newspaper clip file; Arizona index; Chronicle index; Review index; university contracts index. **Remarks:** FAX: (801)585-3464. **Staff:** Ruth Yeaman, Libn.; Walter Jones, Libn.; Clint Bailey, Archv.Rec.Mgr.; Nancy Young, Libn.

★ 19477 ★
University of Utah - Spencer S. Eccles Health Sciences Library (Med)
Bldg. 89
10 N. Medical Dr.   Phone: (801)581-8771
Salt Lake City, UT 84112   Wayne J. Peay, Dir.
Founded: 1906. **Staff:** Prof 9; Other 36. **Subjects:** Medicine, pharmacy, nursing, basic sciences, health. **Special Collections:** Hope Fox Eccles Clinical Library (361 books; 1250 bound periodical volumes); selective documents depository for health sciences (35,634 items). **Holdings:** 43,121 books; 77,098 bound periodical volumes; 3376 AV programs. **Subscriptions:** 1916 journals and other serials. **Services:** Interlibrary loan; copying; SDI; AV loans; CAI; library open to the public with annual permit. **Automated Operations:** Computerized cataloging, acquisitions, serials, circulation, and ILL. **Computerized Information Services:** BRS Information Technologies, MEDLINE, OCLC; BITNET, InterNet (electronic mail services). **Networks/Consortia:** Member of National Network of Libraries of Medicine - Midcontinental Region, Utah Health Sciences Library Consortium (UHSLC). **Publications:** IMS Newsletter, quarterly. **Special Indexes:** MEDOC: Index to U.S. Government Documents in the Health Sciences, quarterly. **Remarks:** FAX: (801)581-3632. **Staff:** Elena Eyzaguirre, Assoc.Dir.; Nina Dougherty, Assoc.Dir., Res. & Educ.; Joan Stoddart, Asst.Dir., Pub.Serv.; Joan Marcotte, Asst.Dir.Tech.Serv.; Kathleen McCloskey, Hd., Clin.Lib.; Mary Youngkin, Asst.Dir., Info.Serv.; Magdeline Quinlan, Hd., Comp. & Media Serv.; Jeanne Le Ber, Ref.Serv.

★ 19478 ★
University of Valencia - Biomedical Documentation and Information Center - Library (Med)
Avda. Blasco Ibanez, 17   Phone: 96 3610654
Valencia 10, Spain   Maria Luz Terrada Ferrandis, Dir.
Founded: 1960. **Staff:** 14. **Subjects:** Biomedicine, medicine, biological sciences, agronomy. **Holdings:** 6500 bound volumes. **Subscriptions:** 320 journals and other serials. **Services:** Copying; SDI; library open to biomedical professionals. **Computerized Information Services:** DIALOG Information Services, NLM, ESA/IRS, other online vendors; Spanish Medical Index, Valencian Science (internal databases). Performs searches. **Publications:** Indice Medico Espanol, 3/year; Cuadernos de Documentacion e Informatica Biomedica. **Remarks:** FAX: 96 3613975.

★ 19479 ★
University of Vermont - Charles A. Dana Medical Library (Med)
Given Bldg.   Phone: (802)656-2200
Burlington, VT 05405   Julie J. McGowan, Dir.
Founded: 1917. **Staff:** Prof 9; Other 17. **Subjects:** Medicine, nursing, and allied health sciences. **Special Collections:** Historical collection, emphasizing Vermont and U.S. history of medicine. **Holdings:** 26,822 books; 65,110 periodical volumes; 3199 AV programs. **Subscriptions:** 1674 journals and other serials. **Services:** Interlibrary loan; copying; library open to the public. **Automated Operations:** Computerized public access catalog, cataloging, acquisitions, serials, circulation, and ILL. **Computerized Information Services:** DIALOG Information Services, BRS Information Technologies, MEDLARS, OCLC, OCLC EPIC, ORBIT Search Service; CD-ROMs (CD-Plus, Compact Cambridge, Silverplatter); BITNET (electronic mail service). Performs searches on fee basis. Contact Person: Marian Farley, Ref.Hd. **Networks/Consortia:** Member of National Network of Libraries of Medicine - New England Region, NELINET, Inc. **Publications:** Resource Library News, irregular - to Vermont and New Hampshire hospital librarians; Dana Medical Library Newsletter, monthly - to user groups. **Remarks:** FAX: (802)863-1136. Electronic mail address(es): UVMVM (BITNET). **Staff:** Dorothy Senghas, Hd., Tech.Serv.; Robert Sekerak, Hd.,Info.,Ed.,Outreach Serv.; Joanna Weinstock, Ref.Libn.; Ellen Hall, Ref.Libn.; Cathy Goddard, Ref.Libn.; Donna Lee, Media Libn.; Lida Douglas, Circ.Supv.; Elizabeth Dow, Outreach Libn.

★ 19480 ★
University of Vermont - Chemistry/Physics Library (Sci-Engr)
Cook Physical Sciences Bldg.   Phone: (802)656-2268
Burlington, VT 05405   Craig A. Robertson, Chem./Physics Libn.
Staff: Prof 1; Other 1. **Subjects:** Chemistry, physics, materials science. **Holdings:** 8500 books; 17,500 bound periodical volumes; 360 reels of microfilm; 1800 microfiche. **Subscriptions:** 351 journals and other serials. **Services:** Interlibrary loan; copying; SDI; library open to the public with restrictions on circulation. **Automated Operations:** Computerized cataloging, acquisitions, and circulation. **Computerized Information Services:** STN International, DIALOG Information Services, Current Contents: Physical, Chemical & Earth Sciences; BITNET (electronic mail service). Performs searches on fee basis. **Publications:** Library Handbook; acquisitions list, monthly - both for internal distribution only. **Remarks:** Electronic mail address(es): CROBERTS@UVMVM (BITNET).

★19481★
University of Vermont - Curriculum Materials Center (Educ)
Bailey/Howe Library   Phone: (802)656-8086
Burlington, VT 05405-0036   Linda Brew MacDonald, Dir.
Founded: 1988. **Staff:** Prof 1; Other 1.5. **Subjects:** Curriculum materials, K-12. **Special Collections:** Reports of school districts; curriculum guides (KCDL microfiche, 1987 to present). **Holdings:** 1200 textbooks and manuals; teaching units; lesson plans; school report forms; educational software. **Services:** Interlibrary loan; center open to the public. **Automated Operations:** Computerized public access catalog, cataloging, acquisitions, serials, and circulation. **Computerized Information Services:** DIALOG Information Services, BRS Information Technologies; BITNET (electronic mail service). Performs searches on fee basis. **Networks/Consortia:** Member of NELINET, Inc. **Remarks:** FAX: (802)656-4038. Electronic mail address(es): LMACDONA@UVMVM (BITNET).

★19482★
University of Vermont - Department of Special Collections (Hist)
Bailey/Howe Library   Phone: (802)656-2138
Burlington, VT 05405   Connell B. Gallagher, Asst. Dir., Res.Coll.
Founded: 1791. **Staff:** Prof 3; Other 4. **Subjects:** Vermontiana, Canadiana, English printer Charles Whittingham, illustrated editions of Ovid, modern fine press books, English poet John Masefield, Vietnam War fiction, poet Diane Wakoski, history of books and printing and photography. **Special Collections:** Wilbur Collection of Vermontiana: manuscripts of Dorothy Canfield Fisher, Warren Austin, John Spargo, Ira Allen, Champlain Transportation Company, Vermont Symphony Orchestra, Vermont governors Roswell Farnham and James Hartness, Civil War Generals William Wells, O.O. Howard, Henry Stevens and family, George P. Marsh; papers of Senators Winston Prouty, George D. Aiken, and Robert T. Stafford, Governor Philip H. Hoff, Congressmen Richard Mallary and William Meyer, Burlington Socialist Mayor Bernard Sanders, and other Vermont public figures, families, and businesses; university archives. **Holdings:** 85,000 books; 900 bound periodical volumes; 8000 linear feet of manuscripts; 7500 maps; census reports, 1810-1880, 1900, on microfilm; 225,000 photographs; university archives. **Subscriptions:** 110 journals and other serials. **Services:** Interlibrary loan; copying; department open to the public. **Automated Operations:** Computerized public access catalog, cataloging, acquisitions, serials, and circulation. **Publications:** Periodic lists of manuscript holdings; oral history lists; Liber (newsletter) - to members. **Special Catalogs:** Catalogs of type and paper specimens, binding samples, and imprints by place and date; catalog of illustrated books by types of illustrations (all on cards); exhibit catalogs; Guides to Manuscripts Collection (card and loose-leaf); Guide to Canadian research collections, 1986; Guide to Photograph Collections, 1990. **Remarks:** FAX: (802)656-4038. **Staff:** J. Kevin Graffagnino, Cur., Wilbur Coll.; Jeffrey Marshall, Archv. & Cur. of Mss.; Nadia Smith, Ref.Spec.; Ingrid Bower, Tech.Spec.

★19483★
University of Vermont - Pringle Herbarium - Library (Biol Sci)
Botany Dept.   Phone: (802)656-3221
Burlington, VT 05405   David S. Barrington, Cur.
Subjects: Plant taxonomy, botany, genetics. **Special Collections:** Memorabilia and collection of Cyrus Guernsey Pringle and Nellie Flynn. **Holdings:** 500 books; 120 bound periodical volumes; 6000 reprints; 331,000 dried plants. **Services:** Interlibrary loan; library not open to the public.

★19484★
University of Veszprem - Central Library (Sci-Engr)
Postafiok 158
Schonherz Z. utca 10   Phone: 80 26016
H-8201 Veszprem, Hungary   Anna Domotor, Gen.Dir.
Founded: 1970. **Staff:** Prof 2; Other 5. **Subjects:** Chemistry, chemical technology, computerized control of processes in the chemical industry, systems organization, teacher training, theology, sociology. **Holdings:** 130,000 bound volumes; 7000 dissertations. **Subscriptions:** 830 journals and other serials. **Services:** Library open to the public. **Computerized Information Services:** Data-Star, DIALOG Information Services, STN International. **Publications:** Hungarian Journal of Industrial Chemistry, quarterly. **Remarks:** FAX: 80 26016. Telex: 32 397 VEGYE H. **Staff:** Marta Egyhazy, Res. Worker.

★19485★
University of Victoria - Curriculum Laboratory (Educ)
P.O. Box 1700   Phone: (604)721-7900
Victoria, BC, Canada V8W 2Y2   Donald E. Hamilton, Educ.Libn.
Founded: 1964. **Staff:** Prof 1; Other 6. **Subjects:** Curriculum-support material, education. **Holdings:** 45,000 volumes; 7000 AV programs; 14 VF drawers of pamphlets; elementary and secondary school textbooks. **Subscriptions:** 80 journals and other serials. **Services:** Interlibrary loan; copying; laboratory open to the public with restrictions. **Automated Operations:** Computerized public access catalog and circulation. **Publications:** Information sheets; resource guide to community for teachers. **Remarks:** FAX: (604)721-7767.

★19486★
University of Victoria - Department of Geography - Cartographic Resource Centre (Geog-Map)
P.O. Box 3050   Phone: (604)721-7356
Victoria, BC, Canada V8W 3P5   Lori Sugden, Lib.Techn.
Founded: 1967. **Staff:** Prof 1. **Subjects:** General reference map collection, with emphasis on Western North America, the Pacific Basin, Oceania, East Asia, Western Europe; aerial photographs, mainly of Vancouver Island. **Holdings:** 3000 books; 650 atlases; 69,000 maps; 80,500 aerial photographs. **Subscriptions:** 80 journals and other serials. **Services:** Interlibrary loan; copying; center open to the public. **Automated Operations:** NOTIS. **Computerized Information Services:** Internal database; electronic mail service. **Remarks:** FAX: (604)721-6216. Center is jointly operated by University Libraries and the Geography Department.

★19487★
University of Victoria - Diana M. Priestly Law Library (Law)
P.O. Box 2300   Phone: (604)721-8562
Victoria, BC, Canada V8W 3B1   John N. Davis, Law Libn.
Staff: Prof 3; Other 13. **Subjects:** Law - Canada, U.S., England, Ireland, Scotland, Australia, New Zealand. **Holdings:** 141,946 volumes; 3345 reels of microfilm; 75,864 microfiche. **Subscriptions:** 800 journals and other serials; 3 newspapers. **Services:** Interlibrary loan; copying; library open to the public. **Computerized Information Services:** QUICKMAIL (electronic mail service). **Remarks:** FAX: (604)477-7413. **Staff:** Joan N. Fraser; Maggie A. Salmond.

★19488★
University of Victoria - McPherson Library - Music & Audio Collection (Mus)
P.O. Box 1800   Phone: (604)721-8232
Victoria, BC, Canada V8W 3H5   Sandra Benet Acker, Mus.Libn.
Staff: Prof 1; Other 4. **Subjects:** Music history and literature, music performance, recorded sound. **Special Collections:** Beethoveniana; William F. Tickle Collection (theater and dance orchestra music, 1919-1960); Charles Haywood Shakespeare Music Collection; Bernard Naylor Archives; Bob Smith Jazz Collection; University of Victoria Audio Archives. **Holdings:** 47,000 books and scores; 42,000 sound recordings; music publisher's catalogs; unbound sheet music. **Subscriptions:** 272 journals and other serials. **Services:** Interlibrary loan; copying; listening facilities; collection open to the public for reference use only. **Automated Operations:** Computerized cataloging, serials, acquisitions, and circulation (NOTIS). **Computerized Information Services:** UTLAS, DIALOG Information Services, BRS Information Technologies, OCLC, MEDLINE, CAN/OLE, QL Systems, Info Globe; CD-ROM; BITNET (electronic mail service). Performs searches on fee basis. Contact Person: Marilyn Berry, 721-8269. **Publications:** Information sheet. **Special Indexes:** Index to record collection by manufacturer's number (card); index to Audio Archives (COM); index to ethnic recordings (card). **Remarks:** FAX: (604)721-8215. Electronic mail address(es): LCIRCSA@UVVM (BITNET).

★19489★
University of Victoria - McPherson Library - Special Collections (Hum, Hist)
Box 1800   Phone: (604)721-8257
Victoria, BC, Canada V8W 3H5   Howard B. Gerwing, Rare Bks.Libn.
Staff: Prof 2; Other 2. **Subjects:** Modern British literature, Vancouver Island studies, Western Canadiana, North American anthropology, Canadian military history, Pacific Rim studies, art. **Special Collections:** Sir Herbert Read Archives (400 books; 6 drawers of manuscripts); Sir John Betjeman (250 books; 45 drawers of manuscripts); Robert Graves Archives (300 books; 3 drawers of manuscripts); Katharine Maltwood Archive (3000

items); University of Victoria Archives (1000 books; 175 meters of manuscripts); Glastonbury Temple of the Stars and Zodiac. **Holdings:** 50,000 volumes; 1000 pieces of sheet music; 10 VF drawers of military maps; 140 drawers of literary manuscripts. **Subscriptions:** 30 journals and other serials. **Services:** Interlibrary loan; copying; SDI; collections open to the public for reference use only. **Automated Operations:** Computerized cataloging and serials. **Computerized Information Services:** Online systems. **Special Indexes:** Indexes to Sir Herbert Read and Robert Graves Archives; Index to Maltwood papers. **Remarks:** FAX: (604)721-8215. **Staff:** Christopher Petter, Archv.

★ 19490 ★

University of Vienna - Botany Library (Biol Sci)
Rennweg 14   Phone: 222 78 71 01
A-1030 Vienna, Austria   Dr. Robert Stangl
Founded: 1754. **Staff:** Prof 1; Other 1. **Subjects:** Electron microscopy, comparative phytochemistry, morphology, cryptogamy, molecular biology, palynology, cytogenetics, systematics, evolution of spermatophytes, tropical botany and geobotany. **Holdings:** 6000 books and monographs; 25,000 bound periodical volumes; 29,000 reprints. **Subscriptions:** 250 journals and other serials. **Services:** Interlibrary loan; copying; library open to the public. **Also Known As:** University of Vienna - Botany Library. **Staff:** Dr. Karin Vetschera, Asst.Libn.

★ 19491 ★

University of the Virgin Islands - Caribbean Research Institute - Library (Env-Cons)
St. Thomas, VI 00802   Phone: (809)776-9200
                    Helen Dookhan, Adm.Spec.
Staff: Prof 1; Other 1. **Subjects:** Water resources, economics, social sciences, ecology, marine sciences, education, energy. **Special Collections:** Maps of the Caribbean, with emphasis on the Virgin Islands (50); Caribbean Shipwreck and other archeological documents (3 VF drawers); Reference/ AV Working Paper Series (Numbers 1 and 2); Microstate Studies Journal (Numbers 1, 2, 3, and 4). **Holdings:** 700 books; 500 documents on energy; 400 pieces of Caribbeana. **Subscriptions:** 53 journals and other serials. **Services:** Copying; library open to the public with restrictions. **Publications:** Covicrier (newsletter), quarterly - free upon request.

★ 19492 ★

University of the Virgin Islands - Cooperative Extension Service - Library (Area-Ethnic)
St. Thomas, VI 00802   Phone: (809)774-0210
                    Dr. Louis Petersen, Dist.Supv.
Subjects: Virgin Islands - agriculture, plants, soils, native arts and crafts, natural resources, medical plants. **Special Collections:** Medical plants; Caribbean plants; Virgin Island soils; Virgin Island architecture; native arts and crafts; native fruits. **Holdings:** 500 books. **Subscriptions:** 25 journals and other serials. **Services:** Copying; library open to the public with restrictions. **Publications:** Cooperative Education Service factsheets. **Remarks:** FAX: (809)776-5610.

★ 19493 ★

University of the Virgin Islands - Melchoir Center for Recent History (Area-Ethnic)
Ralph M. Paiewonsky Library
Charlotte Amalie
St. Thomas, VI 00802   Phone: (809)776-9200
                  David Oettinger, Dir.Libs.
Founded: 1978. **Staff:** Prof 1. **Subjects:** Recent history of the Virgin Islands, social science statistics. **Holdings:** 81 books; 2265 government documents; 371 reels of microfilm; slides. **Subscriptions:** 12 newspapers. **Services:** Copying; center open to qualified researchers. **Computerized Information Services:** DIALOG Information Services. Performs searches free of charge. **Networks/Consortia:** Member of Virgin Islands Library Network (VILINET). **Remarks:** FAX: (809)775-4850. Telex: 3470102 UVI.

★ 19494 ★

University of the Virgin Islands - Ralph M. Paiewonsky Library - Caribbean Collection (Area-Ethnic)
Charlotte Amalie
St. Thomas, VI 00802   Phone: (809)776-9200
                  David Oettinger, Dir.Libs.
Founded: 1963. **Subjects:** History - Caribbean, Virgin Islands, St. Thomas, St. Croix. **Special Collections:** Casper Holstein Collection. **Holdings:** 5310 books; 333 bound periodical volumes; 60 other cataloged items. **Subscriptions:** 14 journals and other serials. **Services:** Copying; library open to qualified researchers. **Automated Operations:** DYNIX. **Computerized Information Services:** OCLC. **Networks/Consortia:** Member of Virgin Islands Library Network (VILINET). **Remarks:** FAX: (809)775-4850.

★ 19495 ★

University of the Virgin Islands - Ralph M. Paiewonsky Library - Foundation Center Regional Collection (Bus-Fin)
St. Thomas, VI 00802   Phone: (809)776-9200
                F. Keith Bingham, Assoc.Libn.
Founded: 1979. **Staff:** Prof 1. **Subjects:** Foundations, grants, fund-raising. **Holdings:** 65 books; 90 microfiche; 50 aperture cards; 165 annual reports and information brochures; 2 VF drawers. **Services:** Interlibrary loan; collection open to the public. **Computerized Information Services:** DIALOG Information Services. **Remarks:** FAX: (809)776-2399.

★ 19496 ★

University of the Virgin Islands - St. Croix Campus Library - Special Collections (Area-Ethnic)
The Library, RR02-Box 10,000
Kingshill   Phone: (809)778-1620
St. Croix, VI 00851   Jennifer Jackson, Univ.Libn.
Founded: 1962. **Staff:** Prof 2. **Subjects:** History - Virgin Islands, St. Croix, Caribbean; rare books. **Holdings:** 27,000 books. **Subscriptions:** 350 journals and other serials. **Services:** Copying; library open to adults only. **Computerized Information Services:** DIALOG Information Services. **Networks/Consortia:** Member of Virgin Islands Library Network (VILINET). **Publications:** New books list; Library newsletter. **Remarks:** FAX: (809)778-9168. **Staff:** Judith Rogers.

★ 19497 ★

University of Virginia - Arthur J. Morris Law Library (Law)
School of Law   Phone: (804)924-3384
Charlottesville, VA 22901   Larry B. Wenger, Law Libn.
Founded: 1826. **Staff:** Prof 10; Other 15. **Subjects:** Law - Anglo-American, international, maritime; historic preservation. **Special Collections:** Newlin Collection on Ocean Law and Policy; John Bassett Moore Collection of International Law. **Holdings:** 139,528 books; 259,124 bound periodical volumes; 176,794 microforms; 71,960 government documents. **Subscriptions:** 9241 journals and other serials; 14 newspapers. **Services:** Interlibrary loan; copying; library open to the public with restrictions. **Automated Operations:** Computerized cataloging, acquisitions, and circulation. **Computerized Information Services:** LEXIS, WESTLAW, OCLC. **Networks/Consortia:** Member of SOLINET, COSELL. **Publications:** Marine Affairs Bibliography. **Remarks:** FAX: (804)982-2232. **Staff:** Barbara G. Murphy, Assoc. Law Libn.; Mary Cooper Gilliam, Intl. Law Libn.; Susan Tulis, Docs.Libn.; Anne Mustain, Cat.Libn.; Micheal Klepper, Media Serv.Libn.; Kent Olson, Pub.Serv.Libn.; Joseph Wynne, Sys.Libn.; Marsha Trimble, Archv.

★ 19498 ★

University of Virginia - Biology/Psychology Library (Biol Sci)
Gilmer Hall   Phone: (804)982-5260
Charlottesville, VA 22903   Sandra Dulaney, Libn.
Staff: 2. **Subjects:** Biological sciences, psychology. **Holdings:** 24,000 volumes. **Subscriptions:** 467 journals and other serials. **Services:** Interlibrary loan; copying; library open to the public. **Remarks:** FAX: (804)924-4338.

★ 19499 ★

University of Virginia - Blandy Experimental Farm Library (Biol Sci)
Box 175   Phone: (703)837-1758
Boyce, VA 22620   Edward F. Connor, Dir.
Founded: 1926. **Subjects:** Plant science, genetics, botany, plant taxonomy, plant collecting, horticulture. **Special Collections:** Manuals of plants of the world. **Holdings:** 2000 books. **Services:** Interlibrary loan; library open to the public with prior permission.

★ 19500 ★

University of Virginia - Chemistry Library (Sci-Engr)
Chemistry Bldg.
McCormick Rd.   Phone: (804)924-3159
Charlottesville, VA 22903   Christine Denton, Libn.
Staff: 1. **Subjects:** Chemistry. **Holdings:** 20,000 volumes. **Subscriptions:** 305 journals and other serials. **Services:** Interlibrary loan; copying; library open to the public. **Remarks:** FAX: (804)924-4338.

★ 19501 ★
University of Virginia - Colgate Darden Graduate School of Business Administration - Library (Bus-Fin)
Box 6550   Phone: (804)924-7321
Charlottesville, VA 22906   Henry Wingate, Libn.
Founded: 1957. **Staff:** Prof 1; Other 5. **Subjects:** Business, management, finance, accounting, economics, marketing, organization behavior. **Special Collections:** Corporation annual and 10K reports (200,000 microfiche). **Holdings:** 80,000 books; 10,000 bound periodical volumes; 2000 reels of microfilm of periodicals. **Subscriptions:** 1100 journals and other serials; 10 newspapers. **Services:** Interlibrary loan; copying; library open to the public. **Computerized Information Services:** DIALOG Information Services, Dow Jones News/Retrieval; CD-ROMs (ABI/INFORM, Lotus One Source). **Remarks:** FAX: (804)924-3533.

★ 19502 ★
University of Virginia - Education Library (Educ)
Ruffner Hall
405 Emmet St.   Phone: (804)924-7040
Charlottesville, VA 22903   Betsy Anthony, Educ.Libn.
Founded: 1973. **Staff:** Prof 2; Other 3. **Subjects:** Education. **Holdings:** 50,000 books; 1300 bound periodical volumes; ERIC microfiche. **Subscriptions:** 800 journals and other serials. **Services:** Interlibrary loan; copying; library open to Virginia residents. **Automated Operations:** Computerized public access catalog (NOTIS). **Computerized Information Services:** Access to 9 Wilson indexes via public access catalog, Abridged Index Medicus, Cumputer Select, PC Globe, PC World; CD-ROMs (ERIC, PsycLIT, Dissertation Abstracts Ondisc, Books in Print Plus, SPORT Discus); BITNET (electronic mail service). **Performs searches.** **Remarks:** Electronic mail address(es): HLASF@VIRGINIA.EDU (BITNET). **Staff:** Kay Cutler, Info.Serv.Libn.

★ 19503 ★
University of Virginia - Fiske Kimball Fine Arts Library (Art)
Bayly Dr.   Phone: (804)924-7024
Charlottesville, VA 22903   Jack Robertson, Libn.
Founded: 1970. **Staff:** Prof 3; Other 4. **Subjects:** Architecture, art, archeology, city planning, theater, landscape architecture, photography, costume. **Special Collections:** Frances Benjamin Johnson Photograph Collection of Virginia Architecture (1000); William Morris Library on Forgery of Works of Art, 15th century to present (700 items); drawings of Charles F. Gillette (landscape architect). **Holdings:** 116,000 volumes; 160,000 architecture slides; 1300 reels of microfilm; 19,000 microfiche. **Subscriptions:** 575 journals and other serials. **Services:** Interlibrary loan; copying; library open to the public with circulation restrictions on some holdings. **Automated Operations:** Computerized public access catalog and cataloging. **Computerized Information Services:** DIALOG Information Services, OCLC; TELNET (electronic mail service). **Networks/Consortia:** Member of SOLINET. **Publications:** Thomas Jefferson & the Arts (bibliography); Notable Additions to the Library Collection (bibliographic newsletter), quarterly. **Special Indexes:** Architectural Papers Produced a the University of Virginia, School of Architecture (bibliography/index). **Remarks:** FAX: (804)982-2678. **Staff:** Christie D. Stephenson, Asst. Fine Arts Libn.; Lynda S. White, Asst. Fine Arts Libn.

★ 19504 ★
University of Virginia - Health Sciences Center - Claude Moore Health Sciences Library (Biol Sci, Med)
Box 234   Phone: (804)924-5464
Charlottesville, VA 22908   Linda Watson, Dir.
Founded: 1825. **Staff:** Prof 14; Other 27. **Subjects:** Biological and medical sciences, nursing, allied health sciences. **Special Collections:** Walter Reed Archives. **Holdings:** 165,081 volumes; 5212 AV programs. **Subscriptions:** 2910 journals and other serials. **Services:** Interlibrary loan; copying; SDI; library open to the public with restrictions. **Automated Operations:** Computerized public access catalog, circulation, serials, acquisitions, and reserves. **Computerized Information Services:** DIALOG Information Services, BRS Information Technologies, NLM, WILSONLINE, miniMEDLINE; CD-ROMs. Performs searches on fee basis. **Networks/Consortia:** Member of National Network of Libraries of Medicine - Southeastern/Atlantic Region, SOLINET. **Publications:** Inside Information, monthly. **Special Catalogs:** Virginia Union List of Biomedical Serials, annual. **Remarks:** FAX: (804)924-0379. **Staff:** Gretchen Naisawald, Assoc.Dir., Pub.Serv.; Jonathan Lord, Online Serv.Coord.; Richard A. Peterson, Asst.Dir., Lrng.Rsrcs.Ctr.; Marylin James, Bibliog.Cont.Libn.; Joan Echtenkamp Klein, Asst.Dir., Hist.Coll. & Serv.; Judith Robinson,

Assoc.Dir., Tech.Serv.; Julia Kochi, Educ.Serv.Coord.; Anne Wood Humphries, Asst.Dir., Info.Serv.; Jonquil D. Feldman, Cons.Serv.Coord.; Inhye K. Son, Cons.Serv.Coord.; Elizabeth Cooley, Asst.Dir., Coll.Serv.; Nadine Ellero, Asst.Dir., Bibliog.Cont.; Daniel Wilson, Asst.Dir., Access Serv.

★ 19505 ★
University of Virginia - Mathematics-Astronomy Library (Sci-Engr)
Mathematics-Astronomy Bldg.   Phone: (804)924-7806
Charlottesville, VA 22903   Roma Reed, Libn.
Staff: 2. **Subjects:** Mathematics, astronomy. **Holdings:** 33,000 volumes. **Subscriptions:** 350 journals and other serials. **Services:** Interlibrary loan; copying; library open to the public. **Remarks:** FAX: (804)924-4338.

★ 19506 ★
University of Virginia - Medical Center - Department of Neurology - Elizabeth J. Ohrstrom Library (Med)
P.O. Box 394   Phone: (804)924-5542
Charlottesville, VA 22908   Barbara White, Lib.Asst.
Staff: 2. **Subjects:** General and pediatric neurology, cardiovascular systems, neuroscience. **Special Collections:** Rare and original neurological texts. **Holdings:** 3000 books; 2000 bound periodical volumes. **Subscriptions:** 35 journals and other serials. **Services:** Library not open to the public. **Computerized Information Services:** DIALOG Information Services, Sci-Mate. **Staff:** Dr. Joel Trugman, Chm., Lib.Comm.

★ 19507 ★
University of Virginia - Music Library (Mus)
Old Cabell Hall   Phone: (804)924-7041
Charlottesville, VA 22903-3298   Diane Parr Walker, Mus.Libn.
Staff: Prof 2; Other 3. **Subjects:** Music. **Special Collections:** Mackay-Smith Collection (18th century imprints); Monticello Music Collection; printed and manuscript collection of the music of John Powell; 19th century American sheet music. **Holdings:** 50,000 volumes; 6060 microfiche; 1500 reels of microfilm; 3120 microcards; 3000 magnetic tapes; 27,000 phonograph records; 2000 compact discs. **Subscriptions:** 576 journals and other serials. **Services:** Interlibrary loan; copying; library open to the public. **Computerized Information Services:** BITNET (electronic mail service). **Publications:** Russian Literature on Music in the Music Library of the University of Virginia (1989). **Special Catalogs:** Computer Catalog of Nineteenth-Century American-Imprint Sheet Music (microfiche). **Remarks:** FAX: (804)924-4337. Electronic mail address(es): DPW@VIRGINIA (BITNET). **Staff:** Jane Edmister Penner, Asst.Mus.Libn.

★ 19508 ★
University of Virginia - Physics Library (Sci-Engr)
Physics Bldg.   Phone: (804)924-6589
Charlottesville, VA 22903   James Shea, Libn.
Staff: 2. **Subjects:** Physics. **Holdings:** 27,000 volumes. **Subscriptions:** 273 journals and other serials. **Services:** Interlibrary loan; copying; library open to the public. **Remarks:** FAX: (804)924-4338.

★ 19509 ★
University of Virginia - Science & Engineering Library (Sci-Engr)
Clark Hall   Phone: (804)924-7209
Charlottesville, VA 22903-3188   Edwina H. Pancake, Dir.
Staff: Prof 4; Other 10. **Subjects:** General science and engineering including reference materials. **Special Collections:** Government technical reports from Atomic Energy Commission, Department of Defense, and NASA. **Holdings:** 245,000 volumes; 166,000 titles of hard copy technical reports; 1,023,000 technical reports on microfiche. **Subscriptions:** 1564 journals and other serials. **Services:** Interlibrary loan; copying; library open to the public. **Automated Operations:** Computerized cataloging, acquisitions, and circulation. **Computerized Information Services:** DIALOG Information Services, PFDS Online, BRS Information Technologies, Questel, Chemical Abstracts Service (CAS), National Environmental Data Referral Service (NEDRES). **Remarks:** FAX: (804)924-4338. **Staff:** Tran Ton-nu, Pub.Serv.Libn.; Fred O'Bryant, Tech.Serv.Libn.; Cristina Sharretts, Electronic Serv.Libn.

★ 19510 ★
University of Virginia - Special Collections Department (Hum)
University of Virginia Library   Phone: (804)924-3025
Charlottesville, VA 22903-2498   Edmund Berkeley, Jr., Dir.
Founded: 1819. **Staff:** Prof 10; Other 9. **Subjects:** American history and literature; Virginia history and literature. **Special Collections:** Mrs. Robert C. Taylor Collection (American best sellers); Clifton Waller Barrett Library (American literature); American Sheet Music Collection; Lee Family papers (American Revolution); Tracy W. McGregor Library (American history); Sherwood Anderson Collection; Matthew Arnold papers; Ann Beattie papers; R.D. Blackmore papers; Jorge Luis Borges Collection; Louis Brownlow papers; William Stanley Braithwaite papers; Bruccoli World War I Collection; Harry F. Byrd, Sr. & Jr., papers; James Branch Cabell Collection; John Canaday papers; Casanova de Seingalt Collection; Phillip K. Crowe Collection (Ceylon); papers of John W. Daniel, W.S. Hillyer, Eppa Hutton, R.M.T. Hunter, John D. Imboden, John S. Mosby, James Lawson Kemper, and Thomas L. Rosser (Civil War and Reconstruction); Martin Julius Hertz Collection (classical studies); Confederate Imprints; Marvin Tatum Collection (contemporary poetry and prose); Stephen Crane Collection; Wilber Cortez Abbott Collection (Oliver Cromwell); Charles Dickens Collection; J. Rives Childs, Hugh S. Cumming, Louis J. Halle, and Murat Williams papers (diplomacy); John Dos Passos Collection; McGregor Library (English literature); papers of Central Virginia Environment Center, Conservation Council of Virginia, U.S. Atomic Energy Commission, and Virginia Electric and Power Company (environment); Victorius Darwin Collection (evolution); Massey Collection and Faulkner Foundation (William Faulkner); Carter Glass papers (finance); Arthur Kyle Davis papers (folklore); Virginia W.P.A. Folklore Collection; Virginia Folklore Society papers; General John Forbes Collection; Douglas H. Gordon Collection (French Renaissance literature); Robert Frost Collection; Garnett and Carter 18th century Libraries; Ellen Glasgow Collection; Sadlier-Black Collection (gothic novels); Nancy Hale papers; Bret Harte Collection; Nathaniel Hawthorne Collection; Lafcadio Hearn Collection; Ernest Hemingway Collection; William Dean Howells Collection; Industrial History of Virginia; John Bassett Moore Collection (international law); Washington Irving Collection; Henry James Collection; Thomas Jefferson papers; Franz Kafka Collection; Rudyard Kipling Collection; papers of Lloyd C. Bird, Borderland Coal Company, William Jett Lauck, Low Moor Iron Company, and John Skelton Williams (labor problems and economics); Vachel Lindsay Collection; James Madison pamphlets and papers; William G. Mather Collection (Mather family of New England); McGregor Library, Rosenthal, Hench, and Stone Collections (Medieval manuscripts); Herman Melville Collection; Middle East Collection; Grinnan, Higgenbottom, and Taylor papers (missionaries); T. Catesby Jones Collection (modern art); John Moffitt Collection; James Monroe Collection; papers of Samuel Barron, Frank F. Fletcher, Hammond Family, Gustavus R.B. Horner, and Whittle Family (naval history); Ma Kiam Library (Oriental collection); P L 480 collection (India and Pakistan); Thomas Nelson Page papers; Poe-Ingram Collection (Edgar Allan Poe); Isabel Mercer Tunstall Collection (poetry); Poland; Political Cartoons Collection; John Powell Music Collection; Thomas W. Streeter Collection (railroads); John Randolph of Roanoke papers; Carl Sandburg Collection; Hugh Scott papers; Edith, Osbert, and Sacheverell Sitwell Collection; Marion duPont Scott Collection (equestrian sporting books); John Steinbeck Collection; Edward R. Stettinius, Sr. & Jr., papers; Sara Teasdale papers; Edgar Finley Shannon, Jr., Collection (Alfred Lord Tennyson); Trollope Collection; Mark Twain Collection; Twin Oaks Community papers; Warren Chappell, Oscar Ogg, Edward L. Stone, Willis W. Tompkins, and Stevens Watts Collections (typography and printing); papers and libraries of Homer S. Cummings, Herbert P. Emmerich, Louis A. Johnson, Guy Moffitt, William B. Spong, Claude Swanson, Oscar W. Underwood, John Warner, Edwin M. Watson, John Skelton Williams, and Walter Wyatt (20th-century U.S. politics and government); University of Virginia Archives Collection; S.S. Van Dine papers; Creole Collection (Venezuela); Virginia Authors Collection (James Branch Cabell, Margaret Haley Carpenter, John Esten Cooke, Hawthorne Daniel, Clifford Dowdey, Murrell Edmunds, George Cary Eggleston, John Fox, Jr., Ellen Glasgow, Nancy Hale, Mary Johnston, John Pendleton Kennedy, Frances Parkinson Keyes, Katie Letcher Lyle, Jane McClary, Harry M. Meacham, Julian Rutherfoord Meade, Harry Edward Neal, Thomas Nelson Page, Agnes Rothery Pratt, Eudora Ramsey Richardson, John Reuben Thompson, Amelie Rives Troubetzkoy, and S.S. Van Dine); Virginia Family papers (Barbour, Berkeley, Bruce, Cabell, Carter-Smith, Cocke, Hubard, Pocket Plantation, Randolph, and Watson; 18th-19th centuries); papers of Allen C. Braxton, Lloyd C. Bird, Edward L. Breeden, Everett R. Combs, Flora Crater, John H. Daniel, E. Griffith Dodson, Patrick Henry Drewry, Charles R. Fenwick, Herbert Harris, Joseph Hutcheson, Martin A. Hutchinson, William A. Jones, J. Harry Michael, Francis P. Miller, Richard H. Poff, Campbell Bascom Slemp, William B. Spong, G. Fred Switzer, and John Warner (Virginia history and politics); papers of Walter S. Copeland, Virginius Dabney, Douglas Southall Freeman, Thomas A. Hanes, Louis I. Jaffe, James J. Kilpatrick, William

Hodges Mann, Philip L. Scruggs, and Louis Spilman (Virginia journalists); Virginiana; Barnard Shipp Collection (voyages and travels); Walt Whitman Collection. **Holdings:** 227,000 books; 8056 reels of microfilm; 105 drawers of maps; 65 oversized boxes of broadsides; 120,000 photographs and prints; 981 phonodiscs; 727 reel-to-reel tapes; 601 cassette tapes; 349 motion picture films; 176 videotapes; 7966 microfiche; 11.6 million cataloged manuscript and archival items. **Subscriptions:** 126 journals and other serials. **Services:** Interlibrary loan (limited); copying; library open to the public. **Automated Operations:** Computerized public access catalog and cataloging. **Computerized Information Services:** OCLC available through main library; BITNET (electronic mail service). **Publications:** Gatherings & Offerings, semiannual; exhibition keepsakes and collection guides, occasional. **Remarks:** FAX: (804)924-4337. **Staff:** Michael F. Plunkett, Cur., Mss. & Univ.Archv.; Kathryn N. Morgan, Cur., Rare Bks.

University of Virginia - Virginia Transportation Research Council
See: **Virginia Transportation Research Council - Library** (19898)

★ 19511 ★
University of Washington - Alcohol & Drug Abuse Institute - Library (Med)
3937 15th Ave., N.E., NL-15   Phone: (206)543-0937
Seattle, WA 98105   Nancy Sutherland, Dir. of Lib.
Founded: 1975. **Staff:** Prof 1.5; Other 1. **Subjects:** Alcohol and drug abuse. **Holdings:** 2000 books; 5000 reprints. **Subscriptions:** 100 journals and other serials. **Services:** Interlibrary loan; SDI; library open to the public. **Automated Operations:** Computerized cataloging and serials. **Computerized Information Services:** DIALOG Information Services, NLM, BRS Information Technologies; ADAI Library database (internal database); InterNet (electronic mail service). **Networks/Consortia:** Member of Substance Abuse Librarians and Information Specialists (SALIS), Regional Alcohol and Drug Abuse Resource Network (RADAR). **Publications:** Current Literature on Alcohol and Drug Abuse, 10/year - limited distribution; subject bibliographies (online). **Remarks:** FAX: (206)543-5473. Electronic mail address(es): ADAILIB@MAX.U.WASHINGTON.EDU (InterNet). **Staff:** Pamela Miles.

★ 19512 ★
University of Washington - Architecture-Urban Planning Library (Art, Plan)
334 Gould Hall, JO-30   Phone: (206)543-4067
Seattle, WA 98195   Betty L. Wagner, Hd.
Founded: 1923. **Staff:** Prof 1; Other 2. **Subjects:** Architecture, urban planning, landscape architecture, building construction. **Holdings:** 33,375 volumes; 1867 ephemeral items; 2355 HUD reports; 7585 microfiche. **Subscriptions:** 327 journals and other serials. **Services:** Interlibrary loan; copying; library open to the public for reference use only. **Computerized Information Services:** OCLC; InterNet (electronic mail service). **Remarks:** FAX: (206)685-8049. Electronic mail address(es): BWAGNER@U.WASHINGTON.EDU(InterNet).

★ 19513 ★
University of Washington - Art Library (Art)
101 Art Bldg., DM-10   Phone: (206)543-0648
Seattle, WA 98195   Connie T. Okada, Hd.
Founded: 1949. **Staff:** Prof 1; Other 2. **Subjects:** Painting, ceramics, printmaking, sculpture, industrial design, fiber arts, metal design, graphic design, photography, history of art. **Holdings:** 39,241 volumes; 70 drawers of pamphlets and clippings; 7500 mounted reproductions. **Subscriptions:** 432 journals and other serials. **Services:** Interlibrary loan; copying; library open to the public for reference use only. **Computerized Information Services:** OCLC; CD-ROM (Art Index). **Remarks:** FAX: (206)685-8049.

★ 19514 ★
University of Washington - Art Slide Collection (Aud-Vis)
120 Art Bldg., DM-10   Phone: (206)543-0649
Seattle, WA 98195   Joan Nilsson, Dir. of Visual Serv.
Staff: 2. **Subjects:** Fine arts and related material. **Holdings:** 250,000 slides. **Services:** Open to faculty in other campus departments and local museum personnel. **Computerized Information Services:** FOX BASE (internal database).

★ 19515 ★
University of Washington - Business Administration Library (Bus-Fin)
100 Balmer Hall, DJ-10   Phone: (206)543-4360
Seattle, WA 98195   Gordon J. Aamot, Hd.Libn.
Founded: 1951. **Staff:** Prof 3; Other 6. **Subjects:** Management, marketing, personnel and labor, accounting, finance, international business, transportation, insurance, real estate, business law. **Holdings:** 50,172 volumes; 213,244 microfiche of U.S. corporation records. **Subscriptions:** 1128 journals and other serials; 11 newspapers. **Services:** Interlibrary loan; copying; library open to the public for reference use only. **Computerized Information Services:** DIALOG Information Services, Knowledge Index, DataTimes, NEXIS, OCLC; CD-ROMs (Compact Disclosure, ABI/INFORM, Business Dateline, National Trade Data Base); InterNet (electronic mail service). **Publications:** Bibliographies, irregular. **Remarks:** FAX: (206)685-9392. Electronic mail address(es): AAMOT@U.WASHINGTON.EDU(InterNet). **Staff:** Siew-Choo Poh, Asst.Libn.; Christian Poehlmann, Ref.Libn.

★ 19516 ★
University of Washington - Center for Law & Justice - CLJ/NCADBIP
   Information Service
DK-40
Seattle, WA 98195
Subjects: Juvenile delinquency and its prevention, juvenile justice, school-based delinquency prevention strategies, criminal justice, social science methodology, violent behavior. **Special Collections:** Juvenile delinquency prevention program questionnaire responses, descriptions, evaluations. **Holdings:** 3000 books; 1000 evaluative reports; 300 microfiche. **Remarks:** NCADBIP stands for National Center for the Assessment of Delinquency Behavior and Its Prevention, which is a federally funded project at the center. Currently inactive.

★ 19517 ★
University of Washington - Center for Studies in Demography and
   Ecology - Library (Soc Sci)
102 Savery Hall, DK-40   Phone: (206)543-9525
Seattle, WA 98195   Muriel Hillson, Lib.Techn.
Staff: 1. **Subjects:** Census, vital statistics, demography, ecology, Southeast Asia. **Holdings:** 2000 books; 4400 government documents; 2200 other publications and papers. **Subscriptions:** 88 journals and other serials. **Services:** Library open to the public. **Automated Operations:** Computerized cataloging.

★ 19518 ★
University of Washington - Chemistry Library (Sci-Engr)
60 Chemistry Library Bldg., BG-10   Phone: (206)543-1603
Seattle, WA 98195   Susanne Redalje, Hd.
Staff: Prof 1; Other 2. **Subjects:** Chemistry, chemical engineering, pharmaceutics, medicinal chemistry. **Holdings:** 50,086 volumes; 7201 microfiche. **Subscriptions:** 915 journals and other serials. **Services:** Interlibrary loan; copying; library open to the public for reference use only. **Automated Operations:** Computerized public access catalog. **Computerized Information Services:** DIALOG Information Services, STN International, Chemical Abstracts Service (CAS), BRS Information Technologies; BITNET, InterNet (electronic mail services). **Remarks:** FAX: (206)685-8049. Electronic mail address(es): chemlib@u.washington.edu. (InterNet); curie@u.washington.edu(InterNet).

★ 19519 ★
University of Washington - Computing Information Center
University Computing Services, HG-45
Seattle, WA 98195   Phone: (206)543-5818
Defunct.

★ 19520 ★
University of Washington - Curriculum Materials and Children's
   Literature Section (Educ)
Suzzallo Library, FM-25   Phone: (206)543-2725
Seattle, WA 98195   Loretta Lopez, Ref./Educ.Libn.
Founded: 1960. **Staff:** Prof 1; Other 2. **Subjects:** Children's literature, elementary and secondary curriculum and instruction, educational and psychological testing, educational games/simulations. **Special Collections:** Children's Literature Archive; Resource Center for Gifted Education.

Holdings: 55,478 books, textbooks, and curriculum guides; 8000 children's literature book jackets, 1920-1965, arranged by author; 3382 standardized tests; 258 games and simulations; 10,841 curriculum guides on microfiche; 27 educational software titles. **Subscriptions:** 75 journals and other serials. **Services:** Interlibrary loan (limited); copying; section open to the public for reference use only. **Computerized Information Services:** OCLC; InterNet (electronic mail service). **Networks/Consortia:** Member of Western Library Network (WLN). **Remarks:** FAX: (206)545-8049. Electronic mail address(es): Wrey@ milton.u.washington.edu(InterNet).

★ 19521 ★
University of Washington - Drama Library (Theater)
145 Hutchinson Hall, DX-20   Phone: (206)543-5148
Seattle, WA 98195   Elizabeth Fugate, Hd.
Founded: 1931. **Staff:** Prof 1; Other 1. **Subjects:** Drama history, dramatic literature, theater history, acting, children's theater, costume, make-up, scene design, creative dramatics, directing, lighting, playwriting, mime, theater buildings and architecture. **Special Collections:** 19th Century Acting Editions (2807). **Holdings:** 19,703 volumes; unbound play collection (14,159 acting editions); 347 phonograph records; 364 audiotapes; 10 video recordings. **Subscriptions:** 177 journals and other serials. **Services:** Interlibrary loan; copying; library open to the public for reference use only. **Computerized Information Services:** OCLC; InterNet (electronic mail service). **Special Catalogs:** Catalog of 19th Century Acting Editions and theses (card). **Special Indexes:** Index of anthologies; sound effects; dialects. **Remarks:** FAX: (206)685-8049. Electronic mail address(es): lvdl@u.washington.edu(InterNet).

★ 19522 ★
University of Washington - East Asia Library (Area-Ethnic)
322 Gowen Hall, DO-27   Phone: (206)543-4490
Seattle, WA 98195   Min-chih Chou, Hd.
Founded: 1937. **Staff:** Prof 7; Other 6.5. **Subjects:** Social sciences, humanities, literature and language, history, religion and philosophy, arts. **Special Collections:** Works in Chinese, Japanese, Korean, Tibetan, Thai, Vietnamese, Mongolian, Manchu, and Indonesian. **Holdings:** 352,781 volumes; 11,054 reels of microfilm; 6688 microfiche; 4589 pamphlets. **Subscriptions:** 3299 serials. **Services:** Interlibrary loan; copying; library open to the public for reference use only. **Computerized Information Services:** OCLC, LC MARC: Contributed CJK Books; electronic mail. **Publications:** Twenty-five Dynastic Histories Full Text Retrieval Database; Current Japanese Serials in East Asia Library; Current Korean Serials in East Asia Library. **Special Catalogs:** University of Washington East Asia Library 1990 catalog of yearbooks on China. **Remarks:** FAX: (206)685-8049. Telex: 206 474 0096 UW UI. **Staff:** Yeen-Mei Wu, China Libn.; Teruko Kyuma Chin, Japan Libn.; Yoon-Whan Choe, Korea Libn.; Fred Kotas, Pub.Serv./Cat.Libn.; Elise Chin, Hd., Cat.

★ 19523 ★
University of Washington - Engineering Library (Sci-Engr, Comp Sci)
Engineering Library Bldg., FH-15   Phone: (206)543-0740
Seattle, WA 98195   Charles R. Lord, Hd.
Founded: 1947. **Staff:** Prof 4; Other 6. **Subjects:** Aeronautics, applied mathematics, applied physics, computer science, energy, engineering, environment, material science, technical communication, theoretical and applied mechanics, transportation. **Special Collections:** Standards; ACM Depository Collection. **Holdings:** 104,976 volumes; 50,635 paper copy technical reports; 2 million technical reports in microform; patent specifications, 1966 to present, on microfilm; patent and trademark depository library. **Subscriptions:** 3031 journals and other serials. **Services:** Interlibrary loan; copying; library open to the public. **Automated Operations:** Computerized public access catalog and circulation. **Computerized Information Services:** DIALOG Information Services, STN International, Chemical Abstracts Service (CAS), U.S. Patent Classification System, MEDLINE, Current Contents; CD-ROMs (NTIS, ASTI, Computer Select, COMPENDEX PLUS, Enviro/Energyline Abstracts Plus, CASSIS, Trademarks); InterNet (electronic mail service). Performs searches on fee basis. **Special Catalogs:** Technical report catalog. **Remarks:** FAX: (206)685-8049. Electronic mail address(es): ENGLIB@U.WASHINGTON.EDU (InterNet). **Staff:** Pamela F. Yorks, Engr.Info.Serv.Libn.; Dorothy D. Smith, Asst.Hd.; Thomas P. Dowling, Engr.Comp. Based Serv.Libn.

★ 19524 ★
University of Washington - Ethnomusicology Archives (Mus)
School of Music, DN-10   Phone: (206)543-0974
Seattle, WA 98195   Laurel Sercombe, Archv.
Founded: 1962. **Staff:** Prof 1. **Subjects:** World music, including classical and indigenous forms. **Special Collections:** Field recordings of Robert Garfias (Burma, Korea, Romania, Mexico, Philippines) and Melville Jacobs (Pacific Northwest Indians); Joe Heaney Collection (Irish songs, stories). **Holdings:** 50 books; 6000 hours of audiotape; 200 videotapes; 150 films; 500 phonograph records; 200 photographs and slides; 300 musical instruments. **Subscriptions:** 10 journals and other serials. **Services:** Copying; listening facility; archives open to researchers. **Automated Operations:** Computerized cataloging. **Computerized Information Services:** Internal database; BITNET (electronic mail service). **Remarks:** Electronic mail address(es): JULIUS@MAX.U.WASHINGTON.EDU(BITNET).

★ 19525 ★
University of Washington - Fisheries-Oceanography Library (Biol Sci, Sci-Engr)
151 Oceanography Teaching Bldg., WB-30   Phone: (206)543-4279
Seattle, WA 98195   Pamela A. Mofjeld, Hd.
Founded: 1950. **Staff:** Prof 2; Other 2. **Subjects:** Fisheries science, marine biology, oceanography, food science and technology, marine policy. **Special Collections:** Canadian translations of fisheries and aquatic sciences on microfiche; Pacific Salmon Literature Compilation. **Holdings:** 60,144 volumes; 344 reels of microfilm; 5976 microcards; 17,481 microfiche; 1750 maps. **Subscriptions:** 1329 journals and other serials. **Services:** Interlibrary loan; copying; library open to the public for reference use only. **Automated Operations:** Computerized public access catalog and circulation. **Computerized Information Services:** DIALOG Information Services, BRS Information Technologies, STN International; CD-ROMs (Aquatic Sciences and Fisheries Abstracts; Selected Water Resources Abstracts; Arctic and Antarctic Regions; NODC, Pacific Ocean Salinity and Temperature Profiles, 1800-1988; West Coast Time Series Coastal Zone Color Scanner Imagery, volume 1, 1979-1981); BITNET, InterNet (electronic mail services). **Special Catalogs:** Selected References to Literature on Marine Expeditions, 1700-1960 (1972). **Remarks:** FAX: (206)685-8049. **Staff:** Louise Richards, Asst.Libn.

★ 19526 ★
University of Washington - Forest Resources Library (Biol Sci, Sci-Engr)
60 Bloedel Hall, AQ-15   Phone: (206)543-2758
Seattle, WA 98195   Carol Green, Hd.
Founded: 1947. **Staff:** Prof 1; Other 2. **Subjects:** Forestry; wood science and technology; wood chemistry; paper and pulp technology; logging engineering; forest management, economics, soils, pathology, hydrology, and entomology; fire control; silvics and silviculture; recreation; urban forestry. **Holdings:** 47,873 volumes. **Subscriptions:** 1724 journals and other serials. **Services:** Interlibrary loan; copying; library open to the public for reference use only. **Automated Operations:** Computerized public access catalog. **Computerized Information Services:** DIALOG Information Services, BRS Information Technologies, STN International, OCLC; CD-ROM (AGRICOLA); InterNet (electronic mail service). **Remarks:** FAX: (206)685-8049. Electronic mail address(es): FORLIB@U.WASHINGTON.EDU (InterNet).

University of Washington - Forest Service Information - FS INFO NW
See: **U.S. Forest Service** (17515)

★ 19527 ★
University of Washington - Friday Harbor Laboratories - Library (Biol Sci)
620 University Rd.   Phone: (206)543-1484
Friday Harbor, WA 98250   Kathy M. Carr, Libn.
Founded: 1921. **Staff:** Prof 1. **Subjects:** Marine biology, invertebrate embryology, invertebrate zoology, algology; fish biology. **Holdings:** 17,436 volumes; 946 microfiche; 242 maps. **Subscriptions:** 152 journals and other serials. **Services:** Interlibrary loan; copying; library open to the public by permission. **Automated Operations:** Computerized public access catalog. **Computerized Information Services:** DIALOG Information Services, BRS Information Technologies; BITNET, SCIENCEnet (electronic mail services). Performs searches on fee basis. **Remarks:** FAX: (206)543-1273. Electronic mail address(es): KCARR@U.WASHINGTON.EDU (BITNET); FRIDAY.HARBOR.LABS (SCIENCEnet). Librarian is available at the Friday Harbor Library only during summer quarter; September through May contact Kathy M. Carr in the Natural Sciences Library at (206)545-2127, ext. 266.

★ 19528 ★
University of Washington - Geography Library (Geog-Map)
415 Smith Hall, DP-10   Phone: (206)543-5244
Seattle, WA 98195   Linda C. Fredericks, Libn.
Founded: 1952. **Staff:** Prof 1; Other 1. **Subjects:** Geography, cartography and GIS, regional science, international relations, foreign areas. **Holdings:** 15,822 volumes. **Subscriptions:** 382 journals and other serials. **Services:** Interlibrary loan; library open to the public for reference use only. **Computerized Information Services:** OCLC; electronic mail. **Remarks:** FAX: (206)685-8049.

★ 19529 ★
University of Washington - Health Sciences Library and Information Center (Med)
T-227 Health Sciences, SB-55   Phone: (206)543-5530
Seattle, WA 98195   Sherrilynne Fuller, Dir.
Founded: 1949. **Staff:** Prof 18.25; Other 46.5. **Subjects:** Medicine, dentistry, nursing, pharmacy, public health. **Special Collections:** Biomedical history (2283 volumes). **Holdings:** 89,376 books; 210,812 bound periodical volumes; 85,712 microfiche. **Subscriptions:** 4354 journals and other serials. **Services:** Interlibrary loan; copying; SDI; library open to the public for reference use only. **Computerized Information Services:** DIALOG Information Services, PFDS Online, NLM, BRS Information Technologies, OCLC; OnTyme Electronic Message Network Service, InterNet (electronic mail services). Performs searches on fee basis. **Networks/Consortia:** Member of Western Library Network (WLN). **Publications:** Books & Bytes, 10/year - to faculty and administrative staff; The Supplement (newsletter of the National Network of Libraries of Medicine, Pacific Northwest Region), quarterly - to libraries in the Pacific Northwest; Resourceline, bimonthly - to health science libraries in Washington. **Remarks:** FAX: (206)543-8066. Electronic mail address(es): UWHSL/GEN (OnTyme Electronic Message Network Service); SFULLER@U.WASHINGTON.EDU (InterNet). Headquarters of National Network of Libraries of Medicine, Pacific Northwest Region (NN/LM, PNR). **Staff:** Carolyn Weaver, Assoc.Dir., Adm.; Elaine Martin, Assoc.Dir.Educ.Clin.Res.Serv.; Colleen Weum, Ser./Acq.Libn.; Lorraine Raymond, Coll.Dev./Cat.Libn.; Leilani St. Anna, Info.Serv.Libn.; Terry Ann Jankowski, Info. Retrieval/Mgmt.Libn.; Janet Schnall, Info.Serv.Libn.; Diana Hall, Res. Funding Libn.; Debra Ketchell, Assoc.Dir., Rsrc.Mgt./Sys.Dev.; Neil Rambo, Assoc.Dir., NN/LM, PNR; Linda Milgrom, Reg.Dev.Coord., NN/LM, PNR; Nancy Press, Rsrc. Sharing Coord., NN/LM, PNR; Mary Ellen Lemon, IAIMS Proj.Coord.Mgr.; Sherry Dodson, Clin.Libn.; Philip Arny, Tchg.Lrng.Ctr.Coord.; Louise Pray, Info.Serv.Libn.

★ 19530 ★
University of Washington - Health Sciences Library and Information Center - K.K. Sherwood Library (Med)
Harborview Medical Center
325 9th Ave., ZA-43   Phone: (206)223-3360
Seattle, WA 98104   Ellen Howard, Libn.
Staff: Prof 1; Other 1. **Subjects:** Core medical collection. **Holdings:** 436 books; 5011 bound periodical volumes. **Subscriptions:** 187 journals and other serials. **Services:** Interlibrary loan; copying; library open to the public for reference use only. **Computerized Information Services:** NLM, BRS Information Technologies, DIALOG Information Services; OnTyme Electronic Message Network Service (electronic mail service). Performs searches on fee basis for primary clientele only. **Remarks:** Electronic mail address(es): UWHSL/KKS (OnTyme Electronic Message Network Service).

★ 19531 ★
University of Washington - Herbarium - Library (Biol Sci)
Seattle, WA 98195   Phone: (206)543-8850
                                     Dr. Melinda F. Denton
Founded: 1880. **Staff:** Prof 2. **Subjects:** Botany - taxonomy, Pacific Northwest; bryophytes. **Special Collections:** Notebooks for Pacific Northwest collectors. **Holdings:** 2100 books; 600 bound periodical volumes; archival material. **Services:** Interlibrary loan; library open to the public for reference use only. **Remarks:** Alternate telephone number(s): (206)543-1682.

★ 19532 ★
University of Washington - Manuscripts and University Archives Division (Hist)
Allen Library, FM-25   Phone: (206)543-1879
Seattle, WA 98195   Karyl Winn, Mss.Libn.
Staff: Prof 2; Other 4.5. **Subjects:** Washington politics and government, congressional papers, public power, labor, forest products, fisheries and

mining, American literature, Pacific Northwest art, urban affairs, ethnic history (especially Jewish and Japanese American), education, health care, University of Washington history and administration. **Holdings:** 41,433 linear feet of archival materials. **Services:** Interlibrary loan (limited); copying; collection open to researchers with restrictions. **Computerized Information Services:** Electronic mail. **Publications:** Guide to the Wilbert McLeod Chapman Collection; microfiche guides to the Warren G. Magnuson and Henry M. Jackson papers. **Special Catalogs:** Comprehensive Guide to the Manuscripts Collections and to the Personal Papers in the University Archives. **Special Indexes:** Inventories of individual accessions. **Remarks:** FAX: (206)545-8049. **Staff:** Kerry Bartels, Univ.Archv.

★ 19533 ★

University of Washington - Map Collection and Cartographic Information Services (Geog-Map)
Suzzallo Library, FM-25   Phone: (206)543-9392
Seattle, WA 98195   Jenny Marie Johnson, Hd.
Founded: 1970. **Staff:** Prof 2; Other 1. **Subjects:** Geologic and topographic maps, nautical charts, aerial photographs, atlases. **Special Collections:** Braille maps and atlases (300). **Holdings:** 3100 books and atlases; 239,787 maps; 56,608 aerial photographs; 317 reels of microfilm; 2816 microfiche. **Subscriptions:** 7 journals and other serials. **Services:** Interlibrary loan; copying; collection open to the public for reference use only. **Automated Operations:** Computerized public access catalog. **Computerized Information Services:** OCLC; CD-ROM (Aerial Photography Summary Record System, SUPERMAP, Electromap World Atlas, Geophysics of North America); BITNET, InterNet (electronic mail services). **Remarks:** FAX: (206)685-8049. Electronic mail address(es): JMJ@U.Washington.edu (BITNET); KWOMBLE@U.Washington.edu (InterNet). **Staff:** Kathryn Womble, Asst. Map Libn.

★ 19534 ★

University of Washington - Marian Gould Gallagher Law Library (Law)
School of Law
1100 N.E. Campus Pkwy., JB-20   Phone: (206)543-4086
Seattle, WA 98105   Penny A. Hazelton, Law Libn.
Founded: 1899. **Staff:** Prof 11.5; Other 20. **Subjects:** Law. **Special Collections:** Japanese legal material; Washington State Bench and Bar biographies (15 file drawers of pictures and biographical sketches). **Holdings:** 442,650 volumes; 135 bound volumes of clippings. **Subscriptions:** 7158 journals and other serials. **Services:** Interlibrary loan; copying; library open to the public for reference use only. **Automated Operations:** Computerized cataloging. **Computerized Information Services:** LEXIS, DIALOG Information Services, OCLC, DataTimes, WESTLAW, NEXIS; InfoTrac; electronic mail. **Networks/Consortia:** Member of Western Library Network (WLN), Northwest Consortium of Law Libraries. **Publications:** Current Index to Legal Periodicals, weekly; Marian Gould Gallagher Law Library Research Studies Series, 1-5; Washington Tort Reform Act Legislative History. **Remarks:** FAX: (206)685-2165. **Staff:** Molly McCluer, Asst.Libn., Pub.Serv.; Richard Jost, Asst.Libn., Tech.Serv.; Reba Turnquist, Acq.Libn.; Peggy Jarrett, Ref.Libn.; Mary Whisner, Hd., Ref.; Martin Cerjan, Ref.Libn.; Mary Louderback, Hd., Circ.; Laura Mahoney, Cat.Libn.; Grace Malson, Docs.Libn.; Ann Nez, Ser.Libn.; Bill McCloy, Asst.Libn., Comparative Law.

★ 19535 ★

University of Washington - Mathematics Research Library (Sci-Engr)
C306 Padelford, GN-50   Phone: (206)543-7296
Seattle, WA 98195   Martha Tucker
Founded: 1930. **Staff:** Prof 1; Other 1. **Subjects:** Pure and theoretical mathematics, pure and applied statistics. **Holdings:** 33,099 volumes. **Subscriptions:** 579 journals and other serials. **Services:** Interlibrary loan; copying; library open to the public for reference use only. **Automated Operations:** Computerized public access catalog. **Computerized Information Services:** DIALOG Information Services, BRS Information Technologies, STN International, OCLC; CD-ROM (MathSci Disc); InterNet, BITNET (electronic mail services). **Remarks:** FAX: (206)543-0397. Electronic mail address(es): MATHLIB@MATH.WASHINGTON.EDU (InterNet, BITNET).

★ 19536 ★

University of Washington - Music Library (Mus)
113 Music Bldg., DN-10   Phone: (206)543-1168
Seattle, WA 98195   David A. Wood, Hd.
Founded: 1950. **Staff:** Prof 3; Other 3. **Subjects:** Music. **Special Collections:** American music center (Kinscella Collection); opera scores, 17th-19th

century; Eric Offenbacher Mozart Collection (recordings); Melvin Harris Collection of Wind Recordings. **Holdings:** 57,305 volumes; 36,703 scores; 1522 reels of microfilm; 41,716 sound recordings; 72 video discs. **Subscriptions:** 503 journals and other serials. **Services:** Interlibrary loan; copying; library open to the public for reference use only. **Computerized Information Services:** OCLC; electronic mail. **Remarks:** FAX: (206)685-8049. **Staff:** John R. Gibbs, Asst.Hd.; Deborah L. Pierce, Mus.Cat./Ref.Libn.

★ 19537 ★

University of Washington - Natural Sciences Library (Biol Sci, Sci-Engr)
Allen Library, FM-25   Phone: (206)543-1243
Seattle, WA 98195   Nancy G. Blase, Hd.
Founded: 1935. **Staff:** Prof 5; Other 4. **Subjects:** Zoology, geology, geophysics, botany, atmospheric sciences, general science, history of science, biology. **Holdings:** 196,443 volumes; 3944 microfiche. **Subscriptions:** 2509 journals and other serials. **Services:** Interlibrary loan; copying; library open to the public for reference use only. **Automated Operations:** Computerized public access catalog and circulation. **Computerized Information Services:** DIALOG Information Services, BRS Information Technologies, STN International, Life Sciences Network, OCLC; CD-ROMs (GeoRef, Biological Abstracts, Birds of America on Disc, Climatedata, Earth Sciences, Hydrodata, Life Sciences Collection, Quality of Water, World Weather Disc); BITNET, InterNet (electronic mail services). **Remarks:** Alternate telephone number(s): 543-1244 (reference). FAX: (206)685-1665. Electronic mail address(es): NATSCI@U.WASHINGTON (BITNET); NATSCI@U.WASHINGTON.EDU (InterNet). **Staff:** Kathy Carr, Natural Sci.Ref.Coord./Friday Harbor Libn.; Doris Jones, Natural Sci.Bibliog.Proj./Ref.Libn.; Thomas Dowling, Natural Sci.Comp.-Based Serv./Ref.Libn.; Kari Anderson, Natural Sci.Ref./User Educ.Libn.; Patricia Carey, Ref.Libn.

★ 19538 ★

University of Washington - Philosophy Library (Rel-Phil)
331 Savery, DK-50   Phone: (206)543-5856
Seattle, WA 98195   Elaine Jennerich, Hd.
Founded: 1948. **Staff:** Prof 1; Other 1. **Subjects:** Philosophy, aesthetics, political and legal philosophy. **Holdings:** 18,002 volumes. **Subscriptions:** 244 journals and other serials. **Services:** Interlibrary loan; copying; library open to the public for reference use only. **Computerized Information Services:** OCLC; CD-ROM (Philosopher's Index); electronic mail. **Remarks:** FAX: (206)685-8049.

★ 19539 ★

University of Washington - Physics-Astronomy Library (Sci-Engr)
219 Physics Bldg., FM-15   Phone: (206)543-2988
Seattle, WA 98195   Martha Austin, Hd.
Founded: 1935. **Staff:** Prof 1; Other 1. **Subjects:** Physics, astronomy, astrophysics. **Holdings:** 24,269 volumes; sky atlases. **Subscriptions:** 352 journals and other serials. **Services:** Interlibrary loan; copying; library open to the public for reference use only. **Automated Operations:** Computerized public access catalog. **Computerized Information Services:** STN International; InterNet (electronic mail service). **Remarks:** FAX: (206)685-8049. Electronic mail address(es): AUSTINM@MILTON.U.WASHINGTON.EDU (InterNet).

★ 19540 ★

University of Washington - Political Science Library (Soc Sci)
220 Smith Hall, DP-25   Phone: (206)543-2389
Seattle, WA 98195   Al Fritz, Hd.
Founded: 1945. **Staff:** Prof 1; Other 2. **Subjects:** Political science, public administration. **Holdings:** 60,178 volumes. **Subscriptions:** 579 journals and other serials; 5 newspapers. **Services:** Interlibrary loan; copying; library open to the public for reference use only. **Computerized Information Services:** DIALOG Information Services, PFDS Online, BRS Information Technologies, OCLC; CD-ROM (PAIS). **Remarks:** FAX: (206)685-8049.

★ 19541 ★

University of Washington - Regional Primate Research Center - Primate Information Center (Biol Sci, Med)
SJ-50   Phone: (206)543-4376
Seattle, WA 98195   Jackie Lee Pritchard, Mgr.
Founded: 1963. **Staff:** 6.25. **Subjects:** Nonhuman primates, biomedical research, behavioral sciences. **Holdings:** 800 books; 100 bound periodical

volumes; 2000 microfiche; microfilm. **Subscriptions:** 60 journals and other serials. **Services:** SDI. **Computerized Information Services:** Internal databases. **Publications:** Current Primate References (bibliographic journal), monthly - by subscription; retrospective bibliographies from extensively indexed reference files - for sale; recurrent bibliographies, monthly - by subscription; list of other publications - available on request. **Remarks:** The Primate Information Center is an indexing service providing bibliographic information to scientists throughout the world. Its staff offers special assistance to those with information needs not met by its standard services. FAX: (206)685-0305. **Staff:** Jean Balch Williams, Res.Lit.Anl.; Cathy Johnson-Delaney, DVM, Res.Lit.Anl.; Stewart Cohen, Ph.D, Res.Lit.Anl.; Chico Otsuka-Gooding, Off.Supv.

★ 19542 ★
University of Washington - Social Work Library (Soc Sci)
Social Work/Speech-Hearing Bldg., JH-30   Phone: (206)685-2180
Seattle, WA 98195   Guela G. Johnson, Hd.
Founded: 1954. **Staff:** Prof 1; Other 2. **Subjects:** Social work; health care; social welfare, policy, and services; human growth and behavior; agency administration and supervision; community organizations; social research. **Holdings:** 28,916 volumes; 5244 pamphlets. **Subscriptions:** 256 journals and other serials. **Services:** Interlibrary loan; copying; reading room with adaptive equipment for disabled persons; library open to the public for reference use only. **Computerized Information Services:** DIALOG Information Services, PFDS Online, BRS Information Technologies, OCLC; CD-ROM (PsycLIT); electronic mail. **Remarks:** FAX: (206)685-8049.

University of Waterloo - Canadian Industrial Innovation Centre/ Waterloo
See: **Canadian Industrial Innovation Centre/Waterloo** (2939)

★ 19543 ★
University of Waterloo - Dana Porter Library (Hum, Soc Sci)
Waterloo, ON, Canada N2L 3G1   Phone: (519)885-1211
   Murray C. Shepherd, Univ.Libn.
Staff: Prof 33.5; Other 106.5. **Subjects:** Humanities, social and behavioral sciences, leisure studies, environmental studies, architecture. **Special Collections:** Works of Eric Gill; Euclid's Elements and History of Mathematics; private presses (Dolmen, Nonesuch, Golden Cockerel); Santayana Collection; D.R. Davis "Southey" Collection; rare materials from Lady Aberdeen Library of the History of Women; Crapo Dance Collection; Breithaupt-Clarke Collection, 1850-1980; K-W Record photograph collection, 1939-1982; Kitchener-Waterloo YWCA papers, 1905-1985. **Holdings:** 871,353 volumes; 214,226 government publications; 874,044 microforms. **Subscriptions:** 6114 journals and other serials. **Services:** Interlibrary loan; copying; facilities for the print-handicapped; library open to the public. **Automated Operations:** Computerized cataloging, acquisitions, serials, and circulation. **Computerized Information Services:** DIALOG Information Services, CAN/OLE, MEDLINE, International Research Development Centre (IRDC), QL Systems, WILSONLINE, Infomart Online, Info Globe, Tourism Reference & Documentation Centre Database (TRDC), OCLC, STN International; CD-ROMs; InterNet, Envoy 100, CoSy, CANET (electronic mail services). Performs searches on fee basis. Contact Person: Faye Abrams, Cord./Indus. & Bus.Info.Serv., 888-4517. **Networks/Consortia:** Member of Ontario Council of University Libraries (OCUL), Association of Research Libraries (ARL). **Publications:** How To, Titles, irregular - for internal distribution only; Bibliographies, Occasional Papers, For Your Information Newsletter, Friends of the Library Newsletter, irregular - external distribution; Library Handbook, annual - for internal distribution only. **Remarks:** FAX: (519)747-4606. Electronic mail address(es): liboff30@WATSERV1.UWATERLOO.CA (InterNet). **Staff:** Bruce MacNeil, Assoc.Libn./Info.; C. David Emery, Assoc.Libn./Coll.; Lorraine Beattie, Coord./Adm.Serv.; Michael Ridley, Assoc.Libn./Sys.

★ 19544 ★
University of Waterloo - Davis Centre Library (Sci-Engr)
Waterloo, ON, Canada N2L 3G1   Phone: (519)885-1211
   Murray C. Shepherd, Univ.Libn.
Staff: Prof 10; Other 24.5. **Subjects:** Engineering, mathematics, sciences, health studies, kinesiology, optometry. **Holdings:** 305,215 volumes; 52,247 microforms; 101,391 government publications; 10,193 maps. **Subscriptions:** 4834 journals and other serials. **Services:** Interlibrary loan; copying; library open to the public. **Automated Operations:** Computerized cataloging,

acquisitions, serials, and circulation. **Computerized Information Services:** DIALOG Information Services, CAN/OLE, MEDLARS, International Development Research Centre (IDRC), QL Systems, WILSONLINE, Infomart Online, Info Globe, STN International, Tourism Reference & Documentation Centre Database; CD-ROMs; InterNet, Envoy 100, CoSy, CANET (electronic mail services). Performs searches on fee basis. Contact Person: Faye Abrams, Coord./Indus. & Bus.Info.Serv., 888-4517. **Networks/Consortia:** Member of Ontario Council of University Libraries (OCUL), Association of Research Libraries (ARL). **Publications:** How To, Titles, irregular - for internal distribution only; bibliography, occasional papers, For Your Information Newsletter, Friends of the Library Newsletter, irregular - external distribution. **Special Indexes:** KWOC Index to IEEE and ACM Conference proceedings (card). **Remarks:** FAX: (519)746-5151. Electronic mail address(es): liboff30@WATSERV1.UWATERLOO.CA (InterNet). **Staff:** D. Morton, Coord., Online Ref.

★ 19545 ★
University of Waterloo - SIRLS - Sport & Leisure Database/Collection
Waterloo, ON, Canada N2L 3G1
Defunct.

★ 19546 ★
University of Waterloo - University Map and Design Library (Geog-Map, Art)
Environmental Studies Bldg., Rm. 246   Phone: (519)885-1211
Waterloo, ON, Canada N2L 3G1   Murray C. Shepherd, Univ.Libn.
Founded: 1965. **Staff:** Prof 2.5; Other 3. **Subjects:** Cartography, architectural design. **Special Collections:** Environmental Studies Honours Essays. **Holdings:** 12,231 books, atlases, and bound periodical volumes; 81,513 maps; 33,395 aerial photographs; 1838 microforms. **Subscriptions:** 98 journals and other serials. **Services:** Interlibrary loan; copying; library open to the public. **Automated Operations:** Computerized cataloging, acquisitions, serials, and circulation. **Computerized Information Services:** DIALOG Information Services, CAN/OLE, MEDLINE, QL Systems, WILSONLINE, Infomart Online, Info Globe, STN International, Tourism Reference & Documentation Centre Database (TRDC); InterNet, Envoy 100, CoSy, CANET (electronic mail services). Performs searches on fee basis. Contact Person: Faye Abrams, Coord./Indus. & Bus.Info.Serv., 888-4517. **Networks/Consortia:** Member of Ontario Council of University Libraries (OCUL), Association of Research Libraries (ARL). **Publications:** Checklist. **Special Indexes:** Map index (microfiche). **Remarks:** FAX: (519)747-4606. Electronic mail address(es): liboff30@WATSERV1.UWATERLOO.CA (InterNet). **Staff:** Richard H. Pinnell, Libn.

★ 19547 ★
University of Waterloo - Waterloo Centre for Groundwater Research - Library (Env-Cons)
Dept. of Earth Sciences
200 University Ave., W.   Phone: (519)885-1211
Waterloo, ON, Canada N2L 3G1   Dr. Robert Gillham, Dir.
Subjects: Groundwater research, resource contamination, resource evaluation, resource protection, resource remediation, groundwater technology. **Holdings:** Figures not available. **Publications:** Scientific publications; newletter; bulletin. **Remarks:** FAX: (519)888-4654. Telex: 069 55259.

★ 19548 ★
University of West Florida - College of Education - Curriculum Materials Library (Educ)
Pensacola, FL 32514-5750   Phone: (904)474-2439
   Ron Toifel, Coord., Educ.Serv.
Founded: 1972. **Staff:** Prof 1; Other 1. **Subjects:** Education - preschool through grade 12. **Holdings:** 11,350 books; 540 filmstrips; 2970 slides; 390 transparencies; 1460 kits and games; 1430 cassette tapes and phonograph records; 5875 curriculum guides on microfiche; 1110 prints, photographs, posters, and charts; 22 videocassettes. **Services:** Library open to the public for reference use only. **Automated Operations:** Computerized public access catalog. **Computerized Information Services:** CD-ROMs (ERIC, Business Index, Academic Index). **Formerly:** Collection housed at John C. Pace Library.

★ 19549 ★

University of West Florida - Human Resource Videotape Library (Aud-Vis)
Dept. of Social Work
College of Arts & Sciences
11000 University Pkwy. Phone: (904)474-2381
Pensacola, FL 32514-5751 Prof. Bonnie Bedics
Founded: 1978. **Staff:** Prof 1; Other 20. **Subjects:** Addiction, child abuse, mental illness and therapy. **Holdings:** 200 videotapes. **Services:** Copying; library open to the public. **Publications:** VRL Connection newsletter, semiannual. **Special Catalogs:** Video Resource Library Catalog, annual.

★ 19550 ★

University of West Florida - John C. Pace Library - Special Collections (Hist)
11000 University Parkway Phone: (904)474-2213
Pensacola, FL 32514-5750 Dean DeBolt, Spec.Coll.Libn.
Founded: 1966. **Staff:** Prof 1; Other 2. **Subjects:** West Florida, 1559 to present, including Florida under Spanish, British, American, and Confederate governments; Pensacola, 1559 to present; Florida Panhandle, southern Alabama and Mississippi; university archives. **Special Collections:** George Washington Sully watercolors, 1833-1839; Governor Sidney Catts papers (5000 items); Eudora Welty Collection; Langston Hughes Collection; James Dickey Collection; Panton-Leslie Papers, 1784-1850 (Spanish-English trading post headquartered in Pensacola). **Holdings:** 5000 rare books and monographs; 500,000 manuscript and archival documents, including personal and family papers, church and business records, and records of organizations; 3000 maps; 10,000 photographs; 300 newspapers. **Subscriptions:** 25 journals and other serials; 30 newspapers. **Services:** Copying; collections open to the public. **Automated Operations:** Computerized public access catalog. **Publications:** Bibliog raphy of West Florida, 1535-1986 (4 volumes). **Special Catalogs:** Separate collection inventories; Guide to the Manuscripts, 1979.

★ 19551 ★

University of the West Indies - Main Library (Agri, Soc Sci, Sci-Engr)
St. Augustine, Trinidad and Tobago Phone: 663-1439
Dr. Alma T. Jordan, Univ.Libn.
Founded: 1926. **Staff:** Prof 19; Other 64. **Subjects:** Agriculture, engineering, social sciences, natural sciences, humanities, education, law. **Special Collections:** West Indian Collection. **Holdings:** 258,416 books; 46,580 bound periodical volumes; 32,557 microforms; 3175 manuscripts; 1201 maps and charts; 146 film strips and multi-media kits; 4696 photographs; 2640 slides; 7195 vertical file items; 298 cassettes; 181 tapes; 1493 records; 85 videocassettes; 12 magnetic tapes; 12 diskettes; 18 compact discs; other AV items. **Subscriptions:** 5698 journals and other serials; 33 newspapers. **Services:** Interlibrary loan; copying; SDI; library open to the public with restrictions. **Automated Operations:** Computerized cataloging and ILL. **Computerized Information Services:** DIALOG Information Services, ORBIT Search Service, WILSONLINE, AGRIS (International Information System for the Agricultural Sciences and Technology), CARBIB, CAGRIS (Caribbean Information System for the Agricultural Sciences), CARSCI (Caribbean Index: Social Sciences and Humanities), Agricola, KIT Abstracts of Tropical Agriculture, CIGAR (Food Agriculture and Science), UWI Theses Index, CARNEW (Caribbean Newspaper Index), UWIPER (Caribbean Agricultural Periodicals); NASCI (publications of the staff of the Faculty of Natural Sciences; internal database). Performs searches on fee basis. Contact Person: Shirley Evelyn, Hd., Rd.Serv. **Publications:** Bibliographic series, irregular; CARIS Caribbean (online); Current Research at the University of the West Indies (St. Augustine), biennial. **Special Indexes:** CARINDEX: Science and Technology; CARINDEX: Social Sciences and Humanities; CAGRINDEX: Abstracts of the agricultural literature of the English-Speaking Caribbean. **Remarks:** Maintains two branch libraries: Faculty of Education Library and Medical Sciences Library. Telex: 24-520 UWI-WG.

★ 19552 ★

University of West Los Angeles - Kelton Law Library (Law)
12201 Washington Pl. Phone: (213)313-1011
Los Angeles, CA 90066 Joseph R. Dreyer, Univ.Libn.
Founded: 1967. **Staff:** Prof 1; Other 12. **Subjects:** Law. **Holdings:** 33,000 books; 3100 bound periodical volumes; 6500 microfiche. **Subscriptions:** 300 journals and other serials. **Services:** Copying; library open to the public. **Computerized Information Services:** WESTLAW, LEXIS.

★ 19553 ★

University of Western Ontario - Allyn and Betty Taylor Library (Biol Sci, Sci-Engr, Med)
Natural Sciences Centre Phone: (519)679-2111
London, ON, Canada N6A 5B7 Lorraine Busby, Hd., Taylor Lib.
Founded: 1881. **Staff:** Prof 6; Other 27. **Subjects:** Anesthesia, anatomy, applied mathematics, astronomy, biochemistry, biology, biophysics, chemistry, clinical neurological sciences, communicative disorders, computer science, dentistry, epidemiology, family medicine, genetics, geology, geophysics, history of medicine and science, mathematics, medicine, microbiology, nursing, obstetrics and gynecology, occupational therapy, ophthalmology, otolaryngology, pediatrics, pathology, pharmacology, physical medicine, physical therapy, physics, physiology, plant sciences, psychiatry, radiation oncology, radiology, statistics, surgery, zoology. **Holdings:** 172,309 books; 158,671 bound periodical volumes; 28,813 microforms; 9652 AV materials; 1399 pamphlets. **Subscriptions:** 4729 journals and other serials. **Services:** Interlibrary loan; copying; Northern Ooutreach Library Service; library open to the public with restrictions. **Automated Operations:** Computerized cataloging, acquisitions, serials, and circulation. **Computerized Information Services:** BRS Information Technologies, CAN/OLE, DIALOG Information Services, NLM, WILSONLINE, Institute for Scientific Information (ISI); internal database; Envoy 100 (electronic mail service). Contact Person: Lila Heilbrunn, Hd., Ref. & Online Serv., 679-2111, ext. 6371. **Remarks:** FAX: (519)661-3880. Electronic mail address(es): ILL.SCI.UWO (Envoy 100). **Formerly:** Its Science Library. **Staff:** Peter Galsworthy; Connie Hoff; Linda Voelker.

★ 19554 ★

University of Western Ontario - Centre for American Studies - Library (Soc Sci)
Social Science Centre Phone: (519)661-3656
London, ON, Canada N6A 5C2 E. H. Redekop, Dir.
Subjects: Canadian perspective on American history, literature, society, and politics. **Holdings:** Figures not available for books, pamphlets, and files. **Remarks:** FAX: (519)661-3292.

★ 19555 ★

University of Western Ontario - D.B. Weldon Library - Department of Special Collections (Hist, Hum)
London, ON, Canada N6A 3K7 Phone: (519)679-2111
John H. Lutman, Libn.
Founded: 1942. **Staff:** Prof 1. **Subjects:** Canadiana - literature from pre-1867 to 1939, history, voyages and travel, black studies; Edwardian writers, 1889-1918; British and European history, 16th and 17th centuries; history of science and medicine; Napoleonic era and the French Revolution. **Special Collections:** G. William Stuart Collection of Milton and Miltonia (850 volumes); 19th century plays of manners and morals (578 volumes); John Galt Collection (150 volumes); Richard Maurice Bucke Collection (515 volumes); 12 linear feet of scrapbooks and pamphlets; 300 items in picture files; diaries; letters; documents; Beatrice Hitchins Memorial Collection of Aviation History (1500 volumes; 91 picture files; 350 vertical files; 50 manuscripts; 15,000 card files); London Free Press Collection of Photographic Negatives (300,000 negatives); Gregory Clark Piscatorial Collection (329 volumes); Hannah Collection on the History of Science and Medicine (1000 volumes); Margaret Atwood Collection of Published and Related Works; Avery Brundage Collection of Olympic History; Carl F. Klinck Collection of Canadiana; Don Gutteridge Collection of Literary Papers; H.G. Wells Collection (140 volumes). **Holdings:** 29,285 volumes; 400 British and American pamphlets of Edwardian era; 250 contemporary Canadian pamphlets. **Services:** Interlibrary loan; copying (both limited); department open to the public. **Automated Operations:** Computerized cataloging and acquisitions. **Computerized Information Services:** Electronic mail. **Special Catalogs:** G.W. Stuart Collection of Milton and Miltonia; Canadian Chronological Imprints; Private Press Holdings; British/American Pamphlets; Canadian Pamphlets; Juvenilia; Beatrice Hitchins Memorial Collection of Aviation History. **Remarks:** FAX: (519)661-3911.

★ 19556 ★

University of Western Ontario - D.B. Weldon Library - Regional Collection (Hist)
London, ON, Canada N6A 3K7 Phone: (519)679-2111
Edward C.H. Phelps, Libn.
Founded: 1942. **Staff:** Prof 1; Other 2. **Subjects:** Canadiana, Ontario regional and local history, historical geography, archives. **Special Collections:** County records (local public archives; business archives; private papers);

Ontario textbook collection (3000). **Holdings:** 47,522 books, bound periodical volumes, U.W.O. dissertations, micromaterials, boxes and volumes of manuscripts and archives, maps, and pictures. **Subscriptions:** 10 journals and other serials. **Services:** Interlibrary loan; copying; collection open to the public with restrictions. **Automated Operations:** Computerized cataloging. **Remarks:** FAX: (519)661-3911. Telex: 064 71 34. Genealogical inquiries are forwarded to the London, ON Genealogical Society.

★ 19557 ★
University of Western Ontario - Department of Geography - Serge A. Sauer Map Library (Geog-Map)
London, ON, Canada N6A 5C2   Phone: (519)661-3424
                                              Cheryl Woods, Map Cur.
Founded: 1966. **Staff:** Prof 2; Other 3. **Subjects:** World, Great Lakes, Canadiana, geography, planning, natural resources. **Special Collections:** Great Lakes. **Holdings:** 223,000 maps; 24,500 aerial photographs; 2300 atlases; 1917 theses. **Subscriptions:** 6 journals and other serials. **Services:** Interlibrary loan; copying; library open to the public. **Computerized Information Services:** Internal database; electronic mail. **Publications:** Theses Bibliography, annual; Newsletter, irregular; facsimile reproductions of historical maps and charts. **Special Catalogs:** Atlas listing (online); Thesis listing (online); urban plans listing (online). **Remarks:** FAX: (519)661-3868. This is regarded as one of the largest university map collections in Canada. The Great Lakes Cartographic Resource Centre is located in the Map Library.

University of Western Ontario - Dr. Joseph Pozsonyi Memorial Library
See: **Dr. Joseph Pozsonyi Memorial Library** (13285)

★ 19558 ★
University of Western Ontario - Education Library (Educ)
Faculty of Education
1137 Western Rd.
London, ON, Canada N6G 1G7   Phone: (519)661-3172
                                              J. Claire Callaghan, Hd.
Founded: 1965. **Staff:** Prof 2; Other 6. **Subjects:** Education. **Special Collections:** Complete ERIC Collection (microfiche). **Holdings:** 85,646 books; 10,285 bound periodical volumes; 464,991 micromaterials; 43,769 AV materials; 20 VF drawers of clippings; 252 computer programs; 1865 curriculum guidelines. **Subscriptions:** 711 journals and other serials. **Services:** Interlibrary loan; library open to the public with restrictions. **Automated Operations:** Computerized cataloging, acquisitions, serials, and circulation. **Computerized Information Services:** BRS Information Technologies; CD-ROMs (ERIC, AVONLINE, CD:Education, Education Index); Envoy 100, NETNORTH (electronic mail services). Performs searches on fee basis. **Special Catalogs:** Curriculum Resource Centre CD-ROM Catalogue. **Remarks:** FAX: (519)661-3833. Electronic mail address(es): EDUC.LIBR.UWO (Envoy 100); CLAIRE.CALLAGHAN@UWO.CA (NETNORTH). **Staff:** Sally McCrae.

★ 19559 ★
University of Western Ontario - Engineering Library (Sci-Engr)
London, ON, Canada N6A 5B9   Phone: (519)661-3958
                                              Jerry Mulcahy, Libn.
Founded: 1959. **Staff:** Prof 1; Other 5. **Subjects:** Engineering - chemical, civil, electrical, materials, mechanical. **Holdings:** 20,524 books; 21,090 bound periodical volumes; 5674 government documents; 601 pamphlets; 2337 microforms. **Subscriptions:** 734 journals and other serials. **Services:** Interlibrary loan; copying; SDI; library open to the public. **Automated Operations:** Computerized cataloging, acquisitions, serials, and circulation. **Computerized Information Services:** CAN/OLE, DIALOG Information Services, BRS Information Technologies, WILSONLINE; CD-ROMs (NTIS, Applied Science and Technology Index, Compendex Plus). **Remarks:** FAX: (519)661-3911.

★ 19560 ★
University of Western Ontario - Faculty of Law Library (Law)
London, ON, Canada N6A 3K7   Phone: (519)661-3171
                                              George Robinson
Founded: 1959. **Staff:** Prof 3; Other 5. **Subjects:** Law. **Holdings:** 161,537 volumes; 700 cassettes; 30,620 microforms; 203 pamphlets. **Subscriptions:** 2302 journals and other serials. **Services:** Interlibrary loan; copying; library open to the public with restrictions. **Automated Operations:** Computerized cataloging, acquisitions, serials, and circulation. **Computerized Information Services:** QL Systems, CAN/LAW, WESTLAW; electronic mail. **Remarks:** FAX: (519)661-2012. **Staff:** Patricia McVeigh; Marianne Welch.

★ 19561 ★
University of Western Ontario - Music Library (Mus)
London, ON, Canada N6A 3K7   Phone: (519)679-2111
                                              William Guthrie, Libn.
Founded: 1963. **Staff:** Prof 3; Other 5. **Subjects:** Music theory, music history, applied music, music education. **Special Collections:** Mahler-Rose Collection (scores by Gustav Mahler, Alfred Rose, and Bruno Walter; 675 letters and documents related to Mahler, including 300 letters written by Mahler); The Opera Collection (200 musical manuscripts; 1900 volumes of contemporary printed scores and librettos of opera titles, 1600-early 20th century). **Holdings:** 81,500 volumes and scores; 380,000 choral, band, and orchestral scores; 29,000 sound recordings; 9800 microforms; 1760 pamphlets. **Subscriptions:** 300 journals and other serials. **Services:** Interlibrary loan; copying; disc and tape recording listening facilities; library open to the public. **Automated Operations:** Computerized acquisitions, serials, and circulation. **Computerized Information Services:** Internal atabases; BITNET (electronic mail service). **Remarks:** Electronic mail address(es): WILLIAM.GUTHRIE@UWO.CA (BITNET).

★ 19562 ★
University of Western Ontario - Occupational Health and Safety Resource Centre - Library (Med)
Bio Engineering Bldg.   Phone: (519)661-3044
London, ON, Canada N6A 5B9   Martin J. Bracken
Founded: 1979. **Subjects:** Occupational health, occupational safety, air pollution. **Holdings:** 600 books; 35 bound periodical volumes; 115 reports. **Subscriptions:** 7 journals and other serials. **Services:** Library not open to the public. **Automated Operations:** Computerized indexing. **Remarks:** FAX: (519)661-3934.

★ 19563 ★
University of Western Ontario - School of Business Administration - Business Library & Information Centre (Bus-Fin)
London, ON, Canada N6A 3K7   Phone: (519)661-3941
                                              Jerry Mulcahy, Libn.
Founded: 1960. **Staff:** Prof 1; Other 5. **Subjects:** International business, finance, marketing, operations research, labor relations, accounting. **Special Collections:** Microfiche collection of Canadian and U.S. company data (120,000 items). **Holdings:** 42,858 books; 13,059 bound periodical volumes; 7965 government documents (coded); 286,969 microforms; 537 pamphlets; 117 cassettes; 23,812 items on companies, industries, and business conditions in Canada. **Subscriptions:** 1458 journals and other serials. **Services:** Interlibrary loan; copying; reference service to academic and business community; library open to the public with borrowing restrictions. **Automated Operations:** Computerized cataloging, acquisitions, serials, and circulation. **Computerized Information Services:** QL Systems, BRS Information Technologies, DIALOG Information Services, Info Globe; CD-ROMs (ABI/INFORM, CIRR, Business Dateline, Worldscope, COMPACT DISCLOSURE, British News Index); electronic mail. **Remarks:** FAX: (519)661-3911.

★ 19564 ★
University of Western Ontario - School of Library & Information Science - Library (Info Sci, Comp Sci)
Elborn College   Phone: (519)661-3542
London, ON, Canada N6G 1H1   Daniel Dorner, Academic
                                              Sup.Serv.Coord.
Founded: 1967. **Staff:** Prof 5; Other 5. **Subjects:** Library and information science, computers and electronic data processing, children's literature, communications. **Special Collections:** Pre-1800 handprinted books (10,000 volumes); dictionaries (500); private press books (600). **Holdings:** 60,000 books; 24,000 bound periodical volumes; 10,000 microforms; 300 tapes. **Subscriptions:** 525 journals and other serials. **Services:** Interlibrary loan; copying; library open to the public. **Automated Operations:** Computerized public access catalog, cataloging, acquisitions, and circulation. **Computerized Information Services:** DIALOG Information Services; Envoy 100 (electronic mail service). **Special Catalogs:** Serials list; special collections catalog. **Special Indexes:** KWOC index to technical reports and ERIC documents on microfiche. **Remarks:** FAX: (519)661-3506. **Staff:** Hanna Marti, Cat.Sys.Libn.; John Fracasso, Automated Sys. & Serv.Coord.; Martie Grof-Iannelli, Asst.Coord.; Charles McClellan, Prog.

University of Western Ontario - Westminster Institute for Ethics and Human Values
See: **Westminster Institute for Ethics and Human Values** (20330)

★ 19565 ★

University of Western Sydney - Hawkesbury Library (Agri, Food-Bev)
Bourke St.   Phone: 45 701364
Richmond, NSW 2753, Australia   Aileen Stevenson
Founded: 1891. **Staff:** Prof 9; Other 17. **Subjects:** Food technology, agriculture, horticulture, business, land economy, environmental health. **Special Collections:** Potts Collection (Australian agriculture books and photographs; pre-1921). **Holdings:** 50,000 books; 20,000 bound periodical volumes. **Subscriptions:** 1500 journals and other serials; 20 newspapers. **Services:** Interlibrary loan; copying; library open to the public for reference use only. **Computerized Information Services:** DIALOG Information Services, STN International, ORBIT Search Service, AUSINET, AUSTRALIS; ILANET (electronic mail service). Contact Person: Erika Redgrove. **Remarks:** FAX: 45 784253. Electronic mail address(es): MLN 205850 (ILANET).

★ 19566 ★

University of Windsor - Faculty of Education Library (Educ)
600 Third Concession Rd.   Phone: (519)969-0520
Windsor, ON, Canada N9E 1A5   Thomas J. Robinson, Educ.Libn.
Founded: 1962. **Staff:** Prof 1; Other 3. **Subjects:** Education. **Special Collections:** School texts; Montessori Memorial Collection; Kraus Curriculum Development Library, 1978-1989 (microfiche). **Holdings:** 61,459 books; 3188 bound periodical volumes; 1175 filmstrips; 15,400 mounted pictures; 2433 unmounted pictures and charts; 25 videocassettes; 433 cassettes; 816 kits; 294 phonograph records; 12 drawers of pamphlets; 6073 public documents; ERIC microfiche, 1966 to present; ONTERIS microfiche, 1972 to present. **Subscriptions:** 200 journals and other serials. **Services:** Interlibrary loan; copying; library open to the public with restrictions. **Automated Operations:** Computerized cataloging and serials. **Computerized Information Services:** Online systems (through Leddy Library). **Remarks:** FAX: (519)969-3646.

★ 19567 ★

University of Windsor - Paul Martin Law Library (Law)
401 Sunset Ave.   Phone: (519)253-2977
Windsor, ON, Canada N9B 3P4   Paul T. Murphy, Law Libn.
Staff: Prof 3; Other 9. **Subjects:** Law. **Holdings:** 148,000 volumes; 120,000 microform volume equivalents. **Subscriptions:** 2700 journals and other serials. **Services:** Interlibrary loan; copying; library open to the public with restrictions. **Computerized Information Services:** QL Systems, DIALOG Information Services, CAN/OLE, WESTLAW; Envoy 100 (electronic mail service). **Staff:** Daniel K.L. Boen, Cat.Libn.; Huey-Min Soong, Ref.Libn.

★ 19568 ★

University of Winnipeg - Library - Special Collections (Area-Ethnic, Rel-Phil)
515 Portage Ave.   Phone: (204)786-9801
Winnipeg, MB, Canada R3B 2E9   Dr. W.R. Converse, Chf.Libn.
Staff: 41. **Special Collections:** Ashdown Collection of Canadian Studies; Newcombe Collection of Theology; Mary Iris Atchison Collection; United Church of Canada; Conference of Manitoba and Northwestern Ontario Archives; University of Winnipeg Archives; George H. Reavis Reading Collection; Drache Law Library. **Holdings:** 495,006 books and bound periodical volumes; 26,963 reels of microfilm; 84,764 microfiche. **Subscriptions:** 2114 journals and other serials. **Services:** Interlibrary loan; copying; SDI; collections open to the public on a fee basis. **Automated Operations:** Computerized cataloging, acquisitions, serials, and circulation. **Computerized Information Services:** DIALOG Information Services, Info Globe, The Financial Post DataGroup, UTLAS, CAN/OLE; Envoy 100 (electronic mail service). Performs searches on fee basis. Contact Person: William Pond, Hd., Pub.Serv., 786-9812. **Remarks:** FAX: (204)786-1824. **Staff:** Coreen Koz, Assoc.Chf.Libn.; Sandra Zuk, Spec.Proj.Libn.; Linwood DeLong, Ref.Libn. (Coll.Dev.); Joan Scanlon, Hd., Tech.Serv.; Linda Dixon, Ref.Libn. (Govt.Docs.); Kam Wing Lee, Cat.Libn.

★ 19569 ★

University of Wisconsin--Eau Claire - Simpson Geographic Research Center - Map Library (Geog-Map)
Department of Geography   Phone: (715)836-3244
Eau Claire, WI 54701   Adam Cahow, Dir.
Founded: 1970. **Staff:** Prof 1; Other 5. **Subjects:** Complete topographic coverage of North America. **Holdings:** 250,000 maps; 200 atlases; 1500 aerial photographs. **Subscriptions:** 5 journals and other serials. **Services:** Interlibrary loan; copying; library open to the public. **Publications:** New Listings - to interested faculty.

★ 19570 ★

University of Wisconsin--Eau Claire - Special Collections - Area Research Center, University Archives, Rare Books (Hist)
McIntyre Library   Phone: (715)836-3715
Eau Claire, WI 54702   Lawrence D. Lynch, Archv.
Staff: Prof 1; Other 1. **Subjects:** History of western Wisconsin, lumbering history, genealogy, university history. **Special Collections:** Wisconsin County Histories and Atlases (44 reels of microfilm). **Holdings:** 1343 linear feet and 498 reels of microfilm of historical manuscripts and local public records; 416 maps and atlases; 1075 linear feet and 666 reels of microfilm of university records; 2913 photographic prints; 144,000 university-related negative frames. **Services:** Interlibrary loan (microfilm only); copying; center open to the public for reference use only. **Automated Operations:** Computerized cataloging. **Networks/Consortia:** Member of Wisconsin Area Research Center Network. **Publications:** Guide to Archives and Manuscripts (prepared for the center by the State Historical Society of Wisconsin, 1990).

★ 19571 ★

University of Wisconsin--Green Bay - Area Research Center (Hist, Soc Sci)
2420 Nicolet Dr.   Phone: (414)465-2539
Green Bay, WI 54311-7001   Debra L. Anderson, Hd. of Spec.Coll.
Staff: Prof 1; Other 1. **Subjects:** Local history, genealogy, radical literature, Belgian Americans. **Special Collections:** Belgian American research material; Leon Kramer Collection of Communist, Socialist and Anarchist Literature (10,000 pamphlets). **Holdings:** 7600 books; 5000 linear feet of local governmental records and private papers; University of Wisconsin - Green Bay, University Archives. **Services:** Interlibrary loan; copying; center open to the public; answers telephone and mail reference questions on a limited basis. **Networks/Consortia:** Member of Wisconsin Area Research Center Network. **Special Indexes:** Belgian American Research Materials; Guide to Archives and Manuscripts in the University of Wisconsin, Green Bay Area Research Center; Guide to Brown County Public Records; Guide to Brown County Manuscript Collections; Guide to Manitowoc County Public Records; Guide to Manitowoc County Manuscript Collections.

★ 19572 ★

University of Wisconsin--Green Bay - Women's Center - Library (Soc Sci)
IS 1144   Phone: (414)465-2582
Green Bay, WI 54302   Michelle Krajnik, Women's Ctr.Coord.
Subjects: Women's history, women's movement, biography, resources available to women. **Holdings:** 400 books; periodicals, information files. **Services:** Library open to the public.

★ 19573 ★

University of Wisconsin--La Crosse - Alice Hagar Curriculum Resource Center (Educ)
213 Morris Hall   Phone: (608)785-8651
La Crosse, WI 54601   Mary Esten, Dir.
Founded: 1972. **Staff:** Prof 1; Other 8. **Subjects:** Curriculum materials for English, foreign languages, art, mathematics, science, social studies, music; literature for children and young adults. **Special Collections:** Standardized test files; district curriculum guides. **Holdings:** 15,000 books; nonprint items; 10 curriculum files; 5 standard test files; 24 vertical files. **Subscriptions:** 50 journals and other serials. **Services:** Copying; center open to the public with valid identification.

★ 19574 ★

University of Wisconsin--La Crosse - Center for Contemporary Poetry (Hum)
Murphy Library
1631 Pine St.   Phone: (608)785-8511
La Crosse, WI 54601   Edwin L. Hill, Spec.Coll.Libn.
Founded: 1970. **Staff:** Prof 1; Other 1. **Subjects:** Contemporary poetry, with emphasis on Midwestern poetry. **Special Collections:** August Derleth (107 volumes); private presses: Prairie, Trovillion, Sumac, Perishable Press, Bieler, Penumbra, Sea Pen, Meadow, Coffee House, Toothpaste, Crepuscular, Arkham House (120 volumes); Skeeters Collection of Gothic, Fantasy, and Science Fiction (1046 volumes); James Bertolino Poetry Collection (manuscripts); Martin Rosenblum Poetry Collection (manuscripts); Edna Meudt Poetry Collection (manuscripts); Margins magazine, 1972-1977; Midwestern Poets, 1960s and 1970s (tape-recorded interviews and readings). **Holdings:** 4900 books. **Subscriptions:** 65 journals and other serials. **Services:** Copying (limited); center open to the public; persons seeking particular information should call in advance. **Computerized Information Services:** Internal database. **Special Indexes:** Index to manuscripts (card).

★ 19575 ★
University of Wisconsin--La Crosse - Media Center - Film Library (Aud-Vis)
1705 State St.   Phone: (608)785-8058
La Crosse, WI 54601   Gary Goorough, Coord., Film Lib.
Founded: 1961. Staff: Prof 1; Other 1. Holdings: 6600 film titles. Services: Library open to the public on a rental basis. Automated Operations: Computerized cataloging, acquisitions, and circulation. Networks/Consortia: Member of Consortium of College and University Media Centers (CCUMC). Special Catalogs: 1985 Film Rental catalog.

★ 19576 ★
University of Wisconsin--La Crosse - Murphy Library (Hum, Hist)
1631 Pine St.   Phone: (608)785-8505
La Crosse, WI 54601   Dale Montgomery, Dir., Lib. and Media Serv.
Founded: 1909. Staff: Prof 11.5; Other 14. Subjects: Humanities, business administration, education, physical education, science, medical technology. Special Collections: Local history and Wisconsiana (4904 volumes; 943 tapes; 93,477 photographs; 450 maps); rare books (11,788); oral history collection (2750 hours of interviews). Holdings: 524,524 volumes; 57,515 bound periodical volumes; 184,026 government documents; 38,576 reels of microfilm; 819,748 microfiche. Subscriptions: 1935 journals and other serials; 59 newspapers. Services: Interlibrary loan; copying; library open to the public. Automated Operations: Computerized cataloging, acquisitions, circulation, and serials. Computerized Information Services: OCLC, OCLC EPIC, DIALOG Information Services, BRS Information Technologies, Knowledge Index, WILSONLINE, STN International, PFDS Online; BITNET, InterNet (electronic mail services). Performs searches on fee basis. Networks/Consortia: Member of Wisconsin Interlibrary Services (WILS), West Central Wisconsin Library Consortium. Remarks: FAX: (608)785-8806. Local cooperative lending with Viterbo College and Western Wisconsin Technical College. Staff: Sandra Sechrest, Doc.; Cristine Berg Prucha, Circ.; Charles Marx, Cat.; Karin Sandvik, Acq.; Cathy Currier, Coord., Tech.Serv./Automation; Randall Hoelzen, B.I./ILL; Anita Evans, Coord., Pub.Serv./Online Serv.; Edwin L. Hill, Archv./Spec.Coll.; Sue Burkhart, Ser.

★ 19577 ★
University of Wisconsin--La Crosse - Steamboat Collection (Hist)
Murphy Library
1631 Pine St.   Phone: (608)785-8511
La Crosse, WI 54601   Edwin L. Hill, Spec.Coll.Libn.
Founded: 1973. Staff: Prof 1; Other 1. Subjects: Inland river steamboats, Mississippi River, river towns, river life. Holdings: 560 books; 150 bound periodical volumes; 40,000 photographs. Subscriptions: 4 journals and other serials. Services: Copying; collection open to the public. Computerized Information Services: Internal database. Special Indexes: Index to inland river steamboat names; index to towns and villages by place name. Remarks: Copy prints of photographs are available for educational and research purposes, and for commercial use with some restrictions. Inquiries before visiting or ordering are recommended.

★ 19578 ★
University of Wisconsin--Madison - African Studies Program - Instructional Materials Center (Area-Ethnic)
1334 Van Hise Hall
1220 Linden Dr.   Phone: (608)263-2171
Madison, WI 53706-1557   Patricia S. Kuntz, Outreach Dir.
Founded: 1973. Staff: Prof 1; Other 3. Subjects: Social studies, music, literature, French, art, anthropology, science, economics, African languages, mathematics, education, history, geography, global issues. Special Collections: Life in African countries slide collection (7000). Holdings: 3000 books; 200 maps; cassettes; discs; filmstrips; transparencies; 3 vertical files. Subscriptions: 10 journals and other serials. Services: Center open to the public. Computerized Information Services: African Studies Bulletin Board System N81. Networks/Consortia: Member of Multitype Advisory Library Committee (MALC). Special Catalogs: Catalog of 35mm slide collection, 1985. Remarks: Maintained by University of Wisconsin, Madison - African Studies Program. Alternate telephone number(s): 262-2380; 262-6003. FAX: (608)262-6998. Electronic mail address(es): KUNTZ@WISCMACC (BITNET) and KUNTZ@MACC.WISC.EDU (InterNet). Electronic bulletin board: (608)262-9689 (24-hour service).

★ 19579 ★
University of Wisconsin--Madison - Archives (Hist)
B134 Memorial Library
728 State St.   Phone: (608)262-5629
Madison, WI 53706   J. Frank Cook, Dir.
Founded: 1957. Staff: Prof 5. Subjects: University archives. Special Collections: Archives of the Society of American Archivists. Holdings: 1000 books; 200 bound periodical volumes; 20,000 cubic feet of archival materials, photographs, microfilm. Subscriptions: 10 journals and other serials; 2 newspapers. Services: Interlibrary loan; copying; archives open to the public with restrictions. Computerized Information Services: InterNet, BITNET (electronic mail services). Publications: Records Management Manual. Remarks: FAX: (608)262-4649. Electronic mail address(es): JFCOOK@VMS.MACC.WISC.EDU (InterNet, BITNET). Staff: Bernard Schermetzler, Archv./Iconographer; Nancy Kunde, Recs.Off.; Steve Masar, Automation; Barry Teicher, Oral Hist.

★ 19580 ★
University of Wisconsin--Madison - Arthur H. Robinson Map Library (Geog-Map)
310 Science Hall
550 N. Park St.   Phone: (608)262-1471
Madison, WI 53706-1491   Mary Galneder, Map Libn.
Staff: Prof 1; Other 3. Subjects: Worldwide coverage of topographic, thematic, and general maps; aerial photographs (primarily Wisconsin); nautical charts. Holdings: 600 books; 245,000 maps; 185,300 aerial photographs; 2470 air photo mosaic indexes. Subscriptions: 30 journals and other serials. Services: Interlibrary loan; library open to the public for reference use only. Computerized Information Services: InterNet, BITNET (electronic mail services). Remarks: Electronic mail address(es): GALNEDER@VMS.MACC.WISC.EDU   (InterNet); GALNEDER@WISC.MACC (BITNET).

★ 19581 ★
University of Wisconsin--Madison - Biology Library (Biol Sci)
Birge Hall
430 Lincoln Dr.   Phone: (608)262-2740
Madison, WI 53706   Elsa Althen, Libn.
Founded: 1907. Staff: Prof 1; Other 1. Subjects: Botany and zoology, with emphasis on organismal biology; ecology; evolutionary biology; taxonomy; ethology. Holdings: 47,000 volumes. Subscriptions: 750 journals and other serials. Services: Library open to the public for reference use. Computerized Information Services: BRS Information Technologies, DIALOG Information Services, OCLC; CD-ROMs; (AGRICOLA, AGRIS (UNFAO), Biological Abstracts, CAB ABSTRACTS, U.S. Department of Agriculture Current Research Information System (CRIS), Food Science and Technology Abstracts (FSTA), MEDLINE, Science Citation Index (SCI), Abstracts on Tropical Agriculture, Abstracts on Rural Development (RURAL)); BITNET (electronic mail service). Performs searches on fee basis. Publications: Acquisitions list, monthly; library use aids. Special Catalogs: Serials file (card). Remarks: FAX: (608)262-9003. Electronic mail address(es): ALTHEN@WISCMACC (BITNET).

★ 19582 ★
University of Wisconsin--Madison - Botany Department - Herbarium Library (Biol Sci)
158 Birge Hall
430 Lincoln Dr.   Phone: (608)262-2792
Madison, WI 53706   H.H. Iltis, Prof., Botany/Dir., Herbarium
Founded: 1849. Staff: 3. Subjects: Taxonomy, biogeography, and evolution of flowering plants, gymnosperms, and ferns, especially corn, lichens, mosses, and parasitic fungi; Wisconsin, United States, Latin American, and world flora. Special Collections: Specimens of pressed dried plants from all over the world (938,000); C.R. Huskins, D.C. Cooper, O.N. and E.K. Allen, and F.J. Hermann reprint collections on cytology and taxonomy; man's need for nature; topographic and vegetation maps (10,000). Holdings: 2000 volumes; 490 bound periodical volumes; 80,000 reprints; 67 dissertations; 155 boxes of microcards. Subscriptions: 18 journals and other serials. Services: Copying; library open to the public with restrictions. Publications: Atlas of the Vascular Flora of Wisconsin Plants; 60 monographic studies on selected Wisconsin plant families; papers on corn evolution; books on lichens. Remarks: FAX: (608)262-7509. Staff: Ted Cochrane, Cur. III; Mark Wetter, Coll.Mgr.

★ 19583 ★
University of Wisconsin--Madison - Bureau of Audiovisual Instruction - Library (Aud-Vis)
1327 University Ave.
Box 2093   Phone: (608)262-1644
Madison, WI 53701   Bruce E. Dewey, Dir.
Staff: Prof 3; Other 15. **Special Collections:** Cooperative Extension Media Collection (agricultural and home economics extension programs; 1200 titles of videotapes and slide/tape sets). **Holdings:** 12,000 prints of video cassettes and 16mm motion picture films (7000 titles). **Services:** Library open to the public. **Automated Operations:** Computerized cataloging, acquisitions, and circulation. **Networks/Consortia:** Member of Consortium of College and University Media Centers (CCUMC). **Special Catalogs:** Bound book catalog, every 2-3 years; interim catalog, annual; special catalogs and lists, irregular. **Remarks:** Maintained by University of Wisconsin Extension. **Remarks:** FAX: (608)262-7568.

★ 19584 ★
University of Wisconsin--Madison - Cast Metals Laboratory - Library (Sci-Engr)
1509 University Ave.   Phone: (608)262-2562
Madison, WI 53706   Prof. Carl R. Loper, Hd., Lab.
Founded: 1946. **Staff:** 5. **Subjects:** Cast metals technology. **Holdings:** 5000 volumes; technical reports. **Subscriptions:** 27 journals and other serials. **Services:** Library not open to the public. **Remarks:** FAX: (608)262-6707; (608)262-8353.

★ 19585 ★
University of Wisconsin--Madison - Center for Demography - Library (Soc Sci)
4457 Social Science Bldg.
1180 Observatory Dr.   Phone: (608)262-2182
Madison, WI 53706   Ruth Sandor, Dir.
Founded: 1962. **Staff:** Prof 1; Other 1. **Subjects:** Demography. **Holdings:** 10,000 books; 200 bound periodical volumes; 200 U.S. census reports; international population censuses, 1945-1967, on microfilm; reprints; documents. **Subscriptions:** 200 journals and other serials. **Services:** Library open to the public with restrictions. **Computerized Information Services:** Internal database; BITNET (electronic mail service). **Networks/Consortia:** Member of APLIC International Census Network. **Publications:** Acquisition List, monthly - free upon request; List of Periodical Holdings. **Remarks:** FAX: (608)262-8400. Electronic mail address(es): SANDOR@WISCSSC (BITNET).

★ 19586 ★
University of Wisconsin--Madison - Center for Health Sciences Libraries (Med)
1305 Linden Dr.   Phone: (608)262-6594
Madison, WI 53706-1593   Virginia Holtz, Dir.
Staff: Prof 17; Other 20. **Subjects:** Health sciences and health care administration. **Special Collections:** History of medicine (15,000 volumes). **Holdings:** 121,400 books; 124,600 bound periodical volumes; 5100 AV programs; 3660 pamphlets and government documents. **Subscriptions:** 4000 journals and other serials. **Services:** Interlibrary loan; copying; SDI; center open to the public. **Automated Operations:** Computerized cataloging, acquisitions, and serials. **Computerized Information Services:** MEDLINE, BRS Information Technologies, TOXLINE; internal database; CD-ROMs; InterNet (electronic mail service). Performs searches on fee basis. **Networks/Consortia:** Member of National Network of Libraries of Medicine - Greater Midwest Region, Wisconsin Interlibrary Services (WILS). **Remarks:** FAX: (608)262-4732. Electronic mail address(es): MEDLIB@MACC.WISC.EDU (InterNet). The Center for Health Sciences Libraries includes the holdings of the William S. Middleton Health Sciences Library at the above address and the Weston Clinical Science Center Library, 600 Highland Ave., Rm. J5/120, Madison, WI 53792-1642. **Staff:** Phyllis Kauffman, Hist.Coll.Libn.; Patricia Wilcox, Weston Coord.; Dorothy Kanter, Coll.Org.Coord.; Judith Hathway, Cat.; Terrence Jones, Cat.; Susan Kirkbride, Hd.Ref.; Cheryl Becker, Ref.Libn.; Blanche Singer, Ref.Libn.; Diana Slater, Assoc.Dir.; Nancy Greene, Cat.; Michele Jacques, Ref.Libn. - Weston; Josephine Crawford, Automation Mgr.; Jacqueline Pratt, Info.Serv.Coord.; Mary Jane Scherdin, Coll.Acc.Coord.; Ann Boyer, Ref.Libn.; Michael Clark, Network Mgr.

★ 19587 ★
University of Wisconsin--Madison - Center for Limnology - Reading Room (Biol Sci)
680 N. Park   Phone: (608)262-4439
Madison, WI 53706   Lynn McElmurry, Libn.
Staff: Prof 1. **Subjects:** Limnology, freshwater ecology, zoology, fishes, oceanography, environmental studies. **Holdings:** 2500 books; 550 bound periodical volumes; 21,000 reprints; 10,000 government documents; 100 microfiche; 300 unbound volumes of journals. **Subscriptions:** 45 journals and other serials. **Services:** Library open to the public for reference use only. **Automated Operations:** Computerized cataloging. **Remarks:** Alternate telephone number(s): 262-2840. **Staff:** Cynthia Robinson, Libn.

University of Wisconsin--Madison - Cereal Crops Research Unit
See: **U.S.D.A. - Agricultural Research Service - Cereal Crops Research Unit** (17180)

★ 19588 ★
University of Wisconsin--Madison - Chemistry Library (Sci-Engr)
Chemistry Bldg.   Phone: (608)262-2942
Madison, WI 53706   Kendall Rouse, Hd.
Founded: 1947. **Staff:** Prof 2; Other 1. **Subjects:** Chemistry - analytical, inorganic, organic, physical, theoretical. **Holdings:** 15,247 books; 24,409 bound periodical volumes. **Subscriptions:** 400 journals and other serials. **Services:** Interlibrary loan; copying; library open to the public. **Computerized Information Services:** Chemical Abstracts Service (CAS), Institute for Scientific Information (ISI); InterNet (electronic mail service). Performs searches on fee basis. **Publications:** New Acquisitions List, monthly. **Remarks:** FAX: (608)262-9002. Electronic mail address(es): KROUSE@MACC.WISC.EDU (InterNet). **Staff:** Gloria Kriewall, Asst.Libn.

★ 19589 ★
University of Wisconsin--Madison - Clinical Research Laboratories - Thorngate Library (Med)
Clinical Science Center, Rm. B4/257
600 Highland Ave.   Phone: (608)263-7507
Madison, WI 53792   Russell Tomar, Div.Dir.
Subjects: Clinical laboratories - instrument design and applications, test development and applications, quality control techniques, computer system design, clinical evaluation of cancer markers. **Holdings:** 450 books. **Subscriptions:** 80 journals and other serials. **Services:** Library not open to the public.

★ 19590 ★
University of Wisconsin--Madison - Cooperative Children's Book Center (CCBC) (Educ)
Helen C. White Hall, Rm. 4290
600 N. Park St.   Phone: (608)263-3720
Madison, WI 53706   Ginny Moore Kruse, Dir.
Founded: 1963. **Staff:** Prof 3; Other 12. **Subjects:** Children's and young adult literature - current trade titles, selected and recommended titles in print, 19th and early 20th century titles; books by Wisconsin authors and illustrators; books by and about people of color; publishing of children's and young adult books; intellectual freedom and book censorship; book reviewing and evaluation; book illustration; biography; children's and young adult literature awards and distinctions. **Special Collections:** Mother Goose Collection (80 titles); Alternative Press Children's Books Collection (1000 titles); Newbery and Caldecott Medal books, including first printings and significant editions; historical and contemporary children's books by Wisconsin authors and illustrators; historical and contemporary pop-up books; winners of the Mildred L. Batchelder Book Award for translated books and of the Coretta Scott King Book Awards for books by Black authors and artists. **Holdings:** 25,000 volumes; 12 VF drawers; manuscripts. **Subscriptions:** 60 journals; 26 newsletters. **Services:** Offers lectures, workshops, conferences, speeches, courses, and special events; open to adult public for reference use only. **Computerized Information Services:** WISCAT (internal database). **Publications:** CCBC Choices, annual - free to Wisconsin residents and for sale to nonresidents; bibliographies - free to Wisconsin residents and for sale to nonresidents; The Book in a Technological Society, 1986; A Directory of Alternative Press Publishers of Children's Books (4th edition, 1992) - for sale; Multicultural Literature for Children and Young Adults (Rev.ed., 1991) - for sale. **Remarks:** Supported by the Wisconsin Department of Public Instruction through the Division for Library Services and by the University of Wisconsin, Madison through the School of Education. Alternate telephone number(s): 263-3721; 262-9503. FAX: (608)262-4933. **Staff:** Kathleen T. Horning, Spec.Coll.Coord.; Merri Lindgren, Libn.

★19591★
University of Wisconsin--Madison - Criminal Justice Reference &
  Information Center (Law, Soc Sci)
L140 Law Library   Phone: (608)262-1499
Madison, WI 53706   Sue L. Center, Asst.Dir.
Founded: 1969. **Staff:** Prof 2; Other 3. **Subjects:** Criminal justice system,
police science, corrections, drug abuse, delinquency, alcoholism. **Special**
Collections: Penal Press Publications. **Holdings:** 22,000 volumes.
Subscriptions: 200 journals and other serials. **Services:** Interlibrary loan;
copying; center open to the public with restrictions. **Publications:** Current
Criminal Justice Literature, bimonthly - to agencies in Wisconsin. **Remarks:**
FAX: (608)262-2775. **Staff:** Virginia Meier, Libn.

★19592★
University of Wisconsin--Madison - Data and Program Library Service
  (Info Sci)
3308 Social Science Bldg.   Phone: (608)262-7962
Madison, WI 53706   Laura A. Guy, Hd.
Founded: 1966. **Staff:** Prof 2. **Subjects:** Political science, sociology,
economics, history, census/demography. **Special Collections:** Slave trade to
the Americas; Florentine census and property survey of 1428; American
fertility surveys; occupational and social mobility. **Holdings:** 300 books;
3500 data files; 80 bound periodical volumes; 1750 codebooks for data; 70
guides to data archival holdings; 2000 magnetic tapes. **Subscriptions:** 32
journals and other serials. **Services:** Interlibrary loan; copying; service open
to the public. **Computerized Information Services:** BITNET (electronic mail
service). **Publications:** Directory of the Machine Readable Data and
Program Holdings of the Data and Program Library Service. **Remarks:**
Electronic mail address(es): GUY@WISCMACC (BITNET). **Staff:** Patrick
Lampani; Lu Chou.

★19593★
University of Wisconsin--Madison - Department of Psychiatry - Lithium
  Information Center (Med)
600 Highland Ave.   Phone: (608)263-6171
Madison, WI 53792   Margaret G. Baudhuin, Libn./Info.Spec.
Founded: 1975. **Staff:** Prof 5; Other 3. **Subjects:** Medical uses of lithium.
Holdings: 20,000 articles, books, abstracts, miscellaneous items stored
online. **Services:** Copying; SDI; center open to the public; direct access to
holdings through a compatible computer terminal. **Automated Operations:**
Computerized cataloging. **Computerized Information Services:** Lithium
Library. Performs searches on fee basis. **Publications:** Lithium and Manic
Depression: A Guide; Carbamazepine and Manic Depression : A Guide;
Lithium Encyclopedia for Clinical Practice - all for sale. **Staff:** James W.
Jefferson, M.D., Co-Dir.; John H. Greist, M.D., Co-Dir.; Bette L. Hartley,
Libn.

★19594★
University of Wisconsin--Madison - Department of Rural Sociology -
  Applied Population Laboratory - Library (Soc Sci)
Agriculture Hall, Rm. 316   Phone: (608)262-1515
Madison, WI 53706   Karen Morgan, Adm.Asst.
Staff: 1. **Subjects:** Demographic material on fertility, mortality, migration.
Holdings: 2000 books; 24 VF drawers of pamphlets. **Services:** Copying;
library open to the public by appointment. **Computerized Information**
Services: WISPOP (internal database).

★19595★
University of Wisconsin--Madison - Department of Urban and Regional
  Planning - Graduate Research Center (Plan)
Music Hall
925 Bascom Mall   Phone: (608)262-1004
Madison, WI 53706   Brenda Pierce, Libn.
Founded: 1965. **Staff:** Prof 1. **Subjects:** Urban and regional planning, land
and water resources, zoning, social services planning, planning in developing
areas. **Holdings:** 7000 books; 25,000 planning reports and documents; 100
theses and dissertations. **Subscriptions:** 120 journals and other serials.
Services: Interlibrary loan; copying; center open to the public.

★19596★
University of Wisconsin--Madison - East Asian Collection (Area-Ethnic,
  Rel-Phil)
728 State St.   Phone: (608)262-0344
Madison, WI 53706   Chester Wang, Bibliog.
Founded: 1964. **Staff:** Prof 4; Other 5. **Subjects:** Chinese and Japanese
literature, history, and sociology. **Special Collections:** Buddhist studies.
Holdings: 150,000 books; 2000 bound periodical volumes. **Subscriptions:**
300 journals and other serials; 16 newspapers. **Services:** Interlibrary loan;
collection open to the public. **Automated Operations:** Computerized
cataloging and serials.

★19597★
University of Wisconsin--Madison - F.B. Power Pharmaceutical Library
  (Med)
School of Pharmacy
425 N. Charter St.   Phone: (608)262-2894
Madison, WI 53706   Dolores Nemec, Libn.
Founded: 1883. **Staff:** Prof 1; Other 1. **Subjects:** Pharmacy and related
subjects. **Special Collections:** Catalogs of drugs and pharmaceutical
equipment, 1860 to present; Kremers Reference Files, 1870 to present
(pamphlets; correspondence; manuscripts; pictures; broadsides; clippings);
Iowa Drug Information Service. **Holdings:** 14,040 books; 19,597 bound
periodical volumes. **Subscriptions:** 957 journals and other serials. **Services:**
Interlibrary loan; copying; library open to the public for reference use only.
Computerized Information Services: CD-ROMs.

★19598★
University of Wisconsin--Madison - Geography Library (Geog-Map)
280 Science Hall   Phone: (608)262-1706
Madison, WI 53706   Miriam E. Kerndt, Hd.
Staff: Prof 1; Other 1. **Subjects:** Geography, cartography. **Holdings:** 50,000
volumes. **Subscriptions:** 600 journals and other serials. **Services:** Interlibrary
loan; library open to the public. **Automated Operations:** Computerized
cataloging. **Computerized Information Services:** DIALOG Information
Services; InterNet, BITNET (electronic mail services). **Networks/**
Consortia: Member of Wisconsin Interlibrary Services (WILS).
Publications: Acquisitions list, 6/yr. **Remarks:** Electronic mail address(es):
Kerndt@VMS.MACC.WISC.EDU (InterNet); KERNDT@WISCMACC
(BITNET).

★19599★
University of Wisconsin--Madison - Geology-Geophysics Library (Sci-
  Engr)
440 Weeks Hall
1215 W. Dayton St.   Phone: (608)262-8956
Madison, WI 53706   Marie Dvorzak, Libn.
Founded: 1974. **Staff:** Prof 1; Other 1. **Subjects:** Geology, geophysics,
oceanography. **Holdings:** 17,000 books; 34,000 bound periodical volumes;
700 department theses, 1970 to present; 2300 maps. **Subscriptions:** 1250
journals and other serials. **Services:** Interlibrary loan; copying; library open
to the public. **Automated Operations:** Computerized public access catalog,
acquisitions, and serials. **Computerized Information Services:** DIALOG
Information Services; BITNET, InterNet (electronic mail services).
Publications: Acquisitions list, monthly. **Remarks:** FAX: (608)262-0693.
Electronic mail address(es): GEOLIB@WISCMACC (BITNET);
GEOLIB@MACC.WISC.EDU (InterNet).

★19600★
University of Wisconsin--Madison - Institute for Research in the
  Humanities - Library (Hum)
Old Observatory
1401 Observatory Dr.   Phone: (608)262-3855
Madison, WI 53706   Loretta Freiling, Prog.Asst.
Founded: 1959. **Staff:** 1. **Subjects:** Humanities - Ancient to Renaissance.
Special Collections: Works by Benedetto Croce (500 volumes). **Holdings:**
1100 books. **Subscriptions:** 50 journals and other serials. **Services:** Library
not open to the public.

★19601★
University of Wisconsin--Madison - Kohler Art Library (Art)
General Library System
800 University Ave.   Phone: (608)263-2256
Madison, WI 53706   William C. Bunce, Dir. & Hd.Libn.
Founded: 1970. **Staff:** Prof 1; Other 2. **Subjects:** Art, architecture, decorative arts, photography. **Holdings:** 108,000 volumes; 28 VF drawers of exhibition catalogs; theses and dissertations; 16,000 microforms. **Subscriptions:** 600 journals and other serials. **Services:** Interlibrary loan; copying; library open to the public with restrictions on circulation. **Automated Operations:** Computerized public access catalog, cataloging, and acquisitions. **Computerized Information Services:** DIALOG Information Services, BRS Information Technologies, WILSONLINE; BITNET, IPNET (electronic mail services). Performs searches on fee basis. **Remarks:** Alternate telephone number(s): 263-2257; 263-2258. Electronic mail address(es): BUNCE@VMS.MACC.WISC.EDU (BITNET).

★19602★
University of Wisconsin--Madison - Land Tenure Center - Library (Agri)
434 Steenbock Memorial Library
550 Babcock Dr.   Phone: (608)262-1240
Madison, WI 53706   Beverly R. Phillips, Sr.Libn.
Founded: 1962. **Staff:** Prof 1.5; Other 2.5. **Subjects:** Land tenure, agrarian reform, agricultural economics, Latin America, Asia, Africa, rural development, developing countries. **Holdings:** 30,000 books; 1200 bound periodical volumes; 36,000 unbound reports, manuscripts, clippings, pamphlets, documents; 8 VF drawers of microfilm and microfiche; 100 titles of Economic Development Plans; 250 titles of dissertations. **Subscriptions:** 350 journals and other serials. **Services:** Interlibrary loan; copying; library open to the public. **Automated Operations:** Computerized cataloging. **Computerized Information Services:** OCLC; NLS (Network Library System; internal database); BITNET, InterNet (electronic mail services). **Publications:** Accessions List, bimonthly - free upon request. **Remarks:** FAX: (608)262-2141. Telex: 265452 Attn: Land Tenure. Electronic mail address(es): PHILLIPS@WISCMACC (BITNET); PHILLIPS@MACC.WISC.EDU (InterNet). **Staff:** Martha Jelinski, Assoc.Libn.

★19603★
University of Wisconsin--Madison - Law School Library (Law)
Madison, WI 53706   Phone: (608)262-1128
S. Blair Kauffman, Dir.
Founded: 1868. **Staff:** Prof 10; Other 8. **Subjects:** Law. **Special Collections:** Criminal justice; foreign law. **Holdings:** 300,000 volumes; 342,993 microforms. **Subscriptions:** 4453 serials; 20 newspapers. **Services:** Interlibrary loan; copying; library open to the public. **Automated Operations:** Computerized cataloging, acquisitions, and serials (NOTIS). **Computerized Information Services:** OCLC, LEXIS, WESTLAW; VAX Mail (electronic mail service). **Networks/Consortia:** Member of Wisconsin Interlibrary Services (WILS). **Publications:** Selected Recent Acquisitions; Current Criminal Justice Literature. **Remarks:** FAX: (608)262-2775. **Staff:** Nancy Paul, Asst.Dir., Tech.Serv.; Cindy May, Cat.Libn.; Gloria Holz, Circ./Reserve Libn.; William Ebbott, Asst.Dir., Info.Serv.; Telle Zoller, Foreign Law Libn.; Virginia Meier, Cat.Libn.; Barbara Meyer, Pub.Serv.Libn.; Sue Center, Asst.Dir., Pub.Serv.; Cheryl O'Connor, Outreach Libn.; Rick Hendricks, Automation Libn.; Carl Christenson, Comp. Lab Dir.

University of Wisconsin--Madison - Law School Library - Criminal Justice Reference & Information Center
See: **University of Wisconsin--Madison - Criminal Justice Reference & Information Center** (19591)

★19604★
University of Wisconsin--Madison - Mathematics Library (Sci-Engr, Comp Sci)
B224 Van Vleck Hall
480 Lincoln Drive   Phone: (608)262-3596
Madison, WI 53706   Shirley Shen, Academic Libn.-Spec.
Founded: 1938. **Staff:** Prof 1. **Subjects:** Mathematics, mathematical statistics, computer sciences, mathematical physics. **Holdings:** 42,340 volumes. **Subscriptions:** 346 journals and other serials. **Services:** Interlibrary loan; copying. **Automated Operations:** Computerized public access catalog, cataloging, acquisitions, and serials. **Computerized Information Services:** DIALOG Information Services, STN International; CD-ROMs; InterNet (electronic mail service). **Publications:** Acquisitions list. **Remarks:** Electronic mail address(es): SHEN@MACC.WISC.EDU (InterNet). **Staff:** Alinda Nelson, Act.Libn.

★19605★
University of Wisconsin--Madison - McArdle Laboratory for Cancer Research - Library (Med)
Madison, WI 53706   Phone: (608)262-2177
Ilse L. Riegel
Founded: 1955. **Subjects:** Cancer, molecular biology, virology. **Holdings:** 500 books; 2000 bound periodical volumes. **Subscriptions:** 100 journals and other serials. **Services:** Interlibrary loan; library open to the public at librarian's discretion. **Remarks:** FAX: (608)262-2824.

★19606★
University of Wisconsin--Madison - Medical Physics Department - Library (Med)
1530 Medical Sciences Center
1300 University Ave.   Phone: (608)262-0878
Madison, WI 53706   Perry Pickhardt, Libn.
Staff: Prof 1. **Subjects:** Medical physics, biomedical engineering, physics, radiology. **Holdings:** 2500 books; 835 bound periodical volumes; 123 audio cassettes. **Subscriptions:** 60 journals and other serials. **Services:** Copying; library open to the public for reference use only. **Automated Operations:** Computerized public access catalog.

★19607★
University of Wisconsin--Madison - Memorial Library - Department of Special Collections (Rare Book, Hum, Publ)
728 State St.   Phone: (608)262-3243
Madison, WI 53706   John Tedeschi, Cur.
Founded: 1946. **Staff:** Prof 2; Other 4. **Subjects:** History of science, 19th and 20th century American literature, English literature, Socialistica, Russian history, 16th-18th century European history and literature, private press books. **Special Collections:** Thordarson Collection (history of science; 5000 volumes); Duveen Collection (history of chemistry; 2900 titles); Cole Collection (history of chemistry; 700 titles); Bassett-Brownell Mark Twain Collection (500 volumes; periodicals; manuscripts); Sukov Collection of Little Magazines (5500 titles); Russian Underground Collection (1800 items); French pamphlet collection (2500 titles); Cairns Collection (American women writers; 4100 titles); Tank Collection (Dutch culture, 16th-18th centuries; 4800 volumes); medieval manuscripts. **Holdings:** 108,000 books; 38,800 periodical volumes. **Subscriptions:** 1200 journals and other serials. **Services:** Department open to the public with restrictions. **Computerized Information Services:** Internal database. **Special Catalogs:** Mongolian and Tibetan Block Books; Irish Manuscripts; Duveen Collection; Russian Underground; Medical and Pharmaceutical Books; Cairns Collection; French Political Pamphlets; Mazarinades; Papyrii; exhibit catalogs, irregular. **Special Indexes:** Chronological and geographical files (book and card); literature in translation and interview indexes. **Remarks:** FAX: (608)262-4648.

★19608★
University of Wisconsin--Madison - Memorial Library - South Asian Collections (Area-Ethnic)
728 State St.   Phone: (608)262-0767
Madison, WI 53706   Jack C. Wells, South Asian Bibliog.
Founded: 1959. **Subjects:** South Asia - social sciences, humanities. **Holdings:** 250,000 books. **Subscriptions:** 2300 journals and other serials. **Services:** Interlibrary loan; copying; library open to the public. **Remarks:** Holdings are in languages of the area (Hindi, Urdu, Telagu, Tamil, and Sanskrit), as well as in English.

★19609★
University of Wisconsin--Madison - Memorial Library - Southeast Asian Collections (Area-Ethnic)
728 State St.   Phone: (608)262-5493
Madison, WI 53706   Carol Mitchell, Southeast Asian Bibliog.
Subjects: Southeast Asia - general, culture, literature. **Special Collections:** Modern Southeast Asian Culture Collections (political and labor tracts; popular literature; religious pamphlets; videotapes; audiocassettes); Southeast Asian Video Archive. **Holdings:** 70,000 books; 600 videotapes; **Subscriptions:** 800 journals and other serials; 7 newspapers. **Services:** Interlibrary loan. **Remarks:** FAX: (608)265-2754. Collections are associated with the University's Center for Southeast Asian Studies. Over half of the holdings are in languages of the area (Indonesian/Malay, Thai, Tagalog, and Vietnamese); other holdings are in colonial languages of the area (Dutch, French, Spanish, and Japanese).

★ 19610 ★
University of Wisconsin--Madison - Mills Music Library (Mus)
B162 Memorial Library
728 State St.   Phone: (608)263-1884
Madison, WI 53706   Geraldine Laudati, Dir.
Staff: Prof 3; Other 7. **Subjects:** Music. **Special Collections:** American music before 1900 (3000 items); Wisconsin Music Archives (2000 items); Stratman-Thomas Collection (Wisconsin folk songs); Civil War band books; Tams-Witmark Collection (American musical theater). **Holdings:** 78,000 scores; 35,000 volumes; 120,000 recordings; 800 reels of microfilm. **Subscriptions:** 418 journals and other serials. **Services:** Interlibrary loan; library open to the public for reference use only. **Automated Operations:** Computerized cataloging. **Special Catalogs:** Catalog of American music collection (card). **Special Indexes:** Indexes to Stratman-Thomas Collection and Tams-Witmark Collection (online).

★ 19611 ★
University of Wisconsin--Madison - Nieman-Grant Journalism Reading Room (Info Sci)
2130 Vilas Communication Hall
821 University Ave.   Phone: (608)263-3387
Madison, WI 53706   G. Marcille Frederick, Hd.Libn.
Founded: 1953. **Staff:** Prof 1. **Subjects:** Journalism and reporting, mass communications methodology and research, public relations, international communications, advertising, photojournalism and photography. **Special Collections:** Thayer Law of Mass Communications Collection (300). **Holdings:** 3500 books; 820 bound periodical volumes; 4 VF drawers of pamphlets and clippings. **Subscriptions:** 125 journals and other serials; 70 newspapers. **Services:** Room open to the public. **Computerized Information Services:** Network Library System (NLS; internal database). **Remarks:** Reading Room is part of the School of Journalism and Mass Communications.

★ 19612 ★
University of Wisconsin--Madison - Physics Library (Sci-Engr)
1150 University Ave.   Phone: (608)262-9500
Madison, WI 53706   Kerry L. Kresse, Assoc. Academic Libn.
Founded: 1974. **Staff:** Prof 1; Other 3. **Subjects:** Experimental and theoretical physics. **Holdings:** 16,000 books; 22,000 bound periodical volumes; 6000 microforms. **Subscriptions:** 450 journals and other serials. **Services:** Interlibrary loan; library open to the public. **Automated Operations:** Computerized public access catalog. **Computerized Information Services:** DIALOG Information Services, STN International; BITNET, DDN Network Information Center; BITNET and Decnet (electronic mail services). Performs searches on fee basis. **Publications:** Acquisitions List and Information Letter, monthly. **Remarks:** Electronic mail address(es): PHYSLIB@WISCMACC (BITNET); WIRCS2::PHYSLIB (Decnet).

★ 19613 ★
University of Wisconsin--Madison - Plant Pathology Memorial Library (Biol Sci)
1630 Linden Dr.   Phone: (608)262-8698
Madison, WI 53706   Patricia J. Herrling, Libn.
Founded: 1911. **Staff:** Prof 1; Other 2. **Subjects:** Phytopathology, plant virology, plant physiology. **Special Collections:** Johnson-Hoggan Memorial Collection of Plant Virus Literature. **Holdings:** 3500 books; 2500 bound periodical volumes; 65,000 reprints; 400 theses and dissertations. **Subscriptions:** 90 journals and other serials. **Services:** Interlibrary loan; library open to the public. **Automated Operations:** Computerized public access catalog. **Computerized Information Services:** DIALOG Information Services; internal databases; VAX Mail (electronic mail service). Performs searches on fee basis. **Special Catalogs:** Catalogs of abstracts of virus and reprint materials in all branches of plant pathology (card). **Remarks:** FAX: (608)263-2626. Electronic mail address(es): PHerrling@UMS.MACC.WISC.EDU. (VAX Mail).

★ 19614 ★
University of Wisconsin--Madison - Poultry Science Department - Halpin Memorial Library (Agri)
Animal Science Bldg., Rm. 214
1675 Observatory Dr.   Phone: (608)262-1243
Madison, WI 53706   Louis C. Arrington, Prof.
Founded: 1960. **Staff:** 2. **Subjects:** Poultry science. **Special Collections:** Radford Collection of poultry literature. **Holdings:** 840 books; 600 bound periodical volumes; 12,000 reprints and pamphlets. **Subscriptions:** 30 journals and other serials. **Services:** Library open to the public.

★ 19615 ★
University of Wisconsin--Madison - School of Education - Instructional Materials Center (Educ)
Teacher Education Bldg.
225 N. Mills St.   Phone: (608)263-4750
Madison, WI 53706   Jo Ann Carr, Dir.
Founded: 1938. **Staff:** Prof 4; Other 13. **Subjects:** Education, print and nonprint instructional materials, children's literature. **Special Collections:** Standardized tests; curriculum guides on microfiche. **Holdings:** 55,000 books and AV programs; 1460 bound periodical volumes; microfiche; ERIC microfiche with indexes. **Subscriptions:** 300 journals and other serials. **Services:** Interlibrary loan; copying; center open to the public with borrower's card. **Automated Operations:** Computerized cataloging. **Computerized Information Services:** CD-ROM (ERIC, SchoolMatch, AV Online); NLS (Network Library System; internal database); Email (electronic mail service). **Networks/Consortia:** Member of Wisconsin Interlibrary Services (WILS). **Publications:** Bibliographies on topics of current interest in education. **Remarks:** Alternate telephone number(s): 263-4755. **Staff:** Michael Cohen, Tech.Serv.Libn.; Kalleen Mortenson, Access Serv.Libn.

★ 19616 ★
University of Wisconsin--Madison - School of Library and Information Studies - Laboratory Library (Info Sci)
600 N. Park St.   Phone: (608)263-2960
Madison, WI 53706   Louise S. Robbins, Asst.Prof. & Dir.
Founded: 1906. **Staff:** Prof 2; Other 3. **Subjects:** Library science, information science, children's literature, young adult literature. **Holdings:** 60,000 books; 5000 bound periodical volumes; 8800 pamphlets; 1800 microforms; 2500 AV programs. **Subscriptions:** 550 journals and other serials. **Services:** Interlibrary loan; copying; library open to the public. **Automated Operations:** Computerized cataloging and circulation. **Computerized Information Services:** CD-ROMs (Library Literature, Library and Information Science Abstracts, ERIC); NLS (Network Library System; internal database); InterNet (electronic mail service). **Networks/Consortia:** Member of Wisconsin Interlibrary Services (WILS). **Remarks:** FAX: (608)263-4849. Electronic mail address(es): lrobbins@wisc.macc.edu (international). **Staff:** Peggy Green, Asst.Libn.; Antonia Samek, Proj.Asst.; Deena Karadsheh, Proj.Asst.; Kathleen Buller, Lib.Serv.Asst. 3.

University of Wisconsin--Madison - School of Social Work - Video Resource Library
See: **University of West Florida - Human Resource Videotape Library** (19549)

★ 19617 ★
University of Wisconsin--Madison - School of Social Work - Virginia L. Franks Memorial Library (Soc Sci)
425 Henry Mall, Rm. 230   Phone: (608)263-3840
Madison, WI 53706   Phyllis Kimbrough, Libn.
Founded: 1972. **Staff:** Prof 1; Other 5. **Subjects:** Social work - education and administration, psychotherapy and behavior modification, corrections, alcoholism and drug abuse, adoption and foster care. **Special Collections:** Unpublished theses and research projects (500); social gerontology books. **Holdings:** 13,073 books; 2130 bound periodical volumes; VF items; pamphlets; AV programs. **Subscriptions:** 174 journals and other serials. **Services:** Interlibrary loan; copying; library open to the public with restrictions. **Publications:** Monthly acquisitions list; current periodicals list.

★ 19618 ★
University of Wisconsin--Madison - Seminary of Medieval Spanish Studies - Library (Area-Ethnic)
1130 Van Hise Hall   Phone: (608)262-2529
Madison, WI 53706   Lloyd A. Kasten, Prof.
Founded: 1931. **Subjects:** Alfonso X of Castille, Old Spanish and Aragonese, Old Spanish literature. **Special Collections:** Photostatic reproduction of works of Alfonso X; vocabulary files of works of Alfonso X and Juan Fernandez de Heredia; Old Spanish dictionaries. **Holdings:** 8500 books; 550 bound periodical volumes; 274 volumes of photostats; 4700 pamphlets and reprints; 38 drawers of notes and research materials; 50 dissertations; 450 reels of microfilm. **Subscriptions:** 25 journals and other serials. **Services:** Copying; library open to the public with restrictions.

★19619★

University of Wisconsin--Madison - Steenbock Memorial Library (Agri, Biol Sci)
550 Babcock Dr.
Madison, WI 53706
Phone: (608)262-9990
Kenneth Frazier, Dir.
Founded: 1904. **Staff:** Prof 10; Other 9. **Subjects:** Life sciences, agriculture, veterinary medicine, biotechnology, food and dairy science, family studies, consumer science, agricultural economics. **Special Collections:** Miller Beekeeping Collection; Swanton Cooperative Collection; Levitan Cookbook Collection. **Holdings:** 111,914 monographs; 64,342 bound periodical volumes; 442,079 documents; 62,915 microforms; 628 AV programs. **Subscriptions:** 2202 journals and other serials. **Services:** Interlibrary loan; copying; document delivery; library open to the public. **Automated Operations:** Computerized cataloging, acquisitions, circulation, and serials. **Computerized Information Services:** OCLC, DIALOG Information Services, BRS Information Technologies, STN International; CD-ROM. **Networks/Consortia:** Member of Center for Research Libraries (CRL), Wisconsin Interlibrary Services (WILS). **Publications:** New Book List, monthly; library guide series, irregular. **Remarks:** FAX: (608)263-3221. **Staff:** Jean Gilbertson, Asst.Dir.; Lois Komai, Coll.Dev.; Robert Sessions, Ref.Libn./Vet.Med.; Carole McEvoy, Hd., Tech.Serv.; Barbara Hamel, Ref.Libn.; Allen Wenzel, Comp. Applications. Barbara Lazewski, Ref.Libn.; John Koch, Ref.Libn.; Patricia Herrling, Ref.Libn.; Gretchen Farwell, Circ.Libn.

★19620★

University of Wisconsin--Madison - Study in Health Care Fiscal Management Organization and Control - Library
1155 Observatory Dr., Rm. 301
Madison, WI 53706
Founded: 1972. **Subjects:** Health care fiscal management, financial management, accounting and internal auditing, sources of funding, reimbursement and related subjects, information systems. **Holdings:** 825 books; 17 bound periodical volumes. **Remarks:** Currently inactive.

★19621★

University of Wisconsin--Madison - Theoretical Chemistry Institute - Theoretical Chemistry Collection (Sci-Engr)
8309 Chemistry Bldg.
1101 University Ave.
Madison, WI 53706
Phone: (608)262-1511
Frank Weinhold, Dir.
Founded: 1962. **Staff:** 1. **Subjects:** Theoretical chemistry, physics, mathematics. **Holdings:** Figures not available. **Services:** Collection not open to the public.

★19622★

University of Wisconsin--Madison - Trace R & D Center - Information Area (Soc Sci)
S157 Waisman Center
1500 Highland Ave.
Madison, WI 53705-2280
Phone: (608)262-6966
Peter Borden, Proj.Dir.
Founded: 1980. **Staff:** Prof 1; Other 1. **Subjects:** Nonvocal communication, computer access for the disabled, rehabilitation engineering, software/hardware for the disabled. **Holdings:** 12 linear feet and 2 filing cabinets of research materials; directories; newsletters; conference proceedings. **Subscriptions:** 10 journals and other serials. **Services:** Library open to the public for reference use only. **Computerized Information Services:** ABLEDATA (CD-ROM). **Publications:** Trace ResourceBook: Assistive Technologies for Communication, Control and Computer Access (1991). **Special Catalogs:** Resource lists. **Remarks:** TDD: (608)263-5408.

★19623★

University of Wisconsin--Madison - University Center for Cooperatives - Cooperative Library (Bus-Fin)
Lowell Hall, Rm. 526
610 Langdon St.
Madison, WI 53703
Phone: (608)262-3981
Ann Hayt, Faculty Coord.
Founded: 1962. **Staff:** 1. **Subjects:** Cooperatives. **Special Collections:** Rochdale Collection (900 early U.S. and English co-op books, European cooperative federations' annual reports); Shaars Collection; Ellerbe Collection; NCBA Archives. **Holdings:** 7000 books; 16 VF drawers of Works Progress Administration (WPA) research on cooperatives; 53 VF drawers of information on all aspects and types of cooperatives worldwide. **Subscriptions:** 350 journals and other serials. **Services:** Interlibrary loan; copying; library open to the public with restrictions. **Publications:** Cooperative Bibliography, 1981. **Remarks:** FAX: (608)262-3251. **Staff:** Abdulla K. Badsha, Libn.

★19624★

University of Wisconsin--Madison - Washburn Observatory - Woodman Astronomical Library (Sci-Engr)
6521 Sterling Hall
475 N. Charter St.
Madison, WI 53706
Phone: (608)262-1320
Pam O'Hara, Libn.
Founded: 1882. **Staff:** Prof 1. **Subjects:** Astronomy, astrophysics. **Special Collections:** Noncommercial astronomical (Society and/or Observatory) publications (800 titles). **Holdings:** 4590 books; 3342 bound periodical volumes; 3500 volumes of noncommercial serials; 4670 charts, plates, photographs; 1150 microfiche. **Subscriptions:** 71 journals and other serials. **Services:** Interlibrary loan; library open to the public. **Computerized Information Services:** InterNet (electronic mail service). **Networks/Consortia:** Member of Multitype Advisory Library Committee (MALC), Wisconsin Interlibrary Services (WILS). **Remarks:** Electronic mail address(es): ASTROLIB@VMS.MACC.WISC.EDU (InterNet).

★19625★

University of Wisconsin--Madison - Water Resources Center - Library (Env-Cons)
1975 Willow Dr.
Madison, WI 53706
Phone: (608)262-3069
JoAnn M. Savoy, Libn.
Founded: 1965. **Staff:** Prof 1; Other 1.5. **Subjects:** Water resources - pollution sources, abatement and control, waste water treatment, limnology, resources management, research and planning, groundwater. **Special Collections:** Eutrophication (7168 reprints and documents); Water Resources Economics Collection (800 reprints). **Holdings:** 25,000 books and technical reports. **Subscriptions:** 22 journals and other serials; 80 newsletters. **Services:** Interlibrary loan; library open to the public. **Automated Operations:** Computerized cataloging and acquisitions. **Computerized Information Services:** DIALOG Information Services, BRS Information Technologies; Current Contents on Diskette; CD-ROM (Selected Water Resources Abstracts); BITNET (electronic mail service). **Publications:** Monthly Acquisitions List - available upon request. **Remarks:** FAX: (608)262-0591. Electronic mail address(es): JOSAVOY@VMS.MACC.WISC.EDU (BITNET).

★19626★

University of Wisconsin--Madison - William A. Scott Business Library (Bus-Fin)
Bascom Hall
Madison, WI 53706
Phone: (608)262-5935
Michael G. Enyart, Dir.
Founded: 1955. **Staff:** Prof 1; Other 1. **Subjects:** Accounting, finance, management, marketing, real estate, insurance, international business. **Special Collections:** Corporate annual reports; Johnson Foundation Collection (productivity). **Holdings:** 20,000 books; 7000 periodical volumes; 104,037 microfiche; 298 reels of microfilm; 970 masters' papers. **Subscriptions:** 500 journals and other serials; 5 newspapers. **Services:** Interlibrary loan; copying; library open to the public. **Computerized Information Services:** CD-ROMs (ABI/INFORM, COMPACT DISCLOSURE, LASERDISCLOSURE). **Networks/Consortia:** Member of Wisconsin Interlibrary Services (WILS). **Remarks:** FAX: (608)262-9001.

★19627★

University of Wisconsin--Madison - Wisconsin Center for Film and Theater Research (Theater)
6040 Vilas Hall
821 University Ave.
Madison, WI 53706
Phone: (608)262-9706
Donald Crafton, Dir.
Founded: 1960. **Staff:** Prof 2; Other 3. **Subjects:** Film, television, theater, radio. **Holdings:** Over 300 manuscript collections of individuals and organizations in the performing arts, including scripts, correspondence, production and promotional materials, legal files, financial records; 15,000 films; 2 million photographs. The largest collection is the United Artists Corporation Collection which contains the corporate records of United Artists from its founding in 1919 through 1951, and includes: 1750 feature films from Warner Brothers, RKO, and Monogram film libraries with related manuscripts; 2000 episodes from the ZIV Library of Television Programs with related manuscripts; 1500 Vitaphone short subjects and 600 Warner and Popeye cartoons with related manuscripts. Other collections include the Rzhevsky Collection (150 post-war Soviet shorts and features) and Hong Kong produced martial arts films (50). **Services:** Copying and photoduplication of stills; center open to the public; original material does not circulate; film archive open to qualified researchers by appointment only. **Publications:** Brochure; guide to collections; feature film list. **Special Catalogs:** Detailed inventories for each processed collection. **Special Indexes:** Production title index for films, stills, and scripts (card). **Remarks:** FAX: (608)262-2150. **Staff:** Maxine Fleckner Ducey, Film Archv.; Ben Brewster, Asst.Dir.

★ 19628 ★
University of Wisconsin--Madison - Wisconsin Regional Primate Research Center - Primate Center Library (Biol Sci, Med)
1223 Capitol Ct.   Phone: (608)263-3512
Madison, WI 53715-1299   Lawrence Jacobsen, Hd.Libn.
Founded: 1973. **Staff:** Prof 2.5; Other 2. **Subjects:** Primatology, neurosciences, reproductive physiology, ethology/ecology, conservation, ethics. **Special Collections:** Primate vocalizations, videotapes, slides, and other nonprint media; Neurosciences Research Program Collection; rare books. **Holdings:** 5600 books; 12,400 bound periodical volumes; 500 unbound volumes; 16,000 topical reprints and bibliographies; 5000 AV programs; 100 masters' and Ph.D. theses. **Subscriptions:** 330 journals and other serials. **Services:** Interlibrary loan; copying; SDI; document delivery; library open to the public. **Automated Operations:** Computerized cataloging and serials. **Computerized Information Services:** MEDLINE, OCLC, BRS Information Technologies; PRIMATELINE, Network Library System (internal databases); PRIMATE-TALK (electronic mail-based forum). Performs searches on fee basis. **Networks/Consortia:** Member of Wisconsin Interlibrary Services (WILS). **Publications:** International Directory of Primatology, biannual; Primate Library Report: Audio-Visual Acquisitions, biennial. **Remarks:** FAX: (608)263-4031. **Staff:** Raymond Hamel, Spec.Coll.Libn.; JoAnne Brown, Tech.Serv.

★ 19629 ★
University of Wisconsin--Madison - Zoological Museum Library (Biol Sci)
L.E. Noland Bldg.
250 N. Mills St.   Phone: (608)262-3766
Madison, WI 53706   Frank A. Iwen, Cur.
Founded: 1887. **Staff:** Prof 1. **Subjects:** Ornithology, mammalogy, anthropology. **Special Collections:** John T. Emlen Reprint Collection; John T. Robinson Book and Reprint Collection. **Holdings:** 5000 volumes; 20,000 reprints; monographs; original field data. **Services:** Interlibrary loan; copying; library open to the public with restrictions. **Computerized Information Services:** BITNET (electronic mail service). **Remarks:** FAX: (608)262-5395. Electronic mail address(es): UWZM@WISCMACC (BITNET).

University of Wisconsin--Milwaukee - American Geographical Society Collection
See: **American Geographical Society Collection of the University of Wisconsin--Milwaukee - Golda Meir Library** (598)

★ 19630 ★
University of Wisconsin--Milwaukee - Center for Economic Education - Library (Educ)
Bolton Hall 824
P.O. Box 413
Milwaukee, WI 53201   Phone: (414)229-1310
                                            Dr. Leon M. Schur, Dir.
Founded: 1964. **Subjects:** Economic education. **Holdings:** 2000 volumes.

★ 19631 ★
University of Wisconsin--Milwaukee - Golda Meir Library - Albert Camus Archives (Rare Book)
2311 E. Hartford Ave.   Phone: (414)229-6119
Milwaukee, WI 53201   Robert F. Roeming
Staff: 1. **Subjects:** Albert Camus. **Holdings:** 20 VF drawers; 6 cases of books and reference materials; 175 reels of microfilm of dissertations and manuscripts; 24 card file drawers of investigators' notes and references to personal contacts abroad; newspapers edited by Camus and in which he was published. **Services:** Archives open to the public with restrictions. **Computerized Information Services:** Internal database. **Publications:** Camus: A Bibliography (9th edition), 1990 - free upon request. **Remarks:** FAX: (414)229-4380.

University of Wisconsin--Milwaukee - Golda Meir Library - Area Research Center
See: **University of Wisconsin--Milwaukee - Golda Meir Library - Milwaukee Urban Archives** (19634)

★ 19632 ★
University of Wisconsin--Milwaukee - Golda Meir Library - Curriculum Collection (Educ, Aud-Vis)
Box 604   Phone: (414)229-4074
Milwaukee, WI 53201   Mary Jo Aman, Educ.Libn.
Founded: 1956. **Staff:** Prof 1; Other 2. **Subjects:** Children's literature, elementary and secondary textbooks and AV media. **Special Collections:** Children's Literature and Textbook Historical Collection (1491). **Holdings:** 21,645 books; 526 bound periodical volumes; 1169 curriculum guides; 7438 K-12 textbooks; 1296 AV programs; 739 seminar papers; 248 tests; ERIC microfiche collection; 1296 kits; 572 phonograph records; 3552 pictures; 2674 slides; 352 magnetic tapes; 504 transparencies. **Subscriptions:** 31 journals and other serials. **Services:** Interlibrary loan; copying; collection open to the public under rules and regulations of the University Library. **Automated Operations:** Computerized cataloging. **Computerized Information Services:** CD-ROM (ERIC; available through Reference Department). **Networks/Consortia:** Member of Wisconsin Interlibrary Services (WILS), Library Council of Metropolitan Milwaukee, Inc. (LCOMM). **Remarks:** Alternate telephone number(s): (414)229-4493 (ILL Department). FAX: (414)229-4380.

★ 19633 ★
University of Wisconsin--Milwaukee - Golda Meir Library - George Hardie Aerospace Collection (Hist)
Box 604   Phone: (414)229-4345
Milwaukee, WI 53201   Ellen M. Murphy, Spec.Coll./Rare Bks.Libn.
Founded: 1987. **Staff:** Prof 1; Other .5. **Subjects:** History of aeronautics, military history. **Holdings:** 1559 books. **Services:** Copying; collection open to the public. **Automated Operations:** Computerized public access catalog. **Remarks:** FAX: (414)229-4380.

★ 19634 ★
University of Wisconsin--Milwaukee - Golda Meir Library - Milwaukee Urban Archives (Hist)
2311 E. Hartford Ave.   Phone: (414)229-5402
Milwaukee, WI 53201   Timothy L. Ericson, Dir.
Founded: 1965. **Staff:** Prof 4; Other 1. **Subjects:** Private papers, records of Milwaukee, Ozaukee, Sheboygan, Washington, and Waukesha counties; University of Wisconsin, Milwaukee Archives; local history, businesses, associations, and churches; history of the quest for social justice in America, 1865-1940. **Special Collections:** Photographic and manuscript holdings relating to Milwaukee's Polish community. **Holdings:** Books; 425 manuscript collections; 142 state, county, and local government record series. **Services:** Copying; center open to the public. **Networks/Consortia:** Member of Wisconsin Area Research Center Network. **Publications:** State Historical Society of Wisconsin Guide to Archives and Manuscripts in the University of Wisconsin - Milwaukee Are Research Center, 1989; Mark A. Vargas, Guide to the Polish-American Holdings in the Milwaukee Urban Archives, 1991. **Remarks:** FAX: (414)229-4380. **Staff:** Barbara Drake; Stanley Mallach; Mark Vargas.

★ 19635 ★
University of Wisconsin--Milwaukee - Golda Meir Library - Music Collection (Mus)
2311 E. Hartford Ave.
Box 604   Phone: (414)229-5529
Milwaukee, WI 53201   Linda B. Hartig, Mus.Libn.
Staff: Prof 2; Other 2. **Subjects:** Music - history, criticism, theory, instruction and study; music bibliography; music librarianship; music sociology; chamber music. **Special Collections:** American Arriaga Archive (52 items); Slovenian Music Collection (1500 items); European-Tradition Music Catalog & Bibliography Collection (4000 items); John Dale Owen Jazz Recordings Collection (10,000 items). **Holdings:** 20,000 books; 2000 bound periodical volumes; 15,000 scores and parts; 43,000 recordings and tapes; 5100 catalogs, pamphlets, bibliographies; 4200 microforms. **Subscriptions:** 152 journals and other serials. **Services:** Interlibrary loan; copying; collection open to the public with restrictions. **Automated Operations:** Computerized cataloging, serials, and circulation. **Computerized Information Services:** OCLC; BITNET (electronic mail service). **Networks/Consortia:** Member of Wisconsin Interlibrary Services (WILS), Library Council of Metropolitan Milwaukee, Inc. (LCOMM). **Remarks:** Alternate telephone number(s): (414)229-4493 (ILL Department). FAX: (414)229-4380. Electronic mail address(es): LHARTIG@CSD4 (BITNET). **Staff:** Lynn Gullickson, Mus.Cat.; Mary Huismann, Asst.Mus.Cat.

★ 19636 ★
University of Wisconsin--Milwaukee - Golda Meir Library - Philip J. Hohlweck Civil War Collection (Hist)
Box 604   Phone: (414)229-4345
Milwaukee, WI 53201   Ellen M. Murphy, Spec.Coll./Rare Bks.Libn.
Founded: 1987. **Staff:** Prof 1; Other .5. **Subjects:** Civil War, military history. **Holdings:** 7150 books. **Services:** Copying; collection open to the public. **Automated Operations:** Computerized public access catalog. **Publications:** The Philip J. Hohlweck Civil War Collection: A Selected Bibliography. **Remarks:** FAX: (414)229-4380.

★ 19637 ★
University of Wisconsin--Milwaukee - Golda Meir Library - Seventeenth-Century Collection (Rare Book)
Box 604   Phone: (414)229-4345
Milwaukee, WI 53201   Ellen M. Murphy, Spec.Coll./Rare Bks.Libn.
Founded: 1976. **Staff:** Prof 1; Other .5. **Subjects:** 17th century English literature, 17th century British history, theology. **Holdings:** 685 books. **Services:** Collection open to the public. **Automated Operations:** Computerized public access catalog. **Special Catalogs:** A Selected Catalog of Books in the Seventeenth-Century Research Collection of the University of Wisconsin - Milwaukee. **Remarks:** FAX: (414)229-4380.

★ 19638 ★
University of Wisconsin--Milwaukee - Golda Meir Library - Shakespeare Research Collection (Theater)
Box 604   Phone: (414)229-6436
Milwaukee, WI 53201   Dr. Virginia Haas, Cur.
Founded: 1970. **Staff:** Prof 2. **Subjects:** Shakespeare, Elizabethan and Jacobean theater. **Holdings:** 3000 books. **Subscriptions:** 18 journals and other serials. **Services:** Interlibrary loan; copying; collection open to the public. **Remarks:** Alternate telephone number(s): (414)229-4493 (ILL Department). FAX: (414)229-4380.

★ 19639 ★
University of Wisconsin--Milwaukee - Graduate School - Office of Research - Information Library (Bus-Fin)
Box 340   Phone: (414)229-4063
Milwaukee, WI 53201   Victor J. Larson, Info.Spec.
Founded: 1967. **Staff:** Prof 1; Other 2. **Special Collections:** Federal and foundation extramural support program information (program announcements; guideline documents; general information items; reference books relating to sources of funds; information and proposal writing guides). **Holdings:** 8000 documents; 2 VF drawers of Senate and House bills and laws; 9 VF drawers of federal program information; 4 VF drawers of foundation and corporate program information; 100 program application kits. **Subscriptions:** 125 journals and other serials. **Services:** Copying; library open to the public by appointment. **Computerized Information Services:** Online systems. Performs searches on fee basis. **Publications:** Acquisitions List, quarterly; Application Deadline List, bimonthly. **Remarks:** FAX: (414)229-6967. Electronic mail address(es): VLARSON@CSD4.CSD.UWM.EDU.

★ 19640 ★
University of Wisconsin--Milwaukee - Greene Memorial Museum - Library
3367 N. Downer Ave.
Milwaukee, WI 53201
Founded: 1913. **Subjects:** Paleontology, mineralogy, geology. **Holdings:** 300 volumes. **Remarks:** This is the personal reference library of Thomas A. Greene, a 19th century collector whose fossil and mineral collections make up the bulk of the museum collection. Presently inactive.

★ 19641 ★
University of Wisconsin--Milwaukee - Institute of World Affairs - Resource Center (Soc Sci)
Garland 202
Box 413
Milwaukee, WI 53201   Gary Shellman, Asst.Dir.
                                                 Phone: (414)229-4251
Founded: 1960. **Staff:** Prof 1. **Subjects:** United States foreign policy, United Nations, regional organizations, international relations, current world problems, international trade and finance, international energy, arms control. **Holdings:** 300 books; 100 bound periodical volumes; 50 other cataloged items. **Subscriptions:** 13 journals and other serials. **Services:** Center open to the public. **Remarks:** FAX: (414)229-6930. Alternate telephone number(s): 229-5716.

★ 19642 ★
University of Wisconsin--Milwaukee - Morris Fromkin Memorial Collection (Soc Sci)
2311 E. Hartford Ave.   Phone: (414)229-5402
Milwaukee, WI 53201   Stanley Mallach, Bibliog.
Founded: 1969. **Staff:** Prof 1. **Subjects:** Socialism in the U.S., 1890-1940; communism in the U.S., 1920-1940; labor movement in the U.S., 1865-1940; social insurance in the U.S. to 1940; reform movements in the U.S., 1865-1940; housing and city planning in the U.S., 1890-1940; materials on European movements and events that affected American Left and Reform movements. **Holdings:** 4500 books; 2000 pamphlets. **Services:** Interlibrary loan; copying; library open to the public for reference use only. **Remarks:** Alternate telephone number(s): (414)229-4493 (ILL Department). FAX: (414)229-4380.

★ 19643 ★
University of Wisconsin--Oshkosh - University Libraries and Learning Resources - Special Collections (Educ)
800 Algoma Blvd.   Phone: (414)424-3334
Oshkosh, WI 54901   Dr. Norma L. Jones, Act.Exec.Dir.
Founded: 1871. **Special Collections:** Rowland Collection (Limited Editions Club); Pare Lorentz Collection (16mm films); archives of the Wisconsin Area Research Center; children's literature collection; A.F. Neumann Collection; J.R. Putney Collection (Wisconsin); government documents depository; Defense Agency map depository. **Services:** Interlibrary loan; copying; collections open to the public for reference use only. **Automated Operations:** Computerized cataloging, acquisitions, and circulation. **Computerized Information Services:** OCLC, DIALOG Information Services, BRS Information Technologies, PFDS Online, LS/2000; PULL (internal database). Performs searches on fee basis. Contact Person: Susheela Rao, Act.Coord., Online Database Searching, 424-2206. **Networks/Consortia:** Member of Wisconsin Interlibrary Services (WILS), Fox Valley Library Council, Wisconsin Interlibrary Services (WILS), Fox River Valley Area Library Consortium (FRVALC). **Publications:** Bridges (newsletter). **Remarks:** FAX: (414)424-2175. **Staff:** Gerald Krueger, Govt.Doc.Coll.; Kathryn Ann Dietz, Educ.Mtls.Coll.

★ 19644 ★
University of Wisconsin--Parkside - University Archives and Area Research Center (Hist)
900 Wood Road, Box 2000   Phone: (414)595-2411
Kenosha, WI 53141-2000   Ellen J. Pedraza, Archv.
Founded: 1972. **Staff:** Prof 1; Other 5. **Subjects:** History - local, state, university; genealogy. **Special Collections:** Irving Wallace; Norman Mailer; David Kherdian; H.O. Teisberg Collection of American Plays; Black Sparrow Collection; Perishable Press Collection. **Holdings:** 1234 books; 3800 cubic feet of manuscripts and archives; 865 reels of microfilm of censuses. **Services:** Interlibrary loan; copying; archives open to the public. **Automated Operations:** Computerized cataloging. **Special Catalogs:** Guide to Archives & Manuscripts in the University of Wisconsin-Parkside Area Research Center. **Remarks:** FAX: (414)595-2545.

★ 19645 ★
University of Wisconsin--Platteville - Karrmann Library - Special Collections (Hist)
1 University Plaza   Phone: (608)342-1688
Platteville, WI 53818   Jerome P. Daniels, Dir.
Founded: 1866. **Staff:** Prof 1; Other 1. **Subjects:** History - local, state, university; genealogy; mining. **Special Collections:** Southwest Wisconsin History and Southwestern Wisconsin Area Research Center (history of the Upper Mississippi Valley lead and zinc mining region). **Holdings:** 2254 books; 585 bound periodical volumes; 919 linear feet of unbound reports, manuscripts, and archival materials; 1575 linear feet of county documents; 7 cubic feet of photographs and negatives; 1919 reels of microfilm; 446 magnetic tapes; 51 films/videotapes; 127 maps; 8 VF drawers. **Subscriptions:** 25 journals and other serials. **Services:** Interlibrary loan; copying; collections open to the public. **Networks/Consortia:** Member of Wisconsin Interlibrary Services (WILS), Wisconsin Area Research Center Network. **Special Indexes:** Southwest Wisconsin Surname index, 1815-1860 (card); Exponent Index, 1925-1955 (online). **Remarks:** FAX: (608)342-1649.

★ 19646 ★
University of Wisconsin--River Falls - Area Research Center (Hist)
Chalmer Davee Library   Phone: (715)425-3567
River Falls, WI 54022   Stephanie Zeman, Act.Dir.
Founded: 1962. **Staff:** Prof 1; Other 8. **Subjects:** History of Western Wisconsin (Pierce, Polk, St. Croix, Washburn, and Burnett Counties); Civil

War history; genealogy; university history. **Special Collections:** Oral History (250 tapes); Wisconsin Census Records, 1836-1910. **Holdings:** 1500 books; 1500 linear feet of manuscript collections; 2400 reels of microfilm; 800 pamphlets; 10,000 photographs; maps; newspaper collection. **Subscriptions:** 5 journals and other serials; 11 newspapers. **Services:** Interlibrary loan; copying; center open to the public for reference use only. **Automated Operations:** OCLC LS/2000. **Networks/Consortia:** Member of Wisconsin Area Research Center Network. **Special Indexes:** Voices of the St. Croix Valley (bound index to Oral History Collections); biographical index for Burnett, Pierce, Polk, St. Croix, and Washburn counties, 1853-1910 (60,000 card entries); university alumni index (25,000 card entries).

★ 19647 ★
University of Wisconsin--River Falls - Chalmer Davee Library (Hist)
120 E. Cascade Ave.   Phone: (715)425-3222
River Falls, WI 54022   Christina Baum, Dir.
Founded: 1875. **Staff:** Prof 8; Other 13. **Subjects:** Education, agriculture. **Special Collections:** Western Americana and frontier history; Pierce and St. Croix county history. **Holdings:** 211,056 books; 43,010 bound periodical volumes; 116,718 government documents; 512,876 microfiche and microcards; 4613 AV programs; 7738 reels of microfilm. **Subscriptions:** 1615 journals and other serials; 33 newspapers. **Services:** Interlibrary loan; copying; library open to the public, deposit required for borrowing. **Automated Operations:** Computerized public access catalog, cataloging, acquisitions, and circulation. **Computerized Information Services:** DIALOG Information Services, BRS Information Technologies, WILSONLINE, OCLC; CD-ROMs (NewsBank Electronic Index, AGRICOLA, ERIC, PsycLIT, Sociofile). **Networks/Consortia:** Member of Wisconsin Interlibrary Services (WILS). **Remarks:** FAX: (715)425-3590. **Staff:** Cindy Riley, Cat.; Linda Olson, Automation Libn.; Kathie Oppegard, Ref.; Stephanie Zeman, Archv.; Michele McKnelly, Govt.Docs.Libn.

★ 19648 ★
University of Wisconsin--Stevens Point - Department of Geography & Geology - Map Collection (Geog-Map)
Science Bldg.   Phone: (715)346-2629
Stevens Point, WI 54481   Dr. Keith Rice, Cur.
Founded: 1964. **Staff:** Prof 2; Other 3. **Subjects:** Maps - U.S. topographic, Defense Mapping Agency (DMA), urban Wisconsin, geologic/oceanographic, aeronautic, Latin America, road, reference/locational. **Holdings:** 300 books; 120,000 maps; drawers of aerial photographs. **Services:** Collection open to the public.

★ 19649 ★
University of Wisconsin--Stevens Point - University Archives (Hist)
Learning Resources Center, 5th Fl. S.   Phone: (715)346-2586
Stevens Point, WI 54481   William G. Paul, Univ.Archv.
Subjects: History and development of the University of Wisconsin, Stevens Point, 1894 to present; individuals and institutions of Stevens Point and central Wisconsin. **Holdings:** 800 linear feet of manuscripts, photographs, tapes, catalogs, bulletins, tapes of events and activities, faculty committee minutes, yearbooks, administrative correspondence and reports, personnel records; 1300 linear feet of county records and manuscripts; Portage County Historical Society records, papers, and photographs. **Services:** Copying; archives open to the public.

★ 19650 ★
University of Wisconsin--Stevens Point - University Library (Educ)
Stevens Point, WI 54481   Phone: (715)346-3038
     Arne J. Arneson, Dir.
Founded: 1894. **Staff:** Prof 16; Other 17. **Subjects:** Natural resources, communicative disorders, home economics, education, communication. **Special Collections:** Federal government document depository; Wisconsin State document depository. **Holdings:** 276,449 books; 55,716 bound periodical volumes; 648,053 microforms; 11,697 AV programs; 503,611 volumes of government documents. **Subscriptions:** 3214 journals and other serials. **Services:** Interlibrary loan; copying; library open to the public. **Automated Operations:** Computerized cataloging. **Computerized Information Services:** OCLC, Faxon, LS/2000, DIALOG Information Services, BRS Information Technologies, WILSONLINE; STARMAIL, InterNet (electronic mail services). **Networks/Consortia:** Member of Wisconsin Interlibrary Services (WILS). **Remarks:** FAX: (715)341-1613. Electronic mail address(es): AARNESON@UWSPMAIL.UWSP.EDU (InterNet). **Staff:** Theresa Chao, Per.Libn.; Marg Whalen, Doc.Libn.; Linette Schuler, Hd.Ref.Libn.; Kathleen Halsey, ILL Libn.; Kate Anderson, Instr.Mtls.Ctr.Libn.; Patricia Paul, Info.Coord.; Carole Van Horn, Data Base Libn.; Margaret Allen, Proc.Coord.

★ 19651 ★
University of Wisconsin--Stout - Library Learning Center (Bus-Fin, Educ)
Menomonie, WI 54751   Phone: (715)232-1215
     John J. Jax, Dir.
Founded: 1908. **Staff:** Prof 11; Other 17. **Subjects:** Industrial technology, hotel and restaurant management, home economics, business, vocational rehabilitation, tourism, hospitality, early childhood education. **Holdings:** 209,500 books; 70,000 volumes on industrial, technical, and vocational education; 988 16mm films; 871,000 microfiche. **Subscriptions:** 1515 journals; 39 newspapers. **Services:** Interlibrary loan; copying; SDI; center open to the public. **Automated Operations:** Computerized public access catalog, cataloging, acquisitions, serials, and circulation. **Computerized Information Services:** DIALOG Information Services, BRS Information Technologies, OCLC. **Networks/Consortia:** Member of Wisconsin Interlibrary Services (WILS). **Publications:** Learning Connection, quarterly. **Special Indexes:** Hospitality Index. **Remarks:** FAX: (715)232-2618. **Staff:** Brooke B. Anson, Coord., INF Access Serv.; Theresa Muraski, Asst. to Dir.; Philip Sawin, Jr., Coll.Dev.Off.; Mary Richards, Hd., Cat.; Philip J. Schwarz, Coord., Bibliog.Serv.; Gayle J. Martinson, Archv.; Jana Reeg-Steidinger, Hd., Ref.; Lela Lugo, Comp. Searches; Carol Hagness, EMC.

★ 19652 ★
University of Wisconsin--Superior - Lake Superior Research Institute - Library (Env-Cons)
1800 Grand Ave.   Phone: (715)394-8315
Superior, WI 54880   J. Barnes
Subjects: Great Lakes, pollution, chemicals, toxicity. **Holdings:** 1200 books. **Services:** Library open to the public. **Remarks:** FAX: (715)394-8420.

★ 19653 ★
University of Wisconsin--Whitewater - Arts Media Center (Art, Mus)
College of the Arts, CA16   Phone: (414)472-1756
Whitewater, WI 53190   Kirby H. Bock, Spec.Libn.
Staff: Prof 1; Other 4. **Subjects:** Music, art, theater. **Holdings:** 6000 phonograph records; 3340 cassettes; 111,000 art slides; 500 compact discs. **Subscriptions:** 4 journals and other serials. **Services:** Copying (limited); center open to the public. **Automated Operations:** OCLC LS/2000. **Computerized Information Services:** OCLC.

★ 19654 ★
University of Wyoming - American Heritage Center (Hist)
P.O. Box 3924, University Sta.   Phone: (307)766-4114
Laramie, WY 82071   Michael Devine, Dir.
Founded: 1945. **Staff:** Prof 5; Other 15. **Subjects:** Western Americana. **Special Collections:** Range cattle industry history; business; conservation; petroleum; mining; performing arts; mountaineering; water resources; transportation history; rare books. **Holdings:** 26,500 books; 1500 bound periodical volumes; 64 file cases of clippings and pamphlets; 80,000 linear feet of manuscripts; 1500 reels of microfilm; 39,485 maps; 500,000 photographs. **Subscriptions:** 62 journals and other serials; 53 newspapers. **Services:** Interlibrary loan; copying; library open to the public. **Computerized Information Services:** OCLC. **Networks/Consortia:** Member of Colorado Alliance of Research Libraries (CARL). **Publications:** News releases; Heritage Highlights (newsletter). **Remarks:** FAX: (307)766-3062. **Staff:** Thomas Wilsted, Assoc.Dir./Oper.; Daniel L. Miller, Dir., Anaconda Coll.; Maxine Trost, Mgr./Arrangement & Description; Lisa Kinney, Doc.Off.

★ 19655 ★
University of Wyoming - Animal Science Division - Wool Library (Biol Sci)
Box 3354, University Sta.   Phone: (307)766-5212
Laramie, WY 82071   Robert Stobart, Dir.
Founded: 1908. **Staff:** Prof 1; Other 2. **Subjects:** Wool science, wool textiles, sheep husbandry. **Special Collections:** W.T. Ritch Collection. **Holdings:** 830 books; 275 bound periodical volumes; 9850 bulletins, articles, and reprints; 900 containers of various specimens of animal and other textile fibers. **Subscriptions:** 18 journals and other serials. **Services:** Library open to the public upon request. **Computerized Information Services:** Internal database. **Remarks:** Alternate telephone number(s): 766-5115. **Staff:** Randy Townsend.

★19656★
University of Wyoming - Family Practice Residency Program at Casper - Lange Memorial Library (Med)
1522 East A St.   Phone: (307)266-3076
Casper, WY 82601   Ginger Nordal, Med.Libn.
Founded: 1980. **Staff:** Prof 1. **Subjects:** Medicine - clinical, family practice, behavioral. **Special Collections:** Clinical geriatrics. **Holdings:** 800 books; 500 video cassettes; 500 audio cassettes; 42 slide/tape programs; 16 slide programs. **Subscriptions:** 53 journals and other serials. **Services:** Interlibrary loan; copying; SDI; center open to the public with restrictions on borrowing. **Automated Operations:** Computerized cataloging and acquisitions. **Computerized Information Services:** MEDLARS, DIALOG Information Services. Performs searches on fee basis. **Remarks:** FAX: (307)235-6202.

★19657★
University of Wyoming - Family Practice Residency Program at Cheyenne - Family Practice Library at Cheyenne (Med)
821 E. 18th St.   Phone: (307)777-7911
Cheyenne, WY 82001-4797   Carol McMurry, Libn.
Founded: 1980. **Staff:** Prof 1. **Subjects:** Clinical medicine. **Holdings:** 300 books; 1500 bound periodical volumes; 1500 current journals on microfilm. **Subscriptions:** 82 journals and other serials. **Services:** Interlibrary loan; copying; library open to medical professionals. **Computerized Information Services:** MEDLARS. **Remarks:** FAX: (307)638-3616.

★19658★
University of Wyoming - Geology Library (Sci-Engr)
S.H. Knight Bldg.
Box 3006, University Sta.   Phone: (307)766-3374
Laramie, WY 82070-3006   Linda R. Zellmer, Geol. & Maps Libn.
Founded: 1956. **Staff:** Prof 1; Other 6. **Subjects:** Geology, geophysics, paleontology, Wyoming and Rocky mountain geology, remote sensing. **Special Collections:** UMI geology dissertations, 1981 to present (microfiche); Wyoming infrared photographs (7000); post-Yellowstone Fire infrared photographs (1000); Wyoming Geological Survey publications. **Holdings:** 56,083 books; 13,000 bound periodical volumes; 16,688 government documents; 29,963 maps; 24,742 titles in microform. **Subscriptions:** 629 journals and other serials. **Services:** Interlibrary loan; copying; library open to the public with restrictions. **Automated Operations:** Computerized public access catalog and serials (CARL). **Computerized Information Services:** Chemical Abstracts Service (CAS), DIALOG Information Services, ORBIT Search Service; CD-ROMs (Earth Science Library, GeoRef). Performs searches on fee basis. **Networks/Consortia:** Member of Bibliographical Center for Research, Rocky Mountain Region, Inc. (BCR), Colorado Alliance of Research Libraries (CARL).

★19659★
University of Wyoming - Law Library (Law)
College of Law
Box 3035, University Sta.   Phone: (307)766-2210
Laramie, WY 82071   Catherine Mealey, Law Libn./Prof.
Founded: 1920. **Staff:** Prof 3; Other 5.7. **Subjects:** Law. **Special Collections:** Blume Collection (Roman law). **Holdings:** 110,787 volumes; 339,022 microfiche. **Subscriptions:** 2945 journals and other serials. **Services:** Interlibrary loan; copying; library open to the public for reference use. **Automated Operations:** Computerized public access catalog, cataloging, circulation, serials, acquisitions and budgeting. **Computerized Information Services:** LEXIS, NEXIS, WESTLAW, DIALOG Information Services, OCLC, LegalTrac; internal database; InterNet, BITNET (electronic mail services). **Networks/Consortia:** Member of Bibliographical Center for Research, Rocky Mountain Region, Inc. (BCR). **Publications:** Self-help guides. **Remarks:** FAX: (307)766-4044. Electronic mail address(es): JEBINDER@CORRAL.UWYO.EDU (InterNet). **Staff:** Joan Binder, Tech.Serv.Libn.; Suzanne Leary, Pub.Serv.Libn.

★19660★
University of Wyoming - Learning Resources Center (Educ)
Box 3374, University Sta.
College of Education Bldg.
Laramie, WY 82071   Phone: (307)766-2527
          Laurn Wilhelm
Founded: 1986. **Staff:** Prof 1. **Subjects:** Children's literature, elementary and secondary education text-book materials, student activities, computer programs, young adult literature, drug education. **Special Collections:** Children/young adult collection (16,000 books); Curriculum collection (15,000 books). **Holdings:** 25,000 books; 100 reports; 250 microfiche; 250 uncataloged items. **Services:** Interlibrary loan; copying; SDI; center open to the public. **Networks/Consortia:** Member of Colorado Alliance of Research Libraries (CARL).

★19661★
University of Wyoming - Science and Technology Library (Sci-Engr)
Box 3262, University Sta.   Phone: (307)766-4264
Laramie, WY 82071   Deborah Dawson, Hd., Sci.Lib. & Ref.Dept.
Founded: 1970. **Staff:** Prof 5; Other 8. **Subjects:** Natural, physical, and health sciences; engineering; mathematics; agriculture. **Holdings:** 319,000 volumes; 10,886 reels of microfilm; 156,947 microfiche. **Subscriptions:** 3000 journals. **Services:** Interlibrary loan; copying; library open to the public. **Automated Operations:** Computerized public access catalog, circulation, and serials (CARL). **Computerized Information Services:** DIALOG Information Services, BRS Information Technologies, MEDLARS, Chemical Abstracts Service (CAS), WILSONLINE, ORBIT Search Service; 7 CD-ROMs. Performs searches on fee basis. Contact Person: Larry Jansen, 766-6538. **Networks/Consortia:** Member of Bibliographical Center for Research, Rocky Mountain Region, Inc. (BCR). **Remarks:** Houses Wyoming Health Sciences Information Network, representing Region IV in the National Library of Medicine's Biomedical Communications Network. **Remarks:** FAX: (307)766-3611; 766-4263 (to verify). **Staff:** Jania Gahagan, Hd., HSIN; Janis Leath, Ref./Coll.Dev.; Barbara Delzell, Ref./Coll.Dev.

★19662★
University of Wyoming - Water Research Center - Library (Sci-Engr)
Laramie, WY 82071   Phone: (307)766-2143
          Pam Murdock, Adm.Asst.
Founded: 1970. **Subjects:** Water resources, evaporation, snow and ice, conservation, irrigation, water law, river basins and water planning, sanitary and civil engineering. **Special Collections:** U.S. Geological Survey water supply papers relating to Wyoming. **Holdings:** 1000 books; 14,000 reports, articles, reprints. **Services:** Copying; library open to the public for reference use only. **Computerized Information Services:** Wyoming Water Bibliography (internal database). **Remarks:** FAX: (307)766-3718.

University of Yaounde - Cameroon Institute of International Relations
See: Cameroon Institute of International Relations (2616)

★19663★
University of Zurich - Institute for Art History - Library (Art)
Ramistr 73   Phone: 1 2572835
CH-8006 Zurich, Switzerland   Thomas Freirogel
Founded: 1954. **Staff:** Prof 3; Other 1. **Subjects:** History of Western art; art - Italian, German, French, and Swiss; gardens; architecture. **Holdings:** 36,000 book. **Subscriptions:** 319 journals and other serials. **Services:** Interlibrary loan; copying; library open to the public. **Automated Operations:** DOBIS-LIBIS. **Remarks:** FAX: 1 2617823. **Also Known As:** Universitat Zurich - Kunstgeschichtliches Seminar - Bibliothek. **Staff:** Pius Sidles.

★19664★
Univerzitet Kiril i Metodij vo Skopje - Matematicki Institut - Biblioteka (Sci-Engr)
Gazibaba   Phone: 91 261330
YU-91000 Skopje, Yugoslavia   Kristina Organdzieva, Libn.
Founded: 1946. **Subjects:** Mathematics. **Holdings:** 17,400 books; 473 bound periodical volumes; doctoral theses. **Subscriptions:** 473 journals and other serials. **Services:** Interlibrary loan; copying; library open to the public with restrictions. **Publications:** Catalogs; Matematicki Bilten (Bulletin Mathematique).

★19665★
Uniwersytet Jagiellonski - Biblioteka Jagiellonska (Hum)
ulica Mickiewicza 22   Phone: 12 336377
PL-30-059 Cracow, Poland   Dr. Jan Pirozynski, Dir.
Founded: 1364. **Staff:** Prof 293. **Subjects:** Culture, literature, linguistics, art, religion, atheism. **Holdings:** 1.4 million; 504,236 bound periodical volumes; 61,192 microfiche and microfilm; 101,447 old prints; 3578 incunabula; 22,883 manuscripts; 32,935 music prints and manuscripts; 42,618 drawings and graphic arts; 11,975 maps and atlases. **Subscriptions:** 5765 journals and other serials. **Services:** Interlibrary loan; copying; library open to the public for reference use only. **Computerized Information Services:** DIALOG Information Services. **Publications:** Inventory of manuscripts of the Jagiellonian Library; collections and works which concern Polish colony from the Jagiellonian Library Collection and from the selected Institute Libraries of the Jagiellonian University; Bulletin of the Jagiellonian Library, annual. **Special Catalogs:** Catalogus Codicum Manuscriptum Medii Aevi Latinorum qui in Bibliotheca Jagellonica Cracoviae Asservantur; The Catalogue of 16th Century Polonica of the Jagiellonian Library. **Remarks:** Telex: 325682 bj pl. **Also Known As:** Biblioteka Jagiellonska. **Staff:** Mgr. Teresa Malik, V.Dir.

★ 19666 ★
Uniwersytet Jagiellonski - Instytut Matematyki - Biblioteka (Sci-Engr)
ul. Reymonta 4   Phone: 12 336377
PL-30-059 Cracow, Poland   Zofia Kalicka, M.A.
Founded: 1874. **Staff:** Prof 3. **Subjects:** Mathematics, computer science. **Special Collections:** Lecture notes in mathematics (683 volumes). **Holdings:** 18,090 books; 1973 bound periodical volumes; 1362 reports; 886 archival items. **Subscriptions:** 40 journals and other serials. **Services:** Interlibrary loan; library open to the public. **Computerized Information Services:** PL-EARN (electronic mail service). **Remarks:** FAX: 12 339781; Electronic mail address(es): UMBIBLIO@PLKRCY11 (PL-EARN).

★ 19667 ★
Uniwersytet Mikolaja Kopernika - Instytut Matematyki - Biblioteka (Sci-Engr)
ul. Chopina 12/18   Phone: 56 26018
PL-87-100 Torun, Poland   Helena Maniakowska
Founded: 1947. **Staff:** Prof 2; Other 1. **Subjects:** Mathematics, mathematics in physics, computer science. **Holdings:** 12,591 books; 4435 bound periodical volumes. **Subscriptions:** 98 journals and other serials. **Services:** Interlibrary loan; library open to the public with restrictions. **Remarks:** Alternate telephone number(s): 26017, 26037.

★ 19668 ★
Uniwersytet Wroclawski - Instytut Matematyczny - Biblioteka (Sci-Engr)
pl. Grundwaldzki 2/4   Phone: 71 211500
PL-50-384 Wroclaw, Poland   Aleksandra Galeczka
Founded: 1945. **Staff:** Prof 4. **Subjects:** Mathematics, harmonic and functional analysis, probability, statistics, differential topology, geometry, differential equations, history, didactics. **Special Collections:** Collected works of famous mathematicians; collections of major journals. **Holdings:** 42,811 books; 21,182 bound periodical volumes; 60 report series. **Subscriptions:** 366 journals and other serials; 6 newspapers. **Services:** Interlibrary loan; copying; library open to the public for reference use only. **Remarks:** FAX: 71 229717.

A.G. Unklesbay Geological Sciences Library
See: **University of Missouri--Columbia - A.G. Unklesbay Geological Sciences Library** (18957)

★ 19669 ★
Unocal Canada Limited - Library (Sci-Engr)
150 6th Ave., S.W.
P.O. Box 999
Calgary, AB, Canada T2P 3Y7   Phone: (403)268-0303
Staff: Prof 1. **Subjects:** Geology, geophysics, law. **Holdings:** 1800 books; 325 bound periodical volumes; 1200 Geological Survey of Canada papers; 1050 reprints; 600 miscellaneous provincial papers. **Subscriptions:** 110 journals and other serials. **Services:** Interlibrary loan; copying; library open to employees and other libraries. **Remarks:** FAX: (403)268-0507. **Staff:** Juile MacInnis, Libn.; Sherry Killen-Smith, Libn.

★ 19670 ★
Unocal Corporation - Corporate Planning Library (Energy, Bus-Fin)
1201 W. 5th St.   Phone: (213)977-7725
Los Angeles, CA 90017   Millie Chong-Dillon, Libn.
Founded: 1974. **Staff:** Prof 1; Other 1. **Subjects:** Petroleum and natural gas industries, business and finance. **Special Collections:** J.S. Herold Oil Industry Comparative Appraisals, 1956 to present; annual reports for major oil companies, 1970 to present. **Holdings:** 1600 books; annual and 10K reports for 1150 companies. **Subscriptions:** 56 journals and other serials; 5 newspapers. **Services:** Interlibrary loan; library not open to the public. **Automated Operations:** Computerized cataloging, acquisitions, and serials. **Computerized Information Services:** DIALOG Information Services, NEXIS, Dow Jones News/Retrieval, Reuters.

★ 19671 ★
Unocal Corporation - International Exploration Library (Sci-Engr)
1201 W. 5th St.   Phone: (213)977-6381
Los Angeles, CA 90017   Keith Globus, Lib.Mgr.
Founded: 1960. **Staff:** Prof 1; Other 1. **Subjects:** Geology, petroleum geology, oceanography, geophysics. **Holdings:** 9000 books; 800 bound periodical volumes. **Subscriptions:** 100 journals and other serials. **Services:** Interlibrary loan; library not open to the public. **Automated Operations:** Computerized cataloging, acquisitions, serials, and circulation. **Computerized Information Services:** NEXIS, DIALOG Information Services, PFDS Online, OCLC. **Remarks:** FAX: (213)977-5185.

★ 19672 ★
Unocal Corporation - Library-File Room (Sci-Engr)
1800 30th St., Suite 200
Box 6176
Bakersfield, CA 93301   Phone: (805)395-5217
Staff: Prof 1. **Subjects:** Geology, geophysics, paleontology. **Holdings:** 640 books; 350 maps; 200 linear feet of company reports; 635 reprints. **Subscriptions:** 10 journals and other serials. **Services:** Library not open to the public.

★ 19673 ★
Unocal Corporation - Molycorp, Inc. - Library
Box 54945
Los Angeles, CA 90054
Defunct.

★ 19674 ★
Unocal Corporation - Science & Technology Division - Technical Information Center (Sci-Engr, Energy)
376 S. Valencia Ave.   Phone: (714)528-7201
Brea, CA 92621   Barbara J. Orosz, Mgr., Tech.Comm.Serv.
Founded: 1922. **Staff:** Prof 3; Other 4. **Subjects:** Petroleum technology, chemistry, geosciences, oceanography, physics, chemical engineering, mathematics, agriculture, geology. **Holdings:** 28,000 books; 28,000 bound periodical volumes; 32,000 documents; 20,000 government documents; 9000 maps. **Subscriptions:** 850 journals and other serials. **Services:** Interlibrary loan; copying; center open to students by appointment for reference use only. **Computerized Information Services:** DIALOG Information Services, ORBIT Search Service, STN International; internal database. **Publications:** List of books and documents, semimonthly - to research center personnel. **Staff:** Gloria Okasako-Oshiro, Sr.Info.Chem.; Robert Powers, Libn.

★ 19675 ★
Unum Life Insurance Co. - Corporate Information Center (Bus-Fin)
2211 Congress St.   Phone: (207)780-2347
Portland, ME 04122   Ann C. Madigan, Supv.
Founded: 1958. **Staff:** Prof 2; Other 2. **Subjects:** Life and health insurance, management, economics, business. **Special Collections:** Corporate archives; legal library; investments library. **Holdings:** 3000 books. **Subscriptions:** 250 journals and other serials; 12 newspapers. **Services:** Interlibrary loan; center open to the public by appointment. **Automated Operations:** Computerized cataloging. **Computerized Information Services:** DIALOG Information Services, BRS Information Technologies, VU/TEXT Information Services, LEXIS, NEXIS, Dow Jones News/Retrieval, InvesText, Trinet, Inc., FYI News. **Publications:** CIC Review, 2/month - for internal distribution only. **Remarks:** FAX: (207)770-2340. **Staff:** Jill Lubiner, Info.Spec.; John Long, Assoc.Res.Anl.

UNYSIS Corporation - Reston Research Library
See: **UNISYS Defense Systems - Reston Research Library** (16684)

UNYSIS Corporation - Technical Information Center
See: **UNISYS Defense Systems - Technical Information Center** (16685)

★ 19676 ★
UOP Research Center - Technical Information Center (Energy)
50 E. Algonquin Rd.   Phone: (708)391-3109
Des Plaines, IL 60017-5016   Suzanne M. Gaumond, Mgr.
Founded: 1926. **Staff:** Prof 5; Other 7. **Subjects:** Petroleum refining processes and technology, petrochemical processes, chemical engineering, air and water conservation, special purpose chemicals, catalysis, patents, trademarks, copyrights. **Special Collections:** American Petroleum Institute project publications; Technical Oil Mission reports (microfilm); official patent publications of Australia, Brazil, Canada, France, Germany, Great Britain, India, South Africa, and United States (150,000 patents). **Holdings:** 20,000 books; 12,250 bound periodical volumes; 25 VF drawers of clippings; 50 VF drawers and 2500 microfiche of government documents; 450,000 U.S. patents. **Subscriptions:** 600 journals and other serials. **Services:** Interlibrary loan; SDI; center open to the public by appointment. **Automated Operations:** Computerized cataloging, acquisitions, serials, and circulation. **Computerized Information Services:** STN International, DIALOG Information Services, PFDS Online, BRS Information Technologies, Reuters Information Services (Canada) Limited, LEXIS, NEXIS, Chemical Information Systems, Inc. (CIS), DRI/McGraw-Hill; Research Reports (internal database); OnTyme Electronic Message Network Service (electronic mail service). **Publications:** What's New/Current Reading List, monthly; Current Awareness Report, weekly - both for internal distribution only. **Special Indexes:** Research Reports. **Remarks:** FAX: (708)391-3330. **Staff:** Else Boland, Group Ldr.; Kay Kim, Sr.Lit. Searcher; Ann Benge, Adm., Lib.Sys.; Betty Aksamit, Sr.Lit. Searcher.

★ 19677 ★
Up Front Drug Information - Library (Med)
5701 Biscayne Blvd., Suite 602   Phone: (305)757-2566
Miami, FL 33137   James N. Hall, Exec.Dir.
Founded: 1973. **Staff:** Prof 3. **Subjects:** Drug information. **Holdings:** 1000 books; 900 unbound periodicals; 12 VF drawers and 100 pamphlet files of drug information. **Subscriptions:** 27 journals and other serials; 5 newspapers. **Services:** Copying; library open to the public. **Automated Operations:** Computerized cataloging, acquisitions, and serials. **Publications:** Street Pharmacologist, quarterly - by subscription; drug abuse brochures. **Staff:** Carlos Zaldivar, Adm.Dir.

★ 19678 ★
Updata Publications, Inc. - Library (Sci-Engr)
1736 Westwood Blvd.   Phone: (213)474-5900
Los Angeles, CA 90024   David P. Hayes, Libn.
Founded: 1973. **Staff:** Prof 1. **Subjects:** Aeronautics, mining, water, fisheries, agriculture, indexes. **Special Collections:** National Advisory Committee for Aeronautics Collection, 1915-1958 (13,914 microfiche); NASA Collection, (complete set; microfiche); U.S. Bureau of Mines Collection, 1910 to present (16,537 microfiche); Mine Safety and Health (400 microfiche); Central Intelligence Agency (2160 microfiche); U.S. Geological Survey Water Supply Papers (8000 microfiche); U.S. Department of Agriculture (30,000 microfiche); U.S. Fisheries documents (4100 microfiche); U.S. Government Indexes of various departments (500 microfiche). **Holdings:** 2000 books; 270,000 microfiche; 60 reels of microfilm. **Subscriptions:** 40 journals and other serials. **Services:** SDI; library open to the public on request. **Computerized Information Services:** DIALOG Information Services; UPDATALINE (internal database); CD-ROMs (400). Performs searches on fee basis. Contact Person: Herbert Sclar, Pres. **Remarks:** FAX: (213)474-4095.

★ 19679 ★
Upjohn Company - Corporate Business Library (Bus-Fin, Med)
Kalamazoo, MI 49001   Phone: (616)323-6352
    Valerie Noble, Mgr.
Founded: 1960. **Staff:** Prof 1; Other 4. **Subjects:** Business and finance, management and supervision, marketing, self-improvement, microcomputer applications, pharmaceuticals and drugs. **Holdings:** 5000 books; SRI-BIP reports; annual reports; microforms; audiocassettes; video cassettes; IBM PC-compatible software; road maps to major U.S. and international cities. **Subscriptions:** 250 journals and other serials. **Services:** Interlibrary loan; copying; SDI; library open to the public by appointment. **Automated Operations:** Computerized acquisitions, circulation, and subscriptions systems. **Computerized Information Services:** DIALOG Information Services, Dow Jones News/Retrieval, OCLC, DataStar, Mead Data Central, Dun & Bradstreet Business Credit Services, Reuter TEXTLINE, Online Information Network. **Publications:** Monthly List of New Materials; descriptive brochures; Guide to Personal Development. **Remarks:** FAX: (616)323-6508. **Staff:** Jan Dommer, Info.Cons.

★ 19680 ★
Upjohn Company - Corporate Patents and Trademarks Library (Law)
301 Henrietta St.   Phone: (616)385-7012
Kalamazoo, MI 49001   Nancy Hord, Off.Supv.
Founded: 1950. **Staff:** 1. **Subjects:** Patents, trademarks, copyrights, licensing, unfair competition. **Special Collections:** U.S. chemical patents (microform); U.S. Official Gazette (microform). **Holdings:** 2000 books; 1500 bound periodical volumes. **Subscriptions:** 83 journals and other serials. **Services:** Library not open to the public. **Automated Operations:** Computerized cataloging, acquisitions, serials, and circulation. **Computerized Information Services:** LEXIS, Derwent, Inc., IMS America, Ltd., Dow Jones News/Retrieval, ORBIT Search Service. **Remarks:** FAX: (616)385-6897. Telex: 224 401 UPJOHN.

★ 19681 ★
Upjohn Company - Corporate Technical Library (Sci-Engr, Med)
7284-267-21   Phone: (616)385-6414
Kalamazoo, MI 49001   Lorraine Schulte, Dir.
Founded: 1941. **Staff:** Prof 17; Other 17. **Subjects:** Chemistry, biotechnology, biochemistry, pharmacology, biomedical and pharmaceutical sciences, statistics, computer science. **Holdings:** 23,500 books; 58,000 bound periodical volumes. **Subscriptions:** 1300 journals and other serials. **Services:** Current awareness; library open to the public with prior approval. **Automated Operations:** Computerized public access catalog,

cataloging, acquisitions, serials, circulation, and document delivery. **Computerized Information Services:** Library Information System (LIS), DIALOG Information Services, PFDS Online, BRS Information Technologies, NLM, OCLC, STN International, WILSONLINE, Questel, Data-Star, REPROTOX, OCLC EPIC; Product Information Retrieval System (PIRSU), Technical Report Electronic Knowledge Base (TREK), TUCO Database, PATS Database (internal databases); OnTyme Electronic Message Network Service (electronic mail service). **Networks/Consortia:** Member of Michigan Library Consortium (MLC). **Publications:** Library Additions, monthly; CTL News, quarterly; Brief Guide to the Corporate Technical Library, irregular; Brief Guide to Using LIS, irregular. **Remarks:** FAX: (616)385-8412. **Staff:** Ruth C.T. Morris, Sabbatical; Dorian Martyn, Info.Spec.; Paula Allred, Info.Spec.; Janet Everitt, Info.Sci.; Mark Rycheck, Info.Sci.; Rein Virkhaus, Info.Sci.; Geneva Williams, Info.Sci.; James Powell, Info.Sci.; June Hauck, Info.Sci.; Kathe Obrig, PIRSU Proj.Ldr.; Suzanne Dankert, Mgr., Info.Rsrcs.; Elin Shallcross, Info.Sci.; Diane Worden, Mgr., Info.Serv.; Chris Adesanya, Info.Spec.

★ 19682 ★
Upjohn Company - Medical Library Services (Med)
Upjohn Laboratories
9184-298-04D   Phone: (616)329-8086
Kalamazoo, MI 49001   L. Pauline Sattler, Mgr.
Founded: 1985. **Staff:** Prof 2; Other 6. **Subjects:** Clinical medicine, drug information, clinical trials. **Holdings:** 700 books; 550 microfilm cartridges. **Subscriptions:** 325 journals and other serials. **Services:** Interlibrary loan; services not open to the public. **Automated Operations:** Computerized public access catalog, serials, and circulation. **Computerized Information Services:** BRS Information Technologies, DIALOG Information Services, PFDS Online, NLM; Product Information Retrieval Service (internal database). **Publications:** Medical Information Newsletter, monthly - for internal distribution only. **Staff:** Audrey J. Pobutsky, Info. Scientist.

Upjohn Library
See: **Kalamazoo College - Upjohn Library** (8528)

★ 19683 ★
W.E. Upjohn Institute for Employment Research - Library (Bus-Fin)
300 S. Westnedge Ave.   Phone: (616)343-5541
Kalamazoo, MI 49007   Christine Clark, Libn.
Founded: 1960. **Staff:** Prof 1. **Subjects:** Unemployment - causes and effects; labor economics; urban affairs. **Holdings:** 6000 books; statistics. **Subscriptions:** 300 journals and other serials; 8 newspapers. **Services:** Interlibrary loan; library not open to the public. **Computerized Information Services:** DIALOG Information Services, OCLC. **Networks/Consortia:** Member of Michigan Library Consortium (MLC). **Remarks:** FAX: (616)343-3308.

Uplands Farm Environmental Center
See: **Nature Conservancy - Long Island Chapter** (11346)

Upper Canada Village Reference Library
See: **St. Lawrence Parks Commission** (14431)

★ 19684 ★
Upper Colorado River Commission - Library (Env-Cons)
355 S. 400th East St.   Phone: (801)531-1150
Salt Lake City, UT 84111   Wayne E. Cook, Exec.Dir.
Staff: 4. **Subjects:** Water and related resource development. **Holdings:** 9000 volumes. **Services:** Library open to the public for reference use only.

★ 19685 ★
Upper Mississippi River Conservation Committee - Library (Env-Cons)
4469 48th Ave.   Phone: (309)793-5800
Rock Island, IL 61201   Jon Duyvejonck, Coord.
Subjects: Mississippi River, fisheries, wildlife, recreation, environmental impacts, aquatic research. **Special Collections:** State Fish and Wildlife Management reports; commercial fishing data for upper Mississippi River. **Holdings:** 3000 books; 1 AV program. **Services:** Library open to the public for reference use only. **Computerized Information Services:** Internal database.

★ 19686 ★
The Upper Room - Devotional Library, Museum and Archives (Rel-Phil)
1908 Grand Ave.
Box 189   Phone: (615)340-7204
Nashville, TN 37202   Sarah Schaller-Linn, Libn.
Founded: 1955. **Staff:** Prof 1. **Subjects:** Devotions, prayers, meditations, spiritual formation, hymns, Methodism. **Special Collections:** Original letters of John Wesley (66 items). **Holdings:** 14,000 books; 200 other cataloged items; 150 feet of archival materials of The Upper Room. **Subscriptions:** 50 journals and other serials. **Services:** Library open to the public for reference use only. **Remarks:** FAX: (615)340-7006.

★ 19687 ★
Upper Savannah Area Health Education Consortium - Library (Med)
Self Memorial Hospital
1325 Spring St.   Phone: (803)227-4851
Greenwood, SC 29646   Thomas W. Hill, Libn.
Founded: 1977. **Staff:** Prof 2; Other 1. **Subjects:** Medicine, health sciences, nursing. **Holdings:** 2000 books; 1000 audio and video cassettes, 16mm films, sound recordings. **Subscriptions:** 300 journals and other serials. **Services:** Interlibrary loan; copying; library open to the public. **Automated Operations:** Computerized public access catalog, cataloging, serials, and ILL (DOCLINE). **Computerized Information Services:** NLM, miniMEDLINE. Performs searches on fee basis. **Networks/Consortia:** Member of South Carolina Health Information Network (SCHIN), Area Health Education Consortium of South Carolina (AHEC), National Network of Libraries of Medicine (NN/LM). **Publications:** Bibliographies. **Special Catalogs:** Audiovisual holdings catalog. **Remarks:** FAX: (803)227-4260. **Staff:** Ellen Dewkett, Asst.Libn.

★ 19688 ★
Upper Snake River Valley Historical Society - Library (Hist)
51 North Center
Box 244   Phone: (208)356-9101
Rexburg, ID 83440   Georgia Ricks, Libn.
Founded: 1965. **Staff:** Prof 1; Other 3. **Subjects:** Idaho history. **Special Collections:** Oral history (600 tapes). **Holdings:** 2300 books; 600 tapes; 20 videotapes; 12 maps. **Subscriptions:** 10 journals and other serials. **Services:** Copying; library open to the public by appointment. **Publications:** Snake River Echoes, annual.

★ 19689 ★
Urban Institute - Library (Soc Sci, Plan)
2100 M St., N.W.   Phone: (202)857-8688
Washington, DC 20037   Camille A. Motta, Dir. of Lib. & Info.Serv.
Founded: 1968. **Staff:** Prof 2; Other 3. **Subjects:** Public policy and economics, housing and urban development, health policy, public finance, human resources research, international housing policy, population studies, economic development, state and local government policy, income and benefits policy. **Special Collections:** Urban Institute archival materials. **Holdings:** 30,000 books and documents; 650 periodical titles; 4600 reels of microfilm. **Subscriptions:** 650 journals. **Services:** Interlibrary loan (fee); SDI; library open to the public by appointment. **Automated Operations:** Computerized cataloging. **Computerized Information Services:** DIALOG Information Services, VU/TEXT Information Services, WILSONLINE, MEDLARS, BRS Information Technologies; Urban Institute Publications Database (internal database); CD-ROMs. Performs searches on fee basis. **Networks/Consortia:** Member of Interlibrary Users Association (IUA), CAPCON Library Network. **Publications:** New Research Papers (Urban Institute), 3/year - free upon request; Books, Bytes and Bits (acquisitions list) - for internal distribution only; Urban Institute bibliographies - free upon request. **Remarks:** FAX: (202)223-3043. **Staff:** Catherine Selden, Asst.Dir.

★ 19690 ★
Urban Land Institute - Library (Plan)
625 Indiana Ave., N.W.   Phone: (202)624-7116
Washington, DC 20004   Joan E. Campbell, Res.Libn.
Founded: 1958. **Staff:** Prof 2; Other 1. **Subjects:** Land use, real estate, urban planning, housing, environment. **Holdings:** 8500 books; U.S. census publications, 1970; ULI publications. **Subscriptions:** 223 journals and other serials. **Services:** Interlibrary loan; copying; library open to the public by appointment. **Computerized Information Services:** DIALOG Information Services, DataTimes, Dow Jones News/Retrieval. **Publications:** Land Use Digest; Urban Land - both monthly - to members. **Remarks:** FAX: (202)624-7141. **Staff:** David A. Mulvihill, Asst.

Urban Mass Transportation Administration
See: U.S. Urban Mass Transportation Administration (17955)

★ 19691 ★
Urbana Municipal Documents Center (Soc Sci)
The Urbana Free Library
201 S. Race St.   Phone: (217)384-0092
Urbana, IL 61801-3283   Jean E. Koch, Dir.
Founded: 1979. **Staff:** Prof 2; Other 1. **Subjects:** Urbana city government. **Holdings:** 38,296 documents on 15,821 microfiche. **Services:** Copying; center open to the public with restrictions. **Automated Operations:** Computerized indexing. **Special Indexes:** Alphabetical, geographical, numerical, and citation indexes (COM). **Remarks:** FAX: (217)367-4061. **Staff:** Howard Grueneberg, Indexer.

★ 19692 ★
Urbana University - Swedenborg Memorial Library - Special Collections (Rel-Phil)
College Way   Phone: (513)652-1301
Urbana, OH 43078-2091   Hugh Durbin, Lib.Dir.
Founded: 1852. **Staff:** 3. **Special Collections:** Swedenborgian Collection (2388 titles). **Holdings:** 2388 books; 200 bound periodical volumes; 100 reports; 25 manuscipts. **Subscriptions:** 5 journals and other serials. **Services:** Copying; collection open to the public. **Automated Operations:** Computerized cataloging. **Computerized Information Services:** EPIE. **Networks/Consortia:** Member of Southwestern Ohio Council for Higher Education (SOCHE), OHIONET. **Remarks:** FAX: (513)652-3835. **Staff:** Jeanne Gamble, Hd., Cat.; Jennifer Midgley, Circ.Supv.

Uris Library and Resource Center
See: Metropolitan Museum of Art (10217)

★ 19693 ★
URS Consultants - Resource Center (Art, Sci-Engr)
3605 Warrensville Center Rd.   Phone: (216)283-4000
Cleveland, OH 44122   Stephanie Eberle, Libn.
Staff: Prof 1; Other 1. **Subjects:** Architecture, engineering, interior design, environment. **Special Collections:** Structural, civil, electrical, mechanical, and environmental engineering; health care. **Holdings:** 5720 books; 50 bound periodical volumes; 15 file cabinets of internal proposals and reports; blueprints on microfiche. **Subscriptions:** 110 journals and other serials. **Services:** Interlibrary loan; copying; center open to the public through ILL. **Automated Operations:** Computerized cataloging, acquisitions, serials, and circulation. **Computerized Information Services:** Internal database. **Networks/Consortia:** Member of OHIONET. **Remarks:** FAX: (216)283-6563.

★ 19694 ★
Ursa Astronomical Association - Library (Sci-Engr)
Laivanvarustajankatu gc 54   Phone: 0 174048
SF-00140 Helsinki 14, Finland   Matti Suhonen, Libn.
Founded: 1921. **Staff:** 5. **Subjects:** Astronomy, astronomical phenomena. **Holdings:** 4500 volumes. **Subscriptions:** 25 journals and other serials. **Services:** Interlibrary loan; copying. **Computerized Information Services:** Internal databases; InterNet (electronic mail service). **Remarks:** FAX: 0 657728. Electronic mail address(es): Ursa@f861.n220.z2.fidonet.org (InterNet). **Also Known As:** Tahtitieteellinen Yhdistys Ursa.

★ 19695 ★
Ursinus College - Myrin Library - Special Collections (Area-Ethnic)
Collegeville, PA 19426-9989   Phone: (215)489-4111
                                        Charles A. Jamison, Lib.Dir.
Founded: 1869. **Subjects:** Pennsylvania German culture; German Reformed Church; Francis Mairs Huntington Wilson diplomatic papers, 1897-1913; Linda Grace Hoyer Updike literary papers. **Holdings:** 179,500 manuscripts; photographs; oral histories; videotapes. **Subscriptions:** 950 journals and other serials; 20 newspapers. **Services:** Interlibrary loan; copying; SDI; collections open to the public. **Automated Operations:** Computerized public access catalog, cataloging, acquisitions, and circulation. **Computerized Information Services:** BRS Information Technologies, DIALOG Information Services, STN International. Performs searches on fee basis. **Contact Person:** David Mill, Info.Serv.Libn. or Judith Fryer, Info.Serv.Libn., 489-4111, ext. 2283. **Networks/Consortia:** Member of PALINET. **Publications:** Friends of the Myrin Library Newsletter, 6/year. **Remarks:** FAX: (215)489-0634. **Staff:** Kim Sando, Media Serv.Supv.; Debbie Malone, Tech.Serv.Libn.

★19696★
Uruguay - Biblioteca Nacional - Centro Nacional de Documentacion Cientifica, Tecnica y Economica (Sci-Engr)
18 de Julio 1790   Phone: 2 484172
Montevideo, Uruguay   Elena Castro De Blengini, Dir.
Subjects: Information science, science and technology. **Holdings:** 1000 books; 200 serial titles. **Services:** Interlibrary loan; copying; SDI; center open to the public with restrictions. **Publications:** Directorio de Servicios de Informacion y Documentacion en el Uruguay. **Special Indexes:** Uruguay: Indice de publicaciones periodicas en ciencia y tecnologia, 1981-1983. **Remarks:** FAX: 2 496902. **Also Known As:** Centro Nacional de Referencia del Uruguay.

US Sprint
See: **United Telecommunications, Inc.** (17964)

★19697★
US West Communications - Learning Systems/Employee Development - Library (Info Sci)
3898 S. Teller St., Rm. 161   Phone: (303)763-1252
Lakewood, CO 80235   Lola C. Sanchez, Rec.Asst.
Founded: 1976. **Staff:** Prof 1. **Subjects:** Communications, management, economics, adult education, pluralism, computer technology. **Holdings:** 3000 books; Bell Company Practices; 150 videotapes; 100 audiocassettes; Bell technical journals. **Subscriptions:** 126 journals and other serials. **Services:** Interlibrary loan; library open to the public for reference use only. **Networks/Consortia:** Member of Colorado Alliance of Research Libraries (CARL). **Remarks:** FAX: (303)985-6496.

★19698★
USA Today - Library (Soc Sci)
1000 Wilson Blvd.   Phone: (703)276-5588
Arlington, VA 22229   Barbara Ellenbogen
Founded: 1982. **Staff:** Prof 11; Other 10. **Subjects:** Demographics, trends, trivia, political science, performing arts, biography, newspaper reference topics. **Holdings:** 5000 books; 500 reports; 2 million color and black-and-white photographs; 1 million clippings. **Subscriptions:** 300 journals and other serials; 60 newspapers. **Services:** Interlibrary loan; copying; library open to news media. **Computerized Information Services:** DIALOG Information Services, DataTimes, VU/TEXT Information Services, NEXIS; annual reports, editorial files (internal databases). Performs searches. Contact Person: Ray Hicks, Ref.Coord. **Publications:** National Source Guide; Libline Newsletter; Ganline Newsletter. **Remarks:** FAX: (703)247-3139. USA Today is a Gannett Co. newspaper.

★19699★
USAFIC International - Library (Law)
Box 136
Wyncote, PA 19095   Phone: (215)657-3976
Founded: 1975. **Subjects:** Security, law enforcement, firearms education and training, security training, forensic videograpy. **Holdings:** 1300 volumes. **Services:** Library open to researchers and other approved users.

★19700★
USCCCN Masters of Philanthropy - Library (Bus-Fin, Rel-Phil)
Box 863   Phone: (908)549-2599
Millburn, NJ 07041   Dr. A. Herbert Peterson, Pres.
Founded: 1986. **Staff:** 1. **Subjects:** Philanthropy, Satanism, the occult, Afro-Carribean studies, cults and intervention, business. **Holdings:** 3000 books; continuously updated reports, publications, videos, and training manuals (intervention and prevention guides). **Subscriptions:** 100 journals and other serials. **Services:** library open to the public by appointment. **Computerized Information Services:** Internal databases. **Publications:** The American Focus on Satanic Crime Series, annual. **Formed by the merger of:** Master of Philanthropy and USCCCN Survival Associates Network.

★19701★
USG Corporation - Research Center Library (Sci-Engr)
700 N. Hwy. 45   Phone: (708)362-9797
Libertyville, IL 60048   Mary Sharpe, Res.Libn.
Founded: 1961. **Staff:** Prof 1; Other 1. **Subjects:** Building materials, gypsum products, engineering, plastics and adhesives, lime, coatings, chemistry,

mineral fibers, paper, fertilizers, acoustical products. **Holdings:** 20,000 books; 1150 bound periodical volumes; 1619 pamphlets; 35,000 laboratory reports; 987 reels of microfilm; 970 microfiche; 60,000 patents; 15 VF drawers of unbound reports, articles, documents. **Subscriptions:** 300 journals and other serials. **Services:** Library open to the public with the approval of the director of research. **Automated Operations:** Computerized public access catalog and serials. **Computerized Information Services:** DIALOG Information Services, STN International. **Networks/Consortia:** Member of North Suburban Library System (NSLS). **Special Indexes:** Gypsum references (computerized). **Remarks:** FAX: (708)362-4871.

USS Arizona Memorial
See: **U.S. Natl. Park Service** (17786)

USS Bowfin Submarine Museum & Park
See: **Pacific Fleet Submarine Memorial Association - USS Bowfin Submarine Museum & Park** (12666)

★19702★
Ustav Vedeckych Informacii a Kniznica - University of Veterinary Medicine (Med, Food-Bev)
Komenskeho 73   Phone: 95 36884
CS-041 81 Kosice, Czechoslovakia   Marta Prosbova, M.V.D., Ph.D.
Founded: 1949. **Staff:** Prof 11; Other 1. **Subjects:** Veterinary medicine, food hygiene, environmental protection, education. **Holdings:** 101,399 books; 10,639 bound periodical volumes; 4425 reports; 20 microfiche. **Subscriptions:** 302 journals and other serials; 26 newspapers. **Services:** Interlibrary loan; copying; library open to the public. **Computerized Information Services:** International Atomic Energy Agency, Excerpta Medica, CA Search, AGRIS; CD-ROM (CAB). Contact Person: Sona Lemakova, M.V.D., Ph.D. **Publications:** Information Retrieval on Fur Animal Production; list of publication activity. **Remarks:** FAX: 95 767675.

Ustav Vedeckych Zdravotnickych Informacii - Slovenska Lekarska Kniznica
See: **Institute of Scientific Health Information - Slovak Medical Library** (7973)

★19703★
USX Corporation - Marathon Oil Company - Law Library (Law, Energy)
539 S. Main St., Rm. 854-M   Phone: (419)421-3376
Findlay, OH 45840   Paul G. Mitchell, Law Libn.
Staff: Prof 1; Other 1. **Subjects:** Law, petroleum industry. **Holdings:** 19,800 books; 19 drawers of microfiche; 16 drawers of microfilm. **Subscriptions:** 250 journals and other serials. **Services:** Interlibrary loan; copying; library open to the public by permission. **Computerized Information Services:** LEXIS, DIALOG Information Services, WESTLAW. **Remarks:** FAX: (419)421-3578.

★19704★
USX Corporation - Marathon Oil Company - Petroleum Technology Center - Technical Information Center (Energy)
Box 269   Phone: (303)794-2601
Littleton, CO 80160   Clarence A. Sturdivant, Supv.
Founded: 1956. **Staff:** Prof 10; Other 1. **Subjects:** Petroleum - exploration, refining, production, transportation, conservation. **Holdings:** 25,000 books; 45,000 bound periodical volumes; 55,000 hardcopy and microfiche technical reports, dissertations, meeting papers; 22,000 patents; 11,000 maps and charts. **Subscriptions:** 1000 journals and other serials; 10 newspapers. **Services:** Center not open to the public. **Computerized Information Services:** Online systems. **Special Catalogs:** Catalog for books, maps, and technical reports (online). **Remarks:** FAX: (303)797-8240.

★19705★
USX Corporation - U.S. Steel Group - Information Resource Center (Sci-Engr)
4000 Tech Center Dr.
MS 88   Phone: (412)825-2344
Monroeville, PA 15146   Angela R. Pollis, Staff Supv.
Founded: 1928. **Staff:** Prof 2; Other 1. **Subjects:** Metallurgy, materials science, steel manufacture and finishing, chemistry and physics, coal and

coke technology, physical chemistry, business. **Holdings:** 25,000 books; 1500 dissertations; 30,000 translations; 10,000 government and university reports; U.S. patents and chemical abstracts on microfilm. **Subscriptions:** 400 journals and other serials; 5 newspapers. **Services:** Interlibrary loan; center not open to the public. **Automated Operations:** Computerized cataloging and serials. **Computerized Information Services:** DIALOG Information Services, Dow Jones News/Retrieval, Dun & Bradstreet Business Credit Services, Inforonics, Inc.; internal database. Performs searches on fee basis. **Publications:** Newsletter, monthly. **Special Indexes:** KWIC and KWOC listings of technical reports. **Remarks:** FAX: (412)825-2050. Alternate telephone number(s): 825-2345. FAX: (412)825-2050. **Staff:** J.A. Richardson, Info.Spec.

★ 19706 ★
Utah Field House of Natural History State Park - Reference Library
(Biol Sci, Sci-Engr)
235 E. Main St.   Phone: (801)789-3799
Vernal, UT 84078   Alden H. Hamblin, Park Mgr.
Founded: 1948. **Staff:** Prof 3; Other 3. **Subjects:** Natural history, geology, paleontology, archeology. **Holdings:** 4000 books. **Services:** Library open to the public. **Remarks:** Maintained by Utah State Division of Parks and Recreation.

★ 19707 ★
Utah Geological Survey - Library (Sci-Engr)
2363 Foothill Dr.   Phone: (801)467-7970
Salt Lake City, UT 84109   Mage Yonetani, Libn.
Staff: 1. **Subjects:** Geology, mineral deposits. **Holdings:** 5000 books. **Subscriptions:** 9 journals and other serials; 2 newspapers. **Services:** Library open to the public for reference use only. **Remarks:** FAX: (801)467-4070. **Formerly:** Utah State Geological and Mineral Survey.

★ 19708 ★
Utah State Archives (Hist)
Archives Bldg.
State Capitol   Phone: (801)538-3012
Salt Lake City, UT 84114   Jeffery O. Johnson, Dir.
Founded: 1951. **Staff:** Prof 11; Other 23. **Subjects:** Public records of the State of Utah and its political subdivisions. **Special Collections:** Military records. **Holdings:** 85,000 cubic feet of semi-active and historically valuable records; 85,000 cubic feet of records in paper copy; 95,000 reels of microfilm; 90,000 microfiche. **Subscriptions:** 35 journals and other serials; 2 newspapers. **Services:** Copying; archives open to the public. **Computerized Information Services:** RLIN. **Publications:** Records Retention Schedule. **Special Catalogs:** Records Series Catalog.

Utah State Geological and Mineral Survey
See: **Utah Geological Survey** (19707)

★ 19709 ★
Utah State Historical Society - Library (Hist)
300 Rio Grande
Salt Lake City, UT 84101   Phone: (801)533-5808
Founded: 1952. **Staff:** Prof 5. **Subjects:** History - Utah, Mormon, Western, Indian. **Special Collections:** Utah water records (200 linear feet); Works Progress Administration records (124 linear feet). **Holdings:** 24,000 books; 50,000 bound periodical volumes; 500,000 photographs; 22,000 pamphlets; 33,000 maps; 1500 oral history tapes; 3500 linear feet of manuscripts; 6000 reels of microfilm; 160 feet of clippings files; 5500 museum objects. **Subscriptions:** 220 journals and other serials. **Services:** Copying; library open to the public. **Automated Operations:** Computerized cataloging. **Computerized Information Services:** RLIN. **Publications:** Guide to Unpublished Materials; Guide to the Women's History Holdings at the USHS Library. **Special Indexes:** Utah History Index (card). **Remarks:** FAX: (801)364-6436. **Staff:** Linda Thatcher, Coord. of Coll.Mgt.; Susan Whetstone, Photo.Libn.

★ 19710 ★
Utah State Hospital - Library (Med)
1300 East Center St.
Box 270   Phone: (801)373-4400
Provo, UT 84601   Janina Chilton, Libn.
Staff: Prof 1. **Subjects:** Medicine, psychology. **Holdings:** 900 volumes; records; tapes. **Subscriptions:** 54 journals and other serials. **Services:** Library not open to the public. **Computerized Information Services:** DIALOG Information Services. **Remarks:** Maintains a patients' collection of 1500 volumes and 14 journal subscriptions.

★ 19711 ★
Utah State Law Library (Law)
125 State Capitol Bldg.   Phone: (801)538-1046
Salt Lake City, UT 84114   Nancy H. Cheng, Law Libn.
Founded: 1914. **Staff:** Prof 1; Other 2. **Subjects:** Law. **Holdings:** 60,000 volumes. **Subscriptions:** 50 journals and other serials, 5 newspapers. **Services:** Copying; library open to the public. **Remarks:** FAX: (801)538-1046.

★ 19712 ★
Utah State Legislature - Office of Legislative Research and General Counsel - Information Center (Law)
436 State Capitol   Phone: (801)538-1032
Salt Lake City, UT 84114   Jane A. Peterson, Info.Coord.
Founded: 1975. **Staff:** 2. **Subjects:** State legislature, state and local government. **Special Collections:** Legislative legal opinions; legislative histories of interim committee meetings. **Holdings:** 2000 books. **Subscriptions:** 90 journals and other serials. **Services:** Center open to the public. **Automated Operations:** Computerized public access catalog and cataloging. **Computerized Information Services:** DIALOG Information Services, WESTLAW, LEGISNET, ISIS, LEGI-SLATE, Deseret News; Utah Code (internal database). **Remarks:** FAX: (801)538-1712.

★ 19713 ★
Utah State Library (Info Sci)
2150 South 300 West, Suite 16   Phone: (801)466-5888
Salt Lake City, UT 84115   Amy Owen, Dir.
Founded: 1957. **Staff:** Prof 15; Other 12. **Subjects:** State and federal government. **Holdings:** 39,811 volumes; 49,987 federal documents; 25,892 state documents. **Subscriptions:** 105 journals and other serials. **Services:** Interlibrary loan; library open to the public with restrictions. **Automated Operations:** Computerized public access catalog (Le Pac), cataloging, and acquisitions. **Computerized Information Services:** DIALOG Information Services, BRS Information Technologies, Mead Data Central, Deseret News; ALANET (electronic mail service). **Networks/Consortia:** Member of Bibliographical Center for Research, Rocky Mountain Region, Inc. (BCR), Utah College Library Council (UCLC). **Publications:** Directions for Utah Libraries, monthly - free upon request; Utah Undercover, annual; Directory of Public Libraries in Utah, annual; Utah Public Library Service, annual. **Remarks:** FAX: (801)533-4657. Electronic mail address(es): ALA1531 (ALANET). Maintained by Utah Department of Community and Economic Development. **Staff:** Douglas Abrams, Dp.Dir.; Gerald Buttars, Dp.Dir.; Edith Blankenship, Prog.Dir., Info.Serv.

★ 19714 ★
Utah State Library - Blind and Physically Handicapped Program - Regional Library (Aud-Vis)
2150 South 300 West, Suite 16   Phone: (801)466-6363
Salt Lake City, UT 84115   Gerald A. Buttars, Prog.Dir.
Founded: 1934. **Staff:** Prof 7; Other 11. **Holdings:** 384,771 talking books and braille books; cassettes; open reel tapes; large print books. **Subscriptions:** 120 journals and other serials. **Services:** Interlibrary loan; copying; radio reading service; library open to blind and physically handicapped. **Automated Operations:** Computerized circulation and braille printer. **Networks/Consortia:** Member of National Library Service for the Blind & Physically Handicapped (NLS). **Publications:** The Ensign, monthly; See Note (newsletter), quarterly. **Special Catalogs:** Mormon literature; Mormon History, Fiction, and Books by L.D.S. Authors; Utah, Wyoming, and the West History and Literature. **Remarks:** This Regional Library for the Blind is the Multi-State Center for 21 Western and mid-western states. FAX: (801)533-4657. **Staff:** Karnell Parry, Multi-State Libn.; Michael Sweeney, Rd.Adv.Libn.; Bessie Oakes, Spec.Serv.Libn.; Robert Wall, Radio Prog.Mgr.; Dennis Hall, Radio Prog.; Sharon Crandall, Volunteer Coord.

★ 19715 ★
Utah State University - Developmental Center for Handicapped Persons - Family Resource Library (Educ)
UMC 9621   Phone: (801)752-0238
Logan, UT 84332   Julia Burnham, Lib.Coord.
Founded: 1972. **Subjects:** Family resources about handicapping conditions and training of the handicapped. **Holdings:** 900 volumes.

★ 19716 ★
Utah Valley Regional Medical Center - Medical Library (Med)
1034 N. 500 W.   Phone: (801)371-7180
Provo, UT 84603   Alan Grosbeck, Media Spec.
Staff: 2. **Subjects:** Medicine. **Holdings:** 1200 books; 135,000 periodicals; 88 drawers of microfilm and microfiche. **Subscriptions:** 500 journals and other serials. **Services:** Interlibrary loan; copying; library open to the public. **Automated Operations:** Computerized cataloging, serials, and circulation. **Computerized Information Services:** MEDLINE, DIALOG Information Services; DOCLINE (electronic mail service). Performs searches on fee basis. **Networks/Consortia:** Member of National Network of Libraries of Medicine - Midcontinental Region, Utah Health Sciences Library Consortium (UHSLC). **Remarks:** FAX: (801)371-7186. **Staff:** Margaret Gatenby.

★ 19717 ★
Utah Water Research Laboratory - Library (Sci-Engr)
Utah State University   Phone: (801)750-3200
Logan, UT 84322-8200   Arthur L. Rivers, Sr.Graphics Techn.
Founded: 1965. **Staff:** Prof 1; Other 2. **Subjects:** Water resources planning, water quality, hydrology, hydraulics. **Special Collections:** UWRL Project Report Series, occasional papers, and proceedings. **Holdings:** 35,000 books. **Subscriptions:** 11 journals and other serials; 6 newspapers. **Services:** Interlibrary loan; copying; library open to the public. **Special Catalogs:** Special catalog of UWRL publications. **Remarks:** FAX: (801)750-3663. Telex: 3729283 UWRL LOGAN UT.

★ 19718 ★
UTDC Inc. - Library (Trans)
Sta. A, Box 220   Phone: (613)384-3100
Kingston, ON, Canada K7M 6R2   Maggie Dorsey, Mgr., Off.Serv.
Founded: 1974. **Staff:** Prof 1. **Subjects:** Urban transportation, engineering, marketing, business. **Special Collections:** Engineering standards and specifications. **Holdings:** 2000 books; 1200 technical reports; 200 documents. **Subscriptions:** 51 journals and other serials. **Services:** Interlibrary loan; library open to the public by appointment with restrictions. **Remarks:** FAX: (613)389-6382; (613)384-8965.

★ 19719 ★
Ute Pass Historical Society - Archives (Hist)
20 W. Hwy. 24
PO Box 6875   Phone: (719)687-3041
Woodland Park, CO 80866   Esther Kroeger, Libn.
Founded: 1976. **Staff:** 4. **Subjects:** Ute Pass; Ute Indians; Pikes Peak; Ute Pass communities; local history; Colorado history; poetry - 1890-1920. **Special Collections:** Colorado Midland Railway Collection (manuscripts and paper materials); glass plate collection on Colorado (300). **Holdings:** 200 books; 6 AV programs; 20 linear feet of manuscripts; school books from 1890. **Services:** Copying; archives open to the public by appointment. **Remarks:** FAX: (719)687-8096. **Formerly:** Located in Cascade, CO.

★ 19720 ★
Utica Mutual Insurance Company - Resource Center (Bus-Fin)
180 Genesee St.   Phone: (315)734-2662
New Hartford, NY 13413   Joan H. Kane, Rsrc.Coord.
Staff: Prof 1. **Subjects:** Law, insurance, business management, history. **Holdings:** 9200 books. **Subscriptions:** 89 journals and other serials. **Services:** Interlibrary loan; copying; center open to the public with approval. **Automated Operations:** Computerized cataloging. **Computerized Information Services:** DIALOG Information Services; internal database. **Remarks:** FAX: (315)735-2662.

★ 19721 ★
(Utica) Observer Dispatch - Library (Publ)
221-3 Oriskany Plaza   Phone: (315)792-5184
Utica, NY 13501   Debbie Dufresne, Libn.
Founded: 1922. **Staff:** 1. **Subjects:** Newspaper reference topics. **Holdings:** 172 VF drawers of clippings; microfilm, 1889 to present. **Subscriptions:** 14 newspapers. **Services:** Library open to scholars and journalists with permission from executive editor.

V

V.I. Lenin Higher Institute of Mechanical and Electrical Engineering
See: **Technical University** (16032)

Vaestoliitto
See: **Finnish Population and Family Welfare Federation** (5719)

★ 19722 ★
Valdez Historical Society, Inc. N-P - Valdez Heritage Archives Alive (Hist)
Royal Center Egan Dr.
Box 6   Phone: (907)835-4367
Valdez, AK 99686   Dorothy I. Clifton, Dir.
Founded: 1959. **Staff:** 2. **Subjects:** Alaska, Valdez, poetry, philately, religion. **Holdings:** 3300 square feet of archival materials; films; slides. **Services:** Copying; free film and slide showings; archives open to the public. **Remarks:** Alternate telephone number(s): 835-4377.

★ 19723 ★
Valencia Province - Service for Prehistoric Research - Library (Hist, Soc Sci)
Calle de la Corona, 36   Phone: 391 7164
E-46003 Valencia, Spain   Consuelo Martin Piera, Libn.
Founded: 1927. **Staff:** Prof 2; Other 4. **Subjects:** Prehistory, archeology. **Holdings:** 20,661 books; 13,042 bound periodical volumes. **Subscriptions:** 761 journals and other serials. **Services:** Interlibrary loan; copying; library open to the public. **Publications:** Serie de Trabajos Varios, irregular; Archivo de Prehistoria Levantina, irregular; La Labor del Servicio de Investigacion Prehistorica y su Museo en el pasado ano, annual. **Also Known As:** Servicio de Investigacion Prehistorica. **Staff:** Carmen Baguena Barrachina, Asst.Libn.

Othon O. Valent Learning Resources Center
See: **U.S. Army - TRADOC - Sergeants Major Academy** (17022)

Curt Valentin Archive
See: **Museum of Modern Art - Department of Rights and Reproductions - Photographic Archives** (10907)

H.A. Valentine Memorial Library
See: **High Street Christian Church** (7192)

★ 19724 ★
Valentine Museum - Library (Hist)
1015 E. Clay St.
Richmond, VA 23219   Phone: (804)649-0711
Founded: 1898. **Staff:** Prof 4. **Subjects:** Life and history of Richmond, fine arts and photography. **Special Collections:** George and Huestis Cook Collection of Photographs (10,000 glass negatives); advertising (chromolithographs, especially tobacco); Hibbs Collection (580 prints); rare book collection (includes parts of the libraries of John Wickham and Valentine family members); manuscripts collection (personal and business papers of Richmond, 1760 to present); papers of the Valentine family, 1786-1920; papers of William James Hubard, artist, 1807-1862; papers of Daniel Call, lawyer, 1772-1844; records of the Richmond Exchange for Women's Work, 1883-1952; minute books of the Richmond Chamber of Commerce, 1867-1980; serials collection (19th century Richmond imprints; 250 volumes); Richmond City directories; Richmond City and Henrico county maps (200); theater collection (19th and 20th century playbills; 100 broadsides); ephemera collection (programs; holiday cards; invitations; miscellaneous printed material); correspondence of Edgar Allan Poe, James Chaffin, and others. **Holdings:** 7000 books; 104 bound periodical volumes; 32 VF drawers; 300 bound volumes of manuscripts; 70 major manuscript collections; 1.5 million photographs. **Subscriptions:** 10 journals and other serials. **Services:** Copying; photographic sales; library open to the public by appointment. **Remarks:** FAX: (804)643-3510. **Staff:** Gregg Kimball, Cur. of Bks. and Mss.; Teresa Roane, Asst.Supv. of Ref.Serv.; Jane Webb Smith, Cur. of Photo.; Barbara C. Batson, Cur. of Fine Arts.

★ 19725 ★
Valero Energy Corporation - Corporate Resource Center (Energy)
530 McCullough
Box 500   Phone: (512)246-2850
San Antonio, TX 78292   Judith A. Kraatz, Supv.
Founded: 1981. **Staff:** Prof 1; Other 2. **Subjects:** Natural gas, petroleum refining, management, accounting, computers. **Holdings:** 4000 books; 1000 bound periodical volumes; 1000 reports on microfiche; 45 VF drawers. **Subscriptions:** 354 journals and other serials. **Services:** Interlibrary loan; copying; SDI; library open to the public with restrictions. **Automated Operations:** Computerized cataloging, serials, and corporate documents. **Computerized Information Services:** DIALOG Information Services, PFDS Online, Dow Jones News/Retrieval, DataTimes, PetroScan, NEXIS. **Networks/Consortia:** Member of Council of Research & Academic Libraries (CORAL). **Publications:** New Acquisitions, monthly - for internal distribution only. **Special Indexes:** Serials list; oil field index (all printouts). **Remarks:** FAX: (512)246-2646.

★ 19726 ★
Validata Computer and Research Corporation - Library (Comp Sci)
428 S. Perry St.
Box 4719   Phone: (205)834-2324
Montgomery, AL 36104   Warren Phillips, Libn.
Subjects: Physical distribution management, microprocessor applications in business. **Holdings:** Figures not available.

★ 19727 ★
Vallejo Naval and Historical Museum - Library (Hist)
734 Marin St.   Phone: (707)643-0077
Vallejo, CA 94590   Dorothy E. Marsden, Libn.
Founded: 1980. **Staff:** Prof 1. **Subjects:** Local history; maritime history - general and of the Bay Area; Mare Island Naval Shipyard; naval philately. **Holdings:** 5000 books; Solano County Historical Society notebooks; 6000 photographs. **Subscriptions:** 16 journals and other serials. **Services:** Library open to the public by appointment. **Publications:** Guide to Social History Resources in the Vallejo Naval and Historical Museum Library; Bibliography of Material Related to World War II: Vallejo Naval and Historical Museum Library.

★ 19728 ★
(Valletta) American Center Library - USIS Library (Educ)
Development House, Fl. 3
St. Ann St., Floriana
P.O. Box 510
Valletta, Malta
Remarks: Maintained or supported by the U.S. Information Agency. Focus is on materials that will assist peoples outside the United States to learn about the United States, its people, history, culture, political processes, and social milieux.

★ 19729 ★
Valley Daily News - Library (Publ)
600 S. Washington St.
Box 130
Kent, WA 98032-0130   Phone: (206)872-6674
Founded: 1970. **Staff:** 1. **Subjects:** Newspaper reference topics. **Special Collections:** Bound volumes of Daily Record Chronicle, Daily News Journal, Daily Globe News, and their predecessors. **Holdings:** Books; microfilm; newspaper clippings; news photos; government documents; maps. **Subscriptions:** 6 newspapers. **Services:** Library not open to the public. **Remarks:** FAX: (206)854-1006.

★ 19730 ★
Valley Forge Christian College - Library (Rel-Phil)
1401 Charleston Rd.   Phone: (215)935-0450
Phoenixville, PA 19460-2399   Dorsey Reynolds, Libn.
Staff: Prof 1; Other 2. **Subjects:** Bible, theology (emphasis on Evangelical and Pentecostal doctrines), church history, Christian education. **Special Collections:** Pentecostalism. **Holdings:** 44,394 books. **Subscriptions:** 260 journals and other serials. **Services:** Interlibrary loan; copying; library open to the public.

★ 19731 ★
Valley Forge Historical Society - Washington Memorial Library (Hist)
Box 122   Phone: (215)783-0535
Valley Forge, PA 19481   Margaret Conner, Off.Mgr.
Founded: 1918. **Staff:** Prof 1; Other 4. **Subjects:** Revolutionary War,
Washingtoniana, American history. **Special Collections:** Writings of
Washington; Pennsylvania archives; Library of Reverend Andrew Hunter,
Chaplain in Continental Army. **Holdings:** 2000 books; 300 manuscripts.
Subscriptions: 700 journals and other serials. **Services:** Library open to the
public by appointment.

★ 19732 ★
Valley Hospital - Medical Library (Med)
223 North Van Dien Ave.   Phone: (201)447-8285
Ridgewood, NJ 07450   Claudia Allocco, Dir., Lib.Serv.
Founded: 1963. **Staff:** Prof 1; Other 2. **Subjects:** Medicine, nursing, hospital
management, allied health sciences. **Holdings:** 1000 books; 3000 bound
periodical volumes; 2 VF drawers of pamphlets. **Subscriptions:** 175 journals
and other serials. **Services:** Interlibrary loan; library not open to the public.
Computerized Information Services: MEDLARS. Performs searches on fee
basis. **Networks/Consortia:** Member of Bergen Passaic Regional Library
Cooperative. **Remarks:** FAX: (201)447-8648.

★ 19733 ★
Valley Medical Center - Library (Med)
400 S. 43rd St.
Renton, WA 98055   Phone: (206)251-5194
Founded: 1969. **Staff:** Prof 1. **Subjects:** Medicine, surgery, allied health
sciences. **Holdings:** 1050 books; 200 bound periodical volumes.
Subscriptions: 210 journals and other serials; 5 newspapers. **Services:**
Interlibrary loan. **Computerized Information Services:** MEDLINE, BRS
Information Technologies, WLN; OnTyme Electronic Message Network
Service (electronic mail service). **Networks/Consortia:** Member of Seattle
Area Hospital Library Consortium (SAHLC), Washington Medical
Librarians' Association. **Remarks:** FAX: (206)575-2593. **Staff:** Nancy
Turrentine, Libn.; Barbara Ivester, Libn.

★ 19734 ★
Valley Medical Center of Fresno - Medical Library (Med)
445 S. Cedar Ave.   Phone: (209)453-5030
Fresno, CA 93702   Vicky Christianson, Hosp.Libn.
Staff: Prof 1; Other 1. **Subjects:** Medicine, dentistry, nursing, hospital
administration. **Holdings:** 5000 volumes. **Subscriptions:** 150 journals and
other serials. **Services:** Interlibrary loan; copying; library open to the public
with restrictions.

★ 19735 ★
Valley National Bank - Library/Information Center (Bus-Fin)
Box 71, A-315   Phone: (602)261-2456
Phoenix, AZ 85001   J.F. Gorman, Mgr.
Founded: 1948. **Staff:** Prof 1. **Subjects:** Banking, business, economics,
management. **Holdings:** 1000 volumes. **Subscriptions:** 250 journals and
other serials. **Services:** Library not open to the public. **Computerized
Information Services:** DIALOG Information Services, Dow Jones News/
Retrieval, DataTimes.

★ 19736 ★
Valley News Dispatch - George D. Stuart Research Library (Publ)
210 Fourth Ave.   Phone: (412)226-4693
Tarentum, PA 15084   G. Louise McCleary, Libn.
Staff: 1. **Subjects:** Newspaper reference topics. **Special Collections:** Valley
News Dispatch, 1891 to present (microfilm). **Holdings:** Microfilm;
newspaper clips (1989 to present). **Services:** Library open to the public by
appointment. **Remarks:** FAX: (412)226-7788.

★ 19737 ★
Valley Presbyterian Hospital - Richard O. Myers Library (Med)
15107 Vanowen St.
Box 9102
Van Nuys, CA 91409-9102   Phone: (818)902-2973
                                    Francine Kubrin, Dir.Lib.Serv.
Founded: 1959. **Staff:** Prof 1; Other 1. **Subjects:** General medicine, general
surgery, nursing, hospital administration. **Holdings:** 5000 volumes; 500
audio cassettes; 1 VF drawer of pamphlets, bibliographies, and reprints; 1
VF drawer of AV catalogs. **Subscriptions:** 365 journals and other serials.
Services: Interlibrary loan; library not open to the public. **Computerized
Information Services:** MEDLINE, BRS Information Technologies.

★ 19738 ★
**Valley Regional Hospital - Education Department - Health Science
  Library** (Med)
Claremont, NH 03743   Phone: (603)542-1839
                                    Theresa Strickland
Subjects: Medicine. **Holdings:** 150 books. **Subscriptions:** 12 journals and
other serials. **Services:** Interlibrary loan; copying; library open to the public.
Remarks: FAX: (603)542-6616.

★ 19739 ★
Valley View Centre - Harrison Memorial Library (Med)
Box 1300   Phone: (306)694-3096
Moose Jaw, SK, Canada S6H 4R2   Diane Gray
Subjects: Special training programs, psychology, nursing. **Holdings:** Figures
not available. **Subscriptions:** 36 journals and other serials. **Services:** Library
not open to the public. **Publications:** In-House Communications
(newsletter), weekly - for internal distribution only.

VALNET
See: **U.S. Dept. of Veterans Affairs** (DC-Washington) (17311)

★ 19740 ★
Valparaiso University - Law Library (Law)
School of Law   Phone: (219)465-783?
Valparaiso, IN 46383   Mary G. Persyn, Law Libn
Founded: 1879. **Staff:** Prof 6; Other 5. **Subjects:** Law. **Special Collections:**
Indiana Supreme Court and Court of Appeals briefs, 1977 to present.
Holdings: 103,730 books; 7000 bound periodical volumes; 95,325 volumes
in microform; CIS legislative histories, 1974 to present, on microfiche;
Supreme Court records and briefs, 1978 to present, on microfiche.
Subscriptions: 2573 journals and other serials. **Services:** Interlibrary loan;
copying; library open to lawyers. **Automated Operations:** Integrated library
system (INNOPAC). **Computerized Information Services:** LEXIS,
WESTLAW, DIALOG Information Services, VU/TEXT Information
Services, LegalTrac, DataTimes. **Networks/Consortia:** Member of
INCOLSA. **Remarks:** FAX: (219)465-7872. **Staff:** Sally Holterhoff,
Doc.Libn.; Tim Watts, Pub.Serv.Libn.; Leslie Schaefer, Asst. Law Libn.;
Naomi Goodman, Cat.; Elaine Moore, Acq.Libn.

Valtionarkisto
See: **Finland - National Archives** (5708)

★ 19741 ★
**Valuation Research Corporation - Corporate Research and Reference
  Library** (Bus-Fin)
411 E. Wisconsin Ave.
Milwaukee, WI 53202   Phone: (414)271-8662
Staff: Prof 1; Other 2. **Subjects:** Appraisal/valuation, property assessment,
real estate, accounting, taxation, industrial technology. **Special Collections:**
Price indexes; machinery and equipment pricing files; real estate
transactions; financial statements of corporations. **Holdings:** 2500 books;
200 bound periodical volumes; catalogs and price lists. **Subscriptions:** 100
journals and other serials. **Services:** Interlibrary loan; copying; library open
to the public with restrictions. **Automated Operations:** Computerized
cataloging. **Networks/Consortia:** Member of Library Council of
Metropolitan Milwaukee, Inc. (LCOMM). **Remarks:** FAX: (414)271-3240.

★ 19742 ★
Value of Life Committee - Library (Med)
637 Cambridge St.
Brighton, MA 02135   Phone: (617)787-4400
Founded: 1970. **Subjects:** Medical and legal aspects of abortion, euthanasia,
ethics, and genetics. **Holdings:** 600 books, newspaper clippings, and other
items. **Subscriptions:** 10 journals and other serials; 7 newspapers. **Services:**
Library open to the public by appointment.

★ 19743 ★
Value Line Inc. - Library (Bus-Fin)
711 Third Ave., 8th Fl.   Phone: (212)687-3965
New York, NY 10017   Roy DeNunzio, Hd.Libn./Dept.Mgr.
Staff: Prof 1; Other 4. **Subjects:** Finance and economics. **Holdings:** 3000
books; 20 bound periodical volumes; 300 reports; 10,000 microfiche.
Subscriptions: 200 journals and other serials. **Services:** Information
provided by written request only; library not open to the public. **Automated
Operations:** Computerized circulation. **Remarks:** FAX: (212)986-3243.

★19744★
Valve Manufacturers Association of America - Library (Sci-Engr)
1050 17th St., N.W., Suite 701   Phone: (202)331-8105
Washington, DC 20036   T. Stephen Larkin, Pres.
Subjects: Industrial and distribution valves, actuators. **Holdings:** 300 volumes of technical and industrial data.

★19745★
Vampire Information Exchange - Library (Hum)
Box 328
Brooklyn, NY 11229-0328   Eric S. Held, Ed./Founder
Founded: 1978. **Subjects:** Vampires in fact and fiction. **Holdings:** 400 books; 150 bound periodical volumes; 56 newsletters. **Subscriptions:** 5 journals and other serials. **Services:** Library not open to the public. **Automated Operations:** Computerized cataloging. **Publications:** Vampire Information Exchange Newsletter, 5/year - for sale. **Special Catalogs:** Vampire Bibliography of Books (printout); catalogs of occasional book sales.

★19746★
Van Buren County Historical Society - Van Buren Historical Library (Hist)
58471 Red Arrow Hwy.   Phone: (616)621-2188
Hartford, MI 49057   Peg Cornish
Founded: 1972. **Staff:** 2. **Subjects:** History of Van Buren County and Michigan. **Holdings:** Books on Van Buren County; family pictures; family histories; oral histories; newspaper clippings; obituaries; township records; cemetery records; photographs. **Services:** Library open to the public with restrictions. **Staff:** LaVern Wolff.

G. Bernard Van Cleve Library
See: **Carnegie Museum of Natural History - Library** (3085)

Van Evera Library
See: **Human Resources Research Organization** (7530)

Van Gorden-Williams Library
See: **Museum of Our National Heritage** (10918)

★19747★
Van Hornesville Community Corporation - Library (Hist)
Box 16   Phone: (315)858-1554
Van Hornesville, NY 13475   Josephine E. Case, Pres.
Subjects: Local and regional New York State history. **Holdings:** Books; rare maps. **Services:** Copying; library open to graduate students holding letters of recommendation. **Remarks:** Alternate telephone number(s): 858-0030. Owen D. Young Collection transferred to St. Lawrence University - Owen D. Young Library.

Robert W. Van Houten Library
See: **New Jersey Institute of Technology** (11504)

★19748★
Van Kampen Merritt Inc. - Research Center (Bus-Fin)
1 Parkview Plaza   Phone: (708)684-6370
Oakbrook Terrace, IL 60181   Joyce L. Miller, Dir. of Info.Serv.
Founded: 1985. **Staff:** Prof 2; Other 3. **Subjects:** Finance, municipal bonds. **Special Collections:** Municipal bond official and financial statements. **Holdings:** 1500 books. **Subscriptions:** 125 journals and other serials; 10 newspapers. **Services:** Center not open to the public. **Computerized Information Services:** LEXIS, NEXIS, DIALOG Information Services, Dun & Bradstreet Business Credit Services, InvesText, VU/TEXT Information Services, Dow Jones News/Retrieval, OCLC; The Merritt System (internal database); CD-ROMs (ABI/INFORM, Business Dateline, Business Periodicals Ondisc). Performs searches on fee basis. **Networks/Consortia:** Member of DuPage Library System. **Publications:** Cutting Edge (table of contents service). **Remarks:** FAX: (708)684-5967. Toll-free telephone number(s): (800)225-2222. **Formerly:** Its Corporate Information Center. **Staff:** Barbara L. Cooke, Info.Spec.

Van Noy Library
See: **U.S. Army Post - Fort Belvoir** (17058)

John Van Oosten Library
See: **U.S. Fish & Wildlife Service - National Fisheries Research Center - Great Lakes** (17500)

J. Robert Van Pelt Library
See: **Michigan Technological University - J. Robert Van Pelt Library** (10344)

John Van Puffelen Library
See: **Appalachian Bible College** (911)

Van Steenberg Library
See: **Kendall College of Art & Design** (8616)

James D. Van Trump Library
See: **Pittsburgh History & Landmarks Foundation** (13085)

Josselyn Van Tyne Memorial Library
See: **Wilson Ornithological Society** (20469)

Van Voorhis Library
See: **Poetry Society of America** (13156)

Jared Van Wagenen, Jr. Learning Resource Center
See: **State University of New York - College of Agriculture and Technology at Cobleskill** (15721)

★19749★
Van Wert County Law Library (Law)
Court of Common Pleas, 3rd Fl.   Phone: (419)238-6935
Van Wert, OH 45891   Richard L. Atwood, Sec./Treas.
Staff: 1. **Subjects:** Law. **Holdings:** 14,000 volumes; Ohio law publications. **Services:** Library open to members of the bar. **Remarks:** Alternate telephone number(s): (419)238-2874.

★19750★
Van Wyck Homestead Museum - Library
PO Box 133
Fishkill, NY 12524
Founded: 1973. **Subjects:** Local and American history, early American crafts, genealogy, American Indian, biography. **Special Collections:** Holland Society of New York yearbooks, 1888-1931. **Holdings:** 700 books; 80 bound periodical volumes; 100 early military documents; clippings and early local newspapers; early business ledgers and schoolbooks. **Remarks:** Maintained by Fishkill Historical Society, Inc. Currently inactive.

★19751★
Ing. Juan C. Van Wyck Center for Research and Development - Library (Sci-Engr)
Berutti y Rio Bamba   Phone: 81-3194
2000 Rosario, Argentina   E. Sisti, Libn.
Subjects: Engineering, material technology, structural analysis, metallurgy, nuclear technology. **Holdings:** 41,175 volumes. **Remarks:** Maintained by Rosario National University - Faculty of Exact Sciences and Engineering. **Also Known As:** Centro de Investigacion y Desarrollo "Ing. Juan C. Van Wyk."

Van Wylen Library
See: **Hope College** (7381)

James E. Van Zandt Medical Center
See: U.S. Dept. of Veterans Affairs (PA-Altoona) (17401)

★ 19752 ★
Vancouver Art Gallery - Library (Art)
750 Hornby St.   Phone: (604)682-4668
Vancouver, BC, Canada V6Z 2H7   Cheryl A. Siegel, Libn.
Founded: 1931. **Staff:** Prof 1. **Subjects:** Painting, sculpture, prints, drawings. **Special Collections:** Canadian exhibition catalogs, artists files, and museum collection catalogs. **Holdings:** 9000 books; 550 bound periodical volumes; 18,000 exhibition catalogs. **Subscriptions:** 125 journals and other serials. **Services:** Interlibrary loan; copying; library open to the public for reference use only. **Automated Operations:** Computerized cataloging. **Publications:** Members Calendar; annual report. **Special Catalogs:** Checklist of biographical files (Canadian artists and artists working in Canada); artists exhibiting at the Vancouver Art Gallery. **Remarks:** FAX: (604)682-1086.

★ 19753 ★
Vancouver Board of Trade/World Trade Centre Vancouver - Information Services Department (Bus-Fin)
999 Canada Place, Suite 400   Phone: (604)681-2111
Vancouver, BC, Canada V6E 3C1   Elizabeth Steele, Info.Serv.Off.
Staff: 1. **Subjects:** Business, economics, international trade. **Special Collections:** International trade. **Holdings:** 350 books; 4 VF drawers of newspapers and pamphlets; 2 VF drawers of annual reports and official publications; Business Opportunities Sourcing System (BOSS) of Canadian manufacturers and trading houses. **Subscriptions:** 50 journals and other serials; 5 newspapers. **Services:** Copying; SDI; library open to the public if material is not available elsewhere. **Computerized Information Services:** Network (electronic mail service). **Publications:** Annual Clerical Salary Survey; Facts and Trends (digest of current industrial relations), biweekly - by subscription. **Remarks:** FAX: (604)681-0437.

★ 19754 ★
Vancouver Botanical Gardens Association - Vandusen Gardens Library (Biol Sci)
5251 Oak St.   Phone: (604)266-7194
Vancouver, BC, Canada V6M 4H1   Barbara Fox, Libn.
Founded: 1975. **Staff:** Prof 1; Other 12. **Subjects:** Horticulture, botany, gardening, plant exploration. **Holdings:** 3600 books; 6 VF drawers of documents. **Subscriptions:** 50 journals and other serials. **Services:** Copying; library open to the public for reference use only.

★ 19755 ★
Vancouver Community College - City Centre Campus Library (Educ)
250 West Pender St.   Phone: (604)443-8340
Vancouver, BC, Canada V6B 1S9   Phyllis Butler, Campus Libn.
Founded: 1974. **Staff:** Prof 2; Other 8. **Subjects:** Business, allied health sciences, drafting, electronics, culinary arts, hairdressing, printing production, tourism and hospitality. **Holdings:** 17,000 books; 600 pamphlet files; 4500 AV programs. **Subscriptions:** 303 journals and other serials. **Services:** Interlibrary loan; copying; library open to the public with restrictions. **Automated Operations:** Computerized cataloging and circulation. **Computerized Information Services:** DIALOG Information Services, UTLAS, BRS Information Technologies; CD-ROMs (ERIC, MEDLINE, CBCA (Canadian Business and Current Affairs), PCOSIG Library); Envoy 100 (electronic mail service). Performs searches on fee basis. **Remarks:** FAX: (604)682-3342. Maintained by Vancouver Community College. **Formerly:** Vancouver Vocational Institute. **Staff:** Eva Sharell.

★ 19756 ★
Vancouver Memorial Hospital - R.D. Wiswall Memorial Library (Med)
3400 Main St.
Box 1600
Vancouver, WA 98668   Phone: (206)696-5143
       Sylvia E. MacWilliams, Dir., Lib.Serv.
Founded: 1965. **Staff:** Prof 1. **Subjects:** Medicine, nursing. **Holdings:** Figures not available. **Services:** Interlibrary loan; library not open to the public. **Automated Operations:** Computerized statistics. **Computerized Information Services:** MEDLARS. **Remarks:** Maintained by Southwest Washington Hospitals.

★ 19757 ★
Vancouver Museum - Library and Resource Centre (Hist)
1100 Chestnut St.   Phone: (604)736-4431
Vancouver, BC, Canada V6J 3J9   Norah J. McLaren, Libn.
Founded: 1968. **Staff:** Prof 1; Other 3. **Subjects:** Local history, decorative arts, ethnology, archaeology, museology, Asian studies. **Holdings:** 8500 books. **Subscriptions:** 30 journals and other serials. **Services:** Library open to the public on a limited schedule. **Remarks:** FAX: (604)736-5417.

Vancouver Pretrial Services Centre
See: British Columbia Ministry of Solicitor General - Vancouver Pretrial Services Centre (2168)

★ 19758 ★
Vancouver Public Aquarium - Library (Biol Sci)
Box 3232   Phone: (604)685-3364
Vancouver, BC, Canada V6B 3X8   Treva Ricou, Libn.
Staff: Prof 1; Other 3. **Subjects:** Marine mammals, fish, reptiles, amphibians, invertebrates, birds. **Holdings:** 4000 books; 850 bound periodical volumes. **Subscriptions:** 124 journals and other serials. **Services:** Copying; library for reference use only. **Automated Operations:** Computerized public access catalog. **Computerized Information Services:** DIALOG Information Services. **Remarks:** FAX: (604)631-2529.

★ 19759 ★
Vancouver Public Library - Business & Economics Division (Bus-Fin)
750 Burrard St.   Phone: (604)665-3365
Vancouver, BC, Canada V6Z 1X5   Sheila Thompson, Hd.
Founded: 1951. **Staff:** Prof 6.5; Other 13. **Subjects:** Industrial economics, transportation, management, marketing, labor, real estate. **Holdings:** 72,000 volumes; 1500 trade directories; 20,000 corporation reports; annual reports; company files; 20,000 pamphlets; 51 cases of clippings. **Subscriptions:** 900 journals and other serials; 10 newspapers. **Services:** Interlibrary loan; division open to the public. **Automated Operations:** Computerized cataloging and circulation. **Computerized Information Services:** Info Globe, Infomart Online, DIALOG Information Services, CAN/OLE, QL Systems; internal databases. **Special Indexes:** Corporation card file; periodical indexing card file. **Remarks:** FAX: (604)665-2265. **Staff:** Linda Woodcock, Libn.; Glenda Guttman, Libn.; Shelagh Flaherty, Libn.; Maureen Matthews, Libn.; Daniela Esparo, Libn.; Marilyn Taylor, Libn.

★ 19760 ★
Vancouver School of Theology - Library (Rel-Phil)
6050 Chancellor Blvd.   Phone: (604)228-0189
Vancouver, BC, Canada V6T 1X3   Elizabeth Hart, Libn.
Founded: 1971. **Staff:** Prof 1; Other 5. **Subjects:** Biblical studies, Christianity, doctrinal and practical theology, Protestant (especially Canadian) denominations and sects, Judaism. **Holdings:** 73,374 books; 4571 bound periodical volumes; 84 kits; 811 microfiche titles; 394 reels of microfilm; 39 phonograph records; 1854 audio cassettes and tapes; 74 filmstrips; 2754 slides; 17 maps; 100 video cassettes. **Subscriptions:** 400 journals and other serials. **Services:** Interlibrary loan; copying; library open to the public. **Computerized Information Services:** Envoy 100 (electronic mail service). **Publications:** Acquisitions list, monthly; periodical abstracts, bimonthly. **Remarks:** FAX: (604)228-0189. Electronic mail address(es): VST.LIBRARY (Envoy 100).

★ 19761 ★
Vancouver Talmud Torah School - Library (Rel-Phil)
998 W. 26th Ave.   Phone: (604)736-7307
Vancouver, BC, Canada V5Z 2G1   Marylile Gill, Teacher/Libn.
Staff: Prof 1. **Subjects:** Hebraica and Judaica. **Holdings:** 5000 books; phonograph records; filmstrips; audio cassettes; kits; transparencies; study prints. **Subscriptions:** 50 journals and other serials. **Services:** Interlibrary loan; library open to the public with restrictions. **Remarks:** FAX: (604)736-9754.

★ 19762 ★
Vancouver Teachers' Professional Library (Educ)
Teacher Centre
123 E. 6th Ave.   Phone: (604)874-2617
Vancouver, BC, Canada V5T 1J6   Linda Dunbar, Lib.Techn.
Founded: 1921. **Staff:** 2. **Subjects:** Education. **Holdings:** 15,000 books; 500 pamphlets; 650 microfiche. **Subscriptions:** 325 journals and other serials. **Services:** Interlibrary loan; library open to the public for reference use only. **Computerized Information Services:** DIALOG Information Services.

Vancouver Vocational Institute
See: Vancouver Community College - City Centre Campus Library (19755)

★ 19763 ★
Vandalia Historical Society - James Hall Library (Hist)
Little Brick House
621 St. Clair St.   Phone: (618)283-0024
Vandalia, IL 62471   Mary Burtschi, V.P.
Founded: 1964. **Staff:** Prof 3; Other 4. **Subjects:** Illinois and local history. **Special Collections:** James Hall Collection, 1793-1868; Abraham Lincoln Collection, 1834-1839; National Road in Illinois Collection (photographs; essays; articles); biographies of Vandalia authors, artists, and statesmen; Joseph Charles Burtschi Collection; Mary Burtschi Collection; Burtschi family archives, 1775-1975; History of the Fayette County Bicentennial of the American Revolution, 1974-1976; Memory Book of the Fayette County Bicentennial of the American Revolution, 1974-1976 (includes photographs of commission members and events; newspaper and magazine articles; printed programs); Badger Collection Featuring Vandalia, Illinois, 1985 (sketches of residences and churches of architectural quality, 1836-1913); Vandalia Historical Society Memory Book, 1954-1987 (photographs; newspaper articles; printed programs); Inventory File of Fifty-five Old Buildings, 1820-1913 (photographs; sketches; architectural, cultural, and historical research survey sheets); Walking Tour A (booklet on the original town of Vandalia, 1819); old Vandalia residences photographs. **Holdings:** 100 books; photographs; manuscripts; reports; letters; scrapbooks. **Services:** Library open to the public by appointment. **Publications:** List of publications - available on request. **Staff:** Josephine Burtschi, Pres.; Candace Zeman, Supv.; Linda Hanabarger, Cat.Libn.

★ 19764 ★
Vanderbilt Family Foundation - Academy of Independent Scholars - Whiteford Memorial Library (Soc Sci)
Box 6317   Phone: (202)362-1588
Washington, DC 20015-0317   Renee K. Boyle, Lib.Dir.
Founded: 1974. **Staff:** 3. **Subjects:** Political science, international relations, humanities, education, post modern age thought, philosophy. **Special Collections:** Prix Teilhard/Londres award manuscripts; Primers for the Age of Inner Space series books. **Holdings:** 2450 books. **Subscriptions:** 19 journals and other serials. **Services:** Interlibrary loan; library open to members and foreign post-graduate scholars awarded grants by the organization or the U.S. State Department only. **Publications:** Primers for the Age of Inner Space, irregular - free upon request to university and public libraries. **Formerly:** Academy of Independent Scholars. **Staff:** Dorsey F. Sheroan; Denise de Faymonville; E.S. Lawrence.

★ 19765 ★
R.T. Vanderbilt Company, Inc. - Library
33 Winfield St.   Phone: (203)853-1400
East Norwalk, CT 06855   Ann Marie Dostilio
Founded: 1956. **Subjects:** Organic chemistry, rubber, plastics, ceramics, paint, mineralogy. **Holdings:** 10,000 books; 4800 bound periodical volumes; 1500 technical reports; 1000 reprints; 22 VF drawers of technical data; 1200 reels of microfilm; Chemical Abstracts and Official Patent Gazette on microfilm.

★ 19766 ★
Vanderbilt University - Alyne Queener Massey Law Library (Law)
School of Law   Phone: (615)322-2568
Nashville, TN 37203   Igor I. Kavass, Dir.
Staff: Prof 8; Other 10. **Subjects:** Law. **Special Collections:** James Cullen Looney Medico-Legal Collection. **Holdings:** 254,469 volumes; 80,036 documents; microforms. **Subscriptions:** 4319 journals and other serials. **Services:** Interlibrary loan; copying; library open to the public for reference use only. **Automated Operations:** Computerized cataloging and acquisitions. **Computerized Information Services:** OCLC, LEXIS, WESTLAW, Information Access Company (IAC). **Networks/Consortia:** Member of SOLINET. **Publications:** Selected bibliographies - available on request. **Remarks:** FAX: (615)322-6631. **Staff:** Howard A. Hood, Legal Info.Spec.

★ 19767 ★
Vanderbilt University - Jean and Alexander Heard Library - Anne Potter Wilson Music Library (Mus)
2400 Blakemore Ave.   Phone: (615)322-7695
Nashville, TN 37212   Shirley Marie Watts, Dir.
Founded: 1948. **Staff:** Prof 1; Other 4. **Subjects:** Music. **Special Collections:** Seminar in piano teaching (lectures, master classes, recitals, 1970-1976; cassette tapes). **Holdings:** 14,160 volumes; 14,262 scores; 12,644 phonograph records; 1163 compact discs; 112 reels of tapes; 542 cassette tapes; 141 videotapes; microforms. **Subscriptions:** 182 journals and other serials. **Services:** Interlibrary loan; copying; library open to visiting scholars for reference use only. **Automated Operations:** Computerized public access catalog, cataloging, acquisitions, serials, and circulation. **Remarks:** FAX: (615)343-0050.

★ 19768 ★
Vanderbilt University - Jean and Alexander Heard Library - Arts Collection (Art)
419 21st Ave., S.   Phone: (615)343-7875
Nashville, TN 37240-0007   Sigrid Docken Mount, Arts Libn.
Founded: 1973. **Subjects:** Art - history, biography, theory, criticism; architectural history; photography; landscape design. **Special Collections:** The Norman L. and Roselea J. Goldberg Research Library (18th and 19th century British landscape art; 400 volumes). **Holdings:** 51,700 books; 5533 bound periodical volumes; 20 VF drawers of art ephemera; 8800 items in arts picture file. **Subscriptions:** 200 journals and other serials. **Networks/Consortia:** Member of Center for Research Libraries (CRL).

★ 19769 ★
Vanderbilt University - Jean and Alexander Heard Library - Divinity Library (Rel-Phil)
419 21st Ave., S.   Phone: (615)322-2865
Nashville, TN 37240   William J. Hook, Dir.
Founded: 1894. **Staff:** Prof 3; Other 1. **Subjects:** Biblical studies, church history, liturgy and homiletics, theology, ethics, history of religion, religion and personality. **Special Collections:** Judaica (7000 volumes); memorabilia. **Holdings:** 151,000 volumes; microforms. **Subscriptions:** 1148 journals and other serials. **Services:** Interlibrary loan; copying; library open to the public on a fee basis. **Automated Operations:** Computerized public access catalog, cataloging, acquisitions, serials, and circulation. **Computerized Information Services:** BRS Information Technologies, OCLC. **Publications:** Library Guide, annual; subject bibliographies for each graduate area in the Divinity School. **Remarks:** FAX: (615)343-7276. **Staff:** Anne Womack, Pub.Serv.Libn.; Dorothy Parks, Coll.Libn.

★ 19770 ★
Vanderbilt University - Jean and Alexander Heard Library - Divinity Library - Kesler Circulating Library (Rel-Phil)
419 21st Ave., S.   Phone: (615)322-2865
Nashville, TN 37240   William J. Hook, Dir.
Founded: 1940. **Staff:** Prof 1; Other 1. **Subjects:** Religion. **Services:** Mail circulation of books to ordained ministry; library open to the public with restrictions. **Publications:** Recent Acquisition Lists, irregular - to members. **Remarks:** Kesler Circulating Library is a continuing education service of the Divinity Library and utilizes its holdings. Membership is open to clergy engaged in ministry (except those based in academic institutions whose needs are met by interlibrary loan) in the continental United States and Canada; nondenominational; free membership upon application. FAX: (615)343-7276. Electronic mail address(es): @CTRVAX.VANDERBILT.EDU. **Staff:** Anne Womack, Pub.Serv.Libn.

★ 19771 ★
Vanderbilt University - Jean and Alexander Heard Library - Dyer Observatory (Sci-Engr)
Sta. B
Box 1803   Phone: (615)373-4897
Nashville, TN 37235   Ellen Ellis, Libn.
Founded: 1953. **Staff:** Prof 1. **Subjects:** Astronomy, astrophysics. **Holdings:** 5000 books; 6600 bound periodical volumes; 10,000 unbound reprints; 43 theses; 1100 slides; 5000 photographs of star fields. **Subscriptions:** 345 journals and other serials. **Services:** Interlibrary loan; observatory open to the public by appointment. **Publications:** Arthur J. Dyer Observatory Reprints, irregular. **Remarks:** The observatory is located at 1000 Oman Dr., Brentwood, TN 37027.

★19772★
Vanderbilt University - Jean and Alexander Heard Library - Education Library (Educ, Info Sci)
Box 325
Peabody Station
Nashville, TN 37203-5601
Phone: (615)322-8095
Mary Beth Blalock, Dir.
Founded: 1875. **Staff:** Prof 3; Other 8. **Subjects:** Education, psychology, special education, child study, human resources, human development, curriculum materials for grades K-12. **Holdings:** 217,322 books; 846 reels of microfilm; 472,001 microfiche; 10,641 microcards; 947 cassettes; 1540 games and kits. **Subscriptions:** 1192 journals and other serials. **Services:** Interlibrary loan; copying; library open to visiting scholars for reference use only. **Automated Operations:** Computerized public access catalog, cataloging, acquisitions, and circulation. **Computerized Information Services:** OCLC, DIALOG Information Services; CD-ROMs (ERIC, GPO, Dissertation Abstracts Ondisc, PsycLIT, International Encyclopedia of Education); BITNET, InterNet (electronic mail services). **Remarks:** FAX: (615)343-7923. Electronic mail address(es): EDUCREF@VUCTRVAX (BITNET); EDUCREF@CTRVAX.VANDERBILT.EDU (InterNet). **Staff:** Jean Reese, Hd. of Info.Serv.; Connie Donley, Pub.Serv.Libn.

★19773★
Vanderbilt University - Jean and Alexander Heard Library - Special Collections Department (Hum)
419 21st Ave., S.
Nashville, TN 37240-0007
Phone: (615)322-2807
Marice Wolfe, Hd.
Founded: 1965. **Staff:** Prof 2; Other 6. **Subjects:** Southern literature, history, and politics; performing arts. **Special Collections:** Sevier and Rand Collections (fine bindings, rare books; 10,000 volumes); Jesse E. Wills Fugitive/Agrarian Collection (American literature and criticism, 1920 to present; 1400 volumes; 2500 cubic feet of manuscripts); Francis Robinson Collection of Theatre, Music and Dance (4000 volumes; 100 cubic feet of manuscripts). **Holdings:** 40,000 books; Vanderbilt theses and dissertations; 2000 cubic feet of manuscripts; 3000 cubic feet of archival materials. **Services:** Copying; department open to the public for reference use only. **Automated Operations:** Computerized cataloging and acquisitions. **Computerized Information Services:** OCLC; University Archives CIS (internal databases). Performs searches on fee basis. Contact Person: Sara Harwell, Libn./Archv.

★19774★
Vanderbilt University - Jean and Alexander Heard Library - Stevenson Science Library (Biol Sci, Sci-Engr)
419 21st Ave., S.
Nashville, TN 37240
Phone: (615)322-2775
Laurie Allen, Hd.
Founded: 1972. **Staff:** Prof 4; Other 5. **Subjects:** Biology, chemistry, engineering, geology, mathematics, physics, astronomy. **Special Collections:** Foreign and State Geological Survey Collections. **Holdings:** 352,308 volumes; Landmarks of Science I and II; AEC Reports through February 1971; NASA Reports, 1976 to present; microfilm of U.S. Patent Official Gazette, 1872 to present; microfilm of U.S. Patent Official Gazette Trademarks, 1971 to present; microfilm of U.S. Annual Report of the Commissioner of Patents, 1790-1871; microfilm of U.S. patents, January 1965 to present; 24 drawers of microfiche of miscellaneous materials; 94,780 maps. **Subscriptions:** 1999 journals and other serials. **Services:** Interlibrary loan; copying; SDI; library open to the public on fee basis. **Automated Operations:** Computerized cataloging, acquisitions, serials, and circulation (NOTIS). **Computerized Information Services:** DIALOG Information Services, OCLC, STN International, U.S. Patent Classification System; CD-ROMs; BITNET (electronic mail service). Performs searches on fee basis. **Networks/Consortia:** Member of Center for Research Libraries (CRL). **Remarks:** FAX: (615)343-7249. Electronic mail address(es): ALLENLC@VUCTRVAX (BITNET). **Staff:** Paul Murphy; Carlin Sappenfield; Cynthia Shabb; Jon Erickson.

★19775★
Vanderbilt University - Jean and Alexander Heard Library - Walker Management Library (Bus-Fin)
401 21st Ave., S.
Nashville, TN 37203
Phone: (615)322-2970
Carol Dickerson, Dir.
Founded: 1970. **Staff:** Prof 6; Other 7. **Subjects:** Management and business, corporate information. **Special Collections:** Career planning and placement resources. **Holdings:** 35,000 volumes; 260 AV programs; 225,000 microfiche; 3004 reels of microfilm. **Subscriptions:** 1360 journals and other serials; 8 newspapers. **Services:** Interlibrary loan; copying; SDI; library open to the public on fee basis. **Automated Operations:** Computerized cataloging

and circulation. **Computerized Information Services:** DIALOG Information Services, NEXIS, OCLC, BRS Information Technologies, DataTimes, Data-Star, WILSONLINE, Dow Jones News/Retrieval, Business Dateline; ACORN (internal database); CD-ROMs (Lotus One Source CD/Corporate, Predicasts F & S Index of Corporate Change, ABI/INFORM, Business Dateline). Performs searches on fee basis. Contact Person: Jill Van der Does or Cindy Boin, Bus.Info.Serv. **Publications:** Newsletter - for internal distribution only. **Remarks:** FAX: (615)343-0061. **Staff:** Sylvia Graham, Asst.Dir.; Rosemary Madill, Supv., Lib.Oper.; William Taylor, Coord., Info.Serv.; Carol McCrary, Info.Serv.Libn.

★19776★
Vanderbilt University - Medical Center Library (Med)
Nashville, TN 37232-2340
Phone: (615)322-2299
T. Mark Hodges, Dir.
Founded: 1906. **Staff:** Prof 12; Other 23. **Subjects:** Health sciences. **Special Collections:** History of Medicine; History of Nutrition (Goldberger-Sebrell Pellagra Collection; Lydia J. Roberts Collection; Helen S. Mitchell Collection; Franklin C. Bing Collection; E. Neige Todhunter Collection); Moll Hypnosis Collection; Vanderbilt Medical Faculty Manuscripts; Archives of Vanderbilt University Medical Center. **Holdings:** 59,138 books and theses; 99,477 bound periodical volumes; 6852 government publications; 659 AV titles; 6495 microforms; 491 linear feet of manuscripts; 144 computer diskettes. **Subscriptions:** 2366 journals and other serials. **Services:** Interlibrary loan (fee); copying; SDI; document delivery; library open to the public with restrictions. **Automated Operations:** Computerized public access catalog, cataloging, acquisitions, serials, and circulation. **Computerized Information Services:** NLM, BRS Information Technologies, DIALOG Information Services, GenBank; CD-ROMs; BITNET, InterNet (electronic mail services). Performs searches on fee basis. Contact Person: Judy Orr, Ref. & Res.Serv.Hd., 322-2291. **Networks/Consortia:** Member of National Network of Libraries of Medicine - Southeastern/Atlantic Region, Consortium of Southern Biomedical Libraries (CONBLS). **Publications:** Catalist, quarterly; Current Serials List, annual; Guide, annual. **Remarks:** Maintains an informatics training Lab. FAX: (615)343-6454. Toll-free telephone number(s): 800-288-0110 (Document Delivery Service). Electronic mail address(es): HODGESTM@CTRVAX.VANDERBILT.EDU (InterNet, Director); MEDLIDDS@CTRVAX.VANDERBILT.EDU (InterNet, Document Delivery Service). **Staff:** Frances H. Lynch, Assoc.Dir.; Mary H. Teloh, Spec.Coll.Libn.; Deborah Broadwater, Acq./Ser.Libn.; Mari Stoddard, Outreach Libn.; Beverly Carlton, Ref.Libn.; Evelyn Forbes, Ref.Libn; B. Faye Green, Ref.Libn.; Mark Kennedy, Ref.Libn.; Gayle Grantham, Mgr., Circ.Supv.; Dan McCollum, DDS Supv.; Dr. William J. Darby, Hon.Cur.

★19777★
Vanderbilt University - Television News Archive (Info Sci)
110 21st Ave. S., Suite 704
Nashville, TN 37203
Phone: (615)322-2927
Scarlett Graham, Dir.
Founded: 1968. **Staff:** Prof 1; Other 12. **Subjects:** Television news, 1968 to present. **Special Collections:** Network evening news programs (videotape); Presidential speeches and press conferences; Democratic and Republican National Conventions; Watergate hearings; impeachment debates and more recent news events. **Holdings:** 21,000 hours of videotape. **Services:** Videotape loan service; copying; archives open to the public. **Publications:** Television News Index and Abstracts, monthly. **Special Catalogs:** News Specials Catalog (online). **Remarks:** FAX: (615)343-8250.

★19778★
Vanderburgh County Law Library (Law)
City-County Courts Bldg., Rm. 207
825 Sycamore
Evansville, IN 47708
Phone: (812)426-5175
Helen S. Reed, Libn.
Founded: 1900. **Staff:** Prof 1. **Subjects:** Law. **Holdings:** 12,000 volumes. **Services:** Copying; library open to the public with restrictions. **Computerized Information Services:** Online systems. **Remarks:** FAX: (812)426-1091. Maintained by Vanderburgh County, Evansville Bar Association, and Vanderburgh Law Library Foundation.

★19779★
Vandercook College of Music - Harry Ruppel Memorial Library (Mus)
3209 S. Michigan Ave.
Chicago, IL 60616
Phone: (312)225-6288
Marguerite J. Krynicki, Chf.Libn.
Founded: 1966. **Staff:** Prof 1. **Subjects:** Music and music education, education. **Special Collections:** Performance Library (12,000 items). **Holdings:** 18,898 books; 1874 phonograph records; 3157 scores; 1841 reels of microfilm. **Subscriptions:** 68 journals and other serials. **Services:** Interlibrary loan; listening facilities; library open to alumni and associates of two neighboring institutions (identification necessary). **Networks/Consortia:** Member of Chicago Library System.

Vandusen Gardens Library
See: **Vancouver Botanical Gardens Association** (19754)

Georges P. Vanier Library
See: **Concordia University - Loyola Campus - Georges P. Vanier Library** (4121)

Vanier Science & Engineering Library
See: **University of Ottawa** (19170)

★19780★
Vantage Consulting and Research Corporation - Library (Info Sci)
357 Warner Milne Rd., No. A
Oregon City, OR 97045-4045   Ray Liere, Dir.Res. & Dev.
Subjects: Computer-oriented topics, administration of government programs. **Holdings:** 3000 books. **Subscriptions:** 80 journals and other serials. **Services:** Library not open to the public. **Computerized Information Services:** More than 600 online databases; internal database; InterNet, UUCCP (electronic mail services). Performs searches on fee basis. **Remarks:** Electronic mail address(es): uunet!nwnexus.WA.COM!vantage!ray (UUCP); ray%vantage@nwnexus.WA.COM (InterNet).

Vida B. Varey Library
See: **Plymouth Congregational Church** (13150)

★19781★
Getulio Vargas Foundation - Library (Soc Sci, Bus-Fin)
C.P. 9052   Phone: 21 5511542
20000 Rio de Janeiro, RJ, Brazil   Guaraciaba Azeredo Coutinho, Libn.
Founded: 1945. **Staff:** 22. **Subjects:** Economics, political science, public administration, management, contemporary Brazilian history, sociology. **Holdings:** 130,000 volumes. **Subscriptions:** 332 journals and other serials. **Services:** Interlibrary loan; copying; library open to the public. **Computerized Information Services:** BIBLIODATA/CALCO (internal database). **Also Known As:** Fundacao Getulio Vargas - Biblioteca Central. **Staff:** Ligia S. Paixao, Automation Div.; Olivia Chermont de Miranda, Ser.Div.; Amanda Lopez Ares, Tech.Proc.Div.; Shirlei S. Patrocinio, Acq.Div.; Ligia Cruz Nogueira, Ref. & Circ.Div.

★19782★
Varian Associates - Technical Library (Sci-Engr)
3075 Hansen Way, K-100   Phone: (415)424-5071
Palo Alto, CA 94304   Joan Murphy, Mgr., Lib.Serv.
Founded: 1961. **Staff:** Prof 2; Other 1. **Subjects:** Electronics, engineering, applied mathematics, chemistry, physics, instrumentation. **Holdings:** 14,000 books; 30,000 bound periodical volumes; 7000 technical reports; microcomputer software; videotapes. **Subscriptions:** 653 journals and other serials. **Services:** Interlibrary loan; SDI; library open to the public with prior approval. **Computerized Information Services:** Dow Jones News/Retrieval, BRS Information Technologies, DataTimes, DTIC, STN International, DIALOG Information Services, RLIN, VU/TEXT Information Services, Socrates; internal database. **Networks/Consortia:** Member of SOUTHNET. **Publications:** Technical Library Bulletin, quarterly. **Remarks:** FAX: (415)424-6988. **Staff:** Joyce Hardy, Libn.

★19783★
Varian Associates, Inc. - Crossed Field & Receiver Protection Products - Technical Library (Sci-Engr)
150 Sohier Rd.   Phone: (508)922-6000
Beverly, MA 01915   Alice Campbell, Libn.
Founded: 1961. **Staff:** Prof 1. **Subjects:** Microwave engineering, physics. **Holdings:** 1200 books; 355 bound periodical volumes; government reports. **Subscriptions:** 75 journals and other serials. **Services:** Interlibrary loan; library not open to the public. **Computerized Information Services:** DIALOG Information Services. **Remarks:** FAX: (508)922-8914.

★19784★
Varian Canada Inc. - Technical Library (Sci-Engr)
45 River Dr.
Georgetown, ON, Canada L7G 2J4   Phone: (416)877-0161
Founded: 1958. **Staff:** Prof 2. **Subjects:** Microwave electronics, metallurgy, chemical analysis, metal working, tool design, management. **Holdings:** 530 books. **Subscriptions:** 60 journals and other serials; 5 newspapers. **Services:** Interlibrary loan; library not open to the public. **Staff:** Harry V. Haylock, Supv.; Kim Rogers, Libn.; Linda Owens, Libn.

★19785★
Varo, Inc. - Integrated Systems Division Library
2800 W. Kingsley
Box 469015   Phone: (214)840-5204
Garland, TX 75046-9015   Brenda Hardin, Libn.
Remarks: No further information was supplied by respondent.

★19786★
Vassar Brothers Hospital - Medical Library (Med)
Reade Place   Phone: (914)437-3121
Poughkeepsie, NY 12601   Mary Jo Russell, Libn.
Founded: 1951. **Staff:** Prof 1. **Subjects:** Internal medicine, surgery, cardiology, pulmonary medicine, orthopedics, obstetrics, gynecology, pediatrics. **Holdings:** 300 books; 50 bound periodical volumes; 1 VF drawer of pamphlets, flyers, and reports; 100 clinical videotapes. **Subscriptions:** 75 journals and other serials. **Services:** Interlibrary loan; copying; library open to the public. **Computerized Information Services:** NLM. **Networks/Consortia:** Member of Southeastern New York Library Resources Council (SENYLRC), Health Information Libraries of Westchester (HILOW). **Remarks:** FAX: (914)437-3120. (Attn: Library).

★19787★
Vassar College - Art Library (Art)
Poughkeepsie, NY 12601   Phone: (914)437-5790
                                 Thomas E. Hill, Art Libn.
Founded: 1864. **Staff:** Prof 1; Other 1. **Subjects:** Western European art and architecture, ancient through contemporary; East Asian art; American art; African art. **Holdings:** 55,000 books and bound periodical volumes. **Subscriptions:** 180 journals and other serials. **Services:** Interlibrary loan; library open to the public with restrictions. **Automated Operations:** Computerized public access catalog, cataloging, acquisitions, circulation, and serials (Innovative Interfaces). **Computerized Information Services:** OCLC, DIALOG Information Services, BRS Information Technologies, WILSONLINE, SCIPIO, Avery Index to Architectural Periodicals, CARL; InterNet, BITNET (electronic mail services). **Networks/Consortia:** Member of Southeastern New York Library Resources Council (SENYLRC). **Remarks:** FAX: (914)437-7187. Electronic mail address(es): THHILL@VASSAR (InterNet, BITNET).

★19788★
Vassar College - George Sherman Dickinson Music Library (Mus)
Ramon Ave.   Phone: (914)437-7000
Poughkeepsie, NY 12601   Sarah B. Canino, Act.Mus.Libn.
Founded: 1908. **Staff:** Prof 2; Other 3. **Subjects:** Music. **Special Collections:** Chittenden Pianoforte Library; historical editions and collected works. **Holdings:** 16,529 books and bound periodical volumes; 30,000 scores; 25,000 phonograph records. **Services:** Interlibrary loan; library open to the public with restrictions. **Computerized Information Services:** OCLC.

★19789★
Vassar College - Library - Department of Special Collections (Hum, Hist)
Box 20   Phone: (914)437-5799
Poughkeepsie, NY 12601   Nancy S. MacKechnie, Cur., Rare Bks./Mss.
Staff: Prof 1; Other 1. **Subjects:** College history, women's history, American and British literature, etiquette and household, fine printing, early atlases and maps. **Special Collections:** Papers of Elizabeth Bishop, Ruth Benedict, Mary McCarthy, John Burroughs, Mark Twain, Maria Mitchell, Lucy Maynard Salmon, Alma Lutz, Elizabeth Cady Stanton, Susan B. Anthony, Hallie Flanagan Davis, Robert Owens; women's suffrage collection; household manuals; cookbooks; Courtesy Books; children's literature; gardening and herbal books; Village Press Collection; Jean Webster McKinney Collection of Mark Twain Manuscripts and Family Papers. **Holdings:** 16,000 books; 1152 linear feet of documents. **Services:** Copying; collection open to the public. **Networks/Consortia:** Member of SUNY/OCLC Library Network, Southeastern New York Library Resources Council (SENYLRC). **Special Indexes:** Manuscript registers for some collections (book).

★ 19790 ★
Vassar Priscilla Anderson Memorial Foundation - L.W. Anderson Genealogical Library (Hist)
P.O. Box 7390   Phone: (601)865-1554
Gulfport, MS 39502   Anne S. Anderson, Dir.
Staff: 2. **Subjects:** Genealogy - Deep South, Eastern Seaboard, New England, Canada. **Special Collections:** Massachusetts Vital Statistics; Mississippi Tax Rolls; Repetoires des Actes de Bapteme, Marriage, Sepulture, et de Recensements du Quebec Ancien; Genealogical Magazine of New Jersey Collection. **Holdings:** 20,000 books; 10,000 nonbook items; military records; census records. **Services:** Copying; library open to the public on a limited schedule on a fee basis. **Publications:** Mississippi Records; Louisiana Records - both quarterly. **Remarks:** Library located at William Carey College on the Coast.

John Vaughan Library/LRC
See: Northeastern Oklahoma State University (11985)

Vaughan Library
See: Acadia University (42)

George A. Vaughn, Jr. Memorial Library
See: College of Aeronautics (3885)

Vedder Memorial Library
See: Greene County Historical Society - Vedder Memorial Library (6726)

★ 19791 ★
Vedder, Price, Kaufman & Kammholz - Library (Law)
222 N. LaSalle St.   Phone: (312)609-7500
Chicago, IL 60601   Kenneth C. Halicki, Libn.
Founded: 1956. **Staff:** Prof 2; Other 3. **Subjects:** Law - labor, employee benefit, tax, corporate. **Holdings:** 22,000 books. **Services:** Interlibrary loan; copying; SDI; library open to the public at librarian's discretion. **Computerized Information Services:** DIALOG Information Services, LEXIS, WESTLAW, LEGI-SLATE, Hannah Information Systems, Information America, Labor Relations Press. **Remarks:** FAX: (312)609-5005.

★ 19792 ★
Vega Precision Laboratories, Inc. - Technical Library (Sci-Engr)
800 Follin Ln.   Phone: (703)938-6300
Vienna, VA 22180   Eileen C. Durham, Libn.
Subjects: Engineering, radio/radar and digital communication, electronics, engineering development. **Holdings:** 200 books; 1500 vendor catalogs; 2000 reports and technical manuals; military specifications and standards on microfiche; Vega technical reports; industry standards. **Services:** Interlibrary loan; library not open to the public. **Publications:** Vega Manuals and Special Reports.

★ 19793 ★
Vegetarian Information Service, Inc. - Information Center (Food-Bev)
Box 5888   Phone: (301)530-1737
Bethesda, MD 20814   Dr. Alex Hershaft, Libn.
Founded: 1976. **Staff:** 4. **Subjects:** Vegetarianism, diet and health, treatment of farm animals, animal rights. **Holdings:** 100 volumes; clipping files. **Subscriptions:** 20 journals and other serials. **Services:** Center open to serious scholars of vegetarianism and animal rights. **Remarks:** FAX: (301)530-5747.

★ 19794 ★
Vehicle Systems Development Corporation - Library (Trans)
1271 W. 9th St.
Upland, CA 91786   Phone: (714)981-3236
Subjects: Transportation, terramechanics, materials science, mobility, ballistics, aerodynamics. **Holdings:** 5000 volumes. **Remarks:** Telex: 804294 (SPEDEX ATL).

Velazquez House
See: France - Ministere de l'Education - Velazquez House (6066)

★ 19795 ★
(Velikiye Luki) Selskochozjajstvennyj Institut - Biblioteka (Agri, Biol Sci, Soc Sci)
nab. A. Matrosova 1   Phone: 36565
Velikiye Luki, Russia   Valentina A. Kozlova
Founded: 1958. **Staff:** Prof 17; Other 12. **Subjects:** Agriculture, biology, economics, social sciences. **Holdings:** 260,000 books; 60,000 bound periodical volumes; 50,000 brochures. **Subscriptions:** 210 journals and other serials; 46 newspapers. **Services:** Interlibrary loan; library open to the public for reference use only.

★ 19796 ★
Venable Baetjer & Howard - Library (Law)
2 Hopkins Plaza   Phone: (301)244-7502
Baltimore, MD 21201   John S. Nixdorff, Libn.
Staff: Prof 1; Other 6. **Subjects:** Law - tax, labor, corporate, securities, environmental, trusts and estates, government contracts, health care, real estate; litigation; international trade; intellectual property; trade regulation. **Holdings:** 38,000 books; 1000 bound periodical volumes. **Subscriptions:** 100 journals and other serials; 5 newspapers. **Services:** Interlibrary loan; library not open to the public. **Computerized Information Services:** NEXIS, LEXIS, DIALOG Information Services, VU/TEXT Information Services, PHINet FedTax Database, CCH ACCESS, DataTimes, LEGI-SLATE. **Remarks:** Maintains branch libraries in Washington, DC, McLean, VA, Rockville, MD, Towson, MD, and Bel Air, MD. FAX: (301)244-7742.

★ 19797 ★
Venango County Law Library (Law)
Court House
Corner 12th & Liberty Sts.   Phone: (814)437-6871
Franklin, PA 16323   Jean Christenson, Libn.
Founded: 1922. **Staff:** Prof 4. **Subjects:** Pennsylvania and United States laws and court reports. **Holdings:** 30,000 volumes. **Services:** Library open to the public for reference use only.

★ 19798 ★
Ventura County Law Library (Law)
800 S. Victoria Ave.   Phone: (805)654-2695
Ventura, CA 93009   Naydean L. Baker, Law Libn.
Founded: 1891. **Staff:** Prof 1; Other 9. **Subjects:** Law. **Holdings:** 55,334 volumes; 105 reels of microfilm of U.S. Statutes; 1796 cassettes; 74,259 pieces of microfiche. **Subscriptions:** 322 journals and other serials. **Services:** Library open to the public for reference use only.

★ 19799 ★
Ventura County Library Services Agency - Government Center Reference Library (Bus-Fin, Env-Cons)
800 S. Victoria Ave.   Phone: (805)654-2480
Ventura, CA 93009   John F. Bluth, Libn.
Founded: 1988. **Staff:** Prof 1; Other 1. **Subjects:** Public administration, management, planning, environment, pollution, building and safety. **Special Collections:** Resource Management Agency Collection. **Holdings:** 400 books; 11,000 other cataloged items. **Subscriptions:** 100 journals and other serials; 10 newspapers. **Services:** Copying; library open to the public for reference use only. **Automated Operations:** Computerized public access catalog, cataloging, and acquisitions. **Computerized Information Services:** DIALOG Information Services. **Remarks:** FAX: (805)654-2424. Contains the holdings of the former Ventura County Resource Management Agency - Technical Library.

★ 19800 ★
Ventura County Museum of History and Art - Library & Archives (Hist)
100 E. Main St.   Phone: (805)653-0323
Ventura, CA 93001   Charles Johnson, Libn.
Founded: 1913. **Staff:** Prof 1. **Subjects:** Local history. **Holdings:** 5000 books; 20,000 photographs; 40,000 negatives; 250 oral histories; 15,000 manuscripts; 400 maps; 750 architectural plans and drawings. **Subscriptions:** 45 journals and other serials. **Services:** Copying; photograph reproduction; library open to the public for reference use only. **Publications:** Ventura County Historical Society Quarterly; Heritage and History (newsletter).

★ 19801 ★
Ventura County Star-Free Press - Library (Publ)
Box 6711   Phone: (805)655-5803
Ventura, CA 93006   Wanda Woessner, Libn.
Staff: Prof 1. **Subjects:** Newspaper reference topics. **Holdings:** 100 books; newspapers, 1897 to present, on microfilm; county government documents; photograph files; clippings. **Subscriptions:** 13 journals and other serials. **Services:** Copying; library open to the public with restrictions. **Special Catalogs:** Divided card file: subject and byline, crime/law suits, accidents. **Special Indexes:** Index to county news items. **Remarks:** FAX: (805)642-3691. Library located at 5250 Ralston, Ventura, CA 93003.

Verein Deutscher Eisenhuttenleute - VDEh
See: **German Iron and Steel Institute - Steel Information Centre and Library (6430)**

Verein Deutscher Zementwerke
See: **German Cement Works Association (6423)**

Verenigde Nederlandse Uitgeversbedrijven - Claritas Corporation
See: **Claritas Corporation (3760)**

★ 19802 ★
Vermont Center for Independent Living (VCIL) - Information and Referral System (Med)
174 River St.   Phone: (802)229-0501
Montpelier, VT 05602   Peter Johnke, Dir.
Founded: 1979. **Staff:** 5. **Subjects:** Disability, adaptive equipment. **Holdings:** 882 books; 24 VF drawers. **Subscriptions:** 25 journals and other serials; 274 newspapers and newsletters. **Services:** Research and referral on disability subjects. **Computerized Information Services:** ABLEDATA. Performs searches free of charge for Vermont residents. **Publications:** Fact sheets; bibliographies, both irregular.

Vermont Environmental Center
See: **Vermont Institute of Natural Sciences - Library (19804)**

★ 19803 ★
Vermont Historical Society - Library (Hist)
Pavilion Office Bldg.
109 State St.   Phone: (802)828-2291
Montpelier, VT 05609   Paul A. Carnahan, Libn.
Founded: 1838. **Staff:** Prof 2; Other 1. **Subjects:** Vermont history and Vermontiana, New England state and local history, genealogy. **Special Collections:** Vermont imprints; Harold G. Rugg Collection of Vermontiana. **Holdings:** 40,000 books and bound periodical volumes; 1000 maps; 30,000 photographs; 200 reels of microfilm; 700 cubic feet of manuscripts; pamphlets; 7000 broadsides. **Subscriptions:** 220 journals and other serials. **Services:** Interlibrary loan (limited); copying; library open to the public. **Computerized Information Services:** Internal database. **Publications:** Vermont History, quarterly; Vermont History News, 6/year; Green Mountaineer, annual - to members. **Staff:** Karl B. Bloom, Asst.Libn.

★ 19804 ★
Vermont Institute of Natural Sciences - Library (Biol Sci)
Church Hill Rd.   Phone: (802)457-2779
Woodstock, VT 05091   Martha L. Williamson, Libn.
Staff: Prof 1.5. **Subjects:** Environmental research, natural history. **Special Collections:** Natural history slides (60,000); Billings-Kittredge Herbarium Collection; Olin Sewall Pellingill Library (collection of 19th and 20th century ornithological publications; 1500 books; 84 bound complete sets of periodicals; 15 unbound complete sets of periodicals). **Holdings:** 5500 books; 3500 bound periodical volumes; 2000 cataloged pamphlets in vertical file. **Subscriptions:** 87 journals and other serials. **Services:** Interlibrary loan; library open to the public for reference use only. **Automated Operations:** Computerized cataloging and acquisitions. **Computerized Information Services:** CD-ROM (BiblioFile). **Publications:** Vermont Natural History, annual; newsletter, quarterly; Bird Records, quarterly. **Remarks:** Includes the holdings of Vermont Environmental Center. **Staff:** Sarah B. Laughlin, Institute Dir.

★ 19805 ★
Vermont Law School - Julian and Virginia Cornell Library (Law)
Box 60   Phone: (802)763-8303
South Royalton, VT 05068   Carl A. Yirka, Assoc.Prof. & Libn.
Founded: 1973. **Staff:** Prof 5; Other 7. **Subjects:** Law. **Special Collections:** Environmental law (6000 volumes); Historic Preservation (1250 volumes); Alternative Dispute Resolution (418 volumes). **Holdings:** 90,000 books; 15,300 bound periodical volumes; 65,780 volumes in microform; government document depository. **Subscriptions:** 1500 journals and other serials; 10 newspapers. **Services:** Interlibrary loan; copying; library open to the public for reference use only. **Automated Operations:** Computerized cataloging, acquisitions, and ILL. **Computerized Information Services:** WESTLAW, OCLC, LEXIS, OCLC EPIC. **Networks/Consortia:** Member of New England Law Library Consortium (NELLCO), NELINET, Inc. **Remarks:** FAX: (802)763-7159. **Staff:** Diane Frake, Assoc.Libn./Pub.Serv.; Victoria Weber, Assoc.Libn./Acq.; Susan Zeigfinger, Assoc.Libn./Tech.Serv.; Christine Ryan, Asst.Libn./Ref.

★ 19806 ★
Vermont State Agency of Administration - Department of General Services - Public Records Division (Hist)
State Administrative Bldg.   Phone: (802)828-3286
Montpelier, VT 05602   A. John Yacavoni, Dir.
Staff: Prof 1; Other 17. **Subjects:** Vermont town and city land records prior to 1850, Vermont town vital records prior to 1850, Vermont probate record volumes prior to 1850. **Special Collections:** Field forms and draft material of Historical Records Survey inventories of Vermont town records and church records; Vermont Vital Record File, 1760-1954 (939 cubic feet). **Holdings:** 1445 boxes of archival holdings; 26,202 reels of microfilm; 201,318 microfiche; 37,677 boxes of semiactive records center material. **Services:** Copying; division open to the public. **Publications:** Information Bulletin, monthly - to Vermont town and city clerks. **Remarks:** FAX: (802)828-3710.

★ 19807 ★
Vermont State Department of Education - Vermont Educational Resource Center (VERC)
120 State St.
Montpelier, VT 05620-2501
Defunct. Holdings absorbed by the Vermont State Department of Libraries.

★ 19808 ★
Vermont State Department of Libraries (Info Sci)
Pavilion Office Bldg.
109 State St.   Phone: (802)828-3261
Montpelier, VT 05602   Patricia E. Klinck, State Libn.
Founded: 1970. **Staff:** Prof 14; Other 33. **Subjects:** Law, Vermontiana, general subjects. **Holdings:** 639,444 books; films; videotapes; microfilm; microfiche; tapes; state and federal documents. **Services:** Interlibrary loan; copying; department open to the public. **Computerized Information Services:** DIALOG Information Services, WESTLAW, BRS Information Technologies, LEXIS, NEXIS, RLIN, OCLC, Vermont Automated Library System; ALANET (electronic mail service). **Networks/Consortia:** Member of NELINET, Inc., Vermont Resource Sharing Network. **Publications:** Biennial Report; Department of Libraries News. **Special Catalogs:** Union Catalog of total holdings of libraries throughout the state, including colleges and universities (author-title card catalog); catalog of major, public, and private academic and state resources (online). **Remarks:** The Department of Libraries maintains regional libraries in Dummerston, Berlin, Rutland, Georgia, and St. Johnsbury. Located at 109 State St., Montpelier, VT 05609. FAX: (802)828-2199. Electronic mail address(es): ALA0770 (ALANET). **Staff:** Sybil B. McShane, Dir., Lib. & Info.Serv.; Marianne K. Cassell, Lib.Dev. & Adult Serv.Cons.; Grace Greene, Ch.Serv.Cons.; Marjorie Zunder, Dir., Ref. & Law Serv.; S. Francis Woods, Spec.Serv.Cons.; Catherine Gravel, Hd., Tech.Serv.; Amy Howlett, Reg.Libn.; Kent Gray, Reg.Libn.; Michael Roche, Reg.Libn.; Lorriane Lanius, Reg.Libn.; Janet Alexander, Reg.Libn.; Paul Donovan, Ref.Libn.; Marian Abajian, Ref.Libn.

★ 19809 ★
Vermont State Hospital - Agency of Human Services - Research Library (Med)
103 S. Main St.   Phone: (802)241-2248
Waterbury, VT 05676   Jane Hull, Libn.
Staff: Prof 1. **Subjects:** Psychiatry, public health, psychology, medicine, alcohol and drug abuse, corrections. **Holdings:** 10,000 books; 2000 bound periodical volumes; 30 cassettes; 60 cases of pamphlets; 45 boxes of government documents. **Subscriptions:** 200 journals and other serials. **Services:** Interlibrary loan; library open to hospital affiliates with restrictions. **Special Catalogs:** Union lists of books and journals.

★ 19810 ★
Vermont (State) Office of the Secretary of State - State Archives
26 Terrace St.
Montpelier, VT 05602   D. Gregory Sanford, State Archv.
Founded: 1777. **Staff:** Prof 2; Other 1. **Subjects:** Governors' official papers, legislative records, surveyors' general papers, original acts and resolves, Vermont state papers, 1744 to present, municipal charters. **Special Collections:** Stevens Collection of Vermontiana (60 feet); Vermont/New Hampshire Boundary Case (30 feet); Vermont Bicentennial Commission (30 feet); Order of Women Legislators (2 feet); Records of the Governor's Commission on the Status of Women (20 feet); Houston Studio/Country Camera Photograph Collection; Agency of Transportation and Department of Agriculture Photograph and Film Collections (35 feet); various state officers' papers (20 feet). **Holdings:** 500 books; 250 volumes of bound manuscripts; 60 volumes of maps, surveys, and charters; 500 cartons of manuscript material; 60 boxes of original acts and resolutions; 57 boxes of legislative committee records. **Services:** Copying; archives open to the public. **Computerized Information Services:** Minaret (internal database). **Publications:** State Papers of Vermont. **Special Catalogs:** Inventories for manuscript collections. **Remarks:** FAX: (802)828-2496. **Staff:** Christie Carter, Asst. State Archv.

Vermont Symphony Orchestra Collection
See: **University of Vermont - Department of Special Collections** (19482)

★ 19811 ★
Vermont Technical College - Hartness Library (Sci-Engr, Agri)
Randolph Center, VT 05061   Phone: (802)728-3391
                           Linda McSweeney, Lib.Dir.
Staff: Prof 2.5; Other 4. **Subjects:** Dairy management; agribusiness; engineering - civil, electrical, electronics, electromechanical, mechanical; surveying; architecture and building; automotive technology. **Holdings:** 55,000 books. **Subscriptions:** 412 journals and other serials; 8 newspapers. **Services:** Copying; CD-ROM workstations; library open to the public with restrictions. **Automated Operations:** Computerized public access catalog. **Computerized Information Services:** DIALOG Information Services, BRS Information Technologies, Vermont Automated Library System. **Networks/Consortia:** Member of NELINET, Inc. **Remarks:** FAX: (802)728-9124. **Staff:** John R. Cocke, Ref.Libn.; Maria Lamson, Ref.Libn.

★ 19812 ★
Vermont Yankee Nuclear Power Corporation - Energy Information Center (Energy)
Governor Hunt Rd.
Box 157   Phone: (802)257-1416
Vernon, VT 05354   Deborah Shader, EIC Asst.
Founded: 1981. **Staff:** Prof 2. **Subjects:** Energy, electricity, nuclear power. **Holdings:** 500 books; 300 bound periodical volumes; technical reports. **Subscriptions:** 4 journals and other serials; 2 newspapers. **Services:** Interlibrary loan; center open to the public.

★ 19813 ★
Verner, Liipfert, Bernhard & McPherson - Library (Law)
901 15th St., N.W.   Phone: (202)371-6000
Washington, DC 20005-2301   Maureen Stellino, Law Libn.
Staff: Prof 3; Other 2. **Subjects:** Law - international, administrative, commercial; legislation. **Special Collections:** Aviation collection; surface transportation collection. **Holdings:** 10,000 books; 129 audio cassettes; 455 microforms; work/product collection. **Subscriptions:** 254 journals and other serials; 30 newspapers. **Services:** Interlibrary loan; copying; library open to the public by appointment. **Computerized Information Services:** LEXIS, Mead Data Central, Disclosure Online Database, Accountants' Index, Mead Data Central. **Publications:** VLBM Weekly; Inside VLBM, biweekly - both for internal distribution only. **Staff:** Christopher Hays, Asst.Libn.; Michael Hill, Asst.Libn.

★ 19814 ★
Verrill and Dana - Law Library (Law)
1 Portland Square
Box 586   Phone: (207)774-4000
Portland, ME 04112   Anne M. Reiman, Libn.
Founded: 1970. **Staff:** 1.5. **Subjects:** Law. **Holdings:** 13,000 books. **Subscriptions:** 100 journals and other serials. **Services:** Library not open to the public. **Computerized Information Services:** LEXIS, WESTLAW, DIALOG Information Services. **Remarks:** FAX: (207)774-7499.

★ 19815 ★
Versar Inc. - Information Services (Env-Cons)
6850 Versar Center
Box 1549   Phone: (703)750-3000
Springfield, VA 22151   David W. Hulvey, Dir., Info.Serv.
Founded: 1981. **Staff:** Prof 1; Other 2. **Subjects:** Environmental research and engineering, consulting, asbestos, PCBs, radon, waste management, risk assessment. **Holdings:** 2000 books; 300 periodical titles; technical reports; government publications. **Subscriptions:** 200 journals and other serials. **Services:** Interlibrary loan; copying; SDI; services open to the public by appointment. **Computerized Information Services:** DIALOG Information Services, BRS Information Technologies, NLM, STN International, Congressional Information Service, Inc. (CIS), DTIC, OCLC. Conducts searches. **Publications:** Journal Holdings, annual. **Remarks:** FAX: (703)642-6807.

Versatec - Technical Information Center
See: **Xerox Engineering Systems - Information Center** (20682)

A.S. Vesic Engineering Library
See: **Duke University** (5039)

★ 19816 ★
Vesterheim Genealogical Center/Norwegian-American Museum - Library (Area-Ethnic)
4909 Sherwood Rd.   Phone: (608)262-2504
Madison, WI 53711   Gerhard B. Naeseth, Dir.
Founded: 1975. **Staff:** Prof 5. **Subjects:** Norwegian-American genealogy and history. **Holdings:** 1260 books; 1711 reels of microfilm; 60 notebooks. **Services:** Copying; library open to the public by appointment. **Publications:** Norwegian Tracks, quarterly - to members. **Staff:** Blaine Hedberg; Shirley Puhl; Margo Hansen; Linda Harvey.

★ 19817 ★
Vesterheim, Norwegian-American Museum - Reference Library (Area-Ethnic)
502 W. Water St.   Phone: (319)382-9681
Decorah, IA 52101   Carol A. Hasvold, Libn.
Founded: 1970. **Staff:** 1. **Subjects:** Norwegian-American history, genealogy, crafts, antiques. **Special Collections:** Norwegian rosemaling. **Holdings:** 9000 books. **Subscriptions:** 15 journals and other serials. **Services:** Library open to the public for reference use only. **Computerized Information Services:** OCLC, CARL.

★ 19818 ★
Vestigia - Library
56 Brookwood Rd.
Stanhope, NJ 07874
Defunct.

Vetco Gray, Inc. - Technical Library
See: **ABB Vetco Gray, Inc. - Technical Library** (9)

Veterans Administration
See: **U.S. Dept. of Veterans Affairs** (17283)

Veterans Affairs Canada
See: **Canada - Veterans Affairs Canada** (2882)

★ 19819 ★
Veterans Home of California - Lincoln Memorial Library (Mil)
P.O. Box 1200   Phone: (707)944-4915
Yountville, CA 94599   Cynthia Hegedus, Libn.
Founded: 1886. **Staff:** Prof 3; Other 16. **Subjects:** Civil War, Spanish American War, World Wars I and II, Korean War, Vietnam conflict. **Special Collections:** Spanish American War papers. **Holdings:** 37,265 books; 353 bound periodical volumes. **Subscriptions:** 160 journals and other serials; 55 newspapers. **Services:** Interlibrary loan; copying; library open to the public for reference use only. **Staff:** Phyllis Bush, Asst.Libn.; Suzel Ho, Asst.Libn.

★ 19820 ★
Veterans Home of California - William K. Murphy Memorial Health Science Library (Med)
Yountville, CA 94599
Phone: (707)944-4715
Cynthia Hegedus, Libn.
Founded: 1978. **Staff:** Prof 1; Other 2. **Subjects:** Medicine. **Holdings:** 1197 books; 118 bound periodical volumes. **Subscriptions:** 128 journals and other serials. **Services:** Interlibrary loan; copying; library open to the public for reference use only. **Networks/Consortia:** Member of Northern California and Nevada Medical Library Group (NCNMLG).

★ 19821 ★
Veterans Memorial Medical Center - Health Sciences Library (Med)
1 King Place
PO Box 1009
Phone: (203)238-8200
Meriden, CT 06450-1009
Ellen C. Sheehan, Libn.
Staff: Prof 1. **Subjects:** Medicine, nursing. **Holdings:** 1000 books; 300 bound periodical volumes. **Subscriptions:** 125 journals and other serials. **Services:** Interlibrary loan; copying; library open to the public for reference use only. **Computerized Information Services:** MEDLARS, BRS Information Technologies. **Networks/Consortia:** Member of Connecticut Association of Health Science Libraries (CAHSL). **Formerly:** Meriden-Wallingford Hospital.

★ 19822 ★
VIA Rail Canada Inc. - Corporate Library (Trans)
2 Place Ville-Marie, Suite 400
Phone: (514)871-6441
Montreal, PQ, Canada H3B 2G6
Barbara Downey, Chf.Libn.
Founded: 1982. **Staff:** Prof 2. **Subjects:** Railroad engineering, passenger rail, high speed rail, management, human resources, quality assurance, law. **Special Collections:** Slide collection (rolling stock and scenery; some historical). **Holdings:** 4000 reports and monographs; 1500 microforms of periodicals, reports, and standards; slides; photographs; videocassettes; audiocassettes. **Subscriptions:** 130 journals and other serials. **Services:** Interlibrary loan; copying; SDI; library open to the public by appointment. **Automated Operations:** Computerized cataloging and circulation. **Computerized Information Services:** DIALOG Information Services, CAN/OLE, Infomart Online, Info Globe. **Remarks:** Alternate telephone number(s): 871-6442. FAX: (514)871-6641. **Staff:** Anne Metras, Info.Res.Anl.

★ 19823 ★
Vibration Institute - Library (Sci-Engr)
6262 S. Kingery Hwy., Suite 212
Phone: (708)654-2254
Willowbrook, IL 60514
Dr. Ronald L. Eshleman, Dir.
Founded: 1972. **Staff:** 8. **Subjects:** Vibration technology, balancing, rotor/bearing dynamics, torsional vibrations, turbomachinery blading, shaft vibrations. **Holdings:** 800 books and journals. **Services:** Library not open to the public. **Publications:** The Shock and Vibration Digest, monthly; Vibrations Magazine, quarterly - free to members. **Special Catalogs:** Publications Catalog. **Remarks:** FAX: (708)654-2271.

Vick Memorial Library
See: **Baptist Bible College** (1496)

★ 19824 ★
Vicksburg Medical Center - Medical Library (Med)
3311 I-20 Frontage Rd.
Phone: (601)636-2611
Vicksburg, MS 39180
Linda Stephenson, Med.Rec.Mgr.
Founded: 1975. **Staff:** Prof 1. **Subjects:** Medicine, surgery, nursing, patient education. **Holdings:** 534 books; 1610 bound periodical volumes; 60 VF folders; 45 cassettes; 9 slide sets; 20 microforms; 2 video cassettes. **Subscriptions:** 70 journals and other serials. **Services:** Interlibrary loan; copying; library open to the public with approval of hospital administrator. **Networks/Consortia:** Member of Central Mississippi Consortium of Medical Libraries.

Vicksburg National Military Park
See: **U.S. Natl. Park Service** (17787)

★ 19825 ★
Vicksburg & Warren County Historical Society - McCardle Library (Hist)
Old Court House Museum
Phone: (601)636-0741
Vicksburg, MS 39180
Blanche Terry, Res.Dir.
Founded: 1948. **Staff:** Prof 2. **Subjects:** Confederacy, local history, genealogy. **Holdings:** 2000 volumes. **Services:** Copying; library open to the public with restrictions.

Michael Victor II Art Library
See: **Springfield Art Association** (15598)

★ 19826 ★
Victoria College/University of Houston, Victoria - Library - Special Collections (Hist)
2602 N. Ben Jordan
Phone: (512)576-3151
Victoria, TX 77901
Dr. Joe F. Dahlstrom, Dir.
Founded: 1949. **Staff:** 31. **Holdings:** Local history (4000 volumes; 4000 slides and photographs); Regional Historical Resource Depository (290 linear feet of archival materials; 280 reels of microfilm); 195 linear feet of other archival materials. **Subscriptions:** 1855 journals and other serials, 14 newspapers. **Services:** Interlibrary loan; copying; collections open to the public with restrictions. **Automated Operations:** Computerized cataloging and circulation. **Computerized Information Services:** DIALOG Information Services, MEDLARS; DataPhase Automated Library Information System (internal database). Performs searches on fee basis. Contact Person: Karen Locker, Govt.Doc.Libn. **Networks/Consortia:** Member of AMIGOS Bibliographic Council, Inc., Circuit Rider Health Information Service (CRHIS), PAISANO Consortium of Libraries. **Remarks:** FAX: (512)573-4401.

★ 19827 ★
Victoria Conservatory of Music - Leon and Thea Koerner Foundation - Music Library (Mus)
839 Academy Close
Phone: (604)386-5311
Victoria, BC, Canada V8V 2X8
Larry De La Haye, Libn.
Founded: 1969. **Staff:** 1. **Subjects:** Instrumental and vocal music. **Special Collections:** Collection of 33 1/3 and 78rpm recordings; 19th-century music (350 pieces). **Holdings:** 2000 books; 50,000 bound periodical volumes. **Subscriptions:** 51 journals and other serials. **Services:** Interlibrary loan; copying; library open to the public on a fee basis. **Remarks:** FAX: (604)386-6602.

Victoria Department of Conservation and Environment - Royal Botanic Gardens & National Herbarium
See: **Royal Botanic Gardens & National Herbarium** (14104)

★ 19828 ★
Victoria General Hospital - Health Sciences Library (Med)
Halifax, NS, Canada B3H 2Y9
Phone: (902)428-2641
Samuel B. King, Libn.
Founded: 1972. **Staff:** Prof 1; Other 5. **Subjects:** Medicine, medical research, nursing, nursing education, allied health sciences, hospital administration and management. **Holdings:** 10,000 books; 5500 bound periodical volumes; 4000 pamphlets. **Subscriptions:** 550 journals and other serials; 10 newspapers. **Services:** Interlibrary loan; library open to the public with restrictions. **Automated Operations:** Computerized cataloging, acquisitions, and ILL. **Computerized Information Services:** DIALOG Information Services, MEDLARS; internal database. **Publications:** Acquisitions list; serials list. **Special Catalogs:** Catalog of Patient Education Resources of the Victoria General Hospital.

(Victoria) State Library of Victoria
See: **State Library of Victoria** (15697)

★ 19829 ★
Victoria Times-Colonist - Library (Publ)
P.O. Box 300
Phone: (604)380-5211
Victoria, BC, Canada V8W 2N4
Corinne Wong, Libn.
Founded: 1955. **Staff:** Prof 1; Other 4. **Subjects:** Newspaper reference topics. **Holdings:** 5000 volumes; newspaper clipping and photograph collection; newspapers on microfilm; newspaper indexes. **Services:** Library for staff use only. **Remarks:** Published by Canadian Newspapers Ltd.

★ 19830 ★
Victoria Union Hospital - Medical Library (Med)
1200 24th St., W.   Phone: (306)953-0291
Prince Albert, SK, Canada S6V 5T4   Joan I. Ryan, Dir.Hea.Rec.
Subjects: Medicine, surgery. **Holdings:** 320 books; 350 bound periodical volumes. **Subscriptions:** 11 journals and other serials. **Services:** Library not open to the public. **Remarks:** FAX: (306)763-2871.

Victoria University
See: **University of Toronto - Victoria University - Library (19463)**

Victoria University Archives
See: **United Church of Canada/Victoria University Archives (16696)**

★ 19831 ★
Victoria University of Technology - Library - Australian Tourism Index (Rec)
P.O. Box 64   Phone: 3 6884413
Footscray, VIC 3011, Australia   Jane Odgers, Coord.
Subjects: Tourism in Australia. **Holdings:** 100,000 volumes; 10,000 AV programs. **Subscriptions:** 2400 journals and other serials. **Services:** Library open to the public. **Computerized Information Services:** AUSTRALIS; produces LEIS. Performs searches on fee basis. **Publications:** Australian Leisure Bibliography - for sale. **Special Indexes:** Australian Leisure Index, semiannual - by subscription; Australian Tourism Index. **Remarks:** FAX: 3 6884801. Telex: AA36596. **Formerly:** Footscray Institute of Technology.

★ 19832 ★
Victorian College of Agriculture and Horticulture - Library (Agri)
Dookie Campus, VIC 3647, Australia   Phone: 58 286371
                  Michael Ferres
Founded: 1886. **Staff:** Prof 1; Other 1.5. **Subjects:** Agriculture. **Holdings:** 14,000 books; 10,000 bound periodical volumes. **Subscriptions:** 150 journals and other serials. **Services:** Interlibrary loan; copying; SDI; library open to the public. **Computerized Information Services:** DIALOG Information Services, AUSTRALIS. **Remarks:** FAX: 58 286475.

Victorian Periodical Library
See: **American Life Foundation and Study Institute - Americana Research Library (670)**

★ 19833 ★
Victory Memorial Hospital - Medical Library (Med)
1324 N. Sheridan Rd.   Phone: (708)360-3000
Waukegan, IL 60085   Mary Anne Zediker, Med.Lib.Techn.
Founded: 1969. **Staff:** Prof 1. **Subjects:** Medicine, nursing, hospitals. **Holdings:** 514 volumes. **Subscriptions:** 45 journals and other serials. **Services:** Interlibrary loan; library not open to the public. **Computerized Information Services:** BRS Information Technologies. **Networks/Consortia:** Member of Northeastern Illinois Library Consortium, North Suburban Library System (NSLS). **Remarks:** FAX: (708)360-4143.

★ 19834 ★
Video-Documentary Clearinghouse - Archives (Aud-Vis)
Harbor Square, Suite 2201
700 Richards St.   Phone: (808)523-2882
Honolulu, HI 96813-4631   Dr. Morton Cotlar, Exec.Dir.
Founded: 1977. **Staff:** Prof 2; Other 1. **Subjects:** Business administration, organizational administration, management, marketing, accounting, finance. **Holdings:** 15 AV programs. **Services:** Interlibrary loan; copying; archives open to the public on fee basis. **Computerized Information Services:** BITNET, InterNet (electronic mail services). **Remarks:** Electronic mail address(es): MORTON@UHUNIX (BITNET); MORTON@UHUNIX.UHCC.HAWAII.EDU (InterNet).

Video In Library
See: **Satellite Video Exchange Society (14877)**

★ 19835 ★
Vienna Institute for Comparative Economic Studies - Library (Bus-Fin)
P.O. Box 87   Phone: 1 782567
A-1103 Vienna, Austria   Sylvia Vondrasek
Founded: 1973. **Staff:** 2. **Subjects:** Comparative economics. **Holdings:** 8775 bound volumes; statistics. **Subscriptions:** 360 journals and other serials. **Services:** Library not open to the public. **Computerized Information Services:** Produces Eastern Bloc Countries Economic Data Base (available online through Reuters Information Services (Canada)). **Remarks:** Alternate telephone number(s): 782468. FAX: 1 787120. **Also Known As:** Wiener Institut fur Internationale Wirtschaftsvergleiche. **Staff:** Barbara Nassler.

★ 19836 ★
Vienna International Centre Library (Sci-Engr, Soc Sci)
Wagramerstr. 5
PO Box 100   Phone: 1 2360
A-1400 Vienna, Austria   Dr. Harriet Z. Gabbert, Hd.
Founded: 1979. **Staff:** Prof 11. **Subjects:** Atomic energy, industrial development, social and humanitarian affairs, drugs. **Holdings:** 95,000 bound volumes; 628,348 technical reports; 1.14 million documents; 412 films. **Subscriptions:** 4335 journals and other serials. **Services:** Interlibrary loan; copying; SDI; library intended primarily for the staffs of the various United Nations organizations located at the Vienna International Centre. **Automated Operations:** Computerized public access catalog and serials. **Computerized Information Services:** DIALOG Information Services, FT PROFILE, Questel, ESA/IRS, BLAISE, INIS, AGRIS, Industrial Development Abstracts; internal databases. Performs searches. **Publications:** Library Accessions List, weekly; Serials Titles. **Special Catalogs:** Film Catalog, irregular. **Special Indexes:** COMIndex, irregular. **Remarks:** FAX: 1 235584. Telex: 112645.

★ 19837 ★
Vienna Municipal Archives (Area-Ethnic)
Rathaus   Phone: 222 400084920
A-1082 Vienna, Austria   Herwig Wurtz, Dir.
Founded: 1856. **Staff:** 40. **Subjects:** Vienna. **Special Collections:** Autograph collection, music collection. **Holdings:** 432,980 books; 103,000 bound periodical volumes; 10,823 nonbook items; 255,000 manuscripts. **Subscriptions:** 3000 journals and other serials. **Services:** Interlibrary loan; copying; library open to the public. **Computerized Information Services:** (internal database). **Special Catalogs:** Kataloge der Wechselausstellungen der Wiener Stadt- und Landesbibliothek. **Remarks:** FAX: 222 40007219. Telex: 114735. **Also Known As:** Wiener Stadt- und Landesbibliothek.

★ 19838 ★
Vietnam - Department of Hygiene and Environment - National AIDS Committee - Library (Med)
Ministry of Health
Hanoi, Vietnam   Phone: 5 6255
Subjects: AIDS, HIV serological surveillance, hygiene, epidemiology. **Holdings:** 45,000 volumes; biographical archival items; statistical materials.

★ 19839 ★
Vietnam Refugee Fund - Library (Soc Sci)
6433 Nothana Dr.
Springfield, VA 22150   Phone: (703)971-9178
Subjects: Vietnam, Asia, resettlement of Vietnamese refugees into the U.S. **Holdings:** 3000 volumes.

★ 19840 ★
Vigo County Historical Society - Historical Museum of the Wabash Valley - Library (Hist)
1411 S. 6th St.   Phone: (812)235-9717
Terre Haute, IN 47802   David Buchanan, Exec.Dir.
Founded: 1958. **Staff:** Prof 1; Other 1. **Subjects:** Local history. **Holdings:** Figures not available. **Services:** Library open to the public by permission. **Publications:** Leaves of Thyme, quarterly.

★ 19841 ★
Vigo County Public Library - Special Collections (Hist)
1 Library Square   Phone: (812)232-1113
Terre Haute, IN 47807   Clarence Brink, Coord., Ref.Serv.
Founded: 1906. **Staff:** Prof 2; Other 4. **Subjects:** State and local history, genealogy. **Special Collections:** Baertich Collection (2 VF drawers); Shriner Collection (4 VF drawers); family files (36 VF drawers); community affairs (116 VF drawers); local club and association records (62 boxes); Dr. Charles N. Combs Memorabilia (1 box); Eugene V. Debs Collection (2 boxes); Jane Dabney Shackelford Collection (10 boxes); Joseph Jenckes Collection (1 box); Theodore Dreiser/Paul Dresser Collection (1 box); J.A. Wickersham Scrapbook (1 box); League of Women Voters of Terre Haute Collection; Rotary Club of Terre Haute Collection; Ida Husted Harper Collection (5 boxes); Terre Haute Chamber of Commerce Collection (30 boxes). **Holdings:** 7200 books; 1440 bound periodical volumes; 425 maps and charts; 244 archival collections; 3744 reels of microfilm. **Subscriptions:** 84 journals and other serials. **Services:** Copying; collections open to the public for reference use only. **Automated Operations:** Computerized cataloging. **Computerized Information Services:** OCLC. **Networks/Consortia:** Member of INCOLSA, Stone Hills Area Library Services Authority. **Special Catalogs:** Main Special Collections (card); Community Archives (card). **Special Indexes:** Surname Index, irregular; Index to the Writings of Ida Husted Harper: The Terre Haute Years (book); Terre Haute Tribune-Star Newspaper Index, 1986 to present. **Staff:** Nancy Sherrill, Geneal.Libn.; Susan Dehler, Spec.Coll.Supv./Archv.

★ 19842 ★
Vigo County School Corporation - Instructional Materials Center (Educ)
3000 College Ave.   Phone: (812)462-4354
Terre Haute, IN 47803   Alice M. Reck, Coord.
Founded: 1966. **Staff:** Prof 2; Other 5. **Subjects:** Curriculum, professional education. **Holdings:** 10,226 books; 6881 transparency masters; 469 framed art prints; 1011 slides; 2545 16mm films; 25 8mm films; 8 filmstrips; 92 sound filmstrips; 162 tapes; 920 videotapes; 24 realia; 72 pieces of sculpture; 53 videodiscs; 44 motion picture loops; 16 kits; 35 computer disks. **Subscriptions:** 12 journals and other serials. **Services:** Copying; center open to the public with restrictions. **Automated Operations:** Computerized cataloging. **Computerized Information Services:** OCLC. **Networks/Consortia:** Member of INCOLSA. **Publications:** Bibliographies, irregular. **Staff:** Lorraine E. Brett, Cat.

Vigyan and Paryavaran Kendra
See: **Center for Science and Environment** (3293)

★ 19843 ★
Vikon Chemical Company, Inc. - Library (Sci-Engr)
P.O. Box 1520   Phone: (919)226-6331
Burlington, NC 27216-1520   Luther B. Arnold, Jr.
Founded: 1948. **Subjects:** Chemistry, business, reference. **Holdings:** 600 books; reports; microfilm. **Subscriptions:** 30 journals and other serials; 2 newspapers. **Services:** Copying; library open to the public at librarian's discretion.

★ 19844 ★
Vikram Sarabhai Space Centre - Library (Sci-Engr)
PO ISRO
                                    Phone: 562281
Trivandrum 695 022, Kerala, India   V. Anjaneyulu
Founded: 1963. **Subjects:** Space science and technology, engineering, physics, chemistry. **Holdings:** 47,133 books; 25,773 bound periodical volumes; 49,177 reports; 23,310 microfiche; 12,505 standards. **Subscriptions:** 801 journals and other serials; 10 newspapers. **Services:** Interlibrary loan; copying; SDI; library open to the public for reference use only. **Automated Operations:** Computerized cataloging. **Publications:** List of additions; bibliography on various subjects related to space technology. **Remarks:** FAX: 471 79795. Telex: 0435 201; 0435 202.

★ 19845 ★
(Vilcea) Casa Corpului Didactic - Biblioteca (Educ)
Hroda H. Balcescu 26   Phone: 947 17520
1000 Vilcea, Romania   Maria Damitrascu, Libn.
Founded: 1974. **Staff:** Prof 1; Other 1. **Subjects:** Pedagogical literature, methodics, literature, technical books, school textbooks. **Holdings:** 24,000 books; 6 bound periodical volumes. **Subscriptions:** 2 journals and other serials; 4 newspapers. **Services:** Library open to the public with restrictions. **Remarks:** Alternate telephone number(s): 947 16218.

Villa Anneslie Archives
See: **Polish Nobility Association** (13184)

Carlos Villalongin Dramatic Company Archives
See: **University of Texas at Austin - Benson Latin American Collection** (19380)

★ 19846 ★
Villanova University - Library Science Library (Info Sci)
Graduate Dept. of Library Science   Phone: (215)645-4672
Villanova, PA 19085   Carolyn C. Walsh, Libn.
Staff: Prof 2; Other 2. **Subjects:** Library and information sciences, children's and young adult's literature, archives, computer science. **Special Collections:** Philadelphia Authors and Illustrators (200 items). **Holdings:** 22,500 items. **Subscriptions:** 415 journals and other serials. **Services:** Interlibrary loan; copying; library open to the public for reference use only. **Publications:** Pennsylvania Authors at a Glance; Philadelphia Children's Authors and Illustrators at a Glance; WINGS. **Staff:** Carol A. Kare, Cat.

★ 19847 ★
Villanova University - School of Law - Pulling Law Library (Law)
Garey Hall   Phone: (215)645-7022
Villanova, PA 19085   William James, Dir.
Founded: 1953. **Staff:** Prof 9; Other 12. **Subjects:** Law. **Special Collections:** Church and State. **Holdings:** 357,893 volumes and microforms. **Subscriptions:** 3795 journals and other serials; 14 newspapers. **Services:** Interlibrary loan; copying; library open to the public on a fee basis. **Automated Operations:** Computerized cataloging. **Computerized Information Services:** LEXIS, WESTLAW, DIALOG Information Services, NEXIS, BRS Information Technologies, VU/TEXT Information Services, OCLC; MCI Mail (electronic mail service). **Networks/Consortia:** Member of Mid-Atlantic Law Library Cooperative (MALLCO). **Publications:** New Acquisitions, monthly. **Staff:** Maura Buri, Circ.Libn.; Steven Elkins, Hd., Tech.Serv.; Margaret Coyne, ILL/Ref.Libn.; Elizabeth Devlin, Assoc. Law Libn. & Hd., Rd.Serv.; Mary Cornelius, Ref.Libn.; Marianne Zajacek, Ref.Libn.; Karen Jordan, Ref.Libn.; Melaine Solon, Hd.Ref.Libn.

★ 19848 ★
Ville Marie Social Service Centre - Library (Soc Sci)
2155 Guy St., Suite 1010   Phone: (514)989-1885
Montreal, PQ, Canada H3H 2R9   Janet Sand Steinhouse, Libn.
Founded: 1976. **Staff:** Prof 1. **Subjects:** Social services, family, youth, aged. **Special Collections:** AIDS; Sexual abuse. **Holdings:** Government publications. **Subscriptions:** 50 journals and other serials. **Services:** Interlibrary loan; copying; library open to the public by appointment. **Networks/Consortia:** Member of McGill Medical and Health Libraries Association (MMHLA). **Remarks:** FAX: (514)939-3609. **Also Known As:** Centre de Services Sociaux Ville Marie.

★ 19849 ★
Vilnius Art Academy - Library (Art)
ul. Tiesos 6   Phone: 611170
Vilnius, Lithuania   D. Simiene
Founded: 1803. **Staff:** Prof 8; Other 7. **Subjects:** Fine arts, decorative arts, art history, philosophy, history, literature. **Special Collections:** Lithuanian-Polish art and history collection (17th-20th centuries; 700 volumes). **Holdings:** 150,000 books; 1000 bound periodical volumes; 400 reports. **Subscriptions:** 26 journals and other serials; 4 newspapers. **Services:** Library open to the public.

Vinal Library
See: **South Shore Natural Science Center** (15434)

★ 19850 ★
Vincennes University - Byron R. Lewis Historical Library (Hist)
Vincennes, IN 47591   Phone: (812)885-4330
                                    Robert R. Stevens, Dir.
Founded: 1967. **Staff:** Prof 1; Other 2. **Subjects:** Political, social, economic and general history of Lower Wabash Valley; university archives; oral history of Depression Era; genealogy. **Holdings:** 7500 volumes; manuscripts; photographs; maps; broadsides; newspapers; pamphlets. **Subscriptions:** 12 journals and other serials. **Services:** Limited area and genealogical research; library open to the public.

D.J. Vincent Medical Library
See: **Riverside Methodist Hospital** (13949)

G. Robert Vincent Voice Library
See: **Michigan State University** (10321)

John Vincent Archive
See: **University of California, Los Angeles - Music Library** (18392)

★ 19851 ★
Vineland Historical and Antiquarian Society - Library (Hist)
108 S. 7th St.
Box 35   Phone: (609)691-1111
Vineland, NJ 08360   Allison L. Smith, Act.Libn.
Founded: 1864. **Staff:** Prof 1. **Subjects:** Genealogy and local history, Americana, antiques. **Special Collections:** Sheppard Genealogical Papers; Autograph Collection; Civil War Official Records; Bureau of American Ethnology Library. **Holdings:** 5000 books; bound local newspapers, 1861-1935; pamphlets and documents; census material on microfilm. **Services:** Copying; library open to the public on a limited schedule.

★ 19852 ★
The Vineyard - Real Estate, Shopping Center & Urban Development Information Center (Bus-Fin, Plan)
50 W. Shaw Ave.   Phone: (209)222-0182
Fresno, CA 93704   Richard Erganian, Info.Dir.
Founded: 1956. **Staff:** Prof 2. **Subjects:** Real estate, shopping centers, urban and regional planning, architecture, mortgage financing, market research, landscaping. **Special Collections:** Shopping center, hotel, and mixed use development. **Holdings:** 3000 books; 500 bound periodical volumes; 2000 other cataloged items; 30 real estate transcripts; 50 shopping center development transcripts; 20 appraisal tapes and cassettes; 25 income property reports and transcripts; 150 video cassettes. **Subscriptions:** 25 journals and other serials; 5 newspapers. **Services:** Library open to real estate developers. **Special Catalogs:** Real Estate Information Sources.

★ 19853 ★
Vinnell Corporation - Reference Center (Mil)
10530 Rosehaven St., Suite 600
Fairfax, VA 22030   Phone: (703)385-4544
Founded: 1932. **Subjects:** Military art and science, military education, vocational/technical education, job corps, specialized marketing information on Saudi Arabia and Southeast Asia. **Special Collections:** Photographs of corporate projects and personnel, 1932 to present (3000). **Holdings:** 250 books; 3000 proposals, reports, contracts; 20,000 military documents; 5000 other government documents; 1500 curriculum resources; 200 slides, cassettes, microfiche. **Services:** Center not open to the public.

★ 19854 ★
Vinson & Elkins - Law Library (Law)
3055 First City Tower
1001 Fannin   Phone: (713)758-2678
Houston, TX 77002-6760   Karl T. Gruben, Libn.
Founded: 1917. **Staff:** Prof 3; Other 8. **Subjects:** Law - Texas, environmental, foreign and international, oil and gas. **Holdings:** 120,000 books; 1800 bound periodical volumes; microforms; audio cassettes; U.S. and Texas documents. **Subscriptions:** 300 journals and other serials. **Services:** Interlibrary loan; copying; library open to researchers with approval of librarian. **Computerized Information Services:** DIALOG Information Services, PFDS Online, LEXIS, WESTLAW, Information America, DataTimes, VU/TEXT Information Services, Dow Jones News/Retrieval. **Remarks:** FAX: (713)758-2346. **Staff:** David Blythe, Asst.Libn.; Patricia Huntsman, Assoc.Libn.

Violin Society of America - Herbert K. Goodkind Collection
See: **Oberlin College - Conservatory of Music Library** (12218)

★ 19855 ★
Virgin Islands Department of Planning and Natural Resources - Division of Libraries, Archives, and Museums (Info Sci)
23 Dronningens Gade
Charlotte Amalie   Phone: (809)774-3407
St. Thomas, VI 00802   Jeannette B. Allis-Bastian, Dir.
Founded: 1920. **Staff:** Prof 17; Other 61. **Subjects:** General and reference topics. **Special Collections:** Von Scholton Collection (Caribbean, West Indian, and Virgin Island materials; 14,000 volumes; periodicals; newspapers; dissertations; manuscripts; maps; documents); Virgin Islands archives, 1655-1933 (on microfilm); newspapers, 1770 to present (on microfilm). **Holdings:** 119,000 books; U.N., U.S., and Virgin Islands government documents depository; manuscripts; clippings; archival materials; ephemera. **Subscriptions:** 354 journals and other serials. **Services:** Interlibrary loan; copying; microfilming; bureau open to the public. **Networks/Consortia:** Member of Virgin Islands Library Network (VILINET). **Publications:** Annual Reports, Virgin Islands Government Documents, quarterly; Caribbeana (union acquisitions list), irregular; occasional papers. **Special Catalogs:** Union List of Periodicals and Newspapers (book); Union Title File (card). **Special Indexes:** Local Newspaper index (card). **Remarks:** Alternate telephone number(s): 774-0630. **Staff:** June A.V. Lindqvist, Cur., Von Scholton Coll.; Martin Gerbens, Hd., Caribbean Coll.

★ 19856 ★
Virgin Islands Energy Office - Library (Energy)
81 Castle Coakley
Christiansted, VI 00820   Phone: (809)772-2616
Subjects: Energy policy. **Holdings:** 5000 books.

★ 19857 ★
Virginia Baptist Historical Society - Library (Hist, Rel-Phil)
University of Richmond
Box 34   Phone: (804)289-8434
Richmond, VA 23173   Fred Anderson, Exec.Dir.
Founded: 1876. **Staff:** Prof 2; Other 2. **Subjects:** History - Virginia Baptist, Baptist, religious, church, Virginia State, Confederate, Colonial Virginia. **Special Collections:** Church manuscripts (2600). **Holdings:** 12,000 books; 650 bound periodical volumes; 95 VF drawers of manuscripts, documents, papers, diaries, journals. **Subscriptions:** 12 journals and other serials. **Services:** Copying; library open to the public by appointment. **Publications:** Virginia Baptist Register, annual - to members and by subscription; The Chronicle, quarterly - to members. **Special Indexes:** Index to Virginia Baptist Register; index to The Religious Herald, 1828-1874 (card).

★ 19858 ★
Virginia Baptist Hospital - Barksdale Medical Library (Med)
3300 Rivermont Ave.   Phone: (804)522-4505
Lynchburg, VA 24503   Anne M. Nurmi, Libn.
Staff: Prof 1. **Subjects:** Obstetrics and gynecology, pediatrics, internal medicine. **Holdings:** 300 books; 1000 bound periodical volumes; video cassettes. **Subscriptions:** 37 journals and other serials. **Services:** Interlibrary loan; copying; library open to the public for reference use only. **Computerized Information Services:** MEDLINE. **Networks/Consortia:** Member of National Network of Libraries of Medicine - Southeastern/Atlantic Region, Lynchburg Area Library Cooperative. **Remarks:** Maintained by Centra Health Inc. **Remarks:** FAX: (804)522-4650.

★ 19859 ★
Virginia Beach Public Library System - Municipal Reference Library (Soc Sci)
Municipal Center   Phone: (804)427-4644
Virginia Beach, VA 23456   Kathleen G. Hevey, Municipal Ref.Coord.
Founded: 1972. **Staff:** Prof 2; Other 1. **Subjects:** Virginia Beach, public administration. **Special Collections:** Governmental and community affairs news clippings. **Holdings:** 2600 books and documents; 80 bound periodical volumes; 259 information files; 4670 microfiche. **Subscriptions:** 94 journals and other serials; 11 newspapers. **Services:** Interlibrary loan; copying; SDI; library open to the public for reference use only. **Automated Operations:** Computerized cataloging, acquisitions, and circulation. **Computerized Information Services:** DIALOG Information Services, LOGIN, Local Exchange (electronic mail services). **Publications:** Information Brief, bimonthly - for internal distribution only. **Special Indexes:** NewsIndex (online). **Remarks:** FAX: (804)427-8240. **Staff:** Helen M. Buonviri, Info.Spec.; Mary Lawrence, Info.Spec.

★ 19860 ★
Virginia Beach Public Library System - Robert S. Wahab, Jr. Public Law Library (Law)
Municipal Center   Phone: (804)427-4419
Virginia Beach, VA 23452   Robert P. Miller, Jr., Law Libn.
Founded: 1975. **Staff:** Prof 1; Other 2. **Subjects:** Law. **Special Collections:** Education. **Holdings:** 9000 books; 200 bound periodical volumes. **Subscriptions:** 29 journals and other serials. **Services:** Interlibrary loan; copying; faxing (fee basis); library open to the public. **Automated Operations:** Computerized public access catalog. **Computerized Information Services:** WESTLAW. Performs searches on fee basis. **Publications:** Information brochure. **Remarks:** FAX: (804)427-8742.

★ 19861 ★
Virginia Commonwealth University - James Branch Cabell Library - Special Collections and Archives Department (Hum)
901 Park Ave.
VCU Box 2033   Phone: (804)367-1108
Richmond, VA 23284-2033   Barbara J. Ford
Founded: 1966. **Staff:** Prof 3; Other 2. **Subjects:** Contemporary Virginia authors, Southeastern American poetry, 20th century American cartoons and caricatures, book art. **Special Collections:** James Branch Cabell Collection (3000 books, notes, and manuscripts); Poetry Society of Virginia Memorial Collection (325 volumes); Richmond authors (250 volumes); Giacomini Collection (Samuel Johnson and James Boswell; 395 volumes); Richmond Area Development Archives (484 feet); multi-cultural archives; Adele Clark papers (100 feet); New Virginia Review Library (600 books and current periodicals); Richmond YWCA Records (30 feet). **Holdings:** 9800 books; 1369 feet of manuscripts; 1450 theses; university archives. **Services:** Copying; photographic reproduction; collections open to the public. **Automated Operations:** Computerized cataloging, acquisitions, and serials. **Computerized Information Services:** OCLC; Black History Archives (internal database). **Networks/Consortia:** Member of SOLINET. **Remarks:** Collection housed in 2 buildings, James Branch Cabell Library and Tompkins-McCaw Library. **Staff:** Jodi Koste, Archv.; Betsy Pittman, Archv.; Dr. John H. Whaley, Dept.Hd.

★ 19862 ★
Virginia Commonwealth University - Medical College of Virginia Campus - Tompkins-McCaw Library (Med)
509 N. 12th St.
P.O. Box 582   Phone: (804)786-0633
Richmond, VA 23298-0582   Barbara J. Ford
Founded: 1913. **Staff:** Prof 10; Other 21. **Subjects:** Medicine, dentistry, pharmacy, nursing, basic sciences, allied health sciences. **Special Collections:** 19th Century Medical History Collection (7046 titles); Archives of the Medical College of Virginia (945.9 feet); Virginia Health Sciences Archives (395.6 feet); Nursing History Collection (247.6 feet); Medical Artifacts Collection (3027 pieces); theses (2400). **Holdings:** 266,605 bound volumes. **Subscriptions:** 2627 journals and other serials. **Services:** Copying, photographic reproduction, library open to the public. **Automated Operations:** Computerized cataloging, serials, circulation, and ILL (DOCLINE). **Computerized Information Services:** DIALOG Information Services, MEDLINE, BRS Information Technologies, NLM, OCLC, VU/TEXT Information Services, WILSONLINE; CD-ROMs. Performs searches on fee basis. **Networks/Consortia:** Member of SOLINET, National Network of Libraries of Medicine - Southeastern/Atlantic Region. **Publications:** Library Online (newsletter), biennial - to Friends of Library; collections and services brochures. **Remarks:** FAX: (804)786-2260.

★ 19863 ★
Virginia Commonwealth University - Virginia Center on Aging - Information Resources Center (Med)
P.O. Box 229, MCV Sta.   Phone: (804)786-1525
Richmond, VA 23298-0229   Ruth B. Finley, IRC Hd.
Founded: 1979. **Subjects:** Gerontology, mental health, sociology and the politics of aging, geriatrics, family relationships, long-term care. **Special Collections:** Alzheimer's Disease collection (books; pamphlets; brochures; videotapes); Second careers and retirement planning collection (books; brochures); Intergenerational relationships collection (books; brochures); Older women collection (books; brochures; bibliography). **Holdings:** 1500 books; 100 reports; 4 archives; 50 AV items. **Subscriptions:** 3 journals and other serials. **Services:** Library open to the public with restrictions. **Automated Operations:** Computerized cataloging. **Publications:** AGE in Action (newsletter), quarterly. **Remarks:** FAX: (804)371-7905.

Virginia Health Sciences Archives
See: Virginia Commonwealth University - Medical College of Virginia Campus (19862)

★ 19864 ★
Virginia Historical Society - Library and Museum (Hist)
428 North Blvd.
Box 7311   Phone: (804)358-4901
Richmond, VA 23221   Charles F. Bryan, Jr., Dir.
Founded: 1831. **Staff:** Prof 11; Other 6. **Subjects:** Virginiana, 16th-19th century Americana. **Special Collections:** Confederate imprints; 17th and 18th century English architecture. **Holdings:** 135,000 volumes; 7 million manuscripts; prints and engravings; maps and printed ephemera; sheet music; newspapers; paintings. **Subscriptions:** 330 journals and other serials. **Services:** Copying; library open to the public. **Remarks:** FAX: (804)355-2399. **Staff:** Robert F. Strohm, Assoc.Dir., Adm.; Frances Pollard, Sr.Libn.; Paulette Thomas, Tech.Serv.; E. Lee Shepard, Mss. & Archv.; Waverly Winfree, Mss. & Archv.; James C. Kelly, Musm.Serv.

★ 19865 ★
Virginia Institute of Marine Science - Library (Biol Sci)
College of William and Mary
School of Marine Science
Gloucester Point, VA 23062   Phone: (804)642-7114
Founded: 1947. **Staff:** Prof 3; Other 1. **Subjects:** Marine and estuarine biology and ecology, oceanography, aquaculture, Chesapeake Bay. **Special Collections:** Sport fishing collection; rare books. **Holdings:** 15,100 books; 24,300 bound periodical volumes; 500 volumes of VIMS Archives. **Subscriptions:** 800 journals and other serials. **Services:** Interlibrary loan; copying; library open to the public. **Automated Operations:** Computerized cataloging and serials. **Computerized Information Services:** DIALOG Information Services, OCLC; SCIENCEnet (electronic mail service). Performs searches. **Networks/Consortia:** Member of SOLINET. **Publications:** Chesapeake Bay Bibliography (book and online); Library Acquisitions List, bimonthly. **Remarks:** Alternate telephone number(s): 642-7115; 642-7116. FAX: (804)642-7113. Electronic mail address(es): VIMS Attn: Library (SCIENCEnet). **Staff:** Marilyn Lewis, Cat./ILL; Diane Walker, Circ., Rd.Serv., VIMS Pubns.

★ 19866 ★
Virginia Marine Science Museum - Library (Biol Sci)
717 General Booth Blvd.   Phone: (804)437-4949
Virginia Beach, VA 23451   Lynn Clements, Educ.Prog.Coord.
Founded: 1985. **Staff:** Prof 14. **Subjects:** Marine science, Chesapeake Bay, museums and aquariums, local maritime history. **Holdings:** Figures not available. **Subscriptions:** 14 journals and other serials. **Services:** Library open to researchers.

Virginia-Maryland Regional College of Veterinary Medicine
See: Virginia Polytechnic Institute and State University (19876)

★ 19867 ★
Virginia Military Institute - Preston Library (Hum, Sci-Engr)
Lexington, VA 24450   Phone: (703)464-7228
                                     James E. Gaines, Jr., Hd.Libn.
Founded: 1839. **Staff:** Prof 6; Other 12. **Subjects:** Engineering, liberal arts, military history. **Special Collections:** Civil War period; Virginia Military Institute archives. **Holdings:** 235,000 volumes; 129,500 government documents. **Subscriptions:** 1054 journals and other serials; 31 newspapers. **Services:** Interlibrary loan; copying; library open to the public. **Computerized Information Services:** DIALOG Information Services, OCLC. **Networks/Consortia:** Member of SOLINET. **Publications:** Friends of Preston Library Newsletter; annual report; New Acquisitions, monthly; list of selected government publications, monthly; Library Guide, annual. **Remarks:** FAX: (703)464-7279. **Staff:** Wylma P. Davis, Ref.Libn.; Janet S. Holly, Asst.Ref.Libn.; Marilyn R. Pearson, Circ. & AV Libn.; Diane B. Jacob, Archv.

★19868★
Virginia Museum of Fine Arts - Library (Art)
2800 Grove Ave.   Phone: (804)367-0827
Richmond, VA 23221-2466   Betty A. Stacy, Libn.
Founded: 1936. **Staff:** Prof 5. **Subjects:** Art history, decorative arts, painting, sculpture, theater. **Special Collections:** John Barton Payne Collection; John Koenig Collection (theater); Ellen Bayard Weedon Collection (Oriental studies); Gordon Strause Collection; Ike Bana Society Collection; John G. Hayes Decorative Arts Collection. **Holdings:** 70,000 books; 2000 bound periodical volumes; VF drawers of clippings; 850 boxes of museum publications; 700 boxes of auction catalogs. **Subscriptions:** 230 journals and other serials. **Services:** Copying; library open to the public for reference use only. **Computerized Information Services:** OCLC; internal database. **Networks/Consortia:** Member of SOLINET. **Remarks:** FAX: (804)367-9393. **Staff:** Margaret Burcham, Lib.Asst.; Elizabeth Yeuich, Lib.Asst.; Kimberly Bishop, Lib.Asst.

★19869★
Virginia Polytechnic Institute and State University - Art & Architecture Library (Art, Plan)
Cowgill Hall   Phone: (703)231-9271
Blacksburg, VA 24061   Annette Burr, Art & Arch.Libn.
Staff: Prof 1; Other 4. **Subjects:** Architecture, art, art history, urban affairs and planning, building construction, landscape architecture. **Holdings:** 60,000 volumes; 50,000 architecture slides. **Subscriptions:** 420 journals and other serials. **Services:** Interlibrary loan; copying; library open to the public. **Automated Operations:** Computerized cataloging, acquisitions, and circulation. **Computerized Information Services:** DIALOG Information Services, OCLC, Knowledge Index, RLIN, MEDLARS, WILSONLINE, STN International, Chemical Abstracts Service (CAS), NASA/RECON, WESTLAW, Dow Jones News/Retrieval, QL Systems; Virginia Tech Library System (VTLS; internal database). Performs searches on fee basis. Contact Person: David Beagle 231-9224. **Networks/Consortia:** Member of SOLINET. **Remarks:** FAX: (703)231-9263; (703)231-9264 (ILL).

★19870★
Virginia Polytechnic Institute and State University - Center for Hospitality Research & Service (Bus-Fin)
Department of Hotel, Restaurant & Institutional Management
Hillcrest Hall   Phone: (703)231-5515
Blacksburg, VA 24061-0429   Michael D. Olsen, Ph.D., Exec.Dir.
Staff: Prof 3; Other 12. **Subjects:** Hospitality service industries. **Holdings:** Figures not available. **Services:** Center not open to the public. **Computerized Information Services:** Computerized Industry Trends (internal database). **Remarks:** FAX: (703)231-7826. Telex: 9103331861.

★19871★
Virginia Polytechnic Institute and State University - Center for the Study of Science in Society - Library (Sci-Engr)
Price House   Phone: (703)231-7687
Blacksburg, VA 24061   Robert A. Paterson, Dir.
Founded: 1980. **Staff:** 2. **Subjects:** Science and technology studies. **Special Collections:** Richard Schallenberg Collection (history of science and technology); Nicholas Mullins Collection (sociology of science and technology). **Holdings:** 2000 books; unbound periodicals, reports, and manuscripts. **Services:** Library open to the public. **Computerized Information Services:** BITNET (electronic mail service). **Remarks:** FAX: (703)231-7013. Electronic mail address(es): STS@VTVM1.CC.VT.EDU (BITNET). **Staff:** Carolyn Furrow, Libn.

★19872★
Virginia Polytechnic Institute and State University - Geology Library (Sci-Engr)
3040 Derring Hall   Phone: (703)231-6101
Blacksburg, VA 24061-0421   Edward F. Lener, Geol.Libn.
Staff: Prof 1; Other 1. **Subjects:** Geology of Virginia, seismic geophysics, geochemistry, paleontology, mineralogy. **Holdings:** 35,000 volumes; 350 reels of microfilm; 13,000 microfiche; 15,500 maps; 35,000 aerial photographs. **Subscriptions:** 500 journals and other serials. **Services:** Interlibrary loan; copying; library open to the public. **Automated Operations:** Computerized circulation. **Computerized Information Services:** DIALOG Information Services, OCLC. Performs searches on fee basis. **Networks/Consortia:** Member of SOLINET. **Publications:** New Acquisitions List, bimonthly - free upon request. **Remarks:** FAX: (703)231-3386.

★19873★
Virginia Polytechnic Institute and State University - International Archive of Women in Architecture (Art)
Special Collections Dept.
University Libraries
P.O. Box 90001   Phone: (703)231-9215
Blacksburg, VA 24062-9001   Laura Katz Smith, Archv.
Founded: 1985. **Staff:** Prof 1. **Subjects:** Architecture, women. **Special Collections:** Papers of Han Schroeder (10 cubic feet), Hilde Westrom (2 cubic feet), Association for Women in Architecture (9 cubic feet), Sena Sekulic (1.5 cubic feet), Elsa Leviseur (6 cubic feet), Susana Torre (3 cubic feet), Diana Lee-Smith (.4 cubic feet). **Holdings:** 120 collections of architectural drawings, photographs, specifications, brochures, and articles. **Services:** Copying; archive open to the public. **Remarks:** FAX: (703)231-9263.

★19874★
Virginia Polytechnic Institute and State University - Libraries - Special Collections Department - Archives of American Aerospace Exploration (Sci-Engr)
P.O. Box 90001   Phone: (703)231-9205
Blacksburg, VA 24062-9001   Glenn L. McMullen, Hd., Spec.Coll.Dept.
Founded: 1986. **Staff:** Prof 3; Other 1. **Subjects:** Aeronautical engineering, space transportation and exploration. **Special Collections:** Papers of Christopher Kraft (30 cubic feet), Samuel Herrick (60 cubic feet), John T. Parsons (200 cubic feet), Melvin Gough (20 cubic feet), Hartley Soule (2 cubic feet), Marjorie R. Townsend (2 cubic feet), Thornton L. Page (2 cubic feet), John D. Clark (4 cubic feet), James Randolph (4 cubic feet), Michael Collins (25 cubic feet), Evert B. Clark (15 cubic feet), John V. Becker (6 cubic feet), Blake W. Corson, Jr. (15 cubic feet), Robert R. Gilruth (1 cubic foot), and Edward C. Polhamus (1 cubic foot). **Services:** Copying; archives open to the public. **Special Catalogs:** Checklist of collections in the Archives of American Aerospace Exploration (pamphlet). **Staff:** Laura H. Katz, Mss.Cur.

★19875★
Virginia Polytechnic Institute and State University - University Libraries (Sci-Engr, Hum)
PO Box 90001   Phone: (703)231-5593
Blacksburg, VA 24062-9001   Paul M. Gherman, Univ.Libn.
Founded: 1872. **Staff:** Prof 50; Other 106. **Subjects:** Agricultural sciences, architecture, biological and physical sciences, engineering, humanities, social sciences. **Special Collections:** Archives of American Aerospace Exploration; Archive of Norfolk & Western Railway; Archive of Southern Railway Predecessors; Sherwood Anderson book collection; Heraldry; Science Fiction Magazines; History of Technology; Southwest Virginiana; Western Americana. **Holdings:** 1.7 million books and bound periodical volumes; 121,000 maps; 5.2 million microforms; 6000 phonograph records; 200 audiotapes; 3000 videotapes. **Subscriptions:** 13,665 journals and other serials; 48 newspapers. **Services:** Interlibrary loan; copying; library open to the public. **Automated Operations:** Computerized cataloging, acquisitions, serials, and circulation. **Computerized Information Services:** DIALOG Information Services, BRS Information Technologies, WESTLAW, LEXIS, NEXIS, OCLC, MEDLARS, Chemical Abstracts Service (CAS); Virginia Tech Library System (VTLS; internal database); CD-ROMs; BITNET (electronic mail service). Performs searches on fee basis (external databases only). **Networks/Consortia:** Member of SOLINET. **Remarks:** FAX: (703)231-9263. **Staff:** M. Cramer, Hd., Acq.Dept.; Glenn McMullen, Hd., Spec.Coll.; A. Burr, Art & Arch.Lib.; Doug Jones, Hd., Bus.Serv.Dept.; M.L. Norstedt, Hd., Cat.Dept.; J. Carlton, N. Virginia Graduate Ctr.; F.O. Painter, Dir., Adm.Serv.Div.; S.R. Glazener, Dir., Tech.Serv.Div.; P. Metz, Prin.Bibliog.; J. Eustis, Chf., Access Serv. Div.; L. Richardson, Act.Chf., Ref.Serv.Div.; W.C. Dougherty, Hd., Sys.Oper.Dept.; V. Kok, Vet.Med.Libn.; D.J. Kenney, Asst. to Univ.Libn.; B. Litchfield, Chf., Libn. Automation Div.; H. Kriz, Automation Libn.

★19876★
Virginia Polytechnic Institute and State University - Virginia-Maryland Regional College of Veterinary Medicine - Veterinary Medical Library (Med)
CVM, Phase II   Phone: (703)231-6610
Blacksburg, VA 24061   Victoria T. Kok, Vet.Med.Libn.
Founded: 1980. **Staff:** Prof 1; Other 2. **Subjects:** Clinical and preclinical veterinary medicine, biomedicine. **Holdings:** 11,878 books; 3574 bound periodical volumes; 480 slide sets and video cassettes. **Subscriptions:** 575 journals and other serials. **Services:** Interlibrary loan; copying; library open

to the public. **Automated Operations:** Computerized public access catalog, cataloging, and circulation. **Computerized Information Services:** DIALOG Information Services, MEDLARS; BITNET (electronic mail service). Performs searches on fee basis. **Remarks:** Alternate telephone number(s): 231-7666. FAX: (703)231-7367. Electronic mail address(es): KOK@VTVM2 (BITNET).

★ 19877 ★
Virginia Power - Research/Records Services (Energy, Sci-Engr)
Box 26666   Phone: (804)771-3657
Richmond, VA 23261   Barbara A. Wichser, Supv.
Founded: 1937. **Staff:** Prof 2; Other 2. **Subjects:** Electric power, nuclear power, environment, management, personal development. **Holdings:** 4221 titles; 7467 volumes; 5876 volumes of association reports; association standards on microfilm; EPRI reports on microfiche; 22 periodicals on microfiche; 308 AV programs. **Subscriptions:** 317 journals and other serials; 7 newspapers. **Services:** Interlibrary loan; SDI; services open to the public by appointment. **Automated Operations:** Computerized cataloging, serials, and circulation. **Computerized Information Services:** DIALOG Information Services, PFDS Online, Dun & Bradstreet Business Credit Services, VU/TEXT Information Services, Mead Data Central; Knight-Ridder Unicom (electronic mail service). **Publications:** Resources Alert, quarterly - available upon request. **Remarks:** FAX: (804)771-3168. **Staff:** Linda G. Royal, Res.Libn.

★ 19878 ★
Virginia (State) Department of Corrections - Academy for Staff Development - Library (Soc Sci, Law)
500 N. Winchester Ave.
Box 2215   Phone: (703)943-3141
Waynesboro, VA 22980   Linda F. Larkin, Libn.
Staff: Prof 1; Other 1. **Subjects:** Criminal justice, management, psychology, juvenile delinquency, family therapy, training and development. **Holdings:** 5800 books; 69 bound periodical volumes; 250 16mm films; 117 filmstrips; 270 videotapes; 5 VF drawers; 34 slide/cassette sets. **Subscriptions:** 90 journals and other serials. **Services:** Interlibrary loan; copying; library open to the public by appointment. **Publications:** Acquisitions list, quarterly; AV resources list; subject bibliographies. **Remarks:** FAX: (703)943-3141, ext. 150.

★ 19879 ★
Virginia (State) Department of Criminal Justice Services - Library (Law, Soc Sci)
805 E. Broad St.   Phone: (804)786-8478
Richmond, VA 23219   Stephen E. Squire, Libn.
Founded: 1982. **Staff:** Prof 1. **Subjects:** Criminal and juvenile justice planning and evaluation; crime prevention programs; domestic violence. **Holdings:** 7000 volumes; 10 VF drawers; 125 videocassettes. **Subscriptions:** 250 journals and other serials. **Services:** Interlibrary loan; copying; library open to the public by appointment. **Networks/Consortia:** Member of Criminal Justice Information Exchange Group. **Publications:** Current Newsletters and Periodicals List, irregular - available upon request; List of Acquisitions, weekly - for internal distribution only. **Remarks:** FAX: (804)371-8981.

★ 19880 ★
Virginia (State) Department of Education - Division of Management Information Services - Data Utilization & Reporting (Educ)
Box 6Q   Phone: (804)225-2100
Richmond, VA 23216   M. Diane Wresinski, Supv.
Founded: 1960. **Staff:** Prof 2; Other 1. **Subjects:** Educational research and statistics. **Holdings:** Statistical reports and documents. **Services:** Copying; open to the public. **Publications:** Facing Up, annual; Membership Report, annual; School Census, triennial.

★ 19881 ★
Virginia (State) Department of General Services - Division of Consolidated Laboratory Services Library (Sci-Engr)
1 N. 14th St.   Phone: (804)786-7905
Richmond, VA 23219   Susan E. Wells, Adm. Staff Spec.
Founded: 1963. **Staff:** Prof 1. **Subjects:** Chemistry, forensic science, microbiology. **Holdings:** 4000 books. **Subscriptions:** 75 journals and other serials. **Services:** Library not open to the public. **Remarks:** FAX: (804)371-7973.

★ 19882 ★
Virginia (State) Department of Health - Bureau of Toxic Substances - Library (Med)
1500 E Main St., Rm. 124   Phone: (804)786-1763
Richmond, VA 23219   Vickie O'Dell, Info.Spec.
Founded: 1980. **Staff:** Prof 1. **Subjects:** Toxicology, occupational health. **Holdings:** 500 books. **Subscriptions:** 10 journals and other serials. **Services:** Interlibrary loan; library not open to the public. **Computerized Information Services:** DIALOG Information Services, BRS Information Technologies, NLM; Dialcom, Inc., Public Health Foundation (electronic mail services). **Remarks:** FAX: (804)786-9510. Electronic mail address(es): PHF45061 (Public Health Foundation).

★ 19883 ★
Virginia (State) Department of Highways and Transportation - Location & Design Plan Library (Plan)
1401 E. Broad St.   Phone: (804)786-2521
Richmond, VA 23219   Deborah D. Easley, Off.Serv.Supv.
Staff: Prof 3. **Subjects:** Highway construction and right of way plans. **Holdings:** 60,000 survey books; 17,000 bound periodical volumes; 2 million cards. **Services:** Library open to the public. **Automated Operations:** Computerized cataloging. **Remarks:** FAX: (804)225-3686. Alternate telephone number(s): 786-2522.

Virginia (State) Department of Highways and Transportation - Virginia Transportation Research Council
See: **Virginia Transportation Research Council - Library** (19898)

★ 19884 ★
Virginia (State) Department of Historic Resources - Archives and Library (Hist, Art)
221 Governor St.   Phone: (804)786-3143
Richmond, VA 23219   Joseph S. White, III, Archv.
Staff: Prof 1. **Subjects:** Virginia - architecture, archeology, local history. **Special Collections:** Mutual Assurance Society of Virginia policies (phtocopies; 16 cf.); unpublished archeological surveys (4300 items); archeological site inventories (24,600 items); architectural site inventories (30,000 items); photograph/slide collection. **Holdings:** 2340 books; 1000 unbound journals; 150,000 images; facsimiles of historic maps (700 items); HABS/HAER measured drawings. **Subscriptions:** 30 journals and other serials. **Services:** Copying; library open to the public by appointment. **Computerized Information Services:** NADB, CRIS, IPS (internal databases).

★ 19885 ★
Virginia (State) Department of Information Technology - Technical Library (Info Sci)
110 S. 7th St.   Phone: (804)344-5775
Richmond, VA 23219   Jane A. Terrell, Lib.Mgr.
Founded: 1984. **Staff:** Prof 1. **Subjects:** Data processing hardware and software, telecommunications, data communications. **Holdings:** 1744 books. **Subscriptions:** 35 journals and other serials. **Services:** Interlibrary loan; library not open to the public. **Automated Operations:** Computerized cataloging, acquisitions, and serials. **Computerized Information Services:** CD-ROM (ADABASE). Performs searches free of charge. **Remarks:** FAX: (804)786-4177.

★ 19886 ★
Virginia (State) Department of Mines, Minerals, and Energy - National Cartographic Information Center (Sci-Engr)
Virginia State Division of Mineral Resources Library
Box 3667   Phone: (804)293-5121
Charlottesville, VA 22903   Christopher B. Devan, Libn.
Staff: 1. **Subjects:** Geology, mineral resources, remote sensing. **Holdings:** 1246 books; 3626 bound periodical volumes; 509 theses; 7693 maps; 24,695 pamphlets; 833 microforms. **Subscriptions:** 54 journals and other serials. **Services:** Center open to the public for reference use only. **Computerized Information Services:** GeoRef. **Remarks:** FAX: (804)293-2239.

★ 19887 ★
Virginia (State) Department of Motor Vehicles - Library (Aud-Vis)
2300 W. Broad St., Rm. 127
P.O. Box 27412   Phone: (804)367-1849
Richmond, VA 23269   Patsy A. Neisz, Hd.Libn.
Founded: 1968. **Staff:** Prof 2. **Subjects:** Transportation and highway safety.
Special Collections: Films and videotapes on all phases of highway safety.
Holdings: 2500 books; 1400 films. **Subscriptions:** 75 journals and other
serials. **Services:** Interlibrary loan; library open to state residents. **Special
Catalogs:** Film/Video Catalog. **Remarks:** Alternate telephone number(s):
(804)367-0034 (film library). **Staff:** Betty Stargardt, Film Libn.

★ 19888 ★
**Virginia (State) Department for Rights of Virginians with Disabilities -
Library** (Med)
James Monroe Bldg.
101 N. 14th St., 17th Fl.   Phone: (804)225-2042
Richmond, VA 23219   Iris S. Judkins, Info. & Referral Mgr.
Founded: 1977. **Staff:** Prof 2; Other 3. **Subjects:** Persons with disabilities -
civil rights, education, training, housing, transportation. **Holdings:** Figures
not available. **Services:** Library open to the public for reference use only.
Computerized Information Services: College, Scan (internal databases).
Remarks: Toll-free telephone number(s): (800)552-3962 (in Virginia). FAX:
(804)225-3221. Main telephone and toll-free telephone numbers can be used
with TDD.

★ 19889 ★
**Virginia (State) Division of Energy - Energy Information and Services
Center** (Energy)
2201 W. Broad St.   Phone: (804)367-1310
Richmond, VA 23220   Jennifer Snead, Prog.Mgr.
Founded: 1975. **Staff:** 1. **Subjects:** Energy. **Special Collections:** Solar energy.
Holdings: 3000 books; 500 subject files. **Subscriptions:** 122 journals and
other serials. **Services:** Center open to the public with restrictions. **Remarks:**
FAX: (804)367-6211.

★ 19890 ★
Virginia (State) Division of Legislative Services - Reference Library (Soc
Sci)
910 Capitol St.
Central Assembly Bldg., 2nd Fl.   Phone: (804)786-3591
Richmond, VA 23219   Grace H. Holmes, Libn.
Founded: 1972. **Staff:** Prof 2. **Subjects:** Energy, taxation, juvenile
delinquency, crime, children, economics, environment. **Special Collections:**
Historical state reports; Virginia Statutes. **Holdings:** 5000 books.
Subscriptions: 45 journals and other serials; 6 newspapers. **Services:**
Copying; library open to the public. **Automated Operations:** Computerized
public access catalog, cataloging, and circulation. **Computerized
Information Services:** LEGISNET, DIALOG Information Services, VU/
TEXT Information Services, WESTLAW, LEXIS; internal databases.
Publications: Topical Studies of the General Assembly of Virginia, irregular
- free upon request. **Remarks:** FAX: (804)371-0169. **Staff:** Cheryl Jackson,
Asst.Libn.

★ 19891 ★
Virginia State Law Library (Law)
Supreme Court Bldg., 2nd Fl.
100 N. 9th St.   Phone: (804)786-2075
Richmond, VA 23219   Gail Warren, State Law Libn.
Staff: 3. **Subjects:** Law. **Holdings:** 90,000 books; 8500 bound periodical
volumes. **Subscriptions:** 329 journals and other serials. **Services:** Copying;
library open to the public with restrictions. **Remarks:** Maintained by
Virginia Supreme Court.

★ 19892 ★
Virginia State Library and Archives (Hist, Info Sci)
11th St. at Capitol Square   Phone: (804)786-8929
Richmond, VA 23219   Dr. John C. Tyson, State Libn.
Founded: 1823. **Staff:** Prof 54; Other 93. **Subjects:** Virginiana, Southern and
Confederate history, genealogy, social sciences, U.S. colonial history.
Special Collections: Virginia newspapers; Virginia public records; Virginia
maps; Confederate imprints. **Holdings:** 640,549 volumes; 86,576 maps;
50,591 cubic feet of manuscripts; 15,522 microforms. **Subscriptions:** 896

journals and other serials; 104 newspapers. **Services:** Interlibrary loan;
copying; library open to the public. **Automated Operations:** Computerized
cataloging and circulation. **Computerized Information Services:** OCLC,
RLIN; Virginia Tech Library System (internal database); ALANET
(electronic mail service). **Networks/Consortia:** Member of SOLINET.
Publications: Virginia Cavalcade, quarterly - available by subscription;
Virginia State Library Publications - available by subscription and exchange;
Statistics of Virginia Public Libraries and Institutional Libraries - free;
Directory of Virginia Libraries - free. **Special Catalogs:** CAVALIR,
statewide union list (microfiche and CD-ROM). **Remarks:** FAX: (804)225-
4035. Electronic mail address(es): ALA1166 (ALANET). **Staff:** Nolan T.
Yelich, Asst. State Libn.; Dr. Louis H. Manarin, State Archv.; Ashby
Wilson, Dir., Automated Sys. and Networking; William R. Chamberlain,
Dir., Gen.Lib.; Anthony Yankus, Dir., Lib.Dev.

★ 19893 ★
Virginia State Library for the Visually and Physically Handicapped
(Aud-Vis)
1901 Roane St.   Phone: (804)786-8016
Richmond, VA 23222   Mary Ruth Halapatz, Lib.Dir.
Founded: 1958. **Staff:** Prof 2; Other 15. **Subjects:** General collection. **Special
Collections:** Association for Research and Enlightenment recordings and
braille. **Holdings:** 3000 large print books; 30,000 talking books; 91,613
cassettes; 8000 braille books. **Subscriptions:** 46 journals and other serials.
Services: Interlibrary loan; copying; volunteer tape recording program;
library open to certified blind and physically handicapped; open to the rest
of the public for reference use only. **Automated Operations:** Computerized
circulation. **Networks/Consortia:** Member of National Library Service for
the Blind & Physically Handicapped (NLS). **Publications:** Visual News
(newsletter), quarterly. **Special Catalogs:** Catalog of large print holdings
(book). **Remarks:** FAX: (804)371-6146. Toll-free telephone number(s): 800-
552-7015 (Virginia only). Main telephone number is also used for TDD.
Staff: Randy French, Asst.Libn.; William Malbon, AV Techn.

Virginia State Office of Emergency & Energy Services
See: **Virginia (State) Division of Energy** (19889)

★ 19894 ★
Virginia State Police Academy - Library (Law)
7700 Midlothian Tpke.   Phone: (804)674-2258
Richmond, VA 23261   Joan Jacobs
Founded: 1989. **Staff:** Prof 1. **Subjects:** Law enforcement, criminal justice,
law. **Holdings:** 1410 books; 6 reports. **Subscriptions:** 45 journals and other
serials. **Services:** Interlibrary loan; library open to the public by appointment
for reference use only.

★ 19895 ★
**Virginia State University - Johnston Memorial Library - Special
Collections** (Educ)
1 Hayden St.
Box 9406   Phone: (804)524-5040
Petersburg, VA 23806   Catherine V. Bland, Act. Dean, Lib.Serv.
Founded: 1882. **Special Collections:** U.S. Government document depository;
black studies; instructional materials; manuscripts. **Holdings:** Figures not
available. **Services:** Interlibrary loan; copying; collections open to the public
with restrictions. **Automated Operations:** Computerized cataloging.
Computerized Information Services: DIALOG Information Services,
OCLC. **Networks/Consortia:** Member of SOLINET.

★ 19896 ★
Virginia (State) Water Control Board - Library (Env-Cons)
PO Box 11143   Phone: (804)527-5215
Richmond, VA 23230   Patricia G. Vanderland, Libn.
Founded: 1974. **Staff:** Prof 1. **Subjects:** Water, water pollution, waste water,
groundwater, toxins in water, environment. **Special Collections:** Virginia
State Water Control Board publications (185); Environmental Protection
Agency publications (2500). **Holdings:** 5000 books; 1800 unbound reports;
6300 microforms; government publications on water and environment.
Subscriptions: 45 journals and other serials. **Services:** Interlibrary loan;
copying; library open to the public for reference use only. **Remarks:** FAX:
(804)527-5313. Library located at 4900 Cox Rd., Glen Allen, VA 23060.

★ 19897 ★
Virginia Theological Seminary - Bishop Payne Library (Rel-Phil)
3737 Seminary Rd. Phone: (703)461-1756
Alexandria, VA 22304 Mitzi M. Jarrett, Libn.
Founded: 1823. **Staff:** Prof 6; Other 2. **Subjects:** Theology. **Holdings:** 124,000 volumes. **Subscriptions:** 863 journals and other serials. **Services:** Interlibrary loan; copying; library open to the public for reference use only. **Automated Operations:** Computerized cataloging and circulation. **Networks/Consortia:** Member of Washington Theological Consortium. **Remarks:** FAX: (703)370-6234. **Staff:** Josephine Dearborn, Asst.Libn.

★ 19898 ★
Virginia Transportation Research Council - Library (Trans)
Box 3817, University Sta. Phone: (804)293-1959
Charlottesville, VA 22903 W.E. Kelsh, Adm. Team Ldr.
Founded: 1949. **Staff:** 1; Other 1. **Subjects:** Road and transportation technology, construction and maintenance, traffic safety, environment. **Special Collections:** American Road and Transportation Archives (1750 pamphlets, maps, documents). **Holdings:** 2200 books; 88 bound periodical volumes; 14,480 reports and documents; 236 videotapes and microfiche; 4 drawers of papers by council authors. **Subscriptions:** 89 journals and other serials. **Services:** Interlibrary loan; copying; library open to the public. **Computerized Information Services:** DIALOG Information Services; VIRGO (University of Virginia Library, internal database). **Remarks:** FAX: (804)293-1990. Council jointly sponsored by Virginia Department of Transportation and University of Virginia. **Staff:** Angela Andrews, Libn.

★ 19899 ★
Virginia Union University - William J. Clark Library - Special Collections (Soc Sci)
1500 N. Lombardy St. Phone: (804)257-5820
Richmond, VA 23220 Vonita W. Dandridge, Libn.
Founded: 1865. **Staff:** 9. **Subjects:** Social sciences, natural sciences, mathematics, education, psychology, business, and humanities. **Special Collections:** African-American materials, with emphasis on Richmond Black history; L.D. Wilder Collection. **Holdings:** 18,941 volumes. **Subscriptions:** 310 journals and other serials; 14 newspapers. **Services:** Interlibrary loan; copying; collections open to the public with special permit for reference use only. **Automated Operations:** Computerized cataloging, acquisitions, circulation, and serials. **Computerized Information Services:** Cooperative College Library Center (CCLC), OCLC. **Publications:** Library Newsletter. **Remarks:** FAX: (804)257-5818. **Staff:** Deborah Dawson; Handsel G. Ingram; Thomas Tillerson; Ronald A. Shelton; Harry Edmonds.

★ 19900 ★
Virginian-Pilot & Ledger-Star - Library (Publ)
150 W. Brambleton Ave. Phone: (804)446-2242
Norfolk, VA 23510 Ann Kinken Johnson, Hd.Libn.
Founded: 1947. **Staff:** Prof 2; Other 5. **Subjects:** Newspaper reference topics. **Holdings:** 2000 books; newspaper clips. **Services:** Library not open to the public except for brief reference questions by phone. **Computerized Information Services:** VU/TEXT Information Services, DataTimes, NEXIS. **Special Indexes:** Index to Virginian-Pilot and Ledger-Star, 1947 to present. **Remarks:** FAX: (804)446-2974. Kirn Memorial Library (Norfolk Public Library) has copies of the newspapers on microfilm and is equipped to make copies.

★ 19901 ★
Visiting Nurse Association of Chicago - Marjorie Montgomery Ward Baker Library (Med)
322 S. Green St., Suite 500 Phone: (312)738-8622
Chicago, IL 60607-3599 Charlene Hudson, Libn.
Founded: 1976. **Staff:** Prof 1; Other 1. **Subjects:** Nursing, medicine. **Special Collections:** Patient Education literature (400 titles). **Holdings:** 2000 books; unbound periodicals; 100 archival items. **Subscriptions:** 100 journals and other serials. **Services:** Interlibrary loan; copying; library open to the public by appointment only. **Automated Operations:** Computerized cataloging and ILL. **Computerized Information Services:** OCLC. **Networks/Consortia:** Member of National Network of Libraries of Medicine - Greater Midwest Region, Chicago Library System, ILLINET.

★ 19902 ★
Visiting Nurse Service, Inc. - Library (Med)
128 E. Olin Ave., Suite 200 Phone: (608)257-6710
Madison, WI 53713-1466 Annette Kreunen, R.N.
Subjects: Nursing, public health, physical therapy, speech therapy, occupational therapy, home health aides, mobile meals, social work, personal care workers. **Holdings:** Figures not available. **Subscriptions:** 6 journals and other serials. **Services:** Library open to the public by appointment.

★ 19903 ★
Viskase Corporation - Technical Information Services (Sci-Engr)
6855 W. 65th St. Phone: (312)496-4286
Chicago, IL 60638 Therese J. Manweiler, Tech.Info.Serv.
Founded: 1945. **Staff:** Prof 1. **Subjects:** Natural and synthetic high polymers; chemistry - food, organic, physical, polymer; packaging; chemical engineering. **Holdings:** 4300 books; 3700 bound periodical volumes; 400 unbound periodical volumes; dissertations; translations. **Subscriptions:** 150 journals and other serials. **Services:** Library not open to the public. **Computerized Information Services:** DIALOG Information Services, STN International, ORBIT Search Service.

★ 19904 ★
Viss Masinno Elektrotechniceski Institut - Biblioteka (Sci-Engr)
ul Chadzi Dimitar 4 Phone: 66 21931
5300 Gabrovo, Bulgaria Ivanka Pangelowa, Lib.Dir.
Founded: 1964. **Staff:** Prof 14. **Subjects:** Engineering - mechanical, electronic, electrical, hydraulic; textile machinery; instruments. **Holdings:** 140,000 books; 14,000 bound periodical volumes. **Subscriptions:** 80 journals and other serials; 10 newspapers. **Services:** Library open to the public.

★ 19905 ★
Visual Communications - Asian Pacific American Photographic Archives (Aud-Vis)
263 S. Los Angeles St., Rm. 307 Phone: (213)680-4462
Los Angeles, CA 90012 Linda Mabalot, Exec.Dir.
Staff: 8. **Subjects:** Asian American studies. **Holdings:** 300,000 historical and contemporary photographs and slides. **Services:** Copying; archives open to the public by appointment for reference use only. **Automated Operations:** Computerized photo indexing (in process).

★ 19906 ★
Visual Studies Workshop - Research Center
31 Prince St. Phone: (716)442-8676
Rochester, NY 14607 Robert Bretz, Libn.
Remarks: No further information was supplied by respondent. **Staff:** John Rudy.

★ 19907 ★
Viterbo College - Zoeller Music Library (Mus)
815 S. 9th Phone: (608)791-0040
La Crosse, WI 54601 Sr. John Hempstead, Libn.
Founded: 1970. **Staff:** 8. **Subjects:** Music. **Holdings:** 9623 scores; 3051 recordings; 268 tapes; 45 compact discs. **Subscriptions:** 50 journals and other serials. **Services:** Library open to the public with restrictions. **Computerized Information Services:** DIALOG Information Services; TECHLIB, Information Dimensions (internal databases). **Networks/Consortia:** Member of Wisconsin Interlibrary Services (WILS). **Formerly:** Zoeller Fine Arts Library. Art and theater holdings have been absorbed by the University's Todd Wehr Memorial Library. **Staff:** Sr. Jeanine Luger, Cat.

★ 19908 ★
(Vitoria) Instituto Brasil-Estados Unidos - USIS Collection (Educ)
Rua Graciano Neves, 62, 1st Andar
29000 Vitoria, Espirito Santo, Brazil
Remarks: Maintained or supported by the U.S. Information Agency. Focus is on materials that will assist peoples outside the United States to learn about the United States, its people, history, culture, political processes, and social milieux.

★ 19909 ★
Vitro Corporation - Library (Sci-Engr)
14000 Georgia Ave.   Phone: (301)231-2553
Silver Spring, MD 20910   Louis M. Morris, Group Supv.
Founded: 1948. **Staff:** Prof 2; Other 8. **Subjects:** Missiles and spacecraft, systems engineering, management, data processing, electronic engineering, ships, underwater acoustics, antisubmarine warfare. **Holdings:** 15,000 books; 1200 bound periodical volumes; 85,000 technical reports; 650,000 standards and specifications, hardcopy and microfilm; 270 nautical charts. **Subscriptions:** 450 journals and other serials; 50 newspapers. **Services:** Interlibrary loan; copying; SDI; library open to the public with restrictions. **Automated Operations:** Computerized cataloging, serials, and circulation. **Computerized Information Services:** DIALOG Information Services, DTIC, Government-Industry Data Exchange Program (GIDEP). **Networks/Consortia:** Member of Interlibrary Users Association (IUA). **Publications:** List of new drawings and technical correspondence, daily; list of new technical reports, weekly; list of new books, monthly - all for internal distribution only. **Special Indexes:** Indexes to drawings of ballistic missiles, guided missiles, missile engineering; technical correspondence index; books, technical reports, and manuals index on COM - for internal distribution only. **Remarks:** FAX: (301)231-2215.

★ 19910 ★
Vizcaya Guides Library (Art)
3251 S. Miami Ave.   Phone: (305)579-2808
Miami, FL 33129   Don Gayer, Lib.Chm.
Staff: 5. **Subjects:** Decorative arts, architecture, furniture, 15th-19th century history. **Special Collections:** James Deering house, furnishings, and gardens (folios; manuscripts; photographs; records; ledgers). **Holdings:** 2500 books; 85 bound periodical volumes; 15,000 slides. **Services:** Library open to the public with written application to the librarian.

★ 19911 ★
The Vocational and Rehabilitation Research Institute - Resource Centre/ Library (Med)
3304 33rd St., N.W.   Phone: (403)284-1121
Calgary, AB, Canada T2L 2A6   Bob McGowan, Libn.
Staff: Prof 1. **Subjects:** Developmental disabilities, rehabilitation, vocational training, residential services. **Holdings:** 2600 books; 2000 manuscripts, reports, dissertations. **Subscriptions:** 80 serials. **Services:** Copying; library open to the public. **Automated Operations:** Computerized public access catalog, cataloging, and serials. **Computerized Information Services:** BRS Information Technologies; Research Database, Library Catalog Database, Reprint Database (internal databases). **Publications:** VRRI Publications and Research Materials; Recent Publications and Research Materials; VRRI Current Awareness Bulletin; Research Highlights; Research Reviews. **Remarks:** FAX: (403)289-6427.

Torah Vodaath Library
See: **Yeshiva Torah Vodaath and Mesifta** (20750)

A.W. Vodges Library of Geology and Paleontology
See: **San Diego Society of Natural History** (14712)

William H. Volck Museum
See: **Pajaro Valley Historical Association** (12692)

★ 19912 ★
Volkskundearchiv Prof. Ernst Burgstoller (Area-Ethnic)
Kulturzentrum Burg Wels   Phone: 7242 235666
A-4601 Wels, Austria   Dr. Wilhelm Rieb, Musm.Dir.
Subjects: Ethnology - Austrian, European, general; history. **Holdings:** Figures not available. **Services:** Copying; library open to the public for academic research. **Remarks:** Alternate telephone number(s): 7242 235 696. FAX: 7242 47477. Maintained by Magistrat Wels. **Staff:** Dr. Jutta Nordone.

★ 19913 ★
Volkswagen AG - Technical Information Library (Sci-Engr)
Postfach   Phone: 5361 924639
W-3180 Wolfsburg 1, Germany   Fritz Schael, Mgr.
Founded: 1971. **Staff:** Prof 10; Other 13. **Subjects:** Motor vehicles, automotive engineering, social and economic factors related to the automotive industry. **Holdings:** 65,000 bound volumes; card file of 150,000 abstracts. **Subscriptions:** 500 journals and other serials. **Services:** SDI; library not open to the public. **Computerized Information Services:** Produces LIDAS database (available online through Data-Star and FIZ Technik); CARS Vehicle Data Bank System (internal database). Performs searches. **Publications:** Referatedienst, abstracts from current literature. **Remarks:** FAX: 5361 929723. Telex: 9 586 533 VWW D.

John A. Volpe National Transportation Systems Center
See: **U.S. Dept. of Transportation - Research and Special Programs Administration** (17281)

★ 19914 ★
Voltarc Technologies, Inc. - Library (Sci-Engr)
Box 688   Phone: (203)255-2633
Fairfield, CT 06430   Evlyn Perkins, Libn.
Founded: 1970. **Staff:** Prof 1. **Subjects:** Lamp manufacturing. **Holdings:** 500 books; 5 VF drawers of patents; 12 VF drawers of clippings. **Subscriptions:** 60 journals and other serials. **Services:** Interlibrary loan; library not open to the public. **Remarks:** FAX: (203)259-1194.

★ 19915 ★
Volunteer Centre of Winnepeg - Library (Soc Sci)
5 Donald St., 3rd Fl.   Phone: (204)477-5180
Winnipeg, MB, Canada R3L 2T4   Jennifer King, Libn.
Subjects: Voluntarism. **Holdings:** 1500 books. **Subscriptions:** 15 journals and other serials. **Services:** Interlibrary loan; copying; library open to the public.

★ 19916 ★
Volunteers in Technical Assistance - Library (Soc Sci)
1815 N. Lynn St., Suite 200   Phone: (703)276-1800
Arlington, VA 22209   Brij Mathur, Dir., Info.Serv.
Staff: 5. **Subjects:** Appropriate technology in the United States and developing countries - agriculture and food processing, renewable energy applications, water supply and sanitation, low-cost construction, reforestation and soil conservation, small business development, and allied subjects; microcomputer applications; international development; volunteerism. **Holdings:** 28,000 documents on microfiche. **Services:** Interlibrary loan; copying; library open to the public by appointment. **Computerized Information Services:** Internal database; BITNET, InterNet (electronic mail services). **Remarks:** FAX: (703)243-1865. Telex: 440192 VITAUI. Cable: VITAINC. Electronic mail address(es): VITA@GMUVAX.GMU.EDU (BITNET, InterNet). **Staff:** Richard Muffley, Info. Sys. Mgr.

★ 19917 ★
Volusia County Law Library (Law)
Courthouse Annex, Rm. 208
125 E. Orange Ave.   Phone: (904)257-6041
Daytona Beach, FL 32114   Rae Mastropierro, Law Libn./Dir.
Staff: Prof 1. **Subjects:** Law. **Holdings:** 22,500 books and periodicals. **Services:** Copying; library open to the public. **Remarks:** This library maintains branch libraries in DeLand and New Smyrna Beach. **Staff:** Deborah A. Patterson, Libn. I; Joseph A. Mastropierro, Libn. II.

★ 19918 ★
Volusia County School Board - Resource Library (Educ)
729 Loomis Ave.
Box 2410   Phone: (904)255-6475
Daytona Beach, FL 32115   Nancy B. Martin, Supv., Media Rsrcs.
Founded: 1967. **Staff:** Prof 1; Other 1. **Subjects:** Education - all subjects K-12. **Special Collections:** Suitcase Museums (60). **Holdings:** 10,000 books; 96 bound periodical volumes; 12,000 AV programs and microfiche; 52 VF drawers; 4000 pamphlets. **Subscriptions:** 133 journals and other serials. **Services:** Interlibrary loan; library not open to the public. **Special Catalogs:** Printed materials and nonprint media catalogs, supplement 2/year.

Dr. Wernher Von Braun Collection
See: **Alabama Space and Rocket Center** (187)

Von Braun-Oberth Memorial Library
See: **National Space Society** (11300)

Eugene Von Brunehenhien Archive
See: **John Michael Kohler Arts Center - Resource Center** (8780)

Von Kleinsmid Library
See: **University of Southern California (19348)**

Leopold Von Ranke Library
See: **Syracuse University - George Arents Research Library for Special Collections (15961)**

Vorhoff Library
See: **Tulane University - Newcomb College Center for Research on Women (16563)**

★ 19919 ★
Vrije Universiteit Amsterdam - Bibliotheek Medische Wetenschappen (Med)
Van der Boechorststraat 7   Phone: 20 5482062
NL-1081 BT Amsterdam, Netherlands   Dr. M.R. Vaillant
Founded: 1959. **Staff:** Prof 17. **Subjects:** Medicine, dentistry, dental surgery, human movement sciences. **Holdings:** 82,000 books; 100,000 bound periodical volumes; 500 microfiche; 200 reels of microfilm. **Subscriptions:** 1350 journals and other serials. **Services:** Interlibrary loan; SDI; library open to the public. **Automated Operations:** LIBS 100 System. **Computerized Information Services:** DIMDI, Data-Star. Contact Person: Dr. S. Bohlken.

★ 19920 ★
VSE Corporation - Corporate Library (Sci-Engr)
2550 Huntington Ave.   Phone: (703)329-4208
Alexandria, VA 22303-1499   Murray L. Howder, Adm.Libn.
Founded: 1959. **Staff:** Prof 1. **Subjects:** Engineering, physics, mathematics, environment, business. **Special Collections:** Total Quality Management (TQM). **Holdings:** 3500 books; 2000 vendor catalogs; Visual Search Microfilm file on military and federal specifications, standards, handbooks, and vendor catalogs. **Subscriptions:** 75 journals and other serials. **Services:** Interlibrary loan; library not open to the public. **Computerized Information Services:** DIALOG Information Services. **Special Catalogs:** Consolidated Master Cross Reference List; Cataloging Handbook H4/H8; Army Adopted List of Reportable Items; Army Master data file (all on microfiche). **Remarks:** FAX: (703)960-3748.

★ 19921 ★
VSE Corporation - Technical Library
1417 N. Battlefield Blvd.
Chesapeake, VA 23320
Founded: 1980. **Subjects:** U.S. Navy ships, marine engineering. **Special Collections:** AFS (auxiliary fast stores) ships (800 technical manuals; 7600 drawings). **Holdings:** 1400 books; 400 vendor catalogs; 5000 aperture cards of drawings; 1600 drawings; 1000 microfiche. **Remarks:** Currently inactive

Vysoka Skola Umeleckoprumyslova - Knihovna
See: **Czechoslovakia - Academy of Applied Arts - Library (4508)**

★ 19922 ★
Vysoka Skola Zemedelska - Ustredni Knihovna (Agri)
Zemedelska 1   Phone: 5 604
CS-613 00 Brno, Czechoslovakia   J. Hegerova, Libn.
Founded: 1919. **Staff:** Prof 10. **Subjects:** Agriculture, forestry, agricultural economics, horticulture. **Holdings:** 95,000 books; 10,000 bound periodical volumes; reports; 312 microfiche; theses. **Subscriptions:** 631 journals and other serials; 15 newspapers. **Services:** Interlibrary loan; copying; library open to the public. **Computerized Information Services:** AGRIS, Pollution Abstracts, Envirolines, FSTA. **Publications:** Acta Universitatis Agriculturae; Information Bulletin. **Remarks:** FAX: 5 678427. Telex: 624 89.

Vyzkumny Ustav Hutnictvi Zeleza, Dobra
See: **Dobra Iron and Steel Research Institute (4932)**

Vyzkumny Ustav Kozedelny
See: **Shoe and Leather Research Institute (15139)**

Vyzkumny Ustav Vodohospodarsky - Informacni Stredisko
See: **Czechoslovakia - Ministry of the Environment - Water Research Institute (4513)**

Vyzkumny a Zkusebni Letecky Ustav
See: **Czechoslovakia - Aeronautical Research and Test Institute (4509)**

W

★19923★
Wabash County Historical Museum - Historical Library (Hist)
Memorial Hall   Phone: (219)563-0661
Wabash, IN 46992   Jack M. Miller, Cur.
Founded: 1923. **Staff:** 2. **Subjects:** Indiana and Wabash County history, Civil War. **Holdings:** 1940 books; Wabash county newspapers (1846 to present); manuscripts; documents; vertical file of genealogies, businesses, churches, and personalities; county records; social club records; maps and atlases; photograph files. **Services:** Library open to the public for research on premises.

★19924★
Wachovia Bank & Trust Company - Library (Bus-Fin)
P.O. Box 3099   Phone: (919)770-5857
Winston-Salem, NC 27150   Edward Greenawald, Libn.
Services: Library not open to the public.

★19925★
Wacker Silicones Corporation - SWS Silicones - Technical Library (Sci-Engr)
3301 Sutton Rd.   Phone: (517)263-5711
Adrian, MI 49221-9397   Ken See, Libn.
Subjects: Siloxanes, electronics, sealants, furniture, automotive products, petroleum, tire construction. **Holdings:** 400 books; 400 bound periodical volumes; 7 VF drawers of government publications and specifications; 3 VF drawers of reprints; 10 VF drawers of patents. **Subscriptions:** 90 journals and other serials; 10 newspapers. **Services:** Copying; library open to the public with prior approval.

★19926★
Waco-McLennan County Library - Special Collections Department (Hist)
1717 Austin Ave.   Phone: (817)750-5941
Waco, TX 76701   Mickey Sparkman, Spec.Coll.Libn.
Staff: Prof 2; Other 2. **Subjects:** Texas and local history, genealogy. **Holdings:** 14,103 books; 15,298 bound periodical volumes; 7502 reels of microfilm; 10 titles on microfiche. **Subscriptions:** 413 journals and other serials; 11 newspapers. **Services:** Copying; department open to the public. **Automated Operations:** Computerized cataloging. **Networks/Consortia:** Member of AMIGOS Bibliographic Council, Inc. **Publications:** Heart of Texas Records, quarterly - by subscription.

★19927★
Waco Tribune-Herald - Library (Publ)
900 Franklin   Phone: (817)757-5757
Waco, TX 76701   Colleen Curran
Founded: 1980. **Staff:** Prof 1. **Subjects:** Newpaper reference topics. **Special Collections:** Waco Tribune-Herald, 1946 to present (microfilm). **Holdings:** 100 books; 50 bound periodical volumes; news clipping files. **Subscriptions:** 4 journals and other serials; 3 newspapers. **Services:** Limited copying; faxing to news agencies for a fee; library open for use by other newspapers. **Remarks:** FAX: (817)757-0302.

★19928★
Waddell and Reed, Inc. - Research Library (Bus-Fin)
6300 Lamar Ave.   Phone: (913)236-2000
Shawnee Mission, KS 66201   Cynthia V Buchanan, Hd.Libn.
Founded: 1962. **Staff:** Prof 1; Other 3. **Subjects:** Stock market, industries, corporation statistics, investments, mutual funds, economics. **Holdings:** 700 books; 100 bound periodical volumes; 4000 corporate files; 300 government documents; 42,000 10K and 10Q reports on microfiche. **Subscriptions:** 200 journals and other serials; 40 newspapers. **Services:** Interlibrary loan; copying; library open to the public for reference use only, with limited access to corporation files. **Remarks:** FAX: (913)236-1885 Telex: 434365.

Marion E. Wade Center
See: Wheaton College (20371)

E.H. Wadewitz Memorial Library
See: Graphic Arts Technical Foundation (6654)

★19929★
Wadhams Hall Seminary - College Library (Rel-Phil)
Riverside Dr.   Phone: (315)393-4231
Ogdensburg, NY 13669   Kim M. Donius, Act.Dir.
Founded: 1924. **Staff:** Prof 1.75; Other 1. **Subjects:** Scholastic philosophy, ascetical theology, classical languages, ecclesiastical history, undergraduate arts. **Holdings:** 79,138 books; 16,566 bound periodical volumes; 916 reels of microfilm; 2467 records; 1738 tapes; 160 videotapes. **Subscriptions:** 513 journals and other serials. **Services:** Interlibrary loan; copying; library open to the public. **Networks/Consortia:** Member of North Country Reference and Research Resources Council (NCRRRC). **Publications:** Monthly Acquisitions List; Patron's Brochure. **Remarks:** FAX: (315)393-4231. **Staff:** Joseph Keenan, Libn.

★19930★
Wadley Institutes of Molecular Medicine - Research Institute Library (Med)
9000 Harry Hines Blvd.   Phone: (214)351-8648
Dallas, TX 75235   Kathryn Manning, Libn.
Founded: 1956. **Staff:** Prof 1. **Subjects:** Cancer, microbiology, hematology, biochemistry, immunology, genetics, interferon. **Holdings:** 11,629 volumes; 73 dissertations; 225 reprints; 6 VF drawers of unbound material. **Subscriptions:** 235 journals and other serials. **Services:** Interlibrary loan; copying; SDI; library open to all medical personnel. **Computerized Information Services:** MEDLINE. **Networks/Consortia:** Member of Health Libraries Information Network (HealthLINE). **Publications:** Journal Clinical Hematology and Oncology, quarterly - to interested medical personnel and libraries. **Remarks:** An alternate telephone number is 351-8649.

★19931★
Wadsworth Atheneum - Auerbach Art Library (Art)
600 Main St.   Phone: (203)278-2670
Hartford, CT 06103   John W. Teahan, Libn.
Staff: Prof 2. **Subjects:** Fine arts, decorative arts, costume, textiles, photography, museology, art education. **Special Collections:** Watkinson Collection (3000 volumes); Lewitt Collection of Artists' Books. **Holdings:** 25,000 volumes; 32 VF drawers; 200 feet of boxes of museum files; 120 feet of sales catalogs; 15 feet of bookplates. **Subscriptions:** 125 journals and other serials. **Services:** Interlibrary loan; copying; library open to the public for reference use only. **Special Indexes:** Index to Wadsworth Atheneum Bulletin; Index to Wadsworth Atheneum Exhibitions, 1910 to present. **Staff:** Anne Lyons, Asst.Libn.

Wadsworth Center for Laboratories and Research Library
See: New York (State) Department of Health (11650)

Wadsworth Learning Resource Center
See: Mount Ida College - Wadsworth Learning Resource Center (10805)

Wadsworth Medical Library
See: U.S. Dept. of Veterans Affairs (CA-Los Angeles) (17297)

★19932★
Wagnalls Memorial Library (Hist)
150 E. Columbus St.   Phone: (614)837-4765
Lithopolis, OH 43136-0217   Mrs. Jo Riegel, Lib.Dir.
Founded: 1924. **Staff:** 9. **Special Collections:** Books written by and belonging to Mabel Wagnalls-Jones; local history; letters written by O. Henry to Mabel Wagnalls-Jones; paintings by John Ward Dunsmore. **Subscriptions:** 160 journals and other serials. **Services:** Library open to the public. **Networks/Consortia:** Member of Columbus Area Libraries Information Council of Ohio (CALICO). **Staff:** Jerry W. Neff, Exec.Dir.; Sue Stebelton, Prog.Coord.

★ 19933 ★
Wagner College - Horrmann Library (Hum)
631 Howard Ave.   Phone: (718)390-3401
Staten Island, NY 10301   Y. John Auh, Dir.
Founded: 1883. **Staff:** 18. **Special Collections:** U.S. Government documents depository; Edwin Markham Collection (10,000 volumes including poems, prose, clippings, Markham's works in translation, musical settings, recordings, and a line by line index to his poems); Early American and German-American Newspapers (118 reels of microfilm); Old English Literature (105,000 microforms). **Holdings:** 237,500 books; 60,000 bound periodical volumes; 1500 reports; 7000 manuscripts; 70,400 microfiche; 9500 reels of microfilm; 17,400 microcards. **Subscriptions:** 1400 journals and other serials; 24 newspapers. **Services:** Interlibrary loan; copying; collections open to the public with library card subscription. **Automated Operations:** Computerized cataloging. **Computerized Information Services:** DIALOG Information Services, BRS Information Technologies. **Networks/Consortia:** Member of New York Metropolitan Reference and Research Library Agency. **Staff:** Mitchael Dakelman; Richard Palumbo; Quain Quain Yang; Carol Bruce.

★ 19934 ★
Wagner Free Institute of Science - Library (Sci-Engr)
17th St. & Montgomery Ave.   Phone: (215)763-6529
Philadelphia, PA 19121   John Parker, Libn.
Founded: 1885. **Subjects:** Natural and physical sciences. **Special Collections:** William Wagner Papers and Museum Archives. **Holdings:** 25,000 volumes; bound periodicals; pamphlets. **Subscriptions:** 10 journals. **Services:** Library open to the public by appointment. **Staff:** Penny Baker, Archv.

Wagner-Kevetter Library
See: **William Carter College & Evangelical Theological Seminary** (3114)

Robert F. Wagner Labor Archives
See: **New York University - Tamiment Library** (11733)

Robert S. Wahab, Jr. Public Law Library
See: **Virginia Beach Public Library System** (19860)

Wahlert Memorial Library
See: **Loras College** (9311)

Wahlquist Library
See: **San Jose State University - Wahlquist Library** (14761)

Magnus Wahlstrom Library
See: **University of Bridgeport** (18252)

Waikiki Aquarium
See: **University of Hawaii** (18630)

★ 19935 ★
Wainwright General Hospital - Medical Library (Med)
Box 820   Phone: (403)842-3324
Wainwright, AB, Canada T0B 4P0   Loretta Haire, Hea.Rec.Adm.
Staff: 1. **Subjects:** Medicine, nursing, hospital administration, allied health sciences. **Holdings:** 500 books. **Subscriptions:** 20 journals and other serials. **Services:** Library open to the public for reference use only. **Computerized Information Services:** Infohealth. **Remarks:** FAX: (403)842-2887.

Waite Agricultural Research Institute
See: **The University of Adelaide - Waite Agricultural Research Institute** (18145)

★ 19936 ★
Wakarusa Public Library - Special Collections (Hist)
124 N. Elkhart St.
P.O. Box 485   Phone: (219)862-2465
Wakarusa, IN 46573   Anne Gottbrath, Lib.Dir.
Founded: 1944. **Staff:** 2. **Subjects:** Local history, family history, genealogy. **Holdings:** Photographs; news clippings; microfilm; bound geneologies and newspapers; McGuffey's Readers; historic journals and ledgers. **Services:** Copying; collections open to the public. **Staff:** Linda Hartman, Geneal.Coord.

★ 19937 ★
Wake County Medical Center - Medical Library (Med)
P. O. Box 14465   Phone: (919)250-8528
Raleigh, NC 27620-4465   Karen K. Grandage, Dir., Lib./Info.Serv.
Staff: Prof 3; Other 3. **Subjects:** Medicine, pediatrics, orthopedics, nursing, hospital administration, allied health sciences. **Special Collections:** Staff development/training collection. **Holdings:** 8000 books; 2988 bound periodical volumes; 1000 AV programs. **Subscriptions:** 300 journals and other serials. **Services:** Interlibrary loan (fee); copying; library open to the public. **Computerized Information Services:** MEDLARS, BRS Information Technologies. Performs searches on fee basis. **Networks/Consortia:** Member of North Carolina Area Health Education Centers Program Library and Information Services Network, Resources for Health Information (REHI). **Staff:** Beverly Richardson, Assoc.Dir., Lib./Info.Serv.; Peggy Adams, Assoc.Dir., Lib./Info.Serv.

★ 19938 ★
Wake Forest University - Babcock Graduate School of Management - Library (Bus-Fin)
Reynolda Sta.,
P.O. Box 7689   Phone: (919)759-5414
Winston-Salem, NC 27109   Jean B. Hopson, Lib.Dir.
Founded: 1970. **Staff:** Prof 1; Other 1. **Subjects:** General management. **Holdings:** 19,919 books; microforms. **Subscriptions:** 721 journals and other serials. **Services:** Interlibrary loan; copying; library open to the public. **Automated Operations:** Computerized cataloging and ILL. **Computerized Information Services:** OCLC, DIALOG Information Services, Dow Jones News/Retrieval; internal database; CD-ROMs (COMPUSTAT Corporate Text, Compact Disclosure, WILSONDISC, ProQuest). **Networks/Consortia:** Member of SOLINET. **Publications:** Management periodicals in university collections. **Remarks:** FAX: (919)759-5830.

★ 19939 ★
Wake Forest University - Baptist Collection (Rel-Phil)
University Library
P.O. Box 7777 Reynolda Sta.   Phone: (919)759-5472
Winston-Salem, NC 27109   John R. Woodard, Jr., Dir.
Founded: 1885. **Staff:** Prof 1; Other 2. **Subjects:** North Carolina Baptist history, Wake Forest University history. **Special Collections:** Manuscript records of 108 North Carolina Baptist churches; microfilm records of 966 North Carolina Baptist churches. **Holdings:** 11,933 books; 1665 bound periodical volumes; 487 private collections of personal papers; 1831 reels of microfilm; vertical file of North Carolina churches; biography file of North Carolina ministers. **Subscriptions:** 84 journals and other serials; 10 newspapers. **Services:** Copying; will answer correspondence relating to Baptist history; collection open to the public. **Publications:** Newsletter, bimonthly; Special Bulletins, irregular. **Special Indexes:** Index to Biblical Recorder, the North Carolina Baptist newspaper (computerized); index to historical information on North Carolina Baptist churches, extant and extinct (computerized); index to Wake Forest College/University photograph sources in the school newspaper and alumni magazine (computerized). **Remarks:** Alternate telephone number(s): 759-5089. FAX: (919)759-9831.

★ 19940 ★
Wake Forest University - Bowman Gray School of Medicine - Coy C. Carpenter Library (Med)
Medical Center Blvd.   Phone: (919)748-4691
Winston-Salem, NC 27157-1069   Michael D. Sprinkle, Dir.
Founded: 1941. **Staff:** Prof 14; Other 23. **Subjects:** Medicine, nursing. **Special Collection:** Hunter Collection; Arts in Medicine; History of Medicine; Samuel Johnson Collection. **Holdings:** 32,568 books; 118,495 bound periodical volumes; 2076 AV programs; 2172 microforms. **Subscriptions:** 3778 journals and other serials. **Services:** Interlibrary loan;

copying; SDI; BioServe (Information Affiliates Program); library open to the public for reference use only. **Automated Operations:** Computerized public access catalog, cataloging, acquisitions, serials, and circulation. **Computerized Information Services:** MEDLARS, DIALOG Information Services, BRS Information Technologies, Data-Star, OCLC, WILSONLINE; CD-ROM (MEDLINE); internal database; OnTyme Electronic Message Network Service, DOCLINE, ALANET (electronic mail services). Performs searches on fee basis. **Networks/Consortia:** Member of SOLINET, Northwest AHEC Library Information Network. **Publications:** FOLIO (newsletter), bimonthly - to the public. **Remarks:** FAX: (919)748-2186. Telex: 806449 BGSM WSL. **Staff:** Sherry Anderson, Dp.Dir.; Sarah-Patsy Knight, Med.Ctr.Archv.; Wesley Byerly, Pharm.D., Drug Info.Serv.Ctr.Dir.; Faye Foltz, Ref.Libn.; Ann Browning, Chf., Biliog. & Coll.Maint.; Rochelle Kramer, Ch., Mktg.; Janine Tillett, Ref.Libn.; Chengren Hu, Sys.Libn.; Molly Barnett, Ref.Libn.; Kathryn Dudley, Chf., Coll.Dev.; Marilyn Summers, Chf., Info. Access & Delivery.

★ 19941 ★
Wake Forest University - Law Library (Law)
Reynolda Sta., Box 7206   Phone: (919)759-5438
Winston-Salem, NC 27109   Thomas M. Steele, Dir./Prof. of Law
Founded: 1894. **Staff:** Prof 6; Other 7. **Subjects:** Law. **Holdings:** 121,560 books; 16,205 bound periodical volumes; 469,210 microfiche; 4576 reels of microfilm. **Subscriptions:** 3354 journals and other serials; 16 newspapers. **Services:** Interlibrary loan; copying; library open to the public. **Automated Operations:** Computerized cataloging, acquisitions, serials, and ILL. **Computerized Information Services:** WESTLAW, OCLC, LEXIS, NEXIS, VU/TEXT Information Services, DIALOG Information Services; BITNET (electronic mail service). **Networks/Consortia:** Member of SOLINET, COSELL. **Remarks:** FAX: (919)759-6077. **Staff:** Mary Louise Cobb, Assoc.Dir.; Miriam A. Murphy, Hd., Pub.Serv.; Martha E. Thomas, Ref.Libn.; John Perkins, Ref.Libn.; Michelle Tsoi, Ser. & Cat.Libn.

★ 19942 ★
Wake Forest University - Z. Smith Reynolds Library - Rare Books & Manuscripts Collection (Hum, Hist, Publ)
PO Box 7777, Reynolda Sta.   Phone: (919)759-5755
Winston-Salem, NC 27109   Sharon Snow, Cur.
Founded: 1966. **Staff:** Prof 2. **Subjects:** American literature, English literature, Irish literature, Americana, North Caroliniana, history of books and printing. **Special Collections:** Maya Angelou personal papers and manuscripts (125 linear feet); Dolmen Press Archives (500 linear feet); W.J. Cash manuscripts (2 linear feet); Harold Hayes personal papers and manuscripts (60 linear feet). **Holdings:** 33,000 books; 300 theatre programs; 200 Confederate broadside verse. **Services:** Copying (limited); collection open to the public. **Computerized Information Services:** InterNet (electronic mail service). **Remarks:** FAX: (919)759-9831. Electronic mail address(es): SNOW@WFUNET.WFU.EDU (InterNet). **Staff:** Megan Mulder, Cat.

Waksman Institute of Microbiology Library
See: **Rutgers University** (14170)

John & Bertha E. Waldmann Memorial Library
See: **New York University - David B. Kriser Dental Center** (11722)

★ 19943 ★
Waldo County General Hospital - Marx Library (Med)
Box 287   Phone: (207)338-2500
Belfast, ME 04915   Lois Dutch, Educ.Asst./Libn.
Staff: Prof 1; Other 1. **Subjects:** Medicine. **Holdings:** 152 books. **Subscriptions:** 44 journals and other serials. **Services:** Interlibrary loan; copying; library open to the public with restrictions and for reference use only. **Networks/Consortia:** Member of Health Science Library and Information Cooperative of Maine (HSLIC).

★ 19944 ★
Waldo County Law Library (Law)
Waldo County Courthouse
73 Church St.
P.O. Box 188   Phone: (207)338-1940
Belfast, ME 04915   Joyce M. Page, Ck. of Courts
Staff: 1. **Subjects:** Law. **Holdings:** 5000 volumes. **Services:** Library open to the public.

Waldo Library
See: **Western Michigan University - Waldo Library - Rare Book Room** (20275)

★ 19945 ★
Waldorf Corporation - Technical Center Library (Sci-Engr)
2250 Wabash Ave.   Phone: (612)641-4125
St. Paul, MN 55114   Bev. Coursolle, Adm.Sec.
Subjects: Paper technology, chemistry, packaging, plastics and polymers. **Special Collections:** Institute of Paper Chemistry (abstracts, 1930 to present; 705 project reports and bibliographies). **Holdings:** 550 books; 129 bound periodical volumes; 100 miscellaneous published reports. **Subscriptions:** 41 journals and other serials. **Services:** Library not open to the public. **Remarks:** FAX: (612)641-4197.

Lionel A. Walford Library
See: **U.S. Natl. Marine Fisheries Service - Sandy Hook Laboratory** (17640)

★ 19946 ★
Walgreen Company - Employee Development Library (Bus-Fin)
200 Wilmot Rd.   Phone: (708)940-3224
Deerfield, IL 60015   Norma Leonard
Staff: 1. **Subjects:** Human resources, performance technology. **Holdings:** 1000 books; 200 archival items. **Subscriptions:** 80 journals and other serials. **Services:** Library not open to the public. **Remarks:** FAX: (708)940-2804.

★ 19947 ★
Walker Art Center - Staff Reference Library (Art)
Vineland Place   Phone: (612)375-7680
Minneapolis, MN 55403   Rosemary Furtak, Libn.
Founded: 1950. **Staff:** 2. **Subjects:** Contemporary art, art history, architecture, design, film, artists' books, graphics, photography, painting, sculpture. **Special Collections:** Artists' catalogs, 1940 to present; Audio/Video Archive; Edmund R. Ruben Film Study Collection. **Holdings:** 8000 books; 550 bound periodical volumes; 30,000 catalogs; vertical files. **Subscriptions:** 140 journals and other serials. **Services:** Copying; library open to the public by appointment. **Automated Operations:** Computerized cataloging. **Computerized Information Services:** OCLC. **Networks/Consortia:** Member of MINITEX Library Information Network. **Publications:** Design Quarterly. **Special Catalogs:** Walker Art Center exhibition catalogs. **Staff:** Susan Lambert, Asst.Libn.; Sue Zimmerman, Slide Libn.

E.F. Walker Memorial Library
See: **First Baptist Church** (5727)

Elisha Walker Staff Library
See: **New York Downtown Hospital** (11575)

Hastings H. Walker Medical Library
See: **Hawaii (State) Department of Health** (7034)

Henry B. Walker, Jr. Memorial Art Library
See: **Evansville Museum of Arts and Science - Library** (5509)

Hiram Walker Historical Museum
See: **Francois Baby House: Windsor's Community Museum** (1397)

John Walker Library
See: **KPMG Peat Marwick Thorne** (8811)

Walker Library
See: **American Council on Alcoholism, Inc.** (546)

Walker Management Library
See: **Vanderbilt University - Jean and Alexander Heard Library** (19775)

Walker Memorial Hospital
See: **Adventist Health Systems Sunbelt - Walker Memorial Hospital** (95)

★ **19948** ★
Wall Street Journal - Library (Bus-Fin, Publ)
World Financial Center
200 Liberty St.   Phone: (212)416-2676
New York, NY 10281   Lottie Lindberg, Libn.
Founded: 1903. **Staff:** Prof 2; Other 7. **Subjects:** Finance, business, investments. **Holdings:** Books; clippings file of The Wall Street Journal (1968-1987). **Services:** Library not open to the public. **Automated Operations:** Computerized cataloging and circulation. **Computerized Information Services:** Dow Jones News/Retrieval. **Special Indexes:** The Wall Street Journal Index, monthly with annual cumulation; Barron's Index, annual.

★ **19949** ★
Walla Walla College - Curriculum Library (Educ)
204 S. College Ave.   Phone: (509)527-2221
College Place, WA 99324   Franice Stirling, Dir.
Founded: 1963. **Staff:** Prof 1; Other 3. **Subjects:** Vocational guidance, curriculum, social sciences, mathematics, science, health and physical education, language arts, administration. **Special Collections:** Teaching kits; career information files; Standardized Test File (300 titles); children's literature (5600 volumes). **Holdings:** 13,000 volumes; 5,800 pamphlets; 535 phonograph records; 4600 pictures; 150 maps and globes; 200 theses; 351 cassettes; 1200 filmstrips; 208 transparencies; 1600 slides; 551 realia. **Subscriptions:** 11 journals and other serials. **Services:** Copying; library open to the public with valid library cards.

★ **19950** ★
Walla Walla College - School of Nursing Professional Library (Med)
10345 S.E. Market   Phone: (503)251-6115
Portland, OR 97216   Shirley A. Cody, Libn.
Founded: 1960. **Staff:** Prof 1; Other .6. **Subjects:** Nursing - administration, medical-surgical, parent-child, public health, psychiatric, mental health. **Holdings:** 8000 books; 1100 bound periodical volumes; 74 tape cassettes; 6 VF drawers of clippings; 2000 pamphlets; 20 slide/tape sets; 125 video cassettes; 60 filmstrips; 10 30mm films. **Subscriptions:** 125 journals and other serials. **Services:** Interlibrary loan; copying; library open to employees of Portland Adventist Medical Center and to the public with librarian's permission.

★ **19951** ★
Walla Walla County Law Library (Law)
315 W. Main   Phone: (509)529-9520
Walla Walla, WA 99362   Ben R. Forcier, Jr., Libn.
Staff: 1. **Subjects:** Law. **Holdings:** 30,000 volumes. **Services:** Library not open to the public.

★ **19952** ★
Walla Walla Union-Bulletin - Library (Publ)
1st & Poplar
Box 1358   Phone: (509)525-3300
Walla Walla, WA 99362   Janet G. Collins, Libn.
Staff: 1. **Subjects:** Newspaper reference topics. **Holdings:** Microfilm. **Subscriptions:** 8 newspapers. **Services:** Library not open to the public. **Remarks:** FAX: (509)525-1232.

DeWitt Wallace Library
See: **Macalester College - DeWitt Wallace Library** (9488)

James A. Wallace Library
See: **Memphis Mental Health Institute** (10062)

Wallace Library
See: **The Criswell College** (4433)

Lila Acheson Wallace Library
See: **Juilliard School** (8491)

Madeleine Clark Wallace Library
See: **Wheaton College** (20370)

Wallace Memorial Library
See: **Rochester Institute of Technology** (13983)

Miriam and Ira D. Wallach Division of Art, Prints & Photographs
See: **New York Public Library** (11624)

★ **19953** ★
Raoul Wallenberg Committee of the United States - Library (Hist)
245 Park Ave., 38th Fl.   Phone: (212)272-7790
New York, NY 10167   Rachel Oestreicher Haspel, Pres.
Founded: 1981. **Staff:** Prof 2; Other 2. **Subjects:** Raoul Wallenberg - biography, efforts to obtain his release, sightings in the USSR; freedom of information; cultural projects; Nobel Prize letters. **Special Collections:** Swedish White Papers collection; FDR Archives collection; Letters to Far Far collection. **Holdings:** Books; bound periodical volumes; reports; audio- and videotapes. **Services:** Library open to the public by appointment. **Publications:** Raoul Wallenberg's Children (newsletter); A Hero for Our Time (booklet). **Remarks:** FAX: (212)272-9720.

Frances L.N. Waller Research Museum and Library
See: **Spotsylvania Historical Association, Inc.** (15594)

★ **19954** ★
Wallingford Historical Society, Inc. - Library (Hist)
180 S. Main St.
Box 73   Phone: (203)269-3172
Wallingford, CT 06492   Mary I. Annis, Pres.
Staff: 1. **Subjects:** Local history, genealogy. **Holdings:** 450 books. **Services:** Library not open to the public.

John Freeman Walls Historic Site & Underground Railroad Museum
See: **Proverbs Heritage Organization** (13439)

Walnut Canyon National Monument
See: **U.S. Natl. Park Service** (17788)

★ **19955** ★
Walnut Creek Historical Society - Shadelands Ranch Historical Museum - History Room (Hist)
2660 Ygnacio Valley Rd.   Phone: (510)935-7871
Walnut Creek, CA 94598   Sherwood Burgess, Libn./Archv.
Founded: 1972. **Subjects:** Walnut Creek history. **Special Collections:** Joseph Reddeford Walker; Albert and Bessie Johnson; Seely-Hodges letters, 1852-1881 (94); Hiram Penniman family letters, 1880-1909; bound collection of Walnut Kernel newspapers (37 years). **Holdings:** 500 books; 62 bound periodical volumes; 6 VF drawers of maps, manuscripts, files, records; 1300 photographs; 25 tapes; 120 unbound newspapers. **Services:** History room open to the public by appointment and on a limited schedule. **Publications:** Shadelands News, bimonthly - to members. **Staff:** Elizabeth Isles, Musm.Dir.

Lewis Walpole Library
See: **Yale University** (20721)

★ 19956 ★
Walsh College of Accountancy and Business Administration - Library
(Bus-Fin)
3838 Livernois
Box 7006   Phone: (313)689-8282
Troy, MI 48007   Gloria B. Ellis, Dir.
Founded: 1965. **Staff:** Prof 4; Other 4. **Subjects:** Accounting, auditing, investments, business law, economics, management, marketing, money and banking, taxation, data processing and statistics. **Special Collections:** Annual reports of 1300 companies. **Holdings:** 21,000 volumes; 500 pamphlets; 500 ultrafiche; 60 C.P.A. audiotapes. **Subscriptions:** 450 journals and other serials; 11 newspapers. **Services:** Interlibrary loan; copying; library open to alumni and area businesses and professionals. **Computerized Information Services:** Dow Jones News/Retrieval, LEXIS, NAARS (National Automated Accounting Research System), WESTLAW, ABI/INFORM, Business Periodicals Index. **Remarks:** FAX: (313)689-9066.

★ 19957 ★
Walsh Wilkins - Law Library (Law)
2800-801 6th Ave., S.W.
Calgary, AB, Canada T2P 4A3   Phone: (403)267-8488
                                                   Frankie Wilson, Libn.
Founded: 1959. **Staff:** Prof 1. **Subjects:** Law. **Holdings:** 700 books; 3300 bound periodical volumes. **Subscriptions:** 120 journals and other serials. **Services:** Interlibrary loan; copying; library open to the public with restrictions. **Automated Operations:** Computerized cataloging. **Computerized Information Services:** QL Systems, CBA. **Remarks:** FAX: (403)264-9400. Telex: 038-22763.

Walson Army Community Hospital
See: U.S. Army Hospitals (17053)

★ 19958 ★
Walter, Conston, Alexander & Green, P.C. - Law Library (Law)
90 Park Ave.   Phone: (212)210-9526
New York, NY 10016   Eric Roberts
Staff: Prof 1; Other 1. **Subjects:** Law - corporate, international, German. **Special Collections:** German law (German and English materials). **Holdings:** 15,000 books. **Subscriptions:** 60 journals and other serials; 5 newspapers. **Services:** Interlibrary loan; copying; SDI; library open to the public with lawyer's permission. **Computerized Information Services:** WESTLAW, DIALOG Information Services, VU/TEXT Information Services, NEXIS, LEXIS, LEGI-SLATE, DataTimes, Data-Star, Dun & Bradstreet Business Credit Services. Performs searches on fee basis. **Remarks:** FAX: (212)210-9444.

★ 19959 ★
Walter, Haverfield, Buescher and Chockley - Law Library (Law)
1215 Terminal Tower   Phone: (216)781-1212
Cleveland, OH 44113   Leon Stevens, Libn.
Founded: 1932. **Staff:** Prof 1. **Subjects:** Law - tax, labor, business, general. **Holdings:** 13,000 books; 250 bound periodical volumes; briefs; memoranda. **Subscriptions:** 200 journals and other serials; 55 newspapers. **Services:** Library not open to the public. **Computerized Information Services:** LEXIS, NEXIS. **Remarks:** FAX: (216)575-0911.

★ 19960 ★
Jim Walter Research Corporation - Technical Information Center (Sci-Engr)
10301 9th St., N.
P.O. Box 42010   Phone: (813)576-4171
St. Petersburg, FL 33716   David Brzana, Info.Spec.
Founded: 1966. **Staff:** Prof 1; Other 1. **Subjects:** Polymer chemistry, specialty chemicals, building materials, materials science, industrial safety, environmental health. **Holdings:** 3500 books; 600 bound periodical volumes; 20 VF drawers of patents. **Subscriptions:** 200 journals and other serials. **Services:** Interlibrary loan; center not open to the public. **Computerized Information Services:** DIALOG Information Services, STN International, PFDS Online, NLM, Chemical Abstracts Service (CAS), OCLC. **Networks/Consortia:** Member of SOLINET, Florida Library Network (FLN).

Joseph C. Walter, Jr. and Elizabeth C. Walter Geology Library
See: University of Texas at Austin - Geology Library (19391)

★ 19961 ★
Walters Art Gallery - Library (Art)
600 N. Charles St.   Phone: (410)547-9000
Baltimore, MD 21201   Muriel L. Toppan, Ref.Libn.
Founded: 1934. **Staff:** Prof 1; Other 1. **Subjects:** Art - European, Greek, Roman, Egyptian, medieval; manuscripts; sculpture. **Holdings:** 80,000 volumes; 700 rare books; 782 illuminated manuscripts; 1400 incunabula. **Subscriptions:** 700 journals and other serials. **Services:** Copying; library open to the public by appointment. **Computerized Information Services:** OCLC. **Remarks:** FAX: (410)783-7969. **Staff:** Elizabeth Fishman, Asst./Slide Libn.; Lilian M.C. Randall, Cur., Mss. & Rare Bks.

Raymond Walters College
See: University of Cincinnati (18481)

★ 19962 ★
Waltham Museum, Inc. - Library (Hist)
17 Noonan St.   Phone: (617)893-8017
Waltham, MA 02154   Albert Arena, Dir.
Founded: 1971. **Subjects:** Waltham, Massachusetts; Metz Automobile Company; Waltham Watch Company; steam engineering of the past. **Holdings:** 5000 books. **Services:** Library open to the public with restrictions.

★ 19963 ★
Waltham Weston Hospital & Medical Center - Medical Library (Med)
Hope Ave.   Phone: (617)647-6261
Waltham, MA 02254-9116   Mr. Frank Landry, Med.Libn.
Staff: Prof 1. **Subjects:** Medicine, surgery, psychiatry, nursing, hospital administration. **Holdings:** 1000 books; 1600 bound periodical volumes; 2 VF drawers of pamphlets; 1200 volumes of unbound periodicals. **Subscriptions:** 153 journals and other serials. **Services:** Interlibrary loan; copying; SDI; library open to the public. **Automated Operations:** Computerized ILL (DOCLINE). **Computerized Information Services:** MEDLINE, MEDLARS. Performs searches on fee basis. **Networks/Consortia:** Member of Consortium for Information Resources (CIR), Massachusetts Health Sciences Libraries Network (MaHSLiN). **Remarks:** FAX: (617)647-6007 (administration office).

★ 19964 ★
Walton Lantaff Schroeder & Carson - Law Library (Law)
One Biscayne Tower, Suite 2500
2 S. Biscayne Blvd.   Phone: (305)379-6411
Miami, FL 33131   Daniel Linehan, Libn.
Founded: 1934. **Staff:** Prof 1. **Subjects:** Law. **Special Collections:** Trinity series of 19th century law; insurance law; public utility law. **Holdings:** 34,000 volumes; monographs and treatises; 2 shelves microfilm. **Subscriptions:** 16 journals and other serials. **Services:** Copying; SDI; library open to the public by appointment. **Computerized Information Services:** WESTLAW; CD-ROMs. **Special Catalogs:** Union Catalog of local loose leaf services; Florida Bar materials; codes of Florida cities and counties. **Special Indexes:** Verdicts and settlements (local). **Remarks:** FAX: (305)577-3875.

★ 19965 ★
Wanderer Press - Library (Rel-Phil, Publ)
201 Ohio St.
St. Paul, MN 55107-2096   Phone: (612)224-5733
Subjects: Catholic religion, theology, and philosophy. **Special Collections:** Papal Encyclicals, 1740 to present; The Wanderer newspaper, 1867 to present. **Holdings:** 2000 books; 25 reels of microfilm. **Subscriptions:** 50 journals and other serials; 50 newspapers. **Services:** Interlibrary loan; library open to the public by appointment. **Remarks:** FAX: (612)224-9666.

Wangenheim Room
See: San Diego Public Library (14711)

Owen H. Wangensteen Historical Library of Biology and Medicine
See: **University of Minnesota - Bio-Medical Library - Owen H.**
   Wangensteen Historical Library of Biology and Medicine (18895)

★19966★
War Memorial Museum of Virginia - Research Library (Mil)
9285 Warwick Blvd.   Phone: (804)247-8523
Newport News, VA 23607   Eliza E. Embrey, Libn.
Founded: 1923. **Staff:** 1. **Subjects:** Military history. **Special Collections:** Rare books and documents on Spanish-American War, Civil War, World Wars I and II; uniform regulations; military manuals. **Holdings:** 14,000 books; 200 bound periodical volumes; 700 newspapers; 5000 items in historical files; 300 microfiche; 600 films; 25 oral history tapes. **Subscriptions:** 60 journals and other serials. **Services:** Copying; library open to the public by appointment for research use. **Special Catalogs:** Film catalog. **Staff:** William C. Baker, Reg./Archv.

★19967★
WAR/WATCH Foundation - Library (Soc Sci)
35 Benton St.
Box 487   Phone: (501)253-8900
Eureka Springs, AR 72632   Richard J. Parker, Exec.Dir.
Founded: 1983. **Subjects:** Conflict resolution, children and war, human cost of war, international law. **Holdings:** 1200 volumes. **Services:** Copying; library open to the public.

Clarence Ward Art Library
See: **Oberlin College** (12216)

Ward Memorial Library
See: **Sacred Heart Major Seminary** (14203)

Robert Ward Archives
See: **Duke University - Music Library** (5047)

Warden's Home Museum
See: **Washington County Historical Society** (19996)

E.G. Ware Library
See: **Garden Grove Historical Society** (6250)

Warne Clinic
See: **Pottsville Hospital and Warne Clinic** (13277)

Thomas Warne Historical Museum and Library
See: **Madison Township Historical Society** (9529)

Warner Bros. Archives
See: **University of Southern California - Library - Cinema-Television**
   Library and Archives of Performing Arts (19336)

★19968★
Warner Brother Studios - Research Library (Art)
5200 Lankershim Blvd., Suite 100   Phone: (818)506-8693
North Hollywood, CA 91601   Anne G. Schlosser, Dir.
Founded: 1929. **Staff:** Prof 2. **Subjects:** Architecture, costume, social life and customs. **Special Collections:** World War II; 19th century illustrated periodicals; period costume; location photographs taken in connection with various movie productions. **Holdings:** 35,000 books; 1.5 million prints, photographs, clippings. **Subscriptions:** 80 journals and other serials. **Services:** Library open for a fee. **Computerized Information Services:** DIALOG Information Services. **Special Indexes:** Index to illustrations and articles useful in motion picture and television production in current periodicals has been maintained for over thirty years. **Remarks:** FAX: (818)506-8079. **Staff:** Barbara M. Poland.

Warner House Library
See: **Constitution Island Association, Inc.** (4232)

★19969★
Warner-Lambert Company - Corporate Library and Literature Services
   (Med)
182 Tabor Rd.   Phone: (201)540-2875
Morris Plains, NJ 07950   Nedra Behringer, Dir., Corp.Lib. and Lit.Serv.
Founded: 1945. **Staff:** Prof 10; Other 4. **Subjects:** Pharmaceuticals, medicine, chemistry, business, marketing, finance, competitive intelligence, confectionery. **Holdings:** 17,000 books; 25,000 bound periodical volumes; 7200 reels of microfilm. **Subscriptions:** 550 journals and other serials. **Services:** Interlibrary loan. **Computerized Information Services:** DIALOG Information Services, NEXIS, MEDLINE, Dow Jones News/Retrieval, NewsNet, Inc., Data-Star. **Remarks:** FAX: (201)540-4756. **Staff:** Verdelle B. Jones, Asst.Libn., Tech.Proc.; Mary Ammann, Sr.Lit.Sci.; Linda Warren, Mgr., Lit.Serv.; Arlene F. Drucker, Mgr., Lib.Serv.; Eric N. Goldschmidt, Sr.Lit.Assoc.; Scott Lawrence, Lit.Sci.; Karen Sattar, Lib.Coord.; Claudia Cuca, Sr.Lit.Sci.; Sara Hagan, Lit.Sci.

★19970★
Warner-Lambert/Parke-Davis - Research Library (Biol Sci, Med)
2800 Plymouth Rd.   Phone: (313)996-7860
Ann Arbor, MI 48105   Sharon Lehman, Dir.
Founded: 1885. **Staff:** Prof 19; Other 5. **Subjects:** Chemistry, pharmacology, medicine, toxicology, microbiology, pathology. **Holdings:** 18,739 books; 14,663 bound periodical volumes; 8319 microfilm cassettes; 98,000 computerized and indexed product documents; 3767 reprints. **Subscriptions:** 1200 journals and other serials. **Services:** Interlibrary loan (limited); library not open to the public. **Automated Operations:** Computerized cataloging, acquisitions, serials, and ILL. **Computerized Information Services:** DIALOG Information Services, PFDS Online, BRS Information Technologies, NLM, Data-Star, STN International; PARDLARS (literature citations on company products; internal database). **Networks/ Consortia:** Member of National Network of Libraries of Medicine - Greater Midwest Region, Michigan Library Consortium (MLC). **Remarks:** FAX: (313)996-7008. **Staff:** Elaine Logan, Mgr., Lib.Serv.; Rose Cygan, Mgr., Lit.Serv.; Beverly Ross, Mgr., Database Serv.; Sandra Robertson, Supv., Doc. Delivery.

★19971★
Warner, Norcross & Judd - Library (Law)
900 Old Kent Bldg.   Phone: (616)459-6121
Grand Rapids, MI 49503   Mary Lou Calvin, Libn.
Staff: Prof 1; Other 1. **Subjects:** Law. **Holdings:** 10,000 books; 750 bound periodical volumes. **Subscriptions:** 175 journals and other serials. **Services:** Library not open to the public. **Automated Operations:** Computerized cataloging and circulation. **Computerized Information Services:** LEXIS, DIALOG Information Services, WESTLAW, VU/TEXT Information Services, Hannah Information Systems, Dow Jones News/Retrieval, Current USC; internal database. **Networks/Consortia:** Member of Michigan Library Consortium (MLC). **Remarks:** FAX: (616)459-2170.

★19972★
Warner-Pacific College - Otto F. Linn Library (Rel-Phil)
2219 S.E. 68th Ave.   Phone: (503)775-4366
Portland, OR 97215   Alice Kienberger, Hd.Libn.
Founded: 1937. **Staff:** Prof 2. **Subjects:** Religion, natural and applied science, education, business, economics, social and behavioral science, music, health, physical education. **Special Collections:** Church of God Collection (Anderson, Indiana). **Holdings:** 52,500 books; 3000 bound periodical volumes; 40 theses and dissertations; 1500 A V programs relating to core program. **Subscriptions:** 185 journals and other serials; 3 newspapers. **Services:** Interlibrary loan; copying; library open to the public. **Computerized Information Services:** Online systems. **Remarks:** FAX: (503)775-4113. **Staff:** Sandra Ajami, Tech.Serv.Libn.

Warner Research Collection
See: **Burbank Public Library** (2363)

★ **19973** ★
Warner & Stackpole - Information Services (Law)
75 State St.   Phone: (617)951-9244
Boston, MA 02109   Sharon E. Sweet, Mgr., Info.Serv.
Staff: Prof 1; Other 4. **Subjects:** Law. **Holdings:** 6000 books. **Subscriptions:** 5 newspapers. **Services:** Library not open to the public. **Computerized Information Services:** DIALOG Information Services, LEXIS. **Publications:** Ex Libris/Tabula. **Remarks:** FAX: (617)951-9151.

Warner and Swasey Observatory - Library
See: **Case Western Reserve University** (3128)

★ **19974** ★
Warren County Historical Society - Library and Archives (Hist)
210 Fourth Ave.
Box 427   Phone: (814)723-1795
Warren, PA 16365   Derek B. McKown, EXEC. DIR.
Founded: 1955. **Staff:** 2. **Subjects:** History - local, state, Indian; genealogy; Quaker records; local authors. **Special Collections:** Harold C. Putnam Collection (local history and the inland rivers of the eastern United States; 95 linear feet); Joseph Wick Collection (background and history of construction of the Kinzua Dam; 9 linear feet); Byron Barnes Horton Collection (history of the Barnes, Hortons, and related families in New England and Pennsylvania; 37 linear feet). **Holdings:** 2000 books; 400 archival boxes of material from local and area families and businesses; 250 boxes of magnetic tapes. **Subscriptions:** 14 journals and other serials. **Services:** Copying; library open to the public with restrictions.

★ **19975** ★
Warren County Historical Society - Museum and Library (Hist)
105 S. Broadway
Box 223   Phone: (513)932-1817
Lebanon, OH 45036   Mary Payne, Dir.
Founded: 1940. **Staff:** Prof 2; Other 35. **Subjects:** Local history, genealogy, archeology, Warren County, Shaker records, agriculture. **Special Collections:** Shaker Library. **Holdings:** 1500 volumes; 1526 family files; 600 general county information files; 75,000 index cards of county residents; 350 reels of microfilm of court records, church census, newspapers, school records; 24 volumes of cemetery, marriage, and birth records; 87 bound copies of Ohio Historical Society quarterlies; Warren County court, census, school, and church records. **Subscriptions:** 20 journals and other serials. **Services:** Copying; library open to the public. **Publications:** Historicalog, quarterly, with monthly update mailer. **Staff:** Mary Klei.

★ **19976** ★
Warren County Historical Society - Warren County Museum and Historical Library (Hist)
Market and Walton
P.O. Box 12
Warrenton, MO 63383   William Frick, Dir.
Subjects: History - Warren County, family, Missouri, Central Wesleyan College. **Holdings:** Church and school records; microfilm of Warren County newspapers. **Subscriptions:** 3 journals and other serials. **Services:** Copying; library open to the public by appointment.

★ **19977** ★
Warren County Law Library (Law)
500 Justice Dr.   Phone: (513)933-1381
Lebanon, OH 45036   Robert Hudson, Libn.
Staff: 2. **Subjects:** Law. **Holdings:** 15,000 volumes. **Services:** Library open to the public.

★ **19978** ★
Warren County Law Library (Law)
Court House   Phone: (814)723-7550
Warren, PA 16365   Sherry Phillips, Law Libn.
Subjects: Law. **Holdings:** 9000 books; 500 bound periodical volumes; microfiche. **Services:** Library open to the public. **Remarks:** FAX: (814)723-8115.

★ **19979** ★
Warren General Hospital - Medical Staff Library (Med)
667 Eastland Ave., S.E.   Phone: (216)373-9818
Warren, OH 44484   Nancy L. Bindas, Med.Libn.
Founded: 1965. **Staff:** 1. **Subjects:** Medicine, surgery, and allied health sciences. **Holdings:** 550 books; 500 bound periodical volumes; 480 Audio-Digest tapes and cassettes; 400 videotapes. **Subscriptions:** 48 journals and other serials. **Services:** Interlibrary loan; library not open to the public. **Remarks:** FAX: (216)373-9819.

★ **19980** ★
Warren Hospital - Medical Library (Med)
185 Roseberry St.   Phone: (201)859-6728
Phillipsburg, NJ 08865   Esther Tews, Dir., Volunteer Serv.
Staff: Prof 1; Other 9. **Subjects:** Medicine. **Holdings:** 700 books. **Subscriptions:** 47 journals and other serials. **Services:** Interlibrary loan; library not open to the public. **Computerized Information Services:** NLM.

★ **19981** ★
Warren Library Association - Library - Special Collections (Mus, Hist)
205 Market St.   Phone: (814)723-4650
Warren, PA 16365   Patricia McElravy, Hd., Ref.
Founded: 1873. **Special Collections:** Petroleum history (450 items); popular American sheet music of show tunes, 1834-1955 (7029 items); Warren County newspapers, 1824 to present, on microfilm; historic Warren County photographs (460); U.S. census for Warren County, on microfilm. **Services:** Interlibrary loan (none on sheet music); copying; collections open to the public. **Automated Operations:** Computerized public access catalog, cataloging, circulation, and ILL. **Computerized Information Services:** OCLC, DIALOG Information Services. **Special Indexes:** Vital statistics index to local newspapers (card). **Remarks:** FAX: (814)723-4521.

★ **19982** ★
Warren State Hospital - Medical Library (Med)
33 Main Dr.   Phone: (814)726-4223
N. Warren, PA 16365-5099   Helen Sweitzer, Lib.Dir.
Founded: 1930. **Staff:** Prof 1. **Subjects:** Psychiatry, neurology, psychology, medicine, nursing, occupational therapy, therapeutic activities, sociology. **Holdings:** 20,000 books; 1600 bound periodical volumes; 1400 audio cassettes. **Subscriptions:** 190 journals and other serials. **Services:** Interlibrary loan; copying; library open to professional and paraprofessional users. **Automated Operations:** Computerized cataloging and serials. **Computerized Information Services:** OCLC, DIALOG Information Services. **Networks/Consortia:** Member of Pennsylvania State Institutional Libraries, Northwest Interlibrary Cooperative of Pennsylvania (NICOP), Erie Area Health Information Library Cooperative (EAHILC). **Remarks:** FAX: (814)726-4562.

★ **19983** ★
(Warren) Tribune Chronicle - Library (Publ)
240 Franklin St.
PO Box 1431   Phone: (216)841-1734
Warren, OH 44482-1431   Kathi A. Kovacic
Founded: 1982. **Staff:** Prof 1. **Subjects:** Newspaper reference topics. **Holdings:** 526 books; 993 reels of microfilm. **Subscriptions:** 8 journals and other serials; 9 newspapers. **Services:** Copying; library open to the public on a limited schedule. **Special Indexes:** Index to the Tribune Chronicle. **Remarks:** FAX: (216)841-1717.

Betty Warrington Memorial
See: **Krotona Institute of Theosophy - Krotona Library** (8819)

★ **19984** ★
(Warsaw) Biblioteka Amerykanska - USIS Library (Educ)
Ambasada Stanow Zjednoczonych Ameryki
Aleje Ujazdowskie 29/31
Warsaw, Poland
Remarks: Maintained or supported by the U.S. Information Agency. Focus is on materials that will assist peoples outside the United States to learn about the United States, its people, history, culture, political processes, and social milieux.

★ 19985 ★
Warsaw Historical Society - Library (Hist)
15 Perry Ave.   Phone: (716)786-2030
Warsaw, NY 14569   D.M. Lane, Pres.
Founded: 1939. **Staff:** 1. **Subjects:** Civil War and Wyoming County history. **Holdings:** 500 books; 100 years of local newspapers bound by years; local publications. **Services:** Library open to the public by appointment.

★ 19986 ★
Warwick Public Library - Central Children's Library (Hum)
600 Sandy Ln.   Phone: (401)739-5440
Warwick, RI 02886   Susan Lepore, Hd., Ch.Serv.
Staff: Prof 2; Other 2. **Subjects:** Children's literature. **Special Collections:** Educational toys (165). **Holdings:** 30,000 books. **Subscriptions:** 10 journals and other serials. **Services:** Interlibrary loan; copying; library open to the public. **Automated Operations:** Computerized circulation. **Networks/Consortia:** Member of Western Interrelated Library System.

Wascana Institute of Applied Arts and Sciences
See: **Saskatchewan Institute of Applied Science & Technology, Wascana Campus - Resource and Information Centre** (14859)

★ 19987 ★
Wascana Rehabilitation Centre - Health Sciences Library (Med)
Ave. G & 23rd Ave.   Phone: (306)359-5650
Regina, SK, Canada S4S 0A5   Donna Cargill, Dir.
Staff: 2. **Subjects:** Rehabilitation, gerontology, pediatrics, physically handicapped. **Holdings:** 2400 books; 1300 bound periodical volumes. **Subscriptions:** 100 journals and other serials. **Services:** Interlibrary loan; copying; library open to the public with restrictions. **Remarks:** FAX: (306)359-5550. **Staff:** Lily Walter-Smith, Libn.

★ 19988 ★
Waseca County Historical Society - Research Library (Hist)
315 2nd Ave., N.E.
Box 314   Phone: (507)835-7700
Waseca, MN 56093   Margaret Sinn, Musm.Dir.
Founded: 1938. **Staff:** 4. **Subjects:** County, community, state, and regional history; genealogy. **Special Collections:** Business and organizational records for local communities; historical photographs; presidential biographies collection. **Holdings:** 1000 books; 750 unbound documents; 70 reels of microfilm. **Services:** Copying; library open to the public with restrictions. **Networks/Consortia:** Member of Southcentral Minnesota Inter-Library Exchange (SMILE), Waseca Interlibrary Resource Exchange (WIRE). **Publications:** Child's History of Waseca County 1854-1904; Waseca Co. Land Atlas, 1874; Vista 1856-1956; Vista 76; History of New Richland and Wilton Villages. **Staff:** Dan Swenson; Martha Waddell; Carol Beetsch.

WASH Information Center
See: **U.S. Agency for International Development - Water & Sanitation for Health Project - Information Center** (16785)

Washburn Observatory
See: **University of Wisconsin--Madison - Washburn Observatory** (19624)

★ 19989 ★
Washburn University of Topeka - School of Law Library (Law)
1700 College Ave.   Phone: (913)231-1088
Topeka, KS 66621   John E. Christensen, Dir.
Founded: 1903. **Staff:** Prof 6.5; Other 9.5. **Subjects:** Law. **Special Collections:** U.S. Government documents depository, 1972 to present; Kansas documents depository; Nuclear Regulatory Commission documents depository. **Holdings:** 145,809 bound volumes; 101,544 titles on microfiche; CIS microfiche, 1974-1982; U.S. Supreme Court records and briefs, 1974 to present, on microfiche. **Subscriptions:** 3225 journals and other serials. **Services:** Interlibrary loan; library open to the public with restrictions. **Computerized Information Services:** Dow Jones News/Retrieval, NEXIS, WESTLAW, DIALOG Information Services, LEXIS, OCLC; InterNet (electronic mail service). **Networks/Consortia:** Member of Mid-America Law School Library Consortium, Bibliographical Center for Research, Rocky Mountain Region, Inc. (BCR). **Remarks:** FAX: (913)232-8087. Electronic mail address(es): wutopll@acc.wuacc.edu (InterNet). **Staff:** Mark Folmsbee, Assoc.Dir.; Paul Arrigo, Doc.Libn.; Virgie Smith, Coll.Dev.Libn.; Martin Wisneski, Hd., Tech.Serv.; Lissa Holzhausen, Ref.Serv.Coord.

E.B. Washburne House State Historic Site
See: **Illinois (State) Historic Preservation Agency - Galena State Historic Sites** (7697)

★ 19990 ★
Washington Adventist Hospital - Health Sciences Library (Med)
7600 Carroll Ave.   Phone: (301)891-5261
Takoma Park, MD 20912   Cathy Cumbo, Libn.
Founded: 1928. **Staff:** Prof 1. **Subjects:** Medicine, nursing, hospital administration. **Holdings:** 1800 volumes; 160 videocassettes. **Subscriptions:** 210 journals and other serials. **Services:** Interlibrary loan; copying; SDI; library open to the public for reference use only. **Automated Operations:** Computerized serials, circulation, and ILL (DOCLINE). **Computerized Information Services:** MEDLARS. Performs searches on fee basis. **Networks/Consortia:** Member of Maryland and D.C. Consortium of Resource Sharing (MADCORS), Maryland Association of Health Science Librarians (MAHSL).

★ 19991 ★
Washington Bible College/Capital Bible Seminary - Oyer Memorial Library (Rel-Phil)
6511 Princess Garden Pkwy.   Phone: (301)552-1400
Lanham, MD 20706   Lyn S. Brown, Dir., Lib.Serv.
Founded: 1937. **Staff:** Prof 1; Other 2. **Subjects:** Evangelical theology, Bible, Christian education, missions and evangelism, Greek and Hebrew language studies, church history. **Holdings:** 61,300 books; 1986 bound periodical volumes; 672 filmstrips; microforms; 2625 cassette tapes; 1624 phonograph records; 140 transparency files; 672 religious teaching aid files; 580 VF folders of pamphlets. **Subscriptions:** 375 journals and other serials; 8 newspapers. **Services:** Interlibrary loan; copying; library open to the public with restrictions. **Automated Operations:** Computerized cataloging. **Computerized Information Services:** OCLC. **Networks/Consortia:** Member of CAPCON Library Network.

Booker T. Washington National Monument
See: **U.S. Natl. Park Service** (17677)

★ 19992 ★
Washington Cathedral Foundation - Cathedral Rare Book Library (Rel-Phil, Rare Book)
Mount St. Alban, N.W.
Washington, DC 20016   Giles E. Dawson, Libn. and Chm., Lib.Comm.
Phone: (202)537-6200
Founded: 1965. **Subjects:** Biblical texts, liturgies, church history, theology, church music, ecclesiastical art and architecture. **Special Collections:** Carson Collection of American Bishops (manuscript material in the hand of most of the Bishops of the Episcopal Church). **Holdings:** 4000 books and manuscripts. **Services:** Library open to the public by appointment. **Special Catalogs:** Catalogs of special exhibitions.

Washington College of Law
See: **American University** (782)

Washington County Free Library - Western Maryland Public Libraries
See: **Western Maryland Public Libraries** (20264)

★ 19993 ★
Washington County Historical Association - Museum Library (Hist)
14th & Monroe Sts.   Phone: (402)468-5740
Fort Calhoun, NE 68023   Agnes Smith, Libn./Cur.
Founded: 1938. **Staff:** 2. **Subjects:** Local and state history, family histories. **Special Collections:** Artifacts and copies of military records of Fort Atkinson, 1819-1827; pioneer documents and letters; Lorenzo Crounse Personal Papers (Governor of Nebraska, 1893). **Holdings:** 600 books; 30 bound periodical volumes; 140 maps and atlases; 54 school reports; 80 manuscripts of letters, genealogies, pioneer reminiscences, and other items; 2600 photographs; 23 photograph albums; 4000 clippings. **Services:** Copying; library open to the public for reference use only. **Publications:** The Story of Fort Atkinson (pamphlet) - for sale; Fort on the Prairie (book) - for sale; History of Washington County, 1876 (reprinted 1985 with index; booklet).

★ 19994 ★
Washington County Historical Society - Jamieson Memorial Library
(Hist)
135 W. Washington St.
PO Box 1281
Hagerstown, MD 21741
Phone: (301)797-8782
Peggy Bledsoe, Lib.Cons.
Founded: 1955. **Subjects:** Washington County and Western Maryland - history, genealogy. **Special Collections:** Mary Mish Collection (historical correspondence). **Holdings:** 1000 books; 30 business ledgers; 1000 files; 1 vertical file; photographs. **Services:** Copying; library open to the public on a limited schedule. **Staff:** Ellen Reed.

★ 19995 ★
Washington County Historical Society - Library (Hist)
Stevens Memorial Museum
307 E. Market St.
Salem, IN 47167
Phone: (812)883-6495
Rae Etta Bordon
Founded: 1915. **Staff:** 3. **Subjects:** Genealogy, history, religion, biography, antiques. **Special Collections:** Newspapers, 1819 to present; The Christian Record, 1843-1884; Quaker Genealogies for Hinshaw and Blue River; family information (VF drawers). **Holdings:** 8000 books; 75 records; 255 genealogies; 36 cemetery record books; 80 church histories; 1340 family files; 206 reels of microfilm; 45 state histories; 60 Daughters of the American Revolution and Colonial Dames records; 400 files of general historical data; 2 Justice of Peace books; 13 records of 1923 survey of Washington County; 25 files of marriage affidavits, applications, and certificates; 1 file of deeds; booklets of clubs and lodges; 61 diaries; 34 account books; 34 township books; war and school records. **Subscriptions:** 5 newspapers. **Services:** Copying; library open to the public on fee basis. **Special Indexes:** Index to Washington County newspapers; 1850 and 1860 census indexes. **Staff:** Willie Harlen, Pres.; J. Ray Clark, Libn.

★ 19996 ★
Washington County Historical Society - Warden's Home Museum - Library (Hist)
602 N. Main St.
Box 167
Stillwater, MN 55082
Phone: (612)439-5956
Joan K. Daniels, Dir.
Staff: 2. **Subjects:** History - Washington County, Minnesota, St. Croix River Valley. **Holdings:** 100 volumes. **Services:** Library open to the public for reference use only.

★ 19997 ★
Washington County Historical Society and Le Moyne House Museum - Library (Hist)
49 E. Maiden St.
Washington, PA 15301
Phone: (412)225-6740
Helen B. Miller, Libn.
Founded: 1900. **Staff:** Prof 1. **Subjects:** Southwestern Pennsylvania history and biography, with emphasis on Washington County. **Special Collections:** Abolitionist correspondence; cemetery records; National Road records; crematory records; military records; personal correspondence of U.S. Grant; Augusta Court records; early indentures; patents and deeds; Le Moyne family records; first settler records; Civil War diaries; church histories; organization histories. **Holdings:** 1300 titles; old newspapers. **Subscriptions:** 10 journals and other serials. **Services:** Library open to the public on a limited schedule for reference use only.

★ 19998 ★
Washington County Hospital - Wroth Memorial Library (Med)
251 E. Antietam St.
Hagerstown, MD 21740
Phone: (301)790-8801
Myra Binau, Coord., Lib.Serv.
Founded: 1953. **Staff:** Prof 1. **Subjects:** Medicine, nursing, and allied health sciences. **Holdings:** 5000 volumes; 8 VF drawers of pamphlets and clippings. **Subscriptions:** 178 journals and other serials. **Services:** Interlibrary loan; copying; library open to the public for reference use only. **Automated Operations:** Computerized ILL (DOCLINE). **Computerized Information Services:** BRS Information Technologies, DIALOG Information Services. Performs searches on fee basis. **Networks/Consortia:** Member of National Network of Libraries of Medicine (NN/LM), Maryland Association of Health Science Librarians (MAHSL).

★ 19999 ★
Washington County Law Library (Law)
Circuit Court House
95 W. Washington St.
Hagerstown, MD 21740
Phone: (301)791-3115
Diane Seltzer, Law Ck./Libn.
Staff: Prof 1. **Subjects:** Law. **Holdings:** Figures not available. **Subscriptions:** 18 journals and other serials. **Services:** Copying; library open to the public for reference use only. **Remarks:** Maintained by Washington County Bar Association.

★ 20000 ★
Washington County Law Library (Law)
County Court House
205 Putnam St.
Marietta, OH 45750
Phone: (614)373-2485
Patricia W. Wheeler, Libn.
Staff: Prof 1; Other 2. **Subjects:** Law. **Special Collections:** Ohio case law (1885 to present). **Holdings:** 15,000 volumes. **Subscriptions:** 8 journals and other serials. **Services:** Library open to the public for reference use only. **Computerized Information Services:** WESTLAW. Performs limited searches on fee basis. **Remarks:** FAX: (614)373-2085.

★ 20001 ★
Washington County Law Library (Law)
230 N.E. 2nd Ave.
Hillsboro, OR 97124
Phone: (503)648-8880
Ann Karlen, Libn.
Founded: 1926. **Staff:** 2. **Subjects:** Law. **Holdings:** 15,000 volumes. **Services:** Copying; library open to the public.

★ 20002 ★
Washington County Law Library (Law)
Courthouse
Washington, PA 15301-6813
Phone: (412)228-6747
Charles G. Stock, Jr., Law Libn.
Founded: 1867. **Staff:** 1. **Subjects:** Law. **Holdings:** 24,000 volumes. **Subscriptions:** 40 journals and other serials. **Services:** Copying; library open to the public. **Automated Operations:** Computerized cataloging and circulation. **Computerized Information Services:** WESTLAW; Cortflo & Land Records. Performs searches on fee basis. **Remarks:** FAX: (412)228-6890.

★ 20003 ★
Washington County Museum - Library (Hist)
17677 N.W. Springville Rd.
Portland, OR 97229
Phone: (503)645-5353
Joan H. Smith, Exec.Dir.
Staff: 2. **Subjects:** History, anthropology, cultural resources management. **Special Collections:** Washington County Collection (manuscripts; pamphlets; ephemera). **Holdings:** 150 books; 16,000 photographs; 72 reels of microfilm of Washington County newspapers; 140 cubic feet of manuscript materials; 40 oral history tapes; 3 cubic feet of clippings; 24 reels of microfilm of Washington County archival materials. **Services:** Copying; library open to the public for reference use only. **Networks/Consortia:** Member of Washington County Cooperative Library Services (WCCLS).

★ 20004 ★
Washington County Museum of Fine Arts - Library (Art)
City Park, Box 423
Hagerstown, MD 21741
Phone: (301)739-5727
Jean Woods, Dir.
Founded: 1931. **Subjects:** Art, art history with emphasis on 19th and 20th century American art. **Holdings:** 4200 volumes. **Subscriptions:** 4 journals and other serials. **Services:** Interlibrary loan; copying; library open to the public for reference use only.

★ 20005 ★
Washington Crossing Historic Park - Library (Hist)
Washington Crossing, PA 18977
Phone: (215)493-4076
Mildred W. Rakus, Libn.
Staff: Prof 1. **Holdings:** 1000 books. **Services:** Library open to the public by appointment.

★ 20006 ★
Washington Gas Light Company - Library (Bus-Fin, Energy)
6801 Industrial Rd.   Phone: (703)750-7927
Springfield, VA 22151   J. Fredic Simms, Libn.
Founded: 1843. **Staff:** Prof 1; Other 1. **Subjects:** Energy, management, natural gas. **Special Collections:** Company history. **Holdings:** 10,000 volumes. **Subscriptions:** 700 journals and other serials; 150 newspapers. **Services:** Interlibrary loan; copying; SDI; clipping service; library open to the public by appointment. **Automated Operations:** Computerized cataloging and serials. **Computerized Information Services:** DIALOG Information Services, BRS Information Technologies, DataTimes, A.G.A. GasNet. Performs searches on fee basis. **Networks/Consortia:** Member of CAPCON Library Network. **Publications:** New in the Library; Corporate Library Bulletin, both monthly; Topical Advisor, quarterly. **Special Indexes:** Index to periodicals collection. **Remarks:** FAX: (703)750-5603.

★ 20007 ★
George Washington University - Medical Center - Paul Himmelfarb Health Sciences Library (Med)
2300 Eye St., N.W.   Phone: (202)994-3528
Washington, DC 20037   Shelley A. Bader, Dir.
Staff: Prof 14; Other 16. **Subjects:** Medicine and allied health sciences. **Holdings:** 25,000 books; 95,000 bound periodical volumes; 1500 titles of AV programs. **Subscriptions:** 2500 journals and other serials. **Services:** Interlibrary loan; copying; SDI; library open to the public with restrictions. **Automated Operations:** Computerized cataloging, serials, circulation, and acquisitions. **Computerized Information Services:** DIALOG Information Services, BRS Information Technologies, NLM, MEDLINE; internal databases. **Networks/Consortia:** Member of National Network of Libraries of Medicine - Southeastern/Atlantic Region, District of Columbia Health Sciences Information Network (DOCHSIN), Consortium of Academic Health Science Libraries of the District of Columbia. **Publications:** Information Interface, 10/year - to Medical Center faculty, staff; to students upon request. **Remarks:** FAX: (202)223-3691. **Staff:** Laurie Thompson, Assoc.Dir., Lib.Oper.; Anne Linton, Assoc.Dir., Info.Instr.Media. Serv.

★ 20008 ★
George Washington University - Melvin Gelman Library - Sino-Soviet Information Center (Area-Ethnic)
2130 H St., N.W., Rm. 603   Phone: (202)994-7105
Washington, DC 20052   Craig H. Seibert, Dir.
Staff: 4. **Subjects:** Soviet Union, China, Eastern Europe - political science, history, economics, geography, military; international communism. **Special Collections:** Joint Publications Research Service (J.P.R.S.); translations from foreign press: USSR, China, Korea; Foreign Broadcast Information Service (F.B.I.S.); China, USSR, Eastern Europe, Western Europe, Middle East, Africa, Southeast Asia, Latin America, Asia and Pacific; map collection. **Holdings:** 5000 books; 500 bound periodical volumes; 2000 other cataloged items; microforms. **Subscriptions:** 200 journals and other serials; 6 newspapers. **Services:** Interlibrary loan; copying; center open to the public. **Automated Operations:** Computerized cataloging, acquisitions, serials, and circulation. **Computerized Information Services:** DIALOG Information Services. Performs searches on fee basis. Contact Person: Lee Anne George, 994-6973. **Networks/Consortia:** Member of Consortium of Universities of the Washington Metropolitan Area. **Staff:** Cathy Zeljak.

George Washington University - National Clearinghouse for Bilingual Education
See: **National Clearinghouse for Bilingual Education** (11116)

★ 20009 ★
George Washington University - National Law Center - Jacob Burns Law Library (Law)
716 20th St., N.W.   Phone: (202)994-6648
Washington, DC 20052   Anita K. Head, Prof. of Law/Law Libn.
Founded: 1865. **Staff:** Prof 13; Other 17. **Subjects:** Law - Anglo-American, international, comparative. **Special Collections:** U.N. publications; records and briefs of U.S. Court of Customs and Patent Appeals; U.S. Supreme Court records and briefs, 1959 to present; selected U.S. Government documents depository. **Holdings:** 400,000 books, microforms, and other volumes. **Subscriptions:** 3800 journals and other serials. **Services:** Interlibrary loan; library reserved for use by University community and law school alumni; government documents open to the public. **Automated Operations:** Computerized cataloging, acquisitions, and serials. **Computerized Information Services:** LEXIS, WESTLAW, VU/TEXT Information Services, DIALOG Information Services, NEXIS, OCLC. **Networks/Consortia:** Member of CAPCON Library Network. **Publications:** Monthly Information Bulletin; Library Guide. **Remarks:** FAX: (202)994-2874.

★ 20010 ★
Washington Hospital - Health Sciences Libraries (Med)
155 Wilson Ave.   Phone: (412)223-3144
Washington, PA 15301-3398   Joan Holloway Frasier,
                                     Hea.Sci.Libn./CME Coord.
Staff: Prof 1; Other 3. **Subjects:** Internal medicine, nursing, cardiology, oncology. **Holdings:** 7800 books; 1500 bound periodical volumes; 1500 AV programs. **Subscriptions:** 277 journals and other serials. **Services:** Interlibrary loan. **Computerized Information Services:** MEDLINE, BRS Information Technologies, DIALOG Information Services; CD-ROMs (MEDLINE, CINAHL, Scientific American Medicine). **Networks/Consortia:** Member of Southeast Pittsburgh Library Consortium, BHSL. **Remarks:** Alternate telephone number(s): (412)223-2020. FAX: (412)223-4096.

★ 20011 ★
Washington Hospital Center - Medical Library (Med)
110 Irving St., N.W., Rm. 2A-21   Phone: (202)877-6221
Washington, DC 20010   Lynne Siemers, Dir.
Founded: 1958. **Staff:** Prof 4; Other 5. **Subjects:** Medicine, nursing, health administration, allied health sciences. **Holdings:** 12,000 books; 22,000 bound periodical volumes; 1500 volumes on microfilm; 800 AV programs; 1 file drawer of pamphlets. **Subscriptions:** 975 journals and other serials. **Services:** Interlibrary loan; library not open to the public. **Automated Operations:** Computerized cataloging. **Computerized Information Services:** MEDLINE, DIALOG Information Services, OCLC, BRS Information Technologies; NEXIS. Performs searches on fee basis. **Networks/Consortia:** Member of District of Columbia Health Sciences Information Network (DOCHSIN). **Publications:** News Log, bimonthly - for internal distribution only; annual report.

★ 20012 ★
Washington and Lee University - Law Library (Law)
Lewis Hall   Phone: (703)463-8540
Lexington, VA 24450   Sarah K. Wiant, Dir.
Staff: Prof 7; Other 9. **Subjects:** Law. **Special Collections:** Extensive early Virginia legal materials; annotated codes and statutes for all states, territories, and possessions, federal government; records and briefs of U.S. Supreme Court, 4th U.S. Circuit Court of Appeals, and Virginia Supreme Court; U.S. Government document depository; John W. Davis papers; Caldwell Butler papers on bankruptcy. **Holdings:** 144,750 volumes; 581,000 microforms; 24,254 documents; 959 AV programs. **Subscriptions:** 3876 journals and other serials; 19 newspapers. **Services:** Interlibrary loan; copying; classroom videotaping; library open to the public. **Automated Operations:** Computerized cataloging. **Computerized Information Services:** VU/TEXT Information Services, DIALOG Information Services, WILSONLINE, NEXIS, LEXIS, WESTLAW, OCLC. **Publications:** Acquisitions List, monthly; Law Library Newsletter; Law Library Users Guide, annual; bibliographies on current legal issues. **Remarks:** FAX: (703)463-8967. **Staff:** Jean Eisenhauer, Acq.Libn.; John P. Bissett, Cat.Libn.; Judy Stinson, Do c./Ref. Libn.; John Doyle, Assoc. Law Libn.; John Jacob, Archv.; Tom Williams, Ref./Media

★ 20013 ★
Washington & Lee University - Special Collections Department (Hist)
University Library   Phone: (703)463-8663
Lexington, VA 24450   Virginia L. Smyers, Spec.Coll.Libn.
Founded: 1939. **Staff:** Prof 1; Other 1. **Subjects:** Local history, genealogy, university history, Civil War, Robert E. Lee. **Special Collections:** Rockbridge Historical Society Collection (local history, genealogy; 130 cubic feet of papers); George West Diehl papers (genealogy, local history, religion; 37 cubic feet of papers); Michael Miley Collection (8000 glass plate negatives); G. William Whitehurst congressional papers (270 cubic feet); Robert E. Lee papers (6 cubic feet of correspondence); University Archives. **Holdings:** 20,000 rare books, 1300 linear feet of manuscripts. **Services:** Copying; department open to the public. **Automated Operations:** Computerized cataloging. **Computerized Information Services:** InterNet (electronic mail service). **Special Indexes:** Guide to the Manuscripts Collection; Guide to the Manuscripts Collection of the Rockbridge Historical Society. **Remarks:** FAX: (703)463-8964. Electronic mail address(es): smyers.g@FS.Library.WLU.EDU (InterNet). **Staff:** Lisa McCown, Spec.Coll.Asst.

★ 20014 ★
Washington Library for the Blind and Physically Handicapped (Aud-Vis)
821 Lenora St.   Phone: (206)464-6930
Seattle, WA 98129   Jan Ames, Dir.
Founded: 1931. **Staff:** 22. **Subjects:** Blindness and disabilities. **Holdings:** 6332 braille books; 124,359 recorded books; 8358 ink print books. **Subscriptions:** 100 journals and other serials. **Services:** Readers' Services; Radio Reading Service; Braille Service; Taping Service; Aids for Print Handicapped. **Computerized Information Services:** BRS Information Technologies; WLN; APH-CARL. **Publications:** Newsletter. **Special Catalogs:** Talking book catalogs, braille catalogs, and cassette catalogs - most prepared by the National Library Service for the Blind and Physically Handicapped at the Library of Congress; Northwest Collection and Large Print catalogs for distribution to eligible borrowers and libraries. **Remarks:** FAX: (206)464-0247. Administered by Seattle Public Library. **Staff:** John Lyall, Mgr.; Phyllis Cairns, Mgr.

★ 20015 ★
Mary Washington Hospital - Gordon W. Jones Medical Library (Med)
2300 Fall Hill Ave.   Phone: (703)899-1597
Fredericksburg, VA 22401   Karen Nelson, Med.Libn.
Staff: Prof 1; Other 1. **Subjects:** Medicine, nursing, biomedical sciences, administration, management. **Special Collections:** Management; History of Medicine. **Holdings:** 1000 books; 3000 bound periodical volumes. **Subscriptions:** 144 journals and other serials. **Services:** Interlibrary loan; copying; current awareness (limited); library open to the public with restrictions. **Computerized Information Services:** MEDLARS. Performs searches on fee basis. **Networks/Consortia:** Member of Northern Virginia Health Sciences Libraries. **Remarks:** FAX: (703)899-1514.

★ 20016 ★
Mary Ball Washington Museum and Library, Inc. (Hist)
Box 97   Phone: (804)462-7280
Lancaster, VA 22503-0097   Ann Lewis Burrows, Exec.Dir.
Founded: 1958. **Staff:** Prof 3; Other 15. **Subjects:** U.S. and Virginia history; county histories; genealogy. **Holdings:** 6000 books; 200 bound periodical volumes; historical research and family papers. **Subscriptions:** 10 journals and other serials. **Services:** Interlibrary loan; copying; library open to the public. **Publications:** Newsletter, quarterly. **Special Indexes:** Surname index; Ball Family Outline. **Staff:** F.W. Jenkins Jr., Res.Dir.

Washington Memorial Library
See: **Valley Forge Historical Society - Washington Memorial Library** (19731)

★ 20017 ★
Washington Memorial Library - Genealogy Department - Middle Georgia Archives (Hist)
1180 Washington Ave.
P.O. Box 6334   Phone: (912)744-0821
Macon, GA 31208-6334   Willard L. Rocker, Chf.Geneal.
Founded: 1923. **Staff:** Prof 3; Other 5. **Subjects:** Genealogy, history, county histories, heraldry, British genealogies. **Special Collections:** Stevens-Davis Memorial Collection (British and pre-Colonial history); J.W. Burke imprints; Macon authors; Porter Horticultural Collection. **Holdings:** 17,270 books; 60 bound periodical titles (1812 volumes); 303 bound volumes of newspapers; 113 city directories; 6541 reels of microfilm; 8338 microfiche; 259 maps; 26 drawers of architectural drawings; 61 boxes of county and family histories. **Subscriptions:** 66 journals and other serials. **Services:** Copying; archives open to the public for reference use only. **Special Indexes:** Index to History of Jones County, Georgia; index to Macon Telegraph (newspaper), 1920-1991. **Remarks:** Alternate telephone numbers are 744-0820 and 744-0851. FAX: (912)742-3161. **Staff:** Peer Ravnan, Archv.

★ 20018 ★
Washington Mutual Savings Bank - Information Center & Dietrich Schmitz Memorial Library (Bus-Fin)
Box 834   Phone: (206)461-2540
Seattle, WA 98111   Chris O'Connor, Info.Ctr.Coord.
Founded: 1970. **Staff:** Prof 1; Other 1. **Subjects:** Banking and finance, economics, investments, management, real estate. **Special Collections:** Seattle History (15 volumes); History of Washington State (6 volumes). **Holdings:** 2000 books; 250 reports; 12 VF drawers of annual reports; 8 VF drawers of ephemera and reports; videotapes. **Subscriptions:** 60 journals and other serials; 5 newspapers. **Services:** Interlibrary loan; library open to the public for reference use by request. **Remarks:** Library located at 1201 3rd Ave., Seattle, WA 98111.

Washington National Records Center
See: **National Archives & Records Administration** (11046)

Washington News Bureau Sound Archive
See: **Broadcast Pioneers Library** (2194)

★ 20019 ★
Washington Park Zoo - Animal Management Division - Library (Biol Sci)
4001 S.W. Canyon Rd.   Phone: (503)226-1561
Portland, OR 97221   Janice Hixson
Staff: Prof 1. **Subjects:** Zoology, animal husbandry, animal behavior, conservation, veterinary medicine, biology. **Special Collections:** Zoo periodicals. **Holdings:** 800 books. **Subscriptions:** 50 journals and other serials. **Services:** Library open to the public by appointment for reference use only. **Remarks:** FAX: (503)226-0074.

★ 20020 ★
Washington Post - News Research Center (Publ)
1150 15th St., N.W.   Phone: (202)334-7341
Washington, DC 20071   Jennifer Belton, Dir., Info.Serv.
Founded: 1933. **Staff:** Prof 17; Other 13. **Subjects:** Politics, government, public policy, health science, religion, sports, finance, foreign affairs, arts, entertainment, local current events. **Holdings:** 15,000 books; 6 million newspaper clippings; 30,000 pamphlets and documents; electronically archived news clippings (400,000 records); 2 million photographs; maps; pictures; microfilm. **Subscriptions:** 250 journals and other serials; 25 newspapers. **Automated Operations:** Computerized cataloging, acquisitions, serials, and circulation (TECHLIBplus). **Computerized Information Services:** NEXIS, DIALOG Information Services, VU/TEXT Information Services, the Washington Post Online, LEGI-SLATE, FT PROFILE, DataTimes, Burrelle's Information Search Service, BASELINE, BLS (U.S. Bureau of Labor Statistics), Washington Alert Service, CompuServe Information Service, Datacall, D.C. Docket, Dow Jones News/Retrieval, FEC Journal of Election Administration, MEDLINE, Info Globe, Lusknet, Maryland Legislature Online, Virginia Legislature Online, PACERS, Presidential CampaignHotline, Spybase, UMI, Periscope Daily News Capsule, Reuters. **Remarks:** FAX: (202)334-5575. **Staff:** Kathy Foley, Dp.Dir.; Margot Williams, Chf. of Res.; Sandy Davis, Post Haste Prod.Chf.; Kim Klein, Photo.Chf.; Rich Ploch, Online Ed.Chf.

Washington Press Club Archives
See: **National Press Club** (11253)

★ 20021 ★
Washington Psychoanalytic Society - Hadley Memorial Library (Med)
4925 MacArthur Blvd., N.W.   Phone: (202)338-5453
Washington, DC 20007   Joyce P. Burke
Staff: Prof 1; Other 2. **Subjects:** Psychoanalysis, psychiatry, psychology. **Holdings:** 3200 books; 950 bound periodical volumes; 1200 unbound journals. **Subscriptions:** 50 journals and other serials. **Services:** Interlibrary loan; copying; library open to professionals in psychoanalysis, psychiatry, and psychology and students in allied disciplines.

★ 20022 ★
Washington Public Power Supply System - Library (Energy)
3000 George Washington Way
Box 968   Phone: (509)372-5120
Richland, WA 99352   Betty J. Hodges, Lib.Spec.
Staff: 2. **Subjects:** Engineering standards, nuclear power, power transmission. **Holdings:** 9100 books; 3800 standards; 3700 reports. **Subscriptions:** 167 journals and other serials. **Services:** Interlibrary loan; copying; library open to the public with restrictions. **Remarks:** FAX: (509)372-5328.

★ 20023 ★
Washington Service Bureau, Inc. - Library (Bus-Fin)
655 15th St., N.W.   Phone: (202)833-9200
Washington, DC 20005   Peggy Marsilii, Sr.Mng.Ed.
Founded: 1967. **Subjects:** Securities, banking, labor, energy, legislature, courts, federal government. **Holdings:** Security and Exchange Commission (SEC) No-Action letters (1971 to present); SEC filings (1979 to present); Dept. of Labor, Pension Benefit Guaranty Coop. opinion letters (1974 to present). **Services:** Copying; library open to the public on fee basis. **Computerized Information Services:** SEC filing (internal database). Contact Person: Linda George, Mgr. SEC Serv. **Publications:** Daily Acquisition Report. **Special Indexes:** SEC No-Action Letters Index and Summaries. **Remarks:** FAX: (202)659-3655.

Washington Star Library
See: District of Columbia Public Library - Washingtoniana Division
(4916)

★ 20024 ★
Washington State Attorney General's Library (Law)
Highways-Licenses Bldg., 7th Fl.   Phone: (206)753-2681
Olympia, WA 98504   Phillip G. Bunker, Law Libn.
Staff: Prof 1. **Subjects:** Law, consumer protection, crime prevention. **Special Collections:** Attorney General's formal opinions with card index; Northwest Indian Law. **Holdings:** 25,000 books; 1620 bound periodical volumes; 150 boxes of Washington State Supreme Court briefs. **Subscriptions:** 25 journals and other serials; 12 newspapers. **Services:** Interlibrary loan; library not open to the public. **Computerized Information Services:** WESTLAW; Legislative Information System. **Publications:** A.G. Reports; consumer brochures. **Remarks:** FAX: (206)753-3490. Offices also maintained in Seattle, Spokane, Tacoma, and Lacey. Figures include holdings for all locations. **Staff:** Jane B. Halligan, Lib.Mgr.

★ 20025 ★
Washington State Department of Ecology - Library Services (Env-Cons)
PO Box 47600   Phone: (206)459-6150
Olympia, WA 98504-7600   Barbara Colquhoun, Tech.Libn.
Founded: 1970. **Staff:** Prof 2; Other 2. **Subjects:** Water resources and quality, air quality, solid waste, environmental legislation, waste treatment, shorelines management, hazardous waste cleanup. **Special Collections:** Radioactive waste (600 items); publications of department and predecessor agencies. **Holdings:** 10,000 books; 12,000 other cataloged items. **Subscriptions:** 700 journals and other serials; 100 newspapers. **Services:** Interlibrary loan; copying; library open to the public. **Automated Operations:** Computerized public access catalog, cataloging, and serials. **Computerized Information Services:** DIALOG Information Services, Chemical Information Systems, Inc. (CIS), LEGI-SLATE, WESTLAW. **Networks/Consortia:** Member of Western Library Network (WLN). **Publications:** Selected New Additions to Ecology Library, bimonthly - for internal distribution only. **Remarks:** FAX: (206)459-6007. This library is a branch of the Washington State Library. **Staff:** Ann Bennett; Judy Hanson; Linda Thompson.

★ 20026 ★
Washington State Department of Natural Resources - Division of Geology and Earth Resources - Library (Sci-Engr)
Bldg. One, Rowe 6
4224 6th Ave., S.E.   Phone: (206)459-6373
Lacey, WA 98503   Connie J. Manson, Sr.Libn.
Founded: 1935. **Staff:** Prof 1; Other 1. **Subjects:** Geology, mining, mineral resources. **Holdings:** 16,000 volumes; 40,000 state and federal documents; 1000 technical reports; 1400 theses; 1400 U.S. Geological Survey topographic quadrangles of Washington; 1500 maps; vertical files. **Subscriptions:** 100 journals and other serials. **Services:** Copying; library open to the public for reference use only. **Computerized Information Services:** Bibliographic Information System (BIS; full bibliography of Washington geology and mineral resources, 1814-1991; internal database). Performs searches on fee basis. **Publications:** List of publications - available on request. **Remarks:** FAX: (206)459-6380.

★ 20027 ★
Washington State Department of Natural Resources - Public Land Survey Office (Geog-Map)
1102 S. Quince St.
Mail Stop EV-11   Phone: (206)753-5337
Olympia, WA 98504   Donnell R. Fitch, Unit Supv./Surveyor
Founded: 1951. **Staff:** Prof 5; Other 1. **Subjects:** Cadastral and geodetic survey information. **Special Collections:** Survey information files. **Holdings:** 200,000 aperture cards of survey maps; 300 reels of microfilm of original government survey notes; 2000 field books from private surveyors. **Services:** Copying; office open to the public for a fee. **Remarks:** FAX: (206)586-5456. **Staff:** Gary Herrick, Asst.Mgr./Surveyor; Ken Brown, Survey Techn.; Ted Smith, Survey Techn.; Jan Phillips, Survey Techn.

★ 20028 ★
Washington State Department of Revenue - Research Section (Bus-Fin, Info Sci)
General Administration Bldg. AX-02   Phone: (206)753-5542
Olympia, WA 98504   Dick Gebhart, Tex.Res.Chf.
Founded: 1960. **Staff:** 13. **Subjects:** Washington state and local government taxation and public finance, analysis of tax legislation, dissemination of statistical tax information. **Holdings:** Data series are maintained including collections and other statistics for state and local tax sources; publications and federal reports containing data on collections, activity levels, and public finance.

★ 20029 ★
Washington State Department of Trade and Economic Development - Tourism Development Division (Rec)
101 General Administration Bldg., AX-13   Phone: (206)753-5600
Olympia, WA 98504-0613   John Savich, Dir.
Founded: 1957. **Subjects:** Promotional material on Washington State. **Holdings:** Maps and brochures. **Services:** Materials are available for promotional use.

★ 20030 ★
Washington State Department of Transportation - Library (Trans, Plan)
Transportation Bldg., KF-01   Phone: (206)753-2107
Olympia, WA 98504-5201   Barbara Russo, Libn.
Founded: 1968. **Staff:** Prof 1; Other 2. **Subjects:** Transportation administration; highway transportation; public transit including the world's largest ferry system; rail and air transportation in the areas of planning, design, construction, maintenance, operations, and safety. **Special Collections:** Comprehensive plans for cities and counties of Washington. **Holdings:** 3000 books; 7555 reports; 1000 microfiche; 880 comprehensive plans. **Subscriptions:** 300 journals and other serials. **Services:** Interlibrary loan; copying; library open to the public for reference use only. **Automated Operations:** Computerized serials and circulation. **Computerized Information Services:** DIALOG Information Services, LEGI-SLATE, OCLC, PRISM, TOXNET, OCLC EPIC; AASHTA, OnTyme Electronic Message Network Service (electronic mail services). **Networks/Consortia:** Member of Western Library Network (WLN). **Publications:** Monthly accessions list - for internal distribution only. **Remarks:** FAX: (206)753-6218. Library is a branch of the Washington State Library. A branch collection of the library is maintained at the Department's Materials Laboratory. **Staff:** Vincent Kueter, Libn.

★ 20031 ★
Washington State Department of Veterans Affairs - Staff & Member Library (Med)
Washington Veterans' Home
P.O. Box 698
Retsil, WA 98378   Phone: (206)895-4700
Founded: 1975. **Staff:** 4. **Subjects:** Geriatric medicine and nursing, long term care, autism, mental retardation, child welfare and abuse, gerontology. **Special Collections:** Aging (45 volumes); autism (38 volumes); mental retardation (35 volumes). **Holdings:** 5200 books; 2000 large print books. **Subscriptions:** 100 journals and other serials. **Services:** Interlibrary loan; library open to the public with restrictions on circulation. **Remarks:** The library is a part of the Washington State Library's Institution Library Services section.

★ 20032 ★
Washington State Energy Office - Library (Energy)
809 Legion Way, S.E. FA-11   Phone: (206)956-2000
Olympia, WA 98504-1211   Gretchen K. Leslie, Sr.Libn.
Founded: 1978. **Staff:** Prof 1; Other 2. **Subjects:** Energy conservation, resources, and planning; alternative sources of energy. **Holdings:** 3000 monographs; 7000 reports and documents. **Subscriptions:** 300 journals and other serials. **Services:** Interlibrary loan; copying; SDI (for state agencies); library open to the public. **Automated Operations:** Computerized cataloging, serials, and circulation. **Computerized Information Services:** DIALOG Information Services, WILSONLINE; OnTyme Electronic Message Network Service (electronic mail service). Performs searches free of charge. **Networks/Consortia:** Member of Western Library Network (WLN). **Publications:** Washington State Energy Use Profile, 1960-1986; WSEO Dispatch (newsletter); Energy Access (newsletter); fact sheets and technical notes on residential, commercial, and agricultural energy conservation; film list. **Remarks:** Alternate telephone number(s): 586-5000. FAX: (206)753-2397.

★ 20033 ★

Washington State Historical Society - Special Collections (Hist)
315 N. Stadium Way
Tacoma, WA 98403
Phone: (206)593-2830
Edward W. Nolan, Cur. of Spec.Coll.
Founded: 1940. **Staff:** 2.5. **Subjects:** Washington State history, Pacific Northwest history. **Special Collections:** Asahel Curtis Negative Collection. **Holdings:** 12,000 books; 250,000 pictures; 4000 manuscripts; 3000 pamphlets; 1017 reels of microfilm. **Subscriptions:** 20 journals and other serials. **Services:** Copying (limited); research by mail (limited); library open to the public by appointment. **Remarks:** FAX: (206)597-4186. **Staff:** Elaine Miller, Asst., Photo.; Joy Werlink, Asst., Mss.

★ 20034 ★

Washington State Law Library (Law)
Temple of Justice, AV-02
P.O. Box 40751
Olympia, WA 98504-0751
Phone: (206)357-2136
Deborah Norwood, Dir.
Founded: 1907. **Staff:** Prof 5; Other 11. **Subjects:** Anglo-American law, government, jurisprudence. **Holdings:** 300,000 books; 45 volumes of State of Washington county maps; 3700 volumes of appellate briefs. **Subscriptions:** 1010 journals; 17 newspapers. **Services:** Interlibrary loan; copying; library open to the public. **Automated Operations:** Computerized cataloging, acquisitions, and serials. **Computerized Information Services:** DIALOG Information Services, WESTLAW, Washington State Legislative Service Center. Performs searches on an individual basis as necessary. Contact Person: Arthur J. Ruffier, Ref. **Networks/Consortia:** Member of Western Library Network (WLN). **Publications:** Washington State legal documents - by exchange; Books Recently Cataloged list, quarterly - free upon request. **Remarks:** FAX: (206)357-2143. **Staff:** James Tsao, Chf. of Tech.Serv.; Cora Morley Eklund, Cat.; Dawn Kendrick, Govt.Docs.

★ 20035 ★

Washington State Library (Info Sci)
PO Box 42460
Olympia, WA 98504-2460
Phone: (206)753-5590
Nancy Zussy, State Libn.
Founded: 1853. **Staff:** Prof 58; Other 70. **Subjects:** Public administration, applied sciences, medicine and health, behavioral sciences, transportation, ecology, energy. **Special Collections:** Pacific Northwest History (13,906 items); Washington authors (13,247 items). **Holdings:** 409,988 books; 75,750 bound periodical volumes; 1.56 million U.S. documents; 117,297 Washington state documents; 20,534 other state documents; 42,734 reels of microfilm; 483,069 microfiche; 26 VF drawers; 8744 AV titles, including 16mm films. **Subscriptions:** 7550 journals and other serials; 160 newspapers. **Services:** Interlibrary loan; copying; library open to the public. **Automated Operations:** Computerized cataloging, acquisitions, circulation, and interlibrary loan search. **Computerized Information Services:** DIALOG Information Services, MEDLARS, WILSONLINE, LEGISNET, Chemical Information Systems, Inc. (CIS), LEGI-SLATE, OCLC; ALANET (electronic mail service). **Networks/Consortia:** Member of Western Library Network (WLN), Research Libraries Information Network (RLIN). **Publications:** List of publications - available on request. **Special Catalogs:** Periodicals Holdings (microfiche). **Remarks:** Alternate telephone number(s): (206)753-5592. FAX: (206)586-7575; (206)753-3546 (ILL). Electronic mail address(es): WSLADMIN ALA0719 (ALANET). **Staff:** David G. Remington, Dp. State Libn.; Mary Moore, Chf., Lib.Plan. & Dev.Div.; Kristy Coomes, Chf., Pub.Serv.Div.; Rosemary Shold, Chf., Tech.Serv.Div.; Debra Crumb, Chf., Instr.Lib.Serv.Div.

★ 20036 ★

Washington State Library - Eastern State Hospital Library (Med)
Box A
Medical Lake, WA 99022
Phone: (509)299-4276
Nancy White, Libn.
Founded: 1968. **Staff:** Prof 1; Other 1. **Subjects:** Psychiatry, nursing, medicine, mental health, social work. **Holdings:** 2283 books; 3 VF drawers. **Subscriptions:** 66 journals and other serials. **Services:** Interlibrary loan; copying; library open to the public. **Computerized Information Services:** DIALOG Information Services. **Networks/Consortia:** Member of Western Library Network (WLN), Inland Northwest Health Sciences Libraries (INWHSL). **Remarks:** FAX: (509)299-4555.

★ 20037 ★

Washington State Library - Lakeland Village Branch Library (Med)
Box 200 B32-25
Medical Lake, WA 99022-0200
Phone: (509)299-5089
Nancy P. White, Libn.
Founded: 1968. **Staff:** Prof 1; Other 1. **Subjects:** Mental retardation, medicine. **Holdings:** 1698 books; back issues of unbound journals (latest 5 years). **Subscriptions:** 66 journals and other serials. **Services:** Interlibrary loan; copying; library open to the public. **Networks/Consortia:** Member of Western Library Network (WLN). **Remarks:** FAX: (209)299-5089.

★ 20038 ★

Washington State Library - Rainier School Branch Library (Med)
Box 600
Buckley, WA 98321
Phone: (206)829-1111
Lynn Red, Module Supv.
Founded: 1965. **Staff:** Prof 1; Other 2. **Subjects:** Mental retardation, developmental psychology, institutionalization, deaf/blind/retarded handicapped. **Holdings:** 3000 books; 1596 bound and unbound periodical volumes; 100 boxes of pamphlets; 15 boxes of periodical, book, and film catalogs in the field of retardation. **Subscriptions:** 163 journals and other serials. **Services:** Interlibrary loan; copying (limited); SDI; library open to state employees. **Computerized Information Services:** DIALOG Information Services. **Networks/Consortia:** Member of Western Library Network (WLN). **Publications:** Bibliographies, irregular. **Remarks:** FAX: (206)829-3008.

★ 20039 ★

Washington State Library - Washington Utilities & Transportation Commission - Library (Trans)
1300 Evergreen Park Dr., S.W., FY-11
Olympia, WA 98504
Phone: (206)586-0900
Mary Lu White, Libn.
Staff: Prof 1; Other 1. **Subjects:** Utilities regulation - electric, gas, water, telecommunications; transportation regulation; regulatory policies and procedures; microeconomics. **Holdings:** 1550 books; 1800 technical reports. **Subscriptions:** 350 journals and other serials. **Services:** Interlibrary loan; copying; library open to the public with restrictions. **Automated Operations:** Computerized serials. **Computerized Information Services:** DIALOG Information Services, LEXIS, NEXIS, WESTLAW; internal database; OnTyme Electronic Message Network Service, Galacticomm (electronic mail services). **Networks/Consortia:** Member of Western Library Network (WLN). **Remarks:** FAX: (206)586-1150. Electronic mail address(es): WAUTC (OnTyme Electronic Message Network Service).

★ 20040 ★

Washington State Library - Western State Hospital Branch Library (Med)
Fort Steilacoom, WA 98494
Phone: (206)756-2715
Neal Van Der Voorn, Libn.
Founded: 1956. **Staff:** Prof 2; Other 2. **Subjects:** Psychiatry, clinical psychology, mental health, psychiatric nursing, psychiatric social work, medicine, occupational therapy, recreational therapy. **Holdings:** 4500 books; 375 tapes. **Subscriptions:** 154 journals and other serials. **Services:** Interlibrary loan; copying; library open to the public if material is not available elsewhere. **Computerized Information Services:** DIALOG Information Services; WLN. **Networks/Consortia:** Member of Western Library Network (WLN). **Publications:** In Touch, monthly - to hospital staff and residents. **Remarks:** FAX: (206)756-2668. Residents' library contains an additional 11,000 volumes. **Staff:** Velta Ashbrook

★ 20041 ★

Washington State Office of Secretary of State - Division of Archives and Record Management (Hist)
Archives & Records Center
12th & Washington
Olympia, WA 98504
Phone: (206)753-5485
Sidney McAlpin, State Archv.
Founded: 1909. **Staff:** Prof 12; Other 12. **Subjects:** State and local government records. **Special Collections:** Governors' Papers, 1854-1980; land records, 1858 to present; election returns; incorporation records, 1854 to present; Supreme Court records, 1854 to present; water rights, 1917 to present; legislative records, 1854 to present; state agency records, 1900 to present. **Holdings:** 8000 bound public records; 50,000 cubic feet of state and local archives; 165,000 cubic feet of records; 180,000 reels of security microfilm. **Services:** Copying; research; division open to the public. **Automated Operations:** Computerized cataloging. **Computerized Information Services:** Gencat Archival Control System (internal database). **Publications:** General Guide to the Washington State Archives; list of other publications - available on request. **Remarks:** FAX: (206)586-9137. Territorial District Court records and other county records are held at five regional depositories operated by the division. **Staff:** David Owens, Dp. State Archv.; Eva Hartley, Rec.Mgt.; Everett Evans, Microfilm Supv.; Wayne Lawson, Reg.Archv.; David Hastings, Chf., Archv.Serv.Sect.; Pat Hopkins, Res.Archv.; James Moore, Reg.Archv.; Tim Eckert, Reg.Archv.; Richard Hobbs, Reg.Archv.; Mike Saunders, Reg.Archv.; Michael Betz, Docs.Cons.

★ 20042 ★
Washington State School for the Deaf - McGill Library (Educ)
611 Grand Blvd.   Phone: (206)696-6113
Vancouver, WA 98661-4918   Ray Ayala, Dir.
Staff: Prof 1; Other 3. **Subjects:** Elementary and secondary education.
Special Collections: Education for the deaf (professional books; 500 titles).
Holdings: 10,672 books; VF drawers; 226 videotapes; 2943 filmstrips; 545
film loops; 369 study prints; 250 microfiche; 44 charts. **Subscriptions:** 89
journals and other serials. **Services:** Interlibrary loan; copying; library open
to the public with restrictions. **Networks/Consortia:** Member of Western
Library Network (WLN). **Remarks:** Library is a part of the Learning
Resource Center, FAX: (206)6966113. **Staff:** Wanda Forcht, Hd.Libn.

★ 20043 ★
Washington State Superintendent of Public Instruction - Educational
  Materials Center (Educ)
PO Box 47200   Phone: (206)753-6731
Olympia, WA 98504-7200   Mrs. Bobbie J. Patterson, Coord.
Founded: 1950. **Staff:** Prof 1. **Subjects:** Education, curriculum materials.
Special Collections: Excellence in education materials; Phi Delta Kappan
Collection. **Holdings:** 200 books; complete ERIC microfiche collections.
Subscriptions: 400 journals and other serials; 5 newspapers. **Services:**
Interlibrary loan (limited); center not open to the public. **Computerized**
Information Services: CD-ROM (ERIC). **Networks/Consortia:** Member of
Western Library Network (WLN). **Publications:** Curriculum guides.

★ 20044 ★
Washington State University - George B. Brain Education Library
  (Educ)
130 Cleveland Hall   Phone: (509)335-1591
Pullman, WA 99164-2112   Ralph Lowenthal, Ref./Coll.Dev.Libn.
Staff: Prof 2; Other 2. **Subjects:** Education. **Holdings:** 43,028 books, juvenile
books, and textbooks; 12,493 bound periodical volumes; 21 cabinets of ERIC
microfiche; 5 cabinets of journals on microfilm; 4 VF cabinets; 3 cabinets of
monographs on microfilm; 9 VF cabinets of tests; 878 masters' projects; 801
kits and records. **Subscriptions:** 800 journals and other serials. **Services:**
Interlibrary loan (fee); copying; SDI; library open to the public by
registration and library card. **Automated Operations:** Computerized
cataloging, acquisitions, circulation, and public access catalog.
Computerized Information Services: DIALOG Information Services, BRS
Information Technologies; CD-ROM (ERIC); internal database; BITNET
(electronic mail service). Performs searches on fee basis. **Networks/**
Consortia: Member of Western Library Network (WLN). **Publications:** List
of recent acquisitions, monthly. **Remarks:** FAX: (509)335-9172. Electronic
mail address(es): LOWENTHA@WSUVM1 (BITNET). **Staff:** Linda
Snook, Supv.; Leslie Liddle-Stamper, Lib.Tech.

Washington State University - Intercollegiate Center for Nursing
  Education
See: Intercollegiate Center for Nursing Education (8033)

★ 20045 ★
Washington State University - Manuscripts, Archives, & Special
  Collections (Hist, Hum)
Pullman, WA 99164-5610   Phone: (509)335-6272
                                         John F. Guido, Hd.
Founded: 1890. **Staff:** Prof 5; Other 5. **Subjects:** History - Pacific Northwest,
agriculture, veterinary medicine; 20th century British literature; wildlife and
outdoor recreation; ethnic history. **Special Collections:** Leonard and
Virginia Woolf Library; Bloomsbury authors; Pacific Northwest
Agricultural History Archives; Veterinary History; Pacific Northwest
Publishers' Archives; 20th Century Music Archives; Angling; Germans
from Russia; Nez Perce (Indian) Music Archives; Small Presses; regional
presses; University archives. **Holdings:** 20,000 volumes; manuscripts;
photographs; audiotapes; maps; broadsides; theses and dissertations.
Services: Copying. **Computerized Information Services:** RLIN; BITNET
(electronic mail service). **Networks/Consortia:** Member of Western Library
Network (WLN). **Publications:** The Record (newsletter). **Remarks:** FAX:
(509)335-0934. **Staff:** Laila Vejzovic, Rare Bks./Spec.Coll.; Tina Oswald,
Mss.; Carol Lichtenberg, Hist.Photo./Vis.Archv.; Lawrence Stark,
Asst.Archv.

★ 20046 ★
Washington State University - Marion Ownbey Herbarium - Library
  (Biol Sci)
Pullman, WA 99164-4309   Phone: (509)335-3250
                                         Joseph E. Laferriere, Act.Dir.
Founded: 1890. **Staff:** Prof 2; Other 1. **Subjects:** Plants of the Northwest,
flora of the U.S. **Holdings:** 1000 books; 3000 bound periodical volumes;
300,000 pressed plant specimens. **Services:** Library open to the public.
Remarks: FAX: (509)335-3517.

★ 20047 ★
Washington State University - Owen Science and Engineering Library
  (Sci-Engr, Biol Sci)
Pullman, WA 99164-3200   Phone: (509)335-4181
                                         Darlene Myers Hildebrandt, Hd.
Founded: 1892. **Staff:** Prof 8; Other 16. **Subjects:** Pure and applied sciences
with special emphasis on computer science, engineering, biological sciences,
chemistry, biochemistry, mathematics, and physical science. **Special**
Collections: Mathematics. **Holdings:** 473,400 volumes; 41 cabinets of
microfilm; 75 cabinets of microfiche; 5 cabinets of microcards.
Subscriptions: 6069 journals and other serials. **Services:** Interlibrary loan;
copying; library open to the public. **Automated Operations:** Computerized
cataloging, acquisitions and circulation. **Computerized Information**
Services: DIALOG Information Services, BRS Information Technologies,
MEDLARS, Chemical Abstracts Service (CAS), BIOSIS Connection,
WILSONLINE; BITNET (electronic mail service). Performs searches on a
cost-recovery basis. **Networks/Consortia:** Member of Western Library
Network (WLN), Center for Research Libraries (CRL), CLASS.
Publications: Palouse Bibliography. **Special Indexes:** Index of Selected
Publications of the WSU College of Agriculture, 1970-1982; Abstracts and
Indexes Section Index; Atlas Index; Biographical Index; Environmental
Impact Statement Index; National Library of Medicine and National
Agriculture Library KWIC Bibliography Index. **Remarks:** FAX: (509)335-
2534. Electronic mail address(es): OWEN@WSUVM1 (BITNET). **Staff:**
Eileen Brady; Elaine Brekke; Janet Chisman; Rita Fisher; Cindy Kaag;
Marilyn Von Seggern.

★ 20048 ★
Washington State University - Owen Science and Engineering Library -
  George W. Fischer Agricultural Sciences Branch Library (Biol Sci,
  Agri)
C-2 Johnson Annex   Phone: (509)335-2266
Pullman, WA 99164-7150   Betty Bienz, Supv.
Founded: 1975. **Staff:** 2. **Subjects:** Plant pathology, agronomy and soils,
horticulture, landscape architecture and regional planning, forestry and
range management, entomology, mycology. **Special Collections:** Plant
pathology reprints (1560 volumes); professional and senior student projects
(360 volumes). **Holdings:** 22,000 volumes; 114 reels of microfilm; 932
microfiche; 430 VF items. **Subscriptions:** 461 journals and other serials.
Services: Interlibrary loan; copying; library open to the public. **Automated**
Operations: Computerized public access catalog and circulation.
Computerized Information Services: Online systems, AGRICOLA;
BITNET (electronic mail service). **Networks/Consortia:** Member of Center
for Research Libraries (CRL), CLASS, Western Library Network (WLN).
Remarks: FAX: (509)335-2534. Electronic mail address(es):
OWEN@WSUVM1 (BITNET).

★ 20049 ★
Washington State University - Tri Cities - Library (Bus-Fin, Sci-Engr,
  Educ)
100 Sprout Rd.   Phone: (509)375-9204
Richland, WA 99352   Harvey Gover, Lib.Dir.
Staff: Prof 1; Other 1. **Subjects:** Business, science, technology, education,
nursing. **Holdings:** 20,000 volumes. **Subscriptions:** 300 journals and other
serials. **Services:** Interlibrary loan; copying; library open to the public.
Computerized Information Services: DIALOG Information Services;
OnTyme Electronic Message Network Service (electronic mail service).
Performs searches on fee basis. **Networks/Consortia:** Member of Western
Library Network (WLN). **Remarks:** FAX: (509)375-5337. Electronic mail
address(es): class.jcgsl (OnTyme).

★ 20050 ★
Washington State University - Veterinary Medical/Pharmacy Library
(Med)
170 Wegner Hall   Phone: (509)335-9556
Pullman, WA 99164-6512   Vicki F. Croft, Hd.
Founded: 1963. **Staff:** Prof 2; Other 2.5. **Subjects:** Veterinary and human medicine, pharmacy and pharmacology. **Holdings:** 22,900 books; 33,500 bound periodical volumes. **Subscriptions:** 860 journals and other serials. **Services:** Interlibrary loan; copying; library open to the public. **Automated Operations:** Computerized cataloging, acquisitions, serials, and circulation. **Computerized Information Services:** DIALOG Information Services, Chemical Abstracts Service (CAS), BRS Information Technologies, NLM; WSU Online Catalog (internal database); CD-ROM (MEDLINE); OnTyme Electronic Message Network Service, BITNET, InterNet (electronic mail services). Performs searches on fee basis. **Networks/Consortia:** Member of Western Library Network (WLN), CLASS, Inland Northwest Health Sciences Libraries (INWHSL). **Remarks:** FAX: (509)335-5158. Electronic mail address(es): VPL@WSUVM1 (BITNET). **Staff:** Joan Campbell, Lib.Supv.; Mary Ann Hughes, Ref.Libn.

★ 20051 ★
Washington State Water Research Center - Library (Env-Cons)
Washington State Univ.   Phone: (509)335-5531
Pullman, WA 99164-3002   Diane L. Weber
Founded: 1964. **Subjects:** Water, Pacific Northwest. **Special Collections:** Pacific Northwest River Basin Commission Library. **Holdings:** 10,000 books. **Subscriptions:** 60 journals and other serials. **Services:** Copying; library open to the public for reference use only.

★ 20052 ★
Washington Theological Union - Library (Rel-Phil)
9001 New Hampshire Ave.   Phone: (301)439-0551
Silver Spring, MD 20903-3699   Dr. John S. Hanson, Libn.
Founded: 1968. **Staff:** Prof 1; Other 2. **Subjects:** Religion. **Special Collections:** Franciscana; Carmelitana; Augustiniana. **Holdings:** 40,000 volumes. **Subscriptions:** 330 journals and other serials. **Services:** Interlibrary loan; copying. **Computerized Information Services:** CD-ROM (Religion Index). **Networks/Consortia:** Member of Washington Theological Consortium. **Publications:** Consortium Guide to Library Resources, updated as needed. **Remarks:** FAX: (301)445-4929.

★ 20053 ★
The Washington Times - Library (Publ)
3600 New York Ave. NE   Phone: (202)636-3000
Washington, DC 20002   Joseph Szadkowski
Founded: 1982. **Staff:** Prof 14. **Subjects:** News - national, world. **Holdings:** 200 books; 2000 microfiche; 800 reels of microfilm; photograph library. **Subscriptions:** 68 journals and other serials; 4 journals and other serials. **Services:** Copying; library open to media and schools. **Computerized Information Services:** VU/TEXT Information Services, DataTimes, NEXIS, LEXIS, DIALOG Information Services, NewsNet, Inc., Federal Election Commission; Personal Librarian (internal database). Contact Person: John Haydon, Res.Libn.

★ 20054 ★
Washington Township Historical Society - Library (Hist)
6 Fairview Ave.
P.O. Box 189   Phone: (201)876-9696
Long Valley, NJ 07853   Dorothy Branney, Pres.
Subjects: Washington Township, genealogy. **Holdings:** Figures not available. **Services:** Library open to the public for reference use only.

★ 20055 ★
Washington University - Art & Architecture Library (Plan, Art)
Steinberg Hall
Campus Box 1061
St. Louis, MO 63130   Phone: (314)935-5268
                                  Dana Beth
Founded: 1879. **Staff:** Prof 1; Other 3. **Subjects:** Art history, classical archeology, architecture, costume design, fine art techniques, East Asian art, building technology, urban planning and design, landscape architecture. **Special Collections:** Bryce Collection (architectural history; 576 volumes); Sorger Collection (historical costume; 243 volumes; 2 VF drawers of plates); Eames and Young Collection (architectural history; 273 volumes); rare

books (2471 volumes). **Holdings:** 73,867 volumes; 52 VF drawers of pamphlets and clippings; 1307 microfiche; 245 microfilm. **Subscriptions:** 380 journals and other serials. **Services:** Interlibrary loan; library open to the public for reference use only. **Automated Operations:** Computerized cataloging. **Computerized Information Services:** BRS Information Technologies, DIALOG Information Services, WILSONLINE, RLIN; BITNET; InterNet (electronic mail services). **Networks/Consortia:** Member of Missouri Library Network Corp. (MLNC), St. Louis Regional Library Network, Center for Research Libraries (CRL). **Special Catalogs:** Washington University Art and Architecture Library List of Serials. **Remarks:** FAX: (314)935-4045. Electronic mail address(es): ARTARCH@WULIBS (BITNET); ARTARCH@WULIBS.WUSTL.EDU (InterNet).

★ 20056 ★
Washington University - Biology Library (Biol Sci)
Campus Box 1061   Phone: (314)935-5405
St. Louis, MO 63130   Ruth Lewis, Libn.
Staff: Prof 1; Other 1.5. **Subjects:** Genetics, mycology, embryology, neurosciences, molecular biology, botany. **Holdings:** 52,255 books; 2982 microfiche. **Subscriptions:** 509 journals and other serials. **Services:** Interlibrary loan; copying; library open to the public. **Automated Operations:** Computerized cataloging. **Computerized Information Services:** MEDLINE, DIALOG Information Services, BRS Information Technologies; BITNET, InterNet (electronic mail services). **Networks/Consortia:** Member of Missouri Library Network Corp. (MLNC), St. Louis Regional Library Network, Center for Research Libraries (CRL). **Publications:** Monthly acquisitions list - to other libraries. **Remarks:** FAX: (314)935-4046. Electronic mail address(es): RUTHL@WULIBS (BITNET); RUTHL@WULIBS.WUSTL.EDU (InterNet).

★ 20057 ★
Washington University - Center for Air Pollution Impact and Trend Analysis - Library (Env-Cons)
Campus Box 1124   Phone: (314)935-6099
St. Louis, MO 63130   Dr. Janja Husar
Staff: 4. **Subjects:** Air pollution. **Holdings:** 1000 reports. **Subscriptions:** 10 journals and other serials; 2 newspapers. **Remarks:** FAX: (314)935-6145.

Washington University - Center for the Study of Data Processing
See: **Washington University - School of Technology and Information Management - STIM/CSDP Library (20072)**

★ 20058 ★
Washington University - Chemistry Library (Sci-Engr)
Louderman Hall   Phone: (314)935-6591
St. Louis, MO 63130   Robert McFarland, Chem.Libn.
Founded: 1905. **Staff:** Prof 1; Other 1. **Subjects:** Chemistry - organic, inorganic, physical, biophysical; nuclear chemistry. **Holdings:** 32,653 volumes; 327 theses; 804 microfiche. **Subscriptions:** 401 journals and other serials. **Services:** Interlibrary loan; copying; document delivery; library open to the public with restrictions. **Computerized Information Services:** DIALOG Information Services, MEDLINE, Chemical Abstracts Service (CAS), STN International; BITNET, InterNet (electronic mail services). Performs searches on fee basis. **Networks/Consortia:** Member of Missouri Library Network Corp. (MLNC), St. Louis Regional Library Network, Center for Research Libraries (CRL). **Remarks:** FAX: (314)935-4778. Electronic mail address(es): ROBMCF@WULIBS (BITNET); ROBMCF@WULIBS.WUSTL.EDU (InterNet).

★ 20059 ★
Washington University - Department of Special Collections (Rare Book, Hum)
Olin Library
1 Brookings Dr., Campus Box 1061 Phone: (314)935-5495
St. Louis, MO 63130   Holly Hall, Hd.
Founded: 1962. **Staff:** Prof 4; Other 1. **Subjects:** 19th and 20th century English and American literature; history of printing and book arts; semeiology; Western Americana; St. Louis political and social welfare history; 16th century French literature, especially Pierre de Ronsard. **Special Collections:** Contemporary American and British writers; distinguished faculty and alumni papers; university records. **Holdings:** 41,289 volumes; 5000 ephemera; 199,385 manuscript items; 5244 linear feet

of archival records. **Subscriptions:** 35 journals and other serials. **Services:** Copying; collections open to the public with restrictions. **Automated Operations:** Computerized cataloging. **Computerized Information Services:** BITNET, InterNet (electronic mail services). **Special Catalogs:** Occasional exhibit catalogs; special subject area catalogs (card); A Guide to the Modern Literary Manuscripts Collections, 1985; The Samuel Beckett Collection, 1986. **Special Indexes:** Manuscript index (card); registers and special finding aids to manuscript collections and archives. **Remarks:** Alternate telephone number(s): (314)935-5444. FAX: (314)935-4045. Electronic mail address(es): SPEC@WULIBS (BITNET); SPEC@WULIBS.WUSTL.EDU (InterNet). **Staff:** Kevin Ray, Cur., Mss.; Carole Prietto, Archv.; Cinda May, Rare Bks.Cat.

★ 20060 ★
Washington University - Earth and Planetary Sciences Library (Sci-Engr)
Wilson Hall   Phone: (314)935-5406
St. Louis, MO 63130   Clara McLeod, Libn.
Founded: 1925. **Staff:** Prof 1; Other 1. **Subjects:** Geology, geophysics, geochemistry, mineralogy, geomorphology, petrology, sedimentation, structural geology, paleontology, planetary geology, remote sensing. **Special Collections:** State Geological Survey Publications; U.S. Geological Survey and Defense Mapping Agency map depository. **Holdings:** 30,098 volumes; 10,234 documents; 446 pamphlets; 95,900 maps; 6 reels of microfilm; 2012 microfiche. **Subscriptions:** 277 journals and other serials. **Services:** Interlibrary loan; copying; library open to qualified users for reference. **Automated Operations:** Computerized public access catalog and map catalog. **Computerized Information Services:** PFDS Online, DIALOG Information Services, Chemical Abstracts Service (CAS), STN International; CD-ROMs; BITNET, InterNet (electronic mail services). **Networks/Consortia:** Member of Missouri Library Network Corp. (MLNC), St. Louis Regional Library Network, Center for Research Libraries (CRL). **Publications:** Monthly acquisitions list. **Remarks:** FAX: (314)935-4800. Electronic mail address(es): CPMCLEOD@WULIBS (BITNET); CPMCLEOD@WULIBS.WUSTL.EDU (InterNet).

★ 20061 ★
Washington University - East Asian Library (Area-Ethnic, Hum)
Box 1061   Phone: (314)935-5155
St. Louis, MO 63130   Sachiko Morrell, Libn.
Founded: 1964. **Staff:** Prof 3. **Subjects:** East Asia - language and literature, history, philosophy and religion, art history, social science, performing arts. **Special Collections:** Rare book collection; Robert S. Elegant Collection (4 cabinets of clippings, magazines, news releases from the Chinese cultural revolution). **Holdings:** 106,150 volumes; 1316 reels of microfilm; 460 microfiche; 21 audiotapes; 6 videotapes; 1 cabinet of pamphlets; Taiwan Government documents. **Subscriptions:** 428 journals and other serials; 11 newspapers. **Services:** Interlibrary loan; copying; library open to the public. **Computerized Information Services:** OCLC, LUIS; BITNET (electronic mail service). **Networks/Consortia:** Member of Missouri Library Network Corp. (MLNC), St. Louis Regional Library Network, Center for Research Libraries (CRL). **Publications:** Guide to Library Resources for Chinese Studies, 1978; Resource Sources for Chinese and Japanese Studies, 1976; List of Serials related to Chinese and Japanese Studies, 1973; A Guide to Library Resources for Japanese Studies, 1987. **Remarks:** FAX: (314)935-4045. Electronic mail address(es): SKM@WULIBS; THC@WULIBS; SUAD@WULIBS (BITNET). **Staff:** Tony Chang, Libn.; Suad Muhammad-Gamal, Libn.

★ 20062 ★
Washington University - Gaylord Music Library (Mus)
6500 Forsyth   Phone: (314)935-5560
St. Louis, MO 63105   Susanne Bell, Mus.Libn.
Founded: 1947. **Staff:** Prof 2; Other 2. **Subjects:** Music. **Special Collections:** Sheet Music (51,000 pieces). **Holdings:** 73,675 books, bound periodical volumes, and scores; 14,122 phonograph records; 3790 audiocassettes; 1000 compact discs; 80 microfiche; 100 videotapes; 392 reels of microfilm; 716 microcards. **Subscriptions:** 536 journals and other serials. **Services:** Interlibrary loan; copying; library open to visiting scholars for research. **Computerized Information Services:** BRS Information Technologies, DIALOG Information Services; BITNET, InterNet (electronic mail services). **Networks/Consortia:** Member of Missouri Library Network Corp. (MLNC), St. Louis Regional Library Network, Center for Research Libraries (CRL). **Special Indexes:** Title index to popular sheet music collection (cards); Composer Index to vocal and piano sheet music collection (cards). **Remarks:** FAX: (314)935-4045. Electronic mail address(es): SUSI@WULIBS (BITNET); SUSI@WULIBS.WUSTL.EDU (InterNet).

★ 20063 ★
Washington University - George Warren Brown School of Social Work - Library & Learning Resources Center (Soc Sci)
Campus Box 1196   Phone: (314)935-6633
St. Louis, MO 63130   Michael E. Powell, Dir.
Staff: Prof 3; Other 1. **Subjects:** Alcoholism, women, women's issues, social work, gerontology, mental health, health, aging, gerontology, minorities, children and youth services, social and economic development, family therapy, management, special populations. **Holdings:** 40,266 volumes; 5000 government documents; 250 theses; 4122 pamphlets; 113 reels of microfilm; 9 films, filmstrips, slides; 496 videotapes; 132 audiotapes. **Subscriptions:** 665 journals and other serials; 14 newspapers. **Services:** Interlibrary loan; copying; library open to those with library cards. **Computerized Information Services:** BRS Information Technologies; CD-ROM (PsycLIT); BITNET, InterNet (electronic mail services). **Publications:** Acquisitions list, monthly; bibliographies. **Remarks:** Maintains computing facility for campus use. FAX: (314)935-8511. Electronic mail address(es): MIKEOP@WULIBS (BITNET); MIKEOP@WULIBS.WUSTL.EDU (InterNet). **Staff:** Shirley Dennis; Carol Gray.

★ 20064 ★
Washington University - Kopolow Business Library (Bus-Fin)
John M. Olin School of Business
Campus Box 1133   Phone: (314)935-6334
St. Louis, MO 63130   Ronald Allen, Dir.
Founded: 1925. **Staff:** Prof 2.5; Other 4.5. **Subjects:** Finance, management, marketing, accounting, production, operations research. **Holdings:** 28,502 books; 1001 bound periodical volumes; 1968 working papers; 334,866 annual reports on microfiche; 39,464 other microforms; 291 dissertations. **Subscriptions:** 711 journals and other serials; 13 newspapers. **Services:** Interlibrary loan; copying; library open to the public for reference use only. **Computerized Information Services:** BRS Information Technologies, DIALOG Information Services, Dow Jones News/Retrieval, NEXIS, National Automated Accounting Research System (NAARS), InfoTrac, Reuters; CD-ROMs (Business Periodicals Ondisc; Compact Disclosure, Worldscope, CD/Corporate, LaserDisclosure). Performs searches on fee basis. Contact Person: Kay Shehan, Asst.Libn., 935-6465. **Networks/Consortia:** Member of Missouri Library Network Corp. (MLNC). **Publications:** Recent Acquisitions, quarterly - available on request. **Remarks:** FAX: (314)935-6332. **Staff:** Nancy O'Connor, Circ.Serv.; Margie Craig, Budget Mgr.

★ 20065 ★
Washington University - Mathematics Library (Sci-Engr)
Campus Box 1146
1 Brookings Dr.   Phone: (314)935-5048
St. Louis, MO 63130   Barbara Luszczynska, Math.Libn.
Founded: 1979. **Staff:** Prof 1. **Subjects:** Advanced mathematics. **Holdings:** 1341 books; 4544 bound periodical volumes; 2 videotapes. **Subscriptions:** 123 journals and other serials. **Services:** Interlibrary loan; library open to the public for reference use only. **Computerized Information Services:** BRS Information Technologies, PFDS Online, DIALOG Information Services, STN International; CD-ROMs; BITNET, InterNet (electronic mail services). **Networks/Consortia:** Member of Missouri Library Network Corp. (MLNC), St. Louis Regional Library Network, Center for Research Libraries (CRL). **Remarks:** FAX: (314)935-4045. Electronic mail address(es): BARBARAL@WULIBS (BITNET); BARBARAL@WULIBS.WUSTL.EDU (InterNet).

★ 20066 ★
Washington University - Pfeiffer Physics Library (Sci-Engr)
Lindell & Skinker Blvds.   Phone: (314)935-6215
St. Louis, MO 63130   H. Sylvia Toombs, Physics Libn.
Staff: Prof 1. **Subjects:** Astrophysics, atomic and nuclear physics, solid state physics, high energy particles, low temperature physics, cosmic rays, quantum mechanics, physical electronics, plasma physics, chemical physics, mathematics, mathematical physics, electronics, electrical and communications engineering, science history, astronomy, space physics. **Holdings:** 34,869 volumes; 5 reels of microfilm; 39 microfiche. **Subscriptions:** 221 journals. **Services:** Interlibrary loan; copying; library open to the public for reference use only. **Computerized Information Services:** BRS Information Technologies, DIALOG Information Services, OCLC EPIC; BITNET, InterNet (electronic mail services). **Remarks:** FAX: (314)935-6219. Electronic mail address(es): SYLVIA@WUPHYS.WUSTL (BITNET); SYLVIA@WUPHYS.WUSTL.EDU (InterNet)

★ 20067 ★
Washington University - Regional Planetary Image Facility - Library (Sci-Engr)
Dept. of Earth & Planetary Sciences
1 Brookings Dr.
Campus Box 1169
St. Louis, MO 63130
Phone: (314)935-5679
Mary A. Dale-Bannister, Libn.
Staff: Prof 1. **Subjects:** Planetary geology, space exploration missions, remote sensing, image processing. **Special Collections:** Space mission (photographs, negatives, slides, digital tapes, videodiscs, and CD-ROMs). **Holdings:** 1500 books; 2000 digital tapes; 100 CD-ROMs; microfiche sets; complete set of U.S. Geological Survey planetary maps. **Subscriptions:** 15 journals and other serials. **Services:** Copying; library open to the public by appointment. **Computerized Information Services:** Image Retrieval and Processing System (IRPS; internal database), Planetary Data System (internal database); NASAMAIL, SprintMail, SPAN, InterNet (electronic mail services). **Remarks:** Alternate telephone number(s): (314)889-6652. FAX: (314)726-7361. Electronic mail address(es): Dale@WURST.WUSTL.EDU (InterNet).

★ 20068 ★
Washington University - School of Law - Freund Law Library (Law)
Mudd Bldg.
1 Brookings Dr.
Box 1120
St. Louis, MO 63130
Phone: (314)935-6459
Bernard D. Reams, Jr., Dir.
Staff: Prof 7; Other 11. **Subjects:** Law, taxation, urban affairs, international law. **Special Collections:** U.S. Supreme Court and Missouri Supreme Court Briefs; Ashman British Collection; Neuhoff Rare Book Collection; U.S. and Missouri documents depository. **Holdings:** 460,773 volumes; 817,358 microfiche; 54 microcards; 6827 reels of microfilm; 410 cassette tapes. **Subscriptions:** 5079 journals and other serials; 20 newspapers. **Services:** Interlibrary loan; copying; library open to the public on a limited schedule. **Automated Operations:** Computerized cataloging. **Computerized Information Services:** LEXIS, WESTLAW, DIALOG Information Services, LEGI-SLATE. **Networks/Consortia:** Member of St. Louis Regional Library Network, Mid-America Law School Library Consortium. **Publications:** Select acquisitions list, quarterly - by request; bi-annual bibliography series - for sale. **Special Indexes:** Index to legislative histories (card). **Remarks:** FAX: (314)935-6493. **Staff:** Mary Ann Nelson, Assoc.Dir.; Rosemary Hamilton, Cat.Libn.; Margaret McDermott, Ref.Libn.; Lisa McNulty, Pub.Serv; Kimberly Martin, Cat.Libn.

★ 20069 ★
Washington University - School of Medicine - Department of Psychiatry Library (Med)
4940 Audubon Ave.
St. Louis, MO 63110
Phone: (314)362-2454
Founded: 1963. **Staff:** 1. **Subjects:** Psychiatry, biochemistry, neurochemical pharmacology, epidemiology, genetics. **Holdings:** 1000 books; 20,000 bound periodical volumes; 3 VF drawers of department reprints. **Subscriptions:** 99 journals and other serials. **Services:** Library not open to the public. **Remarks:** FAX: (314)362-9862.

★ 20070 ★
Washington University - School of Medicine - Mallinckrodt Institute of Radiology Library (Med)
510 S. Kingshighway Blvd.
St. Louis, MO 63110
Phone: (314)362-2978
William Totty, M.D., Lib.Dir.
Staff: Prof 2. **Subjects:** Radiology. **Special Collections:** CIBA, Armed Forces Institute of Pathology, and American College of Radiology syllabi; Saunders monographs; Yearbook of Tumor Radiology. **Holdings:** 1352 books; 1611 bound periodical volumes; 489 videotapes; 106 slide lectures; 5 AV journals. **Subscriptions:** 65 journals and other serials. **Services:** Interlibrary loan; library not open to the public. **Automated Operations:** Computerized cataloging, serials, and circulation. **Computerized Information Services:** Institute for Scientific Information (ISI); BACS (internal database). **Staff:** Harriet Fieweger, Libn.

★ 20071 ★
Washington University - School of Medicine Library (Med)
660 S. Euclid Ave.
Campus Box 8132
St. Louis, MO 63110
Phone: (314)362-7080
Prof. Susan Y. Crawford, Dir.
Founded: 1910. **Staff:** Prof 17; Other 36. **Subjects:** Medicine. **Special Collections:** Becker Ophthalmological Collection, C.I.D. - Max A.

Goldstein Collection in Speech and Hearing (both printed); papers of William Beaumont, Joseph Erlanger, Leo Loeb, Evarts Graham, Helen Treadway Graham, E.V. Cowdry, Wendell Scott; school's early records. **Holdings:** 88,501 books; 150,722 bound periodical volumes; 1780 feet of archives; 2454 nonprint items. **Subscriptions:** 3283 journals and other serials. **Services:** Interlibrary loan; copying; library open to the public. **Automated Operations:** Computerized public access catalog, cataloging, acquisitions, serials, and circulation. **Computerized Information Services:** DIALOG Information Services, OCLC, BRS Information Technologies, NLM, Philnet; BACS (internal database); computer-assisted instruction. Performs searches on fee basis. Contact Person: Linda Mercer, Assoc.Dir., Info.Serv., 362-7084. **Networks/Consortia:** Member of National Network of Libraries of Medicine - Midcontinental Region, St. Louis Regional Library Network. **Publications:** Library Guide; Selection and Acquisitions Manual; Archives Manual; Library Newsletter; Annual Report. **Remarks:** FAX: (314)367-9547. Contains the holdings of the former Washington University - Dentistry Library. **Staff:** Loretta Stucki, Assoc.Dir., Tech.Serv.; Barbara Halbrook, Dp.Dir.; Elizabeth Kelly, AssocDir., Access Serv.; Paul Anderson, Assoc.Dir., Spec.Coll.

★ 20072 ★
Washington University - School of Technology and Information Management - STIM/CSDP Library (Comp Sci)
Prince Hall
Campus Box 1103
1 Brookings Dr.
St. Louis, MO 63130
Phone: (314)935-5366
Daryl Youngman, Libn.
Staff: Prof 1; Other 6. **Subjects:** Data processing, programming languages, systems analysis and design, software engineering, communications, artificial intelligence, computer integrated manufacturing. **Holdings:** 5200 books; 1100 bound periodical volumes; 51 staff seminar notebooks. **Subscriptions:** 405 journals and other serials; 15 newspapers. **Services:** Interlibrary loan; copying; library open to the public for reference use only. **Automated Operations:** Computerized cataloging. **Computerized Information Services:** DIALOG Information Services, Reuter TEXTLINE; CD-ROM (Computer Select); InterNet (electronic mail service). **Publications:** Library Update, bimonthly. **Remarks:** FAX: (314)935-4479. Maintained by the School of Technology and Information Management (STIM) and the Center for the Study of Data Processing (CSDP).

★ 20073 ★
Washington University Medical Center - St. Louis Children's Hospital Library (Med)
400 S. Kingshighway Blvd.
St. Louis, MO 63110
Phone: (314)454-2767
Ileen R. Kendall, Libn.
Founded: 1968. **Staff:** Prof 1; Other 1. **Subjects:** Medicine, pediatrics, nursing. **Holdings:** 1607 books; 1825 bound periodical volumes; 15 dissertations; 43 volumes of staff publications, 1920-1987; AV equipment. **Subscriptions:** 105 journals and other serials. **Services:** Interlibrary loan; copying; SDI; library open to the public for reference use only. **Automated Operations:** Computerized public access catalog, cataloging, acquisitions, serials, and circulation. **Computerized Information Services:** BACS Data Base, MEDLINE, Current Contents Search; internal database; CD-ROM. Performs searches on fee basis. **Special Indexes:** Union List of Serials. **Remarks:** Alternate telephone number(s): (314)454-2768. FAX: (314)454-2037.

Washington Utilities & Transportation Commission
See: **Washington State Library** (20039)

Washington's Headquarters State Historic Site
See: **New York (State) Office of Parks, Recreation and Historic Preservation - Palisades Region** (11682)

★ 20074 ★
Washoe County Law Library (Law)
Court House
Box 11130
Reno, NV 89520
Phone: (702)328-3250
Sandra Marz, Law Lib.Dir.
Founded: 1915. **Staff:** Prof 2; Other 6. **Subjects:** Law. **Special Collections:** Nevada gambling, water rights, and Indian law. **Holdings:** 39,840 books; 3710 bound periodical volumes; 5295 volumes in microform; 85 cassettes. **Subscriptions:** 387 periodicals. **Services:** Interlibrary loan; copying; library open to the public. **Computerized Information Services:** WESTLAW, RLIN. **Publications:** Acquisitions list, monthly. **Remarks:** FAX: (702)323-0601. **Staff:** Wilma Smith, Asst.Libn.

★ 20075 ★
Washoe Medical Center - Medical Library (Med)
77 Pringle Way   Phone: (702)328-5693
Reno, NV 89520   Sherry A. McGee, Dir., Med.Lib.
Founded: 1941. **Staff:** Prof 1; Other 2. **Subjects:** Medicine, nursing, allied health sciences. **Holdings:** 2396 books; 4638 bound periodical volumes. **Subscriptions:** 235 journals and other serials. **Services:** Interlibrary loan; copying; library open to the public for reference use only. **Computerized Information Services:** MEDLARS, DIALOG Information Services. Performs searches on fee basis. **Networks/Consortia:** Member of Northern California and Nevada Medical Library Group (NCNMLG), Nevada Medical Library Group (NMLG). **Publications:** Medical Library News, quarterly - to hospital staff, local libraries, and other interested persons. **Remarks:** FAX: (702)328-4111.

★ 20076 ★
Washtenaw Community College - Learning Resource Center - Special Collections (Educ)
4800 E. Huron River Dr.   Phone: (313)973-3429
Ann Arbor, MI 48106   Adella Blain, Dir., LRC
Founded: 1965. **Staff:** 23.5. **Special Collections:** Professional Collection (higher education); Washtenaw Community College Archives. **Holdings:** 66,500 books. **Subscriptions:** 595 journals; 20 newspapers. **Services:** Interlibrary loan; copying; collections open to the public. 24-Hour computer lab open to students and staff. **Automated Operations:** Computerized public access catalog, cataloging, circulation, and acquisitions (DYNIX). **Computerized Information Services:** DIALOG Information Services. **Networks/Consortia:** Member of Michigan Library Consortium (MLC), Washtenaw-Livingston Library Network (WLLN). **Publications:** Acquisitions List. **Remarks:** FAX: (313)677-2220.

★ 20077 ★
Washtenaw County Metropolitan Planning Commission - Library (Plan)
Court House, Rm. 340
Box 8645   Phone: (313)994-2368
Ann Arbor, MI 48107   Eve Wuttke, Asst. to the Dir.
Founded: 1949. **Staff:** 1. **Subjects:** Planning, census of population and housing, recreation, statistics, transportation, water sewage and drainage, conservation, urban growth and renewal, zoning ordinances, land use plans, development plans, subdivision ordinances. **Holdings:** 5000 books, reports, and bound periodical volumes. **Subscriptions:** 15 journals and other serials. **Services:** Copying; library open to the public at librarian's discretion. **Remarks:** FAX: (313)994-2368.

Wason Collection on East Asia
See: **Cornell University - Wason Collection on East Asia** (4334)

Wasserman Public Affairs Library
See: **University of Texas at Austin** (19408)

Watch & Clock Museum of the NAWCC
See: **National Association of Watch and Clock Collectors, Inc.** (11081)

★ 20078 ★
Water Environment Federation - Library (Env-Cons)
601 Wythe St.   Phone: (703)684-2400
Alexandria, VA 22314-1994   Berinda J. Ross, Dir., Tech. & Educ.Serv.
Founded: 1928. **Staff:** Prof 1; Other 1. **Subjects:** Water pollution control, water supply and resources, wastewater treatment and disposal, sludge treatment and disposal, collection systems, environmental engineering. **Special Collections:** National Commission on Water Quality publications. **Holdings:** 2000 books; 300 bound periodical volumes. **Subscriptions:** 35 journals and other serials. **Services:** Interlibrary loan; copying; library open to the public for reference use only. **Publications:** Journal WPCF; Operations Forum; Highlights; The Bench Sheet; Safety Bulletin; newsletters; manuals of practice; special publications; surveys. **Special Indexes:** Five-year index of Journal WPCF (book). **Remarks:** FAX: (703)684-2492. **Formerly:** Water Pollution Control Federation - Library.

★ 20079 ★
Water Information Center, Inc. (Env-Cons)
125 E. Bethpage Rd.   Phone: (516)249-7634
Plainview, NY 11803   Fred Troise, Pres.
Founded: 1959. **Subjects:** Ground water, water supply, conservation, pollution, chemistry of water, water laws. **Holdings:** 500 books; 2000 bound periodical volumes; 3000 technical reports. **Subscriptions:** 40 journals and other serials. **Services:** Answers general and semi-technical questions, especially on ground water, by phone or mail as a free public service; center not open to general public. **Publications:** Water Newsletter, semimonthly; The Groundwater Newsletter, semimonthly; International Water Report, quarterly - by subscription; Geraghty & Miller's Groundwater Bibliography, 5th Edition; The Water Encyclopedia, 2nd Edition; Drainage of Agricultural Land; Handbook on the Principles of Hydrology. **Remarks:** Division of Geraghty & Miller, Inc., Environmental Services.

Water Pollution Control Federation
See: **Water Environment Federation - Library** (20078)

★ 20080 ★
Water Quality Association - Research Council Library (Env-Cons)
4151 Naperville Rd.   Phone: (708)505-01690
Lisle, IL 60532   Joe Harrison, Tech.Dir.
Staff: 15. **Subjects:** Water quality, water conditioning, home water supply, water usage, industrial water conditioning, water softening, water pollution, geographic water data. **Special Collections:** U.S. Government publications on water quality and usage; water conditioning industry publications; International Water Quality Symposia Proceedings, 1965-1968, 1970, 1972. **Holdings:** 1000 books; industry papers; manuscripts; clippings; committee reports and pamphlets. **Subscriptions:** 40 journals and other serials. **Services:** Copying; library open to the public for reference use only. **Remarks:** FAX: (312)505-9637.

★ 20081 ★
Water Research Centre PLC - Library and Information Services (Env-Cons)
WRC Medmenham Laboratory
P.O. Box 16   Phone: 491 571531
Marlow, Buckinghamshire SL7 2HD, England   Alan C. Jordan, Libn.
Founded: 1974. **Staff:** Prof 1. **Subjects:** Water research and resources - treatment, distribution and supply, quality and health, sewage and industrial waste water treatment, sewerage, sludge disposal, pollution and fish studies, instrumentation, control and automation, water and wastewater distribution. **Holdings:** 15,000 monographs and reports. **Subscriptions:** 600 journals and other serials. **Computerized Information Services:** Produces AQUALINE database (available online through ORBIT Search Service). Performs searches. **Publications:** Aqualine Abstracts, biweekly; Technical Reports - both available for purchase or by subscription. **Remarks:** FAX: 491 579094. Telex: 848632.

★ 20082 ★
Water Resources Association of the Delaware River Basin - Library (Env-Cons)
Davis Rd.
Box 867   Phone: (215)783-0634
Valley Forge, PA 19481   Bruce E. Stewart, Pres.
Founded: 1959. **Staff:** 3. **Subjects:** Water and related land resources. **Holdings:** 1000 volumes. **Subscriptions:** 27 journals and other serials. **Services:** Copying; library open to the public. **Publications:** Newsletter, quarterly; Conference Proceedings, semiannual; Seminar Proceedings - to members. **Remarks:** FAX: (215)783-0635.

Water Resources Scientific Information Center
See: **U.S. Geological Survey - Water Resources Division - National Water Data Exchange and Water Data Storage and Retrieval System** (17545)

Water Resources Scientific Information Center
See: **U.S. Geological Survey - Water Resources Division - Water Resources Scientific Information Center** (17550)

Water & Sanitation for Health Project
See: U.S. Agency for International Development - Water & Sanitation for Health Project - Information Center (16785)

Waterbury Bar Library
See: Connecticut (State) Judicial Department - Law Library at Waterbury (4199)

★ 20083 ★
Waterbury Hospital - Health Center Library (Med)
64 Robbins St.   Phone: (203)573-6136
Waterbury, CT 06721   Joan Ruszkowski, Dir.
Staff: Prof 1; Other 2. **Subjects:** Medicine, nursing, and allied health sciences. **Holdings:** 3196 books; 8332 bound periodical volumes; 4 VF drawers of pamphlets; 800 videotapes; 5 drawers of audiotapes. **Subscriptions:** 281 journals and other serials. **Services:** Interlibrary loan; copying; SDI; library open to the public with permission of librarian. **Automated Operations:** Computerized ILL (DOCLINE). **Computerized Information Services:** MEDLARS, BRS Information Technologies; CD-ROM. **Networks/Consortia:** Member of Northwestern Connecticut Health Science Library Consortium (NW-CT-HSL), Connecticut Association of Health Science Libraries (CAHSL). **Remarks:** FAX: (203)573-7324.

★ 20084 ★
Waterbury Republican-American - Library (Publ)
389 Meadow St.   Phone: (203)574-3636
Waterbury, CT 06722   Anita Bologna, Libn.
Founded: 1926. **Staff:** Prof 1; Other 1. **Subjects:** Newspaper reference topics. **Holdings:** 1000 books; clippings; photographs and negatives; newspapers, 1884 to present, on microfilm. **Subscriptions:** 25 newspapers. **Services:** Copying; library open to the public by appointment. **Remarks:** FAX: (203)597-9344.

★ 20085 ★
Waterford Hospital - Health Services Library (Med)
Waterford Bridge Rd.   Phone: (709)364-0269
St. John's, NF, Canada A1E 4J8   Glenda Gillard, Libn.
Founded: 1969. **Staff:** 1. **Subjects:** Psychiatry, nursing, medicine, social work, psychology, pharmacology. **Holdings:** 2300 books; unbound periodicals; annual reports; manuscripts; pamphlets; AV programs. **Subscriptions:** 156 journals and other serials. **Services:** Interlibrary loan; copying; library open to the public by request.

★ 20086 ★
Waterloo/Cedar Falls Courier - Library (Publ)
W. Park and Commercial   Phone: (319)291-1400
Waterloo, IA 50704   Mary L. Zlabek, Libn.
Founded: 1940. **Staff:** Prof 1; Other 1. **Subjects:** Newspaper reference topics. **Holdings:** Microfilm (1859 to present); newspaper clippings (1940 to 1991); photograph files. **Services:** Copying; library open to the public at librarian's discretion. **Remarks:** FAX: (319)291-2069.

★ 20087 ★
Waterloo Historical Society - Grace Schmidt Room of Local History (Hist)
85 Queen St., N.   Phone: (519)743-0271
Kitchener, ON, Canada N2H 2H1   Susan Hoffman, Local Hist.Libn. & Archv.
Founded: 1984. **Subjects:** History - Kitchener, Waterloo County, Wellington County, general. **Special Collections:** Early issues of Waterloo County newspapers. **Holdings:** 500 books. **Services:** Interlibrary loan; copying; library open to the public. **Publications:** Waterloo Historical Society Annual Volume - to members. **Special Indexes:** Index to annual volumes. **Remarks:** FAX: (519)743-1261. Maintained in cooperation with Kitchener Public Library.

★ 20088 ★
Waterloo Library and Historical Society (Hist)
31 E. Williams St.   Phone: (315)539-3313
Waterloo, NY 13165   C. Phyllis Hudson, Lib.Dir.
Founded: 1875. **Staff:** Prof 2. **Subjects:** Local history, antiques. **Special Collections:** Indian Baskets collection. **Holdings:** 20,917 books; pictures; maps; diaries; letters; organization minute books; 1000 town and county records. **Subscriptions:** 65 journals and other serials. **Services:** Interlibrary loan; copying; library open to the public with restrictions. **Automated Operations:** Computerized public access catalog and cataloging. **Networks/Consortia:** Member of Finger Lakes Library System. **Staff:** Michael Becker, Hd.Libn.

★ 20089 ★
Waterloopkundig Laboratorium - Bibliotheek (Sci-Engr)
Voorsterweg
Postbus 152   Phone: 5274 2922
NL-8316 PT Marknesse, Netherlands   Dr. John D. Vandertuin
Founded: 1963. **Staff:** Prof 3. **Subjects:** Fluid mechanics, hydraulic engineering, water resources management, hydrology, coastal engineering, river engineering. **Holdings:** 17,000 books; 12,000 periodicals; 15,000 reports. **Subscriptions:** 450 journals and other serials; 20 newspapers. **Services:** Interlibrary loan; copying; SDI; library open to the public by appointment. **Automated Operations:** Computerized public access catalog (VOLICAT). **Computerized Information Services:** ESA/IRS Delft Hydro. **Publications:** Hydro Delft. **Remarks:** FAX: 5274 3573. Telex: 42290 hylvo nl.

★ 20090 ★
Watertown Daily Times - Library (Publ)
260 Washington St.   Phone: (315)782-1000
Watertown, NY 13601   Lisa M. Carr-Bourcy, Chf.Libn.
Founded: 1934. **Staff:** Prof 1; Other 3. **Subjects:** Newspaper reference topics, northern New York history. **Holdings:** 109 file cabinets of clippings; 682 reels of microfilm; 100 microfiche. **Services:** Copying; library open to the public on a limited schedule only. **Computerized Information Services:** VU/TEXT Information Services. **Networks/Consortia:** Member of North Country Reference and Research Resources Council (NCRRRC). **Remarks:** FAX: (315)782-2337. Published by Johnson Newspaper Corporation.

★ 20091 ★
Watertown Historical Society - Archives (Hist)
919 Charles St.   Phone: (414)261-2796
Watertown, WI 53094   Judy Quam, Octagon House Mgr.
Staff: 1. **Subjects:** First kindergarten in America, Margarethe Meyer Schurz, Carl Schurz, Octagon House, local history. **Holdings:** 100 volumes; photographs; clippings. **Subscriptions:** 4 journals and other serials. **Services:** Archives open to the public. **Publications:** Octagon House; Froebel gifts; 1st Kindergarten in America (all monographs); John Richards (book); Hill & Mill Publications, 1984 (color illustrations of interior rooms) - for sale; Handi and Pussy Go to Kindergarten, 1990 (a child's story of America's first kindergarten); Biography of Margarethe Meyer Schurz (reprint). **Staff:** Dr. S. Quam.

★ 20092 ★
Watertown Historical Society Inc. - Library (Hist)
22 DeForest St.   Phone: (203)274-4344
Watertown, CT 06795   Florence Crowell, Cur.
Founded: 1968. **Staff:** Prof 1. **Subjects:** Genealogy, local and state history, local authors. **Special Collections:** Collection of diaries of town's residents; town reports; oral histories; Watertown Town Times, 1947-1975, on microfilm. **Holdings:** 1200 books. **Services:** Library open to the public with permission required for circulation. **Remarks:** Alternate telephone number(s): 274-1634. **Staff:** John Pillis, Pres.

★ 20093 ★
Waterville Historical Society - Library and Archives (Hist)
64 Silver St.
Waterville, ME 04901   Phone: (207)872-9439
Founded: 1903. **Subjects:** History - local, regional, state; Civil War. **Special Collections:** Diaries, 1753-1955; early textbooks (200); 19th century apothecary. **Holdings:** 1520 books; local newspaper, 1853-1906; early account books; old documents and letters; maps; old photographs. **Services:** Archives open to the public with restrictions. **Also Known As:** Redington Museum.

★ 20094 ★
Waterville Osteopathic Hospital - M.J. Gerrie, Sr. Medical Library (Med)
Kennedy Memorial Dr.   Phone: (207)873-0731
Waterville, ME 04901   Charlotte S. Gifford, Libn.
Staff: Prof 1. **Subjects:** Medicine, surgery, osteopathy. **Holdings:** 150 books. **Subscriptions:** 40 journals and other serials. **Services:** Interlibrary loan; copying; library open to the public with restrictions. **Networks/Consortia:** Member of Health Science Library and Information Cooperative of Maine (HSLIC).

Jessie Beach Watkins Memorial Library
See: **Seneca Falls Historical Society** (15034)

★ 20095 ★
Watkins Woolen Mill State Historic Site - Research Library (Hist)
26600 Park Rd., N.   Phone: (816)296-3357
Lawson, MO 64062   Ann M. Matthews, Historic Site Adm.
Founded: 1964. **Staff:** Prof 2; Other 3. **Subjects:** 19th century textile industry and farming. **Special Collections:** Watkins family papers; original blankets, fabrics, and yarn produced in 1860s mill. **Holdings:** 500 books; 2000 bound periodical volumes; 5000 pamphlets and letters. **Subscriptions:** 16 journals and other serials. **Services:** Library open to the public for reference use only on request. **Remarks:** Maintained by Missouri State Division of Parks, Recreation, & Historic Preservation. **Staff:** Michael Beckett, Asst.Adm.

Watkinson Library
See: **Trinity College** (16504)

Peter Watne Memorial Library
See: **Crown College** (4446)

Arthur R. Watson Library
See: **Baltimore Zoo** (1457)

★ 20096 ★
Watson Clinic - Medical Library (Med)
Box 95000   Phone: (813)680-7098
Lakeland, FL 33804-5000   Cheryl Dee, Ph.D., Lib.Dir.
Founded: 1945. **Staff:** Prof 1; Other 3. **Subjects:** Medicine. **Holdings:** 1800 books; 3000 bound periodical volumes; 550 cassettes. **Subscriptions:** 400 journals and other serials. **Services:** Interlibrary loan; copying; library open to the public by permission only. **Computerized Information Services:** MEDLINE, DIALOG Information Services. Performs searches on fee basis. Contact: Betty Burgess, Lib.Asst. or Kristy Taggart, Lib.Asst. **Networks/Consortia:** Member of Tampa Bay Library Consortium, Inc. (TBLC), Miami Health Sciences Library Consortium (MHSLC). **Remarks:** FAX: (813)680-7954.

Eugene P. Watson Library
See: **Northwestern State University of Louisiana** (12077)

John Brown Watson Memorial Library
See: **University of Arkansas, Pine Bluff** (18240)

T.J. Watson Research Center Library
See: **IBM Corporation** (7630)

Thomas J. Watson Library
See: **Metropolitan Museum of Art** (10216)

Thomas J. Watson Library of Business and Economics
See: **Columbia University - Thomas J. Watson Library of Business and Economics** (4027)

WATSTORE
See: **U.S. Geological Survey - Water Resources Division - National Water Data Exchange and Water Data Storage and Retrieval System** (17545)

Donald B. Watt Library
See: **Experiment in International Living - School for International Training** (5520)

★ 20097 ★
Watts, Griffis & McOuat, Ltd. - Library (Sci-Engr)
8 King St., E., Suite 400   Phone: (416)364-6244
Toronto, ON, Canada M5C 1B5   Margherita Piazza, Info.Spec.
Subjects: Geology, mining industry, mining engineering. **Holdings:** 6000 books; 2000 reports; federal and provincial geological surveys; U.S. federal and state government geological surveys, maps, and annual reports VF drawers; internal reports. **Subscriptions:** 102 journals and other serials. **Services:** Library open to the public by appointment and for reference use only. **Automated Operations:** Computerized cataloging. **Computerized Information Services:** DIALOG Information Services, Info Globe, InvesText, WILSONLINE; WGMLIB (internal database). **Remarks:** FAX: (416)864-1675

Watts School of Nursing
See: **Durham County Hospital Corporation** (5070)

★ 20098 ★
Watts Street Baptist Church - Library (Rel-Phil)
800 Watts St.   Phone: (919)688-1366
Durham, NC 27705   Tim Dale, Libn.
Founded: 1960. **Staff:** Prof 1; Other 3. **Subjects:** Religion, children's literature. **Holdings:** 1000 books; 200 pamphlets. **Subscriptions:** 12 journals and other serials. **Services:** Library open to the public with restrictions.

★ 20099 ★
Waukegan Historical Society - John Raymond Memorial Library (Hist)
1917 N. Sheridan Rd.
Waukegan, IL 60087   Phone: (708)336-1859
Staff: 3. **Subjects:** Local history. **Special Collections:** Waukegan authors. **Holdings:** 1338 books; 3 bound newspapers; 12 VF drawers of pamphlets; 4 drawer case of slides; 1 cabinet of maps and posters; 4 portfolios of old newspapers; 4 VF drawers of photographs; 1 VF drawer of material on landmark buildings; 3 VF drawers of ephemera. **Services:** Copying; library open to the public for reference use only. **Publications:** Historically Speaking, monthly - to members. **Special Indexes:** Index to books, photographs, and slides (card). **Staff:** Eloise Daydif, Co-Libn.; Beverly Millard, Co-Libn.

★ 20100 ★
Waukegan News-Sun - Library (Publ)
100 Madison St.   Phone: (708)336-7000
Waukegan, IL 60085   Barbara Apple, Hd.Libn.
Staff: Prof 1. **Subjects:** Newspaper reference topics. **Holdings:** 600 books; 3600 reels of microfilm; photographs; newspaper clippings; graphics. **Subscriptions:** 15 journals and other serials. **Services:** Library not open to the public. **Computerized Information Services:** Battelle Automated Search Information System (BASIS). **Special Indexes:** News-Sun Microfilm Index (book); Editorial Index (card; book). **Remarks:** FAX: (708)249-7202.

★ 20101 ★
Waukesha County Freeman Daily Newspaper - Library (Publ)
P.O. Box 7   Phone: (414)542-2501
Waukesha, WI 53187   Wendy Schrank, AM Libn.
Founded: 1965. **Staff:** Prof 1. **Subjects:** Newspaper reference topics. **Holdings:** Clipping files, 1965 to present; photographs and negatives; bound volumes, 1859 to present, in storage; newspapers, 1859 to present, on microfilm. **Subscriptions:** 15 journals and other serials. **Services:** Library open to the public with restrictions. **Special Indexes:** Index of headshot photograph file; index of articles (book and card). **Remarks:** FAX: (414)542-6082.

★ 20102 ★
Waukesha County Historical Museum - Research Center (Hist)
101 W. Main St.   Phone: (414)548-7186
Waukesha, WI 53186   Anita Baerg-Vatndal, Dir. of Musm.
Staff: Prof 2; Other 2. **Subjects:** Local history and genealogy. **Special Collections:** Pioneer Notebooks (unpublished information on early pioneers of city and county; 82 volumes); county naturalization records. **Holdings:** 3000 books; 87 bound periodical volumes; 1 VF drawer of cemetery records; 1 VF drawer of census records; 40 VF drawers of newspaper clippings; 14,000 photographs; 10,000 negatives; 1800 slides; archival material. **Subscriptions:** 36 journals and other serials; 7 newspapers. **Services:** Copying; center open to adults for reference use only. **Publications:** Primary Bibliography for Research in Waukesha History; Family History Research in Waukesha County; Guide to the Waukesha County Museum Research Center; list of other publications - available on request. **Staff:** Terry Becker, Libn.

★ 20103 ★
Waukesha County Technical College - WCTC Library (Educ)
800 Main St.   Phone: (414)691-5316
Pewaukee, WI 53072   Ruth Ahl, Lib.Dir.
Staff: Prof 1; Other 6. **Subjects:** Nursing, allied health sciences, industrial technology, business, police and fire sciences, electronics, food service, automotive technology, accounting, data processing, marketing, financial planning, hospitality management, retailing, real estate, child care, international trade, interior design. **Special Collections:** NEWSBANK, Inc.; international trade; career collection; ERIC microfiche. **Holdings:** 33,893 books; 53,859 unbound periodicals; 495 reels of microfilm; 56 films; 365 videotapes; 805 audiocassettes; SAMS Photofact Service. **Subscriptions:** 433 periodicals; 11 newspapers. **Services:** Interlibrary loan; copying; library open to the public with restrictions. **Automated Operations:** Computerized public access catalog, cataloging, and circulation. **Computerized Information Services:** OCLC, DIALOG Information Services. Performs searches on fee basis. Contact Person: Joyce Laabs, Circ./ILL. **Networks/Consortia:** Member of Library Council of Metropolitan Milwaukee, Inc. (LCOMM), Wisconsin Interlibrary Services (WILS). **Publications:** WCTC film and videotape list, annual; WCTC periodical holdings list, annual. **Remarks:** FAX: (414)691-5593.

★ 20104 ★
Waukesha Memorial Hospital - Medical Library (Med)
725 American Ave.   Phone: (414)544-2150
Waukesha, WI 53186   Linda Oddan, Med.Libn.
Founded: 1958. **Staff:** Prof 1. **Subjects:** Medicine, nursing, hospital administration. **Holdings:** 2100 books; 2500 bound periodical volumes; 9 VF drawers of pamphlets. **Subscriptions:** 200 journals and other serials. **Services:** Interlibrary loan; copying; library open to the public with restrictions. **Computerized Information Services:** DIALOG Information Services, MEDLINE, BRS Information Technologies; DOCLINE (electronic mail service). Performs searches on fee basis. **Networks/Consortia:** Member of National Network of Libraries of Medicine - Greater Midwest Region, Southeastern Wisconsin Health Science Library Consortium (SWHSL). **Remarks:** FAX: (414)544-2514.

★ 20105 ★
Wausau Insurance Companies - Media and Reference Services (Bus-Fin)
2000 Westwood Dr.
Box 8017   Phone: (715)847-8504
Wausau, WI 54402-8017   Douglas H. Lay, Mgr.
Founded: 1935. **Staff:** Prof 2; Other 3. **Subjects:** Insurance, industrial safety and health. **Holdings:** 11,000 books; 130 bound periodical volumes; 185 VF drawers of clippings; 1050 AV programs. **Subscriptions:** 320 journals and other serials; 17 newspapers. **Services:** Interlibrary loan; library open to serious students and researchers. **Automated Operations:** Computerized cataloging, acquisitions, serials, circulation, and media booking. **Computerized Information Services:** DIALOG Information Services, Dun & Bradstreet Business Credit Services, Insurance Information Institute (III), Human Resource Information Network (HRIN). **Networks/Consortia:** Member of Wisconsin Valley Library Service (WVLS). **Publications:** Management Media Scan, quarterly - for internal distribution only. **Remarks:** FAX: (715)847-7405. **Staff:** Lee M. Knutson, Ref.Serv.Spec.

★ 20106 ★
Wauwatosa Presbyterian Church - Library (Rel-Phil)
2366 N. 80th St.
Wauwatosa, WI 53213   Phone: (414)774-5005
Staff: Prof 2; Other 4. **Subjects:** Religion. **Holdings:** 1102 books. **Services:** Library not open to the public.

★ 20107 ★
The Wawel State Collection - Library (Hist, Art)
Wawel 5   Phone: 12 225155
PL-31-001 Cracow, Poland   Anna Mercik
Founded: 1950. **Subjects:** Art history, history of Poland, history of the Wawel Castle. **Holdings:** 10,639 books; 341 bound periodical volumes. **Subscriptions:** 56 journals and other serials. **Services:** Interlibrary loan; library open to historians only. **Remarks:** FAX: 12 221950. **Also Known As:** Panstwowe Zbiory Sztuki na Wawelu - Biblioteka.

Way & Williams Collection
See: University of North Carolina at Greensboro (19090)

★ 20108 ★
Wayne Community College - Learning Resource Center (Educ)
Caller Box 8002   Phone: (919)735-5151
Goldsboro, NC 27533-8002   Dr. Shirley T. Jones, LRC Dean
Founded: 1957. **Staff:** Prof 7; Other 11. **Subjects:** Agriculture and natural resources, health occupations, dental occupations, business, liberal arts, engineering, mechanical vocations, aerospace maintenance technology, mathematics. **Special Collections:** Local genealogy collection. **Holdings:** 35,924 books; 68,399 microforms; 6880 AV programs. **Subscriptions:** 285 journals and other serials; 9 newspapers. **Services:** Interlibrary loan; copying; media production; center open to the public. **Automated Operations:** Computerized public access catalog and circulation (DYNIX). **Remarks:** FAX: (919)736-3204. **Staff:** Dot Elledge, Dir., Lib.Serv.; Malcolm Shearin, Dir., Media Prod.; Sue Potter, Dir., Directed Stud.

★ 20109 ★
Wayne County Historical Museum - Library (Hist)
1150 North A St.   Phone: (317)962-5756
Richmond, IN 47374   Michele Bottorff, Dir.
Founded: 1930. **Staff:** Prof 3. **Subjects:** History - local, Quaker, local families, state. **Special Collections:** Gaar Williams Collection (Chicago Tribune cartoonist); Victorian valentines (500); World War I posters. **Holdings:** 1000 books; 50 scrapbooks; records of the museum. **Subscriptions:** 15 journals and other serials. **Services:** Copying; library open to the public for reference use only. **Also Known As:** Julia Meek Gaar Wayne County Historical Museum. **Staff:** Jim Waechter, Cur.

★ 20110 ★
Wayne County Historical Society - Museum Library (Hist)
Hwy. 2
E. Jefferson St.   Phone: (515)872-2483
Corydon, IA 50060   Wilma West, Libn.
Founded: 1975. **Staff:** 6. **Subjects:** History, genealogy. **Special Collections:** Census records; obituaries, wills, and estates; Dr. Hinkle's birth and death records, 1880-1920; Corydon and Wayne County newspapers, 1894-1986; Wayne and Appanoose Counties, Iowa, and Putnam County, Missouri marriage records; Putnam County cemetery books and estate books; Lucas and Wayne County History; Lucas County marriage and cemetery books; Appanoose County cemetery sections. **Holdings:** Books; family files; microforms. **Subscriptions:** 4 journals and other serials. **Services:** Library open to the public on a limited schedule or by appointment; answers mail queries. **Publications:** List of publications - available on request. **Special Indexes:** Indexes to obituaries, wills, estates, and newspapers. **Staff:** Ruby Couchman; Carol Thomas; Jean Nickel; Velma Cobb; Pauline Vincent.

★ 20111 ★
Wayne County Historical Society Museum - Library (Hist)
21 Butternut St.   Phone: (315)946-4943
Lyons, NY 14489   Marjory Allen Perez, County Hist.
Founded: 1949. **Staff:** 3. **Subjects:** Wayne County history and genealogy, western New York history. **Holdings:** 1800 volumes; 20 VF drawers of clippings, archives, pictures, pamphlets, scrapbooks. **Services:** Copying (limited); library open to the public for reference use only. **Publications:** The Aesthetic Heritage of a Rural Area, 1978; History of Pioneers Settlement of Phelps and Gorham Purchase.

★ 20112 ★
Wayne County Law Library Association (Law)
Wayne County Courthouse
107 W. Liberty St.   Phone: (216)262-5561
Wooster, OH 44691   Betty K. Schuler, Libn.
Founded: 1903. **Subjects:** Law. **Holdings:** 20,000 volumes; microfiche. **Services:** Copying; library open to the public with restrictions. **Computerized Information Services:** LEXIS, DIALOG Information Services.

★ 20113 ★
Wayne County Regional Library for the Blind and Physically
  Handicapped (Aud-Vis)
33030 Van Born Rd.   Phone: (313)274-2600
Wayne, MI 48184   Pat Klemans, Reg.Libn.
Founded: 1931. **Staff:** Prof 4; Other 2. **Holdings:** 110,000 talking books.
Services: Library serves those who are unable to read conventional print
because of a physical disability. **Networks/Consortia:** Member of National
Library Service for the Blind & Physically Handicapped (NLS).

★ 20114 ★
Wayne Historical Museum - Historical Commission Archives (Hist)
1 Town Square   Phone: (313)722-0113
Wayne, MI 48184   Henry Goudy, Fac.Mgr.
Staff: 2. **Subjects:** Local history. **Holdings:** Clippings; manuscripts;
documents; maps; genealogical material; cemetery inscriptions; church,
school, and local government records; local biographies; photographs.
Services: Archives open to the public.

★ 20115 ★
Wayne Presbyterian Church - Library (Rel-Phil)
125 E. Lancaster Ave.
Box 502   Phone: (215)688-8700
Wayne, PA 19087   Mary Augusterfer, Libn.
Founded: 1945. **Staff:** Prof 1; Other 2. **Subjects:** Bible study, Christian
education, biography, fine arts, sociology. **Special Collections:** Hymnals.
Holdings: 7400 books; records; cassettes; filmstrips; 13 rapid reading
program portfolios; 70 college catalogs. **Subscriptions:** 10 journals and other
serials. **Services:** Library open to the public with restrictions.

★ 20116 ★
Wayne State College - U.S. Conn Library (Educ)
200 E. 10   Phone: (402)375-7257
Wayne, NE 68787   Dr. Jack L. Middendorf, Dir.
Founded: 1910. **Staff:** Prof 7; Other 7. **Subjects:** Business, education,
literature, social science. **Holdings:** 100,000 book titles; 3500 AV programs;
30,000 government documents (selective depository); 400,000 microform
titles, including ERIC and U.S. Government microfiche collections.
Subscriptions: 1000 journals and other serials. **Services:** Interlibrary loan;
copying; AV production; library open to the public. **Computerized
Information Services:** DIALOG Information Services. **Networks/
Consortia:** Member of Northeast Library System, NEBASE. **Publications:**
Connformation, weekly - to faculty. **Staff:** Jo Anne Bock, Govt.Doc.; Lois
Spencer, Ref. & Bibliog.Instr.; Marcus Schlichter, Per.; Sue Buryanek, AV
Media Serv./Instr.Rsrcs.; Janet Brumm, Lib. Automation Coord.; Marilyn
Liedorff, Tech.Serv.Coord.

★ 20117 ★
Wayne State University - Archives of Labor and Urban Affairs/
  University Archives (Soc Sci, Bus-Fin)
Walter P. Reuther Library   Phone: (313)577-4024
Detroit, MI 48202   Philip P. Mason, Dir.
Founded: 1960. **Staff:** Prof 12; Other 11. **Subjects:** American labor, urban
affairs, civil rights, civil liberties, economic reform, social reform, history of
Wayne State University. **Special Collections:** Inactive files of United Auto
Workers, American Federation of Teachers, The Newspaper Guild, United
Farm Workers, Industrial Workers of the World, Air Line Pilots
Association, Congress of Industrial Organizations, American Federation of
State, County and Municipal Employees, Association of Flight Attendants,
and other labor and urban groups; personal papers of labor, political, and
community leaders. **Holdings:** 13,000 books; 2600 bound periodical
volumes; 60,000 linear feet of archives; 900,000 still photographs; 10,000
audiotapes; 200 oral histories. **Subscriptions:** 90 journals and other serials;
90 newspapers. **Services:** Copying; archives open to qualified researchers.
Publications: A Guide to the Archives of Labor History and Urban Affairs,
Wayne State University Press, 1974. **Remarks:** FAX: (313)577-4300. **Staff:**
Warner Pflug, Assoc.Dir.; Patricia Bartkowski, Archv.; Raymond
Boryczka, Archv.; Carrolyn Davis, Archv.; Thomas Featherstone, Archv.;
William Gulley, Archv.; William LeFevre, Archv.; Margery Long, Archv.;
Margaret Raucher, Archv.; Kathleen Schmeling, Archv.; Taronda Spencer,
Archv.

★ 20118 ★
Wayne State University - Arthur Neef Law Library (Law)
468 W. Ferry Mall   Phone: (313)577-3925
Detroit, MI 48202   Georgia A. Clark, Law Lib.Dir.
Founded: 1927. **Staff:** Prof 5; Other 7. **Subjects:** Law and allied fields.
Special Collections: Depository for U.S. Government documents (111,000);
Michigan Legal Collection; Alwyn V. Freeman International Law
Collection; U.S. and Michigan Supreme Courts Records and Briefs.
Holdings: 277,681 volumes; 798,583 microform units. **Subscriptions:** 4274
journals and other serials; 35 newspapers. **Services:** Interlibrary loan;
copying (limited); library open to the public. **Automated Operations:**
Computerized cataloging, acquisitions, serials, government documents, and
circulation (NOTIS). **Computerized Information Services:** LEXIS,
WESTLAW, NEXIS, OCLC, QL Systems. **Publications:** Law Library
News, semimonthly; Recent Acquisitions List, semimonthly - both
primarily for faculty distribution. **Remarks:** FAX: (313)577-5478; (313)577-
5498. **Staff:** Heather Simmons, Asst.Dir.; Kanhya Kaul, Ref.Libn./Doc.;
Janice Selberg, Ref.Libn.; M. Christine Chamness, Pub.Serv.Libn./ILL.

★ 20119 ★
Wayne State University - College of Engineering - Machine Tool
  Research Laboratory - Library (Sci-Engr)
Department of Mechanical Engineering
5050 Anthony Wayne Dr.   Phone: (313)577-3898
Detroit, MI 48202   Prof. Eugene I. Rivin, Dir.
Founded: 1988. **Staff:** Prof 3. **Subjects:** Machine tool and tooling structures,
mechanical design and accuracy of robots, advanced machine elements.
Special Collections: Russian mechanical engineering (500 books). **Holdings:**
Books. **Subscriptions:** 3 Russian abstract journals. **Services:** Copying;
library not open to the public. **Computerized Information Services:** Internal
databases. **Remarks:** FAX: (313)577-3881.

★ 20120 ★
Wayne State University - Folklore Archive (Hum, Area-Ethnic)
448 Purdy Library   Phone: (313)577-4053
Detroit, MI 48202   Janet L. Langlois, Dir.
Founded: 1939. **Staff:** Prof 1; Other 2. **Subjects:** Oral, customary, and
material culture of urban, occupational, and ethnic groups. **Special
Collections:** Afro-American Folklore Collections; German and German-
American Folklore Collections; Italian and Italian-American Folklore
Collection; Greek and Greek-American Folklore Collections; Polish and
Polish-American Folklore Collections; Armenian Collection; International
Library of African Music (authentic tribal music); Ivan Walton Collection
of Michigan Folklore (Great Lakes folk music); Michigan State University
Collection of Folk Narrative; Southern Upland Folklife Oral Histories
(Southern whites in Detroit); Greek American Families in Detroit (oral
histories; 75 tapes); Great Lakes Lighthouse Keepers (oral histories; 26
tapes); Bruce L. Harkness Poletown Photographic Exhibit (urban ethnic
neighborhood; 487 black/white photographs); Urban Legends: Video
Anecdotes of Contemporary Folklore; Wayne State University Folklore
Archive Studies Series; recitations and sayings; medical collection; college
folksongs. **Holdings:** 200 books; 3000 manuscripts; 1000 audiotape
recordings; 460 phonograph records; 350 slides; 5 videotapes. **Services:**
Copying; archive open to the public. **Publications:** Triennial Report;
annotated holdings lists; Holiday Pamphlet Series; Archive Study Series (1st
volume: Italian Folktales in America, 1985). **Remarks:** FAX: (313)577-
8618.

★ 20121 ★
Wayne State University - Media Services (Soc Sci)
Purdy/Kresge Library
5265 Cass Ave.   Phone: (313)577-6420
Detroit, MI 48202   Sallie H. Ellison, Dir.
Founded: 1990. **Staff:** Prof 3. **Special Collections:** Mildred Jeffries Collection
of Peace and Conflict Resolution (1294 multimedia items). **Holdings:** 8042
films and videotapes; 4865 audio recordings; 620 computer files. **Services:**
Classroom AV support; graphic design; photography; teleconferencing;
computer literacy laboratory. **Remarks:** FAX: (313)577-4172. **Staff:** John
Stendel, Asst.Dir.; Bennet Crook, Computer Lab.Libn.

★ 20122 ★
Wayne State University - Purdy/Kresge Library (Hum, Soc Sci)
5265 Cass Ave.   Phone: (313)577-6423
Detroit, MI 48202   Sallie H. Ellison, Dir.
Founded: 1973. **Staff:** Prof 12; Other 22. **Subjects:** Business and business
administration, education, humanities, juvenile literature, library science,

social work, social sciences. **Special Collections:** Leonard N. Simons Collection (Detroit and Michigan History); Eloise Ramsey Collection of Literature for Young People (12,500 items). **Holdings:** 1.4 million books; 218,000 bound periodical volumes; 324,984 documents (leaflets and bulletins only); 1.8 million microforms; 7607 curriculum guides; 65 VF drawers of pamphlets and clippings. **Subscriptions:** 8000 journals and other serials; 60 newspapers. **Services:** Interlibrary loan; copying; document delivery (fee); library open to the public. **Automated Operations:** Computerized public access catalog, cataloging, acquisitions, serials, and circulation. **Computerized Information Services:** DIALOG Information Services, BRS Information Technologies, PFDS Online, Wilson Indexes; InfoTrac; CD-ROMs; ALANET, BITNET (electronic mail services). Performs searches on fee basis. Contact Person: Karen Bacsanyi, Database Coord., (313)577-6446 or Patrice Merritt, Asst.Dir., (313)577-5856. **Publications:** WSU Libraries Magazine & Newsletter; (WSU) Library leaflets; undergraduate guides to library use. **Remarks:** FAX: (313)577-4172. **Staff:** Donald Breneau, Libn.; Karen Bacsanyi, Libn.; William Hulsker, Libn.; William Kane, Libn.; Jeffrey Pearson, Circ.Libn.; Joan Reyes, ILL Libn.; Gloria Sniderman, Docs.Libn.; Sally Lawler, Docs.Libn.; Deborah Tucker, Libn.

★ 20123 ★
Wayne State University - Science and Engineering Library (Sci-Engr)
5048 Gullen Mall
Detroit, MI 48202
Phone: (313)577-4068
Lynn Sorensen Sutton, Dir.
Staff: Prof 6; Other 8. **Subjects:** Chemistry, biology, mathematics, engineering, computer science, physics, geology, nursing. **Special Collections:** System on Automotive Safety Information; Samuel Cox Hooker Chemistry Collection. **Holdings:** 213,415 books; 147,141 bound periodical volumes; 123,113 government documents; 97,529 microfiche; 1533 reels of microfilm; 455 microcards; 15,000 microcards. **Subscriptions:** 3000 journals and other serials. **Services:** Interlibrary loan; copying; library open to the public. **Computerized Information Services:** DIALOG Information Services, STN International, BRS Information Technologies, PFDS Online, Chemical Abstracts Service (CAS), MEDLARS; CD-ROMs (Science Citation Index, Nursing & Allied Health (CINAHL)-CD, Biological & Agricultural Index, MathSci); BITNET, PROFS (electronic mail services). Performs searches on fee basis. **Publications:** Recent Additions List. **Remarks:** FAX: (313)577-3613. **Staff:** Dr. James R. Ruffner, Ref.Libn.; Loren Mendelsohn, Ref.Libn.; Nancy Wilmes, Ref.Libn.; Diane Palden, Tech.Serv.Libn.

★ 20124 ★
Wayne State University - Vera Parshall Shiffman Medical Library
(Med)
4325 Brush St.
Detroit, MI 48201
Phone: (313)577-1088
Faith Van Toll, Dir.
Founded: 1949. **Staff:** Prof 5; Other 13. **Subjects:** Clinical medicine, pharmacy, and allied health sciences. **Holdings:** 79,015 books; 123,648 bound periodical volumes. **Subscriptions:** 2924 journals and other serials. **Services:** Interlibrary loan; copying; SDI; library open to the public with restrictions. **Automated Operations:** Computerized public access catalog, cataloging, acquisitions, serials, and circulation. **Computerized Information Services:** NLM, BRS Information Technologies, DIALOG Information Services; CD-ROM (MEDLINE). Performs searches on fee basis. **Remarks:** FAX: (313)577-0706. **Staff:** Ruth Taylor, Pub.Serv.Libn.; Lora Robbins, Pub.Serv.Libn.; John Coffey, Pub.Serv.Libn.; Natalie King, Pub.Serv.Libn.

★ 20125 ★
WCAX-TV - Library (Info Sci)
P.O. Box 608, Joy Dr.
Burlington, VT 05401
Phone: (802)658-6300
Sylvia Sprigg, Libn./Res.
Founded: 1981. **Staff:** 1. **Subjects:** Current events, television news broadcasting. **Special Collections:** News film collection (1950s to present); news video collection (1970s to present). **Holdings:** Films, videotapes, archival material. **Services:** Library open to the public by appointment. **Computerized Information Services:** DIALOG Information Services, NEXIS; news broadcast scripts (1987 to present; internal database). **Special Indexes:** Indexes to video archive library and still store archive library (card file). **Remarks:** FAX: (802)658-6300.

★ 20126 ★
WCO Port Properties, Ltd. - Historical Archives and Resource Center
(Trans, Hist)
Queen Mary & Spruce Goose
Entertainment Center
P.O. Box 8
Long Beach, CA 90801
Phone: (213)435-3511
William M. Winberg, Hist.
Founded: 1967. **Staff:** Prof 3. **Subjects:** RMS Queen Mary, Howard Hughes' Spruce Goose Flying Boat. **Special Collections:** Ship's Logs (145); Radio, Engine, Boiler, and Steam Logs; memoranda, letters, reports, papers for stores, crew, cargo, and drydocking (17 VF drawers and 200 linear feet). **Holdings:** 200 books; 100 bound periodical volumes; 10,000 photographs; 20 VF drawers of plans for mechanical and utilities installations; 250 menus; 45 passenger lists; 400 pieces of memorabilia, pamphlets, booklets, souvenirs; 200 bound reports, test results, plans; 4 VF drawers of plans and documents. **Subscriptions:** 5 journals and other serials; 2 newspapers. **Services:** Center not open to the public; requests for materials and publications should be addressed to the Exhibits Department. **Publications:** Howard Hughes: His Achievements and Legacy; The Queen Mary: The Stateliest Ship - for sale. **Remarks:** Ninety percent of the material in the center was found on the ship. **Remarks:** FAX: (213)437-2914. **Staff:** Ellene Mahoney, Archv.Adm.; Ron Smith, Exhibits Asst.

WCRB Library
See: **Charles River Broadcasting Company** (3439)

Wean Medical Library
See: **Trumbull Memorial Hospital** (16529)

★ 20127 ★
Weather Research Center - Library (Sci-Engr)
3227 Audley
Houston, TX 77098
Phone: (713)529-3076
Jill F. Hasling, Dir., Oper.
Founded: 1988. **Staff:** Prof 3. **Subjects:** Meteorology, oceanography, physics, hydrology, climatology. **Holdings:** 1000 books; government scientific publications; research papers; maps; microfilm. **Subscriptions:** 11 journals and other serials. **Services:** Interlibrary loan; copying; library open to the public for reference use only. **Remarks:** Telex: 3729125. FAX: (713)528-3538.

★ 20128 ★
WeatherData, Inc. - Library (Aud-Vis, Sci-Engr)
825 N. Main St.
Wichita, KS 67203
Phone: (316)265-9127
Janell Johnson, Spec.Serv.Corrd.
Founded: 1981. **Subjects:** Weather. **Special Collections:** Compact disc weather library. **Holdings:** Photographs and slides (most in color); videotapes; films; MacIntosh computer weather graphics library. **Remarks:** FAX: (316)265-0371.

Annie Belle Weaver Special Collections
See: **West Georgia College - Irvine Sullivan Ingram Library** (20192)

Jennie E. Weaver Memorial Library
See: **First United Methodist Church** (5811)

★ 20129 ★
Webb-Deane-Stevens Museum - Library (Hum, Soc Sci)
211 Main St.
Wethersfield, CT 06109
Phone: (203)529-0612
Mrs. William Gaines
Founded: 1975. **Subjects:** Decorative arts, manners and customs, American Revolutionary War history, George Washington. **Holdings:** 1200 books; 40 bound periodical volumes; 15 reports. **Subscriptions:** 3 journals and other serials. **Services:** Library open to the public by appointment.

Del E. Webb Memorial Library
See: **Loma Linda University** (9255)

Del E. Webb Memorial Medical Information Center
See: **Eisenhower Medical Center** (5277)

★ 20130 ★
Webb Institute of Naval Architecture - Livingston Library (Sci-Engr)
Crescent Beach Rd.   Phone: (516)671-0439
Glen Cove, NY 11542-1398   David J. Zaehringer, Libn.
Founded: 1931. **Staff:** Prof 1; Other 1. **Subjects:** Naval architecture, marine engineering, engineering, science, literature, history, fine arts, philosophy, religion, social science. **Holdings:** 46,737 volumes; 5166 engineering reports; 1159 phonograph records; 1516 microforms; clippings and archives of W.H. Webb. **Subscriptions:** 270 journals and other serials; 6 newspapers. **Services:** Interlibrary loan; copying; library open to the public by appointment. **Networks/Consortia:** Member of Long Island Library Resources Council. **Publications:** Accession list, quarterly. **Remarks:** FAX: (516)674-9838.

Webb Memorial Library
See: **Penrose Hospital** (12918)

Webber Resource Center
See: **Field Museum of Natural History** (5685)

★ 20131 ★
Weber County Law Library (Law)
Municipal Bldg., 4th Fl.   Phone: (801)399-8466
Ogden, UT 84401   Jean Ann McMurrin, Libn.
Founded: 1896. **Staff:** Prof 1; Other 2. **Subjects:** Law. **Holdings:** 12,150 volumes. **Services:** Copying; library open to the public with restrictions. **Computerized Information Services:** WESTLAW. **Remarks:** FAX: (801)399-8300.

Weber Memorial Library
See: **San Antonio Community Hospital** (14666)

★ 20132 ★
Daniel Webster College - Library (Sci-Engr, Bus-Fin)
20 University Dr.   Phone: (603)883-3556
Nashua, NH 03063   Mary T. Marks, Lib.Dir.
Founded: 1966. **Staff:** Prof 4; Other 4. **Subjects:** Aeronautics, business administration, computers. **Special Collections:** Aeronautics; aviation history; air traffic control; computer systems; computer science. **Holdings:** 28,000 books. **Subscriptions:** 700 journals and other serials; 10 newspapers. **Services:** Interlibrary loan; copying; library open to the public. **Computerized Information Services:** Newspaper Abstracts, Readers' Guide to Periodical Literature, Business Periodicals Index. **Networks/Consortia:** Member of New Hampshire College & University Council Library Policy Committee (NHCUC). **Staff:** Glenna Rosenstein, Ref.Libn.; Toni Weller, Ref./Acq.Libn.; Maureen Quaglieri, Cat.

★ 20133 ★
Webster Groves Historical Society - History Center (Hist)
1155 S. Rock Hill Rd.   Phone: (314)968-1857
Webster Groves, MO 63119   Charles F. Rehkopf, Archv.
Founded: 1966. **Subjects:** Webster Groves history. **Special Collections:** Kate Moody Collection; Esther Repogle Collection; Laura Parker papers; business papers; Webster Groves newspapers. **Holdings:** 50 books; 27 volumes of local newspapers; 80 lateral file drawers of records and papers. **Services:** Copying; center open to the public by appointment. **Remarks:** Alternate telephone number(s): (314)968-1776; (314)962-8180.

Jerome P. Webster Library of Plastic Surgery
See: **Columbia University - Augustus C. Long Health Sciences Library** (4001)

John P. Webster Library
See: **First Church of Christ Congregational** (5766)

Webster Library
See: **Evanston Hospital** (5508)

★ 20134 ★
Noah Webster Foundation & Historical Society of West Hartford - Library (Hist)
227 S. Main St.   Phone: (203)521-5362
West Hartford, CT 06107   Sally Williams, Dir.
Founded: 1970. **Staff:** Prof 3. **Subjects:** Noah Webster, local history, local architecture and preservation, Connecticut colonial life and culture. **Special Collections:** Noah Webster Collection (rare books; manuscripts; letters); rare book collection (200). **Holdings:** 800 books; 10 VF drawers of West Hartford social history archives; tax records; 6 VF drawers of pictures, clippings, scrapbooks, letters. **Services:** Copying; library open to the public with restrictions. **Computerized Information Services:** Internal database. **Publications:** Noah Webster, David C. Sargent, 1976; From Colonial Parish to Modern Suburb: A Brief Appreciation of West Hartford, Nelson R. Burr, 1976 - for sale; The Spectator, quarterly - to members. **Staff:** Criss Watson, Libn.

★ 20135 ★
Webster & Sheffield - Library
237 Park Ave.
New York, NY 10017
Defunct.

★ 20136 ★
Weekly Reader Corporation - Library (Educ, Publ)
245 Long Hill Rd.   Phone: (203)638-2760
Middletown, CT 06457   Robert Cumming, Sr.Libn.
Staff: Prof 2. **Subjects:** Education, current affairs, social studies, language arts, reading. **Holdings:** 16,000 books; 160 VF drawers of news releases, clippings, pamphlets; 2400 microforms; 137 VF drawers of photographs and illustrations; 2 VF drawers of cartoons. **Subscriptions:** 300 journals and other serials; 10 newspapers. **Services:** Library open to the public for reference use only. **Computerized Information Services:** NEXIS. **Networks/Consortia:** Member of Southern Connecticut Library Council (SCLC). **Remarks:** FAX: (203)638-2787. **Formerly:** Field Corporation - Field Publications - Library. **Staff:** Barbara Wallach, Asst.Libn.

I.D. Weeks Library
See: **University of South Dakota - I.D. Weeks Library** (19317)

★ 20137 ★
Wehran Envirotech - Library (Env-Cons)
666 E. Main St.   Phone: (914)343-0660
Middletown, NY 10940   Virginia Grady, Libn.
Founded: 1978. **Staff:** Prof 1; Other 1. **Subjects:** Solid waste, wastewater, and water management; resource recovery; industrial pollution abatement; environmental monitoring. **Special Collections:** EPA reports on air, water, and waste. **Holdings:** 1480 books; 2000 government reports. **Subscriptions:** 100 journals and other serials. **Services:** Interlibrary loan; library open to the public with restrictions. **Computerized Information Services:** BRS Information Technologies, DIALOG Information Services, IRIS. **Networks/Consortia:** Member of Southeastern New York Library Resources Council (SENYLRC). **Publications:** The Word from WE (newsletter) - for internal distribution only. **Special Catalogs:** Serial holdings (printout). **Remarks:** FAX: (914)692-7376.

A.T. Wehrle Memorial Library
See: **Pontifical College Josephinum** (13211)

G. Weigel Archives
See: **Woodstock Theological Center - Library** (20581)

Weigel Library of Architecture and Design
See: **Kansas State University** (8575)

★ 20138 ★
Weil, Gotshal & Manges - Library (Law)
767 Fifth Ave.   Phone: (212)310-8663
New York, NY 10153   Blanche B. Johnston, Dir., Lib.Serv.
Subjects: Law. **Special Collections:** Business reorganization, customs law, litigation, corporate law, intellectual property, trade regulation, tax, real estate, employment law and ERISA, international trade law. **Holdings:** 70,000 books; 2000 bound periodical volumes. **Subscriptions:** 3500 journals and other serials. **Services:** Interlibrary loan; library not open to the public. **Computerized Information Services:** DIALOG Information Services, Dow Jones News/Retrieval, DataTimes, LEXIS, NewsNet, Inc., WESTLAW, ORBIT Search Service, BRS Information Technologies, ECHO, Data-Star, Information America, InvesText, LEGI-SLATE, RLIN, IDD Information Services, Reuter Country Reports, LRS (Legislative Retrieval System), Dun & Bradstreet Business Credit Services, EXTEL, ICC, IMSMARQ, Info Globe, Infomart Online, Comtext, FT PROFILE, Spectrum, Reuter TEXTLINE; CD-ROMs (Laser D/SEC, Compact D/SEC, Compact D/'33). **Publications:** Access (newsletter). **Remarks:** FAX: (212)310-8786; (212)735-4800. **Staff:** Deborah Cinque, Asst.Dir., Lib.Serv.; Robert M. Berntsen, Corp.Libn.; Kathleen McGee, Tax./Ref.Libn.; Mary Thompson, Res.Libn.; Jim Wagler, Res.Libn.; Shabeer Khan, Ref.Libn.; Joseph Dottavio, Tech.Serv.Libn.

★ 20139 ★
Weinberg & Green, Attorneys-at-Law - Library (Law)
100 S. Charles St.   Phone: (301)332-8651
Baltimore, MD 21201   Sally J. Miles, Libn.
Staff: Prof 2; Other 3. **Subjects:** Law. **Holdings:** 30,000 books; 300 bound periodical volumes. **Subscriptions:** 300 journals and other serials. **Services:** Interlibrary loan; copying; SDI; library open to serious researchers by appointment. **Computerized Information Services:** LEXIS, NEXIS, DIALOG Information Services, Maxwell Macmillan Taxes Online, Dow Jones News/Retrieval, WESTLAW. **Publications:** Acquisitions List, monthly - for internal distribution only. **Staff:** Allyn Simon, Asst.Libn.

Jack Weinberg Library
See: **Illinois State Psychiatric Institute** (7704)

Max and Edith Weinberg Library
See: **Temple Israel** (16112)

★ 20140 ★
Weinberg Nature Center - Library (Biol Sci)
455 Mamaroneck Rd.   Phone: (914)723-4784
Scarsdale, NY 10583   Walter Terrell, Dir.
Founded: 1958. **Subjects:** Botany, ornithology, forestry, geology, environmental education. **Holdings:** 500 books. **Subscriptions:** 10 journals and other serials. **Services:** Library open to the public for reference use only. **Remarks:** Maintained by Village of Scarsdale.

Rabbi Dudley Weinberg Library
See: **Congregation Emanu-El B'ne Jeshurun** (4158)

Weiner Library
See: **Fairleigh Dickinson University** (5569)

Norman D. Weiner Professional Library
See: **Friends Hospital** (6174)

Weinlos Library
See: **Misericordia Hospital** (10503)

Weinreich Library and Archives of Yiddish Linguistics
See: **Yivo Institute for Jewish Research - Library and Archives** (20759)

★ 20141 ★
Robert Weinstein Maritime Historical Collection (Aud-Vis)
1253 S. Stanley Ave.   Phone: (213)936-0558
Los Angeles, CA 90019   Robert Weinstein, Owner
Subjects: Sailing ships of all countries and trades. **Holdings:** 250,000 original and copy photographs, glass negatives, clippings, post cards. **Services:** Library not open to the public.

John A. Weir Memorial Law Library
See: **University of Alberta** (18199)

★ 20142 ★
Paul Weir Company - Library
2340 River Rd., No. 203
Des Plaines, IL 60018
Subjects: Coal, coal geology, mining engineering and laws, coal and mineral benefication. **Holdings:** 1000 books; 18 shelves of technical reports; 24 shelves of foreign publications; 36 shelves of state publications. **Remarks:** Currently inactive.

Theofield G. Weis Library
See: **Columbia Union College** (3999)

Alex F. Weisberg Library
See: **Temple Emanu-El** (16097)

Edward Weiss Reading Center for the Visually Impaired
See: **Temple Beth El of Greater Buffalo - Library** (16088)

★ 20143 ★
Louis A. Weiss Memorial Hospital - L. Lewis Cohen Memorial Medical Library (Med)
4646 N. Marine Dr.   Phone: (312)878-8700
Chicago, IL 60640   Iris Sachs, Med.Libn.
Staff: Prof 1. **Subjects:** Medicine, pre-clinical sciences. **Holdings:** 1100 books; 800 bound periodical volumes. **Subscriptions:** 131 journals and other serials. **Services:** Interlibrary loan; copying; SDI; library open to the public with restrictions. **Computerized Information Services:** NLM; DOCLINE (electronic mail service). Performs searches on fee basis. **Networks/Consortia:** Member of Metropolitan Consortium of Chicago, ILLINET, National Network of Libraries of Medicine - Greater Midwest Region.

★ 20144 ★
Welborn, Dufford, Brown & Tooley, P.C. - Law Library (Law)
1700 Broadway, Suite 1700   Phone: (303)861-8013
Denver, CO 80290-1701   Cori Arsenault, Firm Libn.
Founded: 1981. **Staff:** Prof 1. **Subjects:** Bankruptcy; real estate; law - oil and gas, environmental resources, mining, water. **Holdings:** Figures not available. **Subscriptions:** 129 journals and other serials. **Services:** Interlibrary loan; copying; library open to other law librarians. **Computerized Information Services:** LEXIS, NEXIS. **Networks/Consortia:** Member of Colorado Alliance of Research Libraries (CARL). **Publications:** Library Newsletter, bimonthly - for internal distribution only. **Special Indexes:** Index to local court rule changes. **Remarks:** FAX: (303)832-3804.

William H. Welch Medical Library
See: **Johns Hopkins University** (8432)

★ 20145 ★
Weld County District Court - Law Library (Law)
Weld County Court House
P.O. Box C   Phone: (303)356-4000
Greeley, CO 80362   Oleta B. Weber, Libn.
Founded: 1924. **Staff:** Prof 1. **Subjects:** Law. **Holdings:** 18,000 books; 265 bound periodical volumes; 12,100 reports; 650 laws; 1050 texts. **Services:** Copying; library open to the public.

★ 20146 ★
Weld Library District - Downtown Branch - Special Collections (Area-Ethnic)
919 7th St.　　　　　　　　　　　Phone: (303)350-9210
Greeley, CO 80631　　　　　　　　Charlene Parker, Br.Supv.
Staff: Prof 2; Other 10. **Subjects:** Germans from Russia - history, genealogy, personal reminiscences; history and genealogy - Greeley, Weld County, Colorado. **Special Collections:** Colorado history collection; Greeley Tribune, 1870 to present (487 reels of microfilm). **Holdings:** 1450 books; 33 bound periodical volumes. **Subscriptions:** 13 journals and other serials. **Services:** Interlibrary loan; copying; collections open to the public. **Staff:** Shirley Soenksen, Ref.Libn.

★ 20147 ★
Rob & Bessie Welder Wildlife Foundation - Library (Biol Sci)
Drawer 1400　　　　　　　　　　Phone: (512)364-2643
Sinton, TX 78387　　　　　　　　Vaunda Boscamp, Libn.
Founded: 1954. **Subjects:** Natural history, ornithology, wildlife management, ecology and range management, environment and conservation, science and technology. **Special Collections:** Alexander Wetmore Library (former secretary of the Smithsonian Institution; 5274 volumes); Quillin Egg Collection. **Holdings:** 11,731 books; 2124 bound periodical volumes; 189 bound theses; 396 unbound reports and manuscripts; 500 archival items; 368 vertical files of Welder student contributions; 3267 vertical files of non-Welder reprints. **Subscriptions:** 59 journals and other serials. **Services:** Interlibrary loan; copying; library open to the public by appointment for reference use only. **Computerized Information Services:** Internal database. **Publications:** Reports and newsletters, biennial; Student Symposiums.

★ 20148 ★
Welding Engineers, Inc. - Library (Sci-Engr)
1600 Union Meeting Rd.　　　　　Phone: (215)643-6900
Blue Bell, PA 19422　　　　　　　Bonnie Shipley, Libn.
Subjects: Polymer processing, machine design. **Holdings:** Figures not available. **Remarks:** FAX: (215)825-3891. Telex: 550 286.

★ 20149 ★
Welding Institute of Canada - Technical Information Services (Sci-Engr)
391 Burnhamthorpe Rd., E.　　　　Phone: (416)257-9881
Oakville, ON, Canada L6J 6C9　　　Bruce Bryan, Libn.
Founded: 1973. **Staff:** Prof 1; Other 1. **Subjects:** Welding, nondestructive testing, metallurgy. **Special Collections:** International Institute of Welding (IIW) documents (3500). **Holdings:** 500 books; 550 bound periodical volumes; 3 VF drawers. **Subscriptions:** 45 journals and other serials. **Services:** Interlibrary loan; copying; library open to institute members for reference use. **Computerized Information Services:** DIALOG Information Services, PFDS Online, CAN/OLE; internal database. Performs searches on fee basis. **Publications:** Welding Technology for Canada, quarterly - to corporate members. **Remarks:** FAX: (416)257-9886.

Welding Research Council - American Council of the International Institute of Welding
See: American Council of the International Institute of Welding (550)

D.B. Weldon Library
See: University of Western Ontario (19555)

★ 20150 ★
Weldon Laboratory, Inc. - Library
608 W. 39th St.
Kansas City, MO 64111
Defunct.

Welex Halliburton Company
See: Halliburton Logging Services (6850)

Wellcome Library
See: Royal College of Veterinary Surgeons (14115)

★ 20151 ★
Wellesley College - Archives (Educ)
Wellesley, MA 02181　　　　　　　Phone: (617)235-0320
　　　　　　　　　　　　　　　　Wilma R. Slaight, Archv.
Staff: Prof 1; Other 1. **Subjects:** Wellesley College, women's education. **Holdings:** 4290 linear feet of archival material. **Services:** Copying; archives open to the public. **Automated Operations:** Computerized public access catalog, cataloging, acquisitions, serials, and circulation. **Computerized Information Services:** OCLC. **Networks/Consortia:** Member of NELINET, Inc., Boston Library Consortium (BLC). **Remarks:** FAX: (617)239-1139.

★ 20152 ★
Wellesley College - Art Library (Art)
Jewett Arts Center　　　　　　　Phone: (617)235-0320
Wellesley, MA 02181　　　　　　　Richard McElroy, Art Libn.
Founded: 1883. **Staff:** Prof 1; Other 1. **Subjects:** Art history with emphasis on Western European, American, Far Eastern, and classical art and architecture; photography. **Holdings:** 42,420 volumes. **Subscriptions:** 160 journals and other serials. **Services:** Interlibrary loan; library not open to the public. **Automated Operations:** Computerized public access catalog, cataloging, acquisitions, serials, and circulation. **Computerized Information Services:** OCLC, RLIN. **Networks/Consortia:** Member of NELINET, Inc., Boston Library Consortium (BLC).

★ 20153 ★
Wellesley College - Margaret Clapp Library - Special Collections (Hum, Hist)
Wellesley, MA 02181　　　　　　　Phone: (617)235-0320
　　　　　　　　　　　　　　　　Ruth Rogers, Spec.Coll.Libn.
Staff: Prof 1; Other 2. **Special Collections:** English Poetry Collection (including Robert and Elizabeth Barrett Browning; 12,000 volumes); Durant Collection (19th century America; 10,000 volumes); Plimpton Collection (15th and 16th century Italian literature; 1200 volumes); Book Arts Collection (4600 volumes); Alcove of North American Languages (Indian languages; 280 volumes); Elbert Collection (slavery and Reconstruction; 800 volumes); Juvenile Collection (1000 volumes); John Ruskin Collection (900 volumes); Guy Walker Collection (illustrated books; 350 volumes); Isabel and Charles Goodman Collection (book arts, fine presses, printing history; 2800 volumes). **Holdings:** 41,000 books; 20 linear feet of manuscripts and autographs. **Services:** Copying (limited); microfilming; collections open to the public. **Automated Operations:** Computerized public access catalog, cataloging, acquisitions, serials, and circulation. **Computerized Information Services:** OCLC, RLIN. **Networks/Consortia:** Member of NELINET, Inc., Boston Library Consortium (BLC). **Remarks:** FAX: (617)239-1139.

★ 20154 ★
Wellesley College - Music Library (Mus)
Jewett Arts Center　　　　　　　Phone: (617)235-0320
Wellesley, MA 02181　　　　　　　Ross Wood, Music Libn.
Founded: 1904. **Staff:** Prof 1; Other 1. **Subjects:** Music. **Holdings:** 28,090 volumes; 13,650 sound recordings. **Subscriptions:** 200 journals and other serials. **Services:** Interlibrary loan; library open to the public. **Automated Operations:** Computerized public access catalog, cataloging, acquisitions, serials, and circulation. **Computerized Information Services:** OCLC. **Networks/Consortia:** Member of NELINET, Inc., Boston Library Consortium (BLC), Boston Area Music Libraries (BAML).

★ 20155 ★
Wellesley College - Science Library (Biol Sci, Sci-Engr, Comp Sci)
Science Center　　　　　　　　　Phone: (617)235-0320
Wellesley, MA 02181　　　　　　　Irene S. Laursen, Sci.Libn.
Founded: 1976. **Staff:** Prof 1; Other 2. **Subjects:** Biological sciences, chemistry, computer science, geology, mathematics, physics, psychology. **Holdings:** 95,510 volumes. **Subscriptions:** 700 journals and other serials. **Services:** Interlibrary loan; copying; library open to the public with restrictions. **Automated Operations:** Computerized public access catalog, cataloging, acquisitions, serials, and circulation. **Computerized Information Services:** OCLC, DIALOG Information Services, WILSONLINE. **Networks/Consortia:** Member of NELINET, Inc., Boston Library Consortium (BLC).

★ 20156 ★
Wellesley Hospital - Library (Med)
160 Wellesley St., E.   Phone: (416)926-7071
Toronto, ON, Canada M4Y 1J3   Verla E. Empey, Mgr.
Founded: 1967. **Staff:** Prof 1; Other 3. **Subjects:** Medicine, nursing, and hospital administration. **Holdings:** 10,000 books; 8000 bound periodical volumes; 1 VF drawer of bibliographies; 2 VF drawers of staff publications; 100 AV programs; 4 VF drawers. **Subscriptions:** 400 journals and other serials. **Services:** Interlibrary loan; copying; SDI; library open to the public by appointment. **Computerized Information Services:** MEDLARS. **Remarks:** Electronic mail address(es): Wellesley.Library (Envoy 100).

★ 20157 ★
Wellington American Library - American Chancery - USIS Library
  (Educ)
29 Fitzherbert Terrace
Post Box 1190
Thorndon
Wellington 1, New Zealand   Phone: 4 722068
      Christine Vivian
Staff: 2. **Holdings:** 2500 books; 95 bound periodical volumes; 500 reports; 4 microfiche. **Subscriptions:** 95 journals and other serials; 5 newspapers. **Services:** Interlibrary loan; copying; SDI; library open to the public. **Computerized Information Services:** DIALOG Information Services, LEGI-SLATE, Kiwinet - National Library of New Zealand; CD-ROMs; PDQ (internal database). **Publications:** Spotlight. **Remarks:** FAX: 4 781701. Maintained or supported by the U.S. Information Agency. Focus is on materials that will assist peoples outside the United States to learn about the United States, its people, history, culture, political processes, and social milieux. **Staff:** Kate Hutton.

★ 20158 ★
Wellington County Board of Education - Education Library (Educ)
500 Victoria Rd., N.   Phone: (519)822-4420
Guelph, ON, Canada N1E 6K2   Paola Rowe, Educ.Libn.
Founded: 1973. **Staff:** Prof 1; Other 2. **Subjects:** School librarianship, educational psychology, teaching, children's literature, curriculum support materials, special education. **Holdings:** 14,000 books; 900 bound periodical volumes. **Subscriptions:** 900 journals and other serials. **Services:** Interlibrary loan; periodical routing services; current awareness services; library open to the public by prior arrangement. **Automated Operations:** Computerized public access catalog, cataloging, and circulation. **Computerized Information Services:** DIALOG Information Services, UTLAS, Info Globe, BRS Information Technologies, CAN/OLE; CD-ROMs. **Publications:** Educational Aids. **Remarks:** FAX: (519)763-6870.

★ 20159 ★
Wellington County Board of Education - Teacher Resource Library
  (Educ)
500 Victoria Rd. N.   Phone: (519)822-4420
Guelph, ON, Canada N1E 6K2   Paola Rowe, Educ.Libn.
Founded: 1982. **Staff:** 1. **Subjects:** Special education, reading, life skills, French language, primary education, speech and language. **Special Collections:** AV programs in health education. **Holdings:** 17,000 books. **Services:** Library not open to the public. **Automated Operations:** Computerized catalog and circulation. **Publications:** TRL Bibliographies, irregular. **Remarks:** FAX: (519)822-4487.

★ 20160 ★
Wellington County Museum - Archives (Hist)
R.R. 1   Phone: (519)846-0916
Fergus, ON, Canada N1M 2W3   Bonnie Callen, Archv.
Founded: 1977. **Staff:** 1. **Subjects:** Municipal records, genealogy, maps and plans. **Special Collections:** District of Wellington municipal records; genealogies (600); Couling Collection (13,000 slides and architectural inventories of significant architectural sites in Wellington County). **Holdings:** 2300 books; 750 linear feet of municipal records and manuscripts; 11,000 photographs; 850 maps; 600 reels of microfilm of newspapers, land abstracts, municipal records, and other items. **Subscriptions:** 3 journals and other serials; 11 newspapers. **Services:** Copying; library open to the public. **Computerized Information Services:** Heritage Sentinel (internal database).

★ 20161 ★
Wellington Management Company - Research Library (Bus-Fin)
1201 W. Peachtree St., Suite 3150   Phone: (404)870-2870
Atlanta, GA 30309   Linda Swann Austin, Libn.
Founded: 1970. **Staff:** Prof 1. **Subjects:** Investment information. **Holdings:** 100 volumes; 480 company files on individual companies. **Subscriptions:** 44 journals and other serials. **Services:** Library open to the public by appointment with restrictions. **Special Catalogs:** Catalog of company files (card); catalog of analyst reports published internally (card). **Remarks:** FAX: (404)870-2870. Telex: (404)870-2899.

★ 20162 ★
Wellington Management Company - Research Library (Bus-Fin)
Box 823   Phone: (215)647-6000
Valley Forge, PA 19482   Jeanne Wilmer, Libn.
Staff: Prof 1; Other 1. **Subjects:** Corporate finance, industry. **Holdings:** 72 shelves of annual reports and financial information. **Subscriptions:** 60 journals and other serials; 15 newspapers. **Remarks:** Library located at 1300 Morris Dr., Wayne, PA 19087. FAX: (215)647-3651.

Earl H. Wellman, Sr., Memorial Library of the AFA
See: **Aerophilatelic Federation of the Americas** (108)

★ 20163 ★
A Wellness Center, Inc. - Library
P.O. Box 55
New York, NY 10003
Defunct.

★ 20164 ★
Wells Fargo Bank - History Department 2921 (Hist)
420 Montgomery St., No. 0101-026   Phone: (415)396-4157
San Francisco, CA 94163   Grace A. Evans, Cur./Asst. V.P.
Subjects: Wells Fargo and Company history, California gold rush and mining, staging and western transportation, history of banking and finance, San Francisco history, Californiana. **Special Collections:** Photographic Collection; Wiltsee Memorial Collection of Western Stamps, Franks and Postmarks. **Holdings:** 4000 books. **Subscriptions:** 15 journals and other serials. **Services:** Department open to qualified researchers by appointment.

★ 20165 ★
Wells Fargo Bank - Library 0188-056 (Bus-Fin)
111 Sutter St., 5th Fl.
San Francisco, CA 94163   Phone: (415)399-7357
Founded: 1890. **Staff:** Prof 3; Other 3. **Subjects:** Banking, finance. **Holdings:** 50,000 volumes; 24 drawers of microfiche. **Subscriptions:** 2200 journals and other serials; 32 newspapers. **Services:** Interlibrary loan; copying. **Automated Operations:** Computerized public access catalog, cataloging, acquisitions, serials, and circulation. **Computerized Information Services:** DIALOG Information Services, Dow Jones News/Retrieval, NEXIS, VU/TEXT Information Services, DataTimes, WILSONLINE. **Remarks:** Alternate telephone number(s): 399-7356. **Staff:** Peggy Merbach, Mgr., Ref.Serv.; Paul North, Mgr., Oper./Adm.; Richard Bittner, Ref.Libn.

Wells Freedom Archives
See: **Brigham Young University - Archives and Manuscripts Division**
  (20797)

H.G. Wells Collection
See: **University of Western Ontario** (19555)

W. Keith Welsh Library
See: **North York General Hospital** (11960)

Eudora Welty Collection
See: **University of West Florida** (19550)

Eudora Welty Library
See: **Jackson/Hinds Library System** (8306)

★ 20166 ★
Wenham Museum - Timothy Pickering Library (Hist)
132 Main St.   Phone: (508)468-2377
Wenham, MA 01984   Eleanor E. Thompson, Dir.
Founded: 1952. **Staff:** 7. **Subjects:** Local history, decorative arts, fashions and costumes, herbals and horticulture, agriculture, domestic and farm animals, genealogy and town histories, 19th century ice industry. **Special Collections:** Book collection of Massachusetts Society for Promoting Agriculture, founded 1792. **Holdings:** 2000 volumes; photographs; maps. **Services:** Library open to the public with restrictions.

Wenrich Memorial Library
See: **Landmark Society of Western New York** (8932)

★ 20167 ★
Wentworth Institute of Technology - Alumni Library (Sci-Engr)
550 Huntington Ave.   Phone: (617)442-9010
Boston, MA 02115   Ann Montgomery Smith, Dir. of Libs.
Founded: 1954. **Staff:** Prof 7; Other 5. **Subjects:** Electronics; metals and materials; engineering technology - computer, civil, electrical, mechanical; architecture. **Special Collections:** History of Technology collection; archives of the American Society for Engineering Education - Engineering Technology Divisions. **Holdings:** 77,788 volumes; 950 AV items; 13,300 microforms. **Subscriptions:** 525 journals. **Services:** Interlibrary loan; copying; library open to the public. **Automated Operations:** Computerized public access catalog, cataloging, acquisitions, serials, and circulation. **Computerized Information Services:** DIALOG Information Services; CD-ROMs (Art Index, Applied Science and Technology Index, ACADEMIC INDEX, Boston Globe). **Networks/Consortia:** Member of Fenway Library Consortium (FLC). **Remarks:** FAX: (617)442-5076. **Staff:** Rosemary Walker, Assoc.Libn.; Elizabeth Murray, Info.Serv.LIbn.; Judith Nudelman, Media Serv.Libn.; Michael Logan, Tech.Serv.Libn.; Priscilla Biondi, Arch.; Mary Ellen Flaherty, Archv.

★ 20168 ★
Wentworth Military Academy - Sellers-Coombs Library (Mil)
18th & Washington   Phone: (816)259-2221
Lexington, MO 64067   Fran Rushing, Libn.
Founded: 1879. **Staff:** Prof 1. **Special Collections:** Military history; military science. **Holdings:** 17,000 books; 1200 bound periodical volumes; 4800 microfiche; 350 reels of microfilm. **Subscriptions:** 9 journals and other serials. **Services:** Library not open to the public. **Remarks:** FAX: (816)259-2677.

A.R. Wentz Library
See: **Lutheran Theological Seminary** (9464)

Wentzel Medical Library
See: **Manatee Memorial Hospital** (9584)

Lillie B. Werner Health Sciences Library
See: **Rochester General Hospital** (13978)

★ 20169 ★
Wertheim Schroder and Company, Inc. - Research Library (Bus-Fin)
Equitable Center
787 7th Ave.   Phone: (212)492-6840
New York, NY 10019-6016   Laura Ryder, Hd.Libn.
Founded: 1927. **Staff:** Prof 1; Other 4. **Subjects:** Finance, business, economics, industrial statistics. **Special Collections:** Robert Fisher Manuals of Obsolete Companies; Moody's manuals, 1937 to present; historical Monthly Stock Summary, 1950 to present. **Holdings:** 400 books; 375 reels of microfilm; 60,000 microfiche. **Subscriptions:** 54 journals and other serials. **Services:** Interlibrary loan; library open to clients and students by appointment. **Computerized Information Services:** DIALOG Information Services, Dow Jones News/Retrieval, NEXIS, The Financial Post DataGroup, Reuter TEXTLINE, Data-Star. **Remarks:** FAX: (212)492-6545.

★ 20170 ★
Carl L. Weschcke Library (Rel-Phil)
16363 Norell Ave., N.   Phone: (612)443-2321
Marine-on-St. Croix, MN 55047   Carl L. Weschcke, Pres.
Subjects: Astrology, Tantra, occultism, alchemy, witchcraft, Tarot. **Special Collections:** Bondage fetishism. **Holdings:** 20,000 books; 200 bound periodical volumes. **Subscriptions:** 25 journals and other serials. **Services:** Library open to the public with written application. **Remarks:** The library is associated with Llewellyn Publications.

★ 20171 ★
Wesley Biblical Seminary - Library (Rel-Phil)
Box 9938   Phone: (601)957-1314
Jackson, MS 39286-0938   Wayne W. Woodward, Dir. of Lib.Serv.
Founded: 1974. **Staff:** Prof 1; Other 1. **Subjects:** Theology. **Holdings:** 37,000 books; 89 bound periodical volumes. **Subscriptions:** 167 journals and other serials. **Services:** Interlibrary loan; copying; library open to the public. **Computerized Information Services:** DIALOG Information Services. **Remarks:** FAX: (601)957-1314.

Wesley Collection
See: **United Methodist Church - South Georgia Conference - Commission on Archives and History - Arthur J. Moore Methodist Museum - Library** (16739)

★ 20172 ★
Wesley Medical Center - H.B. McKibbin Health Science Library (Med)
550 N. Hillside
Wichita, KS 67214   Phone: (316)688-2715
Founded: 1956. **Staff:** Prof 2; Other 3. **Subjects:** Medicine and nursing. **Holdings:** 10,000 books; 21,000 bound periodical volumes. **Subscriptions:** 500 journals and other serials. **Services:** Library open to Wesley employees and the local medical community. **Computerized Information Services:** MEDLINE, DIALOG Information Services, BRS Information Technologies, VU/TEXT Information Services; internal database. **Staff:** Jane Tanner, Libn.; Leslie James, Libn.

★ 20173 ★
Wesley Theological Seminary - Library (Rel-Phil)
4500 Massachusetts Ave., N.W.   Phone: (202)885-8691
Washington, DC 20016   Allen W. Mueller, Dir.
Founded: 1882. **Staff:** Prof 3; Other 3. **Subjects:** Theology, Bible, religion, allied fields. **Special Collections:** Materials related to the former Methodist Protestant Church; Wesleyana. **Holdings:** 114,500 books; 14,400 bound periodical volumes; 1298 AV programs; 1228 tapes; 521 microforms. **Subscriptions:** 650 journals; 10 newspapers. **Services:** Interlibrary loan; library open to the public. **Automated Operations:** Computerized cataloging, acquisitions, and ILL. **Computerized Information Services:** OCLC, WILSONDISC. **Networks/Consortia:** Member of Washington Theological Consortium, CAPCON Library Network.

★ 20174 ★
Wesley United Methodist Church - Library (Rel-Phil)
721 King St.   Phone: (608)782-3018
La Crosse, WI 54601   Dorothy Balts, Libn.
Founded: 1966. **Staff:** Prof 1; Other 5. **Subjects:** Religion, philosophy, literature, children's collection, social sciences, fine arts. **Holdings:** 2400 books; 84 filmstrips; 33 phonograph records; 2 VF drawers of pamphlets, study guides. **Services:** Library open to the public.

★ 20175 ★
Wesley United Methodist Church - Resource Library (Rel-Phil)
400 Iowa Ave.
Muscatine, IA 52761   Phone: (319)263-1596
Founded: 1977. **Staff:** Prof 1; Other 1. **Subjects:** Christian education, Bible study, personal development, parenting, family relations, children's literature, Christian biographies and fiction. **Holdings:** 2500 books; phonograph records; media kits; games. **Subscriptions:** 4 journals and other serials. **Services:** Library open to the public. **Networks/Consortia:** Member of Cokesbury Church Library Services (CLS). **Staff:** Judy Kramer, Libn.; Alice Witter.

★ 20176 ★
Wesleyan Church - Archives & Historical Library (Rel-Phil)
8050 Castleway Dr.
Box 50434   Phone: (317)576-1315
Indianapolis, IN 46250   Craig Dunn, Dir. of Archv.
Founded: 1968. **Staff:** 2. **Subjects:** History of The Wesleyan Church, the Wesleyan Methodist Church, Pilgrim Holiness Church, Reformed Baptist Alliance, Methodist church. **Holdings:** 6000 books; 350 bound periodical volumes; 12 filmstrips; 1050 cassettes; 300 reels of microfilm reels; 900 manuscripts, theses, and papers; district journals; conference minute books; journals; photographs; correspondence. **Services:** Interlibrary loan; copying; library open to the public. **Staff:** Donna Watson.

★ 20177 ★
Wesleyan University - Library - Special Collections (Art, Hum)
Middletown, CT 06457   Phone: (203)347-9411
                    Elizabeth A. Swaim, Spec.Coll.Libn./Archv.
Founded: 1831. **Staff:** Prof 1; Other 1. **Subjects:** English and American literature and civilization, history of printing, Methodistica, Wesleyan University and Middletown history. **Special Collections:** Henry Bacon papers (architecture; 30 feet); Wilbur O. Atwater papers (agricultural chemistry; 13.5 feet); Gorham Munson and social credit (33 feet). **Holdings:** 25,029 books; 350 feet of manuscripts and archives. **Services:** Copying; collections open to the public by appointment.

★ 20178 ★
Wesleyan University - Library - World Music Archives (Mus)
Middletown, CT 06457   Phone: (203)347-9411
                    James Farrington, Mus.Libn.
Founded: 1965. **Staff:** Prof 4. **Subjects:** Ethnomusicology, non-Western music, Western nonclassical music. **Special Collections:** Music of North American Indians (especially Navajo ceremonial music), Java (music and language), Bali, Philippines, Japan, Korea, China, South India, British Isles, Greece, Afghanistan, Iran, Turkey, and West Africa. **Holdings:** 4000 audiotapes; 12,000 sound discs; 150 videotapes; 8 VF drawers of indices, translations, and transcriptions. **Services:** Archives open to the public by appointment. **Automated Operations:** Computerized public access catalog. **Computerized Information Services:** BITNET, InterNet (electronic mail services). **Networks/Consortia:** Member of NELINET, Inc., CTW Consortium. **Remarks:** Electronic mail address(es): JFARRINGTON@WESLEYAN (BITNET); jfarrington@eagle.Weslayan.edu (InterNet).

★ 20179 ★
Wesleyan University - Psychology Library (Med)
Judd Hall   Phone: (203)347-9411
Middletown, CT 06457   Shirley Schmottlach, Lib.Asst.
Founded: 1910. **Staff:** 1. **Subjects:** Psychology, psychoanalysis, behavioral sciences, neurosciences, cognitive sciences, women's studies. **Holdings:** 18,200 books; 8801 bound periodical volumes; 295 bound theses. **Subscriptions:** 200 journals and other serials. **Services:** Interlibrary loan; copying; library open to the public with restrictions. **Automated Operations:** Computerized public access catalog and circulation. **Networks/Consortia:** Member of CTW Consortium.

★ 20180 ★
Wesleyan University - Science Library (Biol Sci, Sci-Engr)
Middletown, CT 06457   Phone: (203)347-9411
                    Penny Russman, Sci.Libn.
Founded: 1972. **Staff:** Prof 2; Other 4. **Subjects:** Astronomy, biology, chemistry, earth sciences, mathematics, physics, molecular biology, biochemistry. **Special Collections:** History of Science (early editions; 888 volumes). **Holdings:** 158,806 volumes; 112,792 maps. **Subscriptions:** 927 journals and other serials. **Services:** Interlibrary loan; copying; library open to the public with permission. **Automated Operations:** Computerized public access catalog. **Computerized Information Services:** DIALOG Information Services, BRS Information Technologies, WILSONLINE, Chemical Abstracts Service (CAS). Performs searches on fee basis. **Networks/Consortia:** Member of CTW Consortium. **Publications:** Database Search Services; Science Journals; new books list. **Staff:** Alexa Jaffurs.

George H. Wessel Memorial Library
See: **Hialeah Hospital** (7185)

Nils Yngve Wessell Library
See: **Tufts University - Nils Yngve Wessell Library** (16552)

★ 20181 ★
West Africa Rice Development Association - WARDA Library and Information Services (Food-Bev, Agri)
01 BP 2551
Bouake 01, Cote d'Ivoire   Alassane Diallo, Libn.
Subjects: Rice production, food crops in the tropics. **Holdings:** 15,000 volumes. **Services:** Interlibrary loan; copying; SDI; library open to the public for reference use only. **Computerized Information Services:** West African Rice Bibliography (WARBI; internal database); electronic mail service. **Remarks:** FAX: (225)63-47-14. Telex: 69138 ADRAO CI. **Formerly:** Located in Monrovia, Liberia. **Also Known As:** Association pour le Developpement de la Riziculture en Afrique de l'Ouest (ADRAO).

★ 20182 ★
West Allis Memorial Hospital - Medical Library (Med)
8901 W. Lincoln Ave.   Phone: (414)546-6162
West Allis, WI 53227   Joan A. Clausz, Med.Libn.
Staff: Prof 1. **Subjects:** Medicine. **Special Collections:** NCME videotapes (1984 to present). **Holdings:** 500 books; 900 bound periodical volumes. **Subscriptions:** 100 journals and other serials. **Services:** Interlibrary loan; library not open to the public. **Computerized Information Services:** BRS Information Technologies, MEDLARS; DOCLINE (electronic mail service). **Networks/Consortia:** Member of Southeastern Wisconsin Health Science Library Consortium (SWHSL). **Special Catalogs:** Videotape subject catalog.

★ 20183 ★
West Bend Gallery of Fine Arts - Library (Art)
300 S. 6th Ave.   Phone: (414)334-9638
West Bend, WI 53095   Linda Goetz, Musm.Asst.
Founded: 1987. **Staff:** 1. **Subjects:** Art history, biography reference, value reference, art techniques. **Special Collections:** Letters, sketches, and documents of American-German artist Carl von Marr, 1850-1936; Wisconsin Art History Reference, 1850-1950. **Holdings:** 1000 books; 153 videotapes. **Subscriptions:** 4 journals and other serials. **Services:** Copying; library open to the public. **Special Catalogs:** Carl von Marr catalog.

West Canadian Graphic Industries Ltd.
See: **Commonwealth Microfilm Products** (4066)

★ 20184 ★
West Central Georgia Regional Hospital - Library (Med)
3000 Schatulga Rd.
Box 12435   Phone: (404)568-5236
Columbus, GA 31995-7499   Linda Venuto, Sr.Libn.
Founded: 1976. **Staff:** Prof 1; Other 1. **Subjects:** Alcohol and drug abuse, bibliotherapy, brief and short-term therapy/counseling, consumer/patient education, forensic psychiatry, psychiatric nursing, psychiatric social work, psychology. **Holdings:** 4500 books; 246 bound periodical volumes; 825 AV programs. **Subscriptions:** 60 journals and other serials. **Services:** Interlibrary loan; copying; SDI; library open to the public with restrictions. **Computerized Information Services:** MEDLINE. **Networks/Consortia:** Member of Georgia Health Sciences Library Association (GHSLA), Georgia Online Database (GOLD), Health Science Libraries Consortium of Central Georgia (HSLCG), National Network of Libraries of Medicine - Southeastern/Atlantic Region. **Publications:** Library Manual; brochures; policy statements. **Remarks:** FAX: (404)568-5339. Maintained by the Division of Mental Health, Mental Retardation and Substance Abuse. **Staff:** Linda Ames, Sec.Sr.

★ 20185 ★
West Central Minnesota Historical Center - Library (Hist)
University of Minnesota, Morris   Phone: (612)589-2211
Morris, MN 56267   John Q. Imholte, Dir.
Founded: 1973. **Staff:** 2. **Subjects:** Ethnicity in west central Minnesota, agribusiness, Minnesota politics and government, oral history, church history. **Special Collections:** Stevens County Census Computerization Project; The Great Depression in West Central Minnesota; Powerline Construction Oral History Project; World War II: The Home Front in Central Minnesota (oral history). **Holdings:** 650 linear feet of local history materials; oral history cassettes; microfilm. **Services:** Copying; library open to the public. **Remarks:** FAX: (612)589-3811. Maintained by the University of Minnesota, Morris.

★ 20186 ★
West Chester University - Francis Harvey Green Library - Special Collections (Educ)
West Chester, PA 19383   Phone: (215)436-3456
        R. Gerald Schoelkopf, Spec.Coll.Libn.
Founded: 1871. **Staff:** Prof 1; Other 1. **Subjects:** Botanical history, history of Chester County and Pennsylvania, Chester County and Pennsylvania authors, physical education. **Special Collections:** William Darlington Library (rare scientific and botanical materials); Chester County Cabinet Library; Philips Autograph Library; Shakespeare folios; Ehinger Library (historical material on physical education; 581 items); Staley Weintraub Manuscript and Research Collection; Chester County Collection; university archives (700 boxes). **Holdings:** 9425 books; 200 bound periodical volumes; 5 folio drawers; 40 VF drawers; 100 magnetic tapes; 60 boxes of microfilm; 70 oral history tapes; 4100 photographs; 1800 glass slides. **Services:** Interlibrary loan; copying; collections open to the public for reference use, with borrowing privileges by special arrangement. **Automated Operations:** Computerized cataloging. **Computerized Information Services:** DIALOG Information Services, BRS Information Technologies, PFDS Online, OCLC. **Networks/Consortia:** Member of PALINET, Tri-State College Library Cooperative (TCLC), Interlibrary Delivery Service of Pennsylvania (IDS), State System of Higher Education Libraries Council (SSHELCO). **Special Catalogs:** Periodical list (online). **Special Indexes:** Index to scrapbook, newspaper clippings, and photograph collection; index to classification and finding aides (both online). **Remarks:** FAX: (215)436-2251.

★ 20187 ★
West Chester University - School of Music Library (Mus)
Francis Harvey Green Library
High St. & Rosedale Ave.   Phone: (215)436-2430
West Chester, PA 19383   Paul Emmons, Mus.Libn./Asst.Prof.
Founded: 1960. **Staff:** Prof 1; Other 1. **Subjects:** Music history, opera, instrumental music, jazz, contemporary music, American music. **Special Collections:** Gilbert and Sullivan (100 items). **Holdings:** 24,000 scores; 20,000 phonograph records. **Subscriptions:** 60 journals and other serials. **Services:** Interlibrary loan; copying; library open to the public with restrictions. **Automated Operations:** Computerized, public access catalog, cataloging, serials, and circulation. **Computerized Information Services:** OCLC, DIALOG Information Services, BRS Information Technologies, PFDS Online. **Networks/Consortia:** Member of PALINET, Tri-State College Library Cooperative (TCLC), Interlibrary Delivery Service of Pennsylvania (IDS), State System of Higher Education Libraries Council (SSHELCO). **Special Indexes:** Song title file; record analytic file; piano music file; women composers; early music file.

★ 20188 ★
West Coast Christian College - McBrayer Library (Rel-Phil)
6901 N. Maple Ave.   Phone: (209)299-7201
Fresno, CA 93710   Edward E. Call, Hd.Libn.
Founded: 1949. **Staff:** Prof 1; Other 1. **Subjects:** Religion, philosophy, literature, psychology, social science, science. **Special Collections:** Pentecostal Studies Research; Studies in Seventh Day Adventism; Studies in Christian Scientism. **Holdings:** 52,500 books; 691 bound periodical volumes; 2465 microforms; 5 films; 349 filmstrips; 108 video cassettes; 1102 audio cassettes; 105 reels of microfilm; 61 transparencies; 1344 phonograph records. **Subscriptions:** 712 journals and other serials; 8 newspapers. **Services:** Interlibrary loan; copying; center open to the public for reference use only. **Networks/Consortia:** Member of Area Wide Library Network (AWLNET). **Remarks:** Maintained by the Church of God, Cleveland, TN 37311. **Staff:** William Henry, Circ.Libn.

★ 20189 ★
West Coast University - Elconin Center Library (Sci-Engr, Bus-Fin)
440 Shatto Place   Phone: (213)487-4433
Los Angeles, CA 90020   Kathleen P. Ellison, Dir. of Libs.
Staff: Prof 2. **Subjects:** Business, engineering, computer science. **Holdings:** 15,000 books; unbound periodicals. **Subscriptions:** 300 journals and other serials; 7 newspapers. **Services:** Interlibrary loan; copying; library open to the public with restrictions. **Computerized Information Services:** UCLA ORION User Services. **Remarks:** FAX: (213)380-4362. Maintains branches in Orange County, San Diego County, and Santa Barbara County. **Staff:** Rena Ren

★ 20190 ★
West End Synagogue - Library (Rel-Phil)
3810 West End Ave.   Phone: (615)269-4592
Nashville, TN 37205   Annette Levy Ratkin, Dir.
Staff: Prof 1. **Subjects:** Judaica, children's literature, Yiddish. **Holdings:** 4400 books. **Services:** Interlibrary loan; copying; library open to the public.

★ 20191 ★
West Florida Regional Medical Center - Medical Library (Med)
8383 N. Davis Hwy.
Box 18900   Phone: (904)494-4490
Pensacola, FL 32523-8900   Kay Franklin, Dir./Med.Libn.
Founded: 1954. **Staff:** Prof 1; Other 1. **Subjects:** Clinical medicine, oncology. **Special Collections:** Chadbourne Collection (oncology; 90 books). **Holdings:** 1500 books. **Subscriptions:** 307 journals and other serials. **Services:** Interlibrary loan; library not open to the public. **Automated Operations:** Computerized serials and ILL. **Computerized Information Services:** NLM, BRS Information Technologies, DIALOG Information Services; CD-ROM (MEDLINE). **Remarks:** FAX: (904)494-4826.

★ 20192 ★
West Georgia College - Irvine Sullivan Ingram Library - Annie Belle Weaver Special Collections (Hist)
Carrollton, GA 30118   Phone: (404)836-6495
        Myron W. House, Spec.Coll.Libn.
Founded: 1933. **Staff:** Prof 1. **Subjects:** West Georgia College archives, history of western Georgia, Sacred Harp music. **Special Collections:** Robert H. Claxton papers (5 linear feet); William H. Row papers (5 linear feet); Melvin T. Steely papers (1 linear foot); Alice Nix papers (1 linear foot); W. Benjamin Kennedy papers (1 linear foot); Thomas A. Bryson papers (13 linear feet); Robert D. Tisinger papers (2 linear feet); James E. Boyd papers (13 linear feet); Ward Pafford papers (4 linear feet); Tracy Stallings papers (10 linear feet); Sidney M. Jourard papers (76 linear feet); Association for Humanistic Education (1 linear foot); William G. Roll papers (18 linear feet); Fourth District A & M School Collection (144 items; 19 volumes); Irvine S. Ingram papers (50 linear feet); J. Ebb Duncan papers (4 linear feet); J. Roy Martin papers (2 linear feet); Whatley Family papers (4 linear feet); oral history collection (155 audio cassettes; 102 video cassettes). **Holdings:** 2473 volumes; 20,236 clippings, letters, photographs, maps; 233 feet of manuscript collections. **Services:** Copying; collections open to the public.

★ 20193 ★
West Georgia Regional Library - Genealogy Collection (Hist)
710 Rome St.   Phone: (404)836-6711
Carrollton, GA 30117   James P. Cooper, Dir.
Founded: 1944. **Subjects:** Genealogy, local history, family history. **Holdings:** 3000 books; 2000 nonbook items. **Services:** Interlibrary loan; copying; collection open to the public. **Remarks:** FAX: (404)651-9615. **Staff:** Roni L. Willis, Asst.Dir.

West Indian Reference Library
See: **Trinidad and Tobago - Ministry of Education - Central Library Services** (16499)

★ 20194 ★
West Jersey Health System, Voorhees Division - Staff Medical Library (Med)
101 Carnie Blvd.   Phone: (609)772-5494
Voorhees, NJ 08043   Susan E. Cleveland, Lib.Dir.
Founded: 1976. **Staff:** Prof 1. **Subjects:** Medicine, nursing, administration. **Holdings:** 1000 books; 3000 bound periodical volumes; 15 AV programs. **Subscriptions:** 165 journals and other serials. **Services:** Interlibrary loan; copying; SDI; library open to the public for reference use only. **Computerized Information Services:** MEDLARS; DOCLINE (electronic mail service). **Networks/Consortia:** Member of Southwest New Jersey Consortium for Health Information Services, New Jersey Library Network, Region One Cooperating Library Service Unit, Inc., National Network of Libraries of Medicine (NN/LM), BHSL. **Remarks:** FAX: (609)772-5066.

★ 20195 ★
West Liberty State College - Elbin Library (Educ, Bus-Fin)
West Liberty, WV 26074   Phone: (304)336-8035
      Nancy Sandercox, Coll.Libn.
Founded: 1932. **Staff:** Prof 5; Other 8. **Special Collections:** Krise Rare Book Collection (400 volumes); college archives (10 filing drawers; 130 file boxes; 43 volumes). **Services:** Interlibrary loan; copying; library open to the public. **Computerized Information Services:** DIALOG Information Services; CD-ROM. Performs searches on fee basis. **Networks/Consortia:** Member of Pittsburgh Regional Library Center (PRLC). **Publications:** Accessions List, monthly; Handbook. **Staff:** Jeanne Schramm, Ref.Libn.; Mrs. Francis Stewart, AV Libn.; Rosey Miller, Media Spec.; John Shearer, Acq.Libn.; Jennifer Cross, Asst.Libn. for ILL.

★ 20196 ★
West Park Hospital - Health Disciplines Library (Med)
82 Buttonwood Ave.   Phone: (416)243-3600
Toronto, ON, Canada M6M 2J5   Lois Elliott, Libn.
Founded: 1980. **Staff:** Prof 1. **Subjects:** Medicine, nursing, and allied health sciences, including geriatrics, social services, administration, and rehabilitation. **Special Collections:** Archives dealing with the history of tuberculosis in Toronto. **Holdings:** 600 books; patient records, journals, and other early material on treatment of tuberculosis. **Subscriptions:** 71 journals and other serials. **Services:** Interlibrary loan; library not open to the public. **Remarks:** FAX: (416)243-8947.

Roscoe L. West Library
See: **Trenton State College** (16484)

★ 20197 ★
West Seattle Community Hospital - Library
2600 S.W. Holden St.
Box C26002
Seattle, WA 98126
Defunct.

West Side Medical Center
See: **U.S. Dept. of Veterans Affairs** (IL-Chicago) (17326)

★ 20198 ★
West Suburban Hospital Medical Center - Health Information Center (Med)
Erie at Austin   Phone: (708)383-6200
Oak Park, IL 60302   Constance M. Gibbon, Libn.
Staff: Prof 1; Other 1. **Subjects:** Consumer health. **Holdings:** 900 books; 350 videotapes; pamphlets. **Subscriptions:** 25 journals and other serials. **Services:** Interlibrary loan; copying; center open to the public. **Automated Operations:** Computerized cataloging and acquisitions. **Computerized Information Services:** MEDLINE, BRS Information Technologies. Performs searches on fee basis. **Networks/Consortia:** Member of Suburban Library System (SLS), Metropolitan Consortium of Chicago. **Publications:** Healthinfo - for internal distribution only.

★ 20199 ★
West Suburban Hospital Medical Center - Walter Lawrence Memorial Library (Med)
Erie at Austin   Phone: (708)383-6200
Oak Park, IL 60302   Carol Scherrer, Dir. of Lib. & Info.Serv.
Founded: 1978. **Staff:** Prof 1; Other 1. **Subjects:** Clinical medicine, nursing. **Holdings:** 4000 books; 10 microfiche drawers of journal titles; 400 videotapes. **Subscriptions:** 350 journals and other serials; 5 newspapers. **Services:** Interlibrary loan; copying; SDI; library open to the public by appointment. **Automated Operations:** Computerized acquisitions. **Computerized Information Services:** MEDLINE, BRS Information Technologies. **Networks/Consortia:** Member of National Network of Libraries of Medicine - Greater Midwest Region, Metropolitan Consortium of Chicago, Suburban Library System (SLS). **Publications:** Library News, quarterly - internal distribution and to colleagues upon request. **Remarks:** FAX: (708)383-8783.

★ 20200 ★
West Tennessee Historical Society - Library (Hist)
Memphis State University
Box 111046
Memphis, TN 38111   Phone: (901)567-4518
Founded: 1935. **Staff:** Prof 1; Other 2. **Subjects:** Western Tennessee, Memphis and regional history. **Holdings:** 1000 books; 80 cubic feet of 19th and early 20th century manuscripts, scrapbooks, and articles including archives of the society and its predecessor organizations, 1857 to present. **Subscriptions:** 10 journals and other serials. **Services:** Copying; library open to the public. **Publications:** West Tennessee Historical Society Papers, annual. **Special Indexes:** Composite indexes to WTHS Papers and Guide to West Tennessee Historical Society Publications. **Remarks:** Alternate telephone number(s): 678-2210. Library is part of Memphis State University Libraries - Special Collections. **Staff:** Michele Fagin, Cur.

★ 20201 ★
West Valley Medical Center - Health Information Center (Med)
1717 Arlington   Phone: (208)459-4641
Caldwell, ID 83605   Lesley Woods, Act.Libn.
Staff: 2. **Subjects:** Medicine, consumer health. **Holdings:** 276 books; 60 bound periodical volumes; 200 pamphlets; 300 other cataloged items. **Subscriptions:** 55 journals and other serials; 5 newspapers. **Services:** Interlibrary loan; copying; SDI; library open to the public with restrictions. **Automated Operations:** Computerized cataloging, acquisitions, and circulation. **Computerized Information Services:** MEDLINE; EMS (electronic mail service). **Networks/Consortia:** Member of Boise Valley Health Sciences Library Consortium, National Network of Libraries of Medicine - Pacific Northwest Region.

★ 20202 ★
West Valley Nuclear Services Company, Inc. - Technical Library (Sci-Engr)
10300 Rock Springs Rd.
West Valley, NY 14171-0191   C.M. Schiffhauer
Founded: 1982. **Staff:** Prof 1. **Subjects:** Nuclear waste management; engineering - mechanical, civil, chemical. **Holdings:** 900 books; 4000 government contractor reports. **Subscriptions:** 93 journals and other serials. **Services:** Library not open to the public. **Computerized Information Services:** DIALOG Information Services; Westinghouse Electronic Mail Service (WEMS). **Networks/Consortia:** Member of Western New York Library Resources Council (WNYLRC). **Remarks:** Company is a subsidiary of Westinghouse Electric Corporation.

West Virginia Pulp and Paper Company
See: **Westvaco Corporation** (20350)

★ 20203 ★
West Virginia School of Osteopathic Medicine - WVSOM Library (Med)
400 N. Lee St.   Phone: (304)647-6261
Lewisburg, WV 24901-0827   Mary Frances Bodemuller, Dir., Educ.Rsrcs.
Founded: 1973. **Staff:** Prof 2; Other 4. **Subjects:** Medicine. **Holdings:** 11,000 books; 3000 bound periodical volumes; 4000 AV programs. **Subscriptions:** 512 journals and other serials; 5 newspapers. **Services:** Interlibrary loan; copying; library open to the public with restrictions. **Computerized Information Services:** MEDLINE. Performs searches on fee basis. **Publications:** WVSOM Newsletter, monthly. **Remarks:** FAX: (304)645-4859.

★ 20204 ★
West Virginia Schools for the Deaf and Blind - School for the Blind Library (Aud-Vis)
301 E. Main St.   Phone: (304)822-4894
Romney, WV 26757   Donna See, Coord., Lib.Serv.
Founded: 1963. **Staff:** Prof 2; Other 1. **Subjects:** General collection. **Special Collections:** Education of the visually impaired. **Holdings:** 10,632 talking books; 370 magnetic tapes; 2891 braille books; 4120 print books; 480 commercial sound recordings. **Subscriptions:** 62 journals and other serials; 9 newspapers. **Services:** Interlibrary loan; library not open to the public. **Networks/Consortia:** Member of National Library Service for the Blind & Physically Handicapped (NLS). **Staff:** Cynthia Johnson, Libn.

★ 20205 ★
West Virginia State Attorney General - Law Library (Law)
State Capitol, Rm. 26E
Charleston, WV 25305   Phone: (304)348-2021
Staff: Prof 1. **Subjects:** Law. **Holdings:** 8678 volumes. **Services:** Library not open to the public. **Computerized Information Services:** WESTLAW, LEXIS. **Publications:** Biennial Report & Opinions of Attorney General - for sale. **Remarks:** FAX: (304)348-0140.

★ 20206 ★
West Virginia State Board of Rehabilitation - Division of Rehabilitation Services - Staff Library (Med)
Rehabilitation Center   Phone: (304)766-4644
Institute, WV 25112-1004   Mrs. Jo Skiles, Staff Libn.
Founded: 1966. **Staff:** Prof 1. **Subjects:** Physical and vocational rehabilitation, behavioral sciences, management, medicine. **Special Collections:** Division of Vocational Rehabilitation research and development projects (52). **Holdings:** 12,218 books; 6000 monographs, reports, projects; 93 16mm films; 36 slides and cassettes; 504 videotapes. **Subscriptions:** 56 journals and other serials. **Services:** Interlibrary loan; copying; library open to the public with restrictions. **Special Catalogs:** Film catalog.

★ 20207 ★
West Virginia State Commission on Aging - Resource Center (Soc Sci)
State Capitol
Holly Grove   Phone: (304)348-2917
Charleston, WV 25305   Tom Dudley
Founded: 1980. **Staff:** Prof 1. **Subjects:** Gerontology. **Holdings:** 9063 books; 7 shelves of reports, bulletins; 5 VF drawers of pamphlets. **Subscriptions:** 25 journals and other serials. **Services:** Interlibrary loan; copying; library open to the public. **Computerized Information Services:** Internal database. **Publications:** Annual progress report; brochures.

★ 20208 ★
West Virginia (State) Department of Agriculture - Library (Biol Sci, Agri)
Capitol Bldg.   Phone: (304)348-2212
Charleston, WV 25305   Jean H. Martin, Lib.Dir.
Founded: 1973. **Staff:** Prof 1. **Subjects:** Entomology, plant pathology, regulation and inspection, forestry, animal health and breeding, pesticide regulations. **Special Collections:** Entomology (30,000 items). **Holdings:** 5000 books; 900 bound periodical volumes; 500 boxes of pamphlets. **Subscriptions:** 70 journals and other serials. **Services:** Interlibrary loan; copying; library open to state agencies and college students with permission. **Computerized Information Services:** Internal database. **Publications:** Acquisition List for Books, quarterly; alphabetical and subject lists of journals, monthly.

★ 20209 ★
West Virginia (State) Department of Education and the Arts - Division of Culture and History - Archives and History Library (Hist)
Cultural Center, Capitol Complex
Charleston, WV 25305   Phone: (304)348-0230
Founded: 1905. **Staff:** Prof 6; Other 7. **Subjects:** West Virginia archives, history, genealogy; history - U.S., Civil War, colonial, military. **Special Collections:** Governors' papers (500 linear feet); manuscripts (1189 linear feet); Boyd Stutler-John Brown Collection (50 cubic feet); agency records; state documents (22,200); county court records (5800 reels of microfilm); newspapers (15,000 reels of microfilm and clippings); military and land records (2500 reels of microfilm). **Holdings:** 70,000 books; 10,200 bound periodical volumes; 6838 linear feet of state archives; 174 linear feet of special collections; 25,000 reels of microfilm; 30,000 photographs; 500 stories on newsfilm and videotape from four West Virginia television stations, 1955-1982; 6000 maps; 7500 architectural drawings; 24 VF drawers of clippings. **Subscriptions:** 250 journals and other serials; 95 newspapers. **Services:** Copying; library open to the public for reference use only. **Publications:** West Virginia History, annual; Checklist of State Publications, semiannual. **Remarks:** FAX: (304)348-2779. **Staff:** Fredrick Armstrong, Dir.; Debra Basham, Archv.; Carol Vandevender, Per./Doc.Libn.; Richard Fauss, AV Archv.

★ 20210 ★
West Virginia (State) Department of Health - Office of Laboratory Services - Library (Med)
167 11th Ave.   Phone: (304)348-3530
South Charleston, WV 25303   Jennifer J. Graley, Sec.
Staff: 1. **Subjects:** Public health. **Holdings:** 500 books. **Subscriptions:** 12 journals and other serials. **Services:** Library open to the public with director's permission.

★ 20211 ★
West Virginia (State) Department of Highways - Right of Way Division Library (Trans, Law)
State Capital Complex, Bldg. 5   Phone: (304)348-3195
Charleston, WV 25305   J. Riely, Dir.
Founded: 1963. **Staff:** 1. **Subjects:** Real estate appraisal, eminent domain, highway severance and research studies, building costs, right of way operating manuals. **Holdings:** 1400 volumes; 2 VF drawers of pamphlets; 200 slides; appraisal cassette tapes. **Subscriptions:** 20 journals and other serials. **Services:** Library open to the public at librarian's discretion. **Special Catalogs:** Appraisal subjects on cards.

★ 20212 ★
West Virginia (State) Division of Highways - Planning, Research, and Special Studies Section - Library (Trans)
Capital Complex Bldg. 5, Rm. 803   Phone: (304)348-3181
Charleston, WV 25305   Dale Crouser, Adm.Asst.
Founded: 1963. **Staff:** Prof 2. **Subjects:** Highway maintenance, materials research, highway construction, traffic engineering, planning, environment. **Holdings:** 7000 volumes of reports from the Federal Highway Administration, National Highway Cooperative Research Program, Transportation Research Board, and state research projects. **Subscriptions:** 10 journals and other serials. **Services:** Interlibrary loan; copying; library open to educational institutions and government agencies. **Computerized Information Services:** DIALOG Information Services, Transportation Research Information Services (TRIS). **Publications:** Research reports on state-conducted and sponsored studies. **Special Catalogs:** Listing of completed studies. **Special Indexes:** Catalog of available documents. **Staff:** Dr. T.V. Ramakrishna

★ 20213 ★
West Virginia (State) Legislative Reference Library (Law)
Capitol Bldg., Rm. 206 W.   Phone: (304)348-2153
Charleston, WV 25305   Mary Del Cont, Libn.
Founded: 1957. **Staff:** Prof 1. **Subjects:** Legislation, law, education, government and finance, taxation. **Holdings:** 3150 volumes; 7 VF drawers of legislative reports from other states; 3 vertical files of reports of Council of State Governments; 4 VF drawers of newspaper clippings. **Subscriptions:** 37 journals and other serials. **Services:** Interlibrary loan; library open to the public. **Publications:** Reports of the Legislative Auditor's Office.

★ 20214 ★
West Virginia (State) Library Commission - Film Services Department (Aud-Vis)
Science and Cultural Center   Phone: (304)348-3976
Charleston, WV 25305   Steve Fesenmaier, Hd. Film Serv.
Founded: 1976. **Staff:** Prof 2; Other 3. **Special Collections:** Appalachia (250 films); astronomy (10 films); women (100 films); feature films (2000); Les Blank Collection (30 films); foreign feature films (300); black history and culture (200 films); independent animation (500 titles). **Holdings:** 5000 16mm sound films. **Subscriptions:** 12 journals and other serials. **Services:** Interlibrary loan (within state); department open to the public. **Publications:** WVLC Film Services Newsletter, quarterly - to WV public libraries; Pickflick Papers (online); Library Trustees Manual, 1989. **Special Catalogs:** Video Catalog, 1989. **Special Indexes:** Pickflick Papers III and supplements; filmographies on energy, women, Appalachia, features. **Remarks:** Conducts state and local film workshops and annual film festival. **Staff:** Frani Fesenmaier, Asst.Hd.

★ 20215 ★
West Virginia (State) Library Commission - Reference Library (Info Sci)
Cultural Center   Phone: (304)348-2045
Charleston, WV 25305   Karen E. Goff, Ref.Libn.
Founded: 1929. **Staff:** Prof 2; Other 5. **Subjects:** Political science, public administration, social welfare, economics. **Holdings:** 85,981 volumes; 19,640

reels of microfilm of periodicals; 191,223 microfiche; U.S. Government documents depository. **Subscriptions:** 756 journals and other serials. **Services:** Interlibrary loan; copying; library open to the public. **Automated Operations:** Computerized cataloging, acquisitions, and circulation. **Computerized Information Services:** DIALOG Information Services. **Publications:** West Virginia Library Commission Newsletter, quarterly. **Special Indexes:** Charleston Newspaper Index, annual. **Staff:** Ma Lei Hsieh, Doc.Libn.

★20216★
West Virginia (State) Library Commission - Services for the Blind and Physically Handicapped (Aud-Vis)
Cultural Center
Charleston, WV 25305
Phone: (304)348-4061
Donna Calvert, Hd.
Staff: Prof 1. **Subjects:** General collection. **Special Collections:** Blindness and physical handicaps; West Virginia. **Holdings:** 15,786 large-print books; 102,095 nonbook materials. **Subscriptions:** 55 journals and other serials; 10 newspapers. **Services:** Interlibrary loan; copying; SDI; library open to persons meeting Library of Congress eligibility requirements. **Computerized Information Services:** NLSREADS (internal database). **Publications:** Newsletter (large-print, cassette, braille), quarterly - to patrons. **Remarks:** Collection is composed of 16 percent large-print books, 21 percent Talking Book records, and 63 percent Talking Book cassettes. Toll-free telephone number(s): (800)642-8674.

★20217★
West Virginia (State) Supreme Court of Appeals - State Law Library (Law)
Capitol Bldg., Rm. E-320
Charleston, WV 25305
Phone: (304)348-2607
Marjorie Price, Supreme Court Law Libn.
Founded: 1863. **Staff:** Prof 2; Other 3. **Subjects:** Law. **Special Collections:** State Constitutional Convention Debates; G.P.O. Collection; English and Canadian law; West Virginia documents. **Holdings:** 100,000 books; 25,000 bound periodical volumes; 2500 microfiche. **Subscriptions:** 544 journals and other serials. **Services:** Interlibrary loan; copying; library open to the public. **Computerized Information Services:** WESTLAW. **Publications:** Annual Report to the State Supreme Court; Acquisitions List, irregular. **Special Catalogs:** Periodical Holdings. **Remarks:** FAX: (304)348-3815. **Staff:** Kimberly Crawford, Tech.Serv.Libn.

★20218★
West Virginia State Tax Department - Research & Development Division - Library (Bus-Fin)
Revenue Ctr.
1001 Lee St. E.
Charleston, WV 25301
Phone: (304)348-8730
Subjects: Taxation, energy, economic research. **Holdings:** 1000 books; reports. **Subscriptions:** 53 journals and other serials. **Services:** Library not open to the public. **Computerized Information Services:** Internal databases (tax). **Remarks:** FAX: (304)348-8733.

★20219★
West Virginia University - College of Business and Economics - Bureau of Business Research (Bus-Fin)
328 Business and Economics Bldg.
Box 6025
Morgantown, WV 26506-6025
Phone: (304)293-5837
Linda Culp, Bus.Res.Anl.
Founded: 1949. **Staff:** 10. **Subjects:** Economics, West Virginia economy. **Special Collections:** Association for Business and Economic Research, Bureau of Economic Analysis, Census Data Centers, and Conference Board publications. **Holdings:** 500 books; 2000 other cataloged items. **Subscriptions:** 60 journals and other serials. **Services:** Bureau open to the public. **Computerized Information Services:** Bureau of Economic Analysis (computer tapes, diskettes); census computer tapes, diskettes, and CD-ROM. **Publications:** University Research in Business and Economics, annual - for sale; West Virginia Business and Economic Review, quarterly - free upon request; The Journal of Small Business Management, quarterly - for sale; West Virginia County Data Profiles, annual - for sale. **Remarks:** FAX: (304)293-7061.

★20220★
West Virginia University - College of Creative Arts - Music Library (Mus)
P.O. Box 6111
424-A Creative Arts Center
Morgantown, WV 26506-6111
Phone: (304)293-4505
John Core, Supv.
Staff: Prof 1; Other 12. **Subjects:** Music. **Special Collections:** Fry Jazz Archives (4000 pre-1945 phonograph records). **Holdings:** 14,000 books and bound periodical volumes; 14,500 scores; 950 reels of microfilm; 95 titles on microcards; 12,000 sound recordings. **Subscriptions:** 160 journals and other serials. **Services:** Interlibrary loan; library open to the public with restrictions. **Networks/Consortia:** Member of Pittsburgh Regional Library Center (PRLC). **Special Catalogs:** Fry Archives catalog (card).

★20221★
West Virginia University - Health Sciences Library (Med)
3110 Maccorkle Ave., S.E.
Charleston, WV 25304
Phone: (304)347-1285
Patricia Powell, Hd.Libn.
Founded: 1974. **Staff:** Prof 2; Other 4. **Subjects:** Medicine, nursing. **Holdings:** 19,000 books; 15,000 bound periodical volumes; 1800 AV programs. **Subscriptions:** 525 journals and other serials. **Services:** Interlibrary loan; copying; center open to the public. **Automated Operations:** Computerized cataloging. **Computerized Information Services:** DIALOG Information Services, OCLC, MEDLINE. Performs searches on fee basis. **Networks/Consortia:** Member of Pittsburgh Regional Library Center (PRLC). **Remarks:** Alternate telephone number(s): 347-1282.

★20222★
West Virginia University - Health Sciences Library (Med)
Health Sciences N.
Morgantown, WV 26506-6306
Phone: (304)293-2113
Robert Murphy, Dir.
Founded: 1954. **Staff:** Prof 7; Other 11. **Subjects:** Medicine, dentistry, pharmacy, nursing, hospital administration. **Special Collections:** Medicine in West Virginia; occupational respiratory diseases. **Holdings:** 53,416 books; 147,399 bound periodical volumes; 879 dissertations and theses; 6098 reels of microfilm containing 469 titles; 10,661 microfiche containing 550 titles; 3800 slides and films. **Subscriptions:** 2227 journals and other serials. **Services:** Interlibrary loan; copying; SDI; library open to the public for reference use only. **Automated Operations:** Computerized cataloging and serials union list (NOTIS). **Computerized Information Services:** DIALOG Information Services, BRS Information Technologies, PFDS Online, OCLC, Chemical Abstracts Service (CAS); West Virginia Union List of Serials (internal database). Performs searches on fee basis. **Networks/Consortia:** Member of Pittsburgh Regional Library Center (PRLC), National Network of Libraries of Medicine - Southeastern/Atlantic Region. **Publications:** What's New, irregular. **Remarks:** FAX: (304)293-7319. **Staff:** Marge Abel, Assoc.Dir.; Ellen Sayed, ILL & Network; Judy Lesso, Ref.; Jean Allyson McKee, Hd.Tech.Serv.; Gloria Hwang, Cat.; Lynn Eads, AV.

★20223★
West Virginia University - Law Library (Law)
Law School
Box 6135
Morgantown, WV 26506-6135
Phone: (304)293-5309
Camille M. Riley, Law Libn.
Founded: 1878. **Staff:** Prof 3; Other 8. **Subjects:** Law. **Holdings:** 155,219 volumes; 200,999 microfiche. **Subscriptions:** 2296 journals and other serials. **Services:** Interlibrary loan; copying; library open to the public. **Computerized Information Services:** LEXIS, WESTLAW, OCLC, InfoTrac. **Remarks:** FAX: (304)293-6891. **Staff:** Carol S. Davis, Tech.Serv.Libn.; Malgorzata Pawska, Circ.Libn.

★20224★
West Virginia University - Office of Health Services Research - Library (Med)
Health Sciences South
Morgantown, WV 26506
Phone: (304)293-2601
Stephanie Pratt, Res.Asst. III
Founded: 1979. **Staff:** 1. **Subjects:** Census and vital statistics, hospital discharges, Medicaid and Medicare, employment-related health insurance, small computer systems development, adolescent pregnancy. **Holdings:** Books; reports; census documents for West Virginia and contiguous states; tape files of vital statistics for West Virginia; census tape files for West Virginia. **Subscriptions:** 10 journals and other serials. **Services:** Copying; library open to the public by appointment. **Computerized Information Services:** Internal databases; BITNET (electronic mail service). **Publications:** West Virginia State Census Data Center Newsletter; printed reports and documents containing West Virginia census data. **Remarks:** FAX: (304)293-6685. Electronic mail address(es): U3B50@WVNVM (BITNET).

★ 20225 ★
West Virginia University - West Virginia and Regional History
   Collection (Hist)
University Library
Colson Hall   Phone: (304)293-3536
Morgantown, WV 26506   John A. Cuthbert, Interim Cur.
Founded: 1935. **Staff:** Prof 3; Other 7. **Subjects:** Appalachian, regional,
state, and local history, literature, arts, and genealogy. **Holdings:** 27,000
volumes; 22,810 reels of microfilm; 12,000 linear feet of manuscripts and
archives; 1200 newspapers; 100,000 photographs; oral histories; folk music;
university archives. **Subscriptions:** 200 journals and other serials; 95
newspapers. **Services:** Interlibrary loan; copying; library open to the public.
Computerized Information Services: OCLC. **Publications:** Newsletter,
triannual - to members of West Virginia and Regional History Association.
Staff: Harold M. Forbes, Assoc.Cur.; Kenneth Fones-Wolf, Assoc.Cur.

★ 20226 ★
West Virginia Wesleyan College - Annie Merner Pfeiffer Library (Hist)
College Ave.   Phone: (304)473-8013
Buckhannon, WV 26201   Benjamin F. Crutchfield, Jr., Dir., Lib.Serv.
Founded: 1890. **Staff:** Prof 3; Other 6. **Subjects:** History of Methodist
Church in West Virginia; history of Upshur County, West Virginia;
Lincolniana. **Special Collections:** Charles Aubrey Jones Lincolniana (3000
items); Pearl S. Buck Manuscripts (68 Hollinger boxes; 200 file envelopes).
Holdings: 133,000 volumes; 12,000 unbound periodicals; 7000 volumes in
microform; 6681 AV programs. **Subscriptions:** 642 journals and other
serials; 22 newspapers. **Services:** Interlibrary loan; copying (limited); library
open to the public for reference use only. **Automated Operations:**
Computerized cataloging. **Computerized Information Services:** DIALOG
Information Services, EPIC, ATLAS (internal database). **Networks/
Consortia:** Member of Pittsburgh Regional Library Center (PRLC). **Special
Catalogs:** Media Catalog. **Remarks:** Alternate telephone number(s): 473-
8000. **Staff:** Judith R. Martin, Cat.; David G. Nowak, Ref.Libn.

★ 20227 ★
West Volusia Memorial Hospital - Medical Library (Med)
Box 509   Phone: (904)734-3320
De Land, FL 32721-0509   Carolyn E. Creeron, Med.Libn.
Founded: 1967. **Staff:** Prof 1. **Subjects:** Medicine and allied health sciences.
Holdings: 514 books; 150 bound periodical volumes. **Subscriptions:** 43
journals and other serials. **Services:** Interlibrary loan; library not open to the
public. **Computerized Information Services:** MEDLARS. **Remarks:** FAX:
(904)738-3102.

Wilma L. West Library
See: **American Occupational Therapy Foundation and Association (702)**

★ 20228 ★
Westchester County Department of Parks, Recreation and Conservation -
   Trailside Nature Museum (Area-Ethnic)
Ward Pound Ridge Reservation
Cross River, NY 10518   Phone: (914)763-3993
                                                       Beth Herr, Cur.
Founded: 1977. **Staff:** Prof 3. **Subjects:** Delaware culture, Native American
herbalism, Algonkian tribes of the Eastern United States, Algonkian
linguistics, Northeastern United States archeology, tribes of the greater New
York area. **Special Collections:** Rare books on native cultures of Southern
New York; taped oral history interviews with Delaware elders (50).
Holdings: 1000 books; 500 bound periodical volumes; 10 file boxes of
unbound material. **Services:** Copying; center open to the public by
appointment for reference use only. **Formerly:** Its Delaware Indian
Resource Center. **Staff:** Rebecca McElhinney.

★ 20229 ★
Westchester County Historical Society - Library (Hist)
2199 Saw Mill River Rd.   Phone: (914)592-4323
Elmsford, NY 10523   Elizabeth G. Fuller, Libn.
Founded: 1874. **Staff:** Prof 1. **Subjects:** Genealogy and history of
Westchester County and New York State, history of New York City. **Special
Collections:** French scrapbooks (43); Barron picture collection (New York
City and the Revolutionary War; 225 volumes); Sanchis' Architecture of
Westchester Picture Collection (8 VF drawers). **Holdings:** 5000 books; 350
bound periodical volumes; 8 VF drawers of manuscripts; 6 VF drawers of
photographs; 12 VF drawers of clippings; 10 drawers of maps.
Subscriptions: 27 journals and other serials. **Services:** Copying; library open
to the public.

★ 20230 ★
Westchester County Medical Center - Health Sciences Library (Med)
Eastview Hall   Phone: (914)285-7033
Valhalla, NY 10595   Charlene Sikorski, Med.Libn.
Founded: 1925. **Staff:** Prof 1; Other 1. **Subjects:** Medicine, nursing,
psychiatry, psychology, dentistry. **Holdings:** 12,000 volumes. **Subscriptions:**
190 journals and other serials. **Services:** Interlibrary loan; copying; library
open to the public with permission of librarian. **Computerized Information
Services:** MEDLARS. **Networks/Consortia:** Member of Health
Information Libraries of Westchester (HILOW), BHSL, New York
Metropolitan Reference and Research Library Agency. **Publications:**
Acquisitions List, quarterly; Orientation and Information Manual.

★ 20231 ★
Westcoast Energy Inc. - Library (Energy)
1333 W. Georgia St., 14th Fl.   Phone: (604)691-5517
Vancouver, BC, Canada V6E 3K9   Beatrice P. Yakimchuk, Libn.
Founded: 1970. **Staff:** Prof 2; Other 1.5. **Subjects:** Energy regulation and
law. **Special Collections:** History of Westcoast Energy Inc. (20 books; 2
drawers of clippings). **Holdings:** 10,000 books; 1400 annual reports; 12 VF
drawers; 4 VF drawers of clippings; 200 other cataloged items; 4 drawers
of microfiche. **Subscriptions:** 653 journals and other serials; 20 newspapers.
Services: Interlibrary loan; copying; library open to the public with
restrictions. **Computerized Information Services:** DIALOG Information
Services, Info Globe, CAN/OLE. **Remarks:** FAX: (604)691-5884. Telex:
045 1340. **Staff:** Louise Barre, Asst.Libn.; Susan Neumann, Lib.Techn.

★ 20232 ★
Westerly Hospital - Z.T. Tang Medical Library (Med)
Wells St.   Phone: (401)596-6000
Westerly, RI 02891   Natalie V. Lawton, Libn.
Founded: 1956. **Staff:** Prof 1. **Subjects:** Medicine, surgery. **Holdings:** 686
books; 525 bound periodical volumes. **Subscriptions:** 61 journals and other
serials. **Services:** Interlibrary loan; copying; library open to the public for
reference use only by request. **Computerized Information Services:**
MEDLINE, DOCLINE. **Networks/Consortia:** Member of Association of
Rhode Island Health Sciences Librarians (ARIHSL), BHSL. **Remarks:**
FAX: (401)596-3260.

Western Archeological and Conservation Center
See: **U.S. Natl. Park Service (17789)**

★ 20233 ★
Western Australia - Department of Agriculture - Library (Agri)
Baron Hay Court   Phone: 9 3683201
South Perth, WA 6151, Australia   J. Maughan, Chf.Libn.
Subjects: Agriculture, veterinary science, entomology, botany, food
technology. **Holdings:** 30,000 books; 20,000 pamphlets; 3000 periodical
titles. **Subscriptions:** 1500 journals and other serials. **Services:** Interlibrary
loan; copying; SDI; library open to the public for reference use only.
Computerized Information Services: DIALOG Information Services,
AUSTRALIS, MEDLINE, OZLINE; FARMTI (internal database).
Contact Person: Pat Thorn. **Special Indexes:** Indexes of the W.A.D.A.
Bulletins and Journal Articles. **Remarks:** FAX: 9 3681205.

★ 20234 ★
Western Baptist Memorial Library (Rel-Phil)
2119 Tracy   Phone: (816)842-4195
Kansas City, MO 64108   Floy L. Watson
Founded: 1989. **Subjects:** Religion, philosophy, natural sciences, philology.
Holdings: 7000 books.

★ 20235 ★
Western Canada Aviation Museum - Library/Archives (Sci-Engr)
Hangar T-2
958 Ferry Rd.
Winnipeg, MB, Canada R3H 0Y8   Phone: (204)786-5503
Founded: 1974. **Subjects:** Aircraft and aviation, with emphasis on Canada
and civil history. **Special Collections:** Materials from unpublished sources
(aircraft drawings and blueprints; log books of aircraft and pilots; records
of TransCanada Airlines Overhaul & Engineering Division; oral histories);
aircraft maintenance and overhaul manuals; parts catalogues. **Holdings:**
Books; 20,000 photographs; audio tapes; microfilm, periodicals; reports;
textbooks; videotapes; 16mm films. **Services:** Copying; library/archives
open to researchers by appointment only.

★ 20236 ★
Western Canadian Universities - Marine Biological Society - Devonian Library (Biol Sci)
Bamfield Marine Sta.   Phone: (604)728-3301
Bamfield, BC, Canada V0R 1B0   Leslie Rimmer, Lib.Coord.
Staff: 1. **Subjects:** Marine biology, ecology, plants, and mammals; biological oceanography; fisheries; aquaculture. **Special Collections:** K.D. Hobson Collection (reprints on polychaetes; 4 VF drawers); W.S. Hoar Collection (reprints on fish physiology). **Holdings:** 3000 books; 1061 bound periodical volumes; 1400 unbound journals; 2000 reports and bulletins; 40 VF drawers of reprints; 84 dissertations. **Subscriptions:** 38 journals and other serials. **Services:** Interlibrary loan; copying; library open to the public for reference use only. **Computerized Information Services:** Envoy 100 (electronic mail service). **Remarks:** FAX: (604)728-3452. Electronic mail address(es): BAMFIELD.MARINE (Envoy 100).

★ 20237 ★
Western Carolina University - Hunter Library - Map Room (Geog-Map)
Cullowhee, NC 28723   Phone: (704)227-7316
                                  Anita K. Oser, Hd., Maps
Founded: 1980. **Staff:** Prof 1.25. **Holdings:** 192 books; 100,806 maps; 499 atlases; 78 gazetteers. **Services:** Interlibrary loan; copying; room open to the public. **Automated Operations:** Computerized cataloging. **Computerized Information Services:** BITNET (electronic mail service). **Remarks:** Electronic mail address(es): AOser@WCU VAX1 (BITNET).

★ 20238 ★
Western Carolina University - Hunter Library - Special Collections (Area-Ethnic, Biol Sci)
Cullowhee, NC 28723   Phone: (704)227-7474
                                  George Frizzell, Unit Hd.
Founded: 1953. **Staff:** 2. **Subjects:** Western North Carolina, Cherokee Indians. **Special Collections:** Appalachia (1200 volumes; 220 manuscript collections); spider behavior (200 volumes); Cherokee Documents in Foreign Archives Collection, 1632-1909 (manuscript sources from foreign archives relating specifically to the Cherokee and to southern Indians in general; 821 reels of microfilm). **Services:** Interlibrary loan (Cherokee document microfilm only); copying; collections open to the public. **Automated Operations:** Computerized cataloging and serials. **Computerized Information Services:** Online Manuscript Search Service (internal database). Performs searches free of charge. **Networks/Consortia:** Member of SOLINET.

★ 20239 ★
Western Center on Law and Poverty, Inc. - Library (Soc Sci)
3535 W. 6th St.   Phone: (213)487-7211
Los Angeles, CA 90020   Richard A. Rothschild, Act.Libn.
Staff: Prof 1; Other 1. **Subjects:** Poverty, education, consumer protection, discrimination, employment, housing, health, welfare. **Holdings:** 5000 books; pamphlets; pleadings; reprints. **Subscriptions:** 60 journals and other serials. **Services:** Interlibrary loan; center open to the public with restrictions. **Computerized Information Services:** WESTLAW; internal database. **Remarks:** FAX: (213)487-0242.

★ 20240 ★
Western Connecticut State University - Ruth A. Haas Library - Special Collections (Hist)
181 White St.   Phone: (203)797-4052
Danbury, CT 06810-6885   Ralph W. Holibaugh, Dir. of Lib.Serv.
Founded: 1903. **Staff:** Prof 11. **Special Collections:** Connecticut and Fairfield County history; Instructional Media Center; government documents (1700 linear feet); Young Business Collection. **Services:** Interlibrary loan; copying; collections open to the public for reference use only. **Automated Operations:** Computerized cataloging, acquisitions, and circulation. **Computerized Information Services:** OCLC, DIALOG Information Services, BRS Information Technologies. Performs searches on fee basis. **Networks/Consortia:** Member of NELINET, Inc. **Publications:** Library Handbook.

★ 20241 ★
Western Conservative Baptist Seminary - Cline-Tunnell Library (Rel-Phil)
5511 S.E. Hawthorne Blvd.   Phone: (503)233-8561
Portland, OR 97215   Robert A. Krupp, Lib.Dir.
Founded: 1927. **Staff:** Prof 3; Other 4. **Subjects:** Religion, theology, psychology. **Special Collections:** Oregon Baptist history. **Holdings:** 69,000 books; 1250 bound periodical volumes; 4 VF drawers of pamphlets; 11,550 AV programs; 11,350 titles on microform. **Subscriptions:** 1040 journals and other serials; 10 newspapers. **Services:** Interlibrary loan; copying; library open to the public by registration and with limited loan privileges. **Automated Operations:** Computerized cataloging. **Computerized Information Services:** DIALOG Information Services, OCLC. **Staff:** Karen Arvin, Cat.Libn.; Betty Lu Johnstone, Rd.Serv.Libn.; Audrey Arnst, Per.Libn.; Larry Schumacher, Asst.Lib.Dir.

★ 20242 ★
Western Costume Company - Research Library (Hist)
11041 Vanowen St.   Phone: (818)760-0902
North Hollywood, CA 91605   Sally Nelson-Harb, Dir., Res.
Founded: 1915. **Staff:** Prof 1; Other 1. **Subjects:** Clothing, military and civilian uniforms, insignia, medals and decorations, police uniforms, occupational clothing, sports clothing, ecclesiastical clothing, folk dress. **Special Collections:** Sears, Roebuck and Montgomery Ward clothing catalogs, 1895 to present (70); wardrobe photographs from 20th Century-Fox films, 1930-1975 (800 volumes); London Illustrated News, 1843 to present (bound). **Holdings:** 12,000 volumes; 107 VF drawers; bound periodical volumes. **Subscriptions:** 60 journals and other serials. **Services:** Copying; library open to the public on a fee basis. **Special Indexes:** Index of clothing, especially uniforms, as worn by world police and military, occupational groups, the clergy, ethnic groups, and famous individuals (historical and contemporary). **Remarks:** FAX: (818)508-0468.

★ 20243 ★
Western Curriculum Coordination Center (WCCC) - Resource Center (Educ)
1776 University Ave., Wist 216   Phone: (808)956-6496
Honolulu, HI 96822   Victor W. Harke, Libn.
Founded: 1977. **Staff:** Prof 1; Other 4. **Subjects:** Vocational education and guidance. **Holdings:** 26,000 books; 4 VF drawers of pamphlets and clippings; 350 microfiche; 127 filmstrips; 76 kits; 140 video recordings. **Subscriptions:** 122 journals and other serials. **Services:** Center open to the public with restrictions. **Computerized Information Services:** Internal database. Performs searches. **Special Catalogs:** Special Groups (minorities and women); productivity; small engines; energy; computers and computer-assisted instruction; entrepreneurship; bilingual education; drug education. **Remarks:** Maintained by U.S. Department of Education. Center serves American Samoa, Arizona, California, Guam, Hawaii, Nevada, Northern Marianas, Republic of the Marshall Islands, Republic of Palau, and the Federated States of Micronesia.

★ 20244 ★
Western Evangelical Seminary - George Hallauer Memorial Library (Rel-Phil)
4200 S.E. Jennings Ave.   Phone: (503)654-5182
Milwaukie, OR 97267   Patricia Kuehne, Act.Dir.
Founded: 1947. **Staff:** Prof 2; Other 3. **Subjects:** Religion, theology, philosophy, ethics, marriage, family. **Holdings:** 53,513 books; 7010 bound periodical volumes; 19 filmstrips; 498 cassette tapes; 203 magnetic tapes; 73 reels of microfilm; 19 phonograph records; 150 maps; 308 multimedia kits; 11 videotapes; 82 volumes on microfiche. **Subscriptions:** 446 journals and other serials; 8 newspapers. **Services:** Interlibrary loan; copying. **Automated Operations:** computerized cataloging. **Computerized Information Services:** DIALOG Information Services, OCLC. Performs searches on fee basis. **Networks/Consortia:** Member of Cooperative Library Network of Clackamas County, Northwest Association of Private Colleges & Universities (NAPCU). **Publications:** Selected List of Books Processed, quarterly; Bulletin of the George Hallauer Memorial Library, quarterly - both for internal distribution only; Reference Tools for Theological Students, irregular. **Staff:** Jane Kuizenga, Cat., Per.; Dr. Nobel V. Sack, Archv.

★ 20245 ★
Western Fairs Association - Library (Bus-Fin)
1329 Howe Ave., Suite 202
Sacramento, CA 95825
Phone: (916)927-3100
Stephen J. Chambers, Exec.Dir.
Founded: 1945. **Staff:** 7. **Subjects:** Fair management, fair financing, horse racing, breeding, allied fair and agricultural subjects. **Special Collections:** Lou Merrill Oral History (growth of fairs in California; oral history interviews). **Holdings:** Figures not available. **Services:** Archives open to the public with restrictions. **Remarks:** FAX: (916)927-6397.

Western Federation of Miners Archives
See: **University of Colorado--Boulder - Western Historical Collections/University Archives** (18508)

★ 20246 ★
Western Gas Marketing Ltd. - Library (Sci-Engr, Energy)
530 8th Ave., S.W.
P.O. Box 500, Sta. M
Calgary, AB, Canada T2P 3V6
Phone: (403)269-5792
Elizabeth A. Varsek, Supv., Lib.Serv.
Staff: Prof 1; Other 1. **Subjects:** Geology, petroleum and natural gas technology. **Holdings:** 2000 books; 60 bound periodical volumes; 400 other cataloged items. **Subscriptions:** 400 journals and other serials. **Services:** Interlibrary loan; library open to the public with librarian's permission. **Automated Operations:** Computerized cataloging, acquisitions, and serials. **Computerized Information Services:** DIALOG Information Services, Info Globe, Infomart Online; Envoy 100 (electronic mail service). **Remarks:** FAX: (403)264-7257.

★ 20247 ★
Western Geophysical - R & D Library (Sci-Engr)
Box 2469
Houston, TX 77252
Phone: (713)964-6489
Diane Parker, Dir.
Founded: 1968. **Staff:** 1. **Subjects:** Geophysics, mathematics, geology, computer science, physics, engineering. **Holdings:** 5000 books; 800 bound periodical volumes; technical reports; maps; government documents. **Services:** Interlibrary loan; library not open to the public. **Publications:** New books list, quarterly; newsletter. **Remarks:** Library located at 3600 Briarpark Dr., Houston, TX 77042. FAX: (713)781-2585.

★ 20248 ★
Western Hennepin County Pioneers Association, Inc. - Avery Stubbs Memorial Archives - Library (Hist)
1953 W. Wayzata Blvd.
Box 332
Long Lake, MN 55356
Phone: (612)473-6557
James R. Roehl, Res. Aide
Founded: 1907. **Staff:** Prof 1. **Subjects:** Local and family history. **Holdings:** 2000 books; 25 bound periodical volumes; 1200 family histories; 15 municipal histories; vital records; 7 rolls of microfilm of newspapers; 800 cataloged portraits and photographs; church and business histories; maps. **Subscriptions:** 15 journals and other serials. **Services:** Copying; photograph reproduction; library open to the public on a fee basis. **Publications:** Newsletter, quarterly - to the public.

Western Heritage Center
See: **National Cowboy Hall of Fame & Western Heritage Center** (11146)

★ 20249 ★
Western Highway Institute - Research Library (Trans)
1200 Bayhill Dr., Suite 112
San Bruno, CA 94066
Phone: (415)952-4900
John Paquette, Libn.
Founded: 1970. **Subjects:** Transportation, highway and bridge engineering, motor vehicles, trucking. **Holdings:** 4000 volumes. **Subscriptions:** 20 journals and other serials. **Services:** Interlibrary loan; copying; library open to the public with restrictions. **Remarks:** FAX: (415)588-0424.

★ 20250 ★
Western Historical Manuscript Collection (Hist)
University of Missouri, Columbia
23 Ellis Library
Columbia, MO 65201
Phone: (314)882-6028
Nancy Lankford, Assoc.Dir.
Founded: 1943. **Staff:** Prof 13; Other 3. **Subjects:** History - Missouri, political, economic, agricultural, urban, labor, black, women's, frontier,

religious, literary, social, science, steamboating, social reform and welfare, business. **Holdings:** 12,500 linear feet of manuscripts; 7300 reels of microfilm; 3400 audiotapes and audiocassettes; 675 phonograph records; 190 video materials. **Services:** Interlibrary loan; copying; collection open to the public. **Publications:** Guide to the Western Historical Manuscripts Collection, 1952; supplement, 1956; finding aids (index, shelf list, and chronological file). **Remarks:** Collection contains the manuscript holdings of both the University of Missouri and the State Historical Society of Missouri. Offices are located at the four branches of the University of Missouri. Materials may be loaned among the four branches. **Staff:** Laura Bullion, Asst.Dir.; Cynthia Stewart, Sr.Mss.Spec.; Kathleen Conway, Sr.Mss.Spec.; Paula McNeill, Mss.Spec.; Sharon L. Fleming, Mss.Spec.; Randy Roberts, Sr.Mss.Spec.; Claudia Lane Powell, Doc.Cons.Spec.; James Bantin, Mss.Spec.; Don Radke, Jr., Mss.Spec.; Heather C. Smith, Mss.Spec.; Diane Ayotte, Mss.Spec.

★ 20251 ★
Western Historical Manuscript Collection (Hist)
University of Missouri, Kansas City
302 Newcomb Hall
5100 Rockhill Rd.
Kansas City, MO 64110
Phone: (816)235-1543
David L. Boutros, Assoc.Dir.
Founded: 1980. **Staff:** Prof 2; Other 2. **Subjects:** Kansas City/regional history and architectural records, civic and political leadership, history of citizen action groups. **Holdings:** 5000 cubic feet of manuscripts. **Services:** Copying; collection open to the public with restrictions. **Computerized Information Services:** Electronic mail. **Remarks:** Collection contains the manuscript holdings of both the University of Missouri and the State Historical Society of Missouri. Offices are located at the four branches of the University of Missouri. Materials may be loaned among the four branches. **Remarks:** FAX: (816)235-5191. **Staff:** Ann McFerrin, Sr.Ms.Spec.

★ 20252 ★
Western Historical Manuscript Collection (Hist)
University of Missouri, Rolla
Library, Rm. G-3
Rolla, MO 65401-0249
Phone: (314)341-4874
Mark C. Stauter, Assoc.Dir.
Staff: Prof 2. **Subjects:** History - Missouri, the Ozarks, mining and technology. **Special Collections:** Historical records of St. Joe Minerals Corporation (46 volumes); historical records of American Zinc Company (151 boxes); historical records of St. Louis-San Francisco Railway Company (56 boxes). **Holdings:** 500 historical manuscript collections. **Services:** Interlibrary loan; copying; collection open to the public. **Computerized Information Services:** Electronic mail. **Publications:** Guide to the Historical Records of the St. Louis-San Francisco Railway Company; annual collection summaries. **Remarks:** Collection contains the manuscript holdings of both the University of Missouri and the State Historical Society of Missouri. Offices are located at the four branches of the University of Missouri. Materials may be loaned among the four branches. **Staff:** John F. Bradbury, Jr., Sr.Mss.Spec.

★ 20253 ★
Western Historical Manuscript Collection (Hist, Soc Sci)
Thomas Jefferson Library
University of Missouri, St. Louis
8001 Natural Bridge Rd.
St. Louis, MO 63121
Phone: (314)553-5143
Ann Morris, Assoc.Dir.
Founded: 1968. **Staff:** Prof 3; Other 2. **Subjects:** History - state and local, women's, Afro-American, ethnic, education, immigration; socialism; 19th century science; environment; peace; religion; Missouri politics; social reform and welfare; photography; journalism; business; labor. **Special Collections:** Socialist Party of Missouri records; Oral History Program (1000 tapes); Photograph Collection (200,000 images); League of Women Voters of Missouri; papers of Irving Dilliard, Dr. Thomas A. Dooley, Margaret Hickey, Leo Drey, Judge Noah Weinstein, Charles Guenther, Marlin Perkins, Ernest and Deverne Calloway, Theodore Lentz, Alberta Slavin, Rep. William Hungate, Rep. Robert Young, Rep. James Symington, Lt. Governor Harriet Woods, Paul Preisler, Joseph Pulitzer (copy), Virginia Irwin, and Kay Drey; Coalition for the Environment; Committee for Environmental Information; KETC-TV; Metropolitan Church Federation; Sierra Club - Ozark Chapter; Nuclear Weapons Freeze Campaign; Health and Welfare Council; Bureau for Men; Dismas House; St. Louis Labor Council; Family and Children's Service of Greater St. Louis; Regional Commerce and Growth Association; Missouri Public Interest Research Group; Ethical Society of St. Louis; YMCA and YWCA of St. Louis; Amalgamated Clothing and Textile Workers Union - Southwest Region.

Holdings: 5500 linear feet of manuscripts, photographs, oral history tapes, and university archives. **Services:** Interlibrary loan (limited); copying of manuscripts, tape recordings, and photographs; library open to the public with restricted circulation. **Special Indexes:** Unpublished inventories to collections in repository. **Remarks:** Collection contains the manuscript holdings of both the University of Missouri and the State Historical Society of Missouri. Offices are located at the four branches of the University of Missouri. Materials may be loaned among the four branches. **Staff:** Kenn Thomas, Sr.Mss.Spec.; William Fischetti, Mss.Spec.

★ 20254 ★
Western Illinois Area Agency on Aging - Senior Resource Center (Med)
729 34th Ave.   Phone: (309)793-6800
Rock Island, IL 61201   Erma Dalton, Libn.
Founded: 1988. **Subjects:** Nursing home information, family caregiving, Medicare, Medicaid Social Security, retirement planning, intergenerational programs, housing alternatives. **Special Collections:** Legislation collection. **Holdings:** 1000 books; AV materials. **Subscriptions:** 24 journals and other serials. **Services:** Interlibrary loan; copying; center open to the public. **Computerized Information Services:** Internal database. **Remarks:** FAX: (309)793-6807. Toll-free telephone number(s): (800)322-1051.

★ 20255 ★
Western Illinois University - Geography & Map Library (Geog-Map)
Tillman Hall, Rm. 301   Phone: (309)298-1171
Macomb, IL 61455   Lou Coatney, Map Libn.
Founded: 1968. **Staff:** Prof 1; Other 1. **Subjects:** Maps of Illinois, U.S. topographic maps, thematic maps, geography, area and regional studies. **Special Collections:** Federal and state depositories; U.S. Geological Survey (67,000 maps); Defense Mapping Agency (36,000 maps); Illinois (12,000 maps; 12,000 air photographs, atlases, plat books). **Holdings:** 3300 books; 1000 periodical volumes; 3000 atlases; 170,000 maps; 13,000 air photos; 1000 pamphlets; 120 theses; 120 map information catalogs. **Subscriptions:** 80 journals and other serials. **Services:** Interlibrary loan (limited); copying; library open to the public.

★ 20256 ★
Western Illinois University - Music Library (Mus)
Sallee Hall, Rm. 108   Phone: (309)298-1105
Macomb, IL 61455   Allie Wise Goudy, Mus.Libn.
Founded: 1976. **Staff:** Prof 1; Other 1. **Subjects:** Classical music. **Holdings:** 7000 books; 5000 bound periodical volumes; 5500 volumes of scores; 4700 phonograph records. **Subscriptions:** 100 journals and other serials. **Services:** Copying; library open to the public. **Publications:** Guides to the collection; bibliographies.

★ 20257 ★
Western Illinois University - Physical Sciences Library (Sci-Engr)
Currens Hall, Rm. 201   Phone: (309)298-1407
Macomb, IL 61455   Kenneth Smejkal, Libn.
Founded: 1976. **Staff:** Prof 1; Other 1. **Subjects:** Physics, chemistry. **Holdings:** 20,600 books; 15,500 bound periodical volumes. **Subscriptions:** 465 journals and other serials. **Services:** Interlibrary loan; copying; library open to the public. **Computerized Information Services:** DIALOG Information Services, OCLC.

★ 20258 ★
Western Illinois University - Western Illinois Regional Studies Collections (Hist)
University Library, Special Collections   Phone: (309)298-2718
Macomb, IL 61455   Gordana Rezab, Univ.Archv. & Spec.Coll.Libn.
Founded: 1970. **Staff:** Prof 1; Other 2. **Subjects:** Western Illinois history and literature. **Special Collections:** Papers of Tom Railsback, Elton Fawks, Burl Ives, Phillip D. Jordan; Illinois Regional Archives Depository Collection (public records for the region); Icarian Collection; Regional Authors Collection. **Holdings:** 12,000 books; 10,000 photographs and negatives; 11,500 VF items; 875 linear feet of records. **Subscriptions:** 12 journals and other serials. **Services:** Copying; SDI; center open to the public. **Computerized Information Services:** OCLC, ILLINET ONLINE. **Publications:** Western Illinois Regional Studies; Western Illinois Monograph Series.

★ 20259 ★
Western Interstate Commission for Higher Education - Library (Educ)
Drawer P   Phone: (303)541-0285
Boulder, CO 80301   Eileen Conway, Cons.Dir.
Founded: 1955. **Staff:** Prof 1; Other 1. **Subjects:** Higher education, mental health and human services, nursing, minority education. **Holdings:** 7000 books and documents; 1000 volumes of unbound periodicals; 2000 documents on microfiche. **Subscriptions:** 280 journals and other serials; 10 newspapers. **Services:** Interlibrary loan; copying; SDI; library open to the public. **Automated Operations:** Computerized public access catalog, serials, and circulation. **Computerized Information Services:** DIALOG Information Services. Performs searches on fee basis. **Publications:** Acquisitions List, monthly - for internal distribution only. **Remarks:** FAX: (303)541-0291.

Western Jewish History Center
See: **Judah L. Magnes Memorial Museum** (9538)

★ 20260 ★
Western Kentucky University - Department of Special Collections - Kentucky Library and Museum/University Archives (Hist)
Bowling Green, KY 42101   Phone: (502)745-5083
                                          Riley Handy, Hd., Spec.Coll.Dept.
Founded: 1931. **Staff:** Prof 6; Other 10. **Subjects:** Rare Kentuckiana, Mammoth Cave, Kentucky writers, Civil War, Shakers, Ohio Valley. **Special Collections:** Journals and writers of South Union Shaker Colony; Alice Hegan and Cale Young Rice Collection; McGregor Collection; Janice Holt Giles Collection; Tim Lee Carter Collection. **Holdings:** 35,000 books; 2000 bound periodical volumes; 60 VF drawers; 12,000 photographs; 375 land grants; 10,000 postcards; 510 prints; Kentucky census, 1810-1910, on microfilm; 350 titles of Kentucky sheet music; scrapbooks; broadsides; maps. **Subscriptions:** 55 journals and other serials; 4 newspapers. **Services:** Copying (limited); library open to the public for research and reference. **Publications:** Occasional house organs. **Special Indexes:** Current Kentucky periodicals index. **Staff:** Constance A. Mills, KY Lib.Supv.; Nancy Baird, KY Hist.Spec.; Patricia M. Hodges, Mss./Folklife Archv./ Univ.Archv.Supv.; Sue Lynn McGuire, Mss./FA Libn.; Jonathan Jeffrey, Per.Libn.; Larry Scott, Musm.Dir.

★ 20261 ★
Western Kentucky University - Department of Special Library Collections - Folklife Archives (Soc Sci)
Kentucky Bldg.   Phone: (502)745-6434
Bowling Green, KY 42101   Patricia M. Hodges, Mss. & Archv.Supv.
Staff: Prof 2. **Subjects:** Folklore, folk songs and music, social folk customs, traditional arts, regional oral history. **Holdings:** 3750 cassettes and tapes; 2200 manuscripts; collections of folk songs, beliefs, speech, correspondence. **Services:** Copying (limited); archives open to the public. **Remarks:** FAX: (502)745-5943. **Staff:** Sue Lynn McGuire, Mss.Libn.

★ 20262 ★
Western Life Insurance Company - Library (Bus-Fin)
500 Bielenberg Dr.   Phone: (612)738-4589
Woodbury, MN 55125-1416   Ginger Fleming, Libn.
Founded: 1978. **Staff:** 2. **Subjects:** Insurance, management. **Holdings:** 300 books; annual statements. **Subscriptions:** 120 journals and other serials; 8 newspapers. **Services:** Library not open to the public.

★ 20263 ★
Western Maryland College - Archives (Hist)
Hoover Library   Phone: (301)857-2281
Westminster, MD 21157-4390   Harold D. Neikiak, Lib.Dir.
Founded: 1867. **Subjects:** History of Western Maryland College, 1867 to present. **Holdings:** Photographs; noncurrent working papers; student records on microfilm; college journals and publications; selected faculty and alumni publications. **Services:** Archives open to the public by appointment. **Remarks:** FAX: (301)857-2748.

★ 20264 ★
Western Maryland Public Libraries - Regional Library (Bus-Fin, Educ)
100 S. Potomac St.   Phone: (301)739-3250
Hagerstown, MD 21740   Mary S. Mallery, Reg.Libn.
Founded: 1968. **Staff:** Prof 3; Other 3. **Subjects:** Small business; auto, truck, and motorcycle repair; antiques and collectibles; Civil Service and vocational tests; small scale farming. **Holdings:** 62,000 books; 300 reels of microfilm; 1000 automobile, truck, and motorcycle repair manuals; 2500 videocassettes; 287 talking books. **Services:** Interlibrary loan; copying; library open to the public with restrictions. **Automated Operations:** Computerized public access catalog, circulation, and online 16mm film booking system. **Computerized Information Services:** DIALOG Information Services, WILSONLINE. Performs searches free of charge. **Networks/Consortia:** Member of Maryland Interlibrary Organization (MILO), Maryland Interlibrary Loan Network (MILNET). **Special Catalogs:** Catalogs of videocassettes, and audiocassette and literacy books. **Remarks:** FAX: (301)739-5839. Library is maintained by the Washington County Free Library. **Staff:** Darlene Reimond, ILL.Libn.; David Wolf, Tech.Proc.Libn.

★ 20265 ★
Western Medical Center - Medical Library (Med)
1001 N. Tustin Ave.   Phone: (714)835-3555
Santa Ana, CA 92705   Phyllis Dowling, Dir.
Staff: 1. **Subjects:** Medicine, nursing, surgery. **Holdings:** 4800 books; 5000 bound periodical volumes; 2300 Audio-Digest tapes (9 specialties); video cassettes. **Subscriptions:** 260 journals and other serials. **Services:** Interlibrary loan; copying; SDI; library open to the public with restrictions. **Computerized Information Services:** Online systems.

★ 20266 ★
Western Memorial Regional Hospital - Health Sciences Library (Med)
P.O. Box 2005
Corner Brook, NF, Canada A2H 6J7   Phone: (709)637-5395
Founded: 1968. **Staff:** Prof 1; Other 1. **Subjects:** Medicine, nursing, paramedical fields. **Holdings:** 2500 books; 1150 bound periodical volumes. **Subscriptions:** 167 journals and other serials. **Services:** Interlibrary loan; copying; library open to the public. **Computerized Information Services:** MEDLINE; CD-ROM (CINAHL-CD). **Remarks:** FAX: (709)634-2649.

★ 20267 ★
Western Michigan University - Archives and Regional History Collections (Hist)
East Hall, Rm. 111   Phone: (616)387-8490
Kalamazoo, MI 49008-5081   Wayne C. Mann, Dir.
Founded: 1957. **Staff:** Prof 1; Other 5. **Subjects:** Local and regional history, genealogy, history of Western Michigan University. **Holdings:** 10,327 books; 16,000 linear feet of manuscripts, photographs, and other archival materials. **Subscriptions:** 30 journals and other serials. **Services:** Copying; collection open to the public. **Special Indexes:** Comprehensive index to historic photographs. **Staff:** Susan Husband, Reg.Hist.Cur. & Mss.Cat.; Sharon Carlson, Archv.Cur.

★ 20268 ★
Western Michigan University - Business Library
Kalamazoo, MI 49008
Defunct. Holdings absorbed by Western Michigan University - Waldo Library.

★ 20269 ★
Western Michigan University - Documents Library (Info Sci)
Waldo Library   Phone: (616)387-5208
Kalamazoo, MI 49008   Michael McDonnell, Ref.Libn., Maps & Docs.
Founded: 1963. **Staff:** Prof 1; Other 2. **Subjects:** U.S. Government publications, 1963 to present; United Nations documents, 1946-1981; Michigan documents; U.S. Dept. of Energy documents (microfiche). **Special Collections:** 19th Century Serial Set (microcard). **Holdings:** 488,724 documents. **Services:** Interlibrary loan; copying; library open to the public. **Computerized Information Services:** DIALOG Information Services, OCLC, BRS Information Technologies; OLLI (internal database); BITNET (electronic mail service). Performs searches on fee basis. **Networks/Consortia:** Member of Southwest Michigan Library Cooperative (SMLC), Michigan Library Consortium (MLC), Center for Research Libraries (CRL). **Remarks:** FAX: (616)387-5124. Electronic mail address(es): MCDONNELL@SGW.WMICH.EDU (BITNET).

★ 20270 ★
Western Michigan University - Education Library (Educ)
3300 Sangren Hall   Phone: (616)387-5223
Kalamazoo, MI 49008   David J. Netz, Hd.Libn.
Founded: 1964. **Staff:** Prof 2; Other 4. **Subjects:** Educational research; education - higher, secondary, elementary; educational psychology; educational tests and measurement; educational law; comparative education. **Special Collections:** ERIC documents (350,000 titles; 400,000 microfiche); Curriculum Development Library (12,000 microfiche); children's and young people's books (3778); textbooks (14,701 elementary and secondary). **Holdings:** 49,726 books; 9317 bound periodical volumes; 2500 books on microfilm; 500 producers' catalogs. **Subscriptions:** 600 journals and other serials. **Services:** Interlibrary loan; copying; library open to the public with restrictions on circulation. **Automated Operations:** Computerized public access catalog and circulation. **Computerized Information Services:** DIALOG Information Services, BRS Information Technologies, PFDS Online; InfoTrac. **Networks/Consortia:** Member of Southwest Michigan Library Cooperative (SMLC), Michigan Library Consortium (MLC), Center for Research Libraries (CRL). **Publications:** Monthly Acquisitions List; bibliographies and study guides. **Staff:** Dennis Strasser, Libn.

★ 20271 ★
Western Michigan University - Harper C. Maybee Music & Dance Library (Mus, Theater)
3008 Dalton Center   Phone: (616)387-5237
Kalamazoo, MI 49008   Gregory Fitzgerald, Hd.Libn.
Founded: 1949. **Staff:** Prof 1; Other 1. **Subjects:** Music, dance. **Special Collections:** American vocal sheet music collection (1900 titles); WMU School of Music performance archives (1100 tapes); International Trumpet Guild Archives (400 items). **Holdings:** 14,266 books; 4428 bound periodical volumes; 14,823 scores; 12,685 phonograph records and tapes; 158 reels of microfilm; 225 microfiche; 1250 other cataloged items. **Subscriptions:** 160 journals and other serials. **Services:** Interlibrary loan; copying; library open to the public with restrictions on borrowing. **Automated Operations:** Computerized public access catalog and circulation. **Networks/Consortia:** Member of Southwest Michigan Library Cooperative (SMLC), Michigan Library Consortium (MLC), Center for Research Libraries (CRL). **Publications:** Guides to collection and catalogs; Recent Acquisitions, 2/year; newsletter, semiannual - to faculty and staff. **Special Indexes:** Index to song collections; index to jazz recordings; index to International Trumpet Guild Archives recordings (online).

Western Michigan University - Institute of Cistercian Studies Library
See: **Western Michigan University - Waldo Library - Rare Book Room** (20275)

Western Michigan University - Latvian Studies Center
See: **Latvian Studies Center - Library** (8972)

★ 20272 ★
Western Michigan University - Map Library (Geog-Map)
Waldo Library   Phone: (616)387-5046
Kalamazoo, MI 49008   Michael McDonnell, Ref.Libn., Maps & Docs.
Founded: 1968. **Staff:** Prof 1; Other 2. **Subjects:** Domestic and foreign maps, antique maps of special historical interest, U.S. Geological Survey, U.S. Defense Mapping Agency, National Ocean Survey, U.S. Forest Service, Soil Conservation Service, national parks, city maps, topographic maps, aeronautical and nautical charts. **Special Collections:** Climatological data; historical maps and atlases; soil surveys; gazetteers. **Holdings:** 325 books; 65 bound periodical volumes; 1600 atlases; 186,639 maps. **Subscriptions:** 4 journals and other serials. **Services:** Copying; library open to the public. **Computerized Information Services:** OCLC, DIALOG Information Services, BRS Information Technologies, OLLI (internal database); BITNET (electronic mail service). Performs searches on fee basis. **Networks/Consortia:** Member of Southwest Michigan Library Cooperative (SMLC), Michigan Library Consortium (MLC), Center for Research Libraries (CRL). **Remarks:** FAX: (616)387-5124. Electronic mail address(es): MCDONNEL@GW.WMICH.EDU (BITNET).

★ 20273 ★
Western Michigan University - Physical Sciences Library (Sci-Engr)
3376 Rood Hall   Phone: (616)387-5238
Kalamazoo, MI 49008   Beatrice Sichel, Hd.Libn.
Founded: 1971. **Staff:** Prof 1; Other 1. **Subjects:** Mathematics, physics, geology, computer science, astronomy. **Holdings:** 43,700 books; 26,435 bound periodical volumes; 2485 geological maps; 158 reels of microfilm; 3549 microfiche. **Subscriptions:** 600 journals and other serials. **Services:** Interlibrary loan; copying; library open to the public. **Automated Operations:** Computerized public access catalog and circulation. **Computerized Information Services:** DIALOG Information Services, MATHFILE, ABI/INFORM, ERIC, MathSci. Performs searches on fee basis. **Networks/Consortia:** Member of Southwest Michigan Library Cooperative (SMLC), Michigan Library Consortium (MLC), Center for Research Libraries (CRL).

★ 20274 ★
Western Michigan University - Science for Citizens Center -
   Environmental Resource Center for Community Information (Env-Cons, Plan)
Kalamazoo, MI 49008   Phone: (616)387-2715
                                      Donald J. Brown, Ph.D., Dir.
Founded: 1971. **Staff:** 1. **Subjects:** Environment, public policy, community planning. **Special Collections:** Groundwater management, protection, principles. **Holdings:** 3000 titles; 8 VF drawers of cataloged items. **Services:** Copying; center open to the public for reference use only.

★ 20275 ★
Western Michigan University - Waldo Library - Rare Book Room (Rel-Phil)
Kalamazoo, MI 49008   Phone: (616)387-5221
                                      Beatrice H. Beech, Hd.
Founded: 1973. **Staff:** Prof 1; Other 1. **Subjects:** Cisterciansia, history, monasticism. **Special Collections:** Editions of Bernard of Clairvaux (400 volumes); the rule of St. Benedict; medieval manuscripts; incunabula; early 16th-18th century books. **Holdings:** 6900 books; 34 bound periodical volumes; 96 manuscripts. **Services:** Interlibrary loan; copying; library open to the public. **Networks/Consortia:** Member of Southwest Michigan Library Cooperative (SMLC), Michigan Library Consortium (MLC), Center for Research Libraries (CRL). **Formed by the merger of:** Western Michigan University - Institute of Cistercian Studies Library, and Western Michigan University - Waldo Library - Rare Book Room.

★ 20276 ★
Western Michigan University - Women's Center - Library (Soc Sci)
A-331 Ellsworth Hall   Phone: (616)387-2990
Kalamazoo, MI 49008   Gwen Raaberg, Dir. of Women's Ctr.
Staff: 1. **Subjects:** Women - health, financial status, careers, discrimination; displaced homemakers; nontraditional students and jobs; reentry women; equal pay for equal work. **Special Collections:** Local history of women's groups and causes; sex bias in textbooks in local public schools; local history of women in education. **Holdings:** 1000 books; 9 VF drawers of clippings. **Subscriptions:** 20 journals and other serials. **Services:** Copying; library open to community members.

★ 20277 ★
Western Missouri Mental Health Center - Library (Med)
600 E. 22nd St.   Phone: (816)471-3000
Kansas City, MO 64108   Tyron Emerick, Med.Libn.
Founded: 1954. **Staff:** Prof 1. **Subjects:** Psychiatry, psychology, social science, psychological testing, psychoanalysis, drugs and alcohol. **Special Collections:** Works of Sigmund Freud. **Holdings:** 3400 books; 110 unbound periodical titles; 410 cassette tapes. **Subscriptions:** 90 journals and other serials. **Services:** Interlibrary loan; copying; library open to the public with permission. **Networks/Consortia:** Member of Kansas City Library Network, Inc. (KCLN), Kansas City Metropolitan Library Network (KCMLN).

★ 20278 ★
Western Montana Clinic - Library (Med)
515 W. Front St.
Box 7609
Missoula, MT 59807   Phone: (406)721-5600
                                      Connie Reichelt, Libn.
Staff: Prof 1. **Subjects:** Medicine. **Holdings:** 500 books; 120 bound periodical volumes. **Subscriptions:** 120 journals and other serials. **Services:** Interlibrary loan; copying; library open to those who are referred by a physician. **Computerized Information Services:** MEDLARS; OnTyme Electronic Message Network Service (electronic mail service). **Networks/Consortia:** Member of National Network of Libraries of Medicine - Pacific Northwest Region. **Remarks:** FAX: (406)721-3907.

★ 20279 ★
Western Museum of Mining & Industry - Library (Sci-Engr)
1025 North Gate Rd.   Phone: (719)488-0880
Colorado Springs, CO 80921   Terry Girouard, Cur.
Founded: 1970. **Staff:** Prof 1. **Subjects:** Mining, metallurgy, mechanical engineering, geology, mineralogy. **Holdings:** 7000 books; 400 bound periodical volumes; 45 other items; early engineering periodicals on microfilm. **Subscriptions:** 4 journals and other serials. **Services:** Copying; library open to members and scholars. **Publications:** Newsletter; Annual Report; brochure.

★ 20280 ★
Western New England College - D'Amour Library - Special Collections (Hist)
1215 Wilbraham Rd.   Phone: (413)782-1535
Springfield, MA 01119   May E. Stack, Dir.
Founded: 1983. **Staff:** Prof 3; Other 4. **Subjects:** John F. Kennedy. **Special Collections:** Sprague Collection on John F. Kennedy Assassination (263 volumes; photographs; films; articles; correspondence); Saex Judaica Collection (1500 volumes). **Holdings:** 15,000 books; 1200 bound periodical volumes; 211 microfiche; 9000 reels of microfilm. **Services:** Interlibrary loan; copying (limited); SDI; library open to the public. **Computerized Information Services:** OCLC, ABI/INFORM, NewsBank, Books in Print (BIP) Data Base; CD-ROMs (Compendex, Periodicals Abstracts); BITNET (electronic mail service). **Networks/Consortia:** Member of C/W MARS, Inc. **Publications:** Printed Guide to Sprague Collection; catalog of holdings. **Remarks:** FAX: (413)796-2011. Electronic mail address(es): MSTACK@WNEC (BITNET). **Staff:** Daniel Eckert, Ref.; Suzanne Garber, Ref.; Steve Bobowicz, Tech.Serv.; Nancy Etter, Circ.; Valerie Bolden-Marshall, Circ.; May Stack, Dir.

★ 20281 ★
Western New England College - School of Law Library (Law)
1215 Wilbraham Rd.   Phone: (413)782-1457
Springfield, MA 01119-2693   Donald J. Dunn, Law Libn.
Founded: 1973. **Staff:** Prof 7; Other 8. **Subjects:** Law. **Holdings:** 148,000 books, periodicals, and serials; 114,000 volumes in microform. **Subscriptions:** 3582 journals and other serials; 12 newspapers. **Services:** Interlibrary loan; copying; library open to the public. **Automated Operations:** Computerized cataloging, serials, and interlibrary loan. **Computerized Information Services:** LEXIS, NEXIS, DIALOG Information Services, WESTLAW, MEDIS. **Networks/Consortia:** Member of Cooperating Libraries of Greater Springfield, A CCGS Agency (CLGS), New England Law Library Consortium (NELLCO). **Publications:** Selected List of New Acquisitions; Contents Pages of Legal Periodicals; Slipped Opinions, quarterly; Reader's Guide; Self-Guided Tour, both annual. **Remarks:** FAX: (413)782-1745. **Staff:** Bonnie Koneski-White, Assoc. Law Libn.; Susan C. Wells, Hd., Tech.Serv.; Christine H. Swan, Hd., Rd.Serv.; Michele Dill LaRose, Ref.Libn.; Christine Archambault, Cat.Libn.; Nancy Johnson, Coll.Serv.Libn.

★ 20282 ★
Western New Mexico University - J. Cloyd Miller Library - Special Collections (Hist)
Silver City, NM 88062   Phone: (505)538-6350
                                      Benjamin T. Wakashige, Lib.Dir.
Founded: 1893. **Staff:** 14. **Subjects:** History - American, Southwest, New Mexico. **Holdings:** Newspapers of New Mexico and the Southwest. **Subscriptions:** 838 journals and other serials; 30 newspapers. **Services:** Interlibrary loan; copying; library open to the public. **Automated Operations:** Computerized cataloging and circulation (Galaxy). **Computerized Information Services:** BRS Information Technologies, BRS/After Dark, DIALOG Information Services. Performs searches on fee basis. Contact Person: Katherine Warren, Hd. of Pub.Serv., (505)538-6178. **Networks/Consortia:** Member of AMIGOS Bibliographic Council, Inc. **Publications:** Hilltop Highlights (newsletter). **Remarks:** FAX: (505)538-6178. **Staff:** Louise Leon.

★ 20283 ★
Western New York Genealogical Society, Inc. - Library (Hist)
P.O. Box 338
Hamburg, NY 14075   Betty V. Walter
Founded: 1974. **Subjects:** Genealogy and local history. **Special Collections:** McCabe Collection; Cramer Collection. **Holdings:** 1350 books; 1500 unbound periodicals; 350 pamphlets, paperbacks, manuscripts, articles; genealogical society publications; 200 reels of microfilm. **Services:** Copying; library open to the public. **Remarks:** Library located in the Hamburg Historical Museum, 5859 S. Park Ave., Hamburg, NY.

★ 20284 ★
Western Ontario Breeders, Inc. - Library (Agri)
Hwy. 59 N.
P.O. Box 457   Phone: (519)539-9831
Woodstock, ON, Canada N4S 7Y7 Howard D. Start, Dir. of Advertising
Founded: 1946. **Subjects:** Livestock breeding, veterinary science. **Holdings:**
425 books and bound periodical volumes; breed journals; sire directories;
sales catalogs. **Subscriptions:** 35 journals and other serials; 6 newspapers.
Services: Library not open to the public.

★ 20285 ★
Western Oregon State College - Library - Special Collections (Hist)
345 N. Monmouth Ave.   Phone: (503)838-8418
Monmouth, OR 97361   Dr. Gary D. Jensen, Dir.
Founded: 1856. **Staff:** Prof 6; Other 10. **Holdings:** John C. Higgins Memorial
Collection of Pacific Northwest History and Culture. **Services:** Interlibrary
loan; copying; collections open to the public for reference use only. **Remarks:**
FAX: (503)838-8474.

★ 20286 ★
Western Organization of Resource Councils - Library (Env-Cons)
412 Stapleton Bldg.   Phone: (406)252-9672
Billings, MT 59101   John Smillie
Founded: 1979. **Staff:** 1. **Subjects:** Natural resources, environment, energy,
agriculture. **Holdings:** Figures not available. **Services:** Library not open to
the public. **Computerized Information Services:** MCI Mail (electronic mail
service). **Remarks:** FAX: (406)252-1092. Electronic mail address(es):
Western Organization of Resource Councils (MCI Mail).

Western Pennsylvania Botanical Society Library
See: **Carnegie Museum of Natural History - Library** (3085)

★ 20287 ★
Western Pennsylvania Genealogical Society - Library (Hist)
4338 Bigelow Blvd.   Phone: (412)681-5533
Pittsburgh, PA 15213   Audrey Iacone, Libn.
Staff: Prof 3. **Subjects:** Genealogy, local history. **Special Collections:** Local
manuscript collection. **Holdings:** 2000 volumes; 200 archival items; 10 VF
drawers of local obituaries; 45 feet of newsletters; 2500 pages of obituaries
for persons born in Pennsylvania but living elsewhere; local newspaper
collection. **Subscriptions:** 30 journals and other serials. **Services:** Copying;
library open to the public on fee basis. **Special Indexes:** Index to Members'
Lineage Charts. **Remarks:** Collection is housed at the Historical Society of
Western Pennsylvania. **Staff:** Donald L. Haggerty, Dir., Archv.-Lib.

★ 20288 ★
Western Pentecostal Bible College - Lorne Philip Hudson Memorial
   Library (Rel-Phil)
Box 1700   Phone: (604)853-7491
Abbotsford, BC, Canada V2S 7E7   Rev. Laurence M. Van Kleek, Libn.
Founded: 1941. **Staff:** Prof 1; Other 3. **Subjects:** Humanities, social sciences,
Bible, doctrinal and practical theology, world religions and cults, missions.
Special Collections: Archive for Pentecostal Studies, includes Action, 1970
to present; Pentecostal Testimony, 1920 to present; modern Christian
literature. **Holdings:** 30,185 books; 359 bound periodical volumes; 25
filmstrips; 468 audio recordings; 986 microforms; 855 pamphlets; 75
clippings; 200 yearbooks. **Subscriptions:** 116 journals and other serials.
Services: Copying; library open to the public. **Automated Operations:**
Computerized acquisitions and cataloging. **Computerized Information
Services:** Internal database. **Publications:** WPBC Library Bulletin, irregular
- to faculty, staff, and administration. **Special Indexes:** Indexes to
denominational periodicals (mimeographed). **Remarks:** FAX: (604)853-
8951. **Formerly:** Located in Clayburn, BC, Canada.

Western Psychiatric Institute and Clinic
See: **University of Pittsburgh** (19229)

★ 20289 ★
Western Railroad Association - Library (Trans)
222 S. Riverside Plaza, Suite 1150   Phone: (312)648-7856
Chicago, IL 60606   Michael Wendling, Tarrif Publ.Off.
Founded: 1909. **Subjects:** Railroad tariffs, tariff supplements, division sheets.
Holdings: 600 volumes. **Computerized Information Services:** Internal
databases. **Remarks:** FAX: (312)648-7974.

★ 20290 ★
Western Railway Museum - Library (Trans)
P.O. Box 8136   Phone: (707)374-2978
Berkeley, CA 94707   Vernon J. Sappers, Chf.Libn.
Founded: 1969. **Staff:** Prof 1; Other 3. **Subjects:** Railroad - technology,
history, fiction, maps. **Special Collections:** Vernon J. Sappers Collection
(complete sets of Electric Railway Journal, Electric Traction; negative
collection of 60,000 railroad subjects; bound sets of railroad employees
timetables from major railroads of California); F.M. Smith Memorial
Collection (corporate records of street railways serving Oakland, California,
1863-1946). **Holdings:** 5000 books; 100 bound periodical volumes;
pamphlets; technical railroad newspaper clippings; maps; annual reports;
timetables. **Services:** Library open to the public with recommendation from
outside sources. **Remarks:** Alternate telephone number(s): (510)534-0071.
Maintained by Bay Area Electric Railroad Association. **Staff:** Stephen
Colby, Asst.Libn.; Robert S. Ford, Asst.Libn.

★ 20291 ★
Western Research Institute - Library (Energy, Sci-Engr)
Box 3395, University Sta.   Phone: (307)721-2201
Laramie, WY 82071   Valerie Chilson, Libn.
Founded: 1947. **Staff:** Prof 1. **Subjects:** In-situ recovery research - oil shale,
tar sands, coal gasification; geology; chemistry; hazardous waste
management; engineering. **Special Collections:** Internal publications.
Holdings: 3000 monographs; U.S. Bureau of Mines collection on microfiche;
reports. **Subscriptions:** 70 journals and other serials. **Services:** Interlibrary
loan; library open to the public by appointment. **Computerized Information
Services:** DIALOG Information Services; internal database; DIALMAIL
(electronic mail service). **Remarks:** FAX: (307)721-2345.

★ 20292 ★
Western Reserve Care System - Health Sciences Libraries (Med)
345 Oak Hill Ave.   Phone: (216)740-4689
Youngstown, OH 44501   Patricia L. Augustine, Dir., Hea.Sci.Lib.
Staff: Prof 2; Other 2. **Subjects:** Clinical medicine, science and nursing.
Holdings: 4214 books; 8338 bound periodical volumes; Audio-Digest tapes;
AV slides. **Subscriptions:** 366 journals and other serials; 5 newspapers.
Services: Interlibrary loan; copying; libraries open to college students with
librarian's permission. **Automated Operations:** Computerized cataloging.
Computerized Information Services: DIALOG Information Services,
MEDLINE. **Networks/Consortia:** Member of NEOUCOM Council
Associated Hospital Librarians. **Remarks:** Alternate telephone number(s):
740-4689. Western Reserve Care System maintains libraries at two units:
Southside Medical Center and Northside Medical Center. FAX: (216)740-
4855 (Southside); (216)740-3477 (Northside). **Staff:** Martina Nicholas,
Med.Libn.

★ 20293 ★
Western Reserve Historical Society - Library (Hist)
10825 E. Blvd.   Phone: (216)721-5722
Cleveland, OH 44106   Kermit J. Pike, Dir.
Founded: 1867. **Staff:** Prof 7; Other 7. **Subjects:** Ohio history, American
genealogy, Civil War, slavery and abolitionism, ethnic history, African
Americans. **Special Collections:** Wallace H. Cathcart Shaker Collection;
William P. Palmer Civil War Collection; David Z. Norton Napoleon
Collection. **Holdings:** 234,368 books; 25,000 volumes of newspapers; 50,250
pamphlets; 6 million manuscripts; 27,500 reels of microfilm. **Subscriptions:**
325 journals and other serials; 50 newspapers. **Services:** Interlibrary loan;
copying; library open to the public. **Networks/Consortia:** Member of
OHIONET. **Special Catalogs:** Catalogs to manuscript, genealogy, and
Shaker collections (all on cards). **Remarks:** FAX: (216)721-0645. **Staff:** Ann
Sindelar, Ref.Supv.; John Grabowski, Cur. of Mss.; Marian Sweton, Hd.Cat.

★ 20294 ★
Western Reserve Psychiatric Habilation Center - Staff Library (Med)
1756 Sagamore Rd.
Box 305   Phone: (216)467-7131
Northfield, OH 44067   Pearlie McAlpine, Libn.
Staff: 1. **Subjects:** Psychiatry, psychiatric nursing, psychology, social service. **Holdings:** 500 books. **Subscriptions:** 55 journals and other serials. **Services:** Interlibrary loan; library not open to the public.

★ 20295 ★
Western and Southern Life Insurance Co. - Library (Bus-Fin)
400 Broadway   Phone: (513)629-1393
Cincinnati, OH 45202   Lorraine Dufour
Founded: 1952. **Staff:** Prof 1. **Subjects:** Business, insurance, recreation. **Holdings:** 3523 volumes; 4 VF drawers. **Subscriptions:** 33 journals and other serials. **Services:** Library not open to the public.

★ 20296 ★
Western State Hospital - Library (Med)
Box 1   Phone: (405)766-2311
Fort Supply, OK 73841   Karen Connell, Lib.Techn.
Founded: 1950. **Staff:** Prof 1. **Subjects:** Substance abuse, psychiatry, psychology. **Holdings:** 2778 books; 23 bound periodical volumes; 50 boxes of booklets, pamphlets, and reports; 59 audiotapes; 49 video recordings. **Subscriptions:** 20 journals and other serials; 10 newspapers. **Services:** Interlibrary loan; copying; library open to the public for reference use only. **Remarks:** Maintains a patients' library of 3815 volumes.

★ 20297 ★
Western State Hospital - Medical Library (Med)
Box 2500   Phone: (703)332-8307
Staunton, VA 24401-1405   Richard D. Wills, Med.Libn.
Staff: Prof 1; Other 1. **Subjects:** Psychology, psychiatry, general medicine, nursing. **Holdings:** 3600 books; 600 bound periodical volumes. **Subscriptions:** 117 journals and other serials. **Services:** Interlibrary loan; library open to the public. **Computerized Information Services:** BRS Information Technologies; DOCLINE (electronic mail service).

★ 20298 ★
Western State Hospital - Professional Library (Med)
Russellville Rd.
Box 2200   Phone: (502)886-4431
Hopkinsville, KY 42240   Elizabeth W. Nelson, Staff Libn.
Founded: 1972. **Staff:** Prof 1; Other 1. **Subjects:** Psychiatry, psychology, nursing, medicine, social work, management. **Holdings:** 2500 books; 240 bound periodical volumes. **Subscriptions:** 58 journals and other serials. **Services:** Interlibrary loan; copying; library open to the public with restrictions. **Remarks:** FAX: (502)886-4487.

Western State Hospital Branch Library
See: **Washington State Library** (20040)

★ 20299 ★
Western State University - College of Law - Library (Law)
2121 San Diego Ave.   Phone: (619)297-9700
San Diego, CA 92110   Karla M. Castetter, Assoc.Prof./Libn.
Staff: Prof 2; Other 10. **Subjects:** Law. **Holdings:** 35,000 books; 5000 bound periodical volumes; 26,700 volumes in microform; 150 videotapes; 25 audiotapes. **Subscriptions:** 1057 journals and other serials; 10 newspapers. **Services:** Interlibrary loan; library open to the public. **Computerized Information Services:** LEXIS, WESTLAW, OCLC, NEXIS; CD-ROM (LegalTrac). **Remarks:** FAX: (619)294-4713. **Staff:** Joan Allen-Hart, Assoc. Law Libn.; Norma Dunn, Tech.Serv.Libn.

★ 20300 ★
Western State University - College of Law - Reis Law Library (Law)
1111 N. State College Blvd.   Phone: (714)738-1000
Fullerton, CA 92631   Carol Ebbinghouse, Univ.Libn.
Founded: 1966. **Staff:** Prof 7; Other 19. **Subjects:** California and Anglo-American law. **Holdings:** 44,680 books; 4600 bound periodical volumes; 55,019 volumes in microform. **Subscriptions:** 400 journals; 2097 serials; 12 newspapers. **Services:** Interlibrary loan; copying; SDI; library not open to the public. **Automated Operations:** Computerized cataloging. **Computerized Information Services:** LEXIS, WESTLAW, NEXIS, DIALOG Information Services, ELSS (Electronic Legislative Search System). **Remarks:** FAX: (714)871-4806. **Staff:** Cindy Parkhurst, Ref.Libn.; Doreen Smith, Acq. & Ser.Libn.

★ 20301 ★
Western States Chiropractic College - W.A. Budden Memorial Library (Med)
2900 N.E. 132nd Ave.   Phone: (503)256-3180
Portland, OR 97230   Kay Irvine, Hd.Libn.
Staff: Prof 2; Other 10. **Subjects:** Chiropractic, neurology, orthopedics, radiology, alternative healing. **Holdings:** 9000 books; 3500 bound periodical volumes. **Subscriptions:** 400 journals and other serials. **Services:** Interlibrary loan; copying; library open to the public. **Computerized Information Services:** DIALOG Information Services, MEDLINE, OCLC, EPIC, OnTyme Electronic Message Network Service (electronic mail service). Performs searches on fee basis. **Networks/Consortia:** Member of Chiropractic Library Consortium (CLIBCON), Oregon Health Sciences Libraries Association (OHSLA), Portland Area Health Sciences Librarians, CLASS. **Special Indexes:** Index to Chiropractic Literature. **Remarks:** Electronic mail address(es): CLASS.WSCC (OnTyme Electronic Message Network Service). **Staff:** Patty Turrentine, AV.Techn.; Pam Bjork, AV Libn.

★ 20302 ★
Western Sydney Area Health Services - Westmead Hospital - AMA Library (Med)
Westmead, NSW 2145, Australia   Phone: 02 6336266
    Linda Mulheron, Chf.Libn.
Founded: 1978. **Staff:** Prof 8; Other 5. **Subjects:** Epidemiology, bacteriology, virology, hematology, cytology, cytogenetics, tumors, pathology, medicine, surgery, pediatrics, psychiatry, radiation oncology, radiology. **Special Collections:** New South Wales Department of Health videotape collection; Australian Medical Association Library (5000 books and journals). **Holdings:** 30,000 books; 3000 tapes, slides, films, videotapes, audiocassettes. **Subscriptions:** 1900 journals and other serials. **Services:** Interlibrary loan; copying; SDI; library open to medical professionals and local medical students. **Computerized Information Services:** MEDLINE, DIALOG Information Services, BRS Information Technologies, Data-Star, ABN (Australian Bibliographic Network); OTC Minerva, Dialcom, Inc.; ILANET (electronic mail services). Performs searches on fee basis. Contact Person: Ratnes Singham, Ref.Libn., 633 6261. **Publications:** Journals list. **Special Catalogs:** AV Catalog. **Remarks:** FAX: 02 8938257. Telex: 20298. **Staff:** Mrs. K. Keily, Deputy, Tech.Serv.; Mr. D. Elliot, AV Off.; Mrs. R. Zuther, ILL Off.; Mrs. B. King, Sys./Rd.Serv.Libn.

★ 20303 ★
Western Technologies, Inc. - Library
3737 E. Broadway   Phone: (602)437-3737
Phoenix, AZ 85040   Marlye Logan
Founded: 1955. **Subjects:** Environmental engineering. **Holdings:** Figures not available.

Western Theological Seminary - Archives
See: **(Holland) Joint Archives of Holland** (7328)

★ 20304 ★
Western Theological Seminary - Beardslee Library (Rel-Phil)
Holland, MI 49423   Phone: (616)392-8555
    Paul M. Smith, Libn.
Staff: Prof 2; Other 1. **Subjects:** Theology. **Special Collections:** Henry Bast Preaching Resources Center. **Holdings:** 90,000 books; 11,646 bound periodical volumes; 350 linear feet of archives; 3200 slides; 2330 microforms. **Subscriptions:** 500 journals and other serials. **Services:** Interlibrary loan; copying; library open to the public with restrictions. **Automated Operations:** Computerized cataloging and circulation. **Computerized Information Services:** OCLC; BITNET (electronic mail service). **Networks/Consortia:** Member of Michigan Library Consortium (MLC). **Publications:** Reformed Review, 3/year. **Remarks:** FAX: (616)392-8889. Electronic mail address(es): PSMITH@HOPE (BITNET). Archival material is part of the Joint Archives of Holland. **Staff:** Ann E. Nieuwkoop.

★ 20305 ★
Western Washington University - Center for Pacific Northwest Studies (Hist)
516 High St.   Phone: (206)676-3125
Bellingham, WA 98225   Dr. James W. Scott, Dir.
Founded: 1971. **Staff:** 4. **Subjects:** History - Washington, Pacific Northwest, business. **Holdings:** 1000 books; 100 bound periodical volumes; 600 volumes of bound newspapers; 300 cubic feet and 250 linear feet of business records; 120 cubic feet of manuscripts and personal collections; 90,000 photographs and negatives. **Services:** Copying; center open to the public for reference use only. **Publications:** Occasional Papers series; Guide to the Collections. **Remarks:** An alternate telephone number is 647-4776.

★ 20306 ★

Western Washington University - Department of Geography and Regional Planning - Map Library (Geog-Map)
Arntzen Hall 101   Phone: (206)676-3272
Bellingham, WA 98225   Janet Collins, Map Libn.
Founded: 1957. **Staff:** Prof 1; Other 6. **Subjects:** Maps, atlases. **Special Collections:** Maps emphasizing the Pacific Northwest, Canada, Mexico, and Circum-Pacific. **Holdings:** 915 atlases; 204,182 maps; 22,510 aerial photographs; 55 globes. **Subscriptions:** 6 journals and other serials. **Services:** Copying; library open to the public for reference use only. **Computerized Information Services:** Geologic Maps Database (internal database). **Remarks:** FAX: (206)676-3044.

Western Washington University - Environmental Resource Library
See: **Huxley College of Environmental Studies - Environmental Resource Library** (7596)

★ 20307 ★

Western Wisconsin Technical College - Library (Sci-Engr)
400 N. 6th St.   Phone: (608)785-9142
La Crosse, WI 54602-0908   Patrick J. Brunet, Lib.Mgr.
SFounded: 1966. **Staff:** Prof 2; Other 3. **Subjects:** Technology, health occupations, business administration, legal assistance, distributive education, adult education, home economics, agriculture. **Holdings:** 28,000 books and bound periodical volumes; 750 reels of microfilm; 1200 microfiche; 8 VF drawers of pamphlets. **Subscriptions:** 310 journals and other serials; 15 newspapers. **Services:** Interlibrary loan; copying; library open to the public. **Remarks:** FAX: (608)785-9407. **Staff:** Annette Neiderkorn, Ref.Libn.

★ 20308 ★

Western Wyoming College - Library - Special Collections (Hist)
2500 College Dr.   Phone: (307)382-1700
Rock Springs, WY 82902-0428 Robert Kalabus, Interim Dir. of Lib.Serv.
Founded: 1959. **Staff:** Prof 2; Other 3. **Special Collections:** Wyoming documents (389); Smithsonian Institution annual reports, 1849-1969; Bureau of American Ethnology, 1880-1967; U.S. Government documents. **Holdings:** 50,000 books; 1801 bound periodical volumes; 14,756 microforms; 360 cassettes and AV programs; 24 computer software programs. **Subscriptions:** 316 journals and other serials; 31 newspapers. **Services:** Interlibrary loan; copying; collections open to the public. **Automated Operations:** Computerized cataloging and ILL. **Computerized Information Services:** BRS Information Technologies. Performs searches on fee basis. Contact Person: Pam Hiltner, Pub.Serv. **Networks/Consortia:** Member of Western Wyoming Health Science Library Consortium. **Remarks:** FAX: (307)382-7665.

★ 20309 ★

Westerners International, A Foundation - Library (Hist)
1700 N.E. 63rd St.   Phone: (405)478-8408
Oklahoma City, OK 73111   Donald Reeves, Sec.
Founded: 1944. **Subjects:** Western history. **Holdings:** 500 volumes; publications, documents, and correspondence of more than 100 local units called "Corrals" devoted to research and popularization of Western history. **Subscriptions:** 18 journals and other serials. **Services:** Library open to the public by appointment for reference use only.

★ 20310 ★

Westfield Athenaeum - Edwin Smith Historical Museum - Archives (Hist)
6 Elm St.   Phone: (413)568-7833
Westfield, MA 01085   Patricia Cramer, Dir.
Founded: 1864. **Subjects:** Westfield history. **Special Collections:** Edward Taylor papers (1 reel of microfilm). **Holdings:** 1 reel of microfilm of Westfield town records and early church records; 1 reel of microfilm of local manuscripts; account books. **Services:** Interlibrary loan; copying; archives open to the public by appointment and on a limited schedule.

Westgate Friends Library
See: **Society of Friends - Ohio Yearly Meeting** (15324)

★ 20311 ★

Westinghouse Electric Corporation - Bettis Atomic Power Laboratory - Library (Energy)
Box 79   Phone: (412)462-5000
West Mifflin, PA 15122-0079   Anne H. Liparula, Libn.
Founded: 1949. **Staff:** Prof 4; Other 3. **Subjects:** Nuclear power. **Holdings:** 44,000 books and bound periodical volumes; internal technical reports and correspondence; Atomic Energy Commission reports. **Subscriptions:** 300 journals and other serials. **Services:** Interlibrary loan; library not open to the public. **Remarks:** Westinghouse Electric Corporation operates under contract to the U.S. Department of Energy.

★ 20312 ★

Westinghouse Electric Corporation - Electronic Systems Group - Technical Information Center (Sci-Engr)
7323 Aviation
Box 1693
MS 1138   Phone: (301)765-2858
Baltimore, MD 21203   Joan L. Doerr, Supv.
Founded: 1961. **Staff:** Prof 3; Other 7. **Subjects:** Electronic communication engineering, systems engineering. **Holdings:** 20,000 books; 4000 bound periodical volumes; 100,000 technical reports on microfilm. **Subscriptions:** 450 journals and other serials. **Services:** Interlibrary loan; center not open to the public. **Automated Operations:** Computerized cataloging, acquisitions, serials, and circulation. **Computerized Information Services:** DIALOG Information Services, Integrated Technical Information System (ITIS), DTIC, COMPENDEX, Standard & Poor's; CD-ROM (Computer Library). **Remarks:** FAX: (301)993-7675.

★ 20313 ★

Westinghouse Electric Corporation - Energy Systems - Technical Library (Sci-Engr)
Energy Center East 209   Phone: (412)374-4200
Box 355   Barbara M. Spiegelman, Mgr.,
Pittsburgh, PA 15230   Tech.Info. & Commun.
Founded: 1955. **Staff:** Prof 4; Other 3. **Subjects:** Nuclear power - technology, engineering and industry, physics, business management, marketing, computer applications. **Special Collections:** Three Mile Island and Chernobyl accidents. **Holdings:** 20,000 volumes; 200,000 technical reports in microform; 40,000 technical reports and documents; 2000 AV programs; 2000 pamphlets; 20,000 internal reports. **Subscriptions:** 200 journals and other serials. **Services:** Interlibrary loan; copying; training seminars; AV services. **Automated Operations:** Computerized cataloging, serials, and circulation. **Computerized Information Services:** DIALOG Information Services, BRS Information Technologies, Integrated Technical Information System (ITIS), NEXIS, Dow Jones News/Retrieval, Dun & Bradstreet Business Credit Services, InvesText, NewsNet, Inc., NRC Database, Utility Data Institute, Electronic Newsroom, OCLC, Standard & Poor's COMPUSTAT Services, Inc.; DIALMAIL (electronic mail service). **Networks/Consortia:** Member of Pittsburgh Regional Library Center (PRLC). **Publications:** Video Selection Guide. **Special Indexes:** KWOC Indexes to Nucleonics Week 1968-80, Selected Public Information on Nuclear Energy (SPINDEX) 1969-81, TMI related information. **Remarks:** FAX: (412)374-5744. Telex: 62753525. **Formerly:** Westinghouse Electric Corporation - Power Systems - Information Resource Center. **Staff:** Amy Haugh, Sr.Info.Spec.; Nancy Flury Carlson, Info.Spec.; Jane Singer, Info.Spec.

★ 20314 ★

Westinghouse Electric Corporation - Law Library (Law)
Westinghouse Bldg.
11 Stanwix St.   Phone: (412)642-3588
Pittsburgh, PA 15222   Lynne Serfozo, Mgr., Off.Adm.
Subjects: Law. **Remarks:** No further information was supplied by respondent.

★ 20315 ★

Westinghouse Electric Corporation - Naval Reactor Facility Library (Energy)
Box 2068   Phone: (208)526-0111
Idaho Falls, ID 83401   Donnett Scott, Libn.
Founded: 1956. **Staff:** Prof 1; Other 6. **Subjects:** Atomic power. **Holdings:** 4000 books; 58,000 documents and technical reports. **Subscriptions:** 52 journals and other serials. **Services:** Library not open to the public.

★ 20316 ★
Westinghouse Electric Corporation - Naval Systems Division - Library
Dept. 749, Bldg. 2
18901 Euclid Ave.   Phone: (216)486-8300
Cleveland, OH 44117   Ann McAuliffe, Libn.
Subjects: Military electronics, acoustics, underwater ocean technology, reliability, military science, military computer hardware and software, materials, composites, plastics, metals. **Special Collections:** Military specifications, standards, handbooks; industrial specifications; catalogs; U.S. Government documents. **Holdings:** 2500 books; 200,000 documents.

★ 20317 ★
Westinghouse Electric Corporation - PGBU - Library (Sci-Engr, Comp Sci)
The Quadrangle, MC 235
4400 Alafaya Trail   Phone: (407)281-2170
Orlando, FL 32826-2399   Mary P. Maynard, Sr.Libn.
Founded: 1931. **Staff:** Prof 1; Other 1. **Subjects:** Engineering, mathematics, computers, management, metallurgy. **Special Collections:** Westinghouse Historical Collection. **Holdings:** 3000 books; 2000 bound periodical volumes; 14,000 reports; 8000 microfiche. **Subscriptions:** 104 journals and other serials. **Services:** Interlibrary loan; library not open to the public. **Automated Operations:** Computerized circulation. **Computerized Information Services:** DIALOG Information Services, NEXIS, DataTimes; WCAP (internal database). **Publications:** New Books Listing, monthly; Research Ready, monthly. **Remarks:** FAX: (407)281-2080.

Westinghouse Electric Corporation - Power Systems - Information Resource Center
See: Westinghouse Electric Corporation - Energy Systems - Technical Library (20313)

★ 20318 ★
Westinghouse Electric Corporation - Science & Technology Center (Sci-Engr)
1310 Beulah Rd.   Phone: (412)256-1610
Pittsburgh, PA 15235   Dedrium J. Hanko, Mgr., Adm.Serv.
Founded: 1923. **Staff:** Prof 2; Other 3. **Subjects:** Chemistry, ceramics, electrical engineering, electronics, mathematics, magnetics, mechanical engineering, mechanical sciences, metallurgy, nuclear sciences, space sciences, physics. **Holdings:** 50,000 volumes. **Subscriptions:** 500 journals and other serials. **Services:** Center not open to the public. **Computerized Information Services:** DIALOG Information Services, PFDS Online, BRS Information Technologies, STN International, OCLC, DTIC, WILSONLINE; internal databases. **Networks/Consortia:** Member of Pittsburgh Regional Library Center (PRLC). **Publications:** Library Bulletin, monthly; Keyword Thesaurus, annual; Journal Holdings. **Remarks:** FAX: (412)256-1348. Telex: 4909989013.

★ 20319 ★
Westinghouse Electric Corporation - Training and Operational Services - Information Resource Center (Energy)
2 Energy Dr.   Phone: (708)918-7080
Lake Bluff, IL 60044   Terri Hill
Founded: 1970. **Staff:** 1. **Subjects:** Nuclear power, physics. **Holdings:** 500 books; 600 technical manuals; 150 videotapes; 5000 slides; 300 microfiche. **Subscriptions:** 25 journals and other serials; 6 newspapers. **Services:** Interlibrary loan; center not open to the public. **Remarks:** FAX: (708)918-7081.

★ 20320 ★
Westinghouse Electric Corporation - WIPP Technical Library (Sci-Engr)
Box 2078   Phone: (505)887-8278
Carlsbad, NM 88220   Lata Desai, Libn.
Staff: 1. **Subjects:** Nuclear waste disposal, geology. **Special Collections:** U.S. Department of Energy Waste Isolation Pilot Plant (WIPP) materials. **Holdings:** 500 books; 5500 technical reports. **Subscriptions:** 125 journals and other serials; 10 newspapers. **Services:** Interlibrary loan; library not open to the public. **Computerized Information Services:** Integrated Technical Information System (ITIS), DIALOG Information Services. **Remarks:** FAX: (505)887-1077.

★ 20321 ★
Westinghouse Environmental Management Co. of Ohio - FEMP Library (Sci-Engr, Energy)
P.O. Box 398704   Phone: (513)738-6534
Cincinnati, OH 45239   Rosemary H. Gardewing, Lib.Supv.
Founded: 1951. **Staff:** 3. **Subjects:** Atomic energy, chemistry, metallurgy, radioactive waste. **Holdings:** 9000 books; 2000 bound periodical volumes; 30,000 technical reports; 200,000 technical reports in microform; government publications. **Subscriptions:** 250 journals and other serials. **Services:** Interlibrary loan; library not open to the public. **Computerized Information Services:** DIALOG Information Services. **Publications:** Library Accessions, bimonthly - for internal distribution only. **Remarks:** Operates under contract to the U.S. Department of Energy. **Formerly:** Westinghouse Materials Co. of Ohio - FMPC Library.

★ 20322 ★
Westinghouse Hanford Company - Department of Energy's Public Reading Room, A1-65 (Sci-Engr)
Federal Bldg., Rm. 157
Box 1970   Phone: (509)376-8583
Richland, WA 99352   Terri Traub, Pub.Info.Spec.
Founded: 1976. **Staff:** Prof 1. **Subjects:** Hanford Site, environmental restoration, nuclear waste management. **Holdings:** 50 books; 15,000 technical reports; 3500 microfiche. **Services:** Copying; room open to the public for reference use only. **Automated Operations:** Computerized cataloging. **Remarks:** FAX: (509)376-2071.

Westinghouse Materials Co. of Ohio
See: Westinghouse Environmental Management Co. of Ohio (20321)

★ 20323 ★
Westinghouse Savannah River Co. - Technical Library (Energy, Sci-Engr)
SRS-Bldg. 773A   Phone: (803)725-2940
Aiken, SC 29808   J.M. Stogner, Mgr., Budget & Lib.Sect.
Founded: 1952. **Staff:** Prof 3; Other 6. **Subjects:** Nuclear science, chemistry, physics, metallurgy, engineering, mathematics. **Holdings:** 35,000 books; 45,000 bound periodical volumes. **Subscriptions:** 500 journals and other serials. **Services:** Interlibrary loan; library not open to the public. **Automated Operations:** Computerized cataloging, serials, circulation, and acquisitions. **Computerized Information Services:** DIALOG Information Services, PFDS Online, Integrated Technical Information System (ITIS), NewsNet, Inc., NASA/RECON, STN International, BRS Information Technologies. **Remarks:** FAX: (803)725-1169. The Savannah River site operates under contract to the U.S. Department of Energy. **Staff:** Erminia U. Kauer, Staff Libn.; Judith LeBlanc, Ref.Libn.; C. Tom Sutherland, Sr.Libn.

★ 20324 ★
Westlake Community Hospital - Library (Med)
1225 Lake St.   Phone: (708)681-3000
Melrose Park, IL 60160   Christina E. Rudawski, Libn.
Staff: Prof 1. **Subjects:** Medicine, nursing, hospitals, health administration. **Holdings:** 750 books; 6 VF drawers of pamphlets. **Subscriptions:** 90 journals and other serials. **Services:** Interlibrary loan; library open to the public for reference use only. **Computerized Information Services:** BRS Information Technologies; DOCLINE (electronic mail service). **Networks/Consortia:** Member of Metropolitan Consortium of Chicago, Suburban Library System (SLS). **Publications:** Annual Report. **Remarks:** FAX: (708)681-0151 (Attn: Library).

Westmead Hospital
See: Western Sydney Area Health Services - Westmead Hospital - AMA Library (20302)

★ 20325 ★
Westminister Presbyterian Church - Library (Rel-Phil)
3906 W. Friendly Ave.   Phone: (919)299-3785
Greensboro, NC 27410   Mary G. Harrill, Lib.Chm.
Founded: 1959. **Subjects:** Bible, theology, Christian life, values. **Holdings:** 1468 books. **Subscriptions:** 2 journals and other serials. **Services:** Library open to the public.

★ 20326 ★
Westminster Abbey - Library (Rel-Phil)
Mission, BC, Canada V2V 4J2   Phone: (604)826-8975
            Boniface Aicher, O.S.B., Libn.
Subjects: Theology, church history, scripture, Canadiana. **Special Collections:** Rare book room (manuscripts and volumes from 1540). **Holdings:** 40,000 books; 3000 microfiche. **Subscriptions:** 70 journals and other serials; 15 newspapers. **Services:** Copying; library open to the public with restrictions.

★ 20327 ★
Westminster Choir College - Talbott Library (Mus)
Hamilton Ave. at Walnut Ln.   Phone: (609)921-7100
Princeton, NJ 08540   Mary A. Benton, Act.Dir.
Founded: 1926. **Staff:** Prof 5; Other 7. **Subjects:** Music - choral, organ, keyboard, sacred. **Special Collections:** Choral Music Performance Collection (5500 titles in multiple copy; 35,000 single copy reference collection); Tams-Witmark Collection of Choral Music; American Organ Archives of the Organ Historical Society; Routley Collection (studies in hymnology, special collections of church music); Music Education Resource Center; Media/AV Center. **Holdings:** 24,000 books; 31,300 scores; college archives. **Subscriptions:** 160 journals and other serials. **Services:** Interlibrary loan (fee); copying; library open to the public with fee for circulation for area residents. **Automated Operations:** Computerized cataloging and acquisitions. **Computerized Information Services:** OCLC; MCI Mail (electronic mail service). **Networks/Consortia:** Member of PALINET, (New Jersey) Regional Library Cooperatives. **Remarks:** FAX: (609)921-8829. Electronic mail address(es): 4746586@mcimail.com (MCI Mail). Affiliated with Rider College. **Staff:** Jeanette Jacobson, Hd. of Cat.; Nancy Wicklund, Hd., Rd.Serv.; Mi-Hye Chyun, Acq.; Jane Nowakowski, Cat.; Terry Simpkins, Hd., Media/AV Ctr.; Franceen Hoyt, Hd.Circ.; Andrew Megill, Hd., Performance Coll.

★ 20328 ★
Westminster College - Winston Churchill Memorial and Library (Hist)
7th & Westminster Ave.   Phone: (314)642-3361
Fulton, MO 65251-1299   Judith Pugh, Dir.
Staff: 5. **Subjects:** Sir Winston Churchill; reconstructed Wren Church of St. Mary, Aldermanbury. **Special Collections:** Original oil paintings by Chuchill; World War II and Anglo-American documents; Churchill's life and times (photographs, letters, manuscripts); Sir Christopher Wren, Architect; rare antique maps; 8 section pieces of the Berlin Wall. **Holdings:** 1200 books; 530 reels of microfilm. **Services:** Library open to the public with restrictions. **Automated Operations:** Computerized cataloging. **Publications:** Memorial Memo, quarterly. **Remarks:** An alternate telephone number is 642-6648. **Staff:** Judith Novak Pugh, Dir.

★ 20329 ★
Westminster Historical Society - Library (Hist)
110 Main St.
Box 177
Westminster, MA 01473   Phone: (508)874-5569
         Betsy Hannula, Cur.
Founded: 1921. **Subjects:** Westminster history. **Special Collections:** General Nelson A. Miles Collection (books, news clippings, artifacts). **Holdings:** 200 books; 200 bound periodical volumes; 20 manuscripts. **Services:** Copying; library open to the public.

★ 20330 ★
Westminster Institute for Ethics and Human Values - Library (Soc Sci)
361 Windermere Rd.
London, ON, Canada N6G 2K3   Phone: (519)673-0046
Subjects: Ethics - bioethics, legal, business and professional, philosophical; morality and population. **Holdings:** 1800 volumes; journal article and newspaper clipping files. **Subscriptions:** 51 journals and other serials. **Services:** Copying; library open to the public for reference use only. **Publications:** Westminster Affairs (newsletter), quarterly - free upon request. **Remarks:** The Westminster Institute for Ethics and Human Values is sponsored by Westminster College.

Westminster Law Library
See: **University of Denver - College of Law** (18547)

★ 20331 ★
Westminster Presbyterian Church - John H. Holmes Library (Rel-Phil)
Cleves-Warsaw & Nancy Lee Ln.
Cincinnati, OH 45238   Phone: (513)921-1623
Founded: 1948. **Staff:** 1. **Subjects:** Bible, devotional materials, church work, religious education, family life, children's books, mental health. **Special Collections:** Bibles (including braille). **Holdings:** 6784 books, tapes, records. **Subscriptions:** 5 journals and other serials. **Services:** Library open to church visitors. **Staff:** Emma Reeves, Assoc.Libn.; Carolyn Brinkerhoff, Assoc.Libn.

★ 20332 ★
Westminster Presbyterian Church - Juanita J. Johnson Memorial Library (Rel-Phil)
1502 W. 13th St.   Phone: (302)654-5214
Wilmington, DE 19806   Mrs. Edgell
Staff: Prof 1. **Subjects:** Religion. **Holdings:** 5000. **Subscriptions:** 5 journals and other serials. **Services:** Library open to the public. **Remarks:** (302)654-5706.

★ 20333 ★
Westminster Presbyterian Church - Library (Rel-Phil)
4400 N. Shartel   Phone: (405)524-2204
Oklahoma City, OK 73118   J. Richard Hershberger, Assoc. Minister
Founded: 1950. **Staff:** Prof 1; Other 1. **Subjects:** Religion, church history, biography. **Holdings:** 1200 volumes. **Services:** Library open to the public with restrictions.

★ 20334 ★
Westminster Presbyterian Church - Library (Rel-Phil)
2040 Washington Rd.   Phone: (412)835-6630
Pittsburgh, PA 15241   Betty B. Brown, Lib.Dir.
Staff: Prof 2. **Subjects:** Religion, West Pennsylvania history. **Holdings:** 5000 books. **Services:** Library open to the public.

★ 20335 ★
Westminster Presbyterian Church - Library (Rel-Phil)
2701 Cameron Mills Rd.   Phone: (703)549-4766
Alexandria, VA 22302   Jane Campbell, Coord., Christian Educ.
Founded: 1956. **Staff:** Prof 1; Other 2. **Subjects:** Religion. **Holdings:** 2100 books; phonograph records; audiotapes. **Subscriptions:** 11 journals and other serials. **Services:** Library open to the public. **Staff:** Barbara M. Middleton, Libn.

★ 20336 ★
Westminster Theological Seminary - Montgomery Library (Rel-Phil)
Box 27009   Phone: (215)572-3822
Philadelphia, PA 19118   Grace Mullen, Act.Libn.
Founded: 1929. **Staff:** Prof 3; Other 3. **Subjects:** Biblical studies, theology, church history, patristics. **Special Collections:** Bible texts and versions (1000); Reformed theology of 16th-20th centuries (2500 items). **Holdings:** 100,000 books; 10,000 bound periodical volumes; 600 reels of microfilm. **Subscriptions:** 800 journals and other serials. **Services:** Interlibrary loan; copying; library open to the public. **Automated Operations:** Computerized cataloging and acquisitions. **Computerized Information Services:** OCLC, BRS Information Technologies. **Networks/Consortia:** Member of PALINET, State System of Higher Education Libraries Council (SSHELCO). **Remarks:** Library located at Willow Grove Ave. & Church Rd., Glenside, PA 19038. **Staff:** Jane Patete, Cir.

★ 20337 ★
Westmoreland County Historical Society - Calvin E. Pollins Memorial Library (Hist)
c/o Gbg. Garden Center
951 Old Salem Rd.   Phone: (412)836-1800
Greensburg, PA 15601   Linda E. Forish, Adm.Sec.
Staff: 3. **Subjects:** Local history, genealogy, fine and decorative arts, archeology. **Special Collections:** Early West Pennsylvania manuscript collections dealing with local area and individuals. **Holdings:** 1500 books; 12 VF drawers; 56 bound volumes of local newspapers; 12,000 documents; 50 reels of microfilm; 500 slides; 400 architectural drawings of Westmoreland County. **Services:** Copying; library open to the public on a fee basis. **Publications:** List of publications - available on request. **Special Indexes:** Archival holdings indexes; indexes to fine and decorative arts colllections.

★ 20338 ★
Westmoreland County Law Library (Law)
202 Courthouse Square
Greensburg, PA 15601
Phone: (412)830-3267
Elizabeth Ward, Libn.
Staff: Prof 1; Other 2. **Subjects:** Law. **Holdings:** 19,000 volumes. **Subscriptions:** 20 journals and other serials. **Services:** Interlibrary loan; copying; library open to the public. **Computerized Information Services:** WESTLAW. **Networks/Consortia:** Member of Pittsburgh Regional Library Center (PRLC). **Remarks:** FAX: (412)830-3042.

★ 20339 ★
Westmoreland Hospital - Library and Health Resource Center (Med)
532 W. Pittsburgh St.
Greensburg, PA 15601-2282
Phone: (412)832-4088
Janet C. Petrak, Med.Libn.
Founded: 1959. **Staff:** Prof 1. **Subjects:** Medicine, nursing, surgery. **Special Collections:** History of nursing; Clinical Pastoral Education Program Support Collection. **Holdings:** 4000 books; 1499 bound periodical volumes. **Subscriptions:** 348 journals and other serials. **Services:** Interlibrary loan; copying; library open to the public for reference use only. **Computerized Information Services:** BRS Information Technologies, MEDLARS. **Networks/Consortia:** Member of Southeast Pittsburgh Library Consortium. **Publications:** Library & Health Resource Center Newsletter. **Remarks:** FAX: (412)832-4329 (Attn: Library).

★ 20340 ★
Westmoreland Museum of Art - Art Reference Library (Art)
221 N. Main St.
Greensburg, PA 15601-1898
Phone: (412)837-1500
Founded: 1958. **Staff:** 1. **Subjects:** American and European artists and styles, American architecture, techniques of materials, history. **Holdings:** 10,200 books; 75 bound periodical volumes; 28,000 exhibition catalogs; 15,000 museum exchange bulletins and reports; 50,000 exhibition brochures. **Subscriptions:** 45 journals and other serials. **Services:** Copying; library open to the public for reference use only. **Publications:** Monthly brochures on exhibitions.

Weston Clinical Science Center Library
See: **University of Wisconsin--Madison - Center for Health Sciences Libraries** (19586)

★ 20341 ★
Weston County Historical Society - Anna Miller Museum (Hist)
Box 698
Newcastle, WY 82701
Phone: (307)746-4188
Founded: 1966. **Staff:** 2. **Subjects:** Wyoming and Western history; U.S. Congress. **Special Collections:** Frank W. Mondell, Wyoming Congressman, 1898-1922. **Holdings:** 50 bound periodical volumes; periodicals, 1860 to present; 100 items of ephemera, local history, clippings, pamphlets, booklets, manuscripts; 1900 local history photographs; 30 oral history tapes. **Subscriptions:** 12 journals and other serials. **Services:** Copying; library open to the public for reference use only.

Weston Research Centre - Information Resource Centre
See: **Diversified Research Laboratories, Ltd. - Information Resource Centre** (4922)

★ 20342 ★
Roy F. Weston, Inc. - Weston Information Center (Env-Cons, Energy)
Weston Way
West Chester, PA 19380
Phone: (215)692-3030
Mary Walker, Dir.
Founded: 1963. **Staff:** Prof 2; Other 2. **Subjects:** Pollution; waste - solid, nuclear, hazardous; environmental science; planning; energy. **Holdings:** 5000 books; 700 bound periodical volumes; 10,000 documents; 2500 microfiche. **Subscriptions:** 120 journals and other serials. **Services:** Interlibrary loan; center not open to the public. **Computerized Information Services:** DIALOG Information Services, PFDS Online, MEDLARS, OCLC, Ground Water On-Line, Chemical Information Systems, Inc. (CIS), VU/TEXT Information Services, NewsNet, Inc., Dow Jones News/Retrieval, LEXIS, NEXIS, Occupational Health Services, Inc. (OHS). **Remarks:** FAX: (215)430-3124. **Formerly:** Its Corporate Information Center.

★ 20343 ★
Weston School of Theology - Library (Rel-Phil)
99 Brattle St.
Cambridge, MA 02138
Phone: (617)349-3602
James Dunkly, Dir.
Founded: 1922. **Staff:** Prof 5; Other 8. **Subjects:** Theology, papal and conciliar documents, New Testament, Jesuitica. **Special Collections:** Arabic Collection (4000 volumes). **Holdings:** 260,000 volumes. **Subscriptions:** 1100 journals and other serials. **Services:** Interlibrary loan; copying; library open to the public with restrictions on circulation. **Automated Operations:** Computerized cataloging and ILL. **Computerized Information Services:** OCLC. **Remarks:** Maintained jointly by Weston School of Theology and Episcopal Divinity School. FAX: (617)492-5833. **Staff:** Gayle Pershouse, Pub.Serv.Coord.; Paul LaCharite, Hd., Acq.; Anne Reece, Hd., Cat.; Judith Russell, Cat.Asst.; Richard Brown, Sys.Supv.; Marilyn Brown, Ill.Supv. & Cat.Asst.

★ 20344 ★
Westpoint Pepperell - Research Center - Information Services Library (Sci-Engr)
3300 23rd Dr.
Valley, AL 36854
Phone: (404)645-4658
Debbie Keeble
Founded: 1944. **Staff:** Prof 1; Other 1. **Subjects:** Textiles, chemistry, textile testing, dyeing, fire retardancy, environmental pollution, engineering, industrial hygiene. **Holdings:** 3000 books; 2500 bound periodical volumes; 15 VF drawers of research reports; 4 VF drawers of patents; 4 VF drawers of reprints; 4000 microfiche; 4 VF drawers of catalogs, brochures, and manufacturing technical data. **Subscriptions:** 150 journals and other serials. **Services:** Interlibrary loan; SDI; library open to students. **Computerized Information Services:** DIALOG Information Services, NLM. **Publications:** Recent Accessions, quarterly - to technical supervisors.

★ 20345 ★
Westport Historical Society - Library (Hist)
P.O. Box 3031
Westport, MA 02790
Phone: (508)636-6011
Lincoln S. Tripp
Subjects: Westport and New Bedford, Massachusetts history. **Holdings:** 300 books; documents. **Services:** Copying; library open to the public with restrictions. **Publications:** Newsletter.

★ 20346 ★
Westreco, Inc. - Food Research and Development - Library (Food-Bev)
577 S. 4th St.
Fulton, NY 13069
Phone: (315)593-8402
Jana M. Van der Veer, Res.Libn.
Founded: 1955. **Staff:** Prof 1. **Subjects:** Confectionery industry; food processing; chemistry - industrial, physical, analytical; chemical engineering. **Special Collections:** Chocolate; cocoa. **Holdings:** 1800 books; 24 VF drawers of pamphlets, articles, clippings, newsletters. **Subscriptions:** 130 journals and other serials. **Services:** Interlibrary loan; library not open to the public. **Computerized Information Services:** DIALOG Information Services. **Remarks:** FAX: (315)593-6793. Telex: 755839.

★ 20347 ★
WESTRECO, Inc. - Library (Food-Bev)
8015 Van Nuys Blvd.
Van Nuys, CA 91412
Phone: (818)376-4217
Kathryn A. Stewart, Sr.Libn.
Founded: 1940. **Staff:** Prof 1. **Subjects:** Food science, dairy technology, nutrition, chemistry. **Holdings:** 5000 books; 4000 bound periodical volumes; 7300 patents. **Subscriptions:** 300 journals and other serials. **Services:** Interlibrary loan; library not open to the public. **Computerized Information Services:** DIALOG Information Services. **Remarks:** FAX: (818)904-9746. **Formerly:** CALRECO, Inc.

★ 20348 ★
Westreco, Inc. - Technical Library (Food-Bev)
201 Housatonic Ave.
New Milford, CT 06776
Phone: (203)355-0911
Linda F. Carhuff, Hd.Libn.
Staff: Prof 1. **Subjects:** Food science, analytical chemistry, nutrition, culinary arts, microbiology, packaging. **Special Collections:** Chemical abstracts, 1907 to present (microfilm). **Holdings:** 3700 books; 1500 bound periodical volumes; 3300 patents; 20 VF drawers of pamphlets; 70 reels of microfilm of company records. **Subscriptions:** 300 journals and other serials. **Services:** Interlibrary loan; library open to the public for reference use only by arrangement. **Automated Operations:** Data Trek. **Computerized Information Services:** DIALOG Information Services, Occupational Health Services, Inc. (OHS), OCLC; DIALMAIL (electronic mail service). **Networks/Consortia:** Member of Southwestern Connecticut Library Council (SWLC). **Remarks:** FAX: (203)355-3446.

★ 20349 ★
Westvaco Corporation - Forest Science Laboratory Library (Agri)
Box 1950   Phone: (803)871-5000
Summerville, SC 29484   Roxy Rust, Libn.
Founded: 1982. **Staff:** Prof 1. **Subjects:** Forestry, forestry management, biometrics, forest genetics and soils. **Holdings:** 3500 books; 400 bound periodical volumes; 3000 U.S. Forest Service Experiment Station documents; 3000 clippings; 1100 company reports; 2000 institutional and miscellaneous publications. **Subscriptions:** 100 journals and other serials. **Services:** Interlibrary loan; copying; library open to the public for reference use only. **Automated Operations:** Computerized cataloging and ILL. **Computerized Information Services:** DIALOG Information Services, OCLC. **Networks/Consortia:** Member of SOLINET. **Publications:** FSL Library Book Acquistions List, monthly - for internal distribution only. **Special Indexes:** Information file index (book). **Remarks:** FAX: (803)875-7185.

★ 20350 ★
Westvaco Corporation - Information Services Center (Sci-Engr)
5600 Virginia Ave.
Box 2941105   Phone: (803)745-3719
North Charleston, SC 29411-2905   Elizabeth D. De Liesseline, Info.Spec.
Staff: Prof 2; Other 2. **Subjects:** Papermaking, pulping, forestry, utilization of by-products. **Holdings:** 9000 volumes; 50,000 company reports; 15,000 patents; 2000 clippings. **Subscriptions:** 150 journals and other serials. **Services:** Interlibrary loan; center not open to the public. **Computerized Information Services:** PFDS Online, DIALOG Information Services. **Publications:** Reports Bulletin, monthly. **Remarks:** FAX: (803)745-3768. **Also Known As:** West Virginia Pulp and Paper Company. **Staff:** Barbara McDonald, Info.Spec.

★ 20351 ★
Westvaco Corporation - Laurel Technical Center - Library (Sci-Engr)
11101 Johns Hopkins Rd.   Phone: (301)497-1300
Laurel, MD 20723   Jeanne Lloyd, Res.Libn.
Founded: 1967. **Staff:** Prof 1. **Subjects:** Chemistry - paper, organic; biochemistry; engineering - chemical, corrosion. **Special Collections:** Specialized collection of books, periodicals, theses, reports and bibliographies (210) on paper manufacturing technology and related fields. **Holdings:** 3500 monographs; 2600 bound periodical volumes; 150 technical papers. **Subscriptions:** 140 journals and other serials; 5 newspapers. **Services:** Interlibrary loan; library not open to the public. **Computerized Information Services:** ORBIT Search Service, DIALOG Information Services, STN International. **Networks/Consortia:** Member of National Capitol Area Interlibrary Loan Association. **Remarks:** Alternate telephone number(s): 792-9100 (Baltimore); 497-1307 (Laurel); 953-2575 (Washington, DC). FAX: (301)497-1309.

★ 20352 ★
Westview Christian Reformed Church - Library (Rel-Phil)
2929 Leonard St., N.W.   Phone: (616)453-3105
Grand Rapids, MI 49504   Beatrice Dahnke, Libn.
Founded: 1900. **Staff:** Prof 1; Other 1. **Subjects:** Religion. **Holdings:** 2828 books. **Services:** Library not open to the public.

★ 20353 ★
Westwood First Presbyterian Church - Walter Lorenz Memorial Library (Rel-Phil)
3011 Harrison Ave.   Phone: (513)661-6846
Cincinnati, OH 45211   Marian B. McNair, Libn.
Founded: 1957. **Staff:** Prof 2; Other 9. **Subjects:** Religion, curriculum materials, children's books, fiction, biography. **Special Collections:** Henderson Collection (107 19th century books). **Holdings:** 3900 books; 3 VF drawers; Presbyterian College bulletins. **Subscriptions:** 10 journals and other serials. **Services:** Interlibrary loan; library open to the public. **Publications:** Library Bulletin, monthly; Christian holidays; bibliographies for church school and adult study groups; Sponsored Workshops for Church Libraries in Cincinnati Presbytery.

★ 20354 ★
Wethersfield Historical Society - Old Academy Museum Library (Hist)
150 Main St.   Phone: (203)529-7656
Wethersfield, CT 06109   Elaine St. Onge, Staff Asst.
Founded: 1932. **Staff:** 2. **Subjects:** Wethersfield history, genealogy, maritime history. **Special Collections:** First Church of Christ Archives; The

Connecticut Horticultural Society Library (1000 volumes). **Holdings:** 1000 books; 2000 photographs; 75 linear feet of account books, ship logs, letters, broadsides, maps, sermons, wallpaper, diaries, manuscripts. **Subscriptions:** 2 journals and other serials. **Services:** Copying; library open to the public. **Publications:** Wethersfield Newsletter, quarterly; local history publications. **Staff:** Nora O. Howard, Dir.

Wetland and Water Resources Research Center
See: University of Florida (18590)

★ 20355 ★
Wetlands Institute - Library (Env-Cons)
Stone Harbor Blvd.   Phone: (609)368-1211
Stone Harbor, NJ 08247   Dr. Albert Wood
Founded: 1969. **Subjects:** Ecology, botany, fish, birds. **Holdings:** 1000 books. **Services:** Library not open to the public.

Alexander Wetmore Library
See: Rob & Bessie Welder Wildlife Foundation - Library (20147)

Wey Memorial Library
See: Arnot-Ogden Medical Center (1069)

★ 20356 ★
Weyburn Mental Health Centre - Library (Med)
Box 1056   Phone: (306)848-2800
Weyburn, SK, Canada S4H 2L4   Shirley Biliak
Staff: 1. **Subjects:** Psychiatry, psychology, social work, nursing, child and youth services, occupational therapy, vocational guidance. **Holdings:** 1545 volumes. **Subscriptions:** 37 journals and other serials; 6 newspapers. **Services:** Interlibrary loan; library open to students. **Remarks:** FAX: (306)848-2835.

Carl A. Weyerhaeuser Library
See: Art Complex Museum - Carl A. Weyerhaeuser Library (1074)

★ 20357 ★
Charles A. Weyerhaeuser Memorial Museum - Library (Hist)
Box 239   Phone: (612)632-4007
Little Falls, MN 56345   Jan Warner, Exec.Dir.
Founded: 1975. **Staff:** Prof 1; Other 2. **Subjects:** Local history of Morrison County. **Special Collections:** Swanville News (defunct local newspaper; microfilm); Little Falls Daily Transcript, 1892-1982 (bound volumes); Minnesota State Census, 1865-1904 (microfilm); Works Progress Administration (WPA) Biographies of Morrison County; genealogy files; Pierz Journal; Motley Mercury and Motley Register; Upsala News-Tribune. **Holdings:** 800 books. **Services:** Interlibrary loan; copying; library open to the public for reference use only. **Publications:** News & Notes, quarterly. **Remarks:** Maintained by Morrison County Historical Society.

★ 20358 ★
Weyerhaeuser Company - Archives (Sci-Engr)
Tacoma, WA 98477   Phone: (206)924-5051
         Donnie Crespo, Archv.Mgr.
Staff: Prof 3. **Subjects:** Weyerhaeuser Company, forest products, logging, lumber manufacturing, pulp/paperboard, Pacific Northwest. **Holdings:** 2000 cubic feet and 128 linear feet of archival material including correspondence and office files, 1900-1989, ledgers, journals, annual and financial reports, biographical files, speeches of company executives and personnel, company publications, minute books of the company, photographs of company facilities and operations, photographs of logging in the Northwest, films, oral history interviews, artifacts and memorabilia, maps. **Services:** Copying (limited); archives open to the public with restrictions. **Publications:** Weyerhaeuser Company Archives, 1989; The White River Lumber Company, 1979; Clemons Tree Farm, 1981; Weyerhaeuser Timber Company History 1900-1950. **Special Catalogs:** Shelf lists; content notes; descriptive catalogs. **Remarks:** FAX: (206)924-5052. **Staff:** Pauline Larson, Asst.Archv.; Megan Moholt, Proj.Archv.

★ 20359 ★
Weyerhaeuser Company - Corporate Library and Center for Quality Resources (Bus-Fin)
CH 1-W   Phone: (206)924-3030
Tacoma, WA 98477   Karin H. Williams, Mgr.
Founded: 1952. **Staff:** Prof 11. **Subjects:** Business, economics, forestry, total quality, finance, law/tax, management, marketing. **Special Collections:** Annual reports of major national and foreign companies; Conference Board collection; SRI Business Intelligence Program Audiovisual Collection (700 items). **Holdings:** 10,000 books; 4 drawers of maps; 4 VF drawers. **Subscriptions:** 450 journals and other serials. **Services:** Interlibrary loan; SDI; library open to the public with restrictions. **Automated Operations:** Computerized cataloging, acquisitions, and serials (Datatrek). **Computerized Information Services:** DIALOG Information Services, PFDS Online, BRS Information Technologies, Info Globe, NEXIS, LEXIS, Dow Jones News/Retrieval; OnTyme Electronic Message Network Service, PROFS (electronic mail services). **Publications:** Library Bulletin, bimonthly; CQR News Bulletin, bimonthly. **Remarks:** FAX: (206)924-7407; (206)924-2228. Maintains Law/Tax and Marketing & Economic Research Satellite Libraries. **Staff:** Trish Camozzi-Ebberg, Supv., Tech.Serv.; Linda McBroom, Supv.Res.Dept.; Judi A. Jendrean, Supv., Acq.Dept.

★ 20360 ★
Weyerhaeuser Company - SFRD Technical Information Center (Biol Sci)
Box 1060   Phone: (501)624-8545
Hot Springs, AR 71902   Evelyn Smith, Libn.
Staff: 1. **Subjects:** Forestry and related subjects. **Holdings:** 5000 pamphlets. **Subscriptions:** 75 journals and other serials. **Services:** Center open to the public with restrictions. **Remarks:** FAX: (501)624-8419.

★ 20361 ★
Weyerhaeuser Company - Technical Information Center (Sci-Engr, Biol Sci)
WTC-TIC   Phone: (206)924-6267
Tacoma, WA 98477   L.W. Martinez, Mgr., Tech.Info.Serv.
Founded: 1957. **Staff:** Prof 6; Other 5. **Subjects:** Wood and wood products, forestry, coatings, adhesives, paper chemistry, chemical engineering. **Holdings:** 20,000 books; 30,000 reports. **Subscriptions:** 425 journals and other serials. **Services:** Interlibrary loan; copying (both limited); SDI; center open to the public by permission. **Automated Operations:** Computerized public access catalog, cataloging, acquisitions, serials, and circulation. **Computerized Information Services:** DIALOG Information Services, PFDS Online, STN International, OCLC. Performs searches on fee basis. **Publications:** Accession list, monthly - limited circulation; Journal Holdings list, annual; Patent Digest; Technology Awareness Updates. **Special Catalogs:** Journal subject list (computer printout). **Remarks:** FAX: (206)924-6870. An alternate telephone number is 924-6263.

★ 20362 ★
Weyerhaeuser Company - Western Forestry Research Center - Library (Biol Sci)
Box 420   Phone: (206)736-8241
Centralia, WA 98531   Donna Loucks, Libn.
Founded: 1954. **Staff:** Prof 1; Other 1. **Subjects:** Forestry, biology, zoology, ecology, herbicides, pesticides, agronomy, genetics, physiology, dendrology. **Holdings:** 3000 books; 1000 bound periodical volumes; 40,000 reports; 200 dissertations. **Subscriptions:** 150 journals and other serials. **Services:** Copying; library open to the public for reference use only. **Automated Operations:** Computerized cataloging and serials. **Computerized Information Services:** DIALOG Information Services; internal database. **Publications:** Weyerhaeuser Forestry Paper, irregular. **Remarks:** FAX: (206)736-8241.

★ 20363 ★
Whaling Museum Society, Inc. - Library (Biol Sci)
Main St.
P.O. Box 25
Cold Spring Harbor, NY 11724   Phone: (516)367-3418
                                          Ann M. Gill, Exec.Dir.
Founded: 1936. **Staff:** Prof 7. **Subjects:** Whaling, whales, Cold Spring Harbor, marine mammal conservation, coastwise trade under sail, scrimshaw. **Special Collections:** Manuscript collections on whales, whaling, and Cold Spring Harbor (thousands of documents). **Holdings:** 2800 books; 10 drawers of archives; 6 drawers of photographs and prints; 12 reels of microfilm of logbooks. **Subscriptions:** 12 journals and other serials. **Services:** Copying; library open to the public with written application to director. **Publications:** A Whaling Account (newsletter); annual reports; pamphlets; miscellaneous publications; bibliographies.

★ 20364 ★
James E. Whalley Museum and Library (Rec, Hist)
351 Middle St.   Phone: (603)436-3712
Portsmouth, NH 03801   Lynn J. Sanderson, Pres.
Founded: 1962. **Staff:** Prof 1; Other 1. **Subjects:** Freemasonry; genealogy; history - New Hampshire, New Hampshire seacoast, Portsmouth. **Special Collections:** Masonic proceedings (500 items); published sermons and orations, 1758 to present; New Hampshire state papers (40 volumes); New Hampshire county histories (10); New Hampshire town histories (50); photograph collections (600); town and city directories (60). **Holdings:** 3600 books; 600 bound periodical volumes; 96 file drawers; 100 boxes; 1000 other cataloged items. **Services:** Copying; library open to the public by appointment.

★ 20365 ★
Wheat Ridge Historical Society - Library (Hist)
P.O. Box 1833   Phone: (303)433-6097
Wheat Ridge, CO 80034   Claudia Worth, Pres.
Founded: 1974. **Subjects:** Wheat Ridge history, local government, arts, crafts, tuberculosis sanitariums. **Special Collections:** School collection (VF drawers, manuscripts). **Holdings:** 450 books; 25 bound periodical volumes; 50 AV programs; 30 manuscript collections. **Subscriptions:** 3 newspapers. **Services:** Library open to the public on a limited schedule and by appointment. **Publications:** Guide to the Collections - Wheat Ridge Historical Society. **Remarks:** Library located at 4610 Robb St., Wheat Ridge, CO 80033. **Staff:** Robert J. Olson, Cur.

★ 20366 ★
Wheat Ridge Regional Center - Employee's Library (Med)
10285 Ridge Rd.   Phone: (303)424-7791
Wheat Ridge, CO 80033   Carl Schutter, Sup.Serv.Dir.
Subjects: Mental retardation, behavior modification, developmental disabilities, child development, psychology, sociology, medicine. **Holdings:** 300 books; 25 pamphlets. **Services:** Library not open to the public.

★ 20367 ★
Wheaton College - Billy Graham Center - Archives (Rel-Phil)
Wheaton, IL 60187-5593   Phone: (708)260-5910
                                          Robert Shuster, Dir. of Archv.
Founded: 1975. **Staff:** Prof 3; Other 3. **Subjects:** North American Protestant missions and evangelistic work. **Special Collections:** Billy Graham Evangelistic Association; records of Africa Inland Mission, Evangelical Foreign Mission Association, China Inland Mission, South America Mission, and National Religious Broadcasters; papers of Herbert J. Taylor, Paul Rader, R.A. Torrey, Kathryn Kuhlman, Aimee Semple McPherson, and Billy Sunday; Youth for Christ/USA archival materials. **Holdings:** 400 archival and manuscript collections; 30,000 photographs; 7500 audiotapes; 1400 reels of microfilm. **Services:** Interlibrary loan; copying; archives open to the public. **Automated Operations:** Computerized cataloging and acquisitions. **Publications:** Witness, 3/year - free upon request; guides to special collections. **Staff:** Paul Ericksen, Archv.; Jaynce Nasgowitz, Ref.Archv.

★ 20368 ★
Wheaton College - Billy Graham Center - Library (Rel-Phil)
Wheaton, IL 60187-5593   Phone: (708)752-5194
                                          Ferne L. Weimer, Dir.
Founded: 1976. **Staff:** Prof 3; Other 4. **Subjects:** Christian evangelism and missions; history of revivalism; history of American Evangelicalism; prison ministry. **Special Collections:** Billy Graham Collection; MK (missionary children) Collection; Joint IMC/CBMS Missionary Archives (microfiche); Council for World Mission Archives (microfiche); Moravian Missions to the Indians (microfilm); Early American Imprints; Pamphlets in American History; Human Relations Area Files (microfiche). **Holdings:** 53,000 books; 3500 bound periodical volumes; 1000 theses and dissertations; microforms; imprints and pamphlets. **Subscriptions:** 700 journals and other serials. **Services:** Interlibrary loan; copying; SDI; library open to the public with restrictions. **Automated Operations:** Computerized cataloging. **Computerized Information Services:** OCLC. **Publications:** Researching Modern Evangelism: A Guide to the Holdings of the Billy Graham Center, With Information on Other Collections; Resource Notes (newsletter); occasional papers of conferences; occasional short bibliographies. **Staff:** Judith Franzke, Tech.Serv.; Kenneth Gill, Coll.Dev.

★ 20369 ★
Wheaton College - Buswell Memorial Library (Rel-Phil, Hum)
Franklin and Irving   Phone: (708)752-5101
Wheaton, IL 60187   P. Paul Snezek, Dir.
Founded: 1860. **Staff:** Prof 7; Other 11. **Subjects:** American history, religion and theology, American and English literature, science, education. **Special Collections:** Wheaton College Archives; Mormonism; Hymnals; American Scientific Affiliation; Keswick Movement; Madeleine L'Engle; Malcolm Muggeridge; Frederick Buechner; John Bunyan; Samuel Johnson; James Boswell; Everett Mitchell; Robert Siegel; Norman Stone; Kenneth N. Taylor; Hans Rookmaaker; Calvin Miller; E. Margaret Clarkson; E. Breatrice Batson Shakespeare Collection; Open Doors-Brother Andrew; Kenneth and Margaret Landon Southeast Asia Collection; Sojourners; National Christian Association/Christian Cynosure; Christian Service Brigade; Louis Evans, Sr.; Elizabeth Green; Coleman Luck; Luci Shaw; Cording/Welsh; hymnals; McClatchey Collection (Arthurian and Victorian). **Holdings:** 222,003 books; 31,912 bound periodical volumes; 243,165 microforms; 16,638 documents; 4086 audiotapes; 1831 videotapes; 7662 scores; 7295 phonograph records; 1579 compact discs. **Subscriptions:** 1432 journals and other serials; 20 newspapers. **Services:** Interlibrary loan; library open to visiting scholars. **Automated Operations:** Computerized cataloging (DYNIX). **Computerized Information Services:** DIALOG Information Services, OCLC, BRS/After Dark; CD-ROMs. **Networks/Consortia:** Member of ILLINET, LIBRAS Inc. **Remarks:** FAX: (708)752-5885. **Staff:** John Fawcett, Hd., Pub.Serv.; Larry Thompson, Hd., Spec.Serv.; Joanna Parks, Hd.Tech.Serv.; Larry Reining, Cat.

★ 20370 ★
Wheaton College - Madeleine Clark Wallace Library - Fine Arts Collection (Mus, Art)
Norton, MA 02766   Phone: (508)285-7722
     Linda E. Collins, Circ.Supv.
Founded: 1960. **Staff:** 1. **Subjects:** Art, music. **Holdings:** 30,000 volumes, including scores; 5500 sound recordings; 75,000 slides; 10,000 photographs. **Subscriptions:** 120 journals and other serials. **Services:** Interlibrary loan; copying; collection open to the public for reference use only. **Automated Operations:** Computerized cataloging. **Computerized Information Services:** OCLC, BRS Information Technologies, DIALOG Information Services. **Networks/Consortia:** Member of NELINET, Inc., Southeastern Massachusetts Cooperating Libraries (SMCL). **Remarks:** FAX: (508)285-6329. The Music Library is located in Watson Hall; the Art Collection is located in the Main Library. The Art Department slide and photograph collections are housed in Watson Hall.

★ 20371 ★
Wheaton College - Marion E. Wade Center (Hum)
Wheaton, IL 60187-5593   Phone: (708)752-5908
     Marjorie Lamp Mead, Assoc.Dir.
Founded: 1965. **Staff:** Prof 4; Other 1. **Subjects:** Literature - English, fantasy, detective, Arthurian, Christian; poetry; fiction. **Special Collections:** Owen Barfield; G.K. Chesterton; C.S. Lewis (personal library); George MacDonald; J.R.R. Tolkien; Dorothy L. Sayers; Charles Williams. **Holdings:** 12,250 books; 245 bound periodical volumes; 319 bound dissertations; 49 reels of microfilm; 793 audiotapes; 97 videotapes; 25,000 manuscript letters; 426 file folders of manuscripts; 12 VF drawers of articles; artwork and photographs. **Subscriptions:** 34 journals and other serials. **Services:** Copying (limited); center open to the public. **Remarks:** FAX: (708)752-5855. **Staff:** Marie E. Hass, Asst.Archv.

★ 20372 ★
Wheaton Community Hospital - Medical Library (Med)
401 12th St., N.   Phone: (612)563-8226
Wheaton, MN 56296   Diane Zelka, Med.Libn., ART
Staff: 1. **Subjects:** Medicine. **Holdings:** Figures not available. **Subscriptions:** 90 journals and other serials. **Services:** Interlibrary loan; copying; library open to the public with restrictions. **Networks/Consortia:** Member of Valley Medical Network (VMN).

★ 20373 ★
Wheaton Cultural Alliance, Inc. - Museum of American Glass Research Library (Hist)
Glasstown Rd.
Wheaton Village
Millville, NJ 08332   Phone: (609)825-6800
     Gay Le Cleire Taylor, Cur.
Founded: 1973. **Staff:** Prof 3. **Subjects:** Glass history and manufacture, American and European glass, Victorian life, antiques, American history,

crafts, architecture. **Special Collections:** Charles B. Gardner Library (200 glass photographs and documents; 53 framed glass documents; 75 glass books). **Holdings:** 1800 books; 75 bound periodical volumes; 100 personal papers of T.C. Wheaton; 35 newspapers and pamphlets; 20 glass ledgers and indentures; 200 photographs of glass factories; 2000 glass slides. **Subscriptions:** 35 journals and other serials. **Services:** Copying; library open to the public by appointment. **Remarks:** FAX: (609)825-2410. **Formerly:** Wheaton Historical Association - Library & Research Office. **Staff:** Patricia Martinelli.

Wheaton Historical Association - Library & Research Office
See: **Wheaton Cultural Alliance, Inc. - Museum of American Glass Research Library** (20373)

★ 20374 ★
Whedon Cancer Foundation - Library (Med)
30 S. Scott St.
Box 683   Phone: (307)672-2941
Sheridan, WY 82801-0683   Nancy E. Peterson, Lib.Mgr.
Founded: 1981. **Staff:** 1. **Subjects:** Cancer research, hospice care, medicine, cancer patient education materials. **Special Collections:** American Cancer Society Lending Video and Book Library; Hospice (250 articles); local medical group histories (3). **Holdings:** 100 books. **Subscriptions:** 5 journals and other serials; 2 newspapers. **Services:** Interlibrary loan; copying; library open to the public for reference use only; health professionals and students may borrow materials. **Automated Operations:** Computerized ILL (DOCLINE). **Computerized Information Services:** MEDLARS; electronic mail. Performs cancer-related searches free of charge for local physicians, health care professionals, and area libraries. **Networks/Consortia:** Member of Northeastern Wyoming Medical Library Consortium, National Network of Libraries of Medicine - Midcontinental Region. **Special Catalogs:** Hospice (printout). **Remarks:** FAX: (307)672-7273.

Wheelabrator Technologies, Inc. - Rust International Corporation
See: **Rust International Corporation** (14153)

John M. Wheeler Library
See: **Edward S. Harkness Eye Institute** (6905)

★ 20375 ★
Wheeling Hospital, Inc. - Henry G. Jepson Memorial Library (Med)
Medical Park   Phone: (304)243-3308
Wheeling, WV 26003   Linda E. White
Founded: 1936. **Staff:** Prof 1; Other 1. **Subjects:** Medicine, nursing, allied health sciences. **Holdings:** 2200 books; 118 bound periodical volumes; 612 cassettes; 5 VF drawers; pamphlet file. **Subscriptions:** 113 journals and other serials. **Services:** Copying; library open to physicians, employees and students of health professions. **Computerized Information Services:** MEDLINE; DOCLINE. **Networks/Consortia:** Member of National Network of Libraries of Medicine - Southeastern/Atlantic Region. **Remarks:** FAX: (304)243-3060.

★ 20376 ★
Wheelwright Museum of the American Indian - Mary Cabot Wheelwright Research Library (Area-Ethnic)
704 Camino Lejo
Box 5153   Phone: (505)982-4636
Santa Fe, NM 87502   Steve Rogers, Cur.
Founded: 1937. **Staff:** 1. **Subjects:** Navajo and American Indian - religion, culture, arts; comparative religions; the Southwest. **Special Collections:** Archival material on Navajo religion, sand paintings, chants, and Southwest Indian art. **Holdings:** 2000 books; 2300 periodical volumes; 100 Navajo religion manuscripts; 300 sound recordings; 1000 slides of sandpaintings and reproductions; 100 Navajo music and prayer tapes. **Services:** Copying; library open to the public by appointment. **Publications:** Navajo Figurines Called Dolls; Introduction to Navaho Sandpaintings. **Special Catalogs:** Exhibition Catalogs - Native American Arts and Culture. **Remarks:** FAX: (505)989-7386.

★ 20377 ★
Whidden Memorial Hospital - Medical Library (Med)
103 Garland St.   Phone: (617)389-6270
Everett, MA 02149   Phyllis Perlo, R.N./Educ.Dept.
Subjects: Medicine, nursing, allied health sciences. **Holdings:** 1000 books;
4 shelves of clippings and pamphlets. **Subscriptions:** 69 journals and other
serials. **Services:** Interlibrary loan; copying; library open to the public for
reference use only. **Networks/Consortia:** Member of Massachusetts Health
Sciences Libraries Network (MaHSLiN). **Remarks:** FAX: (617)381-7128.

★ 20378 ★
Whirlpool Corporation - Technical Information Center (Sci-Engr)
Monte Rd.   Phone: (616)926-5325
Benton Harbor, MI 49022   Gene Heileman, Sr.Info.Spec.
Founded: 1954. **Staff:** Prof 1. **Subjects:** Mechanical and electrical
engineering, polymer science, food technology. **Holdings:** 1100 books.
Subscriptions: 105 journals and other serials. **Services:** Interlibrary loan;
center open to the public on request. **Automated Operations:** Computerized
cataloging and circulation. **Computerized Information Services:** DIALOG
Information Services, OCLC, NLM; WIN (Whirlpool Information
Network; internal database). **Networks/Consortia:** Member of Michigan
Library Consortium (MLC), Berrien Library Consortium. **Publications:**
WIN Alert, monthly - for internal distribution only. **Remarks:** FAX:
(616)926-5638.

John C. Whitaker Library
See: **Forsyth Memorial Hospital** (5991)

Mae M. Whitaker Library
See: **St. Louis Conservatory and Schools for the Arts (CASA)** (14439)

★ 20379 ★
White & Case - Library (Law)
1155 Avenue of the Americas   Phone: (212)819-7569
New York, NY 10036   John J. Banta, Chf. Law Libn.
Founded: 1901. **Staff:** Prof 5; Other 8. **Subjects:** Law. **Holdings:** 60,000
volumes. **Services:** Interlibrary loan; library not open to the public.
Computerized Information Services: LEXIS, WESTLAW, Dow Jones
News/Retrieval, DIALOG Information Services, Dun & Bradstreet
Business Credit Services, Information America, Maxwell Macmillan Taxes
Online. **Remarks:** White & Case maintains branch libraries at their offices
in London, Paris, Hong Kong, Singapore, Stockholm, Turkey, Tokyo, Los
Angeles, CA, Miami, FL, and Washington, DC. **Remarks:** Alternate
telephone number(s): 819-8200. FAX: (212)354-8113. **Staff:** Lisa Boice,
Asst.Libn.; Gloria Goldberg, Tax Libn.; Richard E. Cousins, Br.Libn.

Charles E. White Memorial Library
See: **University of Maryland, College Park Libraries** (18812)

E.G. White Research Center
See: **Andrews University - James White Library - Special Collections**
(862)

Ernest Miller White Library
See: **Louisville Presbyterian Theological Seminary** (9401)

G.W. Blunt White Library
See: **Mystic Seaport Museum, Inc.** (10948)

★ 20380 ★
White Haven Center - Staff Library
Oley Valley Rd.
White Haven, PA 18661
Defunct.

James White Library
See: **Andrews University - James White Library - Special Collections**
(862)

James Herbert White Library
See: **Mississippi Valley State University** (10530)

John G. White Collection and Rare Books
See: **Cleveland Public Library - Fine Arts and Special Collections
Department - Special Collections Section - John G. White Collection
and Rare Books** (3823)

★ 20381 ★
White Lung Association - Library (Sci-Engr)
PO Box 1438   Phone: (301)243-5864
Baltimore, MD 21203-1483   Jim Fite, Libn.
Subjects: Asbestos hazards. **Holdings:** 200 books; 800 bound periodical
volumes; 1000 microforms and nonbook items; 20 AV programs; news
clippings; reports. **Services:** Library open to the public.

★ 20382 ★
White Memorial Conservation Center - Nature Library (Env-Cons)
80 Whitehall Rd.
P.O. Box 368   Phone: (203)567-0857
Litchfield, CT 06759   Zoe Greenwood, Lib.Comm.Chm.
Founded: 1972. **Subjects:** Natural history, environmental and outdoor
education, conservation. **Special Collections:** Bird collection (700 books);
special children's section (800 books); educators' section (250 books).
Holdings: 4200 books; 50 bound periodical volumes; 100 nonbook items.
Subscriptions: 30 journals and other serials. **Services:** Library open to the
public for reference use only on a limited schedule. **Staff:** Jeff Greenwood,
Musm.Dir.

★ 20383 ★
White Memorial Medical Center - Courville-Abbott Memorial Library
(Med)
1720 Brooklyn Ave.   Phone: (213)260-5715
Los Angeles, CA 90033   Joyce Marson, Libn.
Founded: 1920. **Staff:** 1. **Subjects:** Medicine, nursing, dietetics, paramedical
sciences. **Special Collections:** Hara History of Medicine Collection.
Holdings: 43,000 volumes; 8 VF drawers of pamphlets; tapes; phonograph
records; filmstrips. **Subscriptions:** 350 journals and other serials. **Services:**
Interlibrary loan; copying; library open to the public for reference use only.
Computerized Information Services: MEDLINE. **Networks/Consortia:**
Member of National Network of Libraries of Medicine - Pacific Southwest
Region. **Remarks:** FAX: (213)260-5748. **Staff:** Mary E. Flake, Ref.Libn.

★ 20384 ★
White Plains Hospital - Medical Library (Med)
White Plains, NY 10601   Phone: (914)681-1231
                                    Rachel Dwyer, Dir.Med.Lib.
Staff: Prof 1. **Subjects:** Medicine, nursing, allied health fields. **Special
Collections:** Patient education (books; pamphlets; journals). **Holdings:** 1000
books; 2900 bound periodical volumes; VF of allied health subjects.
Subscriptions: 160 journals and other serials. **Services:** Interlibrary loan;
SDI; library open to the public for reference use only. **Automated
Operations:** Computerized ILL (DOCLINE). **Computerized Information
Services:** BRS Information Technologies, MEDLINE. **Networks/
Consortia:** Member of Health Information Libraries of Westchester
(HILOW), New York Metropolitan Reference and Research Library
Agency. **Publications:** Medical Library News, quarterly - for internal
distribution only.

★ 20385 ★
White River Valley Historical Society Museum - Library (Hist)
918 H St., S.E.   Phone: (206)939-2783
Auburn, WA 98002   Patricia Cosgrove
Founded: 1970. **Staff:** Prof 1; Other 3. **Subjects:** Local Northwest history
and genealogy, history of local industries. **Special Collections:** Histories of
pioneer families. **Holdings:** 700 volumes; 25 boxes of pamphlets; 100 maps;
25 cassette tapes. **Services:** Library open to the public for reference use only.

Robert J. White Law Library
See: Catholic University of America - School of Law (3164)

Robert M. White Memorial Library
See: Paoli Memorial Hospital (12731)

William Allen White Library
See: Emporia State University (5346)

William M. White Business Library
See: University of Colorado--Boulder (18509)

★ 20386 ★
White & Williams - Library (Law)
1650 Market St.
1 Liberty Pl.　　　　　　　　　　Phone: (215)864-7493
Philadelphia, PA 19103　　　　　　Anne W. Levy, Libn.
Staff: Prof 1; Other 3. Subjects: Law, products liability, insurance, medical malpractice. Holdings: 13,500 volumes. Subscriptions: 80 journals and other serials. Services: Interlibrary loan; library open to the public at librarian's discretion. Computerized Information Services: LEXIS, WESTLAW, DIALOG Information Services, VU/TEXT Information Services, DataTimes, Dow Jones News/Retrieval, Information America. Remarks: FAX: (215)864-7123.

Whiteford Memorial Library
See: Vanderbilt Family Foundation (19764)

Whitehall Library
See: Great Britain - Ministry of Defence (6683)

Whitehall Library
See: Stonington Historical Society (15815)

Alfred Whitehead Memorial Music Library
See: Mount Allison University (10796)

★ 20387 ★
Whitfield-Murray Historical Society - Crown Gardens and Archives (Hist)
715 Chattanooga Ave.　　　　　　Phone: (404)278-0217
Dalton, GA 30720　　　　　　　　Polly Boggess, Exec.Dir.
Founded: 1977. Staff: 1. Subjects: Local history and genealogy. Special Collections: Robert Loveman papers (local poet; 2 linear feet); Malcolm Tarver papers (Congressman; 4 linear feet); Crown Cotton Mill records (ledgers, payrolls, loose papers). Holdings: 500 books; 50 nonbook items. Services: Copying; archives open to the public. Publications: Murray County Heritage, 1987; Official History of Whitfield County, Georgia; WMHS Quarterly. Special Indexes: 1850 Murray County census; 1860 Murray County cenus; 1860 Whitfield County census; 1870 Whitfield County census.

★ 20388 ★
Whiting-Robertsdale Historical Society - Historical Museum (Hist)
1610 119th St.　　　　　　　　　　Phone: (219)659-1432
Whiting, IN 46394　　　　　　　　Elizabeth L. Gehrke, Cur.
Founded: 1976. Subjects: Local history. Holdings: Documents; papers; records; pictures; artifacts; maps; real estate abstracts; local newspapers, 1894 to present. Services: Library open to the public for reference use only. Publications: Whiting Almanac of 1909 (reprint); List of "Whitings" in United States; Whiting Almanac of 1911 (reprint); Story of (local) AMTRAK Station. Staff: Betty Gehrke, Musm.Dir.

★ 20389 ★
Whitman College - Myron Eells Library of Northwest History (Hist)
Penrose Memorial Library
345 Boyer St.　　　　　　　　　　Phone: (509)527-5191
Walla Walla, WA 99362　　　　　　Henry Yaple
Founded: 1960. Subjects: Pacific Northwest - geography, education, politics, government, anthropology, Indians and native peoples, archeology, religion, missions, art, architecture; regional Indian art; historical fiction about the Northwest and Northwesterners; Lewis and Clark; the Oregon Trail. Holdings: 7000 books; 174 periodical titles. Subscriptions: 51 journals and other serials. Services: Interlibrary loan; copying. Automated Operations: Computerized cataloging and acquisitions. Computerized Information Services: DIALOG Information Services, WLN. Remarks: FAX: (509)527-5900.

★ 20390 ★
Whitman College - Northwest and Whitman College Archives (Hist)
Penrose Memorial Library
345 Boyer St.　　　　　　　　　　Phone: (509)527-5922
Walla Walla, WA 99362　　　　　　Lawrence L. Dodd, Archv. & Cur.
Staff: 1. Subjects: History of the city of Walla Walla, Walla Walla County, Whitman College, 1804 to present, and the Pacific Northwest. Special Collections: Papers of American Board of Commissioners for Foreign Missions-affiliated missionaries in the Pacific Northwest; missionary activities on the Skokomish Indian Reservation, 1874-1907; photographs and manuscripts of Indians of the Pacific Northwest coast; Walla Walla area business records; Whitman College archives; photographs of Walla Walla area; WWII aerial photographs of damage to European targets. Holdings: 900 books; 200 periodicals. Services: Copying (limited); archives open to the public for reference use only. Computerized Information Services: Spindex III (Historical Records of Washington State). Publications: The Dorsey Syng Bakee Family Papers Inventory, 1857-1902 (Northwest & Whitman College Archives Inventory Publication No. 1).

★ 20391 ★
Whitman & Ransom - Library (Law)
200 Park Ave.　　　　　　　　　　Phone: (212)351-3000
New York, NY 10166　　　　　　　Lynn Orfe, Libn.
Founded: 1920. Staff: Prof 2; Other 2. Subjects: Law, corporate law. Special Collections: Japanese Law (1600 volumes). Holdings: 15,000 volumes. Services: Interlibrary loan; copying; library open to the public with restrictions. Computerized Information Services: DIALOG Information Services, LEXIS, WESTLAW, Dow Jones News/Retrieval, VU/TEXT Information Services. Remarks: FAX: (212)351-3131. Staff: Robert F. Corallo, Asst.Libn.

★ 20392 ★
Walt Whitman Association - Library (Hum)
326 Mickle St.　　　　　　　　　　Phone: (609)541-8280
Camden, NJ 08102　　　　　　　　Margo Burnette, Dir.
Founded: 1920. Staff: Prof 1; Other 1. Subjects: Walt Whitman. Special Collections: 19th and 20th century American poetry. Holdings: 600 books. Services: Library open to the public by appointment. Automated Operations: Computerized cataloging. Computerized Information Services: RLIN.

★ 20393 ★
Walt Whitman Birthplace Association - Library and Museum (Hum)
246 Old Walt Whitman Rd.　　　　Phone: (516)427-5240
Huntington Station, NY 11746　　　Barbara Bart, Exec.Dir.
Founded: 1949. Staff: 7. Subjects: Books by and about Walt Whitman. Special Collections: Translations and studies in foreign languages including Japanese and Catalan. Holdings: 350 books; artifacts; plaques; portraits; scrapbooks; rare monographs; catalogs; pamphlets; bibliographies; letters; broadsides; photostats of manuscripts; file of Walt Whitman Review; Walt Whitman Fellowship Papers; 600 newspapers. Services: Library open to the public for reference use only. Publications: Broadsides of Whitman prose and poetry - for sale; West Hills Review - A Walt Whitman Journal, 1980-1988 (volumes 1-8). Remarks: FAX: (516)752-0903.

Walt Whitman Collection
See: Brooklyn Public Library - Languages and Literature Division (2244)

★ 20394 ★
Walt Whitman Library - (Guatemala City) Instituto Guatemalteco Americano - USIS Collection (Educ)
Ruta 1, Via 4, Zona 4
Apdo. Postal 691
Guatemala City, Guatemala
Remarks: Maintained or supported by the U.S. Information Agency. Focus is on materials that will assist peoples outside the United States to learn about the United States, its people, history, culture, political processes, and social milieux.

★ 20395 ★
Whitney Communications Company - Research Library (Publ)
Time & Life Bldg., Rm. 4600
110 W. 51st St.   Phone: (212)582-2300
New York, NY 10020   Jean McGoldrick, Off.Mgr.
Founded: 1970. **Staff:** Prof 1. **Subjects:** Communications, finance, business, broadcasting. **Special Collections:** New York Herald Tribune historical material; art collection. **Holdings:** 100 VF drawers of corporate records and archives of Whitney Communications Company. **Subscriptions:** 75 journals and other serials; 50 newspapers. **Services:** Interlibrary loan; library open to the public by appointment. **Computerized Information Services:** Dow Jones News/Retrieval, InvesText, DataTimes. **Special Indexes:** Corporate files. **Remarks:** FAX: (212)582-2310.

Whitney Library
See: **General Electric Company - Corporate Research & Development** (6311)

Whitney Library
See: **New Haven Colony Historical Society** (11500)

★ 20396 ★
Whitney Museum of American Art - Library (Art)
945 Madison Ave.   Phone: (212)570-3649
New York, NY 10021   May Castleberry, Libn.
Founded: 1931. **Staff:** Prof 1; Other 2. **Subjects:** American art, particularly of the 20th century. **Holdings:** 20,000 volumes; 500 periodical titles; 110 VF drawers of clippings on American artists. **Subscriptions:** 100 journals and other serials. **Services:** Library open by appointment to qualified researchers only. **Remarks:** FAX: (212)570-1807.

★ 20397 ★
Whittaker Electronic Systems - Technical Library (Sci-Engr)
1785 Voyager Ave.
Box 8000   Phone: (805)584-8200
Simi Valley, CA 93063-8000   Orlean A. Hinds, Libn.
Founded: 1950. **Staff:** Prof 1. **Subjects:** Engineering, electronics, management, mathematics, computer science. **Holdings:** 3200 books; military specifications and standards; patents; 12,000 unbound reports; 6000 reports on microfiche and microfilm. **Subscriptions:** 165 journals and other serials. **Services:** Library not open to the public. **Computerized Information Services:** DIALOG Information Services. **Remarks:** FAX: (805)527-8332. Contains the holdings of the former Whittaker Electronic Systems - Library, located in Carlsbad, CA.

Whitten Center Library & Media Resource Services
See: **South Carolina (State) Department of Mental Retardation** (15407)

★ 20398 ★
Whittier College - Department of Geology - Fairchild Aerial Photography Collection (Geog-Map)
Whittier, CA 90608   Phone: (310)907-4220
                                                             Dallas D. Rhodes, Dir.
Founded: 1965. **Staff:** Prof 3; Other 7. **Subjects:** Aerial photographs, primarily of California, 1927-1965; partial coverage of 48 states and 29 countries. **Special Collections:** Fairchild Collection including 2350 flights (300,000 prints; 100,000 negatives; 500 photo-mosaic flight indexes; 500 orthophoto maps). **Services:** Copying; collection open to the public on a fee basis. **Computerized Information Services:** Internal database; InterNet (electronic mail service). **Special Indexes:** Inventory of flights (looseleaf); Flight Index Maps. **Remarks:** FAX: (310)693-6117. Electronic mail address(es): drhodes%poets@ymiv.claremont.edu (InterNet). **Staff:** Elizabeth Berry; Pamela Skewes.

★ 20399 ★
Whittier College - School of Law - Library (Law)
5353 W. 3rd St.   Phone: (213)938-3621
Los Angeles, CA 90020   J. Denny Haythorn, Dir./Prof.
Founded: 1975. **Staff:** Prof 9; Other 6. **Subjects:** American law. **Holdings:** 188,000 volumes; 400 cassettes; state and federal depository. **Subscriptions:** 2700 journals and other serials; 21 newspapers. **Services:** Interlibrary loan; copying; student computer lab; library open to attorneys, law students, and others wishing to use legal research materials. **Automated Operations:** Computerized cataloging and serials. **Computerized Information Services:** WESTLAW, LEXIS, NEXIS, DIALOG Information Services, RLIN. **Networks/Consortia:** Member of CLASS. **Publications:** Whittier Law Review, quarterly - by subscription. **Remarks:** FAX: (213)938-3460. **Staff:** Robert Wright, Ref./Circ.; Christa Gowan, Ser.; Virbala Thaker, Govt.Docs.; Rosanne Krikorian, Assoc.Dir.; Billy Nazarro, Cat.; Laurie Carnahan, Sys.Coord.

★ 20400 ★
Whittier Home Association - Library (Hist)
86 Friend St.
P.O. Box 632
Amesbury, MA 01913   Phone: (508)388-1337
Subjects: John Greenleaf Whittier. **Holdings:** Figures not available. **Services:** Library open to the public for reference use only on a limited schedule and for a fee. **Remarks:** The library at the Whittier home consists of books, pamphlets, newspapers, letters, and other documents which belonged to poet and abolitionist John Greenleaf Whittier. **Staff:** Cecile Roaf, Caretaker; George Roaf, Caretaker.

N. Paul Whittier Historical Aviation Library
See: **San Diego Aero-Space Museum - N. Paul Whittier Historical Aviation Library** (14686)

★ 20401 ★
Whittle Communications - Research Center (Bus-Fin)
333 Main Ave.   Phone: (615)595-5130
Knoxville, TN 37902   Martha L. White, Res.Ctr.Mgr.
Founded: 1985. **Staff:** 4. **Subjects:** Marketing, general business. **Holdings:** 1000 books. **Subscriptions:** 100 journals and other serials; 6 newspapers. **Services:** Copying; SDI; center open to the public by appointment. **Computerized Information Services:** DIALOG Information Services, NEXIS. **Networks/Consortia:** Member of SOLINET. **Remarks:** FAX: (615)595-5877.

★ 20402 ★
Whitworth College - Science Library (Sci-Engr)
Spokane, WA 99251   Phone: (509)466-3265
                                                          Hans E. Bynagle, Lib.Dir.
Founded: 1955. **Staff:** 1. **Subjects:** Chemistry, physics, biology. **Holdings:** 2800 books; 2450 bound periodical volumes; 60 filmstrips; 750 microcards. **Subscriptions:** 45 journals and other serials. **Services:** Interlibrary loan; copying; library open to the public for reference use only. **Computerized Information Services:** DIALOG Information Services, STN International. **Networks/Consortia:** Member of Western Library Network (WLN). **Remarks:** FAX: (509)466-3221.

WHO
See: **World Health Organization** (20619)

John L. Whorton Media-Library
See: **First Baptist Church** (5729)

John A. Whyte Medical Library
See: **Delaware Valley Medical Center - John A. Whyte Medical Library** (4739)

Whyte Museum of the Canadian Rockies - Alpine Club of Canada
See: **Alpine Club of Canada** (414)

★ 20403 ★
Whyte Museum of the Canadian Rockies - Archives-Library (Hist, Area-Ethnic)
Box 160   Phone: (403)762-2291
Banff, AB, Canada T0L 0C0   Edward J. Hart, Dir.
Founded: 1965. **Staff:** Prof 3; Other 1. **Subjects:** History, peoples, and natural history of the Canadian Rockies. **Holdings:** 5546 books and pamphlets; 522 bound periodical volumes; 460 manuscript collections; 275,000 photographs; 62 reels of microfilm; 628 audiotapes. **Subscriptions:** 112 journals and other serials. **Services:** Copying; archives open to the public for reference use only. **Publications:** The CAIRN Quarterly, 3/year. **Special Indexes:** Inventory of the Catharine Robb Whyte Collection, 1987; Inventory of the Alpine Club of Canada Collection, 1986; Guide to manuscripts: the fonds and collections of the Archives, Whyte Museum of the Canadian Rockies, 1989; Guide to photographs, the fonds and collections of the Archives, Whyte Museum of the Canadian Rockies, 1990. **Remarks:** The museum also administers the Alpine Club of Canada Library. **Staff:** Mary Andrews, Libn.; Donald Bourdon, Hd.Archv.

Harold E. Wibberley, Jr. Library
See: Brazilian-American Cultural Institute, Inc. (2098)

Wichita Art Association, Inc.
See: Wichita Center for the Arts (20405)

★ 20404 ★
Wichita Art Museum - Library (Art)
619 Stackman Dr.   Phone: (316)268-4921
Wichita, KS 67203   Lois F. Crane, Libn.
Founded: 1935. **Staff:** Prof 1. **Subjects:** American art, general art history. **Holdings:** 4714 books; 18 VF drawers; 5300 slides. **Subscriptions:** 29 journals and other serials. **Services:** Library open to the public for reference use only. **Remarks:** FAX: (316)268-4980.

Wichita Bar Association - Sedgwick County Law Library
See: Sedgwick County Law Library (15013)

★ 20405 ★
Wichita Center for the Arts - Reference Library (Art)
9112 E. Central   Phone: (316)634-2787
Wichita, KS 67206   Janet Murfin, Chm., Lib.Comm.
Founded: 1920. **Staff:** Prof 1; Other 2. **Subjects:** Art. **Holdings:** 3000 volumes. **Subscriptions:** 6 journals and other serials. **Services:** Library open to the public. **Formerly:** Wichita Art Association, Inc.

★ 20406 ★
Wichita Eagle - Library (Publ)
825 E. Douglas
Box 820   Phone: (316)268-6554
Wichita, KS 67201-0820   Allan Tanner, Libn.
Founded: 1872. **Staff:** Prof 1; Other 3. **Subjects:** Newspaper reference topics. **Holdings:** 1000 books; 400,000 clippings; 200,000 photographs; pamphlets; maps; microfilm. **Subscriptions:** 20 journals and other serials. **Services:** Library not open to the public. **Computerized Information Services:** Produces Wichita Eagle database (available online through VU/TEXT Information Services); Dow Jones News/Retrieval, DataTimes, VU/TEXT Information Services, NEXIS, DIALOG Information Services. **Remarks:** FAX: (316)268-6536.

★ 20407 ★
Wichita Falls State Hospital - Thomas J. Galvin Memorial Medical Library (Med)
Box 300   Phone: (817)692-1220
Wichita Falls, TX 76307   Judith A. Morris, Libn.
Staff: 2. **Subjects:** Psychiatry, psychology, surgery and nursing, philosophy, anatomy, education, forensic medicine, history of medicine. **Special Collections:** Bassett Collection (anatomy); Baker and Baker Collection (neurology). **Holdings:** 3500 books; 120 bound periodical volumes; 1050 AV programs; 200 pamphlets; 100 medical reports. **Subscriptions:** 67 journals and other serials. **Services:** Interlibrary loan; copying; library open to the public with restrictions. **Networks/Consortia:** Member of National Network of Libraries of Medicine - South Central Region.

The Wichita Gardens
See: Botanica, The Wichita Gardens (2024)

★ 20408 ★
Wichita General Hospital - Medical Library
1600 8th St.
Wichita Falls, TX 76301
Founded: 1915. **Subjects:** Medicine, nursing. **Holdings:** 1000 books; 25 bound periodical volumes; 10 medical journals; 20 nursing journals. **Remarks:** Currently inactive.

★ 20409 ★
Wichita Public Library - Business and Technology Section (Bus-Fin, Sci-Engr)
223 S. Main   Phone: (316)262-0611
Wichita, KS 67202   Brian Beattie, Hd., Bus. & Tech.Sect.
Founded: 1950. **Staff:** Prof 3; Other 5. **Subjects:** Aeronautics, petroleum, geology, economics, mathematics, taxes, finances, firearms, automobiles, business management. **Holdings:** 90,351 volumes; Patent Gazette, 1872 to present, on microfilm; 22,839 pamphlets; 2800 auto repair manuals; 1350 telephone directories. **Subscriptions:** 304 journals and other serials; 6 newspapers. **Services:** Interlibrary loan; copying. **Automated Operations:** Computerized cataloging and circulation. **Publications:** Occasional book lists and bibliographies. **Staff:** Rhonda K. Inman, Ref.Libn.; Jimmy Hooper, Asst.Sect.Hd.

★ 20410 ★
Wichita-Sedgwick County Historical Museum - Library & Archives (Hist)
204 S. Main   Phone: (316)265-9314
Wichita, KS 67202   Robert A. Puckett, Dir.
Founded: 1939. **Subjects:** Local and state history. **Special Collections:** Wichita city directories, 1877 to present; M.C. Naftzger Collection (books on Wichita and Kansas history); tax records from Sedgwick County and city of Wichita, 1870s (68 volumes); printed material relevant to Wichita and Sedgwick County (5000 items); historic photograph collection relevant to Wichita and Sedgwick County (15,000 items). **Holdings:** 600 books; 50 bound periodical volumes; 4 VF drawers of clippings. **Subscriptions:** 13 journals and other serials. **Services:** Copying; library open to the public with restrictions. **Publications:** Heritage, quarterly.

★ 20411 ★
Wichita State University - Lloyd McKinley Memorial Chemistry Branch Library (Sci-Engr)
Campus Box 68   Phone: (316)689-3764
Wichita, KS 67208   Kathryn Payne, Sci.Libn.
Founded: 1926. **Staff:** 1.5. **Subjects:** Chemistry. **Holdings:** 7700 bound periodicals and serials; reference collection. **Subscriptions:** 70 journals and other serials. **Services:** Interlibrary loan (through main library); library open to university and local community. **Automated Operations:** Computerized public access catalog. **Computerized Information Services:** DIALOG Information Services, BRS Information Technologies, NLM, VU/TEXT Information Services, STN International; BITNET (electronic mail service). **Networks/Consortia:** Member of AMIGOS Bibliographic Council, Inc. **Remarks:** FAX: (316)689-3048. Electronic mail address(es): PAYNE@TWSUM (BITNET).

★ 20412 ★
Wichita State University - Special Collections (Hist)
Abalh Library
Box 68   Phone: (316)689-3590
Wichita, KS 67208   Michael T. Kelly, Cur.
Staff: Prof 1; Other 1. **Subjects:** State and local history, congressional papers, radical pamphlets, history of printing, slavery and abolitionism, university archives, history of hypnotism/mesmerism, World War I aviation. **Special Collections:** Robert T. Aitchison Collection (history of printing; 1582 books); Tinterow Collection (history of hypnotism; 188 books); Merrill Collection of W.L. Garrison papers (abolitionists; 6 linear feet); W.H. Auden Collection (by and about Auden; 600 volumes). **Holdings:** 4500 volumes; 450 Kansas maps; 1000 linear feet of manuscript collections and pamphlets; 2400 theses; 150 linear feet of archival materials. **Services:** Copying; collections open to the public. **Automated Operations:** Computerized public access catalog, cataloging, acquisitions, and circulation. **Publications:** Guide to the Collections, irregular; Illuminator, annual - to Library Associates. **Special Catalogs:** Manuscript registers.

★ 20413 ★
Wichita State University - Thurlow Lieurance Memorial Music Library
(Mus)
Walter Duerksen Fine Arts Center   Phone: (316)689-3029
Wichita, KS 67208   Michele Wolff, Mus.Libn.
Founded: 1926. **Staff:** Prof 1; Other 1. **Subjects:** Music. **Special Collections:**
Kansas Music Teachers' Association Archives. **Holdings:** 16,500 books;
1800 bound periodical volumes; 13,500 phonograph records; 21,500 scores.
Services: Interlibrary loan; library open to the public. **Automated**
Operations: Computerized cataloging, acquisitions, serials, and circulation.
Networks/Consortia: Member of AMIGOS Bibliographic Council, Inc.

★ 20414 ★
Wickes Companies - Marketing Library (Bus-Fin)
26261 Evergreen Rd.
Box 999
Southfield, MI 48037-0999   Phone: (313)355-8517
Founded: 1980. **Subjects:** Business, marketing. **Holdings:** 50 books;
corporate annual and 10K reports. **Subscriptions:** 50 journals and other
serials. **Services:** Interlibrary loan; library not open to the public. **Remarks:**
FAX: (313)355-8385.

★ 20415 ★
Wide World Photos, Inc. (Aud-Vis)
50 Rockefeller Plaza, 6th Fl.   Phone: (212)621-1930
New York, NY 10020   Patricia Lantis, Dir.
Staff: Prof 35. **Subjects:** News, sports, feature, historical, celebrity pictures
- all subjects. **Holdings:** 50 million black and white and color pictures.
Services: Pictures for editorial and commercial use; photography
assignments, distribution, and transmission of pictures; print and
reproduction fees charged. Open to the public. **Remarks:** FAX: (212)621-
1955.

★ 20416 ★
Widener University - School of Law - Harrisburg Campus Library (Law)
3800 Vartan Way   Phone: (717)541-3933
Harrisburg, PA 17110-9450   Eileen B. Cooper, Dir.
Founded: 1989. **Staff:** Prof 4; Other 3. **Subjects:** Law. **Holdings:** 60,425
books; 43,865 volumes in microform. **Subscriptions:** 1703 journals and other
serials; 19 newspapers. **Services:** Interlibrary loan; copying; library open to
the public. **Automated Operations:** Computerized cataloging, acquisitions,
serials, circulation, and ILL. **Computerized Information Services:** LEXIS,
WESTLAW, DIALOG Information Services. **Networks/Consortia:**
Member of Mid-Atlantic Law Library Cooperative (MALLCO), Delaware
Library Consortium (DLC). **Remarks:** FAX: (717)541-3998. **Staff:** Janet
Hirt, Assoc.Dir.; Susan Appleby-Flores, Tech.Proc./Ref.Libn.; Eugene
Shaw-Colyer, Ref.Libn.

★ 20417 ★
Widener University - School of Law - Library (Law)
P.O. Box 7475
Concord Pike
Wilmington, DE 19803   Phone: (302)477-2244
                              Eileen B. Cooper, Dir.
Founded: 1971. **Staff:** Prof 17; Other 30. **Subjects:** Law. **Holdings:** 430,000
books; 126,513 volumes in microform. **Subscriptions:** 7002 journals and
other serials; 19 newspapers. **Services:** Interlibrary loan; copying; library
open to the public. **Automated Operations:** Computerized cataloging,
acquisitions, serials, circulation, and ILL. **Computerized Information**
Services: LEXIS, WESTLAW, DIALOG Information Services. **Networks/**
Consortia: Member of Mid-Atlantic Law Library Cooperative (MALLCO),
Delaware Library Consortium (DLC). **Remarks:** FAX: (302)477-2240.
Maintains a branch library at 3800 Vartan Way, Harrisburg, PA 17110;
telephone, (717)541-3933. FAX: (717)541-3998. The above figures include
the branch library. **Staff:** Janet R. Hirt, Assoc.Dir.; Karin Thurman, Hd.,
Pub.Serv.; Mary Alice Peeling, Hd., Tech.Serv.; Mary Jane Mallonee, Ref./
Govt.Docs.; Mary Marzolla, Ref./State Docs.; David K. King, Ref./
Interdisciplinary; Enza Klotzbucher, ILL; Sandra P. Sadow, Coll.Dev.;
Zona H. Lindsay, Acq.; Ann Kolodzey, Ser.; Jacqueline Paul, Sr.Cat.; Susan
Appleby-Flores, Serv.Coord.; Ann Vigianno, Non Print Coord.

★ 20418 ★
Widener University - Wolfgram Memorial Library (Hum)
17th & Walnut Sts.   Phone: (215)499-4086
Chester, PA 19013   Theresa Taborsky, Dir.
Founded: 1821. **Staff:** Prof 11; Other 24. **Subjects:** Arts and sciences,
behavioral sciences, education, business, hotel management, engineering,
nursing, clinical psychology. **Special Collections:** Wolfgram Collection
(English literature). **Holdings:** 196,000 books and bound periodical volumes;
100,985 microforms; 4668 AV programs; 400 linear feet of archives.
Subscriptions: 2205 journals and other serials. **Services:** Interlibrary loan;
copying; library open to the public with restrictions. **Automated Operations:**
Computerized public access catalog (DYNIX). **Computerized Information**
Services: BRS Information Technologies, DIALOG Information Services,
OCLC; CD-ROM (Indexes). Performs searches on fee basis. Contact
Person: Maria Varki, Ref., 499-4080. **Networks/Consortia:** Member of
PALINET, Tri-State College Library Cooperative (TCLC), Interlibrary
Delivery Service of Pennsylvania (IDS), Consortium for Health Information
& Library Services (CHI). **Publications:** WolfGRAMS, 4/year - to academic
community. **Remarks:** Alternate telephone number(s): 499-4066. FAX:
(215)874-0790. The Wolfgram Memorial Library houses the collection of
the Lindsay Law Library. **Staff:** D. Holl, Tech.Serv.; K.J. Kim, Pub.Serv.;
D. Fidishun, AV.

★ 20419 ★
Widett, Slater & Goldman P.C. - Library (Law)
60 State St.   Phone: (617)227-7200
Boston, MA 02109   Sarah G. Connell, Hd.Libn.
Staff: Prof 1; Other 2. **Subjects:** Law - corporation, real estate, securities,
antitrust, government contracts, banking, estate planning, family, hospital,
probate, tax, bankruptcy, education, labor. **Special Collections:** Memoranda
of Law Archives (200 legal memoranda). **Holdings:** Figures not available.
Subscriptions: 400 journals and other serials; 10 newspapers. **Services:**
Interlibrary loan; SDI; library not open to the public. **Computerized**
Information Services: LEXIS, WESTLAW, Information America,
DIALOG Information Services, Dow Jones News/Retrieval. **Publications:**
WS&G Library News - to attorneys. **Special Catalogs:** Catalog to
Memoranda of Law Archives (card). **Remarks:** FAX: (617)227-0011.

C.M. Wieland Library
See: **Wieland-Museum (20420)**

★ 20420 ★
Wieland-Museum - Bibliothek/Archiv (Hum)
Marktplatz 17   Phone: 7351 51458
W-7950 Biberach, Germany   Mrs. Viia Ottenbacher, Dir.
Founded: 1905. **Subjects:** Works and related works of Christoph Martin
Wieland; 18th century literature and literary life; works and related works
of Sophie von La Roche; Justin Heinrich Knecht. **Special Collections:** C.M.
Wieland Library (1658 volumes); collection of Wieland autographs and
manuscripts (300 items). **Holdings:** 13,235 books and bound periodical
volumes; 1085 manuscripts. **Subscriptions:** 7 journals and other serials.
Services: Interlibrary loan; copying; library open to the public by
appointment. **Publications:** Wieland-Studien I, 1991; Wieland-Museum
Biberach an der Riss 1905-1985 (1985). **Remarks:** Alternate telephone
number(s): 7351 51307. FAX: 7351 51492. Maintained by the City of
Biberach.

Wiener Institut fur Internationale Wirtschaftsvergleiche
See: **Vienna Institute for Comparative Economic Studies (19835)**

Wiener Stadt- und Landesbibliothek
See: **Vienna Municipal Archives (19837)**

★ 20421 ★
Simon Wiesenthal Center - Library/Archives (Area-Ethnic, Hist)
9760 W. Pico Blvd.   Phone: (310)553-9036
Los Angeles, CA 90035   Adaire J. Klein, Coord., Lib./Archv.Serv.
Founded: 1978. **Staff:** 8. **Subjects:** Holocaust, World War II, anti-Semitism,
Jewish life before the Holocaust, human rights, civil rights. **Holdings:** 24,000
volumes; 2000 archival collections. **Subscriptions:** 300 journals and other
serials. **Services:** Interlibrary loan; copying; SDI; library open to the public
for reference use only. **Remarks:** FAX: (310)553-8007. **Staff:** Margo
Gutstein; Cheryl Miller; Bella Sitnyakovsky; Nancy Varat.

Wiggans Health Sciences Library
See: **Norwalk Hospital** (12101)

★ 20422 ★
Wiggin and Dana - Library (Law)
1 Century Tower   Phone: (203)498-4400
New Haven, CT 06508-1832   Ana M. Oman, Libn.
Staff: 2. **Subjects:** Law. **Holdings:** 13,500 books. **Subscriptions:** 250 journals and other serials; 10 newspapers. **Services:** Library not open to the public. **Computerized Information Services:** LEXIS, WESTLAW, DIALOG Information Services, Dow Jones News/Retrieval, DUN, VU/TEXT Information Services. **Remarks:** FAX: (203)782-2889. **Staff:** Rosemarie Kjerulf, Lib.Ck.

★ 20423 ★
Wight Consulting Engineers, Inc. - Technical Library (Sci-Engr)
127 S. Northwest Hwy.   Phone: (708)381-1800
Barrington, IL 60010   Sally M. Trainer, Sec.
Staff: Prof 1; Other 2. **Subjects:** Water, sanitary engineering, city planning, transportation, environment, industrial waste. **Holdings:** 1800 books; 400 bound periodical volumes; 50 directories. **Subscriptions:** 30 journals and other serials; 5 newspapers. **Services:** Interlibrary loan; copying; library open to the public upon request. **Remarks:** FAX: (708)381-1875.

Wiglesworth Ornithological Library
See: **University of Bristol - University Library** (18254)

★ 20424 ★
Wilberforce University - Rembert Stokes Learning Center - Archives and Special Collections (Hist, Area-Ethnic)
Wilberforce, OH 45384-1003   Phone: (513)376-2911
                          Jean Mulhern, Lib.Dir.
Staff: Prof 2; Other 3. **Subjects:** African Methodist Episcopal (A.M.E.) Church history; books by and about blacks, 19th century; history of Wilberforce University. **Special Collections:** A.M.E. Church conference minutes; papers of Bishop Reverdy Cassius Ransom, university president W.S. Scarborough, and Wilberforce professor Milton S.J. Wright. **Holdings:** 2000 books; 20 reels of microfilm; 10,000 uncataloged items. **Services:** Copying; collections open to the public by appointment. **Computerized Information Services:** DIALOG Information Services. **Networks/Consortia:** Member of Southwestern Ohio Council for Higher Education (SOCHE). **Publications:** Printed guides to some parts of collection. **Staff:** Jacqueline Y. Brown, Asst.Libn./Dir., Archv.

Wilbour Library of Egyptology
See: **Brooklyn Museum** (2239)

Peter Wilcock Library
See: **Charles Camsell General Hospital** (2629)

Wilcox Library
See: **William Penn College** (12832)

★ 20425 ★
Wilcox Memorial Hospital - Medical Library (Med)
3420 Kuhio Hwy.   Phone: (808)245-1173
Lihue, HI 96766   Sylvia J. Duarte, Coord., Med. Staff Serv.
Founded: 1971. **Staff:** 1. **Subjects:** General medicine. **Holdings:** Figures not available. **Services:** Interlibrary loan; copying. **Computerized Information Services:** MEDLARS. **Networks/Consortia:** Member of National Network of Libraries of Medicine - Pacific Southwest Region. **Remarks:** FAX: (808)245-1171.

Oscar Wilde Collection
See: **Dalhousie University** (4538)

★ 20426 ★
Laura Ingalls Wilder Museum & Tourist Information (Hist)
Box 58   Phone: (507)859-2358
Walnut Grove, MN 56180   Shirley Knakmuhs, Musm.Cur.
Subjects: Laura Ingalls Wilder. **Special Collections:** Letters from Laura Ingalls Wilder. **Holdings:** 30 books.

★ 20427 ★
Wilderness Leadership International - Outdoor Living Library (Rec)
Wilderness Leadership Center
Box 770
North Fork, CA 93643   Miriam Darnall, Act.Libn.
Founded: 1970. **Subjects:** Wilderness survival, edible wild plants, camping, mountaineering, homestead skills, health, herbs. **Holdings:** 4000 books; 300 magazine articles, pamphlets, reprints; films; slide/tape sets.

★ 20428 ★
Wildlife Information Center - Library (Env-Cons)
629 Green St.   Phone: (215)434-1637
Allentown, PA 18102   Donald S. Heintzelman, Pres.
Founded: 1986. **Subjects:** Wildlife, environment. **Holdings:** 350 books; 111 unbound periodical titles; 1300 VF file folders of magazine and newspaper articles. **Subscriptions:** 11 journals and other serials. **Services:** Library not open to the public. **Computerized Information Services:** Produces Wildlife Protector (available as HyperCard Stack); internal database.

★ 20429 ★
Wildlife Information Service - Library (Biol Sci)
9956 N. Hwy. 85   Phone: (505)527-2547
Las Cruces, NM 88005   Julie L. Moore, Bibliog.
Staff: Prof 2; Other 1. **Subjects:** Game mammals and birds, marine mammals and birds, bats, endangered species, fisheries, fauna, taxonomy. **Special Collections:** Hardcopy files of all SDI profiles created for the databases; retrospective hardcopy files for game, mammals, and birds, 1934-1985. **Holdings:** 1100 books; Zoological Record, 1864-1948, on microfilm; Aves and Mammalia; database tapes of SDI files; biological and technical dictionaries; fauna guides; fauna bibliographies. **Subscriptions:** 12 journals and other serials. **Services:** Library not open to the public. **Computerized Information Services:** DIALOG Information Services, BRS Information Technologies, USFWS (United States Fish and Wildlife Service); HERMAN (Wildlife and Marine Mammals and Birds), Theses in Wildlife (9000 titles on database) (internal databases). Performs searches on fee basis. **Publications:** Bibliography of Wildlife Theses, 1900-1968.

★ 20430 ★
Wildlife Management Institute - Library (Env-Cons)
1101 Fourteenth St., N.W., Suite 725   Phone: (202)347-1774
Washington, DC 20005   Richard E. McCabe, Sec./Dir., Pubns.
Staff: Prof 9. **Subjects:** Wildlife and conservation. **Special Collections:** Complete Transactions of North American Wildlife and Natural Resources Conference; Proceedings of American Game Conference (complete set); American Game Bulletin (complete run). **Holdings:** 1000 volumes. **Subscriptions:** 50 journals and other serials. **Services:** Library open to the public with restrictions. **Special Indexes:** 40-year cumulative index to Transactions of North American Wildlife and Natural Resources Conference. **Remarks:** FAX: (202)408-5059.

Ernest A. Wildman Science Library
See: **Earlham College** (5094)

★ 20431 ★
John Wiley and Sons, Inc. - Information Center (Publ)
605 Third Ave.   Phone: (212)850-6050
New York, NY 10158   Helen Witsenhausen, Info.Serv.Mgr.
Staff: Prof 1. **Subjects:** Publishing, business and management, computers, higher education. **Holdings:** 500 books; 9 VF drawers of clippings. **Subscriptions:** 35 journals and other serials. **Services:** Center not open to the public. **Automated Operations:** Computerized cataloging and acquisitions. **Computerized Information Services:** DIALOG Information Services, NEXIS, Dow Jones News/Retrieval, InvesText/Plus; CD-ROMs; internal databases; electronic mail. Performs searches on fee basis. **Remarks:** FAX: (212)850-6088.

★ 20432 ★
Wilkes, Artis, Hedrick & Lane, Chartered - Law Library (Law)
1666 K St., N.W., 11th Fl.   Phone: (202)457-7344
Washington, DC 20006   Barbara S. Wilson, Law Libn.
Founded: 1926. **Staff:** Prof 1; Other 1. **Subjects:** Law - real estate, tax, communications, eminent domain, zoning; municipal affairs. **Holdings:** 20,000 books; 1260 bound periodical volumes; 2300 microfiche; 2100 ultrafiche; 61 audiotapes; 7 videotapes. **Subscriptions:** 114 journals and other serials. **Services:** Interlibrary loan; SDI; library open to the public by appointment. **Computerized Information Services:** NEXIS, LEXIS, DIALOG Information Services, Dow Jones News/Retrieval, LEGI-SLATE, WESTLAW. **Publications:** Library Report, weekly - for internal distribution only. **Special Indexes:** Index to FCC Daily Releases (book); D.C. Legislative Service (book). **Remarks:** Alternate telephone number(s): 457-7800. FAX: (202)457-7814. **Staff:** Annette Erbrecht, Asst.Libn.

★ 20433 ★
Wilkes-Barre General Hospital - Hospital Library (Med)
Auburn & River Sts.   Phone: (717)820-2180
Wilkes-Barre, PA 18764   Rosemarie Kazda Taylor, Dir., Lib./Commun.
Founded: 1935. **Staff:** Prof 2; Other 1. **Subjects:** Medicine, nursing, allied health sciences, hospital administration. **Holdings:** 3344 books; 249 titles on microfilm; AV programs; 5 VF drawers of pamphlets; periodicals. **Subscriptions:** 382 journals and other serials. **Services:** Interlibrary loan; copying; SDI; library open to health personnel. **Automated Operations:** Computerized serials and circulation. **Computerized Information Services:** MEDLARS, DIALOG Information Services. Performs searches on fee basis. **Networks/Consortia:** Member of Northeastern Pennsylvania Bibliographic Center (NEPBC), Health Information Library Network of Northeastern Pennsylvania (HILNNEP), National Network of Libraries of Medicine - Middle Atlantic Region, BHSL. **Special Indexes:** Medical Index, monthly - for internal distribution, area libraries, and by request. **Remarks:** FAX: (717)820-2269. **Staff:** Marcia Aston, Asst.Dir., Lib.

★ 20434 ★
Wilkes-Barre Law and Library Association (Law)
Courthouse, Rm. 23   Phone: (717)822-6712
Wilkes-Barre, PA 18711   Lawrence H. Sindaco, Libn.
Staff: Prof 3. **Subjects:** Law. **Holdings:** 30,000 books; 200 bound periodical volumes. **Subscriptions:** 20 journals and other serials. **Services:** Copying; library open to the public at librarian's discretion. **Publications:** Luzerne Legal Register, weekly.

Wilkes Library
See: **Strayer College** (15829)

★ 20435 ★
Wilkes University - Institute of Regional Affairs - Library (Soc Sci)
Box 111   Phone: (717)824-4651
Wilkes-Barre, PA 18766   Philip Tuhy, Dir.
Subjects: Government - local, state, in-service training; economic development; legislative reference (state). **Special Collections:** Flood Recovery Collection, 1972 (records of Flood Recovery Task Force, Inc.). **Holdings:** 5000 books; 2000 bound periodical volumes; 3000 pamphlets, studies, reports; 20 file cabinets of news clippings; 500 maps. **Remarks:** FAX: (717)824-2245.

★ 20436 ★
Wilkin County Historical Society - Library (Hist)
Box 212   Phone: (218)643-1303
Breckenridge, MN 56520   Fran Underberg, Sec.
Founded: 1979. **Staff:** 3. **Subjects:** Local history. **Special Collections:** Newspapers, 1881-1970; obituaries; biographies; township books; school records. **Holdings:** 256 books. **Services:** Library open to the public.

Walter L. Wilkins Bio-Medical Library
See: **U.S. Navy - Naval Health Research Center** (17841)

★ 20437 ★
Will County Historical Society - Archives (Hist)
803 S. State St.   Phone: (815)838-5080
Lockport, IL 60441   Rose Bucciferro, Cur.
Subjects: History of Will County, Illinois, and the Illinois and Michigan Canal, 1830-1935; genealogy. **Holdings:** 350,000 archival materials, including property records, surname files, biographies, cemetery records. **Services:** Archives not open to the public. **Remarks:** Manual search services available by written request on a fee basis.

★ 20438 ★
Will County Law Library (Law)
14 W. Jefferson St.
Will County Court House   Phone: (815)727-8536
Joliet, IL 60431   Mr. A.J. Moen, Law Libn.
Founded: 1975. **Staff:** Prof 1. **Subjects:** Illinois law. **Holdings:** 15,000 books; 50 bound periodical volumes; 2000 microfiche. **Subscriptions:** 20 journals and other serials; 4 newspapers. **Services:** Library open to the public. **Computerized Information Services:** LEXIS; internal database. **Publications:** Will County Law Library Title Holdings; Will County Law Library's Materials by Subjects. **Remarks:** Partial Illinois Government Document depository. FAX: (815)722-6342.

★ 20439 ★
Willamette Falls Hospital - Medical Library (Med)
1500 Division St.   Phone: (503)650-6757
Oregon City, OR 97045   Katherine R. Martin, Libn.
Founded: 1978. **Staff:** Prof 1. **Subjects:** Medicine, nursing, consumer health. **Holdings:** 400 books. **Subscriptions:** 86 journals and other serials. **Services:** Interlibrary loan; copying; SDI; library open to the public by appointment. **Computerized Information Services:** DIALOG Information Services, MEDLARS; DOCLINE, OnTyme Electronic Message Network Service (electronic mail services). **Remarks:** FAX: (503)650-6808.

★ 20440 ★
Willamette University - Law Library (Law)
250 Winter St., S.E.   Phone: (503)370-6386
Salem, OR 97301   Richard F. Breen, Jr., Law Libn.
Founded: 1883. **Staff:** Prof 5; Other 4. **Subjects:** Law. **Holdings:** 123,000 volumes. **Subscriptions:** 3000 journals and other serials; 7 newspapers. **Services:** Interlibrary loan; copying; library open to the public. **Automated Operations:** Computerized cataloging. **Computerized Information Services:** WESTLAW, OCLC, LEXIS, NEXIS. **Staff:** Mary Edith Gilbertson, Per.Libn.; Lysa Hall, Law Cat.; Warren Rees, Assoc. Law Libn.; Mary Cleland, Comp.Serv.Libn.

Willan Library of British Association of Dermatologists
See: **Royal College of Physicians of London** (14113)

Frances E. Willard Memorial Library
See: **National Woman's Christian Temperance Union** (11326)

★ 20441 ★
Willard Library of Evansville - Special Collections Department (Hist)
21 1st Ave.   Phone: (812)425-4309
Evansville, IN 47710   Joan Elliott Parker, Spec.Coll.Libn.
Staff: Prof 2; Other 2. **Subjects:** History and genealogy of Evansville, Vanderburgh County, and the surrounding areas in Indiana, Illinois, and Kentucky, 1800 to present. **Special Collections:** Records of Willard Library and its predecessors; Southwest Indiana Historical Society collection; Vanderburgh Historical and Biographical Society collection; papers of Annie Fellows Johnston (author), Albion Fellows Bacon (social reformer), Norman A. Shane, Sr. (businessman and civic leader); radio newscast scripts; U.S. Weather Service, Evansville Station, records; photographic collections of local persons and subjects; Old Evansville, Vanderburgh County Archives (county court records). **Holdings:** 9500 books; 1300 microforms; 3000 linear feet of personal papers, city, township, and county records. **Subscriptions:** 50 journals and other serials; 2 newspapers. **Services:** Interlibrary loan; copying (both limited); department open to the public. **Networks/Consortia:** Member of Four Rivers Area Library Services Authority (ALSA), INCOLSA. **Remarks:** FAX: (812)421-9742. **Staff:** Lyn Martin, Archv.

★ 20442 ★
Willard Psychiatric Center - Hatch Library (Med)
Hatch Bldg.   Phone: (607)869-3111
Willard, NY 14588   Helen Bunting, Sr.Libn.
Founded: 1869. **Staff:** Prof 1. **Subjects:** Psychiatry, medicine, psychology, health sciences, nursing, rehabilitative geriatrics. **Special Collections:** Archives. **Holdings:** 3300 books; 1200 bound periodical volumes; 12 cubic feet of medical files. **Subscriptions:** 80 journals and other serials; 8 newspapers. **Services:** Interlibrary loan; copying; library open to the public with director's written permission. **Computerized Information Services:** New York State Library Data Base (internal database). **Networks/Consortia:** Member of South Central Research Library Council (SCRLC), Finger Lakes Library System. **Publications:** Library Quarterly (acquisitions list). **Special Indexes:** Monthly Journal Index (table of contents of journals received).

★ 20443 ★
Willet Stained Glass Studios - Library (Art)
10 E. Moreland Ave.   Phone: (215)247-5721
Philadelphia, PA 19118   Helene Weis, Libn.
Founded: 1890. **Staff:** Prof 1. **Subjects:** Stained glass - historic and contemporary process; art. **Holdings:** 1000 volumes; 15,350 photographs; 20,000 slides; 4500 microforms; pictures; clippings. **Subscriptions:** 30 journals and other serials. **Services:** Copying; library open to qualified persons. **Remarks:** FAX: (215)247-2951.

★ 20444 ★
Williams Brothers Engineering Company - Technical Information Center (Energy)
P.O. Box 21310   Phone: (918)561-9575
Tulsa, OK 74121-1310   Kay Kittrell, Mgr.
Founded: 1971. **Staff:** Prof 1. **Subjects:** Pipeline engineering, petroleum industry, energy technology, environmental engineering, energy statistics. **Special Collections:** Pipeline maps. **Holdings:** 5000 books; 10,000 company reports; 42 reels of microfilm of association standards; 200 maps. **Subscriptions:** 25 journals and other serials. **Services:** Copying; center open to the public with restrictions. **Computerized Information Services:** DIALOG Information Services. **Special Catalogs:** Technical Reports Catalog (card); catalog of published papers of company personnel (card). **Remarks:** FAX: (918)561-9510. Telex: 158112 WBEC UT. Library located at 119 E. 6th St., Tulsa, OK 74119.

★ 20445 ★
Williams College - Center for Environmental Studies - Matt Cole Memorial Library (Env-Cons)
Box 632   Phone: (413)597-2500
Williamstown, MA 01267   Marcella Rauscher, Res.Coord.
Founded: 1972. **Staff:** Prof 1. **Subjects:** Air pollution, coasts, energy, environmental health, environmental law, land use, natural resources, toxic substances, water resources, local and regional data and planning. **Holdings:** 3500 books; 1700 bound periodical volumes; 3100 EPA documents; 9350 other documents. **Subscriptions:** 250 journals and other serials. **Services:** Library open to the public. **Remarks:** FAX: (413)597-4088.

★ 20446 ★
Williams College - Chapin Library (Rare Book, Hum)
Stetson Hall, 2nd Fl.
Box 426   Phone: (413)597-2462
Williamstown, MA 01267   Robert L. Volz, Custodian
Founded: 1923. **Staff:** Prof 2; Other 1. **Special Collections:** Incunabula (550 volumes); English literature before 1700 (1500 volumes); English 18th and 19th century first editions (2000 volumes); Americana (3000 volumes); History of Science (500 volumes); Ornithology (250 volumes); Classical and European literature (1500 volumes); Bibles and liturgical books (300 volumes); Aldine Press (135 volumes); Graphic Arts and private press books (5000 volumes); Walt Whitman (600 items); William Saroyan (250 items); Edwin Arlington Robinson (400 items); Samuel Butler (1000 items); Rudyard Kipling (700 items); Joseph Conrad (140 items); Theodore Roosevelt (200 items); William Faulkner (450 items); pre-1600 codices (40 volumes); historical and literary manuscripts (1500 items); prints of historical subjects (500 items); English 17th and 18th century broadside ballads (130 items); C.B. Falls (1000 items); performing arts (3000 items); American literature (1000 volumes); English 20th century literature (750 volumes); John Sayles (300 items); bookplates (1000 items); Herman Rosse (500 items). **Holdings:** 37,000 volumes. **Subscriptions:** 25 journals and other

serials. **Services:** Copying; answers correspondence requests for bibliographical information; library open to the public with restrictions. **Automated Operations:** Computerized cataloging. **Networks/Consortia:** Member of SUNY/OCLC Library Network. **Publications:** Exhibition handlists; The Graphic Art of C.B. Falls (1982). **Special Catalogs:** Short-Title List of Books in the Chapin Library (1939); Catalog of the Collection of Samuel Butler (of Erewhon) in the Chapin Library (1945); special card file for printers/place of printing; date of imprint; binders; watermarks in incunabula; provenance; maps and illustrations. **Staff:** Wayne G. Hammond, Asst.Libn.

E.K. Williams Law Library
See: **University of Manitoba** (18788)

Edward Bennett Williams Law Library
See: **Georgetown University** (6376)

★ 20447 ★
Williams International - Library (Sci-Engr)
2280 W. Maple Rd.
Box 200
Walled Lake, MI 48390-0200   Phone: (313)624-5200
Staff: Prof 1; Other 1. **Subjects:** Aerodynamics, gas turbine engines, metallurgy. **Holdings:** 1200 books; 8500 documents; 3000 monographs. **Subscriptions:** 40 journals and other serials. **Services:** Interlibrary loan; library not open to the public. **Computerized Information Services:** Online systems. **Remarks:** FAX: (313)669-1577. **Staff:** Susan L. Chakan; Bonnie Jarvis; Gayla Thompson, Libn.

Jack K. Williams Library
See: **Texas A&M University at Galveston** (16203)

John A. Williams Archive
See: **University of Rochester - Department of Rare Books and Special Collections** (19278)

John Davis Williams Library
See: **University of Mississippi** (18952)

John R. Williams, Sr. Health Sciences Library
See: **Highland Hospital** (7195)

Kemper and Leila Williams Foundation - Historic New Orleans Collection
See: **Historic New Orleans Collection** (7247)

★ 20448 ★
Williams-Kuebelbeck & Associates, Inc. - Library (Bus-Fin)
1301 Shoreway Rd., Suite 317   Phone: (415)593-7600
Belmont, CA 94002   Karen S. Maskel, Libn.
Founded: 1972. **Staff:** Prof 1. **Subjects:** Real estate market, fiscal impact analysis. **Special Collections:** Real estate development; Marina Development (150 volumes). **Holdings:** 1100 books; 1900 unbound reports. **Subscriptions:** 125 journals and other serials. **Services:** Interlibrary loan; library not open to the public. **Computerized Information Services:** DIALOG Information Services. **Publications:** Bibliographies - for internal distribution only. **Special Catalogs:** Internal reports catalog (card). **Remarks:** FAX: (415)593-4147.

Paul Williams Memorial Resource Center
See: **Investigative Reporters and Editors, Inc.** (8215)

★20449★

Roger Williams Hospital - Health Sciences Library (Med)
825 Chalkstone Ave.   Phone: (401)456-2036
Providence, RI 02908   Hadassah Stein, Libn.
Staff: Prof 1. **Subjects:** Medicine, nursing, allied health sciences. **Holdings:** 2200 books; 2800 bound periodical volumes; 600 indexes, clinics. **Subscriptions:** 182 journals and other serials. **Services:** Interlibrary loan; library not open to the public. **Computerized Information Services:** NLM. **Networks/Consortia:** Member of Association of Rhode Island Health Sciences Librarians (ARIHSL). **Formerly:** Roger Williams General Hospital.

★20450★

Roger Williams Park - Museum of Natural History & Planetarium - Museum Library/Resource Center (Hist)
Providence, RI 02905   Phone: (401)785-9450
                                        Marilyn Massaro, Cur.
Founded: 1896. **Staff:** 6. **Subjects:** Natural history, geology, astronomy, Native American and South Pacific ethnology. **Special Collections:** Natural History Library; glassplate negative collection; museum and park archives. **Holdings:** Figures not available. **Services:** Center not open to the public. Special collections research by appointment. **Remarks:** FAX: (401)785-9450. **Staff:** Mary L. Greene.

Ronald Williams Library
See: Northeastern Illinois University (11982)

Samuel C. Williams Library
See: Stevens Institute of Technology - Samuel C. Williams Library (15788)

T.F. Williams Health Sciences Library
See: Monroe Community Hospital (10616)

T.S. Williams Veterinary Medical Library
See: Tuskegee University (16594)

Vaughan Williams Memorial Library
See: English Folk Dance and Song Society (5358)

Dr. George S. Williamson Health Sciences Library
See: Ottawa Civic Hospital (12599)

Jack Williamson Science Fiction Library
See: Eastern New Mexico University - Golden Library - Special Collections (5163)

★20451★

Williamsport Hospital & Medical Center - Learning Resources Center (Med)
777 Rural Ave.   Phone: (717)321-2266
Williamsport, PA 17701-3198   Michael Heyd, Dir.
Staff: Prof 1; Other 3. **Subjects:** Medicine, nursing, allied health sciences. **Special Collections:** Medical textbooks, 1850 to present. **Holdings:** 4726 books; 6044 bound periodical volumes; 127 filmstrip/cassette programs; 219 slide/cassette programs; 2100 video cassette programs; 230 audiocassette programs; 5 16mm films. **Subscriptions:** 220 journals and other serials. **Services:** Interlibrary loan; copying; reference and bibliographic information; center open to the public for reference use only. **Computerized Information Services:** MEDLARS. Performs searches on fee basis. **Networks/Consortia:** Member of Susquehanna Library Cooperative, Central Pennsylvania Health Sciences Library Association (CPHSLA). **Remarks:** FAX: (717)321-2271.

★20452★

Williamstown House of Local History - Library (Hist)
762 Main St.   Phone: (413)458-2160
Williamstown, MA 01267   Nancy Burstein, Cur.
Founded: 1940. **Subjects:** Williamstown history. **Holdings:** Books; documents; photographs; newspapers, artifacts. **Services:** Library open to the public.

★20453★

Willian Brinks Olds Hofer Gilson & Lione Ltd. - Library (Law)
NBC Tower, Suite 3600
455 N. City Front Dr. Plaza   Phone: (312)321-4200
Chicago, IL 60611   Robert Hu, Law Firm Libn.
Founded: 1987. **Staff:** Prof 1; Other 1. **Subjects:** Law - patent, trademark, copyright. **Holdings:** 5000 books; 1000 bound periodical volumes. **Subscriptions:** 50 journals and other serials. **Services:** Library not open to the public. **Computerized Information Services:** DIALOG Information Services, ORBIT Search Service, STN International, BRS Information Technologies, Data-Star, Compu-Mark, Dun & Bradstreet Business Credit Services, LEXIS, WESTLAW, Information America, CompuServe Information Service, DataTimes, VU/TEXT Information Services, Questel, INSMARQ, InvesText, Info Globe, LEGI-SLATE, FT PROFILE, BELINDAS, Dow Jones News/Retrieval, State Net, Current USC, BookQuest, SerialsQuest. **Remarks:** FAX: (312)321-4299.

Jeannie Willis Memorial Library
See: McGill University - Religious Studies Library (9910)

★20454★

Willkie Farr & Gallagher - Library (Law)
153 E. 53rd St.   Phone: (212)935-8000
New York, NY 10022   Debra Glessner, Dir., Lib.Serv.
Staff: Prof 7; Other 10. **Subjects:** Law - corporate, tax, real estate, trusts and estates, general. **Holdings:** 40,000 books; 400 bound periodical volumes; 5 cabinets of microforms. **Subscriptions:** 350 journals and other serials. **Services:** Interlibrary loan; library not open to the public. **Automated Operations:** Computerized cataloging. **Computerized Information Services:** DIALOG Information Services, Dow Jones News/Retrieval, NEXIS, LEXIS, NewsNet, Inc., WESTLAW, OCLC, Spectrum Ownership Profiles Online, TEXTLINE, DataTimes, VU/TEXT Information Services, CompuServe Information Service, Vickers Stock Research Corporation, Invest/Net, Inc., Dun & Bradstreet Business Credit Services, IDD Information Services, LEGI-SLATE, Information America. **Staff:** Felicia Moldovan, Cat.; Elise Lilly, Asst.Libn.; Robin Ahern, Corp.Libn.; Nancy Ciliberti, Br.Libn., DC Off.; Luanne Sarison, Ref.Libn.; Valerie Railey, Ref.Libn.

★20455★

Willmar Public Schools - Early Childhood Family Education/Community Education Toy Library (Educ)
c/o Willmar Public Library
Pioneerland Library System
611 S.W. 5th St.   Phone: (612)231-1100
Willmar, MN 56201   Linda Cogelow, Coord.
Founded: 1980. **Staff:** 4. **Holdings:** 3000 toys; baby furniture. **Services:** Library open to members. **Publications:** Brochures, irregular. **Remarks:** Maintained by Early Childhood Family and Community Education Department.

★20456★

Willmar Regional Treatment Center - Library (Med)
Box 1128   Phone: (612)231-5934
Willmar, MN 56201   Henry L. Wagener, Libn.
Founded: 1917. **Staff:** Prof 1. **Subjects:** Alcoholism, psychiatric nursing, mental retardation. **Special Collections:** Brandes Memorial Library (special collection of books on alcoholism). **Holdings:** 2300 books. **Subscriptions:** 75 journals and other serials. **Services:** Interlibrary loan; copying; library open to the public with restrictions. **Networks/Consortia:** Member of Minnesota Department of Human Services Library Consortium. **Staff:** Peter Thomson.

Bob Wills Memorial Archive of Popular Music
See: **Panhandle-Plains Historical Museum - Research Center (12726)**

★ 20457 ★
Wills Eye Hospital and Research Institute - Arthur J. Bedell Memorial Library (Med)
900 Walnut St.   Phone: (215)928-3288
Philadelphia, PA 19107   Judith Schaeffer Young, Libn.
Founded: 1832. **Staff:** Prof 1; Other 1. **Subjects:** Clinical and historical ophthalmology. **Special Collections:** Ophthalmic history. **Holdings:** 2500 books; 7600 bound periodical volumes; 200 Wills Quarterly Conference Papers; 2 VF drawers of Wills staff reprints; 5 VF drawers; 250,000 audiotapes, cassettes, slides; 78 video cassettes. **Subscriptions:** 125 journals and other serials. **Services:** Interlibrary loan; library open to the public by appointment. **Computerized Information Services:** NLM, DIALOG Information Services; InterNet (electronic mail service). **Networks/Consortia:** Member of Health Sciences Libraries Consortium (HSLC). **Remarks:** FAX: (215)928-3269. Electronic mail address(es): YOUNG@SHRSYS.HSLC.ORG (InterNet).

★ 20458 ★
Wilmer, Cutler & Pickering - Law Library (Law)
2445 M St., N.W.   Phone: (202)663-6760
Washington, DC 20037   Teresa Llewellyn, Dir., Info.Serv.
Staff: Prof 4; Other 7. **Subjects:** Law - antitrust, corporate, securities, tax, administrative. **Special Collections:** Legislative histories (500); bound Senate and House reports. **Holdings:** 50,000 books; 1500 bound periodical volumes. **Subscriptions:** 2000 journals and other serials; 20 newspapers. **Services:** Interlibrary loan; copying; library open to the public with restrictions. **Computerized Information Services:** DRI/McGraw-Hill, DataTimes, VU/TEXT Information Services, LEXIS, PFDS Online, WESTLAW, Dow Jones News/Retrieval, OCLC, NewsNet, Inc., Reuters, EPIC. **Remarks:** Alternate telephone number(s): 663-6015. FAX: (202)293-0074. **Staff:** Richard McClintic, Ref.Libn.; Joan Sherer, Ref.Libn.; M. Elizabeth Hill, Tech.Serv.Supv./Cat.

Wilmer Memorial Medical Library
See: **Abington Memorial Hospital (22)**

Wilmer Ophthalmological Institute
See: **Johns Hopkins Hospital - Wilmer Ophthalmological Institute (8414)**

★ 20459 ★
Wilmette Historical Museum - Library (Hist)
565 Hunter Rd.   Phone: (708)256-5838
Wilmette, IL 60091   E. Ramm, Musm.Dir.
Founded: 1950. **Staff:** 3. **Subjects:** History and institutions of the village of Wilmette. **Holdings:** 500 books; 120 bound periodical volumes; 5000 photographs; 66 VF drawers of archival material. **Subscriptions:** 3 journals and other serials. **Services:** Library open to the public with restrictions. **Special Indexes:** Subject index to photographs; Index to portraits.

★ 20460 ★
Wilmington Area Health Education Center - Learning Resource Center - Library (Med)
2131 S. 17th St.   Phone: (919)343-0161
Wilmington, NC 28402-9990   Donna Flake, Dir.
Staff: Prof 1; Other 6. **Subjects:** Internal medicine, nursing, oncology, cardiology, surgery, obstetrics and gynecology, allied health sciences. **Holdings:** 3000 books; 3000 bound periodical volumes; AV programs. **Subscriptions:** 250 journals and other serials. **Services:** Interlibrary loan; copying; SDI; library open to the public for reference use only. **Automated Operations:** Computerized cataloging, serials, and circulation. **Computerized Information Services:** BRS Information Technologies, NLM; internal database; OnTyme Electronic Message Network Service (electronic mail service). **Networks/Consortia:** Member of North Carolina Area Health Education Centers Program Library and Information Services Network. **Publications:** Newsletter - state distribution. **Remarks:** FAX: (919)762-9203.

★ 20461 ★
Wilmington College of Ohio - Peace Resource Center - Hiroshima/Nagasaki Memorial Collection (Soc Sci)
Pyle Center, Box 1183   Phone: (513)382-5338
Wilmington, OH 45177   Helen Wiegel, Dir.
Founded: 1975. **Staff:** 1. **Subjects:** Atomic bomb development, Hiroshima, Nagasaki, peace education, nonviolence, nuclear war, nuclear testing. **Special Collections:** Hiroshima/Nagasaki Memorial Collection (in Japanese; 600 volumes). **Holdings:** 1500 books; 26 VF drawers; 200 AV programs (videotapes, slide sets, and photograph exhibits). **Subscriptions:** 60 journals and other serials. **Services:** Interlibrary loan; AV rentals; collection open to the public. **Publications:** Newsletter, quarterly - to mailing list. **Special Catalogs:** Peace education resources catalog, irregular.

Wilmington Hospital
See: **Medical Center of Delaware (9991)**

★ 20462 ★
Wilmington Star-News Inc. - Library (Publ)
1103 S. 17th St.
Box 840   Phone: (919)343-2309
Wilmington, NC 28402   Denise J. Henry, Libn.
Staff: Prof 1; Other 1. **Subjects:** Newspaper reference topics. **Holdings:** Morning Star and Sunday Star-News, 1925 to present, on microfilm; clippings; clippings on microfiche; photographs; reference books. **Subscriptions:** 35 journals and other serials; 29 newspapers. **Services:** Library not open to the public. **Computerized Information Services:** DataTimes, NEXIS, DIALOG Information Services. **Remarks:** FAX: (919)343-2227.

Lorette Wilmot Library
See: **Nazareth College of Rochester (11357)**

★ 20463 ★
Wilshire Boulevard Temple - Sigmund Hecht Library (Rel-Phil)
3663 Wilshire Blvd.   Phone: (213)388-2401
Los Angeles, CA 90010   Joan Kropf, Libn.
Staff: Prof 1; Other 1. **Subjects:** Judaica, Bible, philosophy, religion, Jewish history, education, language and literature, arts, sociology. **Special Collections:** World War II, 1939-1945: trials of the major war criminals (complete set). **Holdings:** 17,000 volumes; 100 pamphlets; 12 VF drawers of uncataloged pamphlets; 100 filmstrips. **Subscriptions:** 15 journals and other serials. **Services:** Interlibrary loan; library open to the public for reference use only.

Anne Potter Wilson Music Library
See: **Vanderbilt University - Jean and Alexander Heard Library (19767)**

★ 20464 ★
Wilson & Company, Engineers & Architects - Library (Plan)
P.O. Box 1640   Phone: (913)827-0433
Salina, KS 67402-1640   Linda Newquist, Libn.
Founded: 1932. **Subjects:** Planning - city, regional, industrial; industrial waste. **Holdings:** Figures not available. **Services:** Library not open to the public. **Remarks:** Library located at 631 E. Crawford, Salina, KS, 67401.

★ 20465 ★
Wilson County Historical Society - Museum Library (Hist)
420 N. 7th   Phone: (316)378-3965
Fredonia, KS 66736   C. Jean Vorhees, Musm.Cur.
Founded: 1962. **Staff:** 2. **Subjects:** The West; Kansas; pioneer life; plains agriculture - tools, equipment, facilities. **Special Collections:** Original set of the Offical Records of the Civil War. **Holdings:** 400 books; 300 bound periodical volumes; 1050 indexed pictures; 68 indexed notebooks of clippings; 15 notebooks of clipped obituaries from last 40 years in Wilson County; 110 reels of microfilm of Wilson County newspapers; books of grade school local history essays, 1983-1984. **Services:** Copying; library open to the public for reference use only. **Publications:** Newsletter, 4/year.

Cunningham Wilson Library
See: **St. Vincent's Hospital** (14617)

Curtis Laws Wilson Library
See: **University of Missouri--Rolla** (18980)

Edmund Wilson Library
See: **University of Tulsa - McFarlin Library** (19466)

Evan Wilson Turkish Library
See: **Middle East Institute - George Camp Keiser Library** (10351)

Florence O. Wilson Zoological Library
See: **Oklahoma City Zoo** (12344)

★ 20466 ★
Wilson Foods Corporation - Research Library
4545 Lincoln Blvd.
Oklahoma City, OK 73105
Defunct.

Wilson Hospital
See: **United Health Services/Wilson Hospital** (16715)

★ 20467 ★
Wilson, Ihrig & Associates - Library (Sci-Engr)
5776 Broadway   Phone: (510)658-6719
Oakland, CA 94618   Kash Gill, Mktg.Mgr.
Founded: 1966. **Staff:** 1. **Subjects:** Acoustics theory; acoustics - architectural, industrial, general; rapid transit noise and vibration. **Holdings:** 500 books; 2000 reports; 2400 articles and reprints. **Subscriptions:** 50 journals and other serials. **Services:** Interlibrary loan (limited); copying; library open to the public by appointment. **Automated Operations:** Computerized cataloging. **Computerized Information Services:** DIALOG Information Services. Performs searches on fee basis. **Remarks:** FAX: (510)652-4441.

★ 20468 ★
Wilson Memorial Hospital - Learning Center/Library (Med)
1705 S. Tarboro St.   Phone: (919)399-8253
Wilson, NC 27893   Rosa Edwards, Supv.
Founded: 1964. **Staff:** Prof 1; Other 2. **Subjects:** Medicine, nursing, and allied health sciences. **Special Collections:** University of North Carolina Masters in Public Health Collection. **Holdings:** 613 volumes; 730 video cassettes; 39 slide sets; 293 filmstrips; 269 audiocassettes. **Subscriptions:** 90 journals and other serials. **Services:** Interlibrary loan; copying; library open to the public with restrictions. **Computerized Information Services:** CD-ROMs (MEDLINE, CINAHL-CD). **Networks/Consortia:** Member of North Carolina Area Health Education Centers Program Library and Information Services Network. **Special Catalogs:** Audiovisual Catalog. **Remarks:** FAX: (919)399-8778.

Wilson Memorial Library
See: **Aldersgate College** (334)

★ 20469 ★
Wilson Ornithological Society - Josselyn Van Tyne Memorial Library (Biol Sci)
Museum of Zoology
University of Michigan   Phone: (313)764-0457
Ann Arbor, MI 48109   Janet G. Hinshaw, Libn.
Founded: 1930. **Staff:** 1. **Subjects:** Ornithology. **Holdings:** 1700 books; 2400 bound periodical volumes; 3000 boxes of pamphlets and reprints; 500 translations; 70 dissertations; 50 sound recordings. **Subscriptions:** 193 journals and other serials. **Services:** Interlibrary loan; direct mail loan service to members of Wilson Ornithological Society; library open to University of Michigan staff and students. **Automated Operations:** Computerized public access catalog (MIRLYN). **Computerized Information Services:** RLIN.

Wilson Recordings Collection
See: **University of British Columbia** (18284)

Seth Wilson Library
See: **Ozark Christian College** (12649)

★ 20470 ★
Woodrow Wilson Birthplace Foundation, Inc. - Research Library & Archives (Hist)
20 N. Coalter St.
Box 24   Phone: (703)885-0897
Staunton, VA 24401   Dr. Jean Smith, Libn.
Founded: 1973. **Staff:** Prof 3. **Subjects:** Life and times of President Woodrow Wilson; international affairs during World War I period; Wilson family members; American government, 1902-1921. **Special Collections:** Katherine C. Brand Collection (Life and Times of Woodrow Wilson; 500 volumes); Wallace M. McClure Collection (Woodrow Wilson and International Affairs; 1000 volumes). **Holdings:** 4000 books; 150 bound periodical volumes; 1000 pamphlets; 1000 pieces of Woodrow Wilson and family manuscripts; 10 boxes of period newspaper clippings; 20 boxes of period photographs; 12 drawers and 20 boxes of institutional archives. **Subscriptions:** 20 journals and other serials. **Services:** Library open to the public on request. **Remarks:** FAX: (703)886-9874.

★ 20471 ★
Woodrow Wilson International Center for Scholars - Library (Soc Sci)
1000 Jefferson Dr., S.W.   Phone: (202)357-2567
Washington, DC 20560   Zdenek V. David, Libn.
Founded: 1970. **Staff:** Prof 2; Other 2. **Subjects:** U.S. history and politics; American, East and West European, Latin American, Russian, and Asian studies; international studies. **Special Collections:** Russian/Soviet Collection of the Kennan Institute (10,000 volumes). **Holdings:** 26,000 books; bound periodical volumes. **Subscriptions:** 300 journals and other serials; 25 newspapers. **Services:** Interlibrary loan; copying; library open to the public for reference use only. **Publications:** Scholars' Research and Center Publications: A Bibliography, biennial. **Staff:** Linda Warden.

Woodrow Wilson Library
See: **Library of Congress - Rare Book & Special Collections Division** (9135)

Woodrow Wilson Memorial Library
See: **United Nations Headquarters - Dag Hammarskjold Library** (16772)

Woodrow Wilson School of Public and International Affairs
See: **Princeton University** (13389)

★ 20472 ★
Wilton Historical Society, Inc. - Library (Hist)
249 Danbury Rd.   Phone: (203)762-7257
Wilton, CT 06897   Marilyn Gould, Dir.
Subjects: Connecticut and Wilton history and genealogy. **Special Collections:** Connecticut and New England maps. **Holdings:** 500 volumes; manuscript collection. **Services:** Copying; library open to the public for reference use only. **Remarks:** Library housed at the Wilton Public Library.

E.W. Wimblc Memorial Library
See: **Harlem Valley Psychiatric Center** (6907)

★ 20473 ★
Winchester Historical Society - Solomon Rockwell House - Archive (Hist)
225 Prospect St.   Phone: (203)379-8433
Winsted, CT 06098   Catherine Lipscomb, Cur.
Staff: 2. **Subjects:** Local history. **Holdings:** Books; photographs; maps; documents; 5000 glassplate negatives. **Services:** Archive open to the public on a limited schedule. **Publications:** Brochure; newsletter. **Remarks:** Alternate telephone number(s): 379-6269; 379-4507. **Staff:** Lewella Francis, Asst.Libn.; June Senack, Asst.Libn.

★ 20474 ★
Winchester Medical Center - Health Sciences Library (Med)
Box 3340   Phone: (703)722-8040
Winchester, VA 22601-2540   Mary A. Hyde, Libn.
Staff: Prof 1. **Subjects:** Medicine, nursing, allied health sciences. **Holdings:** 600 books; 1500 bound periodical volumes. **Subscriptions:** 175 journals and other serials. **Services:** Interlibrary loan; copying; library open to the public by appointment. **Computerized Information Services:** BRS Information Technologies, MEDLARS. Performs searches on fee basis. **Networks/Consortia:** Member of Northern Virginia Health Sciences Libraries. **Publications:** Newsletter, bimonthly - for internal distribution only. **Remarks:** FAX: (703)722-8734.

Winchester Repeating Arms Company Archives
See: **Buffalo Bill Historical Center** (2325)

★ 20475 ★
Windels, Marx, Davies & Ives - Library (Law)
156 W. 56th St.   Phone: (212)237-1136
New York, NY 10019   Joel Solomon, Libn.
Staff: Prof 1; Other 1. **Subjects:** Law - corporate, international, securities, tax, trusts and estates, banking. **Holdings:** 18,000 books; 550 bound periodical volumes. **Subscriptions:** 185 journals and other serials; 10 newspapers. **Services:** Interlibrary loan; library open to the public with restrictions. **Computerized Information Services:** LEXIS, DIALOG Information Services, NEXIS, WESTLAW. **Publications:** Library Newsletter, bimonthly. **Remarks:** FAX: (212)262-1215.

★ 20476 ★
Windham Textile and History Museum - Dunham Hall Library (Hist, Art)
157 Union-Main St.   Phone: (203)456-2178
Willimantic, CT 06226   Linda Kate Edgerton, Libn.
Founded: 1989. **Staff:** Prof 1; Other 1. **Subjects:** Textile industrial history, labor history, ethnic studies. **Special Collections:** Architectural and engineering drawings; mill photographs; maps. **Holdings:** 1500 books. **Computerized Information Services:** Internal database.

★ 20477 ★
Windsor Historical Society, Inc. - Library (Hist)
96 Palisado Ave.   Phone: (203)688-3813
Windsor, CT 06095   Robert T. Silliman, Dir.
Founded: 1923. **Staff:** Prof 2; Other 2. **Subjects:** Genealogy, local history, biography. **Special Collections:** Account books; history and genealogy of 17th century founding families; history of 20 daughter towns which were once part of Windsor. **Holdings:** 3500 books; bound Windsor periodicals; 3000 school books, almanacs, early photographs, lantern slides concerning Windsor and its people, and other cataloged items. **Services:** Copying; library open to the public for reference use only. **Publications:** Newsletter, bimonthly. **Staff:** Connie Thomas.

Windsor Public Library - Francois Baby House: Windsor's Community Museum
See: **Francois Baby House: Windsor's Community Museum** (1397)

★ 20478 ★
Windsor Public Library - Special Collections (Hist)
850 Ouellette Ave.   Phone: (519)255-6770
Windsor, ON, Canada N9A 4M9   Marilyn Scasa, Mgr., Main Lib.
Staff: 113.5. **Subjects:** Windsor local history, automotive history. **Special Collections:** Windsor Municipal Archives (1205 linear feet of cataloged records; 1117 cataloged plans and maps; 752 linear feet uncataloged items); local history collection (2000 books, scrapbooks, pamphlets, oral history cassettes, microforms); government documents depository for Windsor, Ontario, and Canada. **Services:** Interlibrary loan; copying; collection open to the public. **Automated Operations:** Computerized public access catalog, acquisitions, and circulation. **Computerized Information Services:** DIALOG Information Services, Info Globe, WILSONLINE, CAN/OLE, Infomart Online, Financial Post Information Service. Performs searches free of charge. **Special Indexes:** Windsor Star Index; index to local French newspapers. **Remarks:** FAX: (519)255-7207. **Staff:** F.C. Israel, Dir., Windsor Pub.Lib.

★ 20479 ★
Windsor Star - Library (Publ)
167 Ferry St.   Phone: (519)255-5711
Windsor, ON, Canada N9A 4M5   Deborah J. Jessop, Chf.Libn.
Founded: 1935. **Staff:** Prof 1; Other 5. **Subjects:** Newspaper reference topics. **Holdings:** 500 books; one million clippings; 1.5 million pictures; 5000 maps; 3 VF drawers of pamphlets; 24 drawers of microfilm of Windsor Star, 1893 to present; 200 other cataloged items. **Subscriptions:** 24 journals and other serials. **Services:** Copying; library open to the public with restrictions. **Computerized Information Services:** Infomart Online, Info Globe, DataTimes, Dow Jones News/Retrieval. **Remarks:** FAX: (519)255-5515.

★ 20480 ★
Wine Institute - Library (Food-Bev)
425 Market St., Suite 1000   Phone: (415)512-0151
San Francisco, CA 94105   Pat McKelvey, Libn.
Founded: 1934. **Staff:** Prof 1. **Subjects:** Wine and winemaking, viticulture. **Special Collections:** California wine industry clippings and brochures spanning 50 years; wine labels; ephemera. **Holdings:** 3000 volumes. **Subscriptions:** 200 journals and other serials. **Services:** Library to members and select others by appointment only. **Remarks:** FAX: (415)442-0742.

★ 20481 ★
Winebrenner Theological Seminary - Library (Rel-Phil)
701 E. Melrose Ave.
Box 478   Phone: (419)422-4824
Findlay, OH 45839-0478   Bur Shilling, Dir., Lib.Serv.
Founded: 1942. **Staff:** Prof 1; Other 2. **Subjects:** Church history, Old and New Testament, contemporary theology, homiletics, Christian education and practical theology, Christian ministries. **Special Collections:** Churches of God old and rare books; Churches of God history; John Winebrenner materials. **Holdings:** 35,388 books; 1803 bound periodical volumes; 398 other cataloged items; 8 VF of pamphlets. **Subscriptions:** 156 journals and other serials. **Services:** Interlibrary loan; copying; library open to the public. **Automated Operations:** Computerized cataloging. **Computerized Information Services:** OCLC. **Staff:** Linda Ewing, Cat.

★ 20482 ★
Winedale Historical Center - Library (Hist)
Box 11   Phone: (409)278-3530
Round Top, TX 78954   Gloria Jaster, Adm.
Founded: 1967. **Staff:** 3. **Subjects:** Historic sites, furniture, decorative arts, agriculture. **Holdings:** 835 books; 75 bound periodical volumes; 200 other cataloged items; historic preservation documentation. **Subscriptions:** 38 journals and other serials. **Services:** Interlibrary loan; copying; library open to the public for reference use only. **Publications:** Quid Nunc (newsletter), quarterly - to friends of Winedale, members, and museums. **Remarks:** Maintained by University of Texas, Austin. **Remarks:** FAX: (409)278-3531.

★ 20483 ★
Winfield State Hospital and Training Center - Professional Library (Med)
Winfield, KS 67156   Phone: (316)221-1200
Founded: 1962. **Staff:** Prof 1. **Subjects:** Mental retardation, psychology, medicine, social work and welfare, education and special education, nursing. **Holdings:** 2200 books; 189 bound periodical volumes; 259 AV programs; 476 unbound periodical volumes; 398 indexes and abstracts in volumes; 15 theses; 2500 pamphlets and clippings. **Subscriptions:** 56 journals and other serials. **Services:** Interlibrary loan; copying; library open to the public. **Networks/Consortia:** Member of National Network of Libraries of Medicine - Midcontinental Region.

★ 20484 ★
Winnebago County Law Library (Law)
Courthouse Bldg., Suite 306
400 W. State St.   Phone: (815)987-2514
Rockford, IL 61101-1221   Robert J. Lindvall, Law Libn.
Founded: 1975. **Staff:** Prof 1; Other 1. **Subjects:** General legal material; law - federal, Illinois, Wisconsin. **Holdings:** 17,000 volumes and microfiche. **Subscriptions:** 26 journals and other serials. **Services:** Interlibrary loan; copying; library open to the public. **Networks/Consortia:** Member of Northern Illinois Library System (NILS).

★ 20485 ★

Winnebago Mental Health Institute - Medical Library (Med)
Box 9   Phone: (414)235-4910
Winnebago, WI 54985-0009   Mary Kotschi, Dir. of Lib.Serv.
Founded: 1873. **Staff:** Prof 2; Other 1. **Subjects:** Psychiatry, psychology, social service, counseling, hospital administration, nursing, sociology. **Holdings:** 6500 volumes; 8 VF drawers of pamphlets; 585 cassette tapes; 15 videotapes. **Subscriptions:** 183 journals and other serials. **Services:** Interlibrary loan; copying; library open to the public. **Computerized Information Services:** MEDLINE. **Networks/Consortia:** Member of Fox River Valley Area Library Consortium (FRVALC), Fox Valley Library Council.

★ 20486 ★

Winnepeg Gay/Lesbian Resource Centre - Library & Archives (Soc Sci)
1 - 222 Osborne St., S.   Phone: (204)474-0212
Winnipeg, MB, Canada R3L 1Z3   Kenneth Steffenson, Dir.
Founded: 1973. **Staff:** Prof 3; Other 4. **Subjects:** Homosexuality, lesbianism, gay liberation, gay-related issues, sexuality, sexual minorities. **Special Collections:** Manitoba Gay and Lesbian Archives (30 meters of files). **Holdings:** 3200 books; 45 VF drawers of correspondence, reports, news clippings; 160 audiotapes; 150 videotapes. **Subscriptions:** 10 journals and other serials; 35 newspapers. **Services:** Interlibrary loan; copying; library open to the public. **Automated Operations:** Computerized cataloging. **Special Catalogs:** Catalog of book and reference file collections (card). **Special Indexes:** Classification index to Reference File Collection (book); Register of Archives (book and online). **Remarks:** FAX: (204)478-1160. **Staff:** Chris Vogel, Dir., Coll.Dev.; Dr. A.E. Millward, Libn.

★ 20487 ★

Winnipeg Art Gallery - Clara Lander Library (Art)
300 Memorial Blvd.
Winnipeg, MB, Canada R3C 1V1   Phone: (204)786-6641
Founded: 1912. **Staff:** Prof 1. **Subjects:** History of art and painting, drawing, sculpture, ceramics, prints, architecture, antiques and photography. **Special Collections:** Canadiana; Inuit art. **Holdings:** 22,000 books; 720 bound periodical volumes; 8500 exhibition catalogs; 844 reports; 800 vertical files; 7000 folders of biographies of artists; 136 binders of archives. **Subscriptions:** 40 journals and other serials. **Services:** Copying; library open to the public for reference use only. **Automated Operations:** Computerized public access catalog. **Special Catalogs:** Exhibition catalogs. **Remarks:** FAX: (204)788-4998. **Staff:** Tamara L. Opar, Libn.

Winnipeg Bible College - Reimer Library
See: **Providence College & Seminary - Library** (13443)

★ 20488 ★

Winnipeg Clinic - Library (Med)
425 St. Mary Ave.   Phone: (204)957-1900
Winnipeg, MB, Canada R3C 0N2   S. Loeppky, Libn.
Staff: Prof 1. **Subjects:** Medicine. **Holdings:** Figures not available. **Subscriptions:** 78 journals and other serials. **Services:** Interlibrary loan; copying; library open to the public with restrictions. **Remarks:** FAX: (204)943-2164.

★ 20489 ★

Winnipeg Free Press - Library (Publ)
1355 Mountain Ave.   Phone: (204)697-7289
Winnipeg, MB, Canada R2X 3B6   Mrs. J. Williamson, Libn.
Founded: 1923. **Staff:** 5. **Subjects:** Newspaper reference topics. **Special Collections:** Selected Canadian and Manitoba government documents. **Holdings:** 6800 volumes. **Subscriptions:** 86 journals and other serials. **Services:** Interlibrary loan; library not open to the public. **Remarks:** FAX: (204)607-7412.

★ 20490 ★

(Winnipeg) Health Sciences Centre - Library Services (Med)
NA110-700 McDermot Ave.   Phone: (204)787-3416
Winnipeg, MB, Canada R3E 0T2   Rilla Edwards, Act.Dir., Educ.Rsrcs.
Founded: 1981. **Staff:** Prof 1; Other 7. **Subjects:** Medicine, surgery, pediatrics, nursing, allied health sciences, hospital administration. **Holdings:** 5344 books; 4893 bound periodical volumes; 725 videotapes; 90 slidetape titles; 16 audiotapes. **Subscriptions:** 463 journals and other serials. **Services:** Interlibrary loan; copying; SDI; services open to the public with restrictions. **Computerized Information Services:** MEDLARS; Envoy 100 (electronic mail service). **Networks/Consortia:** Member of Manitoba Library Consortium, Inc. **Publications:** Library Limelight (newsletter), quarterly - for internal distribution only. **Remarks:** FAX: (204)787-2765. Electronic mail address(es): ILLMWHS (Envoy 100).

★ 20491 ★

Winnipeg School Division No. 1 - Prince Charles Education Resource Centre - Library Media Services (Educ)
1075 Wellington Ave.   Phone: (204)788-0203
Winnipeg, MB, Canada R3E 0J7   Gerald R. Brown, Chf.Libn.
Founded: 1964. **Staff:** Prof 3; Other 27. **Subjects:** Education and audiovisual education, library science, Canadiana, Manitobana. **Special Collections:** Historical curriculum texts. **Holdings:** 27,521 books; 926 bound periodical volumes; 4401 AV programs; 27 VF drawers; 261 reels of microfilm; 2086 16mm film titles; 653 videotape titles. **Subscriptions:** 326 journals and other serials. **Services:** Interlibrary loan; copying; consultant services; center open to the public with restrictions. **Publications:** Newsletter, monthly. **Special Catalogs:** 16mm Film Catalog; Microcomputer Software Catalog. **Remarks:** FAX: (204)772-3911. **Staff:** Mary Green, Hd., Tech.Serv.; Corinne Tellier, Ref.Libn.

★ 20492 ★

Winona Memorial Hospital - Health Sciences Library (Med)
3232 N. Meridian   Phone: (317)927-2248
Indianapolis, IN 46208   Susan Kent, Med.Libn.
Founded: 1971. **Staff:** Prof 1. **Subjects:** Medicine, nursing, hospital administration, allied health sciences. **Holdings:** 1000 books; 600 bound periodical volumes. **Subscriptions:** 75 journals and other serials. **Services:** Interlibrary loan; library not open to the public. **Computerized Information Services:** NLM, BRS Information Technologies. **Networks/Consortia:** Member of Central Indiana Health Science Library Consortium, Central Indiana Area Library Services Authority (CIALSA), National Network of Libraries of Medicine - Greater Midwest Region, INCOLSA. **Remarks:** FAX: (317)927-2241.

★ 20493 ★

Winrock International Institute for Agricultural Development - Library (Agri)
Rte. 3, Box 376   Phone: (501)727-5435
Morrilton, AR 72110   Joan Newton, Libn.
Staff: 2. **Subjects:** Agriculture - education, policy, general; crops/seeds; cropping and farming systems; forestry and agroforestry; irrigation; ruminant livestock; rural development; sustainable agriculture; range management. **Holdings:** 15,000 books; 200 reports on microfiche; 2000 government documents; 10,000 slides; 12 VF drawers of miscellaneous material. **Subscriptions:** 416 journals and other serials; 25 newspapers. **Services:** Interlibrary loan; library open to the public for reference use only. **Computerized Information Services:** Online systems; Dialcom, Inc. (electronic mail service). **Remarks:** FAX: (501)727-5242. Telex: 910 720 6616 WI HQ UD. Electronic mail address(es): 41:TCN400 (Dialcom, Inc.). **Formed by the merger of:** Winrock International, Agricultural Development Council, and International Agricultural Development Service.

Winslow Library
See: **Meadville Medical Center** (9969)

Winspear Business Reference Room
See: **University of Alberta - Humanities and Social Sciences Library - Winspear Business Reference Room** (18198)

★ 20494 ★

Winston-Salem Foundation - Foundation Center Regional Library (Soc Sci)
310 W. 4th St., Suite 229   Phone: (919)725-2382
Winston-Salem, NC 27101-2889   Carolyn McBride, Libn.
Subjects: Foundations. **Special Collections:** North Carolina Foundation IRS Returns. **Holdings:** 35 volumes; 250 annual reports; source book profiles. **Services:** Copying; library open to the public. **Remarks:** FAX: (919)727-0581. **Also Known As:** Donors Forum of Forsyth County.

★ 20495 ★

Winston-Salem Journal - Reference Department (Publ)
418 N. Marshall   Phone: (919)727-7275
Winston-Salem, NC 27102   Marilyn H. Rollins, Ref.Dept.Mgr.
Founded: 1947. **Staff:** Prof 3; Other 4. **Subjects:** Newspaper reference topics. **Holdings:** 1400 books; 50 bound periodical volumes; 3000 pamphlets; 2.5 million newspaper clippings; 370,000 photographs; 1933 reels of microfilm of newspapers; 6 VF drawers of reports. **Subscriptions:** 70 journals and other serials; 53 newspapers. **Services:** Copying; department open to students for academic research by appointment. **Remarks:** Published by Piedmont Publishing Company.

★ 20496 ★
Winston-Salem State University - C.G. O'Kelly Library - Special Collections (Educ)
Winston-Salem, NC 27110
Phone: (919)750-2440
Vicki S. Miller, Ref.Libn.
Founded: 1922. **Special Collections:** Curriculum Materials Center Collection (30,000 items); School of Nursing Library (5000 items). **Services:** Interlibrary loan; copying; collections open to the public with restrictions. **Automated Operations:** Computerized public access catalog, cataloging, acquisitions, serials, and circulation. **Computerized Information Services:** DIALOG Information Services; internal database. Performs searches on fee basis. **Networks/Consortia:** Member of SOLINET. **Remarks:** FAX: (919)750-2459. **Staff:** Boon T. Lee, Acq.Libn.; Mae L. Rodney, Dir., Lib.Serv.; Mary Davis, Cat.Libn.; Michael Hicks, Automation Libn.

★ 20497 ★
Winston & Strawn - Library (Law)
2550 M St., N.W., Suite 500
Phone: (202)371-5843
Washington, DC 20037
Deborah M. Miller, Libn.
Founded: 1970. **Staff:** Prof 1; Other 4. **Subjects:** Law. **Holdings:** 10,000 books; loose-leaf services. **Subscriptions:** 85 journals and other serials; 5 newspapers. **Services:** Interlibrary loan; library not open to the public. **Automated Operations:** Computerized cataloging. **Computerized Information Services:** DIALOG Information Services, OCLC, LEXIS, NEXIS, WESTLAW. **Networks/Consortia:** Member of ILLINET. **Remarks:** FAX: (202)371-5950.

★ 20498 ★
Winston & Strawn - Library (Law)
35 W. Wacker Dr.
Phone: (312)558-5813
Chicago, IL 60601
Yve Griffith, Mgr., Lib. & Info.Serv.
Founded: 1857. **Staff:** Prof 4; Other 5. **Subjects:** Law - securities, antitrust, corporate, tax, labor, real estate, intellectual property. **Holdings:** 30,000 volumes; 10 boxes of ultrafiche; 1 drawer of microfiche; 60 reels of microfilm. **Subscriptions:** 250 journals and other serials. **Services:** Interlibrary loan; library open to lawyers and other professionals for reference use only. **Automated Operations:** Computerized cataloging. **Computerized Information Services:** WESTLAW, Dow Jones News/Retrieval, LEXIS, DIALOG Information Services, VU/TEXT Information Services, OCLC, DataTimes, LEGI-SLATE, Information America; internal database. **Networks/Consortia:** Member of Chicago Library System, ILLINET. **Remarks:** FAX: (312)558-5700.

★ 20499 ★
Winter Haven Hospital - J.G. Converse Memorial Medical Library (Med)
200 Ave. F., N.E.
Phone: (813)293-1121
Winter Haven, FL 33881
Henry Hasse, Media Mgr.
Founded: 1957. **Staff:** Prof 2. **Subjects:** Medicine, nursing, allied health sciences, community mental health. **Holdings:** 835 books; 1300 bound periodical volumes; 500 videocassettes. **Subscriptions:** 110 journals and other serials. **Services:** Interlibrary loan; copying; library open to the public for reference use only. **Computerized Information Services:** MEDLARS. Performs searches on fee basis. Contact Person: Kathryn Bielawa, Med.Libn.

★ 20500 ★
Winter Park Memorial Hospital - Medical Library (Med)
200 N. Lakemont Ave.
Phone: (407)646-7049
Winter Park, FL 32792
Patricia N. Cole, Med.Libn.
Staff: Prof 1; Other 2. **Subjects:** Medicine, surgery, nursing. **Holdings:** 2850 books; 9488 bound periodical volumes; 150 feet of unbound periodicals; 1450 tapes; 1 VF cabinet of pamphlets. **Subscriptions:** 250 journals and other serials. **Services:** Interlibrary loan; copying; library open to the public for reference use only with permission of administration. **Computerized Information Services:** MEDLARS. **Publications:** Report to Chairman of Library Committee, quarterly; New Acquisitions List, monthly - both for internal distribution only; bibliographies - to hospital staff. **Remarks:** FAX: (407)646-7990.

★ 20501 ★
Steven Winter Associates - Library (Plan)
50 Washington St.
Norwalk, CT 06854
Phone: (203)852-0110
Subjects: Housing technology, energy conservation, engineering, construction technology. **Holdings:** Figures not available.

William Winter Marine Library
See: College of Insurance - Insurance Society of New York - Kathryn and Shelby Cullom Davis Library (3897)

★ 20502 ★
Winters Group - Information Center (Bus-Fin)
14 Franklin St., Suite 920
Phone: (716)546-7480
Rochester, NY 14604
Marie Morsheimer, Res.Anl.
Founded: 1984. **Staff:** Prof 1; Other 1. **Subjects:** Corporations, industries, new products, health care, banking, high technology, social services, minority issues. **Holdings:** 50 books. **Subscriptions:** 50 journals and other serials; 10 newspapers. **Services:** Center not open to the public. **Computerized Information Services:** DIALOG Information Services; internal database. **Publications:** Information Advisor, monthly. **Remarks:** Company performs primary and secondary market research.

★ 20503 ★
Winterthur Library (Art, Hist)
Winterthur, DE 19735
Phone: (302)888-4701
Dr. Katharine Martinez, Dir.
Founded: 1951. **Staff:** Prof 8; Other 6. **Subjects:** Art - American, British, European, with emphasis on decorative arts; cultural history. **Special Collections:** Waldron P. Belknap Research Library of American Painting; E.D. Andrews Memorial Shaker Collection; Maxine Waldron Collection of Children's Literature and Toys. **Holdings:** 74,469 volumes; 100,000 manuscripts; 146,000 photographs; 138,231 slides; 12,602 microforms; 2347 linear feet of archival material. **Subscriptions:** 305 journals and other serials. **Services:** Interlibrary loan; copying; library open to the public. **Automated Operations:** Computerized cataloging. **Computerized Information Services:** RLIN; BITNET (electronic mail service). **Publications:** American Cornucopia: Treasures from the Winterthur Library, 1990. **Special Catalogs:** Collection of Printed Books; E.D. Andrews Memorial Shaker Collection; Trade Catalogues at Winterthur. **Remarks:** FAX: (302)888-4870. Electronic mail address(es): BM.WIC@RLG (BITNET). **Staff:** Eleanor M. Thompson, Libn., Print Bk.; E. Richard McKinstry, Libn., Mss. & Print Ephemera; Dr. Paul Hensley, Asst.Dir./Archv.; Maria Fredericks, Assoc.Cons. for Lib.Coll.; Bert Denker, Libn./Vis.Rsrcs.

Winterthur Swiss Insurance Co. - Citadel Assurance
See: Citadel Assurance (3718)

★ 20504 ★
Winthrop, Stimson, Putnam and Roberts - Library (Law)
1 Battery Park Plaza
Phone: (212)858-1675
New York, NY 10004-1490
Nancy J. Haab, Hd.Libn.
Founded: 1948. **Staff:** Prof 4; Other 6. **Subjects:** Law. **Holdings:** 35,000 volumes. **Subscriptions:** 125 journals and other serials. **Services:** Interlibrary loan; library not open to the public. **Remarks:** FAX: (212)858-1500. **Staff:** Paul E. Mitchell, Asst.Libn.; Sonja McDaniel, Cat.

★ 20505 ★
Winthrop-University Hospital - Hollis Health Sciences Library (Med)
259 1st St.
Phone: (516)663-2280
Mineola, NY 11501
Virginia I. Cook, Med.Libn.
Staff: Prof 2; Other 5. **Subjects:** Medicine, surgery, nursing, allied health sciences. **Holdings:** 3800 books; 8800 bound periodical volumes; 515 AV programs; 150 computer-assisted instruction programs; audiotapes; pamphlets. **Subscriptions:** 425 journals and other serials. **Services:** Interlibrary loan; library not open to the public. **Automated Operations:** Computerized ILL (DOCLINE). **Computerized Information Services:** MEDLARS, BRS Information Technologies, BRS/COLLEAGUE, OCLC; CD-ROMs (MEDLINE, CINAHL-CD). **Networks/Consortia:** Member of Medical Library Center of New York (MLCNY), Medical & Scientific Libraries of Long Island (MEDLI). **Publications:** Newsletter, quarterly; acquisition list, quarterly. **Remarks:** FAX: (516)741-9535. **Staff:** Kathy Kwan, Media/Sys.Libn.

Winton Hill Technical Center
See: **Procter & Gamble Company** (13400)

★ 20506 ★
Wire Association International - Technical Information Center (Sci-Engr)
Box H
1570 Boston Post Rd.   Phone: (203)453-2777
Guilford, CT 06437   Phyllis Conon, Tech.Info.Coord.
Founded: 1926. **Staff:** 1. **Subjects:** Wire technology; metallurgy; engineering - electrical, nonferrous, ferrous; fiber optics; fasteners. **Special Collections:** Complete run of Wire Journal (indexed, abstracted); complete run of Wire and Wire Products (48 volumes; indexed, abstracted); Fastener Age. **Holdings:** 600 books; 80 bound periodical volumes. **Services:** Interlibrary loan; copying; center open to the public at director's discretion. **Publications:** Wire Association Conference Proceedings, annual; meeting proceedings; Technical Reports, irregular; technical handbooks and correspondence courses. **Special Indexes:** Wire Index (hardcopy of internal database holdings), updated annually. **Remarks:** FAX: (203)453-8384.

Wirtanen Library
See: **Quincy Historical Society** (13668)

Wisconsin Architectural Archive
See: **Milwaukee Public Library** (10430)

Wisconsin Area Research Center Archives
See: **University of Wisconsin--Oshkosh - University Libraries and Learning Resources - Special Collections** (19643)

Wisconsin Center for Film and Theater Research
See: **University of Wisconsin--Madison - Wisconsin Center for Film and Theater Research** (19627)

★ 20507 ★
Wisconsin Conservatory of Music - Library (Mus)
1584 N. Prospect Ave.   Phone: (414)276-5760
Milwaukee, WI 53202-2394   Raymond Lynn Mueller, Dir.
Founded: 1968. **Staff:** Prof 1. **Subjects:** Music. **Holdings:** 26,000 books and scores; 8225 sound recordings. **Subscriptions:** 10 journals and other serials. **Services:** Interlibrary loan; copying; library open to the public for reference use only. **Publications:** Facsimile reprint of 12 Landler for Two Guitars, Opus 55, by Mauro Giuliani.

★ 20508 ★
Wisconsin Electric Power Company - Library (Sci-Engr)
231 W. Michigan St., Rm. P219   Phone: (414)221-2580
Milwaukee, WI 53203   Mary Ann Barragry, Libn.
Founded: 1974. **Staff:** Prof 1; Other 2. **Subjects:** Electric utility industry - power plants, mechanical and nuclear engineering, nuclear power, business and management. **Holdings:** 10,000 books; 300 bound periodical volumes; 10,000 reports; 25 drawers of newsletters; 1500 cases of unbound periodicals. **Subscriptions:** 600 journals and other serials. **Services:** Interlibrary loan; copying; SDI; library open to the public with restrictions (LCOMM Infopass required). **Automated Operations:** Computerized cataloging, acquisitions, and serials. **Computerized Information Services:** DIALOG Information Services, DataTimes, Utility Information Databases. **Networks/Consortia:** Member of Library Council of Metropolitan Milwaukee, Inc. (LCOMM). **Remarks:** FAX: (414)221-2282.

★ 20509 ★
Wisconsin Gas Company - Corporate and Law Library (Energy)
626 E. Wisconsin Ave.   Phone: (414)291-6666
Milwaukee, WI 53202   Linda J. Nordstrom, Supv., Info.Rsrcs.
Founded: 1930. **Staff:** Prof 2; Other 1. **Subjects:** Natural gas, public utility regulation and law, engineering, gas industries, corporation law, energy statistics. **Holdings:** 2900 books; 15 VF drawers of pamphlets. **Subscriptions:** 300 journals and other serials. **Services:** Interlibrary loan; SDI; library open to the public by appointment. **Automated Operations:** Computerized cataloging. **Computerized Information Services:** DIALOG Information Services, VU/TEXT Information Services, A.G.A. GasNet, WILSONLINE, InvesText; Wisconsin Economic Indicators/Milwaukee Economic Indicators (internal databases); A.G.A. GasNet (electronic mail service). **Networks/Consortia:** Member of Library Council of Metropolitan Milwaukee, Inc. (LCOMM), American Gas Association - Library Services (AGA-LSC). **Publications:** Information Resource Update, irregular. **Remarks:** FAX: (414)291-6672. **Staff:** Patricia Jankowski, Coord., Info.Rsrcs.

★ 20510 ★
Wisconsin Hospital Association - Memorial Library (Med)
5721 Odana Rd.   Phone: (608)274-1820
Madison, WI 53719   Marilyn Johnson, Libn.
Staff: Prof 1. **Subjects:** Health care, hospital administration, health careers, health insurance, hospital law and regulation. **Special Collections:** Archive. **Holdings:** 2100 books. **Subscriptions:** 90 journals and other serials. **Services:** Interlibrary loan; copying; library open to the public for reference use only. **Networks/Consortia:** Member of South Central Wisconsin Health Science Libraries Consortium, South Central Library System. **Remarks:** FAX: (608)274-8554.

★ 20511 ★
Wisconsin Indianhead Technical College, New Richmond Campus - Learning Resource Center (Sci-Engr)
1019 S. Knowles Ave.   Phone: (715)246-6561
New Richmond, WI 54017   Valerie Peltier, Reg.Techn.
Founded: 1969. **Staff:** 2. **Subjects:** Agriculture, business, general education, health occupations, home economics, trade and industry. **Special Collections:** Curriculum Library (1300 volumes; 350 AV programs). **Holdings:** 5980 books; 2300 AV programs. **Subscriptions:** 160 journals and other serials; 16 newspapers. **Services:** Interlibrary loan; center open to the public. **Remarks:** FAX: (715)246-2777. **Also Known As:** Indianhead Technical College; WITC - New Richmond.

★ 20512 ★
Wisconsin Indianhead Technical College, Superior Campus - Library (Educ)
600 N. 21st St.   Phone: (715)394-6677
Superior, WI 54880   Donald Rantala, LRC Spec.
Founded: 1965. **Staff:** Prof 1; Other 2. **Subjects:** Nursing, electronics, business, data processing, marketing and advertising. **Holdings:** 10,000 books; 1500 pamphlets; 50 maps; theses; microfilm; slides; cassettes. **Subscriptions:** 170 journals and other serials; 25 newspapers. **Services:** Copying; library open to the public with restrictions.

Wisconsin Information Service
See: **First Call For Help - Milwaukee** (5754)

★ 20513 ★
Wisconsin Lutheran Seminary - Library (Rel-Phil)
6633 W. Wartburg Circle   Phone: (414)242-7209
Mequon, WI 53092   Rev. Martin O. Westerhaus, Libn.
Founded: 1863. **Staff:** Prof 2; Other 1.5. **Subjects:** Theology - biblical, systematic, practical; church history. **Holdings:** 40,000 books; 2497 bound periodical volumes; 800 other cataloged items. **Subscriptions:** 308 journals and other serials; 5 newspapers. **Services:** Interlibrary loan; copying; library open to the public with restrictions. **Networks/Consortia:** Member of Library Council of Metropolitan Milwaukee, Inc. (LCOMM), Southeastern Wisconsin Information Technology Exchange (SWITCH). **Special Indexes:** Index to Wisconsin Lutheran Quarterly (card). **Remarks:** FAX: (414)242-7255. **Staff:** Rev. Robert M. Oswald, Tech.Serv.Dir.

Wisconsin Music Archives
See: **University of Wisconsin--Madison - Mills Music Library** (19610)

Wisconsin Regional Primate Research Center
See: **University of Wisconsin--Madison** (19628)

★ 20514 ★
Wisconsin School for the Deaf - Evelyn & John R. Gant Library (Educ)
309 W. Walworth Ave.   Phone: (414)728-6477
Delavan, WI 53115   Betty E. Watkins, Libn.
Founded: 1852. **Staff:** Prof 1. **Subjects:** Books of high interest-low vocabulary, professional library, K-12 general collection. **Special Collections:** Education of the deaf; captioned films for the deaf (1100). **Holdings:** 6000 books; 1700 filmstrips; 150 film loops; 500 microfiche; 16 drawers of transparencies. **Subscriptions:** 89 journals and other serials. **Services:** Interlibrary loan; copying; library open to the public with librarian's permission. **Publications:** Wisconsin Times, monthly - to patrons.

★ 20515 ★
Wisconsin (State) Department of Development - Library
123 W. Washington Ave.
Box 7970
Madison, WI 53707
Defunct.

★ 20516 ★
Wisconsin (State) Department of Employee Trust Funds - Library (Bus-Fin)
201 E. Washington Ave., Rm. 171
Box 7931   Phone: (608)266-7387
Madison, WI 53707   Chris Domann, Prog.Asst./Libn.
Staff: Prof 1. **Subjects:** Pensions, insurance, social security. **Special Collections:** Collections of historical materials on various state pension and retirement programs; pamphlets of other states' retirement systems; congressional and state legislative history on retirement bills (12 VF drawers). **Holdings:** 335 books; 5 VF drawers of clippings; 2000 manuscripts and documents. **Subscriptions:** 50 journals and other serials. **Services:** Interlibrary loan; copying; library open to the public. **Automated Operations:** Computerized cataloging and acquisitions. **Publications:** Library summary of new acquisitions, monthly; List of Departmental Publications; Title List of Periodical/Newsletter Holdings. **Remarks:** FAX: (414)267-4549.

★ 20517 ★
Wisconsin (State) Department of Health & Social Services - Library (Med, Soc Sci)
1 W. Wilson St., Rm. 630   Phone: (608)266-7473
Madison, WI 53702   Elisabeth R. Boehnen, Libn.
Staff: Prof 1; Other 1. **Subjects:** Public health and welfare, corrections, community services, mental health, vocational rehabilitation, children and family services. **Holdings:** 10,000 books; 275 periodical titles; pamphlet file. **Subscriptions:** 300 journals and other serials. **Services:** Interlibrary loan. **Automated Operations:** Computerized cataloging and ILL. **Computerized Information Services:** MEDLARS, BRS Information Technologies. Performs searches on fee basis. **Publications:** Acquisition list, monthly; journals and newsletter list. **Remarks:** FAX: (608)266-7882.

★ 20518 ★
Wisconsin (State) Department of Industry, Labor & Human Relations - Employment & Training Library (Bus-Fin)
201 E. Washington Ave.
Box 7944   Phone: (608)266-2832
Madison, WI 53707   Janet D. Pugh, Libn.
Staff: Prof 1; Other 1. **Subjects:** Labor, employment, demographics, Job Training Partnership Act (JTPA), employment and training programs. **Holdings:** 10,000 books; government documents. **Subscriptions:** 80 journals and other serials. **Services:** Interlibrary loan; library open to the public for reference use only. **Publications:** Inform (acquisition list), bimonthly - to interested persons; Labor Market Information: A Reference Guide and Directory of Wisconsin Publications. **Remarks:** FAX: (608)267-0330.

★ 20519 ★
Wisconsin (State) Department of Justice - Law Library (Law)
123 W. Washington, Rm. 349
Box 7857   Phone: (608)266-0325
Madison, WI 53707   Michael F. Bemis, Law Libn.
Founded: 1969. **Staff:** Prof 2; Other 1. **Subjects:** Wisconsin law, general law. **Special Collections:** Antitrust law; consumer protection; law enforcement and criminology; environmental protection. **Holdings:** 30,000 volumes; departmental and divisional publications. **Subscriptions:** 30 journals and other serials; 10 newspapers. **Services:** Library not open to the public, but arrangements may be made with librarian for use of materials. **Computerized Information Services:** LEXIS, NEXIS. **Publications:** Information bulletins, irregular - for internal distribution only. **Special Indexes:** Index to Digest of the Opinions of the Attorney General of Wisconsin, 1845-1972 and 1973 to present (book, with annual updates). **Remarks:** FAX: (608)267-2223. **Staff:** Sara Paul, Asst. Law Libn.

★ 20520 ★
Wisconsin (State) Department of Natural Resources - Bureau of Research - Technical Library (Env-Cons)
1350 Femrite Dr.   Phone: (608)221-6325
Monona, WI 53716-3736   Amy L. Kindschi, Libn.
Founded: 1964. **Staff:** Prof 2; Other 2. **Subjects:** Fish, wildlife, water resources. **Special Collections:** Fish (Dr. Schneberger, Lyle Christensen, Warren Churchill); Wildlife (Richard Hunt, Carroll D. Besadny). **Holdings:** 5000 books; 800 bound periodical volumes; unbound reports; archival materials; dissertations; documents; microfiche; reprints; bureau publications; maps. **Subscriptions:** 122 journals and other serials. **Services:** Interlibrary loan; copying; SDI; library open to the public for reference use only. **Automated Operations:** Computerized cataloging and ILL. **Computerized Information Services:** DIALOG Information Services; CD-ROM. **Networks/Consortia:** Member of Wisconsin Interlibrary Services (WILS). **Publications:** Acquisitions List, quarterly; Periodical Holdings, irregular - both for internal distribution only. **Remarks:** FAX: (608)275-3338. **Formerly:** Located in Fitchburg, WI. **Staff:** Suzanne du Vair, ILL Libn.

★ 20521 ★
Wisconsin (State) Department of Natural Resources - Library (Env-Cons)
Box 7921
Madison, WI 53707   Phone: (608)266-8933
Staff: Prof 1; Other 1. **Subjects:** Environmental protection, air pollution, solid waste and water quality management, natural resources, fish and wildlife. **Holdings:** 6500 books; 100 bound periodical volumes; 4500 other cataloged items. **Subscriptions:** 200 journals and other serials. **Services:** Interlibrary loan; library open to the public by appointment. **Automated Operations:** Computerized cataloging. **Computerized Information Services:** Chemical Information Systems, Inc. (CIS), DIALOG Information Services. **Networks/Consortia:** Member of Multitype Advisory Library Committee (MALC). **Publications:** Shelflife (acquisitions list), irregular. **Staff:** Glenna Carter, Asst.Libn.

★ 20522 ★
Wisconsin (State) Department of Natural Resources - MacKenzie Environmental Education Center (Env-Cons)
W7303 Hwy. CS   Phone: (608)635-4498
Poynette, WI 53955   Robert Wallen, Prog.Spec.
Founded: 1961. **Staff:** 1. **Subjects:** Natural resources, natural sciences, environment. **Special Collections:** Mounted birds and mammals (including 2 passenger pigeons). **Holdings:** 700 books; 12 VF drawers of pamphlets and clippings; 2500 color slides. **Subscriptions:** 5 journals and other serials. **Services:** Center open to the public with restrictions.

★ 20523 ★
Wisconsin (State) Department of Natural Resources - Southeast District Library (Env-Cons)
2300 N. Martin Luther King Jr. Dr.   Phone: (414)263-8493
Milwaukee, WI 53212   Kathleen Schultz, Libn.
Founded: 1979. **Staff:** Prof 1. **Subjects:** Pollution and quality of air and water, fish and wildlife, solid waste management, parks and recreation, forestry. **Special Collections:** Departmental publications (700 technical bulletins, research reports, surface water reports, fish management reports); Environmental Protection Agency documents (1200). **Holdings:** 2900 books; 116 bound periodical volumes. **Subscriptions:** 115 journals and other serials. **Services:** Interlibrary loan; copying; SDI; library open to the public for reference use only. **Remarks:** FAX: (414)263-8483.

Wisconsin (State) Department of Public Instruction - Division of Library Services - Cooperative Children's Book Center
See: **University of Wisconsin--Madison - Cooperative Children's Book Center (CCBC) (19590)**

★ 20524 ★
Wisconsin (State) Department of Public Instruction - Microcomputer Center/Library (Educ, Comp Sci)
125 S. Webster St., 3rd Fl.
Box 7841   Phone: (608)266-2529
Madison, WI 53707   Kay Ihlenfeldt, Libn.
Founded: 1968. **Staff:** Prof 2; Other 1. **Subjects:** Educational administration, handicapped children, curriculum development, public administration,

education and related social sciences, research, professional improvement, instructional materials, educational technology, library and information science. **Holdings:** 300 pamphlets; 300 journals; 4000 monographs; complete ERIC microfiche collection; microcomputer software packages; software reviews. **Subscriptions:** 350 journals and other serials. **Services:** Interlibrary loan; copying; computer demonstration center; library open to the public for reference use only. **Automated Operations:** Computerized cataloging. **Computerized Information Services:** DIALOG Information Services, BRS Information Technologies, LEXIS, NEXIS, WILSONLINE, VU/TEXT Information Services, GTE Education Network. Performs searches on fee basis. **Networks/Consortia:** Member of Multitype Advisory Library Committee (MALC). **Publications:** New Acquisitions, monthly; brochure and request form - on request; subject bibliographies. **Remarks:** FAX: (608)267-1052. **Staff:** Mary Fix, Instr. Software Spec.

★ 20525 ★

Wisconsin (State) Department of Public Instruction - School for the Visually Handicapped - Library (Aud-Vis)
1700 W. State St.   Phone: (608)755-2967
Janesville, WI 53546   Jean Wolski, Libn.
Founded: 1850. **Staff:** Prof 1. **Subjects:** General collection. **Holdings:** 3000 print books; 280 tactile items; 3000 braille books; 5000 talking books; 3000 cassette books. **Subscriptions:** 60 journals and other serials. **Services:** Library services restricted to the visually handicapped and educators serving the visually impaired.

★ 20526 ★

Wisconsin (State) Department of Transportation - Library (Trans)
4802 Sheboygan Ave., Rm. 901
Box 7913   Phone: (608)266-0724
Madison, WI 53707   Debra L. Sommi, Libn.
Founded: 1961. **Staff:** Prof 1; Other 1. **Subjects:** Transportation planning, highways, urban transit, Wisconsin urban planning, transportation economics. **Special Collections:** Transportation (Highway) Research Board. **Holdings:** 4300 books; 200 unbound periodical volumes; 9500 reports; 300 pamphlets. **Subscriptions:** 300 journals and other serials. **Services:** Interlibrary loan; copying; library open to the public. **Computerized Information Services:** DIALOG Information Services, LEXIS, NEXIS, American Association of State Highway & Transportation Officals (AASHTO) Electronic Information Service, OCLC. **Networks/Consortia:** Member of Wisconsin Interlibrary Services (WILS), South Central Library System. **Publications:** Recent Acquisitions, bimonthly - to Department of Transportation staff and others upon request. **Remarks:** FAX: (608)267-0294.

★ 20527 ★

Wisconsin (State) Division for Library Services - Reference and Loan Library (Info Sci)
2109 S. Stoughton Rd.   Phone: (608)221-6161
Madison, WI 53716   Sally J. Drew, Dir.
Founded: 1895. **Staff:** Prof 10.75; Other 15.5. **Subjects:** Biography, geography, religion, education, political science, music, recreation, library science, science and technology, crafts, collectibles, computing, consumer level law and medicine, automobile and appliance repair. **Holdings:** 159,000 volumes; 15,000 phonograph records in English and other languages; 1269 compact discs; 5500 reels of microfilm of periodicals; 22,300 Wisconsin documents; 1050 mixed media kits; 9700 audiotapes; 101 16mm films; 4000 videocassettes; 2600 pamphlets; 174 video discs; Media Resources for Continuing Library Education and Staff Development. **Subscriptions:** 700 journals and other serials. **Services:** Interlibrary loan; copying; library is the state resource center for public and school libraries; other resource center libraries are searched for needed material to which requests are then referred. **Automated Operations:** Computerized cataloging, serials, and acquisitions. **Computerized Information Services:** BRS Information Technologies, WILSONLINE, DIALOG Information Services, OCLC, LEXIS, NEXIS, DataTimes; CD-ROM (WISCAT (Wisconsin Statewide Database)). **Networks/Consortia:** Member of Wisconsin Interlibrary Services (WILS). **Publications:** Manual for Interlibrary Loan Service; selected lists of holdings. **Remarks:** FAX: (608)221-6178. **Staff:** Janice Lang, Tech.Serv.Supv.; Mary Clark, Rsrc. Sharing Tech.Supv.; Mary Struckmeyer, Ref. & ILL Supv.; Willeen Tretheway, AV Libn.

★ 20528 ★

Wisconsin State Journal/Capital Times - Library (Publ)
Box 8058   Phone: (608)252-6112
Madison, WI 53708   Ronald J. Larson, Hd.Libn.
Staff: Prof 2; Other 2. **Subjects:** Newspaper reference topics, local news and history, state news, state government, University of Wisconsin news. **Special Collections:** Joseph McCarthy; Frank Lloyd Wright. **Holdings:** 500 books; newspaper clippings; photographs; Wisconsin State Journal, 1852 to present, on microfilm; Capital Times, 1917 to present, on microfilm. **Subscriptions:** 50 journals and other serials; 10 newspapers. **Services:** Copying; library open to the public on a limited schedule. **Computerized Information Services:** NEXIS, VU/TEXT Information Services; Reference Directory (internal database). **Remarks:** FAX: (608)252-6445. **Staff:** Dennis McCormick, Asst.Libn.

Wisconsin State Law Library
See: **Wisconsin (State) Supreme Court** (20532)

★ 20529 ★

Wisconsin (State) Legislative Reference Bureau - Reference and Library Section (Soc Sci, Law)
100 N. Hamilton St.
P.O. Box 2037   Phone: (608)266-0341
Madison, WI 53701-2037   H. Rupert Theobald, Bureau Chf.
Founded: 1901. **Staff:** Prof 13; Other 7. **Subjects:** State government - public administration, taxation, finance, education, public welfare, labor, conservation, energy, pollution, public health, agriculture, economic development, motor vehicle regulation, highway finance and development, legislative procedure, courts, civil rights, civil service, federal and local governments. **Special Collections:** Wisconsin session laws, statutes, legislative journals, and Supreme Court reports, 1848 to present; Opinions of the Attorney General, 1904 to present; Blue Books, 1858 to present; bound volumes of legislative bills, 1897 to present; archival depository of departmental reports in separate collection of state documents; legislative bill drafting records, 1927 to present. **Holdings:** 100,000 volumes, including an extensive number of unbound and microfiche volumes of clippings. **Subscriptions:** 300 journals and other serials. **Services:** Interlibrary loan; copying; bureau open to the public. **Computerized Information Services:** LEXIS, NEXIS, LEGISNET; ATMS (bill histories), STAIRS (Wisconsin statutes; internal databases). **Publications:** Research Bulletins; Informational Bulletins; Wisconsin Briefs; Wisconsin Facts; Comparative Facts, all irregular; Wisconsin Blue Book, biennial. **Special Catalogs:** State Document Catalog. **Special Indexes:** Index to legislation introduced in the Wisconsin Legislature since 1897. **Remarks:** FAX: (608)266-5648. **Staff:** Lawrence S. Barish, Dir., Ref. & Lib.; Mina Waldie, Supv.Libn.; Rose Arnold, Libn.; Janet Monk, Libn.; Marian Rogers, Libn.; Peter Cannon, Res.Anl.; Patricia Meloy, Res.Anl.; Bette Arey, Res.Anl.; Clark Radatz, Res.Anl.; Richard Roe, Res.Anl.; Gary Watchke, Res.Anl.; Daniel Ritsche, Res.Anl.

★ 20530 ★

Wisconsin State Medical Society - Library (Med)
330 E. Lakeside St.
Box 1109   Phone: (608)257-6781
Madison, WI 53701   Russell King, Pubns.Mgr.
Staff: 5. **Subjects:** Medicine. **Holdings:** 125 volumes. **Subscriptions:** 158 journals and other serials. **Services:** Library not open to the public. **Publications:** Wisconsin Medical Journal, monthly - to members of the Wisconsin State Medical Society. **Remarks:** FAX: (608)283-5401.

★ 20531 ★

Wisconsin State Office of the Commissioner of Insurance - Library (Bus-Fin)
Box 7873   Phone: (608)266-3585
Madison, WI 53707   Beth Miller
Staff: Prof 1. **Subjects:** Insurance. **Special Collections:** Wisconsin Insurance Report, 1870-1989. **Holdings:** 1000 books; 1400 bound periodical volumes; 35 cubic feet of unbound periodicals. **Subscriptions:** 50 journals and other serials. **Services:** Library open to the public with restrictions. **Remarks:** Library located at 121 E. Wilson St., Madison, WI 53702. FAX: (608)266-9935.

★ 20532 ★
Wisconsin (State) Supreme Court - Wisconsin State Law Library (Law)
P.O. Box 7881   Phone: (608)266-1600
Madison, WI 53707-7881   Marcia J. Koslov, State Law Libn.
Founded: 1836. **Staff:** Prof 6; Other 7. **Subjects:** Law. **Special Collections:** Wisconsin Appendices & Briefs, 1836 to present; Wisconsin Court of Appeals Unpublished Opinions. **Holdings:** 140,000 volumes; 10,000 documents; 3600 reels of microfilm; 86,000 microfiche. **Subscriptions:** 675 journals and other serials. **Services:** Copying; library open to the public with restrictions on circulation. **Automated Operations:** Computerized public access catalog, acquisitions, serials, and circulation. **Computerized Information Services:** LEXIS, NEXIS, WESTLAW, DIALOG Information Services, OCLC. Performs searches for attorneys and judges on fee basis. **Remarks:** FAX: (608)267-2319. **Staff:** Dennis Austin, Court Serv.; M. Elaine Sharp, Tech.Serv.; Jane Colwin, Pub.Serv.; Jean Nock, Acq.; Betsy Wright, Ref.

★ 20533 ★
Wisconsin Taxpayers Alliance - Library (Soc Sci)
335 W. Wilson St.   Phone: (608)255-4581
Madison, WI 53703-3694   Beulah Poulter, Libn.
Founded: 1933. **Staff:** 1. **Subjects:** Wisconsin state and local government and taxation. **Holdings:** 600 books. **Subscriptions:** 25 journals and other serials; 4 newspapers. **Services:** Library open to the public with special permission.

★ 20534 ★
Wisconsin Veterans Museum - Archives and Library Division (Mil)
30 W. Mifflin St.   Phone: (608)266-1680
Madison, WI 53203   Dr. Richard Zeitlin, Dir.
Founded: 1901. **Special Collections:** Records of Grand Army of the Republic posts in Wisconsin, 1880-1949; records of the Women's Relief Corps, United Spanish War Veterans, 1883-1960; records of Wisconsin Civil War Regiments, including ledgers, muster rolls, diaries, post-Civil War accounts; records of World Wars I and II and the Vietnam era (total of 200 linear feet). **Holdings:** 6000 books; 15,000 bound periodical volumes. **Services:** Library open to researchers only. **Remarks:** Holdings are in storage until 1992; rare books accessible on a restricted basis. **Formerly:** Grand Army of the Republic Memorial Hall Museum - Archive and Library. **Staff:** Lynnette Wolfe, Coll.Mgr.

★ 20535 ★
Wise County Historical Society, Inc. - Wise County Historical Commission Archive (Hist)
1602 S. Trinity
Box 427   Phone: (817)627-3732
Decatur, TX 76234   Rosalie Gregg, Exec.Dir.
Founded: 1965. **Staff:** 2. **Subjects:** Wise County history, family histories, cemetery records, census. **Special Collections:** Lost Battalion Room (dedicated to members of the 131st Field Artillery and members of the armed forces of Australia, Great Britain, and Holland, who were prisoners of the Japanese for 42 months during World War II); Wise County Messenger and Decatur News (microfilm); Wise County, Tennessee, and Virginia census records; Civil War; Presidents; Texas Heritage Project; county histories. **Holdings:** Books; microfiche; Wise County birth, marriage, and death records. **Subscriptions:** 7 journals and other serials; 6 newspapers. **Services:** Copying; archive open to the public for reference use only; will answer mail inquiries (must enclose self-addressed, legal-sized stamped envelope). **Publications:** Newsletter, monthly. **Remarks:** Alternate telephone number(s): 627-5586.

★ 20536 ★
Isaac M. Wise Temple - Ralph Cohen Memorial Library (Rel-Phil)
8329 Ridge Rd.   Phone: (513)793-2556
Cincinnati, OH 45236   Judith S. Carsch, Libn.
Founded: 1931. **Staff:** Prof 1. **Subjects:** Judaica, Holocaust. **Holdings:** 16,500 books. **Subscriptions:** 23 journals and other serials. **Services:** Library open to the public with restrictions. **Remarks:** FAX: (513)793-3322

★ 20537 ★
Stephen Wise Free Synagogue - Edward Klein Memorial Library (Rel-Phil)
30 W. 68th St.   Phone: (212)877-4050
New York, NY 10023   Annette H. Landau, Dir.
Founded: 1988. **Staff:** Prof 1; Other 4. **Subjects:** Judaica. **Special Collections:** Synagogue archives (1917 to present); Stephen S. Wise Collection (personal letters, articles, books). **Holdings:** 4000 books; 184 volumes of archival materials. **Subscriptions:** 8 journals and other serials; 4 newspapers. **Services:** Interlibrary loan; copying; library open to the public for reference use only. **Automated Operations:** Computerized cataloging and circulation. **Remarks:** FAX: (212)787-7108. **Staff:** Denise Gluck, Archv.

Watson W. Wise Medical Research Library
See: University of Texas Health Science Center at Tyler - Watson W. Wise Medical Research Library (19418)

★ 20538 ★
William N. Wishard Memorial Hospital - Professional Library/Media Services (Med)
1001 W. 10th St.   Phone: (317)630-7028
Indianapolis, IN 46202   Kirsten Quam, Mgr., Lib./Media Serv.Dept.
Founded: 1940. **Staff:** Prof 2; Other 5. **Subjects:** Medicine, nursing, health care administration. **Holdings:** 3500 books; 600 bound periodical volumes; 2500 AV programs. **Subscriptions:** 110 journals and other serials. **Services:** Interlibrary loan; copying; current awareness service; library open to the public for reference use only. **Automated Operations:** Computerized cataloging and ILL (DOCLINE). **Computerized Information Services:** OCLC, DIALOG Information Services, BRS Information Technologies, NLM. **Networks/Consortia:** Member of Central Indiana Health Science Library Consortium, National Network of Libraries of Medicine - Greater Midwest Region, INCOLSA, Central Indiana Area Library Services Authority (CIALSA). **Remarks:** Alternate telephone number(s): 630-7657. **Staff:** Elaine Skopelja, Libn./Search Anl.; Janet Walls, AV Libn.

★ 20539 ★
Wiss, Janney, Elstner Associates, Inc. - Library (Sci-Engr)
330 Pfingsten Rd.   Phone: (708)272-7400
Northbrook, IL 60062   Harriette Bayer, Libn.
Staff: 1. **Subjects:** Engineering, materials, construction technology. **Holdings:** 6000 books. **Subscriptions:** 50 journals and other serials; 2 newspapers. **Services:** Interlibrary loan; copying; library open to the public by appointment. **Computerized Information Services:** OCLC. **Networks/Consortia:** Member of ILLINET. **Remarks:** FAX: (708)291-9599. Telex: 6713036.

Wisser Memorial Library
See: New York Institute of Technology (11584)

★ 20540 ★
Wistar Institute of Anatomy & Biology - Library (Med)
36th & Spruce Sts.   Phone: (215)898-3805
Philadelphia, PA 19104   J.A. Hunter, Libn.
Founded: 1894. **Staff:** Prof 1; Other 1. **Subjects:** Cancer, virus diseases, molecular immunology, molecular genetics, biochemistry. **Special Collections:** Personal library of General Isaac J. Wistar (including English and scientific classics, Americana, and history; 1000 volumes). **Holdings:** 3000 books; 10,000 bound periodical volumes. **Subscriptions:** 170 journals and other serials. **Services:** Interlibrary loan; library open to the public for reference use only. **Computerized Information Services:** NLM, BRS Information Technologies, DIALOG Information Services, PFDS Online, WILSONLINE, Data-Star, OMIM, Brosis Connection; CD-ROM (MEDLINE).

R.D. Wiswall Memorial Library
See: Vancouver Memorial Hospital (19756)

★ 20541 ★
Witches Anti-Discrimination Lobby - Library (Rel-Phil)
Hero Press
153 W. 80th St., Suite 1B   Phone: (212)362-1231
New York, NY 10024   Dr. Leo Louis Martello, Dir.
Subjects: Witchcraft as a religion, historic goddess-worshipping cultures. **Holdings:** 20,000 volumes. **Services:** Library not open to the public.

★ 20542 ★
Witco Chemical Corporation - Golden Bear Division - QC/R & D Library (Sci-Engr)
Ferguson & Manor Rds.
Box 5446   Phone: (805)393-7110
Oildale, CA 93388   Euthene Snell, Libn.
Founded: 1948. **Staff:** 2. **Subjects:** Petroleum refining, lubricants, asphalt pavements, rubber, emulsions, instrumental analyses. **Holdings:** 2200 books; 670 bound periodical volumes; 5 catalogs; 5 VF drawers of internal technical reports; preprints; reprints; instrumental scans; 5 VF drawers of patents, technical documents, product development information; 5 VF drawers of government and industry specifications, qualifications, and contracts. **Subscriptions:** 47 journals and other serials. **Services:** Copying; library open to the public by appointment. **Remarks:** FAX: (805)393-2083.

★ 20543 ★
Witco Corporation - Research & Development Library (Sci-Engr)
3200 Brookfield   Phone: (713)433-7281
Houston, TX 77045   Helen K. Kim, Libn.
Staff: Prof 1. **Subjects:** Chemistry and applied technology. **Holdings:** Books; bound periodical volumes; reprints; reports; technical abstracts. **Subscriptions:** 96 journals and other serials. **Services:** Interlibrary loan; library not open to the public. **Computerized Information Services:** PFDS Online, DIALOG Information Services, STN International. **Publications:** Current Notes, monthly - for internal distribution only; New Acquisitions, semiannual; Selected Subject Bibliographies, irregular; Library Information Bulletin. **Remarks:** FAX: (713)433-0209.

★ 20544 ★
Witco Corporation - Technical Information Center (Sci-Engr)
100 Bauer Dr.   Phone: (201)405-2343
Oakland, NJ 07436   Jo Therese Smith, Mgr., Tech.Info.Serv.
Founded: 1967. **Staff:** Prof 2. **Subjects:** Chemistry - organic, analytic, petroleum; chemical engineering. **Special Collections:** Petroleum technology; surfactant technology. **Holdings:** 14,000 books; 13,500 bound periodical volumes; 15 VF drawers of patents, pamphlets, reprints; 10 drawers of patents and journals on microfiche; Chemical Abstracts, 1917 to present. **Subscriptions:** 154 journals and other serials. **Services:** Interlibrary loan; SDI; center open to the public by appointment. **Computerized Information Services:** DIALOG Information Services, STN International, Chemical Abstracts Service (CAS). **Networks/Consortia:** Member of New Jersey Library Network. **Publications:** Current Holdings List; Articles of Current Interest. **Remarks:** FAX: (201)337-7278.

John Witherspoon Library
See: **Princeton University - Rare Books and Special Collections** (13386)

★ 20545 ★
Withlacoochee Regional Planning Council - Library (Plan)
1241 S.W. 10th St.   Phone: (904)732-1315
Ocala, FL 32674-2798   Vivian A. Whittier, Info.Spec.
Staff: Prof 1. **Subjects:** Statistics, planning, land use, water, energy, criminal justice, census data. **Holdings:** 5000 bound periodical volumes; maps; technical reports. **Subscriptions:** 19 journals and other serials. **Services:** Copying; library open to the public with restrictions on lending. **Publications:** Bulletin; Final Inspection Report, biannual. **Remarks:** Most library materials focus on Citrus, Hernando, Levy, Marion, and Sumter Counties. FAX: (904)732-1319.

B.E. Witkin Editorial Library
See: **Bancroft-Whitney Company** (1462)

Witt Library
See: **Cleveland Museum of Art - Ingalls Library** (3813)

Rabbi Louis Witt Memorial Library
See: **Temple Israel** (16114)

Witte Memorial Museum
See: **San Antonio Museum Association** (14669)

★ 20546 ★
Wittenberg University - Thomas Library (Rel-Phil)
P.O.Box 720   Phone: (513)327-7016
Springfield, OH 45501   John Montag, Dir.
Founded: 1845. **Staff:** Prof 7; Other 12. **Subjects:** Lutheran Church, Martin Luther, Reformation. **Special Collections:** Baltasar Gracian y Morales Collection; Wilhelm C. Berkenmeyer Colonial Parish Library (226 volumes); Susan V. Russell Tape Library (religious sermons); Archives, Ohio Synod Lutheran Church in America; University Archives; 19th century Ohio newspapers; Lutheran Reformation; Goldman Travel Collection (11,080 slides); Cyril F. DosPassos Collection of Lepidoptera (2500 volumes); diaries, papers, and etchings of Walter Tittle, American artist, 1883-1965; correspondence, manuscripts, and books of Dr. Martin C. Fischer, University of Cincinnati professor; Geiger Family papers, 1870-1910; hymnals (3700 volumes). **Holdings:** 340,974 books; 42,362 bound periodical volumes; 16,635 phonograph records; 44,130 AV programs; 35,000 volumes of Library of American Civilization and English Literature on microfiche; 5836 volumes on East Asia. **Subscriptions:** 1601 journals and other serials; 26 newspapers. **Services:** Interlibrary loan; copying; library open to the public. **Automated Operations:** Computerized cataloging. **Computerized Information Services:** DIALOG Information Services, Chemical Abstracts Service (CAS), OCLC. **Networks/Consortia:** Member of OHIONET, Southwestern Ohio Council for Higher Education (SOCHE). **Publications:** Library publications, irregular; selective accessions, semimonthly. **Special Indexes:** Indexes to Martin C. Fischer, Walter Tittle, and Geiger Family Papers collection; University Archives index (card). **Staff:** Sandra Comerforo, Hd., Circ.; Don Gordon, Soc.Sci.Libn.; Regina Entorf, Spec.Coll.Libn.; Kathy Schulz, Hum.Libn.; Robert Klapthor, Sci.Libn.; Norman Pearson, Hd., Tech.Serv.; Lyndon McCurdy, Dir., AV Serv.

Eric D. Wittkower Library
See: **Royal Victoria Hospital - Allan Memorial Institute** (14140)

WNYC Archives
See: **New York Public Library for the Performing Arts** (11638)

★ 20547 ★
Wofford College - Sandor Teszler Library - Archives (Hist)
N. Church St.   Phone: (803)597-4309
Spartanburg, SC 29303-3663   Herbert Hucks, Jr., Archv.
Founded: 1854. **Staff:** Prof 1. **Subjects:** History of Wofford College, its alumni and faculty. **Holdings:** 1450 books; 580 bound periodical volumes; 850 cataloged items; manuscripts of books by faculty members; tape recordings of "From Dr. Snyder's Study" (1948-1949 broadcasts over local radio station WSPA; manuscripts, tapes, and broadcasts contained in 28 legal size filing cabinet drawers); college catalogs; yearbooks; college journals; alumni and faculty publications; Old Gold and Black (student newspaper); memorabilia; photographs. **Services:** Copying; archives open to the public for reference use only.

★ 20548 ★
Wofford College - Sandor Teszler Library - Littlejohn Rare Book Room (Rare Book)
N. Church St.   Phone: (803)597-4300
Spartanburg, SC 29301   Oakley H. Coburn, Lib.Dir.
Founded: 1854. **Staff:** Prof 7; Other 4. **Subjects:** South Caroliniana; private presses, including Wofford Library Press; 16th and 17th century books; Folio Society publications; 19th and 20th century children's books. **Special Collections:** Matthew Carey Collection (100 volumes); Haynes Brown Hymnal Collection (1800 volumes); Leonard Baskin/Gehenna Press Collection (100 volumes); South Carolina Conference of the United Methodist Church materials. **Holdings:** 9000 books; 500 bound periodical volumes. **Services:** Interlibrary loan; copying; room open to the public. **Automated Operations:** DRA Integrated System. **Computerized Information Services:** DIALOG Information Services, BRS Information Technologies. **Publications:** Special Collections Checklists, Numbers 1-7; Wofford Bibliopolist. **Staff:** R. Steve Gonler, Ref.Libn.; Ibrahim Hanif, Coll.Dev.Libn.; Herbert Hucks, Jr., Archv.; Roger O. Niles, Pub.Serv.Libn.; Shirley Sheu, Cat.; Shelley Sperka, Techn.Serv.Libn.; Loren Pinkerman. Ref.Libn.

★ 20549 ★
Alan Wofsy Fine Arts - Reference Library (Art)
401 China Basin St.   Phone: (415)986-3030
San Francisco, CA 94107   Adios Butler, Libn.
Founded: 1969. **Staff:** 1. **Subjects:** Art of the book, graphics, architecture. **Special Collections:** Descriptive catalogs of artists; art reference books; catalogues raisonne's; bibliographies. **Holdings:** 3000 books; 100 bound periodical volumes; monographs on artists. **Services:** Library not open to the public. **Publications:** Catalogues Raisonnes; bibliographies. **Remarks:** FAX: (415)512-0130.

John G. Wolbach Library
See: **Harvard University - Harvard-Smithsonian Center for Astrophysics (CFA) - Library (6971)**

★ 20550 ★
Wolf, Block, Schorr & Solis-Cohen - Library (Law)
Packard Bldg., 12th Fl.   Phone: (215)977-2000
Philadelphia, PA 19102   Susan B. English, Dir. of Lib.Serv.
Founded: 1913. **Staff:** Prof 3; Other 4.75. **Subjects:** Law - corporate, real estate, labor, health, environmental; litigation. **Special Collections:** Tax law. **Holdings:** 20,000 volumes. **Subscriptions:** 1500 journals and other serials. **Services:** Interlibrary loan. **Computerized Information Services:** LEXIS, WESTLAW, VU/TEXT Information Services, DIALOG Information Services, NEXIS, Dun & Bradstreet. **Remarks:** FAX: (215)977-2334. **Staff:** John Duckett, Ref.Libn.; Cheryl Berninger, Tech.Serv.Libn.

WOLF PARK - N.A.W.P.F.
See: **North American Wildlife Park Foundation - WOLF PARK** (11870)

Wolf Trap Foundation for the Performing Arts Archives
See: **George Mason University - Fenwick Library - Special Collections and Archives** (9773)

★ 20551 ★
The Horace L. Wolfe Memorial Library (Mil)
Grand Central Station
Box 3514
Glendale, CA 91221   Phone: (818)241-7284
     Douglas L. Evans, Libn.
Founded: 1954. **Staff:** Prof 2. **Subjects:** Espionage, sabotage, military intelligence, secret services, secret societies, cryptography. **Holdings:** 10,785 books; 3700 clippings. **Subscriptions:** 20 journals and other serials; 12 newspapers. **Services:** Library not open to the public. **Remarks:** Library serves as a reference source for television and motion picture industries and certain government agencies.

Max & Beatrice Wolfe Library
See: **Beth Tzedec Congregation** (1775)

★ 20552 ★
Wolfeboro Historical Society - Library (Hist)
S. Main St.
Box 1066
Wolfeboro, NH 03894   Phone: (603)569-4997
     Joan E. Kimball, Pres.
Staff: 1. **Subjects:** Local history and genealogy, 19th century fire engines. **Holdings:** Books; maps; scrapbooks of local events; town reports; old school records. **Services:** Library open to the public on a limited schedule.

Wolfgram Memorial Library
See: **Widener University** (20418)

Wolfner Library for the Blind & Physically Handicapped
See: **Missouri State Library - Wolfner Library for the Blind & Physically Handicapped** (10551)

Isaac N. Wolfson Library
See: **Letchworth Developmental Diabilities Services** (9070)

Louis Wolfson Media History Center
See: **Miami-Dade Public Library** (10258)

★ 20553 ★
Wollongbar Agricultural Institute - Library (Agri)
Wollongbar, NSW 2480, Australia   Phone: 66 240200
     Des Stewart, Reg.Libn.
Staff: Prof 1; Other 1. **Subjects:** Animal production, crop science, veterinary science. **Holdings:** 3000 books. **Subscriptions:** 300 journals and other serials; 3 newspapers. **Services:** Interlibrary loan; copying; SDI; library open to the public for reference use by appointment only. **Computerized Information Services:** DIALOG Information Services, AUSTRALIS, Australian Bibliographic Network (ABN); FARMTI (internal database); Dialcom, Inc. (electronic mail service). **Remarks:** FAX: (066)283264. Electronic mail address(es): 07.MLN206604 (Dialcom, Inc.).

Womack Army Medical Center
See: **U.S. Army Hospitals** (17056)

★ 20554 ★
Women Artists News/Midmarch Arts - Archives (Art)
Grand Central Sta., Box 3304   Phone: (212)666-6990
New York, NY 10163   L. Greenberg
Founded: 1973. **Staff:** 2. **Subjects:** Art, women artists, women in art, women's organizations, art exhibitions. **Holdings:** 24 VF drawers of archival material on women in the arts; ephemera. **Subscriptions:** 25 journals and other serials. **Services:** Copying; archives open to the public by appointment. **Publications:** Women Artists News, quarterly; Guide to Women's Art Organizations, biennial; Whole Arts Directory, biennial with quarterly update; Voices of Women (criticism, poetry, graphics); Women Artists of the World (essays, photographs, and reproductions of art works of women artists worldwide); Pilgrims & Pioneers: New England Women in the Arts (historical and contemporary; essays and photographs); American Women in Art: Works on Paper; No Bluebonnets, No Yellow Roses: Essays on Texas Women in the Arts (historical and contemporary essays and photographs); California Women in the Arts, 1869-1988 (historical and contemporary; essays and photographs); Camera Fiends & Kodak Girls: Women in Photography, 1840-1930; The Lady Architects: Howe, Manning & Aling, 1843-1937. **Remarks:** Published by Midmarch Associates. **Staff:** Cynthia Navaretta, Exec.Dir.; Judy Seigel, Ed.; Sylvia Moore, Ed.

★ 20555 ★
Women Exploited by Abortion - Library (Med)
International Headquarters
Rte. 1, Box 821   Phone: (214)366-3600
Venus, TX 76084   Kathy Walker, Pres.
Founded: 1982. **Staff:** 6. **Subjects:** Abortion, post abortion syndrome (PAS) counseling, physical and psychological aftereffects of abortion. **Special Collections:** Research and data information on post abortion syndrome; personal stories. **Holdings:** 100 books; 1000 pamphlets and other items. **Services:** Library open to the public. **Publications:** Post-Abortion Newsletter. **Special Catalogs:** Pro-Life items catalog. **Formerly:** Located in Moreno Valley, CA.

★ 20556 ★
Women's Action Alliance, Inc. - Library (Soc Sci)
370 Lexington Ave., Suite 603   Phone: (212)532-8330
New York, NY 10017   Paulette Brill, Info.Serv.
Founded: 1971. **Staff:** Prof 12. **Subjects:** Women's issues - child care, sex discrimination, marriage, divorce, family, health, employment, affirmative action, reproductive rights, legislation, organizations and centers, chemical dependency, AIDS, teenage pregancy. **Special Collections:** Files of national women's organizations and women's centers organized by state. **Holdings:** 2000 books; 2000 bound periodical volumes; 40 VF drawers. **Subscriptions:** 200 journals and other serials. **Services:** Interlibrary loan; library open to the public by appointment. **Automated Operations:** Computerized cataloging. **Publications:** List of publications - available upon request. **Special Indexes:** Employment resource list for New York City. **Remarks:** FAX: (212)779-2846.

Women's American ORT Federation - Bramson ORT Institute
See: **Bramson ORT Technical Institute** (2068)

★ 20557 ★
Women's Centre of Nigeria - Library (Med)
Box 185
Eket, Rivers, Nigeria
Subjects: Women's health and sexuality, AIDS, sexually transmitted diseases, female circumcision. **Holdings:** 1000 volumes. **Also Known As:** Centro de Mujeres de Nigeria.

★ 20558 ★
Women's College Hospital - Medical Library (Med)
76 Grenville St.   Phone: (416)323-6078
Toronto, ON, Canada M5S 1B2   Margaret Robins, Dir.
Founded: 1955. **Staff:** Prof 2; Other 3. **Subjects:** Dermatology, diabetes, perinatal medicine, obstetrics, gynecology, high risk pregnancy. **Holdings:** 4000 books; 4200 periodical volumes; 500 video cassettes. **Subscriptions:** 260 journals and other serials. **Services:** Interlibrary loan (fee); library not open to the public. **Computerized Information Services:** MEDLARS, DIALOG Information Services. **Remarks:** FAX: (416)323-7314.

Women's History Research Center, Inc. - National Clearinghouse on Marital and Date Rape
See: **National Clearinghouse on Marital and Date Rape** (11118)

★ 20559 ★
Women's History Research Center, Inc. - Women's History Library (Hist, Soc Sci)
2325 Oak St.   Phone: (510)524-1582
Berkeley, CA 94708   Laura X, Dir.
Founded: 1968. **Staff:** Prof 2; Other 20. **Subjects:** Women's health and mental health, women and law, black and Third World women, female artists, children, films by and/or about women, Soviet women. **Special Collections:** International Women's History Archive (850 periodical titles on microfilm). **Holdings:** 2000 books; 300 tapes; 54 reels of microfilm on health and law; 90 reels of microfilm of women's periodicals in Herstory Collection. **Services:** Library not open to the public. **Publications:** Directory of Films by and/or about Women; Female Artists Directory; Women & Health/Mental Health, Women & Law, and Herstory serials (microfilm) - all for sale.

★ 20560 ★
Women's International Network (Soc Sci)
187 Grant St.   Phone: (617)862-9431
Lexington, MA 02173   Fran P. Hosken, Ed.
Subjects: Women's development and health, women's economic development, property rights of women worldwide. **Special Collections:** Female circumcision, genital mutilation. **Holdings:** Books; Network publications; foreign journals; uncataloged items. **Subscriptions:** 40 journals and other serials; 10 newspapers. **Services:** Library not open to the public. **Publications:** Childbirth Picture Book/Program; WIN News, quarterly; list of additional publications - available on request. **Remarks:** FAX: (617)862-9431.

★ 20561 ★
Women's League - Library (Soc Sci)
Freedom House
P.O. Box 30302
Lusaka, Zambia   Phone: 1 211062
Subjects: Zambian women - politics, discrimination, education. **Holdings:** 300 volumes.

★ 20562 ★
Women's Resource and Action Center - Sojourner Truth Women's Resource Library (Soc Sci)
130 N. Madison   Phone: (319)335-1486
Iowa City, IA 52242   Cherry Muhanji, Libn.
Founded: 1976. **Staff:** Prof 1; Other 5. **Subjects:** Feminism. **Special Collections:** Complete holdings of Ain't I A Woman, 1970-1973 (feminist periodical). **Holdings:** 1700 books. **Subscriptions:** 100 journals and other serials. **Services:** Library open to the public. **Publications:** Women's Resource & Action Center News, monthly - by subscription and free local distribution.

★ 20563 ★
Women's Resource Center Library (Soc Sci)
250 Golden Bear Ctr.
University of California
Berkeley, CA 94720   Phone: (510)642-4786
    Dorothy Lazard, Lib.Coord.
Founded: 1973. **Staff:** Prof 1; Other 2. **Subjects:** Women's studies, women and work, financial aid, comparable worth, women of color, international issues. **Special Collections:** Catherine Scholten Collection on Women in American History (100 books); Bea Bain Collection on the Women's Movement (100 books); Margaret Monroe Drews Collection of Working Papers (the status of women in the U.S., 1950-1970; 12 VF drawers); Constance Barker Collection on Lesbian History (700 books); women's movement magazines of the 1970s. **Holdings:** 3000 books; 20,000 other uncataloged items. **Subscriptions:** 60 journals and other serials. **Services:** Library open to the public for reference use only. **Computerized Information Services:** GLADIS, MELVYL (internal databases). **Publications:** Acquisitions list, quarterly; bibliographies, irregular. **Special Catalogs:** Tape catalog; journal and newsletter catalog (both on cards). **Special Indexes:** Vertical file index. **Remarks:** Alternate telephone number(s): (510)643-5727.

William C. Wonders Map Collection
See: **University of Alberta - Department of Geography** (18188)

★ 20564 ★
Wood County Law Library (Law)
168 S. Main St.   Phone: (419)353-3921
Bowling Green, OH 43402   Judith L. Gill, Libn.
Staff: 2. **Subjects:** Law. **Holdings:** 19,000 books; 1100 bound periodical volumes; 250 volumes of legal opinions; tapes. **Subscriptions:** 50 journals and other serials. **Services:** Interlibrary loan; copying; library open to the public. **Computerized Information Services:** WESTLAW, VU/TEXT Information Services, DIALOG Information Services, Dow Jones News/Retrieval, LEXIS. **Remarks:** FAX: (419)352-9269.

General Leonard Wood Army Community Hospital
See: **U.S. Army Hospitals** (17042)

Grant Wood Archives
See: **Cedar Rapids Museum of Art - Herbert S. Stamats Art Library** (3186)

★ 20565 ★
Wood Gundy Inc. - Library (Bus-Fin)
425 Lexington Ave., 2nd Fl.   Phone: (212)856-6777
New York, NY 10017   Elvira D'Amore, Libn.
Staff: Prof 1. **Subjects:** Investment securities. **Holdings:** Figures not available.

★ 20566 ★
Wood Gundy Inc. - Library (Bus-Fin)
BCE Place
P.O. Box 500   Phone: (416)594-7716
Toronto, ON, Canada M5J 2S8   Anne Baumann, Libn.
Founded: 1964. **Staff:** Prof 3; Other 4. **Subjects:** Corporations and industry, investments, accounting, economics. **Special Collections:** Wood Gundy publications (145 binders); financial statements of private Canadian companies (8000 microfiche). **Holdings:** 6000 volumes. **Subscriptions:** 434 journals and other serials; 300 Statistics Canada titles. **Services:** Interlibrary loan; copying. **Computerized Information Services:** Info Globe, Infomart Online, STM Systems Corporation, InvesText, The Financial Post DataGroup, PROFILE Information, DIALOG Information Services, Dow Jones News/Retrieval, ADP Network Services, Inc. **Publications:** Acquisitions list, monthly; list of Wood Gundy Research Reports, quarterly; periodicals list, annual - all for internal distribution only. **Special Indexes:** Index of Wood Gundy research reports, 1976 to present. **Remarks:** FAX: (416)594-7618. **Staff:** Cheryl Dhillon, Libn.; Sandra Keys, Libn.; Pino Corigliano, Asst.Libn.

John Penman Wood Library of National Defense
See: **University of Pennsylvania** (19185)

Wood Library-Museum of Anesthesiology
See: **American Society of Anesthesiologists** (743)

Wood Nepal Library
See: **American Nepal Education Foundation - Wood Nepal Library** (696)

Samuel J. Wood Library
See: **Cornell University - Medical College - Samuel J. Wood Library** (4323)

Wood Technical Library
See: **U.S. Army - Medical Research & Development Command - Medical Research Institute of Chemical Defense** (16990)

Woodberry Poetry Room
See: **Harvard University (7000)**

★ 20567 ★
Woodbridge Developmental Center - Library (Med)
Rahway Ave.
P.O. Box 189   Phone: (201)499-5596
Woodbridge, NJ 07095   Margaret DeRidder, Dir. of Educ.
Founded: 1956. **Staff:** 1.5. **Subjects:** Retardation, medicine, education, developmental disabilities, recreation, management. **Holdings:** 1000 books; filmstrips. **Subscriptions:** 20 journals and other serials. **Services:** Interlibrary loan; library open to the public for reference use only.

★ 20568 ★
Woodbury County Bar Association - Woodbury County Law Library
   (Law)
Woodbury County Courthouse, 6th Fl.
7th & Douglas Sts.   Phone: (712)279-6609
Sioux City, IA 51101   Phyllis Christiansen, Libn.
Staff: Prof 1; Other 1. **Subjects:** State, federal and general law. **Holdings:** 12,700 volumes. **Services:** Copying; library open to the public.

★ 20569 ★
Woodbury University - Library (Bus-Fin, Art)
7500 Glenoaks Blvd.
Box 7846   Phone: (818)767-0888
Burbank, CA 91510-7846   Dr. William Stanley, Lib.Dir.
Founded: 1884. **Staff:** Prof 3; Other 3. **Subjects:** Economics, international business, art, architecture, interior design, management, fashion marketing and design, computers. **Holdings:** 62,676 books; 2069 bound periodical volumes; 72,238 microforms; 9205 slides; 384 cassettes; 289 videotapes. **Subscriptions:** 588 journals and other serials; 7 newspapers. **Services:** Interlibrary loan; copying; library open to the public for reference use only. **Automated Operations:** Computerized serials. **Computerized Information Services:** Internal database (serials, slides, student papers). **Remarks:** FAX: (818)504-9320. **Staff:** Lydia Gonzales, Ref.; Martha Pike, Tech.Serv.

Dr. John Woodenlegs Memorial Library
See: **Dull Knife Memorial College (5053)**

★ 20570 ★
Woodhull Medical and Mental Health Center - Health Sciences Library
   (Med)
760 Broadway, Rm. 3A160   Phone: (718)963-8397
Brooklyn, NY 11206   Maria N. Perez, Dept.Sr.Libn.
Founded: 1982. **Staff:** Prof 1; Other 2. **Subjects:** Medicine, allied health sciences. **Holdings:** 1350 books; 250 bound periodical volumes; 300 unbound journals. **Subscriptions:** 154 journals and other serials. **Services:** Interlibrary loan; library not open to the public. **Computerized Information Services:** BRS Information Technologies, NLM. **Networks/Consortia:** Member of Brooklyn-Queens-Staten Island Health Sciences Librarians (BQSI), New York Metropolitan Reference and Research Library Agency, Medical Library Center of New York (MLCNY). **Publications:** Acquisitions list; library handbooks; serials list by title and subject. **Remarks:** Alternate telephone number(s): 963-8000, ext. 5523; 963-8275. FAX: (718)963-8888.

★ 20571 ★
Woodlake Lutheran Church - Library
7525 Oliver Ave., S.
Richfield, MN 55423
Defunct.

★ 20572 ★
Woodland Hills Presbyterian Church - Norman E. Nygaard Library
   (Rel-Phil)
5751 Platt Ave.
Woodland Hills, CA 91367
Founded: 1973. **Staff:** 1. **Subjects:** Bible, philosophy, Christian beliefs and living, children's literature. **Holdings:** 1000 books; 75 audio cassette tapes. **Services:** Library open to the public.

★ 20573 ★
Woodland Park Zoological Gardens - Library (Biol Sci)
5500 Phinney Ave., N.   Phone: (206)684-4040
Seattle, WA 98103   Barbara Glicksberg, Libn.
Founded: 1971. **Staff:** Prof 1. **Subjects:** Wild and captive mammals, birds, reptiles, and amphibians; veterinary medicine; ecology; zoos and zookeeping; conservation; animal behavior. **Special Collections:** Species files; files of information on other zoos. **Holdings:** 1117 books; pamphlets; microforms. **Subscriptions:** 92 journals and other serials. **Services:** Interlibrary loan; copying; library open to the public for reference use only. **Computerized Information Services:** DIALOG Information Services, NEXIS, LOGIN. **Remarks:** FAX: (206)684-4854. **Staff:** Shirley Cotter, Lib.Supv.

Woodman Astronomical Library
See: **University of Wisconsin--Madison - Washburn Observatory (19624)**

★ 20574 ★
Woodmen Accident & Life Company - Library (Bus-Fin)
1526 K St.
Box 82288
Lincoln, NE 68501   Phone: (402)476-6500
Founded: 1969. **Staff:** Prof 1. **Subjects:** Health and life insurance, law, office management, data processing, accounting, finance, economics. **Holdings:** 3500 books; 60 films and filmstrips; 20 VF drawers of clippings, reports, policy forms, pamphlets; 40 videotapes; 300 audio cassettes. **Subscriptions:** 125 journals and other serials. **Services:** Library not open to the public. **Special Indexes:** Index of company magazine and bulletins (card).

★ 20575 ★
Woodmere Art Museum - Library (Art)
9201 Germantown Ave.   Phone: (215)247-0476
Philadelphia, PA 19118   Mary English, Libn.
Subjects: Art. **Remarks:** No further information was supplied by respondent.

Robert W. Woodruff Library
See: **Clark Atlanta University Center (3763)**

D.S. Woods Education Library
See: **University of Manitoba (18786)**

★ 20576 ★
Woods Hole Oceanographic Institution - Research Library (Biol Sci, Sci-Engr)
Woods Hole, MA 02543   Phone: (508)548-1400
                     Carolyn P. Winn, Res.Libn.
Founded: 1932. **Staff:** Prof 2; Other 7. **Subjects:** Oceanography; marine geology, chemistry, and biology; ocean engineering; marine policy. **Special Collections:** Institution Archives and Data Collection (12,000 AV programs; 160,000 underwater photographs; 11,000 charts and atlases; 3000 films; 10,000 slides). **Holdings:** 12,000 books; 20,000 bound periodical volumes; 26,000 technical reports; 250,000 reprints. **Subscriptions:** 1500 journals and other serials. **Services:** Interlibrary loan; copying; library open to the public by permission of librarian. **Computerized Information Services:** DIALOG Information Services, BRS Information Technologies, Chemical Abstracts Service (CAS), WILSONLINE; OMNET (electronic mail service). Performs searches on fee basis. Contact Person: Colleen Hurter, Lib.Asst. **Networks/Consortia:** Member of NELINET, Inc. **Publications:** Monthly accession announcement; Oceanus; annual report; Abstract of Manuscripts - on exchange. **Special Indexes:** Oceanographic Index. **Remarks:** FAX: (508)457-2195. Electronic mail address(es): WHOI.LIBRARY (OMNET). Telex: 951679. Jointly maintained with the Marine Biological Laboratory, where the library's holdings are housed. **Staff:** William Dunkle, Data Libn.

★ 20577 ★
William Woods College - Dulany Library - Special Collections (Hum)
200 W. 12th St.   Phone: (314)592-4289
Fulton, MO 65251   Marjorie J. Pinkerton, Lib.Dir.
Founded: 1870. **Staff:** Prof 3; Other 2. **Special Collections:** Equestrian Science Works Collection (2000 items); Educational Materials Collection (10,000 of print and nonprint materials); Legal Studies Collection (3000 books). **Services:** Interlibrary loan; copying; library open to the public. **Automated Operations:** Computerized indexing. **Computerized Information Services:** BRS/After Dark, Academic Index. **Staff:** P.J. McGinnis, Ref.Libn.; Lori Campbell, Tech.Serv.Libn.

★ 20578 ★
Woodside Hospital - Staff Resource Library/Patients' Library (Med)
800 E. Indianola Ave. Phone: (216)788-8712
Youngstown, OH 44502 Louise M. Mulderig, Libn.
Founded: 1955. **Staff:** Prof 1. **Subjects:** Psychiatry, psychiatric nursing, mental illness, mental health, social services, psychotherapy. **Special Collections:** Large print collection (130 volumes); patients' library (includes the Yale Shakespeare). **Holdings:** 6463 books; 31 bound periodical volumes; 300 boxes of archives; 200 reports; 2000 pamphlets; 22 documents; 200 phonograph records; 10 drawers of filmstrips and cassette tapes; 450 items in picture files; 260 dissertations. **Subscriptions:** 65 journals and other serials. **Services:** Interlibrary loan; copying; library open to visiting state staff and relatives of institution staff. **Networks/Consortia:** Member of NEOUCOM Council Associated Hospital Librarians. **Publications:** Public relations posters and flyers, monthly; acquisitions update, monthly. **Special Catalogs:** Research bibliography catalogs. **Formerly:** Woodside Receiving Hospital.

Carter G. Woodson Library
See: **Association for the Study of Afro-American Life and History - Carter G. Woodson Library** (1169)

Carter G. Woodson Regional Library
See: **Chicago Public Library - Carter G. Woodson Regional Library - Vivian G. Harsh Research Collection of Afro-American History & Literature** (3527)

★ 20579 ★
Leigh Yawkey Woodson Art Museum - Library (Art)
12th & Franklin Sts.
Wausau, WI 54401-5007 Phone: (715)845-7010
Founded: 1976. **Staff:** 3. **Subjects:** Nature art, decorative arts, glass, art history, art techniques. **Holdings:** 1000 books, video recordings, films, and filmstrips. **Subscriptions:** 17 journals and other serials. **Services:** Library open to the public by appointment only; loans are available to museum members and local schools and teachers. **Remarks:** FAX: (715)845-7103.

Woodson Research Center
See: **Rice University - Woodson Research Center** (13897)

Woodstock College Archives
See: **Georgetown University - Special Collections Division - Lauinger Memorial Library** (6379)

★ 20580 ★
Woodstock Historical Society, Inc. - John Cotton Dana Library (Hist)
26 Elm St. Phone: (802)457-1822
Woodstock, VT 05091 Gregory C. Schwarz, Exec.Dir.
Staff: 3. **Subjects:** Woodstock history, antiques, Vermont history, Woodstock genealogy. **Special Collections:** Charles Dana's Account Books (102 volumes); old Woodstock newspapers. **Holdings:** 1500 books; 51 bound periodical volumes; 500 pamphlets; 42 maps; 250 VF folders of papers and manuscripts; account books and records of Woodstock merchants. **Subscriptions:** 2 journals and other serials. **Services:** Library open on a limited schedule to qualified researchers. **Publications:** Woodstock's U.S. Senator Jacob Collamer (1944); Something About Old Woodstock (1952); The Vermont Heritage of George Perkins Marsh (1960); My Grandmother's and Other Tales (1968) - all for sale; The Dana House Collection (1974); Hiram Powers, Vermont Sculptor (1974).

★ 20581 ★
Woodstock Theological Center - Library (Rel-Phil)
Georgetown University
Box 37445
Washington, DC 20013 Rev. Eugene M. Rooney, S.J., Hd.Libn.
Founded: 1869. **Staff:** Prof 2; Other 2. **Subjects:** Roman Catholic theology, patristics, Jesuitica, church history, moral theology, scripture, Catholic Americana. **Special Collections:** Rare Jesuitica; Teilhard de Chardin Collection; Halpern Collection of Engravings (religious art); Woodstock Archives; J.C. Murray Archives; G. Weigel Archives; early printed works. **Holdings:** 183,600 books; 31,700 bound periodical volumes; 17,188 rare books; 984 reels of microfilm; 1683 microfiche. **Subscriptions:** 640 journals and other serials. **Services:** Interlibrary loan; copying; library open to scholars for reference use. **Computerized Information Services:** OCLC. **Networks/Consortia:** Member of Consortium of Universities of the Washington Metropolitan Area. **Remarks:** FAX: (202)687-5835. Maintained by Maryland Province of the Society of Jesus. **Staff:** Paul S. Osmanski, Asst.Libn.

★ 20582 ★
Woodview-Calabasas Psychiatric Hospital - Library (Med)
25100 Calabasas Rd.
Calabasas, CA 91302 Phone: (818)222-1000
Founded: 1958. **Staff:** Prof 1. **Subjects:** Psychiatry, nursing, general medicine. **Holdings:** 2000 books; 500 bound periodical volumes. **Subscriptions:** 25 journals and other serials. **Services:** Interlibrary loan; library open to medical and hospital staff. **Remarks:** Maintained by Hospital Corporation of America.

★ 20583 ★
Woodville State Hospital - Professional Library
Carnegie, PA 15106-3793
Defunct.

Woodward Biomedical Library
See: **University of British Columbia** (18285)

★ 20584 ★
Woodward-Clyde Consultants - Library (Sci-Engr)
2020 E. First St., Ste. 400 Phone: (714)835-6886
Santa Ana, CA 92705 Ute Hertel, Libn.
Founded: 1978. **Staff:** Prof 1. **Subjects:** Geology, geophysics, engineering, waste management. **Holdings:** 13,500 books; 975 unbound periodical volumes; 900 WCC reports; 3100 WCC project files; 15 file cabinets of maps; 2 file cabinets of reprints; microfiche. **Subscriptions:** 62 journals and other serials. **Services:** Interlibrary loan; copying; library open to the public by appointment. **Publications:** New Book List, quarterly. **Special Catalogs:** Project files catalog (card). **Special Indexes:** Large project files. **Remarks:** FAX: (714)667-7147. Telex: 68 3420.

★ 20585 ★
Woodward-Clyde Consultants - Technical Library (Env-Cons)
1550 Hotel Circle N. Phone: (619)294-9400
San Diego, CA 92108 Neil Barron, Libn.
Staff: Prof 1. **Subjects:** Environmental sciences, geology, geotechnical engineering, hydrology. **Holdings:** 1800 books; 1200 reports; 80 microfiche; videotapes; unbound files. **Subscriptions:** 80 journals and other serials. **Services:** Interlibrary loan; library not open to the public. **Computerized Information Services:** DIALOG Information Services, MELVYL. **Publications:** Acquisitions list, monthly. **Remarks:** FAX: (619)293-7920.

★ 20586 ★
Woodward-Clyde Consultants, Eastern Region - WCC Library (Sci-Engr)
201 Willowbrook Blvd.
Box 290 Phone: (201)785-0700
Wayne, NJ 07470 Donna Del Giudice, Libn.
Staff: Prof 1. **Subjects:** Civil and geotechnical engineering, geology, hydrology, environmental science, hazardous waste, seismology. **Special Collections:** Geologic Atlas of the United States. **Holdings:** Figures not available. **Subscriptions:** 60 journals and other serials. **Services:** Library not open to the public. **Computerized Information Services:** DIALOG Information Services. **Remarks:** FAX: (201)785-0023.

★ 20587 ★
Woodward-Clyde Consultants, Western Region - Information Center (Sci-Engr)
500 12th St., Suite 100 Phone: (510)874-3147
Oakland, CA 94607 Margaret Crawford, Libn.
Founded: 1965. **Staff:** Prof 1. **Subjects:** Water, hazardous waste, environmental science, soil mechanics, earthquake engineering, geology, seismology. **Holdings:** 2500 books; 6000 reports; 5000 unbound periodicals; 8 VF drawers of pamphlets. **Subscriptions:** 250 journals and other serials. **Services:** Interlibrary loan; center not open to the public. **Computerized Information Services:** DIALOG Information Services. **Remarks:** FAX: (510)874-3268.

★ 20588 ★
Woodward Governor Co. - Woodward Library (Sci-Engr)
5001 N. 2nd St.   Phone: (815)877-7441
Rockford, IL 61101   Mary Casarotto, Libn.
Founded: 1957. **Staff:** 2. **Subjects:** Prime movers, aircraft,
locomotives, electricity and machine shop practices. **Holdings:** 1200
volumes; 10 VF drawers of technical papers; 1 VF drawer of bulletins.
Subscriptions: 150 journals and other serials. **Services:** Interlibrary loan;
copying; library open to the public for reference use only by request.
Publications: Prime Mover Control - monthly. **Remarks:** FAX: (815)877-
0001.

Roy J. Woodward Memorial Library of Californiana
See: **California State University, Fresno - Henry Madden Library -
Department of Special Collections (2561)**

★ 20589 ★
Woodward State Hospital School - Staff Library
Woodward, IA 50276
Founded: 1962. **Subjects:** Mental retardation, special education, psychology,
training, social services, medicine, nursing, leisure services. **Special
Collections:** Mental retardation. **Holdings:** 6000 books; 8 VF drawers of
pamphlets and reprints; 250 video cassettes. **Remarks:** Currently inactive.

Woolaroc Museum
See: **Frank Phillips Foundation, Inc. (13007)**

Leonard & Virginia Woolf Library
See: **Washington State University - Manuscripts, Archives, & Special
Collections (20045)**

★ 20590 ★
Worcester Art Museum - Library (Art)
55 Salisbury St.   Phone: (508)799-4406
Worcester, MA 01609   Kathy L. Berg, Libn.
Founded: 1909. **Staff:** Prof 2; Other 1. **Subjects:** American and European
painting and prints, photography, Japanese prints. **Holdings:** 38,000
volumes; 132 linear feet of exhibition catalogs; 264 linear feet of sale and
dealer catalogs. **Subscriptions:** 200 journals and other serials. **Services:**
Interlibrary loan; copying; library open to the public for reference use only.
Networks/Consortia: Member of Worcester Area Cooperating Libraries
(WACL). **Special Indexes:** Card index to Worcester Art Museum objects
published in Worcester Art Museum publication (by accession number).
Staff: Cynthia L. Bolshaw, Slide Libn.

★ 20591 ★
Worcester City Hospital - Medical Library (Med)
26 Queen St.   Phone: (508)799-8186
Worcester, MA 01610   Donrue M. Larson, Lib.Asst.
Founded: 1937. **Staff:** 1. **Subjects:** Medicine and allied health sciences.
Special Collections: Burn care and rehabilitation. **Holdings:** 1500 books;
4500 bound periodical volumes. **Subscriptions:** 200 journals and other
serials. **Services:** Interlibrary loan; copying; use of library for reference may
be requested. **Automated Operations:** Computerized cataloging.
Computerized Information Services: NLM, Data-Star, OCLC; DOCLINE
(electronic mail service). **Networks/Consortia:** Member of Worcester Area
Cooperating Libraries (WACL), Central Massachusetts Consortium of
Health Related Libraries (CMCHRL), National Network of Libraries of
Medicine - New England Region. **Remarks:** FAX: (508)799-8314.

Worcester County Historical Society Archives
See: **Worcester County Library (20593)**

★ 20592 ★
Worcester County Horticultural Society - Library (Agri, Biol Sci)
30 Tower Hill Rd.   Phone: (508)869-6111
Boylston, MA 01505-1001   Margot K. Wallin, Libn.
Founded: 1842. **Staff:** 1. **Subjects:** Agriculture, botany, conservation, fruit
culture, general horticulture, landscape design. **Special Collections:** 6
centuries of horticultural literature; 18th and 19th century fruitbooks (250).
Holdings: 7000 books; 1000 bound periodical volumes; 300 seed, tool, plant,
and equipment catalogs. **Subscriptions:** 42 journals and other serials; 30
newspapers. **Services:** Library open to the public for reference use only.
Networks/Consortia: Member of Worcester Area Cooperating Libraries
(WACL). **Publications:** Grow With Us (newsletter), bimonthly. **Remarks:**
FAX: (508)869-0314.

★ 20593 ★
Worcester County Library (Hist)
307 N. Washington St.   Phone: (410)632-2600
Snow Hill, MD 21863   Stewart Wells, Dir.
Founded: 1959. **Staff:** 15. **Subjects:** Worcester County - history,
genealogy. **Special Collections:** William D. Pitts Collection (land survey records; 70
cubic feet); Worcester County Historical Society Archives (9 cubic feet);
Worcester County Extension Service collection (15 cubic feet). **Holdings:**
400 books; 97 bound periodical volumes; 200 documents; 7 AV programs;
50 manuscripts; 95 nonbook items; Worcester County land records.
Services: Interlibrary loan; copying; library open to the public. **Publications:**
Guide to the William D. Pitts Collection - for sale. **Remarks:** FAX:
(410)632-1159. **Staff:** Fay Brooks, Geneal.Res.

Worcester District Medical Society
See: **University of Massachusetts Medical School & Worcester District
Medical Society (18835)**

★ 20594 ★
**Worcester Foundation for Experimental Biology - George F. Fuller
Library** (Biol Sci)
222 Maple St.   Phone: (508)842-8921
Shrewsbury, MA 01545   Barbara Lee, Lib.Dir.
Founded: 1945. **Staff:** Prof 2; Other 2. **Subjects:** Molecular biology,
chemistry, biochemistry, physiology, neurobehavioral sciences. **Holdings:**
8000 books; 25,000 bound periodical volumes; 4 VF drawers of chemical
patents; 4 VF drawers of subject bibliographies; 4 VF drawers of clippings.
Subscriptions: 250 journals and other serials. **Services:** Interlibrary loan;
copying; SDI; library open to staffs and students of institutions of higher
education in the community. **Computerized Information Services:**
DIALOG Information Services, BRS Information Technologies,
MEDLARS; CD-ROM (MEDLINE); BITNET (electronic mail service).
Networks/Consortia: Member of Central Massachusetts Consortium of
Health Related Libraries (CMCHRL). **Publications:** Periodicals list,
annual; bibliographies. **Special Catalogs:** Collected reprints of Worcester
Foundation authors (book); catalog of bound company annual reports, 1945
to present (book). **Remarks:** FAX: (508)842-0342. Electronic mail
address(es): LEE@WFEB2 (BITNET).

★ 20595 ★
Worcester Historical Museum - Library (Hist)
30 Elm St.   Phone: (508)753-8278
Worcester, MA 01609   Beverly Osborn, Res.Libn.
Founded: 1875. **Staff:** Prof 2; Other 3. **Subjects:** Worcester history.
Holdings: 20,000 volumes; photographs; maps; manuscripts; graphics;
newspapers; valentines; ephemera. **Services:** Copying; library open to the
public. **Networks/Consortia:** Member of Worcester Area Cooperating
Libraries (WACL). **Special Indexes:** Manuscript collection (notebook).
Remarks: FAX: (508)753-9070.

★ 20596 ★
Worcester Law Library (Law)
County Court House   Phone: (508)756-2441
Worcester, MA 01608   Suzanne M. Hoey, Law Libn.
Founded: 1842. **Staff:** Prof 1; Other 3. **Subjects:** Law. **Holdings:** 100,000
volumes; periodicals; Reporter series on ultrafiche; Federal Register on
microfiche; Massachusetts Supreme Judicial Court Records and Briefs on
microfiche. **Services:** Interlibrary loan; copying; library open to the public.
Computerized Information Services: OCLC, WESTLAW, LEXIS, Veralex
2. **Remarks:** FAX: (508)754-9933. Part of the Massachusetts State Trial
Court; Marnie Warner, Law Library Coordinator.

★ 20597 ★
Worcester Polytechnic Institute - George C. Gordon Library (Sci-Engr)
West St.   Phone: (508)831-5410
Worcester, MA 01609   Albert G. Anderson, Jr., Hd.Libn.
Founded: 1865. **Staff:** Prof 9; Other 14. **Subjects:** Engineering, chemistry,
environmental science, computer science, physics, life sciences, biomedicine,
mathematics, city planning, fire safety, history of science and technology.
Special Collections: WPI Archives; History of Engineering. **Holdings:**
317,000 books; 51,611 bound periodical volumes; 16,591 technical reports;
2099 maps; 125 boxes and 25 files of archives; 8 VF drawers; 800,000 NASA,
American Engineering Council (AEC), and NASA Test Support microfiche;

2052 recordings; 4800 videotapes, audio cassettes, film loops. **Subscriptions:** 1500 journals and other serials; 25 newspapers. **Services:** Interlibrary loan; copying; microfiche copying; transparencies made; library open to qualified users. **Automated Operations:** Computerized public access catalog, cataloging, serials, and circulation. **Computerized Information Services:** DIALOG Information Services, OCLC; InterNet (electronic mail service). Performs searches on fee basis. Contact Person: Joanne Williams, Ref. **Networks/Consortia:** Member of NELINET, Inc., Worcester Area Cooperating Libraries (WACL), C/W MARS, Inc. **Publications:** New Acquisitions list, monthly; Library Handbook. **Special Catalogs:** Fire Safety Material. **Remarks:** FAX: (508)831-5829. Electronic mail address(es): WPI.WPI.edu (InterNet). **Staff:** Carmen Brown, Hd., Pub.Serv./Ref.; Helen Shuster, Hd., Tech.Serv.; Margaret Riley, Circ.; Diana Johnson, Ref./ILL; Donald Richardson, Tech.Rpt.; Lora Brueck, Spec.Coll.; Martha Gunnarson, Cat.

★ **20598** ★
Worcester Public Library - Reference and Reader Services (Soc Sci, Sci-Engr, Hum)
Salem Square   Phone: (508)799-1655
Worcester, MA 01608   Penelope B. Johnson, Hd.Libn.
Staff: Prof 23; Other 2. **Subjects:** History, art, music, social and political science, literature, travel, science and technology, business, religion, architecture. **Special Collections:** Worcester Collection; Grants Resource Center; U.S. Government documents depository. **Holdings:** 507,826 books; 58,291 bound periodical volumes; 329,634 government documents; 24,108 recordings; Massachusetts State documents. **Subscriptions:** 935 journals and other serials; 65 newspapers. **Services:** Interlibrary loan; copying; services open to the public. **Automated Operations:** Computerized cataloging and circulation. **Computerized Information Services:** DIALOG Information Services, WILSONLINE, VU/TEXT Information Services, BRS Information Technologies. **Networks/Consortia:** Member of C/W MARS, Inc. **Remarks:** FAX: (508)799-1713. **Staff:** Paul Pelletier, Hd., Bus., Sci. & Tech.; Leonard Lucas, Hd., Soc.Sci. & Hist.; Christine Kardokas, Hd., Ref. & Rd.Serv.; Nancy Gaudette, Worcester Coll.Libn.; Dorothy Johnson, Govt.Docs.; 1 C

★ **20599** ★
Worcester State College - Learning Resources Center (Educ)
486 Chandler St.   Phone: (508)793-8027
Worcester, MA 01602   Bruce Plummer, Dir.
Founded: 1874. **Staff:** Prof 7; Other 14. **Subjects:** Education, humanities. **Special Collections:** Education Resources Collection (11,000 elementary and secondary textbooks; 3000 curriculum guides; Kraus curriculum guides on microfiche; 1000 tests); Children's Collection (10,000 juvenile volumes). **Holdings:** 140,000 books; 3000 bound periodical volumes; 57,000 microforms; 20,000 16mm films; 8mm film loops; slides; phonograph records; tapes; video cassettes. **Subscriptions:** 1000 journals and other serials; 10 newspapers. **Services:** Interlibrary loan; copying; television and photography studios; center open to the public. **Computerized Information Services:** DIALOG Information Services, OCLC; CD-ROMs. Performs searches on fee basis. **Networks/Consortia:** Member of Worcester Area Cooperating Libraries (WACL), C/W MARS, Inc., NELINET, Inc. **Publications:** Learning Resources Center Location Guide - to users. **Remarks:** FAX: (508)793-8191. **Staff:** Betsey Brenneman, Acq./ILL; Krishna Das Gupta, Tech.Serv.; Pamela McKay, Ref.; Bill Piekarski, Educ.Rsrcs.; Linda Snodgrass, Per.

★ **20600** ★
Worcester Technical Institute - Library (Educ)
251 Belmont St.   Phone: (508)799-1945
Worcester, MA 01605   Eleanor A. Kingsland, Libn.
Founded: 1990. **Staff:** Prof 1. **Subjects:** Architecture and construction; computer science; industrial electronics; heating; ventilating and refrigeration; mechanical drafting and design; opthalmic dispensing; welding; commerical art and design; dental assisting; medical assisting; practical nursing; surgical technology. **Holdings:** 45,000 books. **Subscriptions:** 85 journals and other serials. **Services:** Library open to the public with restrictions. **Automated Operations:** Computerized cataloging.

★ **20601** ★
Worcester Telegram & Gazette - Library (Publ)
20 Franklin St., Box 15012   Phone: (508)793-9240
Worcester, MA 01615-0012   George H. Labonte, Libn.
Founded: 1913. **Staff:** 6. **Subjects:** Newspaper reference topics; biography. **Special Collections:** Local and state history and biography. **Holdings:** 374

books; 2.3 million clippings; 481,000 graphics; Worcester Telegram, 1884 to 1989, on microfilm; Evening Gazette, 1866 to 1989, on microfilm, Telegram & Gazette 1989 to present, on microfilm. **Services:** Copying; library open to the public on written request only. **Computerized Information Services:** DataTimes. Performs searches on fee basis. **Remarks:** FAX: (508)753-3142.

Worcester Vocational Schools - George I. Alden Library
See: Worcester Technical Institute (20600)

Worden School of Social Service
See: Our Lady of the Lake University (12613)

★ **20602** ★
Work in America Institute, Inc. - Library (Bus-Fin)
700 White Plains Rd.   Phone: (914)472-9600
Scarsdale, NY 10583   Maria Wiencek, Mgr., Info.Serv.
Staff: Prof 2; Other 2. **Subjects:** Productivity, quality of working life, work innovations and design, industrial relations, personnel management. **Special Collections:** Publications of the former National Center for Productivity and Quality of Working Life (52 volumes). **Holdings:** 3000 books; 2200 file documents; 20,000 subject files of clippings, unpublished reports, technical documents. **Subscriptions:** 200 journals and other serials. **Services:** Library open to the public by appointment. **Computerized Information Services:** DIALOG Information Services. **Special Indexes:** Subject Headings Index. **Remarks:** FAX: (914)472-9606. **Staff:** Laura Soifer, Info.Res.Spec.

★ **20603** ★
Working Group Indigenous Peoples - Library (Soc Sci)
Postbus 4098
NL-1009 AB Amsterdam, Netherlands   Phone: 20 938625
Subjects: Rights of indigenous peoples, Amazon Indians, Labrador Indians, Australian aborigines. **Holdings:** 10,000 books, newsletters, clippings, audiovisuals. **Also Known As:** Grupo de Trabajo para los Pueblos Indigenas.

★ **20604** ★
Working Opportunities for Women - W.O.W. Resource Center (Soc Sci)
2700 University Ave. W., Suite 120
St. Paul, MN 55114   Phone: (612)647-9961
Subjects: Women - employment, careers, job seeking skills, networking, occupational resources, divorce, minorities. **Special Collections:** Vocational Biographies (100 booklets). **Holdings:** 700 books; 2 shelves of educational bulletins. **Subscriptions:** 13 journals and other serials. **Services:** Copying; networking and informational interview contacts; job listings; center open to the public.

★ **20605** ★
The Workman and Temple Family Homestead Museum - Library (Hist)
15415 E. Don Julian Rd.   Phone: (818)968-8492
City of Industry, CA 91745-1029   Carol Crilly, Cur.
Subjects: Southern California; California and United States, 1830-1930; architecture; decorative arts; costume. **Holdings:** 960 books; 47 AV programs; 188 nonbook items. **Subscriptions:** 48 journals and other serials. **Services:** Copying; library open to the public at librarian's discretion. **Remarks:** FAX: (818)968-2048.

Workshop in Political Theory & Policy Analysis
See: Indiana University (7805)

★ **20606** ★
World Affairs Council of Northern California - Library (Soc Sci)
312 Sutter St., Suite 200   Phone: (415)982-2541
San Francisco, CA 94108   Lone C. Beeson, Hd.Libn.
Founded: 1947. **Staff:** Prof 2. **Subjects:** International relations, foreign policy, political science, economics, modern history. **Special Collections:** Newsletters and press releases from various embassies and information centers; U.S. Department of State documents. **Holdings:** 6000 books; 200 documents; 3000 pamphlets; 400 cassette tapes; maps. **Subscriptions:** 40 journals and other serials; 5 newspapers. **Services:** Copying; library open to the public with restrictions on borrowing. **Computerized Information Services:** DIALOG Information Services; International Resource Information Service (internal database). **Networks/Consortia:** Member of Bay Area Library and Information Network. **Publications:** Booknotes, monthly - to members. **Remarks:** Alternate telephone number(s): 982-0430. FAX: (415)982-5028. **Staff:** Edith Malamud, Circ.Libn.

★ 20607 ★
World Archeological Society - Information Center (Hist, Soc Sci)
Lake Rd. 65-48
HCR-1-Box 445   Phone: (417)334-2377
Hollister, MO 65672   Ron Miller, Dir.
Founded: 1971. Staff: Prof 2. Subjects: Archeology, anthropology, and art history of the world; Biblical archeology; museum science. Special Collections: Steve Miller Library of American Archaeology (1100 publications); democracy club; career notes; publications commendations; Bible repair project; most interesting old book find contest; anthropological think tank. Holdings: 6500 volumes; 7500 item clipping file; 2000 photographs, tapes, and slides. Subscriptions: 30 journals and other serials; 6 newspapers. Services: Full art service and assistance with brief research queries for researchers, authors, and others; center not open to the public. Publications: W.A.S. Fact Sheet; W.A.S. Newsletter and Special Publications, irregular - to the public. Staff: Mrs. Steve Miller, Asst.Dir.

★ 20608 ★
World Association of Document Examiners - WADE Library (Law)
111 N. Canal St.   Phone: (312)930-9446
Chicago, IL 60606   Lee Arnold, Libn.
Founded: 1973. Staff: Prof 2; Other 3. Subjects: Handwriting, documents, paper and ink, law, trial procedure, psychology. Holdings: 7000 books. Subscriptions: 75 journals and other serials; 25 newspapers. Services: Library not open to the public. Publications: WADE Exchange, monthly; WADE Journal, quarterly. Staff: Martha Lindberg, Libn.

World Association of Harpists
See: **American Harp Society Repository** (603)

★ 20609 ★
World Bank - Sectoral Library (Soc Sci)
1818 H St., N.W., Rm. N 145   Phone: (202)473-8670
Washington, DC 20433   Leighton H. Cumming, Libn.
Founded: 1984. Staff: Prof 9; Other 5. Subjects: Agriculture, population, health, transportation, energy, environment, mining, nutrition, telecommunications, women in development, education, water supply in the developing world. Special Collections: Cartography library (4000 titles). Holdings: 55,000 books; 200,000 microfiche. Subscriptions: 900 journals and other serials; 10 newspapers. Services: Interlibrary loan; copying; library open to the public on a limited basis with permission. Automated Operations: Computerized public access catalog, cataloging, circulation, serials, and acquisitions. Computerized Information Services: DIALOG Information Services, PFDS Online, BRS Information Technologies, NewsNet, Inc., ESA/IRS, Questel, National Ground Water Information Center (NGWIC), WILSONLINE, MEDLARS, International Development Research Centre (IDRC); JOLIS (internal database); All-In-One. Remarks: FAX: (202)334-0564. Staff: Kathryn Scott, Hd., Cat.; Chris Windheuser, Map & Ref.Libn.; Robin Porter, Ref.Libn.; Alcione Amos, Ref. & Acq.Libn.; Laura Harvey, Cat.Libn.; Olga Boemeke, Ref. Libn.; Shewan Workneh, Cat.Libn.; Ana Mukani, Cat.Libn.

World Bank/International Monetary Fund - Joint Bank/Fund Library
See: **International Monetary Fund/World Bank** (8157)

World Baptist Fellowship - Arlington Baptist College
See: **Arlington Baptist College** (1038)

★ 20610 ★
World Book Inc. - Research Library (Publ)
525 W. Monroe   Phone: (312)876-2200
Chicago, IL 60661   MaryAnn Urbashich, Hd., Lib.Serv.
Founded: 1920. Staff: Prof 1; Other 3. Subjects: General reference, area studies, biography, statistics. Holdings: 22,000 volumes; 375 VF drawers of pamphlets and clippings; 3000 maps; 400 government publications. Subscriptions: 600 journals and other serials; 7 newspapers. Services: Interlibrary loan; library not open to the public. Computerized Information Services: DIALOG Information Services, NEXIS, OCLC. Networks/Consortia: Member of ILLINET. Remarks: FAX: (312)245-2867. Telex: 254915.

★ 20611 ★
World Confessional Lutheran Association - Faith Evangelical Lutheran Seminary - Library (Rel-Phil)
3504 N. Pearl St.
Box 7186   Phone: (206)752-2020
Tacoma, WA 98407   John David Hascup, Th.d., Libn.
Founded: 1969. Staff: Prof 1; Other 1. Subjects: Philosophy of religion, theology, church history, hermeneutics, apologetics, homiletics, missiology. Holdings: 10,000 books; 120 bound periodical volumes. Subscriptions: 45 journals and other serials. Services: Interlibrary loan; library open to the public. Remarks: FAX: (206)759-1790.

★ 20612 ★
World Congress of Gay & Lesbian Jewish Organizations - Resource Library (Soc Sci)
Box 18961
Washington, DC 20036   Barret L. Brick, Exec.Dir.
Founded: 1980. Subjects: Gay Jewish ideas, feminism and gay consciousness. Holdings: Journal articles; newsletters; religious and liturgical materials. Services: Library not open to the public.

★ 20613 ★
World Council of Churches - Ecumenical Library (Rel-Phil)
150, route de Ferney
B.P. 2100   Phone: 22 7916111
CH-1211 Geneva 2, Switzerland   Pierre Beffa
Founded: 1946. Staff: 6. Subjects: Ecumenical fellowship of Eastern and Oriental Orthodox, Lutheran, Reformed, Methodist, Anglican, Old Catholic, Pentecostal, Baptist, United, and Independent denominations around the world. Holdings: 95,000 volumes; 10,000 boxes of archival materials. Subscriptions: 519 journals and other serials. Services: Interlibrary loan; library open to the public. Computerized Information Services: Produces URICA (40,000 records); GeoNet, Quest Network International (electronic mail services). Remarks: FAX: 22 7910361. Telex: 415 730 OIK CH. Electronic mail address(es): GEO2:WCC-COE (GeoNet); 141=QNI3601 (Quest Network). Also Known As: Conseil Oecumenique des Eglises.

★ 20614 ★
World Data Center A - Glaciology Information Center (Sci-Engr)
CIRES, Campus Box 449
University of Colorado   Phone: (303)492-5171
Boulder, CO 80309   Ann Brennan Thomas, Info.Spec.
Founded: 1957. Staff: Prof 1; Other 1. Subjects: All aspects of snow and ice, including snow cover, avalanches, glaciers, sea, river, lake ice, polar ice sheets, permafrost, paleoglaciology, ice physics. Special Collections: Historical glacier photograph collections (1880s-1960s). Holdings: 5700 books and technical reports; 12,000 reprints. Subscriptions: 90 journals and other serials. Services: Interlibrary loan; copying; SDI; will answer requests for information by correspondence; center open to the public. Automated Operations: Automated bibliographic file of holdings. Computerized Information Services: DIALOG Information Services, PFDS Online; Citation Data Base, Glacier Photo Index (internal databases); SCIENCEnet (electronic mail service). Performs searches on fee basis. Publications: Quarterly accessions list - free upon request. Remarks: FAX: (303)492-2468. Telex: 7401426 WDCA UC. Electronic mail address(es): [NSIDC/OMNET]MAIL/USA (SCIENCEnet).

★ 20615 ★
World Data Center A - Oceanography (Sci-Engr)
Natl. Oceanic and Atmospheric Adm.   Phone: (202)606-4571
Washington, DC 20235   Ronald E. Moffatt, Assoc.Dir.
Founded: 1957. Staff: Prof 3; Other 1. Subjects: Physical, chemical, and biological oceanographic data; current data; sea surface data. Special Collections: Oceanographic data from the International Geophysical Year, the International Indian Ocean Expedition, and other international cooperative oceanographic expeditions and projects; international data inventory forms. Holdings: Oceanographic data on log sheets, machine listings, and in publications for more than 1 million stations. Services: Copying; utilizes Automatic Data Processing (ADP) facilities of the National Oceanographic Data Center; facility open to qualified scientists and persons interested in oceanography. Computerized Information Services: SCIENCEnet (electronic mail service). Publications: Reports of Oceanographic Data Exchange, annual. Special Catalogs: Catalogue of Data, annual; Catalogue of Accessioned Publications. Remarks: FAX: (202)606-4586. Electronic mail address(es): NODC.WDCA (SCIENCEnet).

★ 20616 ★
World Data Center A - Rockets & Satellites - National Space Science Data Center (Sci-Engr)
Code 933, Goddard Space Flight Ctr.   Phone: (301)286-6695
Greenbelt, MD 20771   Dr. James L. Green, Dir.
Founded: 1966. **Staff:** 125. **Subjects:** Space science. **Special Collections:** Satellite and space probe experiment data. **Holdings:** 472,949 volumes; 30,000 microfiche; 68,292 tapes; 35,000 reels of microfilm; 1.67 million linear feet of photographs. **Services:** Copying; SDI; center open to the public by appointment. **Automated Operations:** Computerized cataloging, acquisitions, and files. **Computerized Information Services:** Astrophysics Data System, NASA Climate Data System, Master Directory, Crustal Dynamics Data Information System; CD-ROMs; Space Physics Analysis Network (SPAN, electronic mail service). **Publications:** NSSDC News; NSSDC Data Listings/Catalogs; A Guide to the National Space Science Data Center. **Remarks:** FAX: (301)286-9803. Telex: 89675 NASACOM GBLT. Electronic mail address(es): SPAN::NSSDCA::REQUEST (SPAN). Maintained by NASA, the NSSDC collects and disseminates scientific data that are obtained from spacecraft and ground-based observations. Disciplines represented include astronomy, astrophysics, atmospheric sciences, ionospheric physics, land sciences, magnetospheric physics, ocean sciences, planetary sciences, and solar-terrestrial physics. The data are contained on magnetic disks, film products, optical, video and magnetic disks, and CD-ROMs. The NSSDC publishes information catalogs and data inventories for the entire archive, a subset of which in maintained online and is accessible through many international computer networks.

★ 20617 ★
World Data Center A - Solar-Terrestrial Physics (Sci-Engr)
Natl. Oceanic and Atmospheric Adm.
E/GC2
325 Broadway   Phone: (303)497-6323
Boulder, CO 80303   Joe H. Allen, Chf., STP Div.
Founded: 1957. **Staff:** Prof 8; Other 9. **Subjects:** Geomagnetism, ionospheric phenomena, solar and interplanetary phenomena, aurora, airglow, cosmic rays. **Special Collections:** Solar-terrestrial data collection. **Holdings:** 19 million feet of 35mm film; station booklets; 12,000 magnetic tapes; microfiche. **Services:** Copying; open to the public. **Automated Operations:** Computerized cataloging and circulation. **Computerized Information Services:** Online systems; SprintMail (electronic mail service). **Publications:** Solar-Geophysical Data, monthly; UAG-Report Series, intermittent. **Special Catalogs:** Catalogs of data (by discipline, periodically). **Remarks:** Is said to maintain the largest collection of solar-terrestrial data in the world. **Also Known As:** National Geophysical Data Center - Solar-Terrestrial Physics Division.

★ 20618 ★
World Forest Institute - Library (Biol Sci)
4033 S.W. Canton Rd.   Phone: (503)228-1367
Portland, OR 97221   Eric Landis, Prog.Dir.
Founded: 1967. **Staff:** 6. **Subjects:** Forestry, wood products, natural resources, international development. **Holdings:** Figures not available. **Services:** Interlibrary loan; copying; library open to the public. **Computerized Information Services:** DIALOG Information Services; Wood PIC (internal database). Performs searches on fee basis. **Publications:** Forestry Business Country Profiles; Wood Design Focus; Forest Perspectives; Forest World. **Remarks:** WFI serves as an information clearinghouse for national and international forestry and wood products inquiries. FAX: (503)228-3624.

World Health Organization - International Agency for Research on Cancer
See: **International Agency for Research on Cancer** (8052)

★ 20619 ★
World Health Organization - Office of Library and Health Literature Services (Med)
Ave. Appia   Phone: 22 7912062
CH-1211 Geneva 27, Switzerland   Dr. Deborah Avriel, Chf.Libn.
Founded: 1948. **Staff:** Prof 9; Other 15. **Subjects:** Public health and allied health sciences; research - promotion, development; medicine; environmental health; education of health personnel. **Special Collections:** World Health Organization Documentation. **Holdings:** 45,000 books; 250,000 documents; 7000 historical items; files (by country). **Subscriptions:** 3000 journals and other serials. **Services:** Interlibrary loan; copying; SDI;

library open to the public for reference use only. **Computerized Information Services:** WHOLIS (database of WHO publications and documents); CD-ROMs. Performs searches. Contact Person: Irene Bertrand; Barbara Aronson. **Publications:** WHODOC (list of recent WHO publications and documents), bimonthly; LIAISON (newsletter). **Remarks:** FAX: 22 7910746; 22 7881836. Telex 415416 OMS. **Also Known As:** WHO; Organisation Mondiale de la Sante; OMS. **Staff:** Edith Certain; Yvonne Grandbois; Carole Modis; Dr. Adrian Senadhira; Mr. Kiyoshi Shibata; Judith Tomero.

World Health Organization - Pan American Health Organization
See: **Pan American Health Organization** (12718)

★ 20620 ★
The World Institute for Advanced Phenomenological Research & Learning - Library and Archives (Rel-Phil)
348 Payson Rd.   Phone: (617)489-3696
Belmont, MA 02178   Anna-Teresa Tymieniecka, Pres.
Subjects: Phenomenology. **Holdings:** 500 books. **Subscriptions:** 15 journals and other serials. **Services:** Library open to the public with restrictions. **Publications:** Phenomenological Inquiry: A Review of Philosophical Ideas and Trends; Les Travaux de Recherches de l'Institut Mondial de Hautes Etudes Phenomologiques, diriges par A-T. **Staff:** Robert Wise, Ed.Asst.

★ 20621 ★
World Intellectual Property Organization - Library (Law)
34, chemin des Colombettes   Phone: 22 7309390
CH-1211 Geneva 20, Switzerland   Mareile Langsdorff-Breitenbach, Hd. of Lib.
Founded: 1960. **Staff:** 3. **Subjects:** Intellectual property - laws, treaties; industrial property - patents, technological inventions, trademarks, industrial designs; copyrights - literary, musical, artistic works. **Holdings:** 35,000 volumes. **Subscriptions:** 350 journals and other serials. **Services:** Library open to the public for reference use only. **Automated Operations:** Computerized public access catalog. **Computerized Information Services:** OASIS. **Publications:** Acquisitions lists, 6/year. **Remarks:** FAX: 22 7335428. Telex: 412 912 OMPI CH. Cable: OMPI. **Also Known As:** Organizacion Mundial de la Propiedad Intelectual; Organisation Mondiale de la Propriete Intellectuelle.

★ 20622 ★
World Jewish Genealogy Organization - Library (Hist, Rel-Phil)
1601 48th St.
Box 420   Phone: (718)435-4400
Brooklyn, NY 11219   Rabbi N. Halberstam, Libn.
Staff: 1. **Subjects:** Judaica. **Holdings:** 10,000 books. **Services:** Library not open to the public. **Publications:** Bibliography and biography journal devoted to genealogy.

★ 20623 ★
World Jurist Association - Information Center (Law)
1000 Connecticut Ave., N.W., Suite 202
Washington, DC 20036   Phone: (202)466-5428
Subjects: International law, law and technology, human rights, international trade, nuclear arms control, aviation and outer space. **Special Collections:** Archives. **Holdings:** 50 books and bound periodical volumes; U.N. documents. **Services:** Library not open to the public. **Automated Operations:** Computerized circulation. **Publications:** List of publications - available on request. **Remarks:** FAX: (202)452-8540. Telex: 440456. **Formerly:** World Jurist Association of the World Peace Through Law Center.

★ 20624 ★
World Life Research Institute - Library (Biol Sci)
23000 Grand Terrace Rd.   Phone: (714)825-4773
Colton, CA 92324   Bruce W. Halstead, Lib.Dir.
Founded: 1959. **Staff:** Prof 1; Other 2. **Subjects:** Marine biotoxins, venomous snakes, plant and insect biotoxins, dangerous marine animals, poisonous and medicinal plants, biomedical history, biologically-active natural products; coverage includes Africa, Asia, and the Americas, with emphasis on Amazonia, Oceania, and China. **Holdings:** 50,000 volumes; 50 manuscripts;

350,000 reprints and pamphlets; bibliographic references on biotoxins; 5000 maps and pictures of poisonous plants and animals. **Subscriptions:** 20 journals and other serials. **Services:** Copying; library open to the public by appointment. **Computerized Information Services:** CompuServe Information Service, MEDLINE; internal database; CompuServe Information Service (electronic mail service). **Publications:** Monographs on poisonous plants and animals; handbooks on immunology and traditional medical therapies worldwide. **Special Indexes:** Plant and animal poisons; traditional herbal medicine; environmental pollution; radiation sickness therapy. **Remarks:** FAX: (714)783-3477. Electronic mail address(es): 76106,3913 (CompuServe Information Service). **Staff:** Carrie Foster.

★ 20625 ★
World Meteorological Organization - WMO Library (Sci-Engr)
PO Box 2300
41, ave. Giuseppe-Motta   Phone: 22 7308411
CH-1211 Geneva 2, Switzerland   Miss Favre, Libn.
Staff: Prof 2. **Subjects:** Weather prediction, world climate, tropical meteorology, monitoring environmental pollution, weather modification, hydrology, atmospheric sciences. **Holdings:** 35,000 volumes. **Subscriptions:** 95 journals and other serials. **Services:** Interlibrary loan (Switzerland only); copying; library open to the public for reference use only. **Remarks:** Organization is a specialized agency of the United Nations. FAX: 22 7342326. Telex: 4141 99A OMNCH.

★ 20626 ★
World Modeling Association - WMA Library (Bus-Fin)
4401 San Pedro Dr., N.E., No. 801   Phone: (505)883-2823
Albuquerque, NM 87109   Kathy Miller, Libn.
Founded: 1961. **Staff:** 3. **Subjects:** Fashion - careers, modeling, and merchandising; personal development. **Special Collections:** Photographic and Professional Modeling Collection. **Holdings:** 275 volumes; 28 manuscripts; clippings. **Subscriptions:** 18 journals and other serials. **Services:** Copying; library open to the public by mail inquiry only. **Remarks:** FAX: (915)658-3180. **Formerly:** Located in San Angelo, TX.

World Music Archives
See: Wesleyan University - Library (20178)

★ 20627 ★
World Nature Association - Orville W. Crowder Memorial Library (Env-Cons)
P.O. Box 673   Phone: (301)593-2522
Silver Spring, MD 20918   Dr. Donald H. Messersmith, Pres.
Founded: 1969. **Subjects:** Birds, mammals, wild flowers, nature, worldwide travel. **Special Collections:** Birdlife of China (30 volumes). **Holdings:** 2000 books; 100 AV programs. **Subscriptions:** 10 journals and other serials. **Services:** Library open to the public with restrictions (written request). **Publications:** World Nature News. **Remarks:** FAX: (301)593-6148.

World Peace Through Law Center - Information Center
See: World Jurist Association - Information Center (20623)

★ 20628 ★
World Research Foundation - Library (Env-Cons, Med)
15300 Ventura Blvd., Suite 405   Phone: (818)907-5483
Sherman Oaks, CA 91403   Lisa Jones
Founded: 1971. **Subjects:** Health and the environment, health tools and technologies available outside the United States. **Holdings:** 10,000 volumes. **Services:** Copying; library open to the public. **Computerized Information Services:** Searches databases in the field of health and environment from over 100 countries. **Remarks:** FAX: (818)907-6044. Acts as a depository for public information.

★ 20629 ★
World Resources Institute - Library (Env-Cons, Agri)
1709 New York Ave., N.W., 7th Fl.   Phone: (202)622-2504
Washington, DC 20006   Susan N. Terry, Libn.
Founded: 1982. **Staff:** Prof 1; Other 1. **Subjects:** Environment, natural resources, agriculture, forestry, climate, energy, biodiversity, sustainable development. **Holdings:** 9000 books and reports; 20 VF drawers of pamphlets and clippings; studies. **Subscriptions:** 350 journals and newsletters. **Services:** Interlibrary loan; library open to the public by appointment. **Automated Operations:** Computerized cataloging, acquisitions, and serials. **Computerized Information Services:** DIALOG Information Services, WILSONLINE; internal databases. **Networks/Consortia:** Member of Interlibrary Users Association (IUA). **Remarks:** FAX: (202)638-0036. Telex: 64414 WRIWASH.

World Shakespeare Bibliography
See: Texas A&M University - Department of English (16193)

World Student Christian Federation - Archives
See: Yale University - Divinity School Library (20708)

★ 20630 ★
World Trade Center of New Orleans - Library
2 Canal St., Suite 2900
New Orleans, LA 70130
Founded: 1946. **Subjects:** Import and export trade, travel, international relations, economics, transportation. **Holdings:** 10,000 volumes; 350 foreign telephone directories; 700 U.S. telephone directories; 700 trade directories; 31 VF drawers of pamphlet material. **Remarks:** Currently inactive.

★ 20631 ★
World Trade Centre Toronto - Library (Bus-Fin)
60 Harbour St.   Phone: (416)863-2008
Toronto, ON, Canada M5J 1B7   Maria A. Escriu Fenn, Libn.
Founded: 1978. **Staff:** Prof 1. **Subjects:** International trade, marketing, importing and exporting, Canadian industries, economics, shipping, ports. **Special Collections:** Foreign indusrial directories; international trade fairs and exhibitions file; international market information and economic reports. **Holdings:** 1000 monographs; country profiles; country reports; commodity reports; annual reports. **Subscriptions:** 350 journals and other serials; 5 newspapers. **Services:** Interlibrary loan (with restrictions), copying; library open to WTC members only. **Computerized Information Services:** DIALOG Information Services, ORBIT Search Service, Info Globe. **Publications:** Focus On (economic country profiles), monthly; Marketplace (business opportunities bulletin), monthly. **Remarks:** FAX: (416)863-4830. Telex: 06 219666. Maintained by Toronto Harbour Commissioners.

World Trade Centre Vancouver
See: Vancouver Board of Trade/World Trade Centre Vancouver (19753)

★ 20632 ★
World Union of Stockholm Pioneers - Library (Env-Cons)
46, rue Raffet
F-75016 Paris, France   Phone: 1 45277876
Subjects: Nature, holistic environment, energy forms. **Holdings:** 350 volumes. **Also Known As:** Union Mondiale des Pioniers de Stockholm.

★ 20633 ★
World University Roundtable - World University Library (Rel-Phil)
Desert Sanctuary Regional Campus
Mescal-Salcido Rd.
Box 2470   Phone: (602)586-2985
Benson, AZ 85602   Howard John Zitko, Pres./Libn.
Founded: 1947. **Staff:** Prof 1; Other 1. **Subjects:** Metaphysics and philosophy, esoteric science, health, astrology, UFO phenomena, poetry. **Special Collections:** Rare books in religious philosophy. **Holdings:** 25,000 books; 250 bound periodical volumes; 100 boxes of unbound magazines, dissertations, essays, paperbacks; 1000 other cataloged items. **Subscriptions:** 25 journals and other serials. **Services:** Library open to the public for reference use only. **Publications:** World University Library, occasional - to members and the public; Liftoff (newsletter), bimonthly.

★ 20634 ★
World Vision International - Information Resource Center (Rel-Phil)
919 W. Huntington Dr.   Phone: (818)303-8811
Monrovia, CA 91016   Lenore A. Beckstrom, Res.Ctr.Spec.
Founded: 1970. **Staff:** 1. **Subjects:** World Christianity, missions, hunger, refugees, development. **Holdings:** 7315 books; 36 periodical titles; 36 VF drawers of geographic material; 2 lateral file drawers on North American mission organizations. **Subscriptions:** 67 journals and other serials. **Services:** Copying (limited); center not open to the public. **Automated Operations:** Computerized circulation. **Computerized Information Services:** The Source Information Network, EasyNet, FYI News; internal database. **Special Indexes:** Index to book collection; index to people and organizations significant to world evangelization (computerized).

World Wide Fund for Nature - International Union for Conservation of Nature and Natural Resources - Library
See: **International Union for Conservation of Nature and Natural Resources - Library** (8202)

★ 20635 ★
World Wide Fund for Nature - Photographic Library (Env-Cons)
c/o World Conservation Centre
Avenue du Mont-Blanc
CH-1196 Gland, Switzerland
Phone: 22 647181
Ms. Michele Depraz
Founded: 1975. **Staff:** 4. **Subjects:** Conservation of the natural environment, ecological processes necessary to life on earth, wildlife. **Holdings:** 10,000 color slides; 10,000 black/white photographs of nature and wildlife. **Services:** Library open to the public on a restricted basis. **Remarks:** Affiliated with International Union for Conservation of Nature and Natural Resources. **Also Known As:** Fonds Mondial pour la Conservation de la Nature.

★ 20636 ★
World Wildlife Fund-U.S. - Conservation Foundation - Library (Env-Cons)
1250 24th St., N.W.
Washington, DC 20037
Phone: (202)293-4800
Barbara K. Rodes, Res.Libn.
Founded: 1949. **Staff:** 2. **Subjects:** Natural resource conservation, environmental quality, pollution, land use planning, wildlife and economic development, habitat preservation, global climate change, international environmental policy. **Holdings:** 10,000 volumes; clippings file. **Subscriptions:** 455 journals and other serials. **Services:** Interlibrary loan; copying; library open to the public by appointment. **Computerized Information Services:** DIALOG Information Services, BRS Information Technologies, OCLC, MEDLARS. Performs searches on fee basis. **Publications:** Acquisitions List, monthly. **Remarks:** FAX: (202)293-9211. Telex: 64505 Panda. **Staff:** Carla Langeveld, Asst.Libn.

★ 20637 ★
World Without War Council - Midwest Library (Soc Sci)
421 S. Wabash
Chicago, IL 60605
Phone: (312)663-9250
Robert Woito, Dir.
Founded: 1970. **Staff:** Prof 1; Other 2. **Subjects:** International relations and organizations, arms race and disarmament, human rights, nonviolence, world economic development, crisis issues, area studies, ethics and war. **Holdings:** 2000 books; reference files on organizations in war/peace field. **Subscriptions:** 10 journals and other serials. **Services:** Library open to the public.

★ 20638 ★
World Zionist Organization - American Section - Zionist Archives and Library (Area-Ethnic, Rel-Phil)
110 E. 59th St.
New York, NY 10022
Phone: (212)753-2167
Cipora Burstein, Dir. & Libn.
Founded: 1939. **Staff:** Prof 3; Other 1. **Subjects:** Israel, Zionism, Middle East, history of the Jews and Jewish life. **Holdings:** 50,000 books and pamphlets; 50,000 photographs; 977 reels of microfilm; slides; filmstrips; nonmusical and musical recordings; symphonic scores; folk music; maps and posters; 137 VF drawers of archival material. **Subscriptions:** 400 journals and other serials. **Services:** Interlibrary loan; copying; library open to the public. **Staff:** Ruth Fergenson, Libn.; Judy Wallach, Libn.

Worldwide Church of God - Ambassador College
See: **Ambassador College** (451)

Sol Worth Ethnographic Film Archive
See: **University of Pennsylvania - Annenberg School for Communication - Library** (19174)

★ 20639 ★
Worthington Historical Society - Library (Hist)
50 W. New England Ave.
Worthington, OH 43085
Phone: (614)885-1247
Lillian Skeele, Libn.
Staff: Prof 1. **Subjects:** Local history and genealogy, historic preservation, decorative arts, pioneer crafts, dolls, lace-making, architecture. **Holdings:** 850 books. **Subscriptions:** 3 journals and other serials. **Services:** Interlibrary loan; copying; library open to the public by appointment.

John Henry Wrenn Library
See: **University of Texas at Austin - Harry Ransom Humanities Research Center** (19392)

★ 20640 ★
Wrestling Review of Western New York - Library (Rec)
1285 Main St.
Buffalo, NY 14209
Phone: (716)885-9016
William S. Hein
Founded: 1989. **Staff:** Prof 1; Other 2. **Subjects:** Wrestling. **Special Collections:** Wrestling Philatelic Collection. **Holdings:** 1070 books; 500 theses and dissertations. **Subscriptions:** 25 journals and other serials. **Services:** Interlibrary loan; copying; library open to the public by appointment. **Computerized Information Services:** Internal databases. Performs searches. Contact Person: Linda Knuutila. **Publications:** Bibliography (under development). **Remarks:** FAX: (716)883-8100. Library is said to contain the largest collection of English language amateur wrestling publications in the Western Hemisphere.

Wright Brothers Aeronautical Engineering Collection
See: **Franklin Institute Science Museum - Library** (6092)

★ 20641 ★
Frank Lloyd Wright Home and Studio Foundation - Research Center (Art)
951 Chicago Ave.
Oak Park, IL 60302
Phone: (708)848-1695
Margaret Klinkow, Res.Ctr.Dir.
Founded: 1974. **Subjects:** Frank Lloyd Wright, Prairie style of architecture, architectural preservation and restoration. **Special Collections:** Restoration of Frank Lloyd Wright's home and studio (1000 drawings; 20,000 photographs and slides; 3000 items in paperwork files; 3500 artifacts); John Drummond Archives; Maginel Wright Barney Archives; John Lloyd Wright Toy Collection Archives; Wright family memorabilia including Japanese prints, books, and photographs from 1905 Wright trip to Japan. **Holdings:** 600 books; unbound periodical volumes; 62 videotapes; 54 sound recordings; 7 manuscripts; 1000 drawings; clipping files; broadsides; 900 historic photographs. **Subscriptions:** 10 journals and other serials. **Services:** Copying; library open to the public. **Publications:** Brochures. **Remarks:** FAX: (708)848-1248. **Staff:** Donna Hawkins.

★ 20642 ★
Wright Information Center - Clearinghouse (Hist)
1511 S.W. 65th Terrace
Boca Raton, FL 33428-7819
Phone: (407)482-7582
Phyllis M. Heiss, Pres.
Founded: 1972. **Staff:** 2. **Subjects:** Genealogy. **Holdings:** 675 volumes. **Services:** Library not open to the public. **Computerized Information Services:** Internal database. **Remarks:** Maintains genealogical information related to the surname Wright.

★ 20643 ★
The Wright Institute (Soc Sci)
2728 Durant Ave.
Berkeley, CA 94704
Phone: (510)841-9230
Dr. James Fu, Libn.
Founded: 1968. **Staff:** Prof 1. **Subjects:** Psychology, sociology, education, research methodology. **Special Collections:** Dr. Abraham Maslow Collection (his complete private collection donated by his widow); Nevitt Sanford Archives. **Holdings:** 10,000 books; 360 Wright Institute dissertations. **Subscriptions:** 64 journals and other serials. **Services:** Interlibrary loan; library open to the public for reference use only. **Computerized Information Services:** BRS Information Technologies.

J.M. Wright Technical School
See: **Connecticut State Board of Education** (4187)

John Lloyd Wright Toy Collection Archives
See: **Frank Lloyd Wright Home and Studio Foundation - Research Center** (20641)

John Shepard Wright Memorial Library
See: **Indiana Academy of Science (7752)**

★ 20644 ★
Wright State University - Archives & Special Collections (Hist)
University Library   Phone: (513)873-2092
Dayton, OH 45435   Robert H. Smith, Hd. of Archv.
Founded: 1964. **Staff:** Prof 4; Other 4. **Subjects:** Aeronautics history, Wright Brothers, Ohio and local history, genealogy, Arthur Rackham. **Special Collections:** Early Aviation (5000 volumes); Miami Valley history (4000 volumes); university archives (150 cubic feet); manuscripts (1500 cubic feet). **Holdings:** 12,000 books and bound periodical volumes; 30 cubic feet of Wright Brothers Papers; 24 cubic feet of James M. Cox Papers; 100 cubic feet of labor union records; 200 cubic feet of local business records; 40 cubic feet of local church records; microfilm. **Services:** Copying; microfilming; collections open to the public. **Automated Operations:** Computerized cataloging. **Computerized Information Services:** Internal database. **Networks/Consortia:** Member of Southwestern Ohio Council for Higher Education (SOCHE), Ohio Network of American History Research Centers (ONARCH). **Publications:** Guide to Manuscripts; Guide to Local Government Records and Newspapers; Microfilm Sales List. **Special Catalogs:** Inventories or registers for manuscript collections; computer guide to local government records; Arthur Rackham Catalog. **Special Indexes:** Naturalization Indexes. **Remarks:** FAX: (513)873-4100. **Staff:** Dorothy Smith, Archv.; John Brannick, Local Rec.Spec.; Julie Orenstein, Microfilm Spec.; Dawn Dewey, Archv.

★ 20645 ★
**Wright State University - School of Medicine - Fordham Health
  Sciences Library (Med)**
3640 Colonel Glenn Hwy.   Phone: (513)873-2266
Dayton, OH 45435   Sarah S. Timmons, Act.Hea.Sci.Libn.
Founded: 1974. **Staff:** Prof 13. **Subjects:** Medicine, human anatomy, microbiology, physiology, psychology, biochemistry. **Special Collections:** Ross A. McFarland Collection in Aerospace Medicine and Human Factors Engineering; Aerospace Medical Association Archives; H.T.E. Hertzburg Collection in Anthropometry. **Holdings:** 44,871 books; 50,367 bound periodical volumes; 2678 AV programs; 191 computer software programs. **Subscriptions:** 1335 journals and other serials. **Services:** Interlibrary loan; copying; SDI; library open to the public with restrictions. **Automated Operations:** Computerized cataloging, acquisitions, serials, circulation, and ILL (DOCLINE). **Computerized Information Services:** MEDLARS, DIALOG Information Services, OCLC, PHILSOM, BRS Information Technologies, NASA/RECON, PaperChase, NLM. **Networks/Consortia:** Member of Southwestern Ohio Council for Higher Education (SOCHE), National Network of Libraries of Medicine - Greater Midwest Region, OHIONET. **Special Catalogs:** Ross A. McFarland Catalogs and Inventory. **Remarks:** FAX: (513)879-2675. **Staff:** Mary Ann Hoffman, Spec. and Gen.Coll.Libn.; Narcissa Baker, Cat.Libn.; Christine Watson, Comp.Serv.Mgr.; Susan Case, Circ.Libn.; Terry Henner, LRC; Jeffrey Wehmeyer, Act.Ref.Libn.; Frances LeSalle, Act.ILL.Libn.

W. Howard Wright Research Center
See: **Schenectady Chemicals, Inc. (14900)**

★ 20646 ★
Wm. Wrigley, Jr. Company - Corporate Library (Bus-Fin)
Wrigley Bldg.
410 N. Michigan Ave.   Phone: (312)644-2121
Chicago, IL 60611-4287   Linda Hanrath, Corp.Libn.
Founded: 1978. **Staff:** Prof 1; Other 1. **Subjects:** Business, chewing gum industry. **Special Collections:** Company history (5 VF drawers). **Holdings:** 2000 volumes; 12 VF drawers. **Subscriptions:** 100 journals and other serials. **Services:** Interlibrary loan; SDI; library open to the public with restrictions. **Computerized Information Services:** DIALOG Information Services. **Networks/Consortia:** Member of Chicago Library System. **Publications:** Serials Holdings List, annual; New Library Acquisitions, quarterly. **Remarks:** FAX: (312)644-7879.

★ 20647 ★
**Wm. Wrigley, Jr. Company - Quality Assurance Branch Library (Sci-
  Engr)**
3535 S. Ashland Ave.   Phone: (312)523-4040
Chicago, IL 60609   Carmen Mendoza, Info.Spec./Tech.Libn.
Staff: Prof 1. **Subjects:** Quality assurance. **Holdings:** 250 titles. **Services:** Interlibrary loan; copying; SDI; library open to the public with restrictions. **Remarks:** The Research & Development Library, located at the same address, staffs and services the Quality Assurance Branch Library.

★ 20648 ★
**Wm. Wrigley, Jr. Company - Research & Development Library (Food-
  Bev)**
3535 S. Ashland Ave.   Phone: (312)650-5587
Chicago, IL 60609   Carmen Mendoza, Info.Spec.
Founded: 1972. **Staff:** Prof 2. **Subjects:** Chewing gum, food science and technology, flavors, chemistry, packaging, chemical engineering. **Special Collections:** Chewing gum patent file, 19th century to present (1300 patents). **Holdings:** 1400 books; 310 volumes of unbound periodicals. **Subscriptions:** 204 journals and other serials. **Services:** Interlibrary loan. **Computerized Information Services:** DIALOG Information Services. **Special Indexes:** Subject index to chewing gum patents (online). **Remarks:** Alternate telephone number(s): 523-4040.

Wroth Memorial Library
See: **Washington County Hospital (19998)**

WSAZ-TV News Film Archive
See: **Marshall University - James E. Morrow Library (9724)**

★ 20649 ★
Wuesthoff Memorial Hospital - Hospital Library (Med)
110 Longwood Ave.
Box 560006
Rockledge, FL 32956   Phone: (407)636-2211
Staff: Prof 1. **Subjects:** Medicine, surgery, nursing, allied health sciences. **Holdings:** 1936 books; 620 bound periodical volumes; 480 audio cassettes; 49 slide carousels; 4 VF drawers of pamphlets. **Subscriptions:** 126 journals and other serials. **Services:** Interlibrary loan; copying; library open to the public with administrative approval.

Wuhan College of Geodesy, Programmetry and Cartography
See: **Wuhan Technical University of Surveying and Mapping - WTUSM
  Library (20650)**

Wuhan Institute of Virology - Documentation and Information Division
See: **Academia Sinica (32)**

★ 20650 ★
**Wuhan Technical University of Surveying and Mapping - WTUSM
  Library (Geog-Map, Sci-Engr)**
39 Lo-Yu Rd.   Phone: 715571
Wuhan, Hubei Province, People's Republic of China   Prof. Lu Kaishu
Founded: 1956. **Staff:** 60. **Subjects:** Surveying, geodesy, photogrammetry, cartography, satellite geodesy, astronomy, gravity, optical instruments, computer hardware and software, lasers, remote sensing, automatic control, civil engineering, printing, mechanics. **Special Collections:** Maps. **Holdings:** 410,989 volumes; 4705 periodicals; 2888 technical reports. **Subscriptions:** 1410 journals and other serials; 100 newspapers. **Services:** Copying. **Computerized Information Services:** GOLEM Information Retrieval System of Surveying and Mapping (internal database). **Remarks:** FAX: 40210. Telex: 6852. **Formerly:** Wuhan College of Geodesy, Programmetry and Cartography, located in Wuchang, Hubei Province, People's Republic of China.

★ 20651 ★
Wuhan University of Hydraulic and Electric Engineering - Library (Sci-Engr)
Luojiashan
Wuchang District
Wuhan 430072, Hubei, People's   Phone: 027 81221247
  Republic of China   Li Yuxin, Prof./Chf.Libn.
Subjects: Engineering - civil, hydraulic, electrical, mechanical, environmental; architecture; electronic and computer science; mathematics; physical science; English language. **Special Collections:** History of Water Conservation (in Chinese; 10,000 items). **Holdings:** 880,000 books; 70,000 bound periodical volumes; 1400 AV programs; 1000 manuscripts; 3000 nonbook items. **Subscriptions:** 3000 journals and other serials; 120 newspapers. **Services:** Interlibrary loan; copying; SDI; library open to the public. **Computerized Information Services:** DIALOG Information Services, ESA/IRS, BRS Information Technologies, Chinese Science & Technology Documentary Data Base. Performs searches on fee basis. Contact Person: Jia Mingxin, Ref.Libn., 027 812212494. **Publications:** Journal of Water Conservancy & Electric Power Technology. **Remarks:** Telex: 40170 WCTEL CN. **Staff:** Xue Lingshan, Assoc.Prof./Vice-Libn.; Hu Jianlin, Libn.

Wupatki National Monument
See: **U.S. Natl. Park Service (17792)**

★ 20652 ★
Wyandot County Historical Society - Wyandot Museum - Library (Hist)
130 S. 7th St.
P.O. Box 372
Upper Sandusky, OH 43351   Phone: (419)294-3857
Subjects: Wyandot Mission, Indian artifacts. **Special Collections:** Normandy Home, 1852 (pioneer and Victorian furniture; toys; musical instruments; clothing; dishes; early history of Wyandot County). **Holdings:** 500 books. **Services:** Library open to the public for reference use only. **Staff:** Paula Cash.

★ 20653 ★
Wyandotte County Historical Society and Museum - Harry M. Trowbridge Research Library (Hist)
631 N. 126th St.   Phone: (913)721-1078
Bonner Springs, KS 66012   Lisa Schwarzenholz, Archv.
Founded: 1956. **Staff:** Prof 1; Other 5. **Subjects:** Wyandotte County and Kansas City history; Wyandot, Shawnee, and Delaware Indians. **Special Collections:** J.R. Kelley Cooperage Company business papers and ledgers, 1903-1916 (36 cubic feet); proceedings of Congresses of mid-19th century; bound magazines and school texts of the late 19th century; Early, Conley, and Farrow Family Collections, 1763-1960 (30 cubic feet of papers, books, photographs). **Holdings:** 4000 books; 1000 bound periodical volumes; clippings; 150 reels of microfilm; 5000 photographs; maps. **Subscriptions:** 10 journals and other serials. **Services:** Copying; library open to the public with restrictions.

★ 20654 ★
Wyandotte County Law Library (Law)
Wyandotte County Courthouse
710 N. 7th St.   Phone: (913)573-2899
Kansas City, KS 66101   Donna Ashley, Law Libn.
Founded: 1925. **Staff:** 2. **Subjects:** Law. **Special Collections:** Blackstones Commentaries, 1761 (4 volumes). **Holdings:** 17,000 books. **Subscriptions:** 12 journals and other serials. **Services:** Copying; library open to students with recommendation from an attorney. **Staff:** Brenda Denver, Asst.

★ 20655 ★
Wyandotte Hospital and Medical Center - Medical/Staff Library (Med)
2333 Biddle   Phone: (313)284-2400
Wyandotte, MI 48192   Diane M. O'Keefe, Libn.
Founded: 1972. **Staff:** Prof 1. **Subjects:** Medicine, nursing, psychology, management, and allied subjects. **Special Collections:** Consumer Health Collection (200 items). **Holdings:** 1200 books; 1500 bound periodical volumes; 500 microfiche. **Subscriptions:** 130 journals and other serials; 3 newspapers. **Services:** Interlibrary loan; copying; SDI; library open to the public for reference use only. **Computerized Information Services:** DIALOG Information Services, MEDLARS, VU/TEXT Information Services. **Remarks:** FAX: (313)246-6069.

Wycliffe College
See: **University of Toronto - Wycliffe College - Leonard Library (19464)**

★ 20656 ★
Wyeth-Ayerst Research - Information Center (Sci-Engr, Med)
64 Maple St.   Phone: (518)297-8294
Rouses Point, NY 12979-9985   George L. Curran, III, Sr.Libn. & Info.Sci.
Founded: 1965. **Staff:** Prof 1; Other 3. **Subjects:** Analytical and pharmaceutical chemistry, pharmacy, pharmacology, business management, quality control. **Special Collections:** Pharmaceutical Sciences Division Archives. **Holdings:** 5500 books; 3500 bound periodical volumes; chemical and world patents, 1970-1989, on microfilm; 1400 volumes on microfilm; 100 cassette programs. **Subscriptions:** 500 serials. **Services:** Interlibrary loan; center not open to the public. **Automated Operations:** Computerized cataloging, acquisitions, serials, circulation, and ILL. **Computerized Information Services:** DIALOG Information Services, BRS Information Technologies, Occupational Health Services, Inc. (OHS), STN International, Chemical Information Systems, Inc. (CIS), OCLC, Data-Star, NLM, ORBIT Search Service, Current Contents; CD-ROMs (MEDLINE, SciTech Reference Plus, CD-CHROM, Materials Safety Data Sheets, ALDRICHCHEM Data Search); DOCLINE (electronic mail service). **Networks/Consortia:** Member of New York State Interlibrary Loan Network (NYSILL), North Country Reference and Research Resources Council (NCRRRC), PALINET. **Publications:** Bulletin, quarterly - for internal distribution only. **Remarks:** FAX: (518)297-8706.

★ 20657 ★
Wyeth-Ayerst Research - Research Library (Biol Sci, Med)
CN 8000   Phone: (908)274-4268
Princeton, NJ 08543-8000   Elaine Harris, Libn.
Subjects: Chemistry, biological sciences, medical sciences. **Holdings:** 4000 books; 25,000 bound periodical volumes; 1500 reels of microfilm. **Subscriptions:** 450 journals and other serials. **Services:** Interlibrary loan; library not open to the public. **Computerized Information Services:** DIALOG Information Services, BRS Information Technologies, STN International, MEDLARS, Data Star, PFDS Online, Questel. **Networks/Consortia:** Member of MEDCORE, PALINET. **Remarks:** FAX: (908)274-4733.

★ 20658 ★
Wyeth, Ltd. - Wyeth Resource Library (Med)
1120 Finch Ave., W., 7th Fl.   Phone: (416)736-4056
Downsview, ON, Canada M3J 3H7   Shamim Jamal-Rajan, Sci.Prod.Info.Off.
Staff: 2. **Subjects:** Pharmacology - general, clinical, hormonal; psychiatry; gynecology; cardiovascular system. **Holdings:** 725 books; 765 bound periodical volumes; 4798 reprints; 10 reports and current awareness publications. **Subscriptions:** 62 journals and other serials. **Services:** Library not open to the public. **Automated Operations:** Computerized cataloging. **Computerized Information Services:** DIALOG Information Services; internal database. **Remarks:** FAX: (416)736-9869.

★ 20659 ★
Wyle Laboratories - Wyle Research Library (Sci-Engr)
128 Maryland St.   Phone: (213)322-1763
El Segundo, CA 90245   Deborah Aber, Info.Dir.
Staff: Prof 1. **Subjects:** Noise control, acoustics. **Holdings:** 12,000 books; 50 bound periodical volumes. **Subscriptions:** 25 journals and other serials. **Services:** Interlibrary loan; library not open to the public. **Automated Operations:** Computerized cataloging. **Computerized Information Services:** DIALOG Information Services. **Remarks:** FAX: (213)322-3603.

★ 20660 ★
Wyoming County Law Library (Law)
Wyoming County Court House   Phone: (717)836-3200
Tunkhannock, PA 18657   Donna N. Clark, Lib.Dir.
Subjects: Law. **Remarks:** No further information was supplied by respondent.

★ 20661 ★
Wyoming Historical and Geological Society - Bishop Memorial Library
(Hist)
49 S. Franklin St.   Phone: (717)823-6244
Wilkes-Barre, PA 18701   Wendy Franklin, Libn./Archv.
Founded: 1858. **Staff:** Prof 1; Other 3. **Subjects:** Wyoming Valley and
Pennsylvania history. **Special Collections:** Manuscripts relating chiefly to
the Wilkes-Barre region of the Wyoming Valley, 1750-1950 (1500 cubic
feet). **Holdings:** 6000 books; 500 bound periodical volumes; 1000 reels of
microfilm of Wilkes-Barre newspapers, 1797-1950; 12,000 photographs.
Subscriptions: 15 journals and other serials. **Services:** Copying; library open
to the public. **Publications:** Susquehanna Company Papers; Proceedings and
Collections, irregular; Newsletter.

★ 20662 ★
Wyoming Medical Center - Medical Library (Med)
1233 E. 2nd St.   Phone: (307)577-2450
Casper, WY 82601   J. Wilbert, Dir.
Staff: Prof 1; Other 1. **Subjects:** Medicine. **Holdings:** 810 books; 800 bound
periodical volumes. **Subscriptions:** 111 journals and other serials. **Services:**
Interlibrary loan; copying; library open to the public for reference use only.
Computerized Information Services: MEDLARS, MEDLINE; DOCLINE
(electronic mail service). Performs searches on fee basis. **Publications:** New
book list, monthly - for internal distribution only. **Remarks:** FAX: (307)237-
1703.

★ 20663 ★
Wyoming Pioneer Home - Library (Hist)
141 Pioneer Home Dr.   Phone: (307)864-3151
Thermopolis, WY 82443   Julie Miller
Founded: 1968. **Subjects:** History, general. **Holdings:** 4500 books.
Subscriptions: 26 journals and other serials; 6 newspapers. **Services:**
Interlibrary loan; library not open to the public.

★ 20664 ★
**Wyoming (State) Department of Commerce - Division of Parks and
Cultural Resources - Historical Research Library** (Hist)
Barrett Bldg.   Phone: (307)777-7016
Cheyenne, WY 82002-0130   Rick Ewig, Sr.Hist.
Founded: 1895. **Staff:** Prof 4; Other 1. **Subjects:** Wyoming and Western
history; collection, preservation, and interpretation of historical,
ethnological, and archeological materials. **Holdings:** 6500 volumes; 38,500
reels of microfilm of Wyoming newspapers, 1867 to present, National
Archives materials, scrapbooks, manuscripts; maps and plats; documents;
letters; ledgers; diaries; research collections; census records; oral histories;
folklore; AV programs; territorial and state government records.
Subscriptions: 75 journals and other serials. **Services:** Copying; department
open to the public. **Publications:** Annals of Wyoming, semiannual; calendar
of Wyoming history; Buffalo Bones, Stories from Wyoming's Past. **Special
Indexes:** Indexes to Annals of Wyoming, 1897-1974; Inventory of WPA
Manuscripts Collection; Oral History index. **Remarks:** Alternate telephone
number(s): 777-7015. **Staff:** Roger Joyce, Hist.; Ann Nelson, Hist.; Jean
Brainerd, Hist.

★ 20665 ★
Wyoming (State) Department of Education - Computer Center (Educ)
Hathaway Bldg.   Phone: (307)777-6670
Cheyenne, WY 82002   Judy Kishman, Educ.Tech.
Staff: Prof 1; Other 1. **Subjects:** K-12 science, mathematics, social studies,
language arts, arts; education. **Holdings:** 20 professional journals; 1150
computer software diskettes. **Subscriptions:** 20 journals and other serials.
Services: Center open to residents of Wyoming. **Computerized Information
Services:** Internal database; WyNet (electronic mail service). **Networks/
Consortia:** Member of Wyoming Libraries Database (WYLD System).
Publications: Wyoming Educator (newsletter), monthly - for internal
distribution only. **Remarks:** FAX: (307)777-6234.

★ 20666 ★
**Wyoming (State) Department of Health - Division of Public Health -
Film Library** (Med, Aud-Vis)
Hathaway Bldg.   Phone: (307)777-7363
Cheyenne, WY 82002-0710   Ramona L. Nelson, Film Libn.
Staff: 2. **Subjects:** Nursing, mental health, childbirth education, venereal
diseases, dental health, school health, AIDS. **Special Collections:** Rape
Prevention; Family Violence. **Holdings:** 431 16mm films; 500 videotape and
filmstrip programs. **Services:** Library open to the public with restrictions.
Special Catalogs: Film Library Catalog.

★ 20667 ★
**Wyoming (State) Department of Transportation - Planning and
Administration Division - Research Library** (Trans)
5300 Bishop Blvd.   Phone: (307)777-4182
Cheyenne, WY 82002-9019   Barry W. Flom, Res.Engr.
Staff: Prof 1; Other 1. **Subjects:** Transportation. **Holdings:** 3 books; 1700
bound periodical volumes; 600 manuscripts; 70 unbound reports. **Services:**
Library not open to the public. **Computerized Information Services:**
DIALOG Information Services, TRIS (Transportation Research
Information Services) Data Base. **Remarks:** FAX: (307)777-4759. **Formerly:**
Wyoming (State) Highway Department.

★ 20668 ★
Wyoming State Game and Fish Department - Library (Env-Cons)
5400 Bishop Blvd.   Phone: (307)777-4541
Cheyenne, WY 82006   Mary E. Link, Sec.
Staff: 1. **Subjects:** Wildlife and fisheries management, conservation. **Special
Collections:** Departmental annual reports, 1898 to present; departmental
publications; Wyoming Wildlife, 1936 to present (magazine). **Holdings:** 100
books; 700 bound periodical volumes; 2300 technical reports; 300 U.S.
Geological Survey maps; 30 film titles; 15 videotape titles; 50,000 color slide
and black/white negatives. **Subscriptions:** 45 journals and other serials; 8
newspapers. **Services:** Interlibrary loan; library not open to the public.
Remarks: FAX: (307)777-4610.

Wyoming (State) Geological Survey
See: Geological Survey of Wyoming (6368)

Wyoming (State) Highway Department
See: Wyoming (State) Department of Transportation (20667)

★ 20669 ★
Wyoming State Hospital - Medical Library (Med)
Box 177   Phone: (307)789-3464
Evanston, WY 82931-0177   William L. Matchinski, Libn.
Staff: Prof 1; Other 1. **Subjects:** Psychiatry, medicine, nursing, social work,
psychology. **Holdings:** 2500 volumes. **Subscriptions:** 155 journals and other
serials; 42 newspapers. **Services:** Interlibrary loan; copying; library open to
the public on a limited schedule. **Networks/Consortia:** Member of Western
Wyoming Health Science Library Consortium. **Remarks:** Alternate
telephone number(s): 789-3785. FAX: (307)789-3737.

★ 20670 ★
Wyoming State Law Library (Law)
Supreme Court Bldg.   Phone: (307)777-7509
Cheyenne, WY 82002   Kathy Carlson, Law Libn.
Founded: 1897. **Staff:** Prof 2; Other 3. **Subjects:** Law. **Special Collections:**
Selective depository for government documents. **Holdings:** 83,000 volumes.
Subscriptions: 425 journals and other serials. **Services:** Interlibrary loan
(limited); copying; library open to the public. **Automated Operations:**
Computerized cataloging. **Computerized Information Services:** OCLC,
OCLC EPIC, WESTLAW. **Networks/Consortia:** Member of
Bibliographical Center for Research, Rocky Mountain Region, Inc. (BCR).
Special Indexes: Quick Index to Wyoming Statutes Annotated. **Remarks:**
FAX: (307)777-7240. **Staff:** Ann Harrington; D.J. DeJong.

★ 20671 ★
Wyoming State Library (Info Sci)
Supreme Court & State Library Bldg.   Phone: (307)777-7281
Cheyenne, WY 82002-0650   Suzanne LeBarron, State Libn.
Founded: 1871. **Staff:** Prof 11; Other 18. **Subjects:** Wyoming, Western
Americana, North American Indians, library science. **Holdings:** 113,000
books; 664 bound periodical volumes; selective depository for U.S.
Government publications (1.5 million); depository for Wyoming
publications (5000). **Subscriptions:** 267 journals and other serials; 48
newspapers. **Services:** Interlibrary loan; library open to the public.
Automated Operations: Computerized cataloging, acquisitions, and
circulation. **Computerized Information Services:** BRS Information
Technologies, WILSONLINE, DIALOG Information Services, CQ
Washington Alert; ALANET (electronic mail service). **Networks/
Consortia:** Member of Bibliographical Center for Research, Rocky

Mountain Region, Inc. (BCR), Health Sciences Information Network (HSIN), Wyoming Libraries Database (WYLD System). **Publications:** Annual Report; Wyoming Public Library Statistics; Outrider (newsletter); Wyoming Public Library Trustees Manual; Wyoming Public Library Guidelines; Wyoming Academic Library Statistics; Wyoming State Library Collection Development Policy. **Special Catalogs:** Wyoming Union List of Periodicals; Wyoming Library Directory; Wyoming Library Laws. **Remarks:** FAX: (307)777-6289. Electronic mail address(es): 0978 (ALANET). **Staff:** Jerome Krois, Dp. State Libn.; Corky Walters, Lib.Dev.Prog.Mgr.; Beth Rulli, State Govt.Info.Serv.Mgr.; Marc Stratton, Automation Sys.Mgr.; Gwen Rice, Chf./Ref. and ILL; Karen Hendrick, Mgr./Acq.; Linn Rounds, Pub.Info.Off.; Joe French, Mgt.Serv.Off.

★ 20672 ★
Wyoming State Library - State Government Information Services Division - Herschler Building Information Center (Plan)
122 W. 25th St., 4th Fl., E.   Phone: (307)777-7641
Cheyenne, WY 82002   Terry Manuel, Libn.
Founded: 1989. **Staff:** Prof 1. **Subjects:** Federal and state agencies, environment, higher education, health and human services, natural resources. **Holdings:** 10,000 federal documents, state documents, and environmental impact statements. **Subscriptions:** 92 journals and other serials. **Services:** Interlibrary loan; library open to the public. **Computerized Information Services:** BRS Information Technologies, DIALOG Information Services, WILSONLINE, CQ Washington Alert. **Remarks:** FAX: (307)777-6289. Direct all correspondence to the Wyoming State Library, Supreme Court & State Library Building, Cheyenne, WY 82002.

★ 20673 ★
Wyoming State Training School - Medical Library (Med)
8204 State Hwy. 789   Phone: (307)332-5302
Lander, WY 82520   Shirley J. Townsend, Libn.
Founded: 1981. **Staff:** Prof 1. **Subjects:** Mental retardation, epilepsy, neurological disorders, pediatric medicine, occupational and physical therapy. **Holdings:** 300 books. **Subscriptions:** 16 journals and other serials. **Services:** Interlibrary loan; copying; library open to state employees. **Computerized Information Services:** MEDLINE. **Remarks:** FAX: (307)332-9632.

★ 20674 ★
Wytheville Community College - Kegley Library - Special Collections (Hist)
1000 E. Main St.   Phone: (703)228-5541
Wytheville, VA 24382   Anna Ray Roberts, Coord., Lib.Serv.
Founded: 1968. **Staff:** Prof 2; Other 1. **Subjects:** Southwest Virginia history and genealogy. **Holdings:** 500 books; 86 bound periodical volumes; 300 historical maps; 500 oral history interviews; data on 162 local cemeteries; 4 VF drawers; 100 volumes of family history; 110 volumes of local history; 137 reels of microfilm. **Services:** Copying; collections open to the public. **Remarks:** FAX: (703)228-6506. **Staff:** George Mattis.

X

Xavier-Damians Christian Life Community Library
See: St. Joseph's University (14422)

★ **20675** ★
Xavier Society for the Blind - National Catholic Press and Library for the Visually Handicapped (Aud-Vis)
154 E. 23rd St.   Phone: (212)473-7800
New York, NY 10010   Rev. Thomas R. Fitzpatrick, S.J., Exec.Dir.
Founded: 1900. **Staff:** 15. **Subjects:** Religion, inspirational. **Holdings:** 647 books in braille; 672 books in large type; 695 books on cassette. **Subscriptions:** 9 journals and other serials. **Services:** Multiple copies of books and periodicals in braille, large-print, and on cassette, available free of charge on a direct basis to visually impaired and print-handicapped people, and through the network of the National Library Service for the Blind and Physically Handicapped. **Publications:** Deaf-Blind News Summary, biweekly (braille); Deaf-Blind Weekly (braille); Sunday Propers, monthly (scriptural readings; braille, large-print, cassette); Deaf-Blind Summary, biweekly (large-print); The Catholic Review, monthly (braille, large-print, cassette); Book of the Month (braille, large-print, cassette); Xavier Review, monthly (newsletter; braille, large-print, cassette).

★ **20676** ★
Xavier University of Louisiana - College of Pharmacy - Library (Med)
7325 Palmetto & Pine Sts.   Phone: (504)486-7411
New Orleans, LA 70125   Yvonne C. Hull, Libn.
Staff: Prof 1; Other 1. **Subjects:** Pharmacy, pharmacology, medicinal chemistry, pharmacognosy, clinical pathology, toxicology, drug interaction, public health, history of pharmacy. **Special Collections:** Collection of volumes dealing with medical and pharmaceutical information from the 19th century (150 volumes including antique chemical handbooks and pharmacopeias). **Holdings:** 4000 books; 2800 bound periodical volumes; 250 audio cassettes; 10 records; 3 films. **Subscriptions:** 100 journals and other serials. **Services:** Interlibrary loan; copying; SDI (limited); library open to the public for reference use only. **Remarks:** Library has initiated a Drug Information Center in cooperation with V.A. Hospital of New Orleans.

★ **20677** ★
Xavier University of Louisiana - Special Collections (Area-Ethnic)
7325 Palmetto St   Phone: (504)483-7304
New Orleans, LA 70125-1098   Robert E. Skinner, Univ.Libn.
Founded: 1937. **Staff:** Prof 10; Other 10. **Special Collections:** African-American History and Culture (1000 volumes; 50 linear feet of manuscripts); Southern Culture and Literature (1000 volumes; 25 linear feet of manuscripts); Southern Catholica and Religion (200 volumes; 15 linear feet of manuscripts). **Services:** Interlibrary loan; copying; SDI; library open to the public. **Automated Operations:** Computerized cataloging (VTLS). **Computerized Information Services:** DIALOG Information Services, NASA/RECON. Performs searches. Contact Person: Laura D. Turner, Hd., Pub.Serv.Div. **Publications:** African-American and Other Historic Serials Held in the Xavier University Archives; pathfinders; information brochures; Xavier Library News, monthly. **Remarks:** FAX: (504)488-3320.

★ **20678** ★
Xerox Corporation - El Segundo Technical Library (Comp Sci)
701 S. Aviation Blvd., ESAE325   Phone: (310)333-5222
El Segundo, CA 90245   Amy Feller, Mrg.
Founded: 1968. **Staff:** Prof 3; Other 2. **Subjects:** Electronics, microelectronics, management, marketing, telecommunications. **Holdings:** 4800 books; 1200 bound periodical volumes; 3000 reports and conference proceedings. **Subscriptions:** 280 journals and other serials; 15 newspapers. **Services:** Interlibrary loan; copying (limited); SDI. **Automated Operations:** Computerized cataloging and serials. **Computerized Information Services:** DIALOG Information Services, OCLC, BRS Information Technologies, PFDS Online, DataTimes; internal databases. **Networks/Consortia:** Member of CLASS, OCLC Pacific Network. **Publications:** Newsletter, monthly; Journal Holdings, annual. **Remarks:** FAX: (310)333-0515. **Staff:** Kay Traylor, Sr.Tech.Info.Asst.; Ellen Chang, Ref.Libn.; Beverly Zuanich Dole, Libn./Doc. Deliveries.

★ **20679** ★
Xerox Corporation - Law Library (Law)
800 Long Ridge Rd.
Stamford, CT 06904   Phone: (203)968-3420
Founded: 1969. **Staff:** 1. **Subjects:** Law. **Holdings:** 10,000 volumes; 6 drawers of annual reports; 2 drawers of foreign materials; 10 drawers of microfiche. **Subscriptions:** 104 journals and other serials. **Services:** Interlibrary loan; library not open to the public at discretion of librarian. **Computerized Information Services:** Dow Jones News/Retrieval, LEXIS, Official Airline Guides, Inc. (OAG), DIALOG Information Services, WESTLAW; internal databases. **Networks/Consortia:** Member of Southwestern Connecticut Library Council (SWLC). **Remarks:** FAX: (203)968-3446.

★ **20680** ★
Xerox Corporation - Palo Alto Research Center - Information Center (Comp Sci, Info Sci)
3333 Coyote Hill Rd.   Phone: (415)812-4042
Palo Alto, CA 94304   Giuliana A. Lavendel, Mgr.
Founded: 1971. **Staff:** Prof 8; Other 7. **Subjects:** Computer and information science, physics, material science, electronics, psychology, education. **Special Collections:** Information systems and materials. **Holdings:** 13,000 books; 5000 bound periodical volumes; 10,000 external reports; 50,000 Xerox reports; microfilm; microfiche. **Subscriptions:** 750 journals and other serials. **Services:** Interlibrary loan; SDI; center open to the public by appointment. **Automated Operations:** Computerized cataloging, serials, and circulation. **Computerized Information Services:** DIALOG Information Services, PFDS Online, BRS Information Technologies, NEXIS, LEXIS, Dow Jones News/Retrieval, RLIN; internal database. **Publications:** Competitive Flyer, weekly; holdings list, annual; Update, weekly; Newsletter, quarterly. **Special Catalogs:** Report list catalog. **Remarks:** FAX: (415)812-4028. **Staff:** Alice Wilder, Supv., User Network; Katherine S. Jarvis, Supv., Tech.Info.; Maia Pindar, Sys.Spec.; Sally Peters, Tech.Serv.Spec.

★ **20681** ★
Xerox Corporation - Technical Information Center (Sci-Engr)
800 Philips
Mail Stop 0105-C   Phone: (716)422-3505
Webster, NY 14580   Michael D. Majcher, Mgr.
Founded: 1960. **Staff:** Prof 18; Other 10. **Subjects:** Xerography, electrophotography, reprography, electronics, chemistry, physics, photography, materials and processes, computer science. **Special Collections:** Corporation Technical Archives. **Holdings:** 35,000 books; 8500 bound periodical volumes; 100,000 internal reports; 20,000 external reports; 45 VF drawers; 5500 reels of microfilm; 305,000 microfiche; 1.5 million patents. **Subscriptions:** 2000 journals and other serials. **Services:** Interlibrary loan; SDI; Xerox Telecopier Facsimile Service; center open to the public by appointment. **Automated Operations:** Computerized cataloging, acquisitions, serials, and circulation. **Computerized Information Services:** OCLC, LEXIS, NEXIS, TEXTLINE, MEDLARS, Dun & Bradstreet Business Credit Services, PFDS Online, NewsNet, Inc., Electronet/1, DIALOG Information Services, BRS Information Technologies, Chemical Abstracts Service (CAS), Dow Jones News/Retrieval, Chemical Information Systems, Inc. (CIS); LINX Courier (electronic mail service). **Networks/Consortia:** Member of Rochester Regional Library Council (RRLC). **Publications:** TIC Users Guide; Internal Reports Accession List; Current Awareness Bulletin. **Remarks:** FAX: (716)422-8297. **Staff:** David A. Mindel, Mgr., Tech.Serv.; Cecelia E. Rice, Mgr., Pub.Serv.; F. Belli, Mgr., Database/Indexing Serv.

★ **20682** ★
Xerox Engineering Systems - Information Center (Sci-Engr)
2710 Walsh   Phone: (408)988-2800
Santa Clara, CA 95051   Ron Katsuranis, Info.Spec.
Founded: 1982. **Staff:** Prof 1; Other 1. **Subjects:** Electronics, computer graphics, paper. **Special Collections:** Standards. **Holdings:** 3000 books. **Subscriptions:** 150 journals and other serials. **Services:** Interlibrary loan; center not open to the public. **Automated Operations:** Computerized cataloging and serials. **Computerized Information Services:** PFDS Online, DIALOG Information Services, RLIN, VU/TEXT Information Services, DataTimes. **Publications:** Periodical holdings; NEWSCAN (current awareness bulletin). **Formerly:** Versatec - Technical Information Center.

★ 20683 ★
Xerox Research Centre of Canada - Technical Information Centre (Sci-Engr)
2660 Speakman Dr.   Phone: (416)823-7091
Mississauga, ON, Canada L5K 2L1 Carolyne Sidey, Tech.Info.Serv.Supv.
Founded: 1974. **Staff:** Prof 1; Other 1. **Subjects:** Polymer chemistry, colloid chemistry, surface science, electrophotography, xerography, chemical engineering, paper science, materials science. **Special Collections:** Internal technical reports (65,000). **Holdings:** 10,000 books; 9000 bound periodical volumes; 3000 reels of microfilm; 70,000 microfiche. **Subscriptions:** 250 journals and other serials; 5 newspapers. **Services:** Interlibrary loan; copying; SDI; center open to the public by appointment. **Automated Operations:** Computerized cataloging, acquisitions, circulation, and current awareness service. **Computerized Information Services:** DIALOG Information Services, ORBIT Search Service, STN International, Info Globe, Infomart Online, CAN/OLE, PFDS Online, UTLAS, WILSONLINE; Ethernet, Envoy 100, BITNET (electronic mail services). **Networks/Consortia:** Member of Sheridan Park Association. **Publications:** TIC Update, monthly; Serials Holdings List, annual. **Remarks:** FAX: (416)695-6988. Electronic mail address(es): SIDEY.XRCC-NS@XEROX.COM (BITNET).

★ 20684 ★
Xerox Special Information Systems - Research Library (Sci-Engr)
250 N. Halstead St., M/S 369   Phone: (818)351-2351
Pasadena, CA 91109   Frances A. McCrary, Res.Libn.
Founded: 1983. **Staff:** Prof 1. **Subjects:** Optics, computer science, engineering. **Holdings:** 1592 books; 500 bound periodical volumes. **Subscriptions:** 107 journals and other serials. **Services:** Interlibrary loan; library not open to the public. **Automated Operations:** Computerized serials and circulation. **Computerized Information Services:** DIALOG Information Services, BRS Information Technologies. **Remarks:** FAX: (818)351-4484.

★ 20685 ★
XI Magnetics, Inc. - Library (Sci-Engr)
Canary Rd.
Unionville, PA 19375   Phone: (215)347-1768
Subjects: Magnetic materials, thin film technology, semiconductors, kinetic energy weapons. **Holdings:** Figures not available. **Subscriptions:** 24 journals and other serials. **Formerly:** Located in Coatesville, PA.

★ 20686 ★
Xicom, Inc. - Library
R.R. 2, Woods Rd.
Tuxedo, NY 10987   Loreen Fennell, Dir. of Mktg.
Subjects: Behavioral science, organizational development, adult learning methods, interpersonal communication, adaption to new technology, organizational change. **Holdings:** 1000 volumes. **Remarks:** Currently inactive.

★ 20687 ★
Xtalonix Products, Inc. - Library
1215 Chesapeake Ave.   Phone: (614)488-5915
Columbus, OH 43212   Rita Wilson, Libn.
Remarks: No further information was supplied by respondent.

Y

★ 20688 ★
Y-ME National Organization for Breast Cancer Information and Support - Library (Med)
18220 Harwood Ave.   Phone: (708)799-8338
Homewood, IL 60430   Kay Mueller
Founded: 1980. **Staff:** Prof 4; Other 5. **Subjects:** Breast cancer - medicine, personal narratives, psychology. **Holdings:** 140 books; clippings. **Subscriptions:** 15 journals and other serials; 15 newsletters. **Services:** Library open to the public. **Remarks:** FAX: (708)799-5937.

★ 20689 ★
Yad Vashem - Library and Archives (Hist)
Har Hazikaron
P.O. Box 3477   Phone: 2 751611
91034 Jerusalem, Israel   Ms. Ora Alcalay, Hd.Libn.
Founded: 1953. **Staff:** 5. **Subjects:** Holocaust, history of anti-Semitism. **Holdings:** 170,000 volumes; 50 million archival items; statistics. **Subscriptions:** 2000 journals and other serials. **Services:** Copying; library open to the public. **Remarks:** FAX: 2 433511. Telex: 26573. **Also Known As:** The Holocaust Martyrs' and Heroes' Remembrance Authority. **Staff:** Ms. Clara Guini; Mr. Yitzhak Len; Ms. Avital Amrani; Ms. Efrat Weinfeld.

★ 20690 ★
Yadkin County Public Library - Paul Price Davis History Room (Hist)
243 E. Main St.
Box 607   Phone: (919)679-8792
Yadkinville, NC 27055   Malinda Sells, Br.Libn.
Founded: 1971. **Staff:** 4.5. **Subjects:** Local and North Carolina history. **Holdings:** 660 volumes; 44 reels of microfilm of census data, marriage records, wills, deeds, estates, court minutes of county, 1851-1950; 12 drawers of family genealogies, local history; The Yadkin Ripple, 1909 to present, 55 reels of microfilm; The Enterprise and The Tribune, both 1981 to present. **Subscriptions:** 2 journals and other serials. **Services:** Interlibrary loan; Copying; room open to the public for reference use only. **Special Indexes:** Index of all surnames (card). **Remarks:** FAX: (919)679-4625.

★ 20691 ★
Yakima County Law Library (Law)
Yakima County Court House   Phone: (509)457-5452
Yakima, WA 98901   Letha Hammer, Law Libn.
Founded: 1932. **Staff:** Prof 1. **Subjects:** Law. **Holdings:** 17,365 volumes. **Subscriptions:** 52 journals and other serials. **Services:** Copying; library open to the public with restrictions. **Automated Operations:** Computerized acquisitions.

★ 20692 ★
Yakima Valley Genealogical Society - Library (Hist)
Box 445   Phone: (509)248-1328
Yakima, WA 98907   Ellen Brzoska, Libn.
Founded: 1967. **Staff:** Prof 2; Other 18. **Subjects:** Genealogy; family, Yakima County, and central Washington history. **Special Collections:** Abstracts from old bound newspapers, 1884-1925; Daughters of the American Revolution, Daughters of Washington Pioneers collections. **Holdings:** 2000 volumes; 3000 bound periodical volumes; 100,000 card Yakima County cemetery file; 50,000 card Klickitat and Kittitas Counties cemetery file; 8 VF drawers of reports, clippings, pamphlets, and documents; 200 reels of microfilm and cassette tapes; 100 family history interview sheets. **Subscriptions:** 200 journals and other serials. **Services:** Interlibrary loan; copying; library open to the public for reference use only. **Publications:** Yakima Valley Genealogical Society Bulletin, quarterly. **Remarks:** The library is located at N. 3rd and East B St., Yakima, WA. **Staff:** Marge Karkau, Asst.Libn.; Wilbur Helm, ILL.

★ 20693 ★
Yakima Valley Museum and Historical Association - Archives (Hist)
2105 Tieton Dr.   Phone: (509)248-0747
Yakima, WA 98902   Martin M. Humphrey, Archv.
Founded: 1956 **Staff:** Prof 1. **Subjects:** Area history and development, Yakima Indians, pioneers, irrigation history. **Special Collections:** Apple and pear box labels; William O. Douglas Collection (1500 books; 11,000 slides; films; photographs); local newspaper, 1889-1952 (bound volumes); records of former Yakima Mayor Betty Edmonson; papers of state legislator and HEW chairwoman Marjorie Lynch; records of Yakima Valley Transportation Co. (railroad). **Holdings:** 6000 books; 6373 photographs; 9 file cabinets of clippings; documents; manuscripts. **Subscriptions:** 25 journals and other serials. **Services:** Copying; archives open to the public only when archivist or assistant is present. **Special Indexes:** Indexes of Douglas Collection (4). **Remarks:** Includes the holdings of the Gannon Museum of Wagons. **Staff:** Jane Glover; Madelyn Sprague.

★ 20694 ★
Yakima Valley Regional Library - Reference Department - Click Relander Collection (Hist)
102 N. 3rd St.   Phone: (509)452-8541
Yakima, WA 98901   Cynthia Garrick, Ref.Coord.
Subjects: Click Relander, Yakima newspaper publisher; Pacific Northwest history; Yakima and Wanapum Indians and their relationship with the U.S. government; Yakima Valley history and agriculture. **Holdings:** 169 boxes of letters, manuscripts, federal documents, photographs. **Services:** Copying; collection open to the public. **Remarks:** FAX: (509)575-2093.

Yale Center for British Art
See: **Yale University** (20734)

★ 20695 ★
Yale Club of New York City - Library (Hum)
550 Vanderbilt Ave.   Phone: (212)661-2070
New York, NY 10017   Seth J. Ramson, Libn.
Founded: 1897. **Staff:** Prof 1; Other 1. **Subjects:** Literature, history, travel, biography, social sciences, art, music. **Special Collections:** Yale memorabilia and publications. **Holdings:** 45,000 volumes. **Subscriptions:** 100 journals and other serials. **Services:** Library not open to the public.

Yale Collection of Historical Sound Recordings
See: **Yale University** (20737)

Yale Editions of the Private Papers of James Boswell
See: **Yale University** (20738)

★ 20696 ★
Yale University - African Collection (Area-Ethnic)
Sterling Memorial Library, Rm. 317   Phone: (203)432-1883
New Haven, CT 06520   J. Moore D. Crossey, Cur.
Founded: 1963. **Staff:** Prof 1; Other 2. **Subjects:** Africa - languages, literature, history, ethnography, anthropology, art, politics, government, religion, education, economics, law, social conditions, civilizations, philosophy, natural history, big game hunting, travel, topography, mining. **Special Collections:** Howell Wright Collection of Rhodesiana and South Africana (5000 volumes). **Holdings:** 100,000 books; 90,000 bound periodical volumes; 460 manuscript collections (original or microform); 3000 reels of microfilm of newspapers, periodicals, pamphlet collections, government documents; photographs; posters; postcards; pamphlets; broadsides; maps. **Subscriptions:** 2000 journals and other serials; 35 newspapers. **Services:** Interlibrary loan; copying; collection open to the public with restrictions. **Automated Operations:** Computerized public access catalog (ORBIS), cataloging, acquisitions, serials, and circulation. **Networks/Consortia:** Member of Research Libraries Information Network (RLIN), Center for Research Libraries (CRL), Hartford Consortium for Higher Education. **Special Catalogs:** Catalog of Africa-related materials (1965-1989) arranged by African countries and/or subjects (card). **Remarks:** FAX: (203)432-7231.

★ 20697 ★
Yale University - American Oriental Society Library (Area-Ethnic)
Sterling Memorial Library, Rm. 329   Phone: (203)432-1842
New Haven, CT 06520   Mary Ann T. Itoga, Libn.
Founded: 1842. **Staff:** Prof 1. **Subjects:** Oriental civilizations - language, literature, history, culture. **Holdings:** 22,774 volumes. **Subscriptions:** 115 journals and other serials. **Services:** Collection open only to members of the society, Yale University personnel, and visiting scholars on application. **Networks/Consortia:** Member of Research Libraries Information Network (RLIN).

★ 20698 ★
Yale University - Anthropology Library (Soc Sci)
Kline Science Library
Box 6666　　　　　　　　　　　　Phone: (203)432-3439
New Haven, CT 06511　　　　　Katherine Branch, Dir. of Sci.Lib.
Subjects: Anthropology. **Holdings:** 18,740 volumes. **Subscriptions:** 134 journals and other serials. **Services:** Interlibrary loan; copying; library open to the public with permission. **Automated Operations:** Computerized public access catalog. **Computerized Information Services:** BITNET (electronic mail service). **Networks/Consortia:** Member of Research Libraries Information Network (RLIN), Center for Research Libraries (CRL), Hartford Consortium for Higher Education. **Remarks:** FAX: (203)432-3441. Electronic mail address(es): KBRANCH@YALEVM (BITNET).

★ 20699 ★
Yale University - Art and Architecture Library (Art)
Art & Architecture Bldg.
Yale Sta., Box 1605A　　　　　　Phone: (203)432-2640
New Haven, CT 06520　　　　　Nancy S. Lambert, Libn.
Staff: Prof 2; Other 6. **Subjects:** History of art, architecture, city planning, photography, painting, sculpture, graphic arts. **Special Collections:** Faber Birren Collection of Books on Color (books; photographs). **Holdings:** 98,557 volumes; 15,843 uncataloged exhibition catalogs; 55 VF drawers of pamphlets; 14 VF drawers of city planning material; 303,471 slides; 176,835 photographs. **Subscriptions:** 498 journals and other serials. **Services:** Interlibrary loan; copying (both limited); library open to the public for reference use only; Special Borrower's Card available on a fee basis. **Computerized Information Services:** RLIN. **Networks/Consortia:** Member of Research Libraries Information Network (RLIN), Center for Research Libraries (CRL), Hartford Consortium for Higher Education. **Remarks:** FAX: (203)432-7175. **Staff:** Helen Chillman, Slide & Photo.Libn.; Christine de Vallet, Asst.Libn.

★ 20700 ★
Yale University - Arts of the Book Collection (Publ, Art)
Sterling Memorial Library　　　　Phone: (203)432-1712
New Haven, CT 06520　　　　　Louis H. Silverstein
Founded: 1967. **Staff:** Prof 1. **Subjects:** Typography, book illustration and design, calligraphy, bookbinding, bookplates, private presses and fine printing. **Special Collections:** Caricature; trade cards; Western Americana prints; engraved views of Vienna; historic printing material including the Bibliographical Press (four presses and an extensive collection of printing types); engraved woodblocks; special archives of Fritz Kredel, Fritz Eichenberg, Carl P. Rollins, and the Overbrook Press. **Holdings:** 14,000 books; 30,000 prints; type specimens; archive of student printing, including masters' theses from School of Graphic Design at Yale; 1 million bookplates. **Subscriptions:** 10 journals and other serials. **Services:** Interlibrary loan; copying; collection open to the public. **Automated Operations:** Computerized public access catalog, cataloging, and acquisitions. **Networks/Consortia:** Member of Research Libraries Information Network (RLIN).

★ 20701 ★
Yale University - Astronomy Library (Sci-Engr)
J.W. Gibbs Laboratory
260 Whitney Ave.
Box 6666　　　　　　　　　　　　Phone: (203)432-3000
New Haven, CT 06511　　　　　Pauline DiGioia, Lib.Serv.Asst.
Founded: 1871. **Staff:** 3. **Subjects:** Astronomy, astrophysics, celestial mechanics, physics, mathematics. **Special Collections:** Extensive collection of domestic and foreign observatory publications. **Holdings:** 23,900 books; 6700 bound periodical volumes; 900 square feet of observatory reprints; slides; charts and atlases. **Subscriptions:** 70 journals. **Services:** Interlibrary loan; copying; library open to the public for reference use only. **Networks/Consortia:** Member of Research Libraries Information Network (RLIN), Center for Research Libraries (CRL), Hartford Consortium for Higher Education. **Publications:** Transactions of Yale University Observatory; Tables of the Motion of the Moon; The Evolution of Galaxies and Stellar Populations, 1977. **Special Catalogs:** Bright Star Catalog, 4th edition; Supplement to the Bright Star Catalog, 1983; General Catalog of Trigonometric Stellar Parallaxes and supplement 1963. **Remarks:** FAX: (203)432-5048.

★ 20702 ★
Yale University - Babylonian Collection (Hist)
Sterling Memorial Library
120 High St.　　　　　　　　　　　Phone: (203)432-1837
New Haven, CT 06520　　　　　William W. Hallo, Cur.
Founded: 1912. **Staff:** Prof 5. **Subjects:** Assyriology; cuneiform; Sumerian, Akkadian, Hittite, Mesopotamian literature, archeology, and history; Semitics. **Special Collections:** Cuneiform texts from the collections of J.B. Nies, Goucher College, J.P. Morgan, Edwin T. Newell, General Theological Seminary, J. Rosen. **Holdings:** 7000 books; 1200 bound periodical volumes; 10,000 reprints; 35,000 cuneiform tablets and inscriptions; 3000 cylinder seals and stamp seals; 1000 other Ancient Near Eastern artifacts. **Subscriptions:** 40 journals and other serials. **Services:** Collection open to the public upon application to the curator. **Computerized Information Services:** BITNET (electronic mail service). **Networks/Consortia:** Member of Research Libraries Information Network (RLIN), Center for Research Libraries (CRL), Hartford Consortium for Higher Education. **Publications:** Yale Oriental Series - Babylonian Texts; Yale Oriental Series - Researches; Babylonian Inscriptions in the Collection of James B. Nies, Yale University; Goucher College Cuneiform Inscriptions; Babylonian Records in the Library of J. Pierpont Morgan; Yale Near Eastern Researches; Texts from the Babylonian Collection. **Remarks:** Electronic mail address(es): WWSTALLO@YALEVM (BITNET). This library includes "the largest collection of cuneiform tablets and cylinder seals in the U.S.A." **Staff:** Gary Beckman, Assoc.Cur.; Ulla Kasten, Musm.Ed.; B.R. Foster, Assyriologist; Paul-Alain Beaulieu, Assyriologist.

★ 20703 ★
Yale University - Beinecke Rare Book and Manuscript Library (Rare Book, Hum)
Wall & High Sts.　　　　　　　　　Phone: (203)432-2977
New Haven, CT 06520　　　　　Ralph W. Franklin, Dir.
Founded: 1963. **Staff:** Prof 20; Other 20. **Subjects:** Alchemy and the occult; Afro-American arts and letters; American, British, and European history and literature; British economic tracts; Congregationalism; exploration and travel; French illustrated books; German literature; Greek and Latin literature; history of education; history of printing; incunabula; Judaica; Latin America; modernism in art and literature; Native American history and languages; Near Eastern manuscripts; early British and American newspapers; ornithology; Oxford; papyri; playing cards; medieval and Renaissance manuscripts; Russian and Slavic books and manuscripts; sporting books; Theatre Guild; theology; Tibet; Western Americana; American children's books. **Special Collections:** Leonie Adams, Aldus Manutius, Matthew Arnold, Asch, Joel Barlow, Barrie, Baskerville, Baskin, William Beckford, S.V. Benet, W.R. Benet, Boccaccio, Boswell, Hermann Broch, Cleanth Brooks, Browning, Buchan, Burney, Byron, Cabell, Carlyle, Rachel Carson, Ernst Cassirer, Sir Winston Churchill, Barrett Clark, Eleanor Clark, Coleridge, Conrad, Cooper, Walter Crane, Dada, Defoe, Dickens, Hilda Doolittle, Norman Douglas, Muriel Draper, Katherine Dreier, Dryden, Jonathan Edwards, George Eliot, Maria Edgeworth, Arthur Davison Ficke, Fielding, Vardis Fisher, John Gould Fletcher, Paul Leicester Ford, Garrick, Jean Giono, Gissing, Goethe, Herman Hagedorn, Hutchins and Neith Boyce Hapgood, Hardy, Marsden Hartley, John Hersey, Hogg, Paul Horgan, Langston Hughes, Joseph Ireland, Washington Irving, Robinson Jeffers, James Weldon Johnson, Samuel Johnson, Joyce, Mary Kennedy, Kipling, Landor, D.H. Lawrence, Sinclair Lewis, Mabel Luhan, George Macdonald, William McFee, MacLeish, Norman MacLeod, Thomas Mann, F.T. Marinetti, Masefield, Mencken, Meredith, Milosz, Milton, George Moore, Sir Thomas More, Robert Nathan, O'Neill, James Gates Percival, Pope, Ezra Pound, Al Poulin, William H. Pratt, James Purdy, Dorothy Richardson, Samuel Richardson, Rilke, Bruce Rogers, Ruskin, Shakespeare, Shaw, Sheridan, Spenser, Spinelli Family Archive, Gertrude Stein, Leo Stein, Stevenson, Stieglitz, Ezra Stiles, Thomas Streeter, Swinburne, Tennyson, Thackeray, Tocqueville, Toklas, Jean Toomer, Trollope, Van Vechten, Verein zum Schutz Deutscher Einwanderer in Texas, Henry R. Wagner, Walton, Robert Penn Warren, Aleksander Wat, Glenway Wescott, Rebecca West, Edith Wharton, Monroe Wheeler, Whitman, Wilder, William Carlos Williams, Edmund Wilson, Kurt Wolff, Wordsworth, Richard Wright, Eleanor Wylie. **Holdings:** 500,000 volumes; 2.25 million manuscripts. **Services:** Copying; library open to the public. **Automated Operations:** Computerized index (ZyIndex). **Computerized Information Services:** Zyindex (internal database). **Networks/Consortia:** Member of Research Libraries Information Network (RLIN), Center for Research Libraries (CRL), Hartford Consortium for Higher Education. **Publications:** Yale University Library Gazette. **Remarks:** FAX: (203)432-4047. **Staff:** Patricia Willis, Cur., Amer.Lit.Coll.; Vincent Giroud, Cur., Modern Bks. & Mss.; Robert Babcock, Cur., Early Bks. & Mss.; George Miles, Cur./W.Americana; Stephen Parks, Cur./Osborn Coll./Mss.; Christa Sammons, Cur./German Coll.; Patricia Middleton, Pub.Serv.Libn.; Suzanne Rutter, Tech.Serv.Libn.; Bruce Stark, Tech.Serv.Libn.

★ 20704 ★
Yale University - Benjamin Franklin Collection (Hist)
Sterling Memorial Library, Rm. 230
Yale Sta., Box 1603A   Phone: (203)432-1814
New Haven, CT 06520   Barbara Oberg, Ed.
Founded: 1935. **Staff:** 4. **Subjects:** Books, portraits, medals, and other memorabilia relating to Benjamin Franklin and the American Revolution. **Holdings:** 16,000 books; 2000 periodicals, reports, and other items. **Subscriptions:** 10 journals and other serials. **Services:** Copying (with restrictions); collection open to the public for reference use only. **Networks/Consortia:** Member of Research Libraries Information Network (RLIN), Center for Research Libraries (CRL), Hartford Consortium for Higher Education. **Remarks:** FAX: (203)432-7231. The manuscripts, broadsides, and a portion of the printed material have been transferred to Beinecke Library.

★ 20705 ★
Yale University - Classics Library (Hum)
Phelps Hall
344 College St.   Phone: (203)432-0854
New Haven, CT 06520   Carla M. Lukas, Lib.Serv.Asst.
Founded: 1892. **Staff:** Prof 1. **Subjects:** Greek and Latin classical literature, ancient history, art, archeology, papyrology. **Holdings:** 21,622 volumes. **Subscriptions:** 161 journals and other serials. **Services:** Interlibrary loan; copying; library open to the public by permission. **Automated Operations:** Computerized public access catalog. **Networks/Consortia:** Member of Research Libraries Information Network (RLIN), Center for Research Libraries (CRL).

★ 20706 ★
Yale University - Collection of the Literature of the American Musical Theatre (Theater, Mus)
Sterling Memorial Library
Box 1603A Yale Sta.   Phone: (203)432-1795
New Haven, CT 06520   Richard Warren, Jr., Cur.
Founded: 1954. **Subjects:** Musical shows produced on Broadway for profit. **Special Collections:** Manuscripts of Cole Porter and E.Y. Harburg. **Holdings:** Books; theater programs; pamphlets and clippings; phonograph records; sheet music; scores. **Services:** Collection open to the public for reference use only by appointment. **Networks/Consortia:** Member of Research Libraries Information Network (RLIN), Center for Research Libraries (CRL), Hartford Consortium for Higher Education.

★ 20707 ★
Yale University - Cowles Foundation for Research in Economics - Library (Bus-Fin)
30 Hillhouse Ave.   Phone: (203)432-3697
New Haven, CT 06520   Karlee Gifford, Lib.Serv.Asst.
Founded: 1932. **Staff:** Prof 1; Other 1. **Subjects:** Economic theory; mathematical econometrics; macroeconomic, microeconomic, monetary, and game theory. **Holdings:** 12,000 volumes; 4000 discussion papers; 1000 Cowles Foundation papers. **Subscriptions:** 161 journals and other serials. **Services:** Interlibrary loan; copying; permission to use library may be requested from director. **Networks/Consortia:** Member of Research Libraries Information Network (RLIN), Center for Research Libraries (CRL), Hartford Consortium for Higher Education. **Remarks:** FAX: (203)432-6167.

★ 20708 ★
Yale University - Divinity School Library (Rel-Phil)
409 Prospect St.   Phone: (203)432-5290
New Haven, CT 06511   Paul F. Stuehrenberg, Act. Divinity Libn.
Founded: 1932. **Staff:** Prof 6; Other 13. **Subjects:** History of doctrine, biblical studies, missions, theology. **Special Collections:** Historical Library of Missions (90,000 items); archives of the Student Volunteer Movement (285 linear feet); archives of the World Student Christian Federation (155 linear feet); papers of American missionaries in China (410 linear feet); papers of John R. Mott (100 linear feet); Missions Pamphlet Collection (250 linear feet); Historical Sermons Collection (75 linear feet); United Board for Christian Higher Education in Asia (475 linear feet); Council for World Mission (23,000 microfiche); Methodist Missionary Society (8700 microfiche); American Home Missionary Society (385 reels of microfilm); International Missionary Council/Conference of British Missionary Societies (2500 microfiche); American Board of Commissioners for Foreign Missions (858 reels of microfilm); International Missionary Council

Archives, 1910-1961 (7000 microfiche). **Holdings:** 385,000 volumes; 350 linear feet of other personal papers and archival collections; 101,000 microform units. **Subscriptions:** 1675 journals and other serials; 8 newspapers. **Services:** Interlibrary loan; copying; library open to the public. **Automated Operations:** Computerized cataloging, acquisitions, and circulation. **Networks/Consortia:** Member of Research Libraries Information Network (RLIN), Center for Research Libraries (CRL). **Staff:** Rolfe Gjellstad, Ser.Libn.; Martha Smalley, Archv.; Susan Burdick, Circ.Supv./ILL; Duane Harbin, Info.Serv.Libn.

★ 20709 ★
Yale University - East Asian Collection (Hum, Area-Ethnic)
Sterling Memorial Library   Phone: (203)432-1790
New Haven, CT 06520   Hideo Kaneko, Cur.
Staff: Prof 7; Other 10.5. **Subjects:** East Asian languages and literature, history, art, politics, government, economics, law, social conditions, religion, education. **Holdings:** 340,000 volumes in Chinese; 180,000 volumes in Japanese; 6500 volumes in Korean; 5950 reels of microfilm. **Subscriptions:** 2500 journals and other serials; 47 newspapers. **Services:** Interlibrary loan; copying; collection open to qualified outside users. **Computerized Information Services:** BITNET (electronic mail service). **Networks/Consortia:** Member of Research Libraries Information Network (RLIN), Center for Research Libraries (CRL), Hartford Consortium for Higher Education. **Remarks:** FAX: (203)432-7231. Electronic mail address(es): BM.YAO@RLG (BITNET). Includes holdings of the Sinological Seminar Library. **Staff:** Wen-Kai Kung, Assoc.Cur.; Boksoon Hahn, Hd.Cat.Libn.; Mitsuko Ichinose, Prin.Cat./Ref.Libn.

★ 20710 ★
Yale University - Economic Growth Center Collection (Soc Sci)
140 Prospect St.   Phone: (203)432-3304
New Haven, CT 06520   Billie I. Salter, Libn. for Soc.Sci.
Founded: 1961. **Staff:** Prof 3; Other 5. **Subjects:** Economic data sources and surveys focusing primarily on the developing countries. **Holdings:** 52,000 volumes. **Subscriptions:** 4481 journals and other serials. **Services:** Interlibrary loan; copying; collection open to the public for reference use only, circulation limited to card holders. **Computerized Information Services:** RLIN; Orbis (internal database). **Networks/Consortia:** Member of Research Libraries Information Network (RLIN), Center for Research Libraries (CRL). **Special Catalogs:** Shelf list, arranged by country and subdivided by subject; subject classified catalog. **Remarks:** Library is a special collection within the Social Science Library. **Staff:** Edita R. Baradi, Acq.Libn. and Coll.Dev.; Nenita A. Fernandez, Cat.Libn.

★ 20711 ★
Yale University - Elizabethan Club Collection (Hum)
459 College St.   Phone: (203)432-2967
New Haven, CT 06511   Stephen R. Parks, Libn.
Founded: 1911. **Subjects:** Elizabethan drama, 16th and 17th century. **Holdings:** 300 volumes, before 1700. **Services:** Copying; collection open to the public by arrangement. **Networks/Consortia:** Member of Research Libraries Information Network (RLIN), Center for Research Libraries (CRL), Hartford Consortium for Higher Education. **Publications:** Newsletter, annual - to members; The Elizabethan Club of Yale University and its Library, 1986. **Remarks:** FAX: (203)432-4047. Readers may consult Elizabethan Club volumes, by arrangement, in the Beinecke Library.

★ 20712 ★
Yale University - Engineering and Applied Science Library (Sci-Engr, Comp Sci)
P.O. Box 2157 Yale Station   Phone: (203)432-2928
New Haven, CT 06520   Jill Newby, Libn.
Founded: 1969. **Staff:** 3. **Subjects:** Applied sciences, engineering, computer sciences. **Holdings:** 36,889 volumes. **Subscriptions:** 400 journals and other serials. **Services:** Interlibrary loan; copying; library open to qualified users. **Computerized Information Services:** DIALOG Information Services, STN International, Current Contents Search; CD-ROMs (Compendex Plus, MathSci, Computing Archive: Bibliography and Reviews from ACM, Sigma-Aldrich Material Safety Data Sheets); InterNet (electronic mail service). Performs searches. **Networks/Consortia:** Member of Research Libraries Information Network (RLIN), Center for Research Libraries (CRL). **Remarks:** FAX: (203)432-3441. Electronic mail address(es): Jill-Newby@yccatsmtp.ycc.yale.edu (InterNet).

★ 20713 ★
Yale University - Fortunoff Video Archive for Holocaust Testimonies
(Hist)
Sterling Memorial Library, Rm. 331C   Phone: (203)432-1879
New Haven, CT 06520-7429   Joanne Rudof, Archv.
Founded: 1981. **Staff:** Prof 1; Other 2. **Subjects:** Holocaust. **Special Collections:** Videotaped oral testimonies from Yale and 28 affiliated projects in North and South America, Europe, and Israel. **Holdings:** 2000 videotaped oral testimonies. **Services:** Archive open to the public. **Automated Operations:** Computerized public access catalog. **Computerized Information Services:** RLIN, AMC. **Publications:** Newsletter, irregular - available on request; Guide to Yale University Library Holocaust Video Testimonies, volume 1. **Special Catalogs:** Testimony inventories (typed).

★ 20714 ★
Yale University - Geology Library (Sci-Engr)
210 Whitney Ave.
P.O. Box 6666   Phone: (203)432-3157
New Haven, CT 06511   Kimberly J. Parker, Libn.
Founded: 1963. **Staff:** Prof 1; Other 2. **Subjects:** Geology, paleontology, oceanography, meteorology, geophysics. **Holdings:** 107,657 volumes; 187,385 maps, including U.S. Geological Survey geologic and topographic series; 14,000 reprints. **Subscriptions:** 2739 journals and other serials. **Services:** Interlibrary loan; copying; library open to public with restrictions. **Computerized Information Services:** DIALOG Information Services, STN International; CD-ROM (GeoRef, Geophysics of North America (National Geophysical Data Center), Marine Geological and Geophysical Data from the DSDP (Joint Oceanographic Institutions), Current Contents); BITNET, InterNet (electronic mail services). **Networks/Consortia:** Member of Research Libraries Information Network (RLIN), Center for Research Libraries (CRL), Hartford Consortium for Higher Education. **Remarks:** FAX: (203)432-3441. Telex: 9102508365 Yale University. Electronic mail address(es): Kimberly–Parker@yccatsmtp.ycc.yale.edu (InterNet).

★ 20715 ★
Yale University - Harvey Cushing/John Hay Whitney Medical Library
(Med)
333 Cedar St.
Box 3333   Phone: (203)785-5354
New Haven, CT 06510   Regina Kenny Fryer, Hd. of Ref.
Founded: 1814. **Staff:** Prof 12; Other 25. **Subjects:** Medicine, nursing, public health, allied health sciences. **Special Collections:** History of medicine (90,000 volumes); George Milton Smith Collection (early ichthyology; 700 volumes); Edward Clark Streeter Collection (early weights and measures; 350 volumes; 3000 artifacts); Clement C. Fry Collection (2000 medical prints and drawings); medical and scientific incunabula. **Holdings:** 369,649 volumes; 50 manuscript codices before 1600. **Subscriptions:** 2511 journals and other serials. **Services:** Interlibrary loan; copying; SDI; library open to the public with restrictions. **Computerized Information Services:** NLM, DIALOG Information Services, RLIN, BRS Information Technologies; OnTyme Electronic Message Network Service, ALANET, BITNET (electronic mail services). **Networks/Consortia:** Member of Research Libraries Information Network (RLIN), Center for Research Libraries (CRL), National Network of Libraries of Medicine - New England Region. **Publications:** Users' Guide; Subject Bibliography; Medical Library Bulletin, all irregular. **Remarks:** FAX: (203)785-4369. Electronic mail address(es): FRYER@YALEEUM (BITNET). **Staff:** Ferenc A. Gyorgyey, Hist.Libn.; Lynn Sette, Act.Hd.Ref.Libn.; Carol Lawrence, Hd., Tech.Serv. & Coll.Dev.; Paula Ball, Asst.Hd., Tech.Serv.; Ann Paietta, Hd., Access Serv.

★ 20716 ★
Yale University - Ira V. Hiscock Epidemiology and Public Health Library (Med)
P.O. Box 3333
60 College St.   Phone: (203)785-5680
New Haven, CT 06510   Carole A. Colter, Libn.
Founded: 1940. **Staff:** 2.5. **Subjects:** Biostatistics, environmental health, epidemiology, health policy and research, public health. **Holdings:** 20,000 books and bound journals. **Subscriptions:** 217 journals and other serials. **Services:** Copying; library open to the public by appointment. **Computerized Information Services:** CD-ROMs (MEDLINE, Occupational Health & Safety, Popline, Health Planning & Administration).

★ 20717 ★
Yale University - John Herrick Jackson Music Library (Mus)
P.O. Box 5469 Yale Station   Phone: (203)432-0492
New Haven, CT 06520   Harold E. Samuel, Libn.
Founded: 1917. **Staff:** Prof 4; Other 10. **Subjects:** Music. **Special Collections:** Complete manuscripts and papers of Richard Donovan, Lehman Engel, Henry Gilbert, Benny Goodman, Thomas de Hartmann, Ralph Kirkpatrick, Vladimir Horowitz, Charles E. Ives, J. Rosamond Johnson, Goddard Lieberson, Armin Loos, Leo Ornstein, Horatio Parker, Quincy Porter, Carl Ruggles, David Stanley Smith; Alec Templeton; Virgil Thomson; Kurt Weill; Deems Taylor; Vladimir Horowitz; Lowell Mason Collection of Church Music (10,000 pieces); Marc Pincherle Collection (musical iconography; 1200 items); Fred Plaut Photograph Collection (35,000 items). **Holdings:** 124,076 volumes; 80,570 pieces of sheet music; 17,321 phonograph records; microfilm. **Subscriptions:** 450 journals and other serials. **Services:** Interlibrary loan; copying; library open to the public for reference use only. **Networks/Consortia:** Member of Research Libraries Information Network (RLIN), Center for Research Libraries (CRL), Hartford Consortium for Higher Education. **Remarks:** FAX: (203)432-7231. **Staff:** Helen Bartlett, Hd.Cat.; Michele Koth, Cat.; Kendall Crilly, Pub.Serv.

★ 20718 ★
Yale University - Kline Science Library (Biol Sci, Sci-Engr)
Kline Biology Tower, Rm. C-8   Phone: (203)432-3439
New Haven, CT 06520   Katherine Branch, Libn.
Staff: Prof 5; Other 6. **Subjects:** Biological sciences, physics, chemistry, conservation, oceanography. **Special Collections:** Evans Collection (bryology and lichenology). **Holdings:** 325,719 volumes; Atomic Energy Commission (AEC) documents on microfiche and microcard. **Subscriptions:** 1600 journals and other serials. **Services:** Interlibrary loan; copying; SDI; library open to qualified users with permission of librarian. **Automated Operations:** Computerized public access catalog, circulation, acquisitions, and serials. **Computerized Information Services:** Current Contents; CD-ROMs (Science Citation Index, Life Sciences Abstracts); BITNET (electronic mail service). **Networks/Consortia:** Member of Research Libraries Information Network (RLIN), Center for Research Libraries (CRL), Hartford Consortium for Higher Education. **Remarks:** FAX: (203)432-3441. Electronic mail address(es): KATHERINE–BRANCH@YCCATSMTP.YCC.YALE.EDU (BITNET). **Staff:** Lori Bronars, Ref.Libn.; Kim Parker, Sci.Bibliog.

★ 20719 ★
Yale University - Latin American Collection (Area-Ethnic)
Sterling Memorial Library, Rm. 316   Phone: (203)432-1835
New Haven, CT 06520   Cesar Rodriguez, Cur.
Founded: 1907. **Staff:** Prof 1; Other 4. **Subjects:** Latin America - languages, literature, history, politics, government, economics, social conditions, religions, education, civilizations, art, law. **Special Collections:** Latin American Pamphlet Collection, 1600-1900 (social, political, and economic conditions in Latin America; 10,000 pamphlets). **Holdings:** 360,000 books. **Subscriptions:** 3000 journals and other serials. **Computerized Information Services:** BITNET (electronic mail service). **Networks/Consortia:** Member of Research Libraries Information Network (RLIN), Center for Research Libraries (CRL), Hartford Consortium for Higher Education. **Special Indexes:** Guide to Latin American Pamphlet Collection (book). **Remarks:** FAX: (203)432-7231. Electronic mail address(es): RODRIG@YALEVM (BITNET).

★ 20720 ★
Yale University - Law Library (Law)
127 Wall St.   Phone: (203)432-1600
New Haven, CT 06520   Diana Vincent-Daviss, Libn.
Founded: 1846. **Staff:** Prof 15; Other 28. **Subjects:** Law - Anglo-American, foreign, comparative, international. **Special Collections:** Blackstone Collection. **Holdings:** 841,758 volumes. **Subscriptions:** 8067 journals and other serials. **Services:** Interlibrary loan; copying; library open to qualified users. **Automated Operations:** Computerized public access catalog, cataloging, acquisitions, and serials. **Computerized Information Services:** LEXIS, WESTLAW. **Networks/Consortia:** Member of Research Libraries Information Network (RLIN), New England Law Library Consortium (NELLCO), Hartford Consortium for Higher Education. **Remarks:** FAX: (203)432-9692. **Staff:** Gene P. Coakley, Fac.Serv.Libn.; Daniel L. Wade, Foreign Law Libn.; Laura Orr-Waters, Hd.Ref.Libn.; Jo-Anne Giammattei, Acq.Libn.; Frances B. Woods, Hd., Cat.Dept.; Lisa Fitzgerald, Ref.Libn.; Mary Jane Kelsey, Asst.Libn., Tech.Serv.; Margaret Chisholm, Pub.Serv.Libn.; Martha Clark, Circ.Libn.; Ann J. Laeuchli, Assoc.Libn.; Fred Shapiro, Asst.Libn., Pub.Serv.

★ 20721 ★

Yale University - Lewis Walpole Library (Hist)
154 Main St.   Phone: (203)677-2140
Farmington, CT 06032   Marie Devine, Libn.
Founded: 1928. **Staff:** Prof 2; Other 3. **Subjects:** Horace Walpole, Earl of
Orford; 18th century caricatures and cartoons; 18th century English history;
Wilmarth Sheldon Lewis; Strawberry Hill and Twickenham; William
Mason; Thomas Gray; Thomas Chatterton. **Special Collections:** Horace
Walpole's Library, 1717-1797 (1314 volumes; 1500 manuscripts);
Strawberry Hill Press (500 volumes); Prints (37,234); Sir Charles Hanbury
Williams papers, 1708-1759 (93 volumes); Edward Weston papers, 1703-
1770 (25 volumes); Keppel Family papers (9 volumes); Henry Seymour
Conway papers, 1721-1795 (14 volumes). **Holdings:** 28,939 volumes; 330
bound manuscripts; 35 linear feet of manuscripts; drawings; paintings.
Subscriptions: 28 journals and other serials. **Services:** Copying; library open
to scholars by appointment. **Networks/Consortia:** Member of Research
Libraries Information Network (RLIN). **Remarks:** FAX: (203)677-6369.
Staff: Joan Hall Sussler.

★ 20722 ★

Yale University - Linguistic Library (Hum)
302 Hall of Graduate Studies
320 York St.
New Haven, CT 06520   Phone: (203)432-2450
Staff: 1. **Subjects:** Indology, descriptive and historical linguistics. **Special
Collections:** Bequest of Franklin Edgerton; Edward E. Salisbury, Professor
of Sanskrit; Warren Cowgill, Professor of Linguistics (300 volumes); James
F. Rettger (200 volumes). **Holdings:** 5596 volumes; 500 offprints.
Subscriptions: 10 journals and other serials; 2 newspapers. **Services:** Library
open to the public by appointment. **Computerized Information Services:**
Orbis (internal database). **Networks/Consortia:** Member of Research
Libraries Information Network (RLIN), Center for Research Libraries
(CRL), Hartford Consortium for Higher Education.

★ 20723 ★

Yale University - Manuscripts and Archives (Hist)
Sterling Memorial Library
P.O. Box 1603A, Yale Station   Phone: (203)432-1744
New Haven, CT 06520-7429   Richard V. Szary, Act.Hd., Mss. & Archv.
Founded: 1701. **Staff:** Prof 10; Other 6. **Subjects:** Yale history; Connecticut
history; religion; World War I and II diplomacy; 19th century science and
writing. **Special Collections:** Papers of Chester Bowles, Henry L. Stimson,
Edward M. House, Jerome Frank, Walter Lippmann, Benjamin Silliman,
John Lindsay, Dwight Macdonald; Crawford Theater Collection;
Contemporary Medical Care and Health Policy Collection; University
Archives. **Holdings:** 52,000 books and bound periodical volumes; 300,000
photographs; 43,300 reels of microfilm; 36,200 microfiche; 33,500 linear feet
of manuscripts. **Services:** Copying; archives open to the public. **Automated
Operations:** Computerized public access catalog. **Computerized Information
Services:** RLIN. **Special Catalogs:** Card catalog for manuscripts. **Special
Indexes:** Registers or indexes to manuscript collections. **Staff:** Richard V.
Szary, Asst.Hd./Univ.Archv.; Judith A. Schiff, Chf.R es.Archv.; Mary C.
La Fogg, Hd., Pub.Serv.; William R. Massa, Jr., Ref.Archv.

★ 20724 ★

Yale University - Map Collection (Geog-Map)
Sterling Memorial Library, Map Rm.   Phone: (203)432-1867
New Haven, CT 06520   Barbara B. McCorkle, Map Cur.
Founded: 1932. **Staff:** Prof 1; Other 1. **Subjects:** Historical map collection
covering the entire world. **Special Collections:** E.L. Stevenson Collection
(glass plates of early maps); Horace Brown Collection of early New England
maps; Karpinski-Thorne Collection of rare and early atlases. **Holdings:** 3000
atlases; 214,679 maps. **Subscriptions:** 18 journals and other serials. **Services:**
Copying; collection open to the public for reference use only. **Networks/
Consortia:** Member of Research Libraries Information Network (RLIN),
Center for Research Libraries (CRL), Hartford Consortium for Higher
Education.

★ 20725 ★

Yale University - Mathematics Library (Sci-Engr)
10 Hillhouse Ave.
P.O. Box 2155, Yale Sta.   Phone: (203)432-4179
New Haven, CT 06520-2155   Paul J. Lukasiewicz, Lib.Serv.Asst.
Staff: 1. **Subjects:** Pure mathematics. **Holdings:** 32,000 volumes.
Subscriptions: 250 journals and other serials. **Services:** Interlibrary loan;

library open to the public for reference use only. **Computerized Information
Services:** InterNet (electronic mail service). **Networks/Consortia:** Member
of Research Libraries Information Network (RLIN), Center for Research
Libraries (CRL), Hartford Consortium for Higher Education. **Remarks:**
FAX: (203)432-7316.   Electronic   mail   address(es):
zdrowic@1oml.math.Yale.edu (InterNet).

★ 20726 ★

Yale University - Ornithology Library (Biol Sci)
310 Bingham Lab., Peabody Museum
170 Whitney Ave.
Box 6666   Phone: (203)432-3797
New Haven, CT 06511   Alfred Mueller, Libn.
Founded: 1959. **Staff:** Prof 1. **Subjects:** Ornithology. **Special Collections:**
William R. Coe Collection. **Holdings:** 6000 books; 3500 Serial volumes;
15,000 reprints. **Subscriptions:** 100 journals and other serials. **Services:**
Interlibrary loan; copying; library open to the public by permission.
Automated Operations: Computerized public access catalog (ORBIS).
Networks/Consortia: Member of Research Libraries Information Network
(RLIN), Center for Research Libraries (CRL), Hartford Consortium for
Higher Education. **Remarks:** FAX: (203)432-9816.

★ 20727 ★

Yale University - School of Drama Library (Theater)
222 York St.
Yale Sta., Box 1903A   Phone: (203)432-1554
New Haven, CT 06520   Pamela C. Jordan, Lib.Serv.Asst.
Founded: 1925. **Staff:** 1. **Subjects:** Plays by American, British, and foreign
playwrights; history of the theater; theater architecture; drama criticism;
costume and set design; stage lighting; acting; direction; production; theater
administration. **Special Collections:** Abel Thomas (1200 books); Rockefeller
Prints Collection (80,000 photographs); George Pierce Baker Collection;
slide collections; History of Costume (1188 slides); Architecture, Interiors
and Furnishings (1893 slides). **Holdings:** 27,000 volumes; 600 production
books; 500 masters' theses; 140 dissertations; 90 scrapbooks of clippings.
Subscriptions: 82 journals and other serials; 12 newspapers. **Services:**
Interlibrary loan; copying; audio and video cassette players; library open to
the public for reference use only, circulation limited to Yale University card
holders. **Automated Operations:** Computerized public access catalog.
Networks/Consortia: Member of Research Libraries Information Network
(RLIN), Center for Research Libraries (CRL), Hartford Consortium for
Higher Education.

★ 20728 ★

**Yale University - Seeley G. Mudd Library - Government Documents
    Center** (Info Sci)
38 Mansfield St.
Yale Sta., Box 2491   Phone: (203)432-3209
New Haven, CT 06520-2491   Sandra K. Peterson, Docs.Libn.
Staff: Prof 2; Other 3. **Subjects:** American history, U.S. foreign relations,
economics, U.S. Congress. **Special Collections:** U.S. federal document
depository, 1859 to present; document depository for Canadian federal
government, United Nations, European Communities, and Food
Agriculture Organization; CIS U.S. Congressional Committee Prints
Microfiche Collection; CIS U.S. House of Representatives Unpublished
Committee Hearings, 1833-1936 (microfiche); CIS U.S. Senate Unpublished
Hearings, 1824-1968 (on microfiche); CIS Index to U.S. Senate Executive
Documents and Reports, 1817-1969 (microfiche); nondepository document
collection from the American Statistics Index and CIS Index to Publications
of the U.S. Congress; Foreign Broadcast Information Service Daily Reports,
1946 to present (all areas); Declassified Documents Reference System (on
microfiche); FAO Comprehensive Collection, 1978 to present (on
microfiche); United Nations Index microprint and microfiche collections,
1946 to present. **Holdings:** 873,955 items; 195 drawers of microfiche.
Services: Copying; center open to the public. **Computerized Information
Services:** CD-ROMs (GPO, NTIS, Congressional Masterfile 1789-1969,
Congressional Masterfile II 1970 to present; Department of Commerce
Economic Bulletin Board); BITNET (electronic mail service). **Networks/
Consortia:** Member of Research Libraries Information Network (RLIN),
Center for Research Libraries (CRL), Hartford Consortium for Higher
Education. **Remarks:** An alternate telephone number is 432-3212. FAX:
(203)432-3214. Electronic mail address(es): PETERSS@YALEVM
(BITNET). **Staff:** Arlene Weible, Asst.Doc.Libn.

★ 20729 ★
Yale University - Semitic Reference Library (Area-Ethnic)
314 Sterling Memorial Library
Yale University Library
New Haven, CT 06520   Phone: (203)432-1707
Founded: 1930. **Subjects:** Comparative Semitics; Hebrew, Arabic, and other Semitic languages (except Akkadian). **Holdings:** 1500 volumes. **Networks/Consortia:** Member of Research Libraries Information Network (RLIN), Center for Research Libraries (CRL), Hartford Consortium for Higher Education.

Yale University - Sinological Seminar Library
See: **Yale University - East Asian Collection** (20709)

★ 20730 ★
Yale University - Slavic & East European Collection (Hum, Area-Ethnic)
Sterling Memorial Library   Phone: (203)432-1861
New Haven, CT 06520   Tatjana Lorkovic, Cur.
Founded: 1961. **Staff:** Prof 1; Other 3. **Subjects:** Slavic and East European social sciences, humanities, linguistics, history. **Special Collections:** Joel Sumner Smith; Harrison Thomson; Mikhail Rostovtseff; George Vernadsky; Vasilii Tutcheff; Pilsudski and Czeslaw Milosz Archives. **Holdings:** 500,000 books in Slavic and East European languages; 80,000 bound periodical volumes; 3 VF drawers of clippings; 41 archival collections; 24,000 titles on microfilm and microfiche; 2.25 aisles of Radio Free Europe material. **Subscriptions:** 501 journals and other serials; 78 newspapers. **Automated Operations:** Computerized public access catalog. **Networks/Consortia:** Member of Research Libraries Information Network (RLIN), Center for Research Libraries (CRL), Hartford Consortium for Higher Education. **Remarks:** FAX: (203)432-7231.

★ 20731 ★
Yale University - Social Science Library (Soc Sci, Bus-Fin)
140 Prospect St.
Yale Sta., Box 1958
New Haven, CT 06520   Phone: (203)432-3304
     Billie I. Salter, Libn.
Founded: 1972. **Staff:** Prof 6; Other 13. **Subjects:** Administrative sciences, business, economics and economic development, finance, organization and management, political science, sociology. **Special Collections:** Economic Growth Center Collection (government reports, surveys, statistical yearbooks, bulletins focusing on developing countries and their economies); Social Science Data Archive (machine-readable data files of political and social surveys, voting records, and economic data sources); Roper Center Archives (public opinion polls). **Holdings:** 121,600 volumes. **Subscriptions:** 6948 journals and other serials. **Services:** Interlibrary loan; copying; library open to the public for reference use only, (circulation limited to card holders). **Automated Operations:** Computerized public access catalog, acquisitions, serials, and cataloging. **Computerized Information Services:** DIALOG Information Services, RLIN, BRS Information Technologies; CD-ROMs. **Networks/Consortia:** Member of Research Libraries Information Network (RLIN), Center for Research Libraries (CRL). **Publications:** Social Science Data Archive's Directory of Data Holdings and Services. **Staff:** JoAnn L. Dionne, Ref.Libn. & Data Archv.; Judith O. Carnes, Ref.Libn. & Coll.Dev.; Edita R. Baradi, Acq.Libn. & Coll.Dev.; Nenita A. Fernandez, Cat.Libn.; Carol Jones, Coll.Serv.Libn.

★ 20732 ★
Yale University - Southeast Asia Collection (Area-Ethnic)
Sterling Memorial Library   Phone: (203)432-1859
New Haven, CT 06520   Charles R. Bryant, Cur.
Staff: Prof 3; Other 3. **Subjects:** Social sciences and humanities of Southeast Asia: Burma, Thailand, Laos, Vietnam, Cambodia, Philippines, Malaysia, Brunei, Singapore, Indonesia. **Holdings:** 200,000 volumes. **Subscriptions:** 750 journals and other serials. **Services:** Interlibrary loan; copying. **Automated Operations:** Computerized cataloging, acquisitions, and serials. **Computerized Information Services:** BITNET (electronic mail service). **Networks/Consortia:** Member of Research Libraries Information Network (RLIN), Center for Research Libraries (CRL), Hartford Consortium for Higher Education. **Publications:** Checklist of Southeast Asian Serials, 1968. **Remarks:** FAX: (203)432-7231. Electronic mail address(es): CBRYANT@YALEVM (BITNET). **Staff:** Ms. Lian Tie Kho, Libn.; Ms. Feng Wang, Proj.Dir.

★ 20733 ★
Yale University - Sterling Chemistry Library (Sci-Engr)
225 Prospect St.
P.O. Box 6666   Phone: (203)432-3960
New Haven, CT 06511   Kimberly J. Parker, Libn.
Founded: 1923. **Staff:** Prof 1. **Subjects:** Chemistry, biochemistry, physical chemistry, organic chemistry, inorganic chemistry. **Holdings:** 13,100 volumes. **Subscriptions:** 117 journals and other serials. **Services:** Interlibrary loan; copying; library open to the public with restrictions. **Computerized Information Services:** DIALOG Information Services, STN International; internal database; BITNET, InterNet (electronic mail services). **Networks/Consortia:** Member of Research Libraries Information Network (RLIN), Center for Research Libraries (CRL), Hartford Consortium for Higher Education. **Remarks:** FAX: (203)432-3441. Telex: 9102508365 Yale University. Electronic mail address(es): Kimberly–parker@yccatsmtp.ycc.yale.edu (InterNet).

★ 20734 ★
Yale University - Yale Center for British Art - Photo Archive (Art)
2120 Yale Sta.   Phone: (203)432-2818
New Haven, CT 06520   Dr. Anne-Marie Logan, Libn./Photo Archv.
Founded: 1977. **Staff:** 3. **Subjects:** British art - paintings, drawings, prints, and sculpture, 1500-1945 (emphasizing works dating before 1900). **Special Collections:** Photographs after works by British artists and foreigners working in Great Britain (100,000 black/white photographs); British School photographs in the Witt Collection, Courtauld Institute, London (4000 microfiche); Harold Jennings Collection (60 volumes containing 150,000 prints, photographs, and reproductions after paintings, drawings, and prints of British sitters). **Services:** Copying; archive open to the public. **Computerized Information Services:** Internal database. **Special Indexes:** Subject thesaurus of British Art (20,000 terms); Artist authority list for British Artists (5300 names); Computerized Census of British Art in North American Collections (12,000 records). **Remarks:** FAX: (203)432-2818.

★ 20735 ★
Yale University - Yale Center for British Art - Rare Book Collection - Department of Prints, Drawings, and Rare Books (Art, Rare Book)
2120 Yale Sta.   Phone: (203)432-2814
New Haven, CT 06520   Elisabeth R. Fairman, Assoc.Cur., Rare Bks.
Founded: 1977. **Staff:** Prof 1; Other 3. **Subjects:** British illustrated books, 15th-19th centuries; visual arts in Great Britain, 17th-19th centuries. **Special Collections:** Major J.R. Abbey Collection of Color-Plate Books; British artists' books, 20th century. **Holdings:** 24,000 rare books and serials. **Services:** Photography; collection open to the public. **Automated Operations:** Computerized cataloging. **Computerized Information Services:** RLIN. **Special Catalogs:** Computerized catalog of illustrators, graphic techniques, provenance, imprints, bookbinding, and chronology; miscellaneous sale catalogs. **Remarks:** FAX: (203)432-9695.

★ 20736 ★
Yale University - Yale Center for British Art - Reference Library (Art)
1080 Chapel St.
Yale Sta., Box 2120   Phone: (203)432-2818
New Haven, CT 06520   Dr. Anne-Marie Logan, Libn./Photo Archv.
Founded: 1977. **Staff:** Prof 1; Other 1. **Subjects:** British art - paintings, drawings, prints, sculpture, and architecture, 1500-1945. **Special Collections:** Sotheby and Christies sales catalogues, 1734-1980; Victoria and Albert Museum oils, watercolors, miniatures, and RIBA architectural drawings; British Museum Satirical Prints; British Museum's Turner Bequest; Huntington Library drawings (all microfilm and photographs). **Holdings:** 11,000 books; 1000 bound periodical volumes; 870 reels of microfilm; 7300 microfiche. **Subscriptions:** 56 journals and other serials. **Services:** Copying; library open to the public. **Automated Operations:** Computerized public access catalog and cataloging. **Computerized Information Services:** Internal database. **Remarks:** FAX: (203)432-9695.

★ 20737 ★
Yale University - Yale Collection of Historical Sound Recordings (Aud-Vis)
Sterling Memorial Library
Box 1603A Yale Station   Phone: (203)432-1795
New Haven, CT 06520   Richard Warren, Jr., Cur.
Founded: 1960. **Staff:** Prof 1. **Subjects:** Phonograph recordings of historical interest in the fields of concert music, jazz, drama, politics, literature, documentary from the end of the 19th century to the present, with emphasis

on history of performance practice in the arts. **Holdings:** 140,000 sound recordings; catalogs; lists; books; photographs; autograph letters, manuscripts, and other documents relating to the history of sound recording. **Subscriptions:** 28 journals and other serials. **Services:** Collection open to the public for reference use only by appointment. **Networks/ Consortia:** Member of Research Libraries Information Network (RLIN), Center for Research Libraries (CRL), Hartford Consortium for Higher Education. **Special Indexes:** The Rigler & Deutsch Record Index - a National Union Catalog of Sound Recordings - Part I; An Index to 78 rpm Sound Recordings in ARSC/AAA member libraries.

★ 20738 ★

Yale University - Yale Editions of the Private Papers of James Boswell (Hum)
Sterling Memorial Library, Rms. 330 and 331A   Phone: (203)432-1864
New Haven, CT 06520   Rachel McClellan, Mgr.
Founded: 1949. **Staff:** Prof 3. **Subjects:** James Boswell. **Special Collections:** The Yale Boswell Collection, 1760-1795 (photostats of manuscript text and proofsheets of Tour to the Hebrides and Life of Johnson; 6000 letters to and from Boswell; original manuscripts held in Beinecke Rare Book and Manuscript Library). **Services:** Collection open to the public by appointment. **Networks/Consortia:** Member of Research Libraries Information Network (RLIN), Hartford Consortium for Higher Education. **Remarks:** Alternate telephone number(s): 432-1863.

★ 20739 ★

Yale University - Yale Forestry Library (Biol Sci)
205 Prospect St.   Phone: (203)432-5130
New Haven, CT 06511   Joseph A. Miller, Libn.
Founded: 1900. **Staff:** Prof 1; Other 2. **Subjects:** Forestry, environmental studies, ecology, natural resources management, conservation, soils, land use, planning. **Holdings:** 130,000 books, bound periodical volumes, government documents, and reports; 125 newsletter titles; 900 dissertations; 500 maps; 2500 microforms. **Subscriptions:** 750 journals and other serials. **Services:** Interlibrary loan; copying; library open to the public for reference use only. **Computerized Information Services:** FESR (Forestry and Environmental Studies Record; internal database). Performs searches on fee basis. **Networks/Consortia:** Member of Research Libraries Information Network (RLIN), Center for Research Libraries (CRL). **Special Catalogs:** Dictionary Catalog, 12 volumes, published in 1962. **Remarks:** FAX: (203)432-5942. **Also Known As:** Henry S. Graves Memorial Library.

★ 20740 ★

Yamaha Motor Corporation USA - Yamaha R&D Minnesota - Research Library (Sci-Engr)
1255 Main St.   Phone: (612)755-2743
Coon Rapids, MN 55448   William B. Seath, Info.Mgr.
Founded: 1979. **Staff:** Prof 1; Other 2. **Subjects:** Engineering, business, management. **Special Collections:** Patent records; Society of Automotive Engineers papers; snowmobile laws; snowmobile accident records. **Holdings:** 500 books; 40 bound periodical volumes; 9 VF drawers. **Subscriptions:** 150 journals and other serials; 5 newspapers. **Services:** Interlibrary loan; library not open to the public. **Computerized Information Services:** Access to online systems.

★ 20741 ★

(Yangon) American Center - USIS Library (Educ)
581 Merchant St.
Yangon 11182, Myanmar   Phone: 82055
Founded: 1986. **Staff:** 3. **Special Collections:** Burma; Southeast Asian Collection. **Holdings:** 4000 books; microfilm. **Subscriptions:** 80 journals and other serials; 3 newspapers. **Services:** Copying; library open to university students and government officials. **Computerized Information Services:** Internal database. **Publications:** Bibliographies. **Remarks:** FAX: 80409. Telex: 083 21230. Maintained or supported by the U.S. Information Agency. Focus is on material. that will assist peoples outside the United States to learn about the United States, its people, history, culture, political processes, and social milieux.

★ 20742 ★

Yankee Atomic Electric Company - Library (Energy)
580 Main St.   Phone: (508)779-6711
Bolton, MA 01740-1398   Delores Markt, Sr.Lib.Techn.
Founded: 1980. **Staff:** 1. **Subjects:** Nuclear power. **Special Collections:** Nuclear Regulatory Commission reports; Electric Power Research Institute

(EPRI) reports (microform); Federal Regulations, 1979 to present (microform); standards from American National Standards Institute (ANSI), American Nuclear Society (ANS), Institute of Electrical and Electronics Engineers (IEEE), American Society for Testing and Materials (ASTM). **Holdings:** 1618 books. **Subscriptions:** 327 journals and other serials. **Services:** Interlibrary loan; copying; SDI; library open to the public with restrictions. **Computerized Information Services:** DIALOG Information Services. **Remarks:** FAX: TWX (710)380-7619.

★ 20743 ★

Yankelovich Clancy Schulman - Information Center (Bus-Fin)
8 Wright St.   Phone: (203)227-2700
Westport, CT 06880   Barbara Maynard Hirsh, Corp.Info.Spec.
Staff: 2. **Subjects:** Marketing, social research, social sciences, industry, public opinion polling, consulting. **Holdings:** Figures not available. **Subscriptions:** 250 journals and other serials; 10 newspapers. **Services:** Interlibrary loan; SDI; library not open to the public. **Computerized Information Services:** DIALOG Information Services, NEXIS, Dow Jones News/Retrieval. **Remarks:** FAX: (203)454-2109. Parent organization is Saatchi & Saatchi.

★ 20744 ★

(Yaounde) American Cultural Center - United States Information Services (Educ)
Ave. de l'Independance
Post Box 817   Phone: 230416
Yaounde, Cameroon   Claudette Bristol, Libn.
Staff: Prof 2; Other 1. **Subjects:** United States - culture, history, geography, literature. **Holdings:** 6000 books. **Subscriptions:** 51 journals and other serials. **Services:** Interlibrary loan; copying; library open to the public. **Remarks:** FAX: 230753. Telex: 8223 KN. Maintained or supported by the U.S. Information Agency. Focus is on materials that will assist peoples outside the United States to learn about the United States, its people, history, culture, political processes, and social milieux. **Staff:** Emmanuel Nwaimah, Asst.Libn.

★ 20745 ★

Yardney Technical Products, Inc. - Technical Information Center (Sci-Engr)
82 Mechanic St.   Phone: (203)599-1100
Pawcatuck, CT 06379   Marian Durfee, Sec.
Founded: 1960. **Staff:** Prof 1. **Subjects:** Batteries, electrochemistry, chemistry, electrical engineering, metallurgy, plastics. **Holdings:** 1000 books. **Subscriptions:** 10 journals and other serials. **Services:** Center not open to the public. **Remarks:** FAX: (203)599-3903.

★ 20746 ★

Yarmouth County Historical Society - Research Library and Archives (Hist)
22 Collins St.   Phone: (902)742-5539
Yarmouth, NS, Canada B5A 3C8   Laura Bradley, Libn./Archv.
Staff: 2. **Subjects:** Local history and genealogy, shipping. **Holdings:** 1300 books; local newspapers, 1833-1980s; 16 VF drawers and 10 shelves of archival materials; manuscripts; maps; charts; clippings; pictures. **Subscriptions:** 20 journals and other serials. **Services:** Copying; library open to the public. **Publications:** Newsletter, monthly; Early Vital Records of the Township of Yarmouth, N.S.; Yarmouth 1821. **Special Indexes:** Index to Shipping of Yarmouth, N.S.

★ 20747 ★

Yavapai County Law Library (Law)
County Courthouse, 2nd Fl.   Phone: (602)771-3309
Prescott, AZ 86301   Pam Mathwig, Law Libn.
Staff: 2. **Subjects:** Law. **Holdings:** 11,986 volumes. **Services:** Copying; library open to the public on a limited schedule.

Alfred A. Yee Division
See: **Leo A. Daly Company** (4572)

Yellowstone Association
See: U.S. Natl. Park Service (17793)

★ 20748 ★

Yellowstone-Bighorn Research Association - Library (Sci-Engr)
P.O. Box 20598   Phone: (406)656-6012
Billings, MT 59104   Dennis McGinnis, Asst.Treas.
Founded: 1936. **Subjects:** Geology. **Special Collections:** N.H. Darton's personal collection. **Holdings:** 2300 volumes; geological manuscripts, reprints, and maps; herbarium contains plants from Montana and Wyoming: 81 families, 381 genera, 1028 species.

★ 20749 ★

Yellowstone Environmental Science, Inc. - Library (Env-Cons)
320 S. Willson Ave.
Bozeman, MT 59715   Phone: (406)586-3905
Founded: 1981. **Subjects:** Environmental engineering and protection, public health, wastewater engineering. **Holdings:** 200 items; patents. **Remarks:** FAX: (406)587-5109.

Yellowstone National Park Library
See: Montana State University - Libraries (10654)

Jean D. Yeomans Memorial Library
See: C.G. Jung Institute of Boston (8493)

Yerkes Observatory Library
See: University of Chicago (18462)

Yerkes Regional Primate Center
See: Emory University (5339)

★ 20750 ★

Yeshiva Torah Vodaath and Mesifta - Torah Vodaath Library (Rel-Phil)
425 E. 9th St.
Brooklyn, NY 11218   Phone: (718)941-8000
Founded: 1918. **Staff:** Prof 1; Other 2. **Subjects:** Biblical exegesis, Talmud (and novellae on), Rabbinical responsa, Halachic literature, liturgy and homiletic literature, Jewish history, Hebrew and Yiddish literature, Hasidic literature. **Holdings:** 23,500 books; 575 bound periodical volumes; 600 unbound periodicals; 280 unbound pamphlets. **Subscriptions:** 65 journals and other serials. **Services:** Copying; library open to the public.

★ 20751 ★

Yeshiva University - Albert Einstein College of Medicine - D. Samuel Gottesman Library (Med)
1300 Morris Park Ave.   Phone: (212)430-3108
Bronx, NY 10461   Judie Malamud, Dir., Lib.
Founded: 1955. **Staff:** Prof 8; Other 17. **Subjects:** Biochemistry, cell biology, psychology, medicine, molecular biology, pharmacology, physiology, genetics, anatomy, oncology, pathology, psychiatry, immunology. **Special Collections:** Gresser Collection (ophthalmology). **Holdings:** 73,424 books; 107,160 bound periodical volumes; 1401 theses; 50 VF drawers of archival materials; 541 dissertations; 10,433 microforms. **Subscriptions:** 2522 journals and other serials. **Services:** Interlibrary loan; copying; SDI; library open to the public with restrictions. **Automated Operations:** Computerized public access catalog, cataloging, serials, acquisitions, and circulation. **Computerized Information Services:** MEDLARS, BRS Information Technologies, miniMEDLINE; CD-ROMs (MEDLINE, PsycLit). Performs searches on fee basis. Contact Person: Norma Nelson, Hd., Ref. **Networks/Consortia:** Member of SUNY/OCLC Library Network, New York Metropolitan Reference and Research Library Agency, Medical Library Center of New York (MLCNY). **Publications:** Newsletter, irregular. **Remarks:** FAX: (212)409-2259. **Staff:** Florence Schreibstein, Asst.Dir.; James Swanton, Sys.Libn.; Racheline Habousha, Hd., Pub.Serv.; Robert Reiss, Cat.; Deborah Stern, Ref.Libn.

★ 20752 ★

Yeshiva University - Albert Einstein College of Medicine - Department of Anesthesiology - Library (Med)
Montefiore Medical Center
Jacobi, Rm. 1226
Pelham Parkway S.   Phone: (212)918-6865
Bronx, NY 10461   Rosemary Vecchio, Adm.
Founded: 1955. **Subjects:** Anesthesiology. **Holdings:** 200 books; 500 bound periodical volumes; 110 slide/tape sets. **Subscriptions:** 30 journals and other serials. **Services:** Library open to the public with restrictions. **Remarks:** FAX: (212)824-0459.

★ 20753 ★

Yeshiva University - Albert Einstein College of Medicine - Department of Psychiatry - J. Thompson Psychiatry Library (Med)
Bronx Municipal Hospital Center
NR 2E7A   Phone: (212)918-4545
Bronx, NY 10461   Mary Nahon Galgan, Libn.
Staff: Prof 1. **Subjects:** Psychiatry, psychoanalysis, social work. **Special Collections:** Philosophy, history, literature, theology, arts. **Holdings:** 8000 books; 3700 bound periodical volumes; 9 VF drawers of reprints; 98 masters' dissertations. **Subscriptions:** 100 journals and other serials. **Services:** Library not open to the public.

★ 20754 ★

Yeshiva University - Albert Einstein College of Medicine - Surgery Library (Med)
Pelham Pkwy. & Eastchester Rd.
Bronx, NY 10461   Phone: (212)918-5371
Founded: 1965. **Subjects:** Surgery, medicine. **Holdings:** 571 books; 1448 bound periodical volumes; 2 drawers of reprints. **Subscriptions:** 21 journals and other serials. **Services:** Interlibrary loan; library not open to the public. **Publications:** Bibliographies - to department members.

★ 20755 ★

Yeshiva University - Hedi Steinberg Library (Rel-Phil)
Stern College for Women
245 Lexington Ave.   Phone: (212)340-7720
New York, NY 10016   Prof. Edith Lubetski, Hd.Libn.
Founded: 1954. **Staff:** Prof 3; Other 5. **Special Collections:** Judaica and Hebraica (15,000 volumes). **Holdings:** 103,296 volumes. **Subscriptions:** 546 journals and other serials; 10 newspapers. **Services:** Interlibrary loan; copying; library open to the public for reference use only. **Automated Operations:** Computerized cataloging and acquisitions. **Computerized Information Services:** DIALOG Information Services, BRS Information Technologies. **Networks/Consortia:** Member of New York Metropolitan Reference and Research Library Agency. **Remarks:** FAX: (212)340-7788. **Staff:** Vivian Moskowitz, Ref.Libn.; Daniel Rosenzweig, Ref.Libn.

★ 20756 ★

Yeshiva University - Mendel Gottesman Library of Hebraica and Judaica (Rel-Phil)
500 W. 185th St.   Phone: (212)960-5382
New York, NY 10033   Pearl Berger, Dean of Libs.
Founded: 1920. **Staff:** Prof 4; Other 2. **Subjects:** Rabbinics; Bible and Jewish commentaries; Hebrew and cognate languages; Jewish history, philosophy, literature. **Special Collections:** Rare books and manuscripts; archives. **Holdings:** 178,866 books; 22,007 bound periodical volumes; 1487 reels of microfilm; 8701 microfiche; 1229 linear feet of manuscripts and archives. **Subscriptions:** 1140 journals and other serials. **Services:** Interlibrary loan; copying; library open to the public for reference use only. **Automated Operations:** Computerized cataloging. **Computerized Information Services:** OCLC, RLIN, BRS Information Technologies, DIALOG Information Services. **Networks/Consortia:** Member of New York Metropolitan Reference and Research Library Agency, Council of Archives and Research Libraries in Jewish Studies (CARLJS). **Publications:** Psalms for the Tsar (1988). **Special Catalogs:** Hebrew Incunabula - Mendel Gottesman Library of Hebraica and Judaica (1984). **Remarks:** FAX: (212)960-0066. **Staff:** Leah Adler, Hd.Libn.; Rabbi B. Mandelbaum, Ref.Libn.; Zalman Alpert, Per.Libn.; Zvi Erenyi, Acq.Dept./ILL.

★ 20757 ★
Yeshiva University - Museum (Area-Ethnic, Hist)
2520 Amsterdam Ave.   Phone: (212)960-5390
New York, NY 10033   Sylvia A. Herskowitz, Musm.Dir.
Staff: 1973. **Staff:** Prof 7; Other 3. **Subjects:** Jewish art, Judaica, Jewish history. **Special Collections:** Jewish history and communities around the world (photographs, documents, ceremonial objects, textiles, manuscripts, books, models of historic synagogues). **Holdings:** Books; bound periodical volumes; reports; documents; photographs; oral histories. **Services:** Copying (with restrictions); museum open on limited schedule. **Special Catalogs:** Exhibition catalogs. **Remarks:** FAX: (212)960-5406. **Staff:** Bonni-Dara Michaels, Reg.; Gabe Goldstein, Asst.Cur.

★ 20758 ★
Yeshiva University - Pollack Library - Landowne-Bloom Collection (Soc Sci)
500 W. 185th St.   Phone: (212)960-5378
New York, NY 10033   John Moryl, Hd.Libn.
Founded: 1975. **Subjects:** Aging, Jewish social welfare. **Holdings:** 13,381 books; 10,000 pamphlets and documents; 2576 dissertations in microform. **Services:** Interlibrary loan; copying; collection open to the public for reference use only. **Automated Operations:** Computerized cataloging. **Computerized Information Services:** BRS Information Technologies, DIALOG Information Services, OCLC. **Networks/Consortia:** Member of New York Metropolitan Reference and Research Library Agency.

★ 20759 ★
Yivo Institute for Jewish Research - Library and Archives (Area-Ethnic, Hist)
1048 Fifth Ave.
New York, NY 10028   Phone: (212)535-6700
Founded: 1925. **Staff:** Prof 19; Other 14. **Subjects:** Yiddish language, literature, drama, folklore; East European Jewry; European Jewry in the 19th and 20th centuries; Jewish history; Jewish immigration to the U.S.; Jews under Nazi rule. **Special Collections:** Rare books; Rabbinics; Vilna Collection of periodicals; Nazi literature; Jewish music; archives of Jewish organizations; archives of ghettoes and concentration camps; captured Nazi documents; manuscripts of Yiddish writers; Weinreich Library and Archives of Yiddish Linguistics; Landsmanshaft Archive. **Holdings:** 320,000 volumes; 10,000 linear feet of manuscript collections, records of institutions, individual collections, general records of the Yivo archives, photograph collections, art collections; 30 linear feet of tapes and recordings; 6000 reels of microfilm. **Subscriptions:** 450 journals and other serials. **Services:** Interlibrary loan; copying; library open to the public on a limited schedule. **Publications:** News of the Yivo, 3/year - to members; bibliographies on certain subjects (mimeographed). **Special Catalogs:** Library catalogs for special collections; guide to major collections in the Yivo Archives; archives' inventories and registers of individual collections. **Remarks:** FAX: (212)879-9763. **Staff:** Samuel Norich, Exec.Dir.; Zachary M. Baker, Hd.Libn.; Marek Web, Chf.Archv.; Dina Abramowicz, Ref.Libn.; Stanley Bergman, Adm.Libn.; Bella Hass Weinberg, Cons.; Fruma Mohrer, Archv.; Eleanor Mlotek, Archv.; Rosaline Schwartz, Dir., Pub.Prog.; Judith Edelstein, Asst.Dir.; Roberta Newman, Photo.Cur.; Henry Sapoznik, Sound Archv.; Beth Feinberg, Hd.Cat.; Leo Greenbaum, Assoc.Archv.; Cecile Kuznitz, Asst.Archv.

★ 20760 ★
YMCA of the USA - Archives (Soc Sci)
2642 University Ave.   Phone: (612)627-4632
St. Paul, MN 55114   Andrea Hinding, Archv.
Founded: 1877. **Staff:** Prof 1; Other 2. **Subjects:** History of the YMCA in the United States, Canada, and abroad, 1850 to present. **Special Collections:** Early Young Men's Societies publications, 1700-1850; biographical files on 200 YMCA leaders, 1850 to present; records of YMCA work in 80 countries, 1890 to present. **Holdings:** 6000 books; 2000 bound periodical volumes; 2000 linear feet of historical records; 125 reels of microfilm; 50,000 photographs; memorabilia. **Services:** Archives open to the public for reference use. **Computerized Information Services:** BITNET (electronic mail service). **Remarks:** FAX: (612)627-4631. Electronic mail address(es): A-HIND@UMINN1 (BITNET). Archives are on deposit in the Social Welfare History Archives of the University of Minnesota Libraries. **Also Known As:** Young Men's Christian Associations of the United States of America - Archives.

P.K. Yonge Laboratory School
See: **University of Florida - P.K. Yonge Laboratory School** (18580)

P.K. Yonge Library of Florida History
See: **University of Florida - Special Collections** (18585)

★ 20761 ★
Yonkers General Hospital - Medical Library (Med)
2 Park Ave.   Phone: (914)964-7300
Yonkers, NY 10701   M. Danber, Libn.
Founded: 1965. **Staff:** 1.5. **Subjects:** Internal medicine, surgery, gynecology, pathology, psychiatry. **Holdings:** 150 books; 250 bound periodical volumes. **Subscriptions:** 42 journals and other serials. **Services:** Interlibrary loan; copying; library open to the public. **Computerized Information Services:** MEDLARS, NLM. **Networks/Consortia:** Member of Health Information Libraries of Westchester (HILOW), National Network of Libraries of Medicine - Middle Atlantic Region, New York Metropolitan Reference and Research Library Agency. **Remarks:** FAX: (914)964-7446.

★ 20762 ★
Yonkers Historical Society - Library (Hist)
7 Odell Plaza
Greystone P.O. Box 885   Phone: (914)965-0401
Yonkers, NY 10703   Olga C. Kourre, Libn.
Founded: 1952. **Subjects:** History - Yonkers, Westchester County, Hudson River; local authors. **Holdings:** 400 books; manuscripts; documents. **Services:** Library open to the public for reference use only.

★ 20763 ★
Yonkers Public Library - Fine Arts Department (Art, Mus)
1500 Central Park Ave.   Phone: (914)337-1500
Yonkers, NY 10710   JoAnn Rochel, Hd., Fine Arts Dept.
Founded: 1962. **Staff:** Prof 3. **Subjects:** History of art, painting, sculpture, architecture, graphic arts, crafts, music, performing arts, photography and film arts, antique collecting. **Holdings:** 13,700 books; 27,000 recordings; 4500 cassettes; 625 compact discs; 7550 pieces of sheet music; 2000 slides; 3 file drawers of film catalogs; 17 file drawers of pictures; 5 file drawers of clippings. **Subscriptions:** 55 journals and other serials. **Services:** Interlibrary loan; copying; department open to the public with restrictions on borrowing. **Networks/Consortia:** Member of Westchester Library System (WLS). **Staff:** Jo Anne Roche; Valerie Schneer.

★ 20764 ★
Yonkers Public Library - Getty Square Information Services (Bus-Fin, Sci-Engr)
7 Main St.   Phone: (914)476-1255
Yonkers, NY 10701   Nedra Biegel, Dept.Hd./Info.Serv.
Founded: 1893. **Staff:** Prof 6; Other 2. **Subjects:** Business and finance. **Special Collections:** Annual corporation reports; U.S. city telephone directories; state, business, and biographical directories; local history. **Holdings:** 19,500 books; 107 bound periodical volumes; Official Patent Gazette, 1925 to present; 7000 government depository publications; 17,000 pamphlets. **Subscriptions:** 240 journals and other serials. **Services:** Interlibrary loan; copying; division open to the public. **Computerized Information Services:** DIALOG Information Services; InfoTrac.

★ 20765 ★
(York Borough) Board of Education for the City of York - Professional Library (Educ)
2 Trethewey Dr.
City of York, ON, Canada M6M 4A8   Phone: (416)394-2168
Founded: 1971. **Staff:** Prof 1; Other 2. **Subjects:** Education, sociology. **Special Collections:** Computer programs preview collection (200). **Holdings:** 15,000 books; 75 files of unbound reports; 1000 filmstrips and media kits; 10 drawers of pamphlets and clippings; 4000 microfiche; 2500 videotapes. **Subscriptions:** 300 journals and other serials; 6 newspapers. **Services:** Interlibrary loan; copying; SDI; library open to the public. **Automated Operations:** Computerized public access catalog, cataloging, acquisitions, serials, and circulation. **Computerized Information Services:** BRS Information Technologies, Info Globe, PFDS Online, EDI News, DIALOG Information Services; internal databases; CD-ROMs (ERIC, Resource/One Ondisc, CCINFOdisc, PC-SIG Library, The Columbia Granger's World of Poetry). **Publications:** New Books and Articles, 4/year. **Special Indexes:** Subject list of computer programs; subject and title guide to media kits. **Remarks:** FAX: (416)394-3397. **Staff:** Pat Steenbergen, Libn.; Sheila Moll, Libn.

★ 20766 ★
York Central Hospital - Douglas Storms Memorial Library (Med)
10 Trench St.   Phone: (416)883-2018
Richmond Hill, ON, Canada L4C 4Z3   Kathy Dedrick, Mgr.
Founded: 1965. **Staff:** Prof 1. **Subjects:** Medicine, nursing, and allied health sciences. **Holdings:** 1500 books. **Subscriptions:** 142 journals and other serials. **Services:** Interlibrary loan. **Computerized Information Services:** MEDLARS. **Remarks:** FAX: (416)883-2293.

★ 20767 ★
York College - Levitt Library - Special Collections (Rel-Phil)
York, NE 68467   Phone: (402)362-4441
                        Charles V. Baucom, Lib.Dir.
Founded: 1956. **Staff:** Prof 1.75; Other 1. **Subjects:** York College, Churches of Christ, Christian Church, York County, Disciples of Christ. **Special Collections:** Restoration Movement Collection (350 books; 200 bound periodical volumes); Yorkana Collection (50 books; 50 bound periodical volumes); York County Oral Collection (58 audiocassettes; 40 transcriptions). **Holdings:** 400 books; 200 bound periodical volumes; archival materials. **Services:** Interlibrary loan; copying; library open to the public. **Publications:** Guide to Selected Archive/Manuscript/Special Collections Holdings in ACU Library, David Lipscomb Library, F-H College Library, Great Lakes Christian College Library, Harding University Library, York College Library.

★ 20768 ★
York College of Pennsylvania - Schmidt Library - Special Collections
(Hist)
York, PA 17405-7199   Phone: (717)846-7788
                      Susan M. Campbell, Lib.Dir.
Staff: Prof 5; Other 12. **Subjects:** Abraham Lincoln. **Special Collections:** Lincoln Collection. **Holdings:** 1356 books. **Services:** Interlibrary loan; copying; collections open to the public with restrictions. **Automated Operations:** Computerized public access catalog, circulation, and ILL. **Computerized Information Services:** DIALOG Information Services, OCLC; CALL (electronic mail service). **Networks/Consortia:** Member of PALINET, Associated College Libraries of Central Pennsylvania (ACLCP). **Remarks:** FAX: (717)846-1274. **Staff:** Susan R. McMillan; William A. Markley, III; Vickie L. Kline; Patricia Bassinger.

★ 20769 ★
York County Law Library (Law)
Court House   Phone: (717)854-0754
York, PA 17401   Susan F. Hedge, Libn.
Founded: 1872. **Staff:** Prof 2. **Subjects:** Law. **Holdings:** 17,748 volumes. **Services:** Interlibrary loan; copying; faxing; library open to the public with restrictions. **Computerized Information Services:** WESTLAW, DIALOG Information Services, VU/TEXT Information Services, DJNS, Maxwell Macmillan Taxes Online, State Net. **Remarks:** FAX: (717)843-7394. **Staff:** Mary Fitzgibbons, Asst.Libn.

★ 20770 ★
York County Planning Commission - Library (Plan)
118 Pleasant Acres Rd.   Phone: (717)771-9550
York, PA 17402   Reed J. Dunn, Jr., Dir. of Plan.
Staff: 1. **Subjects:** Planning, land utilization, transportation, recreation, utilities, natural resources, statistics, housing, social and health planning, computerized information systems. **Holdings:** 6000 books and pamphlets; tapes. **Subscriptions:** 60 journals and other serials. **Services:** Interlibrary loan; copying; library open to the public. **Publications:** Planning Commission Newsletter, quarterly - to interested citizens and municipal officials; Housing Newsletter; Transportation Newsletter, both biennial. **Remarks:** Library is an affiliated data center of the Pennsylvania State Data Center.

★ 20771 ★
York-Finch General Hospital - Thomas J. Malcho Memorial Library
(Med)
2111 Finch Ave., W.   Phone: (416)744-2500
Downsview, ON, Canada M3N 1N1   Mona Frantzke, Med.Libn.
Founded: 1973. **Staff:** Prof 1. **Subjects:** Medicine, nursing, hospital administration. **Holdings:** 2000 books. **Subscriptions:** 210 journals. **Services:** Interlibrary loan; library not open to the public. **Computerized Information Services:** MEDLARS. **Networks/Consortia:** Member of Canadian Health Libraries Association, Ontario Hospital Libraries Association (OHLA). **Remarks:** FAX: (416)747-3883.

The York Gate Geographical and Colonial Library
See: **Royal Geographical Society of Australasia, Inc. - South Australian Branch - Library** (14118)

★ 20772 ★
York Hospital - Health Sciences Library (Med)
15 Hospital Dr.   Phone: (207)363-4321
York, ME 03909   Darryl Hamson, Libn.
Staff: 1. **Subjects:** Medicine, nursing, hospital administration. **Holdings:** 320 books; 480 bound periodical volumes. **Subscriptions:** 90 journals and other serials. **Services:** Interlibrary loan; copying; SDI; library open to the public. **Computerized Information Services:** BRS Information Technologies, WILSONLINE, NLM. Performs searches free of charge for professionals in community. **Networks/Consortia:** Member of Health Science Library and Information Cooperative of Maine (HSLIC). **Publications:** Library News (newsletter), quarterly - for internal distribution only.

★ 20773 ★
York Hospital - Philip A. Hoover, M.D. Library (Med)
1001 S. George St.   Phone: (717)771-2495
York, PA 17405   Beth A. Evitts, Dir., Lib.Serv.
Founded: 1962. **Staff:** Prof 2; Other 4. **Subjects:** Medicine, nursing, health education. **Special Collections:** Health Education Resource Shelf (100 books; pamphlets; periodicals); Chaplaincy Collection (150 books). **Holdings:** 5735 books; 6479 bound periodical volumes. **Subscriptions:** 500 journals and other serials. **Services:** Interlibrary loan; copying; SDI; library open to the public with restrictions on borrowing. **Automated Operations:** Computerized cataloging. **Computerized Information Services:** BRS Information Technologies, MEDLARS; internal database; CD-ROMs (MEDLINE, CINAHL). Performs searches on fee basis. Contact Person: Diane M. Robinson, Asst.Dir. **Networks/Consortia:** Member of Central Pennsylvania Health Sciences Library Association (CPHSLA), BHSL. **Publications:** Library Letter, irregular. **Special Indexes:** Periodical list (book, online). **Remarks:** FAX: (717)771-2487. **Staff:** Diane M. Robinson.

★ 20774 ★
York Institute Museum - Dyer Library (Hist)
371 Main St.   Phone: (207)283-3861
Saco, ME 04072   Emerson W. Baker, PhD., Dir.
Founded: 1881. **Subjects:** History of York County and Maine, 1681-1900. **Holdings:** 100,000 deeds, indentures, letters, public documents, church records, municipal records, logbooks, business records, maps, plans, architectural drawings, photographs, glass negatives, 18th-19th century newspapers, diaries. **Services:** Interlibrary loan; copying; library open to the public. **Computerized Information Services:** Internal database.

★ 20775 ★
York International Corporation - Engineering Library
Box 1592-191A
York, PA 17405-1592
Defunct.

★ 20776 ★
York Minster - Library (Rel-Phil, Hist)
Dean's Park   Phone: 0904 625308
York YO1 2JD, England   C.B.L. Barr, Sub-Libn.
Founded: 1414. **Staff:** 5. **Subjects:** Theology; religion; church history; York Minster - history, work, architecture, art; York and Yorkshire - history, churches, local booktrade; religious literature, art, architecture. **Special Collections:** York and Yorkshire history (30,000 print and manuscript materials); English Civil War (1500 items); music (1250 print and manuscript materials); Minster archives (manuscripts). **Holdings:** 100,000 volumes; 50 microforms; 100 manuscripts. **Subscriptions:** 50 journals and other serials. **Services:** Copying; photography; library open to the public. **Special Catalogs:** Catalog of manuscript music; catalog of printed music. **Staff:** Canon J. Toy, Canon Libn.; M.S. Dorrington, Archv.

★ 20777 ★
York Technical College - Library (Sci-Engr)
452 S. Anderson
U.S. 21 Bypass   Phone: (803)327-8000
Rock Hill, SC 29730   Amanda Yu, Libn.
Founded: 1964. **Staff:** Prof 2; Other 2. **Subjects:** Industrial arts, business, health sciences, engineering, liberal arts. **Holdings:** 23,850 books; 42,000 microforms; 32,000 slides; 3648 cassette tapes; 2763 transparencies; 1200 videotapes; 1716 filmstrips. **Subscriptions:** 230 journals and other serials; 13 newspapers. **Services:** Interlibrary loan; copying; library open to residents of area. **Computerized Information Services:** DIALOG Information Services, CompuServe Information Service. **Remarks:** FAX: (803)327-8059.

★ 20778 ★
York University - Archives and Special Collections (Hum)
Scott Library, Rm. 305
4700 Keele St.   Phone: (416)736-5442
North York, ON, Canada M3J 1P3   Barbara Craig, Archv.
Founded: 1988. **Staff:** Prof 3; Other 2. **Subjects:** Canadian literature, history, politics, fine arts, theater; local history. **Special Collections:** Auden; Day-Lewis; Isherwood; MacNeice; Spender; the Sitwells; Marsh; MacLeish; papers of Louis Applebaum (55 feet); Margaret Avison (1 foot); Bill Bissett (86 feet); Canadian Broadcasting Corporation TV Drama Scripts (485 feet); Canadian Speakers' and Writers' Service (95 feet); Canadian Theatre Review (40 feet); Ramsay Cook (18 feet); Harry Crowe (56 feet); William Esdaile (7 feet); Joseph O. Goodman (100 feet); Allan Grossman (61 feet); Robert Haynes (3 feet); William Jaffe (42 feet); Margaret Laurence (29 feet); Norman Levine (28 feet); Roy Mitchell (5 feet); Mayor Moore (115 feet); Northern Journey (6 feet); Province of Ontario Land Registry Books (916 feet); Operation Life line (24 feet); Joseph Bascom St. John (40 feet); Sitwell Family (9 feet); Richard Storr (36 feet); Toronto Real Estate Board Multiple Listings (450 feet); Toronto Telegram Photograph Collection (1484 feet); United Electrical, Radio and Machine Workers of America, Local 507, Toronto (61 feet); Vaughan Township (45 feet); Ernest Vinci (86 feet); Herman Voaden (72 feet); Waves (9 feet); Lady Victoria Welby (17 feet). **Holdings:** 26,700 books; 4500 feet of manuscripts; 1250 feet of university records; 190 feet of university theses; 6400 Canadian pamphlets. **Services:** Interlibrary loan; copying; archives open to the public. **Automated Operations:** Computerized public access catalog. **Computerized Information Services:** BITNET (electronic mail service). **Publications:** Accession Bulletin, irregular. **Special Catalogs:** Canadian pamphlets collection. Electronic mail address(es): BCRAIG@YORKVM2 (BITNET). **Staff:** Phyllis Platnick, Assoc.Archv.; Grace Heggie, Soc.Sci.Bibliog./Canadiana Coord.

★ 20779 ★
York University - Centre for Research on Latin America and the Caribbean - CERLAC Documentation Centre (Area-Ethnic)
240 York Lanes
4700 Keele St.   Phone: (416)736-5237
North York, ON, Canada M3J 1P3   Liisa North, Fellow CERLAC
Founded: 1979. **Staff:** Prof 2; Other 2. **Subjects:** Latin America and the Caribbean - sociology, economics, political science, history; Canadian-Latin American/Caribbean relations. **Special Collections:** Research reports and working papers from Latin American and Caribbean social science research centers in Argentina, Barbados, Brazil, Chile, Ecuador, Guyana, Jamaica, Mexico, Peru, Trinidad, Uruguay, Venezuela, and Costa Rica; reviews of the Organization for Economic Cooperation and Development (OECD) pertaining to Latin America; United Nations information and statistics; Brazilian government documents. **Holdings:** 1500 volumes; government research reports on microfilm and microfiche; Spanish, Portuguese, Italian journals. **Subscriptions:** 50 journals and other serials. **Services:** Copying; center open to the public by appointment. **Computerized Information Services:** NETNORTH, BITNET (electronic mail services). **Publications:** List of publications - available upon request. **Remarks:** FAX: (416)736-5737. Telex: 065 24736 YORKU.TOR. Electronic mail address(es): CERLAC@YORKVM1 (NETNORTH); YTERM (BITNET).

★ 20780 ★
York University - Centre for the Support of Teaching (Educ)
4700 Keele St.   Phone: (416)736-5754
North York, ON, Canada M3J 1P3   Dr. Pat Rogers, Acad.Dir.
Founded: 1976. **Staff:** Prof 1; Other 2. **Subjects:** Higher and adult education. **Holdings:** 500 books; unbound periodicals. **Subscriptions:** 90 journals and other serials. **Services:** Copying; center open to the public with restrictions. **Automated Operations:** Computerized cataloging. **Publications:** Core (newsletter), quarterly. **Remarks:** FAX: (416)736-5700.

★ 20781 ★
York University - Department of Visual Arts - Slide Library (Art)
Fine Arts Phase II, Rm. 274   Phone: (416)736-5534
Toronto, ON, Canada M3J 1P3   Michele Metraux, Supv.
Founded: 1970. **Staff:** Prof 3; Other 2. **Subjects:** Art history, painting, sculpture, architecture. **Special Collections:** Theodore A. Heinrich Slide Collection. **Holdings:** 250,000 35mm slides. **Subscriptions:** 20 journals and other serials. **Services:** Library open to the public at librarian's discretion. **Staff:** Lillian Heinson, Asst. Slide Libn.; Mika Holubec, Asst. Slide Libn.

York University - Education Development Office - Resource Centre
See: York University - Centre for the Support of Teaching (20780)

★ 20782 ★
York University - Faculty of Arts - Writing Workshop Library (Educ)
208 Stong College
4700 Keele St.   Phone: (416)736-5134
Downsview, ON, Canada M3J 1P3   Lezlie Anderson, Adm.Sec.
Subjects: Composition, how to write and teach special subjects. **Holdings:** 1100 books; 100 bound periodical volumes. **Services:** Interlibrary loan; library open to students and faculty.

★ 20783 ★
York University - Faculty of Education - Education Centre (Educ)
North Tower, Rm. 828 Ross
4700 Keele St.   Phone: (416)736-5259
Downsview, ON, Canada M3J 1P3   Gabrielle O'Reilly, Coord.
Founded: 1974. **Staff:** Prof 2. **Subjects:** Education. **Holdings:** 7000 books; 377 kits; 342 filmstrips; 295 phonograph records; 103 cassette tapes; 118 pictures; 309 multi-media kits; 45 slides; 262 activity files. **Services:** Center open to York University Faculty of Education only.

★ 20784 ★
York University - Film Library (Aud-Vis)
Scott Library
4700 Keele St.   Phone: (416)736-5508
North York, ON, Canada M3J 1P3   Kathryn Elder, Film-Video Libn.
Founded: 1970. **Staff:** Prof 1; Other 3. **Special Collections:** Dance in Canada: Jean A. Chalmers Choreographic Collection (194 video cassettes of work by contemporary Canadian choreographers); Labatt Breweries of Canada Sports Collection (350 films). **Holdings:** 1877 16mm film titles; 1911 video cassettes. **Services:** Films loaned to other Ontario universities. **Automated Operations:** Computerized cataloging. **Special Catalogs:** Annotated catalog with subject index (book). **Remarks:** Provides film reference service and obtains films from outside rental sources.

★ 20785 ★
York University - French Studies Department - Library (Area-Ethnic)
Ross Bldg., Rm. 5556A
4700 Keele St.   Phone: (416)736-5086
Downsview, ON, Canada M3J 1P3   Liliana Guadagnoli, Adm.Asst.
Staff: 3. **Subjects:** French studies. **Special Collections:** Bibliotheque de la Pleiade, 16th-19th centuries (French). **Holdings:** Figures not available. **Services:** Library not open to the public. **Computerized Information Services:** Electronic mail. **Remarks:** FAX: (416)736-5735.

★ 20786 ★
York University - Geography Department - Teaching Resources Centre (Geog-Map)
Ross Bldg., Rm. S405
4700 Keele St.   Phone: (416)736-5107
Downsview, ON, Canada M3J 1P3   Michael Flosznik, Supv.
Staff: Prof 1; Other 6. **Subjects:** Geography - urban and historical Canada, biology, recreation, economic. **Special Collections:** Departmental papers, theses, dissertations; Census of Canada, 1961-1986 (incomplete); airphoto mosaic coverage of Metropolitan Toronto (1988); airphoto coverage of highways and roads in Metro Toronto and area (various years and scales); National Topographic maps series of Canada (various scales, incomplete); Reports of the Royal Commission on the Future of the Toronto Waterfront; thematic maps of Canada. **Holdings:** 200 books; unbound periodicals. **Subscriptions:** 49 journals and other serials. **Services:** Center open to the public for reference use only. **Automated Operations:** Computerized cataloging. **Computerized Information Services:** Internal database. **Special Catalogs:** Map Catalog. **Special Indexes:** Keyword Index of Departmental Theses and Research Papers.

★ 20787 ★
York University - Glendon College - Career Library (Educ)
Glendon Hall
2275 Bayview Ave.   Phone: (416)487-6709
Toronto, ON, Canada M4N 3M6   Marika Kemeny, Career Libn.
Founded: 1982. **Staff:** 3. **Subjects:** Careers for liberal arts graduates.
Holdings: Figures not available. **Services:** Library not open to the public.
Computerized Information Services: Internal database. **Remarks:** FAX: (416)487-6779.

★ 20788 ★
York University - Government Documents/Administrative Studies
    Library (Bus-Fin, Info Sci)
113 Administrative Studies Bldg.
4700 Keele St.   Phone: (416)736-5139
North York, ON, Canada M3J 1P3   Vivienne Monty, Hd.
Staff: Prof 3; Other 9. **Subjects:** Documents of the governments of Canada, Great Britain, United States; documents of United Nations, Organization for Economic Cooperation and Development, European Communities; management; public administration; capital markets; corporations; administrative behavior; arts management; executive development. **Holdings:** 150,000 documents (83,000 bound); 8622 reels of microfilm; 1.06 million microfiche and microcards; 2000 volume reference collection; 15,000 bound periodical volumes; microfiche data file on Canadian and American companies, mid-1950s-1972 for U.S. companies, mid-1950s to present for Canadian companies. **Subscriptions:** 6000 journals and other serials; 12 newspapers. **Services:** Interlibrary loan; copying; library open to the public. **Automated Operations:** Computerized cataloging and acquisitions. **Computerized Information Services:** DIALOG Information Services, CAN/OLE, BRS Information Technologies, The Financial Post DataGroup, Info Globe, International Development Research Centre (IDRC); Envoy 100, BITNET (electronic mail services). **Remarks:** FAX: (416)736-5687. Electronic mail address(es): V.MONTY (Envoy 100); VMONTY@YORKVM2 (BITNET). **Staff:** Elizabeth Watson, Ref.Libn.; D.K. Varma, Adm.Stud.Libn.

★ 20789 ★
York University - Institute for Social Research - Data Archive (Soc Sci)
4700 Keele St.   Phone: (416)736-5061
North York, ON, Canada M3J 1P3   A. Paul Grayson, Dir.
Founded: 1968. **Staff:** Prof 12; Other 8. **Subjects:** Social sciences with Canadian focus; survey research - by mail, telephone, or interview, questionnaire design, measurement, programming, and data analysis. **Holdings:** Reports; archival materials; machine readable survey data. **Services:** Archive open to the public with restrictions. **Computerized Information Services:** Data archives (internal database). **Publications:** List of publications - available on request. **Special Catalogs:** Canadian Social Science Data Catalogue 1985. **Remarks:** FAX: (416)736-5749.

★ 20790 ★
York University - Law Library (Law)
4700 Keele St.   Phone: (416)736-5206
North York, ON, Canada M3J 1P3   Prof. B.J. Halevy, Libn.
Founded: 1892. **Staff:** Prof 6.5; Other 20. **Subjects:** Law. **Holdings:** 279,183 volumes; 117,224 volumes in microform. **Subscriptions:** 2404 journals and other serials. **Services:** Interlibrary loan; copying; library open to the public with fee for borrowing. **Automated Operations:** Computerized public access catalog, acquisitions, circulation, and cataloging. **Computerized Information Services:** QL Systems; CAN/LAW, Info Globe, SOQUIJ (Socite Qebecoise d'Information Juridique), WESTLAW, LEXIS, DIALOG Information Services; Envoy 100, BITNET (electronic mail services). **Publications:** Acquisitions list, monthly; KF Canadian Adaptation Classification Schedule, quarterly. **Remarks:** FAX: (416)736-5298. **Staff:** Judy Ginsberg, Asst. Law Libn.; Trudy Bodak, Cat.Libn.; Marianne Rogers, Hd., Ref.; Karen Foti, Ref.Libn.; Lucie Hamelin-Touloumis, Hd., Acq.; Monica Perot, Hd., Circ.

★ 20791 ★
York University - Map Library (Geog-Map)
Scott Library, Rm. 115
4700 Keele St.   Phone: (416)736-2100
North York, ON, Canada M3J 1P3   Trudy Bodak, Map Libn.
Founded: 1970. **Staff:** Prof 1; Other 2. **Subjects:** Geography, cartography. **Holdings:** 4500 books and atlases; 92,000 maps; clipping file; pamphlet file; 3800 aerial photographs; file of articles on cartography; maps on slides. **Subscriptions:** 30 journals and other serials. **Services:** Interlibrary loan; copying; library open to the public.

★ 20792 ★
York University - Nellie Langford Rowell Library (Soc Sci)
204 Founders College
4700 Keele St.   Phone: (416)736-2100
North York, ON, Canada M3J 1P3   C.M. Donald, Lib.Coord.
Founded: 1970. **Staff:** 9. **Subjects:** Women, women's studies, feminism. **Holdings:** 7000 books; 250 boxes of broadsides and ephemera. **Subscriptions:** 150 journals and other serials. **Services:** Library open to the public. **Publications:** Pamphlet series.

★ 20793 ★
York University - Sound and Moving Image Library (Mus)
Scott Library, Rm. 125
4700 Keele St.   Phone: (416)736-2100
North York, ON, Canada M3J 1P3   Rob van der Bliek, Hd.
Founded: 1970. **Staff:** Prof 1; Other 3. **Subjects:** Music, theater, ethnomusicology, theatre, spoken word. **Special Collections:** Robert and Anne Levine Collection of Archival Jazz and Blues (2500 phonograph records); International Library of African Music (213 phonograph records); Edith Fowke Collection (95 reels of field tapes); Vogt Collection of Popular and Musical Theatre (recordings, books, and memorabilia); CBC Ideas Collection (1750 reels of tape). **Holdings:** 51,500 books and scores; 28,000 phonograph records, compact discs, tapes, cassette tapes; 1000 scores on microfiche. **Subscriptions:** 12 journals and other serials. **Services:** Interlibrary loan; copying (limited); room open to library card holders. **Automated Operations:** Computerized public access catalog, cataloging, acquisitions, serials, and circulation. **Computerized Information Services:** BITNET (electronic mail service). **Publications:** Handbook; discographies on selected topics. **Special Catalogs:** Levine Catalogue (performer, title). **Special Indexes:** Ethnomusicology index. **Remarks:** Electronic mail address(es): STOCKTON@YORKVM2 (BITNET). **Formerly:** Its Sound Recordings Library.

York University - Special Collections
See: York University - Archives and Special Collections (20778)

★ 20794 ★
York University - Steacie Science Library (Sci-Engr, Comp Sci)
4700 Keele St.   Phone: (416)736-5639
North York, ON, Canada M3J 1P3   Brian Wilks, Hd.
Founded: 1970. **Staff:** Prof 2; Other 6. **Subjects:** Mathematics, applied computational mathematics, chemistry, computer science, physics, biology, earth and atmospheric sciences; atmospheric chemistry. **Holdings:** 60,000 books; 68,000 bound periodical volumes; 30,000 microforms. **Subscriptions:** 1800 journals and other serials. **Services:** Interlibrary loan; copying; library open to the public for reference use only. **Automated Operations:** Computerized cataloging, acquisitions, and circulation. **Computerized Information Services:** DIALOG Information Services, BRS Information Technologies, PFDS Online, CAN/SDI, CAN/OLE, The Financial Post DataGroup, QL Systems, MEDLARS, Info Globe, Questel, Infomart Online, WILSONLINE, STN International.

York University - University Archives
See: York University - Archives and Special Collections (20778)

★ 20795 ★
Yorkshire Archaeological Society - Library (Hist)
Claremont 23 Clarendon Rd.   Phone: 457910
Leeds LS2 9NZ, England   Susan Leadbeater
Founded: 1863. **Staff:** Prof 1. **Subjects:** History, archeology, architecture, topography. **Special Collections:** Wakefield Court Rolls, 1274 to 1925; Duke of Leeds Papers. **Holdings:** 40,000 books; 200 bound periodical volumes; 35,000 archives; 350 microfiche. **Subscriptions:** 200 journals and other serials. **Services:** Copying; library open to the public for reference use only. **Publications:** Guides to archives.

Yosemite National Park
See: U.S. Natl. Park Service (17794)

Arthur Young Tax Research Library
See: San Diego State University - Bureau of Business & Economic Research Library (14714)

★ 20796 ★
Brigham Young University - Anthropology Museum Library (Soc Sci)
Allen Hall
Provo, UT 84602
Phone: (801)378-6196
Connie Lamb, Libn.
Staff: Prof 1; Other 5. **Subjects:** Archeology - Mesoamerican, Southwestern, historical. **Holdings:** 4000 books; 1500 bound periodical volumes. **Services:** SDI; library open to the public. **Computerized Information Services:** BITNET (electronic mail service). **Publications:** Publications in Archaeology, annual. **Remarks:** Electronic mail address(es): LIBCXL@BYUVM (BITNET). **Staff:** Joel Janetski, Musm.Dir.

★ 20797 ★
Brigham Young University - Archives and Manuscripts Division (Hist)
5030 Harold B. Lee Library
Provo, UT 84602
Phone: (801)378-2932
Scott H. Duvall, Ch.
Staff: Prof 7; Other 15. **Subjects:** Brigham Young University; Utah and the American West; the Mormon experience; arts and communication; motion pictures; photography; literature; Mesoamerica; politics; history - European, ancient, medieval, renaissance. **Holdings:** 8500 linear feet of manuscripts; 6000 linear feet of archival material. **Services:** Copying; archives open to the public. **Automated Operations:** Computerized public access catalog, cataloging, serials, acquisitions, and circulation. **Computerized Information Services:** RLIN; BITNET (electronic mail service). **Networks/Consortia:** Member of Research Libraries Information Network (RLIN), Utah College Library Council (UCLC). **Remarks:** Electronic mail address(es): LIBEDR@BYUVM (BITNET). **Staff:** Melva H. Richey, Act.Univ.Archv.; Albert L. Winkler, Cat.; David J. Whittaker, Cur.; LeGrand L. Baker, Cur.; Harvard S. Heath, Cur.; James V. D'Arc, Cur.; E. Dennis Rowley, Cur.

★ 20798 ★
Brigham Young University - Archives and Manuscripts Division - Archives of Recorded Sound (Aud-Vis)
5030 Harold B. Lee Library
Provo, UT 84602
Phone: (801)378-2932
Scott H. Duvall, Ch.
Staff: Prof 1; Other 1. **Subjects:** Radio broadcasting, U.S. presidents, movie soundtracks, Utah and university history. **Special Collections:** Oral history interviews (700). **Holdings:** 45,000 tape recordings; 15,000 phonograph records. **Services:** Copying; archives open to the public. **Computerized Information Services:** RLIN.

★ 20799 ★
Brigham Young University - Asian Collection (Area-Ethnic)
1066 Harold B. Lee Library
Provo, UT 84602
Phone: (801)378-4061
Gail King, Cur.
Founded: 1972. **Staff:** Prof 1. **Subjects:** Chinese, Japanese, and Korean materials in the humanities and social sciences. **Holdings:** 57,000 volumes. **Subscriptions:** 102 journals and other serials. **Services:** Interlibrary loan; collection open to the public. **Automated Operations:** Computerized cataloging, serials, and circulation. **Computerized Information Services:** Internal database; BITNET (electronic mail service). Performs searches free of charge. **Networks/Consortia:** Member of Research Libraries Information Network (RLIN). **Remarks:** FAX: (801)378-6347. Electronic mail address(es): LIBGOK@BYUVM (BITNET).

★ 20800 ★
Brigham Young University - Bean Museum - Research Library (Biol Sci)
Provo, UT 84602
Phone: (801)378-4585
Lisa Baer, Bean Musm.Libn.
Founded: 1978. **Staff:** Prof 1; Other 2. **Subjects:** Taxonomy - botany, zoology. **Holdings:** 6000 books; 550 bound periodical volumes; 5000 book titles on microfiche; 10,000 taxonomic offprints. **Subscriptions:** 31 journals and other serials. **Services:** Interlibrary loan (through Harold B. Lee Library); copying; library open to the public. **Automated Operations:** Computerized public access catalog, cataloging, and acquisitions. **Computerized Information Services:** BITNET (electronic mail service). **Networks/Consortia:** Member of Research Libraries Information Network (RLIN), Utah College Library Council (UCLC). **Special Catalogs:** Catalog of offprint collection (online). **Remarks:** Electronic mail address(es): LIBLCB@BYULIB (BITNET).

★ 20801 ★
Brigham Young University - Documents and Map Collection (Geog-Map, Info Sci)
1368 Harold B. Lee Library
Provo, UT 84602
Phone: (801)378-6180
Therrin C. Dahlin, Docs.Libn.
Founded: 1955. **Staff:** Prof 3; Other 1. **Holdings:** Documents - U.S. Federal, state/municipal, Canadian, United Nations, Organization of American States; maps; atlases; gazetteers. **Services:** Interlibrary loan; copying; collection open to the public. **Automated Operations:** Computerized cataloging, acquisitions, serials, and circulation. **Computerized Information Services:** DIALOG Information Services, PFDS Online, WILSONLINE, MEDLINE; BYLINE, Supermap, PC-Globe (internal databases); BITNET (electronic mail service). Performs searches on fee basis. Contact Person: Larry D. Benson, Pol.Sci./Econ.Libn., 378-3800. **Networks/Consortia:** Member of Research Libraries Information Network (RLIN), Utah College Library Council (UCLC). **Remarks:** FAX: (801)378-6347. Electronic mail address(es): LIBTCD@BYUVM (BITNET). **Staff:** Beverly J. Norton, Fed.Docs.Libn.; Richard E. Soares, Map Libn.

★ 20802 ★
Brigham Young University - Glenn and Olive Nielson Library (Bus-Fin)
School of Management
410 N. Eldon Tanner Bldg.
Provo, UT 84602
Phone: (801)378-3924
Gordon C. Casper, Dir.
Founded: 1982. **Staff:** Prof 2; Other 11. **Subjects:** Accounting, business and information management, managerial economics, organizational behavior, public administration. **Special Collections:** Ernst & Young Tax Library. **Holdings:** 5000 books; 450 bound periodical volumes; 40 drawers of microfiche. **Subscriptions:** 500 journals and other serials; 5 newspapers. **Services:** Interlibrary loan; copying; library open to the public. **Automated Operations:** Computerized cataloging, acquisitions, and serials. **Computerized Information Services:** DIALOG Information Services, ABI/INFORM, NEXIS, Nikkei Telecom, Newspaper Abstracts, Bonneville Telecommunications' Market Center; InfoTrac; BITNET (electronic mail service). Performs searches on fee basis. **Networks/Consortia:** Member of Utah College Library Council (UCLC). **Publications:** Subject Bibliographies. **Remarks:** Electronic mail address(es): LIBGCC@BYUVM (BITNET). **Staff:** Kirk Memmott.

★ 20803 ★
Brigham Young University - Humanities and Arts Division Library (Hum)
University Library
Provo, UT 84602
Phone: (801)378-4005
Richard D. Hacken, Dept.Chm.
Staff: Prof 4; Other 8. **Subjects:** Literature, music, art, languages, speech, drama, theater arts, cinematic arts, library science. **Holdings:** Figures not available. **Services:** Interlibrary loan; copying; library open to the public. **Automated Operations:** Computerized cataloging, serials, and circulation. **Computerized Information Services:** DIALOG Information Services, PFDS Online, RLIN, BRS Information Technologies, Mead Data Central, OCLC; CD-ROMs; BITNET (electronic mail service). **Networks/Consortia:** Member of Research Libraries Information Network (RLIN), Utah College Library Council (UCLC). **Remarks:** FAX: (801)378-3221. Electronic mail address(es): LIBRLL@BYUVM (BITNET).

★ 20804 ★
Brigham Young University - J. Reuben Clark Law School Library (Law)
Provo, UT 84602
Phone: (801)378-3593
Constance K. Lundberg, Law Libn.
Founded: 1972. **Staff:** Prof 7; Other 30. **Subjects:** United States, British Commonwealth, foreign, and international law. **Holdings:** 239,599 books; 122,654 bound periodical volumes; 66,388 monographs; 50,557 government documents; 3743 other cataloged items; 95,243 volumes in microform. **Subscriptions:** 3987 journals and other serials; 38 newspapers. **Services:** Interlibrary loan; copying; library open to the public for legal research use only. **Computerized Information Services:** LEXIS, WESTLAW; BITNET (electronic mail service). **Networks/Consortia:** Member of Research Libraries Information Network (RLIN), Utah College Library Council (UCLC). **Publications:** Foreign Law Classification Schedule, Class K (2nd edition); LC Subject Headings - KF: Cross-References; Legal Research Manual. **Remarks:** Electronic mail address(es): LUNDBERG@LAWGATE.BYU.EDU (BITNET). **Staff:** Gary Hill, Assoc. Law Libn.; Dennis Sears, Ref.Libn.; Kory Stahei, Proj.Libn.; Bonnie Geldmacher, Asst.Tech.Serv.Libn.; Lovisa Lyman, Coll.Dev.Libn.; Curt Conklin, Tech.Serv.Libn.; Kerry Lowis, Ser.Libn.; Steven Kenworthy, Circ.Libn.; Karen Newmeyer, Asst.Ref.Libn.

★ 20805 ★
Brigham Young University - Primrose International Viola Archive (Mus)
5222 Harold B. Lee Library   Phone: (801)378-6119
Provo, UT 84602   David A. Day
Founded: 1979. **Staff:** Prof 2; Other 2. **Subjects:** Viola - scores, manuscripts, recordings. **Holdings:** 5000 scores. **Services:** Interlibrary loan; copying; library open to the public. **Computerized Information Services:** OCLC, RLIN; Viola Discography (internal database); BITNET (electronic mail service). Performs searches. **Publications:** Viola Discography (under development); Franz Zeyringer's Literatur fur Viola (revised editions). **Remarks:** Electronic mail address(es): LIBDAD@BYUVM (BITNET).

★ 20806 ★
Brigham Young University - Religion and History Division Library (Hist, Rel-Phil)
University Library   Phone: (801)378-6118
Provo, UT 84602   Gary P. Gillum, Hist./Rel.Libn./Dept.Chm.
Staff: Prof 4; Other 7. **Subjects:** History, religion, genealogy, philosophy, geography, anthropology, archeology. **Holdings:** 500,000 books. **Services:** Interlibrary loan; copying; library open to the public. **Automated Operations:** Computerized cataloging, acquisitions, serials, and circulation. **Computerized Information Services:** DIALOG Information Services, PFDS Online, BRS Information Technologies, NOTIS, RLIN, InfoTrac, OCLC; BITNET (electronic mail service). Performs searches on fee basis. **Networks/Consortia:** Member of Research Libraries Information Network (RLIN), Utah College Library Council (UCLC), Center for Research Libraries (CRL). **Remarks:** Electronic mail address(es): LIBGPG@BYUVM (BITNET). **Staff:** Mark L. Grover, Lat.Amer.Stud.Libn.; Gary P. Gillum, Ancient Stud.Libn.; Connie Lamb, Near Eastern Stud.Libn.; Susan L. Fales, Hist.Libn.

★ 20807 ★
Brigham Young University - Science and Technology Department Library (Sci-Engr)
2222 Harold B. Lee Library   Phone: (801)378-2986
Provo, UT 84602   Richard Jensen, Dept.Chm./Biomed.Agri.Spec.
Founded: 1875. **Staff:** Prof 4; Other 6. **Subjects:** Science and technology. **Holdings:** 500,000 volumes. **Subscriptions:** 6300 journals and other serials. **Services:** Interlibrary loan; copying; SDI; library open to the public. **Automated Operations:** Computerized public access catalog, cataloging, acquisitions, serials, and circulation. **Computerized Information Services:** DIALOG Information Services, STN International, WILSONLINE, BRS Information Technologies, RLIN, NLM, Data-Star; CD-ROMs (WILSONDISC, USGS, Math Reviews, Ulrich, PC-SIG, MEDLINE, NurseSearch, Enviro/Energyline Abstracts Plus, Supertech Abstracts Plus, AGRICOLA, CRIS/ICAR); BITNET (electronic mail service). Performs searches on fee basis. **Networks/Consortia:** Member of Research Libraries Information Network (RLIN), Utah College Library Council (UCLC), Center for Research Libraries (CRL). **Remarks:** FAX: (801)378-6347. Electronic mail address(es): LIBRDJ@BYUVM (BITNET). **Staff:** Mark England, Engr. Subject Spec.; John Christensen, Physical Sci. Subject Spec.; Lisa Baer, Biol. Subject Spec.

★ 20808 ★
Brigham Young University - Social Science Department Library (Soc Sci)
Harold B. Lee Library   Phone: (801)378-6346
Provo, UT 84602   Marvin Wiggins, Dept.Chm.
Staff: Prof 3; Other 7. **Subjects:** Psychology, sociology, family science, education, business/economics, social work, political science, international relations. **Holdings:** Figures not available. **Services:** Interlibrary loan; copying; SDI; library open to the public. **Automated Operations:** Computerized cataloging, acquisitions, serials, and circulation. **Computerized Information Services:** DIALOG Information Services, PFDS Online, WILSONLINE, MEDLINE, NOTIS; CD-ROMs; BITNET (electronic mail service). Performs searches on fee basis. **Networks/Consortia:** Member of Research Libraries Information Network (RLIN), Utah College Library Council (UCLC). **Remarks:** Alternate telephone number(s): 378-3809. Electronic mail address(es): LIBMEW@BYUVM (BITNET). **Staff:** Afton M. Miner, Educ.Libn.; Larry Benson, Political Sci./Intl.Rel.Libn.

★ 20809 ★
Brigham Young University - Special Collections (Hist, Rel-Phil)
Harold B. Lee Library   Phone: (801)378-2932
Provo, UT 84602   Scott H. Duvall, Ch.
Founded: 1956. **Staff:** Prof 3; Other 2. **Subjects:** Renaissance and Reformation; history of printing; Mormonism; Utah and Western history; 19th century American and English literature; typography; 17th century astronomy; 16th century European diplomatics. **Special Collections:** LeRoy Hafen Collection of Western American History; J. Reuben Clark Collection of Law and Religion; Mormon Americana; Victorian book collection; Tyrus Hillway Collection of Herman Melville; Marco Heidner Collection of 15th and 16th century printing. **Holdings:** 185,467 volumes; 25,000 pamphlets. **Subscriptions:** 15 newspapers. **Services:** Interlibrary loan; copying; collections open to the public. **Automated Operations:** Computerized cataloging, acquisitions, and serials. **Computerized Information Services:** DIALOG Information Services, PFDS Online, BRS Information Technologies, Mead Data Central, NOTIS, OCLC; BITNET (electronic mail service). **Networks/Consortia:** Member of Research Libraries Information Network (RLIN), Utah College Library Council (UCLC). **Staff:** Chad J. Flake, Asst.Cur., Spec.Coll.

★ 20810 ★
Brigham Young University - Utah Valley Regional Family History Center and Microfilms Department (Hist)
Harold B. Lee Library, Rm. 4386   Phone: (801)378-6200
Provo, UT 84602   Diane R. Parkinson, Dir./Microforms Libn.
Founded: 1964. **Staff:** 1. **Subjects:** Genealogy. **Special Collections:** Academic microforms. **Holdings:** Genealogical Society of Salt Lake City Library Catalog; primary and secondary source material in microform; 25,000 journals, serials, and newspapers on microfilm. **Subscriptions:** 30 journals and other serials; 85 newspapers. **Services:** Copying; center open to the public. **Automated Operations:** Computerized public access catalog. Computerized family search. **Computerized Information Services:** Internal database; BITNET (electronic mail service). **Publications:** Newsletter and Information Sheet. **Special Catalogs:** Ancestral File; Family History Library Catalog. **Special Indexes:** International Genealogical Index (177 million births, christenings, and marriages arranged by state or country). **Remarks:** Electronic mail address(es): LIBDRP@BYUVM (BITNET). This center is a branch of the Church of Jesus Christ of Latter Day Saints - Family History Library in Salt Lake City and has access to their collection on a loan basis.

★ 20811 ★
Brigham Young University--Hawaii Campus - Joseph F. Smith Library (Rel-Phil, Hum)
55-220 Kulanui St.
BYU-HC Box 1966   Phone: (808)293-3850
Laie, HI 96762   Rex Frandsen, Dir.
Founded: 1955. **Staff:** Prof 10; Other 8. **Special Collections:** Pacific Islands (9500 books); Mormonism (5250 books); children's collection (3750 books); maps (10,000 sheets); government documents (selective depository); archives. **Holdings:** 163,200 books; 730,000 microforms; 1100 films; 2600 videotapes. **Subscriptions:** 1050 journals and other serials; 50 newspapers. **Services:** Interlibrary loan; copying; library open to the public on payment of annual fee. **Automated Operations:** Computerized public access catalog, cataloging, acquisitions, and circulation. **Computerized Information Services:** DIALOG Information Services, OCLC. **Publications:** Library Newsgram. **Special Catalogs:** Serials catalog; book catalog (microfiche). **Remarks:** FAX: (808)293-3877. **Staff:** Marynelle Chew, Cat./Govt.Doc.; Christine Britsch, Cat.; Greg Gubler, Archv.; Anita Henry, Acq.; Ed Jensen, Media; Josephine Bird, Pub.Serv.; Rita Smith, Ref.; Riley Moffat, Ref.; Dwight Miller, Automation; Phil Smith, Ref.

★ 20812 ★
Young, Conaway, Stargatt & Taylor - Library (Law)
Rodney Sq. N., 11th Fl.
Box 391   Phone: (302)571-6680
Wilmington, DE 19899-0391   Christine A. Coffman, Libn.
Staff: Prof 1. **Subjects:** Law. **Holdings:** 10,000 books. **Subscriptions:** 100 journals and other serials. **Services:** Library not open to the public. **Computerized Information Services:** LEXIS, WESTLAW, DIALOG Information Services, Delcat, DIGILAW, LAWCAT. **Remarks:** FAX: (302)571-1253.

Fern Young Memorial Library
See: **First Presbyterian Church** (5787)

★ 20813 ★
Howard Young Medical Center - Health Science Library (Med)
Box 470   Phone: (715)356-8070
Woodruff, WI 54568   Suzanne C. Miller, Med.Libn.
Founded: 1973. **Staff:** Prof 1. **Subjects:** Medicine, nursing. **Holdings:** 1200 volumes; 200 pamphlets; 250 video cassettes; 500 audio cassettes. **Subscriptions:** 150 journals and other serials. **Services:** Interlibrary loan; copying; library open to the public with restrictions. **Computerized Information Services:** MEDLINE, NLM, BRS Information Technologies. Performs searches on fee basis. **Networks/Consortia:** Member of National Network of Libraries of Medicine - Greater Midwest Region. **Remarks:** FAX: (715)356-8064.

★ 20814 ★
Kendall Young Library - MacKinlay Kantor Collection (Hist)
1201 Willson Ave.   Phone: (515)832-2565
Webster City, IA 50595   Cynthia Weiss, Dir.
Founded: 1898. **Staff:** 10. **Subjects:** MacKinlay Kantor - writings, connection with Webster City, family, ancestry. **Holdings:** 150 volumes; 7 boxes of manuscripts; 1 box of nonbook items. **Services:** Copying; collection open to the public. **Publications:** Inventory of the MacKinlay Kantor Collection; Collection Brochure. **Remarks:** FAX: (515)832-2570. **Staff:** Scott Mahoney, Adult Serv.Libn.

★ 20815 ★
Young Men's Christian Association - Library (Soc Sci)
Compania 1360
C.P. 1717
Santiago, Chile   Phone: 2 6965106
Subjects: Juvenile delinquency; young people with special needs; development - physical, cultural, social, ecumenical. **Holdings:** 300 volumes. **Also Known As:** Asociacion Cristiana de Jovenes.

Young Men's Christian Associations of the United States of America - Archives
See: YMCA of the USA - Archives (20760)

★ 20816 ★
Young Men's Mercantile Library Association - Library
414 Walnut St.   Phone: (513)621-0717
Cincinnati, OH 45202   Jean M. Springer, Exec.Dir.
Subjects: General collection. **Holdings:** 200,000 volumes. **Services:** Copying; library open to members only.

★ 20817 ★
Morris N. & Chesley V. Young Mnemonics Library
270 Riverside Dr.
New York, NY 10025
Defunct.

★ 20818 ★
Young Radiator Company - Library (Sci-Engr)
2825 4 Mile Rd.
Racine, WI 53404   Phone: (414)639-1011
Founded: 1945. **Subjects:** Competitive heat transfer material, specifications, and data. **Holdings:** 600 volumes; 300 magazines; 1450 catalogs; 5700 folders; 10 volumes of patents; 1 VF drawer of clippings; 5 VF drawers; house organs; annual reports. **Services:** Library not open to the public.

★ 20819 ★
Young and Rubicam Inc. - Corporate Library (Bus-Fin)
285 Madison Ave., 10th Fl.   Phone: (212)210-3982
New York, NY 10017   Maureen A. Pine, Dir. of Lib.Serv.
Founded: 1953. **Staff:** Prof 4; Other 4. **Subjects:** Advertising, marketing. **Special Collections:** Company histories; annual reports; cookbooks; art books; picture collection; competitive advertisers file. **Holdings:** 7500 volumes. **Subscriptions:** 250 journals and other serials. **Services:** Interlibrary loan; library not open to the public. **Computerized Information Services:** NEXIS, DIALOG Information Services, Market Analysis and Information Database (MAID). **Remarks:** FAX: (212)682-2283. **Staff:** Mary T. Febles, Mgr. Art Lib.; Shelia Parker, Sr.Ref.Libn.; Marie-Josee Fonseca, Ref.Libn.

Whitney M. Young, Jr. Memorial Library of Social Work
See: Columbia University - Whitney M. Young, Jr. Memorial Library of Social Work (4028)

★ 20820 ★
Whitney M. Young, Jr. Resource Center - USIS Library (Educ)
2 Broad St.
P.O. Box 554
Lagos, Nigeria
Remarks: Maintained or supported by the U.S. Information Agency. Focus is on materials that will assist peoples outside the United States to learn about the United States, its people, history, culture, political processes, and social milieux.

★ 20821 ★
Young Women's Christian Association - National Board - Library (Soc Sci)
726 Broadway   Phone: (212)614-2716
New York, NY 10003   Elizabeth D. Norris, Libn./Hist.
Founded: 1959. **Staff:** Prof 1; Other 1. **Subjects:** Women, racism, sexism, civil rights, women's health, youth, voluntarism. **Special Collections:** Womans Press Publications, 1918-1952 (2500 volumes). **Holdings:** 10,000 books; 25 VF drawers of subject files, clippings, pamphlets, reports, catalogs. **Subscriptions:** 175 journals and other serials. **Services:** Interlibrary loan; copying; library open to students and scholars by referral. **Publications:** New Library Books, monthly - for internal distribution only. **Remarks:** FAX: (212)677-9716. **Also Known As:** YWCA.

★ 20822 ★
Young Women's Christian Association of Marin - Resource Center (Educ)
1000 Sir Francis Drake Blvd., Rm. 14   Phone: (415)456-0726
San Anselmo, CA 94960   Ann Kennedy, Ctr.Dir.
Staff: Prof 4; Other 3. **Subjects:** Career planning, self-help law, women's movement, county resources, political issues, health, counseling, children. **Holdings:** 300 books; 10 VF drawers; 4 scrapbooks; 130 tapes. **Subscriptions:** 14 journals and other serials. **Services:** Copying; center open to the public for reference use only.

Barton Kyle Yount Memorial Library
See: American Graduate School of International Management (600)

Youth Liberation Archive
See: Temple University - Central Library System - Contemporary Culture Collection (16133)

★ 20823 ★
Youth Network Council of Chicago, Inc. - Illinois Youth Service Resource Center (Soc Sci)
321 S. 6th St.   Phone: (217)522-2663
Springfield, IL 62701   Kim Hayden, Prog.Adm
Founded: 1983. **Staff:** Prof 3; Other 1. **Subjects:** Youth and social services, community organization, juvenile justice, nonprofit organizations. **Holdings:** Figures not available. **Services:** Interlibrary loan; copying; center open to the public with restrictions. **Publications:** Newsline, quarterly - national distribution.

★ 20824 ★
Youth Network Council, Inc. - Clearinghouse (Soc Sci)
506 S. Wabash Ave.   Phone: (312)427-2710
Chicago, IL 60605   Denis Murstein, Adm.Dir.
Founded: 1972. **Staff:** Prof 15; Other 2. **Subjects:** Alternative youth services, runaway youth, adolescent sexuality, youth employment, substance abuse, grantsmanship, juvenile justice, community development, public relations. **Holdings:** 500 books; 80 VF drawers of pamphlets; Federal Register, 1978 to present; videotapes. **Subscriptions:** 60 journals and other serials; 10 newspapers. **Services:** Interlibrary loan; copying; clearinghouse open to the public by appointment. **Publications:** Newsline, quarterly - by subscription; Reachout, Resource Guide to Substance Abuse in Metropolitan Chicago; Youth Employment & Training Guide; Resources for Youth; A Guide to Advocacy for Youth - all for sale.

★ 20825 ★
Ypsilanti Regional Psychiatric Hospital - Staff Library (Med)
3501 Willis Rd.
Ypsilanti, MI 48197
Defunct.

★ 20826 ★
Yugoslav Center for Technical and Scientific Documentation (Sci-Engr)
Slobodana Penezica-Krcuna 29-31
P.O. Box 724   Phone: 11 644-250
YU-11000 Belgrade, Yugoslavia   Alexsic Miodrag, Dir.
Founded: 1952. **Subjects:** Scientific, technical, and economic information. **Holdings:** 1 million volumes. **Subscriptions:** 5000 journals and other serials. **Services:** Library open to the public. **Publications:** Bibliographies. **Remarks:** Telex: 12497. **Also Known As:** Jugoslovenski Centar za Tehnicku i Naucnu Dokumentaciju.

★ 20827 ★
Yugoslav Press and Cultural Center - Library (Area-Ethnic)
767 3rd Ave., 18th Fl.
New York, NY 10017   Phone: (212)838-2306
Subjects: Yugoslavia. **Holdings:** 5000 volumes.

Yugoslavia - Narodni Muzej - Knjiznica
See: **Yugoslavia - National Museum - Library (20828)**

★ 20828 ★
Yugoslavia - National Museum - Library
ul Presernova 20   Phone: 61 218876
YU-61000 Ljubljana, Yugoslavia   Dr. Branko Reisp
Founded: 1821. **Staff:** Prof 4. **Subjects:** History, numismatics, museology, archeology, cultural history. **Special Collections:** Cabinet of graphic arts (21,000); archives of Sig. Zois, Val. Vodnik, and Fr. Preseren; library of Anastasius Grunn and Joseph K. Erberg. **Holdings:** 50,000 books; 85,000 bound periodical volumes; 8000 reports; 17 reels of microfilm. **Subscriptions:** 420 journals and other serials; 5 newspapers. **Services:** Copying; library open to the public. **Remarks:** FAX: 61 221882. **Also Known As:** Yugoslavia - Narodni Muzej - Knjiznica.

★ 20829 ★
Yugoslavia - National Museum in Belgrade - Library (Hist, Art)
trg Republike 1
YU-11000 Belgrade, Yugoslavia   Phone: 11 624322
Founded: 1844. **Staff:** Prof 3. **Subjects:** Archeology, history of art, numismatics, conservation, museology, history. **Holdings:** 24,250 books; 15,620 bound periodical volumes. **Subscriptions:** 40 journals and other serials. **Services:** Interlibrary loan; copying; library open to researchers and students. **Special Catalogs:** Author and subject catalogs. **Remarks:** 11 627721. **Also Known As:** Narodni Muzej - Biblioteka.

Yukon Chamber of Mines
See: **British Columbia and Yukon Chamber of Mines (2183)**

Yukon Law Library
See: **Yukon Public Law Library (20830)**

★ 20830 ★
Yukon Public Law Library (Law)
Law Courts
P.O. Box 2703
Whitehorse, YT, Canada Y1A 2C6   Phone: (403)667-3086
Staff: 1. **Subjects:** Law. **Holdings:** 19,000 volumes. **Subscriptions:** 200 journals and other serials. **Services:** Interlibrary loan; copying; SDI; library open to the public. **Computerized Information Services:** QL Systems. **Publications:** Monthly new book list and newsletter. **Remarks:** FAX: (403)667-4116. **Formerly:** Yukon Law Library. **Staff:** Tanya Astika, Libn.; Jenny Nesbitt-Dufort, Libn.

★ 20831 ★
Yukon Territory - Department of Education - Yukon Archives (Hist)
Box 2703   Phone: (403)667-5309
Whitehorse, YT, Canada Y1A 2C6   Linda Johnson, Dir.
Founded: 1972. **Staff:** Prof 4; Other 5.5. **Subjects:** Yukon history and current development; Klondike gold rush; Yukon native people; northern pipelines; Alaska Highway; northern hydrocarbon development. **Special Collections:** Yukon Record Group I (central records of Yukon Government, 1894-1951; 500 meters); Dawson Mining Recorder (placer and quartz mining records, 1894-1971; 200 meters); White Pass and Yukon Route Records (transportation company records, 1898-1960; 25 meters); Anglican Church, Diocese of Yukon, 1888-1980 (10.7 meters). **Holdings:** 16,000 books; 215 bound periodical volumes; 1000 meters of territorial, municipal, federal government records; 380 meters of private manuscripts and corporate records; 1431 reels of microfilm; 8500 pamphlets; 8402 maps; 57,507 photographs; 470 films and videos; 2439 sound recordings. **Subscriptions:** 80 journals and other serials. **Services:** Copying; duplic ation of photographs and maps; Public Reading Room open to the public. **Computerized Information Services:** DIALOG Information Services, QL Systems; Envoy 100 (electronic mail service). **Publications:** Checklist of Yukon Newspapers, 1898-1985; Yukon Native History and Culture: A Bibliography of Sources Available at the Yukon Archives; Alaska Highway 1942-1992, Sources of Information in the Yukon Archives; Hydrocarbon Development: A Yukon Perspective; From Sissons to Meyer: The Administrative Development of the Yukon Government, 1948-1979; Yukon Economic Planning Studies, 1965-1985, an annotated bibliography; Archives Information pamphlet; Access to Information (brochure and index); bibliographies and finding aids; visual finding aids for photographs. **Special Indexes:** Inventories of government, private, and corporate records; Index to uncatalogued photographs. **Remarks:** FAX: (403)667-4253. Electronic mail address(es): ILL/Yukon.Govt (Envoy 100). **Staff:** Diane Chisholm, Asst. Territorial Archv.; Clara Rutherford, Archv. Accessions; Peggy D'Orsay, Libn.; Donna McBee, Govt.Rec.Archv.

★ 20832 ★
Yuma County Law Library (Law)
219 W. 2nd St.   Phone: (602)329-2255
Yuma, AZ 85364   Gerrie Regenscheid, Libn.
Staff: Prof 1. **Subjects:** Law. **Holdings:** 14,000 volumes. **Services:** Copying; library open to the public with restrictions.

YWCA
See: **Young Women's Christian Association (20821)**

Z

★ 20833 ★
(Zacatecas) Instituto Mexicano-Norteamericano de Relaciones Culturales - USIS Collection (Educ)
Victor Rosales No. 167
Zacatecas, Zacatecas, Mexico
Remarks: Maintained or supported by the U.S. Information Agency. Focus is on materials that will assist peoples outside the United States to learn about the United States, its people, history, culture, political processes, and social milieux.

★ 20834 ★
H.B. Zachry Company - Central Records and Library (Plan)
Box 21130   Phone: (512)922-1213
San Antonio, TX 78221-0130   Edie McKeown, Dir.
Staff: 1. **Subjects:** Construction specifications, industrial relations, tax laws, electronic data processing, accounting procedures, building codes. **Holdings:** 1500 books; 60 bound periodical volumes; film; maps. **Subscriptions:** 135 journals and other serials. **Services:** Interlibrary loan; copying; library open to the public by permission.

H.B. Zackrison Memorial Library
See: **U.S. Army - Corps of Engineers - Construction Engineering Research Laboratory** (16936)

★ 20835 ★
(Zagreb) Americki Centar - USIS Library (Educ)
Zrinjevac 13
YU-41000 Zagreb, Yugoslavia
Remarks: Maintained or supported by the U.S. Information Agency. Focus is on materials that will assist peoples outside the United States to learn about the United States, its people, history, culture, political processes, and social milieux.

Zahn Library
See: **Temple University** (16141)

Zaklad Antropologii PAN - Biblioteka
See: **Poland - Polish Academy of Sciences - Institute of Anthropology - Library** (13169)

★ 20836 ★
Zanesville Art Center - Library (Art)
620 Military Rd.   Phone: (614)452-0741
Zanesville, OH 43701   Dr. Charles Dietz, Dir., Musm.
Founded: 1936. **Staff:** 5. **Subjects:** Art history, art techniques, aesthetics, world art, antiques, crafts, glass, ceramics. **Holdings:** 7500 books; 3000 filmstrips and slides. **Subscriptions:** 17 journals and other serials. **Services:** Library open to the public. **Publications:** Monthly Bulletin; Gallery Brochure.

D.F. Maza Zavala Library
See: **Inter-American Center for Regional Development** (8023)

Zavod SR Slovenije za Varstvo Naravne in Kulturne Dediscine
See: **Institute for the Protection of the Natural and Cultural Heritage of Slovenia** (7965)

Erich Zeisl Archive
See: **University of California, Los Angeles - Music Library** (18392)

★ 20837 ★
Zeitlin Periodicals Company - Library (Publ)
817 S. La Brea Ave.   Phone: (213)933-7175
Los Angeles, CA 90036   Stanley Zeitlin, Owner
Founded: 1925. **Staff:** Prof 1; Other 4. **Special Collections:** Back-issue periodicals. **Holdings:** 2 million periodicals. **Services:** Library open to the public by appointment.

★ 20838 ★
George A. Zeller Mental Health Center - Professional Library (Med)
5407 N. University   Phone: (309)693-5272
Peoria, IL 61614   Barbara Haun, Libn.
Founded: 1967. **Staff:** Prof 1. **Subjects:** Psychiatry, psychology, community mental health, geriatrics, sociology. **Holdings:** 3200 books; 300 bound periodical volumes; 4 VF drawers. **Subscriptions:** 25 journals and other serials. **Services:** Interlibrary loan; copying; library open to students and professionals in the field. **Networks/Consortia:** Member of Heart of Illinois Library Consortium (HILC), ILLINET, Illinois Valley Library System, Illinois Department of Mental Health and Developmental Disabilities Library Services Network (LISN). **Publications:** New Book List, monthly - for internal distribution only. **Remarks:** FAX: (309)693-5194. Maintained by Illinois State Department of Mental Health and Developmental Disabilities.

Max and Lore Zeller Library
See: **C.G. Jung Institute of Los Angeles, Inc. - Max and Lore Zeller Library** (8495)

★ 20839 ★
Zenith Electronics Corporation - Technical Library (Sci-Engr)
1000 N. Milwaukee Ave.   Phone: (708)391-8452
Glenview, IL 60025   Eleanore L. Berns, Info.Mgr.
Staff: Prof 1; Other 2. **Subjects:** Physics, mathematics, electronics, engineering, chemistry. **Holdings:** 10,500 books; 5000 bound periodical volumes; pamphlet file. **Subscriptions:** 300 journals and other serials. **Services:** Interlibrary loan; library not open to the public. **Computerized Information Services:** Online systems. **Remarks:** FAX: (708)391-7253.

Zenkoku Nogyo Kyodo Kumlai Chuokai - Shiryoshitsu
See: **The Central Union of Agricultural Cooperatives** (3372)

★ 20840 ★
Zentralbibliothek der Landbauwissenschaft und Abteilungsbibliothek fur Naturwissenschaft und Medizin (Agri)
Nussallee 15a
Postfach 2460   Phone: 228 733400
W-5300 Bonn 1, Germany   Christian Jung
Founded: 1847. **Staff:** Prof 21; Other 16. **Subjects:** Agriculture, home economics, nutrition and food science. **Special Collections:** USDA/FAO reports. **Holdings:** 280,000 books and bound periodical volumes; 1138 microfiche and reels of microfilm; 706 maps and charts. **Subscriptions:** 4646 journals and other serials. **Services:** Interlibrary loan; copying; library open to the public. **Computerized Information Services:** DIMDI, STN International, CAB, AGRIS, AGRICOLA, BA (Biological Abstracts), MEDLINE, EMBASE. Contact Person: Jutta Heller, Asst.Libn. **Special Catalogs:** Author catalog (microfiche); subject catalog (microfiche). **Remarks:** FAX: 228 733281.

★ 20841 ★
Zentralbibliothek fur Physik in Wien (Sci-Engr)
Boltzmanngasse 5   Phone: 222 341168
A-1090 Vienna, Austria   Dr. Wolfgang Kerber, Dir
Founded: 1980. **Staff:** Prof 16. **Subjects:** Physics. **Holdings:** 226,775 books and bound periodical volumes; 632,114 reports, microfiche, and other AV media. **Subscriptions:** 770 journals and other serials. **Services:** Interlibrary loan; copying; SDI. **Computerized Information Services:** DIALOG Information Services, ESA/IRS, STN International, BLAISE, DIMDI, InfoDoc; internal databases; InterNet (electronic mail service). Performs searches. Contact persons: Roland Kiesewetter; Juan Gorraiz. **Special Catalogs:** Catalogs on Exhibitions. **Remarks:** Library functions as a depository for the International Geosphere - Biosphere Program. FAX: 222 342630412. Telex: 116 222 PHYSI A. Electronic mail address(es): ZB@Pap.Univie.Ac.AT (InterNet). **Staff:** Erich Nezbeda; Engelbert Tuscher; Ulrike Smola; Gerlinde Fritz; Petra Held; Christian Siegel; Charlotte Allram; Regine Vrtala; Wolfgang Haberbusch; Waltraud Seipka; Gunter Franzl; Klaudia Winkler; Brigitte Zimmel.

Zentralbibliothek der Wirtschaftswissenschaften in der Bundesrepublik Deutschland
See: Germany - National Library of Economics in Germany (6451)

Zilevicius-Kreivenas Lithuanian Music Archive
See: Lithuanian Research and Studies Center, Inc. - Libraries (9211)

★ 20842 ★
Zimbabwe - Parliament of Zimbabwe - Library of Parliament (Area-Ethnic, Soc Sci)
P.O. Box 8055 Causeway　　　　　　　Phone: 700181
Harare, Zimbabwe　　　　　　W.H.C. Gurure, Chf.Libn.
Founded: 1923. **Staff:** Prof 6; Other 4. **Subjects:** Politics and government, social sciences, history and political biography, education, science and technology, English literature. **Special Collections:** Zimbabweana (500 items). **Holdings:** 110,000 volumes; 20,000 legal, official, and parliamentary documents; 70 microforms. **Subscriptions:** 300 journals and other serials; 25 newspapers. **Services:** Interlibrary loan (to libraries in Harare only); library open to members of Parliament and registered users. **Publications:** Library Guide. **Special Indexes:** Newspaper index. **Remarks:** FAX: 795548. Telex: 24064 Zimpar. **Staff:** J.M. Choto; Romana M. Marunda; Angelica Sabau; H. Sambadzai; N.C. Shonhiwa.

★ 20843 ★
Zimpro Passavant Environmental Systems, Inc. - Reference and Resource Center (Sci-Engr)
301 W. Military Rd.　　　　　　　Phone: (715)359-7211
Rothschild, WI 54474　　　　　　Dr. Tipton Randall, Mgr.
Founded: 1960. **Subjects:** Environmental control systems, sewage treatment, hazardous waste treatment. **Holdings:** 2000 books; 200 bound periodical volumes; 500 technical reports; 400 standards; 12 VF drawers of patents; 4 VF drawers of clippings. **Subscriptions:** 155 journals and other serials. **Services:** Interlibrary loan; library not open to the public. **Computerized Information Services:** DIALOG Information Services, STN. **Networks/Consortia:** Member of Wisconsin Valley Library Service (WVLS). **Remarks:** FAX: (715)355-3221. Telex: 29-0495.

Zinbun Kagaku Kenkyusho
See: Kyoto University - Institute for Research in Humanities (8838)

★ 20844 ★
Zion Mennonite Church - Library (Rel-Phil)
149 Cherry Ln.　　　　　　　Phone: (215)723-3592
Souderton, PA 18964　　　　　　Gwen N. Hartzel, Libn.
Founded: 1945. **Staff:** 6. **Subjects:** Bible, Mennonite Church history, books for children and young people. **Holdings:** 5000 books. **Services:** Interlibrary loan; library open to the public.

Zion National Park
See: U.S. Natl. Park Service (17795)

★ 20845 ★
Zion United Church of Christ - Library (Rel-Phil)
415 S. Main St.　　　　　　　Phone: (216)499-8191
North Canton, OH 44720　　　　　　Margaret M. Deibel
Founded: 1964. **Staff:** 2. **Subjects:** Religious literature. **Holdings:** 2000 books. **Subscriptions:** 4 journals and other serials. **Services:** Library not open to the public. **Staff:** Betty Bailey, Asst.Libn.; Edlyn Theiss, Asst.Libn.

Zionist Archives and Library
See: World Zionist Organization - American Section (20638)

Ziskind Memorial Library
See: Temple Beth-El (16086)

Zitek Medical Library
See: La Grange Memorial Hospital (8845)

★ 20846 ★
Zitelman Scout Museum - Library (Rec)
708 Seminary St.　　　　　　　Phone: (815)962-3999
Rockford, IL 61104　　　　　　Mrs. Ralph E. Zitelman, Cur.
Subjects: Boy and Girl Scouts - jamborees, outdoor skills, camping, history, awards; foreign scouting; brigade history. **Holdings:** 3000 books; 1000 bound periodical volumes; 500 AV programs; 2000 manuscripts. **Services:** Interlibrary loan. **Remarks:** Acts as a clearinghouse for information on all phases of scouting (dating from 1910), including Boy and Girl Scouts, Explorers, Sea and Air Scouts, and Cub Scouts.

★ 20847 ★
Zittrer, Siblin, Stein, Levine - Library (Bus-Fin)
1 Place Alexis Nixon, 15th Fl.　　　　　Phone: (514)935-1117
Montreal, PQ, Canada H2E 3E8　　　　　Norman Daitchman
Founded: 1953. **Subjects:** Accounting, auditing, tax. **Holdings:** 200 books. **Subscriptions:** 10 journals and other serials. **Services:** Library not open to the public.

ZIV Library of Television Programs
See: University of Wisconsin--Madison - Wisconsin Center for Film and Theater Research (19627)

Zoeller Music Library
See: Viterbo College (19907)

Zondervan Library
See: Taylor University (16020)

★ 20848 ★
Zoological Society of Philadelphia - Library (Biol Sci)
3400 W. Girard Ave.　　　　　　Phone: (215)243-1100
Philadelphia, PA 19104-1196　　　Kimargret Huller, Zoological Asst.
Founded: 1874. **Staff:** 1. **Subjects:** Zoology, ornithology, mammalogy, herpetology, nutrition, veterinary medicine and pathology, wildlife conservation, ichthyology, natural history, zoos and zoo management, animal behavior, botany, ecology, horticulture. **Special Collections:** Conference proceedings; newsletters; zoo guidebooks; studbooks; pathology reports; animal behavior studies. **Holdings:** 1500 books; 75 bound periodical volumes. **Subscriptions:** 65 journals and other serials. **Services:** Interlibrary loan; copying. **Remarks:** FAX: (215)387-8733.

★ 20849 ★
Zoological Society of San Diego - Ernst Schwarz Library (Biol Sci)
San Diego Zoo
Box 551　　　　　　　Phone: (619)557-3908
San Diego, CA 92112-0551　　　Linda L. Coates, Mgr., Lib.Serv.
Founded: 1916. **Staff:** Prof 1; Other 1. **Subjects:** Vertebrate zoology, animal husbandry, animal behavior, wildlife conservation, veterinary medicine, horticulture. **Special Collections:** Charles E. Shaw Herpetological Library (300 books; 5000 reprints); Ernst Schwarz reprint collection (2000). **Holdings:** 11,000 books; 5000 bound periodical volumes; 15,000 reprints; 60 boxes of zoo annual reports and guidebooks; 54 linear feet of Zoological Society archives; 76 oral history audio- and videotapes. **Subscriptions:** 500 journals and other serials. **Services:** Interlibrary loan; photocopying; current awareness. **Automated Operations:** Computerized cataloging, serials, and ILL. **Computerized Information Services:** OCLC, DIALOG Information Services, NLM. **Networks/Consortia:** Member of CLASS. **Publications:** Acquisitions list - for internal distribution only; Serials Holding List, updated annually; Guide to Library Services. **Remarks:** FAX: (619)595-1717.

Zug Memorial Library
See: Elizabethtown College (5300)

★20850★
Zurich American Insurance Group - Market Research - Business Information Center (Bus-Fin)
1400 American Ln.   Phone: (708)605-7729
Schaumburg, IL 60196   Julianne Josiek, Asst.Libn.
Founded: 1987. **Staff:** Prof 1; Other 1. **Subjects:** Property insurance, casualty insurance. **Holdings:** 350 books; 500 reports; 1200 microfiche. **Subscriptions:** 125 journals and other serials; 10 newspapers. **Services:** Interlibrary loan; library not open to the public. **Automated Operations:** INMAGIC. **Computerized Information Services:** DIALOG Information Services, OCLC, NEXIS, LEXIS, WILSONLINE, BestLink Market Advisor, InvesText, Dow Jones News/Retrieval. **Remarks:** FAX: (708)605-6367.

★20851★
(Zurich) School and Museum of Art and Design - Library (Art)
Ausstellungsstr 60   Phone: 1 2716700
CH-8031 Zurich, Switzerland   Constanza Arvani-Cotta
Founded: 1875. **Staff:** Prof 3; Other 5. **Subjects:** Art, design, visual communication, architecture, fashion, film, photography. **Holdings:** 60,000 books; 7500 bound periodical volumes. **Subscriptions:** 200 journals and other serials. **Services:** Interlibrary loan; copying; library open to the public. **Remarks:** FAX: 1 2716945.

Zwiazek Kompozytorow Polskich
See: **Union of Polish Composers (16664)**

Jacob D. Zylman Memorial Library
See: **Fairfax Hospital (5563)**

Appendix A

Networks and Consortia

Appendix A provides the names, addresses, and telephone numbers of **452** cooperative agencies. A network/consortium is defined for the purposes of this directory as the cooperative effort of a group of information specialists to facilitate, foster, and coordinate the sharing of books, periodicals, and other holdings among member institutions. Union catalogs and shared library systems are excluded because they do not involve the physical interchange of materials. Networks range in scope and sophistication from local, informal arrangements to larger regional and national organizations.

Networks are arranged geographically by state or province. Groups are usually listed under their complete, formal names, although networks better known by an acronym, such as NELINET or ILLINET, are listed under it. When a network is known by more than one name, that information is noted in the entry and the variant name or acronym can be found in the cumulative index following this Appendix.

UNITED STATES

ALABAMA

★N1★
Alabama Health Libraries Association (ALHELA)
c/o Library
Carraway Methodist Medical Center
1600 N. 26th St.   Phone: (205)226-6265
Birmingham, AL 35234   Ms. Bobby Powell, Archv.

★N2★
Jefferson County Hospital Librarians' Association
c/o Library
Brookwood Hospital
2010 Brookwood Medical Center Dr.   Phone: (205)877-1131
Birmingham, AL 35209   Lucy Moor, Coord.
Currently inactive.

★N3★
Alabama Library Exchange, Inc. (ALEX)
Box 443   Phone: (205)532-5965
Huntsville, AL 35804   Lee E. Pike, Dir.

★N4★
Network of Alabama Academic Libraries (NAAL)
Alabama Commission on Higher Education
One Court Square, Suite 221   Phone: (205)269-2700
Montgomery, AL 36197-0001   Dr. Sue O. Medina, Dir.

ALASKA

★N5★
Alaska Library Network (ALN)
c/o Alaska State Library
3600 Denali   Phone: (907)261-2976
Anchorage, AK 99503   Judy Monroe, Coord.

ARIZONA

★N6★
Central Arizona Biomedical Libraries (CABL)
Maricopa County Medical Society Library
326 E. Coronado, Ste. 104   Phone: (602)252-2451
Phoenix, AZ 85004   Patricia Sullivan, Sec./Treas.
FAX: (602)495-8695.

CALIFORNIA

★N7★
Metropolitan Cooperative Library System (MCLS)
2235 N. Lake Ave., Suite 106   Phone: (818)798-1146
Altadena, CA 91001   Linda Katsouleas, Sys.Dir.

★N8★
Northern California and Nevada Medical Library Group (NCNMLG)
2140 Shattuck Ave.
Box 2105
Berkeley, CA 94704   Phone: (916)734-3529

★N9★
Substance Abuse Librarians and Information Specialists (SALIS)
P.O. Box 9513   Phone: (510)642-5208
Berkeley, CA 94709-0513   Andrea Mitchell, Inst. Home Coord.
FAX: (510)642-7175.

★N10★
Consumer Health and Information Programs and Services (CHIPS)
Carson Regional Library
151 E. Carson St.   Phone: (213)830-0909
Carson, CA 90745   Ellen Mulkern, CHIPS Libn.
FAX: (213)830-6181.

★ N11 ★
Los Angeles County Health Sciences Library Consortium
c/o Health Sciences Library, Bldg. 605
Rancho Los Amigos Medical Center
7601 E. Imperial Hwy.   Phone: (310)940-7696
Downey, CA 90242   Evelyn Marks, Act.Dir.

★ N12 ★
Area Wide Library Network (AWLNET)
2420 Mariposa St.   Phone: (209)488-3229
Fresno, CA 93721   Sharon Vandercook, Ref.Coord.
Affiliated with the San Joaquin Valley Library System.

★ N13 ★
San Joaquin Valley Library System (SJVLS)
2420 Mariposa St.   Phone: (209)488-3185
Fresno, CA 93721   John Kallenberg, Sys.Adm.
FAX: (209)488-2965.

★ N14 ★
Inland Empire Medical Library Cooperative (IEMLC)
c/o Medical Library
John F. Kennedy Memorial Hospital
47-111 Monroe St., Drawer LLLL   Phone: (619)347-6191
Indio, CA 92201   Dan Dickinson, Ch.
Address rotates annually.

★ N15 ★
Inland Empire Academic Libraries Cooperative (IEALC)
University of La Verne
Wilson Library
2040 Third St.   Phone: (909)593-3511
La Verne, CA 91750   Marlin Heckman, Dir.
Address rotates biennially. FAX: (909)593-3066.

★ N16 ★
Performing Arts Libraries Network of Greater Los Angeles (PALNET)
University Library
California State University, Long Beach
1250 Bellflower Blvd.
Long Beach, CA 90840-1901   Leslie Kay Swigart, Pres.
Address rotates annually.

★ N17 ★
National Network of Libraries of Medicine - Pacific Southwest Region
c/o Louise Darling Biomedical Library
University of California
10833 Le Conte Ave.   Phone: (213)825-1200
Los Angeles, CA 90024-1798   Beryl Glitz, Assoc.Dir.
Region 7 of the National Network of Libraries of Medicine serves AZ, CA, HI, NV, and United States Territories in the Pacific Basin. It also functions as the Online Center for Regions 6 and 7. FAX: (213)825-5389.

★ N18 ★
State of California Answering Network (SCAN)
Los Angeles Public Library
630 W. 5th St.   Phone: (213)612-3216
Los Angeles, CA 90071   Evelyn Greenwald, Dir.
FAX: (213)612-0546.

★ N19 ★
Merced County Health Information Consortium
Medical Library
Merced Community Medical Center
301 E. 13th St.   Phone: (209)385-7058
Merced, CA 95340   Betty Madalena, Coord.

★ N20 ★
Monterey Bay Area Cooperative Library System (MOBAC)
MPC Library Bldg.
980 Fremont St.   Phone: (408)646-4256
Monterey, CA 93940   Ellen Pastore, Coord.
FAX: (408)646-4111.

★ N21 ★
Research Libraries Information Network (RLIN)
1200 Villa St.   Phone: (415)962-9951
Mountain View, CA 94041-1100   La Vonne Gallo, Mgr., RLIN Trng.
Formerly Research Libraries Group (RLG), Inc. Toll-free telephone number(s): (800)537-RLIN. FAX: (415)964-0943.

★ N22 ★
Bay Area Library and Information System (BALIS)
520 3rd St., Ste. 220   Phone: (510)839-6001
Oakland, CA 94607-3520   Ruth Foley Metz, Sys.Coord.
Affiliated with the Bay Area Library and Information Network (BayNet).
FAX: (510)834-5193.

★ N23 ★
Kaiser Permanente Library System (KPLS) - Northern California
   Region
Kaiser Permanente Medical Ctr.
280 W. MacArthur Blvd.   Phone: (415)596-6158
Oakland, CA 94611   Ysabel Bertolucci

★ N24 ★
Hewlett-Packard Library/Information Network
HP Labs Research Library
Hewlett Packard Company
1501 Page Mill Rd.
Palo Alto, CA 94304   Phone: (415)857-3091

★ N25 ★
Northern California Consortium of Psychology Libraries (NCCPL)
Pacific Graduate School of Psychology
935 E. Meadow Dr.   Phone: (415)494-7477
Palo Alto, CA 94303   Christine Dassoff, Co-Ch.
Formerly Consortium of Psychological Studies Libraries. Address rotates annually. FAX: (415)856-6734.

★ N26 ★
OCLC Pacific Network
9227 Haven Ave., Suite 260   Phone: (714)941-4208
Rancho Cucamonga, CA 91730   Bruce Preslan, Dir.
Toll-free telephone number(s): (800)472-1878 (California only); (800)854-5753 (all others). FAX: (714)948-9803. Maintains branch offices in Portland, OR, and Bremerton, WA.

★ N27 ★
Sacramento Area Health Sciences Librarians (SAHSL)
Roseville Hospital
333 Sunrise Ave.   Phone: (916)781-1580
Roseville, CA 95661   Shirley Lyon, Ch.
Address rotates annually.

★ N28 ★
Mountain Valley Library System
Sacramento Public Library
828 I Street   Phone: (916)552-8400
Sacramento, CA 95814-2589   Gerald Maginnity, Coord.
FAX: (916)441-3425.

★ N29 ★
San Bernardino, Inyo, Riverside Counties United Library Services
   (SIRCULS)
312 W. 20th St., Suite D   Phone: (714)882-7577
San Bernardino, CA 92405   Vaughn Simon, Dir.
FAX: (714)882-6871.

★ N30 ★
Kaiser Permanente Library System (KPLS) - Southern California Region
c/o Health Sciences Library
Kaiser Permanente Medical Center
4647 Zion Ave.
San Diego, CA 92120   Phone: (619)528-7323
Address and phone number given are those of member library.

★ N31 ★
Serra Cooperative Network
5555 Overland Ave., Bldg. 15
San Diego, CA 92123   Phone: (619)278-8090

★ N32 ★
Bay Area Library and Information Network
General Library
Golden Gate University
536 Mission St.   Phone: (415)442-7000
San Francisco, CA 94105   Ann Coder, Vice Ch.
Also known as BayNet and BALIN. Affiliated with the Bay Area Library and Information System (BALIS).

★N33★
San Francisco Biomedical Library Network
c/o Emge Medical Library
Children's Hospital of San Francisco
3700 California St.   Phone: (415)750-6072
San Francisco, CA 94118   Peggy Tahir, Coord.
Address rotates annually.

★N34★
CLASS
1415 Koll Circle, Suite 101   Phone: (800)488-4559
San Jose, CA 95112-4698   Robert A. Drescher, Exec.Dir.
Also known as Cooperative Library Agency for Systems and Services. FAX:
(408)453-5379.

★N35★
Medical Library Consortium of Santa Clara Valley
Planetree Health Resource Center
98 N. 17th St.   Phone: (408)977-4549
San Jose, CA 95112   Candace Ford, Chm.
Address rotates biennially. Also known as Santa Clara County Medical Library Consortium.

★N36★
South Bay Cooperative Library System (SBCLS)
180 W. San Carlos St.   Phone: (408)294-7332
San Jose, CA 95113   Susan Holmer, Ref.Coord.
FAX: (408)295-7388.

★N37★
SOUTHNET
180 W. San Carlos St.   Phone: (415)349-5538
San Jose, CA 95113   Linda Crowe, Dir.
FAX: (415)349-5089.

★N38★
Peninsula Library System (PLS)
25 Tower Rd.   Phone: (415)349-5538
San Mateo, CA 94402-4000   Linda Crowe, Sys.Dir.

★N39★
Santa Clarita InterLibrary Network (SCILNET)
California Institute of the Arts Library
24700 McBean Pkwy.   Phone: (805)253-7885
Santa Clarita, CA 91355   Frederick B. Gardner, Coord.
FAX: (805)254-4561.

★N40★
North Bay Cooperative Library System (NBCLS)
725 3rd St.   Phone: (707)544-0142
Santa Rosa, CA 95404   Annette Milleron
FAX: (707)544-8411.

★N41★
49-99 Cooperative Library System
Centeral Association of Libraries
605 N. El Dorado St.   Phone: (209)944-8204
Stockton, CA 95202   Janet Kase, Sys.Dir.
FAX: (209)944-8292.

★N42★
Total Interlibrary Exchange (TIE)
5574 Everglades St., Suite A   Phone: (805)650-7732
Ventura, CA 93003-6542   Judith Segel, Sys.Dir.
FAX: (805)642-9095.

COLORADO

★N43★
Plains and Peaks Regional Library Service System
1761 S. 8th St., Suite H-2   Phone: (719)473-3417
Colorado Springs, CO 80906   Jeanne Owen, Dir.

★N44★
Bibliographical Center for Research, Rocky Mountain Region, Inc.
  (BCR)
4500 Cherry Creek Dr., S.
Suite 206   Phone: (303)691-0550
Denver, CO 80222   David H. Brunell, Exec.Dir.
Maintains an office in Ames, Iowa; telephone (515)292-1118. See also the library listing for this network in the main section. FAX: (303)691-0112.

★N45★
Colorado Alliance of Research Libraries (CARL)
777 Grant St., Suite 304   Phone: (303)861-5319
Denver, CO 80203   Ward Shaw, Exec.Dir.

★N46★
Colorado Council of Medical Librarians
Denison Memorial Library
University of Colorado Health Science Center
4200 E. 9th Ave.   Phone: (303)393-2821
Denver, CO 80262   Martha Burroughs, Pres.
Address rotates annually.

★N47★
Southwest Regional Library Service System (SWRLSS)
736 Main Ave., No. 200
P.O Drawer B   Phone: (303)247-4782
Durango, CO 81302   S. Jane Ulrich, Dir.

★N48★
High Plains Regional Library Service System
800 8th Ave., Suite 341   Phone: (303)356-4357
Greeley, CO 80631   Nancy Knepel, Dir.

★N49★
Arkansas Valley Regional Library Service System
205 W. Abriendo Ave.   Phone: (303)542-2156
Pueblo, CO 81004   Donna R. Jones, Dir.

★N50★
Central Colorado Library System (CCLS)
4350 Wadsworth, No. 340   Phone: (303)422-1150
Wheat Ridge, CO 80033   Gordon Barhydt, Dir.
FAX: (303)431-9752.

CONNECTICUT

★N51★
Southwestern Connecticut Library Council (SWLC)
Bridgeport Public Library
925 Broad St.   Phone: (203)367-6439
Bridgeport, CT 06604   Ann M. Neary, Adm.
FAX: (203)367-2521.

★N52★
National Network of Libraries of Medicine - New England Region
Lyman Maynard Stowe Library
University of Connecticut
Health Center   Phone: (203)679-4500
Farmington, CT 06034-5370   Linda Walton, Assoc.Dir.
Region 8 of the National Network of Libraries of Medicine (formerly Regional Medical Library in New England) serves CT, MA, ME, NH, RI, and VT. FAX: (203)679-1305.

★N53★
Southern Connecticut Library Council (SCLC)
2405 Whitney Ave., Ste. 3   Phone: (203)284-3641
Hamden, CT 06518-3235   Susan Muro, Exec.Dir.
Formerly located in Wallingford, CT.

★N54★
Hartford Consortium for Higher Education
30 Elizabeth St.   Phone: (203)236-1203
Hartford, CT 06105   Ruth W. Billyou, Coord.

★N55★
CTW Consortium
Olin Memorial Library
Wesleyan University   Phone: (203)347-9411
Middletown, CT 06457-6065   Alan E. Hagyard, Dir.
Consortium is a cooperative effort of the libraries of Connecticut College, Trinity College, and Wesleyan University.

★N56★
Northeast Foreign Law Cooperative Group
Law Library
Yale University
127 Wall St.   Phone: (203)432-1615
New Haven, CT 06520   Dan Wade, Chm.

★ N57 ★
Connecticut Association of Health Science Libraries (CAHSL)
c/o Medical Library
Rockville General Hospital
31 Union St.   Phone: (203)872-5277
Rockville, CT 06066   Laurie Fornes, Pres.
Address rotates biennially. FAX: (203)872-5169.

★ N58 ★
Northwestern Connecticut Health Science Library Consortium (NW-CT-HSL)
Sharon Hospital Health Sciences Library
W. Main St.   Phone: (203)496-6689
Sharon, CT 06069   Robin Ackley, Med.Libn.
Address rotates biennially.

★ N59 ★
Region One Cooperating Library Service Unit, Inc.
c/o Silas Bronson Library
267 Grand St.   Phone: (203)756-6149
Waterbury, CT 06702   Thomas A. Lawrence, Reg.Coord.

★ N60 ★
Capital Region Library Council (CRLC)
599 Matianuck Ave.   Phone: (203)549-0404
Windsor, CT 06095   Ms. Dency Sargent, Coord.

DELAWARE

★ N61 ★
Kent Library Network (KLN)
c/o Dover High School Library
625 Walker Rd.   Phone: (302)739-5578
Dover, DE 19901   Ralph B. Hinzman, Jr., Pres.
Address rotates biennially.

★ N62 ★
Libraries in the New Castle County System (LINCS)
c/o Hockessin Public Library
1041 Valley Rd.   Phone: (302)239-0706
Hockessin, DE 19707   Diedra H. Dodd, Pres.
Address rotates annually. FAX: (302)239-1519.

★ N63 ★
Medical Information Consortium of Kent & Sussex (MEDICKS)
Beebe Medical Center
424 Savannah Rd.   Phone: (302)645-3300
Lewes, DE 19958   Vera C. Reed, Libn.

★ N64 ★
Delaware Library Consortium (DLC)
1925 Lovering Ave.   Phone: (302)656-6398
Wilmington, DE 19806   Gail P. Gill, Pres.
FAX: (302)656-0470.

★ N65 ★
Wilmington Area Biomedical Library Consortium (WABLC)
Delaware Academy of Medicine
1925 Lovering Ave.   Phone: (302)656-6398
Wilmington, DE 19806   Gail P. Gill, Pres.
FAX: (302)656-0470.

DISTRICT OF COLUMBIA

★ N66 ★
American Association of Zoological Parks & Aquariums - Librarians' Special Interest Group (AAZPA/LSIG)
National Zoological Park Branch Library
Smithsonian Institution Libraries
National Zoological Park   Phone: (202)673-4771
Washington, DC 20008   Kay Kenyon, Chf.Libn.

★ N67 ★
CAPCON Library Network
1320 19th St., N.W., Ste. 400   Phone: (202)331-5771
Washington, DC 20036   Dennis Reynolds, Exec.Dir.
Toll-free telephone number(s): (800)543-4599 (Virginia and Maryland).
FAX: (202)797-7719.

★ N68 ★
Consortium of Universities of the Washington Metropolitan Area
1717 Massachussetts Ave., N.W., Suite 101   Phone: (202)332-1894
Washington, DC 20036   Dr. Darrell Lemke, Coord., Lib.

★ N69 ★
District of Columbia Health Sciences Information Network (DOCHSIN)
American College of Obstetricians and Gynecologists
Resource Center
409 12th St., S.W.   Phone: (202)638-5577
Washington, DC 20024   Kathy DeGeorges, Pres.
Address rotates annually.

★ N70 ★
FEDLINK
FLICC (Federal Library and Information Committee)
Library of Congress   Phone: (202)707-4848
Washington, DC 20540   Milton McGee, Coord.
Also known as Federal Library and Information Network. Maintained by FLICC (Federal Library and Information Center Committee). FAX: (202)707-4818.

★ N71 ★
Forest Service Information Network - Forestry Online (FS INFO)
U.S. Forest Service
RPE, Rm. 809
Box 96090   Phone: (703)235-2074
Washington, DC 20090   Seung Ja Sinatra

★ N72 ★
Health Sciences Consortium
c/o Dahlgren Memorial Library
Medical Center
Georgetown University   Phone: (202)687-1176
Washington, DC 20007   Naomi C. Broering, Libn.

★ N73 ★
NASA Aerospace Research Information Network (ARIN)
NASA Headquarters, Code JTT   Phone: (703)271-5644
Washington, DC 20546   Barbara Everidge, Prog.Mgr.
FAX: (703)271-5665.

★ N74 ★
National Library Service for the Blind & Physically Handicapped (NLS)
Library of Congress
1291 Taylor St., N.W.   Phone: (202)707-5104
Washington, DC 20542   Frank Kurt Cylke, Dir.
Regional and subregional libraries in this network are listed in Appendix B. See also the library listing for this network in the main section. Toll-free telephone number(s): (800)424-8567. FAX: (202)707-0712.

★ N75 ★
VALNET
Dept. of Veterans Affairs
810 Vermont Ave., N.W.   Phone: (202)233-2711
Washington, DC 20420   Karen Renninger, Asst.Dir. for Lib. (142A)
Also known as Veterans Administration Library Network.

★ N76 ★
Washington Theological Consortium
487 Michigan Ave., N.E.   Phone: (202)832-2675
Washington, DC 20017   David G. Trickett, Dir.

FLORIDA

★ N77 ★
Tampa Bay Medical Library Network
VA Medical Center
Box 527   Phone: (813)892-4278
Bay Pines, FL 33504   Patricia C. Buchan, Chair.
FAX: (813)892-8557.

★ N78 ★

South East Florida Library Information Network (SEFLIN)
100 S. Andrews Ave.   Phone: (305)357-7318
Fort Lauderdale, FL 33301   Elizabeth Curry, Exec.Dir.
FAX: (305)357-6998.

★ N79 ★

Miami Health Sciences Library Consortium (MHSLC)
c/o Celia Steinberg
Health Sciences Library
South Miami Hospital   Phone: (305)822-8250
Miami, FL 33143   Dolly Farooqi, Ch.

★ N80 ★

Panhandle Library Access Network (PLAN)
4 Harrison Ave., Ste. 5   Phone: (904)763-1950
Panama City, FL 32401   Selma K. Jaskowski, Dir.
FAX: (904)769-0222.

★ N81 ★

Central Florida Library Consortium (CFLC)
Seminole Community College
100 Weldon Blvd.   Phone: (407)323-1304
Sanford, FL 32773-6199   John Dooley, Exec.Dir.
FAX: (407)353-1450, ext. 342.

★ N82 ★

Florida Library Network (FLN)
State Library of Florida
R. A. Gray Bldg.   Phone: (904)487-2651
Tallahassee, FL 32399-0250   Barratt Wilkins, State Libn.
FAX: (904)488-2746. Florida Library Information Network (FLIN) is a
part of Florida Library Network (FLN).

★ N83 ★

Tampa Bay Library Consortium, Inc. (TBLC)
10002 Princess Palm Ave., Ste. 124   Phone: (813)622-8252
Tampa, FL 33619   Barbara J. Stites, Exec.Dir.
FAX: (813)628-4425.

★ N84 ★

Palm Beach Health Sciences Library Consortium (PBHSLC)
Good Samaritan Medical Center
Medical Library
P.O. Box 3166   Phone: (407)650-6315
West Palm Beach, FL 33402   Linda Kressal, Ch.
Address rotates biennially. FAX: (407)650-6239.

GEORGIA

★ N85 ★

Atlanta Health Science Libraries Consortium (AHSLC)
c/o Russell Bellman Memorial Library
St. Joseph's Hospital of Atlanta
5665 Peachtree Dunwoody Rd., N.E.   Phone: (404)851-7040
Atlanta, GA 30342   Beth Poisson
Address rotates annually.

★ N86 ★

CCLC
159 Ralph McGill Blvd., Suite 602   Phone: (404)659-6886
Atlanta, GA 30365   Hillis D. Davis, Dir.
Also known as Cooperative College Library Center, Inc.

★ N87 ★

Consortium of South Eastern Law Libraries
College of Law Library
Georgia State University
University Plaza   Phone: (404)651-2479
Atlanta, GA 30303   Nancy Johnson, Ch.

★ N88 ★

COSELL
College of Law Library
Georgia State University
University Plaza   Phone: (404)651-2479
Atlanta, GA 30303   Nancy Johnson, Pres./Law Libn.

★ N89 ★

Georgia Health Sciences Library Association (GHSLA)
Sauls Memorial Library
Piedmont Hospital
1968 Peachtree Rd., N.W.   Phone: (404)350-3641
Atlanta, GA 30309   Alice DeVierno, Coord.
Address rotates annually.

★ N90 ★

Georgia Online Database (GOLD)
Georgia Department of Education
Division of Public Library Services
156 Trinity Ave., S.W., Rm. 102   Phone: (404)656-2461
Atlanta, GA 30303-3692   JoEllyn Ostendorf, Cons.
Formerly Georgia Library Information Network (GLIN). Toll-free tele-
phone number(s): (800)282-8918. FAX: (404)656-7297.

★ N91 ★

SOLINET
400 Colony Sq. Plaza Level
1201 Peachtree St., N.E.   Phone: (404)892-0943
Atlanta, GA 30361   Frank P. Grisham, Exec.Dir.
Also known as Southeastern Library Network. Toll-free telephone number-
(s): (800)999-8558. FAX: (404)892-7879.

★ N92 ★

University Center in Georgia, Inc.
c/o Georgia State University
University Plaza
Box 1033   Phone: (404)651-2668
Atlanta, GA 30303   Charles B. Bedford, Dir.

★ N93 ★

South Georgia Associated Libraries (SGAL)
Brunswick-Glynn County Regional Library
208 Gloucester St.   Phone: (912)267-1212
Brunswick, GA 31523-0901   Jim Darby, Sec.
Address rotates periodically. FAX: (912)267-9597.

★ N94 ★

Georgia Interactive Network for Medical Information (GaIN)
c/o Medical Library
Mercer University School of Medicine
1550 College St.   Phone: (912)752-2519
Macon, GA 31207   Jocelyn Rankin, Dir.
FAX: (912)752-2051.

★ N95 ★

Health Science Libraries Consortium of Central Georgia (HSLCG)
c/o Medical Library
Mercer University School of Medicine
1550 College St.   Phone: (912)752-2519
Macon, GA 31207   Jocelyn Rankin
FAX: (912)752-2051.

★ N96 ★

Central Georgia Associated Libraries (CGAL)
Pine Mountain Regional Library
P.O. Box 709   Phone: (404)882-7784
Manchester, GA 31816   Charles Gee, Ch.
Address rotates annually.

★ N97 ★

Southwest Georgia Health Sciences Library Consortium
Health Sciences Library
Colquitt Regional Medical Center
P.O. Box 40   Phone: (912)890-3460
Moultrie, GA 31776   Susan Statom
FAX: (912)890-2173.

★ N98 ★

Southeast Georgia Health Sciences Library Consortium (SEGHSLC)
Lane Library
Armstrong State College
11935 Abercorn St.
Savannah, GA 31419-1997   Barbara Heuer
Currently inactive.

HAWAII

★ **N99** ★
Medical Library Group of Hawaii
1221 Punchbowl St.   Phone: (808)536-9302
Honolulu, HI 96813   Beula Horak, Pres.

IDAHO

★ **N100** ★
Boise Valley Health Sciences Library Consortium
Idaho State Library
325 W. State St.   Phone: (208)334-2153
Boise, ID 83702   Nancy Van Dinter, Hea.Info.Cons.
Address is that of member library. FAX: (208)334-4016.

★ **N101** ★
Idaho Health Information Association
c/o Health Sciences Library
St. Alphonsus Regional Medical Center
1055 N. Curtis Rd.   Phone: (208)378-2271
Boise, ID 83706   Judy A. Balcerzak, Libn.
Address rotates annually.

★ **N102** ★
Southeast Idaho Health Information Consortium
c/o Health Sciences Library
Bannock Regional Medical Library
Pocatello, ID 83201   Phone: (208)232-6150
Address rotates annually. Currently inactive.

ILLINOIS

★ **N103** ★
Areawide Hospital Library Consortium of Southwestern Illinois (AHLC)
St. Anthony's Health Center
St. Clare's Hospital
915 E. Fifth St., P.O. Box 340   Phone: (618)463-5645
Alton, IL 62002   Darla A. Reif, Lib.Asst.
FAX: (618)463-5640.

★ **N104** ★
Suburban Library System (SLS)
125 Tower Dr.   Phone: (708)325-6640
Burr Ridge, IL 60521   J. Michael O'Brien, Exec.Dir.
FAX: (708)325-5279.

★ **N105** ★
Illinois Valley Library System
c/o Medical Staff Library
Graham Hospital Association
210 W. Walnut St.   Phone: (309)647-5240
Canton, IL 61520   Moneta Bedwell, Libn.

★ **N106** ★
Shawnee Library System
511 Greenbriar Rd.   Phone: (618)985-3711
Carterville, IL 62918-1600   James A. Ubel, Exec.Dir.
FAX: (618)985-4211.

★ **N107** ★
Lincoln Trail Libraries System (LTLS)
1704 W. Interstate Dr.   Phone: (217)352-0047
Champaign, IL 61821   Jan Ison, Exec.Dir.
FAX: (217)352-7153.

★ **N108** ★
Association of Chicago Theological Schools Library Council
Jesuit-Krauss-McCormick Library
Lutheran School of Theology
1100 E. 55th St.   Phone: (312)753-0735
Chicago, IL 60615   Mary Bischoff, Ch.
Address rotates biennially.

★ **N109** ★
Center for Research Libraries (CRL)
6050 S. Kenwood Ave.   Phone: (312)955-4545
Chicago, IL 60637   Donald B. Simpson, Pres.
FAX: (312)955-4339.

★ **N110** ★
Chicago Library System
400 S. State St., 10S   Phone: (312)747-4013
Chicago, IL 60605   Alice Calabrese, Exec.Dir.
FAX: (312)747-4035.

★ **N111** ★
Consortium of Museum Libraries in the Chicago Area
John G. Shedd Aquarium - Library
1200 S. Lake Shore Dr.   Phone: (312)939-2426
Chicago, IL 60605   Janet E. Powers, Libn.
FAX: (312)939-8069.

★ **N112** ★
Illinois Health Libraries Consortium
Meat Industry Information Center
National Livestock & Meat Board
444 N. Michigan Ave.
Chicago, IL 60611   William D. Siarny, Jr., Coord.

★ **N113** ★
Metropolitan Consortium of Chicago
Joseph G. Stromberg Medical Library
Swedish Covenant Hospital
5145 N. California Ave.
Chicago, IL 60625   Phone: (312)878-8200
Also known as Chicago Metropolitan Consortium.

★ **N114** ★
National Network of Libraries of Medicine - Greater Midwest Region
Library of the Health Sciences
University of Illinois at Chicago
P.O. Box 7509   Phone: (312)996-2462
Chicago, IL 60680   Ann C. Weller, Act.Dir.
Region 3 of the National Network of Libraries of Medicine serves IA, IL,
IN, KY, MI, MN, ND, OH, SD, and WI. FAX: (312)996-2226.

★ **N115** ★
Quad Cities Libraries in Cooperation (Quad-LINC)
220 W. 23rd St.   Phone: (309)799-3155
Coal Valley, IL 61240   Mary Anne Stewart, Automation Mgr.
Maintained by River Bend Library System (RBLS). FAX: (309)799-7916.

★ **N116** ★
Rolling Prairie Library System (RPLS)
345 W. Eldorado
Decatur, IL 62522   Phone: (217)429-2586

★ **N117** ★
Chicago and South Consortium
Medical Library
Good Samaritan Hospital
3815 Highland Ave.   Phone: (708)963-5900
Downers Grove, IL 60515   Susan Marshall, Coord.
Address rotates biennially. FAX: (708)963-1091.

★ **N118** ★
Lewis & Clark Library System
425 Goshen Rd.   Phone: (618)656-3216
Edwardsville, IL 62025   Margaret Stefanak, Exec.Dir.
FAX: (618)656-9041.

★ **N119** ★
**Illinois Department of Mental Health and Developmental Disabilities
Library Services Network (LISN)**
Elgin Mental Health Center
750 S. State St.   Phone: (708)742-1040
Elgin, IL 60123   Jennifer Ford, Coord.

★ **N120** ★
LIBRAS Inc.
A.C. Buehler Library
Elmhurst College
190 Prospect
Elmhurst, IL 60126   Alan Barney, Pres.
Formerly located in Aurora, IL.

★ N121 ★
Cumberland Trail Library System
12th & McCawley St.   Phone: (618)662-2679
Flora, IL 62839   John A. Moorman, Exec.Dir.

★ N122 ★
Western Illinois Library System
1518 S. Henderson   Phone: (309)343-2380
Galesburg, IL 61401   Sherwood Kirk, Exec.Dir.

★ N123 ★
DuPage Library System
127 S. 1st St.
P.O. Box 268   Phone: (708)232-8457
Geneva, IL 60134   Pamela Feather, Exec.Dir.
FAX: (708)232-0699 (Library); (708)232-1584 (ILL).

★ N124 ★
Judaica Library Network of Chicago
1175 Sheridan Rd.   Phone: (708)432-8900
Highland Park, IL 60035   Cheryl Banks, Pres.
Address rotates annually. FAX: (708)432-9242.

★ N125 ★
Capital Area Consortium (CAC)
c/o Sibert Library
Passavant Area Hospital
1600 W. Walnut   Phone: (217)245-9541
Jacksonville, IL 62650   Dorothy Knight, Coord.
Address rotates biennially. FAX: (217)245-9331.

★ N126 ★
East Central Illinois Consortium
Sarah Bush Lincoln Health Center
P.O. Box 372   Phone: (217)258-2262
Mattoon, IL 61938   Nina Pals, Med.Libn.
Address rotates biennially. FAX: (217)258-2111.

★ N127 ★
Corn Belt Library System
1809 W. Hovey Ave.   Phone: (309)452-4485
Normal, IL 61761   Jay Wozny, Exec.Dir.
FAX: (309)452-9192.

★ N128 ★
Northeastern Illinois Library Consortium
c/o Medical Library
V.A. Hospital   Phone: (708)578-3757
North Chicago, IL 60064   William Nielsen, Chf.Libn.

★ N129 ★
Starved Rock Library System
900 Hitt St.   Phone: (815)434-7538
Ottawa, IL 61350-5198   Richard W. Willson, Exec.Dir.

★ N130 ★
Heart of Illinois Library Consortium (HILC)
c/o St. Francis Medical Center
College of Nursing Library
211 Greenleaf St.   Phone: (309)655-2180
Peoria, IL 61603   Joyce Hexdall
Address rotates biennially. FAX: (309)655-2056.

★ N131 ★
Great River Library System (GRLS)
515 York St.   Phone: (217)223-2560
Quincy, IL 62301   Travis Tyler, Exec.Dir.

★ N132 ★
Northern Illinois Library System (NILS)
4034 E. State St.
Rockford, IL 61108   Phone: (815)229-0330
FAX: (815)399-3278.

★ N133 ★
Upstate Consortium of Medical Libraries in Northern Illinois
c/o H. Douglas Singer Mental Health & Development Center
Northern Illinois Library for Mental Health
4402 N. Main St.   Phone: (815)987-7092
Rockford, IL 61103   Pat Ellison, Libn.
Address rotates annually. FAX: (815)987-7075.

★ N134 ★
Bur Oak Library System
405 Earl St.
Shorewood, IL 60436   Phone: (815)729-3345

★ N135 ★
Kaskaskia Library System (KLS)
306 N. Main St.
Box 325   Phone: (618)235-4220
Smithton, IL 62285   Deanna Snowden, Exec.Dir.

★ N136 ★
East Central Curriculum Coordination Center (ECCCC)
Sangamon University
F-2   Phone: (217)786-6163
Springfield, IL 62794   Rebecca Douglass, Dir.

★ N137 ★
ILLINET
300 S. Second St.   Phone: (217)785-5600
Springfield, IL 62701   Bridget L. Lamont, Dir., Illinois State Lib.
FAX: (217)785-4326. Also Known As: Illinois Library and Information Network.

★ N138 ★
Illinois State Data Center Cooperative (ISDCC)
Illinois Bureau of the Budget
605 Stratton Office Bldg.
401 S. Spring St.   Phone: (217)782-1381
Springfield, IL 62706   Sue Ebetsch, Coord.
FAX: (217)524-4876.

★ N139 ★
Sangamon Valley Academic Library Consortium (SVALC)
Medical Library
Southern Illinois University School of Medicine
801 N. Rutledge   Phone: (217)782-2658
Springfield, IL 62708   Roger Guard, Ch.
FAX: (217)782-0988.

★ N140 ★
Fox Valley Health Science Library Consortium (FVHSL)
Marianjoy Rehabilitation Hospital and Clinics
Medical Library
P.O. Box 795   Phone: (708)462-4104
Wheaton, IL 60187   Nalini Mahajan, Libn.
Address rotates periodically. FAX: (708)260-0143.

★ N141 ★
North Suburban Library System (NSLS)
200 W. Dundee Rd.   Phone: (708)459-1300
Wheeling, IL 60090   Dr. Elliott Kanner, Rsrcs.Coord.
FAX: (708)459-0380.

INDIANA

★ N142 ★
Eastern Indiana Area Library Services Authority (EIALSA)
111 E. 12th St.   Phone: (317)641-2471
Anderson, IN 46012   Dr. Harold W. Boyce, Adm.
FAX: (317)641-2468.

★ N143 ★
Stone Hills Area Library Services Authority
112 N. Walnut, Suite 500   Phone: (812)334-8347
Bloomington, IN 47408   Sara Laughlin, Coord.
Also known as Stone Hills Library Network. FAX: (812)334-8378.

★ N144 ★
Northeastern Indiana Health Science Library Consortium
Caylor-Nickel Clinic
311 S. Scott St.   Phone: (219)824-3500
Bluffton, IN 46714   Pat Niblick, Dir.

★ N145 ★
Evansville Area Libraries Consortium
c/o Library
St. Mary Medical Center
3700 Washington Ave.   Phone: (812)479-4151
Evansville, IN 47750   E. Jane Saltzman, Coord.
FAX: (812)473-7564.

★ N146 ★
Four Rivers Area Library Services Authority (ALSA)
201 N.W. 4th St., Ste. 5   Phone: (812)425-1946
Evansville, IN 47708   Ida L. McDowell, Dir.
FAX: (812)425-1969.

★ N147 ★
Tri-ALSA
900 Webster St.
Box 2270
Fort Wayne, IN 46801-2270   Phone: (219)424-6664
                                          Jane Raifsnider, Coord.
Also known as Area 3 Library Services Authority. FAX: (219)422-9762.

★ N148 ★
Central Indiana Area Library Services Authority (CIALSA)
1100 W. 42nd St., Ste. 305   Phone: (317)926-6561
Indianapolis, IN 46208   Judith Ellyn, Exec.Dir.
.FAX: (317)923-3658.

★ N149 ★
Central Indiana Health Science Library Consortium
Indiana Hand Center Library
P.O. Box 80434   Phone: (317)471-4340
Indianapolis, IN 46280-0434   Elaine Skopelja, Pres.
Address rotates annually. FAX: (317)875-8638.

★ N150 ★
INCOLSA
5929 Lakeside Blvd.   Phone: (317)298-6570
Indianapolis, IN 46278-1996   B. Evans Markuson, Exec.Dir.
Also known as Indiana Cooperative Library Services Authority.

★ N151 ★
Wabash Valley Library Network
629 South St.   Phone: (317)429-0250
Lafayette, IN 47901   Dennis Lawson, Adm.
Formerly: Wabash Valley Area Library Services Authority.

★ N152 ★
Area 2 Library Services Authority (ALSA 2)
209 Lincolnway, E.   Phone: (219)255-5262
Mishawaka, IN 46544   James D. Cline, Exec.Dir.
FAX: (219)255-8489.

★ N153 ★
Southeastern Indiana Area Library Services Authority (SIALSA)
128 W. Spring St.   Phone: (812)948-8639
New Albany, IN 47150   Sue Stultz, Exec.Dir.
Toll-free telephone number(s): (800)892-2740.

★ N154 ★
Wabash Valley Health Science Library Consortium
Cunningham Memorial Library
Indiana State University   Phone: (812)237-2540
Terre Haute, IN 47809 Evelyn J. Birkey, Med.Libn./Consortium Coord.
FAX: (812)237-2567.

IOWA

★ N155 ★
Consortium of College and University Media Centers (CCUMC)
Iowa State University
Media Resources Center
121 Pearson Hall   Phone: (515)294-8022
Ames, IA 50011   Dr. Don Rieck, Exec.Dir.
Formerly located in Kent, OH.

★ N156 ★
Linn County Library Consortium (LCLC)
Health Services Library
701 10th St., S.E.   Phone: (319)398-6166
Cedar Rapids, IA 52403   Linda Armtiage, Libn.
Address rotates annually.

★ N157 ★
Quad City Area Biomedical Consortium
United Medical Hospital
1410 N. Fourth St.   Phone: (319)243-5900
Clinton, IA 52732   Kris Paulsen, Lrng.Rsrc.Techn.

★ N158 ★
Chiropractic Library Consortium (CLIBCON)
c/o David D. Palmer Health Sciences Library
Palmer College of Chiropractic
1000 Brady St.   Phone: (319)326-8442
Davenport, IA 52803   Dennis Peterson, Pres.
Address rotates annually. FAX: (319)326-9897.

★ N159 ★
Iowa Computer Assisted Network (ICAN)
State Library
Capitol Complex
E. 12th & Grand   Phone: (515)281-6920
Des Moines, IA 50319   Dan Cates, Networking Coord.

★ N160 ★
Polk County Biomedical Consortium (PCBC)
Iowa Hospital Association Library
100 E. Grand   Phone: (515)288-1955
Des Moines, IA 50309   Roxanna Tovrea, Dir.
Address rotates annually.

★ N161 ★
Siouxland Health Science Library Consortium
Library-Media Ctr.
St. Luke's Regional Medical Center
2720 Stone Park Blvd.
Sioux City, IA 51104

KANSAS

★ N162 ★
Kansas Library Network
Kansas State Library
State Capitol, 3rd Fl.   Phone: (913)296-3296
Topeka, KS 66612-1593   Michael Piper, Exec.Dir.
FAX: (913)296-6650

KENTUCKY

★ N163 ★
Kentucky Library Network, Inc. (KLN)
300 Coffee Tree Rd.
Box 537   Phone: (502)875-7000
Frankfort, KY 40602-0537   Linda Sherrow, Act.Dir.

★ N164 ★
State Assisted Academic Library Council of Kentucky (SAALCK)
Blazer Library
Kentucky State University   Phone: (502)227-6852
Frankfort, KY 40601   Karen McDaniel
Address rotates annually. FAX: (502)564-5068.

★ N165 ★
Bluegrass Medical Libraries Consortium
Dept. of Reference
Medical Center Library
University of Kentucky   Phone: (606)233-6567
Lexington, KY 40536-0084   Mark Ingram, Pres.

★N166★
Kentucky Health Sciences Library Consortium
c/o Library
Alliant Health System
P.O. Box 35070   Phone: (502)629-3191
Louisville, KY 40232-5070   Leslie Pancratz, Pres.
Address rotates biennially. FAX: (502)629-2135.

★N167★
Team-A Librarians
Southern Baptist Theological Seminary
2825 Lexington Rd.   Phone: (502)897-4807
Louisville, KY 40280   Dr. Ronald F. Deering, Libn.
Also known as Theological Education Association of Mid-America Librarians.

★N168★
Eastern Kentucky Health Science Information Network (EKHSIN)
003 Camden-Carroll Library
Morehead State University   Phone: (606)783-2610
Morehead, KY 40351   William J. De Bord, Coord.
FAX: (606)783-5311.

LOUISIANA

★N169★
Health Sciences Library Association of Louisiana
c/o Medical Library
V.A. Medical Center   Phone: (318)473-0010
Alexandria, LA 71301   Nancy Guillet
Address and phone number given are those of member library.

★N170★
LAsernet
State Library of Louisiana
Box 131   Phone: (504)342-3389
Baton Rouge, LA 70821   Sara Taffae, Automation Cons.
FAX: (504)342-3547.

MAINE

★N171★
Health Science Library and Information Cooperative of Maine (HSLIC)
V.A. Medical Center
P.O. Box 3395   Phone: (207)623-8411
Togus, ME 04330   Marjorie Anderson

MARYLAND

★N172★
Maryland Association of Health Science Librarians (MAHSL)
St. Agnes Hospital
900 Caton Ave.   Phone: (410)368-3123
Baltimore, MD 21229   Joanne L. Sullivan, Pres.
Address rotates annually. FAX: (410)368-3298.

★N173★
Maryland Interlibrary Organization (MILO)
State Library Resource Center
Enoch Pratt Free Library
400 Cathedral St.
Baltimore, MD 21201   Phone: (301)396-5328

★N174★
National Network of Libraries of Medicine - Southeastern/Atlantic
  Region
Health Sciences Library
University of Maryland
111 S. Greene St.   Phone: (410)328-2855
Baltimore, MD 21201   Faith Meakin, Exec.Dir.
Services is Region 2 of the National Network of Libraries of Medicine serves AL, DC, FL, GA, MD, MS, NC, SC, TN, VA, WV, Puerto Rico, and the Virgin Islands. Toll-free telephone number(s): (800)638-6093. FAX: (410)328-0099.

★N175★
Interlibrary Users Association (IUA)
c/o Logistics Management Institute
6400 Goldsboro Rd.   Phone: (301)320-7249
Bethesda, MD 20817-5886   Nancy Eichelman Handy, Pres.
Address rotates biennially.

★N176★
National Network of Libraries of Medicine (NN/LM)
8600 Rockville Pike, No. B1E03   Phone: (301)496-4777
Bethesda, MD 20894   Becky Lyon-Hartmann, Hd., NN/LM Off.
The Network, administered by the National Library of Medicine, consists of eight Regional Medical Libraries listed separately. FAX: (301)480-1467.

★N177★
Maryland and D.C. Consortium of Resource Sharing (MADCORS)
Medical Library
Prince George's Hospital Center   Phone: (301)618-2490
Cheverly, MD 20785   Penny Martin

★N178★
Washington Research Library Consortium
4207 Forbes Blvd.   Phone: (301)731-1000
Lanham, MD 20706   Elizabeth A. Payne, Interim Dir.

★N179★
Criminal Justice Information Exchange Group
c/o National Institute of Justic/NCJRS
Box 6000   Phone: (301)251-5500
Rockville, MD 20850   J.H. Anderson, NCJRS Commun.
Toll-free telephone number(s): (800)751-3420.

★N180★
Regional Alcohol and Drug Abuse Resource Network (RADAR)
Natl. Clearinghouse for Alcohol and Other Drug Information
P.O. Box 2345   Phone: (301)468-2600
Rockville, MD 20852   Susan Palmer
Toll-free telephone number(s): (800)729-6686.

MASSACHUSETTS

★N181★
Northeast Consortium of Colleges and Universities in Massachusetts
  (NECCUM)
Middlesex Community College
Springs Rd.   Phone: (617)272-7342
Bedford, MA 01730   Caryl Dundorf, Coord.
Address rotates biennially. FAX: (617)270-9740.

★N182★
North of Boston Library Exchange, Inc. (NOBLE)
112 Sohier Rd., Suite 117   Phone: (508)927-5050
Beverly, MA 01915   Ronald A. Gagnon, Network Adm.
FAX: (508)927-7939.

★N183★
Boston Biomedical Library Consortium
c/o Agoos Medical Library
Beth Israel Hospital
330 Brookline Ave.   Phone: (617)735-4225
Boston, MA 02215   Jay Daly, Chm.
Address rotates annually.

★N184★
Boston Library Consortium (BLC)
Boston Public Library, Rm. 339
666 Boylston St.
Boston, MA 02117   Phone: (617)262-6244
FAX: (617)236-4306.

★N185★
North Atlantic Health Science Libraries (NAHSL)
New England College of Optometry
Library
420 Beacon St.   Phone: (617)236-6265
Boston, MA 02115   Lynne Silvers, Ch.
Address rotates annually.

★ N186 ★
Southeastern Massachusetts Cooperating Libraries (SMCL)
c/o Clement C. Maxwell Library
Bridgewater State College   Phone: (508)697-1256
Bridgewater, MA 02324   William Boyle, Coord.

★ N187 ★
Libraries and Information for Nursing Consortium (LINC)
c/o School of Nursing Library
St. Elizabeth's Hospital
159 Washington St.   Phone: (617)789-2304
Brighton, MA 02135   Robert L. Loud, Libn.

★ N188 ★
Fenway Library Consortium (FLC)
Brookline Public Library   Phone: (617)730-2360
Brookline, MA 02146   Michael Steinfeld, Coord.

★ N189 ★
Boston Area Music Libraries (BAML)
Morse Music Library in Hilles Library
Harvard University
59 Shepard St.   Phone: (617)495-8730
Cambridge, MA 02138   Martin Schreiner, Hd. of Morse Music Lib.
Address rotates annually.

★ N190 ★
Boston Theological Institute Libraries
45 Frances Ave.   Phone: (617)523-9548
Cambridge, MA 02138   Cliff Putney, Lib.Coord.

★ N191 ★
New England Law Library Consortium (NELLCO)
c/o Law School Library
Harvard University
Langdell Hall   Phone: (617)495-9918
Cambridge, MA 02138   Martha B. Crane, Coord.
FAX: (617)495-4449.

★ N192 ★
Digital Library Network
555 Virginia Rd., VR03-3/W5   Phone: (508)371-5465
Concord, MA 01742   Howard William, Dir.

★ N193 ★
Consortium for Information Resources (CIR)
Tedeschi Library and Information Center
MetroWest Medical Center
Framingham Union Campus   Phone: (508)383-1591
Framingham, MA 01701   Sandra Clevesy, Pres.
FAX: (508)879-0471.

★ N194 ★
Cooperating Libraries of Greater Springfield, A CCGS Agency (CLGS)
c/o Learning Resources Center
Holyoke Community College
303 Homestead Ave.   Phone: (413)538-7000
Holyoke, MA 01040   Elizabeth Sheehan, Dir.

★ N195 ★
Massachusetts Health Sciences Libraries Network (MaHSLiN)
c/o Health Science Library
Lowell General Hospital
295 Varnum Ave.   Phone: (508)937-6247
Lowell, MA 01854   Martha Bedard, Pres.
Address rotates annually.

★ N196 ★
Northeastern Consortium for Health Information (NECHI)
c/o Health Science Library
Lawrence Memorial Hospital
170 Governors Ave.   Phone: (617)396-9250
Medford, MA 02155   John Harris, Libn.
Address rotates annually.

★ N197 ★
NELINET, Inc.
2 Newton Executive Park   Phone: (617)969-0400
Newton, MA 02162   Marshall Keys, Exec.Dir.
Also known as New England Library Information Network. Toll-free telephone number(s): (800) NELINET (New England only). FAX: (617)332-9634.

★ N198 ★
C/W MARS, Inc.
1 Sunset Lane   Phone: (508)755-3323
Paxton, MA 01612   David T. Sheehan, Mgr.
FAX: (508)755-3721.

★ N199 ★
Southeastern Massachusetts Consortium of Health Science Libraries (SEMCO)
Quincy Hospital Medical Library
114 Whitwell St.   Phone: (617)773-6100
Qunicy, MA 02169   Carolyn Rubenstein, Pres.
Address rotates annually.

★ N200 ★
Western Massachusetts Health Information Consortium
c/o Health Sciences Library
Mercy Hospital
P.O. Box 9012   Phone: (413)781-9100
Springfield, MA 01102   Roger S. Manahan
Address rotates annually.

★ N201 ★
GTE LIBNET
GTE Laboratories Library
40 Sylvan Rd.   Phone: (617)466-4214
Waltham, MA 02254   Susan Wolfman, Lib.Mgr.
Also Known as GTE Library and Information Center Network. FAX: (617)890-5790.

★ N202 ★
WELEXACOL
c/o Solomon R. Baker Library
Bentley College
175 Forest St.   Phone: (617)891-2917
Waltham, MA 02154   Sherman Hayes, Pres.
Address rotates annually. Also known as Wellesley-Lexington Area Cooperating Libraries. FAX: (617)891-2830.

★ N203 ★
Central Massachusetts Consortium of Health Related Libraries (CMCHRL)
State Mutual Company
Library, G9
440 Lincoln St.   Phone: (508)855-2557
Worcester, MA 01605-1959   Tim Rivard, Pres.
Address rotates annually. FAX: (508)853-6332.

★ N204 ★
Worcester Area Cooperating Libraries (WACL)
Learning Resources Center, Rm. 301
Worcester State College   Phone: (508)754-3964
Worcester, MA 01602   Gladys E. Wood, Coord.
FAX: (508)793-8083.

MICHIGAN

★ N205 ★
Southern Michigan Region of Cooperation
Woodlands Library Cooperative
415 S. Superior, Suite A   Phone: (517)629-9469
Albion, MI 49224   James C. Seidl, Dir.
FAX: (517)629-3812.

★ N206 ★
Northland Interlibrary System (NILS)
Northland Library Cooperative
316 E. Chisholm St.   Phone: (517)356-1622
Alpena, MI 49707   Rebecca E. Cawley
FAX: (517)354-3939.

★ N207 ★
Washtenaw-Livingston Library Network (WLLN)
Huron Valley Library System
4133 Washtenaw Ave.   Phone: (313)971-6056
Ann Arbor, MI 48107   Mary Croteau, Lib.Dir.

★ N208 ★
Mid-Michigan Library League Region of Cooperation
Mid-Michigan Library League
411 S. Lake St.
Box 700   Phone: (616)775-6541
Cadillac, MI 49601   Donald Best

★ N209 ★
Detroit Associated Libraries
Detroit Public Library
5201 Woodward Ave.   Phone: (313)833-3397
Detroit, MI 48202   Jean T. Curtis, Dir.
Formerly Detroit Area Library Service (DALS). FAX: (313)832-0877.

★ N210 ★
Detroit Associated Libraries Region of Cooperation (DALROC)
c/o Detroit Public Library
5201 Woodward Ave.   Phone: (313)833-4036
Detroit, MI 48202   James W. Lawrence, Coord.
FAX: (313)832-0877.

★ N211 ★
Flint Area Health Science Library Network (FAHSLN)
St. Joseph Hospital
302 Kensington   Phone: (313)762-8519
Flint, MI 48502   Ria Lukes, Pres.
Address rotates annually.

★ N212 ★
Michigan Health Sciences Libraries Association (MHSLA)
c/o Health Sciences Library
St. Joseph Hospital
302 Kensington Ave.   Phone: (313)762-8519
Flint, MI 48503-2000   Ria Lukes, Pres.
Address rotates annually.

★ N213 ★
Mideastern Michigan Region of Cooperation
Mideastern Michigan Library Cooperative
1026 E. Kearsley   Phone: (313)232-7119
Flint, MI 48502   Eugene Griffel

★ N214 ★
Lakeland Area Library Network (LAKENET)
c/o Lakeland Library Cooperative
60 Library Plaza, N.E.   Phone: (616)456-3647
Grand Rapids, MI 49503   Harriet Field, Coord.
FAX: (616)454-4517.

★ N215 ★
Michigan Library Consortium (MLC)
6810 S. Cedar St., Suite 8   Phone: (517)694-4242
Lansing, MI 48911   Kevin C. Flaherty, Exec.Dir.
Toll-free telephone number(s): (800)530-9019 (Michigan only). FAX: (517)694-9303.

★ N216 ★
Upper Peninsula Region of Library Cooperation (UPRLC)
1615 Presque Isle Ave.   Phone: (906)228-7697
Marquette, MI 49855   Suzanne Dees

★ N217 ★
Capital Area Library Network (Calnet)
Library Service Center
407 N. Cedar St.   Phone: (517)676-8445
Mason, MI 48854   Kathleen M. Vera
FAX: (517)676-9646.

★ N218 ★
Library Cooperative of Macomb (LCM)
Macomb County Library
16480 Hall Rd.   Phone: (313)286-5750
Mt. Clemens, MI 48044   Carol Windorf, Dp.Dir.
FAX: (313)286-8951.

★ N219 ★
Macomb Region of Cooperation
Macomb County Library
16480 Hall Rd.   Phone: (313)286-6660
Mt. Clemens, MI 48044   Carol Goodwin

★ N220 ★
Southwest Michigan Library Cooperative (SMLC)
200 Kalamazoo St.   Phone: (616)657-4698
Paw Paw, MI 49079   Alida Geppert

★ N221 ★
Southwest Michigan Library Network (SMLN)
200 S. Kalamazoo St.   Phone: (616)657-4698
Paw Paw, MI 49079   Alida Geppert

★ N222 ★
Blue Water Network of Libraries
Blue Water Library Federation
210 McMorran Blvd.   Phone: (313)987-7323
Port Huron, MI 48060   Martha Walker

★ N223 ★
White Pine Library Cooperative
1840 N. Michigan, Ste. 114   Phone: (517)754-9787
Saginaw, MI 48602   Sue Hill, Dir.
FAX: (517)754-9795.

★ N224 ★
Smaller Libraries Information Consortium (SLIC)
Library
Lawrence Technological University
21000 W. 10 Mile Rd.   Phone: (313)356-0200
Southfield, MI 48075   Gary R. Cocozzoli, Ch.

★ N225 ★
Council on Resource Development (CORD)
Oakland Schools
2100 Pontiac Lake Rd.   Phone: (313)858-1969
Waterford, MI 48328   Jenny Cross, Lib.Coord.

★ N226 ★
Oakland Wayne Interlibrary Network (OWIN)
33030 Van Born Rd.   Phone: (313)326-8910
Wayne, MI 48184   Anne Neville, Hd. ILL
FAX: (313)326-3035.

★ N227 ★
Wayne Oakland Library Federation (WOLF)
33030 Van Born Rd.
Wayne, MI 48184   Phone: (313)326-8910
FAX: (313)326-8910.

MINNESOTA

★ N228 ★
Northern Lights Library Network (NLLN)
17th & Jefferson
Box 845   Phone: (612)762-1032
Alexandria, MN 56308-0845   Joan B. Larson, Dir.

★ N229 ★
Southcentral Minnesota Inter-Library Exchange (SMILE)
Box 3031   Phone: (507)389-5108
Mankato, MN 56001   Lucy Lowry, Dir.

★ N230 ★
Honeywell Information Network (HIN)
c/o Corporate Library
Honeywell Inc.
Honeywell Plaza
Minneapolis, MN 55408   Phone: (612)870-2377
Address rotates annually.   Kathy Knauer

★ N231 ★
MINITEX Library Information Network
S-33 Wilson Library
University of Minnesota
309 19th Ave., S.   Phone: (612)624-4002
Minneapolis, MN 55455   William DeJohn, Dir.
Also known as Minnesota Interlibrary Telecommunications Exchange. FAX: (612)624-4508. See also the library listing for this network in the main section.

★ N232 ★
Twin Cities Biomedical Consortium (TCBC)
Riverside Medical Center
Riverside at 25th Ave., S.
Minneapolis, MN 55454
Address rotates annually.
Phone: (612)641-5607
Mary Finnegan, Coord.

★ N233 ★
Central Minnesota Libraries Exchange (CMLE)
c/o Learning Resources, Rm. 61
St. Cloud State University
St. Cloud, MN 56301
FAX: (612)654-5131.
Phone: (612)654-5131
Patricia E. Peterson, Dir.

★ N234 ★
Capital Area Library Consortium (CALCO)
Minnesota Pollution Control Agency Library
520 Lafayette Rd.
St. Paul, MN 55155
Address rotates annually.
Phone: (612)296-7719
Kathy Malec, Libn.

★ N235 ★
Cooperating Libraries in Consortium (CLIC)
1457 Grand Ave., Suite N
St. Paul, MN 55105
Phone: (612)699-9300
Terry Metz, Consortium Mgr.

★ N236 ★
Metronet
226 Metro Square Bldg.
7th & Robert Sts.
St. Paul, MN 55101
FAX: (612)224-4827.
Phone: (612)224-4801
Mary Treacy Birmingham, Dir.

★ N237 ★
Metropolitan Library Service Agency (MELSA)
Griggs-Midway Bldg., Rm. 322 S.
1821 University Ave.
St. Paul, MN 55104-3083
Phone: (612)645-5731
William M. Duncan, Exec.Dir.

★ N238 ★
Minnesota Department of Human Services Library Consortium
DHS Library and Resource Center
444 Lafayette Rd.
St. Paul, MN 55155-3821
Formerly located in Minnetonka, MN. FAX: (612)296-6244.
Phone: (612)297-8708
Colleen Spadaccini, Dir.

★ N239 ★
Minnesota Theological Libraries Association (MTLA)
c/o Luther-Northwestern Seminary Library
2375 Como Ave.
St. Paul, MN 55108
Phone: (612)641-3225
Norman Wente, Dir.

MISSISSIPPI

★ N240 ★
Central Mississippi Consortium of Medical Libraries
Medical Center
U.S. Dept. of Veterans Affairs
1500 E. Woodrow Wilson Dr.
Jackson, MS 39216
Address and phone number given are those of member library.
Phone: (601)362-4471
Rose Anne Tucker, Pres.

★ N241 ★
Mississippi Biomedical Library Consortium (MBLC)
Rowland Medical Library
University of Mississippi Medical Center
2500 N. State St.
Jackson, MS 39216-4505
Address rotates annually.
Phone: (601)385-5751
Connie Machado

★ N242 ★
Central Mississippi Library Council
c o Macklendon Library
Hinds Community College
Raymond, MS 39154
Address rotates annually.
Phone: (601)857-5261
Nancy Baker, Ch.

MISSOURI

★ N243 ★
Kansas City Metropolitan Library Network (KCMLN)
15624 E. 24 Hwy.
Independence, MO 64050
FAX: (816)836-5200.
Phone: (816)836-5200
Sharon Jennings, Network Dir.

★ N244 ★
Missouri Statewide Interlibrary Loan Network
Missouri State Library
Box 387
Jefferson City, MO 65102-0387
Defunct.

★ N245 ★
Kansas City Library Network, Inc. (KCLN)
School of Dentistry Library
University of Missouri, Kansas City
650 E. 25th St.
Kansas City, MO 64108
Address rotates annually.
Phone: (816)276-2063

★ N246 ★
Missouri Library Network Corp. (MLNC)
10332 Old Olive St.
St. Louis, MO 63141
Phone: (314)567-3799
Mary Ann Mercante, Dir.

★ N247 ★
Saint Louis Medical Librarians Consortia
Library
St. Mary's Health Center
6420 Clayton Rd.
St. Louis, MO 63117
Phone: (314)768-8112
Candy Thayer, Chm.

★ N248 ★
St. Louis Regional Library Network
Ursuline Academy Library
341 S. Sappington Rd.
St. Louis, MO 63122
Phone: (314)965-1305
Bernyce Christiansen, Coord.

MONTANA

★ N249 ★
Helena Area Health Sciences Library Consortium (HAHSLC)
c/o Medical Reference Library
Shodair Children's Hospital
840 Helena Ave.
Helena, MT 59604
Phone: (406)444-7534
Suzy Holt, Info.Spec.

NEBRASKA

★ N250 ★
Lincoln Health Science Library Group (LHSLG)
University of Nebraska at Lincoln
Chemistry Library
427 Hamilton Hall
Lincoln, NE 68588-0305
Address rotates biennially.
Phone: (402)472-2739
Richard Voeltz, Dir.

★ N251 ★
NEBASE
Nebraska Library Commission
1420 P St.
Lincoln, NE 68508
NEBASE is Nebraska's OCLC consortium. Toll-free telephone number(s): (800)742-7691 (Nebraska only). FAX: (402)471-2083.
Phone: (402)471-2045
Jacqueline Mundell, Dir.

★ N252 ★
ICON
Creighton University
Health Sciences Library
Omaha, NE 68178
Also known as Midlands Library Consortium for the Health Sciences. Formerly Information Consortium of Omaha, Nebraska. FAX: (402)280-5134.
Phone: (402)280-5108
A. James Bothmer, Pres.

★N253★
National Network of Libraries of Medicine - Midcontinental Region
McGoogan Library of Medicine
University of Nebraska Medical Center
600 S. 42nd St.   Phone: (402)559-4326
Omaha, NE 68198-6706   Claire Gadzikowski, Network Coord.
Region 4 of the National Network of Libraries of Medicine serves CO, KS, MO, NE, UT, and WY. Toll free telephone number: (800)633-7654 (Nebraska residents). FAX: (402)559-5498. It also serves as Online Center for Regions 3, 4, and 5 of the National Network of Libraries of Medicine.

NEVADA

★N254★
Information Nevada
Nevada State Library and Archives
Capitol Complex   Phone: (702)887-2614
Carson City, NV 89710   Joyce C. Lee, Asst.Dir.
FAX: (702)887-2630.

★N255★
Nevada Medical Library Group (NMLG)
Medical Library
Carson Tahoe Hospital
P.O. Box 2168   Phone: (702)885-4358
Carson City, NV 89702   Elaine Laessle, Chm.
Address rotates biennially. FAX: (702)885-4447.

NEW HAMPSHIRE

★N256★
North Country Consortium (NCC)
c/o Littleton Hospital
107 Cottage St.   Phone: (603)444-7731
Littleton, NH 03561   Linda L. Ford, Med.Libn.
Address rotates periodically.

★N257★
New Hampshire College & University Council Library Policy Committee (NHCUC)
Notre Dame College Library
2321 Elm St.   Phone: (603)669-3432
Manchester, NH 03104   James R. Swanson, Sr., Coord.

★N258★
Health Science Libraries of New Hampshire & Vermont (HSL-NH/VT)
c/o Medical Library
New London Hospital   Phone: (603)526-2911
New London, NH 03257   Marion Allen, Pres.
Address rotates bienially. FAX: (603)526-2990.

NEW JERSEY

★N259★
Southwest New Jersey Consortium for Health Information Services
Cooper Hospital/University Medical Center - Library
1 Cooper Plaza
Camden, NJ 08103   Phone: (609)964-0140

★N260★
Northwest Regional Library Cooperative
31 Fairmount Ave.
P.O. Box 486   Phone: (201)879-2442
Chester, NJ 07930   Keith Michael Fiels, Exec.Dir.
This network is Region I of the New Jersey Regional Library Cooperatives. FAX: (908)879-8812.

★N261★
Society for Cooperative Healthcare and Related Education (SCHARE)
MacKay Library
Union County College   Phone: (201)276-5710
Cranford, NJ 07016   Ann Calhoun

★N262★
Cosmopolitan Biomedical Library Consortium (CBLC)
Elizabeth General Medical Center
925 E. Jersey St.   Phone: (908)558-8092
Elizabeth, NJ 07201   Catherine Boss
Address rotates annually. FAX: (908)820-8974.

★N263★
Central Jersey Regional Library Cooperative
55 Schanck Rd., Suite B-15   Phone: (908)409-6484
Freehold, NJ 07728   Dottie Hiebing, Dir.
This network is Region V of the New Jersey Regional Library Cooperatives. FAX: (908)409-6492.

★N264★
Health Sciences Library Association of New Jersey (HSLANJ)
Hackensack Medical Center
30 Prospect Ave.   Phone: (201)996-2326
Hackensack, NJ 07601   Duressa Pujat, Pres.

★N265★
South Jersey Regional Library Cooperative
Midway Professional Center, Suite 102
8 N. White House Pike   Phone: (609)561-4646
Hammonton, NJ 08037   Karen Hyman, Exec.Dir.
This network is Region VI of the New Jersey Regional Library Cooperatives.

★N266★
Bergen Passaic Regional Library Cooperative
326 Lafayette Ave.   Phone: (201)427-3996
Hawthorne, NJ 07506   Clarissa Erwin, Exec.Dir.
This network is Region II of the New Jersey Regional Library Cooperatives.

★N267★
AT & T Library Network
600 Mountain Ave.   Phone: (908)582-4361
Murray Hill, NJ 07974   Ronnye Schreiber, Bus.Dev.Mgr.
FAX: (908)582-3146.

★N268★
Essex Hudson Regional Library Cooperative
350 Scotland Rd., 2nd Fl.   Phone: (201)673-6373
Orange, NJ 07050   Ray Murray, Exec.Dir.
This network is Region III of the New Jersey Regional Library Cooperatives.

★N269★
Union Middlesex Regional Library Cooperative
44 Stelton Rd., Suite 235   Phone: (201)752-7720
Piscataway, NJ 08854   Gail L. Rosenberg, Exec.Dir.
This network is Region IV of the New Jersey Regional Library Cooperatives.

★N270★
MEDCORE
Princeton Medical Center Library
253 Witherspoon St.   Phone: (609)921-7700
Princeton, NJ 08540   Louise Yorke
Also known as Medical Resources Consortium of Central New Jersey.

★N271★
Monmouth-Ocean Biomedical Information Consortium (MOBIC)
c/o Medical Library
Community Medical Center
99 Hwy. 37, W.   Phone: (908)240-8117
Toms River, NJ 08755   Reina Reisler, Med.Libn.
Address rotates annually. FAX: (908)341-8093.

★N272★
Central Jersey Health Science Libraries Association (CJHSLA)
c/o Health Science Library
St. Francis Medical Center
601 Hamilton Ave.   Phone: (609)559-5068
Trenton, NJ 08629   Donna Barlow, Libn.
FAX: (609)599-5773.

★N273★
New Jersey Library Network
Library Development Bureau
New Jersey State Library
CN-520   Phone: (609)984-3293
Trenton, NJ 08625-0520   Marilyn Veldof, Coord. of Lib.Serv.
FAX: (609)984-7898.

★N274★
Pinelands Consortium for Health Information
Kennedy Memorial Hospital
University Medical Center/Washington Township Division
Medical Library   Phone: (609)582-2675
Turnersville, NJ 08012   William Dobkowski, Coord.
FAX: (609)582-3190.

NEW MEXICO

★N275★
New Mexico Consortium of Biomedical and Hospital Libraries
Lovelace Medical Library
5400 Gibson Blvd., S.E.   Phone: (505)262-7158
Albuquerque, NM 87108   Sarah Knox Morley, Coord.

★N276★
New Mexico Consortium of Academic Libraries (NMCAL)
c/o Miller Library
Western New Mexico University   Phone: (505)538-6358
Silver City, NM 88061   Benjamin Wakashige, Pres.
Address rotates annually. FAX: (505)538-6178.

NEW YORK

★N277★
Capital District Library Council for Reference & Research Resources (CDLC)
28 Essex St.   Phone: (518)438-2500
Albany, NY 12206   Charles D. Custer, Exec.Dir.
Formerly located in Schenectady. See also the library listing for this network in the main section. FAX: (518)438-2572.

★N278★
New York State Interlibrary Loan Network (NYSILL)
New York State Library
Cultural Education Center, Rm. 10B41   Phone: (518)474-7890
Albany, NY 12230   Carol Ann Desch
FAX: (518)474-2718.

★N279★
SUNY/OCLC Library Network
Central Administration
State University of New York
State University Plaza   Phone: (518)434-8141
Albany, NY 12246   Glyn T. Evans, Dir.
Toll-free telephone number(s): (800)342-3353 (New York Only).
FAX:(518)432-4346.

★N280★
Suffolk Cooperative Library System
627 N. Sunrise Service Rd.
Bellport, NY 11713   Phone: (516)286-1600

★N281★
Brooklyn-Queens-Staten Island Health Sciences Librarians (BQSI)
c/o Morgan Library
Long Island College Hospital
97 Amity St.   Phone: (718)780-1077
Brooklyn, NY 11201   George Wahlert, Pres.
Address rotates biennially.

★N282★
Medical & Scientific Libraries of Long Island (MEDLI)
c/o Palmer School of Library and Information Science
C.W. Post Campus, L.I.U.   Phone: (516)299-2866
Brookville, NY 11548   Mary L. Westermann, Coord.
FAX: (516)626-2665.

★N283★
Library Consortium of Health Institutions in Buffalo (LCHIB)
Health Sciences Library
Abbott Hall
University of Buffalo   Phone: (716)831-3351
Buffalo, NY 14214   Cynthia Bertuca, Dir.
Consortium consists of eight teaching hospital libraries and the university's Health Sciences Library. FAX: (716)835-4891.

★N284★
Western New York Library Resources Council (WNYLRC)
180 Oak St.   Phone: (716)852-3844
Buffalo, NY 14203   Mary K. Ghikas, Exec.Dir.

★N285★
North Country Reference and Research Resources Council (NCRRRC)
Box 568   Phone: (315)386-4569
Canton, NY 13617   John Hammond, Exec.Dir.

★N286★
Westchester Library System (WLS)
8 Westchester Plaza   Phone: (914)592-8214
Elmsford, NY 10523   Maurice J. Freedman, Dir.
FAX: (914)347-3617.

★N287★
Southeastern New York Library Resources Council (SENYLRC)
220 Rte. 299   Phone: (914)691-2734
Highland, NY 12528-0879   Ellen A. Parravano, Exec.Dir.
Maintains the Southeastern Bibliographic Center (SEBC).

★N288★
American Film & Video Association
Cornell University Resource Center
8 Business and Technology Park   Phone: (607)255-2090
Ithaca, NY 14850   Richard Gray, AV Lib.Coord.
FAX: (607)255-9946.

★N289★
South Central Research Library Council (SCRLC)
215 N. Cayuga St.   Phone: (607)273-9106
Ithaca, NY 14850   Janet E. Steiner, Exec.Dir.
FAX: (607)272-0740.

★N290★
Consortium of Foundation Libraries (CFL)
International Planned Parenthood
902 Broadway   Phone: (212)995-8800
New York, NY 10010   Abigail Hourwich, Ch.
Address rotates biennially. FAX: (212)995-8853.

★N291★
Council of Archives and Research Libraries in Jewish Studies (CARLJS)
330 7th Ave., 21st Fl.   Phone: (212)490-2280
New York, NY 10001   Abraham Atik, Coord.
Affiliated with the World Council on Jewish Archives, Jerusalem.

★N292★
Manhattan-Bronx Health Sciences Library Consortia
Medical Library
Manhattan Eye, Ear and Throat Hospital
210 E. 64th St.   Phone: (212)605-3786
New York, NY 10021   Dede Silverston, Pres.

★N293★
Medical Library Center of New York (MLCNY)
5 E. 102nd St., 7th Fl.   Phone: (212)427-1630
New York, NY 10029   Lois Weinstein, Dir.
See also the library listing for this network in the main section.

★N294★
National Network of Libraries of Medicine - Middle Atlantic Region
New York Academy of Medicine Library
2 E. 103rd St.   Phone: (212)876-8763
New York, NY 10029-5293   Mary Mylenki, Assoc.Dir.
Region 1 of the National Network of Libraries of Medicine serves DE, NJ, NY, and PA. It also functions as the Online Center for Regions 1, 2, and 8. FAX: (212)534-7042.

★ N295 ★
New York Metropolitan Reference and Research Library Agency
57 E. 11th St., 4th Fl.   Phone: (212)228-2320
New York, NY 10003-4605   Joan Neumann, Dir.
Also known as METRO. FAX: (212)228-2598.

★ N296 ★
Research Library Association of South Manhattan
Bobst Library
New York University
70 Washington Square, S.   Phone: (212)998-2566
New York, NY 10012   Joan Grant, Coord.

★ N297 ★
Associated Colleges of the St. Lawrence Valley, Inc. (ACSLV)
Satterlee Hall
SUNY - College at Potsdam   Phone: (315)265-2790
Potsdam, NY 13676   Judy C. Chittenden

★ N298 ★
Rochester Regional Library Council (RRLC)
302 N. Goodman St.   Phone: (716)461-5440
Rochester, NY 14607   Janet M. Welch, Dir.
FAX: (716)461-2721.

★ N299 ★
Long Island Library Resources Council
Melville Library Bldg., Suite 5310   Phone: (516)632-6650
Stony Brook, NY 11794   Judith Newfeld, Asst.Dir.
Formerly Long Island Media Consortium.

★ N300 ★
Central New York Library Resources Council (CENTRO)
763 Butternut St.   Phone: (315)478-6080
Syracuse, NY 13208   Keith E. Washburn, Exec.Dir.
FAX: (315)478-0512.

★ N301 ★
Library Exchange and Resources Network (LEARN)
St. Luke-Memorial Hospital
Box 479
Utica, NY 13503-0479
Defunct.

★ N302 ★
Health Information Libraries of Westchester (HILOW)
c/o Medical Sciences Library
New York Medical College
Basic Sciences Bldg.   Phone: (914)993-4205
Valhalla, NY 10595   Christine Hunter, Pres.

NORTH CAROLINA

★ N303 ★
North Carolina Area Health Education Centers Program Library and Information Services Network
Health Sciences Library, 223H
University of North Carolina
Campus Box 7585   Phone: (919)962-0700
Chapel Hill, NC 27599-7585   Diana McDuffee, Coord.
FAX: (919)966-1537.

★ N304 ★
Triangle Research Libraries Network (TRLN)
University of North Carolina at Chapel Hill
C.B. 3940, Wilson Library   Phone: (919)962-8022
Chapel Hill, NC 27599-0484   David Carlson, Exec.Dir.
TRLN is a cooperative project of Duke University, North Carolina State University, and University of North Carolina at Chapel Hill. FAX: (919)962-0484.

★ N305 ★
Cape Fear Health Sciences Information Consortium (CFHSIC)
Fayetteville Technical Community College Library
2201 Hull Rd.   Phone: (919)678-8400
Fayetteville, NC 28303   Susan S. Rose
Address rotates biennially. FAX: (919)323-3540.

★ N306 ★
South Central Health Information Network of North Carolina (SCHIN of NC)
1601 Owen Dr.   Phone: (919)323-1152
Fayetteville, NC 28304   Barbara A. Wright, Dir.

★ N307 ★
Northwest AHEC Library Information Network
Northwest Area Health Education Center at Hickory
Catawba Memorial Hospital
Fairgrove Church Rd.   Phone: (704)326-3664
Hickory, NC 28602-9643   Phyllis Gillikin, Coord.
FAX: (704)322-2921.

★ N308 ★
Mid-Carolina Academic Library Network (MID-CAL)
Kenan Library
900 Millsborough St.   Phone: (919)839-4038
Raleigh, NC 27603-1689   Dr. Marti Smith
Address rotates biennially.

★ N309 ★
North Carolina Information Network (NCIN)
State Library of North Carolina
109 E. Jones St.   Phone: (919)733-2570
Raleigh, NC 27601-2807   Diana Young, Dir., Network Op.
FAX: (919)733-8748.

★ N310 ★
Resources for Health Information (REHI)
Wake Medical Center/Wake AHEC
Medical Library
P.O. Box 14465   Phone: (919)250-8529
Raleigh, NC 27620-4465   Beverly S. Richardson, Assoc.Dir.
FAX: (919)250-8836.

NORTH DAKOTA

★ N311 ★
North Dakota Network for Knowledge
North Dakota State Library
Liberty Memorial Bldg.
Capitol Grounds   Phone: (701)224-2490
Bismarck, ND 58505-0800   William R. Strader, State Libn.

★ N312 ★
Prairie Library Network
Southeast Clinical Campus Library (142D)
U.S. Dept. of Veterans Affairs
2101 Elm St.
Fargo, ND 58102
Defunct.

★ N313 ★
Valley Medical Network (VMN)
St. Luke's Hospital - Meritcare
720 N. 4th St.   Phone: (701)234-5837
Fargo, ND 58122   Margaret Wagner, Pres.
Address rotates annually. FAX: (701)234-5927.

OHIO

★ N314 ★
Greater Cincinnati Library Consortium (GCLC)
3333 Vine St., Suite 605   Phone: (513)751-4422
Cincinnati, OH 45220   Martha J. McDonald, Exec.Dir.

★ N315 ★
NEOMARL
Cleveland Health Sciences Library
2119 Abington Rd.   Phone: (216)368-3427
Cleveland, OH 44106   Robert G. Cheshier, Chm.
Also known as Northeast Ohio Major Academic and Research Libraries. Address rotates annually.

★ N316 ★
Central Ohio Hospital Library Consortium
D.J. Vincent Medical Library
Riverside Methodist Hospitals
3535 Olentangy River Rd.   Phone: (614)261-5230
Columbus, OH 43214-3998   Ms. Jo Yeoh, Coord.

★ N317 ★
Ohio Network of American History Research Centers (ONARCH)
Ohio Historical Society
1982 Velma Ave.   Phone: (614)297-2500
Columbus, OH 43211-2497   George Parkinson
FAX: (614)297-2411.

★ N318 ★
Ohio Regional Consortium of Law Libraries (ORCLL)
Ohio State University Law Library   Phone: (614)292-6691
1659 High St.   Thomas G. Spaith, Chm. of Board
Columbus, OH 43210-1391   of Trustees
Affiliated with Ohio Regional Association of Law Libraries. FAX: (614)292-3202.

★ N319 ★
OHIONET
1500 West Lane Ave.   Phone: (614)486-2966
Columbus, OH 43221   Robert Busick, Interim Dir.
Also known as Ohio Library Network. Toll-free telephone number(s): (800)686-8975 (Ohio only). FAX: (614)486-1527.

★ N320 ★
Southwestern Ohio Council for Higher Education (SOCHE)
2900 Acosta St., Suite 141   Phone: (513)297-3150
Dayton, OH 45420   Dr. Pressley C. McCoy, Pres.
FAX: (513)297-3163.

★ N321 ★
North Central Library Cooperative (NCLC)
27 N. Main St.
Mansfield, OH 44902   Phone: (419)526-1337

★ N322 ★
NEOUCOM Council Associated Hospital Librarians
Ocasek Regional Medical Information Center   Phone: (216)325-2511
Rootstown, OH 44272   Jean Sayre, Lib.Dir.
Also known as Council of Hospital Librarians.

★ N323 ★
Cleveland Area Metropolitan Library System (CAMLS)
20700 Chagrin Blvd., Ste. 500   Phone: (216)921-3900
Shaker Heights, OH 44122-5334   Victoria Gangloff, Exec.Dir.
FAX: (216)921-7220.

★ N324 ★
Health Science Librarians of Northwest Ohio (HSLNO)
c/o Toledo Hospital
Medical Library
2142 N. Cove Blvd.   Phone: (419)471-3640
Toledo, OH 43606   Deborah Lewis
Address rotates biennially.

★ N325 ★
Columbus Area Libraries Information Council of Ohio (CALICO)
Otterbein College Library
Main and Grove St.   Phone: (614)898-1215
Westerville, OH 43081   Lois Szudy, Pres.
Address rotates annually.

OKLAHOMA

★ N326 ★
BHSL
Library
Children's Hospital of Oklahoma
Box 26307   Phone: (405)271-5699
Oklahoma City, OK 73126   Jean Cavett, Lib.Dir.

★ N327 ★
Greater Oklahoma City Area Health Sciences Library Consortium (GOAL)
Box 60918
Oklahoma City, OK 73106

★ N328 ★
Metropolitan Libraries Network of Central Oklahoma Inc. (MetroNet)
P.O. Box 250   Phone: (405)235-0571
Oklahoma City, OK 73101-0250   Danelle Hall, Chm.

★ N329 ★
Oklahoma Telecommunications Interlibrary System (OTIS)
Oklahoma Department of Libraries
200 N.E. 18th St.   Phone: (405)521-2502
Oklahoma City, OK 73105   Mary Hardin, ILL Libn.
FAX: (405)525-7804 or (800)397-8116.

★ N330 ★
Mid-America Law School Library Consortium
University of Tulsa School of Law
Taliaferro Savage Library
3120 E. 4th Place   Phone: (918)631-2458
Tulsa, OK 74104-3189   Richard E. Ducey, Ch.
Address rotates biennially.

★ N331 ★
Oklahoma Health Sciences Library Association (OHSLA)
c/o Health Sciences Library
St. John Medical Center
1923 S. Utica   Phone: (918)744-2970
Tulsa, OK 74104   James M. Donovan, Pres.
Address rotates annually.

★ N332 ★
Tulsa Area Library Cooperative (TALC)
400 Civic Center   Phone: (918)596-7893
Tulsa, OK 74103   Paula Emmons, Coord.

OREGON

★ N333 ★
Marine-Valley Health Information Network (MarVHIN)
c/o Learning Resources Center
Linn-Benton Community College
6500 S.W. Pacific Blvd.   Phone: (503)928-2361
Albany, OR 97321   Charles Weyant, Dept.Chm.

★ N334 ★
Washington County Cooperative Library Services (WCCLS)
17880 S.W. Blanton St.
Box 5129   Phone: (503)642-1544
Aloha, OR 97006   Peggy Forcier, Coord.

★ N335 ★
Washington County Inter-Library Information Network
P.O. Box 5129
Aloha, OR 97006   Phone: (503)642-1544

★ N336 ★
Oregon Health Sciences Libraries Association (OHSLA)
Tuality Community Hospital Library
P.O. Box 309   Phone: (503)681-1121
Hillsboro, OR 97123   Natalie Norcross, Dir.
Address rotates annually. FAX: (503)681-1729.

★ N337 ★
Southern Oregon Library Federation (SOLF)
Jackson County Library
413 W. Main St.
Medford, OR 97501

★ N338 ★
Association of Visual Science Librarians (AVSL)
Good Samaritan Hospital and Medical Center
Merrill Reeh Ophthalmology Library
1040 N.W. 22nd Ave.   Phone: (503)229-7678
Portland, OR 97210   Madelyn Hall, Ch.
Address rotates periodically. FAX: (503)790-1201.

★ N339 ★
Northwest Association of Private Colleges & Universities (NAPCU)
Wilson W. Clark Memorial Library
University of Portland
5000 N. Willamette Blvd.   Phone: (503)283-7111
Portland, OR 97283-0017   Rev. Joseph P. Browne, C.S.C., Sec.-Treas.
Address rotates periodically. FAX: (503)283-7491.

★ N340 ★
Oregon Health Information Online (ORHION)
Oregon Health Sciences University Library
3181 S.W. Sam Jackson Rd.
Box 573   Phone: (503)494-4739
Portland, OR 97207   Steve Teich, Coord.
Formerly Oregon Health Information Network (OHIN).

★ N341 ★
Portland Area Health Sciences Librarians
c/o Health Sciences Library
Emanuel Hospital
2801 N. Gantenbien   Phone: (503)280-3558
Portland, OR 97227   Kathy Rouzie, Coord.
Address and phone number given are those of member library.

PENNSYLVANIA

★ N342 ★
Cooperating Hospital Libraries of the Lehigh Valley Area
Learning Resource Center
Allentown Osteopathic Medical Center
1736 Hamilton   Phone: (215)770-8355
Allentown, PA 18104   Linda Schwartz, Libn.

★ N343 ★
Lehigh Valley Association of Independent Colleges, Inc. (LVAIC)
Moravian College   Phone: (215)691-6131
Bethlehem, PA 18018   Dr. Galen Godbey, Dir.

★ N344 ★
Philadelphia Regional Interlibrary Loan Group (PRILL)
Technical Information Center
PQ Corporation
280 Cedar Grove Rd.   Phone: (215)686-5360
Conshohocken, PA 19428-2240 Diane Jude McDowell, Pres.
Address rotates annually. FAX: (215)563-3628.

★ N345 ★
Erie Area Health Information Library Cooperative (EAHILC)
c/o Shriner's Hospitals for Crippled Children
1645 W. 8th St.   Phone: (814)452-4164
Erie, PA 16505   Dianne C. Tate, Ch.
Address rotates biennially. FAX: (814)459-0483.

★ N346 ★
Northwest Interlibrary Cooperative of Pennsylvania (NICOP)
c/o Hammermill Library
Mercyhurst College
Erie, PA 16546   David Pinto, Coord.
Address rotates annually.

★ N347 ★
Associated College Libraries of Central Pennsylvania (ACLCP)
Murray Learning Resources Center
Messiah College   Phone: (717)691-6006
Grantham, PA 17027   Jonathan D. Laver, Dir.
Address rotates biennially. FAX: (717)691-6042.

★ N348 ★
Central Pennsylvania Health Sciences Library Association (CPHSLA)
Capital Health System/Harrisburg Hospital
Library Services
S. Front St.   Phone: (717)782-5511
Harrisburg, PA 17101   Cheryl Capitani, Pres.
Address rotates annually. FAX: (717)782-5512.

★ N349 ★
Mid-Atlantic Law Library Cooperative (MALLCO)
State Library of Pennsylvania
Box 1601   Phone: (717)787-3273
Harrisburg, PA 17105   Eugene Smith, Dir.
Address and phone number given are those of member library.

★ N350 ★
Eastern Mennonite Associated Libraries & Archives (EMALA)
2215 Millstrem Rd.   Phone: (717)393-9745
Lancaster, PA 17602   Ray K. Hacker, Ch.

★ N351 ★
Susquehanna Library Cooperative
George B. Stevenson Library
Lock Haven University   Phone: (717)893-2309
Lock Haven, PA 17745-2390   Robert S. Bravard, Dir.
Address rotates biennially. FAX: (717)893-2506.

★ N352 ★
State System of Higher Education Libraries Council (SSHELCO)
Ganser Library
Millersville University   Phone: (717)872-3608
Millersville, PA 17551   Dr. David J. Zubatsky, Coord.
Address rotates biennially. FAX: (717)872-3854.

★ N353 ★
Tri-County Library Consortium
New Castle Public Library
207 E. North St.   Phone: (412)658-6659
New Castle, PA 16101-3691   John Walter, Dir.

★ N354 ★
Health Sciences Libraries Consortium (HSLC)
1001 Sterigere St.   Phone: (215)270-1369
Norristown, PA 19401-5399   Frieda Liem, Libn.
Formerly Confederation of State & State Related Institutions. FAX: (215)270-1370.

★ N355 ★
Delaware Valley Information Consortium (DEVIC)
c/o Health Sciences Library
University of Pennsylvania Medical Center
51 N. 39th St.   Phone: (215)662-9181
Philadelphia, PA 19104   Kathy Ahrens, Coord.

★ N356 ★
Health Sciences Libraries Consortium (HSLC)
3600 Market St., Suite 550   Phone: (215)222-1532
Philadelphia, PA 19104-2646 Joseph C. Scorza, Exec.Dir.
FAX: (215)222-0416.

★ N357 ★
PALINET
3401 Market St., Suite 262   Phone: (215)382-7031
Philadelphia, PA 19104   James E. Rush, Exec.Dir.
See also the library listing for this network in the main section. Toll-free telephone number(s): (800)233-3401 (Pennsylvania only); (800)233-3402 (Delaware, Maryland, and New Jersey). FAX: (215)382-0022.

★ N358 ★
Philadelphia Area Consortium of Special Collections Libraries (PACSCL)
Academy of Natural Sciences Library
1900 Benjamin Franklin Parkway   Phone: (215)898-5240
Philadelphia, PA 19103-1195   Stephen J. Zietz, Proj.Coord.
Address rotates biennially. FAX: (215)573-2036.

★ N359 ★
Southeastern Pennsylvania Theological Library Association (SEPTLA)
Austen K. DeBlois Library
Eastern Baptist Seminary
Lancaster at City Line   Phone: (215)896-5000
Philadelphia, PA 19151-1495   Dr. William J. Hand

★ N360 ★
Association for Library Information (AFLI)
Duquesne University Library
Pittsburgh, PA 15282
Defunct.

★N361★
Oakland Library Consortium
302 Hunt Library
Carnegie Mellon University
Frew St.   Phone: (412)268-2890
Pittsburgh, PA 15213   Sylverna Ford, Exec.Dir.
Consortium consists of the University of Pittsburgh, Carnegie-Mellon University, and Carnegie Library of Pittsburgh. FAX: (412)268-6944.

★N362★
Pittsburgh-East Hospital Library Cooperative
c/o Library
West Penn School of Nursing
4900 Friendship Ave.   Phone: (415)578-5556
Pittsburgh, PA 15224   Christine Matik, Pres.
Address rotates irregularly.

★N363★
Pittsburgh Regional Library Center (PRLC)
103 Yost Blvd.   Phone: (412)825-0600
Pittsburgh, PA 15221   H.E. Broadbent, III, Exec.Dir.
Toll-free telephone number(s): (800)242-3790 (Pennsylvania, West Virginia, and Maryland only). FAX: (412)825-0762.

★N364★
Southeast Pittsburgh Library Consortium
South Hills Health System
P.O. Box 18119   Phone: (412)469-5786
Pittsburgh, PA 15236   Barbara Palso, Med.Libn.
Address rotates biennially. FAX: (412)469-5468.

★N365★
Berks County Library Association (BCLA)
Berks County Law Library
Court House   Phone: (215)378-8189
Reading, PA 19601   Linda Fuerle Fisk, Pres.
Address rotates annually. FAX: (215)378-8913.

★N366★
Tri-State College Library Cooperative (TCLC)
Rosemont College Library   Phone: (215)525-0796
Rosemont, PA 19010   Ellen Gasiewski, Off.Coord.

★N367★
Health Information Library Network of Northeastern Pennsylvania (HILNNEP)
Hospital Library
Community Medical Center
1800 Mulberry St.   Phone: (717)969-8197
Scranton, PA 18510   Ann Duesing, Chm.

★N368★
Interlibrary Delivery Service of Pennsylvania (IDS)
471 Park Lane   Phone: (814)238-0254
State College, PA 16803-3208   Janet C. Phillips, Adm.Dir.
FAX: (814)238-9686. Also known as Pennsylvania Interlibrary Delivery System.

★N369★
Consortium for Health Information & Library Services (CHI)
One Medical Center Blvd.   Phone: (215)447-6163
Upland, PA 19013   Kathleen Vick Kell, Exec.Dir.
FAX: (215)447-6164.

★N370★
Northeastern Pennsylvania Bibliographic Center (NEPBC)
D. Leonard Corgan Library
King's College
14 W. Jackson St.   Phone: (717)826-5841
Wilkes-Barre, PA 18711   Terrence Mech, Dir.

RHODE ISLAND

★N371★
Association of Rhode Island Health Sciences Librarians (ARIHSL)
Health Sciences Library
Mariam Hospital
164 Summit Ave.   Phone: (401)274-3700
Providence, RI 02096   Mary Ann Slocumb, Pres.
Address rotates annually.

★N372★
Consortium of Rhode Island Academic and Research Libraries, Inc. (CRIARL)
Rockefeller Library
Brown University   Phone: (401)863-2162
Providence, RI 02912   Arthur P. Young, Chm.

★N373★
Rhode Island Library Network (RHILINET)
300 Richmond St.   Phone: (401)277-2726
Providence, RI 02903   Barbara Weaver, Dir.
FAX: (401)831-1131.

SOUTH CAROLINA

★N374★
Area Health Education Consortium of South Carolina (AHEC)
Medical University of South Carolina
Charleston, SC 29425   Phone: (803)792-4427

★N375★
Charleston Academic Libraries Consortium
Robert Scott Small Library
College of Charleston   Phone: (803)792-5530
Charleston, SC 29424   David Cohen, Ch.
Address rotates annually.

★N376★
South Carolina Health Information Network (SCHIN)
Medical University of South Carolina Library
171 Ashley Ave.
Charleston, SC 29403
Defunct.

★N377★
Columbia Area Medical Librarians' Association (CAMLA)
Professional Library
William S. Hall Psychiatric Institute
Box 202   Phone: (803)734-7136
Columbia, SC 29202   Neeta N. Shah, Coord.
FAX: (803)734-7078.

★N378★
South Carolina Library Network
South Carolina State Library
1500 Senate St.
Box 11469   Phone: (803)734-8666
Columbia, SC 29211   Lea Walsh, Coord., Network Serv.

SOUTH DAKOTA

★N379★
South Dakota Library Network (SDLN)
800 Governors Dr.
Pierre, SD 57501-2294   Phone: (605)773-3131
FAX: (605)773-4950.

TENNESSEE

★N380★
Consortium of Southern Biomedical Libraries (CONBLS)
c/o Quillen College of Medicine Library
East Tennessee State University
Box 70,693   Phone: (615)929-6252
Johnson City, TN 37617-0693   Janet S. Fisher, Pres.
Address rotates annually. FAX: (615)461-7025.

★N381★
Tri-Cities Area Health Sciences Libraries Consortium
Medical Library
Box 70,693
East Tennessee State University   Phone: (615)929-6252
Johnson City, TN 37614-0693   Janet S. Fisher, Dir.Med.Lib.
FAX: (615)461-7025.

★N382★
Knoxville Area Health Sciences Library Consortium (KAHSLC)
c/o Library
University of Tennessee
College of Nursing   Phone: (615)974-7632
Knoxville, TN 37996-4110   Beth Barrett, Pres.
Address rotates annually.

★N383★
Association of Memphis Area Health Science Libraries (AMAHSL)
Health Sciences Library
University of Tennessee
877 Madison Ave.   Phone: (901)528-5634
Memphis, TN 38163   Glenda Mendina, Coord.
Address rotates annually.

★N384★
Mid-Tennessee Health Sciences Librarians Consortium (MTHSLC)
Medical Library
Meharry Medical College
1005 David Todd Blvd.   Phone: (615)327-6728
Nashville, TN 37208   Mattie McHollin, Pres.

★N385★
Tennessee Health Science Library Association (THeSLA)
Tennessee Hospital Association
500 Interstate Blvd., S.   Phone: (615)322-2291
Nashville, TN 37210   Evelyn H. Forbes, Pres.
Address rotates biennially. FAX: (615)343-6454.

TEXAS

★N386★
APLIC International Census Network
c/o Population Research Center
1800 Main Bldg.
University of Texas
Austin, TX 78712   Phone: (512)471-5514
Also known as Association of Population/Family Planning Libraries and
Information Centers Census Network.

★N387★
Project TexNet Interlibrary Loan Network (TexNet)
Texas State Library
Box 12927   Phone: (512)463-5465
Austin, TX 78711   Edward Seidenberg, Div.Dir.
FAX: (512)463-5436.

★N388★
TAMU Consortium of Medical Libraries
Medical Sciences Library
Texas A & M University   Phone: (409)845-7427
College Station, TX 77843   Dottie Eakir, Dir.

★N389★
Coastal Bend Health Sciences Library Consortium (CBHSLC)
2606 Hospital Blvd.
Box 5280   Phone: (512)881-4198
Corpus Christi, TX 78405   Angelica Hinojosa, Coord.
FAX: (512)881-4198.

★N390★
AMIGOS Bibliographic Council, Inc.
12200 Park Central Dr., Ste. 500   Phone: (214)851-8000
Dallas, TX 75251-2104   Bonnie Jergens, Exec.Dir.
Toll-free telephone number(s): (800)843-8482. FAX: (214)991-6061.

★N391★
Association for Higher Education of North Texas (AHE)
17103 Preston Rd., Ste. 250   Phone: (214)713-8170
Dallas, TX 75248-1373   Dr. Allan Watson, Pres.
FAX: (214)713-8209.

★N392★
Health Libraries Information Network (HealthLINE)
Methodist Hospitals of Dallas
Medical Library
PO Box 655999   Phone: (214)944-8321
Dallas, TX 75265   Janet Cowen, Ch.
Address rotates annually. FAX: (214)944-8006.

★N393★
Health Oriented Libraries of San Antonio (HOLSA)
c/o Headquarters, Health Services Command   Phone: (512)221-6515
Fort Sam Houston, TX 78234-6000   Judith Rinn Knight, Lib.Cons.
Alternate telephone number(s): (512)221-6516. Address rotates annually.

★N394★
Health Services Command Library Network (HSCLN)
Headquarters Health Services Command
Clinical Medical Division (Attn: Staff Libn.)   Phone: (512)221-6515
Fort Sam Houston, TX 78234-6000   Judith Arnn, Staff Libn.
Alternate telephone number(s): 221-6954; 221-6516; 221-6616.

★N395★
South Central Academic Medical Libraries Consortium (SCAMEL)
c/o Health Sciences Library
Texas College of Osteopathic Medicine
Camp Bowie at Montgomery   Phone: (817)735-2464
Fort Worth, TX 76107   Bobby R. Carter, Treas.

★N396★
Northeast Texas Library System (NETLS)
625 Austin   Phone: (214)494-7192
Garland, TX 75040   Elizabeth Crabb, Coord.
Currently inactive.

★N397★
Houston Area Research Library Consortium (HARLIC)
Texas Southern University
Library
3100 Cleburne   Phone: (713)527-7163
Houston, TX 77004   Adele Dendy, Pres.
Address rotates biennially.

★N398★
National Network of Libraries of Medicine - South Central Region
c/o Texas Medical Center Library
Houston Academy of Medicine
1133 M.D. Anderson Blvd.   Phone: (713)790-7053
Houston, TX 77030   Mary L. Ryan, Exec.Dir.
Region 5 of the National Network of Libraries of Medicine serves AR, LA,
NM, OK, and TX. FAX: (713)790-7030.

★N399★
Council of Research & Academic Libraries (CORAL)
Box 290236   Phone: (512)245-2133
San Antonio, TX 78280-1636   Joan Heath, Pres.

★N400★
PAISANO Consortium of Libraries
2602 N. Ben Jordan   Phone: (512)572-6421
Victoria, TX 77901   Dr. Joe F. Dahlstrom, Coord.
FAX: (512)573-4401.

UTAH

★N401★
Utah College Library Council (UCLC)
Dixie College
225 S. 700 E.   Phone: (801)673-4811
St. George, UT 84770   Audrey Shumway, Lib.Dir.

★N402★
Utah Health Sciences Library Consortium (UHSLC)
c/o St. Marks Hospital Library
1200 E. 3900 S.   Phone: (801)268-7004
Salt Lake City, UT 84124   Jane Errion, Pres.
Address rotates annually. FAX: (801)268-7876.

VIRGINIA

★N403★
American Gas Association - Library Services (AGA-LSC)
1515 Wilson Blvd.
Arlington, VA 22219   Phone: (801)841-8400

★ N404 ★
Southside Virginia Library Network
Longwood College
201 High Street   Phone: (804)395-2441
Farmville, VA 23909   Rebecca Laine, Interim Lib.Dir.
FAX: (804)395-2453.

★ N405 ★
TRADOC Library and Information Network (TRALINET)
ATTN: ATBO-N, Bldg. 117   Phone: (804)727-4491
Fort Monroe, VA 23651-5117   James H. Byrn, Dir.
Also known as U.S. Army Training & Doctrine Command (TRADOC) Library & Information Network. FAX: (804)727-2750.

★ N406 ★
Richmond Area Libraries Cooperative
c/o E. Claiborne Robins School of Business Library
University of Richmond   Phone: (804)289-8666
Richmond, VA 23173   Lucretia McCulley, Chm.

★ N407 ★
Virginia Library Network
Virginia State Library
11th St. at Capitol Square   Phone: (804)371-7614
Richmond, VA 23219   Ashby S. Wilson, Jr., Dir, Networking & Auto.

★ N408 ★
Southwestern Virginia Health Information Librarians (SWVAHILI)
VA Medical Center
Medical Library (142D)   Phone: (703)982-2463
Salem, VA 24153   Jean Kennedy, Ch.Libn.
Address rotates biennially.

WASHINGTON

★ N409 ★
Council on Botanical Horticultural Libraries
Lawrence Pierce Library
Rhododendron Species Foundation
2525 S. 336th St.   Phone: (206)927-6960
Federal Way, WA 98063-3798   Mrs. George Harrison, Chm.

★ N410 ★
Western Library Network (WLN)
Washington State Library
AJ-11W   Phone: (206)459-6518
Olympia, WA 98504-0111   Nancy Zussy, State Libn.

★ N411 ★
National Network of Libraries of Medicine - Pacific Northwest Region
Health Sciences Library and Information Center
University of Washington
SB-55   Phone: (206)543-8262
Seattle, WA 98195   Sherrilynne Fuller, Dir.
Region 6 of the National Network of Libraries of Medicine serves AK, ID, MT, OR, and WA. FAX: (206)543-2469.

★ N412 ★
Seattle Area Hospital Library Consortium (SAHLC)
2442 N.W. Market St., No. 326   Phone: (206)883-5431
Seattle, WA 98107   Rhe Jain, Pres.

★ N413 ★
Washington Medical Librarians' Association
Reference Library
Swedish Hospital Medical Center
747 Summit Ave.   Phone: (206)292-2484
Seattle, WA 98104   Jean C. Anderson, Chf.Libn.

★ N414 ★
Inland Northwest Health Sciences Libraries (INWHSL)
Whitworth College
Library   Phone: (509)466-3260
Spokane, WA 99251   Gail Fielding, Ch.
Address rotates annually. FAX: (509)466-3221.

★ N415 ★
Northwest Consortium of Law Libraries
Law School Library
University of Puget Sound
Norton Clapp Law Ctr.
Tacoma, WA 98402-4470
Defunct.

WEST VIRGINIA

★ N416 ★
Huntington Health Science Library Consortium
Health Science Libraries
Marshall University School of Medicine   Phone: (304)696-6426
Huntington, WV 25701   Edward Dzierzak, Chm.

WISCONSIN

★ N417 ★
Fox Valley Library Council
Alleshany-Alpaca Library System Offices
225 N. Oneida St.   Phone: (414)832-6190
Appleton, WI 54911   Mary Brown, Pres.

★ N418 ★
Northwestern Wisconsin Health Science Library Consortium
c/o Medical Library
Luther Hospital
1221 Whipple St.
Eau Claire, WI 54702   Virginia L. Wright, Coord.
Address rotates annually. FAX: (715)839-3289.

★ N419 ★
Northeast Wisconsin Intertype Libraries (NEWIL)
c/o Nicolet Federated Library System
515 Pine St.   Phone: (414)448-4412
Green Bay, WI 54301   Terrie Howe, Lib.Serv.Coord.
FAX: (414)448-4420.

★ N420 ★
Multitype Advisory Library Committee (MALC)
1922 University Ave.   Phone: (608)231-1052
Madison, WI 53705   Lori Belongia-Schneider

★ N421 ★
South Central Library System
201 W. Mifflin St.
Madison, WI 53703   Phone: (608)266-4181

★ N422 ★
South Central Wisconsin Health Science Libraries Consortium
St. Mary's Hospital Medical Center
Medical Library
707 S. Mill St.   Phone: (608)258-6533
Madison, WI 53715   Mary Sanchez, Coord.
Address rotates biennially.

★ N423 ★
Wisconsin Area Research Center Network
State Historical Society of Wisconsin
816 State St.   Phone: (608)264-6480
Madison, WI 53706   Peter Gottlieb

★ N424 ★
Wisconsin Interlibrary Services (WILS)
728 State St., Rm. 464   Phone: (608)263-4962
Madison, WI 53706   Kathy Schneider, Dir.
FAX: (608)263-3684.

★ N425 ★
Library Council of Metropolitan Milwaukee, Inc. (LCOMM)
814 W. Wisconsin Ave.   Phone: (414)271-8470
Milwaukee, WI 53233   Corliss Rice, Exec.Dir.
FAX: (414)278-2137.

★ N426 ★
Southeastern Wisconsin Health Science Library Consortium (SWHSL)
c/o Health Science Learning Center
St. Francis Hospital
3237 S. 16th St.   Phone: (414)647-5156
Milwaukee, WI 53215   Joy Shong, Dir.

★ N427 ★
Southeastern Wisconsin Information Technology Exchange (SWITCH)
6801 N. Yates Rd.   Phone: (414)351-2423
Milwaukee, WI 53217   David Weinberg-Kinsey, Exec.Dir.
FAX: (414)351-7516.

★ N428 ★
Fox River Valley Area Library Consortium (FRVALC)
St. Nicholas Hospital
1601 N. Taylor Dr.   Phone: (414)459-4713
Sheboygan, WI 53081   Kathy Blaser
Address rotates biennially.

★ N429 ★
Arrowhead Professional Libraries Association (APLA)
Hill Library
University of Wisconsin - Superior   Phone: (715)394-8233
Superior, WI 54880   Deb Nordgren
Address rotates biennially.

★ N430 ★
Wisconsin Valley Library Service (WVLS)
400 First St.   Phone: (715)847-5535
Wausau, WI 54401   Heather Eldred, Dir.
FAX: (715)845-4270.

WYOMING

★ N431 ★
Southeast Wyoming Health Science Library Consortium
Family Practice Library
821 E. 18th St.
Cheyenne, WY 82001-4393
Defunct.

★ N432 ★
Wyoming Libraries Database (WYLD System)
c/o Wyoming State Library
Supreme Court & State Library Bldg.   Phone: (307)777-6294
Cheyenne, WY 82002   Marc Stratton, Sys.Mgr.
FAX: (307)777-6289.

★ N433 ★
Northeastern Wyoming Medical Library Consortium
c/o Library
Campbell County Memorial Hospital
P.O. Box 3011   Phone: (307)687-5183
Gillette, WY 82716   Dorothy O'Brien, Chm.
Address rotates annually. FAX: (307)687-5182.

★ N434 ★
Health Sciences Information Network (HSIN)
University of Wyoming
Science Library
PO Box 3262   Phone: (307)766-6537
Laramie, WY 82071-3262   Janice L. Gahagan, HSIN, Coord.
FAX: (307)766-3611.

CANADA

ALBERTA

★ N435 ★
Alberta Government Libraries' Council (AGLC)
c/o Cooperative Government Library Services Section
Alberta Legislature Library
Legislature Annex, 9th Fl.
Edmonton, AB, Canada T5K 2C8   Phone: (403)427-3837
FAX: (403)427-1623.

★ N436 ★
Northern Alberta Health Libraries Association
c/o Weinlos Library
Misericordia Hospital
16940 87th Ave.   Phone: (403)484-8708
Edmonton, AB, Canada T5R 4H5   John Back, Pres.
FAX: (403)486-8774.

MANITOBA

★ N437 ★
Manitoba Government Libraries Council (MGLC)
Robert Fletcher Bldg.
Box 3, Main Fl.
1181 Portage Ave.   Phone: (204)945-7830
Winnipeg, MB, Canada R3G 0T3   Elaine Seepish, Chm.
Address rotates annually. FAX: (204)945-8756.

★ N438 ★
Manitoba Library Consortium, Inc.
c/o Aikins, MacAulay, and Thorvaldson
Commodity Exchange Tower, 30th Fl.
360 Main St.   Phone: (204)632-2232
Winnipeg, MB, Canada R3C 4G1   Patricia Bozyk, Pres.
FAX: (204)697-4791.

ONTARIO

★ N439 ★
Ontario Hospital Libraries Association (OHLA)
c/o Library
Ontario Hospital Association
150 Ferrand Dr.   Phone: (416)429-2661
Don Mills, ON, Canada M3C 1H6   Patricia Johnson, Pres.
Address rotates annually. FAX: (416)429-1363.

★ N440 ★
Canadian Health Libraries Association
Health Sciences Library
McMaster University
1200 Main St., W
Hamilton, ON, Canada L8N 3Z5
Defunct. Merged with Hamilton/Wentworth District Health Library Network.

★ N441 ★
Hamilton/Wentworth District Health Library Network
Health Sciences Library
McMaster University
1200 Main St., W.   Phone: (416)525-9140
Hamilton, ON, Canada L8N 3Z5   Linda Panton, Coord.

★ N442 ★
Southern Ontario Library Service - Escarpment
1133 Central Ave.   Phone: (416)544-2780
Hamilton, ON, Canada L8K 1N7   June E. Wilson, Dir.
Formerly: Ontario Library Service - Escarpment.

★ N443 ★
Sheridan Park Association - Library and Information Science Committee (LISC)
Sheridan Park Research Community
2275 Speakman Dr.   Phone: (416)823-9040
Mississauga, ON, Canada L5K 1B1   Laurie J. Scott, Ch.
FAX: (416)823-6120.

★ N444 ★
Disability Research Library Network
c/o Community Services
North York Public Library
5120 Yonge St.   Phone: (416)733-5581
North York, ON, Canada M2N 5N7   Joanne Bar

★ N445 ★
Canadian Agriculture Library System
930 Carling Ave.   Phone: (613)995-7829
Ottawa, ON, Canada K1A 0C5   Victor Desroches, Dir.
FAX: (613)952-3813.

★ N446 ★
The Bibliocentre
80 Cowdray Court   Phone: (416)299-1515
Scarbourough, ON, Canada M1S 4N1   Doug Wentzel, Dir.

★ N447 ★
Ontario Council of University Libraries (OCUL)
Lakehead University
Library   Phone: (807)343-8205
Thunder Bay, ON, Canada P7B 5E1   Fred McIntosh, Chf.Libn.
Address rotates biennially. FAX: (807)343-8007.

★ N448 ★
Education Libraries Sharing of Resources Network (ELSOR)
Metropolitan Toronto School Board
45 York Mills Rd.   Phone: (416)489-3332
Willowdale, ON, Canada M2P lB6   Martha E. Murphy, Coord.

QUEBEC

★ N449 ★
Association des Bibliotheques de la Sante Affiliees a l'Universite de Montreal (ABSAUM)
c/o Bibliotheque de la Sante
Universite de Montreal
CP 6128, Succursale A   Phone: (514)343-6826
Montreal, PQ, Canada H3C 3J7   Bernard Bedard, Sec.

★ N450 ★
McGill Medical and Health Libraries Association (MMHLA)
Sir Mortimer B. Davis Jewish General Hospital
Medical Library
3755 Cote St. Catherine Rd., Rm. A-200   Phone: (514)340-8222
Montreal, PQ, Canada H3T 1E2   A. Greenberg, Pres.
Address rotates biennially. FAX: (514)340-7552.

★ N451 ★
Montreal Health Libraries Association (MHLA)
Hopital Marie-Enfant
Bibliotheque Medicale
5200 rue Belanger E.   Phone: (514)374-1710
Montreal, PQ, Canada H1T 1C9   Anca Cojocaru, Pres.
Address rotates annually.

INTERNATIONAL

ENGLAND

★ N452 ★
OCLC Europe
Tricorn House, 7th Fl.
51-53 Hagley Rd.   Phone: 21 4564656
Edgbaston, Birmingham B16 8TP, England   Janet Mitchell, Dir.
FAX: 21 4564680. Telex: 335176 ATTN OCLC TESTRS G; 336520 ATTN
OCLC TESTRS G.

All numbers refer to networks and consortia listed in geographic order in Appendix A. An asterisk before an entry number indicates that it has been cross-referenced from another title.

Appendixes

Appendix B

Regional and Subregional Libraries
for the Blind and Physically Handicapped

In cooperation with a network of regional and subregional libraries, the Library of Congress provides free library services to persons who are unable to read or use standard printed materials because of visual or physical impairment. Books and magazines in recorded form (talking books) or in braille are delivered to eligible readers by postage-free mail and are returned in the same manner. Specially designed record players and cassette players are also loaned free to persons borrowing talking books.

This list contains three elements: the addresses, contact numbers, and names of librarians in charge of each of the regional and subregional libraries in the network. The regional library or libraries listed under each state provide a full range of library services to handicapped readers. In many states, readers receive talking books through subregional libraries, which are local public libraries having collections of current materials and direct access to the resources of their regional libraries. In addition, they offer handicapped readers reference and reader's advisory services.

Regional libraries are listed after the state heading. Subregional libraries within the state are listed next, arranged alphabetically by the city in which they are located. Some states contain more than one regional library. In this case, a remark is added to the entry to signify which portion of the state is served by a particular regional library.

United States citizens residing in foreign countries who are certified eligible for such services can receive library service from:

Library of Congress
National Library Service for the Blind and Physically Handicapped
Network Services Section
Washington, DC 20542
Phone: (202)707-9261
FAX: (202)707-0712
Contact: Mr. Yealuri Rathan Raj, Libn.

Alabama

Alabama Public Library Service
Alabama Regional Library for the Blind &
 Physically Handicapped
6030 Monticello Dr.
Montgomery, AL 36130
Phone: (205)277-7330
Toll-free: 800-392-5671
FAX: (205)272-6514
TDD: (205)272-0830
Contact: Mrs. Fara L. Zaleski

Public Library of Anniston & Calhoun
 County
Library for the Blind & Handicapped
PO Box 308
Anniston, AL 36202
Phone: (205)237-8501
FAX: (205)238-0474
Contact: Deenie M. Culver

Houston-Love Memorial Library
Department for the Blind & Physically
 Handicapped
PO Box 1369
Dothan, AL 36302
Phone: (205)793-9767
FAX: (205)793-6645
TDD: (205)793-9767
Contact: Mary Sue Carte

Huntsville Subregional Library for the Blind
 and Physically Handicapped
PO Box 443
Huntsville, AL 35804
Phone: (205)532-5980; (205)532-5981
FAX: (205)532-5994
TDD: (205)532-5968
Contact: Joyce L. Smith

Alabama Institute for the Deaf & Blind
Library and Resource Center for the Blind &
 Physically Handicapped
705 South St.
PO Box 698
Talladega, AL 35160
Phone: (205)761-3287; (205)761-3288
Toll-free: 800-362-1747
FAX: (205)761-3337
Contact: Teresa Lacy

Tuscaloosa Public Library
Tuscaloosa Subregional Library for the Blind
 & Physically Handicapped
1801 River Rd.
Tuscaloosa, AL 35401
Phone: (205)345-3994
FAX: (205)752-8300
TDD: (205)345-3994
Contact: Barbara B. Jordan

Alaska

Alaska State Library
Services for the Blind & Physically
 Handicapped
344 W. 3rd Ave., Suite 125
Anchorage, AK 99518
Phone: (907)272-3033
FAX: (907)272-8484
Contact: Patricia Meek

Arizona

Arizona State Braille and Talking Book
  Library
1030 N. 32nd St.
Phoenix, AZ 85008
Phone: (602)255-5578
Toll-free: 800-255-5578
FAX: (602)255-4312
Contact: Richard C. Peel

Flagstaff City-Coconino County Library
Special Services
300 W. Aspen
Flagstaff, AZ 86001
Phone: (602)779-7670
FAX: (602)774-9573
Contact: Ms. Jimmie Bevill

Prescott Talking Book Library
215 E. Goodwin St.
Prescott, AZ 86303
Phone: (602)445-8110
FAX: (602)445-1851
Contact: Jill North

Arkansas

Library for the Blind & Physically
  Handicapped
One Capitol Mall
Little Rock, AR 72201-1081
Phone: (501)682-1155
FAX: (501)682-1529
Contact: John J.D. Hall

Ozarks Regional Library
Library for the Blind & Handicapped,
  Northwest
217 E. Dickson St.
Fayetteville, AR 72701
Phone: (501)442-6253
Contact: Rachel Anne Ames

Fort Smith Public Library for the Blind &
  Handicapped
61 S. 8th St.
Fort Smith, AR 72901
Phone: (501)783-0229
FAX: (501)782-8571
Contact: Mary Nigh

Crowley Ridge Regional Library
Library for the Blind & Physically
  Handicapped, Northeast
315 W. Oak
Jonesboro, AR 72401
Phone: (501)935-5133
FAX: (501)935-7987
Contact: Ruth Ball

Columbia-Lafayette-Ouachita-Calhoun
  Regional Library
Library for the Blind & Handicapped,
  Southwest
PO Box 668
Magnolia, AR 71753
Phone: (501)234-1991
Contact: Christine McDonald

California

Braille Institute Library Services
741 N. Vermont Ave.
Los Angeles, CA 90029
Phone: (213)663-1111; (213)660-3880
Toll-free: 800-252-9486
FAX: (213)666-5881
Contact: Dr. Henry C. Chang
This regional library serves southern
  California.

California State Library
Braille & Talking Book Library
600 Broadway
Sacramento, CA 95818
Phone: (916)322-4090
Toll-free: 800-952-5666
FAX: (916)324-8121
Contact: Donine Hedrick
This regional library serves northern
  California.

Fresno County Free Library
Blind & Handicapped Services
770 N. San Pablo Ave.
Fresno, CA 93728
Phone: (209)488-3217
Toll-free: 800-742-1011
TDD: (209)488-3209
Contact: Deborah Janzen

San Francisco Public Library for the Blind &
  Print Handicapped
1528 Fillmore St.
San Francisco, CA 94115-3516
Phone: (415)292-2022
TDD: (415)557-4433
Contact: Gloria Hanson, Supv.

Colorado

Library for the Blind & Physically
  Handicapped
Colorado Centennial Bldg.
1313 Sherman St., Level 2B
Denver, CO 80203
Phone: (303)866-2081
Toll-free: 800-332-5852
FAX: (303)830-0793
Contact: Barbara Goral

Connecticut

Connecticut State Library
Library for the Blind & Physically
  Handicapped
198 West St.
Rocky Hill, CT 06067
Phone: (203)566-2151
Toll-free: 800-842-4516
FAX: (203)566-6669
Contact: Carol A. Taylor

Delaware

Delaware Division of Libraries
Library for the Blind & Physically
  Handicapped
43 S. DuPont Hwy.
Dover, DE 19901
Phone: (302)739-4748
Toll-free: 800-282-8676
FAX: (302)739-6787
TDD: (302)739-4739
Contact: Anne E. Norman

District of Columbia

District of Columbia Regional Library for the
  Blind & Physically Handicapped
901 G St., N.W., Rm. 215
Washington, DC 20001
Phone: (202)727-2142
TDD: (202)727-2255
Contact: Grace J. Lyons

Florida

Florida Bureau of Library Services for the
  Blind & Physically Handicapped
420 Platt St.
Daytona Beach, FL 32114-2804
Phone: (904)254-3824
Toll-free: 800-342-5627
FAX: (904)238-3160
TDD: 800-342-5627
Contact: Donald John Weber

Manatee County Central Library System
Talking Book Service
1301 Barcarrota Blvd., W.
Bradenton, FL 34205-7599
Phone: (813)749-7114
FAX: (813)749-7191
TDD: (813)749-7113
Contact: Frederick Duda

Brevard County Library System
Talking Books Library
308 Forrest Ave.
Cocoa, FL 32922-7781
Phone: (407)633-1810; (407)633-1811
FAX: (407)633-1790
Contact: Kay Briley

Broward County Talking Book Library
100 S. Andrews Ave.
Fort Lauderdale, FL 33301
Phone: (305)357-7555; (305)357-7413
TDD: (305)357-7413
Contact: Joann Block

Jacksonville Public Libraries
Talking Book Library
1755 Edgewood Ave., W., Suite 1
Jacksonville, FL 32208-7206
Phone: (904)765-5888
FAX: (904)768-7404
TDD: (904)630-2740
Contact: Susan V. Arthur

Miami-Dade Public Library System
Dade County Talking Book Library
150 N.E. 79th St.
Miami, FL 33138
Phone: (305)751-8687
Toll-free: 800-451-9544
TDD: (305)758-6599
Contact: Barbara L. Moyer

Lee County Subregional Library for the Blind
  & Physically Handicapped
13240 N. Cleveland Ave., No. 5-6
North Fort Meyers, FL 33901-4855
Phone: (813)995-2665
Contact: Barbara Ferris

Orange County Library System
Talking Book Section
101 E. Central Blvd.
Orlando, FL 32801
Phone: (407)425-4694
TDD: (407)425-5668
Contact: Debbie Burbach

West Florida Regional Library
Subregional Talking Book Library
200 W. Gregory St.
Pensacola, FL 32501
Phone: (904)435-1760
FAX: (904)432-9582
Contact: Martha L. Lazor

Palm Beach County Library Annex
Talking Books
7950 Central Industrial Dr., Suite 104
Riviera Beach, FL 33404-9947
Phone: (407)845-4600
Contact: Mrs. Pat Mistretta

Tampa-Hillsborough County Public Library
   System
Hillsborough County Talking Book Library
900 N. Ashley Dr.
Tampa, FL 33602-3788
Phone: (813)223-8349
FAX: (813)223-8278
TDD: (813)223-8858
Contact: Suzanne M. Bell

Georgia

Georgia Library for the Blind & Physically
   Handicapped
1150 Murphy Ave., S.W.
Atlanta, GA 30310
Phone: (404)756-4619
FAX: (404)756-4618
Contact: Mr. Dale Snair

Dougherty County Public Library
Albany Library for the Blind and
   Handicapped
300 Pine Ave.
Albany, GA 31701
Phone: (912)431-2920
FAX: (912)430-4020
Contact: Kathryn R. Sinquefield

Athens Regional Library
Talking Book Center
435 N. Lumpkin St.
Athens, GA 30601
Phone: (404)354-2625
FAX: (404)369-0297
TDD: (404)354-2620
Contact: Janet Wright

Augusta-Richmond County Public Library
Talking Book Center
425 9th St.
Augusta, GA 30901
Phone: (404)821-2625
FAX: (404)724-6762
Contact: Gary Swint

Southwest Georgia Regional Library
Bainbridge Subregional Library for the Blind
   and Physically Handicapped
Shotwell & Monroe Sts.
Bainbridge, GA 31717
Phone: (912)248-2680
FAX: (912)248-2670
Contact: Laura S. Harrison

Brunswick-Glynn County Regional Library
Talking Book Center
208 Gloucester St.
Brunswick, GA 31523
Phone: (912)267-1212
Contact: Betty Ransom

Subregional Library for the Blind & Physically
   Handicapped
Talking Book Center
1120 Bradley Dr.
Columbus, GA 31995
Phone: (404)327-0211
FAX: (404)649-1914
Contact: Crawford B. Pike

Oconee Regional Library
Library for the Blind & Physically
   Handicapped
806 Highland Ave.
PO Box 100
Dublin, GA 31040
Phone: (912)275-3322
Contact: Mr. Chris Campbell Woodburn

Chestatee Regional Library
Library for the Blind and Physically
   Handicapped
127 N. Main St.
Gainesville, GA 30501
Phone: (404)535-5738
FAX: (404)532-4305
Contact: Mrs. Billie Jean Ouellette

La Fayette Subregional Library for the Blind
   and Physically Handicapped
305 S. Duke St.
La Fayette, GA 30728
Phone: (404)638-2992
FAX: (404)638-4028
Contact: Mrs. Lecia Eubanks

Washington Memorial Library
Macon Subregional Library for the Blind and
   Physically Handicapped
1180 Washington Ave.
Macon, GA 31201
Phone: (912)744-0877
FAX: (912)742-3161
TDD: (912)744-0877
Contact: Rebecca M. Sherrill

Sara Hightower Regional Library
Rome Subregional Library for the Blind &
   Physically Handicapped
205 Riverside Pkwy.
Rome, GA 30161-2911
Phone: (404)236-4618
FAX: (404)236-4605
Contact: Sue Frazier

Chatham-Effingham-Liberty (CEL) Regional
   Library
Subregional Library for the Blind and
   Physically Handicapped
2002 Bull St.
Savannah, GA 31499
Phone: (912)234-5127
Toll-free: 800-342-4455
FAX: (912)236-7782
TDD: (912)234-5127
Contact: Linda Stokes

South Georgia Regional Library
Subregional Library for the Blind & Physically
   Handicapped
601 N. Lee St.
Valdosta, GA 31601-4766
Phone: (912)333-5210
Contact: Sharon Bernstein

Guam

Guam Public Library for the Blind &
   Physically Handicapped
Nieves M. Flores Memorial Library
254 Martyr St.
Agana, GU 96910
Phone: (671)472-6417; (671)472-8264
FAX: (671)477-9777
Contact: Joanne Tarpley

Hawaii

Hawaii State Library
Library for the Blind & Physically
   Handicapped
402 Kapahulu Ave.
Honolulu, HI 96815
Phone: (808)732-7767
FAX: (808)732-4158
TDD: (808)732-7767
Contact: Sally Morgan

Idaho

Idaho Regional Library for the Blind &
   Physically Handicapped
325 W. State St.
Boise, ID 83702
Phone: (208)334-2117
Toll-free: 800-233-4931
FAX: (208)334-4016
Contact: Kay H. Salmon

Illinois

Illinois Regional Library for the Blind &
   Physically Handicapped
1055 W. Roosevelt Rd.
Chicago, IL 60608
Phone: (312)746-9210
Toll-free: 800-331-2351
FAX: (312)746-9192
Contact: James Pletz

Shawnee Library System
Southern Illinois Talking Book Center
511 Greenbriar Rd.
Carterville, IL 62918-1600
Phone: (618)985-8375
Toll-free: 800-458-0475
FAX: (618)985-4211
TDD: (618)985-8375
Contact: Joan Laskaris

Chicago Public Library
Talking Book Center
1055 W. Roosevelt Rd.
Chicago, IL 60608
Phone: (312)738-9200
FAX: (312)746-9192
Contact: Mamie Grady

Talking Book Center of Northwest Illinois
PO Box 125
Coal Valley, IL 61240
Phone: (309)799-3137
Toll-free: 800-747-3137
FAX: (309)799-7916
Contact: Dee Canfield

Suburban Audio-Visual Service
Talking Book Center
920 Barnsdale Rd.
La Grange Park, IL 60525
Phone: (708)352-7671
Toll-free: 800-627-0062
FAX: (708)352-7528
Contact: Patti Lang

Illinois Valley Library System
Heart of Illinois Talking Book Center
845 Brenkman Dr.
Pekin, IL 61554
Phone: (309)353-4110
Toll-free: 800-426-0709
FAX: (309)353-8281
Contact: Lori Logsdon

Great River Library System
River Road Talking Book Library
106 N. 5th St.
Quincy, IL 62301
Phone: (217)224-6619
Toll-free: 800-537-1274
TDD: (217)224-6619
Contact: Eileen Shepherd

Indiana

Indiana State Library
Division for the Blind & Physically
  Handicapped
140 N. Senate Ave.
Indianapolis, IN 46204
Phone: (317)232-3684
Toll-free: 800-622-4970
FAX: (317)232-3728
TDD: (317)232-7763
Contact: Lissa Shanahan

Bartholomew County Public Library
Fifth at Lafayette
Columbus, IN 47201
Phone: (812)379-1277
Contact: Wilma J. Perry

Elkhart Public Library
Blind & Physically Handicapped Services
300 S. Second St.
Elkhart, IN 46516-3184
Phone: (219)522-2665
Contact: Pat Ciancio

Evansville-Vanderburgh County Public
  Library
Talking Books Service
22 S.E. 5th St.
Evansville, IN 47708
Phone: (812)428-8235
Contact: Barbara Shanks

Allen County Public Library
Readers' Services Department
Box 2270
Fort Wayne, IN 46801
Phone: (219)424-7241
Contact: Joyce Misner

Lake County Public Library
Northwest Indiana Subregional Library for the
  Blind & Physically Handicapped
1919 W. 81st Ave.
Merrillville, IN 46410
Phone: (219)769-3541
TDD: (219)769-3541
Contact: Joanne Panasuk

Iowa

Iowa Department for the Blind
Library for the Blind & Physically
  Handicapped
524 4th St.
Des Moines, IA 50309-1333
Phone: (515)281-1333
Toll-free: 800-362-2587
FAX: (515)281-1263
TDD: (515)281-1333
Contact: R. Creig Slayton, Dir.

Kansas

Kansas State Library
Kansas Talking Book Service
ESU Memorial Union
1200 Commercial
Emporia, KS 66801
Phone: (316)343-7124
Toll-free: 800-362-0699
Contact: Ms. Arvina Lumley

Central Kansas Library System (CKLS)
  Headquarters
Talking Book Service
1409 Williams
Great Bend, KS 67530
Phone: (316)792-2393
Toll-free: 800-362-2642
FAX: (316)792-5495
Contact: Patsy Arnold

South Central Kansas Library System
Talking Book Subregional
901 N. Main
Hutchinson, KS 67501
Phone: (316)663-5441
Toll-free: 800-234-0529
FAX: (316)663-1215
Contact: Karen Socha

Kansas City, Kansas Public Center
Kansas Braille Library
625 Minnesota Ave.
Kansas City, KS 66101
Phone: (913)621-3073
Toll-free: 800-279-6645
FAX: (913)621-0963
Contact: Joan Gandert
The library is a braille-lending library only.

Manhattan Public Library
Juliette & Poyntz
Manhattan, KS 66502
Phone: (913)776-4741
Toll-free: 800-432-2796
FAX: (913)776-1545
Contact: Lois Hartley

Northwest Kansas Library System
Talking Books
PO Box 446
Norton, KS 67654
Phone: (913)877-5148
Toll-free: 800-432-2858
FAX: (913)877-5697
Contact: Clarice Howard

Topeka Public Library
Talking Books
1515 W. 10th St.
Topeka, KS 66604
Phone: (913)233-2040
Toll-free: 800-432-2925
FAX: (913)233-2055
TDD: (913)233-3277
Contact: Suzanne Bundy

Wichita Public Library
Talking Books Department
223 South Main
Wichita, KS 67202
Phone: (316)262-0611
Toll-free: 800-362-2869
FAX: (316)262-2552
TDD: (316)262-3972
Contact: Betty C. Spriggs

Kentucky

Kentucky Library for the Blind & Physically
  Handicapped
300 Coffee Tree Rd.
PO Box 818
Frankfort, KY 40602
Phone: (502)875-7000
Toll-free: 800-372-2968
FAX: (502)564-5773
Contact: Richard Feindel

Northern Kentucky Talking Book Library
502 Scott St.
Covington, KY 41011
Phone: (606)491-7610
Contact: Alice Manchikes

Louisville Free Public Library
Talking Book Library
301 W. York St.
Louisville, KY 40203
Phone: (502)561-8625
TDD: (502)561-8621
Contact: Maxine Harris Surratt

Louisiana

Louisiana State Library
Section for the Blind & Physically
  Handicapped
760 Riverside, N.
Baton Rouge, LA 70802
Phone: (504)342-4944; (504)342-4943
Toll-free: 800-543-4702
FAX: (504)342-3547
Contact: Jennifer Anjier

Maine

Maine State Library
Library Services for the Blind & Physically
  Handicapped
State House, Sta. 64
Augusta, ME 04333
Phone: (207)289-5650; (207)947-8336
Toll-free: 800-452-8793
Contact: Benita D. Davis
An alternate toll-free telephone number is 800-
  762-7106.

Maryland

Maryland State Library for the Blind &
  Physically Handicapped
1715 N. Charles St.
Baltimore, MD 21201
Phone: (301)333-2668
Toll-free: 800-492-5627
Contact: Lance C. Finney

Montgomery County Department of Public
  Libraries
Special Needs Library
6400 Democracy Blvd.
Bethesda, MD 20817
Phone: (301)493-2555
FAX: (301)530-8941
TDD: (301)493-2554
Contact: Mrs. Devon Skeele Liner

Prince George's County Memorial Library
6530 Adelphi Rd.
Hyattsville, MD 20782
Phone: (301)779-2570
Contact: Shirley J. Tuthill

Massachusetts

Perkins School for the Blind
Braille and Talking Book Library
175 N. Beacon St.
Watertown, MA 02172
Phone: (617)924-3434
Toll-free: 800-852-3133
Contact: Patricia Kirk

Worcester Public Library
Talking Book Library
1 Salem Square
Worcester, MA 01608
Phone: (508)799-1730; (508)799-1661
Toll-free: 800-762-0085
FAX: (508)799-1652
TDD: (508)799-1731
Contact: Marlene Temsky

Michigan

Library of Michigan
Services for the Blind & Physically
Handicapped
Box 30007
Lansing, MI 48909
Phone: (517)373-1590
Toll-free: 800-992-9012
FAX: (517)373-5865
TDD: (517)373-1592
Contact: Margaret Wolfe
This regional library serves the entire state of
Michigan except Wayne County.

Wayne County Regional Library for the Blind
& Physically Handicapped
33030 Van Born Rd.
Wayne, MI 48184
Phone: (313)274-2600
FAX: (313)326-3035
TDD: (313)326-1080
Contact: Ms. Pat Klemans
This regional library serves only Wayne
County.

Northland Library Cooperative
316 E. Chisholm St.
Alpena, MI 49707
Phone: (517)356-1622
Toll-free: 800-446-1580
FAX: (517)354-3939

Washtenaw County Library for the Blind &
Physically Handicapped
PO Box 8645
Ann Arbor, MI 48107
Phone: (313)971-6059
FAX: (313)971-3892
Contact: Mary E. Udoji

Downtown Detroit Subregional Library for
the Blind and Physically Handicapped
121 Gratiot Ave.
Detroit, MI 48226
Phone: (313)224-0580
FAX: (313)965-1977
TDD: (313)224-0584
Contact: Joan Gartland
This subregional library serves only Wayne
County.

Farmington Community Library
Oakland County Library for the Blind &
Physically Handicapped
32737 W. 12 Mile Rd.
Farmington Hills, MI 48334
Phone: (313)553-0300
FAX: (313)553-4037
TDD: (313)553-0320
Contact: Carole Hund

Mideastern Michigan Library Co-op
Library for the Blind & Physically
Handicapped
G-4195 W. Pasadena Ave.
Flint, MI 48504
Phone: (313)732-1120
FAX: (313)732-1715
Contact: Patricia Peterson

Kent County Library for the Blind &
Physically Handicapped
775 Ball Ave., N.E.
Grand Rapids, MI 49503
Phone: (616)774-3262
FAX: (616)774-3256
Contact: Linda Fox

Capital Area Subregional Library for the
Blind & Physically Handicapped
PO Box 30007
Lansing, MI 48909
Phone: (517)373-1590
Toll-free: 800-992-9012
FAX: (517)373-5865
TDD: (517)373-1592
Contact: Edith Darling Heezen

Upper Peninsula Library for the Blind &
Physically Handicapped
1615 Presque Isle Ave.
Marquette, MI 49855
Phone: (906)228-7697
Toll-free: 800-562-8985
FAX: (906)228-5627
Contact: Suzanne Dees

Macomb Library for the Blind & Physically
Handicapped
16480 Hall Rd.
Mt. Clemens, MI 48044-3198
Phone: (313)286-1580
FAX: (313)286-0634
TDD: (313)286-9940
Contact: Linda Champion

Muskegon County Library for the Blind &
Physically Handicapped
635 Ottawa St.
Muskegon, MI 49442
Phone: (616)724-6257
FAX: (616)724-6675
Contact: Linda G. Clapp

Blue Water Library Federation
Blind & Physically Handicapped Library
210 McMorran Blvd.
Port Huron, MI 48060
Phone: (313)982-3600
FAX: (313)987-7327
Contact: Debra Oyler

Grand Traverse Area Library for the Blind
and Physically Handicapped
322 6th St.
Traverse City, MI 49684
Phone: (616)922-4824
FAX: (616)922-4836
TDD: (616)922-4843
Contact: Carol Hubbell

Minnesota

Minnesota Library for the Blind & Physically
Handicapped
Academy for the Blind
Faribault, MN 55021
Phone: (507)332-3279
Toll-free: 800-722-0550
Contact: Myrna Wright

Mississippi

Mississippi Library Commission
Handicapped Services
5455 Executive Place
Jackson, MS 39206
Phone: (601)354-7208
Toll-free: 800-446-0892
FAX: (601)354-6077
Contact: Patricia H. Beard

Missouri

Wolfner Library for the Blind & Physically
Handicapped
PO Box 387
Jefferson City, MO 65102-0387
Phone: (314)751-8720
Toll-free: 800-392-2614
FAX: (314)751-3612
Contact: Elizabeth Eckles

Montana

Montana State Library
Library for the Blind & Physically
Handicapped
1515 E. 6th Ave.
Helena, MT 59620
Phone: (406)444-2064
Toll-free: 800-332-3400
FAX: (406)444-5612
Contact: Sandra Jarvie

Nebraska

Nebraska Library Commission
Library for the Blind & Physically
Handicapped
1420 P St.
Lincoln, NE 68508
Phone: (402)471-2045
Toll-free: 800-742-7691
FAX: (402)471-2083
TDD: (402)471-4038
Contact: David Oertli

North Platte Public Library
Blind & Physically Handicapped Program
120 W. 4th St.
North Platte, NE 69101-3993
Phone: (308)535-8039
Contact: Brenda Behsman

Nevada

Nevada State Library and Archives
Talking Book Program
Capitol Complex
Carson City, NV 89710
Phone: (702)687-5154
Toll-free: 800-922-2880
FAX: (702)887-2630
TDD: (702)687-5160
Contact: Mrs. Leslie M. Peterson

Las Vegas-Clark County Library District
Special Services
1401 E. Flamingo Rd.
Las Vegas, NV 89119
Phone: (702)798-5322.
Contact: Darrell Batson

New Hampshire

New Hampshire State Library
Division of Library Services to the
    Handicapped
17 S. Fruit St.
Concord, NH 03301
Phone: (603)271-3429
Toll-free: 800-592-0300
Contact: Eileen Keim

New Jersey

New Jersey Library for the Blind &
    Handicapped
CN 501
Trenton, NJ 08625-0501
Phone: (609)292-6450
Toll-free: 800-792-8322
TDD: (609)633-7250
Contact: Marya Hunsicker

New Mexico

New Mexico State Library
Talking Book Library
325 Don Gaspar
Santa Fe, NM 87503
Phone: (505)827-3830
Toll-free: 800-432-5515
FAX: (505)827-5515
Contact: Alison P. Glen

New York

New York State Library for the Blind &
    Visually Handicapped
Cultural Education Center
Empire State Plaza
Albany, NY 12230
Phone: (518)474-5935
Toll-free: 800-342-3688
FAX: (518)474-5786
TDD: (518)474-7121
Contact: Jane Somers
This regional library serves the entire state of
    New York except New York City and Long
    Island. The toll-free telephone number for
    state residents is (800)342-3111.

New York Public Library
Andrew Heiskell Library for the Blind &
    Physically Handicapped
40 W. 20th St.
New York, NY 10011
Phone: (212)206-5400
FAX: (212)941-6148
Contact: Barbara Nugent
This regional library serves only New York
    City and Long Island.

Suffolk Cooperative Library System
Talking Books Plus/Outreach Services
627 N. Sunrise Service Rd.
Bellport, NY 11713
Phone: (516)286-1600
FAX: (516)286-1647
TDD: (516)286-4546
Contact: Julie Klauber

Nassau Library System
Talking Books
900 Jerusalem Ave.
Uniondale, NY 11553
Phone: (516)292-8920
FAX: (516)481-4777
TDD: (516)579-8585
Contact: Dorothy Puryear

North Carolina

State Library of North Carolina
North Carolina Library for the Blind &
    Physically Handicapped
Department of Cultural Resources
1811 Capital Blvd.
Raleigh, NC 27635
Phone: (919)733-4376
Toll-free: 800-662-7726
Contact: Charles H. Fox

North Dakota

Served by South Dakota State Library for the
    Handicapped

Ohio

Public Library of Cincinnati and Hamilton
    County
800 Vine St.
Library Square
Cincinnati, OH 45202-2071
Phone: (513)369-6074; (513)369-6075
Toll-free: 800-582-0335
TDD: (513)369-6072
Contact: Donna Faust
This regional library serves southern Ohio.

Cleveland Public Library
Library for the Blind & Physically
    Handicapped
325 Superior Ave.
Cleveland, OH 44114-1271
Phone: (216)623-2911
Toll-free: 800-362-1262
FAX: (216)623-7036
TDD: (216)623-7116
Contact: Barbara T. Mates
This regional library serves northern Ohio.

Oklahoma

Oklahoma Library for the Blind & Physically
    Handicapped
300 N.E. 18th St.
Oklahoma City, OK 73125
Phone: (405)521-3514; (405)521-3833
Toll-free: 800-523-0288
Contact: Gerri Beeson

Tulsa City-County Library System
Special Services
1520 N. Hartford
Tulsa, OK 74106
Phone: (918)596-7922; (918)596-7920
FAX: (918)596-7283
TDD: (918)596-7965
Contact: Ellen Ontko

Oregon

Oregon State Library
Talking Book and Braille Services
State Library Bldg.
Salem, OR 97310-0645
Phone: (503)378-3849
Toll-free: 800-452-0292
FAX: (503)588-7119
Contact: Nancy Stewart
The toll-free telephone number for Portland
    residents is 800-224-0610.

Pennsylvania

Free Library of Philadelphia
Library for the Blind & Physically
    Handicapped
919 Walnut St.
Philadelphia, PA 19107
Phone: (215)925-3213
Toll-free: 800-222-1754
FAX: (215)928-0856
Contact: Vickie Lang Collins
This regional library serves eastern
    Pennsylvania.

Carnegie Library of Pittsburgh
Library for the Blind & Physically
    Handicapped
4724 Baum Blvd.
Pittsburgh, PA 15213
Phone: (412)687-2440
Toll-free: 800-242-0586
FAX: (412)687-2442
Contact: Sue O. Murdock
This regional library serves western
    Pennsylvania.

Puerto Rico

Puerto Rico Regional Library for the Blind &
    Physically Handicapped
520 Ponce de Leon Ave.
San Juan, PR 00901
Phone: (809)723-2519
Toll-free: 800-462-8008
FAX: (809)754-0843
Contact: Irving Figueroa

Rhode Island

Rhode Island Department of State
Library Services
Regional Library for the Blind and Physically
    Handicapped
300 Richmond St.
Providence, RI 02903-4222
Phone: (401)277-2726
Toll-free: 800-662-5141
FAX: 800-662-5141
TDD: (401)277-2726
Contact: Beth Perry

South Carolina

South Carolina State Library
Department for the Blind & Physically
    Handicapped
301 Gervais St.
PO Box 821
Columbia, SC 29202
Phone: (803)737-9970
Toll-free: 800-922-7818
FAX: (803)731-8676
Contact: Frances K. Case

South Dakota

South Dakota State Library for the
    Handicapped
State Library Bldg.
800 Governors Dr.
Pierre, SD 57501-2294
Phone: (605)773-3514
Toll-free: 800-592-1841
FAX: (605)773-4950
TDD: (605)773-4914
Contact: Daniel W. Boyd
This regional library also serves North
    Dakota. Alternate phone number for North
    Dakota residents is (701)781-2604. The toll-
    free telephone number for North Dakota
    residents is 800-843-7927.

Tennessee

Tennessee State Library & Archives
Tennessee Library for the Blind & Physically
  Handicapped
403 7th Ave., N.
Nashville, TN 37243-0313
Phone: (615)741-3915
Toll-free: 800-342-3308
TDD: 800-342-3262
Contact: Miss Francis H. Ezell

Texas

Texas State Library
Division for the Blind & Physically
  Handicapped
PO Box 12927
Austin, TX 78711
Phone: (512)463-5458
Toll-free: 800-252-9605
TDD: (512)463-5449
Contact: Mr. Dale Propp

Utah

Utah State Library Commission
Division for the Blind & Physically
  Handicapped
2150 S. 300 W., Ste. 16
Salt Lake City, UT 84115
Phone: (801)466-6363
Toll-free: 800-662-5540
FAX: (801)533-4657
Contact: Gerald A. Buttars
This regional library also serves Wyoming.
  The toll-free telephone number for residents
  in Wyoming and other western states is
  (800)453-4293.

Vermont

Vermont Department of Libraries
Special Services Unit
Box 1870, RD No. 4
Montpelier, VT 05602
Phone: (802)828-3273
Toll-free: 800-479-1711
FAX: (802)828-2199
Contact: Dewey Patterson

Virgin Islands

Virgin Islands Regional Library for the Blind
  & Physically Handicapped
3012 Golden Rock
Christiansted
St. Croix, VI 00840
Phone: (809)772-2250
Contact: Larry Greco

Virginia

Virginia State Library for the Visually &
  Physically Handicapped
1901 Roane St.
Richmond, VA 23222-4898
Phone: (804)786-8016
Toll-free: 800-552-7015
FAX: (804)371-6146
TDD: (804)786-8863
Contact: Mary Ruth Halapatz

Alexandria Library
Talking Book Service
862 Slaters Ln.
Alexandria, VA 22314
Phone: (703)838-4298
TDD: (703)838-4568
Contact: Patricia Bates

Fairfax County Public Library
Special Services
6209 Rose Hill Dr.
Alexandria, VA 22310
Phone: (703)971-0030
TDD: (703)971-6612
Contact: Jeanette A. Studley

Arlington County Department of Libraries
Talking Book Service
1015 N. Quincy St.
Arlington, VA 22201
Phone: (703)358-7125
FAX: (703)358-4454
TDD: (703)358-6320
Contact: Roxanne Barnes

Central Rappahannock Regional Library
Fredericksburg Area Subregional Library
1201 Caroline St.
Fredericksburg, VA 22401
Phone: (703)372-1144
Toll-free: 800-628-4807
FAX: (703)373-9411
TDD: (703)372-1144
Contact: Nancy Schiff

Hampton Subregional Library for the Blind &
  Physically Handicapped
4207 Victoria Blvd.
Hampton, VA 23669
Phone: (804)727-1900
FAX: (804)727-1152
TDD: (804)727-4900
Contact: Mary Sue Newman

Newport News Public Library System
Library for the Blind & Physically
  Handicapped
112 Main St.
Newport News, VA 23601
Phone: (804)591-7418; (804)886-2828
FAX: (804)591-7465
TDD: (804)591-7418
Contact: Julie M. Hewin

Roanoke City Public Library
Outreach/Extension Services
706 S. Jefferson St.
Roanoke, VA 24016
Phone: (703)981-2921
Contact: Rebecca Cooper

Staunton Public Library
Talking Book Center
19 S. Market St.
Staunton, VA 24401
Phone: (703)885-6215
Contact: Mr. Oakley Pearson

Virginia Beach Public Library
Special Services Division
930 Independence Blvd.
Virginia Beach, VA 23455
Phone: (804)464-9175
FAX: (804)464-6741
TDD: (804)464-9136
Contact: Arleen Wicher

Washington

Washington Library for the Blind &
  Physically Handicapped
821 Lenora St.
Seattle, WA 98129
Phone: (206)464-6930
Toll-free: 800-542-0866
FAX: (206)464-0247
TDD: (206)464-6930
Contact: Ms. Jan Ames

West Virginia

West Virginia Library Commission
Services for the Blind & Physically
  Handicapped
Science & Culture Center
Greenbrier & Washington Sts.
Charleston, WV 25305
Phone: (304)348-4061
FAX: (304)348-2044
Contact: Donna Calvert

Kanawha County Public Library
Services for the Blind & Physically
  Handicapped
123 Capitol St.
Charleston, WV 25301
Phone: (304)343-4646
Toll-free: 800-642-8674
Contact: Mary Penn

Cabell County Public Library
Services for the Blind & Physically
  Handicapped
455 9th St. Plaza
Huntington, WV 25701
Phone: (304)523-9451
FAX: (304)522-4721
Contact: Suzanne L. Coldiron

Parkersburg & Wood County Public Library
Services for the Blind & Physically
  Handicapped
3100 Emerson Ave.
Parkersburg, WV 26104-2414
Phone: (304)485-6564
FAX: (304)485-6580
Contact: Mike Hickman

West Virginia School for the Blind
301 E. Main St.
Romney, WV 26757
Phone: (304)822-3521
Contact: Donna See

Ohio County Public Library
Services for the Blind & Physically
  Handicapped
52 16th St.
Wheeling, WV 26003-3696
Phone: (304)232-0244
Contact: Eleanor Gibson

Wisconsin

Wisconsin Regional Library for the Blind &
  Physically Handicapped
813 W. Wells St.
Milwaukee, WI 53233-1404
Phone: (414)278-3040
Toll-free: 800-242-8822
FAX: (414)278-2137
TDD: (414)278-3062
Contact: Marsha Valance

Wyoming

Served by Utah State Library Commission -
  Division for the Blind & Physically
  Handicapped

Appendixes

Appendix C

Patent and Trademark Depository Libraries

The libraries listed below have been designated as Patent and Trademark Depository Libraries (PTDLs) by the U.S. Patent and Trademark Office. They all receive current issues of U.S. Patents and maintain collections of earlier-issued patents as well as trademarks published for opposition. The scope of these patent and trademark collections varies from library to library, ranging from patents and trademarks of only recent years to all or most patents issued since 1790 and trademarks published since 1872.

The patent and trademark collections, organized in number sequence, are available to the public free of charge. Each of the PTLDs in addition, offers supplemental reference publications of the U.S. Patent Classification System, including the *Manual of Classification*, *Index to the U.S. Patent Classification*, and *Classification Definitions*, and provides technical staff assistance to aid individuals in gaining effective access to information contained in patents and trademarks. CASSIS (Classification And Search Support Information System) and other CD-ROM products for searching patent and trademark information are available at all PTDLs.

Since there are variations in the scope of patent and trademark collections and in their hours of service to the public, it is advisable to contact the particular library in advance to ensure that a meaningful search can be conducted.

Alabama

Auburn University Libraries
Science and Technology Department
Auburn University, AL 36849-5606
Phone: (205)844-1747

Birmingham Public Library
Government Documents Department
2100 Park Place
Birmingham, AL 35203
Phone: (205)226-3680

Alaska

Anchorage Municipal Libraries
Z.J. Loussac Public Library
Reference Services
3600 Denali St.
Anchorage, AK 99503-6903
Phone: (907)261-2916

Arizona

Arizona State University
Daniel E. Noble Science and Engineering
  Library
Tempe, AZ 85287
Phone: (602)965-7010

Arkansas

Arkansas State Library
State Library Services
1 Capitol Mall
Little Rock, AR 72201-1081
Phone: (501)682-2053

California

Los Angeles Public Library
Science, Technology and Patents
630 W. Fifth St.
Los Angeles, CA 90071-2097
Phone: (213)612-3273

California State Library
Government Publications Section
Library-Courts Bldg.
P.O. Box 942837
Sacramento, CA 94237-0001
Phone: (916)654-0069

San Diego Public Library
Science Section
820 E St.
San Diego, CA 92101
Phone: (619)236-5813

Sunnyvale Patent Clearinghouse
1500 Partridge Ave., Bldg. 7
Sunnyvale, CA 94087
Phone: (408)730-7290

Colorado

Denver Public Library
Business, Science and Government
  Publications Department
1357 Broadway
Denver, CO 80203
Phone: (303)640-8874

Connecticut

Patent Library
25 Science Park
New Haven, CT 06511
Phone: (203)786-5447

Delaware

University of Delaware Library
Reference Department
Newark, DE 19717-5267
Phone: (302)451-2965

District of Columbia

Howard University
Undergraduate Library
500 Howard Place, N.W.
Washington, DC 20059
Phone: (202)806-7252

Florida

Broward County Main Library
Government Documents Department
100 S. Andrews Ave.
Fort Lauderdale, FL 33301
Phone: (305)357-7444

Miami-Dade Public Library
Business and Science Department
101 W. Flagler St.
Miami, FL 33130-2585
Phone: (305)375-2665

University of Central Florida Library
Reference Department
P.O. Box 25,000
Orlando, FL 32816-0666
Phone: (407)823-2562

University of South Florida Library
Patent Library
4202 E. Fowler Ave.
Tampa, FL 33620-5400
Phone: (813)974-2726

Georgia

Georgia Institute of Technology
Price Gilbert Memorial Library
Department of Microforms
Atlanta, GA 30332-0900
Phone: (404)894-4508

Hawaii

Hawaii State Public Library System
Federal Documents Section
478 S. King St.
Honolulu, HI 96813
Phone: (808)586-3477

Idaho

University of Idaho
Library
Moscow, ID 83843
Phone: (208)885-6235

Illinois

Chicago Public Library
Business/Science/Technology Division
Science and Technology Information Center
400 S. State St., 35-12
Chicago, IL 60605
Phone: (312)747-4450

Illinois State Library
Reference Department
300 S. 2nd St.
Springfield, IL 62701-1796
Phone: (217)782-5659

Indiana

Indianapolis-Marion County Public Library
Business, Science and Technology Division
P.O. Box 211
Indianapolis, IN 46206
Phone: (317)269-1741

Purdue University
Siegesmund Engineering Library
Potter Center
West Lafayette, IN 47907
Phone: (317)494-2873

Iowa

State Library of Iowa
Information Services and Patent Depository
E. 12th & Grand
Des Moines, IA 50319
Phone: (515)281-4118

Kansas

Wichita State University
Ablah Library
Government Documents
Campus Box 68
Wichita, KS 67208-1595
Phone: (316)689-3155

Kentucky

Louisville Free Public Library
Reference and Adult Services
301 York St.
Louisville, KY 40203-2257
Phone: (502)561-8617

Louisiana

Louisiana State Library
Troy H. Middleton Library
Business Administration/Government
  Documents Department
Baton Rouge, LA 70803
Phone: (504)388-2570

Maryland

University of Maryland, College Park
  Libraries
Engineering and Physical Sciences Library
Reference Services
College Park, MD 20742
Phone: (301)405-9157

Massachusetts

University of Massachusetts, Amherst
Physical Sciences Library
Graduate Research Center
Amherst, MA 01003
Phone: (413)545-1370

Boston Public Library
P.O. Box 286
Boston, MA 02117
Phone: (617)536-5400

Michigan

University of Michigan
Engineering-Transportation Library
312 UGL
Ann Arbor, MI 48109-1185
Phone: (313)764-7494

Ferris State University
Abigail S. Timme Library
901 S. State St.
Big Rapids, MI 49307

Detroit Public Library
Technology and Science Department
5201 Woodward Ave.
Detroit, MI 48202
Phone: (313)833-1450

Minnesota

Minneapolis Public Library and Information
  Center
Technology and Science Department
300 Nicollet Mall
Minneapolis, MN 55401
Phone: (612)372-6570

Mississippi

Mississippi Library Commission
P.O. Box 10700
Jackson, MS 39289-0700
Phone: (601)359-1036

Missouri

Linda Hall Library
Reference Department
5109 Cherry St.
Kansas City, MO 64110
Phone: (816)363-4600

St. Louis Public Library
Applied Sciences Department
1301 Olive St.
St. Louis, MO 63103
Phone: (314)241-2288

Montana

Montana College of Mineral Science and
  Technology Library
Patent Center
Butte, MT 59701
Phone: (406)496-4281

Nebraska

University of Nebraska, Lincoln
Engineering Library
Nebraska Hall, 2nd Fl., W.
Lincoln, NE 68588-0516
Phone: (402)472-3411

Nevada

University of Nevada, Reno
University Library
Government Publications Department
Reno, NV 89557-0044
Phone: (702)784-6579

New Hampshire

University of New Hampshire
University Library
Patent Collection
Durham, NH 03824
Phone: (603)862-1777

New Jersey

Newark Public Library
Social Sciences, Sciences, and U.S.
  Government Publications Division
5 Washington St.
P.O. Box 630
Newark, NJ 07101
Phone: (201)733-7782

Rutgers University
Library of Science and Medicine
Government Documents Department
P.O. Box 1029
Piscataway, NJ 08855-1029
Phone: (903)932-2895

New Mexico

University of New Mexico
Centennial Science and Engineering Library
Albuquerque, NM 87131-1466
Phone: (505)277-4412

New York

New York State Library
Reference Services
Cultural Education Center
Albany, NY 12230
Phone: (518)473-4636

Buffalo and Erie County Public Library
Science and Technology Department
Lafayette Square
Buffalo, NY 14203
Phone: (716)858-7101

New York Public Library Annex
Patents Collection
521 W. 43rd St.
New York, NY 10036-4396
Phone: (212)714-8529

North Carolina

North Carolina State University
D.H. Hill Library
Documents Department
Box 7111
Raleigh, NC 27695-7111
Phone: (919)515-3280

North Dakota

University of North Dakota
Chester Fritz Library
University Sta.
Grand Forks, ND 58202
Phone: (701)777-4888

Ohio

Public Library of Cincinnati and Hamilton
County
Science and Technology Department
800 Vine St.
Cincinnati, OH 45202-2071
Phone: (513)369-6936

Cleveland Public Library
Documents Collection
325 Superior Ave.
Cleveland, OH 44114-1271
Phone: (216)623-2870

Ohio State University Libraries
Information Services Department
1858 Neil Ave. Mall
Columbus, OH 43210
Phone: (614)292-6175

Toledo-Lucas County Public Library
Science/Technology Department
325 Michigan St.
Toledo, OH 43624
Phone: (419)259-5212

Oklahoma

Oklahoma State University
Edmon Low Library
Stillwater, OK 74078-0375
Phone: (405)744-7086

Oregon

Oregon State Library
Documents Section
State Library Bldg.
Salem, OR 97310
Phone: (503)378-4239

Pennsylvania

Free Library of Philadelphia
Government Publications Department
Logan Square
Philadelphia, PA 19103
Phone: (215)686-5331

Carnegie Library of Pittsburgh
Science & Technology Department
4400 Forbes Ave.
Pittsburgh, PA 15213
Phone: (412)622-3138

Pennsylvania State University Libraries
Documents Section
C207 Pattee Library
University Park, PA 16802
Phone: (814)865-4861

Rhode Island

Providence Public Library
Business/Industry/Science/Patent Department
225 Washington St.
Providence, RI 02903
Phone: (401)455-8027

South Carolina

Medical University of South Carolina
Library
171 Ashley Ave.
Charleston, SC 29425
Phone: (803)792-2372

Tennessee

Memphis and Shelby County Public Library
and Information Center
Business/Science Department
1850 Peabody Ave.
Memphis, TN 38104
Phone: (901)725-8877

Vanderbilt University
Stevenson Science Library
419 21st Ave., S.
Nashville, TN 37240-0007
Phone: (615)322-2775

Texas

University of Texas, Austin
McKinney Engineering Library
Rm. 1.3 ECJ
Austin, TX 78712
Phone: (512)495-4500

Texas A&M University
Sterling C. Evans Library
Documents Division
MS 5000
College Station, TX 77843-5000
Phone: (409)845-2551

Dallas Public Library
Government Publications Division
1515 Young St.
Dallas, TX 75201
Phone: (214)670-1468

Rice University
Fondren Library
Division of Government Publications and
Special Resources
Houston, TX 77251-1892
Phone: (713)527-8101

Utah

University of Utah
Marriott Library
Salt Lake City, UT 84112
Phone: (801)581-8394

Virginia

Virginia Commonwealth University
Documents and Interlibrary Loan
901 Park Ave.
Box 2033
Richmond, VA 23284-2033
Phone: (804)367-1104

Washington

University of Washington
Engineering Library, FH-15
Seattle, WA 98195
Phone: (206)543-0740

West Virginia

West Virginia University
Evansdale Library
PO Box 6105
Morgantown, WV 26506-6105
Phone: (304)293-4510

Wisconsin

University of Wisconsin, Madison
Kurt F. Wendt Library
215 N. Randall Ave.
Madison, WI 53706
Phone: (608)262-6845

Milwaukee Public Library
Science, Business, and Technology
Department
814 W. Wisconsin Ave.
Milwaukee, WI 53233
Phone: (414)278-3247

Appendix D

Regional Government Depository Libraries

Free information on a broad range of subjects is available from the federal government to the general public through the U.S. Government Printing Office Depository Library Program. Fifty-one regional depositories receive every unclassified government publication of interest to the public, and have undertaken the responsibility of retaining this material permanently, in paper or microfiche format. Interlibrary loan and reference services are also provided. A listing of regional depositories with their addresses and the telephone numbers follows.

Alabama

Auburn University
Montgomery Library
Documents Department
Montgomery, AL 36117-3650
Phone: (205)244-3650

University of Alabama
Amelia Gayle Gorgas Library
Box 870266
Tuscaloosa, AL 35487-0266
Phone: (205)348-6046

Alaska

Served by Washington State Library -
Document Section

American Samoa

Served by University of Hawaii - Hamilton
Library - Government Documents
Collection

Arizona

Arizona State Department of Library,
Archives, and Public Records
State Capitol, 3rd Fl.
1700 W. Washington
Phoenix, AZ 85007
Phone: (602)542-4121

Arkansas

Arkansas State Library
Documents Service Section
One Capitol Mall
Little Rock, AR 72201
Phone: (501)682-2869

California

California State Library
Government Publications Section
914 Capitol Mall
P.O. Box 942837
Sacramento, CA 94237-0001
Phone: (916)322-4572

Colorado

University of Colorado, Boulder
Norlin Library
Government Publications
Campus Box 184
Boulder, CO 80309
Phone: (303)492-8834

Denver Public Library
Government Publications Department
1357 Broadway
Denver, CO 80203
Phone: (303)571-2135

Connecticut

Connecticut State Library
231 Capitol Ave.
Hartford, CT 06106
Phone: (203)566-4971

Delaware

Served by University of Maryland - Hornbake
Library - Government Documents/Maps
Units

District of Columbia

Served by University of Maryland - Hornbake
Library - Government Documents/Maps
Units

Florida

University of Florida Libraries
Documents Department
Library West
Gainesville, FL 32611
Phone: (904)392-0366

Georgia

University of Georgia Libraries
Government Documents Department
Jackson St.
Athens, GA 30602
Phone: (404)542-8949

Hawaii

University of Hawaii
Hamilton Library
Government Documents Collection
2550 The Mall
Honolulu, HI 96822
Phone: (808)948-8230

Idaho

University of Idaho Library
Documents Section
Moscow, ID 83843
Phone: (208)885-6344

Illinois

Illinois State Library
Reference Department
300 S. 2nd St.
Springfield, IL 62701-1796
Phone: (217)782-7596

Indiana

Indiana State Library
Serials Section
140 N. Senate Ave.
Indianapolis, IN 46204
Phone: (317)232-3678

Iowa

University of Iowa Libraries
Government Publications Department
Washington & Madison Sts.
Iowa City, IA 52242
Phone: (319)335-5926

Kansas

University of Kansas
Government Documents & Map Library
6001 Malatt Hall
Lawrence, KS 66045
Phone: (913)864-4660

Kentucky

University of Kentucky Libraries
Government Publications/Maps Department
Lexington, KY 40506-0039
Phone: (606)257-3139

Louisiana

Louisiana State University
Middleton Library
Government Documents Department
Baton Rouge, LA 70803
Phone: (504)388-2570

Louisiana Technical University
Prescott Memorial Library
Government Documents Department
305 Wisteria St.
Ruston, LA 71270-9985
Phone: (318)257-4962

Maine

University of Maine, Orono
Raymond H. Fogler Library
Government Documents & Microforms
   Department
Orono, ME 04469
Phone: (207)581-1680

Maryland

University of Maryland
Hornbake Library
Government Documents/Maps Units
College Park, MD 20742
Phone: (301)405-3034

Massachusetts

Boston Public Library
Government Documents Department
666 Boylston St.
Boston, MA 02117
Phone: (617)536-5400

Michigan

Detroit Public Library
5201 Woodward Ave.
Detroit, MI 48202-4093
Phone: (313)833-1409

Library of Michigan
Government Documents
735 E. Michigan Ave.
P.O. Box 30007
Lansing, MI 48909
Phone: (517)373-0640

Minnesota

University of Minnesota
Wilson Library
Government Publications
309 19th Ave., S.
Minneapolis, MN 55455
Phone: (612)624-5073

Mississippi

University of Mississippi
J.D. Williams Library
Federal Documents Department
106 Old Gym Bldg.
University, MS 38677
Phone: (601)232-5857

Missouri

University of Missouri, Columbia
Ellis Library
Government Documents
Columbia, MO 65201
Phone: (314)882-6733

Montana

University of Montana
Maureen & Mike Mansfield Library
Documents Division
Missoula, MT 59812-1195
Phone: (406)243-6700

Nebraska

University of Nebraska, Lincoln
Love Memorial Library
Documents Department
Lincoln, NE
Phone: (402)472-2562

Nevada

University of Nevada
Reno Library
Government Publications Department
Reno, NV 89557
Phone: (702)784-6579

New Hampshire

Served by University of Maine, Orono -
   Raymond H. Fogler Library - Government
   Documents & Microforms Department

New Jersey

Newark Public Library
U.S. Documents Division
5 Washington St.
P.O. Box 630
Newark, NJ 07101-0630
Phone: (201)733-7812

New Mexico

University of New Mexico
General Library
Government Publications Department
Albuquerque, NM 87131-1466
Phone: (505)277-5441

New Mexico State Library
325 Don Gaspar Ave.
Santa Fe, NM 87503
Phone: (505)827-3826

New York

New York State Library
Documents/Gift & Exchange Section
Cultural Education Center
Empire State Plaza
Albany, NY 12230
Phone: (518)474-4636

North Carolina

University of North Carolina, Chapel Hill
Davis Library 080 A
BA/SS Division Documents
Chapel Hill, NC 27599
Phone: (919)962-1151

North Dakota

North Dakota State University Library
Documents Office
Fargo, ND 58105
Phone: (701)237-8886

Ohio

State Library of Ohio
Documents Department
65 S. Front St.
Columbus, OH 43266
Phone: (614)644-7051

Oklahoma

Oklahoma Department of Libraries
Government Documents
200 N.E. 18th St.
Oklahoma City, OK 73105-3298
Phone: (405)521-2502

Oklahoma State University Library
Edmon Low Library
Documents Department
Stillwater, OK 74078
Phone: (405)744-6546

Oregon

Portland State University
Millar Library
934 S.W. Harrison
P.O. Box 1151
Portland, OR 97207
Phone: (503)725-3673

Pennsylvania

State Library of Pennsylvania
Government Publications Section
Walnut St. & Commonwealth Ave.
Box 1601
Harrisburg, PA 17105
Phone: (717)787-3752

Puerto Rico

Served by University of Florida Libraries -
   Documents Department

Rhode Island

Served by Connecticut State Library

South Carolina

Clemson University
Cooper Library
Public Documents Unit
Clemson, SC 29634-3001
Phone: (803)656-5174

Tennessee

Memphis State University Libraries
Government Documents
Memphis, TN 38152
Phone: (901)678-2586

Texas

Texas State Library
United States Documents
1201 Brazos
P.O. Box 12927
Austin, TX 78711
Phone: (512)463-5455

Texas Tech University Library
Documents Department
Lubbock, TX 79409
Phone: (806)742-2268

Utah

Utah State University
Merrill Library and Learning Resources
   Center, UMC-3000
Documents Department
Logan, UT 84322-3000
Phone: (801)750-2677

Vermont

Served by University of Maine, Orono -
   Raymond H. Fogler Library - Government
   Documents & Microforms Department

Virgin Islands

Served by Louisiana State University -
   Middleton Library - Government
   Documents Department

Virginia

University of Virginia
Alderman Library
Government Documents
Charlottesville, VA 22903-2498
Phone: (804)924-3133

Washington

Washington State Library
Document Section
MS AJ-11
Olympia, WA 98504-0111
Phone: (206)753-4027

West Virginia

West Virginia University Library
Government Documents Section
P.O. Box 6069
Morgantown, WV 26506
Phone: (304)293-3640

Wisconsin

State Historical Society of Wisconsin Library
Government Publications Section
816 State St.
Madison, WI 53706
Phone: (608)262-2781

Milwaukee Public Library
Documents Division
814 W. Wisconsin Ave.
Milwaukee, WI 53233
Phone: (414)278-2167

Wyoming

Wyoming State Library
Supreme Court and State Library Bldg.
Government Publications
Cheyenne,, WY 82002
Phone: (307)777-5920

Appendixes

Appendix E

United Nations Depository Libraries

The following list contains the names of libraries worldwide that house United Nations documents and publications, with international entries appearing after United States entries. The entries are arranged geographically by state or country, and then by city. Within each city, entries are arranged alphabetically according to the name of the parent institution or library. Users are advised to contact the particular library directly to ascertain the extent of its holdings.

UNITED STATES

American Samoa

The Nelson Memorial Public Library
Apia, AS

California

University of California, Berkeley
General Library
Government Documents Department
Berkeley, CA 94720
Phone: (415)642-2568

Los Angeles Public Library
Serials Division
361 S. Anderson St.
Los Angeles, CA 90033

University of California, Los Angeles
University Research Library
Los Angeles, CA 90024
Phone: (213)825-1323

Stanford University Libraries
Jonsson Library of Government Documents
Stanford, CA 94305
Phone: (415)723-2727

Colorado

University of Colorado—Boulder
Government Publications Library
Campus Box 184
Boulder, CO 80309
Phone: (303)492-8834

Connecticut

Yale University Library
Seeley G. Mudd Library
Government Documents Center
Yale Sta., Box 2491
New Haven, CT 06520
Phone: (203)432-3209

District of Columbia

Library of Congress
Serial & Government Publications Division
Washington, DC 20540
Phone: (202)707-5690

United Nations Information Centre
1889 F St., N.W.
Washington, DC 20006
Phone: (202)289-8670

Florida

Nova University
Law Library
College Ave.
Fort Lauderdale, FL 33314
Phone: (305)760-5766

Florida State University Library
Documents-Maps Department
Tallahasse, FL 32306
Phone: (904)644-6061

Hawaii

University of Hawaii
Library
Honolulu, HI 98622
Phone: (808)956-8230

Illinois

Library of International Relations
77 S. Wacker Dr.
Chicago, IL 60606
Phone: (312)567-5014

University of Chicago
Joseph Regenstein Library
Chicago, IL 60637

Northwestern University Library
Documents Department
Evanston, IL 60201
Phone: (708)491-7658

University of Illinois
Education and Social Sciences Library
100 Library
Urbana, IL 61801
Phone: (217)333-2305

Indiana

Indiana University Libraries
Documents Department
Bloomington, IN 47405
Phone: (812)855-6924

Indiana University
School of Law Library
735 W. New York St.
Indianapolis, IN 46202
Phone: (317)274-4028

Iowa

University of Iowa Libraries
Government Publications Department
Iowa City, IA 52242

Kansas

University of Kansas Libraries
International Documents Collection
Lawrence, KS 66045
Phone: (913)864-4662

Kentucky

University of Kentucky
Margaret I. King Library
Government Publications/Map Department
Lexington, KY 40506
Phone: (606)257-3139

Louisiana

Louisiana State University
Troy H. Middleton Library
Business Administration/Government
   Documents Department
Baton Rouge, LA 70803

Maryland

Johns Hopkins University
Milton S. Eisenhower Library
Government Publications Department
Baltimore, MD 21218

Massachusetts

Boston Public Library
Documents Receipts
Boston, MA 02117
Phone: (617)536-5400

Harvard University
Harvard College Library
Documents Receipts
Cambridge, MA 02138
Phone: (617)495-2479

Michigan

University of Michigan
Harlan Hatcher Graduate Library
Documents Center
Ann Arbor, MI 48109-1205
Phone: (313)764-0410

Minnesota

University of Minnesota
Government Publications Library
409 Wilson Library
Minneapolis, MN 55455
Phone: (612)624-5073

Nevada

University of Nevada—Reno
University Library
Government Publications Department
Reno, NV 89557-0044
Phone: (702)784-6579

New Jersey

Princeton University Library
Documents Division
United Nations Collection
Princeton, NJ 08544
Phone: (609)258-3211

New York

Cornell University Libraries
Serials Department
Ithaca, NY 14853

Columbia University
Law School Library
New York, NY 10027
Phone: (212)854-3737

Council on Foreign Relations, Inc.
New York, NY 10021
Phone: (212)734-0400

New York Public Library
Economic and Public Affairs Division
New York, NY 10017
Phone: (212)930-0724

New York University
Elmer Holmes Bobst Library
70 Washington Sq., S.
New York, NY 10003
Phone: (212)998-2610

North Carolina

University of North Carolina at Chapel Hill
Davis Library CB 3912
BA/SS International Documents
Chapel Hill, NC 27599-3912
Phone: (919)962-1151

Ohio

Cleveland Public Library
Serials Division
325 Superior Ave.
Cleveland, OH 44114-1271
Phone: (216)623-2860

Pennsylvania

University of Pennsylvania
Charles Patterson Van Pelt Library
Philadelphia, PA 19104
Phone: (215)898-7555

Puerto Rico

Universidad Catolica de Puerto Rico
Escuela de Derecho
Biblioteca Mons. Juan Fremio Torres Oliver
Ponce, PR 00731

University of Puerto Rico
General Library
Rio Piedras, PR 00931
Phone: (809)764-0000

Rhode Island

Brown University Library
Documents Department
Providence, RI 02912
Phone: (401)863-2167

Tennessee

Vanderbilt University Library
Government Documents
419 21st Ave., S.
Nashville, TN 37203
Phone: (615)322-2838

Texas

University of Texas at Austin
Perry-Castaneda Library
Documents Unit PCL 2.402 D
Austin, TX 78712
Phone: (512)471-5944

Utah

University of Utah
Marriott Library
International Documents Section
Salt Lake City, UT 84112
Phone: (801)581-8394

Virgin Islands

Enid M. Baa Library and Archives
PO Box 390
Charlotte Amalie
St. Thomas, VI 00801

Virginia

University of Virginia
Alderman Library
Government Documents
Charlottesville, VA 22901
Phone: (804)924-3026

Washington

University of Washington Libraries
Government Documents Center
Serials Division
Seattle, WA 98195
Phone: (206)543-1937

INTERNATIONAL

Afghanistan

Kabul University
Library
Kabul, Afghanistan

United Nations Information Centre
Shah Mahmoud Ghazi Watt
PO Box 5
Kabul, Afghanistan

Algeria

Bibliotheque Nationale d'Algerie
Ave. Dr. Frantz Fanon
Algiers, Algeria

Centre d'Information des Nations Unies
19, ave. Chahid El Ouali Mustapha Sayed
B.P. 823
Algiers, Algeria

Argentina

Centro de Informacion de las Naciones Unidas
Junin 1940, ler piso
1113 **Buenos Aires**, Argentina

Congreso de la Nacion
Direccion de Procesos Tecnicos
Biblioteca
Alsina 1859/61/63
1090 **Buenos Aires**, Argentina

Departamento de Documentacion e
 Informacion Internacional
Paseo Colon 533-7o piso
1063 **Buenos Aires**, Argentina

Universidad Nacional de Cordorba
Biblioteca Mayor
Centro de Documentacion
Casilla de Correos 63
5000 **Cordoba**, Argentina

Biblioteca Depositaria de las Naciones Unidas
9 de julio 733, Casilla de Correo 450
8332 **General Roca**, Rio Negro, Argentina

Municipalidad de Gral Pueyrredon
Biblioteca Depositaria de las Naciones Unidas
Olavarria 2508
CP 7600
7600 **Mar del Plata**, Argentina

Universidad Nacional de Cuyo
Biblioteca Central
Casilla de Correo 420
5500 **Mendoza**, Argentina

Biblioteca Argentina "Dr. Juan Alvarez"
Pasage Dr. Juan Alvarez 1550
2000 **Rosario**, Argentina

Australia

Australian Capital Territory

Australian Parliamentary Library
Parliament House
Canberra, Australian Capital Territory
  2600, Australia

National Library of Australia
Gift and Exchange Section (D139/1)
Canberra, Australian Capital Territory
  2600, Australia

New South Wales

State Library of New South Wales
Government Publications
Macquarie St.
Sydney, New South Wales 2000, Australia

United Nations Information Centre
125 York St., Ste. 1
PO Box 4045
Sydney, New South Wales 2001, Australia

Queensland

State Library of Queensland
Serials Unit
Queensland Cultural Centre
Southbank
PO Box 488
South Brisbane, Queensland 4101, Australia

South Australia

The State Library of South Australia
Acquisitions Section
PO Box 415, GPO
Adelaide, South Australia 5001, Australia

Victoria

State Library of Victoria
Government Publications
328 Swanston St.
Melbourne, Victoria 3000, Australia

Western Australia

The Library Board of Western Australia
Alexander Library Bldg.
Perth Cultural Center
Perth, Western Australia 6000, Australia

Austria

Osterreichische Nationalbibliothek
Josefsplatz 1
A-1015 **Vienna**, Austria

United Nations Information Service
Vienna Information Centre
PO Box 500
A-1400 **Vienna**, Austria

Bahrain

Ministry of Education
Directorate of Public Libraries
Manama Public Library
PO Box 43
Manama, Bahrain

United Nations Information Centre
Road 2803, House No. 131
Segaya 328
PO Box 26004
Manama, Bahrain

Bangladesh

Dhaka University
Library
Dhaka 2, Bangladesh

United Nations Information Centre
Road 11, House 25
Dhanmandi
GPO Box 3658
Dhaka 100, Bangladesh

Barbados

University of the West Indies
Cave Hill Campus
Bridgetown, Barbados

Belarus

Gosudarstvennaya Biblioteka BSSR imeni V.I.
  Lenin
Krasnoarmeiskaya 9
30 **Minsk**, Belarus

Belgium

Bibliotheque du Parlement
Palais de la Nation
Rue de la Loi
B-1040 **Brussels**, Belgium

Bibliotheque Royale Albert 1er
Section des Documents Officiels
Blvd. de l'Empereur 4
B-1000 **Brussels**, Belgium

United Nations Information Centre and
  Liaison Office with the EEC
Ave. de Broqueville 40
B-1200 **Brussels**, Belgium

Katholieke Universiteit Leuven
Bibliotheekcentrale
Mgr. Ladeuzeplein 21
B-3000 **Leuven**, Belgium

Centre General de Documentation de
  l'Universite Catholique de Louvain
Place Cardinal Mercier 31
B-1348 **Louvain-la-neuve**, Belgium

Benin

Universite National du Be
Bibliotheque Universitaire
B.P. 526
Cotonou, Benin

Bhutan

Thimpu Public Library
Thimpu P.O.
Thimpu, Bhutan

Bolivia

Centro de Informacion de las Naciones Unidas
Edificio Naciones Unidas
Plaza Isabel la Catolica
Planta Baja
Apdo. 9072
La Paz, Bolivia

Biblioteca Nacional de Bolivia
Espana 25
Sucre, Bolivia

Botswana

National Library of Botswana
Gaborone, Botswana

Brazil

Biblioteca da Camara dos Deputados
Secao de Colecones Especiais
Centro de Documentacao e Informacao
Palacio do Congreso Nacional
70160 **Brasilia**, DF, Brazil

Universidade Federal do Rio Grande do Sul
Faculdade de Dereito
Biblioteca-Depositaria das Nacoes Unidas
Ave. Joao Passoa 6/No
90000 **Porto Alegre**, Rio Grande do Sul,
  Brazil

Biblioteca Nacional do Rio de Janeiro
Ave. Rio Branco 219
20042 **Rio de Janeiro**, RJ, Brazil

Centro de Informacao das Nacoes Unidas
Palacio Itamaraty
Ave. Marechal Floriano 196
20080 **Rio de Janeiro**, RJ, Brazil

Biblioteca Mario de Andrade
Rueda Consolacao 94
C.P. 8170
01302 **Sao Paulo**, SP, Brazil

Brunei Darussalam

Universiti Brunei Darussalam
University Library
Serials Division (United Nations)
Gadong 3186, Brunei Darussalam

Bulgaria

Sofiiski Universitet "Kliment Ohridsky"
Biblioteca
15 Blvd. Ruski
Sofia, Bulgaria

Burkina Faso

United Nations Information Centre
218, rue de la Gare
Secteur No. 3
B.P. 135
Ouagadougou, Burkina Faso

Burundi

Centre d'Information des Nations Unies
Ave. de la Revolution
7 Place de l'Independence
B.P. 2160
Bujumbura, Burundi

Cameroon

Centre d'Information des Nations Unies
Immeuble Kamden, rue Joseph Clere
B.P. 836
Yaounde, Cameroon

Canada

Alberta

University of Alberta
Library
Government Publications
Edmonton, AB, Canada T6G 2J8
Phone: (403)492-3776

British Columbia

University of British Columbia
Main Library
Government Publications
PO Box 2194
Vancouver, BC, Canada V6B 3V7
Phone: (604)228-2584

Manitoba

Manitoba Legislative Library
Manitoba Archives Bldg.
200 Vaughan St., Main Fl., E.
Winnipeg, MB, Canada R3C 1T5
Phone: (204)945-4330

New Brunswick

University of New Brunswick
Harriet Irving Library
Government Documents Department
PO Box 7500
Fredericton, NB, Canada E3B 5H5
Phone: (506)453-4752

Nova Scotia

Dalhousie University Library
Documents Section
Halifax, NS, Canada B3H 4H8
Phone: (902)494-3634

Ontario

Queen's University at Kingston
Documents Library
Mackintosh-Corry Hall
Kingston, ON, Canada K7L 3N6
Phone: (613)545-6313

University of Ottawa
Bibliotheque Morisset
Documents Officiels
65 Hastey St.
Ottawa, ON, Canada K1N 9A5

University of Toronto Library
Government Publications Division
Toronto, ON, Canada M5S 1A5
Phone: (416)978-3931

Quebec

McGill University
McLennan Library
Government Documents Department
3459 McTavish St.
Montreal, PQ, Canada H3A 1Y1

Universite de Montreal
Bibliotheque des Lettres et Sciences
  Humaines
Publications Officielles
C.P. 6128, Succursale A
Montreal, PQ, Canada H3C 3J2
Phone: (514)343-7920

Saskatchewan

University of Saskatchewan
Murray Memorial Library
Saskatoon, SK, Canada S7N 0W0
Phone: (306)966-5986

Chile

Biblioteca Nacional
Officina de Canje y Donaciones
Ave. Bernardo O'Higgins 651
Santiago, Chile

Comision Economica para America Latina y
  el Caribe
Servicio de Informacion de las Naciones
  Unidas
Edificio Naciones Unidas
Ave. Dag Hammarskjold s/n
Casilla 179-D
Santiago, Chile

Unidad de Organismos Internacionales
Hemeroteca-Biblioteca del Congreso Nacional
Huerfanos 1117 2o piso
Santiago, Chile

China, People's Republic of

National Library of Beijing
United Nations Material Section
Beijing 7, People's Republic of China

Chong-Qing Library
Chang Jiang Rd., No. 1
Chong-Qing, People's Republic of China

Shanghai Library
325 Nanjing Rd., W.
Shanghai 200003, People's Republic of China

Colombia

Biblioteca Nacional
Calle 24, No. 5-60
Apdo. aereo No. 27600
Bogota, Colombia

Centro de Informacion de las Naciones Unidas
Calle 27, no. 12-65, piso 2
Apdo. aereo No. 058964
Bogota, Colombia

Universidad del Valle
Departamento de Bibliotecas
Apdo. aereo No. 25360
Cali, Colombia

Congo

Centre d'Information des Nations Unies
Ave. Foch, Case Ortf 15
BP 13210
Brazzaville, Congo

Costa Rica

Universidad Nacional
Escuela de Relaciones Internacionales
Centro de Documentacion "Luis y Felipe
  Molina"
Apdo. 437
Heredia, Costa Rica

Direccion General de Bibliotecas y Biblioteca
  Nacional
Apdo. 10.008-1000
San Jose, Costa Rica

Cote d'Ivoire

Bibliotheque Nationale
Abidjan, Cote d'Ivoire

Cuba

Biblioteca Nacional "Jose Marti"
Plaza de la Revolucion
Havana, Cuba

Cyprus

Ministry of Education
Library
Nicosia, Cyprus

Czechoslovakia

Univerzitna Kniznica
Michalska 1
CS-814 17 **Bratislava**, Czechoslovakia

Universitni Knihovna
Leninovna 5/7
CS-601 87 **Brno**, Czechoslovakia

Knihovna Federalniho Shromazdeni CSSR
Vinahradska 1
CS-110 02 **Prague**, Czechoslovakia

Narodni Knihovna CSR
Klementinum 190
CS-110 01 **Prague** 1, Czechoslovakia

United Nations Information Centre
Panska 5
CS-110 00 **Prague** 1, Czechoslovakia

Denmark

Statsbiblioteket
Section for International Organisations'
  Publications
Universitetsparken
DK-8000 **Aarhus** C, Denmark

Det Kongelige Bibliotek
Kontoret fur Internationale Publikationer
Christian Brygge 8
DK-1219 **Copenhagen** K, Denmark

United Nations Information Centre
37 H.C. Andersens Blvd.
DK-1533 **Copenhagen** V, Denmark

Dominican Republic

Universidad Autonoma de Santo Domingo
Biblioteca Central
Santo Domingo, Dominican Republic

Ecuador

Biblioteca Nacional
Casa de la Cultura Ecuadoriana
12 de Octubre y av Patria
Quito, Ecuador

Egypt

Universite d'Alexandrie
Faculte de Droit d'Alexandrie
Alexandria, Egypt

Dar-el Kutub al-Wataniyah
Bab-el-Khalk
Cairo, Egypt

United Nations Information Centre
Tagher Bldg. (Garden City)
1 Osoris St.
PO Box 262
Cairo, Egypt

El Salvador

Biblioteca Nacional de El Salvador
8a Ave. Norte 228
San Salvador, El Salvador

Centro de Informacion de las Naciones Unidas
Paseo General Escalon y 87 Ave. Norte
Apdo. Postal 2157
San Salvador, El Salvador

England

Birmingham Central Library
Chamberlain Sq.
Birmingham B3 3HQ, England

The University of Sussex
The Institute of Development Studies
The Library
Falmer
Brighton BN1 9RE, England

Cambridge University
Official Publications Department
Library
West Rd.
Cambridge CB3 9DR, England

Liverpool City Libraries
Liverpool L3 8EW, England

The British Library
Reference Division
Department of Printed Books - Overseas
  English Section
London WC1B 3DG, England

London School of Economic and Political
  Science
British Library of Political and Economic
  Science
London WC2A 2AE, England

United Nations Information Centre
20 Buckingham Gate
London SW1E 6LB, England

Manchester Public Libraries
Book Services Department
Central Library
St. Peter's Sq.
Manchester M2 5PD, England

Oxford University
Bodleian Library
Official Papers
Broad St.
Oxford OX1 3BG, England

Ethiopia

Addis Ababa University
Library
Addis Ababa, Ethiopia

United Nations Information Service
Economic Commission for Africa
Africa Hall
PO Box 3001
Addis Ababa, Ethiopia

Fiji

The University of the South Pacific
Gift and Exchange Library
PO Box 1168
Suva, Fiji

Finland

Abo Akademi
Forenta Nationernas Deposatory
Gezeluingatan 2
SF-20500 **Abo** 50, Finland

Eduskunnan Kirjasto
SF-00102 **Helsinki**, Finland

Tampereen Yliopiston Kirjasto
PO Box 617
SF-33101 **Tampere** 10, Finland

France

Fonds des Nations Unies
Bibliotheque Interuniversitaire d'Aix-
  Marseilles
3, ave. Robert Schuman
F-13626 **Aix-en-Provence**, France

Bibliotheque Interuniversitaire de Lyon
Bureau des Nations Unies
18, quai Claude Bernard
BP No. 0619
F-69365 **Lyon** Cedex 07, France

Universite de Nancy
Bibliotheque
Section Central
11, Pl. Carnot
F-54042 **Nancy** Cedex, France

Bibliotheque Interuniversitaire de Cujas
Service des Publications Internationales
2, rue Cujas
F-75005 **Paris**, France

Bibliotheque de l'Assemblee Nationale
Service de la Documentation Etrangere
126, rue de l'Universite
F-75355 **Paris**, France

Bibliotheque Nationale
Departement des Entrees Francaises
Service des Publications Officielles
2, rue Vivienne
F-75084 **Paris** Cedex 02, France

Centre d'Information des Nations Unies
1, rue Miollis
F-75732 **Paris** Cedex 15, France

Fondation Nationale des Sciences Politique
27, rue Saint Guillaume
F-75006 **Paris**, France

Bibliotheque Nationale et Universitaire
Section Droit
5, rue du Marechal Joffre
BP 1029/F
F-67070 **Strasbourg** Cedex, France

Bibliotheque Interuniversitaire de Bordeaux
Droit et Sciences Economiques
Allee Maine de Biran, Domaine Universitaire
F-33405 **Talence**, France

Gabon

Bibliotheque Nationale Gabonaise
B.P. 1188
Libreville, Gabon

Germany

Freie Universitat Berlin
Universitatsbibliothek
W-1000 **Berlin** 33, Germany

Staatsbibliothek Preussischer Kulturbesitz
Abt. Amtsdruckschriften
Umtausch-Internationale Organisationen
Potsdamer Strasse 30
Postfach 1407
W-1000 **Berlin** 30, Germany

Universitatsbibliothek Bochum
Universitatstrasse 150
Postfach 10 21 48
W-4630 **Bochum** 1, Germany

Deutscher Bundestag
Bibliothek
Internationale Organisationen
Bundeshaus
Gorresstrasse 15
W-5300 **Bonn** 12, Germany

HWWA
Institut fur Wirtschaftsforschung-Hamburg
Bibliothek
Neuer Jungfernstieg 21
W-2000 **Hamburg** 36, Germany

Max Planck-Institut fur Auslandisches
Offentliches Recht und Volkerrecht
Berliner Strasse 48
W-6900 **Heidelberg** 1, Germany

Friedrich-Schiller-Universitat
Institut fur Volkerrecht
O-69 **Jena**, Germany

Institut fur Internationales Recht an der
Universitat Kiel
W-2300 **Kiel** 1, Germany

Deutsche Bucherei
Deutscher Platz
O-7010 **Leipzig**, Germany

Bayerische Staatsbibliothek
Munchen
Postfach 34-0150
W-8000 **Munich** 34, Germany

Ghana

Ghana Library Board
Accra, Ghana

United Nations Information Centre
Gamel Abdul Nassar/Liberia Rds.
Roman Ridge Ambassadorial Estate
Extension Area-Plot N78
Accra, Ghana

University of Ghana
Balme Library
PO Box 24
Legon, Ghana

Greece

Bibliotheque de la Chambre des Deputes
Helleniques
Ancien Palais Royal
Athens, Greece

Bibliotheque Nationale
Athens, Greece

United Nations Information Centre
36 Amalia Ave.
GR-10558 **Athens**, Greece

Institute of International Public Law and
International Relations
Megalou Alexandrou 15 and Hadji Sts.
Thessaloniki, Greece

Guatemala

Biblioteca National
5a Avenida, 7-26 Zona 1
Guatemala City, Guatemala

Guinea

Bibliotheque Nationale
Centre National de Documentation
B.P. 516
Conakry, Guinea

Guinea-Bissau

Instituto Nacional de Estudios e Pesquisa
Bibliotheca
Complexo Escolar 14 de Novembro
Biarro Cobornel
C.P. 112
Bissau, Guinea-Bissau

Guyana

University of Guyana
Library
Georgetown, Guyana

Honduras

Universidad Nacional Autonoma
Sistema Bibliotecario de Honduras
Ciudad Universitaria
Tegucigalpa, Honduras

Hong Kong

Urban Council Public Libraries
Kwong Sang Hong Bldg.
296A Hennessy Rd., 1st Fl.
Hong Kong, Hong Kong

Hungary

Orszaggyulesi Konyvtar
Kossuth Lajos ter 1-3
H-1357 **Budapest**, Hungary

Iceland

Landsbokasafn Islands
Reykjavik, Iceland

India

University of Bombay
Jawaharlal Nehru Library
Vidyanagari, Santacruz E.
Bombay 400098, India

National Library of India
Foreign Official Documents Division
Belvedere
Calcutta 700027, India

Panjab University
Department of Laws
Library
Chandigarth, India

University of Delhi
Delhi School of Economics
Ratan Tata Library
Delhi 110007, India

Karnatak University
Library
Pavate Nagar
Dharwad 580003, India

Osmania University
Library
Hyderabad 500007, Andhra Pradesh, India

Connemara Public Library
Madras 600008, India

Indian Council of World Affairs
Library
Sapru House
Barakhamba Rd.
New Delhi 110001, India

Parliament Library
Acquisition Section
Parliament House
New Delhi 110001, India

United Nations Information Centre
55 Lodi Estate
New Delhi 110003, India

Pondicherry University
University Library
R. Ventakaram Nagar
Kalapet
Pondicherry 605104, India

Servants of India Society
Library
Pune 411004, India

Kerala University
Library
Trivandrum 695034, India

Banares Hindu University
Library
Varanasi 221005, Uttar Pradesh, India

Indonesia

Dewan Perwakilan Rakjat Republik Indonesia
Jakarta, Indonesia

National Library of Indonesia
Jalan Salemba Raya 28
PO Box 3624
10002 **Jakarta**, Indonesia

United Nations Information Centre
Gedung Dewan Pers, 5th Fl.
32-34 Jalan Kebon Sirih
Jakarta, Indonesia

Iran

Shiraz University
College of Literature and Human Science
Mirzaye Shirazi
Shiraz, Iran

Center for Graduate International Studies
Faculty of Law and Political Science
Library
Ave. Enghelab
PO Box 41-155-5779
Teheran 14, Iran

Ketab-Khaneh Majlis - e Showraye Eslami
No. 2 Emam Khomeyni Av.
Teheran 13174, Iran

United Nations Information Centre
Ave. Boharest Maydan
Argantine No. 74
PO Box 15875-4557
Teheran, Iran

Iraq

United Nations Information Service
Economic and Social Commission for Western
  Asia
Amiriya, Airport St.
PO Box 27
Baghdad, Iraq

University of Baghdad
Central Library
Waziriya
Baghdad, Iraq

University of Mosul
Central Library
Mosul, Iraq

Ireland

National Library of Ireland
Kildare St.
Dublin, Ireland

Ireland, Northern

Belfast Public Libraries
Central Library
Belfast BT1 EA, Northern Ireland

Israel

The Jewish National and University Library
General Reading Room
United Nations Collection
PO Box 503
91-004 **Jerusalem**, Israel

Italy

Biblioteca Nazionale Centrale
Piazza Cavalleggeri, 1a
I-50122 **Florence**, Italy

Universita Cattolica del Sacro Cuore
Biblioteca-Ufficio Scambi Periodici
Largo Gemelli 1
I-20123 **Milan**, Italy

Universita di Padova
Istituto di Diritto Pubblico
Seminario de Diritto Internazionale
Via VIII Febbraio 2
I-35122 **Padua**, Italy

Bibliotheque de l'Institut International pour
  l'Unification du Droit Prive (UNIDROIT)
Via Panisperna 28
I-00184 **Rome**, Italy

Centro d'Informazione delle Nazione Unite
Palazzetto Venezia
Piazza San Marco 50
Rome, Italy

Societa Italiana per la Organizzazione
  Internazionale
Via San Marco 3
I-00186 **Rome**, Italy

Istituto di Diritto Internazionale e
  Legislazione Comparata
Facolta de Giurisprudenza
Piazzale Europa 1
I-34127 **Triest**, Italy

Jamaica

National Library of Jamaica
12 East St.
PO Box 823
Kingston, Jamaica

University of the West Indies
Library
Mona, Jamaica

Japan

Fukuoka City Public Library
13-1 Chikkohonmachi
Hakata-ku
Fukuoka 812, Japan

Seinan Gakuin University
Library
Fukuoka 814, Japan

Hiroshima Municipal Central Library
United Nations Depository Library
3-1 Motomachi, Nakaku
Hiroshima 730, Japan

Kobe University
Research Institute for Economics and Business
  Administration
Rokkodai-cho, Nada-ku
Kobe, Japan

Kyoto United Nations Depository Library
c/o Ritsumeikan
28 Kami-Hattchoyanagi-cho
Hiramo, Kita-ku
Kyoto 603, Japan

Nihon University
College of International Relations
Library
2-31-145, Bunkyo-cho
Mishima 411, Shizuoka, Japan

Aichi-Ken Kinro-Kaikan
Aichi Prefectural Library
United Nations Depository Library
9-3, Sannomaru 1-chome
Naka-ku
Nagoya 466, Japan

University of Ryukyus
University Library
Nishihara-Chome
Okinawa 903-01, Japan

Hokkaido University
University Library
Kita-Ru, N.9, W.7
Sapporo, Japan

Tohoku University
Library
United Nations Depository Library
75 Katahira-cho
Kawauchi
Sendai-Shi 980, Japan

National Diet Library
1-10-1 Nagata-cho, Chiyoda-ku
Tokyo 100, Japan

United Nations Information Centre
Shin Aoyama Bldg. Nishikan, 22nd Fl.
1-1 Minami Aoyama 1-chome
Minato-ku
Tokyo 107, Japan

University of Tokyo
Library
United Nations Depository Library
Hongo 7-Chome, Bunkyo-Ku
Tokyo 113, Japan

Jordan

University of Jordan
Library
Amman, Jordan

Kenya

United Nations Information Centre
United Nations Office
Gigiri
PO Box 34135
Nairobi, Kenya

University of Nairobi
Library
PO Box 30197
Nairobi, Kenya

Korea, Republic of

Korea University
Library
1 Anam-dong
Seoul 132-00, Republic of Korea

National Assembly Library
Acquisition and Exchange Division
Yoi-dong 1, Yeongdeungpo-gu
Seoul, Republic of Korea

Kuwait

Kuwait University
United Nations Publications Library
PO Box 5486
Kuwait, Kuwait

Ministry of Foreign Affairs
The Library
Kuwait, Kuwait

Lebanon

United Nations Information Centre
Fakhoury Bldg.
Montee Bain Militaire
Ardati St.
PO Box 4656
Beirut, Lebanon

Lesotho

United Nations Information Centre
Corner Kingsway and Hilton Rds.
Opposite Sanlam Centre
PO Box 301
Maseru 100, Lesotho

National University of Lesotho
Library
Roma 180, Lesotho

Liberia

United Nations Information Centre
LBDI Bldg.
Tubman Blvd.
PO Box 274
Monrovia, Liberia

University of Liberia
Libraries
Monrovia, Liberia

Libyan Arab Jamahiriya

Garyounis University
Central Library Administration
PO Box 1308
Benghazi, Libyan Arab Jamahiriya

Central Bank of Libya
Economic Research Library
King Saud St.
Tripoli, Libyan Arab Jamahiriya

United Nations Information Centre
Muzzafar Al Aftas
Hay El-Andalous 2
PO Box 286
Tripoli, Libyan Arab Jamahiriya

Lithuania

Vilnaius Valstybinis V. Kapsuko vardo
Universitetas
Moksline Biblioteka
232633 **Vilnius**, Lithuania

Luxembourg

Bibliotheque Nationale
37, blvd. F.D. Roosevelt
Luxembourg, Luxembourg

Madagascar

Bibliotheque Universitaire
Antananarivo, Madagascar

Centre d'Information des Nations Unies
22, rue Rainitovo
Antsahavola
B.P. 1348
Antananarivo, Madagascar

Malawi

University of Malawi
Libraries
PO Box 280
Zomba, Malawi

Malaysia

National Library of Malaysia
Legal Deposit, Gifts and Exchange Division
Lot No. G1 E G2, Ground Fl.
Block A, Bukit Naga Complex
Off Jalan Semantan
Damansara Heights
50572 **Kuala Lumpur**, Malaysia

Malta

National Library of Malta
36, Old Treasury St.
Valletta, Malta

Mauritius

The University of Mauritius
Library
Reduit, Mauritius

Mexico

Centro de Informacion de las Naciones Unidas
Presidente Mazaryk No. 29, 7 piso
11570 **Mexico City**, DF, Mexico

Hemeroteca Nacional
Centro Cultural Universitario
Delegacion Coyoacan
Apdo. Postal 22-1999
04510 **Mexico City**, DF, Mexico

Universidad Autonoma de Nuevo Leon
Faculdad de Economia
Biblioteca "Consuelo Meyer L."
Apdo. Postal 288
Monterrey, Nuevo Leon, Mexico

Universidad Veracruzana
Instituto de Investigaciones y Estudios
Superiores Economicos y Sociales
20 de Noviembre Oriente No. 375
Apdo. Postal 67
91030 **Xalapa**, Chiapas, Mexico

Mongolia

Gosudarstvennaia Publichnaia Biblioteka
MNR
Ulan-Bator, Mongolia

Morocco

United Nations Information Centre
Angle Charia Ibnouzaid et Zankat Roundanat
No. 6
B.P. 601
Rabat, Morocco

Universite Mohamed V
Faculte des Sciences Juridiques, Economiques
et Sociales
Blvd. des Nations Unies
Rabat-Agdal, Morocco

Myanmar

National Library
Municipal Bldg., 2nd Fl.
Yangon, Myanmar

United Nations Information Centre
6 Natmauk Rd.
PO Box 230
Yangon, Myanmar

Nepal

Tribhuvan University
Library
Kirtipur
Kathmandu, Nepal

United Nations Information Center
PO Box 107
Pulchowk
Kathmandu, Nepal

Netherlands

Universiteit van Amsterdam
Seminarium voor Volkenrecht en
Internationale Betrekkingen
Bibliotheek Verenigde Naties Doc.
PO Box 19120
NL-1000 GC **Amsterdam**, Netherlands

Bibliotheek der Rijksuniversiteit te Groning
Oude Kijk in 't Jatstraat 5
Postbus 559
NL-9700 AN **Groningen**, Netherlands

Koninklijke
Koninklijke Bibliotheek
Prins Willem Alexanderhof 5
NL-2595 BE **The Hague**, Netherlands

Bibliotheek Rijksuniversiteit Leiden
Tijdschriftenafdeling
PO Box 9501
NL-2300 RA **Leiden**, Netherlands

Katholieke Universiteit
Universiteitsbibliotheek
Erasmuslaan 36
NL-6525 GG **Nijmegen**, Netherlands

New Zealand

Auckland Public Libraries
Documents Library
PO Box 4138
Auckland 1, New Zealand

General Assembly Library
Parliament House
Wellington 1, New Zealand

Victoria University of Wellington
The Library (Periodicals)
United Nations Collection
Private Bag
Wellington, New Zealand

Nicaragua

Biblioteca Nacional
Managua, Nicaragua

Centro de Informacion de las Naciones Unidas
de Plaza Espana
2 Cuadras Abajo, Bolonia
PO Box 3260
Managua, Nicaragua

Niger

Ecole Nationale d'Administration de Niamey
Niamey, Niger

Nigeria

University of Ife
Library
Ife-Ife, Nigeria

National Library of Nigeria
P.M.B. 12626
Lagos, Nigeria

United Nations Information Centre
17 Kingsway Rd., Ikoyi
PO Box 1068
Lagos, Nigeria

University of Nigeria
Nnamdi Azikiwe Library
Nsukka, Nigeria

University of Port Harcourt
P.M.B. 5323
Port Harcourt, Nigeria

Ahmadu Bello University
Kashim Ibrahim Library
Zaria, Nigeria

Norway

Universitetsbiblioteket i Bergen
N-5000 **Bergen**, Norway

Nobelinstituttet
Biblioteket
Drammensveien 19
N-0255 **Oslo** 2, Norway

Universitet Biblioteket
Erling Skakkes GT 47c
N-7000 **Trondheim**, Norway

Pakistan

National Assembly
Library
Ramna-5
Islamabad, Pakistan

Quaid-I-Azam University
Central Library
PO Box 1090
Islamabad, Pakistan

United Nations Information Centre
House No. 26
88th St., Ramna 6/3
PO Box 1107
Islamabad, Pakistan

University of Sind
Central Library
Jamshoro, Pakistan

Karachi University
Dr. Mahmud Husain Library
Karachi 32, Pakistan

Punjab University
Library
1, Shari Al-Biruni
Lahore 2/12, Pakistan

University of Peshawar
Library
Peshawar 1, Pakistan

Panama

Biblioteca Nacional
Panama City, Panama

Centro de Informacion de las Naciones Unidas
Urbanizacion Obarrio
Calle 54 y Ave. Tercesa Sur Case No. 17
PO Box 6-9083 El Dorado
Panama City, Panama

Papua New Guinea

University of Papua New Guinea Library
Periodicals Library
PO Box 319 University P.O.
Boroko, Papua New Guinea

Paraguay

Biblioteca Nacional
PO Box 2931
Asuncion, Paraguay

Centro de Informacion des las Naciones
Unidas
Casilla de Correo 1107
Asuncion, Paraguay

Peru

Biblioteca del Congreso
Camara de Diputados
Plaza Bolivar
Lima, Peru

Biblioteca Nacional
Av. Abancay
Lima, Peru

Centro de Informacion de las Naciones Unidas
Mariscal Blas Cerdena 450, San Isidro
Apdo. Postal 14-0199
Lima, Peru

Philippines

University of Mindanao
Bolton St.
Davao City, Philippines

Central Philippine University
Libraries
Iloilo City 5901, Philippines

The National Library
Acquisition Division
T.M. Kalaw St.
PO Box 2926
Manila, Philippines

United Nations Information Centre
NEDA Bldg., Ground Fl.
106 Amorsollo St.
Legaspi Village, Makati
Manila, Philippines

National Government Center
House of Representatives
Legislative Library
Quezon City, Metro Manila, Philippines

University of the Philippines
College of Law
The Library
Bocobo Hall
Diliman
Quezon City 3004, Philippines

Poland

Biblioteka Sejmowa
PL-00-902 **Warsaw**, Poland

Polski Institut Spraw Miedzynarodowych
Polish Institute of International Affairs
Department of Scientific Information and the
   Library
ul. Warecka 1A
PO Box 1000
PL-00-950 **Warsaw**, Poland

Zaklad Uzupelniania Zbiorow
Biblioteka Narodowa
ul. Hankiewicza 1
PL-00-973 **Warsaw**, Poland

Portugal

Biblioteca Nacional de Lisboa
Lisbon 5, Portugal

Centro de Informacao das Nacoes Unidas
Rua Latino Coelho No. 1
Edificio Aviz Bloco Al-10o
P-1000 **Lisbon**, Portugal

Romania

Academiei Republicii Socialiste Romania
Biblioteca
Bucharest, Romania

Centrul de Informare al ONU
16 rue Aurel Vlaic
PO Box 1-701
Bucharest, Romania

Russia

Gosudarstvennaya Biblioteka SSR imeni V.I.
Lenin
Moscow, Russia

Informatcionnyi Centr OON
4/16 Ulitsa Lunacharskogo 1
121002 **Moscow**, Russia

Institut Nauchnoi Informatzii po
Obschestvennym Naukam
Academii Nauk SSSR
ul. Krassikora, 28/21
117418 **Moscow**, Russia

Leningradskogo Gosudarstvennogo
Universiteta Imeni A.A. Zhdanova
Nauchnaya Biblioteka im. M. Gorky
7/9 Universitetskaia nab.
199164 **St. Petersburg**, Russia

Rwanda

Universite Nationale du Rwanda
Bibliotheque
Butare, Rwanda

Saudi Arabia

King Abdulaziz University
Library
Deanship of Library Affairs - Special
Collections
PO Box 3711
Jeddah 21481, Saudi Arabia

State Public Library
Riyadh, Saudi Arabia

Scotland

National Library of Scotland
Official Papers Unit
George IV Bridge
Edinburgh EH1 1EW, Scotland

The Mitchell Library
Glasgow G3 7DN, Scotland

Senegal

Assemblee Nationale
Secretariat General
Section de la Bibliotheque
Dakar, Senegal

Centre d'Information des Nations Unies
72, Blvd. de la Republique
B.P. 154
Dakar, Senegal

Universite de Dakar
Bibliotheque
Dakar, Senegal

Sierra Leone

University of Sierra Leone
Fourah Bay College Library
Documents Collection
PO Box 87
Freetown, Sierra Leone

Singapore

National Library
Gifts and Exchange Section
Stamford Rd.
Singapore 0617, Singapore

Somalia

University Institute of Somalia
Mogadishu, Somalia

South Africa, Republic of

Library of Parliament
Cape Town, Republic of South Africa

South African Library
PO Box 496
Cape Town 8000, Republic of South Africa

State Library
United Nations Collection
PO Box 397
Pretoria 0001, Republic of South Africa

Spain

Universidad de Barcelona
Facultad de Derecho
Biblioteca Depositaria de las Naciones Unidas
Zona Universitaria-Pedralbes
Diagonal 684
E-08034 **Barcelona**, Spain

Biblioteca de la Escuela Diplomatica
Paseo Juan XXIII, No. 5
E-28040 **Madrid**, Spain

Biblioteca Nacional
Seccion de Publicaciones Oficiales
Paseo de Recoletos, 20
Madrid 1, Spain

Centro de Informacion de las Naciones Unidas
Ave. General Peron, 32-1
PO Box 3400
E-28080 **Madrid**, Spain

Universidad de Valencia
Facultad de Derecho
Biblioteca
Avda. Blasco Ibanez
Valencia, Spain

Sri Lanka

The Bar Association
Hultsdorp
Colombo 12, Sri Lanka

United Nations Information Centre
202-204 Bauddhaloka Mawatha
PO Box 1505
Colombo 7, Sri Lanka

Sudan

University of Juba
Library
PO Box 82
Juba, Sudan

United Nations Information Centre
United Nations Compound
University Ave.
PO Box 1992
Khartoum, Sudan

University of Khartoum
Library
Khartoum, Sudan

Suriname

Anton de Kom Universiteit
United Nations Depository Library
Onaflhandelijkheidshotel
Kleine Waterstraat 10-12
Paramaribo, Suriname

Swaziland

Swaziland National Library Service
Headquarters
PO Box 1461
Mbabane, Swaziland

Sweden

Goteborgs Universitetsbibliotek
PO Box 5096
S-402 22 **Gothenborg**, Sweden

Lunds Universitetsbibliotek
Box 3
S-221 00 **Lund**, Sweden

Riksdagsbiblioteket
S-100 12 **Stockholm**, Sweden

Dag Hammarskjold Library
Box 644
S-751 27 **Uppsala** 1, Sweden

Switzerland

Eidgenossische Parlaments- und
  Zentralbibliothek
Bundeshaus West
CH-3003 **Bern**, Switzerland

Bibliotheque Publique et Universitaire de
  Geneve
CH-1211 **Geneva** 4, Switzerland

Institut Universitaire des Hautes Etudes
  Internationales
Bibliotheque
132, rue de Lausanne
C.P. 36
CH-1211 **Geneva** 21, Switzerland

United Nations Information Service
United Nations Office at Geneva
Palais des Nations
CH-1211 **Geneva** 10, Switzerland

Syrian Arab Republic

Damascus University
United Arab Library
Damascus, Syrian Arab Republic

Tanzania, United Republic of

United Nations Information Centre
Matasalamat Bldg., 1st Fl.
Samora Machel Ave.
PO Box 9224
Dar es Salaam, United Republic of Tanzania

University of Dar es Salaam
Library
PO Box 35092
Dar es Salaam, United Republic of Tanzania

Thailand

National Library
Bangkok 3, Thailand

United Nations Information Service
Economic and Social Commission for Asia
  and the Pacific
United Nations Bldg.
Rajadamnern Ave.
Bangkok, Thailand

Togo

Bibliotheque Nationale du Togo
Lome, Togo

Centre d'Information des Nations Unies
107 Blvd. du 13 Janvier
B.P. 911
Lome, Togo

Trinidad and Tobago

United Nations Information Centre
16 Victoria Ave.
PO Box 130
Port-of-Spain, Trinidad and Tobago

University of the West Indies
Library
St. Augustine, Trinidad and Tobago

Tunisia

Centre d'Information des Nations Unies
61 blvd. Bab Benat
B.P. 863
Tunis, Tunisia

Universite de Tunis
Faculte de Droit et des Sciences Politiques et
  Economiques
Campus universitaire
Tunis, Tunisia

Turkey

Milli Kutuphane Baskanligi
Bahcelievler
Ankara, Turkey

United Nations Information Centre
197 Ataturk Bulvari
P.K. 407
Ankara, Turkey

Istanbul Universitesi Kutuphanesi
University Library
Beyazit, Besim Omer Pasa Cad. No. 15
Istanbul, Turkey

Uganda

Makerere University
Library
Kampala, Uganda

Ukraine

Akademia Nauk Ukrainskoi SSR
Centralnaya Nauchnaya
Biblioteka
Ul. Vladimirskaya 62
17 **Kiev**, Ukraine

United Arab Emirates

United Arab Emirates University
Library
PO Box 1441
Al-Ain, United Arab Emirates

Uruguay

Biblioteca Nacional
Ave. 18 de Julio 1790
Casilla de Correo 452
Montevideo, Uruguay

Venezuela

Biblioteca Nacional
Caracas, Venezuela

Wales

The National Library of Wales
Aberystwyth SY23 3BU, Wales

University College
The Arts and Social Studies Library
United Nations Depository Library
PO Box 78
Cardiff CF1 1XL, Wales

Yemen

Sana'a University
Library
PO Box 1247
Sana'a, Yemen

Yugoslavia

Informacioni Centar Ujedinjenih Nacija
Svetozara Markovica 58
PO Box 157
YU-11001 **Belgrade**, Yugoslavia

Institut za Medjunarodnu Politiku i Privredu
Biblioteka
Makedonsk 25
PO Box 750
YU-11000 **Belgrade**, Yugoslavia

Skupstina SFRJ
Odelenje Inostrane Dokumentacije
TRG Marksa i Engelsa 13
Belgrade, Yugoslavia

Universizitet u Beogradu
Pravni Facultet
Biblioteka
YU-11000 **Belgrade**, Yugoslavia

Univerza v Ljubljani
Pravna Fakulteta
YU-61000 **Ljubljana**, Yugoslavia

Univerzitet "Dzemal Bijedic"
Univerzitetska Biblioteka
Trg "14 Februar"
Postanski Pretinac 168
YU-88000 **Mostar**, Yugoslavia

Univerzitet Kiril I Metodi Skofoje
Praven Fakultet
Depositarna Biblioteka UN
Bul. Krste Misirkov b.b.
Skopje, Yugoslavia

Sveuciliste u Zagrebu
Pravni Fakultet
Biblioteka
YU-41001 **Zagreb**, Yugoslavia

Zaire

Centre d'Information des Nations Unies
Batiment Deuxieme Republique
Blvd. du 30 Juin
B.P. 7248
Kinshasa, Zaire

Zambia

President's Citizenship College
Library
Mulungushi
PO Box 80415
Kabwe, Zambia

United Nations Information Centre
PO Box 32905
Lusaka, Zambia

University of Zambia
Library
PO Box 32379
Lusaka, Zambia

Zimbabwe

United Nations Information Centre
Dolphin House
123 Moffat St./Union Ave.
PO Box 4408
Harare, Zimbabwe

University of Zimbabwe
Library
PO Box MP 167
Mount Pleasant
Harare, Zimbabwe

Appendix F

World Bank Depository Libraries

The institutions listed below have been designated as official World Bank Depository libraries. They provide free public access to books published for the World Bank by university presses, country and economic studies, technical papers, annual reports, statistical publications, and selected public information material. Collections are open to the public during normal business hours and, in most cases, are accessible without charge. Listings are arranged in alphabetical order by country name, and in countries with more than one library, by city name.

Users should address requests for additional information to:

The World Bank
Depository Library Program
Publications Department, J-2191
1818 H St., N.W.
Washington, DC 20433.

Algeria

Institut Superieur de Gestion et de
  Planification
Rue Hadj Messaoud Nourredine
Baha (Ex. Lido) Borg El Kiffane
Algiers, Algeria
Phone: 801761
Telex: 64223
Contact: Mr. Benyagoub Djamila, Biblio.

Argentina

Secretaria de Planificacion
Hipolito Yrigoyen 250
8 piso Of 801-C
1310 **Buenos Aires**, Argentina
Phone: 1 331121; 1 346411
Contact: Prof. Araceli Garcia Acosta, Biblio.

Universidad Nacional del Litoral
Facultad de Ciencias Economicas
25 de Mayo 1783
3000 **Santa Fe**, Argentina
Phone: 42 31127; 42 31128
Telex: 48 153 INLIT AR.
Contact: Beatriz S. Perez Roisso de Costa,
  Dir. de Biblio.

Australia

National Library of Australia
Gift and Exchange Section
Canberra, Australian Capital Territory 2600,
  Australia
Phone: 62 621111
Telex: 62100
Contact: Ross Swindley, Prin.Libn., Ser., Acq.
  & Control

Bahrain

University of Bahrain
Library
P.O. Box 32038
Isa Town, Bahrain
Phone: 681644
Telex: 681465
Contact: Raymond Stobart, Dp.Dir.

Bangladesh

Bangladesh Academy for Rural Development
  (BARD)
Kotbari
Comilla, Bangladesh
Phone: 81 6102; 81 8406
Contact: Mr. Mamtaj Uddin Ahmed,
  Asst.Dir., Lib.

Bangladesh Public Administration Training
  Centre
Library
Savar
Dhaka, Bangladesh
Phone: 2 418102
Contact: Mr. M. Wahiduzzaman, Lib. & Trng.
  Aid

Centre on Integrated Rural Development for
  Asia and the Pacific (CIRDAP)
Documentation and Information Division
Chameli House
17 Topkhana Rd.
GPO Box 2883
Dhaka 1000, Bangladesh
Phone: 2 233141
Telex: 642333 CIRDAP BJ.
Contact: Mr. M.A. Rashid Meah, Libn.

Brazil

Centro de Treinamento para o
  Desenvolvimento Economico (CENDEC)
Library
SGAN quadra 908 Modulo E
DF 70740 **Brasilia**, Brazil
Phone: 61 2744762
Telex: 061-1023
Contact: Mrs. Katia Medeiros Jacobina
  Aieres, Libn.

Burundi

Centre de Perfectionnement et de Formation
  en cours d'Emploi (CPF)
Ministere de la Fonction Publique
10 rte. Rumonge
B.P. 732
Bujumbura, Burundi
Phone: 24801; 23283
Contact: Marie-Louise Nzeyimana, Biblio.

Cameroon

University Center of Dschang
Central Library
B.P. 255
Dschang, Cameroon
Phone: 451134
Contact: Dee F. Baldwin, Libn.

Canada

National Library of Canada
Acquisitions and Bibliographic Services
  Branch
395 Wellington St.
Ottawa, ON, Canada K1A 0N4
Phone: (613)997-7003
Telex: 053-4311
Contact: Ruth Lawless, Asst.Dir.

Chile

Oficina de Planificacion Nacional
  (ODEPLAN)
Ahumada 48 piso 4
Santiago, Chile
Phone: 2 6980104; 2 722033
Telex: OPLAN CL 40767
Contact: Carolina Sanchez E., Jefe Biblio.

Universidad Adolfo Ibanez
Facultad de Economia y Administracion
Escuela de Negocios de Valparaiso
Casilla 846
Balmaceda 1625-Recreo
Vina del Mar, Chile
Phone: 32 662679; 32 660211
Contact: Mrs. Mariza J. de Monardes, Biblio.
  Jefe

China, People's Republic of

Institute of World Economics and Politics
Chinese Academy of Social Sciences
Library
No. 5 Jianguomennei Dajie
Beijing, People's Republic of China
Phone: 1 51773442705
Telex: 22061 CASS CN.
Contact: Mr. Shen Foo-Ken, Libn. of Res.

Ministry of Finance
External Finance Department
World Bank Division - Library
San Li He
Beijing, People's Republic of China
Phone: 1 862361
Telex: 716 22486 MFRPC.ON.
Contact: Mr. Wang Liansheng, Dir.

National Library of China
Section of International Organizations and
  Foreign Government Materials
39 Bai-Shi-Qiao Rd.
Beijing, People's Republic of China
Phone: 1 666331
Contact: Mr. Wu Jing Ying, Hd.

Tsinghua University
School of Economics and Management
Library
Beijing, People's Republic of China
Phone: 1 282451; 1 285451
Telex: 22617 GHTSC CN.
Contact: Prof. Zhao Jiahe, Dp. Dean

Jilin University
Library
International Exchange Section
Jie Fang Da Lu 77
Changchun, People's Republic of China
Phone: 23189
Telex: 1513
Contact: Mr. Xue-Yi Wang, Exchange-Libn.

Guangdong Provincial Academy of Social
  Sciences
222, Yue Xiu Bei Rd.
Guangzhou, People's Republic of China
Phone: 20 34820
Contact: Mr. Cai-Qiong Xie, Libn.

Wuhan University
Department of Economics
Library
Wuchang
Hubei, People's Republic of China
Phone: 812712
Contact: Mr. Chen Yuhwa, Libn.

Fudan University
Institute of World Economy
Library
220 Handan Rd.
Shanghai, People's Republic of China
Phone: 21 484906
Contact: Mr. Lin Peng-xiang, Libn.

Shanghai Academy of Social Sciences
Library
1575 Wan Hang Tu Rd.
Shanghai, People's Republic of China
Phone: 21 522657
Contact: Mr. Chen Qi-Qin, Libn.

Shanghai University of Finance and
  Economics Library
369 N. Zhon-shan Rd. (Northern, No. 1)
Shanghai, People's Republic of China
Phone: 21 421690
Telex: 33462 ETHHH CN.
Contact: Mr. Xia Xian, Dp.Libn.

Colombia

Universidad Externado de Colombia
Biblioteca
Calle 12 No. 1-17 Este
Bogota, Colombia
Phone: 1 2826066
Contact: Mrs. Emilssen Gonzalez De Cancino,
  Dir. de la Biblio.

Universidad del Valle
Seccion Documentos Organismos
  Internacionales
Apdo. Aereo 25360
Cali, Colombia
Phone: 23 39304150
Contact: Isabel Romero de Dulcey, Dir.

Universidad de Antioquia
Centro de Documentacion
Bloque 13 of. 104 Ciudad Universitaria
Apdo. Aereo 1226
Medellin, Colombia
Phone: 4 2330690
Contact: Ms. Lourdes Rodriguez G., Jefe, Ctr.
  de Doc.

Costa Rica

Instituto Centroamericano de Administracion
  de Empresas (INCAE)
Apdo. 960
Alajuela 4050, Costa Rica
Phone: 412255
Telex: 7040
Contact: Thomas Bloch, Chf.Libn.

Cote d'Ivoire

Institut Africain pour le Developpement
  Economique et Social (INADES)
Documentation
15, ave. Jean Mermoz Cocody
08 B.P. 8
Abidjan 08, Cote d'Ivoire
Phone: 441594
Contact: Yves Morel, Biblio./Doc.

Cyprus

Middle East Marketing Research Bureau
  (MEMRB)
Academias Ave.
PO Box 2098
Nicosia, Cyprus
Phone: 2 31133
FAX: 311433
Telex: 2488
Contact: Charles Glover, Libn.

Denmark

Handelshojskolens Bibliotek
Rosenoerns Alle 31
Frederiksberg
DK-1970 **Copenhagen**, Denmark
Phone: 3 31396677; 3 31398881
Contact: Michael von Cotta-Schonberg,
  Chf.Libn.

Egypt

Institute of National Planning
Salah Salem St.
Nasr City
Cairo, Egypt
Phone: 2 603166; 2 603235
Telex: 93261 IPLAN UN.
Contact: Mohamed Abulfath S. Nassar, Dir.,
  Doc. & Pub.Ctr.

El Salvador

Fundacion Salvadorena para el Desarrollo
  Economico y Social (FUSADES)
Biblioteca
Edificio la Centro Americana 6th piso
Apdo. Postal 01-278
San Salvador, El Salvador
Phone: 230655; 234899
Telex: 20438 FUSADES
Contact: Hugo Liborio, Biblio.

Ethiopia

Addis Ababa University Libraries
Documents Department
PO Box 1176
Addis Ababa, Ethiopia
Phone: 1 115673; 1 117786
Telex: 21205
Contact: Mr. Getachew Birru, Univ.Libn.

United Nations
Economic Commission for Africa Library
Africa Hall
PO Box 3001
Addis Ababa, Ethiopia
Phone: 1 447000; 1 447200
Contact: Mr. Abdel-Rahman M. Tahir,
  Chf.Libn.

Fiji

University of the South Pacific
Library
PO Box 1168
Suva, Fiji
Phone: 313900
Telex: 2276

Gambia

National Investment Board
78 Wellington St.
Banjul, Gambia
Phone: 8168; 8868
Telex: GV 2230
Contact: Mr. Musa Ndow, Libn.

Management Development Institute
PO Box 2553
Serrekunda, Gambia
Phone: 92871
Telex: 2204
Contact: Mr. Aedin Ni Bhroithe, Libn.

Germany

Deutscher Bundestag
Bibliothek
Bundeshaus
W-5300 **Bonn** 1, Germany
Phone: 228 162943
Telex: 886529 bthtd.
Contact: Gisela Krischker, Libn.

Ghana

University of Ghana
Balme Library
PO Box 24
Legon
Accra, Ghana
Phone: 21 775381
Contact: Mr. J.K.T. Kafe, Libn.

Ghana Institute of Management & Public
  Administration
Library & Documentation Centre
PO Box 50
Achimota, Ghana
Phone: 667684; 667685
Telex: 2551 GIMPA GH.
Contact: Mr. E. Cabutey Adodoadji, Libn.

University of Cape Coast
Library
University Post Office
Cape Coast, Ghana
Phone: 24409; 24809
Contact: Richard Arkaifie, Acq.Libn.

Greece

Centre of Planning and Economic Research
  (KEPE)
Library
22, Hippokratous St.
GR-106 80 **Athens**, Greece
Phone: 1 3628911; 1 3627321
Contact: Ms. Eleftheria P. Halvadakis,
  Hd.Libn.

Institute of International Public Law and
  International Relations of Thessaloniki
Library
Leof. Megalou Alexandrou 15 & Hadji
GR-546 40 **Thessaloniki**, Greece
Phone: 31 810451; 31 841751
Contact: Prof. Dimitri S. Constantopoulos,
  Dir.

Guyana

Bank of Guyana
Research Department Library
PO Box 1003
Georgetown, Guyana
Phone: 2 632519; 2 632615
Contact: Wenda R. Stephenson, Libn.

Honduras

Secretaria de Planificacion, Coordinacion y
  Presupuesto (SECPLAN)
Apdo. Postal 1327
Tegucigalpa, Honduras
Phone: 220379; 222261
Telex: 1222 CIDAPLAN HO.
Contact: Maria Elena De Guerrero, Jefe
  Biblio.

Hungary

National Bank of Hungary
Library
Szabadsag ter 8-9
H-1850 **Budapest**, Hungary
Phone: 1 322722
Telex: 22 5755 BancoH.
Contact: Mrs. J. Romhanyi, Chf. Libn.

India

Indian Institute of Management, Vastrapur
Vikram Sarabhai Library
Ahmedabad 380 056, Gujarat, India
Phone: 272 407241
Telex: 121 6351
Contact: Mr. Ashok Jambhekar, Libn.

Guru Nanak Dev University
Punjab School of Economics
Amritsar 143 005, Punjab, India
Phone: 183 66067
Contact: Ms. Kewal Singh, Asst. Libn.

Annamalai University Library
S. Arcot District
Annamalainagar 608 002, Tamil Nadu, India
Phone: 2249
Contact: Mr. V. Durairajan, Libn.

Institute for Social and Economic Change
Library
Nagarbhavi
Bangalore 560 072, Karnataka, India
Phone: 812 606274
Contact: Mr. V.K. Jain, Libn.

University of Bombay
Jawaharlal Nehru Library
Vidyanagari Campus
Kalina Santacruz (E)
Bombay 400 098, Maharashtra, India
Phone: 22 6127026
Contact: Prof. A.C. Tikekar, Libn.

Indian Statistical Institute
Library
203 Barrackpore Trunk Rd.
Calcutta 700 035, India
Phone: 33 526694
Telex: 21 2210 STAT IN.
Contact: Dr. Jogesh Misra, Chf. Libn.

Karnatak University
Library
Pavate Nagar
Dharwad 580 003, Karnataka, India
Phone: 8194
Contact: Mr. R.C. Patil, Libn.

Centre for Economic and Social Studies
Library
Nizamia Observatory Campus
Begumpet
Hyderabad 500 016, Andhra Pradesh, India
Phone: 842 227114
Contact: Mr. G. Vijaya Kumar, Libn.

Giri Institute of Developmental Studies
Library
Sector "O"
Aliganj Housing Scheme
Lucknow 226 020, Uttar Pradesh, India
Phone: 73640
Contact: Mr. R.D. Khare, Libn.

Institute for Financial Management &
  Research
H.T. Parekh Library
30 Kothari Rd.
Nungambakkam
Madras 600 034, Tamil Nadu, India
Phone: 44 473801
Contact: Miss K. Indira, Sr.Libn.

Uttar Predesh Academy of Administration
Library
Naintal 263 001, Uttar Pradesh, India
Phone: 2041
Contact: Mr. Prakash Sinha, Joint Dir.

Indian Institute of Public Administration
Library
Indraprastha Estate
Ring Rd.
New Delhi 110 002, Delhi, India
Phone: 11 3317309
Contact: Mr. M.C. Ragavan, Libn.

Institute of Economic Growth
Library
University Enclave
Malkagang Rd.
New Delhi 110 007, Delhi, India
Phone: 11 2522201; 11 2522365
Contact: Mr. S.C. Bhatia, Libn.
Alternate telephone numbers are 11 25225424
  and 11 2522088.

Punjabi University
Department of Economics Library
Patiala 147 002, Punjab, India
Phone: 73261
Contact: Ms. Saroj Bala, Libn.

Gokhale Institute of Politics and Economics
Library
Pune 411 004, Maharashtra, India
Phone: 212 54287
Contact: Mrs. A. Ogale, Doc.Off.

Ravishankar University Library
Raipur 492 010, Madhya Pradesh, India
Phone: 27420
Contact: Mr. Rameshwar Singh, Libn.

University of Kerala Library
Trivandrum 695 034, Kerala, India
Phone: 77844
Contact: Mr. K.C. John, Univ. Libn.

Indonesia

Bandung Institute of Technology
Central Library
Jalan Ganesya 10
40132 **Bandung**, Indonesia
Phone: 22 83814
Telex: 28324 ITB BD.
Contact: Mr. Ai Andaniah, Libn.

Bogor Agricultural University Library
UPT Perpustakaan IPB
Kampus Darmaga
P.O. Box 101
16610 **Bogor**, Indonesia
Contact: Drs. Fahidin, B. SC., Chf.Libn.

Universitas Udayana
Library
Jalan P B Suridam
P.O. Box 105
Denpasar, Bali, Indonesia
Phone: 361 23791
Contact: Mrs. Ida Ayu Alit Asparini, Libn.

Atma Jaya Research Centre Library
Jalan Jenderal Suriman 49A
P.O. Box 2639
10001 **Jakarta**, Indonesia
Phone: 21 5703306
Contact: Paul W. Kartono, Libn.

Dewan Perwakilan Rakyat Republik (DPR-
RI)
Jln. Gatot Subroto
10270 **Jakarta Pusat**, Indonesia
Phone: 21 581223
Telex: 62396 RHM DPR
Contact: Aurora Simandjuntak, Chf. Libn.

Institut Keguruan dan Ilmu
Pendidikan Negeri
Kampus IKIP
95115 **Manado Sulawesi Utara**, Indonesia
Phone: 41741
Contact: Daniel C. Kambey, Libn.

Universitas Hasanuddin
Education and Culture Department
Kampus Unhas
55 **Mesjid Raya** 1, Ujung Pandang, Indonesia
Phone: 3029
Telex: 71179
Contact: Dr. A. Rahman Rahim, Libn.

Institut Telnologi Sepuluh Nopember
Kampus ITS Keputih, Sukolilo
Surabaya Jawa Timur, Indonesia
Phone: 31 597264
Telex: 34224 INTEKS.
Contact: Mrs. Narkanti, Libn.

Jamaica

Planning Institute of Jamaica
39-41 Barbados Ave.
P.O. Box 634
Kingston 5, Jamaica
Phone: 61480
Telex: 3529 PLANJAM JA.
Contact: Arlene Ononaiwu, Chf.Libn.

Japan

National Diet Library
Library Cooperation Department
Nagato-cho, Chiyoda-ku
Tokyo 100, Japan
Phone: 3 5812331
Contact: Mr. Atsumi Kumata, Dir.

Kenya

Moi University Library
P.O. Box 3900
Eldoret, Kenya
Phone: 31660
Telex: 35047 MOIVASITY
Contact: Prof. S.O. Keya, Vice Chancellor

Kenya National Library
P.O. Box 30573
Nairobi, Kenya
Phone: 2 7525569
Contact: Mr. S.C. Otenya, Act.Dir.

Kenyatta University
Moi Library
P.O. Box 43844
Nairobi, Kenya
Phone: 2 810901
Telex: 25483 Ken uni KE
Contact: James Mwangi Nganga, Libn.

Egerton University Library
P.O. Box 536
Njoro, Kenya
Phone: 3761620
Telex: 33075
Contact: Mr. Mutuku Nzioki, Libn.

Korea, Republic of

Korea Development Institute
Informatation Resources Center
207-41 Chungryangri-Dong
Dongdaemun-Ku
Seoul 131, Republic of Korea
Phone: 2 96788116
Telex: KDILINK K25100
Contact: Ms. Young Rhan Ch, Acq.Libn.

Kuwait

The Arab Planning Institute
P.O. Box 5834
Safat 13059, Kuwait
Phone: 4843130
Telex: 22996 KT
Contact: Mr. Abdullatif Al-Khatib,
Controller, Lib. & Docs.

Malawi

Ministry of Agriculture
Chitedze Agricultural Research Station
P.O. Box 158
Lilongwe, Malawi
Phone: 767222
Telex: 4648 MINAGRIC.
Contact: Katherine Wern, Libn.

National Library Service
Headquarters Library
P.O. Box 30314
Capital City
Lilongwe 3, Malawi
Phone: 730788
Contact: Ann B. Kulemeka, Sr. Libn.

Malaysia

Asian and Pacific Development Centre
(APDC)
Persiaran Duta
P.O. Box 12224
50770 **Kuala Lumpur**, Malaysia
Phone: 3 2548088
Telex: MA 30676
Contact: Mrs. Siti Rafeah Shamsudin, Libn.

South East Asian Central Banks Research and
Training Centre (SEACEN)
Lorong Universiti A
591000 **Kuala Lumpur**, Malaysia
Phone: 3 7568622
Telex: MA 30201
Contact: Mr. Baharuddin MD Dali, Chf.Libn.

Malta

Central Bank of Malta
Research Library
Castille Place
Valetta, Malta
Phone: 607480
Telex: MW 262 413
Contact: Joseph R. Grima, Info.Off.

Mauritius

University of Mauritius
Library
Reduit, Mauritius
Phone: 41041
Contact: Mrs. P. Gokulsing, Asst.Libn.

Mexico

Banco de Mexico
Apdo. Postal 98 Bis
06059 **Mexico City**, DF, Mexico
Phone: 5100814
Contact: Ms. Omega Lozada Garcia, Jefe de
Oficina de Serv.Biblio.

Morocco

Ministere du Plan
Centre National de Documentation
Charii Maa Al Ainain
B.P. 826
Haut-Agdal
Rabat, Morocco
Phone: 93 74944
Telex: CND: 310 52M
Contact: Mrs. Mabrouk Zahra, Libn./Dp.Chf.,
Serv. Questions-Responses

Nepal

Tribhuvan University
Central Library
Kirtipur
Kathmandu, Nepal
Phone: 13277
Contact: Mrs. Shanti Mishra, Chf.Libn.

Netherlands

Royal Tropical Institute
Central Library
United Nations Collection
Mauritskade 63
1092 AD **Amsterdam**, Netherlands
Phone: 20 5688711
Telex: 15080 KIT NL
Contact: Dr. A. van der Wal, Libn.

New Zealand

Parliamentary Library
Parliament House
Wellington, New Zealand
Phone: 4 719621
Contact: Katherine Close, International
Docs.Libn.

Nicaragua

Instituto Centroamericano de Administracion
de Empresas (INCAE)
Apdo. Postal 2485
Managua, Nicaragua
Phone: 2 58446
Telex: 2360
Contact: Antonio Acevedo, Assoc.Dir. De
Biblio.

Nigeria

Nigerian Institute of Social and Economic
Research (INCAE)
P.M.B. 5
U I Post Office
Ibadan, Oyo, Nigeria
Phone: 22 400501
Telex: 3119 NISER NG
Contact: Mr. J.A. Akisanya, Libn.

Bayero University Library
P.M.B. 3011
Kano, Nigeria
Phone: 9801
Contact: Dr. H.I. Said, Univ.Libn.

Nigerian Industrial Development Bank
(NIDB)
NIDB House
63-71 Broad St.
P.O. Box 2357
Lagos, Nigeria
Phone: 1 663470
Contact: Mr. S.A. Abiola, Libn.

University of Nigeria
Nnamdi Azikiwe Library
Nsukka, Nigeria
Phone: 48
Contact: Mrs. E.N. Unamba-Oparah, U.N.
Docs.Libn.

The Polytechnic of Sokoto State
College of Administration
Library
P.M.B. 2126
Sokoto, Nigeria
Phone: 232190
Contact: Mohammed Umar B/Magaji, Libn.

Pakistan

University of Agriculture
Library
Faisalabad, Pakistan
Phone: 411 25911
Contact: Mr. Manzur Ahmad, Libn.

Pakistan Institute of Development Economics
(PIDE)
Library
P.O. Box 1091
Islamabad, Pakistan
Phone: 51 812440
Telex: 5602 PIDE PK
Contact: Mr. Zafar Javed, Libn.

University of Karachi
Applied Economic Research Centre
P.O. Box 8043
Karachi 75270, Pakistan
Phone: 21 474384; 21 474749
Telex: 25700 KCC PK ATTN
Contact: Ms. Amtul Wadood
Telex: 25700 KCC PK ATTN 0091 AERC.

Punjab Economic Research Institute
74-B-II Gulberg III
Lahore 11, Pakistan
Phone: 42 876144; 42 873814
Contact: Mrs. K.A. Rehman, Libn.

Pakistan Academy for Rural Development
Academy Town
Peshawar, Pakistan
Phone: 521 40296; 521 40297
Contact: Harold Jonathan, Res.Libn.

University of Baluchistan
Library
Sariab Rd.
Quetta, Pakistan
Phone: 81 41770
Contact: Mr. M.A. Kazmi, Libn.

Papua New Guinea

University of Papua New Guinea
Michael Somare Library
University P.O. Box 319
Goroka
Port Moresby, Papua New Guinea
Phone: 245200
Telex: NE 22366
Contact: Florence Griffin, Univ.Libn.

Paraguay

Universidad Nacional de Asuncion
Facultad de Ingenieria Agronomica
Casilla de Correo No. 1618
Asuncion, Paraguay
Phone: 21 501516; 21 222282
Contact: Ms. Zaida Caballero, Hd.Libn.

Philippines

University of San Carlos
P del Rosario St.
Cebu City 6401, Philippines
Phone: 32 72419
Contact: Marilou P. Tadlip, Dir. of Libs.
Alternate telephone numbers are 32 72410
(information); 32 70874 (library).

University of the Philippines at Los Banos
College
University Library
Laguna 4031, Philippines
Phone: 2235; 2326
Telex: 40904 Searca PM
Contact: Ms. Leonor B. Gregorio, Univ.Libn.

Panay State Polytechnic College
Library
Mambusao Capiz 5706, Philippines
Contact: Mrs. Aurea G. Bernabe, Chm.,
Lib.Serv.

National Economic and Development
Authority (NEDA)
Library
NEDA sa Pasig
Amber Ave.
Pasig, Metro Manila, Philippines
Phone: 6735031; 6735050
Contact: Elenita M. Salvatierra, Chf.
Economic Info. Spec.

University of the Philippines
School of Economics
Library
Diliman
Quezon City, Metro Manila 3004, Philippines
Phone: 989686; 989691
Contact: Rosemarie G. Rosali, Libn.-in-
Charge
An alternate telephone number is 982044.

Poland

Uniwersytet Jagiellonski W Krakowie
Centrum Badan Nad Zadluzeniem i
Rozwojem
32, Slawkowska St.
PL-31-014 **Cracow**, Poland
Phone: 12 213139
Telex: 0326 248 CBZRU PL
Contact: Mrs. Ewa Salkiewicz, Libn.

Narodowy Bank Polski
Central Library
ul. Swietokrzyska 11/21
PL-00-950 **Warsaw**, Poland
Phone: 22 269758; 22 267786
Telex: 12 70
Contact: Mrs. Urszula Suchozebrska,
Hd.Libn.

Portugal

Universidade da Beira Interior
Biblioteca
R. Marques d'Avila e Bolama
P-6200 **Covilha**, Portugal
Phone: 25141; 25144
Telex: 53733
Contact: Dra. Cristina Seabra, Libn.

Universidade do Minho
Braga codex 4719
Largo do Paco, Portugal
Phone: 27021; 27023
Telex: 25235 U MINHO P.
Contact: Dr. Armindo R. Cardoso, Dir., Serv.
de Doc.

Romania

Institutul de Economie Mondiala
Blvd. Republic II 12 Sector 3
70348 **Bucharest**, Romania
Phone: 0 142005; 0 142006
Telex: 429
Contact: Dr. Napoleon Pop, Hd., Foreign
Trade Info. Off.

Saudi Arabia

Ministry of Planning
Library and Documentation Department
Riyadh 11182, Saudi Arabia
Phone: 1 4010417; 1 4049234
Telex: 401075 Plan S.J.
Contact: Mr. Abbas M. Arafat, Dir.

Singapore

National Library of Singapore
Stamford Rd.
Singapore 0617, Singapore
Phone: 3377355
Telex: RS 26620 NAT LIB.
Contact: Mr. R. Ramachandran, Hd., Tech.
Serv. Div.

South Africa, Republic of

State Library
Special Collections
P.O. Box 397
Pretoria 0001, Republic of South Africa
Phone: 12 218931
Telex: 3 22171 SA
Contact: Mrs. M.A. Botha, Asst.Dir.

University of South Africa
Sanlam Library
P.O. Box 392
Pretoria 0001, Republic of South Africa
Phone: 12 4293128
Telex: 350068
Contact: Mrs. A.M. Mouton, Asst.Dir.

Spain

Escuela Superior de Administracion y
Direccion de Empresas (ESADE)
Biblioteca
Avenida de Pedralbes 60-62
E-08034 **Barcelona**, Spain
Phone: 3 2037800
Telex: 98 268
Contact: Mr. Antoni M. Guell, Dir. de la
Biblio.

Sri Lanka

Ceylon Institute of Scientific and Industrial
Research
Technical Library and Information Service
363 Bauddhaloka Mawatha
P.O. Box 787
Colombo 7, Sri Lanka
Phone: 1 598620
Telex: 21248 Minind CE
Contact: Miss C.L.M. Nethsingha, Hd.,
Info.Serv.
Telex: 21248 Minind CE Attention C.I.S.I.R.

Sudan

Arab Organzation for Agricultural
Documentation and Information (ADACI)
4 El Gama'a Ave.
7th Khartoum Extension
P.O. Box 474
Khartoum, Sudan
Phone: 40430; 43425
Telex: 22554 SD.
Contact: Dr. Hassan Fahmi Jumah, Gen.Dir.
(AOAD)
An alternate telephone number is 43389.

Swaziland

University of Swaziland
Private Bag No. 4
Kwaluseni, Swaziland
Phone: 84011
Telex: 2087 WD.
Contact: Mrs. M. Nhlapo, Univ.Libn.

Sweden

Riksdagsbiblioteket
Riksplan
S-100 12 **Stockholm**, Sweden
Phone: 8 7864000
Telex: 10184 Parlbib S.
Contact: Mr. Bengt Alexanderson, Chf.Libn.

Switzerland

United Nations Library
Specialized Agencies Collection
Reader's Services and Documentation Section
Palais des Nations, Rm. B-127
CH-1211 **Geneva** 10, Switzerland
Phone: 22 346011; 22 310211
Telex: 28 96 96
Contact: Nina K. Leneman, Chf.

Tanzania, United Republic of

Eastern and Southern African Management
Institute (ESAMI)
P.O. Box 3030
Arusha, United Republic of Tanzania
Phone: 2881; 2885
Telex: 42076 ESAMI T2
Contact: Mr. G. Maimu, Asst.Libn., Ser.

Institute of Finance Management
Library Services Department
Shaban Robert St.
P.O. Box 3918
Dar es Salaam, United Republic of Tanzania
Phone: 51 27171
Contact: Mohammed H. Mhina, Prin.Libn.

University of Dar es Salaam
P.O. Box 35092
Dar es Salaam, United Republic of Tanzania
Phone: 51 48235
Telex: UNISCIE 41327
Contact: Prof. O.C. Mascarenhas, Dir.

Thailand

National Institute of Development
Administration
Library and Information Center
Klong Chan, Bangkapi
Bangkok 10240, Thailand
Phone: 2 3777400
Contact: Miss Nitaya Berananda, Dir.

Trinidad and Tobago

University of the West Indies
Main Library
St. Augustine, Trinidad and Tobago
Phone: 6631439
Telex: 24 520 UWI Wg.
Contact: Maureen Henry, Libn. II, Tech.Serv.

Tunisia

Faculte des Sciences Economiques et des
Gestion de Tunis
Campus Universitaire
Rte. X
1060 **Tunis**, Tunisia
Phone: 1 510500
Contact: Mr. Lamari Taoufik, Libn.

Turkey

Cukurova Universitesi
Rektorlugu
Adana, Turkey
Phone: 711 33394
Telex: CIIF TR62363
Contact: Dr. Ismet Husrevoglu, Assoc.Dir. of
Lib.

Statistical, Economic and Social Research and
Training Centre for
Islamic Countries (SESRTCIC)
Attar Sokak No. 4
Gazi Osman Pasa
TR-06700 **Ankara**, Turkey
Phone: 4 286105
Telex: 43163 irec tr.
Contact: Ms. Cuna Ekmekcioglu, Libn.

Ege Universitesi
Tarim Fakultesi
Department of Agricultural Economics -
Library
Bornova
TR-35100 **Izmir**, Turkey
Phone: 51 181862
Contact: Miss B. Muserref Kinaci, Chf.Libn.

United Arab Emirates

Sharjah Chamber of Commerce and Industry
Library
Chambers Bldg. No. 14
Al Bourj Ave.
P.O. Box 580
Sharjah, United Arab Emirates
Phone: 6 541444
Telex: 68205 Tijarah Em.
Contact: Mr. Saeed Obeid Al Jarwan,
Dir.Gen.

United Kingdom

British Library
Great Russell St.
London WC1B 3DG, United Kingdom
Phone: 71 6361544
Telex: 21462
Contact: Ilse Sternberg, Hd., Overseas English
Coll.

United States

United Nations
Dag Hammarskjold Library
RM L-221C
New York, NY 10017
Phone: (212)963-4717
Telex: 232422

Library of Congress
Exchange and Gift Division, A-160-IBRD
Washington, DC 20540
Phone: (202)707-9510
Telex: 710 922 0185 LICON
Contact: C. Melvin Flynn, Hd., American-
British Exchange Sect.

Uruguay

Oficina de Planeamiento y Presupuesto
Edificio Libertad, Convencion 1370
Montevideo, Uruguay
Phone: 2 983532
Contact: Silvia Nicola, Biblio.

Vanuatu

Central Bank of Vanuatu
P.O. Box 271
Port Vila, Vanuatu
Phone: 3333
Telex: 1049 VATUBK NH.
Contact: Andrew Kausiama, Prin.Res.Off.

Venezuela

Instituto de Estudios Superiores de
  Administracion (IESA)
Apdo. 1640
Caracas 1010A, Venezuela
Phone: 2 521560; 2 521660
Telex: 28381 IESA VC
Contact: Alicia Curiel, Jefe de la Biblio.

Vietnam

Institute of Economic Research
Information and Library Section
175 Hai Ba Trung St.
District 3
Ho Chi Minh City, Vietnam
Phone: 95498
Contact: Mrs. Anh Nga, Hd.

Thu Vien Khoa Hoc Tong Hop
General Sciences Library
69, Ly Tu Trong QI
Ho Chi Minh City, Vietnam
Contact: Mr. Huynh Ngac Thu, Dir.

Yugoslavia

Institut Ekonomskih Nauka
Zmaj Jovina 12
P.O. Box 611
YU-11001 **Belgrade,** Yugoslavia
Phone: 11 629960
Contact: Mrs. Ljubica Martinovic, Hd.Libn.

Nacionalna Sveucilsna Biblioteka
Marulicev trg 21
YU-41001 **Zagreb,** Yugoslavia
Phone: 41 446322; 41 445928
Telex: 22206 BICH YU.
Contact: Mrs. Zaneta Barsic, Mgr., Info.Rsrcs.

Zaire

Centre d'Etudes pour l'Action Sociale
  (CEPAS)
B.P. 5717
Kinshasa, Zaire
Phone: 12 30066
Contact: Joseph M. Boute, Chf.Libn.

Zambia

University of Zambia
Institute for African Studies
Rural Development Bureau
P.O. Box 30900
Lusaka, Zambia
Phone: 1 282880; 1 282881
Telex: ZA 44370
Contact: Mr. Jairus R. Chanda, Hd., Doc. &
  Reprographic Ctr.

Zimbabwe

National Free Library of Zimbabwe
Dugald Niven Library
12th Ave.
S. Park
P.O. Box 1773
Bulawayo, Zimbabwe
Phone: 9 69827; 9 62359
Telex: 3128
Contact: Miss D.E. Barron, Libn.

Harare City Library
Queen Victoria Memorial Library
Corner of Stanley Ave. & Rotten Row Box
P.O. Box 1087
Harare, Zimbabwe
Phone: 4 704921
Contact: Mrs. M. Ross-Smith, Libn.

Appendix G

European Community Depository Libraries

The following list contains the names of libraries throughout the United States designated as European Community depositories. Users should address requests for additional information to:

Delegation of the Commission of the European Communities
2100 M St., N.W., 7th Fl.
Washington, DC 20037.

Arizona

University of Arizona
International Documents
University Library
Tucson, AZ 85721

Arkansas

University of Arkansas
Documents Department
UALR Library
33rd & University
Little Rock, AR 72204

California

University of California
Documents Department
General Library
Berkeley, CA 94720

University of California
Documents Department
Central Library
La Jolla, CA 92093

University of California
International Documents
Public Affairs Service
Research Library
Los Angeles, CA 90024

University of Southern California
International Documents
Von Kleinschmidt Library
Los Angeles, CA 90089

Stanford University
Central Western European Coll.
The Hoover Institution
Stanford, CA 94305

Colorado

University of Colorado
Government Publications
University Library, Box 184
Boulder, CO 80309-0184

Connecticut

Yale University
Government Documents Center
Seeley G. Mudd Library
38 Mansfield
New Haven, CT 06520

District of Columbia

American University
Law Library
4400 Massachusetts, N.W.
Washington, DC 20016

Library of Congress
Serial Division
Madison Bldg.
10 1st St., S.E.
Washington, DC 20540

Florida

University of Florida
Documents Department
Libraries West
Gainesville, FL 32611

Georgia

University of Georgia
Law Library
Law School
Athens, GA 30602

Emory University
Law Library
School of Law
Atlanta, GA 30322

Hawaii

University of Hawaii
Government Documents
University Library
2550 The Mall
Honolulu, HI 96822

Illinois

University of Illinois
Law Library
School of Law
504 E. Pennsylvania Ave.
Champaign, IL 61820

Illinois Institute of Technology
Law Library
77 South Wacker Dr.
Chicago, IL 60606

University of Chicago
Government Documents
Regenstein Library
1100 E. 57th St.
Chicago, IL 60637

Northwestern University
Government Publications
University Library
Evanston, IL 60201

Indiana

Indiana University
Government Documents
University Library
Bloomington, IN 47405

University of Notre Dame
Document Center
Memorial Library
Notre Dame, IN 46556

Iowa

University of Iowa
Government Publications Library
Iowa City, IA 52242

Kansas

University of Kansas
Government Documents & Maps
University Library
6001 Malott Hall
Lawrence, KS 66045

Kentucky

University of Kentucky
Government Publications
Margaret I. King Library
Lexington, KY 40506

Louisiana

University of New Orleans
Business Reference
Earl K. Long Library
New Orleans, LA 70148

Maine

University of Maine
Law Library
246 Deering Avenue
Portland, ME 04102

Massachusetts

Harvard University
Law School Library
Langdell Hall- Law 431
Cambridge, MA 02138

Michigan

University of Michigan
Serials Department
Law Library
Ann Arbor, MI 48109-1210

Michigan State University
Documents Department
University Library
East Lansing, MI 48824-1048

Minnesota

University of Minnesota
Government Publications
Wilson Library - 409
Minneapolis, MN 55455

Missouri

Washington University
John M. Olin Library
Campub Box 1061
1 Brookings Dr.
St. Louis, MO 63130

Nebraska

University of Nebraska
Acquisitions Division
University Libraries
Lincoln, NE 68588-0410

New Jersey

Princeton University
Documents Division Library
Princeton, NJ 08544

New Mexico

University of New Mexico
Social Science Coll. Dev.
Zimmerman Library
Albuquerque, NM 87131

New York

State University of New York
Government Publications
Library
1400 Washington Ave.
Albany, NY 12222

State University of New York
Governments Documents
Lockwood Library Bldg.
Buffalo, NY 14260

Council on Foreign Relations
Library
58 E. 68th St.
New York, NY 10021

New York Public Library
Research Library, Ecn & Pub Af
Grand Central Station
P.O. Box 2221
New York, NY 10017

New York University
Law Library
School of Law
40 Washington Sq., S.
New York, NY 10012

North Carolina

Duke University
Public Documents Department
University Library
Durham, NC 27706

Ohio

Ohio State University
Documents Division
University Library
1858 Neil Avenue Mall
Columbus, OH 43210

Oklahoma

University of Oklahoma
Government Documents
Bizzell Memorial Library - Rm. 440
401 W. Brooks
Norman, OK 73019

Oregon

University of Oregon
Documents Section
University Library
Eugene, OR 97403

Pennsylvania

University of Pennsylvania
Serial Department
Van Pelt Library
Philadelphia, PA 19104

University of Pittsburgh
Gift and Exchange
Hillman Library G 72
Pittsburgh, PA 15260

Pennsylvania State University
Documents Section
University Library
University Park, PA 16802

Puerto Rico

University of Puerto Rico
Law Library
Law School
Rio Piedras, PR 00931

South Carolina

University of South Carolina
Documents/Microformss
Thomas Cooper Library
Columbia, SC 29208

Texas

University of Texas
Law Library
School of Law
727 E. 26th St.
Austin, TX 78705

Utah

University of Utah
International Documents
Marriott Library
Salt Lake City, UT 84112

Virginia

George Mason University
Center for European Studies
4001 N. Fairfax Dr., Ste. 450
Arlington, VA 22203

University of Virginia
Government Documents
Aldeman Library
Charlottesville, VA 22903

Washington

University of Washington
Government Publications
University Library, FM-25
Seattle, WA 98195

Wisconsin

University of Wisconsin
Documents Department
Memorial Library
728 State St
Madison, WI 53706

Geographic Abbreviations
(State, Province, and Territory)

UNITED STATES & U.S. TERRITORIES

AL	Alabama	MT	Montana
AK	Alaska	NE	Nebraska
AS	American Samoa	NV	Nevada
AZ	Arizona	NH	New Hampshire
AR	Arkansas	NJ	New Jersey
CA	California	NM	New Mexico
CO	Colorado	NY	New York
CT	Connecticut	NC	North Carolina
DE	Delaware	ND	North Dakota
DC	District of Columbia	OH	Ohio
FL	Florida	OK	Oklahoma
GA	Georgia	OR	Oregon
GU	Guam	PA	Pennsylvania
HI	Hawaii	PR	Puerto Rico
ID	Idaho	RI	Rhode Island
IL	Illinois	SC	South Carolina
IN	Indiana	SD	South Dakota
IA	Iowa	TN	Tennessee
KS	Kansas	TX	Texas
KY	Kentucky	UT	Utah
LA	Louisiana	VT	Vermont
ME	Maine	VI	Virgin Islands
MD	Maryland	VA	Virginia
MA	Massachusetts	WA	Washington
MI	Michigan	WV	West Virginia
MN	Minnesota	WI	Wisconsin
MS	Mississippi	WY	Wyoming
MO	Missouri		

CANADA

AB	Alberta	NS	Nova Scotia
BC	British Columbia	ON	Ontario
MB	Manitoba	PE	Prince Edward Island
NB	New Brunswick	PQ	Quebec
NF	Newfoundland	SK	Saskatchewan
NT	Northwest Territories	YT	Yukon Territory

(Continued)

International Country Codes

These abbreviations are used only in the Subject Index.

AFG	Afghanistan		GRC	Greece		PAK	Pakistan
AJN	Azerbaijan		GRE	Grenada		PAN	Panama
ALG	Algeria		GRG	Georgia		PAR	Paraguay
AMA	Armenia		GTM	Guatemala		PER	Peru
ANG	Angola		GUY	Guyana		PHL	Philippines
ARG	Argentina		HKG	Hong Kong		PNG	Papua New Guinea
AUS	Australia		HND	Honduras		POL	Poland
AUT	Austria		HUN	Hungary		PRT	Portugal
BDI	Burundi		ICE	Iceland		ROM	Romania
BEL	Belgium		IDN	Indonesia		RUS	Russia
BEN	Benin		IND	India		RWA	Rwanda
BFA	Burkina Faso		IRL	Ireland		SAF	South Africa, Republic of
BGD	Bangladesh		IRN	Iran		SAU	Saudi Arabia
BHR	Bahrain		IRQ	Iraq		SDN	Sudan
BLR	Belorussia		ISR	Israel		SEN	Senegal
BLZ	Belize		ITA	Italy		SGP	Singapore
BMU	Bermuda		JOR	Jordan		SLE	Sierra Leone
BOL	Bolivia		JPN	Japan		SOM	Somalia
BRN	Brunei Darussalam		KAZ	Kazakhstan		SPA	Spain
BRZ	Brazil		KEN	Kenya		SRI	Sri Lanka
BTN	Bhutan		KGA	Kirgizia		SRM	Suriname
BUL	Bulgaria		KOR	Korea, Republic of		SWE	Sweden
BWA	Botswana		KWT	Kuwait		SWI	Switzerland
CAF	Central African Republic		LAT	Latvia		SWZ	Swaziland
CAN	Canada		LBN	Lebanon		SYC	Seychelles
CHL	Chile		LBR	Liberia		SYR	Syria
CHN	China, People's Republic of		LES	Lesotho		TDN	Tadzhikistan
CMR	Cameroon, United Republic of		LIE	Liechtenstein		TGA	Tonga, Kingdom of
COG	Congo		LIT	Lithuania		TGO	Togo
COL	Colombia		LUX	Luxembourg		THA	Thailand
COT	Cote d'Ivoire		MAL	Malta		TUK	Turkmenistan
CPV	Cape Verde		MDG	Madagascar		TUN	Tunisia
CRI	Costa Rica		MDI	Moldavia		TUR	Turkey
CYP	Cyprus		MEX	Mexico		TWN	Taiwan
CZE	Czechoslovakia		MLI	Mali		TZA	Tanzania
DEN	Denmark		MNC	Monaco		UAE	United Arab Emirates
ECU	Ecuador		MOR	Morocco		UGA	Uganda
EGY	Egypt		MOZ	Mozambique		UKI	United Kingdom
ELS	El Salvador		MRN	Mauritania		URE	Ukraine
EST	Estonia		MUS	Mauritius		URY	Uruguay
ETH	Ethiopia		MWI	Malawi		UZN	Uzbekistan
FGN	French Guiana		MYA	Myanmar		VEN	Venezuela
FIJ	Fiji		MYS	Malaysia		VNM	Vietnam
FIN	Finland		NAM	Namibia		WIN	West Indies
FRA	France		NCG	Nicaragua		WSA	Western Samoa
FRO	French Overseas Territories		NER	Niger		YUG	Yugoslavia
GAB	Gabon		NGA	Nigeria		ZAR	Zaire
GER	Germany		NLD	The Netherlands		ZMB	Zambia
GHA	Ghana		NOR	Norway		ZWE	Zimbabwe
GIN	Guinea		NPL	Nepal			
GMB	The Gambia		NZL	New Zealand			

Subject Index

References to entries are arranged geographically under each subject heading by two-character state, territory, and province codes, or three-character country codes. U.S. entries appear first, followed by Canadian, and then International entries. The geographic codes with definitions may be found on the pages immediately preceding this index. Numbers shown in this index refer to entry numbers, not page numbers.

Abitibi Indians: *Canada:* **PQ** 3191

Abnormalities (Animals and plants): AR 17510 **NC** 11210

Aborigines, Australian See: Australian aborigines

Abortion: AR 9468 **CA** 13920 **DC** 537, 11014, 11277 **IL** 790, 13393 **IN** 13121 **KS** 8180 **KY** 3169 **MA** 19742 **MD** 7528 **MI** 5254, 13921, 13922, 13923, 13924, 13925 **MN** 13126 **MO** 13128 **NC** 3090 **NY** 7006, 9297, 13124, 14794 **OH** 7527 **PA** 4875 **TX** 13125, 20555 **VA** 671 **WA** 11331

Abrasives: MA 12096 **MN** 16338 **NY** 12095 *Canada:* **ON** 12093

Abused wives: NY 11111

Academic advisement (See also Counseling): CA 3632 **DC** 1131 **IA** 11015

Acadians (See also Cajuns; French-Canadians): CT 6143 **MA** 11433 **ME** 1154 *Canada:* **NB** 10797, 18072 **NS** 18484

Accidents—Prevention: IL 11279 **NC** 19062 **NY** 3897 **OH** 14185 *Canada:* **BC** 2182 **ON** 5982, 7831

Accounting: AL 18160 **CA** 845, 1058, 4286, 4287, 4753, 5425, 5724, 8802, 8805, 9074, 13331, 15652, 17528, 18387, 19324 **CO** 16813, 18509 **CT** 846, 5695 **DC** 4289, 4749, 4906, 7479, 8211, 8807, 15829, 17495, 17526, 17561, 17936 **FL** 5862, 13332 **IA** 18706 **IL** 838, 1070, 4282, 4756, 5426, 6653, 7702, 8800, 12923, 13336, 18449, 18666 **IN** 767, 7779, 7819, 13545 **LA** 16555 **MA** 847, 1724, 1995, 4288, 5422, 11801, 13333 **MD** 18246 **MI** 1412, 4043, 4817, 5427, 10316, 13334, 18870, 19956 **MN** 4750, 8803, 18896 **MO** 848, 20064 **NC** 6739 **NH** 11483 **NJ** 3260, 7955, 11745 **NM** 19050 **NY** 633, 849, 2242, 2329, 4290, 4316, 4333, 4747, 4755, 5423, 5428, 8801, 11647, 11732, 12654, 12655, 12728, 13341, 13343, 13422, 13633, 14359, 14360, 19282 **OH** 3818, 5434, 12297, 13483, 13503 **OR** 13337 **PA** 3075, 4283, 12899, 17527, 19186, 19216 **PR** 19238 **RI** 2299 **TX** 842, 4751, 5429, 8804, 8808, 13895 **UT** 20802 **VA** 4430, 15828, 19269, 19501 **WA** 13335, 19515 **WI** 19626, 20103 *Canada:* **AB** 4752, 5431, 8813 **BC** 4754, 13338, 18268 **MB** 6702, 18784 **NB** 11448 **ON** 843, 2831, 2844, 2940, 2941, 4284, 4746, 5433, 8811, 10225, 12500, 13342, 19446, 19563, 20566 **PQ** 2862, 4285, 5205, 5432, 7832, 8810, 9900, 13724, 14664, 20847 *Intl:* **ARG** 5548 **AUS** 1347 **ENG** 7913 **GER** 7890 **IRL** 7912 **JOR** 931 **NLD** 11401 **PAN** 17997 **PRT** 1460 **SCT** 14953

Accreditation (Education): CO 11072 **DC** 553

Acid rain: IL 7690 **MA** 18828 **NC** 50 **NY** 3238, 3239, 5837, 17474, 17547 **OH** 12289 **OR** 17462 **PA** 12904 *Canada:* **PQ** 2721, 13599

Acoustics: AL 16988 **CA** 2482, 18395, 20467, 20659 **DC** 17874 **IN** 1201, 4742, 19111 **MA** 1950, 2598, 4626, 11469 **MD** 5270, 9732, 16018 **MN** 4952 **NJ** 14836 **NY** 3096 **OH** 16725 **PA** 12892 **RI** 13735 **UT** 53 **WA** 392 **WI** 11389 *Canada:* **NS** 7161 **ON** 2821, 2825 *Intl:* **ICE** 7634 **POL** 7940 **RUS** 176

Acquired immune deficiency syndrome: AL 15516 **CA** 14641, 18342 **DC** 3279, 8043, 11237 **FL** 5912 **LA** 16566 **MD** 89, 11209, 17627 **NC** 5588 **NY** 7006, 11650, 20556 **OH** 86, 12282 **PA** 144 **VA** 11152 *Canada:* **AB** 279 *Intl:* **NGA** 20557 **VNM** 19838

Actuarial science See: Insurance—Mathematics

Acuff, Roy: TN 4374

Acupuncture: CA 12672 **MO** 3798 **OR** 11124

Adams, Ansel: AZ 18211

Addams, Jane: PA 15903

Addiction See: Substance abuse

Adhesives: CA 1374, 18321 **CT** 9247 **IL** 19701 **MN** 16334, 16335 **MS** 16967 **NJ** 16987 **OH** 4596, 11842 **PA** 9314 **WA** 20361 **WV** 6273

Adirondack Mountains: NY 75, 3433, 5445, 15712

Adler, Alfred: IL 81

Administrative law (See also Civil service; Public administration; Public contracts): CA 2578 **DC** 83, 4243, 4392, 5624, 8211, 17238, 17247, 17250, 17912, 19813, 20458 **FL** 5891, 5905 **MI** 4246 **NY** 9050, 15098 **PA** 19177 **PR** 8031, 19249 **RI** 7225 *Canada:* **AB** 8165 **ON** 2763, 2829, 2840, 5612, 6565 *Intl:* **GER** 6439, 11806 **ITA** 4344 **SPA** 15565

Adolescence (See also Youth): CT 423 **IN** 6485 **NC** 19058 *Canada:* **ON** 7227, 12456 **PQ** 7402

Adoption (See also Foster home care): CO 3958 **DC** 84, 500, 5590, 11126 **FL** 85 **IL** 5589 **NY** 1179, 11607 **PA** 11018 **WI** 19617 *Canada:* **ON** 12456

Adult education: CA 6159 **CO** 3955 **DC** 4913 **FL** 13069 **GA** 18597 **IL** 844, 3517, 11952, 14793 **IN** 7821 **MI** 9507, 10285, 17171 **MN** 10453, 10478 **MO** 14448 **NY** 8973, 12782, 15961 **OH** 3236, 5395, 16394 **PA** 531 **WI** 20307 *Canada:* **AB** 236 **NS** 14317 **ON** 2694, 20780 **PQ** 3233, 16063 **SK** 14859 *Intl:* **AUT** 5541 **CZE** 13294 **GER** 18022 **MEX** 10240 **NZL** 18245 **SWE** 11840, 15909

Adventists (See also Seventh-Day Adventists): CA 8857 **IL** 1308

Advertising (See also Marketing; Packaging; Public relations): CA 4663, 5606, 5608, 5950, 13269, 15825 **DC** 8588, 15269, 17495 **IL** 59, 1574, 2048, 2384, 2394, 2621, 3551, 4405, 4664, 5949, 6652, 12255, 16012, 16318, 18667 **IN** 7819, 9162, 14878 **KS** 18728 **MA** 1995, 11801 **MD** 2267 **MI** 1578, 4602, 4817, 4954, 5964, 6764, 8616, 9200 **MN** 2620, 3060, 3067, 9740, 18908 **MO** 94, 4603, 6855, 8444, 18966 **NC** 5049 **NJ** 5567, 11745 **NY** 96, 476, 1386, 1399, 1575, 2242, 2329, 2395, 4027, 4333, 4665, 4890, 5611, 6755, 7306, 8051, 8210, 11092, 11608, 11783, 12256, 12684, 13633, 13684, 13740, 14191, 14925, 16319, 20819 **OH**

Advertising (continued)
3818, 10025, 12315, 12922, 13397, 18152 **OR** 467 **PA** 3075, 3601, 8692 **SC** 7132 **TN** 13491 **TX** 16446 **VA** 883, 19724 **WI** 19611 *Canada:* **ON** 9498, 9871, 14190, 15438, 16320 **PQ** 5205 **SK** 14870 *Intl:* **AUS** 1336 **GER** 9983 **SGP** 1120 **SPA** 17980 **SWI** 15939

Advertising, Point-of-sale: **NJ** 13159

Aerial photography See: Photography, Aerial

Aerodynamics: **CA** 103, 10979, 11807, 16073, 16797, 17896, 19342, 19794 **FL** 13776 **KS** 1941, 3399 **MA** 13733, 16287 **MD** 16018, 17889 **MI** 20447 **NJ** 17810 **NM** 14778 **NY** 2582, 6770 **PA** 1939 **TN** 16796, 19372 *Intl:* **AUS** 107 **NLD** 11233, 16043

Aeronautics (See also Flight; Navigation (Aeronautics)): **AL** 181, 16812, 16850, 17007, 17008 **AR** 1033, 16861 **AZ** 405, 987, 9887, 13056, 16864 **CA** 155, 399, 2482, 4410, 4468, 4741, 6298, 7504, 7505, 9883, 10980, 12025, 14012, 14013, 14015, 14041, 14808, 15647, 16073, 16532, 16833, 16868, 16869, 16871, 16878, 16888, 17886, 17904, 17960, 19678 **CO** 16822, 16863, 16881 **CT** 17963 **DC** 110, 15277, 16800, 16825, 17280, 17823 **DE** 6828, 16837 **FL** 5327, 7369, 16794, 16841, 16854 **GA** 6220, 9243, 16875 **IA** 158, 8235, 14011 **IL** 108, 14467, 15871, 18671 **IN** 395, 7775, 13530, 13540, 17825 **KS** 8576, 16872, 20409 **LA** 16826 **MA** 6307, 9795, 9834, 12009, 17133, 18831 **MD** 1408, 5557, 17890, 18813 **ME** 16862 **MI** 12196, 12212, 15259 **MN** 13054 **MO** 9885, 14461, 16923 **MS** 10528 **MT** 16867 **ND** 16874 **NH** 8782, 20132 **NJ** 13372, 17487, 17810 **NM** 16802 **NV** 16877 **NY** 628, 2438, 2582, 3885, 4020, 4493, 7619, 9913, 11630, 13204, 13224, 13633, 15750, 16787 **OH** 3830, 6306, 9307, 10987, 16066, 16805, 16806, 16811 **OK** 470, 14147, 16887, 17485 **OR** 12536, 13228 **PA** 1939, 12903 **SC** 16876 **TN** 16288, 16796, 17821, 19372 **TX** 1682, 7449, 9072, 15535, 16248, 16809, 16829, 16860, 16883, 16884, 17822 **VA** 7923, 10986, 11019, 16922, 19874 **WA** 1938, 10900, 15872, 16870, 19523 *Canada:* **AB** 2866, 2869 **BC** 2877, 2891 **MB** 20235 **ON** 1937, 2773, 2775, 2790, 2822, 2828, 2876, 2878, 2953, 11242, 19451 **PQ** 1951, 2437, 2954, 3890, 8082, 13307 *Intl:* **ARG** 969 **AUS** 107 **CZE** 4509 **DEN** 4768 **ENG** 1378, 16721 **GER** 5546 **ISR** 8266 **NLD** 1381 **POL** 8008

Aeronautics, Commercial: **DC** 152 **NY** 1873 **TX** 469 *Canada:* **AB** 2880

Aeronautics—History: **AL** 17008 **AZ** 13056 **CA** 492, 3754, 14686, 14707, 17909, 19337 **CO** 4784, 16822 **CT** 4175 **DC** 11045, 15271, 15277, 17842 **FL** 5327, 16889 **IA** 158 **IL** 154 **MA** 16801 **NH** 20132 **NY** 957, 4020 **OH** 20644 **TX** 469, 13897, 16521 **WA** 10900, 14997 **WI** 5089, 19633 *Canada:* **ON** 19555

Aeronautics—Law and legislation: **CA** 7190, 15654, 18389 **DC** 152, 4392, 6480, 17254, 19813 **LA** 4835 **NY** 3411, 4129, 6832, 7208 **VA** 149 *Canada:* **ON** 16327 **PQ** 8082, 9902

Aeronautics—Safety measures (See also Air traffic control): **AZ** 1379 **IA** 1377 **NJ** 17487 **OH** 1380 **VA** 16922

Aerosols: **CA** 2488, 2590 **NJ** 13856 **NM** 9404

Aerospace engineering: **AL** 16593 **AZ** 401 **CA** 106, 109, 111, 2482, 6298, 6346, 9244, 9705, 9886, 10979, 10980, 12025, 12026, 12027 **CO** 9733 **CT** 17961, 17962 **DC** 3157, 10984, 16803 **FL** 5876, 9734, 10985 **GA** 6387 **IL** 16807 **IN** 19113 **KS** 1941 **MA** 4999 **MD** 4103, 5557, 9732, 16068, 17866 **MI** 15259, 18851 **MN** 393, 7375 **MO** 18963 **NC** 11899 **NJ** 402 **NY** 2582, 4307, 13203, 15750 **OH** 974, 6306, 12307, 18469 **OK** 12371, 19126 **PA** 6308, 14209, 19194 **TN** 16796 **TX** 6300, 9426, 16217, 19389 **VA** 6301, 10990 *Canada:* **ON** 2674, 19443, 19451 **PQ** 404 *Intl:* **BRZ** 8003 **ENG** 8730, 14093 **GER** 4836 **ISR** 8266 **NLD** 11233

Aerospace medicine See: Space medicine

Aesthetics (See also Art; Color; Painting; Poetry; Sculpture; Surrealism): **CA** 15660 **MI** 5848 **NY** 112 **OH** 20836 **TX** 19390 **WA** 19538 *Intl:* **CZE** 13294 **GER** 8824

Afghanistan: **NE** 19007 *Intl:* **GER** 7926

Africa: **CA** 15650, 18427 **CT** 20696 **DC** 130, 3161, 7477, 9107, 9125, 9126, 12715, 15264, 15286, 16784, 17919 **IL** 8455, 12085 **LA** 810 **MA** 1981, 2005 **MI** 3348, 10312 **NC** 120 **NY** 122, 126, 4314, 7925, 11629, 15708 **OH** 12296 **OK** 8944 **PA** 3183, 9190 **SC** 10924 **WI** 19578, 19602 *Canada:* **PQ** 3216, 4121, 18086 *Intl:* **BEL** 1667, 15194 **COT** 7862 **ETH**

12557 **FRA** 3205 **GER** 18040, 18047, 18052 **GHA** 18608 **ISR** 7102 **LES** 9069 **MOR** 129 **NGA** 11808 **NLD** 131 **POL** 13167 **SAF** 119, 18443 **SEN** 125, 127 **SWE** 14891

Africa, East: *Intl:* **NOR** 10277 **SWE** 15926

Africa—History: **CA** 4380 **CT** 20696 **DC** 12715 **IL** 12085 **MA** 2005 **PA** 16144 **WI** 19578 *Intl:* **ETH** 12557 **GER** 18037 **GHA** 18608 **NGA** 124

Africa, North: **CO** 638 **DC** 10351 **MA** 6955 *Intl:* **ALG** 349 **ENG** 6665 **FRA** 7885

Africa, South See: South Africa

Africa, Southern: *Intl:* **BWA** 2026 **GER** 7863 **SAF** 18443

Africa, West: **AZ** 18208 **MI** 10312 *Intl:* **NGA** 11808

African Americans (See also Blacks): **AL** 192, 15992, 16591 **CA** 18427 **DC** 7477, 7478, 11045 **GA** 1245, 3761, 3763 **IL** 3527, 8455, 15677 **LA** 20677 **MA** 15852, 18827 **MI** 3348 **MO** 14437 **MS** 7338 **NY** 3288, 4020, 4314, 7011, 11049, 11601, 15725 **OH** 20293 **OK** 8944 **PA** 3509, 7282, 9190, 10403, 19200 **TN** 16172 **WA** 14998 *Intl:* **NGA** 124

African Americans—History: **AL** 1835, 16592 **CA** 121, 4100, 4380, 12206, 13913, 18373, 18427 **CT** 4409, 16504 **DC** 9117 **GA** 3763, 8714 **IL** 3527, 5073, 8455, 15677 **IN** 7755, 7778 **KS** 8564, 18729 **LA** 810 **MA** 10198 **MD** 11461, 13359 **ME** 18779 **MO** 17719, 20250, 20253 **MS** 3086, 4924 **NY** 11629, 13630 **OH** 123, 3826, 12296, 20424 **PA** 1728, 3509, 9106, 16144, 19200 **TN** 3300, 5830 **TX** 9931, 16231 **VA** 6880, 17677 **WA** 14998 **WV** 20214

African Americans in medicine: **DC** 7475 **TN** 10021

African Americans in the performing arts: **CA** 18379 **MI** 4825 **NY** 15725 **PA** 9190

African Americans—Religion: **DC** 7480 **GA** 8714 **IL** 3527 **OH** 123 **PA** 5142

African Americans—Social life and customs: **DC** 4905, 18553, 18554 **IL** 3527 **LA** 810 **MD** 13359 **NY** 3047, 11629, 13628 **PA** 19200

African art See: Art, African

African languages and literature: **MA** 2005 **MI** 10312 *Intl:* **ENG** 6665 **GER** 18037, 18047 **NGA** 124 **SAF** 15385

African Methodist Episcopal Zion Church: **NC** 9233 **OH** 12800, 20424

African music See: Music, African

Africana: **DC** 7478 **IL** 3527, 5073, 12085 **MA** 2005 *Intl:* **CZE** 10976 **NAM** 5464 **SAF** 15386, 15387

Afro-Americans See: African Americans

Aged and aging (See also Gerontology): **AZ** 13057 **CA** 135, 420, 1127 **CO** 3958 **DC** 1158, 4054, 4910, 6660, 11137, 17483 **FL** 19320 **IL** 5980, 18459, 20254 **MA** 2011 **MD** 11204 **MI** 967, 15037 **NC** 5041 **NY** 3302, 3310, 4028, 7978, 20758 **OH** 3126, 12280, 14062 **OR** 12534 **PA** 12863, 12983 **TN** 16155 **VA** 11021, 19863 **WI** 3617, 9709 *Canada:* **ON** 12456 **PQ** 3296, 13605, 18097

Aged—Legal status, laws, etc.: **IL** 7674

Agee, James Rufus: **TX** 19392

Agent Orange: **MI** 10306

Agribusiness See: Agriculture—Economic aspects

Agricultural chemicals (See also Fertilizers and manures): **CA** 3497 **CT** 16672, 20177 **DE** 5028 **MI** 1552 **MO** 17499 **NJ** 555, 5933 **PA** 14039 *Intl:* **IND** 7747 **URE** 16618, 16620

Agricultural chemistry (See also Agricultural chemicals): **CA** 13845 **PA** 14039 *Intl:* **CHN** 1655 **GER** 9731, 18033 **HUN** 9542 **MUS** 9852 **TWN** 15987

Alexandria (VA): VA 344

Alexian Brothers: IL 4147

Algae: CA 15651 DC 15272 FL 5896 NC 19067 WA 19527 *Canada:* MB 2731 PQ 18078 *Intl:* IND 7747

Alger, Horatio: MA 11012

Algeria: *Intl:* ALG 349 FRA 7885

Alkali industry and trade: MI 1552

Allen of Hurtwood, Lord: SC 19312

Allen, William Hervey: PA 19225

Allergy: MI 10801 *Intl:* BUL 2347

Alloys (See also Metallurgy): CO 16361 IA 8238 MD 17612 NJ 15989 PA 4452 TX 2614 WV 7727

Alpine regions: CO 18498 *Intl:* ITA 3845

Alternative energy sources See: Renewable energy sources

Alternative press See: Underground press

Aluminum (See also Light metals): CA 8504 DC 431 GA 430 MT 3985 OH 5313 PA 432, 433 TX 13863 VA 13865 *Canada:* ON 322 PQ 321, 323 *Intl:* ITA 434

Alumni See: Universities and colleges—Alumni

Alzheimer's disease: MI 8873 PA 3295 TX 10434

Amazon River Region: *Intl:* BRZ 6519, 11206 PER 3389

Ambulance service: CA 472

America—History See: Americana; United States—History

American Indians See: Indians of North America

American literature: CA 3900, 7572, 9973, 10409, 15658, 18355, 18358, 18382, 18407, 19290, 19338 CO 18507 CT 15633, 20177 DC 6379, 9117 FL 18586, 18846, 19322 GA 18600 IA 6608, 9311, 19108 IL 3528, 9084, 11752, 15492, 18461, 18672, 18689, 20369 IN 1438, 7794, 13542 LA 16844 MA 473, 1999, 2008, 6576, 15841, 17133, 17745 MD 8422, 18820 ME 3872 MN 1293, 10454 MO 490, 20059 NC 11885, 13861, 19075, 19078, 19942 NH 4614, 4860 NJ 5002 NY 460, 2335, 4010, 4023, 9595, 11598, 11616, 11640, 11723, 14360, 15707, 15961, 16994, 19280, 19789 OH 8649, 18155, 18534, 19425 OK 19466 PA 1227, 7811, 8875, 16137, 19197 SC 19312 TN 4417, 19370, 19773 TX 1602, 13897, 16521, 19392 UT 20809 VA 11546 WI 19607 *Canada:* BC 6105 *Intl:* AUT 14658, 18055, 18057 BRZ 16631 COL 1539 DEN 8776 FRA 667, 18070 GER 16039, 18019, 18021, 18024, 18025, 18048, 18050 IND 770 ISR 1521 ITA 18007 JPN 10952

American music: CA 14718, 18335 CT 4179, 16504 IN 2416, 6581 KY 18769 MA 1976, 1981, 11469 MO 18977 NC 10722, 19072 NJ 11744 NY 2193, 2233, 2234, 2334, 19279 PA 3078, 6119, 19212, 20187 RI 2282 SD 15146 TX 1604, 13893 VA 7332, 19507 WA 19536 WI 19610

American Revolution: CA 4293 CT 11519, 20129, 20704 DC 11291, 15314, 17800 IL 6009, 19763 KY 11297 LA 16560 MA 1647, 4962 MD 17860 MI 18888 NC 6800, 17740, 17752 NJ 6489, 11298, 16484, 17753 NY 4953, 5971, 6013, 7289, 8374, 11627, 11682, 14053, 15377, 15849, 15961, 17774, 20229 PA 4636, 7282, 19731 RI 2270 SC 2610, 15402, 17713 WA 20692

American Samoa: CA 11037

Americana (See also United States—History): AL 1862 CA 1390, 2547, 16729, 17909, 17973 CT 4178, 16504, 18519 DC 9134, 17557 FL 5919 IL 4165, 7260, 7698, 11752 KS 14500 LA 16560 MA 473, 1801, 1999, 2008, 13005, 20446 MI 18888 MN 10454 MO 10536, 10537, 18979,

20059 MS 18949 NC 19075, 19942 NE 18995 NJ 13367, 17753, 19851 NY 73, 7499, 11627, 11628, 11640, 11666, 17030, 17922 PA 712, 1227, 6121, 9106, 12858, 14068, 19209 PR 19242 RI 2282 TX 3109 VA 7930, 10628, 15821, 19864 VT 10887 WY 20671 *Canada:* PQ 1830 *Intl:* FRA 18070 GER 18048, 18050 ITA 8280 JPN 10952

Amish (See also Mennonites): IN 10091 OH 1917 PA 8921, 10403

Ammunition (See also Explosives): IL 16921, 16972 IN 17899 PA 8702 VT 6312 *Canada:* MB 14106

Amphibians See: Reptiles

Amphibious warfare: CA 17827 DC 17600 FL 17799 VA 17605, 17828

Anabaptists (See also Baptists; Hutterite Brethren; Mennonites): IN 10091 KS 1784, 3329 OH 1113, 1917 PA 10090 TX 4433 VA 5154 *Canada:* MB 10087 ON 6714 *Intl:* SWI 5480

Anatomy (See also Nervous system; Physiology): AZ 1221 CA 18305 IA 8240 IL 11122, 14919 IN 7795, 13550 MA 5990, 6996 MO 9249 NY 4001, 4313, 20751 OH 20645 PR 13209 SD 19315 TX 20407 *Canada:* AB 14138 ON 19450, 19553 *Intl:* ENG 14114

Ancient art See: Art, Ancient

Ancient history See: History, Ancient

Andersen, Hans Christian: DC 9135

Anderson, Maxwell: TX 19392

Anderson, Sherwood: IL 11752 OH 12337 VA 19510, 19875

Andes: *Intl:* PER 837, 6146

Andrews, Cecily Isobel Fairfield (Dame Rebecca West): CT 20703, 20703 OK 19466

Anesthesiology: AL 18172 CA 6793, 9256 CT 6936 IL 743 KS 18732 KY 18771 ND 19103 NJ 1927 NY 4001, 14056, 20752 PA 6816, 7424, 19211 *Canada:* ON 19553 *Intl:* ENG 14114

Angelou, Maya Marguerita: NC 19942

Anglican Church See: Church of England

Angling See: Fish and game

Animal husbandry See: Livestock

Animal nutrition (See also Pastures): IA 6618 IN 3363, 9163, 13078 MI 10314 MN 3044 MO 13699 NE 17187 *Canada:* ON 2632 SK 2663 *Intl:* AUS 1328 GTM 12717 MEX 15009

Animals (See also Wildlife; names of specific animals, e.g. Cats): CA 18358, 20849 CT 4204 DC 15282 FL 15796, 18569 GA 17193 IL 3553 IN 13544 MA 5107 MD 17203, 17204 MN 18942, 18943 NE 11372 NH 19029 NY 4318 PR 19234 SC 10924 TX 16201 *Canada:* AB 244 MB 4759, 18783 PQ 18088 SK 19299 *Intl:* AUS 18146 CRI 8029

Animals, Aquatic See: Aquatic animals

Animals in art: WI 20579

Animals in research See: Laboratory animals

Animals, Treatment of: CA 875 MA 9827 MD 14948 NY 979 PA 16133 *Intl:* ENG 18142

Annapolis (MD): MD 7237

Anorexia nervosa (See also Eating disorders): IL 5589, 11051

Antarctic regions (See also Polar regions): AK 18181 DC 11045, 11185, 11282 NV 5984, 19013 *Canada:* AB 965 *Intl:* AUS 15689, 15696

Architecture (continued)

19039, 19042, 19047 **NV** 19022 **NY** 670, 2083, 2240, 2251, 2333, 3392, 3731, 4002, 4277, 4309, 5514, 6358, 7243, 7358, 7438, 8932, 10211, 10213, 10216, 10860, 10866, 10909, 11554, 11583, 11584, 11615, 11624, 11666, 11679, 11680, 11724, 11725, 12433, 12768, 13304, 13636, 13818, 13820, 13988, 14984, 15214, 15274, 15707, 15712, 15733, 15761, 15958, 19273, 19276, 19787, 20229, 20763 **OH** 1313, 3809, 3813, 3822, 4032, 4654, 8651, 8734, 8841, 10264, 10266, 12216, 12219, 12307, 12329, 13477, 16392, 18152, 18468, 19693 **OK** 1719, 7488, 12361, 12371, 19121 **OR** 10846, 19141, 19159 **PA** 1227, 2397, 3078, 6109, 9057, 12849, 12893, 12894, 12981, 12987, 12991, 13085, 15595, 16132, 16709, 19182, 20340 **RI** 2274, 11775, 13874, 19264 **SC** 3088, 3442, 3793, 3794, 15252, 15395 **TN** 8773, 10067, 11002, 15701, 19768 **TX** 1087, 1315, 4451, 4561, 5285, 5996, 6021, 7121, 7461, 8433, 13043, 13893, 14670, 18646, 19376 **VA** 954, 1166, 3934, 3938, 6814, 7061, 8475, 19503, 19864, 19869, 19873, 19875, 19884 **VT** 10887, 15108, 19811 **WA** 8817, 14999, 16444, 19512 **WI** 4958, 10426, 10430, 10432, 19601 *Canada:* **AB** 300, 1233, 18292, 18295 **BC** 2141, 2166, 18269 **MB** 9239, 18785, 20487 **NB** 11453 **NS** 16034 **ON** 2713, 2768, 2838, 4740, 19440, 19543, 19546, 20781 **PE** 4136 **PQ** 1622, 3194, 8343, 9892, 10700, 18075 *Intl:* **AUT** 18058, 18702 **CHL** 3167 **CHN** 3603, 3621 **CRI** 17989 **DEN** 4800 **ENG** 950, 8644, 8731, 14120, 20795 **FIN** 7126 **FRA** 3226, 6068 **GER** 6106, 7301, 8824, 9063, 18251 **HUN** 5391, 7541 **ICE** 11240 **IRL** 18485 **NLD** 18206 **NOR** 12592, 16033 **POL** 16035 **RUS** 3198, 3385, 14660, 14945 **SAF** 10276 **SCT** 5233 **SPA** 15565 **SWE** 2423, 11310, 14042, 15910 **SWI** 15937, 15938, 19663, 20851

Architecture, Church See: Church architecture

Architecture and the handicapped: **DC** 953 **NC** 1807 **NY** 8190 **PA** 6909 *Canada:* **BC** 8739

Architecture, Islamic: **MA** 6965, 9817 *Intl:* **EGY** 12562

Architecture, Naval See: Naval architecture

Arctic regions (See also Polar regions): **AK** 209, 211, 213, 963, 11086, 17063, 17068, 17073, 17100, 18175, 18181 **CA** 17830 **CO** 18498 **DC** 11282 **MA** 5266, 9673 **ME** 2033 **NJ** 6489 **NY** 5521 **TX** 5530 **VT** 3276 *Canada:* **AB** 965, 2916, 6496, 18295 **BC** 3011, 18282 **MB** 7500 **NT** 13363 **ON** 2756, 2893, 2963, 6866 *Intl:* **NOR** 12115

Area studies: **AZ** 17013 **CA** 3043, 18328 **DC** 17557 **KS** 18737 **OH** 10266 **PA** 5975, 17080 **TX** 17015 **VA** 15458 **VT** 5520 **WA** 17066 *Intl:* **GER** 13839

Argentina: **DC** 9125 *Intl:* **ARG** 2324, 10884

Arid regions agriculture: **AZ** 18208 **CA** 18403 *Canada:* **PQ** 9904 *Intl:* **IND** 8095 **SYR** 932

Aristotle: **PA** 19197 *Canada:* **ON** 19460 **PQ** 18065

Arizona: **AZ** 985, 987, 988, 989, 1000, 1015, 1864, 3120, 10171, 10587, 11352, 11991, 11992, 13018, 13024, 13026, 13061, 13062, 15081, 16864, 17692, 18215, 18219, 18231 **CA** 11038, 15532 **CO** 11039 **TX** 5285

Arkansas: **AR** 1023, 1029, 1031, 1034, 1037, 1725, 3326, 4445, 5001, 6254, 7133, 12609, 15134, 15167, 15526, 18236, 18237, 18239, 18444 **TX** 11041

Armaments (See also National defense): **MA** 17781 **NJ** 16918 **VT** 6312 *Intl:* **BEL** 11339 **NLD** 18609

Armenia: **CA** 1053, 2560, 6156, 18761 **DC** 1048, 14508 **MA** 1049, 1051, 13415 **MD** 9577 **MI** 18889 **NJ** 1050 **NY** 1047, 11626 **TX** 14426

Armour, Richard Willard: **CA** 3752

Arms and armor: **CA** 16997 **KY** 17020 **MA** 7189, 15242 **NY** 10216 **PA** 12990

Arms control (See also Disarmament): **DC** 3231, 5651, 16917 **IL** 18670 **IN** 7495 **MA** 6956, 7924 **MD** 12164 **NY** 2221, 7931 **OK** 12347 **VA** 11215 *Intl:* **SWE** 15801

Arnold, Matthew: **TX** 16200 **VA** 19510

Art (See also Aesthetics; Architecture; Art museum libraries; Decoration

and ornament; Folk art; Graphic arts; Lithography): **AL** 1851, 1853, 16591 **AR** 1022, 18233 **AZ** 13015, 13024, 13026 **CA** 1741, 1800, 2479, 3900, 4896, 8931, 9281, 9335, 9343, 9418, 9973, 10080, 12158, 12704, 13913, 14699, 14756, 14801, 15472, 15643, 16601, 18355, 18370, 18404, 18426, 20569 **CT** 6937, 7342, 9473, 12688, 15818, 20705 **DC** 3163, 6137, 11177 **FL** 4480, 10250, 13191, 13934, 18844 **GA** 1237, 5333 **HI** 7038, 7378 **IA** 15195, 18704 **ID** 1945, 18649 **IL** 745, 7701, 8490, 15488, 18448, 18450 **IN** 855, 1072, 2417, 5509, 7783, 7814, 7824, 15392, 19120 **KS** 18734, 20405 **KY** 7075, 15580, 18748, 18767 **LA** 16557, 16558 **MA** 3492, 4588, 6253, 6980, 7019, 10896, 10897, 15600, 20370, 20598 **MD** 8420, 9751, 13300, 18811, 19961, 20004 **ME** 13245 **MI** 3228, 4815, 5850, 6632, 10315, 15085 **MN** 10446 **MO** 8547, 11387, 11388, 13268, 14434, 14452 **MS** 18956 **NC** 19077 **NE** 8485, 11370 **NH** 4615, 9586 **NJ** 1050, 6128, 10747, 11516, 11744, 14156 **NM** 527, 19038, 19039, 19042 **NY** 670, 1088, 3392, 4013, 4277, 4309, 4312, 6165, 7598, 8075, 8766, 10213, 10216, 10437, 11583, 11666, 11683, 11724, 12768, 12819, 13627, 13636, 13818, 13993, 14642, 14903, 15714, 15732, 15958, 15961, 19787, 20695 **OH** 3016, 3698, 3813, 3822, 4038, 4654, 4846, 9138, 9402, 10264, 10266, 12216, 12308, 12329, 13477, 15608, 15984, 18533 **OK** 12997, 19127 **OR** 12529, 13236 **PA** 1904, 3078, 5232, 8832, 13748, 15889, 19214 **RI** 13440 **SC** 3088, 3793 **SD** 4419 **TN** 10060, 16154 **TX** 7461, 8708, 18646, 19390, 19414 **UT** 20803 **VA** 1166, 13715, 19503, 19869 **VT** 10887, 15108 **WA** 14991, 14999, 15979 **WI** 8639, 10419, 11429, 11430, 12689, 19601, 19653 *Canada:* **AB** 1464, 18292 **BC** 19489 **NS** 12142 **ON** 1085, 2769, 14427, 14428, 16418 **PE** 4136 **PQ** 9975, 10877, 10880, 15023, 15025, 18108 **SK** 14874, 16616 *Intl:* **ALG** 348 **ARG** 2324 **AUS** 13662, 15697, 16010 **AUT** 8585, 12224, 18058 **BEL** 14121 **CHN** 1657 **CZE** 4508, 4516, 13294 **DEN** 4800 **ENG** 3800, 8644, 9266, 15107 **FRA** 5988, 10881 **GER** 8824, 8825, 14189, 15698, 18251 **HUN** 8719 **ICE** 11240 **ITA** 1821, 15925 **NLD** 18206 **NOR** 12105, 12111, 16033 **POL** 19665 **SPA** 7996, 10610, 15557, 15561 **SWI** 1825, 20851 **THA** 16293

Art, African: **AZ** 16544 **CA** 5703, 18378 **CO** 4774 **CT** 20696 **DC** 15264, 15286 **FL** 18562 **GA** 7191 **IN** 7784 **LA** 810, 11539 **MD** 1452 **MI** 5846 **NC** 11880 **NY** 2238, 10210, 10214, 19787 **OK** 8944 **TX** 4555, 9072 **WI** 19578 *Intl:* **AUS** 1079 **NGA** 124 **SAF** 15385

Art, American: **AL** 1851, 10688 **AZ** 13015, 16544 **CA** 961, 5703, 14699, 16524, 17973, 18378 **CT** 411, 11438 **DC** 959, 4295, 11176, 11178, 11179, 11180, 11181, 15261, 15265, 15266, 15267, 15268, 15271 **DE** 4715, 20503 **FL** 4480 **GA** 7191, 16076 **IA** 4635 **IL** 16181 **KS** 20404 **KY** 18767 **LA** 810, 11539 **MA** 1074, 2442, 3773, 6187, 6199, 13004, 15242, 20152, 20590 **MD** 1452 **ME** 5604 **MI** 1761, 8530 **MN** 10469 **MO** 14434 **NC** 13861, 19081 **NE** 8485 **NJ** 10656, 11743, 14156 **NM** 10912 **NY** 227, 460, 611, 2238, 5514, 6165, 7105, 8624, 8766, 9702, 10210, 10216, 10866, 11016, 11578, 11663, 15703, 16621, 19787, 20396 **OH** 2414, 12308 **OK** 12342 **PA** 2080, 6097, 6121, 12836, 12990, 20340 **SC** 3993 **TN** 7564, 16154 **TX** 1086, 3109, 4394, 9959, 14669 **VT** 10887 **WA** 6189 **WY** 2325 *Canada:* **ON** 1076, 1078

Art, Ancient: **CA** 15643, 18378 **DC** 11180, 11181 **KY** 18767 **MA** 10898 **MD** 19961 **NY** 2239, 4013, 10216, 19787 **TX** 16521 *Intl:* **ISR** 8268

Art, Australian: *Intl:* **AUS** 1079, 1342

Art, British: **CT** 20734, 20735, 20736 **DE** 20503 **VT** 10887 *Canada:* **ON** 1076 *Intl:* **ARG** 1126 **BEL** 2184 **ENG** 3465, 14091, 16011

Art, Canadian: **NY** 2918 *Canada:* **AB** 5238, 6496 **BC** 1075, 19752 **NS** 12132 **ON** 1076, 1077, 1078, 1093, 2813, 9944, 14028, 20778 **PQ** 10700, 18110

Art, Chinese: **IL** 1082 **MO** 11388 **NY** 5514 *Intl:* **CHN** 6789 **HKG** 3615

Art, Decorative See: Decoration and ornament

Art, European: **AL** 1851, 10688 **AZ** 16544 **CA** 14699 **DC** 11176, 11179, 11180, 11181, 15261 **DE** 20503 **FL** 13933 **GA** 7191 **LA** 11539 **MA** 3773, 10898, 20152, 20590 **MD** 19961 **ME** 5604 **MN** 10445 **NE** 8485 **NY** 2238, 6165, 7105, 10215, 10216, 11724, 19787 **OH** 12308 **OK** 12342 **PA** 12990, 20340 **SC** 3993 **TX** 9959 **WA** 6189 *Canada:* **ON** 1078 *Intl:* **BEL** 8785

Art, Folk See: Folk art

Art—Forgeries: **VA** 19503

Art, French: **CA** 5703 **HI** 18627 **MA** 6149 **NY** 6145, 10209 *Canada:* **ON** 7866 *Intl:* **FRA** 6068 **SWI** 19663

Asia, Southeastern (See also Indochina): AL 16815 CA 12678, 18344 CO 638 CT 20732 DC 1116, 9124 HI 18617 IL 11994 MN 5594 NY 4315, 4332 OH 3823, 12333 PA 5232 WI 19609 *Canada:* NS 4535 ON 14130 *Intl:* GER 15794 IDN 9977 KOR 1124 MYS 1115 NOR 10277 SGP 7979 SWE 15926

Asian Americans: CA 4379, 12204, 18301, 18371, 19905 IL 11994

Asimov, Isaac: MA 2008

Asphalt: CA 20542 KY 1130 MD 11048

Assassination (See also Terrorism): CA 2509 DC 1133

Assemblies of God churches: AR 5726 MN 11910 MO 1134, 3330

Assessment: AZ 8179 IL 924, 8053 VA 744 WI 19741 WV 20211 *Canada:* ON 12483, 12489

Associations: DC 746

Assyria: CA 2576 CT 20702 IL 18457 MA 6575 NY 11626 PA 878

Astrology: AZ 577, 20633 CA 13012, 13421 FL 16300 MN 20170 WA 1098 *Intl:* NPL 11391

Astronautics (See also Rockets (Aeronautics); Satellites; Space sciences): AL 10989, 16996 AZ 13056 CA 2491, 4741, 6298, 9886, 14015, 15647, 16532, 17904 CO 16881 DC 110, 15277 IL 14467 IN 9536 MA 9795, 9797, 18831 MD 18813 MO 9885 NJ 6309, 8287, 17810 NY 628, 688, 7619, 11630 OH 16811 OK 14147 TN 16796 TX 16798, 16809 WA 1938 *Canada:* ON 2828 SK 17943 *Intl:* BRZ 8003 GER 5546 JPN 7981

Astronomy (See also Mechanics, Celestial; Planets; Radio astronomy; Satellites): AK 18184 AL 16996, 18173 AZ 8753, 9411, 18229 CA 1182, 2470, 2484, 2491, 3074, 3756, 6759, 9305, 9353, 9353, 10671, 14713, 14718, 14722, 14802, 15657, 18302, 18381, 18412, 18418, 18435, 18438, 19346 CO 1433, 4779, 11098, 17652, 18501 CT 20180, 20701 DC 3073, 4914, 11281, 15277, 17864 DE 10803, 18546 FL 5917, 18577 GA 5669 HI 8464 IA 14790 IL 79, 12088, 18452, 18688 IN 7803, 13539, 13548 KS 18731 KY 18746, 18768, 18770 LA 8877 MA 489, 806, 1999, 3895, 6971, 9797, 9806, 9812, 9820, 9822, 10967, 15232, 16550, 16553, 16801, 18825, 18831 MD 10983, 15556, 17650, 18813 MI 3347, 4408, 10333, 18881, 20273 MN 18928, 18931 MO 6847, 17174, 20066 NC 5045, 19056 NE 19003 NH 4610 NJ 1187, 6874, 13368, 14171 NM 11299 NY 444, 688, 2336, 2340, 4021, 4328, 5034, 10982, 11630, 13986, 15749, 15965, 16994, 19284 OH 3128, 3814, 12222, 12303, 12323, 18478 OK 19137 OR 19158 PA 3080, 6092, 6094, 12912, 13750, 15900, 16136, 19188, 19201 PR 4303, 19247 TN 16796, 19771, 19774 TX 10988, 19402 UT 20809 VA 11258, 16354, 19505 WA 19539 WI 18462, 19624 WV 20214 *Canada:* BC 2816, 2817, 18281 MB 9619, 18795 ON 2674, 2827, 12498, 13659, 14097, 19428, 19553 PQ 18092 *Intl:* BEL 8584, 14127 CHL 3396 CHN 20650 COL 3925 ENG 6669, 14119 FIN 19694 GER 1183, 5546 HUN 7549 ISR 6573 ITA 16498 JPN 11083 NLD 5491, 14126 POL 13177 RUS 10767, 17957 SAF 15382 SPA 7236, 15560, 15567 SWI 15938

Astrophysics (See also Spectrum analysis): CA 2484, 3074, 5439, 6759, 10671, 10980, 15657, 18395 CO 11098, 17652, 18500, 18505 CT 20701 DC 3072, 15277, 17864 DE 10803, 18546 IL 79, 18452, 18688 IN 19111 MA 681, 6971, 9797, 9812, 16550, 16801 MD 15556 MO 20066 NC 5045 NJ 7895, 13368 NY 4021, 5034, 10982, 19284 OH 3128, 12303 OK 19137 PA 19220 TN 19771 TX 10988 VA 10986 WA 19539 WI 18462, 19624 *Canada:* BC 2816, 2817 ON 2827, 13661, 19428 PQ 18092 *Intl:* BEL 14127 GER 1183, 1184, 5546 ITA 16498 NLD 5491 SPA 15560

Atheism: TX 15786 *Intl:* POL 19665

Athletics (See also Coaching (Athletics)): IL 763 KY 5151 *Intl:* GER 5631

Atlanta (GA): GA 1241, 1246, 1247

Atlantic City (NJ): NJ 1251

Atlases See: Maps and atlases

Atmosphere (See also Atmospheric carbon dioxide; Atmospheric physics; **Meteorology):** AK 18184 CA 18381 CO 17652 DC 3157, 11281 FL 18842 MA 6959 NC 11900 PR 4303 RI 19266 VA 10986 WA 19537 *Canada:* AB 2707 NS 4536 ON 2705, 20794 *Intl:* BRZ 8003 ITA 8077 SWI 20625

Atmospheric carbon dioxide: TN 12185

Atmospheric electricity: MA 9160

Atmospheric physics (See also Meteorology): AZ 18214 CA 10506 MD 17650 NV 19013 OH 18470 PA 19220 PR 4303 UT 4406 WA 17649

Atomic power See: Nuclear energy

Atomic transition probabilities: MD 17615

Atomic weapons See: Nuclear weapons

Atwood, Margaret Eleanor: *Canada:* ON 19460, 19555

Auden, Wystan Hugh: KS 20412 TX 16200, 19392 VA 15932 *Canada:* ON 20778

Audio-visual materials (See also Sound recordings): AL 185, 1283, 1860 AZ 18218, 18222 CA 2575, 9346, 13913, 14723, 16786, 16828, 18310, 18410 CO 447, 18489 CT 4184, 4201, 18518 DC 4903, 11027, 11033, 11176, 11184 DE 4726 FL 5497, 10251, 19319, 19549 GA 512, 1239, 6383, 14882 HI 7033, 7038, 7044, 19834 IA 8239 IL 1083, 3523, 3537, 11953 IN 7822, 13541 KS 20128 KY 15461 MA 2012, 9010, 15235, 20599 MD 11042, 13298, 18823 ME 9551 MI 4818, 10326, 18551, 18865, 18882 MN 4884, 10446, 14561, 18912, 18936 MO 14451 MS 10520 MT 18986 NC 11876 ND 11922 NH 19031 NJ 2609, 10774, 14176 NM 46, 893, 5162 NV 19015 NY 956, 1929, 2241, 2331, 4322, 4584, 7086, 11003, 11090, 11605, 13626, 13994, 14356, 15959, 15966 OH 3817, 4658, 8646, 12283, 13482, 18153 OK 12362 OR 13246, 13247, 19151, 19155 PA 1288, 6126, 9642, 12895, 14481, 16995, 19228 RI 2274 TN 16160 TX 7460, 18645, 19104, 19378 UT 14645, 19468, 19471 VA 3933, 6878, 19887 WA 20035 WI 4278, 7858, 19575, 19583 WV 20214 WY 20666 *Canada:* AB 286, 298, 18287 BC 2169, 18258 NB 19023 NS 12145 ON 7719, 10224, 12119, 19166, 19429, 20784 PE 13349 PQ 1829, 18074, 18086, 18109 *Intl:* ENG 2192

Auditing (See also Accounting): AZ 841 CA 4286, 4287, 4748, 4753, 8802, 8805, 9074, 13331, 17528 DC 4289, 17526 FL 13332 IL 4282, 4756, 7702, 8800 MA 847, 1724, 17525 MI 19956 MN 4750 NY 633, 5428, 8801, 13341, 13343 OH 840, 5434 PA 4283 TX 842, 4751, 5429, 8804 VA 5597 WA 13335 *Canada:* AB 4752 BC 13338 NT 12062 ON 843, 2831, 2940, 4284, 8811, 13342 PQ 4285, 5205, 8810, 14664 *Intl:* AUS 1347 ENG 7913 GER 7890

Audubon, John James: LA 12099 RI 13440 SC 19312

Augustinians: MD 20052 PA 1300 *Intl:* BEL 1301

Auroras: CO 20617

Austen, Jane: *Canada:* BC 1309

Australia: DC 1338 NY 1345 *Intl:* AUS 1330, 1333, 1337, 1339, 1346, 1348, 4270, 10712, 14118, 15689, 15690, 15692, 15694, 15696, 15697, 19831

Australian aborigines: NY 1345 *Intl:* AUS 14118 NLD 20603

Australian literature: *Canada:* NS 4530

Austria: DC 9113 NY 1357, 1361 PA 9480 *Intl:* AUT 521, 1352, 1716, 4889, 7919, 7937, 12223, 16372, 19837 GER 1597

Authors: AL 1862, 19305 AR 1033 CA 2568, 9350, 13157, 14741, 19172 CO 11330 CT 4178, 9206 FL 7281, 10254, 10255, 18586 GA 1057, 20017 IA 2323, 4997, 18721 IL 3536, 3538, 7707, 20099, 20258 IN 7769, 13094 KY 9398, 20260 ME 2033, 9564, 18781 MI 10336, 10931 MN 10448, 10454, 18920 MO 490, 14457 MS 18949 ND 11929 NE 19007 NH 4616 NJ 11747, 12787, 14175 NV 19022 NY 73, 166, 3475, 4996, 5360, 7233, 7316, 9591, 15961 OH 3823, 12328, 12337, 13479, 13488, 19425 OR 19159 PA 6111, 19846, 20186 TN 13492, 19302 TX 18643 VA 19861 WA 20035, 20045 *Canada:* AB 18293 ON 2807, 12601 *Intl:* BEL 1155 GER 7110

Biophysics (continued)
4328, 19284 **OH** 12295, 18470 **PA** 12910, 12912, 19206 **WI** 19606 *Canada:* **ON** 2679, 12430, 19553 **PQ** 18092 *Intl:* **GER** 6530

Biosciences See: Life sciences

Biotechnology (See also Bionics; Human engineering; Biomechanics): **CA** 805, 3867 **CO** 11267 **CT** 10389 **IL** 12000 **MA** 8007 **MD** 1847 **NY** 2134 **OR** 15954 **WI** 136 *Canada:* **ON** 8859 **PQ** 7864 **SK** 2661 *Intl:* **AUS** 19053 **BRZ** 2406, 18004 **COL** 3923 **FIN** 355 **ICE** 7638 **IND** 15996 **ISR** 1710 **JPN** 908, 3646 **MEX** 8861 **RUS** 3198

Birds: **CA** 2470, 2577, 6706, 6942, 8065, 9352, 11341, 13160, 14683, 14712, 18390 **CO** 4779, 17199 **CT** 4177, 4204, 16504, 20726 **DC** 15285, 17504 **DE** 4721 **FL** 939, 10888, 17704 **IL** 3512, 5684, 7701, 18661 **IN** 5095 **KS** 18724 **LA** 9390, 12099 **MA** 9637, 18829, 20446 **MD** 1457, 11343, 17505, 20627 **ME** 9549 **MI** 8528, 10341, 18855, 18877, 20469 **MN** 10483, 18893 **MO** 2390 **MS** 10522 **ND** 17503 **NH** 8206 **NJ** 4640 **NY** 687, 2245, 4306, 4313, 4317, 4318, 11085, 15118 **OH** 3814, 6251 **PA** 3085, 7054, 14933, 20848 **SC** 19312 **TN** 13492 **TX** 4341, 4556, 16200, 20147 **WA** 14997 **WI** 7297, 10429, 19629 *Canada:* **AB** 2722 **BC** 14101, 19758 **MB** 4759 **ON** 2716, 2963, 13158, 14105, 19460 **PQ** 2721, 8344, 9893, 13602, 13603 **SK** 2717 *Intl:* **ENG** 11340, 14115, 18254

Birds, Protection of: **WI** 8094 *Intl:* **ENG** 8090

Birmingham (AL): **AL** 1856, 1859

Birth control: **AZ** 13120 **CA** 9356, 18428 **CT** 13123 **DC** 3279, 5590, 8104, 13220, 13222 **FL** 5912 **HI** 5134 **IN** 13121, 13131 **KY** 3169 **MA** 15237 **MD** 7528, 8425, 8429 **MI** 18883 **MN** 13126 **MO** 13128, 5588 **NY** 590, 1174, 4008, 8174, 13124, 13219, 14794, 16776 **OH** 13122 **PA** 7659, 13130 **TX** 13125, 13129 **VA** 671 **WA** 19517 **WI** 13132 *Canada:* **ON** 12578, 14894 *Intl:* **ATG** 3048 **BRZ** 15298 **ENG** 8173

Birth defects: **MD** 8625 **NY** 9655, 11650

Birth, Multiple: **RI** 16605

Bishop, Elizabeth: **NY** 19789

Bituminous materials (See also Asphalt): **IL** 3546 **PA** 4281

Bitzer, Billy (George William): **NY** 10908

Black, Hugo La Fayette: **AL** 18167 **DC** 9129

Black literature See: Literature—Black authors

Black studies See: Blacks—Study and teaching

Black women See: Women, Black

Blackmore, Richard Doddridge: **VA** 19510

Blacks (See also African Americans): **AL** 180, 192 **AR** 18240 **CA** 4380, 12206, 15473 **DC** 8465 **GA** 3762, 3763 **LA** 19052 **MD** 17859 **MI** 7261 **MN** 10454 **MO** 9189 **NC** 9233 **NE** 6700 **NJ** 11746 **NY** 15761 **OH** 12219 **PA** 9413 **RI** 13442 **TN** 5830, 10072 **TX** 7462, 13297, 16231 **VA** 19899

Blacks—Study and teaching: **CA** 18373, 18427 **DC** 4905, 7470, 14420 **IL** 8631 **MO** 6923 **NC** 11876, 20496 **NJ** 11748 **NY** 7129, 11567, 11629, 11719, 14002, 16777, 19280 **OH** 12296, 12800 **PA** 9190 **SC** 16493 **TN** 499 **VA** 19895 *Canada:* **ON** 19555

Blackwell family: **DC** 9129 **MA** 13677

Blaine, James Gillespie: **DC** 9129

Blair, Eric Arthur (George Orwell): **OH** 10270

Blake, William: **CA** 18413 **NY** 73 **TN** 503 *Canada:* **BC** 6105 **PQ** 9895

Blind (See also Braille; Talking books): **AZ** 1005, 13030 **CA** 9158 **CO** 3946 **FL** 5889 **GA** 1243, 6397 **ID** 7651 **IL** 5013, 7681 **KY** 720 **MA** 1896, 12946 **NY** 590, 591, 8392, 11080, 11553, 11622 **OR** 12544 **PR** 19244

RI 7725 **TN** 16167 **TX** 16258 **WA** 20014 **WV** 20216 *Canada:* **BC** 18257 **ON** 1498, 2969 **PQ** 7878, 7879 *Intl:* **ENG** 6685

Blind—Education (See also Vocational education): **AL** 182 **AZ** 1008, 6035 **CA** 2504 **CO** 3946, 3954 **IL** 7681 **KY** 720, 8663 **MA** 12946 **MO** 10540 **NM** 11524 **NY** 591 **OH** 12290 **OK** 12354 **PA** 12631 **PR** 19244 **RI** 7725 **SC** 15397 **WI** 20525 **WV** 20204 *Canada:* **AB** 267, 268

Bloch, Ernest: **CA** 1897

Blood: **CA** 7908 *Canada:* **ON** 2987

Blood pressure: **MD** 11193

Blues (Songs, etc.): **CT** 4179, 16504 **IL** 3540 **LA** 16567 **MS** 3086, 18952 **NJ** 14166 **TN** 10065 *Canada:* **ON** 20793

Boats and boating: **CA** 2555 **MA** 9673 **MD** 3483 **ME** 4696 **NY** 900, 15850 **TN** 12652

Bogan, Louise: **MA** 807 **OH** 10270

Bolivia: **PA** 19217

Bonaparte, Napoleon: **AZ** 13025 **FL** 5919 **IL** 4673 **NM** 11522 **OH** 20293 **PA** 6095 **TX** 4653 *Canada:* **PQ** 9895

Bonds (See also Investments; Securities; Stocks): **AZ** 12244 **IL** 19748 **NY** 10733

Book exchanges See: Exchanges, Literary and scientific

Book industries and trade (See also Publishers and publishing): **CA** 3752, 15658, 18333 **CT** 3337, 4178 **FL** 5919 **HI** 18629 **IL** 3536, 4673 **LA** 9390 **MD** 18820 **ME** 2033 **MI** 18867 **NJ** 3 **NY** 2441, 6088, 6762, 9591 **OH** 3827 **PA** 6123 **TX** 4562, 9960, 19392 **VA** 7930 *Canada:* **AB** 18196 **BC** 18280 **ON** 2807, 2899, 10227 **PQ** 9903 *Intl:* **AUS** 15695 **BRZ** 2099 **ENG** 18441

Book-plates: **CA** 3752, 11341, 14711, 19290 **CT** 20700 **DC** 11244 **IL** 10405 **KY** 18767 **LA** 16560 **MI** 4828 **NH** 4616 **NJ** 10656, 11750 **NY** 2235, 6762, 10866, 11666 **TX** 6021 *Canada:* **ON** 13661 *Intl:* **POL** 13168

Bookbinding: **CA** 1958, 10409, 14711 **CT** 20700 **IA** 6798 **IN** 7772 **MA** 1976, 1981 **MI** 4407, 4809, 4828 **NC** 19075 **NJ** 11750 **NY** 6762, 7316, 10738, 11632 **OH** 12221 *Canada:* **NS** 4538 **ON** 19460 *Intl:* **NLD** 11402

Books, Condensed: **NY** 13743

Books—Conservation and restoration: *Intl:* **AUS** 1334

Booth, Edwin: **CA** 2572 **NY** 6876

Booth, John Wilkes: **MD** 9766 **TN** 16179

Boots and shoes—Trade and manufacture: **DC** 5954 *Intl:* **CZE** 15139

Borden, Lizzie Andrew: **MA** 5582

Borges, Jorge Luis: **VA** 19510

Borglum, Gutzon: **DC** 9129

Boston (MA): **MA** 1981, 1988, 1993, 1998, 2002, 2021, 7938, 9817, 9834

Boswell, James: **CT** 20738 **IL** 20369 **VA** 19861 *Canada:* **ON** 9954

Botanical gardens (See also Arboretums): **AL** 1850 **AZ** 4796 **CA** 13704, 14796, 18306 **CO** 4775 **DC** 17083 **FL** 15018 **GA** 1235 **HI** 11316 **IL** 3516 **KS** 2024 **MI** 18874 **MO** 10535 **NY** 2227, 11554 **PA** 477, 9299 **TN** 3463 **VA** 11844 **WA** 3312 *Canada:* **BC** 19754 **ON** 14105 **PQ** 8343 *Intl:* **AUS** 2023, 14104 **CHN** 10964 **ENG** 14103 **SGP** 15190

Botany (See also Herbaria; Palynology; Phytogeography; Plants): **AZ** 17723, 17789 **CA** 2470, 3071, 3756, 8068, 9328, 11341, 14712, 14796, 14802, 18305, 18346, 18350, 18390, 19329 **CT** 4176, 4177, 18514, 20718 **DC** 3160, 6962, 15272, 15280, 17608 **FL** 939, 4215, 5558, 5917, 14346, 17704, 18558, 18564, 18569 **HI** 1865 **IA** 18707 **ID** 18648 **IL** 5684, 7701,

Carillons (See also Bells; Chimes): CA 18411 MI 6799

Carlyle, Thomas: CA 18435 ME 2033 SC 19312 *Canada:* ON 9954

Carmelites: DC 3064 MD 3065, 20052 VT 3066

Carmichael, Hoagland Howard "Hoagy": IN 7776

Carnap, Rudolf: PA 19225

Carnegie, Andrew: DC 9129 PA 3079

Carriages and carts: NY 10926

Carroll, Lewis   See: Dodgson, Charles Lutwidge (Lewis Carroll)

Carson, Christopher "Kit": NM 3104

Carson, Rachel: CT 20703 MD 3106

Carter, James Earl, Jr. "Jimmy": GA 17926

Cartography (See also Maps and atlases): AL 1858 CA 2566, 18436 CT 18525 DC 9118, 11029, 20609 DE 4733 FL 18576 GA 6393 IL 11752, 13708 IN 7787 KY 18753 LA 9377 MA 3776, 18827 MD 8420, 17175, 17650, 17657 MI 18872 MO 15531 MS 17865 NC 19071 NH 4611 NJ 6874 NY 11612, 11669 OH 2038, 13485 OR 12524, 19153 RI 2270 TX 9014, 19375 VA 17531 WA 19528 WI 598, 19598 *Canada:* AB 18188 BC 2141, 18274, 18282 NS 12134 ON 2199, 2701, 2768, 3055, 9952, 13653, 18611, 19455, 19546, 20791 PQ 2733, 9912, 18115, 18119, 18121, 18123 SK 19262 *Intl:* BRZ 6213, 15044 BUL 2345 CHN 7130, 20650 ENG 6684 FIN 5717 GER 15794 ISR 6831 MEX 12720

Cartoons   See: Caricatures and cartoons

Caruso, Enrico: MD 8424

Carver, George Washington: AL 192, 16592 GA 3763 MO 10542, 17719

Casanova de Seingalt, Giovanni Giacomo: UT 15017

Castaneda, Carlos: TX 19380

Castiglione, Conte Baldassare: OH 3823

Cat family   See: Felidae

Catalysis: CA 3138 IL 19676 KY 16689 NJ 5352 NY 178, 16641 OH 13568 PA 151

Cather, Willa: MN 9488 NE 11381 OH 10270 TX 19106

Catholic Church: AZ 11770 CA 2501, 18355 CO 14600 CT 11, 943, 14208, 14601, 15633 DC 3155, 3165, 9689, 11096, 12229, 17123, 20581 DE 4887 GA 6504, 7343 IA 14227, 14594 IL 3152, 9420, 19287 IN 3151, 12380, 14543, 19110, 19112 KS 14500 KY 3169 MA 20343 MI 5848, 12620, 14423 MN 4884, 15207, 19965 MO 3148, 4110, 8640, 14463 MT 3099 NC 5043 NM 930, 7712 NY 9286, 14419, 15027 OH 13211 OK 14315 PA 944, 4882, 9742, 15203, 19197 RI 14310 TX 356, 12228 WA 15205 WI 7350, 9709, 12701, 14207, 14494 *Canada:* AB 5240, 11771 ON 6869, 8412, 19358 SK 14583 *Intl:* AUT 4889 PAN 17997

Catholic Church—History: CA 517, 946, 14045, 14511 CO 4783, 15551, 18507 DC 3156, 3163, 6379, 14572, 20581 GA 4885 IL 4147 KY 3146 LA 4879, 14361 MA 941, 14394 MI 14203 MN 3913, 14334 NJ 15047, 15050 NY 3143, 4880, 9020, 9595, 14360, 15208 OH 942, 1226, 14507, 15335, 18534 PA 14256, 14604, 15042 TX 945, 4876, 14538, 16206 WA 3147, 15329 WI 4878, 14207, 14314 *Canada:* BC 13663 ON 12227, 18128 PQ 4095, 9566

Catholic schools: *Canada:* ON 6869, 10232

Catlin, Sir George Edward Gordon: *Canada:* ON 9954

Cats: CA 6501 CO 10744

Cattle (See also Livestock): TX 505 *Intl:* EST 5462

Cattle trade: AZ 987 CO 3941 KS 8553 MT 10643 ND 17784 TX 6024, 16278 WY 19654

Catton, Bruce: SC 3719

Caves: AL 11301 MO 3350

Cayce, Edgar: FL 15796 VA 1168

Celebrities: CA 3196 NY 3197, 6513

Celestial mechanics   See: Mechanics, Celestial

Celine, Louis-Ferdinaud: TX 19392

Cello music: AZ 1017 NC 19085 PA 15053

Cellular biology   See: Cytology

Cellulose: AL 8171 NC 6490 NJ 16285 NY 8169, 15722 TN 13395

Celtic Church: HI 3199 IL 20368

Celtic languages and literature: MN 3912 NY 5971 OH 3823 *Canada:* NS 14316 *Intl:* GER 18024

Cement (See also Concrete; Pavements): CO 7339 IL 13237 OH 5080 *Intl:* ENG 2138 GER 6423 ICE 7634

Censorship (See also Freedom of the press): CA 18428 LA 7363 NJ 3 WI 19590 *Canada:* ON 2933

Census (See also Population): AK 215, 17563 AL 1855, 12037 AR 17578, 18237 AZ 16540, 17586 CA 2513, 3667, 14192, 14710, 14804, 17094, 18313, 18336, 19344 CO 4783, 17088 CT 17576 DC 4906, 10234, 13222, 17098, 17219 FL 5888, 5912, 7218, 10253, 10256, 15998, 20545 GA 17086, 17592 HI 5134 IA 15687, 17573, 18713 IL 7685, 7706, 8883, 11981, 17090, 17570 IN 376 KS 8560, 8571, 17093, 18725, 18727 KY 18776 LA 11970, 17583 MA 1993, 6730, 17087 MD 6872, 8429, 9764, 13299, 18805 MI 15522, 17092, 20077 MN 17581, 18919 MO 8545, 18959 MS 7844 MT 3661, 10645 NC 5041, 17089 NE 11382, 19006 NJ 5569, 6874, 10748, 11747, 13381, 13385, 13460, 14161 NM 19040 NY 2329, 5075, 11008, 11608, 11648, 11667, 13221, 17095, 17584, 19280 OH 3821, 12281, 13484, 16395 OR 3658, 8935 PA 11458, 16129, 17096, 17587, 19191 RI 2280, 13876 TN 11000, 16158 TX 7459, 11041, 16224, 17091, 19403, 20535 VA 11847, 17588 WA 11036, 17097, 19517 WI 10428, 19585, 19592, 19646 WV 20224 *Canada:* AB 254, 18204 BC 18259 ON 2812 PQ 13581, 18097 *Intl:* BRZ 6213 ENG 6689 ITA 18013 SRI 15624

Central America (See also Latin America): CA 14908, 19335 CO 15390 KS 18723 LA 16558 MN 3324 TX 3323 VA 562 *Canada:* ON 2886 *Intl:* BLZ 1675 CHL 16759 GTM 6791

Central Europe: DC 9113 NY 13836 OH 7910 *Intl:* GER 7153

Ceramics: CA 15353 GA 6387 IA 4790, 8238 IL 18671, 18671 IN 1435, 13534 MA 9789, 10837, 12096, 12097, 16983 ME 13245 MI 4407, 6331 MN 16334, 16338 MO 8544 NC 10498 NJ 1927 NY 178, 4335, 5514, 6311, 11624, 11645, 15577 OH 519, 5672, 6314, 7305, 12094, 12318, 12636 OR 12529 PA 432, 1271, 1418, 1797, 6109, 6897, 13084, 16149, 20318 WA 19513 *Canada:* AB 257 BC 18265 MB 20487 ON 6901 PQ 2819, 10700 *Intl:* NLD 11412 SAF 10276 SWE 14042

Cereals   See: Grain

Cerebral palsy: MD 8625 MN 3427 NY 16690, 16691

Cerebrovascular disease: CO 11308 TX 607

Cervantes, Miguel de: CA 19335 DC 9135

Chagall, Marc: NE 8391

Chain stores: NY 9038

Chemistry, Physical and theoretical (See also Catalysis; Colloids; Electrochemistry; Fusion; Nuclear physics; Polymers and polymerization; Radiochemistry; Thermodyn CA 18311, 18375 GA 5332 IL 18662, 19903 IN 19111 MA 5066, 13734 MO 20058 NJ 7310, 11304, 13370 NY 4009, 12231 OH 1044, 6314 PA 19179, 19207 TN 13395 WI 19588, 19621 *Canada:* ON 19434 *Intl:* AUS 4701 GER 6530

Chemistry, Textile See: Textile chemistry

Cherokee Indians: GA 7205 NC 10890, 20238 OK 3479, 6475, 11985, 19139

Chesapeake Bay: MD 3483, 17458, 18816 VA 3934, 19865

Chess: CA 9343 CO 3940 NJ 13386 NY 2240, 11609, 16994 OH 3823 PA 6123 *Intl:* AUS 15697 NLD 11402

Chest medicine See: Medicine, Thoracic

Chesterfield, Philip Dormer Stanhope, Earl: CA 14718

Chesterton, Gilbert Keith: DC 6379 IL 20371 IN 19112 MA 1976, 1981 NY 11357 *Canada:* ON 19459 SK 14598

Chewing gum: IL 20646, 20648

Cheyenne Indians: KS 1784 MT 5053

Chicago (IL): IL 3522, 3525, 3533, 3536, 3550, 4053, 8890, 14057

Chicanos See: Mexican Americans

Chickasaw Indians: MS 17757 OK 12349

Child abuse: CA 8079, 10238 CO 620, 8610 DC 3788, 17259 IA 8232 MA 18832 NY 4702 PA 12864 PR 19245 WA 20031 *Canada:* BC 17969 ON 2930, 12456 PQ 3296

Child care: CA 4593, 8079 DC 583 NJ 8450 PA 4841 WI 1883 *Canada:* ON 2749

Child custody See: Custody of children

Child development: CA 3577, 4253, 10238, 13811 CO 3958 DC 3559, 3560, 3579 FL 16477, 18566 IA 13187 IL 5398, 5420, 7673, 8486, 11229, 18676 IN 5510, 6485, 7782, 13538 KS 5345 MD 9748 MI 6418 MN 14567 NE 5840 NY 1488, 6483, 11607 OH 12311 OK 13697 SC 16493 TN 19772 *Canada:* AB 6505 MB 18786 ON 10232, 14893, 19452 *Intl:* NOR 12116 POL 13166

Child, Lydia Maria: MA 9981 NY 4330

Child psychiatry (See also Autism; Child psychology): AZ 1004 CA 12669, 13811, 15803 CT 3558 DC 723 IL 3588 IN 5510 MA 9946 NC 2254 NY 4431, 8377, 10094, 13635 OH 3816 OK 6758 PA 5168 RI 2057 *Canada:* ON 4745 PQ 4974, 7397, 7398, 7402, 10696, 14140

Child psychology (See also Child psychiatry; Educational psychology): CA 3577, 8495, 8949, 10238, 13811 CT 3558 IL 7681 MN 10456 NY 1179, 1930, 8377 OH 3831, 14214 PA 12907 *Canada:* ON 6859, 7227, 12813, 13285, 16310, 19452 PQ 7430, 13438, 18093 *Intl:* DEN 4766

Child support: IA 8232

Child welfare (See also Child abuse; Child support; Foster home care; Juvenile delinquency): AR 3313 CA 19347 CO 3958 CT 3558 DC 500, 3560 FL 13066 IL 18459 IN 7815 KY 8669 MA 1980 MD 8453 MN 10504 MO 20063 NY 11561 OH 3126 PA 11018, 12864, 19224 PR 13516 TX 16243 *Canada:* BC 2167 ON 3563, 12456 PQ 3296 SK 14850 *Intl:* NOR 12116

Children: CT 18517 IN 663 NE 5840 NH 11492 NY 4028 TX 7199 *Canada:* ON 3561 *Intl:* FRA 8080

Children, Exceptional See: Exceptional children

Children, Gifted See: Gifted children

Children—Health and hygiene: CA 8079 CO 3566 IL 463 NY 8174 PA 8022

Children—Legal status, laws, etc.: *Canada:* ON 2930

Children's literature (See also Fairy tales; Story-telling): AK 16842 AL 1857, 18164 AR 1033, 18445 AZ 1019, 13017, 16546 CA 1742, 2369, 3755, 6157, 6159, 9345, 12711, 12937, 13205, 14703, 14723, 14725, 14741, 14743, 15658, 16868, 18317, 18333, 18379, 18400, 18406, 18413, 19327 CO 18507 CT 3337, 4178, 14208, 15482 DC 2194, 4907, 9110, 9135 DE 8178 FL 5914, 5919, 18566, 18583, 19322 GA 1238, 2581, 3761, 6396, 18594 HI 7040, 17601, 18626, 20811 IA 2323, 18708 IL 3289, 3527, 3538, 3544, 5798, 7680, 7707, 10405, 11811, 11994, 14003, 14959, 15487, 18461, 18670 IN 3591, 7794, 7802 KS 5346, 5999, 8563, 18724 KY 10725, 18747 LA 11542 MA 1991, 2014, 5448, 7019, 7092, 9789, 11788, 15177, 15236, 17133, 20153, 20599 MD 14640, 18803 ME 6252 MI 3348, 4166, 4828, 5808, 5853, 6639, 9507, 10367, 10931, 12212, 18867, 20122, 20270 MN 68, 3908, 9633, 10448, 10807, 14074, 18900, 18937 MO 3350, 3359, 6923, 12056, 14450, 15681, 17075, 18983 MS 19354 NC 914, 5738, 11878, 19076, 19083, 19084 NE 4114 NH 11493, 19036 NJ 8370, 10745, 16484 NM 6463, 7109 NY 670, 1488, 3564, 5137, 9296, 10738, 11603, 11606, 11815, 13630, 14358, 14542, 15704, 15757, 15832, 16023, 17922, 19278 OH 2036, 3819, 3823, 4149, 7231, 10270, 12305, 13478, 18536 OK 6261, 12341, 12365, 19136 OR 1180, 19159 PA 1904, 3076, 3493, 5823, 6111, 6122, 8388, 9241, 12854, 15325, 19223, 19846 RI 13440, 13454, 19986 SC 17077, 19312, 20548 TN 16119, 16590, 20190 TX 3650, 4560, 5728, 5746, 5819, 7200, 7463, 14495, 16282, 19106, 19396 VA 3931, 5762 WA 3381, 14998, 19520, 19949 WI 4158, 19573, 19590, 19615, 19616, 19632, 19643 WY 19660 *Canada:* AB 18194, 18288 BC 18258, 18282 NB 19023 NF 10050 NS 10812 ON 2803, 2805, 2808, 2915, 13661, 16414, 16415, 16418, 19564, 20158 PQ 9903 SK 19260, 19291 *Intl:* AUS 15693 GER 6441 HUN 7555 IRN 3565 NOR 12111 SCT 14953 SGP 15189

Children's plays—Presentation, etc.: WA 19521 *Canada:* ON 19460

Chile: *Intl:* CHL 3167, 3598

Chilean literature: CT 18519 *Intl:* CHL 3598

Chimes (See also Bells; Carillons): MI 6799

China: AZ 18227 CA 7914, 15650, 18309, 18316, 18397 CT 20709 DC 9109, 9124, 11185, 17129, 17609, 17842, 20008 KS 18726 MA 5448, 6974, 6978 MD 18814 MI 18854 MN 5594, 10375, 18905 MO 20061 NH 4612 NJ 13374, 14163 NY 3613, 4006, 4334, 9744, 11626, 14352 OH 12302 PA 19210 TX 19388 UT 20799 VA 3217 *Canada:* BC 18255 ON 14130 *Intl:* CHN 3263, 3611, 12929, 12931, 12932, 18703 GER 5630, 10705, 15794 HKG 8123 JPN 8838 KOR 8839 NLD 13928 TWN 12663, 13826

China—History: CA 9355 HI 7021 IL 18451 MN 5594, 10375 NJ 14163 NY 3613, 19274 OH 12302 PA 19180 WI 19596 *Canada:* BC 3614 *Intl:* CHN 30, 3606, 7540, 7929, 10965, 12929, 12932, 15075, 16349 HKG 3615 KOR 1124 NLD 13928 TWN 12663

Chinese Americans: CA 3612, 9355, 18301 HI 7021 NY 11600

Chinese language and literature: AZ 18227 CA 7487, 7914, 9355, 10670, 12204 CO 18495 CT 20709 IL 18451 KS 18726 LA 11542 MD 18814 MN 5594, 18905 NJ 14163 NY 3613, 11556, 19274 PA 3608, 19180 WA 19522 WI 19596 *Canada:* BC 18255 ON 12443, 19439 *Intl:* CHN 1656, 3606, 12929, 12932, 15075, 16349 GER 10705 HKG 3615 ITA 12567 NLD 13928 SGP 11319

Chinese medicine See: Medicine, Oriental

Chippewa Indians: MN 17724

Chiropody See: Podiatry

Chiropractic (See also Naturopathy; Osteopathy): CA 3797, 9152, 9327, 12707, 15465 IA 12706 IL 11122 MN 12069 MO 3798, 9249 NY 11555 OR 20301 SC 15126 TX 16207 *Canada:* ON 2957 *Intl:* ENG 872

Chocolate and cocoa: MA 4962 NY 20346 PA 7164 *Intl:* CRI 8028 GHA 3860

Choctaw Indians: MS 17757 OK 6475

Chodowiecki, Daniel: **NH** 4860

Chopin, Frederic Francois: **OH** 10821

Choral music: **CA** 12203 **DC** 4911 **IL** 18686 **IN** 7818 **KY** 15462 **ME** 1405, 13243 **MI** 8045 **NJ** 20327 **NY** 13185, 19279 **OH** 8654, 13477 **PA** 6120 **PR** 4222 **TX** 14677 *Canada:* **ON** 12431, 19561

Christian art and symbolism (See also Relics and reliquaries): **CA** 3900 **FL** 13933 **IL** 18450 **NE** 9228 **NJ** 13371, 13376 **NY** 4013, 14625 *Canada:* **PQ** 12517 *Intl:* **GER** 15630

Christian education (See also Bible colleges): **AZ** 15539 **CA** 3632, 12661 **CO** 4776, 11355 **FL** 5792 **GA** 3117, 9443, 16383 **IL** 10706, 16508 **IN** 6602 **MA** 6575 **MD** 1793, 19991 **MI** 6595 **MN** 9445 **MO** 11356, 12649 **MS** 13781 **NC** 13434 **NM** 6463 **NY** 7433 **OH** 3640, 7192, 20481 **OR** 10856 **PA** 495, 1288, 1814, 4679, 8916, 8923, 12978, 19730 **SC** 8467 **TN** 10078, 14897 **TX** 3431, 4570, 5749, 5819 **WA** 9444 *Canada:* **AB** 1520, 10829, 12042, 13296 **MB** 1961 **ON** 3328, 12428 **SK** 2123, 2896

Christian ethics: **CA** 6535, 9418 **DC** 6377 **MO** 10379 **OH** 7527 *Canada:* **ON** 866

Christian Reformed Church: **IA** 4963 **MI** 2592, 5764

Christian Science: **CA** 20188 **MA** 5767, 9300

Christianity (See also Ecumenical movement; Missions; Reformation): **CA** 1845, 3632, 9841, 20634 **CO** 7666 **CT** 6940 **DC** 3163 **IL** 5815 **KY** 3169, 13013 **MA** 6575 **MD** 13314 **NC** 5043 **NE** 5796, 20767 **NY** 1047, 9746, 15904 **OK** 13967 **OR** 3979 **TX** 1314 **WA** 9444 *Canada:* **AB** 7215, 11856 **BC** 19760 **ON** 866 **PQ** 2912 **SK** 9466 *Intl:* **IDN** 5074

Chromatographic analysis: **CA** 1642 **MA** 10408 **PA** 1843, 7171

Chronic diseases: **MA** 11313 **NY** 11728, 17381

Chumachan Indians: **CA** 9261, 14802

Church architecture: **DC** 19992 **NC** 5043 **NY** 3143, 16634 **PA** 9465 **WA** 5174 *Canada:* **NB** 4877 *Intl:* **ENG** 4360, 20776

Church of the Brethren: **IL** 1782, 3649 **IN** 6602, 10091 **KS** 9963 **OH** 1113 **PA** 5300 **VA** 2120

Church of Christ, Scientist See: Christian Science

Church of England (See also Puritans): **CO** 14600 **DC** 6073 **IL** 16723 **NY** 6352 *Canada:* **AB** 259, 868 **BC** 870 **NB** 4877 **ON** 866, 867, 871, 19462 **PQ** 869 **YT** 20831 *Intl:* **ENG** 3014, 4360, 9171, 20776

Church, Frederic Edwin: **NY** 12378

Church of God: **GA** 10808 **IN** 12748 **OH** 20481 **OR** 19972 **TX** 451

Church history (See also Fathers of the church; Monasticism and religious orders; Sisterhoods): **CA** 2501, 6535, 6613, 14349 **CT** 11 **DC** 14572, 17123, 19992, 20581 **IL** 8375, 20368 **MA** 2018, 6575, 7116, 14394 **MI** 4802 **MN** 9445, 20185 **MO** 3330, 12649, 14435 **NC** 7380, 13434 **NH** 14232 **NY** 6164, 6352, 10810, 19929 **OH** 20481 **PA** 9464, 13779, 19300, 19730 **TN** 6902, 10078, 19769 **WA** 20611 **WI** 20513 *Canada:* **AB** 1520 **BC** 20326 **ON** 866 **PQ** 7868 *Intl:* **AUT** 7919, 18042 **BEL** 18131 **ENG** 3014, 9171 **SPA** 5465

Church of Jesus Christ of Latter-Day Saints See: Mormon Church

Church music (See also Hymns): **AL** 15448 **CT** 20717 **DC** 19992 **FL** 5870 **GA** 16383 **IL** 3540, 4120, 10706, 12086 **KY** 8662, 15462, 15463 **LA** 11538 **MN** 4113, 11910 **MO** 3330, 4117 **NC** 10722 **NE** 9228 **NJ** 16479, 20327 **NY** 4019, 9595, 14625, 16667 **PA** 6120, 10090 **TN** 10353, 14897, 19303 **TX** 1604 *Canada:* **MB** 15771 **NB** 4877 **PQ** 2892 *Intl:* **ITA** 8275

Church of the Nazarene: **MO** 3685, 11356

Church of the New Jerusalem See: New Jerusalem Church

Church schools: **AL** 5752, 19231 **CA** 9418, 9841, 13157, 20188 **FL** 5869 **IA** 6608 **IL** 12403 **MD** 3999, 5143 **MI** 3928 **MO** 14435 **ND** 18796 **NH**

14232 **NY** 7433 **OH** 12266 **OR** 12043, 19972 **PA** 37 **TN** 15478 **TX** 1038, 4544, 15537 *Canada:* **AB** 2998 **NB** 1250 **PQ** 13316

Church and state: **MD** 791 **NY** 654 **PA** 19847 **TX** 1606, 15786

Church and synagogue libraries See: Libraries, Church and synagogue

Churchill, Sir Winston Leonard Spencer: **CT** 20703 **IL** 18689 **MO** 20328 **OH** 13479 **TX** 16521

Cincinnati (OH): **OH** 3699, 3703, 6704, 10263, 13479, 13482

Cinema See: Motion pictures

Circus: **CA** 9343, 18428 **CT** 2116 **IL** 7707 **MA** 6972 **MI** 4825 **NJ** 13388 **NY** 11634, 15361 **OH** 3715, 13477 **PA** 6125, 7293 **TN** 10076 **TX** 14672, 19393 **WI** 3716

Cistercians (See also Benedictines): **KY** 6455 **MI** 20275

Cities and towns—Study and teaching: **CT** 18515 **DC** 17098 **IL** 18663 **MA** 9816 **MN** 1293, 9634 **NC** 5041 **NJ** 10358 **NY** 3242 **OH** 18464, 18468 **PA** 6695 *Canada:* **ON** 9952, 19433 **PQ** 10703, 18116 **SK** 14845

Citizenship (See also Patriotism): **NY** 11572

Citrus fruits: **CA** 1390, 13205, 18358, 18403, 18413 **FL** 17185, 18564 *Intl:* **ARG** 5460, 12226

City government See: Municipal government

City planning (See also Environmental design; Land use—Planning; Open spaces; Regional planning; Urban policy; Urban renewal; Zoning): **AR** 18233 **AZ** 1009, 13023, 16540, 18212 **CA** 2499, 9349, 10233, 12195, 12507, 13706, 14687, 14804, 15475, 15808, 18300, 18319, 18370, 19331, 19348, 19852 **CO** 13506, 13796, 18490 **CT** 20699 **DC** 629, 715, 4900, 4902, 7472, 12771, 15215, 17241, 19689, 19690 **FL** 10260, 15528, 15998 **GA** 6387, 6388 **HI** 7379 **IA** 15664 **IL** 3525, 10161, 11075, 15540, 18663, 20423 **IN** 1437, 5374 **KS** 3743 **KY** 9089, 18750, 18776 **LA** 16556 **MA** 1975, 2002, 6967, 17717, 20597 **MD** 9753, 18809 **MI** 4824, 4829, 10317, 16491, 18853 **MN** 1545, 10199 **MO** 8545, 14462, 15899, 20055 **NC** 6738, 19059 **NJ** 11513, 14159 **NY** 3731, 4002, 4306, 4309, 4363, 4994, 5075, 11583, 11612, 12765, 13795, 13818, 13988, 15761 **OH** 171, 3829, 8651, 10264, 11974, 12307, 18468 **OR** 8935, 13238, 13790, 19141 **PA** 364, 4213, 10683, 15451, 16140, 19182 **PR** 19248 **SC** 3793, 5855 **TN** 8775, 11000 **TX** 4566, 18646, 19376, 19408 **VA** 9773, 19503, 19869 **WA** 15001, 19512, 20030 **WI** 19595 *Canada:* **AB** 291, 2460, 5242, 15663, 18295 **BC** 6711, 13354 **MB** 18785 **NF** 11760 **NS** 6837, 12134, 12140 **ON** 1925, 2765, 2774, 2838, 5474, 10222, 10226, 11959, 12472, 13402, 14180, 14187, 16409, 19165, 19440 **PQ** 1622, 9892, 10703, 18075, 18105, 18118 **SK** 13788, 19262 *Intl:* **COL** 5349 **ENG** 9270, 14120 **GER** 6106 **IND** 7749 **IRL** 18485 **JPN** 8331 **MOR** 129

Civil defense: **IL** 2058 **MD** 5626 *Intl:* **SWI** 8083, 16754

Civil engineering (See also Earthquake engineering; Excavation; Mining engineering; Transportation engineering): **AL** 14153 **CA** 2272, 4589, 7640, 8626, 9351, 9728, 11828, 14974, 15647, 16962, 17838, 17872, 17877, 18315, 18330 **CO** 3408, 13796 **CT** 6941 **DC** 3157, 16941 **FL** 5865, 5876, 6753, 16789, 16945 **GA** 4575, 6387, 13249, 15479, 16961 **HI** 7050 **IL** 4223, 5927, 6894, 13237, 15836, 16522, 16936, 16954, 18671 **IN** 13540, 19113 **KS** 8576 **KY** 18758, 18770 **MA** 6091, 9796, 10178, 15812, 16069, 16553, 16708, 16949, 18831, 20167 **MD** 4576, 16018, 18813 **ME** 6 **MI** 4830, 10320 **MO** 2386, 15899, 16925, 16956, 18963 **NC** 3091, 5036, 5039 **ND** 19097 **NH** 4609, 11490, 16935, 19032 **NJ** 2387, 5535, 13372, 20586 **NM** 16802 **NV** 19014 **NY** 3734, 3779, 4000, 4307, 4313, 5353, 6919, 7358, 9592, 12433, 12765, 13203, 14984, 15967 **OH** 566, 4459, 5354, 12307, 18158, 18469, 19693 **OK** 1719, 12371, 19126 **OR** 2262 **PA** 1423, 12849, 12977, 12985, 15595, 16132, 16952, 17839, 19194, 19205 **RI** 8698 **SC** 15252 **SD** 15424 **TN** 15701, 16175, 16948 **TX** 966, 1260, 4985, 5533, 6190, 9246, 16939, 16940, 19389 **VA** 3407, 7061 **VT** 19811 **WV** 16943 *Canada:* **AB** 55, 10608 **BC** 1391, 9888, 16348 **MB** 7609, 9616, 18787 **NB** 19024 **NS** 16034 **ON** 56, 2031, 2838, 2874, 13402, 13646, 19443, 19559 **PQ** 9909, 18125 **SK** 19242 *Intl:* **AUS** 11550 **AUT** 18702 **CHN** 7988, 20650 **COL** 17978 **ENG** 8730 **FIN** 7126 **GER** 6106, 6444 **HUN** 5391 **IRL** 4234 **JPN** 19423 **NLD** 7321 **POL** 16035 **SPA** 15565 **SWI** 15937, 15938 **TTO** 3049

Civil law: **AL** 10579 **CA** 64, 3116, 4438, 18331 **CT** 10873 **DC** 13326, 13475,

Civil law: (continued)
17257, 17493 **FL** 8605 **LA** 9381, 16559 **MI** 4856, 10621 **NY** 9048, 9496 **PA** 4085, 8362 **PR** 3168, 8031, 13514, 13518, 13524, 19236 **TX** 165 *Canada:* **AB** 249, 9870 **ON** 2863, 12455, 15175, 19164 **PQ** 1680, 3420, 9902, 13973, 18080 *Intl:* **ENG** 20776 **FIN** 5706 **GER** 11806, 13105, 18051 **GRC** 7118

Civil liberty See: **Liberty**

Civil rights: AL 1856, 15992, 16592 **CA** 2562, 4622, 6733, 9419, 10023, 10237, 12683, 15473, 20421 **CO** 18510 **DC** 525, 3262, 4054, 4905, 7471, 7478, 8025, 8120, 17123, 17255, 17483 **GA** 8714, 15514, 17748, 18602 **LA** 810, 15518 **MA** 3230 **MI** 10298, 20117 **MN** 3324 **MO** 6923 **NY** 652, 653, 654, 897, 3306, 4314, 5962, 11049, 13833, 14983, 20821 **OH** 18154, 18482, 18535 **PA** 8874, 9190 **TN** 11344 **TX** 19408 **VA** 11152 **WI** 15683, 20529 *Canada:* **AB** 285, 8165 **NS** 12147 **ON** 2755, 2886, 2936, 7532 **PQ** 2847, 13583, 18114 *Intl:* **COL** 3926 **ENG** 7969 **FRA** 4364 **SAF** 15389 **SWE** 5487

Civil service (See also **Administrative law**): **CA** 9349 **DC** 12251 **MD** 20264 **NY** 7967, 11559, 11619 **WI** 20529

Civil War (U.S.) (See also **Confederate States of America**): **AL** 1858, 1859, 5858, 7569, 10581, 10925 **AR** 1029, 17762 **CA** 7113, 9184, 9973, 12232, 18413, 18428, 19172, 19819 **CO** 18548 **CT** 11500, 14643, 15360, 16504 **DC** 1063, 9134, 11045 **FL** 7278 **GA** 1246, 3998, 7205, 17689, 17712, 17739, 18600 **IA** 7272, 13557 **IL** 2061, 2365, 3522, 3536, 4629, 7698, 8541, 9945 **IN** 3132, 7283, 7755, 9187, 19923 **KS** 6003, 8559, 20465 **KY** 8659, 20260 **LA** 9390, 16560 **MA** 1999, 4962, 9981 **MD** 9766, 14640, 17657, 17666, 17710, 17860 **ME** 15141, 20093 **MI** 9064, 10338, 10620, 10623, 13151, 16526, 18888 **MN** 9729, 12605 **MO** 8302, 9189, 10536, 14391, 18979 **MS** 19354 **NC** 3139, 6800 **NJ** 1255, 15048, 19851 **NY** 2243, 3175, 3459, 5663, 6044, 7289, 7521, 9595, 11578, 12433, 14053, 15034, 16656, 18483, 19985 **OH** 1648, 7060, 9930, 18534, 20293 **PA** 3747, 6457, 6619, 6725, 9055, 15294, 16657, 17720 **RI** 13454 **SC** 15402, 17713, 19312 **TN** 9185, 10063, 10065, 15133, 15478, 16168, 17665, 17778, 17783 **TX** 5284, 6024, 6927, 7209, 7447, 7463, 8356, 11041, 13897, 14069, 16705, 20535 **VA** 3129, 6015, 7245, 9773, 13680, 15594, 16354, 16704, 17668, 17718, 17747, 17764, 17769, 19867, 19966, 20013 **WA** 15981 **WI** 15103, 19636, 19646, 20534 **WV** 9724, 17730, 20209 *Canada:* **ON** 14107

Clarinet music: CT 18614 **MD** 18821

Clark, Mark Wayne: SC 3719

Classical literature: CT 20705 **DC** 3155, 6953 **IL** 18664 **MA** 20446 **MD** 8420 **MI** 3928 **MN** 18901 **NJ** 7895, 11455 **NY** 4004 **OH** 18473 **PA** 5142, 19197 **TX** 19386 *Canada:* **AB** 18292 **BC** 18271 **ON** 19462 **PQ** 7868, 15023 *Intl:* **ALG** 349 **BEL** 3166 **BRZ** 6214 **GER** 8740, 18054 **ITA** 43 **NLD** 2359

Classification: MD 18804

Clay: GA 16305 **KY** 16689 **NJ** 5352

Cleaning and dyeing industry: MD 8103 **MN** 5203 **NJ** 4927

Clemens, Samuel Langhorne (Mark Twain): CA 4293, 18303 **CT** 3337, 15818, 16599 **HI** 18629 **MI** 4828 **MN** 10454 **MO** 15681, 16598, 16600 **NY** 2335, 19789 **OH** 13479 **PA** 6122, 7811 **TX** 7463, 7465 **VA** 19510 **VT** 10887 **WI** 19607 *Intl:* **CUB** 10882

Clendening, Logan: KS 18732

Cleveland, Grover: NJ 13386

Cleveland (OH): OH 3826, 3829, 13093

Climatology (See also **Meteorology; Weather**): **AZ** 18221 **CA** 9353, 9353, 18314 **CO** 3408, 3968, 18498 **FL** 5890 **GA** 18606 **IL** 7708, 16814 **IN** 13539 **MA** 6959 **MD** 10983, 17650 **MO** 17660, 17796 **NC** 17654 **NH** 4610 **NJ** 16330, 17647 **NY** 3238, 17547 **OK** 17659 **TN** 17646 **UT** 11869 **WA** 17649 *Canada:* **NS** 2703 **ON** 2705, 18611 *Intl:* **AUS** 1332 **BRZ** 2096 **CHN** 7130 **ENG** 6687 **GER** 2360 **HKG** 14128 **SWI** 20625

Clocks and watches (See also **Horology**): **MA** 19962 **NY** 2358 **PA** 11081 **WA** 14997

Clothing and dress (See also **Costume; Fashion; Uniforms**): **CA** 20242 **IL** 13721, 18676 **IN** 13538 **MA** 17027 **NY** 16465 **OH** 12311 **TX** 12726

Clothing trade: CA 5606, 5608, 15825 **NY** 439, 8143 **OR** 1559 **VA** 7984

Club management: VA 3846

Coaching (Athletics): CO 17917 **IN** 7789 **NC** 11871

Coal (See also **Fuel**): **CO** 449 **DC** 17232 **IL** 7690, 7941 **KY** 18745, 18758 **MT** 12008, 17107 **ND** 19096 **OR** 11393 **PA** 4229, 4230, 6474, 8721, 8869, 12860, 12902, 17117, 19705 **TX** 5928, 13682 **WV** 15885, 17237 **WY** 15933, 20291 *Canada:* **AB** 271, 303, 3850, 9580 **ON** 4943 *Intl:* **CHN** 26 **DEN** 13938 **FRA** 11203

Coast Guard: CT 17132 **MD** 17859 **NC** 11884 **NJ** 8409 **NY** 17131

Coastal engineering: CA 2488, 18348 **FL** 5909, 17799, 18565 **MS** 16966 **OR** 12237 **PA** 16952 **SC** 13843 **VA** 16942 *Canada:* **BC** 18261 *Intl:* **NLD** 20089

Coasts (See also **Estuaries**): **AK** 213, 18175 **CT** 18525 **FL** 15426 **MA** 9237, 11464, 20445 **MD** 17670 **NC** 11361, 17681 **RI** 19265 *Canada:* **NS** 4368, 14539 *Intl:* **PHL** 8072

Coatings, Protective See: **Protective coatings**

Cobbett, William: NJ 14175 **NY** 5971

Cocoa and chocolate See: **Chocolate and cocoa**

Cocteau, Jean: CA 15057 **TX** 19392

Cody, William Frederick "Buffalo Bill": CO 2326, 4785 **WY** 2325

Coffee: IN 7589 **NY** 11120 *Intl:* **CRI** 8028 **ENG** 8084 **GHA** 3860

Cohan, George M.: NY 10892

Coinage (See also **Money**): **CO** 699, 18507 **MA** 15600 **MN** 10450 **NH** 12165 **NY** 15629 **WI** 8063 *Intl:* **BEL** 1671 **EGY** 12562 **GER** 6858

Cold regions See: **Polar regions**

Coleridge, Samuel Taylor: CA 2568 **CT** 20703 *Canada:* **ON** 19463

Collective bargaining (See also **Arbitration; Labor and laboring classes; Trade-unions**): **CA** 8149 **DC** 718 **HI** 7022 **MI** 4823, 16687 **MN** 18914 **NJ** 14167 **NY** 439, 582, 4327, 11109, 11672, 12565, 13411, 13474 **WI** 8112 *Canada:* **ON** 2762, 2837, 12499 **PQ** 13582 **SK** 14846

Collective settlements: IL 18678 **IN** 11499, 19350 **ME** 16782 **MO** 5652 **OH** 4092 **PA** 12880

College fraternities See: **Students' societies**

Colleges See: **Universities and colleges**

Colloids: MA 6604 **ME** 5939 **MI** 49 **OH** 13398 **TN** 13395 *Canada:* **ON** 20683

Colonial Williamsburg See: **Williamsburg (VA)**

Colonization: CO 6006 **IN** 7794 **MA** 835 **MN** 18915 **NY** 15731 **RI** 2270 *Intl:* **FRA** 6059 **HTI** 6834 **MOZ** 10834 **NAM** 10960 **PER** 7998

Color: CT 20699 **MD** 14950

Colorado: CO 1128, 1306, 2030, 3940, 3941, 3945, 3947, 3951, 3962, 3965, 4345, 4783, 5995, 6717, 8891, 9218, 10923, 11039, 13046, 13456, 15631, 16472, 18508, 20146

Colorado River: AZ 988, 11992, 13281 **CA** 2514

Colum, Padraic: NY 15731

Columbus, Christopher: CT 8765 **NJ** 8085

Combustion: CA 14932, 19342 **IA** 4712 **IN** 6333 **MD** 17616 **TX** 7311 *Intl:* **CHN** 6790

Comden, Betty: NY 10908

Comic books, strips, etc.: CA 14725, 18379 **CO** 10923 **CT** 8044 **IA** 8239 **MI** 10337 **MN** 18900 **NY** 4044, 10889 **OH** 2040, 3819, 12299

Commerce (See also Foreign trade and employment; International business enterprises; Investments, Foreign): AK 17563 **AL** 17566 **AR** 17578 **AZ** 600, 17586 **CA** 8034, 9344, 12208, 18352 **CT** 6938, 17576 **DC** 2287, 4906, 4991, 5484, 6167, 7483, 8027, 8339, 8742, 12633, 15856, 16783, 17161, 17164, 17219, 17593, 17594 **FL** 10252 **GA** 5632, 17592 **HI** 3414, 7031, 7039 **IA** 17573 **IL** 3141, 3515, 15678, 17570 **LA** 17583 **MA** 17567 **MD** 16447, 19796 **MI** 4856, 10398, 17574 **MN** 7212, 10485, 17581 **MO** 8548, 17589 **NC** 17575 **NM** 17562 **NY** 2402, 8487, 8792, 9646, 15183, 17162, 17568, 17584 **OH** 16391, 17571 **OR** 10851, 13228 **PA** 4228, 17587, 19213 **PR** 17591 **TN** 17582 **TX** 4559, 7458, 14671, 15505, 16240, 17572, 17577 **UT** 17590 **VA** 17588 **WI** 17580 **WV** 17569 *Canada:* **AB** 264, 18195 **BC** 2156, 18271, 19753 **MB** 9603 **NB** 11442 **ON** 2676, 2687, 2724, 2841, 2927, 2938, 5522, 7482, 11873, 12473, 16410, 20631 **PQ** 321, 10693, 13600 *Intl:* **AUT** 521 **BFA** 3416 **CHN** 15152, 18703 **CYP** 4505 **ENG** 6675 **GER** 6450 **GUY** 3046 **HUN** 7544 **IND** 7749 **ISR** 8267 **MUS** 9851 **NLD** 11410 **NOR** 16033 **PAK** 12695 **SRI** 3400 **SWI** 5486, 6292 **THA** 16760, 16761 **TUR** 16647 **TZA** 16005

Commercial law (See also Banking law; Bankruptcy; Business law): AZ 10597 **CA** 9344, 9433 **DC** 7516, 8156, 17254, 19813 **DE** 13901 **ME** 1757 **MI** 10398 **RI** 80 *Canada:* **BC** 5605, 5667 **ON** 1888, 2676, 2941, 6564, 6565, 15132, 16327 **PQ** 3420, 9949 *Intl:* **GER** 13104, 18038 **GRC** 7118

Commercial statistics: CA 1629, 3223, 8323 **CT** 3833 **DC** 17219 **HI** 1480, 3414 **LA** 11970 **MN** 9632 **NY** 10733 **OK** 19124 **TX** 469 *Canada:* **ON** 2927

Commodity exchanges: DC 4060, 8027 **IL** 3515, 3524 **MN** 3044 **NY** 4061

Common law: AL 14661 **CA** 18357 **PR** 13514, 19236 *Canada:* **NB** 19026 **ON** 2863, 19164 **PQ** 1680, 9902

Common Market countries   See: European Economic Community countries

Commonwealth of Nations: DC 5361 **NY** 5360 **PA** 3759 *Intl:* **ENG** 4064, 4068, 19171

Communes   See: Collective settlements

Communicable diseases (See also Biological warfare; Epidemiology; Public health; Venereal diseases): DC 16992, 17222 **GA** 17125 **IN** 7763 **LA** 16566 **MD** 17862 **MT** 17628 **NY** 11004, 11650 **TX** 16242 *Intl:* **BEL** 1969 **CHN** 12930 **GER** 11825

Communication (See also Cybernetics; Journalism; Language arts; Mass media; Radio broadcasting; Telecommunication; Television broadcasting): AZ 10787 **CA** 2491, 4070, 4104, 4249, 6777, 7508, 8185, 9223, 9886, 12013, 12769, 14020, 16003, 16074 **CO** 19697 **CT** 114, 6310 **DC** 8021, 12078, 17166, 17557 **FL** 5085, 5913, 6918 **GA** 16383, 17023 **HI** 5133 **IL** 10786, 18667 **IN** 5404 **KS** 18728 **MA** 830, 3848, 4867, 5328, 6774, 6775, 8532, 13729, 13730 **MD** 7660, 18803, 20312 **MI** 14788 **MO** 1134, 11243 **NC** 7626, 19076 **NJ** 1205, 1207, 1209 **NY** 11584, 11630, 11718, 16023, 16602, 20395 **OH** 3818 **PA** 19174, 19223 **PR** 19250 **TX** 326, 5086, 7623, 16816 **VA** 1614, 3789, 4105, 4704, 5087 **WA** 392 **WI** 19611, 19622, 19650 *Canada:* **ON** 11242, 16442, 16596, 19564 **PQ** 2801, 2902, 3233, 4121, 4142, 13593, 13688, 16063, 18082 **SK** 15012 *Intl:* **AUS** 1326 **BRZ** 18005 **ENG** 8125 **GER** 9983, 14189 **IND** 16767 **MYS** 9568 **NLD** 15792 **NOR** 19161 **SWE** 15918 **SWI** 15939 **THA** 16766

Communication, Intercultural   See: Intercultural communication

Communication law   See: Mass media—Law and legislation

Communication in science: CA 19342 **IA** 14011 **MD** 10983 *Intl:* **HUN** 8147

Communications, Military: CA 17830 **MA** 10559 **MS** 16808 **NJ** 16931 **NY** 16787 **VA** 10558 *Canada:* **PQ** 2785

Communicative disorders (See also Speech, Disorders of): WI 19650

Communism: CA 15650 **CT** 18519 **DC** 20008 **GA** 5338 **IL** 580 **MI** 18854 **NJ** 5567 **NY** 11733, 13833 **WI** 19571, 19642 *Intl:* **DEN** 8862 **GER** 5199, 5630 **KOR** 1124, 8839 **ROM** 7943

Community antenna television   See: Cable television

Community colleges: CA 5402 **PA** 4074

Community development (See also City planning): CA 3043 **CT** 14887 **DC** 11226, 17241, 17919 **GA** 14884 **IL** 18677 **IN** 6016 **KS** 8575, 18727 **MD** 1444, 18246 **MI** 20274 **MS** 7844 **NC** 19059 **NE** 12407 **OH** 3829, 4092 **PA** 2320 *Canada:* **MB** 9628 **NS** 4532, 14317 **PQ** 10693 *Intl:* **FIN** 16030 **ISR** 8126 **JPN** 11145

Community organization: CA 12205, 19347 **DC** 11137 **IN** 7815 **NY** 652, 4028, 5968 **OH** 3126 **TX** 4566 **WA** 19542 *Canada:* **AB** 5244 **ON** 14029

Comparative education: MI 10332, 20270 **MO** 1161 *Intl:* **GER** 6429, 16763 **HUN** 7555

Comparative law (See also Law—History and criticism): CA 2580, 18357 **CT** 20720 **DC** 9121, 17279, 20009 **IL** 12087 **IN** 7801 **LA** 9381, 16559 **MA** 1982, 6980 **NY** 14357 **OH** 18482, 19424 **PR** 8031 *Canada:* **PQ** 9902 *Intl:* **FRA** 15315 **GER** 13102, 13105 **ITA** 8136

Comparative literature   See: Literature, Comparative

Compensation   See: Wages

Composers: CA 18392 **DC** 9131 **IL** 3540 **KY** 18769 **MA** 1997, 9811 **MD** 18821 **ME** 13243 **MI** 4825 **MN** 3453 **NY** 690, 2193, 11637 **OH** 13477 **PA** 6114 **PR** 4222 *Intl:* **FRA** 6062

Composers, Canadian: *Canada:* **AB** 2968 **BC** 2965 **ON** 2809, 2966 **PQ** 2967, 3899

Composition (Music): CA 18411 **MN** 18925 **TX** 19390 **VA** 16915 *Intl:* **AJN** 1388 **POL** 16664

Computer-aided design and manufacturing: CA 7307 **IL** 7663 **MI** 7836 **MO** 20072 **TX** 1084, 4102, 10345 *Canada:* **BC** 2174 **NB** 11454 **PQ** 3890 *Intl:* **GER** 4692

Computer applications in education   See: Educational technology

Computer applications in health   See: Medical electronics

Computer-assisted instruction (See also Programmed instruction): CA 4458, 10667 **MA** 10165 **MI** 10327 **NY** 7618 **PA** 9469 *Canada:* **AB** 18192

Computer crimes: CA 11100 **DC** 17256

Computer graphics: CA 20682 **GA** 1236 **NH** 9245 **NV** 5267 **NY** 7618 **OH** 18152 **OR** 16059, 19141 **PA** 19208 **TX** 16220 *Canada:* **NS** 12134

Computer industry: CA 1972, 7840 **MA** 4864 **MN** 18899

Computer networks: MA 1163, 4867 **NJ** 4621 **PA** 19208 **VA** 6776

Computer programming   See: Programming (Electronic computers)

Computers (See also Information storage and retrieval systems; Programming (Electronic computers)): AL 180, 18163, 18170 **AR** 18232 **AZ** 132, 2355, 6260, 7366, 8018, 16977, 18229 **CA** 109, 455, 918, 2486, 2574, 3502, 3724, 3868, 4257, 4625, 5439, 6298, 6346, 6773, 7076, 7175, 7180, 7183, 7307, 7508, 7512, 7616, 7629, 9145, 9195, 9221, 9223, 9225, 9251, 9253, 9353, 9353, 9434, 10980, 11364, 11365, 14012, 14015, 14017, 14020, 14021, 15327, 15555, 15622, 15645, 15655, 16003, 16074, 16532, 16681, 17520, 17836, 17895, 17900, 18330, 18377, 18381, 18387, 18412, 18418, 18434, 19332, 19346, 20189, 20397, 20569, 20680, 20684 **CO** 1219, 7173, 7179, 7182, 8354, 11099, 16813, 17652, 18505 **CT** 5, 542, 6255, 6310, 6941, 11839, 12100, 14911, 15507, 15508, 17962, 20712 **DC** 4914, 6375, 11281, 16800, 16803, 16974, 17098 **DE** 6542 **FL** 4894, 5347, 5865, 5876, 13672, 18843, 20317 **GA** 1431, 5337, 6387, 6391, 15479, 17023 **IA** 16056 **ID** 975, 5268, 7172 **IL** 851, 1190, 1214, 3529, 4674, 7675, 12088, 14834, 15157, 16790, 18452, 18668, 18671, 18684 **IN** 1201, 7803, 7813, 7819, 13546 **KS** 1941, 8576, 18731 **KY**

Computers (continued)
8657, 9737, 18755, 18770 **MA** 1595, 1950, 2007, 2019, 2071, 2354, 4097, 4125, 4619, 4865, 4999, 5834, 6269, 6313, 6774, 6775, 6778, 6960, 7184, 8047, 8096, 9217, 9796, 9805, 9806, 10557, 10559, 10783, 13346, 13730, 15232, 15812, 16801, 18831, 20155, 20167, 20597 **MD** 3035, 4071, 4103, 4921, 5218, 8415, 9144, 10983, 16933, 17624, 17625, 17650, 17824, 18805, 18813 **ME** 12007 **MI** 6331, 10283, 15259, 16682, 19681, 20123, 20273 **MN** 7375, 10477, 16336, 16337, 16678, 16680, 18896 **MO** 403, 17174, 18967 **MS** 10991, 16808, 16856, 16970 **NC** 327, 1220, 3089, 5037, 5039, 7626, 13847, 19056 **ND** 11920 **NH** 4609, 4866, 11483, 19032, 20132 **NJ** 402, 1189, 1193, 1215, 1216, 1217, 1689, 1690, 1691, 1692, 4126, 4621, 6270, 6271, 6309, 7922, 8596, 13372, 14161, 14165, 14836, 16929 **NM** 11521, 11533, 17001, 17005, 18298 **NV** 19014 **NY** 2336, 2438, 2582, 3734, 3779, 3885, 4000, 4307, 5189, 6317, 7618, 7619, 7620, 7625, 7627, 7630, 7631, 7632, 10393, 11584, 11630, 11863, 12654, 13638, 13983, 15707, 15742, 15748, 15967, 16787, 19275, 19282, 20681 **OH** 4, 1197, 4676, 6306, 6571, 8653, 9307, 11366, 12243, 12307, 16811, 18158, 18469, 18474, 18480 **OK** 817, 12352, 12367, 12369, 14147, 19126 **OR** 7176, 8017, 12521, 12525, 15045, 16057, 17230, 19154, 19158, 19780 **PA** 3080, 6092, 6308, 12849, 12911, 15595, 15900, 16135, 16675, 16683, 17826, 19193, 19208, 19219 **PR** 4303, 19238 **SC** 4772, 11367, 19307 **SD** 4529, 15417 **TN** 16796, 19372 **TX** 4677, 5533, 6178, 7623, 10635, 10784, 10789, 10791, 13896, 16213, 16215, 16217, 16219, 16220, 16662, 16781, 16791, 16795, 19389, 20247 **UT** 572, 16677 **VA** 1045, 1393, 4105, 5364, 5560, 7624, 10986, 11258, 11546, 15582, 15616, 15971, 16354, 16533, 16978, 17016, 17165, 17178 **VT** 7622 **WA** 1938, 4231, 5926, 17905, 19523 **WI** 370, 10432, 19604, 19622 *Canada:* **AB** 300, 7360, 18187, 18192, 18295 **BC** 18276 **MB** 102, 18795 **NB** 19024 **NS** 2680, 4536 **ON** 99, 1684, 2674, 2679, 2681, 2781, 2790, 2828, 4447, 5018, 7613, 7614, 7615, 11833, 12493, 13651, 14137, 19435, 19553, 19564, 20794 **PQ** 2437, 2848, 4124, 9909, 9974, 9975, 13594, 13724, 18085, 18108, 18125 *Intl:* **AUS** 1325, 1326, 1330 **BEL** 11339, 12126 **BRZ** 8003 **CHN** 20651 **COL** 17978 **CRI** 17989 **ENG** 16721 **FRA** 7877, 18124, 18136 **GER** 18053 **HUN** 4888 **IRQ** 933 **ISR** 18613 **ITA** 18011 **JOR** 14134 **KOR** 5293 **MEX** 17994 **NLD** 3267, 5491, 16044, 18130 **POL** 16035 **SAF** 15382 **SAU** 5578, 7966 **SWI** 15937, 15938 **THA** 16292

Computers—Laws and legislation: **AZ** 2258 **CA** 3221, 8246 *Canada:* **ON** 9874

Computers in libraries: **CA** 1641 **MD** 18803 **NC** 19076 **PA** 19846

Computers—Optical equipment: **DC** 7846 **MD** 1160 **NY** 7618 **PA** 3082

Conchology See: Mollusks

Concrete (See also Cement): **CO** 7339 **HI** 4572 **IL** 13237 **MI** 539 **MS** 16967, 16970 **OH** 4429 **WA** 1737 *Intl:* **ENG** 2138 **GER** 6423 **ICE** 7634

Conducting (See also Music—Performance; Orchestra): **TX** 13893 **VA** 16915 *Intl:* **CHN** 3338

Confectionery: **NJ** 10560 **NY** 20346 **PA** 7164 *Intl:* **SCT** 14953

Confederate States of America (See also Civil War (U.S.)): **DC** 9135 **FL** 5919 **GA** 5338 **IL** 18689 **LA** 9372 **MS** 10517, 19354, 19825 **PA** 6123 **SC** 15393 **TX** 7447, 7465, 13897, 16706 **VA** 4134, 19857, 19864, 19892 **WV** 9724

Conflict management: **AR** 19967 **DC** 17559 **MD** 17260 **MI** 20121 **NY** 6510 **OH** 12560 **PA** 4143 **VT** 19805 *Intl:* **NLD** 18609

Confucius: *Intl:* **CHN** 7540, 16349

Congregationalism (See also Puritans): **CT** 5766, 5773, 15414, 20134 **IL** 3547 **MA** 540, 5772, 5774, 6958 **MI** 2399, 5771 **MN** 13047, 13149 **PA** 5504 **WA** 13150 *Canada:* **NS** 16695

Connecticut: **CT** 2116, 3017, 3337, 3875, 4178, 4181, 4192, 4200, 4409, 4583, 4605, 5144, 5566, 6518, 6582, 6749, 7290, 8643, 8645, 9206, 9473, 9523, 9640, 10356, 11456, 11500, 11519, 14023, 14643, 15184, 15318, 15360, 15482, 15634, 15815, 15822, 16400, 16428, 19954, 20092, 20134, 20177, 20240, 20354, 20472, 20473, 20477, 20723 **FL** 12510 **MA** 11034

Connolly, Cyril: **OK** 19466

Conrad, Joseph: **CT** 20703 **MA** 20446 **NH** 4616 **NY** 3880 **PA** 6122 **TX** 16200, 19392 *Intl:* **ENG** 13182

Conscientious objectors (See also Pacifism): **KS** 1784 **PA** 15903

Conservation of natural resources (See also Recycling (Waste, etc.); Water conservation; Wildlife conservation): **AZ** 992 **CA** 2470, 2514, 12823, 13698, 14708, 14765, 14974, 15159, 18322, 18323 **CT** 20718, 20739 **DC** 11250, 17249, 17942, 20430, 20636 **FL** 5871, 5907 **GA** 6384 **IL** 18679 **MA** 9788, 9827, 15434, 20592 **MD** 7238 **MN** 10455, 17119, 18945 **MO** 2390 **NC** 5979 **NY** 3239, 11085, 11346, 11735, 15720, 20137 **OK** 8212 **PA** 4230 **TX** 4217, 11054, 20147 **UT** 17116 **VA** 11325 **WI** 20529 **WY** 19654 *Canada:* **AB** 272, 273, 2711 **BC** 2160 **MB** 5033 **NB** 2715 **NS** 4534 **ON** 2713, 3003, 4216 **PQ** 13596, 13603 **SK** 2834 *Intl:* **CRI** 8028 **ENG** 6671 **GER** 6443 **SWI** 8202, 20635 **TUR** 6821 **YUG** 7965

Constitutional law (See also Administrative law; Eminent domain): **CO** 16821 **DC** 8156, 8355, 17255 **MO** 14465 **NY** 654, 11572 **PA** 8874 **PR** 3168, 8031 **TN** 19367 **TX** 11123 *Canada:* **AB** 249 **BC** 2153 **ON** 12455 **PQ** 18114

Construction industry (See also Building): **CA** 1631, 2499, 2550, 5930, 19799 **DC** 1137, 7472 **FL** 8984 **GA** 13249 **IL** 10867, 16936, 20539 **LA** 11390 **MI** 1136, 9011 **NJ** 6722, 7211 **NY** 5197 **PA** 16709 **SC** 5929 **TX** 2273, 4559, 8470, 20834 **VA** 6051 **WA** 19512 **WI** 10432 *Canada:* **BC** 2171 **NS** 12154 **ON** 2821, 4235 **PQ** 13582, 15290, 16052 *Intl:* **CHN** 3603 **HUN** 5391, 7554 **IRL** 18485 **NOR** 12112 **PRT** 13260 **SWE** 2423

Consulting, Management See: Business consultants

Consumer credit (See also Credit): **NJ** 1717 *Canada:* **SK** 5587

Consumer education (See also Consumers; Consumers' leagues): **KS** 8573 **NJ** 8371, 11749 *Canada:* **AB** 258, 298 **MB** 4245 **ON** 12459 **SK** 5587

Consumer health See: Health education

Consumer protection (See also Product safety): **CA** 11136, 20239 **DC** 4243, 4244, 6348, 13472 **PA** 9059 **WA** 20024 **WI** 20519 *Canada:* **ON** 2676, 12459 **PQ** 18114

Consumers (See also Consumer education; Consumer protection; Consumers' leagues): **DC** 4914, 17495 **IL** 16318, 18676, 18692 **IN** 13538 **LA** 11541 **MA** 5697 **MD** 13299 **NJ** 14175 **NM** 15534 **OH** 7443 **PA** 14421 **WI** 19619

Consumers' goods See: Manufactures

Consumers' leagues (See also Consumer education; Consumers): **NY** 4248

Contact lenses: **CA** 388, 15350 **PA** 12838 **TX** 18640

Contemporary art See: Art, Modern

Continuing education: **GA** 18597 **ME** 5153 **NY** 11619 *Canada:* **PQ** 16063 *Intl:* **GER** 16763

Contraception See: Birth control

Conway, Henry Seymour: **CT** 20721

Conwell, Russell H.: **PA** 16134

Cook, James: **CA** 18379 **HI** 7030, 18626

Cookery: **CA** 3736, 9353, 9353, 14707, 18305 **CO** 18548 **DC** 9135, 11272 **GA** 1246 **IL** 3529, 8614, 11231 **IN** 7819 **KS** 8572 **MA** 13677 **MI** 4828, 10336 **MN** 6327 **MO** 12956 **NJ** 4400 **NY** 1619, 2245, 4333, 4470, 11552, 11630, 12797, 15301 **OH** 3830 **RI** 8461 **TX** 16240, 16279, 16857 **VA** 16354 **WI** 19619 *Canada:* **ON** 10230 **PQ** 7889

Coolidge, Calvin: **DC** 9129 **MA** 5960

Cooper, James Fenimore: **CT** 20703 **NJ** 2373 **NY** 2335, 11663

Cooperative societies: **KS** 8573 **MI** 11866 **MO** 3145, 5602 **OH** 11334 **WI** 19619, 19623 *Canada:* **AB** 258 **NS** 14317 **ON** 2917 **PQ** 4135, 13600 **SK** 3303, 14843 *Intl:* **HUN** 15975 **ISR** 8126 **TWN** 4280

Copland, Aaron: **SC** 4259

Creative ability: NC 3227 NY 981, 4422, 15704 OH 11059 RI 11174

Creative writing: MN 18908

Credit (See also Consumer credit): DC 5649 MI 9240 PA 10750 VA 5597 *Canada:* ON 2941

Credit unions See: Banks and banking, Cooperative

Creek Indians: OK 4425

Creeley, Robert White: NY 15757

Creoles: LA 19356

Cricket: *Intl:* AUS 15694

Crime and criminals (See also Computer crimes; Crime prevention; Juvenile delinquency; Organized crime; Prisons; Victims of crime; White collar crimes): AL 17017 CA 2548, 9354, 12513, 14692, 18326 CO 3958 CT 10862, 18517 DC 3280, 17252, 17259 GA 6395 IL 3525, 12087 IN 7759, 7815 MA 9831 MD 545, 17251, 17260 MI 10336 MN 10462 MO 14445 NJ 14162 NY 4017, 5968, 5971, 11564, 11685 OH 3831, 8649, 12325 WI 10425, 20519 *Canada:* AB 18204 BC 8499 ON 2849, 12460, 12491, 12493, 14108, 19431 PQ 3286, 7881, 13606, 18086, 18095 *Intl:* NLD 11405

Crime and criminals—Identification: CA 8059

Crime prevention (See also Criminal justice, Administration of): FL 579 KY 11147 MD 17260 MN 10462 NJ 14162 VA 19879 WA 20024 *Canada:* AB 262 ON 2849

Criminal insane See: Insane, Criminal and dangerous

Criminal justice, Administration of (See also Criminal law): CA 13706 DC 644, 13391 IL 6705, 7684, 9421 MA 4432, 11108 MD 545, 17260, 19263 ME 9551 MI 5670 MN 8181, 10471 NV 8955 NY 3242, 8345, 11565, 13983, 15702, 15727 OH 10273 OK 12357 PA 15136 TX 7465 VA 11107, 11218, 11285, 17488, 19878, 19879 WI 19591, 19603 *Canada:* AB 262 ON 2849, 14108

Criminal law (See also Criminal justice, Administration of): AL 10579 DC 4920, 13475, 16792, 17163, 17256, 17493 HI 7027 IA 8226 IL 12087 KY 5149, 8673 LA 15518 MA 9921, 11845 MD 9768 MI 10621, 12197 MN 13701 MO 14445, 18971 NJ 7566, 11512 NY 9048, 9050, 11571, 11644, 11685, 15962 OR 8483 PA 17264 PR 3168, 8031, 13518 VA 17903 *Canada:* AB 249, 18201 BC 2168 ON 2763, 12455, 12491, 12494, 13652, 15175 *Intl:* FIN 5706

Criminology See: Crime and criminals

Crisis intervention (Psychiatry): IL 3541 ME 14534 SC 6745

Critical care medicine: MI 17355

Croatian Americans: CA 4435

Croce, Benedetto: WI 19600

Croker, John Wilson: FL 18586

Cromwell, Oliver: VA 19510

Crop protection See: Plants, Protection of

Crops: AR 20493 CA 17198 FL 18569 IA 13071 IL 18657 OH 12292 UT 1650 VA 16712, 19916 WI 742, 17180 *Canada:* AB 2647 BC 2652 ON 2665, 13917 PQ 7888 SK 2661, 2826 *Intl:* ARG 12226 AUS 18145, 20553 BOL 7997 BRZ 7995 CHN 1655, 15413 COL 3923, 8078 COT 20181 GHA 6460 IND 7747 JPN 3646, 7322 NGA 7898, 8135 RUS 8823 SWZ 19361 YUG 8763

Cross-cultural studies: AK 834, 18183 AL 180 CA 1845, 7989 DC 17919 HI 5133 IL 7679 NJ 6512 NY 6510, 9745 *Canada:* AB 1097 MB 9607 NS 12142 PQ 7871 SK 12420, 14864 *Intl:* SAF 119

Crow Indians: MT 12763, 17676

Cruikshank, George: CA 2572 MN 14564 NJ 13386 NY 15958, 18483 OH 13479

Cryogenics: CA 18395 CO 17652 IN 19111 MO 20066 MS 10991 NJ 1927 NY 16646 OH 4502 PA 151, 19220 VA 4797 *Intl:* FRA 8133

Cryptography: CA 1401, 20551 DC 9135 MA 17014 OH 8649 PA 19197 TX 16847

Crystallography (See also Crystals; Geology; Mineralogy): IA 18710 NJ 13373

Crystals (See also Semiconductors): CA 7507 IL 12082 MA 4455 NY 4328 PA 7909 *Canada:* ON 12093

Cuba: CA 19335 DC 4467 FL 10255, 10888, 18846 NY 3229 PA 19217 *Intl:* CUB 4464, 4465, 4466

Cukor, George Dewey: CA 35

Cults (See also Religion): CA 9354 MA 573 NJ 19700

Culture (See also Cross-cultural studies; Education; Humanism; Material culture; Popular culture): DC 4913, 11156, 11158 DE 9484 NJ 11516 PA 9480 VA 7983 *Canada:* ON 14131 *Intl:* AUT 1353 BEL 5517 BRZ 16630 CZE 13294 FIN 15897 FRA 16768 GER 18059 HUN 7546 IND 16767 NLD 11407 PAK 12694 POL 19665 SWI 15941 THA 16766 YUG 20828

cummings, e.e. (Edward Estlin): TX 19392 VA 1490

Cuneiform inscriptions: AZ 13025 CT 20702 DC 3165 IL 18458 MO 8640 NJ 13367 PA 6122 *Intl:* FRA 1833

Currency See: Money

Current events See: Newspaper and periodical libraries

Currier & Ives: DC 9134

Cushman, Charlotte Saunders: DC 9129

Custer, George Armstrong: MI 10620, 10623 MT 5160, 10643, 17697

Custody of children: PA 3557

Customs See: Tariff

Cybernetics (See also Biological control systems; Bionics; Computers; System analysis; Systems engineering): FL 10001 *Intl:* POL 16035

Cycles (See also Business cycles; Time): CA 6050

Cyclones: *Intl:* HKG 14128

Cyprus: NY 13639

Cytology: CA 14973, 15651, 18305, 18388 CO 11221, 18506 CT 17633 GA 513 KY 18744 MA 6949 MI 10334 MN 18942 MT 15138 NC 3471, 11210, 19067, 19068 NJ 16624 NY 3873, 4003, 5837, 5969, 8478, 11566, 11650, 20751 PA 7909, 16130 TX 19374 WI 19582 *Canada:* ON 10279 PQ 9893, 10694 *Intl:* AUS 20302 CHN 12930 FRA 12784 GER 13099

Czech Americans: IL 4456 NE 5161, 19005

Czechoslovakia: DC 9113 IL 4456, 7670 *Canada:* ON 19460 *Intl:* CZE 4512

da Vinci, Leonardo: CA 18370 CT 2382 DC 11179 MA 2072 NJ 15788 NY 19278

Dabney, Virginius: VA 19510

Dentistry (See also Orthodontics): AK 220 AL 16897, 17047, 18171 AZ 15022, 16865 CA 2498, 9255, 9330, 17297, 17846, 18390, 18423, 19734 CO 4778, 18511 CT 18518 DC 4847, 6378, 7475, 16901, 16992 DE 17312 FL 17313, 18572 GA 5336, 9995 HI 17052 IA 18711 IL 564, 7534, 9423, 16910, 17833, 18698 KS 17043 KY 18756, 18771 LA 17340 MA 2017, 5990, 9989, 16549 MD 17629, 18800 ME 17350 MI 8686, 12196 MN 18894 MO 20071 MS 7228, 18953 NC 17056, 19061 ND 17370 NJ 1898 NM 19044 NY 2337, 4001, 5176, 6906, 9289, 10007, 15524, 15737, 15752, 15848, 17389, 20230 OH 3804, 3806, 9996, 12314, 16912 OK 19132 OR 12522 PA 11962, 14608, 19211 PR 19256 SC 10014, 17412 TN 10021, 17417, 17419, 17855, 19371 TX 16798, 16810, 16908, 16909, 17035, 17055, 17420, 19416 VA 17857, 19862 WA 17048, 19529 WI 9713, 10160, 14200, 14305, 17440 WV 20222 *Canada:* AB 18200 BC 18285 NF 10052 NS 4541 ON 2922, 14894, 15033, 19553 PQ 18094 SK 19294 *Intl:* DEN 8777 FRA 18062 GER 10018 ISR 7103 NLD 19919 NOR 19160 SWE 15907 TUR 6821 TWN 8577, 11311

Dentistry—History: CA 19325 IL 12080 MA 5990 MD 18800 NY 11722 OR 12522 PA 19192, 19211 TX 19415

Dentistry—Research: FL 15476 MD 11208 NY 19286 *Canada:* ON 2922

Dentistry—Study and teaching See: Dental school libraries

Dermatology (See also Skin—Diseases): CA 52, 388, 437, 3200, 8506 IL 4490, 14919 LA 17934 MD 6479 NJ 13856 NY 1383, 1599, 2132, 8974, 15793 OH 12264 PA 6611 TX 113, 9743 *Canada:* ON 20558 PQ 9908 *Intl:* ARG 973 BRZ 2084 BUL 2347 ENG 14113

Desalination of water See: Saline water conversion

Desegregation See: Segregation

Deserts: AZ 992, 4796, 18208 CA 2557, 3888, 9230, 17738, 18403, 18405 NV 19013

Design: AL 1278 CA 1073, 2479, 4402, 4896, 12769, 18370 DC 9134, 11156 GA 1236 IL 7675, 13721 IN 19109 KS 18734 MA 1081, 9789, 15234 MD 9747 MI 4407, 4815 MN 10444, 18892, 19947 MO 6855 NC 6219, 11902, 11905 NJ 11744 NY 2240, 10909, 11645, 12768, 13636, 15274, 15614, 15733 OH 4032, 4846, 18464, 19693 PA 6109, 12981 VA 13715 WA 4337 WI 10419 *Canada:* BC 3094 MB 18785 ON 2838, 12432, 19546 PQ 18075, 18110 *Intl:* ENG 3800, 8644, 13200 GER 6424, 9063 NOR 12105 SCT 5233 SWI 20851

Design, Engineering See: Engineering design

Design, Environmental See: Environmental design

Design, Industrial (See also Computer-aided design and manufacturing; Engineering design): AL 1278 AZ 1009 CA 1073, 2473 GA 6388 IL 18690 MA 9789 ME 6 MI 6336 OH 3809, 18468 WA 19513 WI 10424 *Intl:* AUT 1360 FRA 3226 GER 4692 SWI 20621

Design, Theatrical See: Theaters—Stage-setting and scenery

Detergent, Synthetic (See also Soap): NY 15296

Detroit (MI): MI 4684, 4816, 4824, 4834, 20122

Developing countries: CA 11460, 11855, 12683, 18323 CT 20710, 20731 DC 130, 725, 9117, 12634, 16784, 17919, 20609 IN 6175, 7805 KS 8569 MA 1146, 2617, 4274, 14635 MD 4842 MI 10332 NY 9744, 9746, 13630, 16693 RI 13097, 19265 VA 3789, 19916 WI 19602 *Canada:* AB 1097 ON 4839, 6509, 8097, 10225, 14180, 14181, 16309 PQ 3216, 9894 *Intl:* AUS 3277 BEL 5517, 13413 COL 5349 DEN 4590 ENG 926, 6691, 19171 GER 6426, 16308 ISR 8126 ITA 7987, 8276 JPN 16757 KOR 8839 MYS 1115, 1121 NOR 10277, 12107 PHL 1118 SAU 8256 SCT 6690 SEN 125 SWE 14891, 15926 SYR 932 THA 16760 VEN 8023, 8968

Developmental biology (See also Child development; Embryology; Human growth): CA 15651 CO 18506 KY 18744 MA 6949 NE 18994 PA 16130 *Intl:* FRA 12784 NLD 14092

Developmentally disabled (See also Handicapped): AZ 995 CA 2526, 5573 CT 4191 IL 7673, 15079 IN 7790 MD 8625 ME 13065 MI 10293 MO 15612 MT 10648 NJ 8462, 20567 NM 9359 NY 2252, 3343, 9070,

10627, 11678 OH 18147 PA 3076 SD 15420 WI 3382 *Canada:* AB 19911 MB 9610 ON 12456, 14029

Dewey, John: IL 15492

Dewey, Thomas Edmund: NY 19278

Diabetes: CA 13703 MA 8484, 11470 MD 11207 MN 8098 *Canada:* ON 2923, 19430, 20558 PQ 4650

Dickens, Charles: CA 14725 CT 20703 DC 6379 IL 4673 KS 14500 MA 2122 MN 18931 NC 19075 OH 12328, 13479 PA 6122 TX 19392 VA 19510 *Canada:* ON 13661

Dickey, James: FL 19550

Dickinson, Charles Monroe: NY 15731

Dickinson, Emily: MA 807, 8474

Dickson, Gordon Rupert: MN 18920

Dictionaries See: Encyclopedias and dictionaries

Diderot, Denis: ME 2033 *Canada:* NS 6027

Die-casting: IL 11858 OH 4661

Diesel motor: IL 6339 IN 4482 MD 9495 PA 12903 WI 3976

Dietz, Howard: NY 10908

Diffusion (See also Colloids): MD 17620

Digestive organs—Diseases: MD 11148, 11207

Digital electronics: CA 2486

Dime novels: CA 14725 FL 10254 MA 2072 WV 6724

Diplomacy See: International relations

Direct delivery of books: OH 13486

Directories: CA 12774, 14705 DC 9115 FL 10252, 10256 GA 17592 IL 3522, 3529 KS 20409 LA 17583 MA 1993, 1995, 2021, 9833 MD 13299 MI 4817, 5852 MN 10447, 17581 MO 8548 NE 12408 NJ 11745 NY 1386, 2242, 11593, 11667, 13633, 17584, 20764 OH 3818, 13483 PA 3075, 6112 TX 7464 WA 14997 WI 6707 *Canada:* ON 2810, 10227 PQ 9406 *Intl:* CHN 3604

Dirksen, Everett McKinley: IL 4891

Disabled See: Handicapped

Disarmament (See also Peace; Security, International): CA 2562 DC 6169, 16917 IL 20637 NY 3288, 5661 PA 15903, 16133 *Canada:* ON 2790, 16309 *Intl:* BEL 10879 FIN 5718 SWE 15801

Disasters: AZ 6845 CO 18499 DE 18541 MD 5626 *Canada:* BC 8499 *Intl:* SWI 16754

Disciples of Christ: IA 4997 IN 3639 KY 9094 NM 10660 OH 7231 OK 13008 OR 12043 TN 4893, 5763 TX 5118, 16208

Discrimination (See also Segregation; Sexism): CA 20239 DC 4054, 17483 MI 10298, 20276 NY 654, 897, 11049, 20556 TN 16164 TX 19408 *Canada:* ON 2936 *Intl:* BEL 10879

Diseases, Chronic See: Chronic diseases

Diseases, Communicable See: Communicable diseases

Diseases, Infectious See: Communicable diseases

Disney, Walt: CA 4895

Disraeli, Benjamin: **NY** 19278 *Canada:* **ON** 13661

Distribution of goods, Physical   See: Physical distribution of goods

District of Columbia: **DC** 4916, 7291 **MD** 11046 **VA** 1039

Diving, Submarine: **CT** 17885 **FL** 17799 **MD** 17837

Divining rod: **VT** 748

Documentation (See also Information retrieval; Information services): **NC** 19076 **NH** 4869 **NY** 7619 *Canada:* **PQ** 9903 *Intl:* **BRZ** 2095 **DEN** 14133 **GER** 6431 **IRQ** 933 **NLD** 11404 **POL** 7975

Dodgson, Charles Lutwidge (Lewis Carroll): **IL** 10405 **NY** 11723 **OH** 3819 **TX** 7463

Dodsley, Robert: **NY** 4330

Dogs: **ID** 4487 **MO** 12583 **NY** 660 **OH** 3830 **VA** 3918 *Intl:* **AUS** 1343

Dolls: **IL** 7285 **TN** 5126 *Canada:* **ON** 5981

Domestic relations (See also Family): **PA** 9715

Domestic violence   See: Family violence

Dominicans: **CA** 4949 **DC** 4947 **RI** 13442

Donkeys: **TX** 565 **WA** 691

Door knobs: **IL** 902

Dos Passos, John: **MD** 18820 **VA** 19510

Douglas, Melvyn: **IN** 7798

Douglas, William Orville: **DC** 9129 **WA** 20693

Douglass, Frederick: **DC** 9129, 17716 **MD** 15990

Dowden, Edward: **TX** 1602

Down's syndrome: **MN** 3427 **NY** 1152

Dowsing   See: Divining rod

Doyle, Sir Arthur Conan (See also Holmes, Sherlock): *Canada:* **ON** 10229

Drama (See also Theater): **AR** 1022 **CA** 3753, 9104, 9350, 19290 **CT** 12422, 18519, 20711, 20727 **DC** 3163, 4909, 5943, 7474, 9117 **FL** 10255 **IL** 3528, 18461, 18689 **IN** 7818 **MA** 1983, 12416 **MI** 4815, 5850, 18860 **MN** 3910, 10451 **MT** 3099 **NY** 112, 2244, 3735, 8491, 11386, 11635 **OH** 3827, 12328 **OR** 19230 **PA** 19184 **TX** 4568, 7200, 13897, 18643, 19390 **UT** 20803 **WA** 15000, 19521 **WI** 19644 *Canada:* **AB** 18196, 18292 **ON** 2908, 10223, 19460 **SK** 14868 *Intl:* **DEN** 4770

Dramatists: **CT** 12422, 20727 **TX** 19390 *Canada:* **NS** 12142

Drawing: **CA** 9335 **CO** 3949 **CT** 20734, 20736 **DC** 4902, 11179 **IA** 4790 **MA** 1998, 10898 **MD** 9747 **MI** 4815 **MN** 10446 **MO** 11388 **NC** 11880 **NH** 9586 **NY** 6165, 9702, 10216, 10738, 11624, 11724 **PA** 6109, 12894 **TN** 10061 **TX** 4555, 6021, 7461 **WI** 10419, 10426 *Canada:* **BC** 19752 *Intl:* **DEN** 14125 **GER** 6858 **RUS** 14945 **SPA** 15557

Dreiser, Theodore: **IN** 19841 **NY** 4330 **PA** 19197

Dreyfus, Alfred: *Intl:* **FRA** 1826

Drilling muds: **AK** 205

Driver education   See: Automobile driver education

Drug abuse: **AK** 203 **CA** 328 **DC** 17454 **FL** 19677 **GA** 11249, 20184 **IL** 3369, 5980 **IN** 9250, 13547 **KS** 8180 **MA** 9790, 9946, 11916, 17345 **MD** 11115, 17251, 17932, 19263 **MI** 4821 **MN** 18904 **NJ** 14173 **NY** 4028, 10977, 13838, 14356, 14621 **PA** 4213, 5091 **PR** 13512 **SC** 15400, 15405

TX 16246, 19420 **VA** 11152 **VT** 19809 **WI** 13328, 19591, 19617 *Canada:* **AB** 245 **MB** 329 **NS** 12133 **ON** 69, 2750 **SK** 14838 *Intl:* **AUT** 19836 **SWE** 15919

Drugs   See: Pharmacy and pharmacology

Dryden, John: **CA** 18402 **CT** 20703

Dryland farming   See: Arid regions agriculture

Du Bois, William Edward Burghardt: **OH** 12296 **PA** 19200

Du Pont family: **DE** 6828

Dunbar, Paul Laurence: **AR** 18240 **GA** 3763 **OH** 18534

Duncan, Isadora: **CA** 14737 **NY** 11636

Duncan, Robert: **NY** 15757

Durrell, Lawrence George (Charles Norden): **KY** 18768

Dutch Americans: **IA** 4963 **MI** 7328

Dyes and dyeing (See also Batik): **AL** 20344 **MA** 7642 **MI** 1552 **NC** 3693, 14781 **OH** 7221 **PA** 4436 **VA** 7984 *Intl:* **CHN** 3607, 4542

Ear—Diseases (See also Hearing and deafness): **CA** 7439 **NC** 706

Earhart, Amelia Mary: **IN** 13543 **KS** 1224 **PA** 5093

Earp, Wyatt: **IL** 5101

Earth—Rotation: *Intl:* **JPN** 11083

Earth sciences (See also Atmosphere; Climatology; Meteorology; Oceanography): **AK** 18184 **AZ** 992, 17534 **CA** 2489, 6759, 9353, 9353, 15644, 18438 **CT** 18616, 20180 **DC** 4914, 11281, 15277 **ID** 5268 **IN** 13539, 19113 **MA** 3895, 6959 **MD** 8418, 10983 **MO** 17174, 18980 **NH** 4610 **NJ** 10749 **NM** 18298 **NV** 19018 **NY** 628, 2336, 3734, 4307, 11630 **OH** 10265, 12217 **OK** 16571 **PA** 19220 **TX** 1605, 6022 **UT** 19469 **VA** 599, 17531 **WI** 598, 11429 *Canada:* **AB** 2937, 7590, 15111 **BC** 2745 **MB** 18795 **NF** 11759 **NT** 2758 **ON** 2667, 14135, 20794 *Intl:* **AUS** 1327 **BRZ** 6519 **CHN** 7130 **FRA** 6065 **POL** 16035 **SWI** 11348, 15938

Earth sheltered houses: **MN** 18933

Earthquake engineering: **CA** 2487, 4578, 4706, 18315 **MS** 16971 **NY** 15742 *Intl:* **THA** 1119

Earthquakes (See also Tsunamis): **AK** 18184 **AZ** 15041 **CA** 8931, 9785, 14808, 20587 **HI** 8201 **NY** 3897 **WA** 15078 *Intl:* **CZE** 3398

Earths, Rare: **IA** 8238

East Asia: **AZ** 1016 **CA** 4379, 18397, 18416, 18429, 19259, 19326 **CT** 20697, 20709 **DC** 9109, 9124, 20471 **HI** 18617 **IL** 5684, 18659, 18675 **IN** 7781 **MA** 3590 **MI** 18854 **MO** 20061 **NH** 4612 **NJ** 14175 **NY** 9595, 16994 **OH** 12220, 20546 **OR** 19157 **RI** 2278 **TX** 10917 **WA** 19522 *Canada:* **BC** 18255 **ON** 19439 *Intl:* **BEL** 3166 **DEN** 4770 **FRA** 15300 **GER** 1597, 15794 **HUN** 7550 **IND** 1808 **SGP** 15189

East Asia—History: **AZ** 1016 **CT** 20697, 20709 **IL** 18660 **NY** 11626 **OR** 19157 **RI** 2278 **TX** 19388 **WA** 19522

Eastern Europe   See: Europe, Eastern

Eastern Orthodox Church   See: Orthodox Eastern Church, Greek; Orthodox Eastern Church, Russian

Eastland, James O.: **MS** 18955

Eastman, George: **NY** 19278

Eating disorders (See also Anorexia nervosa): **WA** 631 *Canada:* **ON** 2352

Ecology (See also Marine ecology): **AK** 212, 213, 2051, 17100, 17248,

Ecology (continued)
18175, 18185 **AL** 9670, 16177 **AZ** 8408 **CA** 103, 1636, 2470, 2471, 2573, 2574, 4578, 4589, 5102, 5103, 5212, 5255, 5275, 5288, 7610, 8049, 8477, 9353, 9353, 10233, 12507, 12823, 13160, 13681, 14758, 14804, 15159, 15648, 15651, 16377, 16955, 17101, 17480, 17643, 18305, 18388, 18403, 18412, 18434, 19799, 20584, 20585 **CO** 5365, 17199, 17522, 17537, 17771, 18508 **CT** 5, 11345, 11977, 20739 **DC** 709, 726, 1563, 2370, 5235, 6734, 9111, 10234, 11045, 11226, 11281, 13472, 13816, 14943, 15271, 15280, 20609, 20629 **FL** 939, 5379, 5867, 5871, 5875, 5904, 7145, 14346, 15528, 16789, 17463, 17639, 18570, 18590 **GA** 16959, 17461, 18605 **IL** 977, 3529, 7690, 7935, 10161, 10762, 11981, 15670, 16954, 18661, 18679 **IN** 2418, 7062, 7779 **KY** 18744, 18758 **LA** 11390 **MA** 1573, 2006, 3438, 5066, 6960, 9669, 9787, 9788, 10178, 11476, 14635, 16801, 16949, 17472, 17679, 18828, 20597 **MD** 1455, 5088, 5218, 5613, 6851, 15284, 18798, 18802 **ME** 9549 **MI** 4246, 10341, 20274 **MN** 5203, 10455, 10471, 16958 **MO** 8545, 10378, 16653, 16956, 17499, 17660 **MS** 10991, 16970, 17212 **MT** 17722 **NC** 5036, 5040, 11889, 13847, 14910, 17642, 19067, 19068 **ND** 17503, 19095, 19099 **NE** 11375 **NH** 9317 **NJ** 5535, 10358, 13369, 13372, 17466, 17640, 20355 **NM** 6463, 9044, 9322, 11525, 15534 **NV** 5267, 5984, 17122, 17235, 17460 **NY** 58, 2223, 3239, 3288, 5187, 5197, 5213, 5837, 6510, 7358, 7933, 8169, 9000, 11008, 11140, 11346, 11554, 11649, 13995, 15709, 15722, 15751, 15762, 15956, 15967, 16316, 17234, 19283 **OH** 3830, 4652, 6570, 6571, 8195, 12094, 17456 **OK** 17482, 19126 **OR** 3401, 12521, 12531, 12536, 17110, 19148, 19156 **PA** 36, 6092, 6227, 7833, 7974, 12845, 16709, 17475, 19222, 20342 **PR** 19247, 19254 **RI** 1291, 2275 **TN** 2314, 8775, 9736, 11000, 11344, 16174, 16175, 16948 **TX** 1638, 2273, 3362, 4451, 8433, 8470, 9482, 16203, 16583, 16939, 19397, 20147 **VA** 7639, 10558, 11325, 12405, 16942, 17105, 19815, 19877, 19896 **VI** 8259 **VT** 3276, 19804 **WA** 1572, 16960, 19523, 20035, 20362 **WI** 10431, 15581, 19587, 19628 **WV** 16640, 16943 **WY** 16185 *Canada:* **AB** 274, 1097, 2460, 2722, 3495, 7072, 10571, 12127, 12963, 15951, 18290, 18295 **BC** 2146, 2162, 2743, 13354, 16523 **MB** 2710, 4759, 7609 **NF** 2741, 8863 **NS** 2736, 4535, 5211, 12137, 16034 **NT** 2758 **ON** 354, 2644, 2712, 2719, 8489, 12479, 12495, 19543 **PQ** 2739, 8981, 9906, 11836, 13581, 13599, 13602, 13603, 16052, 18077, 18078, 18120, 18125 **SK** 14866 *Intl:* **AUS** 1332, 19028 **AUT** 8124, 18702 **BEL** 1665, 1669 **BRZ** 6519, 11206, 18004 **CHN** 31, 32 **ECU** 5222 **ENG** 8128, 9270 **FIN** 7123 **FRA** 1848, 5206, 5207, 20632 **GER** 6443, 6448, 9731, 13108 **GRC** 5488 **GUY** 3046 **ICE** 7638 **IND** 3293, 15996 **JPN** 8335 **KEN** 16770 **MEX** 5210 **NCG** 1149 **NLD** 11413 **NZL** 11736, 11740 **ROM** 14047 **SAU** 5551 **SCT** 7202, 9490, 14967 **SEN** 4526 **SWE** 2423 **SWI** 8202, 20635 **TUN** 9025 **URE** 7906

Ecology, Forest See: Forest ecology

Ecology—Study and teaching See: Environmental education

Econometrics (See also Statistics): **CT** 20707 **KS** 18727 **MN** 18906 **PA** 54, 19186, 19213, 19216 *Intl:* **GER** 7926, 18026

Economic assistance (See also Technical assistance): **DC** 3262, 16783 **NY** 5962 *Intl:* **GER** 6426 **SWE** 15926

Economic botany See: Botany, Economic

Economic conditions See: Economic history

Economic cycles See: Business cycles

Economic development (See also Developing countries): **AZ** 16540, 16545 **CA** 2522, 11196, 15128, 18328, 18396, 19348 **CT** 20710, 20731 **DC** 8027, 8109, 8157, 12561, 16783, 17216, 17919, 19689, 20636 **FL** 5888 **GA** 3762 **HI** 1480, 7031 **IL** 6705, 7686 **KS** 18727 **KY** 8667 **LA** 19051 **MA** 11473, 16548 **MD** 1455, 1646, 6872, 17209 **MI** 15445 **MN** 10485 **MO** 20063 **NE** 11373 **NJ** 11510 **NY** 7925, 7978, 13219, 14806, 12776 **OH** 11974 **OR** 12537, 13790 **PA** 5215, 19213 **PR** 13517 **RI** 13877 **TN** 8775 **TX** 16241 **WI** 20529 *Canada:* **AB** 965 **BC** 11362 **MB** 9603 **ON** 14181 **PQ** 2670 *Intl:* **AUS** 3277 **BOL** 3415 **BRZ** 522 **CHL** 16759 **COT** 7862 **DEN** 4590 **ENG** 4068, 12641 **FRA** 18099 **GER** 7926 **IND** 7740 **IRQ** 16762 **ISR** 8126 **KEN** 16770 **MYS** 1121 **NCL** 15433 **NLD** 7977 **NOR** 10277 **PER** 837 **PHL** 1118 **SAU** 8256 **SCT** 6690, 7202 **SRI** 6049, 9657 **SWE** 15926 **THA** 16292, 16760 **TZA** 16005 **VEN** 8968

Economic forecasting: **CA** 15620 *Intl:* **FRA** 1848

Economic history: **DC** 5649, 11320, 17282 **IL** 18449 **IN** 13545 **MA** 636, 1724, 5678 **MN** 5640 **MO** 20250 **NY** 4682, 11652, 15961 **OK** 19129

Canada: **ON** 14099 **PQ** 14100 *Intl:* **ENG** 9271 **FRA** 18099 **GER** 5199, 13107 **HUN** 7546 **NLD** 11401

Economic policy (See also Monetary policy; National security; Subsidies; Tariff; Technical assistance; Unemployed): **CA** 7736 **DC** 8465, 19689 *Canada:* **ON** 2687, 2928 *Intl:* **BRZ** 15839 **ECU** 3386 **GRE** 6754 **HUN** 7544 **KWT** 8833 **SWI** 5481

Economic research: **CA** 14714 **MD** 9758 **NY** 2405, 11648 **TX** 15527, 19381 **WV** 20218, 20219

Economics (See also Labor economics; Money): **AL** 180, 18160 **AR** 18237 **AZ** 13027, 18215 **CA** 1058, 1261, 1478, 3223, 4622, 4850, 5647, 9344, 9973, 11149, 14708, 14715, 14804, 15623, 15650, 15652, 16636, 17872, 18307, 18324, 18352, 18387, 19324, 20569, 20606 **CO** 3434, 17112, 18491, 18493, 19697 **CT** 3695, 6938, 11977, 16603, 16643, 18517, 20707, 20731 **DC** 494, 570, 1493, 2225, 2370, 2669, 3417, 4054, 4060, 4170, 4173, 4243, 4289, 4906, 5523, 5649, 6030, 7470, 7473, 8026, 8211, 8416, 9111, 9114, 11150, 11225, 11281, 13851, 16783, 17098, 17135, 17164, 17219, 17269, 17278, 17282, 17484, 17489, 17490, 17494, 17495, 17595, 17916, 17920, 17936, 17938, 17939, 20008 **DE** 5028, 7641 **FL** 5862, 10252 **GA** 5394, 5632, 6014, 6401 **HI** 1480, 5776, 7031, 7039 **IA** 9311 **ID** 18655 **IL** 3141, 4698, 5635, 5784, 9084, 15491, 17570, 18449, 18456, 18666, 18689 **IN** 375, 2136, 7819, 13545, 16495 **KS** 18724, 20409 **LA** 9363, 9393, 9881, 16558 **MA** 636, 1995, 2001, 3438, 5007, 5634, 6969, 6981, 9801, 9824, 11801, 15236, 17927 **MD** 1964, 5218, 5613, 6370, 8422, 13299 **ME** 19675 **MI** 1412, 4043, 4829, 4984, 5852, 6337, 6341, 11359, 17574, 18886, 19956 **MN** 5640, 7212, 10447, 14562, 18906 **MO** 1909, 4931, 5638, 5646, 8548, 10378, 18959, 18960 **MS** 7844 **MT** 10645, 18985 **NC** 5036, 5049, 6739, 11905, 13847 **NE** 12408 **NH** 11483 **NJ** 1207, 13383, 13389 **NM** 19040, 19050 **NY** 582, 1548, 2246, 2329, 2438, 3452, 3470, 3723, 4010, 4023, 4027, 4141, 4316, 4365, 5643, 5700, 6043, 9645, 9646, 9914, 11092, 11151, 11548, 11623, 11666, 11717, 13634, 13989, 15096, 16602, 16772, 19282, 19743 **OH** 174, 3796, 5636, 6099, 6704, 10266, 10273, 12281, 12297, 13483, 13503, 16391, 17518 **OK** 8687, 12372 **OR** 3406, 12536, 19972 **PA** 634, 3241, 5644, 6110, 6132, 6279, 10026, 12852, 12858, 15867, 19186, 19213, 19216, 20418 **PR** 3751, 13522, 13523 **RI** 2299, 17894 **SC** 15252, 15395 **TN** 11000, 16157, 16948 **TX** 1260, 4559, 4707, 5637, 6022, 6771, 7458, 13504, 14671 **UT** 19469, 20802, 20808 **VA** 1490, 3274, 4430, 5560, 5645, 6347, 7923, 9774, 11011, 16986, 17169, 19269, 19501 **VT** 11230 **WA** 1639, 14992, 20359 **WI** 1703, 8112, 10428, 19630 **WV** 20215 *Canada:* **AB** 254, 255, 264, 288, 310, 2053, 18197, 18292 **BC** 2145, 2156, 2743, 6104, 18268, 18271, 19759 **MB** 6702, 9611, 9618 **NB** 11449 **NS** 1257, 12148 **ON** 57, 99, 1483, 1486, 2685, 2693, 2724, 2760, 2764, 2860, 2931, 2938, 4140, 5015, 5433, 5522, 7482, 7720, 7730, 7848, 8979, 9950, 10225, 12483, 12488, 13902, 14099, 16408, 16409, 16410, 17959, 19453, 20566 **PE** 13350 **PQ** 2686, 2696, 5205, 7603, 7888, 9566, 13528, 13575, 13581, 13583, 13593, 13600, 14100, 18086, 18104, 18116, 18118 **SK** 3303, 14598, 14871 *Intl:* **ALG** 350 **ARG** 5548, 7949 **ATG** 12556 **AUT** 19835 **BEL** 1668, 1669, 4056, 11339 **BRZ** 2090, 6213, 6214, 18004, 19781 **CHL** 3167, 3595 **CHN** 1659, 6246, 18703 **COL** 1539 **COT** 7862 **CRI** 17989 **CYP** 4505 **ENG** 9271 **FRA** 3261, 6069, 18099 **GER** 1564, 5543, 5545, 6429, 6448, 6451, 7863 **GHA** 6461 **HUN** 7544, 7545, 7558, 7932, 15975 **ICE** 7635 **IND** 6531, 7749, 15165, 15996 **IRL** 7912 **ISR** 5581 **JOR** 14134 **JPN** 10952 **KEN** 8679 **KOR** 8839 **MEX** 3265 **MUS** 8466 **NLD** 7977, 11401, 11402, 11410 **NOR** 12102, 12106, 19161 **PAK** 12695 **PAN** 17997 **PER** 837 **PHL** 8072 **POL** 13181 **PRT** 1460 **RUS** 3198, 8292, 19795 **SAF** 15387 **SAU** 7966 **SGP** 7979 **SLC** 14469 **SPA** 7891, 7939, 15559, 15562, 15566 **SWI** 3316, 5481, 6292, 7710 **TUR** 16581, 16647 **TWN** 4280 **VEN** 8966 **YUG** 20826

Economics, Energy See: Energy economics

Economics, Medical See: Medical economics

Ecuador (See also Latin America): *Intl:* **ECU** 3386

Ecumenical movement: **DC** 6073, 9117 **GA** 6504 **IA** 18555 **NC** 7380 **NY** 5223, 6164, 6352, 16667 **OH** 14507 **PA** 19300 **VA** 11152 *Canada:* **PQ** 2912 *Intl:* **SWI** 20613

Eddy, Mary Baker: **DE** 5769 **MA** 5767, 9300

Edison, Thomas Alva: **FL** 5236 **MD** 16440 **MI** 5964 **NJ** 17702

Education (See also Education and state; Teaching): **AK** 9412 **AL** 180, 1283, 8057, 16850, 17017, 17019 **AR** 18240 **AZ** 997, 11991, 17586 **CA** 200, 643, 645, 2546, 2573, 3187, 3900, 4458, 8684, 8857, 9283, 9336, 9354,

Educational tests and measurements: CA 645 DC 5409 DE 8178 GA 1243 IA 538 IL 18670 MA 2014, 20599 MI 20270 MN 18907 MO 18983 NJ 5262 NY 5260, 5968, 14356 PA 12995 VA 479 WA 19520, 20044 WI 19615 *Intl:* MYA 10944

Edwards, Jonathan: CT 20703

Eggleston, George Cary: VA 19510

Egypt (See also Africa, North): *Intl:* AUT 18042

Egyptology: AZ 13015 CA 14079 IL 16723, 18457, 18458 LA 19052 ME 5604 NY 2239, 11626 PA 878 TX 15503 *Intl:* AUS 1340 EGY 6148 FRA 10881

Eichenberg, Fritz: CT 20700

Einstein, Albert: CT 2382 *Canada:* ON 19460

Eisenhower, Dwight David: IA 5276 KS 17921 NY 4020 PA 17720

Eisenhower, Mamie Doud: IA 5276

Elastomers: MN 16334, 16335

Elections: CA 3729 DC 8120, 13831, 17491 NY 653, 3730 *Intl:* ENG 18254

Electric apparatus and appliances: AZ 13029 MO 14449

Electric batteries   See: Storage batteries

Electric engineering: AL 14153, 16593, 17019 AZ 16977 CA 1714, 2272, 3868, 6773, 7181, 7629, 8286, 8300, 9145, 9195, 9225, 9351, 9926, 13728, 14012, 14777, 15467, 15647, 17877, 17886, 18330, 18377, 18434 CO 1219, 7179, 10236, 11099, 13498 CT 6295, 6299, 11839, 11976, 12100 DC 3157, 8021, 13272, 17489, 17874 FL 5085, 5347, 5876, 5878, 6918, 7369 GA 6387, 15479 HI 7050 IL 1190, 1932, 5927, 7367, 7370, 14989, 18668, 18671 IN 1201, 13540, 17825, 19113 KS 1941 KY 18758, 18770 MA 827, 1192, 4865, 6091, 6269, 9216, 9481, 9796, 9806, 10557, 10559, 13731, 15812, 16553, 16708, 16801, 18831, 20167 MD 5270, 16018, 18813 MI 4806, 5966, 9011, 10320, 15259, 20378 MN 7373, 16337 MO 2386, 15899, 18963, 20066 NC 3091, 5036, 5039, 15619 ND 19097 NH 4609, 9245, 17879, 19032 NJ 1187, 1189, 1689, 2387, 6271, 8596, 13372, 13500, 16929, 16930 NV 19014 NY 394, 2438, 3096, 3734, 3779, 4000, 4307, 5188, 5353, 6304, 6344, 7627, 9592, 11645, 12765, 13203, 13204, 15750, 15956, 15967 OH 566, 5354, 9738, 12307, 13311, 16811, 18158, 18469, 18480, 19693 OK 1719, 12346, 12371, 13499, 19126 OR 7176, 13239, 17230 PA 819, 4518, 5492, 10200, 12985, 15595, 16132, 17875, 17880, 19193, 19205, 20318 SD 15424 TN 15701, 16175, 19372 TX 1260, 4985, 5533, 6810, 10793, 15535, 16216, 16217, 16535, 16939, 16985, 16985, 19389 VA 1194, 6272, 7061, 13665, 15582 VT 19811 WA 7177 WI 370, 5195, 10432 *Canada:* AB 2455, 5247, 10608 BC 1391, 2682, 18262 MB 9616, 18787 NB 11454, 19024 NS 2680, 16034 ON 56, 325, 2674, 2838, 2874, 2934, 10556, 12442, 13651, 19443, 19559 PQ 2437, 7601, 9909, 18125 SK 19292 *Intl:* BUL 16032, 19904 CHN 25, 7988, 13695, 20651 COL 17978 FIN 7126 GER 5542, 5545 HUN 5391 NLD 7321 POL 16035 SPA 15560 SWI 15937, 15938

Electric power: CA 5288 CO 13141, 13498 CT 11977 DC 5235, 5627, 11278, 17232 FL 5878, 15999 IN 7826 MA 1986, 15812, 20742 MI 4247, 4806 NC 5036 NJ 1256 NY 12515, 13977 OH 3318, 3319, 12267, 13311 PA 6592, 12985 TN 12190, 16174 TX 3362, 13504 VA 19877 VT 6721, 19812 WA 13525 *Canada:* AB 271, 5247 PQ 10609 SK 14863 *Intl:* RUS 3198

Electric railroads (See also Transportation): CA 668, 20290 CT 4180 IL 7678 OR 12520 PA 13696

Electric vehicles: VA 16924

Electricity (See also Magnetism): AZ 14648 CA 2483 CT 2382, 16720 GA 15483 MA 16550 MD 17808 MN 1427 MO 14449 NJ 17702 NV 5267 NY 4225, 11630, 14903 TX 15543, 16226 *Canada:* AB 2999, 16456 ON 6833, 12436 PQ 7602, 8982 *Intl:* CHN 1658, 3621 FRA 6060

Electrochemistry: AL 13864 CA 1642, 13728, 18311 MA 5066 MD 8101 ND 19094 NY 5294 OH 5313, 5512, 6585 RI 16028 TN 12401 TX 11058 WI 13725 *Canada:* ON 317, 4047, 7729 PQ 7602

Electrodes: NY 3039 OH 5313

Electromagnetism: MD 7660 NY 16787

Electron optics: CA 7511, 9145, 9227, 12724 MA 9310 MD 3035 NY 1661, 11863, 13983 OR 16057 *Canada:* PQ 2684 *Intl:* CHN 29 ISR 8269

Electronic data processing (See also Office practice—Automation): CA 455, 1476, 1634, 4104, 5425, 6346, 7629, 9145, 9244, 16003 CO 16813 CT 13021, 18517 DC 13272, 15829, 17831, 17920 FL 571, 15476 KS 18727 MA 2354, 6775, 9101, 15864 MD 17940 MI 4633, 17171, 19956 MN 16678 MO 1365, 9884, 20072 NE 12409, 20574 NJ 1690, 1691, 4621, 7955, 8287 NY 2301, 3452, 4859, 5423, 5641, 7632, 15967 OH 4862, 11366, 15130 PA 10026 SC 15615 TN 11002, 15701 TX 4559, 5086, 7633, 16270 UT 572 VA 15828, 16978, 16986, 17173 WI 3617, 9524, 20103 *Canada:* AB 300, 10571 BC 2178 NS 12150 ON 1482, 1487, 2781, 2844, 2878, 5433, 11363, 12014, 12468, 19564 PQ 1484, 1679, 2862, 8810 SK 14869

Electronic funds transfers: CA 3724 DC 17596

Electronic office machines (See also Office practice—Automation): *Canada:* ON 13014

Electronic warfare: VA 16684

Electronics (See also Cybernetics; Digital electronics; Microelectronics): AK 18184 AZ 6260, 7366, 8018, 10785, 10787, 10790, 13029, 14030, 16977 CA 455, 820, 1373, 3868, 3980, 4468, 4627, 4945, 5439, 5687, 5935, 6297, 6298, 6777, 7076, 7174, 7175, 7183, 7504, 7505, 7506, 7507, 7509, 7510, 7511, 7512, 7629, 8286, 9009, 9145, 9223, 9224, 9225, 9227, 9244, 9253, 9305, 9434, 9535, 9883, 9886, 12724, 13033, 13723, 13728, 14012, 14015, 14017, 14020, 14021, 14777, 14982, 16532, 16820, 17830, 17836, 17876, 17886, 17895, 17896, 17897, 17904, 17908, 18377, 19342, 19782, 20397, 20678, 20680, 20682 CO 1433, 7173, 7179, 7182, 8536, 16863, 17652 CT 852, 6941, 11839, 12943, 13079, 14031, 15508, 17961 DC 5290, 16800, 17166, 17869 DE 5028 FL 5085, 5865, 6320, 6768, 6918, 7147, 9734, 10788, 15476, 16794, 17870 GA 1186, 1295, 9243, 14944, 17023, 17599 IA 14011 ID 5268, 7172 IL 1190, 4674, 4851, 7663, 10786, 14014, 16807, 20839 IN 4742, 7819, 8285, 16324, 17825, 17899 KS 8576 KY 9095 MA 1192, 2354, 4865, 6269, 6313, 6774, 6775, 6960, 7170, 9216, 9226, 9806, 10557, 10559, 10783, 10837, 13729, 13730, 13731, 13733, 16287, 16801, 17014, 20167 MD 2, 400, 3035, 4071, 5218, 5557, 7660, 8415, 9732, 16982, 19909, 20312 MI 4830, 5966, 6302, 10320, 15259 MN 393, 10841, 16333, 16336, 16678, 16680 MO 9885, 10636, 14449, 20066 MS 10991, 16808, 16856 NC 327, 1220 ND 11920, 16874 NH 8782 NJ 402, 1187, 1189, 1193, 1196, 1211, 1215, 1216, 1692, 6270, 6271, 6309, 8287, 8596, 14161, 14836, 16929, 16930, 16931 NM 14778, 17001 NV 5267 NY 146, 2582, 4335, 5188, 5190, 5444, 5969, 6311, 6317, 6915, 7618, 7619, 7620, 7627, 9220, 11584, 11630, 12834, 16029, 16685, 16787, 20681 OH 1197, 1394, 3687, 4676, 4862, 6585, 9307, 11366, 16806 OK 817, 12346, 12369, 14147, 17485 OR 12525, 16057 PA 804, 819, 1198, 1199, 5492, 9306, 12849, 12892, 15595, 16325, 17880, 19193, 20318 PR 19235 RI 13735 SC 16876 TN 15701, 17821 TX 326, 1260, 4677, 5084, 5086, 6300, 7623, 9426, 10345, 10789, 10791, 14913, 16214, 16216, 16217, 16218, 16219, 16270, 16271, 16791, 16809 VA 4105, 5087, 6301, 7624, 7658, 10986, 10990, 17165, 17888, 17906 VT 7622, 19811 WA 392, 1938, 5926, 15872 WI 370, 8438 *Canada:* AB 2683, 15456 BC 2180, 19755 MB 9626 NF 9671 NS 7161 ON 101, 397, 1684, 2674, 2679, 2681, 2775, 2781, 2824, 2828, 2878, 5018, 10556, 12014 PQ 1951, 3194, 3283, 15570 SK 14869 *Intl:* AUS 1330 BUL 16032, 19904 BWA 2027 CHN 25, 13695, 20651 ENG 3863, 16721 JPN 19423 KOR 5293 MEX 17994 NLD 5491 RUS 17957 SPA 15560 TTO 3049

Electronics in aeronautics: AZ 7366 CA 9031, 10979, 15555, 15645 DC 17823 IN 1201 MA 4999, 9795 NJ 17810 NY 2438, 6304, 6770

Electronics in medicine   See: Medical electronics

Electronics in military engineering: CA 9145 GA 6389 NH 9245 NY 9308 TX 16215 *Canada:* ON 4106

Electrophotography: NY 20681 *Canada:* ON 20683

Electroplating (See also Metals—Finishing): NY 4637 OH 9890 PA 819, 1271

Elementary education   See: Education, Elementary

Engineering—History: MA 20597 NY 5353 TX 4985

Engineering, Industrial See: Industrial engineering

Engineering, Marine See: Marine engineering

Engineering, Mechanical See: Mechanical engineering

Engineering, Military See: Military engineering

Engineering, Sanitary See: Sanitary engineering

Engineering standards See: Standards, Engineering

Engineering, Structural See: Structural engineering

Engineering, Traffic See: Traffic engineering

Engines (See also Turbines): IA 4700, 10377 IL 3142, 6339, 11353 NY 9972

England See: Great Britain

English language: DC 17455 IL 11143 IN 5404 MI 18862 NY 13422 *Canada:* ON 2832 *Intl:* AUT 18055, 18057 BEL 2184 CHN 1656 COL 3108 DEN 8776 FRA 18070 GER 2185, 6140, 16039, 18019, 18021, 18031, 18048 MYS 2186

English language—Composition and exercises: CA 18382 *Canada:* ON 20782

English literature: CA 1401, 3900, 6162, 7572, 9973, 10409, 12206, 15658, 18358, 18379, 18382, 18407, 18413, 19290 CO 18507 CT 7342, 18252, 20177 DC 5943, 6379, 9117 FL 18586 GA 5338, 17071, 18600 IA 9311 IL 1297, 3528, 9084, 11752, 11912, 15071, 15492, 18461, 18672, 18689, 20369, 20371 IN 7794, 13542, 19112 KS 18724 KY 18754 MA 807, 1976, 1981, 1999, 2008, 6576, 15236, 15841, 20446 MD 8419, 8420, 8422, 18820 MI 2592 MN 1293 MO 20059 NC 5049, 19075, 19078, 19942 NH 4614, 8600 NJ 5002, 8370, 13386, 14175 NY 347, 2335, 3735, 4010, 4023, 9595, 11598, 11599, 11616, 11723, 12654, 15707, 19278, 19280, 19285, 19789, 19933 OH 8649, 12328, 18155, 18464, 18534, 20546 OK 19466 PA 7811, 14068, 16137, 19184, 19197, 19209, 20418 SC 19312 TX 1602, 19106, 19392 UT 20809 WI 19607 *Canada:* AB 18196 BC 18282, 19489 MB 18794 NS 10812 ON 7585, 9954, 13661, 16418, 19460, 19462, 19555, 20778 SK 2627 *Intl:* ARG 1126 AUT 18055, 18057 DEN 8776 ENG 18254 FRA 18070 GER 2185, 6140, 16039, 18019, 18021, 18024, 18025, 18031, 18048 ISR 1521 MYS 2186 NZL 11739 SCT 14953 WAL 14272 ZWE 20842

English as a second language: AK 834 CA 3043, 6159, 9348, 10670 DC 5403, 11116 FL 13069 IL 7679, 11143 MI 18862 MN 18902 NC 4478 NY 1923, 9208, 11556 OH 4657 *Canada:* AB 231 BC 16317 ON 10229, 12443 *Intl:* AUS 87, 88 AUT 18055 BRZ 16630 GER 18048

Engraving (See also Prints): CT 20700 FL 10895 PA 6122, 8592, 10709 *Canada:* ON 16418 PQ 18110 *Intl:* SPA 15557

Entertainment law See: Performing arts—Law and legislation

Entomology See: Insects

Entrepreneur (See also New business enterprises): CA 2490 *Canada:* ON 2928

Environment See: Ecology

Environmental design: CO 952 DC 7472 IN 13538 NY 12768 OK 19121 PA 2397 TN 11344 VI 8259 *Canada:* NS 12132 *Intl:* ENG 14120 JPN 8331

Environmental education: AL 879 CA 5255, 17767 CT 20382 ID 17695 IL 12002, 15105 IN 19116 MA 6820, 9237, 9788 NH 898 NY 3239, 15762 OH 7323, 11084 PA 14933 TN 16175 WA 7596 WY 16185

Environmental engineering (See also Environmental policy; Work environment): AL 14153 AZ 15041, 20303 CA 2263, 5930, 14974, 16946 DC 16941 FL 5878 IL 5927, 16936 IN 5374 KS 8568 KY 18770 MA 1950, 2617, 5366, 6836, 9796, 13726, 15812 ME 6 MI 3785, 10309, 10320 MN 8181 MO 2386, 15899 MT 10641, 20749 NC 3091, 5039 NH 4609 NY 3779, 9592, 13076 OH 566, 18469, 19693 OK 20444 OR 3406 PA 1423, 5380, 6474, 9058, 16132, 16952, 19194, 19205 RI 8698 TN 15701 TX 3110, 4985, 5928, 8317, 17538 VA 19815, 20078 VI 8259 WI 4958, 13961 *Canada:* AB 15663 NS 2714 ON 56, 6577, 13402 *Intl:* PER 12719 POL 16035 SWE 15921 SWI 15938

Environmental health: AZ 999 CA 3503, 17480, 17841, 18341, 20628 CT 3694, 20716 FL 19960 HI 18622 MA 17027 MD 8428, 16976 MI 5966, 18884 MT 20749 NC 11210 NJ 10566, 14159 NY 7562, 11650, 11726 OH 18467, 18475 PA 3697, 6852 SC 13843 TX 16242 VA 16785 WA 631, 6890 *Canada:* AB 279 ON 2679, 2750, 13658, 14180 PQ 13605, 18091 *Intl:* AUS 19565 CHN 3609 FIJ 5689 GER 7927 SWI 20619

Environmental impact statements: AZ 18208 CA 2536, 11828, 17480 CO 5365 FL 15998 GA 17476 IL 12090 MN 10455 ND 19099 NH 5383 OR 19148 RI 5384 SC 13843 WY 17102, 20672 *Canada:* BC 16523 NB 11444 NS 4534

Environmental law: AR 10868 AZ 10597, 18213 CA 1632, 2538, 2578, 4438, 6659, 12665, 17480 CO 5365, 17469, 20144 CT 10873 DC 4444, 5378, 15097, 17238, 17247, 17257, 17912 IL 7694 KS 17478 LA 66 MA 1840 MD 19796 ME 1757 MI 3770, 5079, 7376 MO 9080 NC 5038 NJ 10120 NY 4333, 9039, 11821, 12656 OH 567, 12268 OK 12646 OR 9076 PA 12887, 17475, 20550 TX 1411, 2271, 19854 VA 3919, 7577, 19272 VT 19805 WA 20025 WI 13571 *Canada:* ON 2719, 2925, 5017 *Intl:* ECU 6170 GER 8091

Environmental policy (See also Conservation of natural resources; Environmental protection; Human ecology; Pollution): DC 9111, 17465 HI 5134 MA 4274 NC 19059 NH 4609 NY 3353 OK 19138 PA 3403, 5351 TX 19408 VA 3727 *Canada:* PQ 2721 *Intl:* FIN 5718 GER 6449, 8091

Environmental protection (See also Conservation of natural resources; Environmental engineering; Environmental law; Water conservation; Wildlife conservation): AZ 16540 CA 14974, 17520, 17829 CO 11160 DC 11119 GA 16496 IL 7694 KY 8668 MA 6610, 17525, 20445 MD 16018 MS 17029 NM 17108 OH 6495 OK 11338 OR 12061 RI 5384 WA 12060 WI 20519, 20521 *Canada:* MB 9609 ON 2818 PQ 18114 *Intl:* CHN 25, 7130, 10964 CZE 4511, 19702 ECU 6170 ENG 6673 FIN 7126 HUN 7551 JPN 8329 NLD 6171 SWI 16769

Enzymes: CT 12159 MA 6357

Epidemiology (See also Communicable diseases): CA 18341 CT 20716 FL 19320 GA 17125 MD 8428 MI 18884 MN 10480 NC 3471 NJ 5527 NY 11650 OK 12358 PA 19195 SC 15403 TN 12182 *Canada:* ON 2750, 19553 PQ 7865, 18091 *Intl:* AUS 20302 FRA 8052 GER 7927

Epigraphy See: Inscriptions

Epilepsy: CA 17297 MD 8625, 11161 VA 3379 *Canada:* ON 12457

Episcopal Church See: Protestant Episcopal Church in the U.S.A.

Ergonomics See: Human engineering

Erie County (NY): NY 2328

Erie County (PA): PA 5416, 10157

Erosion See: Soil conservation

Eschatology: GA 3117

Eskimos (See also Indians of North America): AK 11829, 11951, 18180 WV 5405 *Canada:* NT 13363 ON 2756, 10229

Esperanto: CA 5443 DC 5441 OR 19159 *Intl:* AUT 1354 NLD 17977 SWI 5442

Espionage: CA 20551 DC 17256

Essences and essential oils (See also Perfumes): NJ 3879, 8108 *Intl:* BRZ 2097

Essex County (MA): MA 5448, 9476

Estate planning: **AZ** 10597 **CA** 1461, 6659, 8246 **CO** 16688 **CT** 4192 **FL** 8605 **MA** 20419 **MD** 12215, 19796 **MI** 4856, 5079 **NJ** 9436 **NY** 4843, 6884, 7517, 8606, 9496, 11821, 12752, 13558, 14036, 15098, 15098, 20454, 20475 **RI** 80, 7225 *Canada:* **ON** 5612, 6564, 6565, 11317

Estonia: **DC** 9113 **NY** 5463

Estuaries: **CA** 928 **FL** 10771 **MD** 15284 *Intl:* **ENG** 13152

Ethics (See also Bioethics; Medical ethics; Patriotism; Professional ethics; Spirituality): **CA** 14924 **CO** 7666, 13278 **DC** 5468, 6377, 11158 **FL** 5870 **IL** 3547, 7094, 9968, 11947 **IN** 1139 **MA** 2018, 6072 **MI** 5771 **MN** 18926 **NC** 7380 **NY** 7006, 10109, 13990 **OH** 1226, 3831 **OR** 20244 **TN** 19769 **TX** 5390, 7915 *Canada:* **MB** 1961 **ON** 7897, 8748, 19454, 20330 **PQ** 9910 *Intl:* **GER** 18556

Ethics, Christian See: Christian ethics

Ethics, Medical See: Medical ethics

Ethiopia: *Intl:* **ETH** 5469 **GER** 18052

Ethnic groups—Canada: **MN** 10466 *Canada:* **AB** 2926, 16619 **BC** 10963 **MB** 16612 **NS** 18484 **ON** 10225, 10229 **PQ** 2847, 13592, 18065 **SK** 16616

Ethnic groups—United States: **CA** 1127, 2573, 3744, 7857, 9354, 17521, 18355 **GA** 3761, 6014 **IL** 5470, 14791 **KS** 5999, 8564 **LA** 810, 19052 **MA** 1980, 3230 **MD** 7917 **MI** 9707, 18875, 20120 **MN** 10466, 10488, 18913, 20185 **MO** 9189 **NE** 6844, 19005 **NH** 10998 **NY** 652, 2229, 3270, 11561, 13179, 13640 **OH** 8647, 20293 **PA** 1430, 8869, 10157, 19203 **TX** 19380 **WA** 19532, 20045 **WI** 15684 *Intl:* **ITA** 18007

Ethnology: **AZ** 800, 988, 7085, 10916, 17723, 17789, 17792 **CA** 14701, 18336, 18401 **CO** 17749 **CT** 7529 **DC** 6961, 15263, 15271, 15279 **IA** 17703 **ID** 18653 **MA** 6574, 6999, 12805, 12806 **MI** 4408 **MS** 4924 **NE** 17751 **NJ** 11743, 19851 **NM** 9853, 10911, 14920 **NY** 5521, 7563, 7571, 11335, 11631 **PA** 13748, 19198 **SD** 1906, 15198 **TN** 10069 **TX** 12726 **WY** 20308 *Canada:* **AB** 18193 **BC** 19757 **MB** 9619 **ON** 14131 **PQ** 2962, 18117 *Intl:* **AUS** 15695 **AUT** 19912 **CHN** 3611 **COT** 7862 **CZE** 10976 **FIN** 5711, 15898 **FRA** 6062 **GER** 18040, 18052 **GTM** 6791 **HUN** 7543 **ICE** 11240 **ITA** 2630, 3845 **MOZ** 10834 **NLD** 11412 **NZL** 11740 **POL** 13171 **SPA** 15561 **SWI** 8497 **VEN** 435 **YUG** 7936

Ethnomusicology: **CA** 2567, 18335, 18383, 18392 **CT** 20178 **DC** 9108, 15270 **FL** 18850 **IL** 12086, 18455 **IN** 7776, 7786 **MA** 3894, 16551 **MN** 18925 **NC** 14230 **NY** 4007, 4019 **TX** 19383, 19390 **WA** 19524 *Canada:* **ON** 13657, 20793 *Intl:* **CZE** 15223 **ISR** 7101 **YUG** 7936

Etruscan civilization and culture (See also Italy—History): **MI** 5475

Europe: **CA** 7340, 14716, 15650 **DC** 5484, 9123, 20471 **MA** 6952 **MO** 8205 *Intl:* **BEL** 4056, 5482 **GER** 14046 **SWE** 5487 **SWI** 5486

Europe, Central See: Central Europe

Europe, Eastern (See also Slavic countries): **CA** 15650 **CT** 20730 **DC** 20008 **IL** 1458 **MA** 6991 **NY** 4023, 13686 **PA** 1428, 5065, 9480, 12913 *Canada:* **ON** 3055 **PQ** 13180 *Intl:* **AUT** 1359, 7937 **GER** 1597, 5119, 5630, 13685, 15794 **IND** 6531 **ROM** 7980

Europe—History: **CA** 2572 **IL** 11752, 18675 **MA** 6952, 17133 **WI** 19607 *Canada:* **AB** 18196 **ON** 2771 **PQ** 13580 *Intl:* **AUS** 15688

European Economic Community countries: **DC** 5484 **MA** 1982 **NY** 5970 *Canada:* **ON** 13647, 20788 *Intl:* **BEL** 4056 **ENG** 19360 **FRA** 4364 **IRL** 4057 **LUX** 5489 **POL** 13181 **TUR** 16647

European law: *Intl:* **LUX** 5489

European literature: **IL** 11752 **IN** 1438 **MA** 12416, 17745, 20446 **WI** 19607

Euthanasia: **CA** 13920 **DC** 11277 **IL** 790 **MA** 19742 **MI** 5254, 13921, 13922, 13923, 13924, 13925 **OH** 7527 **OR** 7128 **TX** 3290 **VA** 671 **WA** 11331

Eutrophication (See also Water—Pollution): **WI** 19625

Evangelical Covenant Church: **IL** 5493, 11942

Evangelical Synod Church: **MO** 5502

Evangelical United Brethren (See also United Methodist Church): **MN** 16744 **NJ** 16733 **OH** 17965 **PA** 16734 **VA** 15119

Evangelistic work (See also Missions): **AZ** 5806 **CA** 1845, 9841 **GA** 3117, 6504 **IL** 10706, 16508, 20367, 20368 **MA** 6575 **MD** 19991 **MN** 4446 **MO** 9448 **ND** 16500 **SD** 11857 *Canada:* **ON** 866

Evans, Maurice: **NY** 6876

Evans, Walker: **TN** 3300

Everson, William Oliver: **CA** 19290 **NY** 15757

Evolution: **CA** 7921, 11105, 13704, 18428, 19337 **DC** 11089 **IA** 8239 **IL** 12000 **KY** 18744 **MA** 6984, 18829 **NC** 19068 **NM** 19045 **OH** 12568 **VA** 7983 **WI** 19581 *Canada:* **ON** 2636 **PQ** 18078 *Intl:* **ENG** 9199

Excavation: **MS** 16970

Exceptional children (See also Gifted children; Handicapped children): **OH** 13481

Exceptional children—Education (See also Special education): **CA** 3235 **CO** 13407 **FL** 15977 **IA** 18708 **IL** 3786, 7681 **MA** 9836 **MD** 18806 **MO** 6923 **NJ** 7567 **NY** 1923, 11557 **PA** 12853 **TN** 15477, 16590 **VA** 5399 *Canada:* **AB** 266 **ON** 9174, 10231 **PQ** 9896, 18113

Exchanges, Educational See: Educational exchanges

Exchanges, Literary and scientific (See also Communication in science): **OH** 17976

Executives—Recruitment: **FL** 8913 **IL** 8796

Exercise (See also Physical education and training): **AL** 17945 **CA** 587 **CO** 17917, 18506 **IL** 13565 **PA** 12897 *Canada:* **ON** 14108, 15593

Exhibitions: **IL** 3536 **MA** 1999 **MD** 18809 **WA** 5171

Exploration See: Voyages and travels

Explosives (See also Propellants): **AZ** 909 **CA** 2204, 17896 **DC** 17085 **DE** 6828 **IL** 16972 **IN** 17899 **MD** 17837, 17866, 17889 **MN** 393 **MS** 16970 **NJ** 16918 **NM** 14778 **PA** 1265, 8702 **TX** 8376, 9775 **UT** 7146 **VA** 17898 *Intl:* **AUS** 4701

Eye—Diseases and defects: **MA** 5539

Factory and trade waste See: Solid waste

Fair use (Copyright) (See also Intellectual property; Patents; Trademarks): **CA** 15826, 15876 **DC** 8089, 9112, 17254 **GA** 3857 **IL** 19676, 20453 **MI** 19680 **NY** 3178, 8590, 10732, 12834, 16439 **PA** 16676 **TX** 1067 **WV** 17569 *Canada:* **ON** 2678, 2885, 16327 **PQ** 2677 *Intl:* **GER** 13104 **SWI** 20621 **TTO** 3049

Fairbanks, Douglas: **NY** 10908

Fairs (See also Exhibitions): **CA** 2500, 2561, 7902, 20245 **CT** 3337 **IL** 10920 **MO** 10537 **NY** 11627, 11634 **TN** 8773

Fairy tales: **CA** 1742, 9345, 14703 **IL** 3538, 8494 **MA** 1991 **MI** 5853 **MN** 10448 **MO** 14450 **TX** 4560 *Intl:* **SWI** 8497

Falconry: **CO** 16822 **VA** 11302 *Intl:* **SAU** 5578

Fall River Line: **MA** 5582

Family (See also Foster home care; Marriage; Parent and child; Stepfamily): **CA** 2475, 9354 **GA** 2581 **IL** 18676 **IN** 13538 **KS** 6176 **KY** 3169 **MN** 18943 **MO** 20063 **NC** 19091 **NM** 16700 **NY** 4028, 9845, 15060, 20556 **OH** 12311, 12325 **OR** 20244 **PA** 12907, 19224 **PR** 19245 **TX** 1175 **UT** 20808 **VT** 13127 **WA** 15003 **WI** 19619 *Canada:* **ON** 8412, 16310 **PQ** 4649, 13605 **SK** 5587 *Intl:* **FIN** 5719

Family medicine: AZ 14970 CA 14754, 14898 FL 1598 MI 10370 NJ 7568, 10002 NY 7195, 15524 OH 14283 PA 5958 VA 13954 WI 14255 WY 19656 *Canada:* AB 18294 ON 3891 SK 13786

Family planning See: Birth control

Family psychotherapy: VA 19878

Family violence (See also Child abuse): DC 3790 VA 19879 WY 20666 *Canada:* BC 17969 ON 2749

Fantastic fiction (See also Science fiction): CA 18413 MA 9819 MN 10472 OR 721 PA 16137 TN 4417 VA 16354 WI 19574 *Canada:* ON 16417 *Intl:* ENG 13201

Far East See: East Asia

Fargo (ND): ND 11929

Farm machinery See: Agricultural machinery

Farm management (See also Agriculture): VT 19811 *Intl:* CRI 8028 ENG 18766 JPN 7322 NGA 8135

Farms (See also Agriculture): MD 20264 *Intl:* CUB 4460

Farrell, James Thomas: OH 10270 PA 19197

Fascism: *Intl:* ISR 1145

Fashion (See also Clothing and dress; Costume): CA 33, 5606, 5607, 5608, 5609, 5610, 12769, 20569 MA 9789 MI 15809 NH 11483 NY 2238, 4127, 5611, 10212, 16465 OH 18468 OR 1559 PA 12981 TX 1582, 4561 *Canada:* BC 18269 ON 2268, 3204 *Intl:* ISR 15121 SWI 20851

Fashion designers See: Costume designers

Fashion models See: Models, Fashion

Fasteners: PA 15618

Fathers of the church: CA 6535, 14555 CT 11 DC 4947, 20581 IA 14594 IL 3152, 3535, 20368 LA 14361 MA 7116, 14394 MN 3913 MO 4110, 4117, 8640, 14463 NJ 5002 NY 6352, 14240, 14419, 15027 OH 13211, 14507 OK 14315 PA 878, 9465, 9742, 14256, 19300, 20336 SD 1906 WA 12 WI 14314 *Canada:* PQ 4095, 6642, 7868, 12517

Father's rights: PA 3557

Fats See: Oils and fats

Faulkner, William: CT 4178 LA 16560, 19052 MA 15236, 20446 MD 18820 MN 9488 MS 18949 NY 16994 OH 13479, 19425 TX 16200, 19392 VA 19510

Faure, Gabriel Urbain: TX 19392

Federal government: AL 1855 CA 2493, 11037, 11038, 16871, 17929, 18324, 18408 CO 11039 CT 16603 DC 83, 11024, 11026, 11027, 11029, 11045, 11223, 17484, 17936, 20023 GA 11040 IL 3533, 7700, 11031 MA 1993, 11034 MD 4172, 11046 ME 18780 MI 18888 MO 11030 MS 18954 NJ 11035 NV 19016 NY 11563, 14354, 14355 PA 11032, 16128 TX 1603, 11041 UT 19713 WA 11036 WI 20529 WY 20672 *Canada:* AB 12762 ON 2770, 2835, 17558 *Intl:* NOR 12593 ZWE 20842

Felidae: MD 12249

Feminism (See also Women—Legal status, laws, etc.): FL 10954 GA 1249 IA 20562 IL 12089 MN 10826, 18930 NY 1532, 15034 PA 16133 *Canada:* ON 20792 PQ 3233, 18117 *Intl:* FRA 1826

Fencing: MI 10336 PA 3183

Fermentation: CT 12969 IL 17189 MO 873 WI 17974 *Canada:* PQ 2815

Fermi, Enrico: IL 18461

Ferries: WA 20030 *Canada:* BC 2147

Fertilizers and manures: AL 8106, 16177 DC 5674 MD 17203 *Canada:* SK 13271 *Intl:* CHN 1655 ICE 13711 IND 7747 ISR 16036 URE 16620

Fetishism: MN 20170

Fiber optics: CA 5082 GA 1186 MA 6774 MN 8181 NJ 1215, 6294 NY 3041 *Canada:* PQ 1685 *Intl:* FRA 6071

Fiberglass See: Glass fibers

Fibers: CA 8537 DE 5028 MI 4407 MO 10636 NC 5020, 11898 NJ 7310, 16285 OH 6570 TX 19401 VA 5019 *Intl:* BGD 1467 GER 6432 NGA 7898

Fiedler, Arthur: MA 2015

Field, Eugene: CO 4784 MO 5682, 15681

Fillmore, Millard: NY 2328, 15711

Films See: Motion pictures

Filters and filtration: MI 6280 MN 4952 NY 12700

Finance (See also Banks and banking; Money): AL 18160 AZ 600 CA 1058, 1629, 3032, 5600, 5647, 5724, 9344, 9934, 12667, 12774, 14034, 14708, 15652, 17836, 18387, 19324, 20165 CO 15638, 18509 CT 5695, 8289, 16643, 18515, 20731 DC 1653, 5649, 7479, 8211, 8807, 15226, 17219, 17241, 17490, 17561, 17916, 17936 FL 5862, 5905 GA 1241, 5632 HI 7032 IA 18706 IL 838, 1984, 4251, 5035, 5635, 5784, 7441, 8597, 12016, 14890, 15770, 18449, 18666 IN 2136, 7063, 7779, 9162, 13545 KS 20409 LA 16555 MA 1192, 1724, 2001, 5633, 9801, 11463, 11801 MD 1964 MI 10316, 11359, 18870 MN 3044, 3060, 14562, 18896 MO 5646, 20064 NC 5036 NH 11483 NJ 556, 11745, 13383, 13458, 16480, 19969 NM 19050 NY 633, 675, 1548, 1615, 1618, 2242, 2329, 3452, 3470, 3723, 4027, 4316, 4665, 4682, 4871, 4953, 4990, 5643, 5753, 5959, 6543, 8704, 9002, 9016, 9061, 9295, 9645, 9672, 9938, 10164, 10939, 11647, 11717, 11730, 11732, 12254, 12655, 12691, 12790, 13343, 15020, 15096, 15639, 15728, 15810, 16188, 17953, 19282, 19743, 19948, 20169, 20764 OH 3818, 5636, 9965, 12297, 13483, 13493, 13898 PA 10026, 12899, 14038, 19186, 19216, 20162 PR 13517, 19238 RI 2299 TN 10864, 13491, 16175 TX 4559, 5637, 13895, 16939 VA 2426, 4430, 5560, 5597, 5645, 10565, 17016, 19269, 19501 WA 14210, 14992, 15011, 19515, 20018, 20359 WI 19626 *Canada:* AB 5431 BC 2145, 18268 MB 9611, 18784 ON 1486, 2685, 2693, 2764, 2833, 2836, 2938, 5698, 7730, 8216, 8811, 12488, 13342, 13902, 14099, 14137, 14952, 16410, 19446, 19563 PQ 321, 1679, 2843, 4135, 5205, 5625, 7832, 9900, 13588, 13600, 14100 *Intl:* ENG 3741, 7913 HUN 7932 JOR 931 PAN 17997 THA 16292

Finance, Public: CA 9349, 14692, 14715, 18326 CT 4205 DC 581, 4170, 8830, 11226, 17098, 17282, 19689 FL 5903 GA 14884 HI 7037 IL 3525, 10161, 19748 KY 8675 MA 636, 1988, 5634, 5678, 9835 NJ 14159 NM 11529 NY 3242, 4871, 7056, 7967, 11658, 13411 OH 3829, 12284, 12288 PA 12842, 12874 PR 13522 RI 13872 SC 10861, 19308 SD 19316 TX 19408 WA 15001, 20028 WI 10425, 20529 *Canada:* ON 2841, 2992, 10226, 12472, 12483, 12488 *Intl:* ENG 9270 SAU 7966 SPA 7939

Financial services (See also Estate planning): DC 551 IL 1481, 13868 MA 6885 MN 5640 PA 16452 TX 8446 *Canada:* ON 4447, 15865

Fine arts See: Arts

Finland: DC 9113 MA 5834 MI 15880 *Intl:* FIN 3332, 5705, 5710, 5718, 5719, 15898

Finland—History: MI 5714 *Intl:* FIN 5708, 15897

Finnish Americans: MI 15880 MN 18913, 18937

Fire insurance See: Insurance, Fire

Firearms (See also Ordnance): AL 1861 CA 5722 DC 5257, 11274, 11275, 17085 KS 1224, 20409 MD 17084 OK 4646 PA 8702 TX 7209 VA 11276 WV 7576, 17729 WY 2325 *Canada:* MB 14106 ON 12484

Firearms—Law and legislation: DC 3280

Fires and fire prevention: AZ 6845 CA 3868, 9349, 17886 CT 7835 DC 8058, 17277 FL 15991, 16789 IL 7675, 8366 KY 5149 MA 5547, 8015, 11164, 11472 MD 5626, 17616 MI 1591 NY 647, 2245, 3897, 11657 OH 3829, 18480 PA 4398 RI 382 TX 586 UT 17517 WA 15001, 19526 WI 6262, 11978 *Canada:* BC 2743, 8499 NS 5723 ON 2761, 2821, 12485 *Intl:* AUS 1324 JPN 8331

Fireworks: CA 2204 IN 17899 NJ 16918 PA 19181

Fish and fisheries (See also Salmon): AK 213, 214, 17498, 17519, 17630, 17645, 18175, 18182 AR 17497 CA 928, 2470, 2555, 11341, 17643, 17644, 19678 CO 3964 CT 10948, 17633, 20715 FL 939, 5896, 10168, 10888, 16945, 17639, 17641, 18842 GA 18606 HI 17632 IL 11861, 15105, 19685 MA 9821, 9822, 11464, 17636, 18829 MD 5828, 17637, 17650, 18798 ME 9561, 18777 MI 10304, 17500, 18855, 18877 MN 18944 MS 6808, 10522, 17634 NC 17642, 19064 NE 11376 NJ 17640 NV 5984 NY 686, 687, 12588, 17506 OH 3814, 12321 OK 19122 OR 12059, 12237, 12551 PA 12872, 13090 PR 19253 RI 17464, 19265, 19266 SC 15411 TN 1556 TX 16264 WA 3996, 4577, 8817, 17496, 17638, 19525, 19527 WI 17501, 19587, 20520 WV 17502 WY 20668 *Canada:* AB 270 BC 2729, 2735, 2737, 12676, 16523, 19758, 20236 MB 2731, 9620 NB 2727, 11446 NF 2734, 9671 NS 2736, 4534, 12041, 12138 ON 2732, 12479, 12480 PQ 2733, 13591, 13603 SK 14842, 14849 *Intl:* AUS 1341 BGD 1466 DEN 4592, 8092 ENG 6682, 13152 GER 6447, 18035 ITA 16752 MUS 9850 MYS 18141 PHL 8072 ROM 14047 SCT 7202 SPA 15562 TWN 5518 URE 7906

Fish and game: AK 17063, 17498 CA 2555, 2565 CO 4784 CT 4178 DC 17249 FL 8115 GA 6402 MI 3348 MN 10483 MT 5654 NC 11198 NH 19036 NJ 13386, 17640 NM 20429 PA 6122, 8875, 12873, 19225 TX 16264 VA 11302, 19865 VT 684 WA 20045 WI 20523 *Canada:* BC 2159 NB 1263 PQ 13603 *Intl:* AUT 1351 NLD 15791 POL 13164 SCT 14966 SPA 10883

Fisher, Dorothy Canfield: VT 3010, 19482

Fisheries See: Fish and fisheries

Fishery products: ME 737 *Intl:* SCT 14966

Fishes See: Fish and fisheries

Fishing See: Fish and game

Fitzgerald, F. Scott and Zelda: MN 14564 NJ 13386 PA 6457

Flags: MA 5839 NY 11633 PA 11165 VA 17003

Flagstad, Kirsten: CA 14737

Flavor: NJ 6486, 8108

Flight (See also Aeronautics): CA 10979 IN 13530 *Intl:* NLD 16043

Flight instrumentation See: Electronics in aeronautics

Flight safety See: Aeronautics—Safety measures

Flint (MI): MI 5854

Flood control: CA 12507, 16946, 18348 FL 5907, 16945 IL 6716, 16954 MI 16938 MN 16957 MS 16947, 16968 MT 17543 NJ 12779 NV 17122 TN 16175 TX 16940 VA 16942, 17545 WI 15454

Floor coverings: NJ 4144 VA 2342

Florida: FL 2255, 3663, 3677, 5873, 5888, 5889, 5898, 5919, 6004, 6276, 6840, 7156, 7218, 7252, 7256, 7278, 7281, 8315, 8887, 9416, 10254, 12508, 12510, 12919, 13188, 14245, 14470, 14588, 15686, 16854, 17685, 18585, 18846, 18849, 19322 GA 11040

Flower arrangement: DC 17608 OH 6247 TN 10059 *Canada:* ON 3746 *Intl:* JPN 7665

Flowers: AL 1850 CA 8068, 9281 DC 6962, 17608 DE 13405 IL 588 MA 9793 MI 4808 MO 10535 NY 7414 OH 10271, 12292 WA 14999, 20046 *Intl:* ARG 4618 AUS 2023 CHN 10964 IND 7747 SGP 15190

Flowers, Wild See: Wild flowers

Fluid dynamics (See also Aerodynamics; Gas dynamics; Hydrodynamics; Magnetohydrodynamics): CA 1849 CO 17617 NJ 5000, 17647

Fluid mechanics (See also Fluid dynamics; Hydraulics): CA 2482, 2590, 5082, 7604, 10980, 14021, 19342 CO 3969 ID 5268 IN 6333 MA 333, 9795 MD 9739 MN 4952, 5925, 18927 NH 4420 NY 13204 OH 11842 PA 19194 TN 19372 WI 5924 *Intl:* CHN 7988 ENG 1919, 6687 NLD 20089

Fluid power technology: WI 10432, 11166

Flute music: AZ 18224 DC 9131 PA 15053

Flying saucers See: Unidentified flying objects

Fog-signals (See also Navigation): *Canada:* ON 2874

Folk art: CA 4402, 10441, 14731, 14888, 18401 DC 11178 HI 18627 IN 3591 NC 15485 NM 10913 NY 10885 OH 3824 OR 19146 PA 7293 TX 14669 VA 3931, 5673 VT 10887 WI 8780 *Canada:* AB 16619 *Intl:* GER 15698

Folk dancing: IL 763, 3539 NM 15092 NY 8272 PA 5065 *Intl:* ENG 5358 YUG 7936

Folk music: AL 18169 AZ 18224 CA 2567, 18401 CO 4782, 18504 DC 9108, 15270 IL 3540 IN 7776 KY 15462, 20261 LA 9384 MA 11549 ME 18778 MI 20120 MN 18925 MO 15603 MS 18952 NM 10913 NY 11637, 19279 PA 5065, 19175 SD 627 VA 5673 WI 19610 *Intl:* AUS 15692 ENG 5358

Folklore (See also Material culture; Mythology): AL 10925 AR 1029, 12650, 18236 AZ 16546 CA 9345, 14708, 18355, 18379, 18400, 18401 CO 12234, 18548 CT 16504 DC 4913, 9108, 15270, 15286 FL 5899 HI 7046 ID 314 IL 3538, 18672 IN 7786, 7821 KS 5305, 5999, 8553 KY 17696, 20261 LA 19355, 19356 MA 1976, 1981, 1991, 12416 ME 18778 MI 4815, 12211, 20120 MN 3908, 10448, 10453 MO 14450 MS 18949, 18952 NE 19005 NM 10913 NY 2246, 5445, 10584, 11603, 11609, 11631, 11663, 13634, 13990, 15712 OH 3823, 3823, 3831, 13488 OR 19146 PA 3076, 6111, 6117, 7254, 8721, 10090, 12841, 19175 RI 16085 TN 3300, 5127 TX 19373, 19379, 19383 VA 5673, 13680 *Canada:* NB 18072 NF 10049, 10051, 11764 ON 2805, 2808, 10225, 16418, 19359 PQ 15304, 18065 *Intl:* AUT 12224 FIN 15898 GRC 7117, 7905 HUN 7543 MEX 12720 NLD 8786, 11412 POL 13170 SRI 15626 SWI 8497 YUG 7936

Food: CA 642, 3842, 9353, 10119, 18358 CT 20348 FL 18577 GA 3858 IA 8241 IL 947, 1055, 4624, 13565, 13566, 15632, 16703, 18676 IN 3364, 13538 KY 18743 MA 9216, 9820, 18831 MD 17203 MN 3044, 5203, 6329, 7899, 18938, 18943 NJ 2623, 4400, 13959 NY 4325, 5701, 11552 OH 12293, 12311, 14083 PA 615, 12910, 17181 PR 19234 TX 6179 VA 17016, 19916 WA 19525 WI 7071, 9857, 19619 *Canada:* BC 15181, 18273 MB 9627 NB 11454 ON 2633, 2750, 4922, 10230, 12450, 19450 PQ 2753, 9906, 13591 *Intl:* ARG 17995 AUS 19053, 19258, 20233 BRZ 2097 CHL 8001 DEN 14139 FIN 7123 FRA 1157, 6065, 8100 GER 16042 GTM 12717 GUY 3046 IND 7742 ITA 16752 JAM 12716 MEX 8861 MOR 7876 NLD 11413 POL 161, 162 SAF 19140 SCT 14965 SPA 15562 TTO 3049 TWN 5518

Food, Chemistry of See: Food—Composition

Food—Composition: IL 1055, 4401, 19903 KS 630 MN 13051 NJ 4400, 6797, 14795 NY 4333 TN 8814 *Canada:* BC 2751 ON 2752 PQ 2640, 7864 *Intl:* CHN 1655 ITA 18013 SAF 15382

Food industry and trade: AZ 4848 CA 563, 885, 7560, 11168, 11398, 14211, 17198, 18358, 20347 CT 9500 DC 5948, 11167, 17214, 17508 IL 2621, 8815, 12169, 18657, 20648 LA 17194 MA 17027 MD 9877 MI 6418, 8535, 8607, 20378 MN 6328, 13051 MO 764, 873, 12956, 13699 NE 637, 5072, 9103, 9204, 13959 NY 616, 1966, 6324, 12256, 20346 PA 4737, 7111, 7164, 14421 SC 17631 TX 2624, 6178 WA 17638 WI 8325, 14927 *Canada:* AB 241 BC 19755 MB 18783 NS 2736 ON 12438,

Food industry and trade: (continued)
12451 *Intl:* **AUS** 19565 **BLR** 1707 **BRZ** 18004 **BUL** 2348 **BWA** 2027 **CZE** 19702 **ENG** 9033 **GTM** 3325 **HUN** 7553 **POL** 13164 **ROM** 18061

Food industry and trade—Equipment and supplies: *Intl:* **POL** 160

Food law and legislation: **GA** 3857 *Canada:* **ON** 2752

Food—Packaging (See also Packaging): **CA** 7560 **DC** 11167 **DE** 13405 **IL** 8815 **PA** 7111 **SC** 6606 **TN** 8814 **TX** 13834 **WI** 9857

Food policy   See: Nutrition policy

Food service: **CA** 3736 **DC** 11272 **IL** 16049 **MD** 17207 **NY** 4333, 4470, 15720, 15721 **PA** 12896 **RI** 8461 **VA** 8110 *Canada:* **NF** 2434 **ON** 2990

Football: **OH** 11169, 13392

Footwear   See: Boots and shoes—Trade and manufacture

Ford, Ford Madox: **NY** 4330 **TX** 16200

Ford, Gerald Rudolph: **MI** 17923

Ford, Henry: **MI** 5964

Forecasting (See also Prophecy): **CT** 6221 **DC** 3853, 17914 **HI** 7026 **IN** 7495 **OH** 13503 **PA** 150 **TX** 13134 **VA** 7900 *Intl:* **FRA** 1848, 6222

Foreign affairs   See: International relations

Foreign aid program   See: Economic assistance

Foreign language publications: **AZ** 13028 **CA** 9348, 18316 **FL** 10255 **GA** 17021, 17071 **IL** 3289 **MI** 4819 **NY** 11604, 13631 **OH** 4657, 13488, 17976 *Canada:* **BC** 18255 **PQ** 18088 *Intl:* **CHN** 1659

Foreign law, Pleading and proof of: **AZ** 1012 **CA** 1632, 6733, 9419, 15654, 18331, 18357 **CT** 20720 **DC** 9123, 9124, 9125, 9126, 17279 **FL** 18575, 18847 **IA** 4998 **IL** 4268, 12087, 18447 **IN** 7801 **KS** 8561, 18736 **LA** 9381 **MI** 6340, 18871 **MN** 18918 **NY** 1148, 1420, 4017, 9700, 11667, 14357, 19958, 20391 **OH** 3125 **PA** 4854, 19177 **TX** 16230, 19405, 19854 **VA** 19497 **WA** 19534 **WI** 19603 *Intl:* **BRZ** 6212 **COL** 17983 **FRA** 1833, 15315 **GER** 6429, 13102, 13105, 15794 **GRC** 7118 **NLD** 11402 **NOR** 19160 **PAN** 17997 **SAU** 7966 **SPA** 15559

Foreign policy   See: International relations

Foreign relations   See: International relations

Foreign trade and employment (See also Commerce): **AR** 17578 **AZ** 600 **CA** 1478, 7503 **DC** 17129, 17219, 17594 **IL** 17570 **IN** 375 **MA** 17567 **NY** 5643, 8792, 13224, 17162, 17584 **PA** 17587 **TX** 17572 **WI** 17580 *Canada:* **NB** 11442 **ON** 1925, 3054 *Intl:* **CHN** 3263 **ENG** 6679 **FIN** 3332 **IND** 6531 **ISR** 8270

Forensic medicine   See: Medical jurisprudence

Forensic psychiatry (See also Insane, Criminal and dangerous): **CA** 1223 **GA** 6399 **KS** 10086 **MA** 9946 **MI** 10300 **WI** 10083 *Canada:* **BC** 2164, 13956 **PQ** 7880

Forest ecology: **CO** 17522 **MA** 6970 **PR** 17523 *Canada:* **NB** 2740 **ON** 12477 *Intl:* **ECU** 5222

Forest products (See also Wood): **AL** 8171 **CA** 9940 **DC** 11171 **ID** 1947 **IL** 9784 **LA** 15484 **MN** 18941, 18945 **MT** 18985 **NC** 5979 **OR** 12550 **TN** 8170 **TX** 16254 **WA** 716, 16353, 20358 **WI** 5983, 17513 *Canada:* **AB** 303 **BC** 2146, 18273 **NF** 11756 **ON** 5985 **PQ** 13859 *Intl:* **NZL** 11738

Forester, Cecil Scott: **DC** 6379 **TX** 16200

Forests and forestry: **AK** 17100, 17519 **AL** 17512 **AR** 20360 **AZ** 11991, 18208, 18229 **CA** 2555, 3309, 17520, 17521, 18322 **CO** 3974, 17106, 17522 **CT** 20739 **DC** 589, 11171, 17516 **GA** 1431, 5669, 6407 **IA** 1834 **ID** 18654 **IL** 18657 **IN** 13544 **KY** 18743 **LA** 17524 **MA** 6970, 18829 **MD** 15309, 17203 **MI** 10343, 10344 **MN** 10483, 18945 **MT** 10647, 18987 **NC** 5040, 5979, 11889, 11900, 11905 **ND** 11927 **NH** 11491,

19029 **NY** 1877, 8169, 12797, 15722, 15723 **OH** 4652, 7305, 12293, 17518 **OR** 3921, 12553, 19230, 20618 **PA** 12910, 19189 **SC** 20349, 20350 **TN** 16175, 19363 **TX** 1317, 16252 **UT** 17517 **VA** 731 **WA** 8291, 17515, 19526, 20048, 20359, 20361, 20362 **WI** 17514 **WV** 20208 *Canada:* **AB** 270, 2742, 18189, 18203 **BC** 2162, 2163, 2743, 18273 **MB** 9620 **NB** 2740, 11446, 19024, 19027 **NF** 2741, 11756 **ON** 2738, 2744, 8902, 12477, 12479, 12480, 19438 **PQ** 2739, 3193, 4098, 5978, 11836, 13528, 13596, 18066 **SK** 14842 *Intl:* **ARG** 17995 **AUS** 1327 **AUT** 1351 **BEL** 8583 **BLR** 1707 **CHL** 17987 **CZE** 4511, 19922 **ECU** 5222 **ENG** 6671, 14094 **FIN** 5716 **GER** 11805 **HUN** 5976, 7553 **IND** 15996 **ITA** 16752 **MEX** 17981 **MYS** 18141, 18149 **NZL** 11738 **POL** 161, 13164 **RUS** 8745 **SWE** 15908 **SWI** 15938 **TWN** 5518

Forster, Edward Morgan: **TX** 16200, 19392

Forster, John: **TX** 1602

Forteana: **NJ** 15328 **VA** 8111

Fossil fuels: **AR** 1025 **CT** 5 **DC** 10835 **ND** 19096 **NY** 6465 **PA** 12844, 17117 **WV** 17237 *Canada:* **ON** 2699 *Intl:* **SAF** 6367

Foster home care (See also Adoption): **CO** 3958 **DC** 500 **NY** 1179, 11607 **PA** 11018 **WI** 19617

Foster, Stephen Collins: **PA** 19212

Foundations (Endowments)   See: Endowments

Foundries: **AL** 515 **IL** 592, 11353 **OH** 159 *Intl:* **PRT** 13265

Fox, John W., Jr.: **VA** 19510

France: **DC** 5322, 9113 **MA** 6952 **NH** 10998 **NY** 6142 *Canada:* **BC** 18258 **PQ** 18086 *Intl:* **FRA** 1833, 6069 **GER** 1597

France—History: **MA** 6149 **MD** 18820 **ME** 1560 **MI** 10336 **MN** 3912 **NC** 19075 **NY** 6142, 6145 **PA** 1227 **VA** 8358 *Canada:* **ON** 20785 *Intl:* **FRA** 962, 6059, 6061 **IRL** 13827

Franchises (Retail trade): **DC** 2287, 8113 **TX** 1067

Franciscans: **CA** 14555 **IL** 3152 **MD** 20052 **NY** 6074, 6164, 14240 **OH** 9402 **RI** 14310 **TX** 12612

Frank, Jerome New: **CT** 20723

Frankfurter, Felix: **DC** 9129

Franklin, Benjamin: **CT** 20704 **DC** 9129, 9135 **PA** 712, 16487, 19197

Fraternal benefit societies   See: Friendly societies

Fraternities   See: Students' societies

Free enterprise   See: Laissez-faire

Free Methodist Church: **IN** 6127 **NY** 13969

Free Speech Movement: *Intl:* **SWE** 5487

Freedom   See: Liberty

Freedom of information: **MO** 18964

Freedom of the press (See also Censorship): **IL** 15492 **VA** 883

Freeman, Douglas S.: **VA** 19510

Freemasons: **CA** 6626, 13012, 14968 **DC** 14969 **DE** 9259 **IA** 6627 **IL** 9779, 13759 **IN** 9780 **KS** 6624 **MA** 6629, 10918 **MD** 9783 **NC** 6736 **ND** 9777 **NH** 20364 **NY** 6630 **PA** 9781, 16487 **TX** 9778 **VA** 6631 **WY** 6625 *Canada:* **MB** 6628 **PQ** 4121

Freight and freightage: **CA** 9581

Fremont, Jessie Benton: **CA** 15312

Genealogy (continued)
2561, 3058, 3659, 3667, 3675, 3679, 3680, 4435, 4993, 5109, 6161, 6427, 9280, 9347, 9538, 10104, 10972, 12206, 12775, 13205, 13763, 14710, 14797, 14799, 15376, 15471, 16570, 16579 **CO** 2030, 3951, 4783, 6717, 8737, 15631, 20146 **CT** 2116, 4181, 4186, 4200, 5566, 6143, 6518, 6582, 7748, 8316, 9206, 10356, 11456, 11500, 11519, 15184, 15815, 15822, 16400, 20092, 20354, 20477 **DC** 4904, 9115, 11027, 11291 **DE** 4730, 7266 **FL** 2364, 3663, 3677, 3681, 5898, 8315, 10256, 12510, 12919, 13188, 14245, 14470, 20642 **GA** 1245, 4395, 6286, 6385, 6394, 6785, 7205, 7595, 20017, 20193 **HI** 3664, 7043, 11289 **IA** 803, 2467, 5619, 6769, 8224, 9196, 15679, 15680, 19817 **ID** 7647, 7648 **IL** 1458, 1882, 3421, 3535, 4689, 6230, 7698, 9182, 9688, 13036, 14930, 15436, 20437 **IN** 376, 2265, 3132, 7768, 10091, 13094, 15857, 16370, 19841, 19850, 19936, 19995, 20441 **KS** 3481, 8559, 10376, 13931, 16405 **KY** 3130, 5147, 5694, 8656, 8660, 8671, 11297, 12638 **LA** 9370, 9372, 11543, 16557, 19356 **MA** 473, 1801, 1996, 2001, 2066, 3652, 3682, 4206, 4695, 4962, 5051, 5448, 5451, 5960, 6057, 7019, 7279, 7938, 8474, 11433, 11474, 12382, 13668, 15841 **MD** 8420, 9750, 9756, 9764, 14789, 15990 **ME** 4696, 9552, 9554, 9564, 12395, 12917 **MI** 3656, 3665, 3742, 4684, 4816, 5844, 5854, 6173, 6285, 6289, 6640, 7485, 9141, 9721, 11938, 12199, 16526, 20267 **MN** 10450, 10464, 10466, 10488, 12068, 12108, 12404, 12574, 13217, 15768, 19988, 20248 **MO** 575, 7088, 8066, 8549, 10537, 10542, 11826, 14438, 14442, 14454, 15681 **MS** 8306, 10517, 19354, 19790, 19825 **MT** 3661, 6693, 9086, 10643 **NC** 3139, 3446, 6943, 9716, 11885, 13710, 14089, 20108, 20690 **ND** 15682, 19095 **NE** 2396, 4497, 5161, 11378 **NH** 511, 9587, 11485, 11492, 13251, 14006, 20364, 20552 **NJ** 1251, 1733, 2119, 2608, 4440, 4474, 6290, 6489, 6514, 6824, 7269, 7284, 7565, 9492, 10611, 10748, 11298, 11503, 11514, 12238, 12778, 14175, 14629, 15891, 16482, 19851 **NM** 318, 3651, 3672 **NV** 3653, 3666 **NY** 2235, 2251, 2332, 3433, 3459, 3920, 3981, 4346, 4844, 5076, 5120, 5663, 6354, 6358, 7329, 7521, 7522, 7573, 8394, 8463, 9518, 10442, 11577, 11578, 11633, 11663, 11666, 11667, 12379, 12424, 13556, 13632, 13993, 14053, 14429, 14901, 14917, 14931, 15361, 15523, 15760, 15849, 16368, 17030, 20111, 20229, 20283, 20622 **OH** 372, 1917, 3655, 3703, 3826, 4500, 4657, 4846, 6729, 7060, 7496, 9147, 9930, 12269, 12270, 13484, 15510, 15691, 16395, 16588, 19975, 20293, 20644 **OK** 1544, 12350, 12727 **OR** 3658, 6287, 10849, 16352 **PA** 2318, 2595, 3079, 3487, 3488, 3670, 3757, 4717, 5416, 7258, 7263, 7265, 7282, 7292, 7293, 8754, 8869, 8921, 9035, 9055, 10090, 10619, 11458, 11963, 12841, 12858, 12950, 13849, 14080, 15127, 15294, 15889, 19974, 20287, 20337 **RI** 593, 11775, 13442, 13869 **SC** 2468, 2606, 3442, 7523, 12821, 15395 **TN** 3455, 8773, 10065, 13492, 16162 **TX** 441, 1624, 3429, 3657, 4563, 4653, 5221, 5284, 6024, 7459, 9014, 9866, 14673, 16257, 16259, 19926 **UT** 597, 936, 3660, 3674, 20806, 20810 **VA** 344, 456, 1558, 2120, 2309, 4594, 5154, 5561, 8475, 11183, 11847, 13257, 15594, 19892, 20013, 20016, 20674 **VT** 1723, 13972, 19803, 20580 **WA** 3671, 3676, 9077, 11818, 14993, 15000, 15212, 15981, 20692 **WI** 8636, 10427, 13810, 15684, 19570, 19571, 19644, 19645, 19646, 20102 **WV** 1959, 12381, 20209, 20225 **WY** 3668 *Canada:* **BC** 2148 **MB** 9612 **NB** 12386, 18072 **NF** 10051, 11764 **NS** 18484, 20746 **ON** 2289, 3678, 5981, 6503, 9065, 9268, 10228, 11961, 12439, 12440, 12601, 14431, 15174, 16707, 20160 **PE** 13351 **PQ** 1830, 3916, 4339, 10509, 13574, 15302, 15304 **SK** 14852 *Intl:* **AUS** 15694 **CHN** 12932 **ENG** 18441 **FIN** 5708 **SAF** 15386

Genesee County (NY): NY 13993

Genet, Jean: TX 19392

Genetic engineering: CA 3867 **MD** 17203 *Canada:* **PQ** 2815

Genetics (See also Recombinant DNA): **CA** 14641, 15648 **CO** 3974 **DE** 5014 **GA** 6399 **IL** 3588, 18661 **IN** 19116 **MA** 6357, 6949, 6985 **MD** 11204 **ME** 8309 **MN** 18942 **MO** 20056 **MT** 15138 **NC** 11905, 19067, 19068 **NH** 19029 **NJ** 13369, 16624 **NY** 3873, 4003, 5969, 11566, 11664, 15967, 20751 **OH** 3584, 12295 **PA** 712, 16130, 20540 **SC** 6751, 6848 **TX** 19397, 19930 **VA** 7983 *Canada:* **MB** 9610 **ON** 2632, 8859, 12589, 19553 **PQ** 4650, 9893, 18078 *Intl:* **AUS** 18145 **CHN** 27, 7491, 12930 **FRA** 8052 **GER** 13099 **IND** 15996 **NLD** 14092 **PRT** 13261 **URE** 8820

Geochemistry: CA 2489, 3501, 15644, 18384 **CO** 18494 **DC** 3072 **GA** 18606 **IA** 8238, 18710 **IL** 12082, 18673 **IN** 7788, 13539 **KS** 8557 **KY** 18749 **LA** 9394 **MA** 9807 **MO** 18957, 20060 **MT** 10641 **NJ** 13373, 16072 **NY** 4014, 4016, 15960, 17547, 19283 **OK** 19128 **PA** 2303, 8298 **VA** 19872 **WA** 17649 *Canada:* **ON** 2747 *Intl:* **CHN** 12928 **CZE** 4510 **DEN** 6365 **FIN** 6366 **FRA** 6064 **ICE** 7636 **SAF** 6367

Geodesy: FL 17651 **MD** 17175, 17650, 17655 **MO** 17174 **OH** 12319 **VA** 16964 **WA** 20027 *Canada:* **ON** 2701 **PQ** 13596 *Intl:* **AUT** 18702 **CHN** 20650 **ENG** 6684, 14119 **FIN** 5717 **GER** 2360 **SPA** 15567

Geographical names See: Names, Geographical

Geography (See also Maps and atlases): **AZ** 1013 **CA** 5102, 18314, 18355, 18412, 18434 **CO** 18494 **CT** 7529 **DC** 4908, 9118, 11186, 15263 **GA** 6393 **IL** 6586, 13708, 15491, 18683, 20255 **IN** 7787 **KS** 18730 **LA** 9377, 9387 **MA** 2001, 2006, 18827, 18829 **MI** 4822 **MN** 10450, 14566 **MS** 4924 **NH** 13153, 16935 **NJ** 6874, 11746 **NM** 19041, 19048 **NV** 19018 **NY** 2332, 4015, 5521, 11609, 13628 **OH** 3826, 8652, 10266, 12297, 13484, 16393 **OK** 12372 **OR** 10849 **PA** 3081, 6123, 12859, 16138 **TN** 17821 **UT** 19470, 20806 **VA** 17531 **WA** 19528 **WI** 598, 19598, 20527 *Canada:* **AB** 18188 **BC** 18271 **NS** 12134 **ON** 2698, 2701, 2747, 9952, 10228, 19165, 19455, 19557, 20786, 20791 **PQ** 3194, 9912, 9975, 18083 *Intl:* **AUS** 14118 **CHN** 7130, 15152 **COT** 7862 **CRI** 17789 **FRA** 6059 **GER** 8740 **GHA** 6461 **IND** 7749 **ISR** 316 **ITA** 1821, 3845 **MEX** 12720 **NER** 19054 **NLD** 11402 **PAK** 12694 **PER** 6361 **RUS** 10767 **SPA** 15561

Geology (See also Crystallography; Mineralogy; Paleontology; Petroleum—Geology; Petrology; Sedimentology): **AK** 2051, 17100, 17109, 17248, 17532, 18175, 18184 **AL** 6363 **AR** 1027, 18234 **AZ** 986, 1001, 1014, 1234, 10916, 15041, 17723, 17765, 17789, 18221, 18229 **CA** 1637, 1809, 2470, 2489, 2523, 2524, 2574, 3501, 3756, 4574, 4578, 4706, 6416, 8682, 12233, 14712, 14722, 14802, 15644, 16955, 17536, 18314, 18315, 18356, 18384, 18412, 18419, 18434, 19346, 19671, 19672, 19674, 20584, 20585, 20587 **CO** 133, 450, 921, 3947, 3957, 4506, 4779, 10569, 17106, 17112, 17537, 17706, 18494, 20279 **CT** 3833, 14911, 20714 **DC** 15280 **DE** 4733 **FL** 5890, 5894, 5917, 14346, 18570, 18577 **GA** 5337, 5669, 6403, 16305, 16959, 18604 **HI** 7023 **IA** 13557, 14790, 18710 **ID** 7654, 18650, 18654 **IL** 3512, 5684, 6894, 7696, 7701, 12082, 15836, 18452, 18673, 18700 **IN** 5094, 7773, 7788, 13539, 19350 **KS** 8557, 18731, 20409 **KY** 18749 **LA** 3505, 6761, 10570 **MA** 1979, 2006, 3024, 6836, 6948, 9669, 9807, 15232, 18829, 20155 **MD** 2591, 4576, 8418, 18813 **ME** 12174 **MI** 10322, 10342, 10344, 18859, 18879, 20123, 20273 **MN** 3052, 9062, 10463, 14940, 17119, 18928 **MO** 6847, 10547, 18980, 20060 **MS** 10519, 16970, 19353 **MT** 7295, 10641, 10647, 10651, 17722, 20748 **NC** 5044, 11900, 19060 **ND** 19098 **NE** 18999 **NH** 4611, 7605, 16935 **NJ** 4260, 6415, 11502, 13373, 14169, 17702, 20586 **NM** 9044, 11521, 11527, 17549, 17682, 17684, 20320 **NV** 17114, 17235, 19018 **NY** 346, 687, 2245, 2340, 4014, 5060, 12698, 13638, 15730, 15742, 15749, 15960, 17547, 17548, 17705, 19283 **OH** 2041, 3814, 3830, 8652, 12286, 12322, 18158, 18470 **OK** 485, 817, 8687, 12371, 12377, 13011, 16571, 19126, 19128 **OR** 3401, 12048, 12533, 17694, 19158 **PA** 36, 362, 432, 2303, 3080, 3085, 4230, 6092, 6094, 6227, 6852, 12859, 12860, 12902, 13748, 16138, 17117 **PR** 19247 **SC** 13843 **SD** 15417 **TN** 10951, 19364, 19774 **TX** 816, 1110, 1260, 1605, 3496, 3852, 4298, 4707, 4985, 5297, 5530, 6023, 6190, 6771, 7458, 9482, 10366, 10567, 10568, 12915, 14913, 15116, 15501, 15504, 15535, 16189, 16195, 16198, 16234, 16662, 16666, 18639, 19382, 19391, 19410, 20247 **UT** 17701, 19469, 19706, 19707 **VA** 599, 17539, 17552 **WA** 4577, 17552, 19537, 20026 **WI** 1703, 10431, 19599 **WV** 17237 **WY** 19658, 20291 *Canada:* **AB** 303, 812, 2746, 3495, 6807, 7360, 10571, 12723, 14138, 15111, 16430, 18188, 18289, 18295, 19669, 20246 **BC** 2158, 2183, 2745, 3418, 13092, 16051, 16348, 18266, 18281 **MB** 102, 9619, 18787 **NB** 11446, 11454, 19024, 19027 **NF** 11758 **NS** 4536, 12141, 12154, 16034 **NT** 2758 **ON** 2700, 2747, 6256, 6833, 7730, 9953, 10230, 12482, 13650, 14131, 19438, 19553, 20097 **PQ** 9909, 13596, 15305, 18084, 18112 **SK** 3866, 14866, 19293 *Intl:* **ARG** 972, 6215 **AUS** 16010 **AUT** 6364, 12224 **BMU** 1754 **BRZ** 6213, 10384, 18002 **CHN** 7130, 12928 **COL** 3925 **CRI** 17989 **CZE** 4510 **DEN** 6365 **ENG** 4966, 6669 **FIN** 6366, 7126, 16587 **FRA** 6064, 18101, 18124 **GER** 6530 **HUN** 7551 **ICE** 7634, 7636 **ITA** 3845 **NOR** 12115, 18140 **SAF** 3419, 6367 **SAU** 5551 **SCT** 14955 **SPA** 7236 **THA** 1119

Geology, Stratigraphic: IL 7696, 18673 **IN** 7788, 13539 **MA** 6948 **MO** 18957 **NC** 6029 **NJ** 13373 **NY** 4014 **PA** 2303 *Intl:* **CHN** 12928 **FRA** 6064 **SAF** 6367

Geomagnetism See: Magnetism, Terrestrial

Geomorphology: IA 18718 **IL** 18673 **IN** 7788, 13539 **MO** 18957, 20060 **NY** 15749, 15960 **WY** 8855, 19658 *Canada:* **PQ** 18084 *Intl:* **CHN** 7130, 7988 **FRA** 6064

Geophysics (See also Atmospheric physics): **AK** 17248, 18184 **AL** 6363 **AZ** 15041 **CA** 2489, 3501, 6416, 10980, 14183, 15644, 17536, 18314, 18384, 18412, 19342, 19671 **CO** 20584, 3947, 3957, 10569, 11098, 18494 **DC** 3072, 17864 **GA** 6387 **HI** 7023 **IA** 18710 **IL** 12082, 18452, 18673 **IN** 7788 **KY** 18749 **MA** 681, 1979, 6948, 9807, 16801 **MD** 17650 **MO** 20060 **MS** 10519 **MT** 10641 **NC** 19060 **NJ** 13373 **NM** 11521 **NY** 4014, 4016, 15960 **OH** 18470 **OK** 12347, 19128 **TX** 816, 1260, 3500, 5530, 6023, 6190, 10366, 10567, 12915, 16662, 16666, 18639, 19391, 19395, 20247 **VA** 16070, 19872 **WA** 15078, 19537 **WI** 19599 **WY** 19658

Government publications: (continued)
12058, 15489, 15494, 18669, 18681, 20255 **IN** 375, 1440, 5094, 7768, 7769, 7793, 7801, 7820, 13542 **KS** 8560, 8563, 13082, 18725, 19989 **KY** 3219, 5146, 9397, 18751, 18752 **LA** 9370, 9376, 11541 **MA** 1993, 4488, 6981, 9833, 17525, 20598 **MD** 4172, 5941, 6185, 8421, 9764, 13299, 13303, 14640, 18246, 18801, 18815 **ME** 18780 **MI** 4273, 4829, 5156, 9141, 9507, 10323, 10344, 20118, 20269 **MN** 9634, 10449, 10466, 10490, 11850, 14563, 14566, 18910 **MO** 9189, 10550, 11972, 14453, 18971, 18982, 20068 **MS** 331 **MT** 5160, 10641 **NC** 3446, 11885, 11896, 11897, 11899 **ND** 10497, 11924, 11925 **NE** 11378, 11383, 12408, 20116 **NH** 11483, 11492 **NJ** 5002, 5569, 10658, 11514, 11515, 11749, 13385, 16481 **NM** 11521, 11530 **NV** 11224, 11424, 19016 **NY** 2246, 4015, 11608, 11645, 11665, 11667, 11709, 12656, 13304, 13629, 13820, 14354, 15708, 15962, 19280, 19933 **OH** 175, 3821, 3832, 8650, 12272, 13480, 13483, 15691, 18482 **OK** 11985, 12076, 12359, 12366, 13011, 16571 **OR** 10852, 12553, 19147 **PA** 366, 3183, 5005, 5124, 5232, 6115, 7811, 12858, 17527 **PR** 3168, 19251 **RI** 13442 **SC** 3720, 15409, 19308 **SD** 15422 **TN** 13491, 16173, 19367 **TX** 4565, 5131, 7458, 13894, 16259, 16276, 16521, 19387, 19405, 19411 **UT** 19469, 19713, 20801 **VA** 2120, 6880, 13912, 17220, 17605, 19895 **VI** 19855 **VT** 3136 **WA** 3381, 15001 **WI** 10429, 19650 **WV** 20215 **WY** 20671 *Canada:* **AB** 259, 288, 12398, 18197 **BC** 18270, 18273 **MB** 9618, 18787, 18789 **NB** 11449 **NF** 11762 **NS** 6838 **NT** 12065 **ON** 2676, 2724, 2803, 2812, 2849, 6866, 10225, 10226, 12427, 12446, 12469, 13647, 13655, 19167, 20478, 20788 **PE** 13350 **PQ** 13575, 19848 **SK** 14860 *Intl:* **BUL** 2345 **BWA** 2026 **CHN** 12931 **GER** 15794 **IRL** 13827 **NLD** 11405 **SAF** 15387 **SWZ** 15905

Government purchasing (See also Public contracts): **DC** 5624, 6167, 6349, 17218 **OR** 10848 **VA** 11211

Governors (Machinery): **IL** 20588

Goya y Lucientes, Francisco Jose de: **MA** 1998

Graham, Billy (William Franklin): **IL** 20367, 20368 **KY** 15463 **MN** 6615

Grain: **CA** 17198 **IL** 947 **KS** 8565, 8566, 17200 **MN** 3044, 18942 *Canada:* **AB** 312, 2647 **MB** 2634, 2666, 3002, 16713 **PQ** 2660, 12253 **SK** 2639, 2663 *Intl:* **ARG** 12226 **AUS** 1320 **NGA** 7898 **RUS** 11350

Grain—Harvesting: **KS** 8565 *Intl:* **NZL** 5011

Grain—Milling: **KS** 8566 *Intl:* **NZL** 5011

Grainger, Percy Aldridge: *Intl:* **ENG** 5358

Grand Canyon: **AZ** 11992, 17723

Grant, Cary: **CA** 35

Grant, Ulysses Simpson: **IL** 7697, 15492 **PA** 19997

Grants See: Subsidies

Graphic arts (See also Drawing; Lithography; Photography; Printing): **CA** 1073, 2473, 5608, 5703, 12203, 14702, 14725, 18370, 19290, 20549 **CO** 3949, 16863 **CT** 12688, 16504, 18252, 20699 **DC** 4902, 9134, 11181, 15267, 15268, 15271 **FL** 5865, 13934, 16477, 18586 **IA** 4790 **IL** 1704, 4851, 13708, 14014, 18690 **KS** 18728 **KY** 18767 **LA** 9372, 9382 **MA** 1081, 1992, 1999, 9789, 15234, 20446 **MD** 1452 **MI** 10315, 18853 **MN** 10444, 18900, 19947 **MO** 6855, 14434, 14452, 15599 **NC** 11880 **NJ** 5023, 5567, 11750, 13194, 15863 **NY** 4025, 6655, 6658, 9702, 10710, 11567, 11615, 11625, 12768, 13981, 14925, 19273, 20763 **OH** 2414, 3809, 10264, 12299, 18468 **OK** 12352, 12374 **PA** 5259, 6109, 6654, 12836, 12894, 16149 **PR** 19237 **RI** 19264 **TX** 10583, 14670 **WA** 19513 **WI** 4227, 10417, 10419, 10424 *Canada:* **AB** 257 **MB** 18785 **NS** 12132 **ON** 23 **PQ** 13688 *Intl:* **AUT** 6656 **BUL** 2345 **CZE** 13294 **ENG** 13200, 14091 **FRA** 3226 **GER** 15628

Graphite See: Carbon and graphite

Graphology: **IL** 20608 **MA** 6888 **MN** 12574 *Intl:* **AUT** 1354

Grasses (See also Pastures): **DC** 15272

Grassland ecology: **CO** 3971

Graves, Robert: **CA** 19290 **IL** 15492 **KS** 8572 **NY** 15741 *Canada:* **BC** 19489

Gravity: **PA** 5363 *Canada:* **ON** 2748 *Intl:* **CHN** 20650

Gray, Thomas: **CT** 20721

Grayson, David See: Baker, Ray Stannard (David Grayson)

Great Britain: **DC** 5361 **KS** 18725 **NY** 2187, 5360 **TN** 5830 *Canada:* **ON** 866 *Intl:* **BEL** 2184 **ENG** 4064, 6679, 6680 **FRA** 18070 **GER** 2185

Great Britain—History: **CA** 2547, 2572, 7572, 18358, 18402, 19290 **CT** 8316, 20721 **DC** 5943, 9117 **GA** 18600 **IL** 11752 **KS** 18724 **LA** 16560 **MD** 8420 **MI** 10330, 10336 **MN** 18931 **NC** 5049 **NY** 3735, 7573, 16667 **PA** 16137 **WI** 19637 *Canada:* **ON** 9954, 10601, 13661, 19555 **PQ** 9895 *Intl:* **ARG** 1126 **ENG** 4966, 10905, 14091, 15070, 15310, 20776 **GER** 18018, 18044, 18048 **NIR** 9194

Great Lakes: **IL** 3243 **MD** 17657 **MI** 1590, 6696, 10303, 10304, 10338, 17500, 17648, 18880 **MN** 11971, 16937, 18939 **OH** 3830, 7060, 7106, 12309, 12316, 13093 **WI** 17667 *Canada:* **ON** 8137, 19557

Great Lakes—History: **MI** 4816, 6698, 9707 **OH** 2037, 6697 **WI** 9631, 10427

Great Plains: **KS** 18729 **ND** 15682, 19095 **NE** 60, 11378 **OK** 10901 **SD** 1296, 15421

Greece: **DC** 9113 **OH** 18473 *Intl:* **GRC** 735, 6715, 7117

Greece—History: **DC** 6953 **IL** 18664 **NY** 13639 **TX** 16197, 19386 *Intl:* **GRC** 6419, 6715

Greek language: **CA** 14752 **DC** 3163 **ID** 1946 **IL** 18664 **MD** 19991 **MI** 4802 **NY** 11556 **OH** 3827, 18473 **TX** 19386 *Intl:* **EGY** 6148 **GER** 18054

Greek literature (See also Classical literature): **MA** 7116 **MN** 18931 **NY** 4004, 13639 **OH** 18473 *Intl:* **GER** 18054

Greek Orthodox Church See: Orthodox Eastern Church, Greek

Green, Adolph: **NY** 10908

Greenaway, Kate: **CA** 14711 **IN** 2416 **MI** 4828 **PA** 3084, 6122

Greene, Graham: **CA** 19290 **DC** 6379 **KY** 18768 **MA** 1976, 1981 **TX** 19392

Greenhouse effect: **NY** 3238, 3239 **TN** 12185 **WV** 15885

Greenhouse gardening: **OH** 12292

Greeting cards: **FL** 5919 **IN** 20109 **MO** 6855 **NY** 669 **PA** 6121 **VA** 19724

Gregorian chant See: Chants (Plain, Gregorian, etc.)

Gregory, Lady Isabella Augusta Persse: **FL** 18586 **GA** 5338

Grey, Zane: **AZ** 11992

Grief: **OH** 3700 *Canada:* **ON** 2959

Grierson, Benjamin Henry: **TX** 17707

Griffith, Andy (Andrew): **NC** 9855

Griffith, David Lewelyn Wark: **NY** 10906, 10908

Grocery trade: **CA** 14211 **VA** 11055, 11188

Group medical practice (See also Health maintenance organizations (HMO)): **CO** 10004 **OR** 8508 **WA** 6767

Group relations See: Social interaction

Growth See: Human growth

Guam: **GU** 5859, 6786, 18610

Guatemala: **KS** 18723, 18724 **TX** 19380

Health maintenance organizations (HMO) (See also Group medical practice): **CO** 10004 **DC** 6766 **MI** 10192 **OH** 4089 **OR** 8508

Health manpower See: Medical personnel

Health planning (See also Health services administration): **CA** 15808 **DC** 16783, 19689 **GA** 6408 **IL** 15244 **MD** 17932, 17933 **ME** 9986 **MN** 10480 **OH** 3244, 11973, 18468 **PA** 12910, 20770

Health services administration (See also Health planning): **CA** 11196, 14754 **CO** 4778 **CT** 20716 **DC** 6378, 7479, 17308, 17311 **FL** 5864, 18561 **GA** 6408 **HI** 18622 **IA** 8225, 14475, 19162 **IL** 535, 14149, 16488 **KS** 18735 **MA** 9818 **MD** 17932 **MI** 10131, 14217, 14328, 18884 **MN** 15, 10480 **MO** 3148 **MS** 18951 **NC** 10827, 15873 **NJ** 7080 **NY** 7562, 10662 **OH** 3244, 8695 **PA** 5955 **TN** 10021 **TX** 16281, 16975 **VA** 1172 **WA** 15206 **WI** 19586 *Canada:* **AB** 281, 18200 **BC** 2149 **MB** 9615 **ON** 2749, 13285 **PE** 13350 **PQ** 13605, 18091 *Intl:* **ENG** 6674, 14111 **SAU** 5578

Hearing and deafness (See also Ear—Diseases): **AL** 16988 **AZ** 13030 **CA** 7439, 7440, 18421, 18434 **CO** 3946, 18506 **DC** 1677, 6232, 11201 **FL** 5882 **GA** 1243 **IL** 7680, 18670 **IN** 7762, 13542 **KS** 7953 **KY** 8664 **MD** 765, 16976 **ME** 1584 **MO** 3342, 14443, 20071 **NV** 19017 **NY** 590, 7562, 9093, 11622, 13638, 13982, 13983, 14537, 16023 **OH** 12275, 13481 **OR** 12523, 12544, 12545 **PA** 5537, 12631 **TN** 10077 **TX** 16272 **VT** 1318 **WI** 6262, 20514 *Canada:* **ON** 2921, 2935, 13285 **PQ** 1167, 7882, 18091

Hearn, Lafcadio: **AL** 14663 **KY** 18768 **LA** 16560 **OH** 12328, 13479 **VA** 19510

Hearst, William Randolph: **CA** 2534

Heart—Diseases (See also Cardiology): **MD** 533, 11193 **MI** 17355 **NY** 9782 **TX** 607, 16242, 19418 *Canada:* **AB** 7089

Heat engineering: *Canada:* **ON** 2825 *Intl:* **CHN** 6790 **RUS** 14660

Heat transfer See: Heat—Transmission

Heat—Transmission: **CA** 399, 1849 **ID** 5268 **IL** 18697 **IN** 6333 **NH** 4420 **OH** 1394 **PA** 19194 **WI** 10418, 20818 *Intl:* **ISR** 16038

Heating: **DC** 8099 **MN** 7372 **NJ** 8204 **NY** 3096 **OR** 13240 *Intl:* **CHN** 1658, 3621 **DEN** 13938 **ENG** 2343 **FRA** 8133

Hebraica See: Jewish literature

Hebrew language: **CA** 2069, 14752 **DC** 3165, 9107, 16126 **FL** 3321, 5869, 18573 **MD** 19991 **MI** 4802 **MN** 18922 **NJ** 13380 **NY** 11611, 11815, 20756 **OR** 13248 **TN** 8380

Heine, Heinrich: *Intl:* **GER** 7110

Heinlein, Robert Anson: **CA** 18435

Helicopters: **CA** 14686, 16997 **CT** 17963 **MO** 16923 **PA** 1939 **TX** 1682, 1683 **VA** 608, 7115, 16922

Hellman, Lillian: **TX** 19392

Hematology (See also Blood): **IL** 1586 **KS** 18732 **NJ** 14545 **NY** 7195 **PA** 8359 **TX** 19930 *Canada:* **ON** 34, 14397 *Intl:* **AUS** 20302 **BEL** 1969

Hemingway, Ernest: **CA** 15658 **IL** 8769, 12180 **MA** 15236, 17927 **MD** 18820 **NJ** 13386 **OH** 13479 **VA** 19510 *Intl:* **CUB** 10882

Henley, Beth (Elizabeth Becker): **MS** 18949

Henry, O. See: Porter, William Sidney (O. Henry)

Henry, William M.: **CA** 12232

Heraldry: **AL** 536 **CA** 4435, 6819, 9347 **CO** 4783 **DC** 4904, 9115 **FL** 10256, 12510 **GA** 20017 **IL** 1458 **IN** 376 **MA** 2001, 5839, 10898, 11474 **MI** 6640 **MN** 10450 **MO** 14454 **NM** 3651 **NY** 2332, 11633, 11666, 13184 **OH** 3826 **PA** 3079 **TX** 4563 **VA** 17003, 19875 *Canada:* **ON** 10228, 12439 *Intl:* **FIN** 5708 **FRA** 6061 **SAF** 15386 **SPA** 15557

Herbaria: **AZ** 18220 **CA** 18346 **IL** 18674 **KS** 8567 **MA** 6950 **MO** 10535 **MT** 10653, 20748 **NH** 11491 **OR** 4973, 12552 **TX** 15504 **VT** 3276, 19804 **WA** 20046 *Canada:* **ON** 13158 *Intl:* **NLD** 11409

Herbert, George: **NC** 19082

Herbicides (See also Pesticides; Weed control): **IL** 14782 **WA** 20362 *Canada:* **SK** 2657

Herbs: **CA** 610 **FL** 5919 **ID** 7654 **IL** 8117 **IN** 13547 **ME** 16782 **NY** 7414, 11596 **OH** 3807, 6247, 7144, 8733, 10270 **PA** 3083, 12846 **RI** 19268 **TN** 3458 **WA** 12 *Canada:* **ON** 3746 *Intl:* **SCT** 14102 **TWN** 2126

Herpetology See: Reptiles

Hershey, Lewis Blaine: **IN** 16494

Hibernation: **NV** 8118

High energy physics See: Nuclear physics

High temperatures: **CA** 15353 **IN** 16642 **OH** 16609

Higher education See: Education, Higher

Highway engineering (See also Road construction; Traffic engineering): **CA** 1368, 2536, 2537, 2539, 2540, 20249 **CO** 3961 **DC** 11270, 17280 **IA** 8235 **MA** 9834 **MD** 9763, 11048 **MI** 10309 **MO** 10548 **MS** 10523 **NH** 11490 **OR** 12536 **SD** 15419 **TN** 16163 **TX** 16249, 19384 **WA** 20030 **WI** 20529 **WV** 20212 *Canada:* **AB** 309 **NS** 12143, 12144 **ON** 12487, 16460 **SK** 14845 *Intl:* **GER** 6444

Highway law: **DC** 17492

Highway safety See: Traffic safety

Hillel (Beth Hillel and Beth Shammai): **NY** 347 **OH** 16118

Hindemith, Paul: **OH** 10821

Hindu literature: **CA** 1268, 2480, 18344 **NC** 5043 **NY** 7894, 16724, 19274 **TX** 19406

Hispanic Americans (See also Mexican Americans): **CA** 1127, 11194, 12207, 14761, 19347 **DC** 1131, 18554 **FL** 7252 **MD** 7917 **NY** 11610 **PA** 5142 **TX** 3554, 19380

Historic buildings—Conservation and restoration: **AL** 16591 **AR** 1037 **AZ** 18212 **CA** 6499 **CO** 17771 **DC** 4900, 12771 **DE** 9484 **FL** 6004, 7255 **GA** 17712 **ID** 8958 **IL** 18690 **IN** 1437, 7244 **KS** 8575 **KY** 8347, 18750 **LA** 9382, 16556 **MA** 2600, 3492 **MD** 6872, 7237, 18810 **ME** 6709 **MO** 8933, 13268 **NC** 194 **ND** 15682 **NE** 4940 **NY** 2300, 8932, 11679, 11680 **OH** 2035, 8651, 10263, 11973 **OR** 7251, 15511, 19141 **PA** 5416, 7258, 13085, 19182 **TX** 14069, 14667 **VA** 3934, 10823, 19497, 19884 **VT** 19805 *Canada:* **BC** 2166 **PQ** 10703 **SK** 14842 *Intl:* **ENG** 4360

Historic sites (See also Monuments): **CA** 2534 **DC** 17716 **IL** 6009, 7697 **KS** 17709 **KY** 17661 **MA** 17717, 17773, 17775, 17781 **MD** 17666 **MO** 20095 **MT** 17675, 17726 **NC** 7239, 17683, 17752 **NJ** 17702 **NY** 11680, 11682, 12378 **OH** 17791 **PA** 17663, 17664, 17711, 17733 **RI** 15219 **TN** 17665, 17783 **TX** 17707, 20482 **VA** 17669, 17764 **WA** 17715 **WY** 17708 *Canada:* **ON** 2709

Historical society libraries: **AK** 3599, 4297, 4601, 16404, 19722 **AL** 1835, 2409 **AR** 1686, 1725, 5001, 6254 **AZ** 988, 989, 3120, 13061, 13062, 15081 **CA** 492, 1222, 2477, 3612, 4710, 4993, 5437, 6154, 6250, 7113, 7262, 7271, 8885, 8899, 9514, 9664, 10082, 10717, 10969, 11418, 12772, 12794, 14679, 14695, 14696, 14769, 14799, 14813, 14820, 15176, 15201, 19800, 19955 **CO** 1128, 3941, 9479, 13456, 14025, 14763, 19719, 20365 **CT** 3017, 3875, 4181, 4583, 4605, 5566, 5584, 6582, 7290, 8643, 9206, 9473, 9523, 9640, 10356, 11456, 11500, 11519, 12394, 14023, 14638, 14643, 15184, 15360, 15634, 15815, 15822, 16428, 19954, 20092, 20134, 20354, 20472, 20473, 20477 **DC** 7274, 7291 **DE** 7266 **FL** 5873, 6004, 6840, 7218, 7249, 7278, 7281, 8887, 12919, 13188, 14245, 14588 **GA** 1246, 3449, 5618, 6380, 6385, 6785, 9414, 10352, 20387 **HI** 7051, 9849 **IA** 440, 3184, 3478, 5619, 5922, 7272, 9040, 9544, 10553, 10617, 14957, 15680, 15995, 20110 **ID** 1956, 3135, 7647, 7648, 8958, 12640, 19688 **IL** 2365, 3522, 4793, 5265, 5506, 6205, 6231, 6506, 7197, 7285, 8541, 8618,

Horology (See also Clocks and watches; Time): CA 15019 CT 529, 16504 GA 6382 MA 3440 OH 785 PA 11081

Horowitz, Vladimir: CT 20717

Horror tales: MA 9819 NY 4372

Horse-racing: CA 1593, 2579, 20245 KY 8410, 8601, 8661 NV 19011 NY 11241, 16525 *Canada:* ON 2997 PQ 9360

Horses: AZ 934, 2612 CA 1593, 2551, 2579 CO 935 CT 18519 ID 917 KS 8572 KY 733, 1901, 8601, 8661, 18757 MN 18938 MO 1289, 20577 NV 19017 NY 15720, 16525 OH 12292 OK 12713 PA 4737 TX 771 VA 11302 WA 691 WI 8907 *Canada:* ON 2995, 7537

Horticulture (See also Gardening): AL 1850 AZ 994, 16459 CA 6202, 9328, 13704, 14796, 14808, 15833, 17184, 18306, 18364, 18403, 20849 CO 3974, 4775 CT 18514 DC 6962, 15283, 17083, 17608 FL 5558, 15018, 18569, 18581, 18589, 18845 GA 5669, 20017 IL 3516, 3526, 10762, 15670, 18657 IN 13544 KS 2024 KY 18743 LA 732, 19356 MA 1746, 6950, 9793, 20592 MD 4504, 7238, 9272, 17203 MI 4808, 18874 MN 18917, 18924, 18943 MO 8591, 10535 NC 19067 ND 11927 NE 11372, 11376 NJ 10613 NY 2227, 4304, 6248, 7414, 7933, 10625, 11554, 13137, 15719, 19278 OH 4652, 6247, 6251, 7323, 8733, 12293, 14961 OK 12369 PA 4737, 9299, 12846, 16129, 16137, 19189 SC 2216 TN 3463, 4928, 10059 VA 618, 6881, 11844 WA 3312, 13885, 20048 *Canada:* AB 18191 BC 2662, 19754 NF 2659 ON 3746, 7537, 10230, 11798, 12452, 13917, 14105, 19438 PQ 2637, 2658, 8343 *Intl:* ARG 5460 AUS 1328, 2023, 14104, 18145, 19028, 19565 BEL 7887 BOL 7997 CHN 1655, 10964 CZE 19922 ENG 14103, 18766 GER 16042 IND 7747, 15996, 18148 IRL 8245 MOR 7876 NZL 11737 POL 160, 161 ROM 18061 SCT 5234, 14102, 14965 TWN 1123, 15987

Hosiery: NC 11062, 11898

Hosmer, Chester Craig: CA 19340

Hospices (Terminal care): ME 8622 WY 20374

Hospital libraries (See also Hospitals—Administration; Medicine; Nursing; Surgery): AL 1508, 1511, 1514, 3095, 5538, 7355, 8307, 11827, 11966, 13444, 14617, 15439 AR 1507, 14614, 15571, 18242 AZ 2357, 6559, 8735, 9179, 9662, 10170, 13016, 13020, 14400, 14410, 14488, 14528, 14970, 14971, 16542, 16543 CA 196, 418, 420, 825, 1531, 1592, 1802, 2249, 2497, 2498, 3189, 3320, 3555, 3570, 3574, 3577, 3739, 4078, 4081, 4083, 4351, 4638, 4937, 4948, 5227, 5277, 5321, 6134, 6135, 6498, 7296, 7334, 7348, 7419, 7575, 8506, 8507, 8511, 8513, 8514, 8515, 8516, 8517, 8518, 8519, 8522, 8523, 8589, 8629, 8685, 8865, 8866, 9274, 9276, 9330, 9332, 9338, 9666, 10043, 10102, 10125, 10138, 10147, 10166, 10410, 10411, 10845, 12024, 12245, 12573, 12581, 12672, 12735, 13206, 13620, 13703, 13942, 14075, 14223, 14251, 14295, 14308, 14309, 14339, 14345, 14367, 14384, 14414, 14425, 14473, 14478, 14505, 14529, 14616, 14666, 14678, 14682, 14733, 14746, 14754, 14774, 14811, 14816, 14898, 15051, 15087, 15162, 16323, 16425, 18354, 18363, 18417, 18425, 19734, 19737, 20265, 20383 CO 1792, 2028, 3566, 4777, 9461, 10028, 10154, 10865, 12758, 12918, 13233, 13278, 14064, 14237, 14372, 14476, 14501, 15927 CT 1400, 2115, 4208, 4582, 6265, 6748, 6757, 6934, 7420, 8951, 9590, 10361, 10395, 10813, 11437, 11537, 11769, 12101, 12742, 14008, 14302, 14386, 14513, 14622, 15082, 15635, 18518, 19821, 20083 DC 3579, 3992, 4901, 6378, 6710, 11264, 13445, 15151, 20011 DE 1869, 8642, 9990, 9991, 10396, 13943, 14300 FL 95, 1500, 1504, 1598, 1790, 1928, 3391, 4934, 5826, 5874, 6556, 6579, 6842, 7185, 7330, 7750, 8297, 8900, 8906, 9584, 10139, 10201, 10261, 10818, 11948, 12571, 13136, 14198, 14243, 14296, 14405, 14480, 14515, 14829, 16000, 18513, 18637, 19321, 20191, 20227, 20499, 20500, 20649 GA 940, 3009, 3365, 3975, 4668, 5923, 6381, 6864, 9284, 9987, 12049, 13039, 14406, 14409, 15428, 15862, 18636 GU 6787 HI 7220, 8520, 8578, 14297, 15824, 20425 IA 381, 2195, 2377, 4634, 5250, 8227, 8229, 10129, 10148, 10153, 12608, 14390, 14475, 14490 ID 1841, 5145, 10742, 14225, 14249, 14491, 20201 IL 345, 2207, 3050, 3339, 3519, 3588, 4031, 4128, 4266, 4267, 4390, 4691, 5231, 5264, 5309, 5494, 5507, 5508, 6075, 6136, 6229, 6557, 6583, 6616, 6651, 7198, 7230, 7344, 7351, 7534, 7667, 7677, 7850, 8312, 8845, 8893, 8952, 9423, 9457, 9505, 9658, 10030, 10045, 10127, 10149, 10188, 10189, 10816, 12045, 12072, 12109, 12176, 12621, 12714, 12780, 12951, 13401, 13719, 13853, 13907, 13948, 14004, 14066, 14148, 14234, 14238, 14241, 14242, 14244, 14286, 14287, 14306, 14323, 14324, 14337, 14382, 14385, 14504, 14506, 14514, 15170, 15412, 15917, 15920, 16727, 16779, 19833, 20143, 20198, 20199, 20324 IN 1436, 3173, 3772, 4080, 4681, 7856, 8441, 9458, 9683, 10031, 10185, 10280, 12759, 14254, 14279,

14336, 14388, 14415, 14416, 14492, 14531, 14618, 20492, 20538 KS 1781, 13455, 14312, 15095, 15816, 16367, 18733, 20172 KY 391, 1503, 6552, 7533, 7536, 8395, 9403, 12624, 13792, 14236, 14262, 14282, 14377, 15835, 18756 LA 4263, 6719, 7426, 9285, 9391, 10150, 12242, 12611, 12616, 13714, 14291, 14929, 15460, 16434, 17934 MA 1610, 1750, 1769, 1803, 1977, 1978, 2201, 2602, 3087, 4494, 5614, 6058, 6072, 6516, 7018, 7352, 8879, 8909, 9006, 9010, 9409, 9572, 9703, 9791, 9794, 9989, 10135, 10759, 10798, 10993, 11465, 11470, 11789, 14231, 14290, 14338, 14399, 14486, 14610, 14632, 15090, 15365, 15550, 15840, 16382, 16654, 19963, 20377, 20591 MD 1096, 1448, 1953, 3571, 6108, 6703, 6899, 7347, 7467, 8697, 9097, 9749, 10029, 10039, 10155, 13361, 14201, 14221, 14378, 15185, 16658, 19990, 19998 ME 1071, 1561, 2447, 3119, 3345, 5152, 6096, 7437, 8622, 9555, 10134, 10348, 11993, 13794, 14229, 14534, 15496, 19943, 20094, 20772 MI 1580, 1594, 1625, 1811, 1871, 1899, 1954, 1970, 2025, 2209, 2385, 2422, 3578, 4352, 4810, 4811, 4813, 4832, 5849, 5951, 5963, 6249, 6825, 6910, 6911, 7326, 7583, 7594, 7853, 8947, 9708, 9868, 9943, 10046, 10131, 10132, 10192, 10289, 10302, 10370, 10801, 10802, 11931, 11939, 12201, 12214, 12835, 13210, 13446, 13951, 14217, 14327, 14328, 14373, 14389, 14418, 14430, 14503, 14519, 14830, 15186, 15572, 20655 MN 15, 3572, 4970, 5575, 5576, 6476, 6539, 7138, 9859, 10183, 10374, 10399, 11936, 12747, 13892, 13947, 13984, 14269, 14303, 14318, 14343, 14402, 14477, 14520, 14568, 17972, 20372 MO 1506, 3589, 4397, 4670, 4680, 7090, 7726, 8398, 9462, 10005, 10092, 10533, 10539, 11935, 13842, 14307, 14342, 14344, 14365, 14366, 14460, 14466, 14485, 14512, 16513, 20073 MS 5989, 7228, 11937, 12761, 14273, 15193, 19824 MT 4034, 8533, 14322, 14554, 15138, 20278 NC 195, 3025, 4131, 5046, 5991, 12828, 13319, 13857, 15449, 19937, 20468 ND 4528, 10140, 14411, 14479, 16515, 16716 NE 1729, 2297, 7713, 9178, 11374, 14275 NH 864, 2250, 3149, 3486, 5303, 10599, 10996, 12755, 19738 NJ 1252, 1253, 1398, 1735, 3594, 3602, 3633, 4035, 4275, 5123, 5299, 5356, 6196, 6822, 6823, 6861, 7354, 7418, 7568, 8369, 8372, 8628, 8632, 8633, 9485, 9993, 10037, 10042, 10110, 10615, 10757, 10831, 10844, 11741, 12615, 12632, 12776, 13705, 13717, 13957, 14055, 14247, 14268, 14277, 14304, 14413, 14521, 14545, 14586, 15364, 15430, 16627, 16655, 16719, 19732, 19980, 20194 NM 6236, 6784, 10172, 13321, 14387, 14611, 16366 NV 3107, 7535, 14535, 18836, 20075 NY 230, 1069, 1277, 1557, 1599, 1696, 1770, 1771, 1962, 2213, 2215, 2217, 2236, 2337, 2435, 2588, 3019, 3150, 3340, 3370, 3477, 3568, 4076, 4077, 4079, 4133, 4442, 4503, 4738, 5306, 5387, 5388, 5419, 5617, 5692, 5932, 6090, 6356, 6553, 6906, 7058, 7142, 7195, 7415, 7423, 7574, 7597, 8039, 8040, 8322, 8620, 8726, 8729, 8846, 9007, 9066, 9183, 9275, 9287, 9289, 9291, 9463, 9547, 9838, 10048, 10128, 10136, 10145, 10180, 10203, 10204, 10616, 10662, 10820, 10822, 11006, 11547, 11560, 11575, 11727, 11728, 11933, 11950, 12018, 12172, 12246, 12618, 12623, 12749, 12825, 13226, 13978, 14056, 14264, 14292, 14298, 14325, 14326, 14347, 14375, 14401, 14407, 14412, 14417, 14484, 14526, 14527, 14584, 14620, 14623, 14659, 14832, 14977, 15202, 15432, 15524, 15744, 15745, 15763, 16401, 16714, 16715, 19786, 20230, 20384, 20505, 20570, 20761 OH 170, 172, 1304, 1526, 1787, 1791, 2106, 3567, 3576, 3586, 4082, 4935, 4936, 5317, 5574, 5998, 6549, 6554, 6647, 6650, 7357, 8397, 8509, 8695, 8770, 8894, 8911, 8976, 9149, 9167, 9301, 9460, 9639, 9684, 10133, 10137, 10152, 10158, 10191, 10193, 10272, 10363, 10799, 10817, 12335, 12760, 13447, 13944, 13949, 14224, 14239, 14280, 14283, 14313, 14333, 14383, 14589, 14597, 14603, 14615, 15241, 16364, 16389, 16529, 18476, 18638, 19979, 20292 OK 1510, 3580, 3581, 7216, 10130, 11852, 13320, 14235, 14293, 14329, 14522, 16574 OR 225, 5192, 5320, 6550, 6555, 7325, 8521, 8525, 13451, 14197, 14613, 14633, 16536, 20439 PA 22, 367, 384, 386, 427, 2056, 2079, 2306, 2415, 3057, 3220, 3489, 3494, 3582, 3583, 4086, 4132, 4450, 4739, 4923, 5193, 5274, 5389, 5537, 5836, 5956, 5957, 5958, 6082, 6098, 6166, 6277, 6438, 6551, 6558, 6562, 6611, 6646, 6816, 6875, 6893, 6924, 7070, 8919, 8945, 8971, 9060, 9087, 9533, 9534, 9927, 9969, 9988, 10032, 10126, 10141, 10142, 10143, 10151, 10181, 10349, 10640, 10661, 10685, 10814, 10843, 11358, 11394, 11934, 12334, 12709, 12731, 12757, 12847, 12848, 13155, 13195, 13276, 13277, 13322, 13567, 13746, 13749, 14090, 14202, 14204, 14222, 14260, 14374, 14380, 14481, 14483, 14493, 14608, 15066, 15083, 15120, 15355, 15429, 15604, 16019, 16706, 19221, 20010, 20339, 20433, 20451, 20457, 20773 PR 13513 RI 2057, 8641, 10041, 10501, 11776, 13870, 14368, 14379, 20232, 20449 SC 1509, 6743, 9681, 13793, 13906, 15573 SD 1501, 2224, 9517, 9928, 13713, 14199, 14489, 14523, 15197 TN 1502, 1513, 1905, 5125, 5421, 6012, 7341, 8310, 9017, 10218, 14370, 14424, 14533, 19369 TX 1516, 3587, 4552, 5009, 6561, 6921, 7134, 7196, 7579, 8689, 9992, 10033, 10034, 10044, 10182, 10184, 10186, 11955, 11967, 13317, 14278, 14371, 14474, 14502, 14559, 14675, 14818, 14964, 15148, 15240, 15245, 15589, 16013, 16229, 19374, 19417, 19418, 19421 UT 7345, 8842, 9923, 14250, 14497, 19716 VA 343, 1041, 3573, 3893, 4671, 5563, 7073, 9474, 9769, 10035, 10038, 12225, 13253, 13273, 13908, 13954, 13963, 14005, 14516, 15038, 15525, 19506, 19858, 20015, 20474 VT 377, 2087, 3377, 6471, 11917, 11989, 12071, 13232, 14177, 15546, 15605 WA 3380, 3575, 5341, 5686, 6548, 6929, 7077, 12051, 12673, 13450, 14205, 14284, 14341, 14362, 14376, 14381, 14581, 15923, 19530, 19733, 19756 WI

Humanities: (continued)
19576, 19600 *Canada:* **AB** 18195 **BC** 20288 **MB** 10087, 18789, 18793 **ON** 2803, 2804, 2810, 8979, 14135, 14428, 18612, 19167, 19459, 19463, 19543 **PQ** 3194, 3195, 4121, 7878 *Intl:* **ALG** 348 **CHL** 3167 **COL** 17978, 17983 **DEN** 4770 **ENG** 6665 **FIN** 18635 **FRA** 1833 **HUN** 7550 **IDN** 7830 **ISR** 18613 **ITA** 8280 **JPN** 8838 **MEX** 17990 **NLD** 11402 **NOR** 12113, 19160 **POL** 13161, 13168 **SEN** 15036 **SGP** 11319 **SRI** 15626 **TTO** 19551

Hume, David: **TX** 15503 *Canada:* **PQ** 9895

Hummel, Johann Nepomuk: *Intl:* **AUT** 821

Humor See: Wit and humor

Humphrey, Hubert Horatio, Jr.: **MN** 10466

Hungarian Americans: **IN** 8799

Hungarian language and literature: **MD** 621 *Intl:* **HUN** 7547, 7548

Hungary: **DC** 9113 **IN** 8799 **NY** 622 *Intl:* **BRZ** 16464 **HUN** 7543

Hungary—History: *Intl:* **HUN** 2321, 5664, 7546

Hunger: **CA** 20634 **DC** 2104, 12715 **NY** 7559, 9744

Hunt, Leigh: **NY** 11599

Hunt, Richard Morris: **DC** 629

Hunter, John: *Intl:* **ENG** 14114

Hunting See: Fish and game

Hurricanes: **FL** 17656

Hurston, Zora Neale: **FL** 18586

Huston, John: **CA** 35

Hutterite Brethren (See also Anabaptists; Mennonites): **IN** 10091 **OH** 1917

Huxley, Aldous: **CA** 18379, 18428 **CO** 18507 **IN** 1438 **MI** 4828 **NH** 4616 **NY** 15707 **TX** 18643 *Canada:* **ON** 19460

Hydraulic engineering (See also Hydraulics): **CA** 2272, 2488, 7640 **CO** 3974 **MD** 2 **MS** 16947 **OR** 3406 **TX** 3110, 16583 *Canada:* **MB** 9616 **ON** 56, 2822 *Intl:* **CHN** 7988, 20651 **JPN** 5196 **NLD** 20089

Hydraulics (See also Hydraulic engineering): **AZ** 17197 **CA** 2536, 7604, 16955 **CO** 3969 **IA** 18721 **IL** 6716, 16954 **MA** 18834 **MI** 17648 **MN** 4952, 18927 **MS** 16968, 16970 **NM** 9044 **PA** 7435, 9058 **UT** 19717 **VA** 16942 **WA** 16960 *Canada:* **ON** 2883, 6833 **PQ** 7601 *Intl:* **AMA** 1046 **BUL** 19904 **CHN** 7988 **CZE** 4513 **PRT** 13260

Hydrobiology See: Aquatic biology

Hydrodynamics (See also Mixing): **CA** 2482 **MA** 9798 **MD** 1463 **VA** 4343 *Canada:* **NF** 2823

Hydrography: **CA** 2545 **MD** 17175 **TN** 19364 *Canada:* **BC** 7960 **PQ** 2733 *Intl:* **CHN** 7130, 12928 **GER** 2360

Hydrology (See also Water-supply): **AK** 17100 **AL** 6363 **AZ** 993, 6572, 15041, 18229 **CA** 1637, 2514, 12507, 14687, 16944, 16955 **CO** 3969, 18498 **FL** 5894, 5907, 14346 **GA** 6403 **IL** 7708 **IN** 17542 **KY** 18749 **MA** 16949 **MD** 17650 **MI** 17648 **MN** 1537, 16958, 18927, 18945 **MO** 17796, 18957 **MS** 10519 **NH** 7605, 16935 **NJ** 20586 **NM** 11521, 17549 **NV** 17122, 17235 **NY** 5060, 17547 **OH** 11189, 12286 **OK** 19128 **PA** 16138 **TX** 10366, 17538 **UT** 19717 **WA** 4577 **WV** 16943 *Canada:* **AB** 55, 2742 **BC** 2743 **ON** 6256, 13402, 14187 **PQ** 10609 **SK** 2834, 14866 *Intl:* **CZE** 4513 **FRA** 5206 **ICE** 7636 **NLD** 11403, 20089 **SWI** 20625

Hygiene, Industrial See: Industrial hygiene

Hymns (See also Gospel music): **CA** 3753, 6535, 14924, 16729, 18379 **CO** 3635, 7666 **GA** 5334, 20192 **IA** 18555 **IL** 1308, 4120, 9173, 20369 **IN**

6581, 10091 **KS** 1784 **KY** 15462 **MA** 540, 2018 **MN** 1780, 9442 **MO** 4117, 9448, 18977 **NC** 10722 **NJ** 5002, 13367, 20327 **NY** 16667 **OH** 10821, 16514, 20546 **OR** 12043 **PA** 8921, 9035, 9465, 10719, 12978, 13088, 13318, 20115 **SC** 9467, 20548 **TN** 19686 **TX** 7606, 15503, 15538 *Canada:* **NS** 1264 **ON** 19463 *Intl:* **AUS** 15692

Hypertension: **IL** 14987

Hypnotism (See also Mesmerism; Psychoanalysis): **AZ** 1541, 5412 **CA** 623, 7525 **IL** 743 **KS** 20412 **MN** 1427 **NY** 7972 **PR** 13512 **TN** 19776 *Canada:* **PQ** 2943

Ibsen, Henrik: **OH** 10270

Ice and snow: **CO** 20614 **NH** 16935 **WY** 19662 *Canada:* **AB** 965 **NF** 2823 **ON** 2821 *Intl:* **SWI** 15940

Iceland: **CA** 12712 **DC** 9113 **MN** 15530 **NY** 4310 *Canada:* **MB** 18789 *Intl:* **ICE** 16311 **SWE** 15911

Ichthyology See: Fish and fisheries

Iconography See: Christian art and symbolism

Idaho: **ID** 314, 1956, 7648, 7649, 7650, 8048, 8958, 9085, 10915, 12640, 18656, 19688 **WA** 11036

Illinois: **IL** 2365, 3421, 3422, 3522, 3533, 3550, 4595, 4690, 4793, 5308, 5506, 6230, 6506, 7197, 7285, 7697, 7698, 7703, 8251, 8541, 8618, 8890, 9182, 9420, 9519, 9688, 9945, 10795, 11031, 11752, 11995, 12001, 12079, 12179, 12180, 12259, 12746, 12934, 14791, 15436, 15492, 18678, 19763, 20099, 20258, 20437, 20459 **OH** 16395

Illiteracy See: Literacy

Illumination of books and manuscripts (See also Paleography): **IN** 13541 **MD** 19961 **MI** 10336 **NJ** 13376 **NY** 6165, 10738, 11627, 11632 **PA** 6122, 19214 *Canada:* **ON** 19454 *Intl:* **ENG** 18440 **NLD** 18206 **SAF** 15386

Illustration of books: **CA** 6456, 18364 **CT** 20700, 20735 **DC** 4907 **IL** 1082 **IN** 7772 **MA** 20153 **MD** 13300 **ME** 5604 **MI** 4828 **MN** 18900 **NC** 19087 **NJ** 11744, 11750 **NY** 315, 7316, 10211 **PA** 2304, 6111, 14068 **RI** 13454 **TX** 16200 **VT** 19482 **WI** 10424, 19590 *Canada:* **ON** 1077, 16418, 19449

Illustration, Medical See: Medical illustration

Immigration See: Emigration and immigration

Immortalism: **CA** 7861

Immunology: **CA** 1588, 1752, 3739, 4929, 14973, 15254, 15651, 17296 **CO** 11221 **DC** 16992 **IN** 7795 **LA** 16566, 17934 **MA** 5990 **MD** 1847 **ME** 6036, 8309 **MO** 1934 **MT** 17628 **NE** 18993 **NJ** 10121, 16624 **NY** 8478, 11566, 11664, 15967, 16527, 17191, 20751 **PA** 10122, 20540 **TX** 19930 **VA** 680 *Canada:* **ON** 2631, 4174, 19457 **PQ** 2815, 7864, 7865, 9898, 14780 *Intl:* **ALG** 12785 **AUS** 1344 **BRZ** 2406 **CHL** 3596 **FRA** 12784 **GER** 11825 **KEN** 8141 **POL** 13172 **ROM** 14048

Impressionism (Art): **TN** 4928

Income maintenance programs (See also Insurance, Unemployment; Social security): **DC** 17240, 17939 **NY** 11561 *Canada:* **NS** 12135 **ON** 2694

Incunabula (See also Printing—History): **CA** 7572, 14711, 18303, 19290 **CT** 14601, 16504 **DC** 9135 **IA** 9311 **MA** 6980, 20446 **MD** 19961 **MI** 18860, 18890, 20275 **MN** 3908 **NC** 19075 **NJ** 11750 **NY** 8405 **OH** 12221 **PA** 2304, 3902, 14068, 14256, 14604, 19225 **RI** 2282 **TX** 16200 *Canada:* **NS** 18760 **PQ** 13580 **SK** 10870 *Intl:* **AUT** 1354 **BEL** 1671 **DEN** 4770 **ENG** 18441 **FRA** 1833 **GER** 1597, 15794 **NLD** 11402 **SPA** 15557 **SWE** 15911

Indexing: **OH** 8964

India: **CA** 12657, 18344 **CT** 20722 **DC** 5323 **IL** 18460 **MN** 18891 **NY** 4237, 11626 **OH** 3823 **TX** 19406 **WI** 19608 *Canada:* **ON** 14130 *Intl:* **ENG** 6665 **IND** 1808, 6804, 7744, 15997 **ITA** 12567

Information science (continued)
12151 **ON** 2803, 2806, 8097, 19445, 19564 **PQ** 9903, 18076 *Intl:* **AUS** 1326 **BRZ** 2095 **DEN** 14133 **FRA** 11133 **GER** 6431, 18049 **GRC** 5488 **HUN** 7557, 7932 **IRN** 8242, 8243 **IRQ** 933 **JPN** 8840 **NLD** 11414 **NOR** 18138 **POL** 7975, 13163 **PRT** 13262 **ROM** 14049 **SAU** 7966 **TTO** 3049 **TUN** 16578 **TUR** 16581 **URY** 19696

Information services (See also Data libraries; Documentation; Information storage and retrieval systems; Research): **CA** 4694, 6536, 7845 **DC** 6349 **NC** 5036 *Intl:* **BWA** 2027 **GER** 1564 **JPN** 5392 **KOR** 5293 **POL** 7975

Information storage and retrieval systems (See also Computers; Management information systems; Programming (Electronic computers)): **CA** 1641, 14015, 16022, 18333, 18387, 20680 **CO** 3172, 18509 **CT** 6255, 17130 **MA** 9100, 9217 **MD** 17625 **MI** 18867 **MN** 7375, 16344 **MO** 4675 **NJ** 3881 **NY** 9539, 13629 **OH** 6283 **PA** 4737, 20770 **VA** 3937, 17165 *Canada:* **BC** 2178 **ON** 14137 *Intl:* **BEL** 12126 **FIN** 7126, 16030 **FRA** 6071 **GER** 6431

Infrared technology: **CA** 7511 **MA** 104, 4501, 9310 **MI** 5381, 5382 **OH** 12303

Ink: **IL** 20608 **MI** 1551 *Intl:* **DEN** 14892

Inorganic chemistry See: Chemistry, Inorganic

Insane, Criminal and dangerous (See also Forensic psychiatry): **CA** 1223

Inscriptions (See also Cuneiform inscriptions): **OH** 18473 **TX** 19386 *Intl:* **CHN** 10965 **GER** 6420, 14046 **ISR** 4388, 8268 **TUR** 2188

Inscriptions, Runic: **NY** 4310

Insect pests—Biological control: **CA** 18318 **GA** 17196 *Intl:* **CHN** 38 **TWN** 15988

Insects (See also Beetles; Butterflies): **AK** 17519 **AZ** 994 **CA** 2470, 7643, 11341, 14712, 14779, 17184, 18318, 18403 **CO** 17522 **CT** 4176 **DC** 15276, 15280, 15281, 17222 **FL** 939, 5887, 5904, 7860, 18563, 18564, 18571, 18581, 18589 **GA** 6407, 17196 **HI** 1865, 7053 **ID** 17192, 18654 **IL** 14782, 18661, 18679 **IN** 13544, 19116 **KY** 18743 **MA** 18827, 18829 **MD** 5372, 16989, 17203 **MI** 10336, 10341, 18855, 18877 **MN** 18924, 18944 **MT** 17628 **NC** 11905, 13886 **NE** 18994 **NH** 19029 **NJ** 555 **NY** 687, 4308, 4325, 5969, 15722, 16316 **OH** 3814, 9238, 10267, 12295 **OK** 12371 **PA** 3085, 12905 **SD** 15424 **VA** 6881, 11251 **WA** 19526, 20048 **WV** 20208 *Canada:* **AB** 2742 **BC** 2662, 2664, 2743, 18283 **MB** 2666, 18783 **NF** 2741 **NS** 2653 **ON** 2636, 2643, 2738, 13158 **PE** 2649 **PQ** 2658, 2739, 9906, 13596 **SK** 2661 *Intl:* **AUS** 1322, 18145, 18146, 20233 **AUT** 12224 **BRZ** 2096 **CHN** 38, 1655 **ENG** 6681, 11340 **GER** 11825 **IND** 7747, 15996 **ITA** 18013 **KEN** 8071 **MUS** 9852 **NZL** 5011, 11737 **PAK** 12693 **TZA** 16006

Insects as carriers of disease: **CA** 2528 **GA** 17125 **MD** 5372, 16976 **NC** 11890 **TX** 17186

Instructional materials See: Teaching—Aids and devices

Instrumental music (See also Band music; Chamber music; Orchestral music; Piano music; specific instruments, e.g. Clarinet music): **CA** 18335 **DC** 17602 **IL** 18686 **ME** 1405 **MI** 10331 **MN** 3453, 18925 **MO** 14439 **PA** 1428, 4491, 15053, 19212, 20187 **SD** 15146 **TX** 1604 *Canada:* **BC** 19827 **PQ** 2892

Instrumentation See: Scientific apparatus and instruments

Insulation (Heat): **PA** 3397, 5003

Insurance: **AL** 18160 **AZ** 16607 **CA** 5600, 5724, 7834, 8246 **CO** 18491, 18509 **CT** 114, 10951, 13021, 16467, 18517 **DC** 646, 7479 **GA** 5394 **IA** 3393 **IL** 410, 3847, 7169, 8611, 11063, 15678 **IN** 767, 781, 7779, 7819, 9186, 11070 **KS** 5344, 15010 **LA** 4835 **MA** 1995, 4052, 9100, 9101, 9102, 9824, 15699, 15864 **MD** 5677 **MI** 4483, 4817, 5852 **MN** 14557, 18896, 20262 **MO** 1909, 8011, 8548, 11065 **NE** 10940, 12408 **NJ** 7211, 11745, 13459, 13460 **NY** 649, 856, 2242, 2329, 10207, 11608, 11623, 13422, 13813, 16024, 16436, 19720 **OH** 3818, 11334, 13483, 20295 **OR** 15637 **PA** 531, 634, 3075, 3697, 3930, 4398, 6110, 9099, 10026, 10935, 12830, 19186, 20386 **RI** 382, 10220 **TX** 1142, 16781 **VA** 13408 **VT** 11230 **WA** 14210, 19515 **WI** 574, 8112, 10245, 19626, 20105, 20531

Canada: **AB** 258, 8014 **BC** 8010 **ON** 2833, 2887, 3718, 4139, 8009, 12459, 13772, 15015 **PQ** 7832, 8847, 13588, 15348, 16443

Insurance, Fire: **MA** 8015, 11472 **NY** 3897 *Canada:* **PQ** 18119

Insurance, Health (See also Health maintenance organizations (HMO); Medicare): **CA** 2495 **CT** 114, 115, 3695 **DC** 6766, 8043, 17939 **FL** 1908 **IL** 1489, 1907 **MA** 6885, 8015 **MD** 17940 **ME** 19675 **MN** 12170 **NC** 1910 **NE** 20574 **NY** 3897, 5340, 7359, 10938 **OH** 4089 **PA** 7731 **WI** 143 **WV** 20224 *Canada:* **MB** 6702 **ON** 4447, 10100 **PQ** 4338, 13615

Insurance law: **AZ** 9081, 12244 **CA** 64, 10173, 16457 **CO** 16688 **CT** 3696 **DC** 13326, 15894 **FL** 5891 **GA** 4138 **IL** 3548, 4703, 8611, 9312, 15369 **MA** 9825 **MI** 10398, 13148 **MO** 11065 **NY** 7517, 9039 **WI** 12075 *Canada:* **BC** 5667 **MB** 6702 **ON** 4448, 7718, 8009, 16327 **PQ** 4798, 13973

Insurance, Life: **CT** 3695, 4183, 9153 **DC** 551 **GA** 4138, 9154 **IL** 10406 **MA** 6885, 8015, 11463 **ME** 19675 **MN** 9446, 12170 **NE** 20574 **NY** 3897, 7359, 10938, 10939 **PA** 532 **TX** 13457 **WI** 143, 12073, 15039 *Canada:* **MB** 6702 **ON** 4447, 7718, 9647, 10100, 10937, 11860, 15865

Insurance—Mathematics: **CA** 4748, 16438 **CT** 16467 **GA** 4138 **IL** 7169, 15307 **MA** 15699 **MI** 18873 **MN** 12170 **NE** 11293 **NJ** 13460 **NY** 3897 **PA** 634 **WI** 143 *Canada:* **ON** 4139, 7718, 10116, 15865 **PQ** 10115, 16443

Insurance, Property and casualty: **IL** 15073, 20850 **MA** 8015 **NJ** 4453 **NY** 3092, 3897, 8012 **WI** 15039

Insurance, Social See: Social security

Insurance, Unemployment: **CA** 2542 **IL** 7688 **MI** 10299 **NJ** 11510 **NY** 3897, 8143, 11652 *Canada:* **PQ** 2696

Integrated circuits: **MN** 7374 *Intl:* **CHN** 29

Intellectual property (See also Fair use (Copyright); Industrial property): **IL** 9722, 20498 **MD** 19796 **MI** 5079 **MO** 15140 **NY** 4843, 12834 **OH** 6184 **PA** 4854 **TX** 1411, 8446 **WI** 5942 *Canada:* **ON** 2676, 5017 *Intl:* **GER** 18038 **SWI** 20621

Intelligence service (See also Espionage): **DC** 1133, 6379, 17166 **VA** 1762

Intelligence tests: **NY** 8189

Intensive care See: Critical care medicine

Intercultural communication: **OR** 8036 *Intl:* **TUN** 9025

Intergovernmental relations: **AL** 183 **DC** 97, 11226, 17241 **KY** 4371 **NY** 11667 **OR** 19147 **PA** 12850 **WI** 10425 *Canada:* **AB** 276

Interior decoration: **AR** 18233 **AZ** 1009 **CA** 33, 1800, 5606, 5608, 7122, 12203, 14702, 16601, 20569 **CT** 12688 **DC** 4902, 15215 **FL** 13934, 15476, 18559 **IL** 12947, 18676 **KS** 8575 **KY** 18750 **LA** 9382 **MA** 1975 **MI** 8616, 10400 **MN** 18892 **MO** 7120 **NC** 6219 **NY** 4127, 5611, 7438, 11583, 11624, 15214 **OH** 18468 **OK** 12367, 19121 **OR** 1559, 10846 **PA** 3078, 6109 **TX** 1084, 1582, 6021, 14670 **WI** 10424, 10426, 12689 *Canada:* **MB** 18785 *Intl:* **ENG** 8731 **IRL** 18485 **RUS** 3385 **SAF** 10276

Internal medicine (See also Endocrinology; Gastroenterology): **CA** 9257 **CO** 3943, 14501 **DC** 16901, 16992 **FL** 17314, 17317 **GA** 17038 **IN** 3173 **KS** 8574, 17335 **MD** 8431 **MT** 17364 **NC** 20460 **NJ** 1753, 5356 **NY** 15763 **OH** 6240 **PA** 9988, 10151 **TN** 5421, 11001 *Intl:* **FIJ** 5689

Internal revenue law: **DC** 17561 **IL** 3865

International banking See: Banks and banking, International

International business enterprises (See also Investments, Foreign): **AL** 18160 **CA** 199, 1478, 12678, 14908, 15652, 19324, 20569 **DC** 7479, 8119, 12634 **LA** 16555 **MI** 18870 **NY** 4027, 9646, 11732, 16772 **PA** 12899, 19186 **TX** 326, 15505 **WA** 19515 **WI** 19626 *Canada:* **ON** 2927, 4140, 8216, 19563 **PQ** 9900 *Intl:* **AUT** 7937

International cooperation: **CA** 19348 **DC** 3222 **NY** 16775 *Canada:* **ON** 8097 *Intl:* **RUS** 15676

Italy—History: CA 14742, 18370 **IL** 18689 **MI** 5475, 10336 *Canada:* **PQ** 8278 *Intl:* **ITA** 1821, 8131, 13098

Ives, Charles Edward: CT 20717 **SC** 4259

Ivy: OH 651

Jackson, Andrew: TN 16162

Jackson, Helen Hunt: CO 3940

Jackson, Thomas Jonathan "Stonewall": VA 7245

Jacobites: CT 8316 *Intl:* **SCT** 14953

Jamaica: FL 18846 *Intl:* **JAM** 8321

James, Henry: CA 14718 **NY** 2335, 19278 **TX** 16200 **VA** 19510 *Canada:* **ON** 9954

James, Jesse: MO 8302 **TN** 16179

Jansen, Cornelis: DC 3155

Japan: AZ 18227 **CA** 15650, 18316, 18397, 18416 **CT** 20709 **DC** 8339, 9109, 9124 **FL** 10741 **IL** 18689 **KS** 18726 **KY** 8678 **MA** 6974, 6978, 6989, 18827 **MD** 18814, 18817 **MI** 18854 **MN** 5594, 18905 **NE** 4427 **NH** 4612 **NJ** 13374, 14163 **NY** 4006, 4334, 7208, 8341, 11626, 14352 **OH** 12312 **PA** 19210 **TX** 10917, 19388 **UT** 20799 *Canada:* **AB** 4240 **BC** 18255 **ON** 14130 *Intl:* **GER** 15794 **JPN** 8152, 8334, 8338, 8838, 11145, 13683 **KOR** 1124, 8839

Japan—History: IL 18451 **NJ** 14163 **NY** 19274 **OH** 12312 **VA** 9489 **WI** 19596 *Intl:* **ITA** 12567 **NLD** 13928

Japanese Americans: CA 2572, 4379, 8342, 18379

Japanese language and literature: AK 834 **AZ** 18227 **CA** 6156, 7487, 10670, 12204 **CO** 18495 **CT** 20709 **HI** 18617 **IL** 18451 **KS** 18726 **MD** 18814 **MN** 5594, 18905 **MO** 8544 **NJ** 14163 **NY** 8341, 19274 **PA** 19180 **WA** 19522 **WI** 19596 *Canada:* **BC** 18255 **ON** 19439 *Intl:* **CHN** 1656 **ITA** 12567 **JPN** 8336 **NLD** 13928

Jarrell, Randall: NC 19088

Javits, Jacob Koppel: NY 15757

Jay family: NY 11681

Jazz music (See also Gospel music): AR 1022 **CA** 2567 **CT** 4179, 16504 **FL** 18850 **IL** 11912, 18455 **IN** 7776 **LA** 9384, 16567 **MA** 1743, 3894 **MI** 8045, 10321 **NJ** 6488, 13379, 14166 **NY** 9294, 11605, 11638, 15740 **PA** 3078, 6119, 9643, 20187 **TN** 16172 **TX** 7462 **VA** 16915 **WI** 19635 **WV** 20220 *Canada:* **ON** 20793 *Intl:* **AUS** 15695

Jean Baptiste de la Salle: CA 14511

Jeffers, Robinson: CA 2568, 12232, 18428, 19290

Jefferson, Thomas: DC 9135 **MO** 10536, 10537, 17736 **PA** 16487 **VA** 3919, 8358, 19510

Jennings, Elizabeth: DC 6379

Jensen, Jens Arnold Diederich: CT 20703

Jesuits: CA 2501, 14808 **DC** 3161, 6379, 20581 **IL** 9420 **MA** 20343 **MI** 3928 **MO** 14464 **NY** 5971, 9020 **WA** 15329 **WI** 9709, 9712 *Canada:* **ON** 7587, 19358 **PQ** 4095, 4096 **SK** 2627

Jewelry (See also Gems): CA 6281 **ME** 13245 **NY** 2358 **OK** 12374 *Canada:* **AB** 257

Jewish art and symbolism: AZ 16089 **CA** 9537 **IL** 11947 **MI** 16112 **MO** 2205 **NJ** 10756 **NY** 11815, 12741, 16083, 16088, 16093, 20757 *Canada:* **ON** 139 **PQ** 1920

Jewish law: DC 9126 **NY** 16433 **PA** 4854 *Canada:* **PQ** 1920 *Intl:* **ISR** 5824, 14915, 18613

Jewish literature (See also Talmud): AL 16103 **AZ** 16089, 16099 **CA** 2069, 2368, 2369, 2547, 5117, 7097, 19339, 20463 **CO** 7093, 18548 **FL** 3321, 16081, 16092, 16100, 16108, 16115, 16116, 18573 **IL** 1767, 4160, 5319, 7094, 11811, 11954, 15584, 16117, 16489, 18461 **IN** 4151 **MA** 655, 7092, 16086, 16109, 20280 **ME** 1560 **MI** 4148, 4166, 8384, 10371, 16084, 16112 **MN** 1765, 8382, 16110 **MO** 2205, 16113 **NC** 6041 **NE** 8391 **NJ** 1768, 10756, 16082, 16091 **NY** 1404, 2068, 4157, 7098, 8378, 8405, 9030, 11611, 11815, 13143, 13641, 16083, 16087, 16090, 16093, 16095, 16121, 20537, 20622, 20750, 20755, 20756, 20757 **OH** 1921, 3801, 3823, 5571, 7099, 8500, 15844, 16078, 16118, 20536 **PA** 164, 878, 887, 1764, 4159, 4164, 4737, 6113, 6657, 6895, 9548, 13754, 13777, 14068, 16079 **RI** 16085, 16098 **TN** 8380, 20190 **TX** 3629, 15503, 16097, 16102, 19414 **WA** 16106 **WV** 911 *Canada:* **BC** 19761 **ON** 139, 1775, 2813, 8381, 8970 **PQ** 8403, 9895 *Intl:* **DEN** 4770 **ISR** 8262, 14915, 18613 **LBN** 7961 **WAL** 14272

Jewish music See: Music, Jewish

Jews (See also Hasidism): MA 11332 **MD** 1451, 8383, 8393 **NY** 652, 653, 656, 657, 11814, 20758, 20759 **PA** 878, 3322, 12988 *Canada:* **PQ** 8403 *Intl:* **ISR** 7102, 8265

Jews, Canadian: *Canada:* **MB** 2948 **ON** 2803, 2947 **PQ** 2949, 8403

Jews—Education: CA 2368 **FL** 3321, 16100 **MA** 7092 **MI** 10371 **NY** 1924, 11153 **PA** 164, 3322, 6657 *Canada:* **BC** 19761

Jews, German: NY 1404, 20759 *Intl:* **GER** 3922

Jews—History: CA 2069, 2368, 2369, 7097, 9537, 9538, 15658, 20421, 20463 **CO** 14025 **FL** 16100, 16108, 18573 **IL** 7094, 11947 **IN** 7758 **LA** 16560 **MA** 655, 7092, 16107 **MI** 4148, 16084, 16112 **MN** 68, 8382 **MO** 2205 **NE** 8391 **NJ** 16123 **NY** 1404, 7098, 8394, 8399, 8401, 8405, 11611, 11814, 11815, 11949, 12741, 13143, 16080, 16083, 16087, 16093, 20638, 20750, 20756, 20757, 20759 **OH** 7095, 12750, 16078 **PA** 4161, 4164, 13754 **RI** 13871 **SC** 3442 **TN** 8390, 16119 **TX** 16094 **WA** 16106 *Canada:* **ON** 1775, 8970 **PQ** 1920 *Intl:* **GER** 3922, 9731 **ISR** 7270, 14915

Jews, Russian: CA 1589, 9537 **MA** 7092 **NY** 3291, 11131 *Intl:* **ISR** 7104

Joan of Arc: NY 4023, 12654

Johnson, Andrew: TN 17665

Johnson, Lyndon Baines: TX 17746, 17928

Johnson, Samuel: CT 20703 **IL** 20369 **NC** 19075 **NV** 19022 **NY** 4330 **VA** 19861 *Canada:* **ON** 9954

Johnson, Walter (Thomas Walter): IL 11942

Johnston, Mary: VA 19510

Jones, John Paul: DC 9129

Jones, Mary Harris "Mother": DC 3156

Jones, "Spike" (Lindsay Armstrong): CA 8476

Journalism (See also Broadcast journalism; Communication; Periodicals, Publishing of): CA 2573, 18325 **CT** 20723 **DC** 4909, 11253 **FL** 5863, 10257, 13283 **IL** 15488, 18667 **IN** 7792, 17024 **KS** 18728 **MA** 2010, 15237 **MI** 4820, 5847 **MN** 18908 **MO** 18966 **NY** 2333, 4026, 13992, 15720 **OH** 3827, 12315, 13488 **OK** 12367, 12373 **OR** 721 **PA** 6117, 16145 **PR** 19250 **TX** 4568 **VA** 883 **WI** 19611 *Canada:* **NS** 18760 **ON** 14180 *Intl:* **GER** 7964 **IRQ** 933 **MYS** 9568 **SGP** 1120 **SPA** 17980

Journalism, Pictorial (See also Photography, Journalistic): CA 18325 **NY** 8074 **PA** 16140

Joyce, James: CT 20703 **IL** 15492 **KS** 8572, 18724 **NY** 4330, 9020, 15741 **TX** 15503, 19392

Juarez, Benito Pablo: CA 4293

Labor and laboring classes (continued)
4246, 4829, 5852, 10328, 16687 **MN** 10447, 14562 **MO** 10546 **NJ** 518, 16480 **NY** 439, 582, 2246, 2329, 4027, 4326, 4329, 8143, 11584, 11608, 11652, 13989, 14002, 17267 **OH** 3818, 12300, 13483 **PA** 7811, 19186, 19227 **TN** 16158 **TX** 7458 **WA** 19515 **WI** 10428, 20518, 20529 *Canada:* **AB** 255 **BC** 19759 **NS** 12139 **ON** 2694, 2695, 12474, 17959, 19432 **PQ** 13584, 13593, 13609 *Intl:* **DEN** 8862 **GER** 5198, 6442 **ITA** 8282 **MOR** 10743 **NLD** 7977, 8134

Labor and laboring classes—History: **CA** 2573, 3299, 7838 **CT** 2116 **DC** 3156, 11225, 16711 **GA** 6413 **ID** 10915 **IL** 14059, 14791 **IN** 7772, 7808, 19350 **MA** 10886, 18827 **MD** 19233 **MI** 4823, 20117 **MO** 20250 **NC** 11891 **NY** 3735, 4327, 11733 **OH** 2035 **PA** 1430, 19203 **TN** 16778 **TX** 19375 **WI** 15684, 19642 *Canada:* **BC** 18282 **ON** 2760, 9954, 12437 *Intl:* **DEN** 8862

Labor and laboring classes—Jews: **NY** 8399

Labor laws and legislation: **AL** 8942 **AR** 10868 **AZ** 9660, 12244 **CA** 1632, 2294, 4438, 6659, 8711, 9433, 10173, 10754, 12412, 15061 **CO** 3953, 5280, 10828 **CT** 10873, 16644 **DC** 4392, 5624, 8067, 8139, 8140, 8445, 11225, 13770, 15097, 16322, 17270, 17483, 17902 **DE** 13901 **FL** 18575 **GA** 417, 8718, 13280, 15239 **HI** 7022 **IL** 1070, 7688, 11369, 15062, 19791, 20498 **IN** 7817 **LA** 4835 **MA** 1840, 6569, 20419 **MD** 19796 **ME** 9964 **MI** 3770, 4823, 4856, 5079, 10328, 10398 **MO** 6740, 15140 **NC** 5038, 11891 **NE** 1410 **NJ** 10120, 11510, 13375 **NM** 14027 **NY** 4326, 7517, 8590, 8606, 9496, 9644, 10736, 11155, 11652, 11821, 12752, 13558, 14036, 15063, 15098, 15183, 16439 **OH** 6305, 9723, 19959 **OK** 12646 **PA** 1795, 2310, 6054, 11964, 15819, 16676, 20550 **PR** 13518, 19249 **RI** 80, 7225 **TN** 16778 **TX** 165, 1411, 2407, 8446, 8470 **VA** 7577 **WI** 5942, 10275, 13571, 13809 *Canada:* **AB** 285 **BC** 2179, 5605, 14152 **MB** 2759 **NS** 12139 **ON** 2760, 2762, 4448, 12475, 13652, 15132, 17959, 19432 **PQ** 4798, 9949, 13973, 18114 **SK** 14846 *Intl:* **BEL** 1670 **SWI** 8142

Labor productivity: **AZ** 18215 **CA** 2490 **DC** 19689 **IN** 13543 **MD** 18807 **MO** 9694 **NY** 20602 **TX** 722 **WI** 19626 *Intl:* **IND** 142

Labor relations See: Industrial relations

Laboratory animals: **IN** 13550 **MD** 17204 *Intl:* **CHN** 1655 **ENG** 18142

Labrador: *Canada:* **NF** 8863, 10051, 10055

Lace and lace making: **PA** 3245 **WA** 8163

Lafayette, Marquis de: **GA** 8844 **NC** 10179 **NY** 4330, 8374 **PA** 8875

Lagerkvist, Par: **MN** 18937

Laissez-faire: **ID** 3307 *Canada:* **BC** 6104

Lake Michigan: **IL** 8895, 15105

Lake Superior: **MI** 7434

Lampreys: *Canada:* **ON** 2728

Lamps and lighting: **CT** 19914 **IL** 6913 **MA** 16376 **OH** 6314

Land settlement (See also Human settlements): **TX** 16278 **WI** 19602

Land use (See also Agriculture; Eminent domain; Open spaces; Public lands; Real property; Zoning): **AK** 17100 **AZ** 13023, 13024, 16540 **CA** 2536, 2544, 3309, 6537, 14715, 17121, 18374, 18901 **CO** 13796 **DC** 17214, 17241 **FL** 9583, 15998 **HI** 7031 **IL** 7003, 10161, 16492 **MD** 9753, 9767 **MI** 6355, 6696 **MN** 10471 **MT** 10647, 17107, 18990 **ND** 19099 **NM** 17108 **NY** 5075 **OH** 10273, 11973, 11974 **OR** 17104 **PA** 4720, 10683 **RI** 13876 **TN** 8775 **TX** 8433 **VA** 13679, 17105 **WI** 4587, 15454 *Canada:* **AB** 273, 2460, 2722, 5242 **MB** 9620, 9628 **NB** 11446 **ON** 12451, 12489 *Intl:* **PER** 6361 **SCT** 5234

Land use—Planning (See also City planning; Regional planning): **AK** 217, 18175 **AZ** 13060 **CA** 8477 **CT** 4366, 20739 **DC** 17249, 19690, 20636 **FL** 6276, 12511, 15426, 20545 **HI** 1708 **IA** 15349 **IL** 4688, 8883, 8895 **IN** 6016 **MD** 6872 **NC** 19059 **ND** 11919 **NJ** 10358 **NY** 3353, 12740 **PA** 2320, 20770 **TN** 10064 **VA** 5559 **WI** 19595 *Canada:* **AB** 272, 15663 **BC** 2162, 2166 **ON** 2712, 12479 **PQ** 18119 **SK** 13788 *Intl:* **NLD** 11403 **SWZ** 19361

Landon, Alfred Mossman "Alf": **KS** 8573

Landscape architecture: **AL** 1278, 1850, 1853 **AR** 18233 **AZ** 1009 **CA** 2499, 2500, 7122, 18300, 18319 **CO** 17771, 18490 **DC** 750, 4902, 6962, 15283 **DE** 18543 **FL** 18559 **HI** 1708 **IL** 10762, 18663 **IN** 1437, 19109 **KS** 8575 **KY** 18743, 18750, 18767 **LA** 732, 9382 **MA** 1975, 1999, 3492, 6967, 8435, 9793, 14837, 15234, 17717, 20592 **MI** 10317, 18853 **MN** 18892, 18917 **MO** 20055 **NC** 11902 **ND** 11926 **NY** 3731, 4309, 4363, 6248, 7414, 8932, 11554, 12433, 13818, 15722 **OH** 6247, 8651, 10264, 12292, 12307 **OK** 12361, 19121 **OR** 19141 **PA** 12846, 12893, 13085, 16129, 19182 **RI** 13874 **TN** 3463, 10059, 19768 **TX** 7461 **VA** 3938, 19503, 19869 **WA** 19512, 20048 *Canada:* **MB** 18785 **PQ** 8343, 9892, 18075 *Intl:* **AUS** 14104 **BEL** 7887 **ENG** 14120, 18254 **GER** 6106 **IND** 7747 **NLD** 11403

Language arts (See also Reading; Speech): **AL** 5856 **CA** 4070 **CT** 20136 **DE** 8178, 18542 **WA** 19949 *Canada:* **ON** 20159

Language and languages (See also Linguistics; Philology; Written communication): **AK** 17068, 18180 **AL** 8057, 16850 **AZ** 600, 18227 **CA** 9280, 9348, 10670, 12206, 14702, 14706, 17224, 18344, 18397 **DC** 3155, 3161, 3163, 4909, 5403, 9109, 17227, 17919 **FL** 10255 **GA** 1237, 3117 **HI** 7043 **ID** 18649 **IL** 3528, 11143, 11752, 11982, 15922, 18460, 18659, 18660, 18685 **IN** 7772, 7818 **LA** 11542, 14392 **MA** 1994, 9803, 17745, 20153 **MD** 8420 **MI** 2592, 4815, 4819, 9507, 18862 **MN** 5594, 10451, 14565, 18922 **MO** 14455 **NC** 4478 **NH** 10998 **NJ** 11746, 11748, 13380 **NY** 502, 2244, 2333, 4004, 7129, 10584, 11603, 11604, 11609, 11616, 13631, 13992, 19274 **OH** 3823, 3824, 8655, 16394, 18473 **OK** 12367 **OR** 10849, 19157 **PA** 37, 3077, 6117, 7809, 10403 **TX** 4568, 14674, 16809, 16829, 16847, 17015, 19400 **UT** 19475, 20803 **VA** 15932 **WA** 15000 **WV** 910 *Canada:* **AB** 18292 **BC** 18271 **ON** 2808, 2813, 2832, 10229, 12443 **PQ** 5974, 18067 *Intl:* **AUS** 1340 **AUT** 8122 **BEL** 3166 **CHN** 1659, 18703 **FIN** 15898 **MWI** 9567 **NLD** 8786, 11402, 11404

Language and languages—Study and teaching: **CA** 14641 **DC** 5403 **FL** 10255 **WI** 19573 *Intl:* **AUS** 88 **FRA** 2366 **GER** 18022

Laos: **CT** 20732

Lasers and masers: **AL** 16996 **CA** 7509, 9244, 12028, 12677, 14017, 19342 **CO** 3969, 18500 **CT** 17961 **ID** 5268 **MA** 16286 **MN** 8181 **MO** 10092 **NM** 16802 **NY** 1661, 19281 **OR** 12521 **TN** 19372 **VA** 98 *Intl:* **CHN** 20650 **GER** 13099 **ISR** 8269

Lasers in medicine: **OH** 18475

Latin America (See also Central America; South America): **AZ** 18210, 18213 **CA** 3752, 4622, 12207, 14800, 15650, 18416, 18420, 19344 **CT** 20719 **DC** 3161, 6961, 7477, 8027, 9117, 9119, 9125, 9129, 12558, 17609, 17919, 20471 **FL** 6045, 10255, 14607, 16827, 16866, 17062, 18574, 18586, 18846 **GA** 17021 **IL** 15491, 18675 **IN** 7794 **KS** 18723, 18724 **LA** 16473, 16558 **MA** 6999 **MN** 3324 **MO** 8205, 14464, 18982 **NY** 4492, 7235, 15757 **PA** 14068, 19197, 19217 **PR** 19241 **TX** 16521, 19380 **VA** 14767 **WI** 19602 *Canada:* **ON** 2886, 20779 **PQ** 3216, 18117 *Intl:* **ARG** 7949 **CHL** 16759 **ECU** 8967 **GER** 15795 **ISR** 7102 **MEX** 3265, 10240 **POL** 13167 **SPA** 6066 **VEN** 8023, 8966, 8968

Latin America—History: **CA** 19335 **CT** 20719 **DC** 8026 **TX** 5390 *Intl:* **CHL** 3598 **MEX** 17993 **SPA** 6066

Latin American literature: **AZ** 1011 **CA** 12207, 19335 **CT** 20719 **DC** 3161, 9119 **PR** 13508 **TX** 1175, 5390, 19380 *Intl:* **BRZ** 6212 **PER** 13215 **SPA** 6066

Latin language: **DC** 3163 **IL** 18664 **OH** 3827, 18473 **TX** 19386 *Intl:* **GER** 1597, 18054

Latvia: **DC** 9113 **MI** 8972 **NE** 19005

Laubach, Frank C.: **NY** 8973

Law—Australia: *Intl:* **AUS** 1329

Law—Brazil: *Intl:* **BRZ** 2090

Law—Canada: **FL** 4521 **KS** 18736 **MD** 9105 **MI** 6343, 18552 **OH** 3811, 16390 **SD** 19318 **WV** 20217 *Canada:* **AB** 247, 248, 249, 250, 251, 252, 253, 287, 288, 292, 1722, 1866, 2383, 2456, 2689, 3495, 3862, 4271, 5457, 5683, 7078, 7468, 8988, 8989, 8990, 8991, 8992, 8993, 9501, 9870,

Law—United States: (continued)
9510, 10350, 12933, 12959, 13216, 13666, 14054, 14082, 14144, 15154, 15369, 15678, 16692, 17265, 17935, 17937, 19791, 20484, 20608 **IN** 374, 375, 767, 1413, 1434, 1534, 5116, 7759, 7770, 7821, 8882, 9053, 9054, 9162, 9186, 9679, 13709, 14363, 17024, 19778 **KS** 8440, 8561, 15013, 20654 **KY** 8353, 8676, 9396 **LA** 66, 8479, 8987, 9367, 9369, 15046, 17144 **MA** 1535, 1749, 2128, 2202, 3620, 5052, 5450, 5583, 5833, 6053, 6093, 6835, 6877, 6879, 7207, 9008, 9102, 9410, 9801, 9921, 10360, 10499, 11435, 13732, 14061, 15297, 15699, 15864, 16329, 17137, 19973, 20596 **MD** 360, 1094, 1447, 3100, 3437, 5677, 6078, 6107, 9105, 9757, 9764, 10392, 10677, 11810, 13073, 13303, 13621, 15031, 17940, 19999, 20139 **ME** 1757, 4472, 6883, 9176, 9556, 9563, 12916, 13077, 14213, 19675, 19814, 19944 **MI** 412, 3435, 3738, 4246, 4803, 4829, 4980, 6340, 6353, 6635, 7214, 8529, 9142, 10311, 12197, 14216, 15674, 18552, 19971 **MN** 4967, 5549, 5639, 6330, 6661, 7137, 9013, 10450, 10474, 10489, 12170, 13915, 14043, 14440, 14566, 16345, 17149 **MO** 2295, 6226, 6740, 8304, 8957, 8986, 9052, 9080, 9854, 10543, 10544, 10545, 10549, 10552, 10637, 14441, 17147, 17148 **MS** 6928, 9415, 10524 **MT** 15685 **NC** 3331, 9976, 15230, 15243 **ND** 11925 **NE** 2042, 4498, 4971, 8829, 11382, 13999, 16951 **NH** 11487, 11492, 12576, 13958, 15106 **NJ** 948, 1734, 1892, 1918, 2607, 3717, 3750, 3870, 4454, 4476, 5447, 6225, 6722, 7493, 7566, 9872, 10357, 10612, 10746, 11511, 11512, 11514, 11515, 11853, 12239, 12811, 13080, 13459, 13929, 14630, 15077, 15166, 15362, 15893, 17140, 17263 **NM** 1755, 3461, 11532, 11536 **NV** 3767, 11427, 12173, 20074 **NY** 448, 526, 1420, 1712, 1751, 1836, 2105, 2211, 2226, 2285, 3112, 3298, 3411, 3460, 3722, 3792, 4129, 4355, 4415, 4492, 4685, 4960, 6194, 6884, 7056, 7158, 8492, 8938, 9232, 9521, 9700, 10208, 10842, 10938, 11010, 11565, 11568, 11572, 11573, 11587, 11618, 11646, 11647, 11653, 11654, 11666, 11667, 11686, 11687, 11688, 11689, 11690, 11691, 11692, 11693, 11694, 11695, 11696, 11697, 11698, 11699, 11700, 11701, 11702, 11703, 11704, 11705, 11706, 11707, 11708, 11709, 11710, 11711, 11712, 11713, 11714, 11715, 11718, 11820, 12413, 12595, 12798, 13009, 13292, 13419, 13422, 13634, 13974, 13989, 14072, 15058, 15102, 15211, 15727, 15855, 16180, 16772, 17138, 17162, 17266, 17448, 19720, 20138, 20379, 20391, 20504 **OH** 62, 173, 174, 373, 1229, 1292, 1415, 1700, 2412, 3317, 3423, 3704, 3795, 3803, 3811, 3831, 4030, 4036, 4718, 4874, 5418, 5621, 6184, 6198, 6209, 6275, 6727, 6744, 6795, 6882, 7141, 7194, 7337, 7443, 8301, 8351, 8473, 9003, 9148, 9303, 9522, 9545, 9680, 10017, 10022, 10106, 10247, 10729, 10933, 12277, 12291, 13037, 13234, 13252, 13483, 13503, 13905, 14081, 14785, 15109, 15671, 15672, 15673, 15985, 16390, 16397, 16589, 17145, 19703, 19749, 19977, 20000, 20112, 20564 **OK** 12345, 12359, 16572, 17158 **OR** 3748, 8755, 8937, 8939, 10402, 10855, 12540, 12547, 15806, 16953, 17155, 17230, 17451, 20001 **PA** 63, 366, 661, 1056, 1443, 1538, 1620, 1626, 1744, 1886, 1893, 2319, 2411, 2594, 3038, 3225, 3491, 3771, 3787, 3839, 3871, 4228, 4398, 4416, 4477, 4631, 4693, 4719, 4872, 5008, 5032, 5201, 5301, 5417, 5620, 5977, 6086, 6123, 6208, 6728, 7001, 7570, 7753, 8352, 8362, 8498, 8743, 8760, 8864, 8868, 8918, 9004, 9036, 9056, 9150, 9213, 9471, 9924, 9961, 10107, 10174, 10381, 10622, 10682, 10687, 10691, 10737, 11964, 12032, 12815, 12830, 12851, 12855, 12856, 12857, 12858, 12869, 12886, 12889, 12924, 12935, 12949, 12982, 12984, 13045, 13274, 13771, 14038, 14073, 14880, 14914, 14934, 15363, 15854, 15890, 16369, 16652, 17141, 17142, 19797, 19978, 20002, 20314, 20338, 20386, 20434, 20660, 20769 **PR** 13522 **RI** 10220, 13883, 13884 **SC** 13970, 15398, 15410 **SD** 15423 **TN** 4683, 8771, 10058, 16162, 16165, 16166, 16170, 16171, 16178 **TX** 1804, 2054, 2271, 2286, 3098, 3506, 3775, 4550, 4551, 4567, 5130, 5281, 5362, 5532, 6195, 6568, 6917, 7187, 7450, 7518, 9847, 9947, 10734, 12833, 13275, 13504, 14960, 15059, 15228, 16009, 16235, 16236, 16237, 16238, 16239, 16255, 16256, 16266, 16321, 16939, 16940 **UT** 14646, 19711, 20131, 20804 **VA** 1491, 5564, 5597, 9875, 9919, 10281, 11125, 11228, 11846, 13962, 17143, 19860, 19891 **VT** 1884, 11230, 19808 **WA** 1571, 3768, 6662, 8581, 8712, 8752, 8940, 9078, 12945, 13041, 13327, 15213, 15293, 15590, 16960, 17156, 19951, 20024, 20034, 20691 **WI** 4586, 4972, 5945, 9677, 10422, 12075, 12628, 13674, 15039, 20519, 20532 **WV** 3988, 8308, 12265, 20205, 20213, 20217 **WY** 12744, 20670 *Canada:* **AB** 2383 **BC** 19487 **NS** 4537 **ON** 8999 **PQ** 13575 **SK** 14848 *Intl:* **AUT** 14658

Law—United States Territories: GU 6788 **PA** 9140, 17142 **PR** 3168, 8031, 13514, 13518, 13522, 13523, 13524, 17452, 19236

Law, Water See: Water—Laws and legislation

Law, Welfare See: Public welfare—Law and legislation

Lawrence, David Herbert: CT 20703 **IL** 15492 **MI** 4828 **PA** 2315 **TX** 19392 *Canada:* **AB** 18196 **ON** 9954, 19460

Lawrence, Thomas Edward (Lawrence of Arabia): NH 4616 **VA** 15932

Lawson, Robert: PA 6122

Lawyers: CA 10023

Leacock, Stephen: *Canada:* **ON** 9024

Lead: *Canada:* **ON** 4047

Leadership: DC 11322 **KS** 16928 **MD** 11013 **NC** 3227 **NY** 3137 **PA** 17080 **TX** 2043, 16816, 17022

Leaf, Munro: PA 6122

League of Nations: DC 9117, 11033 **GA** 5331 **MD** 8421 **NY** 4017, 11734, 16772, 16775 **OH** 3831 *Canada:* **ON** 2812 *Intl:* **POL** 13181

Learning disabilities: AZ 13030 **DE** 8178 **MA** 4488 **ME** 9032 **MI** 1382 **NY** 4001, 11622, 15724 **OH** 13481, 18147 **TX** 16258, 19394 **VT** 8930 **WA** 631 *Canada:* **AB** 2463 **PQ** 18113

Learning, Psychology of: DC 5409 **FL** 5872 **MA** 6987 **NY** 4022 *Canada:* **ON** 19442 *Intl:* **MYA** 10944

Leather: PA 7136, 17181 *Intl:* **CZE** 15139

Lee, Robert Edward: VA 4134, 15821, 17669, 20013

Legal aid: HI 9049 **IL** 11117 **MI** 4821 **NY** 3298, 9048, 9050

Legal education See: Law—Study and teaching

Legal ethics: DC 501 *Canada:* **PQ** 9902

Legal medicine See: Medical jurisprudence

Legal services, Prepaid See: Prepaid legal services

Legislation: AK 219 **CA** 7854, 9325, 17528 **DC** 968, 4173, 6376, 13831, 15097, 17213, 17219, 17254, 17257, 17258, 17484, 17555, 17938, 17946, 19813, 20458 **FL** 10253 **GA** 18602 **IL** 7699, 8889, 9722, 15495, 17935, 18669 **IN** 8882 **KS** 8560 **KY** 4371, 8677 **MA** 9835, 17525 **MD** 9105 **MI** 10292 **MN** 10492 **MT** 10649 **NV** 3767 **NY** 7724, 10386, 11667, 14355, 17138 **OH** 12288 **PA** 8362, 12883, 17527, 19177 **PR** 13521 **RI** 13876, 13884 **SC** 15408 **TX** 8446 **UT** 19469 **VA** 5561 **WI** 20529 **WV** 20213 *Canada:* **AB** 288 **NF** 11762 **ON** 5612, 8999, 9955, 12494, 17558 **PQ** 13575 **SK** 14860 *Intl:* **CHL** 3595

Legislative bodies (See also Parliamentary practice): CO 11132 **DC** 9117 **GA** 18599 **KS** 18725 **PA** 8874 **UT** 19712 *Canada:* **MB** 9618 **ON** 2764, 2812, 12446 **PQ** 13575 *Intl:* **ENG** 6679, 6680 **FRA** 4364 **SPA** 15559 **SWI** 8073 **ZWE** 20842

Legislative reference bureaus: AK 209 **CA** 2549 **CT** 4200 **DC** 12251 **DE** 4732 **FL** 5903 **HI** 7037 **IA** 8236 **IL** 7695, 7699 **LA** 9369 **MD** 9761 **ME** 9563 **MI** 10310 **MN** 10490 **MO** 10549 **NC** 11894 **NY** 11559, 11665, 11668 **OK** 12359 **PA** 12885 **RI** 13884 **TN** 16166 **TX** 16256 **VA** 19890 **WI** 10425, 20529 **WV** 20213 *Canada:* **BC** 2153 **NB** 11449 **NS** 12148 **ON** 12446

Legumes: HI 11817 *Canada:* **SK** 2826 *Intl:* **ARG** 12226

Lehman, Herbert Henry: NY 4023

Leiber, Fritz: TX 18643

Leisure (See also Recreation): IL 18658 **KY** 5151 **MD** 14640 **OH** 2040 **OR** 19150 **VA** 11263 *Canada:* **ON** 19543

L'Engle, Madeleine: IL 20369

Lenin, Nikolai: *Intl:* **CHN** 27, 6246

Lenses, Contact See: Contact lenses

Lenski, Lois: AR 1033 **FL** 5919 **KS** 5346 **NC** 19084 **NY** 15704 **OK** 19136

Leprosy: HI 7034 **LA** 17934 **SC** 664 *Intl:* **BRZ** 2084

Lighter-than-air (LTA) craft See: Air-ships

Lighthouses: CA 17678 **ME** 15141 **OH** 6697 **VA** 13257 *Intl:* **AUS** 15695

Lighting See: Lamps and lighting

Limestone: IN 7760

Limnology (See also Eutrophication): AL 1282 **CA** 928 **DC** 15280 **FL** 939 **MI** 10341, 17648, 18855, 18880 **MN** 18944 **NY** 7933, 9000, 15709 **OH** 12309 **OK** 19122 **PA** 19222 **WI** 17501, 19587, 19625 *Canada:* **MB** 2731 **ON** 2883 **PQ** 13602 *Intl:* **ARG** 972 **BRZ** 11206 **GER** 6447, 13108, 18035

Lincoln, Abraham: CA 1390, 9184, 12232, 18428, 19172 **CO** 3940 **CT** 18252 **DC** 9129, 9135, 14969 **GA** 3763 **IA** 6627 **IL** 2061, 3522, 4165, 7670, 7698, 7707, 11912, 11942, 18461, 18675, 19763 **IN** 2416, 7794, 9187, 17744 **KS** 8572, 14500 **KY** 1727, 15580, 17661 **LA** 9390 **MA** 2008, 2122 **MD** 9766 **MI** 4816, 6634, 12211 **MO** 11972 **MT** 10654 **NJ** 1902 **NY** 4330 **OH** 1648, 18534 **PA** 3747, 6095, 16657, 17720, 20768 **RI** 2282 **TN** 9185, 15478 **WA** 15981 **WI** 9712 **WV** 20226

Lind, Jenny: IL 11942 **PA** 772 **TX** 14672

Lindbergh, Charles Augustus: MO 10536 **NJ** 7566

Lindsay, John Vliet: CT 20723

Lindsay, Vachel: IL 9182 **OH** 7231 **VA** 19510

Linguistics (See also Language and languages): AK 18180 **CA** 3043, 17224 **CT** 7004, 20722 **DC** 5403, 6379, 6961, 11158, 15263 **HI** 18623 **IL** 3528, 11994, 15488, 18685 **MA** 6574, 9803 **MI** 4815, 18862 **MN** 18902 **NJ** 13384 **NM** 9853 **NY** 2244, 2333, 7233, 7571, 10584, 11616, 13631 **OH** 3823, 3827, 13488, 16615 **PA** 712, 7809, 19198 **TX** 15859, 19388 **VA** 7983 **VT** 5520 *Canada:* **BC** 18271 **ON** 2832, 2836, 6529, 10229, 12444, 19427 **PQ** 3194, 18085, 18086, 18097, 18108 *Intl:* **AUT** 18057 **BRZ** 6519 **BUL** 2351 **CHN** 15152 **COL** 1539 **ENG** 18441 **FRA** 2366, 18134 **GER** 7942, 16039, 18018, 18024, 18048 **GTM** 6791 **HUN** 1274, 7547 **IND** 7741 **ISR** 1521 **JPN** 8336 **NER** 19054 **NLD** 17977 **PER** 13214 **POL** 19665 **SGP** 11319

Linnaeus, Carolus: DE 4721 **KS** 8572, 18724 **MO** 10535 **PA** 3083 *Canada:* **ON** 2645 *Intl:* **ENG** 9199, 11340, 14103

Lipids: MN 18911

Lippmann, Walter: CT 20723

Liszt, Franz: MA 2015 **NY** 8491 *Intl:* **AUT** 821

Litchfield (CT): CT 9206

Literacy: AK 9207 **CA** 4383, 13913 **GA** 1243, 2581 **MI** 13044 **NC** 19058 **NE** 3190 **NY** 8973 **OH** 4657, 16394 **PA** 3758 *Intl:* **GER** 16763 **MEX** 10240 **THA** 16766

Literature (See also Fairy tales; Philology; Poetry): AL 180, 8057, 16850 **AZ** 13026, 13028 **CA** 2572, 9280, 9348, 9418, 12683, 14706, 14725, 16871, 17973, 18428, 18435, 19259, 20188 **CT** 4178, 6939, 16504, 20703 **DC** 3163, 4909, 5943, 7470 **FL** 10257 **GA** 1237 **HI** 7043 **ID** 18649 **IL** 3528, 11982, 15488, 18685, 20258 **IN** 7818 **KS** 8573 **LA** 14392, 16557 **MA** 1994, 1996, 6976, 9803, 17745, 20598 **MD** 17057 **MI** 4815, 7584, 10321, 10330, 18866 **MN** 10451, 14565, 14566 **MO** 14455 **MS** 4924 **NE** 20116 **NJ** 11746 **NM** 5163, 11530 **NY** 112, 2333, 4004, 4005, 4370, 7316, 10101, 11386, 11603, 11609, 11613, 11667, 12819, 13631, 13992, 15156, 15731, 18483, 20130, 20695 **OH** 3824, 3827, 9138, 10266, 12826, 13488, 16394 **OK** 12367, 19136 **OR** 10849 **PA** 37, 2304, 3077, 3084, 5232, 6117, 8832, 16129 **PR** 19242 **RI** 13440 **SC** 3442 **TX** 14674, 16883 **UT** 19475, 20797, 20803, 20809 **VA** 19510 **WA** 15000, 17066, 20045 **WI** 14248, 19637 *Canada:* **AB** 18205, 18292 **BC** 18271 **NB** 1250 **NS** 10812 **ON** 10229, 14427 **PQ** 3194, 13589, 15025 **SK** 16616 *Intl:* **AMA** 7867 **ARG** 17984 **BEL** 3166 **BEN** 1720 **BRZ** 6214 **CHN** 1657, 6789, 15152 **COT** 4350 **CRI** 17989 **CZE** 4512 **ENG** 4966, 9266 **GER** 18018, 18024, 20420 **GHA** 6461 **IND** 15997 **IRL** 14117 **ISR** 1521 **ITA** 1821 **LIE** 9151 **LIT** 19849 **MEX** 17992 **NLD** 11402 **PAK** 12694 **PER** 13214 **POL** 19665 **ROM** 9652, 16362, 19845 **SLC** 14469 **SPA** 15557, 15561 **SWI** 5946 **THA** 16293

Literature—Black authors: AR 18240 **CA** 12206, 18427 **DC** 4905 **GA** 3763 **IL** 3527, 5073, 8455, 11982 **IN** 7778 **MA** 2008, 15852 **MN** 18931 **MS** 4924, 18949 **NC** 11878 **NJ** 11746 **NY** 11629, 15725 **OH** 12800, 19425, 20424 **PA** 16144, 19200 **VA** 6880 **WA** 14998

Literature, Classical See: Classical literature

Literature, Comparative: DC 3163 *Canada:* **PQ** 18086 *Intl:* **BUL** 2351

Literature—History and criticism (See also Authors): CA 9350, 18364, 18382, 18407 **DC** 4909 **MI** 4815 **MN** 10451 **MO** 20250 **MS** 19354 **MT** 3099 **NH** 10723 **NJ** 11746 **NY** 2244, 2333, 11610, 15156 **OH** 3827, 16394 **PA** 6117 **TX** 4568 *Canada:* **ON** 16408 *Intl:* **AUT** 7303 **CHN** 1659 **GER** 18025 **HUN** 7548, 12607

Literature, Medieval: IL 18672 **NY** 19285 **OH** 3823

Literature, Popular See: Popular literature

Literature, Victorian: AZ 1019 **CA** 14725 **GA** 5338 **MA** 12416 **NJ** 13386 **TN** 7519 **TX** 1602, 5390

Lithium: NC 5938 **WI** 19593

Lithography: CT 12943 **MA** 15236 **NJ** 11750 **PA** 6654, 8592, 16137

Lithuania: DC 9113 **IL** 1458, 9211, 9212 **NH** 10998 **NY** 9210 *Intl:* **LIT** 19849

Lithuanian music See: Music, Lithuanian

Litigation See: Procedure (Law)

Little presses: AZ 13025 **CA** 1806 **CO** 11330 **GA** 18600 **IA** 9311 **KY** 18768 **MA** 1976, 1981 **ME** 2033 **MN** 10451 **NE** 19007 **NY** 73 **PA** 16133, 19225 **TX** 16521 **WA** 20045 **WI** 19644 *Canada:* **AB** 18293 **NS** 4531 **ON** 2807

Littleton, Mark See: Kennedy, John Pendleton (Mark Littleton)

Liturgics (See also Christian art and symbolism; Church music): CA 517 **DC** 19992 **DE** 4887 **KY** 6455 **MO** 4117, 9448 **NE** 9228 **NJ** 15047 **NY** 6352, 8405, 10810, 14419, 15027, 15904 **OH** 13211, 14507 **PA** 9465, 9742, 19300 **RI** 13442 **TN** 19303 *Canada:* **BC** 13663

Livestock (See also Cattle; Pastures; Range management): AR 20493 **CA** 7409, 20849 **ID** 17215 **IL** 18657 **MI** 10314 **MN** 10475 **MO** 11050 **MS** 10526 **MT** 17182 **NE** 17187 **NY** 7925 **OH** 12292, 12293 **PA** 4737, 19196 **TX** 16200, 16240 **WV** 20208 *Canada:* **MB** 2648 **ON** 12451, 12452, 13917, 20284 **PQ** 7888 *Intl:* **AUS** 1327, 18145, 19028, 19053, 20553 **BGD** 1466 **BOL** 7997 **BRZ** 2091, 18002 **BUL** 2348 **CHL** 8001, 17987 **CHN** 1655 **CRI** 8028 **CZE** 4511 **ENG** 14115 **ETH** 8148 **IND** 1132, 18148 **ITA** 16752, 18013 **JPN** 3646, 7322 **KEN** 8679 **MEX** 15009, 17981 **MOR** 7876 **POL** 160, 162 **ROM** 18061 **RUS** 5525, 8823 **SAF** 19140 **TWN** 5518 **YUG** 8763

Lobbying: DC 13326

Local government (See also Municipal government; State and provincial government): AL 1280 **CA** 18326 **DC** 97, 10234 **FL** 10260 **MA** 9835 **MD** 13358 **MS** 18954 **MT** 10649 **NC** 19063 **NY** 3242, 7967 **PA** 12843 **SC** 19308 **SD** 19316 **TN** 16162 **TX** 16227, 16261 **UT** 19712 **WA** 20041 **WI** 13494 *Intl:* **ENG** 9270 **MOR** 129

Locke, John: *Canada:* ON 19460

Locks and keys: CT 9242

Locomotives: CA 2553 **IL** 6339, 7678 **VA** 3484 **WI** 10347 *Intl:* **CHN** 8950, 13695

Logging: CA 13146 **ID** 10915 **MN** 8787 **OR** 3921 **PA** 12881 **WA** 5513, 19526, 20358 **WI** 9653, 12591 *Canada:* **ON** 354, 13573 **PQ** 5978 *Intl:* **SAF** 15382

Logistics: CO 16863 **MD** 9254 **NJ** 719 **OH** 16806, 16811 **PA** 19185 **TX** 16857, 16985 **VA** 11822, 17016 *Canada:* **ON** 2775 *Intl:* **GER** 7976

Mail-order business: CA 6914 OH 174

Mailer, Norman: PA 7811 WI 19644

Maine: MA 11034 MD 15767 ME 10, 863, 1472, 1785, 2033, 2113, 2446, 2611, 6709, 9549, 9550, 9552, 9554, 9557, 9564, 11290, 12395, 12817, 12917, 17662, 18779, 18781, 19351, 20093, 20774 *Canada:* NB 10797

Maize See: Corn

Malacology See: Mollusks

Malaria: *Intl:* PAN 6580

Malawi (See also Africa): *Intl:* MWI 9567, 15331

Malaysia: CA 18344 CT 20732 DC 9109 IL 11994 OH 12333 *Intl:* MYS 9569

Maldives: *Intl:* MDV 9573

Malpractice: IL 1422 MI 13148 NJ 1918 NY 6884, 8492 PA 13720, 20386 *Canada:* AB 7078

Malta: *Intl:* MAL 9576

Mammals (See also Marine mammals): AK 18185 CA 2470, 6706, 11341, 14712, 18390 CO 17199 CT 4177 DE 4721 FL 939 IN 5095 MI 18877 MN 18893 MS 10522 MT 17722 NM 19045 NY 687, 15762 PA 3085, 20848 WA 17635 WI 19629 *Canada:* AB 2722 ON 2716, 2963 PQ 8344, 13602

Man—Migrations: *Intl:* FRA 3273

Management (See also Business; Industrial management; Organizational behavior): AL 184, 16996, 17008, 17019 AR 16861 AZ 405, 600, 991, 2355, 8408, 16607 CA 199, 820, 1058, 1261, 2490, 3737, 4468, 4748, 7505, 7506, 8185, 9223, 9225, 9305, 9331, 9344, 9883, 9886, 9934, 11364, 12026, 12659, 12774, 14017, 15467, 15623, 15652, 16681, 16797, 16820, 16833, 16878, 17895, 17900, 18387, 19324, 19799, 20189, 20245, 20397, 20569, 20678 CO 1219, 3434, 7617, 13278, 13498, 16813, 16881, 18491, 18509, 19697 CT 114, 846, 3695, 9247, 11839, 13021, 14031, 15507, 16467, 16643, 17963, 20731 DC 4906, 6349, 7479, 9937, 10984, 12251, 15226, 15273, 15829, 16803, 16830, 16941, 16974, 17219, 17233, 17249, 17308, 17489, 17526, 17561, 17823, 17831, 17920 DE 5028, 7152 FL 5327, 5862, 5876, 5897, 16841 GA 1241, 5394, 7204, 7944, 9243, 17012, 17059 HI 7022, 7039, 16852 IA 18706 ID 5268 IL 844, 1694, 3141, 3529, 4251, 4698, 5934, 7669, 9935, 11982, 12923, 15678, 16049, 17325, 18449 IN 375, 767, 1434, 2136, 7063, 7779, 9162, 9536, 10391, 13545, 16849, 17024 KS 1941, 8576, 16928, 18735, 20409 KY 8674, 9095, 9737 LA 9380, 9881, 16826 MA 639, 2354, 4865, 4868, 6885, 9100, 9101, 9801, 9829, 11478, 11801, 13333, 13733, 15700, 15864 MD 1454, 17018, 17824, 17866, 17940, 18807, 19263 ME 19675 MI 4806, 5852, 6331, 6334, 9011, 10283, 10307, 11359, 16999, 17171, 19679, 19956 MN 9446, 10459, 12170, 14557, 16341, 16678, 16680, 18896, 18914 MO 9884, 10378, 17174, 20064 MS 7844, 16856 NC 1220, 1553, 2376, 3227, 5036, 6739, 19076, 19938 NE 2297 NH 4609, 11483, 17879 NJ 1193, 1204, 1207, 1218, 1690, 4453, 5696, 7955, 8843, 11504, 13500, 14905 NM 11530, 16853, 19050 NV 5267, 16877 NY 559, 633, 675, 2242, 3470, 3723, 4027, 4141, 4316, 4747, 4859, 5611, 6483, 6770, 9295, 9672, 10207, 11623, 11732, 12655, 13224, 13820, 15728, 16188, 19282, 19720 OH 1044, 1170, 3820, 5434, 11334, 11366, 12262, 12267, 12636, 13503, 13898, 15691, 16674, 16806, 16811, 16895 OK 12372, 16571, 16887, 17010, 19129 OR 7176, 16057, 17081, 17230 PA 433, 531, 1060, 3075, 3697, 7057, 7294, 9099, 9435, 12899, 14038, 14963, 15595, 15780, 19186, 19216, 20313, 20418 PR 19238 RI 2299, 8461 SC 17077 TN 13491, 19775 TX 4543, 4559, 6022, 7453, 7623, 13895, 15115, 16243, 16251, 16781, 16791, 16809, 16816, 16857, 16860, 16883, 16884, 16975, 16985, 17022, 17070 VA 4105, 4430, 5560, 11187, 13364, 13715, 15458, 16152, 16859, 16986, 17011, 17016, 17058, 17165, 17169, 17173, 17882, 17888, 19269, 19501, 19877, 19878, 20006 VT 7622 WA 1938, 8107, 17905, 19515, 20359 WI 143, 4227, 8112, 12073, 15039 WV 6273, 17272, 20206 *Canada:* AB 280, 292, 300, 812, 2880, 2999, 16456 BC 1391, 2167, 2178, 19759 MB 6702, 9603 NB 11448, 11449 ON 99, 1483, 1487, 1681, 2633, 2685, 2694, 2790, 2878, 2888, 4139, 4140, 4447, 5015, 7645, 7720, 8811, 9647, 9936, 10222, 10225, 10937, 12014, 12442, 12473, 12488, 12493, 13342, 14099, 14108, 19446, 20788 PQ 321, 1951, 2862, 2971, 5205, 5625, 7601, 7721, 8847, 9900, 13593, 13604, 13724, 14100, 18104, 18105, 19822 SK 14869 *Intl:* AUS

1330, 3277, 19028 BRZ 19781 ENG 2189, 6677, 6683 GRC 5488 ICE 7638 IND 7749, 9579, 15165 IRL 7912 NLD 8784 PAN 17997 RUS 8292 SAU 7966 SPA 15560 SWI 7710, 8142 TUR 16647 VNM 6892

Management consultants See: Business consultants

Management, Industrial See: Industrial management

Management information systems: DC 7479 IL 8597 MN 18896 NJ 1691 NM 19050 NY 4316, 4859 OH 1170 PA 12899 UT 20802 VA 16978 *Canada:* ON 7615

Manchester (NH): NH 9588

Manfred, Frederick Feikema: MN 18920

Mango: FL 18589

Manistee (MI): MI 9596

Manitoba: *Canada:* MB 9606, 9612, 9618, 9619, 9625, 20491

Mann, Thomas: CA 18364 CT 20703 ME 3872 NJ 13386

Manners and customs: MN 10453

Manning, Henry Edward: GA 5334

Manpower See: Human resources

Manpower planning See: Personnel management

Mansfield, Michael Joseph: MT 18987

Mansfield, Richard: CT 4178

Mantell, Robert Bruce: NY 6876

Manufactures: DC 11069 NY 4248 TX 7458 *Intl:* GER 10777 NLD 82 RUS 8745

Manufacturing processes (See also Computer-aided design and manufacturing): CT 16289 FL 5057 IL 5289 IN 375 KS 1941 MA 4868 MI 15334 MN 16680 MO 403, 14449 OH 6335 PA 1060 *Intl:* AUS 1323 ENG 13406 FIN 16030

Manuscripts: AK 18177 AL 1856, 18169 AR 18236 AZ 11992, 18231 CA 7572, 14711, 15658, 18303, 18402, 19338 CO 18507 CT 2116, 9206, 20723 DC 5943, 9108, 9129, 15314, 19992 DE 6828 FL 7256, 18586 GA 6393, 6413, 18600 HI 7052 IA 9440, 15679, 17925, 18721, 19108 IL 7698, 15492, 18461, 18678, 18693 IN 7257, 7755, 7768, 7769 KS 17921 LA 810, 9371, 16560 MA 473, 6976, 9804, 15338, 17927, 18834 MD 9750, 18820 ME 2033 MI 5964, 17923, 18860, 18875, 20120 MN 10464, 14334, 18920, 18934 MO 14464, 15681, 17924, 20059, 20250, 20251, 20252, 20253 MS 10517, 19354 MT 18987 NC 5049, 19073, 19078 NH 13251, 19036 NJ 5002, 11747, 13380, 14175, 16482 NY 4023, 4306, 7894, 8405, 10738, 11578, 11626, 11627, 11636, 11669, 14002, 15741, 15961, 17922, 19278 OH 7060, 7095, 7099, 16395, 20644 OK 19139 OR 12524, 19159 PA 712, 4852, 7015, 7282, 12875, 15902, 15903, 16134, 16995, 19183, 19203 SC 19310 TN 8773, 10065, 10076, 19302 TX 1609, 7463, 16191, 16279, 18643, 19392, 19414 UT 20797 VA 14651, 17917 VT 19482 WA 19532, 20045 WI 14551, 15683, 19634, 19644 WV 20225 *Canada:* AB 18196, 18293 BC 18282 MB 18789 NB 18072 ON 2807, 19556, 20778 PQ 9893, 13577 SK 19297 *Intl:* BEL 18131 ENG 6664, 6665, 18440 GER 15794 HUN 7550 IRN 8243 NPL 11391

Manuscripts (Papyri): CA 18303 CT 20705 MI 18860 MN 14334 NY 11626 UT 19475 *Intl:* AUT 1354 EGY 6148, 15317 FRA 1833 ITA 8280

Mao Tse-Tung: *Intl:* CHN 27, 6246

Maoris: DC 5324

Maps and atlases (See also Cartography; Geography): AK 17532, 18176 AL 1281, 1858, 14663, 16812, 18168, 18169 AR 18234 AZ 986, 1014, 17534, 18221 CA 2545, 2566, 2569, 3502, 9347, 11341, 12206, 14704, 14946, 17533, 18303, 18314, 18334, 18385, 18409, 18419, 18433, 18436

Maps and atlases (continued)
CO 3947, 17530, 18503 **CT** 3336, 6939, 18525, 20180, 20714, 20724 **DC** 9118, 11029 **FL** 18576 **GA** 6387, 6393, 17012, 18604 **HI** 18621 **IA** 18715 **ID** 18655 **IL** 9957, 11998, 12083, 13708, 15934, 18453, 18683, 18701, 20255 **IN** 1441, 7787, 13543 **KS** 18730 **KY** 18749, 18753 **LA** 9371, 9377 **MA** 2001, 3776, 6982, 8015, 9808, 9833, 14634, 18829 **MD** 541, 8421, 17175, 17657, 18815 **ME** 18780 **MI** 4822, 5159, 9507, 10329, 10344, 18872, 20272 **MN** 9634, 16957, 18916, 18939 **MO** 14453, 14454, 15531, 18957, 18962, 20060 **NC** 5113, 11899, 19060, 19071, 20237 **ND** 10496, 19098 **NE** 11378, 18999 **NH** 4611 **NJ** 6874, 13373 **NV** 11423 **NY** 2243, 4015, 4305, 4320, 10588, 11612, 11659, 11669, 13628, 13820, 13991, 15730, 15753, 15761, 16772, 16994, 19283, 19789 **OH** 2038, 3825, 8652, 10265, 12322, 12331, 13484, 13485, 16393, 16395, 18470 **OK** 3368, 12368, 16571, 19128 **OR** 10849, 12553, 19153 **PA** 6124, 12859, 12901, 12902, 16138, 19187, 19217 **SC** 19311 **TN** 16176, 19364 **TX** 4653, 6023, 15504, 16195, 16224, 16263, 18643, 19398, 19411 **UT** 19473, 20801 **VA** 13679, 17531, 17539, 19724, 19875 **WA** 3381, 5172, 7288, 17552, 19533, 20306 **WI** 598, 19569, 19580, 19599, 19648 **WY** 19658 *Canada:* **AB** 259, 278, 18188 **BC** 2141, 2161, 18263, 18274, 18282, 19486 **NF** 10056 **NS** 4536, 12153, 14539 **ON** 2199, 2698, 2747, 2768, 3055, 8904, 9952, 12427, 12482, 13650, 13653, 18611, 19165, 19455, 19546, 19557, 20160, 20791 **PE** 4369 **PQ** 9895, 9912, 13576, 13578, 18107, 18115, 18119, 18121, 18123 **SK** 19262 *Intl:* **AUT** 1354 **BEL** 1671 **BRZ** 6213 **ENG** 6664 **GER** 1597, 15794 **POL** 13162 **RUS** 17958 **SAF** 15387

Mardi Gras: **AL** 7246 **LA** 11543 **TN** 10065

Marianists: **OH** 15335

Marimba: **MD** 16441

Marine biology (See also Fish and fisheries; Marine ecology): **AK** 18174 **AL** 9670 **CA** 928, 2470, 2577, 9340, 10664, 12660, 14978, 15651, 17643, 17644, 17830, 18419, 19323, 19329, 20624 **CT** 10946, 17633, 18526 **DC** 17653 **DE** 18545 **FL** 5896, 10771, 12157, 17639, 17641, 17704 **GA** 18605 **HI** 1865, 17632 **IL** 15105 **MA** 1573, 9669, 11988, 17636, 20576 **MD** 1715, 17670 **ME** 9561, 18777 **MS** 6808, 17634 **NC** 5044, 11361, 14910, 17642, 19064 **NY** 4016, 4331, 7497, 15754, 17705 **OH** 12309 **OR** 12551, 19156 **PA** 36, 13090 **RI** 19253 **SC** 1547, 15411 **TX** 16203, 16265, 19397 **VA** 19865 **WA** 14990, 17638, 19525, 19527 *Canada:* **BC** 2735, 20236 **NB** 2727, 2730 **NF** 2734 **NS** 41, 12138 **PQ** 2733, 18122 **SK** 14849 *Intl:* **BMU** 1754 **CHN** 3610, 6191 **DEN** 4592 **ENG** 13152 **GER** 6447, 18035 **IND** 7746 **ITA** 2425 **SCT** 14966 **URE** 7906

Marine ecology: **CA** 8151, 10664 **FL** 6898, 17704 **MA** 9237 **MS** 6808 **NC** 19064 **RI** 17464 **SC** 15411 **TX** 3852, 19399 **VA** 19865 *Canada:* **BC** 20236 **NS** 12138 *Intl:* **BMU** 1754 **ENG** 13152 **SEN** 4526 **URE** 7906

Marine engineering (See also Naval architecture): **CA** 2494, 17838 **CT** 6299, 15005, 17130, 17132 **DC** 10835, 17874 **FL** 6898 **MA** 9822 **MD** 1408, 1463, 16018 **ME** 9553 **NH** 17879 **NJ** 7714, 8409 **NY** 6464, 14071, 15086, 15718, 17607, 20130 **OH** 2037 **PA** 17875, 17880 **SC** 17881 **TX** 16203 **VA** 4343, 4744, 16152 **WA** 16960 *Canada:* **BC** 3011 **NF** 9671 **NS** 2872, 2875 **PQ** 2786 *Intl:* **AUS** 1341 **CHN** 12926 **DEN** 6887 **ENG** 1919 **FRA** 15043 **GER** 2360 **NOR** 9678 **PRT** 13259 **SCT** 7154

Marine geology See: Submarine geology

Marine invertebrates: **CA** 18296 **FL** 5896 **MS** 6808 **PR** 19253 **WA** 19527 *Canada:* **ON** 2963

Marine mammals: **CA** 2577, 7490 **HI** 12682 **MA** 11464 **NY** 20363 **PA** 13090 **WA** 4946 *Canada:* **BC** 19758

Marine sciences (See also Ocean engineering): **AK** 18182 **CA** 18420, 18434 **DE** 18542 **FL** 4215, 6898, 18842 **GA** 18606 **MA** 14636 **MD** 11023, 18798, 18802 **ME** 13670 **MS** 6808, 10991 **NC** 1943, 11900 **NH** 19035 **OR** 12553 **PR** 19254 **TX** 2102, 19399 **VA** 17901, 19866 **VI** 6546 *Canada:* **NS** 2820 **ON** 2732 *Intl:* **AUS** 4270 **CHN** 3610, 6191 **DEN** 8092 **GER** 2360 **IND** 7746 **THA** 15440

Marine transportation See: Shipping

Mariology See: Mary, Blessed Virgin, Saint—Theology

Maritime history See: Navigation—History

Maritime law (See also Ocean law): **CA** 13052, 15654 **CT** 4192 **DC** 13326, 17254, 17494, 17800 **FL** 8605, 18575 **IL** 9869 **LA** 66, 4835, 16559 **MA** 1840, 5450, 9822 **MD** 12215, 15031 **NY** 1836, 6832, 7208, 9315, 14983, 16290 **PA** 13720 *Canada:* **NS** 2875, 4537 *Intl:* **GER** 18036 **NOR** 18139 **PRT** 13259

Marketing (See also Commodity exchanges; Consumers; Retail trade; Sales management; Sales promotion): **AL** 18160 **AZ** 16607 **CA** 1058, 5608, 6235, 8323, 12027, 15652, 15825, 16003, 18387, 19324, 20678 **CO** 1219, 18491, 18509 **DC** 4906, 7479, 17219, 17920 **DE** 5028, 13405 **FL** 5862, 14951 **GA** 5394, 9243 **IL** 676, 1481, 2384, 2621, 3141, 3529, 4405, 4664, 5949, 8597, 9649, 12255, 16012, 16318 **IN** 2136, 7779, 9162, 13545, 14878 **LA** 16555 **MA** 1995, 5697, 7170, 11801, 15700 **MI** 4602, 4817, 5964, 9200, 10316, 14084, 18870, 19679, 19956, 20414 **MN** 2401, 3044, 10459, 13050, 16341, 18896 **MO** 94, 12956, 20064 **NC** 6739, 13886 **NH** 11483 **NJ** 1207, 1216, 7314, 11745, 12941, 19969 **NM** 19050 **NY** 476, 675, 1399, 1575, 1965, 4027, 4316, 4665, 4890, 8051, 8210, 9295, 11092, 11608, 12256, 12655, 14191, 15096, 16319, 19282, 20819 **OH** 3818, 3820, 6704, 9965, 10025, 10600, 12297 **OK** 16571 **OR** 467, 8017 **PA** 617, 3930, 4299, 10562, 14038, 15256, 19186, 19216, 19219, 20313 **PR** 19238 **RI** 2299 **TN** 20401 **TX** 7633, 13895, 16213, 16216, 16446 **VA** 16712, 19269, 19501 **WA** 14997, 19515, 20359 **WI** 19626, 20103 *Canada:* **AB** 12963 **BC** 18268, 19759 **MB** 18784 **NF** 5371 **ON** 4139, 5015, 5433, 7720, 9929, 10225, 14137, 16004, 16320, 19446, 19563 **PQ** 2686, 5205, 9900 *Intl:* **BRZ** 18005 **ENG** 7841 **HUN** 7932 **IND** 15165 **ISR** 8270 **SWI** 5481, 15939 **THA** 16292

Marketing research: **CA** 8323, 9697, 19852 **CT** 16643, 20743 **IL** 5312, 6080, 16318 **MA** 3688, 6315 **MI** 4984, 9696 **MN** 6328, 13050 **NJ** 15169 **NY** 96, 2405, 20502 **OH** 12922, 13898 **PA** 3601, 7659, 14962 **PR** 3751 **WI** 17580 *Intl:* **GER** 7872 **SWI** 5481

Markham, Edwin: **NY** 19933

Marquand, John Phillips: **VA** 9704

Marriage (See also Family; Sex): **KY** 3169 **OR** 20244 *Canada:* **ON** 8412

Marshall, Bruce: **DC** 6379

Marshall, George Catlett: **VA** 9720

Martin, Mary: **NY** 10892

Marx Brothers: **PA** 6133

Marx, Karl (See also Socialism): **CA** 15473 *Intl:* **CHN** 27, 6246, 12932 **DEN** 8862 **GER** 5199

Mary, Blessed Virgin, Saint—Theology: **OH** 18533

Mary, Queen of Scots: **NY** 4023 **OH** 1113

Maryknoll Order: **NY** 9745

Maryland: **MD** 1455, 1456, 1542, 2591, 7264, 8393, 8419, 9272, 9750, 9756, 9764, 10680, 11046, 11461, 13298, 13302, 13355, 13360, 14640, 15498, 15990, 18816, 18818, 19994 **PA** 11032

Masaryk, Tomas Garrigue: **PA** 19225

Masefield, John: **AL** 14663 **CO** 18507 **CT** 4178, 20703 **NY** 19278 **VT** 19482 *Canada:* **ON** 13661

Masers See: Lasers and masers

Mason, George: **VA** 6814

Mason, William: **CT** 20721

Masonry (See also Building materials): **CA** 9785 **VA** 2112, 11127

Masons (Secret order) See: Freemasons

Mass media (See also Radio broadcasting; Television broadcasting): **CA** 4070, 9344 **FL** 13283 **HI** 5133 **IL** 18667 **IN** 5404, 7792, 17024 **KS** 18728 **MA** 5328 **MI** 10321 **MN** 18908 **NY** 15961 **OH** 12315 **PA** 19174 **WI** 15683, 19611 *Canada:* **BC** 14877 **ON** 2671, 19429 *Intl:* **BEL** 13689

Mass media (continued)
   BRZ 18005 ENG 8125 GER 7964, 9983 IRQ 933 NOR 12111 NZL 13687 SGP 1120 SPA 17980 SWE 15918

Mass media criticism: NY 3314

Mass media—Law and legislation: DC 2440, 6480, 13770, 20432 NY 3178, 12792 *Intl:* AUS 1336

Mass transit See: Urban transportation

Massachusetts: FL 12510 MA 540, 648, 860, 1647, 1801, 1988, 1993, 2066, 2200, 2600, 2601, 3021, 3464, 4112, 4206, 4962, 5051, 5266, 5582, 5586, 5960, 6057, 6730, 7019, 7242, 7248, 7279, 8474, 9091, 9410, 9476, 9571, 9589, 9654, 9792, 9828, 9833, 9979, 9981, 11012, 11034, 11433, 11474, 11787, 11854, 11872, 12382, 12383, 12392, 12643, 12804, 12958, 13668, 14634, 14787, 14949, 15338, 15799, 15841, 17679, 18827, 19962, 20166, 20595, 20598, 20601

Masters, Edgar Lee: DC 6379

Material culture (See also Folklore): AZ 7085 CA 18401 DC 15286 FL 5899 GA 6055 IN 7786 MD 7253 MI 5964, 20120 NC 916 NY 2228 PA 5065, 7265 TN 3300, 5127 TX 6020 VA 5673 *Canada:* NF 10051 ON 12486 PQ 2962 *Intl:* ENG 5358 POL 13171 SYR 15970

Materials: AK 963 AL 15516 AZ 9887, 10790 CA 105, 399, 2050, 2539, 9001, 9009, 9244, 9434, 9705, 9886, 12025, 14012, 14013, 14021, 14777, 15647, 17877, 17897, 18330, 19342, 20680 CO 8536 CT 2400, 14031, 17961, 17962, 18520 DC 17823, 17869 FL 19960 GA 1186, 9243 ID 5268 IL 693, 977, 4050, 4698, 4699, 5289, 16522, 18671 IN 395, 13540, 16642 MA 228, 1402, 5066, 6307, 6778, 9796, 9820, 10837, 13734, 15182, 16801, 16983, 20167 MD 9739, 16435, 18813 ME 5676 MI 5966, 6302, 6332, 10320, 17000 MN 7621, 10841, 16333 MO 403, 9885, 14449 NC 5039, 17078 NH 17879, 19032 NJ 409, 1193, 3877, 5535 NM 4258, 14778, 18298 NY 178, 4307, 5188, 6770, 9972, 11645, 11863, 15750, 16641, 16919, 20681 OH 974, 1044, 1125, 3705, 5413, 9307, 10987, 12318, 18469 OR 12521, 13309, 16057, 17110 PA 432, 452, 761, 1198, 9314, 12902, 19194, 19205, 19705, 20685 TN 9735 TX 6300, 11058, 15583 VA 1393, 10986, 13866, 17888 VT 19480 WA 19523 WI 8437 *Canada:* AB 7072 MB 102 NS 2680, 12154 ON 101, 322, 2699, 2821, 12487, 19451, 19559, 20683 PQ 3284, 13307, 15570 *Intl:* ARG 19751 AUS 107 BRZ 10384 CHN 7988 ENG 7992, 13406 GER 1564, 4692, 5545, 6449 ICE 7638 JPN 19423 NLD 5491, 16043 POL 16035 SAF 1273, 15382 SAU 5551 SWI 15937, 15938 TTO 3049

Materials handling: KS 1941 MD 2 OH 16363 OR 7608

Materials—Thermal properties: IN 13535, 13536

Mathematics: AK 18184 AL 16996, 17019, 18163 AR 18232 AZ 405, 1013, 1221, 8753, 9411, 16977, 18229 CA 134, 820, 2492, 2574, 3501, 3756, 5439, 6346, 6414, 6773, 6777, 7504, 7505, 7506, 7510, 7629, 9009, 9145, 9225, 9305, 10980, 11364, 14012, 14015, 14722, 15555, 15655, 16797, 16820, 17895, 17904, 18302, 18332, 18356, 18381, 18391, 18418, 18434, 18438, 19332, 19342, 19346, 19674, 19782, 20397 CO 1021, 3947, 8536, 11098, 11099, 17652, 18505, 18507 CT 6938, 11839, 14911, 18616, 20180, 20701, 20725 DC 3157, 4914, 6375, 9846, 11281, 16800, 17823, 17831, 17864 DE 18546 FL 5876, 5917, 7147, 16794, 16841, 17651, 17870, 18577, 20317 GA 5337, 6387 IA 14011, 18716 ID 975, 5268 IL 977, 1190, 2443, 9084, 10786, 12084, 12088, 18452, 18684, 20839 IN 2418, 5094, 7803, 7813, 9536, 13545, 13546, 13548, 17825, 19117 KS 1941, 8570, 18731, 20409 KY 8657, 9095, 9737, 16689, 18755, 18768, 18770 LA 15450, 16561 MA 71, 489, 827, 1999, 2019, 2071, 2072, 3895, 6091, 6774, 6775, 6960, 6966, 6983, 6990, 9796, 9806, 9810, 9820, 10557, 10632, 10967, 13174, 13731, 13733, 15232, 16553, 16801, 18831, 20155, 20597 MD 1964, 5218, 8415, 10983, 16018, 16982, 17624, 17625, 17650, 18805, 18813 MI 677, 5966, 9011, 10339, 10344, 18873, 18881, 20123, 20273 MN 13051, 16678, 18906, 18921 MO 6847, 17174, 18967, 20065, 20066 MS 10516 NC 5045, 19056 ND 19100 NE 12408, 19000 NH 4609, 11483, 16935, 17879, 19032 NJ 402, 1193, 1196, 1217, 1689, 5536, 6270, 6271, 7895, 7922, 8596, 13377, 14165, 14836, 15788, 16930, 17810 NM 11521, 17001, 18298, 19043 NY 2223, 2245, 2336, 2438, 3734, 3779, 3885, 4000, 4018, 4023, 4313, 4321, 5034, 5188, 5969, 6311, 6317, 6612, 6770, 7618, 7619, 7627, 7630, 8768, 11623, 11630, 13203, 13204, 13422, 13633, 13638, 14001, 14542, 15742, 15750, 15755, 15964, 16029, 16787, 19275 OH 1197, 2041, 5271, 5354, 6306, 8653, 9307, 9738, 10265, 12319, 12636, 16805, 16806, 18158, 18474 OK 817, 12346, 12371, 14147, 17485, 18446, 19125 OR 19154 PA 1059, 1199,

1259, 6092, 6094, 7909, 12053, 12908, 12911, 13289, 15900, 16135, 17880, 19188, 19218, 20318 PR 19247 RI 2281 SC 3794, 20323 SD 15417 TN 9736, 16796, 19372, 19774 TX 1260, 5029, 5084, 5533, 6300, 6850, 7458, 10988, 15504, 15535, 16214, 16218, 16829, 19402, 20247 UT 19474 VA 777, 886, 3274, 6347, 7923, 10194, 10990, 11144, 11258, 16152, 16986, 17882, 17888, 17906, 19271, 19505, 19920 VT 7622 WA 1572, 4231, 17066, 17649, 19523, 19535, 20047 WI 9713, 19604, 19621 WY 19661 *Canada:* AB 18187, 18202, 18295 BC 2682, 18276, 18281 MB 102, 18795 NB 19027 NS 16034 ON 101, 2828, 2860, 5018, 9953, 12498, 13654, 14135, 19446, 19456, 19543, 19544, 19553, 20794 PQ 9897, 9909, 18087, 18112, 18125 *Intl:* AJN 7874 AUS 18841 AUT 8124, 18032, 18702 BEL 8584, 18069 BRZ 6214, 8003, 18006 CHN 25, 4542, 7988, 20651 COL 3925 CRI 17989 ENG 6669, 7716, 18442 FIN 7126, 18634 FRA 6065, 7877, 18101, 18124, 18136 GER 5546, 6530, 7872, 13111, 18023, 18028, 18030, 18039, 18045, 18046, 18049, 18053, 18764 HUN 9541 ISR 7100, 16037, 18613 ITA 8077, 13186, 18011, 18015 JPN 10953, 16385 MEX 17994 MYS 15441 NLD 3267, 16044, 18130 NOR 18138 PAN 17997 POL 13193, 16035, 19666, 19667, 19668 RUS 17957 SPA 15560, 15566, 15567 SWI 5208, 15937, 15938, 18064 TWN 28 UZN 7873 VNM 6892 YUG 9843, 19664

Mather, Cotton, Increase, and Richard: MA 540

Maugham, William Somerset: CA 18428 TX 16200, 19392

Maurepas, Jean, Comte de: NY 4330

Mauritius: *Intl:* MUS 6241, 8466, 9851

Maximus, Valerius: NY 4330

Mazursky, Paul: CA 35

Mead, Margaret (Margaret Beteson): DC 9129

Meat industry and trade: IL 1055, 11231 NE 8222, 17187 *Canada:* ON 2955 *Intl:* GER 2362 NZL 9971

Mechanical engineering (See also Power transmission): AL 14153, 15516, 16593 AZ 9887 CA 399, 2272, 3868, 4589, 5935, 5936, 7640, 9145, 9225, 9926, 14777, 15647, 17877, 17886, 17960, 18330, 18434 CO 1219, 3408, 8536, 11099, 16710, 20279 CT 6941, 12100 DC 3157, 11843, 13272, 16941, 17874 FL 5876 GA 6387, 14944, 15479 HI 7050 ID 975 IL 1704, 3142, 5927, 16522, 18671 IN 1201, 13540, 16642, 19113 KS 1941, 8576 KY 18758, 18770 LA 17194 MA 1375, 6091, 9216, 9796, 12009, 15812, 16069, 16553, 16708, 18831, 20167 MD 1408, 8415, 16018, 18813 MI 4806, 4830, 5194, 5966, 6342, 9011, 10320, 20378 MO 2386, 10638, 15899, 18963 NC 3091, 5036, 5039 ND 19097 NH 4609, 19032 NJ 1933, 2387, 5535, 6033, 7714, 10576, 13372, 13500, 17810 NV 19014 NY 2219, 3096, 3734, 3779, 4000, 4307, 5353, 9592, 9972, 11645, 15750, 15967, 16646 OH 566, 974, 2118, 5354, 9738, 12094, 12307, 18158, 18469, 18480, 19693 OK 1719, 12371, 19126 OR 2262, 7176 PA 819, 4518, 12849, 12903, 12985, 15595, 15618, 16132, 17875, 17880, 19194, 19205, 20318 SD 15424 TN 9735, 15701, 16175, 19372 TX 1260, 4985, 5533, 8608, 9246, 15535, 16217, 16939, 16985, 19389 VA 6272, 7061, 15582 VT 19811 WA 12653 WI 10432 *Canada:* AB 3015, 10608 BC 1391 MB 9616, 9626, 18787 NB 11454, 19024 NS 2680, 2872, 7161, 16034 ON 56, 2822, 2838, 13656, 19443, 19559 PQ 2684, 13307, 13528, 15570, 18125 SK 19292 *Intl:* BUL 16032, 19904 CHN 25, 3607, 4542 COL 17978 ENG 7992, 8730 FIN 7126 GER 5542, 5545 ISR 16038 JPN 19423 NLD 7321 POL 16035 RUS 8292 SWI 15937, 15938 TTO 3049

Mechanics (See also Engineering; Soil mechanics; Strains and stresses (Mechanics); Thermodynamics; Vibration): CA 2487, 15647 GA 6387 IA 4700 IL 18671 IN 9536 KY 9095, 18758 MA 6960, 16983 MD 16018 NJ 6033 NY 4307, 7627, 11584, 15750, 16919 OH 1394, 3830, 18469 OK 19137 PA 1797, 9706, 20318 TX 19389 VA 7658, 10986 WA 19523 *Canada:* BC 18264 PQ 3284 *Intl:* CHN 4542, 20650 ITA 13186 JPN 19423 POL 7940 RUS 17957

Mechanics, Celestial: CT 20701 *Intl:* GER 1183 ITA 16498

Mechanization (See also Automation): OH 7892 *Intl:* RUS 3198

Medical care (See also Long-term care of the sick): AZ 990, 1541 CA 10010, 13620, 15808 CO 10004 CT 18527, 20723 DC 11137, 17939 FL 1908 GA 6408 HI 18622 IL 619, 10372, 18459 MA 6993, 9791 MD 17209, 17932, 17933 MI 4821 MO 1909 NC 15873 NJ 1927, 8457 NY 5701,

Medical care (continued)
7188, 11579 OR 8508 PA 1911, 7731, 15613, 19178 WA 19542 WI 20510 *Canada:* AB 280 ON 2749, 12470 PQ 4338 *Intl:* ENG 926

Medical care, Cost of: MA 17525

Medical care—Law and legislation: CA 8510 DC 8043 MD 12215, 19796 MO 6740 PA 2310, 7417, 20550 VA 7577

Medical devices See: Medical instruments and apparatus

Medical economics (See also Medical care, Cost of): CA 2495, 13706 DC 537, 679, 6766 IL 678, 1907 MD 17940 NC 1910 NJ 8457 NY 5340, 7416, 10207 PA 7417 *Canada:* ON 12441, 12449 PQ 13605

Medical electronics: CA 1642, 7175, 16022, 17841 IL 15157 IN 7795 MD 17625 MI 17355 MN 10019 NY 11674 OH 5675 PA 15080

Medical emergencies See: Emergency medical services

Medical entomology See: Insects as carriers of disease

Medical ethics: DC 6377, 17123 FL 3634, 10246 GA 14409 KS 18732 MA 3895, 6993, 19742 MN 18926 NY 7006 PA 5836, 9742, 13746 WA 11331 *Canada:* PQ 4338 *Intl:* SWE 15929

Medical group practice See: Group medical practice

Medical illustration: CT 20715 FL 18849 IL 12081, 12109, 18461 MA 6996 MD 6899, 17629 ME 10134 NY 11552 TX 19419 *Canada:* PQ 9908 *Intl:* ENG 14114

Medical instruments and apparatus: CT 6936 IL 7422 MA 3688, 6992 MD 17507 MN 13702 MO 8146 NJ 1171 NY 6905, 11579 PA 5219 WI 19589 *Intl:* CHN 7491

Medical jurisprudence: CA 1462, 4438, 6158, 12513 FL 9582 GA 13280 IL 9422 KS 8180 MA 6996, 10098 MD 17084 MI 12197 MN 18940 MO 15140 NY 6832, 8345, 11564, 11686 OH 3125 PA 481, 4854 TN 19766 WI 13571 *Canada:* ON 12449, 12484 PQ 4338 *Intl:* ENG 6678 GER 7927

Medical laws and legislation (See also Medical care—Law and legislation): AZ 12244 CA 7005, 9585 DC 17941 FL 1885 GA 417 LA 66 MA 2016 MI 7376 MO 14465 OH 3795 RI 7225 TX 3775 *Canada:* AB 280, 7078 PQ 9902, 18114 *Intl:* CZE 4515

Medical personnel: NJ 8457 NY 15715 *Canada:* AB 280

Medical policy (See also Health planning; Medical laws and legislation): DC 679 *Canada:* ON 2749

Medical records: CA 9984 FL 5864 IL 605 NY 11579 TX 16281

Medical research See: Medicine—Research

Medical school libraries: AK 18182 AL 18162, 18171, 19304 AR 18241 AZ 18209 CA 9255, 12707, 15465, 15653, 18353, 18361, 18390, 18414, 18417, 18423, 19330 CO 18511 CT 18518, 20715 DC 6378, 7475, 20007 FL 15453, 18572, 18848, 18849 GA 5336, 9995, 10112, 10726 IA 12706, 18711, 19162 IL 3518, 12081, 14148, 15486, 18633, 18695, 18696, 18698, 18699 IN 7807 KS 18733 KY 18756, 18771 LA 16564 MA 2017, 6996, 16549, 18835 MD 8432, 17954, 18800 MI 18852, 20124 MN 18894 MO 8744, 18632, 18965, 18974, 20071 NC 5046, 5112, 19061, 19940 ND 19103 NE 4426, 19010 NH 4608 NJ 18837, 18838, 18839, 18840 NM 19044 NV 19021 NY 229, 4323, 10819, 11588, 15737, 15745, 15752, 15848, 19286, 20751 OH 9996, 11984, 12314, 12330, 20645 OK 12364, 19132, 19133 OR 12522, 20301 PA 6830, 8360, 9997, 9999, 12840, 12900, 16147, 19178, 19211 PR 13209, 19256 SC 10014, 19309 SD 19315 TN 5128, 10021, 19369, 19371, 19776 TX 7445, 16196, 16210, 16274, 16275, 16798, 16810, 19416, 19417, 19419, 19421 UT 19477 VA 5170, 19504, 19862 VT 19479 WA 19529, 20050 WI 10000, 19586 WV 9726, 20203 *Canada:* AB 18200, 18294 BC 18285 MB 18790 NF 10052 NS 4541 ON 9951, 13644, 19163 PQ 9899, 18094, 18126 SK 19294 *Intl:* AUS 1344 BEL 18068 BHR 1409 BOL 17982 BRZ 17999, 18001 CHL 13213, 17998 CHN 3605, 3609, 15076 CMR 18129 ENG 18765 FRA 18100 GER 10018, 16041, 18034 HUN 4687, 15030 IDN 6224, 18016 IND 18486 ISR 8263 ITA 18014 JPN 6193,

16387, 16432 KOR 8793 MEX 17991 NLD 19919 PRT 18003 TWN 8577, 11311

Medical social work (See also Psychiatric social work): IL 7916 NY 17387 PR 19245

Medical sociology See: Social medicine

Medical statistics: AZ 999 DC 679 IA 8234 IL 16488 MD 8429, 11103, 17932 MN 10480, 12170 TN 16161 *Intl:* FRA 8052 GER 7927, 8761

Medical technology: CA 7711 DC 752 MA 9818 NV 19017 NY 11004, 15750 PA 15595 SD 19315 TN 10021 WI 19576 *Canada:* ON 10279, 10589, 12471 *Intl:* TWN 8577

Medicare: DC 8043 NY 4020 WV 20224

Medicine (See also Hospital libraries; Medical school libraries; names of medical specialties, e.g. Dermatology): AK 220 AL 16850 AR 18232 AZ 9661, 13027, 16865 CA 1223, 1587, 4384, 4850, 7079, 8257, 9009, 9334, 9353, 9353, 14973, 15974, 18420, 19173 CO 4778, 16823 CT 6936 DC 710, 3160, 4914, 11268, 17308, 17311, 17508 DE 4713 FL 4434, 5876, 5917, 18560, 20096 GA 18603 HI 7024, 7039 IA 15687 IL 13, 705, 977, 1586, 3529, 7333, 15490, 15602, 16614 IN 2136, 7795, 9165 KS 18731 LA 9385, 9391 MA 7178, 8007, 9102, 9820 MD 9765, 9994, 13299, 17507, 17626, 17629 MI 10335, 19970 MN 3008, 9859, 13702, 14562, 16339, 18940 MO 459, 10636 MS 10512, 10526, 18951, 18953 MT 10642, 17628 NC 2391, 2393, 4373, 5622, 6493, 12038, 12039, 12040 NE 12408 NJ 1644, 2133, 3692, 7313, 8458, 8767, 10123, 13559, 14169, 14783, 19969, 20657 NY 223, 1383, 2223, 3734, 7499, 7562, 9865, 10007, 10207, 10393, 11007, 11552, 11569, 11570, 11666, 11667, 12120, 13975, 14001, 15730, 15967 OH 2041, 3799, 3804, 3805, 3806, 9402, 9686, 10265, 11273, 12217 OK 12358, 12371 PA 617, 768, 3902, 9962, 13890, 15257, 15258, 17172 RI 2281 SC 3140, 9408, 19687 TX 1601, 1805, 6022, 16221, 16244 VA 1181, 17079, 17901 WA 10009, 15003, 20035, 20037 WI 20530 WV 20206 *Canada:* AB 2683 BC 2154, 2165, 3903 MB 9601, 9610, 9614, 20488 ON 2750, 2804, 2814, 2956, 3689, 6860, 7315, 10230, 10510, 19450, 19553 PE 10012 PQ 14, 1387, 2392, 3836, 5657, 5658, 7411, 10124, 18066 SK 14853 *Intl:* AMA 7867 AUS 5843, 19053, 20302 BRZ 6214 BUL 2346 CHN 31, 32, 40, 12930, 15074 COL 17983 CRI 17989 DEN 8777 ENG 6669, 14136, 18254 FIN 5710 FRA 1833, 6065, 12784, 18062, 18063, 18102, 18135 GER 6530, 8761 HUN 7556, 7928 IND 6242, 8527 ISR 7103, 15065 ITA 1821 JPN 8602 MEX 17990 NLD 14126 NOR 19160 SAF 10011 SPA 19478 SWE 15907 SWI 20619 TUR 6821, 16581 URE 8820

Medicine, Biochemic: CA 3739, 10388, 16984, 18341, 18403 DC 7476 DE 5028, 5031, 7641 IA 17188 IL 9423, 14148, 18696 LA 9391 MA 16534, 20597 MD 16435, 16990, 17627, 17629 ME 3345 MI 6342, 19681 MN 9858 NC 1645 NJ 10121, 10566, 14904 NM 18298 NY 559, 4311, 10007, 15778 OH 18476 OR 12527 PA 15779 RI 17464 TN 12184 TX 15529 VA 606, 6347 WA 9776, 10009, 19529 WI 8709 *Intl:* CZE 4515, 7973 FIN 355, 16586 FRA 18132 IND 7745 JPN 8152 SPA 15558, 19478

Medicine, Chinese See: Medicine, Oriental

Medicine, Clinical: AL 18162 CA 2474, 3189, 7127, 7419, 8685, 14195, 14768, 15653, 15953, 18363, 18414 CT 1935, 6934, 12969 DE 9990 FL 15453 HI 7034 IA 8240 IL 678, 9457, 12081, 18452 IN 4681, 10391, 13547 KS 18733 KY 17338 MA 3688 MI 10319, 18852, 19682, 20124 MN 7138 NC 10008, 17367 ND 13561 NM 9405 NV 17378 NY 1696, 4001, 5692, 10013, 11588, 12970, 15780, 17390 OH 12314, 13949, 14615, 16912, 18477, 20292 OR 225, 4347 PA 7974, 8456, 14608, 15779 SC 12812 SD 19315 TX 14964, 16196, 16210, 16798 WA 6767, 13450, 15591 WI 3991, 9441 WV 9726 WY 19656, 19657 *Canada:* BC 6712, 18256, 18267 ON 34, 9951 *Intl:* CHN 3609 FIJ 5689 SAU 5578

Medicine, Comparative: CA 20628 IA 8240 IN 13550 KS 8574 NM 9404 OH 12326 PA 19196 *Canada:* PQ 7865 *Intl:* ENG 14115

Medicine, Environmental See: Environmental health

Medicine, Experimental (See also Vivisection): NJ 3113 OH 12314

Medicine—History: AL 18171 AZ 17034 CA 9255, 9334, 14384, 15653, 18361, 18390, 18423, 18424, 18425, 19330 CO 4778, 12918, 18511 CT 6936, 11437, 20715 DC 6378, 17054 FL 18848, 18849 GA 9995 IA 12608, 18711 IL 678, 3518, 8159, 12081, 13719, 15486, 18452, 18461

Medicine—History: (continued)
IN 7761, 7794, 7856 **KS** 7166, 10085, 18732 **KY** 18771 **LA** 16434 **MA** 6996, 9572, 11465, 16549, 18835 **MD** 8432, 9994, 17629, 18800 **ME** 8622, 9555 **MI** 5963, 14519, 15186, 18852 **MN** 9859 **NC** 5046, 19061 **ND** 19103 **NE** 19010 **NJ** 10110, 14586 **NM** 19044 **NY** 2335, 4001, 4313, 9066, 10592, 11552, 11579, 11588, 11727, 13978, 14484, 15737, 15745, 15752, 19286 **OH** 1304, 3807, 8397, 13949, 18464, 18475 **OK** 6758 **OR** 12522 **PA** 427, 2079, 3490, 3902, 6830, 9106, 10685, 12847, 14483, 16147, 19181, 19197, 19211 **PR** 19256 **SC** 10014 **SD** 19315 **TN** 5128, 5421, 19776 **TX** 1601, 18641, 19416, 19419, 19421 **UT** 19716 **VA** 11139 **VT** 19479 **WA** 19529 **WI** 10000, 10416, 14305, 19586 **WV** 9724, 12336 *Canada:* **AB** 18200 **BC** 3903, 6712, 18285 **MB** 18790 **NF** 10052 **NS** 4541 **ON** 34, 9951, 19448, 19460, 19553, 19555 **PQ** 9908 *Intl:* **ENG** 14113, 14114, 14136 **FRA** 18132 **GER** 6530, 7870, 18020, 18027, 18029, 18034, 18059 **ISR** 16062 **ITA** 18010 **MEX** 17991 **NLD** 11408 **SCT** 14102, 14112 **SWE** 15929 **SWI** 18017, 18060

Medicine, Industrial: CA 5368 **DE** 5022 **GA** 483 **MD** 16976 **NY** 5187 **TN** 5183 **TX** 14502 **WA** 1938 *Canada:* **BC** 2182 **ON** 2761 **PQ** 321 *Intl:* **GER** 7927 **SPA** 15564

Medicine, Laser See: Lasers in medicine

Medicine, Legal See: Medical jurisprudence

Medicine, Military (See also Medicine, Naval): CA 17046 **MD** 17954 **OH** 16912 **PA** 19185 **TX** 16975 **VA** 17079 *Canada:* **ON** 2788

Medicine, Naval: MD 17862

Medicine, Oriental: CA 18424 **NJ** 13374 *Canada:* **PQ** 8129 *Intl:* **CHN** 40, 7491 **IND** 15997 **TWN** 2126

Medicine, Physical (See also Rehabilitation): CA 14811 **MI** 13803 **NY** 8070, 11570 **WI** 4484 *Canada:* **BC** 2172, 2173 **PQ** 7883

Medicine, Preventive (See also Public health): CA 9329, 13118 **IA** 8240 **MA** 6993 **ME** 9560 **RI** 13879 *Canada:* **MB** 9614 **ON** 12470 **PQ** 7864, 18091 *Intl:* **CHN** 12930 **GER** 7927

Medicine, Psychosomatic: CA 419 **DC** 723 **IL** 3523 **MA** 9790, 9946

Medicine and religion See: Medicine—Religious aspects

Medicine—Religious aspects: CO 13462 **FL** 3634 **VA** 4672

Medicine—Research: CA 12710, 17841, 18361 **CT** 118, 10389 **FL** 734 **GA** 17125 **IL** 4031 **KS** 15295 **MD** 7515, 11207, 16991, 17862 **MI** 10284 **NC** 13847 **NJ** 1898 **NY** 604, 7562, 9782, 10003, 11650 **OH** 3584 **OK** 12375 **PA** 1931, 7909, 8945 **TX** 16196 **VA** 1491 *Canada:* **MB** 9615 **NS** 19828 **ON** 19430 **PQ** 3836, 4650 *Intl:* **CMR** 2615 **JPN** 13683

Medicine—Study and teaching See: Medical school libraries

Medicine, Submarine See: Submarine medicine

Medicine, Thoracic (See also Heart—Diseases; Respiratory organs—Diseases): CA 1531 **MD** 8432 **NC** 17366 **NY** 14298 **TX** 14675 *Canada:* **PQ** 10695

Medicine, Transportation See: Transportation medicine

Medicine, Veterinary See: Veterinary medicine

Medieval history See: Middle Ages—History

Mediterranean region: *Intl:* **FRA** 3261

Melchior, Lauritz: NE 4580

Melies, Georges: NY 10908

Melville, Herman: CA 3752 **HI** 18629 **IL** 11752 **NH** 4616 **PA** 7811 **UT** 20809 **VA** 19510

Membranes (Technology): MA 8221, 10407 **MN** 18911 **OH** 5313 **OR** 1711 *Canada:* **ON** 2818 *Intl:* **GER** 13099

Memory: NY 4022 **RI** 2276

Memphis (TN): TN 10065, 10072, 10076, 20200

Men: CA 10093 **MA** 9803

Mencken, Henry Louis: CA 14718 **CT** 20703 **KS** 18724 **KY** 18768 **MD** 15990 **NH** 4616 **NY** 2244 **PA** 6457, 19197

Mendelssohn, Felix: *Intl:* **GER** 15794

Mennonites (See also Amish; Anabaptists; Hutterite Brethren): CA 6162 **IN** 1139, 7257, 10091 **KS** 1784, 10088 **OH** 1917 **PA** 2108, 8921, 8929, 10090, 10403, 20844 **VA** 5154 *Canada:* **MB** 2958, 10087, 10089, 15771 **ON** 6714

Mental health: AL 17285 **CA** 19347 **CO** 20259 **DC** 724, 8043 **IA** 8232 **IL** 18459 **IN** 3111, 3269 **KY** 8669 **MA** 1980, 9826 **MD** 8428, 17932 **MI** 14261, 18869 **MO** 20063 **MS** 10521 **NY** 4028, 5968, 10095, 10128, 11580, 11674, 11675, 13270, 17379 **OH** 3708, 12283, 12325, 17393 **PA** 6830 **PR** 13511 **RI** 7956 **TX** 10099, 16246 **VA** 11236 **WA** 631 **WI** 20517 *Canada:* **AB** 279 **BC** 2165 **MB** 9614

Mental health facilities: AR 1030, 1726 **AZ** 1004 **CA** 419, 1223, 2548, 2593, 6263, 6487, 8524, 10221, 10971, 12795, 13231, 15372, 15803, 20582 **CO** 3942, 3943 **CT** 4207, 5565, 6843, 7950, 12121 **DC** 4847 **DE** 4734 **FL** 5901, 5902, 8908, 15427, 19320 **GA** 6392, 6399, 6609, 20184 **HI** 7036 **IA** 7732, 10097, 10809 **IL** 424, 3541, 5298, 7704, 9513, 9889, 15192, 20838 **IN** 3111, 3366, 5510, 9250, 9528, 10874, 11459, 12213, 15541 **KS** 8442, 8954, 12587, 12770, 16406, 20483 **KY** 5167, 12619, 20298 **LA** 3344, 15444 **MA** 2004, 9192, 9823, 9946, 9980, 11475, 13919 **MD** 2214, 4449, 5165, 15596, 15606 **ME** 1470, 10346 **MI** 1577, 8873, 12035, 12193, 13063 **MN** 881, 10716, 20456 **MO** 6210, 14393, 14447, 15446, 20277 **MT** 10096 **NC** 2254, 3482, 4925, 16625 **ND** 11923, 15442 **NE** 7007, 11848 **NH** 11486 **NJ** 836, 5446, 5553, 6756, 9701, 11943, 16483 **NM** 11526 **NV** 11422 **NY** 2339, 3031, 3343, 4424, 4431, 5310, 6587, 6907, 7498, 8723, 8724, 9290, 10205, 10362, 10592, 11581, 11673, 11676, 11677, 11684, 12801, 13048, 13635, 14621, 20442 **OH** 1230, 2603, 4656, 5585, 9168, 13258, 14214, 20294, 20578 **OK** 6758, 20296 **OR** 5164 **PA** 387, 5091, 5168, 6174, 6925, 7016, 7963, 12862, 12863, 12867, 12868, 12994, 19229, 19982 **RI** 2413 **SC** 2296, 6745, 6848, 15404 **TN** 10062 **TX** 1316, 14676, 16183, 16244, 16247, 20407 **UT** 19710 **VA** 3367, 5166, 15547, 20297 **VT** 2088, 19809 **WA** 20036, 20040 **WI** 2266, 10083, 10423, 13997, 20485 **WY** 20669 *Canada:* **AB** 283, 284, 289 **BC** 13956 **MB** 2074, 15021 **NF** 20085 **NS** 12146 **ON** 2203, 3777, 6865, 8732, 9267, 11875, 13624, 14599 **PQ** 3252, 3253, 4649, 4974, 7392, 7398, 7399, 7886, 14140 **SK** 20356

Mental hygiene See: Mental health

Mental retardation: CA 2526, 5573, 8949, 13235, 15372 **CO** 20366 **CT** 4191 **FL** 15977 **GA** 6398, 6609 **IA** 6507, 8232 **IL** 3541, 8314, 9487, 9889, 10872, 15079 **IN** 3366 **KS** 12770, 20483 **MA** 7318 **MD** 8625 **MI** 12193 **MN** 2065, 5595 **MS** 10521 **NE** 1621 **NJ** 7567, 8462 **NM** 9359 **NY** 2252, 3343, 4028, 9070, 10627, 11678 **OH** 919, 18147 **PA** 5316, 6857, 8975 **SC** 15406, 15407 **SD** 15420 **TX** 10099, 16245, 16246 **VA** 3367, 3379 **VT** 2076 **WA** 20031, 20037, 20038 **WI** 1788, 8635, 15520 **WY** 20673 *Canada:* **AB** 18190 **MB** 14226 **ON** 7588, 12423, 12457, 12458, 13348, 14029 **PQ** 7397, 10692 *Intl:* **GER** 7927

Mental tests See: Educational tests and measurements

Mercer, John Francis: VA 6814

Merchant marine: MA 9822 **MD** 16462 **NY** 15718, 16780, 17607 **VA** 9676 *Canada:* **NS** 9691

Meredith, George: VA 15932

Merman, Ethel: NY 10892

Merton, Thomas: KY 1687, 6455 **MO** 8640 **NY** 11357

Mesmerism (See also Hypnotism): MN 1427

Mesoamerica See: Indians of Central America

Metabolism: CA 17296 **CT** 3694 **MD** 11207 *Canada:* **ON** 19430 *Intl:* **GER** 13110

Military engineering: DC 16941 IL 16921 **MA** 17133 **MO** 16925 **NH** 4609 **OH** 20316 **VA** 16924

Military history (See also Naval history): AK 17063, 17068 AL 16815, 17008, 17009, 17017 **AR** 1034 **AZ** 988, 6002, 13056, 17013 **CA** 753, 14686, 16474, 16833, 16869, 16878, 16927, 17909 **CT** 11500 **DC** 1063, 7274, 11190, 16825, 16974, 17226, 17600, 17609 **FL** 16866 **GA** 17012, 17021, 17067, 17071, 17712 **HI** 16852, 16892, 17601 **IL** 5775, 6009, 16818 **KS** 16928, 17124, 17709 **KY** 8659, 17020 **LA** 6011 **MA** 835, 2008, 7189, 12382 **MD** 8154, 16933, 16973, 17018, 17057, 17710, 17824 **MI** 16999 **MN** 10465, 16958 **MO** 10542, 16893, 16925 **MS** 16856, 17787 **MT** 10643 **NC** 5114, 17060 **ND** 16874 **NE** 11379, 15125 **NH** 13254 **NJ** 16931 **NM** 16853, 16858, 17714 **NV** 16877 **NY** 2328, 6013, 11680, 12385, 16993, 16994, 17064, 17131 **OH** 13484 **OK** 17010 **PA** 2316, 12878, 16995, 17711, 19185 **RI** 2282 **SC** 2606, 3719, 17077 **TN** 17821 **TX** 5996, 7209, 7447, 16200, 16809, 16816, 16860, 17004, 17022, 17028, 17070, 17707, 19413, 19414 **VA** 1064, 3129, 4620, 6347, 9720, 11215, 16859, 17003, 17011, 17016, 17025, 17026, 17605, 19867, 19966 **VT** 12122 **WA** 16870, 17693, 17887 **WI** 19633, 19636 **WV** 17729, 20209 **WY** 17708 *Canada:* **NT** 2789 **ON** 10228 *Intl:* **AUS** 1330, 1350 **ENG** 6683, 16722 **POL** 13161 **SPA** 15557

Military intelligence: AZ 17013 CA 20551 CO 16863 DC 16980, 17166, 17861 **MD** 19233 **VA** 1045

Military law: CA 10023 DC 13475, 17163 VA 4620, 17903 *Canada:* **ON** 2784 *Intl:* **NLD** 8784

Military medicine See: Medicine, Military

Military psychology See: Psychology, Military

Military research (See also Ordnance research): CA 17177 NY 13955 TX 16226 *Intl:* **DEN** 4771

Military strategy See: Strategy

Military transportation See: Transportation, Military

Military vehicles See: Vehicles, Military

Milk (See also Dairy products): IL 561 MD 17203

Millay, Edna St. Vincent: DC 9129 RI 19268

Miller, Arthur: TX 19392

Miller, Henry: CA 18379 IL 15492 MN 18931 NH 4616 NY 2244 TX 19392

Milton, John: CT 20703 IL 18689 IN 7794 KY 18754 *Canada:* **AB** 18196 **ON** 19555 *Intl:* **NZL** 11739

Mime: NY 683 WA 19521 *Canada:* **ON** 16416

Mineral industries: MN 17119

Mineralogy (See also Petrology): CA 2489, 2523, 6281, 11341, 14712 **CO** 17106, 17537, 18494, 20279 **DC** 15280 **IA** 18710 **IL** 18673 **IN** 7788, 13539 **KY** 18749 **MA** 6948 **MI** 10342 **MO** 20060 **MS** 10519 **NJ** 13373 **NY** 687, 4014, 19283 **OH** 12286, 12322 **OK** 19128 **PA** 2303, 3085, 19181 **TX** 2102, 6023, 19391 **UT** 19707 **VA** 17539, 19872 *Canada:* **NB** 11454 **ON** 6833, 12482, 14131 **PQ** 18084 *Intl:* **AUS** 15391 **CZE** 4510 **ENG** 11340 **FRA** 6064 **HUN** 7551 **SAF** 6367

Miners: CA 15312 CO 2030, 18508 *Canada:* **BC** 10963 *Intl:* **SAF** 3419

Mines and mineral resources (See also Mining engineering): AK 212, 17109, 17532 **AZ** 986, 988, 1001, 1864, 15081, 18221, 18229 **CA** 1809, 2449, 2523, 2524, 3502, 3744, 8682, 12767, 13146, 14753, 17082, 18330, 19678 **CO** 450, 3408, 3941, 3944, 3947, 4506, 4785, 6006, 13046, 16710, 17271, 17537, 20279 **CT** 3833, 4965 **DC** 17111, 17249, 20609 **DE** 4733 **FL** 5875, 5894 **ID** 18650, 18654 **IL** 7691, 7696, 15358 **IN** 7788 **KS** 8557 **KY** 18745, 18749 **MA** 9796 **MI** 7434, 8249, 10344 **MN** 9062, 10483, 10488, 11971, 18941 **MO** 10547, 17115, 18980, 20252 **MT** 10641, 10643, 17107 **NM** 11521, 17108 **NV** 11421, 19022 **NY** 4000, 5059, 8088, 11630, 15967 **OK** 8687 **OR** 11393 **PA** 1265, 4230, 10435, 10711, 12860, 12902, 17117 **SD** 15417 **TX** 3852, 6597, 15116, 19382 **UT** 17113,

19707 **VA** 17539, 19886 **WA** 5171, 20026 **WI** 19645 **WV** 17272 **WY** 6368, 15933, 19654 *Canada:* **AB** 270, 5458, 10608, 15951 **BC** 1530, 2158, 2174, 2183, 3418, 4045, 13092, 16051, 18266 **MB** 9608 **NB** 11446 **NF** 11759 **NS** 3022, 12141, 16034 **ON** 2289, 2699, 2700, 2963, 6833, 7010, 7730, 11835, 12482, 13935, 20097 **PQ** 4098, 11836, 13596, 15305 **YT** 20831 *Intl:* **AUS** 1332 **AUT** 6364 **CHN** 12928 **ENG** 7993 **FIN** 6366, 7126 **FRA** 6064, 11203 **SAF** 3419, 6367 **SAU** 5551

Mining engineering (See also Petroleum engineering): AZ 15041 CA 2523, 7640, 9926 **CO** 133, 450, 17112 **MN** 17119 **NV** 19018 **NY** 5353 **PA** 19205 **TX** 9482 *Canada:* **BC** 2158 **NS** 3022 **ON** 6540, 13648, 20097 **PQ** 9909 *Intl:* **BOL** 11235 **POL** 13165 **SAF** 3419

Mining law: CA 18331 CO 20144 IL 15489

Minneapolis (MN): MN 7406, 10449, 10452, 10454, 18920

Minnesota: IL 11031 MN 880, 1640, 1913, 2264, 3062, 3349, 3520, 4354, 4443, 4527, 5515, 5691, 6563, 6649, 7139, 7212, 8253, 8284, 8303, 8539, 8787, 8867, 8901, 9023, 9029, 9634, 9729, 10449, 10464, 10465, 10466, 10476, 10483, 10488, 10492, 11803, 11850, 11913, 11971, 12055, 12404, 12574, 12605, 13074, 13217, 13700, 13891, 14564, 14566, 15506, 15530, 15768, 15797, 17724, 19988, 19996, 20185, 20248, 20357

Minorities (See also Segregation): CA 11460, 17812 DC 8465, 17483 IA 18713 **KS** 8563, 8564 **LA** 810 **MI** 10298, 10328, 18885 **MN** 10456 **NY** 5410, 10591, 11049, 13640, 15725 **OH** 3126 **WI** 15684 *Canada:* **NS** 12147 *Intl:* **FRA** 6067

Minorities—Education: CO 20259

Minority business enterprises: PA 16749 TN 16157

Missiles See: Rockets (Ordnance)

Missions (See also Evangelistic work): AL 15448, 15992 AZ 15539 CA 946, 3043, 6200, 6535, 7914, 9840, 12661, 14800, 19290, 20634 **CO** 3635, 4776, 7666 **CT** 4182, 6940, 20708 **DC** 3155 **FL** 5744, 5869 **GA** 3117, 3763, 16383 **HI** 7052 **IA** 18555 **ID** 1946 **IL** 1308, 1782, 3152, 5495, 7422, 8490, 10706, 15008, 20367, 20368 **IN** 1139, 6602 **KY** 1102, 8662 **MA** 6575 **MD** 1793, 19991 **MI** 6595, 13778 **MN** 4446, 5496, 9442, 9445, 11910, 12178 **MO** 1134, 3330, 3334, 3685, 4115, 5758, 11356 **NC** 5114, 10720 **ND** 16500 **NJ** 16733 **NM** 5737, 10079 **NY** 502, 5223, 7433, 9745, 9746, 12171, 16667, 16693 **OH** 3640, 12219 **OK** 12348 **OR** 10856, 12043, 19159 **PA** 496, 497, 1300, 7009, 8916, 10719, 12978 **SC** 3978 **SD** 11857 **TN** 5127, 6902, 10078 **TX** 4570, 5118, 11941, 12612, 13423 **VA** 15457, 15458 **WA** 9444, 15329, 20390, 20611 **WI** 9709, 13362 *Canada:* **AB** 6496, 10829, 13296 **BC** 20288 **NS** 1264 **ON** 867, 9262, 12428, 16696, 19358 **PQ** 5974 **SK** 2896 *Intl:* **BEL** 15194 **GER** 10508 **SWI** 5480

Mississippi: FL 19550 GA 11040 MS 3086, 8306, 10517, 10525, 10527, 10530, 14032, 18949, 18954, 19354, 19825

Mississippi River: IA 13557 IL 1297, 19685 MN 16957 MO 10537 MS 16947 **WI** 19577

Mississippi Valley: MO 10536 TN 10076 WI 19645

Missouri: MO 1915, 3350, 3783, 3874, 8302, 8439, 8546, 8549, 8772, 10536, 10537, 10538, 10542, 10730, 11030, 11972, 12057, 14257, 14391, 14454, 15603, 15681, 18959, 18962, 18979, 20250, 20252, 20253

Mistletoe: CO 17522

Mitchell, Margaret: GA 1245, 18600 TX 4561

Mitchell, Maria: NY 19789

Mixing: NY 9159

Mobile (AL): AL 1835, 7246, 10925

Mobilization: DC 17609

Model railroads See: Railroads—Models

Models, Fashion: NM 20626

Modern art See: Art, Modern

Modern dance: NC 19080 NY 4324, 11636

Modoc Indians: CA 17743

Mogollon Indians: NM 17721

Mohammedanism See: Islam

Molecular biology: AK 18182 CA 805, 1643, 1752, 4929, 14641, 14779, 14973, 15648, 15651, 18305 CO 11221, 18506 CT 20180 IN 19116 KY 18744 MA 5990, 6360, 6949, 20594 MD 89, 11204, 17208 MI 10334 MO 20056 NC 19067, 19068 NJ 13369 NY 4003, 20751 PA 16130 TX 19397 Canada: MB 2666 PQ 2660, 4650, 9893 Intl: CHN 12930 FRA 12784 GER 13099

Mollusks: CA 11341, 14802, 15651, 17644 DE 4721 HI 1865 LA 9387 MI 18877 NC 19064 NY 687, 12698 PA 3085 TX 2102, 4341

Monarchy: Canada: ON 10601

Monasticism and religious orders (See also names of specific orders, e.g. Carmelites): CT 11 DC 9117, 12229, 14572 IL 11266 KY 1687, 6455 LA 14361 MI 20275 MN 14334 MO 4110, 14463 ND 1176 NY 5971, 12782, 14240, 14351 SD 1906 WI 14551 Canada: SK 14583 Intl: BEL 15194

Monetary policy (See also Credit): Intl: MEX 3265 PAK 12695 SWI 6292

Money (See also Banks and banking; Coinage; Credit; Finance; Gold; Silver): DC 5649, 8157 MA 636, 5634 MI 19956 MO 5646 NJ 11745 NY 4027, 12691 PA 5644, 19213 VA 5645

Mongolia: CA 18316 Intl: CHN 9139

Monroe, James: VA 10628, 19510

Montana: CA 18402 CO 11039 MT 1870, 3121, 3892, 5160, 6183, 6693, 10606, 10643, 10650, 10654, 11347, 12745, 12763, 17676, 18985, 18987 WA 11036

Montesquieu, Baron Charles Louis de: NY 4330

Montessori method of education: Canada: ON 19566

Montgomery, Lucy Maud: Canada: ON 18612

Montreal (PQ): Canada: PQ 9975, 15789

Monuments (See also Historic sites): AZ 17692, 17761, 17788 CA 17699, 17743 CO 17706 FL 17685, 17698 GA 17712 IA 17703 IN 17744 MD 17710 MN 17724, 17766 MO 17719, 17736 MT 17697 NE 17732, 17776 NM 17671, 17673, 17682, 17714, 17721 NY 17782 OH 17754, 17763 SC 17713 SD 17756 TX 17687 UT 17701, 17785 VA 17677 Intl: FRA 4761 YUG 7965 ZMB 4059

Moody, Dwight Lyman: IL 10707

Moon: TX 9437

Moore, Clement Clarke: PA 3084

Moore, Henry: Canada: ON 1078

Moore, Marianne Craig: OH 19425 PA 14068

Moore, Thomas: NY 11599

Moran, Thomas: CO 16584 NY 5120

Moravian Church: NC 7239, 10720, 12388 PA 10719, 10721

More, Sir Thomas: CA 19290 CT 20703 MA 1982 NY 14357 Canada: SK 14598

Morgan, Julia: CA 2500

Morgan, Lewis Henry: NY 19278

Morley, Christopher: NY 2300, 13632, 19278 PA 7015

Mormon Church: CA 9841, 14679, 18355 FL 3681 HI 20811 IA 6608 IL 7698 MO 13822 NJ 13386 OH 13479 UT 3662, 3674, 19476, 19709, 20797, 20809 Canada: AB 3654

Morocco: Intl: FRA 7885 MOR 10743

Morse, Samuel Finley Breese: DC 9129

Mortgages: DC 10761, 17241, 17596 NY 2329 PA 16749 WI 10245 Canada: ON 2765

Mortuary science See: Undertakers and undertaking

Moskowitz, Belle: CT 4178

Motel management See: Hotel management

Motion picture actors and actresses: NJ 6005 NY 10833, 11634, 13841 TX 19393 Canada: PQ 3714 Intl: ENG 9730

Motion pictures (See also Silent films): AZ 1019 CA 35, 584, 1800, 2479, 2572, 3980, 4666, 6526, 7335, 7902, 9281, 9343, 9432, 12203, 14702, 14725, 14726, 17973, 18370, 18379, 18399, 19336 CT 6939 DC 6379, 9120, 9130, 11033 FL 10250, 18584 GA 1236 HI 7038 IL 1083, 3539, 6523, 11953, 15493, 18667, 18672, 18685 KY 15580, 18768 MA 6149, 9816 MD 9751 MI 4825, 5850 MN 10444, 10446, 10451, 19947 NH 4616 NJ 380, 2609, 13388, 17702 NY 891, 2240, 2795, 6760, 10057, 10773, 10906, 10908, 10909, 11634, 13626, 13988, 14925, 15726, 15732, 20763 OH 3827, 12329, 13477 OK 12367 OR 10846 PA 3711, 6095, 6125, 16149 PR 19250 TX 15502, 19392, 19393 UT 20797, 20803 VA 19503 WI 1105, 10426, 19627 Canada: AB 18287 BC 2799, 18271 MB 2798 NS 12142 ON 2768, 3712, 10223 PQ 2793, 2797, 2801, 3713, 3714, 4122, 4892, 13589, 13610 SK 2796, 14875 Intl: AUT 7303, 12596 BRZ 18005 CHN 1657 ENG 13200 ITA 8280 MEX 17992 MYS 9568 POL 13170 ROM 39 SGP 1120 SWI 20851

Motivation (Psychology): MA 6987 OH 12273

Motley, Arthur Harrison: MN 18920

Motorcycles: CA 10782 MI 4826 PA 899

Mott, Lucretia: PA 15902

Mount, William Sidney: NY 10927

Mountaineering: CA 15159 CO 18507 IL 10830 MA 912 NY 471 OR 9861 VT 12122 WY 11248, 19654 Canada: AB 414 Intl: ITA 3845 SCT 14953

Moving industry See: Storage and moving trade

Mowat, Farley Mc Gill: Canada: ON 9954

Mozambique (See also Africa, East): Intl: MOZ 10834

Mozart, Wolfgang Amadeus: IL 543 NY 13824 OH 10821 WA 19536

Muggeridge, Malcolm: IL 20369

Muir, John: CA 17737, 19172

Mules: TX 565

Multiple sclerosis: NY 11239

Mumming: PA 11551

Municipal engineering (See also City planning; Sanitary engineering; Water-supply): Canada: AB 15663

Municipal government (See also State and provincial government; Urban policy): AL 183, 10580 AZ 16545 CA 8132, 9325, 9326, 9349, 12208,

Municipal government (continued)
14692 **CO** 13506 **CT** 2114 **DC** 8081, 11213, 11226, 20432 **FL** 12569 **GA** 14884 **HI** 7379 **IA** 9028 **IL** 3525, 12058, 19691 **KY** 8347 **MA** 1988, 6981 **MD** 1444, 9752 **MI** 4824, 10292, 12200 **MN** 9029, 10452, 14556 **NY** 809, 11559, 11563, 13411 **OH** 3829 **PA** 12842 **PR** 13521 **SC** 10861 **TN** 10864 **TX** 1315, 16223 **VA** 19859 **WA** 10863, 15001 **WI** 9527, 10425, 20529 *Canada:* **AB** 291 **MB** 9628 **NS** 12140 **ON** 6867, 10226, 12472, 12488, 20160 **PQ** 13590

Murdoch, Iris: *Canada:* **ON** 9954

Murfree, Mary Noailles (Charles Egbert Craddock): **OH** 18534

Muscles—Diseases: **CA** 416 **MD** 11047

Museum conservation methods: **DC** 15276 **WY** 20664 *Canada:* **ON** 2672, 2673 *Intl:* **BTN** 1810 **YUG** 20829

Museum techniques: **AZ** 18210 **CA** 19331 **CT** 19931 **DC** 482, 15275 **IA** 14790 **IL** 10920 **ME** 9565 **MI** 15085 **MO** 20607 **NM** 9853 **NY** 687, 10588, 13985, 15849, 19276 **OH** 167 **OR** 15511 **PA** 36, 12879 **SC** 10924 **TN** 10063 **TX** 4341, 12726, 15666 **VA** 3934 **WA** 10900, 15675 **WI** 10431, 11429 **WV** 17729 *Canada:* **AB** 14138 **BC** 13227, 14101 **MB** 9619 **NS** 12149 **ON** 2672, 2964, 10227, 14131, 16384 **SK** 14874 *Intl:* **AUS** 13662 **CZE** 2086, 4512 **ENG** 16011 **FIN** 5711 **FRA** 16765 **HUN** 2321 **YUG** 20829

Music (See also Band music; Chamber music; Orchestral music; Piano music; specific instruments, e.g. Clarinet music): **AK** 18176 **AL** 1853 **AR** 12609, 18233 **AZ** 1017, 13026, 18224 **CA** 338, 1741, 2479, 2568, 2572, 3900, 6500, 7902, 9104, 9281, 9343, 11460, 12203, 12683, 14916, 15312, 15656, 15658, 18392, 18426, 19259, 19341 **CO** 11355, 18504 **CT** 4179, 6937, 18516, 18614, 20178, 20717 **DC** 4911, 9120, 9131 **DE** 18540 **FL** 5920, 10250, 18578, 18850, 19322 **GA** 1237, 3763, 18600 **HI** 7038 **IA** 18717 **ID** 18649 **IL** 543, 1083, 3522, 7709, 8490, 11999, 14058, 15488, 18455, 19779, 20256 **IN** 1438, 1442, 2417, 7796, 7818, 14510 **KS** 6176, 18739, 20413 **KY** 5150, 18769 **LA** 9384, 11544, 15450, 16562 **MA** 808, 1983, 1997, 3894, 6946, 6964, 6988, 9811, 11469, 15238, 15600, 18830, 20154, 20370, 20598 **MD** 8422, 8424, 9765, 13300, 16440, 18818, 18821 **ME** 13243 **MI** 862, 4825, 5850, 8045, 18878, 20271 **MN** 1293, 3910, 6815, 10446, 14561, 14561, 18925 **MO** 8547, 10537, 14452, 18976, 18977, 20062 **MS** 1914 **NC** 915, 5047, 5115, 13038, 14230, 19072 **ND** 11924, 18796, 19101 **NH** 4613, 9586 **NJ** 6128, 6488, 9529, 10747, 11750, 13378, 13379, 14157, 16479 **NM** 19042 **NY** 460, 690, 2193, 2234, 2240, 2334, 3733, 4019, 4324, 8491, 9020, 9594, 9636, 10057, 10738, 10866, 11605, 11635, 11637, 11638, 13627, 13824, 13988, 15706, 15707, 15713, 15731, 15732, 15740, 15756, 15958, 19788, 20695, 20763 **OH** 1432, 2039, 3822, 4657, 4846, 8654, 10266, 10268, 12218, 12332, 13477, 14921, 16392, 16398, 18156, 18533 **OK** 12367, 19127 **OR** 10846, 12681, 19972 **PA** 3078, 3183, 6119, 7810, 7811, 12894, 15889, 15901, 18244, 19226 **PR** 19246, 19255 **RI** 1279 **SC** 4259, 8468 **TN** 10073, 19368, 19773 **TX** 4561, 4653, 6021, 6927, 7461, 14670, 15502, 16209, 18644, 19390 **UT** 15519, 20803 **VA** 3934, 7332, 13911, 19270, 19507 **VT** 10354 **WA** 3381, 4337, 5175, 10594, 14999, 19536, 20045 **WI** 19610, 19653, 19907, 20527 **WV** 20220 *Canada:* **AB** 1464 **BC** 18277 **MB** 2907, 10087, 18791 **NB** 1250 **NS** 2904, 12142 **ON** 2803, 2809, 2903, 2969, 8979, 10223, 19168, 20793 **PQ** 2892, 2905, 9907, 13576, 18065, 18089 **SK** 14875 *Intl:* **AJN** 1388 **AUS** 15697 **AUT** 1354 **BRZ** 18005 **BUL** 2345 **CZE** 13294 **DEN** 4770 **ENG** 6664, 19360, 20776 **FRA** 1832, 6063 **GER** 1597, 6441, 8740, 14189, 15794 **MEX** 17992 **NOR** 12111 **POL** 13170, 16664 **ROM** 39 **SPA** 15557 **THA** 16293

Music, African: **NY** 4007 *Intl:* **GER** 18037

Music, British: *Canada:* **ON** 2809 *Intl:* **ENG** 5358 **SCT** 14953

Music, Canadian: *Canada:* **AB** 2968 **BC** 2965 **NB** 10796 **ON** 2809, 2966, 10223, 13661 **PQ** 2967, 13579

Music—Composition See: Composition (Music)

Music, German: **OH** 12320 **PA** 3078 *Intl:* **GER** 6440, 7110

Music, Gospel See: Gospel music

Music—History and criticism: **CA** 14702, 18335 **IL** 3540, 11752 **KY** 15462, 18742 **MA** 2015 **MD** 18821 **MN** 18925 **NC** 10722, 19072 **NE** 19001 **NJ** 6128, 11744 **NY** 4019, 11637, 15706, 15713, 15740 **OH** 10821, 12320, 18465 **PA** 9643, 19226, 20187 **SD** 15146 **TX** 15502 **WA** 10594 **WI**

10426, 19635 *Canada:* **BC** 19488 **MB** 2078, 18791 **NB** 10796 **ON** 19447, 19561 *Intl:* **CZE** 15223 **GER** 7302

Music—Instruction and study (See also Composition (Music); Conducting): **CA** 2567, 14730, 18392 **CO** 8354 **DC** 3159 **FL** 15785, 18578, 18850 **IL** 3540, 7709, 12086, 14058, 18455, 19779 **IN** 2417, 7796 **KS** 20413 **KY** 9395, 18742 **MA** 1743, 1983, 11469, 16551 **MD** 8424, 18821 **MI** 8045 **MN** 18925 **MO** 14439, 18977 **NC** 915, 19085 **NE** 19001 **NJ** 6128, 20327 **NY** 9594, 9636, 15706, 15713, 15740, 15756, 16585, 19279 **OH** 3810, 12218, 12320, 18465 **PA** 4491, 9643, 15053, 16146 **PR** 4222 **TN** 19767 **TX** 1604, 4561, 13893, 19390 **VA** 16915 **WI** 19573, 19635, 20507 *Canada:* **BC** 19827 **NB** 10796 **ON** 13657, 19447, 19561 **PQ** 3899, 4220, 4221, 18111 **SK** 19291 *Intl:* **AUT** 7303 **CHN** 3338 **CZE** 8327

Music, Irish: **IN** 19112

Music, Jewish: **AZ** 16089 **CA** 2369 **MA** 655 **MI** 4166 **NY** 7098, 8272, 11638, 12741, 13143, 16080, 16088, 20759 **OH** 7099 **PA** 1774, 4164, 6657 *Canada:* **PQ** 1920 *Intl:* **ISR** 7101

Music, Lithuanian: **IL** 9211

Music, Medieval: **CA** 18335 **IL** 18686 **MA** 2015 **NY** 10209 **TX** 1604

Music, Oriental: **CA** 18335

Music—Performance (See also Conducting): **CA** 14730, 18411 **DC** 3159 **IL** 12086, 18686, 19779 **MA** 11469, 16551 **MD** 18822 **MI** 20271 **MN** 10470 **NE** 19001 **NJ** 20327 **NY** 15706, 15713, 15740 **OH** 3124, 3810, 12320, 18465 **TX** 13893 *Canada:* **BC** 19488

Music, Popular (See also Gospel music): **AR** 3326 **AZ** 1017, 18224 **CA** 8476, 14702, 18367 **CO** 18504 **DC** 9131 **FL** 18584 **GA** 6413 **IA** 4375 **IL** 3540, 18686 **IN** 2417 **MN** 3453, 10446 **MO** 18977 **NJ** 6488, 13388, 14166 **NY** 955, 9294 **OH** 2039 **PA** 3078, 8592, 9643, 19981 **TN** 4374, 10353 **TX** 3103, 12726 *Canada:* **ON** 2903

Music, Sacred See: Church music

Music—Theory (See also Composition (Music)): **CA** 14702, 18411 **IL** 3540, 12086, 18455 **KY** 18742 **MA** 1997, 2015, 16551 **MN** 10446, 18925 **NC** 19072 **NE** 19001 **NJ** 11744 **NY** 2234, 4019, 11637, 15740 **OH** 10821, 12218, 12320, 18465 **PA** 9643 **TX** 1604, 13893, 19390 **VA** 16915 **WI** 10426, 19635 *Canada:* **MB** 2078, 18791 **NB** 10796 **ON** 19447, 19561 *Intl:* **CHN** 3338 **CZE** 15223

Music therapy: **MN** 18925 **PA** 9643, 12863 *Canada:* **PQ** 18111

Music trade: **IA** 4375 **IL** 3540 **OH** 2039 **PA** 9643 **TN** 4374 *Canada:* **MB** 2907 **PQ** 16475

Musical antiques: **NY** 10929

Musical instruments: **CA** 338 **DC** 9131 **IL** 3540 **IN** 1442 **KY** 15462 **NH** 1989 **NY** 4019, 10216, 11637 **OH** 12221 **SD** 15146 **UT** 20805 *Canada:* **MB** 18791 **ON** 19447 *Intl:* **GER** 6435

Musical theater: **CA** 7902 **CT** 20706 **DC** 12502 **IL** 3540 **MA** 1983 **MI** 960, 1068 **NJ** 6488, 13388 **NY** 10892, 11634 **TX** 19393 **WI** 19610 *Canada:* **MB** 2078

Musicology (See also Ethnomusicology): **CA** 18392, 18411 **CT** 11 **DC** 3159 **IL** 12086, 18455 **MA** 2015, 16551 **MN** 18925 **NC** 19072 **NY** 4324 **OH** 3124, 18465 **PA** 3078 **TX** 1604, 19390 *Canada:* **MB** 18791 **NB** 10796 **ON** 13657 **PQ** 18111 *Intl:* **GER** 15794 **SPA** 15561

Muslims: **CO** 638 **CT** 6940

Mutagenesis See: Chemical mutagenesis

Myanmar: **CT** 20732 **DC** 9109 **IL** 11994

Mycology (See also Fungi): **CO** 3974 **MN** 18946 **MO** 20056 **NC** 19064, 19067 **NY** 11650 **OH** 9238 **OR** 11868 **PA** 12910 **WA** 20048 *Canada:* **AB** 2742 **BC** 2743 **MB** 2666 **ON** 2645 **PQ** 18078 *Intl:* **FRA** 12784 **IND** 7747 **NZL** 11737 **PAK** 12693

Neihardt, John Gneisenau: NE 11380

Neonatology: CA 3577 *Canada:* ON 10279 PQ 7401 SK 13786

Nepal: CA 18344 DC 9109 OR 696 *Intl:* NPL 11391

Neruda, Pablo: NY 15757

Nervous system (See also Biological control systems; Brain; Shock (Physiologic)): *Intl:* GER 13114

Netherlands: DC 9113 MN 18931 WI 19607 *Intl:* NLD 82, 11399

Neurology (See also Nervous system): AZ 14400, 17291 CA 419, 2526, 2593, 3739, 8949, 14641, 14641, 18361, 18372 CT 4207, 7950, 12121, 20179 DC 4847, 11212 FL 17314 GA 3365 IL 11122, 14919, 18698 IN 7761 KS 7953, 17335 LA 16566 MA 2013, 9820, 9823, 9946, 9980, 17346, 20594 MD 11161, 11204, 11209, 15596, 16914 MI 8873, 17353 MN 12069 MO 3342, 9249, 10092, 17359, 18969, 20056 NC 4925 ND 11416 NJ 17376 NY 4001, 4003, 7058, 8726, 10592, 11417, 11664, 11684, 17388 OH 3815, 18147 OK 14235 OR 19158, 20301 PA 9998, 17403, 17407 PR 13512 SC 6848 TN 15032 TX 17429, 20407 VA 19506 WI 14200, 17441, 19628 *Canada:* NS 12146 ON 2957, 19553 PQ 3253, 7430, 10701 *Intl:* AUS 1344 GER 13099, 13113, 13114

Neurosurgery: MA 11470 NY 5692 OH 6549 OK 19131 *Intl:* GER 13114

Nevada: CA 11037, 11038 NV 3666, 3769, 8956, 11421, 11424, 11425, 11426, 11983, 19015, 19022

Nevelson, Louise Berliawsky: ME 5604

New Age Movement: NY 3288

New Brunswick: ME 18780 *Canada:* NB 10797, 11449, 11451, 11453, 12386, 13562, 19025

New business enterprises: CA 199 ME 19352

New England: CT 11, 4181, 11456, 18525 MA 5448, 9792, 11473, 11474, 12392, 13144, 15338, 18827 ME 2033, 9552 MN 10454 MS 19790 NH 4611, 4616, 11485, 14232 RI 13869 VT 3010, 19803

New Guinea   See: Papua New Guinea

New Hampshire: MA 11034 NH 4611, 4616, 8600, 9587, 9588, 10020, 11482, 11483, 11485, 11489, 11492, 11496, 12957, 13154, 13251, 14639, 15827, 19036, 20364, 20552

New Jersey: NJ 1251, 1255, 1733, 1973, 2046, 2119, 2373, 2374, 2608, 3026, 4413, 4440, 4474, 5568, 6489, 6514, 6824, 7269, 7284, 7385, 7565, 8595, 9529, 10611, 10657, 10745, 10748, 10769, 11035, 11503, 11514, 11515, 11545, 11747, 12168, 12236, 12778, 12787, 13386, 14175, 14629, 14631, 15050, 15891, 16026, 16482, 16484, 17753, 19851 NY 7329

New Jerusalem Church: MA 15915

New Mexico: CO 4783, 11039 NM 318, 319, 1090, 5163, 9321, 10910, 10914, 11531, 11534, 16831, 17684, 19040, 19047, 20282 TX 5285, 11041

New Orleans (LA): LA 6234, 7160, 7247, 9371, 11543, 16560, 16567, 19052

New York (City): NY 957, 2212, 2235, 3730, 6630, 9595, 10860, 10891, 11558, 11559, 11578, 11612, 11618, 11633, 11640, 13366, 15435, 16502, 16648, 17064, 20229

New York (State): NJ 11035 NY 166, 227, 361, 2251, 2300, 2328, 2332, 2335, 2338, 3170, 3174, 3175, 3242, 3433, 3459, 3460, 3475, 3880, 3981, 4020, 4305, 4306, 4346, 4844, 5137, 5229, 5415, 5445, 5663, 6013, 6044, 6354, 6358, 6630, 6726, 7129, 7226, 7276, 7286, 7287, 7289, 7316, 7329, 7521, 7573, 7598, 8250, 8348, 8368, 8463, 8932, 9021, 9518, 9591, 10355, 10442, 10588, 10678, 11577, 11578, 11663, 11666, 11667, 11669, 11679, 11680, 11681, 11683, 11796, 12378, 12379, 12385, 12421, 12424, 12425, 12433, 12595, 12690, 13556, 13817, 13985, 13993, 14053, 14429, 14433, 14831, 14901, 14917, 14931, 15118, 15250, 15287, 15523, 15707, 15710, 15711, 15712, 15714, 15715, 15720, 15721, 15760, 15849,

16350, 16368, 19278, 19747, 19985, 20088, 20111, 20228, 20229, 20283, 20762, 20764

New Zealand: DC 5324 *Intl:* NZL 1287, 11739, 11740

Newark (NJ): NJ 11747

Newfoundland: PA 19175 *Canada:* NF 10049, 10051, 10055, 11762, 11764, 11765

Newman, Cardinal John Henry: CA 10811, 14511 CT 11 DC 6379 IA 14594 NY 3144, 14240 *Canada:* ON 19459 *Intl:* BEL 15194

News photography   See: Photography, Journalistic

Newspaper morgues   See: Newspaper and periodical libraries

Newspaper and periodical libraries: AK 832, 5554 AL 1852, 7581, 10675 AZ 985, 13022, 16539 CA 4256, 6153, 7065, 9278, 9339, 9347, 9357, 9667, 10585, 12210, 12512, 13953, 14193, 14196, 14684, 14724, 14727, 14732, 14755, 14803, 14815, 14819, 15804, 16359, 18337, 19340, 19801 CO 2029, 3950, 4780, 13505, 14026 CT 6933, 7143, 11520, 12118, 15481, 15482, 20084 DC 3552, 4916, 17911, 20020, 20053 DE 11780 FL 2055, 5881, 5921, 6228, 10262, 10975, 11159, 12572, 12703, 15868, 16001, 16358 GA 226, 1244, 1247, 1294, 4037, 9511, 14883 HI 7025 IA 3185, 4359, 4792, 9771, 12250, 20086 ID 7655, 9085 IL 425, 1903, 3424, 3532, 3545, 3550, 3551, 4690, 8542, 10596, 10974, 15607, 18687, 20100 IN 6017, 6019, 7769, 7820, 7825, 8781, 8851, 8876, 9741, 10286, 13267 KS 20406 KY 4387, 9090, 12639 LA 1562, 9386, 15144 MA 1748, 1987, 2010, 2200, 3638, 5090, 7008, 9833, 11436, 11779, 15611, 20601 MD 1456, 3029 ME 1468, 6245 MI 877, 1579, 4807, 4812, 5847, 6636, 8948, 10930, 12961, 13225, 14218, 16469 MN 5054, 10457, 10466, 13987, 14560, 19965 MO 3984, 8550, 8551, 14364, 14446, 15447, 15609, 18961 MS 6809, 7013 MT 1838, 10531 NC 120, 1107, 2378, 3448, 5071, 5623, 6737, 11781, 20462, 20495 ND 1868, 4853, 6028, 6622, 10495 NE 9180, 12410 NJ 1101, 2121, 2375, 3352, 6515, 12786, 14175, 16485 NM 319 NV 8956 NY 1140, 1842, 2338, 5311, 5511, 6244, 9286, 10364, 11574, 11590, 11593, 11720, 11782, 11797, 13629, 13741, 13755, 13814, 13996, 14833, 14902, 15955, 19721, 19948, 20090 OH 168, 3702, 3707, 3825, 4033, 4386, 4660, 7096, 9304, 9641, 13093, 15610, 16388, 19983 OK 15028, 16575 OR 9982, 12555, 13798 PA 385, 428, 1627, 2317, 4716, 6112, 8922, 12791, 12992, 13086, 13087, 13745, 14972, 16140, 19736 PR 19251 RI 13449 SC 3444, 6746, 15866 SD 13712, 15196 TN 3457, 3780, 4049, 8313, 8436, 10999, 16153 TX 19, 442, 1310, 1623, 2101, 3109, 4340, 4554, 4571, 4773, 5286, 5287, 5524, 6025, 6932, 7448, 7457, 12248, 14668, 16096, 16606, 19927 UT 4795, 12252, 14647 VA 883, 1064, 4393, 11777, 13910, 16360, 19698, 19900 WA 1698, 3384, 4029, 9298, 12824, 14996, 15004, 15592, 15980, 19729, 19952 WI 6718, 8488, 8638, 13675, 15104, 20101, 20528 WV 1916, 3441 *Canada:* AB 2459, 2464, 5245, 5249, 13760 BC 10962, 12675, 13353, 19829 MB 2075, 20489 NB 10605 NS 6839 ON 1695, 2811, 2983, 6868, 8749, 9019, 9263, 12598, 12604, 16413, 16419, 16421, 20479 PQ 8852, 9018, 10697, 15356 SK 13787, 14876 *Intl:* ENG 6666 KOR 8480 SAF 15386

Newton, Alfred Edward: PA 6122

Newton, Isaac: CA 15658 CT 2382 MA 1396

Nez Perce Indians: ID 17759 MT 17675

Niagara Falls (NY and ON): NY 2328, 2335

Nicaragua: *Intl:* SWE 15926

Nickel and nickel alloys: MN 10455 WV 7727

Nigeria (See also Africa, West): *Intl:* NGA 11808

Nightingale, Florence: CA 18390 MA 2009 NY 4001 *Canada:* ON 16418

Nijinsky, Vaslav: NY 11636

Nitrogen—Fixation: *Canada:* ON 2644

Nixon, Richard Milhous: CA 11038, 13830 DC 11044

Nursing school libraries: (continued)
10156, 20496 **NE** 2298 **NJ** 3626, 5357, 6197, 8371, 9486, 10832, 12617 **NY** 1771, 14288, 14325, 14412, 14619 **OH** 1304, 5574, 13448, 14281, 18477 **OR** 5320, 19950 **PA** 21, 3490, 4087, 6083, 6278, 8326, 8946, 10146, 11980, 12848, 13747, 14090, 14482, 14493, 15084, 16671 **TN** 1515, 10187 **TX** 7451, 16281 **VA** 4672, 10036, 13908 **WI** 3990 *Canada:* **AB** 14096 **NF** 6598, 14266 **NS** 14499 *Intl:* **ENG** 14111

Nutrition (See also Food industry and trade): **AZ** 4848 **CA** 3736, 13118, 13330, 16984, 17198, 17297, 18305, 20347 **CT** 7526, 13903, 14887, 20348 **DC** 15853, 17508, 20609 **FL** 695, 15948 **GA** 3858 **HI** 7039, 18622 **IA** 8228 **IL** 947, 1055, 1586, 8815, 9457, 11231, 13565, 16703, 18676 **IN** 2136, 3364, 13538 **KS** 630 **KY** 18743 **MA** 9409, 9820, 16549, 17202 **MD** 17203, 17207, 18823 **MI** 6418, 8607, 10324 **MN** 6327, 12069, 18943 **MO** 764, 9249, 10092, 12956, 13699 **ND** 19103 **NE** 18994 **NH** 19029 **NJ** 2623, 4400 **NY** 604, 1651, 3268, 4302, 7562, 11584, 16023 **OH** 3804, 3806, 12293, 12311, 14083, 18147 **OR** 11124 **PA** 7111, 7164, 7659, 12910 **PR** 17410 **RI** 8461 **SC** 17631 **TN** 19776 **TX** 6179, 16243, 19385 **VA** 16712, 17016 **WA** 631 *Canada:* **BC** 2165, 18285 **MB** 9627 **ON** 2633, 2750, 2957, 14180, 14894 **PQ** 18091 **SK** 14853, 19298 *Intl:* **AUT** 8934 **BOL** 17982 **BRZ** 17999 **CHN** 3609 **CMR** 2615 **FIJ** 5689 **FIN** 7123 **GER** 11805, 20840 **GTM** 12717 **GUY** 3046 **IND** 7742 **ITA** 16752 **JAM** 12716 **NLD** 11413 **SWE** 15346 **TWN** 1123

Nutrition policy: **DC** 8109

Oakley, Annie (Phoebe Anne Oakley Mozee): **NJ** 12168

Obstetrics: **CA** 437 **DC** 537 **IL** 10149 **IN** 3173 **MI** 7594, 10801 **MN** 18903 **NY** 9463, 9655, 9845, 15202 **OH** 6549 **PA** 367, 8360 **TN** 5421 *Canada:* **BC** 18267 **NS** 6601 **ON** 14894, 19553, 20558 **PQ** 7401, 7402 **SK** 13786 *Intl:* **SCT** 14112

Occult sciences (See also Magic; Witchcraft): **CA** 14706, 16301 **CO** 12234 **CT** 20703 **IL** 7893, 9173, 18670 **MI** 3294 **MN** 20170 **MO** 13466 **NJ** 19700 **NY** 12737 **OH** 3823 **RI** 10177 **WA** 1098, 15003

Occupational health   See: Industrial hygiene

Occupational retraining: **MN** 10478 **OK** 11114

Occupational safety   See: Industrial safety

Occupational therapy (See also Rehabilitation): **CT** 12121 **DC** 4847 **LA** 3344 **MA** 9823 **MD** 702 **OH** 9402, 12278 **SC** 6848 **TX** 16268, 16281 *Canada:* **AB** 280, 283, 6505 **NS** 4541 **ON** 3777, 19553 **PQ** 3282, 7883, 9899

Ocean engineering (See also Marine sciences): **CA** 928, 2272, 17829, 17830, 18348 **FL** 5876, 18842 **MA** 9796, 9821, 9822, 20576 **MD** 17650 **MS** 17865 **NY** 14071 **TX** 16192 **WA** 17649 *Canada:* **BC** 2174 **NF** 10054 **NS** 12138 *Intl:* **ENG** 1919 **IND** 7746

Ocean law: **OR** 12237 *Intl:* **GER** 18036

Oceania: **CA** 4379, 12657, 12671, 18435 **DC** 5324, 17919 **GU** 5859, 18610 **HI** 5133, 5134, 7042, 7051, 9046, 9472, 18623, 18628, 20811 **IN** 2416 *Intl:* **AUS** 1333, 15688, 15689 **FRA** 3205 **NCL** 15433 **NZL** 11739

Oceanography (See also Coasts; Marine biology): **AK** 17630, 18174, 18184 **AL** 9670 **CA** 928, 2577, 3501, 4574, 5082, 8151, 9353, 9353, 10664, 15651, 17536, 17643, 17644, 17830, 17904, 18419, 18434, 19329, 19671, 19674 **CO** 11099, 17652, 18494 **CT** 6299, 18526, 20714, 20718 **DC** 11281, 15280, 17653, 20615 **DE** 18545 **FL** 5876, 6898, 12157, 17639, 17651, 18842 **GA** 18606 **HI** 7023, 12240, 17632, 18630 **IL** 12082, 18452, 18673 **IN** 13539 **LA** 9394 **MA** 1539, 6959, 6984, 9669, 9807, 9822, 11464, 17636, 20576 **MD** 17650, 18798, 18802, 18813 **ME** 9561, 18777 **MI** 17648 **MS** 6808, 17865 **NC** 5044, 17642, 17654, 19060, 19064 **NH** 4611 **NJ** 13373, 17640, 17647 **NY** 3734, 4016, 15749, 15754, 17705 **OK** 19128 **PR** 19253 **RI** 13735, 17464, 17658, 19266 **SC** 1547 **TX** 816, 16194 **VA** 16152, 17801, 19865 **WA** 17638, 17649, 19525 **WI** 19587, 19599 *Canada:* **BC** 2682, 7960, 20236 **NS** 4536, 7161, 12138 **PQ** 2733, 9912, 18122 *Intl:* **ARG** 972 **BMU** 1754 **CHN** 3610 **ENG** 6684, 6687, 13152 **GER** 2360, 18035 **IND** 7746 **ITA** 2425 **SAF** 15382 **SCT** 14966 **SEN** 4526

Ockham, William of: **NY** 6074

O'Connor, Flannery: **GA** 6382

Office management: **MA** 9824 **NE** 20574 **NJ** 13460 *Canada:* **PQ** 7832

Office practice—Automation (See also Electronic data processing; Electronic office machines): **MA** 8035 *Canada:* **ON** 7613 **PQ** 1484 *Intl:* **FRA** 6071

Offshore drilling (Petroleum)   See: Oil well drilling, Submarine

O'Flaherty, Liam: **NJ** 15048

Ohio: **IL** 11031 **OH** 372, 1527, 1648, 2035, 3703, 3765, 3795, 4386, 4500, 6274, 6729, 7060, 7231, 7496, 8886, 8910, 9138, 9302, 9930, 10263, 12219, 12269, 12270, 12271, 12288, 12289, 12328, 12337, 12826, 13093, 13230, 13484, 15247, 15510, 15691, 15994, 16395, 16588, 17754, 18150, 18464, 19932, 19975, 20293, 20639, 20644, 20652 **UT** 597

Ohio Valley: **IL** 18461 **OH** 10270, 13479, 15247 **PA** 19209

Oil (Petroleum)   See: Petroleum

Oil sands: **WY** 20291 *Canada:* **AB** 296, 15951

Oil-shales: **CO** 5365, 17106, 17541 **KY** 18745 **TX** 5928 **WY** 20291 *Intl:* **AUS** 1319

Oil spills: **AK** 12340 **CO** 5365 **MA** 9821 **MI** 15587

Oil well drilling: **AK** 205 **KS** 8558 **OK** 11214 **TX** 12339, 15583, 16234, 16267 *Canada:* **AB** 9933

Oil well drilling fluids   See: Drilling muds

Oil well drilling, Submarine: **CA** 2272, 6454, 7715 **TX** 457 *Canada:* **NF** 2830 *Intl:* **FRA** 6151 **SCT** 7154

Oil well logging: **CT** 14911 **MS** 19353 **TX** 6849, 19382, 19410

Oil wells: **CA** 2558 **MI** 18859

Oils, Essential   See: Essences and essential oils

Oils and fats: **IL** 947, 15632 **LA** 17194 **MN** 3044 **NJ** 3879, 16633 **TN** 8814 *Intl:* **BRZ** 2097

Oilseed plants: *Canada:* **AB** 2647 **SK** 2661, 13266 *Intl:* **BOL** 7997 **NGA** 7898

Ojibwa Indians: *Canada:* **ON** 12486

Oklahoma: **OK** 1544, 3368, 4425, 10901, 12076, 12348, 12350, 12351, 12359, 12373, 12727, 14037, 16573, 19123, 19139 **TX** 11041

Olive: **CA** 2561 *Intl:* **SPA** 8164

Olson, Charles: **CT** 18519 **NY** 15757 *Canada:* **BC** 6105

Olympic games (See also Sports): **CA** 445, 9343 **CO** 17917 **IN** 1232 **NY** 15712, 16356 *Canada:* **ON** 2890 **PQ** 2977

Oman: *Intl:* **GER** 12411 **IRQ** 933

Omar Khayyam: **OH** 3823

Ombudsman: *Canada:* **AB** 295, 8165 **NB** 11452

Oncology   See: Cancer

O'Neill, Eugene: **CT** 4178, 12422, 20703 **NH** 4616 **NY** 10892 **OH** 10270, 13479

Ontario: **WI** 13810 *Canada:* **MB** 19568 **ON** 1397, 2081, 2289, 5981, 6008, 6866, 7587, 8749, 8902, 9065, 9268, 11518, 11959, 11961, 12427, 12439, 12446, 12452, 12477, 12481, 12590, 14253, 14431, 15174, 15175, 15359, 16384, 19358, 19556, 20087, 20160, 20478, 20778

Open spaces (See also City planning; Parks; Regional planning): **IL** 16492 **WI** 15454 *Intl:* **CHN** 1655

Opera: CA 9281, 10928, 14737, 18335 **CT** 4179 **DC** 9131, 12502 **FL** 18584 **IL** 3540 **IN** 7796 **MA** 1983, 2015, 11469 **MI** 10331 **MN** 18925 **MO** 14439 **NC** 19072 **NY** 4324, 8491, 10219, 11637, 11638, 15731, 15958 **OH** 1432, 12218, 14921 **PA** 10403, 20187 **TX** 4561, 14677 **WA** 19536 *Canada:* **ON** 2978, 10223, 19561 *Intl:* **AUT** 7937 **CHN** 3338 **FRA** 6063 **GER** 15794

Operations research (See also Systems engineering): CA 15655, 17868, 18330, 18387 **DC** 16803 **GA** 9243 **MD** 17940 **MO** 20064 **NC** 19056 **NJ** 719, 14165 **NM** 17005 **NY** 4027, 4307, 4316, 19282 **PA** 19186 **VA** 828, 886, 3274, 4105, 6347, 7923, 16978 *Canada:* **ON** 19563 **PQ** 5205, 9900, 18085 *Intl:* **NLD** 3267

Ophthalmology: AL 5538 **CA** 388, 461, 2498, 2884, 4944, 8220, 8502, 8506, 15350, 15466, 15653, 17846, 18338, 18390 **FL** 5877, 15453, 17314, 18848, 18849 **IL** 11295 **LA** 16434 **MA** 6992, 11468 **MD** 8414 **MI** 7594 **MN** 18895 **MO** 8146, 20071 **NH** 4608 **NJ** 16719 **NY** 1583, 3150, 6905, 11576, 20751 **OH** 14603 **OK** 19130 **OR** 6555 **PA** 5537, 6816, 12838, 13287, 20457 **TN** 5421, 15477 **TX** 330, 1600 **WV** 9726 *Canada:* **ON** 19426, 19553 **PQ** 9899, 9908

Oppenheimer, Julius Robert: DC 9129

Optical disks   See: Computers—Optical equipment

Optics (See also Photochemistry): AL 16988 **AZ** 16977, 18226, 18229 **CA** 820, 824, 7509, 7512, 8286, 15466, 18338, 20684 **CO** 1433 **CT** 12505, 12943, 13079, 17961 **ID** 5268 **IL** 2443, 7671, 18688 **MA** 703, 6269, 9226, 9310, 16376 **MN** 7375, 16336 **NH** 8782 **NJ** 14912 **NM** 11299, 16802, 17001 **NY** 1583, 4328, 5188, 6304, 13955, 15724, 16685, 19284 **OH** 3687, 6314, 9096 **PA** 12838, 19193 **TN** 15477, 16796 **TX** 5086, 16215, 18640 **VA** 13665 **WA** 15585 *Canada:* **ON** 2825

Optics, Electronic   See: Electron optics

Optometry: AL 18171 **CA** 15466, 18338 **FL** 15453 **IL** 7671, 11295 **MA** 11468 **MD** 462 **MI** 5670 **MO** 8146 **NY** 15724 **OH** 12314 **PA** 12838 **TN** 15477 **TX** 18640 *Canada:* **ON** 19544 **PQ** 18090

Oral history: AK 11829 **AL** 192, 1856, 16815, 18169 **AZ** 1015, 1864, 11992, 13061, 18211 **CA** 2564, 2568, 2573, 6203, 7340, 9341, 9538, 11234, 14695, 14796, 18303, 18379, 18393, 18437, 20849 **CO** 2030, 3940, 5995, 10923 **CT** 6749, 18529, 20092 **DC** 2194, 4916, 7478, 9108, 17842 **FL** 7256 **GA** 1245, 6055, 20192 **HI** 18623 **IA** 3184, 15680 **ID** 7648, 8958 **IL** 3421, 12179, 12746, 14059, 14791 **IN** 7758, 7769, 7798, 19850 **KS** 5999 **KY** 5151, 12638, 17696, 18775, 20261 **LA** 9372, 16567 **MA** 648, 6730, 9091, 9804, 13677, 17927 **MD** 8393, 17624, 17859 **ME** 9564, 18778 **MI** 5854, 5964, 20120 **MN** 3349, 4443, 8901, 9023, 11913, 11971, 12055, 15530, 20185 **MO** 17924, 20253 **MS** 7338 **MT** 17726, 18987 **NC** 5979, 9716 **ND** 15682, 19095 **NJ** 14166, 16026, 16482, 16484 **NM** 9321, 19047 **NY** 653, 4020, 7011, 9068, 11636, 11733, 13836, 17782, 20228 **OH** 16395 **OK** 12348, 19139 **OR** 19146 **PA** 532, 10157, 16134, 16651, 16995, 17720, 19203 **PR** 19255 **RI** 13442, 19267 **TN** 5830, 8390, 10065, 10076, 16778, 17727 **TX** 1609, 2100, 5132, 7462, 12726, 16191, 17746, 17928, 19105, 19379, 19412, 19414 **UT** 15519, 20798 **VA** 1039, 20674 **WA** 5171, 9077, 11940, 15212 **WI** 19576, 19646 **WV** 9724, 16943, 17729, 20225 **WY** 20664 *Canada:* **MB** 9619 **NF** 10051 **ON** 6714 **PQ** 15304 *Intl:* **AUS** 15694

Orchestra (See also Conducting): CA 10928 **KY** 18774

Orchestral music: AR 12609 **CA** 9343, 14737 **DC** 4911, 17602 **IL** 3540 **MA** 3439, 11987 **MD** 18821 **MI** 4833, 8045, 10331 **MN** 3453, 10470, 18925 **NJ** 16479 **NM** 19042 **NY** 11635, 11637, 13185 **OH** 13482, 15807 **PA** 4491, 6114, 12993 **PR** 4222 **TX** 1604, 14677 **VA** 13911 **VT** 19482 **WI** 1654 *Canada:* **BC** 19488 **ON** 11333, 19561 **PQ** 2892 *Intl:* **CHN** 3338 **DEN** 4770

Orchids: CA 14718, 18364 **FL** 704 *Canada:* **ON** 3746

Ordnance (See also Firearms): CA 5936 **DC** 11045 **FL** 17799 **GA** 17599 **IL** 16921 **MA** 6313 **MD** 2, 17018, 17837 **MI** 6302 **MN** 393, 5937 **MS** 16970 **NM** 14778, 17005 **NY** 16919 **OK** 17010 *Canada:* **MB** 14106 **PQ** 14110 *Intl:* **SWE** 15801

Ordnance, Naval: CA 17830, 17873, 17886, 17897, 17908 **CT** 17893 **DC** 17800, 17843, 17874 **KY** 17867 **MA** 17956 **MD** 17889 **RI** 17892 **VA** 3995, 13255, 17898

Ordnance research: VA 7923

Oregon: OR 3983, 4973, 6287, 8482, 8756, 8936, 9175, 10850, 12524, 12526, 12541, 12546, 13769, 15511, 15512, 16352, 19147, 19159, 20003 **WA** 11036

Organ music: CA 776, 18411 **FL** 15785 **NJ** 20327 **OH** 16392 **PA** 6457 **WI** 1105

Organic chemistry   See: Chemistry, Organic

Organic compounds: NY 407

Organic gardening: MA 11431

Organizational behavior: CA 2505, 2506, 2507, 19324 **DC** 4906 **IN** 7805 **MI** 18870 **MO** 9694 **NC** 3227 **PA** 12899 **UT** 20802 **VA** 19501 *Canada:* **ON** 19446

Organized crime: DC 1133, 17256

Orient   See: East Asia

Oriental art   See: Art, Oriental

Oriental history   See: East Asia—History

Oriental literature: CA 3753, 7487, 12204, 18316, 18344, 18397 **CT** 20697 **DC** 9109 **IL** 18451, 18659, 18660 **KS** 18726 **MD** 18814 **MN** 3908 **MO** 20061 **NH** 4612 **NJ** 15048 **NY** 11626, 14352, 19274 **OH** 3823 **OR** 19157 **RI** 2278 **TX** 19388 **WA** 19522 *Canada:* **BC** 18255 **ON** 19439 *Intl:* **ENG** 18441 **GER** 15794

Oriental medicine   See: Medicine, Oriental

Oriental music   See: Music, Oriental

Oriental philosophy   See: Philosophy, Oriental

Orienteering: *Intl:* **GER** 8167

Orlowski, Alexander: NH 4860

Ornament   See: Decoration and ornament

Ornithology   See: Birds

Orphans: CO 12575

Orthodontics: IL 12080 **MO** 484, 14466

Orthodox Eastern Church, Greek: MA 7116 **NY** 12579 **OH** 12310

Orthodox Eastern Church, Russian: AK 14321 **NY** 12579, 14625 **OK** 14315 **PA** 19300

Orthopedia: CA 196, 2474, 3797, 8506, 12581, 13703 **DE** 5014 **FL** 6556 **IL** 11122, 14306, 14919, 15147 **IN** 9458, 12582 **KS** 7166, 14312 **KY** 391 **MA** 11465 **MD** 16658 **MI** 7594 **MN** 12069, 13947 **MO** 3798, 9249 **MT** 4034 **NC** 17056, 19937 **NE** 9178 **NJ** 16719 **NY** 1771, 2337, 3150, 7058, 7423, 8726, 11570, 17044 **OH** 12264 **OR** 20301 **PA** 10349 **TX** 15148, 16229 *Canada:* **ON** 2957, 12580

Orthopedic apparatus: MD 17310

Orwell, George   See: Blair, Eric Arthur (George Orwell)

Osler, Sir William: CA 9334 **MD** 9994 *Canada:* **PQ** 9908

Osteopathy: AZ 16542 **FL** 15453 **IA** 19162 **IL** 705, 3518 **IN** 10280 **MI** 2025, 4813, 10289, 10319 **MO** 8744, 18632 **NJ** 18840 **NY** 11569 **OH** 2106, 4935, 6647, 12328, 12330, 12760, 14333 **OK** 12364 **PA** 386, 10032, 12979 **TX** 16210 **WV** 20203

Otolaryngology: MA 6992 **MO** 3342 **NY** 11576 **PA** 5537 *Canada:* **ON** 19553

Otology   See: Ear—Diseases

Ottawa (ON):   *Canada:* ON 12601

Oursler, Charles Fulton: DC 6379

Owens, Robert Bowie: NY 19789

Ozarks: AR 1023, 1029, 12650, 18236 MO 3901, 15603, 20252

Ozone: NY 3238

Pacemaker, Artificial (Heart):   MN 10019 TX 8046

Pacific Basin (See also Oceania):   CA 12658 DC 1116 *Intl:* MYS 1121 NZL 11740 THA 16761

Pacific Islands   See: Oceania

Pacific Northwest   See: Northwest, Pacific

Pacifism (See also Conscientious objectors; Nonviolence):   IL 1782 PA 15903 SC 13821 *Canada:* ON 9954

Packaging (See also Food—Packaging):   AL 8171 AZ 4848 CA 6235 GA 16008, 17196 IL 12685, 19903 MA 17027 NJ 14164 NY 1383, 8169 OH 11842 SC 6606 WI 8325 *Intl:* ENG 13075, 13406 FIN 5720 MEX 8861

Page, Thomas Nelson: VA 19510

Pain: AL 18172

Paine, Thomas: PA 712

Paint (See also Protective coatings):   CA 3737 DE 5028 MA 2432 MD 14950 MI 1551 NY 13203 OH 11842 PA 1271, 8822, 13286

Painting (See also Impressionism (Art)):   AL 10688 AZ 13015 CA 12203, 14702, 18378 CO 3949 CT 20699, 20734, 20736 DC 4902, 6137, 11179, 11244, 13006, 15261, 15265, 15267, 15268 DE 20503 FL 12098, 13934, 15319 HI 18627 IA 4790 IN 7824 MA 1992, 6965, 10898, 15234, 20590 MD 1452, 9747 MI 4407, 4809, 8530, 10315 MN 10444, 10445, 10446, 19947 MO 8544, 14434, 14452, 15599 NC 11880 NH 9586 NJ 6128, 11743 NY 2238, 4002, 6165, 6796, 8624, 9702, 10213, 10216, 11624, 11724, 12378, 15832, 19273, 20763 OH 3822 OK 12367 PA 6109, 12836, 12894, 12990 RI 2274 TN 10061, 10067 TX 4555, 4561, 6021, 7461, 10583, 14670 VA 19868 WA 19513 WI 10419, 10424, 10426 *Canada:* AB 257 BC 19752 MB 20487 ON 20781 PQ 10700, 18110 *Intl:* BEL 8785 CHN 6789 DEN 14124 GER 6858 NLD 18206 RUS 14945

Pakistan: DC 9109 *Intl:* PAK 12694

Paleography (See also Illumination of books and manuscripts):   KS 18724 MN 14334 OH 18473 *Canada:* PQ 7868 *Intl:* ENG 3014

Paleontology: AL 6363 AZ 10916, 17765 CA 2470, 3501, 11341, 14712, 14946, 15644, 18314, 18384, 19329 CO 4779, 10923, 17537, 18494 CT 4873, 20714 DC 15280 FL 5894, 18570 IA 14790 ID 7654 IL 5684, 7696, 12082, 18673 IN 7788, 13539 KS 6001 KY 18749 LA 9387 MA 6984, 9669 MD 2591 MI 18877 MN 14940 MO 18957, 20060 MS 10519, 10522 NC 6029, 19060 ND 19098 NJ 13373 NM 6463, 17684 NY 687, 689, 12698, 15749, 15960, 19283 OH 12322, 18470 OK 19128 PA 36, 3085 TX 6023, 19391 UT 17701, 19706 VA 17539, 19872 WI 10431 WY 19658 *Canada:* AB 2746, 14138 ON 2636, 2747, 2963, 14131 PQ 18084 *Intl:* AUS 15391 CHN 12928 CZE 4510 ENG 11340 FRA 6064 ITA 2630

Palestine: *Intl:* GER 3922 LBN 7961

Palynology: OK 19128 *Canada:* AB 14138 *Intl:* ARG 4618 AUT 19490

Panama: FL 12722, 17062 *Intl:* PAN 17997

Panama Canal: CA 14741 CT 14643 DC 14969, 16941 FL 12722 *Canada:* BC 2153

Paper: AL 8171, 14153 CA 8323, 18321 CT 4845, 4965 GA 6390, 7962, 16008 IA 6618 ID 1947 IL 1704, 9784, 12685, 20608 MA 228, 15812 MD 20351 ME 14184 MN 16335, 18945, 19945 NC 3693, 6490, 11900 NH 7851 NJ 8261, 12953, 16638 NY 707, 3426, 8169, 10710, 15722 OH 4, 9967, 10265 OR 1948 PA 6491, 7136, 8168, 13564, 14962, 14963 SC 20350 TN 2314, 8170 WA 8291, 8324, 19526, 20361 WI 4227, 8325, 8709, 17513 *Canada:* BC 9863, 15181 NB 6103 ON 23, 13573, 20683 PQ 2985, 4951, 5226, 8762, 12732, 13528 *Intl:* ENG 13075 FIN 5720 GTM 3325 NLD 11402 NZL 11738

Paper chemicals: MN 16336 NH 10995

Papua New Guinea: *Intl:* PNG 12733

Papyrus manuscripts   See: Manuscripts (Papyri)

Parachutes: CA 17896

Paraguay: CA 18413 KS 18723 *Intl:* BRZ 2092 PAR 12736

Paramedics: CA 6498, 14308, 17845, 20383 FL 7185, 18849 HI 17052 IA 5250 IN 14618 MA 1978 MN 11936 NY 11567 OR 12525 PA 6277, 11394 WA 3380 *Canada:* AB 2458 PQ 7403, 18066 *Intl:* FRA 18062

Paraplegia and paráplegics (See also Handicapped):   *Canada:* ON 2980

Parapsychology   See: Psychical research

Parasites: CA 18318 CO 3974 GA 17126 IL 18694 IN 19116 MA 6996 MI 18855 MO 1934 MS 6808 MT 17628 NE 19004 NY 4308 *Canada:* NF 10053 PQ 9905 *Intl:* CHN 1655 KEN 8141 PAN 6580 ROM 14048 TZA 16006

Parent and child (See also Parenting):   NY 11607

Parent-teacher relationships: IL 11255

Parenting: CA 3235, 10238 IL 5398 IN 7790 LA 16563 MD 13357 MN 5098, 14074 NY 11607 VA 16354 VT 13127 WI 8907

Paris (France):   NY 6145 *Intl:* FRA 1826

Parks (See also National parks and reserves):   AR 1036 CA 2555, 9349, 14692 DC 17249 IN 7789 LA 19052 MD 9753 NY 5075 OH 7305 TX 16264 VA 11263 *Canada:* AB 2460, 2711 BC 2160 MB 9620 NF 11755 ON 2713, 12479 SK 14842

Parks, Gordon Alexander Buchanan: KS 8573

Parliamentary practice: IN 640 MO 11071 *Canada:* ON 2764 *Intl:* LUX 5489

Parliaments   See: Legislative bodies

Parsons, Louella Oettinger: CA 35

Particles (Nuclear physics) (See also Nuclear sciences):   CA 15642, 18395 CO 18500 IL 18144 IN 19111 KS 8570 MD 17619, 17623 MO 20066 NY 4021 OH 18470 *Intl:* GER 6425

Pasadena (CA):   CA 12772, 12775

Passion-music: NE 19001

Passive solar design   See: Solar houses

Pastoral counseling: CA 8185, 14924 IL 9457 MA 2018 NY 7990, 11719 OH 14507 PA 5504, 8923, 9464 SD 11857 TN 6902 TX 5786 *Canada:* AB 12042 ON 3218 PQ 9910

Pastore, John Orlando: RI 13442

Pastures (See also Grasses):   *Intl:* AUS 18145 COL 8078 CRI 8028 JPN 7322 NZL 11736

Patchen, Kenneth: CA 18435 TX 18643

Petroleum (See also Petroleum products): AK 2051, 17532, 18175 AL 6363 CA 1261, 2272, 2523, 2543, 8682, 12233, 19674 CO 3947, 10569, 19704 CT 14911 DC 709, 11150, 17232 IL 814, 7690, 19676 KS 8557, 20409 KY 1112, 16211 LA 5531, 10570, 19356 MA 8365 MT 10641 NJ 1143, 8261 NM 11521 NY 16188 OH 9430 OK 4212, 8212, 8687, 11214, 12377, 12646, 13011, 16571 PA 1259, 15867, 19981 TX 457, 816, 1260, 1957, 4707, 6023, 8162, 8317, 8446, 9482, 10959, 12339, 13010, 15115, 15504, 15583, 16198, 16266 WV 17237 WY 19654 *Canada:* AB 271, 296, 2032, 2053, 2791, 2976, 2982, 4517, 7360, 12128, 12723, 14899, 15951, 16663, 20246 NF 2830, 11758 ON 5456 *Intl:* BRZ 10384 DEN 6365, 13938 FRA 6151 SAU 5551

Petroleum chemicals: CA 2272, 3504 IL 813, 19676 LA 5531 MO 12965 NJ 7, 5536, 10563, 20544 NY 3467 PA 11428, 14039 TX 1957, 3496, 7311, 8317, 15114 WV 6273 *Canada:* AB 12127 ON 5454, 5455, 5456, 12964 *Intl:* BRZ 10384 CHN 1658 FRA 6151

Petroleum engineering: CA 3501, 3502, 15644 CO 16710 ND 19098 NJ 5535 NV 3394 OK 19126 PA 19205 TX 1110, 3989, 4298, 5928, 6771, 6849, 8608, 10366, 14913, 15583, 16189, 16662, 16666, 19389 *Canada:* AB 812, 2937, 3495, 5459, 6807, 7590, 9933, 12963, 15111, 16430 BC 2158 ON 5455 SK 14867

Petroleum—Geology (See also Oil sands; Oil well logging): AZ 1006 CA 3502, 19671 KY 18749 OK 485, 19128 TX 3496, 7458, 16662, 19391 *Canada:* AB 11837, 12963, 18289 BC 3011

Petroleum industry and trade (See also Petroleum products; Petroleum—Refining): CA 1262, 3499, 9279, 19670 CO 10569, 19704 KY 18772 NJ 16072, 20544 OH 19703 OK 817, 20444 PA 12876 TX 45, 3496, 5297, 6597, 10568, 10572, 10575, 12948, 16458, 16662, 19382 *Canada:* AB 292, 812, 5458, 6807, 7590, 15870 BC 16453 NF 2830 ON 5454, 7719, 7720, 12964, 15112 *Intl:* CHN 1658

Petroleum law and legislation: AR 10868 CA 12665 CO 3953, 20144 PA 12924 TX 1411, 2407, 4211, 15505, 19854 WV 3988 *Intl:* NOR 18139

Petroleum products (See also Petroleum chemicals): NJ 5536, 10577

Petroleum—Refining: CA 1261, 3504, 20542 CO 3947 MA 13726 NJ 7, 5536, 10573, 10576, 10577 TX 15114, 19725

Petrology (See also Crystallography; Geochemistry; Geology; Mineralogy): CO 17537 IA 18710 IL 18673 IN 7788, 13539 KY 18749 MA 6948 MO 20060 NJ 13373 NY 4014 PA 2303 VA 17539 *Intl:* CZE 4510 FIN 6366 FRA 6064 SAF 6367

Pets: CA 8959 CO 10744

Pharmacology See: Pharmacy and pharmacology

Pharmacy and pharmacology (See also Psychopharmacology): CA 388, 437, 805, 9353, 9353, 10388, 12710, 15953, 17198, 18423, 19173, 19330 CO 18506 CT 1935, 2135, 3485, 10389, 12969, 13529, 13903, 18527 DC 710, 7476, 11212, 11830, 17164 DE 5027, 5031, 7641 FL 5861, 15453, 17314, 18572, 19677 IA 8223, 8240, 18711 IL 13, 1586, 11052, 13889, 14987, 18463, 18694, 18698 IN 2136, 2416, 2418, 7795, 9165, 9687, 13547 KS 3835, 8574, 18731 KY 18756 LA 20676 MA 5026, 9790, 16547 MD 9754, 11209, 16990, 18800 MI 1106, 5670, 5671, 7853, 18852, 19679, 19681, 19970, 20124 MN 16339, 18894, 18895, 18929 MO 1934, 6847, 9575, 10092, 14436 MS 18951 NC 2391, 2393, 6493, 11210, 11907, 13847, 19061 ND 11930 NE 19010 NJ 1753, 1898, 2129, 2131, 2133, 3113, 3692, 7313, 7314, 8458, 8767, 10121, 10123, 12973, 13856, 14169, 14783, 14784, 14904, 14905, 15431, 19969 NM 19044 NY 223, 559, 2132, 2134, 2337, 3473, 3834, 4001, 4858, 5831, 9293, 9865, 10006, 12120, 12256, 12970, 14353, 15737, 15752, 15758, 15778, 15780, 20656, 20751 OH 9238, 9686, 12324, 12326, 18475, 18476 OK 15542, 19132 PA 617, 8456, 9962, 10122, 12980, 13890, 15256, 15258, 15779, 16147, 17172, 19181, 19211 PR 19256 SC 10014 SD 15424, 19315 TN 3458, 12192, 14906, 19371 TX 330, 7445, 16232, 16810, 16908, 18641, 19397 UT 19477 VA 1181, 19862 WA 6767, 17048, 19518, 19529, 20050 WI 3990, 15683, 17501, 19597 WV 20222 *Canada:* AB 18200 BC 18285 MB 9624, 18795 NF 10052 NS 2619, 4541 ON 2750, 3689, 6492, 7315, 14398, 14986, 15255, 19448, 20658 PQ 2130, 10124, 12968, 14780, 18094, 18120 SK 19294, 19298 *Intl:* BEL 1969 BOL 17982 BRZ 2406 CHN 40, 3609, 7491, 15074 CRI 17989 DEN 8777 FRA 12784, 18063, 18135 GER 6530, 16041 HUN 7928 ISR 7103 JPN 8340 NLD 14126 NZL 76 SPA 15560 SWI 15938 TUR 6821 TWN 2126, 8577, 11311 URE 8820 VEN 17986

Phase diagrams: MD 17622

Phenomenology: MA 20620

Philadelphia (PA): PA 4161, 6121, 6122, 6124, 6437, 6695, 9106, 12975, 12987, 12989, 16140, 16657, 17735

Philanthropy See: Endowments

Philately and philatelists See: Postage-stamps—Collectors and collecting

Philippines: CA 12204, 13001 CT 20732 DC 9109, 9125 GU 18610 IL 11994 MI 18860, 18875 *Canada:* NS 4535

Philology (See also Archeology; Language and languages; Literature; Literature, Comparative): CA 9350 CT 16504 DC 4909 IL 11752, 18672 MO 11356, 20234 NY 2239, 11609 *Intl:* BRZ 6212 CHN 1656, 7540 CRI 17989 CZE 4512 GER 1597, 18054 GRC 5204 ITA 15925 SPA 15561

Philosophy (See also Aesthetics): AL 8057 AZ 11770, 20633 CA 2480, 3187, 3206, 3281, 6162, 6200, 6535, 7097, 8819, 9354, 9418, 12661, 13012, 13421, 14349, 14555, 14706, 15660, 16301, 16701, 19290, 19337, 19343, 20188, 20463 CO 4776, 18507 CT 4178, 6939, 7342, 20696 DC 516, 3163, 3165, 4912, 4947, 6953, 9689, 11158, 13279, 14420, 14572, 14969 DE 15007 FL 5870, 10257, 14332, 14607, 16300 GA 1237 HI 7046 IA 6608, 9543 ID 18649 IL 3535, 7094, 9173, 9968, 11947, 12781, 15488, 15492, 18675 IN 7821, 10724 KY 8657, 15463 LA 14392 MA 1994, 6976, 6990, 9803, 13218, 14394 ME 1471, 1472 MI 2592, 4827, 14203 MN 3913, 10453, 10461, 14334, 14552, 14565, 14566, 16110, 17966, 18926, 18931 MO 1134, 3145, 4110, 5228, 11356, 14455, 18972, 20234 MT 3099 NC 7380, 13038 ND 18796 NE 4427, 11371 NH 10723 NJ 11746, 15047 NM 930 NY 757, 2246, 2330, 4010, 6043, 7098, 8075, 9880, 10109, 11548, 11609, 11618, 11667, 12782, 13143, 13634, 13990, 15156, 16724, 19929, 20130, 20753 OH 3831, 9168, 10266, 12266, 12800, 13211, 13480, 16397 OK 12367, 12372, 14315 OR 10849, 20244 PA 37, 1300, 3077, 5142, 5823, 6113, 13088, 13754, 14256, 19197 TN 6902 TX 4568, 4653, 5390, 5728, 5746, 7915, 14538, 14674 UT 20806 VA 10628 VT 3066 WA 9444, 15000, 19538 WI 9712, 12701, 14207, 14314, 14551 *Canada:* AB 11771, 18292 BC 16298, 18271 MB 1961, 3917, 18794 NB 1250 NS 18760 ON 3889, 7585, 10225, 12227, 13765, 14587, 18128, 19359, 19454, 19460, 19462 PQ 3194, 3285, 4055, 4095, 6642, 7868, 9895, 9910, 9975, 13316, 15023, 18065, 18086 SK 2627, 14598 *Intl:* AMA 7867 ARG 17984 AUT 8585 BRZ 18000 CHN 1659, 6246, 15075 CRI 17989 ENG 9266, 18441 FRA 18134 GER 8740, 18040, 18054, 18556 IDN 5074 IND 8527 LIT 19849 NLD 11402 RUS 17957 SPA 5465, 15561 WAL 14272

Philosophy, Medieval: CA 19290 NY 6074

Philosophy, Oriental: AZ 20633 CA 7487, 7907, 13012 IL 18451 MO 20061 NH 4612 NY 7894, 14352, 19274 OH 3823 RI 2278 WA 19522 *Canada:* BC 18255 *Intl:* CHN 10965, 16349 IDN 5074 IND 15997

Philosophy of science See: Science—Philosophy

Philosophy of teaching See: Education—Philosophy

Phonograph records See: Sound recordings

Phosphates: FL 5875 *Canada:* ON 317

Photochemistry: IN 19111, 19119

Photoelectricity: NJ 14912

Photogrammetry: MD 756, 17650 MN 18945 MS 17865 NY 14070 VA 16964 *Canada:* ON 2701, 12487, 13653 *Intl:* CHN 20650 FIN 5717

Photograph collections: AK 833, 16404, 18181 AL 1856 AZ 987, 988, 1015, 1864, 11992, 17789 CA 35, 1262, 1809, 2470, 2477, 2553, 3744, 6154, 6501, 7271, 9282, 9339, 9347, 11234, 11342, 12772, 13032, 13205, 13767, 14686, 14696, 14740, 14769, 15312, 15650, 15658, 16601, 17533, 18303, 18322, 18370, 18404, 19172, 19340, 19800, 19905, 19968, 20141, 20398 CO 935, 2030, 3941, 3951, 4785, 5995, 10923, 13046, 17537 CT 15634, 17807, 20699, 20727, 20734 DC 2194, 6379, 6963, 7291, 7478, 9108, 9134, 11027, 11045, 11180, 11185, 15263, 15264, 15267, 17214, 17226, 17242, 17504, 17843, 17942 DE 4730, 7266 FL 5898, 6004, 6045, 7256, 10254, 16486, 19550 GA 1246 HI 1865 IA 15680 ID 10915

Phytopathology   See: Plant diseases

Piaget, Jean: MA 13034

Piano music: CA 338 DC 9131, 17602 IL 18686 IN 7796 MA 11469 MD 18821, 18822 ME 1405 MN 3453 NY 11638, 19788 PA 4491 TN 19368, 19767 *Intl:* CHN 3338

Piarists: *Intl:* HUN 13035

Pickford, Mary (Gladys Mary Smith):   CA 35

Pierce, Franklin: ME 2033 NH 11485

Pigments (See also Dyes and dyeing):   DE 5028 MA 2432 MD 14950 MI 1551 NJ 5352 OH 7221 PA 13287

Pikes Peak region: CO 3951, 13046

Pilgrims (New Plymouth Colony):   MA 6350, 13049, 13144

Pinero, Sir Arthur Wing: NY 19278

Pioneering   See: Frontier and pioneer life

Pipe: DC 11134 TX 16629

Pipe lines: AK 17100 AL 15366 CA 2272 DC 5627 IL 7941 OK 20444 TX 10572 VA 595 *Canada:* AB 271, 273, 965, 2791, 2916, 16451 PQ 6267 SK 19296 YT 20831

Pitcairn Islands: CA 6819, 12680

Pittman, Key: WA 15212

Pittsburgh (PA):   PA 3079, 7292, 13085, 19203

Place-names   See: Names, Geographical

Planets (See also Mechanics, Celestial; Satellites):   AZ 18230 CA 2489, 18384 DC 15262 MA 9807 MO 20060, 20067 TX 9437 *Intl:* JPN 7981

Planning (See also Educational planning; Health planning; Social policy):   AK 209 AL 11908, 16591 AR 10195 CA 2544, 4589, 5438, 6499, 8806, 14192, 15371, 15472, 18326, 18374, 19799 CT 4205, 4366 DC 3157 FL 9583, 20545 GU 6786 HI 7031 IL 11981 KS 20464 KY 9400 LA 9382 MA 949, 9834 MD 1095, 1455, 9767, 18246 MI 12200, 20077 MN 10452, 18892 MO 7120 NE 11376, 12407 NJ 4473, 10358, 13387 NY 3728, 11008, 15733, 16623 OH 10273, 13135, 18468 OR 12536, 19147 PA 531, 9057, 10108, 20770 PR 19248 RI 13876 SC 15252 TN 10064, 10072, 16163, 16169 VA 7061 WA 20030 WY 20672 *Canada:* ON 4740, 19557 PE 13350 PQ 13590 *Intl:* ENG 6673 FRA 6222 NOR 12592 SWE 2423, 11310

Planning, City   See: City planning

Planning, Regional   See: Regional planning

Plant diseases: CA 18403 FL 5887, 7860, 18563, 18571, 18589 HI 7053 IN 13544 MN 18924, 18943, 18946 NY 4325, 9593 OH 12293 SD 15424 VA 777 WA 20048 WI 19613 WV 20208 *Canada:* BC 2664, 2743 NS 2653 ON 2643 PQ 2660, 2739 SK 2661 *Intl:* AUS 2023, 18145, 18146 BRZ 2096, 7995 CHN 1655 ENG 6681 GER 6446 MUS 9852 PAK 12693

Plant distribution   See: Phytogeography

Plant genetics: CA 2466, 14779 DC 17608 IA 13071 MN 18942, 18943 VA 19499 WI 17514 *Canada:* MB 2648 ON 2738 SK 2826 *Intl:* ARG 4618 CHN 10964 ENG 14103 GER 13101 NZL 5011, 11736

Plants (See also Botany; Flowers; Gardening; Trees; Weeds):   AK 18182 AZ 4796 CA 3071, 13563, 13704, 14641, 14796, 15833, 18358, 18403 CO 7217 CT 12070 FL 5887, 15018, 15991, 18845 GA 17193, 18607 IN 9163 LA 17194 MA 11480 MD 17203 MN 18942 MO 10535 NC 11903 NH 19029 NY 4003, 4304, 6248, 16316 PA 9299, 17181, 19189 SC 2216 TN 3463 VA 12999 WA 20046 *Canada:* AB 244 MB 18783 ON 12450

PE 2649 PQ 2638, 2660, 18078 SK 2661, 2826 *Intl:* AUS 1327 AUT 1351 BOL 7997 CHN 1655 CZE 4511 ENG 6681, 14103 GER 6446 ICE 13711 IND 7747 MUS 9852 NLD 11409 NZL 11736, 11737 RUS 5525 SCT 9490 TWN 1123, 15987

Plants, Protection of: AZ 4796 *Canada:* ON 2665 *Intl:* BUL 2344 CHN 10964 CRI 8029 CZE 4511 ENG 6670, 14103 GER 6446, 18033 IND 7739 JPN 8330 RUS 5525, 8823 URE 16618 YUG 8763

Plasma (Ionized gases):   CA 18395, 19342 MA 9813, 16286 MO 20066 NJ 13382 NM 10507 NY 19281 OH 6314 *Intl:* ENG 6663 FRA 6060 GER 13112 ITA 8077 NLD 5491

Plastic surgery   See: Surgery, Plastic

Plastics: CO 6259 CT 16455, 16672, 19765 DE 5028 GA 1186 IL 1586, 7370, 13570, 19701 KS 1941 LA 4986 MA 2432, 6315, 6477, 10632 MI 1552, 4982, 4984 MN 16332, 16335 MO 10636 NC 6490 NJ 1933, 4144, 7308, 7310, 10563, 14158, 16645, 16987 NY 3691, 5188, 10564, 13394 OH 175, 2118, 5672, 6284, 6566, 6567, 6570, 10764, 12636 OK 13011 PA 819, 1271, 10562, 13199, 13286, 14039, 16050, 17170 SC 6606 TN 8170 WI 8325 WV 6273 *Canada:* ON 5015, 5018, 16673 PQ 2819, 16639 *Intl:* ENG 13716 GER 6432

Plath, Sylvia: IN 7794 MA 15236

Playwrights   See: Dramatists

Plumbing: MA 11479 *Canada:* SK 14862 *Intl:* ENG 2343

Plymouth (MA):   MA 13049

Plywood (See also Wood):   VA 6904 WI 5983

Podiatry: CA 2474 IA 19162 IL 14919 NJ 14545 NY 11570 OH 12264 PA 12839, 12840 *Canada:* ON 10279

Poe, Edgar Allan: IN 7794 PA 6122, 7811 TX 19392 VA 19510, 19724

Poetry (See also Ballads):   AK 19722 AZ 18228, 18231, 20633 CA 1806, 2499, 2568, 2572, 9345, 9348, 9350, 11460, 18358, 18364, 18382, 18400, 18413, 18420, 19290 CO 10978, 18507 DC 4909 FL 5919, 18586 IL 18461 IN 1438, 2416 KS 8572, 18724 MA 807, 7000, 20153 MN 10448, 10451 MO 3350, 18979 NH 4614 NJ 10658, 11746, 13386, 20392 NV 19022 NY 112, 2244, 3735, 7316, 11609, 11815, 13156, 15156, 15710, 15741, 15757 OH 3827, 12273, 12337, 18471, 19425 PA 3183, 6117, 15325, 16133, 19225 RI 2282 TX 4568, 7200, 16521 VA 19861 WA 15000 WI 19574 *Canada:* BC 6105 ON 2808, 9839 *Intl:* CHN 12932

Point-of-purchase advertising   See: Advertising, Point-of-sale

Poker: LA 9390

Poland: CA 13178 CT 3337 DC 9113 IL 13183 KS 18737 NH 4860 NY 7206, 8798, 13055, 13179, 13184, 15739 PA 7349, 9480 *Canada:* ON 19460 PQ 13180 *Intl:* ENG 13182 GER 5119 LIT 19849 POL 13161, 13162, 13163, 13168, 13171, 13173, 16664, 20107

Polar regions (See also Antarctic regions; Arctic regions):   AK 17109, 18184 DC 11027, 11186, 11281, 17800 NH 4609, 4611, 4616, 16935 OH 717, 12294, 12298 RI 19266 *Canada:* NT 2846 PQ 9911 *Intl:* SCT 14953

Police: CA 2363 DC 17259 IL 12090 MD 1454 ME 9551 MI 4824 MN 10452 NY 8345, 11009 OH 3829, 12287 VA 17488 *Canada:* AB 5246 ON 12814 PQ 7881, 13606 SK 13785 *Intl:* ENG 6678

Police—Study and teaching: AL 17017 CT 10862 IA 8226 IN 7759 MD 9768 MO 14445 NY 11565 OH 7305 OK 12369 WA 15001 WI 10718, 11978, 19591 *Canada:* AB 2461 BC 8499 ON 12491, 12492, 14108

Policy sciences (See also Decision-making):   CA 13706 DC 17484 KS 18727 MA 6977 NE 11373 NY 15956 VA 7923 *Intl:* COL 3927

Poliomyelitis: NH 4608 OH 18475

Polish Americans: CT 3337 IL 13183 NY 15739

Polish art   See: Art, Polish

Power resources (continued)
9009, 9244, 9253, 9785, 11149, 12233, 12664, 12667, 12767, 12823, 14013, 14183, 14721, 14804, 15470, 16532, 17121, 17236, 17829 **CO** 3966, 5365, 11267, 13965, 15811 **CT** 5, 4205, 16720, 17961 **DC** 709, 726, 1563, 4171, 5627, 6030, 7656, 8027, 9937, 11150, 13272, 13851, 14943, 16783, 16803, 17232, 17233, 17249, 20609 **FL** 5880, 5900, 15999 **GA** 6391, 12162, 14885, 15517 **HI** 5134, 7031, 7050 **IA** 8233 **IL** 977, 4063, 5289, 6257, 7003, 7690, 7935, 7941, 10161, 10350, 18697 **IN** 1439, 7766, 7779 **KS** 8563 **KY** 18758 **LA** 9368, 9376 **MA** 2006, 2599, 3438, 4041, 8365, 9214, 9796, 11473, 13726, 13930, 16077 **MD** 5613, 6851, 15311, 16018, 16068 **ME** 3346 **MI** 4246, 5966 **MN** 7735, 8181, 10459, 10485, 12011, 18933 **MT** 12008 **NC** 11899 **NH** 11484, 11494 **NJ** 1256, 5535, 10573 **NM** 9322, 11527, 17229 **NV** 17235 **NY** 2223, 3239, 4307, 5197, 5375, 6311, 11151, 11584, 11662, 11667, 12515, 15751, 15810, 15967, 16188, 17474 **OH** 566, 3318, 10987, 12267 **OK** 8687, 12346, 16571, 20444 **OR** 12059, 12533, 19148 **PA** 6308, 12852, 14775, 15586, 16709, 19205, 20342 **SC** 15252 **TN** 16174 **TX** 1957, 3726, 4559, 6597, 6771, 7453, 9939, 9941, 13504, 15116, 16151, 16195, 16535, 19410 **UT** 13664 **VA** 7639, 10558, 17560, 19889, 19890, 20006 **VT** 3378 **WA** 1572, 17231, 19523, 20032, 20035 **WI** 5983, 20529 *Canada:* **AB** 270, 273, 965, 2791, 5953, 7360, 8813, 12127, 16451 **BC** 2158 **MB** 1846, 9608 **NB** 11446, 11448 **NS** 4534, 5211, 12141, 12154 **ON** 99, 2699, 2700, 5456, 7482, 12465, 12496 **PQ** 7601, 7602, 7603, 10609, 13596 *Intl:* **ALG** 350 **AUS** 1332 **CHN** 6790 **DEN** 13938 **ECU** 8967 **ENG** 9270 **FIN** 7126, 16030 **FRA** 6065 **GER** 1564, 5546, 6449 **GRC** 5488 **GUY** 3046 **HUN** 7551 **ICE** 7636 **IRL** 4057 **MEX** 7934, 10242 **NLD** 11413 **SAU** 5551 **SWI** 5481 **THA** 16760

Power resources—Law and legislation: **AR** 1026 **CA** 12665 **DC** 4444, 10752, 15894, 17233, 17238 **MT** 10644 **NY** 9039 **OK** 19465 **TX** 1411 *Canada:* **AB** 2791 **BC** 20231 **ON** 12436

Power resources—Research: **AL** 6363 **AZ** 18225 **CT** 15878 **ID** 5268 **IL** 976 **NM** 14778 **PA** 6474 **PR** 19255 **TN** 16175 **UT** 19469 **VA** 5476 **WY** 20291 *Canada:* **ON** 13117 **PQ** 3284 *Intl:* **POL** 7940

Power transmission (See also Gearing): **TX** 16535 *Canada:* **AB** 16451 *Intl:* **MEX** 7934

Precious metals: **RI** 16028 *Canada:* **ON** 2946

Pregnancy: **NY** 20556 **PA** 8022 **WV** 20224

Pregnancy, Adolescent See: Pregnancy

Prepaid legal services: **DC** 11271

Pre-Raphaelites (Art): **AZ** 1019 **DE** 4715

Presbyterian Church: **AL** 5580, 5802, 7737 **AZ** 14498 **CA** 4641, 5791, 5804, 14685, 16520 **CO** 5788 **DC** 11252 **DE** 5579 **FL** 5191, 5792, 12773 **IL** 5793, 5798, 8375, 15008 **IN** 5781 **KY** 9401 **MD** 13314 **MI** 5794, 5795, 5801, 10047 **MO** 3359, 4391 **MS** 3358, 13781 **NC** 13315 **NE** 5796 **NJ** 1902, 3360, 13367, 16517 **NM** 5787, 8849, 10079 **NY** 13323 **OH** 10689, 20331, 20353 **PA** 5121, 5797, 5823, 7201, 11397, 12021, 13318, 13780, 15883, 20115, 20334 **TX** 1314, 3361, 5786, 5800, 7199 **VA** 16668, 20335 **WV** 5799 *Canada:* **NS** 16695 **ON** 19454 **PQ** 13316

Preschool education See: Education, Preschool

Preservation of books See: Books—Conservation and restoration

Presidents—United States: **CA** 1390, 4293, 17929 **DC** 9129, 11044, 17484 **GA** 17926 **IA** 17925 **KS** 17921 **MA** 1993, 17927 **MI** 1068, 17923 **MO** 17924 **NY** 3308, 6612, 17922 **OH** 7060 **PA** 6122 **TN** 9185, 19777 **TX** 17928, 17930, 20535 **VA** 10628

Presley, Elvis: **TX** 5314

Press, Underground See: Underground press

Presses, Private See: Private presses

Preventive medicine See: Medicine, Preventive

Priestly, Joseph: **ME** 2033 **PA** 4852, 19181

Primates: **CA** 18353 **GA** 5339 **LA** 16566 **MA** 6985 **MD** 1847 **OR** 12527 **TX** 15529 **WA** 19541 **WI** 19628

Primitive art See: Art, Primitive

Prince Edward Island: *Canada:* **NB** 10797 **PE** 13352, 19232

Printing (See also Graphic arts): **AL** 8171 **CA** 1958, 2565, 2572, 9350, 10409, 15532, 18303, 18333, 18358, 18428, 18435, 19337 **CO** 3949, 4784, 18508 **CT** 18615, 20700 **DC** 6379 **FL** 18586 **GA** 18600 **IL** 4956, 18461, 18667 **IN** 7772, 13543 **KY** 18767 **MA** 6976, 11854 **MD** 9747 **ME** 13245, 14184 **MN** 10445, 16336 **MO** 18966 **NC** 19075 **NH** 9586 **NJ** 4643, 5567, 11744, 13386 **NY** 669, 6655, 11609, 11628, 12768, 13981, 13983, 15757, 19789 **OH** 3827, 13479 **OR** 721 **PA** 6123, 6654 **PR** 13520 **RI** 19268 **TX** 5131 *Canada:* **ON** 9839, 10223, 16418, 19445 **PQ** 9895 *Intl:* **AUT** 1354, 6656 **CHN** 20650 **ENG** 13075 **GER** 6858

Printing—History: **CA** 2478, 3744, 9352, 14088, 14711, 14741, 15352, 18355 **CO** 3940 **CT** 4178, 16504, 20177, 20700, 20703 **IL** 11752, 18461 **KS** 18724, 20412 **KY** 18754 **LA** 9390 **MA** 15236, 20153 **MD** 18820 **MI** 4828, 8528 **MN** 3908, 10454 **MO** 14457, 18972, 20059 **NC** 19087, 19942 **NJ** 3, 11750, 13386 **NV** 19022 **NY** 2335, 3880, 4025, 6762, 9296, 10738, 11626, 13304, 13981, 15731, 18483 **OH** 8649, 12221, 19425 **PA** 3084, 8875, 16137 **RI** 2270, 2283, 13454, 19268 **TX** 4562, 7463, 8356, 15503, 16200 **UT** 20809 **VA** 3918 **VT** 19482 *Canada:* **AB** 18196 **PQ** 9895, 9903 *Intl:* **ENG** 3014 **NZL** 11739

Prints: **CA** 9335, 9343 **CT** 20734, 20736 **DC** 9134, 11179, 11244 **FL** 10895 **IN** 2416 **MA** 1998, 10898, 15600, 20446 **MI** 4407 **MN** 10446 **MO** 8544, 11388 **NC** 11880 **NY** 669, 2238, 10211, 10213, 11625, 11669 **PA** 6109, 6121 **TX** 4555, 4561 **WA** 19513 **WI** 10426 *Canada:* **BC** 19752 **MB** 20487 **PQ** 9895 *Intl:* **AUS** 1342 **DEN** 14125

Prisoners of war: **CA** 17841 **FL** 14186

Prisons: **CO** 17253 **MD** 545 **NY** 8345 **OR** 12543

Private presses: **AZ** 1019, 18231 **CA** 1958, 14711, 18428, 19290 **CO** 18507 **CT** 16504, 20700 **IL** 7707, 15492 **MA** 2008, 20446 **MD** 18820 **ME** 1560 **MI** 8528 **MN** 18931 **NC** 19087 **NH** 4616 **NJ** 2373 **NY** 2335, 7316, 13632, 13981 **PA** 2304 **SC** 20548 **WI** 19574, 19607 *Canada:* **AB** 18196 **ON** 2807, 10223, 19543, 19564 *Intl:* **AUS** 15695

Probate law and practice: **CA** 8246, 8711, 9433 **CO** 5280 **FL** 8605 **IL** 9882 **MA** 6569, 20419 **OH** 9723 **TX** 1411

Procedure (Law): **AL** 15199 **AZ** 10597 **CA** 4438, 6659, 8246, 9433, 10173, 10754, 13052, 14034, 16315 **DC** 4991, 8830, 17256 **GA** 417 **IL** 1376, 4703, 9869, 9882, 11117 **MA** 1840, 6569, 9825 **MD** 12215, 19796 **MI** 5079 **MO** 15798 **NY** 1751, 7517, 11821, 12752, 12792, 15098 **OH** 9723, 14935 **PA** 6054, 20550 **RI** 7225 **TX** 165, 2271, 8446, 8470 **VA** 7577 **WA** 6032 **WI** 13571 *Canada:* **BC** 5605 **ON** 156, 1888, 5612, 6564, 6565, 15132 **PQ** 9949

Process control: **CA** 1374, 2485 **IA** 10634 **PA** 5825 *Intl:* **FIN** 16030

Procurement, Government See: Government purchasing

Produce trade: **CA** 18323 **FL** 17185 **IL** 7668 **MD** 17203 **MN** 3044 **OH** 12292 **PA** 5598, 14421 **VA** 16712 *Canada:* **PQ** 9229 *Intl:* **CRI** 8029 **GER** 18026

Product safety: **CA** 3116 **DC** 4243 **TN** 5184 *Canada:* **ON** 2991

Productivity of labor See: Labor productivity

Products liability (See also Product safety): **CT** 116 **DC** 3214 **IL** 1422 **MI** 4856, 10398, 13148 **MO** 15140 **NJ** 1918 **NY** 856, 6884, 8492, 16439 **OH** 6305 **PA** 3771

Professional ethics: **CA** 3632 **IL** 3304

Profit-sharing (See also Employee ownership): **NY** 16436

Programmed instruction (See also Computer-assisted instruction): **MI** 16470 **NY** 5401

Programming (Electronic computers) (See also Computers; Information storage and retrieval systems): **AL** 18170 **AZ** 132, 2355 **CA** 918, 1476, 4257, 5940, 7076, 7183, 7628, 9251, 9331, 10506, 11365, 16003, 16681 **CO** 7617, 18505 **CT** 6310 **GA** 10981 **IL** 976, 14834 **IN** 19117 **KS** 8576

Public administration (continued)
13895, 19408 **UT** 20802 **VA** 19859 **WA** 15001, 19540, 20035 **WI** 10425, 13494, 20529 **WV** 20215 *Canada:* **AB** 288 **ON** 2685, 2831, 2836, 2837, 2841, 2861, 2888, 7968, 10222, 12446, 14180, 20788 **PQ** 13593, 18104, 18105 *Intl:* **AUS** 1334, 3277 **BEL** 1666 **BRZ** 2090, 19781 **ENG** 6683 **ICE** 7635 **JOR** 931 **NIR** 12005 **SAU** 7966 **SPA** 15565 **THA** 16292

Public contracts (See also Government purchasing): **CA** 601, 13403 **CO** 16821 **DC** 2440, 4444, 7483, 13770, 16803, 17161, 17238, 17254, 17902 **GA** 15239, 16961 **MA** 20419 **OH** 174, 6305, 16391

Public finance See: Finance, Public

Public health (See also Communicable diseases; Health planning; World health): **AK** 212 **AL** 190, 18171 **AZ** 999, 18209 **CA** 2593, 9329, 14692, 14722, 14768, 15653, 18341, 18390 **CT** 20715 **DC** 11272 **FL** 5436, 18560, 19321 **GA** 513, 5336, 17125 **HI** 18622 **IL** 18698 **IN** 7763 **KY** 8669 **LA** 16564 **MA** 2017, 6996, 9832, 18829 **MD** 8432, 13356, 17629, 17932, 17933 **ME** 9555 **MI** 4824, 4829, 10306, 18884 **MN** 10480, 18894, 18895 **NC** 11889, 19061 **NY** 4001, 11005, 11650, 13219, 15724 **OH** 169, 13489 **OK** 19132 **PA** 365, 8946, 19195 **PR** 13511, 19256 **RI** 13879 **SC** 15403 **TN** 11001, 16160 **TX** 1312, 16207, 16242, 18640, 19408 **VT** 19809 **WA** 19529 **WI** 20517, 20529 **WV** 20210 **WY** 20666 *Canada:* **AB** 279 **BC** 2165 **MB** 9614 **NT** 12063 **ON** 2750, 12470 **PQ** 7386 **SK** 14853 *Intl:* **BRZ** 18001 **BUL** 2346 **CHN** 12930 **COL** 5349 **CZE** 4515 **ENG** 6674, 9270 **FRA** 4364 **GER** 7927 **GTM** 12717 **GUY** 3046 **HUN** 7556 **IND** 7743, 7745 **ISR** 7103 **JAM** 12716 **SWI** 20619 **TWN** 8577, 11311 **TZA** 16005, 16006 **URE** 8820

Public hygiene See: Public health

Public interest groups: **DC** 6046

Public interest law: **NJ** 11512 **TX** 5130

Public lands (See also National parks and reserves): **CA** 2545 **CO** 17106 **DC** 17247 **FL** 5895 **MN** 10483 **NE** 17732 **OR** 9076 **VA** 17105

Public law (See also Administrative law; Constitutional law; Criminal law; International law; Military law): **FL** 18575 **MA** 9833 **NC** 19063 **TX** 2271 *Canada:* **ON** 13652 *Intl:* **GER** 13102 **ITA** 4344 **NLD** 16753

Public opinion: **IL** 18456 **NY** 6920 **WI** 19611 *Canada:* **BC** 18259

Public opinion polls: **CA** 18313, 18386 **CT** 18522, 18528, 20731 **IA** 18712 **IL** 18692 **KS** 18727 **KY** 18776 **NC** 19066 **NJ** 13852 *Canada:* **ON** 20789 *Intl:* **ENG** 19360 **GER** 18487

Public policy: **AR** 20493 **CA** 2481, 2507, 4622, 7736, 14720, 18307, 18352 **DC** 17227, 17526, 19689 **FL** 12511 **GA** 3762 **IN** 7495 **LA** 15518 **ME** 9563 **MI** 9141, 20274 **NJ** 3069 **NY** 15727, 16775 **PA** 6132 **PR** 19249 **TN** 16169 **TX** 16259, 19408 *Canada:* **MB** 9603 **ON** 2919, 12446 *Intl:* **JOR** 931

Public relations (See also Advertising; Propaganda): **CT** 2067 **IL** 2394, 7213, 18667 **IN** 17024 **MI** 6341 **MO** 18966 **NY** 2242, 4333, 13497 **OH** 12315 **PR** 19250 *Canada:* **NS** 10812 **ON** 7720 *Intl:* **BRZ** 18005 **SPA** 17980

Public utilities: **AK** 206 **AL** 184, 15366, 15480 **AR** 1025 **AZ** 991, 14648, 16541 **CA** 2543, 9351, 12667, 15467, 15470 **CO** 13498 **CT** 11976, 11977, 16720 **DC** 152, 726, 5235, 13272, 17936 **FL** 5878, 5879, 5880, 15999 **GA** 6391 **HI** 7032, 7049 **IL** 729, 4062, 7672, 7690, 12923 **IN** 7826 **MA** 1986, 11476, 20742 **MD** 1450 **ME** 3346 **MI** 4246, 4247, 4805, 4806, 10287 **MN** 10459, 12011, 12606 **MO** 16653 **NC** 3091, 5036 **NE** 12409 **NH** 11494 **NJ** 1256, 6590, 6591, 13500, 13501, 13502, 14631 **NM** 13764 **NY** 4225, 11151, 11662, 12515, 13977, 15639, 15810 **OH** 566, 3318, 3319, 4226, 12267, 12274, 12289 **OK** 12346, 13499 **OR** 13239, 17230 **PA** 6592, 6594, 10200, 12844, 12977, 12985, 20770 **SC** 15394 **TN** 16170, 16174 **TX** 1411, 3356, 3362, 6810, 7453, 7458, 15543, 16266, 16535 **VA** 19877, 20006 **VT** 3378, 6721, 19812 **WA** 1639, 13525, 15982 **WI** 4524, 20508, 20508, 20509 *Canada:* **AB** 299, 309, 2455, 2791, 2999, 3001, 5247, 16456 **BC** 1391, 13282 **MB** 9616 **NB** 11448 **NS** 12150 **ON** 2934, 12442 **PQ** 7601, 7602, 10609

Public utilities—Law and legislation: **AZ** 15292 **CA** 12665 **DC** 5627, 6030, 17489 **DE** 3986 **MA** 16077 **ME** 3346 **MT** 10644 **NC** 5038 **NJ** 11512 **NY** 1751, 9039, 13808, 15098, 15183 **OH** 13503 **PA** 12852, 12924 **TX** 2271, 6810, 6811, 13504 **VA** 595 **VT** 3378 **WA** 20039 **WI** 20509 *Canada:* **BC** 2181

Public welfare (See also Income maintenance programs; Poverty; Psychiatric social work; Social service): **AL** 185 **AZ** 996 **CA** 2495, 14657, 14692, 18326, 18343, 18396, 19347 **CO** 3958 **CT** 18517 **DC** 3560, 7481, 9111 **FL** 5903 **IA** 8232 **IL** 18459 **IN** 7815 **KS** 8556, 18735 **KY** 8669 **MA** 15177, 15179, 18832 **MD** 1444, 11106 **MN** 18930 **NC** 5112 **NJ** 10614, 14175 **NY** 2330, 3735, 4020, 4028, 4367, 5968, 7563, 11561, 14002, 15727, 15752, 20758 **OH** 3126, 3831 **PA** 12858, 16143 **PR** 19235 **TX** 4567, 19408 **WA** 19542 **WI** 4090, 10420, 20517, 20529 **WV** 20215 *Canada:* **AB** 5244 **BC** 2167 **MB** 2988, 9614 **NS** 4532 **ON** 2749, 2764, 2919, 4084, 12456 **PE** 2882 **SK** 14850 *Intl:* **DOM** 11128 **EGY** 5272 **FRA** 4364 **ITA** 8282 **MOR** 10743 **NLD** 11407 **SWE** 15912

Public welfare—Law and legislation: **IL** 9051, 11117 **IN** 9054 **NY** 3298 *Intl:* **GER** 13106 **SWI** 8086

Public works (See also Municipal engineering): **CA** 9349, 11828, 14692 **GA** 14884 **HI** 7379 **IL** 729 **TX** 16940 **WA** 10863

Publishers and publishing (See also Book industries and trade; Little presses; Periodicals, Publishing of; Private presses): **CA** 16, 70, 155, 1462, 2572, 18333 **CT** 6752, 6763, 20136 **DC** 3643, 4173, 11223, 17911 **FL** 8759, 10954, 16477 **IL** 4617, 5348, 8455, 9714, 14959, 15636, 18667, 20610 **IN** 7794, 14878 **KY** 720 **MA** 71, 7436, 15178 **MD** 13855, 19233 **MI** 801, 8056, 18867, 18890 **MN** 1135, 5501 **MO** 8591 **NC** 19076, 19090 **NE** 8296 **NJ** 6874, 10002, 12941, 13773, 15169 **NV** 11060 **NY** 493, 504, 611, 658, 1386, 2083, 2441, 4023, 4025, 5237, 8487, 8828, 9038, 9914, 11609, 12645, 12734, 13742, 14918, 14938, 16355, 20431 **OH** 93, 818, 3153, 3827, 6497, 12922 **PA** 3601, 5598, 7294, 15613, 16050, 16137 **TN** 16748 **TX** 19392 **VA** 10281, 16354 **WA** 20045 **WI** 8534, 19590 *Canada:* **BC** 1150, 18280 **ON** 2899, 5698, 5699, 9499, 9954, 10223, 19445 **PQ** 13744 *Intl:* **AUS** 1335 **BRZ** 2099, 8194 **CHN** 3604 **SGP** 1120

Puerto Rico: **CT** 18519 **DC** 9125 **NJ** 11035, 11746 **NY** 1971, 2230, 2244, 7561, 11556, 11610 **PR** 3168, 3387, 13508, 13510, 13519, 19235, 19241, 19251, 19252, 19255

Pulp See: Wood-pulp

Puppets and puppet-plays (See also Mime): **CA** 4091 **MI** 4809 **NY** 11634 *Canada:* **ON** 12497, 16416 **PQ** 9895

Purchasing: **AZ** 11074

Puritans (See also Calvinism; Church of England; Congregationalism; Pilgrims (New Plymouth Colony)): **MN** 1786 **MO** 4391 **NJ** 13367 *Canada:* **ON** 12428

Pyle, Ernest Taylor "Ernie": **IN** 7792

Pyle, Howard: **DE** 4715 **PA** 2080, 6122

Pyrotechnics See: Fireworks

Qatar: *Intl:* **IRQ** 933

Quacks and quackery: **PA** 9059

Quakers See: Society of Friends

Quality control (See also Process control): **CA** 3868 **FL** 10639 **ID** 3476 **IL** 20647 **MA** 4868 **MI** 6418 **NJ** 2131 **NM** 9322 **NY** 20656 **OH** 6571 **TX** 16226 **VA** 777 **WA** 20359 **WI** 758, 17974 *Canada:* **ON** 2991 *Intl:* **ENG** 3863 **MEX** 10241

Quality of work life See: Labor productivity

Quantum theory: **MN** 18928 **MO** 20066 **OK** 19137 *Intl:* **GER** 6425

Quebec (Province): **MN** 12068 **WI** 13810 *Canada:* **PQ** 2206, 3191, 3192, 3915, 3916, 4339, 9209, 10509, 13574, 13576, 13580, 13688, 15024, 15303, 15304, 18065, 18106, 18107, 18121

Rabbis: **AZ** 16089 **CA** 7097 **FL** 16092, 18573 **IL** 7094, 11947, 15584 **MA** 7092 **NY** 8405, 20750, 20756, 20759 **OH** 7099 **PA** 878, 13754 **RI** 16085 *Canada:* **ON** 8970 *Intl:* **ISR** 5824

Rabelais, Francois: **OH** 3823

Race relations (See also Racism): **GA** 3763 **MD** 8453 **NC** 15443 **TN** 10076, 16164 *Canada:* **AB** 1097 *Intl:* **CHN** 3611 **ENG** 7969 **SAF** 15389

Rachmaninoff, Sergei W.: **DC** 9131

Racism (See also Anti-Semitism; Race relations): **NY** 20821 *Intl:* **ENG** 7969

Rackham, Arthur: **KY** 18768 **MO** 14450 **OH** 20644 **PA** 6122

Radar: **AL** 5083 **AZ** 10787 **CA** 978, 4468, 6346, 7508, 7512, 8286, 9227, 10506, 12724, 14017, 16067, 16820, 17904 **GA** 6389 **MA** 9822, 13731 **NJ** 6271, 17487 **NY** 3041, 6304, 9308, 9427, 11838, 13955, 16685, 16787 **VA** 13665, 15971, 16533, 19792 *Canada:* **PQ** 15570 *Intl:* **ENG** 16721

Radiation chemistry: **IN** 19119 **NJ** 16072 *Intl:* **ENG** 6688

Radiation dosimetry: *Canada:* **ON** 1272 *Intl:* **ENG** 6688

Radiation—Effect on...: **CA** 15468 **DC** 17465 **MA** 9808 **MD** 17623 **MI** 18880 **NV** 13862, 17235 **TN** 12183 *Canada:* **ON** 13117 *Intl:* **ARG** 972 **JPN** 13683

Radiation—Safety measures: **AL** 17009 **MD** 16976, 17507 **TN** 12191 *Canada:* **ON** 2750 *Intl:* **AUS** 1319 **ENG** 6688 **FIN** 5707 **MEX** 10241

Radio: **CA** 2572, 18370, 18379, 19336 **DC** 11033, 15269 **IL** 15493 **MI** 4825 **MN** 10451 **NJ** 14836 **NY** 906, 2245, 15743 **OH** 175, 3827 **PA** 6125 **PR** 19250 **RI** 11481 **WI** 19627 *Canada:* **ON** 13661 **PQ** 13610 *Intl:* **CHN** 4542 **SWI** 8196

Radio astronomy: **NY** 688 **PR** 4303 *Canada:* **BC** 2817 *Intl:* **GER** 13115 **ITA** 16498

Radio broadcasting (See also Television broadcasting): **AZ** 11865 **CA** 7902, 12683, 18399 **CT** 6939 **DC** 2194, 9120, 9130, 11053, 11256 **IL** 3539 **IN** 2417, 20441 **KY** 9399, 11864 **MA** 958 **MD** 6538 **NY** 3177, 4020, 8401, 11091, 11092, 11634, 11638, 13684 **OH** 2039, 12320, 12603 **OR** 6532 **PA** 16145 **TN** 10074 **UT** 20798 *Canada:* **ON** 2671, 2675, 2906, 2908, 10223 **PQ** 2901, 2902, 13688 *Intl:* **AUS** 1336 **BRZ** 18005 **FRA** 6071 **GER** 4838 **MYS** 1115 **SPA** 17980

Radio waves: **MD** 7660

Radioactive waste disposal: **DC** 17136 **ID** 5268 **MS** 10519, 19353 **NM** 14778, 15534, 17229, 20320 **NV** 17235 **NY** 2222 **PA** 5376 **SC** 3466 **WA** 6541, 20322 *Canada:* **MB** 102 *Intl:* **AUS** 1319

Radiobiology: **GA** 513 **MD** 16914, 17507 **NM** 9404 **TN** 19370 *Intl:* **FRA** 6060

Radiochemistry: **AL** 17459 **VA** 17545

Radiography: **AZ** 6260 **TX** 16226

Radioisotopes: *Intl:* **AUS** 1319

Radiology: **CA** 7575, 8866 **CO** 3974 **FL** 17313 **IA** 17321 **IL** 10149, 11122, 13690 **IN** 3173 **MA** 17511 **MD** 8413, 17507 **MI** 10801 **MN** 12069 **MO** 9249, 20070 **NJ** 12632 **NY** 1599, 11650 **OK** 1403 **OR** 20301 **PA** 16150 **TX** 19374 **WA** 1572 **WI** 19606 *Canada:* **MB** 9601 **ON** 2957 *Intl:* **AUS** 20302

Radiotherapy: *Canada:* **BC** 2142 **ON** 12430 *Intl:* **AUS** 9491

Radon: **VA** 19815

Railroads (See also Eminent domain; Transportation): **AK** 833 **CA** 2553, 9012, 9581, 12232, 20290 **CO** 3941, 3945, 4785, 6006, 10923 **CT** 13768 **DC** 1144, 1525, 17280 **GA** 6385, 11260 **IA** 8235, 15679, 15680 **IL** 730, 7678, 11752, 13708 **IN** 371, 7755, 7775, 13540 **KY** 18774 **MA** 15814, 18834 **MD** 11094 **ME** 2033 **MI** 9707, 9721 **MN** 7212, 8897, 10464, 11259 **MO** 14444 **MS** 19354 **MT** 10643, 12745 **NC** 11905 **NE** 8296, 17751, 19005 **NH** 4616 **NJ** 11641, 13383 **NV** 11426, 19022 **NY** 2246, 6344, 8374, 11262, 15757 **OH** 372, 1648, 7060, 9138 **OK** 2920 **PA** 426, 4228, 8869, 8896, 9425, 11261, 13696, 15451, 17663, 17664 **TN** 5127 **TX** 9014, 13693, 13900, 15499, 15533, 16278 **VA** 3484, 5364, 19875 **WI** 8534, 10347, 10429 *Canada:* **BC** 13227 **ON** 2822, 2942 **PQ** 2971, 2972, 2986, 13608, 19822 *Intl:* **AUT** 1358 **CHN** 8950, 13695 **ENG** 18254 **FRA** 8177

Railroads, Electric   See: Electric railroads

Railroads—Models: **CA** 14698 **NJ** 11641 **PA** 16449 **WI** 8534

Raleigh, Sir Walter: **NC** 19073

Ranch life: **AZ** 988 **CA** 15312 **CO** 6620 **TX** 7155, 12726, 16278

Randolph, Asa Philip: **DC** 9129

Randolph, John (John Randolph of Roanoke): **VA** 19510

Range management (See also Livestock): **AR** 20493 **CO** 17106 **MN** 18945 **MT** 17107, 17182 **TX** 20147 **UT** 17517 **WA** 20048 *Canada:* **BC** 2162 *Intl:* **KEN** 8679

Rankin, Jeannette: **MA** 13677

Rape: **CA** 11118 **WY** 20666

Rapid transit   See: Urban transportation

Rare books (See also Incunabula): **AK** 18176 **AL** 1281, 16591, 18169, 18171 **AR** 15526, 18236 **AZ** 13025, 20633 **CA** 7572, 15352, 18303, 18305, 18316, 18387, 18419 **CT** 16504, 20735 **DC** 6378, 9110, 17227, 17800, 17864, 18553 **DE** 7266 **FL** 5919, 13933, 16100 **GA** 17012, 18600 **HI** 18629 **IA** 18721 **IL** 4267, 4673, 7670, 12080, 12086, 13667, 18451, 18452, 18461, 18689 **IN** 7772, 19112 **KS** 3619, 5346, 8561, 8563 **KY** 1727, 3219, 8678, 10725, 18750, 18768 **LA** 9390, 16560, 19356 **MA** 6253, 6976, 6980, 9804, 17245, 18827 **MD** 1451, 17203, 18820, 19961 **ME** 1472, 12395 **MI** 4828, 18854, 18858, 18860 **MN** 3908, 11850, 14564, 18931 **MO** 6855, 6891, 14457, 14464, 15681, 18972, 20055, 20061 **MS** 19354 **NC** 1699, 19075 **NE** 4426 **NJ** 11750, 14163, 15047, 18837 **NM** 19047 **NY** 347, 2335, 4023, 4313, 5034, 6944, 9020, 9595, 10738, 11599, 11628, 11632, 11669, 15274, 15705, 15708, 15711, 15734, 15741, 15742, 15745, 15961, 16023, 16650, 18483 **OH** 3823, 7099, 12216, 12328, 16078, 18155, 18464, 18471, 20481 **OK** 17010, 19129 **OR** 12529, 19159 **PA** 6457, 7015, 8875, 10403, 11397, 12900, 15136, 16016 **PR** 13520, 19239, 19251 **RI** 13440, 13454, 19268 **SC** 20548 **TX** 451, 9072, 13297, 16521, 17930, 19414 **VA** 344, 3938, 9773, 19724, 20013 **VI** 6546, 19496 **WI** 10429, 19576 **WV** 20195 **WY** 15124, 19654 *Canada:* **MB** 16612, 18789 **NF** 10055 **NS** 42, 4538, 6027, 18760 **ON** 2813, 13661, 14130, 19167 **PQ** 1830, 9975, 10602, 15789, 18098 *Intl:* **AUS** 10712, 15692 **BRZ** 6214, 18000 **CHN** 1659, 10965, 12929, 12932 **COL** 17978 **ENG** 9171, 18440, 19360 **GER** 1597 **GRC** 7905 **IND** 7744 **MEX** 17990 **PHL** 13002 **POL** 13161, 13162 **RUS** 17958 **SCT** 14953 **SWI** 5946

Rare earths   See: Earths, Rare

Rather, Dan: **MA** 2008

Rauschenbush, Walter: **NY** 498

Ravel, Maurice Joseph: **SC** 4259 **TX** 19392

Rawlings, Marjorie Kinnan: **FL** 18586

Rayburn, Sam: **TX** 19404

Reactors (Nuclear physics)   See: Nuclear reactors

Read, Sir Herbert: *Canada:* **BC** 19489

Reading: **CT** 20136 **DC** 17227 **DE** 8178, 18542 **IL** 11982, 14959 **IN** 5404 **KS** 6000 **ME** 9032 **MI** 1382 **NY** 8973, 9208, 14542, 15735 **PA** 12995 **TX** 14674, 16280 *Canada:* **AB** 18194 **ON** 20159

Reagan, Ronald Wilson: CA 13830, 17929

Real estate See: Real property

Real property (See also Eminent domain): AL 18160 AZ 8179, 12244, 15292, 15830 CA 64, 199, 4396, 5216, 6659, 8102, 8246, 9074, 9344, 9433, 10754, 12774, 13052, 14034, 16315, 18374, 19852, 20448 CO 16688, 18491, 18509, 20144 CT 18515 DC 2287, 2341, 4906, 7479, 10761, 17916, 19690, 20432 DE 13901 FL 8605, 18575 GA 8718, 13280 HI 7027 IL 924, 1376, 3865, 9882, 11075, 13752, 20498 IN 13545 MA 1995, 6569, 9825, 20419 MD 19796 MI 3770, 4817, 5852, 7376 MN 13701 MO 8965 NC 6739 NJ 6722 NM 19050 NY 2242, 2329, 4333, 4843, 6168, 6884, 8590, 8926, 9496, 11729, 11821, 12655, 12752, 13422, 13751, 15098, 16290, 20454 OH 567, 3818 OR 8483 PA 3075, 6054, 6481, 19186, 20550 TX 165, 1411, 8446, 8470, 14671 VA 744, 4441, 7577, 9918, 10955, 12017 WA 6032, 19515 WI 5942, 13809, 19626, 19741, 20103 Canada: AB 258 BC 19759 ON 156, 2838, 5612, 6564, 6565, 15865, 16327, 20778 PQ 13590

Realism in art: NY 112

Rearview mirrors See: Automobiles—Rearview mirrors

Recombinant DNA: MA 6360 Intl: NLD 14092

Recording, Magnetic See: Magnetic recorders and recording

Records management: CA 18333 DC 11026 TX 19396 Canada: AB 2460 ON 12427 PQ 9903, 13574, 18076 Intl: AUS 1334 NIR 13496 SRI 15625

Recreation (See also Leisure): AR 1036 CA 2555, 4589, 9343, 9349, 12203, 16840, 16955 CO 17771 CT 4208, 6937, 18517 DC 4911 HI 7035, 7038 IL 15487 IN 510, 10185 LA 11544 MA 15601 MD 13300 MI 4821, 20077 MN 10453, 18930, 18945 MO 16956, 17075 NE 11376 NJ 11746 NY 2240, 15705 OH 2040, 3831, 12306, 13480 OK 12367 PA 20770 TN 16175 TX 16264, 16791, 16940 VA 11263 WA 19526, 20045 WI 20527 Canada: AB 301, 308, 2460 BC 2160, 2166 ON 2713, 3003, 8902, 10230, 12479, 15593 PE 13350 PQ 13603 Intl: ENG 6671 NLD 11403

Recreation—Administration: CT 12070 IN 7789 NC 11900

Recycling (Waste, etc.): DC 7951 MA 5108 NC 50 NJ 14158 Canada: AB 16456 MB 9609

Reed, Walter: VA 19504

Reflexotherapy: CA 466

Reformation: CA 6733, 8857 DC 6073 GA 5334 IL 8375 IN 10091 MO 3287, 4117 NJ 5002 OH 20546 PA 9465, 13779, 14937 UT 20809 Canada: ON 19454 PQ 13316 Intl: SCT 14953

Reformed Church: MI 7383, 13778 MO 5228, 5502 NC 13315 NJ 11455 NY 7329 PA 5503, 20336 Canada: ON 13765

Refractories industry: MA 12096 OH 6314, 6345 PA 1418, 6897 Canada: ON 12093

Refrigeration (See also Air conditioning): IL 13783 MD 13782 MN 16302 NY 3096 Intl: FRA 8133 NZL 9971

Refugees: CA 20634 DC 17134 FL 14186 IL 7679 MN 18913 NY 657, 3270, 15131 VA 11152 Canada: AB 1097 ON 2755 PQ 13592 Intl: SWI 16773

Regional planning (See also City planning; Open spaces): AL 189 CA 2499, 10233, 12195, 18300, 18319, 18396, 19348, 19852 CO 13506 DC 13133 FL 10260, 15426, 15998 IA 15664 IL 6705, 10161, 15540, 18663 KS 8575 MA 9816 MD 6872, 9753 MI 15445, 16491, 18853 MO 5135, 15899 NE 18992 NJ 14159 NY 3353, 4306, 7159, 7497, 7967, 11667, 13795, 13818 OH 4499, 11973, 12307 OR 8935 PA 19182 PR 19248 SC 3793 TN 3456 TX 19376, 19408 WA 13526, 20048 WI 15454, 19595 Canada: AB 291, 18295 BC 6711, 18269 NS 14539 ON 57, 11959, 13402, 14187, 19440 PQ 18118, 18122 SK 14845 Intl: AUT 18702 ENG 6671 GER 6106 IND 6531 IRL 18485 JPN 16757

Rehabilitation (See also Medicine, Physical; Occupational therapy;

Physical therapy; Vocational rehabilitation): AR 1035 AZ 13030 CA 419, 13703, 15372 CT 5140, 5565 DC 11264 FL 5889 GA 14060 HI 18619 IL 7692, 9457, 9658, 13802 IN 3111 KS 17335 LA 17934 MA 8909, 9826 MD 702, 9755, 11265, 17310 MI 13803 MN 7068 MO 10539 MT 10648 NE 9530 NJ 1398, 3594 NY 3343, 4028, 7058, 7531, 8070, 8724, 8726, 11560, 11728 OH 14283, 18147 OK 11114 PA 6909, 9533, 13749, 13801 PR 19245 TX 7970, 16246, 16268 WI 4484 WV 20206 Canada: AB 6505, 15342, 18200, 19911 BC 2172, 2173, 6712, 18285 MB 15333 NF 3593, 7489 ON 3462, 9502, 12456, 13644, 14029 PQ 3282, 7394, 7882, 7883, 8404 SK 19987 Intl: DEN 13804 SCT 19357

Reid, Whitelaw: DC 9129

Reindeer: Intl: RUS 5525

Reinhardt, Max: NY 15731

Reinsurance: CT 10951 KS 5344 NY 3092 Canada: ON 10100

Reliability (Engineering): AZ 13812 MD 983 NY 6304, 7664 TX 16985 VA 16998

Relics and reliquaries: NY 10810 Canada: PQ 9566

Religion (See also Mysticism; Mythology; Theology; Women and religion; Cults): AZ 1541, 4264, 13026 CA 2472, 2480, 2562, 3187, 7097, 8496, 9354, 9418, 9841, 13157, 14706, 16701, 19259, 20188 CO 1298 CT 6939, 15633, 20723 DC 3163, 3213, 11158 DE 20332 FL 10257, 14332 GA 1237, 9443, 10808, 16383 IL 8490, 9968, 12403, 15488, 15602, 16726, 18675, 20369 IN 7821, 14543 KY 8657 LA 14392 MA 540, 861, 1747, 1994, 8493, 9803, 14628, 20598 MI 90 MN 6615, 10453, 14552, 14565 MO 13822, 13823, 14455, 20234 MT 3892 ND 1176 NE 4114, 11371 NJ 11746 NM 6463, 10660 NY 757, 2243, 2330, 3144, 11667, 13143, 13634, 13833, 13990, 14002, 15961, 20130 OH 9168, 9402, 10266, 13480, 16615 OK 1403, 12367 OR 8218, 10849, 19972, 20241, 20244 PA 3077, 6113, 6818, 9464, 10146, 12820, 14078, 14422, 15889, 19300 PR 19242 RI 11775, 14310 TN 499, 19770 TX 4568, 7915, 9429, 10197, 14674, 16205, 16208, 18797 UT 20806 VA 1168, 11130, 14651, 17971 WA 9444, 12044, 15000 WV 911 Canada: AB 2998, 14592, 18292 BC 18271 ON 6869, 8412, 8979, 10225, 13797, 19359 PQ 9566 SK 2627 Intl: ALG 348 AMA 7867 AUS 10712 BRZ 15839 COT 7862 CRI 17989 ENG 9266, 18441, 20776 FRA 18134 GER 9731 HUN 5466 IDN 5074 IND 8527, 15997 ITA 1821 PER 7998 POL 19665 SPA 10610, 15561 SWI 8497

Religion—History: AL 1281 CA 1390, 14752, 14924, 19290 CT 6940 DC 6073 GA 3998 IL 1782, 9968, 16508 KY 8662 MA 540, 16552 MI 15880 MN 17966 MO 18972, 20250 NJ 6489 NY 2330, 10109, 15904, 16667 OR 3979 PA 1814 PR 5505 TN 8434, 19769 TX 4544, 5390, 7463 WI 15684 Canada: AB 10829 ON 3328, 9262, 14246 PQ 4095, 9910, 12517 SK 2896 Intl: BEL 18131 ITA 2630 JPN 8838

Religion and law: DC 3164 UT 20809

Religion and medicine See: Medicine—Religious aspects

Religion and psychiatry See: Psychiatry and religion

Religion—Study and teaching: CT 7342, 14208 DE 4887 MI 6633 MN 4113 MO 3685 NC 13038 NE 4427, 11371 NH 3684 NY 7098 OH 9402 OK 13968 PA 4882, 15325 TN 4604, 6902 TX 16102 WI 1788 Canada: MB 18793 NS 14540 ON 3218, 18128

Religions (See also specific religions, e.g. Bahai Faith; Christianity; Judaism; Islam): AZ 6243, 20633 CA 6613, 8819, 12208, 16301 DC 141, 4912, 16126 FL 15796, 16300 GA 3117 HI 7046 IL 1406, 3535, 4120, 11752, 11947, 16299 KY 6455, 8662, 15463 MD 1451, 11392 ME 1471 MI 4827 MN 1780, 14566 MO 12649, 14435 NE 8391 NJ 5002 NM 5386 NY 7894, 9745, 11609, 11618, 13814, 15904, 16080, 16724 OH 3823, 3831, 16397 PA 3183 RI 16098 WA 19522 WI 14207 Canada: AB 12042 BC 20288 MB 3917 NS 10812 PQ 2912, 8129, 9910 Intl: CHN 3611 ISR 1407 NLD 11402 TUR 10176

Religious art See: Art and religion

Religious Society of Friends See: Society of Friends

Remarque, Erich Maria: NY 11723

Rogers, Bruce: NJ 11750

Rogers, Will: OK 14037

Rolling-stock   See: Locomotives

Rollins, Carl Purlington: CT 20700

Roman Catholic Church   See: Catholic Church

Roman law (See also Civil law): DC 9125, 9126 LA 9381, 16559 MI 18871 NY 4017, 14357 PA 19177 VA 3919 WY 19659

Romania: DC 9113 NY 14051 OH 14536 *Intl:* FRA 6062 ROM 7943

Rome (Italy): DC 3155 *Intl:* ITA 8281

Roofing: MI 4233 PA 3397

Roosevelt, Anna Eleanor: NY 17922

Roosevelt, Franklin Delano: GA 6405 MN 18931 NY 17922 OH 2035

Roosevelt, Theodore: CO 3940 DC 9135 MA 2008, 2122, 20446 ND 4855, 17784 NY 12647

Roses: LA 732 MD 7238 OR 10852

Rosicrucians: CA 1401, 13012, 14079

Rouault, Georges: CT 943

Rousseau, Jean Jacques: ME 2033 *Canada:* ON 19460

Roussel, Albert: TX 19392

Rowlandson, Thomas: MA 1998

Rubber: CA 20542 CO 6259 CT 16672, 19765 MA 6604 MN 16334, 16337 NC 19074 OH 168, 175, 524, 2118, 6284, 6566, 6570, 16674 PA 9314, 17170 WV 6273 *Canada:* ON 13198, 16673 *Intl:* CHN 15413 ENG 13716 GER 6432 MYS 9570

Rugs: DC 16284

Rum: PR 19234

Runic inscriptions   See: Inscriptions, Runic

Running: NY 11639

Rural development: AK 18183 DC 130, 715, 16783 KS 8569, 18727 MD 17203 MO 10378 NY 7925 WI 19602 *Canada:* ON 8042 *Intl:* AUS 3277 AUT 2361 BEL 7887 COL 3923 CRI 8029 ENG 14094, 18766 FRA 3261 IND 7740 ISR 8126 ITA 16752 JPN 7322 MEX 10240 MOR 129 NLD 5478 PAK 12695 PER 3389 SCT 5234 SWE 15926 SWI 14936

Rural education   See: Education, Rural

Rural sociology   See: Sociology, Rural

Ruskin, John: AL 14663 CA 14711 MA 20153 NY 19278 OH 12328

Russell, Bertrand: VT 14150 *Canada:* ON 9954, 19460

Russell, Charles M.: LA 12099 MT 10643, 14151 NE 19005

Russia (See also Soviet Union): AK 211, 14321 CA 2572, 13706 DC 9113, 9117, 20471 IL 18461 KS 18737 LA 16560 NE 19005 NY 4023, 11631 OH 10270 PA 5065, 8832, 9480, 19300 WI 19607

Russian language and literature: CA 10670 DC 17861 MA 11332, 12416 NY 11556 PA 14602 TN 8380

Russian law: KS 18736 NJ 14174

Russian Orthodox Church   See: Orthodox Eastern Church, Russian

Rust   See: Corrosion and anti-corrosives

Ryan, Cornelius John: OH 12328

Sacco-Vanzetti case: MA 2072

Sacramento (CA): CA 3744, 14193

Safety   See: Industrial safety

Safety engineering   See: Industrial safety

Safety, Flight   See: Aeronautics—Safety measures

Safety, Nuclear   See: Nuclear energy—Security measures

Sailing (See also Boats and boating): CA 20141 ME 9553 MS 17865

St. Augustine (FL): FL 7252, 14245

Saint Denis, Ruth: NY 11636

Saint Joseph: *Canada:* PQ 12517

St. Lawrence Seaway: MI 10338 NY 900, 5415 *Canada:* ON 14253, 14432 PQ 18121

St. Louis (MO): MO 10536, 10537, 14438, 14452, 14454, 14457, 14458, 17736, 20059, 20253

St. Paul (MN): MN 14566, 18920

Sales management: IL 4617 IN 2136 OH 3818 *Canada:* BC 18268 *Intl:* SWI 15939

Sales promotion (See also Advertising; Selling): CT 13021 IL 59 NY 4333 *Canada:* PQ 7832

Saline water conversion: MA 15812 *Canada:* PQ 9904 *Intl:* CHN 12927

Salinger, Jerome David: KY 18768

Salmon: CA 17644 WA 17496, 19525 *Canada:* BC 12676 NB 1263 NS 2736

Salt: *Intl:* CHN 12927

Salvage (Waste, etc.) (See also Recycling (Waste, etc.); Solid waste): AL 16177 CA 2445 DC 3851 FL 3409 MA 827, 2617 MD 6851 MI 3785 MN 8181 NC 19079 NY 13076, 20137 OH 13489 PA 6852 TN 5200 TX 6190, 10366 *Canada:* BC 2174 ON 2719, 13402, 13758, 14187 *Intl:* CZE 4513

Samizdat   See: Underground literature—Russia

San Antonio (TX): TX 4628, 14667

San Diego (CA): CA 14695, 14696, 14709, 14718, 14720

San Francisco (CA): CA 199, 8579, 11234, 14732, 14740, 14743, 15312, 20164

San Martin, Jose de: VA 14767

San Mateo County (CA): CA 10084, 14769

Sand, George (Amandine Dudevant): *Intl:* FRA 1826

Sandburg, Carl: IL 6230, 18689 NC 17683 PA 4852 VA 19510

Sandoz, Mari: NE 19005

Sanger, Margaret: MA 15237 MN 13126

Sanitary engineering (See also Municipal engineering): CA 3402, 8626 GA 17461 IL 20423 MD 16976 MT 7295 NC 1879 NY 7358, 11650 OR

Scientific apparatus and instruments: CA 1642, 4627, 7175, 9145, 16820, 16997, 19342, 19782 CO 8536, 16863 CT 12943 IA 10634 IL 15157 IN 5461 MA 9808, 16287 MD 17624 MN 1427 NY 2223 OH 1044, 9428 OK 14147 OR 16057 TN 15701 TX 5533 VA 16998 *Canada:* PQ 2819 *Intl:* CHN 3610 JPN 19423

Scotland (See also Great Britain): CA 3740 FL 5919 MN 3912 NY 736 *Canada:* ON 13661, 18612 *Intl:* SCT 14953

Scott, Paul Mark: OK 19466

Scott, Sir Walter: FL 18586 ID 18656 SC 19312

Sculpture: AL 10688 CA 6500, 12203, 14702, 18378 CO 3949 CT 20699, 20734, 20736 DC 4902, 11179, 11244, 13006, 15261, 15266, 15267, 15268 FL 12098 IA 4790 IN 7824 KY 18767 MA 1992, 3492, 9789, 15234 MD 1452, 9747, 19961 ME 13245 MI 4407, 4809, 10315 MN 10444, 10446, 19947 MO 14434, 14452, 15599 NC 11880, 19089 NJ 6128, 11743 NY 2238, 4002, 5514, 6165, 6796, 8624, 9702, 10213, 10216, 11624, 11645, 11724, 19273, 20763 OH 3822 OK 12367 PA 6109, 12836, 12894 RI 2274 SC 2216 TN 10061, 10067 TX 4555, 4561, 6021, 7461, 10583, 11791, 14670 VA 19868 WA 19513 WI 10419, 10424, 10426 *Canada:* AB 257 BC 19752 MB 20487 ON 10529, 20781 PE 4136 PQ 10700, 18110 *Intl:* BEL 8785 DEN 14124 EGY 12562 GER 6858 RUS 14945

Scurvy: NE 4426

Sealing (Technology) (See also Plastics; Welding): CT 9247 MI 19925 OH 4596

Seattle (WA): WA 7288, 14999, 20018

Secondary education See: Education, Secondary

Securities (See also Bonds; Investments; Stocks): AL 8942 AZ 15292 CA 2525, 7190, 8246, 8711, 10754, 14034 DC 2287, 6167, 8742, 11076, 15856, 15894, 17936, 20023, 20458 DE 15210 FL 5905 GA 417, 13280 IL 1376, 1422, 3865, 8586, 9856, 11369, 17937, 20498 KS 15010 MA 5678, 6569, 9825, 20419 MD 19796 MI 3770, 4817, 5079 NE 1410 NJ 9436, 13459 NY 856, 1618, 1751, 2439, 3722, 4843, 4871, 5753, 6168, 6194, 6884, 7517, 8606, 9039, 10386, 10740, 12752, 13808, 14036, 14644, 15063, 15183, 15231, 15289, 15639, 16439, 17953, 20475, 20565 OH 14935 PA 13720, 15819 TX 165, 2407, 8446, 15505 WA 6032 WI 5942, 13571, 13809 *Canada:* BC 2177, 5667 ON 1888, 1888, 4448, 12459, 13902, 16420

Security, International (See also Arms control; Disarmament; International organization; Peace): DC 44, 20471 MA 6956, 16548 NY 7931 PA 19213 VA 1064, 1762 *Intl:* GER 795, 13839 KOR 1124

Security systems: IL 8062 KY 5149, 11147

Sedimentology: IA 18710 LA 9394 MO 18957, 20060 MS 17212 NY 19283 *Intl:* SAF 6367

Seed industry and trade: DC 739, 15283, 17608 MD 17203 MN 18917 NY 4304, 4325 OH 6247 *Intl:* GER 18033 IND 7747 NZL 11736

Seeger, Pete: MA 11549

Segregation (See also Minorities): MA 10198 NY 13474 OH 3831

Seismology (See also Earthquakes; Volcanoes): CA 2487, 2489, 4706, 14183, 18314, 18315 DC 3072 DE 4733 IL 12082 MA 1979, 9807 NY 4016, 5969 OH 3102 OK 12347 OR 12048 TX 19395 VA 16070, 19872 *Canada:* ON 2748 *Intl:* ARG 972 JPN 19422

Selenology See: Moon

Self-actualization: CT 4208 FL 5872

Self-help groups: NJ 14267 NY 11284

Selling (See also Advertising; Marketing; Sales management): MI 823 NC 6739

Selznick, David Oliver: TX 19392, 19393

Semiconductors: AZ 2389, 8018, 10790 CA 91, 7507, 7509, 7514, 8019, 8020, 9434, 14021, 16679 ID 6584 IN 4742 MA 13734 NJ 14836 NY 7620, 7664 OR 7176, 8016 TX 10789, 16219 *Canada:* ON 2825 *Intl:* CHN 29 GER 13109 KOR 5293

Seminole Indians: FL 12508

Semiotics: CA 15029 MO 20059

Semitic history See: Jews—History

Semitic languages: CT 20729 DC 3165 IL 16723, 18458 NJ 13367 NY 7098 PA 878 *Intl:* NLD 18207

Sendak, Maurice: PA 14068

Senegal (See also Africa, West): NY 7925 *Intl:* SEN 15036

Sennett, Mack: CA 35

Separation (Technology) (See also Membranes (Technology)): TX 16270

Serial publication of books: NY 11595

Servants of Mary: IL 12518

Seton, Ernest Thompson: TX 2043

Seventh-Day Adventists (See also Adventists): CA 9255, 20188 MD 3999, 13855, 15054 MI 862 NE 16649 TN 15478 *Canada:* AB 2998

Seventh-Day Baptists: NY 347 WI 15055

Sewage: MA 10178 NJ 12779 VA 12405 WI 20843 WV 17470 *Canada:* NB 11444 *Intl:* ENG 20081 RUS 14660

Seward, William Henry: NY 19278

Sex: CA 1223, 2572, 7896 IN 7798, 8736 NC 19058 NY 4306, 14794, 15060 VA 671 VT 13127 WA 15003 WI 13132

Sex change: CA 8299

Sex crimes (See also Rape): *Canada:* PQ 19848

Sex instruction: AZ 13120 CT 13123 DC 3279 FL 5902 NC 19058 NY 13124, 15060 OH 7527 TX 13125 VA 671 VT 13127 WI 13132 *Intl:* ENG 8173

Sexism: ME 12563 NY 20821 *Canada:* SK 14846

Sexually transmitted diseases See: Venereal diseases

Shakers: DE 20503 KY 6931, 15068, 15069, 20260 MA 1074, 6187, 6886 ME 16782 NH 19036 NY 757, 2335, 7316, 11627, 11666, 15067 OH 4657, 10270, 13479, 19975, 20293 PA 6725

Shakespeare, William: AZ 13025 CA 1401, 10409, 14706, 15072 CT 20703 DC 5943, 9135 IL 15071, 18689 KS 14500 MA 6574, 6988 MD 18823 MI 15522, 18860 NH 4614, 4616 OH 3827 PA 19184, 20186 TX 16193 UT 15519 WI 1703, 19638 *Canada:* ON 19460 *Intl:* CHN 1659 ENG 15070 GER 18018

Shale: KY 18749

Shale oils See: Oil-shales

Sharks: CA 17644

Shaw, George Bernard: CT 20703 MA 15236 NC 19075 NY 3880, 4330 PA 2315 TX 19392 *Canada:* ON 18612

Sheen, Fulton John, Bishop: NY 15904

Shelley, Mary Wollstonecraft: NY 8114

Shelley, Percy Bysshe: NY 11599

Social medicine: GA 5337 MA 6993 NY 10663 *Canada:* PQ 4338 *Intl:* GER 7927

Social policy (See also Economic policy; Education and state; Nutrition policy; Urban policy): DC 17227 MA 1980 PA 19224 TX 19408 WA 19542 *Intl:* BRZ 15839 ENG 6674 MYS 1121 NLD 7977 SCT 6690

Social protest movements: MA 18832 MI 18860 PA 16133 WI 19642 *Intl:* SPA 18248 SWI 15941

Social sciences: AR 16861 AZ 13027 CA 2492, 2500, 4850, 9354, 14723, 14726, 17909, 17910, 18327, 18386, 20188 CO 16822 CT 11, 6939, 7950, 20731 DC 3160, 4913, 9116, 11281, 12251, 13279, 15273, 16974 DE 4731 FL 8759, 15686, 16880 GA 1241, 3117, 17012 HI 7046, 18623 IA 16056 IL 11982, 16818, 17935 IN 5407, 13532 KY 17337 LA 11541, 14392 MA 24, 13174, 17133 MI 20122 MN 10453, 10461, 14565, 14566 MO 14444, 14455, 17075 MS 4924 NC 13847 NE 20116 NH 19037 NJ 1902, 7895, 11515 NY 3896, 4004, 4010, 4301, 6612, 7316, 9287, 11565, 11613, 11629, 11733, 13221, 13820, 14000, 14215, 15961, 16772, 16994, 20130, 20695 OH 3831, 6099, 12266, 15691, 18532 OK 12363 OR 10852, 12541, 19972 PA 3183, 4213, 6123, 7974, 12053, 12858 PR 3045, 19235 TN 10066 TX 14673, 16838 UT 20799 VA 8130, 11546, 11849, 13912, 16986, 17016, 17058, 17605, 17901, 19875, 19892 VT 5520 WA 9444, 17066 WI 598 *Canada:* AB 2998, 18195, 18205 BC 18259, 20288 MB 3917, 18789 ON 353, 2803, 2804, 2810, 2860, 5472, 6869, 8097, 14135, 14427, 18612, 19167, 19463, 19543, 20789 PQ 2847, 3286, 3383, 4121, 8032, 9566, 9975, 13581, 13583, 18108 SK 3303 *Intl:* ALG 348, 349 AUT 5541, 14658, 19836 BEL 1668, 1670 BEN 1720 BRZ 6214, 18000, 18002 CHL 3595 CHN 6789, 15075 COL 17983 COT 4350 DEN 4770 ENG 6665, 6689, 9271, 18254, 18441 FRA 6069 GER 1564, 6448 HUN 7550 IDN 7830 IND 7740, 7744, 15165 IRN 8242 ISR 18613 ITA 18007 MEX 17979, 17990 NGA 11808 NLD 13927 NOR 12111, 19160 PER 13214 PHL 13002 POL 13161, 13168 RUS 19795 SEN 15036 SGP 11319 SRI 15626 SWI 15941 THA 16293, 16766 TTO 19551 TUR 6821 ZWE 20842

Social sciences—Study and teaching: AL 5856 DC 13707 DE 18542 IN 5407 NJ 11749 NY 1548, 15705 PA 465, 7811 WI 19573 *Intl:* BRZ 2090 CHN 7540

Social security (See also Employee fringe benefits; Income maintenance programs; Pensions): CT 18517 DC 11017, 17939, 17941 MD 17940 NJ 13375 NY 4020, 4326, 8143 VA 1649 *Canada:* PQ 13617, 18114 *Intl:* ENG 6674 GER 13106

Social service (See also Medical social work; Psychiatric social work; Public welfare): AR 17288 CA 2573, 4383, 14657, 14745, 15372, 19347 CO 3958 CT 3558, 5565, 18517 DC 3560, 7481, 17240 FL 19320 IA 8232 IL 7681, 8406, 9421, 9457, 14003, 16692, 17968, 18459, 18670, 20823 IN 3111, 7815 KS 8556, 17335, 18733, 20483 KY 8669 LA 3344 MA 1980, 15179, 15237 MD 1444, 11106, 15596, 18800 MI 4829, 18885, 20122 MN 18930 MO 10550, 20063 MT 3099 ND 11923 NH 11486 NJ 10614 NY 4028, 5968, 7563, 8377, 11561, 11656, 13983, 14652, 17379, 17383, 17390, 20753 OH 3126, 9168, 12273, 12325, 17391, 18147 PA 3183, 8975, 16143, 17407, 19224 PR 13516, 19245 TN 19371 TX 12613, 16243 UT 20808 VA 3367, 3379, 14651, 17967 WA 19542 WI 5592, 5754, 19595, 19617, 20485 *Canada:* AB 234, 275, 2462, 5244 BC 2167, 17969 MB 1961, 9614, 18789 NB 11449 NS 4532, 12135 ON 3204, 8979, 12456, 12458 PE 13350 PQ 3252, 3296, 3297, 13605, 18086, 19848 SK 14850 *Intl:* BEL 5490 ENG 6674, 9270 GER 5543

Social welfare   See: Public welfare

Socialism: CA 3299 CT 18252, 18519 MA 11332 NJ 5567 NY 11733 WI 10421, 10427, 15683, 19571, 19607, 19642 *Intl:* CHN 6246 DEN 8862 FRA 6061 GER 5199 SWI 15941

Society of Friends: DC 15321 IA 7365, 12832 IL 18678 IN 5096, 10091, 13094, 16637, 20109 KS 6176 MA 11433 MD 15990 ME 16782 NC 5043, 6800 NY 166, 7316, 15323 OH 3838, 15324 PA 6436, 7015, 12820, 15325, 15902, 15903, 19974 RI 15322 *Canada:* ON 15320

Society of Jesus   See: Jesuits

Society of St. Vincent de Paul: MO 15340

Sociology (See also Human settlements; Social history): AL 8057 CA 2562, 12208, 12661, 14708, 16833, 18355, 20643 CT 7342, 9156, 18517, 20731 DC 4054, 4913, 8427, 17241 FL 10259 ID 18655 IL 3535, 3542, 3791,

15491, 18456, 18670 IN 7821, 13542 KY 15463 LA 16558 MA 6997, 9801, 14394 MD 1454, 18292 MI 4829 MN 17966 MO 1134 NY 1488, 2246, 2330, 3271, 4015, 7563, 11548, 11618, 11666, 11675, 13634, 13990, 15714 OH 10266, 13480, 16397 OK 12372 PA 5124, 9464, 10403, 12986, 16129 PR 19240 SC 6848 TX 4567, 5390 UT 19470, 20808 VA 16859, 17432 WA 15003 WI 1703, 19592 *Canada:* AB 288, 18197, 18204, 18292 BC 2167, 18271 MB 9614 NS 4532 ON 2783, 11958, 12444, 12491, 14108, 14893, 20765 PQ 3285, 3297, 13583, 13606, 18086, 18118 SK 14598 *Intl:* AUT 18056 BRZ 19781 COT 7862 ENG 9271 FRA 3273, 7875, 18134 GER 7926, 18040, 18487 HUN 7555, 15975 IDN 5074 IND 6531, 7749 ITA 8282 NER 19054 NLD 11402, 13927 NOR 12102, 19161 SGP 7979 SPA 15559, 15563

Sociology, Rural (See also Urbanization): OH 12293 PA 9464 *Canada:* AB 18189 ON 8489 *Intl:* AUT 2361 BOL 7997 FRA 7859 GER 6453 IND 15996 KOR 13829 MEX 17981 SPA 15562 SWI 14936

Soft drinks   See: Carbonated beverages

Softball (See also Baseball): OK 446

Software   See: Programming (Electronic computers)

Soil conservation: AZ 17195 CA 2555 DC 17942 MS 17212 OH 12292 TX 4217 VA 19916 *Canada:* PQ 2660 *Intl:* ECU 5222

Soil mechanics: CA 2539, 4574, 17829, 20587 CO 3974 IL 3142, 6894, 10235, 16954 MS 16970, 16971 NJ 4260 TX 16940 *Canada:* ON 2821 *Intl:* CHN 7988 SWE 15921 THA 1119

Soil science: AK 18179 AL 17190 CA 11828, 18403, 18412 CO 17537 CT 4176, 20739 FL 18569, 18589 IA 15349 ID 17192 IL 18657 IN 13544 MA 6970, 18829 MD 17203 MN 18943 MS 16969 NC 5040 NY 15722 SC 20349 SD 15425 TX 16199 VA 6881 WA 19526, 20048 WI 742 WY 8855 *Canada:* AB 303, 2457, 2647, 2655, 2742, 18188 BC 2652 MB 18783 ON 2644, 13917 PQ 2658 SK 2639, 2663, 2834 *Intl:* AUS 1328, 18145 BEL 1669, 8583 BRZ 7995 CHN 1655, 7130 CUB 4462 FRA 6064 HUN 9542 ICE 13711 IND 7739, 7747 ISR 16036 JPN 3646 MEX 17981 MOR 7876 NGA 7898 NLD 8005, 11403 SAF 15384 SCT 9490 TWN 15988 URE 16618, 16620

Solar energy: AZ 405, 1009, 1013 CA 2543, 13766 CO 11267 FL 5871, 5883 IL 6586, 7690 MA 1975, 11975 MD 2, 15354 MI 8481 MT 11097 NH 11484 NJ 1196 PA 16709, 17944 PR 19254 VA 17560, 19889 *Canada:* AB 18203 MB 1846 *Intl:* CHN 6790 DEN 13938

Solar energy—Research: CT 15878 PA 2397

Solar houses: DC 12783

Solid state physics: AZ 8018 CA 2483, 7174, 7175, 7511, 18395, 19342 CO 11267 IA 8238 IL 18688 IN 13548, 19111 MO 20066 ND 19100 NJ 13372 NM 14778 OH 12303 OR 12521 PA 1198, 19220 *Canada:* ON 2825 *Intl:* GER 13109 ITA 8077

Solid waste: CA 5212, 20584 CO 17479 DC 17465 FL 3409, 5890 GA 17476 IL 729, 4223, 6716, 17477 KS 17478 MA 390, 2611, 17473 MD 15354, 15357, 16989 ME 6 MI 12200 MN 10491 NY 5375, 7358, 13076, 20137 OH 17456 PA 2320, 3403, 12860, 14775, 20342 VA 20078 WA 14995, 20025 WI 13961, 20521 *Canada:* NB 11444 ON 2818, 12467 *Intl:* GER 6443

Sonar: CA 7508 NY 11838 VA 7624, 16533

Sonoran Desert: AZ 992, 17761

Sound recordings (See also Talking books): AZ 18224 CA 12683, 15656, 18411, 19341 CO 18504 CT 18614, 20717, 20737 DC 9130, 15270 FL 18850 IL 11999, 12086, 18686 IN 7776 KS 20413 LA 9384 MA 3439, 20154, 20370 MD 18822 MI 1068, 10321, 20113, 20271 MN 18912, 18925 MO 20062 ND 19101 NJ 13379, 17702, 20327 NY 4318, 4324, 11605, 11638, 15378, 15957, 15959, 19279, 19788 OH 2039, 18465 PA 20187 TN 4374, 10073, 19368 UT 20798 VA 19507 WA 19536 WI 19610 *Canada:* BC 18284, 19488, 19827 MB 2907 NS 2904 ON 2768, 2903, 2906, 19447, 20793 PQ 1831, 2905 *Intl:* FRA 6062

Sound recordings—History: CA 8931 CT 20737 DE 4736 NY 904 OH 12603 PA 6119 SC 3887

Sousa, John Philip: DC 17602 MD 16440

South Africa: AL 15992 CT 20696 IL 12085 WA 15388 *Canada:* ON 2044 *Intl:* GER 18052 NOR 10277 SAF 3027, 15385, 15386, 15387 SWE 15926

South America (See also Latin America): CO 15390 OK 11146 *Intl:* CHL 16759

South Asia: CA 18344 DC 9109 HI 18617 IL 18460, 18659, 18660 MN 6870, 18891 NY 11626 TX 19406 *Canada:* BC 18255 *Intl:* SWE 15926

South Carolina: GA 11040 SC 2610, 3442, 3443, 3719, 3720, 3887, 4607, 6217, 12821, 15393, 15395, 15402, 15408, 15409, 16402, 19308, 19310, 20548

South Dakota: CO 11039 MO 11030 ND 19095 SD 627, 1296, 1876, 4520, 4529, 15198, 15417, 15421, 15422, 17756, 19316, 19317

South Sea Islands See: Oceania

Southeast Asia See: Asia, Southeastern

Southern States: AL 1835, 1859, 14663, 18169 AR 1029 FL 5889, 13188 GA 5338, 6386, 6394, 7205, 15515, 18600 KY 9094 LA 7247, 9390, 16560, 20677 MS 10527, 18949, 19790 NC 5049, 11885, 19078 NY 18483 TN 3300, 8773, 16168, 19302, 19773 TX 16706 VA 4134, 19892

Southey, Robert: NY 19278

Southwest: AZ 800, 987, 988, 1000, 1015, 6002, 7085, 10916, 11992, 13024, 15081, 17761, 17788, 17789, 18210, 18221, 18231 CA 3058, 3752, 4293, 9282, 11341, 15128, 19259 CO 3949, 6006 KS 8563 NM 429, 3210, 3914, 6463, 10079, 10772, 10910, 10911, 11531, 11533, 15052, 16530, 16831, 16853, 16858, 17673, 17686, 17780, 19043, 19047, 20282, 20376 NY 11609 OK 6475, 19123, 19139 TX 443, 4553, 5221, 5993, 12726, 16278, 17004, 19414 UT 597

Soviet Union (See also Russia): CA 15650 DC 9113, 20008, 20471 IL 18461 MA 6991 NH 4611 NY 3314, 4015, 13686 *Canada:* ON 3055 *Intl:* GER 5630, 13685 KOR 8839 RUS 14945

Soviet Union—History: MO 10536 NY 4023, 11631 *Intl:* GER 5119

Soviet Union—Religion: IN 4209

Soybean: CA 15554 IN 3364 MO 764 *Intl:* ARG 12226

Space colonies: NY 11799 TX 9437

Space flight (See also Astronautics): AL 187, 10989 DC 11185 NY 688 OH 10987 PA 17944 TX 10988, 13897 VA 19874 *Canada:* SK 17943 *Intl:* NLD 11233, 16043

Space law: GA 10111 MS 18955 TX 15505 *Canada:* PQ 9902

Space medicine (See also Aviation medicine): CA 10979 FL 17809 OH 16806, 16912, 20645 PA 17826 TX 16798

Space photography: AZ 1018, 18230 CA 17533 CO 17530 MO 20067 NM 19048 VA 17531

Space sciences (See also Astronautics; Astronomy; Geophysics): AK 18184 AL 10989, 16996, 18173 AZ 17534 CA 109, 1182, 2491, 7505, 7512, 9305, 9886, 14015, 15555, 16532, 18384, 19342 CO 1433, 16863, 16881 CT 16689 DC 1563, 11300, 15262, 16800 FL 5876, 18582 IA 14011 IL 79 IN 7819, 16495 MA 6971, 9797, 9806, 16287 MD 8415, 15556, 20616 MI 4830 MS 10991 NJ 8596 NY 146, 628, 3779, 4307, 5034, 6770, 13986, 14070 OH 10987 OK 14018, 14147 PA 17944, 20318 TX 9437, 10988 UT 7146 VA 10986, 16354, 19875 *Canada:* ON 11242 PQ 1951 SK 15012 *Intl:* BRZ 8003 GER 5546 GRC 5488 IND 19844 JPN 7981 NLD 5491 NOR 12110 POL 13177 RUS 10767

Space vehicles: AL 1940 CA 109, 6298, 9244, 16820, 19342 CO 9733 DC 110 TX 10988 *Canada:* SK 17943 *Intl:* JPN 7981 NLD 5491, 16043

Spain: CA 14800, 19335 DC 3161, 9119, 9125 GU 18610 MA 1999 NH 4616 NY 7234, 7235, 15568 TX 4628 *Intl:* MEX 17993 SCT 14953 SPA 6066, 6422, 15559, 18248 TWN 15569

Spain—History—Civil war: CA 2562, 18420 DC 9117 MA 2072 NY 73, 11609 *Intl:* SPA 10610, 18248

Spanish America See: Latin America

Spanish-American War: CA 19819 DC 11045 VA 19966 WI 20534

Spanish civil war See: Spain—History—Civil war

Spanish language: AK 834 CA 3900, 6156, 10670 CT 18519 FL 10255 KS 18723 NY 11556, 11610 TX 14674, 16258, 16283 VT 5520 WI 19618 *Canada:* ON 12443 *Intl:* CHN 1656

Spanish literature: CA 6156, 12207, 19335 DC 9119 IL 3528 LA 11542 MD 18820 NY 7233, 7235, 11610, 11616, 15156 OH 12221 OR 19230 PA 19197, 19225 PR 19252 WI 19618 *Intl:* SPA 6066

Spanish missions: PR 5505 TX 16206

Special education (See also Exceptional children—Education): AK 15575 AL 18164 AZ 13030 CA 5573, 8949, 12506 CO 8354 CT 15574 DC 11200 DE 18542 FL 5866, 5872, 19548 GA 6398 IA 6507 IL 9504 IN 7762 KS 7953, 12587 MA 5834, 7318 ME 1584 MI 1382 NE 18994 NM 11202 NY 1923, 9070, 11582, 13474, 14537, 15707 OH 12290, 18147 PA 3759, 4841, 5168, 5316, 8975, 12853, 12868, 12908, 12995 PR 19235 SC 15406, 15407 SD 1875, 15420 TN 19772 TX 9931 VA 3379, 5399 WI 1788, 4278 *Canada:* ON 3051, 6859, 10232, 14029, 16310, 20158, 20159 PQ 9896, 13438 *Intl:* KWT 6806 SWE 15909

Special libraries See: Libraries, Special

Specifications (See also Standardization): CA 6511 DC 9136 GA 16959 IL 3529 MD 983, 11303, 17621, 19909 MI 15259 NY 766, 11667 TX 326, 7458 VA 19920 WA 8505 *Canada:* ON 15641 *Intl:* ENG 2191

Specifications, Military See: Standards, Military

Spectrum analysis (See also Chemistry, Analytic): CA 1642, 2574, 18412 DE 18544 IL 18700 KS 8562 MA 9820 MD 7660, 17613 MI 18857 MO 15578, 20058 NC 5042 NY 4328, 5969 OH 12217 PA 1843, 19207 TN 5829 TX 16202 *Intl:* FRA 6765 GER 13099, 13115

Speech: CA 18434 CT 7004 DC 1677, 3163 ID 1946 IL 15488, 18670 IN 5404, 13542 MA 5328 MN 3910 MO 20071 NJ 7922 NY 13992, 14537 OH 8655 UT 20803 *Canada:* ON 20159

Speech, Disorders of: CA 2574 CO 18506 DC 4847 FL 5882 IA 18711 KS 7953, 12770 MA 5328 MD 765 MO 3342 NE 18994 NV 19017 NY 7562, 13638, 16023 OH 8655 PA 5537 TN 10077 *Canada:* NS 4541

Speleology (See also Caves): AL 11301 UT 17785 *Intl:* ITA 3845

Spencer, Platt Rogers: OH 5078

Spender, Stephen: *Canada:* ON 20778

Spenser, Edmund: CT 20703

Spices: MD 9877

Spiders: CA 14722 NC 20238

Spinal cord—Wounds and injuries: CO 15927 IL 13802 MD 17310 NY 17386 PA 6909 *Canada:* MB 2981 ON 2980, 9475

Spinoza, Baruch: CA 18379 NY 4023

Spirituality: CA 7985 IA 14594 IL 3152 MA 5104 MD 3065 MI 3928 MN 1786 MO 3330 NY 757, 12782 TN 19686 VT 3066 WA 1098 *Canada:* BC 13663 ON 895, 8412, 12227 PQ 4096, 12517 *Intl:* BEL 18131 ITA 13212

Sports (See also Athletics; Coaching (Athletics); Olympic games; Rodeos; names of specific sports, e.g. Baseball): AL 1281, 17945 CA 445, 9281,

Sports (continued)
9343, 12203, 14702 **CO** 6620, 11247 **FL** 10250 **HI** 7038 **IL** 3535, 4673, 15487, 18658 **IN** 7818, 19112 **LA** 11544 **MA** 2001 **MD** 13300 **MI** 4816, 4820, 10321 **MN** 10453, 14565, 14566 **MO** 17075 **NC** 11871 **NJ** 11746 **NY** 2240, 2332, 9842, 11609, 13627, 13676, 13992, 16356, 18483 **OH** 3831, 13480, 16392 **OK** 12367 **PA** 3077, 6123 **SC** 11077 **TX** 4561, 6021, 7461, 14670 **VA** 11302 **WA** 15003 **WI** 10426 *Canada:* **AB** 301 **BC** 2166 **ON** 2890, 10230, 15593 **PQ** 2977, 18081 **SK** 14842 *Intl:* **BUL** 2350 **ENG** 18441 **GER** 5631

Sports facilities: *Intl:* **GER** 8208

Sports medicine: **AL** 17945 **CA** 587, 2474, 3320 **CO** 17917 **FL** 8193 **IL** 14919 **IN** 7789 **MD** 11047, 16658 **MO** 9249 **NJ** 12776 **NY** 13638 **OH** 12264, 14283 *Canada:* **ON** 2957, 15593 *Intl:* **BUL** 2350 **GER** 5631

Sri Lanka: *Intl:* **SRI** 3400, 6049, 9657, 15625

Stage-setting See: Theaters—Stage-setting and scenery

Stained glass See: Glass painting and staining

Stamp-collecting and stamp-collectors See: Postage-stamps—Collectors and collecting

Standardization (See also Specifications): **CA** 3737, 6511, 9353, 9353, 14707, 18412 **CT** 5 **DC** 4243, 9136, 11843, 17610 **DE** 5028 **FL** 5879, 10985 **IL** 3529, 14016, 14989 **MD** 11303, 17618, 17621, 17624, 19909 **MI** 14009, 15259 **MN** 12418 **MO** 6847, 10638 **NJ** 2387, 6294, 11749, 13501 **NY** 766, 2245, 4248, 6465, 11667 **OH** 3830, 13490 **OR** 10848 **PA** 761, 3080, 16709 **TX** 326, 4559, 6178, 7458, 16272 **VA** 19877 **WA** 8505, 17231 **WI** 10428 *Canada:* **ON** 397, 1684, 2761, 10230, 10556, 12485, 15641 **PQ** 3284, 13611 *Intl:* **ARG** 7904 **AUS** 1323 **ENG** 2191 **FIN** 5721 **FRA** 1157 **GER** 6106 **GTM** 3325 **IDN** 7830 **KEN** 128 **NOR** 16033 **SAU** 5551 **SWE** 15930 **SWI** 8166 **THA** 16291

Standards, Engineering: **CA** 18330 **CT** 16378 **MA** 15812 **MD** 17621 **MN** 16342 **NJ** 6591 **NY** 766 **PA** 6474 **TX** 3110 **WA** 20022 *Canada:* **AB** 5458 **ON** 2991 *Intl:* **ARG** 7904 **ITA** 5369

Standards, Military: **AL** 16065 **AZ** 8018 **CA** 91, 9251, 9252, 11851, 12026, 13033, 17876 **FL** 5879, 6320, 13776 **GA** 17599 **KY** 17867 **MA** 10559 **MD** 4071, 5270, 11303 **MI** 6302 **MO** 5292 **NJ** 1367, 7852, 8409, 16918 **NM** 17001 **NY** 5444, 8768, 9220, 9427 **OH** 974, 10987, 17167 **PA** 1939, 3080 **TX** 5084 **VA** 3995, 5087, 11822, 17173 **VT** 6312 **WA** 392, 8505 **WI** 17168 *Canada:* **AB** 12052 **ON** 10556 **PQ** 2437

Stanton, Elizabeth Cady: **NY** 19789

State law See: Law—State

State and provincial government: **AK** 209, 210, 11028 **AL** 1280 **AZ** 988 **CA** 2509, 2533, 2546, 18324, 18352, 18408 **CO** 18510 **DC** 97, 19689 **DE** 4730 **FL** 15686 **GA** 6401 **HI** 7037 **IA** 15687 **ID** 7648 **IL** 7700, 7702 **IN** 7765, 7771 **KS** 8560 **KY** 4371, 8671, 8677 **LA** 9370, 13470 **MA** 6981, 9828, 9833, 9835 **ME** 9563 **MI** 9141, 10296, 10310 **MN** 3349, 10490, 10492 **MO** 10542, 10549, 10550 **MS** 18954 **MT** 10643, 10649 **NC** 19063 **ND** 11924 **NE** 11373 **NM** 11529 **NV** 11425, 19016 **NY** 11563 **OH** 12288 **OK** 12359 **OR** 12541, 12546 **PA** 12843, 12858, 12884, 12888, 20435 **SC** 15409, 19308 **SD** 19316 **TN** 16162 **TX** 1603, 16227, 16256, 16257 **UT** 19708, 19712, 19713 **VT** 19810 **WA** 19532, 20035, 20041 **WI** 10425, 20529, 20533 **WV** 20213 **WY** 20672 *Canada:* **AB** 259, 295 **BC** 2153 **NB** 11453 **ON** 12427, 12488 **PQ** 13574 **YT** 20831 *Intl:* **ENG** 6673

Staten Island (NY): **NY** 15760, 15761

Statistics (See also Medical statistics): **AL** 1855 **CA** 15655, 17520, 18302, 18313, 18356 **CO** 17199 **CT** 6938 **DC** 4906, 8211, 10761, 17098, 17489, 17863 **GA** 5632, 6406, 17564 **HI** 7031 **IA** 8234, 8239 **IL** 1984, 3141, 4664, 5635, 12084, 18452, 18456, 18684 **IN** 13545, 13546 **KS** 18727 **KY** 8667, 9737, 18755, 18770 **LA** 9881, 17194 **MA** 6966, 6981, 6998, 10632, 18831 **MD** 4172, 17624, 17625, 18805 **MI** 5966, 10339, 18873, 19681, 19956 **MN** 10447, 13051, 18921, 18932 **MO** 5638, 10550, 18967 **MS** 7844 **NC** 5045, 11905, 13847, 19056 **NE** 19000 **NJ** 1189, 1196, 1216, 13377, 14165 **NY** 2329, 4018, 5189, 5969, 11608, 11647, 15728, 15742, 15964, 16772, 19275 **OH** 3821, 12319, 13483, 18467, 18474 **PA** 4213, 12911, 16135, 19186, 19191, 19213, 19218 **PR** 13517, 19238 **TX** 14671, 15504, 16795 **UT** 19469 **VA** 3274, 4430, 5645, 6347, 10194, 13293, 16986 **WA** 17638, 17649, 19535 **WI** 10428, 19604 *Canada:* **AB** 254,

255, 310, 2850, 2859, 18187, 18204 **BC** 1391, 2156, 2851, 18276 **MB** 2852, 9628, 18795 **NF** 2855 **NS** 2853, 12136 **ON** 2693, 2700, 2854, 2856, 2860, 2938, 4140, 5015, 5593, 12444, 12483, 12488, 13654, 19446 **PQ** 2686, 2857, 9897, 9900, 13600, 18087 **SK** 2858 *Intl:* **ARG** 5548 **AUS** 18841 **BEL** 1668, 8584, 18069 **BRZ** 6213, 18006 **CYP** 4505 **ENG** 7716, 18442 **FIN** 5705 **FRA** 3261, 18099 **GER** 6448, 7872, 7926, 18026 **HUN** 7552 **IRL** 8244 **ITA** 13186 **MEX** 17994 **NLD** 3267, 11400 **NOR** 12102 **POL** 19668 **SPA** 15566 **SRI** 15624 **SWE** 15912 **SWI** 5486, 6292, 18064 **THA** 16292, 16761 **TWN** 28

Statutes: **AR** 1032 **CA** 9325, 17101 **CO** 16688 **DC** 5973, 17238 **FL** 4521, 5077, 18575 **IL** 5012 **MA** 6879 **MI** 4246 **OH** 3125, 9522 **TX** 6811, 7187 **VA** 19890 **WV** 3988 *Canada:* **AB** 10414 **MB** 9618 **PQ** 13601

Steam: **MA** 13930, 19962 **NJ** 6033 **PA** 11753 **RI** 11481

Steamboats: **IA** 13557 **ID** 10915 **LA** 9390, 16560 **MD** 15767, 18246 **ME** 4696 **MO** 10537, 20250 **NJ** 10611 **TN** 10065 **WI** 12591, 19577

Steel (See also Iron; Metallurgy): **IL** 8783 **OH** 9428, 16363 **PA** 4452, 19705 *Canada:* **ON** 4943 *Intl:* **CHL** 8969 **GER** 6430

Steel industry and trade: **OH** 159 **PA** 1796, 9435 *Canada:* **ON** 4942 *Intl:* **CZE** 4932

Stein, Gertrude: **CA** 3752, 18379 **CT** 4178, 20703 **TX** 7465 *Canada:* **BC** 6105

Steinbeck, John: **CA** 14637, 14760, 15658 **IN** 1438 **MN** 18931 **NY** 4330 **VA** 19510

Steiner, Rudolph: **NY** 894 *Canada:* **ON** 895

Steinmetz, Charles Proteus: **NY** 14903

Stendhal See: Beyle, Marie Henri (Stendhal)

Stennis, John C.: **MS** 10527

Stepfamily (See also Family): **NY** 15774

Stephens, Alexander Hamilton: **GA** 5338

Stereoscopic photography See: Photography, Stereoscopic

Sterilization (Bacteriology): **NJ** 5467

Sterilization (Birth control) See: Birth control

Stevenson, Adlai Ewing: **IL** 1903 **NJ** 13386 **NY** 4020

Stevenson, Robert Louis: **CA** 15172 **PA** 6122 **SC** 19312

Stieglitz, Alfred: **CT** 20703

Stimson, Henry Lewis: **CT** 20723

Stockbridge (MA): **MA** 15799

Stocks (See also Bonds; Investment banking; Investments; Securities): **CO** 15638 **DC** 5680, 17936 **KS** 19928 **MA** 1995, 5678 **NM** 528 **NY** 769, 10733, 11717, 12503, 20169 *Canada:* **ON** 14952, 16420 **PQ** 11395

Stockton (CA): **CA** 6827, 15805

Stoddard, Charles Warren: **HI** 18629

Stoker, Bram: **NY** 4996

Stokowski, Leopold: **OH** 15807 **PA** 4491

Stone, Harlan Fiske: **DC** 9129

Stonehenge (Megalithic monument): **CA** 15813

Storage batteries: **CT** 20745 **NY** 5294 **OH** 5512 **WI** 8437, 13725

Systems engineering (continued)
9252, 9253, 19333 **DC** 17869 **GA** 6387 **MA** 413, 10557 **MD** 19909, 20312 **MS** 16808 **NJ** 1189, 1196, 1692 **NY** 6344, 16685 **PA** 17826, 19193 **TX** 5533, 7633, 16203 **VA** 828, 10558, 16533 *Canada:* **ON** 1684 *Intl:* **POL** 16035

Tactics (See also Military art and science): **CA** 9252 **NY** 17064 **OH** 1570 **PA** 19185 **VA** 17801

Taft, Lorado: **IL** 12002

Taft, William Howard: **OH** 17791

Tagore, Rabindranath: **DC** 5323

Taiwan: **DC** 9124 **NY** 3613 *Intl:* **TWN** 7723, 15569

Talking books (See also Braille): **CA** 2064 **CT** 4203 **DC** 9132 **DE** 4731 **GA** 6397 **HI** 7044 **IA** 8230 **ID** 7651 **KY** 8670 **MD** 10679 **MI** 9143, 9509, 12198 **MN** 10468, 10473 **MO** 10540, 10551 **NC** 11885, 11886 **NE** 11383 **NJ** 13756 **NY** 8392, 11582, 11592, 11670, 13992 **OK** 12353, 12354 **OR** 12542 **PA** 6116, 12631 **TN** 16167 **UT** 19714 **VA** 2063, 19893 **WI** 20525 **WV** 20204, 20216 *Canada:* **AB** 267, 268 **BC** 18257 **NS** 12151 **ON** 2808, 2969 **SK** 14864

Talmud: **CA** 2069, 7097 **IL** 4169, 11947 **NY** 1924, 20750 **OH** 16078 **PA** 887, 4156 **WI** 4158 *Canada:* **ON** 7897, 8970 *Intl:* **ISR** 5824

Tanganyika See: Tanzania

Tanzania (See also Africa, East): *Intl:* **TZA** 16007

Taoism: **NY** 14352

Tar sand See: Oil sands

Tariff: **DC** 17161, 17254, 17593, 17594 **IL** 20289 **MD** 16447 **NJ** 1688 **NY** 1266, 17162 **TN** 17582 *Canada:* **ON** 2840, 2841 **PQ** 2839 *Intl:* **SWI** 6292

Tarkington, Booth: **OH** 18534

Taste and smell See: Smell and taste

Tattooing: **CA** 16595

Taxation: **AR** 10869, 18237 **AZ** 841 **CA** 3179, 4287, 4438, 4748, 4753, 6372, 6537, 7405, 8802, 8805, 9074, 9325, 9344, 12774, 13331, 14034, 14194, 14714, 18326, 18352, 19324, 19334 **CT** 846 **DC** 97, 2287, 4444, 4906, 8445, 8807, 11312, 16014, 17161, 17261, 17282 **FL** 13067 **GA** 417 **IL** 1422, 4756, 5426, 6653, 8053, 9722, 15062 **IN** 13545 **KS** 20409 **MA** 1724, 1995, 4288, 5422, 9835, 11801, 13333, 15864 **MI** 5427, 13334, 19956 **MN** 839, 4750, 6661, 8803, 10447, 10484, 12170, 18897 **MO** 848, 10546, 10550, 14465, 20068 **NC** 6739 **NE** 18997 **NH** 11483 **NJ** 7566, 8836 **NM** 11529 **NY** 633, 2242, 5423, 5424, 5428, 6884, 8606, 8809, 11658, 12655, 13009, 13341, 13634 **OH** 840, 3818, 9723, 12284, 14935 **OK** 12646 **PA** 531, 1886, 4398, 12883 **RI** 2299, 7225 **TN** 16170 **TX** 165, 842, 4751, 5429, 5534, 8804, 8808, 15505 **UT** 20802 **VA** 12017, 13962, 19890 **WA** 13335, 20028 **WI** 5430, 5942, 20529 **WV** 20218 *Canada:* **AB** 310, 311, 3495, 4752, 8812, 8813 **BC** 4754, 6104 **MB** 6702, 9611 **ON** 2841, 2844, 2992, 4757, 6564, 6565, 9955, 12483 **PQ** 2843, 5432, 8810, 16443 *Intl:* **AUS** 1347 **ENG** 7913 **GER** 5544 **IRL** 7912 **SPA** 7939

Taxation—International aspects: *Intl:* **NLD** 8069

Taxation—Law and legislation: **AL** 8942, 10579, 15199 **AZ** 9660, 10597, 12244, 15292, 15830 **CA** 64, 845, 1461, 2196, 2512, 6502, 6659, 7190, 8246, 8711, 9248, 9433, 10754, 12412, 13052, 16315 **CO** 3953, 5280, 16688 **DC** 2440, 4289, 4392, 4647, 4991, 5624, 6480, 8742, 10752, 13770, 15856, 15894, 17561, 17947, 20432, 20458 **DE** 13901 **FL** 1885, 8605, 9582, 12156, 18575 **GA** 8718, 13280 **IL** 850, 1070, 1376, 3865, 4788, 8586, 9856, 9869, 9882, 11369, 20498 **IN** 7817 **LA** 4835 **MA** 847, 1840, 2016, 6569, 9825, 20419 **MD** 12215, 19796 **ME** 1757 **MI** 3770, 4856, 5079, 6343, 7376, 10398 **MN** 13701 **MO** 6740, 8965, 9080, 15140, 15798 **NE** 1410 **NJ** 4454, 9436 **NM** 14027 **NV** 3767 **NY** 2124, 2439, 4648, 4843, 6168, 7517, 8590, 9039, 9496, 9700, 10386, 10736, 11821, 12406, 12656, 12752, 12792, 13344, 13558, 13808, 14036, 15098, 15183, 15962, 16290, 20454, 20475 **OH** 567, 3795, 19959 **OR** 13337 **PA** 2310, 6054, 11964, 13720, 15819, 20550 **RI** 80 **SD** 19318 **TX** 1411, 2407,

8446, 8470 **VA** 3919, 7577, 9918 **WA** 6032, 20359 **WI** 10275, 12075, 13571, 13809 *Canada:* **ON** 156, 1888, 2864, 4448, 5612, 15175, 16327 **PQ** 4798, 13604, 13973 *Intl:* **GER** 7890

Taxonomy (Biology) See: Biology—Classification

Taxonomy (Botany) See: Botany—Classification

Tay-Sachs disease: **MA** 11313

Taylor, Frederick Winslow: **PA** 7294

Tea: **IN** 7589 **NJ** 9204 *Intl:* **SRI** 15627

Teachers, Training of (See also Comparative education): **CA** 3235 **DC** 5408 **FL** 9682 **GA** 16383 **IL** 11143 **IN** 7767, 19842 **MD** 6185, 18806 **MI** 10325 **NE** 4114 **NH** 8600, 11483 **OH** 5406, 18536 **PA** 3759, 8916 **TX** 5129, 5131, 9429 *Canada:* **NS** 12145 **ON** 6859, 19169, 19566 **PQ** 13597, 18113 *Intl:* **GER** 16763 **KWT** 6806

Teaching (See also Education; Educational psychology; School discipline; School management and organization): **CA** 4255, 12506 **DE** 8178 **FL** 5872 **IL** 11143, 11915 **MI** 7273, 10325 **MN** 4446 **OH** 5406, 12305 **PA** 10403 *Canada:* **AB** 307, 18288 **NF** 11766 **ON** 10232, 12499, 19442, 20158 **PQ** 3234, 9896, 18082 *Intl:* **AUT** 1352, 8585, 18056 **BEL** 2184 **CHN** 7540 **GER** 18022 **HUN** 1274 **KWT** 6806 **MYA** 10944 **NLD** 13927 **ROM** 15845, 16362, 16371

Teaching—Aids and devices (See also Educational technology; Programmed instruction): **AL** 1283 **CA** 2570, 14693, 14719 **CO** 4786 **CT** 5138, 20240 **FL** 5860, 5915, 9682, 18580, 19319, 19548 **HI** 7033 **IL** 585, 3544 **IN** 7774, 15860, 19842 **KS** 6000 **KY** 5148 **MD** 18806 **MI** 862, 5157, 16470, 18882 **MO** 12056 **NJ** 8594, 10747 **NM** 46, 5163, 6237, 19049 **OH** 2036, 8646, 12305, 18466, 18536 **OR** 13246, 19144, 19151 **PA** 16143, 19228 **SC** 20777 **SD** 1875 **TX** 18645 **UT** 19471 **VA** 19895 **VT** 19481 **WA** 19949 **WI** 19615, 19632 *Canada:* **AB** 267, 268, 18288 **BC** 2381, 8943 **MB** 9607, 20491 **NB** 18073 **NF** 10050, 11754 **ON** 6181, 6859, 19558, 19566 **PE** 13349 **PQ** 9896 **SK** 19260, 19291 *Intl:* **FRA** 2366

Teasdale, Sara: **VA** 19510

Technical assistance: **CT** 14887 **DC** 16783 **NY** 5962

Technical education (See also Agricultural education; Apprentices; Employees, Training of; Industrial arts; Occupational retraining): **AZ** 6260 **CA** 1974 **FL** 5911 **IA** 12054 **IL** 3517 **IN** 7816 **KS** 5845 **KY** 9088 **MA** 20600 **ME** 5153, 12007, 15497 **MI** 12091 **MN** 882, 5062, 10458, 14570 **NC** 193, 3331, 5992, 6801, 10676, 20108 **ND** 11920 **NH** 11495, 11496, 11497, 11498 **NJ** 11507 **NM** 17099 **NY** 2068, 11567, 16029 **OH** 4040, 7059 **OK** 12360, 12374 **PA** 8460 **SC** 5857, 6747, 12516, 13040, 15861, 16493, 16497, 20777 **TN** 11002, 12816 **TX** 12092, 16269, 16270, 16271, 16272 **WI** 1883, 3617, 6262, 9516, 10373, 10417, 10418, 10718, 11978, 15536, 19651, 20103, 20307, 20511, 20512 *Canada:* **AB** 15456 **BC** 2150, 19755 **NF** 2433 **NS** 10949, 12160 **ON** 353, 2269, 2597, 3202, 3203, 4137, 5069, 5593, 5841, 9417, 10590, 11794, 14180 **SK** 14857, 14858, 14859 *Intl:* **GER** 6429

Technical writing: **NC** 1220

Technological innovations: **NY** 13197 *Canada:* **ON** 2939, 8980 *Intl:* **HUN** 7551 **PAK** 12696 **SWI** 5481

Technology (See also Appropriate technology; Industry; Inventions; Membranes (Technology)): **AZ** 13027, 17586 **CA** 2500, 4850, 5102, 7181, 8034, 8257, 9353, 9353, 12208, 14757, 16868 **CO** 4781, 16822 **CT** 2117, 2210, 5668, 6938, 16378, 20712 **DC** 1563, 4243, 9136, 10984, 11281, 15285, 16783, 16974, 17861 **FL** 5883, 5917 **GA** 15479, 18603 **HI** 7031, 7039 **IA** 8238, 18709 **IL** 3289, 3529, 7669, 7675, 10920, 14467, 18452 **IN** 7752, 7757, 7813, 13532, 16047 **KS** 8563 **LA** 11541 **MA** 2000, 9216, 9804, 9815, 20598 **MD** 13299, 17624, 17808 **MI** 5852, 6334, 10318, 10335 **MN** 2401, 14562, 14940, 16336 **MO** 9885, 14461 **MS** 7844, 10526 **NC** 11899 **NJ** 1143, 3510, 6271, 10121, 11749, 13365, 13835, 16480 **NM** 19043 **NY** 3734, 9914, 11666, 11667, 13304, 13995, 14903, 15435, 15719, 15730, 15961, 16650, 16772, 16787, 16994, 17162 **OH** 175, 2041, 4995, 5413, 10265, 12217, 13493, 16396 **OK** 18446 **OR** 10852, 12541 **PA** 3080, 6110, 6279, 7974, 8456, 9306, 19219 **RI** 13453, 17834 **SC** 5857 **TN** 10066, 10071, 13491 **TX** 2273, 4411, 4559, 9072, 16151, 16189, 16191, 16198, 16340, 16886, 17004, 20147 **UT** 20807 **VA** 10990, 11849, 16986, 17918, 19871 **WA** 20049 **WI** 20527 *Canada:* **BC**

Theater (See also Burlesque (Theater); Drama; Mumming): AZ 1019 CA 1800, 2479, 2565, 2568, 2572, 3744, 3753, 3980, 6733, 9281, 9350, 10928, 11341, 12203, 13205, 14702, 14737, 15658, 18413, 19336 CT 4178, 6939, 12422, 20703, 20723, 20727 DC 5943, 7474, 9120 FL 10250, 18584 GA 18600 HI 7038 IL 3522, 3536, 3539, 9420, 14057, 15488, 15492, 16295, 18672, 18689 IN 2417, 7798 KY 18748, 18768 MA 807, 1976, 1981, 1999, 5328, 6972, 6976, 15238 MD 9751 MI 4809, 4825, 5850, 10321, 18860 MN 3910, 6817 MO 10537 NC 19065, 19075 NH 4616 NJ 13386, 13388 NM 5163 NY 458, 2240, 6876, 7011, 8199, 10891, 10892, 11386, 11634, 13627, 15731, 15732, 19278 OH 3827, 4846, 12313, 13477, 14921, 16392, 18465, 18535 OK 12367 OR 10849 PA 4496, 6095, 6117, 6125, 6436, 7293, 18244, 19184, 19225 TN 10065, 10076, 19773 TX 4561, 6021, 7461, 9960, 14670, 15502, 16521, 19380, 19390, 19392, 19393 UT 15519, 20803 VA 9773, 19503, 19724, 19868 WA 4337, 19521 WI 10426, 15683, 19627, 19638, 19653 Canada: AB 18196 BC 18271 MB 9597 NS 12142 ON 10223, 15823, 18612, 20778, 20793 PQ 4219, 11314, 13589 SK 14875 Intl: ARG 11216 AUT 7303 BRZ 18005 CZE 8327, 13294 ENG 15070 FRA 1826 ITA 8280 MEX 17992 POL 13170 ROM 39

Theater, Musical See: Musical theater

Theaters—Stage-setting and scenery: CT 12422, 20727 MA 6972 MN 18920 NY 11634, 11636 OH 12313 TX 19393 WA 19521 Canada: ON 10223 Intl: HUN 7541

Theology (See also Bible; Christianity; Ethics; Religion): AL 15448 AZ 14320, 15539 CA 517, 1845, 2472, 3648, 7921, 9841, 12661, 14657, 14752 CO 11355, 12124 CT 11, 943, 7342, 15633 DC 3155, 3163, 3165, 9689, 11281, 17123 FL 5870, 18586 GA 3117 IL 5495, 7670, 10706, 20369 IN 16020 KS 14500 KY 3169, 6455, 8662 MA 540, 1747 ME 1471 MI 6595 MN 1293, 5496, 10461, 14552, 18926, 19965 MO 3145, 3334, 13822 MT 3099 NC 13038, 13434 ND 1176, 16500, 18796 NE 6596, 9228, 11371 NH 3684, 14232 NM 6463 NY 3144, 5223, 7433, 7894, 9880 OH 12266, 13480, 18534 PA 495, 1300, 8916, 8921, 12978, 19300, 19730 RI 13442 SC 19312 SD 13325 TN 4604, 8434, 19769 TX 4433, 4544, 7915, 14671 WA 12 WI 7350, 10994 WV 911 Canada: AB 1520, 2952, 10829 BC 13663, 20288 MB 10087, 18794, 19568 NB 1250, 4877 NS 18760 ON 7585, 12227, 13765, 13797, 19459, 19463 PQ 5974, 18086 Intl: ARG 17984 AUS 1340 AUT 1716, 8585 BEL 15194 DEN 4770 ENG 3014, 20776 FRA 18134 GER 1302, 8740, 9731 ITA 13212 NOR 19160 PER 13214 SCT 14953 SPA 5465, 10610 WAL 14272

Theology—Study and teaching: CA 2496, 6162, 6200, 6535, 6613, 8185, 9840, 14349, 14555, 14924 CO 4776, 7666, 14600 CT 6940, 14601, 20708 DC 3905, 4947, 6073, 7480, 12229, 14420, 14572, 20173, 20581 FL 14332, 14607 GA 3998, 5334, 9443, 16383 IA 18555 IL 1782, 3152, 3547, 7094, 8375, 9173, 9968, 11942, 12781, 15584, 16508, 16723, 19287 IN 1139, 3151, 3639, 4119, 6602, 10724, 14543, 16637 KS 3329 KY 1102, 9094, 9401, 15461, 15463 LA 11538, 14361, 14392 MA 861, 2018, 6575, 6958, 13218, 14350, 14394, 15915, 20343 MD 11392, 19991, 20052 ME 1472 MI 2592, 4802, 5224, 6633, 10290, 14203, 20304 MN 1780, 1786, 3913, 9442, 9445, 14334, 17966 MO 1134, 4110, 4117, 4391, 5228, 8640, 10379, 11356, 14569 MS 4924, 13781, 20171 NC 5043, 7380 NJ 5002, 11455, 13367, 15047 NY 3627, 6352, 8405, 9745, 10109, 10810, 11719, 12171, 12782, 14240, 14419, 14625, 15027, 15904, 16667, 19929 OH 1113, 1226, 10190, 12800, 13211, 14507, 16514, 17965, 20481 OK 13008, 13967 OR 20241, 20244 PA 1814, 2585, 5142, 5504, 8923, 9464, 9465, 9742, 10721, 13088, 13754, 13779, 13780, 14256, 14602, 15834, 20336 PR 5505 SC 9467 SD 1906, 11857 TN 499, 6902, 10078, 19303 TX 1175, 1314, 1517, 3629, 4570, 5390, 7232, 12228, 14538, 15503, 15538, 16205, 16208 VA 16668, 19897 WA 9444, 20611 WI 9712, 14207, 14248, 14314, 14551, 20513 Canada: AB 11771, 11856, 14592 BC 12036, 19760, 20326 MB 13443, 18794 NS 1264 ON 3328, 3889, 7897, 9262, 12428, 14246, 14587, 19454, 19464 PQ 4095, 4096, 6642, 6643, 9910, 15023, 15026 SK 334, 2627, 2896, 9466, 14228, 14583, 14598 Intl: AUS 10712 SWI 5480

Theoretical chemistry See: Chemistry, Physical and theoretical

Theosophy (See also Anthroposophy): AZ 1541 CA 2480, 8819, 13012, 14706, 14744, 16297, 16301 FL 16300 IL 16299 NY 16724 Canada: BC 16298

Therese of Lisieux (Marie-Francoise-Therese Martin): IL 15330

Thermal engineering See: Heat engineering

Thermodynamics (See also Gas dynamics): AL 17118 CA 1849, 9886, 14932, 18311, 19342 GA 14044 MA 6307 MD 17614 NJ 6033 OK 11214 OR 17110 PA 9706 TX 2431, 16202 VA 17560 Intl: FRA 6151

Thermophysical properties See: Materials—Thermal properties

Thin films (See also Protective coatings): DE 5028 ND 19100

Third World See: Developing countries

Thomas, Dylan: NY 15741 TX 19392

Thompson, Francis: MA 1976, 1981

Thompson, John Reuben: VA 19510

Thompson, Stith: IN 7786

Thomson, Virgil: CT 20717 SC 4259

Thoracic medicine See: Medicine, Thoracic

Thoreau, Henry David: MA 16328 ME 18779 RI 2282

Thurmond, James Strom: SC 3794

Tibet: CA 18316 CT 20703 IN 7799 NY 4334, 11626

Tidal waves See: Tsunamis

Tiffany glass: CA 19345

Time (See also Horology): Intl: ENG 14119

Tin: OH 16365 PA 1271 Intl: ENG 8200

Tissue culture: MD 780 NY 5837, 8478

Titanium: PA 4452

Tobacco (See also Smoking): DC 16379, 17085 GA 17128 IL 11326 KY 2284, 18759 MD 17084 NC 5114, 9157, 9319, 11906, 13867 NJ 16380 NY 11596 OH 3823 TN 17950 VA 777, 12999 Canada: ON 2635 PQ 2996, 7721, 7722 Intl: CUB 4461

Tocqueville, Alexis, Comte de: CT 20703

Toilet preparations (See also Cosmetics): CT 3749 IL 313 NJ 2129, 8450, 16633

Tolkien, John Ronald Reuel: IL 20371 WI 9709

Tools (See also Agricultural machinery): CT 3017 NJ 5097 PA 7240

Topographical surveying (See also Maps and atlases): AR 18234 AZ 18221 CA 2545, 18385, 18433, 18436 CO 17530 CT 3336 GA 18604 IL 12083, 18453, 20255 IN 375 KS 18730 MD 17175 MN 18939 NC 5113 ND 10496 NE 12408, 18999 NH 4611 NJ 11502 NY 11612, 15753 OH 8652, 12322 PA 3080, 12901, 16138 TN 16176, 19364 TX 16195, 19398 VA 13679 WA 17552, 19533 WI 19580, 19582 Canada: AB 18188 ON 2199, 2698, 10228 PQ 18107 Intl: ENG 6664, 9266, 20795 GER 15794 ITA 43 NIR 9194

Toponymy See: Names, Geographical

Toronto (ON): Canada: ON 3647, 3745, 4084, 10226, 14896, 16409

Torrey, Reuben Archer: IL 20367

Toscanini, Arturo: NY 11637, 11638

Toulouse-Lautrec, Henri Marie Raymond de: MA 1998

Tourist trade (See also Travel): AZ 1003, 18215 CA 2522, 3736 CO 18492 DC 17952 HI 7031 MA 11473 MI 4633, 10316 MT 10646 NH 11483 NJ 13773 NM 19050 NY 4333, 12728, 15096 TX 12729 WI 19651 Canada: AB 308 BC 2156 MB 9603 NS 10812 ON 2688, 2713, 4140,

Trumpet music: **MI** 20271

Tsunamis (See also Earthquakes): **HI** 8201

Tuba music: **IN** 1442

Tuberculosis (See also Medicine, Thoracic): **CA** 1531 **CT** 6265 **HI** 7034 **MN** 18895 *Canada:* **ON** 15091, 20196 *Intl:* **CHL** 3596

Tumors (See also Cancer): **CA** 14811 **CO** 14476 **FL** 20191 **GA** 513 **IL** 5507 **KS** 7166 **MA** 7352 **MI** 17351 **MN** 18903 **NC** 20460 **NY** 4001, 20751 **OH** 6240 **PA** 427, 9988 **TN** 5421 *Canada:* **AB** 4439 **BC** 2142 **ON** 14397 *Intl:* **AUS** 20302 **BUL** 2347 **CHN** 12930

Tunisia: *Intl:* **FRA** 7885 **TUN** 16578

Tunnels: **NY** 4000 *Canada:* **ON** 858

Turbines: **CA** 399, 15353 **CT** 17962 **IL** 6339 **IN** 6333 **MA** 6307 **MI** 20447 **NJ** 5000, 7714 **OH** 16066 **PA** 5304 *Canada:* **PQ** 13307 *Intl:* **CHN** 4542

Turkey: **CT** 18519 **DC** 10351 **MA** 6955 **MN** 18922 **NY** 480, 16582 **OR** 13248 **UT** 19475 *Intl:* **NLD** 18207 **TUR** 2188, 16647

Turner, Joseph Mallord William: **CO** 16584

Twain, Mark   See: Clemens, Samuel Langhorne (Mark Twain)

Tydings, Millard E.: **MD** 18818

Typography   See: Printing

UFOs   See: Unidentified flying objects

Ukraine: **KS** 18737 **MA** 6973 **MN** 18913 **NY** 15131, 16613 **OH** 16615 **PA** 9480, 9638, 15220 *Canada:* **AB** 14626, 16619 **MB** 6100, 16612 **ON** 12960, 14624, 16617 **SK** 10593, 16616

Ulcers: **CA** 4485 **ND** 13561

Ultrasonics: **TX** 16226 *Canada:* **ON** 10279, 10589

Underdeveloped areas   See: Developing countries

Underground construction: **MN** 18933

Underground literature—Russia: **NY** 13686 **WI** 19607 *Intl:* **GER** 13685

Underground press: **CT** 18519 **DC** 9117 **MD** 422 **MI** 12211

Underground railroad: **PA** 16144 *Canada:* **ON** 13439

Undertakers and undertaking: **CA** 14729 **IL** 11173 **MA** 10805 **OH** 3700 **PA** 11962 **WI** 11175 *Canada:* **ON** 7537

Underwater acoustics: **CA** 1714 **CT** 6299, 17893 **FL** 17799, 17870 **MD** 19909 **VA** 16533 *Canada:* **NS** 2680

Underwater demolition   See: Naval tactics

Underwater weapons   See: Ordnance, Naval

Unemployed (See also Insurance, Unemployment): **MI** 10299, 19683

Unemployment insurance   See: Insurance, Unemployment

Ungerer, Jean Thomas "Tomi": **PA** 6111

Unidentified flying objects: **AZ** 16610, 20633 **CA** 11220, 15218 **FL** 15796 **IL** 7607 **MD** 13416 **MI** 3294 **TX** 10941 **WA** 1098 *Canada:* **ON** 16417 *Intl:* **SPA** 3388

Uniforms (See also Costume): **CA** 20242 *Intl:* **SWE** 15765

Union of Soviet Socialist Republics (USSR)   See: Soviet Union

Unions   See: Trade-unions

Unitarianism: **IL** 9968 **IN** 358 **MA** 6958, 16686

United Arab Emirates: *Intl:* **IRQ** 933

United Brethren   See: Evangelical United Brethren

United Church of Canada: *Canada:* **AB** 259, 14592 **MB** 19568 **NS** 16695 **ON** 16694, 16696

United Church of Christ: **CT** 4182 **IL** 14331 **LA** 810 **MO** 5502, 16518 **OH** 14591, 16698, 20845 **PA** 5503, 8923 **SD** 1296, 16697

United Kingdom   See: Great Britain

United Methodist Church: **AL** 1862, 7569 **CA** 5821, 14924, 16729 **CO** 7666 **CT** 20177 **DC** 10824, 20173 **DE** 11751, 16737 **GA** 5334, 5338, 12031, 16739 **IA** 20175 **IL** 5814, 5815, 16723, 16730 **IN** 4789, 16519 **KS** 1425, 16735 **KY** 1102, 8678 **LA** 5782 **MA** 2018, 16740 **MD** 1793, 16747 **MI** 5808, 14579, 16731 **MN** 16744 **MO** 7501, 11356 **MS** 10412 **MT** 16743 **NC** 5043, 5050 **NE** 16736 **NJ** 4414, 5002, 10758, 16733, 16741 **NM** 3375, 14578, 14580, 14593 **NY** 335, 5811 **OH** 3630, 10190 **OK** 5809 **PA** 3631, 16732, 16734 **SC** 16746 **SD** 16738 **TN** 5756, 14897, 16748, 19686 **TX** 3376, 3431, 5810, 5818, 5819, 5820, 7200, 15503, 16745 **VA** 13854 **WA** 1103 **WI** 1778, 16742, 20174 **WV** 20226 *Canada:* **NS** 16695 **ON** 16696

United Nations: **CA** 9354, 14717 **DC** 1254, 6376, 9117 **FL** 12156 **GA** 5331, 18599 **IL** 18670 **IN** 7801, 13542 **KS** 18725 **LA** 9376 **MA** 1993, 9801, 16548 **MD** 8421, 18815 **MI** 10323, 20269 **MO** 16756 **NJ** 13385 **NV** 19016 **NY** 4017, 4365, 11734, 15734, 16772, 16775 **OH** 3831 **PR** 3168 **TX** 4565, 19405 **UT** 19469 **WA** 3381 **WI** 19641 *Canada:* **MB** 9618 **ON** 2764, 2812, 13647, 20779, 20788 *Intl:* **ETH** 5469 **LBN** 7961 **NAM** 5464 **NLD** 16753 **POL** 13181 **SGP** 15189 **SWZ** 15905

United States: **DC** 17556 *Intl:* **ALG** 351 **ARG** 9172 **AUS** 3007, 10024, 12954, 15946 **AUT** 799 **BDI** 1827 **BEL** 2293 **BEN** 4252 **BFA** 12610 **BGD** 4519 **BOL** 8850 **BRZ** 1662, 1701, 2085, 2626, 4486, 6026, 13250, 13936, 13937, 14650, 14823, 14824, 14825, 14826, 19908 **BWA** 6223 **CHL** 14822 **CMR** 4968, 20744 **COG** 2103 **COL** 1539, 1822, 1942, 2308, 2469, 3108, 9978, 12940 **COT** 18 **CRI** 16597 **CYP** 11804 **DEN** 4292 **DOM** 1823, 14821 **ECU** 6792, 9181 **EGY** 341, 2444 **ENG** 13774 **FIN** 7125 **FRA** 3232 **GAB** 9146 **GER** 792, 793, 794, 795, 796, 797, 798, 1955, 6139, 6141, 7107, 12166, 14188, 16538 **GHA** 8715 **GRC** 1228, 16303 **GTM** 20394 **GUY** 8627 **HKG** 666 **HND** 16054 **HTI** 1828 **ICE** 13860 **IDN** 8318, 8319, 9977, 15884 **IND** 1952, 2451, 2452, 9531, 11462 **ISR** 8373, 16060 **ITA** 10385, 14052 **JAM** 8727 **JOR** 811 **JPN** 6192, 8837, 10952, 12586, 14827, 16386 **KEN** 10956 **KOR** 8835, 13553, 15040, 15983 **LBN** 1660 **LBR** 10630 **LES** 9770 **MAL** 19728 **MDG** 889 **MEX** 1819, 1820, 3556, 6783, 7162, 7999, 8000, 10243, 10244, 10674, 10727, 14649, 14766, 14773, 16002, 16426, 20833 **MLI** 1459 **MOR** 4597, 4598, 4599 **MWI** 9166 **MYA** 20741 **MYS** 9177 **NER** 11800 **NGA** 7612, 8503, 8543, 20820 **NLD** 6829 **NOR** 12593 **NPL** 8582 **NZL** 1286, 3623, 20157 **PAK** 7600, 8254, 8580, 8880, 12955 **PAN** 1817 **PAR** 1185 **PER** 9169 **PHL** 3181, 4632, 8357 **POL** 8816, 13284, 19984 **PRT** 568 **ROM** 2312 **SAF** 3028, 5068, 8411, 15553 **SDN** 8703 **SEN** 4525 **SGP** 15191 **SLE** 6138 **SOM** 10586 **SPA** 1528, 1824 **SRI** 3929, 8540 **SWE** 569 **SWZ** 9864 **SYR** 4573 **TGO** 9260 **THA** 783, 3511 **TTO** 13229 **TUN** 16577 **TUR** 876, 8273, 8295 **TZA** 4600 **URY** 1818 **VEN** 3037, 9651 **YUG** 1674, 9235, 14828, 15217, 16375, 20835 **ZAR** 8738, 9431 **ZMB** 8716 **ZWE** 6896

United States Air Force: **AZ** 16836, 16894

United States Air Force—History: **AL** 16815 **CO** 16822 **DC** 11045 **HI** 16892 **MD** 18823 **NM** 16831 **OH** 16804 **TX** 16838, 16883 **VA** 148

United States—Armed Forces—History: **CA** 16786, 16926 **DC** 11045 **MD** 11046 **TX** 5994

United States—Armed Forces—Women: **MD** 17859

United States Congress: **AZ** 18219 **DC** 1066, 4170, 4173, 9111, 13326, 13472, 17218, 17555, 17938 **GA** 18602 **IL** 4891 **IN** 1440 **MD** 4172 **MI** 10323, 17923 **NY** 3308, 14354 **OH** 3821 **OK** 19123 **TX** 1603, 19404 **WY** 20341

United States—History (See also Americana; specific regions of the U.S., e.g. Southern States): **AL** 1279 **AR** 1034 **AZ** 6002, 18219 **CA** 1845, 7113, 7572, 15650, 15658, 16833, 17929 **CO** 6006, 17771 **DC** 959, 6379,

Veterinary medicine: (continued)
2579, 15953, 18353, 20849 **CO** 3972, 3974, 10744 **DC** 4914, 15282, 16992 **DE** 18543 **FL** 18572 **GA** 18603 **IA** 8239, 8240, 17188 **IL** 784, 18694 **IN** 9163, 13078, 13550 **KS** 8563, 8572, 8574, 10387 **KY** 18743 **LA** 9389, 16566 **MA** 6985, 9827, 16549, 18829 **MD** 1847, 16914, 17203 **MI** 10335, 10336, 10340 **MN** 10493, 18940, 18947 **MO** 1934, 12583, 13699, 18973 **MS** 10526 **MT** 10655 **NC** 3331, 3693, 11905, 11907 **NJ** 555, 10121 **NM** 9404 **NY** 874, 4311, 11650, 15035, 15716, 17191 **OH** 9996, 12326, 16912 **OK** 12375 **PA** 12910, 19196 **TN** 19365 **TX** 16196, 16909, 16975, 17186 **VA** 19876 **WA** 20045, 20050 **WI** 19619 *Canada:* **AB** 244, 2655, 5577 **NB** 2641 **ON** 2631, 2633, 12453, 12454, 18612, 20284 **PQ** 1387, 7865, 13591, 18088 **SK** 19299 *Intl:* **AUS** 1328, 19362, 20233, 20553 **AUT** 8934 **BGD** 1466 **BRZ** 2096, 18002 **BUL** 2348 **CHL** 8001, 17987 **CHN** 1655 **COL** 3923, 17983 **CZE** 4511, 19702 **DEN** 14139 **ENG** 6670, 14115 **EST** 5462 **IND** 1132, 6803, 7002, 7222 **ITA** 18008 **KEN** 8141 **MEX** 15009 **MYS** 18141 **POL** 160 **ROM** 18061 **RUS** 5525, 8823

Vibration: **CA** 2487 **IL** 19823 **MA** 9219 **MD** 16018 **NC** 9313 **NH** 17879 **OH** 13311 **PA** 9314 **VA** 11822 *Canada:* **BC** 18264

Victims of crime (See also Abused wives): **DC** 17259 **MD** 17260 **VA** 11218, 11321

Victorian literature See: Literature, Victorian

Video games: *Canada:* **PQ** 9360

Video tape recorders and recordings: **CA** 584, 11432 **CO** 447 **IL** 3537, 11953 **NY** 891, 2795, 11638 **TX** 4561 *Canada:* **BC** 14877 **PQ** 3714

Vienna (Austria): *Intl:* **AUT** 19837

Viereck, George Sylvester: **VA** 1490

Vietnam: **CA** 9355, 12204 **CT** 20732 **DC** 9109 **MA** 6974 **MI** 10338 **OK** 19466 **VA** 19839 **WI** 20534

Vietnamese conflict: **CA** 4379, 16786, 17827, 19819 **CO** 3973, 3974 **DC** 9117, 11024, 17226 **IL** 5775 **IN** 7257 **MD** 17860 **NH** 13254 **NY** 4020 **OH** 168 **PA** 8856 **TX** 19413

Viola Music: **UT** 20805

Violence—Research: **CA** 13848 **DC** 3280 **MA** 18833 **VA** 671

Violin music: **PA** 15053

Virgin Islands: **NJ** 11035 **VI** 19492, 19493, 19494, 19496, 19855

Virginia: **KY** 5694 **LA** 12099 **MD** 11046 **PA** 11032 **VA** 344, 1039, 1166, 1558, 2120, 3918, 3934, 5154, 5330, 5561, 5673, 6087, 6814, 6930, 8619, 9773, 10628, 11847, 13255, 13257, 13679, 13680, 13964, 15594, 15821, 15842, 17718, 17764, 19857, 19864, 19872, 19875, 19884, 19892, 20013, 20016, 20674

Virology: **AL** 15516 **CA** 14641, 18347 **FL** 5904 **GA** 17125 **KY** 18744 **MD** 1847 **MO** 1934 **MT** 17628 **NY** 3873, 8478, 11566, 11650, 11664, 17191 **OH** 6240 **PA** 20540 *Canada:* **ON** 2631, 4174 **PQ** 7864, 7865 *Intl:* **AUS** 20302 **CHL** 3596 **CHN** 32 **FRA** 8052, 12784 **GER** 11825 **NZL** 11737 **PAN** 6580 **ROM** 14048

Vision: **AL** 16988 **CA** 15246, 15350 **IL** 7671 **IN** 7797 **MO** 8146, 18981 **NY** 4022, 15724 **PA** 12838 *Canada:* **PQ** 7879 *Intl:* **AUS** 1344

Vivisection (See also Laboratory animals): **IL** 11022

Vocal music (See also Ballads): **CA** 18426 **IL** 3540, 18686 **KY** 15462 **ME** 1405 **MI** 10331, 20271 **MN** 3453, 18925 **NY** 4324 **OH** 12218, 16392 **PA** 4491, 19212 **TX** 1604 **WI** 1654, 15337 *Canada:* **BC** 19827 **MB** 18791 **ON** 10223 **PQ** 2892 *Intl:* **CHN** 3338

Vocational education (See also Blind—Education; Career planning; Deaf—Education; Industrial arts; Technical education): **CA** 1974, 7076, 13913, 17812 **DE** 7466, 18542 **FL** 5911 **HI** 20243 **IL** 7679, 14793 **MA** 9836 **MI** 5670, 10285 **MN** 10458 **NC** 6801 **ND** 11920 **NE** 19009 **NJ** 11507 **NM** 17099 **NY** 1923, 11652, 15716, 15725 **OH** 3236, 5395 **OK** 12360 **OR** 12061, 12530, 12545 **PA** 6113 **SC** 8690 **TX** 4547, 16271 **WA**

3844 **WI** 1883, 6262, 9516, 19651 **WV** 9725 *Canada:* **AB** 232, 233, 234, 235, 5572 **ON** 12462, 14427 **PQ** 13582 *Intl:* **AUS** 1331 **FRA** 7875 **GER** 6429 **SCT** 7202 **SWI** 8142 **URY** 8024

Vocational education—Allied health personnel: **AZ** 6260 **CA** 9358 **CT** 4187 **IL** 3517 **IN** 7816 **KS** 5845 **KY** 9088 **MA** 20600 **ME** 859, 1616, 5153, 12007, 15497 **MN** 882, 9635 **NC** 193, 3331, 5992, 6801, 20108 **NH** 11495, 11496 **NY** 2302, 7499, 15719, 15720 **OH** 4040, 7305 **SC** 5857, 6747, 12516, 13040, 15861, 16493, 16497, 20777 **TX** 1312, 7451 **WI** 1883, 3617, 6262, 9516, 10373, 10718, 11978, 20103, 20307, 20512 *Canada:* **AB** 11990, 15456 **BC** 2150, 19755 **NF** 2433, 2434 **NS** 12160 **ON** 353, 2269, 2597, 3204, 4137, 5069, 5593, 5841, 9417, 10589, 10590, 11795, 14180, 14428, 15033 **SK** 14857, 14859

Vocational education—Business: **AZ** 6260 **CA** 9358 **CT** 10760 **DE** 6542 **GA** 1295 **IA** 632 **IL** 3517 **IN** 7757, 7816 **KS** 5845 **KY** 9088 **MA** 6466 **ME** 859, 1616, 5153, 12007 **MI** 12091 **MN** 882, 9635, 14570 **NC** 193, 5992, 10676, 20108 **ND** 16500 **NE** 19009 **NH** 11498 **NY** 2301, 2302, 11567, 12797, 15719, 15721, 16017 **OH** 4040 **OK** 12352, 12374 **PA** 1728, 5414 **SC** 5857, 6747, 12516, 13040, 15861, 16493, 16497, 20777 **SD** 11121 **TN** 11002, 12816 **TX** 12092 **WI** 1883, 3617, 6262, 8907, 9516, 9524, 10373, 10718, 11978, 15536, 20103, 20307, 20511, 20512 *Canada:* **AB** 11990, 15456 **BC** 2150, 19755 **NF** 2433, 2434 **NS** 10949 **ON** 353, 2269, 2597, 3203, 4137, 5069, 5593, 5841, 10590, 14180, 14428 **SK** 14858, 14859

Vocational guidance (See also Counseling; Vocational rehabilitation): **HI** 20243 **IL** 8406 **MD** 13301 **MI** 10299 **MN** 18935 **NE** 19002 **NJ** 8593 **NY** 3042, 5516, 11619, 11652, 14007 **OH** 18147 **OR** 19143 **TX** 16809 **VA** 479 **WA** 19949 *Canada:* **PQ** 18113 *Intl:* **FRA** 7875

Vocational rehabilitation (See also Vocational guidance): **IL** 8406 **MA** 9826 **PA** 5316 **WI** 19651, 20517 **WV** 20206

Volcanoes (See also Seismology): **AK** 18184 **CA** 17743 **HI** 17731 **ID** 17695 **KY** 18749 **NM** 17682 **TX** 19391

Volleyball: **IN** 1438

Voltaire: **ME** 2033 *Canada:* **ON** 19460

Voluntarism: **AL** 17970 **DC** 486, 11322, 15275 **IL** 17968 **MN** 18930 **NY** 1162, 8973, 20821 **SC** 13821 **VA** 6052, 17967, 19916 *Canada:* **MB** 19915 **ON** 2914 *Intl:* **GER** 5485 **JPN** 11145

Von Braun, Wernher: **AL** 187

Voyages and travels (See also Travel): **CA** 2547, 2566, 9352, 12671, 14802, 18420 **CT** 16504, 18252, 20703 **DC** 11186, 17800 **FL** 17698 **HI** 1865, 7051 **IN** 7772 **KS** 8454, 18724 **LA** 9390, 16473 **MA** 2072, 13144 **MD** 8419, 8420 **MI** 3348, 8528, 18888 **MN** 10454 **ND** 15682 **NH** 4616, 13251 **NY** 687, 5521, 11626, 11628, 11640, 13628 **OH** 3826, 18464 **OR** 9861, 12524, 19159 **PA** 1227, 2304, 3183, 6123 **RI** 2270, 13440 **SC** 10924 **TX** 7463 **VA** 9676, 10628 **VT** 3276 **WI** 598 *Canada:* **AB** 965 **NT** 2789, 13363 **ON** 10228, 19555 **PQ** 9895, 13580 *Intl:* **AUS** 14118 **ENG** 14119 **FRA** 15043 **ISR** 6831 **MOZ** 10834 **NOR** 12115 **NZL** 11739 **SPA** 10883

V/STOL aircraft: **CT** 17963 **PA** 1939 **VA** 16922

Wabash Valley (IN): **IN** 19840, 19850

Wages (See also Employee fringe benefits): **IL** 7169 **MA** 2070 **MI** 4823 **NY** 8143, 11652, 16436 **PA** 7057 **VA** 8172 *Canada:* **ON** 4140, 12474, 16442

Wagons: **OK** 10901

Wales (See also Great Britain): **MN** 3912

Wallace, Irving: **WI** 19644

Walpole, Horace: **CT** 20721 **KS** 18724

Walsh, Thomas James: **NY** 2244

Walter, Bruno (Bruno Schlesinger): *Canada:* **ON** 19561

Walton, Izaak: **CT** 20703 **MO** 3350

Welfare See: Public welfare

Well logging, Oil See: Oil well logging

Welles, Orson: IN 7794

Wells: OH 11189

Wells, Herbert George: IL 18689 **OH** 12328 **TX** 7465, 19392 **WI** 10429 *Canada:* **ON** 9954, 19555

Welty, Eudora: FL 19550 **TN** 3300

Werewolves: NY 4372

Wesley, John and Charles: CA 13157 **CO** 11355 **DC** 20173 **GA** 5334, 5338 **IL** 12403, 16723 **IN** 6127 **MA** 16740 **MD** 16747 **MO** 11356 **NC** 5043 **NJ** 5002 **OK** 5809 **TN** 16748, 19686 **TX** 15503 *Canada:* **ON** 16696, 19463 **SK** 334

Wesleyan Church: IN 20176

West, Dame Rebecca See: Andrews, Cecily Isobel Fairfield (Dame Rebecca West)

West Florida: FL 19550

West Indies (See also Caribbean Area): NY 13840 **PA** 19175 **PR** 3387 **VI** 19855 *Intl:* **BRB** 1523 **JAM** 8321 **SLC** 14469 **TTO** 16499, 19551

West Virginia: MD 11046 **PA** 11032 **WV** 6724, 9724, 12258, 12381, 17730, 20209, 20216, 20225, 20226

Westchester County (NY): NY 7289, 11681, 12690

Western States: AZ 989 **CA** 1390, 3753, 9012, 10669, 11342, 12232, 14045, 15532, 17973, 18303, 18355, 18428, 19172, 19337 **CO** 3940, 3941, 4785, 17770, 18508 **DC** 11045 **ID** 18656 **IL** 11752 **IN** 7794 **KS** 5999, 8553, 8559, 8563, 20465 **MI** 10623 **MO** 8549, 10536, 10537, 14444, 17736 **MT** 12763, 17726 **NE** 8485, 11379, 17751, 17776, 18995, 19005 **NJ** 13386 **NM** 3104, 10914, 17714, 17780, 19047 **NY** 17030 **OK** 6475, 11146, 12350, 12727, 19139, 20309 **PA** 1227 **SD** 1876, 19317 **TN** 16179 **TX** 3109, 4394, 14665, 15499, 18643, 19379 **UT** 11292, 15519, 19476, 19709, 20797, 20809 **VA** 16354, 19875 **WI** 19647 **WY** 2325, 15124, 17708, 17725, 19654, 20341, 20664, 20671

Wetlands: DC 5378, 11323 **FL** 18590 **LA** 9394 **NY** 5650 **PA** 17475 *Canada:* **MB** 4759

Whales: CA 520, 12235 **DC** 6734 **HI** 12682 **NY** 20363

Whaling—History: MA 5051, 5266, 8617, 9809, 10966, 11434, 12383 **NY** 8368, 14212, 20363 **RI** 2282, 13454 **VA** 9676

Wharton, Edith (Edith Newbold Jones): CT 20703

Wheat: *Canada:* PQ 12253 *Intl:* **AUS** 1320 **BOL** 7997 **RUS** 11350

Whey products: IL 561

Whiskey: KY 6459

Whistler, James Abbott McNeill: CA 19290 **DC** 9129, 9134 **MA** 1998

White collar crimes (See also Computer crimes): DC 17256, 17259 **MD** 17260

White, Elwyn Brooks: NY 4330

White Mountains: MA 912 **NH** 4616

White, William Allen: KS 5346

Whitehead, Alfred North: CA 3281

Whitman, Walt: CT 20703 **DC** 9129 **MA** 20446 **NJ** 2608, 20392 **NY** 2244, 7129, 11628, 20393 **OH** 10270 **PA** 19197 **RI** 19268 **SC** 19312 **VA** 19510

Whittier, John Greenleaf: MA 5448, 7019, 20400 **MN** 10454 **PA** 7811, 15902

Wieland, Christoph Martin: *Intl:* GER 20420

Wiggin, Kate Douglas: ME 2033

Wilbur, Richard: MA 807

Wild flowers: CO 4775 **KS** 2024 **MA** 11480 **MD** 4504, 20627 **MN** 18917 **NC** 14910 **NJ** 4640 **TX** 11324

Wildcat See: Felidae

Wilde, Oscar: CA 18402, 19290 *Canada:* **NS** 4538

Wilder, Laura Ingalls: CA 13205 **MN** 20426

Wilderness survival: CA 20427

Wildlife: AK 17100, 17498, 17519 **CA** 12823 **CO** 3964, 17199 **DC** 11185, 17249 **FL** 16945, 17704 **ID** 17695 **IL** 9917, 18679 **IN** 11870 **MA** 18829 **MD** 11217, 20627 **MN** 10483 **MT** 18990 **NE** 11376 **NJ** 5377, 16628 **NY** 5315, 5837 **OH** 12321 **PA** 12873, 20428 **TX** 11054, 16264 **UT** 17517 **VA** 11325 **WI** 20520 **WY** 17102 *Canada:* **BC** 2159, 2162 **MB** 9620 **NB** 2715 **NT** 12066 **ON** 3003, 12479, 12480 **SK** 14842 *Intl:* **AUT** 1351 **IND** 1132

Wildlife conservation: AK 213, 18185 **CA** 17520, 18322, 20849 **CO** 3963, 17106 **DC** 15282, 17504, 20430, 20636 **FL** 15991 **IL** 19685 **MA** 9788 **MD** 5828, 17505 **MN** 18944 **MO** 16956 **MT** 17107 **ND** 17503 **NE** 18994 **NY** 7933, 11649, 15722, 15723 **OR** 12059 **PR** 17523 **SD** 15418 **TN** 16175 **TX** 3852, 20147 **UT** 17701 **WY** 20668 *Canada:* **AB** 270, 2722 **MB** 2710 **NB** 11446 **ON** 2712, 2716 **PQ** 13603 *Intl:* **CHN** 38

Wilkins, Roy: DC 9129

Willard, Frances E.: IL 11326

Williams, Tennessee (Thomas Lanier): TX 19392

Williams, William Carlos: CT 20703 **NJ** 10658 **NY** 15741 **OH** 19425 **TX** 19392

Williamsburg (VA): VA 3932, 3933, 3934, 3938

Willkie, Wendell Lewis: IN 7794

Wilson, Earl: OH 12313

Wilson, Edmund: OK 19466

Wilson, Woodrow: NJ 13386 **VA** 20470

Wind power: CO 11267 **MT** 11097 **PR** 19254 *Canada:* **AB** 18203 **MB** 1846 *Intl:* **DEN** 13938

Windows (See also Glass): MN 853

Windsor (ON): *Canada:* ON 1397

Wine and wine making (See also Fermentation): CA 642, 2561, 3736, 6235, 10973, 13205, 18358, 20480 **IN** 7589 **NY** 1619, 4325 **RI** 8461 *Canada:* **ON** 14253, 14981 *Intl:* **AUS** 15695

Wire and cables (See also Barbed wire): CT 20506 **GA** 15549 **NC** 15155 *Intl:* **HUN** 4888

Wisconsin: IL 11031 **MN** 17724 **WI** 1705, 3616, 4969, 5944, 7297, 8488, 8636, 9653, 10421, 10425, 10427, 10429, 10439, 10624, 10629, 11429, 12591, 13673, 13998, 14879, 15103, 15104, 15683, 15684, 17667, 19570, 19571, 19576, 19634, 19643, 19644, 19645, 19646, 19647, 19649, 19650, 20102

Wise, Thomas James: *Canada:* BC 18282

Wister, Owen: DC 9129

Yiddish language and literature: CA 2368, 2369, 9537 **DC** 9107 **FL** 3321, 18573 **IL** 11954, 15584 **MA** 11332 **MI** 4166 **NM** 4155 **NY** 8405, 9030, 11611, 11815, 13641, 20750, 20759 **OH** 7099 **RI** 16085 **TN** 8380, 20190 *Canada:* **PQ** 9895 *Intl:* **ISR** 18613

Yoga: CA 2480 **FL** 16300 **IL** 7893 **PA** 7223 *Canada:* **PQ** 8129 *Intl:* **IND** 8527

York (England): *Intl:* **ENG** 20776

Young adult literature: DC 4917 **HI** 7047 **LA** 9383 **MA** 2014 **MI** 20270 **PA** 6895, 19846 **TX** 19396 **WI** 19573, 19590, 19616 **WY** 19660 *Intl:* **IRN** 3565

Young, Owen D.: NY 14433

Youth (See also Adolescence): DC 788 **FL** 11245 **IL** 20823, 20824 **MD** 11013 **MN** 20760 **NC** 11871 **NE** 5840 **NY** 11606, 20821 **PA** 12864 **TX** 2043 **WA** 9444 *Canada:* **ON** 3561 **PQ** 13619 *Intl:* **FIN** 5713

Yugoslavia: DC 9113 **KS** 18737 **MI** 9494 **NY** 20827

Yukon Territory: DC 11185 *Canada:* **BC** 18263 **YT** 20831

Zablocki, Clement John: WI 9709

Zaire: MI 10312

Zanzibar See: Tanzania

Zen Buddhism: CA 2480 **NY** 506 *Intl:* **SPA** 4107

Zimbabwe: CT 20696 *Intl:* **ZWE** 20842

Zinc: MO 20252 *Canada:* **ON** 4047

Zinneman, Fred: CA 35

Zionism (See also Israel): CA 2069, 2368, 7097 **FL** 18573 **IL** 7094, 11947, 15584 **MA** 16107 **MD** 8383 **MI** 10371 **MN** 68 **NY** 20638 *Canada:* **ON** 8970 **PQ** 1920 *Intl:* **GER** 3922 **LBN** 7961

Zoning: AZ 16540 **CA** 2544, 12507 **DC** 715, 20432 **IN** 6016 **MA** 2002, 9830 **MD** 13358 **MI** 20077 **NJ** 11513 **NY** 11008 **OH** 7443 **OR** 8935 **PA** 364, 4720 **TN** 8775, 11000 **WI** 19595 *Canada:* **BC** 2166 **SK** 13788

Zoology (See also Laboratory animals; Natural history): AZ 17723 **CA** 2470, 3756, 11341, 14712, 14802, 15651, 18390, 19329 **CO** 17199 **DC** 15280, 15282 **FL** 939, 5917, 17639 **HI** 1865, 18630 **IA** 18705 **IL** 5684, 7701, 8884, 9188, 18452, 18661 **IN** 2416, 2418, 7777, 7806 **KY** 18744 **LA** 9394 **MA** 3024, 6984, 9669, 18829 **MI** 10341, 18855 **MS** 6808 **NC** 5040, 19068 **NE** 18993 **NH** 19029 **NJ** 13369 **NY** 687, 2340, 4003, 11735, 15035, 15722, 15746, 15967 **OH** 3814, 9238, 12295 **OK** 12371 **OR** 12527 **PA** 3080, 14933 **PR** 19247 **TX** 19397 **UT** 20800 **WA** 19537 **WI** 10431, 19581, 19587, 19629 **WY** 16185 *Canada:* **AB** 274 **BC** 18285 **MB** 18795 **NB** 2650 **ON** 2963, 12498, 14131, 19437 **PQ** 8344, 9893, 13603, 18077 *Intl:* **ARG** 6215 **AUS** 15391, 16010 **AUT** 12224 **BRZ** 6519 **CHN** 12930 **ENG** 9199, 11340 **FRA** 6065, 12784 **GER** 6530, 18592 **ITA** 18008 **MEX** 5210 **NOR** 18140 **PAN** 6580 **SCT** 14955 **SWI** 11348 **TWN** 15987 **URE** 7906

Zoonoses: CA 2528 **NY** 11650**Zoos:** CA 6706, 20849 **CO** 3508, 4787 **DC** 15282 **IA** 1891 **IL** 3553, 9188 **IN** 7828 **MD** 1457 **MN** 4094, 10493 **MO** 14468 **NY** 11735, 15035, 15764 **OH** 3710, 3812, 16399 **OK** 12344, 16576 **OR** 20019 **PA** 20848 **SD** 6701 **WA** 20573 *Canada:* **AB** 2465